The STANDARD CALIFORNIA CODES 6-in-2®

VOLUME 1

CIVIL—CIVIL PROCEDURE—EVIDENCE—FAMILY—PROBATE

Selected Provisions of the Government Code

VOLUME 2

CALIFORNIA RULES OF COURT

With The

RULES OF PROFESSIONAL CONDUCT

RULES & POLICY DECLARATIONS OF THE
COMMISSION ON JUDICIAL PERFORMANCE

2025 EDITION

As revised by Legislative Enactments
up to and including the
second year of the
2023–2024 Regular Session
and Rules of Court revisions
received from the Judicial Council,
the California Supreme Court, the State Bar
of California, and the Commission
on Judicial Performance
through November 11, 2024

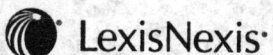

QUESTIONS ABOUT THIS PUBLICATION?

For questions about the **Editorial Content** appearing in these volumes or reprint permission, please call:

E-mail at .... CalCodes@lexisnexis.com

For assistance with replacement pages, shipments, billing or other customer service matters, please call:

Customer Services Department at .... (800) 833-9844
Outside the United States and Canada, please call .... (518) 487-3000
Fax number .... (518) 487-3584
Customer Service Website .... http://www.lexisnexis.com/custserv/

For information on other Matthew Bender Publications, please call
Your account manager .... (877) 394-8826
Outside the United States and Canada, please call .... (518) 487-3000

ISBN 978-1-66338-773-8 (HB)
ISBN 978-1-66338-774-5 (SB)

Copyright 1931, 1933, 1935, 1937, 1939, 1941,
1943, 1945 and 1947 by
CHASE LAW BOOK COMPANY

Copyright 1949 by
STANDARD CODES, LTD.

Copyright 1951, 1953, 1955, 1957, 1959, 1961, 1963 by
HANNA LEGAL PUBLICATIONS

Copyright © 1965–2024
By Matthew Bender & Company, Inc., a member of the LexisNexis Group.

Rules of Professional Conduct
©2024 The State Bar of California. All rights reserved. Reprinted with permission. No part of this work may be reproduced, stored in a retrieval system, or transmitted in any medium without prior written permission of The State Bar of California.

This publication is designed to provide authoritative information in regard to the subject matter covered. It is sold with the understanding that the publisher is not engaged in rendering legal, accounting, or other professional services. If legal advice or other expert assistance is required, the services of a competent professional should be sought.

LexisNexis and the Knowledge Burst logo are registered trademarks of RELX Inc. Matthew Bender and the Matthew Bender Flame Design are registered trademarks of Matthew Bender Properties Inc.

6-in-2 and SIX-IN-TWO are registered trademarks of Matthew Bender & Company, Inc.

Copyright © 2024 Matthew Bender & Company, Inc., a member of LexisNexis.
Originally published in: 1931

All Rights Reserved.

No copyright is claimed by LexisNexis or Matthew Bender & Company, Inc., in the text of statutes, regulations, and excerpts from court opinions quoted within this work. Permission to copy material may be licensed for a fee from the Copyright Clearance Center, 222 Rosewood Drive, Danvers, Mass. 01923, telephone (978) 750-8400. Printed in Canada.

MATTHEW♦BENDER

Editorial Offices
230 Park Ave., 7th Floor, New York, NY 10169
9443 Springboro Pike, Miamisburg, OH 45342
www.lexisnexis.com

PREFACE TO VOLUME 2

This 2025 Edition of the Standard California Codes incorporates all changes required by legislative enactments up to and including ch. 1017 of the second year of the 2023–2024 Regular Session and all changes received from the Judicial Council, the California Supreme Court, the State Bar of California, and the Commission on Judicial Performance through November 11, 2024.

This Edition gives the legislative history of each rule. Amendments made in 2024 are highlighted by printing in boldface type all matter added to a rule and indicating by a figure within brackets, such as [1], each point of deletion. The deleted matter is then shown by footnotes keyed to the corresponding figures. Where changes are extensive, the former rule may be reprinted in full.

The following reproduction of Rule 9.17, as amended effective January 1, 2019, clearly illustrates the "stressed amendment" feature:

> **Rule 9.17. Remand with instructions.**
> [1] The Supreme Court may **at any time** remand [2] **a** matter **filed under this chapter** to the State Bar Court **or the State Bar** with instructions to **take such further actions or** conduct such further proceedings as the Supreme Court deems necessary.
> *Rule 9.17 amended effective January 1, 2019; adopted as rule 953.5 effective February 1, 1991; previously amended and renumbered effective January 1, 2007.*
> **Rule 9.17. 2019 Deletes. [1]** At any time before the final disposition of a decision of the State Bar Court filed under Business and Professions Code section 6081, **[2]** the

To read Rule 9.17 as amended, you read the section as printed, omitting the bracketed figures "[1]" and "[2]":

> **Rule 9.17. Remand with instructions.**
> The Supreme Court may **at any time** remand **a** matter **filed under this chapter** to the State Bar Court **or the State Bar** with instructions to **take such further actions or** conduct such further proceedings as the Supreme Court deems necessary.

To reconstruct the rule as it read before being amended, you read the rule as printed, omitting the words in boldface type and inserting the words appearing in the footnote under Rule 9.17 and referred to by the bracketed figures "[1]" and "[2]" in the rule:

> **Rule 9.17. Remand with instructions.**
> At any time before the final disposition of a decision of the State Bar Court filed under Business and Professions Code section 6081, the Supreme Court may remand the matter to the State Bar Court with instructions to conduct such further proceedings as the Supreme Court deems necessary.

In presenting this Edition of the Standard California Codes, we wish to acknowledge with gratitude the many helpful suggestions received from users of our Codes, and to express the hope that this Edition will serve effectively the needs of bench and bar alike.

THE PUBLISHER

CALIFORNIA RULES OF COURT

2025 EDITION

Rules of practice and procedure promulgated by the Judicial Council and the Supreme Court with amendments received from November 20, 2023 through November 11, 2024.

PREFACE

The California Rules of Court includes all rules of practice and procedure adopted by the Judicial Council and the Supreme Court pursuant to the authority contained in California Constitution, Article VI, Section 6, and in various code sections. The Council originally adopted rules for the superior courts, the Supreme Court, and the courts of appeal shortly after its organization in 1926, and later adopted rules for the appellate departments of the superior court. In 1943, new rules on appeal to the Supreme Court and courts of appeal were adopted. These rules were renumbered and combined into the California Rules of Court adopted April 1, 1962. On June 30, 2006, the Judicial Council of California approved a major reorganization of the California Rules of Court, a group of more than 1,000 rules and 47 standards of judicial administration that govern state court policy and procedure. The reorganization, effective January 1, 2007, involved a major restructuring, reordering, and renumbering of the rules and standards to make them clearer, better organized, and easier to read.

Effective January 1, 2009, the Judicial Council adopted a revision of the rules relating to the superior court appellate divisions to place the rules in a more logical order, reflect current practices, fill in gaps in the rules, eliminate outdated language, and update the remaining language so it is similar to the recently revised rules for the Courts of Appeal.

THE PUBLISHER

Table Showing Changes Received From the Judicial Council
From November 20, 2023 Through November 11, 2024

Rule	Effect	Date	Rule	Effect	Date
4.103	Amended	Jan. 1, 2024	7.2225	Amended	Sept. 1, 2024
4.551(a), (c)	Amended	Sept. 1, 2024	7.2230(a)	Amended	Sept. 1, 2024
4.551(d)	Adopted	Sept. 1, 2024	8.385(f)	Amended	Sept. 1, 2024
4.551(d)	Relettered to (e)	Sept. 1, 2024	8.385(g)	Adopted	Sept. 1, 2024
4.551(e)	Relettered to (f)	Sept. 1, 2024	8.386(f)	Amended	Sept. 1, 2024
4.551(f)	Amended & Relettered to (g)	Sept. 1, 2024	9.9(a), (b)	Amended	Jan. 1, 2024
4.551(g)	Amended & Relettered to (h)	Sept. 1, 2024	9.9(e), (f)	Added	Jan. 1, 2024
4.551(h)	Relettered to (i)	Sept. 1, 2024	9.32	Adopted	Jan. 1, 2024
4.551 Adv. Comment	Amended	Sept. 1, 2024	9.40(e), (f), (h)	Amended	July 24, 2024
4.553	Adopted	Sept. 1, 2024	9.40(i)	Adopted	July 24, 2024
7.2210(b)	Amended	Sept. 1, 2024	9.43(d), (f), (g)	Amended	July 24, 2024
7.2210(c)–(f)	Adopted	Sept. 1, 2024	10.603(c)	Amended	Sept. 1, 2024
7.2210 Adv. Comment	Adopted	Sept. 1, 2024	10.635	Adopted	July 1, 2024
7.2221	Amended	Sept. 1, 2024			

Appendices

Appendix	Effect	Date
A	Amended	Jan. 1, 2024, Apr. 1, 2024, July 12, 2024, July 15, 2024, Sept. 1, 2024, Sept. 21, 2024, Oct. 1, 2024, Jan. 1, 2025, Jan. 1, 2026
F	Amended	Apr. 1, 2024
H	Added	Apr. 1, 2024

California Courts of Appeal

Court of Appeal—First Appellate District

IOPPs	Effect	Date
I–III	Amended	Mar. 18, 2024

Court of Appeal—Fourth Appellate District

Rule	Effect	Date
2	Adopted	Aug. 19, 2024
2	Amended	Nov. 1, 2024

IOPPs	Effect	Date
Div. 1 IOPPs	Amended	June 4, 2024
Div. 3 IOPPs	Amended	June 4, 2024

CONTENTS

Rules

Title 1. Rules Applicable to All Courts
- Chapter 1. Preliminary Rules ... 1.1 – 1.6
- Chapter 2. Timing and Holidays ... 1.10, 1.11
- Chapter 3. Service and Filing ... 1.20, 1.21
- Chapter 4. Judicial Council Forms ... 1.30 – 1.51
- Chapter 5. Accommodations ... 1.100
- Chapter 6. Public Access to Court Proceedings ... 1.150
- Chapter 7. Form and Format of Papers ... 1.200, 1.201
- Chapter 8. Language Access Services ... 1.300

Title 2. Trial Court Rules
- Division 1. General Provisions
  - Chapter 1. Title and Application ... 2.1, 2.2
  - Chapter 2. Definitions and Scope of Rules ... 2.3, 2.10
  - Chapter 3. Timing ... 2.20
  - Chapter 4. Sanctions ... 2.30
- Division 2. Papers and Forms to Be Filed
  - Chapter 1. Papers ... 2.100 – 2.119
  - Chapter 2. General Rules on Forms ... 2.130 – 2.141
  - Chapter 3. Other Forms ... 2.150
- Division 3. Filing and Service
  - Chapter 1. General Provisions ... 2.200, 2.210
  - Chapter 2. Filing and Service by Electronic Means ... 2.250 – 2.261
  - Chapter 3. Filing and Service by Fax ... 2.300 – 2.306
- Division 4. Court Records
  - Chapter 1. General Provisions ... 2.400
  - Chapter 2. Access to Electronic Trial Court Records
    - Article 1. General Provisions ... 2.500 – 2.502
    - Article 2. Public Access ... 2.503 – 2.507
    - Article 3. Remote Access by a Party, Party's Designee, Party's Attorney, Court-Appointed Person, or Authorized Person Working in a Legal Organization or Qualified Legal Services Project ... 2.515 – 2.528
    - Article 4. Remote Access by Government Entities ... 2.540 – 2.545
  - Chapter 3. Sealed Records ... 2.550, 2.551
  - Chapter 4. Records in False Claims Act Cases ... 2.570 – 2.573
  - Chapter 5. Name Change Proceedings Under Address Confidentiality Program ... 2.575 – 2.577
  - Chapter 6. Other Sealed or Closed Records ... 2.580, 2.585
- Division 5. Venue and Sessions
  - Chapter 1. Venue [Reserved] ... 2.700
  - Chapter 2. Sessions [Reserved]
- Division 6. Appointments by the Court or Agreement of the Parties
  - Chapter 1. Court-Appointed Temporary Judges ... 2.810 – 2.819
  - Chapter 2. Temporary Judges Requested by the Parties ... 2.830 – 2.835
  - Chapter 3. Referees [Reserved]
  - Chapter 4. Language Access
    - Article 1. General Provisions ... 2.850, 2.851
    - Article 2. Court Interpreters ... 2.890 – 2.895
- Division 7. Proceedings
  - Chapter 1. General Provisions ... 2.900
  - Chapter 2. Records of Proceedings ... 2.950 – 2.958
- Division 8. Trials
  - Chapter 1. Jury Service ... 2.1000 – 2.1010
  - Chapter 2. Conduct of Trial ... 2.1030 – 2.1036
  - Chapter 3. Testimony and Evidence ... 2.1040
  - Chapter 4. Jury Instructions ... 2.1050 – 2.1058
- Division 9. Judgments ... 2.1100

Title 3. Civil Rules
- Division 1. General Provisions
  - Chapter 1. Preliminary Rules ... 3.1
  - Chapter 2. Scope of the Civil Rules ... 3.10, 3.20
  - Chapter 3. Attorneys ... 3.35 – 3.37
- Division 2. Waiver of Fees and Costs ... 3.50 – 3.58

TABLE OF CONTENTS

Rules

Division 3. Filing and Service
  Chapter 1. Filing 3.100
  Chapter 2. Time for Service 3.110
  Chapter 3. Papers to Be Served . . . . 3.220 – 3.222
  Chapter 4. Miscellaneous . . . . 3.250 – 3.254

Division 4. Parties and Actions
  Chapter 1. [Reserved]
  Chapter 2. Joinder of Parties [Reserved]
  Chapter 3. Related Cases 3.300
  Chapter 4. Consolidated Cases 3.350
  Chapter 5. Complex Cases . . . . 3.400 – 3.403
  Chapter 6. Coordination of Noncomplex Actions 3.500
  Chapter 7. Coordination of Complex Actions
    Article 1. General Provisions . . . . 3.501 – 3.506
    Article 2. Procedural Rules Applicable to All Complex Coordination Proceedings . . . 3.510 – 3.516
    Article 3. Petitions and Proceedings for Coordination of Complex Actions . . . . . 3.520 – 3.532
    Article 4. Pretrial and Trial Rules for Complex Coordinated Actions . . . . . 3.540 – 3.545
    Article 5. Administration of Coordinated Complex Actions 3.550

Division 5. Venue [Reserved]

Division 6. Proceedings
  Chapter 1. General Provisions [Reserved]
  Chapter 2. Stay of Proceedings 3.650
  Chapter 3. Hearings, Conferences, and Proceedings 3.670, 3.672
  Chapter 4. Special Proceedings on Construction-Related Accessibility Claims . . . 3.680, 3.682

Division 7. Civil Case Management
  Chapter 1. General Provisions 3.700
  Chapter 2. Differential Case Management . . . . 3.710 – 3.715
  Chapter 3. Case Management . . . . 3.720 – 3.735
  Chapter 4. Management of Collections Cases 3.740, 3.741
  Chapter 5. Management of Complex Cases 3.750, 3.751
  Chapter 6. Management of Class Actions . . . . 3.760 – 3.771

Division 8. Alternative Dispute Resolution
  Chapter 1. General Provisions 3.800
  Chapter 2. Judicial Arbitration . . . . 3.810 – 3.830
  Chapter 3. General Rules Relating to Mediation of Civil Cases
    Article 1. Procedures for All Court Mediation Programs 3.835, 3.845
    Article 2. Rules of Conduct for Mediators in Court-Connected Mediation Programs for Civil Cases . . . . 3.850 – 3.860
    Article 3. Requirements for Addressing Complaints About Court-Program Mediators . . 3.865 – 3.872
  Chapter 4. Civil Action Mediation Program Rules . . . . 3.890 – 3.898

Division 9. References
  Chapter 1. Reference by Agreement of the Parties Under Code of Civil Procedure Section 638 . . . . 3.900 – 3.907
  Chapter 2. Court-Ordered Reference Under Code of Civil Procedure Section 639 . . . . . 3.920 – 3.926
  Chapter 3. Rules Applicable to References Under Code of Civil Procedure Section 638 or 639 . . . . 3.930 – 3.932

Division 10. Discovery
  Chapter 1. Format of Discovery 3.1000
  Chapter 2. Conduct of Discovery 3.1010

Division 11. Law and Motion
  Chapter 1. General Provisions . . . . 3.1100 – 3.1109
  Chapter 2. Format of Motion Papers . . . . 3.1110 – 3.1116
  Chapter 3. Provisional and Injunctive Relief
    Article 1. General Provisions 3.1130
    Article 2. Writs 3.1140, 3.1142
    Article 3. Injunctions 3.1150, 3.1151
    Article 4. Protective Orders . . . . 3.1160 – 3.1162
    Article 4. Receiverships . . . . 3.1175 – 3.1184
  Chapter 4. Ex Parte Applications . . . . 3.1200 – 3.1207
  Chapter 5. Noticed Motions . . . . 3.1300 – 3.1312
  Chapter 6. Particular Motions
    Article 1. Pleading and Venue Motions . . . . 3.1320 – 3.1327
    Article 2. Procedural Motions . . . . 3.1330 – 3.1335
    Article 3. Motions to Dismiss 3.1340, 3.1342
    Article 4. Discovery Motions . . . . 3.1345 – 3.1348

TABLE OF CONTENTS

		Rules
Article 5.	Summary Judgment Motions	3.1350 – 3.1354
Article 6.	Miscellaneous Motions	3.1360, 3.1362
Chapter 7.	Civil Petitions	3.1365 – 3.1372
Division 12.	Settlement	3.1380 – 3.1385
Division 13.	Dismissal of Actions	3.1390
Division 14.	Pretrial [Reserved]	
Division 15.	Trial	
Chapter 1.	General Provisions [Reserved]	
Chapter 2.	Consolidation or Bifurcation of Cases for Trial [Reserved]	
Chapter 3.	Nonjury Trials [Reserved]	
Chapter 4.	Jury Trials	3.1540
Chapter 4.5.	Expedited Jury Trials	
Article 1.	Applicability	3.1545
Article 2.	Rules Applicable Only to Cases with Mandatory Expedited Jury Trials	3.1546
Article 3.	Rules Applicable Only to Cases with Voluntary Expedited Jury Trials	3.1547, 3.1548
Article 4.	Rules Applicable to All Expedited Jury Trials	3.1549 – 3.1553
Chapter 5.	Testimony and Evidence [Reserved]	
Chapter 6.	Expert Witness Testimony [Reserved]	
Chapter 7.	Jury Instructions	3.1560
Chapter 8.	Special Verdicts	3.1580
Chapter 9.	Statement of Decision	3.1590, 3.1591
Division 16.	Post-trial	3.1600, 3.1602
Division 17.	Attorney's Fees and Costs	3.1700, 3.1702
Division 18.	Judgments	3.1800 – 3.1806
Division 19.	Postjudgment and Enforcement of Judgments	3.1900
Division 20.	Unlawful Detainers	3.2000, 3.2005
Division 21.	Rules for Small Claims Actions	
Chapter 1.	Trial Rules	3.2100 – 3.2110
Chapter 2.	Small Claims Advisors	3.2120
Division 22.	Petitions Under the California Environmental Quality Act	
Chapter 1.	General Provisions	3.2200 – 3.2208
Chapter 2.	California Environmental Quality Act Proceedings Involving Streamlined CEQA Projects	
Article 1.	General Provisions	3.2220 – 3.2231
Article 2.	CEQA Challenges to Approval of Sacramento Arena Project	3.2235 – 3.2237
Article 3.	Trial Court Costs	3.2240
Division 23.	Miscellaneous	3.2300

Title 4. Criminal Rules

Division 1.	General Provisions	4.1 – 4.3
Division 2.	Pretrial	
Chapter 1.	Pretrial Proceedings	4.100 – 4.131
Chapter 2.	Change of Venue	4.150 – 4.155
Division 3.	Trials	4.200 – 4.230
Division 4.	Sentencing	4.305 – 4.336
Division 5.	Felony Sentencing Law	4.401 – 4.480
Division 6.	Postconviction, Postrelease, and Writs	
Chapter 1.	Postconviction	4.510, 4.530
Chapter 2.	Postrelease	4.541
Chapter 3.	Habeas Corpus	
Article 1.	General Provisions	4.545
Article 2.	Noncapital Habeas Corpus Proceedings in the Superior Court	4.550 – 4.552
Article 3.	Death Penalty–Related Habeas Corpus Proceedings in the Superior Court	4.560 – 4.577
Division 7.	Miscellaneous	4.601, 4.700

Title 5. Family and Juvenile Rules

Title		5.1
Division 1.	Family Rules	
Chapter 1.	General Provisions	
Article 1.	General Provisions	5.2, 5.4
Article 2.	Use of Forms	5.7
Article 3.	Appearance by Telephone	5.9
Article 4.	Discovery	5.12
Article 5.	Sanctions	5.14
Chapter 2.	Parties and Joinder of Parties	
Article 1.	Parties to Proceedings	5.16 – 5.18

TABLE OF CONTENTS

		Rules
Article 2.	Joinder of Parties	5.24
Article 3.	Employee Pension Benefit Plan	5.29
Chapter 3.	Filing Fees and Fee Waivers	
Article 1.	Filing Fees and Fee Waivers	5.40, 5.41
Article 2.	Special Procedures	5.43 – 5.46
Chapter 4.	Starting and Responding to a Family Law Case; Service of Papers	
Article 1.	Summonses, Notices, and Declarations	5.50 – 5.52
Article 2.	Initial Pleadings	5.60 – 5.63
Article 3.	Service of Papers	5.66
Article 4.	Manner of Service	5.68, 5.72
Article 5.	Pleadings and Amended Pleadings	5.74
Article 6.	Specific Proceedings	5.76, 5.77
Chapter 5.	Family Centered Case Resolution Plans	5.83
Chapter 6.	Request for Court Orders	
Article 1.	General Provisions	5.90, 5.91
Article 2.	Filing and Service	5.92 – 5.97
Article 3.	Meet-and-Confer Conferences	5.98
Article 4.	Evidence at Hearings	5.111 – 5.115
Article 5.	Reporting and Preparation of Order After Hearing	5.123, 5.125
Article 6.	Special Immigrant Juvenile Findings	5.130
Chapter 7.	Request for Emergency Orders (Ex Parte Orders)	
Article 1.	Request for Emergency Orders (Ex Parte Orders)	5.151
Article 2.	Notice, Service, Appearance	5.165 – 5.169
Article 3.	Procedural Matters Not Requiring Notice (Non-Emergency Orders)	5.170
Chapter 8.	Child Custody and Visitation (Parenting Time) Proceedings	
Article 1.	Child Custody Mediation	5.210, 5.215
Article 2.	Child Custody Investigations and Evaluations	5.220 – 5.230
Article 3.	Ex parte Communication	5.235
Article 4.	Counsel Appointed to Represent a Child	5.240 – 5.242
Article 5.	Children's Participation in Family Court	5.250
Chapter 9.	Child, Spousal, and Domestic Partner Support	
Article 1.	General Provisions	5.260
Article 2.	Certification of Statewide Uniform Guideline Support Calculators	5.275
Chapter 10.	Government Child Support Cases (Title IV-D Support Cases)	5.300 – 5.375
Chapter 11.	Domestic Violence Cases	
Article 1.	Domestic Violence Prevention Act Cases	5.380 – 5.382
Article 2.	Tribal Court Protective Orders	5.386
Chapter 12.	Separate Trials (Bifurcation) and Interlocutory Appeals	
Article 1.	Separate Trials	5.390
Article 2.	Interlocutory Appeals	5.392
Chapter 13.	Trials and Long-Cause Hearings	5.393, 5.394
Chapter 14.	Default Proceedings and Judgments	5.401 – 5.415
Chapter 15.	Settlement Services	5.420
Chapter 16.	Limited Scope Representation; Attorney's Fees and Costs	
Article 1.	Limited Scope Representation	5.425
Article 2.	Attorney's Fees and Costs	5.427
Chapter 17.	Family Law Facilitator	5.430
Chapter 18.	Court Coordination Rules	
Article 1.	Related Cases	5.440, 5.445
Chapter 19.	Minor Marriage or Domestic Partnership	
Article 1.	General Provisions	5.448
Division 2.	Rules Applicable in Family and Juvenile Proceedings	
Chapter 1.	Contact and Coordination	5.451 – 5.475
Chapter 2.	Indian Child Welfare Act	5.480 – 5.488
Chapter 3.	Intercountry Adoptions	5.490 – 5.493
Chapter 4.	Protective Orders	5.496
Division 3.	Juvenile Rules	
Chapter 1.	Preliminary Provisions—Title and Definitions	5.500 – 5.505
Chapter 2.	Commencement of Juvenile Court Proceedings	5.510 – 5.526
Chapter 3.	General Conduct of Juvenile Court Proceedings	5.530 – 5.555
Chapter 4.	Subsequent Petitions and Modifications	5.560 – 5.580
Chapter 5.	Appellate Review	5.585 – 5.595
Chapter 6.	Emancipation	5.605
Chapter 7.	Intercounty Transfers; Out-of-County Placements; Interstate Compact on the Placement of Children	5.610 – 5.619

TABLE OF CONTENTS

Rules

Chapter 8.	Restraining Orders, Custody Orders, and Guardianships General Court Authority	5.620 – 5.630
Chapter 9.	Parentage	5.635, 5.637
Chapter 10.	Medication, Mental Health, and Education	5.640 – 5.652
Chapter 11.	Advocates for Parties	5.655 – 5.664
Chapter 12.	Cases Petitioned Under Section 300	
Article 1.	Initial Hearing	5.667 – 5.678
Article 2.	Jurisdiction	5.682 – 5.684
Article 3.	Disposition	5.690 – 5.705
Article 4.	Reviews, Permanent Planning	5.706 – 5.740
Chapter 13.	Cases Petitioned Under Sections 601 and 602	
Article 1.	Initial Appearance	5.752 – 5.764
Article 2.	Hearing on Transfer of Jurisdiction to Criminal Court	5.766 – 5.770
Article 3.	Jurisdiction	5.774 – 5.782
Article 4.	Disposition	5.785 – 5.805
Article 5.	Reviews and Sealing	5.810 – 5.860
Chapter 14.	Nonminor Dependent	5.900 – 5.906

Title 6. [Reserved]

Title 7. Probate and Mental Health Rules

Division 1. Probate Rules

Chapter 1.	General Provisions	7.1 – 7.10
Chapter 2.	Notices, Publication, and Service	7.50 – 7.55
Chapter 3.	Pleadings	7.101 – 7.104
Chapter 4.	Appointment of Executors and Administrators	7.150
Chapter 5.	Bonding of Personal Representatives, Guardians, Conservators, and Trustees	7.201 – 7.207
Chapter 6.	Independent Administration of Estates	7.250
Chapter 7.	Spousal or Domestic Partner Property Petitions	7.301
Chapter 8.	Petitions for Instructions [Reserved]	
Chapter 9.	Creditors' Claims	7.401 – 7.403
Chapter 10.	Sales of Real and Personal Property	7.451 – 7.454
Chapter 11.	Inventory and Appraisal	7.501
Chapter 12.	Accounts and Reports of Executors, Administrators, Conservators, and Guardians	7.550 – 7.576
Chapter 13.	Taxes [Reserved]	
Chapter 14.	Preliminary and Final Distributions	7.650 – 7.652
Chapter 15.	Compensation of Personal Representatives and Attorneys	7.700 – 7.707
Chapter 16.	Compensation in All Matters Other Than Decedents' Estates	7.750 – 7.776
Chapter 17.	Contested Hearings and Trials	7.801, 7.802
Chapter 18.	Discovery [Reserved]	
Chapter 19.	Trusts	7.901 – 7.903
Chapter 20.	Claims of Minors and Persons With Disabilities	7.950 – 7.955
Chapter 21.	Guardianships	7.1001 – 7.1020
Chapter 22.	Conservatorships	7.1050 – 7.1063
Chapter 23.	Appointed Counsel	7.1101 – 7.1105

Division 2. Mental Health Rules

Chapter 1.	[Reserved]	
Chapter 2.	CARE Act Rules	
Article 1.	Preliminary Provisions	7.2201 – 7.2210
Article 2.	Commencement of Proceedings	7.2221 – 7.2230
Article 3.	Notice and Joinder	7.2235, 7.2240
Article 4.	Accountability	7.2301, 7.2303

Title 8. Appellate Rules

Division 1. Rules Relating to the Supreme Court and Courts of Appeal

Chapter 1.	General Provisions	
Article 1.	In General	8.1 – 8.23
Article 2.	Service, Filing, Filing Fees, Form, and Privacy	8.25 – 8.44
Article 3.	Sealed and Confidential Records	8.45 – 8.47
Article 4.	Applications and Motions; Extending and Shortening Time	8.50 – 8.68
Article 5.	E-filing	8.70 – 8.79
Article 6.	Public Access to Electronic Appellate Court Records	8.80 – 8.85
Article 7.	Privacy	8.90
Chapter 2.	Civil Appeals	
Article 1.	Taking the Appeal	8.100 – 8.116

		Rules
Article 2.	Record on Appeal	8.120 – 8.163
Article 3.	Briefs in the Court of Appeal	8.200 – 8.224
Article 4.	Hearing and Decision in the Court of Appeal	8.240 – 8.278

Chapter 3. Criminal Appeals
- Article 1. Taking the Appeal ... 8.300 – 8.316
- Article 2. Record on Appeal ... 8.320 – 8.346
- Article 3. Briefs, Hearing, and Decision ... 8.360 – 8.368

Chapter 4. Habeas Corpus Appeals and Writs
- Article 1. Habeas Corpus Proceedings Not Related to Judgment of Death ... 8.380 – 8.388
- Article 2. Appeals From Superior Court Decisions in Death Penalty–Related Habeas Corpus Proceedings ... 8.390 – 8.398

Chapter 5. Juvenile Appeals and Writs
- Article 1. General Provisions ... 8.400, 8.401
- Article 2. Appeals ... 8.403 – 8.417
- Article 3. Writs ... 8.450 – 8.456
- Article 4. Hearing and Decision ... 8.470 – 8.474

Chapter 6. Conservatorship and Civil Commitment Appeals ... 8.480, 8.483

Chapter 7. Writs of Mandate, Certiorari, and Prohibition in the Supreme Court and Court of Appeal ... 8.485 – 8.493

Chapter 8. [Reserved]

Chapter 9. Proceedings in the Supreme Court ... 8.500 – 8.552

Division 2. Rules Relating to Death Penalty Appeals and Habeas Corpus Proceedings

Chapter 1. General Provisions ... 8.601

Chapter 2. Automatic Appeals From Judgments of Death
- Article 1. General Provisions ... 8.603, 8.605
- Article 2. Record on Appeal ... 8.608 – 8.622
- Article 3. Briefs, Hearing, and Decision ... 8.630 – 8.642

Chapter 3. Death Penalty–Related Habeas Corpus Proceedings ... 8.652

Division 3. Rules Relating to Miscellaneous Appeals and Writ Proceedings

Chapter 1. Review of California Environmental Quality Act Cases Involving Streamlined CEQA Projects ... 8.700 – 8.705

Chapter 2. Appeals Under Code of Civil Procedure Section 1294.4 From an Order Dismissing or Denying a Petition to Compel Arbitration ... 8.710 – 8.717

Chapter 3. Miscellaneous Writs ... 8.720 – 8.730

Division 4. Rules Relating to the Superior Court Appellate Division

Chapter 1. General Rules Applicable to Appellate Division Proceedings ... 8.800 – 8.819

Chapter 2. Appeals and Records in Limited Civil Cases
- Article 1. Taking Civil Appeals ... 8.820 – 8.825
- Article 2. Record in Civil Appeals ... 8.830 – 8.845

Chapter 3. Appeals and Records in Misdemeanor Cases
- Article 1. Taking Appeals in Misdemeanor Cases ... 8.850 – 8.855
- Article 2. Record in Misdemeanor Appeals ... 8.860 – 8.874

Chapter 4. Briefs, Hearing, and Decision in Limited Civil and Misdemeanor Appeals ... 8.880 – 8.891

Chapter 5. Appeals in Infraction Cases
- Article 1. Taking Appeals in Infraction Cases ... 8.900 – 8.904
- Article 2. Record in Infraction Appeals ... 8.910 – 8.924
- Article 3. Briefs, Hearing, and Decision in Infraction Appeals ... 8.925 – 8.929

Chapter 6. Writ Proceedings ... 8.930 – 8.936

Division 5. Rules Relating to Appeals and Writs in Small Claims Cases

Chapter 1. Trial of Small Claims Cases on Appeals ... 8.950 – 8.966

Chapter 2. Writ Petitions ... 8.970 – 8.977

Division 6. Transfer of Appellate Division Cases to the Court of Appeal ... 8.1000 – 8.1018

Division 7. Publication of Appellate Opinions ... 8.1100 – 8.1125

Title 9. Rules on Law Practice, Attorneys, and Judges

Division 1. General Provisions ... 9.0

Division 2. Attorney Admission and Disciplinary Proceedings and Review of State Bar Proceedings
- Chapter 1. General Provisions ... 9.1, 9.2
- Chapter 2. Attorney Admission ... 9.3 – 9.9.5
- Chapter 3. Attorney Disciplinary Proceedings ... 9.10 – 9.23
- Chapter 4. Legal Education ... 9.30, 9.31

Division 3. Legal Specialists ... 9.35

Division 4. Appearances and Practice by Individuals Who Are Not Licensees of the State Bar of California ... 9.40 – 9.49.1

		Rules
Division 5.	Censure, Removal, Retirement, or Private or Public Admonishment of Judges	9.60, 9.61
Division 6.	Judicial Ethics Opinions	9.80
Division 7.	State Bar Trustees	9.90

Title 10. Judicial Administration Rules

Division 1. Judicial Council
- Chapter 1. The Judicial Council and Internal Committees ... 10.1 – 10.22
- Chapter 2. Judicial Council Advisory Committees and Task Forces ... 10.30 – 10.70
- Chapter 3. Judicial Council Advisory Body Meetings ... 10.75
- Chapter 4. Judicial Council staff ... 10.80, 10.81

Division 2. Administration of the Judicial Branch
- Chapter 1. Budget and Fiscal Management ... 10.101 – 10.106
- Chapter 2. Court Security ... 10.172 – 10.174
- Chapter 3. Court Facilities ... 10.180 – 10.184
- Chapter 4. Management of Claims and Litigation ... 10.201 – 10.203
- Chapter 5. Management of Human Resources ... 10.350, 10.351
- Chapter 6. Court Technology, Information, and Automation ... 10.400
- Chapter 7. Minimum Education Requirements, Expectations, and Recommendations ... 10.451 – 10.493

Division 3. Judicial Administration Rules Applicable to All Courts ... 10.500 – 10.505

Division 4. Trial Court Administration
- Chapter 1. General Rules on Trial Court Management ... 10.601 – 10.630
- Chapter 2. Trial Court Management of Human Resources
  - Article 1. Trial Court Employee Labor Relations ... 10.650 – 10.660
  - Article 2. Other Human Resources Rules ... 10.670
- Chapter 3. Subordinate Judicial Officers ... 10.700 – 10.703
- Chapter 4. Referees [Reserved]
- Chapter 5. Temporary Judges ... 10.740 – 10.746
- Chapter 6. Court Interpreters ... 10.761, 10.762
- Chapter 7. Qualifications of Court Investigators, Probate Attorneys, and Probate Examiners ... 10.776, 10.777
- Chapter 8. Alternative Dispute Resolution Programs ... 10.780 – 10.783
- Chapter 9. Trial Court Budget and Fiscal Management ... 10.800 – 10.830
- Chapter 10. Trial Court Records Management ... 10.850 – 10.856
- Chapter 11. Trial Court Automation ... 10.870
- Chapter 12. Trial Court Management of Civil Cases ... 10.900 – 10.910
- Chapter 13. Trial Court Management of Criminal Cases ... 10.950 – 10.953
- Chapter 14. Management of Self-Help Centers ... 10.960
- Chapter 15. [Reports of Findings and Orders Affecting Voting Rights] ... 10.970

Division 5. Appellate Court Administration
- Chapter 1. Rules Relating to the Supreme Court and Courts of Appeal ... 10.1000 – 10.1030
- Chapter 2. Rules Relating to the Superior Court Appellate Division ... 10.1100 – 10.1108

Standards of Judicial Administration

Title 1.	Standards for All Courts [Reserved]	
Title 2.	Standards for Proceedings in the Trial Courts	2.1 – 2.30
Title 3.	Standards for Civil Cases	3.1 – 3.25
Title 4.	Standards for Criminal Cases	4.10 – 4.42
Title 5.	Standards for Cases Involving Children and Families	5.20 – 5.45
Title 6.	[Reserved]	
Title 7.	Standards for Probate Proceedings	7.10
Title 8.	Standards for the Appellate Courts	8.1
Title 9.	Standards on Law Practice, Attorneys, and Judges [Reserved]	
Title 10.	Standards for Judicial Administration	10.5 – 10.72

	Rules
Ethics Standards for Neutral Arbitrators in Contractual Arbitration	
Appendix A. Judicial Council Legal Forms List	
Appendix B. Liability Limits of a Parent or Guardian Having Custody and Control of a Minor for the Torts of a Minor	
Appendix C. Guidelines for the Operation of Family Law Information Centers and Family Law Facilitator Offices	
Appendix D. Judicial Council Governance Policies	
Appendix E. Guidelines for Determining Financial Eligibility for County Payment of the Cost of Counsel Appointed by the Court in Proceedings Under the Guardianship-Conservatorship Law	
Appendix F. Guidelines for the Juvenile Dependency Counsel Collections Program (JDCCP)	
Appendix G. Parliamentary Procedures for the Judicial Council of California	
Appendix H. Amount of Civil Penalty to Cure Alleged Violation of Proposition 65 for Failure to Provide Certain Warnings (Health & Saf. Code, § 25249.7(k))	
Appendix I. Emergency Rules Related to COVID-19	
California Supreme Court	
California Code of Judicial Ethics	
Supreme Court Committee on Judicial Ethics Opinions Internal Operating Rules and Procedures	
Supreme Court Rules Regarding Electronic Filing	1-13
Internal Operating Practices and Procedures of the California Supreme Court	
Supreme Court Policies Regarding Cases Arising From Judgments of Death	Policy Statements 1-4
Appendix to Supreme Court Policies Regarding Cases Arising From Judgments of Death Concerning Appointed Counsel's Duties	
Payment Guidelines for Appointed Counsel Representing Indigent Criminal Appellants in the California Supreme Court	
Guidelines for Fixed Fee Appointments, On Optional Basis, to Automatic Appeals and Related Habeas Corpus Proceedings in the California Supreme Court	
Guidelines for the Commission on Judicial Appointments	Guidelines 1-8
California Courts of Appeal	
Local Rules and Internal Operating Practices and Procedures of the Courts of Appeal	
First Appellate District	1-21; Internal Operating Practices and Procedures
Second Appellate District	1-9; Internal Operating Practices and Procedures
Third Appellate District	1-6; Internal Operating Practices and Procedures
Fourth Appellate District	1-5; Internal Operating Practices and Procedures, Div. One; Internal Operating Practices and Procedures, Div. Two; Internal Operating Practices and Procedures, Div. Three
Fifth Appellate District	1-8; Local Court Form; Internal Operating Practices and Procedures
Sixth Appellate District	1-4; Internal Operating Practices and Procedures

CALIFORNIA RULES OF COURT

[Approved June 30, 2006. Effective January 1, 2007.]

TITLE 1
Rules Applicable to All Courts

Chap. 1. Preliminary Rules. Rules 1.1–1.6.
Chap. 2. Timing and Holidays. Rules 1.10, 1.11.
Chap. 3. Service and Filing. Rules 1.20, 1.21.
Chap. 4. Judicial Council Forms. Rules 1.30–1.51.
Chap. 5. Accommodations. Rule 1.100.
Chap. 6. Public Access to Court Proceedings. Rule 1.150.
Chap. 7. Form and Format of Papers. Rules 1.200, 1.201.
Chap. 8. Language Access Services. Rule 1.300.

Chapter 1
Preliminary Rules

Rule 1.1. The California Rules of Court
Rule 1.2. Title
Rule 1.3. Authority
Rule 1.4. Contents of the rules
Rule 1.5. Construction of rules and standards
Rule 1.6. Definitions and use of terms

Rule 1.1. The California Rules of Court

These rules are entitled the California Rules of Court.
Rule 1.1 adopted effective January 1, 2007.

Rule 1.2. Title

The rules in this title of the California Rules of Court may be referred to as the Rules Applicable to All Courts.
Rule 1.2 adopted effective January 1, 2007.

Rule 1.3. Authority

The rules in the California Rules of Court are adopted by the Judicial Council of California under the authority of article VI, section 6, of the Constitution of the State of California, unless otherwise indicated. The rules in division 5 of title 8 and in title 9 were adopted by the Supreme Court.
Rule 1.3 amended effective January 1, 2008; adopted effective January 1, 2007.

Rule 1.4. Contents of the rules

(a) The titles
The California Rules of Court includes the following titles:
(1) Title 1. Rules Applicable to All Courts;
(2) Title 2. Trial Court Rules;
(3) Title 3. Civil Rules;
(4) Title 4. Criminal Rules;
(5) Title 5. Family and Juvenile Rules;
(6) Title 6. [Reserved];
(7) Title 7. Probate and Mental Health Rules;
(8) Title 8. Appellate Rules;
(9) Title 9. Rules on Law Practice, Attorneys, and Judges; and
(10) Title 10. Judicial Administration Rules.
(Subd (a) adopted effective January 1, 2007; amended effective September 1, 2023.)

(b) Standards of Judicial Administration
The California Rules of Court includes the Standards of Judicial Administration adopted by the Judicial Council.
(Subd (b) adopted effective January 1, 2007.)

(c) Ethics Standards for Neutral Arbitrators in Contractual Arbitrations
The California Rules of Court includes Ethics Standards for Neutral Arbitrators in Contractual Arbitrations adopted by the Judicial Council under the authority of Code of Civil Procedure section 1281.85.
(Subd (c) repealed and relettered effective January 1, 2008; adopted as subd (d) effective January 1, 2007.)

(d) The appendixes
The California Rules of Court includes the following appendixes:
(1) Appendix A. Judicial Council Legal Forms List;
(2) Appendix B. Liability Limits of a Parent or Guardian Having Custody and Control of a Minor for the Torts of a Minor;
(3) Appendix C. Guidelines for the Operation of Family Law Information Centers and Family Law Facilitator Offices;
(4) Appendix D. Judicial Council Governance Policies;
(5) Appendix E. Guidelines for Determining Financial Eligibility for County Payment of the Cost of Counsel Appointed by the Court in Proceedings Under the Guardianship-Conservatorship Law;
(6) Appendix F. Guidelines for the Juvenile Dependency Counsel Collections Program; and
(7) Appendix G. Parliamentary Procedures for the Judicial Council of California.
(Subd (d) amended effective February 26, 2013; adopted as subd (e) effective January 1, 2007; previously relettered effective January 1, 2008; previously amended effective August 14, 2009, and January 1, 2013.)
Rule 1.4 amended effective September 1, 2023; adopted effective January 1, 2007; previously amended effective January 1, 2008, August 14, 2009, January 1, 2013, and February 26, 2013.

Rule 1.5. Construction of rules and standards

(a) Construction
The rules and standards of the California Rules of Court must be liberally construed to ensure the just and speedy determination of the proceedings that they govern.
(Subd (a) adopted effective January 1, 2007.)

(b) Terminology
As used in the rules and standards:
(1) "Must" is mandatory;
(2) "May" is permissive;
(3) "May not" means not permitted to;
(4) "Will" expresses a future contingency or predicts action by a court or person in the ordinary course of events, but does not signify a mandatory duty; and
(5) "Should" expresses a preference or a nonbinding recommendation.
(Subd (b) adopted effective January 1, 2007.)

(c) Standards
Standards are guidelines or goals recommended by the Judicial Council. The nonbinding nature of standards is indicated by the use of "should" in the standards instead of the mandatory "must" used in the rules.
(Subd (c) adopted effective January 1, 2007.)

(d) Construction of additional terms
In the rules:
(1) Each tense (past, present, or future) includes the others;
(2) Each gender (masculine, feminine, or neuter) includes the others; and
(3) Each number (singular or plural) includes the other.
(Subd (d) adopted effective January 1, 2007.)
Rule 1.5 adopted effective January 1, 2007.

Rule 1.6. Definitions and use of terms

As used in the California Rules of Court, unless the context or subject matter otherwise requires:
(1) "Action" includes special proceeding.
(2) "Case" includes action or proceeding.
(3) "Civil case" means a case prosecuted by one party against another for the declaration, enforcement, or protection of a right or the redress or

prevention of a wrong. Civil cases include all cases except criminal cases and petitions for habeas corpus.

(4) "General civil case" means all civil cases except probate, guardianship, conservatorship, juvenile, and family law proceedings (including proceedings under divisions 6–9 of the Family Code, Uniform Parentage Act, Domestic Violence Prevention Act, and Uniform Interstate Family Support Act; freedom from parental custody and control proceedings; and adoption proceedings), small claims proceedings, unlawful detainer proceedings, and "other civil petitions" described in (5).

(5) "Civil petitions" that are not general civil cases include petitions to prevent civil harassment, elder abuse, and workplace violence; petitions for name change; election contest petitions; and petitions for relief from late claims.

(6) "Unlimited civil cases" and "limited civil cases" are defined in Code of Civil Procedure section 85 et seq.

(7) "Criminal case" means a proceeding by which a party charged with a public offense is accused and prosecuted for the offense.

(8) "Rule" means a rule of the California Rules of Court.

(9) "Local rule" means every rule, regulation, order, policy, form, or standard of general application adopted by a court to govern practice and procedure in that court or by a judge of the court to govern practice or procedure in that judge's courtroom.

(10) "Chief Justice" and "presiding justice" include the Acting Chief Justice and the acting presiding justice, respectively.

(11) "Presiding judge" includes the acting presiding judge or the judicial officer designated by the presiding judge.

(12) "Judge" includes, as applicable, a judge of the superior court, a commissioner, or a temporary judge.

(13) "Temporary judge" means an active or inactive member of the State Bar of California who, under article VI, section 21 of the California Constitution and these rules, serves or expects to serve as a judge once, sporadically, or regularly on a part-time basis under a separate court appointment for each period of service or each case heard.

(14) "Person" includes a corporation or other legal entity as well as a natural person.

(15) "Party" is a person appearing in an action. Parties include both self-represented persons and persons represented by an attorney of record. "Party," "plaintiff," "People of the State of California," "applicant," "petitioner," "defendant," "respondent," "other parent," or any other designation of a party includes the party's attorney of record.

(16) "Attorney" means a member of the State Bar of California.

(17) "Counsel" means an attorney.

(18) "Sheriff" includes marshal.

(19) "Service" means service in the manner prescribed by a statute or rule.

(20) "Memorandum" means a written document containing: a statement of facts; a concise statement of the law, evidence, and arguments relied on; and a discussion of the statutes, cases, rules, and other legal sources relied on in support of the position advanced.

(21) "Declaration" includes "affidavit."

(22) "California Courts Web Site" means the Web site established by the Judicial Council that includes news and information, reference materials, rules and forms, and a self-help center. The address is: www.courts.ca.gov.

Rule 1.6 amended effective January 1, 2014; adopted as rule 200.1 effective January 1, 2003; previously amended and renumbered effective January 1, 2007; previously amended effective July 1, 2007, July 1, 2008, and July 1, 2013.

Chapter 2
Timing and Holidays

Rule 1.10. Time for actions
Rule 1.11. Holiday falling on a Saturday or Sunday

Rule 1.10. Time for actions

(a) Computation of time

The time in which any act provided by these rules is to be performed is computed by excluding the first day and including the last, unless the last day is a Saturday, Sunday, or other legal holiday, and then it is also excluded.

(Subd (a) amended effective January 1, 2007.)

(b) Holidays

Unless otherwise provided by law, if the last day for the performance of any act that is required by these rules to be performed within a specific period of time falls on a Saturday, Sunday, or other legal holiday, the period is extended to and includes the next day that is not a holiday.

(Subd (b) amended effective January 1, 2007.)

(c) Extending or shortening time

Unless otherwise provided by law, the court may extend or shorten the time within which a party must perform any act under the rules.

(Subd (c) amended effective January 1, 2007.)

Rule 1.10 amended and renumbered effective January 1, 2007; adopted as rule 200.3 effective January 1, 2003.

Rule 1.11. Holiday falling on a Saturday or Sunday

When a judicial holiday specified by Code of Civil Procedure section 135 falls on a Saturday, the courts must observe the holiday on the preceding Friday. When a judicial holiday specified by Code of Civil Procedure section 135 falls on a Sunday, the courts must observe the holiday on the following Monday.

Rule 1.11 amended and renumbered effective January 1, 2007; adopted as rule 987 effective January 1, 1986, operative January 1, 1989.

Chapter 3
Service and Filing

Rule 1.20. Effective Date of Filing
Rule 1.21. Service

Rule 1.20. Effective Date of Filing

Unless otherwise provided, a document is deemed filed on the date it is received by the court clerk.

Rule 1.20 amended effective January 1, 2017; adopted effective January 1, 2007; previously amended effective January 1, 2008.

Rule 1.21. Service

(a) Service on a party or attorney

Whenever a document is required to be served on a party, the service must be made on the party's attorney if the party is represented.

(Subd (a) amended effective January 1, 2007.)

(b) "Serve and file"

As used in these rules, unless a statute or rule provides for a different method for filing or service, a requirement to "serve and file" a document means that a copy of the document must be served on the attorney for each party separately represented, on each self-represented party, and on any other person or entity when required by statute, rule, or court order, and that the document and a proof of service of the document must be filed with the court.

(Subd (b) amended effective January 1, 2007.)

(c) "Proof of service"

As used in these rules, "proof of service" means a declaration stating that service has been made as provided in (a) and (b). If the proof of service names attorneys for separately represented parties, it must also state which party or parties each of the attorneys served is representing.

(Subd (c) adopted effective January 1, 2007.)

Rule 1.21 amended effective January 1, 2007; adopted effective January 1, 2007.

Rule 1.22. Recycled paper [Repealed]

Rule 1.22 repealed effective January 1, 2014; adopted effective January 1, 2007.

Chapter 4
Judicial Council Forms

Rule 1.30. Judicial Council forms
Rule 1.31. Mandatory forms
Rule 1.35. Optional forms
Rule 1.37. Use of forms
Rule 1.40. Statutory references on forms
Rule 1.41. Proofs of service on forms
Rule 1.42. Forms not to be rejected
Rule 1.43. Legibility
Rule 1.44. Electronically produced forms
Rule 1.45. Judicial Council pleading forms
Rule 1.51. California Law Enforcement Telecommunications System (CLETS) information form

Rule 1.30. Judicial Council forms

(a) Application

The rules in this chapter apply to Judicial Council forms.

(Subd (a) adopted effective January 1, 2007.)

(b) Mandatory or optional forms

Judicial Council forms are either mandatory or optional.

(Subd (b) relettered effective January 1, 2007; adopted as subd (a) effective January 1, 2003.)

Rule 1.30 amended and renumbered effective January 1, 2007; adopted as rule 982 effective November 10, 1969; previously amended effective November 23, 1969, July 1, 1970, November 23, 1970, January 1, 1971, January 1, 1972, March 4, 1972, July 1, 1972, March 7, 1973, January 1, 1975, July 1, 1975, July 1, 1976, January 1, 1977, July 1, 1977, January 1, 1978, October 1, 1978, January 1, 1979, July 1, 1980, January 1, 1981, July 1, 1983, July 1, 1988, January 1, 1997, and January 1, 2006; amended and renumbered as rule 201.1 effective January 1, 2003.

Rule 1.31. Mandatory forms

(a) Use of mandatory forms and acceptance for filing

Forms adopted by the Judicial Council for mandatory use are forms prescribed under Government Code section 68511. Wherever applicable, they must be used by all parties and must be accepted for filing by all courts. In some areas, alternative mandatory forms have been adopted.

(Subd (a) adopted effective January 1, 2007.)

(b) List of mandatory forms

Each mandatory Judicial Council form is identified as mandatory by an asterisk (*) on the list of Judicial Council forms in Appendix A to the California Rules of Court. The list is available on the California Courts website at www.courts.ca.gov/forms.

(Subd (b) amended effective January 1, 2015; adopted effective January 1, 2007.)

(c) Identification of mandatory forms

Forms adopted by the Judicial Council for mandatory use bear the words "Form Adopted for Mandatory Use," "Mandatory Form," or "Form Adopted for Alternative Mandatory Use" in the lower left corner of the first page.

(Subd (c) adopted effective January 1, 2007.)

(d) Words on forms

Publishers and courts reprinting a mandatory Judicial Council form in effect before July 1, 1999, must add the words "Mandatory Form" to the bottom of the first page.

(Subd (d) adopted effective January 1, 2007.)

(e) No alteration of forms

Except as provided in rule 3.52(6), concerning court fee waiver orders, and rule 5.504, concerning court orders in juvenile court proceedings, courts may not require the use of an altered mandatory Judicial Council form in place of the Judicial Council form. However, a judicial officer may modify a Judicial Council form order as necessary or appropriate to adjudicate a particular case.

(Subd (e) amended effective September 1, 2017; adopted effective January 1, 2007; previously amended effective January 1, 2007, January 1, 2009, and July 1, 2009.)

(f) No colored forms

Courts may not require that any mandatory Judicial Council form be submitted on any color of paper other than white.

(Subd (f) adopted effective January 1, 2007.)

(g) Orders not on mandatory forms

An otherwise legally sufficient court order for which there is a mandatory Judicial Council form is not invalid or unenforceable because the order is not prepared on a Judicial Council form or the correct Judicial Council form.

(Subd (g) adopted effective January 1, 2007.)

Rule 1.31 amended effective September 1, 2017; adopted effective January 1, 2007; previously amended effective January 1, 2007, January 1, 2009, July 1, 2009, and January 1, 2015.

Rule 1.35. Optional forms

(a) Use of optional forms and acceptance for filing

Forms approved by the Judicial Council for optional use, wherever applicable, may be used by parties and must be accepted for filing by all courts.

(Subd (a) adopted effective January 1, 2007.)

(b) List of optional forms

Each optional Judicial Council form appears without an asterisk (*) on the list of Judicial Council forms in Appendix A to the California Rules of Court. The list is available on the California Courts website at www.courts.ca.gov/forms.

(Subd (b) amended effective January 1, 2015; adopted effective January 1, 2007.)

(c) Identification of optional forms

Forms approved by the Judicial Council for optional use bear the words "Form Approved for Optional Use" or "Optional Form" in the lower left corner of the first page.

(Subd (c) adopted effective January 1, 2007.)

(d) Words on forms

Publishers and courts reprinting an optional Judicial Council form in effect before July 1, 1999, must add the words "Optional Form" to the bottom of the first page.

(Subd (d) adopted effective January 1, 2007.)

(e) No alteration of forms

Courts may not require the use of an altered optional Judicial Council form in place of the Judicial Council form. However, a judicial officer may modify a Judicial Council form order as necessary or appropriate to adjudicate a particular case.

(Subd (e) amended effective January 1, 2009; adopted effective January 1, 2007.)

(f) No colored forms

Courts may not require that any optional Judicial Council form be submitted on any color of paper other than white.

(Subd (f) adopted effective January 1, 2007.)

Rule 1.35 amended effective January 1, 2015; adopted effective January 1, 2007; previously amended effective January 1, 2009.

Rule 1.37. Use of forms

A person serving and filing a Judicial Council form must use the current version of the form adopted or approved by the council, unless a rule in the California Rules of Court allows the use of a different form.

Rule 1.37 adopted effective January 1, 2007.

Rule 1.40. Statutory references on forms

The references to statutes and rules at the bottom of Judicial Council forms are advisory only. The presence or absence of a particular reference is not a ground for rejecting a form otherwise applicable in the action or proceeding for the purpose presented.

Rule 1.40 adopted effective January 1, 2007.

Rule 1.41. Proofs of service on forms

Proofs of service are included on some Judicial Council forms solely for the convenience of the parties. A party may use an included proof of service or any other proper proof of service.

Rule 1.41 adopted effective January 1, 2007.

Rule 1.42. Forms not to be rejected

A court must not reject for filing a Judicial Council form for any of the following reasons:

(1) The form lacks the preprinted title and address of the court;

(2) The form lacks the name of the clerk;

(3) The preprinted title and address of another court or its clerk's name is legibly modified;

(4) The form lacks the court's local form number;

(5) The form lacks any other material added by a court, unless the material is required by the Judicial Council;

(6) The form is printed by a publisher or another court;

(7) The form is imprinted with the name or symbol of the publisher, unless the name or symbol replaces or obscures any material on the printed form;

(8) The form is legibly and obviously modified to correct a code section number or to comply with the law under which the form is filed; or

(9) The form is not the latest version of the form adopted or approved by the Judicial Council.

Rule 1.42 amended effective January 1, 2007; adopted effective January 1, 2007.

Rule 1.43. Legibility

A Judicial Council form filed must be a true copy of the original form and must be as legible as a printed form.

Rule 1.43 adopted effective January 1, 2007.

Rule 1.44. Electronically produced forms

A party or attorney may file a duplicate of a Judicial Council form produced by a computer and a printer or similar device with a resolution of at least 300 dots per inch.

Rule 1.44 adopted effective January 1, 2007.

Rule 1.45. Judicial Council pleading forms

(a) Pleading forms

The forms listed under the "Pleading" heading on the list of Judicial Council forms in Appendix A to the California Rules of Court are approved by the Judicial Council.

(Subd (a) amended effective July 1, 2008; previously amended effective July 1, 1999, January 1, 2005, and January 1, 2007.)

(b) Cause of action forms

Any approved cause of action form may be attached to any approved form of complaint or cross-complaint.

(Subd (b) adopted effective January 1, 1982.)

(c) Other causes of action

A cause of action for which no form has been approved may be prepared in the format prescribed by the rules in chapter 1 of division 2 of title 2 and attached to any approved form of complaint or cross-complaint. Each paragraph within a cause of action must be numbered consecutively beginning with one. Each paragraph number must be preceded with one or more identifying letters derived from the title of the cause of action.

(Subd (c) amended effective January 1, 2007; adopted effective January 1, 1982; previously amended effective January 1, 2003.)

Rule 1.45 amended effective July 1, 2008; adopted as rule 982.1 effective January 1, 1982; previously amended effective July 1, 1995, July 1, 1996, January 1, 1997, July 1, 1999, and January 1, 2005; previously amended and renumbered as rule 201.2 effective January 1, 2003; previously amended and renumbered effective January 1, 2007.

Rule 1.51. California Law Enforcement Telecommunications System (CLETS) information form

(a) *Confidential CLETS Information* **form to be submitted to the court**

A person requesting protective orders under Code of Civil Procedure section 527.6, 527.8, or 527.85; Family Code section 6320, 6404, or 6454; Penal Code sections 18100–18205; or Welfare and Institutions Code section 213.5 or 15657.03 must submit to the court with the request a completed *Confidential CLETS Information* form.

(Subd (a) amended effective January 1, 2019; adopted effective January 1, 2011.)

(b) Confidentiality of the form

The *Confidential CLETS Information* form is confidential, and access to the information on the form is limited to the persons listed in (c).

(Subd (b) adopted effective January 1, 2011.)

(c) Access to information on the form

The *Confidential CLETS Information* form must not be included in the court file. After the form is submitted to the court, only the following persons may have access to the information on the form:

(1) Authorized court personnel; and

(2) Law enforcement and other personnel authorized by the California Department of Justice to transmit or receive CLETS information.

(Subd (c) adopted effective January 1, 2011.)

(d) Amendment of the form

A person requesting protective orders or the person's attorney may submit an amended *Confidential CLETS Information* form as a matter of right to provide updated or more complete and accurate information.

(Subd (d) adopted effective January 1, 2011.)

(e) Retention and destruction of the form

(1) When a *Confidential CLETS Information* form is submitted to the court, the court, if a temporary restraining order or order after hearing is entered, may:

(A) Transmit the form to a law enforcement agency for entry into CLETS and not retain any copy; or

(B) Enter the information on the form into CLETS itself and promptly destroy the form or delete it from its records.

(2) If no temporary restraining order or order after hearing is entered, the court may promptly destroy the form or delete it from its records.

(3) Until the court has completed (1) or (2), the form must be retained in a secure manner that prevents access to the information on the form except to those persons identified in (c).

(Subd (e) adopted effective January 1, 2011.)

Rule 1.51 amended effective January 1, 2019; adopted effective January 1, 2011.

Chapter 5
Accommodations

Rule 1.100. Requests for accommodations by persons with disabilities

(a) Definitions

As used in this rule:

(1) "Persons with disabilities" means individuals covered by California Civil Code section 51 et seq.; the Americans With Disabilities Act of 1990 (42 U.S.C. §12101 et seq.); or other applicable state and federal laws. This definition includes persons who have a physical or mental medical condition that limits one or more of the major life activities, have a record of such a condition, or are regarded as having such a condition.

(2) "Applicant" means any lawyer, party, witness, juror, or other person with an interest in attending any proceeding before any court of this state.

(3) "Accommodations" means actions that result in court services, programs, or activities being readily accessible to and usable by persons with disabilities. Accommodations may include making reasonable modifications in policies, practices, and procedures; furnishing, at no charge, to persons with disabilities, auxiliary aids and services, equipment, devices, materials in alternative formats, readers, or certified interpreters for persons who are deaf or hard-of-hearing; relocating services or programs to accessible facilities; or providing services at alternative sites. Although not required where other actions are effective in providing access to court services, programs, or activities, alteration of existing facilities by the responsible entity may be an accommodation.

(Subd (a) amended effective July 1, 2017; adopted as subd (b) effective January 1, 1996; previously amended effective January 1, 2006; previously amended and relettered effective January 1, 2007.)

(b) Policy

It is the policy of the courts of this state to ensure that persons with disabilities have equal and full access to the judicial system. To ensure access to the courts for persons with disabilities, each superior and appellate court must delegate at least one person to be the ADA coordinator, also known as the access coordinator, or designee to address requests for accommodations. This rule is not intended to impose limitations or to invalidate the remedies, rights, and procedures accorded to persons with disabilities under state or federal law.

(Subd (b) adopted effective January 1, 2007.)

(c) Process for requesting accommodations

The process for requesting accommodations is as follows:

(1) Requests for accommodations under this rule may be presented ex parte on a form approved by the Judicial Council, in another written format, or orally. Requests must be forwarded to the ADA coordinator, also known as the access coordinator, or designee, within the time frame provided in (c)(3).

(2) Requests for accommodations must include a description of the accommodation sought, along with a statement of the medical condition that necessitates the accommodation. The court, in its discretion, may require the applicant to provide additional information about the medical condition.

(3) Requests for accommodations must be made as far in advance as possible, and in any event must be made no fewer than 5 court days before the requested implementation date. The court may, in its discretion, waive this requirement.

(4) The court must keep confidential all information of the applicant concerning the request for accommodation, unless confidentiality is waived in writing by the applicant or disclosure is required by law. The applicant's identity and confidential information may not be disclosed to the public or to persons other than those involved in the accommodation process. Confidential information includes all medical information pertaining to the applicant, and all oral or written communication from the applicant concerning the request for accommodation.

(Subd (c) amended effective July 1, 2017; previously amended effective January 1, 2006, and January 1, 2007.)

(d) Permitted communication

Communications under this rule must address only the accommodation requested by the applicant and must not address, in any manner, the subject matter or merits of the proceedings before the court.

(Subd (d) amended effective January 1, 2006.)

(e) Response to accommodation request

The court must respond to a request for accommodation as follows:

(1) In determining whether to grant an accommodation request or provide an appropriate alternative accommodation, the court must consider, but is not limited by, California Civil Code section 51 et seq., the provisions of the Americans With Disabilities Act of 1990 (42 U.S.C. § 12101, et seq.), and other applicable state and federal laws.

(2) The court must promptly inform the applicant of the determination to grant or deny an accommodation request. If the accommodation request is denied in whole or in part, the response must be in writing. On request of the applicant, the court may also provide an additional response in an alternative format. The response to the applicant must indicate:

(A) Whether the request for accommodation is granted or denied, in whole or in part, or an alternative accommodation is granted;

(B) If the request for accommodation is denied, in whole or in part, the reason therefor;

(C) The nature of any accommodation to be provided;

(D) The duration of any accommodation to be provided; and

(E) If the response is in writing, the date the response was delivered in person or sent to the applicant.

(Subd (e) amended effective January 1, 2010; previously amended effective January 1, 2006, and January 1, 2007.)

(f) Denial of accommodation request

A request for accommodation may be denied only when the court determines that:

(1) The applicant has failed to satisfy the requirements of this rule;

(2) The requested accommodation would create an undue financial or administrative burden on the court; or

(3) The requested accommodation would fundamentally alter the nature of the service, program, or activity.

(Subd (f) amended effective January 1, 2007; previously amended effective January 1, 2006.)

(g) Review procedure

(1) If the determination to grant or deny a request for accommodation is made by nonjudicial court personnel, an applicant or any participant in the proceeding may submit a written request for review of that determination to the presiding judge or designated judicial officer. The request for review must be submitted within 10 days of the date the response under (e)(2) was delivered in person or sent.

(2) If the determination to grant or deny a request for accommodation is made by a presiding judge or another judicial officer, an applicant or any participant in the proceeding may file a petition for a writ of mandate under rules 8.485–8.493 or 8.930–8.936 in the appropriate reviewing court. The petition must be filed within 10 days of the date the response under (e)(2) was delivered in person or sent to the petitioner. For purposes of this rule, only those participants in the proceeding who were notified by the court of the determination to grant or deny the request for accommodation are considered real parties in interest in a writ proceeding. The petition for the writ must be served on the respondent court and any real party in interest as defined in this rule.

(3) The confidentiality of all information of the applicant concerning the request for accommodation and review under (g)(1) or (2) must be maintained as required under (c)(4).

(Subd (g) amended effective January 1, 2010; previously amended effective January 1, 2006.)

(h) Duration of accommodations

The accommodation by the court must be provided for the duration indicated in the response to the request for accommodation and must remain in effect for the period specified. The court may provide an accommodation for an indefinite period of time, for a limited period of time, or for a particular matter or appearance.

(Subd (h) amended effective January 1, 2006.)

Rule 1.100 amended effective July 1, 2017; adopted as rule 989.3 effective January 1, 1996; previously amended effective January 1, 2006, and January 1, 2010; previously amended and renumbered effective January 1, 2007.

Advisory Committee Comment

Subdivision (g)(2). Which court is the "appropriate reviewing court" under this rule depends on the court in which the accommodation decision is made and the nature of the underlying case. If the accommodation decision is made by a superior court judicial officer and the underlying case is a limited civil, misdemeanor, or infraction case, the appropriate reviewing court is the appellate division of the superior court. If the accommodation decision is made by a superior court judicial officer and the case is anything other than a limited civil, misdemeanor, or infraction case, such as a family law, unlimited civil, or felony case, the appropriate reviewing court is the Court of Appeal. If the accommodation decision is made by a judicial officer of the Court of Appeal, the appropriate reviewing court is the California Supreme Court.

Chapter 6
Public Access to Court Proceedings

Rule 1.150. Photographing, recording, and broadcasting in court

(a) Introduction

The judiciary is responsible for ensuring the fair and equal administration of justice. The judiciary adjudicates controversies, both civil and criminal, in accordance with established legal procedures in the calmness and solemnity of the courtroom. Photographing, recording, and broadcasting of courtroom proceedings may be permitted as circumscribed in this rule if executed in a manner that ensures that the fairness and dignity of the proceedings are not adversely affected. This rule does not create a presumption for or against granting permission to photograph, record, or broadcast court proceedings.

(Subd (a) adopted effective January 1, 1997.)

(b) Definitions

As used in this rule:

(1) "Media coverage" means any photographing, recording, or broadcasting of court proceedings by the media using television, radio, photographic, or recording equipment.

(2) "Media" or "media agency" means any person or organization engaging in news gathering or reporting and includes any newspaper, radio or television station or network, news service, magazine, trade paper, in-house publication, professional journal, or other news-reporting or news-gathering agency.

(3) "Court" means the courtroom at issue, the courthouse, and its entrances and exits.

(4) "Judge" means the judicial officer or officers assigned to or presiding at the proceeding, except as provided in (e)(1) if no judge has been assigned.

(5) "Photographing" means recording a likeness, regardless of the method used, including by digital or photographic methods. As used in this rule, photographing does not include drawings or sketchings of the court proceedings.

(6) "Recording" means the use of any analog or digital device to aurally or visually preserve court proceedings. As used in this rule, recording does not include handwritten notes on the court record, whether by court reporter or by digital or analog preservation.

(7) "Broadcasting" means a visual or aural transmission or signal, by any method, of the court proceedings, including any electronic transmission or transmission by sound waves.

(Subd (b) amended effective January 1, 2007; adopted as subd (a) effective July 1, 1984; previously amended and relettered as subd (b) effective January 1, 1997; previously amended effective January 1, 2006.)

(c) Photographing, recording, and broadcasting prohibited

Except as provided in this rule, court proceedings may not be photographed, recorded, or broadcast. This rule does not prohibit courts from photographing or videotaping sessions for judicial education or publications and is not intended to apply to closed-circuit television broadcasts solely within the courthouse or between court facilities if the broadcasts are controlled by the court and court personnel.

(Subd (c) amended effective January 1, 2006; adopted effective January 1, 1997.)

(d) Personal recording devices

The judge may permit inconspicuous personal recording devices to be used by persons in a courtroom to make sound recordings as personal notes of the proceedings. A person proposing to use a recording device must obtain advance permission from the judge. The recordings must not be used for any purpose other than as personal notes.

(Subd (d) amended effective January 1, 2007; adopted as subd (c) effective July 1, 1984; previously amended and relettered as subd (d) effective January 1, 1997; previously amended effective January 1, 2006.)

(e) Media coverage

Media coverage may be permitted only on written order of the judge as provided in this subdivision. The judge in his or her discretion may permit, refuse, limit, or terminate media coverage. This rule does not otherwise limit or restrict the right of the media to cover and report court proceedings.

(1) Request for order

The media may request an order on *Media Request to Photograph, Record, or Broadcast* (form MC-500). The form must be filed at least five court days before the portion of the proceeding to be covered unless good cause is shown. A completed, proposed order on *Order on Media Request to Permit Coverage* (form MC-510) must be filed with the request. The judge assigned to the proceeding must rule on the request. If no judge has been assigned, the request will be submitted to the judge supervising the calendar department, and thereafter be ruled on by the judge assigned to the proceeding. The clerk must promptly notify the parties that a request has been filed.

(2) Hearing on request

The judge may hold a hearing on the request or may rule on the request without a hearing.

(3) *Factors to be considered by the judge*

In ruling on the request, the judge is to consider the following factors:

(A) The importance of maintaining public trust and confidence in the judicial system;

(B) The importance of promoting public access to the judicial system;

(C) The parties' support of or opposition to the request;

(D) The nature of the case;

(E) The privacy rights of all participants in the proceeding, including witnesses, jurors, and victims;

(F) The effect on any minor who is a party, prospective witness, victim, or other participant in the proceeding;

(G) The effect on the parties' ability to select a fair and unbiased jury;

(H) The effect on any ongoing law enforcement activity in the case;

(I) The effect on any unresolved identification issues;

(J) The effect on any subsequent proceedings in the case;

(K) The effect of coverage on the willingness of witnesses to cooperate, including the risk that coverage will engender threats to the health or safety of any witness;

(L) The effect on excluded witnesses who would have access to the televised testimony of prior witnesses;

(M) The scope of the coverage and whether partial coverage might unfairly influence or distract the jury;

(N) The difficulty of jury selection if a mistrial is declared;

(O) The security and dignity of the court;

(P) Undue administrative or financial burden to the court or participants;

(Q) The interference with neighboring courtrooms;

(R) The maintenance of the orderly conduct of the proceeding; and

(S) Any other factor the judge deems relevant.

(4) *Order permitting media coverage*

The judge ruling on the request to permit media coverage is not required to make findings or a statement of decision. The order may incorporate any local rule or order of the presiding or supervising judge regulating media activity outside of the courtroom. The judge may condition the order permitting media coverage on the media agency's agreement to pay any increased court-incurred costs resulting from the permitted media coverage (for example, for additional court security or utility service). Each media agency is responsible for ensuring that all its media personnel who cover the court proceeding know and follow the provisions of the court order and this rule.

(5) *Modified order*

The order permitting media coverage may be modified or terminated on the judge's own motion or on application to the judge without the necessity of a prior hearing or written findings. Notice of the application and any modification or termination ordered under the application must be given to the parties and each media agency permitted by the previous order to cover the proceeding.

(6) *Prohibited coverage*

The judge may not permit media coverage of the following:

(A) Proceedings held in chambers;

(B) Proceedings closed to the public;

(C) Jury selection;

(D) Jurors or spectators; or

(E) Conferences between an attorney and a client, witness, or aide; between attorneys; or between counsel and the judge at the bench.

(7) *Equipment and personnel*

The judge may require media agencies to demonstrate that proposed personnel and equipment comply with this rule. The judge may specify the placement of media personnel and equipment to permit reasonable media coverage without disruption of the proceedings.

(8) *Normal requirements for media coverage of proceedings*

Unless the judge in his or her discretion orders otherwise, the following requirements apply to media coverage of court proceedings:

(A) One television camera and one still photographer will be permitted.

(B) The equipment used may not produce distracting sound or light. Signal lights or devices to show when equipment is operating may not be visible.

(C) An order permitting or requiring modification of existing sound or lighting systems is deemed to require that the modifications be installed, maintained, and removed without public expense or disruption of proceedings.

(D) Microphones and wiring must be unobtrusively located in places approved by the judge and must be operated by one person.

(E) Operators may not move equipment or enter or leave the courtroom while the court is in session, or otherwise cause a distraction.

(F) Equipment or clothing must not bear the insignia or marking of a media agency.

(9) *Media pooling*

If two or more media agencies of the same type request media coverage of a proceeding, they must file a joint statement of agreed arrangements. If they are unable to agree, the judge may deny media coverage by that type of media agency.

(Subd (e) amended effective January 1, 2007; adopted as subd (b) effective July 1, 1984; previously amended and relettered as subd (e) effective January 1, 1997; previously amended effective January 1, 2006.)

(f) Sanctions

Any violation of this rule or an order made under this rule is an unlawful interference with the proceedings of the court and may be the basis for an order terminating media coverage, a citation for contempt of court, or an order imposing monetary or other sanctions as provided by law.

(Subd (f) amended and relettered as subd (f) effective January 1, 1997; adopted as subd (e) effective July 1, 1984.)

Rule 1.150 amended and renumbered effective January 1, 2007; adopted as rule 980 effective July 1, 1984; previously amended effective January 1, 1997, and January 1, 2006.)

Chapter 7
Form and Format of Papers

Chapter 7 adopted effective January 1, 2008.

Rule 1.200. Format of citations
Rule 1.201. Protection of privacy

Rule 1.200. Format of citations

Citations to cases and other authorities in all documents filed in the courts must be in the style established by either the *California Style Manual* or *The Bluebook: A Uniform System of Citation*, at the option of the party filing the document. The same style must be used consistently throughout the document.

Rule 1.200 adopted effective January 1, 2008.

Rule 1.201. Protection of privacy

(a) Exclusion or redaction of identifiers

To protect personal privacy and other legitimate interests, parties and their attorneys must not include, or must redact where inclusion is necessary, the following identifiers from all pleadings and other papers filed in the court's public file, whether filed in paper or electronic form, unless otherwise provided by law or ordered by the court:

(1) Social security numbers. If an individual's social security number is required in a pleading or other paper filed in the public file, only the last four digits of that number may be used.

(2) Financial account numbers. If financial account numbers are required in a pleading or other paper filed in the public file, only the last four digits of these numbers may be used.

(Subd (a) adopted effective January 1, 2017.)

(b) Responsibility of the filer

The responsibility for excluding or redacting identifiers identified in (a) from all documents filed with the court rests solely with the parties and their attorneys. The court clerk will not review each pleading or other paper for compliance with this provision.

(Subd (b) adopted effective January 1, 2017.)

(c) Confidential reference list

If the court orders on a showing of good cause, a party filing a document containing identifiers listed in (a) may file, along with the redacted document that will be placed in the public file, a reference list. The reference list is confidential. A party filing a confidential reference list must use *Confidential Reference List of Identifiers* (form MC-120) for that purpose. The confidential list must identify each item of redacted information and specify an appropriate reference that uniquely corresponds to each item of redacted information listed. All references in the case to the redacted identifiers included in the confidential reference list will be understood to refer to the corresponding complete identifier. A party may amend its reference list as of right.

(Subd (c) adopted effective January 1, 2017.)

(d) Scope

The requirements of this rule do not apply to documents or records that by court order or operation of law are filed in their entirety either confidentially or under seal.

(Subd (d) adopted effective January 1, 2017.)
Rule 1.201 adopted effective January 1, 2017.

Chapter 8
Language Access Services

Chapter 8 adopted effective September 1, 2019.

Rule 1.300. Access to programs, services, and professionals

(a) Definitions

As used in this chapter, unless the context or subject matter otherwise requires, the following definitions apply:

(1) "Court-provided programs, services, and professionals" are services offered and provided by court employees or by contractors or vendors under agreement with the court.

(2) "Court litigant" is a person who is a party in a court case or other legal proceeding.

(3) "Language services" are services designed to provide access to the legal system to limited English proficient court litigants and may include in-person interpretation, telephonic interpreter services, video remote interpreting services, and services provided by assigned bilingual employees and bilingual volunteers.

(4) "Limited English proficient" describes a person who speaks English "less than very well" and who, as a result, cannot understand or participate in a court proceeding.

(5) "Private programs, services, and professionals" are services provided by outside agencies, organizations, and persons that court litigants may be required to access by court order.

(Subd (a) adopted effective September 1, 2019.)

(b) Provision of language services in court-ordered and court-provided programs, services, and professionals

As soon as feasible, each court must adopt procedures to enable limited English proficient court litigants to access court-ordered and court-provided programs, services, and professionals to the same extent as persons who are proficient in English.

(Subd (b) adopted effective September 1, 2019.)

(c) Provision of language services in private programs and services, and by private professionals

To the extent feasible, a court should avoid ordering a limited English proficient court litigant to a private program, service, or professional that is not language accessible.

(Subd (c) adopted effective September 1, 2019.)

(d) Delay in access to services

If a limited English proficient court litigant is unable to access a private program, service, or professional within the time period ordered by the court due to limitations in language service availability, the court litigant may submit a statement to the court indicating the reason for the delay, and the court may, for good cause, enter an alternative order or extend the time for completion. Court litigants may use *Service Not Available in My Language: Request to Change Court Order* (form LA-400) for this purpose. The court may respond to the request using *Service Not Available in My Language: Order* (form LA-450).

(Subd (d) adopted effective September 1, 2019.)

(e) Use of technology

Courts should seek out opportunities to collaborate with each other and with community partners in the provision of language services, and should employ technology to promote the sharing of bilingual staff and certified and registered court interpreters among courts, as appropriate.

(Subd (e) adopted effective September 1, 2019.)
Rule 1.300 adopted effective September 1, 2019.

Advisory Committee Comment

Subdivision (b). The goal of this rule is to connect limited English proficient court litigants ordered by courts to access programs or professionals with services in the languages spoken by the litigants. Recognizing that not all program providers will be willing or able to meet the language needs, the rule is intended to help courts become aware of those language services available in the community so that limited English proficient court litigants are not placed in a position where they are unable to comply with court orders because the required services are not available in a language they understand.

To facilitate equal access to justice, when courts order limited English proficient litigants to access court-provided programs, services, and professionals, to the greatest extent possible, courts should ensure that the services are language accessible.

To the extent feasible and as permitted by law, any memorandum of understanding or other written agreement for agency-referred programs, services, and professionals that trial courts enter into or amend after the implementation date of this rule should include the goals of providing language services in the languages spoken by limited English proficient court users and of notifying the court if the language needs of a limited English proficient court litigant referred to the program, service, or professional cannot be accommodated.

Subdivision (c). Courts are encouraged to offer neutral, nonendorsing information about private programs, services, and professionals providing multilingual services or language assistance to enable limited English proficient court litigants to access their programs. Private programs, services, and professionals that would like to be included on a court's informational list may confirm in writing to the court annually that they offer language services, indicating the languages covered by the program, service, or professional. Courts may require providers to use *Notice of Available Language Assistance—Service Provider* (form LA-350) for this purpose.

Subdivision (d). When a defendant is required to participate in a batterer intervention program under section 1203.097(a)(6) of the California Penal Code, the court may order "another appropriate counseling program" if a batterer's program is unavailable in the language spoken by the court litigant. In addition, a judge may, for good cause, excuse the requirement to complete the 52-week program within 18 months. The application of a similar standard to all orders to participate in noncourtroom services, whereby the unavailability of language assistance would constitute good cause to make an alternative order or to excuse delay in completion, would provide the court with flexibility to address situations in which a program or service is unavailable in the language spoken by a limited English proficient court user.

Two optional forms, *Service Not Available in My Language: Request to Change Court Order* (form LA-400) and *Service Not Available in My Language: Order* (form LA-450), were developed to facilitate communication between the court and a limited English proficient court litigant who is unable to comply with a court order because of a lack of language assistance.

Form LA-400 allows the court litigant to notify the court of the unavailability of language assistance in a court-ordered program and to request a modified order or an extension of the time for completion of the program. Form LA-450 allows the court to issue a modified order or to extend the time for completion of a court-ordered program or service. A request may be denied if the court receives information that a program is available in the language of the court litigant or that language assistance is available to help the court litigant access the program, and that the program or service may be accessed within the time mandated by the court for completion. If a request is denied on this basis, the court should provide contact information that will allow the court litigant to access the program. In addition, a request may be denied if the court finds there is good cause to believe that the request was brought for an improper purpose or that the court litigant knowingly provided false information on form LA-400.

Subdivision (e). It is the policy of the California courts to encourage the efficient and effective use of human and technological resources in the provision of language services while ensuring meaningful access for limited English proficient court users. For noncourtroom interpretation events, courts may consult the report, *Technological Options for Providing and Sharing Court Language Access Services Outside the Courtroom* (January 2018) for opportunities to collaborate with other courts and service providers to enhance language access for LEP court users.

TITLE 2
Trial Court Rules

Division 1. General Provisions. Rules 2.1–2.30.
Division 2. Papers and Forms to Be Filed. Rules 2.100–2.150.
Division 3. Filing and Service. Rules 2.200–2.306.
Division 4. Court Records. Rules 2.400–2.585.
Division 5. Venue and Sessions. Rule 2.700.
Division 6. Appointments by the Court or Agreement of the Parties. Rules 2.810–2.895.
Division 7. Proceedings. Rules 2.900–2.958.
Division 8. Trials. Rules 2.1000–2.1058.
Division 9. Judgments. Rule 2.1100.

Division 1
General Provisions

Chap. 1. Title and Application. Rules 2.1, 2.2.
Chap. 2. Definitions and Scope of Rules. Rules 2.3, 2.10.
Chap. 3. Timing. Rule 2.20.
Chap. 4. Sanctions. Rule 2.30.

Chapter 1
Title and Application

Rule 2.1. Title
Rule 2.2. Application

Rule 2.1. Title

The rules in this title may be referred to as the Trial Court Rules.
Rule 2.1 adopted effective January 1, 2007.

Rule 2.2. Application

The Trial Court Rules apply to all cases in the superior courts unless otherwise specified by a rule or statute.
Rule 2.2 amended and renumbered effective January 1, 2007; adopted as rule 200 effective January 1, 2001; previously amended effective January 1, 2002, and January 1, 2003.

Chapter 2
Definitions and Scope of Rules

Rule 2.3. Definitions
Rule 2.10. Scope of rules

Rule 2.3. Definitions

As used in the Trial Court Rules, unless the context or subject matter otherwise requires:

(1) "Court" means the superior court.

(2) "Papers" includes all documents, except exhibits and copies of exhibits, that are offered for filing in any case, but does not include Judicial Council and local court forms, records on appeal in limited civil cases, or briefs filed in appellate divisions. Unless the context clearly provides otherwise, "papers" need not be in a tangible or physical form but may be in an electronic form.

(3) "Written," "writing," "typewritten," and "typewriting" include other methods of printing letters and words equivalent in legibility to typewriting or printing from a word processor.
Rule 2.3 amended effective January 1, 2016; adopted effective January 1, 2007.

Rule 2.10. Scope of rules

These rules apply to documents filed and served electronically as well as in paper form, unless otherwise provided.
Rule 2.10 amended effective January 1, 2016; adopted effective January 1, 2007.

Chapter 3
Timing

Rule 2.20. Application for an order extending time

(a) Application—to whom made

An application for an order extending the time within which any act is required by law to be done must be heard and determined by the judge before whom the matter is pending; provided, however, that in case of the inability, death, or absence of such judge, the application may be heard and determined by another judge of the same court.
(Subd (a) amended effective January 1, 2007.)

(b) Disclosure of previous extensions

An application for an order extending time must disclose in writing the nature of the case and what extensions, if any, have previously been granted by order of court or stipulation of counsel.
(Subd (b) amended effective January 1, 2007.)

(c) Filing and service

An order extending time must be filed immediately and copies served within 24 hours after the making of the order or within such other time as may be fixed by the court.
(Subd (c) amended effective January 1, 2007.)

Rule 2.20 amended and renumbered effective January 1, 2007; adopted as rule 235 effective January 1, 1949.

Chapter 4
Sanctions

Rule 2.30. Sanctions for rules violations in civil cases

(a) Application

This sanctions rule applies to the rules in the California Rules of Court relating to general civil cases, unlawful detainer cases, probate proceedings, civil proceedings in the appellate division of the superior court, and small claims cases.
(Subd (a) amended effective January 1, 2004; adopted effective July 1, 2001.)

(b) Sanctions

In addition to any other sanctions permitted by law, the court may order a person, after written notice and an opportunity to be heard, to pay reasonable monetary sanctions to the court or an aggrieved person, or both, for failure without good cause to comply with the applicable rules. For the purposes of this rule, "person" means a party, a party's attorney, a witness, and an insurer or any other individual or entity whose consent is necessary for the disposition of the case. If a failure to comply with an applicable rule is the responsibility of counsel and not of the party, any penalty must be imposed on counsel and must not adversely affect the party's cause of action or defense thereto.
(Subd (b) amended effective January 1, 2007; adopted as untitled subdivision effective January 1, 1985; amended and relettered effective July 1, 2001; previously amended effective January 1, 1994, and January 1, 2004.)

(c) Notice and procedure

Sanctions must not be imposed under this rule except on noticed motion by the party seeking sanctions or on the court's own motion after the court has provided notice and an opportunity to be heard. A party's motion for sanctions must (1) state the applicable rule that has been violated, (2) describe the specific conduct that is alleged to have violated the rule, and (3) identify the attorney, law firm, party, witness, or other person against whom sanctions are sought. The court on its own motion may issue an order to show cause that must (1) state the applicable rule that has been violated, (2) describe the specific conduct that appears to have violated the rule, and (3) direct the attorney, law firm, party, witness, or other person to show cause why sanctions should not be imposed against them for violation of the rule.
(Subd (c) amended effective January 1, 2007; adopted effective July 1, 2001; previously amended effective January 1, 2004.)

(d) Award of expenses

In addition to the sanctions awardable under (b), the court may order the person who has violated an applicable rule to pay to the party aggrieved by the violation that party's reasonable expenses, including reasonable attorney's fees and costs, incurred in connection with the motion for sanctions or the order to show cause.
(Subd (d) amended effective January 1, 2007; adopted effective July 1, 2001; previously amended effective January 1, 2004.)

(e) Order

An order imposing sanctions must be in writing and must recite in detail the conduct or circumstances justifying the order.

(Subd (e) amended effective January 1, 2004; adopted effective July 1, 2001.)

Rule 2.30 amended and renumbered effective January 1, 2007; adopted as rule 227 effective January 1, 1985; previously amended effective January 1, 1994, July 1, 2001, and January 1, 2004.

Division 2
Papers and Forms to Be Filed

Chap. 1. Papers. Rules 2.100–2.119.
Chap. 2. General Rules on Forms. Rules 2.130–2.141.
Chap. 3. Other Forms. Rule 2.150.

Chapter 1
Papers

Rule 2.100. Form and format of papers presented for filing in the trial courts
Rule 2.102. One-sided paper
Rule 2.103. Size, quality, and color of papers
Rule 2.104. Font size; printing
Rule 2.105. Font style
Rule 2.106. Font color
Rule 2.107. Margins
Rule 2.108. Spacing and numbering of lines
Rule 2.109. Page numbering
Rule 2.110. Footer
Rule 2.111. Format of first page
Rule 2.112. Separate causes of action, counts, and defenses
Rule 2.113. Binding
Rule 2.114. Exhibits
Rule 2.115. Hole punching
Rule 2.116. Changes on face of paper
Rule 2.117. Conformed copies of papers
Rule 2.118. Acceptance of papers for filing
Rule 2.119. Exceptions for forms

Rule 2.100. Form and format of papers presented for filing in the trial courts

(a) Preemption of local rules

The Judicial Council has preempted local rules relating to the form and format of papers to be filed in the trial courts. No trial court, or any division or branch of a trial court, may enact or enforce any local rule concerning the form or format of papers.

(Subd (a) adopted effective January 1, 2007.)

(b) Rules prescribe form and format

The rules in this chapter prescribe the form and format of papers to be filed in the trial courts.

(Subd (b) adopted effective January 1, 2007.)

(c) Electronic format of papers

Papers that are submitted or filed electronically must meet the requirements in rule 2.256(b).

(Subd (c) adopted effective January 1, 2017.)

Rule 2.100 amended effective January 1, 2017; adopted as rule 201 effective January 1, 1949; previously amended effective April 1, 1962, May 1, 1962, July 1, 1964, January 1, 1966, July 1, 1969, July 1, 1971, January 1, 1973, July 1, 1974, January 1, 1976, January 1, 1978, May 6, 1978, January 1, 1984, April 1, 1990, July 1, 1990, January 1, 1992, July 1, 1992, January 1, 1993, July 1, 1993, January 1, 1994, January 1, 1998, January 1, 1999, July 1, 1999, July 1, 2000, January 1, 2001, January 1, 2003, and January 1, 2006; previously amended and renumbered as rule 2.100 effective January 1, 2007.

Rule 2.101. Use of recycled paper; certification by attorney or party [Repealed]

Rule 2.101 repealed effective January 1, 2014; adopted effective January 1, 2007.

Rule 2.102. One-sided paper

When papers are not filed electronically, only one side of each page may be used.

Rule 2.102 amended effective January 1, 2016; adopted effective January 1, 2007.

Rule 2.103. Size, quality, and color of papers

All papers filed must be 8½ by 11 inches. All papers not filed electronically must be on opaque, unglazed paper, white or unbleached, of standard quality not less than 20-pound weight.

Rule 2.103 amended effective January 1, 2017; adopted effective January 1, 2007; previously amended effective January 1, 2016.

Rule 2.104. Font size; printing

Unless otherwise specified in these rules, all papers filed must be prepared using a font size not smaller than 12 points. All papers not filed electronically must be printed or typewritten or be prepared by a photocopying or other duplication process that will produce clear and permanent copies equally as legible as printing.

Rule 2.104 amended effective January 1, 2017; adopted effective January 1, 2007; previously amended effective January 1, 2016.

Rule 2.105. Font style

The font style must be essentially equivalent to Courier, Times New Roman, or Arial.

Rule 2.105 amended effective January 1, 2017; adopted effective January 1, 2007; previously amended effective January 1, 2016.

Rule 2.106. Font color

The font color must be black or blue-black.

Rule 2.106 amended effective January 1, 2016; adopted effective January 1, 2007.

Rule 2.107. Margins

The left margin of each page must be at least one inch from the left edge and the right margin at least ½ inch from the right edge.

Rule 2.107 amended effective January 1, 2016; adopted effective January 1, 2007.

Rule 2.108. Spacing and numbering of lines

The spacing and numbering of lines on a page must be as follows:

(1) The lines on each page must be one and one-half spaced or double-spaced and numbered consecutively.

(2) Descriptions of real property may be single-spaced.

(3) Footnotes, quotations, and printed forms of corporate surety bonds and undertakings may be single-spaced and have unnumbered lines if they comply generally with the space requirements of rule 2.111.

(4) Line numbers must be placed at the left margin and separated from the text by a vertical column of space at least ⅕ inch wide or a single or double vertical line. Each line number must be aligned with a line of type, or the line numbers must be evenly spaced vertically on the page. Line numbers must be consecutively numbered, beginning with the number 1 on each page. There must be at least three line numbers for every vertical inch on the page.

Rule 2.108 amended effective January 1, 2016; adopted effective January 1, 2007.

Rule 2.109. Page numbering

Each page must be numbered consecutively at the bottom unless a rule provides otherwise for a particular type of document. The page numbering must begin with the first page and use only Arabic numerals (e.g., 1, 2, 3). The page number may be suppressed and need not appear on the first page.

Rule 2.109 amended effective January 1, 2017; adopted effective January 1, 2007.

Rule 2.110. Footer

(a) Location

Except for exhibits, each paper filed with the court must bear a footer in the bottom margin of each page, placed below the page number and divided from the rest of the document page by a printed line.

(Subd (a) adopted effective January 1, 2007.)

(b) Contents

The footer must contain the title of the paper (examples: "Complaint," "XYZ Corp.'s Motion for Summary Judgment") or some clear and concise abbreviation.

(Subd (b) adopted effective January 1, 2007.)

(c) Font size

The title of the paper in the footer must be in at least 10-point font.

(Subd (c) amended effective January 1, 2017; adopted effective January 1, 2007.)

Rule 2.110 amended effective January 1, 2017; adopted effective January 1, 2007.

Rule 2.111. Format of first page

The first page of each paper must be in the following form:

(1) In the space commencing 1 inch from the top of the page with line 1, to the left of the center of the page, the name, office address or, if none, residence address or mailing address (if different), telephone number, fax number and e-mail address, and State Bar membership number of the attorney for the party in whose behalf the paper is presented, or of the party if he or she is appearing in person. The inclusion of a fax number or e-mail address on any document does not constitute consent to service by fax or e-mail unless otherwise provided by law.

(2) In the first 2 inches of space between lines 1 and 7 to the right of the center of the page, a blank space for the use of the clerk.

(3) On line 8, at or below 3⅓ inches from the top of the page, the title of the court.

(4) Below the title of the court, in the space to the left of the center of the page, the title of the case. In the title of the case on each initial complaint or cross-complaint, the name of each party must commence on a separate line beginning at the left margin of the page. On any subsequent pleading or paper, it is sufficient to provide a short title of the case (1) stating the name of the first party on each side, with appropriate indication of other parties, and (2) stating that a cross-action or cross-actions are involved (e.g., "and Related Cross-action"), if applicable.

(5) To the right of and opposite the title, the number of the case.

(6) Below the number of the case, the nature of the paper and, on all complaints and petitions, the character of the action or proceeding. In a case having multiple parties, any answer, response, or opposition must specifically identify the complaining, propounding, or moving party and the complaint, motion, or other matter being answered or opposed.

(7) Below the nature of the paper or the character of the action or proceeding, the name of the judge and department, if any, to which the case is assigned.

(8) Below the nature of the paper or the character of the action or proceeding, the word "Referee:" followed by the name of the referee, on any paper filed in a case pending before a referee appointed under Code of Civil Procedure section 638 or 639.

(9) On the complaint, petition, or application filed in a limited civil case, below the character of the action or proceeding, the amount demanded in the complaint, petition, or application, stated as follows: "Amount demanded exceeds $10,000" or "Amount demanded does not exceed $10,000," as required by Government Code section 70613.

(10) In the caption of every pleading and every other paper filed in a limited civil case, the words "Limited Civil Case," as required by Code of Civil Procedure section 422.30(b).

(11) If a case is reclassified by an amended complaint, cross-complaint, amended cross-complaint, or other pleading under Code of Civil Procedure section 403.020 or 403.030, the caption must indicate that the action or proceeding is reclassified by this pleading. If a case is reclassified by stipulation under Code of Civil Procedure section 403.050, the title of the stipulation must state that the action or proceeding is reclassified by this stipulation. The caption or title must state that the case is a limited civil case reclassified as an unlimited civil case, or an unlimited civil case reclassified as a limited civil case, or other words to that effect.

Rule 2.111 amended effective January 1, 2017; adopted effective January 1, 2007; previously amended effective January 1, 2008, and January 1, 2016.

Rule 2.112. Separate causes of action, counts, and defenses

Each separately stated cause of action, count, or defense must specifically state:

(1) Its number (e.g., "first cause of action");

(2) Its nature (e.g., "for fraud");

(3) The party asserting it if more than one party is represented on the pleading (e.g., "by plaintiff Jones"); and

(4) The party or parties to whom it is directed (e.g., "against defendant Smith").

Rule 2.112 adopted effective January 1, 2007.

Rule 2.113. Binding

Each paper not filed electronically must consist entirely of original pages without riders and must be firmly bound together at the top.

Rule 2.113 amended effective January 1, 2016; adopted effective January 1, 2007.

Rule 2.114. Exhibits

Exhibits submitted with papers not filed electronically may be fastened to pages of the specified size and, when prepared by a machine copying process, must be equal to computer-processed materials in legibility and permanency of image. Exhibits submitted with papers filed electronically must meet the requirements in rule 2.256(b).

Rule 2.114 amended effective January 1, 2017; adopted effective January 1, 2007; previously amended effective January 1, 2016.

Rule 2.115. Hole punching

When papers are not filed electronically, each paper presented for filing must contain two prepunched normal-sized holes, centered 2½ inches apart and ⅝ inch from the top of the paper.

Rule 2.115 amended effective January 1, 2016; adopted effective January 1, 2007.

Rule 2.116. Changes on face of paper

Any addition, deletion, or interlineation to a paper must be initialed by the clerk or judge at the time of filing.

Rule 2.116 adopted effective January 1, 2007.

Rule 2.117. Conformed copies of papers

All copies of papers served must conform to the original papers filed, including the numbering of lines, pagination, additions, deletions, and interlineations except that, with the agreement of the other party, a party serving papers by nonelectronic means may serve that other party with papers printed on both sides of the page.

Rule 2.117 amended effective January 1, 2016; adopted effective January 1, 2007; previously amended effective July 1, 2012.

Rule 2.118. Acceptance of papers for filing

(a) Papers not in compliance

The clerk of the court must not accept for filing or file any papers that do not comply with the rules in this chapter, except the clerk must not reject a paper for filing solely on the ground that:

(1) It is handwritten or hand-printed;

(2) The handwriting or hand printing on the paper is in a color other than black or blue-black; or

(3) The font size is not exactly the point size required by rules 2.104 and 2.110(c) on papers submitted electronically in portable document format (PDF). Minimal variation in font size may result from converting a document created using word processing software to PDF.

(Subd (a) amended effective January 1, 2017; adopted effective January 1, 2007.)

(b) Absence of fax number or e-mail address

The clerk must not reject a paper for filing solely on the ground that it does not contain an attorney's or a party's fax number or e-mail address on the first page.

(Subd (b) adopted effective January 1, 2007.)

(c) Filing of papers for good cause

For good cause shown, the court may permit the filing of papers that do not comply with the rules in this chapter.

(Subd (c) adopted effective January 1, 2007.)

Rule 2.118 amended effective January 1, 2017; adopted effective January 1, 2007.

Rule 2.119. Exceptions for forms

Except as provided elsewhere in the California Rules of Court, the rules in this chapter do not apply to Judicial Council forms, local court forms, or forms for juvenile dependency proceedings produced by the California State Department of Social Services Child Welfare Systems Case Management System.

Rule 2.119 adopted effective January 1, 2007.

Advisory Committee Comment

The California Department of Social Services (CDSS) has begun to distribute a new, comprehensive, computerized case management system to county welfare agencies. This system is not able to exactly conform to Judicial Council format in all instances. However, item numbering on the forms will remain the same. The changes allow CDSS computer-generated Judicial Council forms to be used in juvenile court proceedings.

Chapter 2
General Rules on Forms

Rule 2.130. Application
Rule 2.132. True copy certified
Rule 2.133. Hole punching
Rule 2.134. Forms longer than one page
Rule 2.135. Filing of handwritten or hand-printed forms
Rule 2.140. Judicial Council forms
Rule 2.141. Local court forms

Rule 2.130. Application

The rules in this chapter apply to Judicial Council forms, local court forms, and all other official forms to be filed in the trial courts. The rules apply to forms filed both in paper form and electronically, unless otherwise specified.

Rule 2.130 amended effective January 1, 2016; adopted effective January 1, 2007.

Rule 2.131. Recycled paper [Repealed]

Rule 2.131 repealed effective January 1, 2014; adopted effective January 1, 2007.

Rule 2.132. True copy certified

A party or attorney who files a form certifies by filing the form that it is a true copy of the form.

Rule 2.132 adopted effective January 1, 2007.

Rule 2.133. Hole punching

All forms not filed electronically must contain two prepunched normal-sized holes, centered 2½ inches apart and ⅝ inch from the top of the form.

Rule 2.133 amended effective January 1, 2016; adopted effective January 1, 2007.

Rule 2.134. Forms longer than one page
(a) Single side may be used

If a form not filed electronically is longer than one page, the form may be printed on sheets printed only on one side even if the original has two sides to a sheet.

(Subd (a) amended effective January 1, 2016; adopted effective January 1, 2007.)

(b) Two-sided forms must be tumbled

If a form not filed electronically is filed on a sheet printed on two sides, the reverse side must be rotated 180 degrees (printed head to foot).

(Subd (b) amended effective January 1, 2016; adopted effective January 1, 2007.)

(c) Multiple-page forms must be bound

If a form not filed electronically is longer than one page, it must be firmly bound at the top.

(Subd (c) amended effective January 1, 2016; adopted effective January 1, 2007.)

Rule 2.134 amended effective January 1, 2016; adopted effective January 1, 2007.

Rule 2.135. Filing of handwritten or hand-printed forms

The clerk must not reject for filing or refuse to file any Judicial Council or local court form solely on the ground that:

(1) It is completed in handwritten or hand-printed characters; or

(2) The handwriting or hand-printing is a color other than blue-black or black.

Rule 2.135 amended and renumbered effective January 1, 2007; adopted as rule 201.4 effective January 1, 2003.

Rule 2.140. Judicial Council forms

Judicial Council forms are governed by the rules in this chapter and chapter 4 of title 1. Electronic Judicial Council forms must meet the requirements in rule 2.256.

Rule 2.140 amended effective January 1, 2017; adopted effective January 1, 2007.

Rule 2.141. Local court forms

Local court forms are governed by the rules in this chapter and rules 10.613 and 10.614.

Rule 2.141 adopted effective January 1, 2007.

Chapter 3
Other Forms

Rule 2.150. Authorization for computer-generated or typewritten forms for proof of service of summons and complaint

(a) Computer-generated or typewritten forms; conditions

Notwithstanding the adoption of mandatory form *Proof of Service of Summons* (form POS-010), a form for proof of service of a summons and complaint prepared entirely by word processor, typewriter, or similar process may be used for proof of service in any applicable action or proceeding if the following conditions are met:

(1) The form complies with the rules in chapter 1 of this division except as otherwise provided in this rule, but numbered lines are not required.

(2) The left, right, and bottom margins of the proof of service must be at least ½ inch. The top margin must be at least ¾ of an inch. The typeface must be Times New Roman, Courier, Arial, or an equivalent typeface not smaller than 9 points. Text must be single-spaced and a blank line must precede each main numbered item.

(3) The title and all the text of form POS-010 that is not accompanied by a check box must be copied word for word except for any instructions, which need not be copied. In addition, the optional text describing the particular method of service used must be copied word for word, except that the check boxes must not be copied. Any optional text not describing such service need not be included.

(4) The Judicial Council number of the *Proof of Service of Summons* must be typed as follows either in the left margin of the first page opposite the last line of text or at the bottom of each page: "Judicial Council form POS-010."

(5) The text of form POS-010 must be copied in the same order as it appears on form POS-010 using the same item numbers. A declaration of diligence may be attached to the proof of service or inserted as item 5b(5).

(6) Areas marked "For Court Use" must be copied in the same general locations and occupy approximately the same amount of space as on form POS-010.

(7) The telephone number of the attorney or party must appear flush with the left margin and below the attorney's or party's address.

(8) The name of the court must be flush with the left margin. The address of the court is not required.

(9) Material that would have been entered onto form POS-010 must be entered with each line indented 3 inches from the left margin.

(Subd (a) amended effective January 1, 2016; previously amended effective July 1, 1985, January 1, 1986, January 1, 1987, July 1, 1999, January 1, 2004, July 1, 2004, and January 1, 2007.)

(b) Compliance with rule

The act of filing a computer-generated or typewritten form under this rule constitutes a certification by the party or attorney filing the form that it complies with this rule and is a true and correct copy of the form to the extent required by this rule.

(Subd (b) amended effective January 1, 2004; previously amended effective July 1, 1985, January 1, 1987, January 1, 1988, and July 1, 1999; relettered effective January 1, 1986.)

Rule 2.150 amended effective January 1, 2016; adopted as rule 982.9; previously amended effective January 1, 1989, July 1, 1999, January 1, 2004, and July 1, 2004; previously amended and renumbered as rule 2.150 effective January 1, 2007.

Advisory Committee Comment

This rule is intended to permit process servers and others to prepare their own shortened versions of *Proof of Service of Summons* (form POS-010) containing only the information that is relevant to show the method of service used.

Division 3
Filing and Service

Chap. 1. General Provisions. Rules 2.200, 2.210.
Chap. 2. Filing and Service by Electronic Means. Rules 2.250–2.261.
Chap. 3. Filing and Service by Fax. Rules 2.300–2.306.

Chapter 1
General Provisions

Rule 2.200. Service and filing of notice of change of address or other contact information
Rule 2.210. Drop box for filing documents

Rule 2.200. Service and filing of notice of change of address or other contact information

An attorney or self-represented party whose mailing address, telephone number, fax number, or e-mail address (if it was provided under rule 2.111(1)) changes while an action is pending must serve on all parties and file a written notice of the change.

Rule 2.200 amended effective January 1, 2013; adopted as rule 385 effective January 1, 1984; previously amended and renumbered effective January 1, 2007.

Rule 2.210. Drop box for filing documents

(a) Use of drop box

Whenever a clerk's office filing counter is closed at any time between 8:30 a.m. and 4:00 p.m. on a court day, the court must provide a drop box for depositing documents to be filed with the clerk. A court may provide a drop box during other times.

(b) Documents deemed filed on day of deposit

Any document deposited in a court's drop box up to and including 4:00 p.m. on a court day is deemed to have been deposited for filing on that day. A court may provide for same-day filing of a document deposited in its drop box after 4:00 p.m. on a court day. If so, the court must give notice of the deadline for same-day filing of a document deposited in its drop box.

(c) Documents deemed filed on next court day

Any document deposited in a court's drop box is deemed to have been deposited for filing on the next court day if:

(1) It is deposited on a court day after 4:00 p.m. or after the deadline for same-day filing if a court provides for a later time; or

(2) It is deposited on a judicial holiday.

(Subd (c) amended effective January 1, 2007.)

(d) Date and time documents deposited

A court must have a means of determining whether a document was deposited in the drop box by 4:00 p.m., or after the deadline for same-day filing if a court provides for a later time, on a court day.

Rule 2.210 amended and renumbered effective January 1, 2007; adopted as rule 201.6 effective January 1, 2005.

Advisory Committee Comment

The notice required by (b) may be provided by the same means a court provides notice of its clerk's office hours. The means of providing notice may include the following: information on the court's Web site, a local rule provision, a notice in a legal newspaper, a sign in the clerk's office, or a sign near the drop box.

Chapter 2
Filing and Service by Electronic Means

Rule 2.250. Construction and definitions
Rule 2.251. Electronic service
Rule 2.252. General rules on electronic filing of documents
Rule 2.253. Permissive electronic filing, mandatory electronic filing, and electronic filing by court order
Rule 2.254. Responsibilities of court
Rule 2.255. Contracts with electronic filing service providers and electronic filing managers
Rule 2.256. Responsibilities of electronic filer
Rule 2.257. Requirements for signatures on documents
Rule 2.258. Payment of filing fees in civil actions
Rule 2.259. Actions by court on receipt of electronic filing
Rule 2.261. Authorization for courts to continue modifying forms for the purpose of electronic filing and forms generation

Rule 2.250. Construction and definitions

(a) Construction of rules

The rules in this chapter must be construed to authorize and permit filing and service by electronic means to the extent feasible.

(Subd (a) adopted effective January 1, 2011.)

(b) Definitions

As used in this chapter, unless the context otherwise requires:

(1) A "document" is a pleading, a declaration, an exhibit, or another writing submitted by a party or other person, or by an agent of a party or other person on the party's or other person's behalf. A document is also a notice, order, judgment, or other issuance by the court. A document may be in paper or electronic form.

(2) "Electronic service" has the same meaning as defined in Code of Civil Procedure section 1010.6.

(3) "Electronic transmission" has the same meaning as defined in Code of Civil Procedure section 1010.6.

(4) "Electronic notification" has the same meaning as defined in Code of Civil Procedure section 1010.6.

(5) "Electronic service address" means the electronic address at or through which the party or other person has authorized electronic service.

(6) An "electronic filer" is a party or other person filing a document in electronic form directly with the court, by an agent, or through an electronic filing service provider.

(7) "Electronic filing" is the electronic transmission to a court of a document in electronic form. For the purposes of this chapter, this definition concerns the activity of filing and does not include the processing and review of the document, and its entry into the court records, which are necessary for a document to be officially filed.

(8) An "electronic filing service provider" is a person or entity that receives an electronic filing from a party or other person for retransmission to the court or for electronic service on other parties or other persons, or both. In submission of filings, the electronic filing service provider does so on behalf of the electronic filer and not as an agent of the court.

(9) An "electronic filing manager" is a service that acts as an intermediary between a court and various electronic filing service provider solutions certified for filing into California courts.

(10) "Self-represented" means a party or other person who is unrepresented in an action by an attorney and does not include an attorney appearing in an action who represents himself or herself.

(Subd (b) amended effective January 1, 2019; adopted as unlettered subd effective January 1, 2003; previously amended and lettered effective January 1, 2011; previously amended effective July 1, 2013, and January 1, 2018.)

Rule 2.250 amended effective January 1, 2019; adopted as rule 2050 effective January 1, 2003; previously amended and renumbered effective January 1, 2007; previously amended effective January 1, 2006, January 1, 2008, January 1, 2011, July 1, 2013, and January 1, 2018.

Advisory Committee Comment

The definition of "electronic service" has been amended to provide that a party may effectuate service not only by the electronic transmission of a document, but also by providing electronic notification of where a document served electronically may be located and downloaded. This amendment is intended to modify the rules on electronic service to expressly authorize electronic notification as a legally effective alternative means of service to electronic transmission. This rules amendment is consistent with the amendment of Code of Civil Procedure section 1010.6, effective January 1, 2011, to authorize service by electronic notification. (See Stats. 2010, ch. 156 (Sen. Bill 1274).) The amendments change the law on electronic service as understood by the appellate court in *Insyst, Ltd. v. Applied Materials, Inc.* (2009) 170 Cal.App.4th 1129, which interpreted the rules as authorizing electronic transmission as the only effective means of electronic service.

Rule 2.251. Electronic service

(a) Authorization for electronic service

When a document may be served by mail, express mail, overnight delivery, or fax transmission, the document may be served electronically under Code of Civil Procedure section 1010.6, Penal Code section 690.5, and the rules in this chapter. For purposes of electronic service made pursuant to Penal Code section 690.5, express consent to electronic service is required.

(Subd (a) amended effective January 1, 2022; previously amended effective January 1, 2007, January 1, 2008, January 1, 2011, and July 1, 2013.)

(b) Electronic service by express consent

(1) A party or other person indicates that the party or other person agrees to accept electronic service by:

(A) Serving a notice on all parties and other persons that the party or other person accepts electronic service and filing the notice with the court. The notice must include the electronic service address at which the party or other person agrees to accept service; or

(B) Manifesting affirmative consent through electronic means with the court or the court's electronic filing service provider, and concurrently providing the party's electronic service address with that consent for the purpose of receiving electronic service. A party or other person may manifest affirmative consent by serving notice of consent to all parties and other persons and either:

(i) Agreeing to the terms of service with an electronic filing service provider, which clearly state that agreement constitutes consent to receive electronic service; or

(ii) Filing *Consent to Electronic Service and Notice of Electronic Service Address* (form EFS-005-CV).

(2) A party or other person that has consented to electronic service under (1) and has used an electronic filing service provider to serve and file documents in a case consents to service on that electronic filing service provider as the designated agent for service for the party or other person in the case, until such time as the party or other person designates a different agent for service.

(Subd (b) amended effective January 1, 2020; adopted as part of subd (a); previously amended and relettered effective July 1, 2013; previously amended effective January 1, 2007, January 1, 2008, January 1, 2011, January 1, 2018, and January 1, 2019.)

(c) Electronic service required by local rule or court order

(1) A court may require parties to serve documents electronically in specified civil actions by local rule or court order, as provided in Code of Civil Procedure section 1010.6 and the rules in this chapter.

(2) A court may require other persons to serve documents electronically in specified civil actions by local rule, as provided in Code of Civil Procedure section 1010.6 and the rules in this chapter.

(3) Except when personal service is otherwise required by statute or rule, a party or other person that is required to file documents electronically in an action must also serve documents and accept service of documents electronically from all other parties or persons, unless:

(A) The court orders otherwise, or

(B) The action includes parties or persons that are not required to file or serve documents electronically, including self-represented parties or other self-represented persons; those parties or other persons are to be served by non-electronic methods unless they affirmatively consent to electronic service.

(4) Each party or other person that is required to serve and accept service of documents electronically must provide all other parties or other persons in the action with its electronic service address and must promptly notify all other parties, other persons, and the court of any changes under (g).

(Subd (c) amended effective January 1, 2022; adopted effective July 1, 2013; previously amended January 1, 2018.)

(d) Additional provisions for electronic service required by court order

(1) If a court has adopted local rules for permissive electronic filing, then the court may, on the motion of any party or on its own motion, provided that the order would not cause undue hardship or significant prejudice to any party, order all parties in any class action, a consolidated action, a group of actions, a coordinated action, or an action that is

complex under rule 3.403 to serve all documents electronically, except when personal service is required by statute or rule.

(2) A court may combine an order for mandatory electronic service with an order for mandatory electronic filing as provided in rule 2.253(c).

(3) If the court proposes to make any order under (1) on its own motion, the court must mail notice to any parties that have not consented to receive electronic service. The court may electronically serve the notice on any party that has consented to receive electronic service. Any party may serve and file an opposition within 10 days after notice is mailed, electronically served, or such later time as the court may specify.

(4) If the court has previously ordered parties in a case to electronically serve documents and a new party is added that the court determines should also be ordered to do so under (1), the court may follow the notice procedures under (2) or may order the party to electronically serve documents and in its order state that the new party may object within 10 days after service of the order or by such later time as the court may specify.

(Subd (d) adopted effective January 1, 2018.)

(e) Maintenance of electronic service lists

A court that permits or requires electronic filing in a case must maintain and make available electronically to the parties and other persons in the case an electronic service list that contains the parties' or other persons' current electronic service addresses, as provided by the parties or other persons that have filed electronically in the case.

(Subd (e) amended and relettered effective January 1, 2018; adopted as subd (b) effective January 1, 2008; previously amended effective January 1, 2010, and January 1, 2011; previously amended and relettered as subd (d) effective July 1, 2013.)

(f) Service by the parties and other persons

(1) Notwithstanding (e), parties and other persons that have consented to or are required to serve documents electronically are responsible for electronic service on all other parties and other persons required to be served in the case. A party or other person may serve documents electronically directly, by an agent, or through a designated electronic filing service provider.

(2) A document may not be electronically served on a nonparty unless the nonparty consents to electronic service or electronic service is otherwise provided for by law or court order.

(Subd (f) amended and relettered effective January 1, 2018; adopted as subd (c) effective January 1, 2008; previously amended effective January 1, 2011; previously amended and relettered as subd (e) effective July 1, 2013.)

(g) Change of electronic service address

(1) A party or other person whose electronic service address changes while the action or proceeding is pending must promptly file a notice of change of address electronically with the court and must serve this notice electronically on all other parties and all other persons required to be served.

(2) A party's or other person's election to contract with an electronic filing service provider to electronically file and serve documents or to receive electronic service of documents on the party's or other person's behalf does not relieve the party or other person of its duties under (1).

(3) An electronic service address is presumed valid for a party or other person if the party or other person files electronic documents with the court from that address and has not filed and served notice that the address is no longer valid.

(Subd (g) amended and relettered effective January 1, 2018; adopted as subd (d) effective January 1, 2008; previously amended effective January 1, 2011; previously relettered as subd (f) effective July 1, 2013.)

(h) Reliability and integrity of documents served by electronic notification

A party or other person that serves a document by means of electronic notification must:

(1) Ensure that the documents served can be viewed and downloaded using the hyperlink provided;

(2) Preserve the document served without any change, alteration, or modification from the time the document is posted until the time the hyperlink is terminated; and

(3) Maintain the hyperlink until either:

(A) All parties in the case have settled or the case has ended and the time for appeals has expired; or

(B) If the party or other person is no longer in the case, the party or other person has provided notice to all other parties and other persons required to receive notice that it is no longer in the case and that they have 60 days to download any documents, and 60 days have passed after the notice was given.

(Subd (h) amended and relettered effective January 1, 2018; adopted as subd (e) effective January 1, 2011; previously relettered as subd (g) effective July 1, 2013.)

(i) When service is complete

(1) Electronic service of a document is complete as provided in Code of Civil Procedure section 1010.6 and the rules in this chapter.

(2) If an electronic filing service provider is used for service, the service is complete at the time that the electronic filing service provider electronically transmits the document or sends electronic notification of service.

(Subd (i) amended and relettered effective January 1, 2018; adopted as subd (b) effective January 1, 2003; previously amended effective January 1, 2007; previously relettered as subd (e) effective January 1, 2008; previously amended and relettered as subd (f) effective January 1, 2011, and as subd (h) effective July 1, 2013.)

(j) Proof of service

(1) Proof of electronic service shall be made as provided in Code of Civil Procedure section 1013b.

(2) Under rule 3.1300(c), proof of electronic service of the moving papers must be filed at least five court days before the hearing.

(3) If a person signs a printed form of a proof of electronic service, the party or other person filing the proof of electronic service must comply with the provisions of rule 2.257(a).

(Subd (j) amended and relettered effective January 1, 2018; adopted as subd (c) effective January 1, 2003; previously relettered as subd (f) effective January 1, 2008; previously amended effective January 1, 2007, January 1, 2009, July 1, 2009, January 1, 2010, and January 1, 2017; previously amended and relettered as subd (g) effective January 1, 2011; previously relettered as subd (i) effective July 1, 2013.)

(k) Electronic service by or on court

(1) The court may electronically serve documents as provided in Code of Civil Procedure section 1010.6, Penal Code section 690.5, and the rules in this chapter.

(2) A document may be electronically served on a court if the court consents to electronic service or electronic service is otherwise provided for by law or court order. A court indicates that it agrees to accept electronic service by:

(A) Serving a notice on all parties and other persons in the case that the court accepts electronic service. The notice must include the electronic service address at which the court agrees to accept service; or

(B) Adopting a local rule stating that the court accepts electronic service. The rule must indicate where to obtain the electronic service address at which the court agrees to accept service.

(Subd (k) amended effective January 1, 2022; adopted as subd (e) effective January 1, 2003; previously amended effective January 1, 2007, and January 1, 2016; previously relettered as subd (g) effective January 1, 2008, as subd (h) effective January 1, 2011, and as subd (j) effective July 1, 2013; previously amended and relettered as subd (k) effective January 1, 2018.)

Rule 2.251 amended effective January 1, 2022; adopted as rule 2060 effective January 1, 2003; previously amended and renumbered as rule 2.260 effective January 1, 2007, and as rule 2.251 effective January 1, 2011; previously amended effective January 1, 2008, January 1, 2009, July 1, 2009, January 1, 2010, July 1, 2013, January 1, 2016, January 1, 2017, January 1, 2018, January 1, 2019, and January 1, 2020.

Advisory Committee Comment

Subdivision (b)(1)(B). The rule does not prescribe specific language for a provision of a term of service when the filer consents to electronic service, but does require that any such provision be clear. *Consent to Electronic Service and Notice of Electronic Service Address* (form EFS-005-CV) provides an example of language for consenting to electronic service.

Subdivision (c). The subdivision is applicable only to civil actions as defined in rule 1.6. Penal Code section 690.5 excludes mandatory electronic service in criminal cases.

Subdivisions (c)–(d). Court-ordered electronic service is not subject to the provisions in Code of Civil Procedure section 1010.6 requiring that, where mandatory electronic filing and service are established by local rule, the court and the parties must have access to more than one electronic filing service provider.

Rule 2.252. General rules on electronic filing of documents

(a) In general

A court may provide for electronic filing of documents in actions and proceedings as provided under Code of Civil Procedure section 1010.6, Penal Code section 690.5, and the rules in this chapter.

(Subd (a) amended effective January 1, 2022; previously amended effective January 1, 2007, and July 1, 2013.)

(b) Direct and indirect electronic filing

Except as otherwise provided by law, a court may provide for the electronic filing of documents directly with the court, indirectly through one or more approved electronic filing service providers, or through a combination of direct and indirect means.

(Subd (b) adopted effective July 1, 2013.)

(c) No effect on filing deadline

Filing a document electronically does not alter any filing deadline.

(Subd (c) amended effective January 1, 2018; adopted effective July 1, 2013.)

(d) Filing in paper form

When it is not feasible for a party or other person to convert a document to electronic form by scanning, imaging, or another means, a court may allow that party or other person to file the document in paper form.

(Subd (d) amended effective January 1, 2018; adopted effective July 1, 2013.)

(e) Original documents

In a proceeding that requires the filing of an original document, an electronic filer may file an electronic copy of a document if the original document is then filed with the court within 10 calendar days.

(Subd (e) relettered effective July 1, 2013; adopted as subd (b) effective January 1, 2003; previously amended effective January 1, 2011.)

(f) Application for waiver of court fees and costs

The court must permit electronic filing of an application for waiver of court fees and costs in any proceeding in which the court accepts electronic filings.

(Subd (f) amended effective January 1, 2018; adopted as subd (c) effective January 1, 2003; previously amended effective January 1, 2007; previously relettered as subd (f) effective July 1, 2013.)

(g) Orders and judgments

The court may electronically file any notice, order, minute order, judgment, or other document prepared by the court.

(Subd (g) relettered effective July 1, 2013; adopted as subd (d).)

(h) Proposed orders

Proposed orders may be filed and submitted electronically as provided in rule 3.1312.

(Subd (h) relettered effective July 1, 2013; adopted as subd (e) effective January 1, 2011.)

Rule 2.252 amended effective January 1, 2022; adopted as rule 2052 effective January 1, 2003; previously amended and renumbered effective January 1, 2007; previously amended effective January 1, 2011, July 1, 2013, and January 1, 2018.

Rule 2.253. Permissive electronic filing, mandatory electronic filing, and electronic filing by court order

(a) Permissive electronic filing by local rule

A court may permit parties by local rule to file documents electronically in any types of cases, subject to the conditions in Code of Civil Procedure section 1010.6, Penal Code section 690.5, and the rules in this chapter.

(Subd (a) amended effective January 1, 2022; adopted effective July 1, 2013; previously amended effective January 1, 2018.)

(b) Mandatory electronic filing by local rule

A court may require parties by local rule to electronically file documents in civil actions directly with the court, or directly with the court and through one or more approved electronic filing service providers, or through more than one approved electronic filing service provider, subject to the conditions in Code of Civil Procedure section 1010.6, the rules in this chapter, and the following conditions:

(1) The court must specify the types or categories of civil actions in which parties or other persons are required to file and serve documents electronically. The court may designate any of the following as eligible for mandatory electronic filing and service:

(A) All civil cases;

(B) All civil cases of a specific category, such as unlimited or limited civil cases;

(C) All civil cases of a specific case type, including but not limited to, contract, collections, personal injury, or employment;

(D) All civil cases assigned to a judge for all purposes;

(E) All civil cases assigned to a specific department, courtroom or courthouse;

(F) Any class actions, consolidated actions, or group of actions, coordinated actions, or actions that are complex under rule 3.403; or

(G) Any combination of the cases described in subparagraphs (A) to (F), inclusive.

(2) Self-represented parties or other self-represented persons are exempt from any mandatory electronic filing and service requirements adopted by courts under this rule and Code of Civil Procedure section 1010.6.

(3) In civil cases involving both represented and self-represented parties or other persons, represented parties or other persons may be required to file and serve documents electronically; however, in these cases, each self-represented party or other person is to file, serve, and be served with documents by non-electronic means unless the self-represented party or other person affirmatively agrees otherwise.

(4) A party or other person that is required to file and serve documents electronically must be excused from the requirements if the party or other person shows undue hardship or significant prejudice. A court requiring the electronic filing and service of documents must have a process for parties or other persons, including represented parties or other represented persons, to apply for relief and a procedure for parties or other persons excused from filing documents electronically to file them by conventional means.

(5) Any fees charged by the court or an electronic filing service provider shall be consistent with the fee provisions of Code of Civil Procedure section 1010.6.

(6) The effective date of filing any document received electronically is prescribed by Code of Civil Procedure section 1010.6. This provision concerns only the effective date of filing. Any document that is received electronically must be processed and satisfy all other legal filing requirements to be filed as an official court record.

(Subd (b) amended effective January 1, 2023; adopted effective July 1, 2013; previously amended effective January 1, 2018.)

(c) Electronic filing by court order

(1) If a court has adopted local rules for permissive electronic filing, then the court may, on the motion of any party or on its own motion, provided that the order would not cause undue hardship or significant prejudice to any party, order all parties in any class action, a consolidated action, a group of actions, a coordinated action, or an action that is complex under rule 3.403 to file all documents electronically.

(2) A court may combine an order for mandatory electronic filing with an order for mandatory electronic service as provided in rule 2.252(d).

(3) If the court proposes to make any order under (1) on its own motion, the court must mail notice to any parties that have not consented to receive electronic service. The court may electronically serve the notice on any party that has consented to receive electronic service. Any party may serve and file an opposition within 10 days after notice is mailed or electronically served or such later time as the court may specify.

(4) If the court has previously ordered parties in a case to electronically file documents and a new party is added that the court determines should also be ordered to do so under (1), the court may follow the notice procedures under (2) or may order the party to electronically file documents and in its order state that the new party may object within 10 days after service of the order or by such later time as the court may specify.

(5) The court's order may also provide that:

(A) Documents previously filed in paper form may be resubmitted in electronic form; and

(B) When the court sends confirmation of filing to all parties, receipt of the confirmation constitutes service of the filing if the filed document is available electronically.

(Subd (c) amended effective January 1, 2018; adopted as subd (a) and part of subd (b) effective January 1, 2003; previously amended effective January 1, 2007, January 1, 2008, and January 1, 2011; previously repealed, amended and relettered as subd (c) effective July 1, 2013.)

Rule 2.253 amended effective January 1, 2023; adopted as rule 2053 effective January 1, 2003; previously amended and renumbered effective January 1, 2007; previously amended effective January 1, 2008, January 1, 2011, July 1, 2013, January 1, 2018, and January 1, 2022.

Advisory Committee Comment

Subdivision (b)(1). This subdivision allows courts to institute mandatory electronic filing and service in any type of civil case for which the court determines that mandatory electronic filing is appropriate. The scope of this authorization is meant to be broad. It will enable courts to implement mandatory electronic filing in a flexible yet expansive manner. However, in initiating mandatory electronic filing, courts should take into account the fact that some civil case types may be easier and more cost-effective to implement at the outset while other types may require special procedures or other considerations (such as the need to preserve the confidentiality of filed records) that may make them less appropriate for inclusion in initial mandatory e-filing efforts.

Subdivision (b)(2). Although this rule exempts self-represented parties from any mandatory electronic filing and service requirements, these parties are encouraged to participate voluntarily in electronic filing and service. To the extent feasible, courts and other entities should assist self-represented parties to electronically file and serve documents.

Subdivision (c). Court-ordered electronic filing under this subdivision is not subject to the provisions in (b) and Code of Civil Procedure section 1010.6 requiring that, where mandatory electronic filing and service are established by local rule, the court and the parties must have access to more than one electronic filing service provider.

Rule 2.254. Responsibilities of court

(a) Publication of electronic filing requirements

Each court that permits or mandates electronic filing must publish, in both electronic and print formats, the court's electronic filing requirements.

(Subd (a) amended effective July 1, 2013; adopted as subd (b) effective January 1, 2003; previously amended effective January 1, 2007; previously relettered effective January 1, 2011.)

(b) Problems with electronic filing

If the court is aware of a problem that impedes or precludes electronic filing, it must promptly take reasonable steps to provide notice of the problem.

(Subd (b) amended effective January 1, 2018; adopted as subd (c) effective January 1, 2003; previously amended effective January 1, 2007; previously relettered as subd (b) effective January 1, 2011.)

(c) Public access to electronically filed documents

Except as provided in rules 2.250–2.259 and 2.500–2.506, an electronically filed document is a public document at the time it is filed unless it is sealed under rule 2.551(b) or made confidential by law.

(Subd (c) amended and relettered effective January 1, 2011; adopted as subd (d) effective January 1, 2003; previously amended effective January 1, 2007.)

Rule 2.254 amended effective January 1, 2018; adopted as rule 2054 effective January 1, 2003; previously amended and renumbered effective January 1, 2007; previously amended effective January 1, 2011, and July 1, 2013.

Rule 2.255. Contracts with electronic filing service providers and electronic filing managers

(a) Right to contract

(1) A court may contract with one or more electronic filing service providers to furnish and maintain an electronic filing system for the court.

(2) If the court contracts with an electronic filing service provider, it may require electronic filers to transmit the documents to the provider.

(3) A court may contract with one or more electronic filing managers to act as an intermediary between the court and electronic filing service providers.

(4) If the court contracts with an electronic service provider or the court has an in-house system, the provider or system must accept filing from other electronic filing service providers to the extent the provider or system is compatible with them.

(Subd (a) amended effective January 1, 2019; previously amended effective January 1, 2007, and January 1, 2011.)

(b) Provisions of contract

(1) The court's contract with an electronic filing service provider may:

(A) Allow the provider to charge electronic filers a reasonable fee in addition to the court's filing fee;

(B) Allow the provider to make other reasonable requirements for use of the electronic filing system.

(2) The court's contract with an electronic filing service provider must comply with the requirements of Code of Civil Procedure section 1010.6.

(3) The court's contract with an electronic filing manager must comply with the requirements of Code of Civil Procedure section 1010.6.

(Subd (b) amended effective January 1, 2019; previously amended effective January 1, 2018.)

(c) Transmission of filing to court

(1) An electronic filing service provider must promptly transmit any electronic filing, any applicable filing fee, and any applicable acceptance of consent to receive electronic service to the court directly or through the court's electronic filing manager.

(2) An electronic filing manager must promptly transmit an electronic filing, any applicable filing fee, and any applicable acceptance of consent to receive electronic service to the court.

(Subd (c) amended effective January 1, 2020; previously amended effective January 1, 2011, and January 1, 2019.)

(d) Confirmation of receipt and filing of document

(1) An electronic filing service provider must promptly send to an electronic filer its confirmation of the receipt of any document that the filer has transmitted to the provider for filing with the court.

(2) The electronic filing service provider must send its confirmation to the filer's electronic service address and must indicate the date and time of receipt, in accordance with rule 2.259(a).

(3) After reviewing the documents, the court must promptly transmit to the electronic filing service provider and the electronic filer the court's confirmation of filing or notice of rejection of filing, in accordance with rule 2.259.

(Subd (d) amended effective January 1, 2011; previously amended effective January 1, 2007.)

(e) Ownership of information

All contracts between the court and electronic filing service providers or the court and electronic filing managers must acknowledge that the court is the owner of the contents of the filing system and has the exclusive right to control the system's use.

(Subd (e) amended effective January 1, 2019; previously amended effective January 1, 2007.)

(f) Establishing a filer account with an electronic filing service provider

(1) An electronic filing service provider may not require a filer to provide a credit card, debit card, or bank account information to create an account with the electronic filing service provider.

(2) This provision applies only to the creation of an account and not to the use of an electronic filing service provider's services. An electronic filing service provider may require a filer to provide a credit card, debit card, or bank account information before rendering services unless the services are within the scope of a fee waiver granted by the court to the filer.

(Subd (f) adopted effective January 1, 2019.)

(g) Electronic filer not required to consent to electronic service

(1) An electronic filing service provider must allow an electronic filer to proceed with an electronic filing even if the electronic filer does not consent to receive electronic service.

(2) This provision applies only to electronic service by express consent under rule 2.251(b).

(Subd (g) adopted effective January 1, 2021.)

(h) Fees for electronic filing services not chargeable in some criminal actions

(1) Electronic filing service providers and electronic filing managers may not charge a service fee when an electronic filer files a document in a criminal action when the electronic filer is a prosecutor, an indigent defendant, or court appointed counsel for an indigent defendant.

(2) For purposes of this subdivision, "indigent defendant" means a defendant who the court has determined is not financially able to employ counsel pursuant to Penal Code section 987. Pending the court's determination, "indigent defendant" also means a defendant the public defender is representing pursuant to Government Code section 27707.

(Subd (h) adopted effective January 1, 2022.)

Rule 2.255 amended effective January 1, 2022; adopted as rule 2055 effective January 1, 2003; previously amended and renumbered effective January 1, 2007; previously amended effective January 1, 2011, January 1, 2018, January 1, 2019, January 1, 2020, and January 1, 2021.

Rule 2.256. Responsibilities of electronic filer

(a) Conditions of filing

Each electronic filer must:

(1) Comply with any court requirements designed to ensure the integrity of electronic filing and to protect sensitive personal information;

(2) Furnish information the court requires for case processing;

(3) Take all reasonable steps to ensure that the filing does not contain computer code, including viruses, that might be harmful to the court's electronic filing system and to other users of that system;

(4) Furnish one or more electronic service addresses in the manner specified by the court. This only applies when the electronic filer has consented to or is required to accept electronic service;

(5) Immediately provide the court and all parties with any change to the electronic filer's electronic service address. This applies only when the electronic filer has consented to or is required to accept electronic service; and

(6) If the electronic filer uses an electronic filing service provider, provide the electronic filing service provider with the electronic address at

which the filer is to be sent all documents and immediately notify the electronic filing service provider of any change in that address.

(Subd (a) amended effective January 1, 2018; previously amended effective January 1, 2007, January 1, 2011, and July 1, 2013.)

(b) Format of documents to be filed electronically

A document that is filed electronically with the court must be in a format specified by the court unless it cannot be created in that format. The format adopted by a court must meet the following requirements:

(1) The software for creating and reading documents must be in the public domain or generally available at a reasonable cost.

(2) The printing of documents must not result in the loss of document text, format, or appearance.

(3) The document must be text searchable when technologically feasible without impairment of the document's image.

If a document is filed electronically under the rules in this chapter and cannot be formatted to be consistent with a formatting rule elsewhere in the California Rules of Court, the rules in this chapter prevail.

(Subd (b) amended effective January 1, 2017; previously amended effective January 1, 2006, January 1, 2008, and January 1, 2010.)

Rule 2.256 amended effective January 1, 2018; adopted as rule 2056 effective January 1, 2003; previously amended and renumbered effective January 1, 2007; previously amended effective January 1, 2006, January 1, 2008, January 1, 2010, January 1, 2011, July 1, 2013, and January 1, 2017.

Advisory Committee Comment

Subdivision (b)(3). The term "technologically feasible" does not require more than the application of standard, commercially available optical character recognition (OCR) software.

Rule 2.257. Requirements for signatures on documents

(a) Electronic signature

An electronic signature is an electronic sound, symbol, or process attached to or logically associated with an electronic record and executed or adopted by a person with the intent to sign a document or record created, generated, sent, communicated, received, or stored by electronic means.

(Subd (a) adopted effective January 1, 2019.)

(b) Documents signed under penalty of perjury

When a document to be filed electronically provides for a signature under penalty of perjury of any person, the document is deemed to have been signed by that person if filed electronically provided that either of the following conditions is satisfied:

(1) The declarant has signed the document using an electronic signature, and declares under penalty of perjury under the laws of the state of California that the information submitted is true and correct. If the declarant is not the electronic filer, the electronic signature must be unique to the declarant, capable of verification, under the sole control of the declarant, and linked to data in such a manner that if the data are changed, the electronic signature is invalidated; or

(2) The declarant, before filing, has physically signed a printed form of the document. By electronically filing the document, the electronic filer certifies that the original, signed document is available for inspection and copying at the request of the court or any other party. In the event this second method of submitting documents electronically under penalty of perjury is used, the following conditions apply:

(A) At any time after the electronic version of the document is filed, any party may serve a demand for production of the original signed document. The demand must be served on all other parties but need not be filed with the court.

(B) Within five days of service of the demand under (A), the party or other person on whom the demand is made must make the original signed document available for inspection and copying by all other parties.

(C) At any time after the electronic version of the document is filed, the court may order the filing party or other person to produce the original signed document in court for inspection and copying by the court. The order must specify the date, time, and place for the production and must be served on all parties.

(D) Notwithstanding (A)–(C), local child support agencies may maintain original, signed pleadings by way of an electronic copy in the statewide automated child support system and must maintain them only for the period of time stated in Government Code section 68152(a). If the local child support agency maintains an electronic copy of the original, signed pleading in the statewide automated child support system, it may destroy the paper original.

(Subd (b) amended effective January 1, 2020; adopted as subd (a); previously amended effective January 1, 2007, July 1, 2016, and January 1, 2018; previously relettered and amended as subd (b) effective January 1, 2019.)

(c) Documents not signed under penalty of perjury

(1) If a document does not require a signature under penalty of perjury, the document is deemed signed by the person who filed it electronically.

(2) When a document to be filed electronically, such as a stipulation, requires the signatures of opposing parties or persons other than the filer not under penalty of perjury, the following procedures apply:

(A) The opposing party or other person has signed a printed form of the document before, or on the same day as, the date of filing. The electronic filer must maintain the original, signed document and must make it available for inspection and copying as provided in (b)(2) of this rule and Code of Civil Procedure section 1010.6. The court and any other party may demand production of the original signed document in the manner provided in (b)(2)(A)–(C). By electronically filing the document, the electronic filer indicates that all parties have signed the document and that the filer has the signed original in his or her possession; or

(B) The opposing party or other person has signed the document using an electronic signature and that electronic signature is unique to the person using it, capable of verification, under the sole control of the person using it, and linked to data in such a manner that if the data are changed, the electronic signature is invalidated.

(Subd (c) amended effective January 1, 2020; adopted as subd (b); previously amended effective January 1, 2007; previously relettered effective January 1, 2019.)

(d) Digital signature

A party or other person is not required to use a digital signature on an electronically filed document.

(Subd (d) amended and relettered effective January 1, 2020; adopted as subd (d); previously relettered as subd (e) effective January 1, 2019.)

(e) Judicial signatures

If a document requires a signature by a court or a judicial officer, the document may be electronically signed in any manner permitted by law.

(Subd (e) relettered effective January 1, 2020; adopted as subd (e) effective January 1, 2008; previously relettered as subd (f) effective January 1, 2019.)

Rule 2.257 amended effective January 1, 2020; adopted as rule 2057 effective January 1, 2003; previously amended and renumbered effective January 1, 2007; previously amended effective January 1, 2008, July 1, 2016, January 1, 2018, and January 1, 2019.

Advisory Committee Comment

The requirements for electronic signatures that are compliant with the rule do not impair the power of the courts to resolve disputes about the validity of a signature.

Rule 2.258. Payment of filing fees in civil actions

(a) Use of credit cards and other methods

A court may permit the use of credit cards, debit cards, electronic fund transfers, or debit accounts for the payment of civil filing fees associated with electronic filing, as provided in Government Code section 6159, rule 10.820, and other applicable law. A court may also authorize other methods of payment.

(Subd (a) amended effective January 1, 2022; previously amended effective January 1, 2007.)

(b) Fee waivers

Eligible persons may seek a waiver of court fees and costs, as provided in Government Code sections 68630–68641, rule 2.252(f), and division 2 of title 3 of these rules.

(Subd (b) amended effective July 1, 2013; previously amended effective January 1, 2007, and January 1, 2010.)

Rule 2.258 amended effective January 1, 2022; adopted as rule 2058 effective January 1, 2003; previously amended and renumbered effective January 1, 2007; previously amended effective January 1, 2010, and July 1, 2013.

Rule 2.259. Actions by court on receipt of electronic filing

(a) Confirmation of receipt and filing of document

(1) *Confirmation of receipt*

When a court receives an electronically submitted document, the court must promptly send the electronic filer confirmation of the court's receipt of the document, indicating the date and time of receipt. A document is considered received at the date and time the confirmation of receipt is created.

(2) *Confirmation of filing*

If the document received by the court under (1) complies with filing requirements and all required filing fees have been paid, the court must promptly send the electronic filer confirmation that the document has been filed. The filing confirmation must indicate the date and time of filing and is proof that the document was filed on the date and at the time specified. The filing confirmation must also specify:

(A) Any transaction number associated with the filing;
(B) The titles of the documents as filed by the court; and
(C) The fees assessed for the filing.

(3) *Transmission of confirmations*

The court must send receipt and filing confirmation to the electronic filer at the electronic service address the filer furnished to the court under rule 2.256(a)(4). The court must maintain a record of all receipt and filing confirmations.

(4) *Filer responsible for verification*

In the absence of the court's confirmation of receipt and filing, there is no presumption that the court received and filed the document. The electronic filer is responsible for verifying that the court received and filed any document that the electronic filer submitted to the court electronically.

(Subd (a) amended effective January 1, 2011; previously amended effective January 1, 2007, and January 1, 2008.)

(b) Notice of rejection of document for filing

If the clerk does not file a document because it does not comply with applicable filing requirements or because the required filing fee has not been paid, the court must promptly send notice of the rejection of the document for filing to the electronic filer. The notice must state the reasons that the document was rejected for filing.

(Subd (b) amended effective January 1, 2007.)

(c) Delayed delivery

If a technical problem with a court's electronic filing system prevents the court from accepting an electronic filing on a particular court day, and the electronic filer demonstrates that he or she attempted to electronically file the document on that day, the court must deem the document as filed on that day. This subdivision does not apply to the filing of a complaint or any other initial pleading in an action or proceeding.

(Subd (c) repealed, amended and relettered effective January 1, 2018; adopted as subd (d); previously amended effective January 1, 2007.)

(d) Endorsement

(1) The court's endorsement of a document electronically filed must contain the following: "Electronically filed by Superior Court of California, County of _____, on _____ (date)," followed by the name of the court clerk.

(2) The endorsement required under (1) has the same force and effect as a manually affixed endorsement stamp with the signature and initials of the court clerk.

(3) A complaint or another initial pleading in an action or proceeding that is filed and endorsed electronically may be printed and served on the defendant or respondent in the same manner as if it had been filed in paper form.

(Subd (d) relettered effective January 1, 2018; adopted as subd (e); previously amended effective January 1, 2007.)

(e) Issuance of electronic summons

(1) The court may issue an electronic summons in the following circumstances:

(A) On the electronic filing of a complaint, a petition, or another document that must be served with a summons in a civil action, the court may transmit a summons electronically to the electronic filer in accordance with this subdivision and Code of Civil Procedure section 1010.6.

(B) On the electronic filing of an accusatory pleading against a corporation, the court may transmit a summons electronically to the prosecutor in accordance with this subdivision and Penal Code sections 690.5, 1390, and 1391.

(C) When a summons is issued in lieu of an arrest warrant, the court may transmit the summons electronically to the prosecutor or person authorized to serve the summons in accordance with this subdivision and Penal Code sections 690.5, 813, and 816a.

(2) The electronically transmitted summons must contain an image of the court's seal and the assigned case number.

(3) Personal service of the printed form of a summons transmitted electronically to the electronic filer has the same legal effect as personal service of a copy of an original summons.

(Subd (e) amended effective January 1, 2022; adopted as subd (f); previously amended effective January 1, 2007; previously amended and relettered as subd (e) effective January 1, 2018.)

Rule 2.259 amended effective January 1, 2022; adopted as rule 2059 effective January 1, 2003; previously amended and renumbered effective January 1, 2007; previously amended effective January 1, 2008, January 1, 2011, July 1, 2013, and January 1, 2018.

Rule 2.260. Electronic service [Renumbered]

Rule 2.260 renumbered as rule 2.251 effective January 1, 2011.

Rule 2.261. Authorization for courts to continue modifying forms for the purpose of electronic filing and forms generation

Courts that participated in pilot projects for electronic filing and forms generation under former rule 981.5 are authorized to continue to modify Judicial Council forms for the purpose of accepting electronic filing or providing electronic generation of court documents provided that the modification of the forms is consistent with the rules in this chapter.

Rule 2.261 amended and renumbered effective January 1, 2007; adopted as rule 2061 effective July 1, 2004.

Chapter 3
Filing and Service by Fax

Rule 2.300. Application
Rule 2.301. Definitions
Rule 2.302. Compliance with the rules on the form and format of papers
Rule 2.303. Filing through fax filing agency
Rule 2.304. Direct filing
Rule 2.305. Requirements for signatures on documents
Rule 2.306. Service of papers by fax transmission

Rule 2.300. Application

(a) Proceedings to which rules apply

The rules in this chapter apply to civil, probate, and family law proceedings in all trial courts. Rule 5.386 applies to fax filing of a protective order issued by a tribal court. Rule 5.522 applies to fax filing in juvenile law proceedings.

(Subd (a) amended effective July 1, 2012; adopted as part of unlettered subd effective March 1, 1992; previously amended and lettered effective January 1, 2007.)

(b) Documents that may not be issued by fax

Notwithstanding any provision in the rules in this chapter, no will, codicil, bond, or undertaking may be filed by fax nor may a court issue by fax any document intended to carry the original seal of the court.

(Subd (b) amended and lettered effective January 1, 2007; adopted as part of unlettered subd effective March 1, 1992.)

Rule 2.300 amended effective July 1, 2012; adopted as rule 2002 effective March 1, 1992; previously amended effective January 1, 1999; previously amended and renumbered effective January 1, 2007.

Rule 2.301. Definitions

As used in this chapter, unless the context otherwise requires:

(1) "Fax" is an abbreviation for "facsimile" and refers, as indicated by the context, to facsimile transmission or to a document so transmitted.

(2) "Fax transmission" means the transmission of a document by a system that encodes a document into electrical signals, transmits these electrical signals over a telephone line, and reconstructs the signals to print a duplicate of the original document at the receiving end.

(3) "Fax machine" means a machine that can send a facsimile transmission using the international standard for scanning, coding, and transmission established for Group 3 machines by the Consultative Committee of International Telegraphy and Telephone of the International Telecommunications Union (CCITT),[1] in regular resolution. Any fax machine used to send documents to a court under rule 2.305 must send at an initial transmission speed of no less than 4800 baud and be able to generate a transmission record. "Fax machine" includes a fax modem that is connected to a personal computer.

(4) "Fax filing" means the fax transmission of a document to a court that accepts such documents.

(5) "Service by fax" means the transmission of a document to a party or the attorney for a party under the rules in this chapter.

(6) "Transmission record" means the document printed by the sending fax machine, stating the telephone number of the receiving fax machine, the number of pages sent, the transmission time and date, and an indication of any errors in transmission.

(7) "Fax filing agency" means an entity that receives documents by fax for processing and filing with the court.

---

[1] Recommendations T.4 and T.30, Volume VII—Facsimile VII.3, CCITT Red Book, Malaga-Torremolinos, 1984, U.N. Bookstore Code ITU 6731.

Rule 2.301 amended and renumbered effective January 1, 2007; adopted as rule 2003 effective March 1, 1992.

Rule 2.302. Compliance with the rules on the form and format of papers

The document used for transmitting a fax must comply with the rules in division 2, chapter 1 of this title regarding form or format of papers. Any exhibit that exceeds 8-½ by 11 inches must be reduced in size to not more than 8-½ by 11 inches before it is transmitted. The court may require the filing party to file the original of an exhibit that the party has filed by fax.

Rule 2.302 amended and renumbered effective January 1, 2007; adopted as rule 2004 effective March 1, 1992.

Rule 2.303. Filing through fax filing agency

(a) Transmission of document for filing

A party may transmit a document by fax to a fax filing agency for filing with any trial court. The agency acts as the agent of the filing party and not as an agent of the court.

(b) Duties of fax filing agency

The fax filing agency that receives a document for filing must:

(1) Prepare the document so that it complies with the rules in division 2, chapter 1 of this title and any other requirements for filing with the court;

(2) Physically transport the document to the court; and

(3) File the document with the court, paying any applicable filing fee.

(Subd (b) amended effective January 1, 2007.)

(c) Requirement of advance arrangements

A fax filing agency is not required to accept papers for filing from any party unless appropriate arrangements for payment of filing fees and service charges have been made in advance of any transmission to the agency. If an agency receives a document from a party with whom it does not have prior arrangements, the agency may discard the document without notice to the sender.

(Subd (c) amended effective January 1, 2007.)

(d) Confidentiality

A fax filing agency must keep all documents transmitted to it confidential except as provided in the rules in this chapter.

(Subd (d) amended effective January 1, 2007.)

(e) Certification

A fax filing agency, by filing a document with the court, certifies that it has complied with the rules in this chapter and that the document filed is the full and unaltered fax-produced document received by it. The agency is not required to give any additional certification.

(Subd (e) amended effective January 1, 2007.)

(f) Notation of fax filing

Each document filed by a fax filing agency must contain the phrase "By fax" immediately below the title of the document.

(Subd (f) amended effective January 1, 2007.)

Rule 2.303 amended and renumbered effective January 1, 2007; adopted as rule 2005 effective March 1, 1992.

Rule 2.304. Direct filing

(a) Courts in which applicable

A party may file by fax directly to any court that, by local rule, has provided for direct fax filing. The local rule must state that direct fax filing may be made under the rules in this chapter and must provide the fax telephone number for filings and specific telephone numbers for any departments to which fax filings should be made directly. The court must also accept agency filings under rule 2.303.

(Subd (a) amended effective January 1, 2007.)

(b) Mandatory cover sheet

A party filing a document directly by fax must use the *Facsimile Transmission Cover Sheet (Fax Filing)* (form MC-005). The cover sheet must be the first page transmitted, to be followed by any special handling instructions needed to ensure that the document will comply with local rules. Neither the cover sheet nor the special handling instructions are to be filed in the case. The court must ensure that any credit card information on the cover sheet is not publicly disclosed. The court is not required to keep a copy of the cover sheet.

(Subd (b) amended effective January 1, 2007.)

(c) Notation of fax filing

Each document transmitted for direct filing with the court must contain the phrase "By fax" immediately below the title of the document.

(Subd (c) amended effective January 1, 2007.)

(d) Presumption of filing

A party filing by fax must cause the transmitting fax machine to print a transmission record of each filing by fax. If the document transmitted to the court by fax machine is not filed with the court because of (1) an error in the transmission of the document to the court that was unknown to the sending party or (2) a failure to process the document after it has been received by the court, the sending party may move the court for an order filing the document nunc pro tunc. The motion must be accompanied by the transmission record and a proof of transmission in the following form:

"On (date) _____ at (time) _____, I transmitted to the (court name) _____ the following documents (name) _____ by fax machine, under California Rules of Court, rule 2.304. The court's fax telephone number that I used was (fax telephone number) _____. The fax machine I used complied with rule 2.301 and no error was reported by the machine. Under rule 2.304, I caused the machine to print a transmission record of the transmission, a copy of which is attached to this declaration.

"I declare under penalty of perjury under the laws of the State of California that the foregoing is true and correct."

(Subd (d) amended effective July 1, 2013; previously amended effective January 1, 2007.)

(e) Payment of fees by credit card

(1) *Credit or debit card payments*

The court may permit credit cards, debit cards, electronic funds transfers, or debit accounts to be used to pay filing fees for fax filings made directly with the court, as provided in Government Code section 6159, rule 10.820, and other applicable laws. The cover sheet for these filings must include (1) the credit or debit card account number to which the fees may be charged, (2) the signature of the cardholder authorizing the charging of the fees, and (3) the expiration date of the credit or debit card.

(2) *Rejection of charge*

If the charge is rejected by the credit or debit card issuing company, the court must proceed in the same manner as under Code of Civil Procedure section 411.20 relating to returned checks. This provision does not prevent a court from seeking authorization for the charge before the filing and rejecting the filing if the charge is not approved by the issuing company.

(3) *Amount of charge*

The amount charged is the applicable filing fee plus any fee or discount imposed by the card issuer or draft purchaser.

(Subd (e) amended effective January 1, 2007.)

(f) Filing fee accounts

If a court so provides in its local rule establishing a direct fax filing program, an account may be used to pay for documents filed by fax by an attorney or party who has established an account with the court before filing a paper by fax. The court may require the deposit in advance of an amount not to exceed $1,000, or the court may agree to bill the attorney or party not more often than monthly.

(Subd (f) amended effective January 1, 2007.)

Rule 2.304 amended effective July 1, 2013; adopted as rule 2006 effective March 1, 1992; previously amended effective July 1, 2006; previously amended and renumbered effective January 1, 2007.

Rule 2.305. Requirements for signatures on documents

(a) Possession of original document

A party who files or serves a signed document by fax under the rules in this chapter represents that the original signed document is in the party's possession or control.

(Subd (a) amended effective January 1, 2007.)

(b) Demand for original; waiver

At any time after filing or service of a signed fax document, any other party may serve a demand for production of the original physically signed document. The demand must be served on all other parties but not filed with the court.

(Subd (b) amended effective January 1, 2007.)

(c) Examination of original

If a demand for production of the original signed document is made, the parties must arrange a meeting at which the original signed document can be examined.

(Subd (c) amended effective January 1, 2007.)

(d) Fax signature as original

Notwithstanding any provision of law to the contrary, including Evidence Code sections 255 and 260, a signature produced by fax transmission is deemed to be an original.

(Subd (d) amended effective January 1, 2007.)

Rule 2.305 amended and renumbered effective January 1, 2007; adopted as rule 2007 effective March 1, 1992.

Rule 2.306. Service of papers by fax transmission

(a) Service by fax

(1) *Agreement of parties required*

Service by fax transmission is permitted only if the parties agree and a written confirmation of that agreement is made.

(2) *Service on last-given fax number*

Any notice or other document to be served must be transmitted to a fax machine maintained by the person on whom it is served at the fax machine telephone number as last given by that person on any document that the party has filed in the case and served on the party making service.

(Subd (a) amended and lettered effective January 1, 2007; adopted as part of subd (b) effective March 1, 1992.)

(b) Service lists

(1) *Duties of first-named plaintiff or petitioner*

In a case in which the parties have agreed to service by fax, the plaintiff or petitioner named first in the complaint or petition, in addition to its responsibilities under rule 3.254, must:

(A) Maintain a current list of the parties that includes their fax numbers for service of notice on each party; and

(B) Furnish a copy of the list on request to any party or the court.

(2) *Duties of each party*

In a case in which the parties have agreed to service by fax, each party, in addition to its responsibilities under rule 3.254, must:

(A) Furnish the first-named plaintiff or petitioner with the party's current fax number for service of notice when it first appears in the action; and

(B) If the party serves an order, notice, or pleading on a party that has not yet appeared in the action, serve a copy of the service list under (1) at the same time that the order, notice, or pleading is served.

(Subd (b) adopted effective January 1, 2008.)

(c) Transmission of papers by court

A court may serve any notice by fax in the same manner that parties may serve papers by fax.

(Subd (c) relettered effective January 1, 2008; adopted as subd (b) effective January 1, 2007.)

(d) Notice period extended

Except as provided in (e), any prescribed period of notice and any right or duty to do any act or make any response within any prescribed period or on a date certain after the service of a document served by fax transmission is extended by two court days.

(Subd (d) amended effective July 1, 2008; adopted as part of subd (b) effective March 1, 1992; previously amended and lettered as subd (c) effective January 1, 2007; previously relettered as subd (d) effective January 1, 2008.)

(e) Extension inapplicable to certain motions

The extension provided in (d) does not apply to extend the time for the filing of:

(1) A notice of intent to move for new trial;

(2) A notice of intent to move to vacate a judgment under Code of Civil Procedure section 663; or

(3) A notice of appeal.

(Subd (e) amended effective July 1, 2008; adopted as part of subd (b) effective March 1, 1992; previously amended and lettered as subd (d) effective January 1, 2007; previously relettered as subd (e) effective January 1, 2008.)

(f) Availability of fax

A party or attorney agreeing to accept service by fax must make his or her fax machine generally available for receipt of served documents between the hours of 9 a.m. and 5 p.m. on days that are not court holidays under Code of Civil Procedure section 136. This provision does not prevent the party or attorney from sending other documents by means of the fax machine or providing for normal repair and maintenance of the fax machine during these hours.

(Subd (f) relettered effective January 1, 2008; adopted as subd (c) effective March 1, 1992; previously amended and relettered as subd (e) effective January 1, 2007.)

(g) When service complete

Service by fax is complete on transmission of the entire document to the receiving party's fax machine. Service that is completed after 5 p.m. is deemed to have occurred on the next court day. Time is extended as provided by this rule.

(Subd (g) relettered effective January 1, 2008; adopted as subd (d) effective March 1, 1992; previously amended effective July 1, 1997; previously amended and relettered as subd (f) effective January 1, 2007.)

(h) Proof of service by fax

Proof of service by fax may be made by any of the methods provided in Code of Civil Procedure section 1013(a), except that:

(1) The date and sending fax machine telephone number must be used instead of the date and place of deposit in the mail;

(2) The name and fax machine telephone number of the person served must be used instead of the name and address of the person served as shown on the envelope;

(3) A statement that the document was sent by fax transmission and that the transmission was reported as complete and without error must be used instead of the statement that the envelope was sealed and deposited in the mail with the postage thereon fully prepaid;

(4) A copy of the transmission report must be attached to the proof of service and the proof of service must declare that the transmission report was properly issued by the sending fax machine; and

(5) Service of papers by fax is ineffective if the transmission does not fully conform to these provisions.

(Subd (h) amended effective January 1, 2017; adopted as subd (e) effective March 1, 1992; previously amended effective July 1, 1997, and May 1, 1998; previously amended and relettered as subd (g) effective January 1, 2007; previously relettered as subd (h) effective January 1, 2008.)

Rule 2.306 amended effective January 1, 2017; adopted as rule 2008 effective March 1, 1992; previously amended effective July 1, 1997, May 1, 1998, January 1, 2008, and July 1, 2008; previously amended and renumbered effective January 1, 2007.

Division 4
Court Records

Chap. 1. General Provisions. Rule 2.400.
Chap. 2. Access to Electronic Trial Court Records. Rules 2.500–2.545.
Chap. 3. Sealed Records. Rules 2.550, 2.551.
Chap. 4. Records in False Claims Act Cases. Rules 2.570–2.573.
Chap. 5. Name Change Proceedings Under Address Confidentiality Program. Rules 2.575–2.577.
Chap. 6. Other Sealed or Closed Records. Rules 2.580, 2.585.

Chapter 1
General Provisions

Rule 2.400. Court records

(a) Removal of records

Only the clerk may remove and replace records in the court's files. Unless otherwise provided by these rules or ordered by the court, court records may only be inspected by the public in the office of the clerk and released to authorized court personnel or an attorney of record for use in a court facility. No original court records may be used in any location other than a court facility, unless so ordered by the presiding judge or his or her designee.

(Subd (a) amended effective January 1, 2010; previously amended effective July 1, 1993, January 1, 2007, January 1, 2008, and January 1, 2009.)

(b) Original documents filed with the clerk; duplicate documents for temporary judge or referee

(1) All original documents in a case pending before a temporary judge or referee must be filed with the clerk in the same manner as would be required if the case were being heard by a judge, including filing within any time limits specified by law and paying any required fees. The filing party must provide a filed-stamped copy to the temporary judge or referee of each document relevant to the issues before the temporary judge or referee.

(2) If a document must be filed with the court before it is considered by a judge, the temporary judge or referee must not accept or consider any copy of that document unless the document has the clerk's file stamp or is accompanied by a declaration stating that the original document has been submitted to the court for filing.

(3) If a document would ordinarily be filed with the court after it is submitted to a judge or if a party submits an ex parte application, the party that submits the document or application to a temporary judge or referee must file the original with the court no later than the next court day after the document or application was submitted to the temporary judge or referee and must promptly provide a filed-stamped copy of the document or application to the temporary judge or referee.

(4) A party that has submitted a document to a temporary judge or referee must immediately notify the temporary judge or referee if the

document is not accepted for filing by the court or if the filing is subsequently canceled.

(Subd (b) amended effective January 1, 2010; adopted effective July 1, 1993; previously amended effective January 1, 2007.)

(c) Return of exhibits

(1) The clerk must not release any exhibit except on order of the court. The clerk must require a signed receipt for a released exhibit.

(2) If proceedings are conducted by a temporary judge or a referee outside of court facilities, the temporary judge or referee must keep all exhibits and deliver them, properly marked, to the clerk at the conclusion of the proceedings, unless the parties file, and the court approves, a written stipulation providing for a different disposition of the exhibits. On request of the temporary judge or referee, the clerk must deliver exhibits filed or lodged with the court to the possession of the temporary judge or referee, who must not release them to any person other than the clerk, unless the court orders otherwise.

(Subd (c) amended effective January 1, 2010; adopted as subd (b) effective January 1, 1949; previously amended and relettered effective July 1, 1993; previously amended effective January 1, 2007.)

(d) Access to documents and exhibits in matters before temporary judges and referees

(1) Documents and exhibits in the possession of a temporary judge or referee that would be open to the public if filed or lodged with the court must be made available during business hours for inspection by any person within a reasonable time after request and under reasonable conditions.

(2) Temporary judges and referees must file a statement in each case in which they are appointed that provides the name, telephone number, and mailing address of a person who may be contacted to obtain access to any documents or exhibits submitted to the temporary judge or referee that would be open to the public if filed or lodged with the court. The statement must be filed at the same time as the temporary judge's or referee's certification under rule 2.831(b), 3.904(a), or 3.924(a). If there is any change in this contact information, the temporary judge or referee must promptly file a revised statement with the court.

(Subd (d) adopted effective January 1, 2010.)

(e) Definition

For purposes of this rule, "court facility" consists of those areas within a building required or used for court functions.

(Subd (e) adopted effective January 1, 2010.)

Rule 2.400 amended effective January 1, 2010; adopted as rule 243 effective January 1, 1949; previously amended and renumbered effective January 1, 2007; previously amended effective July 1, 1993, January 1, 2008, and January 1, 2009.

Advisory Committee Comment

Subdivision (b)(1). Rules 2.810 and 2.830 provide definitions of temporary judges appointed by the court and temporary judges requested by the parties, respectively.

Subdivision (d)(1). Public access to documents and exhibits in the possession of a temporary judge or referee should be the same as if the case were being heard by a judge. Documents and exhibits are not normally available to the public during a hearing or when needed by the judge for hearing or decision preparation. A temporary judge or referee may direct that access to documents and exhibits be available by scheduled appointment.

Chapter 2
Access to Electronic Trial Court Records

Title 2, Trial Court Rules—Chapter 2, Access to Electronic Trial Court Records; amended effective January 1, 2019.

Art. 1. General Provisions. Rules 2.500–2.502.
Art. 2. Public Access. Rules 2.503–2.507.
Art. 3. Remote Access by a Party, Party's Designee, Party's Attorney, Court-Appointed Person, or Authorized Person Working in a Legal Organization or Qualified Legal Services Project. Rules 2.515–2.528.
Art. 4. Remote Access by Government Entities. Rules 2.540–2.545.

Article 1
General Provisions

Title 2, Trial Court Rules—Chapter 2, Access to Electronic Trial Court Records; Article 1, General Provisions; adopted effective January 1, 2019.

Rule 2.500. Statement of purpose
Rule 2.501. Application, scope, and information to the public
Rule 2.502. Definitions

Rule 2.500. Statement of purpose

(a) Intent

The rules in this chapter are intended to provide the public, parties, parties' attorneys, legal organizations, court-appointed persons, and government entities with reasonable access to trial court records that are maintained in electronic form, while protecting privacy interests.

(Subd (a) amended effective January 1, 2019.)

(b) Benefits of electronic access

Improved technologies provide courts with many alternatives to the historical paper-based record receipt and retention process, including the creation and use of court records maintained in electronic form. Providing access to trial court records that are maintained in electronic form may save the courts, the public, parties, parties' attorneys, legal organizations, court-appointed persons, and government entities time, money, and effort and encourage courts to be more efficient in their operations. Improved access to trial court records may also foster in the public a more comprehensive understanding of the trial court system.

(Subd (b) amended effective January 1, 2019.)

(c) No creation of rights

The rules in this chapter are not intended to give the public, parties, parties' attorneys, legal organizations, court-appointed persons, and government entities a right of access to any record that they are not otherwise legally entitled to access.

(Subd (c) amended effective January 1, 2019; previously amended effective January 1, 2007.)

Rule 2.500 amended effective January 1, 2019; adopted as rule 2070 effective July 1, 2002; previously amended and renumbered effective January 1, 2007.

Advisory Committee Comment

The rules in this chapter acknowledge the benefits that electronic records provide but attempt to limit the potential for unjustified intrusions into the privacy of individuals involved in litigation that can occur as a result of remote access to electronic records. The proposed rules take into account the limited resources currently available in the trial courts. It is contemplated that the rules may be modified to provide greater electronic access as courts' technical capabilities improve and knowledge is gained from the experience of providing electronic access under these rules.

Rule 2.501. Application, scope, and information to the public

(a) Application and scope

The rules in this chapter apply only to trial court records as defined in rule 2.502(3). They do not apply to statutorily mandated reporting between or within government entities, or any other documents or materials that are not court records.

(Subd (a) amended effective January 1, 2019; adopted as subd (b) effective July 1, 2002; amended and relettered effective January 1, 2007.)

(b) Information to the public

The website for each trial court must include a link to information that will inform the public of who may access their electronic records under the rules in this chapter and under what conditions they may do so. This information will be posted publicly on the California Courts website at *www.courts.ca.gov*. Each trial court may post additional information, in plain language, as necessary to inform the public about the level of access that the particular trial court is providing.

(Subd (b) amended effective January 1, 2019; adopted as subd (c) effective July 1, 2002; amended and relettered effective January 1, 2007.)

Rule 2.501 amended effective January 1, 2019; adopted as rule 2017 effective July 1, 2002; amended and renumbered effective January 1, 2007.

Advisory Committee Comment

The rules on remote access do not apply beyond court records to other types of documents, information, or data. Rule 2.502 defines a court record as "any document, paper, or exhibit filed in an action or proceeding; any order or judgment of the court; and any item listed in Government Code section 68151(a)—excluding any reporter's transcript for which the reporter is entitled to receive a fee for any copy—that is maintained by the court in the ordinary course of the judicial process. The term does not include the personal notes or preliminary memoranda of judges or other judicial branch personnel, statutorily mandated reporting between government entities, judicial administrative records, court case information, or compilations of data drawn from court records where the compilations are not themselves contained in a court record." (Cal. Rules of Court, rule 2.502(3).) Thus, courts generate and maintain many types of information that are not court records and to which access may be restricted by law. Such information is not remotely accessible as court records, even to parties and their attorneys. If parties and their attorneys are entitled to access to any such additional information, separate and independent grounds for that access must exist.

Rule 2.502. Definitions

As used in this chapter, the following definitions apply:

(1) "Authorized person" means a person authorized by a legal organization, qualified legal services project, or government entity to access electronic records.

(2) "Brief legal services" means legal assistance provided without, or before, becoming a party's attorney. It includes giving advice, having a consultation, performing research, investigating case facts, drafting documents, and making limited third party contacts on behalf of a client.

(3) "Court record" is any document, paper, or exhibit filed in an action or proceeding; any order or judgment of the court; and any item listed in Government Code section 68151(a)—excluding any reporter's transcript for which the reporter is entitled to receive a fee for any copy—that is maintained by the court in the ordinary course of the judicial process. The term does not include the personal notes or preliminary memoranda of judges or other judicial branch personnel, statutorily mandated reporting between or within government entities, judicial administrative records, court case information, or compilations of data drawn from court records where the compilations are not themselves contained in a court record.

(4) "Court case information" refers to data that is stored in a court's case management system or case histories. This data supports the court's management or tracking of the action and is not part of the official court record for the case or cases.

(5) "Electronic access" means access by electronic means to court records available through public terminals at the courthouse and remotely, unless otherwise specified in the rules in this chapter.

(6) "Electronic record" is a court record that requires the use of an electronic device to access. The term includes both a record that has been filed electronically and an electronic copy or version of a record that was filed in paper form. The term does not include a court record that is maintained only on microfiche, paper, or any other medium that can be read without the use of an electronic device.

(7) "Government entity" means a legal entity organized to carry on some function of the State of California or a political subdivision of the State of California. Government entity also means a federally recognized Indian tribe or a reservation, department, subdivision, or court of a federally recognized Indian tribe.

(8) "Legal organization" means a licensed attorney or group of attorneys, nonprofit legal aid organization, government legal office, in-house legal office of a nongovernmental organization, or legal program organized to provide for indigent criminal, civil, or juvenile law representation.

(9) "Party" means a plaintiff, defendant, cross-complainant, cross-defendant, petitioner, respondent, intervenor, objector, or anyone expressly defined by statute as a party in a court case.

(10) "Person" means a natural human being.

(11) "The public" means a person, a group, or an entity, including print or electronic media, regardless of any legal or other interest in a particular court record.

(12) "Qualified legal services project" has the same meaning under the rules of this chapter as in Business and Professions Code section 6213(a).

(13) "Remote access" means electronic access from a location other than a public terminal at the courthouse.

(14) "User" means an individual person, a group, or an entity that accesses electronic records.

Rule 2.502 amended and renumbered effective January 1, 2019; adopted as rule 2072 effective July 1, 2002; previously amended and renumbered effective January 1, 2007.

Article 2
Public Access

Title 2, Trial Court Rules—Chapter 2, Access to Electronic Trial Court Records; Article 2, Public Access; adopted effective January 1, 2019.

Rule 2.503. Application and scope
Rule 2.504. Limitations and conditions
Rule 2.505. Contracts with vendors
Rule 2.506. Fees for electronic access
Rule 2.507. Electronic access to court calendars, indexes, and registers of actions

Rule 2.503. Application and scope

(a) General right of access by the public

(1) All electronic records must be made reasonably available to the public in some form, whether in electronic or in paper form, except those that are sealed by court order or made confidential by law.

(2) The rules in this article apply only to access to electronic records by the public.

(Subd (a) amended effective January 1, 2019; previously amended effective January 1, 2007.)

(b) Electronic access required to extent feasible

A court that maintains the following records in electronic form must provide electronic access to them, both remotely and at the courthouse, to the extent it is feasible to do so:

(1) Registers of actions (as defined in Gov. Code, § 69845), calendars, and indexes in all cases; and

(2) All court records in civil cases, except those listed in (c)(1)–(11).

(Subd (b) amended effective January 1, 2019; previously amended effective July 1, 2004, January 1, 2007, January 1, 2008, and January 1, 2010.)

(c) Courthouse electronic access only

A court that maintains the following records in electronic form must provide electronic access to them at the courthouse, to the extent it is feasible to do so, but may not provide public remote access to these records:

(1) Records in a proceeding under the Family Code, including proceedings for dissolution, legal separation, and nullity of marriage; child and spousal support proceedings; child custody proceedings; and domestic violence prevention proceedings;

(2) Records in a juvenile court proceeding;

(3) Records in a guardianship or conservatorship proceeding;

(4) Records in a mental health proceeding;

(5) Records in a criminal proceeding;

(6) Records in proceedings to compromise the claims of a minor or a person with a disability;

(7) Records in a civil harassment proceeding under Code of Civil Procedure section 527.6;

(8) Records in a workplace violence prevention proceeding under Code of Civil Procedure section 527.8;

(9) Records in a private postsecondary school violence prevention proceeding under Code of Civil Procedure section 527.85;

(10) Records in an elder or dependent adult abuse prevention proceeding under Welfare and Institutions Code section 15657.03; and

(11) Records in a gun violence prevention proceeding under Penal Code sections 18100–18205.

(Subd (c) amended effective January 1, 2019; previously amended effective July 1, 2004, January 1, 2007, January 1, 2008, January 1, 2010, and January 1, 2012.)

(d) "Feasible" defined

As used in this rule, the requirement that a court provide electronic access to its electronic records "to the extent it is feasible to do so" means that a court is required to provide electronic access to the extent it determines it has the resources and technical capacity to do so.

(Subd (d) amended effective January 1, 2007.)

(e) Remote access allowed in extraordinary criminal cases

Notwithstanding (c)(5), the presiding judge of the court, or a judge assigned by the presiding judge, may exercise discretion, subject to (e)(1), to permit remote access by the public to all or a portion of the public court records in an individual criminal case if (1) the number of requests for access to documents in the case is extraordinarily high and (2) responding to those requests would significantly burden the operations of the court. An individualized determination must be made in each case in which such remote access is provided.

(1) In exercising discretion under (e), the judge should consider the relevant factors, such as:

(A) The privacy interests of parties, victims, witnesses, and court personnel, and the ability of the court to redact sensitive personal information;

(B) The benefits to and burdens on the parties in allowing remote access, including possible impacts on jury selection; and

(C) The burdens on the court in responding to an extraordinarily high number of requests for access to documents.

(2) The court should, to the extent feasible, redact the following information from records to which it allows remote access under (e): driver license numbers; dates of birth; social security numbers; Criminal Identification and Information and National Crime Information numbers; addresses and phone numbers of parties, victims, witnesses, and court personnel; medical or psychiatric information; financial information; account numbers; and other personal identifying information. The court may order any party who files a document containing such information to provide the court with both an original unredacted version of the document for filing in the court file and a redacted version of the document for remote access. No juror names or other juror identifying

information may be provided by remote access. This subdivision does not apply to any document in the original court file; it applies only to documents that are available by remote access.

(3) Five days' notice must be provided to the parties and the public before the court makes a determination to provide remote access under this rule. Notice to the public may be accomplished by posting notice on the court's website. Any person may file comments with the court for consideration, but no hearing is required.

(4) The court's order permitting remote access must specify which court records will be available by remote access and what categories of information are to be redacted. The court is not required to make findings of fact. The court's order must be posted on the court's website and a copy sent to the Judicial Council.

(Subd (e) amended effective January 1, 2019; adopted effective January 1, 2005; previously amended effective January 1, 2007.)

(f) Access only on a case-by-case basis

The court may only grant electronic access to an electronic record when the record is identified by the number of the case, the caption of the case, or the name of a party, and only on a case-by-case basis. This case-by-case limitation does not apply to the court's electronic records of a calendar, register of actions, or index.

(Subd (f) amended effective January 1, 2007; adopted as subd (e) effective July 1, 2002; previously relettered effective January 1, 2005.)

(g) Bulk distribution

The court may provide bulk distribution of only its electronic records of a calendar, register of actions, and index. "Bulk distribution" means distribution of all, or a significant subset, of the court's electronic records.

(Subd (g) amended effective January 1, 2007; adopted as subd (f) effective July 1, 2002; previously relettered effective January 1, 2005.)

(h) Records that become inaccessible

If an electronic record to which the court has provided electronic access is made inaccessible to the public by court order or by operation of law, the court is not required to take action with respect to any copy of the record that was made by the public before the record became inaccessible.

(Subd (h) relettered effective January 1, 2005; adopted as subd (g) effective July 1, 2002.)

(i) Off-site access

Courts should encourage availability of electronic access to court records at public off-site locations.

(Subd (i) relettered effective January 1, 2005; adopted as subd (h) effective July 1, 2002.)

Rule 2.503 amended effective January 1, 2019; adopted as rule 2073 effective July 1, 2002; previously amended and renumbered effective January 1, 2007; previously amended effective July 1, 2004, January 1, 2005, January 1, 2008, January 1, 2010, and January 1, 2012.

Advisory Committee Comment

The rule allows a level of access by the public to all electronic records that is at least equivalent to the access that is available for paper records and, for some types of records, is much greater. At the same time, it seeks to protect legitimate privacy concerns.

Subdivision (c). This subdivision excludes certain records (those other than the register, calendar, and indexes) in specified types of cases (notably criminal, juvenile, and family court matters) from public remote access. The committee recognized that while these case records are public records and should remain available at the courthouse, either in paper or electronic form, they often contain sensitive personal information. The court should not publish that information over the Internet. However, the committee also recognized that the use of the Internet may be appropriate in certain criminal cases of extraordinary public interest where information regarding a case will be widely disseminated through the media. In such cases, posting of selected nonconfidential court records, redacted where necessary to protect the privacy of the participants, may provide more timely and accurate information regarding the court proceedings, and may relieve substantial burdens on court staff in responding to individual requests for documents and information. Thus, under subdivision (e), if the presiding judge makes individualized determinations in a specific case, certain records in criminal cases may be made available over the Internet.

Subdivisions (f) and (g). These subdivisions limit electronic access to records (other than the register, calendars, or indexes) to a case-by-case basis and prohibit bulk distribution of those records. These limitations are based on the qualitative difference between obtaining information from a specific case file and obtaining bulk information that may be manipulated to compile personal information culled from any document, paper, or exhibit filed in a lawsuit. This type of aggregate information may be exploited for commercial or other purposes unrelated to the operations of the courts, at the expense of privacy rights of individuals.

Courts must send a copy of the order permitting remote access in extraordinary criminal cases to Criminal Justice Services, Judicial Council of California, 455 Golden Gate Avenue, San Francisco, CA 94102-3688.

Rule 2.504. Limitations and conditions

(a) Means of access

A court that maintains records in electronic form must provide electronic access to those records by means of a network or software that is based on industry standards or is in the public domain.

(Subd (a) amended effective January 1, 2007.)

(b) Official record

Unless electronically certified by the court, a trial court record available by electronic access is not the official record of the court.

(Subd (b) amended effective January 1, 2007.)

(c) Conditions of use by persons accessing records

A court may condition electronic access to its records on:

(1) The user's consent to access the records only as instructed by the court; and

(2) The user's consent to the court's monitoring of access to its records.

The court must give notice of these conditions, in any manner it deems appropriate. The court may deny access to a member of the public for failure to comply with either of these conditions of use.

(Subd (c) amended effective January 1, 2007.)

(d) Notices to persons accessing records

The court must give notice of the following information to members of the public accessing its records electronically, in any manner it deems appropriate:

(1) The identity of the court staff member to be contacted about the requirements for accessing the court's records electronically.

(2) That copyright and other proprietary rights may apply to information in a case file, absent an express grant of additional rights by the holder of the copyright or other proprietary right. This notice must advise the public that:

(A) Use of such information in a case file is permissible only to the extent permitted by law or court order; and

(B) Any use inconsistent with proprietary rights is prohibited.

(3) Whether electronic records are the official records of the court. The notice must describe the procedure and any fee required for obtaining a certified copy of an official record of the court.

(4) That any person who willfully destroys or alters any court record maintained in electronic form is subject to the penalties imposed by Government Code section 6201.

(Subd (d) amended effective January 1, 2007.)

(e) Access policy

The court must post a privacy policy on its public-access Web site to inform members of the public accessing its electronic records of the information it collects regarding access transactions and the uses that the court may make of the collected information.

(Subd (e) amended effective January 1, 2007.)

Rule 2.504 amended and renumbered effective January 1, 2007; adopted as rule 2074 effective July 1, 2002.

Rule 2.505. Contracts with vendors

(a) Contract must provide access consistent with rules

The court's contract with a vendor to provide public access to its electronic records must be consistent with the rules in this chapter and must require the vendor to provide public access to court records and to protect the confidentiality of court records as required by law or by court order.

(Subd (a) amended and lettered effective January 1, 2007; adopted as part of unlettered subd effective July 1, 2002.)

(b) Contract must provide that court owns the records

Any contract between the court and a vendor to provide public access to the court's electronic records must provide that the court is the owner of these records and has the exclusive right to control their use.

(Subd (b) amended and lettered effective January 1, 2007; adopted as part of unlettered subd effective July 1, 2002.)

Rule 2.505 amended and renumbered effective January 1, 2007; adopted as rule 2075 effective July 1, 2002.

Rule 2.506. Fees for electronic access

(a) Court may impose fees

The court may impose fees for the costs of providing public access to its electronic records, under Government Code section 68150(*l*). On request, the court must provide the public with a statement of the costs on which these fees are based.

(Subd (a) amended effective July 1, 2013; adopted as part of unlettered subd effective July 1, 2002; previously amended and lettered effective January 1, 2007.)

(b) Fees of vendor must be reasonable

To the extent that public access to a court's electronic records is provided exclusively through a vendor, the court must ensure that any fees the vendor imposes for the costs of providing access are reasonable.

(Subd (b) lettered effective January 1, 2007; adopted as part of unlettered subd effective July 1, 2002.)

Rule 2.506 amended effective July 1, 2013; adopted as rule 2076 effective July 1, 2002; previously amended and renumbered effective January 1, 2007.

Rule 2.507. Electronic access to court calendars, indexes, and registers of actions

(a) Intent

This rule specifies information to be included in and excluded from the court calendars, indexes, and registers of actions to which public access is available by electronic means under rule 2.503(b). To the extent it is feasible to do so, the court must maintain court calendars, indexes, and registers of actions available to the public by electronic means in accordance with this rule.

(Subd (a) amended effective January 1, 2007.)

(b) Minimum contents for electronically accessible court calendars, indexes, and registers of actions

(1) The electronic court calendar must include:

(A) Date of court calendar;

(B) Time of calendared event;

(C) Court department number;

(D) Case number; and

(E) Case title (unless made confidential by law).

(2) The electronic index must include:

(A) Case title (unless made confidential by law);

(B) Party names (unless made confidential by law);

(C) Party type;

(D) Date on which the case was filed; and

(E) Case number.

(3) The register of actions must be a summary of every proceeding in a case, in compliance with Government Code section 69845, and must include:

(A) Date case commenced;

(B) Case number;

(C) Case type;

(D) Case title (unless made confidential by law);

(E) Party names (unless made confidential by law);

(F) Party type;

(G) Date of each activity; and

(H) Description of each activity.

(Subd (b) amended effective January 1, 2007.)

(c) Information that must be excluded from court calendars, indexes, and registers of actions

The following information must be excluded from a court's electronic calendar, index, and register of actions:

(1) Social security number;

(2) Any financial information;

(3) Arrest warrant information;

(4) Search warrant information;

(5) Victim information;

(6) Witness information;

(7) Ethnicity;

(8) Age;

(9) Gender;

(10) Government-issued identification card numbers (i.e., military);

(11) Driver's license number; and

(12) Date of birth.

(Subd (c) amended effective January 1, 2007.)

Rule 2.507 amended and renumbered effective January 1, 2007; adopted as rule 2077 effective July 1, 2003.

Article 3
Remote Access by a Party, Party's Designee, Party's Attorney, Court-Appointed Person, or Authorized Person Working in a Legal Organization or Qualified Legal Services Project

Title 2, Trial Court Rules—Chapter 2, Access to Electronic Trial Court Records; Article 3; Remote Access by a Party, Party's Designee, Party's Attorney, Court-Appointed Person, or Authorized Person Working in a Legal Organization or Qualified Legal Services Project; adopted effective January 1, 2019.

Rule 2.515. Application and scope
Rule 2.516. Remote access to extent feasible
Rule 2.517. Remote access by a party
Rule 2.518. Remote access by a party's designee
Rule 2.519. Remote access by a party's attorney
Rule 2.520. Remote access by persons working in the same legal organization as a party's attorney
Rule 2.521. Remote access by a court-appointed person
Rule 2.522. Remote access by persons working in a qualified legal services project providing brief legal services
Rule 2.523. Identity verification, identity management, and user access
Rule 2.524. Security of confidential information
Rule 2.525. Searches; unauthorized access
Rule 2.526. Audit trails
Rule 2.527. Additional conditions of access
Rule 2.528. Termination of remote access

Rule 2.515. Application and scope

(a) No limitation on access to electronic records available under article 2

The rules in this article do not limit remote access to electronic records available under article 2. These rules govern access to electronic records where remote access by the public is not allowed.

(Subd (a) adopted effective January 1, 2019.)

(b) Who may access

The rules in this article apply to remote access to electronic records by:

(1) A person who is a party;

(2) A designee of a person who is a party;

(3) A party's attorney;

(4) An authorized person working in the same legal organization as a party's attorney;

(5) An authorized person working in a qualified legal services project providing brief legal services; and

(6) A court-appointed person.

(Subd (b) adopted effective January 1, 2019.)

Rule 2.515 adopted effective January 1, 2019.

Advisory Committee Comment

Article 2 allows remote access in most civil cases, and the rules in article 3 are not intended to limit that access. Rather, the article 3 rules allow broader remote access—by parties, parties' designees, parties' attorneys, authorized persons working in legal organizations, authorized persons working in a qualified legal services project providing brief services, and court-appointed persons—to those electronic records where remote access by the public is not allowed.

Under the rules in article 3, a party, a party's attorney, an authorized person working in the same legal organization as a party's attorney, or a person appointed by the court in the proceeding basically has the same level of access to electronic records remotely that he or she would have if he or she were to seek to inspect the records in person at the courthouse. Thus, if he or she is legally entitled to inspect certain records at the courthouse, that person could view the same records remotely; on the other hand, if he or she is restricted from inspecting certain court records at the courthouse (e.g., because the records are confidential or sealed), that person would not be permitted to view the records remotely. In some types of cases, such as unlimited civil cases, the access available to parties and their attorneys is generally similar to the public's but in other types of cases, such as juvenile cases, it is much more extensive (see Cal. Rules of Court, rule 5.552).

For authorized persons working in a qualified legal services program, the rule contemplates services offered in high-volume environments on an ad hoc basis. There are some limitations on access under the rule for qualified legal services projects. When an attorney at a qualified legal services project becomes a party's attorney and offers services beyond the scope contemplated under this rule, the access rules for a party's attorney would apply.

Rule 2.516. Remote access to extent feasible

To the extent feasible, a court that maintains records in electronic form must provide remote access to those records to the users described in rule 2.515, subject to the conditions and limitations stated in this article and otherwise provided by law.

Rule 2.516 adopted effective January 1, 2019.

Advisory Committee Comment

This rule takes into account the limited resources currently available in some trial courts. Many courts may not have the financial means, security resources, or technical capabilities necessary to provide the full range of remote access to electronic records authorized by this article. When it is more feasible and courts have had more experience with remote access, these rules may be amended to further expand remote access.

This rule is not intended to prevent a court from moving forward with the limited remote access options outlined in this rule as such access becomes feasible. For example, if it were only feasible for a court to provide remote access to parties who are persons, it could proceed to provide remote access to those users only.

Rule 2.517. Remote access by a party
(a) Remote access generally permitted
A person may have remote access to electronic records in actions or proceedings in which that person is a party.

(Subd (a) adopted effective January 1, 2019.)

(b) Level of remote access
(1) In any action or proceeding, a party may be provided remote access to the same electronic records that he or she would be legally entitled to inspect at the courthouse.

(2) This rule does not limit remote access to electronic records available under article 2.

(3) This rule applies only to electronic records. A person is not entitled under these rules to remote access to documents, information, data, or other materials created or maintained by the courts that are not electronic records.

(Subd (b) adopted effective January 1, 2019.)
Rule 2.517 adopted effective January 1, 2019.

Advisory Committee Comment

Because this rule permits remote access only by a party who is a person (defined under rule 2.501 as a natural human being), remote access would not apply to parties that are organizations, which would need to gain remote access under the party's attorney rule or, for certain government entities with respect to specified electronic records, the rules in article 4.

A party who is a person would need to have the legal capacity to agree to the terms and conditions of a court's remote access user agreement before using a system of remote access. The court could deny access or require additional information if the court knew the person seeking access lacked legal capacity or appeared to lack capacity—for example, if identity verification revealed the person seeking access was a minor.

Rule 2.518. Remote access by a party's designee
(a) Remote access generally permitted
A person who is a party in an action or proceeding may designate other persons to have remote access to electronic records in that action or proceeding.

(Subd (a) adopted effective January 1, 2019.)

(b) Level of remote access
(1) Except for criminal electronic records, juvenile justice electronic records, and child welfare electronic records, a party's designee may have the same access to a party's electronic records that a member of the public would be entitled to if he or she were to inspect the party's court records at the courthouse. A party's designee is not permitted remote access to criminal electronic records, juvenile justice electronic records, and child welfare electronic records.

(2) A party may limit the access to be afforded a designee to specific cases.

(3) A party may limit the access to be afforded a designee to a specific period of time.

(4) A party may modify or revoke a designee's level of access at any time.

(Subd (b) adopted effective January 1, 2019.)

(c) Terms of access
(1) A party's designee may access electronic records only for the purpose of assisting the party or the party's attorney in the action or proceeding.

(2) Any distribution for sale of electronic records obtained remotely under the rules in this article is strictly prohibited.

(3) All laws governing confidentiality and disclosure of court records apply to the records obtained under this article.

(4) Party designees must comply with any other terms of remote access required by the court.

(5) Failure to comply with these rules may result in the imposition of sanctions, including termination of access.

(Subd (c) adopted effective January 1, 2019.)
Rule 2.518 adopted effective January 1, 2019.

Advisory Committee Comment

A party must be a natural human being with the legal capacity to agree to the terms and conditions of a user agreement with the court to authorize designees for remote access. Under rule 2.501, for purposes of the rules, "person" refers to natural human beings. Accordingly, the party's designee rule would not apply to parties that are organizations, which would need to gain remote access under the party's attorney rule or, for certain government entities with respect to specified electronic records, under the rules in article 4.

Rule 2.519. Remote access by a party's attorney
(a) Remote access generally permitted
(1) A party's attorney may have remote access to electronic records in the party's actions or proceedings under this rule or under rule 2.518. If a party's attorney gains remote access under rule 2.518, the requirements of rule 2.519 do not apply.

(2) If a court notifies an attorney of the court's intention to appoint the attorney to represent a party in a criminal, juvenile justice, child welfare, family law, or probate proceeding, the court may grant remote access to that attorney before an order of appointment is issued by the court.

(Subd (a) adopted effective January 1, 2019.)

(b) Level of remote access
A party's attorney may be provided remote access to the same electronic records in the party's actions or proceedings that the party's attorney would be legally entitled to view at the courthouse.

(Subd (b) adopted effective January 1, 2019.)

(c) Terms of remote access applicable to an attorney who is not the attorney of record
An attorney who represents a party, but who is not the party's attorney of record in the party's actions or proceedings, may remotely access the party's electronic records, provided that the attorney:

(1) Obtains the party's consent to remotely access the party's electronic records; and

(2) Represents to the court in the remote access system that he or she has obtained the party's consent to remotely access the party's electronic records.

(Subd (c) adopted effective January 1, 2019.)

(d) Terms of remote access applicable to all attorneys
(1) A party's attorney may remotely access the electronic records only for the purpose of assisting the party with the party's court matter.

(2) A party's attorney may not distribute for sale any electronic records obtained remotely under the rules in this article. Such sale is strictly prohibited.

(3) A party's attorney must comply with any other terms of remote access required by the court.

(4) Failure to comply with these rules may result in the imposition of sanctions, including termination of access.

(Subd (d) adopted effective January 1, 2019.)
Rule 2.519 adopted effective January 1, 2019.

Advisory Committee Comment

Subdivision (c). An attorney of record will be known to the court for purposes of remote access. However, a person may engage an attorney other than the attorney of record for assistance in an action or proceeding in which the person is a party. For example, a party may engage an attorney to (1) prepare legal documents but not appear in the party's action (e.g., provide limited-scope representation); (2) assist the party with dismissal or sealing of a criminal record when the attorney did not represent the party in the criminal proceeding; or (3) represent the party in an appellate matter when the attorney did not represent the party in the trial court. Subdivision (c) provides a mechanism for an attorney not of record to be known to the court for purposes of remote access.

Because the level of remote access is limited to the same court records that an attorney would be entitled to access if he or she were to appear at the courthouse, an attorney providing undisclosed representation would only be able to remotely access electronic records that the public could access at the courthouse. The rule essentially removes the step of the attorney having to go to the courthouse.

Rule 2.520. Remote access by persons working in the same legal organization as a party's attorney
(a) Application and scope
(1) This rule applies when a party's attorney is assisted by others working in the same legal organization.

(2) "Working in the same legal organization" under this rule includes partners, associates, employees, volunteers, and contractors.

(3) This rule does not apply when a person working in the same legal organization as a party's attorney gains remote access to records as a party's designee under rule 2.518.

(Subd (a) adopted effective January 1, 2019.)

(b) Designation and certification
(1) A party's attorney may designate that other persons working in the same legal organization as the party's attorney have remote access.

(2) A party's attorney must certify that the other persons authorized for remote access are working in the same legal organization as the party's attorney and are assisting the party's attorney in the action or proceeding.

(Subd (b) adopted effective January 1, 2019.)

(c) Level of remote access

(1) Persons designated by a party's attorney under (b) must be provided access to the same electronic records as the party.

(2) Notwithstanding (b), when a court designates a legal organization to represent parties in criminal, juvenile, family, or probate proceedings, the court may grant remote access to a person working in the organization who assigns cases to attorneys working in that legal organization.

(Subd (c) adopted effective January 1, 2019.)

(d) Terms of remote access

(1) Persons working in a legal organization may remotely access electronic records only for purposes of assigning or assisting a party's attorney.

(2) Any distribution for sale of electronic records obtained remotely under the rules in this article is strictly prohibited.

(3) All laws governing confidentiality and disclosure of court records apply to the records obtained under this article.

(4) Persons working in a legal organization must comply with any other terms of remote access required by the court.

(5) Failure to comply with these rules may result in the imposition of sanctions, including termination of access.

(Subd (d) adopted effective January 1, 2019.)

Rule 2.520 adopted effective January 1, 2019.

Advisory Committee Comment

Subdivision (b). The designation and certification outlined in this subdivision need only be done once and can be done at the time the attorney establishes his or her remote access account with the court.

Rule 2.521. Remote access by a court-appointed person

(a) Remote access generally permitted

(1) A court may grant a court-appointed person remote access to electronic records in any action or proceeding in which the person has been appointed by the court.

(2) Court-appointed persons include an attorney appointed to represent a minor child under Family Code section 3150; a Court Appointed Special Advocate volunteer in a juvenile proceeding; an attorney appointed under Probate Code section 1470, 1471, or 1474; an investigator appointed under Probate Code section 1454; a probate referee designated under Probate Code section 8920; a fiduciary, as defined in Probate Code section 39; an attorney appointed under Welfare and Institutions Code section 5365; or a guardian ad litem appointed under Code of Civil Procedure section 372 or Probate Code section 1003.

(Subd (a) adopted effective January 1, 2019.)

(b) Level of remote access

A court-appointed person may be provided with the same level of remote access to electronic records as the court-appointed person would be legally entitled to if he or she were to appear at the courthouse to inspect the court records.

(Subd (b) adopted effective January 1, 2019.)

(c) Terms of remote access

(1) A court-appointed person may remotely access electronic records only for purposes of fulfilling the responsibilities for which he or she was appointed.

(2) Any distribution for sale of electronic records obtained remotely under the rules in this article is strictly prohibited.

(3) All laws governing confidentiality and disclosure of court records apply to the records obtained under this article.

(4) A court-appointed person must comply with any other terms of remote access required by the court.

(5) Failure to comply with these rules may result in the imposition of sanctions, including termination of access.

(Subd (c) adopted effective January 1, 2019.)

Rule 2.521 adopted effective January 1, 2019.

Rule 2.522. Remote access by persons working in a qualified legal services project providing brief legal services

(a) Application and scope

(1) This rule applies to qualified legal services projects as defined in Business and Professions Code section 6213(a).

(2) "Working in a qualified legal services project" under this rule includes attorneys, employees, and volunteers.

(3) This rule does not apply to a person working in or otherwise associated with a qualified legal services project who gains remote access to court records as a party's designee under rule 2.518.

(Subd (a) adopted effective January 1, 2019.)

(b) Designation and certification

(1) A qualified legal services project may designate persons working in the qualified legal services project who provide brief legal services, as defined in rule 2.501, to have remote access.

(2) The qualified legal services project must certify that the authorized persons work in their organization.

(Subd (b) adopted effective January 1, 2019.)

(c) Level of remote access

Authorized persons may be provided remote access to the same electronic records that the authorized person would be legally entitled to inspect at the courthouse.

(Subd (c) adopted effective January 1, 2019.)

(d) Terms of remote access

(1) Qualified legal services projects must obtain the party's consent to remotely access the party's electronic records.

(2) Authorized persons must represent to the court in the remote access system that the qualified legal services project has obtained the party's consent to remotely access the party's electronic records.

(3) Qualified legal services projects providing services under this rule may remotely access electronic records only to provide brief legal services.

(4) Any distribution for sale of electronic records obtained under the rules in this article is strictly prohibited.

(5) All laws governing confidentiality and disclosure of court records apply to electronic records obtained under this article.

(6) Qualified legal services projects must comply with any other terms of remote access required by the court.

(7) Failure to comply with these rules may result in the imposition of sanctions, including termination of access.

(Subd (d) adopted effective January 1, 2019.)

Rule 2.522 adopted effective January 1, 2019.

Advisory Committee Comment

The rule does not prescribe any particular method for capturing the designation and certification of persons working in a qualified legal services project. Courts and qualified legal services projects have flexibility to determine what method would work for both entities. For example, the information could be captured in a remote access system if an organizational-level account could be established, or the information could be captured in a written agreement between the court and the qualified legal services project.

The rule does not prescribe any particular method for a qualified legal services project to document the consent it obtained to access a person's electronic records. Qualified legal services projects have flexibility to adapt the requirement to their regular processes for making records.

For example, the qualified legal services project could obtain a signed consent form for its records or could obtain consent over the phone and make an entry to that effect in its records, or the court and the qualified legal services project could enter into an agreement to describe how consent will be obtained and recorded.

Rule 2.523. Identity verification, identity management, and user access

(a) Identity verification required

Except for remote access provided to a party's designee under rule 2.518, before allowing a person who is eligible under the rules in article 3 to have remote access to electronic records, a court must verify the identity of the person seeking access.

(Subd (a) adopted effective January 1, 2019.)

(b) Responsibilities of the court

A court that allows persons eligible under the rules in article 3 to have remote access to electronic records must have an identity verification method that verifies the identity of, and provides a unique credential to, each person who is permitted remote access to the electronic records. The court may authorize remote access by a person only if that person's identity has been verified, the person accesses records using the credential provided to that individual, and the person complies with the terms and conditions of access, as prescribed by the court.

(Subd (b) adopted effective January 1, 2019.)

(c) Responsibilities of persons accessing records

A person eligible to be given remote access to electronic records under the rules in article 3 may be given such access only if that person:

(1) Provides the court with all information it directs in order to identify the person to be a user;

(2) Consents to all conditions for remote access required under article 3 and by the court; and

(3) Is authorized by the court to have remote access to electronic records.

(Subd (c) adopted effective January 1, 2019.)

(d) Responsibilities of the legal organizations or qualified legal services projects

(1) If a person is accessing electronic records on behalf of a legal organization or qualified legal services project, the organization or project must approve granting access to that person, verify the person's identity, and provide the court with all the information it directs in order to authorize that person to have access to electronic records.

(2) If a person accessing electronic records on behalf of a legal organization or qualified legal services project leaves his or her position or for any other reason is no longer entitled to access, the organization or project must immediately notify the court so that it can terminate the person's access.

(Subd (d) adopted effective January 1, 2019.)

(e) Vendor contracts, statewide master agreements, and identity and access management systems

A court may enter into a contract with a vendor to provide identity verification, identity management, or user access services. Alternatively, courts may use a statewide identity verification, identity management, or access management system, if available, or a statewide master agreement for such systems, if available.

(Subd (e) adopted effective January 1, 2019.)
Rule 2.523 adopted effective January 1, 2019.

Advisory Committee Comment

Subdivisions (a) and (d). A court may verify user identities under (a) by obtaining a representation from a legal organization or qualified legal services project that the legal organization or qualified legal services project has verified the user identities under (d). No additional verification steps are required on the part of the court.

Rule 2.524. Security of confidential information

(a) Secure access and encryption required

If any information in an electronic record that is confidential by law or sealed by court order may lawfully be provided remotely to a person or organization described in rule 2.515, any remote access to the confidential information must be provided through a secure platform and any electronic transmission of the information must be encrypted.

(Subd (a) adopted effective January 1, 2019.)

(b) Vendor contracts and statewide master agreements

A court may enter into a contract with a vendor to provide secure access and encryption services. Alternatively, if a statewide master agreement is available for secure access and encryption services, courts may use that master agreement.

(Subd (b) adopted effective January 1, 2019.)
Rule 2.524 adopted effective January 1, 2019.

Advisory Committee Comment

This rule describes security and encryption requirements; levels of access are provided for in rules 2.517–2.522.

Rule 2.525. Searches; unauthorized access

(a) Searches by case number or caption

A user authorized under this article to remotely access a party's electronic records may search for the records by case number or case caption.

(Subd (a) adopted effective January 1, 2019.)

(b) Access level

A court providing remote access to electronic records under this article must ensure that authorized users are able to access the electronic records only at the access levels provided in this article.

(Subd (b) adopted effective January 1, 2019.)

(c) Unauthorized access

If a user gains access to an electronic record that he or she is not authorized to access under this article, the user must:

(1) Report the unauthorized access to the court as directed by the court for that purpose;

(2) Destroy all copies, in any form, of the record; and

(3) Delete from his or her web browser history all information that identifies the record.

(Subd (c) adopted effective January 1, 2019.)
Rule 2.525 adopted effective January 1, 2019.

Rule 2.526. Audit trails

(a) Ability to generate audit trails

The court should have the ability to generate an audit trail that contains one or more of the following elements: what electronic record was remotely accessed, when it was remotely accessed, who remotely accessed it, and under whose authority the user gained access.

(Subd (a) adopted effective January 1, 2019.)

(b) Limited audit trails available to authorized users

(1) A court providing remote access to electronic records under this article should make limited audit trails available to authorized users under this article.

(2) A limited audit trail should identify the user who remotely accessed electronic records in a particular case, but must not identify which specific electronic records were accessed.

(Subd (b) adopted effective January 1, 2019.)
Rule 2.526 adopted effective January 1, 2019.

Advisory Committee Comment

The audit trail is a tool to assist the courts and users in identifying and investigating any potential issues or misuse of remote access. The user's view of the audit trail is limited to protect sensitive information.

To facilitate the use of existing remote access systems, rule 2.526 is currently not mandatory, but may be amended to be mandatory in the future.

Rule 2.527. Additional conditions of access

To the extent consistent with these rules and other applicable law, a court must impose reasonable conditions on remote access to preserve the integrity of its records, prevent the unauthorized use of information, and limit possible legal liability. The court may choose to require each user to submit a signed, written agreement enumerating those conditions before it permits that user to remotely access electronic records. The agreements may define the terms of access, provide for compliance audits, specify the scope of liability, and provide for sanctions for misuse up to and including termination of remote access.

Rule 2.527 adopted effective January 1, 2019.

Rule 2.528. Termination of remote access

(a) Remote access is a privilege

Remote access to electronic records under this article is a privilege and not a right.

(Subd (a) adopted effective January 1, 2019.)

(b) Termination by court

A court that provides remote access may, at any time and for any reason, terminate the permission granted to any person eligible under the rules in article 3 to remotely access electronic records.

(Subd (b) adopted effective January 1, 2019.)
Rule 2.528 adopted effective January 1, 2019.

Article 4
Remote Access by Government Entities

Title 2, Trial Court Rules—Chapter 2, Access to Electronic Trial Court Records; Article 4, Remote Access by Government Entities; adopted effective January 1, 2019.

Rule 2.540. Application and scope
Rule 2.541. Identity verification, identity management, and user access
Rule 2.542. Security of confidential information
Rule 2.543. Audit trails
Rule 2.544. Additional conditions of access
Rule 2.545. Termination of remote access

Rule 2.540. Application and scope

(a) Applicability to government entities

The rules in this article provide for remote access to electronic records by government entities described in (b). The access allowed under these rules is in addition to any access these entities or authorized persons working for such entities may have under the rules in articles 2 and 3.

(Subd (a) adopted effective January 1, 2019.)

(b) Level of remote access

(1) A court may provide authorized persons from government entities with remote access to electronic records as follows:

(A) Office of the Attorney General: criminal electronic records and juvenile justice electronic records.

(B) California Department of Child Support Services: family electronic records, child welfare electronic records, and parentage electronic records.

(C) Office of a district attorney: criminal electronic records and juvenile justice electronic records.

(D) Office of a public defender: criminal electronic records and juvenile justice electronic records.

(E) Office of a county counsel: criminal electronic records, mental health electronic records, child welfare electronic records, and probate electronic records.

(F) Office of a city attorney: criminal electronic records, juvenile justice electronic records, and child welfare electronic records.

(G) County department of probation: criminal electronic records, juvenile justice electronic records, and child welfare electronic records.

(H) County sheriff's department: criminal electronic records and juvenile justice electronic records.

(I) Local police department: criminal electronic records and juvenile justice electronic records.

(J) Local child support agency: family electronic records, child welfare electronic records, and parentage electronic records.

(K) County child welfare agency: child welfare electronic records.

(L) County public guardian: criminal electronic records, mental health electronic records, and probate electronic records.

(M) County agency designated by the board of supervisors to provide conservatorship investigation under chapter 3 of the Lanterman-Petris-Short Act (Welf. & Inst. Code, §§ 5350–5372): criminal electronic records, mental health electronic records, and probate electronic records.

(N) County public conservator: criminal electronic records, mental health electronic records, and probate electronic records.

(O) County public administrator: probate electronic records.

(P) Federally recognized Indian tribe (including any reservation, department, subdivision, or court of the tribe) with concurrent jurisdiction: child welfare electronic records, family electronic records, juvenile justice electronic records, and probate electronic records.

(Q) For good cause, a court may grant remote access to electronic records in particular case types to government entities beyond those listed in (b)(1)(A)–(P). For purposes of this rule, "good cause" means that the government entity requires access to the electronic records in order to adequately perform its legal duties or fulfill its responsibilities in litigation.

(R) All other remote access for government entities is governed by articles 2 and 3.

(2) Subject to (b)(1), the court may provide a government entity with the same level of remote access to electronic records as the government entity would be legally entitled to if a person working for the government entity were to appear at the courthouse to inspect court records in that case type. If a court record is confidential by law or sealed by court order and a person working for the government entity would not be legally entitled to inspect the court record at the courthouse, the court may not provide the government entity with remote access to the confidential or sealed electronic record.

(3) This rule applies only to electronic records. A government entity is not entitled under these rules to remote access to any documents, information, data, or other types of materials created or maintained by the courts that are not electronic records.

(Subd (b) amended effective January 1, 2020; adopted effective January 1, 2019.)

(c) Terms of remote access

(1) Government entities may remotely access electronic records only to perform official duties and for legitimate governmental purposes.

(2) Any distribution for sale of electronic records obtained remotely under the rules in this article is strictly prohibited.

(3) All laws governing confidentiality and disclosure of court records apply to electronic records obtained under this article.

(4) Government entities must comply with any other terms of remote access required by the court.

(5) Failure to comply with these requirements may result in the imposition of sanctions, including termination of access.

(Subd (c) adopted effective January 1, 2019.)

Rule 2.540 amended effective January 1, 2020; adopted effective January 1, 2019.

Advisory Committee Comment

The rule does not restrict courts to providing remote access only to local government entities in the same county in which the court is situated. For example, a court in one county could allow remote access to electronic records by a local child support agency in a different county.

Subdivision (b)(3). As to the applicability of the rules on remote access only to electronic records, see the advisory committee comment to rule 2.501.

Rule 2.541. Identity verification, identity management, and user access

(a) Identity verification required

Before allowing a person or entity eligible under the rules in article 4 to have remote access to electronic records, a court must verify the identity of the person seeking access.

(Subd (a) adopted effective January 1, 2019.)

(b) Responsibilities of the courts

A court that allows persons eligible under the rules in article 4 to have remote access to electronic records must have an identity verification method that verifies the identity of, and provides a unique credential to, each person who is permitted remote access to the electronic records. The court may authorize remote access by a person only if that person's identity has been verified, the person accesses records using the name and password provided to that individual, and the person complies with the terms and conditions of access, as prescribed by the court.

(Subd (b) adopted effective January 1, 2019.)

(c) Responsibilities of persons accessing records

A person eligible to remotely access electronic records under the rules in article 4 may be given such access only if that person:

(1) Provides the court with all of the information it needs to identify the person to be a user;

(2) Consents to all conditions for remote access required by article 4 and the court; and

(3) Is authorized by the court to have remote access to electronic records.

(Subd (c) adopted effective January 1, 2019.)

(d) Responsibilities of government entities

(1) If a person is accessing electronic records on behalf of a government entity, the government entity must approve granting access to that person, verify the person's identity, and provide the court with all the information it needs to authorize that person to have access to electronic records.

(2) If a person accessing electronic records on behalf of a government entity leaves his or her position or for any other reason is no longer entitled to access, the government entity must immediately notify the court so that the court can terminate the person's access.

(Subd (d) adopted effective January 1, 2019.)

(e) Vendor contracts, statewide master agreements, and identity and access management systems

A court may enter into a contract with a vendor to provide identity verification, identity management, or user access services. Alternatively, courts may use a statewide identity verification, identity management, or access management system, if available, or a statewide master agreement for such systems, if available.

(Subd (e) adopted effective January 1, 2019.)

Rule 2.541 adopted effective January 1, 2019.

Rule 2.542. Security of confidential information

(a) Secure access and encryption required

If any information in an electronic record that is confidential by law or sealed by court order may lawfully be provided remotely to a government entity, any remote access to the confidential information must be provided through a secure platform, and any electronic transmission of the information must be encrypted.

(Subd (a) adopted effective January 1, 2019.)

(b) Vendor contracts and statewide master agreements

A court may enter into a contract with a vendor to provide secure access and encryption services. Alternatively, if a statewide master agreement is available for secure access and encryption services, courts may use that master agreement.

(Subd (b) adopted effective January 1, 2019.)

Rule 2.542 adopted effective January 1, 2019.

Rule 2.543. Audit trails

(a) Ability to generate audit trails

The court should have the ability to generate an audit trail that contains one or more of the following elements: what electronic record was remotely accessed, when it was accessed, who accessed it, and under whose authority the user gained access.

(Subd (a) adopted effective January 1, 2019.)

(b) Audit trails available to government entity

(1) A court providing remote access to electronic records under this article should make limited audit trails available to authorized users of the government entity.

(2) A limited audit trail should identify the user who remotely accessed electronic records in a particular case, but must not identify which specific electronic records were accessed.

(Subd (b) adopted effective January 1, 2019.)
Rule 2.543 adopted effective January 1, 2019.

Advisory Committee Comment

The audit trail is a tool to assist the courts and users in identifying and investigating any potential issues or misuse of remote access. The user's view of the audit trail is limited to protect sensitive information.

To facilitate the use of existing remote access systems, rule 2.526 is currently not mandatory, but may be amended to be mandatory in the future.

Rule 2.544. Additional conditions of access

To the extent consistent with these rules and other applicable law, a court must impose reasonable conditions on remote access to preserve the integrity of its records, prevent the unauthorized use of information, and limit possible legal liability. The court may choose to require each user to submit a signed, written agreement enumerating those conditions before it permits that user to access electronic records remotely. The agreements may define the terms of access, provide for compliance audits, specify the scope of liability, and provide for sanctions for misuse up to and including termination of remote access.

Rule 2.544 adopted effective January 1, 2019.

Rule 2.545. Termination of remote access

(a) Remote access is a privilege

Remote access to electronic records under this article is a privilege and not a right.

(Subd (a) adopted effective January 1, 2019.)

(b) Termination by court

A court that provides remote access may, at any time and for any reason, terminate the permission granted to any person or entity eligible under the rules in article 4 to remotely access electronic records

(Subd (b) adopted effective January 1, 2019.)
Rule 2.545 adopted effective January 1, 2019.

Chapter 3
Sealed Records

Rule 2.550. Sealed records
Rule 2.551. Procedures for filing records under seal

Rule 2.550. Sealed records

(a) Application

(1) Rules 2.550–2.551 apply to records sealed or proposed to be sealed by court order.

(2) These rules do not apply to records that are required to be kept confidential by law.

(3) These rules do not apply to discovery motions and records filed or lodged in connection with discovery motions or proceedings. However, the rules do apply to discovery materials that are used at trial or submitted as a basis for adjudication of matters other than discovery motions or proceedings.

(Subd (a) amended effective January 1, 2007.)

(b) Definitions

As used in this chapter:

(1) "Record." Unless the context indicates otherwise, "record" means all or a portion of any document, paper, exhibit, transcript, or other thing filed or lodged with the court, by electronic means or otherwise.

(2) "Sealed." A "sealed" record is a record that by court order is not open to inspection by the public.

(3) "Lodged." A "lodged" record is a record that is temporarily placed or deposited with the court, but not filed.

(Subd (b) amended effective January 1, 2016; previously amended effective January 1, 2007.)

(c) Court records presumed to be open

Unless confidentiality is required by law, court records are presumed to be open.

(d) Express factual findings required to seal records

The court may order that a record be filed under seal only if it expressly finds facts that establish:

(1) There exists an overriding interest that overcomes the right of public access to the record;

(2) The overriding interest supports sealing the record;

(3) A substantial probability exists that the overriding interest will be prejudiced if the record is not sealed;

(4) The proposed sealing is narrowly tailored; and

(5) No less restrictive means exist to achieve the overriding interest.

(Subd (d) amended effective January 1, 2004.)

(e) Content and scope of the order

(1) An order sealing the record must:

(A) Specifically state the facts that support the findings; and

(B) Direct the sealing of only those documents and pages, or, if reasonably practicable, portions of those documents and pages, that contain the material that needs to be placed under seal. All other portions of each document or page must be included in the public file.

(2) Consistent with Code of Civil Procedure sections 639 and 645.1, if the records that a party is requesting be placed under seal are voluminous, the court may appoint a referee and fix and allocate the referee's fees among the parties.

(Subd (e) amended effective January 1, 2007; previously amended effective January 1, 2004.)

Rule 2.550 amended effective January 1, 2016; adopted as rule 243.1 effective January 1, 2001; previously amended effective January 1, 2004; previously amended and renumbered as rule 2.550 effective January 1, 2007.

Advisory Committee Comment

This rule and rule 2.551 provide a standard and procedures for courts to use when a request is made to seal a record. The standard is based on *NBC Subsidiary (KNBC-TV), Inc. v. Superior Court* (1999) 20 Cal.4th 1178. These rules apply to civil and criminal cases. They recognize the First Amendment right of access to documents used at trial or as a basis of adjudication. The rules do not apply to records that courts must keep confidential by law. Examples of confidential records to which public access is restricted by law are records of the family conciliation court (Family Code, § 1818(b)), in forma pauperis applications (Cal. Rules of Court, rules 3.54 and 8.26), and search warrant affidavits sealed under *People v. Hobbs* (1994) 7 Cal.4th 948. The sealed records rules also do not apply to discovery proceedings, motions, and materials that are not used at trial or submitted to the court as a basis for adjudication. (See *NBC Subsidiary, supra,* 20 Cal.4th at pp. 1208–1209, fn. 25.)

Rule 2.550(d)–(e) is derived from *NBC Subsidiary*. That decision contains the requirements that the court, before closing a hearing or sealing a transcript, must find an "overriding interest" that supports the closure or sealing, and must make certain express findings. (*Id.* at pp. 1217–1218.) The decision notes that the First Amendment right of access applies to records filed in both civil and criminal cases as a basis for adjudication. (*Id.* at pp. 1208–1209, fn. 25.) Thus, the *NBC Subsidiary* test applies to the sealing of records.

NBC Subsidiary provides examples of various interests that courts have acknowledged may constitute "overriding interests." (See *id.* at p. 1222, fn. 46.) Courts have found that, under appropriate circumstances, various statutory privileges, trade secrets, and privacy interests, when properly asserted and not waived, may constitute "overriding interests." The rules do not attempt to define what may constitute an "overriding interest," but leave this to case law.

Rule 2.551. Procedures for filing records under seal

(a) Court approval required

A record must not be filed under seal without a court order. The court must not permit a record to be filed under seal based solely on the agreement or stipulation of the parties.

(Subd (a) amended effective January 1, 2007.)

(b) Motion or application to seal a record

(1) *Motion or application required*

A party requesting that a record be filed under seal must file a motion or an application for an order sealing the record. The motion or application must be accompanied by a memorandum and a declaration containing facts sufficient to justify the sealing.

(2) *Service of motion or application*

A copy of the motion or application must be served on all parties that have appeared in the case. Unless the court orders otherwise, any party that already has access to the records to be placed under seal must be served with a complete, unredacted version of all papers as well as a redacted version. Other parties must be served with only the public redacted version. If a party's attorney but not the party has access to the record, only the party's attorney may be served with the complete, unredacted version.

(3) *Procedure for party not intending to file motion or application*

(A) A party that files or intends to file with the court, for the purposes of adjudication or to use at trial, records produced in discovery that are subject to a confidentiality agreement or protective order, and does not intend to request to have the records sealed, must:

(i) Lodge the unredacted records subject to the confidentiality agreement or protective order and any pleadings, memorandums, declarations, and other documents that disclose the contents of the records, in the manner stated in (d);

(ii) File copies of the documents in (i) that are redacted so that they do not disclose the contents of the records that are subject to the confidentiality agreement or protective order; and

(iii) Give written notice to the party that produced the records that the records and the other documents lodged under (i) will be placed in the public court file unless that party files a timely motion or application to seal the records under this rule.

(B) If the party that produced the documents and was served with the notice under (A)(iii) fails to file a motion or an application to seal the records within 10 days or to obtain a court order extending the time to file such a motion or an application, the clerk must promptly transfer all the documents in (A)(i) from the envelope, container, or secure electronic file to the public file. If the party files a motion or an application to seal within 10 days or such later time as the court has ordered, these documents are to remain conditionally under seal until the court rules on the motion or application and thereafter are to be filed as ordered by the court.

(4) *Lodging of record pending determination of motion or application*
The party requesting that a record be filed under seal must lodge it with the court under (d) when the motion or application is made, unless good cause exists for not lodging it or the record has previously been lodged under (3)(A)(i). Pending the determination of the motion or application, the lodged record will be conditionally under seal.

(5) *Redacted and unredacted versions*
If necessary to prevent disclosure, any motion or application, any opposition, and any supporting documents must be filed in a public redacted version and lodged in a complete, unredacted version conditionally under seal. The cover of the redacted version must identify it as "Public—Redacts materials from conditionally sealed record." The cover of the unredacted version must identify it as "May Not Be Examined Without Court Order—Contains material from conditionally sealed record."

(6) *Return of lodged record*
If the court denies the motion or application to seal, the moving party may notify the court that the lodged record is to be filed unsealed. This notification must be received within 10 days of the order denying the motion or application to seal, unless otherwise ordered by the court. On receipt of this notification, the clerk must unseal and file the record. If the moving party does not notify the court within 10 days of the order, the clerk must (1) return the lodged record to the moving party if it is in paper form or (2) permanently delete the lodged record if it is in electronic form.

(Subd (b) amended effective January 1, 2017; previously amended effective January 1, 2004, January 1, 2007, and January 1, 2016.)

(c) References to nonpublic material in public records
A record filed publicly in the court must not disclose material contained in a record that is sealed, conditionally under seal, or subject to a pending motion or an application to seal.

(Subd (c) amended effective January 1, 2004.)

(d) Procedure for lodging of records
(1) A record that may be filed under seal must be transmitted to the court in a secure manner that preserves the confidentiality of the records to be lodged. If the record is transmitted in paper form, it must be put in an envelope or other appropriate container, sealed in the envelope or container, and lodged with the court.

(2) The materials to be lodged under seal must be clearly identified as "CONDITIONALLY UNDER SEAL." If the materials are transmitted in paper form, the envelope or container lodged with the court must be labeled "CONDITIONALLY UNDER SEAL."

(3) The party submitting the lodged record must affix to the electronic transmission, the envelope, or the container a cover sheet that:

(A) Contains all the information required on a caption page under rule 2.111; and

(B) States that the enclosed record is subject to a motion or an application to file the record under seal.

(4) On receipt of a record lodged under this rule, the clerk must endorse the affixed cover sheet with the date of its receipt and must retain but not file the record unless the court orders it filed.

(Subd (d) amended effective January 1, 2016; previously amended effective January 1, 2004, and January 1, 2007.)

(e) Order
(1) If the court grants an order sealing a record and if the sealed record is in paper format, the clerk must substitute on the envelope or container for the label required by (d)(2) a label prominently stating "SEALED BY ORDER OF THE COURT ON *(DATE)*," and must replace the cover sheet required by (d)(3) with a filed-endorsed copy of the court's order. If the sealed record is in electronic form, the clerk must file the court's order, maintain the record ordered sealed in a secure manner, and clearly identify the record as sealed by court order on a specified date.

(2) The order must state whether—in addition to the sealed records—the order itself, the register of actions, any other court records, or any other records relating to the case are to be sealed.

(3) The order must state whether any person other than the court is authorized to inspect the sealed record.

(4) Unless the sealing order provides otherwise, it prohibits the parties from disclosing the contents of any materials that have been sealed in anything that is subsequently publicly filed.

(Subd (e) amended effective January 1, 2017; previously amended effective January 1, 2004, January 1, 2007, and January 1, 2016.)

(f) Custody of sealed records
Sealed records must be securely filed and kept separate from the public file in the case. If the sealed records are in electronic form, appropriate access controls must be established to ensure that only authorized persons may access the sealed records.

(Subd (f) amended effective January 1, 2017; previously amended effective January 1, 2004.)

(g) Custody of voluminous records
If the records to be placed under seal are voluminous and are in the possession of a public agency, the court may by written order direct the agency instead of the clerk to maintain custody of the original records in a secure fashion. If the records are requested by a reviewing court, the trial court must order the public agency to deliver the records to the clerk for transmission to the reviewing court under these rules.

(h) Motion, application, or petition to unseal records
(1) A sealed record must not be unsealed except on order of the court.

(2) A party or member of the public may move, apply, or petition, or the court on its own motion may move, to unseal a record. Notice of any motion, application, or petition to unseal must be filed and served on all parties in the case. The motion, application, or petition and any opposition, reply, and supporting documents must be filed in a public redacted version and a sealed complete version if necessary to comply with (c).

(3) If the court proposes to order a record unsealed on its own motion, the court must give notice to the parties stating the reason for unsealing the record. Unless otherwise ordered by the court, any party may serve and file an opposition within 10 days after the notice is provided and any other party may file a response within 5 days after the filing of an opposition.

(4) In determining whether to unseal a record, the court must consider the matters addressed in rule 2.550(c)–(e).

(5) The order unsealing a record must state whether the record is unsealed entirely or in part. If the court's order unseals only part of the record or unseals the record only as to certain persons, the order must specify the particular records that are unsealed, the particular persons who may have access to the record, or both. If, in addition to the records in the envelope, container, or secure electronic file, the court has previously ordered the sealing order, the register of actions, or any other court records relating to the case to be sealed, the unsealing order must state whether these additional records are unsealed.

(Subd (h) amended effective January 1, 2016; previously amended effective January 1, 2004, and January 1, 2007.)

Rule 2.551 amended effective January 1, 2017; adopted as rule 243.2 effective January 1, 2001; previously amended effective January 1, 2004, and January 1, 2016; previously amended and renumbered as rule 2.551 effective January 1, 2007.

Chapter 4
Records in False Claims Act Cases

Rule 2.570. Filing False Claims Act records under seal
Rule 2.571. Procedures for filing records under seal in a False Claims Act case
Rule 2.572. Ex parte application for an extension of time
Rule 2.573. Unsealing of records and management of False Claims Act cases

Rule 2.570. Filing False Claims Act records under seal

(a) Application
Rules 2.570–2.573 apply to records initially filed under seal pursuant to the False Claims Act, Government Code section 12650 et seq. As to these records, rules 2.550–2.551 on sealed records do not apply.

(Subd (a) amended effective January 1, 2007.)

(b) Definitions
As used in this chapter, unless the context or subject matter otherwise requires:

(1) "Attorney General" means the Attorney General of the State of California.

(2) "Prosecuting authority" means the county counsel, city attorney, or other local government official charged with investigating, filing, and conducting civil legal proceedings on behalf of or in the name of a particular political subdivision.

(3) "*Qui tam* plaintiff" means a person who files a complaint under the False Claims Act.

(4) The definitions in Government Code section 12650 apply to the rules in this chapter.

(Subd (b) amended effective January 1, 2007.)

(c) Confidentiality of records filed under the False Claims Act

Records of actions filed by a *qui tam* plaintiff must initially be filed as confidential and under seal as required by Government Code section 12652(c). Until the seal is lifted, the records in the action must remain under seal, except to the extent otherwise provided in this rule.

(d) Persons permitted access to sealed records in a False Claims Act case

(1) *Public access prohibited*

As long as the records in a False Claims Act case are under seal, public access to the records in the case is prohibited. The prohibition on public access applies not only to filed documents but also to electronic records that would disclose information about the case, including the identity of any plaintiff or defendant.

(2) *Information on register of actions*

As long as the records in a False Claims Act case are under seal, only the information concerning filed records contained on the confidential cover sheet prescribed under rule 2.571(c) may be entered into the register of actions that is accessible to the public.

(3) *Parties permitted access to the sealed court file*

As long as the records in a False Claims Act case are under seal, the only parties permitted access to the court file are:

(A) The Attorney General;

(B) A prosecuting authority for the political subdivision on whose behalf the action is brought, unless the political subdivision is named as a defendant; and

(C) A prosecuting authority for any other political subdivision interested in the matter whose identity has been provided to the court by the Attorney General.

(4) *Parties not permitted access to the sealed court file*

As long as records in a False Claims Act case are under seal, no defendant is permitted to have access to the court records or other information concerning the case. Defendants not permitted access include any political subdivision that has been named as a defendant in a False Claims Act action.

(5) Qui tam *plaintiff's limited access to sealed court file*

The *qui tam* plaintiff in a False Claims Act case may have access to all documents filed by the *qui tam* plaintiff and to such other documents as the court may order.

(Subd (d) amended effective January 1, 2007.)

Rule 2.570 amended and renumbered effective January 1, 2007; adopted as rule 243.5 effective July 1, 2002.

Rule 2.571. Procedures for filing records under seal in a False Claims Act case

(a) No sealing order required

On the filing of an action under the False Claims Act, the complaint, motions for extensions of time, and other papers filed with the court must be kept under seal. Under Government Code section 12652, no order sealing these records is necessary.

(Subd (a) amended effective January 1, 2007.)

(b) Filing a False Claims Act case in a county where filings are accepted in multiple locations

In a county where complaints in civil cases may be filed in more than one location, the presiding judge must designate one particular location where all filings in False Claims Act cases must be made.

(Subd (b) amended effective January 1, 2007.)

(c) Special cover sheet omitting names of the parties

In a False Claims Act case, the complaint and every other paper filed while the case is under seal must have a completed *Confidential Cover Sheet—False Claims Action* (form MC-060) affixed to the first page.

(Subd (c) amended effective January 1, 2007.)

(d) Filing of papers under seal

When the complaint or other paper in a False Claims Act case is filed under seal, the clerk must stamp both the cover sheet and the caption page of the paper.

(Subd (d) amended effective January 1, 2007.)

(e) Custody of sealed records

Records in a False Claims Act case that are confidential and under seal must be securely filed and kept separate from the public file in the case.

(Subd (e) amended effective January 1, 2007.)

Rule 2.571 amended and renumbered effective January 1, 2007; adopted as rule 243.6 effective July 1, 2002.

Rule 2.572. Ex parte application for an extension of time

A party in a False Claims Act case may apply under the ex parte rules in title 3 for an extension of time under Government Code section 12652.

Rule 2.572 amended and renumbered effective January 1, 2007; adopted as rule 243.7 effective July 1, 2002.

Rule 2.573. Unsealing of records and management of False Claims Act cases

(a) Expiration or lifting of seal

(1) Records in a False Claims Act case to which public access has been prohibited under Government Code section 12652(c) must remain under seal until the Attorney General and all local prosecuting authorities involved in the action have notified the court of their decision to intervene or not intervene.

(2) The Attorney General and all local prosecuting authorities involved in the action must give the notice required under (1) within 60 days of the filing of the complaint or before an order extending the time to intervene has expired, unless a new motion to extend time to intervene is pending, in which case the seal remains in effect until a ruling is made on the motion.

(Subd (a) amended effective January 1, 2007.)

(b) Coordination of state and local authorities

The Attorney General and all local prosecuting authorities must coordinate their activities to provide timely and effective notice to the court that:

(1) A political subdivision or subdivisions remain interested in the action and have not yet determined whether to intervene; or

(2) The seal has been extended by the filing or grant of a motion to extend time to intervene, and therefore the seal has not expired.

(Subd (b) amended effective January 1, 2007.)

(c) Designation of lead local prosecuting authority

In a False Claims Act case in which the Attorney General is not involved or has declined to intervene and local prosecuting authorities remain interested in the action, the court may designate a lead prosecuting authority to keep the court apprised of whether all the prosecuting authorities have either intervened or declined to intervene, and whether the seal is to be lifted.

(d) Order unsealing record

The Attorney General or other prosecuting authority filing a notice of intervention or nonintervention must submit a proposed order indicating the documents that are to be unsealed or to remain sealed.

(e) Case management

(1) *Case management conferences*

The court, at the request of the parties or on its own motion, may hold a conference at any time in a False Claims Act case to determine what case management is appropriate for the case, including the lifting or partial lifting of the seal, the scheduling of trial and other events, and any other matters that may assist in managing the case.

(2) *Exemption from case management rules*

Cases under the False Claims Act are exempt from rule 3.110 and the case management rules in title 3, division 7, but are subject to such case management orders as the court may issue.

(Subd (e) amended effective January 1, 2007.)

Rule 2.573 amended and renumbered effective January 1, 2007; adopted as rule 243.8 effective July 1, 2002.

Chapter 5
Name Change Proceedings Under Address Confidentiality Program

Title 2, Trial Court Rules—Division 4, Court Records—Chapter 5, Name Change Proceedings Under Address Confidentiality Program; adopted effective January 1, 2010.

Rule 2.575. Confidential information in name change proceedings under address confidentiality program

Rule 2.576. Access to name of the petitioner

Rule 2.577. Procedures for filing confidential name change records under seal

Rule 2.575. Confidential information in name change proceedings under address confidentiality program

(a) Definitions

As used in this chapter, unless the context or subject matter otherwise requires:

(1) "Confidential name change petitioner" means a petitioner who is a participant in the address confidentiality program created by the Secretary of State under chapter 3.1 (commencing with section 6205) of division 7 of title 1 of the Government Code.

(2) "Record" means all or a portion of any document, paper, exhibit, transcript, or other thing that is filed or lodged with the court.

(3) "Lodged" means temporarily placed or deposited with the court but not filed.

(Subd (a) adopted effective January 1, 2010.)

(b) Application of chapter

The rules in this chapter apply to records filed in a change of name proceeding under Code of Civil Procedure section 1277(b) by a confidential name change petitioner who alleges any of the following reasons or circumstances as a reason for the name change:

(1) The petitioner is seeking to avoid domestic violence, as defined in Family Code section 6211.

(2) The petitioner is seeking to avoid stalking, as defined in Penal Code section 646.9.

(3) The petitioner is, or is filing on behalf of, a victim of sexual assault, as defined in Evidence Code section 1036.2.

(Subd (b) adopted effective January 1, 2010.)

(c) Confidentiality of current name of the petitioner

The current legal name of a confidential name change petitioner must be kept confidential by the court as required by Code of Civil Procedure section 1277(b)(3) and not be published or posted in the court's calendars, indexes, or register of actions, or by any means or in any public forum. Only the information concerning filed records contained on the confidential cover sheet prescribed under (d) may be entered into the register of actions or any other forum that is accessible to the public.

(Subd (c) adopted effective January 1, 2010.)

(d) Special cover sheet omitting names of the petitioner

To maintain the confidentiality provided under Code of Civil Procedure section 1277(b) for the petitioner's current name, the petitioner must attach a completed *Confidential Cover Sheet—Name Change Proceeding Under Address Confidentiality Program (Safe at Home)* (form NC-400) to the front of the petition for name change and every other document filed in the proceedings. The name of the petitioner must not appear on that cover sheet.

(Subd (d) adopted effective January 1, 2010.)

(e) Confidentiality of proposed name of the petitioner

To maintain the confidentiality provided under Code of Civil Procedure section 1277(b) for the petitioner's proposed name, the petitioner must not include the proposed name on the petition for name change or any other record in the proceedings. In any form that requests the petitioner's proposed name, the petitioner and the court must indicate that the proposed name is confidential and on file with the Secretary of State under the provisions of the Safe at Home address confidentiality program.

(Subd (e) adopted effective January 1, 2010.)

Rule 2.575 adopted effective January 1, 2010.

Rule 2.576. Access to name of the petitioner

(a) Termination of confidentiality

The current name of a confidential name change petitioner must remain confidential until a determination is made that:

(1) Petitioner's participation in the address confidentiality program has ended under Government Code section 6206.7; or

(2) The court finds by clear and convincing evidence that the allegations of domestic violence or stalking in the petition are false.

(Subd (a) adopted effective January 1, 2010.)

(b) Procedure to obtain access

A determination under (a) must be made by noticed motion, with service by mail on the confidential name change petitioner in care of the Secretary of State's address confidentiality program as stated in Government Code section 6206(a)(5)(A).

(Subd (b) adopted effective January 1, 2010.)

Rule 2.576 adopted effective January 1, 2010.

Rule 2.577. Procedures for filing confidential name change records under seal

(a) Court approval required

Records in a name change proceeding may not be filed under seal without a court order. A request by a confidential name change petitioner to file records under seal may be made under the procedures in this chapter. A request by any other petitioner to file records under seal must be made under rules 2.550–2.573.

(Subd (a) adopted effective January 1, 2010.)

(b) Application to file records in confidential name change proceedings under seal

An application by a confidential name change petitioner to file records under seal must be filed at the time the petition for name change is submitted to the court. The application must be made on the *Application to File Documents Under Seal in Name Change Proceeding Under Address Confidentiality Program (Safe at Home)* (form NC-410) and be accompanied by a *Declaration in Support of Application to File Documents Under Seal in Name Change Proceeding Under Address Confidentiality Program (Safe at Home)* (form NC-420), containing facts sufficient to justify the sealing.

(Subd (b) amended effective January 1, 2017; adopted effective January 1, 2010.)

(c) Confidentiality

The application to file under seal must be kept confidential by the court until the court rules on it.

(Subd (c) adopted effective January 1, 2010.)

(d) Procedure for lodging of petition for name change

(1) The records that may be filed under seal must be lodged with the court. If they are transmitted on paper, they must be placed in a sealed envelope. If they are transmitted electronically, they must be transmitted to the court in a secure manner that preserves the confidentiality of the documents to be lodged.

(2) If the petitioner is transmitting the petition on paper, the petitioner must complete and affix to the envelope a completed *Confidential Cover Sheet—Name Change Proceeding Under Address Confidentiality Program (Safe at Home)* (form NC-400) and in the space under the title and case number mark it "CONDITIONALLY UNDER SEAL." If the petitioner is transmitting the petition electronically, the first page of the electronic transmission must be a completed *Confidential Cover Sheet—Name Change Proceeding Under Address Confidentiality Program (Safe at Home)* (form NC-400) with the space under the title and case number marked "CONDITIONALLY UNDER SEAL."

(3) On receipt of a petition lodged under this rule, the clerk must endorse the cover sheet with the date of its receipt and must retain but not file the record unless the court orders it filed.

(4) If the court denies the application to seal, the moving party may notify the court that the lodged record is to be filed unsealed. This notification must be received within 10 days of the order denying the motion or application to seal, unless otherwise ordered by the court. On receipt of this notification, the clerk must unseal and file the record. If the moving party does not notify the court within 10 days of the order, the clerk must (1) return the lodged record to the moving party if it is in paper form or (2) permanently delete the lodged record if it is in electronic form.

(Subd (d) amended effective January 1, 2017; adopted effective January 1, 2010; previously amended effective January 1, 2016.)

(e) Consideration of application to file under seal

The court may order that the record be filed under seal if it finds that all of the following factors apply:

(1) There exists an overriding interest that overcomes the right of public access to the record;

(2) The overriding interest supports sealing the record;

(3) A substantial probability exists that the overriding interest will be prejudiced if the record is not sealed;

(4) The proposed order to seal the record is narrowly tailored; and

(5) No less restrictive means exist to achieve the overriding interest.

(Subd (e) adopted effective January 1, 2010.)

(f) Order

(1) The order may be issued on *Order on Application to File Documents Under Seal in Name Change Proceeding Under Address Confidentiality Program (Safe at Home)* (form NC-425).

(2) Any order granting the application to seal must state whether the declaration in support of the application, the order itself, and any other record in the proceeding are to be sealed as well as the petition for name change.

(3) For petitions transmitted in paper form, if the court grants an order sealing a record, the clerk must strike out the notation required by (d)(2)

on the *Confidential Cover Sheet* that the matter is filed "CONDITIONALLY UNDER SEAL," add a notation to that sheet prominently stating "SEALED BY ORDER OF THE COURT ON *(DATE)*," and file the documents under seal. For petitions transmitted electronically, the clerk must file the court's order, maintain the record ordered sealed in a secure manner, and clearly identify the record as sealed by court order on a specified date.

(4) If the court grants the application to file under seal and issues an order under (e), the petition and any associated records may be filed under seal and ruled on by the court immediately.

(5) The order must identify any person other than the court who is authorized to inspect the sealed records.

(Subd (f) amended effective January 1, 2017; adopted effective January 1, 2010; previously amended effective January 1, 2016.)

(g) Custody of sealed records

Sealed records must be securely filed and kept separate from the public file in the case. If the sealed records are in electronic form, appropriate access controls must be established to ensure that only authorized persons may access the sealed records.

(Subd (g) amended effective January 1, 2017; adopted effective January 1, 2010.)

(h) Motion, application, or petition to unseal record

(1) A sealed record may not be unsealed except by order of the court.

(2) Any member of the public seeking to unseal a record or a court proposing to do so on its own motion must follow the procedures described in rule 2.551(h).

(Subd (h) adopted effective January 1, 2010.)

Rule 2.577 amended effective January 1, 2017; adopted effective January 1, 2010; previously amended effective January 1, 2016.

Chapter 6
Other Sealed or Closed Records

Title 2, Trial Court Rules—Division 4, Court Records—Chapter 6, Other Sealed or Closed Record; adopted as Chapter 5 effective January 1, 2007; renumbered effective January 1, 2010.

Rule 2.580. Request for delayed public disclosure
Rule 2.585. Confidential in-camera proceedings

Rule 2.580. Request for delayed public disclosure

In an action in which the prejudgment attachment remedy under Code of Civil Procedure section 483.010 et seq. is sought, if the plaintiff requests at the time a complaint is filed that the records in the action or the fact of the filing of the action be made temporarily unavailable to the public under Code of Civil Procedure section 482.050, the plaintiff must file a declaration stating one of the following:

(1) "This action is on a claim for money based on contract against a defendant who is not a natural person. The claim is not secured within the meaning of Code of Civil Procedure section 483.010(b)."—or—

(2) "This action is on a claim for money based on contract against a defendant who is a natural person. The claim arises out of the defendant's conduct of a trade, business, or profession, and the money, property, or services were not used by the defendant primarily for personal, family, or household purposes. The claim is not secured within the meaning of Code of Civil Procedure section 483.010(b)."

Rule 2.580 renumbered effective January 1, 2007; adopted as rule 243.3 effective January 1, 2001.

Rule 2.585. Confidential in-camera proceedings

(a) Minutes of proceedings

If a confidential in-camera proceeding is held in which a party is excluded from being represented, the clerk must include in the minutes the nature of the hearing and only such references to writings or witnesses as will not disclose privileged information.

(b) Disposition of examined records

Records examined by the court in confidence under (a), or copies of them, must be filed with the clerk under seal and must not be disclosed without court order.

Rule 2.585 renumbered effective January 1, 2007; adopted as rule 243.4 effective January 1, 2001.

Division 5
Venue and Sessions

Chap. 1. Venue [Reserved]. Rule 2.700.

Chap. 2. Sessions [Reserved].

Chapter 1
Venue
[Reserved]

Rule 2.700. Intracounty venue [Reserved]

Rule 2.700 adopted effective January 1, 2007.

Chapter 2
Sessions
[Reserved]

Division 6
Appointments by the Court or Agreement of the Parties

Chap. 1. Court-Appointed Temporary Judges. Rules 2.810–2.819.
Chap. 2. Temporary Judges Requested by the Parties. Rules 2.830–2.835.
Chap. 3. Referees [Reserved].
Chap. 4. Language Access. Rules 2.850–2.895.

Chapter 1
Court-Appointed Temporary Judges

Rule 2.810. Temporary judges appointed by the trial courts
Rule 2.811. Court appointment of temporary judges
Rule 2.812. Requirements for court appointment of an attorney to serve as a temporary judge
Rule 2.813. Contents of training programs
Rule 2.814. Appointment of temporary judge
Rule 2.815. Continuing education
Rule 2.816. Stipulation to court-appointed temporary judge
Rule 2.817. Disclosures to the parties
Rule 2.818. Disqualifications and limitations
Rule 2.819. Continuing duty to disclose and disqualify

Rule 2.810. Temporary judges appointed by the trial courts

(a) Scope of rules

Rules 2.810–2.819 apply to attorneys who serve as court-appointed temporary judges in the trial courts. The rules do not apply to subordinate judicial officers or to attorneys designated by the courts to serve as temporary judges at the parties' request.

(Subd (a) amended effective January 1, 2009; previously amended effective January 1, 2007.)

(b) Definition of "court-appointed temporary judge"

A "court-appointed temporary judge" means an attorney who has satisfied the requirements for appointment under rule 2.812 and has been appointed by the court to serve as a temporary judge in that court.

(Subd (b) amended effective January 1, 2007.)

(c) Appointment of attorneys as temporary judges

Trial courts may appoint an attorney as a temporary judge only if the attorney has satisfied the requirements of rule 2.812.

(Subd (c) amended effective January 1, 2007.)

(d) Exception for extraordinary circumstances

A presiding judge may appoint an attorney who is qualified under rule 2.812(a), but who has not satisfied the other requirements of that rule, only in case of extraordinary circumstances. Any appointment under this subdivision based on extraordinary circumstances must be made before the attorney serves as a temporary judge and must not last more than 10 court days in a three-year period.

(Subd (d) amended effective January 1, 2017; previously amended effective January 1, 2007.)

Rule 2.810 amended effective January 1, 2017; adopted as rule 243.11 effective July 1, 2006; previously amended and renumbered effective January 1, 2007; previously amended effective January 1, 2009.

Rule 2.811. Court appointment of temporary judges

(a) Purpose of court appointment

The purpose of court appointment of attorneys as temporary judges is to assist the public by providing the court with a panel of trained, qualified, and experienced attorneys who may serve as temporary judges at the discretion of the court if the court needs judicial assistance that it cannot provide using its full-time judicial officers.

(b) Appointment and service discretionary

Court-appointed attorneys are appointed and serve as temporary judges solely at the discretion of the presiding judge.

(c) No employment relationship

Court appointment and service of an attorney as a temporary judge do not establish an employment relationship between the court and the attorney.

(d) Responsibility of the presiding judge for appointments

The appointment of attorneys to serve as temporary judges is the responsibility of the presiding judge, who may designate another judge or committee of judges to perform this responsibility. In carrying out this responsibility, the presiding judge is assisted by a Temporary Judge Administrator as prescribed by rule 10.743.

(Subd (d) amended effective January 1, 2007.)

Rule 2.811 amended and renumbered effective January 1, 2007; adopted as rule 243.12 effective July 1, 2006.

Rule 2.812. Requirements for court appointment of an attorney to serve as a temporary judge

(a) Experience required for appointment and service

The presiding judge may not appoint an attorney to serve as a temporary judge unless the attorney has been admitted to practice as a member of the State Bar of California for at least 10 years before the appointment. However, for good cause, the presiding judge may permit an attorney who has been admitted to practice for at least 5 years to serve as a temporary judge.

(b) Conditions for appointment by the court

The presiding judge may appoint an attorney to serve as a temporary judge only if the attorney:

(1) Is a member in good standing of the State Bar and has no disciplinary action pending;

(2) Has not pled guilty or no contest to a felony, or has not been convicted of a felony that has not been reversed;

(3) Has satisfied the education and training requirements in (c);

(4) Has satisfied all other general conditions that the court may establish for appointment of an attorney as a temporary judge in that court; and

(5) Has satisfied any additional conditions that the court may require for an attorney to be appointed as a temporary judge for a particular assignment or type of case in that court.

(c) Education and training requirements

The presiding judge may appoint an attorney to serve as a temporary judge only if the following minimum training requirements are satisfied:

(1) *Mandatory training on bench conduct and demeanor*

Within three years before appointment, the attorney must have attended and successfully completed a course on the subjects identified in rule 2.813(a) approved by the court in which the attorney will serve. This course must be of at least three hours' duration, instructor-led (live remote or in-person), and be taught by a qualified judicial officer approved by the court.

(2) *Mandatory training in ethics*

Within three years before appointment, the attorney must have attended and successfully completed a course on the subjects identified in rule 2.813(b) approved by the court in which the attorney will serve. This course must be of at least three hours' duration and may be taken by any means approved by the court.

(3) *Substantive training*

Within three years before appointment, the attorney must have attended and successfully completed a course on the substantive law in each subject area in which the attorney will serve as a temporary judge. These courses may be taken by any means approved by the court. The substantive courses have the following minimum requirements:

(A) *Small claims*

Within three years before appointment, an attorney serving as a temporary judge in small claims cases must have attended and successfully completed a course on the subjects identified in rule 2.813(c). The course must be at least three hours' duration and approved by the court in which the attorney will serve.

(B) *Traffic*

Within three years before appointment, an attorney serving as a temporary judge in traffic cases must have attended and completed a course on the subjects identified in rule 2.813(d). The course must be at least three hours' duration and approved by the court in which the attorney will serve.

(C) *Other subject areas*

If the court assigns attorneys to serve as temporary judges in other substantive areas such as civil law, family law, juvenile law, unlawful detainers, or case management, the court must determine what additional training is required before an attorney may serve as a temporary judge in each subject area. The training required in each area must be of at least three hours' duration. The court may also require that an attorney possess additional years of practical experience in each substantive area before being assigned to serve as a temporary judge in that subject area.

(D) *Settlement*

An attorney need not be a temporary judge to assist the court in settlement conferences. However, an attorney assisting the court with settlement conferences who performs any judicial function, such as entering a settlement on the record under Code of Civil Procedure section 664.6, must be a qualified temporary judge who has satisfied the training requirements under (c)(1) and (c)(2) of this rule.

(E) The substantive training requirements in (3)(A)–(C) do not apply to courts in which temporary judges are used fewer than 10 times altogether in a calendar year.

(Subd (c) amended effective January 1, 2023; previously amended effective January 1, 2007, and January 1, 2009.)

(d) Requirements for retired judicial officers

Commencing five years after the retired judicial officer last served in a judicial position either as a full-time judicial officer or as an assigned judge, a retired judicial officer serving as a temporary judge must satisfy all the education and training requirements of this rule.

(Subd (d) amended effective January 1, 2023; adopted effective January 1, 2009.)

(e) Additional requirements

The presiding judge in each court should establish additional experience and training requirements for temporary judges beyond the minimum requirements provided in this rule if it is feasible for the court to do so.

(Subd (e) relettered effective January 1, 2009; adopted as subd (d) effective July 1, 2006.)

(f) Records of attendance

A court that uses temporary judges must maintain records verifying that each attorney who serves as a temporary judge in that court has attended and successfully completed the courses required under this rule.

(Subd (f) relettered effective January 1, 2009; adopted as subd (e) effective July 1, 2006.)

(g) Application and appointment

To serve as a temporary judge, an attorney must complete the application required under rule 10.744, must satisfy the requirements prescribed in this rule, and must satisfy such other requirements as the court appointing the attorney in its discretion may determine are appropriate.

(Subd (g) relettered effective January 1, 2009; adopted as subd (f) effective July 1, 2006.)

Rule 2.812 amended effective January 1, 2023; adopted as rule 243.13 effective July 1, 2006; previously amended and renumbered effective January 1, 2007; previously amended effective January 1, 2009.

Advisory Committee Comment

The goal of this rule is to ensure that attorneys who serve as court-appointed temporary judges are qualified and properly trained.

Subdivision (a). If a court determines that there is good cause under (a) to appoint an attorney with less than 10 years of practice as a temporary judge, the attorney must still satisfy the other requirements of the rule before being appointed.

Subdivision (b). "Good standing" means that the attorney is currently eligible to practice law in the State of California. An attorney in good standing may be either an active or a voluntarily inactive member of the State Bar. The rule does not require that an attorney be an active member of the State Bar to serve as a court-appointed temporary judge. Voluntarily inactive members may be appointed as temporary judges if the court decides to appoint them.

Subdivision (c). A court may use attorneys who are not temporary judges to assist in the settlement of cases. For example, attorneys may work under the presiding judge or individual judges and may assist them in settling cases. However, these attorneys may not perform any judicial functions such as entering a settlement on the record under Code of Civil Procedure section 664.6. Settlement attorneys who are not temporary judges are not required to satisfy the requirements of these rules, but they must satisfy any requirements established by the court for attorneys who assist in the settlement of cases.

Rule 2.813. Contents of training programs

(a) Bench conduct

Before the court may appoint an attorney to serve as a temporary judge in any type of case, the attorney must have received training under rule 2.812(c)(1) in the following subjects:

(1) Bench conduct, demeanor, and decorum;
(2) Access, fairness, and elimination of bias; and
(3) Adjudicating cases involving self-represented parties.

(Subd (a) amended effective January 1, 2007.)

(b) Ethics

Before the court may appoint an attorney to serve as a temporary judge in any type of case, the attorney must have received ethics training under rule 2.812(c)(2) in the following subjects:

(1) Judicial ethics generally;
(2) Conflicts;
(3) Disclosures, disqualifications, and limitations on appearances; and
(4) Ex parte communications.

(Subd (b) amended effective January 1, 2007.)

(c) Small claims

Before the court may appoint an attorney to serve as a temporary judge in small claims cases, the attorney must have received training under rule 2.812(c)(3)(A) in the following subjects:

(1) Small claims procedures and practices;
(2) Consumer sales;
(3) Vehicular sales, leasing, and repairs;
(4) Credit and financing transactions;
(5) Professional and occupational licensing;
(6) Tenant rent deposit law;
(7) Contract, warranty, tort, and negotiable instruments law;
(8) The subjects specified in Code of Civil Procedure section 116.240(b); and
(9) Other subjects deemed appropriate by the presiding judge based on local needs and conditions.

In addition, an attorney serving as a temporary judge in small claims cases must be familiar with the publications identified in Code of Civil Procedure section 116.930.

(Subd (c) amended effective January 1, 2023; previously amended effective January 1, 2007.)

(d) Traffic

Before the court may appoint an attorney to serve as a temporary judge in traffic cases, the attorney must have received training under rule 2.812(c)(3)(B) in the following subjects:

(1) Traffic court procedures and practices;
(2) Correctable violations;
(3) Discovery;
(4) Driver licensing;
(5) Failure to appear;
(6) Mandatory insurance;
(7) Notice to appear citation forms;
(8) Red-light enforcement;
(9) Sentencing and court-ordered traffic school;
(10) Speed enforcement;
(11) Settlement of the record;
(12) Uniform bail and penalty schedules;
(13) Vehicle registration and licensing; and
(14) Other subjects deemed appropriate by the presiding judge based on local needs and conditions.

(Subd (d) amended effective January 1, 2007.)

Rule 2.813 amended effective January 1, 2023; adopted as rule 243.14 effective July 1, 2006; previously amended and renumbered effective January 1, 2007.

Advisory Committee Comment

The purpose of this rule is to ensure that all court-appointed temporary judges have proper training in bench conduct and demeanor, ethics, and each substantive area in which they adjudicate cases. Each court is responsible for approving the training and instructional materials for the temporary judges appointed by that court. The training in bench conduct and demeanor must be instructor-led (live remote or in-person), but in other areas each court may determine the approved method or methods by which the training is provided. Courts may offer Minimum Continuing Legal Education (MCLE) credit for courses that they provide and may approve MCLE courses provided by others as satisfying the substantive training requirements under this rule. Courts may work together with other courts, or may cooperate on a regional basis, to develop and provide training programs for court-appointed temporary judges under this rule.

Rule 2.814. Appointment of temporary judge

An attorney may serve as a temporary judge for the court only after the court has issued an order appointing him or her to serve. Before serving, the attorney must subscribe the oath of office and must certify that he or she is aware of and will comply with applicable provisions of canon 6 of the Code of Judicial Ethics and the California Rules of Court.

Rule 2.814 renumbered effective January 1, 2007; adopted as rule 243.15 effective July 1, 2006.

Rule 2.815. Continuing education

(a) Continuing education required

Every three years, each attorney appointed as a temporary judge must attend and successfully complete a course on bench conduct and demeanor, an ethics course, and a course in each substantive area in which the attorney will serve as a temporary judge. The courses must cover the same subjects and be of the same duration as the courses prescribed in rule 2.812(c). These courses must be approved by the court in which the attorney will serve.

(Subd (a) amended effective January 1, 2023; previously amended effective January 1, 2007.)

(b) Records of attendance

A court that uses temporary judges must maintain records verifying that each attorney who serves as a temporary judge in that court has attended and successfully completed the courses required under this rule.

Rule 2.815 amended effective January 1, 2023; adopted as rule 243.17 effective July 1, 2006; previously amended and renumbered effective January 1, 2007.

Rule 2.816. Stipulation to court-appointed temporary judge

(a) Application

This rule governs a stipulation for a matter to be heard by a temporary judge when the court has appointed and assigned an attorney to serve as a temporary judge in that court.

(Subd (a) adopted effective July 1, 2006.)

(b) Contents of notice

Before the swearing in of the first witness at a small claims hearing, before the entry of a plea by the defendant at a traffic arraignment, or before the commencement of any other proceeding, the court must give notice to each party that:

(1) A temporary judge will be hearing the matters for that calendar;
(2) The temporary judge is a qualified member of the State Bar and the name of the temporary judge is provided; and
(3) The party has a right to have the matter heard before a judge, commissioner, or referee of the court.

(Subd (b) amended and relettered effective July 1, 2006; adopted as subd (a) effective January 1, 2001.)

(c) Form of notice

The court may give the notice in (b) by either of the following methods:

(1) A conspicuous sign posted inside or just outside the courtroom, accompanied by oral notification or notification by videotape or audiotape by a court officer on the day of the hearing; or
(2) A written notice provided to each party.

(Subd (c) amended and relettered effective July 1, 2006; adopted as subd (b) effective January 1, 2001.)

(d) Methods of stipulation

After notice has been given under (a) and (b), a party stipulates to a court-appointed temporary judge by either of the following:

(1) The party is deemed to have stipulated to the attorney serving as a temporary judge if the party fails to object to the matter being heard by the temporary judge before the temporary judge begins the proceeding; or
(2) The party signs a written stipulation agreeing that the matter may be heard by the temporary judge.

(Subd (d) amended effective January 1, 2007; adopted effective July 1, 2006.)

(e) Application or motion to withdraw stipulation

An application or motion to withdraw a stipulation for the appointment of a temporary judge must be supported by a declaration of facts establishing good cause for permitting the party to withdraw the stipulation. In addition:

(1) The application or motion must be heard by the presiding judge or a judge designated by the presiding judge.
(2) A declaration that a ruling by a temporary judge is based on an error of fact or law does not establish good cause for withdrawing a stipulation.

(3) The application or motion must be served and filed, and the moving party must provide a copy to the presiding judge.

(4) If the application or motion for withdrawing the stipulation is based on grounds for the disqualification of, or limitation of the appearance by, the temporary judge first learned or arising after the temporary judge has made one or more rulings, but before the temporary judge has completed judicial action in the proceeding, the temporary judge, unless the disqualification or termination is waived, must disqualify himself or herself. But in the absence of good cause, the rulings the temporary judge has made up to that time must not be set aside by the judicial officer or temporary judge who replaces the temporary judge.

(Subd (e) amended effective January 1, 2016; adopted effective July 1, 2006; previously amended effective January 1, 2007.)

Rule 2.816 amended effective January 1, 2016; adopted as rule 1727 effective January 1, 2001; previously amended and renumbered as rule 243.18 effective July 1, 2006; previously amended and renumbered as rule 2.816 effective January 1, 2007.

Rule 2.817. Disclosures to the parties

A temporary judge must make all disclosures required under the Code of Judicial Ethics.

Rule 2.817 renumbered effective January 1, 2007; adopted as rule 243.19 effective July 1, 2006.

Rule 2.818. Disqualifications and limitations

(a) Code of Judicial Ethics

A temporary judge must disqualify himself or herself as a temporary judge in proceedings as provided under the Code of Judicial Ethics.

(Subd (a) lettered effective July 1, 2006; adopted as unlettered subd effective July 1, 2006.)

(b) Limitations on service

In addition to being disqualified as provided in (a), an attorney may not serve as a court-appointed temporary judge:

(1) If the attorney, in any type of case, is appearing on the same day in the same courthouse as an attorney or as a party;

(2) If the attorney, in the same type of case, is presently a party to any action or proceeding in the court; or

(3) If, in a family law or unlawful detainer case, one party is self-represented and the other party is represented by an attorney or is an attorney.

For good cause, the presiding judge may waive the limitations established in this subdivision.

(Subd (b) adopted effective July 1, 2006.)

(c) Waiver of disqualifications or limitations

(1) After a temporary judge who has determined himself or herself to be disqualified under the Code of Judicial Ethics or prohibited from serving under (b) has disclosed the basis for his or her disqualification or limitation on the record, the parties and their attorneys may agree to waive the disqualification or limitation and the temporary judge may accept the waiver. The temporary judge must not seek to induce a waiver and must avoid any effort to discover which attorneys or parties favored or opposed a waiver. The waiver must be in writing, must recite the basis for the disqualification or limitation, and must state that it was knowingly made. The waiver is effective only when signed by all parties and their attorneys and filed in the record.

(2) No waiver is permitted where the basis for the disqualification is any of the following:

(A) The temporary judge has a personal bias or prejudice concerning a party;

(B) The temporary judge has served as an attorney in the matter in controversy; or

(C) The temporary judge has been a material witness in the controversy.

(Subd (c) adopted effective July 1, 2006.)

(d) Late discovery of grounds for disqualification or limitation

In the event that grounds for disqualification or limitation are first learned of or arise after the temporary judge has made one or more rulings in a proceeding, but before the temporary judge has completed judicial action in the proceeding, the temporary judge, unless the disqualification or limitation is waived, must disqualify himself or herself. But in the absence of good cause, the rulings the temporary judge has made up to that time must not be set aside by the judicial officer or temporary judge who replaces the temporary judge.

(Subd (d) amended effective January 1, 2007; adopted effective July 1, 2006.)

(e) Notification of the court

Whenever a temporary judge determines himself or herself to be disqualified or limited from serving, the temporary judge must notify the presiding judge or the judge designated by the presiding judge of his or her withdrawal and must not further participate in the proceeding, unless his or her disqualification or limitation is waived by the parties as provided in (c).

(Subd (e) adopted effective July 1, 2006.)

(f) Requests for disqualifications

A party may request that a temporary judge withdraw on the ground that he or she is disqualified or limited from serving. If a temporary judge who should disqualify himself or herself or who is limited from serving in a case fails to withdraw, a party may apply to the presiding judge under rule 2.816(e) of the California Rules of Court for a withdrawal of the stipulation. The presiding judge or the judge designated by the presiding judge must determine whether good cause exists for granting withdrawal of the stipulation.

(Subd (f) amended effective January 1, 2007; previously adopted effective July 1, 2006.)

Rule 2.818 amended and renumbered effective January 1, 2007; adopted as rule 243.20 effective July 1, 2006; previously amended effective July 1, 2006.

Advisory Committee Comment

Subdivision (a) indicates that the rules concerning the disqualification of temporary judges are provided in the Code of Judicial Ethics. Subdivision (b) establishes additional limitations that prohibit attorneys from serving as court-appointed temporary judges under certain specified circumstances. Under subdivisions (c)–(e), the provisions of Code of Civil Procedure section 170.3 on waiver of disqualifications, the effect of late discovery of the grounds of disqualification, and notification of disqualification of judicial officers are made applicable to temporary judges. Under subdivision (f), requests for disqualification are handled as withdrawals of the stipulation to a temporary judge and are ruled on by the presiding judge. This procedure is different from that for seeking the disqualification of a judge under Code of Civil Procedure section 170.3.

Rule 2.819. Continuing duty to disclose and disqualify

A temporary judge has a continuing duty to make disclosures, to disqualify himself or herself, and to limit his or her service as provided under the Code of Judicial Ethics.

Rule 2.819 renumbered effective January 1, 2007; adopted as rule 243.21 effective July 1, 2006.

Chapter 2
Temporary Judges Requested by the Parties

Rule 2.830. Temporary judges requested by the parties
Rule 2.831. Temporary judge—stipulation, order, oath, assignment, disclosure, and disqualification
Rule 2.832. Compensation
Rule 2.833. Documents and exhibits
Rule 2.834. Open proceedings; notices of proceedings, use of court facilities, and order for hearing site
Rule 2.835. Motions or applications to be heard by the court

Rule 2.830. Temporary judges requested by the parties

(a) Application

Rules 2.830–2.834 apply to attorneys designated as temporary judges under article VI, section 21 of the California Constitution at the request of the parties rather than by prior appointment of the court, including privately compensated temporary judges and attorneys who serve as temporary judges pro bono at the request of the parties.

(Subd (a) amended effective January 1, 2007.)

(b) Definition

"Privately compensated" means that the temporary judge is paid by the parties.

(c) Limitation

These rules do not apply to subordinate judicial officers or to attorneys who are appointed by the court to serve as temporary judges for the court.

Rule 2.830 amended and renumbered effective January 1, 2007; adopted as rule 243.30 effective July 1, 2006.

Rule 2.831. Temporary judge—stipulation, order, oath, assignment, disclosure, and disqualification

(a) Stipulation

When the parties request that an attorney be designated by the court to serve as a temporary judge on a case, the stipulation of the parties that a case may be tried by a temporary judge must be in writing and must state the name and office address of the member of the State Bar agreed on. The stipulation must be submitted for approval to the presiding judge or the judge designated by the presiding judge.

(Subd (a) amended effective July 1, 2006; previously amended and relettered effective July 1, 1993; previously amended effective January 1, 2001, and July 1, 2001.)

(b) Order, oath, and certification

The order designating the temporary judge must be signed by the presiding judge or the presiding judge's designee and refer to the stipulation. The stipulation and order must then be filed. The temporary judge must take and subscribe the oath of office and certify that he or she is aware of and will comply with applicable provisions of canon 6 of the Code of Judicial Ethics and the California Rules of Court.

(Subd (b) amended effective July 1, 2006; previously amended and relettered effective July 1, 1993; previously amended effective July 1, 2001.)

(c) When the temporary judge may proceed The temporary judge may proceed with the hearing, trial, and determination of the cause after the stipulation, order, oath, and certification have been filed.

(Subd (c) amended and relettered effective July 1, 2006; formerly adopted as subd (b).)

(d) Disclosure to the parties

In addition to any other disclosure required by law, no later than five days after designation as a temporary judge or, if the temporary judge is not aware of his or her designation or of a matter subject to disclosure at that time, as soon as practicable thereafter, a temporary judge must disclose to the parties any matter subject to disclosure under the Code of Judicial Ethics.

(Subd (d) amended effective July 1, 2006; adopted as subd (c) effective July 1, 2001; previously amended and relettered effective July 1, 2006.)

(e) Disqualification

In addition to any other disqualification required by law, a temporary judge requested by the parties and designated by the court under this rule must disqualify himself or herself as provided under the Code of Judicial Ethics.

(Subd (e) amended and relettered effective July 1, 2006; adopted as subd (c) effective July 1, 1993; previously amended and relettered as subd (d) effective July 1, 2001.)

(f) Motion to withdraw stipulation

A motion to withdraw a stipulation for the appointment of a temporary judge must be supported by a declaration of facts establishing good cause for permitting the party to withdraw the stipulation, and must be heard by the presiding judge or a judge designated by the presiding judge. A declaration that a ruling is based on error of fact or law does not establish good cause for withdrawing a stipulation. Notice of the motion must be served and filed, and the moving party must provide a copy to the temporary judge. If the motion to withdraw the stipulation is based on grounds for the disqualification of the temporary judge first learned or arising after the temporary judge has made one or more rulings, but before the temporary judge has completed judicial action in the proceeding, the provisions of rule 2.816(e)(4) apply. If a motion to withdraw a stipulation is granted, the presiding judge must assign the case for hearing or trial as promptly as possible.

(Subd (f) amended effective January 1, 2016; adopted as subd (f) effective July 1, 1993; previously amended and relettered as subd (g) effective July 1, 2001, and as subd (f) effective July 1, 2006; previously amended effective January 1, 2007.)

Rule 2.831 amended effective January 1, 2016; adopted as rule 244 effective January 1, 1999; previously amended effective April 1, 1962, July 1, 1981, July 1, 1987, July 1, 1993, July 1, 1995, January 1, 2001, and July 1, 2001; previously amended and renumbered as rule 243.31 effective July 1, 2006 and as rule 2.831 effective January 1, 2007.

Rule 2.832. Compensation

A temporary judge selected by the parties may not be compensated by the parties unless the parties agree in writing on a rate of compensation that they will pay.

Rule 2.832 renumbered effective January 1, 2007; adopted as rule 243.32 effective July 1, 2006.

Rule 2.833. Documents and exhibits

All temporary judges requested by the parties and parties in proceedings before these temporary judges must comply with the applicable requirements of rule 2.400 concerning the filing and handling of documents and exhibits.

Rule 2.833 adopted effective January 1, 2010.

Rule 2.834. Open proceedings; notices of proceedings, use of court facilities, and order for hearing site

(a) Open proceedings

All proceedings before a temporary judge requested by the parties that would be open to the public if held before a judge must be open to the public, regardless of whether they are held in or outside a court facility.

(Subd (a) adopted effective January 1, 2010.)

(b) Notice regarding proceedings before temporary judge requested by the parties

(1) In each case in which he or she is appointed, a temporary judge requested by the parties must file a statement that provides the name, telephone number, and mailing address of a person who may be contacted to obtain information about the date, time, location, and general nature of all hearings and other proceedings scheduled in the matter that would be open to the public if held before a judge. This statement must be filed at the same time as the temporary judge's certification under rule 2.831(b). If there is any change in this contact information, the temporary judge must promptly file a revised statement with the court.

(2) In addition to providing the information required under (1), the statement filed by a temporary judge may also provide the address of a publicly accessible Web site at which the temporary judge will maintain a current calendar setting forth the date, time, location, and general nature of any hearings scheduled in the matter that would be open to the public if held before a judge.

(3) The clerk must post the information from the statement filed by the temporary judge in the court facility.

(Subd (b) amended and relettered effective January 1, 2010; adopted as subd (a) effective July 1, 2006.)

(c) Use of court facilities, court personnel, and summoned jurors

A party who has elected to use the services of a temporary judge requested by the parties is deemed to have elected to proceed outside court facilities. Court facilities, court personnel, and summoned jurors may not be used in proceedings pending before a temporary judge requested by the parties except on a finding by the presiding judge or his or her designee that their use would further the interests of justice.

(Subd (c) amended and relettered effective January 1, 2010; adopted as subd (b) effective July 1, 2006.)

(d) Appropriate hearing site

(1) The presiding judge or his or her designee, on application of any person or on the judge's own motion, may order that a case before a temporary judge requested by the parties must be heard at a site easily accessible to the public and appropriate for seating those who have made known their plan to attend hearings. The application must state facts showing good cause for granting the application, and must be served on all parties and the temporary judge and filed with the court. The proceedings are not stayed while the application is pending unless the presiding judge or his or her designee orders that they be stayed. The issuance of an order for an accessible and appropriate hearing site is not a ground for withdrawal of a stipulation that a case may be heard by a temporary judge.

(2) If a court staff mediator or evaluator is required to attend a hearing before a temporary judge requested by the parties, unless otherwise ordered by the presiding judge or his or her designee, that hearing must take place at a location requiring no more than 15 minutes' travel time from the mediator's or evaluator's work site.

(Subd (d) amended and relettered effective January 1, 2010; adopted as subd (c) effective July 1, 2006.)

Rule 2.834 amended and renumbered effective January 1, 2010; adopted as rule 243.33 effective July 1, 2006; previously renumbered as rule 2.833 effective January 1, 2007.

Rule 2.835. Motions or applications to be heard by the court

(a) Motion or application to seal records

A motion or application to seal records in a case pending before a temporary judge requested by the parties must be filed with the court and must be served on all parties that have appeared in the case and the temporary judge. The motion or application must be heard by the trial court judge to whom the case is assigned or, if the case has not been assigned, by the presiding judge or his or her designee. Rules 2.550–2.551 on sealed records apply to motions or applications filed under this rule.

(Subd (a) amended effective January 1, 2010; previously amended effective January 1, 2007.)

(b) Motion for leave to file complaint for intervention

A motion for leave to file a complaint for intervention in a case pending before a temporary judge requested by the parties must be filed with the court and served on all parties and the temporary judge. The motion must be heard by the trial court judge to whom the case is assigned or, if the case has not been assigned, by the presiding judge or his or her designee. If intervention is allowed, the case must be returned to the trial court docket unless all parties stipulate in the manner prescribed in rule 2.831(a) to proceed before the temporary judge.

(Subd (b) amended effective January 1, 2010; previously amended effective January 1, 2007.)

Rule 2.835 amended and renumbered effective January 1, 2010; adopted as rule 243.34 effective July 1, 2006; previously amended and renumbered as rule 2.834 effective January 1, 2007.

Chapter 3
Referees
[Reserved]

Chapter 4
Language Access

Title 2, Trial Court Rules—Chapter 4, Language Access; adopted effective January 1, 2018.

Art. 1. General Provisions. Rules 2.850, 2.851.
Art. 2. Court Interpreters. Rules 2.890–2.895.

Article 1
General Provisions

Title 2, Trial Court Rules—Chapter 4, Language Access; Article 1, General Provisions; adopted effective January 1, 2018.

Rule 2.850. Language Access Representative
Rule 2.851. Language access services complaints

Rule 2.850. Language Access Representative

(a) Designation of Language Access Representative

The court in each county will designate a Language Access Representative. That function can be assigned to a specific job classification or office within the court.

(Subd (a) adopted effective January 1, 2018.)

(b) Duties

The Language Access Representative will serve as the court's language access resource for all court users, as well as court staff and judicial officers, and should be familiar with all the language access services the court provides; access and disseminate all of the court's multilingual written information as requested; and help limited English proficient (LEP) court users and court staff locate language access resources.

(Subd (b) adopted effective January 1, 2018.)

Rule 2.850 adopted effective January 1, 2018.

Advisory Committee Comment

Subdivision (a). See Recommendation No. 25 of the *Strategic Plan for Language Access in the California Courts*, adopted by the Judicial Council on January 22, 2015.

Rule 2.851. Language access services complaints

(a) Purpose

The purpose of this rule is to ensure that each superior court makes available a form on which court users may submit a complaint about the provision of, or the failure to provide, language access and that each court has procedures for handling those complaints. Courts must implement this rule as soon as reasonably possible but no later than December 31, 2018.

(Subd (a) adopted effective January 1, 2018.)

(b) Complaint form and procedures required

Each superior court must adopt a language access services complaint form and complaint procedures that are consistent with this rule.

(Subd (b) adopted effective January 1, 2018.)

(c) Minimum requirement for complaint form

The language access services complaint form adopted by the court must meet the following minimum requirements:

(1) Be written in plain language;

(2) Allow court users to submit complaints about how the court provided or failed to provide language services;

(3) Allow court users to specify whether the complaint relates to court interpreters, other staff, or local translations;

(4) Include the court's mailing address and an e-mail contact to show court users how they may submit a language access complaint;

(5) Be made available for free both in hard copy at the courthouse and online on the courts' website, where court users can complete the form online and then submit to the court by hand, postal mail, or e-mail; and

(6) Be made available in the languages spoken by significant portions of the county population.

(Subd (c) adopted effective January 1, 2018.)

(d) General requirements for complaint procedures

The complaint procedures adopted by the court must provide for the following:

(1) *Submission and referral of local language access complaints*

(A) Language access complaints may be submitted anonymously.

(B) Language access complaints may be submitted orally or in other written formats; however, use of the court's local form is encouraged to ensure tracking and that complainants provide full information to the court.

(C) Language access complaints regarding local court services should be submitted to the court's designated Language Access Representative.

(D) A complaint submitted to the improper entity must immediately be forwarded to the appropriate court, if that can be determined, or, where appropriate, to the Judicial Council.

(2) *Acknowledgment of complaint*

Except where the complaint is submitted anonymously, within 30 days after the complaint is received, the court's Language Access Representative must send the complainant a written acknowledgment that the court has received the complaint.

(3) *Preliminary review and disposition of complaints*

Within 60 days after receipt of the complaint, the court's Language Access Representative should conduct a preliminary review of every complaint to determine whether the complaint can be informally resolved or closed, or whether the complaint warrants additional investigation. Court user complaints regarding denial of a court interpreter for a courtroom proceeding for pending cases should be given priority.

(4) *Procedure for complaints not resolved through the preliminary review*

If a complaint cannot be resolved through the preliminary review process within 60 days after receipt of the complaint, the court's Language Access Representative should inform the complainant (if identified) that the complaint warrants additional review.

(5) *Notice of outcome*

Except where the complaint is submitted anonymously, the court must send the complainant notice of the outcome taken on the complaint.

(6) *Promptness*

The court must process complaints promptly.

(7) *Records of complaints*

The court should maintain information about each complaint and its disposition. The court must report to the Judicial Council on an annual basis the number and kinds of complaints received, the resolution status of all complaints, and any additional information about complaints requested by Judicial Council staff to facilitate the monitoring of the *Strategic Plan for Language Access in the California Courts*.

(8) *Disagreement (Disputing) Notice of Outcome*

If a complainant disagrees with the notice of the outcome taken on his or her complaint, within 90 days of the date the court sends the notice of outcome, he or she may submit a written follow-up statement to the Language Access Representative indicating that he or she disagrees with the outcome of the complaint. The follow-up statement should be brief, specify the basis of the disagreement, and describe the reasons the complainant believes the court's action lacks merit. For example, the follow-up statement should indicate why the complainant disagrees with the notice of outcome or believes that he or she did not receive an adequate explanation in the notice of outcome. The court's response to any follow-up statement submitted by complainant after receipt of the notice of outcome will be the final action taken by the court on the complaint.

(Subd (d) adopted effective January 1, 2018.)

Rule 2.851 adopted effective January 1, 2018.

Advisory Committee Comment

Subdivision (a). Judicial Council staff have developed a model complaint form and model local complaint procedures, which are available in the Language Access Toolkit at *www.courts.ca.gov/33865.htm*. The model complaint form is posted in numerous languages. Courts are encouraged to base their complaint form and procedures on these models. If a complaint alleges action against a court employee that could lead to discipline, the court will process the complaint consistent with the court's applicable Memoranda of Understanding, personnel policies, and/or rules.

Subdivision (d)(1). Court user complaints regarding language access that relate to Judicial Council meetings, forms, or other translated material hosted on www.courts.ca.gov, should be submitted directly to the Judicial Council at www.courts.ca.gov/languageaccess.htm.

Subdivision (d)(2) and (d)(5). For noncomplicated language access-related complaints that can be resolved quickly, a written response to the complainant indicating that the complaint has been resolved will suffice as both acknowledgement of the complaint and notice of outcome.

Subdivision (d)(5). When appropriate, a written response to the complainant indicating that the language access complaint has been resolved will suffice as notice of outcome. Courts should maintain the privacy of individuals named in the complaint.

Subdivision (d)(7). Reporting to the Judicial Council regarding the overall numbers, kinds, and disposition of language access-related complaints will not include the names of individuals or any other information that may compromise an individual's privacy concerns.

Article 2
Court Interpreters

Title 2, Trial Court Rules—Chapter 4, Language Access; Article 2, Court Interpreters; renumbered from Chapter 4 effective March 5, 2018; adopted effective January 1, 2018.

Rule 2.890. Professional conduct for interpreters
Rule 2.891. Request for court interpreter credential review
Rule 2.892. Guidelines for approval of certification programs for interpreters for deaf and hard-of-hearing persons
Rule 2.893. Appointment of interpreters in court proceedings
Rule 2.894. Reports on appointments of certified and registered interpreters and noncertified and nonregistered interpreters
Rule 2.895. Requests for interpreters

Rule 2.890. Professional conduct for interpreters

(a) Representation of qualifications

An interpreter must accurately and completely represent his or her certifications, training, and relevant experience.

(Subd (a) amended effective January 1, 2007.)

(b) Complete and accurate interpretation

An interpreter must use his or her best skills and judgment to interpret accurately without embellishing, omitting, or editing. When interpreting for a party, the interpreter must interpret everything that is said during the entire proceedings. When interpreting for a witness, the interpreter must interpret everything that is said during the witness's testimony.

(Subd (b) amended effective January 1, 2007.)

(c) Impartiality and avoidance of conflicts of interest

(1) *Impartiality*

An interpreter must be impartial and unbiased and must refrain from conduct that may give an appearance of bias.

(2) *Disclosure of conflicts*

An interpreter must disclose to the judge and to all parties any actual or apparent conflict of interest. Any condition that interferes with the objectivity of an interpreter is a conflict of interest. A conflict may exist if the interpreter is acquainted with or related to any witness or party to the action or if the interpreter has an interest in the outcome of the case.

(3) *Conduct*

An interpreter must not engage in conduct creating the appearance of bias, prejudice, or partiality.

(4) *Statements*

An interpreter must not make statements to any person about the merits of the case until the litigation has concluded.

(Subd (c) amended effective January 1, 2007.)

(d) Confidentiality of privileged communications

An interpreter must not disclose privileged communications between counsel and client to any person.

(Subd (d) amended effective January 1, 2007.)

(e) Giving legal advice

An interpreter must not give legal advice to parties and witnesses, nor recommend specific attorneys or law firms.

(Subd (e) amended effective January 1, 2007.)

(f) Impartial professional relationships

An interpreter must maintain an impartial, professional relationship with all court officers, attorneys, jurors, parties, and witnesses.

(Subd (f) amended effective January 1, 2007.)

(g) Continuing education and duty to the profession

An interpreter must, through continuing education, maintain and improve his or her interpreting skills and knowledge of procedures used by the courts. An interpreter should seek to elevate the standards of performance of the interpreting profession.

(Subd (g) amended effective January 1, 2007.)

(h) Assessing and reporting impediments to performance

An interpreter must assess at all times his or her ability to perform interpreting services. If an interpreter has any reservation about his or her ability to satisfy an assignment competently, the interpreter must immediately disclose that reservation to the court or other appropriate authority.

(Subd (h) amended effective January 1, 2007.)

(i) Duty to report ethical violations

An interpreter must report to the court or other appropriate authority any effort to impede the interpreter's compliance with the law, this rule, or any other official policy governing court interpreting and legal translating.

(Subd (i) amended effective January 1, 2007.)

Rule 2.890 amended and renumbered effective January 1, 2007; adopted as rule 984.4 effective January 1, 1999.

Rule 2.891. Request for court interpreter credential review

Certified and registered court interpreters are credentialed by the Judicial Council under Government Code section 68562. The council, as the credentialing body, has authority to review a credentialed interpreter's performance, skills, and adherence to the professional conduct requirements of rule 2.890, and to impose discipline on interpreters.

(a) Purpose

This rule clarifies the council's authority to adopt disciplinary procedures and to conduct a credential review, as set out in the *California Court Interpreter Credential Review Procedures*.

(Subd (a) adopted effective January 1, 2020.)

(b) Application

Under the *California Court Interpreter Credential Review Procedures*, all court interpreters certified or registered by the council may be subject to a credential review process after a request for a credential review alleging professional misconduct or malfeasance. Nothing in this rule prevents an individual California court from conducting its own review of, and disciplinary process for, interpreter employees under the court's collective bargaining agreements, personnel policies, rules, and procedures, or, for interpreter contractors, under the court's contracting and general administrative policies and procedures.

(Subd (b) adopted effective January 1, 2020.)

(c) Procedure

(1) On a request made to the council by any person, court, or other entity for the review of an interpreter's credential for alleged professional misconduct or malfeasance by an interpreter credentialed by the council, the council will respond in accordance with procedures stated in the *California Court Interpreter Credential Review Procedures*.

(2) On a request by the council in relation to allegations under investigation under the *California Court Interpreter Credential Review Procedures*, a California court is required to forward information to the council regarding a complaint or allegation of professional misconduct by a certified or registered court interpreter.

(Subd (c) adopted effective January 1, 2020.)

(d) Disciplinary action imposed

The appropriateness of disciplinary action and the degree of discipline to be imposed must depend on factors such as the seriousness of the violation, the intent of the interpreter, whether there is a pattern of improper activity, and the effect of the improper activity on others or on the judicial system.

(Subd (d) adopted effective January 1, 2020.)

Rule 2.891 adopted effective January 1, 2020.

Rule 2.892. Guidelines for approval of certification programs for interpreters for deaf and hard-of-hearing persons

Each organization, agency, or educational institution that administers tests for certification of court interpreters for deaf and hard-of-hearing persons under Evidence Code section 754 must comply with the guidelines adopted by the Judicial Council effective February 21, 1992, and any subsequent revisions, and must hold a valid, current approval by the Judicial Council to administer the tests as a certifying organization. The guidelines are stated in the *Judicial Council Guidelines for Approval of Certification Programs for Interpreters for Deaf and Hard-of-Hearing Persons*, published by the Judicial Council.

Rule 2.892 amended effective January 1, 2016; adopted as rule 984.1 effective January 1, 1994; previously amended and renumbered as rule 2.892 effective January 1, 2007.

Rule 2.893. Appointment of interpreters in court proceedings

(a) Application

This rule applies to all trial court proceedings in which the court appoints an interpreter for a Limited English Proficient (LEP) person. This rule applies to spoken language interpreters in languages designated and not designated by the Judicial Council.

(Subd (a) adopted effective January 1, 2018.)

(b) Definitions

As used in this rule:

(1) "Designated language" means a language selected by the Judicial Council for the development of a certification program under Government Code section 68562;

(2) "Certified interpreter" means an interpreter who is certified by the Judicial Council to interpret a language designated by the Judicial Council under Government Code section 68560 et seq.;

(3) "Registered interpreter" means an interpreter in a language not designated by the Judicial Council, who is qualified by the court under the qualification procedures and guidelines adopted by the Judicial Council, and who has passed a minimum of an English fluency examination offered by a testing entity approved by the Judicial Council under Government Code section 68560 et seq.;

(4) "Noncertified interpreter" means an interpreter who is not certified by the Judicial Council to interpret a language designated by the Judicial Council under Government Code section 68560 et seq.;

(5) "Nonregistered interpreter" means an interpreter in a language not designated by the Judicial Council who has not been qualified under the qualification procedures and guidelines adopted by the Judicial Council under Government Code section 68560 et seq.;

(6) "Provisionally qualified" means an interpreter who is neither certified nor registered but has been qualified under the good cause and qualification procedures and guidelines adopted by the Judicial Council under Government Code section 68560 et seq.;

(7) "Temporary interpreter" means an interpreter who is not certified, registered, or provisionally qualified, but is used one time, in a brief, routine matter.

(Subd (b) adopted effective January 1, 2018.)

(c) Appointment of certified or registered interpreters

If a court appoints a certified or registered court interpreter, the judge in the proceeding must require the following to be stated on the record:

(1) The language to be interpreted;

(2) The name of the interpreter;

(3) The interpreter's current certification or registration number;

(4) A statement that the interpreter's identification has been verified as required by statute;

(5) A statement that the interpreter is certified or registered to interpret in the language to be interpreted; and

(6) A statement that the interpreter was administered the interpreter's oath or that he or she has an oath on file with the court.

(Subd (c) adopted effective January 1, 2018.)

(d) Appointment or use of noncertified or nonregistered interpreters

(1) *When permissible*

If after a diligent search a certified or registered interpreter is not available, the judge in the proceeding may either appoint a noncertified or nonregistered interpreter who has been provisionally qualified under (d)(3) or, in the limited circumstances specified in (d)(4), may use a noncertified or nonregistered interpreter who is not provisionally qualified.

(2) *Required record*

In all cases in which a noncertified or nonregistered interpreter is appointed or used, the judge in the proceeding must require the following to be stated on the record:

(A) The language to be interpreted;

(B) A finding that a certified or registered interpreter is not available and a statement regarding whether a *Certification of Unavailability of Certified or Registered Interpreter* (form INT-120) for the language to be interpreted is on file for this date with the court administrator;

(C) A finding that good cause exists to appoint a noncertified or nonregistered interpreter;

(D) The name of the interpreter;

(E) A statement that the interpreter is not certified or registered to interpret in the language to be interpreted;

(F) A finding that the interpreter is qualified to interpret in the proceeding as required in (d)(3) or (d)(4); and

(G) A statement that the interpreter was administered the interpreter's oath.

(3) *Provisional qualification*

(A) A noncertified or nonregistered interpreter is provisionally qualified if the presiding judge of the court or other judicial officer designated by the presiding judge:

(i) Finds the noncertified or nonregistered interpreter to be provisionally qualified following the *Procedures to Appoint a Noncertified or Nonregistered Spoken Language Interpreter as Either Provisionally Qualified or Temporary* (form INT-100-INFO); and

(ii) Signs an order allowing the interpreter to be considered for appointment on *Qualifications of a Noncertified or Nonregistered Spoken Language Interpreter* (form INT-110). The period covered by this order may not exceed a maximum of six months.

(B) To appoint a provisionally qualified interpreter, in addition to the matters that must be stated on the record under (d)(2), the judge in the proceeding must state on the record:

(i) A finding that the interpreter is qualified to interpret the proceeding, following procedures adopted by the Judicial Council (see forms INT-100-INFO, INT-110, and INT-120);

(ii) A finding, if applicable, that good cause exists under (f)(1)(B) for the court to appoint the interpreter beyond the time ordinarily allowed in (f); and

(iii) If a party has objected to the appointment of the proposed interpreter or has waived the appointment of a certified or registered interpreter.

(4) *Temporary use*

At the request of an LEP person, a temporary interpreter may be used to prevent burdensome delay or in other unusual circumstances if:

(A) The judge in the proceeding finds on the record that:

(i) The LEP person has been informed of their right to an interpreter and has waived the appointment of a certified or registered interpreter or an interpreter who could be provisionally qualified by the presiding judge as provided in 15 (d)(3);

(ii) Good cause exists to appoint an interpreter who is not certified, registered, or provisionally qualified; and

(iii) The interpreter is qualified to interpret that proceeding, following procedures adopted by the Judicial Council (see forms INT-100-INFO and INT-140).

(B) The use of an interpreter under this subdivision is limited to a single brief, routine matter before the court. The use of the interpreter in this circumstance may not be extended to subsequent proceedings without again following the procedure set forth in this subdivision.

(Subd (d) adopted effective January 1, 2018.)

(e) Appointment of intermediary interpreters working between two languages that do not include English

An interpreter who works as an intermediary between two languages that do not include English (a relay interpreter) is not eligible to become certified or registered. However, a relay interpreter can become provisionally qualified if the judge finds that he or she is qualified to interpret the proceeding following procedures adopted by the Judicial Council (see forms INT-100-INFO, INT-110, and INT-120). The limitations in (f) below do not apply to relay interpreters.

(Subd (e) adopted effective January 1, 2018.)

(f) Limit on appointment of provisionally qualified noncertified and nonregistered interpreters

(1) A noncertified or nonregistered interpreter who is provisionally qualified under (d)(3) may not interpret in any trial court for more than any four six-month periods, except in the following circumstances:

(A) A noncertified interpreter of Spanish may be allowed to interpret for no more than any two six-month periods in counties with a population greater than 80,000.

(B) A noncertified or nonregistered interpreter may be allowed to interpret more than any four six-month periods, or any two six-month periods for an interpreter of Spanish under (f)(1)(A), if the judge in the proceeding makes a specific finding on the record in each case in which the interpreter is sworn that good cause exists to appoint the interpreter, notwithstanding the interpreter's failure to achieve Judicial Council certification.

(2) Except as provided in (f)(3), each six-month period under (f)(1) begins on the date a presiding judge signs an order under (d)(3)(A)(ii) allowing the noncertified or nonregistered interpreter to be considered for appointment.

(3) If an interpreter is provisionally qualified under (d)(3) in more than one court at the same time, each six-month period runs concurrently for purposes of determining the maximum periods allowed in this subdivision.

(4) Beginning with the second six-month period under (f)(1), a noncertified or nonregistered interpreter may be appointed if he or she meets all of the following conditions:

(A) The interpreter has taken the State of California Court Interpreter Written Exam at least once during the 12 calendar months before the appointment;

(B) The interpreter has taken the State of California's court interpreter ethics course for interpreters seeking appointment as a noncertified or nonregistered interpreter, or is certified or registered in a different language from the one in which he or she is being appointed; and

(C) The interpreter has taken the State of California's online court interpreter orientation course, or is certified or registered in a different language from the one in which he or she is being appointed.

(5) Beginning with the third six-month period under (f)(1), a noncertified or nonregistered interpreter may be appointed if he or she meets all of the following conditions:

(A) The interpreter has taken and passed the State of California Court Interpreter Written Exam with such timing that he or she is eligible to take a Bilingual Interpreting Exam; and

(B) The interpreter has taken either the Bilingual Interpreting Exam or the relevant Oral Proficiency Exam(s) for his or her language pairing at least once during the 12 calendar months before the appointment.

(6) The restrictions in (f)(5)(B) do not apply to any interpreter who seeks appointment in a language pairing for which no exam is available.

(7) The restrictions in (f)(4) and (5) may be waived by the presiding judge for good cause whenever there are fewer than 25 certified or registered interpreters enrolled on the Judicial Council's statewide roster for the language requiring interpretation.

(Subd (f) adopted effective January 1, 2018.)
Rule 2.893 adopted effective January 1, 2018.

Advisory Committee Comment

Subdivisions (c) and (d)(2). When a court reporter is transcribing the proceedings, or an electronic recording is being made of the proceedings, a judge may satisfy the "on the record" requirement by stating the required details of the interpreter appointment in open court. If there is no court reporter and no electronic recording is being made, the "on the record" requirement may be satisfied by stating the required details of the interpreter appointment and documenting them in writing—such as in a minute order, the official clerk's minutes, a formal order, or even a handwritten document—that is entered in the case file.

Subdivision (d)(4). This provision is intended to allow for the one-time use of a noncertified or nonregistered interpreter who is not provisionally qualified to interpret for an LEP person in a courtroom event. This provision is not intended to be used to meet the extended or ongoing interpretation needs of LEP court users.

Subdivision (b)(7) and (d)(4). When determining whether the matter before the court is a "brief, routine matter" for which a noncertified or nonregistered interpreter who has not been provisionally qualified may be used, the judicial officer should consider the complexity of the matter at issue and likelihood of potential impacts on the LEP person's substantive rights, keeping in mind the consequences that could flow from inaccurate or incomplete interpretation of the proceedings.

Rule 2.894. Reports on appointments of certified and registered interpreters and noncertified and nonregistered interpreters

Each superior court must report to the Judicial Council on:

(1) The appointment of certified and registered interpreters under Government Code section 71802, as required by the Judicial Council; and

(2) The appointment of noncertified interpreters of languages designated under Government Code section 68562(a), and registered and nonregistered interpreters of nondesignated languages.

Rule 2.894 amended effective January 1, 2016; adopted as rule 984.3 effective January 1, 1996; previously amended effective March 1, 2003; previously amended and renumbered as rule 2.894 effective January 1, 2007.

Rule 2.895. Requests for interpreters

(a) Publish procedures

Each court must publish procedures for filing, processing, and responding to requests for interpreters consistent with the *Strategic Plan for Language Access in the California Courts* (adopted January 2015). Each court must publish notice of these procedures in English and up to five other languages, based on local community needs.

(Subd (a) adopted effective July 1, 2016.)

(b) Track requests

Each court must track all requests for language services and whether such services were provided. Tracking must include all requests for court interpreters in civil actions, as well as approvals and denials of such requests.

(Subd (b) adopted effective July 1, 2016.)

(c) Notify court if represented party will not be appearing

If a party who has requested an interpreter for herself or himself is represented by counsel, the attorney must notify the court in advance whenever the party will not be appearing at a noticed proceeding.

(Subd (c) adopted effective July 1, 2016.)
Rule 2.895 adopted effective July 1, 2016.

Advisory Committee Comment

The *Request for Interpreter (Civil)* (form INT-300) is concurrently adopted as a model form that will become an optional form, effective January 1, 2018. Until that time, the form can serve as a model that courts may use as part of their procedures, as required under this rule.

This rule shall not be construed in a way that conflicts with Evidence Code section 756.

Subdivision (a). "Local community needs" is described in recommendation 5 of the *Strategic Plan for Language Access in the California Courts* (adopted January 2015).

Subdivision (b). The committee recommends electronic processing of civil interpreter requests to aid the court in data collection about the provision or denial of language services.

Division 7
Proceedings

Chap. 1. General Provisions. Rule 2.900.
Chap. 2. Records of Proceedings. Rules 2.950–2.958.

Chapter 1
General Provisions

Rule 2.900. Submission of a cause in a trial court

(a) Submission

A cause is deemed submitted in a trial court when either of the following first occurs:

(1) The date the court orders the matter submitted; or

(2) The date the final paper is required to be filed or the date argument is heard, whichever is later.

(Subd (a) amended effective January 1, 2007.)

(b) Vacating submission

The court may vacate submission only by issuing an order served on the parties stating reasons constituting good cause and providing for resubmission.

(c) Pendency of a submitted cause

A submitted cause is pending and undetermined unless the court has announced its tentative decision or the cause is terminated. The time required to finalize a tentative decision is not time in which the cause is pending and undetermined. For purposes of this rule only, a motion that has the effect of vacating, reconsidering, or rehearing the cause will be considered a separate and new cause and will be deemed submitted as provided in (a).

(Subd (c) amended effective January 1, 2007.)
Rule 2.900 amended and renumbered effective January 1, 2007; adopted as rule 825 effective January 1, 1989.

Chapter 2
Records of Proceedings

Rule 2.950. Sequential list of reporters
Rule 2.952. Electronic recording as official record of proceedings
Rule 2.954. Specifications for electronic recording equipment
Rule 2.956. Court reporting services in civil cases
Rule 2.958. Assessing fee for official reporter

Rule 2.950. Sequential list of reporters

During any reported court proceeding, the clerk must keep a sequential list of all reporters working on the case, indicating the date the reporter worked and the reporter's name, business address, and Certified Shorthand Reporter license number. If more than one reporter reports a case during one day, the information pertaining to each reporter must be listed with the first reporter designated "A," the second designated "B," etc. If reporter "A" returns during the same day, that reporter will be designated as both reporter "A" and reporter "C" on the list. The list of reporters may be kept in an electronic database maintained by the clerk; however, a hard copy must be available to members of the public within one working day of a request for the list of reporters.

Rule 2.950 amended and renumbered effective January 1, 2007; adopted as rule 980.4 effective July 1, 1991.

Rule 2.952. Electronic recording as official record of proceedings

(a) Application

This rule applies when a court has ordered proceedings to be electronically recorded on a device of a type approved by the Judicial Council or conforming to specifications adopted by the Judicial Council.

(Subd (a) amended effective January 1, 2007; previously amended effective January 1, 1990.)

(b) Definitions

As used in this rule, the following definitions apply:

(1) "Reel" means an individual reel or cassette of magnetic recording tape or a comparable unit of the medium on which an electronic recording is made.

(2) "Monitor" means any person designated by the court to operate electronic recording equipment and to make appropriate notations to identify the proceedings recorded on each reel, including the date and time of the recording. The trial judge, a courtroom clerk, or a bailiff may be the monitor, but when recording is of sound only, a separate monitor without other substantial duties is recommended.

(Subd (b) amended effective January 1, 2007; previously amended effective January 1, 1990.)

(c) Reel numbers

Each reel must be distinctively marked with the date recorded, the department number of the court, if any, and, if possible, a serial number.

(Subd (c) amended effective January 1, 2007; previously amended effective January 1, 1990.)

(d) Certificate of monitor

As soon as practicable after the close of each day's court proceedings, the monitor must execute a certificate for each reel recorded during the day, stating:

(1) That the person executing the certificate was designated by the court as monitor;

(2) The number or other identification assigned to the reel;

(3) The date of the proceedings recorded on that reel;

(4) The titles and numbers of actions and proceedings, or portions thereof, recorded on the reel, and the general nature of the proceedings; and

(5) That the recording equipment was functioning normally, and that all of the proceedings in open court between designated times of day were recorded, except for such matters as were expressly directed to be "off the record" or as otherwise specified.

(Subd (d) amended effective January 1, 2007; previously amended effective January 1, 1990.)

(e) Two or more monitors

If two or more persons acted as monitors during the recording of a single reel, each monitor must execute a certificate as to the portion of the reel that he or she monitored. The certificate of a person other than a judge, clerk, or deputy clerk of the court must be in the form of an affidavit or declaration under penalty of perjury.

(Subd (e) lettered effective January 1, 2007; adopted as part of subd (d) effective January 1, 1976.)

(f) Storage

The monitor's certificate, the recorded reel, and the monitor's notes must be retained and safely stored by the clerk in a manner that will permit their convenient retrieval and use.

(Subd (f) amended and relettered effective January 1, 2007; adopted as subd (e) effective January 1, 1976.)

(g) Transcripts

(1) Written transcripts of electronic recordings may be made by or under the direction of the clerk or a person designated by the court. The person making the transcript must execute a declaration under penalty of perjury that:

(A) Identifies the reel or reels transcribed, or the portions thereof, by reference to the numbers assigned thereto and, where only portions of a reel are transcribed, by reference to index numbers or other means of identifying the portion transcribed; and

(B) States that the transcript is a full, true, and correct transcript of the identified reel or reels or the designated portions thereof.

(2) The transcript must conform, as nearly as possible, to the requirements for a reporter's transcript as provided for in these rules.

(Subd (g) amended and relettered effective January 1, 2007; adopted as subd (f) effective January 1, 1976.)

(h) Use of transcripts

A transcript prepared and certified under (g), and accompanied by a certified copy of the monitor's certificate pertaining to each reel transcribed, is prima facie a true and complete record of the oral proceedings it purports to cover, and satisfies any requirement in the California Rules of Court or in any statute for a reporter's transcript of oral proceedings.

(Subd (h) amended and relettered effective January 1, 2007; adopted as subd (g) effective January 1, 1976.)

(i) Original reels

A reviewing court may order the transmittal to it of the original reels containing electronic recordings of proceedings being reviewed by it, or electronic copies of them.

(Subd (i) relettered effective January 1, 2007; adopted as subd (h) effective January 1, 1976; previously amended effective January 1, 1990.)

(j) Record on appeal

(1) *Stipulation and approval of record without transcription*

On stipulation of the parties approved by the reviewing court, the original reels or electronic copies of them may be transmitted as the record of oral proceedings without being transcribed, in which case the reels or copies satisfy the requirements in the California Rules of Court or in any statute for a reporter's transcript.

(2) *Request for preparation of transcript*

In the absence of a stipulation and approval under (1), the appellant must, within 10 days after filing a notice of appeal in a civil case, serve and file with the clerk directions indicating the portions of the oral proceedings to be transcribed and must, at the same time, deposit with the clerk the approximate cost computed as specified in rule 8.130. Other steps necessary to complete preparation of the record on appeal must be taken following, as nearly as possible, the procedures in rules 8.120 and 8.130.

(3) *Preparation of transcript*

On receiving directions to have a transcript prepared, the clerk may have the material transcribed by a court employee, but should ordinarily send the reels in question to a professional recording service that has been certified by the federal court system or the Judicial Council or verified by the clerk to be skilled in producing transcripts.

(Subd (j) amended effective January 1, 2016; adopted as subd (i) effective January 1, 1990; previously amended effective January 1, 1993; previously amended and relettered as subd (j) effective January 1, 2007.)

Rule 2.952 amended effective January 1, 2016; adopted as rule 980.5 effective January 1, 1976; previously amended effective January 1, 1990, and January 1, 1993; previously amended and renumbered as rule 2.952 effective January 1, 2007.

Rule 2.954. Specifications for electronic recording equipment

(a) Specifications mandated

Electronic recording equipment used in making the official verbatim record of oral courtroom proceedings must conform to the specifications in this rule.

(Subd (a) amended effective January 1, 2007.)

(b) Sound recording only

The following specifications for electronic recording devices and appurtenant equipment apply when only sound is to be recorded:

(1) *Mandatory specifications*

(A) The device must be capable of simultaneously recording at least four separate channels or "tracks," each of which has a separate playback control so that any one channel separately or any combination of channels may be played back.

(B) The device must not have an operative erase head.

(C) The device must have a digital counter or comparable means of logging and locating the place on a reel where specific proceedings were recorded.

(D) Earphones must be provided for monitoring the recorded signal.

(E) The signal going to the earphones must come from a separate playback head, so that the monitor will hear what has actually been recorded on the tape.

(F) The device must be capable of recording at least two hours without interruption. This requirement may be satisfied by a device that automatically switches from one recording deck to another at the completion of a reel of tape of less than two hours in duration.

(G) A separate visual indicator of signal level must be provided for each recording channel.

(H) The appurtenant equipment must include at least four microphones, which should include one at the witness stand, one at the bench, and one at each counsel table. In the absence of unusual circumstances, all microphones must be directional (cardioid).

(I) A loudspeaker must be provided for courtroom playback.

(2) *Recommended features*

The following features are recommended, but not required:

(A) The recording level control should be automatic rather than manual.

(B) The device should be equipped to prevent recording over a previously recorded segment of tape.

(C) The device should give a warning signal at the end of a reel of tape.

(Subd (b) amended effective January 1, 2007.)

(c) Audio-and-video recording

The following specifications for electronic audio-video recording devices and appurtenant equipment apply when audio and video are to be recorded simultaneously.

(1) *Mandatory specifications*

The system must include:

(A) At least five charge-coupled-device color video cameras in fixed mounts, equipped with lenses appropriate to the courtroom. Cameras must conform to EIA standard, accept C-mount lenses, have 2000 lux sensitivity at f4.0 at 3200 degrees Kelvin so as to produce an adequate picture with 30 lux minimum illumination and an f1.4 lens, and be approximately 2.6″ × 2.4″ × 8.0.″

(B) At least eight phase-coherent cardioid (directional) microphones, Crown PCC-160 or equivalent, appropriately placed.

(C) At least two VHS videotape recorders with hi-fi sound on video, specially modified to record 4 channels of audio (2 linear channels with Dolby noise reduction and 2 hi-fi sound on video channels), capable of recording up to 6 hours on T-120 cassettes, modified to prevent automatic rewind at end of tape, and wired for remote control. The two recorders must simultaneously record the same audio and video signals, as selected by the audio-video mixer.

(D) A computer-controlled audio-video mixer and switching system that:

(i) Automatically selects for the VCRs the signal from the video camera that is associated with the active microphone; and

(ii) Compares microphone active signal to ambient noise signal so that microphones are recorded only when a person is speaking, and so that only the microphone nearest a speaker is active, thus minimizing recording of ambient noise.

(E) A sound system that serves both as a sound reinforcement system while recording is in progress, and as a playback amplification system, integrated with other components to minimize feedback.

(F) A time-date generator that is active and records at all times the system is recording.

(G) A color monitor.

(H) Appropriate cables, distribution amplifiers, switches, and the like.

(I) The system must produce:

(i) A signal visible to the judge, the in-court clerk, and counsel indicating that the system is recording;

(ii) An audible signal at end-of-tape or if the tape jams while the controls are set to record; and

(iii) Blanking of the judge's bench monitor when the system is not actually recording.

(2) *Recommended features*

The system should normally include:

(A) A chambers camera and microphone or microphones that, when in use, will override any signals originating in the courtroom, and that will be inactivated when not in use.

(B) Two additional videocassette recorders that will produce tapes with the same video and audio as the main two, but may have fewer channels of sound, for the use of parties in cases recorded.

(Subd (c) amended effective January 1, 2007.)

(d) Substantial compliance

A sound or video and sound system that substantially conforms to these specifications is approved if the deviation does not significantly impair a major function of the system. Subdivision (c)(1)(D)(ii) of this rule describes a specification from which deviation is permissible, if the system produces adequate sound quality.

(Subd (d) amended effective January 1, 2007.)

(e) Previous equipment

The Administrative Director is authorized to approve any electronic recording devices and equipment acquired before the adoption or amendment of this rule that has been found by the court to produce satisfactory recordings of proceedings.

(Subd (e) amended effective January 1, 2016; previously amended effective January 1, 2007.)

Rule 2.954 amended effective January 1, 2016; adopted as rule 980.6 effective January 1, 1990; previously amended and renumbered as rule 2.954 effective January 1, 2007.

Rule 2.956. Court reporting services in civil cases

(a) Statutory reference; application

This rule implements and must be applied so as to give effect to Government Code sections 68086(a)–(c).

(Subd (a) amended effective January 1, 2021; previously amended effective January 31, 1997, and January 1, 2007.)

(b) Notice of availability; parties' request

(1) *Local policy to be adopted and posted*

Each trial court must adopt and post in the clerk's office a local policy enumerating the departments in which the services of official court reporters are normally available, and the departments in which the services of official court reporters are not normally available during regular court hours. If the services of official court reporters are normally available in a department only for certain types of matters, those matters must be identified in the policy.

(2) *Publication of policy*

The court must publish its policy in a newspaper if one is published in the county. Instead of publishing the policy, the court may:

(A) Send each party a copy of the policy at least 10 days before any hearing is held in a case; or

(B) Adopt the policy as a local rule.

(3) *Requests for official court reporter for civil trials and notices to parties*

Unless the court's policy states that all courtrooms normally have the services of official court reporters available for civil trials, the court must require that each party file a statement before the trial date indicating whether the party requests the presence of an official court reporter. If a party requests the presence of an official court reporter and it appears that none will be available, the clerk must notify the party of that fact as soon as possible before the trial. If the services of official court reporters are normally available in all courtrooms, the clerk must notify the parties to a civil trial as soon as possible if it appears that those services will not be available.

(4) *Notice of nonavailability of court reporter for nontrial matters*

If the services of an official court reporter will not be available during a hearing on law and motion or other nontrial matters in civil cases, that fact must be noted on the court's official calendar.

(Subd (b) amended effective January 1, 2007.)

(c) Party may procure reporter or request reporter if granted fee waiver

If the services of an official court reporter are not available for a hearing or trial in a civil case, a party may:

(1) Arrange for the presence of a certified shorthand reporter to serve as an official pro tempore reporter, whom the court must appoint unless there is good cause shown to refuse to do so. It is that party's responsibility to pay the reporter's fee for attendance at the proceedings, but the expense may be recoverable as part of the costs, as provided by law; or

(2) If the party has been granted a fee waiver, request that the court provide an official reporter for attendance at the proceedings. The court must provide an official reporter if the party has been granted a fee waiver and if the court is not electronically recording the hearing or trial.

(A) The request should be made by filing a *Request for Court Reporter by a Party with a Fee Waiver* (form FW-020). If the requesting party has not been granted a fee waiver, a completed *Request to Waive Court Fees* (form FW-001 or form FW-001-GC in guardianship or conservator cases) must be filed at the same time as the request for court reporter.

(B) The party should file the request 10 calendar days before the proceeding for which a court reporter is desired, or as soon as practicable if the proceeding is set with less than 10-days' notice.

(C) If the party has requested a court reporter for a trial, that request remains in effect if the trial is continued to a later date.

(D) The court reporter's attendance is to be provided at no fee or cost to the fee waiver recipient.

(Subd (c) amended effective January 1, 2021; previously amended effective September 1, 2019.)

(d) No additional charge if party arranges for reporter

If a party arranges and pays for the attendance of a certified shorthand reporter at a hearing in a civil case because of the unavailability of the services of an official court reporter, none of the parties may be charged the reporter's attendance fee provided for in Government Code sections 68086(a)(1) or (b)(1).

(Subd (d) amended effective January 1, 2007.)

(e) Definitions

As used in this rule and in Government Code section 68086:

(1) "Civil case" includes all matters other than criminal and juvenile matters.

(2) "Official reporter" and "official reporting services" both include an official court reporter or official reporter as those phrases are used in statutes, including Code of Civil Procedure sections 269 and 274c and Government Code section 69941; and include an official reporter pro tempore as the phrase is used in Government Code section 69945 and other statutes, whose fee for attending and reporting proceedings is paid for by the court or the county, and who attends court sessions as directed by the court, and who was not employed to report specific causes at the request of a party or parties. "Official reporter" and "official reporting services" do not include official reporters pro tempore employed by the court expressly to report only criminal, or criminal and juvenile, matters. "Official reporting services" include electronic recording equipment operated by the court to make the official verbatim record of proceedings where it is permitted.

(Subd (e) amended effective January 1, 2007.)

Rule 2.956 amended effective January 1, 2021; adopted as rule 891 effective January 1, 1994; previously amended effective January 31, 1997, and September 1, 2019; previously amended and renumbered effective January 1, 2007.

Rule 2.958. Assessing fee for official reporter

The half-day fee to be charged under Government Code section 68086 for the services of an official reporter must be established by the trial court as follows: for a proceeding or portion of a proceeding in which a certified shorthand reporter is used, the fee is equal to the average salary and benefit costs of the reporter, plus indirect costs of up to 18 percent of salary and benefits. For purposes of this rule, the daily salary is determined by dividing the average annual salary of temporary and full-time reporters by 225 workdays.

Rule 2.958 amended and renumbered effective January 1, 2007; adopted as rule 892 effective January 1, 1994; previously amended effective January 31, 1997, August 17, 2003, January 1, 2004, and July 1, 2004.

Division 8
Trials

Chap. 1. Jury Service. Rules 2.1000–2.1010.
Chap. 2. Conduct of Trial. Rules 2.1030–2.1036.
Chap. 3. Testimony and Evidence. Rule 2.1040.
Chap. 4. Jury Instructions. Rules 2.1050–2.1058.

Chapter 1
Jury Service

Rule 2.1000. Jury service [Reserved]
Rule 2.1002. Length of juror service
Rule 2.1004. Scheduling accommodations for jurors
Rule 2.1006. Deferral of jury service
Rule 2.1008. Excuses from jury service
Rule 2.1009. Permanent medical excuse from jury service
Rule 2.1010. Juror motion to set aside sanctions imposed by default

Rule 2.1000. Jury service [Reserved]

Rule 2.1000 adopted effective January 1, 2007.

Rule 2.1002. Length of juror service

(a) Purpose

This rule implements Government Code section 68550, which is intended to make jury service more convenient and alleviate the problem of potential jurors refusing to appear for jury duty by shortening the time a person would be required to serve to one day or one trial. The exemptions authorized by the rule are intended to be of limited scope and duration, and they must be applied with the goal of achieving full compliance throughout the state as soon as possible.

(Subd (a) amended effective January 1, 2007.)

(b) Definitions

As used in this rule:

(1) "Trial court system" means all the courts of a county.

(2) "One trial" means jury service provided by a citizen after being sworn as a trial juror.

(3) "One day" means the hours of one normal court working day (the hours a court is open to the public for business).

(4) "On call" means all same-day notice procedures used to inform prospective jurors of the time they are to report for jury service.

(5) "Telephone standby" means all previous-day notice procedures used to inform prospective jurors of their date to report for service.

(Subd (b) amended effective January 1, 2007.)

(c) One-day/one-trial

Each trial court system must implement a juror management program under which a person has fulfilled his or her jury service obligation when the person has:

(1) Served on one trial until discharged;

(2) Been assigned on one day to one or more trial departments for jury selection and served through the completion of jury selection or until excused by the jury commissioner;

(3) Attended court but was not assigned to a trial department for selection of a jury before the end of that day;

(4) Served one day on call; or

(5) Served no more than five court days on telephone standby.

(Subd (c) amended effective January 1, 2007.)

(d) Exemption

(1) *Good cause*

The Judicial Council may grant an exemption from the requirements of this rule for a specified period of time if the trial court system demonstrates good cause by establishing that:

(A) The cost of implementing a one-day/one-trial system is so high that the trial court system would be unable to provide essential services to the public if required to implement such a system; or

(B) The requirements of this rule cannot be met because of the size of the population in the county compared to the number of jury trials.

(2) *Application*

Any application for exemption from the requirements of this rule must be submitted to the Judicial Council no later than September 1, 1999. The application must demonstrate good cause for the exemption sought and must include either:

(A) A plan to fully comply with this rule by a specified date; or

(B) An alternative plan that would advance the purposes of this rule to the extent possible, given the conditions in the county.

(3) *Decision*

If the council finds good cause, it may grant an exemption for a limited period of time and on such conditions as it deems appropriate to further the purposes of this rule.

(Subd (d) amended effective January 1, 2007.)

Rule 2.1002 amended and renumbered effective January 1, 2007; adopted as rule 861 effective July 1, 1999.

Rule 2.1004. Scheduling accommodations for jurors

(a) Accommodations for all jurors

The jury commissioner should accommodate a prospective juror's schedule by granting a prospective juror's request for a one-time deferral of jury service. If the request for a deferral is made under penalty of perjury in writing or through the court's established electronic means, and in accordance with the court's local procedure, the jury commissioner should not require the prospective juror to appear at court to make the request in person.

(b) Scheduling accommodations for peace officers

If a prospective juror is a peace officer, as defined by Penal Code section 830.5, the jury commissioner must make scheduling accommodations on application of the peace officer stating the reason a scheduling accommodation is necessary. The jury commissioner must establish procedures for the form and timing of the application. If the request for special accommodations is made under penalty of perjury in writing or through the court's established electronic means, and in accordance with the court's local procedure, the jury commissioner must not require the prospective juror to appear at court to make the request in person.

(Subd (b) amended effective January 1, 2007.)
Rule 2.1004 amended and renumbered effective January 1, 2007; adopted as rule 858 effective January 1, 2005.

Rule 2.1006. Deferral of jury service

A mother who is breastfeeding a child may request that jury service be deferred for up to one year, and may renew that request as long as she is breastfeeding. If the request is made in writing, under penalty of perjury, the jury commissioner must grant it without requiring the prospective juror to appear at court.

Rule 2.1006 renumbered effective January 1, 2007; adopted as rule 859 effective July 1, 2001.

Rule 2.1008. Excuses from jury service

(a) Duty of citizenship

Jury service, unless excused by law, is a responsibility of citizenship. The court and its staff must employ all necessary and appropriate means to ensure that citizens fulfill this important civic responsibility.

(Subd (a) amended effective January 1, 2007.)

(b) Principles

The following principles govern the granting of excuses from jury service by the jury commissioner on grounds of undue hardship under Code of Civil Procedure section 204:

(1) No class or category of persons may be automatically excluded from jury duty except as provided by law.

(2) A statutory exemption from jury service must be granted only when the eligible person claims it.

(3) Deferring jury service is preferred to excusing a prospective juror for a temporary or marginal hardship.

(4) Inconvenience to a prospective juror or an employer is not an adequate reason to be excused from jury duty, although it may be considered a ground for deferral.

(Subd (b) amended effective January 1, 2007.)

(c) Requests to be excused from jury service

All requests to be excused from jury service that are granted for undue hardship must be put in writing by the prospective juror, reduced to writing, or placed on the court's record. The prospective juror must support the request with facts specifying the hardship and a statement why the circumstances constituting the undue hardship cannot be avoided by deferring the prospective juror's service.

(Subd (c) amended effective January 1, 2007.)

(d) Reasons for excusing a juror because of undue hardship

An excuse on the ground of undue hardship may be granted for any of the following reasons:

(1) The prospective juror has no reasonably available means of public or private transportation to the court.

(2) The prospective juror must travel an excessive distance. Unless otherwise established by statute or local rule, an excessive distance is reasonable travel time that exceeds one-and-one-half hours from the prospective juror's home to the court.

(3) The prospective juror will bear an extreme financial burden. In determining whether to excuse the prospective juror for this reason, consideration must be given to:

(A) The sources of the prospective juror's household income;

(B) The availability and extent of income reimbursement;

(C) The expected length of service; and

(D) Whether service can reasonably be expected to compromise the prospective juror's ability to support himself or herself or his or her dependents, or so disrupt the economic stability of any individual as to be against the interests of justice.

(4) The prospective juror will bear an undue risk of material injury to or destruction of the prospective juror's property or property entrusted to the prospective juror, and it is not feasible to make alternative arrangements to alleviate the risk. In determining whether to excuse the prospective juror for this reason, consideration must be given to:

(A) The nature of the property;

(B) The source and duration of the risk;

(C) The probability that the risk will be realized;

(D) The reason alternative arrangements to protect the property cannot be made; and

(E) Whether material injury to or destruction of the property will so disrupt the economic stability of any individual as to be against the interests of justice.

(5) The prospective juror has a physical or mental disability or impairment, not affecting that person's competence to act as a juror, that would expose the potential juror to undue risk of mental or physical harm. In any individual case, unless the person is aged 70 years or older, the prospective juror may be required to furnish verification or a method of verification of the disability or impairment, its probable duration, and the particular reasons for the person's inability to serve as a juror.

(6) The prospective juror's services are immediately needed for the protection of the public health and safety, and it is not feasible to make alternative arrangements to relieve the person of those responsibilities during the period of service as a juror without substantially reducing essential public services.

(7) The prospective juror has a personal obligation to provide actual and necessary care to another, including sick, aged, or infirm dependents, or a child who requires the prospective juror's personal care and attention, and no comparable substitute care is either available or practical without imposing an undue economic hardship on the prospective juror or person cared for. If the request to be excused is based on care provided to a sick, disabled, or infirm person, the prospective juror may be required to furnish verification or a method of verification that the person being cared for is in need of regular and personal care.

(Subd (d) amended effective January 1, 2007.)

(e) Excuse based on previous jury service

A prospective juror who has served on a grand or trial jury or was summoned and appeared for jury service in any state or federal court during the previous 12 months must be excused from service on request. The jury commissioner, in his or her discretion, may establish a longer period of repose.

(Subd (e) amended effective January 1, 2007.)

Rule 2.1008 amended and renumbered effective January 1, 2007; adopted as rule 860 effective July 1, 1997.

Rule 2.1009. Permanent medical excuse from jury service

(a) Definitions

As used in this rule:

(1) "Applicant" means a "person with a disability" or their authorized representative.

(2) "Authorized representative" means a conservator, agent under a power of attorney (attorney-in-fact), or any other individual designated by the person with a disability.

(3) "Capable of performing jury service" means a person can pay attention to evidence, testimony, and other court proceedings for up to six hours per day, with a lunch break and short breaks in the morning and afternoon, with or without disability-related accommodations, including auxiliary aids and services.

(4) "Health care provider" means a doctor of medicine or osteopathy, podiatrist, dentist, chiropractor, clinical psychologist, optometrist, nurse practitioner, nurse-midwife, clinical social worker, therapist, physician's assistant, Christian Science Practitioner, or any other medical provider, facility, or organization that is authorized and performing within the scope of the practice of their profession in accordance with state or federal law and regulations.

(5) "Permanent medical excuse" means a release from jury service granted by the jury commissioner to a person with a disability whose condition is unlikely to resolve and who, with or without disability-related accommodations, including auxiliary aids or services, is not capable of performing jury service.

(6) "Person with a disability" means an individual covered by Civil Code section 51 et seq., the Americans With Disabilities Act of 1990 (42 U.S.C. § 12101 et seq.), or other applicable state and federal laws. This definition includes a person who has a physical or mental medical condition that limits one or more of the major life activities, has a record of such a condition, or is regarded as having such a condition.

(Subd (a) adopted effective January 1, 2019.)

(b) Policy

(1) This rule is intended to allow a person with a disability whose condition is unlikely to resolve and who is unable for the foreseeable future to serve as a juror to seek a permanent medical excuse from jury service. This rule does not impose limitations on or invalidate the remedies, rights, and procedures accorded to persons with disabilities under state or federal law.

(2) It is the policy of the courts of this state to ensure that persons with disabilities have equal and full access to the judicial system, including the opportunity to serve as jurors. No eligible jurors who can perform jury service, with or without disability-related accommodations, including

auxiliary aids or services, may be excused from jury service due solely to their disability.

(Subd (b) adopted effective January 1, 2019.)

(c) Process for requesting permanent medical excuse

The process for requesting a permanent medical excuse from jury service is as follows:

(1) An applicant must submit to the jury commissioner a written request for permanent medical excuse with a supporting letter, memo, or note from a treating health care provider. The supporting letter, memo, or note must be on the treating health care provider's letterhead, state that the person has a permanent disability that makes the person incapable of performing jury service, and be signed by the provider.

(2) The applicant must submit the request and supporting letter, memo, or note to the jury commissioner on or before the date the person is required to appear for jury service.

(3) In the case of an incomplete application, the jury commissioner may require the applicant to furnish additional information in support of the request for permanent medical excuse.

(4) The jury commissioner must keep confidential all information concerning the request for permanent medical excuse, including any accompanying request for disability-related accommodation, including auxiliary aids or services, unless the applicant waives confidentiality in writing or the law requires disclosure. The applicant's identity and confidential information may not be disclosed to the public but may be disclosed to court officials and personnel involved in the permanent medical excuse process. Confidential information includes all medical information pertaining to the applicant, and all oral or written communication from the applicant concerning the request for permanent medical excuse.

(Subd (c) adopted effective January 1, 2019.)

(d) Response to request

The jury commissioner must respond to a request for a permanent medical excuse from jury service as follows:

(1) The jury commissioner must promptly inform the applicant in writing of the determination to grant or deny a permanent medical excuse request.

(2) If the request is granted, the jury commissioner must remove the person from the rolls of potential jurors as soon as it is practicable to do so.

(3) If the request is denied, the jury commissioner must provide the applicant a written response with the reason for the denial.

(Subd (d) adopted effective January 1, 2019.)

(e) Denial of request

Only when the jury commissioner determines the applicant failed to satisfy the requirements of this rule may the jury commissioner deny the permanent medical excuse request.

(Subd (e) adopted effective January 1, 2019.)

(f) Right to reapply

A person whose request for permanent medical excuse is denied may reapply at any time after receipt of the jury commissioner's denial by following the process in (c).

(Subd (f) adopted effective January 1, 2019.)

(g) Reinstatement

A person who has received a permanent medical excuse from jury service under this rule may be reinstated to the rolls of potential jurors at any time by filing a signed, written request with the jury commissioner that the permanent medical excuse be withdrawn.

(Subd (g) adopted effective January 1, 2019.)
Rule 2.1009 adopted effective January 1, 2019.

Rule 2.1010. Juror motion to set aside sanctions imposed by default

(a) Motion

A prospective juror against whom sanctions have been imposed by default under Code of Civil Procedure section 209 may move to set aside the default. The motion must be brought no later than 60 days after sanctions have been imposed.

(b) Contents of motion

A motion to set aside sanctions imposed by default must contain a short and concise statement of the reasons the prospective juror was not able to attend when summoned for jury duty and any supporting documentation.

(c) Judicial Council form may be used

A motion to set aside sanctions imposed by default may be made by completing and filing *Juror's Motion to Set Aside Sanctions and Order* (form MC-070).

(Subd (c) amended effective January 1, 2007.)

(d) Hearing

The court may decide the motion with or without a hearing.

(Subd (d) amended effective January 1, 2007.)

(e) Good cause required

If the motion demonstrates good cause, a court must set aside sanctions imposed against a prospective juror.

(f) Continuing obligation to serve

Nothing in this rule relieves a prospective juror of the obligation of jury service.

(g) Notice to juror

The court must provide a copy of this rule to the prospective juror against whom sanctions have been imposed.

Rule 2.1010 amended effective January 1, 2010; adopted as rule 862 effective January 1, 2005; previously amended and renumbered effective January 1, 2007.

2009 Note: The sunset provision was repealed to extend the provisions indefinitely.

Chapter 2
Conduct of Trial

Rule 2.1030. Communications from or with jury
Rule 2.1031. Juror note-taking
Rule 2.1032. Juror notebooks in complex civil cases
Rule 2.1033. Juror questions
Rule 2.1035. Preinstruction
Rule 2.1036. Assisting the jury at impasse

Rule 2.1030. Communications from or with jury

(a) Preservation of written jury communications

The trial judge must preserve and deliver to the clerk for inclusion in the record all written communications, formal or informal, received from the jury or from individual jurors or sent by the judge to the jury or individual jurors, from the time the jury is sworn until it is discharged.

(Subd (a) amended and lettered effective January 1, 2007; adopted as part of unlettered subd effective January 1, 1990.)

(b) Recording of oral jury communications

The trial judge must ensure that the reporter, or any electronic recording system used instead of a reporter, records all oral communications, formal or informal, received from the jury or from individual jurors or communicated by the judge to the jury or individual jurors, from the time the jury is sworn until it is discharged.

(Subd (b) amended and lettered effective January 1, 2007; adopted as part of unlettered subd effective January 1, 1990.)
Rule 2.1030 amended and renumbered effective January 1, 2007; adopted as rule 231 effective January 1, 1990.

Rule 2.1031. Juror note-taking

Jurors must be permitted to take written notes in all civil and criminal trials. At the beginning of a trial, a trial judge must inform jurors that they may take written notes during the trial. The court must provide materials suitable for this purpose.

Rule 2.1031 adopted effective January 1, 2007.

Advisory Committee Comment

Several cautionary jury instructions address jurors' note-taking during trial and use of notes in deliberations. (See CACI Nos. 102, 5010 and CALCRIM Nos. 102, 202.)

Rule 2.1032. Juror notebooks in complex civil cases

A trial judge should encourage counsel in complex civil cases to include key documents, exhibits, and other appropriate materials in notebooks for use by jurors during trial to assist them in performing their duties.

Rule 2.1032 adopted effective January 1, 2007.

Advisory Committee Comment

While this rule is intended to apply to complex civil cases, there may be other types of civil cases in which notebooks may be appropriate or useful. Resources, including guidelines for use and recommended notebook contents, are available in *Bench Handbook: Jury Management* (CJER, rev. 2006, p. 59).

Rule 2.1033. Juror questions

A trial judge should allow jurors to submit written questions directed to witnesses. An opportunity must be given to counsel to object to such questions out of the presence of the jury.

Rule 2.1033 adopted effective January 1, 2007.

Advisory Committee Comment

See CACI No. 112 and CALCRIM No. 106. Resources, including a model admonition and a sample form for jurors to use to submit questions to the court, are available in *Bench Handbook: Jury Management* (CJER, rev. 2006, pp. 60–62).

Rule 2.1034. Statements to the jury panel [Repealed]
Rule 2.1034 repealed effective January 1, 2013; adopted effective January 1, 2007.

Rule 2.1035. Preinstruction
Immediately after the jury is sworn, the trial judge may, in his or her discretion, preinstruct the jury concerning the elements of the charges or claims, its duties, its conduct, the order of proceedings, the procedure for submitting written questions for witnesses as set forth in rule 2.1033 if questions are allowed, and the legal principles that will govern the proceeding.
Rule 2.1035 adopted effective January 1, 2007.

Rule 2.1036. Assisting the jury at impasse
(a) Determination
After a jury reports that it has reached an impasse in its deliberations, the trial judge may, in the presence of counsel, advise the jury of its duty to decide the case based on the evidence while keeping an open mind and talking about the evidence with each other. The judge should ask the jury if it has specific concerns which, if resolved, might assist the jury in reaching a verdict.
(Subd (a) adopted effective January 1, 2007.)

(b) Possible further action
If the trial judge determines that further action might assist the jury in reaching a verdict, the judge may:
(1) Give additional instructions;
(2) Clarify previous instructions;
(3) Permit attorneys to make additional closing arguments; or
(4) Employ any combination of these measures.
(Subd (b) adopted effective January 1, 2007.)
Rule 2.1036 adopted effective January 1, 2007.

Advisory Committee Comment
See Judicial Council CACI No. 5013 and Judicial Council CALCRIM No. 3550.

Chapter 3
Testimony and Evidence

Rule 2.1040. Electronic recordings presented or offered into evidence
(a) Electronic recordings of deposition or other prior testimony
(1) Before a party may present or offer into evidence an electronic sound or sound-and-video recording of deposition or other prior testimony, the party must lodge a transcript of the deposition or prior testimony with the court. At the time the recording is played, the party must identify on the record the page and line numbers where the testimony presented or offered appears in the transcript.

(2) Except as provided in (3), at the time the presentation of evidence closes or within five days after the recording in (1) is presented or offered into evidence, whichever is later, the party presenting or offering the recording into evidence must serve and file a copy of the transcript cover showing the witness name and a copy of the pages of the transcript where the testimony presented or offered appears. The transcript pages must be marked to identify the testimony that was presented or offered into evidence.

(3) If the court reporter takes down the content of all portions of the recording in (1) that were presented or offered into evidence, the party offering or presenting the recording is not required to provide a transcript of that recording under (2).
(Subd (a) adopted effective July 1, 2011.)

(b) Other electronic recordings
(1) Except as provided in (2) and (3), before a party may present or offer into evidence any electronic sound or sound-and-video recording not covered under (a), the party must provide to the court and to opposing parties a transcript of the electronic recording and provide opposing parties with a duplicate of the electronic recording, as defined in Evidence Code section 260. The transcript may be prepared by the party presenting or offering the recording into evidence; a certified transcript is not required.

(2) For good cause, the trial judge may permit the party to provide the transcript or the duplicate recording at the time the presentation of evidence closes or within five days after the recording is presented or offered into evidence, whichever is later.

(3) No transcript is required to be provided under (1):
(A) In proceedings that are uncontested or in which the responding party does not appear, unless otherwise ordered by the trial judge;

(B) If the parties stipulate in writing or on the record that the sound portion of a sound-and-video recording does not contain any words that are relevant to the issues in the case; or

(C) If, for good cause, the trial judge orders that a transcript is not required.
(Subd (b) amended and relettered effective July 1, 2011; adopted as part of unlettered subd effective July 1, 1988; amended and lettered as subd (a) effective January 1, 2003.)

(c) Clerk's duties
An electronic recording provided to the court under this rule must be marked for identification. A transcript provided under (a)(2) or (b)(1) must be filed by the clerk.
(Subd (c) amended and relettered effective July 1, 2011; adopted as part of unlettered subd effective July 1, 1988; amended and lettered as subd (a) effective January 1, 2003.)

(d) Reporting by court reporter
Unless otherwise ordered by the trial judge, the court reporter need not take down the content of an electronic recording that is presented or offered into evidence.
(Subd (d) amended and relettered effective July 1, 2011; adopted as part of unlettered subd effective July 1, 1988; amended and lettered as subd (b) effective January 1, 2003.)
Rule 2.1040 amended effective July 1, 2011; adopted as rule 203.5 effective July 1, 1988; previously amended effective January 1, 1997; previously amended and renumbered as rule 243.9 effective January 1, 2003, and as rule 2.1040 effective January 1, 2007.

Advisory Committee Comment
This rule is designed to ensure that, in the event of an appeal, there is an appropriate record of any electronic sound or sound-and-video recording that was presented or offered into evidence in the trial court. The rules on felony, misdemeanor, and infraction appeals require that any transcript provided by a party under this rule be included in the clerk's transcript on appeal (see rules 8.320, 8.861, and 8.912). In civil appeals, the parties may designate such a transcript for inclusion in the clerk's transcript (see rules 8.122(b) and 8.832(a)). The transcripts required under this rule may also assist the court or jurors during the trial court proceedings. For this purpose, it may be helpful for the trial court to request that the party offering an electronic recording provide additional copies of such transcripts for jurors to follow while the recording is played.

Subdivision (a). Note that, under Code of Civil Procedure section 2025.510(g), if the testimony at a deposition is recorded both stenographically and by audio or video technology, the stenographic transcript is the official record of that testimony for the purpose of the trial and any subsequent hearing or appeal.

Subdivision (a)(2). The party offering or presenting the electronic recording may serve and file a copy of the cover and of the relevant pages of the deposition or other transcript; a new transcript need not be prepared.

Subdivision (b). Note that, with the exception of recordings covered by Code of Civil Procedure section 2025.510(g), the recording itself, not the transcript, is the evidence that was offered or presented (see *People v. Sims* (1993) 5 Cal.4th 405, 448). Sometimes, a party may present or offer into evidence only a portion of a longer electronic recording. In such circumstances, the transcript provided to the court and opposing parties should contain only a transcription of those portions of the electronic recording that are actually presented or offered into evidence. If a party believes that a transcript provided under this subdivision is inaccurate, the party can raise an objection in the trial court.

Subdivision (b)(3)(C). Good cause to waive the requirement for a transcript may include such factors as (1) the party presenting or offering the electronic recording into evidence lacks the capacity to prepare a transcript or (2) the electronic recording is of such poor quality that preparing a useful transcript is not feasible.

Subdivision (c). The requirement to file a transcript provided to the court under (a)(2) or (b)(1) is intended to ensure that the transcript is available for inclusion in a clerk's transcript in the event of an appeal.

Subdivision (d). In some circumstances it may be helpful to have the court reporter take down the content of an electronic recording. For example, when short portions of a sound or sound-and-video recording of deposition or other testimony are played to impeach statements made by a witness on the stand, the best way to create a useful record of the proceedings may be for the court reporter to take down the portions of recorded testimony that are interspersed with the live testimony.

Chapter 4
Jury Instructions

Rule 2.1050. Judicial Council jury instructions
Rule 2.1055. Proposed jury instructions
Rule 2.1058. Use of gender-neutral language in jury instructions

Rule 2.1050. Judicial Council jury instructions
(a) Purpose
The California jury instructions approved by the Judicial Council are the official instructions for use in the state of California. The goal of these

instructions is to improve the quality of jury decision making by providing standardized instructions that accurately state the law in a way that is understandable to the average juror.

(b) Accuracy

The Judicial Council endorses these instructions for use and makes every effort to ensure that they accurately state existing law. The articulation and interpretation of California law, however, remains within the purview of the Legislature and the courts of review.

(c) Public access

The Judicial Council must provide copies and updates of the approved jury instructions to the public on the California Courts website. The Judicial Council intends that the instructions be freely available for use and reproduction.

(Subd (c) amended effective April 1, 2023; previously amended effective August 26, 2005, January 1, 2007, and January 1, 2016.)

(d) Publication

The Judicial Council may contract with an official publisher and other publishers to publish the instructions in both paper and electronic formats. The Judicial Council may take appropriate actions to maintain the integrity of the jury instructions, including, without limitation, ensuring that publishers accurately publish the Judicial Council's instructions, accurately credit the Judicial Council as the source of the instructions, and do not claim copyright in the instructions.

(Subd (d) adopted effective April 1, 2023.)

(e) Updating and revisions

The Judicial Council instructions will be regularly updated and maintained through its advisory committees on jury instructions. Revisions to these instructions will be circulated for public comment before publication. Suggestions for revising an instruction or creating new instructions may be submitted in writing, with an explanation of why the change is proposed, to the Judicial Council of California, Legal Services.

(Subd (e) amended and relettered effective April 1, 2023; adopted as subd (d); previously amended effective January 1, 2016.)

(f) Use of instructions

Use of the Judicial Council instructions is strongly encouraged. If the latest edition of the jury instructions approved by the Judicial Council contains an instruction applicable to a case and the trial judge determines that the jury should be instructed on the subject, it is recommended that the judge use the Judicial Council instruction unless the judge finds that a different instruction would more accurately state the law and be understood by jurors. Whenever the latest edition of the Judicial Council jury instructions does not contain an instruction on a subject on which the trial judge determines that the jury should be instructed, or when a Judicial Council instruction cannot be modified to submit the issue properly, the instruction given on that subject should be accurate, brief, understandable, impartial, and free from argument.

(Subd (f) amended and relettered effective April 1, 2023; adopted as subd (e); previously amended effective August 26, 2005.)

Rule 2.1050 amended effective April 1, 2023; adopted as rule 855 effective September 1, 2003; previously amended effective August 26, 2005, and January 1, 2016; previously amended and renumbered as rule 2.1050 effective January 1, 2007.

Rule 2.1055. Proposed jury instructions

(a) Application

(1) This rule applies to proposed jury instructions that a party submits to the court, including:

(A) "Approved jury instructions," meaning jury instructions approved by the Judicial Council of California; and

(B) "Special jury instructions," meaning instructions from other sources, those specially prepared by the party, or approved instructions that have been substantially modified by the party.

(2) This rule does not apply to the form or format of the instructions presented to the jury, which is a matter left to the discretion of the court.

(Subd (a) amended effective August 26, 2005; previously amended effective January 1, 2003, and January 1, 2004.)

(b) Form and format of proposed instructions

(1) All proposed instructions must be submitted to the court in the form and format prescribed for papers in the rules in division 2 of this title.

(2) Each set of proposed jury instructions must have a cover page, containing the caption of the case and stating the name of the party proposing the instructions, and an index listing all the proposed instructions.

(3) In the index, approved jury instructions must be identified by their reference numbers and special jury instructions must be numbered consecutively. The index must contain a checklist that the court may use to indicate whether the instruction was:

(A) Given as proposed;

(B) Given as modified;

(C) Refused; or

(D) Withdrawn.

(4) Each set of proposed jury instructions filed on paper must be bound loosely.

(Subd (b) amended effective January 1, 2016; previously amended effective July 1, 1988, January 1, 2003, January 1, 2004, and January 1, 2007.)

(c) Format of each proposed instruction

Each proposed instruction must:

(1) Be on a separate page or pages;

(2) Include the instruction number and title of the instruction at the top of the first page of the instruction; and

(3) Be prepared without any blank lines or unused bracketed portions, so that it can be read directly to the jury.

(Subd (c) amended effective January 1, 2004; previously amended effective July 1, 1988, April 1, 1962, and January 1, 2003.)

(d) Citation of authorities

For each special instruction, a citation of authorities that support the instruction must be included at the bottom of the page. No citation is required for approved instructions.

(Subd (d) adopted effective January 1, 2004.)

(e) Form and format are exclusive

No local court form or rule for the filing or submission of proposed jury instructions may require that the instructions be submitted in any manner other than as prescribed by this rule.

(Subd (e) adopted effective January 1, 2004.)

Rule 2.1055 amended effective January 1, 2016; adopted as rule 229 effective January 1, 1949; previously amended effective April 1, 1962, July 1, 1988, January 1, 2003, January 1, 2004, and August 26, 2005; previously amended and renumbered as rule 2.1055 effective January 1, 2007.

Advisory Committee Comment

This rule does not preclude a judge from requiring the parties in an individual case to transmit the jury instructions to the court electronically.

Rule 2.1058. Use of gender-neutral language in jury instructions

All instructions submitted to the jury must be written in gender-neutral language. If standard jury instructions (*CALCRIM* and *CACI*) are to be submitted to the jury, the court or, at the court's request, counsel must recast the instructions as necessary to ensure that gender-neutral language is used in each instruction.

Rule 2.1058 amended and renumbered effective January 1, 2007; adopted as rule 989 effective January 1, 1991.

Division 9
Judgments

Rule 2.1100. Notice when statute or regulation declared unconstitutional

Within 10 days after a court has entered judgment in a contested action or special proceeding in which the court has declared unconstitutional a state statute or regulation, the prevailing party, or as otherwise ordered by the court, must serve a copy of the judgment and a notice of entry of judgment on the Attorney General and file a proof of service with the court.

Rule 2.1100 amended effective January 1, 2016; adopted as rule 826 effective January 1, 1999; previously amended and renumbered as rule 2.1100 effective January 1, 2007.

TITLE 3
Civil Rules

Division 1. General Provisions. Rules 3.1–3.37.
Division 2. Waiver of Fees and Costs. Rules 3.50–3.58.
Division 3. Filing and Service. Rules 3.100–3.254.
Division 4. Parties and Actions. Rules 3.300–3.550.
Division 5. Venue [Reserved].
Division 6. Proceedings. Rules 3.650–3.682.
Division 7. Civil Case Management. Rules 3.700–3.771.
Division 8. Alternative Dispute Resolution. Rules 3.800–3.898.
Division 9. References. Rules 3.900–3.932.
Division 10. Discovery. Rules 3.1000, 3.1010.
Division 11. Law and Motion. Rules 3.1100–3.1372.
Division 12. Settlement. Rules 3.1380–3.1385.
Division 13. Dismissal of Actions. Rule 3.1390.
Division 14. Pretrial [Reserved].
Division 15. Trial. Rules 3.1540–3.1591.
Division 16. Post-trial. Rules 3.1600, 3.1602.
Division 17. Attorney's Fees and Costs. Rules 3.1700, 3.1702.
Division 18. Judgments. Rules 3.1800–3.1806.
Division 19. Postjudgment and Enforcement of Judgments. Rule 3.1900.
Division 20. Unlawful Detainers. Rule 3.2000, 3.2005.
Division 21. Rules for Small Claims Actions. Rules 3.2100–3.2120.
Division 22. Petitions Under the California Environmental Quality Act. Rules 3.2200–3.2237.
Division 23. Miscellaneous. Rule 3.2300.

Division 1
General Provisions

Chap. 1. Preliminary Rules. Rule 3.1.
Chap. 2. Scope of the Civil Rules. Rules 3.10, 3.20.
Chap. 3. Attorneys. Rules 3.35–3.37.

Chapter 1
Preliminary Rules

Rule 3.1. Title

The rules in this title may be referred to as the Civil Rules.
Rule 3.1 adopted effective January 1, 2007.

Chapter 2
Scope of the Civil Rules

Rule 3.10. Application
Rule 3.20. Preemption of local rules

Rule 3.10. Application

The Civil Rules apply to all civil cases in the superior courts, including general civil, family, juvenile, and probate cases, unless otherwise provided by a statute or rule in the California Rules of Court.
Rule 3.10 adopted effective January 1, 2007.

Rule 3.20. Preemption of local rules

(a) Fields occupied

The Judicial Council has preempted all local rules relating to pleadings, demurrers, ex parte applications, motions, discovery, provisional remedies, and the form and format of papers. No trial court, or any division or branch of a trial court, may enact or enforce any local rule concerning these fields. All local rules concerning these fields are null and void unless otherwise permitted or required by a statute or a rule in the California Rules of Court.

(Subd (a) amended effective January 1, 2007; adopted as untitled subd effective July 1, 1997; previously amended effective July 1, 2000.)

(b) Application

This rule applies to all matters identified in (a) except:

(1) Trial and post-trial proceedings including but not limited to motions in limine (see rule 3.1112(f));

(2) Proceedings under Code of Civil Procedure sections 527.6, 527.7, and 527.8; the Family Code; the Probate Code; the Welfare and Institutions Code; and the Penal Code and all other criminal proceedings;

(3) Eminent domain proceedings; and

(4) Local court rules adopted under the Trial Court Delay Reduction Act.

(Subd (b) amended effective January 1, 2015; adopted effective July 1, 2000; previously amended effective July 1, 2000, January 1, 2002, and January 1, 2007.)
Rule 3.20 amended effective January 1, 2015; adopted as rule 302 effective July 1, 1997; previously amended effective January 1, 2002; previously amended and renumbered as rule 981.1 effective July 1, 2000, and as rule 3.20 effective January 1, 2007.

Chapter 3
Attorneys

Rule 3.35. Definition of limited scope representation; application of rules
Rule 3.36. Notice of limited scope representation and application to be relieved as attorney
Rule 3.37. Nondisclosure of attorney assistance in preparation of court documents

Rule 3.35. Definition of limited scope representation; application of rules

(a) Definition

"Limited scope representation" is a relationship between an attorney and a person seeking legal services in which they have agreed that the scope of the legal services will be limited to specific tasks that the attorney will perform for the person.

(Subd (a) adopted effective January 1, 2007.)

(b) Application

Rules 3.35 through 3.37 apply to limited scope representation in civil cases, except in family law cases. Rule 5.425 applies to limited scope representation in family law cases.

(Subd (b) amended effective January 1, 2016; adopted effective January 1, 2007.)

(c) Types of limited scope representation

These rules recognize two types of limited scope representation:

(1) *Noticed representation*

Rule 3.36 provides procedures for cases in which an attorney and a party notify the court and other parties of the limited scope representation.

(2) *Undisclosed representation*

Rule 3.37 applies to cases in which the limited scope representation is not disclosed.

(Subd (c) adopted effective January 1, 2007.)
Rule 3.35 amended effective January 1, 2016; adopted effective January 1, 2007.

Rule 3.36. Notice of limited scope representation and application to be relieved as attorney

(a) Notice of limited scope representation

A party and an attorney may provide notice of their agreement to limited scope representation by serving and filing a *Notice of Limited Scope Representation* (form CIV-150).

(Subd (a) amended effective September 1, 2018; adopted effective January 1, 2007.)

(b) Notice and service of papers

After the notice in (a) is received and until either a substitution of attorney or an order to be relieved as attorney is filed and served, papers in the case must be served on both the attorney providing the limited scope representation and the client.

(Subd (b) adopted effective January 1, 2007.)

(c) Procedures to be relieved as counsel on completion of representation

Notwithstanding rule 3.1362, an attorney who has completed the tasks specified in the *Notice of Limited Scope Representation* (form CIV-150) may use the procedures in this rule to request that he or she be relieved as attorney in cases in which the attorney has appeared before the court as an attorney of record and the client has not signed a *Substitution of Attorney—Civil* (form MC-050).

(Subd (c) amended effective September 1, 2018; adopted effective January 1, 2007.)

(d) Application

An application to be relieved as attorney on completion of limited scope representation under Code of Civil Procedure section 284(2) must be directed to the client and made on the *Application to Be Relieved as Attorney on Completion of Limited Scope Representation* (form CIV-151).

(Subd (d) amended effective September 1, 2018; adopted effective January 1, 2007.)

(e) Filing and service of application

The application to be relieved as attorney must be filed with the court and served on the client and on all other parties or attorneys for parties in the case. The client must also be served with a blank *Objection to Application to Be Relieved as Attorney on Completion of Limited Scope Representation* (form CIV-152).

(Subd (e) amended effective September 1, 2018; adopted effective January 1, 2007.)

(f) No objection

If no objection is served and filed with the court within 15 days from the date that the *Application to Be Relieved as Attorney on Completion of Limited Scope Representation* (form CIV-151) is served on the client, the attorney making the application must file an updated form CIV-151 indicating the lack of objection, along with a proposed *Order on Application to Be Relieved as Attorney on Completion of Limited Scope Representation* (form CIV-153). The clerk must then forward the order for judicial signature.

(Subd (f) amended effective September 1, 2018; adopted effective January 1, 2007.)

(g) Objection

If an objection to the application is served and filed within 15 days, the clerk must set a hearing date on the *Objection to Application to Be Relieved as Attorney on Completion of Limited Scope Representation* (form CIV-152). The hearing must be scheduled no later than 25 days from the date the objection is filed. The clerk must send the notice of the hearing to the parties and the attorney.

(Subd (g) amended effective September 1, 2018; adopted effective January 1, 2007.)

(h) Service of the order

If no objection is served and filed and the proposed order is signed under (f), the attorney who filed the *Application to Be Relieved as Attorney on Completion of Limited Scope Representation* (form CIV-151) must serve a copy of the signed order on the client and on all parties or the attorneys for all parties who have appeared in the case. The court may delay the effective date of the order relieving the attorney until proof of service of a copy of the signed order on the client has been filed with the court.

(Subd (h) amended effective September 1, 2018; adopted effective January 1, 2007.)

Rule 3.36 amended effective September 1, 2018; adopted effective January 1, 2007.

Rule 3.37. Nondisclosure of attorney assistance in preparation of court documents

(a) Nondisclosure

In a civil proceeding, an attorney who contracts with a client to draft or assist in drafting legal documents, but not to make an appearance in the case, is not required to disclose within the text of the documents that he or she was involved in preparing the documents.

(Subd (a) adopted effective January 1, 2007.)

(b) Attorney's fees

If a litigant seeks a court order for attorney's fees incurred as a result of document preparation, the litigant must disclose to the court information required for a proper determination of the attorney's fees, including:

(1) The name of the attorney who assisted in the preparation of the documents;

(2) The time involved or other basis for billing;

(3) The tasks performed; and

(4) The amount billed.

(Subd (b) adopted effective January 1, 2007.)

(c) Application of rule

This rule does not apply to an attorney who has made a general appearance in a case.

(Subd (c) adopted effective January 1, 2007.)

Rule 3.37 adopted effective January 1, 2007.

Division 2
Waiver of Fees and Costs

Rule 3.50. Application of rules
Rule 3.51. Method of application
Rule 3.52. Procedure for determining application
Rule 3.53. Application granted unless acted on by the court
Rule 3.54. Confidentiality
Rule 3.55. Court fees and costs included in all initial fee waivers
Rule 3.56. Additional court fees and costs that may be included in initial fee waiver
Rule 3.57. Amount of lien for waived fees and costs
Rule 3.58. Posting notice

Rule 3.50. Application of rules

(a) Application

The rules in this division govern applications in the trial court for an initial waiver of court fees and costs because of the applicant's financial condition. As provided in Government Code sections 68631 and following, any waiver may later be ended, modified, or retroactively withdrawn if the court determines that the applicant is not eligible for the waiver. As provided in Government Code sections 68636 and 68637, the court may, at a later time, determine that the previously waived fees and costs be paid.

(Subd (a) amended and lettered effective July 1, 2009; adopted as unlettered subd effective January 1, 2007.)

(b) Definitions

For purpose of the rules in this division, "initial fee waiver" means the initial waiver of court fees and costs that may be granted at any stage of the proceedings and includes both the fees and costs specified in rule 3.55 and any additional fees and costs specified in rule 3.56.

(Subd (b) adopted effective July 1, 2009.)

(c) Probate fee waivers

Initial fee waivers in decedents' estate, probate conservatorship, and probate guardianship proceedings or involving guardians or conservators as parties on behalf of their wards or conservatees are governed by rule 7.5.

(Subd (c) adopted effective September 1, 2015.)

Rule 3.50 amended effective September 1, 2015; adopted effective January 1, 2007; previously amended effective July 1, 2009.

Rule 3.51. Method of application

(a) An application for initial fee waiver under rule 3.55 must be made on *Request to Waive Court Fees* (form FW-001). An application for initial fee waiver under rule 3.56 must be made on *Request to Waive Additional Court Fees (Superior Court)* (form FW-002). The clerk must provide the forms and the *Information Sheet on Waiver of Superior Court Fees and Costs* (form FW-001-INFO) without charge to any person who requests any fee waiver application or indicates that he or she is unable to pay any court fee or cost.

(Subd (a) lettered effective September 1, 2015; adopted as unlettered subd effective January 1, 2007.)

(b) Applications involving (proposed) wards and conservatees

An application for initial fee waiver under rules 3.55 and 7.5 by a probate guardian or probate conservator or a petitioner for the appointment of a probate guardian or probate conservator for the benefit of a (proposed) ward or conservatee, in the guardianship or conservatorship proceeding or in a civil action or proceeding in which the guardian or conservator is a party on behalf of the ward or conservatee, must be made on *Request to Waive Court Fees (Ward or Conservatee)* (form FW-001-GC). An application for initial fee waiver under rule 3.56 by a guardian or conservator or a petitioner for the appointment of a guardian or conservator for the benefit of a (proposed) ward or conservatee must be made on *Request to Waive Additional Court Fees (Superior Court) (Ward or Conservatee)* (form FW-002-GC).

(Subd (b) adopted effective September 1, 2015.)

Rule 3.51 amended effective September 1, 2015; adopted effective January 1, 2007; previously amended effective January 1, 2007, and July 1, 2009.

Rule 3.52. Procedure for determining application

The procedure for determining an application is as follows:

(1) The trial court must consider and determine the application as required by Government Code sections 68634 and 68635.

(2) An order determining an application for an initial fee waiver without a hearing must be made on *Order on Court Fee Waiver (Superior Court)* (form FW-003) or, if the application is made for the benefit of a (proposed) ward or conservatee, on *Order on Court Fee Waiver (Superior Court) (Ward or Conservatee)* (form FW-003-GC), except as provided in (6) below.

(3) An order determining an application for an initial fee waiver after a hearing in the trial court must be made on *Order on Court Fee Waiver After Hearing (Superior Court)* (form FW-008) or, if the application is made for the benefit of a (proposed) ward or conservatee, on *Order on Court Fee Waiver After Hearing (Superior Court) (Ward or Conservatee)* (form FW-008-GC).

(4) Any order granting a fee waiver must be accompanied by a blank *Notice of Improved Financial Situation or Settlement* (form FW-010) or, if the application is made for the benefit of a (proposed) ward or conservatee, a *Notice to Court of Improved Financial Situation or Settlement (Ward or Conservatee)* (form FW-010(GC).

(5) Any order denying an application without a hearing on the ground that the information on the application conclusively establishes that the applicant is not eligible for a waiver must be accompanied by a blank *Request for Hearing About Fee Waiver Order (Superior Court)* (form FW-006) or, if the application is made for the benefit of a (proposed) ward or conservatee, a *Request for Hearing About Court Fee Waiver Order (Superior Court) (Ward or Conservatee)* (form FW-006-GC).

(6) Until January 1, 2016, a court with a computerized case management system may produce electronically generated court fee waiver orders as long as:

(A) The document is substantively identical to the mandatory Judicial Council form it is replacing;

(B) Any electronically generated form is identical in both language and legally mandated elements, including all notices and advisements, to the mandatory Judicial Council form it is replacing; and

(C) The order is an otherwise legally sufficient court order, as provided in rule 1.31(g), concerning orders not on Judicial Council mandatory forms.

Rule 3.52 amended effective September 1, 2015; adopted as rule 3.56 effective January 1, 2007; previously amended and renumbered as rule 3.52 effective July 1, 2009; previously amended effective January 1, 2007, and July 1, 2015.

Rule 3.53. Application granted unless acted on by the court

The application for initial fee waiver is deemed granted unless the court gives notice of action on the application within five court days after it is filed. If the application is deemed granted under this provision, the clerk must prepare and serve a *Notice: Waiver of Court Fees (Superior Court)* (form FW-005) or, if the application is made for the benefit of a (proposed) ward or conservatee, a *Notice: Waiver of Court Fees (Superior Court) (Ward or Conservatee)* (form FW-005-GC), five court days after the application is filed.

Rule 3.53 amended effective September 1, 2015; adopted as rule 3.57 effective January 1, 2007; previously amended effective January 1, 2007; previously amended and renumbered as rule 3.53 effective July 1, 2009.

Rule 3.54. Confidentiality

(a) Confidential records

No person may have access to an application for an initial fee waiver except the court and authorized court personnel, any persons authorized by the applicant, and any persons authorized by order of the court. No person may reveal any information contained in the application except as authorized by law or order of the court.

(Subd (a) amended and lettered effective July 1, 2009; adopted as unlettered subd effective January 1, 2007.)

(b) Request for access to confidential records

Any person seeking access to an application or financial information provided to the court by an applicant must make the request by noticed motion, supported by a declaration showing good cause regarding why the confidential information should be released.

(Subd (b) adopted effective July 1, 2009.)

(c) Order

An order granting access to an application or financial information may include limitations on who may access the information and on the use of the information after it has been released.

(Subd (c) adopted effective July 1, 2009.)

Rule 3.54 amended and renumbered effective July 1, 2009; adopted as rule 3.60 effective January 1, 2007; previously amended effective January 1, 2008.

Rule 3.55. Court fees and costs included in all initial fee waivers

Court fees and costs that must be waived upon granting an application for an initial fee waiver include:

(1) Clerk's fees for filing papers;

(2) Clerk's fees for reasonably necessary certification and copying;

(3) Clerk's fees for issuance of process and certificates;

(4) Clerk's fees for transmittal of papers;

(5) Sheriff's and marshal's fees under article 7 of chapter 2 of part 3 of division 2 of title 3 of the Government Code (commencing with section 26720);

(6) Reporter's fees for attendance at hearings and trials;

(7) The court fee for a telephone appearance;

(8) Clerk's fees for preparing, copying, certifying, and transmitting the clerk's transcript on appeal to the reviewing court and the party. A party proceeding under an initial fee waiver must specify with particularity the documents to be included in the clerk's transcript on appeal;

(9) The fee under rule 8.130(b) or rule 8.834(b) for the court to hold in trust the deposit for a reporter's transcript on appeal; and

(10) The clerk's fee for preparing a transcript of an official electronic recording under rule 8.835 or a copy of such an electronic recording.

Rule 3.55 amended effective January 1, 2023; adopted as rule 3.61 effective January 1, 2007; previously amended and renumbered as rule 3.55 effective July 1, 2009; previously amended effective January 1, 2009, July 1, 2015, and September 1, 2019.

Advisory Committee Comment

The inclusion of court reporter's fees in the fees waived upon granting an application for an initial fee waiver is intended to provide a fee waiver recipient with an official court reporter or other valid means to create an official verbatim record, for purposes of appeal, on a request. (See *Jameson v. Desta* (2018) 5 Cal.5th 594.). It is intended to include within a waiver all fees mandated under the Government Code for the cost of court reporting services provided by a court.

Rule 3.56. Additional court fees and costs that may be included in initial fee waiver

Necessary court fees and costs that may be waived upon granting an application for an initial fee waiver, either at the outset or upon later application, include:

(1) Jury fees and expenses;

(2) Court-appointed interpreter's fees for witnesses;

(3) Witness fees of peace officers whose attendance is reasonably necessary for prosecution or defense of the case;

(4) Witness fees of court-appointed experts; and

(5) Other fees or expenses as itemized in the application.

Rule 3.56 amended effective July 1, 2015; adopted as rule 3.62 effective January 1, 2007; previously amended and renumbered as rule 3.56 effective July 1, 2009.

Rule 3.57. Amount of lien for waived fees and costs

To determine the amount of the court lien for waived fees and costs, any party to a civil action in which an initial fee waiver has been granted may ask the clerk to calculate the total amount of court fees and costs that have been waived as of the date of the request.

Rule 3.57 adopted effective July 1, 2009.

Rule 3.58. Posting notice

Each trial court must post in a conspicuous place near the filing window or counter a notice, 8½ by 11 inches or larger, advising litigants in English and Spanish that they may ask the court to waive court fees and costs. The notice must be substantially as follows:

"NOTICE: If you are unable to pay fees and costs, you may ask the court to permit you to proceed without paying them. Ask the clerk for the *Information Sheet on Waiver of Superior Court Fees and Costs* or *Information Sheet on Waiver of Court Fees and Costs for Appeal or Writ Proceedings* and the *Request to Waive Court Fees.*"

Rule 3.58 amended and renumbered effective July 1, 2009; adopted as rule 3.63 effective January 1, 2007.

Rule 3.59. Changed circumstances [Repealed]

Rule 3.59 repealed effective July 1, 2009; adopted effective January 1, 2007.

Rule 3.60. Confidentiality [Renumbered]

Rule 3.60 renumbered as rule 3.54 effective July 1, 2009.

Rule 3.61. Court fees and costs waived by initial application [Renumbered]

Rule 3.61 renumbered as rule 3.55 effective July 1, 2009.

Rule 3.62. Additional court fees and costs waived [Renumbered]

Rule 3.62 renumbered as rule 3.56 effective July 1, 2009.

Rule 3.63. Posting notice [Renumbered]

Rule 3.63 renumbered as rule 3.58 effective July 1, 2009.

Division 3
Filing and Service

Chap. 1. Filing. Rule 3.100.
Chap. 2. Time for Service. Rule 3.110.
Chap. 3. Papers to Be Served. Rules 3.220–3.222.
Chap. 4. Miscellaneous. Rules 3.250–3.254.

Chapter 1
Filing

Rule 3.100. Payment of filing fees by credit or debit card

A party may pay a filing fee by credit or debit card provided the court is authorized to accept payment by this method under Government Code section 6159, rule 10.820, and other applicable law.

Rule 3.100 adopted effective January 1, 2007.

Chapter 2
Time for Service

Rule 3.110. Time for service of complaint, cross-complaint, and response

(a) Application

This rule applies to the service of pleadings in civil cases except for collections cases under rule 3.740(a), unlawful detainer actions, proceedings under the Family Code, and other proceedings for which different service requirements are prescribed by law.

(Subd (a) amended effective July 1, 2007; previously amended effective January 1, 2007.)

(b) Service of complaint

The complaint must be served on all named defendants and proofs of service on those defendants must be filed with the court within 60 days after the filing of the complaint. When the complaint is amended to add a defendant, the added defendant must be served and proof of service must be filed within 30 days after the filing of the amended complaint.

(c) Service of cross-complaint

A cross-complaint against a party who has appeared in the action must be accompanied by proof of service of the cross-complaint at the time it is filed. If the cross-complaint adds new parties, the cross-complaint must be served on all parties and proofs of service on the new parties must be filed within 30 days of the filing of the cross-complaint.

(d) Timing of responsive pleadings

The parties may stipulate without leave of court to one 15-day extension beyond the 30-day time period prescribed for the response after service of the initial complaint.

(e) Modification of timing; application for order extending time

The court, on its own motion or on the application of a party, may extend or otherwise modify the times provided in (b)–(d). An application for a court order extending the time to serve a pleading must be filed before the time for service has elapsed. The application must be accompanied by a declaration showing why service has not been completed, documenting the efforts that have been made to complete service, and specifying the date by which service is proposed to be completed.

(Subd (e) amended effective January 1, 2007.)

(f) Failure to serve

If a party fails to serve and file pleadings as required under this rule, and has not obtained an order extending time to serve its pleadings, the court may issue an order to show cause why sanctions shall not be imposed.

(Subd (f) amended effective January 1, 2007.)

(g) Request for entry of default

If a responsive pleading is not served within the time limits specified in this rule and no extension of time has been granted, the plaintiff must file a request for entry of default within 10 days after the time for service has elapsed. The court may issue an order to show cause why sanctions should not be imposed if the plaintiff fails to timely file the request for the entry of default.

(Subd (g) amended effective January 1, 2007.)

(h) Default judgment

When a default is entered, the party who requested the entry of default must obtain a default judgment against the defaulting party within 45 days after the default was entered, unless the court has granted an extension of time. The court may issue an order to show cause why sanctions should not be imposed if that party fails to obtain entry of judgment against a defaulting party or to request an extension of time to apply for a default judgment within that time.

(Subd (h) amended effective January 1, 2007.)

(i) Order to show cause

Responsive papers to an order to show cause issued under this rule must be filed and served at least 5 calendar days before the hearing.

(Subd (i) amended effective January 1, 2007.)

Rule 3.110 amended effective July 1, 2007; adopted as rule 201.7 effective July 1, 2002; previously amended and renumbered effective January 1, 2007.

Chapter 3
Papers to Be Served

Rule 3.220. Case cover sheet
Rule 3.221. Information about alternative dispute resolution
Rule 3.222. Papers to be served on cross-defendants

Rule 3.220. Case cover sheet

(a) Cover sheet required

The first paper filed in an action or proceeding must be accompanied by a case cover sheet as required in (b). The cover sheet must be on a form prescribed by the Judicial Council and must be filed in addition to any cover sheet required by local court rule. If the plaintiff indicates on the cover sheet that the case is complex under rule 3.400 et seq. or a collections case under rule 3.740, the plaintiff must serve a copy of the cover sheet with the complaint. In all other cases, the plaintiff is not required to serve the cover sheet. The cover sheet is used for statistical purposes and may affect the assignment of a complex case.

(Subd (a) amended effective January 1, 2009; previously amended effective January 1, 2000, January 1, 2002, and January 1, 2007.)

(b) List of cover sheets

(1) *Civil Case Cover Sheet* (form CM-010) must be filed in each civil action or proceeding, except those filed in small claims court or filed under the Probate Code, Family Code, or Welfare and Institutions Code.

(2) [**Note:** Case cover sheets will be added for use in additional areas of the law as the data collection program expands.]

(Subd (b) amended effective January 1, 2007; previously amended effective July 1, 2002, and July 1, 2003.)

(c) Failure to provide cover sheet

If a party that is required to provide a cover sheet under this rule or a similar local rule fails to do so or provides a defective or incomplete cover sheet at the time the party's first paper is submitted for filing, the clerk of the court must file the paper. Failure of a party or a party's counsel to file a cover sheet as required by this rule may subject that party, its counsel, or both, to sanctions under rule 2.30.

(Subd (c) amended effective January 1, 2007; adopted effective January 1, 2002.)

Rule 3.220 amended effective January 1, 2009; adopted as rule 982.2 effective July 1, 1996; previously amended and renumbered as rule 201.8 effective July 1, 2002, and as rule 3.220 effective January 1, 2007; previously amended effective January 1, 2000, January 1, 2002, and July 1, 2003.

Rule 3.221. Information about alternative dispute resolution

(a) Court to provide information package

Each court must make available to the plaintiff, at the time the complaint is filed in all general civil cases, an alternative dispute resolution (ADR) information package that includes, at a minimum, all of the following:

(1) General information about the potential advantages and disadvantages of ADR and descriptions of the principal ADR processes. Judicial Council staff have prepared model language that the courts may use to provide this information.

(2) Information about the ADR programs available in that court, including citations to any applicable local court rules and directions for contacting any court staff responsible for providing parties with assistance regarding ADR.

(3) In counties that are participating in the Dispute Resolution Programs Act (DRPA), information about the availability of local dispute resolution programs funded under the DRPA. This information may take the form of a list of the applicable programs or directions for contacting the county's DRPA coordinator.

(4) An ADR stipulation form that parties may use to stipulate to the use of an ADR process.

(Subd (a) amended effective January 1, 2016; previously amended effective July 1, 2002, and January 1, 2007.)

(b) Court may make package available on Web site

A court may make the ADR information package available on its Web site as long as paper copies are also made available in the clerk's office.

(Subd (b) adopted effective July 1, 2002.)

(c) Plaintiff to serve information package

In all general civil cases, the plaintiff must serve a copy of the ADR information package on each defendant together with the complaint. Cross-complainants must serve a copy of the ADR information package on any new parties to the action together with the cross-complaint.

(Subd (c) amended effective January 1, 2007; adopted as subd (b) effective January 1, 2001; previously amended and relettered effective July 1, 2002.)

Rule 3.221 amended effective January 1, 2016; adopted as rule 1590.1 effective January 1, 2001; previously amended and renumbered as rule 201.9 effective July 1, 2002, and as rule 3.221 effective January 1, 2007.

Rule 3.222. Papers to be served on cross-defendants

A cross-complainant must serve a copy of the complaint or, if it has been amended, the most recently amended complaint and any answers thereto on cross-defendants who have not previously appeared.

Rule 3.222 amended and renumbered effective January 1, 2007; adopted as rule 202 effective January 1, 1985; previously amended effective January 1, 2003.

Chapter 4
Miscellaneous

Rule 3.250. Limitations on the filing of papers
Rule 3.252. Service of papers on the clerk when a party's address is unknown
Rule 3.254. List of parties

Rule 3.250. Limitations on the filing of papers

(a) Papers not to be filed

The following papers, whether offered separately or as attachments to other documents, may not be filed unless they are offered as relevant to the determination of an issue in a law and motion proceeding or other hearing or are ordered filed for good cause:

(1) Subpoena;

(2) Subpoena duces tecum;

(3) Deposition notice, and response;

(4) Notice to consumer or employee, and objection;

(5) Notice of intention to record testimony by audio or video tape;

(6) Notice of intention to take an oral deposition by telephone, videoconference, or other remote electronic means;

(7) Agreement to set or extend time for deposition, agreement to extend time for response to discovery requests, and notice of these agreements;

(8) Interrogatories, and responses or objections to interrogatories;

(9) Demand for production or inspection of documents, things, and places, and responses or objections to demand;

(10) Request for admissions, and responses or objections to request;

(11) Agreement for physical and mental examinations;

(12) Demand for delivery of medical reports, and response;

(13) Demand for exchange of expert witnesses;

(14) Demand for production of discoverable reports and writings of expert witnesses;

(15) List of expert witnesses whose opinion a party intends to offer in evidence at trial and declaration;

(16) Statement that a party does not presently intend to offer the testimony of any expert witness;

(17) Declaration for additional discovery;

(18) Stipulation to enlarge the scope of number of discovery requests from that specified by statute, and notice of the stipulation;

(19) Demand for bill of particulars or an accounting, and response;

(20) Request for statement of damages, and response, unless it is accompanied by a request to enter default and is the notice of special and general damages;

(21) Notice of deposit of jury fees;

(22) Notice to produce party, agent, or tangible things before a court, and response; and

(23) Offer to compromise, unless accompanied by an original proof of acceptance and a written judgment for the court's signature and entry of judgment.

(Subd (a) amended effective January 1, 2003; previously amended effective January 1, 2001.)

(b) Retaining originals of papers not filed

(1) Unless the paper served is a response, the party who serves a paper listed in (a) must retain the original with the original proof of service affixed. If served electronically under rule 2.251, the proof of electronic service must meet the requirements in rule 2.251(i).

(2) The original of a response must be served, and it must be retained by the person upon whom it is served.

(3) An original must be retained under (1) or (2) in the paper or electronic form in which it was created or received.

(4) All original papers must be retained until six months after final disposition of the case, unless the court on motion of any party and for good cause shown orders the original papers preserved for a longer period.

(Subd (b) amended effective January 1, 2017; previously amended effective January 1, 2003, and January 1, 2007.)

(c) Papers defined

As used in this rule, papers include printed forms furnished by the clerk, but do not include notices filed and served by the clerk.

Rule 3.250 amended effective January 1, 2017; adopted as rule 201.5 effective July 1, 1987; previously amended effective January 1, 2001, and January 1, 2003; previously amended and renumbered effective January 1, 2007.

Rule 3.252. Service of papers on the clerk when a party's address is unknown

(a) Service of papers

When service is made under Code of Civil Procedure section 1011(b) and a party's residence address is unknown, the notice or papers delivered to the clerk, or to the judge if there is no clerk, must be enclosed in an envelope addressed to the party in care of the clerk or the judge.

(Subd (a) amended and lettered effective January 1, 2003.)

(b) Information on the envelope

The back of the envelope delivered under (a) must bear the following information:

"Service is being made under Code of Civil Procedure section 1011(b) on a party whose residence address is unknown."

[Name of party whose residence address is unknown]

[Case name and number]

(Subd (b) amended and lettered effective January 1, 2003.)

Rule 3.252 renumbered effective January 1, 2007; adopted as rule 202.5 effective July 1, 1997; previously amended effective January 1, 2003.

Rule 3.254. List of parties

(a) Duties of first-named plaintiff or petitioner

Except as provided under rule 2.251 for electronic service, if more than two parties have appeared in a case and are represented by different counsel, the plaintiff or petitioner named first in the complaint or petition must:

(1) Maintain a current list of the parties and their addresses for service of notice on each party; and

(2) Furnish a copy of the list on request to any party or the court.

(Subd (a) amended effective January 1, 2016; adopted as part of unlettered subd effective July 1, 1984; previously amended and lettered as subd (a) effective January 1, 2007.)

(b) Duties of each party

Except as provided under rule 2.251 for electronic service, each party must:

(1) Furnish the first-named plaintiff or petitioner with its current address for service of notice when it first appears in the action;

(2) Furnish the first-named plaintiff or petitioner with any changes in its address for service of notice; and

(3) If it serves an order, notice, or pleading on a party who has not yet appeared in the action, serve a copy of the list required under (a) at the same time as the order, notice, or pleading is served.

(Subd (b) amended effective January 1, 2016; adopted as part of unlettered subd effective July 1, 1984; previously amended and lettered as subd (b) effective January 1, 2007.)

Rule 3.254 amended effective January 1, 2016; adopted as rule 387 effective July 1, 1984; previously amended and renumbered as rule 202.7 effective January 1, 2003, and as rule 3.254 effective January 1, 2007.

Division 4
Parties and Actions

Chap. 1. [Reserved].
Chap. 2. Joinder of Parties [Reserved].
Chap. 3. Related Cases. Rule 3.300.
Chap. 4. Consolidated Cases. Rule 3.350.
Chap. 5. Complex Cases. Rules 3.400–3.403.
Chap. 6. Coordination of Noncomplex Actions. Rule 3.500.
Chap. 7. Coordination of Complex Actions. Rules 3.501–3.550.

Chapter 1
[Reserved]

Chapter 2
Joinder of Parties
[Reserved]

Chapter 3
Related Cases

Rule 3.300. Related cases

(a) Definition of "related case"

A pending civil case is related to another pending civil case, or to a civil case that was dismissed with or without prejudice, or to a civil case that was disposed of by judgment, if the cases:

(1) Involve the same parties and are based on the same or similar claims;

(2) Arise from the same or substantially identical transactions, incidents, or events requiring the determination of the same or substantially identical questions of law or fact;

(3) Involve claims against, title to, possession of, or damages to the same property; or

(4) Are likely for other reasons to require substantial duplication of judicial resources if heard by different judges.

(Subd (a) adopted effective January 1, 2007.)

(b) Duty to provide notice

Whenever a party in a civil action knows or learns that the action or proceeding is related to another action or proceeding pending, dismissed, or disposed of by judgment in any state or federal court in California, the party must serve and file a Notice of Related Case.

(Subd (b) amended and relettered effective January 1, 2007; adopted as part of subd (a) effective January 1, 1996; previously amended effective January 1, 2007.)

(c) Contents of the notice

The Notice of Related Case must:

(1) List all civil cases that are related by court, case name, case number, and filing date;

(2) Identify the case that has the earliest filing date and the court and department in which that case is pending; and

(3) Describe the manner in which the cases are related.

(Subd (c) repealed and adopted effective January 1, 2007.)

(d) Service and filing of notice

The Notice of Related Case must be filed in all pending cases listed in the notice and must be served on all parties in those cases.

(Subd (d) adopted effective January 1, 2007.)

(e) Time for service

The Notice of Related Case must be served and filed as soon as possible, but no later than 15 days after the facts concerning the existence of related cases become known.

(Subd (e) adopted effective January 1, 2007.)

(f) Continuing duty to provide notice

The duty under (b)–(e) is a continuing duty that applies when a party files a case with knowledge of a related action or proceeding, and that applies thereafter whenever a party learns of a related action or proceeding.

(Subd (f) amended and relettered effective January 1, 2007; adopted as part of subd (a) effective January 1, 1996; previously adopted as subd (b) effective January 1, 2007.)

(g) Response

Within 5 days after service on a party of a Notice of Related Case, the party may serve and file a response supporting or opposing the notice. The response must state why one or more of the cases listed in the notice are not related or why other good cause exists for the court not to transfer the cases to or from a particular court or department. The response must be filed in all pending cases listed in the notice and must be served on all parties in those cases.

(Subd (g) amended and relettered effective January 1, 2007; adopted as subd (c) effective January 1, 1996; previously amended and relettered subd (d) effective January 1, 2007.)

(h) Judicial action

(1) *Related cases pending in one superior court*

If all the related cases have been filed in one superior court, the court, on notice to all parties, may order that the cases, including probate and family law cases, be related and may assign them to a single judge or department. In a superior court where there is a master calendar, the presiding judge may order the cases related. In a court in which cases are assigned to a single judge or department, cases may be ordered related as follows:

(A) Where all the cases listed in the notice are unlimited civil cases, or where all the cases listed in the notice are limited civil cases, the judge who has the earliest filed case must determine whether the cases must be ordered related and assigned to his or her department;

(B) Where the cases listed in the notice include both unlimited and limited civil cases, the judge who has the earliest filed unlimited civil case must determine whether the cases should be ordered related and assigned to his or her department;

(C) Where the cases listed in the notice contain a probate or family law case, the presiding judge or a judge designated by the presiding judge must determine whether the cases should be ordered related and, if so, to which judge or department they should be assigned;

(D) In the event that any of the cases listed in the notice are not ordered related under (A), (B), or (C), any party in any of the cases listed in the notice may file a motion to have the cases related. The motion must be filed with the presiding judge or the judge designated by the presiding judge; and

(E) If the procedures for relating pending cases under this rule do not apply, the procedures under Code of Civil Procedure section 1048 and rule 3.350 must be followed to consolidate cases pending in the same superior court.

(2) *Related cases pending in different superior courts*

(A) If the related cases are pending in more than one superior court on notice to all parties, the judge to whom the earliest filed case is assigned may confer informally with the parties and with the judges to whom each related case is assigned, to determine the feasibility and desirability of joint discovery orders and other informal or formal means of coordinating proceedings in the cases.

(B) If it is determined that related cases pending in different superior courts should be formally coordinated, the procedures in Code of Civil Procedure section 403 and rule 3.500 must be followed for noncomplex cases, and the procedures in Code of Civil Procedure section 404 et seq. and rules 3.501 et seq. must be followed for complex cases.

(3) *Complex cases*

The provisions in (1) of this subdivision do not apply to cases that have been designated as complex by the parties or determined to be complex by the court.

(Subd (h) amended effective January 1, 2008; adopted as subd (d) effective January 1, 1996; previously amended and relettered as subd (e) effective January 1, 2007.)

(i) Ruling on related cases

The court, department, or judge issuing an order relating cases under this rule must either:

(1) File a notice of the order in all pending cases and serve a copy of the notice on all parties listed in the Notice of Related Case; or

(2) Direct counsel for a party to file the notice in all pending cases and serve a copy on all parties.

(Subd (i) adopted effective January 1, 2007.)

(j) Cases not ordered related

If for any reason a case is not ordered related under this rule, that case will remain assigned to the court, judge, or department where it was pending at the time of the filing and service of the Notice of Related Case.

(Subd (j) adopted effective January 1, 2007.)

(k) Exception

A party is not required to serve and file Notice of Related Case under this rule if another party has already filed a notice and served all parties under this rule on the same case.

(Subd (k) adopted effective January 1, 2007.)

Rule 3.300 amended effective January 1, 2008; adopted as rule 804 effective January 1, 1996; previously amended and renumbered effective January 1, 2007.

Chapter 4
Consolidated Cases

Rule 3.350. Consolidation of cases

(a) Requirements of motion

(1) A notice of motion to consolidate must:

(A) List all named parties in each case, the names of those who have appeared, and the names of their respective attorneys of record;

(B) Contain the captions of all the cases sought to be consolidated, with the lowest numbered case shown first; and

(C) Be filed in each case sought to be consolidated.

(2) The motion to consolidate:

(A) Is deemed a single motion for the purpose of determining the appropriate filing fee, but memorandums, declarations, and other supporting papers must be filed only in the lowest numbered case;

(B) Must be served on all attorneys of record and all nonrepresented parties in all of the cases sought to be consolidated; and

(C) Must have a proof of service filed as part of the motion.

(Subd (a) amended effective January 1, 2007; adopted effective July 1, 1999.)

(b) Lead case

Unless otherwise provided in the order granting the motion to consolidate, the lowest numbered case in the consolidated case is the lead case.

(Subd (b) amended effective January 1, 2007; adopted effective July 1, 1999.)

(c) Order

An order granting or denying all or part of a motion to consolidate must be filed in each case sought to be consolidated. If the motion is granted for all purposes including trial, any subsequent document must be filed only in the lead case.

(Subd (c) amended effective January 1, 2007; adopted effective July 1, 1999.)

(d) Caption and case number

All documents filed in the consolidated case must include the caption and case number of the lead case, followed by the case numbers of all of the other consolidated cases.

(Subd (d) amended effective January 1, 2007; adopted effective July 1, 1999.)

Rule 3.350 amended and renumbered effective January 1, 2007; adopted as rule 367 effective January 1, 1984; previously amended effective July 1, 1999.

Chapter 5
Complex Cases

Rule 3.400. Definition
Rule 3.401. Complex case designation
Rule 3.402. Complex case counterdesignations
Rule 3.403. Action by court

Rule 3.400. Definition

(a) Definition

A "complex case" is an action that requires exceptional judicial management to avoid placing unnecessary burdens on the court or the litigants and to expedite the case, keep costs reasonable, and promote effective decision making by the court, the parties, and counsel.

(b) Factors

In deciding whether an action is a complex case under (a), the court must consider, among other things, whether the action is likely to involve:

(1) Numerous pretrial motions raising difficult or novel legal issues that will be time-consuming to resolve;

(2) Management of a large number of witnesses or a substantial amount of documentary evidence;

(3) Management of a large number of separately represented parties;

(4) Coordination with related actions pending in one or more courts in other counties, states, or countries, or in a federal court; or

(5) Substantial postjudgment judicial supervision.

(Subd (b) amended effective January 1, 2007.)

(c) Provisional designation

Except as provided in (d), an action is provisionally a complex case if it involves one or more of the following types of claims:

(1) Antitrust or trade regulation claims;

(2) Construction defect claims involving many parties or structures;

(3) Securities claims or investment losses involving many parties;

(4) Environmental or toxic tort claims involving many parties;

(5) Claims involving mass torts;

(6) Claims involving class actions; or

(7) Insurance coverage claims arising out of any of the claims listed in (c)(1) through (c)(6).

(Subd (c) amended effective January 1, 2007.)

(d) Court's discretion

Notwithstanding (c), an action is not provisionally complex if the court has significant experience in resolving like claims involving similar facts and the management of those claims has become routine. A court may declare by local rule that certain types of cases are or are not provisionally complex under this subdivision.

(Subd (d) amended effective January 1, 2007.)

Rule 3.400 amended and renumbered effective January 1, 2007; adopted as rule 1800 effective January 1, 2000.

Rule 3.401. Complex case designation

A plaintiff may designate an action as a complex case by filing and serving with the initial complaint the *Civil Case Cover Sheet* (form CM-010) marked to indicate that the action is a complex case.

Rule 3.401 renumbered effective January 1, 2007; adopted as rule 1810 effective January 1, 2000; previously amended effective July 1, 2002, and July 1, 2004.

Rule 3.402. Complex case counterdesignations

(a) Noncomplex counterdesignation

If a *Civil Case Cover Sheet* (form CM-010) designating an action as a complex case has been filed and served and the court has not previously declared the action to be a complex case, a defendant may file and serve no later than its first appearance a counter *Civil Case Cover Sheet* (form CM-010) designating the action as not a complex case. The court must decide, with or without a hearing, whether the action is a complex case within 30 days after the filing of the counterdesignation.

(Subd (a) amended effective January 1, 2007; previously amended effective July 1, 2004.)

(b) Complex counterdesignation

A defendant may file and serve no later than its first appearance a counter *Civil Case Cover Sheet* (form CM-010) designating the action as a complex case. The court must decide, with or without a hearing, whether the action is a complex case within 30 days after the filing of the counterdesignation.

(Subd (b) amended effective January 1, 2007; previously amended effective July 1, 2004.)

(c) Joint complex designation

A defendant may join the plaintiff in designating an action as a complex case.

Rule 3.402 amended and renumbered effective January 1, 2007; adopted as rule 1811 effective January 1, 2000; previously amended effective July 1, 2004.

Rule 3.403. Action by court

(a) Decision on complex designation

Except as provided in rule 3.402, if a *Civil Case Cover Sheet* (form CM-010) that has been filed and served designates an action as a complex case or checks a case type described as provisionally complex civil litigation, the court must decide as soon as reasonably practicable, with or without a hearing, whether the action is a complex case.

(Subd (a) amended effective January 1, 2007; previously amended effective July 1, 2004.)

(b) Court's continuing power

With or without a hearing, the court may decide on its own motion, or on a noticed motion by any party, that a civil action is a complex case or that an action previously declared to be a complex case is not a complex case.

Rule 3.403 amended effective January 1, 2007; adopted as rule 1812 effective January 1, 2000; previously amended effective July 1, 2004; previously amended and renumbered effective January 1, 2007.

Chapter 6
Coordination of Noncomplex Actions

Rule 3.500. Transfer and consolidation of noncomplex common-issue actions filed in different courts

(a) Application

This rule applies when a motion under Code of Civil Procedure section 403 is filed requesting transfer and consolidation of noncomplex cases involving a common issue of fact or law filed in different courts.

(Subd (a) amended and lettered effective January 1, 2007; adopted as unlettered subd effective September 21, 1996.)

(b) Preliminary step

A party that intends to file a motion under Code of Civil Procedure section 403 must first make a good-faith effort to obtain agreement of all parties to each case to the proposed transfer and consolidation.

(Subd (b) amended and relettered effective January 1, 2007; adopted as subd (a) effective September 21, 1996.)

(c) Motion and hearing

A motion to transfer an action under Code of Civil Procedure section 403 must conform to the requirements generally applicable to motions, and must be supported by a declaration stating facts showing that:

(1) The actions are not complex;

(2) The moving party has made a good-faith effort to obtain agreement to the transfer and consolidation from all parties to the actions; and

(3) The moving party has notified all parties of their obligation to disclose to the court any information they may have concerning any other motions requesting transfer of any case that would be affected by the granting of the motion before the court.

(Subd (c) amended and relettered effective January 1, 2007; adopted as subd (b) effective September 21, 1996.)

(d) Findings and order

If the court orders that the case or cases be transferred from another court, the order must specify the reasons supporting a finding that the transfer will promote the ends of justice, with reference to the following standards:

(1) The actions are not complex;

(2) Whether the common question of fact or law is predominating and significant to the litigation;

(3) The convenience of the parties, witnesses, and counsel;

(4) The relative development of the actions and the work product of counsel;

(5) The efficient utilization of judicial facilities and staff resources;

(6) The calendar of the courts;

(7) The disadvantages of duplicative and inconsistent rulings, orders, or judgments; and

(8) The likelihood of settlement of the actions without further litigation should coordination be denied.

(Subd (d) amended and relettered effective January 1, 2007; adopted as subd (c) effective September 21, 1996.)

(e) Moving party to provide copies of order

If the court orders that the case or cases be transferred from another court, the moving party must promptly serve the order on all parties to each case and send it to the Judicial Council and to the presiding judge of the court from which each case is to be transferred.

(Subd (e) amended and relettered effective January 1, 2007; adopted as subd (d) effective September 21, 1996.)

(f) Moving party to take necessary action to complete transfer and consolidation

If the court orders a case or cases transferred, the moving party must promptly take all appropriate action necessary to assure that the transfer takes place and that proceedings are initiated in the other court or courts to complete consolidation with the case pending in that court.

(Subd (f) amended and relettered effective January 1, 2007; adopted as subd (e) effective September 21, 1996.)

(g) Conflicting orders

The Judicial Council's coordination staff must review all transfer orders submitted under (e) and must promptly confer with the presiding judges of any courts that have issued conflicting orders under Code of Civil Procedure section 403. The presiding judges of those courts must confer with each other and with the judges who have issued the orders to the extent necessary to resolve the conflict. If it is determined that any party to a case has failed to disclose information concerning pending motions, the court may, after a duly noticed hearing, find that the party's failure to disclose is an unlawful interference with the processes of the court.

(Subd (g) amended effective January 1, 2016; adopted as subd (f) effective September 21, 1996; previously amended and relettered as subd (g) effective January 1, 2007.)

(h) Alternative disposition of motion

If after considering the motion the judge determines that the action or actions pending in another court should not be transferred to the judge's court but instead all the actions that are subject to the motion to transfer should be transferred and consolidated in another court, the judge may order the parties to prepare, serve, and file a motion to have the actions transferred to the appropriate court.

(Subd (h) amended and relettered effective January 1, 2007; adopted as subd (g) effective September 21, 1996.)

Rule 3.500 amended effective January 1, 2016; adopted as rule 1500 effective September 21, 1996; previously amended and renumbered as rule 3.500 effective January 1, 2007.

Chapter 7
Coordination of Complex Actions

Art. 1. General Provisions. Rules 3.501–3.506.
Art. 2. Procedural Rules Applicable to All Complex Coordination Proceedings. Rules 3.510–3.516.
Art. 3. Petitions and Proceedings for Coordination of Complex Actions. Rules 3.520–3.532.
Art. 4. Pretrial and Trial Rules for Complex Coordinated Actions. Rules 3.540–3.545.
Art. 5. Administration of Coordinated Complex Actions. Rule 3.550.

Article 1
General Provisions

Rule 3.501. Definitions
Rule 3.502. Complex case—determination
Rule 3.503. Requests for extensions of time or to shorten time
Rule 3.504. General law applicable
Rule 3.505. Appellate review
Rule 3.506. Liaison counsel

Rule 3.501. Definitions

As used in this chapter, unless the context or subject matter otherwise requires:

(1) "Action" means any civil action or proceeding that is subject to coordination or that affects an action subject to coordination.

(2) "Add-on case" means an action that is proposed for coordination, under Code of Civil Procedure section 404.4, with actions previously ordered coordinated.

(3) "Assigned judge" means any judge assigned by the Chair of the Judicial Council or by a presiding judge authorized by the Chair of the Judicial Council to assign a judge under Code of Civil Procedure section 404 or 404.3, including a "coordination motion judge" and a "coordination trial judge."

(4) "Clerk," unless otherwise indicated, means any person designated by an assigned judge to perform any clerical duties required by the rules in this chapter.

(5) "Coordinated action" means any action that has been ordered coordinated with one or more other actions under chapter 3 (commencing with section 404) of title 4 of part 2 of the Code of Civil Procedure and the rules in this chapter.

(6) "Coordination attorney" means an attorney with the Judicial Council staff appointed by the Chair of the Judicial Council to perform such administrative functions as may be appropriate under the rules in this chapter, including but not limited to the functions described in rules 3.524 and 3.550.

(7) "Coordination motion judge" means an assigned judge designated under Code of Civil Procedure section 404 to determine whether coordination is appropriate.

(8) "Coordination proceeding" means any procedure authorized by chapter 3 (commencing with section 404) of title 4 of part 2 of the Code of Civil Procedure and by the rules in this chapter.

(9) "Coordination trial judge" means an assigned judge designated under Code of Civil Procedure section 404.3 to hear and determine coordinated actions.

(10) "Expenses" means all necessary costs that are reimbursable under Code of Civil Procedure section 404.8, including the compensation of the assigned judge and other necessary judicial officers and employees, the costs of any necessary travel and subsistence determined under rules of the State Board of Control, and all necessarily incurred costs of facilities, supplies, materials, and telephone and mailing expenses.

(11) "Included action" means any action or proceeding included in a petition for coordination.

(12) "Liaison counsel" means an attorney of record for a party to an included action or a coordinated action who has been appointed by an assigned judge to serve as representative of all parties on a side with the following powers and duties, as appropriate:

(A) To receive on behalf of and promptly distribute to the parties for whom he or she acts all notices and other documents from the court;

(B) To act as spokesperson for the side that he or she represents at all proceedings set on notice before trial, subject to the right of each party to present individual or divergent positions; and

(C) To call meetings of counsel for the purpose of proposing joint action.

(13) "Party" includes all parties to all included actions or coordinated actions, and the word "party," "petitioner," or any other designation of a party includes that party's attorney of record. When a notice or other paper is required to be given or served on a party, the notice or paper must be given to or served on the party's attorney of record, if any.

(14) "Petition for coordination" means any petition, motion, application, or request for coordination of actions submitted to the Chair of the Judicial Council or to a coordination trial judge under rule 3.544.

(15) "Remand" means to return a coordinated action or a severable claim or issue in a coordinated action from a coordination proceeding to the court in which the action was pending at the time the coordination of that action was ordered. If a remanded action or claim had been transferred by the coordination trial judge under rule 3.543 from the court in which the remanded action or claim was pending, the remand must include the retransfer of that action or claim to that court.

(16) "Serve and file" means that a paper filed in a court must be accompanied by proof of prior service of a copy of the paper on each party required to be served under the rules in this chapter.

(17) "Serve and submit" means that a paper to be submitted to an assigned judge under the rules in this chapter must be submitted to that judge at a designated court address. Every paper so submitted must be accompanied by proof of prior service on each party required to be served under the rules in this chapter. If there is no assigned judge or if the paper is of a type included in rule 3.511(a), the paper must be submitted to the Chair of the Judicial Council.

(18) "Side" means all parties to an included or a coordinated action who have a common or substantially similar interest in the issues, as determined by the assigned judge for the purpose of appointing liaison counsel or of allotting peremptory challenges in jury selection, or for any other appropriate purpose. Except as defined in rule 3.515, a side may include less than all plaintiffs or all defendants.

(19) "Transfer" means to remove a coordinated action or severable claim in that action from the court in which it is pending to any other court under rule 3.543, without removing the action or claim from the coordination proceeding. "Transfer" includes "retransfer."

Rule 3.501 amended effective January 1, 2016; adopted as rule 1501 effective January 1, 1974; previously amended effective July 1, 1974, and January 1, 2005; previously amended and renumbered as rule 3.501 effective January 1, 2007.

Rule 3.502. Complex case—determination

The court must consider rule 3.400 et seq. in determining whether a case is or is not a complex case within the meaning of Code of Civil Procedure sections 403 and 404.

Rule 3.502 amended and renumbered effective January 1, 2007; adopted as rule 1501.1 effective September 21, 1996; previously amended effective January 1, 2000; previously amended and renumbered as rule 1502 effective January 1, 2005.

Rule 3.503. Requests for extensions of time or to shorten time

(a) Assigned judge may grant request

The assigned judge, on terms that are just, may shorten or extend the time within which any act is permitted or required to be done by a party. Unless otherwise ordered, any motion or application for an extension of time to perform an act required by these rules must be served and submitted in accordance with rule 3.501(17).

(Subd (a) amended effective January 1, 2007; adopted as part of unlettered subd effective January 1, 1974; previously amended and lettered effective January 1, 2005.)

(b) Stipulation requires consent of assigned judge

A stipulation for an extension of time for the filing and service of documents required by the rules in this chapter requires approval of the assigned judge.

(Subd (b) amended and lettered effective January 1, 2005; adopted as part of unlettered subd effective January 1, 1974.)

(c) Extension does not extend time for bringing action to trial

Nothing in this rule extends the time within which a party must bring an action to trial under Code of Civil Procedure section 583.310.

(Subd (c) adopted effective January 1, 2005.)

Rule 3.503 amended and renumbered effective January 1, 2007; adopted as rule 1503 effective January 1, 1974; previously amended effective January 1, 2005.

Rule 3.504. General law applicable

(a) General law applicable

Except as otherwise provided in the rules in this chapter, all provisions of law applicable to civil actions generally apply to an action included in a coordination proceeding.

(Subd (a) amended effective January 1, 2005.)

(b) Rules prevail over conflicting general provisions of law

To the extent that the rules in this chapter conflict with provisions of law applicable to civil actions generally, the rules in this chapter prevail, as provided by Code of Civil Procedure section 404.7.

(Subd (b) amended and lettered effective January 1, 2005; adopted as part of subd (a) effective January 1, 1974.)

(c) Manner of proceeding may be prescribed by assigned judge

If the manner of proceeding is not prescribed by chapter 3 (commencing with section 404) of title 4 of part 2 of the Code of Civil Procedure or by the rules in this chapter, or if the prescribed manner of proceeding cannot, with reasonable diligence, be followed in a particular coordination proceeding, the assigned judge may prescribe any suitable manner of proceeding that appears most consistent with those statutes and rules.

(Subd (c) amended and relettered effective January 1, 2005; adopted as subd (b) effective January 1, 1974.)

(d) Specification of applicable local rules

At the beginning of a coordination proceeding, the assigned judge must specify, subject to rule 3.20, any local court rules to be followed in that proceeding, and thereafter all parties must comply with those rules. Except as otherwise provided in the rules in this chapter or as directed by the assigned judge, the local rules of the court designated in the order appointing the assigned judge apply in all respects if they would otherwise apply without reference to the rules in this chapter.

(Subd (d) amended effective January 1, 2007; adopted as subd (c) effective January 1, 1974; previously amended and relettered effective January 1, 2005.)

Rule 3.504 amended and renumbered effective January 1, 2007; adopted as rule 1504 effective January 1, 1974; previously amended effective January 1, 2005.

Rule 3.505. Appellate review

(a) Coordination order to specify reviewing court

If the actions to be coordinated are within the jurisdiction of more than one reviewing court, the coordination motion judge must select and the order granting a petition for coordination must specify, in accordance with Code of Civil Procedure section 404.2, the court having appellate jurisdiction of the coordinated actions.

(Subd (a) amended and lettered effective January 1, 2005; adopted as part of unlettered subd effective January 1, 1974.)

(b) Court for review of order granting or denying coordination

A petition for a writ relating to an order granting or denying coordination may be filed, subject to the provisions of rule 10.1000, in any reviewing court having jurisdiction under the rules applicable to civil actions generally.

(Subd (b) amended effective January 1, 2007; adopted as part of unlettered subd effective January 1, 1974; previously amended and lettered effective January 1, 2005.)

Rule 3.505 amended and renumbered effective January 1, 2007; adopted as rule 1505 effective January 1, 1974; previously amended effective January 1, 2005.

Rule 3.506. Liaison counsel

(a) Selection and appointment

An assigned judge may at any time request that the parties on each side of the included or coordinated actions select one or more of the attorneys of record on that side for appointment as liaison counsel, and may appoint liaison counsel if the parties are unable to agree.

(Subd (a) amended effective January 1, 2005.)

(b) Duration of appointment by coordination motion judge

Unless otherwise stipulated to or directed by an assigned judge, the appointment of a liaison counsel by a coordination motion judge terminates on the final determination of the issue whether coordination is appropriate. For good cause shown, the coordination motion judge, on the court's own motion or on the motion of any party, may remove previously appointed counsel as liaison counsel.

(Subd (b) amended and lettered effective January 1, 2005; adopted as part of subd (a) effective January 1, 1974.)

(c) Service on party that has requested special notice

Except as otherwise directed by the assigned judge, any party that has made a written request for special notice must be served with a copy of any document thereafter served on the party's liaison counsel.

(Subd (c) amended effective January 1, 2007; adopted as subd (b) effective January 1, 1974.) amended and relettered effective January 1, 2005.)

Rule 3.506 amended and renumbered effective January 1, 2007; adopted as rule 1506 effective January 1, 1974; previously amended effective January 1, 2005.)

Article 2
Procedural Rules Applicable to All Complex Coordination Proceedings

Rule 3.510. Service of papers
Rule 3.511. Papers to be submitted to the Chair of the Judicial Council
Rule 3.512. Electronic submission of documents to the Chair of the Judicial Council
Rule 3.513. Service of memorandums and declarations
Rule 3.514. Evidence presented at court hearings
Rule 3.515. Motions and orders for a stay
Rule 3.516. Motions under Code of Civil Procedure section 170.6

Rule 3.510. Service of papers

(a) Proof of service

Except as otherwise provided in the rules in this chapter, all papers filed or submitted must be accompanied by proof of prior service on all other parties to the coordination proceeding, including all parties appearing in all included actions and coordinated actions. Service and proof of such service must be made as provided for in civil actions generally.

(Subd (a) amended and lettered effective January 1, 2005; adopted as part of unlettered subd effective January 1, 1974.)

(b) Service on liaison counsel

Except as provided in rule 3.506(c), any party for whom liaison counsel has been designated may be served by serving the liaison counsel.

(Subd (b) amended effective January 1, 2007; adopted as part of unlettered subd effective January 1, 1974; previously amended and lettered effective January 1, 2005.)

(c) Effect of failure to serve

Failure to serve any defendant with a copy of the summons and of the complaint, or failure to serve any party with any other paper or order as required by the rules in this chapter, will not preclude the coordination of the actions, but the unserved defendant or party may assert the failure to serve as a basis for appropriate relief.

(Subd (c) amended and lettered effective January 1, 2005; adopted as part of unlettered subd effective January 1, 1974.)

Rule 3.510 amended and renumbered effective January 1, 2007; adopted as rule 1510 effective January 1, 1974; previously amended effective January 1, 2005.)

Rule 3.511. Papers to be submitted to the Chair of the Judicial Council

(a) Types of papers

A copy of the following papers must be submitted to the Chair of the Judicial Council at the Judicial Council's San Francisco office:

(1) Petition for coordination, including a petition for coordination of add-on cases;

(2) Notice of submission of petition for coordination, along with the caption page of the original action;

(3) Order assigning coordination motion judge, if made by a presiding judge;

(4) Order assigning coordination trial judge, if made by a presiding judge;

(5) Notice of opposition;

(6) Response in opposition to or in support of a petition for coordination;

(7) Motion for a stay order;

(8) Notice of hearing on petition;

(9) Order granting or denying coordination, including coordination of add-on cases;

(10) Order of remand;

(11) Order of transfer;

(12) Order terminating a coordination proceeding in whole or in part;

(13) Order dismissing an included or coordinated action;

(14) Notice of appeal; and

(15) Notice of disposition of appeal.

(Subd (a) adopted effective January 1, 2005.)

(b) Obligation of party

The papers listed in (a) are to be submitted by the party that filed or submitted and served the papers or that was directed to give notice of entry of the order. Notice of submission must be filed with the court as part of the proof of service.

(Subd (b) adopted effective January 1, 2005.)

Rule 3.511 amended and renumbered effective January 1, 2007; adopted as rule 1511 effective January 1, 1974; previously amended effective January 1, 2005.

Rule 3.512. Electronic submission of documents to the Chair of the Judicial Council

(a) Documents that may be submitted electronically

Any paper listed in rule 3.511(a) may be submitted electronically to coordination@jud.ca.gov.

(Subd (a) amended effective January 1, 2008; previously amended effective January 1, 2007.)

(b) Responsibilities of party submitting documents electronically

A party submitting a document electronically must:

(1) Take all reasonable steps to ensure that the submission does not contain computer code, including viruses, that might be harmful to the Judicial Council's electronic system and to other users of that system; and

(2) Furnish one or more electronic notification addresses and immediately provide any change to his or her electronic notification addresses.

(c) Format of documents to be submitted electronically

A document that is submitted electronically must meet the following requirements:

(1) The software for creating and reading the document must be in the public domain or generally available at a reasonable cost; and

(2) The printing of documents must not result in the loss of document text, format, or appearance.

(d) Signature on documents under penalty of perjury

(1) When a document to be submitted electronically requires a signature under penalty of perjury, the document is deemed signed by the declarant if, before submission, the declarant has signed a printed form of the document.

(2) By electronically submitting the document, the party submitting it indicates that he or she has complied with subdivision (d)(1) of this rule and that the original, signed document is available for review and copying at the request of the court or any party.

(3) At any time after the document is submitted, any other party may serve a demand for production of the original signed document. The demand must be served on all other parties but need not be filed with the court.

(4) Within five days of service of the demand, the party on whom the demand is made must make the original signed document available for review and copying by all other parties.

(e) Signature on documents not under penalty of perjury

If a document does not require a signature under penalty of perjury, the document is deemed signed by the party if the document is submitted electronically.

(f) Digital signature

A party is not required to use a digital signature on an electronically submitted document.

Rule 3.512 amended effective January 1, 2008; adopted as rule 1511.5 effective July 1, 2005; previously amended and renumbered effective January 1, 2007.

Rule 3.513. Service of memorandums and declarations

Unless otherwise provided in the rules in this chapter or directed by the assigned judge, all memorandums and declarations in support of or opposition to any petition, motion, or application must be served and submitted at least nine court days before any hearing on the matter at issue.

Rule 3.513 amended effective January 1, 2007; adopted as rule 1512 effective January 1, 1974; previously amended effective January 1, 2005; previously amended and renumbered effective January 1, 2007.

Rule 3.514. Evidence presented at court hearings

All factual matters to be heard on any petition for coordination, or on any other petition, motion, or application under the rules in this chapter, must be initially presented and heard on declarations, answers to interrogatories or requests for admissions, depositions, or matters judicially noticed. Oral testimony will not be permitted at a hearing except as the assigned judge may permit to resolve factual issues shown by the declarations, responses to discovery, or matters judicially noticed to be in dispute. Only parties that have submitted a petition or motion, or a written response or opposition to a petition or motion, will be permitted to appear at the hearing, except the assigned judge may permit other parties to appear, on a showing of good cause.

Rule 3.514 renumbered effective January 1, 2007; adopted as rule 1513 effective January 1, 1974; previously amended effective January 1, 2005.

Rule 3.515. Motions and orders for a stay

(a) Motion for stay

Any party may file a motion for an order under Code of Civil Procedure section 404.5 staying the proceedings in any action being considered for, or affecting an action being considered for, coordination, or the court may stay the proceedings on its own motion. The motion for a stay may be included with a petition for coordination or may be served and submitted to the Chair of the Judicial Council and the coordination motion judge by any party at any time prior to the determination of the petition.

(Subd (a) amended effective January 1, 2005.)

(b) Contents of motion

A motion for a stay order must:

(1) List all known pending related cases;

(2) State whether the stay order should extend to any such related case; and

(3) Be supported by a memorandum and by declarations establishing the facts relied on to show that a stay order is necessary and appropriate to effectuate the purposes of coordination.

(Subd (b) amended and lettered effective January 1, 2005; adopted as part of subd (a) effective January 1, 1974.)

(c) Service requirements for certain motions for stay orders

If the action to be stayed is not included in the petition for coordination or any response to that petition, the motion for a stay order and all supporting documents must be served on each party to the action to be stayed and any such party may serve and submit opposition to the motion for a stay order.

(Subd (c) amended and lettered effective January 1, 2005; adopted as part of subd (a) effective January 1, 1974.)

(d) Opposition to motion for stay order

Any memorandums and declarations in opposition to a motion for a stay order must be served and submitted within 10 days after service of the motion.

(Subd (d) amended and lettered effective January 1, 2005; adopted as part of subd (a) effective January 1, 1974.)

(e) Hearing on motion for stay order

A stay order may be issued with or without a hearing. A party filing a motion for a stay order or opposition thereto may request a hearing to determine whether the stay order should be granted. A request for hearing should be made at the time the requesting party files the motion or opposition. If the coordination motion judge grants the request for a hearing, the requesting party must provide notice.

(Subd (e) amended and lettered effective January 1, 2005; adopted as part of subd (a) effective January 1, 1974.)

(f) Determination of motion for stay order

In ruling on a motion for a stay order, the assigned judge must determine whether the stay will promote the ends of justice, considering the imminence of any trial or other proceeding that might materially affect the status of the action to be stayed, and whether a final judgment in that action would have a res judicata or collateral estoppel effect with regard to any common issue of the included actions.

(Subd (f) amended and relettered effective January 1, 2005; adopted as subd (e) effective January 1, 1974.)

(g) Issuance of stay order and termination of stay

If a stay order is issued, the party that requested the stay must serve and file a copy of the order in each included action that is stayed. Thirty or more days following issuance of the stay order, any party that is subject to the stay order may move to terminate the stay.

(Subd (g) amended and relettered effective January 1, 2005; adopted as subd (b) effective January 1, 1974.)

(h) Effect of stay order

Unless otherwise specified in the order, a stay order suspends all proceedings in the action to which it applies. A stay order may be limited by its terms to specified proceedings, orders, motions, or other phases of the action to which the order applies.

(Subd (h) amended and relettered effective January 1, 2005; adopted as subd (c) effective January 1, 1974.)

(i) Effect of absence of stay order

In the absence of a stay order, a court receiving an order assigning a coordination motion judge may continue to exercise jurisdiction over the included action for purposes of all pretrial and discovery proceedings, but no trial may be commenced and no judgment may be entered in that action unless trial of the action had commenced before the assignment of the coordination motion judge.

(Subd (i) amended and relettered effective January 1, 2005; adopted as subd (d) effective January 1, 1974; previously amended effective July 1, 1974.)

(j) Effect of stay order on dismissal for lack of prosecution

The time during which any stay of proceedings is in effect under the rules in this chapter must not be included in determining whether the action stayed should be dismissed for lack of prosecution under chapter 1.5 (§ 583.110 et seq.) of title 8 of part 2 of the Code of Civil Procedure.

(Subd (j) amended and relettered effective January 1, 2005; adopted as subd (f) effective January 1, 1974; previously amended effective January 1, 1986.)

Rule 3.515 renumbered effective January 1, 2007; adopted as rule 1514 effective January 1, 1974; previously amended effective July 1, 1974, January 1, 1986, and January 1, 2005.

Rule 3.516. Motions under Code of Civil Procedure section 170.6

A party making a peremptory challenge by motion or affidavit of prejudice regarding an assigned judge must submit it in writing to the assigned judge within 20 days after service of the order assigning the judge to the coordination proceeding. All plaintiffs or similar parties in the included or coordinated actions constitute a side and all defendants or similar parties in such actions constitute a side for purposes of applying Code of Civil Procedure section 170.6.

Rule 3.516 renumbered effective January 1, 2007; adopted as rule 1515 effective January 1, 1974; previously amended effective June 19, 1982, and January 1, 2005.

Article 3
Petitions and Proceedings for Coordination of Complex Actions

Rule 3.520. Motions filed in the trial court
Rule 3.521. Petition for coordination
Rule 3.522. Notice of submission of petition for coordination
Rule 3.523. Service of notice of submission on party
Rule 3.524. Order assigning coordination motion judge
Rule 3.525. Response in opposition to petition for coordination
Rule 3.526. Response in support of petition for coordination
Rule 3.527. Notice of hearing on petition for coordination
Rule 3.528. Separate hearing on certain coordination issues
Rule 3.529. Order granting or denying coordination
Rule 3.530. Site of coordination proceedings
Rule 3.531. Potential add-on case
Rule 3.532. Petition for coordination when cases already ordered coordinated

Rule 3.520. Motions filed in the trial court

(a) General requirements

A motion filed in the trial court under this rule must specify the matters required by rule 3.521(a) and must be made in the manner provided by law for motions in civil actions generally.

(Subd (a) amended effective January 1, 2007; previously amended effective January 1, 1983, and January 1, 2005.)

(b) Permission to submit a petition for coordination

(1) *Request for permission to submit coordination petition*

If a direct petition is not authorized by Code of Civil Procedure section 404, a party may request permission from the presiding judge of the court in which one of the included actions is pending to submit a petition for coordination to the Chair of the Judicial Council. The request must be made by noticed motion accompanied by a proposed order. The proposed order must state that the moving party has permission to submit a petition for coordination to the Chair of the Judicial Council under rules 3.521–3.523.

(2) *Order to be prepared*

If permission to submit a petition is granted, the moving party must serve and file the signed order and submit it to the Chair of the Judicial Council.

(3) *Stay permitted pending preparation of petition*

To provide sufficient time for a party to submit a petition, the presiding judge may stay all related actions pending in that court for a reasonable time not to exceed 30 calendar days.

(Subd (b) amended effective January 1, 2007; previously amended effective January 1, 1983, January 1, 2005, and July 1, 2006.)

Rule 3.520 amended and renumbered effective January 1, 2007; adopted as rule 1520 effective January 1, 1974; previously amended effective January 1, 1983, January 1, 2005, and July 1, 2006.

Rule 3.521. Petition for coordination

(a) Contents of petition

A request submitted to the Chair of the Judicial Council for the assignment of a judge to determine whether the coordination of certain actions is appropriate, or a request that a coordination trial judge make such a determination concerning an add-on case, must be designated a "Petition for Coordination" and may be made at any time after filing of the complaint. The petition must state whether a hearing is requested and must be supported by a memorandum and declarations showing:

(1) The name of each petitioner or, when the petition is submitted by a presiding or sole judge, the name of each real party in interest, and the name and address of each party's attorney of record, if any;

(2) The names of the parties to all included actions, and the name and address of each party's attorney of record, if any;

(3) If the party seeking to submit a petition for coordination is a plaintiff, whether the party's attorney has served the summons and complaint on all parties in all included actions in which the attorney has appeared;

(4) For each included action, the complete title and case number, the date the complaint was filed, and the title of the court in which the action is pending;

(5) The complete title and case number of any other action known to the petitioner to be pending in a court of this state that shares a common question of fact or law with the included actions, and a statement of the reasons for not including the other action in the petition for coordination or a statement that the petitioner knows of no other actions sharing a common question of fact or law;

(6) The status of each included action, including the status of any pretrial or discovery motions or orders in that action, if known to petitioner;

(7) The facts relied on to show that each included action meets the coordination standards specified in Code of Civil Procedure section 404.1; and

(8) The facts relied on in support of a request that a particular site or sites be selected for a hearing on the petition for coordination.

(Subd (a) amended effective January 1, 2005.)

(b) Submit proof of filing and service

Within five court days of submitting the petition for coordination, the petitioner must submit to the Chair of the Judicial Council proof of filing of the notice of submission of petition required by rule 3.522, and proof of service of the notice of submission of petition and of the petition required by rule 3.523.

(Subd (b) amended effective January 1, 2007; previously amended effective January 1, 2005, and January 1, 2007.)

(c) Copies of pleadings in lieu of proof by declaration

In lieu of proof by declaration of any fact required by (a)(2), (4), (7), and (8), a certified or endorsed copy of the respective pleadings may be attached to the petition for coordination, provided that the petitioner specifies with particularity the portions of the pleadings that are relied on to show the fact.

(Subd (c) amended effective January 1, 2005.)

(d) Effect of imminent trial date

The imminence of a trial in any action otherwise appropriate for coordination may be a ground for summary denial of a petition for coordination, in whole or in part.

(Subd (d) amended effective January 1, 2005.)

Rule 3.521 amended effective January 1, 2007; adopted as rule 1521 effective January 1, 1974; previously amended effective January 1, 2005; previously amended and renumbered effective January 1, 2007.

Rule 3.522. Notice of submission of petition for coordination

(a) Contents of notice of submission

In each included action, the petitioner must file a "Notice of Submission of Petition for Coordination" and the petition for coordination. Each notice must bear the title of the court in which the notice is to be filed and the title and case number of each included action that is pending in that court. Each notice must include:

(1) The date that the petition for coordination was submitted to the Chair of the Judicial Council;

(2) The name and address of the petitioner's attorney of record;

(3) The title and case number of each included action to which the petitioner is a party and the title of the court in which each action is pending; and

(4) The statement that any written opposition to the petition must be submitted and served at least nine court days before the hearing date.

(Subd (a) amended effective January 1, 2007; adopted as part of unlettered subd effective January 1, 1974; previously amended and lettered effective January 1, 2005; previously amended effective January 1, 2006.)

(b) Copies of notice

The petitioner must submit the notice and proof of filing in each included action to the Chair of the Judicial Council within five court days of submitting the petition for coordination.

(Subd (b) amended effective January 1, 2007; adopted as part of unlettered subd effective January 1, 1974; previously amended and lettered effective January 1, 2005.)

Rule 3.522 amended and renumbered effective January 1, 2007; adopted as rule 1522 effective January 1, 1974; previously amended effective January 1, 2005, and January 1, 2006.

Rule 3.523. Service of notice of submission on party

The petitioner must serve the notice of submission of petition for coordination that was filed in each included action, the petition for coordination, and supporting documents on each party appearing in each included action and submit the notice to the Chair of the Judicial Council within five court days of submitting the petition for coordination.

Rule 3.523 amended effective January 1, 2007; adopted as rule 1523 effective January 1, 1974; previously amended effective January 1, 2005; previously amended and renumbered effective January 1, 2007.

Rule 3.524. Order assigning coordination motion judge

(a) Contents of order

An order by the Chair of the Judicial Council assigning a coordination motion judge to determine whether coordination is appropriate, or authorizing the presiding judge of a court to assign the matter to judicial officers of the court to make the determination in the same manner as assignments are made in other civil cases, must include the following:

(1) The special title and number assigned to the coordination proceeding; and

(2) The court's address or electronic service address for submitting all subsequent documents to be considered by the coordination motion judge.

(Subd (a) amended effective January 1, 2016; adopted as part of unlettered subd effective January 1, 1974; previously amended and lettered as subd (a) effective January 1, 2005.)

(b) Service of order

The petitioner must serve the order described in (a) on each party appearing in an included action and send it to each court in which an included action is pending with directions to the clerk to file the order in the included action.

(Subd (b) amended and lettered effective January 1, 2005; adopted as part of unlettered subd effective January 1, 1974.)

Rule 3.524 amended effective January 1, 2016; adopted as rule 1524 effective January 1, 1974; previously amended effective January 1, 2005; previously renumbered as rule 3.524 effective January 1, 2007.

Rule 3.525. Response in opposition to petition for coordination

Any party to an included action that opposes coordination may serve and submit a memorandum and declarations in opposition to the petition. Any response in opposition must be served and filed at least nine court days before the date set for hearing.

Rule 3.525 amended effective January 1, 2007; adopted as rule 1525 effective January 1, 1974; previously amended effective January 1, 2005; previously amended and renumbered effective January 1, 2007.

Rule 3.526. Response in support of petition for coordination

Any party to an included action that supports coordination may serve and submit a written statement in support of the petition. Any response in support must be served and filed at least nine court days before the date set for hearing. If a party that supports coordination does not support the particular site or sites requested by the petitioner for the hearing on the petition for coordination, that party may request that a different site or sites be selected and include in his or her response the facts relied on in support thereof.

Rule 3.526 amended effective January 1, 2007; adopted as rule 1526 effective January 1, 1974; previously amended effective January 1, 2005; previously amended and renumbered effective January 1, 2007.

Rule 3.527. Notice of hearing on petition for coordination

(a) Timing and notice of hearing

The coordination motion judge must set a hearing date on a petition for coordination within 30 days of the date of the order assigning the coordination motion judge. When a coordination motion judge is assigned to decide a petition for coordination that lists additional included actions sharing a common question of law or fact with included actions in a petition for coordination already pending before the judge, the judge may continue the hearing date on the first petition no more than 30 calendar days in order to hear both petitions at the same time. The petitioner must provide notice of the hearing to each party appearing in an included action. If the coordination motion judge determines that a party that should be served with notice of the petition for coordination has not been served with notice, the coordination motion judge must order the petitioner to promptly serve that party. If the coordination motion judge determines that a hearing is not required under (b), the hearing date must be vacated and notice provided to the parties.

(Subd (a) amended and relettered effective January 1, 2005; adopted as subd (b) effective January 1, 1974.)

(b) Circumstances in which hearing required

A hearing must be held to decide a petition for coordination if a party opposes coordination. A petition for coordination may not be denied unless a hearing has been held.

(Subd (b) adopted effective January 1, 2005.)

(c) Report to the Chair of the Judicial Council

If the petition for coordination has not been decided within 30 calendar days after the hearing, the coordination motion judge must promptly submit to the Chair of the Judicial Council a written report describing:

(1) The present status of the petition for coordination proceeding;

(2) Any factors or circumstances that may have caused undue or unanticipated delay in the decision on the petition for coordination; and

(3) Any stay orders that are in effect.

(Subd (c) amended effective January 1, 2005.)

Rule 3.527 renumbered effective January 1, 2007; adopted as rule 1527 effective January 1, 1974; previously amended effective January 1, 2005.

Rule 3.528. Separate hearing on certain coordination issues

When a petition for coordination may be disposed of on the determination of a specified issue or issues, without a hearing on all issues raised by the petition and any opposition, the assigned judge may order that the specified issue or issues be heard and determined before a hearing on the remaining issues.

Rule 3.528 renumbered effective January 1, 2007; adopted as rule 1528 effective January 1, 1974; previously amended effective January 1, 2005.

Rule 3.529. Order granting or denying coordination

(a) Filing, service, and submittal

When a petition for coordination is granted or denied, the petitioner must promptly file the order in each included action, serve it on each party appearing in an included action, and submit it to the Chair of the Judicial Council.

(Subd (a) amended effective January 1, 2007; previously amended effective January 1, 2005.)

(b) Stay of further proceedings

When an order granting coordination is filed in an included action, all further proceedings in that action are automatically stayed, except as directed by the coordination trial judge or by the coordination motion judge under (c). The stay does not preclude the court in which the included action is pending from accepting and filing papers with proof of submission of a copy to the assigned judge or from exercising jurisdiction over any severable claim that has not been ordered coordinated.

(Subd (b) amended effective January 1, 2005.)

(c) Authority of coordination motion judge pending assignment of coordination trial judge

After a petition for coordination has been granted and before a coordination trial judge has been assigned, the coordination motion judge may for good cause make any appropriate order as the ends of justice may require but may not commence a trial or enter judgment in any included action. Good cause includes a showing of an urgent need for judicial action to preserve the rights of a party pending assignment of a coordination trial judge.

(Subd (c) amended effective January 1, 2005.)

(d) Order denying coordination

The authority of a coordination motion judge over an included action terminates when an order denying a petition for coordination is filed in the included action and served on the parties to the action. A stay ordered by the coordination motion judge terminates 10 days after the order denying coordination is filed.

(Subd (d) amended effective January 1, 2005.)

Rule 3.529 amended and renumbered effective January 1, 2007; adopted as rule 1529 effective January 1, 1974; previously amended effective June 19, 1982, and January 1, 2005.

Rule 3.530. Site of coordination proceedings

(a) Recommendation by coordination motion judge

If a petition for coordination is granted, the coordination motion judge must, in the order granting coordination, recommend to the Chair of the Judicial Council a particular superior court for the site of the coordination proceedings.

(b) Factors to consider

The coordination motion judge may consider any relevant factors in making a recommendation for the site of the coordination proceedings, including the following:

(1) The number of included actions in particular locations;

(2) Whether the litigation is at an advanced stage in a particular court;

(3) The efficient use of court facilities and judicial resources;

(4) The locations of witnesses and evidence;

(5) The convenience of the parties and witnesses;

(6) The parties' principal places of business;

(7) The office locations of counsel for the parties; and

(8) The ease of travel to and availability of accommodations in particular locations.

Rule 3.530 renumbered effective January 1, 2007; adopted as rule 1530 effective January 1, 2005.

Rule 3.531. Potential add-on case

(a) Notice

Any party to an included action in a pending petition for coordination must promptly provide notice of any potential add-on cases in which that party is also named or in which that party's attorney has appeared. The party must submit notice to the coordination motion judge and the Chair of the Judicial Council and serve it on each party appearing in the included actions in the pending petition and each party appearing in the potential add-on cases.

(b) Stipulation or order

By stipulation of all parties or order of the coordination motion judge, each potential add-on case will be deemed an included action for purposes of the hearing on the petition for coordination.

Rule 3.531 renumbered effective January 1, 2007; adopted as rule 1531 effective January 1, 2005.

Rule 3.532. Petition for coordination when cases already ordered coordinated

(a) Assignment of coordination trial judge

If it appears that included actions in a petition for coordination share a common question of law or fact with cases already ordered coordinated, the Chair of the Judicial Council may assign the petition to the coordination trial judge for the existing coordinated cases to decide the petition as a request to coordinate an add-on case under rule 3.544.

(Subd (a) amended effective January 1, 2007.)

(b) Order

The coordination trial judge's order must specify that the request to coordinate an add-on case is either granted or denied.

(c) Filing and service

The petitioner must promptly file the order in each included action, serve it on each party appearing in an included action, and submit a copy to the Chair of the Judicial Council.

(Subd (c) amended effective January 1, 2007.)

(d) Cases added on and right to peremptory challenge

If the coordination trial judge grants the petition, the included actions will be coordinated as add-on cases and the right to file a peremptory challenge under Code of Civil Procedure section 170.6 will be limited by rule 3.516.

(Subd (d) amended effective January 1, 2007.)

(e) Assignment of coordination motion judge if cases not added on

If the coordination trial judge denies the petition as a request to coordinate an add-on case under rule 3.544, the Chair of the Judicial Council must assign a coordination motion judge to determine whether coordination is appropriate under rule 3.524.

(Subd (e) amended effective January 1, 2007.)

Rule 3.532 amended and renumbered effective January 1, 2007; adopted as rule 1532 effective January 1, 2005.

Article 4
Pretrial and Trial Rules for Complex Coordinated Actions

Rule 3.540. Order assigning coordination trial judge
Rule 3.541. Duties of the coordination trial judge
Rule 3.542. Remand of action or claim
Rule 3.543. Transfer of action or claim
Rule 3.544. Add-on cases
Rule 3.545. Termination of coordinated action

Rule 3.540. Order assigning coordination trial judge

(a) Assignment by the Chair of the Judicial Council

When a petition for coordination is granted, the Chair of the Judicial Council must either assign a coordination trial judge to hear and determine the coordinated actions or authorize the presiding judge of a court to assign the matter to judicial officers of the court in the same manner as assignments are made in other civil cases, under Code of Civil Procedure section 404.3. The order assigning a coordination trial judge must designate an address for submission of papers to that judge.

(Subd (a) amended and lettered effective January 1, 2005; adopted as part of unlettered subd effective January 1, 1974.)

(b) Powers of coordination trial judge

Immediately on assignment, the coordination trial judge may exercise all the powers over each coordinated action that are available to a judge of the court in which that action is pending.

(Subd (b) amended effective January 1, 2007; adopted as part of unlettered subd effective January 1, 1974; previously amended and lettered effective January 1, 2005.)

(c) Filing and service of copies of assignment order

The petitioner must file the assignment order in each coordinated action and serve it on each party appearing in each action, and, if the assignment was made by the presiding judge, submit it to the Chair of the Judicial Council. Every paper filed in a coordinated action must be accompanied by proof of submission of a copy of the paper to the coordination trial judge at the designated address. A copy of the assignment order must be included in any subsequent service of process on any defendant in the action.

(Subd (c) amended effective January 1, 2011; adopted as part of unlettered subd; previously amended and lettered effective January 1, 2005.)

Rule 3.540 amended effective January 1, 2011; adopted as rule 1540 effective January 1, 1974; previously amended effective January 1, 2005; previously amended and renumbered effective January 1, 2007.

Rule 3.541. Duties of the coordination trial judge

(a) Initial case management conference

The coordination trial judge must hold a case management conference within 45 days after issuance of the assignment order. Counsel and all self-represented persons must attend the conference and be prepared to discuss all matters specified in the order setting the conference. At any time following the assignment of the coordination trial judge, a party may serve and submit a proposed agenda for the conference and a proposed form of order covering such matters of procedure and discovery as may be appropriate. At the conference, the judge may:

(1) Appoint liaison counsel under rule 3.506;

(2) Establish a timetable for filing motions other than discovery motions;

(3) Establish a schedule for discovery;

(4) Provide a method and schedule for the submission of preliminary legal questions that might serve to expedite the disposition of the coordinated actions;

(5) In class actions, establish a schedule, if practicable, for the prompt determination of matters pertinent to the class action issue;

(6) Establish a central depository or depositories to receive and maintain for inspection by the parties evidentiary material and specified documents that are not required by the rules in this chapter to be served on all parties; and

(7) Schedule further conferences if appropriate.

(Subd (a) amended effective January 1, 2007; previously amended effective January 1, 2005.)

(b) Management of proceedings by coordination trial judge

The coordination trial judge must assume an active role in managing all steps of the pretrial, discovery, and trial proceedings to expedite the just determination of the coordinated actions without delay. The judge may, for the purpose of coordination and to serve the ends of justice:

(1) Order any coordinated action transferred to another court under rule 3.543;

(2) Schedule and conduct hearings, conferences, and a trial or trials at any site within this state that the judge deems appropriate with due consideration to the convenience of parties, witnesses, and counsel; to the relative development of the actions and the work product of counsel; to the efficient use of judicial facilities and resources; and to the calendar of the courts; and

(3) Order any issue or defense to be tried separately and before trial of the remaining issues when it appears that the disposition of any of the coordinated actions might thereby be expedited.

(Subd (b) amended effective January 1, 2007; previously amended effective January 1, 2005.)

Rule 3.541 amended and renumbered effective January 1, 2007; adopted as rule 1541 effective January 1, 1974; previously amended effective January 1, 2005.

Rule 3.542. Remand of action or claim

The coordination trial judge may at any time remand a coordinated action or any severable claim or issue in that action to the court in which the action was pending at the time the coordination of that action was ordered. Remand may be made on the stipulation of all parties or on the basis of evidence received at a hearing on the court's own motion or on the motion of any party to any coordinated action. No action or severable claim or issue in that action may be remanded over the objection of any party unless the evidence demonstrates a material change in the circumstances that are relevant to the criteria for coordination under Code of Civil Procedure section 404.1. If the order of remand requires that the action be transferred, the provisions of rule 3.543(c)–(e) are applicable to the transfer. A remanded action is no longer part of the coordination proceedings for purposes of the rules in this chapter.

Rule 3.542 amended and renumbered effective January 1, 2007; adopted as rule 1542 effective January 1, 1974; previously amended effective January 1, 2005, and July 1, 2006.

Rule 3.543. Transfer of action or claim

(a) Court may transfer coordinated action

The coordination trial judge may order any coordinated action or severable claim in that action transferred from the court in which it is pending to another court for a specified purpose or for all purposes. Transfer may be made by the court on its own motion or on the motion of any party to any coordinated action.

(Subd (a) amended effective January 1, 2005.)

(b) Hearing on motion to transfer

If a party objects to the transfer, the court must hold a hearing on at least 10 days' written notice served on all parties to that action. At any hearing to determine whether an action or claim should be transferred, the court must consider the convenience of parties, witnesses, and counsel; the relative development of the actions and the work product of counsel; the efficient use of judicial facilities and resources; the calendar of the courts; and any other relevant matter.

(Subd (b) amended effective January 1, 2007; adopted as part of subd (a) effective January 1, 1974; previously amended and lettered effective January 1, 2005.)

(c) Order transferring action

The order transferring the action or claim must designate the court to which the action is transferred and must direct that a copy of the order of transfer be filed in each coordinated action. The order must indicate whether the action remains part of the coordination proceedings for purposes of the rules in this chapter.

(Subd (c) amended and lettered effective January 1, 2005; adopted as part of subd (b) effective January 1, 1974.)

(d) Duties of transferor and transferee courts

(1) *Duty of transferor court*

The clerk of the court in which the action was pending must immediately prepare and transmit to the court to which the action is transferred a certified copy of the order of transfer and of the pleadings and proceedings in the transferred action and must serve a copy of the order of transfer on each party appearing in that action.

(2) *Duty of transferee court*

The court to which the action is transferred must file the action as if the action had been commenced in that court. No fees may be required for such transfer by either court.

(3) *Transmission of papers*

If it is necessary to have any of the original pleadings or other papers in the transferred action before the coordination trial judge, the clerk of the court from which the action was transferred must, on written request of a party to that action or of the coordination trial judge, transmit such papers or pleadings to the court to which the action is transferred and must retain a certified copy.

(Subd (d) amended effective January 1, 2007; adopted as part of subd (b) effective January 1, 1974; previously amended and lettered effective January 1, 2005.)

(e) Transferee court to exercise jurisdiction

On receipt of a transfer order, the court to which the action is transferred may exercise jurisdiction over the action in accordance with the orders and directions of the coordination trial judge, and no other court may exercise jurisdiction over that action except as provided in this rule.

(Subd (e) amended and lettered effective January 1, 2005; adopted as part of subd (b) effective January 1, 1974.)

Rule 3.543 amended and renumbered effective January 1, 2007; adopted as rule 1543 effective January 1, 1974; previously amended effective January 1, 2005.

Rule 3.544. Add-on cases

(a) Request to coordinate add-on case

A request to coordinate an add-on case must comply with the requirements of rules 3.520 through 3.523, except that the request must be submitted to the coordination trial judge under Code of Civil Procedure section 404.4, with proof of service of one copy on the Chair of the Judicial Council and proof of service as required by rule 3.510.

(Subd (a) amended effective January 1, 2016; previously amended effective January 1, 2005, and January 1, 2007.)

(b) Opposition to request to coordinate an add-on case

Within 10 days after the service of a request, any party may serve and submit a notice of opposition to the request. Thereafter, within 15 days after submitting a notice of opposition, the party must serve and submit a memorandum and declarations in opposition to the request. Failure to serve and submit a memorandum and declarations in opposition may be a ground for granting the request to coordinate an add-on case.

(Subd (b) amended and lettered effective January 1, 2005; adopted as part of subd (a) effective January 1, 1974.)

(c) Hearing on request to coordinate an add-on case

The coordination trial judge may order a hearing on a request to coordinate an add-on case under rules 3.527 and 3.528 and may allow the parties to serve and submit additional written materials in support of or opposition to the request. In deciding the request to coordinate, the court must consider the relative development of the actions and the work product of counsel, in addition to any other relevant matter. An application for an order staying the add-on case must be made to the coordination trial judge under rule 3.515.

(Subd (c) amended effective January 1, 2007; adopted as subd (b) effective January 1, 1974; previously amended and relettered effective January 1, 2005.)

(d) Order on request to coordinate an add-on case

If no party has filed a notice of opposition within the time required under (b), the coordination trial judge may enter an order granting or denying the request without a hearing. An order granting or denying a request to coordinate an add-on case must be prepared and served under rule 3.529, and an order granting such request automatically stays all further proceedings in the add-on case under rule 3.529.

(Subd (d) amended effective January 1, 2007; adopted as subd (c) effective January 1, 1974; previously amended and relettered effective January 1, 2005.)

Rule 3.544 amended effective January 1, 2016; adopted as rule 1544 effective January 1, 1974; previously amended effective January 1, 2005; previously amended and renumbered as rule 3.544 effective January 1, 2007.

Rule 3.545. Termination of coordinated action

(a) Coordination trial judge may terminate action

The coordination trial judge may terminate any coordinated action by settlement or final dismissal, summary judgment, or judgment, or may transfer the action so that it may be dismissed or otherwise terminated in the court where it was pending when coordination was ordered.

(Subd (a) amended and lettered effective January 1, 2005; adopted as part of unlettered subd effective January 1, 1974.)

(b) Copies of order dismissing or terminating action and judgment

A certified copy of the order dismissing or terminating the action and of any judgment must be transmitted to:

(1) The clerk of the court in which the action was pending when coordination was ordered, who shall promptly enter any judgment and serve notice of entry of the judgment on all parties to the action and on the Chair of the Judicial Council; and

(2) The appropriate clerks for filing in each pending coordinated action.

(Subd (b) amended and lettered effective January 1, 2005; adopted as part of unlettered subd effective January 1, 1974.)

(c) Judgment in coordinated action

The judgment entered in each coordinated action must bear the title and case number assigned to the action at the time it was filed.

(Subd (c) amended and lettered effective January 1, 2005; adopted as part of unlettered subd effective January 1, 1974.)

(d) Proceedings in trial court after judgment

Until the judgment in a coordinated action becomes final or until a coordinated action is remanded, all further proceedings in that action to be determined by the trial court must be determined by the coordination trial judge. Thereafter, unless otherwise ordered by the coordination trial judge, all such proceedings must be conducted in the court where the action was pending when coordination was ordered. The coordination trial judge must also specify the court in which any ancillary proceedings will be heard and determined. For purposes of this rule, a judgment is final when it is no longer subject to appeal.

(Subd (d) amended and lettered effective January 1, 2005; adopted as part of unlettered subd effective January 1, 1974.)

Rule 3.545 renumbered effective January 1, 2007; adopted as rule 1545 effective January 1, 1974; previously amended effective January 1, 2005.

Article 5
Administration of Coordinated Complex Actions

Rule 3.550. General administration by Judicial Council staff

(a) Coordination attorney

Except as otherwise provided in the rules in this chapter, all necessary administrative functions under this chapter will be performed at the direction of the Chair of the Judicial Council by a coordination attorney.

(Subd (a) amended effective January 1, 2016; previously amended effective January 1, 2005, and January 1, 2007.)

(b) Duties of coordination attorney

The coordination attorney must at all times maintain:

(1) A list of active and retired judges who are qualified and currently available to conduct coordination proceedings; and

(2) A register of all coordination proceedings and a file for each proceeding, for public inspection during regular business hours at the San Francisco office of the Judicial Council.

(Subd (b) amended and lettered effective January 1, 2005; previously adopted as part of subd (a) effective January 1, 2005.)

(c) Coordination proceeding title and case number

The coordination attorney must assign each coordination proceeding a special title and coordination proceeding number. Thereafter all papers in that proceeding must bear that title and number.

(Subd (c) amended and relettered effective January 1, 2005; adopted as subd (b) effective January 1, 1974.)

Rule 3.550 amended effective January 1, 2016; adopted as rule 1550 effective January 1, 1974; previously amended effective January 1, 2005; previously amended and renumbered as rule 3.550 effective January 1, 2007.

Division 5
Venue
[Reserved]

Division 6
Proceedings

Chap. 1. General Provisions [Reserved].
Chap. 2. Stay of Proceedings. Rule 3.650.
Chap. 3. Hearings, Conferences, and Proceedings. Rules 3.670, 3.672.
Chap. 4. Special Proceedings on Construction-Related Accessibility Claims. Rules 3.680, 3.682.

Chapter 1
General Provisions
[Reserved]

Chapter 2
Stay of Proceedings

Rule 3.650. Duty to notify court and others of stay
(a) Notice of stay

The party who requested or caused a stay of a proceeding must immediately serve and file a notice of the stay and attach a copy of the order or other document showing that the proceeding is stayed. If the person who requested or caused the stay has not appeared, or is not subject to the jurisdiction of the court, the plaintiff must immediately file a notice of the stay and attach a copy of the order or other document showing that the proceeding is stayed. The notice of stay must be served on all parties who have appeared in the case.

(b) When notice must be provided

The party responsible for giving notice under (a) must provide notice if the case is stayed for any of the following reasons:

(1) An order of a federal court or a higher state court;

(2) Contractual arbitration under Code of Civil Procedure section 1281.4;

(3) Arbitration of attorney fees and costs under Business and Professions Code section 6201; or

(4) Automatic stay caused by a filing in another court, including a federal bankruptcy court.

(Subd (b) amended effective January 1, 2007.)

(c) Contents of notice

The notice must state whether the case is stayed with regard to all parties or only certain parties. If it is stayed with regard to only certain parties, the notice must specifically identify those parties. The notice must also state the reason that the case is stayed.

(Subd (c) amended effective January 1, 2006.)

(d) Notice that stay is terminated or modified

When a stay is vacated, is no longer in effect, or is modified, the party who filed the notice of the stay must immediately serve and file a notice of termination or modification of stay. If that party fails to do so, any other party in the action who has knowledge of the termination or modification of the stay must serve and file a notice of termination or modification of stay. Once one party in the action has served and filed a notice of termination or modification of stay, other parties in the action are not required to do so.

(Subd (d) amended effective January 1, 2006.)

Rule 3.650 amended and renumbered effective January 1, 2007; adopted as rule 224 effective January 1, 2004; previously amended effective January 1, 2006.

Chapter 3
Hearings, Conferences, and Proceedings

Chapter 3 amended effective July 1, 2008.

Rule 3.670. Telephone appearance
Rule 3.672. Remote proceedings

Rule 3.670. Telephone appearance
(a) Policy favoring telephone appearances

The intent of this rule is to promote uniformity in the practices and procedures relating to telephone appearances in civil cases. To improve access to the courts and reduce litigation costs, courts should permit parties, to the extent feasible, to appear by telephone at appropriate conferences, hearings, and proceedings in civil cases.

(Subd (a) adopted effective January 1, 2008.)

(b) Application

Subdivisions (c) through (i) of this rule are suspended from January 1, 2022, to January 1, 2026, during which time the provisions in rule 3.672 apply in their place. This rule applies to all general civil cases as defined in rule 1.6 and to unlawful detainer and probate proceedings.

(Subd (b) amended effective August 4, 2023; previously repealed and adopted as subd (a) effective July 1, 1998; previously relettered effective January 1, 2008; previously amended effective January 1, 1999, January 1, 2001, January 1, 2003, January 1, 2007, and January 1, 2022.)

(c) General provision authorizing parties to appear by telephone

Except as ordered by the court under (f)(2) and subject to (d) (regarding ex parte applications) and (h) (regarding notice), all parties, including moving parties, may appear by telephone at all conferences, hearings, and proceedings other than those where personal appearances are required under (e).

(Subd (c) amended effective January 1, 2014; previously repealed and adopted as subd (b) effective July 1, 1998; previously amended effective July 1, 1999, and January 1, 2003; previously amended and relettered effective January 1, 2008.)

(d) Provisions regarding ex parte applications

(1) *Applicants*

Except as ordered by the court under (f)(2) and subject to (h), applicants seeking an ex parte order may appear by telephone provided that the moving papers have been filed and a proposed order submitted by at least 10:00 a.m. two court days before the ex parte appearance and, if required by local rule, copies have been provided directly to the department in which the matter is to be considered.

(2) *Opposing Parties*

Even if the applicant has not complied with (1), except as ordered by the court under (f)(2) and subject to the provisions in (h), parties opposing an ex parte order may appear by telephone.

(Subd (d) adopted effective January 1, 2014.)

(e) Required personal appearances

(1) Except as permitted by the court under (f)(3), a personal appearance is required for the following hearings, conferences, and proceedings:

(A) Trials, hearings, and proceedings at which witnesses are expected to testify;

(B) Hearings on temporary restraining orders;

(C) Settlement conferences;

(D) Trial management conferences;

(E) Hearings on motions in limine; and

(F) Hearings on petitions to confirm the sale of property under the Probate Code.

(2) In addition, except as permitted by the court under (f)(3), a personal appearance is required for the following persons:

(A) Persons ordered to appear to show cause why sanctions should not be imposed for violation of a court order or a rule; or

(B) Persons ordered to appear in an order or citation issued under the Probate Code.

At the proceedings described under (2), parties who are not required to appear in person under this rule may appear by telephone.

(Subd (e) amended and relettered effective January 1, 2014; adopted as subd (c) effective July 1, 1998; previously amended effective July 1, 2002, and January 1, 2003; previously amended and relettered as subd (d) effective January 1, 2008.)

(f) Court discretion to modify rule

(1) *Policy favoring telephone appearances in civil cases*

In exercising its discretion under this provision, the court should consider the general policy favoring telephone appearances in civil cases.

(2) *Court may require personal appearances*

The court may require a party to appear in person at a hearing, conference, or proceeding listed in (c) or (d) if the court determines on a hearing-by-hearing basis that a personal appearance would materially assist in the determination of the proceedings or in the effective management or resolution of the particular case.

(3) *Court may permit appearances by telephone*

The court may permit a party to appear by telephone at a hearing, conference, or proceeding under (e) if the court determines that a telephone appearance is appropriate.

(Subd (f) amended and relettered effective January 1, 2014; adopted as subd (e) effective January 1, 2008.)

(g) Need for personal appearance

If, at any time during a hearing, conference, or proceeding conducted by telephone, the court determines that a personal appearance is necessary, the court may continue the matter and require a personal appearance.

(Subd (g) relettered effective January 1, 2014; adopted as subd (f) effective January 1, 2014.)

(h) Notice by party

(1) Except as provided in (6), a party choosing to appear by telephone at a hearing, conference, or proceeding, other than on an ex parte application, under this rule must either:

(A) Place the phrase "Telephone Appearance" below the title of the moving, opposing, or reply papers; or

(B) At least two court days before the appearance, notify the court and all other parties of the party's intent to appear by telephone. If the notice is oral, it must be given either in person or by telephone. If the notice is in writing, it must be given by filing a "Notice of Intent to Appear by Telephone" with the court at least two court days before the appearance and by serving the notice by any means authorized by law and reasonably calculated to ensure delivery to the parties at least two court days before the appearance.

(2) If after receiving notice from another party as provided under (1) a party that has not given notice also decides to appear by telephone, the

party may do so by notifying the court and all other parties that have appeared in the action, no later than noon on the court day before the appearance, of its intent to appear by telephone.

(3) An applicant choosing to appear by telephone at an ex parte appearance under this rule must:

(A) Place the phrase "Telephone Appearance" below the title of the application papers;

(B) File and serve the papers in such a way that they will be received by the court and all parties by no later than 10:00 a.m. two court days before the ex parte appearance; and

(C) If provided by local rule, ensure that copies of the papers are received in the department in which the matter is to be considered.

(4) Any party other than an applicant choosing to appear by telephone at an ex parte appearance under this rule must notify the court and all other parties that have appeared in the action, no later than 2:00 p.m. or the "close of business" (as that term is defined in rule 2.250(b)(10)), whichever is earlier, on the court day before the appearance, of its intent to appear by telephone. If the notice is oral, it must be given either in person or by telephone. If the notice is in writing, it must be given by filing a "Notice of Intent to Appear by Telephone" with the court and by serving the notice on all other parties by any means authorized by law reasonably calculated to ensure delivery to the parties no later than 2:00 p.m. or "the close of business" (as that term is defined in rule 2.250(b)(10)), whichever is earlier, on the court day before the appearance.

(5) If a party that has given notice that it intends to appear by telephone under (1) subsequently chooses to appear in person, the party may appear in person.

(6) A party may ask the court for leave to appear by telephone without the notice provided for under (1)–(4). The court should permit the party to appear by telephone upon a showing of good cause or unforeseen circumstances.

(Subd (h) amended effective January 1, 2016; adopted as subd (d) effective July 1, 1998; previously amended effective January 1, 1999, July 1, 1999, January 1, 2003, and January 1, 2007; previously amended and relettered subd (g) effective January 1, 2008, and subd (h) effective January 1, 2014.)

(i) Notice by court

After a party has requested a telephone appearance under (h), if the court requires the personal appearance of the party, the court must give reasonable notice to all parties before the hearing and may continue the hearing if necessary to accommodate the personal appearance. The court may direct the court clerk, a court-appointed vendor, a party, or an attorney to provide the notification. In courts using a telephonic tentative ruling system for law and motion matters, court notification that parties must appear in person may be given as part of the court's tentative ruling on a specific law and motion matter if that notification is given one court day before the hearing.

(Subd (i) amended and relettered effective January 1, 2014; adopted as subd (e) effective July 1, 1998; previously amended effective January 1, 1999, and January 1, 2003; previously amended and relettered as subd (h) effective January 1, 2008.)

(j) Fee waivers

(1) *Effect of fee waiver*

A party that has received a fee waiver must not be charged fees for telephone appearances.

(2) *Responsibility of requesting party*

To obtain telephone services without payment of a telephone appearance fee from a vendor or a court that provides telephone appearance services, a party must advise the vendor or the court that he or she has received a fee waiver from the court. If a vendor requests, the party must transmit a copy of the order granting the fee waiver to the vendor.

(3) *Lien on judgment*

If a party based on a fee waiver receives telephone appearance services under this rule without payment of a fee, the vendor or court that provides the telephone appearance services has a lien on any judgment, including a judgment for costs, that the party may receive, in the amount of the fee that the party would have paid for the telephone appearance. There is no charge for filing the lien.

(Subd (j) amended and relettered effective January 1, 2023; adopted as subd (k) effective July 1, 2011; previously amended and relettered as subd (l) effective January 1, 2014.)

(k) Title IV-D proceedings

(1) *Court-provided telephone appearance services*

If a court provides telephone appearance services in a proceeding for child or family support under Title IV-D of the Social Security Act brought by or otherwise involving a local child support agency, the court must not charge a fee for those services.

(2) *Responsibility of requesting party*

When a party in a Title IV-D proceeding requests telephone appearance services from a court or a vendor, the party requesting the services must advise the court or the vendor that the requester is a party in a proceeding for child or family support under Title IV-D brought by or otherwise involving a local child support agency.

(3) *Fee waivers applicable*

The fee waiver provisions in (j) apply to a request by a party in a Title IV-D proceeding for telephone appearance services from a vendor.

(Subd (k) amended and relettered effective January 1, 2023; adopted as subd (l) effective July 1, 2011; previously amended and relettered as subd (m) effective January 1, 2014; previously amended effective July 1, 2013, and January 1, 2019.)

(l) Audibility and procedure

The court must ensure that the statements of participants are audible to all other participants and the court staff and that the statements made by a participant are identified as being made by that participant.

(Subd (l) relettered effective January 1, 2023; adopted as subd (f); previously amended effective January 1, 2003, and January 1, 2007; previously amended and relettered as subd (j) effective January 1, 2008; previously relettered as subd (c) effective January 1, 1989, as subd (g) effective July 1, 1998, as subd (m) effective July 1, 2011, and as subd (n) effective January 1, 2014.)

(m) Reporting

All proceedings involving telephone appearances must be reported to the same extent and in the same manner as if the participants had appeared in person.

(Subd (m) relettered effective January 1, 2023; adopted as subd (h) effective July 1, 1998; previously amended effective January 1, 2003; previously relettered as subd (k) effective January 1, 2008, as subd (n) effective July 1, 2011, and as subd (o) effective January 1, 2014.)

(n) Conference call vendor or vendors

A court, by local rule, may designate the conference call vendor or vendors that must be used for telephone appearances.

(Subd (n) relettered effective January 1, 2023; adopted as subd (i) effective July 1, 1998; previously amended effective January 1, 1999, and January 1, 2003; previously relettered as subd (l) effective January 1, 2008, and as subd (p) effective January 1, 2014; previously amended and relettered as subd (o) effective July 1, 2011.)

(o) Information on telephone appearances

The court must publish notice providing parties with the particular information necessary for them to appear by telephone at conferences, hearings, and proceedings in that court under this rule.

(Subd (o) relettered effective January 1, 2023; adopted as subd (j); previously amended effective January 1, 2003, and January 1, 2007; previously amended and relettered as subd (m) effective January 1, 2008; previously relettered as subd (p) effective July 1, 2011, and as subd (q) effective January 1, 2014.)

Rule 3.670 amended effective August 4, 2023; adopted as rule 298 effective March 1, 1988; previously amended and renumbered as rule 3.670 effective January 1, 2007; previously amended effective January 1, 1989, July 1, 1998, January 1, 1999, July 1, 1999, January 1, 2001, July 1, 2002, January 1, 2003, January 1, 2008, July 1, 2011, July 1, 2013, January 1, 2014, January 1, 2016, January 1, 2019, January 1, 2022, and January 1, 2023.

Advisory Committee Comment

This rule does not apply to criminal or juvenile matters, and it also does not apply to family law matters, except in certain respects as provided in rule 5.324 relating to telephone appearances in proceedings for child or family support under Title IV-D of the Social Security Act. (See Cal. Rules of Court, rule 3.670(b) [rule applies to general civil cases and unlawful detainer and probate proceedings]; rule 5.324(j) [subdivisions (j)–(q) of rule 3.670 apply to telephone appearances in Title IV-D proceedings].)

Subdivision (d). The inclusion of ex parte applications in this rule is intended to address only the way parties may appear and is not intended to alter the way courts handle ex parte applications.

Subdivision (h). Under subdivision (h)(6), good cause should be construed consistent with the policy in (a) and in Code of Civil Procedure section 367.5(a) favoring telephone appearances. Some examples of good cause to appear by telephone without notice include personal or family illness, death in the family, natural disasters, and unexpected transportation delays or interruption.

Rule 3.672. Remote proceedings

(a) Purpose

The intent of this rule is to promote greater consistency in the practices and procedures relating to remote appearances and proceedings in civil cases subject to Code of Civil Procedure section 367.75. To improve access to the courts and reduce litigation costs, to the extent feasible courts should permit parties to appear remotely at conferences, hearings, and proceedings in civil cases consistent with Code of Civil Procedure section 367.75.

(Subd (a) amended effective August 4, 2023; adopted effective January 1, 2022.)

(b) Application

(1) This rule applies to all civil cases subject to Code of Civil Procedure section 367.75. Provisions that apply specifically to juvenile dependency proceedings are set out in (i). This rule does not apply to proceedings in matters subject to Code of Civil Procedure section 367.76 or Welfare and Institutions Code section 679.5.

(2) Nothing in this rule limits a requirement or right established by statute or case law to an appearance in one manner, either remote or in person, to the exclusion of the other.

(3) Nothing in this rule modifies current rules, statutes, or case law regarding confidentiality or access to confidential proceedings.

(Subd (b) amended effective August 4, 2023; adopted effective January 1, 2022.)

(c) Definitions

As used in this rule:

(1) "Civil case" is any case subject to Code of Civil Procedure section 367.75.

(2) "Evidentiary hearing or trial" is any proceeding at which oral testimony may be provided.

(3) "Oral testimony" is a spoken statement provided under oath and subject to examination.

(4) "Party" is, except in (i), as defined in rule 1.6(15), meaning any person appearing in an action and that person's counsel, as well as any nonparty who is subject to discovery in the action.

(5) "Proceeding" means a conference, hearing, or any other matter before the court, including an evidentiary hearing or trial.

(6) "Remote appearance" or "appear remotely" means the appearance of a party at a proceeding through the use of remote technology.

(7) "Remote proceeding" means a proceeding conducted in whole or in part through the use of remote technology.

(8) "Remote technology" means technology that provides for the transmission of video and audio signals or audio signals alone. This phrase is meant to be interpreted broadly and includes a computer, tablet, telephone, cellphone, or other electronic or communications device.

(Subd (c) amended effective August 4, 2023; adopted effective January 1, 2022.)

(d) Court discretion to require in-person appearance

Notwithstanding the other provisions of this rule and except as otherwise required by law, the court may require a party to appear in person at a proceeding subject to this rule in any of the following circumstances:

(1) If the court determines on a hearing-by-hearing basis that an in-person appearance would materially assist in the determination of the proceeding or in the effective management or resolution of the case.

(2) If the court does not have the technology to conduct the proceeding remotely, or if the quality of the technology prevents the effective management or resolution of the proceeding.

(3) If, at any time during a remote proceeding, the court determines that an in-person appearance is necessary, the court may continue the matter and require such an appearance. Such determination may be based on the factors listed in Code of Civil Procedure section 367.75(b).

(Subd (d) amended effective August 4, 2023; adopted effective January 1, 2022.)

(e) Local court rules for remote proceedings

(1) Except for juvenile dependency cases, a court may by local rule prescribe procedures for remote proceedings subject to this rule, so long as the procedures are consistent with the requirements of Code of Civil Procedure section 367.75, posted on the court's website, and include the following provisions:

(A) A requirement that notice of intent to appear remotely be given to the court and to all parties or persons entitled to receive notice of the proceedings;

(B) A clear description of the amount of notice required; and

(C) For evidentiary hearing and trials, an opportunity for parties to oppose the remote proceedings.

(2) If local procedures include written notice, any mandatory Judicial Council forms must be used.

(3) For juvenile dependency cases, a court may by local rule prescribe procedures for remote proceedings as long as the procedures are posted on the court's website and consistent with Code of Civil Procedure section 367.75 and subdivision (i).

(4) Notwithstanding the requirements of rule 10.613, courts may adopt or amend a local rule under this subdivision for an effective date other than January 1 or July 1 and without a 45-day comment period if the court:

(A) Posts notice of the adoption of the new or amended rule prominently on the court's website, along with a copy of the rule and the effective date of the new or amended rule;

(B) Distributes the rule to the organizations identified in rule 10.613(g)(2) on or before the effective date of the new rule or amendment; and

(C) Provides a copy of the rule to the Judicial Council.

No litigant's substantive rights may be prejudiced for failing to comply with a rule adopted or amended under this paragraph until at least 20 days after the rule change has been posted and distributed.

(5) Notwithstanding (1) and rule 10.613, any local court procedures consistent with Code of Civil Procedure section 367.75 and posted on the court's website may continue in effect until March 31, 2022, or until such earlier date by which a court has adopted a local rule under (1)-(3).

(Subd (e) amended effective August 4, 2023; adopted effective January 1, 2022.)

(f) Notice and waiver for duration of case

(1) *Notice for remote appearances for duration of case*

At any time during a case subject to this rule, a party may provide notice to the court and all other parties or persons who are entitled to receive notice of the proceedings that the party intends to appear remotely for the duration of a case. Such notice must be provided with at least as much advance notice as required in (g), (h), or (i), or by local court rules or procedures.

(A) *Notice process*

Notice must be given either orally during a court proceeding or by service on all other parties or persons who are entitled to receive notice of the proceedings and filing with the court a *Notice of Remote Appearance* (form RA-010). If any party appears in the case after this notice has been given, form RA-010 must be served on that party. Service may be by any means authorized by law.

(B) *Court's local procedures*

This notice does not exempt a party from following a court's local procedures, as posted on its website, for providing notice of intent to appear remotely at a particular proceeding, if the court has such a procedure.

(2) *Waiver of Notice*

At any time during a case, all parties to an action may stipulate to waive notice of any other participants' remote appearance. This stipulation may be made orally during a court proceeding or in writing filed with the court.

(Subd (f) amended effective August 4, 2023; adopted effective January 1, 2022.)

(g) Remote proceedings other than an evidentiary hearing or trial

(1) *Applicable rules*

This subdivision applies to any proceeding subject to this rule other than an evidentiary hearing or trial, unless one of the following applies:

(A) The court has applicable local procedures or local rules under (e);

(B) The proceeding is a juvenile dependency proceeding governed by (i);

(C) The person intending to appear remotely has provided a notice for remote appearances for the duration of the case or all parties have stipulated to a waiver of notice under (f);

(D) The court permits a party to appear remotely under (j)(2).

(2) *Required notice*

(A) *Hearing with at least three court days' notice*

(i) *Notice to appear remotely*

A party choosing to appear remotely in a proceeding under this subdivision for which a party gives or receives notice of the proceeding at least three court days before the hearing date, must provide notice of the party's intent to appear remotely at least two court days before the proceeding.

(ii) *Notice process*

Notice to the court must be given by filing a *Notice of Remote Appearance* (form RA-010). Notice to the other parties may be provided in writing, electronically, or orally in a way reasonably calculated to ensure notice is received no later than two court days before the proceeding.

(B) *Hearing with less than three court days' notice*

(i) *Notice by moving party*

a. *Notice to appear remotely*

A moving party or applicant choosing to appear remotely in a proceeding under this subdivision for which a party gives or receives notice of less than three court days must provide notice of the party's intent to appear remotely at the same time as providing notice of the application or other moving papers.

b. *Notice process*

Notice to the court must be given by filing a *Notice of Remote Appearance* (form RA-010). Notice to the other parties may be provided in writing, electronically, or orally in a way reasonably calculated to ensure notice is received with notice of the moving papers.

(ii) *Notice by other parties*

a. *Notice to appear remotely*

Any party choosing to appear remotely at a hearing governed by (B), other than an applicant or moving party, must provide notice of their intent to appear remotely to the court and all other parties that have appeared in the action, no later than 2:00 p.m. on the court day before the proceeding.

b. *Notice process*

The notice to the court may be given orally or in writing by filing *Notice of Remote Appearance* (form RA-010). Notice to the other parties may be in writing, electronically, or orally in a way reasonably calculated to ensure notice is received no later than 2:00 p.m. on the court day before the proceeding.

(C) *Proof of notice*

A party may use *Notice of Remote Appearance* (form RA-010) to provide proof to the court that notice to other parties was given.

(D) *Delivery to courtroom*

If required by local rule, a party must ensure a copy of any written notice filed under (A) or (B) is received in the department in which the proceeding is to be held.

(*Subd (g) amended effective August 4, 2023; adopted effective January 1, 2022.*)

(h) *Remote proceedings for an evidentiary hearing or trial*

(1) *Court notice of remote proceeding*

A court intending to conduct an evidentiary hearing or trial remotely in a case subject to this rule must provide notice by one of the following means:

(A) By providing notice to all parties who have appeared in the action or who are entitled to receive notice of the proceedings, at least 10 court days before the hearing or trial date, unless the hearing or trial is on less than 10 court days' notice, in which case at least two court days' notice of remote proceedings is required; or

(B) By local rule providing that certain evidentiary hearings or trials are to be held remotely, so long as the court procedure includes a process for self-represented parties to agree to their remote appearance and for parties to show why remote appearances or testimony should not be allowed.

(2) *Party notice of remote proceeding*

(A) *Applicable rules*

This subdivision applies to all evidentiary hearings and trials in a case subject to this rule unless one of the following applies:

(i) The court has applicable local procedures or local rules under (e);

(ii) The proceeding is a juvenile dependency proceeding governed by (i);

(iii) The person intending to appear remotely has provided a notice for remote appearances for the duration of the case or all parties have stipulated to a waiver of notice under (f);

(iv) The court permits a party to appear remotely under (j)(2).

(B) *Motion*

The notice described in this subdivision serves as the motion by a party under Code of Civil Procedure section 367.75(d).

(C) *Hearings or trials with at least 15 court days' notice and small claims trials*

(i) *Time of notice*

A party choosing to appear remotely at a small claims trial or an evidentiary hearing or trial for which a party gives or receives notice of the proceeding at least 15 court days before the hearing or trial date must provide notice of the party's intent to appear remotely at least 10 court days before the hearing or trial.

(ii) *Notice process*

Notice to the court must be given by filing a *Notice of Remote Appearance* (form RA-010). Notice to the other parties may be in writing, electronically, or orally in a way reasonably calculated to ensure notice is received at least 10 court days before the proceeding. A party may use *Notice of Remote Appearance* (form RA-010) to provide proof to the court that notice to other parties was given.

(D) *Hearings or trials held on less than 15 court days' notice*

A party choosing to appear remotely in an evidentiary hearing or trial for which a party gives or receives notice of the proceeding less than 15 court days before the hearing or trial date, including hearings on restraining orders or protective orders, must provide notice of the party's intent to appear remotely in one of the following ways:

(i) As provided in (g)(2)(B); or

(ii) By filing a *Notice of Remote Appearance* (form RA-010) and providing notice to the other parties in writing, electronically, or orally in a way reasonably calculated to ensure notice is received at least five court days before the proceeding.

(3) *Opposition to remote proceedings*

(A) *Filing and serving opposition*

In response to notice of a remote proceeding for an evidentiary hearing or trial in a case subject to this rule, whether set by local rule or otherwise noticed under (h)(1) or (2), or to obtain a court order for in-person appearance, a party may make a showing to the court as to why a remote appearance or remote testimony should not be allowed, by serving and filing an *Opposition to Remote Proceeding at Evidentiary Hearing or Trial* (form RA-015) by:

(i) At least five court days before the proceeding if for an evidentiary hearing or trial for which a party gives or receives at least 15 court days' notice; or

(ii) At least noon the court day before the proceeding if for an evidentiary hearing or trial for which a party gives or receives less than 15 court days' notice.

(iii) If required by local rule, a party must ensure a copy of any opposition is received in the department in which the proceeding is to be held.

(B) *Court determination on opposition*

In determining whether to conduct an evidentiary hearing or trial in whole or in part through the use of remote technology over opposition, the court must consider the factors in section 367.75(b) and (f), and any limited access to technology or transportation asserted by a party. The court may not require a party to appear through remote technology.

(*Subd (h) amended effective August 4, 2023; adopted effective January 1, 2022.*)

(i) *Remote proceedings in juvenile dependency*

(1) *General provisions*

(A) This subdivision applies to any juvenile dependency proceeding. A court may adopt local rules as provided in (e) to prescribe procedures for remote juvenile dependency proceedings.

(B) The definitions in (c) apply, except that, for purposes of this subdivision, a "party" is any of the following persons and that person's counsel:

(i) A child or nonminor dependent subject to the proceeding;

(ii) Any parent, Indian custodian, or guardian of a child subject to the proceeding;

(iii) The social worker who filed the petition to commence the juvenile dependency proceedings on behalf of the county child welfare department;

(iv) The tribe of an Indian child subject to the proceeding if the tribe has intervened; and

(v) A de facto parent of a child subject to the proceeding to whom the court has granted party status.

(C) This subdivision does not apply to a juvenile justice proceeding. The provisions in Welfare and Institutions Code section 679.5 and any rules implementing that statute govern a remote appearance in a juvenile justice proceeding.

(2) *Conducting a remote proceeding*

Any juvenile dependency proceeding may be conducted as a remote proceeding, as long as the following conditions are met:

(A) The court provides an opportunity for any person authorized to be present to request to appear remotely;

(B) All statutory confidentiality requirements applicable to a juvenile dependency proceeding held in person apply equally to a remote proceeding.

(C) The court does not require any party to appear remotely.

(3) *Option to appear remotely*

(A) If a proceeding is conducted as a remote proceeding, any person entitled to be present under rule 5.530(b) may appear remotely without submitting a request.

(B) Except as provided in (ii), any person entitled under rule 5.530(b) or authorized by court order to be present at a proceeding may request to appear remotely using any means, oral or written, that is reasonably calculated to ensure receipt by the court no later than the time the case is called for hearing.

(i) If the request is in writing, *Request to Appear Remotely—Juvenile Dependency* (form RA-025) may be used.

(ii) A request for a remote appearance by a witness must be made in writing by counsel for the party calling the witness or, if the party does not have counsel, by the party, by filing the request with the court and serving a copy of the request on counsel for all other parties or, if a party does not have counsel, on the party, by any means authorized by law reasonably calculated to ensure receipt no later than close of business three court days before the proceeding.

(4) *Request to compel physical presence*

Any party may ask the court to compel the physical presence of a witness or a party by filing the request in writing with the court and serving a copy of the request on counsel for each party by any means authorized by law reasonably calculated to ensure receipt no later than close of business two court days before the proceeding. *Request to Compel Physical Presence—Juvenile Dependency* (form RA-030) may be used for this purpose.

(5) *Determination of request*

(A) The court must require a witness to appear in person unless all parties to the proceeding have consented to the witness's remote appearance.

(B) The court may require any person to appear in person if the court determines that:

(i) One or more of the factors listed in Code of Civil Procedure section 367.75(b) or (f) or in this rule, including the person's limited access to technology, requires the person's physical presence;

(ii) The court cannot ensure that the person's remote appearance will have the privacy and security necessary to preserve the confidentiality of the proceeding; or

(iii) A remote appearance by the person is likely to cause undue prejudice to a party.

(C) The court must consider a person's ability to appear in person at a proceeding, including any limits to the person's access to transportation, before ordering the person to appear in person.

(Subd (i) amended effective August 4, 2023; adopted effective January 1, 2022.)

(j) Other rules regarding notice

(1) Any party, including a party that has given notice that it intends to appear remotely under (f)-(h) or a person authorized to appear remotely under (i), may choose to appear in person.

(2) Notwithstanding the other provisions of this rule, a party may ask the court for leave to appear remotely without the notice provided for under (f)-(h). The court may permit the party to appear remotely upon a finding of good cause, unforeseen circumstances, or that the remote appearance would promote access to justice.

(Subd (j) adopted effective January 1, 2022.)

(k) Remote appearance fees

(1) *Parties not charged fees*

Parties who, by statute, are not charged filing fees or fees for court services may not be charged a videoconference fee under Government Code section 70630.

(2) *Parties with fee waiver*

(A) When a party has received a fee waiver, that party may not be charged fees for remote appearances.

(B) To obtain remote appearance services without payment of a fee from a vendor or a court that provides such services, a party must advise the vendor or the court that they have received a fee waiver from the court. If a vendor requests, the party must transmit a copy of the order granting the fee waiver to the vendor.

(C) If a party, based on a fee waiver, receives remote appearance services under this rule without payment of a fee, the vendor or court that provides the remote appearance services has a lien on any judgment, including a judgment for costs, that the party may receive, in the amount of the fee that the party would have paid for the remote appearance. There is no charge for filing the lien.

(Subd (k) adopted effective January 1, 2022.)

(*l*) Vendor or platform

A court, by local rule, may designate the vendors or platforms that must be used for remote appearances or the location on its website where such information may be found.

(Subd (l) adopted effective January 1, 2022.)

(m) Court information on remote appearances

The court must publish notice online providing parties with the information necessary to appear remotely at proceedings in that court under this rule. The notice should include information regarding in which departments, types of proceedings, or types of cases the court has the technological capability to allow remote appearances, and the vendors or platforms that must be used, including whether there are limitations to using them concurrently.

(Subd (m) adopted effective January 1, 2022.)

Rule 3.672 amended effective August 4, 2023; adopted effective January 1, 2022.

Advisory Committee Comment

Subdivision (h). Nothing in this rule, including time frames provided in subdivision (h), is intended to preclude a court or party from discussing the use of remote appearances and testimony at any time during an action, including at case management conferences and status conferences.

Subdivision (k). Statutes currently provide that courts are not to charge fees to certain types of parties, such as governmental entities; representatives of tribes in cases covered by the Indian Child Welfare Act; and parties in certain types of cases, such as juvenile cases or actions to prevent domestic violence. This rule would preclude courts from charging videoconference fees to such parties as well.

Chapter 4
Special Proceedings on Construction-Related Accessibility Claims

Title 3, Civil Rules—Division 6, Proceedings—Chapter 4, Special Proceedings on Construction-Related Accessibility Claims; adopted effective July 1, 2013.

Rule 3.680. Service of Notice of Stay and Early Evaluation Conference
Rule 3.682. Notice of Mandatory Evaluation Conferences

Rule 3.680. Service of Notice of Stay and Early Evaluation Conference

(a) Service of Application and Notice

The defendant who requested a stay and early evaluation conference on a construction-related claim under Civil Code section 55.54 must, within 10 days of issuance of the notice, serve on all other parties the application for stay and any *Notice of Stay of Proceedings and Early Evaluation Conference* (form DAL-010) issued by the court.

(Subd (a) adopted effective July 1, 2013.)

(b) Filing Proof of Service

A proof of service must be filed with the court 15 days before the date set for the early evaluation conference. *Proof of Service—Disability Access Litigation* (form DAL-012) may be used to show service of the documents.

(Subd (b) adopted effective July 1, 2013.)

Rule 3.680 adopted effective July 1, 2013.

Rule 3.682. Notice of Mandatory Evaluation Conferences

(a) Service of Application and Notice

The party who requested a mandatory evaluation conference on a construction-related accessibility claim under Civil Code section 55.545 must, within 10 days of issuance of the notice, serve on all other parties the application and any *Notice of Mandatory Evaluation Conference* (form DAL-020) issued by the court.

(Subd (a) adopted effective July 1, 2013.)

(b) Filing Proof of Service

A proof of service must be filed with the court 15 days before the date set for the early evaluation conference. *Proof of Service—Disability Access Litigation* (form DAL-012) may be used to show service of the documents.

(Subd (b) adopted effective July 1, 2013.)

Rule 3.682 adopted effective July 1, 2013.

Division 7
Civil Case Management

Chap. 1. General Provisions. Rule 3.700.
Chap. 2. Differential Case Management. Rules 3.710–3.715.
Chap. 3. Case Management. Rules 3.720–3.735.
Chap. 4. Management of Collections Cases. Rules 3.740, 3.741.
Chap. 5. Management of Complex Cases. Rules 3.750, 3.751.
Chap. 6. Management of Class Actions. Rules 3.760–3.771.

Chapter 1
General Provisions

Rule 3.700. Scope and purpose of the case management rules

The rules in this division are to be construed and administered to secure the fair, timely, and efficient disposition of every civil case. The rules are to be applied in a fair, practical, and flexible manner so as to achieve the ends of justice.

Rule 3.700 amended and renumbered effective January 1, 2007; adopted as rule 204 effective January 1, 2004.

Chapter 2
Differential Case Management

Rule 3.710. Authority
Rule 3.711. Local court rules
Rule 3.712. Application and exceptions
Rule 3.713. Delay reduction goals
Rule 3.714. Differentiation of cases to achieve goals
Rule 3.715. Case evaluation factors

Rule 3.710. Authority

The rules in this chapter implement Government Code section 68603(c) under the Trial Court Delay Reduction Act of 1990.

Rule 3.710 amended and renumbered effective January 1, 2007; adopted as rule 2101 effective July 1, 1991; previously amended and renumbered as rule 205 effective July 1, 2002.

Rule 3.711. Local court rules

Each court must adopt local rules on differential case management as provided in this chapter consistent with the rules on case management in chapter 3 of this division and standard 2.1 of the California Standards of Judicial Administration.

Rule 3.711 amended and renumbered effective January 1, 2007; adopted as rule 2102 effective July 1, 1991; previously amended effective January 1, 1994, and January 1, 2000; previously amended and renumbered as rule 206 effective July 1, 2002.

Rule 3.712. Application and exceptions

(a) General application

The rules in this chapter apply to all general civil cases filed in the trial courts except those specified in (b), (c), and (d) and except those specified types or categories of general civil cases that have been exempted from the case management rules under rule 3.720(b).

(Subd (a) amended effective February 26, 2013; previously amended effective January 1, 1994, July 1, 2002, January 1, 2007, and July 1, 2007.)

(b) Uninsured motorist cases

To allow for arbitration of the plaintiff's claim, the rules in this chapter do not apply to a case designated by the court as "uninsured motorist" until 180 days after the designation.

(Subd (b) amended and relettered effective January 1, 2007; adopted as subd (c) effective July 1, 1991; previously amended effective July 1, 2002.)

(c) Coordinated cases

The rules in this chapter do not apply to any case included in a petition for coordination. If the petition is granted, the coordination trial judge may establish a case progression plan for the cases, which may be assigned for review under the case management rules in chapter 3 of this division or, after appropriate findings, for treatment as an exceptional case.

(Subd (c) amended and relettered effective January 1, 2007; adopted as subd (d) effective July 1, 1991; previously amended effective July 1, 2002.)

(d) Collections cases

The rules in this chapter do not apply to a collections case, as defined in rule 3.740(a), unless a defendant files a responsive pleading.

(Subd (d) adopted effective July 1, 2007.)

Rule 3.712 amended effective February 26, 2013; adopted as rule 2103 effective July 1, 1991; previously amended and renumbered as rule 207 effective July 1, 2002, and amended and renumbered effective January 1, 2007; previously amended effective January 1, 1994, and July 1, 2007.

Rule 3.713. Delay reduction goals

(a) Case management goals

The rules in this chapter are adopted to advance the goals of Government Code section 68607 and standard 2.1 of the California Standards of Judicial Administration.

(Subd (a) amended effective January 1, 2007; previously amended effective July 1, 2002.)

(b) Case disposition time goals

The goal of the court is to manage general civil cases from filing to disposition as provided under standard 2.2 of the California Standards of Judicial Administration.

(Subd (b) amended effective January 1, 2007; previously amended effective January 1, 1994, July 1, 2002, and January 1, 2004.)

(c) Judges' responsibility

It is the responsibility of judges to achieve a just and effective resolution of each general civil case through active management and supervision of the pace of litigation from the date of filing to disposition.

(Subd (c) amended effective July 1, 2002.)

Rule 3.713 amended and renumbered effective January 1, 2007; adopted as rule 2104 effective July 1, 1991; previously amended and renumbered as rule 208 effective July 1, 2003; previously amended effective January 1, 1994, and January 1, 2004.

Rule 3.714. Differentiation of cases to achieve goals

(a) Evaluation and assignment

The court must evaluate each case on its own merits as provided in rule 3.715, under procedures adopted by local court rules. After evaluation, the court must:

(1) Assign the case to the case management program for review under the case management rules in chapter 3 of this division for disposition under the case disposition time goals in (b) of this rule;

(2) Exempt the case as an exceptional case under (c) of this rule from the case disposition time goals specified in rule 3.713(b) and monitor it with the goal of disposing of it within three years; or

(3) Assign the case under (d) of this rule to a local case management plan for disposition within six to nine months after filing.

(Subd (a) amended effective January 1, 2007; previously amended effective July 1, 2002, and January 1, 2004.)

(b) Civil case disposition time goals

Civil cases assigned for review under the case management rules in chapter 3 of this division should be managed so as to achieve the following goals:

(1) *Unlimited civil cases*

The goal of each trial court should be to manage unlimited civil cases from filing so that:

(A) 75 percent are disposed of within 12 months;
(B) 85 percent are disposed of within 18 months; and
(C) 100 percent are disposed of within 24 months.

(2) *Limited civil cases*

The goal of each trial court should be to manage limited civil cases from filing so that:

(A) 90 percent are disposed of within 12 months;
(B) 98 percent are disposed of within 18 months; and
(C) 100 percent are disposed of within 24 months.

(3) *Individualized case management*

The goals in (1) and (2) are guidelines for the court's disposition of all unlimited and limited civil cases filed in that court. In managing individual civil cases, the court must consider each case on its merits. To enable the fair and efficient resolution of civil cases, each case should be set for trial as soon as appropriate for that individual case consistent with rule 3.729.

(Subd (b) amended effective January 1, 2007; previously amended effective July 1, 2002, and January 1, 2004.)

(c) Exemption of exceptional cases

(1) The court may in the interest of justice exempt a general civil case from the case disposition time goals under rule 3.713(b) if it finds the case involves exceptional circumstances that will prevent the court and the parties from meeting the goals and deadlines imposed by the program. In making the determination, the court is guided by rules 3.715 and 3.400.

(2) If the court exempts the case from the case disposition time goals, the court must establish a case progression plan and monitor the case to ensure timely disposition consistent with the exceptional circumstances, with the goal of disposing of the case within three years.

(Subd (c) amended effective January 1, 2007; adopted as subd (d) effective July 1, 1991; previously amended effective January 1, 2000, and July 1, 2002; previously amended and relettered as subd (c) effective January 1, 2004.)

(d) Local case management plan for expedited case disposition

(1) For expedited case disposition, the court may by local rule adopt a case management plan that establishes a goal for disposing of appropriate cases within six to nine months after filing. The plan must establish a procedure to identify the cases to be assigned to the plan.

(2) The plan must be used only for uncomplicated cases amenable to early disposition that do not need a case management conference or review or similar event to guide the case to early resolution.

(Subd (d) amended and relettered effective January 1, 2004; adopted as subd (e) effective July 1, 1991; previously amended effective January 1, 1994, and July 1, 2002.)

Rule 3.714 amended and renumbered effective January 1, 2007; adopted as rule 2105 effective July 1, 1991; amended and renumbered as rule 209 effective July 1,

2002; previously amended effective January 1, 1994, January 1, 2000, and January 1, 2004.

Rule 3.715. Case evaluation factors

(a) Time estimate

In applying rule 3.714, the court must estimate the maximum time that will reasonably be required to dispose of each case in a just and effective manner. The court must consider the following factors and any other information the court deems relevant, understanding that no one factor or set of factors will be controlling and that cases may have unique characteristics incapable of precise definition:

(1) Type and subject matter of the action;
(2) Number of causes of action or affirmative defenses alleged;
(3) Number of parties with separate interests;
(4) Number of cross-complaints and the subject matter;
(5) Complexity of issues, including issues of first impression;
(6) Difficulty in identifying, locating, and serving parties;
(7) Nature and extent of discovery anticipated;
(8) Number and location of percipient and expert witnesses;
(9) Estimated length of trial;
(10) Whether some or all issues can be arbitrated or resolved through other alternative dispute resolution processes;
(11) Statutory priority for the issues;
(12) Likelihood of review by writ or appeal;
(13) Amount in controversy and the type of remedy sought, including measures of damages;
(14) Pendency of other actions or proceedings that may affect the case;
(15) Nature and extent of law and motion proceedings anticipated;
(16) Nature and extent of the injuries and damages;
(17) Pendency of underinsured claims; and
(18) Any other factor that would affect the time for disposition of the case.

(Subd (a) amended and lettered effective January 1, 2007; adopted as untitled subd effective July 1, 1991.)

Rule 3.715 amended and renumbered effective January 1, 2007; adopted as rule 2106 effective July 1, 1991; previously amended and renumbered as rule 210 effective July 1, 2002.

Chapter 3
Case Management

Rule 3.720. Application
Rule 3.721. Case management review
Rule 3.722. Case management conference
Rule 3.723. Additional case management conferences
Rule 3.724. Duty to meet and confer
Rule 3.725. Case Management Statement
Rule 3.726. Stipulation to alternative dispute resolution
Rule 3.727. Subjects to be considered at the case management conference
Rule 3.728. Case management order
Rule 3.729. Setting the trial date
Rule 3.730. Case management order controls
Rule 3.734. Assignment to one judge for all or limited purposes
Rule 3.735. Management of short cause cases

Rule 3.720. Application

(a) General application

The rules in this chapter prescribe the procedures for the management of all applicable court cases. These rules may be referred to as "the case management rules."

(Subd (a) amended and lettered effective February 26, 2013; adopted as unlettered subd effective January 1, 2007.)

(b) Suspension of rules

A court by local rule may exempt specified types or categories of general civil cases from the case management rules in this chapter, provided that the court has in place alternative procedures for case processing and trial setting for such actions, including, without limitation, compliance with Code of Civil Procedure sections 1141.10 et seq. and 1775 et seq. The court must include the alternative procedures in its local rules.

(Subd (b) amended effective January 1, 2020; adopted effective February 26, 2013; previously amended effective January 1, 2016.)

(c) Rules when case management conference set

In any case in which a court sets an initial case management conference, the rules in this chapter apply.

(Subd (c) adopted effective February 26, 2013.)

Rule 3.720 amended effective January 1, 2020; adopted effective January 1, 2007; previously amended effective February 26, 2013, and January 1, 2016.

Rule 3.721. Case management review

In every general civil case except complex cases and cases exempted under rules 3.712(b)–(d), 3.714(c)–(d), 3.735(b), 2.573(e), and 3.740(c), the court must review the case no later than 180 days after the filing of the initial complaint.

Rule 3.721 amended effective July 1, 2007; adopted effective January 1, 2007.

Rule 3.722. Case management conference

(a) The initial conference

In each case, the court must set an initial case management conference to review the case. At the conference, the court must review the case comprehensively and decide whether to assign the case to an alternative dispute resolution process, whether to set the case for trial, and whether to take action regarding any of the other matters identified in rules 3.727 and 3.728. The initial case management conference should generally be the first case management event conducted by court order in each case, except for orders to show cause.

(Subd (a) adopted effective January 1, 2007.)

(b) Notice of the initial conference

Notice of the date of the initial case management conference must be given to all parties no later than 45 days before the conference, unless otherwise ordered by the court. The court may provide by local rule for the time and manner of giving notice to the parties.

(Subd (b) adopted effective January 1, 2007.)

(c) Preparation for the conference

At the conference, counsel for each party and each self-represented party must appear in person or remotely as provided in rule 3.672; must be familiar with the case; and must be prepared to discuss and commit to the party's position on the issues listed in rules 3.724 and 3.727.

(Subd (c) amended effective January 21, 2022; adopted effective January 1, 2007; previously amended effective January 1, 2008.)

(d) Case management order without appearance

If, based on its review of the written submissions of the parties and such other information as is available, the court determines that appearances at the conference are not necessary, the court may issue a case management order and notify the parties that no appearance is required.

(Subd (d) adopted effective January 1, 2007.)

(e) Option to excuse attendance at initial conferences in limited civil cases

By local rule the court may provide that counsel and self-represented parties are not to attend an initial case management conference in limited civil cases unless ordered to do so by the court.

(Subd (e) adopted effective January 1, 2007.)

Rule 3.722 amended effective January 21, 2022; adopted effective January 1, 2007; previously amended effective January 1, 2008.

Rule 3.723. Additional case management conferences

The court on its own motion may order, or a party or parties may request, that an additional case management conference be held at any time. A party should be required to appear at an additional conference only if an appearance is necessary for the effective management of the case. In determining whether to hold an additional conference, the court must consider each case individually on its own merits.

Rule 3.723 adopted effective January 1, 2007.

Advisory Committee Comment

Regarding additional case management conferences, in many civil cases one initial conference and one other conference before trial will be sufficient. But in other cases, including complicated or difficult cases, the court may order an additional case management conference or conferences if that would promote the fair and efficient administration of the case.

Rule 3.724. Duty to meet and confer

Unless the court orders another time period, no later than 30 calendar days before the date set for the initial case management conference, the parties must meet and confer, in person or by telephone, to consider each of the issues identified in rule 3.727 and, in addition, to consider the following:

(1) Resolving any discovery disputes and setting a discovery schedule;
(2) Identifying and, if possible, informally resolving any anticipated motions;
(3) Identifying the facts and issues in the case that are uncontested and may be the subject of stipulation;
(4) Identifying the facts and issues in the case that are in dispute;

(5) Determining whether the issues in the case can be narrowed by eliminating any claims or defenses by means of a motion or otherwise;

(6) Determining whether settlement is possible;

(7) Identifying the dates on which all parties and their attorneys are available or not available for trial, including the reasons for unavailability;

(8) Any issues relating to the discovery of electronically stored information, including:

(A) Issues relating to the preservation of discoverable electronically stored information;

(B) The form or forms in which information will be produced;

(C) The time within which the information will be produced;

(D) The scope of discovery of the information;

(E) The method for asserting or preserving claims of privilege or attorney work product, including whether such claims may be asserted after production;

(F) The method for asserting or preserving the confidentiality, privacy, trade secrets, or proprietary status of information relating to a party or person not a party to the civil proceedings;

(G) How the cost of production of electronically stored information is to be allocated among the parties;

(H) Any other issues relating to the discovery of electronically stored information, including developing a proposed plan relating to the discovery of the information; and

(9) Other relevant matters.

Rule 3.724 amended effective August 14, 2009; adopted effective January 1, 2007.

Rule 3.725. Case Management Statement

(a) Timing of statement

No later than 15 calendar days before the date set for the case management conference or review, each party must file a case management statement and serve it on all other parties in the case.

(b) Joint statement

In lieu of each party's filing a separate case management statement, any two or more parties may file a joint statement.

(c) Contents of statement

Parties must use the mandatory *Case Management Statement* (form CM-110). All applicable items on the form must be completed.

Rule 3.725 adopted effective January 1, 2007.

Rule 3.726. Stipulation to alternative dispute resolution

If all parties agree to use an alternative dispute resolution (ADR) process, they must jointly complete the ADR stipulation form provided for under rule 3.221 and file it with the court.

Rule 3.726 adopted effective January 1, 2007.

Rule 3.727. Subjects to be considered at the case management conference

In any case management conference or review conducted under this chapter, the parties must address, if applicable, and the court may take appropriate action with respect to, the following:

(1) Whether there are any related cases;

(2) Whether all parties named in the complaint or cross-complaint have been served, have appeared, or have been dismissed;

(3) Whether any additional parties may be added or the pleadings may be amended;

(4) Whether, if the case is a limited civil case, the economic litigation procedures under Code of Civil Procedure section 90 et seq. will apply to it or the party intends to bring a motion to exempt the case from these procedures;

(5) Whether any other matters (e.g., the bankruptcy of a party) may affect the court's jurisdiction or processing of the case;

(6) Whether the parties have stipulated to, or the case should be referred to, judicial arbitration in courts having a judicial arbitration program or to any other form of alternative dispute resolution (ADR) process and, if so, the date by which the judicial arbitration or other ADR process must be completed;

(7) Whether an early settlement conference should be scheduled and, if so, on what date;

(8) Whether discovery has been completed and, if not, the date by which it will be completed;

(9) What discovery issues are anticipated;

(10) Whether the case should be bifurcated or a hearing should be set for a motion to bifurcate under Code of Civil Procedure section 598;

(11) Whether there are any cross-complaints that are not ready to be set for trial and, if so, whether they should be severed;

(12) Whether the case is entitled to any statutory preference and, if so, the statute granting the preference;

(13) Whether a jury trial is demanded, and, if so, the identity of each party requesting a jury trial;

(14) If the trial date has not been previously set, the date by which the case will be ready for trial and the available trial dates;

(15) The estimated length of trial;

(16) The nature of the injuries;

(17) The amount of damages, including any special or punitive damages;

(18) Any additional relief sought;

(19) Whether there are any insurance coverage issues that may affect the resolution of the case; and

(20) Any other matters that should be considered by the court or addressed in its case management order.

Rule 3.727 adopted effective January 1, 2007.

Rule 3.728. Case management order

The case management conference must be conducted in the manner provided by local rule. The court must enter a case management order setting a schedule for subsequent proceedings and otherwise providing for the management of the case. The order may include appropriate provisions, such as:

(1) Referral of the case to judicial arbitration or other alternative dispute resolution process;

(2) A date for completion of the judicial arbitration process or other alternative dispute resolution process if the case has been referred to such a process;

(3) In the event that a trial date has not previously been set, a date certain for trial if the case is ready to be set for trial;

(4) Whether the trial will be a jury trial or a nonjury trial;

(5) The identity of each party demanding a jury trial;

(6) The estimated length of trial;

(7) Whether all parties necessary to the disposition of the case have been served or have appeared;

(8) The dismissal or severance of unserved or not-appearing defendants from the action;

(9) The names and addresses of the attorneys who will try the case;

(10) The date, time, and place for a mandatory settlement conference as provided in rule 3.1380;

(11) The date, time, and place for the final case management conference before trial if such a conference is required by the court or the judge assigned to the case;

(12) The date, time, and place of any further case management conferences or review; and

(13) Any additional orders that may be appropriate, including orders on matters listed in rules 3.724 and 3.727.

Rule 3.728 adopted effective January 1, 2007.

Rule 3.729. Setting the trial date

In setting a case for trial, the court, at the initial case management conference or at any other proceeding at which the case is set for trial, must consider all the facts and circumstances that are relevant. These may include:

(1) The type and subject matter of the action to be tried;

(2) Whether the case has statutory priority;

(3) The number of causes of action, cross-actions, and affirmative defenses that will be tried;

(4) Whether any significant amendments to the pleadings have been made recently or are likely to be made before trial;

(5) Whether the plaintiff intends to bring a motion to amend the complaint to seek punitive damages under Code of Civil Procedure section 425.13;

(6) The number of parties with separate interests who will be involved in the trial;

(7) The complexity of the issues to be tried, including issues of first impression;

(8) Any difficulties in identifying, locating, or serving parties;

(9) Whether all parties have been served and, if so, the date by which they were served;

(10) Whether all parties have appeared in the action and, if so, the date by which they appeared;

(11) How long the attorneys who will try the case have been involved in the action;

(12) The trial date or dates proposed by the parties and their attorneys;

(13) The professional and personal schedules of the parties and their attorneys, including any conflicts with previously assigned trial dates or other significant events;

(14) The amount of discovery, if any, that remains to be conducted in the case;

(15) The nature and extent of law and motion proceedings anticipated, including whether any motions for summary judgment will be filed;

(16) Whether any other actions or proceedings that are pending may affect the case;

(17) The amount in controversy and the type of remedy sought;

(18) The nature and extent of the injuries or damages, including whether these are ready for determination;

(19) The court's trial calendar, including the pendency of other trial dates;

(20) Whether the trial will be a jury or a nonjury trial;

(21) The anticipated length of trial;

(22) The number, availability, and locations of witnesses, including witnesses who reside outside the county, state, or country;

(23) Whether there have been any previous continuances of the trial or delays in setting the case for trial;

(24) The achievement of a fair, timely, and efficient disposition of the case; and

(25) Any other factor that would significantly affect the determination of the appropriate date of trial.

Rule 3.729 adopted effective January 1, 2007.

Rule 3.730. Case management order controls

The order issued after the case management conference or review controls the subsequent course of the action or proceeding unless it is modified by a subsequent order.

Rule 3.730 adopted effective January 1, 2007.

Rule 3.734. Assignment to one judge for all or limited purposes

The presiding judge may, on the noticed motion of a party or on the court's own motion, order the assignment of any case to one judge for all or such limited purposes as will promote the efficient administration of justice.

Rule 3.734 amended and renumbered effective January 1, 2007; adopted as rule 213 effective January 1, 1985; previously amended effective July 1, 2002.

Rule 3.735. Management of short cause cases

(a) Short cause case defined

A short cause case is a civil case in which the time estimated for trial by all parties or the court is five hours or less. All other civil cases are long cause cases.

(Subd (a) amended effective January 1, 2007.)

(b) Exemption for short cause case and setting of case for trial

The court may order, upon the stipulation of all parties or the court's own motion, that a case is a short cause case exempted from the requirements of case management review and set the case for trial.

(c) Mistrial

If a short cause case is not completely tried within five hours, the judge may declare a mistrial or, in the judge's discretion, may complete the trial. In the event of a mistrial, the case will be treated as a long cause case and must promptly be set either for a new trial or for a case management conference.

Rule 3.735 amended and renumbered effective January 1, 2007; adopted as rule 214 effective July 1, 2002.

Chapter 4
Management of Collections Cases

Chapter 4 adopted effective July 1, 2008.

Rule 3.740. Collections cases
Rule 3.741. Settlement of collections case

Rule 3.740. Collections cases

(a) Definition

"Collections case" means an action for recovery of money owed in a sum stated to be certain that is not more than $25,000, exclusive of interest and attorney fees, arising from a transaction in which property, services, or money was acquired on credit. A collections case does not include an action seeking any of the following:

(1) Tort damages;

(2) Punitive damages;

(3) Recovery of real property;

(4) Recovery of personal property; or

(5) A prejudgment writ of attachment.

(Subd (a) adopted effective July 1, 2007.)

(b) Civil Case Cover Sheet

If a case meets the definition in (a), a plaintiff must check the case type box on the *Civil Case Cover Sheet* (form CM-010) to indicate that the case is a collections case under rule 3.740 and serve the *Civil Case Cover Sheet* (form CM-010) with the initial complaint.

(Subd (b) amended effective January 1, 2009; adopted effective July 1, 2007.)

(c) Exemption from general time-for-service requirement and case management rules

A collections case is exempt from:

(1) The time-for-service requirement of rule 3.110(b); and

(2) The case management rules that apply to all general civil cases under rules 3.712–3.715 and 3.721–3.730, unless a defendant files a responsive pleading.

(Subd (c) adopted effective July 1, 2007.)

(d) Time for service

The complaint in a collections case must be served on all named defendants, and proofs of service on those defendants must be filed, or the plaintiff must obtain an order for publication of the summons, within 180 days after the filing of the complaint.

(Subd (d) adopted effective July 1, 2007.)

(e) Effect of failure to serve within required time

If proofs of service on all defendants are not filed or the plaintiff has not obtained an order for publication of the summons within 180 days after the filing of the complaint, the court may issue an order to show cause why reasonable monetary sanctions should not be imposed. If proofs of service on all defendants are filed or an order for publication of the summons is filed at least 10 court days before the order to show cause hearing, the court must continue the hearing to 360 days after the filing of the complaint.

(Subd (e) adopted effective July 1, 2007.)

(f) Effect of failure to obtain default judgment within required time

If proofs of service of the complaint are filed or service by publication is made and defendants do not file responsive pleadings, the plaintiff must obtain a default judgment within 360 days after the filing of the complaint. If the plaintiff has not obtained a default judgment by that time, the court must issue an order to show cause why reasonable monetary sanctions should not be imposed. The order to show cause must be vacated if the plaintiff obtains a default judgment at least 10 court days before the order to show cause hearing.

(Subd (f) adopted effective July 1, 2007.)

Rule 3.740 amended effective January 1, 2009; adopted effective July 1, 2007.

Rule 3.741. Settlement of collections case

If the plaintiff or other party seeking affirmative relief in a case meeting the definition of "collections case" in rule 3.740(a) files a notice of settlement under rule 3.1385, including a conditional settlement, the court must vacate all hearing, case management conference, and trial dates.

Rule 3.741 adopted effective July 1, 2007.

Chapter 5
Management of Complex Cases

Chapter 5 renumbered effective July 1, 2008; adopted as chapter 4 effective January 1, 2007.

Rule 3.750. Initial case management conference
Rule 3.751. Electronic service

Rule 3.750. Initial case management conference

(a) Timing of conference

The court in a complex case should hold an initial case management conference with all parties represented at the earliest practical date.

(b) Subjects for consideration

At the conference, the court should consider the following subjects:

(1) Whether all parties named in the complaint or cross-complaint have been served, have appeared, or have been dismissed;

(2) Whether any additional parties may be added or the pleadings may be amended;

(3) The deadline for the filing of any remaining pleadings and service of any additional parties;

(4) Whether severance, consolidation, or coordination with other actions is desirable;

(5) The schedule for discovery proceedings to avoid duplication and whether discovery should be stayed until all parties have been brought into the case;

(6) The schedule for settlement conferences or alternative dispute resolution;

(7) Whether to appoint liaison or lead counsel;

(8) The date for the filing of any dispositive motions;

(9) The creation of preliminary and updated lists of the persons to be deposed and the subjects to be addressed in each deposition;

(10) The exchange of documents and whether to establish an electronic document depository;

(11) Whether a special master should be appointed and the purposes for such appointment;

(12) Whether to establish a case-based Web site and other means to provide a current master list of addresses and telephone numbers of counsel; and

(13) The schedule for further conferences.

(c) Objects of conference

Principal objects of the initial case management conference are to expose at an early date the essential issues in the litigation and to avoid unnecessary and burdensome discovery procedures in the course of preparing for trial of those issues.

(d) Meet and confer requirement

The court may order counsel to meet privately before the initial case management conference to discuss the items specified in (a) and to prepare a joint statement of matters agreed upon, matters on which the court must rule at the conference, and a description of the major legal and factual issues involved in the litigation.

Rule 3.750 adopted effective January 1, 2007.

Rule 3.751. Electronic service

Parties may consent to electronic service, or the court may require electronic 36 service by local rule or court order, under rule 2.251. The court may provide in a case management order that documents filed electronically in a central electronic depository available to all parties are deemed served on all parties.

Rule 3.751 amended effective January 1, 2017; adopted as rule 1830 effective January 1, 2000; previously renumbered effective January 1, 2007.

Chapter 6
Management of Class Actions

Chapter 6 renumbered effective July 1, 2008; adopted as chapter 5 effective January 1, 2007.

Rule 3.760. Application
Rule 3.761. Form of complaint
Rule 3.762. Case conference
Rule 3.763. Conference order
Rule 3.764. Motion to certify or decertify a class or amend or modify an order certifying a class
Rule 3.765. Class action order
Rule 3.766. Notice to class members
Rule 3.767. Orders in the conduct of class actions
Rule 3.768. Discovery from unnamed class members
Rule 3.769. Settlement of class actions
Rule 3.770. Dismissal of class actions
Rule 3.771. Judgment

Rule 3.760. Application

(a) Class actions

The rules in this chapter apply to each class action brought under Civil Code section 1750 et seq. or Code of Civil Procedure section 382 until the court finds the action is not maintainable as a class action or revokes a prior class certification.

(Subd (a) amended effective January 1, 2007.)

(b) Relief from compliance with rules

The court, on its own motion or on motion of any named party, may grant relief from compliance with the rules in this chapter in an appropriate case.

(Subd (b) amended effective January 1, 2007.)

Rule 3.760 amended and renumbered effective January 1, 2007; adopted as rule 1850 effective January 1, 2002.

Rule 3.761. Form of complaint

(a) Caption of pleadings

A complaint for or against a class party must include in the caption the designation "CLASS ACTION." This designation must be in capital letters on the first page of the complaint, immediately below the case number but above the description of the nature of the complaint.

(b) Heading and class action allegations

The complaint in a class action must contain a separate heading entitled "CLASS ACTION ALLEGATIONS," under which the plaintiff describes how the requirements for class certification are met.

Rule 3.761 renumbered effective January 1, 2007; adopted as rule 1851 effective January 1, 2002.

Rule 3.762. Case conference

(a) Purpose

One or more conferences between the court and counsel for the parties may be held to discuss class issues, conduct and scheduling of discovery, scheduling of hearings, and other matters. No evidence may be presented at the conference, but counsel must be fully prepared to discuss class issues and must possess authority to enter into stipulations.

(b) Notice by the parties

Notice of the conference may be given by any party. If notice is given by a named plaintiff, notice must be served on all named parties to the action. If notice is given by a defendant, notice must be served only on the parties who have appeared. Within 10 calendar days after receipt of the notice, the plaintiff must serve a copy on each named party who has not appeared in the action and must file a declaration of service. If the plaintiff is unable to serve any party, the plaintiff must file a declaration stating the reasons for failure of service.

(Subd (b) amended effective January 1, 2007.)

(c) Notice by the court

The court may give notice of the conference to the plaintiff. Within 10 calendar days after receipt of the notice given by the court, the plaintiff must serve a copy of the notice on all parties who have been served in the action, whether they have appeared or not, and must file a declaration of service. If the plaintiff is unable to serve any party, the plaintiff must file a declaration stating the reasons for failure of service.

(Subd (c) amended effective January 1, 2007.)

(d) Timing of notice

The notice must be filed and served on the parties at least 20 calendar days before the scheduled date of the conference.

(Subd (d) amended effective January 1, 2007.)

(e) Timing of conference

A conference may be held at any time after the first defendant has appeared. Before selecting a conference date, the party noticing the conference must:

(1) Obtain prior approval from the clerk of the department assigned to hear the class action; and

(2) Make reasonable efforts to accommodate the schedules of all parties entitled to receive notice under (b).

(Subd (e) amended effective January 1, 2007.)

Rule 3.762 amended and renumbered effective January 1, 2007; adopted as rule 1852 effective January 1, 2002.

Rule 3.763. Conference order

At the conclusion of the conference, the court may make an order:

(1) Approving any stipulations of the parties;

(2) Establishing a schedule for discovery;

(3) Setting the date for the hearing on class certification;

(4) Setting the dates for any subsequent conferences; and

(5) Addressing any other matters related to management of the case.

Rule 3.763 renumbered effective January 1, 2007; adopted as rule 1853 effective January 1, 2002.

Rule 3.764. Motion to certify or decertify a class or amend or modify an order certifying a class

(a) Purpose

Any party may file a motion to:

(1) Certify a class;

(2) Determine the existence of and certify subclasses;

(3) Amend or modify an order certifying a class; or

(4) Decertify a class.

(b) Timing of motion, hearing, extension, deferral

A motion for class certification should be filed when practicable. In its discretion, the court may establish a deadline for the filing of the motion, as part of the case conference or as part of other case management proceedings. Any such deadline must take into account discovery proceedings that may be necessary to the filing of the motion.

(c) Format and filing of motion

(1) *Time for service of papers*

Notice of a motion to certify or decertify a class or to amend or modify a certification order must be filed and served on all parties to the action at least 28 calendar days before the date appointed for hearing. Any opposition to the motion must be served and filed at least 14 calendar days before the noticed or continued hearing, unless the court for good cause orders otherwise. Any reply to the opposition must be served and filed at least 5 calendar days before the noticed or continued date of the hearing, unless the court for good cause orders otherwise. The provisions of Code of Civil Procedure section 1005 otherwise apply.

(2) *Length of papers*

An opening or responding memorandum filed in support of or in opposition to a motion for class certification must not exceed 20 pages. A reply memorandum must not exceed 15 pages. The provisions of rule 3.1113 otherwise apply.

(3) *Documents in support*

The documents in support of a motion for class certification consist of the notice of motion; a memorandum; evidence in support of the motion in the form of declarations of counsel, class representatives, or other appropriate declarants; and any requests for judicial notice.

(4) *Documents in opposition*

The documents in opposition to the motion consist of the opposing party's memorandum; the opposing party's evidence in opposition to the motion, including any declarations of counsel or other appropriate declarants; and any requests for judicial notice.

(Subd (c) amended effective January 1, 2007.)

(d) Presentation of evidence

Evidence to be considered at the hearing must be presented in accordance with rule 3.1306.

(Subd (d) amended effective January 1, 2007.)

(e) Stipulations

The parties should endeavor to resolve any uncontroverted issues by written stipulation before the hearing. If all class issues are resolved by stipulation of the named parties and approved by the court before the hearing, no hearing on class certification is necessary.

Rule 3.764 amended and renumbered effective January 1, 2007; adopted as rule 1854 effective January 1, 2002.

Rule 3.765. Class action order

(a) Class described

An order certifying, amending, or modifying a class must contain a description of the class and any subclasses.

(b) Limited issues and subclasses

When appropriate, an action may be maintained as a class action limited to particular issues. A class may be divided into subclasses.

Rule 3.765 renumbered effective January 1, 2007; adopted as rule 1855 effective January 1, 2002.

Rule 3.766. Notice to class members

(a) Party to provide notice

If the class is certified, the court may require either party to notify the class of the action in the manner specified by the court.

(b) Statement regarding class notice

The class proponent must submit a statement regarding class notice and a proposed notice to class members. The statement must include the following items:

(1) Whether notice is necessary;

(2) Whether class members may exclude themselves from the action;

(3) The time and manner in which notice should be given;

(4) A proposal for which parties should bear the costs of notice; and,

(5) If cost shifting or sharing is proposed under subdivision (4), an estimate of the cost involved in giving notice.

(c) Order

Upon certification of a class, or as soon thereafter as practicable, the court must make an order determining:

(1) Whether notice to class members is necessary;

(2) Whether class members may exclude themselves from the action;

(3) The time and manner of notice;

(4) The content of the notice; and

(5) The parties responsible for the cost of notice.

(d) Content of class notice

The content of the class notice is subject to court approval. If class members are to be given the right to request exclusion from the class, the notice must include the following:

(1) A brief explanation of the case, including the basic contentions or denials of the parties;

(2) A statement that the court will exclude the member from the class if the member so requests by a specified date;

(3) A procedure for the member to follow in requesting exclusion from the class;

(4) A statement that the judgment, whether favorable or not, will bind all members who do not request exclusion; and

(5) A statement that any member who does not request exclusion may, if the member so desires, enter an appearance through counsel.

(e) Manner of giving notice

In determining the manner of the notice, the court must consider:

(1) The interests of the class;

(2) The type of relief requested;

(3) The stake of the individual class members;

(4) The cost of notifying class members;

(5) The resources of the parties;

(6) The possible prejudice to class members who do not receive notice; and

(7) The res judicata effect on class members.

(f) Court may order means of notice

If personal notification is unreasonably expensive or the stake of individual class members is insubstantial, or if it appears that all members of the class cannot be notified personally, the court may order a means of notice reasonably calculated to apprise the class members of the pendency of the action—for example, publication in a newspaper or magazine; broadcasting on television, radio, or the Internet; or posting or distribution through a trade or professional association, union, or public interest group.

(Subd (f) lettered effective January 1, 2007; adopted as part of subd (e) effective January 1, 2002.)

Rule 3.766 amended and renumbered effective January 1, 2007; adopted as rule 1856 effective January 1, 2002.

Rule 3.767. Orders in the conduct of class actions

(a) Court orders

In the conduct of a class action, the court may make orders that:

(1) Require that some or all of the members of the class be given notice in such manner as the court may direct of any action in the proceeding, or of their opportunity to seek to appear and indicate whether they consider the representation fair and adequate, or of the proposed extent of the judgment;

(2) Impose conditions on the representative parties or on intervenors;

(3) Require that the pleadings be amended to eliminate allegations as to representation of absent persons, and that the action proceed accordingly;

(4) Facilitate the management of class actions through consolidation, severance, coordination, bifurcation, intervention, or joinder; and

(5) Address similar procedural matters.

(Subd (a) amended effective January 1, 2007.)

(b) Altered or amended orders

The orders may be altered or amended as necessary.

(Subd (b) amended effective January 1, 2007.)

Rule 3.767 amended and renumbered effective January 1, 2007; adopted as rule 1857 effective January 1, 2002.

Rule 3.768. Discovery from unnamed class members

(a) Types of discovery permitted

The following types of discovery may be sought, through service of a subpoena and without a court order, from a member of a class who is not a party representative or who has not appeared:

(1) An oral deposition;

(2) A written deposition; and

(3) A deposition for production of business records and things.

(b) Motion for protective order

A party representative, deponent, or other affected person may move for a protective order to preclude or limit the discovery.

(c) Interrogatories require court order

A party may not serve interrogatories on a member of a class who is not a party representative or who has not appeared, without a court order.

(d) Determination by court

In deciding whether to allow the discovery requested under (a) or (c), the court must consider, among other relevant factors:

(1) The timing of the request;
(2) The subject matter to be covered;
(3) The materiality of the information being sought;
(4) The likelihood that class members have such information;
(5) The possibility of reaching factual stipulations that eliminate the need for such discovery;
(6) Whether class representatives are seeking discovery on the subject to be covered; and
(7) Whether discovery will result in annoyance, oppression, or undue burden or expense for the members of the class.

(Subd (d) amended effective January 1, 2007.)
Rule 3.768 amended and renumbered effective January 1, 2007; adopted as rule 1858 effective January 1, 2002.

Rule 3.769. Settlement of class actions

(a) Court approval after hearing
A settlement or compromise of an entire class action, or of a cause of action in a class action, or as to a party, requires the approval of the court after hearing.

(Subd (a) amended effective January 1, 2007.)

(b) Attorney's fees
Any agreement, express or implied, that has been entered into with respect to the payment of attorney's fees or the submission of an application for the approval of attorney's fees must be set forth in full in any application for approval of the dismissal or settlement of an action that has been certified as a class action.

(Subd (b) amended effective January 1, 2007.)

(c) Preliminary approval of settlement
Any party to a settlement agreement may serve and file a written notice of motion for preliminary approval of the settlement. The settlement agreement and proposed notice to class members must be filed with the motion, and the proposed order must be lodged with the motion.

(Subd (c) amended effective January 1, 2007.)

(d) Order certifying provisional settlement class
The court may make an order approving or denying certification of a provisional settlement class after the preliminary settlement hearing.

(e) Order for final approval hearing
If the court grants preliminary approval, its order must include the time, date, and place of the final approval hearing; the notice to be given to the class; and any other matters deemed necessary for the proper conduct of a settlement hearing.

(f) Notice to class of final approval hearing
If the court has certified the action as a class action, notice of the final approval hearing must be given to the class members in the manner specified by the court. The notice must contain an explanation of the proposed settlement and procedures for class members to follow in filing written objections to it and in arranging to appear at the settlement hearing and state any objections to the proposed settlement.

(Subd (f) amended effective January 1, 2007.)

(g) Conduct of final approval hearing
Before final approval, the court must conduct an inquiry into the fairness of the proposed settlement.

(h) Judgment and retention of jurisdiction to enforce
If the court approves the settlement agreement after the final approval hearing, the court must make and enter judgment. The judgment must include a provision for the retention of the court's jurisdiction over the parties to enforce the terms of the judgment. The court may not enter an order dismissing the action at the same time as, or after, entry of judgment.

(Subd (h) amended effective January 1, 2009.)
Rule 3.769 amended effective January 1, 2009; adopted as rule 1859 effective January 1, 2002; previously amended and renumbered effective January 1, 2007.

Rule 3.770. Dismissal of class actions

(a) Court approval of dismissal
A dismissal of an entire class action, or of any party or cause of action in a class action, requires court approval. The court may not grant a request to dismiss a class action if the court has entered judgment following final approval of a settlement. Requests for dismissal must be accompanied by a declaration setting forth the facts on which the party relies. The declaration must clearly state whether consideration, direct or indirect, is being given for the dismissal and must describe the consideration in detail.

(Subd (a) amended effective January 1, 2009; adopted as untitled subd effective January 1, 1984; previously amended and lettered as subd (a) effective January 1, 2002; previously amended effective January 1, 2007.)

(b) Hearing on request for dismissal
The court may grant the request without a hearing. If the request is disapproved, notice of tentative disapproval must be sent to the attorneys of record. Any party may seek, within 15 calendar days of the service of the notice of tentative disapproval, a hearing on the request. If no hearing is sought within that period, the request for dismissal will be deemed denied.

(Subd (b) amended effective January 1, 2007; adopted as untitled subd effective January 1, 1984; previously amended and lettered as subd (b) effective January 1, 2002.)

(c) Notice to class of dismissal
If the court has certified the class, and notice of the pendency of the action has been provided to class members, notice of the dismissal must be given to the class in the manner specified by the court. If the court has not ruled on class certification, or if notice of the pendency of the action has not been provided to class members in a case in which such notice was required, notice of the proposed dismissal may be given in the manner and to those class members specified by the court, or the action may be dismissed without notice to the class members if the court finds that the dismissal will not prejudice them.

(Subd (c) amended effective January 1, 2007; adopted effective January 1, 2002.)
Rule 3.770 amended effective January 1, 2009; adopted as rule 365 effective January 1, 1984; previously amended and renumbered as rule 1860 effective January 1, 2002, and as rule 3.770 effective January 1, 2007.

Rule 3.771. Judgment

(a) Class members to be included in judgment
The judgment in an action maintained as a class action must include and describe those whom the court finds to be members of the class.

(Subd (a) amended and lettered effective January 1, 2007; adopted as unlettered subd effective January 1, 2002.)

(b) Notice of judgment to class
Notice of the judgment must be given to the class in the manner specified by the court.

(Subd (b) amended and lettered effective January 1, 2007; adopted as unlettered subd effective January 1, 2002.)
Rule 3.771 amended and renumbered effective January 1, 2007; adopted as rule 1861 effective January 1, 2002.

Division 8
Alternative Dispute Resolution

Chap. 1. General Provisions. Rule 3.800.
Chap. 2. Judicial Arbitration. Rules 3.810–3.830.
Chap. 3. General Rules Relating to Mediation of Civil Cases. Rules 3.835–3.872.
Chap. 4. Civil Action Mediation Program Rules. Rules 3.890–3.898.

Chapter 1
General Provisions

Rule 3.800. Definitions
As used in this division:
(1) "Alternative dispute resolution process" or "ADR process" means a process, other than formal litigation, in which a neutral person or persons resolve a dispute or assist parties in resolving their dispute.
(2) "Mediation" means a process in which a neutral person or persons facilitate communication between disputants to assist them in reaching a mutually acceptable agreement. As used in this division, mediation does not include a settlement conference under rule 3.1380.

Rule 3.800 amended and renumbered effective January 1, 2007; adopted as rule 1580 effective January 1, 2001; previously amended effective July 1, 2002.

Chapter 2
Judicial Arbitration

Rule 3.810. Application
Rule 3.811. Cases subject to and exempt from arbitration
Rule 3.812. Assignment to arbitration
Rule 3.813. Arbitration program administration
Rule 3.814. Panels of arbitrators
Rule 3.815. Selection of the arbitrator
Rule 3.816. Disqualification for conflict of interest
Rule 3.817. Arbitration hearings; notice; when and where held
Rule 3.818. Continuances
Rule 3.819. Arbitrator's fees

Rule 3.820. Communication with the arbitrator
Rule 3.821. Representation by counsel; proceedings when party absent
Rule 3.822. Discovery
Rule 3.823. Rules of evidence at arbitration hearing
Rule 3.824. Conduct of the hearing
Rule 3.825. The award
Rule 3.826. Trial after arbitration
Rule 3.827. Entry of award as judgment
Rule 3.828. Vacating judgment on award
Rule 3.829. Settlement of case
Rule 3.830. Arbitration not pursuant to rules

Rule 3.810. Application

The rules in this chapter (commencing with this rule) apply if Code of Civil Procedure, part 3, title 3, chapter 2.5 (commencing with section 1141.10) is in effect.

Rule 3.810 amended and renumbered effective January 1, 2007; adopted as rule 1600.1 effective January 1, 1988; previously amended effective July 1, 1999, and January 1, 2000; previously amended and renumbered as rule 1600 effective January 1, 2004.

Rule 3.811. Cases subject to and exempt from arbitration

(a) Cases subject to arbitration

Except as provided in (b), the following cases must be arbitrated:

(1) In each superior court with 18 or more authorized judges, all unlimited civil cases where the amount in controversy does not exceed $50,000 as to any plaintiff;

(2) In each superior court with fewer than 18 authorized judges that so provides by local rule, all unlimited civil cases where the amount in controversy does not exceed $50,000 as to any plaintiff;

(3) All limited civil cases in courts that so provide by local rule;

(4) Upon stipulation, any limited or unlimited civil case in any court, regardless of the amount in controversy; and

(5) Upon filing of an election by all plaintiffs, any limited or unlimited civil case in any court in which each plaintiff agrees that the arbitration award will not exceed $50,000 as to that plaintiff.

(Subd (a) amended effective January 1, 2004.)

(b) Cases exempt from arbitration

The following cases are exempt from arbitration:

(1) Cases that include a prayer for equitable relief that is not frivolous or insubstantial;

(2) Class actions;

(3) Small claims cases or trials de novo on appeal from the small claims court;

(4) Unlawful detainer proceedings;

(5) Family Law Act proceedings except as provided in Family Code section 2554;

(6) Any case otherwise subject to arbitration that is found by the court not to be amenable to arbitration on the ground that arbitration would not reduce the probable time and expense necessary to resolve the litigation;

(7) Any category of cases otherwise subject to arbitration but excluded by local rule as not amenable to arbitration on the ground that, under the circumstances relating to the particular court, arbitration of such cases would not reduce the probable time and expense necessary to resolve the litigation; and

(8) Cases involving multiple causes of action or a cross-complaint if the court determines that the amount in controversy as to any given cause of action or cross-complaint exceeds $50,000.

(Subd (b) adopted effective January 1, 2004.)

Rule 3.811 renumbered effective January 1, 2007; adopted as rule 1600 effective July 1, 1979; previously amended effective January 1, 1982, January 1, 1986, January 1, 1988, and July 1, 1999; previously amended and renumbered as rule 1601 effective January 1, 2004.

Rule 3.812. Assignment to arbitration

(a) Stipulations to arbitration

When the parties stipulate to arbitration, the case must be set for arbitration forthwith. The stipulation must be filed no later than the time the initial case management statement is filed, unless the court orders otherwise.

(Subd (a) amended effective January 1, 2004; previously amended effective July 1, 1979, January 1, 1999, and January 1, 2003.)

(b) Plaintiff election for arbitration

Upon written election of all plaintiffs to submit a case to arbitration, the case must be set for arbitration forthwith, subject to a motion by defendant for good cause to delay the arbitration hearing. The election must be filed no later than the time the initial case management statement is filed, unless the court orders otherwise.

(Subd (b) amended effective January 1, 2004; adopted effective July 1, 1979; previously amended effective January 1, 1982, January 1, 1986, January 1, 1988, and January 1, 2003.)

(c) Cross-actions

A case involving a cross-complaint where all plaintiffs have elected to arbitrate must be removed from the list of cases assigned to arbitration if, upon motion of the cross-complainant made within 15 days after notice of the election to arbitrate, the court determines that the amount in controversy relating to the cross-complaint exceeds $50,000.

(Subd (c) amended effective January 1, 2004; adopted as part of subd (b) effective July 1, 1979; amended and lettered effective January 1, 2003.)

(d) Case management conference

Absent a stipulation or an election by all plaintiffs to submit to arbitration, cases must be set for arbitration when the court determines that the amount in controversy does not exceed $50,000. The amount in controversy must be determined at the first case management conference or review under the rules on case management in division 7 of this title that takes place after all named parties have appeared or defaulted.

(Subd (d) amended effective January 1, 2007; adopted as subd (c) effective July 1, 1976; previously amended effective July 1, 1979, January 1, 1982, and January 1, 2004; previously amended and relettered effective January 1, 2003.)

Rule 3.812 amended and renumbered effective January 1, 2007; adopted as rule 1601 effective July 1, 1976; previously amended effective July 1, 1979, January 1, 1982, January 1, 1985, January 1, 1986, January 1, 1988, January 1, 1991, and January 1, 2003; previously amended and renumbered as rule 1602 effective January 1, 2004.

Rule 3.813. Arbitration program administration

(a) Arbitration administrator

The presiding judge must designate the ADR administrator selected under rule 10.783 to serve as arbitration administrator. The arbitration administrator must supervise the selection of arbitrators for the cases on the arbitration hearing list, generally supervise the operation of the arbitration program, and perform any additional duties delegated by the presiding judge.

(Subd (a) amended effective January 1, 2007; previously amended effective January 1, 2004.)

(b) Responsibilities of ADR committee

The ADR committee established under rule 10.783 is responsible for:

(1) Appointing the panels of arbitrators provided for in rule 3.814;

(2) Removing a person from a panel of arbitrators;

(3) Establishing procedures for selecting an arbitrator not inconsistent with these rules or local court rules; and

(4) Reviewing the administration and operation of the arbitration program periodically and making recommendations to the Judicial Council as the committee deems appropriate to improve the program, promote the ends of justice, and serve the needs of the community.

(Subd (b) amended effective January 1, 2007; adopted as subd (d) effective July 1, 1976; previously amended and relettered as subd (b) effective January 1, 2004.)

Rule 3.813 amended and renumbered effective January 1, 2007; adopted as rule 1603 effective July 1, 1976; previously amended effective July 1, 1979, July 1, 1999, and January 1, 2004.

Rule 3.814. Panels of arbitrators

(a) Creation of panels

Every court must have a panel of arbitrators for personal injury cases, and such additional panels as the presiding judge may, from time to time, determine are needed.

(Subd (a) amended effective January 1, 2004; previously amended effective July 1, 1979, and July 1, 2001.)

(b) Composition of panels

The panels of arbitrators must be composed of active or inactive members of the State Bar, retired court commissioners who were licensed to practice law before their appointment as commissioners, and retired judges. A former California judicial officer is not eligible for the panel of arbitrators unless he or she is an active or inactive member of the State Bar.

(Subd (b) amended effective January 1, 2007; previously amended effective July 1, 1979, January 1, 1996, July 1, 2001, and January 1, 2004.)

(c) Responsibilities of ADR committee

The ADR committee is responsible for determining the size and composition of each panel of arbitrators. The personal injury panel, to the extent feasible, must contain an equal number of those who usually represent plaintiffs and those who usually represent defendants.

(Subd (c) amended effective January 1, 2004; previously amended effective July 1, 2001.)

(d) Service on panel

Each person appointed serves as a member of a panel of arbitrators at the pleasure of the ADR committee. A person may be on arbitration panels in more than one county. An appointment to a panel is effective when the person appointed:

(1) Agrees to serve;

(2) Certifies that he or she is aware of and will comply with applicable provisions of canon 6 of the Code of Judicial Ethics and these rules; and

(3) Files an oath or affirmation to justly try all matters submitted to him or her.

(Subd (d) amended effective January 1, 2004; previously amended effective January 1, 1996, and July 1, 2001.)

(e) Panel lists

Lists showing the names of panel arbitrators available to hear cases must be available for public inspection in the ADR administrator's office.

(Subd (e) amended effective January 1, 2007; previously amended effective July 1, 2001, and January 1, 2004.)

Rule 3.814 amended and renumbered effective January 1, 2007; adopted as rule 1604 effective July 1, 1976; previously amended effective July 1, 1979, January 1, 1996, July 1, 2001, and January 1, 2004.

Rule 3.815. Selection of the arbitrator

(a) Selection by stipulation

By stipulation, the parties may select any person to serve as arbitrator. If the parties select a person who is not on the court's arbitration panel to serve as the arbitrator, the stipulation will be effective only if:

(1) The selected person completes a written consent to serve and the oath required of panel arbitrators under these rules; and

(2) Both the consent and the oath are attached to the stipulation.

A stipulation may specify the maximum amount of the arbitrator's award. The stipulation to an arbitrator must be served and filed no later than 10 days after the case has been set for arbitration under rule 3.812.

(Subd (a) amended effective January 1, 2007; adopted effective January 1, 2004.)

(b) Selection absent stipulation or local procedures

If the arbitrator has not been selected by stipulation and the court has not adopted local rules or procedures for the selection of the arbitrator as permitted under (c), the arbitrator will be selected as follows:

(1) Within 15 days after a case is set for arbitration under rule 3.812, the administrator must determine the number of clearly adverse sides in the case; in the absence of a cross-complaint bringing in a new party, the administrator may assume there are two sides. A dispute as to the number or identity of sides must be decided by the presiding judge in the same manner as disputes in determining sides entitled to peremptory challenges of jurors.

(2) The administrator must select at random a number of names equal to the number of sides, plus one, and send the list of randomly selected names to counsel for the parties.

(3) Each side has 10 days from the date on which the list was sent to file a rejection, in writing, of no more than one name on the list; if there are two or more parties on a side, they must join in the rejection of a single name.

(4) Promptly on the expiration of the 10-day period, the administrator must appoint, at random, one of the persons on the list whose name was not rejected, if more than one name remains.

(5) The administrator must assign the case to the arbitrator appointed and must give notice of the appointment to the arbitrator and to all parties.

(Subd (b) amended effective January 1, 2016; adopted as subd (a) effective July 1, 1976; previously amended and relettered as subd (b) effective January 1, 2004; previously amended effective July 1, 1979, January 1, 1982, January 1, 1984, and January 1, 2007.)

(c) Local selection procedures

Instead of the procedure in (b), a court that has an arbitration program may, by local rule or by procedures adopted by its ADR committee, establish any fair method of selecting an arbitrator that:

(1) Affords each side an opportunity to challenge at least one listed arbitrator peremptorily; and

(2) Ensures that an arbitrator is appointed within 30 days from the submission of a case to arbitration.

The local rule or procedure may require that all steps leading to the selection of the arbitrator take place during or immediately following the case management conference or review under the rules on case management in division 7 of this title at which the court determines the amount in controversy and the suitability of the case for arbitration.

(Subd (c) amended effective January 1, 2007; adopted effective January 1, 2004.)

(d) Procedure if first arbitrator declines to serve

If the first arbitrator selected declines to serve, the administrator must vacate the appointment of the arbitrator and may either:

(1) Return the case to the top of the arbitration hearing list, restore the arbitrator's name to the list of those available for selection to hear cases, and appoint a new arbitrator; or

(2) Certify the case to the court.

(Subd (d) amended and relettered effective January 1, 2004; adopted as subd (b) effective July 1, 1976; previously amended effective January 1, 1991, and January 1, 1994.)

(e) Procedure if second arbitrator declines to serve or hearing is not timely held

If the second arbitrator selected declines to serve or if the arbitrator does not complete the hearing within 90 days after the date of the assignment of the case to him or her, including any time due to continuances granted under rule 3.818, the administrator must certify the case to the court.

(Subd (e) amended effective January 1, 2007; adopted as subd (c) effective July 1, 1976; previously amended effective January 1, 1991; previously amended and relettered effective January 1, 2004.)

(f) Cases certified to court

If a case is certified to the court under either (d) or (e), the court must hold a case management conference. If the inability to hold an arbitration hearing is due to the neglect or lack of cooperation of a party who elected or stipulated to arbitration, the court may set the case for trial and may make any other appropriate orders. In all other circumstances, the court may reassign the case to arbitration or make any other appropriate orders to expedite disposition of the case.

(Subd (f) amended effective January 1, 2007; adopted as part of subd (c) effective July 1, 1976; previously amended and relettered as subd (f) effective January 1, 2004.)

Rule 3.815 amended effective January 1, 2016; adopted as rule 1605 effective July 1, 1976; previously amended effective July 1, 1979, January 1, 1982; January 1, 1984, January 1, 1991, January 1, 1994, and January 1, 2004; previously amended and renumbered as rule 3.815 effective January 1, 2007.

Rule 3.816. Disqualification for conflict of interest

(a) Arbitrator's duty to disqualify himself or herself

The arbitrator must determine whether any cause exists for disqualification upon any of the grounds set forth in Code of Civil Procedure section 170.1 governing the disqualification of judges. If any member of the arbitrator's law firm would be disqualified under subdivision (a)(2) of section 170.1, the arbitrator is disqualified. Unless the ground for disqualification is disclosed to the parties in writing and is expressly waived by all parties in writing, the arbitrator must promptly notify the administrator of any known ground for disqualification and another arbitrator must be selected as provided in rule 3.815.

(Subd (a) amended effective January 1, 2007; previously amended effective July 1, 1979, July 1, 1990, July 1, 2001, January 1, 2004, and July 1, 2004.)

(b) Disclosures by arbitrator

In addition to any other disclosure required by law, no later than five days before the deadline for parties to file a motion for disqualification of the arbitrator under Code of Civil Procedure section 170.6 or, if the arbitrator is not aware of his or her appointment or of a matter subject to disclosure at that time, as soon as practicable thereafter, an arbitrator must disclose to the parties:

(1) Any matter subject to disclosure under subdivisions (D)(5)(a) and (D)(5)(b) of canon 6 of the Code of Judicial Ethics; and

(2) Any significant personal or professional relationship the arbitrator has or has had with a party, attorney, or law firm in the instant case, including the number and nature of any other proceedings in the past 24 months in which the arbitrator has been privately compensated by a party, attorney, law firm, or insurance company in the instant case for any services, including service as an attorney, expert witness, or consultant or as a judge, referee, arbitrator, mediator, settlement facilitator, or other alternative dispute resolution neutral.

(Subd (b) amended effective January 1, 2008; adopted effective July 1, 2001; previously amended effective January 1, 2007.)

(c) Request for disqualification

A copy of any request by a party for the disqualification of an arbitrator under Code of Civil Procedure section 170.1 or 170.6 must be sent to the ADR administrator.

(Subd (c) amended effective January 1, 2007; adopted as subd (b) effective July 1, 1976; previously amended and relettered effective July 1, 2001; previously amended effective July 1, 1979, July 1, 1990, and January 1, 2004.)

(d) Arbitrator's failure to disqualify himself or herself

On motion of any party, made as promptly as possible under Code of Civil Procedure sections 170.1 and 1141.18(d) and before the conclusion of arbitration proceedings, the appointment of an arbitrator to a case must be vacated if the court finds that:

(1) The party has demanded that the arbitrator disqualify himself or herself;

(2) The arbitrator has failed to do so; and

(3) Any of the grounds specified in section 170.1 exists.

The ADR administrator must return the case to the top of the arbitration hearing list and appoint a new arbitrator. The disqualified arbitrator's name must be returned to the list of those available for selection to hear cases, unless the court orders that the circumstances of the disqualification be reviewed by the ADR administrator, the ADR committee, or the presiding judge for appropriate action.

(Subd (d) amended effective January 1, 2007; adopted as subd (c) effective January 1, 1994; previously amended and relettered effective July 1, 2001; previously amended effective January 1, 2004.)

Rule 3.816 amended effective January 1, 2008; adopted as rule 1606 effective July 1, 1976; previously amended effective July 1, 1979, July 1, 1990, January 1, 1994, July 1, 2001, January 1, 2004, and July 1, 2004; previously amended and renumbered effective January 1, 2007.

Rule 3.817. Arbitration hearings; notice; when and where held

(a) Setting hearing; notice

Within 15 days after the appointment of the arbitrator, the arbitrator must set the time, date, and place of the arbitration hearing and notify each party and the administrator in writing of the time, date, and place set.

(Subd (a) amended and lettered effective January 1, 2004; adopted as part of unlettered subd effective July 1, 1976.)

(b) Date of hearing; limitations

Except upon the agreement of all parties and the arbitrator, the arbitration hearing date must not be set:

(1) Earlier than 30 days after the date the arbitrator sends the notice of the hearing under (a); or

(2) On Saturdays, Sundays, or legal holidays.

(Subd (b) amended and lettered effective January 1, 2004; adopted as part of unlettered subd effective July 1, 1976.)

(c) Hearing completion deadline

The hearing must be scheduled so as to be completed no later than 90 days from the date of the assignment of the case to the arbitrator, including any time due to continuances granted under rule 3.818.

(Subd (c) amended effective January 1, 2007; adopted as part of unlettered subd effective July 1, 1976; previously amended and relettered effective January 1, 2004.)

(d) Hearing location

The hearing must take place in appropriate facilities provided by the court or selected by the arbitrator.

(Subd (d) amended effective January 1, 2004.)

Rule 3.817 amended and renumbered effective January 1, 2007; adopted as rule 1611 effective July 1, 1976; previously amended effective July 1, 1979, and January 1, 1992; previously amended and renumbered as rule 1607 effective January 1, 2004.

Rule 3.818. Continuances

(a) Stipulation to continuance; consent of arbitrator

Except as provided in (c), the parties may stipulate to a continuance in the case, with the consent of the assigned arbitrator. An arbitrator must consent to a request for a continuance if it appears that good cause exists. Notice of the continuance must be sent to the ADR administrator.

(Subd (a) amended effective January 1, 2004; previously amended effective January 1, 1984, and January 1, 1992.)

(b) Court grant of continuance

If the arbitrator declines to give consent to a continuance, upon the motion of a party and for good cause shown, the court may grant a continuance of the arbitration hearing. In the event the court grants the motion, the party who requested the continuance must notify the arbitrator and the arbitrator must reschedule the hearing, giving notice to all parties to the arbitration proceeding.

(Subd (b) amended effective January 1, 2007; previously amended effective July 1, 1979, and January 1, 2004.)

(c) Limitation on length of continuance

An arbitration hearing must not be continued to a date later than 90 days after the assignment of the case to the arbitrator, including any time due to continuances granted under this rule, except by order of the court upon the motion of a party as provided in (b).

(Subd (c) amended effective January 1, 2004; previously amended effective January 1, 1991 and January 1, 1994.)

Rule 3.818 amended and renumbered effective January 1, 2007; adopted as rule 1607 effective July 1, 1976; previously amended effective July 1, 1979, January 1, 1984, January 1, 1991, January 1, 1992, and January 1, 1994; previously amended and renumbered as rule 1608 effective January 1, 2004.

Rule 3.819. Arbitrator's fees

(a) Filing of award required

Except as provided in (b), the arbitrator's award must be timely filed with the clerk of the court under rule 3.825(b) before a fee may be paid to the arbitrator.

(Subd (a) amended effective January 1, 2013; previously amended effective July 1, 1979, January 1, 2004, and January 1, 2007.)

(b) Exceptions for good cause

On the arbitrator's verified ex parte application, the court may for good cause authorize payment of a fee:

(1) If the arbitrator devoted a substantial amount of time to a case that was settled without a hearing or without an award being filed. For this purpose, a case is considered settled when one of the following is filed:

(A) A notice of settlement of the entire case, under rule 3.1385; or

(B) A *Request for Dismissal* (form CIV-110) of the entire case or as to all parties to the arbitration is filed; or

(2) If the award was not timely filed.

(Subd (b) amended effective January 1, 2013; previously amended effective July 1, 1979, January 1, 1987, and January 1, 2004.)

(c) Arbitrator's fee statement

The arbitrator's fee statement must be submitted to the administrator promptly upon the completion of the arbitrator's duties and must set forth the title and number of the cause arbitrated, the date of any arbitration hearing, and the date the award, notice of settlement, or request for dismissal was filed.

(Subd (c) amended effective January 1, 2013; previously amended effective July 1, 1979, January 1, 2004, and January 1, 2007.)

Rule 3.819 amended effective January 1, 2013; adopted as rule 1608 effective July 1, 1976; previously amended effective July 1, 1979, and January 1, 1987; previously amended and renumbered as rule 1609 effective January 1, 2004; previously amended and renumbered effective January 1, 2007.

Rule 3.820. Communication with the arbitrator

(a) Disclosure of settlement offers prohibited

No disclosure of any offers of settlement made by any party may be made to the arbitrator prior to the filing of the award.

(Subd (a) amended and relettered effective January 1, 2004; adopted as part of unlettered subd effective July 1, 1976.)

(b) Ex parte communication prohibited

An arbitrator must not initiate, permit, or consider any ex parte communications or consider other communications made to the arbitrator outside the presence of all of the parties concerning a pending arbitration, except as follows:

(1) An arbitrator may communicate with a party in the absence of other parties about administrative matters, such as setting the time and place of hearings or making other arrangements for the conduct of the proceedings, as long as the arbitrator reasonably believes that the communication will not result in a procedural or tactical advantage for any party. When such a discussion occurs, the arbitrator must promptly inform the other parties of the communication and must give the other parties an opportunity to respond before making any final determination concerning the matter discussed.

(2) An arbitrator may initiate or consider any ex parte communication when expressly authorized by law to do so.

(Subd (b) amended effective January 1, 2007; adopted as part of unlettered subd effective July 1, 1976; previously amended and lettered effective January 1, 2004.)

Rule 3.820 amended and renumbered effective January 1, 2007; adopted as rule 1609 effective July 1, 1976; previously amended and renumbered as rule 1610 effective January 1, 2004.

Rule 3.821. Representation by counsel; proceedings when party absent

(a) Representation by counsel

A party to the arbitration has a right to be represented by an attorney at any proceeding or hearing in arbitration, but this right may be waived.

A waiver of this right may be revoked, but if revoked, the other party is entitled to a reasonable continuance for the purpose of obtaining counsel.

(*Subd (a) amended effective January 1, 2004.*)

(b) Proceedings when party absent

The arbitration may proceed in the absence of any party who, after due notice, fails to be present and to obtain a continuance. An award must not be based solely on the absence of a party. In the event of a default by defendant, the arbitrator must require the plaintiff to submit such evidence as may be appropriate for the making of an award.

(*Subd (b) amended effective January 1, 2007; previously amended effective January 1, 2004.*)

Rule 3.821 amended and renumbered effective January 1, 2007; adopted as rule 1610 effective July 1, 1976; previously amended and renumbered as rule 1611 effective January 1, 2004.

Rule 3.822. Discovery

(a) Right to discovery

The parties to the arbitration have the right to take depositions and to obtain discovery, and to that end may exercise all of the same rights, remedies, and procedures, and are subject to all of the same duties, liabilities, and obligations as provided in part 4, title 3, chapter 3 of the Code of Civil Procedure, except as provided in (b).

(*Subd (a) amended and lettered effective January 1, 2007; adopted as part of unlettered subd effective July 1, 1976.*)

(b) Completion of discovery

All discovery must be completed not later than 15 days before the date set for the arbitration hearing unless the court, upon a showing of good cause, makes an order granting an extension of the time within which discovery must be completed.

(*Subd (b) amended and lettered effective January 1, 2007; adopted as part of unlettered subd effective July 1, 1976.*)

Rule 3.822 amended and renumbered effective January 1, 2007; adopted as rule 1612 effective July 1, 1976; previously amended effective July 1, 1979, and January 1, 2004.

Rule 3.823. Rules of evidence at arbitration hearing

(a) Presence of arbitrator and parties

All evidence must be taken in the presence of the arbitrator and all parties, except where any of the parties has waived the right to be present or is absent after due notice of the hearing.

(*Subd (a) amended effective January 1, 2004.*)

(b) Application of civil rules of evidence

The rules of evidence governing civil cases apply to the conduct of the arbitration hearing, except:

(1) *Written reports and other documents*

Any party may offer written reports of any expert witness, medical records and bills (including physiotherapy, nursing, and prescription bills), documentary evidence of loss of income, property damage repair bills or estimates, police reports concerning an accident that gave rise to the case, other bills and invoices, purchase orders, checks, written contracts, and similar documents prepared and maintained in the ordinary course of business.

(A) The arbitrator must receive them in evidence if copies have been delivered to all opposing parties at least 20 days before the hearing.

(B) Any other party may subpoena the author or custodian of the document as a witness and examine the witness as if under cross-examination.

(C) Any repair estimate offered as an exhibit, and the copies delivered to opposing parties, must be accompanied by:

(i) A statement indicating whether or not the property was repaired, and, if it was, whether the estimated repairs were made in full or in part; and

(ii) A copy of the receipted bill showing the items of repair made and the amount paid.

(D) The arbitrator must not consider any opinion as to ultimate fault expressed in a police report.

(2) *Witness statements*

The written statements of any other witness may be offered and must be received in evidence if:

(A) They are made by declaration under penalty of perjury;

(B) Copies have been delivered to all opposing parties at least 20 days before the hearing; and

(C) No opposing party has, at least 10 days before the hearing, delivered to the proponent of the evidence a written demand that the witness be produced in person to testify at the hearing. The arbitrator must disregard any portion of a statement received under this rule that would be inadmissible if the witness were testifying in person, but the inclusion of inadmissible matter does not render the entire statement inadmissible.

(3) *Depositions*

(A) The deposition of any witness may be offered by any party and must be received in evidence, subject to objections available under Code of Civil Procedure section 2025.410, notwithstanding that the deponent is not "unavailable as a witness" within the meaning of Evidence Code section 240 and no exceptional circumstances exist, if:

(i) The deposition was taken in the manner provided for by law or by stipulation of the parties and within the time provided for in these rules; and

(ii) Not less than 20 days before the hearing the proponent of the deposition delivered to all opposing parties notice of intention to offer the deposition in evidence.

(B) The opposing party, upon receiving the notice, may subpoena the deponent and, at the discretion of the arbitrator, either the deposition may be excluded from evidence or the deposition may be admitted and the deponent may be further cross-examined by the subpoenaing party. These limitations are not applicable to a deposition admissible under the terms of Code of Civil Procedure section 2025.620.

(*Subd (b) amended effective January 1, 2008; previously amended effective July 1, 1979, January 1, 1984, January 1, 1988, July 1, 1990, January 1, 2004, and January 1, 2007.*)

(c) Subpoenas

(1) *Compelling witnesses to appear*

The attendance of witnesses at arbitration hearings may be compelled through the issuance of subpoenas as provided in the Code of Civil Procedure, in section 1985 and elsewhere in part 4, title 3, chapters 2 and 3. It is the duty of the party requesting the subpoena to modify the form of subpoena so as to show that the appearance is before an arbitrator and to give the time and place set for the arbitration hearing.

(2) *Adjournment or continuances*

At the discretion of the arbitrator, nonappearance of a properly subpoenaed witness may be a ground for an adjournment or continuance of the hearing.

(3) *Contempt*

If any witness properly served with a subpoena fails to appear at the arbitration hearing or, having appeared, refuses to be sworn or to answer, proceedings to compel compliance with the subpoena on penalty of contempt may be had before the superior court as provided in Code of Civil Procedure section 1991 for other instances of refusal to appear and answer before an officer or commissioner out of court.

(*Subd (c) amended effective January 1, 2007; previously amended effective July 1, 1979, and January 1, 2004.*)

(d) Delivery of documents

For purposes of this rule, "delivery" of a document or notice may be accomplished manually, by electronic means under Code of Civil Procedure section 1010.6 and rule 2.251, or in the manner provided by Code of Civil Procedure section 1013. If service is by electronic means, the times prescribed in this rule for delivery of documents, notices, and demands are increased as provided by Code of Civil Procedure section 1010.6. If service is in the manner provided by Code of Civil Procedure section 1013, the times prescribed in this rule are increased as provided by that section.

(*Subd (d) amended effective January 1, 2017; adopted effective January 1, 1988; previously amended effective January 1, 2004, and January 1, 2016.*)

Rule 3.823 amended effective January 1, 2017; adopted as rule 1613 effective July 1, 1976; previously amended and renumbered as rule 3.823 effective January 1, 2007; previously amended effective July 1, 1979, January 1, 1984, January 1, 1988, July 1, 1990, January 1, 2004, January 1, 2008, and January 1, 2016.

Rule 3.824. Conduct of the hearing

(a) Arbitrator's powers

The arbitrator has the following powers; all other questions arising out of the case are reserved to the court:

(1) To administer oaths or affirmations to witnesses;

(2) To take adjournments upon the request of a party or upon his or her own initiative when deemed necessary;

(3) To permit testimony to be offered by deposition;

(4) To permit evidence to be offered and introduced as provided in these rules;

(5) To rule upon the admissibility and relevancy of evidence offered;

(6) To invite the parties, on reasonable notice, to submit arbitration briefs;

(7) To decide the law and facts of the case and make an award accordingly;

(8) To award costs, not to exceed the statutory costs of the suit; and

(9) To examine any site or object relevant to the case.

(Subd (a) amended effective January 1, 2007; previously amended effective January 1, 2004.)

(b) Record of proceedings

(1) *Arbitrator's record*

The arbitrator may, but is not required to, make a record of the proceedings.

(2) *Record not subject to discovery*

Any records of the proceedings made by or at the direction of the arbitrator are deemed the arbitrator's personal notes and are not subject to discovery, and the arbitrator must not deliver them to any party to the case or to any other person, except to an employee using the records under the arbitrator's supervision or pursuant to a subpoena issued in a criminal investigation or prosecution for perjury.

(3) *No other record*

No other record may be made, and the arbitrator must not permit the presence of a stenographer or court reporter or the use of any recording device at the hearing, except as expressly permitted by (1).

(Subd (b) amended effective January 1, 2007; previously amended effective January 1, 2004.)

Rule 3.824 amended and renumbered effective January 1, 2007; adopted as rule 1614 effective July 1, 1976; previously amended effective January 1, 2004.

Rule 3.825. The award

(a) Form and content of the award

(1) *Award in writing*

The award must be in writing and signed by the arbitrator. It must determine all issues properly raised by the pleadings, including a determination of any damages and an award of costs if appropriate.

(2) *No findings or conclusions required*

The arbitrator is not required to make findings of fact or conclusions of law.

(Subd (a) amended effective January 1, 2007; previously amended effective January 1, 2004.)

(b) Filing the award or amended award

(1) *Time for filing the award*

Within 10 days after the conclusion of the arbitration hearing, the arbitrator must file the award with the clerk, with proof of service on each party to the arbitration. On the arbitrator's application in cases of unusual length or complexity, the court may allow up to 20 additional days for the filing and service of the award.

(2) *Amended award*

Within the time for filing the award, the arbitrator may file and serve an amended award.

(Subd (b) amended effective January 1, 2007; previously amended effective January 1, 1995, and January 1, 2004.)

Rule 3.825 amended and renumbered effective January 1, 2007; adopted as rule 1615 effective July 1, 1976; previously amended effective January 1, 1983, January 1, 1985, January 1, 1995, January 1, 2003, and January 1, 2004.

Rule 3.826. Trial after arbitration

(a) Request for trial; deadline

Within 60 days after the arbitration award is filed with the clerk of the court, a party may request a trial by filing with the clerk a request for trial, with proof of service of a copy upon all other parties appearing in the case. A request for trial filed after the parties have been served with a copy of the award by the arbitrator, but before the award has been filed with the clerk, is valid and timely filed. The 60-day period within which to request trial may not be extended.

(Subd (a) amended effective January 1, 2012; previously amended effective January 1, 1985, July 1, 1990, January 1, 2004, and January 1, 2007.)

(b) Prosecution of the case

If a party makes a timely request for a trial, the case must proceed as provided under an applicable case management order. If no pending order provides for the prosecution of the case after a request for a trial after arbitration, the court must promptly schedule a case management conference.

(Subd (b) amended effective January 1, 2007; previously amended effective January 1, 2004.)

(c) References to arbitration during trial prohibited

The case must be tried as though no arbitration proceedings had occurred. No reference may be made during the trial to the arbitration award, to the fact that there had been arbitration proceedings, to the evidence adduced at the arbitration hearing, or to any other aspect of the arbitration proceedings, and none of the foregoing may be used as affirmative evidence, or by way of impeachment, or for any other purpose at the trial.

(Subd (c) amended effective January 1, 2004.)

(d) Costs after trial

In assessing costs after the trial, the court must apply the standards specified in Code of Civil Procedure section 1141.21.

(Subd (d) amended effective January 1, 2007; previously amended effective July 1, 1979, and January 1, 2004.)

Rule 3.826 amended effective January 1, 2012; adopted as rule 1616 effective July 1, 1976; previously amended effective July 1, 1979, July 1, 1990, and January 1, 2004; previously amended and renumbered effective January 1, 2007.

Rule 3.827. Entry of award as judgment

(a) Entry of award as judgment by clerk

The clerk must enter the award as a judgment immediately upon the expiration of 60 days after the award is filed if no party has, during that period, served and filed either:

(1) A request for trial as provided in these rules; or

(2) A *Request for Dismissal* (form CIV-110) of the entire case or as to all parties to the arbitration. The *Request for Dismissal* must be fully completed. If the request is for dismissal of the entire case, it must include the signatures of all parties. If the request is for dismissal as to all parties to the arbitration, it must include the signatures of all those parties.

(Subd (a) amended effective January 1, 2013; adopted effective January 1, 2007; previously amended effective January 1, 2012.)

(b) Notice of entry of judgment

Promptly upon entry of the award as a judgment, the clerk must serve notice of entry of judgment on all parties who have appeared in the case and must execute a certificate of service and place it in the court's file in the case.

(Subd (b) amended effective January 1, 2016.)

(c) Effect of judgment

The judgment so entered has the same force and effect in all respects as, and is subject to all provisions of law relating to, a judgment in a civil case or proceeding, except that it is not subject to appeal and it may not be attacked or set aside except as provided in rule 3.828. The judgment so entered may be enforced as if it had been rendered by the court in which it is entered.

Rule 3.827 amended effective January 1, 2016; adopted effective January 1, 2007; previously amended effective January 1, 2012, and January 1, 2013.

Rule 3.828. Vacating judgment on award

(a) Motion to vacate

A party against whom a judgment is entered under an arbitration award may, within six months after its entry, move to vacate the judgment on the ground that the arbitrator was subject to a disqualification not disclosed before the hearing and of which the arbitrator was then aware, or upon one of the grounds set forth in Code of Civil Procedure sections 473 or 1286.2(a)(1), (2), and (3), and on no other grounds.

(b) Notice and grounds for granting motion

The motion must be heard upon notice to the adverse parties and to the arbitrator, and may be granted only upon clear and convincing evidence that the grounds alleged are true, and that the motion was made as soon as practicable after the moving party learned of the existence of those grounds.

Rule 3.828 adopted effective January 1, 2007.

Rule 3.829. Settlement of case

If a case is settled, each plaintiff or other party seeking affirmative relief must notify the arbitrator and the court as required in rule 3.1385.

Rule 3.829 amended and renumbered effective January 1, 2007; adopted as rule 1618 effective January 1, 1992; previously amended effective January 1, 2004.

Rule 3.830. Arbitration not pursuant to rules

These rules do not prohibit the parties to any civil case or proceeding from entering into arbitration agreements under part 3, title 9 of the Code of Civil Procedure. Neither the ADR committee nor the ADR administrator may take any part in the conduct of an arbitration under an agreement not in conformity with these rules except that the administrator may, upon joint request of the parties, furnish the parties to the agreement with a randomly selected list of at least three names of members of the appropriate panel of arbitrators.

Rule 3.830 amended and renumbered effective January 1, 2007; adopted as rule 1617 effective July 1, 1976; previously amended effective January 1, 2004.

Chapter 3
General Rules Relating to Mediation of Civil Cases

Art. 1. Procedures for All Court Mediation Programs. Rules 3.835, 3.845.
Art. 2. Rules of Conduct for Mediators in Court-Connected Mediation Programs for Civil Cases. Rules 3.850–3.860.
Art. 3. Requirements for Addressing Complaints About Court-Program Mediators. Rules 3.865–3.872.

Article 1
Procedures for All Court Mediation Programs

Division 8, Alternative Dispute Resolution—Chapter 3, General Rules Relating to Mediation of Civil Cases—Article 1, Procedures for All Court Mediation Programs; adopted effective July 1, 2012.

Rule 3.835. Application
Rule 3.845. Form of mediator statements and reports

Rule 3.835. Application

The rules in this article apply to all court mediation programs for general civil cases, as defined in rule 1.6, unless otherwise specified.
Rule 3.835 adopted effective July 1, 2012.

Rule 3.845. Form of mediator statements and reports

If a mediator is required to submit a statement or report to the court concerning the status or result of the mediation, the statement or report must be submitted on the Judicial Council *Statement of Agreement or Nonagreement* (form ADR-100). The mediator's completed form ADR-100 must not disclose the terms of any agreement or any other communications or conduct that occurred in the course of the mediation, except as allowed in Evidence Code sections 1115–1128.
Rule 3.845 adopted effective July 1, 2012.

Advisory Committee Comment

This rule does not preclude courts from asking mediators to provide other information about court-program mediations on separate forms or surveys that do not request any information that will allow identification of a specific case or mediation participant and that will not become part of the court's case file.

Article 2
Rules of Conduct for Mediators in Court-Connected Mediation Programs for Civil Cases

Rule 3.850. Purpose and function
Rule 3.851. Application
Rule 3.852. Definitions
Rule 3.853. Voluntary participation and self-determination
Rule 3.854. Confidentiality
Rule 3.855. Impartiality, conflicts of interest, disclosure, and withdrawal
Rule 3.856. Competence
Rule 3.857. Quality of mediation process
Rule 3.858. Marketing
Rule 3.859. Compensation and gifts
Rule 3.860. Attendance sheet and agreement to disclosure

Rule 3.850. Purpose and function

(a) Standards of conduct

The rules in this article establish the minimum standards of conduct for mediators in court-connected mediation programs for general civil cases. These rules are intended to guide the conduct of mediators in these programs, to inform and protect participants in these mediation programs, and to promote public confidence in the mediation process and the courts. For mediation to be effective, there must be broad public confidence in the integrity and fairness of the process. Mediators in court-connected programs are responsible to the parties, the public, and the courts for conducting themselves in a manner that merits that confidence.
(Subd (a) amended effective January 1, 2007.)

(b) Scope and limitations

These rules are not intended to:

(1) Establish a ceiling on what is considered good practice in mediation or discourage efforts by courts, mediators, or others to educate mediators about best practices;

(2) Create a basis for challenging a settlement agreement reached in connection with mediation; or

(3) Create a basis for a civil cause of action against a mediator.

(Subd (b) amended effective January 1, 2007.)
Rule 3.850 amended and renumbered effective January 1, 2007; adopted as rule 1620 effective January 1, 2003.

Rule 3.851. Application

(a) Circumstances applicable

The rules in this article apply to mediations in which a mediator:

(1) Has agreed to be included on a superior court's list or panel of mediators for general civil cases and is notified by the court or the parties that he or she has been selected to mediate a case within that court's mediation program; or

(2) Has agreed to mediate a general civil case pending in a superior court after being notified by the court or the parties that he or she was recommended, selected, or appointed by that court or will be compensated by that court to mediate a case within that court's mediation program. A mediator who is not on a superior court list or panel and who is selected by the parties is not "recommended, selected, or appointed" by the court within the meaning of this subdivision simply because the court approves the parties' agreement to use this mediator or memorializes the parties' selection in a court order.

(Subd (a) amended effective January 1, 2010; previously amended effective January 1, 2007, and January 1, 2009.)

(b) Application to listed firms

If a court's panel or list includes firms that provide mediation services, all mediators affiliated with a listed firm are required to comply with the rules in this article when they are notified by the court or the parties that the firm was selected from the court list to mediate a general civil case within that court's mediation program.

(Subd (b) amended effective July 1, 2007; previously amended effective January 1, 2007.)

(c) Time of applicability

Except as otherwise provided in these rules, the rules in this article apply from the time the mediator agrees to mediate a case until the end of the mediation in that case.

(Subd (c) amended effective January 1, 2007.)

(d) Inapplicability to judges

The rules in this article do not apply to judges or other judicial officers while they are serving in a capacity in which they are governed by the Code of Judicial Ethics.

(Subd (d) amended effective January 1, 2007.)

(e) Inapplicability to settlement conferences

The rules in this article do not apply to settlement conferences conducted under rule 3.1380.

(Subd (e) amended effective January 1, 2007.)
Rule 3.851 amended effective January 1, 2010; adopted as rule 1620.1 effective January 1, 2003; previously amended and renumbered effective January 1, 2007; previously amended effective July 1, 2007, and January 1, 2009.

Advisory Committee Comment

Subdivision (d). Although these rules do not apply to them, judicial officers who serve as mediators in their courts' mediation programs are nevertheless encouraged to be familiar with and observe these rules when mediating, particularly the rules concerning subjects not covered in the Code of Judicial Ethics such as voluntary participation and self-determination.

Rule 3.852. Definitions

As used in this article, unless the context or subject matter requires otherwise:

(1) "Mediation" means a process in which a neutral person or persons facilitate communication between the disputants to assist them in reaching a mutually acceptable agreement.

(2) "Mediator" means a neutral person who conducts a mediation.

(3) "Participant" means any individual, entity, or group, other than the mediator taking part in a mediation, including but not limited to attorneys for the parties.

(4) "Party" means any individual, entity, or group taking part in a mediation that is a plaintiff, a defendant, a cross-complainant, a cross-defendant, a petitioner, a respondent, or an intervenor in the case.

Rule 3.852 amended and renumbered effective January 1, 2007; adopted as rule 1620.2 effective January 1, 2003.

Advisory Committee Comment

The definition of "mediator" in this rule departs from the definition in Evidence Code section 1115(b) in that it does not include persons designated by the mediator to assist in the mediation or to communicate with a participant in preparation for the mediation. However, these definitions are applicable only to these rules of conduct and do not limit or expand mediation confidentiality under the Evidence Code or other law.

The definition of "participant" includes insurance adjusters, experts, and consultants as well as the parties and their attorneys.

Rule 3.853. Voluntary participation and self-determination

A mediator must conduct the mediation in a manner that supports the principles of voluntary participation and self-determination by the parties. For this purpose a mediator must:

(1) Inform the parties, at or before the outset of the first mediation session, that any resolution of the dispute in mediation requires a voluntary agreement of the parties;

(2) Respect the right of each participant to decide the extent of his or her participation in the mediation, including the right to withdraw from the mediation at any time; and

(3) Refrain from coercing any party to make a decision or to continue to participate in the mediation.

Rule 3.853 amended and renumbered effective January 1, 2007; adopted as rule 1620.3 effective January 1, 2003.

Advisory Committee Comment

Voluntary participation and self-determination are fundamental principles of mediation that apply both to mediations in which the parties voluntarily elect to mediate and to those in which the parties are required to go to mediation in a mandatory court mediation program or by court order. Although the court may order participants to attend mediation, a mediator may not mandate the extent of their participation in the mediation process or coerce any party to settle the case.

After informing the parties of their choices and the consequences of those choices, a mediator can invoke a broad range of approaches to assist the parties in reaching an agreement without offending the principles of voluntary participation and self-determination, including (1) encouraging the parties to continue participating in the mediation when it reasonably appears to the mediator that the possibility of reaching an uncoerced, consensual agreement has not been exhausted and (2) suggesting that a party consider obtaining professional advice (for example, informing an unrepresented party that he or she may consider obtaining legal advice). Conversely, examples of conduct that violate the principles of voluntary participation and self-determination include coercing a party to continue participating in the mediation after the party has told the mediator that he or she wishes to terminate the mediation, providing an opinion or evaluation of the dispute in a coercive manner or over the objection of the parties, using abusive language, and threatening to make a report to the court about a party's conduct at the mediation.

Rule 3.854. Confidentiality

(a) Compliance with confidentiality law

A mediator must, at all times, comply with the applicable law concerning confidentiality.

(b) Informing participants of confidentiality

At or before the outset of the first mediation session, a mediator must provide the participants with a general explanation of the confidentiality of mediation proceedings.

(c) Confidentiality of separate communications; caucuses

If, after all the parties have agreed to participate in the mediation process and the mediator has agreed to mediate the case, a mediator speaks separately with one or more participants out of the presence of the other participants, the mediator must first discuss with all participants the mediator's practice regarding confidentiality for separate communications with the participants. Except as required by law, a mediator must not disclose information revealed in confidence during such separate communications unless authorized to do so by the participant or participants who revealed the information.

(d) Use of confidential information

A mediator must not use information that is acquired in confidence in the course of a mediation outside the mediation or for personal gain.

Rule 3.854 renumbered effective January 1, 2007; adopted as rule 1620.4 effective January 1, 2003.

Advisory Committee Comment

Subdivision (a). The general law concerning mediation confidentiality is found in Evidence Code sections 703.5 and 1115–1128 and in cases interpreting those sections. (See, e.g., *Foxgate Homeowners' Association, Inc. v. Bramalea California, Inc.* (2001) 26 Cal.4th 1; *Rinaker v. Superior Court* (1998) 62 Cal.App.4th 155; and *Gilbert v. National Corp. for Housing Partnerships* (1999) 71 Cal.App.4th 1240.)

Rule 3.855. Impartiality, conflicts of interest, disclosure, and withdrawal

(a) Impartiality

A mediator must maintain impartiality toward all participants in the mediation process at all times.

(b) Disclosure of matters potentially affecting impartiality

(1) A mediator must make reasonable efforts to keep informed about matters that reasonably could raise a question about his or her ability to conduct the proceedings impartially, and must disclose these matters to the parties. These matters include:

(A) Past, present, and currently expected interests, relationships, and affiliations of a personal, professional, or financial nature; and

(B) The existence of any grounds for disqualification of a judge specified in Code of Civil Procedure section 170.1.

(2) A mediator's duty to disclose is a continuing obligation, from the inception of the mediation process through its completion. Disclosures required by this rule must be made as soon as practicable after a mediator becomes aware of a matter that must be disclosed. To the extent possible, such disclosures should be made before the first mediation session, but in any event they must be made within the time required by applicable court rules or statutes.

(Subd (b) amended effective January 1, 2007.)

(c) Proceeding if there are no objections or questions concerning impartiality

Except as provided in (f), if, after a mediator makes disclosures, no party objects to the mediator and no participant raises any question or concern about the mediator's ability to conduct the mediation impartially, the mediator may proceed.

(Subd (c) amended effective January 1, 2007.)

(d) Responding to questions or concerns concerning impartiality

If, after a mediator makes disclosures or at any other point in the mediation process, a participant raises a question or concern about the mediator's ability to conduct the mediation impartially, the mediator must address the question or concern with the participants. Except as provided in (f), if, after the question or concern is addressed, no party objects to the mediator, the mediator may proceed.

(Subd (d) amended effective January 1, 2007.)

(e) Withdrawal or continuation upon party objection concerning impartiality

In a two-party mediation, if any party objects to the mediator after the mediator makes disclosures or discusses a participant's question or concern regarding the mediator's ability to conduct the mediation impartially, the mediator must withdraw. In a mediation in which there are more than two parties, the mediator may continue the mediation with the nonobjecting parties, provided that doing so would not violate any other provision of these rules, any law, or any local court rule or program guideline.

(f) Circumstances requiring mediator recusal despite party consent

Regardless of the consent of the parties, a mediator either must decline to serve as mediator or, if already serving, must withdraw from the mediation if:

(1) The mediator cannot maintain impartiality toward all participants in the mediation process; or

(2) Proceeding with the mediation would jeopardize the integrity of the court or of the mediation process.

Rule 3.855 amended and renumbered effective January 1, 2007; adopted as rule 1620.5 effective January 1, 2003.

Advisory Committee Comment

Subdivision (b). This subdivision is intended to provide parties with information they need to help them determine whether a mediator can conduct the mediation impartially. A mediator's overarching duty under this subdivision is to make a "reasonable effort" to identify matters that, in the eyes of a reasonable person, could raise a question about the mediator's ability to conduct the mediation impartially, and to inform the parties about those matters. What constitutes a "reasonable effort" to identify such matters varies depending on the circumstances, including whether the case is scheduled in advance or received on the spot, and the information about the participants and the subject matter that is provided to the mediator by the court and the parties.

The interests, relationships, and affiliations that a mediator may need to disclose under (b)(1)(A) include: (1) prior, current, or currently expected service as a mediator in another mediation involving any of the participants in the present mediation; (2) prior, current, or currently expected business relationships or transactions between the mediator and any of the participants; and (3) the mediator's ownership of stock or any other significant financial interest involving any participant in the mediation. Currently expected interests, relationships, and affiliations may include, for example, an intention to form a partnership or to enter into a future business relationship with one of the participants in the mediation.

Although (b)(1) specifies interests, relationships, affiliations, and matters that are grounds for disqualification of a judge under Code of Civil Procedure section 170.1, these are only examples of common matters that reasonably could raise a question about a mediator's ability to conduct the mediation impartially and, thus, must be disclosed. The absence of particular interests, relationships, affiliations, and section 170.1 matters does not necessarily mean that there is no matter that could reasonably raise a question about the mediator's ability to conduct the mediation impartially. A mediator must make determinations concerning disclosure on a case-by-case basis, applying the general criteria for disclosure under (b)(1).

Attorney mediators should be aware that under the section 170.1 standard, they may need to make disclosures when an attorney in their firm is serving or has served as a lawyer for any of the parties in the mediation. Section 170.1 does not specifically address whether a mediator must disclose when another member of the mediator's dispute resolution services firm is providing or has provided services to any of the parties in the mediation. Therefore, a mediator must evaluate such circumstances under the general criteria for disclosure under (b)(1)—that is, is it a matter that, in the eyes of a reasonable person, could raise a question about the mediator's ability to conduct the mediation impartially?

If there is a conflict between the mediator's obligation to maintain confidentiality and the mediator's obligation to make a disclosure, the mediator must determine whether he or she can make a general disclosure of the circumstance without revealing any confidential information, or must decline to serve.

Rule 3.856. Competence

(a) Compliance with court qualifications
A mediator must comply with experience, training, educational, and other requirements established by the court for appointment and retention.

(b) Truthful representation of background
A mediator has a continuing obligation to truthfully represent his or her background to the court and participants. Upon a request by any party, a mediator must provide truthful information regarding his or her experience, training, and education.

(c) Informing court of public discipline and other matters
A mediator must also inform the court if:

(1) Public discipline has been imposed on the mediator by any public disciplinary or professional licensing agency;

(2) The mediator has resigned his or her membership in the State Bar or another professional licensing agency while disciplinary or criminal charges were pending;

(3) A felony charge is pending against the mediator;

(4) The mediator has been convicted of a felony or of a misdemeanor involving moral turpitude; or

(5) There has been an entry of judgment against the mediator in any civil action for actual fraud or punitive damages.

(d) Assessment of skills; withdrawal
A mediator has a continuing obligation to assess whether or not his or her level of skill, knowledge, and ability is sufficient to conduct the mediation effectively. A mediator must decline to serve or withdraw from the mediation if the mediator determines that he or she does not have the level of skill, knowledge, or ability necessary to conduct the mediation effectively.

Rule 3.856 renumbered effective January 1, 2007; adopted as rule 1620.6 effective January 1, 2003.

Advisory Committee Comment

Subdivision (d). No particular advanced academic degree or technical or professional experience is a prerequisite for competence as a mediator. Core mediation skills include communicating clearly, listening effectively, facilitating communication among all participants, promoting exploration of mutually acceptable settlement options, and conducting oneself in a neutral manner.

A mediator must consider and weigh a variety of issues in order to assess whether his or her level of skill, knowledge, and ability is sufficient to make him or her effective in a particular mediation. Issues include whether the parties (1) were involved or had input in the selection of the mediator; (2) had access to information about the mediator's background or level of skill, knowledge, and ability; (3) have a specific expectation or perception regarding the mediator's level of skill, knowledge, and ability; (4) have expressed a preference regarding the style of mediation they would like or expect; or (5) have expressed a desire to discuss legal or other professional information, to hear a personal evaluation of or opinion on a set of facts as presented, or to be made aware of the interests of persons who are not represented in mediation.

Rule 3.857. Quality of mediation process

(a) Diligence
A mediator must make reasonable efforts to advance the mediation in a timely manner. If a mediator schedules a mediation for a specific time period, he or she must keep that time period free of other commitments.

(b) Procedural fairness
A mediator must conduct the mediation proceedings in a procedurally fair manner. "Procedural fairness" means a balanced process in which each party is given an opportunity to participate and make uncoerced decisions. A mediator is not obligated to ensure the substantive fairness of an agreement reached by the parties.

(c) Explanation of process
In addition to the requirements of rule 3.853 (voluntary participation and self-determination), rule 3.854(a) (confidentiality), and (d) of this rule (representation and other professional services), at or before the outset of the mediation the mediator must provide all participants with a general explanation of:

(1) The nature of the mediation process;

(2) The procedures to be used; and

(3) The roles of the mediator, the parties, and the other participants.

(Subd (c) amended effective January 1, 2007.)

(d) Representation and other professional services
A mediator must inform all participants, at or before the outset of the first mediation session, that during the mediation he or she will not represent any participant as a lawyer or perform professional services in any capacity other than as an impartial mediator. Subject to the principles of impartiality and self-determination, a mediator may provide information or opinions that he or she is qualified by training or experience to provide.

(e) Recommending other services
A mediator may recommend the use of other services in connection with a mediation and may recommend particular providers of other services. However, a mediator must disclose any related personal or financial interests if recommending the services of specific individuals or organizations.

(f) Nonparticipants' interests
A mediator may bring to the attention of the parties the interests of others who are not participating in the mediation but who may be affected by agreements reached as a result of the mediation.

(g) Combining mediation with other ADR processes
A mediator must exercise caution in combining mediation with other alternative dispute resolution (ADR) processes and may do so only with the informed consent of the parties and in a manner consistent with any applicable law or court order. The mediator must inform the parties of the general natures of the different processes and the consequences of revealing information during any one process that might be used for decision making in another process, and must give the parties the opportunity to select another neutral for the subsequent process. If the parties consent to a combination of processes, the mediator must clearly inform the participants when the transition from one process to another is occurring.

(h) Settlement agreements
Consistent with (d), a mediator may present possible settlement options and terms for discussion. A mediator may also assist the parties in preparing a written settlement agreement, provided that in doing so the mediator confines the assistance to stating the settlement as determined by the parties.

(Subd (h) amended effective January 1, 2007.)

(i) Discretionary termination and withdrawal
A mediator may suspend or terminate the mediation or withdraw as mediator when he or she reasonably believes the circumstances require it, including when he or she suspects that:

(1) The mediation is being used to further illegal conduct;

(2) A participant is unable to participate meaningfully in negotiations; or

(3) Continuation of the process would cause significant harm to any participant or a third party.

(j) Manner of withdrawal
When a mediator determines that it is necessary to suspend or terminate a mediation or to withdraw, the mediator must do so without violating the obligation of confidentiality and in a manner that will cause the least possible harm to the participants.

Rule 3.857 amended and renumbered effective January 1, 2007; adopted as rule 1620.7 effective January 1, 2003.

Advisory Committee Comment

Subdivision (c). The explanation of the mediation process should include a description of the mediator's style of mediation.

Subdivision (d). Subject to the principles of impartiality and self-determination, and if qualified to do so, a mediator may (1) discuss a party's options, including a range of possible outcomes in an adjudicative process; (2) offer a personal evaluation of or opinion on a set of facts as presented, which should be clearly identified as a personal evaluation or opinion; or (3) communicate the mediator's opinion or view of what the law is or how it applies to the subject of the mediation, provided that the mediator does not also advise any participant about how to adhere to the law or on what position the participant should take in light of that opinion.

One question that frequently arises is whether a mediator's assessment of claims, defenses, or possible litigation outcomes constitutes legal advice or the practice of law. Similar questions may arise when accounting, architecture, construction, counseling, medicine, real estate, or other licensed professions are relevant to a mediation. This rule does not determine what constitutes the practice of law or any other licensed profession. A mediator should be cautious when providing any information or opinion related to any field for which a professional license is required, in order to avoid doing so in a manner that may constitute the practice of a profession for which the mediator is not licensed, or in a manner that may violate the regulations of a profession that the mediator is licensed to practice. A mediator should exercise particular caution when discussing the law with unrepresented parties and should inform such parties that they may seek independent advice from a lawyer.

Subdivision (i). Subdivision (i)(2) is not intended to establish any new responsibility or diminish any existing responsibilities that a mediator may have, under the Americans With Disabilities Act or other similar law, to attempt to accommodate physical or mental disabilities of a participant in mediation.

Rule 3.858. Marketing
(a) Truthfulness
A mediator must be truthful and accurate in marketing his or her mediation services. A mediator is responsible for ensuring that both his or her own marketing activities and any marketing activities carried out on his or her behalf by others comply with this rule.

(b) Representations concerning court approval
A mediator may indicate in his or her marketing materials that he or she is a member of a particular court's panel or list but, unless specifically permitted by the court, must not indicate that he or she is approved, endorsed, certified, or licensed by the court.

(c) Promises, guarantees, and implications of favoritism
In marketing his or her mediation services, a mediator must not:

(1) Promise or guarantee results; or

(2) Make any statement that directly or indirectly implies bias in favor of one party or participant over another.

(d) Solicitation of business
A mediator must not solicit business from a participant in a mediation proceeding while that mediation is pending.

Rule 3.858 renumbered effective January 1, 2007; adopted as rule 1620.8 effective January 1, 2003.

Advisory Committee Comment

Subdivision (d). This rule is not intended to prohibit a mediator from accepting other employment from a participant while a mediation is pending, provided that there was no express solicitation of this business by the mediator and that accepting that employment does not contravene any other provision of these rules, including the obligations to maintain impartiality, confidentiality, and the integrity of the process. If other employment is accepted from a participant while a mediation is pending, however, the mediator may be required to disclose this to the parties under rule 3.855.

This rule also is not intended to prohibit a mediator from engaging in general marketing activities. General marketing activities include, but are not limited to, running an advertisement in a newspaper and sending out a general mailing (either of which may be directed to a particular industry or market).

Rule 3.859. Compensation and gifts
(a) Compliance with law
A mediator must comply with any applicable requirements concerning compensation established by statute or the court.

(b) Disclosure of and compliance with compensation terms
Before commencing the mediation, the mediator must disclose to the parties in writing any fees, costs, or charges to be paid to the mediator by the parties. A mediator must abide by any agreement that is reached concerning compensation.

(c) Contingent fees
The amount or nature of a mediator's fee must not be made contingent on the outcome of the mediation.

(Subd (c) amended effective January 1, 2007.)

(d) Gifts and favors
A mediator must not at any time solicit or accept from or give to any participant or affiliate of a participant any gift, bequest, or favor that might reasonably raise a question concerning the mediator's impartiality.

Rule 3.859 amended and renumbered effective January 1, 2007; adopted as rule 1620.9 effective January 1, 2003.

Advisory Committee Comment

Subdivision (b). It is good practice to put mediation fee agreements in writing, and mediators are strongly encouraged to do so; however, nothing in this rule is intended to preclude enforcement of a compensation agreement for mediation services that is not in writing.

Subdivision (d). Whether a gift, bequest, or favor "might reasonably raise a question concerning the mediator's impartiality" must be determined on a case-by-case basis. This subdivision is not intended to prohibit a mediator from accepting other employment from any of the participants, consistent with rule 3.858(d).

Rule 3.860. Attendance sheet and agreement to disclosure
(a) Attendance sheet
In each mediation to which these rules apply under rule 3.851(a), the mediator must request that all participants in the mediation complete an attendance sheet stating their names, mailing addresses, and telephone numbers; retain the attendance sheet for at least two years; and submit it to the court on request.

(Subd (a) amended effective January 1, 2007.)

(b) Agreement to disclosure
The mediator must agree, in each mediation to which these rules apply under rule 3.851(a), that if an inquiry or a complaint is made about the conduct of the mediator, mediation communications may be disclosed solely for purposes of a complaint procedure conducted pursuant to rule 3.865 to address that complaint or inquiry.

(Subd (b) amended effective January 1, 2011; previously amended effective January 1, 2007.)

Rule 3.860 amended effective January 1, 2011; adopted as rule 1621 effective January 1, 2006; previously amended and renumbered effective January 1, 2007.

Rule 3.865. Complaint procedure required [Renumbered]
Rule 3.865 amended and renumbered to rule 3.868 effective July 1, 2009, effective date extended to January 1, 2010; adopted as rule 1622 effective January 1, 2003; previously amended effective January 1, 2006, and January 1, 2007.

2009 Note: Another Rule 3.865 follows in Article 3.

Rule 3.866. Designation of person to receive inquiries and complaints [Renumbered]
Rule 3.866 amended and renumbered to rule 3.867 effective July 1, 2009, effective date extended to January 1, 2010; adopted as rule 1622.1 effective January 1, 2006; previously amended and renumbered effective January 1, 2007.

2009 Note: Another Rule 3.866 follows in Article 3.

Rule 3.867. Confidentiality of complaint procedures, information, and records [Renumbered]
Rule 3.867 amended and renumbered to rule 3.871 effective July 1, 2009, effective date extended to January 1, 2010; adopted as rule 1622.2 effective January 1, 2006; previously amended and renumbered effective January 1, 2007; previously amended effective January 1, 2008.

2009 Note: Another Rule 3.867 follows in Article 3.

Rule 3.868. Disqualification from subsequently serving as an adjudicator [Renumbered]
Rule 3.868 amended and renumbered to rule 3.872 effective July 1, 2009, effective date extended to January 1, 2010; adopted as rule 1622.3 effective January 1, 2006; previously amended and renumbered effective January 1, 2007.

2009 Note: Another Rule 3.868 follows in Article 3.

Article 3
Requirements for Addressing Complaints About Court-Program Mediators

Title 3, Civil Rules—Division 8, Alternative Dispute Resolution—Chapter 3, General Rules Relating to Mediation of Civil Cases—Article 3, Requirements for Addressing Complaints About Court-Program Mediators adopted effective July 1, 2009, effective date extended to January 1, 2010.

Rule 3.865. Application and purpose
Rule 3.866. Definitions
Rule 3.867. Complaint coordinator
Rule 3.868. Complaint procedure required
Rule 3.869. General requirements for complaint procedures and complaint proceedings
Rule 3.870. Permissible court actions on complaints
Rule 3.871. Confidentiality of complaint proceedings, information, and records
Rule 3.872. Disqualification from subsequently serving as an adjudicator

Rule 3.865. Application and purpose

(a) Application

The rules in this article apply to each superior court that makes a list of mediators available to litigants in general civil cases or that recommends, selects, appoints, or compensates a mediator to mediate any general civil case pending in that court. A court that approves the parties' agreement to use a mediator who is selected by the parties and who is not on the court's list of mediators or that memorializes the parties' agreement in a court order has not thereby recommended, selected, or appointed that mediator within the meaning of this rule.

(Subd (a) amended and lettered effective January 1, 2010; previously adopted as part of unlettered subd effective January 1, 2010.)

(b) Purpose

These rules are intended to promote the resolution of complaints that mediators in court-connected mediation programs for civil cases may have violated a provision of the rules of conduct for such mediators in article 2. They are intended to help courts promptly resolve any such complaints in a manner that is respectful and fair to the complainant and the mediator and consistent with the California mediation confidentiality statutes.

(Subd (b) lettered effective January 1, 2010; previously adopted as part of unlettered subd effective January 1, 2010.)
Rule 3.865 amended effective January 1, 2010; adopted effective July 1, 2009, effective date extended to January 1, 2010.

Advisory Committee Comment

As used in this article, complaint means a written communication presented to a court's complaint coordinator indicating that a mediator may have violated a provision of the rules of conduct for mediators in article 2.

Complaints about mediators are relatively rare. To ensure the quality of court mediation panels and public confidence in the mediation process and the courts, it is, nevertheless, important to ensure that any complaints that do arise are resolved through procedures that are consistent with California mediation confidentiality statutes (Evid. Code, §§ 703.5 and 1115 et seq.), as well as fair and respectful to the interested parties.

The requirements and procedures in this article do not abrogate or limit a court's inherent or other authority, in its sole and absolute discretion, to determine who may be included on or removed from a court list of mediators; to approve or revoke a mediator's eligibility to be recommended, selected, appointed, or compensated by the court; or to follow other procedures or take other actions to ensure the quality of mediators who serve in the court's mediation program in contexts other than when addressing a complaint. The failure to follow a requirement or procedure in this article will not invalidate any action taken by the court in addressing a complaint.

2009 Note: Another Rule 3.865 precedes in Article 2.

Rule 3.866. Definitions

As used in this article, unless the context or subject matter requires otherwise:

(1) "The rules of conduct" means rules 3.850–3.860 of the California Rules of Court in article 2.

(2) "Court-program mediator" means a person subject to the rules of conduct under rule 3.851.

(3) "Inquiry" means an unwritten communication presented to the court's complaint coordinator indicating that a mediator may have violated a provision of the rules of conduct.

(4) "Complaint" means a written communication presented to the court's complaint coordinator indicating that a mediator may have violated a provision of the rules of conduct.

(5) "Complainant" means the person who makes or presents a complaint.

(6) "Complaint coordinator" means the person designated by the presiding judge under rule 3.867(a) to receive complaints and inquiries about the conduct of mediators.

(7) "Complaint committee" means a committee designated or appointed to investigate and make recommendations concerning complaints under rule 3.869(d)(2).

(8) "Complaint procedure" means a procedure for presenting, receiving, reviewing, responding to, investigating, and acting on any inquiry or complaint.

(9) "Complaint proceeding" means all of the proceedings that take place as part of a complaint procedure concerning a specific inquiry or complaint.

(10) "Mediation communication" means any statement that is made or any writing that is prepared for the purpose of, in the course of, or pursuant to a mediation or a mediation consultation, as defined in Evidence Code section 1115, and includes any communications, negotiations, and settlement discussions between participants in the course of a mediation or a mediation consultation.

Rule 3.866 adopted effective July 1, 2009, effective date extended to January 1, 2010.

Advisory Committee Comment

Paragraph (2). Under rule 3.851, the rules of conduct apply when a mediator, or a firm with which a mediator is affiliated, has agreed to be included on a superior court's list or panel of mediators for general civil cases and is notified by the court or the parties that he or she has been selected to mediate a case within that court's mediation program or when a mediator has agreed to mediate a general civil case after being notified that he or she was recommended, selected, or appointed by a court, or will be compensated by a court, to mediate a case within a court's mediation program.

Paragraphs (3) and (4). The distinction between "inquiries" and "complaints" is significant because some provisions of this article apply only to complaints (i.e., written communications presented to the court's complaint coordinator indicating that a mediator may have violated a provision of the rules of conduct) and not to inquiries.

2009 Note: Another Rule 3.866 precedes in Article 2.

Rule 3.867. Complaint coordinator

(a) Designation of the complaint coordinator

The presiding judge must designate a person who is knowledgeable about mediation to serve as the complaint coordinator.

(Subd (a) amended and lettered effective July 1, 2009, effective date extended to January 1, 2010; adopted as unlettered subd effective January 1, 2006.)

(b) Identification of the complaint coordinator

The court must make the complaint coordinator's identity and contact information readily accessible to litigants and the public.

(Subd (b) adopted effective July 1, 2009, effective date extended to January 1, 2010.)
Rule 3.867 amended and renumbered effective July 1, 2009, effective date extended to January 1, 2010; adopted as rule 1622.1 effective January 1, 2006; previously amended and renumbered as rule 3.866 effective January 1, 2007.

Advisory Committee Comment

The alternative dispute resolution program administrator appointed under rule 10.783(a) may also be appointed as the complaint coordinator if that person is knowledgeable about mediation.

2009 Note: Another Rule 3.867 precedes in Article 2.

Rule 3.868. Complaint procedure required

Each court to which this article applies under rule 3.865 must establish a complaint procedure by local rule of court that is consistent with this article.

(Subd amended and unlettered effective July 1, 2009, effective date extended to January 1, 2010; adopted as subd (a) effective January 1, 2003; previously amended effective January 1, 2006, and January 1, 2007.)
Rule 3.868 amended and renumbered effective July 1, 2009, effective date extended to January 1, 2010; adopted as rule 1622 effective January 1, 2003; previously amended effective January 1, 2006; previously amended and renumbered as rule 3.865 effective January 1, 2007.

2009 Note: Another Rule 3.868 precedes in Article 2.

Rule 3.869. General requirements for complaint procedures and complaint proceedings

(a) Submission and referral of inquiries and complaints to the complaint coordinator

All inquiries and complaints should be submitted or referred to the complaint coordinator.

(Subd (a) adopted effective July 1, 2009, effective date extended to January 1, 2010.)

(b) Acknowledgment of complaint

The complaint coordinator must send the complainant a written acknowledgment that the court has received the complaint.

(Subd (b) adopted effective July 1, 2009, effective date extended to January 1, 2010.)

(c) Preliminary review and disposition of complaints

The complaint coordinator must conduct a preliminary review of all complaints to determine whether the complaint can be informally resolved or closed, or whether the complaint warrants investigation.

(Subd (c) adopted effective July 1, 2009, effective date extended to January 1, 2010.)

(d) Procedure for complaints not resolved through the preliminary review

The following procedures are required only if a complaint is not resolved or closed through the preliminary review.

(1) *Mediator's notice and opportunity to respond*

The mediator must be given notice of the complaint and an opportunity to respond.

(2) *Investigation and recommendation*

(A) Except as provided in (B), the complaint must be investigated and a recommendation concerning court action on the complaint must be made by either an individual who has experience as a mediator and who is familiar with the rules of conduct stated in article 2 or a complaint committee that has at least one such individual as a member.

(B) A court with eight or fewer authorized judges may waive the requirement in (A) for participation by an individual who has experience as a mediator in conducting the investigation and making the recommendation if the court cannot find a suitable qualified individual to perform the functions described in (A) or for other grounds of hardship.

(3) *Final decision*

The final decision on the complaint must be made by the presiding judge or his or her designee, who must not be the complaint coordinator or an individual who investigated the complaint before its submission for final decision.

(Subd (d) adopted effective July 1, 2009, effective date extended to January 1, 2010.)

(e) Notice of final action

(1) The court must send the complainant notice of the final action taken by the court on the complaint.

(2) If the complaint was not closed during the preliminary review, the court must send notice of the final action to the mediator.

(Subd (e) adopted effective July 1, 2009, effective date extended to January 1, 2010.)

(f) Promptness

The court must process complaints promptly at all stages.

(Subd (f) adopted effective July 1, 2009, effective date extended to January 1, 2010.)

(g) Records of complaints

The court should maintain sufficient information about each complaint and its disposition to identify any history or patterns of complaints submitted under these rules.

(Subd (g) adopted effective July 1, 2009, effective date extended to January 1, 2010.)

Rule 3.869 adopted effective July 1, 2009, effective date extended to January 1, 2010.

Advisory Committee Comment

Judicial Council staff have developed model local rules that satisfy the requirements of this rule. These model local rules were developed with input from judicial officers, court administrators, alternative dispute resolution (ADR) program administrators, court-program mediators, and public commentators and are designed so that they can be readily adapted to the circumstances of individual courts and specific complaints. Courts are encouraged to adopt rules that follow the model rules, to the extent feasible. Courts can obtain copies of these model rules from the Judicial Council's civil ADR program staff.

Subdivision (a). Coordination of inquiries and complaints by a person knowledgeable about mediation is important to help ensure that the requirements of this article are followed and that mediation confidentiality is preserved.

Subdivision (c). Courts are encouraged to resolve inquiries and complaints about mediators using the simplest, least formal procedures that are appropriate under the circumstances, provided that they meet the requirements stated in this article.

Most complaints can be appropriately resolved during the preliminary review stage of the complaint process, through informal discussions between or among the complaint coordinator, the complainant, and the mediator. Although complaint coordinators are not required to communicate with the mediator during the preliminary review, they are encouraged to consider doing so. For example, some complaints may arise from a misunderstanding of the mediator's role or from behavior that would not violate the standards of conduct. These types of complaints might appropriately be addressed by providing the complainant with additional information or by informing the mediator that certain behavior was upsetting to a mediation participant.

The circumstances under which a complaint coordinator might informally resolve or close a complaint include, for example, when (1) the complaint is withdrawn; (2) no violation of the rules of conduct appears to have occurred; (3) the alleged violation of the rules of conduct is very minor and the mediator has provided an acceptable explanation or response; and (4) the complainant, the mediator, and the complaint coordinator have agreed on a resolution. In determining whether to close a complaint, the complaint coordinator might also consider whether there are or have been other complaints about the mediator.

Subdivision (d). At the investigation and recommendation stage, all courts are encouraged to consider using a complaint committee comprised of members with a variety of backgrounds, including at least one person with experience as a mediator, to investigate and make recommendations concerning those rare complaints that are not resolved during the preliminary review.

Courts are also encouraged to have a judicial officer who is knowledgeable about mediation, or a committee that includes another person who is knowledgeable about mediation, make the final decision on complaints that are not resolved through the preliminary review.

Rule 3.870. Permissible court actions on complaints

After an investigation has been conducted, the presiding judge or his or her designee may do one or more of the following:

(1) Direct that no action be taken on the complaint;

(2) Counsel, admonish, or reprimand the mediator;

(3) Impose additional training requirements as a condition of the mediator remaining on the court's panel or list;

(4) Suspend the mediator from the court's panel or list or otherwise temporarily prohibit the mediator from receiving future mediation referrals from the court; or

(5) Remove the mediator from the court's panel or list or otherwise prohibit the mediator from receiving future mediation referrals from the court.

Rule 3.870 adopted effective July 1, 2009, effective date extended to January 1, 2010.

Advisory Committee Comment

This rule does not abrogate or limit any existing legal right or duty of the court to take other actions, including interim suspension of a mediator pending final action by the court on a complaint.

2009 Note: Another Rule 3.870 follows in Chapter 4.

Rule 3.871. Confidentiality of complaint proceedings, information, and records

(a) Intent

This rule is intended to:

(1) Preserve the confidentiality of mediation communications as required by Evidence Code sections 1115–1128;

(2) Promote cooperation in the reporting, investigation, and resolution of complaints about court-program mediators; and

(3) Protect mediators against damage to their reputations that might result from the disclosure of unfounded complaints against them.

(Subd (a) amended effective July 1, 2009, effective date extended to January 1, 2010; previously amended effective January 1, 2007.)

(b) Preserving the confidentiality of mediation communications

All complaint procedures and complaint proceedings must be designed and conducted in a manner that preserves the confidentiality of mediation communications, including but not limited to the confidentiality of any communications between the mediator and individual mediation participants or subgroups of mediation participants.

(Subd (b) amended effective July 1, 2009, effective date extended to January 1, 2010.)

(c) Confidentiality of complaint proceedings

All complaint proceedings must occur in private and must be kept confidential. No information or records concerning the receipt, investigation, or resolution of an inquiry or a complaint may be open to the public or disclosed outside the course of the complaint proceeding except as provided in (d) or as otherwise required by law.

(Subd (c) amended effective July 1, 2009, effective date extended to January 1, 2010; previously amended effective January 1, 2007.)

(d) Authorized disclosures

After the decision on a complaint, the presiding judge, or a person whom the presiding judge designates to do so, may authorize the public disclosure of information or records concerning the complaint proceeding that do not reveal any mediation communications. The disclosures that may be authorized under this subdivision include the name of a mediator against whom action has been taken under rule 3.870, the action taken, and the general basis on which the action was taken. In determining whether to authorize the disclosure of information or records under this subdivision, the presiding judge or the designee should consider the purposes of the confidentiality of complaint proceedings stated in (a)(2) and (a)(3).

(Subd (d) amended effective July 1, 2009, effective date extended to January 1, 2010; previously amended effective January 1, 2007.)

(e) Disclosures required by law

In determining whether the disclosure of information or records concerning a complaint proceeding is required by law, courts should consider the purposes of the confidentiality of complaint proceedings stated in (a). If it appears that the disclosure of information or records concerning a complaint proceeding that would reveal mediation communications is required by law, before the information or records are disclosed, notice should be given to any person whose mediation communications may thereby be revealed.

(Subd (e) amended effective July 1, 2009, effective date extended to January 1, 2010; previously amended effective January 1, 2007.)

Rule 3.871 amended and renumbered effective July 1, 2009, effective date extended to January 1, 2010; adopted as rule 1622.2 effective January 1, 2006; previously amended and renumbered as rule 3.867 effective January 1, 2007.

Advisory Committee Comment

Under rule 3.866(9), the complaint proceedings covered by this rule include proceedings to address inquiries as well as complaints (i.e., to unwritten as well as written communications indicating that a mediator may have violated a provision of the rules of conduct).

Subdivision (a). See Evidence Code sections 1115 and 1119 concerning the scope and types of mediation communications protected by mediation confidentiality. Rule 3.871 is intended to supplement the confidentiality of mediation communications established by the Evidence Code by ensuring that disclosure of information or records about a complaint proceeding does not reveal confidential mediation communications. Rule 3.871 is not intended to supersede or abrogate the confidentiality of mediation communications established by the Evidence Code.

Subdivision (b). Private meetings, or "caucuses," between a mediator and subgroups of participants are common in court-connected mediations, and it is frequently understood that these communications will not be disclosed to other participants in the mediation. (See Cal. Rules of Court, rule 3.854(c).) It is important to protect the confidentiality of these communications in complaint proceedings so that one participant in the mediation does not learn what another participant discussed in confidence with the mediator without the consent of the participants in the caucus communication.

Subdivisions (c)–(e). The provisions of (c)–(e) that authorize the disclosure of information and records related to complaint proceedings do not create any new exceptions to mediation confidentiality. Although public disclosure of information and records about complaint proceedings that do not reveal mediation communications may be authorized under (d), information and records that *would* reveal mediation communications may be publicly disclosed only as required by law (e.g., in response to a subpoena or court order) and consistent with the statutes and case law governing mediation confidentiality. A person who is knowledgeable about California's mediation confidentiality laws should determine whether the disclosure of mediation communications is required by law.

Evidence Code sections 915 and 1040 establish procedures and criteria for deciding whether information acquired in confidence by a public employee in the course of his or her duty is subject to disclosure. These sections may be applicable or helpful in determining whether the disclosure of information or records acquired by judicial officers, court staff, and other persons in the course of a complaint proceeding is required by law or should be authorized in the discretion of the presiding judge.

2009 Note: Another Rule 3.871 follows in Chapter 4.

Rule 3.872. Disqualification from subsequently serving as an adjudicator

A person who has participated in a complaint proceeding or otherwise received information about the substance of a complaint, other than information that is publicly disclosed under rule 3.871(d), must not subsequently hear or determine any contested issue of law, fact, or procedure concerning the dispute that was the subject of the underlying mediation or any other dispute that arises from the mediation, as a judge, an arbitrator, a referee, or a juror, or in any other adjudicative capacity, in any court action or proceeding.

Rule 3.872 amended and renumbered effective July 1, 2009, effective date extended to January 1, 2010; adopted as rule 1622.3 effective January 1, 2006; previously amended and renumbered as rule 3.868 effective January 1, 2007.

Advisory Committee Comment

Persons who participated in a complaint proceeding are prohibited from subsequently adjudicating the dispute that was the subject of the underlying mediation or any other dispute that arises from the mediation because they may have learned confidential mediation communications that were disclosed in the complaint proceeding or may have been influenced by what transpired in that proceeding. Because the information that can be disclosed publicly under rule 3.871(d) is limited and excludes mediation communications, it is unnecessary to disqualify persons who received only publicly disclosed information from subsequently adjudicating the dispute.

2009 Note: Another Rule 3.872 follows in Chapter 4.

Chapter 4
Civil Action Mediation Program Rules

Rule 3.890. Application
Rule 3.891. Actions subject to mediation
Rule 3.892. Panels of mediators
Rule 3.893. Selection of mediators
Rule 3.894. Attendance, participant lists, and mediation statements
Rule 3.895. Filing of *Statement of Agreement or Nonagreement* by mediator
Rule 3.896. Coordination with Trial Court Delay Reduction Act
Rule 3.898. Educational material

Rule 3.870. Application [Renumbered]

Rule 3.870 renumbered to rule 3.890 effective July 1, 2009; adopted as rule 1630 effective March 1, 1994; previously amended and renumbered effective January 1, 2007.

2008 Note: Another Rule 3.870 precedes in Article 3.

Rule 3.871. Actions subject to mediation [Renumbered]

Rule 3.871 renumbered to rule 3.891 effective July 1, 2009; adopted as rule 1631 effective March 1, 1994; previously amended and renumbered effective January 1, 2007.

2008 Note: Another Rule 3.871 precedes in Article 3.

Rule 3.872. Panels of mediators [Renumbered]

Rule 3.872 renumbered to rule 3.892 effective July 1, 2009; adopted as rule 1632 effective March 1, 1994; previously amended and renumbered effective January 1, 2007.

2008 Note: Another Rule 3.872 precedes in Article 3.

Rule 3.873. Selection of mediators [Renumbered]

Rule 3.873 renumbered to rule 3.893 effective July 1, 2009; adopted as rule 1633 effective March 1, 1994; previously amended and renumbered effective January 1, 2007.

Rule 3.874. Attendance, participant lists, and mediation statements [Renumbered]

Rule 3.874 renumbered to rule 3.894 effective July 1, 2009; adopted as rule 1634 effective March 1, 1994; previously amended and renumbered effective January 1, 2007; previously amended effective January 1, 2007.

Rule 3.875. Filing of statement by mediator [Renumbered]

Rule 3.875 renumbered to rule 3.895 effective July 1, 2009; adopted as rule 1635 effective March 1, 1994; previously amended and renumbered effective January 1, 2007.

Rule 3.876. Coordination with Trial Court Delay Reduction Act [Renumbered]

Rule 3.876 renumbered to rule 3.896 effective July 1, 2009; adopted as rule 1637 effective March 1, 1994; previously amended and renumbered effective January 1, 2007.

Rule 3.877. Statistical information [Renumbered]

Rule 3.877 renumbered to rule 3.897 effective July 1, 2009; adopted as rule 1638 effective March 1, 1994; previously amended effective February 9, 1999; previously amended and renumbered effective January 1, 2007.

Rule 3.878. Educational material [Renumbered]

Rule 3.878 renumbered to rule 3.898 effective July 1, 2009; adopted as rule 1639 effective March 1, 1994; amended and renumbered effective January 1, 2007.

Rule 3.890. Application

The rules in this chapter implement the Civil Action Mediation Act, Code of Civil Procedure section 1775 et seq. Under section 1775.2, they apply in the Superior Court of California, County of Los Angeles and in other courts that elect to apply the act.

Rule 3.890 renumbered effective July 1, 2009; adopted as rule 1630 effective March 1, 1994; previously amended and renumbered as rule 3.870 effective January 1, 2007.

Rule 3.891. Actions subject to mediation

(a) Actions that may be submitted to mediation

The following actions may be submitted to mediation under these provisions:

(1) By court order

Any action in which the amount in controversy, independent of the merits of liability, defenses, or comparative negligence, does not exceed $50,000 for each plaintiff. The court must determine the amount in controversy under Code of Civil Procedure section 1775.5. Determinations to send a case to mediation must be made by the court after consideration of the expressed views of the parties on the amenability of the case to mediation. The court must not require the parties or their counsel to personally appear in court for a conference held solely to determine whether to send their case to mediation.

(2) *By stipulation*

Any other action, regardless of the amount of controversy, in which all parties stipulate to such mediation. The stipulation must be filed not later than 90 days before trial unless the court permits a later time.

(Subd (a) amended effective January 1, 2007.)

(b) Case-by-case determination

Amenability of a particular action for mediation must be determined on a case-by-case basis, rather than categorically.

(Subd (b) amended effective January 1, 2007.)

Rule 3.891 renumbered effective July 1, 2009; adopted as rule 1631 effective March 1, 1994; previously amended and renumbered as rule 3.871 effective January 1, 2007.

Rule 3.892. Panels of mediators

Each court, in consultation with local bar associations, ADR providers, and associations of providers, must identify persons who may be appointed as mediators. The court must consider the criteria in standard 10.72 of the Standards of Judicial Administration and California Code of Regulations, title 16, section 3622, relating to the Dispute Resolution Program Act.

Rule 3.892 renumbered effective July 1, 2009; adopted as rule 1632 effective March 1, 1994; previously amended and renumbered as rule 3.872 effective January 1, 2007.

Rule 3.893. Selection of mediators

The parties may stipulate to any mediator, whether or not the person selected is among those identified under rule 3.892, within 15 days of the date an action is submitted to mediation. If the parties do not stipulate to a mediator, the court must promptly assign a mediator to the action from those identified under rule 3.892.

Rule 3.893 amended effective January 1, 2011; adopted as rule 1633 effective March 1, 1994; previously amended and renumbered as rule 3.873 effective January 1, 2007; previously renumbered effective July 1, 2009.

Rule 3.894. Attendance, participant lists, and mediation statements

(a) Attendance

(1) All parties and attorneys of record must attend all mediation sessions in person unless excused or permitted to attend by telephone as provided in (3). If a party is not a natural person, a representative of that party with authority to resolve the dispute or, in the case of a governmental entity that requires an agreement to be approved by an elected official or a legislative body, a representative with authority to recommend such agreement, must attend all mediation sessions in person, unless excused or permitted to attend by telephone as provided in (3).

(2) If any party is insured under a policy of insurance that provides or may provide coverage for a claim that is a subject of the action, a representative of the insurer with authority to settle or recommend settlement of the claim must attend all mediation sessions in person, unless excused or permitted to attend by telephone as provided in (3).

(3) The mediator may excuse a party, attorney, or representative from the requirement to attend a mediation session under (1) or (2) or permit attendance by telephone. The party, attorney, or representative who is excused or permitted to attend by telephone must promptly send a letter or an electronic communication to the mediator and to all parties confirming the excuse or permission.

(4) Each party may have counsel present at all mediation sessions that concern the party.

(Subd (a) amended and lettered effective January 1, 2007; adopted as untitled subd effective March 1, 1994.)

(b) Participant lists and mediation statements

(1) At least five court days before the first mediation session, each party must serve a list of its mediation participants on the mediator and all other parties. The list must include the names of all parties, attorneys, representatives of a party that is not a natural person, insurance representatives, and other persons who will attend the mediation with or on behalf of that party. A party must promptly serve a supplemental list if the party subsequently determines that other persons will attend the mediation with or on behalf of the party.

(2) The mediator may request that each party submit a short mediation statement providing information about the issues in dispute and possible resolutions of those issues and other information or documents that may appear helpful to resolve the dispute.

(Subd (b) adopted effective January 1, 2007.)

Rule 3.894 renumbered effective July 1, 2009; adopted as rule 1634 effective March 1, 1994; previously amended and renumbered as rule 3.874 effective January 1, 2007.

Rule 3.895. Filing of *Statement of Agreement or Nonagreement* by mediator

Within 10 days after conclusion of the mediation, or by another date set by the court, the mediator must complete, serve on all parties, and file a *Statement of Agreement or Nonagreement* (form ADR-100). If the mediation has not ended when the report is filed, the mediator must file a supplemental form ADR-100 within 10 days after the mediation is concluded or by another date set by the court. The completed form ADR-100 must not disclose the terms of any agreement or any other communications or conduct that occurred in the course of the mediation, except as allowed in Evidence Code sections 1115–1128.

Rule 3.895 amended effective July 1, 2012; adopted as rule 1635 effective March 1, 1994; previously amended and renumbered as rule 3.875 effective January 1, 2007; previously renumbered effective July 1, 2009.

Rule 3.896. Coordination with Trial Court Delay Reduction Act

(a) Effect of mediation on time standards

Submission of an action to mediation under the rules in this chapter does not affect time periods specified in the Trial Court Delay Reduction Act (Gov. Code, § 68600 et seq.), except as provided in this rule.

(Subd (a) amended effective January 1, 2007.)

(b) Exception to delay reduction time standards

On written stipulation of the parties filed with the court, the court may order an exception of up to 90 days to the delay reduction time standards to permit mediation of an action. The court must coordinate the timing of the exception period with its delay reduction calendar.

(Subd (b) amended effective January 1, 2007.)

(c) Time for completion of mediation

Mediation must be completed within 60 days of a reference to a mediator, but that period may be extended by the court for up to 30 days on a showing of good cause.

(Subd (c) amended and lettered effective January 1, 2007; adopted as part of subd (b) effective March 1, 1994.)

(d) Restraint in discovery

The parties should exercise restraint in discovery while a case is in mediation. In appropriate cases to accommodate that objective, the court may issue a protective order under Code of Civil Procedure section 2017(c) and related provisions.

(Subd (d) amended and lettered effective January 1, 2007; adopted as part of subd (b) effective March 1, 1994.)

Rule 3.896 renumbered effective July 1, 2009; adopted as rule 1637 effective March 1, 1994; previously amended and renumbered as rule 3.876 effective January 1, 2007.

Rule 3.897. Statistical information [Repealed]

Rule 3.897 repealed effective July 1, 2012; adopted as rule 1638 effective March 1, 1994; previously amended effective February 9, 1999; previously amended and renumbered as rule 3.877 effective January 1, 2007; previously renumbered effective July 1, 2009.

Rule 3.898. Educational material

Each court must make available educational material, adopted by the Judicial Council, or from other sources, describing available ADR processes in the community.

Rule 3.898 renumbered effective July 1, 2009; adopted as rule 1639 effective March 1, 1994; previously amended and renumbered as rule 3.878 effective January 1, 2007.

Division 9
References

Chap. 1. Reference by Agreement of the Parties Under Code of Civil Procedure Section 638. Rules 3.900–3.907.

Chap. 2. Court-Ordered Reference Under Code of Civil Procedure Section 639. Rules 3.920–3.926.

Chap. 3. Rules Applicable to References Under Code of Civil Procedure Section 638 or 639. Rules 3.930–3.932.

Chapter 1
Reference by Agreement of the Parties Under Code of Civil Procedure Section 638

Rule 3.900. Purposes of reference

Rule 3.901. Application for order appointing referee
Rule 3.902. Order appointing referee
Rule 3.903. Selection and qualifications of referee
Rule 3.904. Certification and disclosure by referee
Rule 3.905. Objections to the appointment
Rule 3.906. Motion to withdraw stipulation
Rule 3.907. Use of court facilities and court personnel

Rule 3.900. Purposes of reference

A court must not use the reference procedure under Code of Civil Procedure section 638 to appoint a person to conduct a mediation.
Rule 3.900 adopted effective January 1, 2007.

Advisory Committee Comment

Rule 3.900 is not intended to prohibit a court from appointing a referee to conduct a mandatory settlement conference or, following the conclusion of a reference, from appointing a person who previously served as a referee to conduct a mediation.

Rule 3.901. Application for order appointing referee

(a) Stipulation or motion for appointment

A written stipulation or motion for an order appointing a referee under Code of Civil Procedure section 638 must be presented to the judge to whom the case is assigned, or to the presiding judge or law and motion department if the case has not been assigned.

(b) Contents of application

The stipulation or motion for the appointment of a referee under section 638 must:

(1) Clearly state whether the scope of the requested reference includes all issues or is limited to specified issues;

(2) State whether the referee will be privately compensated;

(3) If authorization to use court facilities or court personnel is requested, describe the use requested and state the reasons that this would further the interests of justice;

(4) If the applicant is requesting or the parties have stipulated to the appointment of a particular referee, be accompanied by the proposed referee's certification as required by rule 3.904(a); and

(5) Be accompanied by a proposed order that includes the matters specified in rule 3.902.

Rule 3.901 adopted effective January 1, 2007.

Rule 3.902. Order appointing referee

An order appointing a referee under Code of Civil Procedure section 638 must be filed with the clerk or entered in the minutes and must specify:

(1) The name, business address, and telephone number of the referee and, if he or she is a member of the State Bar, the referee's State Bar number;

(2) Whether the scope of the reference covers all issues or is limited to specified issues;

(3) Whether the referee will be privately compensated; and

(4) Whether the use of court facilities and court personnel is authorized.

Rule 3.902 amended effective January 1, 2010; adopted effective January 1, 2007.

Rule 3.903. Selection and qualifications of referee

The court must appoint the referee or referees as provided in the Code of Civil Procedure section 640. If the proposed referee is a former judicial officer, he or she must be an active or an inactive member of the State Bar.
Rule 3.903 adopted effective January 1, 2007.

Rule 3.904. Certification and disclosure by referee

(a) Certification by referee

Before a referee begins to serve:

(1) The referee must certify in writing that he or she consents to serve as provided in the order of appointment and is aware of and will comply with applicable provisions of canon 6 of the Code of Judicial Ethics and with the California Rules of Court; and

(2) The referee's certification must be filed with the court.

(Subd (a) adopted effective January 1, 2007.)

(b) Disclosure by referee

In addition to any other disclosure required by law, no later than five days before the deadline for parties to file a motion for disqualification of the referee under Code of Civil Procedure section 170.6 or, if the referee is not aware of his or her appointment or of a matter subject to disclosure at that time, as soon as practicable thereafter, a referee must disclose to the parties:

(1) Any matter subject to disclosure under either canon 6D(5)(a) or 6D(5)(b) of the Code of Judicial Ethics; and

(2) Any significant personal or professional relationship the referee has or has had with a party, attorney, or law firm in the current case, including the number and nature of any other proceedings in the past 24 months in which the referee has been privately compensated by a party, attorney, law firm, or insurance company in the current case for any services. The disclosure must include privately compensated service as an attorney, expert witness, or consultant or as a judge, referee, arbitrator, mediator, settlement facilitator, or other alternative dispute resolution neutral.

(Subd (b) adopted effective January 1, 2007.)
Rule 3.904 adopted effective January 1, 2007.

Rule 3.905. Objections to the appointment

A stipulation or an agreement for an order appointing a referee does not constitute a waiver of grounds for objection to the appointment of a particular person as referee under Code of Civil Procedure section 641. Any objection to the appointment of a person as a referee must be made with reasonable diligence and in writing. The objection must be served on all parties and the referee and filed with the court. The objection must be heard by the judge to whom the case is assigned or by the presiding judge or law and motion judge if the case has not been assigned.
Rule 3.905 adopted effective January 1, 2007.

Rule 3.906. Motion to withdraw stipulation

(a) Good cause requirement

A motion to withdraw a stipulation for the appointment of a referee must be supported by a declaration of facts establishing good cause for permitting the party to withdraw the stipulation. The following do not constitute good cause for withdrawing a stipulation:

(1) A declaration that a ruling is based on an error of fact or law.

(2) The issuance of an order for an appropriate hearing site under rule 3.910.

(Subd (a) adopted effective January 1, 2007.)

(b) Service, filing and hearing of motion

Notice of the motion must be served on all parties and the referee and filed with the court. The motion must be heard by the judge to whom the case is assigned or by the presiding judge or law and motion judge. If the motion is granted, the case must be transferred to the trial court docket.

(Subd (b) adopted effective January 1, 2007.)
Rule 3.906 adopted effective January 1, 2007.

Rule 3.907. Use of court facilities and court personnel

A party who has elected to use the services of a referee appointed under Code of Civil Procedure section 638 is deemed to have elected to proceed outside court facilities. Court facilities, court personnel, and summoned jurors may not be used in proceedings pending before such a referee except on a finding by the presiding judge or his or her designee that their use would further the interests of justice.
Rule 3.907 amended and renumbered effective January 1, 2010; adopted as rule 3.909 effective January 1, 2007.

Rule 3.908. Motion for leave to file complaint for intervention [Repealed]

Rule 3.908 repealed effective January 1, 2010; adopted effective January 1, 2007.

Rule 3.909. Proceedings before privately compensated referees [Renumbered]

Rule 3.909 amended and renumbered to rule 3.907 effective January 1, 2010; adopted as rule 3.909 effective January 1, 2007.

Rule 3.910. Request and order for appropriate and accessible hearing site [Repealed]

Rule 3.910 repealed effective January 1, 2010; adopted effective January 1, 2007.

Chapter 2
Court-Ordered Reference Under Code of Civil Procedure Section 639

Rule 3.920. Purposes and conditions for appointment of referee
Rule 3.921. Motion for appointment of a referee
Rule 3.922. Form and contents of order appointing referee
Rule 3.923. Selection and qualification of referee
Rule 3.924. Certification and disclosure by referee
Rule 3.925. Objection to reference
Rule 3.926. Use of court facilities

Rule 3.920. Purposes and conditions for appointment of referee

(a) Purposes prescribed by statute

A court may order the appointment of a referee under Code of Civil Procedure section 639 only for the purposes specified in that section.

(Subd (a) adopted effective January 1, 2007.)

(b) No references for mediation

A court must not use the reference procedure under Code of Civil Procedure section 639 to appoint a person to conduct a mediation.

(Subd (b) adopted effective January 1, 2007.)

(c) Conditions for appointment of discovery referee

A discovery referee must not be appointed under Code of Civil Procedure section 639(a)(5) unless the exceptional circumstances of the particular case require the appointment.

(Subd (c) adopted effective January 1, 2007.)

Rule 3.920 adopted effective January 1, 2007.

Advisory Committee Comment

Rule 3.920(b) is not intended to prohibit a court from appointing a referee to conduct a mandatory settlement conference in a complex case or, following the conclusion of a reference, from appointing a person who previously served as a referee to conduct a mediation.

Rule 3.921. Motion for appointment of a referee

(a) Filing and contents

A motion by a party for the appointment of a referee under Code of Civil Procedure section 639 must be served and filed. The motion must specify the matter or matters to be included in the requested reference. If the applicant is requesting the appointment of a particular referee, the motion must be accompanied by the proposed referee's certification as required by rule 3.924(a).

(Subd (a) adopted effective January 1, 2007.)

(b) Hearing

The motion must be heard by the judge to whom the case is assigned, or by the presiding judge or law and motion judge if the case has not been assigned.

(Subd (b) adopted effective January 1, 2007.)

Rule 3.921 adopted effective January 1, 2007.

Rule 3.922. Form and contents of order appointing referee

(a) Written order required

An order appointing a referee under Code of Civil Procedure section 639, on the motion of a party or on the court's own motion, must be in writing and must address the matters set forth in (b) through (g).

(Subd (a) amended effective January 1, 2010; adopted effective January 1, 2007.)

(b) Referee information

The order must state the name, business address, and telephone number of the referee and, if he or she is a member of the State Bar, the referee's State Bar number.

(Subd (b) adopted effective January 1, 2007.)

(c) Basis for reference

The order must specify whether the referee is appointed under paragraph (1), (2), (3), (4), or (5) of subdivision (a) of section 639 and:

(1) If the referee is appointed under section 639(a)(1)–(a)(4), the order must state the reason the referee is being appointed.

(2) If the referee is appointed under section 639(a)(5) to hear and determine discovery motions and disputes relevant to discovery, the order must state the exceptional circumstances of the particular case that require the reference.

(Subd (c) adopted effective January 1, 2007.)

(d) Subject matter and scope of reference

(1) The order must specify the subject matter or matters included in the reference.

(2) If the referee is appointed under section 639(a)(5) to hear and determine discovery motions and disputes relevant to discovery, the order must state whether the discovery referee is appointed for all purposes or only for limited purposes.

(Subd (d) adopted effective January 1, 2007.)

(e) Authority of discovery referee

If the referee is appointed under section 639(a)(5) to hear and determine discovery motions and disputes relevant to discovery, the order must state that the referee is authorized to set the date, time, and place for all hearings determined by the referee to be necessary; direct the issuance of subpoenas; preside over hearings; take evidence; and rule on objections, motions, and other requests made during the course of the hearing.

(Subd (e) adopted effective January 1, 2007.)

(f) Referee fees; apportionment

If the referee will be appointed at a cost to the parties, the order must:

(1) Specify the maximum hourly rate the referee may charge and, if any party so requests, the maximum number of hours for which the referee may charge;

(2) Include a finding that either:

(A) No party has established an economic inability to pay a pro rata share of the referee's fee; or

(B) One or more parties has established an economic inability to pay a pro rata share of the referee's fees and another party has agreed voluntarily to pay that additional share of the referee's fees.

(3) When the issue of economic hardship is raised before the referee begins performing services, the court must determine a fair and reasonable apportionment of reference costs. The court may modify its apportionment order and may consider a recommendation by the referee as a factor in determining any modification.

(Subd (f) adopted effective January 1, 2007.)

(g) Use of court facilities and court personnel

The order must specify the extent, if any, to which court facilities and court personnel may be used in connection with the reference.

(Subd (g) adopted effective January 1, 2007.)

Rule 3.922 amended effective January 1, 2010; adopted effective January 1, 2007.

Rule 3.923. Selection and qualification of referee

The court must appoint the referee or referees as provided in Code of Civil Procedure section 640. If the referee is a former California judicial officer, he or she must be an active or inactive member of the State Bar.

Rule 3.923 adopted effective January 1, 2007.

Rule 3.924. Certification and disclosure by referee

(a) Certification by referee

Before a referee begins to serve:

(1) The referee must certify in writing that he or she consents to serve as provided in the order of appointment and is aware of and will comply with applicable provisions of canon 6 of the Code of Judicial Ethics and with the California Rules of Court; and

(2) The referee's certification must be filed with the court.

(Subd (a) adopted effective January 1, 2007.)

(b) Disclosure by referee

In addition to any other disclosure required by law, no later than five days before the deadline for parties to file a motion for disqualification of the referee under Code of Civil Procedure section 170.6 or, if the referee is not aware of his or her appointment or of a matter subject to disclosure at that time, as soon as practicable thereafter, a referee must disclose to the parties:

(1) Any matter subject to disclosure under subdivisions (D)(5)(a) and (D)(5)(b) of canon 6 of the Code of Judicial Ethics; and

(2) Any significant personal or professional relationship the referee has or has had with a party, attorney, or law firm in the current case, including the number and nature of any other proceedings in the past 24 months in which the referee has been privately compensated by a party, attorney, law firm, or insurance company in the current case for any services. The disclosure must include privately compensated service as an attorney, expert witness, or consultant or as a judge, referee, arbitrator, mediator, settlement facilitator, or other alternative dispute resolution neutral.

(Subd (b) amended effective January 1, 2008; adopted effective January 1, 2007.)

Rule 3.924 amended effective January 1, 2008; adopted effective January 1, 2007.

Rule 3.925. Objection to reference

The filing of a motion for an order appointing a referee does not constitute a waiver of grounds for objection to the appointment of a particular person as referee under Code of Civil Procedure section 641, or objection to the rate or apportionment of compensation of the referee. Any objection to the appointment of a particular person as a referee must be made with reasonable diligence and in writing. The objection must be heard by the judge to whom the case is assigned, or by the presiding judge or the law and motion judge.

Rule 3.925 adopted effective January 1, 2007.

Rule 3.926. Use of court facilities

A reference ordered under Code of Civil Procedure section 639 entitles the parties to the use of court facilities and court personnel to the extent provided in the order of reference. The proceedings may be held in a private facility, but, if so, the private facility must be open to the public as provided in rule 3.931.

Rule 3.926 amended effective January 1, 2010; adopted effective January 1, 2007.

Rule 3.927. Circumstances required for appointment of discovery referee [Repealed]

Rule 3.927 repealed effective January 1, 2010; adopted effective January 1, 2007.

Chapter 3
Rules Applicable to References Under Code of Civil Procedure Section 638 or 639

Title 3, Civil Rules—Division 9, References—Chapter 3, Rules Applicable to References Under Code of Civil Procedure Section 638 or 639; adopted effective January 1, 2010.

Rule 3.930. Documents and exhibits
Rule 3.931. Open proceedings, notice of proceedings, and order for hearing site
Rule 3.932. Motions or applications to be heard by the court

Rule 3.930. Documents and exhibits

All referees and parties in proceedings before a referee appointed under Code of Civil Procedure section 638 or 639 must comply with the applicable requirements of rule 2.400 concerning the filing and handling of documents and exhibits.

Rule 3.930 adopted effective January 1, 2010.

Rule 3.931. Open proceedings, notice of proceedings, and order for hearing site

(a) Open proceedings

All proceedings before a referee that would be open to the public if held before a judge must be open to the public, regardless of whether they are held in a court facility or in another location.

(Subd (a) adopted effective January 1, 2010.)

(b) Notice regarding proceedings before referee

(1) In each case in which he or she is appointed, a referee must file a statement that provides the name, telephone number, e-mail address, and mailing address of a person who may be contacted to obtain information about the date, time, location, and general nature of all hearings scheduled in matters pending before the referee that would be open to the public if held before a judge. This statement must be filed at the same time as the referee's certification under rule 3.904(a) or 3.924(a). If there is any change in this contact information, the referee must promptly file a revised statement with the court.

(2) In addition to providing the information required under (1), the statement filed by a referee may also provide the address of a publicly accessible website at which the referee will maintain a current calendar setting forth the date, time, location, and general nature of any hearings scheduled in the matter that would be open to the public if held before a judge.

(3) The clerk must post the information from the statement filed by the referee in the court facility.

(Subd (b) amended effective January 1, 2016; adopted effective January 1, 2010.)

(c) Appropriate hearing site

(1) The presiding judge or his or her designee, on application of any person or on the judge's own motion, may order that a case before a referee must be heard at a site easily accessible to the public and appropriate for seating those who have made known their plan to attend hearings. The application must state facts showing good cause for granting the application, must be served on all parties and the referee, and filed with the court. The proceedings are not stayed while the application is pending unless the presiding judge or his or her designee orders that they be stayed. The issuance of an order for an accessible and appropriate hearing site is not grounds for withdrawal of a stipulation for the appointment of a referee.

(2) If a court staff mediator or evaluator is required to attend a hearing before a referee, unless otherwise ordered by the presiding judge or his or her designee, that hearing must take place at a location requiring no more than 15 minutes' travel time from the mediator's or evaluator's work site.

(Subd (c) adopted effective January 1, 2010.)

Rule 3.931 amended effective January 1, 2016; adopted effective January 1, 2010.

Rule 3.932. Motions or applications to be heard by the court

(a) Motion or application to seal records

A motion or application to seal records in a case pending before a referee must be filed with the court and served on all parties that have appeared in the case and the referee. The motion or application must be heard by the trial court judge to whom the case is assigned or, if the case has not been assigned, by the presiding judge or his or her designee. Rules 2.550 and 2.551 apply to the motion or application to seal the records.

(Subd (a) adopted effective January 1, 2010.)

(b) Motion for leave to file complaint for intervention

A motion for leave to file a complaint for intervention in a case pending before a referee must be filed with the court and served on all parties and the referee. The motion must be heard by the trial court judge to whom the case is assigned or, if the case has not been assigned, by the presiding judge or his or her designee. If intervention is allowed, the case must be returned to the trial court docket unless all parties stipulate in the manner prescribed in rule 3.901 to proceed before the referee.

(Subd (b) adopted effective January 1, 2010.)

Rule 3.932 adopted effective January 1, 2010.

Division 10
Discovery

Chap. 1. Format of Discovery. Rule 3.1000.
Chap. 2. Conduct of Discovery. Rule 3.1010.

Chapter 1
Format of Discovery

Rule 3.1000. Format of supplemental and further discovery

(a) Supplemental interrogatories and responses, etc.

In each set of supplemental interrogatories, supplemental responses to interrogatories, amended answers to interrogatories, and further responses to interrogatories, inspection demands, and admission requests, the following must appear in the first paragraph immediately below the title of the case:

(1) The identity of the propounding, demanding, or requesting party;
(2) The identity of the responding party;
(3) The set number being propounded or responded to; and
(4) The nature of the paper.

(Subd (a) amended effective January 1, 2007; previously amended effective January 1, 1986, and July 1, 1987.)

(b) Identification of responses

Each supplemental or further response and each amended answer must be identified by the same number or letter and be in the same sequence as the corresponding interrogatory, inspection demand, or admission request, but the text of the interrogatory, demand, or request need not be repeated.

(Subd (b) amended effective January 1, 2007; previously amended effective January 1, 1986, and July 1, 1987.)

Rule 3.1000 amended and renumbered effective January 1, 2007; adopted as rule 331 effective January 1, 1984; previously amended effective January 1, 1986, and January 1, 1987.

Chapter 2
Conduct of Discovery

Rule 3.1010. Oral depositions by telephone, videoconference, or other remote electronic means

(a) Taking depositions

Any party may take an oral deposition by telephone, videoconference, or other remote electronic means, provided:

(1) Notice is served with the notice of deposition or the subpoena;
(2) That party makes all arrangements for any other party to participate in the deposition in an equivalent manner. However, each party so appearing must pay all expenses incurred by it or properly allocated to it;
(3) Any party or attorney of record may be physically present at the deposition at the location of the deponent with written notice of such appearance served by personal delivery, email, or fax, at least five court days before the deposition, and subject to Code of Civil Procedure section 2025.420. An attorney for the deponent may be physically present with the deponent without notice.

(Subd (a) amended effective January 1, 2022.)

(b) Appearing and participating in depositions

Any party, other than the deponent, or attorney of record may appear and participate in an oral deposition by telephone, videoconference, or other remote electronic means, provided:

(1) Written notice of such appearance is served by personal delivery, email, or fax at least five court days before the deposition;

(2) The party so appearing makes all arrangements and pays all expenses incurred for the appearance.

(Subd (b) amended effective January 1, 2022; previously amended effective January 1, 2007, and January 1, 2016.)

(c) Deponent's appearance

A deponent must appear as required by statute or as agreed to by the parties and deponent.

(Subd (c) amended effective January 1, 2022.)

(d) Court orders

On motion by any person, the court in a specific action may make such other orders as it deems appropriate.

(Subd (d) relettered effective January 1, 2022; adopted as subd (e) effective January 1, 2003; previously amended effective January 1, 2007.)

Rule 3.1010 amended effective January 1, 2022; adopted as rule 333 effective January 1, 2003; previously amended and renumbered as rule 3.1010 effective January 1, 2007; previously amended effective January 1, 2016.

Rule 3.1015. Discovery in action pending outside of California [Repealed]

Rule 3.1015 repealed on its own provisions effective January 1, 2010; adopted effective March 13, 2009.

Chapter 3
Discovery Motions
[Repealed]

Chapter 3 repealed effective January 1, 2009.

Rule 3.1020. Format of discovery motions [Renumbered]

Rule 3.1020 renumbered to rule 3.1345 effective January 1, 2009; adopted as rule 335 effective January 1, 1984; previously amended effective July 1, 1987, January 1, 1992, January 1, 1997, and July 1, 2001; previously amended and renumbered effective January 1, 2007.

Rule 3.1025. Service of motion papers on nonparty deponent [Renumbered]

Rule 3.1025 renumbered to rule 3.1346 effective January 1, 2009; adopted as rule 337 effective January 1, 1984; previously amended effective July 1, 1987; previously amended and renumbered effective January 1, 2007.

Rule 3.1030. Sanctions for failure to provide discovery [Renumbered]

Rule 3.1030 renumbered to rule 3.1348 effective January 1, 2009; adopted as rule 341 effective July 1, 2001; previously renumbered effective January 1, 2007.

Division 11
Law and Motion

Chap. 1. General Provisions. Rules 3.1100–3.1109.
Chap. 2. Format of Motion Papers. Rules 3.1110–3.1116.
Chap. 3. Provisional and Injunctive Relief. Rules 3.1130–3.1184.
Chap. 4. Ex Parte Applications. Rules 3.1200–3.1207.
Chap. 5. Noticed Motions. Rules 3.1300–3.1312.
Chap. 6. Particular Motions. Rules 3.1320–3.1362.
Chap. 7. Civil Petitions. Rules 3.1365–3.1372.

Chapter 1
General Provisions

Rule 3.1100. Application
Rule 3.1103. Definitions and construction
Rule 3.1109. Notice of determination of submitted matters

Rule 3.1100. Application

The rules in this division apply to proceedings in civil law and motion, as defined in rule 3.1103, and to discovery proceedings in family law and probate.

Rule 3.1100 amended and renumbered effective January 1, 2007; adopted as rule 301 effective January 1, 1984; previously amended effective July 1, 1984, July 1, 1997, and January 1, 2002.

Rule 3.1103. Definitions and construction

(a) Law and motion defined

"Law and motion" includes any proceedings:

(1) On application before trial for an order, except for causes arising under the Welfare and Institutions Code, the Probate Code, the Family Code, or Code of Civil Procedure sections 527.6, 527.7, 527.8, and 527.85; or

(2) On application for an order regarding the enforcement of judgment, attachment of property, appointment of a receiver, obtaining or setting aside a judgment by default, writs of review, mandate and prohibition, a petition to compel arbitration, and enforcement of an award by arbitration.

(Subd (a) amended effective January 1, 2011; previously amended effective July 1, 1997.)

(b) Application of rules on extending or shortening time

Rules 1.10(c) and 2.20 on extending or shortening time apply to proceedings under this division.

(Subd (b) amended effective January 1, 2007.)

(c) Application to demurrers

Unless the context or subject matter otherwise requires, the rules in this division apply to demurrers.

(Subd (c) amended effective January 1, 2007.)

Rule 3.1103 amended effective January 1, 2011; adopted as rule 303 effective January 1, 1984; previously amended effective July 1, 1984; previously amended and renumbered effective January 1, 2007.

Rule 3.1109. Notice of determination of submitted matters

(a) Notice by clerk

When the court rules on a motion or makes an order or renders a judgment in a matter it has taken under submission, the clerk must immediately notify the parties of the ruling, order, or judgment. The notification, which must specifically identify the matter ruled on, may be given by serving electronically or mailing the parties a copy of the ruling, order, or judgment, and it constitutes service of notice only if the clerk is required to give notice under Code of Civil Procedure section 664.5.

(Subd (a) amended effective January 1, 2016; adopted as part of untitled subd effective January 1, 1984; previously amended and lettered subd (a) effective January 1, 2007.)

(b) Notice in a case involving more than two parties

In a case involving more than two parties, a clerk's notification made under this rule, or any notice of a ruling or order served by a party, must name the moving party, and the party against whom relief was requested, and specifically identify the particular motion or other matter ruled upon.

(Subd (b) amended and lettered effective January 1, 2007; adopted as part of untitled subd effective January 1, 1984.)

(c) Time not extended by failure of clerk to give notice

The failure of the clerk to give the notice required by this rule does not extend the time provided by law for performing any act except as provided in rules 8.104(a) or 8.822(a).

(Subd (c) amended effective January 1, 2016; adopted effective January 1, 2007.)

Rule 3.1109 amended effective January 1, 2016; adopted as rule 309 effective January 1, 1984; previously amended and renumbered as rule 3.1109 effective January 1, 2007.

Chapter 2
Format of Motion Papers

Rule 3.1110. General format
Rule 3.1112. Motions—and other pleadings
Rule 3.1113. Memorandum
Rule 3.1114. Applications, motions, and petitions not requiring a memorandum
Rule 3.1115. Declarations
Rule 3.1116. Deposition testimony as an exhibit

Rule 3.1110. General format

(a) Notice of motion

A notice of motion must state in the opening paragraph the nature of the order being sought and the grounds for issuance of the order.

(Subd (a) amended effective January 1, 2007.)

(b) Date of hearing and other information

The first page of each paper must specify immediately below the number of the case:

(1) The date, time, and location, if ascertainable, of any scheduled hearing and the name of the hearing judge, if ascertainable;

(2) The nature or title of any attached document other than an exhibit;

(3) The date of filing of the action; and

(4) The trial date, if set.

(Subd (b) amended effective January 1, 2007; previously amended effective July 1, 1997.)

(c) Pagination of documents

Documents must be consecutively paginated. The page numbering must begin with the first page and use only Arabic numerals (e.g., 1, 2, 3). The page number may be suppressed and need not appear on the first page.

(Subd (c) amended effective January 1, 2017; adopted as part of subd (b) effective January 1, 1984; previously amended and lettered effective January 1, 2007.)

(d) Reference to previously filed papers

Any paper previously filed must be referred to by date of execution and title.

(Subd (d) amended and relettered effective January 1, 2007; adopted as subd (c) effective January 1, 1984.)

(e) Binding

For motions filed on paper, all pages of each document and exhibit must be attached together at the top by a method that permits pages to be easily turned and the entire content of each page to be read.

(Subd (e) amended effective January 1, 2016; adopted as subd (d) effective July 1, 1997; previously amended and relettered as subd (e) effective January 1, 2007.)

(f) Format of exhibits

(1) An index of exhibits must be provided. The index must briefly describe the exhibit and identify the exhibit number or letter and page number.

(2) Pages from a single deposition must be designated as a single exhibit.

(3) Each paper exhibit must be separated by a hard 8½ × 11 sheet with hard paper or plastic tabs extending below the bottom of the page, bearing the exhibit designation.

(4) Electronic exhibits must meet the requirements in rule 2.256(b). Unless they are submitted by a self-represented party, electronic exhibits must include electronic bookmarks with links to the first page of each exhibit and with bookmark titles that identify the exhibit number or letter and briefly describe the exhibit.

(Subd (f) amended effective January 1, 2017; adopted as subd (e) effective July 1, 1997; previously amended and relettered effective January 1, 2007.)

(g) Translation of exhibits

Exhibits written in a foreign language must be accompanied by an English translation, certified under oath by a qualified interpreter.

(Subd (g) amended and lettered effective January 1, 2007; adopted as part of subd (e) effective July 1, 1997.)

Rule 3.1110 amended effective January 1, 2017; adopted as rule 311 effective January 1, 1984; previously amended effective July 1, 1997, and January 1, 2016; previously amended and renumbered as rule 3.1110 effective January 1, 2007.

Advisory Committee Comment

Subdivision (f)(4). Under current technology, software programs that allow users to apply electronic bookmarks to electronic documents are available for free.

Rule 3.1112. Motions—and other pleadings

(a) Motions required papers

Unless otherwise provided by the rules in this division, the papers filed in support of a motion must consist of at least the following:

(1) A notice of hearing on the motion;

(2) The motion itself; and

(3) A memorandum in support of the motion or demurrer.

(Subd (a) amended effective January 1, 2007.)

(b) Other papers

Other papers may be filed in support of a motion, including declarations, exhibits, appendices, and other documents or pleadings.

(Subd (b) adopted effective January 1, 2007.)

(c) Form of motion papers

The papers filed under (a) and (b) may either be filed as separate documents or combined in one or more documents if the party filing a combined pleading specifies these items separately in the caption of the combined pleading.

(Subd (c) amended and lettered effective January 1, 2007 adopted as part of subd (a) effective July 1, 1997.)

(d) Motion—required elements

A motion must:

(1) Identify the party or parties bringing the motion;

(2) Name the parties to whom it is addressed;

(3) Briefly state the basis for the motion and the relief sought; and

(4) If a pleading is challenged, state the specific portion challenged.

(Subd (d) amended and relettered effective January 1, 2007; adopted as subd (b) effective July 1, 1997.)

(e) Additional requirements for motions

In addition to the requirements of this rule, a motion relating to the subjects specified in chapter 6 of this division must comply with any additional requirements in that chapter.

(Subd (e) amended effective July 1, 2008; previously amended effective January 1, 2007.)

(f) Motion in limine

Notwithstanding (a), a motion in limine filed before or during trial need not be accompanied by a notice of hearing. The timing and place of the filing and service of the motion are at the discretion of the trial judge.

(Subd (f) adopted effective January 1, 2007.)

Rule 3.1112 amended effective July 1, 2008; adopted as rule 312 effective July 1, 1997; previously amended and renumbered effective January 1, 2007.

Rule 3.1113. Memorandum

(a) Memorandum in support of motion

A party filing a motion, except for a motion listed in rule 3.1114, must serve and file a supporting memorandum. The court may construe the absence of a memorandum as an admission that the motion or special demurrer is not meritorious and cause for its denial and, in the case of a demurrer, as a waiver of all grounds not supported.

(Subd (a) amended effective January 1, 2007; previously amended effective January 1, 2004.)

(b) Contents of memorandum

The memorandum must contain a statement of facts, a concise statement of the law, evidence and arguments relied on, and a discussion of the statutes, cases, and textbooks cited in support of the position advanced.

(Subd (b) amended effective January 1, 2004.)

(c) Case citation format

A case citation must include the official report volume and page number and year of decision. The court must not require any other form of citation.

(Subd (c) amended effective January 1, 2007; previously amended effective July 1, 1984, January 1, 1992, and January 1, 2004.)

(d) Length of memorandum

Except in a summary judgment or summary adjudication motion, no opening or responding memorandum may exceed 15 pages. In a summary judgment or summary adjudication motion, no opening or responding memorandum may exceed 20 pages. No reply or closing memorandum may exceed 10 pages. The page limit does not include the caption page, the notice of motion and motion, exhibits, declarations, attachments, the table of contents, the table of authorities, or the proof of service.

(Subd (d) amended effective January 1, 2017; adopted as part of a longer subd (d); previously amended effective July 1, 1984, January 1, 1992, and January 1, 2004.)

(e) Application to file longer memorandum

A party may apply to the court ex parte but with written notice of the application to the other parties, at least 24 hours before the memorandum is due, for permission to file a longer memorandum. The application must state reasons why the argument cannot be made within the stated limit.

(Subd (e) amended and relettered effective January 1, 2004; adopted as part of subd (d).)

(f) Format of longer memorandum

A memorandum that exceeds 10 pages must include a table of contents and a table of authorities. A memorandum that exceeds 15 pages must also include an opening summary of argument.

(Subd (f) amended and lettered effective January 1, 2007; adopted as part of subd (d); subd (d) previously amended and relettered as subd (e) effective January 1, 2004.)

(g) Effect of filing an oversized memorandum

A memorandum that exceeds the page limits of these rules must be filed and considered in the same manner as a late-filed paper.

(Subd (g) amended and lettered effective January 1, 2007; adopted as part of subd (d); previously amended and relettered as subd (e) effective January 1, 2004.)

(h) Pagination of memorandum

The pages of a memorandum must be numbered consecutively beginning with the first page and using only Arabic numerals (e.g., 1, 2, 3). The page number may be suppressed and need not appear on the first page.

(Subd (h) amended effective January 1, 2017; previously amended and relettered as subd (f) effective January 1, 2004, and as subd (h) effective January 1, 2007; adopted as subd (e) effective July 1, 2000.)

(i) Copies of authorities

(1) A judge may require that if any authority other than California cases, statutes, constitutional provisions, or state or local rules is cited, a copy of the authority must be lodged with the papers that cite the authority. If in paper form, the authority must be tabbed or separated as required by rule 3.1110(f)(3). If in electronic form, the authority must be electronically bookmarked as required by rule 3.1110(f)(4).

(2) If a California case is cited before the time it is published in the advance sheets of the Official Reports, the party must include the title, case number, date of decision, and, if from the Court of Appeal, district of the Court of Appeal in which the case was decided. A judge may require that a copy of that case must be lodged. If in paper form, the copy must be tabbed or separated as required by rule 3.1110(f)(3). If in electronic form, the copy must be electronically bookmarked as required by rule 3.1110(f)(4).

(3) Upon the request of a party to the action, any party citing any authority other than California cases, statutes, constitutional provisions, or state or local rules must promptly provide a copy of such authority to the requesting party.

(Subd (i) amended effective January 1, 2017; adopted as part of subd (e) effective January 1, 1992; previously relettered as part of subd (f) effective July 1, 2000; previously amended and relettered as subd (h) effective January 1, 2004, and as subd (j) effective January 1, 2007; repealed and relettered as subd (i) effective January 1, 2008; previously amended effective July 1, 1997, July 1, 2011, and January 1, 2016.)

(j) Attachments

To the extent practicable, all supporting memorandums and declarations must be attached to the notice of motion.

(Subd (j) relettered effective January 1, 2008; adopted as subd (f) effective July 1, 1997; previously relettered as subd (g) effective July 1, 2000; previously amended and relettered as subd (i) effective January 1, 2004, and as subd (k) effective January 1, 2007.)

(k) Exhibit references

All references to exhibits or declarations in supporting or opposing papers must reference the number or letter of the exhibit, the specific page, and, if applicable, the paragraph or line number.

(Subd (k) relettered effective January 1, 2008; adopted as subd (g) effective July 1, 1997; previously relettered as subd (h) effective July 1, 2000, and as subd (l) effective January 1, 2007; previously amended and relettered as subd (j) effective January 1, 2004.)

(l) Requests for judicial notice

Any request for judicial notice must be made in a separate document listing the specific items for which notice is requested and must comply with rule 3.1306(c).

(Subd (l) relettered effective January 1, 2008; adopted as subd (h) effective July 1, 1997; relettered as subd (i) effective July 1, 2000; previously amended effective January 1, 2003; previously amended and relettered as subd (k) effective January 1, 2004, and as subd (m) effective January 1, 2007.)

(m) Proposed orders or judgments

If a proposed order or judgment is submitted, it must be lodged and served with the moving papers but must not be attached to them. The requirements for proposed orders, including the requirements for submitting proposed orders by electronic means, are stated in rule 3.1312.

(Subd (m) amended effective January 1, 2016; adopted as subd (i) effective July 1, 1997; previously amended and relettered as subd (l) effective January 1, 2004; previously relettered as subd (j) effective July 1, 2000, as subd (n) effective January 1, 2007, and as subd (m) effective January 1, 2008.)

Rule 3.1113 amended effective January 1, 2017; adopted as rule 313 effective January 1, 1984; previously amended and renumbered as rule 3.1113 effective January 1, 2007; previously amended effective July 1, 1984, January 1, 1992, July 1, 1997, July 1, 2000, January 1, 2003, January 1, 2004, January 1, 2008, July 1, 2011, and January 1, 2016.)

Advisory Committee Comment

See also rule 1.200 concerning the format of citations.

Rule 3.1114. Applications, motions, and petitions not requiring a memorandum

(a) Memorandum not required

Civil motions, applications, and petitions filed on Judicial Council forms that do not require a memorandum include the following:

(1) Application for appointment of guardian ad litem in a civil case;

(2) Application for an order extending time to serve pleading;

(3) Motion to be relieved as counsel;

(4) Motion filed in small claims case;

(5) Petition for change of name or gender;

(6) Petition for declaration of emancipation of minor;

(7) Petition for injunction prohibiting harassment;

(8) Petition for protective order to prevent elder or dependent adult abuse;

(9) Petition for order to prevent postsecondary school violence;

(10) Petition of employer for injunction prohibiting workplace violence;

(11) Petition for order prohibiting abuse (transitional housing);

(12) Petition to approve compromise of claim of a minor or a person with a disability; and

(13) Petition for withdrawal of funds from blocked account.

(Subd (a) amended effective January 1, 2011; previously amended effective January 1, 2007.)

(b) Submission of a memorandum

Notwithstanding (a), if it would further the interests of justice, a party may submit, or the court may order the submission of, a memorandum in support of any motion, application, or petition. The memorandum must comply with rule 3.1113.

(Subd (b) amended effective January 1, 2007.)

Rule 3.1114 amended effective January 1, 2011; adopted as rule 314 effective January 1, 2004; previously amended and renumbered effective January 1, 2007.

Rule 3.1115. Declarations

The caption of a declaration must state the name of the declarant and must specifically identify the motion or other proceeding that it supports or opposes.

Rule 3.1115 amended and renumbered effective January 1, 2007; adopted as rule 315 effective January 1, 1984.

Rule 3.1116. Deposition testimony as an exhibit

(a) Title page

The first page of any deposition used as an exhibit must state the name of the deponent and the date of the deposition.

(Subd (a) amended effective January 1, 2007.)

(b) Deposition pages

Other than the title page, the exhibit must contain only the relevant pages of the transcript. The original page number of any deposition page must be clearly visible.

(Subd (b) amended effective January 1, 2007.)

(c) Highlighting of testimony

The relevant portion of any testimony in the deposition must be marked in a manner that calls attention to the testimony.

(Subd (c) amended effective January 1, 2007.)

Rule 3.1116 amended and renumbered effective January 1, 2007; adopted as rule 316 effective January 1, 1992.

Chapter 3
Provisional and Injunctive Relief

Art. 1. General Provisions. Rule 3.1130.
Art. 2. Writs. Rules 3.1140, 3.1142.
Art. 3. Injunctions. Rules 3.1150, 3.1151.
Art. 4. Protective Orders. Rules 3.1160–3.1162.
Art. 5. Receiverships. Rules 3.1175–3.1184.

Article 1
General Provisions

Rule 3.1130. Bonds and undertakings

(a) Prerequisites to acceptance of corporate sureties

A corporation must not be accepted or approved as surety on a bond or undertaking unless the following conditions are met:

(1) The Insurance Commissioner has certified the corporation as being admitted to do business in the state as a surety insurer;

(2) There is filed in the office of the clerk a copy, duly certified by the proper authority, of the transcript or record of appointment entitling or authorizing the person or persons purporting to execute the bond or undertaking for and in behalf of the corporation to act in the premises; and

(3) The bond or undertaking has been executed under penalty of perjury as provided in Code of Civil Procedure section 995.630, or the fact of execution of the bond or undertaking by the officer or agent of the corporation purporting to become surety has been duly acknowledged before an officer of this state authorized to take and certify acknowledgements.

(Subd (a) amended effective January 1, 2007.)

(b) Certain persons not eligible to act as sureties

An officer of the court or member of the State Bar may not act as a surety.

(Subd (b) amended effective January 1, 2007.)

(c) Withdrawal of bonds and undertakings

An original bond or undertaking may be withdrawn from the files and delivered to the party by whom it was filed on order of the court only if all parties interested in the obligation so stipulate, or upon a showing that the purpose for which it was filed has been abandoned without any liability having been incurred.

Rule 3.1130 amended and renumbered effective January 1, 2007; adopted as rule 381 effective January 1, 1984.

Article 2
Writs

Rule 3.1140. Lodging of record in administrative mandate cases
Rule 3.1142. Stay of driving license suspension

Rule 3.1140. Lodging of record in administrative mandate cases

The party intending to use a part of the administrative record in a case brought under Code of Civil Procedure section 1094.5 must lodge that part of the record at least five days before the hearing.

Rule 3.1140 amended and renumbered effective January 1, 2007; adopted as rule 347 effective January 1, 1984.

Rule 3.1142. Stay of driving license suspension

A request for a stay of a suspension of a driving license must be accompanied by a copy of the petitioner's driving record from the Department of Motor Vehicles.

Rule 3.1142 amended and renumbered effective January 1, 2007; adopted as rule 355 effective January 1, 1984.

Article 3
Injunctions

Rule 3.1150. Preliminary injunctions and bonds
Rule 3.1151. Requirements for injunction in certain cases

Rule 3.1150. Preliminary injunctions and bonds

(a) Manner of application and service

A party requesting a preliminary injunction may give notice of the request to the opposing or responding party either by serving a noticed motion under Code of Civil Procedure section 1005 or by obtaining and serving an order to show cause (OSC). An OSC must be used when a temporary restraining order (TRO) is sought, or if the party against whom the preliminary injunction is sought has not appeared in the action. If the responding party has not appeared, the OSC must be served in the same manner as a summons and complaint.

(Subd (a) amended effective January 1, 2007; adopted effective July 1, 1997; previously amended effective July 1, 1999.)

(b) Filing of complaint or obtaining of court file

If the action is initiated the same day a TRO or an OSC is sought, the complaint must be filed first. The moving party must provide a file-stamped copy of the complaint to the judge who will hear the application. If an application for a TRO or an OSC is made in an existing case, the moving party must request that the court file be made available to the judge hearing the application.

(Subd (b) amended effective January 1, 2007; adopted effective July 1, 1997; previously amended effective July 1, 1999.)

(c) Form of OSC and TRO

The OSC and TRO must be stated separately, with the OSC stated first. The restraining language sought in an OSC and a TRO must be separately stated in the OSC and the TRO and may not be incorporated by reference. The OSC must describe the injunction to be sought at the hearing. The TRO must describe the activities to be enjoined pending the hearing. A proposed OSC must contain blank spaces for the time and manner of service on responding parties, the date on which the proof of service must be delivered to the court hearing the OSC, a briefing schedule, and, if applicable, the expiration date of the TRO.

(Subd (c) amended effective January 1, 2007; adopted effective July 1, 1997; previously amended effective July 1, 1999.)

(d) Personal attendance

The moving party or counsel for the moving party must be personally present when the request for a TRO is made.

(Subd (d) amended effective January 1, 2007; adopted as subd (e) effective July 1, 1997; amended as [Proof of service] effective July 1, 1999; previously relettered effective July 1, 1999.)

(e) Previous applications

An application for a TRO or an OSC must state whether there has been any previous application for similar relief and, if so, the result of the application.

(Subd (e) amended effective January 1, 2007; adopted as subd (f) effective July 1, 1997; previously amended and relettered effective July 1, 1999.)

(f) Undertaking

Notwithstanding rule 3.1312, whenever an application for a preliminary injunction is granted, a proposed order must be presented to the judge for signature, with an undertaking in the amount ordered, within one court day after the granting of the application or within the time ordered. Unless otherwise ordered, any restraining order previously granted remains in effect during the time allowed for presentation for signature of the order of injunction and undertaking. If the proposed order and the undertaking required are not presented within the time allowed, the TRO may be vacated without notice. All bonds and undertakings must comply with rule 3.1130.

(Subd (f) amended effective January 1, 2007; previously amended and relettered effective July 1, 1997.)

(g) Ex parte temporary restraining orders

Applications for ex parte temporary restraining orders are governed by the ex parte rules in chapter 4 of this division.

(Subd (g) amended effective January 1, 2007; adopted effective July 1, 1999.)
Rule 3.1150 amended and renumbered effective January 1, 2007; adopted as rule 359 effective January 1, 1984; previously amended effective July 1, 1997, and July 1, 1999.

Rule 3.1151. Requirements for injunction in certain cases

A petition for an injunction to limit picketing, restrain real property encroachments, or protect easements must depict by drawings, plot plans, photographs, or other appropriate means, or must describe in detail the premises involved, including, if applicable, the length and width of the frontage on a street or alley, the width of sidewalks, and the number, size, and location of entrances.

Rule 3.1151 amended and renumbered effective January 1, 2007; adopted as rule 361 effective January 1, 1984.

Rule 3.1152. Requests for protective orders to prevent civil harassment, workplace violence, private postsecondary school violence, and elder or dependent adult abuse [Renumbered]

Rule 3.1152 renumbered as rule 3.1160 effective January 1, 2019; adopted as rule 363 effective January 1, 1984; previously amended effective January 1, 1993, July 1, 1995, January 1, 2000, January 1, 2002, and January 1, 2012; previously amended and renumbered effective January 1, 2007.

Rule 3.1153. Minors may appear without counsel to seek specified restraining orders [Repealed]

Rule 3.1153 repealed effective January 1, 2012; adopted as rule 364 effective July 1, 1995; previously amended and renumbered effective January 1, 2007.

Article 4
Protective Orders

Title 3, Civil Rules—Division 11, Law and Motion—Chapter 3, Provisional and Injunctive Relief; Article 4, Protective Orders; adopted effective January 1, 2019.

Rule 3.1160. Requests for protective orders to prevent civil harassment, workplace violence, private postsecondary school violence, and elder or dependent adult abuse
Rule 3.1161. Request to make minor's information confidential in civil harassment protective order proceedings
Rule 3.1162. Service requirement for respondents who appear remotely

Rule 3.1160. Requests for protective orders to prevent civil harassment, workplace violence, private postsecondary school violence, and elder or dependent adult abuse

(a) Application

This rule applies to requests for protective orders under Code of Civil Procedure sections 527.6, 527.8, and 527.85, and Welfare and Institutions Code section 15657.03.

(Subd (a) repealed and adopted effective January 1, 2012; previously amended effective July 1, 1995, and January 1, 2007.)

(b) No memorandum required

Unless ordered by the court, no memorandum is required in support of or in opposition to a request for a protective order.

(Subd (b) repealed and adopted effective January 1, 2012; previously amended effective July 1, 1995, January 1, 2002, and January 1, 2007.)

(c) Service of requests, notices, and orders

(1) Except as provided in (2), the request for a protective order, notice of hearing, and any temporary restraining order, must be personally served on the respondent at least five days before the hearing, unless the court for

good cause orders a shorter time. Service must be made in the manner provided by law for personal service of summons in civil actions.

(2) The court may specify another method of service for a request for a civil harassment protective order brought under Code of Civil Procedure section 527.6 if the court determines that the petitioner has been unable to accomplish personal service, and that there is reason to believe that the respondent is evading service or cannot be located.

(Subd (c) amended effective September 1, 2022; previously amended effective January 1, 1993, January 1, 2007, and January 1, 2012.)

(d) Response

The response to a request for a protective order may be written or oral, or both. If a written response is served on the petitioner or, if the petitioner is represented, on the petitioner's attorney at least two days before the hearing, the petitioner is not entitled to a continuance on account of the response.

(Subd (d) amended effective January 1, 2012; previously amended effective January 1, 2007.)

(e) Continuance

A respondent may request continuance of the hearing upon a showing of good cause. If the court in its discretion grants the continuance, any temporary restraining order that has been granted remains in effect until the end of the continued hearing unless otherwise ordered by the court.

(Subd (e) adopted effective January 1, 2012.)

Rule 3.1160 amended effective September 1, 2022; adopted as rule 363 effective January 1, 1984; previously amended effective January 1, 1993, July 1, 1995, January 1, 2000, January 1, 2002, and January 1, 2012; previously amended and renumbered as rule 3.1152 effective January 1, 2007; previously renumbered effective January 1, 2019.

Rule 3.1161. Request to make minor's information confidential in civil harassment protective order proceedings

(a) Application of rule

This rule applies to requests and orders made under Code of Civil Procedure section 527.6(v) to keep a minor's information confidential in a civil harassment protective order proceeding.

Wherever used in this rule, "legal guardian" means either parent if both parents have legal custody, or the parent or person having legal custody, or the guardian, of a minor.

(Subd (a) adopted effective January 1, 2019.)

(b) Information that may be made confidential

The information that may be made confidential includes:

(1) The minor's name;

(2) The minor's address;

(3) The circumstances surrounding the protective order with respect to the minor. These include the allegations in the *Request for Civil Harassment Retraining Orders* (form CH-100) that involve conduct directed, in whole or in part, toward the minor; and

(4) Any other information that the minor or legal guardian believes should be confidential.

(Subd (b) adopted effective January 1, 2019.)

(c) Requests for confidentiality

(1) *Person making request*

A request for confidentiality may be made by a minor or legal guardian.

(2) *Number of minors*

A request for confidentiality by a legal guardian may be made for more than one minor. "Minor," as used in this rule, refers to all minors for whom a request for confidentiality is made.

(Subd (c) adopted effective January 1, 2019.)

(d) Procedures for making request

(1) *Timing of requests*

A request for confidentiality may be made at any time during the case.

(2) *Submission of request*

The person submitting a request must complete and file *Request to Keep Minor's Information Confidential* (form CH-160), a confidential form.

(3) *Ruling on request*

(A) *Ruling on request without notice*

The court must determine whether to grant a request for confidentiality without requiring that any notice of the request be given to the other party, or both parties if the minor is not a party in the proceeding. No adversarial hearing is to be held.

(B) *Request for confidentiality submitted at the same time as a request for restraining orders*

If a request for confidentiality is submitted at the same time as a request for restraining orders, the court must consider both requests consistent with Code of Civil Procedure section 527.6(e) and must consider and rule on the request for confidentiality before the request for restraining order is filed.

Documents submitted with the restraining order request must not be filed until after the court has ruled on the request for confidentiality and must be consistent with (C) below.

(C) *Withdrawal of request for restraining order*

If a request for confidentiality under (B) made by the person asking for the restraining order is denied and the requester seeks to withdraw the request for restraining orders, all of the following apply:

(i) The court must not file the request for restraining order and the accompanying proposed order forms and must return the documents to the requester personally, destroy the documents, or delete the documents from any electronic files;

(ii) The order denying confidentiality must be filed and maintained in a public file; and

(iii) The request for confidentiality must be filed and maintained in a confidential file.

(4) *Need for additional facts*

If the court finds that the request for confidentiality is insufficiently specific to meet the requirements under Code of Civil Procedure section 527.6(v)(2) for granting the request, the court may take testimony from the minor, or legal guardian, the person requesting a protective order, or other competent witness, in a closed hearing in order to determine if there are additional facts that would support granting the request.

(Subd (d) adopted effective January 1, 2019.)

(e) Orders on request for confidentiality

(1) *Rulings*

The court may grant the entire request, deny the entire request, or partially grant the request for confidentiality.

(2) *Order granting request for confidentiality*

(A) *Applicability*

An order made under Code of Civil Procedure section 527.6(v) applies in this case and in any other civil case to all registers of actions, indexes, court calendars, pleadings, discovery documents, and other documents filed or served in the action, and at hearings, trial, and other court proceedings that are open to the public.

(B) *Minor's name*

If the court grants a request for confidentiality of the minor's name and:

(i) If the minor is a party to the action, the court must use the initials of the minor or other initials, at the discretion of the court. In addition, the court must use only initials to identify both parties to the action if using the other party's name would likely reveal the identity of the minor.

(ii) If the minor is not a party to the action, the court must not include any information that would likely reveal the identity of the minor, including whether the minor lives with the person making the request for confidentiality.

(C) *Circumstances surrounding protective order (statements related to minor)*

If the court grants a request for confidentiality, the order must specifically identify the information about the minor in *Request for Civil Harassment Restraining Orders* (form CH-100) and any other applicable document that must be kept confidential. Information about the minor ordered confidential by the court must not be made available to the public.

(D) *Service*

The other party, or both parties if the person making the request for confidentiality is not a party to the action, must be served with a copy of the *Request to Keep Minor's Information Confidential* (form CH-160), *Order on Request to Keep Minor's Information Confidential* (form CH-165) and *Notice of Order Protecting Information of Minor* (form CH-170), redacted if required under (f)(4).

(3) *Order denying request for confidentiality*

(A) The order denying confidentiality must be filed and maintained in a public file. The request for confidentiality must be filed and maintained in a confidential file.

(B) Notwithstanding denial of a request to keep the minor's address confidential, the address may be confidential under other statutory provisions.

(C) *Service*

(i) If a request for confidentiality is denied and the request for restraining order has been withdrawn, and if no other action is pending before the court in the case, then the *Request to Keep Minor's Information*

Confidential (form CH-160) and *Order on Request to Keep Minor's Information Confidential* (form CH-165) must not be served on the other party, or both parties if the person making the request for confidentiality is not a party to the action.

(ii) If a request for confidentiality is denied and the request for restraining order has not been withdrawn, or if an action between the same parties is pending before the court, then the *Request to Keep Minor's Information Confidential* (form CH-160) and *Order on Request to Keep Minor's Information Confidential* (form CH-165) must be served on the other party, or both parties if the person making the request for confidentiality is not a party to the action.

(Subd (e) adopted effective January 1, 2019.)

(f) Procedures to protect confidential information when request is granted

(1) If a request for confidentiality is granted in whole or in part, the court, in its discretion, and taking into consideration the factors stated in (g), must ensure that the order granting confidentiality is maintained in the most effective manner by:

(A) The judicial officer redacting all information to be kept confidential from all applicable documents;

(B) Ordering the requesting party or the requesting party's attorney to prepare a redacted copy of all applicable documents and submit all redacted copies to the court for review and filing; or

(C) Ordering any other procedure that facilitates the prompt and accurate preparation of a redacted copy of all applicable documents in compliance with the court's order granting confidentiality, provided the selected procedure is consistent with (g).

(2) The redacted copy or copies must be filed and maintained in a public file, and the unredacted copy or copies must be filed and maintained in a confidential file.

(3) Information that is made confidential from the public and the restrained person must be filed in a confidential file accessible only to the minor or minors who are subjects of the order of confidentiality, or the legal guardian who requested confidentiality, law enforcement for enforcement purposes only, and the court.

(4) Any information that is made confidential from the restrained person must be redacted from the copy that will be served on the restrained person.

(Subd (f) adopted effective January 1, 2019.)

(g) Factors in selecting redaction procedures

In determining the procedure to follow under (f), the court must consider the following factors:

(1) Whether the requesting party is represented by an attorney;

(2) Whether the requesting party has immediate access to a self-help center or other legal assistance;

(3) Whether the requesting party is capable of preparing redacted materials without assistance;

(4) Whether the redactions to the applicable documents are simple or complex; and

(5) When applicable, whether the selected procedure will ensure that the orders on the request for restraining order and the request for confidentiality are issued and redacted in an expeditious and timely manner.

(Subd (g) amended effective September 1, 2020; adopted effective January 1, 2019.)

(h) Releasing minor's confidential information

(1) *To respondent*

Information about a protected minor must be released to the respondent only as provided in Code of Civil Procedure section 527.6(v)(4)(A)(ii), limited to information necessary to allow the respondent to respond to the request for the protective order and to comply with the confidentiality order and the protective order.

(2) *To law enforcement*

Information about a minor must be shared with law enforcement as provided in Code of Civil Procedure section 527.6(v)(4)(A)(i) or by court order.

(3) *To other persons*

If the court finds it is necessary to prevent harassment or is in the best interest of the minor, the court may release confidential information on the request of any person or entity or on the court's own motion.

(A) *Request for release of confidential information*

(i) Any person or entity may request the release of confidential information by filing *Request for Release of Minor's Confidential Information* (form CH-176) and a proposed, *Order on Request for Release of Minor's Confidential Information* (form CH-179), with the court.

(ii) Within 10 days after filing form CH-176 with the clerk, the clerk must serve, by first-class mail, the following documents on the minor or legal guardian who made the request to keep the minor's information confidential:

a. *Cover Sheet for Confidential Information* (form CH-175);

b. *Request for Release of Minor's Confidential Information* (form CH-176);

c. *Notice of Request for Release of Minor's Confidential Information* (form CH-177);

d. *Response to Request for Release of Minor's Confidential Information* (form CH-178) (blank copy);

e. *Order on Request for Release of Minor's Confidential Information* (form CH-179).

(B) *Opportunity to object*

(i) The person who made the request for confidentiality has the right to object by filing form CH-178 within 20 days from the date of the mailing of form CH-177, or verbally objecting at a hearing, if one is held.

(ii) The person filing a response must serve a copy of the response (form CH-178) on the person requesting release of confidential information. Service must occur before filing the response form with the court unless the response form contains confidential information. If the response form contains confidential information, service must be done as soon as possible after the response form has been redacted.

(iii) If the person who made the request for confidentiality objects to the release of information, the court may set the matter for a closed hearing.

(C) *Rulings*

The request may be granted or denied in whole or in part without a hearing. Alternatively, the court may set the matter for hearing on at least 10 days' notice to the person who made the request for release of confidential information and the person who made the request for confidential information. Any hearing must be confidential.

(i) *Order granting release of confidential information*

a. The order (form CH-179) granting the release of confidential information must be prepared in a manner consistent with the procedures outlined in (f).

b. A redacted copy of the order (form CH-179) must be filed in a public file and an unredacted copy of the order must be filed in a confidential file.

c. *Service*

If the court grants the request for release of information based on the pleadings, the court must mail a copy of form CH-179 to the person who filed form CH-176 and the person who made the request to keep the minor's information confidential. Parties may be served in court if present at the hearing.

(ii) *Order denying request to release minor's confidential information*

a. The court may deny a request to release confidential information based on the request alone.

b. The order (form CH-179) denying the release of confidential information must be filed in a public file and must not include any confidential information.

c. *Service*

If the court denies the request for release of information based on the pleadings, the court must mail a copy of form CH-179 to the person who filed form CH-176 and the person who made the request to keep the minor's information confidential. Parties may be served in court if present at the hearing.

(iii) If the court finds that the request to release confidential information is insufficiently specific to meet the requirements under Code of Civil Procedure section 527.6(v)(4)(C), the court may conduct a closed hearing to determine if there are additional facts that would support granting the request. The court may receive any relevant evidence, including testimony from the person requesting the release of a minor's confidential information, the minor, the legal guardian, the person who requested the restraining order, or other competent witness.

(Subd (h) amended effective September 1, 2020; adopted effective January 1, 2019.)

(i) Protecting information in subsequent filings and other civil cases

(1) *Filings made after an order granting confidentiality*

(A) A party seeking to file a document or form after an order for confidentiality has been made must submit the *Cover Sheet for Confidential Information* (form CH-175) attached to the front of the document to be filed.

(B) Upon receipt of form CH-175 with attached documents, the court must:

(i) Order a procedure for redaction consistent with the procedures stated in (f);

(ii) File the unredacted document in the confidential file pending receipt of the redacted document if the redacted document is not prepared on the same court day; and

(iii) File the redacted document in the public file after it has been reviewed and approved by the court for accuracy.

(2) *Other civil case*

(A) Information subject to an order of confidentiality issued under Code of Civil Procedure section 527.6(v) must be kept confidential in any other civil case with the same parties.

(B) The minor or person making the request for confidentiality and any person who has been served with a notice of confidentiality must submit a copy of the order of confidentiality (form CH-165) in any other civil case with the same parties.

(Subd (i) amended effective September 1, 2020; adopted effective January 1, 2019.)

Rule 3.1161 amended effective September 1, 2020; adopted effective January 1, 2019.

Advisory Committee Comment

Subdivisions (a)–(e). The process described in this rule need not be used for minors if the request for confidentiality is merely to keep an address confidential and a petitioning minor has a mailing address which need not be kept private that can be listed on the forms. The restraining order forms do not require the address of a nonpetitioning minor.

This rule and rule 2.551 provide a standard and procedures for courts to follow when a request is made to seal a record. The standard as reflected in Code of Civil Procedure section 527.6(v)(2) is based on *NBC Subsidiary (KNBC-TV), Inc. v. Superior Court* (1999) 20 Cal.4th 1178. The standard recognizes the First Amendment right of access to documents used at trial or as a basis of adjudication.

Rule 3.1162. Service requirement for respondents who appear remotely

(a) Application of rule

This rule applies to protective orders issued under Code of Civil Procedure sections 527.6, 527.8, and 527.85; Penal Code sections 18100–18205; and Welfare and Institutions Code section 15657.03.

(Subd (a) adopted effective January 1, 2024.)

(b) No additional proof of service required

If the respondent named in an order issued after hearing appears at that hearing through the use of remote technology, and through that appearance has received actual notice of the existence and substance of the restraining order after hearing, no additional proof of service is required for enforcement of the order.

(Subd (b) adopted effective January 1, 2024.)

Rule 3.1162 adopted effective January 1, 2024.

Article 5
Receiverships

Rule 3.1175. Ex parte application for appointment of receiver
Rule 3.1176. Confirmation of ex parte appointment of receiver
Rule 3.1177. Nomination of receivers
Rule 3.1178. Amount of undertakings
Rule 3.1179. The receiver
Rule 3.1180. Employment of attorney
Rule 3.1181. Receiver's inventory
Rule 3.1182. Monthly reports
Rule 3.1183. Interim fees and objections
Rule 3.1184. Receiver's final account and report

Rule 3.1175. Ex parte application for appointment of receiver

(a) Application

In addition to any other matters supporting an application for the ex parte appointment of a receiver, the applicant must show in detail by verified complaint or declaration:

(1) The nature of the emergency and the reasons irreparable injury would be suffered by the applicant during the time necessary for a hearing on notice;

(2) The names, addresses, and telephone numbers of the persons in actual possession of the property for which a receiver is requested, or of the president, manager, or principal agent of any corporation in possession of the property;

(3) The use being made of the property by the persons in possession; and

(4) If the property is a part of the plant, equipment, or stock in trade of any business, the nature and approximate size or extent of the business and facts sufficient to show whether the taking of the property by a receiver would stop or seriously interfere with the operation of the business.

If any of the matters listed above are unknown to the applicant and cannot be ascertained by the exercise of due diligence, the applicant's declaration or verified complaint must fully state the matters unknown and the efforts made to acquire the information.

(Subd (a) amended effective January 1, 2007; previously amended effective January 1, 2002.)

Rule 3.1175 amended and renumbered effective January 1, 2007; adopted as rule 349 effective January 1, 1984; previously amended and renumbered as rule 1900 effective January 1, 2002.

Rule 3.1176. Confirmation of ex parte appointment of receiver

(a) Order to show cause

Whenever a receiver is appointed without notice, the matter must be made returnable upon an order to show cause why the appointment should not be confirmed. The order to show cause must be made returnable on the earliest date that the business of the court will admit, but not later than 15 days or, if good cause appears to the court, 22 days from the date the order is issued.

(Subd (a) amended effective January 1, 2002.)

(b) Service of complaint, order to show cause, declarations, and memorandum

The applicant must serve on each of the adverse parties:

(1) A copy of the complaint if not previously served;

(2) The order to show cause stating the date, time, and place of the hearing;

(3) Any declarations supporting the application; and

(4) A memorandum supporting the application.

Service must be made as soon as reasonably practical, but no later than 5 days after the date on which the order to show cause is issued, unless the court orders another time for service.

(Subd (b) amended effective January 1, 2007; previously amended effective January 1, 2002.)

(c) Failure to proceed or serve adverse party

When the matter first comes on for hearing, the party that obtained the appointment must be ready to proceed. If that party is not ready to proceed or has failed to exercise diligence to effect service upon the adverse parties as provided in (b), the court may discharge the receiver.

(Subd (c) amended effective January 1, 2007; previously amended effective January 1, 2002.)

(d) Continuance

The adverse parties are entitled to one continuance to enable them to oppose the confirmation. If a continuance is granted under this subdivision, the order to show cause remains in effect until the date of the continued hearing.

(Subd (d) amended effective January 1, 2002.)

Rule 3.1176 amended and renumbered effective January 1, 2007; adopted as rule 351 effective January 1, 1984; previously amended and renumbered as rule 1901 effective January 1, 2002.

Rule 3.1177. Nomination of receivers

At the hearing of an application for appointment of a receiver on notice or at the hearing for confirmation of an ex parte appointment, each party appearing may, at the time of the hearing, suggest in writing one or more persons for appointment or substitution as receiver, stating the reasons. A party's suggestion is without prejudice to its objection to the appointment or confirmation of a receiver.

Rule 3.1177 renumbered effective January 1, 2007; adopted as rule 353 effective January 1, 1984; previously amended and renumbered as rule 1902 effective January 1, 2002.

Rule 3.1178. Amount of undertakings

At the hearing of an application for appointment of a receiver on notice or ex parte, the applicant must, and other parties may, propose and state the reasons for the specific amounts of the undertakings required from (1) the applicant by Code of Civil Procedure section 529, (2) the applicant by Code of Civil Procedure section 566(b), and (3) the receiver by Code of Civil Procedure section 567(b), for any injunction that is ordered in or with the order appointing a receiver.

Rule 3.1178 amended and renumbered effective January 1, 2007; adopted as rule 1902.5 effective January 1, 2004.

Rule 3.1179. The receiver

(a) Agent of the court

The receiver is the agent of the court and not of any party, and as such:

(1) Is neutral;

(2) Acts for the benefit of all who may have an interest in the receivership property; and

(3) Holds assets for the court and not for the plaintiff or the defendant.

(b) Prohibited contracts, agreements, arrangements, and understandings

The party seeking the appointment of the receiver may not, directly or indirectly, require any contract, agreement, arrangement, or understanding with any receiver whom it intends to nominate or recommend to the court, and the receiver may not enter into any such contract, arrangement, agreement, or understanding concerning:

(1) The role of the receiver with respect to the property following a trustee's sale or termination of a receivership, without specific court permission;

(2) How the receiver will administer the receivership or how much the receiver will charge for services or pay for services to appropriate or approved third parties hired to provide services;

(3) Who the receiver will hire, or seek approval to hire, to perform necessary services; or

(4) What capital expenditures will be made on the property.

Rule 3.1179 renumbered effective January 1, 2007; adopted as rule 1903 effective January 1, 2002.

Rule 3.1180. Employment of attorney

A receiver must not employ an attorney without the approval of the court. The application for approval to employ an attorney must be in writing and must state:

(1) The necessity for the employment;

(2) The name of the attorney whom the receiver proposes to employ; and

(3) That the attorney is not the attorney for, associated with, nor employed by an attorney for any party.

Rule 3.1180 amended and renumbered effective January 1, 2007; adopted as rule 1904 effective January 1, 2002.

Rule 3.1181. Receiver's inventory

(a) Filing of inventory

A receiver must, within 30 days after appointment, or within such other time as the court may order, file an inventory containing a complete and detailed list of all property of which the receiver has taken possession by virtue of the appointment.

(Subd (a) lettered effective January 1, 2007; adopted as part of untitled subd effective January 1, 2002.)

(b) Supplemental inventory

The receiver must promptly file a supplementary inventory of all subsequently obtained property.

(Subd (b) lettered effective January 1, 2007; adopted as part of untitled subd effective January 1, 2002.)

Rule 3.1181 amended and renumbered effective January 1, 2007; adopted as rule 1905 effective January 1, 2002.

Rule 3.1182. Monthly reports

(a) Content of reports

The receiver must provide monthly reports to the parties and, if requested, to nonparty client lien holders. These reports must include:

(1) A narrative report of events;

(2) A financial report; and

(3) A statement of all fees paid to the receiver, employees, and professionals showing:

(A) Itemized services;

(B) A breakdown of the services by 1/10 hour increments;

(C) If the fees are hourly, the hourly fees; and

(D) If the fees are on another basis, that basis.

(Subd (a) amended effective January 1, 2007.)

(b) Reports not to be filed

The monthly reports are not to be filed with the court unless the court so orders.

Rule 3.1182 amended effective January 1, 2007; adopted as rule 1906 effective January 1, 2002; previously renumbered effective January 1, 2007.

Rule 3.1183. Interim fees and objections

(a) Interim fees

Interim fees are subject to final review and approval by the court. The court retains jurisdiction to award a greater or lesser amount as the full, fair, and final value of the services received.

(b) Objections to interim accounts and reports

Unless good cause is shown, objections to a receiver's interim report and accounting must be made within 10 days of notice of the report and accounting, must be specific, and must be delivered to the receiver and all parties entitled to service of the interim report and accounting.

Rule 3.1183 renumbered effective January 1, 2007; adopted as rule 1907 effective January 1, 2002.

Rule 3.1184. Receiver's final account and report

(a) Motion or stipulation

A receiver must present by noticed motion or stipulation of all parties:

(1) A final account and report;

(2) A request for the discharge; and

(3) A request for exoneration of the receiver's surety.

(Subd (a) amended and relettered effective January 1, 2004; adopted as part of unlettered subd effective January 1, 2002.)

(b) No memorandum required

No memorandum needs to be submitted in support of the motion or stipulation served and filed under (a) unless the court so orders.

(Subd (b) adopted effective January 1, 2004.)

(c) Notice

Notice of the motion or of the stipulation must be given to every person or entity known to the receiver to have a substantial, unsatisfied claim that will be affected by the order or stipulation, whether or not the person or entity is a party to the action or has appeared in it.

(Subd (c) adopted effective January 1, 2004.)

(d) Claim for compensation for receiver or attorney

If any allowance of compensation for the receiver or for an attorney employed by the receiver is claimed in an account, it must state in detail what services have been performed by the receiver or the attorney and whether previous allowances have been made to the receiver or attorney and the amounts.

(Subd (d) amended and relettered effective January 1, 2007; adopted as part of unlettered subd effective January 1, 2002; amended and lettered effective January 1, 2004.)

Rule 3.1184 amended and renumbered effective January 1, 2007; adopted as rule 1908 effective January 1, 2002; previously amended effective January 1, 2004.

Chapter 4
Ex Parte Applications

Rule 3.1200. Application
Rule 3.1201. Required documents
Rule 3.1202. Contents of application
Rule 3.1203. Time of notice to other parties
Rule 3.1204. Contents of notice and declaration regarding notice
Rule 3.1205. Filing and presentation of the ex parte application
Rule 3.1206. Service of papers
Rule 3.1207. Appearance requirements

Rule 3.1200. Application

The rules in this chapter govern ex parte applications and orders in civil cases, unless otherwise provided by a statute or a rule. These rules may be referred to as "the ex parte rules."

Rule 3.1200 adopted effective January 1, 2007.

Rule 3.1201. Required documents

A request for ex parte relief must be in writing and must include all of the following:

(1) An application containing the case caption and stating the relief requested;

(2) A declaration in support of the application making the factual showing required under rule 3.1202(c);

(3) A declaration based on personal knowledge of the notice given under rule 3.1204;

(4) A memorandum; and

(5) A proposed order.

Rule 3.1201 adopted effective January 1, 2007.

Rule 3.1202. Contents of application

(a) Identification of attorney or party

An ex parte application must state the name, address, e-mail address, and telephone number of any attorney known to the applicant to be an attorney for any party or, if no such attorney is known, the name, address, e-mail address, and telephone number of the party if known to the applicant.

(Subd (a) amended effective January 1, 2016.)

(b) Disclosure of previous applications

If an ex parte application has been refused in whole or in part, any subsequent application of the same character or for the same relief, although made upon an alleged different state of facts, must include a full disclosure of all previous applications and of the court's actions.

(c) Affirmative factual showing required

An applicant must make an affirmative factual showing in a declaration containing competent testimony based on personal knowledge of irreparable harm, immediate danger, or any other statutory basis for granting relief ex parte.

(Subd (c) amended effective January 1, 2007.)

Rule 3.1202 amended effective January 1, 2016; adopted effective January 1, 2007; previously amended effective January 1, 2007.

Rule 3.1203. Time of notice to other parties

(a) Time of notice

A party seeking an ex parte order must notify all parties no later than 10:00 a.m. the court day before the ex parte appearance, absent a showing of exceptional circumstances that justify a shorter time for notice.

(Subd (a) amended effective January 1, 2008; adopted effective January 1, 2007.)

(b) Time of notice in unlawful detainer proceedings

A party seeking an ex parte order in an unlawful detainer proceeding may provide shorter notice than required under (a) provided that the notice given is reasonable.

(Subd (b) adopted effective January 1, 2007.)

Rule 3.1203 amended effective January 1, 2008; adopted effective January 1, 2007.

Rule 3.1204. Contents of notice and declaration regarding notice

(a) Contents of notice

When notice of an ex parte application is given, the person giving notice must:

(1) State with specificity the nature of the relief to be requested and the date, time, and place for the presentation of the application; and

(2) Attempt to determine whether the opposing party will appear to oppose the application.

(Subd (a) adopted effective January 1, 2007.)

(b) Declaration regarding notice

An ex parte application must be accompanied by a declaration regarding notice stating:

(1) The notice given, including the date, time, manner, and name of the party informed, the relief sought, any response, and whether opposition is expected and that, within the applicable time under rule 3.1203, the applicant informed the opposing party where and when the application would be made;

(2) That the applicant in good faith attempted to inform the opposing party but was unable to do so, specifying the efforts made to inform the opposing party; or

(3) That, for reasons specified, the applicant should not be required to inform the opposing party.

(Subd (b) adopted effective January 1, 2007.)

(c) Explanation for shorter notice

If notice was provided later than 10:00 a.m. the court day before the ex parte appearance, the declaration regarding notice must explain:

(1) The exceptional circumstances that justify the shorter notice; or

(2) In unlawful detainer proceedings, why the notice given is reasonable.

(Subd (c) adopted effective January 1, 2007.)

Rule 3.1204 adopted effective January 1, 2007.

Rule 3.1205. Filing and presentation of the ex parte application

Notwithstanding the failure of an applicant to comply with the requirements of rule 3.1203, the clerk must not reject an ex parte application for filing and must promptly present the application to the appropriate judicial officer for consideration.

Rule 3.1205 adopted effective January 1, 2007.

Rule 3.1206. Service of papers

Parties appearing at the ex parte hearing must serve the ex parte application or any written opposition on all other appearing parties at the first reasonable opportunity. Absent exceptional circumstances, no hearing may be conducted unless such service has been made.

Rule 3.1206 adopted effective January 1, 2007.

Rule 3.1207. Appearance requirements

An applicant for an ex parte order must appear, either in person or remotely under rule 3.672, except in the following cases:

(1) Applications to file a memorandum in excess of the applicable page limit;

(2) Applications for extensions of time to serve pleadings;

(3) Setting of hearing dates on alternative writs and orders to show cause; and

(4) Stipulations by the parties for an order.

Rule 3.1207 amended effective January 21, 2022; adopted effective January 1, 2007; previously amended effective January 1, 2008, and January 1, 2014.

Chapter 5
Noticed Motions

Rule 3.1300. Time for filing and service of motion papers
Rule 3.1302. Place and manner of filing
Rule 3.1304. Time of hearing
Rule 3.1306. Evidence at hearing
Rule 3.1308. Tentative rulings
Rule 3.1310. Reporting of proceedings on motions
Rule 3.1312. Preparation and submission of proposed order

Rule 3.1300. Time for filing and service of motion papers

(a) In general

Unless otherwise ordered or specifically provided by law, all moving and supporting papers must be served and filed in accordance with Code of Civil Procedure section 1005 and, when applicable, the statutes and rules providing for electronic filing and service.

(Subd (a) amended effective January 1, 2016; previously amended effective January 1, 2000, and January 1, 2007.)

(b) Order shortening time

The court, on its own motion or on application for an order shortening time supported by a declaration showing good cause, may prescribe shorter times for the filing and service of papers than the times specified in Code of Civil Procedure section 1005.

(Subd (b) adopted effective January 1, 2000.)

(c) Time for filing proof of service

Proof of service of the moving papers must be filed no later than five court days before the time appointed for the hearing.

(Subd (c) amended effective January 1, 2007; adopted as subd (b) effective January 1, 1984; previously relettered effective January 1, 2000.)

(d) Filing of late papers

No paper may be rejected for filing on the ground that it was untimely submitted for filing. If the court, in its discretion, refuses to consider a late filed paper, the minutes or order must so indicate.

(Subd (d) amended effective January 1, 2007; adopted as subd (c) effective January 1, 1992; previously amended and relettered effective January 1, 2000.)

(e) Computation of time

A paper submitted before the close of the clerk's office to the public on the day the paper is due is deemed timely filed. Under rules 2.253(b)(7) and 2.259(c), a court may provide by local rule that a paper that is required to be filed electronically and that is received electronically by the court before midnight on a court day is deemed filed on that court day.

(Subd (e) amended effective January 1, 2016; adopted as subd (d) effective January 1, 1992; previously relettered as subd (e) effective January 1, 2000.)

Rule 3.1300 amended effective January 1, 2016; adopted as rule 317 effective January 1, 1984; previously amended effective January 1, 1992, and January 1, 2000; previously amended and renumbered as rule 3.1300 effective January 1, 2007.

Rule 3.1302. Place and manner of filing

(a) Papers filed in clerk's office

Unless otherwise provided by local rule or specified in a court's protocol for electronic filing, all papers relating to a law and motion proceeding must be filed in the clerk's office.

(Subd (a) amended effective January 1, 2016; previously amended effective January 1, 2007.)

(b) Requirements for lodged material

Material lodged physically with the clerk must be accompanied by an addressed envelope with sufficient postage for mailing the material. Material lodged electronically must clearly specify the electronic address to which a notice of deletion may be sent. After determination of the matter, the clerk may mail or send the material if in paper form back to the party lodging it. If the lodged material is in electronic form, the clerk may permanently delete it after sending notice of the deletion to the party who lodged the material.

(Subd (b) amended effective January 1, 2017; previously amended effective January 1, 2007, and January 1, 2016.)

Rule 3.1302 amended effective January 1, 2017; adopted as rule 319 effective January 1, 1984; previously amended and renumbered as rule 3.1302 effective January 1, 2007; previously amended effective January 1, 2016.

Rule 3.1304. Time of hearing

(a) General schedule

The clerk must post electronically and at the courthouse a general schedule showing the days and departments for holding each type of law and motion hearing.

(Subd (a) amended effective January 1, 2016; previously amended effective January 1, 2003.)

(b) Duty to notify if matter not to be heard

The moving party must immediately notify the court if a matter will not be heard on the scheduled date.

(Subd (b) amended effective January 1, 2003.)

(c) Notice of nonappearance

A party may give notice that he or she will not appear at a law and motion hearing and submit the matter without an appearance unless the court orders otherwise. The court must rule on the motion as if the party had appeared.

(Subd (c) amended effective January 1, 2003; previously amended effective January 1, 1992.)

(d) Action if no party appears

If a party fails to appear at a law and motion hearing without having given notice under (c), the court may take the matter off calendar, to be reset only upon motion, or may rule on the matter.

(Subd (d) amended effective January 1, 2003; previously amended and relettered effective January 1, 1992.)

Rule 3.1304 amended effective January 1, 2016; adopted as rule 321 effective January 1, 1984; previously amended effective January 1, 1992, and January 1, 2003; amended and renumbered as rule 3.1304 effective January 1, 2007.

Rule 3.1306. Evidence at hearing

(a) Restrictions on oral testimony

Evidence received at a law and motion hearing must be by declaration or request for judicial notice without testimony or cross-examination, unless the court orders otherwise for good cause shown.

(Subd (a) amended effective January 1, 2007; previously amended effective January 1, 2003.)

(b) Request to present oral testimony

A party seeking permission to introduce oral evidence, except for oral evidence in rebuttal to oral evidence presented by the other party, must file, no later than three court days before the hearing, a written statement stating the nature and extent of the evidence proposed to be introduced and a reasonable time estimate for the hearing. When the statement is filed less than five court days before the hearing, the filing party must serve a copy on the other parties in a manner to assure delivery to the other parties no later than two days before the hearing.

(Subd (b) amended and relettered effective January 1, 2003; adopted as part of subd (a) effective January 1, 1984.)

(c) Judicial notice

A party requesting judicial notice of material under Evidence Code sections 452 or 453 must provide the court and each party with a copy of the material. If the material is part of a file in the court in which the matter is being heard, the party must:

(1) Specify in writing the part of the court file sought to be judicially noticed; and

(2) Either make arrangements with the clerk to have the file in the courtroom at the time of the hearing or confirm with the clerk that the file is electronically accessible to the court.

(Subd (c) amended effective January 1, 2017; adopted as subd (b) effective January 1, 1984; previously amended and relettered effective January 1, 2003; previously amended effective January 1, 2007.)

Rule 3.1306 amended effective January 1, 2017; adopted as rule 323 effective January 1, 1984; previously amended effective January 1, 2003; previously amended and renumbered effective January 1, 2007.

Rule 3.1308. Tentative rulings

(a) Tentative ruling procedures

A trial court that offers a tentative ruling procedure in civil law and motion matters must follow one of the following procedures:

(1) *Notice of intent to appear required*

The court must make its tentative ruling available by telephone and also, at the option of the court, by any other method designated by the court, by no later than 3:00 p.m. the court day before the scheduled hearing. If the court desires oral argument, the tentative ruling must so direct. The tentative ruling may also note any issues on which the court wishes the parties to provide further argument. If the court has not directed argument, oral argument must be permitted only if a party notifies all other parties and the court by 4:00 p.m. on the court day before the hearing of the party's intention to appear. A party must notify all other parties by telephone or in person. The court must accept notice by telephone and, at its discretion, may also designate alternative methods by which a party may notify the court of the party's intention to appear. The tentative ruling will become the ruling of the court if the court has not directed oral argument by its tentative ruling and notice of intent to appear has not been given.

(2) *No notice of intent to appear required*

The court must make its tentative ruling available by telephone and also, at the option of the court, by any other method designated by the court, by a specified time before the hearing. The tentative ruling may note any issues on which the court wishes the parties to provide further argument at the hearing. This procedure must not require the parties to give notice of intent to appear, and the tentative ruling will not automatically become the ruling of the court if such notice is not given. The tentative ruling, or such other ruling as the court may render, will not become the final ruling of the court until the hearing.

(Subd (a) amended effective January 1, 2007; previously amended effective July 1, 2000.)

(b) No other procedures permitted

Other than following one of the tentative ruling procedures authorized in (a), courts must not issue tentative rulings except:

(1) By posting a calendar note containing tentative rulings on the day of the hearing; or

(2) By announcing the tentative ruling at the time of oral argument.

(Subd (b) amended effective January 1, 2007; previously repealed and adopted effective July 1, 2000.)

(c) Notice of procedure

A court that follows one of the procedures described in (a) must so state in its local rules. The local rule must specify the telephone number for obtaining the tentative rulings and the time by which the rulings will be available.

(Subd (c) amended effective January 1, 2007; previously amended effective July 1, 2000.)

(d) Uniform procedure within court or branch

If a court or a branch of a court adopts a tentative ruling procedure, that procedure must be used by all judges in the court or branch who issue tentative rulings.

(Subd (d) amended and lettered effective January 1, 2007; adopted as part of subd (c) effective July 1, 1992.)

(e) Tentative rulings not required

This rule does not require any judge to issue tentative rulings.

(Subd (e) amended and lettered effective January 1, 2007; adopted as part of subd (c) effective July 1, 1992.)

Rule 3.1308 amended and renumbered effective January 1, 2007; adopted as rule 324 effective July 1, 1992; previously amended effective July 1, 2000.

Rule 3.1310. Reporting of proceedings on motions

A court that does not regularly provide for reporting or electronic recording of hearings on motions must so state in its local rules. The rules must also provide a procedure by which a party may obtain a reporter or a recording of the proceedings in order to provide an official verbatim transcript.

Rule 3.1310 amended and renumbered effective January 1, 2007; adopted as rule 324.5 effective January 1, 1992.

Rule 3.1312. Preparation and submission of proposed order

(a) Prevailing party to prepare

Unless the parties waive notice or the court orders otherwise, the party prevailing on any motion must, within five days of the ruling, serve by any means authorized by law and reasonably calculated to ensure delivery to the other party or parties no later than the close of the next business day a proposed order for approval as conforming to the court's order. Within five days after service, the other party or parties must notify the prevailing party as to whether or not the proposed order is so approved. The opposing party or parties must state any reasons for disapproval. Failure to notify the prevailing party within the time required shall be deemed an approval. The extensions of time based on a method of service provided under any statute or rule do not apply to this rule.

(Subd (a) amended effective January 1, 2011; previously amended effective July 1, 2000, and January 1, 2007.)

(b) Submission of proposed order to court

The prevailing party must, upon expiration of the five-day period provided for approval, promptly transmit the proposed order to the court together with a summary of any responses of the other parties or a statement that no responses were received.

(Subd (b) amended effective January 1, 2007; previously amended effective July 1, 2000.)

(c) Submission of proposed order by electronic means

If a proposed order is submitted to the court electronically in a case in which the parties are electronically filing documents under rules 2.250–2.261, two versions of the proposed order must be submitted:

(1) A version of the proposed order must be attached to a completed *Proposed Order (Cover Sheet)* (form EFS-020), and the combined document in Portable Document Format (PDF) must be filed electronically; and

(2) A version of the proposed order in an editable word-processing format must also be sent electronically to the court, with a copy of the e-mail and proposed order also being sent to all parties in the action.

Each court that provides for electronic filing must provide an electronic address or addresses to which the editable versions of proposed orders are to be sent and must specify any particular requirements regarding the editable word-processing format for proposed orders.

(Subd (c) adopted effective January 1, 2011.)

(d) Failure of prevailing party to prepare proposed order

If the prevailing party fails to prepare and submit a proposed order as required by (a) and (b) above, any other party may do so.

(Subd (d) amended and relettered effective January 1, 2011; adopted as subd (c); previously amended effective July 1, 2000.)

(e) Motion unopposed

This rule does not apply if the motion was unopposed and a proposed order was submitted with the moving papers, unless otherwise ordered by the court.

(Subd (e) relettered effective January 1, 2011; adopted as subd (d) effective July 1, 2000; previously amended effective January 1, 2007.)
Rule 3.1312 amended effective January 1, 2011; adopted as rule 391 effective July 1, 1992; previously amended effective July 1, 2000; previously amended and renumbered effective January 1, 2007.

Chapter 6
Particular Motions

Art. 1. Pleading and Venue Motions. Rules 3.1320–3.1327.
Art. 2. Procedural Motions. Rules 3.1330–3.1335.
Art. 3. Motions to Dismiss. Rules 3.1340, 3.1342.
Art. 4. Discovery Motions. Rules 3.1345–3.1348.
Art. 5. Summary Judgment Motions. Rules 3.1350–3.1354.
Art. 6. Miscellaneous Motions. Rules 3.1360, 3.1362.

Article 1
Pleading and Venue Motions

Rule 3.1320. Demurrers
Rule 3.1322. Motions to strike
Rule 3.1324. Amended pleadings and amendments to pleadings
Rule 3.1326. Motions for change of venue
Rule 3.1327. Motions to quash or to stay action in summary proceeding involving possession of real property

Rule 3.1320. Demurrers

(a) Grounds separately stated

Each ground of demurrer must be in a separate paragraph and must state whether it applies to the entire complaint, cross-complaint, or answer, or to specified causes of action or defenses.

(Subd (a) amended effective January 1, 2007.)

(b) Demurrer not directed to all causes of action

A demurrer to a cause of action may be filed without answering other causes of action.

(Subd (b) adopted effective January 1, 2007.)

(c) Notice of hearing

A party filing a demurrer must serve and file therewith a notice of hearing that must specify a hearing date in accordance with the provisions of Code of Civil Procedure section 1005 and, if service is by electronic means, in accordance with the requirements of Code of Civil Procedure section 1010.6(a)(4) and rule 2.251(h)(2).

(Subd (c) amended effective January 1, 2016; adopted as subd (b) effective January 1, 1984; previously amended effective July 1, 2000; previously amended and relettered as subd (c) effective January 1, 2007.)

(d) Date of hearing

Demurrers must be set for hearing not more than 35 days following the filing of the demurrer or on the first date available to the court thereafter. For good cause shown, the court may order the hearing held on an earlier or later day on notice prescribed by the court.

(Subd (d) amended and lettered effective January 1, 2007; adopted as part of subd (b) effective January 1, 1984.)

(e) Caption

A demurrer must state, on the first page immediately below the number of the case, the name of the party filing the demurrer and the name of the party whose pleading is the subject of the demurrer.

(Subd (e) amended and relettered effective January 1, 2007; adopted as subd (c) effective January 1, 1984.)

(f) Failure to appear at hearing

When a demurrer is regularly called for hearing and one of the parties does not appear, the demurrer must be disposed of on the merits at the request of the party appearing unless for good cause the hearing is continued. Failure to appear in support of a special demurrer may be construed by the court as an admission that the demurrer is not meritorious and as a waiver of all grounds thereof. If neither party appears, the demurrer may be disposed of on its merits or dropped from the calendar, to be restored on notice or on terms as the court may deem proper, or the hearing may be continued to such time as the court orders.

(Subd (f) amended and relettered effective January 1, 2007; adopted as subd (d) effective January 1, 1984.)

(g) Leave to answer or amend

Following a ruling on a demurrer, unless otherwise ordered, leave to answer or amend within 10 days is deemed granted, except for actions in forcible entry, forcible detainer, or unlawful detainer in which case 5 calendar days is deemed granted.

(Subd (g) amended and relettered effective January 1, 2007; adopted as subd (e) effective January 1, 1984.)

(h) Ex parte application to dismiss following failure to amend

A motion to dismiss the entire action and for entry of judgment after expiration of the time to amend following the sustaining of a demurrer may be made by ex parte application to the court under Code of Civil Procedure section 581(f)(2).

(Subd (h) amended and relettered effective January 1, 2007; adopted as subd (f) effective January 1, 1984; previously amended effective July 1, 1995.)

(i) Motion to strike late-filed amended pleading

If an amended pleading is filed after the time allowed, an order striking the amended pleading must be obtained by noticed motion under Code of Civil Procedure section 1010.

(Subd (i) amended effective January 1, 2009; adopted as part of subd (f) effective January 1, 1984; previously amended effective July 1, 1995; previously amended and lettered effective January 1, 2007.)

(j) Time to respond after demurrer

Unless otherwise ordered, defendant has 10 days to answer or otherwise plead to the complaint or the remaining causes of action following:

(1) The overruling of the demurrer;

(2) The expiration of the time to amend if the demurrer was sustained with leave to amend; or

(3) The sustaining of the demurrer if the demurrer was sustained without leave to amend.

(Subd (j) amended effective January 1, 2011; adopted as subd (g) effective July 1, 1984; previously amended and relettered effective January 1, 2007.)
Rule 3.1320 amended effective January 1, 2016; adopted as rule 325 effective January 1, 1984; previously amended and renumbered as rule 3.1320 effective January 1, 2007; previously amended effective July 1, 1984, July 1, 1995, July 1, 2000, January 1, 2009, and January 1, 2011.

Rule 3.1322. Motions to strike

(a) Contents of notice

A notice of motion to strike a portion of a pleading must quote in full the portions sought to be stricken except where the motion is to strike an entire paragraph, cause of action, count, or defense. Specifications in a notice must be numbered consecutively.

(Subd (a) amended and lettered effective January 1, 2007; adopted as part of untitled subd effective January 1, 1984.)

(b) Timing

A notice of motion to strike must be given within the time allowed to plead, and if a demurrer is interposed, concurrently therewith, and must be noticed for hearing and heard at the same time as the demurrer.

(Subd (b) amended and lettered effective January 1, 2007; adopted as part of untitled subd effective January 1, 1984.)

Rule 3.1322 amended and renumbered effective January 1, 2007; adopted as rule 329 effective January 1, 1984.

Rule 3.1324. Amended pleadings and amendments to pleadings

(a) Contents of motion

A motion to amend a pleading before trial must:

(1) Include a copy of the proposed amendment or amended pleading, which must be serially numbered to differentiate it from previous pleadings or amendments;

(2) State what allegations in the previous pleading are proposed to be deleted, if any, and where, by page, paragraph, and line number, the deleted allegations are located; and

(3) State what allegations are proposed to be added to the previous pleading, if any, and where, by page, paragraph, and line number, the additional allegations are located.

(Subd (a) amended effective January 1, 2002.)

(b) Supporting declaration

A separate declaration must accompany the motion and must specify:

(1) The effect of the amendment;

(2) Why the amendment is necessary and proper;

(3) When the facts giving rise to the amended allegations were discovered; and

(4) The reasons why the request for amendment was not made earlier.

(Subd (b) adopted effective January 1, 2002.)

(c) Form of amendment

The court may deem a motion to file an amendment to a pleading to be a motion to file an amended pleading and require the filing of the entire previous pleading with the approved amendments incorporated into it.

(Subd (c) adopted effective January 1, 2002.)

(d) Requirements for amendment to a pleading

An amendment to a pleading must not be made by alterations on the face of a pleading except by permission of the court. All alterations must be initialed by the court or the clerk.

(Subd (d) amended and relettered effective January 1, 2002; adopted as subd (b) effective January 1, 1984.)

Rule 3.1324 renumbered effective January 1, 2007; adopted as rule 327 effective January 1, 1984; previously amended effective January 1, 2002.

Rule 3.1326. Motions for change of venue

Following denial of a motion to transfer under Code of Civil Procedure section 396b, unless otherwise ordered, 30 calendar days are deemed granted defendant to move to strike, demur, or otherwise plead if the defendant has not previously filed a response. If a motion to transfer is granted, 30 calendar days are deemed granted from the date the receiving court sends notice of receipt of the case and its new case number.

Rule 3.1326 amended effective January 1, 2016; adopted as rule 326 effective January 1, 1984; previously amended effective July 1, 1984; previously amended and renumbered as rule 3.1326 effective January 1, 2007.

Rule 3.1327. Motions to quash or to stay action in summary proceeding involving possession of real property

(a) Notice

In an unlawful detainer action or other action brought under chapter 4 of title 3 of part 3 of the Code of Civil Procedure (commencing with section 1159), notice of a motion to quash service of summons on the ground of lack of jurisdiction or to stay or dismiss the action on the ground of inconvenient forum must be given in compliance with Code of Civil Procedure sections 1010.6 or 1013 and 1167.4.

(Subd (a) amended effective January 1, 2016; adopted effective January 1, 2009.)

(b) Opposition and reply at hearing

Any opposition to the motion and any reply to an opposition may be made orally at the time of hearing or in writing as set forth in (c).

(Subd (b) adopted effective January 1, 2009.)

(c) Written opposition in advance of hearing

If a party seeks to have a written opposition considered in advance of the hearing, the written opposition must be filed and served on or before the court day before the hearing. Service must be by personal delivery, electronic service, fax transmission, express mail, or other means consistent with Code of Civil Procedure sections 1010, 1010.6, 1011, 1012, and 1013, and reasonably calculated to ensure delivery to the other party or parties no later than the close of business on the court day before the hearing. The court, in its discretion, may consider written opposition filed later.

(Subd (c) amended effective January 1, 2016; adopted effective January 1, 2009.)

Rule 3.1327 amended effective January 1, 2016; adopted effective January 1, 2009.

Article 2
Procedural Motions

Rule 3.1330. Motion concerning arbitration
Rule 3.1332. Motion or application for continuance of trial
Rule 3.1335. Motion or application to advance, specially set, or reset trial date

Rule 3.1330. Motion concerning arbitration

A petition to compel arbitration or to stay proceedings pursuant to Code of Civil Procedure sections 1281.2 and 1281.4 must state, in addition to other required allegations, the provisions of the written agreement and the paragraph that provides for arbitration. The provisions must be stated verbatim or a copy must be physically or electronically attached to the petition and incorporated by reference.

Rule 3.1330 amended effective January 1, 2016; adopted as rule 371 effective January 1, 1984; previously amended and renumbered as rule 3.1330 effective January 1, 2007.

Rule 3.1332. Motion or application for continuance of trial

(a) Trial dates are firm

To ensure the prompt disposition of civil cases, the dates assigned for a trial are firm. All parties and their counsel must regard the date set for trial as certain.

(Subd (a) repealed and adopted effective January 1, 2004; amended effective January 1, 1995.)

(b) Motion or application

A party seeking a continuance of the date set for trial, whether contested or uncontested or stipulated to by the parties, must make the request for a continuance by a noticed motion or an ex parte application under the rules in chapter 4 of this division, with supporting declarations. The party must make the motion or application as soon as reasonably practical once the necessity for the continuance is discovered.

(Subd (b) amended effective January 1, 2007; previously amended effective January 1, 1995.)

(c) Grounds for continuance

Although continuances of trials are disfavored, each request for a continuance must be considered on its own merits. The court may grant a continuance only on an affirmative showing of good cause requiring the continuance. Circumstances that may indicate good cause include:

(1) The unavailability of an essential lay or expert witness because of death, illness, or other excusable circumstances;

(2) The unavailability of a party because of death, illness, or other excusable circumstances;

(3) The unavailability of trial counsel because of death, illness, or other excusable circumstances;

(4) The substitution of trial counsel, but only where there is an affirmative showing that the substitution is required in the interests of justice;

(5) The addition of a new party if:

(A) The new party has not had a reasonable opportunity to conduct discovery and prepare for trial; or

(B) The other parties have not had a reasonable opportunity to conduct discovery and prepare for trial in regard to the new party's involvement in the case;

(6) A party's excused inability to obtain essential testimony, documents, or other material evidence despite diligent efforts; or

(7) A significant, unanticipated change in the status of the case as a result of which the case is not ready for trial.

(Subd (c) amended effective January 1, 2007; adopted effective January 1, 2004.)

(d) Other factors to be considered

In ruling on a motion or application for continuance, the court must consider all the facts and circumstances that are relevant to the determination. These may include:

(1) The proximity of the trial date;
(2) Whether there was any previous continuance, extension of time, or delay of trial due to any party;
(3) The length of the continuance requested;
(4) The availability of alternative means to address the problem that gave rise to the motion or application for a continuance;
(5) The prejudice that parties or witnesses will suffer as a result of the continuance;
(6) If the case is entitled to a preferential trial setting, the reasons for that status and whether the need for a continuance outweighs the need to avoid delay;
(7) The court's calendar and the impact of granting a continuance on other pending trials;
(8) Whether trial counsel is engaged in another trial;
(9) Whether all parties have stipulated to a continuance;
(10) Whether the interests of justice are best served by a continuance, by the trial of the matter, or by imposing conditions on the continuance; and
(11) Any other fact or circumstance relevant to the fair determination of the motion or application.

(Subd (d) adopted effective January 1, 2004.)

Rule 3.1332 amended and renumbered effective January 1, 2007; adopted as rule 375 effective January 1, 1984; previously amended effective January 1, 1985, January 1, 1995, and January 1, 2004.

Rule 3.1335. Motion or application to advance, specially set, or reset trial date

(a) Noticed motion or application required

A party seeking to advance, specially set, or reset a case for trial must make this request by noticed motion or ex parte application under the rules in chapter 4 of this division.

(Subd (a) amended effective January 1, 2007.)

(b) Grounds for motion or application

The request may be granted only upon an affirmative showing by the moving party of good cause based on a declaration served and filed with the motion or application.

Rule 3.1335 amended and renumbered effective January 1, 2007; adopted as rule 375.1 effective January 1, 2004.

Article 3
Motions to Dismiss

Rule 3.1340. Motion for discretionary dismissal after two years for delay in prosecution
Rule 3.1342. Motion to dismiss for delay in prosecution

Rule 3.1340. Motion for discretionary dismissal after two years for delay in prosecution

(a) Discretionary dismissal two years after filing

The court on its own motion or on motion of the defendant may dismiss an action under Code of Civil Procedure sections 583.410–583.430 for delay in prosecution if the action has not been brought to trial or conditionally settled within two years after the action was commenced against the defendant.

(Subd (a) amended effective January 1, 2007.)

(b) Notice of court's intention to dismiss

If the court intends to dismiss an action on its own motion, the clerk must set a hearing on the dismissal and send notice to all parties at least 20 days before the hearing date.

(Subd (b) amended effective January 1, 2016; adopted as part of subd (a) effective January 1, 1990; previously amended and lettered as subd (b) effective January 1, 2007.)

(c) Definition of "conditionally settled"

"Conditionally settled" means:
(1) A settlement agreement conditions dismissal on the satisfactory completion of specified terms that are not to be fully performed within two years after the filing of the case; and
(2) Notice of the settlement is filed with the court as provided in rule 3.1385.

(Subd (c) amended and lettered effective January 1, 2007; adopted as part of subd (a) effective January 1, 1990.)

Rule 3.1340 amended effective January 1, 2016; adopted as rule 372 effective January 1, 1990; previously amended and renumbered as rule 3.1340 effective January 1, 2007.

Rule 3.1342. Motion to dismiss for delay in prosecution

(a) Notice of motion

A party seeking dismissal of a case under Code of Civil Procedure sections 583.410–583.430 must serve and file a notice of motion at least 45 days before the date set for hearing of the motion. The party may, with the memorandum, serve and file a declaration stating facts in support of the motion. The filing of the notice of motion must not preclude the opposing party from further prosecution of the case to bring it to trial.

(Subd (a) amended effective January 1, 2009; previously amended effective January 1, 1986, and January 1, 2007.)

(b) Written opposition

Within 15 days after service of the notice of motion, the opposing party may serve and file a written opposition. The failure of the opposing party to serve and file a written opposition may be construed by the court as an admission that the motion is meritorious, and the court may grant the motion without a hearing on the merits.

(Subd (b) amended effective January 1, 2007.)

(c) Response to opposition

Within 15 days after service of the written opposition, if any, the moving party may serve and file a response.

(Subd (c) amended effective January 1, 2007.)

(d) Reply

Within five days after service of the response, if any, the opposing party may serve and file a reply.

(e) Relevant matters

In ruling on the motion, the court must consider all matters relevant to a proper determination of the motion, including:
(1) The court's file in the case and the declarations and supporting data submitted by the parties and, where applicable, the availability of the moving party and other essential parties for service of process;
(2) The diligence in seeking to effect service of process;
(3) The extent to which the parties engaged in any settlement negotiations or discussions;
(4) The diligence of the parties in pursuing discovery or other pretrial proceedings, including any extraordinary relief sought by either party;
(5) The nature and complexity of the case;
(6) The law applicable to the case, including the pendency of other litigation under a common set of facts or determinative of the legal or factual issues in the case;
(7) The nature of any extensions of time or other delay attributable to either party;
(8) The condition of the court's calendar and the availability of an earlier trial date if the matter was ready for trial;
(9) Whether the interests of justice are best served by dismissal or trial of the case; and
(10) Any other fact or circumstance relevant to a fair determination of the issue.

The court must be guided by the policies set forth in Code of Civil Procedure section 583.130.

(Subd (e) amended effective January 1, 2007; previously amended effective January 1, 1986.)

(f) Court action

The court may grant or deny the motion or, where the facts warrant, the court may continue or defer its ruling on the matter pending performance by either party of any conditions relating to trial or dismissal of the case that may be required by the court to effectuate substantial justice.

Rule 3.1342 amended effective January 1, 2009; adopted as rule 373 effective January 1, 1984; previously amended effective January 1, 1986; previously amended and renumbered effective January 1, 2007.

Article 4
Discovery Motions

Title 3, Civil Rules—Division 11, Law and Motion—Chapter 6, Particular Motions—Article 4, Discovery Motions adopted effective January 1, 2009.

Rule 3.1345. Format of discovery motions
Rule 3.1346. Service of motion papers on nonparty deponent
Rule 3.1347. Discovery motions in summary proceeding involving possession of real property
Rule 3.1348. Sanctions for failure to provide discovery

Rule 3.1345. Format of discovery motions

(a) Separate statement required

Except as provided in (b), any motion involving the content of a discovery request or the responses to such a request must be accompanied by a separate statement. The motions that require a separate statement include a motion:
(1) To compel further responses to requests for admission;

(2) To compel further responses to interrogatories;

(3) To compel further responses to a demand for inspection of documents or tangible things;

(4) To compel answers at a deposition;

(5) To compel or to quash the production of documents or tangible things at a deposition;

(6) For medical examination over objection; and

(7) For issue or evidentiary sanctions.

(Subd (a) amended effective January 1, 2020; previously amended effective July 1, 1987, January 1, 1992, January 1, 1997, July 1, 2001, and January 1, 2007.)

(b) Separate statement not required

A separate statement is not required under the following circumstances:

(1) When no response has been provided to the request for discovery; or

(2) When a court has allowed the moving party to submit—in place of a separate statement—a concise outline of the discovery request and each response in dispute.

(Subd (b) amended effective January 1, 2020; adopted effective July 1, 2001.)

(c) Contents of separate statement

A separate statement is a separate document filed and served with the discovery motion that provides all the information necessary to understand each discovery request and all the responses to it that are at issue. The separate statement must be full and complete so that no person is required to review any other document in order to determine the full request and the full response. Material must not be incorporated into the separate statement by reference. The separate statement must include—for each discovery request (e.g., each interrogatory, request for admission, deposition question, or inspection demand) to which a further response, answer, or production is requested—the following:

(1) The text of the request, interrogatory, question, or inspection demand;

(2) The text of each response, answer, or objection, and any further responses or answers;

(3) A statement of the factual and legal reasons for compelling further responses, answers, or production as to each matter in dispute;

(4) If necessary, the text of all definitions, instructions, and other matters required to understand each discovery request and the responses to it;

(5) If the response to a particular discovery request is dependent on the response given to another discovery request, or if the reasons a further response to a particular discovery request is deemed necessary are based on the response to some other discovery request, the other request and the response to it must be set forth; and

(6) If the pleadings, other documents in the file, or other items of discovery are relevant to the motion, the party relying on them must summarize each relevant document.

(Subd (c) amended effective January 1, 2007; previously repealed and adopted effective July 1, 2001.)

(d) Identification of interrogatories, demands, or requests

A motion concerning interrogatories, inspection demands, or admission requests must identify the interrogatories, demands, or requests by set and number.

(Subd (d) amended effective January 1, 2007; adopted as subd (b) effective January 1, 1984; previously amended effective July 1, 1987; previously relettered effective July 1, 2001.)

Rule 3.1345 amended effective January 1, 2020; adopted as rule 335 effective January 1, 1984; previously amended effective July 1, 1987, January 1, 1992, January 1, 1997, and July 1, 2001; previously amended and renumbered as rule 3.1020 effective January 1, 2007; previously renumbered as rule 3.1345 effective January 1, 2009.

Rule 3.1346. Service of motion papers on nonparty deponent

A written notice and all moving papers supporting a motion to compel an answer to a deposition question or to compel production of a document or tangible thing from a nonparty deponent must be personally served on the nonparty deponent unless the nonparty deponent agrees to accept service by mail or electronic service at an address or electronic service address specified on the deposition record.

Rule 3.1346 amended effective January 1, 2016; adopted as rule 337 effective January 1, 1984; previously amended effective July 1, 1987; previously amended and renumbered as rule 3.1025 effective January 1, 2007; previously renumbered as rule 3.1346 effective January 1, 2009.

Rule 3.1347. Discovery motions in summary proceeding involving possession of real property

(a) Notice

In an unlawful detainer action or other action brought under chapter 4 of title 3 of part 3 of the Code of Civil Procedure (commencing with section 1159), notice of a discovery motion must be given in compliance with Code of Civil Procedure sections 1010.6 or 1013 and 1170.8.

(Subd (a) amended effective January 1, 2016; adopted effective January 1, 2009.)

(b) Opposition and reply at hearing

Any opposition to the motion and any reply to an opposition may be made orally at the time of hearing or in writing as set forth in (c).

(Subd (b) adopted effective January 1, 2009.)

(c) Written opposition in advance of hearing

If a party seeks to have a written opposition considered in advance of the hearing, the written opposition must be served and filed on or before the court day before the hearing. Service must be by personal delivery, electronic service, fax transmission, express mail, or other means consistent with Code of Civil Procedure sections 1010, 1010.6, 1011, 1012, and 1013, and reasonably calculated to ensure delivery to the other party or parties no later than the close of business on the court day before the hearing. The court, in its discretion, may consider written opposition filed later.

(Subd (c) amended effective January 1, 2016; adopted effective January 1, 2009.)

Rule 3.1347 amended effective January 1, 2016; adopted effective January 1, 2009.

Rule 3.1348. Sanctions for failure to provide discovery

(a) Sanctions despite no opposition

The court may award sanctions under the Discovery Act in favor of a party who files a motion to compel discovery, even though no opposition to the motion was filed, or opposition to the motion was withdrawn, or the requested discovery was provided to the moving party after the motion was filed.

(b) Failure to oppose not an admission

The failure to file a written opposition or to appear at a hearing or the voluntary provision of discovery shall not be deemed an admission that the motion was proper or that sanctions should be awarded.

Rule 3.1348 renumbered effective January 1, 2009; adopted as rule 341 effective July 1, 2001; previously renumbered as rule 3.1030 effective January 1, 2007.

Article 5
Summary Judgment Motions

Title 3, Civil Rules—Division 11, Law and Motion—Chapter 6, Particular Motions—Article 5, Summary Judgment Motions renumbered effective January 1, 2009; adopted as article 4 effective January 1, 2007.

Rule 3.1350. Motion for summary judgment or summary adjudication
Rule 3.1351. Motions for summary judgment in summary proceeding involving possession of real property
Rule 3.1352. Objections to evidence
Rule 3.1354. Written objections to evidence

Rule 3.1350. Motion for summary judgment or summary adjudication

(a) Definitions

As used in this rule:

(1) "Motion" refers to either a motion for summary judgment or a motion for summary adjudication.

(2) "Material facts" are facts that relate to the cause of action, claim for damages, issue of duty, or affirmative defense that is the subject of the motion and that could make a difference in the disposition of the motion.

(Subd (a) amended effective January 1, 2016.)

(b) Motion for summary adjudication

If made in the alternative, a motion for summary adjudication may make reference to and depend on the same evidence submitted in support of the summary judgment motion. If summary adjudication is sought, whether separately or as an alternative to the motion for summary judgment, the specific cause of action, affirmative defense, claims for damages, or issues of duty must be stated specifically in the notice of motion and be repeated, verbatim, in the separate statement of undisputed material facts.

(Subd (b) amended effective January 1, 2007; previously amended effective January 1, 2002.)

(c) Documents in support of motion

Except as provided in Code of Civil Procedure section 437c(r) and rule 3.1351, the motion must contain and be supported by the following documents:

(1) Notice of motion by *[moving party]* for summary judgment or summary adjudication or both;

(2) Separate statement of undisputed material facts in support of *[moving party's]* motion for summary judgment or summary adjudication or both;

(3) Memorandum in support of *[moving party's]* motion for summary judgment or summary adjudication or both;

(4) Evidence in support of *[moving party's]* motion for summary judgment or summary adjudication or both; and

(5) Request for judicial notice in support of *[moving party's]* motion for summary judgment or summary adjudication or both (if appropriate).

(Subd (c) amended effective January 1, 2009; previously amended effective January 1, 2002, and January 1, 2007.)

(d) Separate statement in support of motion

(1) The Separate Statement of Undisputed Material Facts in support of a motion must separately identify:

(A) Each cause of action, claim for damages, issue of duty, or affirmative defense that is the subject of the motion; and

(B) Each supporting material fact claimed to be without dispute with respect to the cause of action, claim for damages, issue of duty, or affirmative defense that is the subject of the motion.

(2) The separate statement should include only material facts and not any facts that are not pertinent to the disposition of the motion.

(3) The separate statement must be in the two-column format specified in (h). The statement must state in numerical sequence the undisputed material facts in the first column followed by the evidence that establishes those undisputed facts in that same column. Citation to the evidence in support of each material fact must include reference to the exhibit, title, page, and line numbers.

(Subd (d) amended effective January 1, 2016; previously amended effective January 1, 2002, January 1, 2007, and January 1, 2008.)

(e) Documents in opposition to motion

Except as provided in Code of Civil Procedure section 437c(r) and rule 3.1351, the opposition to a motion must consist of the following separate documents, titled as shown:

(1) *[Opposing party's]* memorandum in opposition to *[moving party's]* motion for summary judgment or summary adjudication or both;

(2) *[Opposing party's]* separate statement in opposition to *[moving party's]* motion for summary judgment or summary adjudication or both;

(3) *[Opposing party's]* evidence in opposition to *[moving party's]* motion for summary judgment or summary adjudication or both (if appropriate); and

(4) *[Opposing party's]* request for judicial notice in opposition to *[moving party's]* motion for summary judgment or summary adjudication or both (if appropriate).

(Subd (e) amended effective January 1, 2016; previously amended effective January 1, 2002, January 1, 2007, and January 1, 2009.)

(f) Content of separate statement in opposition to motion

The Separate Statement in Opposition to Motion must be in the two-column format specified in (h).

(1) Each material fact claimed by the moving party to be undisputed must be set out verbatim on the left side of the page, below which must be set out the evidence said by the moving party to establish that fact, complete with the moving party's references to exhibits.

(2) On the right side of the page, directly opposite the recitation of the moving party's statement of material facts and supporting evidence, the response must unequivocally state whether that fact is "disputed" or "undisputed." An opposing party who contends that a fact is disputed must state, on the right side of the page directly opposite the fact in dispute, the nature of the dispute and describe the evidence that supports the position that the fact is controverted. Citation to the evidence in support of the position that a fact is controverted must include reference to the exhibit, title, page, and line numbers.

(3) If the opposing party contends that additional material facts are pertinent to the disposition of the motion, those facts must be set forth in the separate statement. The separate statement should include only material facts and not any facts that are not pertinent to the disposition of the motion. Each fact must be followed by the evidence that establishes the fact. Citation to the evidence in support of each material fact must include reference to the exhibit, title, page, and line numbers.

(Subd (f) amended effective January 1, 2016; previously amended effective January 1, 2002.)

(g) Documentary evidence

If evidence in support of or in opposition to a motion exceeds 25 pages, the evidence must be separately bound and must include a table of contents.

(Subd (g) amended effective January 1, 2007; previously amended effective January 1, 2002.)

(h) Format for separate statements

Supporting and opposing separate statements in a motion for summary judgment must follow this format:

Supporting statement:

Moving Party's Undisputed Material Facts and Supporting Evidence:	Opposing Party's Response and Supporting Evidence:
1. Plaintiff and defendant entered into a written contract for the sale of widgets. Jackson declaration, 2:17–21; contract, Ex. A to Jackson declaration.	
2. No widgets were ever received. Jackson declaration, 3:7–21.	

Opposing statement:

Moving Party's Undisputed Material Facts and Alleged Supporting Evidence:	Opposing Party's Response and Evidence:
1. Plaintiff and defendant entered into a written contract for the sale of widgets. Jackson declaration, 2:17–21; contract, Ex. A to Jackson declaration.	Undisputed.
2. No widgets were ever received. Jackson declaration, 3:7–21.	Disputed. The widgets were received in New Zealand on August 31, 2001. Baygi declaration, 7:2–5.

Supporting and opposing separate statements in a motion for summary adjudication must follow this format:

Supporting statement:

ISSUE 1—THE FIRST CAUSE OF ACTION FOR NEGLIGENCE IS BARRED BECAUSE PLAINTIFF EXPRESSLY ASSUMED THE RISK OF INJURY

Moving Party's Undisputed Material Facts and Supporting Evidence:	Opposing Party's Response and Supporting Evidence:
1. Plaintiff was injured while mountain climbing on a trip with Any Company USA. Plaintiff's deposition, 12:3–4.	

2. Before leaving on the mountain climbing trip, plaintiff signed a waiver of liability for acts of negligence. Smith declaration, 5:4–5; waiver of liability, Ex. A to Smith declaration.

Opposing statement:

ISSUE 1—THE FIRST CAUSE OF ACTION FOR NEGLIGENCE IS BARRED BECAUSE PLAINTIFF EXPRESSLY ASSUMED THE RISK OF INJURY

Moving Party's Undisputed Material Facts and Alleged Supporting Evidence:

1. Plaintiff was injured while mountain climbing on a trip with Any Company USA. Plaintiff's deposition, 12:3–4.

2. Before leaving on the mountain climbing trip, plaintiff signed a waiver of liability for acts of negligence. Smith declaration, 5:4–5; waiver of liability, Ex. A to Smith declaration.

Opposing Party's Response and Evidence:

Undisputed.

Disputed. Plaintiff did not sign the waiver of liability; the signature on the waiver is forged. Jones declaration, 3:6–7.

(Subd (h) amended effective July 1, 2008; previously amended effective January 1, 1999, January 1, 2002, and January 1, 2008.)

(i) Request for electronic version of separate statement

On request, a party must within three days provide to any other party or the court an electronic version of its separate statement. The electronic version may be provided in any form on which the parties agree. If the parties are unable to agree on the form, the responding party must provide to the requesting party the electronic version of the separate statement that it used to prepare the document filed with the court. Under this subdivision, a party is not required to create an electronic version or any new version of any document for the purpose of transmission to the requesting party.

(Subd (i) amended effective January 1, 2007; adopted effective January 1, 2002.)
Rule 3.1350 amended effective January 1, 2016; adopted as rule 342 effective July 1, 1997; previously amended and renumbered as rule 3.1350 effective January 1, 2007; previously amended effective January 1, 1999, January 1, 2002, January 1, 2008, July 1, 2008, and January 1, 2009.

Advisory Committee Comment

Subdivision (a)(2). This definition is derived from statements in *L.A. Nat. Bank v. Bank of Canton* (1991) 229 Cal. App. 3d 1267, 1274 ("In order to prevent the imposition of a summary judgment, the disputed facts must be 'material,' i.e., relate to a claim or defense in issue which could make a difference in the outcome.") and *Reid v. Google, Inc.* (2010) 50 Cal.4th 512, 532-533 (Parties are encouraged "to raise only meritorious objections to items of evidence that are legitimately in dispute and pertinent to the disposition of the summary judgment motion.")

Subdivisions (d)(2) and (f)(3). Consistent with *Reid, supra*, these provisions are intended to eliminate from separate statements facts that are not material, and, thereby reduce the number of unnecessary objections to evidence.

Rule 3.1351. Motions for summary judgment in summary proceeding involving possession of real property

(a) Notice

In an unlawful detainer action or other action brought under chapter 4 of title 3 of part 3 of the Code of Civil Procedure (commencing with section 1159), notice of a motion for summary judgment must be given in compliance with Code of Civil Procedure sections 1010.6 or 1013 and 1170.7.

(Subd (a) amended effective January 1, 2016; adopted effective January 1, 2009.)

(b) Opposition and reply at hearing

Any opposition to the motion and any reply to an opposition may be made orally at the time of hearing or in writing as set forth in (c).

(Subd (b) adopted effective January 1, 2009.)

(c) Written opposition in advance of hearing

If a party seeks to have a written opposition considered in advance of the hearing, the written opposition must be filed and served on or before the court day before the hearing. Service must be by personal delivery, electronic service, fax transmission, express mail, or other means consistent with Code of Civil Procedure sections 1010, 1010.6, 1011, 1012, and 1013, and reasonably calculated to ensure delivery to the other party or parties no later than the close of business on the court day before the hearing. The court, in its discretion, may consider written opposition filed later.

(Subd (c) amended effective January 1, 2016; adopted effective January 1, 2009.)
Rule 3.1351 amended effective January 1, 2016; adopted effective January 1, 2009.

Rule 3.1352. Objections to evidence

A party desiring to make objections to evidence in the papers on a motion for summary judgment must either:

(1) Submit objections in writing under rule 3.1354; or

(2) Make arrangements for a court reporter to be present at the hearing.

Rule 3.1352 amended and renumbered effective January 1, 2007; adopted as rule 343 effective January 1, 1984; previously amended effective January 1, 2002.

Rule 3.1354. Written objections to evidence

(a) Time for filing and service of objections

Unless otherwise excused by the court on a showing of good cause, all written objections to evidence in support of or in opposition to a motion for summary judgment or summary adjudication must be served and filed at the same time as the objecting party's opposition or reply papers are served and filed.

(Subd (a) repealed, amended, and relettered effective January 1, 2007; adopted as untitled subd effective January 1, 1984; previously amended and lettered subd (b) effective January 1, 2007.)

(b) Format of objections

All written objections to evidence must be served and filed separately from the other papers in support of or in opposition to the motion. Objections to specific evidence must be referenced by the objection number in the right column of a separate statement in opposition or reply to a motion, but the objections must not be restated or reargued in the separate statement. Each written objection must be numbered consecutively and must:

(1) Identify the name of the document in which the specific material objected to is located;

(2) State the exhibit, title, page, and line number of the material objected to;

(3) Quote or set forth the objectionable statement or material; and

(4) State the grounds for each objection to that statement or material.

Written objections to evidence must follow one of the following two formats:

(First Format):

Objections to Jackson Declaration

Objection Number 1

"Johnson told me that no widgets were ever received." (Jackson declaration, page 3, lines 7–8.)

Grounds for Objection 1: Hearsay (Evid. Code, § 1200); lack of personal knowledge (Evid. Code, § 702(a)).

(Second Format):

Objections to Jackson Declaration

Material Objected to:	**Grounds for Objection:**
1. Jackson declaration, page 3, lines 7–8: "Johnson told me that no widgets were ever received."	Hearsay (Evid. Code, § 1200); lack of personal knowledge (Evid. Code, § 702(a)).

(Subd (b) amended effective January 1, 2016; adopted effective January 1, 2007.)

(c) Proposed order

A party submitting written objections to evidence must submit with the objections a proposed order. The proposed order must include places for the court to indicate whether it has sustained or overruled each objection. It must also include a place for the signature of the judge. The court may require that the proposed order be provided in electronic form. The proposed order must be in one of the following two formats:

(First Format):

Objections to Jackson Declaration

Objection Number 1

"Johnson told me that no widgets were ever received." (Jackson declaration, page 3, lines 7–8.)

Grounds for Objection 1: Hearsay (Evid. Code, § 1200); lack of personal knowledge (Evid. Code, § 702(a)).

Court's Ruling on Objection 1:

Sustained: _____
Overruled: _____

(Second Format):

Objections to Jackson Declaration

Material Objected to:	**Grounds for Objection:**	**Ruling on the Objection:**
1. Jackson declaration, page 3, lines 7–8: "Johnson told me that no widgets were ever received."	Hearsay (Evid. Code, §1200); lack of personal knowledge (Evid. Code, § 702(a)).	Sustained: _____ Overruled: _____

Date: _____

Judge

(Subd (c) amended effective January 1, 2016; adopted effective January 1, 2007.)

Rule 3.1354 amended effective January 1, 2016; adopted as rule 345 effective January 1, 1984; previously amended and renumbered as rule 3.1354 effective January 1, 2007; previously amended effective January 1, 2002, and January 1, 2007.

Article 6
Miscellaneous Motions

Title 3, Civil Rules—Division 11, Law and Motion—Chapter 6, Particular Motions—Article 6, Miscellaneous Motions renumbered effective January 1, 2009; adopted as article 5 effective January 1, 2007.

Rule 3.1360. Motion to grant lien on cause of action
Rule 3.1362. Motion to be relieved as counsel

Rule 3.1360. Motion to grant lien on cause of action

A motion that a lien be granted on a cause of action, right to relief, or judgment must be accompanied by an authenticated record of the judgment on which the judgment creditor relies and a declaration as to the identity of the party involved and the amount due.

Rule 3.1360 amended and renumbered effective January 1, 2007; adopted as rule 369 effective January 1, 1984.

Rule 3.1362. Motion to be relieved as counsel

(a) Notice

A notice of motion and motion to be relieved as counsel under Code of Civil Procedure section 284(2) must be directed to the client and must be made on the *Notice of Motion and Motion to Be Relieved as Counsel—Civil* (form MC-051).

(Subd (a) amended effective January 1, 2007; previously amended effective July 1, 2000.)

(b) Memorandum

Notwithstanding any other rule of court, no memorandum is required to be filed or served with a motion to be relieved as counsel.

(Subd (b) amended effective January 1, 2007; adopted effective July 1, 2000.)

(c) Declaration

The motion to be relieved as counsel must be accompanied by a declaration on the *Declaration in Support of Attorney's Motion to Be Relieved as Counsel—Civil* (form MC-052). The declaration must state in general terms and without compromising the confidentiality of the attorney-client relationship why a motion under Code of Civil Procedure section 284(2) is brought instead of filing a consent under Code of Civil Procedure section 284(1).

(Subd (c) amended effective January 1, 2007; adopted as subd (b) effective July 1, 1984; previously relettered and amended effective July 1, 2000.)

(d) Service

The notice of motion and motion, the declaration, and the proposed order must be served on the client and on all other parties who have appeared in the case. The notice may be by personal service, electronic service, or mail.

(1) If the notice is served on the client by mail under Code of Civil Procedure section 1013, it must be accompanied by a declaration stating facts showing that either:

(A) The service address is the current residence or business address of the client; or

(B) The service address is the last known residence or business address of the client and the attorney has been unable to locate a more current address after making reasonable efforts to do so within 30 days before the filing of the motion to be relieved.

(2) If the notice is served on the client by electronic service under Code of Civil Procedure section 1010.6 and rule 2.251, it must be accompanied by a declaration stating that the electronic service address is the client's current electronic service address.

As used in this rule, "current" means that the address was confirmed within 30 days before the filing of the motion to be relieved. Merely demonstrating that the notice was sent to the client's last known address and was not returned or no electronic delivery failure message was received is not, by itself, sufficient to demonstrate that the address is current. If the service is by mail, Code of Civil Procedure section 1011(b) applies.

(Subd (d) amended effective January 1, 2017; adopted as subd (c) effective July 1, 1984; previously amended effective July 1, 1991, January 1, 1996, January 1, 2007, and January 1, 2009; previously relettered and amended effective July 1, 2000.)

(e) Order

The proposed order relieving counsel must be prepared on the *Order Granting Attorney's Motion to Be Relieved as Counsel—Civil* (form MC-053) and must be lodged with the court with the moving papers. The order must specify all hearing dates scheduled in the action or proceeding, including the date of trial, if known. If no hearing date is presently scheduled, the court may set one and specify the date in the order. After the order is signed, a copy of the signed order must be served on the client and on all parties that have appeared in the case. The court may delay the effective date of the order relieving counsel until proof of service of a copy of the signed order on the client has been filed with the court.

(Subd (e) amended effective January 1, 2009; adopted as subd (d) effective July 1, 1984; previously amended effective January 1, 1996, and January 1, 2007; previously amended and relettered effective July 1, 2000.)

Rule 3.1362 amended effective January 1, 2017; adopted as rule 376 effective July 1, 1984; previously amended effective July 1, 1991, January 1, 1996, July 1, 2000, and January 1, 2009; previously amended and renumbered effective January 1, 2007.

Chapter 7
Civil Petitions

Title 3, Civil Rules—Division 11, Law and Motion—Chapter 7, Civil Petitions; repealed and renumbered from Chapter 8 effective July 1, 2014; adopted as Chapter 7, Petitions Under the California Environmental Quality Act, effective January 1, 2007.

Rule 3.1365. Petitions under the California Environmental Quality Act
Rule 3.1370. Emancipation of minors
Rule 3.1372. Petitions for relief from financial obligations during military service

Rule 3.1365. Petitions under the California Environmental Quality Act

Rules for petitions for relief brought under the California Environmental Quality Act have been renumbered and moved to division 22 of these rules, beginning with rule 3.2200.

Rule 3.1365 adopted effective July 1, 2014.

Advisory Committee Comment

Former rule 3.1365 on the form and format of administrative record lodged in a CEQA proceeding has been renumbered as rule 3.2205.

Rule 3.1366. Lodging and service [Renumbered]

Rule 3.1366 amended and renumbered as rule 3.2206 effective July 1, 2014; adopted effective January 1, 2010.

Rule 3.1367. Electronic format [Renumbered]

Rule 3.1367 amended and renumbered as rule 3.2207 effective July 1, 2014; adopted effective January 1, 2010.

Rule 3.1368. Paper format [Renumbered]

Rule 3.1368 renumbered as rule 3.2208 effective July 1, 2014; adopted effective January 1, 2010; previously amended effective January 1, 2014.

Rule 3.1370. Emancipation of minors

A petition for declaration of the emancipation of a minor must comply with rule 5.605.

Rule 3.1370 amended and renumbered effective January 1, 2007; adopted as rule 270 effective July 1, 1994.

Rule 3.1372. Petitions for relief from financial obligations during military service

(a) Application

This rule applies to petitions for relief from financial obligations made by a servicemember under Military and Veterans Code section 409.3.

(Subd (a) adopted effective January 1, 2012.)

(b) Service of petition

Service of the petition for relief and all supporting papers must be made in the manner provided by law for service of summons in civil actions.

(Subd (b) adopted effective January 1, 2012.)

(c) No memorandum required

Unless ordered by the court, no memorandum is required in support of or opposition to a petition for relief.

(Subd (c) adopted effective January 1, 2012.)

Rule 3.1372 adopted effective January 1, 2012.

Chapter 8
Other Civil Petitions [Renumbered]

Title 3, Civil Rules—Division 11, Law and Motion—Chapter 8, Other Civil Petitions; amended and renumbered to Chapter 7 effective July 1, 2014; previously renumbered as Chapter 8 effective January 1, 2010; adopted as Chapter 7 effective January 1, 2007.

Division 12
Settlement

Rule 3.1380. Mandatory settlement conferences
Rule 3.1382. Good faith settlement and dismissal
Rule 3.1384. Petition for approval of compromise of claim of minor or person with a disability; order for deposit of funds; and petition for withdrawal
Rule 3.1385. Duty to notify court and others of settlement of entire case

Rule 3.1380. Mandatory settlement conferences

(a) Setting conferences

On the court's own motion or at the request of any party, the court may set one or more mandatory settlement conferences.

(Subd (a) amended effective January 1, 2008; previously amended effective January 1, 1995, and July 1, 2002.)

(b) Persons attending

Trial counsel, parties, and persons with full authority to settle the case must personally attend the conference, unless excused by the court for good cause. If any consent to settle is required for any reason, the party with that consensual authority must be personally present at the conference.

(Subd (b) amended and relettered effective July 1, 2002; adopted as subd (c) effective January 1, 1985; previously amended effective January 1, 1995.)

(c) Settlement conference statement

No later than five court days before the initial date set for the settlement conference, each party must submit to the court and serve on each party a mandatory settlement conference statement containing:

(1) A good faith settlement demand;

(2) An itemization of economic and noneconomic damages by each plaintiff;

(3) A good faith offer of settlement by each defendant; and

(4) A statement identifying and discussing in detail all facts and law pertinent to the issues of liability and damages involved in the case as to that party.

The settlement conference statement must comply with any additional requirement imposed by local rule.

(Subd (c) amended effective January 1, 2008; adopted as subd (d) effective January 1, 1985; previously amended effective January 1, 1995 and January 1, 2007; previously amended and relettered effective July 1, 2002.)

(d) Restrictions on appointments

A court must not:

(1) Appoint a person to conduct a settlement conference under this rule at the same time as that person is serving as a mediator in the same action; or

(2) Appoint a person to conduct a mediation under this rule.

(Subd (d) adopted effective January 1, 2008.)

Rule 3.1380 amended effective January 1, 2008; adopted as rule 222 effective January 1, 1985; previously amended effective January 1, 1995, July 1, 2001, and July 1, 2002; previously amended and renumbered effective January 1, 2007.

Advisory Committee Comment

Subdivision (d). This provision is not intended to discourage settlement conferences or mediations. However, problems have arisen in several cases, such as *Jeld-Wen v. Superior Court of San Diego County* (2007) 146 Cal.App.4th 536, when distinctions between different ADR processes have been blurred. To prevent confusion about the confidentiality of the proceedings, it is important to clearly distinguish between settlement conferences held under this rule and mediations. The special confidentiality requirements for mediations established by Evidence Code sections 1115–1128 expressly do not apply to settlement conferences under this rule. This provision is not intended to prohibit a court from appointing a person who has previously served as a mediator in a case to conduct a settlement conference in that case following the conclusion of the mediation.

Rule 3.1382. Good faith settlement and dismissal

A motion or application for determination of good faith settlement may include a request to dismiss a pleading or a portion of a pleading. The notice of motion or application for determination of good faith settlement must list each party and pleading or portion of pleading affected by the settlement and the date on which the affected pleading was filed.

Rule 3.1382 amended and renumbered effective January 1, 2007; adopted as rule 330 effective July 1, 1999.

Rule 3.1384. Petition for approval of compromise of claim of minor or person with a disability; order for deposit of funds; and petition for withdrawal

(a) Petition for approval of compromise of claim

A petition for court approval of a compromise or covenant not to sue under Code of Civil Procedure section 372 must comply with rules 7.950 or 7.950.5, 7.951, and 7.952.

(Subd (a) amended effective January 1, 2021.)

(b) Order for the deposit of funds and petition for withdrawal

An order for the deposit of funds of a minor or a person with a disability, and a petition for the withdrawal of such funds, must comply with rules 7.953 and 7.954.

(Subd (b) amended effective January 1, 2007.)

Rule 3.1384 amended effective January 1, 2021; adopted as rule 378 effective January 1, 2002; previously amended and renumbered effective January 1, 2007.

Rule 3.1385. Duty to notify court and others of settlement of entire case

(a) Notice of settlement

(1) *Court and other persons to be notified*

If an entire case is settled or otherwise disposed of, each plaintiff or other party seeking affirmative relief must immediately file written notice of the settlement or other disposition with the court and serve the notice on all parties and any arbitrator or other court-connected alternative dispute resolution (ADR) neutral involved in the case. Each plaintiff or other party seeking affirmative relief must also immediately give oral notice to all of the above if a hearing, conference, or trial is scheduled to take place within 10 days.

(2) *Compensation for failure to provide notice*

If the plaintiff or other party seeking affirmative relief does not notify an arbitrator or other court-connected ADR neutral involved in the case of a settlement at least 2 days before the scheduled hearing or session with that arbitrator or neutral, the court may order the party to compensate the arbitrator or other neutral for the scheduled hearing time. The amount of compensation ordered by the court must not exceed the maximum amount of compensation the arbitrator would be entitled to receive for service as an arbitrator under Code of Civil Procedure section 1141.18(b) or that the neutral would have been entitled to receive for service as a neutral at the scheduled hearing or session.

(Subd (a) amended effective January 1, 2007; previously amended effective January 1, 1989, July 1, 2001, July 1, 2002, January 1, 2004, and January 1, 2006.)

(b) Dismissal of case

Except as provided in (c) or (d), each plaintiff or other party seeking affirmative relief must serve and file a request for dismissal of the entire case within 45 days after the date of settlement of the case. If the plaintiff or other party required to serve and file the request for dismissal does not do so, the court must dismiss the entire case 45 days after it receives notice of settlement unless good cause is shown why the case should not be dismissed.

(Subd (b) amended effective January 1, 2009; adopted effective January 1, 1989; previously amended effective July 1, 2002, January 1, 2004, and January 1, 2006.)

(c) Conditional settlement

(1) *Notice*

If the settlement agreement conditions dismissal of the entire case on the satisfactory completion of specified terms that are not to be performed within 45 days of the settlement, including payment in installment payments, the notice of conditional settlement served and filed by each plaintiff or other party seeking affirmative relief must specify the date by which the dismissal is to be filed.

(2) *Dismissal*

If the plaintiff or other party required to serve and file a request for dismissal within 45 days after the dismissal date specified in the notice does not do so, the court must dismiss the entire case unless good cause is shown why the case should not be dismissed.

(3) *Hearings vacated*

(A) Except as provided in (B), on the filing of the notice of conditional settlement, the court must vacate all hearings and other proceedings requiring the appearance of a party and may not set any hearing or other proceeding requiring the appearance of a party earlier than 45 days after the dismissal date specified in the notice, unless requested by a party.

(B) The court need not vacate a hearing on an order to show cause or other proceeding relating to sanctions, or for determination of good faith settlement at the request of a party under Code of Civil Procedure section 877.6.

(4) *Case disposition time*

Under standard 2.2(n)(1)(A), the filing of a notice of conditional settlement removes the case from the computation of time used to determine case disposition time.

(Subd (c) amended effective July 1, 2013; adopted effective January 1, 1989; previously amended effective July 1, 2002, January 1, 2004, and January 1, 2006.)

(d) Compromise of claims of a minor or disabled person

If the settlement of the case involves the compromise of the claim of a minor or person with a disability, the court must not hold an order to show cause hearing under (b) before the court has held a hearing to approve the settlement, provided the parties have filed appropriate papers to seek court approval of the settlement.

(Subd (d) adopted effective January 1, 2009.)

(e) Request for additional time to complete settlement

If a party who has served and filed a notice of settlement under (a) determines that the case cannot be dismissed within the prescribed 45 days, that party must serve and file a notice and a supporting declaration advising the court of that party's inability to dismiss the case within the prescribed time, showing good cause for its inability to do so, and proposing an alternative date for dismissal. The notice and a supporting declaration must be served and filed at least 5 court days before the time for requesting dismissal has elapsed. If good cause is shown, the court must continue the matter to allow additional time to complete the settlement. The court may take such other actions as may be appropriate for the proper management and disposition of the case.

(Subd (e) adopted effective January 1, 2009.)

Rule 3.1385 amended effective July 1, 2013; adopted as rule 225 effective January 1, 1985; previously amended effective January 1, 1989, January 1, 1992, July 1, 2001, July 1, 2002, January 1, 2004, January 1, 2006, and January 1, 2009; previously amended and renumbered effective January 1, 2007.

Division 13
Dismissal of Actions

Rule 3.1390. Service and filing of notice of entry of dismissal

A party that requests dismissal of an action must serve on all parties and file notice of entry of the dismissal.

Rule 3.1390 amended and renumbered effective January 1, 2007; adopted as rule 383 effective January 1, 1984.

Division 14
Pretrial
[Reserved]

Division 15
Trial

Chap. 1. General Provisions [Reserved].
Chap. 2. Consolidation or Bifurcation of Cases for Trial [Reserved].
Chap. 3. Nonjury Trials [Reserved].
Chap. 4. Jury Trials. Rule 3.1540.
Chap. 4.5. Expedited Jury Trials. Rules 3.1545–3.1553.
Chap. 5. Testimony and Evidence [Reserved].
Chap. 6. Expert Witness Testimony [Reserved].
Chap. 7. Jury Instructions. Rule 3.1560.
Chap. 8. Special Verdicts. Rule 3.1580.
Chap. 9. Statement of Decision. Rules 3.1590, 3.1591.

Chapter 1
General Provisions
[Reserved]

Chapter 2
Consolidation or Bifurcation of Cases for Trial
[Reserved]

Chapter 3
Nonjury Trials
[Reserved]

Chapter 4
Jury Trials

Rule 3.1540. Examination of prospective jurors in civil cases

(a) Application

This rule applies to all civil jury trials.

(Subd (a) amended and lettered effective January 1, 2007; adopted as part of untitled subd effective January 1, 1949.)

(b) Examination of jurors by the trial judge

In examining prospective jurors in civil cases, the judge should consider the policies and recommendations in Standard 3.25 of the Standards of Judicial Administration.

(Subd (b) amended effective January 1, 2013; adopted as part of untitled subd effective January 1, 1949; previously amended and lettered effective January 1, 2007.)

(c) Additional questions and examination by counsel

On completion of the initial examination, the trial judge must permit counsel for each party that so requests to submit additional questions that the judge will put to the jurors.

(Subd (c) amended effective January 1, 2013; adopted as part of untitled subd effective January 1, 1949; previously amended and lettered effective January 1, 2007.)

Rule 3.1540 amended effective January 1, 2013; adopted as rule 228 effective January 1, 1949; previously amended effective January 1, 1972, January 1, 1974, January 1, 1975, January 1, 1988, January 1, 1990, June 6, 1990, and July 1, 1993; previously amended and renumbered effective January 1, 2007.

Chapter 4.5
Expedited Jury Trials

Division 15, Trial—Chapter 4.5, Expedited Jury Trials, adopted effective January 1, 2011.

Art. 1. Applicability. Rule 3.1545.
Art. 2. Rules Applicable Only to Cases with Mandatory Expedited Jury Trials. Rule 3.1546.
Art. 3. Rules Applicable Only to Cases with Voluntary Expedited Jury Trials. Rules 3.1547, 3.1548.
Art. 4. Rules Applicable to All Expedited Jury Trials. Rules 3.1549–3.1553.

Article 1
Applicability

Title 3, Civil Rules—Division 15, Trial—Chapter 4.5, Expedited Jury Trials—Article 1, Applicability; adopted effective July 1, 2016.

Rule 3.1545. Expedited jury trials

(a) Application

The rules in this chapter apply to civil actions in which the parties either:

(1) Agree to a voluntary expedited jury trial under chapter 4.5 (commencing with section 630.01) of title 8 of part 2 of the Code of Civil Procedure, or

(2) Are required to take part in an expedited jury trial under chapter 4.6 (commencing with section 630.20) of title 8 of part 2 of the Code of Civil Procedure.

(Subd (a) amended effective July 1, 2016; adopted effective January 1, 2011.)

(b) Definitions

As used in this chapter, unless the context or subject matter otherwise requires:

(1) "Consent order" means the consent order granting an expedited jury trial described in Code of Civil Procedure section 630.03.

(2) "Expedited jury trial" is a short jury trial before a reduced jury panel, and may be either a "mandatory expedited jury trial" or a "voluntary expedited jury trial".

(3) "Mandatory expedited jury trial" has the same meaning as stated in Code of Civil Procedure section 630.21.

(4) "Voluntary expedited jury trial" has the same meaning as stated for "expedited jury trial" in Code of Civil Procedure section 630.01.

(5) "High/low agreement" and "posttrial motions" have the same meanings as stated in Code of Civil Procedure section 630.01.

(Subd (b) amended effective July 1, 2016; adopted effective January 1, 2011.)

(c) Other programs

This chapter does not limit the adoption or use of other expedited trial or alternative dispute resolution programs or procedures.

(Subd (c) adopted effective January 1, 2011.)

Rule 3.1545 amended effective July 1, 2016; adopted effective January 1, 2011.

Article 2
Rules Applicable Only to Cases with Mandatory Expedited Jury Trials

Title 3, Civil Rules—Division 15, Trial—Chapter 4.5, Expedited Jury Trials—Article 2, Rules Applicable Only to Cases with Mandatory Expedited Jury Trials; adopted effective July 1, 2016.

Rule 3.1546. Pretrial procedures for mandatory expedited jury trials

(a) Pretrial procedures

The pretrial procedures for limited civil actions set out in Code of Civil Procedure sections 90–100 are applicable to all cases with mandatory expedited jury trials. The statutory procedures include limited discovery, optional case questionnaires, optional requests for pretrial statements identifying trial witnesses and exhibits, and the possibility of presenting testimony in the form of affidavits or declarations.

(Subd (a) adopted effective July 1, 2016.)

(b) Case management

The case management rules in chapter 3 of division 7 of these rules, starting at rule 3.720, are applicable to all cases with mandatory expedited jury trials, except to the extent the rules have been modified by local court rules applicable to limited civil cases.

(Subd (b) adopted effective July 1, 2016.)

(c) Opting out of mandatory expedited jury trial procedures

(1) Parties seeking to opt out of mandatory expedited jury trial procedures on grounds stated in Code of Civil Procedure section 630.20(b) must file a *Request to Opt Out of Mandatory Expedited Jury Trial Procedures* (form EJT-003).

(2) Except on a showing of good cause, the request to opt out must be served and filed at least 45 days before the date first set for trial or, in cases in which the date first set for trial occurred before July 1, 2016, 45 days before the first trial date after July 1, 2016.

(3) Except on a showing of good cause, any objection to the request must be served and filed within 15 days after the date of service of the request, on an *Objection to Request to Opt Out of Mandatory Expedited Jury Trial Procedures* (form EJT-004).

(4) If the grounds on which a party or parties have opted out of mandatory expedited jury trial procedures no longer apply to a case, the parties must promptly inform the court, and the case may be tried as a mandatory expedited jury trial.

(Subd (c) amended effective September 1, 2017; adopted effective July 1, 2016.)

(d) Agreements regarding pretrial and trial procedures

Parties are encouraged to agree to procedures or limitations on pretrial procedures and on presentation of information at trial that could streamline the case, including but not limited to those items described in rule 3.1547(b). The parties may use *Agreement of Parties (Mandatory Expedited Jury Trial Procedures)* (form EJT-018) and the attachment (form EJT-022A) to describe such agreements.

(Subd (d) adopted effective July 1, 2016.)

Rule 3.1546 amended effective September 1, 2017; adopted effective July 1, 2016.

Advisory Committee Comment

Because Code of Civil Procedure section 630.20, which becomes operative July 1, 2016, applies to cases already on file and possibly already set for trial, as well as cases filed after the statutory provisions go into effect, the deadlines in rule 3.1546(c) for opt outs and objections may be problematic as applied to cases set for trial within the first couple of months after the rule goes into effect. It is expected that the good cause provisions within the rules regarding deadlines, along with judicious use of continuances as appropriate, will be liberally used to permit courts to manage those cases fairly, appropriately, and efficiently.

Article 3
Rules Applicable Only to Cases with Voluntary Expedited Jury Trials

Title 3, Civil Rules—Division 15, Trial—Chapter 4.5, Expedited Jury Trials—Article 3, Rules Applicable Only to Cases with Voluntary Expedited Jury Trials; adopted effective July 1, 2016.

Rule 3.1547. Consent order for voluntary expedited jury trial
Rule 3.1548. Pretrial submissions for voluntary expedited jury trials

Rule 3.1547. Consent order for voluntary expedited jury trial

(a) Submitting proposed consent order to the court

(1) Unless the court otherwise allows, to be eligible to participate in a voluntary expedited jury trial, the parties must submit to the court, no later than 30 days before any assigned trial date, a proposed consent order granting an expedited jury trial.

(2) The parties may enter into written stipulations regarding any high/low agreements or other matters. Only in the following circumstances may a high/low agreement be submitted to the court with the proposed consent order or disclosed later in the action:

(A) Upon agreement of the parties;

(B) In any case involving either

(i) A self-represented litigant, or

(ii) A minor, an incompetent person, or a person for whom a conservator has been appointed; or

(C) If necessary for entry or enforcement of the judgment.

(Subd (a) amended effective July 1, 2016; adopted effective January 1, 2011.)

(b) Optional content of proposed consent order

In addition to complying with the provisions of Code of Civil Procedure section 630.03(e), the proposed consent order may include other agreements of the parties, including the following:

(1) Modifications of the requirements or timelines for pretrial submissions required by rule 3.1548;

(2) Limitations on the number of witnesses per party, including expert witnesses;

(3) Modification of statutory or rule provisions regarding exchange of expert witness information and presentation of testimony by such witnesses;

(4) Allocation of the time periods stated in rule 3.1550 including how arguments and cross-examination may be used by each party in the five-hour time frame;

(5) Any evidentiary matters agreed to by the parties, including any stipulations or admissions regarding factual matters;

(6) Any agreements about what constitutes necessary or relevant evidence for a particular factual determination;

(7) Agreements about admissibility of particular exhibits or demonstrative evidence that are presented without the legally required authentication or foundation;

(8) Agreements about admissibility of video or written depositions and declarations;

(9) Agreements about any other evidentiary issues or the application of any of the rules of evidence;

(10) Agreements to use photographs, diagrams, slides, electronic presentations, overhead projections, notebooks of exhibits, or other methods for presenting information to the jury;

(11) Agreements concerning the time frame for filing and serving motions in limine; and

(12) Agreements concerning numbers of jurors required for jury verdicts in cases with fewer than eight jurors.

(Subd (b) amended effective July 1, 2016; adopted effective January 1, 2011.)

Rule 3.1547 amended effective July 1, 2016; adopted effective January 1, 2011.

Rule 3.1548. Pretrial submissions for voluntary expedited jury trials

(a) Service

Service under this rule must be by a means consistent with Code of Civil Procedure sections 1010.6, 1011, 1012, and 1013 or rule 2.251 and be reasonably calculated to assure delivery to the other party or parties no later than the close of business on the last allowable day for service as specified below.

(Subd (a) adopted effective January 1, 2011.)

(b) Pretrial exchange for voluntary expedited jury trials

Unless otherwise agreed by the parties, no later than 25 days before trial, each party must serve on all other parties the following:

(1) Copies of any documentary evidence that the party intends to introduce at trial (except for documentary evidence to be used solely for impeachment or rebuttal), including, but not limited to, medical bills, medical records, and lost income records;

(2) A list of all witnesses whom the party intends to call at trial, except for witnesses to be used solely for impeachment or rebuttal, and designation of whether the testimony will be in person, by video, or by deposition transcript;

(3) A list of depositions that the party intends to use at trial, except for depositions to be used solely for impeachment or rebuttal;

(4) A copy of any audiotapes, videotapes, digital video discs (DVDs), compact discs (CDs), or other similar recorded materials that the party intends to use at trial for evidentiary purposes, except recorded materials to be used solely for impeachment or rebuttal and recorded material intended to be used solely in closing argument;

(5) A copy of any proposed jury questionnaires (parties are encouraged to agree in advance on a questionnaire);

(6) A list of proposed approved introductory instructions, preinstructions, and instructions to be read by the judge to the jury;

(7) A copy of any proposed special jury instructions in the form and format described in rule 2.1055;

(8) Any proposed verdict forms;

(9) A special glossary, if the case involves technical or unusual vocabulary; and

(10) Motions in limine.

(Subd (b) amended effective July 1, 2016; adopted effective January 1, 2011.)

(c) Supplemental exchange for voluntary expedited jury trials

No later than 20 days before trial, a party may serve on any other party any additional documentary evidence and a list of any additional witnesses whom the party intends to use at trial in light of the exchange of information under subdivision (b).

(Subd (c) amended effective July 1, 2016; adopted effective January 1, 2011.)

(d) Submissions to court for voluntary expedited jury trials

No later than 20 days before trial, each party must file all motions in limine and must lodge with the court any items served under (b)(2)–(9) and (c).

(Subd (d) amended effective July 1, 2016; adopted effective January 1, 2011.)

(e) Preclusionary effect

Unless good cause is shown for any omission, failure to serve documentary evidence as required under this rule will be grounds for preclusion of the evidence at the time of trial.

(Subd (e) adopted effective January 1, 2011.)

(f) Pretrial conference for voluntary expedited jury trials

No later than 15 days before trial, unless that period is modified by the consent order, the judicial officer assigned to the case must conduct a pretrial conference, at which time objections to any documentary evidence previously submitted will be ruled on. If there are no objections at that time, counsel must stipulate in writing to the admissibility of the evidence. Matters to be addressed at the pretrial conference, in addition to the evidentiary objections, include the following:

(1) Any evidentiary matters agreed to by the parties, including any stipulations or admissions regarding factual matters;

(2) Any agreement of the parties regarding limitations on necessary or relevant evidence, including any limitations on expert witness testimony;

(3) Any agreements of the parties to use photographs, diagrams, slides, electronic presentations, overhead projections, notebooks of exhibits, or other methods of presenting information to the jury;

(4) Admissibility of any exhibits or demonstrative evidence without legally required authentication or foundation;

(5) Admissibility of video or written depositions and declarations and objections to any portions of them;

(6) Objections to and admissibility of any recorded materials that a party has designated for use at trial;

(7) Jury questionnaires;

(8) Jury instructions;

(9) Special verdict forms;

(10) Allocation of time for each party's case;

(11) Motions in limine filed before the pretrial conference; and

(12) The parties' intention on how any high/low agreement will affect an award of fees and costs.

(Subd (f) amended effective July 1, 2016; adopted effective January 1, 2011.)

(g) Expert witness documents

Any documents produced at the deposition of an expert witness are deemed to have been timely exchanged for the purpose of (c) above.

(Subd (g) adopted effective January 1, 2011.)

Rule 3.1548 amended effective July 1, 2016; adopted effective January 1, 2011.

Article 4
Rules Applicable to All Expedited Jury Trials

Title 3, Civil Rules—Division 15, Trial—Chapter 4.5, Expedited Jury Trials—Article 4, Rules Applicable to All Expedited Jury Trials; adopted effective July 1, 2016.

Rule 3.1549. Voir dire
Rule 3.1550. Time limits
Rule 3.1551. Case presentation
Rule 3.1552. Presentation of evidence
Rule 3.1553. Assignment of judicial officers

Rule 3.1549. Voir dire

Parties are encouraged to submit a joint form questionnaire to be used with prospective jurors to help expedite the voir dire process.

Rule 3.1549 amended effective July 1, 2016; adopted effective January 1, 2011.

Rule 3.1550. Time limits

Including jury voir dire, each side will be allowed five hours to present its case, including opening statements and closing arguments, unless the court, upon a finding of good cause, allows additional time. The amount of time allotted for each side includes the time that the side spends on cross-examination. The parties are encouraged to streamline the trial process by limiting the number of live witnesses. The goal is to complete an expedited jury trial within two trial days.

Rule 3.1550 amended effective July 1, 2016; adopted effective January 1, 2011.

Rule 3.1551. Case presentation

(a) Methods of presentation

Upon agreement of the parties and with the approval of the judicial officer, the parties may present summaries and may use photographs, diagrams, slides, electronic presentations, overhead projections, individual notebooks of exhibits for submission to the jurors, or other innovative methods of presentation approved at the pretrial conference.

(Subd (a) adopted effective January 1, 2011.)

(b) Exchange of items

Anything to be submitted to the jury under (a) as part of the evidentiary presentation of the case in chief must be exchanged 20 days in advance of the trial, unless that period is modified by the consent order or agreement of the parties. This rule does not apply to items to be used solely for closing argument.

(Subd (b) amended effective July 1, 2016; adopted effective January 1, 2011.)

(c) Stipulations regarding facts

The parties should stipulate to factual and evidentiary matters to the greatest extent possible.

(Subd (c) adopted effective January 1, 2011.)

Rule 3.1551 amended effective July 1, 2016; adopted effective January 1, 2011.

Rule 3.1552. Presentation of evidence

(a) Stipulations regarding rules of evidence

The parties may offer such evidence as is relevant and material to the dispute. An agreement to modify the rules of evidence for the trial made pursuant to the expedited jury trial statutes commencing with Code of Civil Procedure section 630.01 may be included in the consent order or agreement of the parties. To the extent feasible, the parties should stipulate to modes and methods of presentation that will expedite the process, either in the consent order or at the pretrial conference.

(Subd (a) amended effective July 1, 2016; adopted effective January 1, 2011.)

(b) Objections

Objections to evidence and motions to exclude evidence must be submitted in a timely manner. Except as provided in rule 3.1548(f), failure to raise an objection before trial does not preclude making an objection or motion to exclude at trial.

(Subd (b) adopted effective January 1, 2011.)

Rule 3.1552 amended effective July 1, 2016; adopted effective January 1, 2011.

Rule 3.1553. Assignment of judicial officers

The presiding judge is responsible for the assignment of a judicial officer to conduct an expedited jury trial. The presiding judge may assign a temporary judge appointed by the court under rules 2.810–2.819 to conduct an expedited jury trial. A temporary judge requested by the parties under rules 2.830–2.835, whether or not privately compensated, may not be appointed to conduct a voluntary expedited jury trial.

Rule 3.1553 amended and renumbered effective July 1, 2016; adopted as rule 3.1546 effective January 1, 2011.

Chapter 5
Testimony and Evidence
[Reserved]

Chapter 6
Expert Witness Testimony
[Reserved]

Chapter 7
Jury Instructions

Rule 3.1560. Application

The rules on jury instructions in chapter 4 of division 8 of title 2 of these rules apply to civil cases.

Rule 3.1560 adopted effective January 1, 2007.

Chapter 8
Special Verdicts

Rule 3.1580. Request for special findings by jury

Whenever a party desires special findings by a jury, the party must, before argument, unless otherwise ordered, present to the judge in writing the issues or questions of fact on which the findings are requested, in proper form for submission to the jury, and serve copies on all other parties.

Rule 3.1580 amended and renumbered effective January 1, 2007; adopted as rule 230 effective January 1, 1949.

Chapter 9
Statement of Decision

Rule 3.1590. Announcement of tentative decision, statement of decision, and judgment
Rule 3.1591. Statement of decision, judgment, and motion for new trial following bifurcated trial

Rule 3.1590. Announcement of tentative decision, statement of decision, and judgment

(a) Announcement and service of tentative decision

On the trial of a question of fact by the court, the court must announce its tentative decision by an oral statement, entered in the minutes, or by a written statement filed with the clerk. Unless the announcement is made in open court in the presence of all parties that appeared at the trial, the clerk must immediately serve on all parties that appeared at the trial a copy of the minute entry or written tentative decision.

(Subd (a) amended effective January 1, 2010; previously amended effective January 1, 1969, July 1, 1973, January 1, 1982, January 1, 1983, and January 1, 2007.)

(b) Tentative decision not binding

The tentative decision does not constitute a judgment and is not binding on the court. If the court subsequently modifies or changes its announced tentative decision, the clerk must serve a copy of the modification or change on all parties that appeared at the trial.

(Subd (b) amended effective January 1, 2010; adopted as part of subd (a) effective January 1, 1949; previously amended and lettered effective January 1, 2007; previously amended effective January 1, 2007.)

(c) Provisions in tentative decision

The court in its tentative decision may:

(1) State that it is the court's proposed statement of decision, subject to a party's objection under (g);

(2) Indicate that the court will prepare a statement of decision;

(3) Order a party to prepare a statement of decision; or

(4) Direct that the tentative decision will become the statement of decision unless, within 10 days after announcement or service of the tentative decision, a party specifies those principal controverted issues as to which the party is requesting a statement of decision or makes proposals not included in the tentative decision.

(Subd (c) amended effective January 1, 2010; adopted as part of subd (a) effective January 1, 1949; previously amended and lettered effective January 1, 2007.)

(d) Request for statement of decision

Within 10 days after announcement or service of the tentative decision, whichever is later, any party that appeared at trial may request a statement of decision to address the principal controverted issues. The principal controverted issues must be specified in the request.

(Subd (d) adopted effective January 1, 2010.)

(e) Other party's response to request for statement of decision

If a party requests a statement of decision under (d), any other party may make proposals as to the content of the statement of decision within 10 days after the date of request for a statement of decision.

(Subd (e) amended and relettered effective January 1, 2010; adopted as subd (b) effective January 1, 1949; previously amended effective January 1, 1969, and January 1, 1982; previously amended and relettered as subd (d) effective January 1, 2007.)

(f) Preparation and service of proposed statement of decision and judgment

If a party requests a statement of decision under (d), the court must, within 30 days of announcement or service of the tentative decision, prepare and serve a proposed statement of decision and a proposed judgment on all parties that appeared at the trial, unless the court has ordered a party to prepare the statement. A party that has been ordered to prepare the statement must within 30 days after the announcement or service of the tentative decision, serve and submit to the court a proposed statement of decision and a proposed judgment. If the proposed statement of decision and judgment are not served and submitted within that time, any other party that appeared at the trial may within 10 days thereafter: (1) prepare, serve, and submit to the court a proposed statement of decision and judgment or (2) serve on all other parties and file a notice of motion for an order that a statement of decision be deemed waived.

(Subd (f) amended and relettered effective January 1, 2010; adopted as subd (c) effective January 1, 1949; previously amended effective January 1, 1969, July 1, 1973, and January 1, 1982; previously amended and relettered as subd (e) effective January 1, 2007.)

(g) Objections to proposed statement of decision

Any party may, within 15 days after the proposed statement of decision and judgment have been served, serve and file objections to the proposed statement of decision or judgment.

(Subd (g) amended and relettered effective January 1, 2010; adopted as subd (d) effective January 1, 1949; previously amended effective January 1, 1969, and January 1, 1982; previously relettered as subd (f) effective January 1, 2007.)

(h) Preparation and filing of written judgment when statement of decision not prepared

If no party requests or is ordered to prepare a statement of decision and a written judgment is required, the court must prepare and serve a proposed judgment on all parties that appeared at the trial within 20 days after the announcement or service of the tentative decision or the court may order a party to prepare, serve, and submit the proposed judgment to the court within 10 days after the date of the order.

(Subd (h) amended and relettered effective January 1, 2010; previously amended effective January 1, 1969; previously amended and relettered as subd (e) effective January 1, 1982, and as subd (g) effective January 1, 2007.)

(i) Preparation and filing of written judgment when statement of decision deemed waived

If the court orders that the statement of decision is deemed waived and a written judgment is required, the court must, within 10 days of the order deeming the statement of decision waived, either prepare and serve a proposed judgment on all parties that appeared at the trial or order a party to prepare, serve, and submit the proposed judgment to the court within 10 days.

(Subd (i) adopted effective January 1, 2010.)

(j) Objection to proposed judgment

Any party may, within 10 days after service of the proposed judgment, serve and file objections thereto.

(Subd (j) adopted effective January 1, 2010.)

(k) Hearing

The court may order a hearing on proposals or objections to a proposed statement of decision or the proposed judgment.

(Subd (k) amended and relettered effective January 1, 2010; adopted as subd (f) effective January 1, 1982; previously relettered as subd (i) effective January 1, 2007.)

(l) Signature and filing of judgment

If a written judgment is required, the court must sign and file the judgment within 50 days after the announcement or service of the tentative decision, whichever is later, or, if a hearing was held under (k), within 10 days after the hearing. An electronic signature by the court is as effective as an original signature. The judgment constitutes the decision on which judgment is to be entered under Code of Civil Procedure section 664.

(Subd (l) amended effective January 1, 2016; adopted as part of subd (e) effective January 1, 1949; previously amended and lettered as subd (h) effective January 1, 2007, and as subd (l) effective January 1, 2010.)

(m) Extension of time; relief from noncompliance

The court may, by written order, extend any of the times prescribed by this rule and at any time before the entry of judgment may, for good cause shown and on such terms as may be just, excuse a noncompliance with the time limits prescribed for doing any act required by this rule.

(Subd (m) relettered effective January 1, 2010; previously amended effective January 1, 1969, and July 1, 1973; previously amended and relettered as subd (g) effective January 1, 1982, and as subd (j) effective January 1, 2007.)

(n) Trial within one day

When a trial is completed within one day or in less than eight hours over more than one day, a request for statement of decision must be made before the matter is submitted for decision and the statement of decision may be made orally on the record in the presence of the parties.

(Subd (n) amended and relettered effective January 1, 2010; adopted as subd (h) effective January 1, 1983; previously amended and relettered as subd (k) effective January 1, 2007.)

Rule 3.1590 amended effective January 1, 2016; adopted as rule 232 effective January 1, 1949; previously amended and renumbered as rule 3.1590 effective January 1, 2007; previously amended effective January 1, 1969, July 1, 1973, January 1, 1982, January 1, 1983, January 1, 2007, and January 1, 2010.

Rule 3.1591. Statement of decision, judgment, and motion for new trial following bifurcated trial

(a) Separate trial of an issue

When a factual issue raised by the pleadings is tried by the court separately and before the trial of other issues, the judge conducting the separate trial must announce the tentative decision on the issue so tried and must, when requested under Code of Civil Procedure section 632, issue a statement of decision as prescribed in rule 3.1590; but the court must not prepare any proposed judgment until the other issues are tried, except when an interlocutory judgment or a separate judgment may otherwise be properly entered at that time.

(Subd (a) amended and lettered effective January 1, 2007; adopted as part of untitled subd effective January 1, 1975.)

(b) Trial of issues by a different judge

If the other issues are tried by a different judge or judges, each judge must perform all acts required by rule 3.1590 as to the issues tried by that judge and the judge trying the final issue must prepare the proposed judgment.

(Subd (b) amended and lettered effective January 1, 2007; adopted as part of untitled subd effective January 1, 1975.)

(c) Trial of subsequent issues before issuance of statement of decision

A judge may proceed with the trial of subsequent issues before the issuance of a statement of decision on previously tried issues. Any motion for a new trial following a bifurcated trial must be made after all the issues are tried and, if the issues were tried by different judges, each judge must hear and determine the motion as to the issues tried by that judge.

(Subd (c) amended and lettered effective January 1, 2007; adopted as part of untitled subd effective January 1, 1975.)

Rule 3.1591 amended and renumbered effective January 1, 2007; adopted as rule 232.5 effective January 1, 1975; previously amended effective January 1, 1982, and January 1, 1985.

Division 16
Post-trial

Rule 3.1600. Notice of intention to move for new trial
Rule 3.1602. Hearing of motion to vacate judgment

Rule 3.1600. Notice of intention to move for new trial

(a) Time for service of memorandum

Within 10 days after filing notice of intention to move for a new trial in a civil case, the moving party must serve and file a memorandum in support of the motion, and within 10 days thereafter any adverse party may serve and file a memorandum in reply.

(Subd (a) amended and lettered effective January 1, 2007; adopted as part of untitled subd effective January 1, 1949.)

(b) Effect of failure to serve memorandum

If the moving party fails to serve and file a memorandum within the time prescribed in (a), the court may deny the motion for a new trial without a hearing on the merits.

(Subd (b) amended and lettered effective January 1, 2007; adopted as part of untitled subd effective January 1, 1949.)

Rule 3.1600 amended and renumbered effective January 1, 2007; adopted as rule 203 effective January 1, 1949; previously amended effective April 1, 1962, January 1, 1971, January 1, 1984, and January 1, 1987; previously amended and renumbered as rule 236.5 effective January 1, 2003.

Rule 3.1602. Hearing of motion to vacate judgment

A motion to vacate judgment under Code of Civil Procedure section 663 must be heard and determined by the judge who presided at the trial; provided, however, that in case of the inability or death of such judge or if at the time noticed for the hearing thereon he is absent from the county where the trial was had, the motion may be heard and determined by another judge of the same court.

Rule 3.1602 amended and renumbered effective January 1, 2007; adopted as rule 236 effective January 1, 1949.

Division 17
Attorney's Fees and Costs

Rule 3.1700. Prejudgment costs
Rule 3.1702. Claiming attorney's fees

Rule 3.1700. Prejudgment costs

(a) Claiming costs

(1) *Trial costs*

A prevailing party who claims costs must serve and file a memorandum of costs within 15 days after the date of service of the notice of entry of judgment or dismissal by the clerk under Code of Civil Procedure section 664.5 or the date of service of written notice of entry of judgment or dismissal, or within 180 days after entry of judgment, whichever is first. The memorandum of costs must be verified by a statement of the party, attorney, or agent that to the best of his or her knowledge the items of cost are correct and were necessarily incurred in the case.

(2) *Costs on default*

A party seeking a default judgment who claims costs must request costs on the *Request for Entry of Default (Application to Enter Default)* (form CIV-100) at the time of applying for the judgment.

(Subd (a) amended effective January 1, 2016; previously amended effective January 1, 2007, and July 1, 2007.)

(b) Contesting costs

(1) *Striking and taxing costs*

Any notice of motion to strike or to tax costs must be served and filed 15 days after service of the cost memorandum. If the cost memorandum was served by mail, the period is extended as provided in Code of Civil Procedure section 1013. If the cost memorandum was served electronically, the period is extended as provided in Code of Civil Procedure section 1010.6(a)(4).

(2) *Form of motion*

Unless objection is made to the entire cost memorandum, the motion to strike or tax costs must refer to each item objected to by the same number and appear in the same order as the corresponding cost item claimed on the memorandum of costs and must state why the item is objectionable.

(3) *Extensions of time*

The party claiming costs and the party contesting costs may agree to extend the time for serving and filing the cost memorandum and a motion to strike or tax costs. This agreement must be confirmed in writing, specify the extended date for service, and be filed with the clerk. In the absence of an agreement, the court may extend the times for serving and filing the cost memorandum or the notice of motion to strike or tax costs for a period not to exceed 30 days.

(4) *Entry of costs*

After the time has passed for a motion to strike or tax costs or for determination of that motion, the clerk must immediately enter the costs on the judgment.

(Subd (b) amended effective January 1, 2016; previously amended effective January 1, 2007.)

Rule 3.1700 amended effective January 1, 2016; adopted as rule 870 effective January 1, 1987; previously amended and renumbered as rule 3.1700 effective January 1, 2007; previously amended effective July 1, 2007.

Rule 3.1702. Claiming attorney's fees

(a) Application

Except as otherwise provided by statute, this rule applies in civil cases to claims for statutory attorney's fees and claims for attorney's fees provided for in a contract. Subdivisions (b) and (c) apply when the court determines entitlement to the fees, the amount of the fees, or both, whether the court makes that determination because the statute or contract refers to "reasonable" fees, because it requires a determination of the prevailing party, or for other reasons.

(Subd (a) amended effective January 1, 2007.)

(b) Attorney's fees before trial court judgment

(1) *Time for motion*

A notice of motion to claim attorney's fees for services up to and including the rendition of judgment in the trial court—including attorney's fees on an appeal before the rendition of judgment in the trial court—must be served and filed within the time for filing a notice of appeal under rules 8.104 and 8.108 in an unlimited civil case or under rules 8.822 and 8.823 in a limited civil case.

(2) *Stipulation for extension of time*

The parties may, by stipulation filed before the expiration of the time allowed under (b)(1), extend the time for filing a motion for attorney's fees:

(A) Until 60 days after the expiration of the time for filing a notice of appeal in an unlimited civil case or 30 days after the expiration of the time in a limited civil case; or

(B) If a notice of appeal is filed, until the time within which a memorandum of costs must be served and filed under rule 8.278(c) in an unlimited civil case or under rule 8.891(c)(1) in a limited civil case.

(Subd (b) amended effective July 1, 2013; previously amended effective January 1, 1999, January 1, 2006, January 1, 2007, January 1, 2009, and January 1, 2011.)

(c) Attorney's fees on appeal

(1) *Time for motion*

A notice of motion to claim attorney's fees on appeal—other than the attorney's fees on appeal claimed under (b)—under a statute or contract requiring the court to determine entitlement to the fees, the amount of the fees, or both, must be served and filed within the time for serving and filing the memorandum of costs under rule 8.278(c)(1) in an unlimited civil case or under rule 8.891(c)(1) in a limited civil case.

(2) *Stipulation for extension of time*

The parties may by stipulation filed before the expiration of the time allowed under (c)(1) extend the time for filing the motion up to an additional 60 days in an unlimited civil case or 30 days in a limited civil case.

(Subd (c) amended effective January 1, 2011; previously amended effective January 1, 1999, January 1, 2006, January 1, 2007, and July 1, 2008.)

(d) Extensions

For good cause, the trial judge may extend the time for filing a motion for attorney's fees in the absence of a stipulation or for a longer period than allowed by stipulation.

(Subd (d) amended effective January 1, 2007; adopted effective January 1, 1999.)

(e) Attorney's fees fixed by formula

If a party is entitled to statutory or contractual attorney's fees that are fixed without the necessity of a court determination, the fees must be claimed in the memorandum of costs.

(Subd (e) amended effective January 1, 2007; adopted as subd (d) effective January 1, 1994; previously relettered effective January 1, 1999.)

Rule 3.1702 amended effective July 1, 2013; adopted as rule 870.2 effective January 1, 1994; previously amended and renumbered effective January 1, 2007; previously amended effective January 1, 1999, January 1, 2006, July 1, 2008, January 1, 2009, and January 1, 2011.

Division 18
Judgments

Rule 3.1800. Default judgments
Rule 3.1802. Inclusion of interest in judgment
Rule 3.1804. Periodic payment of judgments against public entities
Rule 3.1806. Notation on written instrument of rendition of judgment

Rule 3.1800. Default judgments

(a) Documents to be submitted

A party seeking a default judgment on declarations must use mandatory *Request for Entry of Default (Application to Enter Default)* (form CIV-100), unless the action is subject to the Fair Debt Buying Practices Act, Civil Code section 1788.50 et seq., in which case the party must use mandatory *Request for Entry of Default (Fair Debt Buying Practices Act)* (form CIV-105). In an unlawful detainer case, a party may, in addition, use optional *Declaration for Default Judgment by Court* (form UD-116) when seeking a court judgment based on declarations. The following must be included in the documents filed with the clerk:

(1) Except in unlawful detainer cases, a brief summary of the case identifying the parties and the nature of plaintiff's claim;

(2) Declarations or other admissible evidence in support of the judgment requested;

(3) Interest computations as necessary;

(4) A memorandum of costs and disbursements;

(5) A declaration of nonmilitary status for each defendant against whom judgment is sought;

(6) A proposed form of judgment;

(7) A dismissal of all parties against whom judgment is not sought or an application for separate judgment against specified parties under Code of Civil Procedure section 579, supported by a showing of grounds for each judgment;

(8) Exhibits as necessary; and

(9) A request for attorney fees if allowed by statute or by the agreement of the parties.

(Subd (a) amended effective January 1, 2018; previously amended effective January 1, 2005, January 1, 2007, and July 1, 2007.)

(b) Fee schedule

A court may by local rule establish a schedule of attorney's fees to be used by that court in determining the reasonable amount of attorney's fees to be allowed in the case of a default judgment.

(Subd (b) amended effective January 1, 2007.)

Rule 3.1800 amended effective January 1, 2018; adopted as rule 388 effective July 1, 2000; previously amended effective January 1, 2005, and July 1, 2007; previously amended and renumbered effective January 1, 2007.

Rule 3.1802. Inclusion of interest in judgment

The clerk must include in the judgment any interest awarded by the court.

Rule 3.1802 amended effective January 1, 2014; adopted as rule 875 effective January 1, 1987; previously amended and renumbered effective January 1, 2007.

Rule 3.1804. Periodic payment of judgments against public entities

(a) Notice of election or hearing

A public entity electing to pay a judgment against it by periodic payments under Government Code section 984 must serve and file a notice of election stipulating to the terms of such payments, or a notice of hearing on such terms, by the earlier of:

(1) 30 days after the clerk sends, or a party serves, notice of entry of judgment; or

(2) 60 days after entry of judgment.

(b) Time for hearing

Notwithstanding any contrary local rule or practice, a hearing under (a) must be held within 30 days after service of the notice. The court must make an order for periodic payments at the hearing.

(Subd (b) amended effective January 1, 2007.)

Rule 3.1804 amended and renumbered effective January 1, 2007; adopted as rule 389 effective January 1, 2002.

Rule 3.1806. Notation on written instrument of rendition of judgment

In all cases in which judgment is rendered upon a written obligation to pay money, the clerk must, at the time of entry of judgment, unless otherwise ordered, note over the clerk's official signature and across the face of the writing the fact of rendition of judgment with the date of the judgment and the title of the court and the case.

Rule 3.1806 amended and renumbered effective January 1, 2007; adopted as rule 234 effective January 1, 1949.

Division 19
Postjudgment and Enforcement of Judgments

Rule 3.1900. Notice of renewal of judgment

A copy of the application for renewal of judgment must be physically or electronically attached to the notice of renewal of judgment required by Code of Civil Procedure section 683.160.

Rule 3.1900 amended effective January 1, 2016; adopted as rule 986 effective July 1, 1983; previously amended and renumbered as rule 3.1900 effective January 1, 2007.

Division 20
Unlawful Detainers

Rule 3.2000. Unlawful detainer—supplemental costs
Rule 3.2005. Settlement opportunities

Rule 3.2000. Unlawful detainer—supplemental costs

(a) Time for filing supplemental cost memorandum

In unlawful detainer proceedings, the plaintiff who has complied with Code of Civil Procedure section 1034.5 may, no later than 10 days after being advised by the sheriff or marshal of the exact amount necessarily used and expended to effect the eviction, file a supplemental cost memorandum claiming the additional costs and specifying the items paid and the amount.

(Subd (a) amended and lettered effective January 1, 2007; adopted as part of untitled subd effective January 1, 1987.)

(b) Motion to tax costs

The defendant may move to tax those costs within 10 days after service of the supplemental cost memorandum.

(Subd (b) amended and lettered effective January 1, 2007; adopted as part of untitled subd effective January 1, 1987.)

(c) Entry of judgment for costs and enforcement

After costs have been fixed by the court, or on failure of the defendant to file a timely notice of motion to tax costs, the clerk must immediately enter judgment for the costs. The judgment may be enforced in the same manner as a money judgment.

(Subd (c) amended and lettered effective January 1, 2007; adopted as part of untitled subd effective January 1, 1987.)

Rule 3.2000 amended and renumbered effective January 1, 2007; adopted as part of rule 870.4 effective January 1, 1987.

Rule 3.2005. Settlement opportunities

(a) Policy favoring an opportunity for resolution without trial

The intent of this rule is to promote opportunities for resolution of unlawful detainer cases before trial. Courts should encourage participation, to the extent feasible, in at least one opportunity for resolution before trial, including but not limited to a settlement conference, mediation, or another alternative dispute resolution process.

(Subd (a) adopted effective January 1, 2024.)

(b) Exemption for mandatory settlement conference statement deadline

The court may exempt the parties in an unlawful detainer case participating in a mandatory settlement conference from the five-court-day deadline for submitting a settlement conference statement set out in rule 3.1380(c).

(Subd (b) adopted effective January 1, 2024.)

Rule 3.2005 adopted effective January 1, 2024.

Advisory Committee Comment

The Judicial Council has adopted an optional form—*Eviction Case (Unlawful Detainer) Stipulation* (form UD-155)—that can be used to advise the court about any settlement that has been reached before trial.

Subdivision (a). The committee notes that parties may choose but cannot be required to participate in for-cost mediation or alternative dispute resolution (ADR). This rule is not intended in any way to mandate for-cost mediation or ADR.

Subdivision (b). Because unlawful detainer cases generally proceed on an expedited basis, this exemption allows parties in unlawful detainer cases to participate in and complete mandatory settlement conferences on shorter timelines. Nothing in this rule, including the exemption set out in subdivision (b), is intended to preclude a court from shortening other deadlines related to alternative dispute resolution processes.

Division 21
Rules for Small Claims Actions

Chap. 1. Trial Rules. Rules 3.2100–3.2110.
Chap. 2. Small Claims Advisors. Rule 3.2120.

Chapter 1
Trial Rules

Rule 3.2100. Compliance with fictitious business name laws
Rule 3.2102. Substituted service
Rule 3.2104. Defendant's claim
Rule 3.2106. Venue challenge
Rule 3.2107. Request for court order
Rule 3.2108. Form of judgment
Rule 3.2110. Role of clerk in assisting small claims litigants

Rule 3.2100. Compliance with fictitious business name laws

(a) Filing of declaration of compliance

A claimant who is required to file a declaration of compliance with the fictitious business name laws under Code of Civil Procedure section 116.430 must file the declaration in each case filed.

(Subd (a) amended and lettered effective January 1, 2007; adopted as untitled subd effective January 1, 1986.)

(b) Available methods

The clerk must make the declaration of compliance available to the claimant in any one of the following ways:

(1) The declaration of compliance may be placed on a separate form approved by the Judicial Council;

(2) The approved Judicial Council form may be placed on the reverse of the Plaintiff's Statement to the Clerk or on the back of any Judicial Council small claims form with only one side; or

(3) The precise language of the declaration of compliance that appears on the approved Judicial Council form may be incorporated into the Plaintiff's Statement to the Clerk.

(Subd (b) amended and lettered effective January 1, 2007; adopted as part of untitled subd effective January 1, 1986.)

Rule 3.2100 amended and renumbered effective January 1, 2007; adopted as rule 1701 effective January 1, 1986; previously amended effective July 1, 1991.

Rule 3.2102. Substituted service

If substituted service is authorized by Code of Civil Procedure section 116.340 or other provisions of law, no due diligence is required in a small claims court action.

Rule 3.2102 renumbered effective January 1, 2007; adopted as rule 1702 effective July 1, 1991.

Rule 3.2104. Defendant's claim

A defendant may file a claim against the plaintiff even if the claim does not relate to the same subject or event as the plaintiff's claim, so long as the claim is within the jurisdictional limit of the small claims court.

Rule 3.2104 renumbered effective January 1, 2007; adopted as rule 1703 effective July 1, 1991.

Rule 3.2106. Venue challenge

A defendant may challenge venue by writing to the court. The defendant is not required to personally appear at the hearing on the venue challenge. If the court denies the challenge and the defendant is not present, the hearing must be continued to another appropriate date. The parties must be given notice of the venue determination and hearing date.

Rule 3.2106 amended and renumbered effective January 1, 2007; adopted as rule 1704 effective July 1, 1991.

Rule 3.2107. Request for court order

(a) Request before trial

If a party files a written request for a court order before the hearing on the claim, the requesting party must mail, personally deliver, or if agreed on by the parties electronically serve a copy to all other parties in the case. The other parties must be given an opportunity to answer or respond to the request before or at the hearing. This subdivision does not apply to a request to postpone the hearing date if the plaintiff's claim has not been served.

(Subd (a) amended effective January 1, 2016; adopted effective January 1, 2007.)

(b) Request after trial

If a party files a written request for a court order after notice of entry of judgment, the clerk must send a copy of the request to all other parties in the action. A party has 10 calendar days from the date on which the clerk sent the request to file a response before the court makes an order. The court may schedule a hearing on the request, except that if the request is to vacate the judgment for lack of appearance by the plaintiff, the court must hold a hearing. The court may give notice of any scheduled hearing with notice of the request, but the hearing must be scheduled at least 11 calendar days after the clerk has sent the request.

(Subd (b) amended effective January 1, 2016; adopted effective January 1, 2007.)

Rule 3.2107 amended effective January 1, 2016; adopted effective January 1, 2007.

Rule 3.2108. Form of judgment

The court may give judgment for damages, equitable relief, or both, and may make other orders as the court deems just and equitable for the resolution of the dispute. If specific property is referred to in the judgment, whether it be personal or real, tangible or intangible, the property must be identified with sufficient detail to permit efficient implementation or enforcement of the judgment.

Rule 3.2108 amended and renumbered effective January 1, 2007; adopted as rule 1705 effective July 1, 1991.

Rule 3.2110. Role of clerk in assisting small claims litigants

(a) Provision of forms and pamphlets

The clerk must provide forms and pamphlets from the Judicial Council.

(Subd (a) amended and lettered effective January 1, 2007; adopted as part of untitled subd effective July 1, 1991.)

(b) Provision of Department of Consumer Affairs materials

The clerk must provide materials from the Department of Consumer Affairs when available.

(Subd (b) amended and lettered effective January 1, 2007; adopted as part of untitled subd effective July 1, 1991.)

(c) Information about small claims advisory service

The clerk must inform litigants of the small claims advisory service.

(Subd (c) amended and lettered effective January 1, 2007; adopted as part of untitled subd effective July 1, 1991.)

(d) Answering questions

The clerk may answer questions relative to filing and service of the claim, designation of the parties, scheduling of hearings, and similar matters.

(Subd (d) amended and lettered effective January 1, 2007; adopted as part of untitled subd effective July 1, 1991.)

Rule 3.2110 amended and renumbered effective January 1, 2007; adopted as rule 1706 effective July 1, 1991.

Chapter 2
Small Claims Advisors

Rule 3.2120. Advisor assistance

(a) Notice to parties

The clerk must inform the parties, orally or in writing, about:

(1) The availability of advisors to assist small claims litigants at no additional charge as provided in Code of Civil Procedure sections 116.260 and 116.940; and

(2) The provisions of Government Code section 818.9.

(Subd (a) amended effective January 1, 2007; previously amended effective July 1, 1991.)

(b) Training

All small claims advisors must receive training sufficient to ensure competence in the areas of:

(1) Small claims court practice and procedure;

(2) Alternative dispute resolution programs;

(3) Consumer sales;

(4) Vehicular sales, leasing, and repairs;

(5) Credit and financing transactions;

(6) Professional and occupational licensing;

(7) Landlord-tenant law; and

(8) Contract, warranty, tort, and negotiable instruments law.

It is the intent of this rule that the county must provide this training.

(Subd (b) amended effective January 1, 2007; previously adopted effective January 1, 1986; previously repealed and adopted effective July 1, 1991.)

(c) Qualifications

In addition to the training required in subdivision (b), each county may establish additional qualifications for small claims advisors.

(Subd (c) adopted effective July 1, 1991.)

(d) Conflict of interest

A small claims advisor must disclose any known direct or indirect relationship the advisor may have with any party or witness in the action. An advisor must not disclose information obtained in the course of the advisor's duties or use the information for financial or other advantage.

(Subd (d) amended effective January 1, 2007; adopted as subd (c) effective January 1, 1986; previously relettered effective July 1, 1991.)

Rule 3.2120 amended and renumbered effective January 1, 2007; adopted as rule 1725 effective January 1, 1986; previously amended effective July 1, 1991.

Division 22
Petitions Under the California Environmental Quality Act

Title 3, Civil Rules—Division 22, Petitions Under the California Environmental Quality Act; adopted effective July 1, 2014.

Chap. 1. General Provisions. Rules 3.2200–3.2208.

Chap. 2. California Environmental Quality Act Proceedings Under Public Resources Code Sections 21168.6, 21178–21189.3, and 21189.50–21189.57. Rules 3.2220–3.2240.

Chapter 1
General Provisions

Title 3, Civil Rules—Division 22, Petitions Under the California Environmental Quality Act—Chapter 1, General Provisions; adopted effective July 1, 2014.

Rule 3.2200. Application

Rule 3.2205. Form and format of administrative record lodged in a CEQA proceeding

Rule 3.2206. Lodging and service
Rule 3.2207. Electronic format
Rule 3.2208. Paper format

Rule 3.2200. Application

Except as otherwise provided in chapter 2 of the rules in this division, which govern actions under Public Resources Code sections 21168.6.6–21168.6.9, 21178–21189.3, 21189.50–21189.57, and 21189.70–21189.70.10, the rules in this chapter apply to all actions brought under the California Environmental Quality Act (CEQA) as stated in division 13 of the Public Resources Code.

Rule 3.2200 amended effective January 1, 2023; adopted effective July 1, 2014; previously amended effective January 1, 2017, and March 11, 2022.

Rule 3.2205. Form and format of administrative record lodged in a CEQA proceeding

(a) Organization

(1) *Order of documents*

Except as permitted in (a)(3), the administrative record must be organized in the following order, as applicable:

(A) The Notice of Determination;

(B) The resolutions or ordinances adopted by the lead agency approving the project;

(C) The findings required by Public Resources Code section 21081, including any statement of overriding considerations;

(D) The final environmental impact report, including the draft environmental impact report or a revision of the draft, all other matters included in the final environmental impact report, and other types of environmental impact documents prepared under the California Environmental Quality Act, such as a negative declaration, mitigated negative declaration, or addenda;

(E) The initial study;

(F) Staff reports prepared for the administrative bodies providing subordinate approvals or recommendations to the lead agency, in chronological order;

(G) Transcripts and minutes of hearings, in chronological order; and

(H) The remainder of the administrative record, in chronological order.

(2) *List not limiting*

The list of documents in (1) is not intended to limit the content of the administrative record, which is prescribed in Public Resources Code section 21167.6(e).

(3) *Different order permissible*

The documents may be organized in a different order from that set out in (1) if the court so orders on:

(A) A party's motion;

(B) The parties' stipulation; or

(C) The court's own motion.

(4) *Oversized documents*

Oversized documents included in the record must be presented in a manner that allows them to be easily unfolded and viewed.

(5) *Use of tabs or electronic bookmarks*

The administrative record must be separated by tabs or marked with electronic bookmarks that identify each part of the record listed above.

(Subd (a) adopted effective January 1, 2010.)

(b) Index

A detailed index must be placed at the beginning of the administrative record. The index must list each document in the administrative record in the order presented, or in chronological order if ordered by the court, including title, date of the document, brief description, and the volume and page where it begins. The index must list any included exhibits or appendixes and must list each document contained in the exhibit or appendix (including environmental impact report appendixes) and the volume and page where each document begins. A copy of the index must be filed in the court at the time the administrative record is lodged with the court.

(Subd (b) adopted effective January 1, 2010.)

(c) Appendix of excerpts

A court may require each party filing a brief to prepare and lodge an appendix of excerpts that contains the documents or pages of the record cited in that party's brief.

(Subd (c) adopted effective January 1, 2010.)

Rule 3.2205 renumbered effective July 1, 2014; adopted as rule 3.1365 effective January 1, 2010.

Rule 3.2206. Lodging and service

The party preparing the administrative record must lodge it with the court and serve it on each party. A record in electronic format must comply with rule 3.2207. A record in paper format must comply with rule 3.2208. If the party preparing the administrative record elects, is required by law, or is ordered to prepare an electronic version of the record, (1) a court may require the party to lodge one copy of the record in paper format, and (2) a party may request the record in paper format and pay the reasonable cost or show good cause for a court order requiring the party preparing the administrative record to serve the requesting party with one copy of the record in paper format.

Rule 3.2206 renumbered and amended effective July 1, 2014; adopted as rule 3.1366 effective January 1, 2010.

Rule 3.2207. Electronic format

(a) Requirements

The electronic version of the administrative record lodged in the court in a proceeding brought under the California Environmental Quality Act must be:

(1) In compliance with rule 3.2205;

(2) Created in portable document format (PDF) or other format for which the software for creating and reading documents is in the public domain or generally available at a reasonable cost;

(3) Divided into a series of electronic files and include electronic bookmarks that identify each part of the record and clearly state the volume and page numbers contained in each part of the record;

(4) Contained on a CD-ROM, DVD, or other medium in a manner that cannot be altered; and

(5) Capable of full text searching.

The electronic version of the index required under rule 3.2205(b) may include hyperlinks to the indexed documents.

(Subd (a) amended effective July 1, 2014; adopted effective January 1, 2010.)

(b) Documents not included

Unless otherwise required by law, any document that is part of the administrative record and for which it is not feasible to create an electronic version may be provided in paper format only. Not feasible means that it would be reduced in size or otherwise altered to such an extent that it would not be easily readable.

(Subd (b) amended effective July 1, 2014; adopted effective January 1, 2010.)

Rule 3.2207 renumbered and amended effective July 1, 2014; adopted as rule 3.1367 effective January 1, 2010.

Rule 3.2208. Paper format

(a) Requirements

In the paper format of the administrative record lodged in the court in a proceeding brought under the California Environmental Quality Act:

(1) Both sides of each page must be used;

(2) The paper must be opaque, unglazed, white or unbleached, 8 ½ by 11 inches, and of standard quality no less than 20-pound weight, except that maps, charts, and other demonstrative materials may be larger; and

(3) Each page must be numbered consecutively at the bottom.

(Subd (a) amended effective January 1, 2014; adopted effective January 1, 2010.)

(b) Binding and cover

The paper format of the administrative record must be bound on the left margin or contained in three-ring binders. Bound volumes must contain no more than 300 pages, and binders must contain no more than 400 pages. If bound, each page must have an adequate margin to allow unimpaired readability. The cover of each volume must contain the information required in rule 2.111, be prominently entitled "ADMINISTRATIVE RECORD," and state the volume number and the page numbers included in the volume.

(Subd (b) adopted effective January 1, 2010.)

Rule 3.2208 renumbered effective July 1, 2014; adopted as rule 3.1368 effective January 1, 2010; previously amended effective January 1, 2014.

Chapter 2
California Environmental Quality Act Proceedings Involving Streamlined CEQA Projects

Title 3, Civil Rules—Division 22, Petitions Under the California Environmental Quality Act—Chapter 2, California Environmental Quality Act Proceedings Involving Streamlined CEQA Projects; amended effective March 11, 2022; adopted effective July 1, 2014; previously amended effective January 1, 2017.

Art. 1. General Provisions. Rules 3.2220–3.2231.
Art. 2. CEQA Challenges to Approval of Sacramento Arena Project. Rules 3.2235–3.2237.

Article 1
General Provisions

Title 3, Civil Rules—Division 22, Petitions Under the California Environmental Quality Act—Chapter 2, California Environmental Quality Act Proceedings Under Public Resources Code Sections 21168.6.6 and 21178–21189.3—Article 1, General Provisions; adopted effective July 1, 2014.

Rule 3.2220. Definitions and application
Rule 3.2221. Time
Rule 3.2222. Filing and service
Rule 3.2223. Petition
Rule 3.2224. Response to petition
Rule 3.2225. Administrative record
Rule 3.2226. Initial case management conference
Rule 3.2227. Briefing and Hearing
Rule 3.2228. Judgment
Rule 3.2229. Notice of settlement
Rule 3.2230. Settlement procedures and statement of issues
Rule 3.2231. Postjudgment motions

Rule 3.2220. Definitions and application

(a) Definitions

As used in this chapter:

(1) A "streamlined CEQA project" means any project within the definitions stated in (2) through (8).

(2) An "environmental leadership development project" or "leadership project" means a project certified by the Governor under Public Resources Code sections 21182–21184.

(3) The "Sacramento entertainment and sports center project" or "Sacramento arena project" means an entertainment and sports center project as defined by Public Resources Code section 21168.6.6, for which the proponent provided notice of election to proceed under that statute described in section 21168.6.6(j)(1).

(4) An "Oakland sports and mixed-use project" or "Oakland ballpark project" means a project as defined in Public Resources Code section 21168.6.7 and certified by the Governor under that section.

(5) An "Inglewood arena project" means a project as defined in Public Resources Code section 21168.6.8 and certified by the Governor under that section.

(6) An "expanded capitol building annex project" means a state capitol building annex project, annex project-related work, or state office building project as defined by Public Resources Code section 21189.50.

(7) An "Old Town Center transit and transportation facilities project" or "Old Town Center project" means a project as defined in Public Resources Code section 21189.70.

(8) An "environmental leadership transit project" means a project as defined in Public Resources Code section 21168.6.9.

(Subd (a) amended effective January 1, 2023; adopted effective July 1, 2014; previously amended effective January 1, 2017, and March 11, 2022.)

(b) Proceedings governed

The rules in this chapter govern actions or proceedings brought to attack, review, set aside, void, or annul the certification of the environmental impact report or the grant of any project approvals for a streamlined CEQA project. Except as otherwise provided in Public Resources Code sections 21168.6.6–21168.6.9, 21178–21189.3, 21189.50–21189.57, and 21189.70–21189.70.10 and these rules, the provisions of the Public Resources Code and the CEQA Guidelines adopted by the Natural Resources Agency (Cal. Code Regs., tit. 14, § 15000 et seq.) governing judicial actions or proceedings to attack, review, set aside, void, or annul acts or decisions of a public agency on the grounds of noncompliance with the California Environmental Quality Act and the rules of court generally apply in proceedings governed by this rule.

(Subd (b) amended effective January 1, 2023; adopted effective July 1, 2014; previously amended effective January 1, 2017, and March 11, 2022.)

(c) Complex case rules

Any action or proceeding governed by these rules is exempted from the rules regarding complex cases.

(Subd (c) adopted effective July 1, 2014.)

Rule 3.2220 amended effective January 1, 2023; adopted effective July 1, 2014; previously amended effective January 1, 2017, and March 11, 2022.

Rule 3.2221. Time

(a) Extensions of time

The court may order extensions of time only for good cause and in order to promote the interests of justice.

(Subd (a) adopted effective July 1, 2014.)

(b) Extensions of time by parties

If the parties stipulate to extend the time for performing any acts in actions governed by these rules, they are deemed to have agreed that the statutorily prescribed time for resolving the action may be extended by the stipulated number of days of the extension, and to that extent to have waived any objection to noncompliance with the deadlines for completing review stated in Public Resources Code sections 21168.6.6–21168.6.9, 21185, 21189.51, and 21189.70.3. Any such stipulation must be approved by the court.

(Subd (b) amended effective January 1, 2023; adopted effective July 1, 2014; previously amended effective January 1, 2017, and March 11, 2022.)

(c) Sanctions for failure to comply with rules

If a party fails to comply with any time requirements provided in these rules or ordered by the court, the court may issue an order to show cause as to why one of the following sanctions should not be imposed:

(1) Reduction of time otherwise permitted under these rules for the performance of other acts by that party;

(2) If the failure to comply is by petitioner or plaintiff, dismissal of the petition;

(3) If the failure to comply is by respondent or a real party in interest, removal of the action from the expedited procedures provided under Public Resources Code sections 21168.6.6–21168.6.9, 21185, 21189.51, and 21189.70.3, and these rules; or

(4) Any other sanction that the court finds appropriate.

(Subd (c) amended effective January 1, 2023; adopted effective July 1, 2014; previously amended effective January 1, 2017, and March 11, 2022.)

Rule 3.2221 amended effective January 1, 2023; adopted effective July 1, 2014; previously amended effective January 1, 2017, and March 11, 2022.

Rule 3.2222. Filing and service

(a) Electronic filing

All pleadings and other documents filed in actions or proceedings governed by this chapter must be filed electronically, unless the action or proceeding is in a court that does not provide for electronic filing of documents.

(Subd (a) adopted effective July 1, 2014.)

(b) Service

Other than the petition, which must be served personally, all documents that the rules in this chapter require be served on the parties must be served personally or electronically. All parties represented by counsel are deemed to have agreed to accept electronic service. All self-represented parties may agree to such service.

(Subd (b) adopted effective July 1, 2014.)

(c) Service of petition in action regarding Sacramento arena project

Service of the petition or complaint in an action governed by these rules and relating to a Sacramento arena project must be made according to the rules in article 2.

(Subd (c) adopted effective July 1, 2014.)

(d) Service of petition in action regarding streamlined CEQA project other than the Sacramento arena project

If the petition or complaint in an action governed by these rules and relating to a streamlined CEQA project other than the Sacramento arena project is not personally served on any respondent public agency, any real party in interest, and the Attorney General within three court days following filing of the petition, the time for filing petitioner's briefs on the merits provided in rule 3.2227(a) and rule 8.702(f) will be decreased by one day for every additional two court days in which service is not completed, unless otherwise ordered by the court for good cause shown.

(Subd (d) amended effective March 11, 2022; adopted effective July 1, 2014; previously amended effective January 1, 2017.)

(e) Exemption from extension of time

The extension of time provided in Code of Civil Procedure section 1010.6 for service completed by electronic means does not apply to any service in actions governed by these rules.

(Subd (e) adopted effective July 1, 2014.)

Rule 3.2222 amended effective March 11, 2022; adopted effective July 1, 2014; previously amended effective January 1, 2017.

Advisory Committee Comment

Parties should note that, while Public Resources Code section 21167 provides the statute of limitations for filing petitions under the California Environment Quality

Act, these rules provide an incentive for parties to file actions governed by these rules more quickly, in the form of extra briefing time for petitioners who file within 10 days of the issuance of a Notice of Determination. See rule 3.2227(a).

Rule 3.2223. Petition

In addition to any other applicable requirements, the petition must:

(1) On the first page, directly below the case number, indicate that the matter is a "Streamlined CEQA Project";

(2) State one of the following:

(A) The proponent of the project at issue provided notice to the lead agency that it was proceeding under Public Resources Code section 21168.6.6, 21168.6.7, 21168.6.8, or 21168.6.9 (whichever is applicable) and is subject to this rule; or

(B) The project at issue was certified by the Governor as an environmental leadership development project under Public Resources Code sections 21182–21184 and is subject to this rule; or

(C) The project at issue is an expanded capitol building annex project as defined by Public Resources Code section 21189.50 and is subject to this rule; or

(D) The project at issue is an Old Town Center project as defined by Public Resources Code section 21189.70 and is subject to this rule.

(3) If an environmental leadership development, Oakland ballpark, or Inglewood arena project, provide notice that the person or entity that applied for certification of the project as such a project must make the payments required by rule 3.2240 and, if the matter goes to the Court of Appeal, the payments required by rule 8.705;

(4) If an environmental leadership transit project, provide notice that the project applicant must make the payments required by rule 3.2240 and, if the matter goes to the Court of Appeal, the payments required by rule 8.705; and

(5) Be verified.

Rule 3.2223 amended effective January 1, 2023; adopted effective July 1, 2014; previously amended effective January 1, 2017, and March 11, 2022.

Rule 3.2224. Response to petition

(a) Responsive pleadings and motions

Respondent and any real party in interest must serve and file any answer to the petition; any motion challenging the sufficiency of the petition, including any motion to dismiss the petition; any other response to the petition; any motion to change venue; or any motion to intervene within 10 days after service of petition or complaint on that party or within the time ordered by the court. Any such answer, motion, or other response from the same party must be filed concurrently.

(Subd (a) adopted effective July 1, 2014.)

(b) Opposition

Any opposition or other response to a motion challenging the sufficiency of the petition or to change venue must be served and filed within 10 days after the motion is served.

(Subd (b) adopted effective July 1, 2014.)
Rule 3.2224 adopted effective July 1, 2014.

Rule 3.2225. Administrative record

(a) Lodging and service

Within 10 days after the petition is served on the lead public agency, that agency must lodge the certified final administrative record in electronic form with the court and serve notice on petitioner and real party in interest that the record has been lodged with the court. Within that same time, the agency must serve a copy of the administrative record in electronic form on any petitioner and real party in interest who has not already been provided a copy.

(Subd (a) adopted effective July 1, 2014.)

(b) Paper copy of record

(1) On request of the court, the lead agency shall provide the court with the record in paper format.

(2) On request and payment of the reasonable cost of preparation, or on order of the court for good cause shown, the lead agency shall provide a party with the record in paper format.

(Subd (b) adopted effective July 1, 2014.)

(c) Motions regarding the record

Unless otherwise ordered by the court:

(1) Any request to augment or otherwise change the contents of the administrative record must be made by motion served and filed no later than the filing of that party's initial brief.

(2) Any opposition or other response to the motion must be served and filed within 10 days after the motion is filed.

(3) Any motion regarding the record will be heard at the time of the hearing on the merits of the petition unless the court orders otherwise.

(Subd (c) adopted effective July 1, 2014.)
Rule 3.2225 adopted effective July 1, 2014.

Rule 3.2226. Initial case management conference

(a) Timing of conference

The court should hold an initial case management conference within 30 days of the filing of the petition or complaint.

(Subd (a) adopted effective July 1, 2014.)

(b) Notice

Petitioner must provide notice of the case management conference to respondent, real party in interest, and any responsible agency or party to the action who has been served before the case management conference, within one court day of receiving notice from the court or at time of service of the petition or complaint, whichever is later.

(Subd (b) adopted effective July 1, 2014.)

(c) Subjects for consideration

At the conference, the court should consider the following subjects:

(1) Whether all parties named in the petition or complaint have been served;

(2) Whether a list of responsible agencies has been provided, and notice provided to each;

(3) Whether all responsive pleadings have been filed, and if not, when they must be filed, and whether any hearing is required to address them;

(4) Whether severance, bifurcation, or consolidation with other actions is desirable, and if so, a relevant briefing schedule;

(5) Whether to appoint a liaison or lead counsel, and either a briefing schedule on this issue or the actual appointment of counsel;

(6) Whether the administrative record has been certified and served on all parties, whether there are any issues with it, and whether the court wants to receive a paper copy;

(7) Whether the parties anticipate any motions before the hearing on the merits concerning discovery, injunctions, or other matters, and if so, a briefing schedule for these motions;

(8) What issues the parties intend to raise in their briefs on the merits, and whether any limitation of issues to be briefed and argued is appropriate;

(9) Whether a schedule for briefs on the merits different from the schedule provided in these rules is appropriate;

(10) Whether the submission of joint briefs on the merits is appropriate, and the page limitations on all briefs, whether aggregate per side or per brief;

(11) When the hearing on the merits of the petition will be held, and the amount of time appropriate for it;

(12) The potential for settlement, and whether a schedule for settlement conferences or alternative dispute resolution should be set;

(13) Any stipulations between the parties;

(14) Whether a further case management conference should be set; and

(15) Any other matters that the court finds appropriate.

(Subd (c) adopted effective July 1, 2014.)

(d) Joint case management conference statements

At least three court days before the case management conference, petitioner and all parties that have been served with the petition must serve and file a joint case management conference statement that addresses the issues identified in (c) and any other pertinent issues.

(Subd (d) adopted effective July 1, 2014.)

(e) Preparation for the conference

At the conference, lead counsel for each party and each self-represented party must appear in person or remotely, must be familiar with the case, and must be prepared to discuss and commit to the party's position on the issues listed in (c).

(Subd (e) amended effective January 21, 2022; adopted effective July 1, 2014.)
Rule 3.2226 amended effective January 21, 2022; adopted effective July 1, 2014.

Rule 3.2227. Briefing and Hearing

(a) Briefing schedule

Unless otherwise ordered by the court:

(1) Within 5 days after filing its brief, each party must submit an electronic version of the brief that contains hyperlinks to material cited in the brief, including electronically searchable copies of the administrative record, cited decisions, and any other brief in the case filed electronically by the parties. Such briefs must comply with any local requirements of the reviewing court relating to e-briefs.

(2) The petitioner must serve and file its brief within 25 days after the case management conference, unless petitioner served and filed the petition within 10 days of the public agency's issuance of its Notice of Determination, in which case petitioner must file and serve its brief within 35 days after the case management conference.

(3) Within 25 days after the petitioner's brief is filed, the respondent public agency must—and any real party in interest may—serve and file a respondent's brief. Respondents and real parties must file a single joint brief, unless otherwise ordered by the court.

(4) Within 5 days after the respondent's brief is filed, the parties must jointly file an appendix of excerpts that contain the documents or pertinent excerpts of the documents cited in the parties' briefs.

(5) Within 10 days after the respondent's brief is filed, the petitioner may serve and file a reply brief.

(Subd (a) adopted effective July 1, 2014.)

(b) Hearing

(1) The hearing should be held within 80 days of the case management conference, extended by the number of days to which the parties have stipulated to extend the briefing schedule.

(2) If the court has, within 90 days of the filing of the petition or complaint, set a hearing date, the provision in Public Resources Code section 21167.4 that petitioner request a hearing date within 90 days is deemed to have been met, and no further request is required.

(Subd (b) adopted effective July 1, 2014.)
Rule 3.2227 adopted effective July 1, 2014.

Rule 3.2228. Judgment

The court should issue its decision and final order, writ, or judgment within 30 days of the completion of the hearing in the action. The court must include a written statement of the factual and legal basis for its decision. Code of Civil Procedure section 632 does not apply to actions governed by the rules in this division.
Rule 3.2228 adopted effective July 1, 2014.

Rule 3.2229. Notice of settlement

The petitioner or plaintiff must immediately notify the court if the case is settled.
Rule 3.2229 adopted effective July 1, 2014.

Rule 3.2230. Settlement procedures and statement of issues

In cases governed by the rules in this chapter, unless otherwise ordered by the court, the procedures described in Public Resources Code section 21167.8, including the filing of a statement of issues, are deemed to have been met by the parties addressing the potential for settlement and narrowing of issues within the case management conference statement and discussing those points as part of the case management conference.
Rule 3.2230 adopted effective July 1, 2014.

Rule 3.2231. Postjudgment motions

(a) Exemption from statutory provisions

In any actions governed by the rules in this article, any postjudgment motion except for a motion for attorney's fees and costs is governed by this rule. Such motions are exempt from the timing requirements otherwise applicable to postjudgment motions under Code of Civil Procedure section 1005. Motions in Sacramento arena project cases are also exempt from the timing and procedural requirements of Code of Civil Procedure sections 659 and 663.

(Subd (a) adopted effective July 1, 2014.)

(b) Time for postjudgment motions

(1) *Time for motions under Code of Civil Procedure section 473*

Moving party must serve and file any motion before the earlier of:

(A) Five days after the court clerk mails to the moving party a document entitled "Notice of Entry" of judgment or a file-stamped copy of the judgment, showing the date either was served; or

(B) Five days after the moving party is served by any party with a written notice of judgment or a file-stamped copy of the judgment, accompanied by a proof of service.

(2) *Time for motions for new trial or motions to vacate judgment*

Moving party in Sacramento arena project cases must serve and file motion before the earlier of:

(A) Five days after the court clerk mails to the moving party a document entitled "Notice of Entry" of judgment or a file-stamped copy of the judgment, showing the date either was served; or

(B) Five days after the moving party is served by any party with a written notice of judgment or a file-stamped copy of the judgment, accompanied by a proof of service.

(Subd (b) adopted effective July 1, 2014.)

(c) Memorandum

A memorandum in support of a postjudgment motion may be no longer than 15 pages.

(Subd (c) adopted effective July 1, 2014.)

(d) Opposition to motion

Any opposition to the motion must be served and filed within five days of service of the moving papers and may be no longer than 15 pages.

(Subd (d) adopted effective July 1, 2014.)

(e) Reply

Any reply brief must be served and filed within two court days of service of the opposition papers and may be no longer than 5 pages.

(Subd (e) adopted effective July 1, 2014.)

(f) Hearing and decision

The court may set a hearing on the motion at its discretion. The court should issue its decision on the motion within 15 days of the filing of the motion.

(Subd (f) adopted effective July 1, 2014.)
Rule 3.2231 adopted effective July 1, 2014.

Article 2
CEQA Challenges to Approval of Sacramento Arena Project

Title 3, Civil Rules—Division 22, Petitions Under the California Environmental Quality Act—Chapter 2, California Environmental Quality Act Proceedings Under Public Resources Code Sections 21168.6.6 and 21178–21189.3—Article 2, CEQA Challenges to Approval of Sacramento Arena Project; adopted effective July 1, 2014.

Rule 3.2235. Application
Rule 3.2236. Service of Petition
Rule 3.2237. List of responsible parties

Rule 3.2235. Application

This article governs any action or proceeding brought to attack, review, set aside, void, or annul the certification of the environmental impact report or any project approvals for the Sacramento arena project.
Rule 3.2235 adopted effective July 1, 2014.

Rule 3.2236. Service of Petition

(a) Respondent

Unless the respondent public agency has agreed to accept service of summons electronically, the petitioner or plaintiff must personally serve the petition or complaint on the respondent public agency within three court days after the date of filing.

(Subd (a) adopted effective July 1, 2014.)

(b) Real parties in interest

The petitioner or plaintiff must serve the petition or complaint on any real party in interest named in the pleading within three court days after the date of filing.

(Subd (b) adopted effective July 1, 2014.)

(c) Attorney General

The petitioner or plaintiff must serve the petition or complaint on the Attorney General within three court days after the date of filing.

(Subd (c) adopted effective July 1, 2014.)

(d) Responsible agencies

The petitioner or plaintiff must serve the petition or complaint on any responsible agencies or public agencies with jurisdiction over a natural resource affected by the project within two court days of receipt of a list of such agencies from respondent public agency.

(Subd (d) adopted effective July 1, 2014.)

(e) Proof of service

The petitioner or plaintiff must file proof of service on each respondent, real party in interest, or agency within one court day of completion of service.

(Subd (e) adopted effective July 1, 2014.)
Rule 3.2236 adopted effective July 1, 2014.

Rule 3.2237. List of responsible parties

Respondent public agency must provide the petitioner or plaintiff, not later than three court days following service of the petition or complaint on the public agency, with a list of responsible agencies and any public agency having jurisdiction over a natural resource affected by the project.
Rule 3.2237 adopted effective July 1, 2014.

Article 3
Trial Court Costs

Title 3, Civil Rules—Division 22, Petitions Under the California Environmental Quality Act—Chapter 2, California Environmental Quality Act Proceedings Under

Public Resources Code Sections 21168.6.6 and 21178–21189.3—Article 3, Trial Court Costs; adopted effective January 1, 2023.

Rule 3.2240. Trial court costs in certain streamlined CEQA projects

In fulfillment of the provisions in Public Resources Code sections 21168.6.7, 21168.6.8, 21168.6.9, and 21183 regarding payment of trial court costs with respect to cases concerning environmental leadership development, environmental leadership transit, Oakland ballpark, and Inglewood arena projects:

(1) Within 10 days after service of the petition or complaint in a case concerning an environmental leadership development project, the person or entity that applied for certification of the project as an environmental leadership development project must pay a fee of $180,000 to the court.

(2) Within 10 days after service of the petition or complaint in a case concerning an environmental leadership transit project, the project applicant must pay a fee of $180,000 to the court.

(3) Within 10 days after service of the petition or complaint in a case concerning an Oakland ballpark project or an Inglewood arena project, the person or entity that applied for certification of the project as a streamlined CEQA project must pay a fee of $120,000 to the court.

(4) If the court incurs the costs of any special master appointed by the court in the case or of any contract personnel retained by the court to work on the case, the person or entity that applied for certification of the project or the project applicant must also pay, within 10 days of being ordered by the court, those incurred or estimated costs.

(5) If the party fails to timely pay the fee or costs specified in this rule, the court may impose sanctions that the court finds appropriate after notifying the party and providing the party with an opportunity to pay the required fee or costs.

(6) Any fee or cost paid under this rule is not recoverable.

Rule 3.2240 amended effective January 1, 2023; adopted effective March 11, 2022.

Division 23
Miscellaneous

Title 3, Civil Rules—Division 23, Miscellaneous; adopted effective January 20, 2017.

Rule 3.2300. Review under Penal Code section 186.35 of law enforcement agency denial of request to remove name from shared gang database

(a) Proceedings governed

This rule applies to proceedings under Penal Code section 186.35 to seek review of a local law enforcement agency's denial of a request under Penal Code section 186.34 to remove a person's name from a shared gang database.

(Subd (a) adopted effective January 20, 2017.)

(b) Definitions

For purposes of this rule:

(1) "Request for review" or "petition" means a "notice of appeal" under Penal Code section 186.35 requesting review of a law enforcement agency's decision denying a person's request under Penal Code section 186.34 to remove a person's name from a shared gang database.

(2) "Law enforcement agency" means the local law enforcement agency that denied the request under Penal Code section 186.34 to remove a person's name from a shared gang database.

(Subd (b) adopted effective January 20, 2017.)

(c) Designated judge

The presiding judge of each superior court must designate one or more judges to handle any petitions governed by this rule that are filed in the court.

(Subd (c) adopted effective January 20, 2017.)

(d) Petition

(1) *Form*

(A) Except as provided in (i) and (ii), *Petition for Review of Denial of Request to Remove Name From Gang Database* (form MC-1000) must be used to seek review under Penal Code section 186.35 of a law enforcement agency's decision denying a request to remove a person's name from a shared gang database.

(i) A petition filed by an attorney need not be on form MC-1000. For good cause the court may also accept a petition from a nonattorney that is not on form MC-1000.

(ii) Any petition that is not on form MC-1000 must contain the information specified in form MC-1000 and must bear the name "Petition for Review of Denial of Request to Remove Name From Gang Database."

(B) The person seeking review must attach to the petition under (A) either:

(i) The law enforcement agency's written verification, if one was received, of its decision denying the person's request under Penal Code section 186.34 to remove his or her name—or, if the request was filed by a parent or guardian on behalf of a child under 18, the name of the child—from the shared gang database; or

(ii) If the law enforcement agency did not provide written verification responding to the person's request under Penal Code section 186.34 within 30 days of submission of the request, a copy of the request and written documentation submitted to the law enforcement agency contesting the designation.

(2) *Time for filing*

The petition must be filed within 90 calendar days of the date the law enforcement agency mails or personally serves the person filing the petition with written verification of the agency's decision denying that person's request under Penal Code section 186.34 to remove the name from the shared gang database.

(3) *Where to file*

The petition must be filed in either the superior court of the county in which the law enforcement agency is located or, if the person filing the petition resides in California, in the superior court of the county in which that person resides.

(4) *Fee*

The fee for filing the petition is $25, as specified in Government Code section 70615.

(5) *Service*

A copy of the petition with the attachment required under (1)(B) must be served either personally or by mail on the law enforcement agency, as provided in Code of Civil Procedure sections 1011–1013a. Proof of this service must be filed in the superior court with the petition.

(Subd (d) amended effective January 1, 2019; adopted effective January 20, 2017.)

(e) Record

(1) *Filing*

(A) The law enforcement agency must serve the record on the person filing the petition and must file the record in the superior court in which the petition was filed.

(B) The record must be served and filed within 15 days after the date the petition is served on the law enforcement agency as required by subdivision (d)(5) of this rule.

(C) If the record contains any documents that are part of a juvenile case file or are confidential under Welfare and Institutions Code section 827 or have been sealed, the law enforcement agency must include a coversheet that states "Confidential Filing – Juvenile Case File Enclosed."

(D) The procedures set out in rules 2.550 and 2.551 apply to any record sought to be filed under seal in a proceeding under this rule.

(2) *Contents*

The record is limited to the documents required by Penal Code section 186.35(c).

(3) *Format*

(A) The cover or first page of the record must:

(i) Clearly identify it as the record in the case;

(ii) Clearly indicate if the record includes any documents that are confidential under Welfare and Institutions Code section 827 or have been sealed;

(iii) State the title and court number of the case; and

(iv) Include the name, mailing address, telephone number, fax number (if available), e-mail address (if available), and California State Bar number (if applicable) of the attorney or other person filing the record on behalf of the law enforcement agency. The court will use this as the name, mailing address, telephone number, fax number, and e-mail address of record for the agency unless the agency informs the court otherwise in writing.

(B) All documents in the record must have a page size of 8.5 by 11 inches;

(C) The text must be reproduced as legibly as printed matter;

(D) The contents must be arranged chronologically;

(E) The pages must be consecutively numbered; and

(F) The record must be stapled and two-hole punched at the top of the page.

(4) *Failure to file the record*

If the law enforcement agency does not timely file the required record, the superior court clerk must serve the law enforcement agency with a notice indicating that the agency must file the record within five court days of service of the clerk's notice or the court may order the law enforcement agency to remove the name of the person from the shared gang database.

(Subd (e) amended effective January 1, 2019; adopted effective January 20, 2017.)

(f) Written argument

(1) *Contents*

(A) The person filing the petition may include in the petition or separately serve and file a written argument about why, based on the record specified in Penal Code section 186.35(c), the law enforcement agency has failed to establish by clear and convincing evidence the active gang membership, associate status, or affiliate status of the person so designated or to be so designated by the law enforcement agency in the shared gang database.

(B) The law enforcement agency may serve and file a written argument about why, based on the record specified in Penal Code section 186.35(c), it has established by clear and convincing evidence the active gang membership, associate status, or affiliate status of the person.

(C) If an argument refers to something in the record, it must provide the page number of the record where that thing appears or, if the record has not yet been filed, the page number of the relevant document.

(D) Except for any required attachment to a petition, when an argument is included in the petition, nothing may be attached to an argument and an argument must not refer to any evidence that is not in the record.

(2) *Time to serve and file*

Any written argument must be served and filed within 15 days after the date the record is served.

(3) *Format and length of argument*

(A) The cover or first page of any argument must:

(i) Clearly identify it as the argument of the person filing the petition or of the law enforcement agency;

(ii) State the title and, if assigned, court number of the case; and

(iii) Include the name, mailing address, telephone number, fax number (if available), e-mail address (if available), and California State Bar number (if applicable) of the attorney or other person filing the argument.

(B) An argument must not exceed 10 pages.

(C) The pages must be consecutively numbered.

(Subd (f) amended effective January 1, 2019; adopted effective January 20, 2017.)

(g) Oral argument

(1) *Setting oral argument*

The court may set the case for oral argument at the request of either party or on its own motion.

(2) *Requesting or waiving oral argument*

The person filing the petition or the law enforcement agency may request oral argument or inform the court that they do not want to participate in oral argument. Any such request for or waiver of oral argument must be served and filed within 15 days after the date the record is served.

(3) *Sending notice of oral argument*

If oral argument is set, the clerk must send notice at least 20 days before the oral argument date. The court may shorten the notice period for good cause; in that event, the clerk must immediately notify the parties by telephone or other expeditious method.

(4) *Sealed or confidential records*

If the responding party indicates that the record contains information from a juvenile case file or documents that are sealed or confidential under Welfare and Institutions Code section 827, the argument must be closed to the public unless the crime charged allows for public access under Welfare and Institutions Code section 676.

(Subd (g) adopted effective January 20, 2017.)

(h) Decision

As provided in Penal Code section 186.35, if, on de novo review and any arguments presented to the court, the court finds that the law enforcement agency has failed to establish by clear and convincing evidence the active gang membership, associate status, or affiliate status of the person so designated in the shared gang database, the court must order the law enforcement agency to remove the name of the person from the shared gang database.

(Subd (h) adopted effective January 20, 2017.)

(i) Service on the Attorney General

The court must serve on the Attorney General a copy of any order under (e)(4) or (h) to remove a name from a shared gang database.

(Subd (i) adopted effective January 20, 2017.)

Rule 3.2300 amended effective January 1, 2019; adopted effective January 20, 2017.

Advisory Committee Comment

Subdivision (d)(1)(B). Penal Code section 186.34(f) provides that if a person to be designated as a suspected gang member, associate, or affiliate, or his or her parent or guardian, submits written documentation to the local law enforcement agency contesting the designation, the local law enforcement agency "shall provide the person and his or her parent or guardian with written verification of the agency's decision within 30 days of submission of the written documentation contesting the designation. If the law enforcement agency denies the request for removal, the notice of its determination shall state the reason for the denial."

Subdivision (e)(2). Penal Code section 186.35(b) provides that the evidentiary record for this review proceeding "shall be limited to the agency's statement of basis of its designation made pursuant to subdivision (e) of Section 186.34, and the documentation provided to the agency by the appellant pursuant to subdivision (f) of Section 186.34."

Penal Code section 186.34(e)(1) provides that "[a] person, or, if the person is under 18 years of age, his or her parent or guardian, or an attorney working on behalf of the person may request information of any law enforcement agency as to whether the person is designated as a suspected gang member, associate, or affiliate in a shared gang database" and, if the person is so designated, "information as to the basis for the designation for the purpose of contesting the designation as described in subdivision (f)." Section 186.35(e)(2) provides that "[t]he law enforcement agency shall provide information requested under paragraph (1), unless doing so would compromise an active criminal investigation or compromise the health or safety of the person if the person is under 18 years of age."

Penal Code section 186.34(f) provides that "the person to be designated as a suspected gang member, associate, or affiliate, or his or her parent or guardian, may submit written documentation to the local law enforcement agency contesting the designation."

Penal Code section 186.34(g) also provides that "[n]othing in this section shall require a local law enforcement agency to disclose any information protected under Section 1040 or 1041 of the Evidence Code or Section 6254 of the Government Code."

TITLE 4
Criminal Rules

Division 1. General Provisions. Rules 4.1–4.3.
Division 2. Pretrial. Rules 4.100–4.155.
Division 3. Trials. Rules 4.200–4.230.
Division 4. Sentencing. Rules 4.305–4.336.
Division 5. Felony Sentencing Law. Rules 4.401–4.480.
Division 6. Postconviction, Postrelease, and Writs. Rules 4.510–4.577.
Division 7. Miscellaneous. Rules 4.601, 4.700.

Division 1
General Provisions

Rule 4.1. Title
Rule 4.2. Application
Rule 4.3. Reference to Penal Code

Rule 4.1. Title

The rules in this title may be referred to as the Criminal Rules.

Rule 4.1 adopted effective January 1, 2007.

Rule 4.2. Application

The Criminal Rules apply to all criminal cases in the superior courts unless otherwise provided by a statute or rule in the California Rules of Court.

Rule 4.2 adopted effective January 1, 2007.

Rule 4.3. Reference to Penal Code

All statutory references are to the Penal Code unless stated otherwise.

Rule 4.3 adopted effective January 1, 2007.

Division 2
Pretrial

Chap. 1. Pretrial Proceedings. Rules 4.100–4.131.
Chap. 2. Change of Venue. Rules 4.150–4.155.

Chapter 1
Pretrial Proceedings

Rule 4.100. Arraignments
Rule 4.101. Bail in criminal cases
Rule 4.102. Uniform bail and penalty schedules—traffic, boating, fish and game, forestry, public utilities, parks and recreation, business licensing
Rule 4.103. Notice to appear forms
Rule 4.104. Procedures and eligibility criteria for attending traffic violator school
Rule 4.105. Appearance without deposit of bail in infraction cases
Rule 4.106. Failure to appear or failure to pay for a *Notice to Appear* issued for an infraction offense
Rule 4.107. Mandatory reminder notice—traffic procedures
Rule 4.108. Installment Payment Agreements
Rule 4.110. Time limits for criminal proceedings on information or indictment
Rule 4.111. Pretrial motions in criminal cases
Rule 4.112. Readiness conference
Rule 4.113. Motions and grounds for continuance of criminal case set for trial
Rule 4.114. Certification under Penal Code section 859a
Rule 4.115. Criminal case assignment
Rule 4.116. Certification to juvenile court
Rule 4.117. Qualifications for appointed trial counsel in capital cases
Rule 4.119. Additional requirements in pretrial proceedings in capital cases
Rule 4.130. Mental competency proceedings
Rule 4.131. Probable cause determinations under section 1368.1(a)(2)

Rule 4.100. Arraignments

At the arraignment on the information or indictment, unless otherwise ordered for good cause, and on a plea of not guilty, including a plea of not guilty by reason of insanity;

(1) The court must set dates for:

(A) Trial, giving priority to a case entitled to it under law; and

(B) Filing and service of motions and responses and hearing thereon;

(2) A plea of not guilty must be entered if a defendant represented by counsel fails to plead or demur; and

(3) An attorney may not appear specially.

Rule 4.100 amended effective January 1, 2007; adopted as rule 227.4 effective January 1, 1985; previously amended effective June 6, 1990; previously renumbered and amended effective January 1, 2001.

Advisory Committee Comment

Cross reference: Penal Code section 987.1.

Rule 4.101. Bail in criminal cases

The fact that a defendant in a criminal case has or has not asked for a jury trial must not be taken into consideration in fixing the amount of bail and, once set, bail may not be increased or reduced by reason of such fact.

Rule 4.101 amended effective January 1, 2007; adopted as rule 801 effective July 1, 1964; previously renumbered effective January 1, 2001.

Rule 4.102. Uniform bail and penalty schedules—traffic, boating, fish and game, forestry, public utilities, parks and recreation, business licensing

The Judicial Council of California has established the policy of promulgating uniform bail and penalty schedules for certain offenses in order to achieve a standard of uniformity in the handling of these offenses.

In general, bail is used to ensure the presence of the defendant before the court. Under Vehicle Code sections 40512 and 13103, bail may also be forfeited and forfeiture may be ordered without the necessity of any further court proceedings and be treated as a conviction for specified Vehicle Code offenses. A penalty in the form of a monetary sum is a fine imposed as all or a portion of a sentence imposed.

To achieve substantial uniformity of bail and penalties throughout the state in traffic, boating, fish and game, forestry, public utilities, parks and recreation, and business licensing cases, the trial court judges, in performing their duty under Penal Code section 1269b to annually revise and adopt a schedule of bail and penalties for all misdemeanor and infraction offenses except Vehicle Code infractions, must give consideration to the Uniform Bail and Penalty Schedules approved by the Judicial Council. The Uniform Bail and Penalty Schedule for infraction violations of the Vehicle Code will be established by the Judicial Council in accordance with Vehicle Code section 40310. Judges must give consideration to requiring additional bail for aggravating or enhancing factors.

After a court adopts a countywide bail and penalty schedule, under Penal Code section 1269b, the court must, as soon as practicable, mail or e-mail a copy of the schedule to the Judicial Council with a report stating how the revised schedule differs from the council's uniform traffic bail and penalty schedule, uniform boating bail and penalty schedule, uniform fish and game bail and penalty schedule, uniform forestry bail and penalty schedule, uniform public utilities bail and penalty schedule, uniform parks and recreation bail and penalty schedule, or uniform business licensing bail and penalty schedule.

The purpose of this uniform bail and penalty schedule is to:

(1) Show the standard amount for bail, which for Vehicle Code offenses may also be the amount used for a bail forfeiture instead of further proceedings; and

(2) Serve as a guideline for the imposition of a fine as all or a portion of the penalty for a first conviction of a listed offense where a fine is used as all or a portion of the penalty for such offense. The amounts shown for the misdemeanors on the boating, fish and game, forestry, public utilities, parks and recreation, and business licensing bail and penalty schedules have been set with this dual purpose in mind.

Unless otherwise shown, the maximum penalties for the listed offenses are six months in the county jail or a fine of $1,000, or both. The penalty amounts are intended to be used to provide standard fine amounts for a first offense conviction of a violation shown where a fine is used as all or a portion of the sentence imposed.

Note:

Courts may obtain copies of the Uniform Bail and Penalty Schedules by contacting:

Criminal Justice Services

Judicial Council of California
455 Golden Gate Avenue
San Francisco, CA 94102-3688
or
www.courts.ca.gov/7532.htm

Rule 4.102 amended effective January 1, 2018; adopted as rule 850 effective January 1, 1965; previously renumbered as rule 4.102 and amended effective January 1, 2001; previously amended effective January 1, 1970, January 1, 1971, July 1, 1972, January 1, 1973, January 1, 1974, July 1, 1975, July 1, 1979, July 1, 1980, July 1, 1981, January 1, 1983, July 1, 1984, July 1, 1986, January 1, 1989, January 1, 1990, January 1, 1993, January 1, 1995, January 1, 1997, July 1, 2004, January 1, 2007, July 1, 2013, and January 1, 2016.

Rule 4.103. Notice to appear forms

(a) Traffic offenses

A printed or electronic notice to appear that is issued for any violation of the Vehicle Code other than a felony or for a violation of an ordinance of a city or county relating to traffic offenses must be prepared and filed with the court on *Automated Traffic Enforcement System Notice to Appear* (form TR-115) [1] **or** *Traffic/Nontraffic Notice to Appear* (form TR-130), [2] must comply with the requirements in the current version of the Judicial Council's instructions, *Notice to Appear and Related Forms* (form TR-INST).

(Subd (a) amended effective January 1, 2024; previously amended effective January 1, 2007, and June 26, 2015.)

Rule 4.103(a) 2024 Deletes. [1] , [2] *Electronic Traffic/Nontraffic Notice to Appear* (4-inch format) (form TR-135), or *Electronic Traffic/Nontraffic Notice to Appear* (3-inch format) (form TR-145), and

(b) Nontraffic offenses

A notice to appear issued for a nontraffic infraction or misdemeanor offense that is prepared on *Nontraffic Notice to Appear* (form TR-120) [1] **or** *Traffic/Nontraffic Notice to Appear* (form TR-130), [2] and that complies with the requirements in the current version of the Judicial Council's instructions, *Notice to Appear and Related Forms* (form TR-INST), may be filed with the court and serve as a complaint as provided in Penal Code section 853.9 or 959.1.

(Subd (b) amended effective January 1, 2024; previously amended effective January 1, 2007, and June 26, 2015.)

Rule 4.103(b) 2024 Deletes. [1] , [2] *Electronic Traffic/Nontraffic Notice to Appear* (4-inch format) (form TR-135), or *Electronic Traffic/Nontraffic Notice to Appear* (3-inch format) (form TR-145),

(c) Corrections

Corrections to citations previously issued on *Continuation of Notice to Appear* (form TR-106), *Continuation of Citation* (form TR-108), *Automated Traffic Enforcement System Notice to Appear* (form TR-115), *Nontraffic Notice to Appear* (form TR-120) [1] **or** *Traffic/Nontraffic Notice to Appear* (form TR-130) [2] must be made on a *Notice of Correction and Proof of Service* (form TR-100).

(Subd (c) amended effective January 1, 2024; previously amended effective January 1, 2007, and June 26, 2015.)

Rule 4.103(c) 2024 Deletes. [1] , [2] , *Electronic Traffic/Nontraffic Notice to Appear* (4-inch format) (form TR-135), or *Electronic Traffic/Nontraffic Notice to Appear* (3-inch format) (form TR-145)

(d) Electronic citation forms

A law enforcement agency that uses an electronic citation device to issue notice to appear citations on the Judicial Council's [1] *Traffic/Nontraffic Notice to Appear* (form TR-130) must submit to the Judicial Council an exact printed copy of the agency's current citation form that complies with the requirements in the most recent version of the Judicial Council's instructions, *Notice to Appear and Related Forms* (form TR-INST).

(Subd (d) amended effective January 1, 2024.)

Rule 4.103(d) 2024 Deletes. [1] *Electronic Traffic/Nontraffic Notice to Appear* (4-inch format) (form TR-135) or *Electronic Traffic/Nontraffic Notice to Appear* (3-inch format) (form TR-145)

Rule 4.103 amended effective January 1, 2024; adopted effective January 1, 2004; previously amended effective January 1, 2007, and June 26, 2015.

Rule 4.104. Procedures and eligibility criteria for attending traffic violator school

(a) Purpose

The purpose of this rule is to establish uniform statewide procedures and criteria for eligibility to attend traffic violator school.

(Subd (a) amended effective January 1, 2003; previously amended effective July 1, 2001.)

(b) Authority of a court clerk to grant a request to attend traffic violator school

(1) *Eligible offenses*

Except as provided in (2), a court clerk is authorized to grant a request to attend traffic violator school when a defendant with a valid driver's license requests to attend an 8-hour traffic violator school under Vehicle Code sections 41501(a) and 42005 for any infraction under divisions 11 and 12 (rules of the road and equipment violations) of the Vehicle Code if the violation is reportable to the Department of Motor Vehicles.

(2) *Ineligible offenses*

A court clerk is not authorized to grant a request to attend traffic violator school for a misdemeanor or any of the following infractions:

(A) A violation that carries a negligent operator point count of more than one point under Vehicle Code section 12810 or one and one-half points or more under Vehicle Code section 12810.5(b)(2);

(B) A violation that occurs within 18 months after the date of a previous violation and the defendant either attended or elected to attend a traffic violator school for the previous violation (Veh. Code, §§ 1808.7 and 1808.10);

(C) A violation of Vehicle Code section 22406.5 (tank vehicles);

(D) A violation related to alcohol use or possession or drug use or possession;

(E) A violation on which the defendant failed to appear under Vehicle Code section 40508(a) unless the failure-to-appear charge has been adjudicated and any fine imposed has been paid;

(F) A violation on which the defendant has failed to appear under Penal Code section 1214.1 unless the civil monetary assessment has been paid;

(G) A speeding violation in which the speed alleged is more than 25 miles over a speed limit as stated in Chapter 7 (commencing with section 22348) of Division 11 of the Vehicle Code; and

(H) A violation that occurs in a commercial vehicle as defined in Vehicle Code section 15210(b).

(Subd (b) amended effective January 1, 2013; previously amended effective January 1, 2003, September 20, 2005, January 1, 2007, January 1, 2007, and July 1, 2011.)

(c) Judicial discretion

(1) A judicial officer may in his or her discretion order attendance at a traffic violator school in an individual case as permitted under Vehicle Code section 41501(a) or 42005 or for any other purpose permitted by law. A defendant having a class A, class B, or commercial class C driver's license may request to attend traffic violator school if the defendant was operating a vehicle requiring only a noncommercial class C or class M license. The record of conviction after completion of traffic violator school by a driver who holds a class A, class B, or commercial class C license must not be reported as confidential. A defendant charged with a violation that occurs in a commercial vehicle, as defined in Vehicle Code section 15210(b), is not eligible to attend traffic violator school under Vehicle Code sections 41501 or 42005 in lieu of adjudicating an offense, to receive a confidential conviction, or to avoid violator point counts.

(2) A defendant who is otherwise eligible for traffic violator school is not made ineligible by entering a plea other than guilty or by exercising his or her right to trial. A traffic violator school request must be considered based on the individual circumstances of the specific case. The court is not required to state on the record a reason for granting or denying a traffic violator school request.

(Subd (c) amended effective January 1, 2013; amended and relettered as part of subd (b) effective January 1, 2003; previously amended effective January 1, 1998, September 20, 2005, January 1, 2007, January 1, 2007, and July 1, 2011.)

Rule 4.104 amended effective January 1, 2013; adopted as rule 851 effective January 1, 1997; previously amended effective January 1, 1998, July 1, 2001, January 1, 2003, September 20, 2005, January 1, 2007, and July 1, 2011; previously amended and renumbered effective January 1, 2007.

Advisory Committee Comment

Subdivision (c)(1). Rule 4.104(c)(1) reflects that under Vehicle Code sections 1808.10, 41501, and 42005, the record of a driver with a class A, class B, or commercial class C license who completes a traffic violator school program is not confidential and must be reported to and disclosed by the Department of Motor Vehicles for purposes of Title 49 of the Federal Code of Regulations and to insurers for underwriting and rating purposes.

Subdivision (c)(2). Rule 4.104(c)(2) reflects court rulings in cases where defendants wished to plead not guilty and have the court order attendance of traffic violator school if found guilty after trial. A court has discretion to grant or not grant traffic violator school. (*People v. Schindler* (1993) 20 Cal.App.4th 431, 433; *People* *v. Levinson* (1984) 155 Cal.App.3d Supp. 13, 21.) However, the court may not arbitrarily refuse to consider a request for traffic violator school because a defendant pleads not guilty. (*Schindler, supra*, at p. 433; *People v. Wozniak* (1987) 197 Cal.App.3d Supp. 43, 44; *People v. Enochs* (1976) 62 Cal.App.3d Supp. 42, 44.) If a judicial officer believes that a defendant's circumstances indicate that a defendant would benefit from attending school, such attendance should be authorized and should not be affected by the order in which the plea, explanation, and request for traffic violator school are presented. (*Enochs, supra*, at p. 44.) A court is not required to state its reasons for granting or denying traffic violator school following a defendant's conviction for a traffic violation. (*Schindler, supra*, at p. 433.)

Rule 4.105. Appearance without deposit of bail in infraction cases

(a) Application

This rule applies to any infraction for which the defendant has received a written notice to appear.

(Subd (a) amended effective December 1, 2015; adopted effective June 8, 2015.)

(b) Appearance without deposit of bail

Except as provided in (c), courts must allow a defendant to appear for arraignment and trial without deposit of bail.

(Subd (b) adopted effective June 8, 2015.)

(c) Deposit of bail

(1) Courts must require the deposit of bail when the defendant elects a statutory procedure that requires the deposit of bail.

(2) Courts may require the deposit of bail when the defendant does not sign a written promise to appear as required by the court.

(3) Courts may require a deposit of bail before trial if the court determines that the defendant is unlikely to appear as ordered without a deposit of bail and the court expressly states the reasons for the finding.

(4) In determining the amount of bail set under (2) and (3), courts must consider the totality of the circumstances.

(Subd (c) amended effective January 1, 2017; adopted effective June 8, 2015; previously amended effective December 1, 2015.)

(d) Notice

Courts must inform defendants of the option to appear in court without the deposit of bail in any instructions or other materials courts provide for the public that relate to bail for infractions, including any website information, written instructions, courtesy notices, and forms.

(Subd (d) amended effective December 1, 2015; adopted effective June 8, 2015.)

(e) Local Website Information

The website for each trial court must include a link to the traffic self-help information posted at: *http://www.courts.ca.gov/selfhelp-traffic.htm*.

(Subd (e) adopted effective January 1, 2017.)

Rule 4.105 amended effective January 1, 2017; adopted effective June 8, 2015; previously amended effective December 1, 2015.

Advisory Committee Comment

Subdivision (a). The rule is intended to apply only to an infraction violation for which the defendant has received a written notice to appear and has appeared by the appearance date or an approved extension of that date. The rule does not apply to postconviction matters or cases in which the defendant seeks an appearance in court after a failure to appear or pay.

Subdivision (c). This subdivision takes into account the distinct statutory purposes and functions that bail and related considerations serve in infraction cases, including, for example, the posting and forfeiting of bail in uncontested cases and the use of bail to satisfy later judgments, as distinguished from felony and most misdemeanor cases.

Subdivision (c)(1). Various statutory provisions authorize infraction defendants who have received a written notice to appear to elect to deposit bail in lieu of appearing in court or in advance of the notice to appear date. (See, e.g., Veh. Code, §§ 40510 [authorizing defendants to deposit bail before the notice to appear date]; 40519(a) [authorizing defendants who have received a written notice to appear to declare the intention to plead not guilty and deposit bail before the notice to appear date for purposes of electing to schedule an arraignment and trial on the same date or on separate dates]; 40519(b) [authorizing defendants who have received a written notice to appear to deposit bail and plead not guilty in writing in lieu of appearing in person]; and 40902 [authorizing trial by written declaration].)

This rule is not intended to modify or contravene any statutorily authorized alternatives to appearing in court. (See, e.g., Pen. Code, §§ 853.5, 853.6; Veh. Code, §§ 40510, 40512, and 40512.5 [authorizing defendants to post and forfeit bail in lieu of appearing for arraignment].) The purpose of this rule is to clarify that if the defendant declines to use a statutorily authorized alternative, courts must allow the defendant to appear *without* prior deposit of bail as provided above.

Subdivision (c)(2). As used in this subdivision, the phrase "written promise to appear as required by the court" refers to a signed promise, made by a defendant who has appeared in court, to return to court on a future date and time as ordered by the court.

Subdivision (c)(3). In exercising discretion to require deposit of bail on a particular case, courts should consider, among other factors, whether previous failures to pay or appear were willful or involved adequate notice.

Subdivision (c)(4). In considering the "totality of the circumstances" under this subdivision, courts may consider whether the bail amount would impose an undue hardship on the defendant.

Rule 4.106. Failure to appear or failure to pay for a *Notice to Appear* issued for an infraction offense

(a) Application

This rule applies to infraction offenses for which the defendant has received a written notice to appear and has failed to appear or failed to pay.

(Subd (a) adopted effective January 1, 2017.)

(b) Definitions

As used in this rule, "failure to appear" and "failure to pay" mean failure to appear and failure to pay as defined in section 1214.1(a).

(Subd (b) adopted effective January 1, 2017.)

(c) Procedure for consideration of good cause for failure to appear or pay

(1) A notice of a civil assessment under section 1214.1(b) must inform the defendant of his or her right to petition that the civil assessment be vacated for good cause and must include information about the process for vacating or reducing the assessment.

(2) When a notice of civil assessment is given, a defendant may, within the time specified in the notice, move by written petition to vacate or reduce the assessment.

(3) When a court imposes a civil assessment for failure to appear or pay, the defendant may petition that the court vacate or reduce the civil assessment without paying any bail, fines, penalties, fees, or assessments.

(4) A petition to vacate an assessment does not stay the operation of any order requiring the payment of bail, fines, penalties, fees, or assessment unless specifically ordered by the court.

(5) The court must vacate the assessment upon a showing of good cause under section 1214.1(b)(1) for failure to appear or failure to pay.

(6) If the defendant does not establish good cause, the court may still exercise its discretion under section 1214.1(a) to reconsider:

(A) Whether a civil assessment should be imposed; and

(B) If so, the amount of the assessment.

(7) In exercising its discretion, the court may consider such factors as a defendant's due diligence in appearing or paying after notice of the assessment has been given under section 1214.1(b)(1) and the defendant's financial circumstances.

(Subd (c) adopted effective January 1, 2017.)

(d) Procedure for unpaid bail referred to collection as delinquent debt in unadjudicated cases

(1) When a case has not been adjudicated and a court refers it to a comprehensive collection program as provided in section 1463.007(b)(1) as delinquent debt, the defendant may schedule a hearing for adjudication of the underlying charge(s) without payment of the bail amount.

(2) The defendant may request an appearance date to adjudicate the underlying charges by written petition or alternative method provided by the court. Alternatively, the defendant may request or the court may direct a court appearance.

(3) A court may require a deposit of bail before adjudication of the underlying charges if the court finds that the defendant is unlikely to appear as ordered without a deposit of bail and the court expressly states the reasons for the finding. The court must not require payment of the civil assessment before adjudication.

(Subd (d) adopted effective January 1, 2017.)

(e) Procedure for failure to pay or make a payment under an installment payment plan

(1) When a defendant fails to pay a fine or make a payment under an installment plan as provided in section 1205 or Vehicle Code sections 40510.5, 42003, or 42007, the court must permit the defendant to appear by written petition to modify the payment terms. Alternatively, the defendant may request or the court may direct a court appearance.

(2) The court must not require payment of bail, fines, penalties, fees, or assessments to consider the petition.

(3) The petition to modify the payment terms does not stay the operation of any order requiring the payment of bail, fines, penalties, fees, or assessments unless specifically ordered by the court.

(4) If the defendant petitions to modify the payment terms based on an inability to pay, the procedures stated in rule 4.335 apply.

(5) If the petition to modify the payment terms is not based on an inability to pay, the court may deny the defendant's request to modify the payment terms and order no further proceedings if the court determines that:

(A) An unreasonable amount of time has passed; or

(B) The defendant has made an unreasonable number of requests to modify the payment terms.

(Subd (e) adopted effective January 1, 2017.)

(f) Procedure after a trial by written declaration in absentia for a traffic infraction

When the court issues a judgment under Vehicle Code section 40903 and a defendant requests a trial de novo within the time permitted, courts may require the defendant to deposit bail.

(Subd (f) adopted effective January 1, 2017.)

(g) Procedure for referring a defendant to the Department of Motor Vehicles (DMV) for license suspension for failure to pay a fine

Before a court may notify the DMV under Vehicle Code sections 40509(b) or 40509.5(b) that a defendant has failed to pay a fine or an installment of bail, the court must provide the defendant with notice of and an opportunity to be heard on the inability to pay. This notice may be provided on the notice required in rule 4.107, the civil assessment notice, or any other notice provided to the defendant.

(Subd (g) adopted effective January 1, 2017.)

Rule 4.106 adopted effective January 1, 2017.

Advisory Committee Comment

Subdivision (a). The rule is intended to apply only to an infraction offense for which the defendant (1) has received a written notice to appear and (2) has failed to appear by the appearance date or an approved extension of that date or has failed to pay as required.

Subdivision (c)(3). Circumstances that indicate good cause may include, but are not limited to, the defendant's hospitalization, incapacitation, or incarceration; military duty required of the defendant; death or hospitalization of the defendant's dependent or immediate family member; caregiver responsibility for a sick or disabled dependent or immediate family member of the defendant; or an extraordinary reason, beyond the defendant's control, that prevented the defendant from making an appearance or payment on or before the date listed on the notice to appear.

Subdivision (e)(1). A court may exercise its discretion to deny a defendant's request to modify the payment terms. If the court chooses to grant the defendant's request, the court may modify the payment terms by reducing or suspending the base fine, lowering the payments, converting the remaining balance to community service, or otherwise modifying the payment terms as the court sees fit.

Subdivision (g). A hearing is not required unless requested by the defendant or directed by the court.

Rule 4.107. Mandatory reminder notice—traffic procedures

(a) Mandatory reminder notice

(1) Each court must send a reminder notice to the address shown on the *Notice to Appear*, unless the defendant otherwise notifies the court of a different address.

(2) The court may satisfy the requirement in paragraph (1) by sending the notice electronically, including by e-mail or text message, to the defendant. By providing an electronic address or number to the court or to a law enforcement officer at the time of signing the promise to appear, a defendant consents to receiving the reminder notice electronically at that electronic address or number.

(3) The failure to receive a reminder notice does not relieve the defendant of the obligation to appear by the date stated in the *Notice to Appear*.

(Subd (a) adopted effective January 1, 2017.)

(b) Minimum information in reminder notice

In addition to information obtained from the *Notice to Appear*, the reminder notice must contain at least the following information:

(1) An appearance date and location;

(2) Whether a court appearance is mandatory or optional;

(3) The total bail amount and payment options;

(4) The notice about traffic school required under Vehicle Code section 42007, if applicable;

(5) Notice that a traffic violator school will charge a fee in addition to the administrative fee charged by the court;

(6) The potential consequences for failure to appear, including a driver's license hold or suspension, a civil assessment of up to $300, a new charge for failure to appear, a warrant of arrest, or some combination of these consequences, if applicable;

(7) The potential consequences for failure to pay a fine, including a driver's license hold or suspension, a civil assessment of up to $300, a new charge for failure to pay a fine, a warrant of arrest, or some combination of these consequences, if applicable;

(8) The right to request an ability-to-pay determination;

(9) Notice of the option to pay bail through community service (if available) and installment plans (if available);

(10) Contact information for the court, including the court's website;

(11) Information regarding trial by declaration, informal trial (if available), and telephone or website scheduling options (if available); and

(12) Correction requirements and procedures for correctable violations.

(Subd (b) adopted effective January 1, 2017.)

Rule 4.107 adopted effective January 1, 2017.

Advisory Committee Comment

Subdivision (a)(2). The court may provide a means for obtaining the defendant's consent and designated electronic address or number on its local website. Because notices to appear state the website address for the superior court in each county, this location may increase the number of defendants who become aware and take advantage of this option. To obtain the defendant's electronic address or number at the time of signing the promise to appear, the court may need to collaborate with local law enforcement agencies.

Subdivision (b). While not required, some local court websites may provide information about local court processes and local forms related to the information on the reminder notice. If in electronic form, the reminder notice should include direct links to any information and forms on the local court website. If in paper form, the reminder notice may include the website addresses for any information and forms on the local court website.

Rule 4.108. Installment Payment Agreements

(a) Online interface for installment payment agreements

(1) A court may use an online interface to enter into installment payment agreements with traffic infraction defendants under Vehicle Code sections 40510.5 and 42007.

(2) Before entering into an installment payment agreement, an online interface must provide defendants with the Advisement of Rights stated in Attachment 1 of *Online Agreement to Pay and Forfeit Bail in Installments* (form TR-300 (online)), and *Online Agreement to Pay Traffic Violator School Fees in Installments* (form TR-310 (online)).

(Subd (a) adopted effective January 1, 2017.)

(b) Alternative mandatory forms

(1) The Judicial Council has adopted the following alternative mandatory forms for use in entering into installment payment agreements under Vehicle Code sections 40510.5 and 42007:

(A) *Agreement to Pay and Forfeit Bail in Installments* (form TR-300); and *Online Agreement to Pay and Forfeit Bail in Installments* (form TR-300 (online)); and

(B) *Agreement to Pay Traffic Violator School Fees in Installments* (form TR-310); and *Online Agreement to Pay Traffic Violator School Fees in Installments* (form TR-310 (online)).

(2) Forms TR-300 (online) and TR-310 (online) may be used only in online interfaces for installment payment agreements as provided in subdivision (a).

(Subd (b) adopted effective January 1, 2017.)

Rule 4.108 adopted effective January 1, 2017.

Rule 4.110. Time limits for criminal proceedings on information or indictment

Time limits for criminal proceedings on information or indictment are as follows:

(1) The information must be filed within 15 days after a person has been held to answer for a public offense;

(2) The arraignment of a defendant must be held on the date the information is filed or as soon thereafter as the court directs; and

(3) A plea or notice of intent to demur on behalf of a party represented by counsel at the arraignment must be entered or made no later than seven days after the initial arraignment, unless the court lengthens time for good cause.

Rule 4.110 amended effective January 1, 2007; adopted as rule 227.3 effective January 1, 1985; previously amended effective June 6, 1990; previously renumbered and amended effective January 1, 2001.

Rule 4.111. Pretrial motions in criminal cases

(a) Time for filing papers and proof of service

Unless otherwise ordered or specifically provided by law, all pretrial motions, accompanied by a memorandum, must be served and filed at least 10 court days, all papers opposing the motion at least 5 court days, and all reply papers at least 2 court days before the time appointed for hearing. Proof of service of the moving papers must be filed no later than 5 court days before the time appointed for hearing.

(Subd (a) amended effective January 1, 2010; previously amended effective January 1, 2007.)

(b) Failure to serve and file timely points and authorities

The court may consider the failure without good cause of the moving party to serve and file a memorandum within the time permitted as an admission that the motion is without merit.

(Subd (b) amended effective January 1, 2007.)

Rule 4.111 amended effective January 1, 2010; adopted as rule 227.5 effective January 1, 1985; previously renumbered effective January 1, 2001; previously amended effective January 1, 2007.

Rule 4.112. Readiness conference

(a) Date and appearances

The court may hold a readiness conference in felony cases within 1 to 14 days before the date set for trial. At the readiness conference:

(1) All trial counsel must appear and be prepared to discuss the case and determine whether the case can be disposed of without trial;

(2) The prosecuting attorney must have authority to dispose of the case; and

(3) The defendant must be present in court.

(Subd (a) amended effective January 1, 2007; adopted as rule 227.6 effective January 1, 1985; previously amended and relettered effective January 1, 2001; previously amended effective January 1, 2005.)

(b) Motions

Except for good cause, the court should hear and decide any pretrial motion in a criminal case before or at the readiness conference.

(Subd (b) adopted effective January 1, 2001.)

Rule 4.112 amended effective January 1, 2007; subd (a) adopted as rule 227.6 effective January 1, 1985; subd (b) adopted as section 10.1 of the Standards of Judicial Administration effective January 1, 1985; previously amended and renumbered effective January 1, 2001; previously amended effective January 1, 2005.

Rule 4.113. Motions and grounds for continuance of criminal case set for trial

Motions to continue the trial of a criminal case are disfavored and will be denied unless the moving party, under Penal Code section 1050, presents affirmative proof in open court that the ends of justice require a continuance.

Rule 4.113 amended effective January 1, 2007; adopted as rule 227.7 effective January 1, 1985 previously renumbered effective January 1, 2001.

Rule 4.114. Certification under Penal Code section 859a

When a plea of guilty or no contest is entered under Penal Code section 859a, the magistrate must:

(1) Set a date for imposing sentence; and

(2) Refer the case to the probation officer for action as provided in Penal Code sections 1191 and 1203.

Rule 4.114 amended effective January 1, 2007; adopted as rule 227.9 effective January 1, 1985; previously amended and renumbered effective January 1, 2001.

Rule 4.115. Criminal case assignment

(a) Master calendar departments

To ensure that the court's policy on continuances is firm and uniformly applied, that pretrial proceedings and trial assignments are handled consistently, and that cases are tried on a date certain, each court not operating on a direct calendaring system must assign all criminal matters to one or more master calendar departments. The presiding judge of a master calendar department must conduct or supervise the conduct of all arraignments and pretrial hearings and conferences and assign to a trial department any case requiring a trial or dispositional hearing.

(Subd (a) lettered effective January 1, 2008; adopted as unlettered subd effective January 1, 1985.)

(b) Trial calendaring and continuances

Any request for a continuance, including a request to trail the trial date, must comply with rule 4.113 and the requirement in section 1050 to show good cause to continue a hearing in a criminal proceeding. Active management of trial calendars is necessary to minimize the number of statutory dismissals. Accordingly, courts should avoid calendaring or trailing criminal cases for trial to the last day permitted for trial under section 1382. Courts must implement calendar management procedures, in accordance with local conditions and needs, to ensure that criminal cases are assigned to trial departments before the last day permitted for trial under section 1382.

(Subd (b) adopted effective January 1, 2008.)

Rule 4.115 amended effective January 1, 2008; adopted as section 10 of the Standards of Judicial Administration effective January 1, 1985; amended and renumbered effective January 1, 2001; previously amended effective January 1, 2007.

Advisory Committee Comment

Subdivision (b) clarifies that the "good cause" showing for a continuance under section 1050 applies in all criminal cases, whether or not the case is in the 10-day grace period provided for in section 1382. The Trial Court Presiding Judges Advisory Committee and Criminal Law Advisory Committee observe that the "good cause" requirement for a continuance is separate and distinct from the "good cause" requirement to avoid dismissals under section 1382. There is case law stating that the prosecution is not required to show good cause to avoid a dismissal under section 1382 during the 10-day grace period because a case may not be dismissed for delay during that 10-day period. (See, e.g., *Bryant v. Superior Court* (1986) 186 Cal.App.3d 483, 488.) Yet, both the plain language of section 1050 and case law show that there must be good cause for a continuance under section 1050 during the 10-day grace period. (See, e.g., section 1050 and *People v. Henderson* (2004) 115 Cal.App.4th 922, 939–940.) Thus, a court may not dismiss a case during the 10-day grace period under section 1382, but the committees believe that the court must deny a request for a continuance during the 10-day grace period that does not comply with the good cause requirement under section 1050.

The decision in *Henderson* states that when the prosecutor seeks a continuance but fails to show good cause under section 1050, the trial court "must nevertheless postpone the hearing to another date within the statutory period." (115 Cal.App.4th at p. 940.) That conclusion, however, may be contrary to the plain language of section 1050, which requires a court to deny a continuance if the moving party fails to show good cause. The conclusion also appears to be dicta, as it was not a contested issue on appeal. Given this uncertainty, the rule is silent as to the remedy for failure to show good cause for a requested continuance during the 10-day grace period. The committees note that the remedies under section 1050.5 are available and, but for the *Henderson* dicta, a court would appear to be allowed to deny the continuance request and commence the trial on the scheduled trial date.

Rule 4.116. Certification to juvenile court

(a) Application

This rule applies to all cases not filed in juvenile court in which the person charged by an accusatory pleading appears to be under the age of 18, except when jurisdiction over the child has been transferred from the juvenile court under Welfare and Institutions Code section 707.

(Subd (a) amended effective May 22, 2017; adopted effective January 1, 2001; previously amended effective January 1, 2007.)

(b) Procedure to determine whether certification is appropriate

If an accusatory pleading is pending, and it is suggested or it appears to the court that the person charged was under the age of 18 on the date the offense is alleged to have been committed, the court must immediately suspend proceedings and conduct a hearing to determine the true age of the person charged. The burden of proof of establishing the age of the accused person is on the moving party. If, after examination, the court is satisfied by a preponderance of the evidence that the person was under the age of 18 on the date the alleged offense was committed, the court must immediately certify the matter to the juvenile court and state on the certification order:

(1) The crime with which the person named is charged;

(2) That the person was under the age of 18 on the date of the alleged offense;

(3) The date of birth of the person;

(4) The date of suspension of criminal proceedings; and

(5) The date and time of certification to juvenile court.

(Subd (b) amended effective January 1, 2007; adopted as untitled subd effective January 1, 1991; previously amended and lettered effective January 1, 2001.)

(c) Procedure on certification

If the court determines that certification to the juvenile court is appropriate under (b), copies of the certification, the accusatory pleading, and any police reports must immediately be transmitted to the clerk of the juvenile court. On receipt of the documents, the clerk of the juvenile court must immediately notify the probation officer, who must immediately investigate the matter to determine whether to commence proceedings in juvenile court.

(Subd (c) amended effective January 1, 2007; adopted as untitled subd effective January 1, 1991; previously amended and lettered effective January 1, 2001.)

(d) Procedure if child is in custody

If the person is under the age of 18 and is in custody, the person must immediately be transported to the juvenile detention facility.

(Subd (d) amended effective January 1, 2007; adopted as untitled subd effective January 1, 1991; previously amended and lettered effective January 1, 2001.)
Rule 4.116 amended effective May 22, 2017; adopted as rule 241.2 effective January 1, 1991; previously amended and renumbered effective January 1, 2001; previously amended effective July 1, 1991, and January 1, 2007.

Rule 4.117. Qualifications for appointed trial counsel in capital cases

(a) Purpose

This rule defines minimum qualifications for attorneys appointed to represent persons charged with capital offenses in the superior courts. These minimum qualifications are designed to promote adequate representation in death penalty cases and to avoid unnecessary delay and expense by assisting the trial court in appointing qualified counsel. Nothing in this rule is intended to be used as a standard by which to measure whether the defendant received effective assistance of counsel.

(b) General qualifications

In cases in which a person is charged with a capital offense, the court must assign qualified trial counsel to represent the defendant unless the district attorney has made an affirmative statement on the record that the prosecution will not be seeking the death penalty. The attorney may be appointed only if the court, after reviewing the attorney's background, experience, and training, determines that the attorney has demonstrated the skill, knowledge, and proficiency to diligently and competently represent the defendant. An attorney is not entitled to appointment simply because he or she meets the minimum qualifications.

(Subd (b) amended effective January 1, 2024.)

(c) Designation of counsel

(1) If the court appoints more than one attorney, one must be designated lead counsel and meet the qualifications stated in (d) or (f), and at least one other must be designated associate counsel and meet the qualifications stated in (e) or (f).

(2) If the court appoints only one attorney, that attorney must meet the qualifications stated in (d) or (f).

(Subd (c) amended effective January 1, 2007.)

(d) Qualifications of lead counsel

To be eligible to serve as lead counsel, an attorney must:

(1) Be an active member of the State Bar of California;

(2) Be an active trial practitioner with at least 10 years' litigation experience in the field of criminal law;

(3) Have prior experience as lead counsel in either:

(A) At least 10 serious or violent felony jury trials, including at least 2 murder cases, tried to argument, verdict, or final judgment; or

(B) At least 5 serious or violent felony jury trials, including at least 3 murder cases, tried to argument, verdict, or final judgment;

(4) Be familiar with the practices and procedures of the California criminal courts;

(5) Be familiar with and experienced in the use of expert witnesses and evidence, including psychiatric and forensic evidence;

(6) Have completed within two years before appointment at least 15 hours of capital case defense training approved for Minimum Continuing Legal Education credit by the State Bar of California; and

(7) Have demonstrated the necessary proficiency, diligence, and quality of representation appropriate to capital cases.

(Subd (d) amended effective January 1, 2007.)

(e) Qualifications of associate counsel

To be eligible to serve as associate counsel, an attorney must:

(1) Be an active member of the State Bar of California;

(2) Be an active trial practitioner with at least three years' litigation experience in the field of criminal law;

(3) Have prior experience as:

(A) Lead counsel in at least 10 felony jury trials tried to verdict, including 3 serious or violent felony jury trials tried to argument, verdict, or final judgment; or

(B) Lead or associate counsel in at least 5 serious or violent felony jury trials, including at least 1 murder case, tried to argument, verdict, or final judgment;

(4) Be familiar with the practices and procedures of the California criminal courts;

(5) Be familiar with and experienced in the use of expert witnesses and evidence, including psychiatric and forensic evidence;

(6) Have completed within two years before appointment at least 15 hours of capital case defense training approved for Minimum Continuing Legal Education credit by the State Bar of California; and

(7) Have demonstrated the necessary proficiency, diligence, and quality of representation appropriate to capital cases.

(Subd (e) amended effective January 1, 2007.)

(f) Alternative qualifications

The court may appoint an attorney even if he or she does not meet all of the qualifications stated in (d) or (e) if the attorney demonstrates the ability to provide competent representation to the defendant. If the court appoints counsel under this subdivision, it must state on the record the basis for finding counsel qualified. In making this determination, the court must consider whether the attorney meets the following qualifications:

(1) The attorney is an active member of the State Bar of California or admitted to practice *pro hac vice* under rule 9.40;

(2) The attorney has demonstrated the necessary proficiency, diligence, and quality of representation appropriate to capital cases;

(3) The attorney has had extensive criminal or civil trial experience;

(4) Although not meeting the qualifications stated in (d) or (e), the attorney has had experience in death penalty trials other than as lead or associate counsel;

(5) The attorney is familiar with the practices and procedures of the California criminal courts;

(6) The attorney is familiar with and experienced in the use of expert witnesses and evidence, including psychiatric and forensic evidence;

(7) The attorney has had specialized training in the defense of persons accused of capital crimes, such as experience in a death penalty resource center;

(8) The attorney has ongoing consultation support from experienced death penalty counsel;

(9) The attorney has completed within the past two years before appointment at least 15 hours of capital case defense training approved for Minimum Continuing Legal Education credit by the State Bar of California; and

(10) The attorney has been certified by the State Bar of California's Board of Legal Specialization as a criminal law specialist.

(Subd (f) amended effective January 1, 2007.)

(g) Public defender appointments

When the court appoints the Public Defender under Penal Code section 987.2, the Public Defender should assign an attorney from that office or agency as lead counsel who meets the qualifications described in (d) or assign an attorney that he or she determines would qualify under (f). If associate counsel is designated, the Public Defender should assign an attorney from that office or agency who meets the qualifications described in (e) or assign an attorney he or she determines would qualify under (f).

(Subd (g) amended effective January 1, 2007.)

(h) Standby or advisory counsel

When the court appoints standby or advisory counsel to assist a self-represented defendant, the attorney must qualify under (d) or (f).

(Subd (h) amended effective January 1, 2007.)

(i) Order appointing counsel

When the court appoints counsel to a capital case, the court must complete *Order Appointing Counsel in Capital Case* (form CR-190), and counsel must complete *Declaration of Counsel for Appointment in Capital Case* (form CR-191).

(Subd (i) amended effective January 1, 2007; adopted effective January 1, 2004.)
Rule 4.117 amended effective January 1, 2024; adopted effective January 1, 2003; previously amended effective January 1, 2004, and January 1, 2007.

Rule 4.119. Additional requirements in pretrial proceedings in capital cases

(a) Application

This rule applies only in pretrial proceedings in cases in which the death penalty may be imposed.

(Subd (a) adopted effective April 25, 2019.)

(b) Checklist

Within 10 days of counsel's first appearance in court, primary counsel for each defendant and the prosecution must each acknowledge that they have reviewed *Capital Case Attorney Pretrial Checklist* (form CR-600) by signing and submitting this form to the court. Counsel are encouraged to keep a copy of this checklist.

(Subd (b) adopted effective April 25, 2019.)

(c) Lists of appearances, exhibits, and motions

(1) Primary counsel for each defendant and the prosecution must each prepare the lists identified in (A)–(C):

(A) A list of all appearances made by that party during the pretrial proceedings. *Capital Case Attorney List of Appearances* (form CR-601) must be used for this purpose. The list must include all appearances, including ex parte appearances; the date of each appearance; the department in which it was made; the name of counsel making the appearance; and a brief description of the nature of the appearance. A separate list of Penal Code section 987.9 appearances must be maintained under seal for each defendant.

(B) A list of all exhibits offered by that party during the pretrial proceedings. *Capital Case Attorney List of Exhibits* (form CR-602) must be used for this purpose. The list must indicate whether the exhibit was admitted in evidence, refused, lodged, or withdrawn.

(C) A list of all motions made by that party during the pretrial proceedings, including ex parte motions. *Capital Case Attorney List of Motions* (form CR-603) must be used for this purpose. The list must indicate if a motion is awaiting resolution.

(2) In the event of any substitution of attorney during the pretrial proceedings, the relieved attorney must provide the lists of all appearances, exhibits, and motions to substituting counsel within five days of being relieved.

(3) No later than 21 days after the clerk notifies trial counsel that it must submit the lists to the court, counsel must submit the lists to the court and serve on all parties a copy of all the lists except the list of Penal Code section 987.9 appearances. Unless otherwise provided by local rule, the lists must be submitted to the court in electronic form.

(Subd (c) adopted effective April 25, 2019.)

(d) Electronic recordings presented or offered into evidence

Counsel must comply with the requirements of rule 2.1040 regarding electronic recordings presented or offered into evidence, including any such recordings that are part of a digital or electronic presentation.

(Subd (d) adopted effective April 25, 2019.)

Rule 4.119 adopted effective April 25, 2019.

Advisory Committee Comment

Subdivision (b). *Capital Case Attorney Pretrial Checklist* (form CR-600) is designed to be a tool to assist pretrial counsel in identifying and fulfilling all their record preparation responsibilities. Counsel are therefore encouraged to keep a copy of this form and to use it to monitor their own progress.

Subdivision (c)(1). To facilitate preparation of complete and accurate lists, counsel are encouraged to add items to the lists at the time appearances or motions are made or exhibits offered.

Subdivision (c)(3). Rule 8.613(d) requires the clerk to notify counsel to submit the lists of appearances, exhibits, and motions.

Rule 4.130. Mental competency proceedings

(a) Application

(1) This rule applies to proceedings in the superior court under Penal Code section 1367 et seq. to determine the mental competency of a criminal defendant.

(2) The requirements of subdivision (d)(2) apply only to a formal competency evaluation ordered by the court under Penal Code section 1369(a).

(3) The requirements of subdivision (d)(2) do not apply to a brief preliminary evaluation of the defendant's competency if:

(A) The parties stipulate to a brief preliminary evaluation; and

(B) The court orders the evaluation in accordance with a local rule of court that specifies the content of the evaluation and the procedure for its preparation and submission to the court.

(Subd (a) amended effective January 1, 2018; adopted effective January 1, 2007.)

(b) Initiation of mental competency proceedings

(1) The court must initiate mental competency proceedings if the judge has a reasonable doubt, based on substantial evidence, about the defendant's competence to stand trial.

(2) The opinion of counsel, without a statement of specific reasons supporting that opinion, does not constitute substantial evidence. The court may allow defense counsel to present his or her opinion regarding the defendant's mental competency in camera if the court finds there is reason to believe that attorney-client privileged information will be inappropriately revealed if the hearing is conducted in open court.

(3) In a felony case, if the judge initiates mental competency proceedings prior to the preliminary examination, counsel for the defendant may request a preliminary examination as provided in Penal Code section 1368.1(a)(1), or counsel for the People may request a determination of probable cause as provided in Penal Code section 1368.1(a)(2) and rule 4.131.

(Subd (b) amended effective January 1, 2020; adopted effective January 1, 2007.)

(c) Effect of initiating mental competency proceedings

(1) If mental competency proceedings are initiated, criminal proceedings are suspended and may not be reinstated until a trial on the competency of the defendant has been concluded and the defendant is found mentally competent at a trial conducted under Penal Code section 1369, at a hearing conducted under Penal Code section 1370(a)(1)(G), or at a hearing following a certification of restoration under Penal Code section 1372.

(2) In misdemeanor cases, speedy trial requirements are tolled during the suspension of criminal proceedings for mental competency evaluation and trial. If criminal proceedings are later reinstated and time is not waived, the trial must be commenced within 30 days after the reinstatement of the criminal proceedings, as provided by Penal Code section 1382(a)(3).

(3) In felony cases, speedy trial requirements are tolled during the suspension of criminal proceedings for mental competency evaluation and trial. If criminal proceedings are reinstated, unless time is waived, time periods to commence the preliminary examination or trial are as follows:

(A) If criminal proceedings were suspended before the preliminary hearing had been conducted, the preliminary hearing must be commenced within 10 days of the reinstatement of the criminal proceedings, as provided in Penal Code section 859b.

(B) If criminal proceedings were suspended after the preliminary hearing had been conducted, the trial must be commenced within 60 days of the reinstatement of the criminal proceedings, as provided in Penal Code section 1382(a)(2).

(Subd (c) amended effective January 1, 2020; adopted effective January 1, 2007.)

(d) Examination of defendant after initiation of mental competency proceedings

(1) On initiation of mental competency proceedings, the court must inquire whether the defendant, or defendant's counsel, seeks a finding of mental incompetence.

(A) If the defense informs the court that the defendant is seeking a finding of mental incompetence, the court must appoint at least one expert to examine the defendant.

(B) If the defense informs the court that the defendant is not seeking a finding of mental incompetence, the court must appoint two experts to examine the defendant. The defense and the prosecution may each name one expert from the court's list of approved experts.

(2) Any court-appointed experts must examine the defendant and advise the court on the defendant's competency to stand trial. Experts' reports are to be submitted to the court, counsel for the defendant, and the prosecution. The report must include the following:

(A) A brief statement of the examiner's training and previous experience as it relates to examining the competence of a criminal defendant to stand trial and preparing a resulting report;

(B) A summary of the examination conducted by the examiner on the defendant, including a summary of the defendant's mental status, a diagnosis under the most recent version of the *Diagnostic and Statistical Manual of Mental Disorders*, if possible, of the defendant's current mental health disorder or disorders, and a statement as to whether symptoms of the mental health disorder or disorders which motivated the defendant's behavior would respond to mental health treatment;

(C) A detailed analysis of the competence of the defendant to stand trial using California's current legal standard, including the defendant's ability or inability to understand the nature of the criminal proceedings or assist counsel in the conduct of a defense in a rational manner as a result of a mental health disorder;

(D) A summary of an assessment—conducted for malingering or feigning symptoms, if clinically indicated—which may include, but need not be limited to, psychological testing;

(E) Under Penal Code section 1369, a statement on whether treatment with antipsychotic or other medication is medically appropriate for the defendant and whether the defendant has capacity to make decisions regarding antipsychotic or other medication as outlined in Penal Code section 1370. If a licensed psychologist examines the defendant and opines that treatment with antipsychotic medication may be appropriate, the psychologist's opinion must be based on whether the defendant has a mental disorder that is typically known to benefit from that treatment. A licensed psychologist's opinion must not exceed the scope of their license. If a psychiatrist examines the defendant and opines that treatment with antipsychotic medication is appropriate, the psychiatrist must inform the court of their opinion as to the likely or potential side effects of the medication, the expected efficacy of the medication, and possible alternative treatments, as outlined in Penal Code section 1370;

(F) A list of all sources of information considered by the examiner, including legal, medical, school, military, regional center, employment, hospital, and psychiatric records; the evaluations of other experts; the results of psychological testing; police reports; criminal history; statement of the defendant; statements of any witnesses to the alleged crime; booking information, mental health screenings, and mental health records following the alleged crime; consultation with the prosecutor and defendant's attorney; and any other collateral sources considered by the examiner in reaching a conclusion;

(G) If the defendant is charged with a felony offense, a recommendation, if possible, for a placement or type of placement or treatment program that is most appropriate for restoring the defendant to competency; and

(H) If the defendant is charged only with a misdemeanor offense, an opinion based on present clinical impressions and available historical data as to whether the defendant, regardless of custody status, appears to be gravely disabled, as defined in Welfare and Institutions Code section 5008(h)(1)(A).

(3) Statements made by the defendant during the examination to experts appointed under this rule, and products of any such statements, may not be used in a trial on the issue of the defendant's guilt or in a sanity trial should defendant enter a plea of not guilty by reason of insanity.

(Subd (d) amended effective May 15, 2023; adopted effective January 1, 2007; previously amended effective January 1, 2018, January 1, 2020, September 1, 2020, and May 13, 2022.)

(e) Trial on mental competency

(1) Regardless of the conclusions or findings of the court-appointed expert, the court must conduct a trial on the mental competency of the defendant if the court has initiated mental competency proceedings under (b).

(2) At the trial, the defendant is presumed to be mentally competent, and it is the burden of the party contending that the defendant is not mentally competent to prove the defendant's mental incompetence by a preponderance of the evidence.

(3) In addition to the testimony of the experts appointed by the court under (d), either party may call additional experts or other relevant witnesses.

(4) After the presentation of the evidence and closing argument, the trier of fact is to determine whether the defendant is mentally competent or mentally incompetent.

(A) If the matter is tried by a jury, the verdict must be unanimous.

(B) If the parties have waived the right to a jury trial, the court's findings must be made in writing or placed orally in the record.

(Subd (e) adopted effective January 1, 2007.)

(f) Posttrial procedure

(1) If the defendant is found mentally competent, the court must reinstate the criminal proceedings.

(2) If the defendant in a felony case is found to be mentally incompetent under section 1370 or the defendant in any criminal action is found to be mentally incompetent under section 1370.1 due to a developmental disability, the criminal proceedings remain suspended and the court either:

(A) Must issue an order committing the person for restoration treatment under the provisions of the governing statute; or

(B) In the case of a person eligible for commitment under section 1370, if the person is found incompetent due to a mental disorder, may consider placing the person on a program of diversion under section 1001.36 in lieu of commitment.

(3) If the defendant is found to be mentally incompetent in a misdemeanor case under section 1370.01, the criminal proceedings remain suspended, and the court may dismiss the case under section 1385 or conduct a hearing to consider placing the person on a program of diversion under section 1001.36.

(Subd (f) amended effective May 13, 2022; adopted effective January 1, 2007; previously amended effective January 1, 2020.)

(g) Reinstatement of felony proceedings under section 1001.36(g)

If a defendant eligible for commitment under section 1370 is granted diversion under section 1001.36, and during the period of diversion the court determines that criminal proceedings should be reinstated under section 1001.36(g), the court must, under section 1369, appoint a psychiatrist, licensed psychologist, or any other expert the court may deem appropriate, to examine the defendant and return a report opining on the defendant's competence to stand trial. The expert's report must be provided to counsel for the People and to the defendant's counsel.

(1) On receipt of the evaluation report, the court must conduct an inquiry into the defendant's current competency, under the procedures set forth in (h)(2) of this rule.

(2) If the court finds by a preponderance of the evidence that the defendant is mentally competent, the court must hold a hearing as set forth in Penal Code section 1001.36(g).

(3) If the court finds by a preponderance of the evidence that the defendant is mentally incompetent, criminal proceedings must remain suspended, and the court must order that the defendant be committed and placed for restoration treatment.

(4) If the court concludes, based on substantial evidence, that the defendant is mentally incompetent and is not likely to attain competency within the time remaining before the defendant's maximum date for returning to court, and has reason to believe the defendant may be gravely disabled, within the meaning of Welfare and Institutions Code section 5008(h)(1), the court may, instead of issuing a commitment order under section 1370, refer the matter to the conservatorship investigator of the county of commitment to initiate conservatorship proceedings for the defendant under Welfare and Institutions Code section 5350 et seq.

(Subd (g) amended effective May 15, 2023; adopted effective January 1, 2020; previously amended effective September 1, 2020, and May 13, 2022.)

(h) Posttrial hearings on competence under section 1370

(1) If, at any time after the court has declared a defendant incompetent to stand trial, and counsel for the defendant, or a jail medical or mental health staff provider, provides the court with substantial evidence that the defendant's psychiatric symptoms have changed to such a degree as to create a doubt in the mind of the judge as to the defendant's current mental incompetence, the court may appoint a psychiatrist or a licensed psychologist to examine the defendant and, in an examination with the court, opine as to whether the defendant has regained competence.

(2) On receipt of an evaluation report under (h)(1) or an evaluation by the State Department of State Hospitals under Welfare and Institutions Code section 4335.2, the court must direct the clerk to serve a copy on counsel for the People and counsel for the defendant. If, in the opinion of the appointed expert or the department's expert, the defendant has regained competence, the court must conduct a hearing as if a certificate of restoration of competence had been filed under section 1372(a)(1). At the hearing, the court may consider any evidence, presented by any party, that is relevant to the question of the defendant's current mental competency.

(A) At the conclusion of the hearing, if the court finds that it has been established by a preponderance of the evidence that the defendant is mentally competent, the court must reinstate criminal proceedings.

(B) At the conclusion of the hearing, if the court finds that it has not been established by a preponderance of the evidence that the defendant is mentally competent, criminal proceedings must remain suspended.

(C) The court's findings on the defendant's mental competency must be stated on the record and recorded in the minutes.

(Subd (h) amended effective May 15, 2023; adopted effective January 1, 2020; previously amended effective May 13, 2022.)

Rule 4.130 amended effective May 15, 2023; adopted effective January 1, 2007; previously amended effective January 1, 2018, January 1, 2020, September 1, 2020, and May 13, 2022.

Advisory Committee Comment

The case law interpreting Penal Code section 1367 et seq. established a procedure for judges to follow in cases where there is a concern whether the defendant is legally competent to stand trial, but the concern does not necessarily rise to the level of a reasonable doubt based on substantial evidence. Before finding a reasonable doubt as to the defendant's competency to stand trial and initiating competency proceedings under Penal Code section 1368 et seq., the court may appoint an expert to assist the court in determining whether such a reasonable doubt exists. As noted in *People v. Visciotti* (1992) 2 Cal.4th 1, 34–36, the court may appoint an expert when it is concerned about the mental competency of the defendant, but the concern does not rise to the level of a reasonable doubt, based on substantial evidence, required by Penal Code section 1367 et seq. Should the results of this examination present substantial evidence of mental incompetency, the court must initiate competency proceedings under (b).

Once mental competency proceedings under Penal Code section 1367 et seq. have been initiated, the court is to appoint at least one expert to examine the defendant under (d). Under no circumstances is the court obligated to appoint more than two experts. (Pen. Code, § 1369(a).) The costs of the experts appointed under (d) are to be paid for by the court as the expert examinations and reports are for the benefit or use of the court in determining whether the defendant is mentally incompetent. (See Cal. Rules of Court, rule 10.810, function 10.)

Subdivision (d)(3), which provides that the defendant's statements made during the examination cannot be used in a trial on the defendant's guilt or a sanity trial in a not guilty by reason of sanity trial, is based on the California Supreme Court holdings in *People v. Arcega* (1982) 32 Cal.3d 504 and *People v. Weaver* (2001) 26 Cal.4th 876.

Although the court is not obligated to appoint additional experts, counsel may nonetheless retain their own experts to testify at a trial on the defendant's competency. (See *People v. Mayes* (1988) 202 Cal.App.4th 908, 917–918.) These experts are not for the benefit or use of the court, and their costs are not to be paid by the court. (See Cal. Rules of Court, rule 10.810, function 10.)

Both the prosecution and the defense have the right to a jury trial. (See *People v. Superior Court (McPeters)* (1995) 169 Cal.App.3d 796.) Defense counsel may waive this right, even over the objection of the defendant. (*People v. Masterson* (1994) 8 Cal.4th 965, 970.)

Either defense counsel or the prosecution (or both) may argue that the defendant is not competent to stand trial. (*People v. Stanley* (1995) 10 Cal.4th 764, 804 [defense counsel may advocate that defendant is not competent to stand trial and may present evidence of defendant's mental incompetency regardless of defendant's desire to be found competent].) If the defense declines to present evidence of the defendant's mental incompetency, the prosecution may do so. (Pen. Code, § 1369(b)(2).) If the prosecution elects to present evidence of the defendant's mental incompetency, it is the prosecution's burden to prove the incompetency by a preponderance of the evidence. (*People v. Mixon* (1990) 225 Cal.App.3d 1471, 1484, fn. 12.)

Should both parties decline to present evidence of defendant's mental incompetency, the court may do so. In those cases, the court is not to instruct the jury that a party has the burden of proof. "Rather, the proper approach would be to instruct the jury on the legal standard they are to apply to the evidence before them without allocating the burden of proof to one party or the other." (*People v. Sherik* (1991) 229 Cal.App.3d 444, 459–460.)

Rule 4.131. Probable cause determinations under section 1368.1(a)(2)

(a) Notice of a request for a determination of probable cause

The prosecuting attorney must serve and file notice of a request for a determination of probable cause on the defense at least 10 court days before the time appointed for the proceeding.

(Subd (a) adopted effective January 1, 2019.)

(b) Judge requirement

A judge must hear the determination of probable cause unless there is a stipulation by both parties to having the matter heard by a subordinate judicial officer.

(Subd (b) adopted effective January 1, 2019.)

(c) Defendant need not be present

A defendant need not be present for a determination of probable cause to proceed.

(Subd (c) adopted effective January 1, 2019.)

(d) Application of section 861

The one-session requirement of section 861 does not apply.

(Subd (d) adopted effective January 1, 2019.)

(e) Transcript

A transcript of the determination of probable cause must be provided to the prosecuting attorney and counsel for the defendant consistent with the manner in which a transcript is provided in a preliminary examination.

(Subd (e) adopted effective January 1, 2019.)

Rule 4.131 adopted effective January 1, 2019.

Chapter 2
Change of Venue

Rule 4.150. Change of venue: application and general provisions
Rule 4.151. Motion for change of venue
Rule 4.152. Selection of court and trial judge
Rule 4.153. Order on change of venue
Rule 4.154. Proceedings in the receiving court
Rule 4.155. Guidelines for reimbursement of costs in change of venue cases—criminal cases

Rule 4.150. Change of venue: application and general provisions

(a) Application

Rules 4.150 to 4.155 govern the change of venue in criminal cases under Penal Code section 1033.

(Subd (a) adopted effective January 1, 2006.)

(b) General provisions

When a change of venue has been ordered, the case remains a case of the transferring court. Except on good cause to the contrary, the court must follow the provisions below:

(1) Proceedings before trial must be heard in the transferring court.

(2) Proceedings that are not to be heard by the trial judge must be heard in the transferring court.

(3) Postverdict proceedings, including sentencing, if any, must be heard in the transferring court.

(Subd (b) amended effective January 1, 2007; adopted effective January 1, 2006.)

(c) Appellate review

Review by the Court of Appeal, either by an original proceeding or by appeal, must be heard in the appellate district in which the transferring court is located.

(Subd (c) adopted effective January 1, 2006.)

Rule 4.150 amended effective January 1, 2007; adopted as rule 840 effective March 4, 1972; previously amended and renumbered effective January 1, 2001; previously amended effective January 1, 2006.

Advisory Committee Comment

Subdivision (b)(1). This subdivision is based on Penal Code section 1033(a), which provides that all proceedings before trial are to be heard in the transferring court, except when a particular proceeding must be heard by the trial judge.

Subdivision (b)(2). This subdivision addresses motions heard by a judge other than the trial judge, such as requests for funds under Penal Code section 987.9 or a challenge or disqualification under Code of Civil Procedure section 170 et seq.

Subdivision (b)(3). Reflecting the local community interest in the case, (b)(3) clarifies that after trial the case is to return to the transferring court for any posttrial proceedings. There may be situations where the local interest is outweighed, warranting the receiving court to conduct posttrial hearings. Such hearings may include motions for new trial where juror testimony is necessary and the convenience to the jurors outweighs the desire to conduct the hearings in the transferring court.

Subdivision (c). This subdivision ensures that posttrial appeals and writs are heard in the same appellate district as any writs that may have been heard before or during trial.

Rule 4.151. Motion for change of venue

(a) Motion procedure

A motion for change of venue in a criminal case under Penal Code section 1033 must be supported by a declaration stating the facts supporting the application. Except for good cause shown, the motion must be filed at least 10 days before the date set for trial, with a copy served on the adverse party at least 10 days before the hearing. At the hearing counterdeclarations may be filed.

(Subd (a) amended effective January 1, 2007; adopted effective January 1, 2006; formerly part of an unlettered subd.)

(b) Policy considerations in ruling on motion

Before ordering a change of venue in a criminal case, the transferring court should consider impaneling a jury that would give the defendant a fair and impartial trial.

(Subd (b) adopted effective January 1, 2006.)

Rule 4.151 amended effective January 1, 2008; adopted as rule 841 effective March 4, 1972; previously amended and renumbered effective January 1, 2001; previously amended effective January 1, 2006, and January 1, 2007.

Advisory Committee Comment

Rule 4.151(b) is not intended to imply that the court should attempt to impanel a jury in every case before granting a change of venue.

Rule 4.152. Selection of court and trial judge

When a judge grants a motion for change of venue, he or she must inform the presiding judge of the transferring court. The presiding judge, or his or her designee, must:

(1) Notify the Administrative Director of the change of venue. After receiving the transferring court's notification, the Administrative Director, in order to expedite judicial business and equalize the work of the judges, must advise the transferring court which courts would not be unduly burdened by the trial of the case.

(2) Select the judge to try the case, as follows:

(A) The presiding judge, or his or her designee, must select a judge from the transferring court, unless he or she concludes that the transferring court does not have adequate judicial resources to try the case.

(B) If the presiding judge, or his or her designee, concludes that the transferring court does not have adequate judicial resources to try the case, he or she must request that the Chief Justice of California determine whether to assign a judge to the transferring court. If the Chief Justice determines not to assign a judge to the transferring court, the presiding judge, or his or her designee, must select a judge from the transferring court to try the case.

Rule 4.152 amended effective January 1, 2016; adopted as rule 842 effective March 4, 1972; previously amended and renumbered as rule 4.152 effective January 1, 2001; previously amended effective January 1, 2006.

Rule 4.153. Order on change of venue

After receiving the list of courts from the Administrative Director, the presiding judge, or his or her designee, must:

(1) Determine the court in which the case is to be tried. In making that determination, the court must consider, under Penal Code section 1036.7, whether to move the jury rather than to move the pending action. In so doing, the court should give particular consideration to the convenience of the jurors.

(2) Transmit to the receiving court a certified copy of the order of transfer and any pleadings, documents, or other papers or exhibits necessary for trying the case.

(3) Enter the order for change of venue in the minutes of the transferring court. The order must include the determinations in (1).

Rule 4.153 amended effective January 1, 2016; adopted as rule 843 effective March 4, 1972; previously amended and renumbered as rule 4.153 effective January 1, 2001; previously amended effective January 1, 2006.

Advisory Committee Comment

Rules 4.152 and 4.153 recognize that, although the determination of whether to grant a motion for change of venue is judicial in nature, the selection of the receiving court and the decision whether the case should be tried by a judge of the transferring court are more administrative in nature. Thus, the rules provide that the presiding judge of the transferring court is to make the latter decisions. He or she may delegate those decisions to the trial judge, the supervising judge of the criminal division, or any other judge the presiding judge deems appropriate. If, under the particular facts of the case, the latter decisions are both judicial and administrative, those decisions may be more properly made by the judge who heard the motion for change of venue.

Rule 4.154. Proceedings in the receiving court

The receiving court must conduct the trial as if the case had been commenced in the receiving court. If it is necessary to have any of the original pleadings or other papers before the receiving court, the transferring court must transmit such papers or pleadings. If, during the trial, any original papers or pleadings are submitted to the receiving court, the receiving court is to file the original. After sentencing, all original papers and pleadings are to be retained by the transferring court.

Rule 4.154 amended effective January 1, 2006; adopted as rule 844 effective March 4, 1972; previously amended and renumbered effective January 1, 2001.

Rule 4.155. Guidelines for reimbursement of costs in change of venue cases—criminal cases

(a) General

Consistent with Penal Code section 1037, the court in which an action originated must reimburse the court receiving a case after an order for change of venue for any ordinary expenditure and any extraordinary but reasonable and necessary expenditure that would not have been incurred by the receiving court but for the change of venue.

(Subd (a) amended effective September 1, 2017; previously amended effective January 1, 2001, and January 1, 2006.)

(b) Reimbursable ordinary expenditures—court related

Court-related reimbursable ordinary expenses include:

(1) For prospective jurors on the panel from which the jury is selected and for the trial jurors and alternates seated:

(A) Normal juror per diem and mileage at the rates of the receiving court. The cost of the juror should only be charged to a change of venue case if the juror was not used in any other case on the day that juror was excused from the change of venue case.

(B) If jurors are sequestered, actual lodging, meals, mileage, and parking expenses up to state Board of Control limits.

(C) If jurors are transported to a different courthouse or county, actual mileage and parking expenses.

(2) For court reporters:

(A) The cost of pro tem reporters, even if not used on the change of venue trial, but not the salaries of regular official reporters who would have been paid in any event. The rate of compensation for pro tem reporters should be that of the receiving court.

(B) The cost of transcripts requested during trial and for any new trial or appeal, using the folio rate of the receiving court.

(C) The cost of additional reporters necessary to allow production of a daily or expedited transcript.

(3) For assigned judges: The assigned judge's per diem, travel, and other expenses, up to state Board of Control limits, if the judge is assigned to the receiving court because of the change of venue case, regardless of whether the assigned judge is hearing the change of venue case.

(4) For interpreters and translators:

(A) The cost of the services of interpreters and translators, not on the court staff, if those services are required under Evidence Code sections 750 through 754. Using the receiving court's fee schedule, this cost should be paid whether the services are used in a change of venue trial or to cover staff interpreters and translators assigned to the change of venue trial.

(B) Interpreters' and translators' actual mileage, per diem, and lodging expenses, if any, that were incurred in connection with the trial, up to state Board of Control limits.

(5) For maintenance of evidence: The cost of handling, storing, or maintaining evidence beyond the expenses normally incurred by the receiving court.

(6) For services and supplies: The cost of services and supplies incurred only because of the change of venue trial, for example, copying and printing charges (such as for juror questionnaires), long-distance telephone calls, and postage. A pro rata share of the costs of routine services and supplies should not be reimbursable.

(7) For court or county employees:

(A) Overtime expenditures and compensatory time for staff incurred because of the change of venue case.

(B) Salaries and benefit costs of extra help or temporary help incurred either because of the change of venue case or to replace staff assigned to the change of venue case.

(Subd (b) amended effective January 1, 2007; previously amended effective January 1, 1998, and January 1, 2006.)

(c) Reimbursable ordinary expenses—defendant related

Defendant-related reimbursable ordinary expenses include the actual costs incurred for guarding, keeping, and transporting the defendant, including:

(1) Expenses related to health care: Costs incurred by or on behalf of the defendant such as doctors, hospital expenses, medicines, therapists, and counseling for diagnosis, evaluation, and treatment.

(2) Cost of food and special clothing for an in-custody defendant.

(3) Transportation: Nonroutine expenses, such as transporting an in-custody defendant from the transferring court to the receiving court. Routine transportation expenses if defendant is transported by usual means used for other receiving court prisoners should not be reimbursable.

(Subd (c) amended effective January 1, 2006.)

(d) Reimbursable ordinary expenditures—defense expenses

Reimbursable ordinary expenses related to providing defense for the defendant include:

(1) Matters covered by Penal Code section 987.9 as determined by the transferring court or by a judge designated under that section.

(2) Payment of other defense costs in accordance with policies of the court in which the action originated, unless good cause to the contrary is shown to the trial court.

(3) Unless Penal Code section 987.9 applies, the receiving court may, in its sound discretion, approve all trial-related expenses including:

(A) Attorney fees for defense counsel and, if any, co-counsel and actual travel-related expenses, up to state Board of Control limits, for staying in the county of the receiving court during trial and hearings.

(B) Paralegal and extraordinary secretarial or office expenditures of defense counsel.

(C) Expert witness costs and expenses.

(D) The cost of experts assisting in preparation before trial or during trial, for example, persons preparing demonstrative evidence.

(E) Investigator expenses.

(F) Defense witness expenses, including reasonable-and-necessary witness fees and travel expenses.

(Subd (d) amended effective January 1, 2006; previously amended effective January 1, 1998.)

(e) Extraordinary but reasonable-and-necessary expenses

Except in emergencies or unless it is impracticable to do so, a receiving court should give notice before incurring any extraordinary expenditures to the transferring court, in accordance with Penal Code section 1037(d). Extraordinary but reasonable-and-necessary expenditures include:

(1) Security-related expenditures: The cost of extra security precautions taken because of the risk of escape or suicide or threats of, or the potential for, violence during the trial. These precautions might include, for example, extra bailiffs or correctional officers, special transportation to the courthouse for trial, television monitoring, and security checks of those entering the courtroom.

(2) Facility remodeling or modification: Alterations to buildings or courtrooms to accommodate the change of venue case.

(3) Renting or leasing of space or equipment: Renting or leasing of space for courtrooms, offices, and other facilities, or equipment to accommodate the change of venue case.

(Subd (e) amended effective January 1, 2006; previously amended effective January 1, 1998.)

(f) Nonreimbursable expenses

Nonreimbursable expenses include:

(1) Normal operating expenses including the overhead of the receiving court, for example:

(A) Salary and benefits of existing court staff that would have been paid even if there were no change of venue case.

(B) The cost of operating the jail, for example, detention staff costs, normal inmate clothing, utility costs, overhead costs, and jail construction costs. These expenditures would have been incurred whether or not the case was transferred to the receiving court. It is, therefore, inappropriate to seek reimbursement from the transferring court.

(2) Equipment that is purchased and then kept by the receiving court and that can be used for other purposes or cases.

(Subd (f) amended effective January 1, 2006.)

(g) Miscellaneous

(1) Documentation of costs: No expense should be submitted for reimbursement without supporting documentation, such as a claim, invoice, bill, statement, or time sheet. In unusual circumstances, a declaration under penalty of perjury may be necessary. The declaration should describe the cost and state that it was incurred because of the change of venue case. Any required court order or approval of costs also should be sent to the transferring court.

(2) Timing of reimbursement: Unless both courts agree to other terms, reimbursement of all expenses that are not questioned by the transferring court should be made within 60 days of receipt of the claim for reimbursement. Payment of disputed amounts should be made within 60 days of the resolution of the dispute.

(Subd (g) amended effective January 1, 2007; previously amended effective January 1, 2006.)

Rule 4.155 amended effective September 1, 2017; adopted as section 4.2 of the Standards of Judicial Administration effective July 1, 1989; amended and renumbered as rule 4.162 effective January 1, 2001; previously amended effective January 1, 1998, January 1, 2006, and January 1, 2007.

Division 3
Trials

Rule 4.200. Pre-voir dire conference in criminal cases
Rule 4.201. Voir dire in criminal cases
Rule 4.202. Statements to the jury panel
Rule 4.210. Traffic court—trial by written declaration
Rule 4.230. Additional requirements in capital cases

Rule 4.200. Pre-voir dire conference in criminal cases

(a) The conference

Before jury selection begins in criminal cases, the court must conduct a conference with counsel to determine:

(1) A brief outline of the nature of the case, including a summary of the criminal charges;

(2) The names of persons counsel intend to call as witnesses at trial;

(3) The People's theory of culpability and the defendant's theories;

(4) The procedures for deciding requests for excuse for hardship and challenges for cause;

(5) The areas of inquiry and specific questions to be asked by the court and by counsel and any time limits on counsel's examination;

(6) The schedule for the trial and the predicted length of the trial;

(7) The number of alternate jurors to be selected and the procedure for selecting them; and

(8) The procedure for making objections pursuant to Code of Civil Procedure 231.7(b).

The judge must, if requested, excuse the defendant from then disclosing any defense theory.

(Subd (a) amended effective March 14, 2022; previously amended effective January 1, 2006, and January 1, 2007.)

(b) Written questions

The court may require counsel to submit in writing, and before the conference, all questions that counsel requests the court to ask of prospective jurors. This rule applies to questions to be asked either orally or by written questionnaire. The *Juror Questionnaire for Criminal Cases* (form MC-002) may be used.

(Subd (b) amended effective January 1, 2006.)

Rule 4.200 amended effective March 14, 2022; adopted as rule 228.1 effective June 6, 1990; previously amended and renumbered effective January 1, 2001; previously amended effective January 1, 2006, and January 1, 2007.

Advisory Committee Comment

This rule is to be used in conjunction with standard 4.30.

Rule 4.201. Voir dire in criminal cases

To select a fair and impartial jury, the judge must conduct an initial examination of the prospective jurors orally, or by written questionnaire, or by both methods. The *Juror Questionnaire for Criminal Cases* (form MC-002) may be used. After completion of the initial examination, the court must permit counsel to conduct supplemental questioning as provided in Code of Civil Procedure section 223.

Rule 4.201 amended effective January 1, 2008; adopted as rule 228.2 effective June 6, 1990; previously amended and renumbered effective January 1, 2001; previously amended effective January 1, 2006.

Advisory Committee Comment

Although Code of Civil Procedure section 223 creates a preference for nonsequestered voir dire (*People v. Roldan* (2005) 35 Cal.4th 646, 691), a judge may conduct sequestered voir dire on questions concerning media reports of the case and on any other issue deemed advisable. (See, e.g., Cal. Stds. Jud. Admin., std. 4.30(a)(3).) To determine whether such issues are present, a judge may consider factors including the charges, the nature of the evidence that is anticipated to be presented, and any other relevant factors. To that end, a judge should always inform jurors of the possibility of sequestered voir dire if the voir dire is likely to elicit answers that the juror may believe are sensitive in nature. It should also be noted that when written questionnaires are used, jurors must be advised of the right to request a hearing in chambers on sensitive questions rather than answering them on the questionnaire. (*Copley Press Inc. v. Superior Court* (1991) 228 Cal.App.3d 77, 87.)

Rule 4.202. Statements to the jury panel

Prior to the examination of prospective jurors, the trial judge may, in his or her discretion, permit brief opening statements by counsel to the panel.

Rule 4.202 adopted effective January 1, 2013.

Advisory Committee Comment

This statement is not a substitute for opening statements. Its purpose is to place voir dire questions in context and to generate interest in the case so that prospective jurors will be less inclined to claim marginal hardships.

Rule 4.210. Traffic court—trial by written declaration

(a) Applicability

This rule establishes the minimum procedural requirements for trials by written declaration under Vehicle Code section 40902. The procedures established by this rule must be followed in all trials by written declaration under that section.

(Subd (a) amended effective January 1, 2007.)

(b) Procedure

(1) *Definition of due date*

As used in this subdivision, "due date" means the last date on which the defendant's appearance is timely.

(2) *Extending due date*

If the clerk receives the defendant's written request for a trial by written declaration by the appearance date indicated on the *Notice to Appear*, the clerk must, within 15 calendar days after receiving the defendant's written request, extend the appearance date 25 calendar days and must give or mail notice to the defendant of the extended due date on the *Request for Trial by Written Declaration* (form TR-205) with a copy of the *Instructions to Defendant* (form TR-200) and any other required forms.

(3) *Election*

The defendant must file a *Request for Trial by Written Declaration* (form TR-205) with the clerk by the appearance date indicated on the *Notice to Appear* or the extended due date as provided in (2). The *Request for Trial by Written Declaration* (form TR-205) must be filed in addition to the defendant's written request for a trial by written declaration, unless the defendant's request was made on the election form.

(4) *Bail*

The defendant must deposit bail with the clerk by the appearance date indicated on the *Notice to Appear* or the extended due date as provided in (2).

(5) *Instructions to arresting officer*

If the clerk receives the defendant's *Request for Trial by Written Declaration* (form TR-205) and bail by the due date, the clerk must deliver or mail to the arresting officer's agency *Notice and Instructions to Arresting Officer* (form TR-210) and *Officer's Declaration* (form TR-235) with a copy of the *Notice to Appear* and a specified return date for receiving the officer's declaration. After receipt of the officer's declaration, or at the close of the officer's return date if no officer's declaration is filed, the clerk must submit the case file with all declarations and other evidence received to the court for decision.

(6) *Court decision*

After the court decides the case and returns the file and decision, the clerk must immediately deliver or mail the *Decision and Notice of Decision* (form TR-215) to the defendant and the arresting agency.

(7) *Trial de novo*

If the defendant files a *Request for New Trial (Trial de Novo)* (form TR-220) within 20 calendar days after the date of delivery or mailing of the *Decision and Notice of Decision* (form TR-215), the clerk must set a trial date within 45 calendar days of receipt of the defendant's written request for a new trial. The clerk must deliver or mail to the defendant and to the arresting officer's agency the *Order and Notice to Defendant of New Trial (Trial de Novo)* (form TR-225). If the defendant's request is not timely received, no new trial may be held and the case must be closed.

(8) *Case and time standard*

The clerk must deliver or mail the *Decision and Notice of Decision* (form TR-215) within 90 calendar days after the due date. Acts for which no specific time is stated in this rule must be performed promptly so that the *Decision and Notice of Decision* can be timely delivered or mailed by the clerk. Failure of the clerk or the court to comply with any time limit does not void or invalidate the decision of the court, unless prejudice to the defendant is shown.

(Subd (b) amended effective January 1, 2007; previously amended effective January 1, 2000, and July 1, 2000.)

(c) Due dates and time limits

Due dates and time limits must be as stated in this rule, unless changed or extended by the court. The court may extend any date, but the court need not state the reasons for granting or denying an extension on the record or in the minutes.

(Subd (c) amended effective January 1, 2007.)

(d) Ineligible defendants

If the defendant requests a trial by written declaration and the clerk or the court determines that the defendant is not eligible for a trial by written declaration, the clerk must extend the due date 25 calendar days and notify the defendant by mail of the determination and due date.

(Subd (d) amended effective January 1, 2007.)

(e) Noncompliance

If the defendant does not comply with this rule (including submitting the required bail amount, signing and filing all required forms, and complying with all time limits and due dates), the court may deny a trial by written declaration and may proceed as otherwise provided by statute and court rules.

(Subd (e) amended effective January 1, 2007.)

(f) Evidence

Testimony and other relevant evidence may be introduced in the form of a *Notice to Appear* issued under Vehicle Code section 40500; a business record or receipt; a sworn declaration of the arresting officer; and, on behalf of the defendant, a sworn declaration of the defendant.

(Subd (f) amended effective January 1, 2007.)

(g) Fines, assessments, or penalties

The statute and the rules do not prevent or preclude the court from imposing on a defendant who is found guilty any lawful fine, assessment, or other penalty, and the court is not limited to imposing money penalties in the bail amount, unless the bail amount is the maximum and the only lawful penalty.

(Subd (g) amended effective January 1, 2007.)

(h) Additional forms and procedures

The clerk may approve and prescribe forms, time limits, and procedures that are not in conflict with or not inconsistent with the statute or this rule.

(i) Forms

The following forms are to be used to implement the procedures under this rule:

(1) *Instructions to Defendant* (form TR-200)

(2) *Request for Trial by Written Declaration* (form TR-205)

(3) *Notice and Instructions to Arresting Officer* (form TR-210)

(4) *Officer's Declaration* (form TR-235)

(5) *Decision and Notice of Decision* (form TR-215)

(6) *Request for New Trial (Trial de Novo)* (form TR-220)

(7) *Order and Notice to Defendant of New Trial (Trial de Novo)* (form TR-225)

(Subd (i) amended effective January 1, 2007; previously amended effective January 1, 2000.)

(j) Local forms

A court may adopt additional forms as may be required to implement this rule and the court's local procedures not inconsistent with this rule.

(Subd (j) amended effective January 1, 2007.)

Rule 4.210 amended and renumbered effective January 1, 2007; adopted as rule 828 effective January 1, 1999; previously amended effective January 1, 2000, and July 1, 2000.

Rule 4.220. Remote video proceedings in traffic infraction cases [Repealed]

Rule 4.220 repealed effective May 13, 2022; adopted effective February 1, 2013; previously amended effective September 1, 2015.

Rule 4.230. Additional requirements in capital cases

(a) Application

This rule applies only in trials in cases in which the death penalty may be imposed.

(Subd (a) adopted effective April 25, 2019.)

(b) Checklist

Within 10 days of counsel's first appearance in court, primary counsel for each defendant and the prosecution must each acknowledge that they have reviewed *Capital Case Attorney Trial Checklist* (form CR-605) by signing and submitting this form to the court. Counsel is encouraged to keep a copy of this checklist.

(Subd (b) adopted effective April 25, 2019.)

(c) Review of daily transcripts by counsel during trial

During trial, counsel must call the court's attention to any errors or omissions they may find in the daily transcripts. The court must periodically ask counsel for lists of any such errors or omissions and may hold hearings to verify them. Immaterial typographical errors that cannot conceivably cause confusion are not required to be brought to the court's attention.

(Subd (c) adopted effective April 25, 2019.)

(d) Lists of appearances, exhibits, motions, and jury instructions

(1) Primary counsel for each defendant and the prosecution must each prepare the lists identified in (A)–(D).

(A) A list of all appearances made by that party. *Capital Case Attorney List of Appearances* (form CR-601) must be used for this purpose. The list must include all appearances, including ex parte appearances, the date of each appearance, the department in which it was made, the name of counsel making the appearance, and a brief description of the nature of the appearance. A separate list of Penal Code section 987.9 appearances must be maintained under seal for each defendant. In the event of any substitution of attorney at any stage of the case, the relieved attorney must provide the list of all appearances to substituting counsel within five days of being relieved.

(B) A list of all exhibits offered by that party. *Capital Case Attorney List of Exhibits* (form CR-602) must be used for this purpose. The list must indicate whether the exhibit was admitted in evidence, refused, lodged, or withdrawn.

(C) A list of all motions made by that party, including ex parte motions. *Capital Case Attorney List of Motions* (form CR-603) must be used for this purpose.

(D) A list of all jury instructions submitted in writing by that party. *Capital Case Attorney List of Jury Instructions* (form CR-604) must be used for this purpose. The list must indicate whether the instruction was given, given as modified, refused, or withdrawn.

(2) No later than 21 days after the imposition of a sentence of death, counsel must submit the lists to the court and serve on all parties a copy of all the lists except the list of Penal Code section 987.9 appearances. Unless otherwise provided by local rule, the lists must be submitted to the court in electronic form.

(Subd (d) adopted effective April 25, 2019.)

(e) Electronic recordings presented or offered into evidence

Counsel must comply with the requirements of rule 2.1040 regarding electronic recordings presented or offered into evidence, including any such recordings that are part of a digital or electronic presentation.

(Subd (e) adopted effective April 25, 2019.)

(f) Copies of audio and visual aids

Primary counsel must provide the clerk with copies of any audio or visual aids not otherwise subject to the requirements of (e) that are used during jury selection or in presentations to the jury, including digital or electronic presentations. If a visual aid is oversized, a photograph of that visual aid must be provided in place of the original. For digital or electronic presentations, counsel must supply both a copy of the presentation in its native format and printouts showing the full text of each slide or image. Photographs and printouts provided under this subdivision must be on 8-1/2 by 11 inch paper.

(Subd (f) adopted effective April 25, 2019.)
Rule 4.230 adopted effective April 25, 2019.

Advisory Committee Comment

Subdivision (b). *Capital Case Attorney List of Appearances* (form CR-601), *Capital Case Attorney List of Exhibits* (form CR-602), *Capital Case Attorney List of Motions* (form CR-603), and *Capital Case Attorney List of Jury Instructions* (form CR-604) must be used to comply with the requirements in this subdivision.

Subdivision (d). To facilitate preparation of complete and accurate lists, counsel are encouraged to add items to the lists at the time appearances or motions are made, exhibits are offered, or jury instructions are submitted.

Division 4
Sentencing

Rule 4.305. Notification of appeal rights in felony cases
Rule 4.306. Notification of appeal rights in misdemeanor and infraction cases
Rule 4.310. Determination of presentence custody time credit
Rule 4.315. Setting date for execution of death sentence
Rule 4.320. Records of criminal convictions (Gov. Code, §§ 69844.5, 71280.5)
Rule 4.325. Ignition interlock installation orders: "interest of justice" exceptions
Rule 4.330. Misdemeanor hate crimes
Rule 4.335. Ability-to-pay determinations for infraction offenses
Rule 4.336. Confidential Can't Afford to Pay Fine Forms

Rule 4.300. Commitments to nonpenal institutions [Repealed]

Rule 4.300 repealed effective March 14, 2022; adopted as rule 453 effective July 1, 1977; previously amended and renumbered effective January 1, 2001; previously amended effective July 28, 1977, January 1, 2006, and January 1, 2007.

Rule 4.305. Notification of appeal rights in felony cases

After imposing sentence or making an order deemed to be a final judgment in a criminal case on conviction after trial, or after imposing sentence following a revocation of probation, except where the revocation is after the defendant's admission of violation of probation, the court must advise the defendant of his or her right to appeal, of the necessary steps and time for taking an appeal, and of the right of an indigent defendant to have counsel appointed by the reviewing court.

Rule 4.305 amended effective January 1, 2013; adopted as rule 250 effective January 1, 1972; previously amended effective July 1, 1972, January 1, 1977, and January 1, 2007; previously amended and renumbered as rule 470 effective January 1, 1991; previously renumbered effective January 1, 2001.

Rule 4.306. Notification of appeal rights in misdemeanor and infraction cases

After imposing sentence or making an order deemed to be a final judgment in a misdemeanor case on conviction after trial or following a revocation of probation, the court must orally or in writing advise a defendant not represented by counsel of the right to appeal, the time for filing a notice of appeal, and the right of an indigent defendant to have counsel appointed on appeal. This rule does not apply to infractions or when a revocation of probation is ordered after the defendant's admission of a violation of probation.

Rule 4.306 amended effective January 1, 2007; adopted as rule 535 effective July 1, 1981; previously renumbered effective January 1, 2001.

Rule 4.310. Determination of presentence custody time credit

At the time of sentencing, the court must cause to be recorded on the judgment or commitment the total time in custody to be credited on the sentence under Penal Code sections 2900.5, 2933.1(c), and 2933.2(c). On referral of the defendant to the probation officer for an investigation and report under Penal Code section 1203(b) or 1203(g), or on setting a date for sentencing in the absence of a referral, the court must direct the sheriff, probation officer, or other appropriate person to report to the court and notify the defendant or defense counsel and prosecuting attorney within a reasonable time before the date set for sentencing as to the number of days that defendant has been in custody and for which he or she may be entitled to credit. Any challenges to the report must be heard at the time of sentencing.

Rule 4.310 amended effective January 1, 2007; adopted as rule 252 effective January 1, 1977; previously amended and renumbered as rule 472 effective January 1, 1991; previously amended and renumbered effective January 1, 2001; previously amended effective July 1, 2004.

Rule 4.315. Setting date for execution of death sentence

(a) Open session of court; notice required

A date for execution of a judgment of death under Penal Code section 1193 or 1227 must be set at a public session of the court at which the defendant and the People may be represented.

At least 10 days before the session of court at which the date will be set, the court must mail notice of the time and place of the proceeding by first-class mail, postage prepaid, to the Attorney General, the district attorney, the defendant at the prison address, the defendant's counsel or, if none is known, counsel who most recently represented the defendant on appeal or in postappeal legal proceedings, and the executive director of the California Appellate Project in San Francisco. The clerk must file a certificate of mailing copies of the notice. The court may not hold the proceeding or set an execution date unless the record contains a clerk's certificate showing that the notices required by this subdivision were timely mailed.

Unless otherwise provided by statute, the defendant does not have a right to be present in person.

(Subd (a) amended effective January 1, 2007; previously amended effective July 1, 1990.)

(b) Selection of date; notice

If, at the announced session of court, the court sets a date for execution of the judgment of death, the court must mail certified copies of the order setting the date to the warden of the state prison and to the Governor, as required by statute; and must also, within five days of the making of the order, mail by first-class mail, postage prepaid, certified copies of the order setting the date to each of the persons required to be given notice by (a). The clerk must file a certificate of mailing copies of the order.

(Subd (b) amended effective January 1, 2007.)

Rule 4.315 amended effective January 1, 2007; adopted as rule 490 effective July 1, 1989; previously amended effective July 1, 1990; previously renumbered effective January 1, 2001.

Rule 4.320. Records of criminal convictions (Gov. Code, §§ 69844.5, 71280.5)

(a) Information to be submitted

In addition to the information that the Department of Justice requires from courts under Penal Code section 13151, each trial court must also report, electronically or manually, the following information, in the form and manner specified by the Department of Justice:

(1) Whether the defendant was represented by counsel or waived the right to counsel; and

(2) In the case of a guilty or nolo contendere plea, whether:

(A) The defendant was advised of and understood the charges;

(B) The defendant was advised of, understood, and waived the right to a jury trial, the right to confront witnesses, and the privilege against self-incrimination; and

(C) The court found the plea was voluntary and intelligently made.

For purposes of this rule, a change of plea form signed by the defendant, defense counsel if the defendant was represented by counsel, and the judge, and filed with the court is a sufficient basis for the clerk or deputy clerk to report that the requirements of (2) have been met.

(Subd (a) amended effective January 1, 2007; previously amended January 1, 2001.)

(b) Certification required

The reporting clerk or a deputy clerk must certify that the report submitted to the Department of Justice under Penal Code section 13151 and this rule is a correct abstract of the information contained in the court's records in the case.

(Subd (b) amended effective January 1, 2007.)

Rule 4.320 amended effective January 1, 2007; adopted as rule 895 effective July 1, 1998; previously amended and renumbered effective January 1, 2001.

Rule 4.325. Ignition interlock installation orders: "interest of justice" exceptions

If the court finds that the interest of justice requires an exception to the Vehicle Code sections 14601(e), 14601.1(d), 14601.4(c), or 14601.5(g) requirements for installation of an ignition interlock device under Vehicle Code section 23575, the reasons for the finding must be stated on the record.

Rule 4.325 amended and renumbered effective January 1, 2001; adopted as rule 530 effective January 1, 1995.

Rule 4.330. Misdemeanor hate crimes

(a) Application

This rule applies to misdemeanor cases where the defendant is convicted of either (1) a substantive hate crime under section 422.6 or (2) a misdemeanor violation and the facts of the crime constitute a hate crime under section 422.55.

(Subd (a) adopted effective January 1, 2007.)

(b) Sentencing consideration

In sentencing a defendant under (a), the court must consider the goals for hate crime sentencing stated in rule 4.427(e).

(Subd (b) adopted effective January 1, 2007.)

Rule 4.330 adopted effective January 1, 2007.

Rule 4.335. Ability-to-pay determinations for infraction offenses

(a) Application

This rule applies to any infraction offense for which the defendant has received a written *Notice to Appear.*

(Subd (a) adopted effective January 1, 2017.)

(b) Required notice regarding an ability-to-pay determination

Courts must provide defendants with notice of their right to request an ability-to-pay determination and make available instructions or other materials for requesting an ability-to-pay determination.

(Subd (b) adopted effective January 1, 2017.)

(c) Procedure for determining ability to pay

(1) The court, on request of a defendant, must consider the defendant's ability to pay.

(2) A defendant may request an ability-to-pay determination at adjudication, or while the judgment remains unpaid, including when a case is delinquent or has been referred to a comprehensive collection program.

(3) The court must permit a defendant to make this request by written petition unless the court directs a court appearance. The request must include any information or documentation the defendant wishes the court to consider in connection with the determination. The judicial officer has the discretion to conduct the review on the written record or to order a hearing.

(4) Based on the ability-to-pay determination, the court may exercise its discretion to:

(A) Provide for payment on an installment plan (if available);

(B) Allow the defendant to complete community service in lieu of paying the total fine (if available);

(C) Suspend the fine in whole or in part;

(D) Offer an alternative disposition.

(5) A defendant ordered to pay on an installment plan or to complete community service may request to have an ability-to-pay determination at any time during the pendency of the judgment.

(6) If a defendant has already had an ability-to-pay determination in the case, a defendant may request a subsequent ability-to-pay determination only based on changed circumstances.

(Subd (c) adopted effective January 1, 2017.)

Rule 4.335 adopted effective January 1, 2017.

Advisory Committee Comment

Subdivision (b). This notice may be provided on the notice required by rule 4.107, the notice of any civil assessment under section 1214.1, a court's website, or any other notice provided to the defendant.

Subdivision (c)(1). In determining the defendant's ability to pay, the court should take into account factors including: (1) receipt of public benefits under Supplemental Security Income (SSI), State Supplementary Payment (SSP), California Work Opportunity and Responsibility to Kids (CalWORKS), Federal Tribal Temporary Assistance for Needy Families (Tribal TANF), Supplemental Nutrition Assistance Program, California Food Assistance Program, County Relief, General Relief (GR), General Assistance (GA), Cash Assistance Program for Aged, Blind, and Disabled Legal Immigrants (CAPI), In Home Supportive Services (IHSS), or Medi-Cal; and (2) a monthly income of 125 percent or less of the current poverty guidelines, updated periodically in the Federal Register by the U.S. Department of Health and Human Services under 42 U.S.C. § 9902(2).

Subdivision (c)(4). The amount and manner of paying the total fine must be reasonable and compatible with the defendant's financial ability. Even if the defendant has not demonstrated an inability to pay, the court may still exercise discretion. Regardless of whether the defendant has demonstrated an inability to pay, the court in exercising its discretion under this subdivision may consider the severity of the offense, among other factors. While the base fine may be suspended in whole or in part in the court's discretion, this subdivision is not intended to affect the imposition of any mandatory fees.

Rule 4.336. Confidential Can't Afford to Pay Fine Forms

(a) Use of request and order forms

(1) A court uses the information on *Can't Afford to Pay Fine: Traffic and Other Infractions* (form TR-320/CR-320) to determine an infraction defendant's ability to pay under rule 4.335.

(2) A court may use *Can't Afford to Pay Fine: Traffic and Other Infractions (Court Order)* (form TR-321/CR-321) to issue an order in response to an infraction defendant's request for an ability-to-pay determination under rule 4.335.

(Subd (a) adopted effective April 1, 2018.)

(b) Confidential request form

Can't Afford to Pay Fine: Traffic and Other Infractions (form TR-320/CR-320), the information it contains, and any supporting documentation are confidential. The clerk's office must maintain the form and supporting documentation in a manner that will protect and preserve their confidentiality. Only the parties and the court may access the form and supporting documentation.

(Subd (b) adopted effective April 1, 2018.)

(c) Optional request and order forms

Can't Afford to Pay Fine: Traffic and Other Infractions (form TR-320/CR-320) and *Can't Afford to Pay Fine: Traffic and Other Infractions (Court Order)* (form TR-321/CR-321) are optional forms under rule 1.35.

(Subd (c) adopted effective April 1, 2018.)

Rule 4.336 adopted effective April 1, 2018.

Division 5
Felony Sentencing Law

Rule 4.401. Authority
Rule 4.403. Application
Rule 4.405. Definitions
Rule 4.406. Reasons
Rule 4.408. Listing of factors not exclusive; sequence not significant
Rule 4.409. Consideration of relevant factors
Rule 4.410. General objectives in sentencing
Rule 4.411. Presentence investigations and reports
Rule 4.411.5. Probation officer's presentence investigation report
Rule 4.412. Reasons—agreement to punishment as an adequate reason and as abandonment of certain claims
Rule 4.413. Grant of probation when defendant is presumptively ineligible for probation
Rule 4.414. Criteria affecting probation
Rule 4.415. Criteria affecting the imposition of mandatory supervision
Rule 4.420. Selection of term of imprisonment for offense
Rule 4.421. Circumstances in aggravation
Rule 4.423. Circumstances in mitigation
Rule 4.424. Consideration of applicability of section 654
Rule 4.425. Factors affecting concurrent or consecutive sentences
Rule 4.426. Violent sex crimes
Rule 4.427. Hate crimes
Rule 4.428. Factors affecting imposition of enhancements
Rule 4.431. Proceedings at sentencing to be reported
Rule 4.433. Matters to be considered at time set for sentencing
Rule 4.435. Sentencing on revocation of probation, mandatory supervision, and postrelease community supervision
Rule 4.437. Statements in aggravation and mitigation
Rule 4.447. Sentencing of enhancements

Rule 4.451. Sentence consecutive to or concurrent with indeterminate term or term in other jurisdiction
Rule 4.452. Determinate sentence consecutive to prior determinate sentence
Rule 4.472. Determination of presentence custody time credit
Rule 4.480. Judge's statement under section 1203.01

Rule 4.401. Authority

The rules in this division are adopted under Penal Code section 1170.3 and under the authority granted to the Judicial Council by the Constitution, article VI, section 6, to adopt rules for court administration, practice, and procedure.

Rule 4.401 amended effective January 1, 2007; adopted as rule 401 effective July 1, 1977; previously renumbered effective January 1, 2001.

Rule 4.403. Application

These rules apply only to criminal cases in which the defendant is convicted of one or more offenses punishable as a felony by (1) a determinate sentence imposed under Penal Code part 2, title 7, chapter 4.5 (commencing with section 1170) and (2) an indeterminate sentence imposed under section 1168(b) only if it is imposed relative to other offenses with determinate terms or enhancements.

Rule 4.403 amended effective January 1, 2018; adopted as rule 403 effective July 1, 1977; previously amended and renumbered effective January 1, 2001; previously amended effective July 1, 2003, and January 1, 2007.

Advisory Committee Comment

The operative portions of section 1170 deal exclusively with prison sentences; and the mandate to the Judicial Council in section 1170.3 is limited to criteria affecting the length of prison sentences, sentences in county jail under section 1170(h), and the grant or denial of probation.

Rule 4.405. Definitions

As used in this division, unless the context otherwise requires:

(1) "These rules" means the rules in this division.

(2) "Base term" is the determinate or indeterminate sentence imposed for the commission of a crime, not including any enhancements that carry an additional term of imprisonment.

(3) When a person is convicted of two or more felonies, the "principal term" is the greatest determinate term of imprisonment imposed by the court for any of the crimes, including any term imposed for applicable count-specific enhancements.

(4) When a person is convicted of two or more felonies, the "subordinate term" is the determinate term imposed for an offense, plus any count-specific enhancements applicable to the offense ordered to run consecutively to the principal term.

(5) "Enhancement" means an additional term of imprisonment added to the base term.

(6) "Offense" means the offense of conviction unless a different meaning is specified or is otherwise clear from the context. The term "instant" or "current" is used in connection with "offense" or "offense of conviction" to distinguish the violation for which the defendant is being sentenced from an enhancement, prior or subsequent offense, or from an offense before another court.

(7) "Aggravation," or "circumstances in aggravation" means factors that justify the imposition of the upper prison term referred to in section 1170(b) and 1170.1, or factors that the court may consider in exercising discretion authorized by statute and under these rules including imposing the middle term instead of a low term, denying probation, ordering consecutive sentences, or determining whether to exercise discretion pursuant to section 1385(c).

(8) "Mitigation" or "circumstances in mitigation" means factors that the court may consider in its broad discretion authorized by statute and under these rules.

(9) "Sentence choice" means the selection of any disposition of the case that does not amount to a dismissal, acquittal, or grant of a new trial.

(10) "Section" means a section of the Penal Code.

(11) "Imprisonment" means confinement in a state prison or county jail under section 1170(h).

(12) "Charged" means charged in the indictment or information.

(13) "Found" means admitted by the defendant or found to be true by the trier of fact upon trial.

(14) "Mandatory supervision" means the period of supervision defined in section 1170(h)(5)(A), (B).

(15) "Postrelease community supervision" means the period of supervision governed by section 3451 et seq.

(16) "Risk/needs assessment" means a standardized, validated evaluation tool designed to measure an offender's actuarial risk factors and specific needs that, if successfully addressed, may reduce the likelihood of future criminal activity.

(17) "Evidence-based practices" means supervision policies, procedures, programs, and practices demonstrated by scientific research to reduce recidivism among individuals under probation, parole, or postrelease supervision.

(18) "Community-based corrections program" means a program consisting of a system of services for felony offenders under local supervision dedicated to the goals stated in section 1229(c)(1)–(5).

(19) "Local supervision" means the supervision of an adult felony offender on probation, mandatory supervision, or postrelease community supervision.

(20) "County jail" means local county correctional facility.

Rule 4.405 amended effective March 14, 2022; adopted as rule 405 effective July 1, 1977; previously renumbered effective January 1, 2001; previously amended effective July 28, 1977, January 1, 1991, July 1, 2003, January 1, 2007, May 23, 2007, January 1, 2017, and January 1, 2018.

Advisory Committee Comment

The Legislature amended the determinate sentencing law to require courts to order imposition of a sentence or enhancement not to exceed the middle term unless factors in aggravation justify imposition of the upper term and are stipulated to by the defendant or found true beyond a reasonable doubt at trial by the jury or by the judge in a court trial. (See Sen. Bill 567; Stats. 2021, ch. 731.) However, in determining whether to impose the upper term for a criminal offense, the court may consider as an aggravating factor that a defendant has suffered one or more prior convictions, based on certified records of conviction. This exception may not be used to select the upper term of an enhancement.

The court may exercise its judicial discretion in imposing the middle term or low term and must state the facts and reasons on the record for choosing the sentence imposed. In exercising this discretion between the middle term and the low term, the court may rely on aggravating factors that have not been stipulated to by the defendant or proven beyond a reasonable doubt. (*People v. Black* (2007) 41 Cal.4th 799.)

The Legislature also amended the determinate sentencing law to require courts to order imposition of the low term when the court finds that certain factors contributed to the commission of the crime unless the court finds that it would not be in the interests of justice to do so because the aggravating factors outweigh the mitigating factors. (Pen. Code, § 1170(b)(6).)

Rule 4.406. Reasons

(a) How given

If the sentencing judge is required to give reasons for a sentence choice, the judge must state in simple language the primary factor or factors that support the exercise of discretion. The statement need not be in the language of the statute or these rules. It must be delivered orally on the record. The court may give a single statement explaining the reason or reasons for imposing a particular sentence or the exercise of judicial discretion, if the statement identifies the sentencing choices where discretion is exercised and there is no impermissible dual use of facts.

(Subd (a) amended effective January 1, 2018; previously amended effective January 1, 2007.)

(b) When reasons required

Sentence choices that generally require a statement of a reason include, but are not limited to:

(1) Granting probation when the defendant is presumptively ineligible for probation;

(2) Denying probation when the defendant is presumptively eligible for probation;

(3) Selecting a term for either an offense or an enhancement;

(4) Imposing consecutive sentences;

(5) Imposing full consecutive sentences under section 667.6(c) rather than consecutive terms under section 1170.1(a), when the court has that choice;

(6) Waiving a restitution fine;

(7) Granting relief under section 1385; and

(8) Denying mandatory supervision in the interests of justice under section 1170(h)(5)(A).

(Subd (b) amended effective March 14, 2022; previously amended effective January 1, 2001, July 1, 2003, January 1, 2006, January 1, 2007, May 23, 2007, January 1, 2017, and January 1, 2018.)

Rule 4.406 amended effective March 14, 2022; adopted as rule 406 effective January 1, 1991; previously amended and renumbered effective January 1, 2001; previously amended effective July 1, 2003, January 1, 2006, January 1, 2007, May 23, 2007, January 1, 2017, and January 1, 2018.

Advisory Committee Comment

This rule is not intended to expand the statutory requirements for giving reasons, and is not an independent interpretation of the statutory requirements.

The court is not required to separately state the reasons for making each sentencing choice so long as the record reflects the court understood it had discretion on a particular issue and its reasons for making the particular choice. For example, if the court decides to deny probation and impose the upper term of punishment, the court may simply state: "I am denying probation and imposing the upper term because of the extensive losses to the victim and because the defendant's record is increasing in seriousness." It is not necessary to state a reason after exercising each decision.

The court must be mindful of impermissible dual use of facts in stating reasons for sentencing choices. For example, the court is not permitted to use a reason to impose a greater term if that reason also is either (1) the same as an enhancement that will be imposed, or (2) an element of the crime. The court should not use the same reason to impose a consecutive sentence and to impose an upper term of imprisonment. (*People v. Avalos* (1984) 37 Cal.3d 216, 233.) It is not improper to use the same reason to deny probation and to impose the upper term. (*People v. Bowen* (1992) 11 Cal.App.4th 102, 106.)

Whenever relief is *granted* under section 1385, the court's reasons for exercising that discretion must be stated orally on the record and entered in the minutes if requested by a party or if the proceedings are not recorded electronically or reported by a court reporter. (Pen. Code, § 1385(a).) Although no legal authority requires the court to state reasons for *denying* relief, such a statement may be helpful in the appellate review of the exercise of the court's discretion.

Rule 4.407. [Repealed 2007]

Rule 4.407 repealed effective January 1, 2007; adopted as rule 407 effective July 1, 1977; previously amended effective January 1, 1991; previously renumbered effective January 1, 2001. The repealed rule related to rules of construction.

Rule 4.408. Listing of factors not exclusive; sequence not significant

(a) The listing of factors in these rules for making discretionary sentencing decisions is not exhaustive and does not prohibit a trial judge from using additional criteria reasonably related to the decision being made. Any such additional criteria must be stated on the record by the sentencing judge.

(Subd (a) amended effective January 1, 2018; previously amended effective January 1, 2007.)

(b) The order in which criteria are listed does not indicate their relative weight or importance.

Rule 4.408 amended effective January 1, 2018; adopted as rule 408 effective July 1, 1977; previously renumbered effective January 1, 2001; previously amended effective January 1, 2007.

Advisory Committee Comment

The variety of circumstances presented in felony cases is so great that no listing of criteria could claim to be all-inclusive. (Cf. Evid. Code, § 351.)

The court may impose a sentence or enhancement exceeding the middle term only if the facts underlying the aggravating factor were stipulated to by the defendant or found true beyond a reasonable doubt at trial by the jury or by the judge in a court trial. (Pen. Code, § 1170(b)(2).)

However, in determining whether to impose the upper term for a criminal offense, the court may consider as an aggravating factor that a defendant has suffered one or more prior convictions, based on certified records of conviction. This exception may not be used to select the upper term of an enhancement. (Pen. Code, § 1170(b)(3).)

The Legislature also amended the determinate sentencing law to require courts to order imposition of the low term when the court finds that certain factors contributed to the commission of the crime unless the court finds that it would not be in the interests of justice to do so because the aggravating factors outweigh the mitigating factors. (Pen. Code, § 1170(b)(6).)

Rule 4.409. Consideration of relevant factors

Relevant factors enumerated in these rules must be considered by the sentencing judge, and will be deemed to have been considered unless the record affirmatively reflects otherwise.

Rule 4.409 amended effective January 1, 2018; adopted as rule 409 effective July 1, 1977; previously renumbered effective January 1, 2001; previously amended effective January 1, 2007.

Advisory Committee Comment

Relevant factors are those applicable to the facts in the record of the case; not all factors will be relevant to each case. The judge's duty is similar to the duty to consider the probation officer's report. Section 1203.

In deeming the sentencing judge to have considered relevant factors, the rule applies the presumption of Evidence Code section 664 that official duty has been regularly performed. (See *People v. Moran* (1970) 1 Cal.3d 755, 762 [trial court presumed to have considered referring eligible defendant to California Youth Authority in absence of any showing to the contrary, citing Evidence Code section 664].)

Rule 4.410. General objectives in sentencing

(a) General objectives of sentencing include:

(1) Protecting society;

(2) Punishing the defendant;

(3) Encouraging the defendant to lead a law-abiding life in the future and deterring him or her from future offenses;

(4) Deterring others from criminal conduct by demonstrating its consequences;

(5) Preventing the defendant from committing new crimes by isolating him or her for the period of incarceration;

(6) Securing restitution for the victims of crime;

(7) Achieving uniformity in sentencing; and

(8) Increasing public safety by reducing recidivism through community-based corrections programs and evidence-based practices.

(Subd (a) amended effective January 1, 2017; previously amended effective July 1, 2003, and January 1, 2007.)

(b) Because in some instances these objectives may suggest inconsistent dispositions, the sentencing judge must consider which objectives are of primary importance in the particular case. The sentencing judge should be guided by statutory statements of policy, the criteria in these rules, and any other facts and circumstances relevant to the case.

(Subd (b) amended effective January 1, 2018; adopted as part of unlettered subd effective July 1, 1977; former subd (b) amended and relettered as part of subd (a) effective July 1, 2003; lettered as subd (b) effective July 1, 2003.)

Rule 4.410 amended effective January 1, 2018; adopted as rule 410 effective July 1, 1977; previously renumbered effective January 1, 2001; previously amended effective July 1, 2003, January 1, 2007, and January 1, 2017.

Advisory Committee Comment

Statutory expressions of policy include:

Section 1170(a)(1) expresses the policies of uniformity, proportionality of terms of imprisonment to the seriousness of the offense, and the use of imprisonment as punishment. It also states that "the purpose of sentencing is public safety achieved through punishment, rehabilitation, and restorative justice."

Sections 17.5, 1228, and 3450 express the policies promoting reinvestment of criminal justice resources to support community-based corrections programs and evidence-based practices to improve public safety through a reduction in recidivism.

Rule 4.411. Presentence investigations and reports

(a) When required

As provided in subdivision (b), the court must refer the case to the probation officer for:

(1) A presentence investigation and report if the defendant:

(A) Is statutorily eligible for probation or a term of imprisonment in county jail under section 1170(h); or

(B) Is not eligible for probation but a report is needed to assist the court with other sentencing issues, including the determination of the proper amount of restitution fine;

(2) A supplemental report if a significant period of time has passed since the original report was prepared.

(Subd (a) amended effective January 1, 2018; previously amended effective January 1, 2007, and January 1, 2015.)

(b) Waiver of the investigation and report

The parties may stipulate to the waiver of the probation officer's investigation and report in writing or in open court and entered in the minutes, and with the consent of the court. In deciding whether to consent to the waiver, the court should consider whether the information in the report would assist in the resolution of any current or future sentencing issues, or would assist in the effective supervision of the person. A waiver under this section does not affect the requirement under section 1203c that a probation report be created when the court commits a person to state prison.

(Subd (b) amended effective January 1, 2018; previously amended effective January 1, 2015.)

Rule 4.411 amended effective January 1, 2018; adopted as rule 418 effective July 1, 1977; previously amended and renumbered as rule 411 effective January 1, 1991; previously renumbered effective January 1, 2001; previously amended effective January 1, 2006, January 1, 2007, and January 1, 2015.

Advisory Committee Comment

Section 1203 requires a presentence report in every felony case in which the defendant is eligible for probation. Subdivision (a) requires a presentence report in every felony case in which the defendant is eligible for a term of imprisonment in county jail under section 1170(h).

When considering whether to waive a presentence investigation and report, courts should consider that probation officers' reports are used by (1) courts in determining the appropriate term of imprisonment in prison or county jail under section 1170(h); (2) courts in deciding whether probation is appropriate, whether a period of mandatory supervision should be denied in the interests of justice under section 1170(h)(5)(A), and the appropriate length and conditions of probation and mandatory supervision; (3) the probation department in supervising the defendant; and (4) the Department of Corrections and Rehabilitation, Division of Adult Operations, in deciding on the type of facility and program in which to place a defendant.

Subdivision (a)(2) is based on case law that generally requires a supplemental report if the defendant is to be resentenced a significant time after the original sentencing, as, for example, after a remand by an appellate court, or after the apprehension of a defendant who failed to appear at sentencing. The rule is not intended to expand on the requirements of those cases.

The rule does not require a new investigation and report if a recent report is available and can be incorporated by reference and there is no indication of changed circumstances. This is particularly true if a report is needed only for the Department of Corrections and Rehabilitation because the defendant has waived a report and agreed to a prison sentence. If a full report was prepared in another case in the same or another jurisdiction within the preceding six months, during which time the defendant was in custody, and that report is available to the Department of Corrections and Rehabilitation, it is unlikely that a new investigation is needed.

This rule does not prohibit pre-conviction, pre-plea reports as authorized by section 1203.7.

Rule 4.411.5. Probation officer's presentence investigation report

(a) Contents

A probation officer's presentence investigation report in a felony case must include at least the following:

(1) A face sheet showing at least:

(A) The defendant's name and other identifying data;

(B) The case number;

(C) The crime of which the defendant was convicted, and any enhancements which were admitted or found true;

(D) Any factors in aggravation including whether the factors were stipulated to by the defendant, found true beyond a reasonable doubt at trial by a jury, or found true beyond a reasonable doubt by a judge in a court trial;

(E) The date of commission of the crime, the date of conviction, and any other dates relevant to sentencing;

(F) The defendant's custody status; and

(G) The terms of any agreement on which a plea of guilty was based.

(2) The facts and circumstances of the crime and the defendant's arrest, including information concerning any co-defendants and the status or disposition of their cases. The source of all such information must be stated.

(3) A summary of the defendant's record of prior criminal conduct, including convictions as an adult and sustained petitions in juvenile delinquency proceedings. Records of an arrest or charge not leading to a conviction or the sustaining of a petition may not be included unless supported by facts concerning the arrest or charge.

(4) Any statement made by the defendant to the probation officer, or a summary thereof, including the defendant's account of the circumstances of the crime.

(5) Information concerning the victim of the crime, including:

(A) The victim's statement or a summary thereof, if available;

(B) Any physical or psychological injuries suffered by the victim;

(C) The amount of the victim's monetary loss, and whether or not it is covered by insurance; and

(D) Any information required by law.

(6) Any relevant facts concerning the defendant's social history, including those categories enumerated in section 1203.10, organized under appropriate subheadings, including, whenever applicable, "Family," "Education," "Employment and income," "Military," "Medical/psychological," "Record of substance abuse or lack thereof," and any other relevant subheadings. This includes:

(A) Facts relevant to whether the defendant may be suffering from sexual trauma, traumatic brain injury, post-traumatic stress disorder, substance abuse, or mental health problems as a result of his or her U.S. military service; and

(B) Factors listed in section 1170(b)(6) and whether the current offense is connected to those factors.

(7) Collateral information, including written statements from:

(A) Official sources such as defense and prosecuting attorneys, police (subsequent to any police reports used to summarize the crime), probation and parole officers who have had prior experience with the defendant, and correctional personnel who observed the defendant's behavior during any period of presentence incarceration; and

(B) Interested persons, including family members and others who have written letters concerning the defendant.

(8) The defendant's relevant risk factors and needs as identified by a risk/needs assessment, if such an assessment is performed, and such other information from the assessment as may be requested by the court.

(9) An evaluation of factors relating to disposition. This section must include:

(A) A reasoned discussion of the defendant's suitability and eligibility for probation, and, if probation is recommended, a proposed plan including recommendations for the conditions of probation and any special need for supervision;

(B) If a prison sentence or term of imprisonment in county jail under section 1170(h) is recommended or is likely to be imposed, a reasoned discussion of aggravating and mitigating factors affecting the sentence length;

(C) If denial of a period of mandatory supervision in the interests of justice is recommended, a reasoned discussion of the factors prescribed by rule 4.415(b);

(D) If a term of imprisonment in county jail under section 1170(h) is recommended, a reasoned discussion of the defendant's suitability for specific terms and length of period of mandatory supervision, including the factors prescribed by rule 4.415(c); and

(E) A reasoned discussion of the defendant's ability to make restitution, pay any fine or penalty that may be recommended, or satisfy any special conditions of probation that are proposed.

Discussions of factors (A) through (D) must refer to any sentencing rule directly relevant to the facts of the case, but no rule may be cited without a reasoned discussion of its relevance and relative importance.

(10) Any mitigating factors pursuant to section 1385(c).

(11) The probation officer's recommendation. When requested by the sentencing judge or by standing instructions to the probation department, the report must include recommendations concerning the length of any prison or county jail term under section 1170(h) that may be imposed, including the base term, the imposition of concurrent or consecutive sentences, and the imposition or striking of the additional terms for enhancements charged and found.

(12) Detailed information on presentence time spent by the defendant in custody, including the beginning and ending dates of the period or periods of custody; the existence of any other sentences imposed on the defendant during the period of custody; the amount of good behavior, work, or participation credit to which the defendant is entitled; and whether the sheriff or other officer holding custody, the prosecution, or the defense wishes that a hearing be held for the purposes of denying good behavior, work, or participation credit.

(13) A statement of mandatory and recommended restitution, restitution fines, and other fines, fees, assessments, penalties, and costs to be assessed against the defendant; a recommendation whether any restitution order should become a judgment under section 1203(j) if unpaid; and, when appropriate, any finding concerning the defendant's ability to pay.

(14) Information pursuant to section 29810(c):

(A) Whether the defendant has properly complied with Penal Code section 29810 by relinquishing all firearms identified by the probation officer's investigation or declared by the defendant on the Prohibited Persons Relinquishment Form, and

(B) Whether the defendant has timely submitted a completed Prohibited Persons Relinquishment Form.

(Subd (a) amended effective March 14, 2022; previously amended effective January 1, 1991, July 1, 2003, January 1, 2007, January 1, 2015, January 1, 2017, and January 1, 2018.)

(b) Format

The report must be on paper 8-½ by 11 inches in size and must follow the sequence set out in (a) to the extent possible.

(Subd (b) amended effective January 1, 2007; previously amended effective January 1, 1991.)

(c) Sources

The source of all information must be stated. Any person who has furnished information included in the report must be identified by name or official capacity unless a reason is given for not disclosing the person's identity.

(*Subd (c) amended effective January 1, 2007; previously amended effective January 1, 1991.*)

Rule 4.411.5 amended effective March 14, 2022; adopted as rule 419 effective July 1, 1981; previously amended and renumbered as rule 411.5 effective January 1, 1991; previously renumbered effective January 1, 2001; previously amended effective July 1, 2003, January 1, 2007, January 1, 2015, January 1, 2017, and January 1, 2018.

Rule 4.412. Reasons—agreement to punishment as an adequate reason and as abandonment of certain claims

(a) Defendant's agreement as reason

It is an adequate reason for a sentence or other disposition that the defendant, personally and by counsel, has expressed agreement that it be imposed and the prosecuting attorney has not expressed an objection to it. The agreement and lack of objection must be recited on the record. This section does not authorize a sentence that is not otherwise authorized by law.

(*Subd (a) amended effective January 1, 2007; previously amended effective January 1, 2001.*)

(b) Agreement to sentence abandons section 654 claim

By agreeing to a specified term in prison or county jail under section 1170(h) personally and by counsel, a defendant who is sentenced to that term or a shorter one abandons any claim that a component of the sentence violates section 654's prohibition of double punishment, unless that claim is asserted at the time the agreement is recited on the record.

(*Subd (b) amended effective January 1, 2017; previously amended effective January 1, 2007.*)

Rule 4.412 amended effective January 1, 2017; adopted as rule 412 effective January 1, 1991; previously amended and renumbered effective January 1, 2001; previously amended effective January 1, 2007.

Advisory Committee Comment

Subdivision (a). This subdivision is intended to relieve the court of an obligation to give reasons if the sentence or other disposition is one that the defendant has accepted and to which the prosecutor expresses no objection. The judge may choose to give reasons for the sentence even though not obligated to do so.

Judges should also be aware that there may be statutory limitations on "plea bargaining" or on the entry of a guilty plea on the condition that no more than a particular sentence will be imposed. Such limitations appear, for example, in sections 1192.5 and 1192.7.

Subdivision (b). This subdivision is based on the fact that a defendant who, with the advice of counsel, expresses agreement to a specified term of imprisonment normally is acknowledging that the term is appropriate for his or her total course of conduct. This subdivision applies to both determinate and indeterminate terms.

Rule 4.413. Grant of probation when defendant is presumptively ineligible for probation

(a) Consideration of eligibility

The court must determine whether the defendant is eligible for probation. In most cases, the defendant is presumptively eligible for probation; in some cases, the defendant is presumptively ineligible; and in some cases, probation is not allowed.

(*Subd (a) amended effective January 1, 2018; previously amended effective January 1, 2007.*)

(b) Probation in cases when defendant is presumptively ineligible

If the defendant comes under a statutory provision prohibiting probation "except in unusual cases where the interests of justice would best be served," or a substantially equivalent provision, the court should apply the criteria in (c) to evaluate whether the statutory limitation on probation is overcome; and if it is, the court should then apply the criteria in rule 4.414 to decide whether to grant probation.

(*Subd (b) amended effective January 1, 2018; previously amended effective July 1, 2003, and January 1, 2007.*)

(c) Factors overcoming the presumption of ineligibility

The following factors may indicate the existence of an unusual case in which probation may be granted if otherwise appropriate:

(1) *Factors relating to basis for limitation on probation*

A factor or circumstance indicating that the basis for the statutory limitation on probation, although technically present, is not fully applicable to the case, including:

(A) The factor or circumstance giving rise to the limitation on probation is, in this case, substantially less serious than the circumstances typically present in other cases involving the same probation limitation, and the defendant has no recent record of committing similar crimes or crimes of violence; and

(B) The current offense is less serious than a prior felony conviction that is the cause of the limitation on probation, and the defendant has been free from incarceration and serious violation of the law for a substantial time before the current offense.

(2) *Factors limiting defendant's culpability*

A factor or circumstance not amounting to a defense, but reducing the defendant's culpability for the offense, including:

(A) The defendant participated in the crime under circumstances of great provocation, coercion, or duress not amounting to a defense, and the defendant has no recent record of committing crimes of violence;

(B) The crime was committed because of a mental condition not amounting to a defense, and there is a high likelihood that the defendant would respond favorably to mental health care and treatment that would be required as a condition of probation; and

(C) The defendant is youthful or aged, and has no significant record of prior criminal offenses.

(3) *Results of risk/needs assessment*

Along with all other relevant information in the case, the court may consider the results of a risk/needs assessment of the defendant, if one was performed. The weight of a risk/needs assessment is for the court to consider in its sentencing discretion.

(*Subd (c) amended effective January 1, 2018; previously amended effective January 1, 2007.*)

Rule 4.413 amended effective January 1, 2018; adopted as rule 413 effective January 1, 1991; previously renumbered effective January 1, 2001; previously amended effective July 1, 2003, and January 1, 2007.

Advisory Committee Comment

Subdivision (c)(3). Standard 4.35 of the California Standards of Judicial Administration provides courts with additional guidance on using the results of a risk/needs assessment at sentencing.

Rule 4.414. Criteria affecting probation

Criteria affecting the decision to grant or deny probation include facts relating to the crime and facts relating to the defendant.

(a) Facts relating to the crime

Facts relating to the crime include:

(1) The nature, seriousness, and circumstances of the crime as compared to other instances of the same crime;

(2) Whether the defendant was armed with or used a weapon;

(3) The vulnerability of the victim;

(4) Whether the defendant inflicted physical or emotional injury;

(5) The degree of monetary loss to the victim;

(6) Whether the defendant was an active or a passive participant;

(7) Whether the crime was committed because of an unusual circumstance, such as great provocation, which is unlikely to recur;

(8) Whether the manner in which the crime was carried out demonstrated criminal sophistication or professionalism on the part of the defendant; and

(9) Whether the defendant took advantage of a position of trust or confidence to commit the crime.

(*Subd (a) amended effective January 1, 2007; previously amended effective January 1, 1991.*)

(b) Facts relating to the defendant

Facts relating to the defendant include:

(1) Prior record of criminal conduct, whether as an adult or a juvenile, including the recency and frequency of prior crimes; and whether the prior record indicates a pattern of regular or increasingly serious criminal conduct;

(2) Prior performance and present status on probation, mandatory supervision, postrelease community supervision, or parole;

(3) Willingness to comply with the terms of probation;

(4) Ability to comply with reasonable terms of probation as indicated by the defendant's age, education, health, mental faculties, history of alcohol or other substance abuse, family background and ties, employment and military service history, and other relevant factors;

(5) The likely effect of imprisonment on the defendant and his or her dependents;

(6) The adverse collateral consequences on the defendant's life resulting from the felony conviction;

(7) Whether the defendant is remorseful; and

(8) The likelihood that if not imprisoned the defendant will be a danger to others.

(*Subd (b) amended effective January 1, 2017; previously amended effective January 1, 1991, July 1, 2003, and January 1, 2007.*)

(c) Suitability for probation

In determining the suitability of the defendant for probation, the court may consider factors in aggravation and mitigation, whether or not the factors have been stipulated to by the defendant or found true beyond a reasonable doubt at trial by a jury or the judge in a court trial.

(Subd (c) adopted effective March 14, 2022.)

Rule 4.414 amended effective March 14, 2022; adopted as rule 414 effective July 1, 1977; previously amended effective January 1, 1991; previously renumbered effective January 1, 2001; previously amended effective July 1, 2003, January 1, 2007, and January 1, 2017.

Advisory Committee Comment

The sentencing judge's discretion to grant probation is unaffected by the Uniform Determinate Sentencing Act (section 1170(a)(3)).

The decision whether to grant probation is normally based on an overall evaluation of the likelihood that the defendant will live successfully in the general community. Each criterion points to evidence that the likelihood of success is great or small. A single criterion will rarely be determinative; in most cases, the sentencing judge will have to balance favorable and unfavorable facts.

Under criteria (b)(3) and (b)(4), it is appropriate to consider the defendant's expressions of willingness to comply and his or her apparent sincerity, and whether the defendant's home and work environment and primary associates will be supportive of the defendant's efforts to comply with the terms of probation, among other factors.

Rule 4.415. Criteria affecting the imposition of mandatory supervision

(a) Presumption

Except where the defendant is statutorily ineligible for suspension of any part of the sentence, when imposing a term of imprisonment in county jail under section 1170(h), the court must suspend execution of a concluding portion of the term to be served as a period of mandatory supervision unless the court finds, in the interests of justice, that mandatory supervision is not appropriate in a particular case. Because section 1170(h)(5)(A) establishes a statutory presumption in favor of the imposition of a period of mandatory supervision in all applicable cases, denials of a period of mandatory supervision should be limited.

(Subd (a) amended effective January 1, 2017; adopted effective January 1, 2015.)

(b) Criteria for denying mandatory supervision in the interests of justice

In determining that mandatory supervision is not appropriate in the interests of justice under section 1170(h)(5)(A), the court's determination must be based on factors that are specific to a particular case or defendant. Factors the court may consider include:

(1) Consideration of the balance of custody exposure available after imposition of presentence custody credits;

(2) The defendant's present status on probation, mandatory supervision, postrelease community supervision, or parole;

(3) Specific factors related to the defendant that indicate a lack of need for treatment or supervision upon release from custody; and

(4) Whether the nature, seriousness, or circumstances of the case or the defendant's past performance on supervision substantially outweigh the benefits of supervision in promoting public safety and the defendant's successful reentry into the community upon release from custody.

(Subd (b) adopted effective January 1, 2015.)

(c) Criteria affecting conditions and length of mandatory supervision

In exercising discretion to select the appropriate period and conditions of mandatory supervision, factors the court may consider include:

(1) Availability of appropriate community corrections programs;

(2) Victim restitution, including any conditions or period of supervision necessary to promote the collection of any court-ordered restitution;

(3) Consideration of length and conditions of supervision to promote the successful reintegration of the defendant into the community upon release from custody;

(4) Public safety, including protection of any victims and witnesses;

(5) Past performance and present status on probation, mandatory supervision, postrelease community supervision, and parole;

(6) The balance of custody exposure after imposition of presentence custody credits;

(7) Consideration of the statutory accrual of post-sentence custody credits for mandatory supervision under section 1170(h)(5)(B) and sentences served in county jail under section 4019(a)(6);

(8) The defendant's specific needs and risk factors identified by a risk/needs assessment, if available; and

(9) The likely effect of extended imprisonment on the defendant and any dependents.

(Subd (c) amended effective January 1, 2018; adopted effective January 1, 2015.)

(d) Statement of reasons for denial of mandatory supervision

Notwithstanding rule 4.412(a), when a court denies a period of mandatory supervision in the interests of justice, the court must state the reasons for the denial on the record.

(Subd (d) adopted effective January 1, 2015.)

Rule 4.415 amended effective January 1, 2018; adopted effective January 1, 2015; previously amended effective January 1, 2017.

Advisory Committee Comment

Penal Code section 1170.3 requires the Judicial Council to adopt rules of court that prescribe criteria for the consideration of the court at the time of sentencing regarding the court's decision to "[d]eny a period of mandatory supervision in the interests of justice under paragraph (5) of subdivision (h) of Section 1170 or determine the appropriate period of and conditions of mandatory supervision."

Subdivision (a). Penal Code section 1170(h)(5)(A): "Unless the court finds, in the interests of justice, that it is not appropriate in a particular case, the court, when imposing a sentence pursuant to paragraph (1) or (2) of this subdivision, shall suspend execution of a concluding portion of the term for a period selected at the court's discretion." Under *People v. Borynack* (2015) 238 Cal.App.4th 958, review denied, courts may not impose mandatory supervision when the defendant is statutorily ineligible for a suspension of part of the sentence.

Subdivisions (b)(3), (b)(4), and (c)(3). The Legislature has declared that "[s]trategies supporting reentering offenders through practices and programs, such as standardized risk and needs assessments, transitional community housing, treatment, medical and mental health services, and employment, have been demonstrated to significantly reduce recidivism among offenders in other states." (Pen. Code, § 17.7(a).)

Subdivision (c)(7). Under Penal Code section 1170(h)(5)(B), defendants serving a period of mandatory supervision are entitled to day-for-day credits: "During the period when the defendant is under such supervision, unless in actual custody related to the sentence imposed by the court, the defendant shall be entitled to only actual time credit against the term of imprisonment imposed by the court." In contrast, defendants serving terms of imprisonment in county jails under Penal Code section 1170(h) are entitled to conduct credits under Penal Code section 4019(a)(6).

Subdivision (c)(8). Standard 4.35 of the California Standards of Judicial Administration provides courts with additional guidance on using the results of a risk/needs assessment at sentencing.

Rule 4.420. Selection of term of imprisonment for offense

(a) When a judgment of imprisonment is imposed, or the execution of a judgment of imprisonment is ordered suspended, the sentencing judge must, in their sound discretion, order imposition of a sentence not to exceed the middle term, except as otherwise provided in paragraph (b).

(Subd (a) amended effective March 14, 2022; previously amended effective July 28, 1977, January 1, 1991, January 1, 2007, and May 23, 2007.)

(b) The court may only choose an upper term when (1) there are circumstances in aggravation of the crime that justify the imposition of an upper term, and (2) the facts underlying those circumstances have been (i) stipulated to by the defendant, (ii) found true beyond a reasonable doubt at trial by a jury, or (iii) found true beyond a reasonable doubt by the judge in a court trial.

(Subd (b) adopted effective March 14, 2022.)

(c) Notwithstanding paragraphs (a) and (b), the court may consider the fact of the defendant's prior convictions based on a certified record of conviction without it having been stipulated to by the defendant or found true beyond a reasonable doubt at trial by a jury or the judge in a court trial. This exception does not apply to the use of the record of a prior conviction in selecting the upper term of an enhancement.

(Subd (c) adopted effective March 14, 2022.)

(d) In selecting between the middle and lower terms of imprisonment, the sentencing judge may consider circumstances in aggravation or mitigation, and any other factor reasonably related to the sentencing decision. The court may consider factors in aggravation and mitigation, whether or not the factors have been stipulated to by the defendant or found true beyond a reasonable doubt at trial by a jury or the judge in a court trial. The relevant circumstances may be obtained from the case record, the probation officer's report, other reports and statements properly received, statements in aggravation or mitigation, and any evidence introduced at the sentencing hearing.

(Subd (d) relettered and amended effective March 14, 2022; adopted as subd (b); previously amended effective July 28, 1977, January 1, 1991, January 1, 2007, May 23, 2007, January 1, 2008, and January 1, 2017.)

(e) Notwithstanding section 1170(b)(1), and unless the court finds that the aggravating circumstances outweigh the mitigating circumstances such that imposition of the lower term would be contrary to the interests of justice, the court must order imposition of the lower term if any of the following was a contributing factor in the commission of the offense:

(1) The defendant has experienced psychological, physical, or childhood trauma, including, but not limited to, abuse, neglect, exploitation, or sexual violence;

(2) The defendant is a youth, or was a youth as defined under section 1016.7(b) at the time of the commission of the offense; or

(3) Prior to the instant offense, or at the time of the commission of the offense, the defendant is or was a victim of intimate partner violence or human trafficking.

(Subd (e) adopted effective March 14, 2022.)

(f) Paragraph (e) does not preclude the court from imposing the lower term even if there is no evidence of the circumstances listed in paragraph (e).

(Subd (f) adopted effective March 14, 2022.)

(g) To comply with section 1170(b)(5), a fact charged and found as an enhancement may be used as a reason for imposing a particular term only if the court has discretion to strike the punishment for the enhancement and does so. The use of a fact of an enhancement to impose the upper term of imprisonment is an adequate reason for striking the additional term of imprisonment, regardless of the effect on the total term.

(Subd (g) relettered and amended effective March 14, 2022; adopted as subd (c) effective January 1, 1991; previously amended effective January 1, 2018.)

(h) A fact that is an element of the crime on which punishment is being imposed may not be used to impose a particular term.

(Subd (h) relettered effective March 14, 2022; adopted as subd (d) effective January 1, 1991; previously amended effective January 1, 2007, May 23, 2007, January 1, 2008, and January 1, 2018.)

(i) The reasons for selecting one of the three authorized terms of imprisonment referred to in section 1170(b) must be stated orally on the record.

(Subd (i) relettered effective March 14, 2022; previously amended and relettered as subd (e) effective January 1, 1991; previously amended effective July 28, 1977, January 1, 2007, May 23, 2007, and January 1, 2017.)

Rule 4.420 amended effective March 14, 2022; adopted as rule 439 effective July 1, 1977; previously amended and renumbered as rule 420 effective January 1, 1991; previously renumbered effective January 1, 2001; previously amended effective July 28, 1977, January 1, 2007, May 23, 2007, January 1, 2008, January 1, 2017, and January 1, 2018.

Advisory Committee Comment

It is not clear whether the reasons stated by the judge for selecting a particular term qualify as "facts" for the purposes of the rule prohibition on dual use of facts. Until the issue is clarified, judges should avoid the use of reasons that may constitute an impermissible dual use of facts. For example, the court is not permitted to use a reason to impose a greater term if that reason also is either (1) the same as an enhancement that will be imposed, or (2) an element of the crime. The court should not use the same reason to impose a consecutive sentence as to impose an upper term of imprisonment. (*People v. Avalos* (1984) 37 Cal.3d 216, 233.) It is not improper to use the same reason to deny probation and to impose the upper term. (*People v. Bowen* (1992) 11 Cal.App.4th 102, 106.)

The rule makes it clear that a fact charged and found as an enhancement may, in the alternative, be used as a factor in aggravation.

People v. Riolo (1983) 33 Cal.3d 223, 227 (and note 5 on 227) held that section 1170.1(a) does not require the judgment to state the base term (upper, middle, or lower) and enhancements, computed independently, on counts that are subject to automatic reduction under the one-third formula of section 1170.1(a).

Even when sentencing is under section 1170.1, however, it is essential to determine the base term and specific enhancements for each count independently, in order to know which is the principal term count. The principal term count must be determined before any calculation is made using the one-third formula for subordinate terms.

In addition, the base term (upper, middle, or lower) for each count must be determined to arrive at an informed decision whether to make terms consecutive or concurrent; and the base term for each count must be stated in the judgment when sentences are concurrent or are fully consecutive (i.e., not subject to the one-third rule of section 1170.1(a)).

Case law suggests that in determining the "interests of justice" the court should consider the constitutional rights of the defendant and the interests of society represented by the people; the defendant's background and prospects, including the presence or absence of a record; the nature and circumstances of the crime and the defendant's level of involvement; the factors in aggravation and mitigation including the specific factors in mitigation of Penal Code section 1170(b)(6); and the factors that would motivate a "reasonable judge" in the exercise of their discretion. The court should not consider whether the defendant has simply pled guilty, factors related to controlling the court's calendar, or antipathy toward the statutory scheme. (See *People v. Romero* (1996) 13 Cal.4th 947; *People v. Dent* (1995) 38 Cal.App.4th 1726; *People v. Kessel* (1976) 61 Cal.App.3d 322; *People v. Orin* (1975) 13 Cal.3d 937.)

Rule 4.421. Circumstances in aggravation

Circumstances in aggravation include factors relating to the crime and factors relating to the defendant.

(a) Factors relating to the crime

Factors relating to the crime, whether or not charged or chargeable as enhancements include that:

(1) The crime involved great violence, great bodily harm, threat of great bodily harm, or other acts disclosing a high degree of cruelty, viciousness, or callousness;

(2) The defendant was armed with or used a weapon at the time of the commission of the crime;

(3) The victim was particularly vulnerable;

(4) The defendant induced others to participate in the commission of the crime or occupied a position of leadership or dominance of other participants in its commission;

(5) The defendant induced a minor to commit or assist in the commission of the crime;

(6) The defendant threatened witnesses, unlawfully prevented or dissuaded witnesses from testifying, suborned perjury, or in any other way illegally interfered with the judicial process;

(7) The defendant was convicted of other crimes for which consecutive sentences could have been imposed but for which concurrent sentences are being imposed;

(8) The manner in which the crime was carried out indicates planning, sophistication, or professionalism;

(9) The crime involved an attempted or actual taking or damage of great monetary value;

(10) The crime involved a large quantity of contraband; and

(11) The defendant took advantage of a position of trust or confidence to commit the offense.

(12) The crime constitutes a hate crime under section 422.55 and:

(A) No hate crime enhancements under section 422.75 are imposed; and

(B) The crime is not subject to sentencing under section 1170.8.

(Subd (a) amended effective May 23, 2007; previously amended effective January 1, 1991, and January 1, 2007.)

(b) Factors relating to the defendant

Factors relating to the defendant include that:

(1) The defendant has engaged in violent conduct that indicates a serious danger to society;

(2) The defendant's prior convictions as an adult or sustained petitions in juvenile delinquency proceedings are numerous or of increasing seriousness;

(3) The defendant has served a prior term in prison or county jail under section 1170(h);

(4) The defendant was on probation, mandatory supervision, postrelease community supervision, or parole when the crime was committed; and

(5) The defendant's prior performance on probation, mandatory supervision, postrelease community supervision, or parole was unsatisfactory.

(Subd (b) amended effective January 1, 2017; previously amended effective January 1, 1991, January 1, 2007, and May 23, 2007.)

(c) Other factors

Any other factors statutorily declared to be circumstances in aggravation or that reasonably relate to the defendant or the circumstances under which the crime was committed.

(Subd (c) amended effective January 1, 2018; adopted effective January 1, 1991; previously amended effective January 1, 2007, and May 23, 2007.)

Rule 4.421 amended effective January 1, 2018; adopted as rule 421 effective July 1, 1977; previously renumbered effective January 1, 2001; previously amended effective January 1, 1991, January 1, 2007, May 23, 2007, and January 1, 2017.

Advisory Committee Comment

Courts may not impose a sentence greater than the middle term except when aggravating factors justifying the imposition of the upper term have been stipulated to by the defendant or found true beyond a reasonable doubt at trial by the jury or the judge in a court trial. These requirements do not apply to consideration of aggravating factors for the lower or middle term. If the court finds that any of the factors listed in section 1170(b)(6)(A-C) were a contributing factor to the commission of the offense, the court must impose the lower term (see rule 4.420(e)) unless the court finds that the aggravating factors outweigh the mitigating factors to such a degree that imposing the lower term would be contrary to the interests of justice. In this instance, since the court is not addressing the imposition of the upper term, the court may consider factors in aggravation that have not been stipulated to by the defendant or found true beyond a reasonable doubt at trial by the jury or the judge in a court trial.

In determining whether to impose the upper term for a criminal offense, the court may consider as an aggravating factor that a defendant has suffered one or more prior convictions, based on a certified record of conviction. This exception may not be used to select the upper term of an enhancement.

This rule does not deal with the dual use of the facts; the statutory prohibition against dual use is included, in part, in the comment to rule 4.420.

Refusal to consider the personal characteristics of the defendant in imposing sentence may raise serious constitutional questions. The California Supreme Court has held that sentencing decisions must take into account "the nature of the offense and/or the offender, with particular regard to the degree of danger both present to society." (*In re Rodriguez* (1975) 14 Cal.3d 639, 654, quoting *In re Lynch* (1972) 8 Cal.3d 410, 425.) In *Rodriguez* the court released petitioner from further incarceration because "it appears that neither the circumstances of his offense *nor his personal characteristics* establish a danger to society sufficient to justify such a prolonged period of imprisonment." (*Id.* at p. 655, fn. omitted, italics added.) "For the determination of sentences, justice generally requires … that there be taken into account the circumstances of the offense together with the character and propensities of the offender." (*Pennsylvania ex rel. Sullivan v. Ashe* (1937) 302 U.S. 51, 55, quoted with approval in *Gregg v. Georgia* (1976) 428 U.S. 153, 189.)

Other statutory factors in aggravation are listed, for example, in sections 422.76, 1170.7, 1170.71, 1170.8, and 1170.85, and may be considered to impose the upper term if stipulated to by the defendant or found true beyond a reasonable doubt at trial by a jury or the judge in a court trial.

Rule 4.423. Circumstances in mitigation

Circumstances in mitigation include factors relating to the crime and factors relating to the defendant.

(a) Factors relating to the crime

Factors relating to the crime include that:

(1) The defendant was a passive participant or played a minor role in the crime;

(2) The victim was an initiator of, willing participant in, or aggressor or provoker of the incident;

(3) The crime was committed because of an unusual circumstance, such as great provocation, that is unlikely to recur;

(4) The defendant participated in the crime under circumstances of coercion or duress, or the criminal conduct was partially excusable for some other reason not amounting to a defense;

(5) The defendant, with no apparent predisposition to do so, was induced by others to participate in the crime;

(6) The defendant exercised caution to avoid harm to persons or damage to property, or the amounts of money or property taken were deliberately small, or no harm was done or threatened against the victim;

(7) The defendant believed that he or she had a claim or right to the property taken, or for other reasons mistakenly believed that the conduct was legal;

(8) The defendant was motivated by a desire to provide necessities for his or her family or self; and

(9) The defendant suffered from repeated or continuous physical, sexual, or psychological abuse inflicted by the victim of the crime, and the victim of the crime, who inflicted the abuse, was the defendant's spouse, intimate cohabitant, or parent of the defendant's child; and the abuse does not amount to a defense.

(10) If a firearm was used in the commission of the offense, it was unloaded or inoperable.

(Subd (a) amended effective March 14, 2022; previously amended effective January 1, 1991, July 1, 1993, January 1, 2007, and May 23, 2007.)

(b) Factors relating to the defendant

Factors relating to the defendant include that:

(1) The defendant has no prior record, or has an insignificant record of criminal conduct, considering the recency and frequency of prior crimes;

(2) The defendant was suffering from a mental or physical condition that significantly reduced culpability for the crime;

(3) The defendant experienced psychological, physical, or childhood trauma, including, but not limited to, abuse, neglect, exploitation, or sexual violence and it was a factor in the commission of the crime;

(4) The commission of the current offense is connected to the defendant's prior victimization or childhood trauma, or mental illness as defined by section 1385(c);

(5) The defendant is or was a victim of intimate partner violence or human trafficking at the time of the commission of the offense, and it was a factor in the commission of the offense;

(6) The defendant is under 26 years of age, or was under 26 years of age at the time of the commission of the offense;

(7) The defendant was a juvenile when they committed the current offense;

(8) The defendant voluntarily acknowledged wrongdoing before arrest or at an early stage of the criminal process;

(9) The defendant is ineligible for probation and but for that ineligibility would have been granted probation;

(10) Application of an enhancement could result in a sentence over 20 years;

(11) Multiple enhancements are alleged in a single case;

(12) Application of an enhancement could result in a discriminatory racial impact;

(13) An enhancement is based on a prior conviction that is over five years old;

(14) The defendant made restitution to the victim; and

(15) The defendant's prior performance on probation, mandatory supervision, postrelease community supervision, or parole was satisfactory.

(Subd (b) amended effective March 14, 2022; previously amended effective January 1, 1991, January 1, 2007, May 23, 2007, and January 1, 2017.)

(c) Other factors

Any other factors statutorily declared to be circumstances in mitigation or that reasonably relate to the defendant or the circumstances under which the crime was committed.

(Subd (c) adopted effective January 1, 2018.)

Rule 4.423 amended effective March 14, 2022; adopted as rule 423 effective July 1, 1977; previously renumbered effective January 1, 2001; previously amended effective January 1, 1991, July 1, 1993, January 1, 2007, May 23, 2007, January 1, 2017, and January 1, 2018.

Advisory Committee Comment

See comment to rule 4.421.

This rule applies both to mitigation for purposes of section 1170(b) and to circumstances in mitigation justifying the court in striking the additional punishment provided for an enhancement.

Some listed circumstances can never apply to certain enhancements; for example, "the amounts taken were deliberately small" can never apply to an excessive taking under section 12022.6, and "no harm was done" can never apply to infliction of great bodily injury under section 12022.7. In any case, only the facts present may be considered for their possible effect in mitigation.

See also rule 4.409; only relevant criteria need be considered.

Since only the fact of restitution is considered relevant to mitigation, no reference to the defendant's financial ability is needed. The omission of a comparable factor from rule 4.421 as a circumstance in aggravation is deliberate.

Rule 4.424. Consideration of applicability of section 654

Before determining whether to impose either concurrent or consecutive sentences on all counts on which the defendant was convicted, the court must determine whether the proscription in section 654 against multiple punishments for the same act or omission requires a stay of execution of the sentence imposed on some of the counts. If a stay of execution is required due to the prohibition against multiple punishments for the same act, the court has discretion to choose which act or omission will be punished and which will be stayed.

Rule 4.424 amended effective March 14, 2022; adopted as rule 424 effective January 1, 1991; previously renumbered effective January 1, 2001; previously amended effective January 1, 2007, and January 1, 2011.

Rule 4.425. Factors affecting concurrent or consecutive sentences

Factors affecting the decision to impose consecutive rather than concurrent sentences include:

(a) Facts relating to crimes

Facts relating to the crimes, including whether or not:

(1) The crimes and their objectives were predominantly independent of each other;

(2) The crimes involved separate acts of violence or threats of violence; or

(3) The crimes were committed at different times or separate places, rather than being committed so closely in time and place as to indicate a single period of aberrant behavior.

(Subd (a) amended effective January 1, 2018; previously amended effective January 1, 1991, and January 1, 2007.)

(b) Other facts and limitations

Any circumstances in aggravation or mitigation, whether or not the factors have been stipulated to by the defendant or found true beyond a reasonable doubt at trial by a jury or the judge in a court trial, may be considered in deciding whether to impose consecutive rather than concurrent sentences, except:

(1) A fact used to impose the upper term;

(2) A fact used to otherwise enhance the defendant's sentence in prison or county jail under section 1170(h); and

(3) A fact that is an element of the crime.

(Subd (b) amended effective March 14, 2022; previously amended effective January 1, 1991, January 1, 2007, January 1, 2017, and January 1, 2018.)

Rule 4.425 amended effective March 14, 2022; adopted as rule 425 effective July 1, 1977; previously amended effective January 1, 1991, January 1, 2007, January 1, 2017, and January 1, 2018; previously renumbered effective January 1, 2001.

Advisory Committee Comment

The sentencing judge should be aware that there are some cases in which the law mandates consecutive sentences.

Rule 4.426. Violent sex crimes

(a) Multiple violent sex crimes

When a defendant has been convicted of multiple violent sex offenses as defined in section 667.6, the sentencing judge must determine whether the crimes involved separate victims or the same victim on separate occasions.

(1) *Different victims*

If the crimes were committed against different victims, a full, separate, and consecutive term must be imposed for a violent sex crime as to each victim, under section 667.6(d).

(2) *Same victim, separate occasions*

If the crimes were committed against a single victim, the sentencing judge must determine whether the crimes were committed on separate occasions. In determining whether there were separate occasions, the sentencing judge must consider whether, between the commission of one sex crime and another, the defendant had a reasonable opportunity to reflect on his or her actions and nevertheless resumed sexually assaultive behavior. A full, separate, and consecutive term must be imposed for each violent sex offense committed on a separate occasion under section 667.6(d).

(Subd (a) amended effective January 1, 2007.)

(b) Same victim, same occasion; other crimes

If the defendant has been convicted of multiple crimes, including at least one violent sex crime, as defined in section 667.6, or if there have been multiple violent sex crimes against a single victim on the same occasion and the sentencing court has decided to impose consecutive sentences, the sentencing judge must then determine whether to impose a full, separate, and consecutive sentence under section 667.6(c) for the violent sex crime or crimes instead of including the violent sex crimes in the computation of the principal and subordinate terms under section 1170.1(a). A decision to impose a fully consecutive sentence under section 667.6(c) is an additional sentence choice that requires a statement of reasons separate from those given for consecutive sentences, but which may repeat the same reasons. The sentencing judge is to be guided by the criteria listed in rule 4.425, which incorporates rules 4.421 and 4.423, as well as any other reasonably related criteria as provided in rule 4.408.

(Subd (b) amended effective January 1, 2007; previously amended effective July 1, 2003.)

Rule 4.426 amended effective January 1, 2007; adopted as rule 426 effective January 1, 1991; previously renumbered effective January 1, 2001; previously amended effective July 1, 2003.

Advisory Committee Comment

Section 667.6(d) requires a full, separate, and consecutive term for each of the enumerated violent sex crimes that involve separate victims, or the same victim on separate occasions. Therefore, if there were separate victims or the court found that there were separate occasions, no other reasons are required.

If there have been multiple convictions involving at least one of the enumerated violent sex crimes, the court may impose a full, separate, and consecutive term for each violent sex crime under section 667.6(c). (See *People v. Coleman* (1989) 48 Cal.3d 112, 161.) A fully consecutive sentence under section 667.6(c) is a sentence choice, which requires a statement of reasons. The court may not use the same fact to impose a sentence under section 667.6(c) that was used to impose an upper term. (See rule 4.425(b).) If the court selects the upper term, imposes consecutive sentences, and uses section 667.6(c), the record must reflect three sentencing choices with three separate statements of reasons, but the same reason may be used for sentencing under section 667.6(c) and to impose consecutive sentences. (See *People v. Belmontes* (1983) 34 Cal.3d 335, 347-349.)

Rule 4.427. Hate crimes

(a) Application

This rule is intended to assist judges in sentencing in felony hate crime cases. It applies to:

(1) Felony sentencing under section 422.7;

(2) Convictions of felonies with a hate crime enhancement under section 422.75; and

(3) Convictions of felonies that qualify as hate crimes under section 422.55.

(Subd (a) adopted effective January 1, 2007.)

(b) Felony sentencing under section 422.7

If one of the three factors listed in section 422.7 is pled and proved, a misdemeanor conviction that constitutes a hate crime under section 422.55 may be sentenced as a felony. The punishment is imprisonment in state prison or county jail under section 1170(h) as provided by section 422.7.

(Subd (b) amended effective January 1, 2017; adopted effective January 1, 2007.)

(c) Hate crime enhancement

If a hate crime enhancement is pled and proved, the punishment for a felony conviction must be enhanced under section 422.75 unless the conviction is sentenced as a felony under section 422.7.

(1) The following enhancements apply:

(A) An enhancement of a term in state prison as provided in section 422.75(a). Personal use of a firearm in the commission of the offense is an aggravating factor that must be considered in determining the enhancement term.

(B) An additional enhancement of one year in state prison for each prior felony conviction that constitutes a hate crime as defined in section 422.55.

(2) The court may strike enhancements under (c) if it finds mitigating circumstances under rule 4.423, or pursuant to section 1385(c) and states those mitigating circumstances on the record.

(3) The punishment for any enhancement under (c) is in addition to any other punishment provided by law.

(Subd (c) amended effective March 14, 2022; adopted effective January 1, 2007.)

(d) Hate crime as aggravating factor

If the defendant is convicted of a felony, and the facts of the crime constitute a hate crime under section 422.55, that fact must be considered a circumstance in aggravation in determining the appropriate punishment under rule 4.421 unless:

(1) The court imposed a hate crime enhancement under section 422.75; or

(2) The defendant has been convicted of an offense subject to sentencing under section 1170.8.

(Subd (d) adopted effective January 1, 2007.)

(e) Hate crime sentencing goals

When sentencing a defendant under this rule, the judge must consider the principal goals for hate crime sentencing.

(1) The principal goals for hate crime sentencing, as stated in section 422.86, are:

(A) Punishment for the hate crime committed;

(B) Crime and violence prevention, including prevention of recidivism and prevention of crimes and violence in prisons and jails; and

(C) Restorative justice for the immediate victims of the hate crimes and for the classes of persons terrorized by the hate crimes.

(2) Crime and violence prevention considerations should include educational or other appropriate programs available in the community, jail, prison, and juvenile detention facilities. The programs should address sensitivity or similar training or counseling intended to reduce violent and antisocial behavior based on one or more of the following actual or perceived characteristics of the victim:

(A) Disability;

(B) Gender;

(C) Nationality;

(D) Race or ethnicity;

(E) Religion;

(F) Sexual orientation; or

(G) Association with a person or group with one or more of these actual or perceived characteristics.

(3) Restorative justice considerations should include community service and other programs focused on hate crime prevention or diversity sensitivity. Additionally, the court should consider ordering payment or other compensation to programs that provide services to violent crime victims and reimbursement to the victim for reasonable costs of counsel-

ing and other reasonable expenses that the court finds are a direct result of the defendant's actions.

(Subd (e) adopted effective January 1, 2007.)

Rule 4.427 amended effective March 14, 2022; adopted effective January 1, 2007; previously amended effective January 1, 2017.

Advisory Committee Comment

Multiple enhancements for prior convictions under subdivision (c)(1)(B) may be imposed if the prior convictions have been brought and tried separately. (Pen. Code, § 422.75(d)).

In order to impose the upper term based on section 422.75, the fact of the enhancement pursuant to sections 422.55 or 422.6 must be stipulated to by the defendant or found true beyond a reasonable doubt at trial by the jury or the judge in a court trial.

Any enhancement alleged pursuant to this section may be dismissed pursuant to section 1385(c).

Rule 4.428. Factors affecting imposition of enhancements

(a) Enhancements punishable by one of three terms

If an enhancement is punishable by one of three terms, the court must, in its sound discretion, order imposition of a sentence not to exceed the middle term, unless there are circumstances in aggravation that justify the imposition of a term of imprisonment exceeding the middle term, and the facts underlying those circumstances have been stipulated to by the defendant, or have been found true beyond a reasonable doubt at trial by the jury or by the judge in a court trial.

(Subd (a) amended effective March 14, 2022; previously lettered and amended effective January 1, 2018.)

(b) Striking or dismissing enhancements under section 1385

If the court has discretion under section 1385(a) to strike an enhancement in the interests of justice, the court also has the authority to strike the punishment for the enhancement under section 1385(b). In determining whether to strike the entire enhancement or only the punishment for the enhancement, the court may consider the effect that striking the enhancement would have on the status of the crime as a strike, the accurate reflection of the defendant's criminal conduct on his or her record, the effect it may have on the award of custody credits, and any other relevant consideration.

(Subd (b) amended effective March 14, 2022; adopted effective January 1, 2018.)

(c) Dismissing enhancements under section 1385(c)

(1) The court shall exercise the discretion to dismiss an enhancement if it is in the furtherance of justice to do so, unless the dismissal is prohibited by initiative statute.

(2) In exercising its discretion under section 1385(c), the court must consider and afford great weight to evidence offered by the defendant to prove that any of the mitigating circumstances in section 1385(c) are present.

(A) Proof of the presence of one or more of these circumstances weighs greatly in favor of dismissing the enhancement, unless the court finds that dismissal of the enhancement would endanger public safety.

(B) The circumstances listed in 1385(c) are not exclusive.

(C) "Endanger public safety" means there is a likelihood that the dismissal of the enhancement would result in physical injury or other serious danger to others.

(3) If the court dismisses the enhancement pursuant to 1385(c), then both the enhancement and its punishment must be dismissed.

(Subd (c) adopted effective March 14, 2022.)

Rule 4.428 amended effective March 14, 2022; adopted as rule 428 effective January 1, 1991; previously renumbered effective January 1, 2001; previously amended effective January 1, 1998, July 1, 2003, January 1, 2007, May 23, 2007, January 1, 2008, January 1, 2011, and January 1, 2018.

Advisory Committee Comment

Case law suggests that in determining the "furtherance of justice" the court should consider the constitutional rights of the defendant and the interests of society represented by the people; the defendant's background and prospects, including the presence or absence of a record; the nature and circumstances of the crime and the defendant's level of involvement; the factors in aggravation and mitigation including the specific factors in mitigation of section 1385(c); and the factors that would motivate a "reasonable judge" in the exercise of their discretion. The court should not consider whether the defendant has simply pled guilty, factors related to controlling the court's calendar, or antipathy toward the statutory scheme. (See *People v. Romero* (1996) 13 Cal.4th 947; *People v. Dent* (1995) 38 Cal.App.4th 1726; *People v. Kessel* (1976) 61 Cal.App.3d 322; *People v. Orin* (1975) 13 Cal.3d 937.)

How to afford great weight to a mitigating circumstance is not further explained in section 1385. The court is not directed to give conclusive weight to the mitigating factors, and must still engage in a weighing of both mitigating and aggravating factors. A review of case law suggests that the court can find great weight when there is an absence of "substantial evidence of countervailing considerations of sufficient weight to overcome" the presumption of dismissal when the mitigating factors are present. (*People v. Martin* (1996) 42 Cal.3d 437.) In exercising this discretion, the court may rely on aggravating factors that have not been stipulated to by the defendant or proven beyond a reasonable doubt at trial by a jury or a judge in a court trial. (*People v. Black* (2007) 41 Cal.4th 799.)

Rule 4.431. Proceedings at sentencing to be reported

All proceedings at the time of sentencing must be reported.

Rule 4.431 amended effective January 1, 2007; adopted as rule 431 effective July 1, 1977; previously renumbered effective January 1, 2001.

Advisory Committee Comment

Reporters' transcripts of the sentencing proceedings are required on appeal (rule 8.320, except in certain cases under subdivision (d) of that rule), and when the defendant is sentenced to prison (section 1203.01).

Rule 4.433. Matters to be considered at time set for sentencing

(a) In every case, at the time set for sentencing under section 1191, the sentencing judge must hold a hearing at which the judge must:

(1) Hear and determine any matters raised by the defendant under section 1201;

(2) Determine whether a defendant who is eligible for probation should be granted or denied probation, unless consideration of probation is expressly waived by the defendant personally and by counsel; and

(3) Determine whether to deny a period of mandatory supervision in the interests of justice under section 1170(h)(5)(A).

(Subd (a) amended effective January 1, 2017; previously amended effective January 1, 2007.)

(b) If the imposition of a sentence is to be suspended during a period of probation after a conviction by trial, the trial judge must identify and state circumstances that would justify imposition of one of the three authorized terms of imprisonment referred to in section 1170(b), or any enhancement, if probation is later revoked. The circumstances identified and stated by the judge must be based on evidence admitted at the trial or other circumstances properly considered under rule 4.420(b).

(Subd (b) amended effective January 1, 2018; previously amended effective July 28, 1977, January 1, 2007, May 23, 2007, January 1, 2008, and January 1, 2017.)

(c) If a sentence of imprisonment is to be imposed, or if the execution of a sentence of imprisonment is to be suspended during a period of probation, the sentencing judge must:

(1) Determine, under section 1170(b), whether to impose one of the three authorized terms of imprisonment referred to in section 1170(b), or any enhancement, and state on the record the reasons for imposing that term;

(2) Determine whether any additional term of imprisonment provided for an enhancement charged and found will be stricken;

(3) Determine whether the sentences will be consecutive or concurrent if the defendant has been convicted of multiple crimes;

(4) Determine any issues raised by statutory prohibitions on the dual use of facts and statutory limitations on enhancements, as required in rules 4.420(c) and 4.447; and

(5) Pronounce the court's judgment and sentence, stating the terms thereof and giving reasons for those matters for which reasons are required by law.

(Subd (c) amended effective January 1, 2018; previously amended effective July 28, 1977, July 1, 2003, January 1, 2007, May 23, 2007, and January 1, 2017.)

(d) All these matters must be heard and determined at a single hearing unless the sentencing judge otherwise orders in the interests of justice.

(Subd (d) amended effective January 1, 2007.)

(e) When a sentence of imprisonment is imposed under (c) or under rule 4.435, the sentencing judge must inform the defendant:

(1) Under section 1170(c) of the parole period provided by section 3000 to be served after expiration of the sentence in addition to any period of incarceration for parole violation;

(2) Of the period of postrelease community supervision provided by section 3456 to be served after expiration of the sentence, in addition to any period of incarceration for a violation of postrelease community supervision; or

(3) Of any period of mandatory supervision imposed under section 1170(h)(5)(A) and (B), in addition to any period imprisonment for a violation of mandatory supervision.

(Subd (e) amended effective January 1, 2018; previously amended effective July 28, 1977; January 1, 1979, July 1, 2003, January 1, 2007, and January 1, 2017.)
Rule 4.433 amended effective January 1, 2018; adopted as rule 433 effective July 1, 1977; previously renumbered effective January 1, 2001; previously amended effective July 28, 1977, January 1, 1979, July 1, 2003, January 1, 2007, May 23, 2007, January 1, 2008, and January 1, 2017.

Advisory Committee Comment

This rule summarizes the questions that the court is required to consider at the time of sentencing, in their logical order.

Subdivision (a)(2) makes it clear that probation should be considered in every case, without the necessity of any application, unless the defendant is statutorily ineligible for probation.

Under subdivision (b), when imposition of sentence is to be suspended, the sentencing judge is not to make any determinations as to possible length of a term of imprisonment on violation of probation (section 1170(b)). If there was a trial, however, the judge must state on the record the circumstances that would justify imposition of one of the three authorized terms of imprisonment based on the trial evidence.

Subdivision (d) makes it clear that all sentencing matters should be disposed of at a single hearing unless strong reasons exist for a continuance.

Rule 4.435. Sentencing on revocation of probation, mandatory supervision, and postrelease community supervision

(a) When the defendant violates the terms of probation, mandatory supervision, or postrelease community supervision or is otherwise subject to revocation of supervision, the sentencing judge may make any disposition of the case authorized by statute. In deciding whether to permanently revoke supervision, the judge may consider the nature of the violation and the defendant's past performance on supervision.

(Subd (a) amended effective January 1, 2018; previously amended effective January 1, 1991.)

(b) On revocation and termination of supervision under section 1203.2, when the sentencing judge determines that the defendant will be committed to prison or county jail under section 1170(h):

(1) If the imposition of sentence was previously suspended, the judge must impose judgment and sentence after considering any findings previously made and hearing and determining the matters enumerated in rule 4.433(c).

The length of the sentence must be based on circumstances existing at the time supervision was granted, and subsequent events may not be considered in selecting the base term or in deciding whether to strike the additional punishment for enhancements charged and found.

(2) If the execution of sentence was previously suspended, the judge must order that the judgment previously pronounced be in full force and effect and that the defendant be committed to the custody of the Secretary of the Department of Corrections and Rehabilitation or local county correctional administrator or sheriff for the term prescribed in that judgment.

(Subd (b) amended effective January 1, 2018; previously amended effective July 1, 2003, January 1, 2006, January 1, 2007, and January 1, 2017.)
Rule 4.435 amended effective January 1, 2018; adopted as rule 435 effective July 1, 1977; previously renumbered effective January 1, 2001; previously amended effective January 1, 1991, July 1, 2003, January 1, 2006, January 1, 2007, and January 1, 2017.

Advisory Committee Comment

Subdivision (a) makes it clear that there is no change in the court's power, on finding cause to revoke and terminate supervision under section 1203.2(a), to continue the defendant on supervision.

The restriction of subdivision (b)(1) is based on *In re Rodriguez* (1975) 14 Cal.3d 639, 652: "[T]he primary term must reflect the circumstances existing at the time of the offense."

A judge imposing imprisonment on revocation of probation will have the power granted by section 1170(d) to recall the commitment on his or her own motion within 120 days after the date of commitment, and the power under section 1203.2(e) to set aside the revocation of probation, for good cause, within 30 days after the court has notice that execution of the sentence has commenced.

Consideration of conduct occurring after the granting of probation should be distinguished from consideration of preprobation conduct that is discovered after the granting of an order of probation and before sentencing following a revocation and termination of probation. If the preprobation conduct affects or nullifies a determination made at the time probation was granted, the preprobation conduct may properly be considered at sentencing following revocation and termination of probation. (See *People v. Griffith* (1984) 153 Cal.App.3d 796, 801.) While *People v. Griffith* refers only to probation, this rule likely will apply to any form of supervision.

Rule 4.437. Statements in aggravation and mitigation

(a) Time for filing and service

Statements in aggravation and mitigation referred to in section 1170(b) must be filed and served at least four days before the time set for sentencing under section 1191 or the time set for pronouncing judgment on revocation of probation under section 1203.2(c) if imposition of sentence was previously suspended.

(Subd (a) amended effective January 1, 2007.)

(b) Combined statement

A party seeking consideration of circumstances in aggravation or mitigation may file and serve a statement under section 1170(b) and this rule.

(Subd (b) amended effective January 1, 2007.)

(c) Contents of statement

A statement in aggravation or mitigation must include:

(1) A summary of evidence that the party relies on as circumstances justifying the imposition of a particular term; and

(2) Notice of intention to dispute facts or offer evidence in aggravation or mitigation at the sentencing hearing. The statement must generally describe the evidence to be offered, including a description of any documents and the names and expected substance of the testimony of any witnesses. No evidence in aggravation or mitigation may be introduced at the sentencing hearing unless it was described in the statement, or unless its admission is permitted by the sentencing judge in the interests of justice.

(Subd (c) amended effective May 23, 2007; previously amended effective January 1, 2007.)

(d) Support required for assertions of fact

Assertions of fact in a statement in aggravation or mitigation must be disregarded unless they are supported by the record in the case, the probation officer's report or other reports properly filed in the case, or other competent evidence.

(Subd (d) amended effective January 1, 2007.)

(e) Disputed facts

In the event the parties dispute the facts on which the conviction rested, the court must conduct a presentence hearing and make appropriate corrections, additions, or deletions in the presentence probation report or order a revised report.

(Subd (e) amended effective January 1, 2007; adopted effective January 1, 1991.)
Rule 4.437 amended effective January 1, 2008; adopted as rule 437 effective July 1, 1977; previously renumbered effective January 1, 2001; previously amended effective July 28, 1977, January 1, 1991, January 1, 2007, and May 23, 2007.

Advisory Committee Comment

Section 1170(b)(4) states in part:

"At least four days prior to the time set for imposition of judgment, either party or the victim, or the family of the victim if the victim is deceased, may submit a statement in aggravation or mitigation to dispute facts in the record or the probation officer's report, or to present additional facts."

This provision means that the statement is a document giving notice of intention to dispute evidence in the record or the probation officer's report, or to present additional facts.

The statement itself cannot be the medium for presenting new evidence, or for rebutting competent evidence already presented, because the statement is a unilateral presentation by one party or counsel that will not necessarily have any indicia of reliability. To allow its factual assertions to be considered in the absence of corroborating evidence would, therefore, constitute a denial of due process of law in violation of the United States (14th Amend.) and California (art. I, § 7) Constitutions.

The requirement that the statement include notice of intention to rely on new evidence will enhance fairness to both sides by avoiding surprise and helping to ensure that the time limit on pronouncing sentence is met. This notice may include either party's intention to provide evidence to prove or contest the existence of a factor in mitigation that would require imposition of the low term for the underlying offense or dismissal of an enhancement.

Rule 4.447. Sentencing of enhancements

(a) Enhancements resulting in unlawful sentences

Except pursuant to section 1385(c), a court may not strike or dismiss an enhancement solely because imposition of the term is prohibited by law or exceeds limitations on the imposition of multiple enhancements. Instead, the court must:

(1) Impose a sentence for the aggregate term of imprisonment computed without reference to those prohibitions and limitations; and

(2) Stay execution of the part of the term that is prohibited or exceeds the applicable limitation. The stay will become permanent once the

defendant finishes serving the part of the sentence that has not been stayed.

(Subd (a) amended effective March 14, 2022; previously lettered and amended effective January 1, 2018.)

(b) Multiple enhancements

Notwithstanding section 1385(c), if a defendant is convicted of multiple enhancements of the same type, the court must either sentence each enhancement or, if authorized, strike the enhancement or its punishment. While the court may strike an enhancement, the court may not stay an enhancement except as provided in (a) or as authorized by section 654.

(Subd (b) amended effective March 14, 2022; adopted effective January 1, 2018.)
Rule 4.447 amended effective March 14, 2022; adopted as rule 447 effective July 1, 1977; previously amended and renumbered effective January 1, 2001; previously amended effective July 28, 1977, January 1, 1991, July 1, 2003, January 1, 2007, and January 1, 2018.

Advisory Committee Comment

Subdivision (a). Statutory restrictions may prohibit or limit the imposition of an enhancement in certain situations. (See, for example, sections 186.22(b)(1), 667(a)(2), 667.61(f), 1170.1(f) and (g), 12022.53(e)(2) and (f), and Vehicle Code section 23558.)

Section 1385(c) requires that in the furtherance of justice certain enhancements be dismissed unless dismissal is prohibited by any initiative statute.

Present practice of staying execution is followed to avoid violating a statutory prohibition or exceeding a statutory limitation, while preserving the possibility of imposition of the stayed portion should a reversal on appeal reduce the unstayed portion of the sentence. (See *People v. Gonzalez* (2008) 43 Cal.4th 1118, 1129–1130; *People v. Niles* (1964) 227 Cal.App.2d 749, 756.)

Only the portion of a sentence or component thereof that exceeds a limitation is prohibited, and this rule provides a procedure for that situation. This rule applies to both determinate and indeterminate terms.

Subdivision (b). A court may stay an enhancement if section 654 applies. (See *People v. Bradley* (1998) 64 Cal.App.4th 386; *People v. Haykel* (2002) 96 Cal.App.4th 146, 152.)

Rule 4.451. Sentence consecutive to or concurrent with indeterminate term or term in other jurisdiction

(a) When a defendant is sentenced under section 1170 and the sentence is to run consecutively to or concurrently with a sentence imposed under section 1168(b) in the same or another proceeding, the judgment must specify the determinate term imposed under section 1170 computed without reference to the indeterminate sentence, must order that the determinate term be served consecutively to or concurrently with the sentence under section 1168(b), and must identify the proceedings in which the indeterminate sentence was imposed. The term under section 1168(b), and the date of its completion or date of parole or postrelease community supervision, and the sequence in which the sentences are deemed or served, will be determined by correctional authorities as provided by law.

(Subd (a) amended effective January 1, 2018; previously amended effective January 1, 1979, July 1, 2003, and January 1, 2007.)

(b) When a defendant is sentenced under sections 1168 or 1170 and the sentence is to run consecutively to or concurrently with a sentence imposed by a court of the United States or of another state or territory, the judgment must specify the term imposed under sections 1168(b) or 1170 computed without reference to the sentence imposed by the other jurisdiction, must identify the other jurisdiction and the proceedings in which the other sentence was imposed, and must indicate whether the sentences are imposed concurrently or consecutively. If the term imposed is to be served consecutively to the term imposed by the other jurisdiction, the court must order that the California term be served commencing on the completion of the sentence imposed by the other jurisdiction.

(Subd (b) amended effective January 1, 2018; previously amended effective January 1, 2007.)
Rule 4.451 amended effective January 1, 2018; adopted as rule 451 effective July 1, 1977; previously renumbered effective January 1, 2001; previously amended effective January 1, 1979, July 1, 2003, and January 1, 2007.

Advisory Committee Comment

Subdivision (a). The provisions of section 1170.1(a), which use a one-third formula to calculate subordinate consecutive terms, can logically be applied only when all the sentences are imposed under section 1170. Indeterminate sentences are imposed under section 1168(b). Since the duration of the indeterminate term cannot be known to the court, subdivision (a) states the only feasible mode of sentencing. (See *People v. Felix* (2000) 22 Cal.4th 651, 654–657; *People v. McGahuey* (1981) 121 Cal.App.3d 524, 530–532.)

Subdivision (b). On the authority to sentence consecutively to the sentence of another jurisdiction and the effect of such a sentence, see *In re Helpman* (1968) 267 Cal.App.2d 307 and cases cited at page 310, footnote 3. The mode of sentencing required by subdivision (b) is necessary to avoid the illogical conclusion that the total of the consecutive sentences will depend on whether the other jurisdiction or California is the first to pronounce judgment.

Rule 4.452. Determinate sentence consecutive to prior determinate sentence

(a) If a determinate sentence is imposed under section 1170.1(a) consecutive to one or more determinate sentences imposed previously in the same court or in other courts, the court in the current case must pronounce a single aggregate term, as defined in section 1170.1(a), stating the result of combining the previous and current sentences. In those situations:

(1) The sentences on all determinately sentenced counts in all of the cases on which a sentence was or is being imposed must be combined as though they were all counts in the current case.

(2) The court in the current case must make a new determination of which count, in the combined cases, represents the principal term, as defined in section 1170.1(a). The principal term is the term with the greatest punishment imposed including conduct enhancements. If two terms of imprisonment have the same punishment, either term may be selected as the principal term.

(3) Discretionary decisions of courts in previous cases may not be changed by the court in the current case. Such decisions include the decision to impose one of the three authorized terms of imprisonment referred to in section 1170(b), making counts in prior cases concurrent with or consecutive to each other, or the decision that circumstances in mitigation or in the furtherance of justice justified striking the punishment for an enhancement. However, if a previously designated principal term becomes a subordinate term after the resentencing, the subordinate term will be limited to one-third the middle base term as provided in section 1170.1(a).

(4) If all previously imposed sentences and the current sentence being imposed by the second or subsequent court are under section 1170(h), the second or subsequent court has the discretion to specify whether a previous sentence is to be served in custody or on mandatory supervision and the terms of such supervision, but may not, without express consent of the defendant, modify the sentence on the earlier sentenced charges in any manner that will (i) increase the total length of the sentence imposed by the previous court; (ii) increase the total length of the custody portion of the sentence imposed by the previous court; (iii) increase the total length of the mandatory supervision portion of the sentence imposed by the previous court; or (iv) impose additional, more onerous, or more restrictive conditions of release for any previously imposed period of mandatory supervision.

(5) If the second or subsequent court imposes a sentence to state prison because the defendant is ineligible for sentencing under section 1170(h), the jurisdiction of the second or subsequent court to impose a prison sentence applies solely to the current case. The defendant must be returned to the original sentencing court for potential resentencing on any previous case or cases sentenced under section 1170(h). The original sentencing court must convert all remaining custody and mandatory supervision time imposed in the previous case to state prison custody time and must determine whether its sentence is concurrent with or consecutive to the state prison term imposed by the second or subsequent court and incorporate that sentence into a single aggregate term as required by this rule. (A)(4) does not apply—and the consent of the defendant is not required—for this conversion and resentencing.

(6) In cases in which a sentence is imposed under the provisions of section 1170(h) and the sentence has been imposed by courts in two or more counties, the second or subsequent court must determine the county or counties of incarceration or supervision, including the order of service of such incarceration or supervision. To the extent reasonably possible, the period of mandatory supervision must be served in one county and after completion of any period of incarceration. In accordance with rule 4.472, the second or subsequent court must calculate the defendant's remaining custody and supervision time.

(7) In making the determination under (a)(6), the court must exercise its discretion after consideration of the following factors:

(A) The relative length of custody or supervision required for each case;

(B) Whether the cases in each county are to be served concurrently or consecutively;

(C) The nature and quality of treatment programs available in each county, if known;

(D) The nature and extent of the defendant's current enrollment and participation in any treatment program;

(E) The nature and extent of the defendant's ties to the community, including employment, duration of residence, family attachments, and property holdings;

(F) The nature and extent of supervision available in each county, if known;

(G) The factors listed in rule 4.530(f); and

(H) Any other factor relevant to such determination.

(8) If after the court's determination in accordance with (a)(6) the defendant is ordered to serve only a custody term without supervision in another county, the defendant must be transported at such time and under such circumstances as the court directs to the county where the custody term is to be served. The defendant must be transported with an abstract of the court's judgment as required by section 1213(a), or other suitable documentation showing the term imposed by the court and any custody credits against the sentence. The court may order the custody term to be served in another county without also transferring jurisdiction of the case in accordance with rule 4.530.

(9) If after the court's determination in accordance with (a)(6) the defendant is ordered to serve a period of supervision in another county, whether with or without a term of custody, the matter must be transferred for the period of supervision in accordance with provisions of rule 4.530(f), (g), and (h).

(Subd (a) amended effective January 1, 2021; previously adopted as unlettered subdivisions effective January 1, 1991; previously lettered and amended effective July 1, 2019.)

Rule 4.452 amended effective January 1, 2021; adopted as rule 452 effective January 1, 1991; previously renumbered effective January 1, 2001; previously amended effective July 1, 2003, January 2, 2007, May 23, 2007, January 1, 2017, January 1, 2018, and July 1, 2019.

Advisory Committee Comment

The restrictions of (a)(3) do not apply to circumstances where a previously imposed base term is made a consecutive term on resentencing. If the court selects a consecutive sentence structure, and since there can be only one principal term in the final aggregate sentence, if a previously imposed full base term becomes a subordinate consecutive term, the new consecutive term normally will become one-third the middle term by operation of law (section 1170.1(a)).

Rule 4.453. Commitments to nonpenal institutions [Repealed]

Rule 4.453 repealed effective March 14, 2022; adopted as rule 453 effective July 1, 1977; previously amended and renumbered effective January 1, 2001; previously amended effective July 28, 1977, January 1, 2006, and January 1, 2007.

Rule 4.470. Notification of appeal rights in felony cases [Repealed]

Rule 4.470 repealed effective January 1, 2013; adopted as rule 250 effective January 1, 1972; previously amended effective July 1, 1972, January 1, 1977, and January 1, 2007; previously amended and renumbered as rule 470 effective January 1, 1991; previously renumbered effective January 1, 2001.

Rule 4.472. Determination of presentence custody time credit

At the time of sentencing, the court must cause to be recorded on the judgment or commitment the total time in custody to be credited on the sentence under sections 2900.5, 2933.1(c), 2933.2(c), and 4019. On referral of the defendant to the probation officer for an investigation and report under section 1203(b) or 1203(g), or on setting a date for sentencing in the absence of a referral, the court must direct the sheriff, probation officer, or other appropriate person to report to the court and notify the defendant or defense counsel and prosecuting attorney within a reasonable time before the date set for sentencing as to the number of days that defendant has been in custody and for which he or she may be entitled to credit. Any challenges to the report must be heard at the time of sentencing.

Rule 4.472 amended effective January 1, 2017; adopted as rule 252 effective January 1, 1977; previously amended and renumbered as rule 472 effective January 1, 1991; previously amended and renumbered effective January 1, 2001; previously amended effective July 1, 2003, and January 1, 2007.

Rule 4.480. Judge's statement under section 1203.01

A sentencing judge's statement of his or her views under section 1203.01 respecting a person sentenced to the Department of Corrections and Rehabilitation, Division of Adult Operations is required only in the event that no probation report is filed. Even though it is not required, however, a statement should be submitted by the judge in any case in which he or she believes that the correctional handling and the determination of term and parole should be influenced by information not contained in other court records.

The purpose of a section 1203.01 statement is to provide assistance to the Department of Corrections and Rehabilitation, Division of Adult Operations in its programming and institutional assignment and to the Board of Parole Hearings with reference to term fixing and parole release of persons sentenced indeterminately, and parole and postrelease community supervision waiver of persons sentenced determinately. It may amplify any reasons for the sentence that may bear on a possible suggestion by the Secretary of the Department of Corrections and Rehabilitation or the Board of Parole Hearings that the sentence and commitment be recalled and the defendant be resentenced. To be of maximum assistance to these agencies, a judge's statements should contain individualized comments concerning the convicted offender, any special circumstances that led to a prison sentence rather than local incarceration, and any other significant information that might not readily be available in any of the accompanying official records and reports.

If a section 1203.01 statement is prepared, it should be submitted no later than two weeks after sentencing so that it may be included in the official Department of Corrections and Rehabilitation, Division of Adult Operations case summary that is prepared during the time the offender is being processed at the Reception-Guidance Center of the Department of Corrections and Rehabilitation, Division of Adult Operations.

Rule 4.480 amended effective January 1, 2017; adopted as section 12 of the Standards of Judicial Administration effective January 1, 1973; previously amended and renumbered effective January 1, 2001; previously amended effective July 1, 1978, July 1, 2003, January 1, 2006, and January 1, 2007.

Division 6
Postconviction, Postrelease, and Writs

Title 4, Criminal Rules—Division 6, Postconviction, Postrelease, and Writs; amended effective October 28, 2011.

Chap. 1. Postconviction. Rules 4.510, 4.530.
Chap. 2. Postrelease. Rule 4.541.
Chap. 3. Habeas Corpus. Rules 4.545–4.577.

Chapter 1
Postconviction

Rule 4.510. Reverse remand
Rule 4.530. Intercounty transfer of probation and mandatory supervision cases

Rule 4.510. Reverse remand

(a) Minor prosecuted under Welfare and Institutions Code section 602(b) or 707(d) and convicted of offense listed in Welfare and Institutions Code section 602(b) or 707(d) (Penal Code, § 1170.17)

If the prosecuting attorney lawfully initiated the prosecution as a criminal case under Welfare and Institutions Code section 602(b) or 707(d), and the minor is convicted of a criminal offense listed in those sections, the minor must be sentenced as an adult.

(Subd (a) amended effective January 1, 2007.)

(b) Minor convicted of an offense not listed in Welfare and Institutions Code section 602(b) or 707(d) (Penal Code, § 1170.17)

(1) If the prosecuting attorney lawfully initiated the prosecution as a criminal case and the minor is convicted of an offense not listed in Welfare and Institutions Code section 602(b) or 707(d), but one that would have raised the presumption of unfitness under juvenile court law, the minor may move the court to conduct a postconviction fitness hearing.

(A) On the motion by the minor, the court must order the probation department to prepare a report as required in rule 5.768.

(B) The court may conduct a fitness hearing or remand the matter to the juvenile court for a determination of fitness.

(C) The minor may receive a disposition hearing under the juvenile court law only if he or she is found to be fit under rule 5.772. However, if the court and parties agree, the minor may be sentenced in adult court.

(D) If the minor is found unfit, the minor must be sentenced as an adult, unless all parties, including the court, agree that the disposition be conducted under juvenile court law.

(2) If the minor is convicted of an offense not listed in Welfare and Institutions Code section 602(b) or 707(d), but one for which the minor would have been presumed fit under the juvenile court law, the minor must have a disposition hearing under juvenile court law, and consistent with the provisions of Penal Code section 1170.19, either in the trial court or on remand to the juvenile court.

(A) If the prosecuting attorney objects to the treatment of the minor as within the juvenile court law and moves for a fitness hearing to be conducted, the court must order the probation department to prepare a report as required by rule 5.768.

(B) The court may conduct a fitness hearing or remand the matter to the juvenile court for a determination of fitness.

(C) If found to be fit under rule 5.770, the minor will be subject to a disposition hearing under juvenile court law and Penal Code section 1170.19.

(D) If the minor is found unfit, the minor must be sentenced as an adult, unless all parties, including the court, agree that the disposition be conducted under juvenile court law.

(3) If the minor is convicted of an offense that would not have permitted a fitness determination, the court must remand the matter to juvenile court for disposition, unless the minor requests sentencing in adult court and all parties, including the court, agree.

(4) Fitness hearings held under this rule must be conducted as provided in title 5, division 3, chapter 14, article 2.

(Subd (b) amended effective January 1, 2007.)

Rule 4.510 amended effective January 1, 2007; adopted effective January 1, 2001.

Rule 4.530. Intercounty transfer of probation and mandatory supervision cases

(a) Application

This rule applies to intercounty transfers of probation and mandatory supervision cases under Penal Code section 1203.9.

(Subd (a) amended effective February 20, 2014; adopted effective July 1, 2010; previously amended effective November 1, 2012.)

(b) Definitions

As used in this rule:

(1) "Transferring court" means the superior court of the county in which the supervised person is supervised on probation or mandatory supervision.

(2) "Receiving court" means the superior court of the county to which transfer of the case and probation or mandatory supervision is proposed.

(Subd (b) amended effective November 1, 2012; adopted effective July 1, 2010.)

(c) Motion

Transfers may be made only after noticed motion in the transferring court.

(Subd (c) adopted effective July 1, 2010.)

(d) Notice

(1) If transfer is requested by the probation officer of the transferring county, the probation officer must provide written notice of the date, time, and place set for hearing on the motion to:

(A) The presiding judge of the receiving court or his or her designee;

(B) The probation officer of the receiving county or his or her designee;

(C) The prosecutor of the transferring county;

(D) The victim (if any);

(E) The supervised person; and

(F) The supervised person's last counsel of record (if any).

(2) If transfer is requested by any other party, the party must first request in writing that the probation officer of the transferring county notice the motion. The party may make the motion to the transferring court only if the probation officer refuses to do so. The probation officer must notify the party of his or her decision within 30 days of the party's request. Failure by the probation officer to notify the party of his or her decision within 30 days is deemed a refusal to make the motion.

(3) If the party makes the motion, the motion must include a declaration that the probation officer has refused to bring the motion, and the party must provide written notice of the date, time, and place set for hearing on the motion to:

(A) The presiding judge of the receiving court or his or her designee;

(B) The probation officers of the transferring and receiving counties or their designees;

(C) The prosecutor of the transferring county;

(D) The supervised person; and

(E) The supervised person's last counsel of record (if any).

Upon receipt of notice of a motion for transfer by a party, the probation officer of the transferring county must provide notice to the victim, if any.

(4) Notice of a transfer motion must be given at least 60 days before the date set for hearing on the motion.

(5) Before deciding a transfer motion, the transferring court must confirm that notice was given to the receiving court as required by (1) and (3).

(Subd (d) amended effective November 1, 2012; adopted effective July 1, 2010.)

(e) Comment

(1) No later than 10 days before the date set for hearing on the motion, the receiving court may provide comments to the transferring court regarding the proposed transfer.

(2) Any comments provided by the receiving court must be in writing and signed by a judge and must state why transfer is or is not appropriate.

(3) Before deciding a transfer motion, the transferring court must state on the record that it has received and considered any comments provided by the receiving court.

(Subd (e) adopted effective July 1, 2010.)

(f) Factors

The transferring court must consider at least the following factors when determining whether transfer is appropriate:

(1) The permanency of the supervised person's residence. As used in this subdivision, "residence" means the place where the supervised person customarily lives exclusive of employment, school, or other special or temporary purpose. A supervised person may have only one residence. The fact that the supervised person intends to change residence to the receiving county, without further evidence of how, when, and why this is to be accomplished, is insufficient to transfer supervision;

(2) The availability of appropriate programs for the supervised person, including substance abuse, domestic violence, sex offender, and collaborative court programs;

(3) Restitution orders, including whether transfer would impair the ability of the receiving court to determine a restitution amount or impair the ability of the victim to collect court-ordered restitution; and

(4) Victim issues, including:

(A) The residence and places frequented by the victim, including school and workplace; and

(B) Whether transfer would impair the ability of the court, law enforcement, or the probation officer of the transferring county to properly enforce protective orders.

(Subd (f) amended effective November 1, 2012; adopted effective July 1, 2010.)

(g) Transfer

(1) If the transferring court determines that the permanent residence of the supervised person is in the county of the receiving court, the transferring court must transfer the case unless it determines that transfer would be inappropriate and states its reasons on the record.

(2) To the extent possible, the transferring court must establish any amount of restitution owed by the supervised person before it orders the transfer.

(3) Transfer is effective the date the transferring court orders the transfer. Upon transfer of the case, the receiving court must accept the entire jurisdiction over the case.

(4) The orders for transfer must include an order committing the supervised person to the care and custody of the probation officer of the receiving county.

(5) Upon transfer of the case, the transferring court must transmit the entire original court file to the receiving court in all cases in which the supervisee is the sole defendant, except the transferring court shall not transfer (A) exhibits or (B) any records of payments. If transfer is ordered in a case involving more than one defendant, the transferring court must transmit certified copies of the entire original court file, except exhibits and any records of payments, to the receiving court upon transfer of the case.

(6) A certified copy of the entire court file may be electronically transmitted if an original paper court file does not exist. Upon receipt of an electronically transmitted certified copy of the entire court file from the transferring court, the receiving court must deem it an original file.

(7) Upon transfer the probation officer of the transferring county must transmit, at a minimum, any court orders, probation or mandatory supervision reports, and case plans to the probation officer of the receiving county.

(8) Upon transfer of the case, the probation officer of the transferring county must notify the supervised person of the transfer order. The

supervised person must report to the probation officer of the receiving county no later than 30 days after transfer unless the transferring court orders the supervised person to report sooner. If the supervised person is in custody at the time of transfer, the supervised person must report to the probation officer of the receiving county no later than 30 days after being released from custody unless the transferring court orders the supervised person to report sooner. Any jail sentence imposed as a condition of probation or mandatory supervision prior to transfer must be served in the transferring county unless otherwise authorized by law.

(9) Upon transfer of the case, only the receiving court may certify copies from the case file.

(Subd (g) amended effective March 14, 2022; adopted effective July 1, 2010; previously amended effective November 1, 2012, January 1, 2017, and January 1, 2021.)

(h) Court-ordered debt

(1) In accordance with Penal Code section 1203.9(d) and (e):

(A) If the transferring court has ordered the defendant to pay fines, fees, forfeitures, penalties, assessments, or restitution, the transfer order must require that those and any other amounts ordered by the transferring court that are still unpaid at the time of transfer be paid by the defendant to the collection program for the transferring court for proper distribution and accounting once collected.

(B) The receiving court and receiving county probation department may not impose additional local fees and costs.

(C) Upon approval of a transferring court, a receiving court may elect to collect all of the court-ordered payments from a defendant attributable to the case under which the defendant is being supervised.

(2) Policies and procedures for implementation of the collection, accounting, and disbursement of court-ordered debt under this rule must be consistent with Judicial Council fiscal procedures available at www.courts.ca.gov.

(Subd (h) amended effective March 14, 2022; adopted effective January 1, 2017.)
Rule 4.530 amended effective March 14, 2022; adopted effective July 1, 2010; previously amended effective November 1, 2012, February 20, 2014, January 1, 2017, and January 1, 2021.

Advisory Committee Comment

Subdivision (g)(5) requires the transferring court to transmit the entire original court file, except exhibits and any records of payments, to the court of the receiving county in all cases in which the supervisee is the sole defendant. Before transmitting the entire original court file, transferring courts should consider retaining copies of the court file in the event of an appeal or a writ. In cases involving more than one defendant, subdivision (g)(5) requires the transferring court to transmit certified copies of the entire original court file to ensure that transferring courts are able to properly adjudicate any pending or future codefendant proceedings. Only documents related to the transferring defendant must be transmitted to the receiving court.

Subdivision (g)(7) clarifies that any jail sentence imposed as a condition of probation or mandatory supervision before transfer must be served in the transferring county unless otherwise authorized by law. For example, Penal Code section 1208.5 authorizes the boards of supervisors of two or more counties with work furlough programs to enter into agreements to allow work-furlough-eligible persons sentenced to or imprisoned in one county jail to transfer to another county jail.

Subdivision (h) requires defendants still owing fines, fees, forfeitures, penalties, assessments, or restitution to pay the transferring court's collection program. In counties where the county probation department collects this court-ordered debt, the term "collection program" is intended to include the county probation department.

Chapter 2
Postrelease

Title 4, Criminal Rules—Division 6, Postconviction, Postrelease, and Writs—Chapter 2, Postrelease; adopted effective October 28, 2011.

Rule 4.540. Revocation of postrelease community supervision [Repealed]

Rule 4.540 repealed effective November 1, 2012; adopted effective October 28, 2011.

Rule 4.541. Minimum contents of supervising agency reports

(a) Application

This rule applies to supervising agency petitions for revocation of formal probation, parole, mandatory supervision under Penal Code section 1170(h)(5)(B), and postrelease community supervision under Penal Code section 3455.

(Subd (a) amended effective July 1, 2013; adopted effective October 28, 2011; previously amended effective November 1, 2012.)

(b) Definitions

As used in this rule:

(1) "Supervised person" means any person subject to formal probation, parole, mandatory supervision under Penal Code section 1170(h)(5)(B), or community supervision under Penal Code section 3451.

(2) "Formal probation" means the suspension of the imposition or execution of a sentence and the order of conditional and revocable release in the community under the supervision of a probation officer.

(3) "Court" includes any hearing officer appointed by a superior court and authorized to conduct revocation proceedings under Government Code section 71622.5.

(4) "Supervising agency" includes the county agency designated by the board of supervisors under Penal Code section 3451.

(Subd (b) amended effective July 1, 2013; adopted effective November 1, 2012.)

(c) Minimum contents

Except as provided in (d), a petition for revocation of supervision must include a written report that contains at least the following information:

(1) Information about the supervised person, including:

(A) Personal identifying information, including name and date of birth;

(B) Custody status and the date and circumstances of arrest;

(C) Any pending cases and case numbers;

(D) The history and background of the supervised person, including a summary of the supervised person's record of prior criminal conduct; and

(E) Any available information requested by the court regarding the supervised person's risk of recidivism, including any validated risk-needs assessments;

(2) All relevant terms and conditions of supervision and the circumstances of the alleged violations, including a summary of any statement made by the supervised person, and any victim information, including statements and type and amount of loss;

(3) A summary of any previous violations and sanctions; and

(4) Any recommended sanctions.

(Subd (c) amended and relettered effective November 1, 2012; adopted as subd (b) effective October 28, 2011.)

(d) Subsequent reports

If a written report was submitted as part of the original sentencing proceeding or with an earlier revocation petition, a subsequent report need only update the information required by (c). A subsequent report must include a copy of the original report if the original report is not contained in the court file.

(Subd (d) amended and relettered effective November 1, 2012; adopted as subd (c) effective October 28, 2011.)

(e) Parole and Postrelease Community Supervision Reports

In addition to the minimum contents described in (c), a report filed by the supervising agency in conjunction with a petition to revoke parole or postrelease community supervision must include the reasons for that agency's determination that intermediate sanctions without court intervention as authorized by Penal Code sections 3000.08(f) or 3454(b) are inappropriate responses to the alleged violations.

(Subd (e) amended effective July 1, 2013; adopted effective November 1, 2012.)
Rule 4.541 amended effective July 1, 2013; adopted effective October 28, 2011; previously amended effective November 1, 2012.

Advisory Committee Comment

Subdivision (c). This subdivision prescribes minimum contents for supervising agency reports. Courts may require additional contents in light of local customs and needs.

Subdivision (c)(1)(D). The history and background of the supervised person may include the supervised person's social history, including family, education, employment, income, military, medical, psychological, and substance abuse information.

Subdivision (c)(1)(E). Penal Code section 3451(a) requires postrelease community supervision to be consistent with evidence-based practices, including supervision policies, procedures, programs, and practices demonstrated by scientific research to reduce recidivism among supervised persons. "Evidence-based practices" refers to "supervision policies, procedures, programs, and practices demonstrated by scientific research to reduce recidivism among individuals under probation, parole, or postrelease supervision." (Pen. Code, § 3450(b)(9).).

Subdivision (e). Penal Code sections 3000.08(d) and 3454(b) authorize supervising agencies to impose appropriate responses to alleged violations of parole and postrelease community supervision without court intervention, including referral to a reentry court under Penal Code section 3015 or flash incarceration in a county jail. Penal Code sections 3000.08(f) and 3455(a) require the supervising agency to determine that the intermediate sanctions authorized by sections 3000.08(d) and 3454(b) are inappropriate responses to the alleged violation *before* filing a petition to revoke parole or postrelease community supervision.

Chapter 3
Habeas Corpus

Title 4, Criminal Rules—Division 6, Postconviction, Postrelease, and Writs—Chapter 3, Habeas Corpus; renumbered effective October 28, 2011; adopted as Chapter 2.

Art. 1. General Provisions. Rule 4.545.
Art. 2. Noncapital Habeas Corpus Proceedings in the Superior Court. Rules 4.550–4.552.
Art. 3. Death Penalty–Related Habeas Corpus Proceedings in the Superior Court. Rules 4.560–4.577.

Article 1
General Provisions

Title 4, Criminal Rules—Division 6, Postconviction, Postrelease, and Writs—Chapter 3, Habeas Corpus—Article 1, General Provisions; adopted effective April 25, 2019.

Rule 4.545. Definitions

In this chapter, the following definitions apply:

(1) A "petition for writ of habeas corpus" is the petitioner's initial filing that commences a proceeding.

(2) An "order to show cause" is an order directing the respondent to file a return. The order to show cause is issued if the petitioner has made a prima facie showing that he or she is entitled to relief; it does not grant the relief requested. An order to show cause may also be referred to as "granting the writ."

(3) The "return" is the respondent's statement of reasons that the court should not grant the relief requested by the petitioner.

(4) The "denial" is the petitioner's pleading in response to the return. The denial may be also referred to as the "traverse."

(5) An "evidentiary hearing" is a hearing held by the trial court to resolve contested factual issues.

(6) An "order on writ of habeas corpus" is the court's order granting or denying the relief sought by the petitioner.

(7) The definitions in rule 8.601 also apply to this chapter.

Rule 4.545 adopted effective April 25, 2019.

Article 2
Noncapital Habeas Corpus Proceedings in the Superior Court

Title 4, Criminal Rules—Division 6, Postconviction, Postrelease, and Writs—Chapter 3, Habeas Corpus—Article 2, Noncapital Habeas Corpus Proceedings in the Superior Court; adopted effective April 25, 2019.

Rule 4.550. Habeas corpus application
Rule 4.551. Habeas corpus proceedings
Rule 4.552. Habeas corpus jurisdiction
Rule 4.553. Qualifications for appointed counsel for claims under section 1473(e) in noncapital case

Rule 4.550. Habeas corpus application

This article applies to habeas corpus proceedings in the superior court under Penal Code section 1473 et seq. or any other provision of law authorizing relief from unlawful confinement or unlawful conditions of confinement, except for death penalty–related habeas corpus proceedings, which are governed by rule 4.560 et seq.

Rule 4.550 amended effective April 25, 2019; adopted effective January 1, 2002; previously amended effective January 1, 2007.

Rule 4.551. Habeas corpus proceedings

(a) Petition; form and court ruling

(1) Except as provided in (2), the petition must be on the *Petition for Writ of Habeas Corpus* (form HC-001).

(2) For good cause, a court may also accept for filing a petition that does not comply with (a)(1). A petition submitted by an attorney need not be on the Judicial Council form. However, a petition that is not on the Judicial Council form must comply with Penal Code section 1474 and must contain the pertinent information specified in the *Petition for Writ of Habeas Corpus* (form HC-001), including the information required regarding other petitions, motions, or applications filed in any court with respect to the conviction, commitment, or issue.

(3) If a petition raises a claim under Penal Code section 745(a), the petition must include whether the petitioner requests appointment of counsel and whether the petitioner can afford counsel.

(4) If a petitioner has an unadjudicated habeas corpus petition pending in the superior court, the petitioner may amend the existing petition with a claim the petitioner's conviction or sentence was in violation of Penal Code section 745(a).

[1] **(5)** (A) On filing, the clerk of the court must immediately deliver the petition to the presiding judge or [2] **their** designee. The court must rule on a petition for writ of habeas corpus within 60 days after the petition is filed.

(B) When an unadjudicated habeas corpus petition is amended to include a claim under section 745, or otherwise amended with leave of court, the time to rule on a petition for writ of habeas corpus is extended to 60 days from the date the amended petition was filed.

[3] **(6)** If the court fails to rule on the petition **(or amended petition)** within 60 days of its filing, the petitioner may file a notice and request for ruling.

[4] **(A)** The petitioner's notice and request for ruling must include a declaration stating the date [5] **on which any** petition **or amended petition** was filed, [6] the date of the notice and request for ruling, and [7] **the fact** that the petitioner has not received a ruling on the petition. A copy of the original **(and the amended)** petition must be attached to the notice and request for ruling.

[8] **(B)** If the presiding judge or [9] **their** designee determines that the notice is complete and the court has failed to rule, the presiding judge or [10] **their** designee must assign the petition to a judge and calendar the matter for a decision without appearances within 30 days of the filing of the notice and request for ruling. If the judge assigned by the presiding judge rules on the petition before the date the petition is calendared for decision, the matter may be taken off calendar.

(7) If a petition raises a claim under Penal Code section 745(a) that is based on conduct or statements by a judge, the judge must disqualify themselves from proceedings under section 745.

[11] **(8)** For the purposes of [12] **(a)(5)**, the court rules on the petition by:

(A) Issuing an order to show cause under (c);
(B) Denying the petition for writ of habeas corpus; or
(C) Requesting an informal response to the petition for writ of habeas corpus under (b).

[13] **(9)** The court must issue an order to show cause or deny the petition within 45 days after receipt of an informal response requested under (b).

(Subd (a) amended effective September 1, 2024; previously amended effective January 1, 2002, January 1, 2004, January 1, 2007, January 1, 2009, and January 22, 2019.)

Rule 4.551(a) 2024 Deletes. [1] (3) [2] his or her [3] (B) [4] (i) [5] the [6] and [7] indicating [8] (ii) [9] his or her [10] his or her [11] (4) [12] (a)(3) [13] (5)

(b) Informal response

(1) Before passing on the petition, the court may request an informal response from:

(A) The respondent or real party in interest; or
(B) The custodian of any record pertaining to the petitioner's case, directing the custodian to produce the record or a certified copy to be filed with the clerk of the court.

(2) A copy of the request must be sent to the petitioner. The informal response, if any, must be served on the petitioner by the party of whom the request is made. The informal response must be in writing and must be served and filed within 15 days. If any informal response is filed, the court must notify the petitioner that he or she may reply to the informal response within 15 days from the date of service of the response on the petitioner. If the informal response consists of records or copies of records, a copy of every record and document furnished to the court must be furnished to the petitioner.

(3) After receiving an informal response, the court may not deny the petition until the petitioner has filed a timely reply to the informal response or the 15-day period provided for a reply under (b)(2) has expired.

(Subd (b) amended effective January 1, 2007; adopted effective January 1, 2002.)

(c) Order to show cause

(1) The court must issue an order to show cause if the petitioner has made a prima facie showing that [1] **the petitioner** is entitled to relief. In doing so, the court takes petitioner's factual allegations as true and makes a preliminary assessment regarding whether the petitioner would be

entitled to relief if [2] **the petitioner's** factual allegations were proved. If so, the court must issue an order to show cause.

[3] **(2)** An order to show cause is a determination that the petitioner has made a showing that [4] **they** may be entitled to relief. It does not grant the relief sought in the petition.

(Subd (c) amended effective September 1, 2024; adopted effective January 1, 2002; previously amended effective January 1, 2007.)

Rule 4.551(c) 2024 Deletes. [1] he or she **[2]** his or her **[3]** (2) On issuing an order to show cause, the court must appoint counsel for any unrepresented petitioner who desires but cannot afford counsel. (3) **[4]** he or she

(d) Appointment of counsel

(1) On issuing an order to show cause, the court must appoint counsel for any unrepresented petitioner who desires but cannot afford counsel.

(2) When a petition raises a claim under Penal Code section 745(a) and requests appointment of counsel, the court must appoint counsel if the petitioner cannot afford counsel and either the petition alleges facts that would establish a violation of section 745(a) or the State Public Defender requests that counsel be appointed. Newly appointed counsel may amend a petition filed before their appointment.

(Subd (d) adopted effective September 1, 2024.)

(e) Return

If an order to show cause is issued as provided in (c), the respondent may, within 30 days thereafter, file a return. Any material allegation of the petition not controverted by the return is deemed admitted for purposes of the proceeding. The return must comply with Penal Code section 1480 and must be served on the petitioner.

(Subd (e) relettered effective September 1, 2024; repealed and adopted as subd (d) effective January 1, 2002; previously amended effective January 1, 2004.)

(f) Denial

Within 30 days after service and filing of a return, the petitioner may file a denial. Any material allegation of the return not denied is deemed admitted for purposes of the proceeding. Any denial must comply with Penal Code section 1484 and must be served on the respondent.

(Subd (f) relettered effective September 1, 2024; adopted as subd (b) effective January 1, 1982; previously amended and relettered as subd (e) effective January 1, 2002.)

(g) Evidentiary hearing; when required

[1] (1) Except as provided in (2), within 30 days after the filing of any denial or, if none is filed, after the expiration of the time for filing a denial, the court must either grant or deny the relief sought by the petition or order an evidentiary hearing. An evidentiary hearing is required if, after considering the verified petition, the return, any denial, any affidavits or declarations under penalty of perjury, and matters of which judicial notice may be taken, the court finds there is a reasonable likelihood that the petitioner may be entitled to relief and the petitioner's entitlement to relief depends on the resolution of an issue of fact. The petitioner must be produced at the evidentiary hearing unless the court, for good cause, directs otherwise.

(2) If the court issues an order to show cause on a claim raised under Penal Code section 745(a), the court must hold an evidentiary hearing, unless the state declines to show cause. The defendant may appear remotely, and the court may conduct the hearing with remote technology, unless counsel indicates the defendant's presence in court is needed.

(Subd (g) amended and relettered effective September 1, 2024; adopted as subd (c) effective January 1, 1982; previously amended and relettered as subd (f) effective January 1, 2002.)

Rule 4.551(g) 2024 Deletes. [1] Within

(h) Reasons for denial of petition

[1] (1) Except as provided in (2), any order denying a petition for writ of habeas corpus must contain a brief statement of the reasons for the denial. An order only declaring the petition to be "denied" is insufficient.

(2) If the court determines that the petitioner has not established a prima facie showing of entitlement to relief for a claim raised under Penal Code section 745(a), the court must state the factual and legal basis for its conclusion on the record or issue a written order detailing the factual and legal basis for its conclusion.

(Subd (h) amended and relettered effective September 1, 2024; adopted as subd (e) effective January 1, 1982; previously amended and relettered as subd (g) effective January 1, 2002.)

Rule 4.551(h) 2024 Deletes. [1] Any

(i) Extending or shortening time

On motion of any party or on the court's own motion, for good cause stated in the order, the court may shorten or extend the time for doing any act under this rule. A copy of the order must be mailed to each party.

(Subd (i) relettered effective September 1, 2024; adopted as subd (f) effective January 1, 1982; previously amended and relettered as subd (h) effective January 1, 2002.)

Rule 4.551 amended effective September 1, 2024; adopted as rule 260 effective January 1, 1982; previously renumbered as rule 4.500 effective January 1, 2001; previously amended and renumbered effective January 1, 2002; previously amended effective January 1, 2004, January 1, 2007, January 1, 2009, and January 22, 2019.

Advisory Committee Comment

The court must appoint counsel on the issuance of an order to show cause. (*In re Clark* (1993) 5 Cal.4th 750, 780 and *People v. Shipman* (1965) 62 Cal.2d 226, 231-232.) The Court of Appeal has held that under Penal Code section 987.2, counties bear the expense of appointed counsel in a habeas corpus proceeding challenging the underlying conviction. (*Charlton v. Superior Court* (1979) 93 Cal.App.3d 858, 862.) Penal Code section 987.2 authorizes appointment of the public defender, or private counsel if there is no public defender available, for indigents in criminal proceedings.

The issue of whether the prima facie showing for a petition for writ of habeas corpus under section 1473(e) is the same as in section 745(h)(2) or defined in subdivision (c)(1) of this rule (see *In re Marquez* (2007) 153 Cal.App.4th 1, 11) is unresolved.

Subdivision (a)(4) and (7). The committee's revisions reflect the language in section 1473(e) and are not intended to limit a court's discretion and authority in habeas corpus proceedings that do not include claims under section 745.

Rule 4.552. Habeas corpus jurisdiction

(a) Proper court to hear petition

Except as stated in (b), the petition should be heard and resolved in the court in which it is filed.

(Subd (a) amended effective January 1, 2012; previously amended effective January 1, 2006, and January 1, 2007.)

(b) Transfer of petition

(1) The superior court in which the petition is filed must determine, based on the allegations of the petition, whether the matter should be heard by it or in the superior court of another county.

(2) If the superior court in which the petition is filed determines that the matter may be more properly heard by the superior court of another county, it may nonetheless retain jurisdiction in the matter or, without first determining whether a prima facie case for relief exists, order the matter transferred to the other county. Transfer may be ordered in the following circumstances:

(A) If the petition challenges the terms of a judgment, the matter may be transferred to the county in which judgment was rendered.

(B) If the petition challenges the conditions of an inmate's confinement, it may be transferred to the county in which the petitioner is confined. A change in the institution of confinement that effects a change in the conditions of confinement may constitute good cause to deny the petition.

(C) If the petition challenges the denial of parole or the petitioner's suitability for parole and is filed in a superior court other than the court that rendered the underlying judgment, the court in which the petition is filed should transfer the petition to the superior court in which the underlying judgment was rendered.

(3) The transferring court must specify in the order of transfer the reason for the transfer.

(4) If the receiving court determines that the reason for transfer is inapplicable, the receiving court must, within 30 days of receipt of the case, order the case returned to the transferring court. The transferring court must retain and resolve the matter as provided by these rules.

(Subd (b) amended effective January 1, 2012; previously amended effective January 1, 2006.)

(c) Single judge must decide petition

A petition for writ of habeas corpus filed in the superior court must be decided by a single judge; it must not be considered by the appellate division of the superior court.

(Subd (c) repealed and relettered effective January 1, 2012; adopted as subd (c) effective January 1, 2002; previously relettered as subd (d) effective January 1, 2006.)

Rule 4.552 amended effective January 1, 2012; adopted effective January 1, 2002; previously amended effective January 1, 2006, and January 1, 2007.

Advisory Committee Comment

Subdivision (b)(2)(C). This subdivision is based on the California Supreme Court decision in *In re Roberts* (2005) 36 Cal.4th 575, which provides that petitions for writ of habeas corpus challenging denial or suitability for parole should first be adjudicated in the trial court that rendered the underlying judgment.

Rule 4.553. Qualifications for appointed counsel for claims under section 1473(e) in noncapital case

(a) Purpose

This rule defines the minimum qualifications for appointment of counsel for a petition for writ of habeas corpus claim filed under section 1473(e) in a noncapital case in the superior court. These minimum qualifications are designed to promote competent representation in habeas corpus proceedings related to the California Racial Justice Act of 2020 and to avoid unnecessary delay and expense by assisting the courts in appointing qualified counsel. Nothing in this rule is intended to be used as a standard by which to measure whether a person received effective assistance of counsel. An attorney is not entitled to appointment simply because the attorney meets the minimum requirements.

(Subd (a) effective September 1, 2024.)

(b) Qualifications

To be eligible as appointed counsel, an attorney must:

(1) Be an active member of the State Bar of California.

(2) Have experience as one of the following:

(A) Counsel of record for a petitioner in at least two habeas corpus proceedings filed in the Supreme Court, a Court of Appeal, a superior court, or a federal court.

(B) Counsel of record in at least two criminal appeals filed in the Supreme Court, a Court of Appeal, or a federal appellate court.

(C) Have the experience required to have represented the individual in the underlying class of criminal case.

(3) Be familiar with the practices and procedures of California criminal courts.

(4) Demonstrate proficiency in investigation, issue identification, legal research, analysis, writing, and advocacy.

(5) Have completed a minimum requirement of 10 hours of training on the California Racial Justice Act of 2020, including training on implicit bias and on habeas corpus procedure, approved for Minimum Continuing Legal Education credit by the State Bar of California.

(Subd (b) effective September 1, 2024.)

(c) Alternative requirements

The court may appoint an attorney who does not meet all the qualifications stated in (b)(1)–(4) if the attorney meets the qualifications of (b)(5) and demonstrates the ability to provide competent representation to the petitioner. If the court appoints counsel under this subdivision, it should state on the record the basis for finding counsel qualified.

(Subd (a) effective September 1, 2024.)

(d) Public defender appointments

When the court appoints the public defender under section 987.2, the public defender should assign an attorney from that office or agency who meets the qualifications described in (b) or assign an attorney who the public defender determines would qualify under (c).

(Subd (d) effective September 1, 2024.)

Rule 4.553 adopted effective September 1, 2024.

Article 3
Death Penalty–Related Habeas Corpus Proceedings in the Superior Court

Title 4, Criminal Rules—Division 6, Postconviction, Postrelease, and Writs—Chapter 3, Habeas Corpus—Article 3, Death Penalty–Related Habeas Corpus Proceedings in the Superior Court; adopted effective April 25, 2019.

Rule 4.560. Application of article
Rule 4.561. Superior court appointment of counsel in death penalty–related habeas corpus proceedings
Rule 4.562. Recruitment and determination of qualifications of attorneys for appointment in death penalty–related habeas corpus proceedings
Rule 4.571. Filing of petition in the superior court
Rule 4.572. Transfer of petitions
Rule 4.573. Proceedings after the petition is filed
Rule 4.574. Proceedings following an order to show cause
Rule 4.575. Decision on death penalty–related habeas corpus petition
Rule 4.576. Successive petitions
Rule 4.577. Transfer of files

Rule 4.560. Application of article

This article governs procedures for death penalty–related habeas corpus proceedings in the superior courts.

Rule 4.560 adopted effective April 25, 2019.

Rule 4.561. Superior court appointment of counsel in death penalty–related habeas corpus proceedings

(a) Purpose

This rule, in conjunction with rule 4.562, establishes a mechanism for superior courts to appoint qualified counsel to represent indigent persons in death penalty–related habeas corpus proceedings. This rule governs the appointment of counsel by superior courts only, including when the Supreme Court or a Court of Appeal has transferred a habeas corpus petition without having appointed counsel for the petitioner. It does not govern the appointment of counsel by the Supreme Court or a Court of Appeal.

(Subd (a) adopted effective April 25, 2019.)

(b) Prioritization of oldest judgments

In the interest of equity, both to the families of victims and to persons sentenced to death, California courts, whenever possible, should appoint death penalty–related habeas corpus counsel first for those persons subject to the oldest judgments of death.

(Subd (b) adopted effective April 25, 2019.)

(c) List of persons subject to a judgment of death

The Habeas Corpus Resource Center must maintain a list of persons subject to a judgment of death, organized by the date the judgment was entered by the sentencing court. The list must indicate whether death penalty–related habeas corpus counsel has been appointed for each person and, if so, the date of the appointment. The list must also indicate for each person whether a petition is pending in the Supreme Court.

(Subd (c) adopted effective April 25, 2019.)

(d) Notice of oldest judgments without counsel

(1) Within 30 days of the effective date of this rule, the Habeas Corpus Resource Center must identify the persons on the list required by (c) with the 25 oldest judgments of death for whom death penalty–related habeas corpus counsel have not been appointed.

(2) The Habeas Corpus Resource Center must notify the presiding judges of the superior courts in which these 25 judgments of death were entered that these are the oldest cases in which habeas corpus counsel have not been appointed. The Habeas Corpus Resource Center will send a copy of the notice to the administrative presiding justice of the appellate district in which the superior court is located.

(3) The presiding judge must identify the appropriate judge within the court to make an appointment and notify the judge that the case is among the oldest cases in which habeas corpus appointments are to be made.

(4) If qualified counsel is available for appointment to a case for which a petition is pending in the Supreme Court, the judge must provide written notice to the Supreme Court that counsel is available for appointment.

(5) On entry of an order appointing death penalty–related habeas corpus counsel, the appointing court must promptly send a copy of the appointment order to the Habeas Corpus Resource Center, which must update the list to reflect that counsel was appointed, and to the clerk/executive officer of the Supreme Court, the Attorney General, and the district attorney. The court must also send notice to the Habeas Corpus Resource Center, clerk/executive officer of the Supreme Court, Attorney General, and district attorney if, for any reason, the court determines that it does not need to make an appointment.

(6) When a copy of an appointment order, or information indicating that an appointment is for any reason not required, has been received by the Habeas Corpus Resource Center for 20 judgments, the center will identify the next 20 oldest judgments of death in cases in which death penalty–related habeas corpus counsel have not been appointed and send out a notice identifying these 20 judgments, and the procedures required by paragraphs (3) through (6) of this subdivision must be repeated.

(7) The presiding judge of a superior court may designate another judge within the court to carry out his or her duties in this subdivision.

(Subd (d) adopted effective April 25, 2019.)

(e) Appointment of counsel

(1) After the court receives a notice under (d)(2) and has made the findings required by Government Code section 68662, the appropriate judge must appoint a qualified attorney or attorneys to represent the person in death penalty–related habeas corpus proceedings.

(2) The superior court must appoint an attorney or attorneys from the statewide panel of counsel compiled under rule 4.562(d)(4); an entity that employs qualified attorneys, including the Habeas Corpus Resource Center, the local public defender's office, or alternate public defender's office; or if the court has adopted a local rule under 4.562(g), an attorney determined to be qualified under that court's local rules. The court must at this time also designate an assisting entity or counsel, unless the appointed counsel is employed by the Habeas Corpus Resource Center.

(3) When the court appoints counsel to represent a person in a death penalty–related habeas corpus proceeding under this subdivision, the court must complete and enter an *Order Appointing Counsel in Death Penalty–Related Habeas Corpus Proceeding* (form HC-101).

(Subd (e) adopted effective April 25, 2019.)
Rule 4.561 adopted effective April 25, 2019.

Rule 4.562. Recruitment and determination of qualifications of attorneys for appointment in death penalty–related habeas corpus proceedings

(a) Purpose

This rule provides for a panel of attorneys from which superior courts may appoint counsel in death penalty–related habeas corpus proceedings.

(Subd (a) adopted effective April 25, 2019.)

(b) Regional habeas corpus panel committees

Each Court of Appeal must establish a death penalty–related habeas corpus panel committee as provided in this rule.

(Subd (b) adopted effective April 25, 2019.)

(c) Composition of regional habeas corpus panel committees

(1) The administrative presiding justice of the Court of Appeal appoints the members of each committee. Each committee must be composed of:

(A) One justice of the Court of Appeal to serve as the chair of the committee;

(B) A total of three judges from among those nominated by the presiding judges of the superior courts located within the appellate district; and

(C) A total of three attorneys from among those nominated by the entities in the six categories below. At least two of those appointed must have experience representing a petitioner in a death penalty–related habeas corpus proceeding.

(i) An attorney nominated by the Habeas Corpus Resource Center;

(ii) An attorney nominated by the California Appellate Project–San Francisco;

(iii) An attorney nominated by the appellate project with which the Court of Appeal contracts;

(iv) An attorney nominated by any of the federal public defenders' offices of the federal districts in which the participating courts are located;

(v) An attorney nominated by any of the public defenders' offices in a county where the participating courts are located; and

(vi) An attorney nominated by any entity not listed in this subparagraph, if the administrative presiding justice requests such a nomination.

(2) Each committee may also include advisory members, as authorized by the administrative presiding justice.

(3) The term of the chair and committee members is three years. Terms are staggered so that an approximately equal number of each committee's members changes annually. The administrative presiding justice has the discretion to remove or replace a chair or committee member for any reason.

(4) Except as otherwise provided in this rule, each committee is authorized to establish the procedures under which it is governed.

(Subd (c) adopted effective April 25, 2019.)

(d) Regional habeas corpus panel committee responsibilities

The committee has the following responsibilities:

(1) *Support superior court efforts to recruit applicants*

Each committee must assist the participating superior courts in their efforts to recruit attorneys to represent indigent petitioners in death penalty–related habeas corpus proceedings in the superior courts.

(2) *Accept applications*

Each committee must accept applications from attorneys who seek to be included on the panel of attorneys qualified for appointment in death penalty–related habeas corpus proceedings in the superior courts.

(A) The application must be on a *Declaration of Counsel re Minimum Qualifications for Appointment in Death Penalty–Related Habeas Corpus Proceedings* (form HC-100).

(B) Except as provided in (C), each committee must accept applications from attorneys whose principal place of business is within the appellate district and from only those attorneys.

(C) In addition to accepting applications from attorneys whose principal place of business is in its district, the First Appellate District committee must also accept applications from attorneys whose principal place of business is outside the state.

(3) *Review qualifications*

Each committee must review the applications it receives and determine whether the applicant meets the minimum qualifications stated in this division to represent persons in death penalty–related habeas corpus proceedings in the superior courts.

(4) *Provide names of qualified counsel for statewide panel*

(A) If a committee determines by a majority vote that an attorney is qualified to represent persons in death penalty–related habeas corpus proceedings in the superior court, it must include the name of the attorney on a statewide panel of qualified attorneys.

(B) Committees will provide to the Habeas Corpus Resource Center the names of attorneys who the committees determine meet the minimum qualifications. The Habeas Corpus Resource Center must consolidate the names into a single statewide panel, update the names on the panel at least quarterly, and make the most current panel available to superior courts on its website.

(C) Unless removed from the panel under (d)(6), an attorney included on the panel may remain on the panel for up to six years without submitting a renewed application.

(D) Inclusion on the statewide panel does not entitle an attorney to appointment by a superior court, nor does it compel an attorney to accept an appointment.

(5) *Match qualified attorneys to cases*

Each committee must assist a participating superior court in matching one or more qualified attorneys from the statewide panel to a person for whom counsel must be appointed under Government Code section 68662, if the court requests such assistance.

(6) *Remove attorneys from panel*

Suspension or disbarment of an attorney will result in removal of the attorney from the panel. Other disciplinary action, or a finding that counsel has provided ineffective assistance of counsel, may result in a reevaluation of the attorney's inclusion on the panel by the committee that initially determined the attorney to have met minimum qualifications.

(Subd (d) adopted effective April 25, 2019.)

(e) Consolidated habeas corpus panel committees

The administrative presiding justices of two or more Courts of Appeal may elect, following consultation with the presiding judges of the superior courts within their respective appellate districts, to operate a single committee to collectively fulfill the committee responsibilities for the superior courts in their appellate districts.

(Subd (e) adopted effective April 25, 2019.)

(f) Recruitment of qualified attorneys

The superior courts in which a judgment of death has been entered against an indigent person for whom habeas corpus counsel has not been appointed must develop and implement a plan to identify and recruit qualified counsel who may apply to be appointed.

(Subd (f) adopted effective April 25, 2019.)

(g) Local rule

A superior court may, by adopting a local rule, authorize appointment of qualified attorneys who are not members of the statewide panel. The local rule must establish procedures for submission and review of a *Declaration of Counsel re Minimum Qualifications for Appointment in Death Penalty–Related Habeas Corpus Proceedings* (form HC-100) and require attorneys to meet the minimum qualifications under rule 8.652(c).

(Subd (g) adopted effective April 25, 2019.)
Rule 4.562 adopted effective April 25, 2019.

Advisory Committee Comment

Subdivisions (d) and (f). In addition to the responsibilities identified in subdivisions (d) and (f), courts and regional committees are encouraged to support activities to expand the pool of attorneys that are qualified to represent petitioners in death penalty–related habeas corpus proceedings. Examples of such activities include providing mentoring and training programs and encouraging the use of supervised counsel.

Rule 4.571. Filing of petition in the superior court

(a) Petition

(1) A petition and supporting memorandum must comply with this rule and, except as otherwise provided in this rule, with rules 2.100–2.117 relating to the form of papers.

(2) A memorandum supporting a petition must comply with rule 3.1113(b), (c), (f), (h), (i), and (l).

(3) The petition and supporting memorandum must support any reference to a matter in the supporting documents or declarations, or other supporting materials, by a citation to its index number or letter and page and, if applicable, the paragraph or line number.

(Subd (a) adopted effective April 25, 2019.)

(b) Supporting documents

(1) The record prepared for the automatic appeal, including any exhibits admitted in evidence, refused, or lodged, and all briefs, rulings, and other documents filed in the automatic appeal are deemed part of the supporting documents for the petition.

(2) The petition must be accompanied by a copy of any petition, excluding exhibits, pertaining to the same judgment and petitioner that was previously filed in any state court or any federal court, along with any order in a proceeding on such a petition that disposes of any claim or portion of a claim.

(3) If the petition asserts a claim that was the subject of a hearing, the petition must be accompanied by a certified transcript of that hearing.

(4) If any supporting documents have previously been filed in the same superior court in which the petition is filed and the petition so states and identifies the documents by case number, filing date and title of the document, copies of these documents need not be included in the supporting documents.

(5) Rule 8.486(c)(1) governs the form of any supporting documents accompanying the petition.

(6) If any supporting documents accompanying the petition or any subsequently filed paper are sealed, rules 2.550 and 2.551 govern. Notwithstanding rule 8.45(a), if any supporting documents accompanying the petition or any subsequently filed papers are confidential records, rules 8.45(b), (c), and 8.47 govern, except that rules 2.550 and 2.551 govern the procedures for making a motion or application to seal such records.

(7) When other laws establish specific requirements for particular types of sealed or confidential records that differ from the requirements in this subdivision, those specific requirements supersede the requirements in this subdivision.

(Subd (b) adopted effective April 25, 2019.)

(c) Filing and service

(1) If the petition is filed in paper form, an original and one copy must be filed, along with an original and one copy of the supporting documents.

(2) A court that permits electronic filing must specify any requirements regarding electronically filed petitions as authorized under rules 2.250 et seq.

(3) Petitioner must serve one copy of the petition and supporting documents on the district attorney, the Attorney General, and on any assisting entity or counsel.

(Subd (c) adopted effective April 25, 2019.)

(d) Noncomplying filings

The clerk must file an attorney's petition not complying with this rule if it otherwise complies with the rules of court, but the court may notify the attorney that it may strike the petition or impose a lesser sanction if the petition is not brought into compliance within a stated reasonable time of not less than five court days.

(Subd (d) adopted effective April 25, 2019.)

(e) Ruling on the petition

(1) The court must rule on the petition within 60 days after the petition is filed with the court or transferred to the court from another superior court.

(2) For purposes of this subdivision, the court rules on a petition by:

(A) Requesting an informal response to the petition;

(B) Issuing an order to show cause; or

(C) Denying the petition.

(3) If the court requests an informal response, it must issue an order to show cause or deny the petition within 30 days after the filing of the reply, or if none is filed, after the expiration of the time for filing the reply under rule 4.573(a)(3).

(Subd (e) adopted effective April 25, 2019.)
Rule 4.571 adopted effective April 25, 2019.

Rule 4.572. Transfer of petitions

Unless the court finds good cause for it to consider the petition, a petition subject to this article that is filed in a superior court other than the court that imposed the sentence must be transferred to the court that imposed the sentence within 21 days of filing. The court in which the petition was filed must enter an order with the basis for its transfer or its finding of good cause for retaining the petition.
Rule 4.572 adopted effective April 25, 2019.

Rule 4.573. Proceedings after the petition is filed

(a) Informal response and reply

(1) If the court requests an informal written response, it must serve a copy of the request on the district attorney, the Attorney General, the petitioner and on any assisting entity or counsel.

(2) The response must be served and filed within 45 days of the filing of the request, or a later date if the court so orders. One copy of the informal response and any supporting documents must be served on the petitioner and on any assisting entity or counsel. If the response and supporting documents are served in paper form, two copies must be served on the petitioner.

(3) If a response is filed, the court must notify the petitioner that a reply may be served and filed within 30 days of the filing of the response, or a later date if the court so orders. The court may not deny the petition until that time has expired.

(4) If a reply is filed, the petitioner must serve one copy of the reply and any supporting documents on the district attorney, the Attorney General, and on any assisting entity or counsel.

(5) The formatting of the response, reply, and any supporting documents must comply with the applicable requirements for petitions in rule 4.571(a) and (b). The filing of the response, reply, and any supporting documents must comply with the requirements for petitions in rule 4.571(c)(1) and (2).

(6) On motion of any party or on the court's own motion, for good cause stated in the order, the court may extend the time for a party to perform any act under this subdivision. If a party requests extension of a deadline in this subdivision, the party must explain the additional work required to meet the deadline.

(Subd (a) adopted effective April 25, 2019.)

(b) Order to show cause

If the petitioner has made the required prima facie showing that petitioner is entitled to relief, the court must issue an order to show cause. An order to show cause does not grant the relief sought in the petition.

(Subd (b) adopted effective April 25, 2019.)
Rule 4.573 adopted effective April 25, 2019.

Rule 4.574. Proceedings following an order to show cause

(a) Return

(1) Any return must be served and filed within 45 days after the court issues the order to show cause, or a later date if the court so orders.

(2) The formatting of the return and any supporting documents must comply with the applicable requirements for petitions in rule 4.571(a) and (b). The filing of the return and any supporting documents must comply with the requirements for petitions in rule 4.571(c)(1) and (2).

(3) A copy of the return and any supporting documents must be served on the petitioner and on any assisting entity or counsel. If the return is served in paper form, two copies must be served on the petitioner.

(4) Any material allegation of the petition not controverted by the return is deemed admitted for purposes of the proceeding.

(Subd (a) adopted effective April 25, 2019.)

(b) Denial

(1) Unless the court orders otherwise, within 30 days after the return is filed, or a later date if the court so orders, the petitioner may serve and file a denial.

(2) The formatting of the denial and any supporting documents must comply with the applicable requirements for petitions in rule 4.571(a) and (b). The filing of the denial and any supporting documents must comply with the requirements for petitions in rule 4.571(c)(1) and (2).

(3) A copy of the denial and any supporting documents must be served on the district attorney, the Attorney General, and on any assisting entity or counsel.

(4) Any material allegation of the return not controverted in the denial is deemed admitted for purposes of the proceeding.

(Subd (b) amended effective September 1, 2021; adopted effective April 25, 2019.)

(c) Ruling on the petition

Within 60 days after filing of the denial, or if none is filed, after the expiration of the deadline for filing the denial under (b)(1), the court must either grant or deny the relief sought by the petition or set an evidentiary hearing.

(Subd (c) adopted effective April 25, 2019.)

(d) Evidentiary hearing

(1) An evidentiary hearing is required if, after considering the verified petition, the return, any denial, any affidavits or declarations under penalty of perjury, exhibits, and matters of which judicial notice may be taken, the court finds there is a reasonable likelihood that the petitioner may be entitled to relief and the petitioner's entitlement to relief depends on the resolution of an issue of fact.

(2) The court must assign a court reporter who uses computer-aided transcription equipment to report all proceedings under this subdivision.

(A) All proceedings under this subdivision, whether in open court, in conference in the courtroom, or in chambers, must be conducted on the record with a court reporter present. The court reporter must prepare and certify a daily transcript of all proceedings.

(B) Any computer-readable transcript produced by court reporters under this subdivision must conform to the requirements of Code of Civil Procedure section 271.

(3) Rule 3.1306(c) governs judicial notice.

(Subd (d) adopted effective April 25, 2019.)

(e) Additional briefing

The court may order additional briefing during or following the evidentiary hearing.

(Subd (e) adopted effective April 25, 2019.)

(f) Submission of cause

For purposes of article VI, section 19, of the California Constitution, a death penalty–related habeas corpus proceeding is submitted for decision at the conclusion of the evidentiary hearing, if one is held. If there is supplemental briefing after the conclusion of the evidentiary hearing, the matter is submitted when all supplemental briefing is filed with the court.

(Subd (f) adopted effective April 25, 2019.)

(g) Extension of deadlines

On motion of any party or on the court's own motion, for good cause stated in the order, the court may extend the time for a party to perform any act under this rule. If a party requests extension of a deadline in this rule, the party must explain the additional work required to meet the deadline.

(Subd (g) adopted effective April 25, 2019.)

Rule 4.574 amended effective September 1, 2021; adopted effective April 25, 2019.

Rule 4.575. Decision on death penalty–related habeas corpus petition

On decision of the initial petition, the court must prepare and file a statement of decision specifying its order and explaining the factual and legal basis for its decision. The clerk of the court must serve a copy of the decision on the petitioner, the district attorney, the Attorney General, the clerk/executive officer of the Supreme Court, the clerk/executive officer of the Court of Appeal, and on any assisting entity or counsel.

Rule 4.575 adopted effective April 25, 2019.

Rule 4.576. Successive petitions

(a) Notice of intent to dismiss

Before dismissing a successive petition under Penal Code section 1509(d), a superior court must provide notice to the petitioner and an opportunity to respond.

(Subd (a) adopted effective April 25, 2019.)

(b) Certificate of appealability

The superior court must grant or deny a certificate of appealability concurrently with the issuance of its decision denying relief on a successive death penalty–related habeas corpus petition. Before issuing its decision, the superior court may order the parties to submit arguments on whether a certificate of appealability should be granted. If the superior court grants a certificate of appealability, the certificate must identify the substantial claim or claims for relief shown by the petitioner and the substantial claim that the requirements of Penal Code section 1509(d) have been met. The superior court clerk must send a copy of the certificate to the petitioner, the Attorney General, the district attorney, the clerk/executive officer of the Court of Appeal and the district appellate project for the appellate district in which the superior court is located, the assisting counsel or entity, and the clerk/executive officer of the Supreme Court. The superior court clerk must send the certificate of appealability to the Court of Appeal when it sends the notice of appeal under rule 8.392(c).

(Subd (b) adopted effective April 25, 2019.)

Rule 4.576 adopted effective April 25, 2019.

Rule 4.577. Transfer of files

Counsel for the petitioner must deliver all files counsel maintained related to the proceeding to the attorney representing petitioner in any appeal taken from the proceeding.

Rule 4.577 adopted effective April 25, 2019.

Division 7
Miscellaneous

Rule 4.601. Judicial determination of factual innocence form
Rule 4.700. Firearm relinquishment procedures for criminal protective orders

Rule 4.601. Judicial determination of factual innocence form

(a) Form to be confidential

Any *Certificate of Identity Theft: Judicial Finding of Factual Innocence* (form CR-150) that is filed with the court is confidential. The clerk's office must maintain these forms in a manner that will protect and preserve their confidentiality.

(Subd (a) amended effective January 1, 2007.)

(b) Access to the form

Notwithstanding (a), the court, the identity theft victim, the prosecution, and law enforcement agencies may have access to the *Certificate of Identity Theft: Judicial Finding of Factual Innocence* (form CR-150). The court may allow access to any other person on a showing of good cause.

(Subd (b) amended effective January 1, 2007.)

Rule 4.601 amended effective January 1, 2007; adopted effective January 1, 2002.

Rule 4.700. Firearm relinquishment procedures for criminal protective orders

(a) Application of rule

This rule applies when a court issues a criminal protective order under Penal Code section 136.2 during a criminal case or as a condition of probation under Penal Code section 1203.097(a)(2) against a defendant charged with a crime of domestic violence as defined in Penal Code section 13700 and Family Code section 6211.

(Subd (a) amended effective January 22, 2019; adopted effective July 1, 2010.)

(b) Purpose

This rule is intended to:

(1) Assist courts issuing criminal protective orders to determine whether a defendant subject to such an order owns, possesses, or controls any firearms; and

(2) Assist courts that have issued criminal protective orders to determine whether a defendant has complied with the court's order to relinquish or sell the firearms under Code of Civil Procedure section 527.9.

(Subd (b) adopted effective July 1, 2010.)

(c) Setting review hearing

(1) At any hearing where the court issues a criminal protective order, the court must consider all credible information, including information provided on behalf of the defendant, to determine if there is good cause to believe that the defendant has a firearm within his or her immediate possession or control.

(2) If the court finds good cause to believe that the defendant has a firearm within his or her immediate possession or control, the court must set a review hearing to ascertain whether the defendant has complied with the requirement to relinquish the firearm as specified in Code of Civil Procedure section 527.9. Unless the defendant is in custody at the time, the review hearing should occur within two court days after issuance of the criminal protective order. If circumstances warrant, the court may extend the review hearing to occur within 5 court days after issuance of the criminal protective order. The court must give the defendant an opportunity to present information at the review hearing to refute the allegation that he or she owns any firearms. If the defendant is in custody at the time the criminal protective order is issued, the court should order the defendant to appear for a review hearing within two court days after the defendant's release from custody.

(3) If the proceeding is held under Penal Code section 136.2, the court may, under Penal Code section 977(a)(2), order the defendant to person-

ally appear at the review hearing. If the proceeding is held under Penal Code section 1203.097, the court should order the defendant to personally appear.

(Subd (c) adopted effective July 1, 2010.)

(d) Review hearing

(1) If the court has issued a criminal protective order under Penal Code section 136.2, at the review hearing:

(A) If the court finds that the defendant has a firearm in or subject to his or her immediate possession or control, the court must consider whether bail, as set, or defendant's release on own recognizance is appropriate.

(B) If the defendant does not appear at the hearing and the court orders that bail be revoked, the court should issue a bench warrant.

(2) If the criminal protective order is issued as a condition of probation under Penal Code section 1203.097, and the court finds at the review hearing that the defendant has a firearm in or subject to his or her immediate possession or control, the court must proceed under Penal Code section 1203.097(a)(12).

(3) In any review hearing to determine whether a defendant has complied with the requirement to relinquish firearms as specified in Code of Civil Procedure section 527.9, the burden of proof is on the prosecution.

(Subd (d) adopted effective July 1, 2010.)

Rule 4.700 amended effective January 22, 2019; adopted effective July 1, 2010.

Advisory Committee Comment

When issuing a criminal protective order under Penal Code section 136.2 or 1203.097(a)(2), the court is required to order a defendant "to relinquish any firearm in that person's immediate possession or control, or subject to that person's immediate possession or control …." (Code Civ. Proc., § 527.9(b).) Mandatory Judicial Council form CR-160, *Criminal Protective Order—Domestic Violence*, includes a mandatory order in bold type that the defendant "must surrender to local law enforcement or sell to a licensed gun dealer any firearm owned or subject to his or her immediate possession or control within 24 hours after service of this order and must file a receipt with the court showing compliance with this order within 48 hours of receiving this order."

Courts are encouraged to develop local procedures to calendar review hearings for defendants in custody beyond the two-court-day time frame to file proof of firearms relinquishment with the court under Code of Civil Procedure section 527.9.

TITLE 5
Family and Juvenile Rules

Title. Rule 5.1.
Division 1. Family Rules. Rules 5.2–5.445.
Division 2. Rules Applicable in Family and Juvenile Proceedings. Rules 5.451–5.493.
Division 3. Juvenile Rules. Rules 5.500–5.906.

Rule 5.1. Title

The rules in this title may be referred to as the Family and Juvenile Rules.

Rule 5.1 adopted effective January 1, 2007.

Division 1
Family Rules

Chap. 1. General Provisions. Rules 5.2–5.14.
Chap. 2. Parties and Joinder of Parties. Rules 5.16–5.29.
Chap. 3. Filing Fees and Fee Waivers. Rules 5.40–5.46.
Chap. 4. Starting and Responding to a Family Law Case; Service of Papers. Rules 5.50–5.77.
Chap. 5. Family Centered Case Resolution Plans. Rule 5.83.
Chap. 6. Request for Court Orders. Rules 5.90–5.130.
Chap. 7. Request for Emergency Orders (Ex Parte Orders). Rules 5.151–5.170.
Chap. 8. Child Custody and Visitation (Parenting Time) Proceedings. Rules 5.210–5.250.
Chap. 9. Child, Spousal, and Domestic Partner Support. Rules 5.260, 5.275.
Chap. 10. Government Child Support Cases (Title IV-D Support Cases). Rules 5.300–5.375.
Chap. 11. Domestic Violence Cases. Rules 5.380–5.386.
Chap. 12. Separate Trials (Bifurcation) and Interlocutory Appeals. Rules 5.390, 5.392.
Chap. 13. Trials and Long-Cause Hearings. Rules 5.393, 5.394.
Chap. 14. Default Proceedings and Judgments. Rules 5.401–5.415.
Chap. 15. Settlement Services. Rule 5.420.
Chap. 16. Limited Scope Representation; Attorney's Fees and Costs. Rules 5.425, 5.427.
Chap. 17. Family Law Facilitator. Rule 5.430.
Chap. 18. Court Coordination Rules. Rules 5.440, 5.445.
Chap. 19. Minor Marriage or Domestic Partnership. Rule 5.448.

Chapter 1
General Provisions

Art. 1. General Provisions. Rules 5.2, 5.4.
Art. 2. Use of Forms. Rule 5.7.
Art. 3. Appearance by Telephone. Rule 5.9.
Art. 4. Discovery. Rule 5.12.
Art. 5. Sanctions. Rule 5.14.

Article 1
General Provisions

Title 5, Family and Juvenile Rules—Division 1, Family Rules—Chapter 1, General Provisions—Article 1, General Provisions; adopted effective January 1, 2013.

Rule 5.2. Division title; definitions; application of rules and laws
Rule 5.4. Preemption; local rules and forms

Rule 5.2. Division title; definitions; application of rules and laws

(a) Division title

The rules in this division may be referred to as the Family Rules.

(Subd (a) adopted effective January 1, 2013.)

(b) Definitions and use of terms

As used in this division, unless the context or subject matter otherwise requires, the following definitions apply:

(1) "Family Code" means that code enacted by chapter 162 of the Statutes of 1992 and any subsequent amendments to that code.

(2) "Action" is also known as a lawsuit, a case, or a demand brought in a court of law to defend or enforce a right, prevent or remedy a harm, or punish a crime. It includes all the proceedings in which a party requests orders that are available in the lawsuit.

(3) "Proceeding" is a court hearing in an action under the Family Code, including a hearing that relates to the dissolution or nullity of a marriage or domestic partnership, legal separation, custody and support of minor children, a parent and child relationship, adoptions, local child support agency actions under the Family Code, contempt proceedings relating to family law or local child support agency matters, and any action filed under the Domestic Violence Prevention Act, Uniform Parentage Act, Uniform Child Custody Jurisdiction and Enforcement Act, Indian Child Welfare Act, or Uniform Interstate Family Support Act.

(4) "Dissolution" is the legal term used for "divorce." "Divorce" commonly refers to a marriage that is legally ended.

(5) "Attorney" means a member of the State Bar of California. "Counsel" means an attorney.

(6) "Party" is a person appearing in an action. Parties include both self-represented persons and persons represented by an attorney of record. Any designation of a party encompasses the party's attorney of record, including "party," "petitioner," "plaintiff," "People of the State of California," "applicant," "defendant," "respondent," "other parent," "other parent/party," "protected person," and "restrained person."

(7) "Best interest of the child" is described in Family Code section 3011.

(8) "Parenting time," "visitation," and "visitation (parenting time)" refer to how parents share time with their children.

(9) "Property" includes assets and obligations.

(10) "Local rule" means every rule, regulation, order, policy, form, or standard of general application adopted by a court to govern practice and procedure in that court.

(11) "Reschedule the hearing" means the same as "continue the hearing" under the Family Code and refers to moving a hearing to another date and time.

(Subd (b) amended effective July 1, 2020; adopted effective January 1, 2013.)

(c) Application of rules

The rules in this division apply to every action and proceeding to which the Family Code applies and, unless these rules elsewhere explicitly make them applicable, do not apply to any other action or proceeding that is not found in the Family Code.

(Subd (c) adopted effective January 1, 2013.)

(d) General law applicable

Except as otherwise provided in these rules, all provisions of law applicable to civil actions generally apply to a proceeding under the Family Code if they would otherwise apply to such proceeding without reference to this rule. To the extent that these rules conflict with provisions in other statutes or rules, these rules prevail.

(Subd (d) adopted effective January 1, 2013.)

(e) Law applicable to other proceedings

In any action under the Family Code that is not considered a "proceeding" as defined in (b), all provisions of law applicable to civil actions generally apply. Such an action must be commenced by filing an appropriate petition, and the respondent must file an appropriate response within 30 days after service of the summons and a copy of the petition.

(Subd (e) adopted effective January 1, 2013.)

(f) Extensions of time

The time within which any act is permitted or required to be done by a party under these rules may be extended by the court upon such terms as may be just.

(Subd (f) adopted effective January 1, 2013.)

(g) Implied procedures

In the exercise of the court's jurisdiction under the Family Code, if the course of proceeding is not specifically indicated by statute or these rules, any suitable process or mode of proceeding may be adopted by the court that is consistent with the spirit of the Family Code and these rules.

(Subd (g) adopted effective January 1, 2013.)

Rule 5.2 amended effective July 1, 2020; adopted effective January 1, 2013.

Rule 5.4. Preemption; local rules and forms

Each local court may adopt local rules and forms regarding family law actions and proceedings that are not in conflict with or inconsistent with California law or the California Rules of Court. Effective January 1, 2013, local court rules and forms must comply with the Family Rules.

Rule 5.4 adopted effective January 1, 2013.

Advisory Committee Comment

The Family and Juvenile Law Advisory Committee agrees with the *Elkins Family Law Task Force: Final Report and Recommendations* (final report) regarding local rules of court (see final report at pages 31–32). The final report is available at *www.courts.ca.gov/elkins-finalreport.pdf*.

The advisory committee encourages local courts to continue piloting innovative family law programs and practices using local rules that are consistent with California law and the California Rules of Court.

Courts must not adopt local rules that create barriers for self-represented litigants or parties represented by counsel in getting their day in court. Further, courts should not adopt general rules for a courtroom as they pose substantial barriers to a party's access to justice.

Rule 5.5. Division title [Repealed]

Rule 5.5 repealed effective January 1, 2013; adopted effective January 1, 2007.

Article 2
Use of Forms

Title 5, Family and Juvenile Rules—Division 1, Family Rules—Chapter 1, General Provisions—Article 2, Use of Forms; adopted effective January 1, 2013.

Rule 5.7. Use of forms

(a) Status of family law and domestic violence forms

All forms adopted or approved by the Judicial Council for use in any proceeding under the Family Code, including any form in the FL, ADOPT, DV, and EJ series, are adopted as rules of court under the authority of Family Code section 211; article VI, section 6 of the California Constitution; and other applicable law.

(Subd (a) adopted effective January 1, 2013.)

(b) Forms in nonfamily law proceedings

The forms specified by this division may be used, at the option of the party, in any proceeding involving a financial obligation growing out of the relationship of parent and child or husband and wife or domestic partners, to the extent they are appropriate to that proceeding.

(Subd (b) adopted effective January 1, 2013.)

(c) Interstate forms

Notwithstanding any other provision of these rules, all Uniform Interstate Family Support Act forms approved by either the National Conference of Commissioners on Uniform State Laws or the U.S. Department of Health and Human Services are adopted for use in family law and other support actions in California.

(Subd (c) adopted effective January 1, 2013.)

Rule 5.7 adopted effective January 1, 2013.

Article 3
Appearance by Telephone

Title 5, Family and Juvenile Rules—Division 1, Family Rules—Chapter 1, General Provisions—Article 3, Appearance by Telephone; adopted effective January 1, 2013.

Rule 5.9. Appearance by telephone

(a) Application

Subdivisions (b) through (d) of this rule are suspended from January 1, 2022, to January 1, 2026. During that time, the provisions in rule 3.672 apply in their place. This rule applies to all family law cases, except for actions for child support involving a local child support agency and cases governed by the Indian Child Welfare Act. Rule 5.324 governs telephone appearances in governmental child support cases. Welfare and Institutions Code section 224.2(k) governs telephone appearances in cases under the Indian Child Welfare Act.

(Subd (a) amended effective August 4, 2023; adopted effective January 1, 2013; previously amended January 1, 2021, and January 1, 2022.)

(b) Telephone appearance

The court may permit a party to appear by telephone at a hearing, conference, or proceeding if the court determines that a telephone appearance is appropriate.

(Subd (b) adopted effective January 1, 2013.)

(c) Need for personal appearance

(1) At its discretion, the court may require a party to appear in person at a hearing, conference, or proceeding if the court determines that a personal appearance would materially assist in the determination of the proceedings or in the effective management or resolution of the particular case.

(2) If, at any time during a hearing, conference, or proceeding conducted by telephone, the court determines that a personal appearance is necessary, the court may continue the matter and require a personal appearance.

(Subd (c) adopted effective January 1, 2013.)

(d) Local rules

Courts may develop local rules to specify procedures regarding appearances by telephone.

(Subd (d) adopted effective January 1, 2013.)

Rule 5.9 amended effective August 4, 2023; adopted effective January 1, 2013; previously amended January 1, 2021, and January 1, 2022.

Rule 5.10. Definitions and use of terms [Repealed]

Rule 5.10 repealed effective January 1, 2013; adopted as rule 1201 effective January 1, 1970; previously amended effective January 1, 1994, January 1, 1999; previously amended and renumbered effective January 1, 2003; previously amended effective January 1, 2007, and January 1, 2008.

Article 4
Discovery

Title 5, Family and Juvenile Rules—Division 1, Family Rules—Chapter 1, General Provisions—Article 4, Discovery; adopted effective January 1, 2013.

Rule 5.12. Request for order regarding discovery

(a) Use of terms

In a family law proceeding, the term "request for order" has the same meaning as the terms "motion" or "notice of motion" when they are used in the Code of Civil Procedure.

(Subd (a) adopted effective July 1, 2016.)

(b) Applicable law

A request for order regarding discovery in family court is subject to the provisions for discovery motions under Code of Civil Procedure sections 2016.010 through 2036.050 and Family Code sections 2100 through 2113 regarding disclosure of assets and liabilities.

(Subd (b) amended and relettered effective July 1, 2016; adopted as subd (a).)

(c) Applicable rules

Discovery proceedings brought in a case under the Family Code must comply with applicable civil rules for motions, including:

(1) The format of supplemental and further discovery (rule 3.1000);

(2) Oral deposition by telephone, videoconference, or other remote electronic means (rule 3.1010);

(3) Separate statement requirements (rule 3.1345);

(4) Service of motion papers on nonparty deponent (rule 3.1346); and

(5) Sanctions for failure to provide discovery (rule 3.1348).

(Subd (c) amended and relettered effective July 1, 2016; adopted as subd (b).)

Rule 5.12 amended effective July 1, 2016; adopted effective January 1, 2013.

Article 5
Sanctions

Title 5, Family and Juvenile Rules—Division 1, Family Rules—Chapter 1, General Provisions—Article 5, Sanctions; adopted effective January 1, 2013.

Rule 5.14. Sanctions for violations of rules of court in family law cases

(a) Application

This sanctions rule applies to any action or proceeding brought under the Family Code.

(Subd (a) adopted effective January 1, 2013.)

(b) Definition

For purposes of the rules in this division:

(1) "Sanctions" means a monetary fine or penalty ordered by the court.

(2) "Person" means a party, a party's attorney, a law firm, a witness, or any other individual or entity whose consent is necessary for the disposition of the case.

(Subd (b) adopted effective January 1, 2013.)

(c) Sanctions imposed on a person

In addition to any other sanctions permitted by law, the court may order a person, after written notice and an opportunity to be heard, to pay reasonable monetary sanctions to the court or to an aggrieved person, or both, for failure without good cause to comply with the applicable rules. The sanction must not put an unreasonable financial burden on the person ordered to pay.

(Subd (c) adopted effective January 1, 2013.)

(d) Notice and procedure

Sanctions must not be imposed under this rule except on a request for order by the person seeking sanctions or on the court's own motion after the court has provided notice and an opportunity to be heard.

(1) A party's request for sanctions must:

(A) State the applicable rule of court that has been violated;

(B) Describe the specific conduct that is alleged to have violated the rule; and

(C) Identify the party, attorney, law firm, witness, or other person against whom sanctions are sought.

(2) The court on its own motion may issue an order to show cause that must:

(A) State the applicable rule of court that has been violated;

(B) Describe the specific conduct that appears to have violated the rule; and

(C) Direct the attorney, law firm, party, witness, or other person to show cause why sanctions should not be imposed for violation of the rule.

(Subd (d) adopted effective January 1, 2013.)

(e) Award of expenses

In addition to the sanctions awardable under this rule, the court may order the person who has violated an applicable rule of court to pay to the party aggrieved by the violation that party's reasonable expenses, including reasonable attorney's fees and costs, incurred in connection with the motion or request for order for sanctions.

(Subd (e) adopted effective January 1, 2013.)

(f) Order

A court order awarding sanctions must be in writing and must recite in detail the conduct or circumstances justifying the order.

(Subd (f) adopted effective January 1, 2013.)
Rule 5.14 adopted effective January 1, 2013.

Rule 5.15. Extensions of time [Repealed]

Rule 5.15 repealed effective January 1, 2013; adopted as rule 1203 effective January 1, 1970; previously renumbered effective January 1, 2003.

Chapter 2
Parties and Joinder of Parties

Title 5, Family and Juvenile Rules—Division 1, Family Rules—Chapter 2, Parties and Joinder of Parties; adopted effective January 1, 2013.

Art. 1.   Parties to Proceedings. Rules 5.16–5.18.
Art. 2.   Joinder of Parties. Rule 5.24.
Art. 3.   Employee Pension Benefit Plan. Rule 5.29.

Article 1
Parties to Proceedings

Title 5, Family and Juvenile Rules—Division 1, Family Rules—Chapter 2, Parties and Joinder of Parties—Article 1, Parties to Proceedings; adopted effective January 1, 2013.

Rule 5.16. Designation of parties
Rule 5.17. Other causes of action
Rule 5.18. Injunctive relief and reservation of jurisdiction

Rule 5.16. Designation of parties

(a) Designation of parties

(1) In cases filed under the Family Code, the party starting the case is referred to as the "petitioner," and the other party is the "respondent."

(2) In local child support agency actions, the local child support agency starts the case and is the petitioner or plaintiff in the case. The parent sued by the child support agency is the "respondent" or "defendant," and the parent who is not the defendant is referred to as the "Other Parent." Every other proceeding must be prosecuted and defended in the names of the real parties in interest.

(Subd (a) adopted effective January 1, 2013.)

(b) Parties to proceeding

(1) The only persons permitted to be parties to a proceeding for dissolution, legal separation, or nullity of marriage are the spouses, except as provided in (3), a third party who is joined in the case under rule 5.24, or a local child support agency that intervenes in the case.

(2) The only persons permitted to be parties to a proceeding for dissolution, legal separation, or nullity of domestic partnership are the domestic partners, except as provided in (3), a third party who is joined in the case under rule 5.24, or a local child support agency that intervenes in the case.

(3) In a nullity proceeding, the case can be started by the spouses or domestic partners. The case may also be started by a parent or guardian, conservator, or other person specified in Family Code section 2211. For this type of case, the person starting the case is a party and the caption on all papers must be appropriately changed to reflect that fact.

(4) The only persons permitted to be parties to a proceeding under the Domestic Violence Prevention Act are those identified in Family Code section 6211.

(5) The only persons permitted to be parties to a family law proceeding to establish parentage are the presumed or putative parents of the minor child, the minor child, a third party who is joined in the case under rule 5.24, or a local child support agency that intervenes in the case.

(Subd (b) adopted effective January 1, 2013.)
Rule 5.16 adopted effective January 1, 2013.

Rule 5.17. Other causes of action

A party in a family law proceeding may only ask that the court make orders against or involving the other party, or any other person, that are available to the party in these rules, Family Code sections 17400, 17402, and 17404, or other sections of the California Family Code.
Rule 5.17 adopted effective January 1, 2013.

Rule 5.18. Injunctive relief and reservation of jurisdiction

(a) Injunctive relief

When a party in a family law case applies for a court order under rule 5.92, the court may grant injunctive or other relief against or for the following persons to protect the rights of either or both parties:

(1) A person who has or claims an interest in the case;

(2) A person who would be a necessary party to a complete disposition of the issues in the case, but is not permitted to be a party under rule 5.16; or

(3) A person who is acting as a trustee, agent, custodian, or similar fiduciary with respect to any property subject to disposition by the court in the proceeding, or other matter subject to the jurisdiction of the court in the proceeding.

(Subd (a) adopted effective January 1, 2013.)

(b) Reservation of jurisdiction

If the court is unable to resolve the issue in the proceeding under the Family Code, the court may reserve jurisdiction over the particular issue until such time as the rights of such person and the parties to the proceeding under the Family Code have been determined in a separate action or proceeding.

(Subd (b) adopted effective January 1, 2013.)
Rule 5.18 adopted effective January 1, 2013.

Rule 5.20. Application of rules [Repealed]

Rule 5.20 repealed effective January 1, 2013; adopted as rule 1205 effective January 1, 1970; previously amended effective January 1, 1979, January 1, 1994, and January 1, 1999; previously amended and renumbered effective January 1, 2003; previously amended effective January 1, 2007.

Rule 5.21. General law applicable [Repealed]

Rule 5.21 repealed effective January 1, 2013; adopted as rule 1206 effective January 1, 1970; previously amended effective January 1, 1994; previously amended and renumbered effective January 1, 2003.

Rule 5.22. Other proceedings [Repealed]

Rule 5.22 repealed effective January 1, 2013; adopted as rule 1207 effective January 1, 1970; previously amended effective January 1, 1994; previously amended and renumbered effective January 1, 2003; previously amended effective January 1, 2007.

Article 2
Joinder of Parties

Title 5, Family and Juvenile Rules—Division 1, Family Rules—Chapter 2, Parties and Joinder of Parties—Article 2, Joinder of Parties; adopted effective January 1, 2013.

Rule 5.24. Joinder of persons claiming interest

A person who claims or controls an interest in any matter subject to disposition in the proceeding may be joined as a party to the family law case only as provided in this chapter.

(a) Applicable rules

(1) All provisions of law relating to joinder of parties in civil actions generally apply to the joinder of a person as a party to a family law case, except as otherwise provided in this chapter.

(2) The law applicable to civil actions generally governs all pleadings, motions, and other matters pertaining to that portion of the proceeding as to which a claimant has been joined as a party to the proceeding in the same manner as if a separate action or proceeding not subject to these rules had been filed, except as otherwise provided in this chapter or by the court in which the proceeding is pending.

(b) "Claimant" defined

For purposes of this rule, a "claimant" is an individual or an entity joined or sought or seeking to be joined as a party to the family law proceeding.

(c) Persons who may seek joinder

(1) The petitioner or the respondent may apply to the court for an order joining a person as a party to the case who has or claims custody or physical control of any of the minor children subject to the action, or visitation rights with respect to such children, or who has in his or her possession or control or claims to own any property subject to the jurisdiction of the court in the proceeding.

(2) A person who has or claims custody or physical control of any of the minor children subject to the action, or visitation rights with respect to such children, may apply to the court for an order joining himself or herself as a party to the proceeding.

(3) A person served with an order temporarily restraining the use of property that is in his or her possession or control or that he or she claims to own, or affecting the custody of minor children subject to the action, or visitation rights with respect to such children, may apply to the court for an order joining himself or herself as a party to the proceeding.

(d) Form of joinder application

(1) All applications for joinder other than for an employee pension benefit plan must be made by serving and filing form a *Notice of Motion and Declaration for Joinder* (form FL-371). The hearing date must be less than 30 days from the date of filing the notice. The completed form must state with particularity the claimant's interest in the proceeding and the relief sought by the applicant, and it must be accompanied by an appropriate pleading setting forth the claim as if it were asserted in a separate action or proceeding.

(2) A blank copy of *Responsive Declaration to Motion for Joinder and Consent Order for Joinder* (form FL-373) must be served with the *Notice of Motion* and accompanying pleading.

(e) Court order on joinder

(1) *Mandatory joinder*

(A) The court must order that a person be joined as a party to the proceeding if the court discovers that person has physical custody or claims custody or visitation rights with respect to any minor child of the marriage, domestic partnership, or to any minor child of the relationship.

(B) Before ordering the joinder of a grandparent of a minor child in the proceeding under Family Code section 3104, the court must take the actions described in section 3104(a).

(2) *Permissive joinder*

The court may order that a person be joined as a party to the proceeding if the court finds that it would be appropriate to determine the particular issue in the proceeding and that the person to be joined as a party is either indispensable for the court to make an order about that issue or is necessary to the enforcement of any judgment rendered on that issue.

In deciding whether it is appropriate to determine the particular issue in the proceeding, the court must consider its effect upon the proceeding, including:

(A) Whether resolving that issue will unduly delay the disposition of the proceeding;

(B) Whether other parties would need to be joined to make an effective judgment between the parties;

(C) Whether resolving that issue will confuse other issues in the proceeding; and

(D) Whether the joinder of a party to determine the particular issue will complicate, delay, or otherwise interfere with the effective disposition of the proceeding.

(3) *Procedure upon joinder*

If the court orders that a person be joined as a party to the proceeding under this rule, the court must direct that a summons be issued on *Summons (Joinder)* (form FL-375) and that the claimant be served with a copy of *Notice of Motion and Declaration for Joinder* (form FL-371), the pleading attached thereto, the order of joinder, and the summons. The claimant has 30 days after service to file an appropriate response.

(Subd (e) amended effective January 1, 2017; adopted effective January 1, 2013.)

Rule 5.24 amended effective January 1, 2017; adopted effective January 1, 2013.

Rule 5.25. Status of family law and domestic violence forms [Repealed]

Rule 5.25 repealed effective January 1, 2013; adopted as rule 1278 effective January 1, 2001; previously amended and renumbered effective January 1, 2003.

Rule 5.26. Use of forms in nonfamily law proceedings [Repealed]

Rule 5.26 repealed effective January 1, 2013; adopted as rule 1275 effective July 1, 1985; previously amended and renumbered effective January 1, 2003.

Rule 5.27. Use of interstate forms [Repealed]

Rule 5.27 repealed effective January 1, 2013; adopted as rule 1276 effective July 1, 1988; previously amended effective January 1, 1998; previously renumbered effective January 1, 2003.

Rule 5.28. Domestic partnerships [Repealed]

Rule 5.28 repealed effective January 1, 2013; adopted effective January 1, 2005; previously amended effective January 1, 2007.

Article 3
Employee Pension Benefit Plan

Title 5, Family and Juvenile Rules—Division 1, Family Rules—Chapter 2, Parties and Joinder of Parties—Article 3, Employee Pension Benefit Plan; adopted effective January 1, 2013.

Rule 5.29. Joinder of employee pension benefit plan

(a) Request for joinder

Every request for joinder of employee pension benefit plan and order and every pleading on joinder must be submitted on *Request for Joinder of Employee Benefit Plan and Order* (form FL-372) and *Pleading on Joinder—Employee Benefit Plan* (form FL-370).

(Subd (a) adopted effective January 1, 2013.)

(b) Summons

Every summons issued on the joinder of employee pension benefit plan must be on *Summons (Joinder)* (form FL-375).

(Subd (b) adopted effective January 1, 2013.)

(c) Notice of Appearance

Every notice of appearance of employee pension benefit plan and responsive pleading filed under Family Code section 2063(b) must be given on *Notice of Appearance and Response of Employee Benefit Plan* (form FL-374).

(Subd (c) adopted effective January 1, 2013.)

Rule 5.29 adopted effective January 1, 2013.

Rule 5.30. Judicial education for family court judicial officers [Renumbered]

Rule 5.30 renumbered as rule 10.463 effective January 1, 2008.

Rule 5.35. Minimum standards for the Office of the Family Law Facilitator [Renumbered]

Rule 5.35 renumbered as rule 5.430 effective January 1, 2013.

Chapter 3
Filing Fees and Fee Waivers

Title 5, Family and Juvenile Rules—Division 1, Family Rules—Chapter 3, Filing Fees and Fee Waivers; adopted effective January 1, 2013.

Art. 1. Filing Fees and Fee Waivers. Rules 5.40, 5.41.
Art. 2. Special Procedures. Rules 5.43–5.46.

Article 1
Filing Fees and Fee Waivers

Title 5, Family and Juvenile Rules—Division 1, Family Rules—Chapter 3, Filing Fees and Fee Waivers—Article 1, Filing Fees and Fee Waivers; adopted effective January 1, 2013.

Rule 5.40. Filing Fees
Rule 5.41. Waiver of fees and costs

Rule 5.40. Filing Fees

(a) Filing fees

Parties must pay filing fees to the clerk of the court at the time the parties file papers with the court.

(Subd (a) adopted effective January 1, 2013.)

(b) Authority

The amount of money required to pay filing fees in family court is established by the Uniform Civil Fees and Standard Fee Schedule Act of 2005 under Government Code section 70670 et seq. and is subject to change. The act covers fees the court may charge parties to file the first papers in a family law proceeding, motions, or other papers requiring a hearing. It also covers filing fees that courts may charge in proceedings relating to child custody or visitation (parenting time) to cover the costs of maintaining mediation services under Family Code section 3160 et seq.

(Subd (b) adopted effective January 1, 2013.)

Rule 5.41

(c) Other fees

(1) The court must not charge filing fees that are inconsistent with law or with the California Rules of Court and may not impose any tax, charge, or penalty upon a proceeding, or the filing of any pleading allowed by law, as provided by Government Code section 68070.

(2) In the absence of a statute or rule authorizing or prohibiting a fee by the superior court for a particular service or product, the court may charge a reasonable fee not to exceed the costs of providing the service or product, if the Judicial Council approves the fee, as provided by Government Code section 70631. Approved fees must be clearly posted and accessible to the public.

(Subd (c) adopted effective January 1, 2013.)
Rule 5.40 adopted effective January 1, 2013.

Rule 5.41. Waiver of fees and costs

If unable to afford the costs to file an action in family court, a party may request that the court waive fees and costs. The procedure and forms needed to request an initial fee waiver in a family law action are the same as for all other civil actions, unless otherwise provided by a statute or the California Rules of Court.

(a) Forms

The forms required to request a fee waiver may be obtained from the clerk of the court, the public law library, or online at the California Courts website.

(b) Rules

Rules 3.50–3.56 of the California Rules of Court (title 3, division 2) govern fee waivers in family law cases. Parties may refer to the civil rules for information about:

(1) Applying for a fee waiver (rule 3.51);

(2) Forms for requesting a fee waiver (rule 3.51);

(3) How the court makes an order on a fee waiver application (rule 3.52);

(4) The time required for the court to grant a fee waiver (rule 3.53);

(5) The confidentiality of fee waiver applications and hearings (rule 3.54);

(6) Court fees and costs included in an initial fee waiver (rule 3.55); and

(7) Additional court fees and costs that may be included in the fee waiver (rule 3.56).

Rule 5.41 adopted effective January 1, 2013.

Article 2
Special Procedures

Title 5, Family and Juvenile Rules—Division 1, Family Rules—Chapter 3, Filing Fees and Fee Waivers—Article 2, Special Procedures; adopted effective January 1, 2013.

Rule 5.43. Fee waiver denials; voided actions; dismissal
Rule 5.45. Repayment of waived court fees and costs in family law support actions
Rule 5.46. Waiver of fees and costs—Supreme Court or Court of Appeal

Rule 5.43. Fee waiver denials; voided actions; dismissal

(a) Voided paperwork

The clerk of the court must void the papers that were filed with a petitioner's or respondent's fee waiver application if 10 days pass after notice of the fee waiver denial and petitioner or respondent has not:

(1) Paid the fees owed;

(2) Submitted a new *Request to Waive Court Fees* (form FW-001) if the fee waiver was denied because the first form was incomplete; or

(3) Requested a hearing using *Request for Hearing About Court Fee Waiver Order (Superior Court)* (form FW-006).

(Subd (a) adopted effective January 1, 2013.)

(b) Effect of voided petition or complaint; dismissal or continuation of case

(1) *No response or notice of appearance filed*

If a petition or complaint is voided under (a) and a response to the petition or complaint has not been filed, or respondent has not appeared in the action, the court may dismiss the case without prejudice. If the court dismisses the case, the clerk of the court must notify the parties.

(2) *Response or notice of appearance filed; case continuation or dismissal*

If a petition or complaint is voided and a response has been filed with the court, or respondent has appeared in the action, the court must:

(A) Review the response, or documents constituting respondent's appearance, to determine whether or how the case will proceed based on the relief requested;

(B) Notify the parties of the court's determination; and

(C) Refund filing fees paid by the respondent if the court dismisses the case.

(Subd (b) adopted effective January 1, 2013.)
Rule 5.43 adopted effective January 1, 2013.

Rule 5.45. Repayment of waived court fees and costs in family law support actions

(a) Determination of repayment required

When a judgment or support order is entered in a family law case, the court may order either party to pay all or part of the fees and costs that the court waived under Government Code section 68637. The court must consider and determine the repayment of waived fees as required by Government Code section 68637(d) and (e). The rule does not apply to actions initiated by a local child support agency.

(Subd (a) adopted effective January 1, 2013.)

(b) Required forms

(1) An order determining repayment of waived initial fees must be made on *Order to Pay Waived Court Fees and Costs (Superior Court)* (form FL-336). An order for payment of waived court fees must be accompanied by a blank *Application to Set Aside Order to Pay Waived Court Fees—Attachment* (form FL-337).

(2) An order granting or denying a request to set aside an order to pay waived court fees and costs must be made on *Order After Hearing on Motion to Set Aside Order to Pay Waived Court Fees (Superior Court)* (form FL-338).

(Subd (b) adopted effective January 1, 2013.)
Rule 5.45 adopted effective January 1, 2013.

Rule 5.46. Waiver of fees and costs—Supreme Court or Court of Appeal

(a) Application

Rule 8.26 of the appellate rules specifies the procedure and forms for applying for an initial waiver of court fees and costs in the Supreme Court or Court of Appeal.

(Subd (a) adopted effective January 1, 2013.)

(b) Information

Parties may refer to rule 8.26 for information about:

(1) Applying for a fee waiver in appeals, writ proceedings, and petitions for review;

(2) Required forms requesting a fee waiver;

(3) The confidentiality of fee waiver applications and hearings;

(4) Time required for the court to grant a fee waiver; and

(5) Denial of a fee waiver application.

(Subd (b) adopted effective January 1, 2013.)
Rule 5.46 adopted effective January 1, 2013.

Chapter 4
Starting and Responding to a Family Law Case; Service of Papers

Title 5, Family and Juvenile Rules—Division 1, Family Rules—Chapter 4, Starting and Responding to a Family Law Case; Service of Papers; adopted effective January 1, 2013.

Art. 1. Summonses, Notices, and Declarations. Rules 5.50–5.52.
Art. 2. Initial Pleadings. Rules 5.60–5.63.
Art. 3. Service of Papers. Rule 5.66.
Art. 4. Manner of Service. Rules 5.68, 5.72.
Art. 5. Pleadings and Amended Pleadings. Rule 5.74.
Art. 6. Specific Proceedings. Rules 5.76, 5.77.

Article 1
Summonses, Notices, and Declarations

Title 5, Family and Juvenile Rules—Division 1, Family Rules—Chapter 4, Starting and Responding to a Family Law Case; Service of Papers—Article 1, Summonses, Notices, and Declarations; adopted effective January 1, 2013.

Rule 5.50. Papers issued by the court
Rule 5.51. Confidential cover sheet for parentage actions or proceedings involving assisted reproduction; other requirements
Rule 5.52. Declaration Under Uniform Child Custody Jurisdiction and Enforcement Act (UCCJEA)

Rule 5.50. Papers issued by the court

(a) Issuing the summons; form

If a summons is required to commence a family law case, the clerk of the court must issue the summons using the same procedure for issuing a summons in civil actions, generally.

(1) The clerk of the court must:

(A) Issue a *Summons (Family Law)* (form FL-110) for divorces, legal separations, or annulment cases involving married persons or domestic partnerships;

(B) Issue a *Summons (Uniform Parentage—Petition for Custody and Support)* (form FL-210) for parentage or custody and support cases;

(C) Issue a *Summons (UIFSA)* (form FL-510) when a party seeks to establish or enforce child support orders from other states; and

(D) Process a *Summons and Complaint or Supplemental Complaint Regarding Parental Obligations* (form FL-600) as specified in rule 5.325.

(2) The clerk of the court must not give the original summons to the petitioner, but must maintain it in the court file, except for support cases initiated by a local child support agency.

(Subd (a) adopted effective January 1, 2013.)

(b) Automatic temporary family law restraining order in summons; handling by clerk

Under Family Code section 233, in proceedings for dissolution, legal separation, or nullity of a marriage or domestic partnership and in parentage proceedings, the clerk of the court must issue a summons that includes automatic temporary (standard) restraining orders.

(1) The summons and standard restraining orders must be issued and filed in the same manner as a summons in a civil action and must be served and enforced in the manner prescribed for any other restraining order.

(2) If service is by publication, the publication need not include the standard restraining orders.

(Subd (b) amended effective January 1, 2016; adopted effective January 1, 2013.)

(c) Individual restraining order

(1) On application of a party and as provided in the Family Code, a court may issue any individual restraining order that appears to be reasonable or necessary, including those automatic temporary restraining orders in (b) included in the family law summons under Family Code section 233.

(2) Individual restraining orders supersede the standard family law restraining orders in the Family Law and Uniform Parentage Act summonses.

(Subd (c) amended effective January 1, 2016.)
Rule 5.50 amended effective January 1, 2016; adopted effective January 1, 2013.

Rule 5.51. Confidential cover sheet for parentage actions or proceedings involving assisted reproduction; other requirements

(a) Application

This rule applies to actions or proceedings filed with the court after January 1, 2023, involving assisted reproduction, in which the parties seek to determine a parental relationship under Family Code section 7613 or 7630, or sections 7960–7962.

(Subd (a) adopted effective January 1, 2023.)

(b) Filing Requirement

To comply with Family Code section 7643.5, for all actions in (a):

(1) Petitioner must complete a *Confidential Cover Sheet—Parentage Action Involving Assisted Reproduction* (form FL-211) and attach it to the initial papers being filed with the court; and

(2) The court clerk must maintain form FL-211, the initial papers, and all subsequent papers—other than the final judgment—in a confidential court file.

(Subd (b) adopted effective January 1, 2023.)
Rule 5.51 adopted effective January 1, 2023.

Rule 5.52. Declaration Under Uniform Child Custody Jurisdiction and Enforcement Act (UCCJEA)

(a) Filing requirements; application

(1) Petitioner and respondent must each complete, serve, and file a *Declaration Under Uniform Child Custody Jurisdiction and Enforcement Act (UCCJEA)* (form FL-105/GC-120) if there are children of their relationship under the age of 18 years.

(2) The form is a required attachment to the petition and response in actions for divorce, to establish parentage, or actions for custody and support of minor children.

(Subd (a) adopted effective January 1, 2013.)

(b) Duty to update information

In any action or proceeding involving custody of a minor child, a party has a continuing duty to inform the court if he or she obtains further information about a custody proceeding in a California court or any other court concerning a child who is named in the petition, complaint, or response. To comply with this duty, a party must file an updated UCCJEA form with the court and have it served on the other party.

(Subd (b) adopted effective January 1, 2013.)
Rule 5.52 adopted effective January 1, 2013.

Article 2
Initial Pleadings

Title 5, Family and Juvenile Rules—Division 1, Family Rules—Chapter 4, Starting and Responding to a Family Law Case; Service of Papers—Article 2, Initial Pleadings; adopted effective January 1, 2013.

Rule 5.60. Petition or complaint; alternative relief
Rule 5.62. Appearance by respondent
Rule 5.63. Request for order to quash proceeding or responsive relief

Rule 5.60. Petition or complaint; alternative relief

(a) Format

A party starting a family law case must file an appropriate petition or complaint using a form approved by the Judicial Council. Where the Judicial Council has not approved a specific petition or complaint form, the party must submit the petition or complaint in an appropriate format under Trial Court Rules, rules 2.100 through 2.119.

(Subd (a) adopted effective January 1, 2013.)

(b) Request for alternative relief

The petitioner or respondent may request alternative relief when filing a family law action. The request for alternative relief must be indicated in the petition or response.

(Subd (b) adopted effective January 1, 2013.)
Rule 5.60 adopted effective January 1, 2013.

Rule 5.62. Appearance by respondent

(a) Use of terms

In a family law proceeding, the term "request for order" has the same meaning as the terms "motion" or "notice of motion" when they are used in the Code of Civil Procedure.

(Subd (a) adopted effective July 1, 2016.)

(b) Appearance

Except as provided in Code of Civil Procedure section 418.10 and Family Code sections 2012 and 3409, a respondent is deemed to have made a general appearance in a proceeding when he or she files:

(1) A response or answer;

(2) A request for order to strike, under section 435 of the Code of Civil Procedure;

(3) A request for order to transfer the proceeding under section 395 of the Code of Civil Procedure; or

(4) A written notice of his or her appearance.

(Subd (b) amended and relettered effective July 1, 2016; adopted as subd (a) effective January 1, 2013.)

(c) Notice required after appearance

After appearance, the respondent or his or her attorney is entitled to notice of all subsequent proceedings of which notice is required to be given by these rules or in civil actions generally.

(Subd (c) amended and relettered effective July 1, 2016; adopted as subd (b) effective January 1, 2013.)

(d) No notice required

Where a respondent has not appeared, notice of subsequent proceedings need not be given to the respondent except as provided in these rules.

(Subd (d) amended and relettered effective January 1, 2016; adopted as subd (c) effective January 1, 2013.)
Rule 5.62 amended effective July 1, 2016; adopted effective January 1, 2013.

Rule 5.63. Request for order to quash proceeding or responsive relief

(a) Use of terms

In a family law proceeding, the term "request for order" has the same meaning as the terms "motion" or "notice of motion" when they are used in the Code of Civil Procedure.

(Subd (a) adopted effective July 1, 2016.)

(b) Respondent's application

Within the time permitted to file a response, the respondent may move to quash the proceeding, in whole or in part, for any of the following reasons:

(1) Lack of legal capacity to sue;

(2) Prior judgment or another action pending between the same parties for the same cause;

(3) Failure to meet the residence requirement of Family Code section 2320; or

(4) Statute of limitations in Family Code section 2211.

(Subd (b) relettered effective July 1, 2016; adopted as subd (a) effective January 1, 2013.)

(c) Service of respondent's request for order to quash

The request for order to quash must be served in compliance with Code of Civil Procedure section 1005(b). If the respondent files a request for order to quash, no default may be entered, and the time to file a response will be extended until 15 days after service of the court's order denying the request for order to quash.

(Subd (c) amended and relettered effective July 1, 2016; adopted as subd (b) effective January 1, 2013.)

(d) Petitioner's application

Within 15 days after the filing of the response, the petitioner may move to quash, in whole or in part, any request for affirmative relief in the response for the grounds set forth in (a).

(Subd (d) relettered effective July 1, 2016; adopted as subd (c) effective January 1, 2013.)

(e) Waiver

The parties are deemed to have waived the grounds set forth in (b) if they do not file a request for order to quash within the time frame set forth.

(Subd (e) amended and relettered effective July 1, 2016; adopted as subd (d) effective January 1, 2013.)

(f) Relief

When a request for order to quash is granted, the court may grant leave to amend the petition or response and set a date for filing the amended pleadings. The court may also dismiss the action without leave to amend. The action may also be dismissed if the request for order has been sustained with leave to amend and the amendment is not made within the time permitted by the court.

(Subd (f) amended and relettered effective July 1, 2016; adopted as subd (e) effective January 1, 2013.)

Rule 5.63 amended effective July 1, 2016; adopted effective January 1, 2013.

Article 3
Service of Papers

Title 5, Family and Juvenile Rules—Division 1, Family Rules—Chapter 4, Starting and Responding to a Family Law Case; Service of Papers—Article 3, Service of Papers; adopted effective January 1, 2013.

Rule 5.66. Proof of service

(a) Requirements to file proof of service

Parties must file with the court a completed form to prove that the other party received the petition or complaint or response to petition or complaint.

(Subd (a) amended and lettered effective January 1, 2017; adopted as unlettered subd.)

(b) Methods of proof of service

(1) The proof of service of summons may be on a form approved by the Judicial Council or a document or pleading containing the same information required in *Proof of Service of Summons* (form FL-115).

(2) The proof of service of response to petition or complaint may be on a form approved by the Judicial Council or a document or pleading containing the same information required in *Proof of Service by Mail* (form FL-335), *Proof of Personal Service* (form FL-330), or *Proof of Electronic Service* (form POS-050/EFS-050).

(Subd (b) amended and lettered effective January 1, 2017; adopted as unlettered subd.)

Rule 5.66 amended effective January 1, 2017; adopted effective January 1, 2013.

Article 4
Manner of Service

Title 5, Family and Juvenile Rules—Division 1, Family Rules—Chapter 4, Starting and Responding to a Family Law Case; Service of Papers—Article 4, Manner of Service; adopted effective January 1, 2013.

Rule 5.68. Manner of service of summons and petition; response; jurisdiction
Rule 5.72. Court order for service by publication or posting when respondent's address is unknown

Rule 5.68. Manner of service of summons and petition; response; jurisdiction

(a) Service of summons and petition

The petitioner must arrange to serve the other party with a summons, petition, and other papers as required by one of the following methods:

(1) Personal service (Code Civ. Proc., § 415.10);

(2) Substituted service (Code Civ. Proc., § 415.20);

(3) Service by mail with a notice and acknowledgment of receipt (Code Civ. Proc., § 415.30);

(4) Service on person outside of the state (Code Civ. Proc., § 415.40);

(5) Service on a person residing outside of the United States, which must be done in compliance with service rules of the following:

(A) Hague Convention on the Service Abroad of Judicial and Extrajudicial Documents in Civil or Commercial Matters; or

(B) Inter-American Convention on Letters Rogatory and the Additional Protocol to the Inter-American Convention on Letters Rogatory.

(6) Service by posting or publication (Code Civ. Proc., §§ 415.50 and 413.30).

(Subd (a) amended effective January 1, 2014; adopted effective January 1, 2013.)

(b) Service of response to petition

A response to a family law petition may be served by the methods described in (a) but may also be served by mail without notice and acknowledgment of receipt.

(Subd (b) adopted effective January 1, 2013.)

(c) Continuing jurisdiction

The court has jurisdiction over the parties and control of all subsequent proceedings from the time of service of the summons and a copy of the petition. A general appearance of the respondent is equivalent to personal service within this state of the summons and a copy of the petition upon him or her.

(Subd (c) adopted effective January 1, 2013.)

Rule 5.68 amended effective January 1, 2014; adopted effective January 1, 2013.

Rule 5.70. Nondisclosure of attorney assistance in preparation of court documents [Repealed]

Rule 5.70 repealed effective January 1, 2013; adopted as rule 5.170 effective July 1, 2003; previously renumbered effective January 1, 2004; previously amended effective January 1, 2007.

Rule 5.71. Application to be relieved as counsel on completion of limited scope representation [Repealed]

Rule 5.71 repealed effective January 1, 2013; adopted as rule 5.171 effective July 1, 2003; previously renumbered effective January 1, 2004; previously amended effective January 1, 2007, and July 1, 2007.

Rule 5.72. Court order for service by publication or posting when respondent's address is unknown

If the respondent cannot be found to be served a summons by any method described in Code of Civil Procedure sections 415.10 through 415.40, the petitioner may request an order for service of the summons by publication or posting under Code of Civil Procedure sections 415.50 and 413.30, respectively.

(a) Service of summons by publication or posting; forms

To request service of summons by publication or posting, the petitioner must complete and submit to the court *Application for Order for Publication or Posting* (form FL-980) and *Order for Publication or Posting* (form FL-982). Alternatively, petitioner may complete and submit to the court pleadings containing the same information as forms FL-980 and FL-982. The petitioner must list all the reasonable diligent efforts that have been made to find and serve the respondent.

(Subd (a) adopted effective January 1, 2013.)

(b) Service of summons by posting; additional requirements

Service of summons by posting may be ordered only if the court finds that the petitioner is eligible for a waiver of court fees and costs.

(1) To request service by posting, the petitioner must have obtained an order waiving court fees and costs. If the petitioner's financial situation has improved since obtaining the approved order on court fee waiver, the petitioner must file a *Notice to Court of Improved Financial Situation or Settlement* (form FW-010). If the court finds that the petitioner no longer qualifies for a fee waiver, the court may order service by publication of the documents.

(2) *Proof of Service by Posting* (form FL-985) (or a pleading containing the same information as form FL-985) must be completed by the person who posted the documents and then filed with the court once posting is completed.

(Subd (b) amended effective January 1, 2014; adopted effective January 1, 2013.)

Rule 5.72 amended effective January 1, 2014; adopted effective January 1, 2013.

Article 5
Pleadings and Amended Pleadings

Title 5, Family and Juvenile Rules—Division 1, Family Rules—Chapter 4, Starting and Responding to a Family Law Case; Service of Papers—Article 5, Pleadings and Amended Pleadings; adopted effective January 1, 2013.

Rule 5.74. Pleadings and amended pleadings

(a) Definitions

(1) "Pleading" means a petition, complaint, application, objection, answer, response, notice, request for orders, statement of interest, report, or account filed in proceedings under the Family Code.

(2) "Amended pleading" means a pleading that completely restates and supersedes the pleading it amends for all purposes.

(3) "Amendment to a pleading" means a pleading that modifies another pleading and alleges facts or requests relief materially different from the facts alleged or the relief requested in the modified pleading. An amendment to a pleading does not restate or supersede the modified pleading but must be read together with that pleading.

(4) "Supplement to a pleading" and "supplement" mean a pleading that modifies another pleading but does not allege facts or request relief materially different from the facts alleged or the relief requested in the supplemented pleading. A supplement to a pleading may add information to or may correct omissions in the modified pleading.

(Subd (a) adopted effective January 1, 2013.)

(b) Forms of pleading

(1) The forms of pleading and the rules by which the sufficiency of pleadings is to be determined are solely those prescribed in these rules.

(2) Demurrers, motions for summary adjudication, and motions for summary judgment must not be used in family law actions.

(Subd (b) amended effective January 1, 2014; adopted effective January 1, 2013.)

(c) Amendment to pleadings

(1) Amendments to pleadings, amended pleadings, and supplemental pleadings may be served and filed in conformity with the provisions of law applicable to such matters in civil actions generally, but the petitioner is not required to file a reply if the respondent has filed a response.

(2) If both parties have filed initial pleadings (petition and response), there may be no default entered on an amended pleading of either party.

(Subd (c) adopted effective January 1, 2013.)

Rule 5.74 amended effective January 1, 2014; adopted effective January 1, 2013.

Article 6
Specific Proceedings

Title 5, Family and Juvenile Rules—Division 1, Family Rules—Chapter 4, Starting and Responding to a Family Law Case; Service of Papers—Article 6, Specific Proceedings; adopted effective January 1, 2013.

Rule 5.76. Domestic partnerships
Rule 5.77. Summary dissolution

Rule 5.76. Domestic partnerships

To obtain a dissolution, a legal separation, or an annulment of a domestic partnership:

(1) Persons who qualify for a summary dissolution as described in the booklet *Summary Dissolution Information* (form FL-810) may act to dissolve their partnership through the California Secretary of State using forms found at www.sos.ca.gov or in the superior court following the procedures described in form FL-810.

(2) For persons who do not qualify for a summary dissolution proceeding, all forms and procedures used for the dissolution, legal separation, or annulment of a domestic partnership are the same as those used for the dissolution, legal separation, or annulment of a marriage.

Rule 5.76 amended effective January 1, 2015; adopted effective January 1, 2013.

Rule 5.77. Summary dissolution

(a) Declaration of disclosure

To comply with the preliminary disclosure requirements of chapter 9 (beginning with section 2100) of part 1 of division 6 of the Family Code in proceedings for summary dissolution, each joint petitioner must complete and give each other copies of the following documents before signing a property settlement agreement or completing a divorce:

(1) An *Income and Expense Declaration* (form FL-150).

(2) Either of the following documents listing separate and community property assets and obligations:

(A) *Declaration of Disclosure* (form FL-140) and either a *Schedule of Assets and Debts* or a *Property Declaration* (form FL-160) with all attachments; or

(B) The completed worksheet pages indicated in *Summary Dissolution Information* (form FL-810).

(3) A written statement of all investment, business, or other income-producing opportunities that came up after the date of separation based on investments made or work done during the marriage or domestic partnership and before the date of separation.

(4) All tax returns filed by the spouse or domestic partner in the two year period before exchanging the worksheets or forms described in (2).

(Subd (a) amended effective July 1, 2013; adopted effective January 1, 2013.)

(b) Fee for filing

The joint petitioners must pay one fee for filing a *Joint Petition for Summary Dissolution of Marriage* (form FL-800) unless both parties are eligible for a fee waiver order. The fee is the same as that charged for filing a *Petition—Marriage* (form FL-100). No additional fee may be charged for the filing of any form prescribed for use in a summary dissolution proceeding.

(Subd (b) adopted effective January 1, 2013.)

Rule 5.77 amended effective July 1, 2013; adopted effective January 1, 2013.

Chapter 5
Family Centered Case Resolution Plans

Title 5, Family and Juvenile Rules—Division 1, Family Rules—Chapter 5, Family Centered Resolution Plans; adopted effective January 1, 2013.

Rule 5.83. Family centered case resolution

(a) Purpose

This rule establishes processes and procedures for courts to manage cases from initial filing to final disposition in an effective and timely manner. It is intended to advance the goals of Family Code section 2450(a) and Standards of Judicial Administration, standard 5.30.

(Subd (a) adopted effective January 1, 2012.)

(b) Definitions

(1) "Family centered case resolution process" refers to the process employed by the court to ensure that family law cases move through the court process from filing to final disposition in a timely, fair, and effective manner.

(2) "Disposition" refers to final judgment, dismissal, change of venue, or consolidation of the case into a lead case. Courts may continue a case in, or return a case to, the family centered case resolution process after disposition.

(3) "Status conference" refers to court events scheduled with the parties and attorneys for the purpose of identifying the current status of the case and determining the next steps required to reach disposition.

(4) "Family centered case resolution conference" refers to a conference scheduled with parties, attorneys, and a judicial officer to develop and implement a family centered case resolution plan under Family Code section 2451.

(Subd (b) adopted effective January 1, 2012.)

(c) Family centered case resolution process

(1) Beginning January 1, 2012, courts must develop a family centered case resolution process which must be fully implemented by January 1, 2013. The family centered case resolution process must identify and assist all dissolution, legal separation, nullity, and parentage cases to progress through the court process toward disposition effectively in a timely manner. The court may identify other family law case types to include in the family centered case resolution process.

(2) For cases filed on or after January 1, 2013, the court must include as part of the family centered case resolution process a review of all dissolution, legal separation, nullity, and parentage cases within at least 180 days from the date of the initial filing and at a minimum, at least every 180 days thereafter until disposition in order to determine the most appropriate next steps to help ensure an effective, fair, and timely resolution. Unless the court determines that procedural milestones are being met, the review must include at least one of the following: (1) a status conference or (2) a family centered case resolution conference. Nothing in this section prohibits courts from setting more frequent review dates.

(3) If, after 18 months from the date the petition was filed, both parties have failed to participate in the case resolution process as determined by the court, the court's obligation for further review of the case is relieved until the case qualifies for dismissal under Code of Civil Procedure section 583.210 or 583.310, or until the parties reactivate participation in the case, and the case is not counted toward the goals for disposition set out in (c)(5).

(4) In deciding whether a case is progressing in an effective and timely manner, the court should consider procedural milestones including the following:

(A) A proof of service of summons and petition should be filed within 60 days of case initiation;

(B) If no response has been filed, and the parties have not agreed on an extension of time to respond, a request to enter default should be submitted within 60 days after the date the response was due;

(C) The petitioner's preliminary declaration of disclosure should be served within 60 days of the filing of the petition;

(D) When a default has been entered, a judgment should be submitted within 60 days of the entry of default;

(E) Whether a trial date has been requested or scheduled; and

(F) When the parties have notified the court that they are actively negotiating or mediating their case, a written agreement for judgment is submitted within six months of the date the petition was filed, or a request for trial date is submitted.

(5) For dissolution, legal separation, and nullity cases initially filed on or after January 1, 2014, the goals of any family centered case resolution process should be to finalize dispositions as follows:

(A) At least 20 percent are disposed within 6 months from the date the petition was filed;

(B) At least 75 percent are disposed within 12 months from the date the petition was filed; and

(C) At least 90 percent are disposed within 18 months from the date the petition was filed.

(6) The court may select various procedural milestones at which to assist cases in moving toward disposition in an effective and timely manner. Types of assistance that can be provided include the following:

(A) Notifying the parties and attorneys by mail, telephone, e-mail, or other electronic method of communication of the current status of the case and the next procedural steps required to reach disposition;

(B) Implementing a schedule of status conferences for cases to identify the status of the case and determine the next steps required to progress toward disposition;

(C) Providing assistance to the parties at the time scheduled for hearings on requests for orders to identify the status of the case and determine the next steps required to reach disposition;

(D) Providing financial and property settlement opportunities to the parties and their attorneys with judicial officers or qualified attorney settlement officers;

(E) Scheduling a family centered case resolution conference to develop and implement a family centered case resolution plan under Family Code section 2451.

(7) In deciding that a case requires a family centered case resolution conference, the court should consider, in addition to procedural milestones, factors including the following:

(A) Difficulty in locating and serving the respondent;

(B) Complexity of issues;

(C) Nature and extent of anticipated discovery;

(D) Number and locations of percipient and expert witnesses;

(E) Estimated length of trial;

(F) Statutory priority for issues such as custody and visitation of minor children;

(G) Extent of property and support issues in controversy;

(H) Existence of issues of domestic violence, child abuse, or substance abuse;

(I) Pendency of other actions or proceedings that may affect the case; and

(J) Any other factor that would affect the time for disposition.

(Subd (c) adopted effective January 1, 2012.)

(d) Family centered case resolution conferences

(1) The court may hold an initial family centered case resolution conference to develop a specific case resolution plan. The conference is not intended to be an evidentiary hearing.

(2) Family centered case resolution conferences must be heard by a judicial officer. On the court's initiative or at the request of the parties, to enhance access to the court, the conference may be held in person, by telephone, by videoconferencing, or by other appropriate means of communication.

(3) At the conference, counsel for each party and each self-represented litigant must be familiar with the case and must be prepared to discuss the party's positions on the issues.

(4) With the exception of mandatory child custody mediation and mandatory settlement conferences, before alternative dispute resolution (ADR) is included in a family centered case resolution plan under Family Code section 2451(a)(2), the court must inform the parties that their participation in any court recommended ADR services is voluntary and that ADR services can be part of a plan only if both parties voluntarily opt to use these services. Additionally, the court must:

(A) Inform the parties that ADR may not be appropriate in cases involving domestic violence and provide information about separate sessions; and

(B) Ensure that all court-connected providers of ADR services that are part of a family centered case resolution plan have been trained in assessing and handling cases that may involve domestic violence.

(5) Nothing in this rule prohibits an employee of the court from reviewing the file and notifying the parties of any deficiencies in their paperwork before the parties appear in front of a judicial officer at a family centered case resolution conference. This type of assistance can occur by telephone, in person, in writing, or by other means approved by the court, on or before each scheduled family centered case resolution conference. However, this type of procedural assistance is not intended to replace family centered case resolution plan management or to create a barrier to litigants' access to a judicial officer.

(Subd (d) amended effective January 1, 2016; adopted effective January 1, 2012.)

(e) Family centered case resolution plan order

(1) Family centered case resolution plans as ordered by the court must comply with Family Code sections 2450(b) and 2451.

(2) The family centered case resolution plan order should set a schedule for subsequent family centered case resolution conferences and otherwise provide for management of the case.

(Subd (e) adopted effective January 1, 2012.)

(f) Family centered case resolution order without appearance

If the court determines that appearances at a family centered case resolution conference are not necessary, the court may notify the parties and, if stipulated, issue a family centered case resolution order without an appearance at a conference.

(Subd (f) adopted effective January 1, 2012.)

(g) Family centered case resolution information

(1) Upon the filing of first papers in dissolution, legal separation, nullity, or parentage actions the court must provide the filing party with the following:

(A) Written information summarizing the process of a case through disposition;

(B) A list of local resources that offer procedural assistance, legal advice or information, settlement opportunities, and domestic violence services;

(C) Instructions for keeping the court informed of the person's current address and phone number, and e-mail address;

(D) Information for self-represented parties about the opportunity to meet with court self-help center staff or a family law facilitator; and

(E) Information for litigants on how to request a status conference, or a family centered case resolution conference earlier than or in addition to, any status conference or family centered case resolution conferences scheduled by the court.

(Subd (g) adopted effective January 1, 2012.)

Rule 5.83 amended effective January 1, 2016; adopted effective January 1, 2012.

Chapter 6
Request for Court Orders

Title 5, Family and Juvenile Rules—Division 1, Family Rules—Chapter 6, Request for Court Orders; adopted effective January 1, 2013.

Art. 1. General Provisions. Rules 5.90, 5.91.
Art. 2. Filing and Service. Rules 5.92–5.97.
Art. 3. Meet-and-Confer Conferences. Rule 5.98.
Art. 4. Evidence at Hearings. Rules 5.111–5.115.
Art. 5. Reporting and Preparation of Order After Hearing. Rules 5.123, 5.125.
Art. 6. Special Immigrant Juvenile Findings. Rule 5.130.

Article 1
General Provisions

Title 5, Family and Juvenile Rules—Division 1, Family Rules—Chapter 6, Request for Court Orders—Article 1, General Provisions; adopted effective January 1, 2013.

Rule 5.90. Format of papers
Rule 5.91. Individual restraining order

Rule 5.90. Format of papers

The rules regarding the format of a request for order are the same as the rules for format of motions in civil rules 3.1100 through 3.1116, except as otherwise provided in these Family Rules.

Rule 5.90 adopted effective January 1, 2013.

Rule 5.91. Individual restraining order

On a party's request for order and as provided in the Family Code, a court may issue any individual restraining order that appears to be reasonable or necessary, including those automatic temporary restraining orders included in the family law summons. Individual orders supersede the standard family law restraining orders in the Family Law and Uniform Parentage Act summonses.

Rule 5.91 amended effective January 1, 2016; adopted effective January 1, 2013.

Article 2
Filing and Service

Title 5, Family and Juvenile Rules—Division 1, Family Rules—Chapter 6, Request for Court Orders—Article 2, Filing and Service; adopted effective January 1, 2013.

Rule 5.92. Request for court order; responsive declaration
Rule 5.94. Order shortening time; other filing requirements; failure to serve request for order
Rule 5.95. Request to reschedule hearing
Rule 5.96. Place and manner of filing
Rule 5.97. Time frames for transferring jurisdiction

Rule 5.92. Request for court order; responsive declaration

(a) Application

(1) In a family law proceeding under the Family Code:

(A) The term "request for order" has the same meaning as the terms "motion" or "notice of motion" when they are used in the Code of Civil Procedure;

(B) A *Request for Order* (form FL-300) must be used to ask for court orders, unless another Judicial Council form has been adopted or approved for the specific request; and

(C) A *Responsive Declaration to Request for Order* (form FL-320) must be used to respond to the orders sought in form FL-300, unless another Judicial Council form has been adopted or approved for the specific purpose.

(2) In an action under the Domestic Violence Prevention Act, a *Request for Order* (form FL-300) must be used to request a modification or termination of all orders made after a hearing on *Restraining Order After Hearing* (form DV-130).

(3) In a local child support action under the Family Code, any party other than the local child support agency must use *Request for Order* (form FL-300) to ask for court orders.

(Subd (a) adopted effective July 1, 2016; previous subd (a) repealed effective July 1, 2016.)

(b) Request for order; required forms and filing procedure

(1) The *Request for Order* (form FL-300) must set forth facts sufficient to notify the other party of the moving party's contentions in support of the relief requested.

(2) When a party seeks orders for spousal or domestic partner support, attorney's fees and costs, or other orders relating to the parties' property or finances:

(A) The party must complete an *Income and Expense Declaration* (form FL-150) and file it with the *Request for Order* (form FL-300); and

(B) The *Income and Expense Declaration* (form FL-150) must be current, as described in rule 5.260 and include the documents specified in form FL-150 that demonstrate the party's income.

(3) When seeking child support orders:

(A) A party must complete an *Income and Expense Declaration* (form FL-150) and file it with the *Request for Order* (form FL-300);

(B) The *Income and Expense Declaration* (form FL-150) must be current, as described in rule 5.260 and include the documents specified in the form that demonstrate the party's income; and

(C) A party may complete a current *Financial Statement (Simplified)* (form FL-155) instead of a current *Income and Expense Declaration* (form FL-150) only if the party meets the requirements listed in form FL-155.

(4) The moving party may be required to complete, file and have additional forms or attachments served along with a *Request for Order* (form FL-300) when seeking court orders for child custody and visitation (parenting time), attorney's fees and costs, support, and other financial matters. For more information, see *Information Sheet for Order* (form FL-300-INFO).

(5) The moving party must file the documents with the court clerk to obtain a court date and then have a filed copy served on all parties in the case within the timelines required by law.

(6) No memorandum of points and authorities need to be filed with a *Request for Order* (form FL-300) unless required by the court on a case-by-case basis.

(Subd (b) adopted effective July 1, 2016; previous subd (b) repealed effective July 1, 2016.)

(c) Request for temporary emergency (ex parte) orders

If the moving party seeks temporary emergency orders pending the hearing, the moving party must:

(1) Comply with rules 5.151 through 5.169 of the California Rules of Court;

(2) Complete and include a proposed *Temporary Emergency (Ex Parte) Orders* (form FL-305) with the *Request for Order* (form FL-300); and

(3) Comply with specified local court procedures and/or local court rules about reserving the day for the temporary emergency hearing, submitting the paperwork to the court, and use of local forms.

(Subd (c) adopted effective July 1, 2016; previous subd (c) repealed effective July 1, 2016.)

(d) Request for order shortening time (for service or time until the hearing)

If the moving party seeks an order for a shorter time to serve documents or a shorter time until the hearing:

(1) The moving party must submit the request as a temporary emergency order on form FL-300 and comply with the requirements of rules 5.151 through 5.169 of the California Rules of Court; and

(2) The moving party's request must be supported by a declaration or a statement of facts showing good cause for the court to prescribe shorter times for the filing and service of the *Request for Order* (form FL-300) than the times specified in Code of Civil Procedure section 1005.

(3) The court may issue the order shortening time in the "Court Orders" section of the *Request for Order* (form FL-300).

(Subd (d) adopted effective July 1, 2016; previous subd (d) repealed effective July 1, 2016.)

(e) Issuance by court clerk

The court clerk's authority to issue a *Request for Order* (form FL-300) as a ministerial act is limited to those orders or notices:

(1) For the parties to attend orientation and confidential mediation or child custody recommending counseling; and

(2) That may be delegated by a judicial officer and do not require the use of judicial discretion.

(Subd (e) adopted effective July 1, 2016.)

(f) Request for order; service requirements

(1) The *Request for Order* (form FL-300) and appropriate documents or orders must be served in the manner specified for the service of a summons in Code of Civil Procedure sections 415.10 through 415.95, including personal service, if:

(A) The court granted temporary emergency orders pending the hearing;

(B) The responding party has not yet appeared in the case as described in rule 5.62; or

(C) The court ordered personal service on the other party.

(2) A *Request for Order* (form FL-300) must be served as specified in Family Code section 215 if filed after entry of a family law judgment or after a permanent order was made in any proceeding in which there was at issue the custody, visitation (parenting time), or support of a child.

(A) Requests to change a judgment or permanent order for custody, visitation (parenting time), or support of a child may be served by mail on the other party or parties only if the moving party can verify the other parties' current address.

(B) *Declaration Regarding Address Verification* (form FL-334) may be used as the address verification required by Family Code section 215. The completed form, or a declaration that includes the same information, must be filed with the proof of service of the *Request for Order*.

(3) All other requests for orders and appropriate documents may be served as specified in Code of Civil Procedure section 1010 et seq., including service by mail.

(4) The following blank forms must be served with a *Request for Order* (form FL-300):

(A) *Responsive Declaration to Request for Order* (form FL-320); and

(B) *Income and Expense Declaration* (form FL-150), when the requesting party is serving a completed FL-150 or FL-155.

(Subd (f) adopted effective July 1, 2016.)

(g) Responsive declaration to request for order; procedures

To respond to the issues raised in the *Request for Order* (form FL-300) and accompanying papers, the responding party must complete, file, and have a *Responsive Declaration to Request for Order* (form FL-320) served on all parties in the case.

(1) The *Responsive Declaration to Request for Order* (form FL-320) must set forth facts sufficient to notify the other party of the declarant's contentions in response to the request for order and in support of any relief requested.

(2) The responding party may request relief related to the orders requested in the moving papers. However, unrelated relief must be sought by scheduling a separate hearing using *Request for Order* (form FL-300) and following the filing and service requirements for a *Request for Order* described in this rule.

(3) A completed *Income and Expense Declaration* (form 150) must be filed with the *Responsive Declaration to Request for Order* (form FL-320) following the same requirements specified above in rule 5.92(b)(2) and (b)(3).

(4) The responding party may be required to complete, file, and serve additional forms or attachments along with a *Responsive Declaration to Request for Order* (form FL-320) when responding to a *Request for Order* (form FL-300) about child custody and visitation (parenting time), attorney fees and costs, support, and other financial matters. For more information, read *Information Sheet: Responsive Declaration to Request for Order* (form FL-320-INFO).

(5) No memorandum of points and authorities need be filed with a *Responsive Declaration to Request for Order* (form FL-320) unless required by the court on a case-by-case basis.

(6) A *Responsive Declaration to Request for Order* (form FL-320) may be served on the parties by mail, unless otherwise required by court order.

(Subd (g) adopted effective July 1, 2016.)
Rule 5.92 amended effective July 1, 2016; adopted effective July 1, 2012.

Advisory Committee Comment

The Family and Juvenile Law Advisory Committee and the Elkins Implementation Task Force developed rule 5.92 and *Request for Order* (form FL-300) in response to *Elkins Family Law Task Force: Final Report and Recommendations (April 2010)* for one comprehensive form and related procedures to replace the *Order to Show Cause* (form FL-300) and *Notice of Motion* (form FL-301). (See page 35 of the final report online at www.courts.ca.gov/elkins-finalreport.pdf.)

Rule 5.93. Attorney's fees and costs [Renumbered]
Rule 5.93 renumbered as rule 5.427 effective January 1, 2013.

Rule 5.94. Order shortening time; other filing requirements; failure to serve request for order

(a) Order shortening time

The court, on its own motion or on application for an order shortening time supported by a declaration showing good cause, may prescribe shorter times for the filing and service of papers than the times specified in Code of Civil Procedure section 1005.

(Subd (a) adopted effective January 1, 2013.)

(b) Time for filing proof of service

Proof of service of the *Request for Order* (FL-300) and supporting papers should be filed five court days before the hearing date.

(Subd (b) adopted effective January 1, 2013.)

(c) Filing of late papers

No papers relating to a request for order or responsive declaration to the request may be rejected for filing on the ground that they were untimely submitted for filing. If the court, in its discretion, refuses to consider a late filed paper, the minutes or order must so indicate.

(Subd (c) amended and relettered effective July 1, 2016; adopted as subd (d) effective January 1, 2013.)

(d) Timely submission to court clerk

The papers requesting an order or responding to the request are deemed timely filed if they are submitted:

(1) Before the close of the court clerk's office to the public; and

(2) On or before the day the papers are due.

(Subd (d) amended and relettered effective July 1, 2016; adopted as subd (e) effective January 1, 2013.)

(e) Failure to serve request for order

The *Request for Order* (form FL-300) or other moving papers such as an order to show cause, along with any temporary emergency (ex parte) orders, will expire on the date and time of the scheduled hearing if the requesting party fails to:

(1) Have the other party served before the hearing with the *Request for Order* (form FL-300) or other moving papers, such as an order to show cause; supporting documents; and any temporary emergency (ex parte) orders; or

(2) Obtain a court order to reschedule the hearing, as described in rule 5.95.

(Subd (e) amended effective July 1, 2020; adopted as subd (c) effective January 1, 2013; previously amended and relettered as subd (e) effective July 1, 2016; previously amended effective September 1, 2017.)
Rule 5.94 amended effective July 1, 2020; adopted effective January 1, 2013; previously amended effective July 1, 2016, and September 1, 2017.

Rule 5.95. Request to reschedule hearing

(a) Application

The rules in this chapter govern requests to reschedule a hearing in family law cases, unless otherwise provided by statute or rule. Unless specifically stated, these rules do not apply to ex parte applications for domestic violence restraining orders under the Domestic Violence Prevention Act.

(Subd (a) adopted effective July 1, 2020.)

(b) Reschedule a hearing because the other party was not served

If a *Request for Order* (form FL-300) (with or without temporary emergency [ex parte] orders), order to show cause, or other moving paper is not served on the other party as described in rule 5.92 or as ordered by the court and the requesting party still wishes to proceed with the hearing, the party must ask the court to reschedule the hearing date.

(1) To request that the court reschedule the hearing to serve papers on the other party, the party must take one of the following actions:

(A) *Before the date of the hearing*

(i) The party must complete and file with the court a written request and a proposed order. The following forms may be used for this purpose: *Request to Reschedule Hearing* (form FL-306) or *Request to Reschedule Hearing Involving Temporary Emergency (Ex Parte) Orders* (form FL-307), whichever form is appropriate for the case, and *Order on Request to Reschedule Hearing* (form FL-309); and

(ii) The party should submit the request to the court no later than five court days before the hearing set on the *Request for Order* (form FL-300), order to show cause, or other moving paper.

(B) *On the date of the hearing*

The party may appear and orally ask the court to reschedule the hearing. The party is not required to file a written request but must complete and submit a proposed *Order on Request to Reschedule Hearing* (form FL-309).

(2) The court may do any of the following:

(A) Grant or deny the request to reschedule the hearing.

(B) Delegate to the court clerk the authority to reschedule the hearing if:

(i) The request to reschedule the hearing is required to allow more time to serve the other party with notice of the hearing; and

(ii) The party asking to reschedule the hearing does not request a change to any temporary emergency (ex parte) orders issued with the *Request for Order* (form FL-300).

(3) If the court reschedules the hearing:

(A) The court, on a showing of good cause, may modify or terminate any temporary emergency (ex parte) orders initially granted with the *Request for Order* (form FL-300), order to show cause, or other moving papers.

(B) The requesting party must serve the *Order on Request to Reschedule Hearing* (form FL-309) on the other party in the case, along with the *Request for Order* (form FL-300) or other moving papers such as an order to show cause, any temporary emergency (ex parte) orders, and supporting documents.

(C) If the other party has not been served with the papers in (B) after the court granted the request to reschedule, the party must repeat the procedures in this rule, unless the court orders otherwise.

(Subd (b) adopted effective July 1, 2020.)

(c) Written agreements (stipulations) to reschedule a hearing

The court may reschedule the hearing date of a *Request for Order* (FL-300), order to show cause, or other moving paper based on a written agreement (stipulation) between the parties and/or their attorneys.

(1) The parties may complete *Agreement and Order to Reschedule Hearing* (form FL-308) for this purpose.

(2) The parties may agree to reschedule the hearing to a date that must be provided by the court clerk. Parties should follow the court's local rules and procedures for obtaining a new hearing date.

(3) Any temporary emergency orders will remain in effect until after the end of the new hearing date, unless modified by the court.

(4) The parties should submit the agreement to the court no later than five days before the hearing set on the *Request for Order* (form FL-300), order to show cause, or other moving paper.

(5) The court must approve and sign the agreement to make it a court order.

(6) The court may limit the number of times that parties can agree to reschedule a hearing.

(Subd (c) adopted effective July 1, 2020.)

(d) Reschedule a hearing after the other party was served with the request for order or other moving papers

The procedures in this section apply when a *Request for Order* (form FL-300), order to show cause, or other moving paper was served on the other party as described in rule 5.92 or as ordered by the court and either party seeks to reschedule the hearing date, and the parties are unable to reach an agreement about rescheduling the hearing.

(1) To reschedule a hearing, either party must submit a written request to reschedule before the hearing date as described below in (A) or appear in court on the date of the hearing and orally ask the court to reschedule, as described below in (B):

(A) *Before the date of the hearing*

(i) The party asking to reschedule the hearing must complete a written request and a proposed order. The following forms may be used for this purpose: *Request to Reschedule Hearing* (form FL-306) or *Request to Reschedule Hearing Involving Temporary Emergency (Ex Parte) Orders* (form FL-307), whichever form is appropriate for the case, and *Order on Request to Reschedule Hearing* (form FL-309).

(ii) The party must first notify and serve the other party. Notice and service to the other party of the documents in (i) must be completed as required by rules 5.151 through 5.169.

(iii) The party must file or submit to the court the forms in (i), along with a declaration describing how the other party was notified of the request to reschedule and served the documents. *Declaration Regarding Notice and Service of Request for Temporary Emergency (Ex Parte) Orders* (form FL-303), a local form, or a declaration that contains the same information as form FL-303 may be used for this purpose.

(iv) The party should submit the forms in (iii) to the court no later than five court days before the hearing date set on the *Request for Order* (form FL-300), order to show cause, or other moving paper.

(v) The party responding to a written request to reschedule may file and serve a responsive declaration to the request to reschedule before the court considers the written request. *Responsive Declaration to Request to Reschedule Hearing* (form FL-310) may be used for this purpose.

(B) *On the date of the hearing*

The party asking to reschedule the hearing may appear in court and orally request to reschedule the hearing. The party is not required to file a written request but must complete and submit a proposed *Order on Request to Reschedule Hearing* (form FL-309).

(2) The court may do any of the following:

(A) Grant the request to reschedule the hearing on a showing of good cause or as required by law.

(B) Deny the request to reschedule absent a showing of good cause.

(C) Modify or terminate any temporary emergency (ex parte) orders initially granted with the *Request for Order* (form FL-300), order to show cause, or other moving paper.

(Subd (d) adopted effective July 1, 2020.)

(e) Reschedule a hearing to attend mediation or child custody recommending counseling

(1) When parties need to reschedule a hearing relating to child custody and visitation (parenting time) because they have been unable to attend the family court services appointment, they should follow their local court rules and procedures for requesting and obtaining an order to reschedule the hearing.

(2) If the local court has no local rules and procedures for rescheduling hearings under (1), the parties may:

(A) Complete and file a written agreement (stipulation) for the court to sign as described in (c) of this rule; or

(B) Follow the procedures in (d) to ask for a court order to reschedule the hearing.

(Subd (e) adopted effective July 1, 2020.)

Rule 5.95 adopted effective July 1, 2020.

Rule 5.96. Place and manner of filing

(a) Papers filed in clerk's office

All papers relating to a request for order proceeding must be filed in the clerk's office, unless otherwise provided by local rule or court order.

(Subd (a) adopted effective January 1, 2013.)

(b) General schedule

The clerk must post a general schedule showing the days and departments for hearing the matters indicated in the *Request for Order* (form FL-300).

(Subd (b) adopted effective January 1, 2013.)

(c) Duty to notify court of settlement

If the matter has been settled before the scheduled court hearing date, the moving party must immediately notify the court of the settlement.

(Subd (c) adopted effective January 1, 2013.)

Rule 5.96 adopted effective January 1, 2013.

Rule 5.97. Time frames for transferring jurisdiction

(a) Application

This rule applies to family law actions or family law proceedings for which a transfer of jurisdiction has been ordered under part 2 of title 4 of the Code of Civil Procedure.

(Subd (a) adopted effective January 1, 2019.)

(b) Payment of fees; fee waivers

Responsibility for the payment of court costs and fees for the transfer of jurisdiction as provided in Government Code section 70618 is subject to the following provisions:

(1) If a transfer of jurisdiction is ordered in response to a motion made under title 4 of the Code of Civil Procedure by a party, the responsibility for costs and fees is subject to Code of Civil Procedure section 399(a). If the fees are not paid within the time specified in section 399(a), the court may, on a duly noticed motion by any party or on its own motion, dismiss the action without prejudice to the cause of action. Except as provided in (e), no other action on the cause may be commenced in another court before satisfaction of the court's order for fees and costs or a court-ordered waiver of such fees and costs.

(2) If a transfer of jurisdiction is ordered by the court on its own motion, the court must specify in its order which party is responsible for the Government Code section 70618 fees. If that party has not paid the fees within five days of service of notice of the transfer order, any other party interested in the action or proceeding may pay the costs and fees and the clerk must transmit the case file. If the fees are not paid within the time period set forth in Code of Civil Procedure section 399, the court may, on a duly noticed motion by any party or on its own motion, dismiss the action without prejudice to the cause or enter such other orders as the court deems appropriate. Except as provided in (e), no other action on the cause may be commenced in the original court or another court before satisfaction of the court's order for fees and costs or a court-ordered waiver of such fees and costs.

(3) If the party responsible for the fees has been granted a fee waiver by the sending court, the case file must be transmitted as if the fees and costs were paid and the fee waiver order must be transmitted with the case file in lieu of the fees and costs. If a partial fee waiver has been granted, the party responsible for the fees and costs must pay the required portion of the fees and costs before the case will be transmitted. In any case involving a fee waiver, the court receiving the case file has the authority under Government Code section 68636 to review the party's eligibility for a fee waiver based on additional information available to the court or pursuant to a hearing at final disposition of the case.

(4) At the hearing to transfer jurisdiction, the court must address any issues regarding fees. If a litigant indicates they cannot afford to pay the fees, a fee waiver request form should be provided by the clerk and the court should promptly rule on that request.

(Subd (b) adopted effective January 1, 2019.)

(c) Time frame for transfer of jurisdiction

After a court orders the transfer of jurisdiction over the action or proceeding, the clerk must transmit the case file to the clerk of the court to which the action or proceeding is transferred within five court days of the date of expiration of the 20-day time period to petition for a writ of mandate. If a writ is filed, the clerk must transmit the case file within five court days of the notice that the order is final. The clerk must send notice stating the date of the transmittal to all parties who have appeared in the action or proceeding and the court receiving the transfer.

(Subd (c) adopted effective January 1, 2019.)

(d) Time frame to assume jurisdiction over transferred matter

Within 20 court days of the date of the transmittal, the clerk of the court receiving the transferred action or proceeding must send notice to all parties who have appeared in the action or proceeding and the court that ordered the transfer stating the date of the filing of the case and the number assigned to the case in the court.

(Subd (d) adopted effective January 1, 2019.)

(e) Emergency orders while transfer is pending

Until the clerk of the receiving court sends notice of the date of filing, the transferring court retains jurisdiction over the matter to make orders designed to prevent immediate danger or irreparable harm to a party or the children involved in the matter, or immediate loss or damage to property subject to disposition in the matter. When an emergency order is requested, the transferring court must send notice to the receiving court that it is exercising its jurisdiction and must inform the receiving court of the action taken on the request. If the court makes a new order in the case, it must send a copy of the order to the receiving court if the case file has already been transmitted. The transferring court retains jurisdiction over the request until it takes action on it.

(Subd (e) adopted effective January 1, 2019.)

Rule 5.97 adopted effective January 1, 2019.

Article 3
Meet-and-Confer Conferences

Title 5, Family and Juvenile Rules—Division 1, Family Rules—Chapter 6, Request for Court Orders—Article 3, Meet-and-Confer Conferences; adopted effective January 1, 2013.

Rule 5.98. Meet-and-confer requirements; document exchange

(a) Meet and confer

All parties and all attorneys are required to meet and confer in person, by telephone, or as ordered by the court, before the date of the hearing relating to a *Request for Order* (FL-300). During this time, parties must discuss and make a good faith attempt to settle all issues, even if a complete settlement is not possible and only conditional agreements are made. The requirement to meet and confer does not apply to cases involving domestic violence.

(Subd (a) adopted effective January 1, 2013.)

(b) Document exchange

Before or while conferring, parties must exchange all documentary evidence that is to be relied on for proof of any material fact at the hearing. At the hearing, the court may decline to consider documents that were not given to the other party before the hearing as required under this rule. The requirement to exchange documents does not relate to documents that are submitted primarily for rebuttal or impeachment purposes.

(Subd (b) adopted effective January 1, 2013.)

Rule 5.98 adopted effective January 1, 2013.

Rule 5.100. Designation of parties [Repealed]

Rule 5.100 repealed effective January 1, 2013; adopted as rule 1210 effective January 1, 1970; previously amended effective January 1, 1999; previously amended and renumbered effective January 1, 2003.

Rule 5.102. Parties to proceeding [Repealed]

Rule 5.102 repealed effective January 1, 2013; adopted as rule 1211 effective January 1, 1970; previously amended effective January 1, 1977, January 1, 1994, and January 1, 1999; previously amended and renumbered effective January 1, 2003; previously amended effective January 1, 2005.

Rule 5.104. Other causes of action [Repealed]

Rule 5.104 repealed effective January 1, 2013; adopted as rule 1212 effective January 1, 1970; previously amended effective January 1, 1994, and January 1, 1999; previously amended and renumbered effective January 1, 2003.

Rule 5.106. Injunctive relief and reservation of jurisdiction [Repealed]

Rule 5.106 repealed effective January 1, 2013; adopted as rule 1213 effective January 1, 1970; previously amended effective January 1, 1994; previously amended and renumbered effective January 1, 2003; previously amended effective January 1, 2007.

Rule 5.108. Pleadings [Repealed]

Rule 5.108 repealed effective January 1, 2013; adopted as rule 1215 effective January 1, 1970; previously amended effective January 1, 1999; previously amended and renumbered effective January 1, 2003; previously amended effective January 1, 2007.

Rule 5.110. Summons; restraining order [Repealed]

Rule 5.110 repealed effective January 1, 2013; adopted as rule 1216 effective January 1, 1970; previously amended effective July 1, 1990, January 1, 1994, January 1, 1999; previously amended and renumbered effective January 1, 2003; previously amended effective January 1, 2007.

Article 4
Evidence at Hearings

Title 5, Family and Juvenile Rules—Division 1, Family Rules—Chapter 6, Request for Court Orders—Article 4, Evidence at Hearings; adopted effective January 1, 2013.

Rule 5.111. Declarations supporting and responding to a request for court order
Rule 5.112.1. Declaration page limitation; exemptions
Rule 5.113. Live testimony
Rule 5.115. Judicial notice

Rule 5.111. Declarations supporting and responding to a request for court order

Along with a *Request for Order* (form FL-300) or a *Responsive Declaration* (form FL-320), a party must file a supporting declaration with the court clerk and serve it on the other party. The declarations must comply with the following requirements:

(a) Length of declarations

A declaration included with a request for court order or a responsive declaration must not exceed 10 pages in length. A reply declaration must not exceed 5 pages in length, unless:

(1) The declaration is of an expert witness; or

(2) The court grants permission to extend the length of a declaration.

(b) Form, format, and content of declarations

(1) The form and format of each declaration submitted in a case filed under the Family Code must comply with the requirements set out in California Rules of Court, rule 2.100 et seq.

(2) A declaration must be based on personal knowledge and explain how the person has acquired that knowledge. The statements in the declaration must be admissible in evidence.

(c) Objections to declarations

(1) If a party thinks that a declaration does not meet the requirements of (b)(2) the party must file their objections in writing at least 2 court days before the time of the hearing, or any objection will be considered waived, and the declaration may be considered as evidence. Upon a finding of good cause, objections may be made in writing or orally at the time of the hearing.

(2) If the court does not specifically rule on the objection raised by a party, the objection is presumed overruled. If an appeal is filed, any presumed overrulings can be challenged.

Rule 5.111 adopted effective January 1, 2013.

Rule 5.112. Continuing jurisdiction [Repealed]

Rule 5.112 repealed effective January 1, 2013; adopted as rule 1217 effective January 1, 1970; previously amended and renumbered effective January 1, 2003.

Rule 5.112.1. Declaration page limitation; exemptions

The Judicial Council form portion of a declaration does not count toward the page limitation for declarations specified in rule 5.111. In addition, the following documents may be attached to a *Request for Order* (form FL-300) or *Responsive Declaration* (form FL-320) without being counted toward the page limitation for declarations:

(1) An *Income and Expense Declaration* (form FL-150) and its required attachments;

(2) A *Financial Statement (Simplified)* (form FL-155) and its required attachments;

(3) A *Property Declaration* (form FL-160) and required attachments;

(4) Exhibits attached to declarations; and

(5) A memorandum of points and authorities.

Rule 5.112.1 adopted effective January 1, 2013.

Rule 5.113. Live testimony

(a) Purpose

Under Family Code section 217, at a hearing on any request for order brought under the Family Code, absent a stipulation of the parties or a finding of good cause under (b), the court must receive any live, competent, and admissible testimony that is relevant and within the scope of the hearing.

(Subd (a) adopted effective January 1, 2013.)

(b) Factors

In addition to the rules of evidence, a court must consider the following factors in making a finding of good cause to refuse to receive live testimony under Family Code section 217:

(1) Whether a substantive matter is at issue—such as child custody, visitation (parenting time), parentage, child support, spousal support, requests for restraining orders, or the characterization, division, or temporary use and control of the property or debt of the parties;

(2) Whether material facts are in controversy;

(3) Whether live testimony is necessary for the court to assess the credibility of the parties or other witnesses;

(4) The right of the parties to question anyone submitting reports or other information to the court;

(5) Whether a party offering testimony from a non-party has complied with Family Code section 217(c); and

(6) Any other factor that is just and equitable.

(Subd (b) adopted effective January 1, 2013.)

(c) Findings

If the court makes a finding of good cause to exclude live testimony, it must state its reasons on the record or in writing. The court is required to state only those factors on which the finding of good cause is based.

(Subd (c) adopted effective January 1, 2013.)

(d) Minor children

When receiving or excluding testimony from minor children, in addition to fulfilling the requirements of Evidence Code section 765, the court must follow the procedures in Family Code section 3042 and rule 5.250 of the California Rules of Court governing children's testimony.

(Subd (d) adopted effective January 1, 2013.)

(e) Witness lists

Witness lists required by Family Code section 217(c) must be served along with the request for order or responsive papers in the manner required for the service of those documents (*Witness List* (form FL-321) may be used for this purpose). If no witness list has been served, the court may require an offer of proof before allowing any nonparty witness to testify.

(Subd (e) adopted effective January 1, 2013.)

(f) Continuance

The court must consider whether or not a brief continuance is necessary to allow a litigant adequate opportunity to prepare for questioning any witness for the other parties. When a brief continuance is granted to allow time to prepare for questioning witnesses, the court should make appropriate temporary orders.

(Subd (f) adopted effective January 1, 2013.)

(g) Questioning by court

Whenever the court receives live testimony from a party or any witness it may elicit testimony by directing questions to the parties and other witnesses.

(Subd (g) adopted effective January 1, 2013.)

Rule 5.113 adopted effective January 1, 2013.

Rule 5.114. Alternative relief [Repealed]

Rule 5.114 repealed effective January 1, 2013; adopted as rule 1221 effective January 1, 1970; previously amended and renumbered effective January 1, 2003.

Rule 5.115. Judicial notice

A party requesting judicial notice of material under Evidence Code section 452 or 453 must provide the court and each party with a copy of the material. If the material is part of a file in the court in which the matter is being heard, the party must specify in writing the part of the court file sought to be judicially noticed and make arrangements with the clerk to have the file in the courtroom at the time of the hearing.

Rule 5.115 adopted effective January 1, 2013.

Rule 5.116. Stipulation for judgment [Repealed]

Rule 5.116 repealed effective January 1, 2013; adopted as rule 1223 effective January 1, 1970; previously amended effective January 1, 1972; previously amended and renumbered effective January 1, 2003.

Rule 5.118. Declarations supporting and responding to a request for court order [Repealed]

Rule 5.118 repealed effective January 1, 2013; adopted as rule 1225 effective January 1, 1970; previously amended effective January 1, 1972, July 1, 1977, January 1, 1980, and January 1, 1999; previously amended and renumbered effective January 1, 2003; previously amended effective January 1, 2004, January 1, 2007, July 1, 2011, and July 1, 2012.

Rule 5.119. Live testimony [Repealed]

Rule 5.119 repealed effective January 1, 2013; adopted effective July 1, 2011.

Rule 5.120. Appearance [Repealed]

Rule 5.120 repealed effective January 1, 2013; adopted as rule 1236 effective January 1, 1970; previously amended effective January 1, 1972, and January 1, 1999; previously amended and renumbered effective January 1, 2003; previously amended effective January 1, 2004, and January 1, 2006.

Rule 5.121. Motion to quash proceeding or responsive relief [Repealed]

Rule 5.121 repealed effective January 1, 2013; adopted effective January 1, 2004; previously amended effective January 1, 2006.

Rule 5.122. Default [Repealed]

Rule 5.122 repealed effective January 1, 2013; adopted as rule 1237 effective January 1, 1970; previously amended effective January 1, 1972, and January 1, 1980; previously amended and renumbered effective January 1, 2003; previously amended effective January 1, 2007.

Article 5
Reporting and Preparation of Order After Hearing

Title 5, Family and Juvenile Rules—Division 1, Family Rules—Chapter 6, Request for Court Orders—Article 5, Reporting and Preparation of Order After Hearing; adopted effective January 1, 2013.

Rule 5.123. Reporting of hearing proceedings
Rule 5.125. Preparation, service, and submission of order after hearing

Rule 5.123. Reporting of hearing proceedings

A court that does not regularly provide for reporting of hearings on a request for order or motion must so state in its local rules. The rules must also provide a procedure by which a party may obtain a court reporter in order to provide the party with an official verbatim transcript.

Rule 5.123 adopted effective January 1, 2013.

Rule 5.124. Request for default [Repealed]

Rule 5.124 repealed effective January 1, 2013; adopted as rule 1240 effective January 1, 1970; previously amended effective January 1, 1979, and January 1, 1980; previously amended and renumbered effective January 1, 2003.

Rule 5.125. Preparation, service, and submission of order after hearing

The court may prepare the order after hearing and serve copies on the parties or their attorneys. Alternatively, the court may order one of the parties or attorneys to prepare the proposed order as provided in these rules. The court may also modify the timelines and procedures in this rule when appropriate to the case.

(a) In general

The term "party" or "parties" includes both self-represented persons and persons represented by an attorney of record. The procedures in this rule requiring a party to perform action related to the preparation, service, and submission of an order after hearing include the party's attorney of record.

(b) Submission of proposed order after hearing to the court

Within 10 calendar days of the court hearing, the party ordered to prepare the proposed order must:

(1) Serve the proposed order to the other party for approval; or

(2) If the other party did not appear at the hearing or the matter was uncontested, submit the proposed order directly to the court without the other party's approval. A copy must also be served to the other party or attorney.

(c) Other party approves or rejects proposed order after hearing

(1) Within 20 calendar days from the court hearing, the other party must review the proposed order to determine if it accurately reflects the orders made by the court and take one of the following actions:

(A) Approve the proposed order by signing and serving it on the party or attorney who drafted the proposed order; or

(B) State any objections to the proposed order and prepare an alternate proposed order. Any alternate proposed order prepared by the objecting party must list the findings and orders in the same sequence as the proposed order. After serving any objections and the alternate proposed order to the party or attorney, both parties must follow the procedure in (e).

(2) If the other party does not respond to the proposed order within 20 calendar days of the court hearing, the party ordered to prepare the proposed order must submit the proposed order to the court without approval within 25 calendar days of the hearing date. The correspondence to the court and to the other party must include:

(A) The date the proposed order was served on the other party;

(B) The other party's reasons for not approving the proposed order, if known;

(C) The date and results of any attempts to meet and confer, if relevant; and

(D) A request that the court sign the proposed order.

(d) Failure to prepare proposed order after hearing

(1) If the party ordered by the court to prepare the proposed order fails to serve the proposed order to the other party within 10 calendar days from the court hearing, the other party may prepare the proposed order and serve it to the party or attorney whom the court ordered to prepare the proposed order.

(2) Within 5 calendar days from service of the proposed order, the party who had been ordered to prepare the order must review the proposed order to determine if it accurately reflects the orders made by the court and take one of the following actions:

(A) Approve the proposed order by signing and serving it to the party or attorney who drafted the proposed order; or

(B) State any objections to the proposed order and prepare an alternate proposed order. Any alternate proposed order by the objecting party must list the findings and orders in the same sequence as the proposed order. After serving any objections and the alternate proposed order to the other party or attorney, both parties must follow the procedure in (e).

(3) If the party does not respond as described in (2), the party who prepared the proposed order must submit the proposed order to the court without approval within 5 calendar days. The cover letter to the court and to the other party or attorney must include:

(A) The facts relating to the preparation of the order, including the date the proposed order was due and the date the proposed order was served to the party whom the court ordered to draft the proposed order;

(B) The party's reasons for not preparing or approving the proposed order, if known;

(C) The date and results of any attempts to meet and confer, if relevant; and

(D) A request that the court sign the proposed order.

(e) Objections to proposed order after hearing

(1) If a party objects to the proposed order after hearing, both parties have 10 calendar days following service of the objections and the alternate proposed order after hearing to meet and confer by telephone or in person to attempt to resolve the disputed language.

(2) If the parties reach an agreement, the proposed findings and order after hearing must be submitted to the court within 10 calendar days following the meeting.

(3) If the parties fail to resolve their disagreement after meeting and conferring, each party will have 10 calendar days following the date of the meeting to submit to the court and serve on each other the following documents:

(A) A proposed *Findings and Order After Hearing* (FL-340) (and any form attachments);

(B) A copy of the minute order or official transcript of the court hearing; and

(C) A cover letter that explains the objections, describes the differences in the two proposed orders, references the relevant sections of the transcript or minute order, and includes the date and results of the meet-and-confer conferences.

(f) Unapproved order signed by the court; requirements

Before signing a proposed order submitted to the court without the other party's approval, the court must first compare the proposed order after hearing to the minute order; official transcript, if available; or other court record.

(g) Service of order after hearing signed by the court

After the proposed order is signed by the court, the court clerk must file the order. The party who prepared the order must serve an endorsed-filed copy to the other party.

Rule 5.125 adopted effective January 1, 2013.

Rule 5.126. Alternate date of valuation [Repealed]

Rule 5.126 repealed effective January 1, 2013; adopted as rule 1242.5 effective July 1, 1995; previously amended and renumbered effective January 1, 2003; previously amended effective July 1, 2003.

Rule 5.128. Financial declaration [Repealed]

Rule 5.128 repealed effective January 1, 2013; adopted as rule 1243 effective January 1, 1970; previously amended effective January 1, 1972, January 1, 1980, July 1, 1985, and January 1, 1999; previously amended and renumbered effective January 1, 2003.

Article 6
Special Immigrant Juvenile Findings

Title 5, Family and Juvenile Rules—Division 1, Family Rules—Chapter 6, Request for Court Orders—Article 6, Special Immigrant Juvenile Findings; adopted effective July 1, 2016.

Rule 5.130. Request for Special Immigrant Juvenile findings

(a) Application

This rule applies to a request by or on behalf of a minor child who is a party or the child of a party in a proceeding under the Family Code for the judicial findings needed as a basis for filing a federal petition for classification as a Special Immigrant Juvenile (SIJ). This rule also applies to an opposition to such a request, a hearing on such a request or opposition, and judicial findings in response to such a request.

(Subd (a) adopted effective July 1, 2016.)

(b) Request for findings

Unless otherwise required by law or this rule, the rules in this chapter governing a request for court orders in family law proceedings also apply to a request for SIJ findings in those proceedings.

(1) *Who may file*

Any person—including the child's parent, the child if authorized by statute, the child's guardian ad litem, or an attorney appointed to represent the child—authorized by the Family Code to file a petition, response, request for order, or responsive declaration to a request for order in a proceeding to determine custody of a child may file a request for SIJ findings with respect to that child.

(2) *Form of request*

A request for SIJ findings must be made using *Confidential Request for Special Immigrant Juvenile Findings—Family Law* (form FL-356). The completed form may be filed in any proceeding under the Family Code in which a party is requesting sole physical custody of the child who is the subject of the requested findings:

(A) At the same time as, or any time after, the petition or response;

(B) At the same time as, or any time after, a *Request for Order* (form FL-300) or a *Responsive Declaration to Request for Order* (form FL-320) requesting sole physical custody of the child; or

(C) In an initial action under the Domestic Violence Prevention Act, at the same time as, or any time after, a *Request for Domestic Violence Restraining Order (Domestic Violence Prevention)* (form DV-100) or *Response to Request for Domestic Violence Restraining Order (Domestic Violence Prevention)* (form DV-120) requesting sole physical custody of the child.

(3) *Separate filing*

A request on form FL-356 filed at the same time as any of the papers in (A), (B), or (C) must be filed separately from, and not as an attachment to, that paper.

(4) *Separate form for each child*

A separate form FL-356 must be filed for each child for whom SIJ findings are requested.

(Subd (b) adopted effective July 1, 2016.)

(c) Notice of hearing

Notice of a hearing on a request for SIJ findings must be served with a copy of the request and all supporting papers in the appropriate manner specified in rule 5.92(f)(1), (2) or (3), as applicable, on the following persons:

(1) All parties to the underlying family law case;

(2) All alleged, biological, and presumed parents of the child who is the subject of the request; and

(3) Any other person who has physical custody or is likely to claim a right to physical custody of the child who is the subject of the request.

(Subd (c) amended effective September 1, 2017; adopted effective July 1, 2016.)

(d) Response to request

Any person entitled under (c) to notice of a request for SIJ findings with respect to a child may file and serve a response to such a request using *Confidential Response to Request for Special Immigrant Juvenile Findings* (form FL-358).

(Subd (d) adopted effective July 1, 2016.)

(e) Hearing on request

To obtain a hearing on a request for SIJ findings, a person must file and serve a *Confidential Request for Special Immigrant Juvenile Findings—*

Family Law (form FL-356) for each child who is the subject of such a request.

(1) A request for SIJ findings and a request for an order of sole physical custody of the same child may be heard and determined together.

(2) The court may consolidate into one hearing separate requests for SIJ findings for more than one sibling or half sibling named in the same family law case or in separate family law cases.

(3) If custody proceedings relating to siblings or half siblings are pending in multiple departments of a single court or in the courts of more than one California county, the departments or courts may communicate about consolidation consistent with the procedures and limits in Family Code section 3410(b)–(e).

(Subd (e) adopted effective July 1, 2016.)

(f) Separate findings for each child

The court must make separate SIJ findings with respect to each child for whom a request is made, and the clerk must issue a separate *Special Immigrant Juvenile Findings* (form FL-357) for each child with respect to whom the court makes SIJ findings.

(Subd (f) adopted effective July 1, 2016.)

(g) Confidentiality (Code Civ. Proc., § 155(c))

The forms *Confidential Request for Special Immigrant Juvenile Findings—Family Law* (form FL-356), *Confidential Response to Request for Special Immigrant Juvenile Findings* (form FL-358), and *Special Immigrant Juvenile Findings* (form FL-357) must be kept in a confidential part of the case file or, alternatively, in a separate, confidential file. Any information regarding the child's immigration status contained in a record related to a request for SIJ findings kept in the public part of the file must be redacted to prevent its inspection by any person not authorized under Code of Civil Procedure section 155(c).

(Subd (g) adopted effective July 1, 2016.)

Rule 5.130 amended effective September 1, 2017; adopted effective July 1, 2016.

Rule 5.134. Notice of entry of judgment [Repealed]

Rule 5.134 repealed effective January 1, 2013; adopted as rule 1247 effective January 1, 1970; previously amended effective January 1, 1972, January 1, 1982, and January 1, 1999; previously amended and renumbered effective January 1, 2003; previously amended effective January 1, 2007.

Rule 5.136. Completion of notice of entry of judgment [Repealed]

Rule 5.136 repealed effective January 1, 2013; adopted as rule 1248 effective January 1, 1970; previously amended effective January 1, 1972, January 1, 1980, July 1, 1982, and January 1, 1999; previously amended and renumbered effective January 1, 2003; previously amended effective January 1, 2007.

Rule 5.140. Implied procedures [Repealed]

Rule 5.140 repealed effective January 1, 2013; adopted as rule 1249 effective January 1, 1970; previously amended effective January 1, 1994; previously amended and renumbered effective January 1, 2003.

Rule 5.146. Judgment checklists [Renumbered]

Rule 5.146 renumbered as rule 5.405 effective January 1, 2013; adopted effective July 1, 2012.

Rule 5.147. Review of judgments based on default and uncontested judgments submitted by declaration under Family Code section 2336 [Renumbered]

Rule 5.147 renumbered as rule 5.407 effective January 1, 2013; adopted effective July 1, 2012.

Rule 5.148. Default and uncontested hearings on judgments submitted on the basis of declarations under Family Code section 2336 [Renumbered]

Rule 5.148 renumbered as rule 5.409 effective January 1, 2013; adopted effective July 1, 2012.

Rule 5.150. Joinder of persons claiming interest [Repealed]

Rule 5.150 repealed effective January 1, 2013; adopted as rule 1250 effective November 23, 1970; previously amended effective January 1, 1978; previously renumbered effective January 1, 2003.

Chapter 7
Request for Emergency Orders (Ex Parte Orders)

Title 5, Family and Juvenile Rules—Division 1, Family Rules—Chapter 7, Request for Emergency Orders (Ex Parte Orders); adopted effective January 1, 2013.

Art. 1. Request for Emergency Orders (Ex Parte Orders). Rule 5.151.
Art. 2. Notice, Service, Appearance. Rules 5.165–5.169.
Art. 3. Procedural Matters Not Requiring Notice (Non-Emergency Orders). Rule 5.170.

Article 1
Request for Emergency Orders (Ex Parte Orders)

Title 5, Family and Juvenile Rules—Division 1, Family Rules—Chapter 7, Request for Emergency Orders (Ex Parte Orders)—Article 1, Request for Emergency Orders (Ex Parte Orders); adopted effective January 1, 2013.

Rule 5.151. Request for temporary emergency (ex parte) orders; application; required documents

(a) Application

The rules in this chapter govern applications for emergency orders (also known as ex parte applications) in family law cases, unless otherwise provided by statute or rule. These rules may be referred to as "the emergency orders rules." Unless specifically stated, these rules do not apply to ex parte applications for domestic violence restraining orders under the Domestic Violence Prevention Act.

(Subd (a) adopted effective January 1, 2013.)

(b) Purpose

The purpose of a request for emergency orders is to address matters that cannot be heard on the court's regular hearing calendar. In this type of proceeding, notice to the other party is shorter than in other proceedings. Notice to the other party can also be waived under exceptional and other circumstances as provided in these rules. The process is used to request that the court:

(1) Make orders to help prevent an immediate danger or irreparable harm to a party or to the children involved in the matter;

(2) Make orders to help prevent immediate loss or damage to property subject to disposition in the case; or

(3) Make orders about procedural matters, including the following:

(A) Setting a date for a hearing on the matter that is sooner than that of a regular hearing (granting an order shortening time for hearing);

(B) Shortening or extending the time required for the moving party to serve the other party with the notice of the hearing and supporting papers (grant an order shortening time for service); and

(C) Rescheduling a hearing or trial.

(Subd (b) amended effective July 1, 2020; adopted effective January 1, 2013.)

(c) Required documents

(1) *Request for order*

A request for emergency orders must be in writing and must include all of the following completed documents:

(A) *Request for Order* (form FL-300) that identifies the relief requested.

(B) When relevant to the relief requested, a current *Income and Expense Declaration* (form FL-150) or *Financial Statement (Simplified)* (form FL-155) and *Property Declaration* (form FL-160).

(C) *Temporary Emergency (Ex Parte) Orders* (form FL-305) to serve as the proposed temporary order.

(D) A written declaration regarding notice of application for emergency orders based on personal knowledge. *Declaration Regarding Notice and Service of Request for Temporary Emergency (Ex Parte) Orders* (form FL-303), a local court form, or a declaration that contains the same information as form FL-303 may be used for this purpose.

(E) A memorandum of points and authorities only if required by the court.

(2) *Request to reschedule hearing*

A request to reschedule a hearing must comply with the requirements of rule 5.95.

(Subd (c) amended effective July 1, 2020; adopted effective January 1, 2013; previously amended effective July 1, 2016.)

(d) Contents of application and declaration

(1) *Identification of attorney or party*

An application for emergency orders must state the name, address, and telephone number of any attorney known to the applicant to be an attorney for any party or, if no such attorney is known, the name, address, and telephone number of the party, if known to the applicant.

(2) *Affirmative factual showing required in written declarations*

The declarations must contain facts within the personal knowledge of the declarant that demonstrate why the matter is appropriately handled as an emergency hearing, as opposed to being on the court's regular hearing calendar.

An applicant must make an affirmative factual showing of irreparable harm, immediate danger, or any other statutory basis for granting relief without notice or with shortened notice to the other party.

(3) *Disclosure of previous applications and orders*

An applicant should submit a declaration that fully discloses all previous applications made on the same issue and whether any orders were made on any of the applications, even if an application was previously made upon a different state of facts. Previous applications include an order to shorten time for service of notice or an order shortening time for hearing.

(4) *Disclosure of change in status quo*

The applicant has a duty to disclose that an emergency order will result in a change in the current situation or status quo. Absent such disclosure, attorney's fees and costs incurred to reinstate the status quo may be awarded.

(5) *Applications regarding child custody or visitation (parenting time)*

Applications for emergency orders involving child custody or visitation (parenting time) under Family Code section 3064 must:

(A) Provide a full, detailed description of the most recent incidents showing:

(i) Immediate harm to the child as defined in Family Code section 3064(b); or

(ii) Immediate risk that the child will be removed from the state of California.

(B) Specify the date of each incident described in (A);

(C) Advise the court of the existing custody and visitation (parenting time) arrangements and how they would be changed by the request for emergency orders;

(D) Include a copy of the current custody orders, if they are available. If no orders exist, explain where and with whom the child is currently living; and

(E) Include a completed *Declaration Under Uniform Child Custody Jurisdiction and Enforcement Act (UCCJEA)* (FL-105) if the form was not already filed by a party or if the information has changed since it was filed.

(6) *Applications for child custody or visitation (parenting time) when child is in the state for gender-affirming health care or gender-affirming mental health care*

Notwithstanding the requirements in Family Code section 3064, when a child is in the state for the purpose of obtaining gender-affirming health care or gender-affirming mental health care, applications for emergency orders for child custody or visitation (parenting time) under Family Code sections 3427, 3428, and 3453.5 must:

(A) Be filed with, or after filing, either:

(i) A petition appropriate for the case type (for example, a petition for dissolution of marriage or legal separation, a petition to determine parental relationship, or a petition for custody and support); or

(ii) *Registration of Out-of-State Custody Order* (form FL-580) if there is a previous custody determination in another state and the party does not intend to file a petition under (i).

(B) Include the documents listed in (c) of this rule.

(C) Include the information specified in (d)(5)(C)–(E) of this rule.

(Subd (d) amended effective January 1, 2024; adopted effective January 1, 2013.)

(e) **Contents of notice and declaration regarding notice of emergency hearing**

(1) *Contents of notice*

When notice of a request for emergency orders is given, the person giving notice must:

(A) State with specificity the nature of the relief to be requested;

(B) State the date, time, and place for the presentation of the application;

(C) State the date, time, and place of the hearing, if applicable; and

(D) Attempt to determine whether the opposing party will appear to oppose the application (if the court requires a hearing) or whether the opposing party will submit responsive pleadings before the court rules on the request for emergency orders.

(2) *Declaration regarding notice*

An application for emergency orders must be accompanied by a completed declaration regarding notice that includes one of the following statements:

(A) The notice given, including the date, time, manner, and name of the party informed, the relief sought, any response, and whether opposition is expected and that, within the applicable time under rule 5.165, the applicant informed the opposing party where and when the application would be made;

(B) That the applicant in good faith attempted to inform the opposing party but was unable to do so, specifying the efforts made to inform the opposing party; or

(C) That, for reasons specified, the applicant should not be required to inform the opposing party.

(Subd (e) amended effective January 1, 2024; adopted effective January 1, 2013.)

Rule 5.151 amended effective January 1, 2024; adopted effective January 1, 2013; previously amended effective July 1, 2016, and July 1, 2020.

Advisory Committee Comment

Applications for child custody or visitation (parenting time), including applications involving a child who is present in this state to obtain gender-affirming health care or gender-affirming mental health care under Family Code sections 3427, 3428, and 3453.5, may also be requested under the Domestic Violence Prevention Act (DVPA) (Fam. Code, §§ 6200–6460). Different forms and procedures apply to DVPA cases.

Rule 5.152. "Claimant" defined [Repealed]

Rule 5.152 repealed effective January 1, 2013; adopted as rule 1251 effective November 23, 1970; previously amended effective January 1, 1972; previously renumbered effective January 1, 2003.

Rule 5.154. Persons who may seek joinder [Repealed]

Rule 5.154 repealed effective January 1, 2013; adopted as rule 1252 effective November 23, 1970; previously amended and renumbered effective January 1, 2003; previously amended effective July 1, 1975, January 1, 2006, and January 1, 2007.

Rule 5.156. Form of joinder application [Repealed]

Rule 5.156 repealed effective January 1, 2013; adopted as rule 1253 effective November 23, 1970; previously amended effective January 1, 1972, January 1, 1978, January 1, 1979, July 1, 1985, January 1, 1994, and January 1, 2001; previously amended and renumbered effective January 1, 2003; previously amended effective January 1, 2007.

Rule 5.158. Determination on joinder [Repealed]

Rule 5.158 repealed effective January 1, 2013; adopted as rule 1254 effective November 23, 1970; previously amended effective July 1, 1997; previously amended and renumbered effective January 1, 2003; previously amended effective July 1, 2003, and January 1, 2007.

Rule 5.160. Pleading rules applicable [Repealed]

Rule 5.160 repealed effective January 1, 2013; adopted as rule 1255 effective November 23, 1970; previously amended and renumbered effective January 1, 2003.

Rule 5.162. Joinder of employee pension benefit plan [Repealed]

Rule 5.162 repealed effective January 1, 2013; adopted as rule 1256 effective January 1, 1979; previously amended effective January 1, 1994; previously amended and renumbered effective January 1, 2003; previously amended effective January 1, 2007.

Article 2
Notice, Service, Appearance

Title 5, Family and Juvenile Rules—Division 1, Family Rules—Chapter 7, Request for Emergency Orders (Ex Parte Orders)—Article 2, Notice, Service, Appearance; adopted effective January 1, 2013.

Rule 5.165. Requirements for notice
Rule 5.167. Service of application; temporary restraining orders
Rule 5.169. Personal appearance at hearing for temporary emergency orders

Rule 5.165. Requirements for notice

(a) **Method of notice**

Notice of appearance at a hearing to request emergency orders may be given personally or by telephone, voicemail, fax transmission, electronic means (if permitted), overnight mail, or other overnight carrier.

(Subd (a) amended effective July 1, 2020; adopted effective January 1, 2013.)

(b) **Notice to parties**

A party seeking emergency orders under this chapter must give notice to all parties or their attorneys so that it is received no later than 10:00 a.m. on the court day before the matter is to be considered by the court. After providing notice, each party must be served with the documents requesting emergency orders as described in rule 5.167 or as required by local rule. This rule does not apply to a party seeking emergency orders under the Domestic Violence Prevention Act.

(1) *Explanation for shorter notice*

If a party provided notice of the request for emergency orders to all parties and their attorneys later than 10:00 a.m. the court day before the appearance, the party must request in a declaration regarding notice that the court approve the shortened notice. The party must provide facts in the declaration that show exceptional circumstances that justify the shorter notice.

(2) *Explanation for waiver of notice (no notice)*

A party may ask the court to waive notice to all parties and their attorneys of the request for emergency orders. To make the request, the party must file a written declaration signed under penalty of perjury that includes facts showing good cause not to give the notice. A judicial officer may approve a waiver of notice for good cause, which may include that:

(A) Giving notice would frustrate the purpose of the order;

(B) Giving notice would result in immediate and irreparable harm to the applicant or the children who may be affected by the order sought;

(C) Giving notice would result in immediate and irreparable damage to or loss of property subject to disposition in the case;

(D) The parties agreed in advance that notice will not be necessary with respect to the matter that is the subject of the request for emergency orders; and

(E) The party made reasonable and good faith efforts to give notice to the other party, and further efforts to give notice would probably be futile or unduly burdensome.

(Subd (b) adopted effective January 1, 2013.)

(c) Notice to the court

The court may adopt a local rule requiring that the party provide additional notice to the court that he or she will be requesting emergency orders the next court day. The local rule must include a method by which the party may give notice to the court by telephone.

(Subd (c) adopted effective January 1, 2013.)

Rule 5.165 amended effective July 1, 2020; adopted effective January 1, 2013.

Rule 5.167. Service of application; temporary restraining orders

(a) Service of documents requesting emergency orders

A party seeking emergency orders and a party providing written opposition must serve the papers on the other party or on the other party's attorney at the first reasonable opportunity before the hearing. Absent exceptional circumstances, no hearing may be conducted unless such service has been made. The court may waive this requirement in extraordinary circumstances if good cause is shown that imminent harm is likely if documents are provided to the other party before the hearing. This rule does not apply in cases filed under the Domestic Violence Prevention Act.

(Subd (a) adopted effective January 1, 2013.)

(b) Service of temporary emergency orders

If the judicial officer signs the applicant's proposed emergency orders, the applicant must obtain and have the conformed copy of the orders personally served on all parties.

(Subd (b) adopted effective January 1, 2013.)

Rule 5.167 adopted effective January 1, 2013.

Rule 5.169. Personal appearance at hearing for temporary emergency orders

Courts may require all parties to appear at a hearing before ruling on a request for emergency orders. Courts may also make emergency orders based on the documents submitted without requiring the parties to appear at a hearing.

Rule 5.169 adopted effective January 1, 2013.

Article 3
Procedural Matters Not Requiring Notice (Non-Emergency Orders)

Title 5, Family and Juvenile Rules—Division 1, Family Rules—Chapter 7, Request for Emergency Orders (Ex Parte Orders)—Article 3, Procedural Matters Not Requiring Notice (Non-Emergency Orders); adopted effective January 1, 2013.

Rule 5.170. Matters not requiring notice to other parties

The courts may consider a party's request for order on the following issues without notice to the other parties or personal appearance at a hearing:

(1) Applications to restore a former name after judgment;

(2) Stipulations by the parties;

(3) An order or judgment after a default court hearing;

(4) An earnings assignment order based on an existing support order;

(5) An order for service of summons by publication or posting;

(6) An order or judgment that the other party or opposing counsel approved or agreed not to oppose; and

(7) Application for an order waiving filing fees.

Rule 5.170 adopted effective January 1, 2013.

Rule 5.175. Bifurcation of issues [Repealed]

Rule 5.175 repealed effective January 1, 2013; adopted as rule 1269 effective July 1, 1989; previously amended effective January 1, 1994; previously amended and renumbered effective January 1, 2003; previously amended effective July 1, 2009.

Rule 5.180. Interlocutory appeals [Renumbered]

Rule 5.180 renumbered as rule 5.392 effective January 1, 2013; adopted as rule 1269.5 effective July 1, 1989; previously amended effective January 1, 1994, and January 1, 2002; amended and renumbered effective January 1, 2003; previously amended effective January 1, 2007.

Chapter 8
Child Custody and Visitation (Parenting Time) Proceedings

Title 5, Family and Juvenile Rules—Division 1, Family Rules—Chapter 8, Child Custody and Visitation (Parenting Time) Proceedings; adopted effective January 1, 2013.

Art. 1. Child Custody Mediation. Rules 5.210, 5.215.
Art. 2. Child Custody Investigations and Evaluations. Rules 5.220–5.230.
Art. 3. Ex parte Communication. Rule 5.235.
Art. 4. Counsel Appointed to Represent a Child. Rules 5.240–5.242.
Art. 5. Children's Participation in Family Court. Rule 5.250.

Article 1
Child Custody Mediation

Title 5, Family and Juvenile Rules—Division 1, Family Rules—Chapter 8, Child Custody and Visitation (Parenting Time) Proceedings—Article 1, Child Custody Mediation; adopted effective January 1, 2013.

Rule 5.210. Court-connected child custody mediation
Rule 5.215. Domestic violence protocol for Family Court Services

Rule 5.210. Court-connected child custody mediation

(a) Authority

This rule of court is adopted under article VI, section 6 of the California Constitution and Family Code sections 211, 3160, and 3162(a).

(b) Purpose

This rule sets forth standards of practice and administration for court-connected child custody mediation services that are consistent with the requirements of Family Code section 3161.

(c) Definitions

(1) "Best interest of the child" is defined in Family Code section 3011.

(2) "Parenting plan" is a plan describing how parents or other appropriate parties will share and divide their decision making and caretaking responsibilities to protect the health, safety, welfare, and best interest of each child who is a subject of the proceedings.

(d) Responsibility for mediation services

(1) Each court must ensure that:

(A) Mediators are impartial, competent, and uphold the standards of practice contained in this rule of court.

(B) Mediation services and case management procedures implement state law and allow sufficient time for parties to receive orientation, participate fully in mediation, and develop a comprehensive parenting plan without unduly compromising each party's right to due process and a timely resolution of the issues.

(C) Mediation services demonstrate accountability by:

(i) Providing for acceptance of and response to complaints about a mediator's performance;

(ii) Participating in statewide data collection efforts; and

(iii) Disclosing the use of interns to provide mediation services.

(D) The mediation program uses a detailed intake process that screens for, and informs the mediator about, any restraining orders or safety-related issues affecting any party or child named in the proceedings to allow compliance with relevant law or court rules before mediation begins.

(E) Whenever possible, mediation is available from bilingual mediators or other interpreter services that meet the requirements of Evidence Code sections 754(f) and 755(a) and section 18 of the California Standards of Judicial Administration.

(F) Mediation services protect, in accordance with existing law, party confidentiality in:

(i) Storage and disposal of records and any personal information accumulated during the mediation process;

(ii) Interagency coordination or cooperation regarding a particular family or case; and

(iii) Management of child abuse reports and related documents.

(G) Mediation services provide a written description of limitations on the confidentiality of the process.

(H) Within one year of the adoption of this rule, the court adopts a local court rule regarding ex parte communications.

(2) Each court-connected mediator must:

(A) Maintain an overriding concern to integrate the child's best interest within the family context;

(B) Inform the parties and any counsel for a minor child if the mediator will make a recommendation to the court as provided under Family Code section 3184; and

(C) Use reasonable efforts and consider safety issues to:

(i) Facilitate the family's transition and reduce acrimony by helping the parties improve their communication skills, focus on the child's needs and areas of stability, identify the family's strengths, and locate counseling or other services;

(ii) Develop a comprehensive parenting agreement that addresses each child's current and future developmental needs; and

(iii) Control for potential power imbalances between the parties during mediation.

(3) If so informed by the child at any point, each child custody recommending counselor must notify the parties, other professionals serving on the case, and then the judicial officer:

(A) About the child's desire to provide input and address the court; and

(B) As soon as feasible, that the child has changed their choice about addressing the court.

(Subd (d) amended effective January 1, 2023; previously amended effective January 1, 2002, January 1, 2003, and January 1, 2007.)

(e) Mediation process

All court-connected mediation processes must be conducted in accordance with state law and include:

(1) Review of the intake form and court file, if available, before the start of mediation;

(2) Oral or written orientation or parent education that facilitates the parties' informed and self-determined decision making about:

(A) The types of disputed issues generally discussed in mediation and the range of possible outcomes from the mediation process;

(B) The mediation process, including the mediator's role; the circumstances that may lead the mediator to make a particular recommendation to the court; limitations on the confidentiality of the process; and access to information communicated by the parties or included in the mediation file;

(C) How to make best use of information drawn from current research and professional experience to facilitate the mediation process, parties' communication, and co-parenting relationship; and

(D) How to address each child's current and future developmental needs;

(3) Interviews with children at the mediator's discretion and consistent with Family Code section 3180(a). The mediator may interview the child alone or together with other interested parties, including stepparents, siblings, new or step-siblings, or other family members significant to the child. If interviewing a child, the mediator must:

(A) Inform the child in an age-appropriate way of the mediator's obligation to disclose suspected child abuse and neglect and the local policies concerning disclosure of the child's statements to the court; and

(B) With parental consent, coordinate interview and information exchange among agency or private professionals to reduce the number of interviews a child might experience;

(4) Assistance to the parties, without undue influence or personal bias, in developing a parenting plan that protects the health, safety, welfare, and best interest of the child and that optimizes the child's relationship with each party by including, as appropriate, provisions for supervised visitation in high-risk cases; designations for legal and physical custody; a description of each party's authority to make decisions that affect the child; language that minimizes legal, mental health, or other jargon; and a detailed schedule of the time a child is to spend with each party, including vacations, holidays, and special occasions, and times when the child's contact with a party may be interrupted;

(5) Extension of time to allow the parties to gather additional information if the mediator determines that such information will help the discussion proceed in a fair and orderly manner or facilitate an agreement;

(6) Suspension or discontinuance of mediation if allegations of child abuse or neglect are made until a designated agency performs an investigation and reports a case determination to the mediator;

(7) Termination of mediation if the mediator believes that he or she is unable to achieve a balanced discussion between the parties;

(8) Conclusion of mediation with:

(A) A written parenting plan summarizing the parties' agreement or mediator's recommendation that is given to counsel or the parties before the recommendation is presented to the court; and

(B) A written or oral description of any subsequent case management or court procedures for resolving one or more outstanding custody or visitation issues, including instructions for obtaining temporary orders;

(9) Return to mediation to resolve future custody or visitation disputes.

(Subd (e) amended effective January 1, 2007; previously amended effective January 1, 2003.)

(f) Training, continuing education, and experience requirements for mediator, mediation supervisor, and family court services director

As specified in Family Code sections 1815 and 1816:

(1) All mediators, mediation supervisors, and family court service directors must:

(A) Complete a minimum of 40 hours of custody and visitation mediation training within the first six months of initial employment as a court-connected mediator;

(B) Annually complete 8 hours of related continuing education programs, conferences, and workshops. This requirement is in addition to the annual 4-hour domestic violence update training described in rule 5.215; and

(C) Participate in performance supervision and peer review.

(2) Each mediation supervisor and family court services director must complete at least 24 hours of additional training each calendar year. This requirement may be satisfied in part by the domestic violence training required by Family Code section 1816.

(Subd (f) amended effective January 1, 2005; previously amended effective January 1, 2003.)

(g) Education and training providers

Only education and training acquired from eligible providers meet the requirements of this rule. "Eligible providers" includes the Judicial Council and may include educational institutions, professional associations, professional continuing education groups, public or private for-profit or not-for-profit groups, and court-connected groups.

(1) Eligible providers must:

(A) Ensure that the training instructors or consultants delivering the education and training programs either meet the requirements of this rule or are experts in the subject matter;

(B) Monitor and evaluate the quality of courses, curricula, training, instructors, and consultants;

(C) Emphasize the importance of focusing child custody mediations on the health, safety, welfare, and best interest of the child;

(D) Develop a procedure to verify that participants complete the education and training program; and

(E) Distribute a certificate of completion to each person who has completed the training. The certificate must document the number of hours of training offered, the number of hours the person completed, the dates of the training, and the name of the training provider.

(2) Effective July 1, 2005, all education and training programs must be approved by Judicial Council staff in consultation with the Family and Juvenile Law Advisory Committee.

(Subd (g) amended effective January 1, 2016; adopted effective January 1, 2005.)

(h) Ethics

Mediation must be conducted in an atmosphere that encourages trust in the process and a perception of fairness. To that end, mediators must:

(1) Meet the practice and ethical standards of the Code of Ethics for the Court Employees of California and of related law;

(2) Maintain objectivity, provide and gather balanced information for both parties, and control for bias;

(3) Protect the confidentiality of the parties and the child in making any collateral contacts and not release information about the case to any individual except as authorized by the court or statute;

(4) Not offer any recommendations about a party unless that party has been evaluated directly or in consultation with another qualified neutral professional;

(5) Consider the health, safety, welfare, and best interest of the child in all phases of the process, including interviews with parents, extended family members, counsel for the child, and other interested parties or collateral contacts;

(6) Strive to maintain the confidential relationship between the child who is the subject of an evaluation and his or her treating psychotherapist;

(7) Operate within the limits of his or her training and experience and disclose any limitations or bias that would affect his or her ability to conduct the mediation;

(8) Not require children to state a custodial preference;

(9) Not disclose any recommendations to the parties, their attorneys, or the attorney for the child before having gathered the information necessary to support the conclusion;

(10) Disclose to the court, parties, attorneys for the parties, and attorney for the child conflicts of interest or dual relationships and not accept any appointment except by court order or the parties' stipulation;

(11) Be sensitive to the parties' socioeconomic status, gender, race, ethnicity, cultural values, religion, family structures, and developmental characteristics; and

(12) Disclose any actual or potential conflicts of interest. In the event of a conflict of interest, the mediator must suspend mediation and meet and confer in an effort to resolve the conflict of interest to the satisfaction of all parties or according to local court rules. The court may order mediation to continue with another mediator or offer the parties alternatives. The mediator cannot continue unless the parties agree in writing to continue mediation despite the disclosed conflict of interest.

(Subd (h) amended effective January 1, 2007; adopted as subd (g) effective July 1, 2001; previously amended effective January 1, 2003; previously relettered effective January 1, 2005.)

Rule 5.210 amended effective January 1, 2023; adopted as rule 1257.1 effective July 1, 2001; amended and renumbered as rule 5.210 effective January 1, 2003; previously amended effective January 1, 2003, January 1, 2005, January 1, 2007, and January 1, 2016.

Rule 5.215. Domestic violence protocol for Family Court Services

(a) Authority

This rule of court is adopted under Family Code sections 211, 1850(a), and 3170(b).

(Subd (a) amended effective January 1, 2007.)

(b) Purpose

This rule sets forth the protocol for Family Court Services' handling of domestic violence cases consistent with the requirement of Family Code section 3170(b).

(c) Definitions

(1) "Domestic violence" is used as defined in Family Code sections 6203 and 6211.

(2) "Protective order" is used as defined in Family Code section 6215, "Emergency protective order"; Family Code section 6218, "Protective order"; and Penal Code section 136.2 (orders by court). "Domestic violence restraining order" is synonymous with "protective order."

(3) "Mediation" refers to proceedings described in Family Code section 3161.

(4) "Evaluation" and "investigation" are synonymous terms.

(5) "Family Court Services" refers to court-connected child custody services and child custody mediation made available by superior courts under Family Code section 3160.

(6) "Family Court Services staff" refers to contract and employee mediators, evaluators, investigators, and counselors who provide services on behalf of Family Court Services.

(7) "Differential domestic violence assessment" is a process used to assess the nature of any domestic violence issues in the family so that Family Court Services may provide services in such a way as to protect any victim of domestic violence from intimidation, provide services for perpetrators, and correct for power imbalances created by past and prospective violence.

(Subd (c) amended effective January 1, 2003.)

(d) Family Court Services: Description and duties

(1) *Local protocols*

Family Court Services must handle domestic violence cases in accordance with pertinent state laws and all applicable rules of court and must develop local protocols in accordance with this rule.

(2) *Family Court Services duties relative to domestic violence cases*

Family Court Services is a court-connected service that must:

(A) Identify cases in Family Court Services that involve domestic violence, and code Family Court Services files to identify such cases;

(B) Make reasonable efforts to ensure the safety of victims, children, and other parties when they are participating in services provided by Family Court Services;

(C) Make appropriate referrals; and

(D) Conduct a differential domestic violence assessment in domestic violence cases and offer appropriate services as available, such as child custody evaluation, parent education, parent orientation, supervised visitation, child custody mediation, relevant education programs for children, and other services as determined by each superior court.

(3) *No negotiation of violence*

Family Court Services staff must not negotiate with the parties about using violence with each other, whether either party should or should not obtain or dismiss a restraining order, or whether either party should cooperate with criminal prosecution.

(4) *Domestic violence restraining orders*

Notwithstanding the above, to the extent permitted under Family Code section 3183(c), in appropriate cases, Family Court Services staff may recommend that restraining orders be issued, pending determination of the controversy, to protect the well-being of the child involved in the controversy.

(5) *Providing information*

Family Court Services staff must provide information to families accessing their services about the effects of domestic violence on adults and children. Family Court Services programs, including but not limited to orientation programs, must provide information and materials that describe Family Court Services policy and procedures with respect to domestic violence. Whenever possible, information delivered in video or audiovisual format should be closed-captioned.

(6) *Separate sessions*

In a Family Court Services case in which there has been a history of domestic violence between the parties or in which a protective order as defined in Family Code section 6218 is in effect, at the request of the party who is alleging domestic violence in a written declaration under penalty of perjury or who is protected by the order, the Family Court Services mediator, counselor, evaluator, or investigator must meet with the parties separately and at separate times. When appropriate, arrangements for separate sessions must protect the confidentiality of each party's times of arrival, departure, and meeting with Family Court Services. Family Court Services must provide information to the parties regarding their options for separate sessions under Family Code sections 3113 and 3181. If domestic violence is discovered after mediation or evaluation has begun, the Family Court Services staff member assigned to the case must confer with the parties separately regarding safety-related issues and the option of continuing in separate sessions at separate times. Family Court Services staff, including support staff, must not respond to a party's request for separate sessions as though it were evidence of his or her lack of cooperation with the Family Court Services process.

(7) *Referrals*

Family Court Services staff, where applicable, must refer family members to appropriate services. Such services may include but are not limited to programs for perpetrators, counseling and education for children, parent education, services for victims, and legal resources, such as family law facilitators.

(8) *Community resources*

Family Court Services should maintain a liaison with community-based services offering domestic violence prevention assistance and support so that referrals can be made based on an understanding of available services and service providers.

(Subd (d) amended effective January 1, 2016; previously amended effective January 1, 2003.)

(e) Intake

(1) *Court responsibility*

Each court must ensure that Family Court Services programs use a detailed intake process that screens for, and informs staff about, any restraining orders, dependency petitions under Welfare and Institutions Code section 300, and other safety-related issues affecting any party or child named in the proceedings.

(2) *Intake form*

Any intake form that an agency charged with providing family court services requires the parties to complete before the commencement of mediation or evaluation must state that, if a party alleging domestic violence in a written declaration under penalty of perjury or a party protected by a protective order so requests, the Family Court Services staff must meet with the parties separately and at separate times.

(3) *Review of intake form and case file*

All Family Court Services procedures must be conducted in accordance with state law and must include review of intake forms and court files, when available, by appropriate staff.

(f) Screening

(1) *Identification of domestic violence*

Screening for a history of domestic violence incidents must be done throughout the Family Court Services process. As early in the case as possible, Family Court Services staff should make every effort to identify cases in which incidents of domestic violence are present. The means by which Family Court Services elicits screening information may be determined by each program. Screening techniques may include but are not limited to questionnaires, telephone interviews, standardized screening devices, and face-to-face interviews.

(2) *Procedures for identification*

Procedures for identifying domestic violence may include, but are not limited to: (a) determination of an existing emergency protective order or domestic violence restraining order concerning the parties or minor; (b) review of court papers and declarations; (c) telephone interviews; (d) use of an intake form; (e) orientation; (f) information from attorneys, shelters, hospital reports, Child Protective Services, police reports, and criminal background checks; and (g) other collateral sources. Questions specific to incidents of domestic violence should request the following information: date of the parties' separation, frequency of domestic violence, most recent as well as past incidents of domestic violence, concerns about future domestic violence, identities of children and other individuals present at domestic violence incidents or otherwise exposed to the domestic violence, and severity of domestic violence.

(3) *Context for screening*

In domestic violence cases in which neither party has requested separate sessions at separate times, Family Court Services staff must confer with the parties separately and privately to determine whether joint or separate sessions are appropriate.

(g) Safety issues

(1) *Developing a safety plan*

When domestic violence is identified or alleged in a case, Family Court Services staff must consult with the party alleging domestic violence away from the presence of the party against whom such allegations are made and discuss the existence of or need for a safety plan. Safety planning may include but is not limited to discussion of safe housing, workplace safety, safety for other family members and children, access to financial resources, and information about local domestic violence agencies.

(2) *Safety procedures*

Each Family Court Services office should develop safety procedures for handling domestic violence cases.

(3) *Confidential addresses*

Where appropriate, Family Court Services staff must make reasonable efforts to keep residential addresses, work addresses, and contact information—including but not limited to telephone numbers and e-mail addresses—confidential in all cases and on all Family Court Services documents.

(Subd (g) amended effective January 1, 2007.)

(h) Support persons

(1) *Support person*

Family Court Services staff must advise the party protected by a protective order of the right to have a support person attend any mediation orientation or mediation sessions, including separate mediation sessions, under Family Code section 6303.

(2) *Excluding support person*

A Family Court Services staff person may exclude a domestic violence support person from a mediation session if the support person participates in the mediation session or acts as an advocate or the presence of a particular support person disrupts the process of mediation. The presence of the support person does not waive the confidentiality of the process, and the support person is bound by the confidentiality of the process.

(Subd (h) amended effective January 1, 2003.)

(i) Accessibility of services

To effectively address domestic violence cases, the court must make reasonable efforts to ensure the availability of safe and accessible services that include, but are not limited to:

(1) *Language accessibility*

Whenever possible, Family Court Services programs should be conducted in the languages of all participants, including those who are deaf. When the participants use only a language other than spoken English and the Family Court Services staff person does not speak their language, an interpreter—certified whenever possible—should be assigned to interpret at the session. A minor child of the parties must not be used as an interpreter. An adult family member may act as an interpreter only when appropriate interpreters are not available. When a family member is acting as an interpreter, Family Court Services staff should attempt to establish, away from the presence of the potential interpreter and the other party, whether the person alleging domestic violence is comfortable with having that family member interpret for the parties.

(2) *Facilities design*

To minimize contact between the parties and promote safety in domestic violence cases, courts must give consideration to the design of facilities. Such considerations must include but are not limited to the following: separate and secure waiting areas, separate conference rooms for parent education and mediation, signs providing directions to Family Court Services, and secure parking for users of Family Court Services.

(j) Training and education

(1) *Training, continuing education, and experience requirements for Family Court Services staff*

All Family Court Services staff must participate in programs of continuing instruction in issues related to domestic violence, including child abuse, as may be arranged for and provided to them, under Family Code section 1816(a).

(2) *Advanced domestic violence training*

Family Court Services staff must complete 16 hours of advanced domestic violence training within the first 12 months of employment and 4 hours of domestic violence update training each year thereafter. The content of the 16 hours of advanced domestic violence training and 4 hours of domestic violence update training must be the same as that required for court-appointed child custody investigators and evaluators as stated in rule 5.230. Those staff members employed by Family Court Services on January 1, 2002, who have not already fulfilled the requirements of rule 5.230 must participate in the 16-hour training within one year of the rule's effective date.

(3) *Support staff*

Family Court Services programs should, where possible, enable support staff, including but not limited to clerical staff, to participate in training on domestic violence and in handling domestic violence cases appropriately.

(Subd (j) amended effective January 1, 2003.)

Rule 5.215 amended effective January 1, 2016; adopted as rule 1257.2 effective January 1, 2002; previously amended and renumbered as rule 5.215 effective January 1, 2003; previously amended effective January 1, 2007.

Article 2
Child Custody Investigations and Evaluations

Title 5, Family and Juvenile Rules—Division 1, Family Rules—Chapter 8, Child Custody and Visitation (Parenting Time) Proceedings—Article 2, Child Custody Investigations and Evaluations; adopted effective January 1, 2013.

Rule 5.220. Court-ordered child custody evaluations
Rule 5.225. Appointment requirements for child custody evaluators
Rule 5.230. Domestic violence training standards for court-appointed child custody investigators and evaluators

Rule 5.220. Court-ordered child custody evaluations

(a) Authority

This rule of court is adopted under Family Code sections 211 and 3117.

(Subd (a) amended effective January 1, 2007.)

(b) Purpose

Courts order child custody evaluations, investigations, and assessments to assist them in determining the health, safety, welfare, and best interests of children with regard to disputed custody and visitation issues. This rule governs both court-connected and private child custody evaluators appointed under Family Code section 3111, Family Code section 3118, Evidence Code section 730, or chapter 15 (commencing with section 2032.010) of title 4, part 4 of the Code of Civil Procedure.

(Subd (b) amended effective January 1, 2021; previously amended effective January 1, 2003.)

(c) Definitions

For purposes of this rule:

(1) A "child custody evaluator" is a court-appointed investigator as defined in Family Code section 3110.

(2) The "best interest of the child" is as defined in Family Code section 3011.

(3) A "child custody evaluation" is an expert investigation and analysis of the health, safety, welfare, and best interest of children with regard to disputed custody and visitation issues.

(4) A "full evaluation, investigation, or assessment" is a comprehensive examination of the health, safety, welfare, and best interest of the child.

(5) A "partial evaluation, investigation, or assessment" is an examination of the health, safety, welfare, and best interest of the child that is limited by court order in either time or scope.

(6) "Evaluation," "investigation," and "assessment" are synonymous.

(Subd (c) amended effective January 1, 2003.)

(d) Responsibility for evaluation services

(1) Each court must:

(A) Adopt a local rule by January 1, 2000, to:

(i) Implement this rule of court;

(ii) Determine whether a peremptory challenge to a court-appointed evaluator is allowed and when the challenge must be exercised. The rules must specify whether a family court services staff member, other county employee, a mental health professional, or all of them may be challenged;

(iii) Allow evaluators to petition the court to withdraw from a case;

(iv) Provide for acceptance of and response to complaints about an evaluator's performance; and

(v) Address ex parte communications.

(B) Give the evaluator, before the evaluation begins, a copy of the court order that specifies:

(i) The appointment of the evaluator under Evidence Code section 730, Family Code section 3110, or Code of Civil Procedure 2032; and

(ii) The purpose and scope of the evaluation.

(C) Require child custody evaluators to adhere to the requirements of this rule.

(D) Determine and allocate between the parties any fees or costs of the evaluation.

(2) The child custody evaluator must:

(A) Consider the health, safety, welfare, and best interest of the child within the scope and purpose of the evaluation as defined by the court order;

(B) Strive to minimize the potential for psychological trauma to children during the evaluation process;

(C) Include in the initial meeting with each child an age-appropriate explanation of the evaluation process, including limitations on the confidentiality of the process;

(D) Inform the parties, other professionals serving on the case, and then the judicial officer about the child's desire to provide input and address the court; and

(E) If so informed by the child at any point, provide notice that the child has changed their choice about addressing the court. Notice must be provided as soon as feasible to the parties or their attorneys, other professionals serving on the case, and then to the judicial officer.

(Subd (d) amended effective January 1, 2023; previously amended effective January 1, 2003, and January 1, 2007.)

(e) Scope of evaluations

All evaluations must include:

(1) A written explanation of the process that clearly describes the:

(A) Purpose of the evaluation;

(B) Procedures used and the time required to gather and assess information and, if psychological tests will be used, the role of the results in confirming or questioning other information or previous conclusions;

(C) Scope and distribution of the evaluation report;

(D) Limitations on the confidentiality of the process; and

(E) Cost and payment responsibility for the evaluation.

(2) Data collection and analysis that are consistent with the requirements of Family Code section 3118; that allow the evaluator to observe and consider each party in comparable ways and to substantiate (from multiple sources when possible) interpretations and conclusions regarding each child's developmental needs; the quality of attachment to each parent and that parent's social environment; and reactions to the separation, divorce, or parental conflict. This process may include:

(A) Reviewing pertinent documents related to custody, including local police records;

(B) Observing parent-child interaction (unless contraindicated to protect the best interest of the child);

(C) Interviewing parents conjointly, individually, or both conjointly and individually (unless contraindicated in cases involving domestic violence), to assess:

(i) Capacity for setting age-appropriate limits and for understanding and responding to the child's needs;

(ii) History of involvement in caring for the child;

(iii) Methods for working toward resolution of the child custody conflict;

(iv) History of child abuse, domestic violence, substance abuse, and psychiatric illness; and

(v) Psychological and social functioning;

(D) Conducting age-appropriate interviews and observation with the children, both parents, stepparents, step- and half-siblings conjointly, separately, or both conjointly and separately, unless contraindicated to protect the best interest of the child;

(E) Collecting relevant corroborating information or documents as permitted by law; and

(F) Consulting with other experts to develop information that is beyond the evaluator's scope of practice or area of expertise.

(Subd (e) amended effective January 1, 2021; previously amended effective January 1, 2003, July 1, 2003, and January 1, 2007.)

(f) Presentation of findings

All evaluations must include a written or oral presentation of findings that is consistent with Family Code section 3111, Family Code section 3118, or Evidence Code section 730. In any presentation of findings, the evaluator must do all of the following:

(1) Summarize the data-gathering procedures, information sources, and time spent, and present all relevant information, including information that does not support the conclusions reached;

(2) Describe any limitations in the evaluation that result from unobtainable information, failure of a party to cooperate, or the circumstances of particular interviews;

(3) Only make a custody or visitation recommendation for a party who has been evaluated. This requirement does not preclude the evaluator from making an interim recommendation that is in the best interests of the child; and

(4) Provide clear, detailed recommendations that are consistent with the health, safety, welfare, and best interests of the child if making any recommendations to the court regarding a parenting plan.

(Subd (f) adopted effective January 1, 2021.)

(g) Confidential written report; requirements

(1) *Family Code section 3111 evaluations.* An evaluator appointed under Family Code section 3111 must do all of the following:

(A) File and serve a report on the parties or their attorneys and any attorney appointed for the child under Family Code section 3150; and

(B) Attach a *Notice Regarding Confidentiality of Child Custody Evaluation Report Under Family Code Section 3111* (form FL-328) as the first page of the child custody evaluation report when a court-ordered child custody evaluation report is filed with the clerk of the court and served on the parties or their attorneys, and any counsel appointed for the child, to inform them of the confidential nature of the report and the potential consequences for the unwarranted disclosure of the report.

(2) *Family Code section 3118 evaluations.* An evaluator appointed to conduct a child custody evaluation, investigation, or assessment based on (1) a serious allegation of child sexual abuse or (2) an allegation of child abuse under Family Code section 3118 must do all of the following:

(A) Provide a full and complete analysis of the allegations raised in the proceeding and address the health, safety, welfare, and best interests of the child, as ordered by the court; and

(B) Complete, file, and serve *Confidential Child Custody Evaluation Report Under Family Code Section 3118* (form FL-329) on the parties or their attorneys and any attorney appointed for the child under Family Code section 3150.

(Subd (g) amended effective September 1, 2022; adopted effective January 1, 2021.)

(h) Cooperation with professionals in another jurisdiction

When one party resides in another jurisdiction, the custody evaluator may rely on another qualified neutral professional for assistance in gathering information. In order to ensure a thorough and comparably reliable out-of-jurisdiction evaluation, the evaluator must:

(1) Make a written request that includes, as appropriate:

(A) A copy of all relevant court orders;

(B) An outline of issues to be explored;

(C) A list of the individuals who must or may be contacted;

(D) A description of the necessary structure and setting for interviews;

(E) A statement as to whether a home visit is required;

(F) A request for relevant documents such as police records, school reports, or other document review; and

(G) A request that a written report be returned only to the evaluator and that no copies of the report be distributed to parties or attorneys;

(2) Provide instructions that limit the out-of-jurisdiction report to factual matters and behavioral observations rather than recommendations regarding the overall custody plan; and

(3) Attach and discuss the report provided by the professional in another jurisdiction in the evaluator's final report.

(Subd (h) relettered effective January 1, 2021; adopted as subd (f); previously amended effective January 1, 2003.)

(i) Requirements for evaluator qualifications, training, continuing education, and experience

All child custody evaluators must meet the qualifications, training, and continuing education requirements specified in Family Code sections 1815, 1816, and 3111, and rules 5.225 and 5.230.

(Subd (i) repealed and relettered effective January 1, 2021; adopted as subd (g); previously amended effective July 1, 1999, January 1, 2003, and January 1, 2004.)

(j) Ethics

In performing an evaluation, the child custody evaluator must:

(1) Maintain objectivity, provide and gather balanced information for both parties, and control for bias;

(2) Protect the confidentiality of the parties and children in collateral contacts and not release information about the case to any individual except as authorized by the court or statute;

(3) Not offer any recommendations about a party unless that party has been evaluated directly or in consultation with another qualified neutral professional;

(4) Consider the health, safety, welfare, and best interest of the child in all phases of the process, including interviews with parents, extended family members, counsel for the child, and other interested parties or collateral contacts;

(5) Strive to maintain the confidential relationship between the child who is the subject of an evaluation and his or her treating psychotherapist;

(6) Operate within the limits of the evaluator's training and experience and disclose any limitations or bias that would affect the evaluator's ability to conduct the evaluation;

(7) Not pressure children to state a custodial preference;

(8) Inform the parties of the evaluator's reporting requirements, including, but not limited to, suspected child abuse and neglect and threats to harm one's self or another person;

(9) Not disclose any recommendations to the parties, their attorneys, or the attorney for the child before having gathered the information necessary to support the conclusion;

(10) Disclose to the court, parties, attorney for a party, and attorney for the child conflicts of interest or dual relationships; and not accept any appointment except by court order or the parties' stipulation; and

(11) Be sensitive to the socioeconomic status, gender, race, ethnicity, cultural values, religion, family structures, and developmental characteristics of the parties.

(Subd (j) relettered effective January 1, 2021; adopted as subd (h); previously amended effective January 1, 2003, and January 1, 2007.)

(k) Cost-effective procedures for cross-examination of evaluators

Each local court must develop procedures for expeditious and cost-effective cross-examination of evaluators, including, but not limited to, consideration of the following:

(1) Videoconferences;

(2) Telephone conferences;

(3) Audio or video examination; and

(4) Scheduling of appearances.

(Subd (k) relettered effective January 1, 2021; adopted as subd (i) effective January 1, 1999; previously amended effective January 1, 2003; previously relettered to subd (j) effective January 1, 2010.)

Rule 5.220 amended effective January 1, 2023; adopted as rule 1257.3 effective January 1, 1999; previously amended and renumbered effective January 1, 2003; previously amended effective July 1, 1999, July 1, 2003, January 1, 2004, January 1, 2007, January 1, 2010, January 1, 2021, and September 1, 2022.

Rule 5.225. Appointment requirements for child custody evaluators

(a) Purpose

This rule provides the licensing, education and training, and experience requirements for child custody evaluators who are appointed to conduct full or partial child custody evaluations under Family Code sections 3111 and 3118, Evidence Code section 730, or chapter 15 (commencing with section 2032.010) of title 4 of part 4 of the Code of Civil Procedure. This rule is adopted as mandated by Family Code section 3110.5.

(Subd (a) amended and relettered effective January 1, 2007; adopted as subd (b).)

(b) Definitions

For purposes of this rule:

(1) A "child custody evaluator" is a court-appointed investigator as defined in Family Code section 3110.

(2) A "child custody evaluation" is an investigation and analysis of the health, safety, welfare, and best interest of a child with regard to disputed custody and visitation issues conducted under Family Code sections 3111 and 3118, Evidence Code section 730, or Code of Civil Procedure section 2032.010 et seq.

(3) A "full evaluation, investigation, or assessment" is a child custody evaluation that is a comprehensive examination of the health, safety, welfare, and best interest of the child.

(4) A "partial evaluation, investigation, or assessment" is a child custody evaluation that is limited by the court in terms of its scope.

(5) The terms "evaluation," "investigation," and "assessment" are synonymous.

(6) "Best interest of the child" is described in Family Code section 3011.

(7) A "court-connected evaluator" is a superior court employee or a person under contract with a superior court who conducts child custody evaluations.

(Subd (b) amended and relettered effective January 1, 2007; adopted as subd (c).)

(c) Licensing requirements

A person appointed as a child custody evaluator meets the licensing criteria established by Family Code section 3110.5(c)(1)–(5) if:

(1) The person is licensed as a:

(A) Physician and either is a board-certified psychiatrist or has completed a residency in psychiatry;

(B) Psychologist;

(C) Marriage and family therapist;

(D) Clinical social worker; or

(E) Professional clinical counselor qualified to assess couples and families.

(2) A person may be appointed as an evaluator even if he or she does not have a license as described in (c)(1) if:

(A) The court certifies that the person is a court-connected evaluator who meets all the qualifications specified in (j); or

(B) The court finds that all the following criteria have been met:

(i) There are no licensed or certified evaluators who are willing and available, within a reasonable period of time, to perform child custody evaluations;

(ii) The parties stipulate to the person; and

(iii) The court approves the person.

(Subd (c) amended effective January 1, 2020; adopted effective January 1, 2007; previously amended effective January 1, 2015.)

(d) Education and training requirements

Before appointment, a child custody evaluator must complete 40 hours of education and training, which must include all the following topics:

(1) The psychological and developmental needs of children, especially as those needs relate to decisions about child custody and visitation;

(2) Family dynamics, including, but not limited to, parent-child relationships, blended families, and extended family relationships;

(3) The effects of separation, divorce, domestic violence, child sexual abuse, child physical or emotional abuse or neglect, substance abuse, and interparental conflict on the psychological and developmental needs of children and adults;

(4) The assessment of child sexual abuse issues required by Family Code section 3118; local procedures for handling child sexual abuse cases; the effect that court procedures may have on the evaluation process

when there are allegations of child sexual abuse; and the areas of training required by Family Code section 3110.5(b)(2)(A)–(F), as listed below:

(A) Children's patterns of hiding and disclosing sexual abuse in a family setting;

(B) The effects of sexual abuse on children;

(C) The nature and extent of sexual abuse;

(D) The social and family dynamics of child sexual abuse;

(E) Techniques for identifying and assisting families affected by child sexual abuse; and

(F) Legal rights, protections, and remedies available to victims of child sexual abuse;

(5) The significance of culture and religion in the lives of the parties;

(6) Safety issues that may arise during the evaluation process and their potential effects on all participants in the evaluation;

(7) When and how to interview or assess adults, infants, and children; gather information from collateral sources; collect and assess relevant data; and recognize the limits of data sources' reliability and validity;

(8) The importance of addressing issues such as general mental health, medication use, and learning or physical disabilities;

(9) The importance of staying current with relevant literature and research;

(10) How to apply comparable interview, assessment, and testing procedures that meet generally accepted clinical, forensic, scientific, diagnostic, or medical standards to all parties;

(11) When to consult with or involve additional experts or other appropriate persons;

(12) How to inform each adult party of the purpose, nature, and method of the evaluation;

(13) How to assess parenting capacity and construct effective parenting plans;

(14) Ethical requirements associated with the child custody evaluator's professional license and rule 5.220;

(15) The legal context within which child custody and visitation issues are decided and additional legal and ethical standards to consider when serving as a child custody evaluator;

(16) The importance of understanding relevant distinctions among the roles of evaluator, mediator, and therapist;

(17) How to write reports and recommendations, where appropriate;

(18) Mandatory reporting requirements and limitations on confidentiality;

(19) How to prepare for and give court testimony;

(20) How to maintain professional neutrality and objectivity when conducting child custody evaluations; and

(21) The importance of assessing the health, safety, welfare, and best interest of the child or children involved in the proceedings.

(Subd (d) repealed, amended, and relettered effective January 1, 2007; adopted as subd (e); previously amended effective January 1, 2005.)

(e) Additional training requirements

In addition to the requirements described in this rule, before appointment, child custody evaluators must comply with the basic and advanced domestic violence training requirements described in rule 5.230.

(Subd (e) adopted effective January 1, 2007.)

(f) Authorized education and training

The education and training described in (d) must be completed:

(1) After January 1, 2000;

(2) Through an eligible provider under this rule; and

(3) By either:

(A) Attending and participating in an approved course; or

(B) Serving as an instructor in an approved course. Each course taught may be counted only once. Instructors may claim and receive credit for only actual classroom time.

(Subd (f) adopted effective January 1, 2007.)

(g) Experience requirements

To satisfy the experience requirements of this rule, persons appointed as child custody evaluators must have participated in the completion of at least four partial or full court-appointed child custody evaluations within the preceding three years, as described below. Each of the four child custody evaluations must have resulted in a written or an oral report.

(1) The child custody evaluator participates in the completion of the child custody evaluations if the evaluator:

(A) Independently conducted and completed the child custody evaluation; or

(B) Materially assisted another child custody evaluator who meets all the following criteria:

(i) Licensing or certification requirements in (c);

(ii) Education and training requirements in (d);

(iii) Basic and advanced domestic violence training in (e);

(iv) Experience requirements in (g)(1)(A) or (g)(2); and

(v) Continuing education and training requirements in (h).

(2) The court may appoint an individual to conduct the child custody evaluation who does not meet the experience requirements described in (1), if the court finds that all the following criteria have been met:

(A) There are no evaluators who meet the experience requirements of this rule who are willing and available, within a reasonable period of time, to perform child custody evaluations;

(B) The parties stipulate to the person; and

(C) The court approves the person.

(3) Those who supervise court-connected evaluators meet the requirements of this rule by conducting or materially assisting in the completion of at least four partial or full court-connected child custody evaluations in the preceding three years.

(Subd (g) amended effective January 1, 2011; adopted as subd (f); previously amended and relettered effective January 1, 2007.)

(h) Appointment eligibility

After completing the licensing requirements in (c), the initial education and training requirements described in (d) and (e), and the experience requirements in (g), a person is eligible for appointment as a child custody evaluator.

(Subd (h) amended effective January 1, 2011; adopted as subd (g); previously amended and relettered effective January 1, 2005; previously amended effective January 1, 2007.)

(i) Continuing education and training requirements

(1) After a child custody evaluator completes the initial education and training requirements described in (d) and (e), the evaluator must complete these continuing education and training requirements to remain eligible for appointment:

(A) Domestic violence update training described in rule 5.230; and

(B) Eight hours of update training covering the subjects described in (d).

(2) The time frame for completing continuing education and training in (1) is as follows:

(A) A newly trained court-connected or private child custody evaluator who recently completed the education and training in (d) and (e) must:

(i) Complete the continuing education and training requirements of this rule within 18 months from the date he or she completed the initial education and training; and

(ii) Specify on form FL-325 or FL-326 the date by which he or she must complete the continuing education and training requirements of this rule.

(B) All other court-connected or private child custody evaluators must complete the continuing education and training requirements in (1) as follows:

(i) Court-connected child custody evaluators must complete the continuing education and training requirements within the 12-month period immediately preceding the date he or she signs the *Declaration of Court-Connected Child Custody Evaluator Regarding Qualifications* (form FL-325), which must be submitted as provided by (*l*) of this rule.

(ii) Private child custody evaluators must complete the continuing education and training requirements within the 12-month period immediately preceding his or her appointment to a case.

(3) Compliance with the continuing education and training requirements of this rule is determined at the time of appointment to a case.

(Subd (i) adopted effective January 1, 2011.)

(j) Court-connected evaluators

A court-connected evaluator who does not meet the education and training requirements in (d) may conduct child custody evaluations if, before appointment, he or she:

(1) Completed at least 20 of the 40 hours of education and training required by (d);

(2) Completes the remaining hours of education and training required by (d) within 12 months of conducting his or her first evaluation as a court-connected child custody evaluator;

(3) Complied with the basic and advanced domestic violence training requirements under Family Code sections 1816 and 3110.5 and rule 5.230;

(4) Complies with the experience requirements in (g); and

(5) Is supervised by a court-connected child custody evaluator who meets the requirements of this rule.

(Subd (j) relettered effective January 1, 2011; adopted as subd (h); previously relettered as subd (i) effective January 1, 2005; previously amended effective January 1, 2007.)

(k) Responsibility of the courts

Each court:

(1) Must develop local court rules that:

(A) Provide for acceptance of and response to complaints about an evaluator's performance; and

(B) Establish a process for informing the public about how to find qualified evaluators in that jurisdiction;

(2) Must use an *Order Appointing Child Custody Evaluator* (form FL-327) to appoint a private child custody evaluator or a court-connected evaluation service. Form FL-327 may be supplemented with local court forms;

(3) Must provide the Judicial Council with a copy of any local court forms used to implement this rule;

(4) As feasible and appropriate, may confer with education and training providers to develop and deliver curricula of comparable quality and relevance to child custody evaluations for both court-connected and private child custody evaluators; and

(5) Must use form *Declaration of Court-Connected Child Custody Evaluator Regarding Qualifications* (form FL-325) to certify that court-connected evaluators have met all the qualifications for court-connected evaluators under this rule for a given year. Form FL-325 may be supplemented with local court rules or forms.

(Subd (k) relettered effective January 1, 2011; adopted as subd (l); previously amended and relettered as subd (k) effective January 1, 2005, and as subd (j) effective January 1, 2007.)

(l) Child custody evaluator

A person appointed as a child custody evaluator must:

(1) Submit to the court a declaration indicating compliance with all applicable education, training, and experience requirements:

(A) Court-connected child custody evaluators must submit a *Declaration of Court-Connected Child Custody Evaluator Regarding Qualifications* (form FL-325) to the court executive officer or his or her designee. Court-connected child custody evaluators practicing as of January 1 of a given year must submit the form by January 30 of that year. Court-connected evaluators beginning practice after January 1 must submit the form before any work on the first child custody evaluation has begun and by January 30 of every year thereafter; and

(B) Private child custody evaluators must complete a *Declaration of Private Child Custody Evaluator Regarding Qualifications* (form FL-326) and file it with the clerk's office no later than 10 days after notification of each appointment and before any work on each child custody evaluation has begun;

(2) At the beginning of the child custody evaluation, inform each adult party of the purpose, nature, and method of the evaluation, and provide information about the evaluator's education, experience, and training;

(3) Use interview, assessment, and testing procedures that are consistent with generally accepted clinical, forensic, scientific, diagnostic, or medical standards;

(4) Have a license in good standing if licensed at the time of appointment, except as described in (c)(2) and Family Code section 3110.5(d);

(5) Be knowledgeable about relevant resources and service providers; and

(6) Before undertaking the evaluation or at the first practical moment, inform the court, counsel, and parties of possible or actual multiple roles or conflicts of interest.

(Subd (l) amended and relettered effective January 1, 2011; adopted as subd (m); previously amended and relettered as subd (l) effective January 1, 2005, and as subd (k) effective January 1, 2007.)

(m) Use of interns

Court-connected and court-appointed child custody evaluators may use interns to assist with the child custody evaluation, if:

(1) The evaluator:

(A) Before or at the time of appointment, fully discloses to the parties and attorneys the nature and extent of the intern's participation in the evaluation;

(B) Obtains the written agreement of the parties and attorneys as to the nature and extent of the intern's participation in the evaluation after disclosure;

(C) Ensures that the extent, kind, and quality of work performed by the intern being supervised is consistent with the intern's training and experience;

(D) Is physically present when the intern interacts with the parties, children, or other collateral persons in the evaluation; and

(E) Ensures compliance with all laws and regulations governing the professional practice of the supervising evaluator and the intern.

(2) The interns:

(A) Are enrolled in a master's or doctorate program or have obtained a graduate degree qualifying for licensure or certification as a clinical social worker, marriage and family therapist, psychiatrist, or psychologist;

(B) Are currently completing or have completed the coursework necessary to qualify for their degree in the subjects of child abuse assessment and spousal or partner abuse assessment; and

(C) Comply with the applicable laws related to the practice of their profession in California when interns are:

(i) Accruing supervised professional experience as defined in the California Code of Regulations; and

(ii) Providing professional services for a child custody evaluator that fall within the lawful scope of practice as a licensed professional.

(Subd (m) relettered effective January 1, 2011; adopted as subd (l) effective January 1, 2007.)

(n) Education and training providers

"Eligible providers" includes the Judicial Council and may include educational institutions, professional associations, professional continuing education groups, public or private for-profit or not-for-profit groups, and court-connected groups. Eligible providers must:

(1) Ensure that the training instructors or consultants delivering the training and education programs either meet the requirements of this rule or are experts in the subject matter;

(2) Monitor and evaluate the quality of courses, curricula, training, instructors, and consultants;

(3) Emphasize the importance of focusing child custody evaluations on the health, safety, welfare, and best interest of the child;

(4) Develop a procedure to verify that participants complete the education and training program;

(5) Distribute a certificate of completion to each person who has completed the training. The certificate must document the number of hours of training offered, the number of hours the person completed, the dates of the training, and the name of the training provider; and

(6) Meet the approval requirements described in (o).

(Subd (n) amended effective January 1, 2016; adopted as subd (n); previously amended and relettered as subd (m) effective January 1, 2005; previously amended effective January 1, 2007; previously amended and relettered as subd (n) effective January 1, 2011.)

(o) Program approval required

All education and training programs must be approved by Judicial Council staff in consultation with the Family and Juvenile Law Advisory Committee. Education and training courses that were taken between January 1, 2000, and July 1, 2003, may be applied toward the requirements of this rule if they addressed the subjects listed in (d) and either were certified or approved for continuing education credit by a professional provider group or were offered as part of a related postgraduate degree or licensing program.

(Subd (o) amended effective January 1, 2016; adopted as subd (o); previously amended and relettered as subd (n) effective January 1, 2005; previously amended effective January 1, 2007; relettered as subd (o) effective January 1, 2011.)

Rule 5.225 amended effective January 1, 2020; adopted as rule 1257.4 effective January 1, 2002; renumbered as rule 5.225 effective January 1, 2003; previously amended effective January 1, 2005, January 1, 2007, January 1, 2011, January 1, 2015, and January 1, 2016.

Rule 5.230. Domestic violence training standards for court-appointed child custody investigators and evaluators

(a) Authority

This rule of court is adopted under Family Code sections 211 and 3111(d) and (e).

(Subd (a) amended effective January 1, 2007.)

(b) Purpose

Consistent with Family Code sections 3020 and 3111, the purposes of this rule are to require domestic violence training for all court-appointed persons who evaluate or investigate child custody matters and to ensure that this training reflects current research and consensus about best practices for conducting child custody evaluations by prescribing standards that training in domestic violence must meet. Effective January 1, 1998, no person may be a court-appointed investigator under Family Code section 3111(d) or Evidence Code section 730 unless the person has completed domestic violence training described here and in Family Code section 1816.

(Subd (b) amended effective January 1, 2003.)

(c) Definitions

For purposes of this rule, "court-appointed investigator" is considered to be synonymous with "court-appointed evaluator" as defined in Family Code section 3110.

(d) Mandatory training

Persons appointed as child custody investigators under Family Code section 3110 or Evidence Code section 730, and persons who are professional staff or trainees in a child custody or visitation evaluation or investigation, must complete basic training in domestic violence issues as described in Family Code section 1816 and, in addition:

(1) *Advanced training*

Sixteen hours of advanced training must be completed within a 12-month period. The training must include the following:

(A) Twelve hours of instruction, as approved by Judicial Council staff, in:

(i) The appropriate structuring of the child custody evaluation process, including, but not limited to, maximizing safety for clients, evaluators, and court personnel; maintaining objectivity; providing and gathering balanced information from both parties and controlling for bias; providing for separate sessions at separate times (as specified in Family Code section 3113); and considering the impact of the evaluation report and recommendations with particular attention to the dynamics of domestic violence;

(ii) The relevant sections of local, state, and federal law or rules;

(iii) The range, availability, and applicability of domestic violence resources available to victims, including, but not limited to, battered women's shelters, specialized counseling, drug and alcohol counseling, legal advocacy, job training, parenting classes, battered immigrant victims, and welfare exceptions for domestic violence victims;

(iv) The range, availability, and applicability of domestic violence intervention available to perpetrators, including, but not limited to, arrest, incarceration, probation, applicable Penal Code sections (including Penal Code section 1203.097, which describes certified treatment programs for batterers), drug and alcohol counseling, legal advocacy, job training, and parenting classes; and

(v) The unique issues in family and psychological assessment in domestic violence cases, including the following concepts:

a. The effects of exposure to domestic violence and psychological trauma on children; the relationship between child physical abuse, child sexual abuse, and domestic violence; the differential family dynamics related to parent-child attachments in families with domestic violence; intergenerational transmission of familial violence; and manifestations of post-traumatic stress disorders in children;

b. The nature and extent of domestic violence, and the relationship of gender, class, race, culture, and sexual orientation to domestic violence;

c. Current legal, psychosocial, public policy, and mental health research related to the dynamics of family violence, the impact of victimization, the psychology of perpetration, and the dynamics of power and control in battering relationships;

d. The assessment of family history based on the type, severity, and frequency of violence;

e. The impact on parenting abilities of being a victim or perpetrator of domestic violence;

f. The uses and limitations of psychological testing and psychiatric diagnosis in assessing parenting abilities in domestic violence cases;

g. The influence of alcohol and drug use and abuse on the incidence of domestic violence;

h. Understanding the dynamics of high-conflict relationships and abuser/victim relationships;

i. The importance of, and procedures for, obtaining collateral information from probation departments, children's protective services, police incident reports, restraining order pleadings, medical records, schools, and other relevant sources;

j. Accepted methods for structuring safe and enforceable child custody and parenting plans that assure the health, safety, welfare, and best interest of the child, and safeguards for the parties; and

k. The importance of discouraging participants in child custody matters from blaming victims of domestic violence for the violence and from minimizing allegations of domestic violence, child abuse, or abuse against any family member.

(B) Four hours of community resource networking intended to acquaint the evaluator with domestic violence resources in the geographical communities where the families being evaluated may reside.

(2) *Annual update training*

Four hours of update training are required each year after the year in which the advanced training is completed. These four hours must consist of instruction focused on, but not limited to, an update of changes or modifications in local court practices, case law, and state and federal legislation related to domestic violence, and an update of current social science research and theory, particularly in regard to the impact on children of exposure to domestic violence.

(Subd (d) amended effective January 1, 2016; previously amended effective January 1, 2002, January 1, 2003, January 1, 2004, and January 1, 2005.)

(e) Education and training providers

Only education and training acquired from eligible providers meets the requirements of this rule. "Eligible providers" includes the Judicial Council and may include educational institutions, professional associations, professional continuing education groups, public or private for-profit or not-for-profit groups, and court-connected groups.

(1) Eligible providers must:

(A) Ensure that the training instructors or consultants delivering the education and training programs either meet the requirements of this rule or are experts in the subject matter;

(B) Monitor and evaluate the quality of courses, curricula, training, instructors, and consultants;

(C) Emphasize the importance of focusing child custody evaluations on the health, safety, welfare, and best interest of the child;

(D) Develop a procedure to verify that participants complete the education and training program; and

(E) Distribute a certificate of completion to each person who has completed the training. The certificate must document the number of hours of training offered, the number of hours the person completed, the dates of the training, and the name of the training provider.

(2) Effective July 1, 2005, all education and training programs must be approved by Judicial Council staff in consultation with the Family and Juvenile Law Advisory Committee.

(Subd (e) amended effective January 1, 2016; previously amended effective January 1, 2005.)

(f) Local court rules

Each local court may adopt rules regarding the procedures by which child custody evaluators who have completed the training in domestic violence as mandated by this rule will notify the local court. In the absence of such a local rule of court, child custody evaluators must attach copies of their certificates of completion of the initial 12 hours of advanced instruction and of the most recent annual 4-hour update training in domestic violence to each child custody evaluation report.

(Subd (f) relettered effective January 1, 2005; adopted as subd (g) effective January 1, 1999; amended effective January 1, 2003, and January 1, 2004.)

(g) Previous training accepted

Persons attending training programs offered after January 1, 1996, that meet all of the requirements set forth in subdivision (d)(1)(A) of this rule are deemed to have met the minimum standards set forth in subdivision (d)(1)(A) of this rule, but they must still meet the minimum standards listed in subdivisions (d)(1)(B) and (d)(2) of this rule.

(Subd (g) amended effective January 1, 2007; adopted as subd (h) effective January 1, 1999; relettered effective January 1, 2005.)

Rule 5.230 amended effective January 1, 2016; adopted as rule 1257.7 effective January 1, 1999; amended and renumbered as rule 5.230 effective January 1, 2003; previously amended effective January 1, 2004, January 1, 2005, and January 1, 2007.

Article 3
Ex Parte Communication

Title 5, Family and Juvenile Rules—Division 1, Family Rules—Chapter 8, Child Custody and Visitation (Parenting Time) Proceedings—Article 3, Ex Parte Communication; adopted effective January 1, 2013.

Rule 5.235. Ex parte communication in child custody proceedings

(a) Purpose

Generally, ex parte communication is prohibited in legal proceedings. In child custody proceedings, Family Code section 216 recognizes specific circumstances in which ex parte communication is permitted between court-connected or court-appointed child custody mediators or evaluators and the attorney for any party, the court-appointed counsel for a child, or the court. This rule of court establishes mandatory statewide standards of practice relating to when, and between whom, ex parte communication is permitted in child custody proceedings. This rule applies to all court-ordered child custody mediations or evaluations. As in Family Code section 216, this rule of court does not restrict communications between a court-connected or court-appointed child custody mediator or evaluator and a party in a child custody proceeding who is self-represented or represented by counsel.

(b) Definitions

For purposes of this rule,

(1) "Communication" includes any verbal statement made in person, by telephone, by voicemail, or by videoconferencing; any written statement, illustration, photograph, or other tangible item, contained in a letter, document, e-mail, or fax; or other equivalent means, either directly or through third parties.

(2) "Ex parte communication" is a direct or indirect communication on the substance of a pending case without the knowledge, presence, or consent of all parties involved in the matter.

(3) A "court-connected mediator or evaluator" is a superior court employee or a person under contract with a superior court who conducts child custody evaluations or mediations.

(4) A "court-appointed mediator or evaluator" is a professional in private practice appointed by the court to conduct a child custody evaluation or mediation.

(c) Ex parte communication prohibited

In any child custody proceeding under the Family Code, ex parte communication is prohibited between court-connected or court-appointed mediators or evaluators and the attorney for any party, a court-appointed counsel for a child, or the court, except as provided by this rule.

(d) Exception for parties' stipulation

The parties may enter into a stipulation either in open court or in writing to allow ex parte communication between a court-connected or court-appointed mediator or evaluator and:

(1) The attorney for any party; or

(2) The court.

(e) Ex parte communication permitted

In any proceeding under the Family Code, ex parte communication is permitted between a court-connected or court-appointed mediator or evaluator and (1) the attorney for any party, (2) the court-appointed counsel for a child, or (3) the court, only if:

(1) The communication is necessary to schedule an appointment;

(2) The communication is necessary to investigate or disclose an actual or potential conflict of interest or dual relationship as required under rule 5.210(h)(10) and (h)(12);

(3) The court-appointed counsel for a child is interviewing a mediator as provided by Family Code section 3151(c)(5);

(4) The court expressly authorizes ex parte communication between the mediator or evaluator and court-appointed counsel for a child in circumstances other than described in (3); or

(5) The mediator or evaluator is informing the court of the belief that a restraining order is necessary to prevent an imminent risk to the physical safety of the child or party.

(Subd (e) amended effective January 1, 2007.)

(f) Exception for mandated duties and responsibilities

This rule does not prohibit ex parte communication for the purpose of fulfilling the duties and responsibilities that:

(1) A mediator or evaluator may have as a mandated reporter of suspected child abuse;

(2) A mediator or evaluator may have to warn of threatened violent behavior against a reasonably identifiable victim or victims;

(3) A mediator or evaluator may have to address a case involving allegations of domestic violence under Family Code sections 3113, 3181, and 3192 and rule 5.215; and

(4) The court may have to investigate complaints.

(Subd (f) amended effective January 1, 2007.)
Rule 5.235 amended effective January 1, 2007; adopted effective July 1, 2006.

Article 4
Counsel Appointed to Represent a Child

Title 5, Family and Juvenile Rules—Division 1, Family Rules—Chapter 8, Child Custody and Visitation (Parenting Time) Proceedings—Article 4, Counsel Appointed to Represent a Child; adopted effective January 1, 2013.

Rule 5.240. Appointment of counsel to represent a child in family law proceedings

Rule 5.241. Compensation of counsel appointed to represent a child in a family law proceeding

Rule 5.242. Qualifications, rights, and responsibilities of counsel appointed to represent a child in family law proceedings

Rule 5.240. Appointment of counsel to represent a child in family law proceedings

(a) Appointment considerations

In considering appointing counsel under Family Code section 3150, the court should take into account the following factors, including whether:

(1) The issues of child custody and visitation are highly contested or protracted;

(2) The child is subjected to stress as a result of the dispute that might be alleviated by the intervention of counsel representing the child;

(3) Counsel representing the child would be likely to provide the court with relevant information not otherwise readily available or likely to be presented;

(4) The dispute involves allegations of physical, emotional, or sexual abuse or neglect of the child;

(5) It appears that one or both parents are incapable of providing a stable, safe, and secure environment;

(6) Counsel is available for appointment who is knowledgeable about the issues being raised regarding the child in the proceeding;

(7) The best interest of the child appears to require independent representation; and

(8) If there are two or more children, any child would require separate counsel to avoid a conflict of interest.

(Subd (a) adopted effective January 1, 2008.)

(b) Request for appointment of counsel

The court may appoint counsel to represent the best interest of a child in a family law proceeding on the court's own motion or if requested to do so by:

(1) A party;

(2) The attorney for a party;

(3) The child, or any relative of the child;

(4) A mediator under Family Code section 3184;

(5) A professional person making a custody recommendation under Family Code sections 3111 and 3118, Evidence Code section 730, or Code of Civil Procedure section 2032.010 et seq.;

(6) A county counsel, district attorney, city attorney, or city prosecutor authorized to prosecute child abuse and neglect or child abduction cases under state law; or

(7) A court-appointed guardian ad litem or special advocate;

(8) Any other person who the court deems appropriate.

(Subd (b) adopted effective January 1, 2008.)

(c) Orders appointing counsel for a child

The court must issue written orders when appointing and terminating counsel for a child.

(1) The appointment orders must specify the:

(A) Appointed counsel's name, address, and telephone number;

(B) Name of the child for whom counsel is appointed; and

(C) Child's date of birth.

(2) The appointment orders may include the:

(A) Child's address, if appropriate;

(B) Issues to be addressed in the case;

(C) Tasks related to the case that would benefit from the services of counsel for the child;

(D) Responsibilities and rights of the child's counsel;

(E) Counsel's rate or amount of compensation;

(F) Allocation of fees payable by each party or the court;

(G) Source of funds and manner of reimbursement for counsel's fees and costs;

(H) Allocation of payment of counsel's fees to one party subject to reimbursement by the other party;

(I) Terms and amount of any progress or installment payments; and

(J) Ability of the court to reserve jurisdiction to retroactively modify the order on fees and payment.

(3) Courts may use *Order Appointing Counsel for a Child* (form FL-323) or may supplement form FL-323 with local forms developed under rule 10.613.

(Subd (c) amended effective January 1, 2013; adopted effective January 1, 2008.)

(d) Panel of counsel eligible for appointment

(1) Each court may create and maintain a list or panel of counsel meeting the minimum qualifications of this rule for appointment.

(2) If a list or panel of counsel is maintained, a court may appoint counsel not on the list or panel in special circumstances, taking into consideration factors including language, culture, and the special needs of a child in the following areas:

(A) Child abuse;

(B) Domestic violence;

(C) Drug abuse of a parent or the child;

(D) Mental health issues of a parent or the child;

(E) Particular medical issues of the child; and

(F) Educational issues.

(3) If the court maintains a panel of counsel eligible for appointment and the court appoints counsel who is not on the panel, the court must state the reason for not appointing a panel counsel in writing or on the record.

(4) Any lists maintained from which the court might appoint counsel should be reviewed at least annually to ensure that those on the list meet the education and training requirements. Courts should ask counsel annually to update their information and to notify the court if any changes would make them unable to be appointed.

(Subd (d) amended effective January 1, 2013; adopted effective January 1, 2008.)

(e) Complaint procedures

By January 1, 2010, each court must develop local court rules in accordance with rule 10.613 that provide for acceptance and response to complaints about the performance of the court-appointed counsel for a child.

(Subd (e) adopted effective January 1, 2008.)

(f) Termination of appointment

On entering an appearance on behalf of a child, counsel must continue to represent that child until:

(1) The conclusion of the proceeding for which counsel was appointed;

(2) Relieved by the court;

(3) Substituted by the court with other counsel;

(4) Removed on the court's own motion or request of counsel or parties for good cause shown; or

(5) The child reaches the age of majority or is emancipated.

(Subd (f) adopted effective January 1, 2008.)

Rule 5.240 amended effective January 1, 2013; adopted effective January 1, 2008.

Rule 5.241. Compensation of counsel appointed to represent a child in a family law proceeding

(a) Determination of counsel's compensation

The court must determine the reasonable sum for compensation and expenses for counsel appointed to represent the child in a family law proceeding, and the ability of the parties to pay all or a portion of counsel's compensation and expenses.

(1) The court must set the compensation for the child's counsel:

(A) At the time of appointment;

(B) At the time the court determines the parties' ability to pay; or

(C) Within a reasonable time after appointment.

(2) No later than 30 days after counsel is relieved as attorney of record, the court may make a redetermination of counsel's compensation:

(A) On the court's own motion;

(B) At the request of a party or a party's counsel; or

(C) At the request of counsel for the child.

(Subd (a) adopted effective January 1, 2008.)

(b) Determination of ability to pay

The court must determine the respective financial ability of the parties to pay all or a portion of counsel's compensation.

(1) Before determining the parties' ability to pay:

(A) The court should consider factors such as the parties' income and assets reasonably available at the time of the determination, and eligibility for or existence of a fee waiver under Government Code section 68511.3; and

(B) The parties must have on file a current *Income and Expense Declaration* (form FL-150) or *Financial Statement (Simplified)* (form FL-155).

(2) The court should determine the parties' ability to pay:

(A) At the time counsel is appointed;

(B) Within 30 days after appointment; or

(C) At the next subsequent hearing.

(3) No later than 30 days after counsel is relieved as attorney of record, the court may redetermine the parties' ability to pay:

(A) On the court's own motion; or

(B) At the request of counsel or the parties.

(Subd (b) adopted effective January 1, 2008.)

(c) Payment to counsel

(1) If the court determines that the parties have the ability to pay all or a portion of the fees, the court must order that the parties pay in any manner the court determines to be reasonable and compatible with the parties' financial ability, including progress or installment payments.

(2) The court may use its own funds to pay counsel for a child and seek reimbursement from the parties.

(3) The court must inform the parties that the failure to pay fees to the appointed counsel or to the court may result in the attorney or the court initiating legal action against them to collect the money.

(Subd (c) adopted effective January 1, 2008.)

(d) Parties' inability to pay

If the court finds that the parties are unable to pay all or a portion of the cost of the child's counsel, the court must pay the portion the parties are unable to pay.

(Subd (d) adopted effective January 1, 2008.)

Rule 5.241 adopted effective January 1, 2008.

Rule 5.242. Qualifications, rights, and responsibilities of counsel appointed to represent a child in family law proceedings

(a) Purpose

This rule governs counsel appointed to represent the best interest of the child in a custody or visitation proceeding under Family Code section 3150.

(Subd (a) adopted effective January 1, 2008.)

(b) General appointment requirements

To be eligible for appointment as counsel for a child, counsel must:

(1) Be an active member in good standing of the State Bar of California;

(2) Have professional liability insurance or demonstrate to the court that he or she is adequately self-insured; and

(3) Meet the education, training, and experience requirements of this rule.

(Subd (b) adopted effective January 1, 2008.)

(c) Education and training requirements

Effective January 1, 2009, before being appointed as counsel for a child in a family law proceeding, counsel must have completed at least 12 hours of applicable education and training which must include all the following subjects:

(1) Statutes, rules of court, and case law relating to child custody and visitation litigation;

(2) Representation of a child in custody and visitation proceedings;

(3) Special issues in representing a child, including the following:

(A) Various stages of child development;

(B) Communicating with a child at various developmental stages and presenting the child's view;

(C) Recognizing, evaluating and understanding evidence of child abuse and neglect, family violence and substance abuse, cultural and ethnic diversity, and gender-specific issues;

(D) The effects of domestic violence and child abuse and neglect on children; and

(E) How to work effectively with multidisciplinary experts.

(Subd (c) adopted effective January 1, 2008.)

(d) Annual education and training requirements

Effective January 1, 2010, to remain eligible for appointment as counsel for a child, counsel must complete during each calendar year a minimum of eight hours of applicable education and training in the subjects listed in (c).

(Subd (d) adopted effective January 1, 2008.)

(e) Applicable education and training

(1) Education and training that addresses the subjects listed in (c) may be applied toward the requirements of this rule if completed through:

(A) A professional continuing education group;

(B) An educational institution;

(C) A professional association;

(D) A court-connected group; or

(E) A public or private for-profit or not-for-profit group.

(2) A maximum of two of the hours may be by self-study under the supervision of an education provider that provides evidence of completion.

(3) Counsel may complete education and training courses that satisfy the requirements of this rule offered by the education providers in (1) by means of video presentations or other delivery means at remote locations. Such courses are not self-study within the meaning of this rule.

(4) Counsel who serve as an instructor in an education and training course that satisfies the requirements of this rule may receive 1.5 hours of course participation credit for each hour of course instruction. All other counsel may claim credit for actual time he or she attended the education and training course.

(Subd (e) adopted effective January 1, 2008.)

(f) Experience requirements

(1) Persons appointed as counsel for a child in a family law proceeding must have represented a party or a child in at least six proceedings involving child custody within the preceding five years as follows:

(A) At least two of the six proceedings must have involved contested child custody and visitation issues in family law; and

(B) Child custody proceedings in dependency or guardianship cases can count for no more than three of the six required for appointment.

(2) Courts may develop local rules that impose additional experience requirements for persons appointed as counsel for a child in a family law proceeding.

(Subd (f) adopted effective January 1, 2008.)

(g) Alternative experience requirements

Counsel who does not meet the initial experience requirements in (f) may be appointed to represent a child in a family law proceeding if he or she meets one of the following alternative experience requirements. Counsel must:

(1) Be employed by a legal services organization, a governmental agency, or a private law firm that has been approved by the presiding or supervising judge of the local family court as qualified to represent a child in family law proceedings and be directly supervised by an attorney in an organization, an agency, or a private law firm who meets the initial experience requirements in (f);

(2) Be an attorney working in consultation with an attorney approved by the presiding or supervising judge of the local family court as qualified to represent a child in family law proceedings; or

(3) Demonstrate substantial equivalent experience as determined by local court rule or procedure.

(Subd (g) adopted effective January 1, 2008.)

(h) Compliance with appointment requirements

A person appointed as counsel for a child must:

(1) File a declaration with the court indicating compliance with the requirements of this rule no later than 10 days after being appointed and before beginning work on the case. Counsel may complete the *Declaration of Counsel for a Child Regarding Qualifications* (form FL-322) or other local court forms for this purpose; and

(2) Notify the court within five days of any disciplinary action taken by the State Bar of California, stating the basis of the complaint, result, and notice of any reproval, probation, or suspension.

(Subd (h) adopted effective January 1, 2008.)

(i) Rights of counsel for a child

Counsel has rights relating to the representation of a child's best interest under Family Code sections 3111, 3151, 3151.5, 3153, and Welfare and Institutions Code section 827, which include the right to:

(1) Reasonable access to the child;

(2) Seek affirmative relief on behalf of the child;

(3) Notice to any proceeding, and all phases of that proceeding, including a request for examination affecting the child;

(4) Take any action that is available to a party to the proceeding, including filing pleadings, making evidentiary objections, and presenting evidence;

(5) Be heard in the proceeding, which may include presenting motions and orders to show cause and participating in settlement conferences and trials, seeking writs, appeals, and arbitrations;

(6) Access the child's medical, dental, mental health, and other health-care records, and school and educational records;

(7) Inspect juvenile case files subject to the provisions of Welfare and Institutions Code section 827;

(8) Interview school personnel, caretakers, health-care providers, mental health professionals, and others who have assessed the child or provided care to the child; however, the release of this information to counsel does not constitute a waiver of the confidentiality of the reports, files, and any disclosed communications;

(9) Interview mediators, subject to the provisions of Family Code sections 3177 and 3182;

(10) Receive reasonable advance notice of and the right to refuse any physical or psychological examination or evaluation, for purposes of the proceeding, that has not been ordered by the court;

(11) Assert or waive any privilege on behalf of the child;

(12) Seek independent psychological or physical examination or evaluation of the child for purposes of the proceeding on approval by the court;

(13) Receive child custody evaluation reports;

(14) Not be called as a witness in the proceedings;

(15) Request the court to authorize release of relevant reports or files, concerning the child represented by the counsel, of the relevant local child protective services agency; and

(16) Receive reasonable compensation and expenses for representing the child, the amount of which will be determined by the court.

(Subd (i) adopted effective January 1, 2008.)

(j) Responsibilities of counsel for a child

Counsel is charged with the representation of the child's best interest. The role of the child's counsel is to gather evidence that bears on the best interest of the child and present that admissible evidence to the court in any manner appropriate for the counsel of a party. If the child so desires, the child's counsel must present the child's wishes to the court.

(1) Counsel's duties, unless under the circumstances it is inappropriate to exercise the duties, include those under Family Code section 3151:

(A) Interviewing the child;

(B) Reviewing the court files and all accessible relevant records available to both parties; and

(C) Making any further investigations that counsel considers necessary to ascertain the facts relevant to the custody or visitation hearings.

(2) Counsel must serve notices and pleadings on all parties consistent with the requirements for parties.

(3) Counsel may introduce and examine witnesses, present arguments to the court concerning the child's welfare, and participate further in the proceeding to the degree necessary to represent the child adequately.

(4) In any case in which counsel is representing a child who is called to testify in the proceeding, counsel must:

(A) Provide information to the child in an age-appropriate manner about the limitations on confidentiality and the possibility that information provided to the court may be on the record and provided to the parties in the case;

(B) Allow but not require the child to state a preference regarding custody or visitation and, in an age-appropriate manner, provide information about the process by which the court will make a decision;

(C) Provide procedures relevant to the child's participation and, if appropriate, provide an orientation to the courtroom where the child will be testifying;

(D) Inform the parties, other professionals serving on the case, and then the judicial officer about the client's desire to provide input and address the court; and

(E) If so informed by the child at any point, provide notice that the child has changed their choice about addressing the court. Notice must be provided as soon as feasible to the parties or their attorneys, other professionals serving on the case, and then to the judicial officer.

(Subd (j) amended effective January 1, 2023; adopted effective January 1, 2008; previously amended effective January 1, 2012.)

(k) Other considerations

Counsel is not required to assume the responsibilities of a social worker, probation officer, child custody evaluator, or mediator and is not expected to provide nonlegal services to the child. Subject to the terms of the court's order of appointment, counsel for a child may take the following actions to implement his or her statutory duties in representing a child in a family law proceeding:

(1) Interview or observe the child as appropriate to the age and circumstances of the child. In doing so, counsel should consider all possible interview or observation environments and select a location most conducive to both conducting a meaningful interview of the child and investigating the issues relevant to the case at that time.

(2) In a manner and to the extent consistent with the child's age, level of maturity, and ability to understand, and consistent with the order of appointment for the case:

(A) Explain to the child at their first meeting counsel's role and the nature of the attorney-client relationship (including confidentiality issues); and

(B) Advise the child on a continuing basis of possible courses of action and of the risks and benefits of each course of action.

(3) Actively participate in the representation of the child at any hearings that affect custody and visitation of the child and attend and participate in any other hearings relevant to the child. In doing so, counsel may, as appropriate:

(A) Take positions relevant to the child on legal issues before the court;

(B) Seek and advocate for services for the child;

(C) Prepare for any hearings or trials;

(D) Work to settle contested issues and to define trial issues;

(E) Prepare witnesses, including the child if the child is to testify;

(F) Introduce and examine witnesses on behalf of the child;

(G) Cross-examine other witnesses;

(H) Make appropriate evidentiary objections;

(I) Review court files and other pertinent records;

(J) Prepare motions to advance the child's interest, including motions to quash subpoenas for the child and other protective orders;

(K) Present arguments to advance the child's interest;

(L) Prepare trial briefs and other documents if appropriate; and

(M) Request appointment of separate appellate counsel.

(4) Conduct thorough, continuing, and independent investigations and discovery to protect the child's interest, which may include:

(A) Obtaining necessary authorizations for the release of information.

(B) Reviewing the child's social services, mental health, drug and alcohol, medical, law enforcement, education, and other records relevant to the case;

(C) Reviewing the court files of the child and his or her siblings, case-related records of the social service agency, and case-related records of other service providers;

(D) Contacting attorneys for the parties and nonlawyer guardians ad litem, Court Appointed Special Advocates (CASAs), and other service professionals, to the extent permitted by local rule, for background information;

(E) Contacting and meeting with the child's parents, legal guardians, or caretakers, with permission of their attorneys;

(F) Interviewing witnesses and individuals involved with the child, including school personnel, child welfare caseworkers, foster parents and other caretakers, neighbors, relatives, coaches, clergy, mental health professionals, physicians, law enforcement officers, and other potential witnesses;

(G) Reviewing relevant photographs, video- or audio recordings, and other evidence;

(H) Documenting the results of these investigations;

(I) Monitoring compliance with court orders as appropriate, including the provision for and effectiveness of any court-ordered services;

(J) Promoting the timely progression of the case through the judicial system;

(K) Investigating the interests of the child beyond the scope of the proceeding and reporting to the court other interests of the child that may need to be protected by the institution of other administrative or judicial proceedings; however, counsel is not responsible for instituting those proceedings or representing the child in them unless expressly appointed by the court for that purpose; and

(L) After learning of other existing administrative or judicial proceedings involving the child, communicating and cooperating with others to the extent necessary and appropriate to protect the child's interest.

(5) Taking all other steps to represent the child adequately as appropriate to the case, including becoming knowledgeable in other areas affecting minors including:

(A) The Indian Child Welfare Act;

(B) Information about local experts who can provide evaluation, consultation, and testimony; and

(C) Delinquency, dependency, probate, family law, and other proceedings.

(Subd (k) amended effective January 1, 2016; adopted effective January 1, 2008.)

Rule 5.242 amended effective January 1, 2023; adopted effective January 1, 2008; previously amended effective January 1, 2012, and January 1, 2016.

Article 5
Children's Participation in Family Court

Title 5, Family and Juvenile Rules—Division 1, Family Rules—Chapter 8, Child Custody and Visitation (Parenting Time) Proceedings—Article 5, Children's Participation in Family Court; adopted effective January 1, 2013.

Rule 5.250. Children's participation and testimony in family court proceedings

(a) Authority and overview

This rule is intended to implement Family Code section 3042. No statutory mandate, rule, or practice requires children to participate in court or prohibits them from doing so.

(Subd (a) amended effective January 1, 2023; adopted effective January 1, 2012.)

(b) Children's participation

When a child wishes to participate in a court proceeding involving child custody and visitation (parenting time):

(1) The court should find a balance between protecting the child, the statutory duty to consider the wishes of and input from the child, and the probative value of the child's input while ensuring all parties' due process rights to be aware of and to challenge evidence relied on by the court in making custody decisions.

(2) The court must:

(A) Consider a child's participation in family law matters on a case-by-case basis; and

(B) Not permit a child addressing the court about child custody or visitation (parenting time) to do so in the presence of the parties. The court must provide an alternative to having the child address the court in the presence of the parties to obtain input directly from the child.

(3) Notwithstanding the prohibition in (b)(2)(B), the court:

(A) May permit the child addressing the court about child custody or visitation (parenting time) to do so in the presence of the parties if the court determines that doing so is in the child's best interests and states its reasons for that finding on the record; and

(B) Must, in determining the best interests of the child under (b)(2)(A), consider whether addressing the court regarding child custody or visitation (parenting time) in the presence of the parties is likely to be detrimental to the child.

(Subd (b) adopted effective January 1, 2023.)

(c) Determining if the child wishes to address, or has changed their choice about addressing, the court

(1) The following persons must notify the persons in (c)(2) if they have information indicating that a child in a custody or visitation (parenting time) matter either wishes to address the court or has changed their choice about addressing the court:

(A) An attorney appointed to represent the child in the case;

(B) An evaluator;

(C) An investigator;

(D) A child custody recommending counselor who provides recommendations to the judicial officer under Family Code section 3183; and

(E) Other professionals serving on the case.

(2) The notice described in (c)(1) must be given, as soon as feasible, to the following:

(A) The parties or their attorneys;

(B) The attorney appointed to represent the child;

(C) Other professionals serving on the case; and then

(D) The judicial officer.

(3) The following persons may inform the court if they have information indicating that a child wishes to address the court:

(A) A party; and

(B) A party's attorney.

(4) In the absence of information indicating a child wishes to address the court, the judicial officer may inquire whether the child wishes to do so.

(Subd (c) amended and relettered effective January 1, 2023; adopted as subd (b) effective January 1, 2012.)

(d) Guidelines for determining whether addressing the court is in the child's best interest

(1) When a child indicates that he or she wishes to address the court, the judicial officer must consider whether involving the child in the proceedings is in the child's best interest.

(2) If the child indicating an interest in addressing the court is 14 years old or older, the judicial officer must hear from that child unless the court makes a finding that addressing the court is not in the child's best interest and states the reasons on the record.

(3) In determining whether addressing the court is in a child's best interest, the judicial officer should consider the following:

(A) Whether the child is of sufficient age and capacity to reason to form an intelligent preference as to custody or visitation (parenting time);

(B) Whether the child is of sufficient age and capacity to understand the nature of testimony;

(C) Whether information has been presented indicating that the child may be at risk emotionally if he or she is permitted or denied the opportunity to address the court or that the child may benefit from addressing the court;

(D) Whether the subject areas about which the child is anticipated to address the court are relevant to the court's decisionmaking process; and

(E) Whether any other factors weigh in favor of or against having the child address the court, taking into consideration the child's desire to do so.

(Subd (d) relettered effective January 1, 2023; adopted as subd (c) effective January 1, 2012.)

(e) Guidelines for receiving testimony and other input

(1) If the court precludes the calling of a child as a witness, alternatives for the court to obtain information or other input from the child may include, but are not limited to:

(A) The child's participation in child custody mediation under Family Code section 3180;

(B) Appointment of a child custody evaluator or investigator under Family Code section 3110 or Evidence Code section 730;

(C) Admissible evidence provided by the parents, parties, or witnesses in the proceeding;

(D) Information provided by a child custody recommending counselor authorized to provide recommendations under Family Code section 3183(a); and

(E) Information provided from a child interview center or professional so as to avoid unnecessary multiple interviews.

(2) If the court precludes the calling of a child as a witness and specifies one of the other alternatives, the court must require that the information or evidence obtained by alternative means and provided by a professional or nonparty:

(A) Be in writing and fully document the child's views on the matters on which the child wished to express an opinion;

(B) Describe the child's input in sufficient detail to assist the court in its adjudication process;

(C) Be provided to the court and to the parties by an individual who will be available for testimony and cross-examination; and

(D) Be filed in the confidential portion of the family law file.

(3) On deciding to take the testimony of a child, the judicial officer should balance the necessity of taking the child's testimony in the courtroom with parents and attorneys present with the need to create an environment in which the child can be open and honest. In each case in which a child's testimony will be taken, courts should consider:

(A) Where the testimony will be taken, including the possibility of closing the courtroom to the public or hearing from the child on the record in chambers;

(B) Who should be present when the testimony is taken, such as: both parents and their attorneys, only attorneys in the case in which both parents are represented, the child's attorney and parents, or only a court reporter with the judicial officer;

(C) How the child will be questioned, such as whether only the judicial officer will pose questions that the parties have submitted, whether attorneys or parties will be permitted to cross-examine the child, or whether a child advocate or expert in child development will ask the questions in the presence of the judicial officer and parties or a court reporter; and

(D) Whether a court reporter is available in all instances, but especially when testimony may be taken outside the presence of the parties and their attorneys and, if not, whether it will be possible to provide a listening device so that testimony taken in chambers may be heard simultaneously by the parents and their attorneys in the courtroom or to otherwise make a record of the testimony.

(4) In taking testimony from a child, the court must take special care to protect the child from harassment or embarrassment and to restrict the unnecessary repetition of questions. The court must also take special care to ensure that questions are stated in a form that is appropriate to the witness's age or cognitive level. If the child is not represented by an attorney, the court must inform the child in an age-appropriate manner about the limitations on confidentiality and that the information provided to the court will be on the record and provided to the parties in the case. In the process of listening to and inviting the child's input, the court must allow but not require the child to state a preference regarding custody or visitation and should, in an age-appropriate manner, provide information about the process by which the court will make a decision.

(5) In any case in which a child will be called to testify, the court may consider the appointment of minor's counsel for that child. The court may consider whether such appointment will cause unnecessary delay or otherwise interfere with the child's ability to participate in the process. In addition to adhering to the requirements for minor's counsel under Family Code section 3151 and rules 5.240, 5.241, and 5.242, and subdivision (c) of this rule, minor's counsel must:

(A) Provide information to the child in an age-appropriate manner about the limitations on confidentiality and indicate to the child the possibility that information provided to the court will be on the record and provided to the parties in the case;

(B) Allow but not require the child to state a preference regarding custody or visitation (parenting time) and, in an age-appropriate manner, provide information about the process by which the court will make a decision;

(C) Provide procedures relevant to the child's participation and, if appropriate, provide an orientation to the courtroom where the child will be testifying.

(6) No testimony of a child may be received without such testimony being heard on the record or in the presence of the parties. This requirement may not be waived by stipulation.

(Subd (e) amended and relettered effective January 1, 2023; adopted as subd (d) effective January 1, 2012.)

(f) Additional responsibilities of court-connected or appointed professionals

In addition to the duties in (c), a child custody evaluator, a child custody recommending counselor, or an investigator assigned to meet with a child in a family court proceeding must:

(1)–(3) * * *

(Subd (f) amended and relettered effective January 1, 2023; adopted as subd (e) effective January 1, 2012.)

(g) Methods of providing information to parents and supporting children

Courts should provide information to parties and parents and support for children when children want to participate or testify or are otherwise involved in family law proceedings. Such methods may include but are not limited to:

(1) Having court-connected professionals meet jointly or separately with the parents or parties to discuss alternatives to having a child provide direct testimony;

(2) Providing an orientation for a child about the court process and the role of the judicial officer in making decisions, how the courtroom or chambers will be set up, and what participating or testifying will entail;

(3) Providing information to parents or parties before and after a child participates or testifies so that they can consider the possible effect on their child of participating or not participating in a given case;

(4) Including information in child custody mediation orientation presentations and publications about a child's participation in family law proceedings;

(5) Providing a children's waiting room; and

(6) Providing an interpreter for the child, if needed.

(Subd (g) relettered effective January 1, 2023; adopted as subd (f) effective January 1, 2012.)

(h) Education and training

Education and training content for court staff and judicial officers should include information on children's participation in family court processes, methods other than direct testimony for receiving input from children, and procedures for taking children's testimony.

(*Subd (h) relettered effective January 1, 2023; adopted as subd (g) effective January 1, 2012.*)

Rule 5.250 amended effective January 1, 2023; adopted effective January 1, 2012.

Advisory Committee Comment

Rule 5.250 does not apply to probate guardianships except as and to the extent that the rule is incorporated or expressly made applicable by a rule of court in title 7 of the California Rules of Court.

Chapter 9
Child, Spousal, and Domestic Partner Support

Title 5, Family and Juvenile Rules—Division 1, Family Rules—Chapter 9, Child, Spousal, and Domestic Partner Support; adopted effective January 1, 2013.

Art. 1. General Provisions. Rule 5.260.
Art. 2. Certification of Statewide Uniform Guideline Support Calculators. Rule 5.275.

Article 1
General Provisions

Title 5, Family and Juvenile Rules—Division 1, Family Rules—Chapter 9, Child, Spousal, and Domestic Partner Support—Article 1, General Provisions; adopted effective January 1, 2013.

Rule 5.260. General provisions regarding support cases

(a) Financial declarations

Except as provided below, for all hearings involving child, spousal, or domestic partner support, both parties must complete, file, and serve a current *Income and Expense Declaration* (form FL-150) on all parties.

(1) A party requesting support orders must include a current, completed *Income and Expense Declaration* (form FL-150) with the *Request for Order* (form FL-300) that is filed with the court and served on all parties.

(2) A party responding to a request for support orders must include a current, completed *Income and Expense Declaration* (form FL-150) with the *Responsive Declaration to Request for Order* (form FL-320) that is filed with the court and served on all parties.

(3) "Current" means the form has been completed within the past three months providing no facts have changed. The form must be sufficiently completed to allow the court to make an order.

(4) In child support hearings, a party may complete a current *Financial Statement (Simplified)* (form FL-155) instead of a current *Income and Expense Declaration* (form FL-150) if he or she meets the requirements allowing submission of a *Financial Statement (Simplified)* (form FL-155).

(5) *Financial Statement (Simplified)* (form FL-155) is not appropriate for use in proceedings to determine or modify spousal or domestic partner support, to determine or modify family support, or to determine attorney's fees and costs.

(*Subd (a) adopted effective January 1, 2013.*)

(b) Deviations from guideline child support in orders and judgments

(1) If a party contends that the amount of support as calculated under the statewide uniform guideline formula is inappropriate, that party must file a declaration stating the amount of support alleged to be proper and the factual and legal bases justifying a deviation from guideline support under Family Code section 4057.

(2) In its discretion, for good cause shown, the court may deviate from the amount of guideline support resulting from the computer calculation. If the court finds good cause to deviate from the statewide uniform guideline formula for child support, the court must state its findings in writing or on the record as required by Family Code sections 4056, 4057, and 4065.

(3) Stipulated agreements for child support that deviate from the statewide uniform guideline must include either a *Non-Guideline Child Support Findings Attachment* (form FL-342(A)) or language in the agreement or judgment conforming with Family Code sections 4056 and 4065.

(*Subd (b) adopted effective January 1, 2013.*)

(c) Request to change prior support orders

The supporting declaration submitted in a request to change a prior child, spousal, or domestic partner support order must include specific facts demonstrating a change of circumstances. No change of circumstances must be shown to change a previously agreed upon child support order that was below the child support guidelines.

(*Subd (c) adopted effective January 1, 2013.*)

(d) Notification to the local child support agency

The party requesting court orders must provide the local child support agency timely notice of any request to establish, change, or enforce any child, spousal, or domestic partner support order if the agency is providing support enforcement services or has intervened in the case as described in Family Code section 17400.

(*Subd (d) adopted effective January 1, 2013.*)

(e) Judgment for support

(1) If child support is an issue in a judgment:

(A) Each party should file a proposed support calculation with the proposed judgment that sets forth the party's assumptions with regard to gross income, tax filing status, time-share, add-on expenses, and any other factor relevant to the support calculation.

(B) The moving party should file the documents in (A) with the proposed judgment if the judgment is based on respondent's default or a stipulation of the parties.

(C) The court may use and must permit parties or their attorneys to use any software certified by the Judicial Council to present support calculations to the court.

(2) If spousal or domestic partner support is an issue in a judgment:

(A) Use of support calculation software is not appropriate when requesting a judgment or modification of a judgment for spousal or domestic partner support.

(B) Petitioner or the parties may use *Spousal or Partnership Support Declaration Attachment* (form FL-157) to address the issue of spousal or domestic partner support under Family Code section 4320 when relevant to the case.

(*Subd (e) adopted effective January 1, 2013.*)

Rule 5.260 adopted effective January 1, 2013.

Article 2
Certification of Statewide Uniform Guideline Support Calculators

Title 5, Family and Juvenile Rules—Division 1, Family Rules—Chapter 9, Child, Spousal, and Domestic Partner Support—Article 2, Certification of Statewide Uniform Guideline Support Calculators; amended effective January 1, 2013; adopted as Chapter 6.

Rule 5.275. Standards for computer software to assist in determining support

(a) Authority

This rule is adopted under Family Code section 3830.

(*Subd (a) amended effective January 1, 2007; previously amended effective January 1, 2003.*)

(b) Standards

The standards for computer software to assist in determining the appropriate amount of child or spousal support are:

(1) The software must accurately compute the net disposable income of each parent as follows:

(A) Permit entry of the "gross income" of each parent as defined by Family Code section 4058;

(B) Either accurately compute the state and federal income tax liability under Family Code section 4059(a) or permit the entry of a figure for this amount; this figure, in the default state of the program, must not include the tax consequences of any spousal support to be ordered;

(C) Ensure that any deduction for contributions to the Federal Insurance Contributions Act or as otherwise permitted by Family Code section 4059(b) does not exceed the allowable amount;

(D) Permit the entry of deductions authorized by Family Code sections 4059(c) through (f); and

(E) Permit the entry of deductions authorized by Family Code section 4059(g) (hardship) while ensuring that any deduction subject to the limitation in Family Code section 4071(b) does not exceed that limitation.

(2) Using examples provided by the Judicial Council, the software must calculate a child support amount, using its default settings, that is accurate to within 1 percent of the correct amount. In making this determination, the Judicial Council must calculate the correct amount of

support for each example and must then calculate the amount for each example using the software program. Each person seeking certification of software must supply a copy of the software to the Judicial Council. If the software does not operate on a standard Windows 95 or later compatible or Macintosh computer, the person seeking certification of the software must make available to the Judicial Council any hardware required to use the software. The Judicial Council may delegate the responsibility for the calculation and determinations required by this rule.

(3) The software must contain, either on the screen or in written form, a glossary defining each term used on the computer screen or in printed hard copy produced by the software.

(4) The software must contain, either on the screen or in written form, instructions for the entry of each figure that is required for computation of child support using the default setting of the software. These instructions must include but not be limited to the following:

(A) The gross income of each party as provided for by Family Code section 4058;

(B) The deductions from gross income of each party as provided for by Family Code section 4059 and subdivision (b)(1) of this rule;

(C) The additional items of child support provided for in Family Code section 4062; and

(D) The following factors rebutting the presumptive guideline amount: Family Code section 4057(b)(2) (deferred sale of residence) and 4057(b)(3) (income of subsequent partner).

(5) In making an allocation of the additional items of child support under subdivision (b)(4)(C) of this rule, the software must, as its default setting, allocate the expenses one-half to each parent. The software must also provide, in an easily selected option, the alternative allocation of the expenses as provided for by Family Code section 4061(b).

(6) The printout of the calculator results must display, on the first page of the results, the range of the low-income adjustment as permitted by Family Code section 4055(b)(7), if the low-income adjustment applies. If the software generates more than one report of the calculator results, the range of the low-income adjustment only must be displayed on the report that includes the user inputs.

(7) The software or a license to use the software must be available to persons without restriction based on profession or occupation.

(8) The sale or donation of software or a license to use the software to a court or a judicial officer must include a license, without additional charge, to the court or judicial officer to permit an additional copy of the software to be installed on a computer to be made available by the court or judicial officer to members of the public.

(Subd (b) amended effective January 1, 2020; previously amended effective January 1, 2003, and January 1, 2007.)

(c) Expiration of certification

Any certification provided by the Judicial Council under Family Code section 3830 and this rule must expire one year from the date of its issuance unless another expiration date is set forth in the certification. The Judicial Council may provide for earlier expiration of a certification if (1) the provisions involving the calculation of tax consequences change or (2) other provisions involving the calculation of support change.

(Subd (c) amended effective January 1, 2003.)

(d) Statement of certified public accountant

If the software computes the state and federal income tax liability as provided in subdivision (b)(1)(B) of this rule, the application for certification, whether for original certification or for renewal, must be accompanied by a statement from a certified public accountant that

(1) The accountant is familiar with the operation of the software;

(2) The accountant has carefully examined, in a variety of situations, the operation of the software in regard to the computation of tax liability;

(3) In the opinion of the accountant the software accurately calculates the estimated actual state and federal income tax liability consistent with Internal Revenue Service and Franchise Tax Board procedures;

(4) In the opinion of the accountant the software accurately calculates the deductions under the Federal Insurance Contributions Act (FICA), including the amount for social security and for Medicare, and the deductions for California State Disability Insurance and properly annualizes these amounts; and

(5) States which calendar year the statement includes and must clearly indicate any limitations on the statement. The Judicial Council may request a new statement as often as it determines necessary to ensure accuracy of the tax computation.

(Subd (d) amended effective January 1, 2003.)

(e) Renewal of certification

At least three months prior to the expiration of a certification, a person may apply for renewal of the certification. The renewal must include a statement of any changes made to the software since the last application for certification. Upon request, the Judicial Council will keep the information concerning changes confidential.

(Subd (e) amended effective January 1, 2003.)

(f) Modifications to the software

The certification issued by the Judicial Council under Family Code section 3830 and this rule imposes a duty upon the person applying for the certification to promptly notify the Judicial Council of all changes made to the software during the period of certification. Upon request, the Judicial Council will keep the information concerning changes confidential. The Judicial Council may, after receipt of information concerning changes, require that the software be recertified under this rule.

(Subd (f) amended effective January 1, 2003.)

(g) Definitions

As used in this chapter:

(1) "Software" refers to any program or digital application used to calculate the appropriate amount of child or spousal support.

(2) "Default settings" refers to the status in which the software first starts when it is installed on a computer system. The software may permit the default settings to be changed by the user, either on a temporary or a permanent basis, if (1) the user is permitted to change the settings back to the default without reinstalling the software; (2) the computer screen prominently indicates whether the software is set to the default settings; and (3) any printout from the software prominently indicates whether the software is set to the default settings.

(3) "Contains" means, with reference to software, that the material is either displayed by the program code itself or is found in written documents supplied with the software.

(Subd (g) amended effective January 1, 2016; previously amended effective January 1, 2003.)

(h) Explanation of discrepancies

Before the Judicial Council denies a certificate because of failure to comply with the standards in paragraph (b)(1) or (b)(2) of this rule, the Judicial Council may request the person seeking certification to explain the differences in results.

(i) Application

A person seeking certification of software must apply in writing to the Judicial Council.

(Subd (i) amended effective January 1, 2020; previously amended effective January 1, 2003.)

(j) Acceptability in the courts

(1) In all actions for child or family support brought by or otherwise involving the local child support agency under title IV-D of the Social Security Act, the Department of Child Support Services' California Guideline Child Support Calculator software program must be used by:

(A) Parties and attorneys to present support calculations to the court; and

(B) The court to prepare support calculations.

(2) In all non-title IV-D proceedings, the court may use and must permit parties or attorneys to use any software certified by the Judicial Council under this rule.

(Subd (j) amended effective January 1, 2009; adopted as subd (k) effective January 1, 2000; previously relettered effective January 1, 2003.)

Rule 5.275 amended effective January 1, 2020; adopted as rule 1258 effective December 1, 1993; previously amended and renumbered as rule 5.275 effective January 1, 2003; previously amended effective January 1, 2000, January 1, 2007, January 1, 2009, and January 1, 2016.

Chapter 10
Government Child Support Cases (Title IV-D Support Cases)

Title 5, Family and Juvenile Rules—Division 1, Family Rules—Chapter 10, Government Child Support Cases (Title IV-D Support Cases); adopted effective January 1, 2013.

Rule 5.300. Purpose, authority, and definitions

Rule 5.305. Hearing of matters by a judge under Family Code sections 4251(a) and 4252(b)(7)

Rule 5.310. Use of existing family law forms

Rule 5.311. Implementation of new and revised governmental forms by local child support agencies

Rule 5.315. Memorandum of points and authorities

Rule 5.320. Attorney of record in support actions under title IV-D of the Social Security Act
Rule 5.324. Telephone appearance in title IV-D hearings and conferences
Rule 5.325. Procedures for clerk's handling of combined summons and complaint
Rule 5.330. Procedures for child support case registry form
Rule 5.335. Procedures for hearings on interstate income withholding orders
Rule 5.340. Judicial education for child support commissioners
Rule 5.350. Procedures for hearings to cancel (set aside) voluntary declarations of parentage or paternity when no previous action has been filed
Rule 5.355. Minimum standards of training for court clerk staff whose assignment includes title IV-D child support cases
Rule 5.360. Appearance by local child support agency
Rule 5.365. Procedure for consolidation of child support orders
Rule 5.370. Party designation in interstate and intrastate cases
Rule 5.372. Transfer of title IV-D cases between tribal court and state court
Rule 5.375. Procedure for a support obligor to file a motion regarding mistaken identity

Rule 5.300. Purpose, authority, and definitions

(a) Purpose

The rules in this chapter are adopted to provide practice and procedure for support actions under title IV-D of the Social Security Act and under California statutory provisions concerning these actions.

(Subd (a) amended effective January 1, 2007.)

(b) Authority

These rules are adopted under Family Code sections 211, 3680(b), 4251(a), 4252(b), 10010, 17404, 17432, and 17400.

(Subd (b) amended effective January 1, 2007; previously amended effective January 1, 2003.)

(c) Definitions

As used in these rules, unless the context requires otherwise, "title IV-D support action" refers to an action for child or family support that is brought by or otherwise involves the local child support agency under title IV-D of the Social Security Act.

(Subd (c) amended effective January 1, 2007; previously amended effective January 1, 2003.)

Rule 5.300 amended effective January 1, 2007; adopted as rule 1280 effective January 1, 1977; previously amended and renumbered effective January 1, 2003.

Rule 5.305. Hearing of matters by a judge under Family Code sections 4251(a) and 4252(b)(7)

(a) Exceptional circumstances

The exceptional circumstances under which a judge may hear a title IV-D support action include:

(1) The failure of the judge to hear the action would result in significant prejudice or delay to a party including added cost or loss of work time;

(2) Transferring the matter to a commissioner would result in undue consumption of court time;

(3) Physical impossibility or difficulty due to the commissioner being geographically separate from the judge presently hearing the matter;

(4) The absence of the commissioner from the county due to illness, disability, death, or vacation; and

(5) The absence of the commissioner from the county due to service in another county and the difficulty of travel to the county in which the matter is pending.

(Subd (a) amended effective January 1, 2007; previously amended January 1, 2003.)

(b) Duty of judge hearing matter

A judge hearing a title IV-D support action under this rule and Family Code sections 4251(a) and 4252(b)(7) may make an order or may make an interim order and refer the matter to the commissioner for further proceedings when appropriate. As long as a local child support agency is a party to the action, any future proceedings must be heard by a commissioner, unless the commissioner is unavailable because of exceptional circumstances.

(Subd (b) amended effective January 1, 2020; previously amended effective January 1, 2003, and January 1, 2007.)

(c) Discretion of the court

Notwithstanding (a) and (b) of this rule, a judge may, in the interests of justice, transfer a case to a commissioner for hearing.

(Subd (c) amended effective January 1, 2007.)

Rule 5.305 amended effective January 1, 2020; adopted as rule 1280.1 effective July 1, 1997; previously amended and renumbered effective January 1, 2003; previously amended effective January 1, 2007.

Rule 5.310. Use of existing family law forms

When an existing family law form is required or appropriate for use in a title IV-D support action, the form may be used notwithstanding the absence of a notation for the other parent as a party under Family Code section 17404. The caption of the form must be modified by the person filing it by adding the words "Other parent:" and the name of the other parent to the form.

Rule 5.310 amended effective January 1, 2007; adopted as rule 1280.2 effective July 1, 1997; previously amended and renumbered effective January 1, 2003.

Rule 5.311. Implementation of new and revised governmental forms by local child support agencies

(a) General extended implementation

A local child support agency providing services as required by Family Code section 17400 must implement any new or revised form approved or adopted by the Judicial Council for support actions under title IV-D of the Social Security Act, and under California statutory provisions concerning these actions, within six months of the effective date of the form. During that six-month period, the local child support agency may properly use and file the immediately prior version of the form.

(Subd (a) amended effective January 1, 2007.)

(b) Judgment regarding parental obligations

When the local child support agency files a proposed judgment or proposed supplemental judgment in any action using *Judgment Regarding Parental Obligations (Governmental)* (form FL-630), a final judgment or supplemental judgment may be filed on:

(1) The same version of the form that was used with the initial action or that was filed as an amended proposed judgment; or

(2) The most current version of the form, unless there have been amendments to the form that result in substantial changes from the filed version. If the most current version of the form has been substantially changed from the filed version, then the filed version must be used for the final judgment. A substantial change is one that would change the relief granted in a final judgment from that noticed in a proposed or amended proposed judgment.

(Subd (b) amended effective January 1, 2007.)

Rule 5.311 amended effective January 1, 2007; adopted effective January 1, 2004.

Rule 5.315. Memorandum of points and authorities

Notwithstanding any other rule, including rule 313, a notice of motion in a title IV-D support action must not be required to contain points and authorities if the notice of motion uses a form adopted or approved by the Judicial Council. The absence of points and authorities under these circumstances may not be construed by the court as an admission that the motion is not meritorious and cause for its denial.

Rule 5.315 amended effective January 1, 2007; adopted as rule 1280.3 effective July 1, 1997; previously amended and renumbered effective January 1, 2003.

Rule 5.320. Attorney of record in support actions under title IV-D of the Social Security Act

The attorney of record on behalf of a local child support agency appearing in any action under title IV-D of the Social Security Act is the director of the local child support agency, or if the director of that agency is not an attorney, the senior attorney of that agency or an attorney designated by the director for that purpose. Notwithstanding any other rule, including but not limited to rule 2.100–2.119, the name, address, and telephone number of the county child support agency and the name of the attorney of record are sufficient for any papers filed by the child support agency. The name of the deputy or assistant district attorney or attorney of the child support agency, who is not attorney of record, and the State Bar number of the attorney of record or any of his or her assistants are not required.

Rule 5.320 amended effective January 1, 2007; adopted as rule 1280.4 effective July 1, 1997; previously amended effective January 1, 2001; previously amended and renumbered effective January 1, 2003.

Rule 5.324. Telephone appearance in title IV-D hearings and conferences

(a) Purpose

This rule is suspended from January 1, 2022, to January 1, 2026. During that time, the provisions in rule 3.672 apply in its place.

(Subd (a) amended effective August 4, 2023; previously amended effective January 1, 2022.)

(b) Definition

"Telephone appearance," as used in this rule, includes any appearance by telephonic, audiovisual, videoconferencing, digital, or other electronic means.

(c) Permissibility of telephone appearances

Upon request, the court, in its discretion, may permit a telephone appearance in any hearing or conference related to an action for child support when the local child support agency is providing services under title IV-D of the Social Security Act.

(d) Exceptions

A telephone appearance is not permitted for any of the following except as permitted by Family Code section 5700.316:

(1) Contested trials, contempt hearings, orders of examination, and any matters in which the party or witness has been subpoenaed to appear in person; and

(2) Any hearing or conference for which the court, in its discretion on a case-by-case basis, decides that a personal appearance would materially assist in a determination of the proceeding or in resolution of the case.

(Subd (d) amended effective January 1, 2017; previously amended effective January 1, 2008.)

(e) Request for telephone appearance

(1) A party, an attorney, a witness, a parent who has not been joined to the action, or a representative of a local child support agency or government agency may request permission of the court to appear and testify by telephone. The local child support agency may request a telephone appearance on behalf of a party, a parent, or a witness when the local child support agency is appearing in the title IV-D support action, as defined by rule 5.300(c). The court may also, on its own motion, allow a telephone appearance.

(2) A party, an attorney, a witness, a parent who has not been joined to the action, or a representative of a local child support agency or government agency who wishes to appear by telephone at a hearing must file a request with the court clerk at least 12 court days before the hearing. A local child support agency that files the request for telephone appearance on behalf of a party, a parent, or a witness must file the request with the court clerk at least 12 court days before the hearing. This request must be served on the other parties, the local child support agency, and attorneys, if any. Service must be by personal delivery, fax, express mail, or other means reasonably calculated to ensure delivery by the close of the next court day.

(3) The mandatory *Request for Telephone Appearance (Governmental)* (form FL-679) must be filed to request a telephone appearance.

(Subd (e) amended effective January 1, 2008.)

(f) Opposition to telephone appearance

Any opposition to a request to appear by telephone must be made by declaration under penalty of perjury under the laws of the State of California. It must be filed with the court clerk and served at least eight court days before the court hearing. Service on the person or agency requesting the telephone appearance; all parties, including the other parent, a parent who has not been joined to the action, the local child support agency; and attorneys, if any, must be accomplished using one of the methods listed in (e)(2).

(Subd (f) amended effective January 1, 2007.)

(g) Shortening time

The court may shorten the time to file, submit, serve, respond, or comply with any of the procedures specified in this rule.

(h) Notice by court

At least five court days before the hearing, the court must notify the person or agency requesting the telephone appearance, the parties, and attorneys, if any, of its decision. The court may direct the court clerk, the court-approved vendor, the local child support agency, a party, or an attorney to provide the notification. This notice may be given in person or by telephone, fax, express mail, e-mail, or other means reasonably calculated to ensure notification no later than five court days before the hearing date.

(Subd (h) amended effective January 1, 2007.)

(i) Need for personal appearance

If, at any time during the hearing, the court determines that a personal appearance is necessary, the court may continue the matter and require a personal appearance.

(j) Vendors, procedure, audibility, reporting, and information

Rule 3.670(j)–(q) applies to telephone appearances under this rule.

(Subd (j) amended effective January 1, 2014; previously amended effective January 1, 2007, July 1, 2008, and July 1, 2011.)

(k) Technical equipment

Courts that lack the technical equipment to implement telephone appearances are exempt from the rule.

Rule 5.324 amended effective August 4, 2023; adopted effective July 1, 2005; previously amended effective January 1, 2007, January 1, 2008, July 1, 2008, July 1, 2011, January 1, 2014, January 1, 2017, and January 1, 2022.

Rule 5.325. Procedures for clerk's handling of combined summons and complaint

(a) Purpose

This rule provides guidance to court clerks in processing and filing the *Summons and Complaint or Supplemental Complaint Regarding Parental Obligations (Governmental)* (form FL-600) for actions under Family Code section 17400 or 17404.

(Subd (a) amended effective January 1, 2007; previously amended effective January 1, 2003.)

(b) Filing of complaint and issuance of summons

The clerk must accept the *Summons and Complaint or Supplemental Complaint Regarding Parental Obligations (Governmental)* (form FL-600) for filing under Code of Civil Procedure section 411.10. The clerk must issue the original summons in accordance with Code of Civil Procedure section 412.20 by filing the original form FL-600 and affixing the seal of the court. The original form FL-600 must be retained in the court's file.

(Subd (b) amended effective January 1, 2003.)

(c) Issuance of copies of combined summons and complaint

Upon issuance of the original summons, the clerk must conform copies of the filed form FL-600 to reflect that the complaint has been filed and the summons has been issued. A copy of form FL-600 so conformed must be served on the defendant in accordance with Code of Civil Procedure section 415.10 et seq.

(Subd (c) amended effective January 1, 2003.)

(d) Proof of service of summons

Proof of service of the *Summons and Complaint or Supplemental Complaint Regarding Parental Obligations (Governmental)* (form FL-600) must be on the form prescribed by rule 2.150 or any other proof of service form that meets the requirements of Code of Civil Procedure section 417.10.

(Subd (d) amended effective January 1, 2007; previously amended effective January 1, 2003.)

(e) Filing of proposed judgment and amended proposed judgment

The proposed judgment must be an attachment to the *Summons and Complaint or Supplemental Complaint Regarding Parental Obligations (Governmental)* (form FL-600) and must not be file-endorsed separately. An amended proposed judgment submitted for filing must be attached to the *Declaration for Amended Proposed Judgment* (form FL-616), as required by Family Code section 17430(c), and a proof of service by mail, if appropriate. Upon filing, the *Declaration for Amended Proposed Judgment* may be file-endorsed. The amended proposed judgment must not be file-endorsed.

(Subd (e) amended effective January 1, 2007; previously amended effective January 1, 2003.)

Rule 5.325 amended effective January 1, 2007; adopted as rule 1280.5 effective July 1, 1998; previously amended and renumbered effective January 1, 2003.

Rule 5.330. Procedures for child support case registry form

(a) Purpose

This rule provides guidance to court clerks in processing the *Child Support Case Registry Form* (form FL-191).

(Subd (a) amended effective January 1, 2007; previously amended effective January 1, 2003.)

(b) Application

This rule applies to any action or proceeding in which there is an order for child support or family support except for cases in which the local child support agency provides support enforcement services under Family Code section 17400. This rule does not apply to cases in which the local child support agency provides support enforcement services under Family Code section 17400.

(Subd (b) amended effective January 1, 2003.)

(c) Requirement that form be filed

The court must require that a *Child Support Case Registry Form* (form FL-191), completed by one of the parties, be filed each time an initial court order for child support or family support or a modification of a court order for child support or family support is filed with the court. A party attempting to file an initial judgment or order for child support or family support or a modification of an order for child or family support without a completed *Child Support Case Registry Form* (form FL-191) must be given a blank form to complete. The form must be accepted if legibly handwritten in ink or typed. No filing fees may be charged for filing the form.

(Subd (c) amended effective January 1, 2007; previously amended effective January 1, 2003.)

(d) Distribution of the form

Copies of the *Child Support Case Registry Form* (form FL-191) must be made available by the clerk's office and the family law facilitator's office to the parties without cost. A blank copy of the *Child Support Case Registry Form* (form FL-191) must be sent with the notice of entry of judgment to the party who did not submit the judgment or order.

(Subd (d) amended effective January 1, 2003.)

(e) Items on form that must be completed

A form must be considered complete if items 1b, 1c, 2, 5, and 6 are completed. Either item 3 or item 4 must also be completed as appropriate. If the form is submitted with the judgment or order for court approval, the clerk must complete item 1a once the judgment or order has been signed by the judicial officer and filed.

(Subd (e) amended effective January 1, 2003.)

(f) Clerk handling of form

The completed *Child Support Case Registry Form* (form FL-191) must not be stored in the court's file. It should be date and time stamped when received and stored in an area to which the public does not have access. At least once per month all forms received must be mailed to the California Department of Social Services.

(Subd (f) amended effective January 1, 2003.)

(g) Storage of confidential information

Provided that all information is kept confidential, the court may keep either a copy of the form or the information provided on the form in an electronic format.

Rule 5.330 amended effective January 1, 2007; adopted as rule 1280.6 effective July 1, 1999; previously amended and renumbered effective January 1, 2003.

Rule 5.335. Procedures for hearings on interstate income withholding orders

(a) Purpose

This rule provides a procedure for a hearing under Family Code section 5700.506 in response to an income withholding order.

(Subd (a) amended effective September 1, 2021; previously amended effective January 1, 2003.)

(b) Filing of request for hearing

A support obligor may contest the validity or enforcement of an income withholding order by filing a completed request for hearing. A copy of the income withholding order must be attached.

(c) Filing fee

The court must not require a filing fee to file the request for hearing under this rule.

(Subd (c) amended effective January 1, 2003.)

(d) Creation of court file

Upon receipt of the completed request for hearing and a copy of the income withholding order, the clerk must assign a case number and schedule a court date. The court date must be no earlier than 30 days from the date of filing and no later than 45 days from the date of filing.

(Subd (d) amended effective January 1, 2003.)

(e) Notice of hearing

The support obligor must provide the clerk with envelopes addressed to the obligor, the support enforcement agency that sent the income withholding order, and the obligor's employer. The support obligor must also provide an envelope addressed to the person or agency designated to receive the support payments if that person or agency is different than the support enforcement agency that sent the income withholding order. The support obligor must provide sufficient postage to mail each envelope provided. Upon scheduling the hearing, the clerk must mail a copy of the request for hearing in each envelope provided by the support obligor.

(Subd (e) amended effective January 1, 2007; previously amended effective January 1, 2003.)

(f) Use of court file in subsequent proceedings

Any subsequent proceedings filed in the same court that involve the same parties and are filed under the Uniform Interstate Family Support Act (UIFSA) must use the file number created under this rule.

(Subd (f) amended effective January 1, 2007; previously amended effective January 1, 2003.)

(g) Definitions

As used in this rule:

(1) An "income withholding order" is the *Order/Notice to Withhold Income for Child Support* (form FL-195) issued by a child support enforcement agency in another state; and

(2) A "request for hearing" is the *Request for Hearing Regarding Wage and Earnings Assignment (Family Law—Governmental—UIFSA)* (form FL-450).

(Subd (g) amended effective January 1, 2007; previously amended effective January 1, 2003.)

Rule 5.335 amended effective September 1, 2021; adopted as rule 1280.7 effective July 1, 1999; previously amended and renumbered effective January 1, 2003; previously amended effective January 1, 2007.

Rule 5.340. Judicial education for child support commissioners

Every commissioner whose principal judicial assignment is to hear child support matters must attend the following judicial education programs:

(1) *Basic child support law education*

Within one year of beginning an assignment as a child support commissioner, the judicial officer must attend a basic educational program on California child support law and procedure designed primarily for judicial officers. The training program must include instruction on both state and federal laws concerning child support. A judicial officer who has completed the basic educational program need not attend the basic educational program again.

(2) *Continuing education*

The judicial officer must attend an update on new developments in child support law and procedure at least once each calendar year.

(3) *Other child support education*

To the extent that judicial time and resources are available, the judicial officer is encouraged to attend additional educational programs on child support and other related family law issues.

(4) *Other judicial education*

The requirements of this rule are in addition to and not in lieu of the requirements of rule 10.462.

Rule 5.340 amended effective January 1, 2023; adopted as rule 1280.8 effective July 1, 1999; previously amended and renumbered effective January 1, 2003; previously amended effective January 1, 2007, and January 1, 2017.

Rule 5.350. Procedures for hearings to cancel (set aside) voluntary declarations of parentage or paternity when no previous action has been filed

(a) Purpose

This rule provides a procedure for a hearing to cancel (set aside) a voluntary declaration of parentage or paternity under Family Code sections 7576 and 7577.

(Subd (a) amended effective January 1, 2020.)

(b) Filing of request for hearing

A person who has signed a voluntary declaration of parentage or paternity, or another interested party, may ask that the declaration be canceled (set aside) by filing a completed *Request for Hearing and Application to Cancel (Set Aside) Voluntary Declaration of Parentage or Paternity* (form FL-280).

(Subd (b) amended effective January 1, 2020; previously amended effective January 1, 2003, and January 1, 2006.)

(c) Creation of court file

On receipt of the completed request for hearing, the clerk must assign a case number and schedule a court date. The court date must be no earlier than 31 days after the date of filing and no later than 45 days after the date of filing.

(Subd (c) amended effective January 1, 2007; previously amended effective January 1, 2003.)

(d) Notice of hearing

The person who is asking that the voluntary declaration of parentage or paternity be canceled (set aside) must serve, either by personal service or by mail, a copy of the request for hearing and a blank *Responsive Declaration to Application to Cancel (Set Aside) Voluntary Declaration of Parentage or Paternity* (form FL-285) on the other person or people who signed the voluntary declaration of parentage or paternity. If the local child support agency is providing services in the case, the person requesting the set-aside must also serve a copy of the request for hearing on the agency.

(Subd (d) amended effective January 1 2020; previously amended effective January 1, 2003.)

(e) Order after hearing

The decision of the court must be written on the *Order After Hearing on Motion to Cancel (Set Aside) Voluntary Declaration of Parentage or Paternity* (form FL-290). If the voluntary declaration of parentage or paternity is canceled (set aside), the clerk must mail a copy of the order to the Department of Child Support Services in order that the voluntary declaration of parentage or paternity be purged from the records.

(*Subd (e) amended effective January 1, 2020; previously amended effective January 1, 2003.*)

(f) Use of court file in subsequent proceedings

Pleadings in any subsequent proceedings, including but not limited to proceedings under the Uniform Parentage Act, that involve the parties and child named in the voluntary declaration of parentage or paternity must be filed in the court file that was initiated by the filing of the *Request for Hearing and Application to Cancel (Set Aside) Voluntary Declaration of Parentage or Paternity* (form FL-280).

(*Subd (f) amended effective January 1, 2020; previously amended effective January 1, 2003.*)

Rule 5.350 amended effective January 1, 2020; adopted as rule 1280.10 effective July 1, 2000; previously amended and renumbered effective January 1, 2003; previously amended effective January 1, 2006, and January 1, 2007.

Rule 5.355. Minimum standards of training for court clerk staff whose assignment includes title IV-D child support cases

Any court clerk whose assignment includes title IV-D child support cases must participate in a minimum of six hours of continuing education annually in federal and state laws concerning child support and related issues.

Rule 5.355 amended effective January 1, 2007; adopted as rule 1280.11 effective July 1, 2000; previously amended and renumbered effective January 1, 2003.

Rule 5.360. Appearance by local child support agency

When a local child support agency is providing services as required by Family Code section 17400, that agency may appear in any action or proceeding that it did not initiate by giving written notice to all parties, on *Notice Regarding Payment of Support* (form FL-632), that it is providing services in that action or proceeding under title IV-D of the Social Security Act. The agency must file the original of the notice in the action or proceeding with proof of service by mail on the parties. On service and filing of the notice, the court must not require the local child support agency to file any other notice or pleading before that agency appears in the action or proceeding.

Rule 5.360 amended effective January 1, 2007; adopted as rule 1280.12 effective January 1, 2001; previously amended and renumbered effective January 1, 2003.

Rule 5.365. Procedure for consolidation of child support orders

(a) When an order of consolidation of actions has been made under section 1048(a) of the Code of Civil Procedure in cases in which a local child support agency is appearing under section 17400 of the Family Code, or when a motion to consolidate or combine two or more child support orders has been made under section 17408 of the Family Code, the cases in which those orders were entered must be consolidated as follows:

(1) *Priority of consolidation*

The order consolidating cases that contain child support orders must designate the primary court file into which the support orders must be consolidated and must also designate the court files that are subordinate. Absent an order upon showing of good cause, the cases or child support orders must be consolidated into a single court file according to the following priority, including those cases or orders initiated or obtained by a local child support agency under division 17 of the Family Code that are consolidated under either section 1048(a) of the Code of Civil Procedure or section 17408 of the Family Code:

(A) If one of the cases or child support orders to be consolidated is in an action for nullity, dissolution, or legal separation brought under division 6 of the Family Code, all cases and orders so consolidated must be consolidated into that action, which must be the primary file.

(B) If none of the cases or child support orders to be consolidated is in an action for nullity, dissolution, or legal separation, but one of the child support orders to be consolidated has been issued in an action under the Uniform Parentage Act (Fam. Code, div. 12, pt. 3), all orders so consolidated must be consolidated into that action, which must be the primary file.

(C) If none of the cases or child support orders to be consolidated is in an action for nullity, dissolution, or legal separation or in an action under the Uniform Parentage Act, but one of the child support orders to be consolidated has been issued in an action commenced by a *Petition for Custody and Support of Minor Children* (form FL-260), all orders so consolidated must be consolidated into that action, which must be the primary file.

(D) If none of the cases or child support orders to be consolidated is in an action for nullity, dissolution, or legal separation or in an action under the Uniform Parentage Act, the case or cases with the higher number or numbers must be consolidated into the case with the lowest number, which must be the primary file. Child support orders in cases brought under the Domestic Violence Protection Act (Fam. Code, div. 10, pt. 4) or any similar law may be consolidated under this rule. However, a domestic violence case must not be designated as the primary file.

(2) *Notice of consolidation*

Upon issuance of the consolidation order, the local child support agency must prepare and file in each subordinate case a *Notice of Consolidation* (form FL-920), indicating that the support orders in those actions are consolidated into the primary file. The notice must state the date of the consolidation, the primary file number, and the case number of each of the cases so consolidated. If the local child support agency was not a participant in the proceeding in which the consolidation was ordered, the court must designate the party to prepare and file the notice.

(*Subd (a) amended effective January 1, 2007; previously amended effective January 1, 2003.*)

(b) Subsequent filings in consolidated cases

Notwithstanding any other rule, including but not limited to rule 367, upon consolidation of cases with child support orders, all filings in those cases, whether dealing with child support or not, must occur in the primary court action and must be filed under that case, caption, and number only. All further orders must be issued only in the primary action, and no further orders may be issued in a subordinate court file. All enforcement and modification of support orders in consolidated cases must occur in the primary court action regardless of in which action the order was originally issued.

(*Subd (b) amended effective January 1, 2007; previously amended effective January 1, 2003.*)

Rule 5.365 amended effective January 1, 2007; adopted as rule 1285.13 effective January 1, 2001; previously amended and renumbered effective January 1, 2003.

Rule 5.370. Party designation in interstate and intrastate cases

When a support action that has been initiated in another county or another state is filed, transferred, or registered in a superior court of this state under the Uniform Interstate Family Support Act (Fam. Code, div. 9, pt. 5, ch. 6, commencing with § 4900), the intercounty support enforcement provisions of the Family Code (div. 9, pt. 5, ch. 8, art. 9, commencing with § 5600), or any similar law, the party designations in the caption of the action in the responding court must be as follows:

(1) *New actions initiated under the Uniform Interstate Family Support Act*

The party designation in the superior court of this state, responding to new actions initiated under the Uniform Interstate Family Support Act (Fam. Code, div. 9, pt. 5, ch. 6, commencing with § 4900), must be the party designation that appears on the first page of *the Uniform Support Petition* (form FL-500/OMB 0970-0085) in the action.

(2) *Registered orders under the Uniform Interstate Family Support Act or state law*

The party designation in all support actions registered for enforcement or modification must be the one that appears in the original (earliest) order being registered.

Rule 5.370 amended effective January 1, 2007; adopted as rule 1285.14 effective January 1, 2001; previously amended and renumbered effective January 1, 2003.

Rule 5.372. Transfer of title IV-D cases between tribal court and state court

(a) Purpose

This rule is intended to define the procedure for transfer of title IV-D child support cases between a California superior court and a tribal court.

(*Subd (a) amended effective January 1, 2018; adopted effective January 1, 2014.*)

(b) Definitions

(1) "Tribal court" means any tribal court of a federally recognized Indian tribe located in California that is receiving funding from the federal government to operate a child support program under title IV-D of the Social Security Act (42 U.S.C. § 654 et seq.).

(2) "Superior court" means a superior court of the state of California.

(3) "Title IV-D child support cases" include all cases where title IV-D services are being provided whether the case originates from the local child support agency's filing of a summons and complaint or later becomes a title IV-D cases when the local child support agency registers a child support order or intervenes in a child support action by filing a change of payee.

(Subd (b) adopted effective January 1, 2014.)

(c) Disclosure of related case

A party must disclose in superior court whether there is any related action in tribal court in the first pleading, in an attached affidavit, or under oath. A party's disclosure of a related action must include the names and addresses of the parties to the action, the name and address of the tribal court where the action is filed, the case number of the action, and the name of judge assigned to the action, if known.

(Subd (c) adopted effective January 1, 2014.)

(d) Notice of intent to transfer case

Before filing a motion for case transfer of a child support matter from a superior court to a tribal court, the party requesting the transfer, the state title IV-D agency, or the tribal IV-D agency must provide the parties with notice of their right to object to the case transfer and the procedures to make such an objection.

(Subd (d) adopted effective January 1, 2014.)

(e) Determination of concurrent jurisdiction by a superior court

(1) The superior court may, on its own motion or on the motion of any party and after notice to the parties of their right to object, transfer a child support and custody provision of an action in which the state is providing services under Family Code section 17400 to a tribal court, as defined in (a). This provision applies to both prejudgment and postjudgment cases.

(2) The motion for transfer to a tribal court must include the following information:

(A) Whether the child is a tribal member or eligible for tribal membership;

(B) Whether one or both of the child's parents are tribal members or eligible for tribal membership;

(C) Whether one or both of the child's parents live on tribal lands or in tribal housing, work for the tribe, or receive tribal benefits or services;

(D) Whether there are other children of the obligor subject to child support obligations;

(E) Any other factor supporting the child's or parents' connection to the tribe.

(3) When ruling on a motion to transfer, the superior court must first make a threshold determination that concurrent jurisdiction exists. Evidence to support this determination may include:

(A) Evidence contained within the motion for transfer;

(B) Evidence agreed to by stipulation of the parties; and

(C) Other evidence submitted by the parties or by the tribe.

The court may request that the tribal child support agency or the tribal court submit information concerning the tribe's jurisdiction.

(4) There is a presumption of concurrent jurisdiction if the child is a tribal member or eligible for tribal membership. If concurrent jurisdiction is found to exist, the transfer to tribal court will occur unless a party has objected within 20 days after service of notice of the right to object referenced in subdivision (e)(1) above. On the filing of a timely objection to the transfer, the superior court must conduct a hearing on the record considering all the relevant factors set forth in (f). The objecting party has the burden of proof to establish good cause not to transfer to tribal court.

(Subd (e) amended effective January 1, 2018; adopted effective January 1, 2014.)

(f) Evidentiary considerations

(1) In making a determination on the motion for case transfer, the superior court must consider:

(A) The identities of the parties;

(B) The convenience of the parties and witnesses;

(C) The remedy available in the superior court or tribal court; and

(D) Any other factors deemed necessary by the superior court.

(2) In making a determination on the motion for case transfer, the superior court may not consider the perceived adequacy of tribal justice systems.

(3) The superior court may, after notice to all parties, attempt to resolve any procedural issues by contacting the tribal court concerning a motion to transfer. The superior court must allow the parties to participate in, and must prepare a record of, any communication made with the tribal court judge.

(Subd (f) amended effective January 1, 2018; adopted effective January 1, 2014.)

(g) Order on request to transfer

If the superior court denies the request for transfer, the court must state on the record the basis for denying the request. If the superior court grants the request for transfer, it must issue a final order on the request to transfer including a determination of whether concurrent jurisdiction exists.

(Subd (g) amended effective January 1, 2018; adopted effective January 1, 2014.)

(h) Proceedings after order granting transfer

Once the superior court has granted the application to transfer and has received confirmation that the tribal court has accepted jurisdiction, the superior court clerk must deliver a copy of the entire file, including all pleadings and orders, to the clerk of the tribal court within 20 days of confirmation that the tribal court has accepted jurisdiction. With the exception of a filing by a tribal court as described by subdivision (i) of this rule, the superior court may not accept any further filings in the state court action in relation to the issues of child support and custody that were transferred to the tribal court.

(Subd (h) amended effective January 1, 2018; adopted effective January 1, 2014.)

(i) Transfer of proceedings from tribal court

(1) If a tribal court determines that it is not in the best interest of the child or the parties for the tribal court to retain jurisdiction of a child support case, the tribe may, upon noticed motion to all parties and the state child support agency, file a motion with the superior court to transfer the case to the jurisdiction of the superior court along with copies of the tribal court's order transferring jurisdiction and the entire file.

(2) The superior court must notify the tribal court upon receipt of the materials and the date scheduled for the hearing of the motion to transfer.

(3) If the superior court has concurrent jurisdiction, it must not reject the case.

(4) No filing fee may be charged for the transfer of a title IV-D child support case from a tribal court.

(Subd (i) adopted effective January 1, 2018.)

Rule 5.372 amended effective January 1, 2018; adopted effective January 1, 2014.

Advisory Committee Comment

This rule applies only to title IV-D child support cases. In the normal course, transfers from tribal court are initiated by the local child support agencies. Under Government Code sections 6103.9 and 70672, local child support agencies are exempt from payment of filing fees. The rule makes it clear that this exemption also applies when an eligible case is being transferred from a tribal court.

Rule 5.375. Procedure for a support obligor to file a motion regarding mistaken identity

(a) Purpose

This rule applies to a support obligor who claims that support enforcement actions have erroneously been taken against him or her by the local child support agency because of a mistake in the support obligor's identity. This rule sets forth the procedure for filing a motion in superior court to establish the mistaken identity under Family Code section 17530 after the support obligor has filed a claim of mistaken identity with the local child support agency and the claim has been denied.

(Subd (a) amended effective January 1, 2003.)

(b) Procedure for filing motion in superior court

The support obligor's motion in superior court to establish mistaken identity must be filed on *Request for Order* (form FL-300) with appropriate attachments. The support obligor must also file as exhibits to the request for order a copy of the claim of mistaken identity that he or she filed with the local child support agency and a copy of the local child support agency's denial of the claim.

(Subd (b) amended effective January 1, 2013; previously amended effective January 1, 2003, and January 1, 2007.)

Rule 5.375 amended effective January 1, 2013; adopted as rule 1280.15 effective January 1, 2001; previously amended and renumbered effective January 1, 2003; previously amended effective January 1, 2007.

Chapter 11
Domestic Violence Cases

Title 5, Family and Juvenile Rules—Division 1, Family Rules—Chapter 11, Domestic Violence Cases; adopted effective January 1, 2013.

2012 Note: Chapter 11, effective January 1, 2013 was originally adopted as Chapter 8, effective July 1, 2012.

Art. 1. Domestic Violence Prevention Act Cases. Rules 5.380–5.382.
Art. 2. Tribal Court Protective Orders. Rule 5.386.

Article 1
Domestic Violence Prevention Act Cases

Title 5, Family and Juvenile Rules—Division 1, Family Rules—Chapter 11, Domestic Violence Cases—Article 1, Domestic Violence Prevention Act Cases; adopted effective January 1, 2013.

2012 Note: Article 1 of Chapter 11, effective January 1, 2013 was originally adopted as Article 1 of Chapter 8, effective July 1, 2012.

Rule 5.380. Agreement and judgment of parentage in Domestic Violence Prevention Act cases
Rule 5.381. Modification of child custody, visitation, and support orders in Domestic Violence Prevention Act cases
Rule 5.382. Request to make minor's information confidential in domestic violence protective order proceedings

Rule 5.380. Agreement and judgment of parentage in Domestic Violence Prevention Act cases

(a) No requirement to open separate case; no filing fee

(1) If the court accepts the agreement of parentage and issues a judgment of parentage, the court may not require a party to open a separate parentage or other type of case in which to file the judgment. The court may open a separate type of case, but the court must not charge a fee for filing the judgment of parentage in the new case.

(2) When a judgment of parentage is filed in a Domestic Violence Prevention Act case in which a restraining order is currently in effect, no filing fee may be charged.

(Subd (a) adopted effective January 1, 2012.)

(b) Retention

The judgment must be retained by the court as a paternity record under Government Code section 68152.

(Subd (b) adopted effective January 1, 2012.)

(c) Notice of Entry of Judgment

When an *Agreement and Judgment of Parentage* (form DV-180) is filed, the court must serve a *Notice of Entry of Judgment* (form FL-190) on the parties.

(Subd (c) amended effective January 1, 2017; adopted effective January 1, 2012.)

Rule 5.380 amended effective January 1, 2017; adopted effective January 1, 2012.

Rule 5.381. Modification of child custody, visitation, and support orders in Domestic Violence Prevention Act cases

(a) Application of rule

This rule addresses court procedures for the modification of child custody, visitation, and support orders in accordance with Family Code section 6340(a).

(Subd (a) adopted effective January 1, 2012.)

(b) Filing fees

A filing fee may be charged on a request to modify a child custody, visitation, or support order only after a protective order, as defined in Family Code section 6218, is no longer in effect. The filing fee, if charged, is the same as the filing fee for a motion, application, or any other paper requiring a hearing after the first paper.

(Subd (b) adopted effective January 1, 2012.)

(c) Retention

The court must retain any child custody, visitation, or support order filed in a Domestic Violence Prevention Act as a Family Law order under Government Code section 68152(c)(5).

(Subd (c) adopted effective January 1, 2012.)

Rule 5.381 adopted effective January 1, 2012.

Rule 5.382. Request to make minor's information confidential in domestic violence protective order proceedings

(a) Application of rule

This rule applies to requests and orders made under Family Code section 6301.5 to keep a minor's information confidential in a domestic violence protective order proceeding.

Wherever used in this rule, "legal guardian" means either parent if both parents have legal custody, or the parent or person having legal custody, or the guardian, of a minor.

(Subd (a) adopted effective January 1, 2019.)

(b) Information that may be made confidential

The information that may be made confidential includes:

(1) The minor's name;
(2) The minor's address;
(3) The circumstances surrounding the protective order with respect to the minor. These include the allegations in the *Request for Domestic Violence Retraining Order* (form DV-100) that involve conduct directed, in whole or in part, toward the minor; and
(4) Any other information that the minor or legal guardian believes should be confidential.

(Subd (b) adopted effective January 1, 2019.)

(c) Requests for confidentiality

(1) *Person making request*

A request for confidentiality may be made by a minor or legal guardian.

(2) *Number of minors*

A request for confidentiality by a legal guardian may be made for more than one minor. "Minor," as used in this rule, refers to all minors for whom a request for confidentiality is made.

(Subd (c) adopted effective January 1, 2019.)

(d) Procedures for making request

(1) *Timing of requests*

A request for confidentiality may be made at any time during the case.

(2) *Submission of request*

The person submitting a request must complete and file *Request to Keep Minor's Information Confidential* (form DV-160), a confidential form.

(3) *Ruling on request*

(A) *Ruling on request without notice*

The court must determine whether to grant a request for confidentiality without requiring that any notice of the request be given to the other party, or both parties if the minor is not a party in the proceeding. No adversarial hearing is to be held.

(B) *Request for confidentiality submitted at the same time as a request for restraining orders*

If a request for confidentiality is submitted at the same time as a request for restraining orders, the court must consider both requests consistent with Family Code section 6326, and must consider and rule on the request for confidentiality before the request for restraining order is filed.

Documents submitted with the restraining order request must not be filed until after the court has ruled on the request for confidentiality and must be consistent with (C) below.

(C) *Withdrawal of request*

If a request for confidentiality under (B) made by the person asking for the restraining order is denied and the requester seeks to withdraw the request for restraining orders, all of the following apply:

(i) The court must not file the request for restraining order and the accompanying proposed order forms and must return the documents to the requester personally, destroy the documents, or delete the documents from any electronic files;

(ii) The order denying confidentiality must be filed and maintained in a public file; and

(iii) The request for confidentiality must be filed and maintained in a confidential file.

(4) *Need for additional facts*

If the court finds that the request for confidentiality is insufficiently specific to meet the requirements under Family Code section 6301.5(b) for granting the request, the court may take testimony from the minor, or legal guardian, the person requesting a protective order, or other competent witness, in a closed hearing in order to determine if there are additional facts that would support granting the request.

(Subd (d) adopted effective January 1, 2019.)

(e) Orders on request for confidentiality

(1) *Rulings*

The court may grant the entire request, deny the entire request, or partially grant the request for confidentiality.

(2) *Order granting request for confidentiality*

(A) *Applicability*

An order made under Family Code section 6301.5 applies in this case and in any other civil case to all registers of actions, indexes, court calendars, pleadings, discovery documents, and other documents filed or served in the action, and at hearings, trial, and other court proceedings that are open to the public.

(B) *Minor's name*

If the court grants a request for confidentiality of the minor's name and:

(i) If the minor is a party to the action, the court must use the initials of the minor, or other initials at the discretion of the court. In addition, the court must use only initials to identify both parties to the action if using the other party's name would likely reveal the identity of the minor.

(ii) If the minor is not a party to the action, the court must not include any information that would likely reveal the identity of the minor, including whether the minor lives with the person making the request for confidentiality.

(C) *Circumstances surrounding protective order (statements related to minor)*

If the court grants a request for confidentiality, the order must specifically identify the information about the minor in *Request for Domestic Violence Restraining Order* (form DV-100) and any other applicable document that must be kept confidential. Information about the minor ordered confidential by the court must not be made available to the public.

(D) *Service and copies*

The other party, or both parties if the person making the request for confidentiality is not a party to the action, must be served with a copy of the *Request to Keep Minor's Information Confidential* (form DV-160), *Order on Request to Keep Minor's Information Confidential* (form DV-165), and *Notice of Order Protecting Information of Minor* (form DV-170), redacted if required under (f)(4).

The protected person and the person requesting confidentiality (if not the protected person) must be provided up to three copies of redacted and unredacted copies of any request or order form.

(3) *Order denying request for confidentiality*

(A) The order denying confidentiality must be filed and maintained in a public file. The request for confidentiality must be filed and maintained in a confidential file.

(B) Notwithstanding denial of a request to keep the minor's address confidential, the address may be confidential under other statutory provisions

(C) Service

(i) If a request for confidentiality is denied and the request for restraining order has been withdrawn, and if no other action is pending before the court in the case, then the *Request to Keep Minor's Information Confidential* (form DV-160) and *Order on Request to Keep Minor's Information Confidential* (form DV-165) must not be served on the other party, or both parties if the person making the request for confidentiality is not a party to the action.

(ii) If a request for confidentiality is denied and the request for restraining order has not been withdrawn, or if an action between the same parties is pending before the court, then the *Request to Keep Minor's Information Confidential* (form DV-160) and *Order on Request to Keep Minor's Information Confidential* (form DV-165) must be served on the other party, or both parties if the person making the request for confidentiality is not a party to the action.

(Subd (e) amended effective September 1, 2020; adopted effective January 1, 2019.)

(f) Procedures to protect confidential information when order is granted

(1) If a request for confidentiality is granted in whole or in part, the court, in its discretion, and taking into consideration the factors stated in (g), must ensure that the order granting confidentiality is maintained in the most effective manner by:

(A) The judicial officer redacting all information to be kept confidential from all applicable documents;

(B) Ordering the requesting party or the requesting party's attorney to prepare a redacted copy of all applicable documents and submit all redacted copies to the court for review and filing; or

(C) Ordering any other procedure that facilitates the prompt and accurate preparation of a redacted copy of all applicable documents in compliance with the court's order granting confidentiality, provided the selected procedure is consistent with (g).

(2) The redacted copy or copies must be filed and maintained in a public file, and the unredacted copy or copies must be filed and maintained in a confidential file.

(3) Information that is made confidential from the public and the restrained person must be filed in a confidential file accessible only to the minor or minors who are subjects of the order of confidentiality, or legal guardian who requested confidentiality, law enforcement for enforcement purposes only, and the court.

(4) Any information that is made confidential from the restrained person must be redacted from the copy that will be served on the restrained person.

(Subd (f) adopted effective January 1, 2019.)

(g) Factors in selecting redaction procedures

In determining the procedures to follow under (f), the court must consider the following factors:

(1) Whether the requesting party is represented by an attorney;

(2) Whether the requesting party has immediate access to a self-help center or other legal assistance;

(3) Whether the requesting party is capable of preparing redacted materials without assistance;

(4) Whether the redactions to the applicable documents are simple or complex; and

(5) When applicable, whether the selected procedure will ensure that the orders on the request for restraining order and the request for confidentiality are entered in an expeditious and timely manner.

(Subd (g) adopted effective January 1, 2019.)

(h) Releasing minor's confidential information

(1) *To respondent*

Information about a minor must be shared with the respondent only as provided in Family Code section 6301.5(d)(1)(B), limited to information necessary to allow the respondent to respond to the request for the protective order and to comply with the confidentiality order and the protective order.

(2) *To law enforcement*

Information about a minor must be shared with law enforcement as provided in Family Code section 6301.5(d)(1)(A) or by court order.

(3) *To other persons*

If the court finds it is necessary to prevent abuse within the meaning of Family Code section 6220, or is in the best interest of the minor, the court may release confidential information on the request of any person or entity or on the court's own motion.

(A) *Request for release of confidential information*

(i) Any person or entity may request the release of confidential information by filing *Request for Release of Minor's Confidential Information* (form DV-176) and a proposed order, *Order on Request for Release of Minor's Confidential Information* (form DV-179), with the court.

(ii) Within 10 days after filing form DV-176 with the clerk, the clerk must serve, by first-class mail, the following documents on the minor or legal guardian who made the request to keep the minor's information confidential:

a. *Cover Sheet for Confidential Information* (form DV-175);

b. *Request for Release of Minor's Confidential Information* (form DV-176);

c. *Notice of Request for Release of Minor's Confidential Information* (form DV-177);

d. *Response to Request for Release of Minor's Confidential Information* (form DV-178) (blank copy);

e. *Order on Request for Release of Minor's Confidential Information* (form DV-179).

(B) *Opportunity to object*

(i) The person who made the request for confidentiality has the right to object by filing form DV-178 within 20 days from the date of the mailing of form DV-177, or verbally objecting at a hearing, if one is held.

(ii) The person filing a response must serve a copy of the response (form DV-178) on the person requesting release of confidential information. Service must occur before filing the response form with the court unless the response form contains confidential information. If the response form contains confidential information, service must be done as soon as possible after the response form has been redacted.

(iii) If the person who made the request for confidentiality objects to the release of information, the court may set the matter for a closed hearing.

(C) *Rulings*

The request may be granted or denied in whole or in part without a hearing. Alternatively, the court may set the matter for hearing on at least 10 days' notice to the person who made the request for release of confidential information and the person who made the request for confidential information. Any hearing must be confidential.

(i) *Order granting release of confidential information*

a. The order (form DV-179) granting the release of confidential information must be prepared in a manner consistent with the procedures outlined in (f).

b. A redacted copy of the order (form DV-179) must be filed in a public file and an unredacted copy of the order must be filed in a confidential file.

c. *Service*

If the court grants the request for release of information based on the pleadings, the court must mail a copy of form DV-179 to the person who filed form DV-176 and the person who made the request to keep the minor's information confidential. Parties may be served in court if present at the hearing.

(ii) *Order denying request to release minor's confidential information*

a. The court may deny a request to release confidential information based on the request alone.

b. The order (form DV-179) denying the release of confidential information must be filed in a public file and must not include any confidential information.

c. *Service*

If the court denies the request for release of information based on the pleadings, the court must mail a copy of form DV-179 to the person who filed form DV-176 and the person who made the request to keep the minor's information confidential. Parties may be served in court if present at the hearing.

(iii) If the court finds that the request to release confidential information is insufficiently specific to meet the requirements under Family Code section 6301.5(d)(3), the court may conduct a closed hearing to determine if there are additional facts that would support granting the request. The court may receive any relevant evidence, including testimony from the person requesting release of the minor's confidential information, the minor, the legal guardian, the person who requested the restraining order, or other competent witness.

(Subd (h) amended effective September 1, 2020; adopted effective January 1, 2019.)

(i) Protecting information in subsequent filings and other civil cases

(1) *Filings made after an order granting confidentiality*

(A) A party seeking to file a document or form after an order for confidentiality has been made must submit the *Cover Sheet for Confidential Information* (form DV-175) attached to the front of the document to be filed.

(B) Upon receipt of form DV-175 with attached documents, the court must:

(i) Order a procedure for redaction consistent with the procedures stated in (f);

(ii) File the unredacted document in the confidential file pending receipt of the redacted document if the redacted document is not prepared on the same court day; and

(iii) File the redacted document in the public file after it has been reviewed and approved by the court for accuracy.

(2) *Other civil case*

(A) Information subject to an order of confidentiality issued under Family Code section 6301.5 must be kept confidential in any family law case and any other civil case with the same parties.

(B) The minor or person making the request for confidentiality and any person who has been served with a notice of confidentiality must submit a copy of the order of confidentiality (form DV-165) in any family law case and any other civil case with the same parties.

(Subd (i) amended effective September 1, 2020; adopted effective January 1, 2019.)

Rule 5.382 amended effective September 1, 2020; adopted effective January 1, 2019.

Advisory Committee Comment

Subdivisions (a), (b), (d), and (e). The process described in this rule need not be used if the request for confidentiality is merely to keep an address confidential and the minor has a mailing address which does not need to be kept private that can be listed on the forms, or if the minor's address can be made confidential under Family Code section 3429. In addition, the address need not be listed on the protective order for enforcement purposes under Family Code section 6225. The restraining order forms do not require the address of the nonpetitioning minor.

This rule and rule 2.551 provide a standard and procedures for courts to follow when a request is made to seal a record. The standard as reflected in Family Code section 6301.5 is based on *NBC Subsidiary (KNBC-TV), Inc. v. Superior Court* (1999) 20 Cal.4th 1178. The standard recognizes the First Amendment right of access to documents used at trial or as a basis of adjudication.

Article 2
Tribal Court Protective Orders

Title 5, Family and Juvenile Rules—Division 1, Family Rules—Chapter 11, Domestic Violence Cases—Article 2, Tribal Court Protective Orders; adopted effective January 1, 2013.

2012 Note: Article 2 of Chapter 11, effective January 1, 2013 was originally adopted as Article 2 of Chapter 8, effective July 1, 2012.

Rule 5.386. Procedures for filing a tribal court protective order

(a) Request for written procedures for filing a tribal court protective order

At the request of any tribal court located within the county, a court must adopt a written procedure or local rule to permit the fax or electronic filing of any tribal court protective order that is entitled to be registered under Family Code section 6404.

(Subd (a) adopted effective July 1, 2012.)

(b) Process for registration of order

The written procedure or local rule developed in consultation with the local tribal court or courts must provide a process for:

(1) The tribal court or courts to contact a representative of the superior court to inform him or her that a request for registration of a tribal court protective order will be made;

(2) Confirmation of receipt of the request for registration of the order; and

(3) Return of copies of the registered order to the tribal court or the protected person.

(Subd (b) adopted effective July 1, 2012.)

(c) No filing fee required

In accordance with Family Code section 6404(b), no fee may be charged for the fax or electronic filing registration of a tribal court protective order.

(Subd (c) adopted effective July 1, 2012.)

(d) Facsimile coversheet

The *Fax Transmission Cover Sheet for Registration of Tribal Court Protective Order* (form DV-610) or similar cover sheet established by written procedure or local rule must be used when fax filing a tribal court protective order. The cover sheet must be the first page transmitted, to be followed by any special handling instructions needed to ensure that the document will comply with local rules. Neither the cover sheet nor the special handling instructions are to be filed in the case. The court is not required to keep a copy of the cover sheet.

(Subd (d) adopted effective July 1, 2012.)

Rule 5.386 adopted effective July 1, 2012.

Chapter 12
Separate Trials (Bifurcation) and Interlocutory Appeals

Title 5, Family and Juvenile Rules—Division 1, Family Rules—Chapter 12, Separate Trials (Bifurcation) and Interlocutory Appeals; adopted effective January 1, 2013.

Art. 1. Separate Trials. Rule 5.390.
Art. 2. Interlocutory Appeals. Rule 5.392.

Article 1
Separate Trials

Title 5, Family and Juvenile Rules—Division 1, Family Rules—Chapter 12, Separate Trials (Bifurcation) and Interlocutory Appeals—Article 1, Separate Trials; adopted effective January 1, 2013.

Rule 5.390. Bifurcation of issues

(a) Request for order to bifurcate

As part of the noticed *Request for Order* (FL-300) of a party, the stipulation of the parties, case management, or the court's own motion, the court may bifurcate one or more issues to be tried separately before other issues are tried. A party requesting a separate trial or responding to a request for a separate trial must complete *Application or Response to Application for Separate Trial* (form FL-315).

(Subd (a) adopted effective January 1, 2013.)

(b) When to bifurcate

The court may separately try one or more issues before trial of the other issues if resolution of the bifurcated issue is likely to simplify the

determination of the other issues. Issues that may be appropriate to try separately in advance include:
(1) Validity of a postnuptial or premarital agreement;
(2) Date of separation;
(3) Date to use for valuation of assets;
(4) Whether property is separate or community;
(5) How to apportion increase in value of a business;
(6) Existence or value of business or professional goodwill;
(7) Termination of status of a marriage or domestic partnership;
(8) Child custody and visitation (parenting time);
(9) Child, spousal, or domestic partner support;
(10) Attorney's fees and costs;
(11) Division of property and debts;
(12) Reimbursement claims; or
(13) Other issues specific to a family law case.
(Subd (b) adopted effective January 1, 2013.)

(c) Alternate date of valuation

Requests for separate trial regarding alternate date of valuation under Family Code section 2552(b) must be accompanied by a declaration stating the following:
(1) The proposed alternate valuation date;
(2) Whether the proposed alternate valuation date applies to all or only a portion of the assets and, if the *Request for Order* (FL-300) is directed to only a portion of the assets, the declaration must separately identify each such asset; and
(3) The reasons supporting the alternate valuation date.
(Subd (c) adopted effective January 1, 2013.)

(d) Separate trial to terminate status of marriage or domestic partnership

(1) All pension plans that have not been divided by court order that require joinder must be joined as a party to the case before a petitioner or respondent may file a request for a separate trial to terminate marital status or the domestic partnership. Parties may refer to *Retirement Plan Joinder—Information Sheet* (form FL-318-INFO) to help determine whether their retirement benefit plans must be joined.
(2) The party not requesting termination of status may ask the court:
(A) To order that the judgment granting a dissolution include conditions that preserve his or her claims in retirement benefit plans, health insurance, and other assets; and
(B) For other orders made as conditions to terminating the parties' marital status or domestic partnership.
(3) The court must use *Bifurcation of Status of Marriage or Domestic Partnership—Attachment* (form FL-347) as an attachment to the order after hearing in these matters.
(4) In cases involving division of pension benefits acquired by the parties during the marriage or domestic partnership, the court must use *Pension Benefits—Attachment to Judgment* (form FL-348) to set out the orders upon severance of the status of marriage or domestic partnership. The form serves as a temporary qualified domestic relations order and must be attached to the status-only judgment and then served on the plan administrator. It can also be attached to a judgment to allow the parties time to prepare a qualified domestic relations order.
(Subd (d) adopted effective January 1, 2013.)

(e) Notice by clerk

Within 10 days after the order deciding the bifurcated issue and any statement of decision under rule 3.1591 have been filed, the clerk must serve copies to the parties and file a certificate of mailing or a certificate of electronic service.
(Subd (e) amended effective January 1, 2017; adopted effective January 1, 2013.)
Rule 5.390 amended effective January 1, 2017; adopted effective January 1, 2013.

Article 2
Interlocutory Appeals

Title 5, Family and Juvenile Rules—Division 1, Family Rules—Chapter 12, Separate Trials (Bifurcation) and Interlocutory Appeals—Article 2, Interlocutory Appeals; adopted effective January 1, 2013.

Rule 5.392. Interlocutory appeals

(a) Applicability

This rule does not apply to appeals from the court's termination of marital status as a separate issue, or to appeals from other orders that are separately appealable.
(Subd (a) amended effective January 1, 2003; previously amended effective January 1, 1994.)

(b) Certificate of probable cause for appeal

(1) The order deciding the bifurcated issue may include an order certifying that there is probable cause for immediate appellate review of the issue.
(2) If it was not in the order, within 10 days after the clerk serves the order deciding the bifurcated issue, a party may notice a motion asking the court to certify that there is probable cause for immediate appellate review of the order. The motion must be heard within 30 days after the order deciding the bifurcated issue is served.
(3) The clerk must promptly serve notice of the decision on the motion to the parties. If the motion is not determined within 40 days after serving the order on the bifurcated issue, it is deemed granted on the grounds stated in the motion.
(Subd (b) amended effective January 1, 2017; previously amended effective January 1, 2002, and January 1, 2003.)

(c) Content and effect of certificate

(1) A certificate of probable cause must state, in general terms, the reason immediate appellate review is desirable, such as a statement that final resolution of the issue:
(A) Is likely to lead to settlement of the entire case;
(B) Will simplify remaining issues;
(C) Will conserve the courts' resources; or
(D) Will benefit the well-being of a child of the marriage or the parties.
(2) If a certificate is granted, trial of the remaining issues may be stayed. If trial of the remaining issues is stayed, unless otherwise ordered by the trial court on noticed motion, further discovery must be stayed while the certification is pending. These stays terminate upon the expiration of time for filing a motion to appeal if none is filed, or upon the Court of Appeal denying all motions to appeal, or upon the Court of Appeal decision becoming final.
(Subd (c) amended effective January 1, 2003; previously amended effective January 1, 2002.)

(d) Motion to appeal

(1) If the certificate is granted, a party may, within 15 days after the court serves the notice of the order granting it, serve and file in the Court of Appeal a motion to appeal the decision on the bifurcated issue. On ex parte application served and filed within 15 days, the Court of Appeal or the trial court may extend the time for filing the motion to appeal by not more than an additional 20 days.
(2) The motion must contain:
(A) A brief statement of the facts necessary to an understanding of the issue;
(B) A statement of the issue; and
(C) A statement of why, in the context of the case, an immediate appeal is desirable.
(3) The motion must include or have attached:
(A) A copy of the decision of the trial court on the bifurcated issue;
(B) Any statement of decision;
(C) The certification of the appeal; and
(D) A sufficient partial record to enable the Court of Appeal to determine whether to grant the motion.
(4) A summary of evidence and oral proceedings, if relevant, supported by a declaration of counsel may be used when a transcript is not available.
(5) The motion must be accompanied by the filing fee for an appeal under rule 8.100(c) and Government Code sections 68926 and 68926.1.
(6) A copy of the motion must be served on the trial court.
(Subd (d) amended effective January 1, 2017; previously amended effective January 1, 2002, January 1, 2003, and January 1, 2007.)

(e) Proceedings to determine motion

(1) Within 10 days after service of the motion, an adverse party may serve and file an opposition to it.
(2) The motion to appeal and any opposition will be submitted without oral argument, unless otherwise ordered.
(3) The motion to appeal is deemed granted unless it is denied within 30 days from the date of filing the opposition or the last document requested by the court, whichever is later.
(4) Denial of a motion to appeal is final forthwith and is not subject to rehearing. A party aggrieved by the denial of the motion may petition for review by the Supreme Court.
(Subd (e) amended effective January 1, 2007; previously amended effective January 1, 2002, and January 1, 2003.)

(f) Proceedings if motion to appeal is granted

(1) If the motion to appeal is granted, the moving party is deemed an appellant, and the rules governing other civil appeals apply except as provided in this rule.

(2) The partial record filed with the motion will be considered the record for the appeal unless, within 10 days from the date notice of the grant of the motion is served, a party notifies the Court of Appeal of additional portions of the record that are needed for a full consideration of the appeal.

(3) If a party notifies the court of the need for an additional record, the additional material must be secured from the trial court by augmentation under rule 8.155, unless it appears to the Court of Appeal that some of the material is not needed.

(4) Briefs must be filed under a schedule set for the matter by the Court of Appeal.

(Subd (f) amended effective January 1, 2017; previously amended effective January 1, 2002, January 1, 2003, and January 1, 2007.)

(g) Review by writ or appeal

The trial court's denial of a certification motion under (b) does not preclude review of the decision on the bifurcated issue by extraordinary writ.

(Subd (g) amended effective January 1, 2003; previously amended effective January 1, 2002.)

(h) Review by appeal

None of the following precludes review of the decision on the bifurcated issue upon appeal of the final judgment:

(1) A party's failure to move for certification under (b) for immediate appeal;

(2) The trial court's denial of a certification motion under (b) for immediate appeal;

(3) A party's failure to move to appeal under (d); and

(4) The Court of Appeals denial of a motion to appeal under (d).

Rule 5.392 amended effective January 1, 2017; adopted as rule 1269.5 effective July 1, 1989; previously amended and renumbered as rule 5.180 effective January 1, 2003; previously renumbered as rule 5.392 effective January 1, 2013; previously amended effective January 1, 1994, January 1, 2002, and January 1, 2007.

Chapter 13
Trials and Long-Cause Hearings

Title 5, Family and Juvenile Rules—Division 1, Family Rules—Chapter 13, Trials and Long-Cause Hearings; adopted effective January 1, 2013.

Rule 5.393. Setting trials and long-cause hearings
Rule 5.394. Trial or hearing brief

Rule 5.393. Setting trials and long-cause hearings

(a) Definitions

For purposes of this rule:

(1) A "trial day" is defined as a period no less than two and a half hours of a single court day.

(2) A "long-cause hearing" is defined as a hearing on a request for order that extends more than a single court day.

(3) A "trial brief" or "hearing brief" is a written summary or statement submitted by a party that explains to a judge the party's position on particular issues that will be part of the trial or hearing.

(Subd (a) adopted effective January 1, 2013.)

(b) Conference with judge before trial or long-cause hearing

The judge may schedule a conference with the parties and their attorneys before any trial or long-cause hearing.

(1) *Time estimates*

During the conference, each party must provide an estimate of the amount of time that will be needed to complete the trial or long-cause hearing. The estimate must take into account the time needed to examine witnesses and introduce evidence at the trial.

(2) *Trial or hearing brief*

The judge must determine at the conference whether to require each party to submit a trial or hearing brief. If trial briefs will be required, they must comply with the requirements of rule 5.394. Any additional requirements to the brief must be provided to the parties in writing before the end of the conference.

(Subd (b) adopted effective January 1, 2013.)

(c) Sequential days

Consistent with the goal of affording family law litigants continuous trials and long-cause hearings without interruption, when trials or long-cause hearings are set, they must be scheduled on as close to sequential days as the calendar of the trial judge permits.

(Subd (c) adopted effective January 1, 2013.)

(d) Intervals between trial or hearing days

When trials or long-cause hearings are not completed in the number of days originally scheduled, the court must schedule the remaining trial days as soon as possible on the earliest available days with the goal of minimizing intervals between days for trials or long-cause hearings.

(Subd (d) adopted effective January 1, 2013.)
Rule 5.393 adopted effective January 1, 2013.

Rule 5.394. Trial or hearing brief

(a) Contents of brief

For cases in which the judge orders each party to complete a trial or hearing brief or other pleading, the contents of the brief must include at least:

(1) The statistical facts and any disputes about the statistical facts. Statistical facts that may apply to the case could include:

(A) Date of the marriage or domestic partnership;

(B) Date of separation;

(C) Length of marriage or domestic partnership in years and months; and

(D) Names and ages of the parties' minor children;

(2) A brief summary of the case;

(3) A statement of any issues that need to be resolved at trial;

(4) A brief statement summarizing the contents of any appraisal or expert report to be offered at trial;

(5) A list of the witnesses to be called at trial and a brief description of the anticipated testimony of each witness, as well as name, business address, and statement of qualifications of any expert witness;

(6) Any legal arguments on which a party intends to rely; and

(7) Any other matters determined by the judge to be necessary and provided to the parties in writing.

(Subd (a) adopted effective January 1, 2013.)

(b) Service of brief

The parties must serve the trial or hearing brief on all parties and file the brief with the court a minimum of 5 court days before the trial or long-cause hearing.

(Subd (b) adopted effective January 1, 2013.)
Rule 5.394 adopted effective January 1, 2013.

Chapter 14
Default Proceedings and Judgments

Title 5, Family and Juvenile Rules—Division 1, Family Rules—Chapter 14, Default Proceedings and Judgments; adopted effective January 1, 2013.

Rule 5.401. Default
Rule 5.402. Request for default; forms
Rule 5.405. Judgment checklists
Rule 5.407. Review of default and uncontested judgments submitted on the basis of declaration under Family Code section 2336
Rule 5.409. Default and uncontested judgment hearings on judgments submitted on the basis of declarations under Family Code section 2336
Rule 5.411. Stipulated judgments
Rule 5.413. Notice of entry of judgment
Rule 5.415. Completion of notice of entry of judgment

Rule 5.400. Contact after adoption agreement [Renumbered]

Rule 5.400 renumbered as rule 5.451 effective January 1, 2013; adopted as rule 1180 effective July 1, 1998; previously amended effective July 1, 2001; previously amended and renumbered effective January 1, 2003; previously amended effective July 1, 2003, and January 1, 2007.

Rule 5.401. Default

(a) Entry of default

Upon proper application of the petitioner, the clerk must enter a default if the respondent or defendant fails within the time permitted to:

(1) Make an appearance as stated in rule 5.62;

(2) File a notice of motion to quash service of summons under section 418.10 of the Code of Civil Procedure; or

(3) File a petition for writ of mandate under section 418.10 of the Code of Civil Procedure.

(Subd (a) adopted effective January 1, 2013.)

(b) Proof of facts

(1) The petitioner may apply to the court for the relief sought in the petition at the time default is entered. The court must require proof to be made of the facts stated in the petition and may enter its judgment based on that proof.

(2) The court may permit the use of a completed *Income and Expense Declaration* (form FL-150) or *Financial Statement (Simplified)* (form FL-155) and *Property Declaration* (form FL-160) for all or any part of the proof required or permitted to be offered on any issue to which they are relevant.

(Subd (b) adopted effective January 1, 2013.)

(c) Disposition of all matters required

A judgment based on a default must include disposition of all matters subject to the court's jurisdiction for which a party seeks adjudication or an explicit reservation of jurisdiction over any matter not proposed for disposition at that time.

(Subd (c) adopted effective January 1, 2013.)

Rule 5.401 adopted effective January 1, 2013.

Rule 5.402. Request for default; forms

(a) Forms

No default may be entered in any proceeding unless a request has been completed on a *Request to Enter Default* (form FL-165) and filed by the petitioner. However, an *Income and Expense Declaration* (form FL-150) or *Financial Statement (Simplified)* (form FL-155) are not required if the petition contains no request for support, costs, or attorney's fees. A *Property Declaration* (form FL-160) is not required if the petition contains no request for property.

(Subd (a) adopted effective January 1, 2013.)

(b) Service address required

For the purpose of completing the declaration of mailing, unless service was by publication and the address of respondent is unknown, it is not sufficient to state that the address of the party to whom notice is given is unknown or unavailable.

(Subd (b) adopted effective January 1, 2013.)

Rule 5.402 adopted effective January 1, 2013.

Rule 5.405. Judgment checklists

The *Judgment Checklist—Dissolution/Legal Separation* (form FL-182) lists the forms that courts may require to complete a judgment based on default or uncontested judgment in dissolution or legal separation cases based on a declaration under Family Code section 2336. The court may not require any additional forms or attachments.

Rule 5.405 renumbered effective January 1, 2013; adopted as rule 5.146 effective July 1, 2012.

Rule 5.407. Review of default and uncontested judgments submitted on the basis of declaration under Family Code section 2336

Once a valid proof of service of summons has been filed with the court or respondent has made a general appearance in the case:

(a) Court review

The court must conduct a procedural review of all the documents submitted for judgment based on default or uncontested judgments submitted under Family Code section 2336 and notify the attorneys or self-represented litigants who submitted them of all identified defects.

(b) Notice of errors and omissions

Basic information for correction of the defects must be included in any notification to attorneys or self-represented litigants made under (a).

Rule 5.407 amended and renumbered effective January 1, 2013; adopted as rule 5.147 effective July 1, 2012.

Rule 5.409. Default and uncontested judgment hearings on judgments submitted on the basis of declarations under Family Code section 2336

The decision to hold a hearing in a case in which a judgment has been submitted on the basis of a declaration under Family Code section 2336 should be made on a case-by-case basis at the discretion of the court or request of a party. Courts must allow judgments in default and uncontested cases to be submitted by declaration pursuant to section 2336 and must not require that a hearing be conducted in all such cases.

Rule 5.409 renumbered effective January 1, 2013; adopted as rule 5.148 effective July 1, 2012.

Rule 5.410. Request for sibling contact information under Family Code section 9205 [Renumbered]

Rule 5.410 renumbered as rule 5.460 effective January 1, 2013; adopted effective January 1, 2008.

Rule 5.411. Stipulated judgments

(a) Format

A stipulated judgment (which must be attached to form FL-180 or form FL-250) may be submitted to the court for signature as an uncontested matter or at the time of the hearing on the merits and must contain the exact terms of any judgment proposed to be entered in the case. At the end, immediately above the space reserved for the judge's signature, the stipulated judgment must contain the following:

The foregoing is agreed to by:

_____   _____
(Petitioner)   (Respondent)

Approved as conforming to the agreement of the parties:

_____   _____
(Attorney for Petitioner)   (Attorney for Respondent)

(Subd (a) adopted effective January 1, 2013.)

(b) Disposition of all matters required

A stipulated judgment must include disposition of all matters subject to the court's jurisdiction for which a party seeks adjudication or an explicit reservation of jurisdiction over any matter not proposed for disposition at that time. A stipulated judgment constitutes a written agreement between the parties as to all matters covered by the stipulation.

(Subd (b) adopted effective January 1, 2013.)

Rule 5.411 adopted effective January 1, 2013.

Rule 5.413. Notice of entry of judgment

(a) Notice by clerk

Notwithstanding Code of Civil Procedure section 664.5, the clerk must give notice of entry of judgment, using *Notice of Entry of Judgment* (form FL-190), to the attorney for each party or to the party if self-represented, of the following:

(1) A judgment of legal separation;

(2) A judgment of dissolution;

(3) A judgment of nullity;

(4) A judgment establishing parental relationship (on form FL-190); or

(5) A judgment regarding custody or support.

(Subd (a) adopted effective January 1, 2013.)

(b) Notice to local child support agency form

This rule applies to local child support agency proceedings except that the notice of entry of judgment must be on *Notice of Entry of Judgment and Proof of Service by Mail* (form FL-635).

(Subd (b) adopted effective January 1, 2013.)

Rule 5.413 adopted effective January 1, 2013.

Rule 5.415. Completion of notice of entry of judgment

(a) Required attachments

Every person who submits a judgment for signature by the court must submit:

(1) Stamped envelopes addressed to the parties (if they do not have attorneys), or to the attorneys of record (if the parties are represented) that show the address of the court clerk as the return address; and

(2) An original and at least two additional copies of the *Notice of Entry of Judgment* (form FL-190).

(Subd (a) adopted effective January 1, 2013.)

(b) Fully completed

Form FL-190 must be fully completed except for the designation of the date entered, the date of mailing, and signatures. It must specify in the certificate of mailing the place where notices have been given to the other party.

(Subd (b) adopted effective January 1, 2013.)

(c) Address of respondent or defendant

If there has been no appearance by the other party, the address stated in the affidavit of mailing in part 3 of the *Request to Enter Default* (form FL-165) must be the party's last known address and must be used for mailing form FL-190 to that party. In support proceedings initiated by the local child support agency, an envelope addressed to the child support agency need not be submitted. If service was by publication and the address of respondent or defendant is unknown, those facts must be stated in place of the required address.

(Subd (c) adopted effective January 1, 2013.)

(d) Consequences of failure to comply

Failure to complete the form or to submit the envelopes is cause for refusal to sign the judgment until compliance with the requirements of this rule.

(Subd (d) adopted effective January 1, 2013.)

(e) Application to local child support agencies

This rule applies to local child support agency proceedings filed under the Family Code except that:

(1) The local child support agency must use form *Notice of Entry of Judgment and Proof of Service by Mail* (form FL-635);

(2) The local child support agency may specify in the certificate of mailing that the address where the *Notice of Entry of Judgment* (form FL-190) was mailed is on file with the local child support agency; and

(3) An envelope addressed to the local child support agency need not be submitted.

(Subd (e) adopted effective January 1, 2013.)

Rule 5.415 adopted effective January 1, 2013.

Chapter 15
Settlement Services

Title 5, Family and Juvenile Rules—Division 1, Family Rules—Chapter 15, Settlement Services; adopted effective January 1, 2013.

Rule 5.420. Domestic violence procedures for court-connected settlement service providers

(a) Purpose

This rule sets forth the protocol for court-connected settlement service providers handling cases involving domestic violence and not involving child custody or visitation (parenting time).

(Subd (a) adopted effective January 1, 2013.)

(b) Definitions

(1) "Domestic violence" is used as defined in Family Code sections 6203 and 6211.

(2) "Protective order" is synonymous with "domestic violence restraining order" as well as the following:

(A) "Emergency protective order" under Family Code section 6215;

(B) "Protective order" under Family Code section 6218;

(C) "Restraining order" under Welfare and Institutions Code section 213.5; and

(D) "Orders by court" under Penal Code section 136.2.

(3) "Settlement service(s)" refers to voluntary procedures in which the parties in a family law case agree to meet with a neutral third party professional for the purpose of identifying the issues involved in the case and attempting to reach a resolution of those issues by mutual agreement.

(Subd (b) adopted effective January 1, 2013.)

(c) Duties of settlement service providers

Courts providing settlement services must develop procedures for handling cases involving domestic violence. In developing these procedures, courts should consider:

(1) Reviewing court files or, if available, intake forms, to inform the person providing settlement services of any existing protective orders or history of domestic violence;

(2) Making reasonable efforts to ensure the safety of parties when they are participating in services;

(3) Avoiding negotiating with the parties about using violence with each other, whether either party should or should not obtain or dismiss a restraining order, or whether either party should cooperate with criminal prosecution;

(4) Providing information and materials that describe the settlement services and procedures with respect to domestic violence;

(5) Meeting first with the parties separately to determine whether joint meetings are appropriate in a case in which there has been a history of domestic violence between the parties or in which a protective order is in effect;

(6) Conferring with the parties separately regarding safety-related issues and the option of continuing in separate sessions at separate times if domestic violence is discovered after services have begun;

(7) Protecting the confidentiality of each party's times of arrival, departure, and meeting for separate sessions when appropriate; and

(8) Providing information to parties about support persons participating in joint or separate sessions.

(Subd (c) adopted effective January 1, 2013.)

(d) Training and education

All settlement service providers should participate in programs of continuing instruction in issues related to domestic violence, including child abuse.

(Subd (d) adopted effective January 1, 2013.)

Rule 5.420 adopted effective January 1, 2013.

Chapter 16
Limited Scope Representation; Attorney's Fees and Costs

Title 5, Family and Juvenile Rules—Division 1, Family Rules—Chapter 16, Limited Scope Representation; Attorney's Fees and Costs; adopted effective January 1, 2013.

Art. 1. Limited Scope Representation. Rule 5.425.
Art. 2. Attorney's Fees and Costs. Rule 5.427.

Article 1
Limited Scope Representation

Title 5, Family and Juvenile Rules—Division 1, Family Rules—Chapter 16, Limited Scope Representation; Attorney's Fees and Costs—Article 1, Limited Scope Representation; adopted effective January 1, 2013.

Rule 5.425. Limited scope representation; application of rules

(a) Definition

"Limited scope representation" is a relationship between an attorney and a person seeking legal services in which they have agreed that the scope of the legal services will be limited to specific tasks that the attorney will perform for the person.

(Subd (a) adopted effective January 1, 2013.)

(b) Application

This rule applies to limited scope representation in family law cases. Rules 3.35 through 3.37 apply to limited scope representation in civil cases.

(Subd (b) adopted effective January 1, 2013.)

(c) Types of limited scope representation

These rules recognize two types of limited scope representation:

(1) *Noticed representation*

This type occurs when an attorney and a party notify the court and other parties of the limited scope representation. The procedures in (d) and (e) apply only to cases involving noticed limited scope representation.

(2) *Undisclosed representation*

In this type of limited scope representation, a party contracts with an attorney to draft or assist in drafting legal documents, but the attorney does not make an appearance in the case. The procedures in (f) apply to undisclosed representation.

(Subd (c) adopted effective January 1, 2013.)

(d) Noticed limited scope representation

(1) A party and an attorney must provide the required notice of their agreement for limited scope representation by serving other parties and filing with the court a *Notice of Limited Scope Representation* (form FL-950).

(2) After the notice in (1) is received and until a *Substitution of Attorney—Civil* (form MC-050), or a *Notice of Completion of Limited Scope Representation* (form FL-955) with the "Final" box checked, or an order to be relieved as attorney is filed and served:

(A) The attorney must be served only with documents that relate to the issues identified in the *Notice of Limited Scope Representation* (form FL-950); and

(B) Documents that relate to all other issues outside the scope of the attorney's representation must be served directly on the party or the attorney representing the party on those issues.

(3) Electronic service of notices and documents described in this rule is permitted if the client previously agreed in writing to accept service of documents electronically from the attorney.

(4) Before being relieved as counsel, the limited scope attorney must file and serve the order after hearing or judgment following the hearing or trial at which he or she provided representation unless:

(A) Otherwise directed by the court; or

(B) The party agreed in the *Notice of Limited Scope Representation* (form FL-950) that completion of the order after hearing is not within the scope of the attorney's representation.

(Subd (d) amended effective September 1, 2017; adopted effective January 1, 2013.)

(e) Procedures to be relieved as counsel on completion of limited scope representation if client has not signed a substitution of attorney

An attorney who has completed the tasks specified in the *Notice of Limited Scope Representation* (form FL-950) may use the following procedures to request that he or she be relieved as attorney if the client has not signed a *Substitution of Attorney—Civil* (form MC-050):

(1) *Notice of completion of limited scope representation*

The limited scope attorney must serve the client with the following documents:

(A) A *Notice of Completion of Limited Scope Representation* (form FL-955) with the "Proposed" box marked and the deadline for the client to file the objection completed by the attorney;

(B) *Information for Client About Notice of Completion of Limited Scope Representation* (form FL-955-INFO); and

(C) A blank *Objection to Proposed Notice of Completion of Limited Scope Representation* (form FL-956).

(2) *No objection*

If the client does not file and serve an *Objection to Proposed Notice of Completion of Limited Scope Representation* (form FL-956) within 10 calendar days from the date that the *Notice of Completion of Limited Scope Representation* (form FL-955) was served, the limited scope attorney:

(A) Must serve the client and the other parties or, if represented, their attorneys, with a *Notice of Completion of Limited Scope Representation* (form FL-955) with the "Final" box marked;

(B) Must file the final *Notice of Completion of Limited Scope Representation* (form FL-955) with the court, and attach the proofs of service of both the "Proposed" and "Final" notices of completion;

(C) May not be charged a fee to file the final notice of completion, even if the attorney has not previously made an appearance in the case; and

(D) Is deemed to be relieved as attorney on the date that the final notice of completion is served on the client.

(3) *Objection*

If the client files the *Objection to Proposed Notice of Completion of Limited Scope Representation* (form FL-956) within 10 calendar days from the date that the proposed notice of completion was served, the following procedures apply:

(A) The clerk must set a hearing date on the *Objection to Proposed Notice of Completion of Limited Scope Representation* (form FL-956) to be conducted no later than 25 court days from the date the objection is filed.

(B) The court may charge a motion fee to file the objection and schedule the hearing.

(C) The objection—including the date, time, and location of the hearing—must be served on the limited scope attorney and all other parties in the case (or on their attorneys, if they are represented). Unless the court orders a different time for service, the objection must be served by the deadline specified in *Information for Client About Notice of Completion of Limited Scope Representation* (form FL-955-INFO).

(D) If the attorney wishes, he or she may file and serve a *Response to Objection to Proposed Notice of Completion of Limited Scope Representation* (form FL-957). Unless otherwise directed by the court, any response should be filed with the court and served on the client and other parties, or their attorneys, at least nine court days before the hearing.

(E) Unless otherwise directed by the court, the attorney must prepare the *Order on Completion of Limited Scope Representation* (form FL-958) and obtain the judge's signature.

(F) The attorney is responsible for filing and serving the order on the client and other parties after the hearing, unless the court directs otherwise.

(G) If the court finds that the attorney has completed the agreed-upon work, the representation is concluded on the date determined by the court in the *Order on Completion of Limited Scope Representation* (form FL-958).

(Subd (e) amended effective January 1, 2018; adopted effective January 1, 2013; previously amended and renumbered effective September 1, 2017.)

(f) Nondisclosure of attorney assistance in preparation of court documents

(1) *Nondisclosure*

In a family law proceeding, an attorney who contracts with a client to draft or assist in drafting legal documents, but does not make an appearance in the case, is not required to disclose within the text of the document that he or she was involved in preparing the documents.

(2) *Attorney's fees*

If a litigant seeks a court order for attorney's fees incurred as a result of document preparation, the litigant must disclose to the court information required for a proper determination of attorney's fees, including the name of the attorney who assisted in the preparation of the documents, the time involved or other basis for billing, the tasks performed, and the amount billed.

(3) *Applicability*

This rule does not apply to an attorney who has made a general appearance or has contracted with his or her client to make an appearance on any issue that is the subject of the pleadings.

(Subd (f) adopted effective January 1, 2013.)

Rule 5.425 amended effective January 1, 2018; adopted effective January 1, 2013; previously amended effective September 1, 2017.

Article 2
Attorney's Fees and Costs

Title 5, Family and Juvenile Rules—Division 1, Family Rules—Chapter 16, Limited Scope Representation; Attorney's Fees and Costs—Article 2, Attorney's Fees and Costs; adopted effective January 1, 2013.

Rule 5.427. Attorney's fees and costs

(a) Application

This rule applies to attorney's fees and costs based on financial need, as described in Family Code sections 2030, 2032, 3121, 3557, and 7605.

(Subd (a) adopted effective January 1, 2012.)

(b) Request

(1) Except as provided in Family Code section 2031(b), to request attorney's fees and costs, a party must complete, file, and serve the following documents:

(A) *Request for Order* (form FL-300);

(B) *Request for Attorney's Fees and Costs Attachment* (form FL-319) or a comparable declaration that addresses the factors covered in form FL-319;

(C) A current *Income and Expense Declaration* (form FL-150);

(D) A personal declaration in support of the request for attorney's fees and costs, either using *Supporting Declaration for Attorney's Fees and Costs Attachment* (form FL-158) or a comparable declaration that addresses the factors covered in form FL-158; and

(E) Any other papers relevant to the relief requested.

(2) The party requesting attorney's fees and costs must provide the court with sufficient information about the attorney's hourly billing rate; the nature of the litigation; the attorney's experience in the particular type of work demanded; the fees and costs incurred or anticipated; and why the requested fees and costs are just, necessary, and reasonable.

(Subd (b) amended effective July 1, 2012; adopted effective January 1, 2012.)

(c) Response to request

To respond to the request for attorney's fees and costs, a party must complete, file, and serve the following documents:

(1) *Responsive Declaration to Request for Order* (form FL-320);

(2) A current *Income and Expense Declaration* (form FL-150);

(3) A personal declaration responding to the request for attorney's fees and costs, either using *Supporting Declaration for Attorney's Fees and Costs Attachment* (form FL-158) or a comparable declaration that addresses the factors covered in form FL-158; and

(4) Any other papers relevant to the relief requested.

(Subd (c) amended effective July 1, 2012; adopted effective January 1, 2012.)

(d) Income and expense declaration

Both parties must complete, file, and serve a current *Income and Expense Declaration* (form FL-150). A *Financial Statement (Simplified)* (form FL-155) is not appropriate for use in proceedings to determine or modify attorney's fees and costs.

(1) "Current" is defined as being completed within the past three months, provided that no facts have changed. The form must be sufficiently completed to allow determination of the issues.

(2) When attorney's fees are requested by either party, the section on the *Income and Expense Declaration* (form FL-150) related to the amount in savings, credit union, certificates of deposit, and money market accounts must be fully completed, as well as the section related to the amount of attorney's fees incurred, currently owed, and the source of money used to pay such fees.

(Subd (d) adopted effective January 1, 2012.)

(e) Court findings and order

The court may make findings and orders regarding attorney's fees and costs by using *Attorney's Fees and Costs Order Attachment* (form FL-346). This form is an attachment to *Findings and Order After Hearing* (form FL-340), *Judgment* (form FL-180), and *Judgment (Uniform Parentage—Custody and Support)* (form FL-250).

(Subd (e) adopted effective January 1, 2012.)

Rule 5.427 renumbered effective January 1, 2013; adopted as rule 5.93 effective January 1, 2012; previously amended effective July 1, 2012.

Chapter 17
Family Law Facilitator

Title 5, Family and Juvenile Rules—Division 1, Family Rules—Chapter 17, Family Law Facilitator; adopted effective January 1, 2013.

Rule 5.430. Minimum standards for the Office of the Family Law Facilitator

(a) Authority

These standards are adopted under Family Code section 10010.

(Subd (a) amended effective January 1, 2003.)

(b) Family law facilitator qualifications

The Office of the Family Law Facilitator must be headed by at least one attorney, who is an active member of the State Bar of California, known as the family law facilitator. Each family law facilitator must possess the following qualifications:

(1) A minimum of five years experience in the practice of law, which must include substantial family law practice including litigation and/or mediation;

(2) Knowledge of family law procedures;

(3) Knowledge of the child support establishment and enforcement process under Title IV-D of the federal Social Security Act (42 U.S.C. § 651 et seq.);

(4) Knowledge of child support law and the operation of the uniform state child support guideline; and

(5) Basic understanding of law and psychological issues related to domestic violence.

(Subd (b) amended effective January 1, 2003.)

(c) Substituted experience

Courts may substitute additional experience, skills, or background appropriate to their community for the qualifications listed above.

(d) Desirable experience

Additional desirable experience for a family law facilitator may include experience in working with low-income, semiliterate, self-represented, or non-English-speaking litigants.

(Subd (d) amended effective January 1, 2007.)

(e) Service provision

Services may be provided by other paid and volunteer members of the Office of the Family Law Facilitator under the supervision of the family law facilitator.

(f) Protocol required

Each court must develop a written protocol to provide services when a facilitator deems himself or herself disqualified or biased.

(g) Grievance procedure

Each court must develop a written protocol for a grievance procedure for processing and responding to any complaints against a family law facilitator.

(Subd (g) adopted effective January 1, 2003.)

(h) Training requirements

Each family law facilitator should attend at least one training per year for family law facilitators provided by the Judicial Council.

(Subd (h) relettered effective January 1, 2003; adopted as subd (g) effective January 1, 2000.)

Rule 5.430 renumbered effective January 1, 2013; adopted as rule 1208 effective January 1, 2000; previously amended and renumbered as rule 5.35 effective January 1, 2003; previously amended effective January 1, 2007.

Chapter 18
Court Coordination Rules

Title 5, Family and Juvenile Rules—Division 1, Family Rules—Chapter 18, Court Coordination Rules; adopted effective January 1, 2013.

Article 1
Related Cases

Title 5, Family and Juvenile Rules—Division 1, Family Rules—Chapter 18, Court Coordination Rules—Article 1, Related Cases; adopted effective January 1, 2013.

Rule 5.440. Related cases
Rule 5.445. Court communication protocol for domestic violence and child custody orders

Rule 5.440. Related cases

Where resources permit, courts should identify cases related to a pending family law case to avoid issuing conflicting orders and make effective use of court resources.

(a) Definition of "related case"

For purposes of this rule, a pending family law case is related to another pending case, or to a case that was dismissed with or without prejudice, or to a case that was disposed of by judgment, if the cases:

(1) Involve the same parties or the parties' minor children;

(2) Are based on issues governed by the Family Code or by the guardianship provisions of the Probate Code; or

(3) Are likely for other reasons to require substantial duplication of judicial resources if heard by different judges.

(Subd (a) adopted effective January 1, 2013.)

(b) Confidential information

Other than forms providing custody and visitation (parenting time) orders to be filed in the family court, where the identification of a related case includes a disclosure of information relating to a juvenile dependency or delinquency matter involving the children of the parties in the pending family law case, the clerk must file that information in the confidential portion of the court file.

(Subd (b) adopted effective January 1, 2013.)

(c) Coordination of title IV-D cases

To the extent possible, courts should coordinate title IV-D (government child support) cases with other related family law matters.

(Subd (c) adopted effective January 1, 2013.)

Rule 5.440 adopted effective January 1, 2013.

Rule 5.445. Court communication protocol for domestic violence and child custody orders

(a) Definitions

For purposes of this rule:

(1) "Criminal court protective order" means any court order issued under California Penal Code section 136.2 arising from a complaint, an information, or an indictment in which the victim or witness and the defendant have a relationship as defined in Family Code section 6211.

(2) "Court" means all departments and divisions of the superior court of a single county.

(3) "Cases involving child custody and visitation" include family, juvenile, probate, and guardianship proceedings.

(Subd (a) amended effective January 1, 2007.)

(b) Purpose

(1) This rule is intended to:

(A) Encourage courts to share information about the existence and terms of criminal court protective orders and other orders regarding child custody and visitation that involve the defendant and the victim or witness named in the criminal court protective orders.

(B) Encourage courts hearing cases involving child custody and visitation to take every action practicable to ensure that they are aware of the existence of any criminal court protective orders involving the parties to the action currently before them.

(C) Encourage criminal courts to take every action practicable to ensure that they are aware of the existence of any child custody or visitation court orders involving the defendant in the action currently before them.

(D) Permit appropriate visitation between a criminal defendant and his or her children under civil court orders, but at the same time provide for the safety of the victim or witness by ensuring that a criminal court protective order is not violated.

(E) Protect the rights of all parties and enhance the ability of law enforcement to enforce orders.

(F) Encourage courts to establish regional communication systems with courts in neighboring counties regarding the existence of and terms of criminal court protective orders.

(2) This rule is not intended to change the procedures, provided in Family Code section 6380, for the electronic entry of domestic violence restraining orders into the Domestic Violence Restraining Order System.

(Subd (b) amended effective January 1, 2007.)

(c) Local rule required

Every superior court must, by January 1, 2004, adopt local rules containing, at a minimum, the following elements:

(1) *Court communication*

A procedure for communication among courts issuing criminal court protective orders and courts issuing orders involving child custody and visitation, regarding the existence and terms of criminal protective orders and child custody and visitation orders, including:

(A) A procedure requiring courts issuing any orders involving child custody or visitation to make reasonable efforts to determine whether there exists a criminal court protective order that involves any party to the action; and

(B) A procedure requiring courts issuing criminal court protective orders to make reasonable efforts to determine whether there exist any child custody or visitation orders that involve any party to the action.

(2) *Modification*

A procedure by which the court that has issued a criminal court protective order may, after consultation with a court that has issued a subsequent child custody or visitation order, modify the criminal court protective order to allow or restrict contact between the person restrained by the order and his or her children.

(3) *Penal Code section 136.2*

The requirements of Penal Code section 136.2(f)(1) and (2).

(*Subd (c) amended effective January 1, 2007; previously amended effective January 1, 2005.*)

Rule 5.445 renumbered effective January 1, 2013; adopted as rule 5.500 effective January 1, 2003; previously amended effective January 1, 2005; previously amended and renumbered as rule 5.450 effective January 1, 2007.

Chapter 19
Minor Marriage or Domestic Partnership

Title 5, Family and Juvenile Rules—Division 1, Family Rules—Chapter 19, Minor Marriage or Domestic Partnership; adopted effective January 1, 2020.

Article 1
General Provisions

Title 5, Family and Juvenile Rules—Division 1, Family Rules—Chapter 19, Minor Marriage or Domestic Partnership—Article 1, General Provisions; adopted effective January 1, 2020.

Rule 5.448. Minor's request to marry or establish a domestic partnership

(a) Application

(1) This rule implements Family Code sections 297.1, 303, and 304, allowing a person under 18 years of age (a minor) to seek a court order for permission to marry or establish a domestic partnership.

(2) The responsibilities of Family Court Services under (c) apply equally to courts that adopt a confidential child custody mediation program, recommending child custody counseling, or a tiered/hybrid program.

(3) For the purpose of this rule, the terms "parent" and "parent with legal authority" are used interchangeably.

(*Subd (a) adopted effective January 1, 2020.*)

(b) Required initial filings

(1) The minor and the minor's proposed spouse or domestic partner must complete and file with the court clerk a *Request of Minor to Marry or Establish a Domestic Partnership* (form FL-910).

(2) Unless the minor has no parent or legal guardian capable of consenting, each minor must file, in addition to form FL-910, the written consent from a parent with legal authority to provide consent or a legal guardian. *Consent for Minor to Marry or Establish a Domestic Partnership* (form FL-912) may be used for this purpose.

(*Subd (b) adopted effective January 1, 2020.*)

(c) Responsibilities of Family Court Services

Unless the minor is 17 years of age and has achieved a high school diploma or a high school equivalency certificate, Family Court Services must:

(1) Interview the parties intending to marry or establish a domestic partnership.

(A) The parties must initially be interviewed separately; and

(B) The parties may subsequently be interviewed together.

(2) Interview at least one of the parents or the legal guardian of each party who is a minor, if the minor has a parent or legal guardian. If more than one parent or legal guardian is interviewed, the parents or guardians must be interviewed separately.

(3) Inform the parties that Family Court Services must:

(A) Prepare a written report, including recommendations for granting or denying the parties permission to marry or establish a domestic partnership;

(B) Provide the parties and the court with a copy of the report; and

(C) Submit a report of known or suspected child abuse or neglect to the county child protective services agency if Family Court Services knows or reasonably suspects that either party is a victim of child abuse or neglect.

(4) Prepare a written report, which must:

(A) Include an assessment of any potential force, threat, persuasion, fraud, coercion, or duress by either of the parties or their family members relating to the intended marriage or domestic partnership;

(B) Include recommendations for granting or denying the parties permission to marry or establish a domestic partnership; and

(C) Be submitted to the parties and the court.

(5) Protect party confidentiality in:

(A) Storage and disposal of records and any personal information gathered during the interviews; and

(B) Management of written reports containing recommendations for either granting or denying permission for a minor to marry or establish a domestic partnership.

(*Subd (c) adopted effective January 1, 2020.*)

(d) Responsibilities of judicial officer

In determining whether to issue a court order granting permission for the minor to marry or establish a domestic partnership:

(1) The judicial officer must:

(A) If Family Court Services is required to interview the parties, do the following before making a final determination:

(i) Separately and privately interview each of the parties; and

(ii) Consider whether there is any evidence of coercion or undue influence on the minor.

(B) Complete *Order and Notices to Minor on Request to Marry or Establish a Domestic Partnership* (form FL-915).

(2) The judicial officer may order that the parties:

(A) Appear at a hearing to consider whether it is in the best interest of the minor to marry or establish a domestic partnership.

(B) Participate in counseling concerning the social, economic, and personal responsibilities incident to the marriage or domestic partnership before the marriage or domestic partnership is established. The judicial officer:

(i) Must not require the parties to confer with counselors provided by religious organizations of any denomination;

(ii) Must consider, among other factors, the ability of the parties to pay for the counseling in determining whether to order the parties to participate in counseling;

(iii) May impose a reasonable fee to cover the cost of any counseling provided by the county or the court; and

(iv) May require the parties to file a certificate of completion of counseling before granting permission to marry or establish a domestic partnership.

(*Subd (d) adopted effective January 1, 2020.*)

(e) Waiting period

After obtaining a court order granting a minor permission to marry or establish a domestic partnership, the parties must wait 30 days from the date the court made the order before filing a marriage license or filing a declaration of domestic partnership. This waiting period is not required if the minor is:

(1) 17 years of age and has a high school diploma or a high school equivalency certificate; or

(2) 16 or 17 years of age and is pregnant or whose prospective spouse or domestic partner is pregnant.

(*Subd (e) adopted effective January 1, 2020.*)

Rule 5.448 adopted effective January 1, 2020.

Division 2
Rules Applicable in Family and Juvenile Proceedings

Chap. 1. Contact and Coordination. Rules 5.451–5.475.
Chap. 2. Indian Child Welfare Act. Rules 5.480–5.488.
Chap. 3. Intercountry Adoptions. Rules 5.490–5.493.

Chapter 1
Contact and Coordination

Chapter 1 adopted effective January 1, 2008.

Rule 5.451. Contact after adoption agreement
Rule 5.460. Request for sibling contact information
Rule 5.475. Custody and visitation orders following termination of a juvenile court proceeding or probate court guardianship proceeding

Rule 5.450. Court communication protocol for domestic violence and child custody orders [Renumbered]

Rule 5.450 renumbered as rule 5.445 effective January 1, 2013; adopted as rule

5.500 effective January 1, 2003; previously amended effective January 1, 2005; previously amended and renumbered effective January 1, 2007.

2012 Note: Rule 5.445 appears under Division 1, Chapter 18.

Rule 5.451. Contact after adoption agreement

(a) Applicability of rule

This rule applies to any adoption of a child filed under Family Code section 8714, 8714.5, 8802, 8912, or 9000.

(Subd (a) amended effective January 1, 2024; previously amended effective January 1, 2007, and January 1, 2013.)

(b) Preparing the agreement

Any agreement must be prepared and submitted on *Contact After Adoption Agreement* (form ADOPT-310) and include all terms required under section 8616.5.

(Subd (b) relettered and amended effective January 1, 2024; adopted as subd (c); previously amended effective January 1, 2003, and January 2013.)

(c) Enforcement, modification, or termination of the agreement

(1) The court that grants the petition for adoption and approves the contact after adoption agreement retains jurisdiction over the agreement.

(2) Any petition for enforcement of an agreement must be filed on *Request to: Enforce, Change, End Contact After Adoption Agreement* (form 16 ADOPT-315).

(3) Any petition for modification or termination of an agreement must be filed on *Request to: Enforce, Change, End Contact After Adoption Agreement* (form ADOPT-315).

(Subd (c) amended effective January 1, 2024; adopted as subd (d); previously amended effective July 1, 2001, January 1, 2003, July 1, 2003, January 1, 2007, and January 1, 2013.)

(d) Costs and fees

The fee for filing *Request to: Enforce, Change, End Contact After Adoption Agreement* (form ADOPT-315) must not exceed the fee assessed for the filing of an adoption petition.

(Subd (d) relettered and amended effective January 1, 2024; adopted as subd (e) previously amended effective July 1, 2001, January 1, 2003, July 1, 2003, and January 1, 2013.)

(f) Form and provisions of the agreement [Repealed]

(Subd (f) repealed effective January 1, 2024; previously amended effective July 1, 2001, January 1, 2003, January 1, 2007, and January 1, 2013.)

(g) Report to the court [Repealed]

(Subd (g) repealed effective January 1, 2024; previously amended effective July 1, 2001, January 1, 2003, July 1, 2003, and January 1, 2013.)

(h) Enforcement of the agreement [Repealed]

(Subd (h) repealed effective January 1, 2024; previously amended effective July 1, 2001, January 1, 2003, July 1, 2003, January 1, 2007, and January 1, 2013.)

(i) Modification or termination of agreement [Repealed]

(Subd (i) repealed effective January 1, 2024; previously amended effective July 1, 2001, January 1, 2003, July 1, 2003, January 1, 2007, and January 1, 2013.)

(j) Costs and fees [Repealed]

(Subd (j) repealed effective January 1, 2024; previously amended effective July 1, 2001, January 1, 2003, July 1, 2003, January 1, 2007, and January 1, 2013.)

(k) Adoption final [Repealed]

(Subd (k) repealed effective January 1, 2024; previously amended effective January 1, 2013.)

Rule 5.451 amended effective January 1, 2024; adopted as rule 1180 effective July 1, 1998; previously amended and renumbered as rule 5.400 effective January 1, 2003; previously amended effective July 1, 2001, July 1, 2003, January 1, 2007, and January 1, 2018; previously renumbered effective January 1, 2013.

Rule 5.460. Request for sibling contact information

(a) Applicability of rule

This rule applies to all persons wishing to exchange contact information with their adopted siblings and all adopted persons wishing to have contact with their siblings, regardless of whether the adoption occurred in juvenile or family court.

(Subd (a) adopted effective January 1, 2008.)

(b) Definitions

As used in this rule:

(1) "Adoptee" means any person adopted under California law.

(2) "Department" means the California Department of Social Services (CDSS).

(3) "Licensed adoption agency" means an agency licensed by the department to provide adoption services and includes a licensed county adoption agency and a licensed private adoption agency under Family Code sections 8521, 8530, and 8533.

(4) "Confidential intermediary" means either the department or a licensed adoption agency that provided adoption services for either sibling.

(5) "Alternate confidential intermediary" means a named entity or person designated by the court in place of a licensed adoption agency when the court finds that the agency would experience economic hardship by serving as confidential intermediary.

(6) "Sibling" means a biological sibling, half-sibling, or stepsibling of the adoptee.

(7) "Waiver" means *Waiver of Rights to Confidentiality for Siblings*, department form AD 904A (used for adoptees or siblings over the age of 18 years) or AD 904B (used for adoptees or siblings under the age of 18).

(8) "Consent" means the consent contained within the Department form AD 904B. It is the approval of the filing of a waiver by a person under the age of 18 years obtained from an adoptive parent, a legal parent, a legal guardian, or a dependency court when a child is currently a dependent of the court.

(9) "Petition" means Judicial Council form *Request for Appointment of Confidential Intermediary* (form ADOPT-330).

(10) "Order" means Judicial Council form *Order for Appointment of Confidential Intermediary* (form ADOPT-331).

(Subd (b) adopted effective January 1, 2008.)

(c) Waiver submitted by person under the age of 18 years

(1) *Adoptee or sibling waiver*

Each adoptee or sibling under the age of 18 years may submit a waiver to the department or the licensed adoption agency, provided that a consent is also completed.

(2) *Court consent*

If the sibling is currently under the jurisdiction of the juvenile court and his or her parent or legal guardian is unable or unavailable to sign the consent, the court may sign it.

(Subd (c) amended effective January 1, 2013; adopted effective January 1, 2008.)

(d) No waiver on file—sibling requesting contact

If, after contacting the department or licensed adoption agency, the sibling who is seeking contact learns that no waiver is on file for the other sibling, the sibling seeking contact should use the following procedure to ask the court that finalized the adoption of either sibling to designate a confidential intermediary to help locate the other sibling:

(1) *Sibling's request*

(A) A sibling requesting contact under Family Code section 9205 must file a petition and submit a blank order to the court that finalized the adoption of either sibling.

(B) If the sibling requesting contact is under the age of 18 years, the petition must be filed through the sibling's duly appointed guardian ad litem under Code of Civil Procedure section 373 or through the sibling's attorney.

(2) *Appointment of a confidential intermediary*

(A) The court must grant the petition unless the court finds that it would be detrimental to the adoptee or sibling with whom contact is sought. The court may consider any and all relevant information in making this determination, including, but not limited to, a review of the court file.

(B) The court will appoint the department or licensed adoption agency that provided adoption services for either sibling as the confidential intermediary.

(C) If the court finds that the licensed adoption agency that conducted the adoptee's adoption is unable to serve as the intermediary, owing to economic hardship, the court may then appoint any one of the following who agrees to serve as an alternate confidential intermediary:

(i) A CASA volunteer or CASA program staff member;

(ii) A court-connected mediator;

(iii) An adoption service provider as defined in Family Code section 8502(a);

(iv) An attorney; or

(v) Another California licensed adoption agency or the California Department of Social Services' Adoptions Support Bureau when no other individuals are available.

(D) When an alternate confidential intermediary is appointed, the licensed adoption agency must provide to the court all records related to the adoptee or sibling for inspection by the alternate confidential intermediary.

(3) *Role of the confidential intermediary*

(A) The confidential intermediary must:

(i) Have access to all records of the adoptee or the sibling, including the court adoption file and adoption agency or CDSS files of either sibling;

(ii) Make all reasonable efforts to locate the adoptee, the sibling, or the adoptive or birth parent;

(iii) Attempt to obtain the consent of the adoptee, the sibling, or the adoptive or birth parent; and

(iv) Notify any located adoptee, sibling, or adoptive or birth parent that consent is optional, not required by law, and does not affect the status of the adoption.

(B) The confidential intermediary must not make any further attempts to obtain consent if the individual denies the request for consent.

(C) The confidential intermediary must use information found in the records of the adoptee or the sibling for authorized purposes only and must not disclose any information obtained in this procedure unless specifically authorized.

(4) *Adopted sibling seeking contact with a sibling who is a dependent child*

An adoptee seeking contact with his or her sibling who is a dependent child must follow the procedure set forth under Welfare and Institutions Code section 388(b) to seek contact with the sibling.

(*Subd (d) amended effective January 1, 2013; adopted effective January 1, 2008.*)

Rule 5.460 amended and renumbered effective January 1, 2013; adopted as rule 5.410 effective January 1, 2008.

Rule 5.475. Custody and visitation orders following termination of a juvenile court proceeding or probate court guardianship proceeding

(a) Custody and visitation order from other courts or divisions

On termination of juvenile court jurisdiction under rule 5.700 or termination of a probate guardianship under rule 7.1008, the juvenile court or probate court will direct the transmission of its custody or visitation orders to any superior court in which a related family law custody proceeding or probate guardianship proceeding is pending for filing in that proceeding.

If no such proceeding is pending, the court terminating jurisdiction will direct the transmission of its order to the superior court of, in order of preference, the county in which the parent with sole physical custody resides; if none, the county where the child's primary residence is located; or, if neither exists, a county or location where any custodial parent resides.

(1) *Procedure for filing custody or visitation orders from juvenile or probate court*

(A) Except as directed in subparagraph (B), on receiving the custody or visitation order of a juvenile court or probate court, the clerk of the receiving court must file the order in any pending nullity, dissolution, legal separation, Uniform Parentage Act, Domestic Violence Prevention Act, or other family law custody proceeding, or in any probate guardianship proceeding that affects custody or visitation of the child.

(B) If the only pending proceeding related to the child in the receiving court is filed under Family Code section 17400 et seq., the clerk must proceed as follows:

(i) If the receiving court has issued a custody or visitation order in the pending proceeding, the clerk must file the received order in that proceeding.

(ii) If the receiving court has not issued a custody or visitation order in the pending proceeding, the clerk must not file the received order in that proceeding, but must instead proceed under subparagraph (C).

(C) If no dependency, family law, or guardianship proceeding affecting custody or visitation of the child is pending, the order must be used to open a new custody proceeding in the receiving court. The clerk must immediately open a family law file without charging a filing fee, assign a case number, and file the order in the new case file.

(2) *Endorsed filed copy—clerk's certificate of mailing*

Within 15 court days of receiving the order, the clerk must send an endorsed filed copy of the order showing the case number assigned by the receiving court by first-class mail to each of the child's parents and to the court that issued the order, with a completed clerk's certificate of mailing, for inclusion in the issuing court's file.

(*Subd (a) amended effective January 1, 2016; previously amended effective January 1, 2007.*)

(b) Modification of former guardian visitation orders—custodial parent

When a parent has custody of the child following termination of a probate guardianship, a former guardian's request for modification of the probate court visitation order, including an order denying visitation, must be brought in a proceeding under the Family Code.

(*Subd (b) amended effective January 1, 2016; previously amended effective January 1, 2007.*)

(c) Independent action for former guardian visitation

(1) If the court terminated a guardianship under the Probate Code and did not issue a visitation order, the former guardian may maintain an independent action for visitation if a dependency proceeding is not pending. The former guardian may bring the action without the necessity of a separate joinder action.

(2) If the child has at least one living parent and has no guardian, visitation must be determined in a proceeding under the Family Code. If the child does not have at least one living parent, visitation must be determined in a guardianship proceeding, which may be initiated for that purpose.

(3) *Declaration Under Uniform Child Custody Jurisdiction and Enforcement Act (UCCJEA)* (form FL-105/GC-120) must be filed with a petition or motion for visitation by a former guardian.

(*Subd (c) amended effective January 1, 2007.*)

Rule 5.475 amended effective January 1, 2016; adopted effective January 1, 2006; previously amended effective January 1, 2007.

Chapter 2
Indian Child Welfare Act

Chapter 2 adopted effective January 1, 2008.

Rule 5.480. Application
Rule 5.481. Inquiry and notice
Rule 5.482. Proceedings after notice
Rule 5.483. Dismissal and transfer of case
Rule 5.484. Emergency proceedings involving an Indian child
Rule 5.485. Placement of an Indian child
Rule 5.486. Termination of parental rights
Rule 5.487. Petition to invalidate orders
Rule 5.488. Adoption record keeping

Rule 5.480. Application

This chapter addressing the Indian Child Welfare Act (25 U.S.C. § 1901 et seq.) as codified in various sections of the Family Code, Probate Code, and Welfare and Institutions Code, applies to most proceedings involving Indian children that may result in an involuntary foster care placement; guardianship or conservatorship placement; custody placement under Family Code section 3041; declaration freeing a child from the custody and control of one or both parents; termination of parental rights; preadoptive placement; or adoptive placement. This chapter applies to:

(1) Proceedings under Welfare and Institutions Code section 300 et seq.;

(2) Proceedings under Welfare and Institutions Code sections 601 and 602 et seq., whenever the child is either in foster care or at risk of entering foster care. In these proceedings, inquiry is required in accordance with rule 5.481(a). The other requirements of this chapter contained in rules 5.481 through 5.487 apply only if:

(A) The court's jurisdiction is based on conduct that would not be criminal if the child were 18 years of age or over;

(B) The court has found that placement outside the home of the parent or legal guardian is based entirely on harmful conditions within the child's home. Without a specific finding, it is presumed that placement outside the home is based at least in part on the child's criminal conduct, and this chapter shall not apply; or

(C) The court is setting a hearing to terminate parental rights of the child's parents.

(3) Proceedings under Family Code section 3041;

(4) Proceedings under the Family Code resulting in adoption or termination of parental rights; and

(5) Proceedings listed in Probate Code section 1459.5 and rule 7.1015.

This chapter does not apply to voluntary foster care and guardianship placements where the child can be returned to the parent or Indian custodian on demand.

Rule 5.480 amended effective January 1, 2020; adopted effective January 1, 2008; previously amended effective January 1, 2013, and July 1, 2013.

Rule 5.481. Inquiry and notice

(a) Inquiry

The court, court-connected investigator, and party seeking a foster-care placement, guardianship, conservatorship, custody placement under Family Code section 3041, declaration freeing a child from the custody or control of one or both parents, termination of parental rights, preadoptive placement, or adoption have an affirmative and continuing duty to inquire whether a child is or may be an Indian child in all proceedings identified in rule 5.480. The court, court-connected investigator, and party include the county welfare department, probation department, licensed adoption agency, adoption service provider, investigator, petitioner, appointed guardian or conservator of the person, and appointed fiduciary.

(1) The party seeking a foster-care placement, guardianship, conservatorship, custody placement under Family Code section 3041, declaration freeing a child from the custody or control of one or both parents, termination of parental rights, preadoptive placement, or adoption must ask the child, if the child is old enough, and the parents, Indian custodian, or legal guardians, extended family members, others who have an interest in the child, and where applicable the party reporting child abuse or neglect, whether the child is or may be an Indian child and whether the residence or domicile of the child, the parents, or Indian custodian is on a reservation or in an Alaska Native village, and must complete the *Indian Child Inquiry Attachment* (form ICWA-010(A)) and attach it to the petition unless the party is filing a subsequent petition and there is no new information.

(2) At the first appearance by a parent, Indian custodian, or guardian, and all other participants in any dependency case; or in juvenile wardship proceedings in which the child is at risk of entering foster care or is in foster care; or at the initiation of any guardianship, conservatorship, proceeding for custody under Family Code section 3041, proceeding to terminate parental rights, proceeding to declare a child free of the custody and control of one or both parents, preadoptive placement, or adoption proceeding; and at each hearing that may culminate in an order for foster care placement, termination of parental rights, preadoptive placement or adoptive placement, as described in Welfare and Institutions Code section 224.1(d)(1), or that may result in an order for guardianship, conservatorship, or custody under Family Code section 3041; the court must:

(A) Ask each participant present whether the participant knows or has reason to know the child is an Indian child;

(B) Instruct the parties to inform the court if they subsequently receive information that provides reason to know the child is an Indian child; and

(C) Order the parent, Indian custodian, or guardian, if available, to complete *Parental Notification of Indian Status* (form ICWA-020).

(3) If the parent, Indian custodian, or guardian does not appear at the first hearing, or is unavailable at the initiation of a proceeding, the court must order the person or entity that has the inquiry duty under this rule to use reasonable diligence to find and inform the parent, Indian custodian, or guardian that the court has ordered the parent, Indian custodian, or guardian to complete *Parental Notification of Indian Status* (form ICWA-020).

(4) If the social worker, probation officer, licensed adoption agency, adoption service provider, investigator, or petitioner knows or has reason to know or believe that an Indian child is or may be involved, that person or entity must make further inquiry as soon as practicable by:

(A) Interviewing the parents, Indian custodian, and "extended family members" as defined in 25 United States Code section 1903, to gather the information listed in Welfare and Institutions Code section 224.3(a)(5), Family Code section 180(b)(5), or Probate Code section 1460.2(b)(5);

(B) Contacting the Bureau of Indian Affairs and the California Department of Social Services for assistance in identifying the names and contact information of the tribes in which the child may be a member or eligible for membership; and

(C) Contacting the tribes and any other person who reasonably can be expected to have information regarding the child's membership status or eligibility. These contacts must at a minimum include the contacts and sharing of information listed in Welfare and Institutions Code section 224.2(e)(3).

(5) The petitioner must on an ongoing basis include in its filings a detailed description of all inquiries, and further inquiries it has undertaken, and all information received pertaining to the child's Indian status, as well as evidence of how and when this information was provided to the relevant tribes. Whenever new information is received, that information must be expeditiously provided to the tribes.

(Subd (a) amended effective January 1, 2020; adopted effective January 1, 2008; previously amended effective January 1, 2013.)

(b) Reason to know the child is an Indian child

(1) There is reason to know a child involved in a proceeding is an Indian child if:

(A) A person having an interest in the child, including the child, an officer of the court, a tribe, an Indian organization, a public or private agency, or a member of the child's extended family informs the court the child is an Indian child;

(B) The residence or domicile of the child, the child's parents, or Indian custodian is on a reservation or in an Alaska Native village;

(C) Any participant in the proceeding, officer of the court, Indian tribe, Indian organization, or agency informs the court that it has discovered information indicating that the child is an Indian child;

(D) The child who is the subject of the proceeding gives the court reason to know he or she is an Indian child;

(E) The court is informed that the child is or has been a ward of a tribal court; or

(F) The court is informed that either parent or the child possesses an identification card indicating membership or citizenship in an Indian tribe.

(2) When there is reason to know the child is an Indian child, but the court does not have sufficient evidence to determine that the child is or is not an Indian child, the court must confirm, by way of a report, declaration, or testimony included in the record that the agency or other party used due diligence to identify and work with all of the tribes of which there is reason to know the child may be a member, or eligible for membership, to verify whether the child is in fact a member or whether a biological parent is a member and the child is eligible for membership. Due diligence must include the further inquiry and tribal contacts discussed in (a)(4) above.

(3) Upon review of the evidence of due diligence, further inquiry, and tribal contacts, if the court concludes that the agency or other party has fulfilled its duty of due diligence, further inquiry, and tribal contacts, the court may:

(A) Find there is no reason to know the child is an Indian child and the Indian Child Welfare Act does not apply. Notwithstanding this determination, if the court or a party subsequently receives information that was not previously available relevant to the child's Indian status, the court must reconsider this finding; or

(B) Find it is known the child is an Indian child, and that the Indian Child Welfare Act applies, and order compliance with the requirements of the act, including notice in accordance with (c) below; or

(C) Find there is reason to know the child is an Indian child, order notice in accordance with (c) below, and treat the child as an Indian child unless and until the court determines on the record that the child is not an Indian child.

(4) A determination by an Indian tribe that a child is or is not a member of, or eligible for membership in, that tribe, or testimony attesting to that status by a person authorized by the tribe to provide that determination, must be conclusive. Information that the child is not enrolled, or is not eligible for enrollment in, the tribe is not determinative of the child's membership status unless the tribe also confirms in writing that enrollment is a prerequisite for membership under tribal law or custom.

(Subd (b) adopted effective January 1, 2020.)

(c) Notice

(1) If it is known or there is reason to know an Indian child is involved in a proceeding listed in rule 5.480, except for a wardship proceeding under Welfare and Institutions Code sections 601 and 602 et seq., the social worker, petitioner, or in probate guardianship and conservatorship proceedings, if the petitioner is unrepresented, the court, must send *Notice of Child Custody Proceeding for Indian Child* (form ICWA-030) to the parent or legal guardian and Indian custodian of an Indian child, and the Indian child's tribe, in the manner specified in Welfare and Institutions Code section 224.3, Family Code section 180, and Probate Code section 1460.2 for all initial hearings that may result in the foster care placement, termination of parental rights, preadoptive placement, or adoptive placement, or an order of guardianship, conservatorship, or custody under Family Code section 3041. For all other hearings, and for continued hearings, notice must be provided to the child's parents, legal guardian or Indian custodian, and tribe in accordance with Welfare and Institutions Code sections 292, 293, and 295.

(2) If it is known or there is reason to know that an Indian child is involved in a wardship proceeding under Welfare and Institutions Code sections 601 and 602 et seq., the probation officer must send *Notice of Child Custody Proceeding for Indian Child* (form ICWA-030) to the

parent or legal guardian, Indian custodian, if any, and the child's tribe, in accordance with Welfare and Institutions Code section 727.4(a)(2) in any case described by rule 5.480(2)(A)–(C).

(3) The circumstances that may provide reason to know the child is an Indian child include the circumstances specified in (b)(1).

(4) Notice to an Indian child's tribe must be sent to the tribal chairperson unless the tribe has designated another agent for service.

(Subd (c) relettered and amended effective January 1, 2020; adopted as subd (b) effective January 1, 2008; previously amended effective January 1, 2013, and July 1, 2013.)

Rule 5.481 amended effective January 1, 2020; adopted effective January 1, 2008; previously amended effective January 1, 2013, and July 1, 2013.

Advisory Committee Comment

Federal regulations (25 C.F.R. § 23.105) and state law (Welf. & Inst. Code, § 224.2(e)) contain detailed recommendations for contacting tribes to fulfill the obligations of inquiry, due diligence, information sharing, and notice under the Indian Child Welfare Act and state law.

Except for purposes of inquiry, the requirements of the Indian Child Welfare Act (ICWA) and related provisions of state law do not apply to most cases adjudicated under section 602 of the Welfare and Institutions Code for conduct that would be criminal if committed by an adult (see *In re W.B.* (2012) 55 Cal.4th 30). But in those cases where ICWA does not apply, following inquiry and receipt of information about Indian ancestry, the court is encouraged to communicate with and voluntarily provide informal or formal notice to the Indian child's tribe regarding resources and services to benefit the Indian child and his or her family. Such notice should particularly be encouraged wherever the Indian child's tribe has previously intervened or participated in other proceedings involving the child, such as earlier dependency or probate guardianship proceedings. The California Legislature has stated: "[i]t is in the interest of an Indian child that the child's membership in the child's Indian tribe and connection to the tribal community be encouraged and protected...." (See Welf. & Inst. Code, §§ 224(a)(2), 306.6.) Further, Welfare and Institutions Code section 727.1(a) mandates that in selecting a placement for a child under the supervision of a probation officer, the court "shall consider, in order of priority, placement with relatives, *tribal members*, and foster family...." (Emphasis added.) This mandate applies even if the case is not governed by ICWA.

As a matter of policy and best practice, culturally appropriate placements and services provide psychological benefit for the Indian child and family. By engaging the Indian child's tribe, tribal members, Indian Health Services, or other agencies and organizations providing services to Native Americans, additional resources and culturally appropriate services are often identified to assist in case planning. (See Welf. & Inst. Code, §§ 727.4(d)(5),(6) & 16501.1(c)(1) for information on services and case planning for children adjudicated under section 602.) Outreach to these entities is also an important part of family finding and engagement efforts for Indian children and of finding appropriate placements. By contacting the child's tribe, placement options and services—such as substance abuse treatment, counseling, and other services—may be available to Indian children and their families. A list of available services can be found on the California Courts website at Program, Tribal/State Programs, ICWA, Statewide Directory of Services for Native American Families, at *www.courts.ca.gov/5807.htm*.

Rule 5.482. Proceedings after notice

(a) Timing of Proceedings

(1) If it is known or there is reason to know a child is an Indian child, a court hearing that may result in a foster care placement, termination of parental rights, preadoptive placement, or adoptive placement must not proceed until at least 10 days after the parent, Indian custodian, the tribe, or the Bureau of Indian Affairs has received notice, except as stated in sections (a)(2) and (3).

(2) The detention hearing in dependency cases and in delinquency cases in which the probation officer has assessed that the child is in foster care or it is probable the child will be entering foster care described by rule 5.480(2)(A)–(C) may proceed without delay, provided that:

(A) Notice of the detention hearing must be given as soon as possible after the filing of the petition initiating the proceeding; and

(B) Proof of notice must be filed with the court within 10 days after the filing of the petition.

(3) The parent, Indian custodian, or tribe must be granted a continuance, if requested, of up to 20 days to prepare for the proceeding, except for specified hearings in the following circumstances:

(A) The detention hearing in dependency cases and in delinquency cases described by rule 5.480(2)(A)–(C);

(B) The jurisdiction hearing in a delinquency case described by rule 5.480(2)(A)–(C) in which the court finds the continuance would not conform to speedy trial considerations under Welfare and Institutions Code section 657; and

(C) The disposition hearing in a delinquency case described by rule 5.480(2)(A)–(C) in which the court finds good cause to deny the continuance under Welfare and Institutions Code section 682. A good cause reason includes when probation is recommending the release of a detained child to his or her parent or to a less restrictive placement. The court must follow the placement preferences under rule 5.485 when holding the disposition hearing.

(Subd (a) amended effective January 1, 2020; adopted effective January 1, 2008; previously amended effective January 1, 2013, and July 1, 2013.)

(b) Proof of notice

Proof of notice in accordance with this rule must be filed with the court in advance of the hearing, except for those excluded by (a)(2) and (3), and must include *Notice of Child Custody Proceeding for Indian Child* (form ICWA-030), return receipts, and any responses received from the Bureau of Indian Affairs and tribes.

(Subd (b) amended effective January 1, 2020; adopted effective January 1, 2008; previously amended effective January 1, 2013.)

(c) Determination of applicability of the Indian Child Welfare Act

(1) If the court finds that proper and adequate inquiry, further inquiry, and due diligence were conducted under Welfare and Institutions Code section 224.2 and, if applicable, notice provided under Welfare and Institutions Code section 224.3, and the court determines there is no reason to know the child is an Indian child, the court may make a finding that the Indian Child Welfare Act does not apply to the proceedings.

(2) The determination of the court that the Indian Child Welfare Act does not apply in (c)(1) is subject to reversal based on sufficiency of the evidence. The court must reverse its determination if it subsequently receives information providing reason to believe that the child is an Indian child and order the social worker or probation officer to conduct further inquiry under Welfare and Institutions Code section 224.3.

(Subd (c) amended effective January 1, 2020; adopted as subd (d) effective January 1, 2008; previously amended effective January 1, 2013; previously repealed and relettered effective August 15, 2016.)

(d) Intervention

(1) The Indian child's tribe and Indian custodian are entitled to intervene, orally or in writing, at any point in the proceedings. The tribe may, but is not required to, file with the court *Notice of Designation of Tribal Representative in a Court Proceeding Involving an Indian Child* (form ICWA-040) to give notice of its intent to intervene.

(2) A tribe that is not entitled to intervene may request permission to participate in the proceedings in accordance with rule 5.530(g).

(Subd (d) amended effective January 1, 2024; adopted as subd (e) effective January 1, 2008; previously amended effective January 1, 2013, and January 1, 2020; previously relettered as subd (d) effective August 15, 2016.)

(e) Posthearing actions

Whenever an Indian child is removed from a guardian, conservator, other custodian, foster home, or institution for placement with a different guardian, conservator, custodian, foster home, institution, or preadoptive or adoptive home, the placement must comply with the placement preferences and standards specified in Welfare and Institutions Code section 361.31.

(Subd (e) relettered effective August 15, 2016; adopted as subd (f) effective January 1, 2008; previously amended effective January 1, 2013.)

(f) Consultation with tribe

Any person or court involved in the placement of an Indian child in a proceeding described by rule 5.480 must use the services of the Indian child's tribe, whenever available through the tribe, in seeking to secure placement within the order of placement preference specified in rule 5.485.

(Subd (f) amended effective January 1, 2020; adopted as subd (g) effective January 1, 2008; previously amended effective July 1, 2013; previously relettered as subd (f) effective August 15, 2016.)

(g) Tribal appearance by telephone or other remote means

In proceedings governed by the Indian Child Welfare Act, the child's tribe must be allowed to appear remotely as provided in Welfare and Institutions Code section 224.2(k). No fee may be charged to a tribe for a telephonic or other remote appearance.

(Subd (g) amended effective August 4, 2023; adopted effective January 1, 2021; previously amended effective January 1, 2022.)

Rule 5.482 amended effective January 1, 2024; adopted effective January 1, 2008; previously amended effective January 1, 2013, July 1, 2013, August 15, 2016, January 1, 2020, January 1, 2021, January 1, 2022, and August 4, 2023.

Rule 5.483. Dismissal and transfer of case

(a) Dismissal when tribal court has exclusive jurisdiction

Subject to the terms of any agreement between the state and the tribe under 25 United States Code section 1919:

(1) If the court receives information at any stage of the proceeding suggesting that the Indian child is already the ward of the tribal court or is domiciled or resides within a reservation of an Indian tribe that has exclusive jurisdiction over Indian child custody proceedings under 25 United States Code section 1911 or 1918, the court must expeditiously notify the tribe and the tribal court that it intends to dismiss the case upon receiving confirmation from the tribe or tribal court that the child is a ward of the tribal court or subject to the tribe's exclusive jurisdiction.

(2) When the court receives confirmation that the child is already a ward of a tribal court or is subject to the exclusive jurisdiction of an Indian tribe, the state court must dismiss the proceeding and ensure that the tribal court is sent all information regarding the proceeding, including, but not limited to, the pleadings and any state court record. If the local agency has not already transferred physical custody of the Indian child to the child's tribe, the state court must order that the local agency do so forthwith and hold in abeyance any dismissal order pending confirmation that the Indian child is in the physical custody of the tribe.

(3) This section does not preclude an emergency removal consistent with 25 United States Code section 1922, 25 Code of Federal Regulations part 23.113, and Welfare and Institutions Code section 319 to protect the child from risk of imminent physical damage or harm and if more time is needed to facilitate the transfer of custody of the Indian child from the county welfare department to the tribe.

(Subd (a) amended effective January 1, 2020; adopted effective January 1, 2008.)

(b) Presumptive transfer of case to tribal court with concurrent state and tribal jurisdiction

Unless the court finds good cause under subdivision (d), the court must order transfer of a case to the tribal court of the child's tribe if the parent, the Indian custodian, or the child's tribe requests.

(Subd (b) adopted effective January 1, 2008.)

(c) Documentation of request to transfer a case to tribal court

(1) The parent, the Indian custodian, or the child's tribe may request transfer of the case, either orally or in writing or by filing *Notice of Petition and Petition to Transfer Case Involving an Indian Child to Tribal Jurisdiction* (form ICWA-050).

If the request is made orally, the court must document the request and make it part of the record.

(2) Upon receipt of a transfer petition, the state court must ensure that the tribal court is promptly notified in writing of the transfer petition. This notification may request a timely response regarding whether the tribal court wishes to decline the transfer.

(Subd (c) amended effective January 1, 2020; adopted effective January 1, 2008.)

(d) Cause to deny a request to transfer to tribal court with concurrent state and tribal jurisdiction

(1) Either of the following circumstances constitutes mandatory good cause to deny a request to transfer:

(A) One or both of the child's parents objects to the transfer in open court or in an admissible writing for the record; or

(B) The tribal court of the child's tribe declines the transfer.

(2) In assessing whether good cause to deny the transfer exists, the court must not consider:

(A) Socioeconomic conditions and the perceived adequacy of tribal social services or judicial systems;

(B) Whether the child custody proceeding is at an advanced stage if the Indian child's parent, Indian custodian, or tribe did not receive notice of the child custody proceeding until an advanced stage. It must not, in and of itself, be considered an unreasonable delay for a party to wait until reunification efforts have failed and reunification services have been terminated before filing a petition to transfer;

(C) Whether there have been prior proceedings involving the child for which no transfer petition was filed;

(D) Whether transfer could affect the placement of the child; or

(E) Whether the Indian child has cultural connections with the tribe or its reservation.

(3) If it appears that there is good cause to deny a transfer, the court must hold an evidentiary hearing on the transfer and make its findings on the record.

(Subd (d) amended effective January 1, 2020; adopted effective January 1, 2008; previously amended effective January 1, 2013.)

(e) Evidentiary burdens

(1) The burden of establishing good cause to deny a request to transfer is on the party opposing the transfer.

(2) If the court believes, or any party asserts, that good cause to deny the request exists, the reasons for that belief or assertion must be stated orally on the record or in writing, in advance of the hearing, and made available to all parties who are requesting the transfer, and the petitioner must have the opportunity to provide information or evidence in rebuttal of the belief or assertion.

(Subd (e) repealed, relettered and amended effective January 1, 2020; adopted as subd (f) effective January 1, 2008; previously amended effective January 1, 2013.)

(f) Order on request to transfer

(1) The court must issue its final order on the *Order on Petition to Transfer Case Involving an Indian Child to Tribal Jurisdiction* (form ICWA-060).

(2) When a matter is being transferred from the jurisdiction of a juvenile court, the order must include:

(A) All of the findings, orders, or modifications of orders that have been made in the case;

(B) The name and address of the tribe to which jurisdiction is being transferred;

(C) Directions for the agency to release the child case file to the tribe having jurisdiction under section 827.15 of the Welfare and Institutions Code;

(D) Directions that all papers contained in the child case file must be transferred to the tribal court; and

(E) Directions that a copy of the transfer order and the findings of fact must be maintained by the transferring court.

(Subd (f) relettered effective January 1, 2020; adopted as subd (g) effective January 1, 2008; previously amended effective January 1, 2016.)

(g) Advisement when transfer order granted

When the court grants a petition transferring a case to tribal court under Welfare and Institutions Code section 305.5, Family Code section 177(a), or Probate Code section 1459.5(b) and rule 5.483, the court must advise the parties orally and in writing that any appeal to the order for transfer to a tribal court must be made before the transfer to tribal jurisdiction is finalized and that failure to request and obtain a stay of the order for transfer will result in a loss of appellate jurisdiction.

(Subd (g) relettered effective January 1, 2020; adopted as subd (h) effective January 1, 2016.)

(h) Proceeding after transfer

When, under Welfare and Institutions Code section 305.5, Family Code section 177(a), or Probate Code section 1459.5(b), the court transfers any proceeding listed in rule 5.480, the court must proceed as follows:

(1) Dismiss the proceeding or terminate jurisdiction if the court has received proof that the tribal court has accepted the transfer of jurisdiction;

(2) Make an order transferring the physical custody of the child to a designated representative of the tribal court (not necessarily the same "designated representative" identified in the *Notice of Designation of Tribal Representative and Notice of Intervention in a Court Proceeding Involving an Indian Child* (form ICWA-040)); and

(3) Include in the *Order on Petition to Transfer Case Involving an Indian Child to Tribal Jurisdiction* (form ICWA-060) all contact information for the designated tribal court representative.

(Subd (h) relettered effective January 1, 2020; adopted as subd (h) effective January 1, 2008; previously relettered as subd (i) effective January 1, 2016.)

Rule 5.483 amended effective January 1, 2020; adopted effective January 1, 2008; previously amended effective January 1, 2013, and January 1, 2016.

Advisory Committee Comment

Once a transfer to tribal court is finalized as provided in rule 5.483(h), the appellate court lacks jurisdiction to order the case returned to state court (*In re M.M.* (2007) 154 Cal.App.4th 897).

As stated by the Court of Appeal in *In re M.M.*, the juvenile court has the discretion to stay the provisions of a judgment or order awarding, changing, or affecting custody of a minor child "pending review on appeal or for any other period or periods that it may deem appropriate" (Code Civ. Proc., § 917.7), and the party seeking review of the transfer order should first request a stay in the lower court. (See *Nuckolls v. Bank of California, Nat. Assn.* (1936) 7 Cal.2d 574, 577 [61 P.2d 927] ["Inasmuch as the [L]egislature has provided a method by which the trial court, in a proper case, may grant the stay, the appellate courts, assuming that they have the power, should not, except in some unusual emergency, exercise their power until the petitioner has first presented the matter to the trial court"].) If the juvenile court should deny the stay request, the aggrieved party may then petition this court for a writ of supersedeas pending appeal. (Cal. Rules of Court, rule 8.112).

Subdivision (g) and this advisory committee comment are added to help ensure that an objecting party does not inadvertently lose the right to appeal a transfer order.

Rule 5.484. Emergency proceedings involving an Indian child

(a) Standards for removal

Whenever it is known or there is reason to know the case involves an Indian child, the court may not order an emergency removal or placement of the child without a finding that the removal or placement is necessary to prevent imminent physical damage or harm to the child. The petition requesting emergency removal or continued emergency placement of the child or its accompanying documents must contain the following:

(1) A statement of the risk of imminent physical damage or harm to the child and any evidence that the emergency removal or placement continues to be necessary to prevent such imminent physical damage or harm to the child;

(2) The name, age, and last known address of the Indian child;

(3) The name and address of the child's parents and Indian custodian, if any;

(4) The steps taken to provide notice to the child's parents, Indian custodian, and tribe about the emergency proceeding;

(5) If the child's parents and Indian custodian are unknown, a detailed explanation of what efforts have been made to locate and contact them;

(6) The residence and the domicile of the Indian child;

(7) If either the residence or the domicile of the Indian child is believed to be on a reservation or in an Alaska Native village, the name of the tribe affiliated with that reservation or village;

(8) The tribal affiliation of the child and of the parents or Indian custodian;

(9) A specific and detailed account of the circumstances that led to the emergency removal of the child;

(10) If the child is believed to reside or be domiciled on a reservation where the tribe exercises exclusive jurisdiction over child custody matters, a statement of efforts that have been made and are being made to contact the tribe and transfer the child to the tribe's jurisdiction; and

(11) A statement of the efforts that have been taken to assist the parents or Indian custodian so the Indian child may safely be returned to their custody.

(Subd (a) adopted effective January 1, 2020.)

(b) Return of Indian child when emergency situation has ended

(1) Whenever it is known or there is reason to know the child is an Indian child and there has been an emergency removal of the child from parental custody, any party who asserts that there is new information indicating that the emergency situation has ended may request an ex parte hearing by filing a request on *Request for Ex Parte Hearing to Return Physical Custody of an Indian Child* (form ICWA-070) to determine whether the emergency situation has ended.

(2) If the request provides evidence of new information establishing that the emergency placement is no longer necessary, the court must promptly schedule a hearing. At the hearing the court must consider whether the child's removal and placement is still necessary to prevent imminent physical damage or harm to the child. If the court determines that the child's emergency removal or placement is no longer necessary to prevent imminent physical damage or harm to the child, the court must order the child returned to the physical custody of the parents or Indian custodian.

(3) In accordance with rules 3.10 and 3.20, this procedure is governed by the provisions of division 6, chapter 3 and division 11, chapter 4 of title 3 of the California Rules of Court.

(Subd (b) adopted effective January 1, 2020.)

(c) Time limitation on emergency proceedings

An emergency removal must not continue for more than 30 days unless the court makes the following determinations:

(1) Restoring the child to the parent or Indian custodian would subject the child to imminent physical damage or harm;

(2) The court has been unable to transfer the proceeding to the jurisdiction of the appropriate Indian tribe; and

(3) It has not been possible to have a hearing that complies with the substantive requirements of the Indian Child Welfare Act for a foster care placement proceeding.

(Subd (c) adopted effective January 1, 2020.)
Rule 5.484 adopted effective January 1, 2020.

Rule 5.485. Placement of an Indian child

(a) Evidentiary burdens

The court may only terminate parental rights to an Indian child or declare an Indian child free of the custody and control of one or both parents if at the hearing terminating parental rights or declaring the child free of the custody and control of one or both parents, the court:

(1) Finds by clear and convincing evidence that active efforts to provide remedial services and rehabilitative programs designed to prevent the breakup of the Indian family were made; and

(2) Makes a determination, supported by evidence beyond a reasonable doubt, including testimony of one or more "qualified expert witnesses" as defined in Welfare and Institutions Code section 224.6 and Family Code section 177(a), that the continued custody of the child by the parent is likely to result in serious emotional or physical damage to the child.

(Subd (a) adopted effective January 1, 2008.)

(b) Standards and preferences in placement of an Indian child

(1) All placements of an Indian child must be in the least restrictive setting that most approximates a family situation and in which the child's special needs, if any, may be met.

(2) Unless the court finds by clear and convincing evidence that there is good cause to deviate from them, whenever it is known or there is reason to know the child is an Indian child, all placements in any proceeding listed in rules 5.480 and 5.484 must follow the specified placement preferences in Family Code section 177(a), Probate Code section 1459(b), and Welfare and Institutions Code section 361.31.

(3) The court must analyze the availability of placements within the placement preferences in descending order without skipping. The court may deviate from the preference order only for good cause, which may include the following considerations:

(A) The requests of the parent or Indian custodian if they attest that they have reviewed the placement options, if any, that comply with the order of preference;

(B) The requests of the Indian child, when of sufficient age and capacity to understand the decision being made;

(C) The presence of a sibling attachment that can be maintained only through a particular placement;

(D) The extraordinary physical, mental, or emotional needs of the Indian child, including specialized treatment services that may be unavailable in the community where families who meet the placement preferences live; or

(E) The unavailability of a suitable placement within the placement preferences based on a documented diligent effort to identify placements meeting the preference criteria. The standard for determining whether a placement is unavailable must conform to the prevailing social and cultural standards of the Indian community in which the Indian child's parent or extended family resides or with which the Indian child's parent or extended family members maintain social and cultural ties.

(4) The placement preferences must be analyzed and considered each time there is a change in the child's placement. A finding that there is good cause to deviate from the placement preferences does not affect the requirement that a diligent search be made for a subsequent placement within the placement preferences.

(5) The burden of establishing good cause for the court to deviate from the preference order is on the party requesting that the preference order not be followed. A placement may not depart from the preferences based on the socioeconomic status of any placement relative to another or solely on the basis of ordinary bonding or attachment that flowed from time spent in a nonpreferred placement that was made in violation of the Indian Child Welfare Act.

(6) The tribe, by resolution, may establish a different preference order, which must be followed if it provides for the least restrictive setting.

(7) The preferences and wishes of the Indian child, when of sufficient age, and the parent must be considered, and weight given to a consenting parent's request for anonymity.

(8) When no preferred placement is available, active efforts must be made and documented to place the child with a family committed to enabling the child to have visitation with "extended family members," as defined in 25 United States Code section 1903(2), and participation in the cultural and ceremonial events of the child's tribe.

(Subd (b) amended effective January 1, 2020; adopted effective January 1, 2008; previously amended effective January 1, 2013.)

(c) Active efforts

In addition to any other required findings to place an Indian child with someone other than a parent or Indian custodian, or to terminate parental rights, the court must find that active efforts have been made, in any proceeding listed in rule 5.480, to provide remedial services and rehabilitative programs designed to prevent the breakup of the Indian family, and must find that these efforts were unsuccessful. These active efforts must include affirmative, active, thorough, and timely efforts intended primarily to maintain or reunite the child with his or her family, must be tailored to the facts and circumstances of the case, and must be consistent with the requirements of Welfare and Institutions Code section 224.1(f).

(1) The active efforts must be documented in detail in the record.

(2) The court must consider whether active efforts were made in a manner consistent with the prevailing social and cultural conditions and way of life of the Indian child's tribe.

(3) Active efforts to provide services must include pursuit of any steps necessary to secure tribal membership for a child if the child is eligible for membership in a given tribe, as well as attempts to use the available resources of extended family members, the tribe, tribal and other Indian social service agencies, and individual Indian caregivers.

(Subd (c) amended effective January 1, 2020; adopted effective January 1, 2008; previously amended effective January 1, 2013.)

Rule 5.485 renumbered and amended effective January 1, 2020; adopted as rule 5.484 effective January 1, 2008; previously amended effective January 1, 2013.

Rule 5.486. Termination of parental rights

(a) Evidentiary burdens

The court may only terminate parental rights to an Indian child or declare an Indian child free of the custody and control of one or both parents if at the hearing terminating parental rights or declaring the child free of the custody and control of one or both parents, the court:

(1) Finds by clear and convincing evidence that active efforts to provide remedial services and rehabilitative programs designed to prevent the breakup of the Indian family were made; and

(2) Makes a determination, supported by evidence beyond a reasonable doubt, including testimony of one or more "qualified expert witnesses" as defined in Welfare and Institutions Code section 224.6 and Family Code section 177(a), that the continued custody of the child by the parent is likely to result in serious emotional or physical damage to the child.

(Subd (a) adopted effective January 1, 2008.)

(b) When parental rights may not be terminated

The court may not terminate parental rights to an Indian child or declare a child free from the custody and control of one or both parents if the court finds a compelling reason for determining that termination of parental rights would not be in the child's best interest. Such a reason may include:

(1) The child is living with a relative who is unable or unwilling to adopt the child because of circumstances that do not include an unwillingness to accept legal or financial responsibility for the child, but who is willing and capable of providing the child with a stable and permanent environment through legal guardianship, and the removal of the child from the custody of his or her relative would be detrimental to the emotional well-being of the child. For purposes of an Indian child, "relative" must include an "extended family member," as defined in the Indian Child Welfare Act (25 U.S.C. § 1903(2));

(2) Termination of parental rights would substantially interfere with the child's connection to his or her tribal community or the child's tribal membership rights; or

(3) The child's tribe has identified tribal customary adoption, guardianship, long-term foster care with a fit and willing relative, or another planned permanent living arrangement for the child.

(Subd (b) amended effective January 1, 2020; adopted effective January 1, 2008.)

Rule 5.486 renumbered and amended effective January 1, 2020; adopted as rule 5.485 effective January 1, 2008; previously amended effective January 1, 2013.

Rule 5.487. Petition to invalidate orders

(a) Who may petition

Any Indian child who is the subject of any action for foster-care placement, guardianship or conservatorship placement, custody placement under Family Code section 3041, declaration freeing a child from the custody and control of one or both parents, preadoptive placement, adoptive placement, or termination of parental rights; any parent or Indian custodian from whose custody such child was removed; and the Indian child's tribe may petition the court to invalidate the action on a showing that the action violated the Indian Child Welfare Act.

(Subd (a) amended effective January 1, 2020; adopted effective January 1, 2008.)

(b) Court of competent jurisdiction

If the Indian child is a dependent child or ward of the juvenile court or the subject of a pending petition, the juvenile court is a court of competent jurisdiction with the authority to hear the request to invalidate the foster placement or termination of parental rights.

(Subd (b) adopted effective January 1, 2008.)

(c) Request to return custody of the Indian child

If a final decree of adoption is vacated or set aside, or if the adoptive parents voluntarily consent to the termination of their parental rights, a biological parent or prior Indian custodian may request a return of custody of the Indian child.

(1) The court must reinstate jurisdiction.

(2) In a juvenile case, the juvenile court must hold a new disposition hearing in accordance with 25 United States Code section 1901 et seq. where the court may consider all placement options as stated in Welfare and Institutions Code sections 361.31(b), (c), (d), and (h).

(3) The court may consider placement with a biological parent or prior Indian custodian if the biological parent or prior Indian custodian can show that placement with him or her is not detrimental to the child and that the placement is in the best interests of the child.

(4) The hearing on the request to return custody of an Indian child must be conducted in accordance with statutory requirements and the relevant sections of this rule.

(Subd (c) adopted effective January 1, 2008.)

Rule 5.487 amended and renumbered effective January 1, 2020; adopted effective January 1, 2008; previously amended effective January 1, 2013.

Rule 5.488. Adoption record keeping

(a) Copies of adoption decree and other information to the Secretary of the Interior

After granting a decree of adoption of an Indian child, the court must provide the Secretary of the Interior with a copy of the decree and the following information:

(1) The name and tribal affiliation of the Indian child;

(2) The names and addresses of the biological parents;

(3) The names and addresses of the adoptive parents; and

(4) The agency maintaining files and records regarding the adoptive placement.

(Subd (a) adopted effective January 1, 2008.)

(b) Affidavit of confidentiality to the Bureau of Indian Affairs

If a biological parent has executed an affidavit requesting that his or her identity remain confidential, the court must provide the affidavit to the Bureau of Indian Affairs, which must ensure the confidentiality of the information.

(Subd (b) adopted effective January 1, 2008.)

Rule 5.488 renumbered effective January 1, 2020; adopted as rule 5.487 effective January 1, 2008; previously amended effective January 1, 2013.

Advisory Committee Comment

This chapter was adopted, effective January 1, 2008, as the result of the passage of Senate Bill 678 (Ducheny; Stats. 2006, ch. 838), which codified the federal Indian Child Welfare Act into California's Family, Probate, and Welfare and Institutions Codes affecting all proceedings listed in rule 5.480. Rule 5.664, which applied the Indian Child Welfare Act but was limited in its effect to juvenile proceedings, was repealed effective January 1, 2008, and was replaced by this chapter.

As of January 1, 2008, only the Washoe Tribe of Nevada and California is authorized under the Indian Child Welfare Act to exercise exclusive jurisdiction as discussed in rule 5.483.

Chapter 3
Intercountry Adoptions

Title 5, Family and Juvenile Rules—Division 2, Rules Applicable in Family and Juvenile Proceedings—Chapter 3, Intercountry Adoptions; amended effective January 1, 2021; adopted effective July 1, 2013.

Rule 5.490. Adoption of a child resident in the United States by a resident of a foreign country party to the Convention of 29 May 1993 on Protection of Children and Cooperation in Respect of Intercountry Adoption (Convention or Hague Adoption Convention)

Rule 5.491. Adoption of a child resident in the United States by a resident of a foreign country not party to the Hague Adoption Convention

Rule 5.492. Adoption by a United States resident of a child resident in a foreign country that is party to the Hague Adoption Convention

Rule 5.493. Requirement to request adoption under California law of a child born in a foreign country when the adoption is finalized in the foreign country (Fam. Code, §§ 8912, 8919)

Rule 5.490. Adoption of a child resident in the United States by a resident of a foreign country party to the Convention of 29 May 1993 on Protection of Children and Cooperation in Respect of Intercountry Adoption (Convention or Hague Adoption Convention)

(a) Purpose

The rules in this chapter are adopted to provide practice and procedure for intercountry adoptions conducted under the Hague Adoption Convention and applicable California law.

(Subd (a) adopted effective July 1, 2013.)

(b) Applicability of rule

This rule applies to any adoption of a child resident in the United States by an individual or individuals residing in a convention country, as defined in Family Code section 8900.5(f), if, in connection with the adoption, the child has moved or will move between the United States and the convention country.

(Subd (b) adopted effective July 1, 2013.)

(c) Adoption request and attachments

(1) The *Adoption Request* (form ADOPT-200) and *Verification of Compliance with Hague Adoption Convention Attachment* (ADOPT-216) must allege specific facts about the applicability of the Hague Adoption Convention and whether the petitioner is seeking a California adoption, will be petitioning for a Hague Adoption Certificate, or will be seeking a Hague Custody Declaration.

(2) The court must determine whether a child resident in the United States has been or will be moved to a convention country in connection with an adoption by an individual or individuals residing in a convention country.

(Subd (c) adopted effective July 1, 2013.)

(d) Evidence required to verify compliance with the Hague Adoption Convention

If the Hague Adoption Convention applies to the case, and the court is asked to issue findings and an order supporting a request for the U.S. Department of State to issue a Hague Adoption Certificate or a Hague Custody Declaration for the adoption placement, the court must receive sufficient evidence to conclude that the child is eligible for adoption and find that the placement is in the best interest of the child. The court must receive evidence of all of the following:

(1) The adoption agency or provider is accredited by the Council on Accreditation, is supervised by an accredited primary provider, or is acting as an exempted provider, as defined in Family Code section 8900.5(g), to provide intercountry adoption services for convention cases;

(2) A child background study has been completed and transmitted to a foreign authorized entity in accordance with the regulations governing convention adoptions with proof that the necessary consents have been obtained and the reason for its determination that the proposed placement is in the child's best interest, based on the home study and child background study and giving due consideration to the child's upbringing and his or her ethnic, religious, and cultural background;

(3) The child is eligible for adoption under California law;

(4) The adoption agency or provider has made reasonable efforts, as described under 22 Code of Federal Regulations section 96.54(a), to place the child in the United States, but was unable to do so, or an exception to this requirement applies to the case. Such reasonable efforts include: (1) disseminating information on the child and his or her availability for adoption through print, media, and Internet resources designed to communicate with potential prospective adoptive parents in the United States; (2) listing information about the child on a national or state adoption exchange or registry for at least 60 calendar days after the birth of the child; (3) responding to inquiries about adoption of the child; and (4) providing a copy of the child background study to potential U.S. prospective adoptive parent(s);

(5) The agency has determined that the placement is in the child's best interest;

(6) A home study on the petitioner(s) has been completed, which includes:

(A) Information on the petitioner(s), such as identity, eligibility and suitability to adopt, background, family and medical history, social environment, reasons for adoption, ability to undertake an intercountry adoption, an assessment of their ability to care for the child, and the characteristics of the child for whom they would be qualified to care;

(B) Confirmation that a competent authority has determined that the petitioner is eligible and suited to adopt and has ensured that the petitioner has been counseled as necessary; and

(C) The results of criminal background checks;

(7) The Hague Adoption Convention authority designated by the receiving country has declared that the child will be permitted to enter and reside permanently or on the same basis as the adopting parent(s) in the receiving country, and has consented to the adoption;

(8) All appropriate consents have been obtained in writing in accordance with the following standards:

(A) Counseling was provided to any biological or legal parent or legal guardian consenting to the adoption;

(B) All biological or legal parents or legal guardians were informed of the legal effect of adoption;

(C) Such consent was freely given without inducement by compensation;

(D) Such consent was not subsequently withdrawn; and

(E) Consents were taken only after the birth of the child.

(9) As appropriate in light of the child's age and maturity, the child has been counseled and informed of the effects of the adoption and the child's views have been considered. If the child's consent is required, the child has also been counseled and informed of the effects of granting consent and has freely given consent expressed or evidenced in writing in the required legal form without any inducement by compensation of any kind;

(10) The adoption agency or provider has committed to taking all steps to ensure the secure transfer of the child, including obtaining permission for the child to leave the United States;

(11) The adoption agency or provider has agreed to keep the receiving country's designated Hague Adoption Convention authority informed about the status of the case;

(12) The petitioner consents to adoption or has agreed to accept custody of the child for purposes of adoption;

(13) The adoption agency or provider demonstrates that any contact between the birth family and the adoptive family complies with applicable state law and federal regulations governing the timing of such communications; and

(14) The adoption agency or provider certifies that no one is deriving improper financial gain from the adoption and describes the financial arrangement with the prospective adoptive family.

(Subd (d) adopted effective July 1, 2013.)

(e) Court findings required to support the application for a Hague Adoption Certificate or Hague Custody Declaration

The court must make findings relating to the application for a Hague Adoption Certificate or Hague Custody Declaration from the Department of State. To meet the requirements for issuance of the certificate or declaration, the findings must include that:

(1) The adoption is in the child's best interest;

(2) The substantive regulatory requirements set forth in 22 Code of Federal Regulations sections 97.3(a)–(k) have been met; and

(3) The adoption services provider meets the requirements of 22 Code of Federal Regulations part 96.

(Subd (e) adopted effective July 1, 2013.)

(f) Court findings to verify that all Hague Adoption Convention requirements have been met

If the court is satisfied that all Hague Adoption Convention requirements have been met, the court must make findings of fact and order the following:

(1) The child is eligible for adoption;

(2) The grant of custody with respect to the proposed adoption is in the child's best interest; and

(3) The court grants custody of the child to the named family for purposes of adoption, as applicable.

(Subd (f) adopted effective July 1, 2013.)

(g) Petitioner's intent to finalize adoption

If the adoption is not finalized in California, a petition for a Hague Custody Declaration must state specific facts indicating that the petitioner intends to finalize the adoption in petitioner's country of residence or that petitioner will return to California after any required post-placement supervisory period to finalize the adoption in a superior court of California.

(Subd (g) adopted effective July 1, 2013.)
Rule 5.490 adopted effective July 1, 2013.

Advisory Committee Comment

The Hague Adoption Convention (HAC) is a treaty that entered into force with respect to the United States on April 1, 2008. The HAC strengthens protections for children, birth parents, and prospective adoptive parents and establishes internationally agreed-upon rules and procedures for adoptions between countries that have a treaty relationship under the HAC. It provides a framework for countries party to the Convention to work together to ensure that children are provided with permanent, loving homes; that adoptions take place in the best interest of a child; and that the abduction, sale, or traffic of children is prevented. This rule expands procedurally on Family Code sections 8900 through 8925, which address intercountry adoptions, by specifying the findings and evidence set forth in 22 Code of Federal Regulations section 97.3 that are required by a state court when the HAC applies to an adoption.

Rule 5.491. Adoption of a child resident in the United States by a resident of a foreign country not party to the Hague Adoption Convention

The adoption of a child resident in the United States by a resident of a foreign country not party to the Hague Adoption Convention must conform to the law governing California adoptions.

Rule 5.491 adopted effective July 1, 2013.

Rule 5.492. Adoption by a United States resident of a child resident in a foreign country that is party to the Hague Adoption Convention

A United States resident who plans to adopt, in California, a child resident in a foreign country that is party to the Hague Adoption Convention must provide to the California court the required proof, in the form of a Hague Custody Declaration, that all required Hague Adoption Convention findings have been made by the child's country of residence.

Rule 5.492 adopted effective July 1, 2013.

Rule 5.493. Requirement to request adoption under California law of a child born in a foreign country when the adoption is finalized in the foreign country (Fam. Code, §§ 8912, 8919)

(a) Responsibility to file request

(1) A resident of California who has finalized an intercountry adoption in a foreign country must:

(A) File a request to adopt the child in California within the earlier of 60 days from the adoptee's entry into the United States or the adoptee's 16th birthday; and

(B) Provide a copy of the adoption request to each adoption agency that provided the adoption services to the adoptive parent or parents.

(2) If the adopting parent fails to timely file a request to adopt the child under California law, the adoption agency that facilitated the adoption must:

(A) File the request within 90 days of the child's entry into the United States; and

(B) Provide a file-marked copy of the request to the adoptive parent and to any other adoption agency that provided services to the adoptive parent within five business days of filing.

(3) If an adoption agency files a request in accordance with (2), the adoptive parent or parents will be liable to the adoption agency for all costs and fees incurred as a result of good faith actions taken by the adoption agency to fulfill the requirement set forth in this rule.

(Subd (a) adopted effective January 1, 2021.)

(b) Contents of request

(1) A request to adopt under California law a child born in a foreign country whose adoption was finalized in a foreign country must include all of the following:

(A) A certified or otherwise official copy of the foreign decree, order, or certification of adoption that reflects finalization of the adoption in the foreign country;

(B) A certified or otherwise official copy of the child's foreign birth certificate;

(C) A certified translation of all documents described in this subdivision that are not written in English;

(D) Proof that the child was granted lawful entry into the United States as an immediate relative of the adoptive parent or parents;

(E) A report from at least one postplacement home visit by an intercountry adoption agency or a contractor of that agency licensed to provide intercountry adoption services in the state of California; and

(F) A copy of the home study report previously completed for the international finalized adoption by an adoption agency authorized to provide intercountry adoption services, in accordance with Family Code section 8900.

(2) If an adoption agency initiates a request in accordance with (a)(2), the filing must consist of the following:

(A) A signed cover sheet containing the name, date of birth, and date of entry to the United States of the child, the name and address of the adoptive parent or parents, and the name and contact information for the adoption agency;

(B) Blank copies of all forms required to initiate the request for adoption under California law; and

(C) Any document required in (b)(1) that is in the possession of the adoption agency.

(Subd (b) adopted effective January 1, 2021.)

(c) Clerk's notice of request and order

(1) When a request for adoption under California law of a child whose adoption was finalized in a foreign country is filed, the court clerk must immediately notify the California Department of Social Services in Sacramento in writing of the pendency of the proceeding and of any subsequent action taken.

(2) If a request for adoption under California law is initiated under (a)(2), the clerk of the court must file-stamp the request to allow the adoption agency to fulfill its obligations under (a)(2)(B).

(3) Within 10 business days of an order granting a request for adoption under California law, the clerk of the court must submit to the State Registrar the order granting the request.

(Subd (c) adopted effective January 1, 2021.)
Rule 5.493 adopted effective January 1, 2021.

Chapter 4
Protective Orders

Title 5, Family and Juvenile Rules—Division 2, Rules Applicable in Family and Juvenile Proceedings—Chapter 4, Protective Orders; adopted effective January 1, 2024.

Rule 5.495. Firearm relinquishment procedures [Repealed]
Rule 5.495 repealed effective January 1, 2023; adopted effective July 1, 2014.

Rule 5.496. Service requirement for proposed restrained persons who appear remotely

(a) Application of rule

This rule applies to orders issued under part 4 of division 10 (Domestic Violence Prevention Act) of the Family Code and Welfare and Institutions Code section 213.5.

(Subd (a) adopted effective January 1, 2024.)

(b) No additional proof of service required

If the proposed restrained person named in an order issued after hearing appears at that hearing through the use of remote technology, and through that appearance has received actual notice of the existence and substance of the restraining order after hearing, no additional proof of service is required for enforcement of the order.

(Subd (b) adopted effective January 1, 2024.)
Rule 5.496 adopted effective January 1, 2024.

Division 3
Juvenile Rules

Chap. 1. Preliminary Provisions—Title and Definitions. Rules 5.500–5.505.
Chap. 2. Commencement of Juvenile Court Proceedings. Rules 5.510–5.526.
Chap. 3. General Conduct of Juvenile Court Proceedings. Rules 5.530–5.555.
Chap. 4. Subsequent Petitions and Modifications. Rules 5.560–5.580.
Chap. 5. Appellate Review. Rules 5.585–5.595.
Chap. 6. Emancipation. Rule 5.605.
Chap. 7. Intercounty Transfers; Out-of-County Placements; Interstate Compact on the Placement of Children. Rules 5.610–5.619.
Chap. 8. Restraining Orders, Custody Orders, and Guardianships General Court Authority. Rules 5.620–5.630.
Chap. 9. Parentage. Rules 5.635, 5.637.

Chap. 10. Medication, Mental Health, and Education. Rules 5.640–5.652.
Chap. 11. Advocates for Parties. Rules 5.655–5.664.
Chap. 12. Cases Petitioned Under Section 300. Rules 5.667–5.740.
Chap. 13. Cases Petitioned Under Sections 601 and 602. Rules 5.752–5.860.
Chap. 14. Nonminor Dependent. Rules 5.900–5.906.

Chapter 1
Preliminary Provisions—Title and Definitions

Rule 5.500. Division title
Rule 5.501. Preliminary provisions
Rule 5.502. Definitions and use of terms
Rule 5.504. Judicial Council forms
Rule 5.505. Juvenile dependency court performance measures

Rule 5.500. Division title

The rules in this division may be referred to as the Juvenile Rules.

Rule 5.500 adopted effective January 1, 2007.

Rule 5.501. Preliminary provisions

(a) Application of rules (§§ 200–945)

The rules in this division solely apply to every action and proceeding to which the juvenile court law (Welf. & Inst. Code, div. 2, pt. 1, ch. 2, § 200 et seq.) applies, unless they are explicitly made applicable in any other action or proceeding. The rules in this division do not apply to an action or proceeding heard by a traffic hearing officer, nor to a rehearing or appeal from a denial of a rehearing following an order by a traffic hearing officer.

(Subd (a) amended effective January 1, 2007.)

(b) Authority for and purpose of rules (Cal. Const., art. VI, §§ 6, 265)

The Judicial Council adopted the rules in this division under its constitutional and statutory authority to adopt rules for court administration, practice, and procedure that are not inconsistent with statute. These rules implement the purposes of the juvenile court law by promoting uniformity in practice and procedure and by providing guidance to judicial officers, attorneys, social workers, probation officers, and others participating in the juvenile court.

(Subd (b) amended effective January 1, 2007.)

(c) Rules of construction

Unless the context otherwise requires, these preliminary provisions and the following rules of construction govern the construction of these rules:

(1) Insofar as these rules are substantially the same as existing statutory provisions relating to the same subject matter, these rules must be construed as restatements of those statutes; and

(2) Insofar as these rules may add to existing statutory provisions relating to the same subject matter, these rules must be construed so as to implement the purposes of the juvenile court law.

(Subd (c) amended effective January 1, 2007.)

(d) Severability clause

If a rule or a subdivision of a rule in this division is invalid, all valid parts that are severable from the invalid part remain in effect. If a rule or a subdivision of a rule in this division is invalid in one or more of its applications, the rule or subdivision remains in effect in all valid applications that are severable from the invalid applications.

Rule 5.501 amended and renumbered effective January 1, 2007; adopted as rule 1400 effective January 1, 1990.

Rule 5.502. Definitions and use of terms

Definitions (§§ 202(e), 303, 319, 361, 361.5(a)(3), 450, 628.1, 636, 726, 727.3(c)(2), 727.4(d), 4512(j), 4701.6(b), 11400(v), 11400(y), 16501(f)(16); 20 U.S.C. § 1415; 25 U.S.C. § 1903(2))

As used in these rules, unless the context or subject matter otherwise requires:

(1) "Affinity" means the connection existing between one spouse or domestic partner and the blood or adoptive relatives of the other spouse or domestic partner.

(2) "At risk of entering foster care" means that conditions within a child's family may require that the child be removed from the custody of a parent or guardian and placed in foster care unless or until those conditions are resolved.

(3) "CASA" means Court Appointed Special Advocate as defined in rule 5.655.

(4) "Child Abuse Prevention and Treatment Act (CAPTA) guardian ad litem for a child subject to a juvenile dependency petition" is defined in rule 5.662.

(5) "Child" means a person under the age of 18 years.

(6) "Clerk" means the clerk of the juvenile court.

(7) "Court" means the juvenile court and includes any judicial officer of the juvenile court.

(8) "Court-ordered services" or "court-ordered treatment program" means child welfare services or services provided by an appropriate agency ordered at a dispositional hearing at which the child is declared a dependent child or ward of the court, and any hearing thereafter, for the purpose of maintaining or reunifying a child with a parent or guardian.

(9) "Date the child entered foster care" means:

(A) In dependency, the date on which the court sustained the petition filed under section 300 or 60 days after the "initial removal" of the child as defined below, whichever is earlier; or

(B) In delinquency, the date 60 days after the date on which the child was initially removed from the home, unless one of the following exceptions applies:

(i) If the child is detained pending foster care placement and remains detained for more than 60 days, then the "date the child entered foster care" means the date the court declares the child a ward and orders the child placed in foster care under the supervision of the probation officer;

(ii) If, before the child is placed in foster care, the child is committed to a ranch, camp, school, or other institution pending placement, and remains in that facility for more than 60 days, then the "date the child entered foster care" is the date the child is physically placed in foster care; or

(iii) If, at the time the wardship petition was filed, the child was a dependent of the juvenile court and in out-of-home placement, then the "date the child entered foster care" is the date defined in (A).

(10) "De facto parent" means a person who has been found by the court to have assumed, on a day-to-day basis, the role of parent, fulfilling both the child's physical and psychological needs for care and affection, and who has assumed that role for a substantial period.

(11) "Detained" means any removal of the child from the person or persons legally entitled to the child's physical custody, or any release of the child on home supervision under section 628.1 or 636. A child released or placed on home supervision is not detained for the purposes of federal foster care funding.

(12) "Domestic partner" means one of two adults who have chosen to share one another's lives in an intimate and committed relationship of mutual caring as described in Family Code section 297.

(13) "Educational rights holder" means the adult identified or appointed by the court to make educational or developmental-services decisions for a child, nonminor, or nonminor dependent. If the court limits a parent's or guardian's decisionmaking rights and appoints an educational rights holder, the appointed rights holder acts as the child's or youth's parent, spokesperson, decision maker, and "authorized representative" as described in sections 4512(j) and 4701.6(b) in regard to all matters related to educational or developmental-services needs, including those described in sections 319, 361, 726, 4512, 4646–4648, and 4700–4731; Education Code sections 56028(b)(2), 56050, and 56055; Government Code sections 7579.5 and 7579.6; chapter 33 (commencing with section 1400) of title 20 of the United States Code; and part 300 (commencing with section 300.1) of title 34 of the Code of Federal Regulations, unless the court orders otherwise. An appointed educational rights holder is entitled to access to educational and developmental-services records and information to the extent permitted by law, including by sections 4514 and 5328, and to the same extent as a parent, as that term is used in title 20 United States Code section 1232g and defined in title 34 Code of Federal Regulations part 99.3.

(14) "Foster care" means residential care provided in any of the settings described in section 11402.

(15) "Foster parent" includes a relative with whom the child is placed.

(16) "General jurisdiction" means the jurisdiction the juvenile court maintains over a nonminor under section 303(b) at the time of the dismissal of dependency jurisdiction, delinquency jurisdiction, or transition jurisdiction for the purpose of considering a request to resume its dependency jurisdiction or to assume or resume its transition jurisdiction over the person as a nonminor dependent.

(17) "Guardian" means legal guardian of the child.

(18) "Hearing" means a noticed proceeding with findings and orders that are made on a case-by-case basis, heard by either of the following:

(A) A judicial officer, in a courtroom, in which the proceedings are recorded by a court reporter; or

(B) An administrative panel, provided that the hearing meets the conditions described in section 366.3(d) and (e) for dependents and section 727.4(d)(7)(B) for delinquents.

(19) "Indian child" means any unmarried person under 18 years of age who is either (a) a member of an Indian tribe or (b) eligible for membership in an Indian tribe and is the biological child of a member of an Indian tribe. In a court proceeding defined in section 224.1(d), the term also means a youth who satisfies the conditions in either (a) or (b), above, is 18 years of age but not yet 21 years of age, and remains under the jurisdiction of the juvenile court, unless that youth, directly or through his or her attorney, chooses not to be considered an Indian child for purposes of the proceeding.

(20) "Indian child's tribe" means (a) the Indian tribe of which the Indian child is a member or is eligible for membership, or (b), if an Indian child is a member of, or eligible for membership in, more than one tribe, the Indian tribe with which the Indian child has the more significant contacts, as determined under section 224.1(e).

(21) "Initial removal" means the date on which the child, who is the subject of a petition filed under section 300 or 600, was taken into custody by the social worker or a peace officer, or was deemed to have been taken into custody under section 309(b) or 628(c), if removal results in the filing of the petition before the court.

(22) "Member of the household," for purposes of section 300 proceedings, means any person continually or frequently found in the same household as the child.

(23) "Modification of parental rights" means a modification of parental rights through a tribal customary adoption under Welfare and Institutions Code section 366.24.

(24) "90-day Transition Plan" means the personalized plan developed at the direction of a child currently in a foster care placement during the 90-day period before the child's planned exit from foster care when she or he attains 18 years of age or, if applicable, developed at the direction of a nonminor during the 90-day period prior to his or her anticipated exit from foster care. A 90-day Transition Plan must also be developed for and at the direction of a former foster child who remains eligible for Independent Living Program services during the 90-day period before he or she attains 18 years of age. The plan is as detailed as the child or nonminor chooses and includes information about a power of attorney for health care and specific options regarding housing, health insurance, education, local opportunities for mentors and continuing support services, workforce supports, and employment services. Inclusion of information in the plan relating to sexual health, services, and resources to ensure the child or nonminor is informed and prepared to make healthy decisions about his or her life is encouraged.

(25) "Nonminor" means a youth at least 18 years of age and not yet 21 years of age who remains subject to the court's dependency, delinquency, or general jurisdiction under section 303 but is not a "nonminor dependent."

(26) "Nonminor dependent" means a youth who is a dependent or ward of the court, or a nonminor under the transition jurisdiction of the court, is at least 18 years of age and not yet 21 years of age, and:

(A) Was under an order of foster care placement on the youth's 18th birthday;

(B) Is currently in foster care under the placement and care authority of the county welfare department, the county probation department, or an Indian tribe that entered into an agreement under section 10553.1; and

(C) Is participating in a current Transitional Independent Living Case Plan as defined in this rule.

(27) "Notice" means a paper to be filed with the court accompanied by proof of service on each party required to be served in the manner prescribed by these rules. If a notice or other paper is required to be given to or served on a party, the notice or service must be given to or made on the party's attorney of record, if any.

(28) "Notify" means to inform, either orally or in writing.

(29) "Petitioner," in section 300 proceedings, means the county welfare department; "petitioner," in section 601 and 602 proceedings, means the probation officer or prosecuting attorney.

(30) "Preadoptive parent" means a licensed foster parent who has been approved to adopt a child by the California State Department of Social Services, when it is acting as an adoption agency, or by a licensed adoption agency, or, in the case of an Indian child for whom tribal customary adoption is the permanent plan, the individual designated by the child's identified Indian tribe as the prospective adoptive parent.

(31) "Probation officer," in section 300 proceedings, includes a social worker in the county agency responsible for the administration of child welfare.

(32) "Punishment" means the imposition of sanctions, as defined in section 202(e), on a child declared a ward of the court after a petition under section 602 is sustained. A court order to place a child in foster care must not be used as punishment.

(33) "Reasonable efforts" or "reasonable services" means those efforts made or services offered or provided by the county welfare agency or probation department to prevent or eliminate the need for removing the child, or to resolve the issues that led to the child's removal in order for the child to be returned home, or to finalize the permanent placement of the child.

(34) "Relative" means

(A) An adult who is related to the child by blood, adoption, or affinity within the fifth degree of kinship. This term includes:

(i) A parent, sibling, grandparent, aunt, uncle, nephew, niece, great-grandparent, great-aunt or -uncle (grandparents' sibling), first cousin, great-great-grandparent, great-great-aunt or -uncle (great-grandparents' sibling), first cousin once removed (parents' first cousin), and great-great-great-grandparent;

(ii) A stepparent or stepsibling; and

(iii) The spouse or domestic partner of any of the persons described in subparagraphs (A)(i) and (ii), even if the marriage or partnership was terminated by death or dissolution; or

(B) An extended family member as defined by the law or custom of an Indian child's tribe. (25 U.S.C. § 1903(2).)

(35) "Removal" means a court order that takes away the care, custody, and control of a dependent child or ward from the child's parent or guardian, and places the care, custody, and control of the child with the court, under the supervision of the agency responsible for the administration of child welfare or the county probation department.

(36) "Section" means a section of the Welfare and Institutions Code unless stated otherwise.

(37) "Sibling group" means two or more children related to each other by blood, adoption, or affinity through a common legal or biological parent.

(38) "Social study," in section 300, 601, or 602 proceedings, means any written report provided to the court and all parties and counsel by the social worker or probation officer in any matter involving the custody, status, or welfare of a child in a dependency or wardship proceeding.

(39) "Social worker," in section 300 proceedings, means an employee of the county child welfare agency and includes a probation officer performing the child welfare duties.

(40) "Subdivision" means a subdivision of the rule in which the term appears.

(41) "Transition dependent" means a ward of the court at least 17 years and five months of age but not yet 18 years of age who is subject to the court's transition jurisdiction under section 450.

(42) "Transition jurisdiction" means the juvenile court's jurisdiction over a child or nonminor described in Welfare and Institutions Code section 450.

(43) "Transitional independent living case plan" means a child's case plan submitted for the last review hearing held before he or she turns 18 years of age or a nonminor dependent's case plan, developed with the child or nonminor dependent and individuals identified as important to him or her, signed by the child or nonminor dependent and updated every six months, that describes the goals and objectives of how the child or nonminor will make progress in the transition to living independently and assume incremental responsibility for adult decision making; the collaborative efforts between the child or nonminor dependent and the social worker, probation officer, or Indian tribe and the supportive services as described in the Transitional Independent Living Plan (TILP) to ensure the child's or nonminor dependent's active and meaningful participation in one or more of the eligibility criteria described in subdivision (b) of section 11403; the child or nonminor dependent's appropriate supervised placement setting; the child or nonminor dependent's permanent plan for transition to living independently; and the steps the social worker, probation officer, or Indian tribe is taking to ensure the child or nonminor

dependent achieves permanence, including maintaining or obtaining permanent connections to caring and committed adults, as set forth in paragraph (16) of subdivision (f) of section 16501.1.

(44) "Transitional Independent Living Plan" means the written unique, individualized service delivery plan for a child or nonminor mutually agreed upon by the child or nonminor and the social worker or probation officer that identifies the child's or nonminor's current level of functioning, emancipation goals, and the specific skills needed to prepare the child or nonminor to live independently upon leaving foster care.

(45) "Tribal customary adoption" means adoption by and through the tribal custom, traditions, or law of an Indian child's tribe as defined in Welfare and Institutions Code section 366.24 and to which a juvenile court may give full faith and credit under 366.26(e)(2). Termination of parental rights is not required to effect a tribal customary adoption.

(46) "Youth" means a person who is at least 14 years of age and not yet 21 years of age.

Rule 5.502 amended effective January 1, 2021; adopted as rule 1401 effective January 1, 1990; previously amended and renumbered as rule 5.502 effective January 1, 2007; previously amended effective July 1, 1992, July 1, 1997, January 1, 1998, January 1, 1999, January 1, 2001, July 1, 2002, January 1, 2003, January 1, 2008, July 1, 2010, January 1, 2011, January 1, 2012, July 1, 2012, January 1, 2014, and January 1, 2016.

Rule 5.504. Judicial Council forms

(a) Explanation of Judicial Council legal forms

Rules 1.30–1.37 and 2.131–2.134 apply to Judicial Council legal forms, including forms applicable to the juvenile court.

(Subd (a) amended effective January 1, 2007; repealed and adopted effective January 1, 2001.)

(b) Electronically produced forms

The forms applicable to juvenile court may be produced entirely by computer, word-processor printer, or similar process, or may be produced by the California State Department of Social Services Child Welfare Systems Case Management System.

(Subd (b) amended effective July 1, 2006; adopted as subd (c) effective July 1, 1991; amended and relettered effective January 1, 2001; previously amended effective January 1, 1993, January 1, 1998, and January 1, 2006.)

(c) Implementation of new and revised mandatory forms

To help implement mandatory Judicial Council juvenile forms:

(1) New and revised mandatory forms produced by computer, word-processor printer, or similar process must be implemented within one year of the effective date of the form. During that one-year period the court may authorize the use of a legally accurate alternative form, including any existing local form or the immediate prior version of the Judicial Council form.

(2) A court may produce court orders in any form or format as long as:

(A) The document is substantively identical to the mandatory Judicial Council form it is modifying;

(B) Any electronically generated form is identical in both language and legally mandated elements, including all notices and advisements, to the mandatory Judicial Council form it is modifying;

(C) The order is an otherwise legally sufficient court order, as provided in rule 1.31(g), concerning orders not on Judicial Council mandatory forms; and

(D) The court sends written notice of its election to change the form or format of the mandatory form to the Family and Juvenile Law Advisory Committee and submits additional informational reports as requested by the committee.

(Subd (c) amended effective January 1, 2019; adopted effective January 1, 2006; previously amended effective January 1, 2007, January 1, 2012, and January 1, 2017.)

Rule 5.504 amended effective January 1, 2019; adopted as rule 1402 effective January 1, 1991; previously amended and renumbered effective January 1, 2007; previously amended effective July 1, 1991, January 1, 1992, July 1, 1992, January 1, 1993, January 1, 1994, January 1, 1998, January 1, 2001, January 1, 2006, July 1, 2006, January 1, 2012, and January 1, 2017.

Rule 5.505. Juvenile dependency court performance measures

(a) Purpose

The juvenile dependency court performance measures and related procedures set forth in this rule are intended to:

(1) Protect abused and neglected children by assisting courts in promoting children's placement in safe and permanent homes, enhancing their well-being and that of their families, and ensuring that all participants receive timely and fair treatment;

(2) Assist trial courts in meeting the mandated timelines for dependency hearings, securing due process for all litigants, and, in collaboration with the child welfare agency, improving safety, permanency, and well-being outcomes for children and families under the jurisdiction of the juvenile dependency court; and

(3) Assist courts in making well-informed resource allocation decisions.

(Subd (a) adopted effective January 1, 2009.)

(b) Performance measures

Detailed definitions of the performance measures and descriptions of the methods for producing the performance measures in accordance with (c)(2) and (3) are contained in the Judicial Council–approved *Implementation Guide to Juvenile Dependency Court Performance Measures*.

The juvenile dependency court performance measures are:

(1) Hearing timeliness:

(A) Percentage of children for whom the initial hearing is completed within the statutory time frame following the filing of the initial petition;

(B) Percentage of children for whom the jurisdictional hearing is completed within the statutory time frame following the initial hearing;

(C) Percentage of children for whom the disposition hearing is completed within the statutory time frame following the finding of jurisdiction;

(D) Percentage of children for whom a 3-month or other interim review hearing is held;

(E) Percentage of children for whom the 6-month review hearing is completed within 6 months of the date the child entered foster care;

(F) Percentage of children for whom the 12-month permanency hearing is completed within 12 months of the date the child entered foster care;

(G) Percentage of children for whom the 18-month review hearing is completed within 18 months of the date of original protective custody;

(H) Percentage of children for whom the first section 366.26 hearing is completed within 120 days of the termination of reunification services;

(I) Percentage of children whose postpermanency hearing is completed within 6 months of the section 366.26 hearing or the last postpermanency hearing;

(J) Percentage of children in long-term foster care whose subsequent section 366.26 hearing is completed within 12 months of the previous section 366.26 hearing;

(K) Percentage of children whose adoption is finalized within 180 days after termination of parental rights;

(L) Median time from disposition or section 366.26 hearing to order establishing guardianship;

(M) Percentage of children for whom the first and subsequent postpermanency review hearings are completed within the statutory time frame;

(N) Percentage of hearings delayed by reasons for delay and hearing type;

(O) Median time from filing of original petition to implementation of a permanent plan by permanent plan type; and

(P) Median time from filing of original petition to termination of jurisdiction by reason for termination of jurisdiction.

(2) Court procedures and due process:

(A) Percentage of cases in which all hearings are heard by one judicial officer;

(B) Percentage of cases in which all parties and other statutorily entitled individuals are served with a copy of the original petition;

(C) Percentage of hearings in which notice is given to all statutorily entitled parties and individuals within the statutory time frame;

(D) Percentage of hearings in which child or parents are present if statutorily entitled to be present;

(E) Percentage of hearings in which a judicial inquiry is made when a child 10 years of age or older is not present at hearing;

(F) Percentage of hearings in which other statutorily entitled individuals who are involved in the case (e.g., CASA volunteers, caregivers, de facto parents, others) are present;

(G) Percentage of cases in which legal counsel for parents, children, and the child welfare agency are present at every hearing;

(H) Point at which children and parents are assigned legal counsel;

(I) Percentage of cases in which legal counsel for children or parents changes;

(J) Percentage of cases in which no reunification services are ordered and reasons;

(K) Percentage of cases for which youth have input into their case plans; and

(L) Cases in compliance with the requirements of the Indian Child Welfare Act (ICWA).

(3) Child safety in the child welfare system:

(A) Percentage of children who are not victims of another substantiated maltreatment allegation within 6 and 12 months after the maltreatment incident that led to the filing of the initial petition; and

(B) For all children served in foster care during the year, percentage of children who were not victims of substantiated maltreatment by a foster parent or facility staff member.

(4) Child permanency:

(A) Percentage of children reunified in less than 12 months;

(B) Percentage of children who were reunified but reentered foster care within 12 months;

(C) Percentage of children who were discharged from foster care to a finalized adoption within 24 months;

(D) Percentage of children in foster care who were freed for adoption;

(E) Percentage of children in long-term foster care who were discharged to a permanent home before their 18th birthdays;

(F) Of children discharged to emancipation or aging out of foster care, percentage who were in foster care 3 years or longer;

(G) Percentage of children with multiple foster-care placements;

(5) Child and family well-being:

(A) Percentage of children 14 years of age or older with current transitional independent living plans;

(B) Percentage of children for whom a section 391 termination of jurisdiction hearing was held;

(C) Percentage of section 391 termination of jurisdiction hearings that did not result in termination of jurisdiction and reasons jurisdiction did not terminate;

(D) Percentage of youth present at section 391 termination of jurisdiction hearing with judicial confirmation of receipt of all services and documents mandated by section 391(b)(1–5);

(E) Percentage of children placed with all siblings who are also under court jurisdiction, as appropriate;

(F) Percentage of children placed with at least one but not all siblings who are also under court jurisdiction, as appropriate;

(G) For children who have siblings under court jurisdiction but are not placed with all of them, percentage of cases in which sibling visitation is not ordered and reasons;

(H) Percentage of cases in which visitation is not ordered for parents and reasons;

(I) Number of visitation orders for adults other than parents and siblings, (e.g., grandparents, other relatives, extended family members, others) as appropriate;

(J) Number of cases in which the court has requested relative-finding efforts from the child welfare agency;

(K) Percentage of children placed with relatives;

(L) For children 10 years of age or older and in foster care for at least 6 months, percentage for whom the court has inquired whether the social worker has identified persons important to the child; and

(M) For children 10 years of age or older in foster care for at least 6 months, percentage for whom the court has made orders to enable the child to maintain relationships with persons important to that child.

(Subd (b) adopted effective January 1, 2009.)

(c) **Data collection**

(1) California's Court Case Management System (CCMS) family and juvenile law module must be capable of collecting the data described in the *Implementation Guide to Juvenile Dependency Court Performance Measures* in order to calculate the performance measures and to produce performance measure reports.

(2) Before implementation of the CCMS family and juvenile law module, each local court must collect and submit to the Judicial Council the subset of juvenile dependency data described in (b) and further delineated in the *Implementation Guide to Juvenile Dependency Court Performance Measures* that it is reasonably capable of collecting and submitting with its existing court case management system and resources.

(3) On implementation of the CCMS family and juvenile law module in a local court, and as the necessary data elements become electronically available, the local court must collect and submit to the Judicial Council the juvenile dependency data described in (b) and further delineated in the *Implementation Guide to Juvenile Dependency Court Performance Measures*. For the purposes of this subdivision, "implementation of the CCMS family and juvenile law module" in a local court means that the CCMS family and juvenile law module has been deployed in that court, is functioning, and has the ability to capture the required data elements and that local court staff has been trained to use the system.

(Subd (c) amended effective January 1, 2016; adopted effective January 1, 2009.)

(d) **Use of data and development of measures before CCMS implementation**

Before CCMS implementation, the Judicial Council must:

(1) Establish a program to assist the local courts in collecting, preparing, analyzing, and reporting the data required by this rule;

(2) Establish a procedure to assist the local courts in submitting the required data to the Judicial Council;

(3) Use the data submitted under (c)(2) to test and refine the detailed definitions of the performance measures and descriptions of the methods for producing the performance measures described in the *Implementation Guide to Juvenile Dependency Court Performance Measures*;

(4) Consult with local courts about the accuracy of the data submitted under (c)(2). After such consultation, use data to generate aggregate data reports on performance measures, consistent with section 16543, while not disclosing identifying information about children, parents, judicial officers, and other individuals in the dependency system; and

(5) Assist the courts in using the data to achieve improved outcomes for children and families in the dependency system, make systemic improvements, and improve resource allocation decisions.

(Subd (d) amended effective January 1, 2016; adopted effective January 1, 2009.)

(e) **Use of data after CCMS implementation**

On implementation of CCMS, the Judicial Council must:

(1) Use the data submitted under (c)(3) to conduct ongoing testing, refining, and updating of the information in the *Implementation Guide to Juvenile Dependency Court Performance Measures*;

(2) Use the data submitted under (c)(3) to generate aggregate data reports on performance measures, consistent with section 16543, while not disclosing identifying information about children, parents, judicial officers, and other individuals in the dependency system;

(3) Upon the request of any local court, extract data from the system and prepare county-level reports to meet data reporting requirements; and

(4) Assist the courts in using the data to achieve improved outcomes for children and families in the dependency system, make systemic improvements, and improve resource allocation decisions.

(Subd (e) amended effective January 1, 2016; adopted effective January 1, 2009.)

Rule 5.505 amended effective January 1, 2016; adopted effective January 1, 2009.

Advisory Committee Comment

The juvenile dependency court performance measures and related procedures set forth in this rule fulfill the requirements of the Child Welfare Leadership and Accountability Act of 2006 (Welf. & Inst. Code, §§ 16540–16545).

Consistent with section 16545, the Child Welfare Council and the secretary of the California Health and Human Services Agency were consulted in adopting these performance measures. The appropriate court technology groups have also been consulted.

The *Implementation Guide to Juvenile Dependency Court Performance Measures* is a companion publication to this rule, approved by the Judicial Council.

It is anticipated that the Judicial Council will update the *Implementation Guide to Juvenile Dependency Court Performance Measures*, as appropriate, to stay current with Court Case Management System (CCMS) requirements, local court needs, and the most recent versions of the relevant state and federal child welfare measures. Proposed updates other than those that are purely technical will be circulated for public comment prior to publication.

Chapter 2
Commencement of Juvenile Court Proceedings

Rule 5.510. Proper court; determination of child's residence; exclusive jurisdiction
Rule 5.512. Joint assessment procedure
Rule 5.514. Intake; guidelines
Rule 5.516. Factors to consider
Rule 5.518. Court-connected child protection/dependency mediation
Rule 5.520. Filing the petition; application for petition
Rule 5.522. Remote filing
Rule 5.523. Electronic service (§ 212.5)
Rule 5.524. Form of petition; notice of hearing

Rule 5.526. Citation to appear; warrants of arrest; subpoenas

Rule 5.510. Proper court; determination of child's residence; exclusive jurisdiction

(a) Proper court (§§ 327, 651)

The proper court in which to commence proceedings to declare a child a dependent or ward of the court is the juvenile court in the county:

(1) In which the child resides;

(2) In which the child is found; or

(3) In which the acts take place or the circumstances exist that are alleged to bring the child within the provisions of section 300 or 601 or 602.

(Subd (a) amended effective January 1, 2007.)

(b) Determination of residence—general rule (§ 17.1)

Unless otherwise provided in the juvenile court law or in these rules, the residence of a child must be determined under section 17.1.

(c) Exclusive jurisdiction (§§ 304, 316.2, 726.4)

(1) Once a petition has been filed under section 300, the juvenile court has exclusive jurisdiction of the following:

(A) All issues regarding custody and visitation of the child, including legal guardianship; and

(B) All issues and actions regarding the parentage of the child under rule 5.635 and Family Code section 7630.

(2) Once a petition has been filed under section 601 or 602, the juvenile court has exclusive jurisdiction to hear an action filed under Family Code section 7630.

(Subd (c) amended effective January 1, 2021; adopted effective January 1, 1999; previously amended effective January 1, 2007, and January 1, 2015.)

Rule 5.510 amended effective January 1, 2021; adopted as rule 1403 effective January 1, 1991; previously amended effective January 1, 1999, and January 1, 2015; previously amended and renumbered effective January 1, 2007.

Rule 5.512. Joint assessment procedure

(a) Joint assessment requirement (§ 241.1)

Whenever a child appears to come within the description of section 300 and either section 601 or section 602, the responsible child welfare and probation departments must conduct a joint assessment to determine which status will serve the best interest of the child and the protection of society.

(1) The assessment must be completed as soon as possible after the child comes to the attention of either department.

(2) Whenever possible, the determination of status must be made before any petition concerning the child is filed.

(3) The assessment report need not be prepared before the petition is filed but must be provided to the court for the hearing as stated in (e).

(4) If a petition has been filed, on the request of the child, parent, guardian, or counsel, or on the court's own motion, the court may set a hearing for a determination under section 241.1 and order that the joint assessment report be made available as required in (f).

(Subd (a) amended effective January 1, 2007.)

(b) Proceedings in same county

If the petition alleging jurisdiction is filed in a county in which the child is already a dependent or ward, the child welfare and probation departments in that county must assess the child under a jointly developed written protocol and prepare a joint assessment report to be filed in that county.

(Subd (b) amended effective January 1, 2007.)

(c) Proceedings in different counties

If the petition alleging jurisdiction is filed in one county and the child is already a dependent or ward in another county, a joint assessment must be conducted by the responsible departments of each county. If the departments cannot agree on which will prepare the joint assessment report, then the department in the county where the petition is to be filed must prepare the joint assessment report.

(1) The joint assessment report must contain the recommendations and reasoning of both the child welfare and the probation departments.

(2) The report must be filed at least 5 calendar days before the hearing on the joint assessment in the county where the second petition alleging jurisdictional facts under sections 300, 601, or 602 has been filed.

(Subd (c) amended effective January 1, 2007.)

(d) Joint assessment report

The joint assessment report must contain the joint recommendation of the probation and child welfare departments if they agree on the status that will serve the best interest of the child and the protection of society, or the separate recommendation of each department if they do not agree. The report must also include:

(1) A description of the nature of the referral;

(2) The age of the child;

(3) The history of any physical, sexual, or emotional abuse of the child;

(4) The prior record of the child's parents for abuse of this or any other child;

(5) The prior record of the child for out-of-control or delinquent behavior;

(6) The parents' cooperation with the child's school;

(7) The child's functioning at school;

(8) The nature of the child's home environment;

(9) The history of involvement of any agencies or professionals with the child and his or her family;

(10) Any services or community agencies that are available to assist the child and his or her family;

(11) A statement by any counsel currently representing the child; and

(12) A statement by any CASA volunteer currently appointed for the child.

(Subd (d) amended effective January 1, 2007.)

(e) Hearing on joint assessment

If the child is detained, the hearing on the joint assessment report must occur as soon as possible after or concurrent with the detention hearing, but no later than 15 court days after the order of detention and before the jurisdictional hearing. If the child is not detained, the hearing on the joint assessment must occur before the jurisdictional hearing and within 30 days of the date of the petition. The juvenile court must conduct the hearing and determine which type of jurisdiction over the child best meets the child's unique circumstances.

(Subd (e) amended effective January 1, 2007.)

(f) Notice and participation

At least 5 calendar days before the hearing, notice of the hearing and copies of the joint assessment report must be provided to the child, the child's parent or guardian, all attorneys of record, any CASA volunteer, and any other juvenile court having jurisdiction over the child. The notice must be directed to the judicial officer or department that will conduct the hearing.

(Subd (f) amended effective January 1, 2007.)

(g) Conduct of hearing

All parties and their attorneys must have an opportunity to be heard at the hearing. The court must make a determination regarding the appropriate status of the child and state its reasons on the record or in a written order.

(h) Notice of decision after hearing

Within 5 calendar days after the hearing, the clerk of the juvenile court must transmit the court's findings and orders to any other juvenile court with current jurisdiction over the child.

(i) Local protocols

On or before January 1, 2004, the probation and child welfare departments of each county must adopt a written protocol for the preparation of joint assessment reports, including procedures for resolution of disagreements between the probation and child welfare departments, and submit a copy to the Judicial Council.

Rule 5.512 amended and renumbered effective January 1, 2007; adopted as rule 1403.5 effective January 1, 2003.

Rule 5.514. Intake; guidelines

(a) Role of juvenile court

It is the duty of the presiding judge of the juvenile court to initiate meetings and cooperate with the probation department, welfare department, prosecuting attorney, law enforcement, and other persons and agencies performing an intake function. The goal of the intake meetings is to establish and maintain a fair and efficient intake program designed to promote swift and objective evaluation of the circumstances of any referral and to pursue an appropriate course of action.

(Subd (a) amended effective January 1, 2007.)

(b) Purpose of intake program

The intake program must be designed to:

(1) Provide for settlement at intake of:

(A) Matters over which the juvenile court has no jurisdiction;

(B) Matters in which there is insufficient evidence to support a petition; and

(C) Matters that are suitable for referral to a nonjudicial agency or program available in the community;

(2) Provide for a program of informal supervision of the child under sections 301 and 654; and

(3) Establish a process for a judge to witness the consent of the parent or Indian custodian to a placement of an Indian child under section 16507.4(b) before a judge in accordance with section 16507.4(b)(3) that ensures the placement is consistent with the federal Indian Child Welfare Act and corresponding state law and all of the rights and protections of the Indian parent are respected, using *Agreement of Parent or Indian Custodian to Temporary Custody of Indian Child* (form ICWA-101). This process must ensure that the witnessing of the consent is scheduled within 72 hours of the request having been made. The original completed *Agreement of Parent or Indian Custodian to Temporary Custody of Indian Child* (form ICWA-101) must be retained by the court with a copy to the agency; and

(4) Provide for the commencement of proceedings in the juvenile court only when necessary for the welfare of the child or protection of the public.

(Subd (b) amended effective January 1, 2021; previously amended effective January 1, 1995, and January 1, 2007.)

(c) Investigation at intake (§§ 309, 652.5)

The probation officer or the social worker must conduct an investigation and determine whether:

(1) The matter should be settled at intake by:

(A) Taking no action;

(B) Counseling the child and any others involved in the matter; or

(C) Referring the child, the child's family, and any others involved to other agencies and programs in the community for the purpose of receiving services to prevent or eliminate the need for removal;

(2) A program of informal supervision should be undertaken for not more than six months under section 301 or 654; or

(3) A petition should be filed under section 300 or 601, or the prosecuting attorney should be requested to file a petition under section 602.

(Subd (c) amended effective January 1, 2007; previously amended effective January 1, 1994, January 1, 1995, and January 1, 2001.)

(d) Mandatory referrals to the prosecuting attorney (§ 653.5)

Notwithstanding (c), the probation officer must refer to the prosecuting attorney, within 48 hours, all affidavits requesting that a petition be filed under section 602 if it appears to the probation officer that:

(1) The child, regardless of age:

(A) Is alleged to have committed an offense listed in section 707(b);

(B) Has been referred for the sale or possession for sale of a controlled substance under chapter 2 of division 10 of the Health and Safety Code;

(C) Has been referred for a violation of Health and Safety Code section 11350 or 11377 at a school, or for a violation of Penal Code sections 245.5, 626.9, or 626.10;

(D) Has been referred for a violation of Penal Code section 186.22;

(E) Has previously been placed on informal supervision under section 654; or

(F) Has been referred for an alleged offense in which restitution to the victim exceeds $1,000;

(2) The child was 16 years of age or older on the date of the alleged offense and the referral is for a felony offense; or

(3) The child was under 16 years of age on the date of the alleged offense and the referral is not the first referral for a felony offense.

Except for the offenses listed in (1)(C), the provisions of this subdivision do not apply to narcotics and drug offenses listed in Penal Code section 1000.

(Subd (d) amended effective January 1, 2007; previously amended effective January 1, 1994, and January 1, 1995.)

(e) Informal supervision (§§ 301, 654)

(1) If the child is placed on a program of informal supervision for not more than six months under section 301, the social worker may file a petition at any time during the six-month period. If the objectives of a service plan under section 301 have not been achieved within six months, the social worker may extend the period up to an additional six months, with the consent of the parent or guardian.

(2) If a child is placed on a program of informal supervision for not more than six months under section 654, the probation officer may file a petition under section 601, or request that the prosecuting attorney file a petition under section 602, at any time during the six-month period, or within 90 days thereafter. If a child on informal supervision under section 654 has not participated in the specific programs within 60 days, the probation officer must immediately file a petition under section 601, or request that the prosecuting attorney file one under section 602, unless the probation officer determines that the interests of the child and the community can be adequately protected by continuing under section 654.

(Subd (e) amended effective January 1, 2007; previously amended effective January 1, 1995.)

Rule 5.514 amended effective January 1, 2021; adopted as rule 1404 effective January 1, 1991; previously amended effective January 1, 1994, January 1, 1995, and January 1, 2001; previously amended and renumbered effective January 1, 2007.

Rule 5.516. Factors to consider

(a) Settlement at intake (§ 653.5)

In determining whether a matter not described in rule 5.514(d) should be settled at intake, the social worker or probation officer must consider:

(1) Whether there is sufficient evidence of a condition or conduct to bring the child within the jurisdiction of the court;

(2) If the alleged condition or conduct is not considered serious, whether the child has previously presented significant problems in the home, school, or community;

(3) Whether the matter appears to have arisen from a temporary problem within the family that has been or can be resolved;

(4) Whether any agency or other resource in the community is available to offer services to the child and the child's family to prevent or eliminate the need to remove the child from the child's home;

(5) The attitudes of the child, the parent or guardian, and any affected persons;

(6) The age, maturity, and capabilities of the child;

(7) The dependency or delinquency history, if any, of the child;

(8) The recommendation, if any, of the referring party or agency; and

(9) Any other circumstances that indicate that settling the matter at intake would be consistent with the welfare of the child and the protection of the public.

(Subd (a) amended effective January 1, 2007; previously amended effective January 1, 2001.)

(b) Informal supervision

In determining whether to undertake a program of informal supervision of a child not described by rule 5.514(d), the social worker or probation officer must consider:

(1) If the condition or conduct is not considered serious, whether the child has had a problem in the home, school, or community that indicates that some supervision would be desirable;

(2) Whether the child and the parent or guardian seem able to resolve the matter with the assistance of the social worker or probation officer and without formal court action;

(3) Whether further observation or evaluation by the social worker or probation officer is needed before a decision can be reached;

(4) The attitudes of the child and the parent or guardian;

(5) The age, maturity, and capabilities of the child;

(6) The dependency or delinquency history, if any, of the child;

(7) The recommendation, if any, of the referring party or agency;

(8) The attitudes of affected persons; and

(9) Any other circumstances that indicate that a program of informal supervision would be consistent with the welfare of the child and the protection of the public.

(Subd (b) amended effective January 1, 2007.)

(c) Filing of petition

In determining whether to file a petition under section 300 or 601 or to request the prosecuting attorney to file a petition under section 602, the social worker or probation officer must consider:

(1) Whether any of the statutory criteria listed in rules 5.770 and 5.772 relating to the fitness of the child are present;

(2) Whether the alleged conduct would be a felony;

(3) Whether the alleged conduct involved physical harm or the threat of physical harm to person or property;

(4) If the alleged condition or conduct is not serious, whether the child has had serious problems in the home, school, or community that indicate that formal court action is desirable;

(5) If the alleged condition or conduct is not serious, whether the child is already a ward or dependent of the court;

(6) Whether the alleged condition or conduct involves a threat to the physical or emotional health of the child;

(7) Whether a chronic, serious family problem exists after other efforts to resolve the problem have been made;

(8) Whether the alleged condition or conduct is in dispute and, if proven, whether court-ordered disposition appears desirable;

(9) The attitudes of the child and the parent or guardian;

(10) The age, maturity, and capabilities of the child;

(11) Whether the child is on probation or parole;

(12) The recommendation, if any, of the referring party or agency;

(13) The attitudes of affected persons;

(14) Whether any other referrals or petitions are pending; and

(15) Any other circumstances that indicate that the filing of a petition is necessary to promote the welfare of the child or to protect the public.

(Subd (c) amended effective January 1, 2007.)

(d) Certification to juvenile court

Copies of the certification, the accusatory pleading, any police reports, and the order of a superior court, certifying that the accused person was under the age of 18 on the date of the alleged offense, must immediately be delivered to the clerk of the juvenile court.

(1) On receipt of the documents, the clerk must immediately notify the probation officer, who must immediately investigate the matter to determine whether to commence proceedings in juvenile court.

(2) If the child is under the age of 18 and is in custody, the child must immediately be transported to the juvenile detention facility.

(Subd (d) amended effective January 1, 2007.)

Rule 5.516 amended effective January 1, 2007; adopted as rule 1405 effective January 1, 1991; previously amended effective January 1, 2001.

Rule 5.518. Court-connected child protection/dependency mediation

(a) Purpose (§ 350)

This rule establishes mandatory standards of practice and administration for court-connected dependency mediation services in accordance with section 350. This rule is intended to ensure fairness, accountability, and a high quality of service to children and families and to improve the safety, confidentiality, and consistency of dependency mediation programs statewide.

(Subd (a) amended effective January 1, 2007.)

(b) Definitions

(1) "Dependency mediation" is a confidential process conducted by specially trained, neutral third-party mediators who have no decision-making power. Dependency mediation provides a nonadversarial setting in which a mediator assists the parties in reaching a fully informed and mutually acceptable resolution that focuses on the child's safety and best interest and the safety of all family members. Dependency mediation is concerned with any and all issues related to child protection.

(2) "Safety and best interest of the child" refers to the child's physical, psychological, and emotional well-being. Determining the safety and best interest of the child includes consideration of all of the following:

(A) The preservation and strengthening of the family and family relationships whenever appropriate and possible;

(B) The manner in which the child may be protected from the risk of future abuse or neglect;

(C) The child's need for safety, stability, and permanency;

(D) The ongoing need of the child to cope with the issues that caused his or her involvement in the juvenile dependency system;

(E) The child's need for continuity of care and the effect that removal and subsequent placements have had, or may have, on the child; and

(F) The child's education, which includes the child's participation, progress, need for assistance, cognitive development and, if applicable, early childhood education and care, the need for special education and related services, and the extent to which the child has or has had limited English proficiency (LEP).

(3) "Safety of family members" refers to the physical, psychological, and emotional well-being of all family members, with consideration of the following:

(A) The role of domestic violence in creating a perceived or actual threat for the victim; and

(B) The ongoing need of family members to feel safe from physical, emotional, and psychological abuse.

(4) "Differential domestic violence assessment" is a process used to assess the nature of any domestic violence issues in the family so that the mediator may conduct the mediation in such a way as to protect any victim of domestic violence from intimidation and to correct for power imbalances created by past violence and the fear of prospective violence.

(5) "Protocols" refer to any local set of rules, policies, and procedures developed and implemented by juvenile dependency mediation programs. All protocols must be developed in accordance with pertinent state laws, California Rules of Court, and local court rules.

(Subd (b) amended effective January 1, 2008; previously amended effective January 1, 2007.)

(c) Responsibility for mediation services

(1) Each court that has a dependency mediation program must ensure that:

(A) Dependency mediators are impartial, are competent, and uphold the standards established by this rule;

(B) Dependency mediators maintain an appropriate focus on issues related to the child's safety and best interest and the safety of all family members;

(C) Dependency mediators provide a forum for all interested persons to develop a plan focused on the best interest of the child, emphasizing family preservation and strengthening and the child's need for permanency;

(D) Dependency mediation services and case management procedures are consistent with applicable state law without compromising each party's right to due process and a timely resolution of the issues;

(E) Dependency mediation services demonstrate accountability by:

(i) Providing for the processing of complaints about a mediator's performance; and

(ii) Participating in any statewide and national data-collection efforts;

(F) The dependency mediation program uses an intake process that screens for and informs the mediator about any restraining orders, domestic violence, or safety-related issues affecting the child or any other party named in the proceedings;

(G) Whenever possible, dependency mediation is conducted in the shared language of the participants. When the participants speak different languages, interpreters, court-certified when possible, should be assigned to translate at the mediation session; and

(H) Dependency mediation services preserve, in accordance with pertinent law, party confidentiality, whether written or oral, by the:

(i) Storage and disposal of records and any personal information accumulated by the mediation program; and

(ii) Management of any new child abuse reports and related documents.

(2) Each dependency mediator must:

(A) Attempt to assist the mediation participants in reaching a settlement of the issues consistent with preserving the safety and best interest of the child, first and foremost, and the safety of all family members and participants;

(B) Discourage participants from blaming the victim and from denying or minimizing allegations of child abuse or violence against any family member;

(C) Be conscious of the values of preserving and strengthening the family as well as the child's need for permanency;

(D) Not make any recommendations or reports of any kind to the court, except for the terms of any agreement reached by the parties;

(E) Treat all mediation participants in a manner that preserves their dignity and self-respect;

(F) Promote a safe and balanced environment for all participants to express and advocate for their positions and interests;

(G) Identify and disclose potential grounds on which a mediator's impartiality might reasonably be challenged through a procedure that allows for the selection of another mediator within a reasonable time. If a dependency mediation program has only one mediator and the parties are unable to resolve the conflict, the mediator must inform the court;

(H) Identify and immediately disclose to the participants any reasonable concern regarding the mediator's continuing capacity to be impartial, so they can decide whether the mediator should withdraw or continue;

(I) Promote the participants' understanding of the status of the case in relation to the ongoing court process, what the case plan requires of them, and the terms of any agreement reached during the mediation; and

(J) Conduct an appropriate review to evaluate the viability of any agreement reached, including the identification of any provision that depends on the action or behavior of any individual who did not participate in creating the agreement.

(Subd (c) amended effective January 1, 2007.)

(d) Mediation process

The dependency mediation process must be conducted in accordance with pertinent state laws, applicable rules of court, and local protocols. All local protocols must include the following:

(1) The process by which cases are sent to mediation, including:

(A) Who may request mediation;

(B) Who decides which cases are to be sent to mediation;

(C) Whether mediation is voluntary or mandatory;

(D) How mediation appointments are scheduled; and

(E) The consequences, if any, to a party who fails to participate in the mediation process.

(2) A policy on who participates in the mediation, according to the following guidelines:

(A) When at all possible, dependency mediation should include the direct and active participation of the parties, including but not limited to the child, the parents or legal guardian, a representative of the child protective agency, and, at some stage, their respective attorneys.

(B) The child has a right to participate in the dependency mediation process accompanied by his or her attorney. If the child makes an informed choice not to participate, then the child's attorney may participate. If the child is unable to make an informed choice, then the child's attorney may participate.

(C) Any attorney who has not participated in the mediation must have an opportunity to review and agree to any proposal before it is submitted to the court for approval.

(D) As appropriate, other family members and any guardian ad litem, CASA volunteer, or other involved person or professional may participate in the mediation.

(E) A mediation participant who has been a victim of violence allegedly perpetrated by another mediation participant has the right to be accompanied by a support person. Unless otherwise invited or ordered to participate under the protocols developed by the court, a support person may not actively participate in the mediation except to be present as a source of emotional support for the alleged victim.

(3) A method by which the mediator may review relevant case information before the mediation.

(4) A protocol for providing mediation in cases in which domestic violence or violence perpetrated by any other mediation participant has, or allegedly has, occurred. This protocol must include specialized procedures designed to protect victims of domestic violence from intimidation by perpetrators. The protocol must also appropriately address all family violence issues by encouraging the incorporation of appropriate safety and treatment interventions in any settlement. The protocol must require:

(A) A review of case-related information before commencing the mediation;

(B) The performance of a differential domestic violence assessment to determine the nature of the violence, for the purposes of:

(i) Assessing the ability of the victim to fully and safely participate and to reach a noncoerced settlement;

(ii) Clarifying the history and dynamics of the domestic violence issue in order to determine the most appropriate manner in which the mediation can proceed; and

(iii) Assisting the parties, attorneys, and other participants in formulating an agreement following a discussion of appropriate safeguards for the safety of the child and family members; and

(C) A mediation structure designed to meet the need of the victim of violence for safety and for full and noncoerced participation in the process, which structure must include:

(i) An option for the victim to attend the mediation session without the alleged perpetrator being present; and

(ii) Permission for the victim to have a support person present during the mediation process, whether he or she elects to be seen separately from or together with the alleged perpetrator.

(5) An oral or written orientation that facilitates participants' safe, productive, and informed participation and decision making by educating them about:

(A) The mediation process, the typical participants, the range of disputes that may be discussed, and the typical outcomes of mediation;

(B) The importance of keeping confidential all communications, negotiations, or settlement discussions by and between the participants in the course of mediation;

(C) The mediator's role and any limitations on the confidentiality of the process; and

(D) The right of a participant who has been a victim of violence allegedly perpetrated by another mediation participant to be accompanied by a support person and to have sessions with the mediators separate from the alleged perpetrator.

(6) Protocols related to the inclusion of children in the mediation, including a requirement that the mediator explain in an age-appropriate way the mediation process to a participating child. The following information must be explained to the child:

(A) How the child may participate in the mediation;

(B) What occurs during the mediation process;

(C) The role of the mediator;

(D) What the child may realistically expect from the mediation, and the limits on his or her ability to affect the outcome;

(E) Any limitations on the confidentiality of the process;

(F) The child's right to be accompanied, throughout the mediation, by his or her attorney and other support persons; and

(G) The child's right to leave the mediation session if his or her emotional or physical well-being is threatened.

(7) Policy and procedures for scheduling follow-up mediation sessions.

(8) A procedure for suspending or terminating the process if the mediator determines that mediation cannot be conducted in a safe or an appropriately balanced manner or if any party is unable to participate in an informed manner for any reason, including fear or intimidation.

(9) A procedure for ensuring that each participant clearly understands any agreement reached during the mediation, and a procedure for presenting the agreement to the court for its approval. This procedure must include the requirement that all parties and the attorneys who participate in the agreement review and approve it and indicate their agreement in writing before its submission to the court.

(Subd (d) amended effective January 1, 2007; previously amended effective January 1, 2005.)

(e) Education, experience, and training requirements for dependency mediators

Dependency mediators must meet the following minimum qualifications:

(1) Possession of one or more of the following:

(A) A master's or doctoral degree in psychology, social work, marriage and family therapy, conflict resolution, or another behavioral science substantially related to family relationships, family violence, child development, or conflict resolution from an accredited college or university; or

(B) A juris doctorate or bachelor of laws degree;

(2) At least two years of experience as an attorney, a referee, a judicial officer, a mediator, or a child welfare worker in juvenile dependency court, or at least three years of experience in mediation or counseling, preferably in a setting related to juvenile dependency or domestic relations; and

(3) Completion of at least 40 hours of initial dependency mediation training before or within 12 months of beginning practice as a dependency mediator. Currently practicing dependency mediators must complete the required 40 hours of initial training by January 1, 2006. The training must cover the following subject areas as they relate to the practice of dependency mediation:

(A) Multiparty, multi-issue, multiagency, and high-conflict cases, including:

(i) The roles and participation of parents, other family members, children, attorneys, guardians ad litem, children's caregivers, the child welfare agency staff, CASA volunteers, law enforcement, mediators, the court, and other involved professionals and interested participants in the mediation process;

(ii) The impact that the mediation process can have on a child's well-being, and when and how to involve the child in the process;

(iii) The methods to help parties collaboratively resolve disputes and jointly develop plans that consider the needs and best interest of the child;

(iv) The disclosure, recantation, and denial of child abuse and neglect;

(v) Adult mental health issues; and

(vi) The rights to educational and developmental services recognized or established by state and federal law and strategies for appropriately addressing the individual needs of persons with disabilities;

(B) Physical and sexual abuse, exploitation, emotional abuse, endangerment, and neglect of children, and the impacts on children, including safety and treatment issues related to child abuse, neglect, and family violence;

(C) Family violence, its relevance to child abuse and neglect, and its effects on children and adult victims, including safety and treatment issues related to child abuse, neglect, and family violence;

(D) Substance abuse and its impact on children;

(E) Child development and its relevance to child abuse, neglect, and child custody and visitation arrangements;

(F) Juvenile dependency and child welfare systems, including dependency law;

(G) Interfamilial relationships and the psychological needs of children, including, but not limited to:

(i) The effect of removal or nonremoval of children from their homes and family members; and

(ii) The effect of terminating parental rights;

(H) The effect of poverty on parenting and familial relationships;

(I) Awareness of differing cultural values, including cross-generational cultural issues and local demographics;

(J) An overview of the special needs of dependent children, including their educational, medical, psychosocial, and mental health needs; and

(K) Available community resources and services for dealing with domestic and family violence, substance abuse, and housing, educational, medical, and mental health needs for families in the juvenile dependency system.

(Subd (e) amended effective January 1, 2014; previously amended effective January 1, 2005, January 1, 2007, and January 1, 2008.)

(f) Substitution for education or experience

The court, on a case-by-case basis, may approve substitution of experience for the education, or education for the experience, required by (e)(1) and (e)(2).

(Subd (f) amended effective January 1, 2007.)

(g) Continuing education requirements for mediators

In addition to the 40 hours of training required by (e)(3), all dependency mediators, mediation supervisors, program coordinators and directors, volunteers, interns, and paraprofessionals must participate in at least 12 hours per year of continuing instruction designed to enhance dependency mediation practice, skills, and techniques, including at least 4 hours specifically related to the issue of family violence.

(Subd (g) amended effective January 1, 2007.)

(h) Volunteers, interns, or paraprofessionals

Dependency mediation programs may use volunteers, interns, or paraprofessionals as mediators, but only if they are supervised by a professional mediator who is qualified to act as a professional dependency mediator as described in (e). They must meet the training and continuing education requirements in (e)(3) and (g) unless they co-mediate with another professional who meets the requirements of this rule. They are exempt from meeting the education and experience requirements in (e)(1) and (e)(2).

(Subd (h) amended effective January 1, 2007.)

(i) Education and training providers

Only education and training acquired from eligible providers meet the requirements of this rule. "Eligible providers" includes the Judicial Council and may include educational institutions, professional associations, professional continuing education groups, public or private for-profit or not-for-profit groups, and court-connected groups.

(1) Eligible providers must:

(A) Ensure that the training instructors or consultants delivering the education and training programs either meet the requirements of this rule or are experts in the subject matter;

(B) Monitor and evaluate the quality of courses, curricula, training, instructors, and consultants;

(C) Emphasize the importance of focusing dependency mediations on the health, safety, welfare, and best interest of the child;

(D) Develop a procedure to verify that participants complete the education and training program; and

(E) Distribute a certificate of completion to each person who has completed the training. The certificate must document the number of hours of training offered, the number of hours the person completed, the dates of the training, and the name of the training provider.

(2) Effective July 1, 2005, all education and training programs must be approved by Judicial Council staff in consultation with the Family and Juvenile Law Advisory Committee.

(Subd (i) amended effective January 1, 2016; adopted effective January 1, 2005; previously amended effective January 1, 2007.)

(j) Ethics/standards of conduct

Mediators must:

(1) Meet the standards of the applicable code of ethics for court employees.

(2) Maintain objectivity, provide information to and gather information from all parties, and be aware of and control their own biases.

(3) Protect the confidentiality of all parties, including the child. Mediators must not release information or make any recommendations about the case to the court or to any individual except as required by statute (for example, the requirement to make mandatory child abuse reports or reports to authorities regarding threats of harm or violence). Any limitations to confidentiality must be clearly explained to all mediation participants before any substantive issues are discussed in the mediation session.

(4) Maintain the confidential relationship between any family member or the child and his or her treating counselor, including the confidentiality of any psychological evaluations.

(5) Decline to provide legal advice.

(6) Consider the health, safety, welfare, and best interest of the child and the safety of all parties and other participants in all phases of the process and encourage the formulation of settlements that preserve these values.

(7) Operate within the limits of their training and experience and disclose any limitations or bias that would affect their ability to conduct the mediation.

(8) Not require the child to state a preference for placement.

(9) Disclose to the court, to any participant, and to the participant's attorney any conflicts of interest or dual relationships, and not accept any referral except by court order or the parties' stipulation. In the event of a conflict of interest, the mediator must suspend mediation and meet and confer in an effort to resolve the conflict of interest either to the satisfaction of all parties or according to local court rules. The court may order mediation to continue with another mediator or offer the parties an alternative method of resolving the issues in dispute.

(10) Not knowingly assist the parties in reaching an agreement that would be unenforceable for a reason such as fraud, duress, illegality, overreaching, absence of bargaining ability, or unconscionability.

(11) Protect the integrity of the mediation process by terminating the mediation when a party or participant has no genuine interest in resolving the dispute and is abusing the process.

(12) Terminate any session in which an issue of coercion, inability to participate, lack of intention to resolve the issues at hand, or physical or emotional abuse during the mediation session is involved.

(Subd (j) amended effective January 1, 2007; adopted as subd (i) effective January 1, 2004; previously relettered effective January 1, 2005.)

Rule 5.518 amended effective January 1, 2016; adopted as rule 1405.5 effective January 1, 2004; previously amended and renumbered as rule 5.518 effective January 1, 2007; previously amended effective January 1, 2005, January 1, 2008, and January 1, 2014.

Rule 5.520. Filing the petition; application for petition

(a) Discretion to file (§§ 325, 650)

Except as provided in sections 331, 364, 604, 653.5, 654, and 655, the social worker or probation officer has the sole discretion to determine whether to file a petition under section 300 and 601. The prosecuting attorney has the sole discretion to file a petition under section 602.

(Subd (a) amended effective January 1, 2007.)

(b) Filing the petition (§§ 325, 650)

A proceeding in juvenile court to declare a child a dependent or a ward of the court is commenced by the filing of a petition.

(1) In proceedings under section 300, the social worker must file the petition;

(2) In proceedings under section 601, the probation officer must file the petition; and

(3) In proceedings under section 602, the prosecuting attorney must file the petition. The prosecuting attorney may refer the matter back to the probation officer for appropriate action.

(Subd (b) amended effective January 1, 2007.)

(c) Application for petition (§§ 329, 331, 653, 653.5, 655)

Any person may apply to the social worker or probation officer to commence proceedings. The application must be in the form of an affidavit alleging facts showing the child is described in sections 300, 601, or 602. The social worker or probation officer must proceed under sections 329, 653, or 653.5. The applicant may seek review of a decision not to file a petition by proceeding under section 331 or 655.

(Subd (c) amended effective January 1, 2007.)

Rule 5.520 amended and renumbered effective January 1, 2007; adopted as rule 1406 effective January 1, 1991.

Rule 5.522. Remote filing

(a) Applicability and definitions

(1) This rule applies to juvenile court proceedings in courts that permit fax or electronic filing by local rule.

(2) As used in this rule, "fax," "fax transmission," "fax machine," and "fax filing" are defined in rule 2.301. A fax machine also includes any electronic device capable of receiving a fax transmission, as defined in rule 2.301.

(3) As used in this rule, "electronic filing" is defined in rule 2.250. Rule 2.250 also defines other terms used in this rule related to electronic filing, such as "document," "electronic filer," and "electronic filing service provider."

(Subd (a) amended effective January 1, 2019; previously amended effective January 1, 2007, and January 1, 2015.)

(b) Electronic filing

A court may allow for the electronic filing of documents in juvenile proceedings in accordance with section 212.5.

(Subd (b) amended effective January 1, 2019; adopted effective January 1, 2015.)

(c) Fax filing

(1) *Juvenile court documents that may be filed by fax*

The following documents may be filed in juvenile court by the use of a fax machine: petitions filed under sections 300, 342, 387, 388, 601, 602, 777, and 778; Tribal Information Form (form ICWA-100); and other documents, may be filed by the use of a fax machine if permitted by local rule as specified in (a).

(2) *Persons and agencies that may file by fax*

Only the following persons and agencies may file documents by the use of a fax machine, as stated in (c)(1):

(A) Any named party to the proceeding;

(B) Any attorney of record in the proceeding;

(C) The county child welfare department;

(D) The probation department;

(E) The office of the district attorney;

(F) The office of the county counsel;

(G) A Court Appointed Special Advocate (CASA) volunteer appointed in the case; and

(H) An Indian tribe.

(3) *Procedures for fax filing*

A person described in (c)(2) may file by fax directly to any juvenile court that has provided for fax filing by local rule. The local rule or other written instruction must provide the fax telephone number or numbers for filings and the business hours during which fax filings will be accepted.

(4) *Mandatory cover sheet*

A fax filing must be accompanied by *Fax Filing Cover Sheet* (form JV-520). The cover sheet must be the first page of the transferred document. The court is not required to retain or file a copy of the cover sheet.

(5) *Signatures*

Notwithstanding any provision of law to the contrary, a signature produced by fax transmission is an original signature.

(6) *Confidentiality requirements*

To secure the confidentiality of the documents subject to filing by fax, the following procedures are required:

(A) The clerk's office designated to receive such documents must have either a separate fax machine dedicated solely to the receipt of the documents described in (c)(1) or a fax machine that is set up with a protocol to preserve the confidentiality of the documents described in (c)(1); and

(B) Any document received for fax filing must be filed or submitted to the court immediately on receipt and must not be placed or stored where anyone not entitled to access may examine it.

(Subd (c) amended effective January 1, 2021; adopted and amended effective January 1, 2015; previously subd (b)–(g); previously amended effective January 1, 2007.)

Rule 5.522 amended effective January 1, 2021; adopted as rule 1406.5 effective January 1, 1999; previously amended and renumbered effective January 1, 2007; previously amended effective January 1, 2015, and January 1, 2019.

Rule 5.523. Electronic service (§ 212.5)

(a) Electronic service—General provisions

(1) Electronic service is authorized only if the court and county agencies required to serve in juvenile court permit electronic service.

(2) Unless otherwise provided by law, a document in a juvenile court matter may be served electronically as prescribed by Code of Civil Procedure section 1010.6 and in accordance with Welfare and Institutions Code section 212.5.

(3) If the noticing entity knows or should know that a child or nonminor who has consented to electronic service is in custody at the time that a notice will issue, the entity must also provide service of the notice by first-class mail.

(Subd (a) adopted effective January 1, 2019.)

(b) Consent to electronic service by a child, age 10 to 15

Electronic service is permitted on a child who is 10 to 15 years of age only upon express consent of the child and the child's attorney by completing the appropriate Judicial Council form.

(Subd (b) adopted effective January 1, 2019.)

(c) Consent to electronic service by a child, age 16 or 17

Electronic service is permitted on a child who is 16 or 17 years of age only if the child, after consultation with his or her attorney, expressly consents by completing the appropriate Judicial Council form.

(Subd (c) adopted effective January 1, 2019.)

(d) Required consultation with attorney for child, age 16 or 17

In a consultation with a child who is 16 or 17 years old and who seeks to consent to electronic service in a juvenile matter, the child's attorney must discuss and encourage the child to consider the following:

(1) Whether the child has regular and reliable access to a means of electronic communication for purposes of communication regarding his or her case;

(2) The importance of maintaining confidentiality and what means of electronic communication the child intends to use to communicate about his or her case and whether it is private and secure; and

(3) Whether the child understands his or her rights with respect to the provision and withdrawal of consent to electronic service.

(Subd (d) adopted effective January 1, 2019.)

(e) Required notification to child, age 16 or 17

In addition to the required factors for consideration in consultation described in (d), the child's attorney must also notify the child who seeks to provide consent to electronic service of the following:

(1) Electronic service of medical or psychological documentation related to a child is prohibited, with the exception of the summary required under Welfare and Institutions Code section 16010 when included as part of a required report to the court.

(2) Electronic service on a party or other person is permitted only if the party or other person has expressly consented, as provided in Code of Civil Procedure section 1010.6.

(3) A party or other person may subsequently withdraw his or her consent to electronic service by completing the appropriate Judicial Council form.

(Subd (e) adopted effective January 1, 2019.)

Rule 5.523 adopted effective January 1, 2019.

Rule 5.524. Form of petition; notice of hearing

(a) Form of petition—dependency (§§ 332, 333)

The petition to declare a child a dependent of the court must be verified and may be dismissed without prejudice if not verified. The petition must contain the information stated in section 332.

(Subd (a) amended effective January 1, 2007; previously amended effective January 1, 1995, and January 1, 2006.)

(b) Form of petition—delinquency (§§ 656, 656.1, 656.5, 661)

The petition to declare a child a ward of the court must be verified and may be dismissed without prejudice if not verified. The petition must contain the information stated in sections 656, 656.1, 656.5, 661, and, if applicable, the intent to aggregate other offenses under section 726.

(Subd (b) amended effective January 1, 2007; adopted effective January 1, 2006.)

(c) Use of forms

Dependency petitions must be filed on a Judicial Council form. The filing party must use *Juvenile Dependency Petition (Version One)* (form JV-100) with the *Additional Children Attachment (Juvenile Dependency Petition)* (form JV-101(A)) when appropriate, or *Juvenile Dependency Petition (Version Two)* (form JV-110) as prescribed by local rule or practice. Rules 1.31 and 1.35 govern the use of mandatory and optional forms, respectively.

(Subd (c) amended effective January 1, 2019; adopted as subd (b) effective January 1, 1991; previously amended and relettered effective January 1, 2006; previously amended effective January 1, 2007.)

(d) Amending the petition (§§ 348, 678)

Chapter 8 of title 6 of part 2 of the Code of Civil Procedure, beginning at section 469, applies to variances and amendments of petitions and proceedings in the juvenile court.

(Subd (d) amended and relettered effective January 1, 2006; adopted as subd (c) effective January 1, 1991.)

(e) Notice of hearing—dependency (§§ 290.1, 290.2, 297, 338)

(1) When the petition is filed, the probation officer or social worker must serve a notice of hearing under section 290.1, with a copy of the petition attached. On filing of the petition, the clerk must issue and serve notice as prescribed in section 290.2, along with a copy of the petition. CASA volunteers are entitled to the same notice as stated in sections 290.1 and 290.2. Notice under sections 290.1 and 290.2 may not be served electronically.

(2) If the county and the court choose to allow notice by electronic service of hearings under sections 291–295, the court must develop a process for obtaining consent from persons entitled to notice that complies with Welfare and Institutions Code section 212.5 and ensures that notice can be effectuated according to statutory timelines.

(Subd (e) amended effective January 1, 2019; adopted as subd (d) effective January 1, 1991; previously amended and relettered effective January 1, 2006; previously amended effective January 1, 2007, and July 1, 2016.)

(f) Notice of hearing—delinquency (§§ 630, 630.1, 658, 659, 660)

(1) Immediately after the filing of a petition to detain a child, the probation officer or the prosecuting attorney must issue and serve notice as prescribed in section 630.

(2) When a petition is filed, the clerk must issue and serve a notice of hearing in accordance with sections 658, 659, and 660 with a copy of the petition attached.

(3) After reasonable notification by counsel representing the child, or representing the child's parents or guardian, the clerk must notify such counsel of the hearings as prescribed in section 630.1.

(Subd (f) amended effective January 1, 2019; adopted effective January 1, 2006; previously amended effective January 1, 2007.)

(g) Waiver of service (§§ 290.2, 660)

A person may waive service of notice by a voluntary appearance noted in the minutes of the court, or by a written waiver of service filed with the clerk.

(Subd (g) amended and relettered effective January 1, 2006; adopted as subd (h) effective January 1, 1991.)

(h) Oral notice (§§ 290.1, 630)

Notice required by sections 290.1 and 630 may be given orally. The social worker or probation officer must file a declaration stating that oral notice was given and to whom.

(Subd (h) amended effective January 1, 2007; adopted as subd (j) effective January 1, 1991; previously amended and relettered effective January 1, 2006.)
Rule 5.524 amended effective January 1, 2019; adopted as rule 1407 effective January 1, 1991; previously amended effective January 1, 1992, January 1, 1995, January 1, 2001, January 1, 2006, and July 1, 2016; previously amended and renumbered as rule 5.524 effective January 1, 2007.

Rule 5.526. Citation to appear; warrants of arrest; subpoenas

(a) Citation to appear (§§ 338, 661)

In addition to the notice required under rule 5.524, the court may issue a citation directing a parent or guardian to appear at a hearing as specified in section 338 or 661.

(Subd (a) amended effective January 1, 2019; previously amended effective January 1, 2006, and January 1, 2007.)

(b) Warrant of arrest (§§ 339, 662)

The court may order a warrant of arrest to issue against the parent, guardian, or present custodian of the child as specified in section 339 or 662.

(Subd (b) amended effective January 1, 2019.)

(c) Protective custody or warrant of arrest for child (§§ 340, 663)

The court may order a protective custody warrant or a warrant of arrest for a child as specified in section 340 or 663.

(Subd (c) amended effective January 1, 2019.)

(d) Subpoenas (§§ 341, 664)

On the court's own motion or at the request of the petitioner, child, parent, guardian, or present caregiver, the clerk must issue subpoenas as specified in section 341 or 664.

(Subd (d) amended effective January 1, 2019; previously amended effective January 1, 2006.)
Rule 5.526 amended effective January 1, 2019; adopted as rule 1408 effective January 1, 1991; previously amended effective January 1, 2006; previously amended and renumbered effective January 1, 2007.

Chapter 3
General Conduct of Juvenile Court Proceedings

Rule 5.530. Persons present
Rule 5.531. Appearance by telephone (§ 388; Pen. Code, § 2625)
Rule 5.532. Court reporter; transcripts
Rule 5.534. General provisions—all proceedings
Rule 5.536. General provisions—proceedings held before referees
Rule 5.538. Conduct of proceedings held before a referee not acting as a temporary judge
Rule 5.540. Orders of referees not acting as temporary judges
Rule 5.542. Rehearing of proceedings before referees
Rule 5.544. Prehearing motions (§ 700.1)
Rule 5.546. Prehearing discovery
Rule 5.548. Granting immunity to witnesses
Rule 5.550. Continuances
Rule 5.552. Confidentiality of records (§§ 827, 827.12, 828)
Rule 5.553. Juvenile case file of a deceased child
Rule 5.555. Hearing to consider termination of juvenile court jurisdiction over a nonminor—dependents or wards of the juvenile court in a foster care placement and nonminor dependents (§§ 224.1(b), 303, 366.31, 391, 451, 452, 607.2, 607.3, 16501.1(g)(16))

Rule 5.530. Persons present

(a) Separate session; restriction on persons present (§§ 345, 675)

All juvenile court proceedings must be heard at a special or separate session of the court, and no other matter may be heard at that session. No person on trial, awaiting trial, or accused of a crime, other than a parent, de facto parent, guardian, or relative of the child, may be present at the hearing, except while testifying as a witness.

(Subd (a) amended effective January 1, 2005.)

(b) Persons present (§§ 280, 290.1, 290.2, 332, 347, 349, 353, 656, 658, 677, 679, 681, 700; 25 U.S.C. §§ 1911, 1931–1934)

The following persons are entitled to be present:

(1) The child or nonminor dependent;

(2) All parents, de facto parents, Indian custodians, and guardians of the child or, if no parent or guardian resides within the state or their places of residence are not known, any adult relative residing within the county or, if none, the adult relative residing nearest the court;

(3) Counsel representing the child or the parent, de facto parent, guardian, adult relative, or Indian custodian or the tribe of an Indian child;

(4) The probation officer or social worker;

(5) The prosecuting attorney, as provided in (c) and (d);

(6) Any CASA volunteer;

(7) In a proceeding described by rule 5.480, a representative of the Indian child's tribe;

(8) The court clerk;

(9) The official court reporter, as provided in rule 5.532;

(10) At the court's discretion, a bailiff; and

(11) Any other persons entitled to notice of the hearing under sections 290.1 and 290.2.

(Subd (b) amended effective July 1, 2013; previously amended effective January 1, 1995, January 1, 1997, January 1, 2005, January 1, 2007, and January 1, 2012.)

(c) Presence of prosecuting attorney—section 601–602 proceedings (§ 681)

In proceedings brought under section 602, the prosecuting attorney must appear on behalf of the people of the State of California. In proceedings brought under section 601, the prosecuting attorney may appear to assist in ascertaining and presenting the evidence if:

(1) The child is represented by counsel; and

(2) The court consents to or requests the prosecuting attorney's presence, or the probation officer requests and the court consents to the prosecuting attorney's presence.

(Subd (c) amended effective January 1, 2007.)

(d) Presence of petitioner's attorney—section 300 proceedings (§ 317)

In proceedings brought under section 300, the county counsel or district attorney must appear and represent the petitioner if the parent or guardian is represented by counsel and the juvenile court requests the attorney's presence.

(Subd (d) amended effective January 1, 2007.)

(e) Others who may be admitted (§§ 346, 676, 676.5)

Except as provided below, the public must not be admitted to a juvenile court hearing. The court may admit those whom the court deems to have a direct and legitimate interest in the case or in the work of the court.

(1) If requested by a parent or guardian in a hearing under section 300, and consented to or requested by the child, the court may permit others to be present.

(2) In a hearing under section 602:

(A) If requested by the child and a parent or guardian who is present, the court may admit others.

(B) Up to two family members of a prosecuting witness may attend to support the witness, as authorized by Penal Code section 868.5.

(C) Except as provided in section 676(b), members of the public must be admitted to hearings concerning allegations of the offenses stated in section 676(a).

(D) A victim of an offense alleged to have been committed by the child who is the subject of the petition, and up to two support persons chosen by the victim, are entitled to attend any hearing regarding the offense.

(E) Any persons, including the child, may move to exclude a victim or a support person and must demonstrate a substantial probability that overriding interests will be prejudiced by the presence of the individual sought to be excluded. On such motion, the court must consider reasonable alternatives to the exclusion and must make findings as required under section 676.5.

(Subd (e) amended effective January 1, 2007; previously amended effective January 1, 2001.)

(f) Participation of incarcerated parent in dependency proceedings (§§ 290.1–294, 316.2, 349, 361.5(e); Pen. Code § 2625)

The incarcerated parent of a child on behalf of whom a petition under section 300 has been filed may appear and participate in dependency proceedings as provided in this subdivision.

(1) Notice must be sent to an incarcerated parent of a detention hearing under section 319 as required by sections 290.1 and 290.2; a jurisdictional hearing under section 355 or a dispositional hearing under section 358 or 361 as required by section 291; a review hearing under section 366.21, 366.22, or 366.25 as required by section 293; or a permanency planning hearing under section 366.26 as required by section 294.

(A) Notice to an incarcerated parent of a jurisdictional hearing, a dispositional hearing, or a section 366.26 permanency planning hearing at which termination of parental rights is at issue must inform the incarcerated parent of his or her right to be physically present at the hearing and explain how the parent may secure his or her presence or, if he or she waives the right to be physically present, appearance and participation.

(B) Notice to an incarcerated parent of a detention hearing, a review hearing, or any other hearing in a dependency proceeding must inform the incarcerated parent of his or her options for requesting physical or telephonic appearance at and participation in the hearing.

(C) The county welfare department must use the prisoner location system developed by the Department of Corrections and Rehabilitation to facilitate timely and effective notice of hearings to incarcerated parents.

(2) The court must order an incarcerated parent's temporary removal from the institution where he or she is confined and production before the court at the time appointed for any jurisdictional hearing held under section 355 or dispositional hearing held under section 358 or 361, and any permanency planning hearing held under section 366.26 in which termination of parental rights is at issue.

(3) For any other hearing in a dependency proceeding, including but not limited to a detention hearing or a review hearing, the court may order the temporary removal of the incarcerated parent from the institution where he or she is confined and the parent's production before the court at the time appointed for that hearing.

(4) No hearing described in (2) may be held without the physical presence of the incarcerated parent and the parent's attorney unless the court has received:

(A) A knowing waiver of the right to be physically present signed by the parent; or

(B) A declaration, signed by the person in charge of the institution in which the parent is incarcerated, or his or her designated representative, stating that the parent has, by express statement or action, indicated an intent not to be physically present at the hearing.

(5) When issuing an order under (2) or (3), the court must require that *Order for Prisoner's Appearance at Hearing Affecting Parental Rights* (form JV-450) and a copy of *Prisoner's Statement Regarding Appearance at Hearing Affecting Parental Rights* (form JV-451) be attached to the notice of hearing and served on the parent, the parent's attorney, the person in charge of the institution, and the sheriff's department of the county in which the order is issued by the person responsible for giving notice of the hearing at issue not less than 15 days before the date of the hearing.

(6) The court may, at the request of any party or on its own motion, permit an incarcerated parent, who has waived his or her right to be physically present at a hearing described in (2) or who has not been ordered to appear before the court, to appear and participate in a hearing by videoconference consistent with the requirements of rule 5.531. If video technology is not available, the court may permit the parent to appear by telephone consistent with the requirements of rule 5.531. The court must inform the parent that, if no technology complying with rule 5.531 is available, the court may proceed without his or her appearance and participation.

(7) The presiding judge of the juvenile court in each county should convene representatives of the county welfare department, the sheriff's department, parents' attorneys, and other appropriate entities to develop:

(A) Local procedures or protocols to ensure an incarcerated parent's notification of, transportation to, and physical presence at court hearings involving proceedings affecting his or her child as required or authorized by Penal Code section 2625 and this rule unless he or she has knowingly waived the right to be physically present; and

(B) Local procedures or protocols, consistent with (f)(6) and rule 5.531, to facilitate the appearance and participation by videoconference or telephone of an incarcerated parent who has knowingly waived the right to be physically present.

(Subd (f) adopted effective January 1, 2012.)

(g) Discretionary tribal participation (§§ 224, 306.6, 346, 676, 827, 16001.9)

(1) The tribe of a child may request to participate in a case, using *Request for Tribal Participation* (form ICWA-042). The court should exercise its discretion as follows:

(A) In a proceeding involving an Indian child, the child's tribe may request permission to participate in the proceedings under section 346 or 676. Consistent with sections 224 and 16001.9, there is a presumption that the tribe has a direct and legitimate interest in the proceedings under section 346 or 676 and the request should be approved absent a finding by the court that the tribe's participation would not assist the court in making decisions that are in the best interest of the child.

(B) In a proceeding involving a child described by section 306.6, the tribe from which the child is descended may request permission to participate in the proceedings. Consistent with sections 224 and 16001.9, the request should be approved absent a finding by the court that the tribe's participation would not assist the court in making decisions that are in the best interest of the child.

(C) When a child does not meet the definition of an Indian child but either of the child's parents is a member of a tribe and the tribe wishes to participate in juvenile proceedings involving the child, the parent's tribe may request permission to participate in the proceedings under section 346 or 676. Consistent with sections 224 and 16001.9, there is a presumption that the tribe has a direct and legitimate interest in the proceedings under section 346 or 676 and the request should be approved absent a finding by the court that the tribe's participation would not assist the court in making decisions that are in the best interest of the child.

(2) Upon approval of a request, the court must instruct the tribe as to the confidentiality of the proceedings and, although the tribe does not become a party unless the court orders otherwise, the tribe is authorized to:

(A) Be present at the hearing;

(B) Address the court;

(C) Request and receive notices of hearings;

(D) Request to examine court documents relating to the proceeding consistent with section 827;

(E) Present information to the court that is relevant to the proceeding;

(F) Submit written reports and recommendations to the court; and

(G) Perform other duties and responsibilities as requested or approved by the court.

(Subd (g) adopted effective January 1, 2024.)

Rule 5.530 amended effective January 1, 2024; adopted as rule 1410 effective January 1, 1990; previously amended and renumbered effective January 1, 2007; previously amended effective January 1, 1995, January 1, 1997, January 1, 2001, January 1, 2005, January 1, 2012, and July 1, 2013.

Rule 5.531. Appearance by telephone (§ 388; Pen. Code, § 2625)

(a) Application

Subdivisions (b) and (c) of this rule are suspended from January 1, 2022, to January 1, 2026. During that time, the applicable provisions in rule 3.672 or Welfare and Institutions Code sections 224.2(k) or 679.5, and any rules implementing those statutes govern remote appearances and proceedings in juvenile court. The standards in (b) apply to any appearance or participation in court by telephone, videoconference, or other digital or electronic means authorized by law.

(Subd (a) amended effective August 4, 2023; adopted effective January 1, 2012; previously amended effective January 1, 2022.)

(b) Standards for local procedures or protocols

Local procedures or protocols must be developed to ensure the fairness and confidentiality of any proceeding in which a party is permitted by statute, rule of court, or judicial discretion to appear by telephone. These procedures or protocols must, at a minimum:

(1) Allow an Indian child's tribe to appear by telephone or other computerized remote means at no charge in accordance with rule 5.482(g). The method of appearance may be determined by the court consistent with court capacity and contractual obligations, and taking account of the capacity of the tribe, as long as a method of effective remote appearance and participation sufficient to allow the tribe to fully exercise its rights is provided;

(2) Ensure that the party appearing by telephone can participate in the hearing in real time, with no delay in aural or, if any, visual transmission or reception;

(3) Ensure that the statements of participants are audible to all other participants and court staff and that the statements made by a participant are identified as being made by that participant;

(4) Ensure that the proceedings remain confidential as required by law;

(5) Establish a deadline of no more than three court days before the proceeding for notice to the court by the party or party's attorney (if any) of that party's intent to appear by telephone, and permit that notice to be conveyed by any method reasonably calculated to reach the court, including telephone, fax, or other electronic means;

(6) Permit the party, on a showing of good cause, to appear by telephone even if he or she did not provide timely notice of intent to appear by telephone;

(7) Permit a party to appear in person for a proceeding at the time and place for which the proceeding was noticed, even if that party had previously notified the court of an intent to appear by telephone;

(8) Ensure that any hearing at which a party appears by telephone is recorded and reported to the same extent and in the same manner as if he or she had been physically present;

(9) Ensure that the party appearing by telephone is able to communicate confidentially with his or her attorney (if any) during the proceeding and provide timely notice to all parties of the steps necessary to secure confidential communication; and

(10) Provide for the development of the technological capacity to accommodate appearances by telephone that comply with the requirements of this rule.

(Subd (b) amended effective January 1, 2021; adopted effective January 1, 2012.)

(c) No independent right

Nothing in this rule confers on any person an independent right to appear by telephone, videoconference, or other electronic means in any proceeding.

(Subd (c) adopted effective January 1, 2012.)

Rule 5.531 amended effective August 4, 2023; adopted effective January 1, 2012; previously amended January 1, 2021, and January 1, 2022.

Rule 5.532. Court reporter; transcripts

(a) Hearing before judge (§§ 347, 677)

If the hearing is before a judge or a referee acting as a temporary judge by stipulation, an official court reporter or other authorized reporting procedure must record all proceedings.

(Subd (a) amended effective January 1, 2007.)

(b) Hearing before referee (§§ 347, 677)

If the hearing is before a referee not acting as a temporary judge, the judge may direct an official court reporter or other authorized reporting procedure to record all proceedings.

(c) Preparation of transcript (§§ 347, 677)

If directed by the judge or if requested by a party or the attorney for a party, the official court reporter or other authorized transcriber must prepare a transcript of the proceedings within such reasonable time after the hearing as the judge designates and must certify that the proceedings have been correctly reported and transcribed. If directed by the judge, the official court reporter or authorized transcriber must file the transcript with the clerk of the court.

(Subd (c) amended effective January 1, 2007.)

Rule 5.532 amended and renumbered effective January 1, 2007; adopted as rule 1411 effective January 1, 1990.

Rule 5.534. General provisions—all proceedings

(a) De facto parents

On a sufficient showing, the court may recognize the child's present or previous custodian as a de facto parent and grant him or her standing to participate as a party in the dispositional hearing and any hearing thereafter at which the status of the dependent child is at issue. The de facto parent may:

(1) Be present at the hearing;

(2) Be represented by retained counsel or, at the discretion of the court, by appointed counsel; and

(3) Present evidence.

(Subd (a) relettered effective January 1, 2017; adopted as subd (e) effective January 1, 1991; previously amended effective January 1, 2007, and January 1, 2014.)

(b) Relatives

(1) On a sufficient showing, the court may permit a relative of the child or youth to:

(A) Be present at the hearing; and

(B) Address the court.

(2) A relative of the child has the right to submit information about the child to the court at any time. Written information about the child may be submitted to the court using *Relative Information* (form JV-285) or in a letter to the court.

(3) When a relative is located through the investigation required by rule 5.637, the social worker or probation officer must give that relative:

(A) The written notice required by section 309 or 628 and the "Important Information for Relatives" document as distributed in California Department of Social Services All County Letter No. 09-86;

(B) A copy of *Relative Information* (form JV-285), with the county and address of the court, the child's name and date of birth, and the case number already entered in the appropriate caption boxes by the social worker; and

(C) A copy of *Confidential Information* (form JV-287).

(4) When form JV-285 or a relative's letter is received by the court, the clerk must provide the social worker or probation officer, all self-represented parties, and all attorneys with a copy of the completed form or letter.

(5) When form JV-287 is received by the court, the clerk must place it in a confidential portion of the case file.

(Subd (b) relettered effective January 1, 2017; adopted as subd (f) effective January 1, 1991; previously amended effective January 1, 2007, January 1, 2011, and January 1, 2014.)

(c) Right to counsel (§§ 317, 633, 634, 700)

At each hearing, the court must advise any self-represented child, parent, or guardian of the right to be represented by counsel and, if applicable, of the right to have counsel appointed, subject to a claim by the court or the county for reimbursement as provided by law.

(Subd (c) relettered effective January 1, 2017; adopted as subd (g) effective January 1, 1991; previously amended effective July 1, 2002, January 1, 2007, and January 1, 2014.)

(d) Appointment of counsel (§§ 317, 353, 633, 634, 700)

(1) In cases petitioned under section 300:

(A) The court must appoint counsel for the child unless the court finds that the child would not benefit from the appointment and makes the findings required by rule 5.660(b); and

(B) The court must appoint counsel for any parent or guardian unable to afford counsel if the child is placed in out-of-home care or the recommendation of the petitioner is for out-of-home care, unless the court finds the parent or guardian has knowingly and intelligently waived the right to counsel.

(2) In cases petitioned under section 601 or 602:

(A) The court must appoint counsel for any child who appears without counsel, unless the child knowingly and intelligently waives the right to counsel. If the court determines that the parent or guardian can afford counsel but has not retained counsel for the child, the court must appoint counsel for the child and order the parent or guardian to reimburse the county;

(B) The court may appoint counsel for a parent or guardian who desires but cannot afford counsel; and

(C) If the parent has retained counsel for the child and a conflict arises, the court must take steps to ensure that the child's interests are protected.

(Subd (d) relettered effective January 1, 2017; adopted as subd (h) effective January 1, 1991; previously amended effective July 1, 2002, January 1, 2007, and January 1, 2014.)

(e) Tribal representatives (25 U.S.C. §§ 1911, 1931–1934)

The tribe of an Indian child is entitled to intervene as a party at any stage of a dependency proceeding concerning the Indian child.

(1) The tribe may appear by counsel or by a representative of the tribe designated by the tribe to intervene on its behalf. When the tribe appears as a party by a representative of the tribe, the name of the representative and a statement of authorization for that individual or agency to appear as the tribe must be submitted to the court in the form of a tribal resolution or other document evidencing an official act of the tribe.

(2) If the tribe of the Indian child does not intervene as a party, the court may permit an individual affiliated with the tribe or, if requested by the tribe, a representative of a program operated by another tribe or Indian organization to:

(A) Be present at the hearing;

(B) Address the court;

(C) Receive notice of hearings;

(D) Examine all court documents relating to the dependency case;

(E) Submit written reports and recommendations to the court; and

(F) Perform other duties and responsibilities as requested or approved by the court.

(Subd (e) relettered effective January 1, 2017; adopted as subd (i) effective January 1, 1997; previously amended effective July 1, 2002, and January 1, 2007.)

(f) Appointment of educational rights holder (§§ 319, 361, 366, 366.27, 726, 727.2; Gov. Code, §§ 7579.5–7579.6)

(1) If the court limits, even temporarily, the rights of a parent or guardian to make educational or developmental-services decisions for a child under rule 5.649, the court must immediately proceed under rule 5.650 to appoint a responsible adult as educational rights holder for the child.

(2) If a nonminor or nonminor dependent youth chooses not to make educational or developmental-services decisions for him- or herself or is deemed by the court to be incompetent, and the court also finds that the appointment of an educational rights holder would be in the best interests of the youth, then the court must immediately proceed under rule 5.650 to appoint or continue the appointment of a responsible adult as educational rights holder for the youth.

(Subd (f) relettered effective January 1, 2017; adopted as subd (j) effective January 1, 2008; previously amended effective January 1, 2014.)

(g) Advisement of hearing rights (§§ 301, 311, 341, 630, 702.5, 827)

(1) The court must advise the child, parent, and guardian in section 300 cases, and the child in section 601 or section 602 cases, of the following rights:

(A) The right to assert the privilege against self-incrimination;

(B) The right to confront and cross-examine the persons who prepared reports or documents submitted to the court by the petitioner and the witnesses called to testify at the hearing;

(C) The right to use the process of the court to bring in witnesses; and

(D) The right to present evidence to the court.

(2) The child, parent, guardian, and their attorneys have:

(A) The right to receive probation officer or social worker reports; and

(B) The right to inspect the documents used by the preparer of the report.

(3) Unless prohibited by court order, the child, parent, guardian, and their attorneys also have the right to receive all documents filed with the court.

(Subd (g) amended and relettered effective January 1, 2017; adopted as subd (i) effective January 1, 1991; previously relettered as subd (j) effective January 1, 1997, and as subd (k) effective January 1, 2008; previously amended effective July 1, 2002, and January 1, 2007.)

(h) Notice

At each hearing under section 300 et seq., the court must determine whether notice has been given as required by law and must make an appropriate finding noted in the minutes.

(Subd (h) relettered effective January 1, 2017; adopted as subd (j) effective January 1, 1991; previously relettered as subd (k) effective January 1, 1997, and as subd (l) effective January 1, 2008; previously amended effective July 1, 2002, and January 1, 2007.)

(i) Mailing address of parent or guardian (§ 316.1)

At the first appearance by a parent or guardian in proceedings under section 300 et seq., the court must order each parent or guardian to provide a mailing address.

(1) The court must advise that the mailing address provided will be used by the court, the clerk, and the social services agency for the purposes of notice of hearings and the mailing of all documents related to the proceedings.

(2) The court must advise that until and unless the parent or guardian, or the attorney of record for the parent or guardian, submits written notification of a change of mailing address, the address provided will be used, and notice requirements will be satisfied by appropriate service at that address.

(3) *Notification of Mailing Address* (form JV-140) is the preferred method of informing the court and the social services agency of the mailing address of the parent or guardian and change of mailing address.

(A) The form must be delivered to the parent or guardian, or both, with the petition.

(B) The form must be available in the courtroom, in the office of the clerk, and in the offices of the social services agency.

(C) The form must be printed and made available in both English and Spanish.

(Subd (i) amended effective January 1, 2019; adopted as subd (k) effective January 1, 1994; previously relettered as subd (l) effective January 1, 1997, as subd (m) effective January 1, 2008, and as subd (i) effective January 1, 2017; previously amended effective July 1, 2002, January 1, 2007, and July 1, 2016.)

(j) Electronic service address (§ 316.1)

At the first appearance by a party or person before the court, each party or person entitled to notice who consents to electronic service under section 212.5 must provide the court with an electronic service address by completing the appropriate Judicial Council form.

(1) The court must advise the party or person entitled to notice that the electronic service address will be used to serve notices and documents in the case, unless and until the party or person notifies the court of a new electronic service address in writing or unless the party or person withdraws consent to electronic service.

(2) A party or person entitled to notice may indicate his or her consent and provide his or her electronic service address or may withdraw his or her consent to electronic service or change his or her electronic service address by filing *Electronic Service: Consent, Withdrawal of Consent, Address Change (Juvenile)* (form EFS-005-JV/JV-141).

(3) If a person under 18 years old files form EFS-005-JV/JV-141, he or she must ask his or her attorney or another adult to serve the document on the other parties and persons required to be served in the case.

(4) The persons required to be served form EFS-005-JV/JV-141 are all legal parties to the action and their attorneys of record, including, but not limited to, the social services agency, the child, any parent, a legal guardian, a Court Appointed Special Advocate, and a guardian ad litem. In the case of an Indian child, the Indian custodian, if any, and the child's tribe must be served pursuant to section 224.2. The judge may order service to be made on additional parties or persons.

(Subd (j) adopted effective January 1, 2019.)

(k) Caregiver notice and right to be heard (§§ 290.1–297, 366.21)

For cases filed under section 300 et seq.:

(1) For any child who has been removed from the home, the court must ensure that notice of statutory review hearings, permanency hearings, and section 366.26 hearings has been provided to the current caregiver of the child, including foster parents, preadoptive parents, relative caregivers, and nonrelative extended family members. Notice of dispositional hearings also must be provided to these individuals when the dispositional hearing is serving as a permanency hearing under section 361.5(f).

(2) The current caregiver has the right to be heard in each proceeding listed in paragraph (1), including the right to submit information about the child to the court before the hearing. Written information about the child may be submitted to the court using the *Caregiver Information Form* (form JV-290) or in the form of a letter to the court.

(3) At least 10 calendar days before each hearing listed in paragraph (1), the social worker must provide to the current caregiver:

(A) A summary of his or her recommendations for disposition, and any recommendations for change in custody or status;

(B) *Caregiver Information Form* (form JV-290); and

(C) *Instruction Sheet for Caregiver Information Form* (form JV-290-INFO).

(4) If the caregiver chooses to provide written information to the court using form JV-290 or by letter, the caregiver must follow the procedures set forth below. The court may waive any element of this process for good cause.

(A) If filing in person, the caregiver must bring the original document and 8 copies to the court clerk's office for filing no later than five calendar days before the hearing.

(B) If filing by mail, the caregiver must mail the original document and 8 copies to the court clerk's office for filing no later than seven calendar days before the hearing.

(5) When form JV-290 or a caregiver letter is received by mail the court clerk must immediately file it.

(6) When form JV-290 or a caregiver letter is filed, the court clerk must provide the social worker, all unrepresented parties, and all attorneys with a copy of the completed form or letter immediately upon receipt. The clerk also must complete, file, and distribute *Proof of Service—Juvenile* (form JV-510). The clerk may use any technology designed to speed the distribution process, including drop boxes in the courthouse, e-mail, fax, or other electronic transmission, as defined in rule 2.250, to distribute the JV-290 form or letter and proof of service form.

(Subd (k) relettered effective January 1, 2019; adopted as subd (m) effective October 1, 2007; previously relettered as subd (n) effective January 1, 2008, and as subd (j) effective January 1, 2017; previously amended effective January 1, 2016.)

Rule 5.534 amended effective January 1, 2019; adopted as rule 1412 effective January 1, 1991; previously amended and renumbered as rule 5.534 effective January 1, 2007; previously amended effective January 1, 1994, July 1, 1995, January 1, 1997, January 1, 2000, July 1, 2002, January 1, 2005, October 1, 2007, January 1, 2008, January 1, 2010, January 1, 2011, January 1, 2014, January 1, 2016, July 1, 2016, and January 1, 2017.

Advisory Committee Comment

Because the intent of subdivision (j) is to expand access to the courts for caregivers of children in out-of-home care, the rule should be liberally construed. To promote caregiver participation and input, judicial officers are encouraged to permit caregivers to orally address the court when caregivers would like to share information about the child. In addition, court clerks should allow filings by caregivers even if the caregiver has not strictly adhered to the requirements in the rule regarding number of copies and filing deadlines.

Rule 5.536. General provisions—proceedings held before referees

(a) Referees—appointment; powers (Cal. Const., art. VI, § 22)

One or more referees may be appointed under section 247 to perform subordinate judicial duties assigned by the presiding judge of the juvenile court.

(Subd (a) amended effective January 1, 2007.)

(b) Referee as temporary judge (Cal. Const., art. VI, § 21)

If the referee is an attorney admitted to practice in this state, the parties may stipulate under rule 2.816 that the referee is acting as a temporary judge with the same powers as a judge of the juvenile court. An official court reporter or other authorized reporting procedure must record all proceedings.

(Subd (b) amended effective January 1, 2007.)

Rule 5.536 amended and renumbered effective January 1, 2007; adopted as rule 1415 effective January 1, 1990.

Rule 5.538. Conduct of proceedings held before a referee not acting as a temporary judge

(a) General conduct (§§ 248, 347, 677)

Proceedings heard by a referee not acting as a temporary judge must be conducted in the same manner as proceedings heard by a judge, except:

(1) An official court reporter or other authorized reporting procedure must record the proceedings if directed by the court; and

(2) The referee must inform the child and parent or guardian of the right to seek review by a juvenile court judge.

(Subd (a) amended effective January 1, 2007.)

(b) Furnishing and serving findings and order; explanation of right to review (§§ 248, 248.5)

After each hearing before a referee, the referee must make findings and enter an order as provided elsewhere in these rules. In each case, the referee must furnish and serve the findings and order and provide an explanation of the right to review the order in accordance with sections 248 and 248.5.

(Subd (b) amended effective January 1, 2019; previously amended effective January 1, 2007, and January 1, 2016.)

Rule 5.538 amended effective January 1, 2019; adopted as rule 1416 effective January 1, 1990; previously amended and renumbered as rule 5.538 effective January 1, 2007; previously amended effective January 1, 2016.

Rule 5.540. Orders of referees not acting as temporary judges

(a) Effective date of order (§ 250)

Except as provided in (b) and subject to the right of review provided for in rule 5.542, all orders of a referee become effective immediately and continue in effect unless vacated or modified on rehearing by order of a juvenile court judge.

(Subd (a) amended effective January 1, 2007.)

(b) Orders requiring express approval of judge (§§ 249, 251)

The following orders made by a referee do not become effective unless expressly approved by a juvenile court judge within two court days:

(1) Any order removing a child from the physical custody of the person legally entitled to custody; or

(2) Any order the presiding judge of the juvenile court requires to be expressly approved.

(Subd (b) amended effective January 1, 2007.)

(c) Finality date of order

An order of a referee becomes final 10 calendar days after service of a copy of the order and findings under rule 5.538, if an application for rehearing has not been made within that time or if the judge of the juvenile court has not within the 10 days ordered a rehearing on the judge's own motion under rule 5.542.

(Subd (c) amended effective January 1, 2007.)

Rule 5.540 amended and renumbered effective January 1, 2007; adopted as rule 1417 effective January 1, 1990.

Rule 5.542. Rehearing of proceedings before referees

(a) Application for rehearing (§ 252)

An application for a rehearing of a proceeding before a referee not acting as a temporary judge may be made by the child, parent, or guardian at any time before the expiration of 10 calendar days after service of a copy of the order and findings. The application may be directed to all, or any specified part of, the order or findings and must contain a brief statement of the factual or legal reasons for requesting the rehearing.

(Subd (a) amended effective January 1, 2007.)

(b) If no formal record (§ 252)

A rehearing must be granted if proceedings before the referee were not recorded by an official court reporter or other authorized reporting procedure.

(Subd (b) amended effective January 1, 2007.)

(c) Hearing with court reporter (§ 252)

If the proceedings before the referee have been recorded by an official court reporter or other authorized reporting procedure, the judge of the juvenile court may, after reading the transcript of the proceedings, grant or deny the application for rehearing. If the application is not denied within 20 calendar days following the date of receipt of the application, or within 45 calendar days if the court for good cause extends the time, the application must be deemed granted.

(Subd (c) amended effective January 1, 2007.)

(d) Rehearing on motion of judge (§ 253)

Notwithstanding (a), at any time within 20 court days after a hearing before a referee, the judge, on the judge's own motion, may order a rehearing.

(Subd (d) amended effective January 1, 2007.)

(e) Hearing de novo (§ 254)

Rehearings of matters heard before a referee must be conducted de novo before a judge of the juvenile court. A rehearing of a detention hearing must be held within two court days after the rehearing is granted. A rehearing of other matters heard before a referee must be held within 10 court days after the rehearing is granted.

(Subd (e) amended effective January 1, 2007.)

(f) Advisement of appeal rights—rule 5.590

If the judge of the juvenile court denies an application for rehearing directed in whole or in part to issues arising during a contested jurisdiction hearing, the judge must advise, either orally or in writing, the child and the parent or guardian of all of the following:

(1) The right of the child, parent, or guardian to appeal from the court's judgment;

(2) The necessary steps and time for taking an appeal;

(3) The right of an indigent appellant to have counsel appointed by the reviewing court; and

(4) The right of an indigent appellant to be provided a free copy of the transcript.

(Subd (f) amended effective January 1, 2007.)

Rule 5.542 amended and renumbered effective January 1, 2007; adopted as rule 1418 effective January 1, 1991.

Rule 5.544. Prehearing motions (§ 700.1)

Unless otherwise ordered or specifically provided by law, prehearing motions and accompanying points and authorities must, absent a waiver, be served on the child and opposing counsel and filed with the court:

(1) At least 5 judicial days before the date the jurisdiction hearing is set to begin if the child is detained or the motion is one to suppress evidence obtained as a result of an unlawful search and seizure; or

(2) At least 10 judicial days before the date the jurisdiction hearing is set to begin if the child is not detained and the motion is other than one to suppress evidence obtained as a result of an unlawful search and seizure.

Prehearing motions must be specific, noting the grounds, and supported by points and authorities.

Rule 5.544 amended and renumbered effective January 1, 2007; adopted as rule 1419 effective January 1, 1991.

Rule 5.546. Prehearing discovery

(a) General purpose

This rule must be liberally construed in favor of informal disclosures, subject to the right of a party to show privilege or other good cause not to disclose specific material or information.

(Subd (a) amended effective January 1, 2007.)

(b) Duty to disclose police reports

After filing the petition, petitioner must promptly deliver to or make accessible for inspection and copying by the child and the parent or guardian, or their counsel, copies of the police, arrest, and crime reports relating to the pending matter. Privileged information may be omitted if notice of the omission is given simultaneously.

(Subd (b) amended effective January 1, 2007.)

(c) Affirmative duty to disclose

Petitioner must disclose any evidence or information within petitioner's possession or control favorable to the child, parent, or guardian.

(Subd (c) amended effective January 1, 2007.)

(d) Material and information to be disclosed on request

Except as provided in (g) and (h), petitioner must, after timely request, disclose to the child and parent or guardian, or their counsel, the following material and information within the petitioner's possession or control:

(1) Probation reports prepared in connection with the pending matter relating to the child, parent, or guardian;

(2) Records of statements, admissions, or conversations by the child, parent, or guardian;

(3) Records of statements, admissions, or conversations by any alleged coparticipant;

(4) Names and addresses of witnesses interviewed by an investigating authority in connection with the pending matter;

(5) Records of statements or conversations of witnesses or other persons interviewed by an investigating authority in connection with the pending matter;

(6) Reports or statements of experts made regarding the pending matter, including results of physical or mental examinations and results of scientific tests, experiments, or comparisons;

(7) Photographs or physical evidence relating to the pending matter; and

(8) Records of prior felony convictions of the witnesses each party intends to call.

(Subd (d) amended effective January 1, 2007.)

(e) Disclosure in section 300 proceedings

Except as provided in (g) and (h), the parent or guardian must, after timely request, disclose to petitioner relevant material and information within the parent's or guardian's possession or control. If counsel represents the parent or guardian, a disclosure request must be made through counsel.

(Subd (e) amended effective January 1, 2007.)

(f) Motion for prehearing discovery

If a party refuses to disclose information or permit inspection of materials, the requesting party or counsel may move the court for an order requiring timely disclosure of the information or materials. The motion must specifically and clearly designate the items sought, state the relevancy of the items, and state that a timely request has been made for the items and that the other party has refused to provide them. Each court may by local rule establish the manner and time within which a motion under this subdivision must be made.

(Subd (f) amended effective January 1, 2007.)

(g) Limits on duty to disclose—protective orders

On a showing of privilege or other good cause, the court may make orders restricting disclosures. All material and information to which a party is entitled must be disclosed in time to permit counsel to make beneficial use of them.

(h) Limits on duty to disclose—excision

When some parts of the materials are discoverable under (d) and (e) and other parts are not discoverable, the nondiscoverable material may be excised and need not be disclosed if the requesting party or counsel has been notified that the privileged material has been excised. Material ordered excised must be sealed and preserved in the records of the court for review on appeal.

(Subd (h) amended effective January 1, 2007.)

(i) Conditions of discovery

An order of the court granting discovery under this rule may specify the time, place, and manner of making the discovery and inspection and may prescribe terms and conditions. Discovery must be completed in a timely manner to avoid the delay or continuance of a scheduled hearing.

(Subd (i) amended effective January 1, 2007.)

(j) Failure to comply; sanctions

If at any time during the course of the proceedings the court learns that a person has failed to comply with this rule or with an order issued under this rule, the court may order the person to permit the discovery or inspection of materials not previously disclosed, grant a continuance, prohibit a party from introducing in evidence the material not disclosed, dismiss the proceedings, or enter any other order the court deems just under the circumstances.

(Subd (j) amended effective January 1, 2007.)

(k) Continuing duty to disclose

If subsequent to compliance with these rules or with court orders a party discovers additional material or information subject to disclosure, the party must promptly notify the child and parent or guardian, or their counsel, of the existence of the additional matter.

(Subd (k) amended effective January 1, 2007.)

Rule 5.546 amended and renumbered effective January 1, 2007; adopted as rule 1420 effective January 1, 1990.

Rule 5.548. Granting immunity to witnesses

(a) Privilege against self-incrimination

If a person is called as a witness and it appears to the court that the testimony or other evidence being sought may tend to incriminate the witness, the court must advise the witness of the privilege against self-incrimination and of the possible consequences of testifying. The court must also inform the witness of the right to representation by counsel and, if indigent, of the right to have counsel appointed.

(Subd (a) amended effective January 1, 2007.)

(b) Authority of judge to grant immunity

If a witness refuses to answer a question or to produce evidence based on a claim of the privilege against self-incrimination, a judge may grant immunity to the witness under (c) or (d) and order the question answered or the evidence produced.

(Subd (b) amended effective January 1, 2007.)

(c) Request for immunity—section 602 proceedings

In proceedings under section 602, the prosecuting attorney may make a written or oral request on the record that the court order a witness to answer a question or produce evidence. The court must then proceed under Penal Code section 1324.

(1) After complying with an order to answer a question or produce evidence and if, but for those Penal Code sections or this rule, the witness would have been privileged to withhold the answer given or the evidence produced, no testimony or other information compelled under the order or information directly or indirectly derived from the testimony or other

information may be used against the witness in any criminal case, including any juvenile court proceeding under section 602.

(2) The prosecuting attorney may request an order granting the witness use or transactional immunity.

(Subd (c) amended effective January 1, 2007; previously amended effective January 1, 1998.)

(d) Request for immunity—section 300 or 601 proceedings

In proceedings under section 300 or 601, the prosecuting attorney or petitioner may make a written or oral request on the record that the judge order a witness to answer a question or produce evidence. They may also make the request jointly.

(1) If the request is not made jointly, the other party must be given the opportunity to show why immunity is not to be granted and the judge may grant or deny the request as deemed appropriate.

(2) If jointly made, the judge must grant the request unless the judge finds that to do so would be clearly contrary to the public interest. The terms of a grant of immunity must be stated in the record.

(3) After complying with the order and if, but for this rule, the witness would have been privileged to withhold the answer given or the evidence produced, any answer given, evidence produced, or information derived there from must not be used against the witness in a juvenile court or criminal proceeding.

(Subd (d) amended effective January 1, 2007.)

(e) No immunity from perjury or contempt

Notwithstanding (c) or (d), a witness may be subject to proceedings under the juvenile court law or to criminal prosecution for perjury, false swearing, or contempt committed in answering or failing to answer or in producing or failing to produce evidence in accordance with the order.

(Subd (e) amended effective January 1, 2007.)

Rule 5.548 amended and renumbered effective January 1, 2007; adopted as rule 1421 effective January 1, 1990; previously amended effective January 1, 1998.

Rule 5.550. Continuances

(a) Cases petitioned under section 300 (§§ 316.2, 352, 354)

(1) The court must not continue a hearing beyond the time set by statute unless the court determines the continuance is not contrary to the interest of the child. In considering the child's interest, the court must give substantial weight to a child's needs for stability and prompt resolution of custody status, and the damage of prolonged temporary placements.

(2) Continuances may be granted only on a showing of good cause, and only for the time shown to be necessary. Stipulation between counsel of parties, convenience of parties, and pending criminal or family law matters are not in and of themselves good cause.

(3) If a child has been removed from the custody of a parent or guardian, the court must not grant a continuance that would cause the disposition hearing under section 361 to be completed more than 60 days after the detention hearing unless the court finds exceptional circumstances. In no event may the disposition hearing be continued more than six months after the detention hearing.

(4) In order to obtain a continuance, written notice with supporting documents must be filed and served on all parties at least two court days before the date set for hearing, unless the court finds good cause for hearing an oral motion.

(5) The court must state in its order the facts requiring any continuance that is granted.

(Subd (a) amended effective July 1, 2016; previously amended effective January 1, 1999, July 1, 2002, and January 1, 2007.)

(b) Cases petitioned under section 601 or 602 (§ 682)

(1) A continuance may be granted only on a showing of good cause and only for the time shown to be necessary. Stipulation between counsel or parties and convenience of parties are not in and of themselves good cause.

(2) In order to obtain a continuance, written notice with supporting documents must be filed and served on all parties at least two court days before the date set for the hearing, unless the court finds good cause for failure to comply with these requirements.

(3) The court must state in its order the facts requiring any continuance that is granted.

(4) If the child is represented by counsel, failure of counsel or the child to object to an order continuing a hearing beyond the time limit is deemed a consent to the continuance.

(Subd (b) amended effective January 1, 2007; previously amended effective July 1, 2002.)

(c) Continuances of detention hearings (§§ 319, 322, 635, 636, 638)

(1) On the motion of the child, parent, or guardian, the court must continue the detention hearing for one court day or for a reasonable period to permit the moving party to prepare any relevant evidence on the issue of detention. Unless otherwise ordered by the court, the child must remain in custody pending the continued hearing.

(2) At the initial detention hearing, if the court continues the hearing under (c)(1) or for any other reason, or sets the matter for rehearing, the court must either find that the continuance of the child in the parent's or guardian's home is contrary to the child's welfare or order the child released to the custody of the parent or guardian. The court may enter this finding on a temporary basis, without prejudice to any party, and reevaluate the finding at the time of the continued detention hearing.

(3) When the court knows or has reason to know the child is an Indian child, the detention hearing may not be continued beyond 30 days unless the court makes the findings required by section 319(e)(2).

(Subd (c) amended effective January 1, 2020; adopted effective January 1, 1998; previously amended effective July 1, 2002, and January 1, 2007.)

(d) Continuances of a dispositional hearing when the court knows or has reason to know the child is an Indian child (§ 352(b))

(1) When the court knows or has reason to know that the case involves an Indian child, no continuance of a dispositional may be granted that would result in the hearing being held longer than 30 days after the hearing at which the minor was ordered removed or detained unless the court finds that there are exceptional circumstances requiring a continuance.

(2) The absence of an opinion from a qualified expert witness must not, in and of itself, support a finding that exceptional circumstances exist.

(Subd (d) adopted effective January 1, 2020.)

Rule 5.550 amended effective January 1, 2020; adopted effective January 1, 1991; previously amended effective January 1, 1998, January 1, 1999, July 1, 2002, and July 1, 2016; previously amended and renumbered as rule 5.550 effective January 1, 2007.

Rule 5.552. Confidentiality of records (§§ 827, 827.12, 828)

(a) Definitions

For the purposes of this rule, "juvenile case file" includes:

(1) All documents filed in a juvenile court case;

(2) Reports to the court by probation officers, social workers of child welfare services programs, and CASA volunteers;

(3) Documents made available to probation officers, social workers of child welfare services programs, and CASA volunteers in preparation of reports to the court;

(4) Documents relating to a child concerning whom a petition has been filed in juvenile court that are maintained in the office files of probation officers, social workers of child welfare services programs, and CASA volunteers;

(5) Transcripts, records, or reports relating to matters prepared or released by the court, probation department, or child welfare services program; and

(6) Documents, video or audio tapes, photographs, and exhibits admitted into evidence at juvenile court hearings.

(Subd (a) amended effective January 1, 2007; previously amended effective January 1, 2001.)

(b) Petition

Juvenile case files may be obtained or inspected only in accordance with sections 827, 827.12, and 828. They may not be obtained or inspected by civil or criminal subpoena. With the exception of those persons permitted to inspect juvenile case files without court authorization under sections 827 and 828, and the specific requirements for accessing juvenile case files provided in section 827.12(a)(1), every person or agency seeking to inspect or obtain juvenile case files must petition the court for authorization using *Petition for Access to Juvenile Case File* (form JV-570). A chief probation officer seeking juvenile court authorization to access and provide data from case files in the possession of the probation department under section 827.12(a)(2) must comply with the requirements in (e) of this rule.

(1) The specific files sought must be identified based on knowledge, information, and belief that such files exist and are relevant to the purpose for which they are being sought.

(2) Petitioner must describe in detail the reasons the files are being sought and their relevancy to the proceeding or purpose for which petitioner wishes to inspect or obtain the files.

(Subd (b) amended effective September 1, 2020; adopted as subd (c); previously amended effective July 1, 1997, January 1, 2007, September 1, 2018, and January 1, 2019; previously repealed, amended and relettered effective January 1, 2018.)

(c) Notice of petition for access

(1) At least 10 days before the petition is submitted to the court, the petitioner must personally or by first-class mail serve *Petition for Access to Juvenile Case File* (form JV-570), *Notice of Petition for Access to Juvenile Case File* (form JV-571), and a blank copy of *Objection to Release of Juvenile Case File* (form JV-572) on the following:

(A) The county counsel, city attorney, or any other attorney representing the petitioning agency in a dependency action if the child's petition was filed under section 300;

(B) The district attorney if the child's petition was filed under section 601 or 602;

(C) The child if the child is 10 years of age or older;

(D) The attorney of record for the child who remains a ward or dependent of the court;

(E) The parents of the child if:

(i) The child is under 18 years of age; or

(ii) The child's petition was filed under section 300;

(F) The guardians of the child if:

(i) The child is under 18 years of age; or

(ii) The child's petition was filed under section 300;

(G) The probation department or child welfare agency, or both, if applicable;

(H) The Indian child's tribe; and

(I) The child's CASA volunteer.

(2) The petitioner must complete *Proof of Service—Petition for Access to Juvenile Case File* (form JV-569) and file it with the court.

(3) If the petitioner or the petitioner's counsel does not know or cannot reasonably determine the identity or address of any of the parties in (c)(1) above, the clerk must:

(A) Serve personally or by first-class mail to the last known address a copy of *Petition for Access to Juvenile Case File* (form JV-570), *Notice of Petition for Access to Juvenile Case File* (form JV-571), and a blank copy of *Objection to Release of Juvenile Case File* (form JV-572); and

(B) Complete *Proof of Service—Petition for Access to Juvenile Case File* (form JV-569) and file it with the court.

(4) For good cause, the court may, on the motion of the person seeking the order or on its own motion, shorten the time for service of the petition for access.

(Subd (c) amended effective September 1, 2020; adopted as subd (d); previously amended effective January 1, 2007, and January 1, 2009; previously amended and relettered effective January 1, 2018.)

(d) Procedure

(1) The court must review the petition and, if petitioner does not show good cause, deny it summarily.

(2) If petitioner shows good cause, the court may set a hearing. The clerk must notice the hearing to the persons and entities listed in (c)(1) above.

(3) Whether or not the court holds a hearing, if the court determines that there may be information or documents in the records sought to which the petitioner may be entitled, the juvenile court judicial officer must conduct an in camera review of the juvenile case file and any objections and assume that all legal claims of privilege are asserted.

(4) In determining whether to authorize inspection or release of juvenile case files, in whole or in part, the court must balance the interests of the child and other parties to the juvenile court proceedings, the interests of the petitioner, and the interests of the public.

(5) If the court grants the petition, the court must find that the need for access outweighs the policy considerations favoring confidentiality of juvenile case files. The confidentiality of juvenile case files is intended to protect the privacy rights of the child.

(6) The court may permit access to juvenile case files only insofar as is necessary, and only if petitioner shows by a preponderance of the evidence that the records requested are necessary and have substantial relevance to the legitimate need of the petitioner.

(7) If, after in camera review and review of any objections, the court determines that all or a portion of the juvenile case file may be accessed, the court must make appropriate orders, specifying the information that may be accessed and the procedure for providing access to it.

(8) The court may issue protective orders to accompany authorized disclosure, discovery, or access.

(Subd (d) amended effective September 1, 2020; adopted as subd (e); previously amended effective January 1, 2007, and January 1, 2009; previously amended and relettered effective January 1, 2018.)

(e) Release of case file information for research (§ 872.12(a)(2))

The court may authorize a chief probation officer to access and provide data contained in juvenile delinquency case files and related juvenile records in the possession of the probation department for the purpose of data sharing or conducting or facilitating research on juvenile justice populations, practices, policies, or trends if the court finds the following:

(1) The research, evaluation, or study includes a sound method for the appropriate protection of the confidentiality of an individual whose juvenile delinquency case file is accessed for this purpose. In considering whether a method is sound, the court must have information on:

(A) The names and qualifications of any nonprobation personnel who will have access to personally identifying information as defined in Civil Code section 1798.79.8(b);

(B) Procedures to mask personally identifying information that is shared electronically; and

(C) Data security protocols to ensure that access to the information is limited to those people authorized by the court.

(2) No further release, dissemination, or publication of personally identifying information by the probation department or a program evaluator, researcher, or research organization that is retained by the probation department will take place for research or evaluation purposes.

(3) The disclosure requirements of section 10850 are met if any dependency information in a delinquency file may be disclosed.

(4) A date for destruction of records containing personally identifying information in the possession of nonprobation department personnel has been set to prevent inappropriate disclosure of the records.

If the information is being released for human subject research as defined in 45 Code of Federal Regulations part 46, the probation department must provide notice to the office of the public defender 30 days before the court authorizes the release of the information so that the office has an opportunity to file an objection to the release with the court. If such an objection is filed within the 30 day period the court must set a hearing on the objection within 30 days of the filing of the objection to consider the objection and make a determination on whether and how release of information should be accomplished. Upon receiving authorization, but prior to the release of information, the probation department must enter into a formal agreement with the entity or entities conducting the research that specifies what may and may not be done with the information disclosed.

(Subd (e) adopted effective September 1, 2018.)

(f) Reports of law enforcement agencies (§ 828)

Except as authorized under section 828, all others seeking to inspect or obtain information gathered and retained by a law enforcement agency regarding the taking of a child into custody must petition the juvenile court for authorization using *Petition to Obtain Report of Law Enforcement Agency* (form JV-575).

(Subd (f) relettered effective September 1, 2018; adopted as subd (f) effective January 1, 1994; previously relettered as subd (g) effective January 1, 2001, and as subd (f) effective January 1, 2009; previously amended effective January 1, 2007; previously amended and relettered as subd (e) effective January 1, 2018.)

(g) Other applicable statutes

Under no circumstances must this rule or any section of it be interpreted to permit access to or release of records protected under any other federal or state law, including Penal Code section 11165 et seq., except as provided in those statutes, or to limit access to or release of records permitted under any other federal or state statute.

(Subd (g) relettered effective September 1, 2018; adopted as subd (f); previously amended and relettered as subd (h) effective July 1, 1995; previously relettered as subd (g) effective January 1, 1994, as subd (i) effective January 1, 2001, and as subd (h) effective January 1, 2009; previously amended effective January 1, 2007; previously amended and relettered as subd (f) effective January 1, 2018.)

Rule 5.552 amended effective September 1, 2020; adopted as rule 1423 effective July 1, 1992; previously amended effective January 1, 1994, July 1, 1995, July 1, 1997, January 1, 2001, January 1, 2004, January 1, 2009, January 1, 2018, September 1, 2018, and January 1, 2019; previously amended and renumbered effective January 1, 2007.

Rule 5.553. Juvenile case file of a deceased child

When the juvenile case file of a deceased child is sought, the court must proceed as follows:

(1) Under section 827(a)(2) if the request is made by a member of the public; or

(2) Under section 16502.5 if the request is made by a county board of supervisors.

Rule 5.553 adopted effective January 1, 2009.

Rule 5.555. Hearing to consider termination of juvenile court jurisdiction over a nonminor—dependents or wards of the juvenile court in a foster care placement and nonminor dependents (§§ 224.1(b), 303, 366.31, 391, 451, 452, 607.2, 607.3, 16501.1(g)(16))

(a) Applicability

(1) This rule applies to any hearing during which the termination of the juvenile court's jurisdiction over the following nonminors will be considered:

(A) A nonminor dependent as defined in section 11400(v);

(B) A ward or dependent of the juvenile court who is 18 years of age or older and subject to an order for a foster care placement; or

(C) A ward who was subject to an order for foster care placement at the time the ward attained 18 years of age, or a dependent of the juvenile court who is 18 years of age or older and is living in the home of the parent or former legal guardian.

(2) Nothing in the Welfare and Institutions Code or the California Rules of Court restricts the ability of the juvenile court to maintain dependency jurisdiction or delinquency jurisdiction over a person 18 years of age or older, who does not meet the eligibility requirements for status as a nonminor dependent and to proceed as to that person under the relevant sections of the Welfare and Institutions Code and California Rules of Court.

(3) This rule does not apply to a hearing on a petition for a nonminor to exit and reenter care to establish eligibility for federal financial participation under section 388(f). Those petitions may be decided with or without a hearing using mandatory forms *Petition and Order to Exit and Reenter Jurisdiction—Nonminor Dependent* (form JV-469) and *Findings and Orders Regarding Exit and Reentry of Jurisdiction—Nonminor Dependent* (form JV-471).

(Subd (a) amended effective September 1, 2022; adopted effective January 1, 2012; previously amended effective July 1, 2012, and January 1, 2014.)

(b) Setting a hearing

(1) A court hearing must be placed on the appearance calendar and completed before juvenile court jurisdiction is terminated.

(2) The hearing under this rule may be held during any regularly scheduled review hearing or a hearing on a petition filed under section 388 or section 778.

(3) Notice of the hearing must be given as required by section 295.

(4) Notice of the hearing to the parent of a nonminor dependent as defined in section 11400(v) is not required, unless the parent is receiving court-ordered family reunification services or the nonminor is living in the home of the parent or former legal guardian.

(5) If juvenile court jurisdiction was resumed after having previously been terminated, a hearing under this rule must be held if the nonminor dependent wants juvenile court jurisdiction terminated again. The social worker or probation officer is not required to file the 90-day Transition Plan, and the court need not make the findings described in (d)(1)(L)(iii) or (d)(2)(E)(vi).

(6) The hearing must be continued for no more than five court days for the submission of additional information as ordered by the court if the court determines that the report, the Transitional Independent Living Plan, the Transitional Independent Living Case Plan, if required, or the 90-day Transition Plan submitted by the social worker or probation officer does not provide the information required by (c) and the court is unable to make the findings and orders required by (d).

(Subd (b) amended effective January 1, 2017; adopted effective January 1, 2012; previously amended effective July 1, 2012, and January 1, 2014.)

(c) Reports

(1) The report prepared by the social worker or probation officer for a hearing under this rule must, in addition to any other elements required by law, include:

(A) Whether remaining under juvenile court jurisdiction is in the nonminor's best interests and the facts supporting the conclusion reached;

(B) The specific criteria in section 11403(b) met by the nonminor that make the nonminor eligible to remain under juvenile court jurisdiction as a nonminor dependent as defined in section 11400(v);

(C) For a nonminor to whom the Indian Child Welfare Act applies, when and how the nonminor was provided with information about the right to continue to be considered an Indian child for the purposes of the ongoing application of the Indian Child Welfare Act to the nonminor;

(D) Whether the nonminor has applied for title XVI Supplemental Security Income benefits and, if so, the status of that application, and whether remaining under juvenile court jurisdiction until a final decision has been issued is in the nonminor's best interests;

(E) Whether the nonminor has applied for Special Immigrant Juvenile status or other immigration relief and, if so, the status of that application, and whether an active juvenile court case is required for that application;

(F) When and how the nonminor was provided with information about the potential benefits of remaining under juvenile court jurisdiction as a nonminor dependent, and the social worker's or probation officer's assessment of the nonminor's understanding of those benefits;

(G) When and how the nonminor was informed that if juvenile court jurisdiction is terminated, the court maintains general jurisdiction over the nonminor for the purpose of resuming jurisdiction and the nonminor has the right to file a request to return to foster care and have the juvenile court resume jurisdiction over the nonminor as a nonminor dependent until the nonminor has attained the age of 21 years;

(H) When and how the nonminor was informed that if juvenile court dependency jurisdiction or transition jurisdiction is continued, the nonminor has the right to have that jurisdiction terminated;

(I) If the social worker or probation officer has reason to believe that the nonminor will not appear at the hearing, documentation of the basis for that belief, including:

(i) Documentation of the nonminor's statement that the nonminor does not wish to appear in person or by telephone for the hearing; or

(ii) Documentation of reasonable efforts to find the nonminor when the nonminor's location is unknown;

(J) Verification that the nonminor was provided with the information, documents, and services as required under section 391(d); and

(K) When and how a nonminor who is under delinquency jurisdiction was provided with the notices and information required under section 607.5.

(2) The social worker or probation officer must file with the report a completed *Termination of Juvenile Court Jurisdiction—Nonminor* (form JV-365).

(3) The social worker or probation officer must also file with the report the nonminor's:

(A) Transitional Independent Living Case Plan when recommending continuation of juvenile court jurisdiction;

(B) Most recent Transitional Independent Living Plan; and

(C) Completed 90-day Transition Plan.

(4) The social worker's or probation officer's report and all documents required by (2)–(3) must be filed with the court at least 10 calendar days before the hearing, and the social worker or probation officer must provide copies of the report and other documents to the nonminor, the nonminor's parent, and all attorneys of record. If the nonminor is under juvenile court jurisdiction as a nonminor dependent, the social worker or probation officer is not required to provide copies of the report and other documents to the nonminor dependent's parent, unless the parent is receiving court-ordered family reunification services.

(Subd (c) amended effective September 1, 2022; adopted effective January 1, 2012; previously amended effective July 1, 2012, January 1, 2014, January 1, 2017, and January 1, 2021.)

(d) Findings and orders

The court must, in addition to any other determinations required by law, make the following findings and orders and include them in the written documentation of the hearing:

(1) *Findings*

(A) Whether the nonminor had the opportunity to confer with the nonminor's attorney about the issues currently before the court;

(B) Whether remaining under juvenile court jurisdiction is in the nonminor's best interests and the facts in support of the finding made;

(C) Whether the nonminor meets one or more of the eligibility criteria in section 11403(b) to remain in foster care as a nonminor dependent under juvenile court jurisdiction and, if so, the specific criteria in section 11403(b) met by the nonminor;

(D) For a nonminor to whom the Indian Child Welfare Act applies, whether the nonminor was provided with information about the right to continue to be considered an Indian child for the purposes of the ongoing application of the Indian Child Welfare Act to the nonminor;

(E) Whether the nonminor has an application pending for title XVI Supplemental Security Income benefits, and if so, whether it is in the nonminor's best interests to continue juvenile court jurisdiction until a final decision has been issued to ensure that the nonminor receives continued assistance with the application process;

(F) Whether the nonminor has an application pending for Special Immigrant Juvenile status or other immigration relief, and whether an active juvenile court case is required for that application;

(G) Whether the nonminor understands the potential benefits of remaining in foster care under juvenile court jurisdiction;

(H) Whether the nonminor has been informed that if juvenile court jurisdiction is continued, the nonminor may have the right to have juvenile court jurisdiction terminated and that the court will maintain general jurisdiction over the nonminor for the purpose of resuming dependency jurisdiction or assuming or resuming transition jurisdiction over the nonminor as a nonminor dependent;

(I) Whether the nonminor has been informed that if juvenile court jurisdiction is terminated, the nonminor has the right to file a request to return to foster care and have the juvenile court resume jurisdiction over the nonminor as a nonminor dependent until the nonminor has attained the age of 21 years;

(J) Whether the nonminor was provided with the information, documents, and services as required under section 391(d) and, if not, whether juvenile court jurisdiction should be continued to ensure that all information, documents, and services are provided;

(K) Whether a nonminor who is under delinquency jurisdiction was provided with the notices and information required under section 607.5; and

(L) Whether the nonminor's:

(i) Transitional Independent Living Case Plan, if required, includes a plan for a placement the nonminor believes is consistent with the nonminor's need to gain independence, reflects the agreements made between the nonminor and social worker or probation officer to obtain independent living skills, and sets out the benchmarks that indicate how both will know when independence can be achieved;

(ii) Transitional Independent Living Plan identifies the nonminor's level of functioning, emancipation goals, and specific skills needed to prepare for independence and successful adulthood on leaving foster care; and

(iii) 90-day Transition Plan is a concrete individualized plan that specifically covers the following areas: housing, health insurance, education, local opportunities for mentors and continuing support services, workforce supports and employment services, and information that explains how and why to designate a power of attorney for health care.

(M) For a nonminor who does not appear in person or by telephone for the hearing, whether:

(i) The nonminor expressed a wish not to appear for the hearing; or

(ii) The nonminor's location remains unknown and, if so, whether reasonable efforts were made to find the nonminor.

(N) For a nonminor who has attained 21 years of age the court is only required to find that:

(i) Notice was given as required by law.

(ii) The nonminor was provided with the information, documents, and services required under section 391(e), and a completed *Termination of Juvenile Court Jurisdiction—Nonminor* (form JV-365) was filed with the court.

(iii) The 90-day Transition Plan is a concrete, individualized plan that specifically covers the following areas: housing, health insurance, education, local opportunities for mentoring and continuing support services, workforce supports and employment services, and information that explains how and why to designate a power of attorney for health care.

(iv) The nonminor has attained 21 years of age and is no longer subject to the jurisdiction of the court under section 303.

(2) *Orders*

(A) For a nonminor who meets one or more of the eligibility criteria in section 11403(b) to remain in placement under dependency jurisdiction as a nonminor dependent or under transition jurisdiction as a nonminor dependent, the court must order the continuation of juvenile court jurisdiction unless the court finds that:

(i) The nonminor does not wish to remain under juvenile court jurisdiction as a nonminor dependent;

(ii) The nonminor is not participating in a reasonable and appropriate Transitional Independent Living Case Plan; or

(iii) Reasonable efforts were made to locate the nonminor whose current location is unknown.

(B) When juvenile court jurisdiction is continued for the nonminor to remain in placement as a nonminor dependent:

(i) Order a permanent plan consistent with the nonminor's Transitional Independent Living Plan or Transitional Independent Living Case Plan;

(ii) Continue the nonminor's status as an Indian child for the purposes of the ongoing application of the Indian Child Welfare Act unless the nonminor has elected not to have the nonminor's status as an Indian child continued; and

(iii) Set a status review hearing under rule 5.903 within six months of the date of the nonminor's most recent status review hearing.

(C) For a nonminor who does not meet and does not intend to meet the eligibility requirements for nonminor dependent status but who is otherwise eligible to and will remain under juvenile court jurisdiction in a foster care placement, the court must set an appropriate statutory review hearing within six months of the date of the nonminor's most recent status review hearing.

(D) For a nonminor whose current location is unknown, the court may enter an order for termination of juvenile court jurisdiction only after finding that reasonable efforts were made to locate the nonminor;

(E) For a nonminor who does not meet one or more of the eligibility criteria of section 11403(b) and is not otherwise eligible to remain under juvenile court jurisdiction or, alternatively, who meets one or more of the eligibility criteria of section 11403(b) but either does not wish to remain under the jurisdiction of the juvenile court as a nonminor dependent or is not participating in a reasonable and appropriate Transitional Independent Living Case Plan, the court may order the termination of juvenile court jurisdiction only after entering the following findings:

(i) The nonminor was provided with the information, documents, and services as required under section 391(d);

(ii) The nonminor was informed of the options available to assist with the transition from foster care to independence;

(iii) The nonminor was informed that if juvenile court jurisdiction is terminated, the nonminor has the right to file a request to return to foster care and have the juvenile court resume jurisdiction over the nonminor as a nonminor dependent until the nonminor has reached 21 years of age;

(iv) The nonminor was provided with a copy of *How to Return to Juvenile Court Jurisdiction and Foster Care* (form JV-464-INFO), *Request to Return to Juvenile Court Jurisdiction and Foster Care* (form JV-466), *Confidential Information—Request to Return to Juvenile Court Jurisdiction and Foster Care* (form JV-468), and an endorsed filed copy of the *Termination of Juvenile Court Jurisdiction—Nonminor* (form JV-365);

(v) The nonminor had an opportunity to confer with the nonminor's attorney regarding the issues currently before the court;

(vi) The nonminor's 90-day Transition Plan includes specific options regarding housing, health insurance, education, local opportunities for mentors and continuing support services, workforce supports and employment services, and information that explains how and why to designate a power of attorney for health care.

(F) For a nonminor who has attained 21 years of age and is no longer subject to the jurisdiction of the juvenile court under section 303, the court must enter an order that juvenile court jurisdiction is dismissed and that the attorney for the nonminor dependent is relieved 60 days from the date of the order.

(Subd (d) amended effective September 1, 2022; adopted effective January 1, 2012; previously amended effective July 1, 2012, July 1, 2013, January 1, 2014, January 1, 2016, January 1, 2017, and January 1, 2021.)

Rule 5.555 amended effective September 1, 2022; adopted effective January 1, 2012; previously amended effective July 1, 2012, July 1, 2013, January 1, 2014, January 1, 2016, January 1, 2017, and January 1, 2021.

Chapter 4
Subsequent Petitions and Modifications

Rule 5.560. General provisions
Rule 5.565. Hearing on subsequent and supplemental petitions (§§ 342, 364, 386, 387)
Rule 5.570. Request to change court order (petition for modification)
Rule 5.575. Joinder of Agencies
Rule 5.580. Hearing on violation of probation (§ 777)

Rule 5.560. General provisions

(a) General authority of the court (§ 385)

Subject to the procedural requirements prescribed by this chapter, an order made by the court may at any time be changed, modified, or set aside.

(Subd (a) amended effective January 1, 2001.)

(b) Subsequent petitions (§§ 297, 342, 360(b), 364)

All procedures and hearings required for an original petition are required for a subsequent petition. Petitioner must file a subsequent petition if:

(1) A child has previously been found to be a person described by section 300 and the petitioner alleges new facts or circumstances, other than those sustained in the original petition, sufficient to again describe the child as a person under section 300 based on these new facts or circumstances;

(2) At or after the disposition hearing the court has ordered that a parent or guardian retain custody of the dependent child and the petitioner receives information providing reasonable cause to believe the child is now, or once again, described by section 300(a), (d), or (e); or

(3) The family is unwilling or unable to cooperate with services previously ordered under section 301.

(Subd (b) amended effective July 1, 2007; previously amended effective January 1, 2001, January 1, 2006, and January 1, 2007.)

(c) Supplemental petition (§§ 297, 387)

A supplemental petition must be used if petitioner concludes that a previous disposition has not been effective in the protection of a child declared a dependent under section 300 and seeks a more restrictive level of physical custody. For purposes of this chapter, a more restrictive level of custody, in ascending order, is

(1) Placement in the home of the person entitled to legal custody;

(2) Placement in the home of a noncustodial parent;

(3) Placement in the home of a relative or friend;

(4) Placement in a foster home; or

(5) Commitment to a private institution.

(Subd (c) amended effective January 1, 2007; previously amended effective January 1, 2001, and January 1, 2006.)

(d) Petition for modification hearing (§§ 297, 388, 778)

A petition for modification hearing must be used if there is a change of circumstances or new evidence that may require the court to:

(1) Change, modify, or set aside an order previously made; or

(2) Terminate the jurisdiction of the court over the child.

(Subd (d) amended effective January 1, 2007; adopted as subd (e) effective January 1, 1991; previously amended and relettered effective January 1, 2001; previously amended effective January 1, 2006.)

(e) Filing of petition (§§ 297, 388, 778)

A petition for modification hearing may be filed by:

(1) The probation officer, the parent, the guardian, the child, the attorney for the child, or any other person having an interest in a child who is a ward if the requested modification is not for a more restrictive level of custody;

(2) The social worker, regarding a child who is a dependent, if the requested modification is not for a more restrictive level of custody; or

(3) The parent, the guardian, the child, the attorney for the child, or any other person having an interest in a child who is a dependent.

(Subd (e) amended effective January 1, 2007; adopted as subd (f) effective January 1, 1991; previously amended and relettered effective January 1, 2001; previously amended effective January 1, 2006.)

(f) Clerical errors

Clerical errors in judgments, orders, or other parts of the record may be corrected by the court at any time on the court's own motion or on motion of any party and may be entered nunc pro tunc.

(Subd (f) relettered effective January 1, 2001; adopted as subd (g) effective January 1, 1991.)

Rule 5.560 amended effective July 1, 2007; adopted as rule 1430 effective January 1, 1991; previously amended and renumbered effective January 1, 2007; previously amended effective January 1, 2001, and January 1, 2006.

Rule 5.565. Hearing on subsequent and supplemental petitions (§§ 342, 364, 386, 387)

(a) Contents of subsequent and supplemental petitions (§§ 342, 364, 387)

A subsequent petition and a supplemental petition must be verified and, to the extent known to the petitioner, contain the information required in an original petition as described in rule 5.524. A supplemental petition must also contain a concise statement of facts sufficient to support the conclusion that the previous disposition has not been effective in the protection of the child or, in the case of a dependent child placed with a relative, that the placement is not appropriate in view of the criteria in section 361.3.

(Subd (a) amended effective January 1, 2007; repealed and adopted effective January 1, 1990; previously amended effective January 1, 1992, January 1, 1999, January 1, 2001, and January 1, 2006.)

(b) Setting the hearing (§§ 334, 342, 364, 386, 387)

When a subsequent or supplemental petition is filed, the clerk must immediately set it for hearing within 30 days of the filing date. The hearing must begin within the time limits prescribed for jurisdiction hearings on original petitions under rule 5.670.

(Subd (b) amended effective January 1, 2007; adopted as subd (c) effective January 1, 1990; previously amended and relettered effective January 1, 2001; previously amended effective January 1, 1992, July 1, 1995, and January 1, 2006.)

(c) Notice of hearing (§§ 292, 297)

(1) For petitions filed under section 342 or section 387, notice must be provided in accordance with section 297.

(2) For petitions filed under section 364, notice must be provided in accordance with section 292.

(Subd (c) amended effective January 1, 2019; adopted effective January 1, 2006.)

(d) Initial hearing (§ 387)

Chapter 12, article 1 of these rules applies to the case of a child who is the subject of a supplemental or subsequent petition.

(Subd (d) amended effective July 1, 2010; adopted as subd (d) effective January 1, 1990; previously amended and relettered as subd (c) effective January 1, 2001; previously amended and relettered effective January 1, 2006; previously amended effective January 1, 2007.)

(e) Requirement for bifurcated hearing

The hearing on a subsequent or supplemental petition must be conducted as follows:

(1) The procedures relating to jurisdiction hearings prescribed in chapter 12, article 2 apply to the determination of the allegations of a subsequent or supplemental petition. At the conclusion of the hearing on a subsequent petition the court must make a finding that the allegations of the petition are or are not true. At the conclusion of the hearing on a supplemental petition the court must make findings that:

(A) The factual allegations are or are not true; and

(B) The allegation that the previous disposition has not been effective is or is not true.

(2) The procedures relating to disposition hearings prescribed in chapter 12, article 3 apply to the determination of disposition on a subsequent or supplemental petition. If the court finds under a subsequent petition that the child is described by section 300(a), (d), or (e), the court must remove the child from the physical custody of the parent or guardian, if removal was not ordered under the previous disposition.

(Subd (e) amended effective July 1, 2010; adopted as subd (e) effective January 1, 1990; previously amended and relettered as subd (d) effective January 1, 2001; previously relettered effective January 1, 2006; previously amended effective January 1, 2007.)

(f) Supplemental petition (§ 387)—permanency planning

If a dependent child was returned to the custody of a parent or guardian at the 12-month review or the 18-month review or at an interim review between 12 and 18 months and a 387 petition is sustained and the child removed once again, the court must set a hearing under section 366.26 unless the court finds there is a substantial probability of return within the next 6 months or, if more than 12 months had expired at the time of the prior return, within whatever time remains before the expiration of the maximum 18-month period.

(Subd (f) amended effective January 1, 2007; adopted as subd (f) effective January 1, 1990; relettered as subd (e) effective January 1, 2001; previously amended and relettered effective January 1, 2006.)

Rule 5.565 amended effective January 1, 2019; adopted as rule 1431 effective January 1, 1990; previously amended effective January 1, 1992, July 1, 1995, January 1, 1999, July 1, 1999, January 1, 2001, January 1, 2006, and July 1, 2010; previously amended and renumbered effective January 1, 2007.

Rule 5.570. Request to change court order (petition for modification)

(a) Contents of petition (§§ 388, 778)

A petition for modification must be liberally construed in favor of its sufficiency. The petition must be verified and, to the extent known to the petitioner, must contain the following:

(1) The name of the court to which the petition is addressed;

(2) The title and action number of the original proceeding;

(3) The name and age of the child, nonminor, or nonminor dependent;

(4) The address of the child, nonminor, or nonminor dependent, unless confidential under (c);

(5) The name and address of the parent or guardian of the child or nonminor;

(6) The date and general nature of the order sought to be modified;

(7) A concise statement of any change of circumstance or new evidence that requires changing the order or, for requests under section 388(c)(1)(B), a concise statement of the relevant action or inaction of the parent or guardian;

(8) A concise statement of the proposed change of the order;

(9) A statement of the petitioner's relationship or interest in the child, nonminor, or nonminor dependent, if the petition is made by a person other than the child, nonminor, or nonminor dependent; and

(10) A statement whether or not all parties agree to the proposed change.

(Subd (a) amended effective January 1, 2014; previously amended effective July 1, 2002, January 1, 2007, January 1, 2009, and January 1, 2010.)

(b) 388 petition

A petition under Welfare and Institutions Code section 388 must be made on form *Request to Change Court Order* (form JV-180).

(Subd (b) adopted effective January 1, 2007.)

(c) Confidentiality

The addresses and telephone numbers of the person requesting to change the court order; the child, nonminor, or nonminor dependent; and the caregiver may be kept confidential by filing *Confidential Information (Request to Change Court Order)* (form JV-182) with form JV-180. Form JV-182 must be kept in the court file under seal, and only the court, the agency, and the attorney for the child, nonminor, or nonminor dependent may have access to this information.

(Subd (c) amended effective January 1, 2014; adopted effective January 1, 2007.)

(d) Denial of hearing

The court may deny the petition ex parte if:

(1) The petition filed under section 388(a) or section 778(a) fails to state a change of circumstance or new evidence that may require a change of order or termination of jurisdiction or fails to show that the requested modification would promote the best interest of the child, nonminor, or nonminor dependent.

(2) The petition filed under section 388(b) fails to demonstrate that the requested modification would promote the best interest of the dependent child;

(3) The petition filed under section 388(b) or 778(b) requests visits with a nondependent child and demonstrates that sibling visitation is contrary to the safety and well-being of any of the siblings;

(4) The petition filed under section 388(b) or 778(b) requests visits with a nondependent sibling who remains in the custody of a mutual parent who is not subject to the court's jurisdiction; or

(5) The petition filed under section 388(c) fails to state facts showing that the parent has failed to visit the child or that the parent has failed to participate regularly and make substantive progress in a court-ordered treatment plan or fails to show that the requested termination of services would promote the best interest of the child.

(Subd (d) amended effective January 1, 2016; adopted as subd (b); previously amended and relettered as subd (d) effective January 1, 2007; previously amended effective January 1, 2010, and January 1, 2014.)

(e) Grounds for grant of petition (§§ 388, 778)

(1) If the petition filed under section 388(a) or section 778(a) states a change of circumstance or new evidence and it appears that the best interest of the child, nonminor, or nonminor dependent may be promoted by the proposed change of order or termination of jurisdiction, the court may grant the petition after following the procedures in (f), (g), and (h), or (i).

(2) If the petition is filed under section 388(b) and it appears that the best interest of the child, nonminor, or nonminor dependent may be promoted by the proposed recognition of a sibling relationship or other requested orders, the court may grant the petition after following the procedures in (f), (g), and (h).

(3) If the petition is filed under section 388(b), the request is for visitation with a sibling who is not a dependent of the court and who is in the custody of a parent subject to the court's jurisdiction, and that sibling visitation is not contrary to the safety and well-being of any of the siblings, the court may grant the request after following the procedures in (f), (g), and (h).

(4) If the petition is filed under section 778(b), the request is for visitation with a sibling who is not a dependent of the court and who is in the custody of a parent subject to the court's jurisdiction, and that sibling visitation is not contrary to the safety and well being of the ward or any of the siblings, the court may grant the request after following the procedures in (f), (g), and (i).

(5) For a petition filed under section 388(c)(1)(A), the court may terminate reunification services during the time periods described in section 388(c)(1) only if the court finds by a preponderance of evidence that reasonable services have been offered or provided, and, by clear and convincing evidence, that the change of circumstance or new evidence described in the petition satisfies a condition in section 361.5(b) or (e). In the case of an Indian child, the court may terminate reunification services only if the court finds by clear and convincing evidence that active efforts have been made to provide remedial services and rehabilitative programs designed to prevent the breakup of the Indian family within the meaning of sections 224.1(f) and 361.7 and that these efforts have proved unsuccessful. The court may grant the petition after following the procedures in (f), (g), and (h).

(6) For a petition filed under section 388(c)(1)(B), the court may terminate reunification services during the time periods described in section 388(c)(1) only if the court finds by a preponderance of evidence that reasonable services have been offered or provided, and, by clear and convincing evidence, that action or inaction by the parent or guardian creates a substantial likelihood that reunification will not occur. Such action or inaction includes, but is not limited to, failure to visit the child or failure to participate regularly and make substantive progress in a court-ordered treatment program. In determining whether the parent or guardian has failed to visit the child or to participate regularly or make progress in a court-ordered treatment plan, the court must consider factors including, but not limited to, the parent or guardian's incarceration, institutionalization, or participation in a residential substance abuse treatment program. In the case of an Indian child, the court may terminate reunification services only if the court finds by clear and convincing evidence that active efforts have been made to provide remedial services and rehabilitative programs designed to prevent the breakup of the Indian family within the meaning of sections 224.1(f) and 361.7 and that these efforts have proved unsuccessful. The court may grant the petition after following the procedures in (f), (g), and (h).

(7) If the petition filed under section 388(a) is filed before an order terminating parental rights and is seeking to modify an order that reunification services need not be provided under section 361.5(b)(4), (5), or (6) or to modify any orders related to custody or visitation of the child for whom reunification services were not ordered under section 361.5(b)(4), (5), or (6), the court may modify the orders only if the court finds by clear and convincing evidence that the proposed change is in the best interests of the child. The court may grant the petition after following the procedures in (f), (g), and (h).

(Subd (e) amended effective January 1, 2020; adopted as subd (c); previously amended and relettered as subd (e) effective January 1, 2007; previously amended effective January 1, 2010, January 1, 2014, and January 1, 2016.)

(f) Hearing on petition

If all parties stipulate to the requested modification, the court may order modification without a hearing. If there is no such stipulation and the petition has not been denied ex parte under section (d), the court must either:

(1) order that a hearing on the petition be held within 30 calendar days after the petition is filed; or

(2) order a hearing for the parties to argue whether an evidentiary hearing on the petition should be granted or denied. If the court then grants an evidentiary hearing on the petition, that hearing must be held within 30 calendar days after the petition is filed.

(Subd (f) amended effective January 1, 2016; adopted as subd (d); previously relettered as subd (f) effective January 1, 2007; previously amended effective July 1, 2002, and January 1, 2010.)

(g) Notice of petition and hearing (§§ 388, 778)

(1) If a petition is filed under section 388 or section 778 to terminate juvenile court jurisdiction over a nonminor, notice of the hearing must be given as required by section 295.

(2) For hearings on all other petitions filed under section 388 or section 778, notice of the hearing must be provided as required under section 297, or sections 776 and 779, except that notice to parents or former guardians of a nonminor must be provided only if the nonminor requests, in writing on the face of the petition, that such notice be provided, or if the parent or legal guardian is receiving court-ordered family reunification services.

(Subd (g) amended effective January 1, 2019; repealed and adopted as subd (e); previously amended effective January 1, 1992, July 1, 1995, July 1, 2000, July 1,

2002, and January 1, 2014; previously amended and relettered as subd (g) effective January 1, 2007.)

(h) Conduct of hearing (§ 388)

(1) The petitioner requesting the modification under section 388 has the burden of proof.

(A) If the request is for the removal of the child from the child's home, the petitioner must show by clear and convincing evidence that the grounds for removal in section 361(c) exist.

(B) If the request is for termination of court-ordered reunification services, the petitioner must show by clear and convincing evidence that one of the conditions in section 388(c)(1)(A) or (B) exists and must show by a preponderance of the evidence that reasonable services have been offered or provided. In the case of an Indian child, the court may terminate reunification services only if the court finds by clear and convincing evidence that active efforts have been made to provide remedial services and rehabilitative programs designed to prevent the breakup of the Indian family within the meaning of sections 224.1(f) and 361.7 and that these efforts have proved unsuccessful.

(C) If the request is to modify an order that reunification services were not ordered under section 361.5(b)(4), (5), or (6) or to modify any orders related to custody or visitation of the child for whom reunification services were not ordered under section 361.5(b)(4), (5), or (6), the petitioner must show by clear and convincing evidence that the proposed change is in the best interests of the child.

(D) All other requests require a preponderance of the evidence to show that the child's welfare requires such a modification.

(E) If the request is for visitation with a sibling who is not a dependent of the court, the court may grant the request unless the court determines that the sibling remains in the custody of a mutual parent who is not subject to the court's jurisdiction or that sibling visitation is contrary to the safety and well-being of any of the siblings.

(2) The hearing must be conducted as a dispositional hearing under rules 5.690 and 5.695 if:

(A) The request is for termination of court-ordered reunification services; or

(B) There is a due process right to confront and cross-examine witnesses.

Otherwise, proof may be by declaration and other documentary evidence, or by testimony, or both, at the discretion of the court.

(Subd (h) amended effective January 1, 2020; adopted as subd (f); previously amended and relettered as subd (h) effective January 1, 2007; previously amended effective July 1, 2000, July 1, 2002, January 1, 2003, January 1, 2010, January 1, 2014, and January 1, 2016.)

(i) Conduct of hearing (§ 778)

(1) The petitioner requesting the modification under section 778(a) has the burden of proving by a preponderance of the evidence that the ward's welfare requires the modification. Proof may be by declaration and other documentary evidence, or by testimony, or both, at the discretion of the court.

(2) If the request is for sibling visitation under section 778(b), the court may grant the request unless the court determines that the sibling remains in the custody of a mutual parent who is not subject to the court's jurisdiction or that sibling visitation is contrary to the safety and well-being of any of the siblings.

(Subd (i) amended effective January 1, 2016; adopted as subd (g); previously amended effective July 1, 2002; previously amended and relettered as subd (i) effective January 1, 2007.)

(j) Petitions for juvenile court to resume jurisdiction over nonminors (§§ 388(e), 388.1)

A petition filed by or on behalf of a nonminor requesting that the court resume jurisdiction over the nonminor as a nonminor dependent is not subject to this rule. Petitions filed under section 388(e) or section 388.1 are subject to rule 5.906.

(Subd (j) amended effective January 1, 2016; adopted effective January 1, 2014.)

(k) Petitions for juvenile court to exit and reenter jurisdiction over nonminors (§ 388(f))

This rule does not apply to a hearing on a petition for a nonminor to exit and reenter care to establish eligibility for federal financial participation under section 388(f). Those petitions may be decided with or without a hearing using mandatory forms *Petition and Order to Exit and Reenter Jurisdiction—Nonminor Dependent* (form JV-469) and *Findings and Orders Regarding Exit and Reentry of Jurisdiction—Nonminor Dependent* (form JV-471).

(Subd (k) adopted effective September 1, 2022.)

Rule 5.570 amended effective September 1, 2022; adopted as rule 1432 effective January 1, 1991; previously amended and renumbered as rule 5.570 effective January 1, 2007; previously amended effective January 1, 1992, July 1, 1995, July 1, 2000, July 1, 2002, January 1, 2003, January 1, 2009, January 1, 2010, January 1, 2014, January 1, 2016, January 1, 2019, and January 1, 2020.)

Rule 5.575. Joinder of Agencies

(a) Basis for joinder (§§ 362, 365, 727)

The court may, at any time after a petition has been filed, following notice and a hearing, join in the proceedings any agency (as defined in section 362) that the court determines has failed to meet a legal obligation to provide services to a child or a nonminor or nonminor dependent youth for whom a petition has been filed under section 300, 601, or 602. The court may not impose duties on an agency beyond those required by law.

(Subd (a) amended effective January 1, 2014; previously amended effective January 1, 2007.)

(b) Notice and Hearing

On application by a party, counsel, or CASA volunteer, or on the court's own motion, the court may set a hearing and require notice to the agency or provider subject to joinder.

(1) Notice of the hearing must be given to the agency on *Notice of Hearing on Joinder—Juvenile* (form JV-540). The notice must clearly describe the legal obligation at issue, the facts and circumstances alleged to constitute the agency's failure to meet that obligation, and any issues or questions the court expects the agency to address at the hearing.

(2) The hearing must be set to occur within 30 calendar days of the signing of the notice by the court. The hearing will proceed under the provisions of rule 5.570(h) or (i), as appropriate.

(3) The clerk must cause the notice to be served on the agency and all parties, attorneys of record, the CASA volunteer, any other person or entity entitled to notice under section 291 or 658, and, if the hearing might address educational or developmental-services issues, the educational rights holder by first-class mail within 5 court days of the signing of the notice.

(4) Nothing in this rule prohibits agencies from meeting before the hearing to coordinate the delivery of services. The court may request, using section 8 of form JV-540, that agency representatives meet before the hearing and that the agency or agencies submit a written response to the court at least 5 court days before the hearing.

(Subd (b) amended effective January 1, 2014; previously amended effective January 1, 2006, and January 1, 2007.)

Rule 5.575 amended effective January 1, 2014; adopted as rule 1434 effective January 1, 2002; previously amended effective January 1, 2006; amended and renumbered effective January 1, 2007.

Rule 5.580. Hearing on violation of probation (§ 777)

(a) Notice of hearing (§§ 656, 658, 660)

Notice of a hearing to be held under section 777 must be issued and served as provided in sections 658, 660, and 777 and prepared:

(1) By the probation officer if the child has been declared a ward under section 601; or

(2) By the probation officer or the district attorney if the child is a ward or is on probation under section 602, and the alleged violation of probation is not a crime.

(Subd (a) amended effective January 1, 2007; adopted effective January 1, 2001; previously amended effective January 1, 2006.)

(b) Motion to dismiss

If the probation officer files the notice of hearing, before jeopardy attaches the prosecuting attorney may move the court to dismiss the notice and request that the matter be referred to the probation officer for appropriate action under section 777(a)(3).

(Subd (b) adopted effective January 1, 2001.)

(c) Detention hearing

If the child has been brought into custody, the procedures described in rules 5.524 and 5.752 through 5.764 must be followed.

(Subd (c) amended effective January 1, 2007; adopted as subd (d) effective January 1, 2001; amended and relettered effective January 1, 2006.)

(d) Report of probation officer

Before every hearing the probation officer must prepare a report on those matters relevant to a determination of whether the child has violated a condition of probation. The report must be furnished to all parties at least 48 hours, excluding noncourt days, before the beginning of the hearing unless the child is represented by counsel and waives the right to service of the report.

(Subd (d) amended and relettered effective January 1, 2006; adopted as subd (b) effective January 1, 1990; amended and relettered as subd (e) effective January 1, 2001.)

(e) Evidence considered

The court must consider the report prepared by the probation officer and other relevant and material evidence offered by the parties to the proceeding.

(1) The court may admit and consider reliable hearsay evidence as defined by section 777(c).

(2) The probation officer or prosecuting attorney must prove the alleged violation by a preponderance of the evidence.

(Subd (e) amended and relettered effective January 1, 2006; adopted as subd (e) effective January 1, 1990; amended and relettered as subd (f) effective January 1, 2001.)

Rule 5.580 amended and renumbered effective January 1, 2007; adopted as rule 1433 effective January 1, 1990; previously amended effective January 1, 1992, January 1, 2001, and January 1, 2006.

Chapter 5
Appellate Review

Title 5, Family and Juvenile Rules—Division 3, Juvenile Rules—Chapter 5, Appellate Review; adopted effective January 1, 2007; amended effective July 1, 2010.

Rule 5.585. Rules governing appellate review
Rule 5.590. Advisement of right to review in section 300, 601, or 602 cases
Rule 5.595. Stay pending appeal

Rule 5.585. Rules governing appellate review

The rules in title 8, chapter 5 govern appellate review of judgments and orders in cases under Welfare and Institutions Code section 300, 601, or 602.

Rule 5.585 adopted effective July 1, 2010.

Advisory Committee Comment

Rules 8.450 and 8.452 describe how a party, including the petitioner, child, and parent or guardian, must proceed if seeking appellate court review of findings and orders of the juvenile court made at a hearing at which the court orders that a hearing under Welfare and Institutions Code section 366.26 be held.

Rule 5.590. Advisement of right to review in section 300, 601, or 602 cases

(a) Advisement of right to appeal

If at a contested hearing on an issue of fact or law the court finds that the child is described by Welfare and Institutions Code section 300, 601, or 602 or sustains a supplemental or subsequent petition, the court after making its disposition order other than orders covered in (b) must advise, orally or in writing, the child, if of sufficient age, and the parent or guardian of:

(1) The right of the child, parent, and guardian to appeal from the court order if there is a right to appeal;

(2) The necessary steps and time for taking an appeal;

(3) The right of an indigent appellant to have counsel appointed by the reviewing court; and

(4) The right of an indigent appellant to be provided with a free copy of the transcript.

If the parent or guardian is not present at the hearing, the advisement must be made by the clerk of the court by first-class mail to the last known address of the party or by electronic service in accordance with section 212.5.

(Subd (a) amended effective January 1, 2020; adopted as subd (d) effective January 1, 1990; previously amended effective January 1, 2007; previously amended and relettered as subd (a) effective July 1, 2010.)

(b) Advisement of requirement for writ petition to preserve appellate rights when court orders hearing under section 366.26

When the court orders a hearing under section 366.26, the court must advise all parties and, if present, the child's parent, guardian, or adult relative, that if the party wishes to preserve any right to review on appeal of the order setting the hearing under section 366.26, the party is required to seek an extraordinary writ by filing a *Notice of Intent to File Writ Petition and Request for Record (California Rules of Court, Rule 8.450)* (form JV-820) or other notice of intent to file a writ petition and request for record and a *Petition for Extraordinary Writ (California Rules of Court, Rules 8.452, 8.456)* (form JV-825) or other petition for extraordinary writ.

(1) The advisement must be given orally to those present when the court orders the hearing under section 366.26.

(2) If a party is not present when the court orders a hearing under section 366.26, within 24 hours of the hearing, the advisement must be made by the clerk of the court by first-class mail to the last known address of the party or by electronic service in accordance with section 212.5. If the notice is for a hearing at which the social worker will recommend the termination of parental rights, the notice may be electronically served in accordance with section 212.5, but only in addition to service of the notice by first-class mail.

(3) The advisement must include the time for filing a notice of intent to file a writ petition.

(4) Copies of *Petition for Extraordinary Writ (California Rules of Court, Rules 8.452, 8.456)* (form JV-825) and *Notice of Intent to File Writ Petition and Request for Record (California Rules of Court, Rule 8.450)* (form JV-820) must be available in the courtroom and must accompany all mailed and electronically served notices informing the parties of their rights.

(Subd (b) amended effective January 1, 2019; adopted as subd (e) effective January 1, 1995; previously amended effective January 1, 2007; previously repealed, amended and relettered effective July 1, 2010.)

(c) Advisement requirements for appeal of order to transfer to tribal court

When the court grants a petition transferring a case to tribal court under Welfare and Institutions Code section 305.5, Family Code section 177(a), or Probate Code section 1459.5(b), and rule 5.483, the court must advise the parties orally and in writing, that an appeal of the order must be filed before the transfer to tribal jurisdiction is finalized, and that failure to request and obtain a stay of the order for transfer will result in a loss of appellate jurisdiction.

(Subd (c) adopted effective January 1, 2016.)

Rule 5.590 amended effective January 1, 2020; adopted as rule 1435 effective January 1, 1990; previously amended effective January 1, 1992, January 1, 1993, January 1, 1994, January 1, 1995, July 1, 1999, January 1, 2016, and January 1, 2019; previously amended and renumbered as rule 5.585 effective January 1, 2007; previously amended and renumbered as rule 5.590 effective July 1, 2010.

Advisory Committee Comment

Subdivision (a). The right to appeal in Welfare and Institutions Code section 601 or 602 (juvenile delinquency) cases is established by Welfare and Institutions Code section 800 and case law (see, for example, *In re Michael S.* (2007) 147 Cal.App.4th 1443, *In re Jeffrey M.* (2006) 141 Cal.App.4th 1017, and *In re Sean R.* (1989) 214 Cal.App.3d 662). The right to appeal in Welfare and Institutions Code section 300 (juvenile dependency) cases is established by Welfare and Institutions Code section 395 and case law (see, for example, *In re Aaron R.* (2005) 130 Cal.App.4th 697, and *In re Merrick V.* (2004) 122 Cal.App.4th 235).

Subdivision (b). Welfare and Institutions Code section 366.26(*l*) establishes important limitations on appeals of judgments, orders, or decrees setting a hearing under section 366.26, including requirements for the filing of a petition for an extraordinary writ and limitations on the issues that can be raised on appeal.

Rule 5.595. Stay pending appeal

The court must not stay an order or judgment pending an appeal unless suitable provision is made for the maintenance, care, and custody of the child.

Rule 5.595 amended effective July 1, 2010; adopted as rule 1436 effective January 1, 1993; previously amended effective January 1, 1994, January 1, 1995, and January 1, 2006; previously amended and renumbered effective January 1, 2007.

Rule 5.600. Writ petition after orders setting hearing under section 366.26; appeal [Repealed]

Rule 5.600 repealed effective July 1, 2010; adopted as rule 1436.5 effective January 1, 1995; previously amended effective July 1, 1995, January 1, 1996, July 1, 2006, and January 1, 2009; previously amended and renumbered effective January 1, 2007.

Chapter 6
Emancipation

Rule 5.605. Emancipation of minors

(a) Petition

A petition for declaration of emancipation of a minor must be submitted on *Petition for Declaration of Emancipation of Minor, Order Prescribing Notice, Declaration of Emancipation, and Order Denying Petition* (form MC-300). Only the minor may petition the court for emancipation, and the petition may be filed in the county in which the minor can provide a verifiable residence address. The petitioner must complete and attach to the petition *Emancipation of Minor—Income and Expense Declaration* (form MC-306).

(Subd (a) amended effective January 1, 2007.)

(b) Dependents and wards of the juvenile court

Petitions to emancipate a child who is a dependent or ward of the juvenile court must be filed and heard in juvenile court.

(Subd (b) amended effective January 1, 2007; previously amended effective January 1, 1995.)

(c) Court

The petition to emancipate a minor other than a dependent or ward of the juvenile court must be filed and will be heard in juvenile court or other superior court department so designated by local rule or by order of the presiding judge.

(Subd (c) amended effective January 1, 2007.)

(d) Filing fee

Unless waived, the petitioner must pay the filing fee as specified. The ability or inability to pay the filing fee is not in and of itself evidence of the financial responsibility of the minor as required for emancipation.

(Subd (d) amended effective January 1, 2007.)

(e) Declaration of emancipation without hearing

If the court finds that all notice and consent requirements have been met or waived, and that emancipation is not contrary to the best interest of the petitioner, the court may grant the petition without a hearing. The presiding judge of the superior court must develop a protocol for the screening, evaluation, or investigation of petitions.

(Subd (e) amended effective January 1, 2007.)

(f) Time limits

The clerk of the court in which the petition is filed must immediately provide or direct the petitioner to provide the petition to the court. Within 30 days from the filing of the petition, the court must (1) grant the petition, (2) deny the petition, or (3) set a hearing on the petition to be conducted within 30 days thereafter. The clerk must immediately provide the petitioner with an endorsed-filed copy of the court's order.

(Subd (f) amended effective January 1, 2007.)

(g) Notice

If the court orders the matter set for hearing, the clerk must notify the district attorney of the time and date of the hearing, which must be within 30 days of the order prescribing notice and setting for hearing. The petitioner is responsible for notifying all other persons to whom the court requires notice.

(Subd (g) amended effective January 1, 2007.)

Rule 5.605 amended and renumbered effective January 1, 2007; adopted as rule 1437 effective July 1, 1994; previously amended effective January 1, 1995.

Chapter 7
Intercounty Transfers; Out-of-County Placements; Interstate Compact on the Placement of Children

Title 5, Family and Juvenile Rules—Division 3, Juvenile Rules—Chapter 7, Intercounty Transfers; Out-of-County Placements; Interstate Compact on the Placement of Children; amended effective January 1, 2020; previously amended effective January 1, 2019.

Rule 5.610. Transfer-out hearing
Rule 5.612. Transfer-in hearing
Rule 5.613. Transfer of nonminor dependents
Rule 5.614. Out-of-county placements
Rule 5.616. Interstate Compact on the Placement of Children
Rule 5.618. Placement in short-term residential therapeutic program or community treatment facility (§§ 361.22, 727.12)
Rule 5.619. Voluntary placement in psychiatric residential treatment facility (Welf. & Inst. Code, §§ 361.23, 727.13)

Rule 5.610. Transfer-out hearing

(a) Determination of residence—special rule on intercounty transfers (§§ 375, 750)

(1) For purposes of rules 5.610, 5.612, and 5.614, the residence of the child is the residence of the person who has the legal right to physical custody of the child according to prior court order, including:

(A) A juvenile court order under section 361.2; and

(B) An order appointing a guardian of the person of the child.

(2) If there is no order determining custody, both parents are deemed to have physical custody.

(3) The juvenile court may make a finding of paternity under rule 5.635. If there is no finding of paternity, the mother is deemed to have physical custody.

(4) For the purposes of transfer of wardship, residence of a ward may be with the person with whom the child resides with approval of the court.

(Subd (a) amended effective January 1, 2019; previously amended effective January 1, 2004, and January 1, 2007.)

(b) Verification of residence

The residence of the person entitled to physical custody may be verified by declaration of a social worker or probation officer in the transferring or receiving county.

(Subd (b) amended effective January 1, 2017; previously amended effective January 1, 2004, and January 1, 2007.)

(c) Transfer to county of child's residence (§§ 375, 750)

(1) After making its jurisdictional finding, the court may order the case transferred to the juvenile court of the child's residence as specified in section 375 or section 750.

(2) If the court decides to transfer a delinquency case, the court must order the transfer before beginning the disposition hearing without adjudging the child to be a ward.

(3) If the court decides to transfer a dependency case, the court may order the transfer before or after the disposition hearing.

(Subd (c) amended effective January 1, 2019; previously amended effective January 1, 2004, and January 1, 2007.)

(d) Transfer on subsequent change in child's residence (§§ 375, 750)

If, after the child has been placed under a program of supervision, the residence is changed to another county, the court may, on an application for modification under rule 5.570, transfer the case to the juvenile court of the other county.

(Subd (d) amended effective January 1, 2007; previously amended effective January 1, 2004.)

(e) Conduct of hearing

(1) The request for transfer must be made on *Motion for Transfer Out* (form JV-548), which must include all required information.

(2) After the court determines the identity and residence of the child's custodian, the court must consider whether transfer of the case would be in the child's best interest. The court may not transfer the case unless it determines that the transfer will protect or further the child's best interest.

(Subd (e) amended effective January 1, 2017; repealed and adopted effective January 1, 1990; previously amended effective January 1, 1993, January 1, 2004, and January 1, 2007.)

(f) Date of transfer-in hearing

(1) If the transfer-out motion is granted, the sending court must set a date certain for the transfer-in hearing in the receiving court: within 5 court days of the transfer-out order if the child is in custody, and within 10 court days of the transfer-out order if the child is out of custody. The sending court must state on the record the date, time, and location of the hearing in the receiving court.

(2) The website for every court must include up-to-date contact information for the court clerks handling dependency and delinquency matters, as well as up-to-date information on when and where transfer-in hearings are held.

(Subd (f) adopted effective January 1, 2017.)

(g) Order of transfer (§§ 377, 752)

The order of transfer must be entered on *Juvenile Court Transfer-Out Orders* (form JV-550), which must include all required information and findings.

(Subd (g) amended and relettered effective January 1, 2017; repealed and adopted as subd (f) effective January 1, 1990; previously amended effective January 1, 1993, January 1, 2004, and January 1, 2007.)

(h) Modification of form JV-550

Juvenile Court Transfer Orders (form JV-550) may be modified as follows:

(1) Notwithstanding the mandatory use of form JV-550, the form may be modified for use by a formalized regional collaboration of courts to facilitate the efficient processing of transfer cases among those courts if the modification has been approved by the Judicial Council of California.

(2) The mandatory form must be used by a regional collaboration when transferring a case to a court outside the collaboration or when accepting a transfer from a court outside the collaboration.

(Subd (h) relettered effective January 1, 2017; adopted as subd (g) effective January 1, 2007; previously amended effective January 1, 2015.)

(i) Transport of child and transmittal of documents (§§ 377, 752)

(1) If the child is ordered transported in custody to the receiving county, the child must be delivered to the receiving county at least two business days before the transfer-in hearing, and the clerk of the court of the transferring county must prepare a certified copy of the complete case file so that it may be transported with the child to the court of the receiving county.

(2) If the child is not ordered transported in custody, the clerk of the transferring court must transmit to the clerk of the court of the receiving county within five court days a certified copy of the complete case file.

(3) The file may be transferred electronically, if possible. A certified copy of the complete case file is deemed an original.

(Subd (i) amended and relettered effective January 1, 2017; repealed and adopted as subd (g) effective, January 1, 1990; previously amended effective January 1, 1992, January 1, 1993, July 1, 1999, and January 1, 2004; previously amended and relettered as subd (h) effective January 1, 2007.)

(j) Appeal of transfer order (§§ 379, 754)

The order of transfer may be appealed by the transferring or receiving county and notice of appeal must be filed in the transferring county, under rule 8.400. Notwithstanding the filing of a notice of appeal, the receiving county must assume jurisdiction of the case on receipt and filing of the order of transfer.

(Subd (j) relettered effective January 1, 2017; repealed and adopted as subd (h) effective January 1, 1990; previously amended effective January 1, 1992, and January 1, 2004; previously amended and relettered as subd (i) effective January 1, 2007.)

Rule 5.610 amended effective January 1, 2019; adopted as rule 1425 effective January 1, 1990; previously amended and renumbered effective January 1, 2007; previously amended effective January 1, 1992, January 1, 1993, July 1, 1999, January 1, 2004, January 1, 2015, and January 1, 2017.

Advisory Committee Comment

Juvenile court judicial officers throughout the state have expressed concern that in determining whether or not to transfer a juvenile court case, the best interest of the subject child is being overlooked or at least outweighed by a desire to shift the financial burdens of case management and foster care. The advisory committee has clarified rule 5.610 in order to stress that in considering an intercounty transfer, as in all matters relating to children within its jurisdiction, the court has a mandate to act in the best interest of the subject children.

Juvenile Court Transfer-Out Orders (form JV-550) was adopted for mandatory use commencing January 1, 1992. Although the finding regarding the best interest of the child was noted on the original form, the language has been emphasized on the amended form.

Rule 5.612. Transfer-in hearing

(a) Procedure on transfer (§§ 378, 753)

On receipt and filing of a certified copy of a transfer order, the receiving court must accept jurisdiction of the case. The receiving court may not reject the case. The clerk of the receiving court must confirm the transfer-in hearing date scheduled by the sending court and ensure that date is on the receiving court's calendar. The receiving court must notify the transferring court on receipt and filing of the certified copies of the transfer order and complete case file.

(Subd (a) amended effective January 1, 2017; repealed and adopted effective January 1, 1990; previously amended effective January 1, 1992, July 1, 1999, January 1, 2004, and January 1, 2007.)

(b) Conduct of hearing

At the transfer-in hearing, the court must:

(1) Advise the child and the parent or guardian of the purpose and scope of the hearing;

(2) Provide for the appointment of counsel if appropriate; and

(3) If the child was transferred to the county in custody, determine whether the child must be further detained under rule 5.667.

(Subd (b) amended effective January 1, 2007; previously amended effective January 1, 2004.)

(c) Subsequent proceedings

The proceedings in the receiving court must commence at the same phase as when the case was transferred. The court may continue the hearing for an investigation and report to a date not to exceed 10 court days if the child is in custody or 15 court days if the child is not detained in custody.

(Subd (c) amended effective January 1, 2004; previously amended effective July 1, 1999.)

(d) Limitation on more restrictive custody (§§ 387, 777)

If a disposition order has already been made in the transferring county, a more restrictive level of physical custody may not be ordered in the receiving county, except after a hearing on a supplemental petition under rule 5.565.

(Subd (d) amended effective January 1, 2007; previously amended effective January 1, 2004.)

(e) Setting six-month review (§ 366)

When an order of transfer is received and filed relating to a child who has been declared a dependent, the court must set a date for a six-month review within six months of the disposition or the most recent review hearing.

(Subd (e) amended effective January 1, 2004.)

(f) Change of circumstances or additional facts (§§ 388, 778)

If the receiving court believes that a change of circumstances or additional facts indicate that the child does not reside in the receiving county, a transfer-out hearing must be held under rules 5.610 and 5.570. The court may direct the department of social services or the probation department to seek a modification of orders under section 388 or 778 and under rule 5.570.

(Subd (f) amended effective January 1, 2007; adopted effective January 1, 1992; previously amended effective July 1, 1999, and January 1, 2004.)

Rule 5.612 amended effective January 1, 2017; adopted as rule 1426 effective January 1, 1990; previously amended effective January 1, 1992, July 1, 1999, and January 1, 2004; previously amended and renumbered as rule 5.612 effective January 1, 2007.

Rule 5.613. Transfer of nonminor dependents

(a) Purpose

This rule applies to requests to transfer the county of jurisdiction of a nonminor dependent as allowed by Welfare and Institutions Code section 375. This rule sets forth the procedures that a court is to follow when it seeks to order a transfer of a nonminor dependent and those to be followed by the court receiving the transfer. All other intercounty transfers of juveniles are subject to rules 5.610 and 5.612.

(Subd (a) adopted effective January 1, 2017.)

(b) Transfer-out hearing

(1) *Determination of residence—special rule on intercounty transfers (§§ 17.1, 375)*

(A) For purposes of this rule, the residence of a nonminor dependent who is placed in a planned permanent living arrangement may be either the county in which the court that has jurisdiction over the nonminor is located or the county in which the nonminor has resided continuously for at least one year as a nonminor dependent and the nonminor dependent has expressed his or her intent to remain.

(B) If a nonminor dependent's dependency jurisdiction has been resumed, or if transition jurisdiction has been assumed or resumed by the juvenile court that retained general jurisdiction over the nonminor under section 303, the county that the nonminor dependent is residing in may be deemed the county of residence of the nonminor dependent. The court may make this determination if the nonminor has established a continuous physical presence in the county for one year as a nonminor and has expressed his or her intent to remain in that county after the court grants the petition to resume jurisdiction. The period of continuous physical presence includes any period of continuous residence immediately before filing the petition.

(2) *Verification of residence*

The residence of a nonminor may be verified by declaration of a social worker or probation officer in the transferring or receiving county.

(3) *Transfer to county of nonminor's residence (§ 375)*

If the court is resuming dependency jurisdiction or assuming or resuming transition jurisdiction of a nonminor for whom the court has retained general jurisdiction under section 303(b) as a result of a petition filed under section 388(e), after granting the petition, the court may order the transfer of the case to the juvenile court of the county in which the nonminor is living if the nonminor establishes residency in that county as provided in (b)(1) and the court finds that the transfer is in the minor's best interest.

(4) *Transfer on change in nonminor's residence (§ 375)*

If a nonminor dependent under the dependency or transition jurisdiction of the court is placed in a planned permanent living arrangement in a county other than the county with jurisdiction over the nonminor, the court may, on an application for modification under rule 5.570, transfer the case to the juvenile court of the county in which the nonminor is living if the nonminor establishes residency in that county as provided in (b)(1).

(5) *Conduct of hearing*

(A) The request for transfer must be made on *Motion for Transfer Out* (form JV-548), which must include all required information.

(B) After the court determines whether a nonminor has established residency in another county as required in (b)(1), the court must consider whether transfer of the case would be in the nonminor's best interest. The court may not transfer the case unless it determines that the nonminor supports the transfer and that the transfer will protect or further the nonminor's best interest.

(C) If the transfer-out motion is granted, the sending court must set a date certain for the transfer-in hearing in the receiving court, which must be within 10 court days of the transfer-out order. The sending court must state on the record the date, time, and location of the hearing in the receiving court.

(6) *Order of transfer (§ 377)*

The order of transfer must be entered on *Juvenile Court Transfer-Out Orders—Nonminor Dependent* (form JV-552), which must include all required information and findings.

(7) *Modification of form JV-552*

Juvenile Court Transfer-Out Orders—Nonminor Dependent (form JV-552) may be modified as follows:

(A) Notwithstanding the mandatory use of form JV-552, the form may be modified for use by a formalized regional collaboration of courts to facilitate the efficient processing of transfer cases among those courts if the modification has been approved by the Judicial Council.

(B) The mandatory form must be used by a regional collaboration when transferring a case to a court outside the collaboration or when accepting a transfer from a court outside the collaboration.

(8) *Transmittal of documents (§ 377)*

The clerk of the transferring court must transmit to the clerk of the court of the receiving county no later than five court days from the date of the transfer-out order a certified copy of the entire nonminor file and, at a minimum, all documents associated with the last status review hearing held before the nonminor reached majority, including the court report and all findings and orders. The files may be transferred electronically, if possible. A certified copy of the complete case file is deemed an original.

(9) *Appeal of transfer order (§ 379)*

The order of transfer may be appealed by the transferring or receiving county, and notice of appeal must be filed in the transferring county, under rule 8.400. Notwithstanding the filing of a notice of appeal, the receiving county must assume jurisdiction of the case on receipt and filing of the order of transfer.

(Subd (b) adopted effective January 1, 2017.)

(c) Transfer-in hearing

(1) *Procedure on transfer (§ 378)*

On receipt and filing of a certified copy of a transfer order, the receiving court must accept jurisdiction of the case. The receiving court may not reject the case. The receiving court must notify the transferring court on receipt and filing of the certified copies of the transfer order and complete case file. The clerk of the receiving court must confirm the transfer-in hearing date scheduled by the sending court and ensure that date is on the receiving court's calendar.

(2) *Conduct of hearing*

At the transfer-in hearing, the court must:

(A) Advise the nonminor of the purpose and scope of the hearing; and

(B) Provide for the appointment of counsel, if appropriate.

(3) *Subsequent proceedings*

The proceedings in the receiving court must commence at the same phase as when the case was transferred. The court may continue the hearing for an investigation and a report to a date not to exceed 15 court days.

(4) *Setting six-month review (§ 366.31)*

When an order of transfer is received and filed relating to a nonminor dependent, the court must set a date for a six-month review within six months of the most recent review hearing or, if the sending court transferred the case immediately after assuming or resuming jurisdiction, within six months of the date a voluntary reentry agreement was signed.

(5) *Change of circumstances or additional facts (§§ 388, 778)*

If the receiving court believes that a change of circumstances or additional facts indicate that the nonminor does not reside in the receiving county, a transfer-out hearing must be held under this rule and rule 5.570. The court may direct the department of social services or the probation department to seek a modification of orders under section 388 or section 778 and under rule 5.570.

(Subd (c) adopted effective January 1, 2017.)

Rule 5.613 adopted effective January 1, 2017.

Rule 5.614. Out-of-county placements

(a) Procedure

Whenever a social worker intends to place a dependent child outside the child's county of residence, the procedures in section 361.2(h) must be followed.

(Subd (a) adopted effective January 1, 2019.)

(b) Required notices

Unless the requirements for emergency placement in section 361.4 are met or the circumstances in section 361.2(h)(2)(A) exist, before placing a child out of county, the agency must notify the following of the proposed removal:

(1) The persons listed in section 361.2(h);

(2) The Indian child's identified Indian tribe, if any;

(3) The Indian child's Indian custodian, if any; and

(4) The child's CASA program, if any.

(Subd (b) amended effective January 1, 2020; adopted effective January 1, 2019.)

(c) Form of notice

The social worker may provide the required written notice to the participants in (b) on *Notice of Intent to Place Child Out of County* (form JV-555). If form JV-555 is used, the social worker must also provide a blank copy of *Objection to Out-of-County Placement and Notice of Hearing* (form JV-556).

(Subd (c) adopted effective January 1, 2019.)

(d) Method of Service

The agency must serve notice of its intent to place the child out of county as follows:

(1) Notice must be served by either first-class mail, sent to the last known address of the person to be noticed; electronic service in accordance with Welfare and Institutions Code section 212.5; or personal service at least 14 days before the placement, unless the child's health or well-being is endangered by delaying the action or would be endangered if prior notice were given;

(2) Notice to the child's identified Indian tribe and Indian custodian must comply with the requirements of section 224.3; and

(3) *Proof of Notice* (form JV-326) must be filed with the court before any hearing on the proposed out-of-county placement.

(Subd (d) amended effective January 1, 2020; adopted effective January 1, 2019.)

(e) Objection to proposed out-of-county placement

Each participant who receives notice under (b)(1)–(3) may object to the proposed removal of the child, and the court must set a hearing as required by section 361.2(h).

(1) An objection to the proposed out-of-county placement may be made by using *Objection to Out-of-County Placement and Notice of Hearing* (form JV-556).

(2) An objection must be filed within the time frames in section 361.2(h).

(Subd (e) amended effective January 1, 2020; adopted effective January 1, 2019.)

(f) Notice of hearing on proposed removal

If an objection is filed, the clerk must set a hearing, and notice of the hearing must be as follows:

(1) If the party objecting to the removal is not represented by counsel, the clerk must provide notice of the hearing to the agency and the participants listed in (b);

(2) If the party objecting to the removal is represented by counsel, that counsel must provide notice of the hearing to the agency and the participants listed in (b);

(3) Notice must be by either first-class mail, sent to the last known address of the person to be noticed; electronic service in accordance with Welfare and Institutions Code section 212.5; or personal service;

(4) Notice to the child's identified Indian tribe and Indian custodian must comply with the requirements of section 224.3; and

(5) *Proof of Notice* (form JV-326) must be filed with the court before the hearing on the proposed removal.

(Subd (f) amended effective January 1, 2020; adopted effective January 1, 2019.)

(g) Burden of proof

At a hearing on an out-of-county placement, the agency intending to move the child must prove by a preponderance of the evidence that the standard in section 361.2(h) is met.

(Subd (g) adopted effective January 1, 2019.)

(h) Emergency placements

If the requirements for emergency placement in section 361.4 are met, the agency must provide notice as required in section 16010.6.

(Subd (h) adopted effective January 1, 2019.)

Rule 5.614 amended effective January 1, 2020; adopted effective January 1, 2019.

Rule 5.616. Interstate Compact on the Placement of Children

(a) Applicability of rule (Fam. Code, § 7900 et seq.)

This rule implements the purposes and provisions of the Interstate Compact on the Placement of Children (ICPC, or the compact). California juvenile courts must apply this rule when placing children who are dependents or wards of the juvenile court and for whom placement is indicated in any other state, the District of Columbia, or the U.S. Virgin Islands.

(1) This rule applies to expedited placements as described in (h).

(2) This rule does not apply to placements made under the Interstate Compact for Juveniles (Welf. & Inst. Code, § 1400 et seq.).

(Subd (a) amended effective January 1, 2013; previously amended effective January 1, 2007.)

(b) Definitions (Fam. Code, § 7900 et seq.; ICPC Regulations)

(1) "Placement" is defined in article 2(d) of the compact. It includes placements with a relative, as defined in Regulation No. 3, paragraph 4, item 56; a legal guardian of the child; a placement recipient who is not related to the child; or a residential facility or group home as defined in Regulation No. 4.

(A) A court's directing or making an award of custody to a parent of the child or placing a child with his or her parent is not a placement requiring compliance with this rule.

(B) The following situations each constitute a placement, and the compact must be applied:

(i) An order causing a child to be sent or brought to a person, other than a parent, in a compact jurisdiction without a specific date of return to the sending jurisdiction;

(ii) An order causing a child to be sent or brought to a person, other than a parent, in a compact jurisdiction with a return date more than 30 days from the start of the visit or beyond the ending date of a school vacation period, under Regulation No. 9;

(iii) An out-of-state placement for the purpose of an anticipated adoption, whether independent, private, or public;

(iv) An out-of-state placement with a related or unrelated caregiver in a licensed or approved foster home;

(v) An out-of-state placement with relatives, except when a parent or relative sends or brings the child to the relative's home in the receiving state, as defined in article 8(a) of the ICPC; or

(vi) An out-of-state group home or residential placement of any child, including a child adjudicated delinquent.

(2) "Child," for the purposes of ICPC placement, includes nonminor dependents up to age 21. If a California nonminor dependent is to be placed out of state, the placing county may request supervision from the receiving state, but such services are discretionary. If the receiving state will not supervise the nonminor dependent, the sending county must make other supervision arrangements, which may include contracting with a private agency to provide the supervision.

(3) "Parent," as used in this rule, does not include de facto parents or legal guardians.

(4) ICPC Regulations Nos. 3, 4, 5, 9, 10, 11, and 12 contain additional definitions that apply to California ICPC cases, except where inconsistent with this rule or with California law.

(Subd (b) amended effective January 1, 2014; previously amended effective January 1, 2007, and January 1, 2013.)

(c) Compact requirements (Fam. Code, § 7901; ICPC Regulations)

Whenever the juvenile court makes a placement in another jurisdiction included in the compact or reviews a placement plan, the court must adhere to the provisions and regulations of the compact.

(1) Cases in which out-of-state placement is proposed in order to place a child for public adoption, in foster care, or with relatives, and where the criteria for expedited placement are not met, must meet all requirements of Regulation No. 2, except where inconsistent with California law.

(2) Expedited placement cases must meet the requirements in (h) and of Regulation No. 7, except where the requirements of Regulation No. 7 are inconsistent with California law.

(3) Cases in which out-of-state placement is proposed in order to place a child in a residential facility or group home must meet all the requirements of Regulation No. 4, except where inconsistent with California law.

(Subd (c) amended effective January 1, 2014; previously amended effective January 1, 2007, and January 1, 2013.)

(d) Notice of intention; authorization (Fam. Code, § 7901)

A sending jurisdiction must provide to the designated receiving jurisdiction written notice of intention to place the child, using Form ICPC-100A: Interstate Compact on the Placement of Children Request.

(1) The representative of the receiving jurisdiction may request and receive additional information as the representative deems necessary.

(2) The child must not be placed until the receiving jurisdiction has determined that the placement is not contrary to the interest of the child and has so notified the sending jurisdiction in writing.

(Subd (d) amended effective January 1, 2013; previously amended effective January 1, 2007.)

(e) Placement of delinquent children in institutional care (Fam. Code, §§ 7901, art. 6, and 7908; ICPC Reg. No. 4, § 2)

A child declared a ward of the court under Welfare and Institutions Code section 602 may be placed in an institution in another jurisdiction under the compact only when:

(1) Before the placement, the court has held a properly noticed hearing at which the child, parent, and guardian have had an opportunity to be heard;

(2) The court has found that equivalent facilities for the child are not available in the sending jurisdiction; and

(3) Institutional care in the other jurisdiction is in the best interest of the child and will not produce undue hardship for the child or his or her family.

(Subd (e) amended effective January 1, 2014; previously amended effective January 1, 2007, and January 1, 2013.)

(f) Relocation of Family Units (ICPC Reg. No. 1)

(1) The ICPC applies to family relocation cases when the child has been placed and continues to live with a family approved by California, the family relocates to another state with the child, and supervision by California is ongoing.

(2) The ICPC does not apply when the family with whom the child is placed relocates to another state and there will be no ongoing supervision by the sending state or the relocation will be temporary (90 days or less) and will not recur.

(3) Additional procedural requirements for cases involving relocation of family units are in ICPC Regulation No. 1.

(Subd (f) adopted effective January 1, 2013.)

(g) Placing a Child With an Out-of-State Parent (Fam. Code, §§ 7901, art. 5(b), and 7906; ICPC Reg. No. 2, § 3)

When a child will be placed with his or her parent in another state, compliance with the requirements of the ICPC is not required. However, the court has discretion to take the steps it deems necessary to ensure the child's safety and well-being in that placement. Those steps may include:

(1) Directing the child welfare agency to request an independent, non-ICPC home study or courtesy check;

(2) Directing the child welfare agency to enter into a contract with a public or private agency in the receiving state to obtain a home study or other needed information;

(3) Directing the child welfare agency to enter into an informal agreement with a public or private agency in the receiving state, or requesting a courtesy check from such an agency, to obtain needed information; or

(4) Any other steps that the court deems necessary to ensure the child's safety and well-being.

(Subd (g) adopted effective January 1, 2013.)

(h) Expedited placement (ICPC Reg. No. 7)

When seeking expedited approval of an out-of-state placement of a child with a relative or guardian, a California court may designate a proposed placement as an expedited placement by using procedures described in this section.

(1) Expedited placement under Regulation No. 7 does not apply to any situation in which a California child is being placed with his or her parent in another state.

(2) Before the court orders an expedited placement, the court must make express findings that the child is a dependent child removed from and no longer residing in the home of a parent and now being considered for placement in another state with a stepparent, grandparent, adult aunt or uncle, adult sibling, or legal guardian. In addition, the court must find that the child to be placed meets at least one of the following criteria:

(A) Unexpected dependency due to the sudden or recent incarceration, incapacitation, or death of a parent or guardian. *Incapacitation* means the parent or guardian is unable to care for the child due to the parent's medical, mental, or physical condition;

(B) The child is 4 years of age or younger;

(C) The child is part of a group of siblings who will be placed together, where one or more of the siblings is 4 years of age or younger;

(D) The child to be placed, or any of the child's siblings in a sibling group to be placed, has a substantial relationship with the proposed placement resource as defined in section 5(c) of Regulation No. 7; or

(E) The child is in an emergency placement.

(3) Before the court orders an expedited placement, the child welfare agency must provide to the court, at a minimum, the documents required by section 7(a) and (b) of Regulation No. 7:

(A) A signed statement of interest from the potential placement, or a written statement from the assigned case manager affirming that the potential placement resource confirms appropriateness for the ICPC expedited placement decision process. The statement must include all items listed in Regulation No. 7, section 7(a); and

(B) A statement from the assigned case manager or other child welfare agency representative stating that he or she knows of no reason why the child could not be placed with the proposed placement and that the agency has completed and is prepared to send all required paperwork.

(4) On findings of the court under (h)(2) and (3) that the child meets the criteria for an expedited placement and that the required statements have been provided to the court, the case must proceed as follows:

(A) The court must enter an order for expedited placement, stating on the record or in the written order the factual basis for that order. If the court is also requesting provisional approval of the proposed placement, the court must so order, and must state on the record or in the written order the factual basis for that request.

(B) The court's findings and orders must be noted in a written order using *Expedited Placement Under the Interstate Compact on the Placement of Children: Findings and Orders* (form JV-567), which must include the name, address, e-mail address, telephone number, and fax number of the clerk of court or designated court administrator.

(C) The order must be transmitted by the court to the sending agency of the court's jurisdiction within 2 business days of the hearing or consideration of the request.

(D) The sending child welfare agency must be ordered to transmit to the county ICPC Liaison in the sending jurisdiction within 3 business days of receipt of the order the following:

(i) A copy of the completed *Expedited Placement Under the Interstate Compact on the Placement of Children: Findings and Orders* (form JV-567); and

(ii) A completed Interstate Compact on the Placement of Children Request (form ICPC-100A), along with form ICPC-101, the statements required under section (h)(3), above, and all required supporting documentation.

(E) Within 2 business days after receipt of the paperwork, the county ICPC Liaison of the sending jurisdiction must transmit the documents described in (D) to the compact administrator of the receiving jurisdiction with a request for an expedited placement decision, as well as any request for provisional placement.

(5) The compact administrator of the receiving jurisdiction must determine immediately, and no later than 20 business days after receipt, whether the placement is approved and must transmit the completed written report and form ICPC 100A, as required by Regulation 7, section 9, to the county ICPC Liaison in the sending jurisdiction.

(6) The transmission of any documentation, request for information, or decision may be by overnight mail, fax, e-mail, or other recognized, secure method of communication. The receiving state may also request original documents or certified copies if it considers them necessary for a legally sufficient record.

(7) When California is the sending state and there appears to be a lack of compliance with Regulation No. 7 requirements by state officials or the local child welfare agency in the receiving state regarding the expedited placement request, the California judicial officer may communicate directly with the judicial officer in the receiving state.

(A) This communication may be by telephone, e-mail, or any other recognized, secure communication method.

(B) The California judicial officer may do any one or more of the following:

(i) Contact the appropriate judicial officer in the receiving state to discuss the situation and possible solutions.

(ii) Provide, or direct someone else to provide, the judicial officer of the receiving state with copies of relevant documents and court orders.

(iii) Request assistance with obtaining compliance.

(iv) Use *Request for Assistance With Expedited Placement Under the Interstate Compact on the Placement of Children* (form JV-565) to communicate the request for assistance to the receiving state judicial officer. When this form is used, a copy should be provided to the county ICPC Liaison in the sending jurisdiction.

(8) All other requirements, exceptions, timelines, and instructions for expedited placement cases, along with procedures for provisional approval or denial of a placement and for removal of a child from the placement, are stated in Regulation No. 7.

(Subd (h) amended and relettered effective January 1, 2013; previously amended as subd (f) effective January 1, 2007.)

(i) Authority of sending court or agency to place child; timing (ICPC Reg. No. 2, § 8(d), and Reg. No. 4, § 8)

(1) When the receiving state has approved a placement resource, the sending court has the final authority to determine whether to use the approved placement resource. The sending court may delegate that decision to the sending state child welfare agency or probation department.

(2) For proposed placements of children for adoption, in foster care, or with relatives, the receiving state's approval expires six months from the date form ICPC-100A was signed by the receiving state.

(3) For proposed placements of children in residential facilities or group homes, the receiving state's approval expires 30 calendar days from the date form ICPC-100A was signed by the receiving state. The 30-day time frame can be extended by mutual agreement between the sending and receiving states.

(Subd (i) amended effective January 1, 2014; adopted effective January 1, 2013.)

(j) Ongoing jurisdiction

If a child is placed in another jurisdiction under the terms of the compact, the sending court must not terminate its jurisdiction until the child is adopted, reaches majority, or is emancipated, or the dependency is terminated with the concurrence of the receiving state authority.

(Subd (j) relettered effective January 1, 2013; previously amended as subd (g) effective January 1, 2007.)

Rule 5.616 amended effective January 1, 2014; adopted as rule 1428 effective January 1, 1999; previously amended and renumbered effective January 1, 2007; previously amended effective January 1, 2013.

Advisory Committee Comment

Urgency of ICPC Matters. Implementation of the ICPC has long frustrated judicial officers and other professionals. The overriding concern is that the process takes too long, and children cannot wait. In all ICPC actions, there should be a sense of urgency, and all professionals involved should take action as quickly as possible.

Subdivision (h)(7). Judicial officers requesting assistance under subdivision (h)(7) from the receiving state judge or judicial officer should be cognizant of ethical concerns raised by such ex parte communication. These concerns can be addressed in various ways, including but not limited to using form JV-565, obtaining a stipulation from all parties to permit judge-to-judge phone or e-mail contact, or conducting the discussion by phone with parties and a court reporter present.

Validity of California Placements in Receiving Jurisdictions. When a California child is placed with an out-of-state parent, and the placement is consistent with California law, the receiving jurisdiction may consider the placement invalid if it does not comply with the law of the receiving jurisdiction. In this situation, the receiving jurisdiction would have no obligation to provide services.

Regulations and Forms. The ICPC regulations and forms can be found on the website of the Association of Administrators of the Interstate Compact on the Placement of Children at *http://icpc.aphsa.org/*.

Rule 5.618. Placement in short-term residential therapeutic program or community treatment facility (§§ 361.22, 727.12)

(a) Applicability

This rule applies to the court's review under section 361.22 or 727.12 following the placement of a child or nonminor dependent in a short-term residential therapeutic program or community treatment facility.

(Subd (a) amended effective January 1, 2023; adopted effective October 1, 2021.)

(b) Service of request for hearing

The social worker or probation officer must use *Placing Agency's Request for Review of Placement in Short-Term Residential Therapeutic Program or Community Treatment Facility* (form JV-235) to request a hearing and notify the following parties that a hearing is requested under section 361.22(b) or 727.12(b), and serve a copy of the form and a blank copy of *Input on Placement in Short-Term Residential Therapeutic Program or Community Treatment Facility* (form JV-236) within five calendar days of each placement of a child or nonminor dependent in a short-term residential therapeutic program or community treatment facility on:

(1) The child's parents and their attorneys of record, if parental rights have not been terminated, or a nonminor dependent's parents and their attorneys of record, if the parent is receiving family reunification services;

(2) The child's legal guardians, if applicable, and their attorneys of record or the nonminor dependent's legal guardians and their attorneys of record, if the legal guardian is receiving family reunification services;

(3) The attorney of record for the child or nonminor dependent, or their CAPTA guardian ad litem as defined by rule 5.662, and the child, if 10 years of age or older, or the nonminor dependent;

(4) The child's or nonminor dependent's Indian tribe and any Indian custodian, in the case of an Indian child, and their attorneys of record;

(5) The district attorney, if the youth is a ward of the juvenile court;

(6) The child's or nonminor dependent's Court Appointed Special Advocate volunteer, if applicable; and

(7) A nonminor dependent's guardian ad litem, if one has been appointed under Code of Civil Procedure section 372 and Probate Code sections 810–813.

(Subd (b) amended effective January 1, 2023; adopted effective October 1, 2021.)

(c) Setting the hearing

After receiving a request for a hearing, the court must set a hearing under section 361.22(d) or 727.12(d) to be held within 45 days of the start of the short-term residential therapeutic program or community treatment facility placement. The court must provide notice of the hearing to the following:

(1) The child's parents and their attorneys of record, if parental rights have not been terminated, or a nonminor dependent's parents and their attorneys of record, if the parent is receiving family reunification services;

(2) The child's legal guardians, if applicable, and their attorneys of record or a nonminor dependent's legal guardians and their attorneys of record, if the legal guardian is receiving family reunification services;

(3) The attorney of record for the child or nonminor dependent, or their CAPTA guardian ad litem as defined by rule 5.662, and the child if 10 years of age or older, or the nonminor dependent;

(4) A nonminor dependent's guardian ad litem if one has been appointed under Code of Civil Procedure section 372 and Probate Code sections 810–813;

(5) The child's or nonminor dependent's Indian tribe and any Indian custodian, in the case of an Indian child, and their attorneys of record;

(6) The social worker or probation officer;

(7) The district attorney, if the youth is a ward of the juvenile court;

(8) The county counsel, if the youth is a dependent of the juvenile court; and

(9) The child's or nonminor dependent's Court Appointed Special Advocate volunteer, if applicable.

(Subd (c) amended effective January 1, 2023; adopted effective October 1, 2021.)

(d) Report for the hearing

(1) The social worker or probation officer must submit a report to the court that includes the information required by section 361.22(c) or 727.12(c) no later than seven calendar days before the hearing.

(2) The report must be served on the individuals listed in (c) of this rule no later than seven calendar days before the hearing.

(3) The documentation required by section 361.22(c)(1)(A) or 727(c)(1)(A) must not contain information that is privileged or confidential under existing state law or federal law or regulation without the appropriate waiver or consent.

(Subd (d) amended effective January 1, 2023; adopted effective October 1, 2021.)

(e) Input on placement

(1) The following parties who object to the placement may inform the court of the objection by filing *Input on Placement in Short-Term Residential Therapeutic Program or Community Treatment Facility* (form JV-236):

(A) The child's parents and their attorneys of record, if parental rights have not been terminated, or a nonminor dependent's parents and their attorneys of record, if the parent is receiving family reunification services;

(B) The child's legal guardians, if applicable, and their attorneys of record or the nonminor dependent's legal guardians and their attorneys of record, if the legal guardian is receiving family reunification services;

(C) The attorney of record for the child or nonminor dependent, or their CAPTA guardian ad litem as defined by rule 5.662, and the child, if 10 years of age or older, or the nonminor dependent;

(D) A nonminor dependent's guardian ad litem, if one has been appointed under Code of Civil Procedure section 372 and Probate Code sections 810–813;

(E) The child's or nonminor dependent's Indian tribe and any Indian custodian, in the case of an Indian child, and their attorneys of record; and

(F) The district attorney, if the youth is a ward of the juvenile court.

(2) The individuals listed in (1) and other individuals with an interest in the child or nonminor dependent may use form JV-236 to provide input to the court on the child's or nonminor dependent's placement in the short-term residential therapeutic program or community treatment facility.

(3) Input from a Court Appointed Special Advocate volunteer can also be by a court report under local rule.

(4) Local county practice and local rules of court determine the procedures for completing, filing, and serving form JV-236, except as otherwise provided in this rule.

(Subd (e) amended effective January 1, 2023; adopted effective October 1, 2021.)

(f) Approval without a hearing

(1) After the court receives a request for a hearing, the court may approve the placement without a hearing if the following conditions are met:

(A) The service requirements of (b) were met;

(B) No later than 5 court days before the hearing date, the placing agency has filed *Proof of Service—Short-Term Residential Therapeutic Program Placement or Community Treatment Facility* (JV-237) verifying that the parties listed in (e)(1) were served, no later than 10 court days before the hearing date, a copy of the report described in section 361.22(c) or 727.12(c) and a completed *Notice of Request for Approval of Short-Term Residential Therapeutic Program or Community Treatment Facility Without a Hearing* (form JV-240);

(C) No party listed in (e)(1) has notified the court of their objection to the placement within 5 court days of receiving the report described in section 361.22(c) or 727.12(c). Code of Civil Procedure section 1013(a) does not apply to this deadline; and

(D) Based on the information before the court, the court intends to approve the placement consistent with section 361.22(e) or 727.12(e) and (g) of this rule.

(2) If the court approves the placement without a hearing, it must notify the individuals in (c) of the court's decision to approve the placement and vacate the hearing set under section 361.22(d) or 727.12(d).

(3) Nothing in this subdivision precludes the court from holding a hearing when no objection to the placement is received.

(4) Notwithstanding (1)–(3), the court may approve the placement without a hearing under a local rule of court if the local rule is adopted under the procedures in rule 10.613 and meets the following requirements:

(A) The rule ensures that, before the hearing date, the placing agency has filed form JV-237 verifying that the parties listed in (e)(1) were served, no later than 10 court days before the hearing date, a copy of the report described in section 361.22(c) or 727.12(c) and form JV-240;

(B) The rule ensures the court does not approve the placement until all the parties listed in (e)(1), after receiving the report, have been given an opportunity to indicate to the court their position on the placement through form JV-236; and

(C) The rule ensures that the approval occurs no later than 60 days from the start of the placement.

(Subd (f) amended effective January 1, 2023; adopted effective October 1, 2021.)

(g) Conduct of the hearing

(1) In addition to the report described in section 361.22(c) or 727.12(c), the court must consider all evidence relevant to the court's determinations required under section 361.22(e)(2), (3) and (4) or 727.12(e)(2), (3) and (4) and whether the placement in the short-term residential therapeutic program or community treatment facility is consistent with the child's or nonminor dependent's best interest.

(2) The court must make the determinations in section 361.22(e)(2) and (3) or 727.12(e)(2) and (3) by a preponderance of the evidence.

(3) The court must approve or disapprove the placement based on the determinations required by section 361.22(e)(2), (3) and (4) or 727.12(e)(2), (3) and (4) and whether it appears that the child's or nonminor dependent's best interest will be promoted by the placement.

(4) If the court continues the hearing for good cause, including for an evidentiary hearing, in no event may the hearing be continued beyond 60 days after the start of the placement.

(Subd (g) amended effective January 1, 2023; adopted effective October 1, 2021.)

Rule 5.618 amended effective January 1, 2023; adopted effective October 1, 2021.

Advisory Committee Comment

The exception to Code of Civil Procedure section 1013(a) in subdivision (f)(1)(C) was created because of the exigency required by the timelines of sections 361.22 and 727.12 and the need for a prompt resolution of the youth's placement status in a short-term residential therapeutic program or community treatment facility.

Rule 5.619. Voluntary placement in psychiatric residential treatment facility (Welf. & Inst. Code, §§ 361.23, 727.13)

(a) Applicability

This rule applies to the court's review under section 361.23 or 727.13 when a voluntary admission into a psychiatric residential treatment facility is sought for a child, nonminor, or nonminor dependent, as defined in rule 5.502.

(Subd (a) adopted effective January 1, 2024.)

(b) Notice and setting of hearing on application

(1) The social worker or probation officer must use *Ex Parte Application for Voluntary Admission to Psychiatric Residential Treatment Facility* (form JV-172) to request an order authorizing the voluntary admission into a psychiatric residential treatment facility.

(2) After receiving an ex parte application for an order, the court must set a hearing under section 361.23 or 727.13 for the next judicial day. The court must immediately notify the social worker or probation officer and the child, nonminor, or nonminor dependent's counsel of the date, time, and location of the hearing.

(3) The social worker or probation officer must orally notify the parties identified in section 361.23(b)(3), 361.23(e)(3), 727.13(b)(3), or 727.13(e)(3) of the date, time, and location of the hearing.

(4) The social worker or probation officer must complete and file *Proof of Notice of Hearing on Application for Voluntary Admission to Psychiatric Residential Treatment Facility* (form JV-173).

(Subd (b) adopted effective January 1, 2024.)

(c) Conduct of hearing on application

(1) The court must consider all evidence required by section 361.23(c)(1), 361.23(e)(4), 727.13(b)(1), or 727.13(e)(4), and all evidence relevant to the court's determinations required under section 361.23(d), 361.23(e)(5), 727.13(d), or 727.13(e)(5).

(2) The court must use *Order on Application for Voluntary Admission to Psychiatric Residential Treatment Facility* (form JV-174) to document its findings and orders.

(3) If the court authorizes the admission of the child, nonminor, or nonminor dependent, the court must set a hearing to review the placement in the facility no later than 60 days following the admission.

(Subd (c) adopted effective January 1, 2024.)

(d) Notice of hearing on review of placement

At least 10 days before the hearing, the child welfare agency or probation department must provide notice of the date, time, and location of the hearing to review the placement to all parties identified in section 361.23(b)(3), 361.23(e)(3), 727.13(b)(3), or 727.13(e)(3).

(Subd (d) adopted effective January 1, 2024.)

(e) Conduct of hearing on review of placement

(1) The court must consider all evidence required by section 361.23(f)(1)(C), 361.23(f)(2)(C), 727.13(f)(1)(C), or 727.13(f)(2)(C) and all evidence relevant to the court's determinations required under section 361.23(d), 361.23(e)(5), 727.13(d), or 727.13(e)(5).

(2) The court must use *Review of Voluntary Admission of Child to Psychiatric Residential Treatment Facility* (form JV-175) or *Review of Voluntary Admission of Nonminor or Nonminor Dependent to Psychiatric Residential Treatment Facility* (form JV-176) to document its findings and orders.

(3) If the court authorizes the continued admission of the child, nonminor, or nonminor dependent, the court must set a review hearing on the child's placement in the facility no later than 30 days from the date of the review hearing.

(4) If the court does not authorize the continued admission of the child, nonminor, or nonminor dependent, the court must set a hearing in no later than 30 days to verify that the child, nonminor, or nonminor dependent has been discharged.

(Subd (e) adopted effective January 1, 2024.)

(f) Placement by consent of conservator

(1) At any review hearing under section 364, 366.21, 366.22, 366.3, or 366.31, if a child or nonminor dependent has been admitted to a psychiatric residential treatment facility by the consent of a conservator, the court must review the child's case plan. The court must make findings and orders as required by section 361.23(h).

(2) The court must use *Admission to Psychiatric Residential Treatment Facility by Consent of Conservator—Additional Findings and Orders* (form JV-177) to document its findings and orders, and attach the form to the findings and orders document used for the review hearing.

(Subd (f) adopted effective January 1, 2024.)

Rule 5.619 adopted effective January 1, 2024.

Chapter 8
Restraining Orders, Custody Orders, and Guardianships General Court Authority

Rule 5.620. Orders after filing under section 300
Rule 5.625. Orders after filing of petition under section 601 or 602
Rule 5.630. Restraining orders

Rule 5.620. Orders after filing under section 300

(a) Exclusive jurisdiction (§ 304)

Once a petition has been filed alleging that a child is described by section 300, and until the petition is dismissed or dependency is terminated, the juvenile court has exclusive jurisdiction to hear proceedings relating to the custody of the child and visitation with the child and establishing a legal guardianship for the child.

(Subd (a) amended effective January 1, 2021; previously amended effective January 1, 2016.)

(b) Restraining orders (§ 213.5)

After a petition has been filed under section 300, and until the petition is dismissed or dependency is terminated, the court may issue restraining orders as provided in rule 5.630. A temporary restraining order must be prepared on *Notice of Court Hearing and Temporary Restraining Order—Juvenile* (form JV-250). An order after hearing must be prepared on *Juvenile Restraining Order After Hearing* (form JV-255).

(Subd (b) amended effective January 1, 2023; previously amended effective January 1, 2007, and January 1, 2014.)

(c) Custody and visitation (§ 361.2)

If the court sustains a petition, finds that the child is described by section 300, and removes physical custody from a parent or guardian, it may order the child placed in the custody of a previously noncustodial parent as described in rule 5.695(a)(7)(A) or (B).

(1) This order may be entered at the dispositional hearing, at any subsequent review hearing under rule 5.708(k), or on granting a request under section 388 for custody and visitation orders.

(2) If the court orders legal and physical custody to the previously noncustodial parent and terminates dependency jurisdiction under rule 5.695(a)(7)(A), the court must proceed under rule 5.700.

(3) If the court orders custody to the noncustodial parent subject to the continuing supervision of the court, the court may order services provided to either parent or to both parents under section 361.2(b)(3). If the court orders the provision of services, it must review its custody determination at each subsequent hearing held under section 366 and rule 5.708.

(Subd (c) amended effective January 1, 2016; previously amended effective January 1, 2007.)

(d) Appointment of a legal guardian (§§ 360, 366.26)

If the court finds that the child is described by section 300, it may appoint a legal guardian at the disposition hearing, as described in section 360(a) and rule 5.695(a), or at the hearing under section 366.26, as described in that section and rule 5.735. The juvenile court maintains jurisdiction over the guardianship, and a petition to terminate or modify that guardianship must be heard in juvenile court under rule 5.740(c).

(Subd (d) amended effective January 1, 2021; previously amended effective January 1, 2007.)

(e) Termination or modification of previously established probate guardianships (§ 728)

At any time after the filing of a petition under section 300 and until the petition is dismissed or dependency is terminated, the court may terminate or modify a guardianship of the person previously established under the Probate Code.

The social worker may recommend to the court in a report accompanying an initial or supplemental petition that an existing probate guardianship be modified or terminated. The probate guardian or the child's attorney may also file a motion to modify or terminate an existing probate guardianship.

(1) The hearing on the petition or motion may be held simultaneously with any regularly scheduled hearing regarding the child. The notice requirements in section 294 apply.

(2) If the court terminates or modifies a previously established probate guardianship, the court must provide notice of the order to the probate court that made the original appointment. The clerk of the probate court must file the notice in the probate file and send a copy of the notice to all parties of record identified in that file.

(Subd (e) amended effective January 1, 2021; previously amended effective January 1, 2007.)

Rule 5.620 amended effective January 1, 2023; adopted as rule 1429.1 effective January 1, 2000; previously amended and renumbered as rule 5.620 effective January 1, 2007; previously amended effective January 1, 2014, January 1, 2016, and January 1, 2021.

Rule 5.625. Orders after filing of petition under section 601 or 602

(a) Restraining orders (§ 213.5)

After a petition has been filed under section 601 or 602, and until the petition is dismissed or wardship is terminated, the court may issue restraining orders as provided in rule 5.630. A temporary restraining order must be prepared on *Notice of Court Hearing and Temporary Restraining Order—Juvenile* (form JV-250) or, if the restrained person is the subject of a petition under section 601 or 602, on *Notice of Court Hearing and Temporary Restraining Order Against a Child* (form JV-260). An order after hearing must be prepared on *Juvenile Restraining Order After Hearing* (form JV-255) or, if the restrained person is the subject of a petition under section 601 or 602, on *Juvenile Restraining Order After Hearing—Against a Child* (form JV-265).

(Subd (a) amended effective January 1, 2023; previously amended effective January 1, 2003, January 1, 2007, and January 1, 2014.)

(b) Appointment of a legal guardian (§§ 727.3, 728)

At any time during wardship of a child under 18 years of age, the court may appoint a legal guardian of the person for the child in accordance with the requirements in section 366.26 and rule 5.815.

(1) On appointment of a legal guardian, the court may continue wardship and conditions of probation or may terminate wardship.

(2) The juvenile court retains jurisdiction over the guardianship. All proceedings to modify or terminate the guardianship must be held in juvenile court.

(Subd (b) amended effective January 1, 2021; adopted as subd (c) effective January 1, 2000; previously amended effective January 1, 2003; previously amended and relettered as subd (b) effective January 1, 2007.)

(c) Termination or modification of previously established probate guardianships (§ 728)

At any time after the filing of a petition under section 601 or 602 and until the petition is dismissed or wardship is terminated, the court may terminate or modify a guardianship of the person previously established under the Probate Code. The probation officer may recommend to the court in a report accompanying an initial or supplemental petition that an existing probate guardianship be modified or terminated. The guardian or the child's attorney may also file a motion to modify or terminate the guardianship.

(1) The hearing on the petition or motion may be held simultaneously with any regularly scheduled hearing regarding the child. The notice requirements in section 294 apply.

(2) If the court terminates or modifies a previously established probate guardianship, the court must provide notice of the order to the probate court that made the original appointment. The clerk of the probate court must file the notice in the probate file and send a copy of the notice to all parties of record identified in that file.

(Subd (c) adopted effective January 1, 2021.)

Rule 5.625 amended effective January 1, 2023; adopted as rule 1429.3 effective January 1, 2000; previously amended and renumbered effective January 1, 2007; previously amended effective January 1, 2003, January 1, 2014, and January 1, 2021.

Rule 5.630. Restraining orders

(a) Court's authority (§§ 213.5, 304)

(1) After a petition has been filed under section 300, 601, or 602, and until the petition is dismissed or dependency or wardship is terminated, or the ward is no longer on probation, the court may issue restraining orders as provided in section 213.5. The juvenile court has exclusive jurisdiction under section 213.5 to issue a restraining order to protect the child who is the subject of a petition under section 300, or any other child in the household.

(2) The juvenile court, on its own motion, may issue an order as provided for in section 213.5, or as described in Family Code section 6218.

(Subd (a) amended effective January 1, 2023; adopted effective January 1, 2003; previously amended effective January 1, 2012.)

(b) Definition of abuse

The definition of abuse in Family Code section 6203 applies to restraining orders issued under Welfare and Institutions Code section 213.5.

(Subd (b) relettered effective January 1, 2023; adopted as subd (c) effective January 1, 2012.)

(c) Application for restraining orders

(1) Application for restraining orders may be made orally at any scheduled hearing regarding the child who is the subject of a petition under section 300, 601, or 602, or may be made by written application, or may be made on the court's own motion.

(2) If the application is made orally and the court grants a temporary order, the court may direct the requesting party to prepare a temporary order, as directed in (8) below, obtain the judicial officer's signature, file the order with the court, and serve the order on the restrained person.

(3) If the application is made in writing, it must be submitted on *Request for Juvenile Restraining Order* (form JV-245) or, if the request is for a restraining order against the child or youth who is the subject of a petition under section 601 or 602, on *Request for Juvenile Restraining Order Against a Child* (form JV-258).

(4) A person applying for a restraining order in writing must submit to the court with the application a completed *Confidential CLETS Information* (form CLETS-001) under rule 1.51.

(5) If the application is related to domestic violence, the application may be submitted without notice, and the court may grant the request and issue a temporary order.

(6) If the application is not related to domestic violence, the notice requirements in Code of Civil Procedure section 527 apply.

(7) In determining whether or not to issue the temporary restraining order, the court must consider all documents submitted with the application and may review the contents of the juvenile court file regarding the child.

(8) The temporary restraining order must be prepared on *Notice of Court Hearing and Temporary Restraining Order—Juvenile* (form JV-250) or, if the restrained person is the subject of a petition under section 601 or 602, on *Notice of Court Hearing and Temporary Restraining Order Against a Child* (form JV-260), and must state on its face the date of expiration of the order.

(Subd (c) amended and relettered effective January 1, 2023; adopted as subd (b); previously amended effective January 1, 2003, January 1, 2004, January 1, 2007, and January 1, 2012.)

(d) Continuance

(1) The court may grant a continuance under section 213.5.

(2) The court must grant one request for continuance by the restrained party for a reasonable period of time to respond to the petition.

(3) A written request for a continuance must be made on *Request to Reschedule Restraining Order Hearing* (form JV-251).

(4) Either *Order on Request to Reschedule Restraining Order Hearing* (form JV-253) or a new *Notice of Court Hearing and Temporary Restraining Order—Juvenile* (form JV-250) must be used to grant or deny a request for continuance. If the restrained person is the subject of a petition under section 601 or 602, either form JV-253 or a new *Notice of Court Hearing and Temporary Restraining Order Against a Child* (form JV-260) must be used.

(Subd (d) amended and relettered effective January 1, 2023; adopted as subd (g) effective January 1, 2003; amended and relettered as subd (e) effective January 1, 2012; previously amended effective January 1, 2004, January 1, 2007, January 1, 2014, and July 1, 2016.)

(e) Hearing on application for restraining order

(1) Proof may be by the application and any attachments, additional declarations or documentary evidence, the contents of the juvenile court file, testimony, or any combination of these.

(2) The restraining order hearing may be held at the same time as any hearing to declare the child a dependent or ward of the juvenile court

under section 300, 601, or 602, or subsequent hearings regarding the dependent or ward.

(3) The restraining order hearing must be held within the timelines in section 213.5(c)(1).

(4) The order after hearing must be prepared on *Juvenile Restraining Order After Hearing* (form JV-255) or, if the restrained person is the subject of a petition under section 601 or 602, *Juvenile Restraining Order After Hearing—Against a Child* (form JV-265), and must state on its face the date of expiration of the order.

(Subd (e) amended and relettered effective January 1, 2023; adopted as subd (d) effective January 1, 2000; previously amended and relettered as subd (h) effective January 1, 2003, and as subd (f) effective January 1, 2012; previously amended effective January 1, 2007, and January 1, 2014.)

(f) Service of restraining order

When service of *Notice of Court Hearing and Temporary Restraining Order—Juvenile* (form JV-250), *Notice of Court Hearing and Temporary Restraining Order Against a Child* (form JV-260), *Juvenile Restraining Order After Hearing* (form JV-255), or *Juvenile Restraining Order After Hearing—Against a Child* (form JV-265) is made, it must be served with a blank *Receipt for Firearms, Firearm Parts, and Ammunition* (form DV-800/JV-270) and *How Do I Turn In, Sell, or Store Firearms, Firearm Parts, and Ammunition?* (form DV-800-INFO/JV-270-INFO). Failure to serve form JV-270 or JV-270-INFO does not make service of form JV-250, form JV-255, form JV-260, or form JV-265 invalid.

(Subd (f) amended and relettered effective January 1, 2023; adopted as subd (g) effective January 1, 2012; previously amended effective January 1, 2014, and July 1, 2014.)

(g) Firearm relinquishment

The firearm and ammunition relinquishment procedures in Family Code sections 6322.5 and 6389 also apply to restraining orders issued under section 213.5.

(Subd (g) amended and relettered effective January 1, 2023; adopted as subd (h) effective July 1, 2014.)

(h) Expiration of restraining order

If the juvenile case is dismissed, the restraining order remains in effect until it expires or is terminated.

(Subd (h) relettered effective January 1, 2023; adopted as subd (h) effective January 1, 2012; previously relettered as subd (i) effective July 1, 2014.)

(i) Criminal records search (§ 213.5(k))

(1) Before any hearing on the issuance or denial of a restraining order, the court must ensure that a criminal records search is or has been conducted as described in Family Code section 6306(a). Before deciding whether to issue a restraining order, the court must consider the information obtained from the search.

(2) If the results of the search indicate that an outstanding warrant exists against the subject of the search, or that the subject of the search is currently on parole or probation, the court must proceed under section 213.5(k)(3).

(Subd (i) amended and relettered effective January 1, 2023; adopted as subd (i) effective January 1, 2003; previously amended effective January 1, 2007, and January 1, 2012; previously relettered as subd (j) effective July 1, 2014.)

(j) Modification of restraining order

(1) A restraining order may be modified on the court's own motion or in the manner provided for in section 388 or 778, as appropriate, and rule 5.570.

(2) A termination or modification order must be made on *Change to Restraining Order After Hearing* (form JV-257). A new *Juvenile Restraining Order After Hearing* (form JV-255) or, if the restrained person is the subject of a petition under section 601 or 602, a new *Juvenile Restraining Order After Hearing—Against a Child* (form JV-265), may be prepared in addition to form JV-257.

(Subd (j) amended and relettered effective January 1, 2023; adopted as subd (j) effective January 1, 2012; previously amended effective January 1, 2014; previously relettered as subd (k) effective July 1, 2014.)

Rule 5.630 amended effective January 1, 2023; adopted as rule 1429.5 effective January 1, 2000; amended and renumbered effective January 1, 2007; previously amended effective January 1, 2003, January 1, 2004, January 1, 2012, January 1, 2014, July 1, 2014, and July 1, 2016.

Chapter 9
Parentage

Rule 5.635. Parentage
Rule 5.637. Family finding (§§ 309(e), 628(d))

Rule 5.635. Parentage

(a) Authority to declare; duty to inquire (§§ 316.2, 726.4)

The juvenile court has a duty to inquire about and to attempt to determine the parentage of each child who is the subject of a petition filed under section 300, 601, or 602. The court may establish and enter a judgment of parentage under the Uniform Parentage Act. (Fam. Code, § 7600 et seq.) Once a petition has been filed to declare a child a dependent or ward, and until the petition is dismissed or dependency or wardship is terminated, the juvenile court with jurisdiction over the action has exclusive jurisdiction to hear an action filed under Family Code section 7630.

(Subd (a) amended effective January 1, 2015; previously amended effective January 1, 2001, January 1, 2006, and January 1, 2007.)

(b) Parentage inquiry (§§ 316.2, 726.4)

At the initial hearing on a petition filed under section 300 or at the dispositional hearing on a petition filed under section 601 or 602, and at hearings thereafter until or unless parentage has been established, the court must inquire of the child's parents present at the hearing and of any other appropriate person present as to the identity and address of any and all presumed or alleged parents of the child. Questions, at the discretion of the court, may include the following and others that may provide information regarding parentage:

(1) Has there been a judgment of parentage?

(2) Was the mother married or did she have a registered domestic partner at or after the time of conception?

(3) Did the mother believe she was married or believe she had a registered domestic partner at or after the time of conception?

(4) Was the mother cohabiting with another adult at the time of conception?

(5) Has the mother received support payments or promises of support for the child or for herself during her pregnancy or after the birth of the child?

(6) Has a man formally or informally acknowledged parentage, including the execution and filing of a voluntary declaration of parentage or paternity under Family Code section 7570 et seq., and agreed to have his name placed on the child's birth certificate?

(7) Has genetic testing been administered, and, if so, what were the results?

(8) Has the child been raised jointly with another adult or in any other co-parenting arrangement?

(Subd (b) amended effective January 1, 2020; adopted effective January 1, 2001; previously amended effective January 1, 2006, January 1, 2007, and January 1, 2015.)

(c) Voluntary declaration

If a voluntary declaration as described in Family Code section 7570 et seq. has been executed and filed with the California Department of Child Support Services, the declaration establishes the parentage of a child and has the same force and effect as a judgment of parentage by a court. A person is presumed to be the parent of the child under Family Code section 7611 if the voluntary declaration has been properly executed and filed.

(Subd (c) amended effective January 1, 2020; adopted effective January 1, 2001; previously amended effective January 1, 2006, July 1, 2006, January 1, 2007, and January 1, 2015.)

(d) Issue raised; inquiry

If, at any proceeding regarding the child, the issue of parentage is addressed by the court:

(1) The court must ask the parent or the person alleging parentage, and others present, whether any parentage finding has been made, and, if so, what court made it, or whether a voluntary declaration has been executed and filed under the Family Code;

(2) The court must direct the court clerk to prepare and transmit *Parentage Inquiry—Juvenile* (form JV-500) to the local child support agency requesting an inquiry regarding whether parentage has been established through any superior court order or judgment or through the execution and filing of a voluntary declaration under the Family Code;

(3) The office of child support enforcement must prepare and return the completed *Parentage Inquiry—Juvenile* (form JV-500) within 25 judicial days, with certified copies of any such order or judgment or proof of the filing of any voluntary declaration attached; and

(4) The juvenile court must take judicial notice of the prior determination of parentage.

(Subd (d) amended effective January 1, 2015; adopted as subd (b) effective July 1, 1995; previously amended and relettered effective January 1, 2001; previously amended effective January 1, 2006, and January 1, 2007.)

(e) No prior determination

If the local child support agency states, or if the court determines through statements of the parties or other evidence, that there has been no prior determination of parentage of the child, the juvenile court must take appropriate steps to make such a determination.

(1) Any alleged father and his counsel must complete and submit *Statement Regarding Parentage (Juvenile)* (form JV-505). Form JV-505 must be made available in the courtroom.

(2) To determine parentage, the juvenile court may order the child and any alleged parents to submit to genetic tests and proceed under Family Code section 7550 et seq.

(3) The court may make its determination of parentage or nonparentage based on the testimony, declarations, or statements of the alleged parents. The court must advise any alleged parent that if parentage is determined, the parent will have responsibility for the financial support of the child, and, if the child receives welfare benefits, the parent may be subject to an action to obtain support payments.

(Subd (e) amended effective January 1, 2015; adopted as subd (c) effective July 1, 1995; previously amended and relettered effective January 1, 2001; previously amended effective January 1, 2006, and January 1, 2007.)

(f) Notice to office of child support enforcement

If the court establishes parentage of the child, the court must sign *Parentage—Finding and Judgment (Juvenile)* (form JV-501) and direct the clerk to transmit the signed form to the local child support agency.

(Subd (f) amended effective January 1, 2015; adopted as subd (d) effective July 1, 1995; previously amended and relettered effective January 1, 2001; previously amended effective January 1, 2006, and January 1, 2007.)

(g) Dependency and delinquency; notice to alleged parents

If, after inquiry by the court or through other information obtained by the county welfare department or probation department, one or more persons are identified as alleged parents of a child for whom a petition under section 300, 601, or 602 has been filed, the clerk must provide to each named alleged parent, at the last known address, by certified mail, return receipt requested, a copy of the petition, notice of the next scheduled hearing, and *Statement Regarding Parentage (Juvenile)* (form JV-505) unless:

(1) The petition has been dismissed;

(2) Dependency or wardship has been terminated;

(3) The alleged parent has previously filed a form JV-505 denying parentage and waiving further notice; or

(4) The alleged parent has relinquished custody of the child to the county welfare department.

(Subd (g) amended effective January 1, 2015; adopted as subd (e) effective July 1, 1995; previously amended and relettered effective January 1, 2001; previously amended effective January 1, 2006, and January 1, 2007.)

(h) Dependency and delinquency; alleged parents (§§ 316.2, 726.4)

If a person appears at a hearing in dependency matter or at a hearing under section 601 or 602 and requests a judgment of parentage on form JV-505, the court must determine:

(1) Whether that person is the biological parent of the child; and

(2) Whether that person is the presumed parent of the child, if that finding is requested.

(Subd (h) amended effective January 1, 2007; adopted as subd (f) effective January 1, 1999; previously amended and relettered effective January 1, 2001; previously amended effective January 1, 2006.)

Rule 5.635 amended effective January 1, 2020; adopted as rule 1413 effective July 1, 1995; previously amended effective January 1, 1999, January 1, 2001, January 1, 2006, July 1, 2006, January 1, 2007, and January 1, 2015.

Rule 5.637. Family finding (§§ 309(e), 628(d))

(a) Definition

(1) "Family finding" means conducting an investigation to identify kin and connect the child with those kin in an effort to provide family support and possible placement. For an Indian child, family finding also includes contacting the child's Indian tribe to identify kin.

(2) "Kin" means any relative as defined in rule 5.502(34), and any nonrelative extended family member of the child or the child's relatives.

(3) "Nonrelative extended family member" means an adult who has an established familial or mentoring relationship with a child or a familial relationship with a relative of the child. These adults may include but are not limited to the following people: godparents, teachers, clergy, neighbors, parents of a sibling, and family friends.

(Subd (a) adopted effective January 1, 2024.)

(b) Juvenile dependency proceedings

(1) No later than 30 days after a child is removed from their parent or guardian and detained in a juvenile dependency proceeding, the social worker must use due diligence in conducting family finding, including an investigation to identify, locate, and provide notification and information as required in paragraph (2) to the child's parents or alleged parents, all the child's adult kin, parents with legal custody of the child's siblings, any adult siblings, and in the case of an Indian child, any extended family members of the child's tribe.

(2) After locating persons specified in paragraph (1), the social worker must provide to them, within 30 days of removal, the following:

(A) Written notification that the child has been removed from the parent, guardian, or Indian custodian's custody;

(B) An explanation in writing of the available options to participate in the child's care and placement, including the information set forth in section 309(e)(1)(B); and

(C) A copy of *Relative Information* (form JV-285) for providing information to the social worker and the court regarding the child's needs and to request permission to address the court, if desired.

Oral notification in person or by telephone of the information must also be provided to the child's kin, when appropriate.

(Subd (b) amended and relettered effective January 1, 2024; adopted as subd (a) effective January 1, 2011.)

(c) Juvenile delinquency proceedings

(1) No later than 30 days after a child is detained in a juvenile delinquency proceeding, if the probation officer has reason to believe that the child may be at risk of entering a foster care placement or within 30 days of the court order placing the child into foster care, the probation officer must use due diligence to conduct family finding, including an investigation to identify, locate, and provide notification and information as required in paragraph (2) to the child's parents or alleged parents, all of the child's adult kin, parents with legal custody of the child's siblings, any adult siblings, and in the case of an Indian child, any extended family members of the child's tribe.

(2) After locating the child's kin and other persons specified in paragraph (1), the probation officer must provide within 30 days of the date on which the child is detained, to all kin who are located, the following:

(A) Written notification that the child has been removed from the parent, guardian, or Indian custodian's custody; and

(B) An explanation in writing of the available options to participate in the child's care and placement, including the information set forth in section 628(d)(2)(B).

Oral notification in person or by telephone of the information must also be provided to the child's kin, when appropriate.

(Subd (c) adopted effective January 1, 2024.)

(d) Due diligence (§§ 309, 628, Fam. Code, § 7950)

(1) §During the time the child is removed from the child's parent, guardian, or Indian custodian, the social worker and probation officer have an ongoing responsibility to exercise due diligence to engage in family finding until the time the child is placed for adoption.

(2) The court must find whether the social worker or probation officer has exercised due diligence in family finding by:

(A) Asking the child, in an age-appropriate manner and consistent with the child's best interests, about the identity and location of kin;

(B) Using a computer-based search engine and internet-based search tools to locate kin identified as support for the child and their family; and

(C) If it is known or there is reason to know the child is an Indian child as defined by section 224.1, contacting the Indian child's tribe to identify kin.

(3) When making the finding of due diligence, the court may also consider other efforts, including whether the social worker or probation officer has done any of the following:

(A) Obtained information regarding the location of the child's kin;

(B) Reviewed the child's case file for any information regarding kin;

(C) Telephoned, emailed, or visited all identified kin;

(D) Asked located kin for the names and locations of other kin; or

(E) Developed tools—including a genogram, family tree, family map, or other diagram of family relationships—to help the child, parent, guardian, or Indian custodian to identify kin.

(4) In cases involving a dual-status child, the duty to exercise due diligence in family finding must be assigned in accordance with the written protocols required by section 241.1(b)(4).

(Subd (d) adopted effective January 1, 2024.)

(e) When notification of kin is inappropriate

The social worker or probation officer is not required to notify a relative whose personal history of family or domestic violence would make notification inappropriate. A social worker or probation officer who determines that notification of kin is inappropriate under this subdivision must notify the court that kin has not been notified and explain the reasoning underlying that lack of notification.

(Subd (e) amended and relettered effective January 1, 2024; adopted as subd (b) effective January 1, 2011.)

Rule 5.637 amended effective January 1, 2024; adopted effective January 1, 2011.

Advisory Committee Comment

This rule initially restated the original requirements of section 103 of the federal Fostering Connections to Success and Increasing Adoptions Act (Pub. L. No. 110-351, § 103 (Oct. 7, 2008) 122 Stat. 3949, 3956, codified at 42 U.S.C. § 671(a)(29)) as implemented by California Assembly Bill 938 (Com. on Judiciary; Stats. 2009, ch. 261, codified at Welf. & Inst. Code §§ 309(e) and 628(d)). These statutes enacted elements of the child welfare practice known as family finding and engagement, which has been recommended to improve outcomes for children by the Judicial Council's California Blue Ribbon Commission on Children in Foster Care and the California Child Welfare Council. (*See* Cal. Blue Ribbon Com. on Children in Foster Care, *Fostering a New Future for California's Children*, pp. 30–31 (Admin. Off. of Cts., May 2009) (final report and action plan); www.courts.ca.gov; Permanency Committee Recommendations to the Child Welfare Council, pp. 1–4 (Sept. 10, 2009), www.chhs.ca.gov.)

The rule was amended to reflect Senate Bill 384 (Cortese; Stats. 2022, ch. 811), which revised Welfare and Institutions Code sections 309 and 628 regarding the obligation of the social worker and probation officer to engage in family finding in dependency and delinquency cases.

Chapter 10
Medication, Mental Health, and Education

Rule 5.640. Psychotropic medications

Rule 5.642. Authorization to release psychotropic medication prescription information to Medical Board of California

Rule 5.643. Mental health or condition of child; court procedures

Rule 5.645. Mental health or condition of child; competency evaluations

Rule 5.647. Medi-Cal: Presumptive Transfer of Specialty Mental Health Services

Rule 5.649. Right to make educational or developmental-services decisions

Rule 5.650. Appointed educational rights holder

Rule 5.651. Educational and developmental-services decisionmaking rights

Rule 5.652. Access to pupil records for truancy purposes

Rule 5.640. Psychotropic medications

(a) Definition (§§ 369.5(d), 739.5(d))

For the purposes of this rule, "psychotropic medication" means those medications prescribed to affect the central nervous system to treat psychiatric disorders or illnesses. They may include, but are not limited to, anxiolytic agents, antidepressants, mood stabilizers, antipsychotic medications, anti-Parkinson agents, hypnotics, medications for dementia, and psychostimulants.

(Subd (a) amended effective January 1, 2009; previously amended effective January 1, 2007.)

(b) Authorization to administer (§§ 369.5, 739.5)

(1) Once a child is declared a dependent child of the court and is removed from the custody of the parents, guardian, or Indian custodian, only a juvenile court judicial officer is authorized to make orders regarding the administration of psychotropic medication to the child, unless, under (e), the court orders that the parent or legal guardian is authorized to approve or deny the medication.

(2) Once a child is declared a ward of the court, removed from the custody of the parents, guardian, or Indian custodian, and placed into foster care, as defined in Welfare and Institutions Code section 727.4, only a juvenile court judicial officer is authorized to make orders regarding the administration of psychotropic medication to the child, unless, under (e), the court orders that the parent or legal guardian is authorized to approve or deny the medication.

(Subd (b) amended effective September 1, 2020; previously amended effective January 1, 2009, July 1, 2016, and January 1, 2018.)

(c) Procedure to obtain authorization

(1) To obtain authorization to administer psychotropic medication to a dependent child of the court who is removed from the custody of the parents, legal guardian, or Indian custodian, or to a ward of the court who is removed from the custody of the parents, legal guardian, or Indian custodian and placed into foster care, the following forms must be completed and filed with the court:

(A) *Application for Psychotropic Medication* (form JV-220);

(B) *Physician's Statement—Attachment* (form JV-220(A)), unless the request is to continue the same medication and maximum dosage by the same physician who completed the most recent JV-220(A); then the physician may complete *Physician's Request to Continue Medication—Attachment* (form JV-220(B)); and

(C) *Proof of Notice of Application* (form JV-221).

(2) The child, caregiver, parents, legal guardians, or Indian custodian, child's Indian tribe, and Court Appointed Special Advocate, if any, may provide input on the medications being prescribed.

(A) Input can be by *Child's Opinion About the Medicine* (form JV-218) or *Statement About Medicine Prescribed* (form JV-219); letter; talking to the judge at a court hearing; or through the social worker, probation officer, attorney of record, or Court Appointed Special Advocate.

(B) If form JV-218 or form JV-219 is filed, it must be filed within four court days after receipt of notice of the pending application for psychotropic medication. If a hearing is set on the application, form JV-218 and form JV-219 may be filed at any time before, or at, the hearing.

(C) Input from a Court Appointed Special Advocate can also be by a court report under local rule.

(3) *Input on Application for Psychotropic Medication* (form JV-222) may be filed by a parent, guardian, or Indian custodian, their attorney of record, a child's attorney of record, a child's Child Abuse Prevention and Treatment Act guardian ad litem appointed under rule 5.662 of the California Rules of Court, or the Indian child's tribe. If form JV-222 is filed, it must be filed within four court days of receipt of notice of the application.

(4) Additional information may be provided to the court through the use of local forms that are consistent with this rule.

(5) Local county practice and local rules of court determine the procedures for completing and filing the forms, except as otherwise provided in this rule.

(6) *Application for Psychotropic Medication* (form JV-220) may be completed by the prescribing physician, medical office staff, child welfare services staff, probation officer, or the child's caregiver. If the applicant is the social worker or probation officer, he or she must complete all items on form JV-220. If the applicant is the prescribing physician, medical office staff, or child's caregiver, he or she must complete and sign only page one of form JV-220.

(7) The physician prescribing the administration of psychotropic medication for the child must complete and sign *Physician's Statement—Attachment* (form JV-220(A)) or, if it is a request to continue the same medication by the same physician who completed the most recent JV-220(A), then the physician must complete and sign *Physician's Statement—Attachment* (form JV-220(A)) or *Physician's Request to Continue Medication—Attachment* (form JV-220(B)).

(8) The court must approve, deny, or set the matter for a hearing within seven court days of the receipt of the completed form JV-220 and form JV-220(A) or form JV-220(B).

(9) The court must grant or deny the application using *Order on Application for Psychotropic Medication* (form JV-223).

(10) Notice of the application must be provided to the parents, legal guardians, or Indian custodian, their attorneys of record, the child's attorney of record, the child's Child Abuse Prevention and Treatment Act guardian ad litem, the child's current caregiver, the child's Court Appointed Special Advocate, if any, and where a child has been determined to be an Indian child, the Indian child's tribe (see also 25 U.S.C. § 1903(4)–(5); Welf. & Inst. Code, §§ 224.1(a) and (e) and 224.3).

(A) If the child is living in a group home or short-term residential therapeutic program, notice to the caregiver must be by notice to the facility administrator as defined in California Code of Regulations, title 22, section 84064, or to the administrator's designee.

(B) Local county practice and local rules of court determine the procedures for the provision of notice, except as otherwise provided in this rule and in section 212.5. Psychological or medical documentation related to a minor may not be served electronically. The person or persons responsible for providing notice as required by local court rules or local practice protocols are encouraged to use the most expeditious legally authorized manner of service possible to ensure timely notice.

(C) Notice must be provided as follows:

(i) Notice to the parents or legal guardians and their attorneys of record must include:

a. A statement that a physician is asking to treat the child's emotional or behavioral problems by beginning or continuing the administration of psychotropic medication to the child and the name of the psychotropic medication;

b. A statement that an *Application for Psychotropic Medication* (form JV-220) and a *Physician's Statement—Attachment* (form JV-220(A)) or *Physician's Request to Continue Medication—Attachment* (form JV-220(B)) are pending before the court;

c. A copy of *Guide to Psychotropic Medication Forms* (form JV-217-INFO);

d. A blank copy of *Statement About Medicine Prescribed* (form JV-219); and

e. A blank copy of *Input on Application for Psychotropic Medication* (form JV-222).

(ii) Notice to the child's current caregiver and Court Appointed Special Advocate, if one has been appointed, must include only:

a. A statement that a physician is asking to treat the child's emotional or behavioral problems by beginning or continuing the administration of psychotropic medication to the child and the name of the psychotropic medication;

b. A statement that an *Application for Psychotropic Medication* (form JV-220) and a *Physician's Statement—Attachment* (form JV-220(A)) or *Physician's Request to Continue Medication—Attachment* (form JV-220(B)) are pending before the court;

c. A copy of *Guide to Psychotropic Medication Forms* (form JV-217-INFO);

d. A blank copy of *Child's Opinion About the Medicine* (form JV-218); and

e. A blank copy of *Statement About Medicine Prescribed* (form JV-219).

(iii) Notice to the child's attorney of record and any Child Abuse Prevention and Treatment Act guardian ad litem for the child must include:

a. A completed copy of *Application for Psychotropic Medication* (form JV-220);

b. A completed copy of *Physician's Statement—Attachment* (form JV-220(A)) or *Physician's Request to Continue Medication—Attachment* (form JV-220(B));

c. A copy of *Guide to Psychotropic Medication Forms* (form JV-217-INFO) or information on how to obtain a copy of the form;

d. A blank copy of *Input on Application for Psychotropic Medication* (form JV-222) or information on how to obtain a copy of the form;

e. A blank copy of *Child's Opinion About the Medicine* (form JV-218) or information on how to obtain a copy of the form; and

f. If the application could result in the authorization of three or more psychotropic medications for 90 days or longer, notice must also include a blank copy of *Position on Release of Information to Medical Board of California* (form JV-228), a copy of *Background on Release of Information to Medical Board of California* (form JV-228-INFO), a blank copy of *Withdrawal of Release of Information to Medical Board of California* (form JV-229), and the procedures in rule 5.642 must be followed.

(iv) Notice to the Indian child's tribe must include:

a. A statement that a physician is asking to treat the child's emotional or behavioral problems by beginning or continuing the administration of psychotropic medication to the child, and the name of the psychotropic medication;

b. A statement that an *Application for Psychotropic Medication* (form JV-220) and a *Physician's Statement—Attachment* (form JV-220(A)) or *Physician's Request to Continue Medication—Attachment* (form JV-220(B)) are pending before the court;

c. A copy of *Guide to Psychotropic Medication Forms* (form JV-217-INFO) or information on how to obtain a copy of the form;

d. A blank copy of *Input on Application for Psychotropic Medication* (form JV-222) or information on how to obtain a copy of the form; and

e. A blank copy of *Child's Opinion About the Medicine* (form JV-218) or information on how to obtain a copy of the form.

f. A blank copy of *Statement About Medicine Prescribed* (form JV-219) or information on how to obtain a copy of the form.

(v) Proof of notice of the application regarding psychotropic medication must be filed with the court using *Proof of Notice of Application* (form JV-221).

(11) If all the required information is not included in the request for authorization, the court must order the applicant to provide the missing information and set a hearing on the application.

(12) The court may grant the application without a hearing or may set the matter for hearing at the court's discretion. If the court sets the matter for a hearing, the clerk of the court must provide notice of the date, time, and location of the hearing to the parents, legal guardians, or Indian custodian, their attorneys of record, the dependent child if 12 years of age or older, a ward of the juvenile court of any age, the child's attorney of record, the child's current caregiver, the child's social worker or probation officer, the social worker's or probation officer's attorney of record, the child's Child Abuse Prevention and Treatment Act guardian ad litem, the child's Court Appointed Special Advocate, if any, and the Indian child's tribe at least two court days before the hearing. Notice must be provided to the child's probation officer and the district attorney, if the child is a ward of the juvenile court.

(Subd (c) amended effective September 1, 2020; previously amended effective January 1, 2007, January 1, 2008, January 1, 2009, January 1, 2014, July 1, 2016, January 1, 2018, and January 1, 2019.)

(d) Conduct of hearing on application

At the hearing on the application, the procedures described in rule 5.570 and section 349 must be followed. The court may deny, grant, or modify the application for authorization. If the court grants or modifies the application for authorization, the court must set a date for review of the child's progress and condition. This review must occur at every status review hearing and may occur at any other time at the court's discretion.

(Subd (d) amended effective July 1, 2016; previously amended effective January 1, 2007.)

(e) Delegation of authority (§§ 369.5, 739.5)

If a child is removed from the custody of his or her parent, legal guardian, or Indian custodian, the court may order that the parent, legal guardian, or Indian custodian is authorized to approve or deny the administration of psychotropic medication. The order must be based on the findings in section 369.5 or section 739.5, which must be included in the order. The court may use *Order Delegating Judicial Authority Over Psychotropic Medication* (form JV-216) to document the findings and order.

(Subd (e) amended effective September 1, 2020; previously amended effective January 1, 2008, and January 1, 2018.)

(f) Continued treatment

If the court grants the request or modifies and then grants the request, the order for authorization is effective until terminated or modified by court order or until 180 days from the order, whichever is earlier.

(Subd (f) amended effective July 1, 2016.)

(g) Progress review

(1) After approving any application for authorization, regardless of whether the approval is made at a hearing, the court must set a progress review.

(2) A progress review must occur at every status review hearing and may occur at any other time at the court's discretion.

(3) If the progress review is held at the time of the status review hearing, notice must be provided as required under section 293 or 295, except that electronic service of psychological or medical documentation related to a child is not permitted. The notice must include a statement that the hearing will also be a progress review on previously ordered psychotropic medication, and must include a blank copy of *Child's Opinion About the Medicine* (form JV-218) and a blank copy of *Statement About Medicine Prescribed* (form JV-219).

(4) If the progress review is not held at the time of the status review hearing, notice must be provided as required under section 293 or 295, except that electronic service of psychological or medical documentation related to a child is not permitted. The notice must include a statement that the hearing will be a progress review on previously ordered psychotropic medication; and must include a blank copy of *Child's Opinion About the Medicine* (form JV-218) and a blank copy of *Statement About Medicine Prescribed* (form JV-219).

(5) Before each progress review, the social worker or probation officer must file a completed *County Report About Psychotropic Medication* (form JV-224) at least 10 calendar days before the hearing. If the progress review is set at the same time as a status review hearing, form JV-224 must be attached to and filed with the report.

(6) The child, caregiver, parents, legal guardians, or Indian custodian, and Court Appointed Special Advocate, if any, may provide input at the progress review as stated in (c)(2).

(7) At the progress review, the procedures described in section 349 must be followed.

(Subd (g) amended effective September 1, 2020; adopted effective July 1, 2016; previously amended effective January 1, 2018, and January 1, 2019.)

(h) Copy of order to caregiver

(1) Upon the approval or denial of the application, the county child welfare agency, probation department, or other person or entity who submitted the request must provide the child's caregiver with a copy of the court order approving or denying the request.

(2) The copy of the order must be provided in person or mailed within two court days of when the order is signed.

(3) If the court approves the request, the copy of the order must include the last two pages of form JV-220(A) or the last two pages of form JV-220(B) and all medication information sheets (medication monographs) that were attached to form JV-220(A) or form JV-220(B).

(4) If the child resides in a group home or short-term residential therapeutic program, a copy of the order, the last two pages of form JV-220(A) or the last two pages of form JV-220(B), and all medication information sheets (medication monographs) that were attached to form JV-220(A) or form JV-220(B) must be provided to the facility administrator, as defined in California Code of Regulations, title 22, section 84064, or to the administrator's designee.

(5) If the child changes placement, the social worker or probation officer must provide the new caregiver with a copy of the order, the last two pages of form JV-220(A) or the last two pages of form JV-220(B), and the medication information sheets (medication monographs) that were attached to form JV-220(A) or form JV-220(B).

(Subd (h) amended effective January 1, 2019; adopted effective July 1, 2016; previously amended effective January 1, 2018.)

(i) Emergency treatment

(1) Psychotropic medications may be administered without court authorization in an emergency situation. An emergency situation occurs when:

(A) A physician finds that the child requires psychotropic medication to treat a psychiatric disorder or illness; and

(B) The purpose of the medication is:

(i) To protect the life of the child or others, or

(ii) To prevent serious harm to the child or others, or

(iii) To treat current or imminent substantial suffering; and

(C) It is impractical to obtain authorization from the court before administering the psychotropic medication to the child.

(2) Court authorization must be sought as soon as practical but in no case more than two court days after the emergency administration of the psychotropic medication.

(Subd (i) relettered effective July 1, 2016; adopted as subd (g); previously amended effective January 1, 2007, and January 1, 2008.)

(j) Section 601–602 wardships; local rules

A local rule of court may be adopted providing that authorization for the administration of such medication to a child declared a ward of the court under sections 601 or 602 and removed from the custody of the parent or guardian for placement in a facility that is not considered a foster-care placement may be similarly restricted to the juvenile court. If the local court adopts such a local rule, then the procedures under this rule apply; any reference to social worker also applies to probation officer.

(Subd (j) amended and relettered effective July 1, 2016; adopted as subd (i) effective January 1, 2001; previously relettered as subd (h) effective January 1, 2008; previously amended effective January 1, 2007, and January 1, 2009.)

(k) Public health nurses

Information may be provided to public health nurses as governed by Civil Code section 56.103.

(Subd (k) adopted effective July 1, 2016.)

Rule 5.640 amended effective September 1, 2020; adopted as rule 1432.5 effective January 1, 2001; previously amended and renumbered effective January 1, 2007; previously amended effective January 1, 2003, January 1, 2008, January 1, 2009, January 1, 2014, July 1, 2016, January 1, 2018, and January 1, 2019.

Rule 5.642. Authorization to release psychotropic medication prescription information to Medical Board of California

(a) Providing authorization forms

Whenever there is an *Application for Psychotropic Medication* (form JV-220) filed with the court under rule 5.640, the applicant must review the *Physician's Statement—Attachment* (form JV-220(A)) or *Physician's Request to Continue Medication—Attachment* (form JV-220(B)) to determine if the request would result in the child being prescribed three or more concurrent psychotropic medications for 90 days or more, as described in section 14028. If the request would result in the child being prescribed three or more psychotropic medications for 90 days or more, the applicant must provide blank copies of *Position on Release of Information to Medical Board of California* (form JV-228), *Background on Release of Information to Medical Board of California* (form JV-228-INFO), and *Withdrawal of Release of Information to Medical Board of California* (form JV-229) to the child and the child's attorney.

(Subd (a) adopted effective September 1, 2020.)

(b) Signing authorization form

(1) Form JV-228 may be signed by either the child, nonminor dependent, or the attorney, with the informed consent of the child if the child is found by the court to be of sufficient age and maturity to consent. Sufficient age and maturity to consent must be presumed, subject to rebuttal by clear and convincing evidence, if the child is 12 years of age or over. If the child does not want to sign form JV-228, the child's attorney may not sign it. The child's attorney may sign form JV-228 with the approval of a child 12 years of age or older, if the child is under 12 years of age, or if the court finds the child not to be of sufficient age and maturity to consent.

(2) The authorization is for the release of medical records only. It is not an authorization for the release of juvenile court case files as described in section 827.

(Subd (b) adopted effective September 1, 2020.)

(c) Filing and sending authorization form

(1) The child's attorney must review form JV-228 with the child and file it with the superior court.

(2) Within three court days of filing, the clerk of the superior court must send form JV-228 to the California Department of Social Services at the address indicated on the form.

(Subd (c) adopted effective September 1, 2020.)

(d) Withdrawal of authorization

At any time, the child, nonminor dependent, or attorney may withdraw the authorization to release information to the Medical Board of California.

(1) Withdrawal may be made by filing *Withdrawal of Release of Information to Medical Board of California* (form JV-229) or by written letter to the California Department of Social Services.

(2) The child, nonminor dependent, or attorney may sign (as specified in (b)) form JV-229.

(3) Within three court days of filing, the clerk of the superior court must send form JV-229 to the California Department of Social Services at the address indicated on the form.

(Subd (d) adopted effective September 1, 2020.)

(e) Notice of release of information to medical board

If the California Department of Social Services releases identifying information to the Medical Board of California, the California Department of Social Services must notify the child, nonminor dependent, or former dependent or ward, at the last known address. The California Department of Social Services must also notify the child's, nonminor dependent's, or former dependent's or ward's attorney, including in cases when jurisdiction has been terminated.

(Subd (e) adopted effective September 1, 2020.)

Rule 5.642 adopted effective September 1, 2020.

Rule 5.643. Mental health or condition of child; court procedures

(a) Doubt concerning the mental health of a child (§§ 357, 705, 6550, 6551)

Whenever the court believes that the child who is the subject of a petition filed under section 300, 601, or 602 is mentally disabled or may be mentally ill, the court may stay the proceedings and order the child taken to a facility designated by the court and approved by the State Department of Mental Health as a facility for 72-hour treatment and evaluation. The professional in charge of the facility must submit a written evaluation of the child to the court.

(Subd (a) amended effective January 1, 2007.)

(b) Findings regarding a mental disorder (§ 6551)

Article 1 of chapter 2 of part 1 of division 5 (commencing with section 5150) applies.

(1) If the professional reports that the child is not in need of intensive treatment, the child must be returned to the juvenile court on or before the

expiration of the 72-hour period, and the court must proceed with the case under section 300, 601, or 602.

(2) If the professional in charge of the facility finds that the child is in need of intensive treatment for a mental disorder, the child may be certified for not more than 14 days of involuntary intensive treatment according to the conditions of sections 5250(c) and 5260(b). The stay of the juvenile court proceedings must remain in effect during this time.

(A) During or at the end of the 14 days of involuntary intensive treatment, a certification may be sought for additional treatment under sections commencing with 5270.10 or for the initiation of proceedings to have a conservator appointed for the child under sections commencing with 5350. The juvenile court may retain jurisdiction over the child during proceedings under sections 5270.10 et seq. and 5350 et seq.

(B) For a child subject to a petition under section 602, if the child is found to be gravely disabled under sections 5300 et seq., a conservator is appointed under those sections, and the professional in charge of the child's treatment or of the treatment facility determines that proceedings under section 602 would be detrimental to the child, the juvenile court must suspend jurisdiction while the conservatorship remains in effect. The suspension of jurisdiction may end when the conservatorship is terminated, and the original 602 matter may be calendared for further proceedings.

(Subd (b) amended effective January 1, 2007.)

(c) Findings regarding developmental disability (§ 6551)

Article 1 of chapter 2 of part 1 of division 5 (commencing with section 5150) applies.

(1) If the professional finds that the child has a developmental disability and recommends commitment to a state hospital, the court may direct the filing in the appropriate court of a petition for commitment of a child who has a developmental disability to the State Department of Developmental Services for placement in a state hospital.

(2) If the professional finds that the child does not have a developmental disability, the child must be returned to the juvenile court on or before the expiration of the 72-hour period, and the court must proceed with the case under section 300, 601, or 602.

(3) The jurisdiction of the juvenile court must be suspended while the child is subject to the jurisdiction of the appropriate court under a petition for commitment of a person who has a developmental disability, or under remand for 90 days for intensive treatment or commitment ordered by that court.

(Subd (c) amended effective January 1, 2020; previously amended effective January 1, 2007, and January 1, 2009.)

Rule 5.643 amended and renumbered effective January 1, 2020; adopted as rule 1498 effective January 1, 1999; previously amended and renumbered as rule 5.645 effective January 1, 2007; previously amended effective January 1, 2009, and January 1, 2012.

Rule 5.645. Mental health or condition of child; competency evaluations

(a) Doubt as to child's competency (§§ 601, 602, 709)

(1) If the court finds that there is substantial evidence regarding a child who is the subject of a petition filed under section 601 or 602 that raises a doubt as to the child's competency as defined in section 709, the court must suspend the proceedings and conduct a hearing regarding the child's competency.

(2) Unless the parties have stipulated to a finding of incompetency, the court must appoint an expert to evaluate the child and determine whether the child suffers from a mental illness, mental disorder, developmental disability, developmental immaturity, or other condition affecting competency and, if so, whether the child is incompetent as defined in section 709(a)(2).

(3) Following the hearing on competency, the court must proceed as directed in section 709.

(Subd (a) adopted effective January 1, 2020.)

(b) Expert qualifications

(1) To be appointed as an expert, an individual must be a:

(A) Licensed psychiatrist who has successfully completed four years of medical school and either four years of general psychiatry residency, including one year of internship and two years of child and adolescent fellowship training, or three years of general psychiatry residency, including one year of internship and one year of residency that focus on children and adolescents and one year of child and adolescent fellowship training; or

(B) Clinical, counseling, or school psychologist who has received a doctoral degree in psychology from an educational institution accredited by an organization recognized by the Council for Higher Education Accreditation and who is licensed as a psychologist.

(2) The expert, whether a licensed psychiatrist or psychologist, must:

(A) Possess demonstrable professional experience addressing child and adolescent developmental issues, including the emotional, behavioral, and cognitive impairments of children and adolescents;

(B) Have expertise in the cultural and social characteristics of children and adolescents;

(C) Possess a curriculum vitae reflecting training and experience in the forensic evaluation of children and adolescents;

(D) Be familiar with juvenile competency standards and accepted criteria used in evaluating juvenile competence;

(E) Be familiar with effective interventions, as well as treatment, training, and programs for the attainment of competency available to children and adolescents;

(F) Be proficient in the language preferred by the child, or if that is not feasible, employ the services of a certified interpreter and use assessment tools that are linguistically and culturally appropriate for the child; and

(G) Be familiar with juvenile competency remediation services available to the child.

(3) Nothing in this rule precludes involvement of clinicians with other professional qualifications from participation as consultants or witnesses or in other capacities relevant to the case.

(Subd (b) adopted effective January 1, 2020.)

(c) Interview of child

The expert must attempt to interview the child face-to-face. If an in-person interview is not possible because the child refuses an interview, the expert must try to observe and make direct contact with the child to attempt to gain clinical observations that may inform the expert's opinion regarding the child's competency.

(Subd (c) adopted effective January 1, 2020.)

(d) Review of records

(1) The expert must review all the records provided as required by section 709.

(2) The written protocol required under section 709(i) must include a description of the process for obtaining and providing the records to the expert to review, including who will obtain and provide the records to the expert.

(Subd (d) adopted effective January 1, 2020.)

(e) Consult with the child's counsel

(1) The expert must consult with the child's counsel as required by section 709. This consultation must include, but is not limited to, asking the child's counsel the following:

(A) If the child's counsel raised the question of competency, why the child's counsel doubts that the child is competent;

(B) What has the child's counsel observed regarding the child's behavior; and

(C) A description of how the child interacts with the child's counsel.

(2) No waiver of the attorney-client privilege will be deemed to have occurred from the child's counsel report of the child's statements to the expert, and all such statements are subject to the protections in (g)(2) of this rule.

(Subd (e) adopted effective January 1, 2020.)

(f) Developmental history

The expert must gather a developmental history of the child as required by section 709. This history must be documented in the report and must include the following:

(1) Whether there were complications or drug use during pregnancy that could have caused medical issues for the child;

(2) When the child achieved developmental milestones such as talking, walking, and reading;

(3) Psychosocial factors such as abuse, neglect, or drug exposure;

(4) Adverse childhood experiences, including early disruption in the parent-child relationship;

(5) Mental health services received during childhood and adolescence;

(6) School performance, including an Individualized Education Plan, testing, achievement scores, and retention;

(7) Acculturation issues;

(8) Biological and neurological factors such as neurological deficits and head trauma; and

(9) Medical history including significant diagnoses, hospitalizations, or head trauma.

(Subd (f) adopted effective January 1, 2020.)

(g) Written report

(1) Any court-appointed expert must examine the child and advise the court on the child's competency to stand trial. The expert's report must be submitted to the court, to the counsel for the child, to the probation department, and to the prosecution. The report must include the following:

(A) A statement identifying the court referring the case, the purpose of the evaluation, and the definition of competency in the state of California.

(B) A brief statement of the expert's training and previous experience as it relates to evaluating the competence of a child to stand trial.

(C) A statement of the procedure used by the expert, including:

(i) A list of all sources of information considered by the expert including those required by section 709(b)(3);

(ii) A list of all sources of information the expert tried or wanted to obtain but, for reasons described in the report, could not be obtained;

(iii) A detailed summary of the attempts made to meet the child face to-face and a detailed account of any accommodations made to make direct contact with the child; and

(iv) All diagnostic and psychological tests administered, if any.

(D) A summary of the developmental history of the child as required by this rule.

(E) A summary of the evaluation conducted by the expert on the child, including the current diagnosis or diagnoses that meet criteria under the most recent version of the *Diagnostic and Statistical Manual of Mental Disorders*, when applicable, and a summary of the child's mental or developmental status.

(F) A detailed analysis of the competence of the child to stand trial under section 709, including the child's ability or inability to understand the nature of the proceedings or assist counsel in the conduct of a defense in a rational manner as a result of a mental or developmental impairment.

(G) An analysis of whether and how the child's mental or developmental status is related to any deficits in abilities related to competency.

(H) If the child has significant deficits in abilities related to competency, an opinion with explanation as to whether treatment is needed to restore or attain competency, the nature of that treatment, its availability, and whether restoration is likely to be accomplished within the statutory time limit.

(I) A recommendation, as appropriate, for a placement or type of placement, services, and treatment that would be most appropriate for the child to attain or restore competence. The recommendation must be guided by the principle of section 709 that services must be provided in the least restrictive environment consistent with public safety.

(J) If the expert is of the opinion that a referral to a psychiatrist is appropriate, the expert must inform the court of this opinion and recommend that a psychiatrist examine the child.

(2) Statements made to the appointed expert during the child's competency evaluation and statements made by the child to mental health professionals during the remediation proceedings, and any fruits of these statements, must not be used in any other hearing against the child in either juvenile or adult court.

(Subd (g) adopted effective January 1, 2020.)

Rule 5.645 adopted effective January 1, 2020.

2019 Note: Subdivisions (a) and (b) were derived from former rule 5.645(d).

Rule 5.647. Medi-Cal: Presumptive Transfer of Specialty Mental Health Services

(a) Applicability

This rule applies to the court's review under Welfare and Institutions Code section 14717.1 of the presumptive transfer of responsibility to arrange and provide for a child's or nonminor's specialty mental health services to the child's or nonminor's county of residence. The rule applies to presumptive transfer following any change of placement within California for a child or nonminor to a placement that is outside the county of original jurisdiction, including the initial placement. Nothing in this rule relieves the placing agency of the reporting requirements and duties under section 14717.1 when no hearing under this rule is held.

(Subd (a) adopted effective September 1, 2018.)

(b) Requesting a hearing to review the request for waiver of presumptive transfer (§ 14717.1)

(1) The following persons or agencies may make a request to the placing agency that presumptive transfer be waived and that the responsibility for providing specialty mental health services remain in the child's or nonminor's county of original jurisdiction:

(A) The foster child or nonminor;

(B) The person or agency that is responsible for making mental health care decisions on behalf of the foster child or nonminor;

(C) The child welfare services agency or the probation agency with responsibility for the care and placement of the child or nonminor; and

(D) Any other interested party who owes a legal duty to the child or nonminor involving the child's or nonminor's health or welfare, as defined by the department.

(2) The person or agency who requested the waiver, or any other party to the case who disagrees with the placing agency's determination on the request for the waiver of presumptive transfer, may request a judicial review of the placing agency's determination.

(3) A request for a hearing must be made by filing a *Request for Hearing on Waiver of Presumptive Transfer* (form JV-214). If a hearing is requested, form JV-214 must be provided to the placing agency within seven court days of the petitioner's being noticed of the placing agency's determination on the request for waiver of presumptive transfer.

(4) When a hearing is requested in (b)(3), the transfer of the responsibility for providing specialty mental health services cannot occur until the court makes a ruling as required in (c)(1).

(Subd (b) adopted effective September 1, 2018.)

(c) Setting of a hearing (§ 14717.1)

(1) The court on its own motion may direct the clerk to set a hearing no later than five court days after the request for a hearing was filed, or may deny the request for a hearing without ruling on the transfer of jurisdiction.

(2) If the court sets a hearing, the clerk must provide notice of the hearing date to:

(A) The parents—unless parental rights have been terminated—or guardians of the child;

(B) The petitioner;

(C) The social worker or probation officer;

(D) The mental health care decision maker for the child or nonminor, if one has been appointed under section 361(a)(1);

(E) The Indian child's tribe, if applicable, as defined in rule 5.502;

(F) The child—if 10 years of age or older—or nonminor; and

(G) All other persons entitled to notice under section 293 or section 727.4(a).

(3) If the court grants a hearing under (c)(1), responsibility for providing specialty mental health services cannot be transferred until the court makes a ruling as required in (e)(2) and section 14717.1(d)(4).

(Subd (c) adopted effective September 1, 2018.)

(d) Reports

When a hearing is granted under (c)(1), the social worker or probation officer must provide a report including discussion or documentation of the following:

(1) The placing agency's rationale for its decision on the request for a waiver of presumptive transfer, including:

(A) Any requests for waiver, and the exceptions claimed as the basis for those requests;

(B) The placing agency's determination of whether waiver of presumptive transfer is appropriate under section 14717.1(d)(5)(A)–(D);

(C) Any objections to the placing agency's determination in (B); and

(D) The ways that the child's or nonminor's best interests will be promoted by the placing agency's presumptive transfer determination.

(2) That the child or nonminor, his or her parents if applicable, the child and family team, and others who serve the child or nonminor as appropriate—such as the therapist, mental health care decision maker for the child or nonminor if one has been appointed under section 361(a)(1), and Court Appointed Special Advocate volunteer—were consulted regarding the waiver determination.

(3) That notice of the placing agency's determination of whether to waive presumptive transfer was provided to the individual who requested waiver of presumptive transfer, along with all parties to the case.

(4) Whether the mental health plan in the county of original jurisdiction demonstrates an existing contract with a specialty mental health care provider, or the ability to enter into a contract with a specialty mental health care provider within 30 days of the waiver decision, and the ability to deliver timely specialty mental health services directly to the foster child or nonminor.

(5) The child's or nonminor's current provision of specialty mental health services, and how those services will be affected by the placing agency's presumptive transfer determination.

(Subd (d) adopted effective September 1, 2018.)

(e) Conduct at the hearing

(1) The social worker or probation officer must provide the report in (d) to the court, all parties to the case, and the person or agency that requested the waiver no later than two court days after the hearing is set under (c)(1).

(2) At the hearing, the court may confirm or deny the transfer of jurisdiction or application of an exception based on the best interests of the child or nonminor. A waiver of presumptive transfer is contingent on the mental health plan in the county of original jurisdiction demonstrating an existing contract with a specialty mental health care provider, or the ability to enter into such a contract within 30 days of the waiver decision, and the ability to deliver timely specialty mental health services directly to the child or nonminor.

(3) The person or agency that requested the waiver of presumptive transfer bears the burden to show that an exception to presumptive transfer is in the best interests of the child or nonminor by a preponderance of the evidence.

(4) The hearing must conclude within five court days of the initial hearing date, unless a showing of good cause consistent with section 352 or section 682 supports a continuance of the hearing beyond five days.

(5) When considering whether it is in the child's or nonminor's best interests to confirm or deny the request for a waiver of presumptive transfer, the court may consider the following in addition to any other factors the court deems relevant:

(A) The child's or nonminor's access to specialty mental health services, the current provision of specialty mental health services to the child or nonminor, and whether any important service relationships will be affected by the transfer of jurisdiction or a waiver of presumptive transfer;

(B) If reunification services are being provided, the impact that the transfer of jurisdiction would have on reunification services;

(C) The anticipated length of stay in the child's or nonminor's new placement;

(D) The position of the child or nonminor, or of the child's or nonminor's attorney, on presumptive transfer; and

(E) The ability to maintain specialty mental health services in the county of original jurisdiction or to arrange for specialty mental health services in the county of residence after the child or nonminor changes placements.

(6) Findings and orders must be made on *Order after Hearing on Waiver of Presumptive Transfer* (form JV-215).

(Subd (e) adopted effective September 1, 2018.)

(f) Existing out-of-county placement

This rule applies to presumptive transfer for any child or nonminor who resided in a county other than the county of original jurisdiction after June 30, 2017, and who continues to reside outside his or her county of original jurisdiction after December 31, 2017, and has not had a presumptive transfer determination as required under Welfare and Institutions Code section 14717.1(c)(2). Unless amended by Judicial Council action effective after the effective date of this rule, this subdivision will be repealed effective January 1, 2020.

(Subd (f) adopted effective September 1, 2018.)

Rule 5.647 adopted effective September 1, 2018.

Advisory Committee Comment

The exceptions to the presumptive transfer of the responsibility to provide for and arrange for specialty mental health services to the county of the child's or nonminor's out-of-county residence are found in Welfare and Institutions Code section 14717.1(d)(5)(A–D). A court review hearing under this rule may not necessarily be common, but under section 14717.1(d)(7), for all cases, a request for waiver, the exceptions claimed as the basis for the request, a determination whether a waiver is appropriate under Welfare and Institutions Code section 14717.1, and any objections to the determination must be documented in the child's or nonminor's case plan under Welfare and Institutions Code section 16501.1. The Department of Health Care Services and California Department of Social Services are responsible for providing policy guidance and regulations to implement Assembly Bill 1299 (Ridley-Thomas; Stats. 2016, ch. 603). The policy guidance and regulations should be used during the administrative process related to presumptive transfer. This would include determining who is entitled to make a request for waiver under (b)(1)(D) of the rule and section 14717.1(d)(2), where "department" refers to the Department of Health Care Services. In the policy guidance and regulations, the Department of Health Care Services and California Department of Social Services will determine who owes a legal duty to the child or nonminor and thus may request a waiver of presumptive transfer. In addition, the policy guidance and regulations will address the timelines for the period to request a hearing. Presumptive transfer cannot occur until the court has made a ruling on the request for a hearing, and if a hearing is granted, makes a ruling as required in (c)(3). In accordance with the policy guidance issued by the Department of Health Care Services and California Department of Social Services, the delivery of existing specialty mental health services to the child or nonminor must however continue without interruption, and be provided or arranged for, and paid for by the Mental Health Plan in the county of original jurisdiction until the court makes a ruling on the request for a hearing or makes a ruling as required in (c)(3) if a hearing is granted.

Rule 5.649. Right to make educational or developmental-services decisions

The court must identify the educational rights holder for the child at each hearing in a juvenile dependency or juvenile justice proceeding. At any hearing, where the court limits, restores, or modifies educational rights, or where there are updates to any contact or other information, in any juvenile proceeding, the findings and orders must be documented on form JV-535. Unless the rights of the parent, guardian, or Indian custodian have been limited by the court under this rule, the parent, guardian, or Indian custodian holds the educational and developmental-services decisionmaking rights for the child. In addition, a nonminor or nonminor dependent youth holds the rights to make educational and developmental-services decisions for the youth and should be identified on form JV-535, unless rule 5.650(b) applies.

(a) Order (§§ 361, 366, 366.27, 366.3, 726, 727.2; 20 U.S.C. § 1415; 34 C.F.R. § 300.300)

At the dispositional hearing and each subsequent review or permanency hearing, the court must determine whether the rights of a parent, guardian, or Indian custodian to make educational or developmental-services decisions for the child should be limited.

If necessary to protect a child who is adjudged a dependent or ward of the court under section 300, 601, or 602, the court may limit the rights of a parent, guardian, or Indian custodian to make educational or developmental-services decisions for the child by making appropriate, specific orders on *Order Designating Educational Rights Holder* (form JV-535).

(Subd (a) amended effective September 1, 2020; adopted effective January 1, 2014.)

(b) Temporary order (§ 319)

At the initial hearing on a petition filed under section 325 or at any time before a child is adjudged a dependent or the petition is dismissed, the court may, on making the findings required by section 319(g)(1), use form JV-535 to temporarily limit the rights of a parent, guardian, or Indian custodian to make educational or developmental-services decisions for the child. An order made under section 319(g) expires on dismissal of the petition, but in no circumstances later than the conclusion of the hearing held under section 361.

If the court does temporarily limit the rights of a parent, guardian, or Indian custodian to make educational or developmental-services decisions, the court must, at the dispositional hearing, reconsider the need to limit those rights and must identify the authorized educational rights holder on form JV-535.

(Subd (b) amended effective September 1, 2020; adopted effective January 1, 2014.)

(c) No delay of initial assessment

The child's initial assessment to determine any need for special education or developmental services need not be delayed to obtain parental or guardian consent or for the appointment of an educational rights holder if one or more of the following circumstances is met:

(1) The court has limited, even temporarily, the educational or developmental-services decisionmaking rights of the parent, guardian, or Indian custodian, and consent for an initial assessment has been given by an individual appointed by the court to represent the child;

(2) The local educational agency or regional center, after reasonable efforts, cannot locate the parent, guardian, or Indian custodian; or

(3) Parental rights have been terminated or the guardianship has been set aside.

(Subd (c) amended September 1, 2020; adopted effective January 1, 2014.)

(d) Judicial determination

If the court determines that the child is in need of any assessments, evaluations, or services—including special education, mental health, developmental, and other related services—the court must direct an appropriate person to take the necessary steps to request those assessments, evaluations, or services.

(Subd (d) amended effective September 1, 2020; adopted effective January 1, 2014.)

(e) Filing of order

Following the dispositional hearing and each statutory review hearing, the party that has requested a modification, limitation, or restoration of educational or developmental-services decisionmaking rights must complete form JV-535 and any required attachments to reflect the court's orders and submit the completed form within five court days for the court's review and signature. If there has been no request for modification, limitation, or restoration of educational or developmental-services decisionmaking rights, or there are no required updates to contact or other information, there is no need to file a new form JV-535. If a new form JV-535 is filed, the most recent *Attachment to Order Designating Educational Rights Holder* (form JV-535(A)) must be attached. The court may instead direct the appropriate party to attach a new form JV-535(A) to document the court's findings and orders.

(Subd (e) amended effective September 1, 2020; adopted effective January 1, 2014.)

(f) Service of process

After each hearing where a party has requested a modification, limitation, or restoration of educational or developmental-services decisionmaking rights, the court clerk must serve the most current forms JV-535 and JV-535(A) on each applicable party.

(Subd (f) adopted effective September 1, 2020.)

Rule 5.649 amended effective September 1, 2020; adopted effective January 1, 2014.

Rule 5.650. Appointed educational rights holder

(a) Order and appointment (§§ 319, 361, 366, 366.27, 366.3, 726, 727.2; Gov. Code, §§ 7579.5–7579.6; 20 U.S.C. § 1415; 34 C.F.R. § 300.519)

Whenever it limits, even temporarily, the rights of a parent or guardian to make educational or developmental-services decisions for a child, the court must use form JV-535 to appoint a responsible adult as educational rights holder or to document that one of the following circumstances exists:

(1) The child is a dependent child or ward of the court and has a court-ordered permanent plan of placement in a planned permanent living arrangement. The caregiver may, without a court order, exercise educational decisionmaking rights under Education Code section 56055 and developmental-services decisionmaking rights under section 361 or 726, and is not prohibited from exercising those rights by section 361, 726, or 4701.6(b), or by 34 Code of Federal Regulations section 300.519 or 303.422; or

(2) The court cannot identify a responsible adult to serve as the child's educational rights holder under section 319, 361, or 726 or under Education Code section 56055; and

(A) The child is a dependent child or ward of the court and is or may be eligible for special education and related services or already has a valid individualized education program, and the court:

(i) Refers the child to the local educational agency for the appointment of a surrogate parent under section 361 or 726, Government Code section 7579.5, and title 20 United States Code section 1415; and

(ii) Will, with the input of any interested person, make developmental-services decisions for the child; or

(B) The appointment of a surrogate parent is not warranted, and the court will, with the input of any interested person, make educational and developmental-services decisions for the child.

(C) If the court must temporarily make educational or developmental-services decisions for a child before disposition, it must order that every effort be made to identify a responsible adult to make future educational or developmental-services decisions for the child.

(Subd (a) amended and relettered effective January 1, 2014; adopted as subd (b) effective January 1, 2004; previously amended effective January 1, 2007, and January 1, 2008.)

(b) Nonminor and nonminor dependent youth (§§ 361, 726, 366.3)

The court may, using form JV-535, appoint or continue the appointment of an educational rights holder to make educational or developmental-services decisions for a nonminor or nonminor dependent youth if:

(1) The youth has chosen not to make educational or developmental-services decisions for himself or herself or is deemed by the court to be incompetent; and

(2) With respect to developmental-services decisions, the court also finds that the appointment or continuance of a rights holder would be in the best interests of the youth.

(Subd (b) adopted effective January 1, 2014.)

(c) Limits on appointment (§§ 319, 361, 726; Ed. Code, § 56055; Gov. Code, § 7579.5(i)–(j); 34 C.F.R. §§ 300.519, 303.422)

(1) The court must determine whether a responsible adult relative, nonrelative extended family member, or other adult known to the child is available and willing to serve as the educational rights holder and, if one of those adults is available and willing to serve, should consider appointing that person before appointing or temporarily appointing a responsible adult not known to the child.

(2) The court may not appoint any individual as the educational rights holder if that person is excluded under, or would have a conflict of interest as defined by, section 361(a) or 726(c), Education Code section 56055, Government Code section 7579.5(i)–(j), 20 United States Code section 1415(b)(2), or 34 Code of Federal Regulations section 300.519 or 303.422.

(Subd (c) amended effective January 1, 2014; adopted effective January 1, 2004; previously amended effective January 1, 2007, and January 1, 2008.)

(d) Referral for appointment of surrogate parent (§§ 361, 726; Gov. Code, § 7579.5; 20 U.S.C. § 1415)

(1) If the court has limited a parent's or guardian's right to make educational decisions for a child and cannot identify a responsible adult to act as the educational rights holder, and the child is or may be eligible for special education and related services or already has an individualized education program, the court must use form JV-535 to refer the child to the responsible local educational agency for prompt appointment of a surrogate parent under Government Code section 7579.5.

(2) If the court refers a child to the local educational agency for appointment of a surrogate parent, the court must order that *Local Educational Agency Response to JV-535—Appointment of Surrogate Parent* (form JV-536) be attached to form JV-535 and served by first-class mail on the local educational agency no later than five court days from the date the order is signed.

(3) The court must direct the local educational agency that when the agency receives form JV-535 requesting prompt appointment of a surrogate parent, the agency must make reasonable efforts to identify and appoint a surrogate parent within 30 calendar days of service of the referral.

(A) Whenever the local educational agency appoints a surrogate parent for a dependent or ward under Government Code section 7579.5(a)(1), it must notify the court on form JV-536 within five court days of the appointment and, at the same time, must send copies of the notice to the child's attorney and to the social worker or probation officer identified on the form.

(B) If the local educational agency does not appoint a surrogate parent within 30 days of receipt of a judicial request, it must notify the court within the next five court days on form JV-536 of the following:

(i) Its inability to identify and appoint a surrogate parent; and

(ii) Its continuing reasonable efforts to identify and appoint a surrogate parent.

(4) Whenever a surrogate parent resigns or the local educational agency terminates the appointment of a surrogate parent, replaces a surrogate parent, or appoints another surrogate parent, it must notify the court, the child's attorney, and the social worker or probation officer on form JV-536 within five court days of the resignation, termination, replacement, or appointment. The child's attorney, the social worker, or the probation officer may request a hearing for appointment of a new educational rights holder by filing *Request for Hearing Regarding Child's Access to Services* (form JV-539) and must provide notice of the hearing as provided in (g)(2). The court may, on its own motion, direct the clerk to set a hearing.

(Subd (d) amended effective January 1, 2014; adopted as subd (b) effective July 1, 2002; previously amended and relettered effective January 1, 2004; previously amended effective January 1, 2007, and January 1, 2008.)

(e) Transfer of parent's or guardian's educational or developmental-services decisionmaking rights to educational rights holder

When the court appoints an educational rights holder after limiting a parent's or guardian's educational or developmental-services decisionmaking rights, those parental decisionmaking rights including the right to notice of educational or developmental-services meetings and activities, to participation in educational or developmental-services meetings and activities, and to decisionmaking authority regarding the child's education or developmental services, including the authority under sections 4512 and 4701.6, Education Code section 56028, 20 United States Code sections 1232g and 1401(23), and 34 Code of Federal Regulations section 300.30 are transferred to the educational rights holder unless the court specifies otherwise in its order.

(1) When returning a child to a parent or guardian, the court must consider the child's educational and developmental-services needs. The parent's or guardian's educational and developmental-services decisionmaking rights are reinstated when the court returns custody to the parent or guardian unless the court finds specifically that continued limitation of parental decisionmaking rights is necessary to protect the child.

(2) If the court appoints a guardian for the child under rule 5.735 or 5.815, all of the parent's or previous guardian's educational and developmental-services decisionmaking rights transfer to the newly appointed guardian unless the court determines that limitation of the new guardian's decisionmaking rights is necessary to protect the child.

(Subd (e) amended effective January 1, 2014; adopted effective January 1, 2004; previously amended effective January 1, 2007, and January 1, 2008.)

(f) Authority and responsibilities (§§ 317, 319, 360, 361, 635, 706.5, 726, 4514, 4646–4648, 4700–4731, 5328; Ed. Code, §§ 56055, 56340, 56345; Gov. Code, §§ 7579.5, 95014–95020; 34 C.F.R. § 300.519)

(1) The educational rights holder acts as and holds the rights of the parent or guardian with respect to all decisions regarding the child's education and developmental services, and is entitled:

(A) To access records and to authorize the disclosure of information to the same extent as a parent or guardian under the Family Educational Rights and Privacy Act (FERPA), 20 United States Code section 1232g;

(B) To be given notice of and participate in all meetings or proceedings relating to school discipline;

(C) To advocate for the interests of a child or youth with exceptional needs in matters relating to:

(i) The identification and assessment of those needs;

(ii) Instructional or service planning and program development—including the development of an individualized family service plan, an individualized educational program, an individual program plan, or the provision of other services and supports, as applicable;

(iii) Placement in the least restrictive program appropriate to the child's or youth's educational or developmental needs;

(iv) The review or revision of the individualized family service plan, the individualized education program, or the individual program plan; and

(v) The provision of a free, appropriate public education.

(D) To attend and participate in the child's or youth's individualized family service plan, individualized education program, individual program plan, and other educational or service planning meetings; to consult with persons involved in the provision of the child's or youth's education or developmental services; and to sign any written consent to educational or developmental services and plans; and

(E) Notwithstanding any other provision of law, to consent to the child's or youth's individualized family service plan, individualized education program, or individual program plan, including any related nonemergency medical services, mental health treatment services, and occupational or physical therapy services provided under sections 7570–7587 of the Government Code.

(2) The educational rights holder is responsible for investigating the child's or youth's educational and developmental-services needs, determining whether those needs are being met, and acting on behalf of the child or youth in all matters relating to the provision of educational or developmental services, as applicable, to ensure:

(A) The stability of the child's or youth's school placement. At any hearing following a change of educational placement, the educational rights holder must submit a statement to the court indicating whether the proposed change of placement is in the child's or youth's best interest and whether any efforts have been made to keep the pupil in the school of origin;

(B) Placement in the least restrictive educational program appropriate to the child's or youth's individual needs;

(C) The child's or youth's access to academic resources, services, and extracurricular and enrichment activities;

(D) The child's or youth's access to any educational and developmental services and supports needed to meet state standards for academic achievement and functional performance or, with respect to developmental services, to promote community integration, an independent, productive, and normal life, and a stable and healthy environment;

(E) The prompt and appropriate resolution of school disciplinary matters;

(F) The provision of any other elements of a free, appropriate public education; and

(G) The provision of any appropriate early intervention or developmental services required by law, including the California Early Intervention Services Act or the Lanterman Developmental Disabilities Services Act.

(3) The educational rights holder is also responsible for:

(A) Meeting with the child or youth at least once and as often as necessary to make educational or developmental-services decisions that are in the best interest of the child or youth;

(B) Being culturally sensitive to the child or youth;

(C) Complying with all federal and state confidentiality laws, including, but not limited to, sections 362.5, 827, 4514, and 5328, as well as Government Code section 7579.5(f);

(D) Participating in, and making decisions regarding, all matters affecting the child's or youth's educational or developmental-services needs—including, as applicable, the individualized family service planning process, the individualized education program planning process, the individual program planning process, the fair hearing process (including mediation and any other informal dispute resolution meetings), and as otherwise specified in the court order—in a manner consistent with the child's or youth's best interest; and

(E) Maintaining knowledge and skills that ensure adequate representation of the child's or youth's needs and interests with respect to education and developmental services.

(4) Before each statutory review hearing, the educational rights holder must do one or more of the following:

(A) Provide information and recommendations concerning the child's or youth's educational or developmental-services needs to the assigned social worker or probation officer;

(B) Make written recommendations to the court concerning the child's or youth's educational or developmental-services needs;

(C) Attend the review hearing and participate in any part of the hearing that concerns the child's or youth's education or developmental services.

(5) The educational rights holder may provide the contact information for the child's or youth's attorney to the local educational agency.

(Subd (f) amended effective January 1, 2014; adopted effective January 1, 2008.)

(g) Term of service; resignation (§§ 319, 361, 726; Gov. Code § 7579.5)

(1) An appointed educational rights holder must make educational or developmental-services decisions for the child or youth until:

(A) The dismissal of the petition or the conclusion of the dispositional hearing, if the rights holder is appointed under section 319(g);

(B) The rights of the parent or guardian to make educational or developmental-services decisions for the child are fully restored;

(C) The dependent or ward reaches 18 years of age, unless he or she chooses not to make his or her own educational or developmental-services decisions or is deemed incompetent by the court, in which case the court may, if it also finds that continuation would be in the best interests of the youth, continue the appointment until the youth reaches 21 years of age or the court's jurisdiction is terminated;

(D) The court appoints another responsible adult as educational rights holder for the child or youth under this rule;

(E) The court appoints a successor guardian or conservator; or

(F) The court designates an identified foster parent, relative caregiver, or nonrelative extended family member to make educational or developmental-services decisions because:

(i) Reunification services have been terminated and the child is placed in a planned permanent living arrangement with the identified caregiver under section 366.21(g)(5), 366.22, 366.26, 366.3(i), 727.3(b)(5), or 727.3(b)(6); and

(ii) The foster parent, relative caregiver, or nonrelative extended family member is not otherwise excluded from making education or developmental-services decisions by the court, by section 361 or 726, or by 34 Code of Federal Regulations section 300.519 or 303.422.

(2) If an appointed educational rights holder resigns his or her appointment, he or she must give notice to the court and to the child's attorney and may use *Educational Rights Holder Statement* (form JV-537)

to provide this notice. Once notice is received, the child's or youth's attorney, or the social worker or probation officer may request a hearing for appointment of a new educational rights holder by filing form JV-539.

The attorney for the party requesting the hearing must provide notice of the hearing to:

(A) The parents or guardians, unless otherwise indicated on the most recent form JV-535, parental rights have been terminated, or the child has reached 18 years of age;

(B) Each attorney of record;

(C) The social worker or probation officer;

(D) The CASA volunteer; and

(E) All other persons or entities entitled to notice under section 293.

The hearing must be set within 14 days of receipt of the request for hearing. The court may, on its own motion, direct the clerk to set a hearing.

(Subd (g) amended effective January 1, 2014; adopted effective January 1, 2008.)

(h) Service of order

Whenever the order identifies or appoints a new or different educational rights holder or includes any other changes, the clerk will provide a copy of the completed and signed form JV-535, form JV-535(A) if attached, and any received form JV-536 or JV-537 to:

(1) The child, if 10 years or older, or youth;

(2) The attorney for the child or youth;

(3) The social worker or probation officer;

(4) The Indian child's tribe, if applicable, as defined in rule 5.502;

(5) The local foster youth educational liaison, as defined in Education Code section 48853.5;

(6) The county office of education foster youth services coordinator;

(7) The regional center service coordinator, if applicable; and

(8) The educational rights holder.

The completed and signed form must be provided no later than five court days from the date the order is signed. The clerk must also ensure that any immediately preceding educational rights holder, surrogate parent, or authorized representative, if any, is notified that the previous court order has been vacated and their appointment terminated.

The clerk will make copies of the form available to the parents or guardians, unless otherwise indicated on the form, parental rights have been terminated, or the child has reached 18 years of age and reunification services have been terminated; to the CASA volunteer; and, if requested, to all other persons or entities entitled to notice under section 293.

(Subd (h) amended effective January 1, 2014; adopted effective January 1, 2008.)

(i) Education and training of educational rights holder

If the educational rights holder, including a parent or guardian, asks for assistance in obtaining education and training in the laws incorporated in rule 5.651(a), the court must direct the clerk, social worker, or probation officer to inform the educational rights holder of all available resources, including resources available through the California Department of Education, the California Department of Developmental Services, the local educational agency, and the local regional center.

(Subd (i) amended effective January 1, 2015; adopted effective January 1, 2008; previously amended effective January 1, 2014.)

(j) Notice of and participation in hearings

(1) The educational rights holder must receive notice of all regularly scheduled juvenile court hearings and other judicial hearings that might affect the child's or youth's education and developmental services, including joint assessment hearings under rule 5.512 and joinder proceedings under rule 5.575.

(2) The educational rights holder may use form JV-537 to explain any educational or developmental-services needs to the court. The court must permit the educational rights holder to attend and participate in those portions of a court hearing, nonjudicial hearing, or mediation that concern education or developmental services.

(Subd (j) amended effective January 1, 2014; adopted effective January 1, 2008.)
Rule 5.650 amended effective January 1, 2015; adopted as rule 1499 effective July 1, 2002; previously amended and renumbered effective January 1, 2007; previously amended effective January 1, 2004, January 1, 2008, and January 1, 2014.

Advisory Committee Comment

Under the Individuals With Disabilities Education Act (IDEA), the court may appoint a surrogate parent to speak and act on behalf of a pupil in all matters relating to the identification, evaluation, and educational placement of the child and to the provision of the child's free, appropriate public education. (20 U.S.C. § 1415(b)(2); 34 C.F.R. § 300.519.) Under Welfare and Institutions Code sections 361 and 726, the court must appoint a responsible adult as an educational representative or rights holder to make decisions regarding the child's educational or developmental-services needs when the parent's rights to make those decisions have been limited. A court-appointed educational rights holder is responsible for protecting the child's rights and interests with respect to educational or developmental services, including any special education and related services.

If the court limits the parent's decisionmaking rights and cannot identify a responsible adult to appoint as educational rights holder, and the appointment of a surrogate parent is not warranted, sections 361 and 726 authorize the court to make educational or developmental-services decisions for the child with the input of interested persons. If, however, the court cannot identify a responsible adult to appoint as educational rights holder and there is reason to believe that the child needs special education and related services, the court must refer the child to the local educational agency (LEA) for the appointment of a surrogate parent. Sections 361 and 726 do not authorize the court to make *educational* decisions for a child in these circumstances. The surrogate parent appointed by the LEA acts as a parent for the purpose of making decisions with respect to special education and related services and the provision of a free, appropriate public education on behalf of the child. (Gov. Code, § 7579.5(c); Ed. Code, § 56028; 34 C.F.R. § 300.30(b)(2); see 20 U.S.C. §§ 1401(9), 1414(d).) If, however, the LEA does not appoint a surrogate parent in a timely manner, the court has the authority to join the LEA in the dependency proceedings under section 362 and rule 5.575. In the period between the setting of the joinder hearing and the appointment of a surrogate parent by the LEA, the court may make educational decisions for the child under the general authority granted by section 362(a). The appointment of a surrogate parent notwithstanding, the court holds the authority under sections 361 and 726 to make *developmental-services* decisions if it cannot identify a responsible adult to do so.

Rule 5.651. Educational and developmental-services decisionmaking rights

(a) Applicability (§§ 213.5, 319(g), 358, 358.1, 361(a), 362(a), 364, 366.21, 366.22, 366.23, 366.26, 366.27(b), 366.3(e), 726, 727.2(e), 4500 et seq., 11404.1; Ed. Code, §§ 48645 et seq., 48850 et seq., 49069.5, 56028, 56055, and 56155 et seq.; Gov. Code, §§ 7573–7579.6; 20 U.S.C. § 1400 et seq.; 29 U.S.C. § 794; 42 U.S.C. § 12101 et seq.)

This rule incorporates all rights with respect to education or developmental services recognized or established by state or federal law and applies:

(1) To any child, or any nonminor or nonminor dependent youth, for whom a petition has been filed under section 300, 601, or 602 until the petition is dismissed or the court has terminated dependency, delinquency, or transition jurisdiction over that person; and

(2) To every judicial hearing related to, or that might affect, the child's or youth's education or receipt of developmental services.

(Subd (a) amended effective January 1, 2014; adopted effective January 1, 2008.)

(b) Conduct of hearings

(1) To the extent the information is available, at the initial or detention hearing the court must consider:

(A) Who holds educational and developmental-services decisionmaking rights, and identify the rights holder or holders;

(B) Whether the child or youth is enrolled in, and is attending, the child's or youth's school of origin, as that term is defined in Education Code section 48853.5(f);

(C) If the child or youth is at risk of removal from or is no longer attending the school of origin, whether:

(i) In accordance with the child's or youth's best interest, the educational liaison, as described in Education Code section 48853.5(b), (d), and (e), in consultation with, and with the agreement of, the child or youth and the parent, guardian, or other person holding educational decisionmaking rights, recommends the waiver of the child's or youth's right to attend the school of origin;

(ii) Before making any recommendation to move a foster child or youth from his or her school of origin, the educational liaison provided the child or youth and the person holding the right to make educational decisions for the child or youth with a written explanation of the basis for the recommendation and how this recommendation serves the foster child's or youth's best interest as provided in Education Code section 48853.5(e)(7);

(iii) If the child or youth is no longer attending the school of origin, the local educational agency obtained a valid waiver of the child's or youth's right to continue in the school of origin under Education Code section 48853.5(e)(1) before moving the child or youth from that school; and

(iv) The child or youth was immediately enrolled in the new school as provided in Education Code section 48853.5(e)(8).

(D) In a dependency proceeding, whether the parent's or guardian's educational or developmental-services decisionmaking rights should be temporarily limited and an educational rights holder temporarily appointed using form JV-535; and

(E) Taking into account other statutory considerations regarding placement, whether the out-of-home placement:

(i) Is the environment best suited to meet the exceptional needs of a child or youth with disabilities and to serve the child's or youth's best interest if he or she has a disability; and

(ii) Promotes educational stability through proximity to the child's or youth's school of origin.

(2) At the dispositional hearing and at all subsequent hearings described in (a)(2), the court must:

(A) Consider and determine whether the child's or youth's educational, physical, mental health, and developmental needs, including any need for special education and related services, are being met;

(B) Identify the educational rights holder on form JV-535; and

(C) Direct the rights holder to take all appropriate steps to ensure that the child's or youth's educational and developmental needs are met.

The court's findings and orders must address the following:

(D) Whether the child's or youth's educational, physical, mental health, and developmental-services needs are being met;

(E) What services, assessments, or evaluations, including those for developmental services or for special education and related services, the child or youth may need;

(F) Who must take the necessary steps for the child or youth to receive any necessary assessments, evaluations, or services;

(G) If the child's or youth's educational placement changed during the period under review, whether:

(i) The child's or youth's educational records, including any evaluations of a child or youth with a disability, were transferred to the new educational placement within two business days of the request for the child's or youth's enrollment in the new educational placement; and

(ii) The child or youth is enrolled in and attending school.

(H) Whether the parent's or guardian's educational or developmental-services decisionmaking rights should be limited or, if previously limited, whether those rights should be restored.

(i) If the court finds that the parent's or guardian's educational or developmental-services decisionmaking rights should not be limited or should be restored, the court must explain to the parent or guardian his or her rights and responsibilities in regard to the child's education and developmental services as provided in rule 5.650(e), (f), and (j); or

(ii) If the court finds that the parent's or guardian's educational or developmental-services decisionmaking rights should be or remain limited, the court must designate the holder of those rights. The court must explain to the parent or guardian why the court is limiting his or her educational or developmental-services decisionmaking rights and must explain the rights and responsibilities of the educational rights holder as provided in rule 5.650(e), (f), and (j); and

(I) Whether, in the case of a nonminor or nonminor dependent youth who has chosen not to make educational or developmental-services decisions for himself or herself or has been deemed incompetent, it is in the best interests of the youth to appoint or to continue the appointment of an educational rights holder.

(Subd (b) amended effective January 1, 2014; adopted effective January 1, 2008.)

(c) **Reports for hearings related to, or that may affect, education or developmental services**

This subdivision applies at all hearings, including dispositional and joint assessment hearings. The court must ensure that, to the extent the information was available, the social worker or the probation officer provided the following information in the report for the hearing:

(1) The child's or youth's age, behavior, educational level, and developmental status and any discrepancies between that person's age and his or her level of achievement in education or level of cognitive, physical, and emotional development;

(2) The child's or youth's educational, physical, mental health, or developmental needs;

(3) Whether the child or youth is participating in developmentally appropriate extracurricular and social activities;

(4) Whether the child or youth is attending a comprehensive, regular, public or private school;

(5) Whether the child or youth may have physical, mental, or learning-related disabilities or other characteristics indicating a need for developmental services or special education and related services as provided by state of federal law;

(6) If the child is 0 to 3 years old, whether the child may be eligible for or is already receiving early intervention services or services under the California Early Intervention Services Act (Gov. Code, § 95000 et seq.) and, if the child is already receiving services, the specific nature of those services;

(7) If the child is between 3 and 5 years old and is or may be eligible for special education and related services, whether the child is receiving the early educational opportunities provided by Education Code section 56001 and, if so, the specific nature of those opportunities;

(8) Whether the child or youth is receiving special education and related services or any other services through a current individualized education program and, if so, the specific nature of those services;

(i) A copy of the current individualized education program should be attached to the report unless disclosure would create a risk of harm. In that case, the report should explain the risk.

(9) Whether the child or youth is receiving services under section 504 of the Rehabilitation Act of 1973 (29 U.S.C. § 701 et seq.) and, if so, the specific nature of those services;

(i) A copy of any current Section 504 plan should be attached to the report unless disclosure would create a risk of harm. In that case, the report should explain the risk.

(10) Whether the child or youth is or may be eligible for developmental services or is already receiving developmental services and, if that person is already receiving services, the specific nature of those services;

(i) A copy of any current individualized family service plan or individual program plan should be attached to the report unless disclosure would create a risk of harm. In that case, the report should explain the risk.

(11) Whether the parent's or guardian's educational or developmental-services decisionmaking rights have been or should be limited or restored;

(12) If the social worker or probation officer recommends that the court limit the parent's or guardian's rights to make educational or developmental-services decisions, the reasons those rights should be limited and the actions that the parent or guardian may take to restore those rights if they are limited;

(13) If the parent's or guardian's educational or developmental-services decisionmaking rights have been limited, the identity of the designated or appointed educational rights holder or surrogate parent;

(14) Recommendations and case plan goals to meet the child's or youth's identified educational, physical, mental health, and developmental-services needs, including all related information listed in section 16010(a) as required by section 16010(b);

(15) Whether any orders to direct an appropriate person to take the necessary steps for the child to receive assessments, evaluations, or services, including those for developmental services or for special education and related services, are requested; and

(16) In the case of a joint assessment, separate statements by the child welfare department and the probation department, each addressing whether the child or youth may have a disability and whether the child or youth needs developmental services or special education and related services or qualifies for any assessment or evaluation required by state or federal law.

(Subd (c) amended effective January 1, 2014; adopted effective January 1, 2008.)

(d) **Continuance, stay, or suspension (§§ 357, 358, 702, 705)**

If the court continues the dispositional hearing under rule 5.686 or 5.782 or stays the proceedings or suspends jurisdiction under rule 5.645, the child must continue to receive all services or accommodations required by state or federal law.

(Subd (d) amended effective January 1, 2014; adopted effective January 1, 2008.)

(e) **Change of placement affecting the child's or youth's educational stability (§§ 16010, 16010.6; Ed. Code §§ 48850–48853.5)**

This subdivision applies to all changes of placement, including the initial placement and any subsequent change of placement.

(1) At any hearing to which this rule applies that follows a decision to change the child's or youth's placement to a location that could lead to removal from the school of origin, the placement agency must demonstrate that, and the court must determine whether:

(A) The social worker or probation officer notified the court, the child's or youth's attorney, and the educational rights holder or surrogate parent, no more than one court day after making the placement decision, of the proposed placement decision.

(B) If the child or youth had a disability and an active individualized education program before removal, the social worker or probation officer, at least 10 days before the change of placement, notified in writing the local educational agency that provided a special education program for the child or youth before removal and the receiving special education local plan area, as described in Government Code section 7579.1, of the impending change of placement.

(2) After receipt of the notice in (1):

(A) The child's or youth's attorney must, as appropriate, discuss the proposed placement change and its effect on the child's or youth's right to attend the school of origin with the child or youth and the person who holds educational rights. The child's or youth's attorney may request a hearing by filing form JV-539. If requesting a hearing, the attorney must:

(i) File form JV-539 no later than two court days after receipt of the notice in (1); and

(ii) Provide notice of the hearing date, which will be no later than five court days after the form was filed, to the parents or guardians, unless otherwise indicated on form JV-535, parental rights have been terminated, or the youth has reached 18 years of age and reunification services have been terminated; the social worker or probation officer; the educational rights holder or surrogate parent; the foster youth educational liaison; the Court Appointed Special Advocate (CASA) volunteer; and all other persons or entities entitled to notice under section 293.

(B) The person who holds educational rights may request a hearing by filing form JV-539 no later than two court days after receipt of the notice in (1). After receipt of the form, the clerk must notify the persons in (e)(2)(A)(ii) of the hearing date.

(C) The court on its own motion may direct the clerk to set a hearing.

(3) If removal from the school of origin is disputed, the child or youth must be allowed to remain in the school of origin pending this hearing and pending the resolution of any disagreement between the child or youth, the parent, guardian, or educational rights holder, and the local educational agency.

(4) If the court sets a hearing, the social worker or probation officer must provide a report no later than two court days after the hearing is set that includes the information required by (b)(1)(C) as well as the following:

(A) Whether the foster child or youth has been allowed to continue his or her education in the school of origin to the extent required by Education Code section 48853.5(e)(1);

(B) Whether a dispute exists regarding the request of a foster child or youth to remain in the school of origin and whether the foster child or youth has been allowed to remain in the school of origin pending resolution of the dispute;

(C) Information addressing whether the information-sharing and other requirements in section 16501.1(c)(4) and Education Code section 49069.5 have been met;

(D) Information addressing how the proposed change serves the best interest of the child or youth;

(E) The responses of the child, if over 10 years old, or youth; the child's or youth's attorney; the parent, guardian, or other educational rights holder; the foster youth educational liaison; and the child's or youth's CASA volunteer to the proposed change of placement, specifying whether each person agrees or disagrees with the proposed change and, if any person disagrees, stating the reasons; and

(F) A statement from the social worker or probation officer confirming that the child or youth has not been segregated in a separate school, or in a separate program within a school, because the child or youth is placed in foster care.

(Subd (e) amended effective January 1, 2014; adopted effective January 1, 2008.)

(f) Court review of proposed change of placement affecting the right to attend the school of origin

(1) At a hearing set under (e)(2), the court must:

(A) Determine whether the placement agency and other relevant parties and advocates have fulfilled their obligations under section 16000(b), 16010(a), and 16501.1(f)(8);

(B) Determine whether the proposed school placement meets the requirements of this rule and Education Code sections 48853.5 and 49069.5, and whether the placement is in the best interest of the child or youth;

(C) Determine what actions are necessary to ensure the protection of the child's or youth's educational and developmental-services rights; and

(D) Make any findings and orders needed to enforce those rights, which may include an order to set a hearing under section 362 to join the necessary agencies regarding provision of services, including the provision of transportation services, so that the child or youth may remain in his or her school of origin.

(2) When considering whether it is in the child's or youth's best interest to remove him or her from the school of origin, the court must consider the following:

(A) Whether the parent, guardian, or other educational rights holder believes that removal from the school of origin is in the child's or youth's best interest;

(B) How the proposed change of placement will affect the stability of the child's or youth's school placement and the child's or youth's access to academic resources, services, and extracurricular and enrichment activities;

(C) Whether the proposed school placement would allow the child or youth to be placed in the least restrictive educational program; and

(D) Whether the child or youth has the educational and developmental services and supports, including those for special education and related services, necessary to meet state academic achievement standards.

(3) The court may make its findings and orders on *Findings and Orders Regarding Transfer From School of Origin* (form JV-538).

(Subd (f) amended effective January 1, 2014; adopted effective January 1, 2008.)
Rule 5.651 amended effective January 1, 2014; adopted effective January 1, 2008.

Advisory Committee Comment

A child or youth in, or at risk of entering, foster care has a statutory right to a meaningful opportunity to meet the state's academic achievement standards. To protect this right, the juvenile court, advocates, placing agencies, care providers, educators, and service providers must work together to maintain stable school placements and ensure that the child or youth is placed in the least restrictive educational programs and has access to the academic resources, services, and extracurricular and enrichment activities that are available to other pupils. This rule, sections 362 and 727, and rule 5.575 provide procedures for coordinating the provision of services to ensure that the child's or youth's educational and developmental-services needs are met.

Congress has found that improving the educational performance of children with disabilities is an essential prerequisite to ensuring their equality of opportunity, full participation in education, and economic self-sufficiency. Children and youth in foster care are disproportionately represented in the population of pupils with disabilities and face systemic challenges to attaining self-sufficiency. Children and youth in foster care have rights arising out of federal and state law, including the IDEA, the ADA, and section 504 of the Rehabilitation Act of 1973. To comply with federal requirements regarding the identification of children and youth with disabilities and the provision of services to those children and youth who qualify, the court, parent or guardian, placing agency, attorneys, CASA volunteer, local educational agencies, and educational rights holders must affirmatively address the child's or youth's educational and developmental-services needs. The court must continually inquire about the educational and developmental-services needs of the child or youth and the progress being made to enforce any rights the child or youth has under these laws.

Rule 5.652. Access to pupil records for truancy purposes

(a) Conditions of access (Ed. Code, § 49076)

Education Code section 49076 authorizes a school district to permit access to pupil records, including accurate copies, to any judicial officer or probation officer without consent of the pupil's parent or guardian and without a court order for the purposes of:

(1) Conducting a truancy mediation program for the pupil; or

(2) Presenting evidence in a truancy proceeding under section 681(b).

(Subd (a) amended effective January 1, 2007.)

(b) Written certification

The judicial officer or probation officer may request pupil records but must certify in writing that the requested information will be used only for purposes of truancy mediation or a truancy petition. A judicial officer or probation officer must complete and file *Certified Request for Pupil Records—Truancy* (form JV-530) and serve it with *Local Educational Agency Response to JV-530* (form JV-531), by first-class mail to the local educational agency.

(Subd (b) amended effective January 1, 2007.)

(c) Local educational agency response

Form JV-531 must be completed by the local educational agency and returned to the requesting judicial officer or probation officer within 15 calendar days of receipt of the request with copies of any responsive pupil records attached. After receipt the judicial officer or probation officer must file form JV-531 and the attached pupil records in the truancy proceedings.

(1) The school district must inform by telephone or other means, or provide written notification to, the child's parent or guardian within 24 hours of the release of the information.

(2) If a parent's or guardian's educational rights have been terminated, the school must notify the child's surrogate parent, relative, or other individual responsible for the child's education.

(Subd (c) amended effective January 1, 2007.)

Rule 5.652 amended and renumbered effective January 1, 2007; adopted as rule 1499.5 effective July 1, 2002.

Chapter 11
Advocates for Parties

Rule 5.655. Program requirements for Court Appointed Special Advocate programs
Rule 5.660. Attorneys for parties (§§ 317, 317.5, 317.6, 353, 366.26, 16010.6)
Rule 5.661. Representation of the child on appeal
Rule 5.662. Child Abuse Prevention and Treatment Act (CAPTA) guardian ad litem for a child subject to a juvenile dependency petition
Rule 5.663. Responsibilities of children's counsel in delinquency proceedings (§§ 202, 265, 633, 634, 634.3, 634.6, 679, 700)
Rule 5.664. Training requirements for children's counsel in delinquency proceedings (§ 634.3)

Rule 5.655. Program requirements for Court Appointed Special Advocate programs

(a) General provisions

(1) A Court Appointed Special Advocate (CASA) program is a child advocacy program that recruits, screens, selects, trains, supervises, and supports lay volunteers for appointment by the court to help define the best interest of children and nonminors under the jurisdiction of the juvenile court, including the dependency and delinquency courts.

(2) To be authorized to serve children and nonminors in a county, the CASA program must be designated by the presiding judge of the juvenile court.

(3) A CASA program must comply with this rule to be eligible to receive Judicial Council funding.

(Subd (a) amended effective January 1, 2019; adopted effective January 1, 2005.)

(b) CASA program administration and management

(1) The court's designation of the CASA program must take the form of a memorandum of understanding (MOU) between the CASA program and the designating court.

(A) The MOU must state that the relationship between the CASA program and the designating court can be terminated for convenience by either the CASA program or the designating court.

(B) A CASA program may serve children and nonminors in more than one court if the program executes an MOU with each court.

(C) The CASA program and the designating court must be the only parties to the MOU.

(D) The MOU must indicate when and how the CASA program will have access to the juvenile case file and the nonminor dependent court file if applicable.

(2) A CASA program must function as a nonprofit organization or under the auspices of a public agency or nonprofit organization, and must adopt and adhere to a written plan for program governance and evaluation. The plan must include the following, as applicable:

(A) Articles of incorporation, a board of directors, and bylaws that specify a clear administrative relationship with the parent organization and clearly delineated delegations of authority and accountability.

(B) A clear statement of the purpose or mission of the CASA program that express goals and objectives to further that purpose. Where the CASA program is not an independent organization, but instead functions under the auspices of a public agency or a nonprofit organization, an active advisory council must be established. The role of the advisory council for CASA programs functioning under the auspices of a public agency or a nonprofit organization includes but is not limited to developing and approving policies for CASA, developing the CASA program's budget, promoting a collaborative relationship with the umbrella organization, monitoring and evaluating program operations, and developing and implementing fundraising activities to benefit the CASA program. The board of directors for the nonprofit organization or management of the public agency will function as the governing body for the CASA program, with guidance from the advisory council.

(C) A procedure for the recruitment, selection, hiring, and evaluation of an executive director for the CASA program.

(D) An administrative manual containing personnel policies, recordkeeping practices, and data collection practices.

(E) Local juvenile court rules developed in consultation with the presiding judge of the juvenile court or a designee, as specified in section 100. One local rule must specify when CASA reports are to be submitted to the court, who is entitled to receive a copy of the report, and who will copy and distribute the report. This rule must also specify that the CASA court report must be distributed to the persons entitled to receive it at least two court days before the hearing for which the report was prepared.

(3) No CASA program may function under the auspices of a probation department or department of social services. CASA programs may receive funds from probation departments, local child welfare agencies, and the California Department of Social Services if:

(A) The CASA program and the contributing agency develop an MOU stating that the funds will be used only for general operating expenses as determined by the receiving CASA program, and the contributing agency will not oversee or monitor the funds;

(B) A procedure resolving any conflict between the CASA program and contributing agency is implemented so that conflict between the two agencies does not affect funding or the CASA program's ability to retain an independent evaluation separate from that of the contributing agency's; and

(C) Any MOU between a CASA program and the contributing agency is submitted to and approved by Judicial Council staff.

(4) If a CASA program serves more than one county, the CASA program is encouraged to seek representation on the board of directors and/or advisory council from each county it serves.

(Subd (b) repealed and adopted effective January 1, 2019.)

(c) Finance, facility, and risk management

(1) A CASA program must adopt a written plan for fiscal control. The fiscal plan must include an annual audit, conducted by a qualified professional, that is consistent with generally accepted accounting principles and the audit protocols in the program's Judicial Council contract.

(2) The fiscal plan must include a written budget with projections that guide the management of financial resources and a strategy for obtaining necessary funding for program operations.

(3) When the program has accounting oversight, it must adhere to written operational procedures in regard to accounting control.

(4) The CASA program's board of directors must set policies for and exercise control over fundraising activities carried out by its employees and volunteers.

(5) The CASA program must have the following insurance coverage for its staff and volunteers:

(A) General liability insurance with liability limits of not less than $1million ($1,000,000) for each person per occurrence/aggregate for bodily injury, and not less than $1million ($1,000,000) per occurrence/aggregate for property damage;

(B) Nonowned automobile liability insurance and hired vehicle coverage with liability limits of not less than $1million ($1,000,000) combined single limit per occurrence and in the aggregate;

(C) Automobile liability insurance meeting the minimum state automobile liability insurance requirements, if the program owns a vehicle; and

(D) Workers' compensation insurance with a minimum limit of $500,000.

(6) The CASA program must require staff, volunteers, and members of the governing body, when applicable, to immediately notify the CASA program of any criminal charges against themselves.

(7) The nonprofit CASA program must plan for the disposition of property and confidential records in the event of its dissolution.

(Subd (c) adopted effective January 1, 2019.)

(d) Confidentiality

The presiding juvenile court judge and the CASA program director must adopt a written plan governing confidentiality of case information, case records, and personnel records. The plan must be included in the MOU or a local rule. The written plan must include the following provisions:

(1) All information concerning children and families, including nonminors, in the juvenile court process is confidential. Volunteers must

not give case information to anyone other than the court, the parties and their attorneys, and CASA staff.

(2) CASA volunteers are required by law (Pen. Code, § 11166 et seq.) to report any reasonable suspicion that a child is a victim of child abuse or serious neglect as described by Penal Code section 273a.

(3) The child's original case file must be maintained in the CASA office by a custodian of records and must remain there. Copies of documents needed by a volunteer must be restricted to those actually needed to conduct necessary business outside of the office. No one may have access to the child's original case file except on the approval of the CASA program director or presiding judge of the juvenile court. Controls must be in place to ensure that records can be located at any time. The office must establish a written procedure for the maintenance of case files.

(4) If the nonminor provides consent for the CASA volunteer to obtain his or her nonminor dependent court file, the procedures stated in paragraph (3) related to maintenance of the case file must be followed.

(5) The volunteer's personnel file is confidential. No one may have access to the personnel file except the volunteer, the CASA program director or a designee, or the presiding judge of the juvenile court.

(Subd (d) adopted effective January 1, 2019.)

(e) Recruiting, screening, and selecting CASA volunteers

(1) A CASA volunteer is a person who has been recruited, screened, selected, and trained; is being supervised and supported by a local CASA program; and has been appointed by the juvenile court as a sworn officer of the court to help define the best interest of children or nonminors in juvenile court dependency and wardship proceedings.

(2) A CASA program must adopt and adhere to a written plan for the recruitment of potential CASA volunteers. The program staff, in its recruitment effort, must address the demographics of the jurisdiction by making all reasonable efforts to ensure that individuals representing all racial, ethnic, linguistic, and economic sectors of the community are recruited and made available for appointment as CASA volunteers.

(3) A CASA program must adopt and adhere to the following minimum written procedures for screening potential CASA volunteers under section 102(e):

(A) A written application that generates minimum identifying data; information regarding the applicant's education, training, and experience; minimum age requirements; and current and past employment.

(B) Notice to the applicant that a formal security check will be made, including inquiries through appropriate law enforcement agencies—including but not limited to the Department of Justice, Federal Bureau of Investigations, and Child Abuse Index—regarding any criminal record, driving record, or other record of conduct that would disqualify the applicant from service as a CASA volunteer. The security check must include fingerprinting. Refusal to consent to a formal security check is grounds for rejecting an applicant.

(C) A minimum of three completed references regarding the character, competence, and reliability of the applicant and his or her suitability for assuming the role of a CASA volunteer.

(4) If a CASA program allows its volunteers to transport children, the program must ensure that each volunteer transporting children:

(A) Possesses a valid and current driver's license;

(B) Possesses personal automobile insurance that meets the minimum state personal automobile insurance requirements;

(C) Obtains permission from the child's guardian or custodial agency; and

(D) Provides the CASA program with a Department of Motor Vehicles driving record report annually.

(5) A CASA program must adopt a written preliminary procedure for selecting CASA candidates to enter the CASA training program. The selection procedure must state that any applicant found to have been convicted of or to have current charges pending for a felony or misdemeanor involving a sex offense, child abuse, or child neglect must not be accepted as a CASA volunteer. This policy must be stated on the volunteer application form.

(6) An adult otherwise qualified to act as a CASA must not be discriminated against based on marital status, socioeconomic factors, race, national origin, ethnic group identification, religion, age, sex, sexual orientation, color, or disability or because of any other characteristic listed or defined in Government Code section 11135 or Welfare and Institutions Code section 103.

(Subd (e) amended and relettered effective January 1, 2019; adopted as subd (b) effective July 1, 1994; previously amended and relettered as subd (c) effective January 1, 2005; previously amended effective January 1, 1995, January 1, 2007, and January 1, 2010.)

(f) Initial training of CASA volunteers (§ 102(d))

A CASA program must adopt and adhere to a written plan for the initial training of CASA volunteers.

(1) The initial training curriculum must include at least 30 hours of formal instruction. This curriculum must include mandatory training topics as listed in section 102(d). The curriculum may also include additional appropriate topics, such as those stated in California Rules of Court, rule 5.664.

(2) The final selection process is contingent on the successful completion of the initial training program, as determined by the presiding judge of the juvenile court or designee.

(Subd (f) amended and relettered effective January 1, 2019; adopted as subd (c) effective July 1, 1994; previously amended and relettered as subd (d) effective January 1, 2005; previously amended effective January 1, 1995, and January 1, 2007.)

(g) Oath

At the completion of training, and before assignment to any child or nonminor's case, the CASA volunteer must take a court-administered oath describing the duties and responsibilities of the advocate under section 103(f). The CASA volunteer must also sign a written affirmation of that oath. The signed affirmation must be retained in the volunteer's file.

(Subd (g) amended and relettered effective January 1, 2019; adopted as subd (d) effective July 1, 1994; previously amended and relettered to subd (e) effective January 1, 2005; previously amended effective January 1, 2007.)

(h) Duties and responsibilities

CASA volunteers serve at the discretion of the court having jurisdiction over the proceeding in which the volunteer has been appointed. A CASA volunteer is an officer of the court and is bound by all court rules under section 103(e). A CASA program must develop and adopt a written description of duties and responsibilities, consistent with local court rules.

(Subd (h) amended and relettered effective January 1, 2019; adopted as subd (e) effective July 1, 1994; previously amended and relettered as subd (f) effective January 1, 2005; previously amended effective January 1, 1995, and January 1, 2007.)

(i) Prohibited activities

A CASA program must develop and adopt a written description of activities that are prohibited for CASA volunteers. The specified prohibited activities must include:

(1) Taking a child or nonminor to the CASA volunteer's home;

(2) Giving legal advice or therapeutic counseling;

(3) Giving money or expensive gifts to the child, nonminor, or family of the child or nonminor;

(4) Being related to any parties involved in a case or being employed in a position and/or agency that might result in a conflict of interest; and

(5) Any other activities prohibited by the local juvenile court.

(Subd (i) amended and relettered effective January 1, 2019; adopted as subd (g) effective January 1, 2005.)

(j) The appointment of CASA volunteers

The CASA program director must develop, with the approval of the presiding juvenile court judge, a written procedure for the selection of cases and the appointment of CASA volunteers for children and nonminors in juvenile court proceedings.

(Subd (j) amended and relettered effective January 1, 2019; adopted as subd (f) effective July 1, 1994; previously amended effective January 1, 1995; previously amended and relettered as subd (h) effective January 1, 2005.)

(k) Oversight, support, and supervision of CASA volunteers

A CASA program must adopt and adhere to a written plan, approved by the presiding juvenile court judge, for the oversight, support, and supervision of CASA volunteers in the performance of their duties. The plan must:

(1) Include a grievance procedure that covers grievances by any person against a volunteer or CASA program staff and grievances by a volunteer against a CASA program or program staff. The grievance procedure must:

(A) Be incorporated into a document that contains a description of the roles and responsibilities of CASA volunteers. This document must be provided:

(i) When a copy of the court order that appointed the CASA volunteer is provided to any adult involved with the child's or nonminor's case, including but not limited to teachers, foster parents, therapists, and health-care workers;

(ii) To the nonminor upon appointment of the CASA; and

(iii) To any person, including a volunteer, who has a grievance against a volunteer or a CASA program employee.

(B) Include a provision that documentation of any grievance filed by or against a volunteer must be retained in the volunteer's personnel file.

(2) Include a provision for the ongoing training and continuing education of CASA volunteers. Ongoing training opportunities must be provided at least monthly under section 103(a). CASA volunteers must participate in a minimum of 12 hours of continuing education in each year of service.

(Subd (k) repealed, amended and relettered effective January 1, 2019; adopted as subd (g) effective July 1, 1994; previously amended and relettered as subd (i) effective January 1, 2005; previously amended effective January 1, 1995, and January 1, 2007.)

(*l*) Removal, resignation, and termination of a CASA volunteer

The CASA program must adopt a written plan for the removal, resignation, or involuntary termination of a CASA volunteer, including the following provisions:

(1) A volunteer may resign or be removed from an individual case at any time by the order of the juvenile court presiding judge or designee.

(2) A volunteer may be involuntarily terminated from the program by the program director.

(3) The volunteer has the right to appeal termination by the program director under the program's grievance procedure.

(Subd (l) repealed and relettered effective January 1, 2019; adopted as subd (h) effective July 1, 1994; previously amended and relettered as subd (j) effective January 1, 2005; previously amended effective January 1, 1995, and January 1, 2007.)

Rule 5.655 amended effective January 1, 2019; adopted as rule 1424 effective July 1, 1994; previously amended and renumbered as rule 5.655 effective January 1, 2007; previously amended effective January 1, 1995, January 1, 2000, January 1, 2001, January 1, 2005, January 1, 2010, and January 1, 2016.

Advisory Committee Comment

These 1995 guidelines implement the requirements of section 100, which establishes a grant program administered by the Judicial Council to establish or expand CASA programs to assist children involved in juvenile dependency proceedings, including guardianships, adoptions, and actions to terminate parental rights to custody and control.

CASA programs provide substantial benefits to children appearing in dependency proceedings and to the juvenile court having responsibility for these children. Child advocates improve the quality of judicial decision making by providing information to the court concerning the child. Advocates help identify needed services for the children they are assisting and provide a consistent friend and support person for children throughout the long and complex dependency process.

The CASA concept was first implemented in Seattle in 1977. As of 1994, there were more than 30,000 volunteers working in more than 525 CASA programs in nearly every state. The programs recruit, screen, select, train, and supervise lay volunteers to become effective advocates in the juvenile court.

Currently, numerous jurisdictions in California use some variation of the CASA concept. These programs have developed over the past several years under the supervision of local juvenile courts under sections 356.5 and 358. Each program is unique and was designed to respond to the specific needs of the local jurisdiction and community it serves.

These guidelines provide a framework for ensuring the excellence of California CASA programs and volunteers. They are intended to be consistent with the guidelines established by the National CASA Association and to conform with the requirements of California law and procedure. The California CASA Association has assisted in developing these guidelines, which are meant to give the local bench, bar, child welfare professionals, children's advocates, and other interested citizens full rein to adapt the CASA concept to the special needs and circumstances of local communities.

Central to the intent of these guidelines is the effort to provide a vehicle for the presiding judge of the local juvenile court to exercise fully informed and effective oversight of the local CASA program and CASA volunteers. These guidelines are also intended to help CASA programs and juvenile courts develop local court rules. Nothing in these guidelines should limit or restrict the local juvenile court from developing and supporting multiple branches of a CASA program within the community to enable a county to offer comprehensive volunteer advocacy programs for children.

Rule 5.660. Attorneys for parties (§§ 317, 317.5, 317.6, 353, 366.26, 16010.6)

(a) Local rules

On or before January 1, 2002, the superior court of each county must amend its local rules regarding the representation of parties in dependency proceedings.

(1) The local rules must be amended after consultation by the court with representatives of the State Bar of California; local offices of the county counsel, district attorney, public defender, and other attorneys appointed to represent parties in these proceedings; county welfare departments; child advocates; current or recent foster youth; and others selected by the court in accordance with standard 5.40(c) of the Standards of Judicial Administration.

(2) The amended rules must address the following as needed:

(A) Representation of children in accordance with other sections of this rule;

(B) Timelines and procedures for settlements, mediation, discovery, protocols, and other issues related to contested matters;

(C) Procedures for the screening, training, and appointment of attorneys representing parties, with particular attention to the training requirements for attorneys representing children;

(D) Establishment of minimum standards of experience, training, and education of attorneys representing parties, including additional training and education in the areas of substance abuse and domestic violence as required;

(E) Establishment of procedures to determine appropriate caseloads for attorneys representing children;

(F) Procedures for reviewing and resolving complaints by parties regarding the performance of attorneys;

(G) Procedures for informing the court of interests of the dependent child requiring further investigation, intervention, or litigation; and

(H) Procedures for appointment of a Child Abuse Prevention and Treatment Act (CAPTA) guardian ad litem, who may be an attorney or a CASA volunteer, in cases in which a prosecution is initiated under the Penal Code arising from neglect or abuse of the child.

(3) Appropriate local forms may be used.

(Subd (a) amended effective January 1, 2007; previously amended effective July 1, 2001, and January 1, 2003.)

(b) Attorneys for children

The court must appoint counsel for a child who is the subject of a petition under section 300 and is unrepresented by counsel, unless the court finds that the child would not benefit from the appointment of counsel.

(1) In order to find that a child would not benefit from the appointment of counsel, the court must find all of the following:

(A) The child understands the nature of the proceedings;

(B) The child is able to communicate and advocate effectively with the court, other counsel, other parties, including social workers, and other professionals involved in the case; and

(C) Under the circumstances of the case, the child would not gain any benefit by being represented by counsel.

(2) If the court finds that the child would not benefit from representation by counsel, the court must make a finding on the record as to each of the criteria in (1) and state the reasons for each finding.

(3) If the court finds that the child would not benefit from representation by counsel, the court must appoint a CASA volunteer for the child, to serve as the CAPTA guardian ad litem, as required in section 326.5.

(Subd (b) amended effective January 1, 2007; adopted effective July 1, 2001; previously amended effective January 1, 2003.)

(c) Conflict of interest guidelines for attorneys representing siblings

(1) *Appointment*

(A) The court may appoint a single attorney to represent a group of siblings involved in the same dependency proceeding.

(B) An attorney must decline to represent one or more siblings in a dependency proceeding, and the court must appoint a separate attorney to represent the sibling or siblings, if, at the outset of the proceedings:

(i) An actual conflict of interest exists among those siblings; or

(ii) Circumstances specific to the case present a reasonable likelihood that an actual conflict of interest will arise among those siblings.

(C) The following circumstances, standing alone, do not necessarily demonstrate an actual conflict of interest or a reasonable likelihood that an actual conflict of interest will arise:

(i) The siblings are of different ages;

(ii) The siblings have different parents;

(iii) There is a purely theoretical or abstract conflict of interest among the siblings;

(iv) Some of the siblings appear more likely than others to be adoptable; or

(v) The siblings may have different permanent plans.

(2) *Withdrawal from appointment or continued representation*

(A) An attorney representing a group of siblings has an ongoing duty to evaluate the interests of each sibling and assess whether there is an actual conflict of interest.

(B) The following circumstances, standing alone, do not necessarily demonstrate an actual conflict of interest:

(i) The siblings are of different ages;

(ii) The siblings have different parents;

(iii) There is a purely theoretical or abstract conflict of interest among the siblings;

(iv) Some of the siblings are more likely to be adopted than others;

(v) The siblings have different permanent plans;

(vi) The siblings express conflicting desires or objectives, but the issues involved are not material to the case; or

(vii) The siblings give different or contradictory accounts of the events, but the issues involved are not material to the case.

(C) It is not necessary for an attorney to withdraw from representing some or all of the siblings if there is merely a reasonable likelihood that an actual conflict of interest will develop.

(D) If an attorney believes that an actual conflict of interest existed at appointment or developed during representation, the attorney must take any action necessary to ensure that the siblings' interests are not prejudiced, including:

(i) Notifying the juvenile court of the existence of an actual conflict of interest among some or all of the siblings; and

(ii) Requesting to withdraw from representation of some or all of the siblings.

(E) If the court determines that an actual conflict of interest exists, the court must relieve an attorney from representation of some or all of the siblings.

(F) After an actual conflict of interest arises, the attorney may continue to represent one or more siblings whose interests do not conflict only if:

(i) The attorney has successfully withdrawn from the representation of all siblings whose interests conflict with those of the sibling or siblings the attorney continues to represent;

(ii) The attorney has exchanged no confidential information with any sibling whose interest conflicts with those of the sibling or siblings the attorney continues to represent; and

(iii) Continued representation of one or more siblings would not otherwise prejudice the other sibling or siblings.

(Subd (c) amended effective January 1, 2007; adopted effective January 1, 2006.)

(d) Competent counsel

Every party in a dependency proceeding who is represented by an attorney is entitled to competent counsel.

(1) *Definition*

"Competent counsel" means an attorney who is a member in good standing of the State Bar of California, who has participated in training in the law of juvenile dependency, and who demonstrates adequate forensic skills, knowledge and comprehension of the statutory scheme, the purposes and goals of dependency proceedings, the specific statutes, rules of court, and cases relevant to such proceedings, and procedures for filing petitions for extraordinary writs.

(2) *Evidence of competency*

The court may require evidence of the competency of any attorney appointed to represent a party in a dependency proceeding.

(3) *Experience and education*

(A) Only those attorneys who have completed a minimum of eight hours of training or education in the area of juvenile dependency, or who have sufficient recent experience in dependency proceedings in which the attorney has demonstrated competency, may be appointed to represent parties. Attorney training must include:

(i) An overview of dependency law and related statutes and cases;

(ii) Information on child development, child abuse and neglect, substance abuse, domestic violence, family reunification and preservation, and reasonable efforts; and

(iii) For any attorney appointed to represent a child, instruction on cultural competency and sensitivity relating to, and best practices for, providing adequate care to lesbian, gay, bisexual, and transgender youth in out-of-home placement.

(B) Within every three years, attorneys must complete at least eight hours of continuing education related to dependency proceedings.

(4) *Standards of representation*

Attorneys or their agents are expected to meet regularly with clients, including clients who are children, regardless of the age of the child or the child's ability to communicate verbally, to contact social workers and other professionals associated with the client's case, to work with other counsel and the court to resolve disputed aspects of a case without contested hearing, and to adhere to the mandated timelines. The attorney for the child must have sufficient contact with the child to establish and maintain an adequate and professional attorney-client relationship. The attorney for the child is not required to assume the responsibilities of a social worker and is not expected to perform services for the child that are unrelated to the child's legal representation.

(5) *Attorney contact information*

The attorney for a child for whom a dependency petition has been filed must provide his or her contact information to the child's caregiver no later than 10 days after receipt of the name, address, and telephone number of the child's caregiver. If the child is 10 years of age or older, the attorney must also provide his or her contact information to the child for whom a dependency petition has been filed no later than 10 days after receipt of the caregiver's contact information. The attorney may give contact information to a child for whom a dependency petition has been filed who is under 10 years of age. At least once a year, if the list of educational liaisons is available online from the California Department of Education, the child's attorney must provide, in any manner permitted by section 317(e)(4), his or her contact information to the educational liaison of each local educational agency serving the attorney's clients in foster care in the county of jurisdiction.

(6) *Caseloads for children's attorneys*

The attorney for a child must have a caseload that allows the attorney to perform the duties required by section 317(e) and this rule, and to otherwise adequately counsel and represent the child. To enhance the quality of representation afforded to children, attorneys appointed under this rule must not maintain a maximum full-time caseload that is greater than that which allows them to meet the requirements stated in (3), (4), and (5).

(Subd (d) amended effective January 1, 2015; adopted as subd (b) effective January 1, 1996; amended and relettered as subd (c) effective July 1, 2001; previously relettered effective January 1, 2006; previously amended effective July 1, 1999, January 1, 2005, January 1, 2007, and January 1, 2014.)

(e) Client complaints

The court must establish a process for the review and resolution of complaints or questions by a party regarding the performance of an appointed attorney. Each party must be informed of the procedure for lodging the complaint. If it is determined that an appointed attorney has acted improperly or contrary to the rules or policies of the court, the court must take appropriate action.

(Subd (e) relettered effective January 1, 2006; adopted as subd (c) effective January 1, 1996; previously amended and relettered as subd (d) effective July 1, 2001.)

(f) CASA volunteer as CAPTA guardian ad litem (§ 326.5)

If the court makes the findings as outlined in (b) and does not appoint an attorney to represent the child, the court must appoint a CASA volunteer as the CAPTA guardian ad litem of the child.

(1) The required training of CASA volunteers is stated in rule 5.655.

(2) The caseload of a CASA volunteer acting as a CAPTA guardian ad litem must be limited to 10 cases. A case may include siblings, absent a conflict.

(3) CASA volunteers must not assume the responsibilities of attorneys for children.

(4) The appointment of an attorney to represent the child does not prevent the appointment of a CASA volunteer for that child, and courts are encouraged to appoint both an attorney and a CASA volunteer for the child in as many cases as possible.

(Subd (f) amended effective January 1, 2007; adopted as subd (e) effective July 1, 2001; previously amended effective January 1, 2003; previously relettered effective January 1, 2006.)

(g) Interests of the child

At any time following the filing of a petition under section 300 and until juvenile court jurisdiction is terminated, any interested person may advise the court of information regarding an interest or right of the child to be protected or pursued in other judicial or administrative forums.

(1) *Juvenile Dependency Petition (Version One)* (form JV-100) and *Request to Change Court Order* (form JV-180) may be used.

(2) If the attorney for the child, or a CASA volunteer acting as a CAPTA guardian ad litem, learns of any such interest or right, the attorney or CASA volunteer must notify the court immediately and seek instructions from the court as to any appropriate procedures to follow.

(3) If the court determines that further action on behalf of the child is required to protect or pursue any interests or rights, the court must appoint an attorney for the child, if the child is not already represented by counsel, and do one or all of the following:

(A) Refer the matter to the appropriate agency for further investigation and require a report to the court within a reasonable time;

(B) Authorize and direct the child's attorney to initiate and pursue appropriate action;

(C) Appoint a guardian ad litem for the child. The guardian may be the CASA volunteer already appointed as a CAPTA guardian ad litem or a person who will act only if required to initiate appropriate action; or

(D) Take any other action to protect or pursue the interests and rights of the child.

(Subd (g) amended effective January 1, 2007; adopted as subd (d) effective January 1, 1996; previously amended and relettered as subd (f) effective July 1, 2001; amended effective January 1, 2003; previously relettered effective January 1, 2006.)

Rule 5.660 amended effective January 1, 2015; adopted as rule 1438 effective January 1, 1996; previously amended and renumbered effective January 1, 2007; previously amended effectively July 1, 1999, July 1, 2001, January 1, 2003, January 1, 2005, January 1, 2006, and January 1, 2014.

Advisory Committee Comment

The court should initially appoint a single attorney to represent all siblings in a dependency matter unless there is an actual conflict of interest or a reasonable likelihood that an actual conflict of interest will arise. (*In re Celine R.* (2003) 31 Cal.4th 45, 58.) After the initial appointment, the court should relieve an attorney from representation of multiple siblings only if an actual conflict of interest arises. (*Ibid.*) Attorneys have a duty to use their best judgment in analyzing whether, under the particular facts of the case, it is necessary to decline appointment or request withdrawal from appointment due to a purported conflict of interest.

Nothing in this rule is intended to extend the permissible scope of any judicial inquiry into an attorney's reasons for declining to represent one or more siblings or requesting to withdraw from representation of one or more siblings, due to an actual or reasonably likely conflict of interest. (See State Bar Rules Prof. Conduct, rule 3-310(C).) While the court has the duty and authority to inquire as to the general nature of an asserted conflict of interest, it cannot require an attorney to disclose any privileged communication, even if such information forms the basis of the alleged conflict. (*In re James S.* (1991) 227 Cal.App.3d 930, 934; *Aceves v. Superior Court* (1996) 51 Cal.App.4th 584, 592–593.)

Rule 5.661. Representation of the child on appeal

(a) Definition

For purposes of this rule, "guardian ad litem" means a person designated as the child's Child Abuse Prevention and Treatment Act (CAPTA) guardian ad litem as defined in rule 5.662.

(Subd (a) adopted effective July 1, 2007.)

(b) Child as appellant

A notice of appeal on behalf of the child must be filed by the child's trial counsel, guardian ad litem, or the child if the child is seeking appellate relief from the trial court's judgment or order.

(Subd (b) adopted effective July 1, 2007.)

(c) Recommendation from child's trial counsel or guardian ad litem

(1) In any juvenile dependency proceeding in which a party other than the child files a notice of appeal, if the child's trial counsel or guardian ad litem concludes that, for purposes of the appeal, the child's best interests cannot be protected without the appointment of separate counsel on appeal, the child's trial counsel or guardian ad litem must file a recommendation in the Court of Appeal requesting appointment of separate counsel.

(2) A child's trial counsel or guardian ad litem who recommends appointment of appellate counsel for a child who is not an appellant must follow the procedures outlined in (d)–(g).

(Subd (c) adopted effective July 1, 2007.)

(d) Time for trial counsel or guardian ad litem to file the recommendation with the Court of Appeal

A recommendation from the child's trial counsel or guardian ad litem may be filed at any time after a notice of appeal has been filed, but absent good cause, must be filed in the Court of Appeal no later than 20 calendar days after the filing of the last appellant's opening brief.

(Subd (d) adopted effective July 1, 2007.)

(e) Service of recommendation

The child's trial counsel or guardian ad litem must serve a copy of the recommendation filed in the Court of Appeal on the district appellate project and the trial court.

(Subd (e) amended effective January 1, 2015; adopted effective July 1, 2007.)

(f) Factors to be considered

The following are factors to be considered by a child's trial counsel or guardian ad litem in making a recommendation to the Court of Appeal:

(1) An actual or potential conflict exists between the interests of the child and the interests of any respondent;

(2) The child did not have an attorney serving as his or her guardian ad litem in the trial court;

(3) The child is of a sufficient age or development such that he or she is able to understand the nature of the proceedings and,

(A) The child expresses a desire to participate in the appeal, or

(B) The child's wishes differ from his or her trial counsel's position;

(4) The child took a legal position in the trial court adverse to that of one of his or her siblings, and an issue has been raised in an appellant's opening brief regarding the siblings' adverse positions;

(5) The appeal involves a legal issue regarding a determination of parentage, the child's inheritance rights, educational rights, privileges identified in division 8 of the Evidence Code, consent to treatment, or tribal membership;

(6) Postjudgment evidence completely undermines the legal underpinnings of the juvenile court's judgment under review, and all parties recognize this and express a willingness to stipulate to reversal of the juvenile court's judgment;

(7) The child's trial counsel or guardian ad litem, after reviewing the appellate briefs, believes that the legal arguments contained in the respondents' briefs do not adequately represent or protect the best interests of the child; and

(8) The existence of any other factors relevant to the child's best interests.

(Subd (f) adopted effective July 1, 2007.)

(g) Form of recommendation

The child's trial counsel, the guardian ad litem, or the child may use *Recommendation for Appointment of Appellate Attorney for Child* (form JV-810). Any recommendation for an appellate attorney for the child must state a factual basis for the recommendation, include the information provided on form JV-810, and be signed under penalty of perjury.

(Subd (g) adopted effective July 1, 2007.)

Rule 5.661 amended effective January 1, 2015; adopted effective July 1, 2007.

Advisory Committee Comment

Generally, separate counsel for a nonappealing child will not be appointed for the purpose of introducing postjudgment evidence. See California Code Civ. Proc., § 909; *In re Zeth S.* (2003) 31 Cal.4th 396; *In re Josiah Z.* (2005) 36 Cal.4th 664. For further discussion, see *In re Mary C.* (1995) 41 Cal.App.4th 71.

Rule 5.662. Child Abuse Prevention and Treatment Act (CAPTA) guardian ad litem for a child subject to a juvenile dependency petition

(a) Authority

This rule is adopted under section 326.5.

(Subd (a) amended effective January 1, 2007.)

(b) Applicability

The definition of the role and responsibilities of a CAPTA guardian ad litem in this rule applies exclusively to juvenile dependency proceedings and is distinct from the definitions of guardian ad litem in all other juvenile, civil, and criminal proceedings. No limitation period for bringing an action based on an injury to the child commences running solely by reason of the appointment of a CAPTA guardian ad litem under section 326.5 and this rule.

(Subd (b) amended effective January 1, 2007.)

(c) Appointment

A CAPTA guardian ad litem must be appointed for every child who is the subject of a juvenile dependency petition under section 300. An attorney appointed under rule 5.660 will serve as the child's CAPTA guardian ad litem under section 326.5. If the court finds that the child would not benefit from the appointment of counsel, the court must appoint a CASA volunteer to serve as the child's CAPTA guardian ad litem. The court must identify on the record the person appointed as the child's CAPTA guardian ad litem.

(Subd (c) amended effective January 1, 2007.)

(d) General duties and responsibilities

The general duties and responsibilities of a CAPTA guardian ad litem are:

(1) To obtain firsthand a clear understanding of the situation and needs of the child; and

(2) To make recommendations to the court concerning the best interest of the child as appropriate under (e) and (f).

(e) Attorney as guardian ad litem

The specific duties and responsibilities of the child's court-appointed attorney who is appointed to serve as the child's CAPTA guardian ad litem are stated in section 317(e) and rule 5.660.

(Subd (e) amended effective January 1, 2007.)

(f) CASA volunteer as CAPTA guardian ad litem

The specific duties and responsibilities of the child's CASA volunteer who is appointed to serve as the child's CAPTA guardian ad litem are stated in section 102(c) and rule 5.655.

(Subd (f) amended effective January 1, 2007.)

Rule 5.662 amended and renumbered effective January 1, 2007; adopted as rule 1448 effective January 1, 2003.

Rule 5.663. Responsibilities of children's counsel in delinquency proceedings (§§ 202, 265, 633, 634, 634.3, 634.6, 679, 700)

(a) Purpose

This rule is designed to ensure public safety and the protection of the child's best interest at every stage of the delinquency proceedings by clarifying the role of the child's counsel in delinquency proceedings. This rule is not intended to affect any substantive duty imposed on counsel by existing civil standards or professional discipline standards.

(b) Responsibilities of counsel

A child's counsel is charged with providing effective, competent, diligent, and conscientious advocacy and making rational and informed decisions founded on adequate investigation and preparation. Counsel must maintain a confidential relationship with the child and provide legal representation based on the child's expressed interests.

(Subd (b) amended effective July 1, 2023.)

(c) Right to representation

A child is entitled to have their interests represented by counsel at every stage of the proceedings, including in the postdispositional phase. Counsel must continue to represent the child unless relieved by the court upon the substitution of other counsel, or for cause.

(Subd (c) amended effective July 1, 2023; previously amended effective January 1, 2007.)

(d) Limits to responsibilities

A child's counsel is not required:

(1) To assume the responsibilities of a probation officer, social worker, parent, or guardian;

(2) To provide nonlegal services to the child; or

(3) To represent the child in any proceedings outside of the delinquency proceedings.

(Subd (d) amended effective January 1, 2007.)

Rule 5.663 amended effective July 1, 2023; adopted as rule 1479 effective July 1, 2004; previously amended and renumbered effective January 1, 2007.

Rule 5.664. Training requirements for children's counsel in delinquency proceedings (§ 634.3)

(a) Definition

"Competent counsel" means an attorney who is a member, in good standing, of the State Bar of California, who provides representation in accordance with Welfare and Institutions Code section 634.3(a)(1)–(3), and who has participated in training in the law and practice of juvenile delinquency as defined in this rule.

(Subd (a) adopted effective July 1, 2016.)

(b) Education and training requirements

(1) Only those attorneys who, during each of the most recent three calendar years, have dedicated at least 50 percent of their practice to juvenile delinquency and demonstrated competence or who have completed a minimum of 12 hours of training or education during the most recent 12-month period in the area of juvenile delinquency, may be appointed to represent youth.

(2) Attorney training must include:

(A) An overview of delinquency law and related statutes and cases;

(B) Trial skills, including drafting and filing pretrial motions, introducing evidence at trial, preserving the record for appeal, filing writs, notices of appeal, and posttrial motions;

(C) Advocacy at the detention phase;

(D) Advocacy at the dispositional phase;

(E) Child and adolescent development, including training on interviewing and working with adolescent clients;

(F) Competence and mental health issues, including capacity to commit a crime and the effects of trauma, child abuse, and family violence, as well as crossover issues presented by youth involved in the dependency system;

(G) Police interrogation methods, suggestibility of juveniles, and false confessions;

(H) Counsel's ethical duties, including racial, ethnic, and cultural understanding and addressing bias;

(I) Cultural competency and sensitivity relating to, and best practices for, providing adequate care to lesbian, gay, bisexual, and transgender youth;

(J) Understanding of the effects of and how to work with victims of human trafficking and commercial sexual exploitation of children and youth;

(K) Immigration consequences and the requirements of Special Immigrant Juvenile Status;

(L) General and special education, including information on school discipline;

(M) Extended foster care;

(N) Substance abuse;

(O) How to secure effective rehabilitative resources, including information on available community-based resources;

(P) Direct and collateral consequences of court involvement;

(Q) Transfer of jurisdiction to criminal court hearings and advocacy in adult court;

(R) Appellate advocacy; and

(S) Advocacy in the postdispositional phase.

(Subd (b) amended effective May 22, 2017; adopted effective July 1, 2016.)

(c) Continuing education requirements

(1) To remain eligible for appointment to represent delinquent youth, attorneys must engage in annual continuing education in the areas listed in (b)(2), as follows:

(A) Attorneys must complete at least 8 hours per calendar year of continuing education, for a total of 24 hours, during each MCLE compliance period.

(B) An attorney who is eligible to represent delinquent youth for only a portion of the corresponding MCLE compliance period must complete training hours in proportion to the amount of time the attorney was eligible. An attorney who is eligible to represent delinquent youth for only a portion of a calendar year must complete two hours of training for every three months of eligibility.

(C) The 12 hours of initial training may be applied toward the continuing training requirements for the first compliance period.

(2) Each individual attorney is responsible for complying with the training requirements in this rule; however, offices of the public defender and other agencies that work with delinquent youth are encouraged to provide MCLE training that meets the training requirements in (b)(2).

(3) Each individual attorney is encouraged to participate in policy meetings or workgroups convened by the juvenile court and to participate in local trainings designed to address county needs.

(Subd (c) adopted effective July 1, 2016.)

(d) Evidence of competency

The court may require evidence of the competency of any attorney appointed to represent a youth in a delinquency proceeding, including requesting documentation of trainings attended. The court may also require attorneys who represent youth in delinquency proceedings to complete *Declaration of Eligibility for Appointment to Represent Youth in Delinquency Court* (JV-700).

(Subd (d) adopted effective July 1, 2016.)

Rule 5.664 amended effective May 22, 2017; adopted effective July 1, 2016.

Chapter 12
Cases Petitioned Under Section 300

Chapter 12 renumbered effective January 1, 2008; Adopted as Chapter 7 effective July, 1989; previously renumbered as Chapter 8 effective July 1, 1994, and as Chapter 9 effective January 1, 2000; previously renumbered and amended as Chapter 13 effective January 1, 2007.

Art. 1. Initial Hearing. Rules 5.667–5.678.

Art. 2. Jurisdiction. Rules 5.682, 5.684.
Art. 3. Disposition. Rules 5.690–5.705.
Art. 4. Reviews, Permanent Planning. Rules 5.706–5.740.

Article 1
Initial Hearing

Rule 5.667. Service and notice
Rule 5.668. Commencement of hearing—explanation of proceedings (§§ 316, 316.2)
Rule 5.670. Initial hearing; detention hearings; time limit on custody; setting jurisdiction hearing; visitation (§§ 309, 311, 313, 315, 362.1)
Rule 5.672. Continuances
Rule 5.674. Conduct of hearing; admission, no contest, submission
Rule 5.676. Requirements for detention
Rule 5.678. Findings in support of detention; factors to consider; reasonable efforts; active efforts; detention alternatives

Rule 5.667. Service and notice

(a) In court order of notice (§ 296)

The court may order the child, or any parent or guardian or Indian custodian of the child who is present in court, to appear again before the court, social worker, probation officer, or county financial officer at a specified time and place as stated in the order.

(Subd (a) amended effective January 1, 2007; previously amended effective January 1, 2006.)

(b) Language of notice

If it appears that the parent or guardian does not read English, the social worker must provide notice in the language believed to be spoken by the parent or guardian.

(Subd (b) amended effective January 1, 2006.)

Rule 5.667 amended and renumbered effective January 1, 2007; repealed and adopted as rule 1440 effective January 1, 1998; previously amended effective January 1, 2006.

Rule 5.668. Commencement of hearing—explanation of proceedings (§§ 316, 316.2)

(a) Commencement of hearing

At the beginning of the initial hearing on the petition, whether the child is detained or not detained, the court must give advisement as required by rule 5.534 and must inform each parent and guardian present, and the child, if present:

(1) Of the contents of the petition;

(2) Of the nature of, and possible consequences of, juvenile court proceedings;

(3) If the child has been taken into custody, of the reasons for the initial detention and the purpose and scope of the detention hearing; and

(4) If the petition is sustained and the child is declared a dependent of the court and removed from the custody of the parent or guardian, the court-ordered reunification services must be considered to have been offered or provided on the date the petition is sustained or 60 days after the child's initial removal, whichever is earlier. The time for services must not exceed 12 months for a child three years of age or older at the time of the initial removal and must not exceed 6 months for a child who was under three years of age or who is in a sibling group in which one sibling was under three years of age at the time of the initial removal if the parent or guardian fails to participate regularly and make substantive progress in any court-ordered treatment program.

(Subd (a) amended effective January 1, 2017; adopted effective January 1, 1999; previously amended effective January 1, 2001, and January 1, 2007.)

(b) Parentage inquiry

The court must also inquire of the child's mother and of any other appropriate person present as to the identity and address of any and all presumed or alleged parents of the child as set forth in section 316.2.

(Subd (b) amended effective January 1, 2017; adopted effective January 1, 1999; previously amended effective January 1, 2007, and January 1, 2015.)

(c) Indian Child Welfare Act inquiry (§ 224.2(c) & (g))

(1) At the first appearance in court of each party, the court must ask each participant present at the hearing whether:

(A) The participant knows or has reason to know the child is an Indian child;

(B) The residence or domicile of the child, the child's parents, or Indian custodian is on a reservation or in an Alaska Native village;

(C) The child is or has ever been a ward of a tribal court; and

(D) Either parent or the child possess an identification card indicating membership or citizenship in an Indian tribe.

(2) The court must also instruct all parties to inform the court if they subsequently receive information that provides reason to know the child is an Indian child, and order the parents, Indian custodian, or guardian, if available, to complete *Parental Notification of Indian Status* (form ICWA-020).

(3) If there is reason to believe that the case involves an Indian child, the court must require the agency to proceed in accordance with section 224.2(e).

(4) If it is known, or there is reason to know, the case involves an Indian child, the court must proceed in accordance with rules 5.481 et seq. and treat the child as an Indian child unless and until the court determines on the record after review of the report of due diligence described in section 224.2(g) that the child does not meet the definition of an Indian child.

(Subd (c) adopted effective January 1, 2020.)

(d) Health and education information (§ 16010)

The court must order each parent and guardian present either to complete *Your Child's Health and Education* (form JV-225) or to provide the information necessary for the social worker or probation officer, court staff, or representative of the local child welfare agency to complete the form. The social worker or probation officer assigned to the dependency matter must provide the child's attorney with a copy of the completed form. Before each periodic status review hearing, the social worker or probation officer must obtain and include in the reports prepared for the hearing all information necessary to maintain the accuracy of form JV-225.

(Subd (d) relettered effective January 1, 2020; adopted as subd (c) effective January 1, 2002; previously amended effective January 1, 2007, and January 1, 2008.)

Rule 5.668 amended effective January 1, 2020; repealed and adopted as rule 1441 effective January 1, 1998; previously amended and renumbered effective January 1, 2007; previously amended effective January 1, 1999, January 1, 2001, January 1, 2002, January 1, 2008, January 1, 2015, and January 1, 2017.

Rule 5.670. Initial hearing; detention hearings; time limit on custody; setting jurisdiction hearing; visitation (§§ 309, 311, 313, 315, 362.1)

(a) Child not detained; filing petition, setting hearing

If the social worker does not take the child into custody but determines that a petition concerning the child should be filed, the social worker must file a petition with the clerk of the juvenile court as soon as possible. The clerk must set an initial hearing on the petition within 15 court days.

(Subd (a) amended effective January 1, 2007.)

(b) Detention hearing—warrant cases, transfers in, changes in placement

Notwithstanding section 309(b), and unless the child has been released sooner, a detention hearing must be held as soon as possible, but no later than 48 hours, excluding noncourt days, after the child arrives at a facility within the county if:

(1) The child was taken into custody in another county and transported in custody to the requesting county under a protective custody warrant issued by the juvenile court;

(2) The child was taken into custody in the county in which a protective custody warrant was issued by the juvenile court; or

(3) The matter was transferred from the juvenile court of another county under rule 5.610 and the child was ordered transported in custody.

At the hearing the court must determine whether the child is to continue to be detained in custody. If the hearing is not commenced within that time, the child must be immediately released from custody.

(Subd (b) amended and relettered effective January 1, 2017; adopted as subd (e) effective January 1, 1998; previously amended effective January 1, 2007.)

(c) Visitation

(1) The court must consider the issue of visitation between the child and other persons, determine if contact pending the jurisdiction hearing would be beneficial or detrimental to the child, and make appropriate orders.

(2) The court must consider the issue of visitation between the child and any sibling who was not placed with the child, and who was taken into custody with the child or is otherwise under the court's jurisdiction, and enter an order for sibling visitation pending the jurisdiction hearing, unless the court finds by clear and convincing evidence that sibling interaction between the child and the sibling is contrary to the safety or well-being of either child.

(Subd (c) relettered effective January 1, 2017; adopted as subd (g) effective January 1, 1998; previously amended effective January 1, 2007, and July 1, 2011.)
Rule 5.670 amended effective January 1, 2017; repealed and adopted as rule 1442 effective January 1, 1998; previously amended and renumbered effective January 1, 2007; previously amended effective July 1, 2011.

Rule 5.672. Continuances

(a) Detention hearing; right to one-day continuance; custody pending continued hearing (§§ 319, 322)

On motion of the child, parent, or guardian, the court must continue the detention hearing for one court day. Unless otherwise ordered by the court, the child must remain detained pending completion of the detention hearing or a rehearing. The court must either find that continuance in the home of the parent or guardian is contrary to the child's welfare or order the child released to the custody of the parent or guardian. The court may enter this finding on a temporary basis, without prejudice to any party, and reevaluate the finding at the time of the continued detention hearing.

(Subd (a) amended effective January 1, 2007; previously amended effective July 1, 2002.)

(b) Initial hearing; child not detained

If the child is not detained, motions for continuances of the initial hearing must be made and ruled on under rule 5.550.

(Subd (b) amended effective January 1, 2007; previously amended effective July 1, 2002.)

Rule 5.672 amended and renumbered effective January 1, 2007; repealed and adopted as rule 1443 effective January 1, 1998; previously amended effective July 1, 2002.

Rule 5.674. Conduct of hearing; admission, no contest, submission

(a) Admission, no contest, submission

(1) At the initial hearing, whether or not the child is detained, the parent or guardian may admit the allegations of the petition, plead no contest, or submit the jurisdictional determination to the court based on the information provided to the court and waive further jurisdictional hearing.

(2) If the court accepts an admission, a plea of no contest, or a submission from each parent and guardian with standing to participate as a party, the court must then proceed according to rules 5.682 and 5.686.

(Subd (a) amended effective January 1, 2007; previously amended effective July 1, 2002.)

(b) Detention hearing; general conduct (§ 319; 42 U.S.C. § 600 et seq.)

(1) The court must read, consider, and reference any reports submitted by the social worker and any relevant evidence submitted by any party or counsel. All detention findings and orders must appear in the written orders of the court.

(2) The findings and orders that must be made on the record are:

(A) Continuance in the home is contrary to the child's welfare;

(B) Temporary placement and care are vested with the social services agency;

(C) Reasonable efforts, or when it is known or there is reason to know the child is an Indian child, active efforts, have been made to prevent removal;

(D) The findings and orders required to be made on the record under section 319; and

(E) When it is known or there is reason to know the case involves an Indian child, that detention is necessary to prevent imminent physical damage or harm to the child, and there are no reasonable means by which the child can be protected if maintained in the physical custody of his or her parent or parents or Indian custodian.

(Subd (b) amended effective January 1, 2020; adopted effective July 1, 2002; previously amended effective January 1, 2007, and January 1, 2016.)

(c) Detention hearing; rights of child, parent, Indian custodian, or guardian (§§ 311, 319)

At the detention hearing, the child, the parent, Indian custodian, and the guardian have the right to assert the privilege against self-incrimination and the right to confront and cross-examine:

(1) The preparer of a police report, probation or social worker report, or other document submitted to the court; and

(2) Any person examined by the court under section 319. If the child, parent, Indian custodian, Indian child's tribe, or guardian asserts the right to cross-examine preparers of documents submitted for court consideration, the court may not consider any such report or document unless the preparer is made available for cross-examination.

(Subd (c) amended effective January 1, 2020; adopted as subd (c) effective January 1, 1998; previously amended and relettered as subd (d) effective July 1, 2002, amended and relettered as subd (c) effective January 1, 2017; previously amended effective January 1, 2007.)

(d) No parent, Indian custodian, or Indian child's tribe or guardian present and not noticed (§ 321)

If the court orders the child detained at the detention hearing and no parent, Indian custodian, or Indian child's tribe or guardian is present and no parent, Indian custodian, or Indian child's tribe or guardian has received actual notice of the detention hearing, a parent, Indian custodian, or Indian child's tribe or guardian may file an affidavit alleging the failure of notice and requesting a detention rehearing. The clerk must set the rehearing for a time within 24 hours of the filing of the affidavit, excluding noncourt days. At the rehearing the court must proceed under rules 5.670–5.678.

(Subd (d) amended effective January 1, 2020; adopted effective January 1, 2017.)

(e) Hearing for further evidence; prima facie case (§ 321)

If the court orders the child detained, and the child, a parent, an Indian custodian, an Indian child's tribe, a guardian, or counsel requests that evidence of the prima facie case be presented, the court must set a prima facie hearing for a time within 3 court days to consider evidence of the prima facie case or set the matter for jurisdiction hearing within 10 court days. If at the hearing the petitioner fails to establish the prima facie case, the child must be released from custody.

(Subd (e) amended effective January 1, 2020; adopted effective January 1, 2017.)

Rule 5.674 amended effective January 1, 2020; repealed and adopted as rule 1444 effective January 1, 1998; previously amended and renumbered as rule 5.674 effective January 1, 2007; previously amended effective July 1, 2002, January 1, 2016, and January 1, 2017.

Rule 5.676. Requirements for detention

(a) Requirements for detention (§ 319)

No child may be ordered detained by the court unless the court finds that:

(1) A prima facie showing has been made that the child is described by section 300;

(2) Continuance in the home of the parent, Indian custodian, or guardian is contrary to the child's welfare; and

(3) One or more of the grounds for detention in rule 5.678 is found.

(Subd (a) amended effective January 1, 2020; previously amended effective July 1, 2002, and January 1, 2007.)

(b) Additional requirements for detention of Indian child

If it is known, or there is reason to know the child is an Indian child, the child may not be ordered detained unless the court also finds that detention is necessary to prevent imminent physical damage or harm to the child. The court must state the facts supporting this finding on the record.

(Subd (b) adopted effective January 1, 2020.)

(c) Evidence required at detention hearing

In making the findings required to support an order of detention, the court may rely solely on written police reports, probation or social worker reports, or other documents.

The reports relied on must include:

(1) A statement of the reasons the child was removed from the parent's custody;

(2) A description of the services that have been provided, including those under section 306, and of any available services or safety plans that would prevent or eliminate the need for the child to remain in custody;

(3) If a parent is enrolled in a certified substance abuse treatment facility that allows a dependent child to reside with his or her parent, information and a recommendation regarding whether the child can be returned to the custody of that parent.

(4) Identification of the need, if any, for the child to remain in custody; and

(5) If continued detention is recommended, information about any parent or guardian of the child with whom the child was not residing at the time the child was taken into custody and about any relative or nonrelative extended family member as defined under section 362.7 with whom the child may be detained.

(Subd (c) relettered effective January 1, 2020; adopted as subd (b); previously amended effective July 1, 2002, January 1, 2007, and January 1, 2016.)

(d) Additional evidence required at detention hearing for Indian child

If it is known, or there is reason to know the child is an Indian child, the reports relied on must also include:

(1) A statement of the risk of imminent physical damage or harm to the Indian child and any evidence that the emergency removal or placement continues to be necessary to prevent the imminent physical damage or harm to the child;

(2) The steps taken to provide notice to the child's parents, Indian custodian, and tribe about the hearing under section 224.3;

(3) If the child's parents and Indian custodian are unknown, a detailed explanation of what efforts have been made to locate and contact them, including contact with the appropriate Bureau of Indian Affairs regional director;

(4) The residence and the domicile of the Indian child;

(5) If either the residence or the domicile of the Indian child is believed to be on a reservation or in an Alaska Native village, the name of the tribe affiliated with that reservation or village;

(6) The tribal affiliation of the child and of the parents or Indian custodian;

(7) A specific and detailed account of the circumstances that caused the Indian child to be taken into temporary custody;

(8) If the child is believed to reside or be domiciled on a reservation in which the tribe exercises exclusive jurisdiction over child custody matters, a statement of efforts that have been made and that are being made to contact the tribe and transfer the child to the tribe's jurisdiction; and

(9) A statement of the efforts that have been taken to assist the parents or Indian custodian so the Indian child may safely be returned to their custody.

(Subd (d) adopted effective January 1, 2020.)

Rule 5.676 amended effective January 1, 2020; repealed and adopted as rule 1445 effective January 1, 1998; previously amended effective July 1, 2002, and January 1, 2016; previously amended and renumbered as rule 5.676 effective January 1, 2007.

Rule 5.678. Findings in support of detention; factors to consider; reasonable efforts; active efforts; detention alternatives

(a) Findings in support of detention (§ 319; 42 U.S.C. § 672)

The court must order the child released from custody unless the court makes findings as specified in section 319(c), and where it is known, or there is reason to know the child is an Indian child, the additional finding specified in section 319(d).

(Subd (a) amended effective January 1, 2020; previously amended effective July 1, 2002, January 1, 2007, and January 1, 2019.)

(b) Factors to consider

In determining whether to release or detain the child under (a), the court must consider the factors in section 319(f).

(Subd (b) amended effective January 1, 2020; previously amended effective July 1, 2002, January 1, 2007, January 1, 2016, and January 1, 2019.)

(c) Findings of the court—reasonable or active efforts (§ 319; 42 U.S.C. § 672)

(1) Whether the child is released or detained at the hearing, the court must determine whether reasonable efforts have been made to prevent or eliminate the need for removal and must make one of the following findings:

(A) Reasonable efforts have been made; or

(B) Reasonable efforts have not been made.

(2) Where it is known or there is reason to know the child is an Indian child, whether the child is released or detained at the hearing, the court must determine whether active efforts have been made to provide remedial services and rehabilitative programs designed to prevent the breakup of the Indian family and whether those efforts have been successful. Those active efforts must be documented in detail in the record, and the court must make one of the following findings:

(A) Active efforts have been made and were successful; or

(B) Active efforts have been made and were not successful; or

(C) Active efforts have not been made; and

(D) The court orders the department to initiate or continue services in accordance with section 358.

(3) The court must also determine whether services are available that would prevent the need for further detention.

(4) The court must not order the child detained unless the court, after inquiry regarding available services, finds that there are no reasonable services, or where it is known or there is reason to know the child is an Indian child, active efforts to provide remedial services and rehabilitative programs designed to prevent the breakup of the Indian family that would prevent or eliminate the need to detain the child or that would permit the child to return home.

(5) If the court orders the child detained, the court must proceed under section 319(g)–(h) and where it is known, or there is reason to know the child is an Indian child, subdivision (f) of this rule.

(Subd (c) amended effective January 1, 2020; adopted as subd (d) effective January 1, 1998; previously amended and relettered effective July 1, 2002; previously amended effective January 1, 2007, and January 1, 2019.)

(d) Orders of the court (§ 319; 42 U.S.C. § 672)

If the court orders the child detained, the court must order that temporary care and custody of the child be vested with the county welfare department pending disposition or further order of the court and must make the other findings and orders specified in section 319(g) and (h)(3).

(Subd (d) amended effective January 1, 2020; adopted effective July 1, 2002; previously amended effective January 1, 2019.)

(e) Detention alternatives (§ 319)

The court may order the child detained as specified in section 319(h).

(Subd (e) amended effective January 1, 2020; adopted effective January 1, 1999; previously amended effective July 1, 2002, January 1, 2007, and January 1, 2019.)

(f) Additional requirements regarding detention of Indian child (§ 319)

(1) If it is known, or there is reason to know the child is an Indian child, the child must be detained in a home that complies with the placement preferences in section 361.31 unless the court finds by clear and convincing evidence good cause exists not to follow the placement preferences in accordance with rule 5.485.

(2) If it is known, or there is reason to know the child is an Indian child, the detention hearing may not be continued beyond 30 days unless the court finds all of the following:

(A) Restoring the child to the parent, parents, or Indian custodian would subject the child to imminent physical damage or harm;

(B) The court is unable to transfer the proceeding to the jurisdiction of the appropriate Indian tribe; and

(C) It is not possible to initiate an Indian child custody proceeding as defined in section 224.1.

(Subd (f) adopted effective January 1, 2020.)

(g) Hearing for return of custody of Indian child after emergency removal when emergency has ended (§ 319.4)

If it is known or there is reason to know the child is an Indian child, a party may request a hearing under rule 5.484(b) for return of the child before disposition if the party asserts that there is new evidence that the emergency removal or placement is no longer necessary to prevent imminent physical damage or harm to the child.

(Subd (g) adopted effective January 1, 2020.)

Rule 5.678 amended effective January 1, 2020; repealed and adopted as rule 1446 effective January 1, 1998; previously amended and renumbered as rule 5.678 effective January 1, 2007; previously amended effective January 1, 1999, July 1, 2002, January 1, 2016, and January 1, 2019.

Rule 5.680. Detention rehearings; prima facie hearings [Repealed]

Rule 5.680 repealed effective January 1, 2017; repealed and adopted as rule 1447 effective January 1, 1998; previously amended and renumbered effective January 1, 2007.

Article 2
Jurisdiction

Rule 5.682. Commencement of jurisdiction hearing—advisement of trial rights; admission, no contest, submission

Rule 5.684. Contested hearing on petition

Rule 5.682. Commencement of jurisdiction hearing—advisement of trial rights; admission, no contest, submission

(a) Rights explained (§§ 341, 353, 361.1)

After giving the advisement required by rule 5.534, the court must advise the parent or guardian of the following rights:

(1) The right to a hearing by the court on the issues raised by the petition; and

(2) The right, if the child has been removed, to have the child returned to the parent or guardian within two working days after a finding by the court that the child does not come within the jurisdiction of the juvenile

court under section 300, unless the parent or guardian and the child welfare agency agree that the child will be released on a later date.

(Subd (a) amended and relettered effective January 1, 2017; adopted as subd (b) effective January 1, 1991; previously amended effective January 1, 2005, and January 1, 2007.)

(b) Admission of allegations; prerequisites to acceptance

The court must then inquire whether the parent or guardian intends to admit or deny the allegations of the petition. If the parent or guardian neither admits nor denies the allegations, the court must state on the record that the parent or guardian does not admit the allegations. If the parent or guardian wishes to admit the allegations, the court must first find and state on the record that it is satisfied that the parent or guardian understands the nature of the allegations and the direct consequences of the admission, and understands and waives the rights in (a) and (e)(3).

(Subd (b) amended and relettered effective January 1, 2017; adopted as subd (c) effective January 1, 1991; previously amended effective January 1, 2007.)

(c) Parent or guardian must admit

An admission by the parent or guardian must be made personally by the parent or guardian.

(Subd (c) relettered effective January 1, 2017; adopted as subd (d) effective January 1, 1991; previously amended effective January 1, 2007.)

(d) Admission, no contest, submission

The parent or guardian may elect to admit the allegations of the petition or plead no contest and waive further jurisdictional hearing. The parent or guardian may elect to submit the jurisdictional determination to the court based on the information provided to the court and choose whether to waive further jurisdictional hearing. If the parent or guardian submits to the jurisdictional determination in writing, *Waiver of Rights—Juvenile Dependency* (form JV-190) must be completed by the parent or guardian and counsel and submitted to the court.

(Subd (d) amended and relettered effective January 1, 2017; adopted as subd (e) effective January 1, 1991; previously amended effective January 1, 2007.)

(e) Findings of court (§ 356)

After admission, plea of no contest, or submission, the court must make the following findings noted in the order of the court:

(1) Notice has been given as required by law;

(2) The birthdate and county of residence of the child;

(3) The parent or guardian has knowingly and intelligently waived the right to a trial on the issues by the court, the right to assert the privilege against self-incrimination, and the right to confront and to cross-examine adverse witnesses and to use the process of the court to compel the attendance of witnesses on the parent or guardian's behalf;

(4) The parent or guardian understands the nature of the conduct alleged in the petition and the possible consequences of an admission, plea of no contest, or submission;

(5) The admission, plea of no contest, or submission by the parent or guardian is freely and voluntarily made;

(6) There is a factual basis for the parent or guardian's admission;

(7) Those allegations of the petition as admitted are true as alleged; or

(8) Whether the allegations of the petition as submitted are true as alleged; and

(9) The child is described by one or more specific subdivisions of section 300.

(Subd (e) amended and relettered effective January 1, 2017; adopted as subd (f) effective January 1, 1991; previously amended effective January 1, 2007.)

(f) Disposition

After accepting an admission, plea of no contest, or submission, the court must proceed to a disposition hearing under rule 5.690 or rule 5.697, if the youth will attain 18 years of age before the holding of the disposition hearing.

(Subd (f) amended effective January 1, 2021; adopted as subd (g) effective January 1, 1991; previously amended effective January 1, 2007; previously amended and relettered as subd (f) effective January 1, 2017.)

Rule 5.682 amended effective January 1, 2021; adopted as rule 1449 effective January 1, 1991; previously amended effective January 1, 2005, and January 1, 2017; previously amended and renumbered as rule 5.682 effective January 1, 2007.

Rule 5.684. Contested hearing on petition

(a) Contested jurisdiction hearing (§ 355)

If the parent or guardian denies the allegations of the petition, the court must hold a contested hearing and determine whether the allegations in the petition are true.

(Subd (a) amended effective January 1, 2007.)

(b) Admissibility of evidence—general (§§ 355, 355.1)

Except as provided in sections 355(c) and 355.1 and (c) and (d) of this rule, the admission and exclusion of evidence must be in accordance with the Evidence Code as it applies to civil cases.

(Subd (b) amended effective January 1, 2017; previously amended effective July 1, 1997, and January 1, 2007.)

(c) Reports

(1) A social study, with hearsay evidence contained in it, is admissible as provided in section 355.

(2) The social study must be provided to all parties and their counsel by the county welfare department within a reasonable time before the hearing.

(Subd (c) amended effective January 1, 2017; previously amended effective July 1, 1997, and January 1, 2007.)

(d) Inapplicable privileges (Evid. Code, §§ 972, 986)

The privilege not to testify or to be called as a witness against a spouse or domestic partner, and the confidential marital communication privilege, does not apply to dependency proceedings.

(Subd (d) relettered effective January 1, 2017; adopted as subd (e) effective January 1, 1991; previously amended effective July 1, 1997, and January 1, 2007.)

(e) Findings of court—allegations true (§ 356)

If the court determines by a preponderance of the evidence that the allegations of the petition are true, the court must make findings on each of the following, noted in the minutes:

(1) Notice has been given as required by law;

(2) The birthdate and county of residence of the child;

(3) The allegations of the petition are true; and

(4) The child is described by one or more subdivisions of section 300.

(Subd (e) amended and relettered effective January 1, 2017; adopted as subd (f) effective January 1, 1991; previously amended effective January 1, 2007.)

(f) Disposition and continuance pending disposition hearing (§§ 356, 358)

After making the findings in (e), the court must proceed to a disposition hearing under rule 5.690 or rule 5.697, if the youth will attain 18 years of age before the holding of the disposition hearing. The court may continue the disposition hearing as provided in section 358.

(Subd (f) amended effective January 1, 2021; adopted as subd (g) effective January 1, 1991; previously amended effective July 1, 1997, and January 1, 2007; previously amended and relettered as subd (f) effective January 1, 2017.)

(g) Findings of court—allegations not proved (§§ 356, 361.1)

If the court determines that the allegations of the petition have not been proved by a preponderance of the evidence, the court must dismiss the petition and terminate any detention orders relating to the petition. The court must order that the child be returned to the physical custody of the parent or guardian immediately but, in any event, not more than two working days following the date of that finding, unless the parent or guardian and the agency with custody of the child agree to a later date for the child's release. The court must make the following findings, noted in the order of the court:

(1) Notice has been given as required by law;

(2) The birthdate and county of residence of the child; and

(3) The allegations of the petition are not proved.

(Subd (g) relettered effective January 1, 2017; adopted as subd (h) effective January 1, 1991; previously amended effective July 1, 1997, January 1, 2005, and January 1, 2007.)

Rule 5.684 amended effective January 1, 2021; adopted as rule 1450 effective January 1, 1991; previously amended effective July 1, 1997, January 1, 2005, and January 1, 2017; previously amended and renumbered as rule 5.684 effective January 1, 2007.

Rule 5.686. Continuance pending disposition hearing [Repealed]

Rule 5.686 repealed effective January 1, 2017; adopted as rule 1451 effective January 1, 1990; previously amended and renumbered as rule 5.684 effective January 1, 2007.

Rule 5.688. Failure to cooperate with services (§ 360(b)) [Repealed]

Rule 5.688 repealed effective January 1, 2017; adopted as rule 1452 effective January 1, 1990; previously amended effective July 1, 2000; previously amended and renumbered effective January 1, 2007.

Article 3
Disposition

Rule 5.690. General conduct of disposition hearing
Rule 5.695. Findings and orders of the court—disposition

Rule 5.697. Disposition hearing for a nonminor (Welf. & Inst. Code, §§ 224.1, 295, 303, 358, 358.1, 361, 361.6, 366.31, 390, 391)

Rule 5.700. Termination of jurisdiction—custody and visitation orders (§§ 302, 304, 361.2, 362.4, 726.5)

Rule 5.705. Setting a hearing under section 366.26

Rule 5.690. General conduct of disposition hearing

(a) Social study (§§ 280, 309, 358, 358.1, 360, 361.5, 16002(b))

The petitioner must prepare a social study of the child. The social study must include a discussion of all matters relevant to disposition and a recommendation for disposition.

(1) The petitioner must comply with the following when preparing the social study:

(A) If petitioner recommends that the court appoint a legal guardian, petitioner must prepare an assessment under section 360(a), to be included in the social study report prepared for disposition or in a separate document.

(B) If petitioner recommends removal of the child from the home, the social study must include:

(i) A discussion of the reasonable efforts made to prevent or eliminate removal, or if it is known or there is reason to know the child is an Indian child, the active efforts to provide remedial services and rehabilitative programs designed to prevent the breakup of the Indian family, and a recommended plan for reuniting the child with the family, including a plan for visitation;

(ii) A plan for achieving legal permanence for the child if efforts to reunify fail; and

(iii) A statement that each parent has been advised of the option to participate in adoption planning and to voluntarily relinquish the child if an adoption agency is willing to accept the relinquishment, and the parent's response.

(C) The social study must include a discussion of the social worker's efforts to comply with section 309(e) and rule 5.637, including but not limited to:

(i) The number of relatives identified and the relationship of each to the child;

(ii) The number and relationship of those relatives described by item (i) who were located and notified;

(iii) The number and relationship of those relatives described by item (ii) who are interested in ongoing contact with the child;

(iv) The number and relationship of those relatives described by item (ii) who are interested in providing placement for the child; and

(v) If it is known or there is reason to know the child is an Indian child, efforts to locate extended family members as defined in section 224.1, and evidence that all individuals contacted have been provided with information about the option of obtaining approval for placement through the tribe's license or approval procedure.

(D) If siblings are not placed together, the social study must include an explanation of why they have not been placed together in the same home, what efforts are being made to place the siblings together, or why making those efforts would be contrary to the safety and well-being of any of the siblings.

(E) If petitioner alleges that section 361.5(b) applies, the social study must state why reunification services should not be provided.

(F) All other relevant requirements of sections 358 and 358.1.

(2) The petitioner must submit the social study and copies of it to the clerk at least 48 hours before the disposition hearing is set to begin, and the clerk must make the copies available to the parties and attorneys. A continuance within statutory time limits must be granted on the request of a party who has not been furnished a copy of the social study in accordance with this rule.

(Subd (a) amended effective January 1, 2020; previously amended effective July 1, 1995, January 1, 2000, January 1, 2007, January 1, 2011, and January 1, 2017.)

(b) Evidence considered (§§ 358, 360)

The court must receive in evidence and consider the social study, a guardianship assessment, the report of any CASA volunteer, the case plan, and any relevant evidence offered by petitioner, the child, or the parent or guardian. The court may require production of other relevant evidence on its own motion. In the order of disposition, the court must state that the social study and the study or evaluation by the CASA volunteer, if any, have been read and considered by the court.

(Subd (b) amended effective January 1, 2007; previously amended effective July 1, 1995.)

(c) Case plan (§ 16501.1)

Whenever child welfare services are provided, the social worker must prepare a case plan.

(1) A written case plan must be completed and filed with the court by the date of disposition or within 60 calendar days of initial removal or of the in-person response required under section 16501(f) if the child has not been removed from his or her home, whichever occurs first.

(2) For a child of any age, the court must consider the case plan and must find as follows:

(A) The case plan meets the requirements of section 16501.1; or

(B) The case plan does not meet the requirements of section 16501.1, in which case the court must order the agency to comply with the requirements of section 16501.1; and

(C) The social worker solicited and integrated into the case plan the input of the child; the child's family; the child's identified Indian tribe, including consultation with the child's tribe on whether tribal customary adoption as defined in section 366.24 is an appropriate permanent plan for the child if reunification is unsuccessful; and other interested parties; or

(D) The social worker did not solicit and integrate into the case plan the input of the child, the child's family, the child's identified Indian tribe, and other interested parties, in which case the court must order that the social worker solicit and integrate into the case plan the input of the child, the child's family, the child's identified Indian tribe, and other interested parties, unless the court finds that each of these participants was unable, unavailable, or unwilling to participate.

(3) For a child 12 years of age or older and in a permanent placement, the court must consider the case plan and must also find as follows:

(A) The child was given the opportunity to review the case plan, sign it, and receive a copy; or

(B) The child was not given the opportunity to review the case plan, sign it, and receive a copy, in which case the court must order the agency to give the child the opportunity to review the case plan, sign it, and receive a copy.

(Subd (c) amended effective January 1, 2019; adopted effective January 1, 2007; previously amended effective January 1, 2009, July 1, 2010, and January 1, 2017.)

(d) Timing

Notwithstanding any other law, if a minor has been removed from the custody of the parents or Indian custodians or guardians, a continuance may not be granted that would result in the dispositional hearing, held under section 361, being completed more than 60 days, or 30 days in the case of an Indian child, after the hearing at which the minor was ordered removed or detained, unless the court finds that there are exceptional circumstances requiring a continuance. If the court knows or has reason to know that the child is an Indian child, the absence of the opinion of a qualified expert witness must not, in and of itself, support a finding that exceptional circumstances exist.

(Subd (d) adopted effective January 1, 2020.)

Rule 5.690 amended effective January 1, 2020; adopted as rule 1455 effective January 1, 1991; previously amended and renumbered effective January 1, 2007; previously amended effective July 1, 1995, January 1, 2000, January 1, 2009, July 1, 2010, January 1, 2011, January 1, 2017, and January 1, 2019.

Rule 5.695. Findings and orders of the court—disposition

(a) Orders of the court (§§ 245.5, 358, 360, 361, 361.2, 390)

At the disposition hearing, the court may:

(1) Dismiss the petition with specific reasons stated in the minutes;

(2) Place the child under a program of supervision for a time period consistent with section 301 and order that services be provided;

(3) If the requirements of section 360(a) are met, appoint a legal guardian for the child without declaring dependency and order the clerk, as soon as the guardian has signed the required affirmation, to issue letters of guardianship, which are not subject to the confidential protections of juvenile court documents in section 827;

(4) If the requirements of section 360(a) are met, declare dependency, appoint a legal guardian for the child, and order the clerk, as soon as the guardian has signed the required affirmation, to issue letters of guardianship, which are not subject to the confidential protections of juvenile court documents in section 827;

(5) Declare dependency, permit the child to remain at home, and order that services be provided;

(6) Declare dependency, permit the child to remain at home, limit the control to be exercised by the parent or guardian, and order that services be provided; or

(7) Declare dependency, remove physical custody from the parent or guardian, and:

(A) After stating on the record or in writing the factual basis for the order, order custody to a noncustodial parent, terminate jurisdiction, and direct that *Custody Order—Juvenile—Final Judgment* (form JV-200) be prepared and filed under rule 5.700;

(B) After stating on the record or in writing the factual basis for the order, order custody to a noncustodial parent with services to one or both parents; or

(C) Make a placement order and consider granting specific visitation rights to the child's grandparents.

(Subd (a) amended effective January 1, 2021; previously amended effective July 1, 1995, January 1, 2007, January 1, 2015, and January 1, 2017.)

(b) Limitations on parental control (§§ 245.5, 361, 362; Gov. Code, § 7579.5)

(1) If a child is declared a dependent, the court may clearly and specifically limit the control over the child by a parent or guardian.

(2) If the court orders that a parent or guardian retain physical custody of the child subject to court-ordered supervision, the parent or guardian must be ordered to participate in child welfare services or services provided by an appropriate agency designated by the court.

(3) The court must consider whether it is necessary to limit the rights of the parent or guardian to make educational or developmental-services decisions for the child or youth. If the court limits those rights, it must follow the procedures in rules 5.649–5.651.

(Subd (b) relettered effective January 1, 2017; adopted as subd (b) effective January 1, 1991; relettered as subd (c) effective July 1, 1995; previously amended effective July 1, 2002, January 1, 2004, January 1, 2007, January 1, 2008, and January 1, 2014.)

(c) Removal of custody—required findings (§ 361)

(1) The court may not order a dependent removed from the physical custody of a parent or guardian with whom the child resided at the time the petition was filed, unless the court makes one or more of the findings in section 361(c) by clear and convincing evidence.

(2) The court may not order a dependent removed from the physical custody of a parent with whom the child did not reside at the time the petition was initiated unless the juvenile court makes both of the findings in section 361(d) by clear and convincing evidence.

(Subd (c) amended effective January 1, 2019; adopted as subd (c) effective January 1, 1991; previously relettered as subd (d) effective July 1, 1995; previously amended effective July 1, 1997, July 1, 1999, July 1, 2002, and January 1, 2007; previously amended and relettered effective January 1, 2017.)

(d) Reasonable efforts finding

The court must consider whether reasonable efforts to prevent or eliminate the need for removal have been made and make one of the following findings:

(1) Reasonable efforts have been made to prevent removal; or

(2) Reasonable efforts have not been made to prevent removal.

(Subd (d) amended and relettered effective January 1, 2017; adopted as subd (d) effective January 1, 1991; relettered as subd (e) effective July 1, 1995; amended effective July 1, 2002, and January 1, 2006.)

(e) Family-finding determination (§ 309)

(1) If the child is removed, the court must consider and determine whether the social worker has exercised due diligence in conducting the required investigation to identify, locate, and notify the child's kin. The court must consider the mandatory activities listed in rule 5.637(d)(2) and may consider the additional activities listed in rule 5.637(d)(3) in determining whether the agency has exercised due diligence in family finding. The court must document its determination by making a finding on the record.

If the dispositional hearing is continued, the court may set a hearing to be held 30 days from the date of removal or as soon as possible thereafter to consider and determine whether the social worker has exercised due diligence in conducting the required investigation to identify, locate, and notify the child's kin.

(2) If the court finds that the social worker has not exercised due diligence, the court may order the social worker to exercise due diligence in conducting an investigation to identify, locate, and notify the child's kin—except for any individual the social worker identifies as inappropriate to notify under rule 5.637(e)—and may require a written or oral report to the court.

(Subd (e) amended effective January 1, 2024; adopted as subd (f) effective January 1, 2011; previously amended effective January 1, 2014, and January 1, 2015; previously amended and relettered effective January 1, 2017.)

(f) Provision of reunification services (§ 361.5)

(1) Unless the court makes a finding that reunification services need not be provided under subdivision (b) of section 361.5 if a child is removed from the custody of a parent or legal guardian, the court must order the county welfare department to provide reunification services to the child and the child's mother and statutorily presumed parent, or the child's legal guardian, to facilitate reunification of the family as required in section 361.5.

(2) On a finding and declaration of paternity by the juvenile court or proof of a prior declaration of paternity by any court of competent jurisdiction, the juvenile court may order services for the child and the biological father, if the court determines that such services will benefit the child.

(3) If a child is removed from the custody of a parent or guardian, and reunification services are ordered, the court must order visitation between the child and the parent or guardian for whom services are ordered. Visits are to be as frequent as possible, consistent with the well-being of the child.

(4) Reunification services must not be provided when the parent has voluntarily relinquished the child and the relinquishment has been filed with the State Department of Social Services, or if the court has appointed a guardian under section 360.

(5) Except when the order is made under paragraph (1) of subdivision (b) of section 361.5, if the court orders no reunification services for every parent otherwise eligible for such services, the court must conduct a hearing under section 366.26 within 120 days and:

(A) Order that the social worker provide a copy of the child's birth certificate to the caregiver consistent with sections 16010.4(e)(5) and 16010.5(b)–(c); and

(B) Order that the social worker provide a child or youth 16 years of age or older with a certified copy of his or her birth certificate unless the court finds that provision of the birth certificate would be inappropriate.

(6) A judgment, order, or decree setting a hearing under section 366.26 is not an immediately appealable order. Review may be sought only by filing a *Notice of Intent to File Writ Petition and Request for Record (California Rules of Court, Rule 8.450)* (form JV-820) or other notice of intent to file a writ petition and request for record, and a *Petition for Extraordinary Writ (California Rules of Court, Rules 8.452, 8.456)* (form JV-825) or other petition for extraordinary writ. If a party wishes to preserve any right to review on appeal of the findings and orders made under this rule, the party must seek an extraordinary writ under rules 8.450 and 8.452.

(7) A judgment, order, or decree setting a hearing under section 366.26 may be reviewed on appeal following the order of the 366.26 hearing only if the following have occurred:

(A) An extraordinary writ was sought by the timely filing of a *Notice of Intent to File Writ Petition and Request for Record (California Rules of Court, Rule 8.450)* (form JV-820) or other notice of intent to file a writ petition and request for record and a *Petition for Extraordinary Writ (California Rules of Court, Rules 8.452, 8.456)* (form JV-825) or other petition for extraordinary writ; and

(B) The petition for extraordinary writ was summarily denied or otherwise not decided on the merits.

(8) Review on appeal of the order setting a hearing under section 366.26 is limited to issues raised in a previous petition for extraordinary writ that were supported by an adequate record.

(9) Failure to file a notice of intent to file a writ petition and request for record and a petition for extraordinary writ review within the period specified by rules 8.450 and 8.452 to substantively address the issues challenged, or to support the challenge by an adequate record, precludes subsequent review on appeal of the findings and orders made under this rule.

(10) When the court orders a hearing under section 366.26, the court must advise orally all parties present, and by first-class mail or by electronic service in accordance with section 212.5 for parties not present, that if the party wishes to preserve any right to review on appeal of the order setting the hearing under section 366.26, the party must seek an extraordinary writ by filing a *Notice of Intent to File Writ Petition and Request for Record (California Rules of Court, Rule 8.450)* (form JV-820) or other notice of intent to file a writ petition and request for record and a *Petition for Extraordinary Writ (California Rules of Court, Rules 8.452, 8.456)* (form JV-825) or other petition for extraordinary writ.

(A) Within 24 hours of the hearing, notice by first-class mail or by electronic service in accordance with section 212.5 must be provided by the clerk of the court to the last known address of any party who is not present when the court orders the hearing under section 366.26.

(B) Copies of *Petition for Extraordinary Writ (California Rules of Court, Rules 8.452, 8.456)* (form JV-825) and *Notice of Intent to File Writ Petition and Request for Record (California Rules of Court, Rule 8.450)* (form JV-820) must be available in the courtroom and must accompany all mailed notices informing the parties of their rights.

(C) If the notice is for a hearing at which the social worker will recommend the termination of parental rights, the notice may be electronically served in accordance with section 212.5, but only in addition to service of the notice by first-class mail.

(Subd (g) amended and relettered effective January 1, 2024; adopted as subd (e) effective January 1, 1991; previously relettered as subd (f) effective July 1, 1995, and as subd (h) effective January 1, 2011; previously amended effective January 1, 1993, July 1, 1993, January 1, 1994, January 1, 1995, January 1, 1996, July 1, 1997, January 1, 1999, July 1, 1999, January 1, 2001, July 1, 2001, July 1, 2002, January 1, 2007, January 1, 2010, January 1, 2014, January 1, 2015, and January 1, 2019; previously amended and relettered effective January 1, 2017.)

(g) Information regarding termination of parent-child relationship (§§ 361, 361.5)

If a child is removed from the physical custody of the parent or guardian under either section 361 or 361.5, the court must:

(1) State the facts on which the decision is based; and

(2) Notify the parents that their parental rights may be terminated if custody is not returned within 6 months of the dispositional hearing or within 12 months of the date the child entered foster care, whichever time limit is applicable.

(Subd (g) relettered effective January 1, 2024; adopted as subd (f); previously relettered as subd (g) effective July 1, 1995, as subd (i) effective January 1, 2011, and as subd (h) effective January 1, 2017; previously amended effective January 1, 2001, July 1, 2002, January 1, 2015.)

(h) Setting a hearing under section 366.26

At the disposition hearing, the court may not set a hearing under section 366.26 to consider termination of the rights of only one parent unless that parent is the only surviving parent, or the rights of the other parent have been terminated by a California court of competent jurisdiction or by a court of competent jurisdiction of another state under the statutes of that state, or the other parent has relinquished custody of the child to the county welfare department.

(Subd (h) relettered effective January 1, 2024; adopted as subd (j) effective July 1, 1997; previously amended effective July 1, 2002; previously relettered as subd (l) effective January 1, 2011, and as subd (i) effective January 1, 2017.)

Rule 5.695 amended effective January 1, 2024; adopted as rule 1456 effective January 1, 1991; previously amended and renumbered effective January 1, 2007; previously amended effective January 1, 1993, July 1, 1993, January 1, 1994, January 1, 1995, July 1, 1995, January 1, 1996, January 1, 1997, July 1, 1997, January 1, 1999, July 1, 1999, January 1, 2001, July 1, 2001, July 1, 2002, January 1, 2004, January 1, 2006, January 1, 2008, January 1, 2010, January 1, 2011, January 1, 2014, January 1, 2015, January 1, 2017, January 1, 2019, and January 1, 2021.

Rule 5.697. Disposition hearing for a nonminor (Welf. & Inst. Code, §§ 224.1, 295, 303, 358, 358.1, 361, 361.6, 366.31, 390, 391)

(a) Purpose

This rule provides the procedures that must be followed when a disposition hearing for a nonminor is set under Welfare and Institutions Code section 358(d).

(Subd (a) adopted effective January 1, 2021.)

(b) Notice of hearing (§§ 291, 295)

(1) The social worker must serve written notice of the hearing in the manner provided in section 291 to all persons required to receive notice under section 295, including the nonminor's parent or guardian.

(2) The social worker must serve a copy of the *Nonminor's Informed Consent to Hold Disposition Hearing* (form JV-463) with the notice to the youth.

(Subd (b) adopted effective January 1, 2021.)

(c) Informed consent (§§ 317, 358)

(1) Unless the court has appointed a guardian ad litem for the nonminor or the nonminor is not locatable after reasonable and documented efforts have been made to locate the nonminor, the court must find that the nonminor:

(A) Understands the potential benefits of continued dependency;

(B) Has been informed of their right to seek termination of dependency jurisdiction under section 391 if the court establishes dependency;

(C) Has been informed of their right to have dependency reinstated under section 388(e) if the court establishes dependency; and

(D) Has had the opportunity to confer with their attorney regarding providing informed consent.

(2) The youth must give informed consent to the disposition hearing by completing and signing *Nonminor's Informed Consent to Hold Disposition Hearing* (form JV-463). The youth or their attorney must file the form with the court at or before the scheduled disposition hearing.

(3) If the nonminor is not competent to direct counsel and give informed consent in accordance with Code of Civil Procedure section 372 and Probate Code sections 810 thru 813, the court must appoint a guardian ad litem to determine whether to provide informed consent on the nonminor's behalf by completing and signing *Nonminor's Informed Consent to Hold Disposition Hearing* (form JV-463) and filing it with the court at or before the scheduled disposition hearing.

(Subd (c) adopted effective January 1, 2021.)

(d) Conduct of the hearing (§§ 295, 303, 358, 361)

(1) The hearing may be attended, as appropriate, by participants invited by the nonminor in addition to those entitled to notice under (b).

(2) The nonminor may appear by telephone as provided in rule 5.900(e).

(3) If the nonminor or the nonminor's guardian ad litem does not provide informed consent, the court must vacate the temporary orders made under section 319, and dependency or general jurisdiction must not be retained. Before dismissing jurisdiction, the court must make the following findings:

(A) Notice was given as required by law;

(B) The requirements of (c)(1) have been met unless a guardian ad litem has been appointed for the nonminor or the nonminor could not be located after reasonable and documented efforts have been made to locate the nonminor;

(C) If the reason the nonminor did not give informed consent is because the social worker could not locate the nonminor, the court must find that after reasonable and documented efforts the nonminor could not be located.

(4) If the nonminor or the nonminor's guardian ad litem does provide informed consent, the court must proceed to a disposition hearing consistent with this rule and section 358(d). The parent or guardian of the nonminor may participate as a party in the disposition hearing, receive the social study and other evidence submitted for the hearing, and present evidence. The parent's participation is limited to addressing the court's consideration of whether one of the conditions of section 361(c) existed immediately before the nonminor attained 18 years of age.

(Subd (d) adopted effective January 1, 2021.)

(e) Social study (§§ 358, 358.1, 361.6, 366.31)

(1) The petitioner must prepare a social study of the nonminor if the court proceeds to a disposition hearing. The social study must include a discussion of all matters relevant to disposition and a recommendation for disposition. The petitioner's social study must include the following information:

(A) Whether one of the conditions of section 361(c) existed immediately before the youth attained 18 years of age.

(B) The reasonable efforts that were made to prevent or eliminate the need for removal.

(C) A plan for achieving legal permanence or successful adulthood, if reunification is not being considered.

(D) If reunification services are being considered:

(i) A plan for reuniting the nonminor with the family, including a plan of visitation, developed in collaboration with the nonminor, parent or guardian, and child and family team;

(ii) Whether the nonminor and parent or guardian were actively involved in the development of the case plan;

(iii) The extent of progress the parent or guardian has made toward alleviating or mitigating the causes necessitating placement in foster care;

(iv) Whether the nonminor and parent, parents, or guardian agree to court-ordered reunification services;

(v) Whether reunification services are in the best interest of the nonminor; and

(vi) Whether there is a substantial probability that the nonminor will be able to safely reside in the home of the parent or guardian by the next review hearing date.

(E) The social worker's efforts to comply with rule 5.637, including but not limited to:

(i) The number of relatives identified and the relationship of each to the nonminor;

(ii) The number and relationship of those relatives described by (i) who were located and notified;

(iii) The number and relationship of those relatives described by (ii) who are interested in ongoing contact with the nonminor;

(iv) The number and relationship of those relatives described by (ii) who are interested in providing placement for the nonminor; and

(v) If it is known or there is reason to know that the nonminor is an Indian child, efforts to locate extended family members as defined in section 224.1, and evidence that all individuals contacted have been provided with information about the option of obtaining approval for placement through the tribe's license or approval procedure.

(F) If siblings are not placed together, an explanation of why they have not been placed together in the same home, what efforts are being made to place the siblings together, or why making those efforts would be contrary to the safety and well-being of any of the siblings.

(G) How and when the Transitional Independent Living Case Plan was developed, including the nature and the extent of the nonminor's participation in its development and, for an Indian child who has elected to have the Indian Child Welfare Act apply to them, the extent of consultation with the tribal representative.

(H) All other relevant information as required in sections 358 and 358.1.

(I) The requirements of section 366.31(b).

(J) If the recommendation is to consider the findings in (h)(3)(C) at the disposition hearing:

(i) the requirements of section 366.31(d), if reunification services under section 361.6 are recommended, or

(ii) information addressing the required judicial determinations of section 366.31(e).

(2) The petitioner must submit the social study and copies of it to the court clerk at least 48 hours before the disposition hearing is set to begin, and the clerk must make the copies available to the parties and attorneys. A continuance within statutory time limits must be granted on the request of a party who has not been furnished with a copy of the social study in accordance with this rule.

(Subd (e) amended effective January 1, 2023; adopted effective January 1, 2021; previously amended effective September 1, 2021, and October 1, 2021.)

(f) Case plan and Transitional Independent Living Case Plan (§§ 11401, 16501.1)

(1) Whenever court-ordered services are provided, the social worker must prepare a case plan consistent with section 16501.1 and the requirements of rule 5.690(c).

(2) At least 48 hours before the hearing, the nonminor's Transitional Independent Living Case Plan must be submitted with the report that the social worker prepared for the hearing and must include:

(A) The individualized plan for the nonminor to satisfy one or more of the criteria in section 11403(b) and the nonminor's anticipated placement as specified in section 11402; and

(B) The nonminor's alternate plan for their transition to independence—including housing, education, employment, and a support system—in the event that the nonminor does not remain under juvenile court jurisdiction.

(Subd (f) adopted effective January 1, 2021.)

(g) Evidence considered (§§ 358, 360)

At a hearing held under this rule, the court must receive in evidence and consider the following:

(1) The social study described in (e), the report of any CASA volunteer, and any relevant evidence offered by the petitioner, nonminor, or parent or guardian. The court may require production of other relevant evidence on its own motion. In the order of disposition, the court must state that the social study and the study or evaluation by the CASA volunteer, if any, have been read and considered by the court.

(2) The case plan, if applicable, and the Transitional Independent Living Case Plan.

(Subd (g) adopted effective January 1, 2021.)

(h) Findings and orders (§§ 358, 358.1, 361, 361.6, 390)

After the nonminor or the nonminor's guardian ad litem provides informed consent, the court must consider the safety of the nonminor, determine if notice was given as required by law, and determine if by clear and convincing evidence one of the conditions of section 361(c) existed immediately before the nonminor attained 18 years of age.

(1) If the court does not find by clear and convincing evidence that one of the conditions of section 361(c) existed immediately before the nonminor attained 18 years of age, the court must vacate the temporary orders made under section 319 and dismiss dependency jurisdiction.

(2) If the court finds by clear and convincing evidence that one of the conditions of section 361(c) existed immediately before the nonminor attained 18 years of age, the court must declare dependency and:

(A) Order the continuation of juvenile court jurisdiction and, consistent with (3), set a nonminor dependent review hearing under section 366.31 and rule 5.903 within 60 days or six months, or

(B) Set a hearing to consider termination of juvenile court jurisdiction over the nonminor dependent under rule 5.555 within 30 days, if the nonminor dependent chooses not to remain in foster care.

(3) If the court makes the finding in (2), the following findings and orders must be made and included in the written court documentation of the hearing, with the exception of those findings and orders stated in (C) that may be made at the nonminor disposition hearing or at a nonminor dependent status review hearing under section 366.31 and rule 5.903 to be held within 60 days:

(A) Findings

(i) Whether reasonable efforts have been made to prevent or eliminate the need for removal;

(ii) Whether the social worker has exercised due diligence in conducting the required investigation to identify, locate, and notify the nonminor dependent's relatives consistent with section 309(e); and

(iii) Whether a nonminor who is an Indian child chooses to have the Indian Child Welfare Act apply to them as a nonminor dependent.

(B) Orders

(i) Order that placement and care is vested with the placing agency.

(ii) Order the county agency to comply with rule 5.481, if there was no inquiry or determination of whether the nonminor dependent was an Indian child before the nonminor dependent attained 18 years of age and the nonminor dependent requests an Indian Child Welfare Act determination.

(iii) The court may order family reunification services under 361.6 for the nonminor and the parent or legal guardian. Court-ordered reunification services must not exceed the time frames as stated in section 361.5.

(C) The following findings and orders must be made either at the nonminor disposition hearing held under this rule and section 358(d), or at a nonminor dependent status review hearing under rule 5.903 and section 366.31 held within 60 days of the nonminor disposition hearing:

(i) The findings and orders required by rule 5.903(e);

(ii) For a nonminor dependent whose case plan is court-ordered family reunification services, a determination of the following:

a. The extent of the agency's compliance with the case plan in making reasonable efforts or, in the case of an Indian child, active efforts, as described in section 361.7, to create a safe home of the parent or guardian for the nonminor dependent to reside in or to complete whatever steps are necessary to finalize the permanent placement of the nonminor dependent; and

b. The extent of progress the parents or legal guardians have made toward alleviating or mitigating the causes necessitating placement in foster care.

(Subd (h) amended effective January 1, 2023; adopted effective January 1, 2021.)

Rule 5.697 amended effective January 1, 2023; adopted effective January 1, 2021; previously amended effective September 1, 2021, and October 1, 2021.

Rule 5.700. Termination of jurisdiction—custody and visitation orders (§§ 302, 304, 361.2, 362.4, 726.5)

When the juvenile court terminates its jurisdiction over a dependent or ward of the court and places the child in the home of a parent, it may issue an order determining the rights to custody of and visitation with the child. The court may also issue protective orders as provided in section 213.5 or as described in Family Code section 6218.

(a) Effect of order

Any order issued under this rule continues in effect until modified or terminated by a later order of a superior court with jurisdiction to make determinations about the custody of the child. The order may be modified or terminated only if the superior court finds both that:

(1) There has been a significant change of circumstances since the juvenile court issued the order; and

(2) Modification or termination of the order is in the best interest of the child.

(Subd (a) adopted effective January 1, 2016.)

(b) Preparation and transmission of order

The order must be prepared on *Custody Order—Juvenile—Final Judgment* (form JV-200). The court must direct either the parent, parent's attorney, county counsel, or clerk to:

(1) Prepare the order for the court's signature; and

(2) Transmit the order within 10 calendar days after the order is signed to any superior court where a proceeding described in (c)(1) is pending or, if no such proceeding exists, to the superior court of, in order of preference:

(A) The county in which the parent who has been given sole physical custody resides;

(B) The county in which the children's primary residence is located if no parent has been given sole physical custody; or

(C) A county or other location where any parent resides.

(Subd (b) amended and relettered effective January 1, 2016; adopted as part of subd (a).)

(c) Procedures for filing order—receiving court

On receiving a juvenile court custody order transmitted under (b)(2), the clerk of the receiving court must immediately file the juvenile court order as follows.

(1) Except as provided in paragraph (2), the juvenile court order must be filed in any pending nullity, dissolution, legal separation, guardianship, Uniform Parentage Act, Domestic Violence Prevention Act, or other family law custody proceeding and, when filed, becomes a part of that proceeding.

(2) If the only pending proceeding related to the child in the receiving court is filed under Family Code section 17400 et seq., the clerk must proceed as follows.

(A) If the receiving court has issued a custody or visitation order in the pending proceeding, the clerk must file the received order in that proceeding.

(B) If the receiving court has not issued a custody or visitation order in the pending proceeding, the clerk must not file the received order in that proceeding, but must instead proceed under paragraph (3).

(3) If no dependency, family law, or guardianship proceeding affecting custody or visitation of the child is pending, the order must be used to open a new custody proceeding in the receiving court. The clerk must immediately open a family law file without charging a filing fee, and assign a case number, and file the order in the new case file.

(Subd (c) amended and relettered effective January 1, 2016; adopted as part of subd (a).)

(d) Endorsed filed copy—clerk's certificate of service

Within 15 court days of receiving the order, the clerk of the receiving court must send an endorsed filed copy of the order showing the case number assigned by the receiving court by first-class mail or by electronic means in accordance with section 212.5 to the child's parents and the originating juvenile court, with a completed clerk's certificate of service, for inclusion in the child's file.

(Subd (d) amended effective January 1, 2019; adopted as part of subd (a); previously amended and relettered effective January 1, 2016.)

Rule 5.700 amended effective January 1, 2019; adopted as rule 1457 effective January 1, 1990; previously amended effective January 1, 1994, January 1, 2001, and January 1, 2016; previously amended and renumbered as rule 5.700 effective January 1, 2007.

Rule 5.705. Setting a hearing under section 366.26

At a disposition hearing, a review hearing, or at any other hearing regarding a dependent child, the court must not set a hearing under section 366.26 to consider termination of the rights of only one parent unless that parent is the only surviving parent, or the rights of the other parent have been terminated by a California court of competent jurisdiction or by a court of competent jurisdiction of another state under the statutes of that state, or the other parent has relinquished custody of the child to the county welfare department.

Rule 5.705 amended and renumbered effective January 1, 2007; adopted as rule 1459 effective July 1, 1990; previously amended effective January 1, 1994, and July 1, 1997.

Article 4
Reviews, Permanent Planning

Rule 5.706. Family maintenance review hearings (§ 364)
Rule 5.707. Review or dispositional hearing requirements for child approaching majority (§§ 224.1, 366(a)(1)(F), 366.3, 366.31, 16501.1(f)(16))
Rule 5.708. General review hearing requirements
Rule 5.710. Six-month review hearing
Rule 5.715. Twelve-month permanency hearing
Rule 5.720. Eighteen-month permanency review hearing
Rule 5.722. Twenty-four-month subsequent permanency review hearing
Rule 5.725. Selection of permanent plan (§§ 366.24, 366.26, 727.3, 727.31)
Rule 5.726. Prospective adoptive parent designation (§§ 366.26(n), 16010.6)
Rule 5.727. Proposed removal (§ 366.26(n))
Rule 5.728. Emergency removal (§ 366.26(n))
Rule 5.730. Adoption (§§ 366.24, 366.26(e), Fam. Code, § 8600 et seq.)
Rule 5.735. Legal guardianship
Rule 5.740. Hearings after selection of a permanent plan (§§ 366.26, 366.3, 16501.1)

Rule 5.706. Family maintenance review hearings (§ 364)

(a) Notice (§ 292)

The petitioner or the court clerk must give notice of review hearings on *Notice of Review Hearing* (form JV-280), in the manner provided in section 292, to all persons required to receive notice under section 292 and to any CASA volunteer that has been appointed on the case.

(Subd (a) relettered effective January 1, 2017; adopted as subd (b) effective January 1, 2010.)

(b) Release of Information to the Medical Board of California

If the child has signed *Position on Release of Information to Medical Board of California* (form JV-228), the social worker must provide the child with a blank copy of *Withdrawal of Release of Information to Medical Board of California* (form JV-229) before the hearing if it is the last hearing before the child turns 18 years of age or if the social worker is recommending termination of juvenile court jurisdiction.

(Subd (b) adopted effective September 1, 2020.)

(c) Court considerations and findings

(1) The court must consider the report prepared by the petitioner, the report of any CASA volunteer, and the case plan submitted for this hearing.

(2) In considering the case plan submitted for the hearing, the court must find as follows:

(A) The child was actively involved in the development of his or her own case plan as age and developmentally appropriate; or

(B) The child was not actively involved in the development of his or her own case plan. If the court makes such a finding, the court must order the agency to actively involve the child in the development of his or her own case plan, unless the court finds that the child is unable, unavailable, or unwilling to participate; and

(C) Each parent was actively involved in the development of the case plan; or

(D) Each parent was not actively involved in the development of the case plan. If the court makes such a finding, the court must order the agency to actively involve each parent in the development of the case plan, unless the court finds that each parent is unable, unavailable, or unwilling to participate.

(Subd (c) relettered effective September 1, 2020; adopted as subd (d) effective January 1, 2010; previously relettered as subd (b) effective January 1, 2017.)

(d) Conduct of hearing (§ 364)

If the court retains jurisdiction, the court must order continued services and set a review hearing within six months. The court must determine whether continued supervision is necessary under section 364(c).

(Subd (d) relettered effective September 1, 2020; adopted as subd (e) effective January 1, 2010; previously amended and relettered as subd (c) effective January 1, 2017.)

(e) Reasonable cause (§ 364)

In any case in which the court has ordered that a parent or legal guardian retain physical custody of a child subject to supervision by a social worker, and the social worker subsequently receives a report of acts or circumstances that indicate there is reasonable cause to believe that the child is a person described under section 300(a), (d), or (e), the social worker must file a subsequent petition under section 342 or a supplemental petition under section 387. If, as a result of the proceedings under the section 342 or 387 petition, the court finds that the child is a person described in section 300(a), (d), or (e), the court must remove the child from the care, custody, and control of the child's parent or legal guardian and must commit the child to the care, custody, and control of the social worker under section 361.

(Subd (e) relettered effective September 1, 2020; adopted as subd (f) effective January 1, 2010; previously relettered as subd (d) effective January 1, 2017.)

(f) Child's education (§§ 361, 366, 366.1)

The court must consider the child's education, including whether it is necessary to limit the right of the parent or legal guardian to make educational or developmental-services decisions for the child, following the requirements and procedures in rules 5.649, 5.650, and 5.651 and in section 361(a).

(Subd (f) relettered effective September 1, 2020; adopted as subd (g) effective January 1, 2010; previously amended and relettered as subd (e) effective January 1, 2017.)

Rule 5.706 amended effective September 1, 2020; adopted effective January 1, 2010; previously amended effective January 1, 2017.

Rule 5.707. Review or dispositional hearing requirements for child approaching majority (§§ 224.1, 366(a)(1)(F), 366.3, 366.31, 16501.1(f)(16))

(a) Reports

At the last review hearing before the child attains 18 years of age held under section 366.21, 366.22, 366.25, or 366.3, or at the dispositional hearing held under section 360 if no review hearing will be set before the child attains 18 years of age, in addition to complying with all other statutory and rule requirements applicable to the report prepared by the social worker for the hearing, the report must include a description of:

(1) The child's plans to remain under juvenile court jurisdiction as a nonminor dependent including the criteria in section 11403(b) that he or she plans to meet;

(2) The efforts made by the social worker to help the child meet one or more of the criteria in section 11403(b);

(3) For an Indian child to whom the Indian Child Welfare Act applies, his or her plans to continue to be considered an Indian child for the purposes of the ongoing application of the Indian Child Welfare Act to him or her as a nonminor dependent;

(4) Whether the child has applied for and, if so, the status of any in-progress application pending for title XVI Supplemental Security Income benefits and, if such an application is pending, whether it will be in the child's best interest to continue juvenile court jurisdiction until a final decision is issued to ensure that the child receives continued assistance with the application process;

(5) Whether the child has an in-progress application pending for Special Immigrant Juvenile Status or other applicable application for legal residency and whether an active dependency case is required for that application;

(6) The efforts made by the social worker toward providing the child with the written information, documents, and services described in section 391(b) and (c), and to the extent that the child has not yet been provided with them, the barriers to providing the information, documents, or services and the steps that will be taken to overcome those barriers by the date the child attains 18 years of age;

(7) When and how the child was informed of his or her right to have juvenile court jurisdiction terminated when he or she attains 18 years of age;

(8) When and how the child was provided with information about the potential benefits of remaining under juvenile court jurisdiction as a nonminor dependent and the social worker's assessment of the child's understanding of those benefits; and

(9) When and how the child was informed that if juvenile court jurisdiction is terminated after he or she attains 18 years of age, he or she has the right to file a request to return to foster care and have the juvenile court resume jurisdiction over him or her as a nonminor dependent.

(Subd (a) amended effective January 1, 2021; adopted effective January 1, 2012; previously amended effective July 1, 2012, and January 1, 2016.)

(b) Transitional Independent Living Case Plan

At the last review hearing before the child attains 18 years of age held under section 366.21, 366.22, 366.25, or 366.3, or at the dispositional hearing held under section 360 if no review hearing will be set before the child attains 18 years of age, the child's Transitional Independent Living Case Plan:

(1) Must be submitted with the social worker's report prepared for the hearing at least 10 calendar days before the hearing; and

(2) Must include:

(A) The individualized plan for the child to satisfy one or more of the criteria in section 11403(b) and the child's anticipated placement as specified in section 11402; and

(B) The child's alternate plan for his or her transition to independence, including housing, education, employment, and a support system in the event the child does not remain under juvenile court jurisdiction after attaining 18 years of age.

(Subd (b) amended effective January 1, 2016; adopted effective January 1, 2012.)

(c) Findings

(1) At the last review hearing before the child attains 18 years of age held under section 366.21, 366.22, 366.25, or 366.3, or at the dispositional hearing held under section 360 if no review hearing will be set before the child attains 18 years of age, in addition to complying with all other statutory and rule requirements applicable to the hearing, the court must make the following findings in the written court documentation of the hearing:

(A) Whether the child's Transitional Independent Living Case Plan includes a plan for the child to satisfy one or more of the criteria in section 11403(b) and the specific criteria it is anticipated the child will satisfy;

(B) Whether there is included in the child's Transitional Independent Living Case Plan an alternative plan for the child's transition to independence, including housing, education, employment, and a support system in the event the child does not remain under juvenile court jurisdiction after attaining 18 years of age;

(C) For an Indian child to whom the Indian Child Welfare Act applies, whether he or she intends to continue to be considered an Indian child for the purposes of the ongoing application of the Indian Child Welfare Act to him or her as a nonminor dependent;

(D) Whether the child has an in-progress application pending for title XVI Supplemental Security Income benefits and, if such an application is pending, whether it is in the child's best interest to continue juvenile court jurisdiction until a final decision has been issued to ensure that the child receives continued assistance with the application process;

(E) Whether the child has an in-progress application pending for Special Immigrant Juvenile Status or other applicable application for legal residency and whether an active dependency case is required for that application;

(F) Whether all the information, documents, and services in sections 391(b) and (c) were provided to the child, and whether the barriers to providing any missing information, documents, or services can be overcome by the date the child attains 18 years of age;

(G) Whether the child has been informed of his or her right to have juvenile court jurisdiction terminated when he or she attains 18 years of age;

(H) Whether the child understands the potential benefits of remaining under juvenile court jurisdiction as a nonminor dependent; and

(I) Whether the child has been informed that if juvenile court jurisdiction is terminated after he or she attains 18 years of age, he or she has the right to file a request to return to foster care and have the juvenile court resume jurisdiction over him or her as a nonminor dependent.

(2) The hearing must be continued for no more than five court days for the submission of additional information as ordered by the court if the court finds that the report and Transitional Independent Living Case Plan submitted by the social worker do not provide the information required by (a) and (b) and the court is unable to make all the findings required by (c)(1).

(Subd (c) amended effective January 1, 2021; adopted effective January 1, 2012; previously amended effective July 1, 2012, January 1, 2014, and January 1, 2016.)

(d) Orders

(1) For a child who intends to remain under juvenile court jurisdiction as a nonminor dependent, as defined in section 11400(v), after attaining 18 years of age, the court must set a nonminor dependent status review hearing under rule 5.903 within six months from the date of the current hearing.

(2) For a child who does not intend to remain under juvenile court as a nonminor dependent, as defined in section 11400(v), after attaining 18 years of age, the court must:

(A) Set a hearing under rule 5.555 for a date within one month after the child's 18th birthday, for the child who requests that the juvenile court terminate its jurisdiction after he or she attains 18 years of age; or

(B) Set a hearing under section 366.21, 366.22, 366.25, or 366.3 no more than six months from the date of the current hearing, for a child who will remain under juvenile court jurisdiction in a foster care placement.

(Subd (d) amended effective July 1, 2012; adopted effective January 1, 2012.)

Rule 5.707 amended effective January 1, 2021; adopted effective January 1, 2012; previously amended effective July 1, 2012, January 1, 2014, and January 1, 2016.

Rule 5.708. General review hearing requirements

(a) Notice of hearing (§ 293)

The petitioner or the clerk must serve written notice of review hearings on *Notice of Review Hearing* (form JV-280), in the manner provided in sections 224.2 or 293 as appropriate, to all persons or entities entitled to notice under sections 224.2 and 293 and to any CASA volunteer, educational rights holder, or surrogate parent appointed to the case.

(Subd (a) amended and relettered effective January 1, 2017; adopted as subd (b) effective January 1, 2010; previously amended effective January 1, 2014.)

(b) Reports (§§ 366.05, 366.1, 366.21, 366.22, 366.25, 16022)

Before the hearing, the social worker must investigate and file a report describing the services offered to the family, progress made, and, if relevant, the prognosis for return of the child to the parent or legal guardian.

(1) The report must include:

(A) Recommendations for court orders and the reasons for those recommendations;

(B) A description of the efforts made to achieve legal permanence for the child if reunification efforts fail;

(C) A factual discussion of each item listed in sections 366.1 and 366.21(c); and

(D) A factual discussion of the information required by section 16002(b).

(2) At least 10 calendar days before the hearing, the social worker must file the report and provide copies to the parent or legal guardian and his or her counsel, to counsel for the child, to any CASA volunteer, and, in the case of an Indian child, to the child's identified Indian tribe. The social worker must provide a summary of the recommendations to any foster parents, relative caregivers, or certified foster parents who have been approved for adoption.

(3) The court must read and consider, and state on the record that it has read and considered, the report of the social worker, the report of any CASA volunteer, the case plan submitted for the hearing, any report submitted by the child's caregiver under section 366.21(d), and any other evidence.

(Subd (b) relettered effective January 1, 2017; adopted as subd (c) effective January 1, 2010; previously amended effective July 1, 2010, and January 1, 2016.)

(c) Release of Information to the Medical Board of California

If the child has signed *Position on Release of Information to Medical Board of California* (form JV-228), the social worker must provide the child with a blank copy of *Withdrawal of Release of Information to Medical Board of California* (form JV-229) before the hearing if it is the last hearing before the child turns 18 years of age or if the social worker is recommending termination of juvenile court jurisdiction.

(Subd (c) adopted effective September 1, 2020.)

(d) Reasonable services (§§ 366, 366.21, 366.22, 366.25, 366.3)

(1) If the child is not returned to the custody of the parent or legal guardian, the court must consider whether reasonable services have been offered or provided. The court must find that reasonable services have been offered or provided or have not been offered or provided.

(2) If the child is not returned to the custody of the parent or legal guardian, the court must consider the safety of the child and make the findings listed in sections 366(a) and 16002.

(Subd (d) relettered effective September 1, 2020; adopted as subd (e) effective January 1, 2010; previously amended and relettered as subd (c) effective January 1, 2017.)

(e) Educational and developmental-services needs (§§ 361, 366, 366.1, 366.3)

The court must consider the educational and developmental-services needs of each child and nonminor or nonminor dependent, including whether it is necessary to limit the rights of the parent or legal guardian to make educational or developmental-services decisions for the child. If the court limits those rights or, in the case of a nonminor or nonminor dependent who has chosen not to make educational or developmental-services decisions for him- or herself or has been deemed incompetent, finds that appointment would be in the best interests of the nonminor or nonminor dependent, the court must appoint a responsible adult as the educational rights holder as defined in rule 5.502. Any limitation on the rights of a parent or guardian to make educational or developmental-services decisions for the child must be specified in the court order. The court must follow the procedures in rules 5.649–5.651.

(Subd (e) relettered effective September 1, 2020; adopted as subd (f) effective January 1, 2010; previously amended effective January 1, 2014, and January 1, 2016; previously relettered as subd (d) effective January 1, 2017.)

(f) Case plan (§§ 16001.9, 16501.1)

The court must consider the case plan submitted for the hearing and must find as follows:

(1) The case plan meets the requirements of section 16501.1; or

(2) The case plan does not meet the requirements of section 16501.1, in which case the court must order the agency to comply with the requirements of section 16501.1; and

(3) The child was actively involved, as age- and developmentally appropriate, in the development of the case plan and plan for permanent placement; or

(4) The child was not actively involved, as age- and developmentally appropriate, in the development of the case plan and plan for permanent placement, in which case the court must order the agency to actively involve the child in the development of the case plan and plan for permanent placement, unless the court finds the child is unable, unavailable, or unwilling to participate; and

(5) Each parent or legal guardian was actively involved in the development of the case plan and plan for permanent placement; or

(6) Each parent or legal guardian was not actively involved in the development of the case plan and plan for permanent placement, in which case the court must order the agency to actively involve that parent or legal guardian in the development of the case plan and plan for permanent placement, unless the court finds that the parent or legal guardian is unable, unavailable, or unwilling to participate; and

(7) In the case of an Indian child, the agency consulted with the Indian child's tribe, as defined in rule 5.502, and the tribe was actively involved in the development of the case plan and plan for permanent placement, including consideration of tribal customary adoption as an appropriate permanent plan for the child if reunification is unsuccessful; or

(8) The agency did not consult with the Indian child's tribe, as defined in rule 5.502, and the tribe was not actively involved in the development of the case plan and plan for permanent placement, including consideration of tribal customary adoption as an appropriate permanent plan for the child if reunification is unsuccessful, in which case the court must order the agency to do so, unless the court finds that the tribe is unable, unavailable, or unwilling to participate; and

(9) For a child 12 years of age or older in a permanent placement, the child was given the opportunity to review the case plan, sign it, and receive a copy; or

(10) The child was not given the opportunity to review the case plan, sign it, and receive a copy, in which case the court must order the agency to give the child the opportunity to review the case plan, sign it, and receive a copy.

(Subd (f) relettered effective September 1, 2020; adopted as subd (g) effective January 1, 2010; previously amended effective July 1, 2010, January 1, 2014, January 1, 2016, and January 1, 2019; amended and relettered as subd (e) effective January 1, 2016.)

(g) Sibling findings; additional findings (§§ 366, 16002)

(1) The court must determine whether the child has other siblings under the court's jurisdiction. If so, the court must make the additional determinations required by section 366(a)(1)(D); and

(2) The court must enter any additional findings as required by section 366 and section 16002.

(Subd (g) relettered effective September 1, 2020; adopted as subd (j) effective January 1, 2010; previously amended effective January 1, 2016; previously relettered as subd (f) effective January 1, 2017.)

(h) Placement with noncustodial parent (§ 361.2)

If at any review hearing the court places the child with a noncustodial parent, or if the court has previously made such a placement, the court may, after stating on the record or in writing the factual basis for the order:

(1) Continue supervision and reunification services;

(2) Order custody to the noncustodial parent, continue supervision, and order family maintenance services; or

(3) Order custody to the noncustodial parent, terminate jurisdiction, and direct that *Custody Order—Juvenile—Final Judgment* (form JV-200) be prepared and filed under rule 5.700.

(Subd (h) relettered effective September 1, 2020; adopted as subd (k) effective January 1, 2010; previously relettered as subd (g) effective January 1, 2017.)

(i) Setting a hearing under section 366.26 for one parent

The court may not set a hearing under section 366.26 to consider termination of the rights of only one parent unless:

(1) That parent is the only surviving parent;

(2) The rights of the other parent have been terminated by a California court of competent jurisdiction or by a court of competent jurisdiction of another state under the statutes of that state; or

(3) The other parent has relinquished custody of the child to the county welfare department.

(Subd (i) relettered effective September 1, 2020; adopted as subd (l) effective January 1, 2010; previously relettered as subd (h) effective January 1, 2017.)

(j) Requirements on setting a section 366.26 hearing (§§ 366.21, 366.22, 366.25)

The court must make the following orders and determinations when setting a hearing under section 366.26:

(1) The court must ensure that notice is provided as required by section 294.

(2) The court must follow all procedures in rule 5.590 regarding writ petition rights, advisements, and forms.

(Subd (j) relettered effective September 1, 2020; adopted as subd (n) effective January 1, 2010; previously amended effective July 1, 2010, January 1, 2014, January 1, 2015, January 1, 2016, and July 1, 2016; previously amended and relettered as subd (i) effective January 1, 2017.)

(k) Appeal of order setting section 366.26 hearing

An appeal of any order setting a hearing under section 366.26 is subject to the limitation stated in subdivision (l) of section 366.26 and must follow the procedures in rules 8.400–8.416.

(Subd (k) relettered effective September 1, 2020; adopted as subd (o) effective January 1, 2010; relettered as subd (j) effective January 1, 2017; previously amended effective January 1, 2019.)

Rule 5.708 amended effective September 1, 2020; adopted effective January 1, 2010; previously amended effective July 1, 2010, January 1, 2014, January 1, 2015, January 1, 2016, July 1, 2016, January 1, 2017, and January 1, 2019.

Rule 5.710. Six-month review hearing

(a) Determinations and conduct of hearing (§§ 364, 366, 366.1, 366.21)

At the hearing, the court and all parties must comply with all relevant requirements and procedures in rule 5.708, General review hearing requirements. The court must make all appropriate findings and orders specified in rule 5.708 and proceed under section 366.21(e) and (g), and as follows:

(1) *Order return of the child or find that return would be detrimental*

If the child is returned, the court may order the termination of dependency jurisdiction or order continued dependency services and set a review hearing within 6 months.

(2) *Place with noncustodial parent*

If the court has previously placed or at this hearing places the child with a noncustodial parent, the court must follow the procedures in rule 5.708(g) and section 361.2.

(3) *Set a section 366.26 hearing*

If the court does not return custody of the child to the parent or legal guardian, the court may set a hearing under section 366.26 within 120 days, as provided in (b).

(4) *Continue the case for a 12-month permanency hearing*

If the child is not returned and the court does not set a section 366.26 hearing, the court must order that any reunification services previously ordered will continue to be offered to the parent or legal guardian, if appropriate. The court may modify those services as appropriate or order additional services reasonably believed to facilitate the return of the child to the parent or legal guardian. The court must set a date for the next hearing no later than 12 months from the date the child entered foster care as defined in section 361.49.

(Subd (a) amended effective January 1, 2018; repealed and adopted as subd (d) effective January 1, 1990; relettered as subd (e) effective January 1, 1992; previously amended effective January 1, 1999, July 1, 1999, January 1, 2001, July 1, 2002, January 1, 2004, January 1, 2005, and January 1, 2007; previously repealed, amended and relettered as subd (b) effective January 1, 2010 and as subd (a) effective January 1, 2017.)

(b) Setting a section 366.26 hearing (§§ 366.21, 366.215)

(1) The court may set a hearing under section 366.26 within 120 days if any of the conditions in section 366.21(e) are met; or the parent is deceased.

(2) At the hearing, the court and all parties must comply with all relevant requirements and procedures related to section 366.26 hearings in rule 5.708, General review hearing requirements. The court must make all appropriate findings and orders specified in rule 5.708.

(Subd (b) amended and relettered effective January 1, 2017; repealed and adopted as subd (e); previously amended and relettered as subd (f) effective January 1, 1992, and as subd (c) effective January 1, 2010; previously amended effective January 1, 1993, January 1, 1995, July 1, 1997, January 1, 1999, July 1, 1999, January 1, 2000, January 1, 2001, July 1, 2002, January 1, 2004, January 1, 2005, January 1, 2006, January 1, 2007, January 1, 2010, January 1, 2011, January 1, 2014, and January 1, 2015.)

Rule 5.710 amended effective January 1, 2018; adopted as rule 1460 effective January 1, 1990; previously amended and renumbered effective January 1, 2007; previously amended effective January 1, 1992, January 1, 1993, January 1, 1995, July 1, 1995, July 1, 1997, January 1, 1999, July 1, 1999, January 1, 2000, January 1, 2001, July 1, 2002, January 1, 2004, January 1, 2005, January 1, 2006, January 1, 2010, January 1, 2011, January 1, 2014, January 1, 2015, and January 1, 2017.

Rule 5.715. Twelve-month permanency hearing

(a) Requirement for 12-month review; setting of hearing (§§ 293, 366.21)

The case of any dependent child whom the court has removed from the custody of the parent or legal guardian must be set for a permanency hearing within 12 months of the date the child entered foster care, as defined in section 361.49, and no later than 18 months from the date of the initial removal.

(Subd (a) amended effective January 1, 2017; previously amended effective January 1, 2001, January 1, 2004, January 1, 2006, January 1, 2007, and January 1, 2010.)

(b) Determinations and conduct of hearing (§§ 309(e), 361.5, 366, 366.1, 366.21)

At the hearing, the court and all parties must comply with all relevant requirements and procedures in rule 5.708, General review hearing requirements. The court must make all appropriate findings and orders specified in rule 5.708 and proceed under section 366.21(f) and (g), and as follows:

(1) The requirements in rule 5.708(c) must be followed in entering a reasonable services finding.

(2) If the court has previously placed or at this hearing places the child with a noncustodial parent, the court must follow the procedures in rule 5.708(g) and section 361.2.

(3) The court may order that the name and address of the foster home remain confidential.

(4) In the case of an Indian child, if the child is not returned to his or her parent or legal guardian, the court must determine whether:

(A) The agency has consulted the child's tribe about tribal customary adoption;

(B) The child's tribe concurs with tribal customary adoption; and

(C) Tribal customary adoption is an appropriate permanent plan for the child.

(5) If the child is not returned to his or her parent or legal guardian and the court terminates reunification services, the court must find as follows:

(A) The agency has made diligent efforts to locate an appropriate relative; or

(B) The agency has not made diligent efforts to locate an appropriate relative. If the court makes such a finding, the court or administrative review panel must order the agency to make diligent efforts to locate an appropriate relative; and

(C) Each relative whose name has been submitted to the agency as a possible caregiver has been evaluated as an appropriate placement resource; or

(D) Each relative whose name has been submitted to the agency as a possible caregiver has not been evaluated as an appropriate placement resource. If the court makes such a finding, the court must order the agency to evaluate as an appropriate placement resource, each relative whose name has been submitted to the agency as a possible caregiver.

(Subd (b) amended effective January 1, 2018; repealed and adopted as subd (c)(2) effective January 1, 1990; previously amended and relettered as subd (c) effective July 1, 1999, as subd (d) effective January 1, 2002, as subd (c) effective January 1, 2001, and as subd (b) effective January 1, 2010; previously amended effective January 1, 1992, January 1, 1993, January 1, 1995, July 1, 1995, July 1, 1997, January 1, 1999, January 1, 2004, January 1, 2005, January 1, 2007, July 1, 2010, January 1, 2014, and January 1, 2017.)

Rule 5.715 amended effective January 1, 2018; adopted as rule 1461 effective January 1, 1990; previously amended and renumbered effective January 1, 2007; previously amended effective January 1, 1992, January 1, 1993, January 1, 1994, January 1, 1995, July 1, 1995, July 1, 1997, January 1, 1999, July 1, 1999, January 1, 2000, January 1, 2001, January 1, 2004, January 1, 2005, January 1, 2006, January 1, 2010, July 1, 2010, January 1, 2014, and January 1, 2017.

Rule 5.720. Eighteen-month permanency review hearing

(a) Determinations and conduct of hearing (§§ 309(e), 361.5, 366.22)

At the hearing the court and all parties must comply with all relevant requirements and procedures in rule 5.708, General review hearing requirements. The court must make all appropriate findings and orders specified in rule 5.708, and proceed under section 366.22 and as follows:

(1) If the court has previously placed or at this hearing places the child with a noncustodial parent, the court must follow the procedures in rule 5.708(g) and section 361.2.

(2) The court may order that the name and address of the foster home remain confidential.

(3) In the case of an Indian child, if the child is not returned to his or her parent or legal guardian, the court must determine whether:

(A) The agency has consulted the child's tribe about tribal customary adoption;

(B) The child's tribe concurs with tribal customary adoption; and

(C) Tribal customary adoption is an appropriate permanent plan for the child.

(4) If the child is not returned to his or her parent or legal guardian and the court terminates reunification services, the court must find as follows:

(A) The agency has made diligent efforts to locate an appropriate relative; or

(B) The agency has not made diligent efforts to locate an appropriate relative. If the court makes such a finding, the court must order the agency to make diligent efforts to locate an appropriate relative; and

(C) Each relative whose name has been submitted to the agency as a possible caregiver has been evaluated as an appropriate placement resource; or

(D) Each relative whose name has been submitted to the agency as a possible caregiver has not been evaluated as an appropriate placement resource. If the court makes such a finding, the court must order the agency to evaluate as an appropriate placement resource, each relative whose name has been submitted to the agency as a possible caregiver.

(Subd (a) amended and relettered effective January 1, 2017; repealed and adopted as subd (b) effective January 1, 1990; previously amended and relettered as subd (c) effective January 1, 2005, and as subd (b) effective January 1, 2010; previously amended effective July 1, 1991, January 1, 1992, January 1, 1993, January 1, 1995, July 1, 1995, January 1, 1999, July 1, 1999, January 1, 2006, July 1, 2006, January 1, 2007, July 1, 2007, July 1, 2010, January 1, 2014, and January 1, 2015.)

Rule 5.720 amended effective January 1, 2017; repealed and adopted as rule 1462 effective January 1, 1990; previously amended and renumbered effective January 1, 2007; previously amended effective July 1, 1991, January 1, 1992, January 1, 1993, January 1, 1994, January 1, 1995, July 1, 1995, July 1, 1997, January 1, 1999, July 1, 1999, January 1, 2001, January 1, 2005, January 1, 2006, July 1, 2006, July 1, 2007, January 1, 2010, July 1, 2010, January 1, 2014, and January 1, 2015.

Rule 5.722. Twenty-four-month subsequent permanency review hearing

(a) Determinations and conduct of hearing (§§ 309(e), 366, 366.1, 366.25)

At the hearing, the court and all parties must comply with all relevant requirements and procedures in rule 5.708, General review hearing requirements. The court must make all appropriate findings and orders specified in rule 5.708, and proceed under section 366.25 and as follows:

(1) The requirements in rule 5.708(c) must be followed in entering a reasonable services finding.

(2) If the court does not order the return of the child to the custody of the parent or legal guardian, the court must specify the factual basis for its finding of risk of detriment.

(3) The court may order that the name and address of the foster home remain confidential. The court and all parties must comply with all relevant requirements, procedures, findings, and orders related to section 366.26 hearings in rule 5.708(h)–(j).

(4) In the case of an Indian child, if the child is not returned to his or her parent or legal guardian, the court must determine whether:

(A) The agency has consulted the child's tribe about tribal customary adoption;

(B) The child's tribe concurs with tribal customary adoption; and

(C) Tribal customary adoption is an appropriate permanent plan for the child.

(5) If the child is not returned to his or her parent or legal guardian and the court terminates reunification services, the court must find as follows:

(A) The agency has made diligent efforts to locate an appropriate relative; or

(B) The agency has not made diligent efforts to locate an appropriate relative. If the court makes such a finding, the court must order the agency to make diligent efforts to locate an appropriate relative; and

(C) Each relative whose name has been submitted to the agency as a possible caregiver has been evaluated as an appropriate placement resource; or

(D) Each relative whose name has been submitted to the agency as a possible caregiver has not been evaluated as an appropriate placement resource. If the court makes such a finding, the court must order the agency to evaluate as an appropriate placement resource, each relative whose name has been submitted to the agency as a possible caregiver.

(Subd (a) amended and relettered effective January 1, 2017; adopted as subd (b) effective January 1, 2010; previously amended effective July 1, 2010.)

Rule 5.722 amended effective January 1, 2017; adopted effective January 1, 2010; previously amended effective July 1, 2010.

Rule 5.725. Selection of permanent plan (§§ 366.24, 366.26, 727.3, 727.31)

(a) Application of rule

This rule applies to children who have been declared dependents or wards of the juvenile court.

(1) The court may not terminate the rights of only one parent under section 366.26 unless that parent is the only surviving parent; or unless the rights of the other parent have been terminated by a California court of competent jurisdiction or by a court of competent jurisdiction of another state under the statutes of that state; or unless the other parent has relinquished custody of the child to the welfare department.

(2) Sections 360, 366.26, 727.3, 727.31, and 728 provide the exclusive authority and procedures for the juvenile court to establish a legal guardianship for a dependent child or ward of the court.

(3) For termination of the parental rights of an Indian child, the procedures in this rule and in rule 5.485 must be followed.

(Subd (a) amended effective January 1, 2021; previously amended effective January 1, 1994, July 1, 2002, January 1, 2007, January 1, 2009, and January 1, 2017.)

(b) Notice of hearing (§ 294)

In addition to the requirements stated in section 294, notice must be given to any CASA volunteer, Indian custodian, and de facto parent on *Notice of Hearing on Selection of a Permanent Plan* (form JV-300).

(Subd (b) amended effective January 1, 2017; previously amended effective January 1, 1992, July 1, 1992, July 1, 1995, July 1, 2002, January 1, 2005, January 1, 2006, and January 1, 2007.)

(c) Report

Before the hearing, petitioner must prepare an assessment under section 366.21(i). At least 10 calendar days before the hearing, the petitioner must file the assessment, provide copies to each parent or guardian and all counsel of record, and provide a summary of the recommendations to the present custodians of the child, to any CASA volunteer, and to the tribe of an Indian child.

(Subd (c) amended effective January 1, 2007; adopted effective January 1, 1992; previously amended effective July 1, 1995, and July 1, 2002.)

(d) Conduct of hearing

At the hearing, the court must state on the record that the court has read and considered the report of petitioner, the report of any CASA volunteer, the case plan submitted for this hearing, any report submitted by the child's caregiver under section 366.21(d), and any other evidence, and must proceed under section 366.26 and as follows:

(1) In the case of an Indian child, after the agency has consulted with the tribe, when the court has determined with the concurrence of the tribe that tribal customary adoption is the appropriate permanent plan for the child, order a tribal customary adoption in accordance with section 366.24.

(2) The party claiming that termination of parental rights would be detrimental to the child has the burden of proving the detriment.

(3) If the court finds that section 366.26(c)(1)(A) or section 366.26(c)(2)(A) applies, the court must appoint the present custodian or other appropriate person to become the child's legal guardian or must order the child to remain in foster care.

(A) If the court orders that the child remain in foster care, it may order that the name and address of the foster home remain confidential.

(B) If the court finds that removal of the child from the home of a foster parent or relative who is not willing to become a legal guardian for the child would be seriously detrimental to the emotional well-being of the child, then the child must not be removed. The foster parent or relative must be willing to provide, and capable of providing, a stable and permanent home for the child and must have substantial psychological ties with the child.

(4) The court must consider the case plan submitted for this hearing and must make the required findings and determinations in rule 5.708(e).

(Subd (d) amended effective January 1, 2017; repealed and adopted as subd (c) effective January 1, 1991; previously amended and relettered as subd (d) effective January 1, 1992, and as subd (e) effective January 1, 2005; previously relettered as subd (d) effective January 1, 2010; previously amended effective July 1, 1994, January 1, 1999, July 1, 1999, July 1, 2002, January 1, 2006, January 1, 2007, January 1, 2009, July 1, 2010, and January 1, 2015.)

(e) Procedures—adoption

(1) The court must follow the procedures in section 366.24 or 366.26, as appropriate.

(2) An order of the court terminating parental rights, ordering adoption under section 366.26 or, in the case of an Indian child, ordering tribal customary adoption under section 366.24, is conclusive and binding on the child, the parent, and all other persons who have been served under the provisions of section 294. Once a final order of adoption has issued, the order may not be set aside or modified by the court, except as provided in section 366.26(e)(3) and (i)(3) and rules 5.538, 5.540, and 5.542 with regard to orders by a referee.

(Subd (e) amended effective January 1, 2020; adopted as subd (d) effective January 1, 1991; previously relettered as subd (e) effective January 1, 1992, as subd (f) effective January 1, 2005, and as subd (e) effective January 1, 2010; previously amended effective July 1, 1992, January 1, 1995, July 1, 2002, January 1, 2006, January 1, 2007, July 1, 2010, January 1, 2015, and January 1, 2017.)

(f) Purpose of termination of parental rights

The purpose of termination of parental rights is to free the child for adoption. Therefore, the court must not terminate the rights of only one parent unless that parent is the only surviving parent, or the rights of the other parent have been terminated by a California court of competent jurisdiction or by a court of competent jurisdiction of another state under the statutes of that state, or the other parent has relinquished custody of the child to the county welfare department. The rights of all parents—whether natural, presumed, biological, alleged, or unknown—must be terminated in order to free the child for adoption.

(Subd (f) repealed and relettered effective January 1, 2021; adopted as subd (g) effective July 1, 1997; previously amended and relettered as subd (h) effective January 1, 2005; previously amended effective July 1, 2002, and July 1, 2015; previously relettered as subd (g) effective January 1, 2010.)

(g) Advisement of appeal rights

The court must advise all parties of their appeal rights as provided in rule 5.585 and section 366.26(l).

(Subd (g) relettered effective January 1, 2021; repealed and adopted as subd (f) effective January 1, 1991; previously relettered as subd (g) effective January 1, 1992; amended and relettered as subd (h) effective July 1, 1997; previously relettered as subd (i) effective January 1, 2005; previously relettered as subd (h) effective January 1, 2010; previously amended effective July 1, 2002, January 1, 2006, and January 1, 2007.)

Rule 5.725 amended effective January 1, 2021; repealed and adopted as rule 1463 effective January 1, 1991; previously amended and renumbered effective January 1, 2007; previously amended effective January 1, 1992, July 1, 1992, January 1, 1994, July 1, 1994, January 1, 1995, July 1, 1995, July 1, 1997, January 1, 1999, July 1, 1999, July 1, 2002, January 1, 2005, January 1, 2006, January 1, 2009, January 1, 2010, July 1, 2010, January 1, 2015, January 1, 2017, and January 1, 2020.

Rule 5.726. Prospective adoptive parent designation (§§ 366.26(n), 16010.6)

(a) Request procedure

A dependent child's caregiver may be designated as a prospective adoptive parent. The court may make the designation on its own motion or on a request by a caregiver, the child, a social worker, the child's identified Indian tribe, or the attorney for any of these parties.

(1) A request for designation as a prospective adoptive parent may be made at a hearing where parental rights are terminated or a plan of tribal customary adoption is ordered or thereafter, whether or not the child's removal from the home of the prospective adoptive parent is at issue.

(2) A request may be made orally.

(3) If a request for prospective adoptive parent designation is made in writing, it must be made on *Request for Prospective Adoptive Parent Designation* (form JV-321).

(4) The address and telephone number of the caregiver and the child may be kept confidential by filing *Confidential Information—Prospective Adoptive Parent* (form JV-322), with form JV-321. Form JV-322 must be kept in the court file under seal, and only the court, the child's attorney, the agency, and the child's CASA volunteer may have access to this information.

(Subd (a) amended effective July 1, 2010; previously amended effective January 1, 2007, and January 1, 2008.)

(b) Facilitation steps

Steps to facilitate the adoption process include those listed in section 366.26(n)(2) and, in the case of an Indian child when tribal customary adoption has been identified as the child's permanent plan, the child's identified Indian tribe has designated the caregiver as the prospective adoptive parent.

(Subd (b) amended effective January 1, 2017; previously amended effective January 1, 2007, and July 1, 2010.)

(c) Hearing on request for prospective adoptive parent designation

(1) The court must determine whether the caregiver meets the criteria in section 366.26(n)(1).

(2) If the court finds that the caregiver does not meet the criteria in section 366.26(n)(1), the court may deny the request without a hearing.

(3) If the court finds that the caregiver meets the criteria in section 366.26(n)(1), the court must set a hearing as set forth in (4) below.

(4) If it appears to the court that the request for designation as a prospective adoptive parent will be contested, or if the court wants to receive further evidence on the request, the court must set a hearing.

(A) If the request for designation is made at the same time a petition is filed to object to removal of the child from the caregiver's home, the court must set a hearing as follows:

(i) The hearing must be set as soon as possible and not later than five court days after the petition objecting to removal is filed with the court.

(ii) If the court for good cause cannot set the matter for hearing five court days after the petition objecting to removal is filed, the court must set the matter for hearing as soon as possible.

(iii) The matter may be set for hearing more than five court days after the petition objecting to removal is filed if this delay is necessary to allow participation by the child's identified Indian tribe or the child's Indian custodian.

(B) If the request for designation is made before the agency serves notice of a proposed removal or before an emergency removal has occurred, the court must set a hearing within 30 calendar days after the request for designation is made.

(5) If all parties stipulate to the designation of the caregiver as a prospective adoptive parent, the court may order the designation without a hearing.

(Subd (c) amended effective January 1, 2017; previously amended effective January 1, 2007.)

(d) Notice of designation hearing

After the court has ordered a hearing on a request for prospective-adoptive-parent designation, notice of the hearing must be as described below.

(1) The following participants must be noticed:

(A) The adoption agency;

(B) The current caregiver;

(C) The child's attorney;

(D) The child, if the child is 10 years of age or older;

(E) The child's identified Indian tribe if any;

(F) The child's Indian custodian if any; and

(G) The child's CASA program if any.

(2) If the request for designation is made at the same time as a request for hearing on a proposed or emergency removal, notice of the designation hearing must be provided with notice of the hearing on proposed removal, as stated in rule 5.727(f).

(3) If the request for designation is made before the agency serves notice of a proposed removal or before an emergency removal occurred, notice must be as follows:

(A) Service of the notice must be either by first-class mail or electronic service in accordance with section 212.5 sent at least 15 calendar days before the hearing date to the last known address of the person to be noticed, or by personal service on the person at least 10 calendar days before the hearing.

(B) *Prospective Adoptive Parent Designation Order* (form JV-327) must be used to provide notice of a hearing on the request for prospective adoptive parent designation.

(C) The clerk must provide notice of the hearing to the participants listed in (1) above, if the court, caregiver, or child requested the hearing.

(D) The child's attorney must provide notice of the hearing to the participants listed in (1) above, if the child's attorney requested the hearing.

(E) *Proof of Notice Under Section 366.26(n)* (form JV-326) must be filed with the court before the hearing on the request for prospective adoptive parent designation.

(Subd (d) amended effective January 1, 2019; previously amended effective January 1, 2007, January 1, 2008, and January 1, 2017.)

(e) Termination of designation

If the prospective adoptive parent no longer meets the criteria in section 366.26(n)(1), a request to vacate the order designating the caregiver as a prospective adoptive parent may be filed under section 388 and rule 5.570.

(Subd (e) amended effective January 1, 2017; previously amended effective January 1, 2007.)

(f) Confidentiality

If the telephone or address of the caregiver or the child is confidential, all forms must be kept in the court file under seal. Only the court, the child's attorney, the agency, and the child's CASA volunteer may have access to this information.

Rule 5.726 amended effective January 1, 2019; adopted as rule 1463.1 effective July 1, 2006; previously amended and renumbered effective January 1, 2007; previously amended effective January 1, 2008, July 1, 2010, and January 1, 2017.

Rule 5.727. Proposed removal (§ 366.26(n))

(a) Application of rule

This rule applies, after termination of parental rights or, in the case of tribal customary adoption, modification of parental rights, to the removal by the Department of Social Services (DSS) or a licensed adoption agency of a dependent child from a prospective adoptive parent or from a caregiver who may meet the criteria for designation as a prospective adoptive parent in section 366.26(n)(1). This rule does not apply if the caregiver requests the child's removal.

(Subd (a) amended effective January 1, 2017; previously amended effective January 1, 2007, and July 1, 2010.)

(b) Participants to be served with notice

Before removing a child from the home of a prospective adoptive parent as defined in section 366.26(n)(1) or from the home of a caregiver who may meet the criteria of a prospective adoptive parent in section 366.26(n)(1), and as soon as possible after a decision is made to remove the child, the agency must notify the following participants of the proposed removal:

(1) The court;

(2) The current caregiver, if that caregiver either is a designated prospective adoptive parent or, on the date of service of the notice, meets the criteria in section 366.26(n)(1);

(3) The child's attorney;

(4) The child, if the child is 10 years of age or older;

(5) The child's identified Indian tribe if any;

(6) The child's Indian custodian if any;

(7) The child's CASA program if any; and

(8) The child's sibling's attorney, if the change in placement of a dependent child will result in the separation of siblings currently placed together. Notice must be made in accordance with Code of Civil Procedure section 1010.6.

(Subd (b) amended effective January 1, 2019; previously amended effective January 1, 2007, and January 1, 2017.)

(c) Form of notice

DSS or the agency must provide notice on *Notice of Intent to Remove Child* (form JV-323). A blank copy of *Objection to Removal* (form JV-325) and *Request for Prospective Adoptive Parent Designation* (form JV-321) must also be provided to all participants listed in (b) except the court.

(Subd (c) amended effective January 1, 2017; previously amended effective January 1, 2007, and January 1, 2008.)

(d) Service of notice

DSS or the agency must serve notice of its intent to remove a child as follows:

(1) DSS or the agency must serve notice either by first-class mail or by electronic service in accordance with section 212.5, sent to the last known address of the person to be noticed, or by personal service.

(2) If service is by first-class mail, service is completed and time to respond is extended by five calendar days.

(3) If service is made through electronic means, service is completed and time to respond is extended in accordance with Code of Civil Procedure section 1010.6.

(4) Notice to the child's identified Indian tribe and Indian custodian must comply with the requirements of section 224.2.

(5) *Proof of Notice Under Section 366.26(n)* (form JV-326) must be filed with the court before the hearing on the proposed removal.

(Subd (d) amended effective January 1, 2019; previously amended effective January 1, 2007, January 1, 2008, January 1, 2011, and January 1, 2017.)

(e) Objection to proposed removal

Each participant who receives notice under (b) may object to the proposed removal of the child and may request a hearing.

(1) A request for hearing on the proposed removal must be made on *Objection to Removal* (form JV-325).

(2) A request for hearing on the proposed removal must be made within five court or seven calendar days from the date of notification, whichever is longer. If service of the notification is by mail, time to request a hearing is extended by five calendar days. If service of the notification is by electronic means, time to request a hearing is extended in accordance with Code of Civil Procedure section 1010.6.

(3) The court must set a hearing as follows:

(A) The hearing must be set as soon as possible and not later than five court days after the objection is filed with the court.

(B) If the court for good cause is unable to set the matter for hearing five court days after the petition is filed, the court must set the matter for hearing as soon as possible.

(C) The matter may be set for hearing more than five court days after the objection is filed if this delay is necessary to allow participation by the child's identified Indian tribe or the child's Indian custodian.

(Subd (e) amended effective January 1, 2019; previously amended effective January 1, 2007, January 1, 2008, and January 1, 2017.)

(f) Notice of hearing on proposed removal

After the court has ordered a hearing on a proposed removal, notice of the hearing must be as follows:

(1) The clerk must provide notice of the hearing to the agency and the participants listed in (b) above, if the court, caregiver, or child requested the hearing.

(2) The child's attorney must provide notice of the hearing to the agency and the participants listed in (b) above, if the child's attorney requested the hearing.

(3) Notice must be by personal service or by telephone. Notice by personal service must include a copy of the completed forms *Notice of Intent to Remove Child* (form JV-323) and *Objection to Removal* (form JV-325). Telephone notice must include the reasons for and against the removal, as indicated on forms JV-323 and JV-325.

(4) *Proof of Notice Under 366.26(n)* (form JV-326) must be filed with the court before the hearing on the proposed removal.

(Subd (f) amended effective January 1, 2019; previously amended effective January 1, 2007, January 1, 2008, and January 1, 2017.)

(g) Burden of proof

At a hearing on an intent to remove the child, the agency intending to remove the child must prove by a preponderance of the evidence that the proposed removal is in the best interest of the child.

(h) Confidentiality

If the telephone or address of the caregiver or the child is confidential, all forms must be kept in the court file under seal. Only the court, the child's attorney, the agency, and the child's CASA volunteer may have access to this information.

(i) Appeal

If the court order made after a hearing on an intent to remove a child is appealed, the appeal must be brought as petition for writ review under rules 8.454 and 8.456.

(Subd (i) amended effective January 1, 2017; previously amended effective January 1, 2007.)

Rule 5.727 amended effective January 1, 2019; adopted as rule 1463.3 effective July 1, 2006; previously amended and renumbered effective January 1, 2007; previously amended effective January 1, 2008, July 1, 2010, January 1, 2011, and January 1, 2017.

Rule 5.728. Emergency removal (§ 366.26(n))

(a) Application of rule

This rule applies, after termination of parental rights or, in the case of tribal customary adoption, modification of parental rights, to the removal by the Department of Social Services (DSS) or a licensed adoption agency of a dependent child from the home of a prospective adoptive parent or a caregiver who may meet the criteria for designation as a prospective adoptive parent in section 366.26(n)(1) when the DSS or the licensed adoption agency has determined a removal must occur immediately due to a risk of physical or emotional harm. This rule does not apply if the child is removed at the request of the caregiver.

(Subd (a) amended effective January 1, 2017; previously amended effective January 1, 2007, and July 1, 2010.)

(b) Participants to be noticed

After removing a child from the home of a prospective adoptive parent, or from the home of a caregiver who may meet the criteria of a prospective adoptive parent in section 366.26(n)(1), because of risk of physical or emotional harm, the agency must notify the following participants of the emergency removal:

(1) The court;

(2) The caregiver, who is a prospective adoptive parent or who, on the date of service of the notice, may meet the criteria in section 366.26(n)(1);

(3) The child's attorney;

(4) The child if the child is 10 years of age or older;

(5) The child's identified Indian tribe if any;

(6) The child's Indian custodian if any;

(7) The child's CASA program if any; and

(8) The child's sibling's attorney, if the change in placement of a dependent child will result in the separation of siblings currently placed together. Notice must be made in accordance with section 1010.6 of the Code of Civil Procedure.

(Subd (b) amended effective January 1, 2019; previously amended effective January 1, 2007, and January 1, 2017.)

(c) Form and service of notice

Notice of Emergency Removal (form JV-324) must be used to provide notice of an emergency removal, as described below.

(1) The agency must provide notice of the emergency removal as soon as possible but no later than two court days after the removal.

(2) Notice must be either by telephone or by personal service of the form.

(3) Telephone notice must include the reasons for removal as indicated on the form, and notice of the right to object to the removal.

(4) Whenever possible, the agency, at the time of the removal, must give a blank copy of *Request for Prospective Adoptive Parent Designation* (form JV-321) and a blank copy of *Objection to Removal* (form JV-325) to the caregiver and, if the child is 10 years of age or older, to the child.

(5) Notice to the court must be served by filing *Notice of Emergency Removal* (form JV-324) and *Proof of Notice Under 366.26(n)* (form JV-326) with the court.

(6) *Proof of Notice Under Section 366.26(n)* (form JV-326) must be filed with the court before the hearing on the proposed removal.

(Subd (c) amended effective January 1, 2019; previously amended effective January 1, 2007, January 1, 2008, and January 1, 2017.)

(d) Objection to emergency removal

Each participant who receives notice under (b) may object to the removal of the child and may request a hearing.

(1) A request for hearing on the emergency removal must be made on *Objection to Removal* (form JV-325).

(2) The court must set a hearing as follows:

(A) The hearing must be set as soon as possible and not later than five court days after the petition objecting to removal is filed with the court.

(B) If the court for good cause cannot set the matter for hearing within five court days after the petition objecting to removal is filed, the court must set the matter for hearing as soon as possible.

(C) The matter may be set for hearing more than five court days after the petition objecting to removal is filed if this delay is necessary to allow participation by the child's identified Indian tribe or the child's Indian custodian.

(Subd (d) amended effective January 1, 2017; previously amended effective January 1, 2007, and January 1, 2008.)

(e) Notice of hearing on emergency removal

After the court has ordered a hearing on an emergency removal, notice of the hearing must be as follows:

(1) The clerk must provide notice of the hearing to the agency and the participants listed in (b) above, if the court, caregiver, or child requested the hearing.

(2) The child's attorney must provide notice of the hearing to the agency and the participants listed in (b) above, if the child's attorney requested the hearing.

(3) Notice must be by personal service or by telephone. Notice by personal service must include a copy of the completed *Notice of Emergency Removal* (form JV-324). Telephone notice must include the reasons for and against the removal, as indicated on forms JV-324 and JV-325.

(4) *Proof of Notice Under Section 366.26(n)* (form JV-326) must be filed with the court before the hearing on the emergency removal.

(Subd (e) amended effective January 1, 2019; previously amended effective January 1, 2007, January 1, 2008, and January 1, 2012.)

(f) Burden of proof

At a hearing on an emergency removal, the agency that removed the child must prove by a preponderance of the evidence that the removal is in the best interest of the child.

(g) Confidentiality

If the telephone or address of the caregiver or the child is confidential, all forms must be kept in the court file under seal. Only the court, the child's attorney, the agency, and the child's CASA volunteer and program may have access to this information.

Rule 5.728 amended effective January 1, 2019; adopted as rule 1463.5 effective July 1, 2006; previously amended and renumbered effective January 1, 2007; previously amended effective January 1, 2008, July 1, 2010, and January 1, 2017.

Rule 5.730. Adoption (§§ 366.24, 366.26(e), Fam. Code, § 8600 et seq.)

(a) Procedures—adoption

(1) The petition for the adoption of a dependent child who has been freed for adoption may be filed in the juvenile court with jurisdiction over the dependency.

(2) All adoption petitions must be completed on *Adoption Request* (form ADOPT-200) and must be verified. In addition, the petitioner must complete *Adoption Agreement* (form ADOPT-210) and *Adoption Order* (form ADOPT-215).

(3) A petitioner seeking to adopt an Indian child must also complete *Adoption of Indian Child* (form ADOPT-220). If applicable, *Parent of Indian Child Agrees to End Parental Rights* (form ADOPT-225) may be filed.

(4) The clerk must open a confidential adoption file for each child and this file must be separate and apart from the dependency file, with an adoption case number different from the dependency case number.

(Subd (a) amended effective January 1, 2007; previously amended effective January 1, 1996, January 1, 1999, and January 1, 2004.)

(b) Notice

The clerk of the court must give notice of the adoption hearing to:

(1) Any attorney of record for the child;

(2) Any CASA volunteer;

(3) The child welfare agency;

(4) The tribe of an Indian child; and

(5) The California Department of Social Services. The notice to the California Department of Social Services must include a copy of the completed *Adoption Request* (form ADOPT-200) and a copy of any adoptive placement agreement or agency joinder filed in the case.

(Subd (b) amended effective January 1, 2007; previously amended effective January 1, 2004.)

(c) Hearing

If the petition for adoption is filed in the juvenile court, the proceeding for adoption must be heard in juvenile court once appellate rights have been exhausted. Each petitioner and the child must be present at the hearing. The hearing may be heard by a referee if the referee is acting as a temporary judge.

(Subd (c) amended effective January 1, 2007; previously amended effective January 1, 1999, and January 1, 2004.)

(d) Record

The record must reflect that the court has read and considered the assessment prepared for the hearing held under section 366.26 and as required by section 366.22(b), the report of any CASA volunteer, and any other reports or documents admitted into evidence.

(Subd (d) amended effective January 1, 2007; previously amended effective January 1, 2004.)

(e) Assessment

The preparer of the assessment may be called and examined by any party to the adoption proceeding.

(f) Consent

(1) At the hearing, each adoptive parent must execute *Adoption Agreement* (form ADOPT-210) in the presence of and with the acknowledgment of the court.

(2) If the child to be adopted is 12 years of age or older, he or she must also execute *Adoption Agreement* (form ADOPT-210), except in the case of a tribal customary adoption.

(Subd (f) amended effective July 1, 2010; previously amended effective January 1, 1999, January 1, 2004, and January 1, 2007.)

(g) Dismissal of jurisdiction

If the petition for adoption is granted, the juvenile court must dismiss the dependency, terminate jurisdiction over the child, and vacate any previously set review hearing dates. A completed *Termination of Dependency (Juvenile)* (form JV-364) must be filed in the child's juvenile dependency file.

(*Subd (g) amended effective January 1, 2007; previously amended effective January 1, 1999, and January 1, 2004.*)

Rule 5.730 amended effective January 1, 2017; adopted as rule 1464 effective July 1, 1995; previously amended effective January 1, 1996, January 1, 1999, January 1, 2004, and July 1, 2010; previously amended and renumbered effective January 1, 2007.

Advisory Committee Comment

Family Code section 8600.5 exempts tribal customary adoption from various provisions of the Family Code applicable to adoptions generally, including section 8602, which requires the consent of a child over the age of 12 to an adoption. However, under Welfare and Institutions Code section 366.24(c)(7), "[t]he child, birth parents, or Indian custodian and the tribal customary adoptive parents and their counsel, if applicable, may present evidence to the tribe regarding the tribal customary adoption and the child's best interest." Under Welfare and Institutions Code section 317(e), for all children over 4 years of age, the attorney for the child must determine the child's wishes and advise the court of the child's wishes. Welfare and Institutions Code section 361.31(e) provides that "[w]here appropriate, the placement preference of the Indian child, when of sufficient age, … shall be considered." This is consistent with Guideline F-3 of the *Guidelines for State Courts; Indian Child Custody Proceedings* issued by the Bureau of Indian Affairs on November 26, 1979, which recognizes that the request and wishes of a child of sufficient age are important in making an effective placement. The committee concludes, therefore, that while the consent of a child over the age of 12 is not required for a tribal customary adoption, the wishes of a child are still an important and appropriate factor for the court to consider and for children's counsel to ascertain and present to the court when determining whether tribal customary adoption is the appropriate permanent plan for an Indian child.

Rule 5.735. Legal guardianship

(a) Proceedings in juvenile court (§§ 360, 366.26)

The proceedings for the appointment of a legal guardian for a dependent child must be held in the juvenile court. The recommendation for appointment of a guardian must be included in the social study report prepared by the county welfare department or in the assessment prepared for the hearing under section 366.26. Neither a separate petition nor a separate hearing is required.

(*Subd (a) amended effective January 1, 2021; previously amended effective July 1, 1997, July 1, 1999, January 1, 2006, and January 1, 2007.*)

(b) Notice; hearing

Unless the court proceeds under section 360(a) at the dispositional hearing, notice of the hearing at which the court considers appointing a legal guardian must be given under section 294, and the hearing must be conducted under the procedures in section 366.26.

(*Subd (b) amended effective January 1, 2021; previously amended effective July 1, 1999, and January 1, 2006.*)

(c) Findings and orders

(1) If the court finds that legal guardianship is the appropriate permanent plan, the court must appoint the guardian and order the clerk to issue letters of guardianship (*Letters of Guardianship (Juvenile)* (form JV-330)) as soon as the guardian has signed the required affirmation. These letters are not subject to the confidentiality protections in section 827.

(2) The court must issue orders regarding visitation of the child by a parent or former guardian, unless the court finds that visitation would be detrimental to the physical or emotional well-being of the child.

(3) The court may issue orders regarding visitation of the child by a relative.

(4) Except as provided in (5), on appointment of a legal guardian under section 360 or 366.26, the court may retain dependency jurisdiction or terminate dependency jurisdiction and retain jurisdiction over the child as a ward of the guardianship under section 366.4.

(5) If the court appoints a relative or nonrelative extended family member as the child's legal guardian and the other requirements in section 366.3(a)(3) apply, the court must terminate dependency jurisdiction and retain jurisdiction over the child under section 366.4 unless the guardian objects or the court finds that exceptional circumstances require it to retain dependency jurisdiction.

(*Subd (c) amended effective January 1, 2021; adopted as subd (d) effective January 1, 1991; previously amended effective July 1, 1999, and January 1, 2006; previously amended and relettered as subd (c) effective January 1, 2017.*)

(d) Notification of appeal rights

The court must advise all parties of their appeal rights as provided in rule 5.590.

(*Subd (d) amended and relettered effective January 1, 2017; adopted as subd (e) effective January 1, 1991; previously amended effective January 1, 2006, and January 1, 2007.*)

Rule 5.735 amended effective January 1, 2021; adopted as rule 1464 effective January 1, 1991; renumbered as rule 1465 effective July 1, 1995; previously amended effective July 1, 1999, January 1, 2006, and January 1, 2017; previously amended and renumbered effective January 1, 2007.

Rule 5.740. Hearings after selection of a permanent plan (§§ 366.26, 366.3, 16501.1)

(a) Review hearings—adoption and guardianship

Following an order for termination of parental rights or, in the case of tribal customary adoption, modification of parental rights, or a plan for the establishment of a legal guardianship under section 366.26, the court must retain jurisdiction and conduct review hearings at least every 6 months to ensure the expeditious completion of the adoption or guardianship.

(1) At the review hearing, the court must consider the report of the petitioner required by section 366.3(g), the report of any CASA volunteer, the case plan submitted for this hearing, and any report submitted by the child's caregiver under section 366.21(d); inquire about the progress being made to provide a permanent home for the child; consider the safety of the child; and enter findings as required by section 366.3(e).

(2) The court or administrative review panel must consider the case plan and make the findings and determinations concerning the child in rule 5.708(e).

(3) When adoption is granted, the court must terminate its jurisdiction.

(4) After a legal guardianship is established, the court may continue dependency jurisdiction or may terminate dependency jurisdiction and retain jurisdiction over the child as a ward of the guardianship under section 366.4. If the court appoints a relative or nonrelative extended family member as the child's guardian and the other requirements in section 366.3(a)(3) apply, the court must terminate dependency jurisdiction and retain jurisdiction over the child under section 366.4 unless the guardian objects or the court finds that exceptional circumstances require it to retain dependency jurisdiction.

(5) Notice of the hearing must be given as provided in section 295.

(6) If the child is not placed for adoption, the court or administrative review panel must find as follows:

(A) Whether the agency has made diligent efforts to locate an appropriate relative. If the court or administrative review panel finds the agency has not made diligent efforts to locate an appropriate relative, the court or administrative review panel must order the agency to do so.

(B) Whether each relative whose name has been submitted to the agency as a possible caregiver has been evaluated as an appropriate placement resource. If the court or administrative review panel finds the agency has not evaluated each relative whose name has been submitted as a possible caregiver, the court or administrative review panel must order the agency to do so.

(*Subd (a) amended effective January 1, 2021; repealed and adopted effective January 1, 1991; previously amended effective January 1, 1992, January 1, 1993, July 1, 1999, January 1, 2005, January 1, 2006, January 1, 2007, July 1, 2010, January 1, 2015, and January 1, 2017.*)

(b) Review hearings—relative care or foster care

Following the establishment of a plan other than those provided for in (a), review hearings must be conducted at least every 6 months by the court or by a local administrative review panel.

(1) At the review hearing, the court or administrative review panel must consider the report of the petitioner, the report of any CASA volunteer, the case plan submitted for this hearing, and any report submitted by the child's caregiver under section 366.21(d); inquire about the progress being made to provide a permanent home for the child; consider the safety of the child; and enter findings as required by section 366.3(e).

(2) The court or administrative review panel must consider the case plan submitted for this hearing and make the findings and determinations concerning the child in rule 5.708(e).

(3) If the child is not placed for adoption, the court or administrative review panel must find as follows:

(A) Whether the agency has made diligent efforts to locate an appropriate relative. If the court or administrative review panel finds the agency has not made diligent efforts to locate an appropriate relative, the court or administrative review panel must order the agency to do so.

(B) Whether each relative whose name has been submitted to the agency as a possible caregiver has been evaluated as an appropriate placement resource. If the court or administrative review panel finds the agency has not evaluated each relative whose name has been submitted as a possible caregiver, the court or administrative review panel must order the agency to do so.

(4) No less frequently than once every 12 months, the court must conduct a review of the previously ordered permanent plan to consider whether the plan continues to be appropriate for the child. The review of the permanent plan may be combined with the 6-month review.

(5) If circumstances have changed since the permanent plan was ordered, the court may order a new permanent plan under section 366.26 at any subsequent hearing, or any party may seek a new permanent plan by a motion filed under section 388 and rule 5.570.

(6) Notice of the hearing must be given as provided in section 295.

(7) The court must continue the child in foster care unless the parents prove, by a preponderance of the evidence, that further efforts at reunification are the best alternative for the child. In those cases, the court may order reunification services for a period not to exceed 6 months.

(Subd (b) amended effective January 1, 2017; repealed and adopted effective January 1, 1991; previously amended effective January 1, 1992, January 1, 1994, January 1, 1998, January 1, 1999, July 1, 1999, January 1, 2005, January 1, 2006, and January 1, 2007.)

(c) Review hearings—youth 16 years of age and older

If the youth is 16 years of age or older, the procedures in section 391 must be followed.

(1) If it is the first review hearing after the youth turns 16 years of age, the social worker must provide the information, documents, and services required by section 391(a) and must use *First Review Hearing After Youth Turns 16 years of Age—Information, Documents, and Services* (form JV-361).

(2) If it is the last review hearing before the youth turns 18 years of age, the social worker must provide the information, documents, and services required by section 391(b)–(c) and must use *Review Hearing for Youth Approaching 18 Years of Age—Information, Documents, and Services* (form JV-362).

(3) If it is a review hearing after the youth turns 18 years of age, the social worker must provide the information, documents, and services required by section 391(c) and must use *Review Hearing for Youth 18 Years of Age or Older—Information, Documents, and Services* (form JV-363). If the court is terminating jurisdiction at this review hearing, the social worker must also provide the information, documents, and services required by section 391(h), must follow the procedures in rule 5.555, and must use *Termination of Juvenile Court Jurisdiction—Nonminor* (form JV-365).

(Subd (c) adopted effective January 1, 2021.)

(d) Hearing on petition to terminate guardianship or modify guardianship orders

A petition to terminate a guardianship established by the juvenile court, to appoint a successor guardian, or to modify or supplement orders concerning a guardianship must be filed in the juvenile court. The procedures described in rule 5.570 must be followed, and *Request to Change Court Order* (form JV-180) must be used.

(1) Proceedings on a petition to terminate a guardianship established under section 366.26 must be heard in the juvenile court. If dependency was terminated at the time of or subsequent to the appointment of the guardian, and dependency is later declared in another county, proceedings to terminate the guardianship may be held in the juvenile court with current dependency jurisdiction.

(2) Not less than 15 court days before the hearing date, the clerk must cause notice of the hearing to be given to the department of social services; the guardian; the child, if 10 years or older; parents whose parental rights have not been terminated; the court that established the guardianship, if in another county; and counsel of record for those entitled to notice.

(3) At the hearing on the petition to terminate the guardianship, the court may do one of the following:

(A) Deny the petition to terminate guardianship;

(B) Deny the petition and request the county welfare department to provide services to the guardian and the ward for the purpose of maintaining the guardianship, consistent with section 301; or

(C) Grant the petition to terminate the guardianship.

(4) If the petition is granted and the court continues or resumes dependency, the court must order that a new plan be developed to provide stability and permanency to the child. Unless the court has already scheduled a hearing to review the child's status, the court must conduct a hearing within 60 days. Parents whose parental rights have not been terminated must be notified of the hearing on the new plan. The court may consider further efforts at reunification only if the parent proves, by a preponderance of the evidence, that the efforts would be the best alternative for the child.

(5) If the court terminates a guardianship established in another county, the clerk of the county of current dependency jurisdiction must transmit a certified copy of the order terminating guardianship within 15 days to the court that established the original guardianship.

(Subd (d) relettered effective January 1, 2021; adopted as subd (c); previously amended effective January 1, 1993, July 1, 1994, July 1, 1999, January 1, 2007, and January 1, 2017.)

Rule 5.740 amended effective January 1, 2021; adopted as rule 1465 effective January 1, 1991; previously renumbered as rule 1466 effective July 1, 1995; previously amended and renumbered effective January 1, 2007; previously amended effective January 1, 1992, January 1, 1993, January 1, 1994, July 1, 1994, January 1, 1998, January 1, 1999, July 1, 1999, July 1, 2002, January 1, 2005, January 1, 2006, July 1, 2010, January 1, 2012, January 1, 2015, and January 1, 2017.)

Chapter 13
Cases Petitioned Under Sections 601 and 602

Chapter 13 renumbered effective January 1, 2008; adopted as Chapter 11 effective July 1, 2002; previously amended and renumbered as Chapter 14, effective January 1, 2007.

Art. 1. Initial Appearance. Rules 5.752–5.764.
Art. 2. Hearing on Transfer of Jurisdiction to Criminal Court. Rules 5.766–5.770.
Art. 3. Jurisdiction. Rules 5.774–5.782.
Art. 4. Disposition. Rules 5.785–5.808.
Art. 5. Reviews and Sealing. Rules 5.810–5.860.

Article 1
Initial Appearance

Rule 5.752. Initial hearing; detention hearings; time limit on custody; setting jurisdiction hearing
Rule 5.754. Commencement of initial hearing—explanation, advisement, admission
Rule 5.756. Conduct of detention hearing
Rule 5.758. Requirements for detention; prima facie case
Rule 5.760. Detention hearing; report; grounds; determinations; findings; orders; factors to consider for detention; restraining orders
Rule 5.762. Detention rehearings
Rule 5.764. Prima facie hearings

Rule 5.752. Initial hearing; detention hearings; time limit on custody; setting jurisdiction hearing

(a) Child not detained; filing petition, setting hearing

If the child is not taken into custody and the authorized petitioner (district attorney or probation officer) determines that a petition or notice of probation violation concerning the child should be filed, the petition or notice must be filed with the clerk of the juvenile court as soon as possible. The clerk must set an initial hearing on the petition within 15 court days.

(Subd (a) amended effective January 1, 2007.)

(b) Time limit on custody; filing petition (§§ 604, 631, 631.1)

A child must be released from custody within 48 hours, excluding noncourt days, after first being taken into custody unless a petition or notice of probation violation has been filed either within that time or before the time the child was first taken into custody.

(Subd (b) amended effective January 1, 2007.)

(c) Time limit on custody—willful misrepresentation of age (§ 631.1)

If the child willfully misrepresents the child's age to be 18 years or older, and this misrepresentation causes an unavoidable delay in investigation that prevents the filing of a petition or of a criminal complaint within 48 hours, excluding noncourt days, after the child has been taken into custody, the child must be released unless a petition or complaint has been filed within 48 hours, excluding noncourt days, from the time the true age is determined.

(Subd (c) amended effective January 1, 2007.)

(d) Time limit on custody—certification of child detained in custody (§ 604)

A child must be released from custody within 48 hours, excluding noncourt days, after certification to juvenile court under rules 4.116 and 5.516(d) unless a petition has been filed.

(Subd (d) amended effective January 1, 2007.)

(e) Time limit for detention hearing—warrant or nonward charged with nonviolent misdemeanor (§ 632)

A detention hearing must be set and commenced as soon as possible, but no later than 48 hours, excluding noncourt days, after the child has been taken into custody, if:

(1) The child has been taken into custody on a warrant or by the authority of the probation officer; or

(2) The child is not on probation or parole and is alleged to have committed a misdemeanor not involving violence, the threat of violence, or the possession or use of a weapon.

(Subd (e) amended effective January 1, 2007.)

(f) Time limit for detention hearing—felony, violent misdemeanor, or ward (§ 632)

A detention hearing must be set and commenced as soon as possible, but no later than the expiration of the next court day after the petition or notice of probation violation has been filed, if:

(1) The child is alleged to have committed a felony;

(2) The child is alleged to have committed a misdemeanor involving violence, the threat of violence, or the possession or use of a weapon; or

(3) The child is a ward currently on probation or parole.

(Subd (f) amended effective January 1, 2007.)

(g) Time limit for hearing—arrival at detention facility (§ 632)

A detention hearing must be set and commenced as soon as possible, but no later than 48 hours, excluding noncourt days, after the child arrives at a detention facility within the county if:

(1) The child was taken into custody in another county and transported in custody to the requesting county;

(2) The child was ordered transported in custody when transferred by the juvenile court of another county under rule 5.610; or

(3) The child is a ward temporarily placed in a secure facility pending a change of placement.

(Subd (g) amended effective January 1, 2007.)

(h) Time limit for hearing—violation of home supervision (§§ 628.1, 636)

A child taken into custody for a violation of a written condition of home supervision, which the child has promised in writing to obey under section 628.1 or 636, must be brought before the court for a detention hearing as soon as possible, but no later than 48 hours, excluding noncourt days, after the child was taken into custody.

(Subd (h) amended effective January 1, 2007.)

(i) Time limits—remedy for not observing (§§ 632, 641)

If the detention hearing is not commenced within the time limits, the child must be released immediately, or, if the child is a ward under section 602 awaiting a change of placement, the child must be placed in a suitable, nonsecure facility.

(Subd (i) amended effective January 1, 2007.)

Rule 5.752 amended and renumbered effective January 1, 2007; repealed and adopted as rule 1471 effective January 1, 1998.

Rule 5.754. Commencement of initial hearing—explanation, advisement, admission

(a) Explanation of proceedings (§ 633)

At the beginning of the initial hearing, whether the child is detained or not detained, the court must give the advisement required by rule 5.534 and must inform the child and each parent and each guardian present of the following:

(1) The contents of the petition;

(2) The nature and possible consequences of juvenile court proceedings; and

(3) If the child has been taken into custody, the reasons for the initial detention and the purpose and scope of the initial hearing.

(Subd (a) amended effective January 1, 2007.)

(b) Admission of allegations; no contest plea

If the child wishes to admit the allegations of the petition or enter a no contest plea at the initial hearing, the court may accept the admission or plea of no contest and must proceed according to rule 5.778.

(Subd (b) amended effective January 1, 2007.)

Rule 5.754 amended and renumbered effective January 1, 2007; repealed and adopted as rule 1472 effective January 1, 1998.

Rule 5.756. Conduct of detention hearing

(a) Right to inspect (§ 827)

The child, the parent, the guardian, and counsel are permitted to inspect and receive copies of police reports, probation reports, and any other documents filed with the court or made available to the probation officer in preparing the probation recommendations.

(Subd (a) amended effective January 1, 2007.)

(b) Examination by court (§ 635)

Subject to the child's privilege against self-incrimination, the court may examine the child, the parent, the guardian, and any other person present who has knowledge or information relevant to the issue of detention and must consider any relevant evidence that the child, the parent, the guardian, or counsel presents.

(Subd (b) amended effective January 1, 2007.)

(c) Evidence required

The court may base its findings and orders solely on written police reports, probation reports, or other documents.

Rule 5.756 amended and renumbered effective January 1, 2007; repealed and adopted as rule 1473 effective January 1, 1998.

Rule 5.758. Requirements for detention; prima facie case

(a) Requirements for detention (§§ 635, 636)

The court must release the child unless the court finds that:

(1) A prima facie showing has been made that the child is described by section 601 or 602;

(2) Continuance in the home is contrary to the child's welfare; and

(3) One or more of the grounds for detention stated in rule 5.760 exist.

However, except as provided in sections 636.2 and 207, no child taken into custody solely on the basis of being a person described in section 601 may be detained in juvenile hall or any other secure facility.

(Subd (a) amended effective January 1, 2007; previously amended effective July 1, 2002.)

(b) Detention in adult facility

A child must not be detained in a jail or lockup used for the confinement of adults, except as provided in section 207.1.

(Subd (b) amended effective July 1, 2002.)

Rule 5.758 amended and renumbered effective January 1, 2007; repealed and adopted as rule 1474 effective January 1, 1998; previously amended effective July 1, 2002.

Rule 5.760. Detention hearing; report; grounds; determinations; findings; orders; factors to consider for detention; restraining orders

(a) Conduct of detention hearing (§§ 635, 636)

The court must consider the written report of the probation officer and any other evidence and may examine the child, any parent or guardian, or any other person with relevant knowledge of the child.

(Subd (a) adopted effective January 1, 2007.)

(b) Written detention report (§§ 635, 636)

If the probation officer has reason to believe that the child is at risk of entering foster care placement, the probation officer must submit a written report to the court that includes the following:

(1) The reasons the child has been removed;

(2) Any prior referral for abuse or neglect of the child and any prior filing of a petition regarding the child under section 300;

(3) The need, if any, for continued detention;

(4) Available services to facilitate the return of the child;

(5) Whether there are any relatives able and willing to provide effective care and control over the child;

(6) Documentation that continuance in the home is contrary to the child's welfare; and

(7) Documentation that reasonable efforts were made to prevent or eliminate the need for removal of the child from the home and documentation of the nature and results of the services provided.

(Subd (b) amended and relettered effective January 1, 2007; adopted as subd (a) effective January 1, 2001; previously amended effective July 1, 2002.)

(c) Grounds for detention (§§ 625.3, 635, 636)

(1) The child must be released unless the court finds that continuance in the home of the parent or legal guardian is contrary to the child's welfare, and one or more of the following grounds for detention exist:

(A) The child has violated an order of the court;

(B) The child has escaped from a commitment of the court;

(C) The child is likely to flee the jurisdiction of the court;

(D) It is a matter of immediate and urgent necessity for the protection of the child; or

(E) It is reasonably necessary for the protection of the person or property of another.

(2) If the child is a dependent of the court under section 300, the court's decision to detain must not be based on the child's status as a dependent of the court or the child welfare services department's inability to provide a placement for the child.

(3) The court may order the child placed on home supervision under the conditions stated in sections 628.1 and 636, or detained in juvenile hall, or in a suitable place designated by the court.

(4) If the court orders the release of a child who is a dependent of the court under section 300, the court must order the child welfare services department either to ensure that the child's current caregiver takes physical custody of the child or to take physical custody of the child and place the child in a licensed or approved placement.

(Subd (c) amended effective January 1, 2016; adopted as subd (a); previously amended effective July 1, 2002; previously amended and relettered as subd (b) effective January 1, 2001, and as subd (c) effective January 1, 2007.)

(d) Required determinations before detention

Before detaining the child, the court must determine whether continuance in the home of the parent or legal guardian is contrary to the child's welfare and whether there are available services that would prevent the need for further detention. The court must make these determinations on a case-by-case basis and must state the evidence relied on in reaching its decision.

(1) If the court determines that the child can be returned to the home of the parent or legal guardian through the provision of services, the court must release the child to the parent or guardian and order that the probation department provide the required services.

(2) If the child cannot be returned to the home of the parent or legal guardian, the court must state the facts on which the detention is based.

(Subd (d) amended effective January 1, 2016; adopted as subd (c) effective July 1, 2002; previously amended and relettered as subd (d) effective January 1, 2007.)

(e) Required findings to support detention (§ 636)

If the court orders the child detained, the court must make the following findings on the record and in the written order. The court must reference the probation officer's report or other evidence relied on to make its determinations:

(1) Continuance in the home of the parent or guardian is contrary to the child's welfare;

(2) Temporary placement and care is the responsibility of the probation officer pending disposition or further order of the court; and

(3) Reasonable efforts have been made to prevent or eliminate the need for removal of the child, or reasonable efforts were not made.

(Subd (e) amended effective January 1, 2016; adopted as subd (b); previously relettered as subd (c) effective January 1, 2001; previously amended and relettered as subd (d) effective July 1, 2002, and as subd (e) effective January 1, 2007.)

(f) Required orders to support detention (§ 636)

If the court orders the child detained, the court must make the following additional orders:

(1) As soon as possible, the probation officer must provide services that will enable the child's parent or legal guardian to obtain such assistance as may be needed to effectively provide the care and control necessary for the child to return home; and

(2) The child's placement and care must be the responsibility of the probation department pending disposition or further order of the court.

(Subd (f) relettered effective January 1, 2007; adopted as subd (e) effective July 1, 2002.)

(g) Factors—violation of court order

Regarding the ground for detention in (c)(1)(A), the court must consider:

(1) The specificity of the court order alleged to have been violated;

(2) The nature and circumstances of the alleged violation;

(3) The severity and gravity of the alleged violation;

(4) Whether the alleged violation endangered the child or others;

(5) The prior history of the child as it relates to any failure to obey orders or directives of the court or probation officer;

(6) Whether there are means to ensure the child's presence at any scheduled court hearing without detaining the child;

(7) The underlying conduct or offense that brought the child before the juvenile court; and

(8) The likelihood that if the petition is sustained, the child will be ordered removed from the custody of the parent or guardian at disposition.

(Subd (g) amended effective July 1, 2023; adopted as subd (c) effective January 1, 1998; previously relettered as subd (d) effective January 1, 2001; previously amended and relettered as subd (f) effective July 1, 2002, and as subd (g) effective January 1, 2007.)

(h) Factors—escape from commitment

Regarding the ground for detention in (c)(1)(B), the court must consider whether or not the child:

(1) Was committed to a county juvenile home, ranch, camp, forestry camp, secure youth treatment facility, or juvenile hall; and

(2) Escaped from the facility or the lawful custody of any officer or person in which the child was placed during commitment.

(Subd (h) amended effective July 1, 2023; adopted as subd (d) effective January 1, 1998; previously relettered as subd (e) effective January 1, 2001; amended and relettered as subd (g) effective July 1, 2002, and as subd (h) effective January 1, 2007; previously amended effective January 1, 2006.)

(i) Factors—likely to flee

Regarding the ground for detention in (c)(1)(C), the court must consider whether or not:

(1) The child has previously fled the jurisdiction of the court or failed to appear in court as ordered;

(2) There are means to ensure the child's presence at any scheduled court hearing without detaining the child;

(3) The child promises to appear at any scheduled court hearing;

(4) The child has a prior history of failure to obey orders or directions of the court or the probation officer;

(5) The child is a resident of the county;

(6) The nature and circumstances of the alleged conduct or offense make it appear likely that the child would flee to avoid the jurisdiction of the court;

(7) The child's home situation is so unstable as to make it appear likely that the child would flee to avoid the jurisdiction of the court; and

(8) Absent a danger to the child, the child would be released on modest bail or own recognizance were the child appearing as an adult in adult court.

(Subd (i) amended effective July 1, 2023; adopted as subd (e) effective January 1, 1998; previously relettered as subd (f) effective January 1, 2001; previously amended and relettered as subd (h) effective July 1, 2002, and as subd (i) effective January 1, 2007.)

(j) Factors—protection of child

Regarding the ground for detention in (c)(1)(D), the court must consider whether or not:

(1) There are means to ensure the care and protection of the child until the next scheduled court appearance;

(2) The child is addicted to or is in imminent danger from the use of a controlled substance or alcohol; and

(3) There exist other compelling circumstances that make detention reasonably necessary.

(Subd (j) amended effective July 1, 2023; adopted as subd (f) effective January 1, 1998; previously relettered as subd (g) effective January 1, 2001; previously amended and relettered as subd (i) effective July 1, 2002, and as subd (j) effective January 1, 2007.)

(k) Factors—protection of person or property of another

Regarding the ground for detention in (c)(1)(E), the court must consider whether or not:

(1) The alleged offense involved physical harm to the person or property of another;

(2) The prior history of the child reveals that the child has caused physical harm to the person or property of another or has posed a substantial threat to the person or property of another; and

(3) There exist other compelling circumstances that make detention reasonably necessary.

(Subd (k) amended effective July 1, 2023; adopted as subd (g) effective January 1, 1998; previously relettered as subd (h) effective January 1, 2001; previously amended and relettered as subd (j) effective July 1, 2002, and as subd (k) effective January 1, 2007.)

(*l*) Restraining orders

As a condition of release or home supervision, the court may issue restraining orders as stated in rule 5.630 or orders restraining the child from any or all of the following:

(1) Molesting, attacking, striking, sexually assaulting, or battering, or from any contact whatsoever with an alleged victim or victim's family;

(2) Presence near or in a particular area or building; or

(3) Associating with or contacting in writing, by phone, or in person any adult or child alleged to have been a companion in the alleged offense.

(Subd (l) amended effective January 1, 2016; adopted as subd (i) effective January 1, 1998; previously relettered as subd (j) effective January 1, 2001; previously amended and relettered as subd (k) effective July 1, 2002, and as subd (l) effective January 1, 2007.)

Rule 5.760 amended effective July 1, 2023; repealed and adopted as rule 1475 effective January 1, 1998; previously amended effective January 1, 2001, July 1, 2002, January 1, 2006, and January 1, 2016; previously amended and renumbered as rule 5.760 effective January 1, 2007.

Rule 5.762. Detention rehearings

(a) No parent or guardian present and not noticed

If the court orders the child detained at the detention hearing and no parent or guardian is present and no parent or guardian has received actual notice of the detention hearing, a parent or guardian may file an affidavit alleging the failure of notice and requesting a detention rehearing. The clerk must set the rehearing within 24 hours of the filing of the affidavit, excluding noncourt days. At the rehearing, the court must proceed under rules 5.752–5.760.

(Subd (a) amended effective January 1, 2007.)

(b) Parent or guardian noticed; parent or guardian not present (§ 637)

If the court determines that the parent or guardian has received adequate notice of the detention hearing, and the parent or guardian fails to appear at the hearing, a request from the parent or guardian for a detention rehearing must be denied, absent a finding that the failure was due to good cause.

(Subd (b) amended effective January 1, 2007.)

(c) Parent or guardian noticed; preparers available (§ 637)

If a parent or guardian received notice of the detention hearing, and the preparers of any reports or other documents relied on by the court in its order detaining the child are present at court or otherwise available for cross-examination, there is no right to a detention rehearing.

(Subd (c) amended effective January 1, 2007.)

Rule 5.762 amended and renumbered effective January 1, 2007; repealed and adopted as rule 1476 effective January 1, 1998.

Rule 5.764. Prima facie hearings

(a) Hearing for further evidence; prima facie case (§ 637)

If the court orders the child detained, and the child or the child's attorney requests that evidence of the prima facie case be presented, the court must set a prima facie hearing for a time within three court days to consider evidence of the prima facie case.

(b) Continuance (§ 637)

If the court determines that a prima facie hearing cannot be held within three court days because of the unavailability of a witness, a reasonable continuance not to exceed five court days may be granted. If at the hearing petitioner fails to establish the prima facie case, the child must be released from custody.

Rule 5.764 adopted effective January 1, 2007.

Article 2
Hearing on Transfer of Jurisdiction to Criminal Court

Title 5, Family and Juvenile Rules—Division 3, Juvenile Rules—Chapter 13, Cases Petitioned Under Sections 601 and 602—Article 2, Hearing on Transfer of Jurisdiction to Criminal Court; amended effective January 1, 2019.

Rule 5.766. General provisions
Rule 5.768. Report of probation officer
Rule 5.770. Conduct of transfer of jurisdiction hearing under section 707

Rule 5.766. General provisions

(a) Hearing on transfer of jurisdiction to criminal court (§ 707)

A youth who is the subject of a petition under section 602 and who was 14 years or older at the time of the alleged felony offense may be considered for prosecution under the general law in a court of criminal jurisdiction. The district attorney or other appropriate prosecuting officer may make a motion to transfer the youth from juvenile court to a court of criminal jurisdiction, in one of the following circumstances:

(1) The youth was 14 or 15 years of age at the time of the alleged offense listed in section 707(b) and was not apprehended before the end of juvenile court jurisdiction.

(2) The youth was 16 years or older at the time of the alleged felony offense.

(Subd (a) amended effective January 1, 2023; previously amended effective January 1, 1996, January 1, 2001, and May 22, 2017.)

(b) Notice (§ 707)

Notice of the transfer hearing must be given at least five judicial days before the hearing. In no case may notice be given following the attachment of jeopardy.

(Subd (b) amended effective May 22, 2007; previously amended effective January 1, 2007.)

(c) Prima facie showing

On the youth's motion, the court must determine whether a prima facie showing has been made that the offense alleged is an offense that makes the youth subject to transfer as set forth in subdivision (a).

(Subd (c) amended effective January 1, 2023; adopted effective May 22, 2017.)

(d) Time of transfer hearing—rules 5.774, 5.776

The transfer of jurisdiction hearing must be held and the court must rule on the request to transfer jurisdiction before the jurisdiction hearing begins. Absent a continuance under rule 5.776 or the youth's waiver of the statutory time period to commence the jurisdiction hearing, the jurisdiction hearing must begin within the time limits under rule 5.774.

(Subd (d) amended effective January 1, 2023; adopted as subd (c); previously amended effective January 1, 2007; previously amended and relettered effective May 22, 2017.)

Rule 5.766 amended effective January 1, 2023; adopted as rule 1486 effective January 1, 1991; previously amended and renumbered effective January 1, 2007; previously amended effective May 22, 2017.

Rule 5.768. Report of probation officer

(a) Contents of report (§ 707)

The probation officer must prepare and submit to the court a report on the behavioral patterns and social history of the youth being considered. The report must include information relevant to the determination of whether the youth should be retained under the jurisdiction of the juvenile court or transferred to the jurisdiction of the criminal court, including information regarding all of the criteria in section 707(a)(3). The report must also include any written or oral statement offered by the victim pursuant to section 656.2.

(Subd (a) amended effective January 1, 2023; previously amended effective January 1, 2007, and May 22, 2017.)

(b) Recommendation of probation officer (§§ 281, 707)

If the court, under section 281, orders the probation officer to include a recommendation, the probation officer must make a recommendation to the court as to whether the youth should be retained under the jurisdiction of the juvenile court or transferred to the jurisdiction of the criminal court.

(Subd (b) amended effective January 1, 2023; previously amended effective January 1, 2007, and May 22, 2017.)

(c) Copies furnished

The probation officer's report on the behavioral patterns and social history of the youth must be furnished to the youth, the parent or guardian, and all counsel at least two court days before commencement of the hearing on the motion. A continuance of at least 24 hours must be granted on the request of any party who has not been furnished the probation officer's report in accordance with this rule.

(Subd (c) amended effective January 1, 2023; previously amended effective January 1, 2007, and May 22, 2017.)

Rule 5.768 amended effective January 1, 2023; adopted as rule 1481 effective January 1, 1991; previously amended and renumbered effective January 1, 2007; previously amended effective May 22, 2017.

Rule 5.770. Conduct of transfer of jurisdiction hearing under section 707

(a) Burden of proof (§ 707)

In a transfer of jurisdiction hearing under section 707, the burden of proving that there should be a transfer of jurisdiction to criminal court jurisdiction is on the petitioner, by clear and convincing evidence.

(Subd (a) amended effective September 1, 2023; previously amended effective January 1, 1996, January 1, 2001, July 1, 2002, and May 22, 2017.)

(b) Criteria to consider (§ 707)

Following receipt of the probation officer's report and any other relevant evidence, the court may order that the youth be transferred to the jurisdiction of the criminal court if the court finds by clear and convincing evidence each of the following:

(1) The youth was 16 years or older at the time of any alleged felony offense, or the youth was 14 or 15 years of age at the time of an alleged felony offense listed in section 707(b) and was not apprehended prior to the end of juvenile court jurisdiction; and

(2) The youth should be transferred to the jurisdiction of the criminal court based on an evaluation of all the criteria in section 707(a)(3)(A)-(E) as provided in that section; and

(3) The youth is not amenable to rehabilitation while under the jurisdiction of the juvenile court.

(Subd (b) amended effective September 1, 2023; adopted as subd (b) effective January 1, 1991; previously amended and relettered as subd (c) effective January

1, 1996; previously amended and relettered effective January 1, 2001; previously amended effective January 1, 2007, May 22, 2017, January 1, 2021, and January 1, 2023.)

(c) Basis for order of transfer

If the court orders a transfer of jurisdiction to the criminal court, the court must recite the basis for its decision in an order entered on the minutes. The court must state on the record the basis for its decision, including how it weighed the evidence and identifying the specific factors on which the court relied to reach its decision. This statement must include the reasons supporting the court's finding that the minor is not amenable to rehabilitation while under the jurisdiction of the juvenile court.

(Subd (c) amended effective September 1, 2023; adopted as subd (c) effective January 1, 1991; previously amended and relettered as subd (d) effective January 1, 1996; amended and relettered effective January 1, 2001; previously amended effective July 1, 2002, January 1, 2007, and May 22, 2017.)

(d) Procedure following findings

(1) If the court finds the youth should be retained within the jurisdiction of the juvenile court, the court must proceed to jurisdiction hearing under rule 5.774.

(2) If the court finds the youth should be transferred to the jurisdiction of the criminal court, the court must make orders under section 707.1 relating to bail and to the appropriate facility for the custody of the youth, or release on own recognizance pending prosecution. The court must set a date for the youth to appear in criminal court and dismiss the petition without prejudice upon the date of that appearance.

(3) When the court rules on the request to transfer the youth to the jurisdiction of the criminal court, the court must advise all parties present regarding appellate review of the order as provided in subdivision (g) of this rule. The advisement may be given orally or in writing when the court makes the ruling. The advisement must include the time for filing the notice of appeal or the petition for extraordinary writ as set forth in subdivision (g) of this rule. The court must advise the youth of the right to appeal, of the necessary steps and time for taking an appeal, of the right to the appointment of counsel if the youth is unable to retain counsel, and the right to a stay.

(Subd (d) amended effective January 1, 2023; adopted as subd (d) effective January 1, 1991; previously relettered as subd (g) effective January 1, 1996, and as subd (f) effective January 1, 2001; previously amended effective July 1, 2002, and January 1, 2007; previously amended and relettered effective May 22, 2017.)

(e) Continuance or stay pending review

(1) If the prosecuting attorney informs the court orally or in writing that a review of the court's decision not to transfer jurisdiction to the criminal court will be sought and requests a continuance of the jurisdiction hearing, the court must grant a continuance for not less than two judicial days to allow time within which to obtain a stay of further proceedings from the reviewing judge or appellate court.

(2) If the youth informs the court orally or in writing that a notice of appeal of the court's decision to transfer jurisdiction to the criminal court will be filed and requests a stay, the court must issue a stay of the criminal court proceedings until a final determination of the appeal. The court retains jurisdiction to modify or lift the stay upon request of the youth.

(Subd (e) amended effective January 1, 2023; adopted as subd (e) effective January 1, 1991; previously relettered as subd (h) effective January 1, 1996, and as subd (g) effective January 1, 2001; previously amended effective July 1, 2002, and January 1, 2007; previously amended and relettered effective May 22, 2017.)

(f) Subsequent role of judicial officer

Unless the youth objects, the judicial officer who has conducted a hearing on a motion to transfer jurisdiction may participate in any subsequent contested jurisdiction hearing relating to the same offense.

(Subd (f) amended effective January 1, 2023; adopted as subd (f) effective January 1, 1991; relettered as subd (i) effective January 1, 1996; previously amended and relettered as subd (h) effective January 1, 2001, and as subd (f) effective May 22, 2017.)

(g) Review of determination on a motion to transfer jurisdiction to criminal court

(1) An order granting a motion to transfer jurisdiction of a youth to the criminal court is an appealable order subject to immediate review. A notice of appeal must be filed within 30 days of the order transferring jurisdiction or 30 days after the referee's order becomes final under rule 5.540(c) or after the denial of an application for rehearing of the referee's decision to transfer jurisdiction of the youth to the criminal court. If a notice of appeal is timely filed, the court must prepare and submit the record to the Court of Appeal within 20 days.

(2) An order denying a motion to transfer jurisdiction of a youth to the criminal court is not an appealable order. Appellate review of the order is by petition for extraordinary writ. Any petition for review of a judge's order denying a motion to transfer jurisdiction of the child to the criminal court, or denying an application for rehearing of the referee's determination not to transfer jurisdiction of the child to the criminal court, must be filed no later than 20 days after the judge's order is entered, or the referee's order becomes final under rule 5.540(c).

(Subd (g) amended effective January 1, 2023; adopted as subd (g) effective January 1, 1991; previously relettered as subd (j) effective January 1, 1996; amended and relettered effective 1, 2001; previously amended as subd (i) effective July 1, 2002; previously amended and relettered as subd (g) effective May 22, 2017.)

(h) Postponement of plea prior to transfer hearing

If a hearing for transfer of jurisdiction has been noticed under section 707, the court must postpone the taking of a plea to the petition until the conclusion of the transfer hearing, and no pleas that may have been entered already may be considered as evidence at the hearing.

(Subd (h) adopted effective May 22, 2017.)

Rule 5.770 amended effective September 1, 2023; adopted as rule 1482 effective January 1, 1991; previously amended effective January 1, 1996, January 1, 2001, July 1, 2002, May 22, 2017, January 1, 2021, and January 1, 2023; previously amended and renumbered effective January 1, 2007.

Advisory Committee Comment

Subdivision (b). This subdivision reflects changes to section 707 as a result of the passage of Senate Bill 382 (Lara; Stats. 2015, ch. 234); Proposition 57, the Public Safety and Rehabilitation Act of 2016; and Assembly Bill 2361 (Bonta, Mia; Stats. 2022, ch. 330). SB 382 was intended to clarify the factors for the juvenile court to consider when determining whether a case should be transferred to criminal court by emphasizing the unique developmental characteristics of children and their prior interactions with the juvenile justice system. Proposition 57 provided that its intent was to promote rehabilitation for juveniles and prevent them from reoffending, and to ensure that a judge makes the determination that a youth should be tried in a criminal court. Consistent with this intent, the committee urges juvenile courts—when evaluating the statutory criteria to determine if transfer is appropriate—to look at the totality of the circumstances, taking into account the specific statutory language guiding the court in its consideration of the criteria.

Subdivision (c). The court must state on the record the basis for its decision. The statement of decision must fully explain the court's reasoning to allow for meaningful appellate review. See, 15 e.g., *C.S. v. Superior Court* (2018) 29 Cal.App.5th 1009.

Although this rule and section 707 only require the juvenile court to recite the basis for its decision when the transfer motion is granted, the advisory committee believes that juvenile courts should, as a best practice, state the basis for their decisions on these motions in all cases so that the parties have an adequate record from which to seek subsequent review.

Rule 5.772. Conduct of fitness hearings under sections 707(a)(2) and 707(c) [Repealed]

Rule 5.772 repealed effective May 22, 2017; adopted as rule 1483 effective January 1, 1991; previously amended effective January 1, 1996, and January 1, 2001; previously amended and renumbered effective January 1, 2007; previously amended effective January 1, 2009.

Article 3
Jurisdiction

Rule 5.774. Setting petition for hearing—detained and nondetained cases; waiver of hearing
Rule 5.776. Grounds for continuance of jurisdiction hearing
Rule 5.778. Commencement of hearing on section 601 or section 602 petition; right to counsel; advisement of trial rights; admission, no contest
Rule 5.780. Contested hearing on section 601 or section 602 petition
Rule 5.782. Continuance pending disposition hearing

Rule 5.774. Setting petition for hearing—detained and nondetained cases; waiver of hearing

(a) Nondetention cases (§ 657)

If the child is not detained, the jurisdiction hearing on the petition must begin within 30 calendar days from the date the petition is filed.

(Subd (a) amended effective January 1, 2007.)

(b) Detention cases (§ 657)

If the child is detained, the jurisdiction hearing on the petition must begin within 15 judicial days from the date of the order of the court directing detention. If the child is released from detention before the jurisdiction hearing, the court may reset the jurisdiction hearing within the time limit in (a).

(Subd (b) amended effective January 1, 2007.)

(c) Tolling of time period

Any period of delay caused by the child's unavailability or failure to appear must not be included in computing the time limits of (a) and (b).

(Subd (c) amended effective January 1, 2007.)

(d) Dismissal

Absent a continuance under rule 5.776, when a jurisdiction hearing is not begun within the time limits of (a) and (b), the court must order the petition dismissed. This does not bar the filing of another petition based on the same allegations as in the original petition, but the child must not be detained.

(Subd (d) amended effective January 1, 2007.)

(e) Waiver of hearing (§ 657)

At the detention hearing, or at any time thereafter, a child may admit the allegations of the petition or plead no contest and waive further jurisdiction hearing. The court may accept the admission or no contest plea and proceed according to rules 5.778 and 5.782.

(Subd (e) amended effective January 1, 2007.)

Rule 5.774 amended and renumbered effective January 1, 2007; adopted as rule 1485 effective January 1, 1991.

Rule 5.776. Grounds for continuance of jurisdiction hearing

(a) Request for continuance; consent (§ 682)

A continuance may be granted only on a showing of good cause and only for the time shown to be necessary. Stipulation between counsel or parties and convenience of parties are not in and of themselves good cause.

(1) In order to obtain a continuance, written notice with supporting documents must be filed and served on all parties at least two court days before the date set for the hearing, unless the court finds good cause for failure to comply with these requirements. Absent a waiver of time, a child may not be detained beyond the statutory time limits.

(2) The court must state in its order the facts requiring any continuance that is granted.

(3) If the child is represented by counsel and no objection is made to an order setting or continuing the jurisdiction hearing beyond the time limits of rule 5.774, consent must be implied.

(Subd (a) amended effective January 1, 2007.)

(b) Grounds for continuance—mandatory (§ 700)

The court must continue the jurisdiction hearing for:

(1) A reasonable period to permit the child and the parent, guardian, or adult relative to prepare for the hearing; and

(2) No more than seven calendar days:

(A) For appointment of counsel;

(B) To enable counsel to become acquainted with the case; or

(C) To determine whether the parent, guardian, or adult relative can afford counsel.

(Subd (b) amended effective January 1, 2007.)

(c) Grounds for continuance—discretionary (§§ 700.5, 701)

The court may continue the jurisdiction hearing for no more than seven calendar days to enable the petitioner to subpoena witnesses if the child has made an extrajudicial admission and denies it, or has previously indicated to the court or petitioner an intention to admit the allegations of the petition, and at the time set for jurisdiction hearing denies the allegations.

(d) Grounds for continuance—section 654.2 (§§ 654.2, 654.3, 654.4)

In a case petitioned under section 602, the court may, with the consent of the child and the parent or guardian, continue the jurisdiction hearing for six months. If the court grants the continuance, the court must order the child and the parent or guardian to participate in a program of supervision under section 654, and must order the parent or guardian to participate with the child in a program of counseling or education under section 654.

(Subd (d) amended effective January 1, 2007.)

Rule 5.776 amended and renumbered effective January 1, 2007; adopted as rule 1486 effective January 1, 1991.

Rule 5.778. Commencement of hearing on section 601 or section 602 petition; right to counsel; advisement of trial rights; admission, no contest

(a) Petition read and explained (§ 700)

At the beginning of the jurisdiction hearing, the petition must be read to those present. On request of the child, or the parent, guardian, or adult relative, the court must explain the meaning and contents of the petition, the nature of the hearing, the procedures of the hearing, and possible consequences.

(Subd (a) amended effective January 1, 2007.)

(b) Rights explained (§ 702.5)

After giving the advisement required by rule 5.534, the court must advise those present of each of the following rights of the child:

(1) The right to a hearing by the court on the issues raised by the petition;

(2) The right to assert the privilege against self-incrimination;

(3) The right to confront and to cross-examine any witness called to testify against the child; and

(4) The right to use the process of the court to compel the attendance of witnesses on the child's behalf.

(Subd (b) amended effective January 1, 2007.)

(c) Admission of allegations; prerequisites to acceptance

The court must then inquire whether the child intends to admit or deny the allegations of the petition. If the child neither admits nor denies the allegations, the court must state on the record that the child does not admit the allegations. If the child wishes to admit the allegations, the court must first find and state on the record that it is satisfied that the child understands the nature of the allegations and the direct consequences of the admission, and understands and waives the rights in (b).

(Subd (c) amended effective January 1, 2007.)

(d) Consent of counsel—child must admit

Counsel for the child must consent to the admission, which must be made by the child personally.

(Subd (d) amended effective January 1, 2007.)

(e) No contest

The child may enter a plea of no contest to the allegations, subject to the approval of the court.

(f) Findings of the court (§ 702)

On an admission or plea of no contest, the court must make the following findings noted in the minutes of the court:

(1) Notice has been given as required by law;

(2) The birthdate and county of residence of the child;

(3) The child has knowingly and intelligently waived the right to a hearing on the issues by the court, the right to confront and cross-examine adverse witnesses and to use the process of the court to compel the attendance of witnesses on the child's behalf, and the right to assert the privilege against self-incrimination;

(4) The child understands the nature of the conduct alleged in the petition and the possible consequences of an admission or plea of no contest;

(5) The admission or plea of no contest is freely and voluntarily made;

(6) There is a factual basis for the admission or plea of no contest;

(7) Those allegations of the petition as admitted are true as alleged;

(8) The child is described by section 601 or 602; and

(9) In a section 602 matter, the degree of the offense and whether it would be a misdemeanor or felony had the offense been committed by an adult. If any offense may be found to be either a felony or misdemeanor, the court must consider which description applies and expressly declare on the record that it has made such consideration and must state its determination as to whether the offense is a misdemeanor or a felony. These determinations may be deferred until the disposition hearing.

(Subd (f) amended effective January 1, 2007; previously amended effective January 1, 1998.)

(g) Disposition

After accepting an admission or plea of no contest, the court must proceed to disposition hearing under rules 5.782 and 5.785.

(Subd (g) amended effective January 1, 2007.)

Rule 5.778 amended and renumbered effective January 1, 2007; adopted as rule 1487 effective January 1, 1991; previously amended effective January 1, 1998.

Rule 5.780. Contested hearing on section 601 or section 602 petition

(a) Contested jurisdiction hearing (§ 701)

If the child denies the allegations of the petition, the court must hold a contested hearing to determine whether the allegations in the petition are true.

(Subd (a) amended effective January 1, 2007.)

(b) Admissibility of evidence—general (§ 701)

In a section 601 matter, the admission and exclusion of evidence must be in accordance with the Evidence Code as it applies in civil cases. In a section 602 matter, the admission and exclusion of evidence must be in accordance with the Evidence Code as it applies in criminal cases.

(Subd (b) amended effective January 1, 2007.)

(c) Probation reports

Except as otherwise provided by law, the court must not read or consider any portion of a probation report relating to the contested petition before or during a contested jurisdiction hearing.

(Subd (c) amended effective January 1, 2007.)

(d) Unrepresented children (§ 701)

If the child is not represented by counsel, objections that could have been made to the evidence must be deemed made.

(Subd (d) amended effective January 1, 2007.)

(e) Findings of court—allegations true (§ 702)

If the court determines by a preponderance of the evidence in a section 601 matter, or by proof beyond a reasonable doubt in a section 602 matter, that the allegations of the petition are true, the court must make findings on each of the following, noted in the order:

(1) Notice has been given as required by law;

(2) The birthdate and county of residence of the child;

(3) The allegations of the petition are true;

(4) The child is described by section 601 or 602; and

(5) In a section 602 matter, the degree of the offense and whether it would be a misdemeanor or a felony had the offense been committed by an adult. If any offense may be found to be either a felony or a misdemeanor, the court must consider which description applies and expressly declare on the record that it has made such consideration, and must state its determination as to whether the offense is a misdemeanor or a felony. These determinations may be deferred until the disposition hearing.

(Subd (e) amended effective January 1, 2007; previously amended effective January 1, 1998.)

(f) Disposition

After making the findings in (e), the court must then proceed to disposition hearing under rules 5.782 and 5.785.

(Subd (f) amended effective January 1, 2007.)

(g) Findings of court—allegations not proved (§ 702)

If the court determines that the allegations of the petition have not been proved by a preponderance of the evidence in a 601 matter, or beyond a reasonable doubt in a 602 matter, the court must make findings on each of the following, noted in the order:

(1) Notice has been given as required by law;

(2) The birthdate and county of residence of the child; and

(3) The allegations of the petition have not been proved.

The court must dismiss the petition and terminate detention orders related to this petition.

(Subd (g) amended effective January 1, 2007.)

Rule 5.780 amended and renumbered effective January 1, 2007; adopted as rule 1488 effective January 1, 1991; previously amended effective January 1, 1998.

Rule 5.782. Continuance pending disposition hearing

(a) Continuance pending disposition hearing (§ 702)

If the court finds that the child is described by section 601 or 602, it must proceed to a disposition hearing. The court may continue the disposition hearing up to 10 judicial days if the child is detained. If the child is not detained, the court may continue the disposition hearing up to 30 calendar days from the date of the filing of the petition and up to an additional 15 calendar days for good cause shown.

(Subd (a) amended effective January 1, 2007.)

(b) Detention pending hearing (§ 702)

The court may release or detain the child during the period of the continuance.

(c) Observation and diagnosis (§ 704)

If the child is eligible for commitment to the Youth Authority, the court may continue the disposition hearing up to 90 calendar days and order the child to be placed temporarily at a Youth Authority diagnostic and treatment center for observation and diagnosis. The court must order the Youth Authority to submit a diagnosis and recommendation within 90 days, and the probation officer or any other peace officer designated by the court must place the child in the diagnostic and treatment center and return the child to the court. After return from the diagnostic and treatment center, the child must be brought to court within 2 judicial days. A disposition hearing must be held within 10 judicial days thereafter.

(Subd (c) amended effective January 1, 2007.)

Rule 5.782 amended and renumbered effective January 1, 2007; adopted as rule 1489 effective January 1, 1991.

Article 4
Disposition

Rule 5.785. General conduct of hearing
Rule 5.790. Orders of the court
Rule 5.795. Required determinations
Rule 5.800. Deferred entry of judgment
Rule 5.804. Commitment to secure youth treatment facility
Rule 5.806. Secure youth treatment facility baseline term
Rule 5.807. Secure youth treatment facility progress review process
Rule 5.808. Discharge from secure youth treatment facility (§ 875(e)(3) & (4))

Rule 5.785. General conduct of hearing

(a) Social study (§§ 280, 702, 706.5)

The probation officer must prepare a social study of the child, which must contain all matters relevant to disposition, including any parole status information, and a recommendation for disposition.

(1) In any case in which the probation officer is recommending placement in foster care or in which the child is already in foster care placement or pending placement under an earlier order, the social study must include a case plan as described in (c).

(2) The probation officer must submit the social study and copies of it to the clerk at least 48 hours before the disposition hearing is set to begin, and the clerk must make the copies available to the parties and attorneys. A continuance of up to 48 hours must be granted on the request of a party who has not been furnished a copy of the social study in accordance with this rule.

(Subd (a) amended effective January 1, 2007; previously amended effective July 1, 2002.)

(b) Evidence considered (§ 706)

The court must receive in evidence and consider the social study and any relevant evidence offered by the petitioner, the child, or the parent or guardian. The court may require production of other relevant evidence on its own motion. In the order of disposition the court must state that the social study has been read and considered by the court.

(Subd (b) amended effective July 1, 2002.)

(c) Case plan

When a child is detained and is at risk of entering foster care placement, the probation officer must prepare a case plan.

(1) The plan must be completed and filed with the court by the date of disposition or within 60 calendar days of initial removal, whichever occurs first.

(2) The court must consider the case plan and must find as follows:

(A) The probation officer solicited and integrated into the case plan the input of the child, the child's family, in a case described by rule 5.480(2)(A)–(C) the child's identified Indian tribe, and other interested parties; or

(B) The probation officer did not solicit and integrate into the case plan the input of the child, the child's family, in a case described by rule 5.480(2)(A)–(C) the child's identified Indian tribe, and other interested parties. If the court finds that the probation officer did not solicit and integrate into the case plan the input of the child, the child's family, the child's identified Indian tribe, and other interested parties, the court must order that the probation officer solicit and integrate into the case plan the input of the child, the child's family, in a case described by rule 5.480(2)(A)–(C) the child's identified Indian tribe, and other interested parties, unless the court finds that each of these participants was unable, unavailable, or unwilling to participate.

(3) For a child 12 years of age or older and in a permanent placement, the court must consider the case plan and must find as follows:

(A) The child was given the opportunity to review the case plan, sign it, and receive a copy; or

(B) The child was not given the opportunity to review the case plan, sign it, and receive a copy. If the court makes such a finding, the court must order the probation officer to give the child the opportunity to review the case plan, sign it, and receive a copy, unless the court finds that the child was unable, unavailable, or unwilling to participate.

(4) If the probation officer believes that the child will be able to return home through reasonable efforts by the child, the parents or guardian, and the probation officer, the case plan must include the elements described in section 636.1(b).

(5) If the probation officer believes that foster care placement is the most appropriate disposition for the child, the case plan must include all of the information required by section 706.6.

(Subd (c) amended effective January 1, 2021; adopted effective July 1, 2002; previously amended effective January 1, 2007, and July 1, 2013.)

Rule 5.785 amended effective January 1, 2021; adopted as rule 1492 effective January 1, 1991; previously amended effective July 1, 2002, and July 1, 2013; previously amended and renumbered effective January 1, 2007.

Rule 5.790. Orders of the court

(a) Findings and orders of the court (§§ 654, 654.1, 654.2, 654.3, 654.4, 725, 725.5, 782)

At the disposition hearing:

(1) If the court has not previously considered whether any offense is a misdemeanor or felony, the court must do so at this time and state its finding on the record. If the offense may be found to be either a felony or a misdemeanor, the court must consider which description applies and must expressly declare on the record that it has made such consideration and must state its finding as to whether the offense is a misdemeanor or a felony.

(2) The court may then:

(A) Dismiss the petition in the interests of justice and the welfare of the child or, if the child does not need treatment or rehabilitation, with the specific reasons stated in the minutes;

(B) Place the child on probation for no more than six months, without declaring the child a ward; or

(C) Declare the child a ward of the court.

(Subd (a) amended effective January 1, 2007; previously amended effective January 1, 1998, and July 1, 2002.)

(b) Conditions of probation (§§ 725, 726, 727, 729.2, 729.9, 729.10)

If the child is placed on probation, with or without wardship, the court must set reasonable terms and conditions of probation. Unless the court finds and states its reasons on the record that any of the following conditions is inappropriate, the court must:

(1) Require the child to attend school;

(2) Require the parent to participate with the child in a counseling or education program; and

(3) Require the child to be at the child's residence between 10:00 p.m. and 6:00 a.m. unless accompanied by a parent or a guardian or an adult custodian.

(Subd (b) amended effective January 1, 2014; previously amended effective July 1, 2002, and January 1, 2007.)

(c) Custody and visitation (§ 726.5)

(1) At any time when a child is a ward of the juvenile court, the court may issue an order determining the custody of or visitation with the child. An order issued under this subdivision continues in effect until modified or terminated by a later order of the juvenile court.

(2) At the time wardship is terminated, the court may issue an order determining custody of or visitation with the child, as described in rule 5.700.

(Subd (c) amended effective January 1, 2016; adopted effective January 1, 2007.)

(d) Removal of custody—required findings (§ 726)

The court must not order a ward removed from the physical custody of a parent or guardian unless the court finds:

(1) The parent or guardian has failed or neglected to provide, or is incapable of providing, proper maintenance, training, and education for the child;

(2) The child has been on probation in the custody of the parent or guardian and during that time has failed to reform; or

(3) The welfare of the child requires that physical custody be removed from the parent or guardian.

(Subd (d) amended and relettered effective January 1, 2007; adopted as subd (c) effective January 1, 1991; previously amended effective July 1, 2002.)

(e) Removal of custody—orders regarding reunification services (§ 727.2)

(1) Whenever the court orders the care, custody, and control of the child to be under the supervision of the probation officer for placement, the court must order the probation department to ensure the provision of reunification services to facilitate the safe return of the child to his or her home or the permanent placement of the child and to address the needs of the child while in foster care.

(2) Reunification services need not be provided to the parent or guardian if the court finds, by clear and convincing evidence, that one or more of the exceptions listed in section 727.2(b) is true.

(Subd (e) amended and relettered effective January 1, 2007; adopted as subd (d) effective July 1, 2002; previously amended effective January 1, 2004.)

(f) Family-finding determination (§ 628(d))

(1) If the child is detained and at risk of entering foster care placement or within 30 days of the court order placing the child into foster care, the court must consider and determine whether the probation officer has exercised due diligence in conducting the required investigation to identify, locate, and provide notification and information as required in paragraph (2) of rule 5.637(c) to the child's kin. Due diligence in family finding requires that the probation officer engaged in the mandatory activities listed in rule 5.637(d)(2). The court may also consider the additional activities listed in rule 5.637(d)(3). The court must document its determination by making a finding on the record.

If the dispositional hearing is continued, the court may set a hearing to be held 30 days from the date of detention or as soon as possible thereafter to consider and determine whether the probation officer has exercised due diligence in conducting the required investigation to identify, locate, and notify the child's kin.

(2) If the court finds that the probation officer has not exercised due diligence, the court may order the probation officer to exercise due diligence in conducting an investigation to identify, locate, and notify the child's kin—except for any individual the probation officer identifies who is inappropriate to notify under rule 5.637(e)—and may require a written or oral report to the court.

(Subd (f) amended effective January 1, 2024; adopted effective January 1, 2014; previously amended effective January 1, 2015.)

(g) Wardship orders (§§ 726, 727, 727.1, 730, 731)

The court may make any reasonable order for the care, supervision, custody, conduct, maintenance, support, and medical treatment of a child adjudged a ward of the court.

(1) Subject to the provisions of section 727, the court may order the ward to be on probation without the supervision of the probation officer and may impose on the ward reasonable conditions of behavior.

(2) The court may order the care, custody, control, and conduct of the ward to be under the supervision of the probation officer in the home of a parent or guardian.

(3) If the court orders removal of custody under (d), it must authorize the probation officer to place the ward with a person or organization described in section 727. The decision regarding choice of placement must take into account the following factors:

(A) That the setting is safe;

(B) That the setting is the least restrictive or most family-like environment that is appropriate for the child and available;

(C) That the setting is in close proximity to the parent's home; and

(D) That the setting is the environment best suited to meet the child's special needs and best interest.

The selection must consider, in order of priority, placement with relatives, tribal members, and foster family, group care, and residential treatment under Family Code section 7950.

(4) If the child was declared a ward under section 602, the court may order treatment or commitment of the child under section 730 or 731.

(5) The court may limit the control exercised over the ward by a parent or guardian. Orders must clearly specify all limitations. In particular, the court must consider whether it is necessary to limit the rights of the parent or guardian to make educational or developmental-services decisions for the child. If the court limits those rights, it must follow the procedures in rules 5.649–5.651.

(Subd (g) relettered effective January 1, 2024; adopted as subd (d); previously amended and relettered as subd (e) effective July 1, 2002, and as subd (f) effective January 1, 2007; and as subd (h) effective January 1, 2014; previously amended effective January 1, 2004, and January 1, 2008.)

(h) Fifteen-day reviews (§ 737)

If the child or nonminor is detained pending the implementation of a dispositional order, the court must review the case at least every 15 days as long as the child is detained. The review must meet all the requirements in section 737.

(Subd (h) relettered effective January 1, 2024; adopted as subd (e); previously amended effective January 1, 2006; previously amended and relettered as subd (f) effective July 1, 2002, and as subd (g) effective January 1, 2007; previously relettered as subd (j) effective January 1, 2014, and as subd (i) effective July 1, 2023.)

Rule 5.790 amended effective January 1, 2024; adopted as rule 1493 effective January 1, 1991; previously amended and renumbered as rule 5.790 effective January 1, 2007; previously amended effective January 1, 1998, July 1, 2002, January 1, 2004, January 1, 2006, January 1, 2008, January 1, 2014, January 1, 2015, January 1, 2016, and July 1, 2023.

Rule 5.795. Required determinations

(a) Felony or misdemeanor (§ 702)

Unless determined previously, the court must find and note in the minutes the degree of the offense committed by the youth, and whether it would be a felony or a misdemeanor had it been committed by an adult. If any offense may be found to be either a felony or a misdemeanor, the court must consider which description applies and expressly declare on the record that it has made such consideration and must state its determination as to whether the offense is a misdemeanor or a felony.

(Subd (a) amended effective January 1, 2007; previously amended effective January 1, 2003.)

(b) Physical confinement (§ 726)

If the youth is declared a ward under section 602 and ordered removed from the physical custody of a parent or guardian, the court must specify and note in the minutes the maximum period of confinement under section 726.

(Subd (b) amended effective January 1, 2007; previously amended effective January 1, 2003.)

Rule 5.795 amended and renumbered effective January 1, 2007; adopted as rule 1494 effective January 1, 1991; previously amended effective January 1, 2001, and January 1, 2003.

Rule 5.800. Deferred entry of judgment

(a) Eligibility (§ 790)

A child who is the subject of a petition under section 602 alleging violation of at least one felony offense may be considered for a deferred entry of judgment if all of the following apply:

(1) The child is 14 years or older at the time of the hearing on the application for deferred entry of judgment;

(2) The offense alleged is not listed in section 707(b);

(3) The child has not been previously declared a ward of the court based on the commission of a felony offense;

(4) The child has not been previously committed to the California Department of Corrections and Rehabilitation, Division of Juvenile Justice;

(5) If the child is presently or was previously a ward of the court, probation has not been revoked before completion; and

(6) The child meets the eligibility standards stated in Penal Code section 1203.06.

(Subd (a) amended effective July 1, 2010; previously amended effective January 1, 2006.)

(b) Procedures for consideration (§ 790)

(1) Before filing a petition alleging a felony offense, or as soon as possible after filing, the prosecuting attorney must review the child's file to determine if the requirements of (a) are met. If the prosecuting attorney's review reveals that the requirements of (a) have been met, the prosecuting attorney must file *Determination of Eligibility—Deferred Entry of Judgment—Juvenile* (form JV-750) with the petition.

(2) If the court determines that the child is eligible and suitable for a deferred entry of judgment, and would derive benefit from education, treatment, and rehabilitation efforts, the court may grant deferred entry of judgment.

(Subd (b) amended effective July 1, 2010; previously amended effective January 1, 2007.)

(c) Citation (§ 792)

The court must issue *Citation and Written Notification for Deferred Entry of Judgment—Juvenile* (form JV-751) to the child's custodial parent, guardian, or foster parent. The form must be personally served on the custodial adult at least 24 hours before the time set for the appearance hearing.

(Subd (c) amended effective January 1, 2007.)

(d) Determination without a hearing; supplemental information (§ 791)

(1) The court may grant a deferred entry of judgment as stated in (2) or (3).

(2) If the child admits each allegation contained in the petition as charged and waives the right to a speedy disposition hearing, the court may summarily grant the deferred entry of judgment.

(3) When appropriate, the court may order the probation department to prepare a report with recommendations on the suitability of the child for deferred entry of judgment or set a hearing on the matter, with or without the order to the probation department for a report.

(A) The probation report must address the following:

(i) The child's age, maturity, educational background, family relationships, motivation, any treatment history, and any other relevant factors regarding the benefit the child would derive from education, treatment, and rehabilitation efforts; and

(ii) The programs best suited to assist the child and the child's family.

(B) The probation report must be submitted to the court, the child, the prosecuting attorney, and the child's attorney at least 48 hours, excluding noncourt days, before the hearing.

(Subd (d) amended effective July 1, 2010; previously amended effective January 1, 2007.)

(e) Written notification of ineligibility (§ 790)

If it is determined that the child is ineligible for deferred entry of judgment, the prosecuting attorney must complete and provide to the court, the child, and the child's attorney *Determination of Eligibility—Deferred Entry of Judgment—Juvenile* (form JV-750).

(Subd (e) amended effective January 1, 2007.)

(f) Conduct of hearing (§§ 791, 794)

At the hearing, the court must consider the declaration of the prosecuting attorney, any report and recommendations from the probation department, and any other relevant material provided by the child or other interested parties.

(1) If the child consents to the deferred entry of judgment, the child must enter an admission as stated in rule 5.778(c) and (d). A no-contest plea must not be accepted.

(2) The child must waive the right to a speedy disposition hearing.

(3) After acceptance of the child's admission, the court must set a date for review of the child's progress and a date by which the probation department must submit to the court, the child, the child's parent or guardian, the child's attorney, and the prosecuting attorney a report on the child's adherence to the conditions set by the court. Although the date set may be any time within the following 36 months, consideration of dismissal of the petition may not occur until at least 12 months have passed since the court granted the deferred entry of judgment.

(4) If the court grants the deferred entry of judgment, the court must order search-and-seizure probation conditions and may order probation conditions regarding the following:

(A) Education;

(B) Treatment;

(C) Testing for alcohol and other drugs, if appropriate;

(D) Curfew and school attendance requirements;

(E) Restitution; and

(F) Any other conditions consistent with the identified needs of the child and the factors that led to the conduct of the child.

(Subd (f) amended effective July 1, 2010; previously amended effective January 1, 2007.)

(g) Compliance with conditions; progress review

Twelve months after the court granted the deferred entry of judgment and on receipt of the progress report ordered at the hearing on the deferred entry of judgment, the court may:

(1) Find that the child has complied satisfactorily with the conditions imposed, dismiss the petition, seal the court records in compliance with section 793(c), and vacate the date set for review hearing; or

(2) Confirm the review hearing. At the hearing the court must:

(A) Find that the child has complied satisfactorily with the conditions imposed, dismiss the petition, and seal the court records in compliance with section 793(c); or

(B) Find that the child has not complied satisfactorily with the conditions imposed, lift the deferred entry of judgment, and set a disposition hearing.

(Subd (g) amended effective January 1, 2007.)

(h) Failure to comply with conditions (§ 793)

(1) Before the date of the progress hearing, if the child is found to have committed a misdemeanor offense or more than one misdemeanor offense on a single occasion, the court may schedule a hearing within 15 court days.

(A) At the hearing, the court must follow the procedure stated in rule 5.580(d) and (e) to determine if the deferred entry of judgment should be lifted, with a disposition hearing to be conducted thereafter.

(B) The disposition hearing must be conducted as stated in rules 5.785 through 5.795.

(C) The child's admission of the charges under a deferred entry of judgment must not constitute a finding that a petition has been sustained unless a judgment is entered under section 793(b).

(2) Before the date of the progress hearing, on the court's own motion, or if the court receives a declaration from the probation department or the prosecuting attorney alleging that the child has not complied with the conditions imposed or that the conditions are not benefiting the child, or if the child is found to have committed a felony offense or two or more misdemeanor offenses on separate occasions, the court must schedule a hearing within 10 court days.

(A) At the hearing, the court must follow the procedure stated in rule 5.580(d) and (e) to determine if the deferred entry of judgment should be lifted, with a disposition hearing to be conducted thereafter.

(B) The disposition hearing must be conducted as stated in rules 5.785 through 5.795.

(C) The child's admission of the charges under a deferred entry of judgment must not constitute a finding that a petition has been sustained unless a judgment is entered under section 793(b).

(3) If the child is found to have committed a felony offense or two or more misdemeanor offenses on separate occasions, the court must schedule a disposition hearing within 10 court days. The disposition hearing must be conducted as stated in rules 5.785 through 5.795.

(4) If the judgment previously deferred is imposed and a disposition hearing is scheduled under section 793(a), the juvenile court must report the complete criminal history of the child to the Department of Justice under section 602.5.

(Subd (h) amended effective January 1, 2007.)

Rule 5.800 amended effective July 1, 2010; adopted as rule 1495 effective January 1, 2001; previously amended effective January 1, 2006; previously amended and renumbered effective January 1, 2007.

Rule 5.804. Commitment to secure youth treatment facility

As provided in Welfare and Institutions Code section 875, the following applies if a court orders a youth to a secure youth treatment facility.

(a) Eligibility (§ 875(a))

A youth may be committed to a secure youth treatment facility as defined in section 875 if:

(1) The youth committed an offense listed in section 707(b) when the youth was 14 years of age or older; and

(2) The offense is the most recent offense for which the youth has been adjudicated; and

(3) The court finds on the record that a less restrictive alternative disposition is unsuitable for the youth after considering all relevant and material evidence, including the recommendations of counsel, the probation department, and any other agency or individual designated by the court to advise on the appropriate disposition of the case. To make this finding the court must consider each of the criteria set forth in section 875(a)(3)(A)–(E).

(Subd (a) adopted effective July 1, 2023.)

(b) Setting baseline term (§ 875(b))

The court must set a baseline term for the youth as provided in rule 5.806.

(Subd (b) adopted effective July 1, 2023.)

(c) Setting the maximum term of confinement (§ 875(c))

The court must set a maximum term of confinement as provided in section 875(c) based on the facts and circumstances of the matter or matters that brought or continued the youth under the jurisdiction of the court and as deemed appropriate to achieve rehabilitation. The court must apply the youth's precommitment credits to the maximum term.

(Subd (c) adopted effective July 1, 2023.)

(d) Individualized rehabilitation plan (§ 875(d))

The court must, at the time of the commitment, order the probation department to prepare a proposed individualized rehabilitation plan for the youth as provided by section 875(d). The court must approve a plan for the youth no later than 30 court days after the order of commitment.

(1) The court must set a hearing to review and approve the plan no later than 30 court days from the date of the commitment order.

(2) The proposed plan must be filed with the court and a copy of the plan must be provided to the prosecuting attorney, the youth, and counsel for the youth at least 5 calendar days before the hearing.

(Subd (d) adopted effective July 1, 2023.)

(e) Setting the progress review hearing (§ 875(e))

The court must set a progress review hearing no later than six months from the date of the commitment order to evaluate the youth's progress in relation to the rehabilitation plan and to determine whether the baseline term of confinement is to be modified.

(Subd (e) adopted effective July 1, 2023.)

Rule 5.804 adopted effective July 1, 2023.

Rule 5.805. California Department of Corrections and Rehabilitation, Division of Juvenile Justice, commitments [Repealed]

Rule 5.805 repealed effective July 1, 2023; adopted as rule 1494.5 effective January 1, 2003; previously amended effective January 1, 2006, and January 1, 2014; previously amended and renumbered effective January 1, 2007.

Rule 5.806. Secure youth treatment facility baseline term

(a) Category for baseline term based on most serious recent offense

If the court orders the youth committed to a secure youth treatment facility, the court must set a baseline term of months, years, or months and years falling within the range for the offense category, based on the most serious recent offense that is the basis for the youth's commitment to the secure youth treatment facility, as provided in the matrix contained in (d) of this rule.

(Subd (a) adopted effective July 1, 2023.)

(b) Selecting the baseline term with the range for the offense category

The baseline term must be set by the court based on the individual facts and circumstances of the case. In its selection of the individual baseline term, the court must review and consider each of the criteria listed in paragraphs (1) through (4). When evaluating each of the criteria, the court may give weight to any relevant factor, including but not limited to the factors listed below each one. The court must select a baseline term that is no longer than necessary to meet the developmental needs of the youth and to prepare the youth for discharge to a period of probation supervision in the community. Enumerated factors listed below that are outside the youth's control must not result in a longer baseline term than otherwise needed to meet this objective. The court must state on the record its reasons for selecting a particular term, referencing each of the criteria and any factors the court deemed relevant.

(1) *The circumstances and gravity of the commitment offense*

(A) The severity and statutory degree of the offense for which the youth has been committed to the secure youth treatment facility;

(B) The extent of harm to victims occurring as a result of the offense;

(C) The role and behavior of the youth in the commission of the offense;

(D) The role of co-participants or victims in relation to the offense; and

(E) Any exculpatory circumstances related to the commission of the offense including peer influence, immaturity or developmental delays, mental or physical impairment, or drug or alcohol impairment.

(2) *The youth's prior history in the juvenile justice system*

(A) The youth's offense and commitment history;

(B) The success of prior efforts to rehabilitate the youth; and

(C) The effects of the youth's family, community environment, and childhood trauma on the youth's previous behavior that resulted in contact with the juvenile justice system.

(3) *The confinement time considered reasonable and necessary to achieve the rehabilitation of the youth*

(A) The amount of time the youth has already spent in custody for the current offense and any progress made by the youth in programming and development;

(B) The capacity of the secure youth treatment facility to provide suitable treatment and education for the youth;

(C) Special needs the youth may have in relation to mental health, intellectual development, academic or learning disability, substance use recovery, and other special needs that must be addressed during the term of confinement;

(D) Whether the youth is pregnant, is a parent, or is a primary caregiver for children; and

(E) The availability of programs and services in the community to which the youth may be transitioned from secure commitment to less restrictive alternatives.

(4) *The youth's developmental history*

(A) The age and overall maturity of the youth;

(B) Developmental challenges the youth may have in relation to mental health, intellectual capacity, educational progress or learning disability, or other developmental deficits, including specific medical or health challenges;

(C) The youth's child welfare and foster care history including abandonment or abuse by parents or caregivers or the incarceration of parents;

(D) Harmful childhood experiences including trauma and exposure to domestic or community violence, poverty, and other harmful experiences; and

(E) Discrimination experienced by the ward based on gender, race, ethnicity, sexual orientation, or other factors.

(*Subd (b) adopted effective July 1, 2023.*)

(c) Adjusting the baseline term at review hearings

As provided in Welfare and Institutions Code section 875(e)(1), the court must review the progress of a youth committed to a secure youth treatment facility at least every six months, and may modify the baseline term downward by up to six months at each hearing. To provide an incentive for each youth to engage productively with the individual rehabilitation plan approved by the court under section 875(b)(1), each probation department operating a secure youth treatment facility must implement a system to track the positive behavior of the youth in a regular and systematic way and report to the court at every progress hearing on the youth's positive behavior, including a recommendation to the court on any downward adjustment that should be made to the baseline term in recognition of the youth's positive behavior and development. In developing this recommendation, the probation department must consult with and report on the input of all other agencies or entities providing services to the youth.

(*Subd (c) adopted effective July 1, 2023.*)

(d) Secure youth treatment facility offense-based classification matrix

The court must select a baseline term within the range set for the category that has been assigned to the Welfare and Institutions Code section 707(b) commitment offense as provided in this matrix:

Category	Offense (*Listed with reference to paragraph within section 707(b)*)	Term
A	(1) Murder. (11) Kidnapping with bodily harm involving death or substantial injury. (23) Torture, as described in Penal Code sections 206 and 206.1.	4 to 7 years
B	(4) Rape with force, violence, or threat of great bodily harm. (5) Sodomy by force, violence, duress, menace, or threat of great bodily harm. (7) Oral copulation by force, violence, duress, menace, or threat of great bodily harm. (8) An offense specified in Penal Code section 289(a). (9) Kidnapping for ransom. (10) Kidnapping for purposes of robbery. (11) Kidnapping with bodily harm not involving death or substantial injury. (12) Attempted murder. (24) Aggravated mayhem, as described in Penal Code section 205. (26) Kidnapping for purposes of sexual assault, as punishable in Penal Code section 209(b). (27) Kidnapping, as punishable in Penal Code section 209.5. (29) The offense described in Penal Code section 18745. (30) Voluntary manslaughter, as described in Penal Code section 192(a).	3 to 5 years
C	(2) Arson, as provided in Penal Code section 451(a) or (b). (3) Robbery. (6) A lewd or lascivious act, as provided in Penal Code section 288(b). (13) Assault with a firearm or destructive device. (14) Assault by any means of force likely to produce great bodily injury. (15) Discharge of a firearm into an inhabited or occupied building. (16) An offense described in Penal Code section 1203.09. (17) An offense described in Penal Code section 12022.5 or 12022.53. (18) A felony offense in which the minor personally used a weapon described in any provision listed in Penal Code section 16590. (21) A violent felony, as defined in Penal Code section 667.5, that also would constitute a felony violation of Penal Code section 186.22(b). (22) Escape, by the use of force or violence, from a county juvenile hall, home, ranch, camp, or forestry camp in violation of Penal Code section 871(b) if great bodily injury is intentionally inflicted on an employee of the juvenile facility during the commission of the escape. (25) Carjacking, as described in Penal Code section 215, while armed with a dangerous or deadly weapon. (28) The offense described in Penal Code section 26100(c).	2 to 4 years
D	(19) A felony offense described in Penal Code section 136.1 or 137.	1 to 2 years

(20) Manufacturing, compounding, or selling one-half ounce or more of a salt or solution of a controlled substance specified in Health and Safety Code section 11055(e).

(Subd (d) adopted effective July 1, 2023.)
Rule 5.806 adopted effective July 1, 2023.

Advisory Committee Comment

In developing the matrix for baseline terms required by Welfare and Institutions Code section 875, the committee sought to accomplish three primary goals that should serve as objectives for the court when setting a baseline term: positive youth development, public and community safety, and the establishment of flexible and fair commitment terms.

A primary objective of a commitment to a secure youth treatment facility must be an evidence-based and trauma-responsive effort to promote healthy adolescent development. This objective will be achieved by providing positive incentives for prosocial behavior, focusing on the treatment needs of the youth to ensure healing and rehabilitation, and with a persistent focus on the end goal of successful reentry into the community. The flexibility inherent in the matrix is intended to result in a baseline term of commitment that is no longer than necessary to protect the public but is of sufficient length to assure the victim and the community that the harm committed can be redressed by the juvenile justice system in a developmentally appropriate manner and thus reduce the need for the youth to be transferred to criminal court.

A baseline term should be based on the needs of the individual being committed and not simply the seriousness of the offense for which the youth was adjudicated. This individualized approach must be balanced with the goal of fair and just application of the matrix across California jurisdictions and an awareness that racial and ethnic disproportionality has been a failing of our juvenile justice system that all stakeholders must seek to remedy at each decision point. To advance this goal the advisory committee encourages juvenile courts and probation departments to monitor implementation of this rule to ensure that it is fairly and consistently applied.

Rule 5.807. Secure youth treatment facility progress review process

(a) Application

This rule sets forth the statutory requirements for the court's review of a youth's progress under section 875(e) and (f) and rule 5.806(c) for youth committed to secure youth treatment facilities to evaluate the youth's progress in relation to the rehabilitation plan approved under section 875(d) and rule 5.804(d).

(Subd (a) adopted effective July 1, 2023.)

(b) Setting a progress review hearing (§ 875(e))

The court must, during the term of commitment, set and hold a progress review hearing for the youth not less frequently than once every six months.

(Subd (b) adopted effective July 1, 2023.)

(c) Findings and orders (§ 875(e))

At the progress review hearing, after having considered the recommendations of the probation department and any recommendations of counsel and any behavioral, educational, or other specialists having information relevant to the youth's progress, the court must:

(1) Make a finding on the record supporting an order as to whether the youth is to remain committed to the secure youth treatment facility for the remainder of the baseline term or if the baseline term is to be reduced after considering:

(A) the progress of the youth in relation to the rehabilitation plan in light of the programming made available to the youth, and

(B) the recommendations of probation concerning the youth's positive behavior in the secure youth treatment facility program as required by rule 5.806(c); and

(2) Set a progress review hearing or, if the baseline term remaining is six months or less, a discharge hearing, no more than six months from the date of the current hearing.

(Subd (c) adopted effective July 1, 2023.)

(d) Transfer to a less restrictive program (§ 875(f))

(1) Upon a motion by the probation department or the youth that the youth be transferred from the secure youth treatment facility to a less restrictive program, the court must consider such a transfer at the youth's next progress review hearing or may set a separate hearing to consider the motion. The moving party must serve the motion on the prosecution, the youth if the youth is not the moving party, and the probation department if the probation department is not the moving party.

(2) In making its determination, the court must consider:

(A) The youth's overall progress in relation to the rehabilitation plan in light of the programming made available to the youth during the period of confinement in a secure youth treatment facility; and

(B) The programming and community transition services to be provided, or coordinated by the less restrictive program, including any educational, vocational, counseling, housing, or other services made available through the program.

(3) If the court orders the youth transferred to a less restrictive program:

(A) The court must set the length of time the youth is to remain in a less restrictive program, not to exceed the remainder of the baseline or modified baseline term, prior to a discharge hearing; and

(B) The court may require the youth to observe any conditions of performance or compliance with the program that are reasonable and appropriate in the individual case and that are within the capacity of the youth to perform.

(4) If, after transfer to a less restrictive program, the court determines that the youth has materially failed to comply with the court-ordered conditions of the program, the court may:

(A) Modify the terms and conditions of placement in the program; or

(B) Order the youth to be returned to a secure youth treatment facility for the remainder of the baseline term, or modified baseline term, subject to further progress review hearings as required in this rule.

(5) If the court orders a youth returned to a secure youth treatment facility from a less restrictive program the court must adjust the youth's baseline or modified baseline term to include credit for the time served by the youth in the less restrictive program.

(Subd (d) adopted effective July 1, 2023.)
Rule 5.807 adopted effective July 1, 2023.

Rule 5.808. Discharge from secure youth treatment facility (§ 875(e)(3) & (4))

(a) Application

This rule sets forth the statutory provisions that apply to any youth committed to a secure youth treatment facility, or who has been transferred from a secure youth treatment facility to a less restrictive program under section 875(f) and rule 5.807(d), and who has reached the end of their baseline term, including any modifications to that term made during progress review hearings.

(Subd (a) adopted effective July 1, 2023.)

(b) Conduct of the hearing

At the discharge hearing the court must review the progress of the youth toward meeting the goals of the individual rehabilitation plan and the recommendations of counsel, the probation department, and any other agencies or individuals having information the court deems necessary.

(Subd (b) adopted effective July 1, 2023.)

(c) Findings and orders

(1) The court must order that the youth be discharged to a period of probation supervision in the community, unless the court finds that the youth poses a substantial risk of imminent harm to others in the community if released from custody. If a discharge is ordered, the court:

(A) Must determine and order the reasonable conditions of probation that are suitable to meet the developmental needs and circumstances of the youth and that will facilitate the youth's successful reentry into the community.

(B) Must periodically review the youth's progress under probation supervision and make any additional orders deemed necessary to modify the program of supervision in order to facilitate the provision of services or to otherwise support the youth's successful reentry into the community.

(C) May, if the court finds that the youth has failed materially to comply with the reasonable orders of probation imposed by the court, order that the youth be returned to a juvenile facility or to a less restrictive program for a period not to exceed either the remainder of the baseline term, including any court-ordered modifications, or six months, whichever is longer, subject to the maximum confinement limits of section 875(c).

(2) If the court finds that the youth poses a substantial risk of imminent harm to others in the community if released from custody, the court must recite the basis for that finding on the record and may order that the youth

be retained in custody in a secure youth treatment facility for up to one additional year of confinement, subject to the maximum confinement provisions of section 875(c). If the court orders that the youth is to be confined, it must set a progress review hearing under section 875(d) and rule 5.807, or if the period of confinement is six months or less, a discharge hearing under section 875(e) and this rule for a date not to exceed six months from the date of the initial discharge hearing.

(Subd (c) adopted effective July 1, 2023.)

Rule 5.808 adopted effective July 1, 2023.

Article 5
Reviews and Sealing

Rule 5.810. Reviews, hearings, and permanency planning

Rule 5.811. Modification to transition jurisdiction for a ward older than 17 years and 5 months with a petition subject to dismissal (Welf. & Inst. Code, §§ 450, 451, 727.2(i)–(j), 778; Pen. Code, § 236.14)

Rule 5.812. Additional requirements for any hearing to terminate jurisdiction over child in foster care and for status review or dispositional hearing for child approaching majority (§§ 450, 451, 727.2(i)–(j), 778)

Rule 5.813. Modification to transition jurisdiction for a ward older than 18 years and younger than 21 years of age (§§ 450, 451)

Rule 5.814. Modification to transition jurisdiction for a ward older than 17 years, 5 months of age and younger than 18 years of age (§§ 450, 451)

Rule 5.815. Legal guardianship—wards (§§ 366.26, 727.3, 728)

Rule 5.820. Termination of parental rights for child in foster care for 15 of the last 22 months

Rule 5.825. Freeing wards for adoption

Rule 5.830. Sealing records (§ 781)

Rule 5.840. Dismissal of petition and sealing of records (§ 786)

Rule 5.850. Sealing of records by probation in diversion cases (§ 786.5)

Rule 5.860. Prosecuting attorney request to access sealed juvenile case files

Rule 5.810. Reviews, hearings, and permanency planning

(a) Six-month status review hearings (§§ 727.2, 11404.1)

For any ward removed from the custody of his or her parent or guardian under section 726 and placed in a home under section 727, the court must conduct a status review hearing no less frequently than once every six months from the date the ward entered foster care. The court may consider the hearing at which the initial order for placement is made as the first status review hearing.

(1) *Consideration of reports (§ 727.2(d))*

The court must review and consider the social study report and updated case plan submitted by the probation officer and the report submitted by any CASA volunteer, and any other reports filed with the court under section 727.2(d).

(2) *Return of child if not detrimental (§ 727.2(f))*

At any status review hearing before the first permanency hearing, the court must order the return of the ward to the parent or guardian unless it finds the probation department has established by a preponderance of evidence that return would create a substantial risk of detriment to the safety, protection, or physical or emotional well-being of the ward. The probation department has the burden of establishing that detriment. In making its determination, the court must review and consider all reports submitted to the court and must consider the efforts and progress demonstrated by the child and the family and the extent to which the child availed himself or herself of the services provided.

(3) *Findings and orders (§ 727.2(e))*

The court must consider the safety of the ward and make findings and orders that determine the following:

(A) The continuing necessity for and appropriateness of the placement;

(B) The extent of the probation department's compliance with the case plan in making reasonable efforts to safely return the child to the child's home and to complete whatever steps are necessary to finalize the permanent placement of the child;

(C) Whether it is necessary to limit the rights of the parent or guardian to make educational or developmental-services decisions for the child. If the court limits those rights or, if the ward is 18 years of age or older and has chosen not to make educational or developmental-services decisions for him- or herself or has been deemed incompetent, finds that it is in the best interests of the ward, the court must appoint a responsible adult as the educational rights holder as defined in rule 5.502. Any limitation on the rights of a parent or guardian to make educational or developmental-services decisions for a ward must be specified in the court order. The court must follow the procedures in rules 5.649–5.651;

(D) The extent of progress that has been made by the child and parent or guardian toward alleviating or mitigating the causes necessitating placement in foster care;

(E) The likely date by which the child may return to and be safely maintained in the home or placed for adoption, legal guardianship, or another permanent plan;

(F) In the case of a child who is 16 years of age or older, the services needed to assist the child in making the transition from foster care to independent living;

(G) Whether the child was actively involved, as age- and developmentally appropriate, in the development of his or her own case plan and plan for permanent placement. If the court finds that the child was not appropriately involved, the court must order the probation department to actively involve the child in the development of his or her own case plan and plan for permanent placement, unless the court finds that the child is unable, unavailable, or unwilling to participate;

(H) Whether each parent was actively involved in the development of the case plan and plan for permanent placement. If the court finds that any parent was not actively involved, the court must order the probation department to actively involve that parent in the development of the case plan and plan for permanent placement, unless the court finds that the parent is unable, unavailable, or unwilling to participate; and

(I) If sibling interaction has been suspended and will continue to be suspended, that sibling interaction is contrary to the safety or well-being of either child.

(4) *Basis for Findings and Orders (§ 727.2(e))*

The determinations required by (a)(3) must be made on a case-by-case basis, and the court must reference, in its written findings, the probation officer's report and any other evidence relied on in reaching its decision.

(Subd (a) amended effective January 1, 2016; previously amended effective January 1, 1998, January 1, 2001, January 1, 2003, January 1, 2004, January 1, 2007, and January 1, 2014.)

(b) Permanency planning hearings (§§ 727.2, 727.3, 11404.1)

A permanency planning hearing for any ward who has been removed from the custody of a parent or guardian and not returned at a previous review hearing must be held within 12 months of the date the ward entered foster care as defined in section 727.4(d)(4). However, when no reunification services are offered to the parents or guardians under section 727.2(b), the first permanency planning hearing must occur within 30 days of disposition.

(1) *Consideration of reports (§ 727.3)*

The court must review and consider the social study report and updated case plan submitted by the probation officer and the report submitted by any CASA volunteer, and any other reports filed with the court under section 727.3(a)(2).

(2) *Findings and orders (§§ 727.2(e), 727.3(a))*

At each permanency planning hearing, the court must consider the safety of the ward and make findings and orders regarding the following:

(A) The continuing necessity for and appropriateness of the placement;

(B) The extent of the probation department's compliance with the case plan in making reasonable efforts to safely return the child to the child's home and to complete whatever steps are necessary to finalize the permanent placement of the child;

(C) The extent of progress that has been made by the child and parent or guardian toward alleviating or mitigating the causes necessitating placement in foster care;

(D) The permanent plan for the child, as described in (3);

(E) Whether the child was actively involved, as age- and developmentally appropriate, in the development of his or her own case plan and plan for permanent placement. If the court finds that the child was not appropriately involved, the court must order the probation officer to actively involve the child in the development of his or her own case plan and plan for permanent placement, unless the court finds that the child is unable, unavailable, or unwilling to participate;

(F) Whether each parent was actively involved in the development of the case plan and plan for permanent placement. If the court finds that any parent was not actively involved, the court must order the probation department to actively involve that parent in the development of the case plan and plan for permanent placement, unless the court finds that the parent is unable, unavailable, or unwilling to participate;

(G) If sibling interaction has been suspended and will continue to be suspended, that sibling interaction is contrary to the safety or well-being of either child; and

(H) Whether the probation officer has exercised due diligence under rule 5.637 in conducting the required investigation to identify, locate, and provide notification and information as required in paragraph (2) of rule 5.637(c) to the child's kin. The court must consider the mandatory activities listed in rule 5.637(d)(2) and may consider the additional activities listed in rule 5.637(d)(3) in determining whether the department has exercised due diligence in family finding. The court must document its determination by making a finding on the record.

(3) *Selection of a permanent plan (§ 727.3(b))*

At the first permanency planning hearing, the court must select a permanent plan. At subsequent permanency planning hearings that must be held under section 727.2(g) and rule 5.810(c), the court must either make a finding that the current permanent plan is appropriate or select a different permanent plan, including returning the child home, if appropriate. The court must choose from one of the permanent plans listed in section 727.3(b).

(4) *Involvement of parents or guardians*

If the child has a continuing involvement with his or her parents or legal guardians, they must be involved in the planning for permanent placement. The permanent plan order must include an order regarding the nature and frequency of visitation with the parents or guardians.

(Subd (b) amended effective January 1, 2024; adopted effective January 1, 2001; previously amended effective January 1, 2003, January 1, 2007, January 1, 2014, January 1, 2016, and January 1, 2018.)

(c) Postpermanency status review hearings (§ 727.2)

A postpermanency status review hearing must be conducted for wards in placement no less frequently than once every six months.

(1) *Consideration of reports (§ 727.2(d))*

The court must review and consider the social study report and updated case plan submitted for this hearing by the probation officer and the report submitted by any CASA volunteer, and any other reports filed with the court under section 727.2(d).

(2) *Findings and orders (§ 727.2(g))*

At each postpermanency status review hearing, the court must consider the safety of the ward and make findings and orders regarding the following:

(A) Whether the current permanent plan continues to be appropriate. If not, the court must select a different permanent plan, including returning the child home, if appropriate. If the plan is another planned permanent living arrangement, the court must meet the requirements stated in Welfare and Institutions Code section 727.3(a)(5);

(B) The continuing necessity for and appropriateness of the placement;

(C) The extent of the probation department's compliance with the case plan in making reasonable efforts to complete whatever steps are necessary to finalize the permanent plan for the child;

(D) Whether the child was actively involved, as age- and developmentally appropriate, in the development of his or her own case plan and plan for permanent placement. If the court finds that the child was not appropriately involved, the court must order the probation department to actively involve the child in the development of his or her own case plan and plan for permanent placement, unless the court finds that the child is unable, unavailable, or unwilling to participate;

(E) If sibling interaction has been suspended and will continue to be suspended, sibling interaction is contrary to the safety or well-being of either child; and

(F) Whether the probation officer has exercised due diligence under rule 5.637 in conducting the required investigation to identify, locate, and provide notification and information as required in paragraph (2) of rule 5.637(c) to the child's kin. The court must consider the mandatory activities listed in rule 5.637(d)(2) and may consider the additional activities listed in rule 5.637(d)(3) in determining whether the department has exercised due diligence in family finding. The court must document its determination by making a finding on the record.

(3) *Information, Documents, and Services (§ 391)*

If the youth is 16 years of age or older, the procedures in section 391 must be followed.

(A) If it is the first review hearing after the youth turns 16 years of age, the probation officer must provide the information, documents, and services required by section 391(a) and must use *First Review Hearing After Youth Turns 16 Years of Age—Information, Documents, and Services* (form JV-361).

(B) If it is the last review hearing before the youth turns 18 years of age, the probation officer must provide the information, documents, and services required by section 391(b)–(c) and must use *Review Hearing for Youth Approaching 18 Years of Age—Information, Documents, and Services* (form JV-362).

(C) If it is a review hearing after the youth turns 18 years of age, the probation officer must provide the information, documents, and services required by section 391(c) and must use *Review Hearing for Youth 18 Years of Age or Older—Information, Documents, and Services* (form JV-363). If the court is terminating jurisdiction at this review hearing, the probation officer must also provide the information, documents, and services required by section 391(h), must follow the procedures in rule 5.555, and must use *Termination of Juvenile Court Jurisdiction—Nonminor* (form JV-365).

(Subd (c) amended effective January 1, 2024; adopted effective January 1, 2001; previously amended effective January 1, 2003, January 1, 2007, January 1, 2014, January 1, 2016, January 1, 2018, and January 1, 2021.)

(d) Notice of hearings; service; contents (§ 727.4)

No earlier than 30 nor later than 15 calendar days before each hearing date, the probation officer must serve written notice on all persons entitled to notice under section 727.4, as well as the current caregiver, any CASA volunteer or educational rights holder, and all counsel of record. A *Notice of Hearing—Juvenile Delinquency Proceeding* (form JV-625) must be used.

(Subd (d) amended effective January 1, 2014; adopted effective January 1, 2001; previously amended effective January 1, 2003, January 1, 2006, and January 1, 2007.)

(e) Report (§§ 706.5, 706.6, 727.2(c), 727.3(a)(1), 727.4(b), 16002)

Before each hearing described above, the probation officer must investigate and prepare a social study report that must include an updated case plan and all of the information required in sections 706.5, 706.6, 727.2, 727.3, and 16002.

(1) The report must contain recommendations for court findings and orders and must document the evidentiary basis for those recommendations.

(2) At least 10 calendar days before each hearing, the probation officer must file the report and provide copies of the report to the ward, the parent or guardian, all attorneys of record, and any CASA volunteer.

(Subd (e) amended effective January 1, 2016; adopted as subd (b) effective January 1, 1991; previously amended and relettered as subd (e) effective January 1, 2001; previously amended effective January 1, 1998, January 1, 2003, January 1, 2007, and January 1, 2014.)

(f) Release of Information to the Medical Board of California

If the child has signed *Position on Release of Information to Medical Board of California* (form JV-228), the probation officer must provide the child with a blank copy of *Withdrawal of Release of Information to Medical Board of California* (form JV-229) before the hearing if it is the last hearing before the child turns 18 years of age or if the social worker is recommending termination of juvenile court jurisdiction.

(Subd (f) adopted effective September 1, 2020.)

Rule 5.810 amended effective January 1, 2024; adopted as rule 1496 effective January 1, 1991; previously amended and renumbered as rule 5.810 effective January 1, 2007; previously amended effective January 1, 1998, January 1, 2001, January 1, 2003, January 1, 2004, January 1, 2006, January 1, 2014, January 1, 2016, January 1, 2018, September 1, 2020, and January 1, 2021.

Rule 5.811. Modification to transition jurisdiction for a ward older than 17 years and 5 months with a petition subject to dismissal (Welf. & Inst. Code, §§ 450, 451, 727.2(i)–(j), 778; Pen. Code, § 236.14)

(a) Purpose

This rule provides the procedures that must be followed to modify delinquency jurisdiction to transition jurisdiction for a young person who is older than 17 years, 5 months of age and:

(1) Is under a foster care placement order;

(2) Wants to remain in extended foster care under the transition jurisdiction of the juvenile court;

(3) Is not receiving reunification services;

(4) Does not have a hearing set for termination of parental rights or establishment of guardianship; and

(5) The underlying adjudication establishing wardship over the young person is subject to vacatur under Penal Code section 236.14.

(Subd (a) adopted effective January 1, 2019.)

(b) Setting and conduct of hearing

(1) The probation officer must request a hearing for the court to modify delinquency jurisdiction to transition jurisdiction and vacate the underlying adjudication.

(2) The hearing must be held before a judicial officer and recorded by a court reporter.

(3) The hearing must be continued for no more than five court days for the submission of additional evidence if the court finds that the report and, if required, the Transitional Independent Living Case Plan submitted by the probation officer do not provide the information required by (d), and the court is unable to make all the findings required by (e).

(Subd (b) adopted effective January 1, 2019.)

(c) Notice of hearing

(1) The probation officer must serve written notice of the hearing in the manner provided in section 295.

(2) Proof of service of notice must be filed by the probation officer at least five court days before the hearing.

(Subd (c) adopted effective January 1, 2019.)

(d) Reports

At least 10 calendar days before the hearing, the probation officer must submit a report to the court that includes information regarding:

(1) Whether the young person is subject to an order for foster care placement and is older than 17 years, 5 months of age and younger than 18 years of age;

(2) Whether the young person is a nonminor who was subject to an order for foster care placement on the day of the young person's 18th birthday and is within the age eligibility requirements for extended foster care;

(3) Whether the young person was removed from the physical custody of his or her parents, adjudged to be within the jurisdiction of the juvenile court under section 725, and ordered into foster care placement; or whether the young person was removed from the custody of his or her parents as a dependent of the court with an order for foster care placement in effect at the time the court adjudged him or her to be within the jurisdiction of the juvenile court under section 725 and was ordered into a foster care placement, including the date of the initial removal findings—"continuance in the home is contrary to the child's welfare" and "reasonable efforts were made to prevent removal"—as well as whether the young person continues to be removed from the parents or legal guardian from whom the young person was removed under the original petition;

(4) Whether each parent or legal guardian is currently able to provide the care, custody, supervision, and support the child requires in a safe and healthy environment;

(5) Whether the young person signed a mutual agreement with the probation department or social services agency for placement in a supervised setting as a transition dependent and, if so, a recommendation as to which agency should be responsible for placement and care of the transition dependent;

(6) Whether the young person plans to meet at least one of the conditions in section 11403(b) and what efforts the probation officer has made to help the young person meet any of these conditions;

(7) When and how the young person was informed of the benefits of remaining under juvenile court jurisdiction as a transition dependent and the probation officer's assessment of the young person's understanding of those benefits;

(8) When and how the young person was informed that he or she may decline to become a transition dependent and have the juvenile court terminate jurisdiction at a hearing under section 391 and rule 5.555; and

(9) When and how the young person was informed that if juvenile court jurisdiction is terminated, he or she can file a request to return to foster care and have the court resume jurisdiction over him or her as a nonminor.

(Subd (d) adopted effective January 1, 2019.)

(e) Findings

At the hearing, the court must make the following findings:

(1) Whether notice has been given as required by law;

(2) Whether the underlying adjudication is subject to vacatur under Penal Code section 236.14;

(3) Whether the young person has been informed that he or she may decline to become a transition dependent and have juvenile court jurisdiction terminated at a hearing set under rule 5.555;

(4) Whether the young person intends to sign a mutual agreement with the probation department or social services agency for placement in a supervised setting as a nonminor dependent;

(5) Whether the young person was informed that if juvenile court jurisdiction is terminated, the young person can file a request to return to foster care and may have the court resume jurisdiction over the young person as a nonminor dependent;

(6) Whether the benefits of remaining under juvenile court jurisdiction as a nonminor dependent were explained and whether the young person understands them;

(7) Whether the young person's Transitional Independent Living Case Plan includes a plan for the young person to satisfy at least one of the conditions in section 11403(b); and

(8) Whether the young person has had an opportunity to confer with his or her attorney.

In addition to the findings listed above, for children who are older than 17 years, 5 months of age but younger than 18 years of age, the court must make the following findings:

(A) Whether the young person's return to the home of his or her parent or legal guardian would create a substantial risk of detriment to the young person's safety, protection, or physical or emotional well-being—the facts supporting this finding must be stated on the record;

(B) Whether reunification services have been terminated; and

(C) Whether the young person's case has been set for a hearing to terminate parental rights or establish a guardianship.

(Subd (e) adopted effective January 1, 2019.)

(f) Orders

The court must enter the following orders:

(1) An order adjudging the young person a transition dependent as of the date of the hearing or pending his or her 18th birthday and granting status as a nonminor dependent under the general jurisdiction of the court. The order modifying the court's jurisdiction must contain all of the following provisions:

(A) A statement that "continuance in the home is contrary to the child or nonminor's welfare" and that "reasonable efforts have been made to prevent or eliminate the need for removal";

(B) A statement that the child continues to be removed from the parents or legal guardian from whom the child was removed under the original petition; and

(C) Identification of the agency that is responsible for placement and care of the child based on the modification of jurisdiction.

(2) An order vacating the underlying adjudication and dismissing the associated delinquency petition under Penal Code section 236.14.

(3) An order directing the Department of Justice and any law enforcement agency that has records of the arrest to seal those records and, three years from the date of the arrest or one year after the order to seal, whichever occurs later, destroy them.

(4) An order continuing the appointment of the attorney of record, or appointing a new attorney as the attorney of record for the nonminor dependent.

(5) An order setting a nonminor dependent status review hearing under section 366.31 and rule 5.903 within six months of the last hearing held under section 727.2 or 727.3.

(Subd (f) adopted effective January 1, 2019.)

Rule 5.811 adopted effective January 1, 2019.

Rule 5.812. Additional requirements for any hearing to terminate jurisdiction over child in foster care and for status review or dispositional hearing for child approaching majority (§§ 450, 451, 727.2(i)–(j), 778)

(a) Hearings subject to this rule

The following hearings are subject to this rule:

(1) The last review hearing under section 727.2 or 727.3 before the child turns 18 years of age and a dispositional hearing under section 702 for a child under an order of foster care placement who will attain 18 years of age before a subsequent review hearing will be held. If the hearing is the last review hearing under section 727.2 or 727.3, the hearing must be set at least 90 days before the child attains his or her 18th birthday and within six months of the previous hearing held under section 727.2 or 727.3.

(2) Any review hearing held under section 727.2 or 727.3 for a child less than 18 years of age during which a recommendation to terminate juvenile court jurisdiction will be considered;

(3) Any hearing to terminate juvenile court jurisdiction over a child less than 18 years of age who is subject to an order for foster care placement; and

(4) Any hearing to terminate juvenile court jurisdiction over a child less than 18 years of age who is not currently subject to an order for foster care placement but was previously removed from the custody of his or her parents or legal guardian as a dependent of the juvenile court and an order for a foster care placement as a dependent of the juvenile court was in effect at the time the juvenile court adjudged the child to be a ward of the juvenile court under section 725.

(Subd (a) amended effective January 1, 2016; adopted effective January 1, 2012; previously amended effective July 1, 2012.)

(b) Conduct of the hearing

(1) The hearing must be held before a judicial officer and recorded by a court reporter.

(2) The hearing must be continued for no more than five court days for the submission of additional information as ordered by the court if the court finds that the report and, if required, the Transitional Independent Living Case Plan and Transitional Independent Living Plan submitted by the probation officer do not provide the information required by (c) and the court is unable to make all the findings required by (d).

(Subd (b) amended effective July 1, 2012; adopted effective January 1, 2012.)

(c) Reports

(1) In addition to complying with all other statutory and rule requirements applicable to the report prepared by the probation officer for a hearing described in (a)(1)–(4), the report must state whether the child was provided with the notices and information required under section 607.5 and include a description of:

(A) The child's progress toward meeting the case plan goals that will enable him or her to be a law-abiding and productive member of his or her family and the community. This information is not required if dismissal of delinquency jurisdiction and vacatur of the underlying adjudication is based on Penal Code section 236.14.

(B) If reunification services have not been previously terminated, the progress of each parent or legal guardian toward participating in case plan service activities and meeting the case plan goals developed to resolve his or her issues that were identified and contributed to the child's removal from his or her custody.

(C) The current ability of each parent or legal guardian to provide the care, custody, supervision, and support the child requires in a safe and healthy environment.

(D) For a child previously determined to be a dual status child for whom juvenile court jurisdiction as a dependent was suspended under section 241.1(e)(5)(A), a joint assessment by the probation department and the child welfare services agency under section 366.5 regarding the detriment, if any, to the child of a return to the home of his or her parents or legal guardian and a recommendation on the resumption of dependency jurisdiction. The facts in support of the opinions expressed and the recommendations made must be included in the joint assessment section of the report. If the probation department and the child welfare services agency do not agree, the child welfare services agency must file a separate report with facts in support of its opinions and recommendations.

(E) For a child previously determined to be a dual status child for whom the probation department was designated the lead agency under section 241.1(e)(5)(B), the detriment, if any, to the child of a return to the home of his or her parents or legal guardian and the probation officer's recommendation regarding the modification of the court's jurisdiction over the child from that of a dual status child to that of a dependent under section 300 and the facts in support of the opinion expressed and the recommendation made.

(F) For a child other than a dual status child, including a child whose underlying adjudication is subject to vacatur under Penal Code section 236.14, the probation officer's recommendation regarding the modification of the juvenile court's jurisdiction over the child from that of a ward under section 601 or 602 to that of a dependent under section 300 or to that of a transition dependent under section 450 and the facts in support of his or her recommendation.

(2) For the review hearing held on behalf of a child approaching majority described in (a)(1) and any hearing described in (a)(2) or (a)(3) held on behalf of a child more than 17 years, 5 months old and less than 18 years of age, in addition to complying with all other report requirements set forth in (c)(1), the report prepared by the probation officer must include:

(A) The child's plans to remain under juvenile court jurisdiction as a nonminor dependent including the criteria in section 11403(b) that he or she plans to meet;

(B) The efforts made by the probation officer to help the child meet one or more of the criteria in section 11403(b);

(C) For an Indian child, his or her plans to continue to be considered an Indian child for the purposes of the ongoing application of the Indian Child Welfare Act to him or her as a nonminor dependent;

(D) Whether the child has applied for and, if so, the status of any in-progress application pending for title XVI Supplemental Security Income benefits and, if such an application is pending, whether it is in the child's best interest to continue juvenile court jurisdiction until a final decision has been issued to ensure that the child receives continued assistance with the application process;

(E) Whether the child has an in-progress application pending for Special Immigrant Juvenile Status or other applicable application for legal residency and whether an active juvenile court case is required for that application;

(F) The efforts made by the probation officer toward providing the child with the written information, documents, and services described in section 391 and, to the extent that the child has not yet been provided with them, the barriers to providing the information, documents or services and the steps that will be taken to overcome those barriers by the date the child attains 18 years of age;

(G) When and how the child was informed that upon reaching 18 years of age he or she may request the dismissal of juvenile court jurisdiction over him or her under section 778;

(H) When and how the child was provided with information regarding the potential benefits of remaining under juvenile court jurisdiction as a nonminor dependent and the probation officer's assessment of the child's understanding of those benefits;

(I) When and how the child was informed that if juvenile court jurisdiction is terminated after he or she attains 18 years of age, he or she has the right to file a request to return to foster care and have the juvenile court assume or resume transition jurisdiction over him or her as a nonminor dependent; and

(J) The child's Transitional Independent Living Case Plan and Transitional Independent Living Plan, which must include:

(i) The individualized plan for the child to satisfy one or more of the criteria in section 11403(b) and the child's anticipated placement as specified in section 11402; and

(ii) The child's alternate plan for his or her transition to independence, including housing, education, employment, and a support system in the event the child does not remain under juvenile court jurisdiction after attaining 18 years of age.

(Subd (c) amended effective January 1, 2019; adopted effective January 1, 2012; previously amended effective July 1, 2012.)

(d) Findings

(1) At the hearing described in (a)(1)–(4), in addition to complying with all other statutory and rule requirements applicable to the hearing, the court must make the following findings in the written documentation of the hearing:

(A) Whether the rehabilitative goals for this child have been met and juvenile court jurisdiction over the child as a ward is no longer required. The facts supporting the finding must be stated on the record. This finding is not required where dismissal of delinquency jurisdiction is based on Penal Code section 236.14.

(B) For a dual status child for whom dependency jurisdiction was suspended under section 241.1(e)(5)(A), whether the return to the home of the parents or legal guardian would be detrimental to the minor. The facts supporting the finding must be stated on the record.

(C) For a child previously determined to be a dual status child for whom the probation department was designated the lead agency under section 241.1(e)(5)(B), whether the return to the home of the parents or legal guardian would be detrimental to the minor. The facts supporting the finding must be stated on the record.

(D) For a child other than a dual status child:

(i) Who was not subject to the court's dependency jurisdiction at the time he or she was adjudged a ward and is currently subject to an order for a foster care placement, including a child whose underlying adjudication is subject to vacatur under Penal Code section 236.14, whether the child appears to come within the description of section 300 and cannot be returned home safely. The facts supporting the finding must be stated on the record;

(ii) Who was subject to an order for a foster care placement as a dependent of the court at the time he or she was adjudged a ward, whether the child remains within the description of a dependent child under section 300 and whether the return to the home of the parents or legal guardian would create a substantial risk of detriment to the child's safety, protection, or physical or emotional well-being. The facts supporting the findings must be stated on the record;

(iii) Whether reunification services have been terminated;

(iv) Whether the matter has been set for a hearing to terminate parental rights or establish a guardianship; and

(v) Whether the minor intends to sign a mutual agreement for a placement in a supervised setting as a nonminor dependent.

(2) At the review hearing held on behalf of a child approaching majority described in (a)(1) and any hearing under (a)(2) or (a)(3) held on behalf of a child more than 17 years, 5 months old and less than 18 years of age, in addition to complying with all other statutory and rule requirements applicable to the hearing, the court must make the following findings in the written documentation of the hearing:

(A) Whether the child's Transitional Independent Living Case Plan, if required, or Transitional Independent Living Plan includes:

(i) A plan specific to the child for him or her to satisfy one or more of the criteria in section 11403(b) and the specific criteria in section 11403(b) it is anticipated the child will satisfy; and

(ii) The child's alternate plan for his or her transition to independence, including housing, education, employment, and a support system in the event the child does not remain under juvenile court jurisdiction after attaining 18 years of age.

(B) For an Indian child to whom the Indian Child Welfare Act applies, whether he or she intends to continue to be considered an Indian child for the purposes of the ongoing application of the Indian Child Welfare Act to him or her as a nonminor dependent;

(C) Whether the child has an in-progress application pending for title XVI Supplemental Security Income benefits and, if such an application is pending, whether it is in the child's best interest to continue juvenile court jurisdiction until a final decision has been issued to ensure that the child receives continued assistance with the application process;

(D) Whether the child has an in-progress application pending for Special Immigrant Juvenile Status or other applicable application for legal residency and whether an active juvenile court case is required for that application;

(E) Whether the child has been informed that he or she may decline to become a nonminor dependent;

(F) Whether the child has been informed that upon reaching 18 years of age he or she may request the dismissal of juvenile court jurisdiction over him or her under section 778;

(G) Whether the child understands the potential benefits of remaining under juvenile court jurisdiction as a nonminor dependent;

(H) Whether the child has been informed that if after reaching 18 years of age juvenile court jurisdiction is terminated, he or she has the right to file a request to return to foster care and have the juvenile court assume or resume transition jurisdiction over him or her as a nonminor dependent;

(I) Whether all the information, documents, and services in sections 391(e) were provided to the child, and whether the barriers to providing any missing information, documents, or services can be overcome by the date the child attains 18 years of age; and

(J) Whether the notices and information required under section 607.5 were provided to a child who is or was subject to an order for foster care placement.

(Subd (d) amended effective January 1, 2019; adopted effective January 1, 2012; previously amended effective July 1, 2012, and January 1, 2014.)

(e) Orders

(1) For a child previously determined to be a dual status child for whom dependency jurisdiction was suspended under section 241.1(e)(5)(A), dependency jurisdiction must be resumed if the court finds that the child's rehabilitative goals have been achieved and a return to the home of the parents or legal guardian would be detrimental to the child.

(2) For a child previously determined to be a dual status child for whom the probation department was designated the lead agency under section 241.1(e)(5)(B), the court must terminate dual status, dismiss delinquency jurisdiction, and continue dependency jurisdiction with the child welfare services department responsible for the child's placement if the court finds that the child's rehabilitative goals have been achieved and a return to the home of the parents or legal guardian would be detrimental to the child.

(3) For a child who comes within the description of section 450(a), other than a child described in (e)(1) or (e)(2), the court must enter an order modifying its jurisdiction over him or her from delinquency jurisdiction to transition jurisdiction and set a nonminor dependent status review hearing under rule 5.903 within six months of the last hearing held under section 727.2.

(4) For a child who was not subject to the court's dependency jurisdiction at the time he or she was adjudged a ward and is currently subject to an order for a foster care placement, including a child whose underlying adjudication is subject to vacatur under Penal Code section 236.14, the court must:

(A) Order the probation department or the child's attorney to submit an application under section 329 to the county child welfare services department to commence a proceeding to declare the child a dependent of the court by filing a petition under section 300 if the court finds:

(i) The child does not come within the description of section 450(a);

(ii) The rehabilitative goals for the child included in his or her case plan have been met and delinquency jurisdiction is no longer required, or the underlying adjudication is subject to vacatur under Penal Code section 236.14; and

(iii) The child appears to come within the description of section 300 and a return to the home of the parents or legal guardian may be detrimental to his or her safety, protection, or physical or emotional well-being.

(B) Set a hearing to review the county child welfare services department's decision within 20 court days of the date the order to file an application under section 329 was entered and at that hearing:

(i) Affirm the county child welfare services department's decision not to file a petition under section 300; or

(ii) Order the county child welfare services department to file a petition under section 300.

(C) If the court affirms the decision not to file a petition under section 300 or a petition filed under section 300 is not sustained, the court may:

(i) Return the child to the home of the parents or legal guardian and set a progress report hearing within the next six months;

(ii) Return the child to the home of the parents or legal guardian and terminate juvenile court jurisdiction over the child; or

(iii) Continue the child's foster care placement and set a hearing under section 727.2 no more than six months from the date of the most recent hearing held under 727.2.

(5) For a child who was subject to an order for foster care placement as a dependent of the court at the time he or she was adjudged a ward, the court must modify its delinquency jurisdiction over the child by vacating the order terminating jurisdiction over the child as a dependent of the court and resuming dependency jurisdiction over him or her if the court finds that:

(A) The child does not come within the description of section 450(a);

(B) The rehabilitative goals for the child included in his or her case plan have been met and delinquency jurisdiction may not be required; and

(C) The child remains within the description of a dependent child under section 300 and a return to the home of a parents or legal guardian would create a substantial risk of detriment to his or her safety, protection, or physical or emotional well-being.

(6) At a hearing described in (a)(1) for a child approaching majority or at any hearing described in (a)(2) or (a)(3) held on behalf of a child more than 17 years, 5 months old and less than 18 years old that did not result in modification of jurisdiction over the child from delinquency jurisdiction to dependency jurisdiction or transition jurisdiction, the court must:

(A) Return the child to the home of the parents or legal guardian and set a progress report hearing within the next six months; or

(B) Return the child to the home of the parents or legal guardian and terminate juvenile court jurisdiction over the child; or

(C) Continue the child's foster care placement and:

(i) For the child who intends to meet the eligibility requirements for status as a nonminor dependent after attaining 18 years of age, set a nonminor dependent status review hearing under rule 5.903 no more than six months from the most recent hearing held under section 727.2; or

(ii) For the child who does not intend to meet the eligibility requirements for nonminor dependent status after attaining 18 years of age:

a. Set a hearing to terminate delinquency jurisdiction under section 607.2(b)(4) and section 607.3 for a date within one month after the child's 18th birthday; or

b. Set a hearing under section 727.2 no more than six months from the date of the most recent hearing held under section 727.2 for the child who will remain under delinquency jurisdiction in a foster care placement.

(7) At any hearing under (a)(2) or (a)(3) held on behalf of a child 17 years, 5 months old or younger that did not result in modification of jurisdiction over the child from delinquency jurisdiction to dependency jurisdiction, the court must:

(A) Return the child to the home of the parents or legal guardian and set a progress report hearing within the next six months;

(B) Return the child to the home of the parents or legal guardian and terminate juvenile court jurisdiction over the child; or

(C) Continue the child's out-of-home placement and set a hearing under section 727.2 to occur within six months of the most recent hearing under section 727.2.

(8) At any hearing under (a)(4) on behalf of a child less than 18 years of age that did not result in modification of jurisdiction over the child from delinquency jurisdiction to dependency jurisdiction, the court must:

(A) Return the child to the home of the parents or legal guardian and set a progress report hearing within the next six months;

(B) Return the child to the home of the parents or legal guardian and terminate juvenile court jurisdiction over the child; or

(C) Continue the child's out-of-home placement and set a progress report hearing within the next six months.

(Subd (e) amended effective January 1, 2019; adopted effective January 1, 2012; previously amended effective July 1, 2012.)

(f) Modification of jurisdiction—conditions

(1) Whenever the court modifies its jurisdiction over a dependent or ward under section 241.1, 607.2, or 727.2, the court must ensure that all of the following conditions are met:

(A) The petition under which jurisdiction was taken at the time the dependent or ward was originally removed from his or her parents or legal guardian and placed in foster care is not dismissed until after the new petition is sustained; and

(B) The order modifying the court's jurisdiction contains all of the following provisions:

(i) A reference to the original removal findings, the date those findings were made, and a statement that the finding "continuation in the home is contrary to the child's welfare" and the finding "reasonable efforts were made to prevent removal" made at that hearing remain in effect;

(ii) A statement that the child continues to be removed from the parents or legal guardian from whom the child was removed under the original petition; and

(iii) Identification of the agency that is responsible for placement and care of the child based upon the modification of jurisdiction.

(2) Whenever the court modifies jurisdiction over a young person under section 450(a)(1)(B), the court must ensure that all of the following conditions are met:

(A) The order modifying the court's jurisdiction must be made before the underlying petition is vacated;

(B) The order modifying jurisdiction must contain the following provisions:

(i) Continuance in the home is contrary the child's welfare, and reasonable efforts were made to prevent removal;

(ii) The child continues to be removed from the parents or legal guardians;

(iii) Identification of the agency that is responsible for placement and care of the young person based on modification of jurisdiction;

(iv) A statement that the underlying adjudication is vacated and the arrest upon which it was based is expunged; and

(v) An order directing the Department of Justice and any law enforcement agency that has records of the arrest to seal those records and destroy them three years from the date of the arrest or one year after the order to seal, whichever occurs later.

(Subd (f) amended effective January 1, 2019; adopted effective January 1, 2012; previously amended effective July 1, 2012.)

Rule 5.812 amended effective January 1, 2019; adopted effective January 1, 2012; previously amended effective July 1, 2012, January 1, 2014, and January 1, 2016.

Rule 5.813. Modification to transition jurisdiction for a ward older than 18 years and younger than 21 years of age (§§ 450, 451)

(a) Purpose

This rule provides the procedures that must be followed when it appears to a probation officer that a ward who is at least 18 years of age and younger than 21 years of age has met his or her rehabilitative goals and wants to remain in extended foster care under the jurisdiction of the court.

(Subd (a) adopted effective January 1, 2014.)

(b) Setting and conduct of hearing

(1) The probation officer must request a hearing for the court to consider modifying delinquency jurisdiction to transition jurisdiction.

(2) The hearing must be held before a judicial officer and recorded by a court reporter.

(3) The hearing must be continued for no more than five court days for the submission of additional evidence as ordered by the court if the court finds that the report and, if required, the Transitional Independent Living Case Plan submitted by the probation officer do not provide the information required by (d) and the court is unable to make all the findings required by (e).

(Subd (b) adopted effective January 1, 2014.)

(c) Notice of hearing

(1) The probation officer must serve written notice of the hearing in the manner provided in section 295.

(2) Proof of service of notice must be filed by the probation officer at least five court days before the hearing.

(Subd (c) adopted effective January 1, 2014.)

(d) Reports

At least 10 calendar days before the hearing, the probation officer must submit a report to the court that includes information regarding:

(1) Whether the ward is a nonminor who was subject to an order for foster care placement on the day of the ward's 18th birthday and is within the age eligibility requirements for extended foster care;

(2) Whether the ward was removed from the physical custody of his or her parents, adjudged to be a ward of the juvenile court under section 725, and ordered into foster care placement as a ward; or whether the ward was removed from the custody of his or her parents as a dependent of the court with an order for foster care placement in effect at the time the court adjudged him or her to be a ward of the juvenile court under section 725 and was ordered into a foster care placement as a ward, including the date of the initial removal findings—"continuance in the home is contrary to the child's welfare" and "reasonable efforts were made to prevent removal"—as well as whether the ward continues to be removed from the parents or legal guardian from whom the child was removed under the original petition;

(3) Whether the ward's rehabilitative goals as stated in the case plan have been met and whether juvenile court jurisdiction over the ward is no longer required;

(4) Whether the probation officer recommends the modification of juvenile court jurisdiction over the ward from that of a ward under section 601 or 602 to that of a nonminor dependent under section 450 and the facts in support of that recommendation;

(5) Whether the ward signed a mutual agreement with the probation department or social services agency for placement in a supervised setting as a nonminor dependent and, if so, a recommendation as to which agency should be responsible for placement and care of the nonminor dependent;

(6) Whether the ward plans to meet at least one of the conditions in section 11403(b) and what efforts the probation officer has made to help the ward meet any of the conditions;

(7) When and how the ward was informed of the benefits of remaining under juvenile court jurisdiction as a nonminor dependent and the probation officer's assessment of the ward's understanding of those benefits;

(8) When and how the ward was informed that he or she may decline to become a nonminor dependent and have the juvenile court terminate jurisdiction at a hearing under section 391 and rule 5.555; and

(9) When and how the ward was informed that if juvenile court jurisdiction is terminated, he or she can file a request to return to foster care and have the court resume jurisdiction over him or her as a nonminor.

(Subd (d) adopted effective January 1, 2014.)

(e) Findings

At the hearing described in (a), the court must make the following findings:

(1) Whether notice has been given as required by law;

(2) Whether the nonminor comes within the description of section 450;

(3) Whether the ward has been informed that he or she may decline to become a nonminor dependent and have juvenile court jurisdiction terminated at a hearing set under rule 5.555;

(4) Whether the ward was informed that if juvenile court jurisdiction is terminated, the ward can file a request to return to foster care and may have the court resume jurisdiction over the ward as a nonminor;

(5) Whether the benefits of remaining under juvenile court jurisdiction as a nonminor dependent were explained and whether the ward understands them;

(6) Whether the ward has signed a mutual agreement with the probation department for placement in a supervised setting as a nonminor dependent;

(7) Whether the ward's Transitional Independent Living Case Plan includes a plan for the ward to satisfy at least one of the conditions in section 11403(b); and

(8) Whether the ward has had an opportunity to confer with his or her attorney.

(Subd (e) adopted effective January 1, 2014.)

(f) Orders

For a child who comes within the description of section 450(a), the court must enter the following orders:

(1) An order modifying the court's jurisdiction over the child from delinquency to transition jurisdiction and setting a nonminor dependent status review hearing under section 366.31 and rule 5.903 within six months of the last hearing held under section 727.2 or 366.31. The order modifying the court's jurisdiction must contain all of the following provisions:

(A) A reference to the initial removal findings, the date those findings were made, and a statement that the findings—"continuance in the home is contrary to the child's welfare" and "reasonable efforts were made to prevent removal"—made at that hearing remain in effect;

(B) A statement that the nonminor dependent continues to be removed from the parents or legal guardian from whom the nonminor dependent was removed under the original petition; and

(C) Identification of the agency that is responsible for placement and care of the nonminor dependent based on the modification of jurisdiction.

(2) An order continuing the appointment of the attorney of record or appointing a new attorney as the attorney of record for the nonminor dependent.

(Subd (f) adopted effective January 1, 2014.)

Rule 5.813 adopted effective January 1, 2014.

Rule 5.814. Modification to transition jurisdiction for a ward older than 17 years, 5 months of age and younger than 18 years of age (§§ 450, 451)

(a) Purpose

This rule provides the procedures that must be followed to modify delinquency jurisdiction to transition jurisdiction for a ward who is older than 17 years, 5 months of age, younger than 18 years of age, and:

(1) Has met his or her rehabilitative goals;

(2) Is under a foster care placement order;

(3) Wants to remain in extended foster care under the transition jurisdiction of the juvenile court;

(4) Is not receiving reunification services; and

(5) Does not have a hearing set for termination of parental rights or establishment of guardianship.

(Subd (a) adopted effective January 1, 2014.)

(b) Setting and conduct of hearing

(1) The probation officer must request a hearing for the court to consider modifying delinquency jurisdiction to transition jurisdiction.

(2) The hearing must be held before a judicial officer and recorded by a court reporter.

(3) The hearing must be continued for no more than five court days for the submission of additional evidence as ordered by the court if the court finds that the report and, if required, the Transitional Independent Living Case Plan submitted by the probation officer, do not provide the information required by (d) and the court is unable to make all the findings required by (e).

(Subd (b) adopted effective January 1, 2014.)

(c) Notice of hearing

(1) The probation officer must serve written notice of the hearing in the manner provided in section 295.

(2) Proof of service of notice must be filed by the probation officer at least five court days before the hearing.

(Subd (c) adopted effective January 1, 2014.)

(d) Reports

At least 10 calendar days before the hearing, the probation officer must submit a report to the court that includes information regarding:

(1) Whether the ward is subject to an order for foster care placement and is older than 17 years, 5 months of age and younger than 18 years of age;

(2) Whether the ward was removed from the physical custody of his or her parents, adjudged to be a ward of the juvenile court under section 725, and ordered into foster care placement as a ward; or whether the ward was removed from the custody of his or her parents as a dependent of the court with an order for foster care placement in effect at the time the court adjudged him or her to be a ward of the juvenile court under section 725 and was ordered into a foster care placement as a ward, including the date of the initial removal findings—"continuance in the home is contrary to the child's welfare" and "reasonable efforts were made to prevent removal"—as well as whether the ward continues to be removed from the parents or legal guardian from whom the child was removed under the original petition;

(3) Whether the ward's rehabilitative goals as stated in the case plan have been met and whether juvenile court jurisdiction over the ward is no longer required;

(4) Whether each parent or legal guardian is currently able to provide the care, custody, supervision, and support the child requires in a safe and healthy environment;

(5) Whether the probation officer recommends the modification of the juvenile court's jurisdiction over the ward from that of a ward under section 601 or 602 to that of a transition dependent under section 450;

(6) Whether the ward signed a mutual agreement with the probation department or social services agency for placement in a supervised setting as a transition dependent and, if so, a recommendation as to which agency should be responsible for placement and care of the transition dependent;

(7) Whether the ward plans to meet at least one of the conditions in section 11403(b) and what efforts the probation officer has made to help the ward meet any of these conditions;

(8) When and how the ward was informed of the benefits of remaining under juvenile court jurisdiction as a transition dependent and the probation officer's assessment of the ward's understanding of those benefits;

(9) When and how the ward was informed that he or she may decline to become a transition dependent and have the juvenile court terminate jurisdiction at a hearing under section 391 and rule 5.555; and

(10) When and how the ward was informed that if juvenile court jurisdiction is terminated, he or she can file a request to return to foster care and have the court resume jurisdiction over him or her as a nonminor.

(Subd (d) adopted effective January 1, 2014.)

(e) Findings

At the hearing, the court must make the following findings:

(1) Whether notice has been given as required by law;

(2) Whether the ward comes within the description of section 450;

(3) Whether the ward has been informed that he or she may decline to become a transition dependent and have juvenile court jurisdiction terminated at a hearing set under rule 5.555;

(4) Whether the ward's return to the home of his or her parent or legal guardian would create a substantial risk of detriment to the ward's safety, protection, or physical or emotional well-being. The facts supporting this finding must be stated on the record;

(5) Whether reunification services have been terminated;

(6) Whether the ward's case has been set for a hearing to terminate parental rights or establish a guardianship;

(7) Whether the ward intends to sign a mutual agreement with the probation department or social services agency for placement in a supervised setting as a nonminor dependent;

(8) Whether the ward was informed that if juvenile court jurisdiction is terminated, the ward can file a request to return to foster care and may have the court resume jurisdiction over the ward as a nonminor dependent;

(9) Whether the benefits of remaining under juvenile court jurisdiction as a nonminor dependent were explained and whether the ward understands them;

(10) Whether the ward's Transitional Independent Living Case Plan includes a plan for the ward to satisfy at least one of the conditions in section 11403(b); and

(11) Whether the ward has had an opportunity to confer with his or her attorney.

(Subd (e) adopted effective January 1, 2014.)

(f) Orders

For a child who comes within the description of section 450(a), the court must enter the following orders:

(1) An order modifying the court's jurisdiction over the child from delinquency to transition jurisdiction and adjudging the ward a transition dependent pending his or her 18th birthday and status as a nonminor dependent under the transition jurisdiction of the court. The order modifying the court's jurisdiction must contain all of the following provisions:

(A) A reference to the initial removal findings, the date those findings were made, and a statement that the findings—"continuance in the home is contrary to the child's welfare" and "reasonable efforts were made to prevent removal"—made at that hearing remain in effect;

(B) A statement that the child continues to be removed from the parents or legal guardian from whom the child was removed under the original petition; and

(C) Identification of the agency that is responsible for placement and care of the child based on the modification of jurisdiction.

(2) An order continuing the appointment of the attorney of record, or appointing a new attorney, as the attorney of record for the nonminor dependent.

(3) An order setting a nonminor dependent status review hearing under section 366.31 and rule 5.903 within six months of the last hearing held under section 727.2 or 727.3.

(Subd (f) adopted effective January 1, 2014.)
Rule 5.814 adopted effective January 1, 2014.

Rule 5.815. Legal guardianship—wards (§§ 366.26, 727.3, 728)

(a) Proceedings in juvenile court

Proceedings for the appointment of a legal guardian for a child who is a ward of the juvenile court may be held in the juvenile court under the procedures specified in section 366.26.

(Subd (a) amended effective January 1, 2021; previously amended effective January 1, 2007.)

(b) Hearing to consider guardianship

On the recommendation of the probation officer supervising the child in the social study and case plan required by sections 706.5(c)–(d) and 706.6(n), the motion of the child's attorney under section 778, or the court's determination under section 727.3 that a legal guardianship is the appropriate permanent plan for the child, the court must set a hearing to consider the establishment of a legal guardianship and must order the probation officer to prepare an assessment that includes:

(1) All the elements required to be addressed in the assessment prepared under Welfare and Institutions Code section 727.31(b); and

(2) A statement confirming that the proposed guardian has been provided with a copy of *Becoming a Child's Guardian in Juvenile Court* (form JV-350-INFO) or *La función de un tutor nombrado por la corte de menores* (form JV-350-INFO S).

(Subd (b) amended effective January 1, 2021; previously amended effective January 1, 2007.)

(c) Probation officer's recommendation

The probation officer's recommendation for appointment of a legal guardian may be included in the social study report and case plan submitted under sections 706.5 and 706.6. Neither a separate petition nor a separate hearing is required.

(Subd (c) amended effective January 1, 2021; previously amended effective January 1, 2007.)

(d) Notice (§ 728(c))

The clerk must provide notice of the hearing to the child, the child's parents, and other individuals as required by section 294.

(Subd (d) amended effective July 1, 2016.)

(e) Conduct of hearing

The proceedings for appointment of a legal guardian must be conducted according to the procedural requirements of section 366.26, except for subdivision (j). The court must read and consider the assessment prepared by the probation officer and any other relevant evidence. The preparer of the assessment must be available for examination by the court or any party to the proceedings.

(Subd (e) amended effective January 1, 2021.)

(f) Findings and orders

If the court makes the necessary findings under section 366.26(c)(4)(A), the court must appoint a legal guardian for the child and order the clerk to issue letters of guardianship *(Letters of Guardianship (Juvenile)* (form JV-330)) as soon as the appointed guardian has signed them. These letters are not subject to the confidentiality protections in section 827.

(1) The court may issue orders regarding visitation and contact between the child and a parent or other relative.

(2) After the appointment of a legal guardian, the court may continue juvenile court wardship and supervision or may terminate wardship.

(Subd (f) amended effective January 1, 2021; previously amended effective July 1, 2006, and January 1, 2007.)

(g) Modification or termination of juvenile court guardianship

A petition to modify or terminate a legal guardianship established by the juvenile court, including a petition to appoint a co-guardian or successor guardian, must be filed and heard in juvenile court. The procedures described in rule 5.570 must be followed, and *Request to Change Court Order* (form JV-180) must be used. The hearing on the petition may be held concurrently with any regularly scheduled hearing regarding the child.

(Subd (g) amended effective January 1, 2021; previously amended effective January 1, 2007.)
Rule 5.815 amended effective January 1, 2021; adopted as rule 1496.2 effective January 1, 2004; previously amended effective July 1, 2006, and July 1, 2016; previously amended and renumbered as rule 5.815 effective January 1, 2007.

Rule 5.820. Termination of parental rights for child in foster care for 15 of the last 22 months

(a) Requirement (§§ 727.32(a), 16508.1)

Whenever a child has been declared a ward and has been in any foster care placement for 15 of the most recent 22 months, the probation department must follow the procedures described in section 727.31 to terminate the parental rights of the child's parents. The probation department is not required to follow these procedures if it has documented a compelling reason in the probation file, as defined in section 727.3(c), for determining that termination of parental rights would not be in the child's best interest, or if it has not provided the family with reasonable efforts necessary to achieve reunification.

(1) If the probation department sets a hearing under section 727.31, it must also make efforts to identify an approved family for adoption.

(2) If the probation department has determined that a compelling reason exists, it must document that reason in the case file. The documentation may be a separate document or may be included in another court document, such as the social study prepared for a permanency planning hearing.

(Subd (a) amended effective January 1, 2007.)

(b) Calculating time in foster care (§ 727.32(d))

The following guidelines must be used to determine if the child has been in foster care for 15 of the most recent 22 months:

(1) Determine the date the child entered foster care, as defined in rule 5.502(a)(9). In some cases, this will be the date the child entered foster care as a dependent.

(2) Calculate the total number of months since the date in (1) that the child has spent in foster care. Do not start over if a new petition is filed or for any other reason.

(3) If the child is in foster care for a portion of a month, calculate the total number of days in foster care during that month. Add one month to the total number of months for every 30 days the child is in foster care.

(4) Exclude time during which the child was detained in the home of a parent or guardian; the child was living at home on formal or informal probation, at home on a trial home visit, or at home with no probationary status; the child was a runaway or "absent without leave" (AWOL); or the child was out of home in a non–foster care setting, including juvenile hall, a ranch, a camp, a school, a secure youth treatment facility, or any other locked facility.

(5) Once the total number of months in foster care has been calculated, determine how many of those months occurred within the most recent 22 months. If that number is 15 or more, the requirement in (a) applies.

(6) If the requirement in (a) has been satisfied once, there is no need to take additional action or provide additional documentation after any subsequent 22-month period.

(Subd (b) amended effective July 1, 2023; previously amended effective January 1, 2006, and January 1, 2007.)

Rule 5.820 amended effective July 1, 2023; adopted as rule 1496.3 effective January 1, 2003; previously amended effective January 1, 2006; previously amended and renumbered as rule 5.820 effective January 1, 2007.

Rule 5.825. Freeing wards for adoption

(a) Applicable law (§§ 294, 366.26, 727.2, 727.3, 727.31)

Except as provided in section 727.31, the procedures for termination of parental rights to free children described in that section for adoption are stated in sections 294 and 366.26. Rules 5.725 and 5.730 are applicable to these proceedings.

(Subd (a) amended effective January 1, 2007; previously amended effective January 1, 2006.)

(b) Joint county protocol

In each county, the county probation department and the county child welfare department must jointly develop a protocol for freeing wards for adoption. The protocol should address questions such as:

(1) When and how will wards be referred to the licensed county adoption agency, or State Department of Social Services when it is acting as the adoption agency, for a determination of whether the ward is adoptable, as described by section 727.3(i)(2)?

(2) Once a finding has been made that the permanent plan for the ward must be adoption and the case is set for a section 727.31 hearing, how will the referral be made to the licensed county adoption agency, or to the State Department of Social Services when it is acting as the adoption agency, to prepare an adoption assessment, as required by section 727.3(j)?

(3) Will the probation department continue to have ongoing case management and supervision of the case, pending the termination of parental rights hearing?

(4) Will the probation department or the child welfare department prepare the notices and other legal documents required before a termination of parental rights hearing?

(5) In counties in which different judicial officers hear delinquency and dependency matters, what procedure will be used to ensure that the dependency judge will hear each 727.31 hearing?

(6) Will the probation department or the child welfare department prepare the petition for adoption and other forms needed after the 727.31 hearing to complete the adoption process?

(Subd (b) amended effective January 1, 2007.)

Rule 5.825 amended and renumbered effective January 1, 2007; adopted as rule 1496.5 effective January 1, 2001; previously amended effective January 1, 2006.

Rule 5.830. Sealing records (§ 781)

(a) Sealing records—former wards

(1) A former ward of the court may apply to petition the court to order juvenile records sealed. Determinations under section 781 may be made by the court in any county in which wardship was terminated. A court may seal the records of another court when it determines that it is appropriate to do so, and must make a determination on sealing those records if the case has been transferred to its jurisdiction under rules 5.610 and 5.612.

(2) At the time jurisdiction is terminated or the case is dismissed, the court must provide or instruct the probation department to provide form JV-595-INFO, *How to Ask the Court to Seal Your Records*, and form JV-595, *Request to Seal Juvenile Records*, to the ward if the court does not seal the ward's records under section 786. If the court does seal the ward's records under section 786, the court must provide or instruct the probation department to provide form JV-596-INFO, *Sealing of Records for Satisfactory Completion of Probation*, and a copy of the sealing order as provided in rule 5.840.

(3) *Application—submission*

(A) The application for a petition to seal records must be submitted to the probation department in the county in which wardship was terminated.

(B) The application for a petition to seal juvenile records may be submitted on form JV-595, *Request to Seal Juvenile Records*, or on another form that includes all required information.

(4) *Investigation*

If the applicant is at least 18 years of age, or if it has been at least five years since the applicant's probation was last terminated or since the applicant was cited to appear before a probation officer or was taken before a probation officer under section 626 or before any officer of a law enforcement agency, the probation officer must do all of the following:

(A) Prepare the petition;

(B) Conduct an investigation under section 781 and compile a list of cases and contact addresses of every agency or person that the probation department knows has a record of the ward's case—including the date of each offense, case number(s), and date when the case was closed—to be attached to the sealing petition;

(C) Prepare a report to the court with a recommendation supporting or opposing the requested sealing; and

(D) Within 90 days from receipt of the application if only the records of the investigating county are to be reviewed, or within 180 days from receipt of the application if records of other counties are to be reviewed:

(i) File the petition;

(ii) Set the matter for a hearing, which may be nonappearance; and

(iii) Notify the prosecuting attorney of the hearing.

(5) The court must review the petition and the report of the probation officer, and the court must grant or deny the petition.

(6) If the petition is granted, the court must order the sealing of all records described in section 781 using form JV-590, *Order to Seal Juvenile Records—Welfare and Institutions Code Section 781*, or a similar form. The order must apply in the county of the court hearing the petition and in all other counties in which there are juvenile records concerning the petitioner. If the court determines that sealing the records of another court for a petition that has not been transferred is inappropriate, it must inform the petitioner that a petition to seal those records can be filed in the county where the other court is located.

(Subd (a) amended effective July 1, 2016; previously amended effective January 1, 2007.)

(b) Sealing—nonwards

(1) For all other persons described in section 781, application may be submitted to the probation department in any county in which there is a juvenile record concerning the petitioner, and the procedures of (a) must be followed.

(2) When jurisdiction is terminated or the case is closed, the probation department must provide the following forms to individuals described under section 781(h)(1)(A) and (B):

(A) If the individual's records have not been sealed under section 786, form JV-595-INFO, *How to Ask the Court to Seal Your Records*, and form JV-595, *Request to Seal Juvenile Records*; or

(B) If the individual's records have been sealed under section 786, form JV-596-INFO, *Sealing of Records for Satisfactory Completion of Probation*, and a copy of the sealing order.

(Subd (b) amended effective July 1, 2016; previously amended effective January 1, 2007.)

(c) Destruction of records

All records sealed must be destroyed according to section 781(d).

(Subd (c) amended effective January 1, 2007.)

(d) Distribution of order

The clerk of the issuing court must:

(1) Send a copy of the order to each agency and official listed in the order; and

(2) Send a certified copy of the order to the clerk in each county in which a record is ordered sealed.

(Subd (d) amended effective January 1, 2007.)

(e) Deadline for sealing

Each agency and official notified must immediately seal all records as ordered.

(Subd (e) amended effective January 1, 2007.)

Rule 5.830 amended effective July 1, 2016; adopted as rule 1499 effective January 1, 1991; previously renumbered as rule 1497 effective January 1, 1999; previously amended and renumbered as rule 5.830 effective January 1, 2007.

Advisory Committee Comment

This rule is intended to describe the legal process by which a person may apply to petition the juvenile court to order the sealing—that is, the prohibition of access and inspection—of the records related to specified cases in the custody of the juvenile court, the probation department, and other agencies and public officials. This rule establishes minimum legal standards but does not prescribe procedures for managing physical or electronic records or methods for preventing public inspection of the records at issue. These procedures remain subject to local discretion. Procedures may, but are not required to, include the actual sealing of physical records or files. Other permissible methods of sealing physical records pending their destruction under section 781(d) include, but are not limited to, storing sealed records separately from publicly accessible records, placing sealed records in a folder or sleeve of a color different from that in which publicly accessible records are kept, assigning a distinctive file number extension to sealed records, or designating them with a special stamp. Procedures for sealing electronic records must accomplish the same objectives as the procedures used to seal physical records, and appropriate access controls must be established to ensure that only authorized persons may access the sealed records.

Rule 5.840. Dismissal of petition and sealing of records (§ 786)

(a) Applicability

This rule states the procedures to dismiss and seal the records of minors who are subject to section 786.

(Subd (a) adopted effective July 1, 2016.)

(b) Dismissal of petition

If the court finds that a minor subject to this rule has satisfactorily completed his or her informal or formal probation supervision, the court must order the petition dismissed. The court must not dismiss a petition if it was sustained based on the commission of an offense listed in subdivision (b) of section 707 when the minor was 14 or older unless the finding on that offense has been dismissed or was reduced to a misdemeanor or an offense not listed in subdivision (b) of section 707. The court may also dismiss prior petitions filed or sustained against the minor if they appear to the satisfaction of the court to meet the sealing and dismissal criteria in section 786. An unfulfilled order, condition, or restitution or an unpaid restitution fee must not be deemed to constitute unsatisfactory completion of probation supervision. The court may not extend the period of supervision or probation solely for the purpose of deferring or delaying eligibility for dismissal and sealing under section 786.

(Subd (b) amended effective September 1, 2018; adopted effective July 1, 2016.)

(c) Sealing of records

For any petition dismissed by the court under section 786, including any petition dismissed before adjudication, the court must also order sealed all records in the custody of the court, law enforcement agencies, the probation department, and the Department of Justice pertaining to those dismissed petition(s) using form JV-596, *Dismissal and Sealing of Records—Welfare and Institutions Code Section 786*, or a similar form. The court may also seal records pertaining to these cases in the custody of other public agencies upon a request by an individual who is eligible to have records sealed under section 786, if the court determines that sealing the additional record(s) will promote the successful reentry and rehabilitation of the individual. The prosecuting attorney, probation officer, and court must have access to these records as specifically provided in section 786. Access to the records for research purposes must be provided as required in section 787.

(Subd (c) amended effective September 1, 2018; adopted effective July 1, 2016.)

(d) Destruction of records

The court must specify in its order the date by which all sealed records must be destroyed. For court records this date may be no earlier than the date the subject of the order attains age 21 and no later than the end of the time frame set forth in section 781(d). For all other records, the date may be no earlier than the date the subject of the order attains age 18, and no later than the time frame set forth in section 781(d) unless that time frame expires prior to the date the subject attains 18 years of age.

(Subd (d) adopted effective July 1, 2016.)

(e) Distribution of order

The clerk of the issuing court must send a copy of the order to each agency and official listed in the order and provide a copy of the order to the individual whose records have been sealed and his or her attorney. The court shall also provide or instruct the probation department to provide the individual with form JV-596-INFO, *Sealing of Records for Satisfactory Completion of Probation*.

(Subd (e) adopted effective July 1, 2016.)

(f) Deadline for sealing

Each agency, individual, and official notified must immediately seal all records as ordered and advise the court that its sealing order has been completed using form JV-591, *Acknowledgment of Juvenile Record Sealed*, or another means.

(Subd (f) adopted effective July 1, 2016.)

Rule 5.840 amended effective September 1, 2018; adopted effective July 1, 2016.

Rule 5.850. Sealing of records by probation in diversion cases (§ 786.5)

(a) Applicability

This rule states the procedures to seal the records of persons who are subject to section 786.5.

(Subd (a) adopted effective September 1, 2018.)

(b) Determination of satisfactory completion

Within 60 days of the completion of a program of diversion or supervision under a referral by the probation officer or the prosecutor instead of filing a petition to adjudge the person a ward of the juvenile court, including a program of informal supervision under section 654, the probation department must determine whether the participant satisfactorily completed a program subject to this rule.

(Subd (b) adopted effective January 1, 2022.)

(c) Review of unsatisfactory completion of program by the juvenile court

If the probation department determines that the program has not been completed satisfactorily, it must notify the person in writing of the reason or reasons for not sealing the record and provide the person with a copy of the *Petition to Review Denial of Sealing of Records After Diversion Program* (form JV-598) or similar local form to allow the person to seek court review of the probation department's determination within 60 days of making that determination, as well as a copy of *How to Ask the Court to Seal Your Records* (form JV-595-INFO) or other information on how to petition the court directly to seal arrest and other related records. A person who receives notice from the probation department that the program has not been satisfactorily completed and that the records have not been sealed may seek review of that determination by the court by submitting a petition to the probation department on the *Petition to Review Denial of Sealing of Records After Diversion Program* (form JV-598) or similar local form, and the probation department must file that petition with the court for a hearing to review whether the satisfactory completion requirement has been met and the records are eligible for sealing by the probation department. The petition must be provided to the probation department within 60 days of the date the notice from the probation department was sent, and must include a copy of that notice. The probation department must file the petition with the juvenile court in the county that issued the notice within 30 days of receiving it. The clerk of the court must set the matter for hearing and notify the petitioner and the probation department of the date, time, and location of the hearing. The court must appoint counsel to represent the youth before or at the hearing unless the court finds that the youth has made an intelligent waiver of the right to counsel under section 634 or is already represented. If the court finds after the hearing that the petitioner is eligible to have the records sealed under section 786.5, it must order the probation department to promptly comply with the sealing and notice requirements of this rule.

(Subd (c) adopted effective January 1, 2022.)

(d) Sealing of records

Upon satisfactory completion of a program of diversion or supervision subject to this rule, the probation department must seal the arrest and other records in its custody relating to the arrest or referral and participation in the program. The probation department must notify the arresting law enforcement agency to seal the records relating to the arrest and referral, and the arresting law enforcement agency must seal the records in its custody relating to the arrest, no later than 60 days from the date of the notification. Upon sealing, the law enforcement agency must notify the probation department that the records have been sealed. The probation department must also notify the public or private agency operating the diversion program to which the person has been referred to seal any records in its custody relating to the arrest or referral and participation in the program, and the operator of the program must do so no later than 60 days from the date of the notification by the probation department. Upon sealing, the public or private agency must notify the probation department that the records have been sealed.

(Subd (d) amended and relettered effective January 1, 2022; adopted as subd (b) effective September 1, 2018.)

(e) Notice to participant

Within 30 days from receipt of the notification by the arresting law enforcement agency that the records have been sealed, the probation department must notify the person in writing that the records have been sealed.

(Subd (e) amended and relettered effective January 1, 2022; adopted as subd (c) effective September 1, 2018.)

Rule 5.850 amended effective January 1, 2022; adopted effective September 1, 2018.

Rule 5.860. Prosecuting attorney request to access sealed juvenile case files

(a) Applicability

This rule applies when a prosecuting attorney is seeking to access, inspect, utilize, or disclose a record that has been sealed by the court under sections 781, 786, or 793, or Penal Code section 851.7, and the attorney has reason to believe that access to the record is necessary to meet the attorney's statutory or constitutional obligation to disclose favorable or exculpatory evidence to a defendant in a criminal case.

(Subd (a) adopted effective January 1, 2021.)

(b) Contents of the request

Any request filed with the juvenile court under this rule must include the prosecuting attorney's rationale for believing that access to the information in the record may be necessary to meet the disclosure obligation and the date by which the records are needed. The date must allow for sufficient time to meet the notice and hearing requirements of this rule. Form JV-592, *Prosecutor Request for Access to Sealed Juvenile Case File*, may be used for this purpose.

(Subd (b) adopted effective January 1, 2021.)

(c) Notice and opportunity to respond

(1) *Notice requirements*

(A) The request must include a form for the court to notify the person whose records are to be accessed as well as that person's attorney of record, and a form for those individuals to respond in writing and to request an appearance before the juvenile court. Forms JV-593, *Notice of Prosecutor Request for Access to Sealed Juvenile Case File*, and JV-594, *Response to Prosecutor Request for Access to Sealed Juvenile Case File*, may be used for this purpose.

(B) The juvenile court must notify the person with the sealed record and that person's attorney of record using the documents prepared by the prosecuting attorney within two court days of the request being filed.

(2) *Requirements if a response is filed*

(A) If a written response is filed no more than 10 days after the date the notice was issued and no appearance has been requested, the clerk of the court must provide that response to the juvenile court for its consideration as it reviews the prosecuting attorney's request.

(B) If a response is filed no more than 10 days after the date the notice was issued and an appearance is requested, the clerk of the court must set a hearing and provide notice of the hearing to the person with the sealed record, the attorney of record for that person, and the prosecuting attorney who filed the request.

(Subd (c) adopted effective January 1, 2021.)

(d) Juvenile court review and order

The court must review the case file and records that have been referenced by the prosecuting attorney's request as well as any response provided as set forth in subdivision (c)(2). The court must approve the request, in whole or in part, if it determines that access to a specific sealed record or portion of a sealed record is necessary to enable the prosecuting attorney to comply with the disclosure obligation. If the court approves the request, the order must include appropriate limits on the access, inspection, utilization, and disclosure of the sealed record information in order to protect the confidentiality of the person whose sealed record is at issue. Such limits may include protective orders to accompany authorized disclosure, discovery, or access, including an order that the prosecuting attorney first submit the records to be disclosed to the court for its review and possible redaction to protect confidentiality. The court must make its initial order within 21 court days of when the request is filed, unless an appearance has been requested under subdivision (c)(2), in which case the court must act within five court days of the date set for the appearance.

(Subd (d) adopted effective January 1, 2021.)

Rule 5.860 adopted effective January 1, 2021.

Chapter 14
Nonminor Dependent

Title 5, Family and Juvenile Rules—Division 3, Juvenile Rules—Chapter 14, Nonminor Dependent; adopted effective January 1, 2012.

Rule 5.900. Nonminor dependent—preliminary provisions (§§ 224.1(b), 295, 303, 366, 366.3, 388, 391, 607(a))

Rule 5.903. Nonminor dependent status review hearing (§§ 224.1(b), 295, 366.1, 366.3, 366.31, 391, 11403)

Rule 5.906. Request by nonminor for the juvenile court to resume jurisdiction (§§ 224.1(b), 303, 388(e), 388.1)

Rule 5.900. Nonminor dependent—preliminary provisions (§§ 224.1(b), 295, 303, 366, 366.3, 388, 391, 607(a))

(a) Applicability

(1) The provisions of this chapter apply to nonminor dependents as defined in section 11400(v).

(2) Nothing in the Welfare and Institutions Code or in the California Rules of Court restricts the ability of the juvenile court to maintain dependency jurisdiction or delinquency jurisdiction over a person, 18 years of age and older, who does not meet the eligibility requirements for status as a nonminor dependent and to proceed as to that person under the relevant sections of the Welfare and Institutions Code and California Rules of Court.

(Subd (a) adopted effective January 1, 2012.)

(b) Purpose

(1) Maintaining juvenile court jurisdiction under sections 300 or 450 over a person as a nonminor dependent is the result of a consensual agreement between the person and child welfare services agency or the probation department for a voluntary placement in a supervised setting and includes the agreement between the social worker or probation officer and the person to work together to implement the mutually developed supervised placement agreement or reentry agreement.

(2) Maintaining juvenile court jurisdiction and supervision by the child welfare services agency or probation department under sections 300, 450, 601, or 602 over a person as a nonminor dependent is for the purpose of implementing the mutually developed Transitional Independent Living Case Plan and providing support, guidance, and foster care services to the person as a nonminor dependent so he or she is able to successfully achieve independence, including relationships with caring and committed adults who can serve as lifelong connections.

(Subd (b) amended effective January 1, 2014; adopted effective January 1, 2012.)

(c) Legal status

(1) Nothing in the Welfare and Institutions Code, including sections 340, 366.2, and 369.5, or in the California Rules of Court provides legal custody of a nonminor dependent to the child welfare services agency or the probation department or abrogates any right the nonminor dependent, as a person who has attained 18 years of age, may have as an adult under California law.

(2) A nonminor dependent retains all his or her legal decisionmaking authority as an adult. The decisionmaking authority of a nonminor dependent under delinquency jurisdiction may be limited by and subject to the care, supervision, custody, conduct, and maintenance orders in section 727.

(Subd (c) amended effective January 1, 2014; adopted effective January 1, 2012.)

(d) Conduct of hearings

(1) All hearings involving a person who is a nonminor dependent must be conducted in a manner that respects the person's legal status as an adult.

(2) Unless there is a contested issue of fact or law, the hearings must be informal and nonadversarial and all parties must work collaboratively with the nonminor dependent as he or she moves toward the achievement of his or her Transitional Independent Living Case Plan goals.

(3) The nonminor dependent may designate his or her attorney to appear on his or her behalf at a hearing under this chapter.

(Subd (d) adopted effective January 1, 2012.)

(e) Telephone appearance

Paragraph (1) below is suspended from January 1, 2022, to January 1, 2026. During that period, the juvenile dependency provisions in rule 3.672 apply in its place.

(1) The person who is the subject of the hearing may appear, at his or her request, by telephone at a hearing to terminate juvenile court jurisdiction held under rule 5.555, a status review hearing under rule 5.903, or a hearing on a request to have juvenile court jurisdiction resumed held under rule 5.906. Rule 5.531 applies to telephone appearances under this paragraph.

(2) The court may require the nonminor dependent or the person requesting to return to juvenile court jurisdiction and foster care to appear personally on a showing of good cause and a showing that the personal appearance will not create an undue hardship for him or her.

(3) The telephone appearance must be permitted at no cost to the nonminor dependent or the person requesting to return juvenile court jurisdiction and foster care.

(Subd (e) amended effective August 4, 2023; adopted effective January 1, 2012; previously amended effective January 1, 2022.)

(f) Separate court file

The clerk of the superior court must open a separate court file for nonminor dependents under the dependency, delinquency, or transition jurisdiction of the court that ensures the confidentiality of the nonminor dependent and allows access only to those listed in section 362.5.

(Subd (f) adopted effective January 1, 2014.)

Rule 5.900 amended effective August 4, 2023; adopted effective January 1, 2012; previously amended January 1, 2014, and January 1, 2022.

Advisory Committee Comment

A nonminor is entitled to be represented by an attorney of his or her choice rather than by a court-appointed attorney in proceedings under this chapter and under rule 5.555. (See Welf. & Inst. Code, § 349(b); *In re Akkiko M.* (1985) 163 Cal.App.3d 525.) Any fees for an attorney retained by the nonminor are the nonminor's responsibility.

Rule 5.903. Nonminor dependent status review hearing (§§ 224.1(b), 295, 366.1, 366.3, 366.31, 391, 11403)

(a) Purpose

The primary purpose of the nonminor dependent status review hearing is to focus on the goals and services described in the nonminor dependent's Transitional Independent Living Case Plan and the efforts and progress made toward achieving independence and establishing lifelong connections with caring and committed adults.

(Subd (a) adopted effective January 1, 2012.)

(b) Setting and conduct of a nonminor dependent status review hearing

(1) A status review hearing for a nonminor dependent conducted by the court or by a local administrative review panel must occur no less frequently than once every 6 months.

(2) The hearing must be placed on the appearance calendar, held before a judicial officer, and recorded by a court reporter under any of the following circumstances:

(A) The hearing is the first hearing following the nonminor dependent's 18th birthday;

(B) The hearing is the first hearing following the resumption of juvenile court jurisdiction over a person as a nonminor dependent under rule 5.906;

(C) The nonminor dependent or the nonminor dependent's attorney requests that the hearing be conducted by the court; or

(D) It has been 12 months since the hearing was conducted by the court.

(3) The hearing may be attended, as appropriate, by participants invited by the nonminor dependent in addition to those entitled to notice under (c). If delinquency jurisdiction is dismissed in favor of transition jurisdiction under Welfare and Institutions Code section 450, the prosecuting attorney is not permitted to appear at later review hearings for the nonminor dependent.

(4) The nonminor dependent may appear by telephone as provided in rule 5.900 at a hearing conducted by the court.

(5) The hearing must be continued for no more than five court days for the social worker, probation officer, or nonminor dependent to submit additional information as ordered by the court if the court determines that the report and Transitional Independent Living Case Plan submitted by the social worker or probation officer do not provide the information required by (d)(1) and the court is unable to make all the findings and orders required by (e).

(Subd (b) amended effective January 1, 2019; adopted effective January 1, 2012.)

(c) Notice of hearing (§ 295)

(1) The social worker or probation officer must serve written notice of the hearing in the manner provided in section 295, and to all persons required to receive notice under section 295, except notice to the parents of the nonminor dependent is not required.

(2) The written notice served on the nonminor dependent must include:

(A) A statement that he or she may appear for the hearing by telephone; and

(B) Instructions about the local court procedures for arranging to appear and appearing at the hearing by telephone.

(3) Proof of service of notice must be filed by the social worker or probation officer at least five court days before the hearing.

(Subd (c) adopted effective January 1, 2012.)

(d) Reports

(1) The social worker or probation officer must submit a report to the court that includes the information required by section 366.31, as applicable, and section 391. The following additional information must also be included:

(A) How and when the Transitional Independent Living Case Plan was developed, including the nature and the extent of the nonminor dependent's participation in its development, and for the nonminor dependent who has elected to have the Indian Child Welfare Act continue to apply, the extent of consultation with the tribal representative;

(B) Progress made toward meeting the Transitional Independent Living Case Plan goals and the need for any modifications to assist the nonminor dependent in attaining the goals;

(2) The social worker or probation officer must submit with his or her report the Transitional Independent Living Case Plan.

(3) The social worker or probation officer must file with the court the report prepared for the hearing and the Transitional Independent Living Case Plan at least 10 calendar days before the hearing, and provide copies of the report and other documents to the nonminor dependent, all attorneys of record, and for the nonminor dependent who has elected to have the Indian Child Welfare Act continue to apply, the tribal representative.

(Subd (d) amended effective January 1, 2023; adopted effective January 1, 2012; previously amended effective January 1, 2014.)

(e) Findings and orders

The court must consider the safety of the nonminor dependent, make the judicial findings and issue the orders required by section 366.31, and include them in the written court documentation of the hearing, along with the following:

(1) *Findings*

(A) Whether notice was given as required by law;

(B) Whether the Transitional Independent Living Case Plan includes a plan for the nonminor dependent to satisfy one or more of the criteria in section 11403(b);

(C) The specific criteria in section 11403(b) the nonminor dependent satisfied since the last hearing held under this rule;

(D) The specific criteria in section 11403(b) it is anticipated the nonminor dependent will satisfy during the next six months;

(E) Whether reasonable efforts were made and assistance provided by the social worker or probation officer to help the nonminor dependent establish and maintain compliance with section 11403(b);

(F) Whether the Transitional Independent Living Case Plan was developed jointly by the nonminor dependent and the social worker or probation officer, reflects the living situation and services that are consistent in the nonminor dependent's opinion with what he or she needs to gain independence, and sets out the benchmarks that indicate how both will know when independence can be achieved;

(G) For the nonminor dependent who has elected to have the Indian Child Welfare Act continue to apply, whether the representative from his or her tribe was consulted during the development of the Transitional Independent Living Case Plan;

(H) Whether the Transitional Independent Living Case Plan includes appropriate and meaningful independent living skill services that will assist him or her with the transition from foster care to successful adulthood;

(I) Whether the nonminor dependent signed and received a copy of his or her Transitional Independent Living Case Plan;

(J) The extent of progress made by the nonminor dependent toward meeting the Transitional Independent Living Case Plan goals and any modifications needed to assist in attaining the goals; and

(K) For a nonminor who has returned to the home of the parent or former legal guardian, whether continued juvenile court jurisdiction is necessary.

(2) *Orders*

(A) Order the continuation of juvenile court jurisdiction and set a nonminor dependent review hearing under this rule within six months, and:

(i) Order a permanent plan consistent with the nonminor dependent's Transitional Independent Living Case Plan, and

(ii) Specify the likely date by which independence is anticipated to be achieved; and

(iii) For a nonminor dependent whose parents are receiving court-ordered family reunification services:

a. Order the continuation of reunification services;

b. Order the termination of reunification services; or

c. Order that the nonminor may reside in the home of the parent or former legal guardian and that juvenile court jurisdiction is terminated or that juvenile court jurisdiction is continued under section 303(a) and a status review hearing is set for within six months.

(B) Order the continuation of juvenile court jurisdiction and set a hearing to consider termination of juvenile court jurisdiction over a nonminor under rule 5.555 within 30 days; or

(C) Order termination of juvenile court jurisdiction pursuant to rule 5.555 if this nonminor dependent status review hearing was heard at the same time as a hearing under rule 5.555.

(Subd (e) amended effective January 1, 2023; adopted effective January 1, 2012; previously amended effective January 1, 2014.)

Rule 5.903 amended effective January 1, 2023; adopted effective January 1, 2012; previously amended effective January 1, 2014, and January 1, 2019.

Rule 5.906. Request by nonminor for the juvenile court to resume jurisdiction (§§ 224.1(b), 303, 388(e), 388.1)

(a) Purpose

(1) Except as provided in (2), this rule provides the procedures that must be followed when a nonminor wants to have juvenile court jurisdiction assumed or resumed over the nonminor as a nonminor dependent as defined in subdivisions (v) or (aa) of section 11400.

(2) This rule does not apply to a petition for a nonminor to exit and reenter care to establish eligibility for federal financial participation under section 388(f). Those petitions may be decided with or without a hearing using mandatory forms *Petition and Order to Exit and Reenter Jurisdiction—Nonminor Dependent* (form JV-469) and *Findings and Orders Regarding Exit and Reentry of Jurisdiction—Nonminor Dependent* (form JV-471).

(Subd (a) amended effective September 1, 2022; adopted effective January 1, 2012; previously amended effective July 1, 2012, January 1, 2014, and January 1, 2016.)

(b) Contents of the request

(1) The request to have the juvenile court assume or resume jurisdiction must be made on the *Request to Return to Juvenile Court Jurisdiction and Foster Care* (form JV-466).

(2) The request must be liberally construed in favor of its sufficiency. It must be verified by the nonminor or if the nonminor is unable to provide verification due to a medical condition, the nonminor's representative, and to the extent known to the nonminor or the nonminor's representative, must include the following information:

(A) The nonminor's name and date of birth;

(B) The nonminor's address and contact information, unless the nonminor requests that this information be kept confidential from those persons entitled to access to the juvenile court file, including his or her parents, by filing *Confidential Information—Request to Return to Juvenile Court Jurisdiction and Foster Care* (form JV-468). Form JV-468 must be kept in the court file under seal, and only the court, the child welfare services agency, the probation department, or the Indian tribe with an agreement under section 10553.1 to provide child welfare services to Indian children (Indian tribal agency), the attorney for the child welfare services agency, the probation department, or the Indian tribe, and the nonminor's attorney may have access to this information;

(C) The name and action number or court file number of the nonminor's case and the name of the juvenile court that terminated its dependency jurisdiction, delinquency jurisdiction, or transition jurisdiction;

(D) The date the juvenile court entered the order terminating its dependency jurisdiction, delinquency jurisdiction, or transition jurisdiction;

(E) If the nonminor wants the nonminor's parents or former legal guardians to receive notice of the filing of the request and the hearing, the name and residence addresses of the nonminor's parents or former guardians;

(F) The name and telephone number of the court-appointed attorney who represented the nonminor at the time the juvenile court terminated its dependency jurisdiction, delinquency jurisdiction, or transition jurisdiction if the nonminor wants that attorney to be appointed to represent the nonminor for the purposes of the hearing on the request;

(G) If the nonminor is an Indian child within the meaning of the Indian Child Welfare Act and chooses to have the Indian Child Welfare Act apply to the nonminor, the name of the tribe and the name, address, and telephone number of tribal representative;

(H) If the nonminor had a Court Appointed Special Advocate (CASA) when the nonminor was a dependent or ward of the court and wants the CASA to receive notice of the filing of the request and the hearing, the CASA's name;

(I) The condition or conditions under section 11403(b) that the nonminor intends to satisfy; and

(J) Whether the nonminor requires assistance to maintain or secure an appropriate, supervised placement, or is in need of immediate placement and will agree to a supervised placement under a voluntary reentry agreement.

(3) The court may dismiss without prejudice a request filed under this rule that is not verified.

(Subd (b) amended effective September 1, 2022; adopted effective January 1, 2012; previously amended effective July 1, 2012, and January 1, 2016.)

(c) Filing the request

(1) The form JV-466 must be completed and verified by the nonminor or the nonminor's representative if the nonminor is unable to provide verification due to a medical condition, and may be filed by the nonminor or the county child welfare services, probation department, or Indian tribe (placing agency) on behalf of the nonminor.

(2) For the convenience of the nonminor, the form JV-466 and, if the nonminor wishes to keep the nonminor's contact information confidential, the *Confidential Information—Request to Return to Juvenile Court Jurisdiction and Foster Care* (form JV-468) may be:

(A) Filed with the juvenile court that maintained general jurisdiction or for cases petitioned under section 388.1, in the court that established the guardianship or had jurisdiction when the adoption was finalized; or

(B) Submitted to the juvenile court in the county in which the nonminor currently resides, after which:

(i) The court clerk must record the date and time received on the face of the originals submitted and provide a copy of the originals marked as received to the nonminor at no cost to the nonminor.

(ii) To ensure receipt of the original form JV-466 and, if submitted, the form JV-468 by the court of general jurisdiction within five court days as required in section 388(e), the court clerk must forward those originals to the clerk of the court of general jurisdiction within two court days of submission of the originals by the nonminor.

(iii) The court in the county in which the nonminor resides is responsible for all costs of processing, copying, and forwarding the form JV-466 and form JV-468 to the clerk of the court of general jurisdiction.

(iv) The court clerk in the county in which the nonminor resides must retain a copy of the documents submitted.

(v) The form JV-466 and, if submitted, the form JV-468 must be filed immediately upon receipt by the clerk of the juvenile court of general jurisdiction.

(C) For a nonminor living outside the state of California, the form JV-466 and, if the nonminor wishes to keep the nonminor's contact information confidential, the form JV-468 must be filed with the juvenile court of general jurisdiction.

(3) If form JV-466 is filed by the nonminor, within two court days of its filing with the clerk of the court in the county of general jurisdiction, the clerk of that court must notify the placing agency that was supervising the nonminor when juvenile court jurisdiction was terminated that the nonminor has filed form JV-466 and provide the placing agency with the nonminor's contact information. The notification must be by telephone, fax, e-mail, or other method approved by the presiding juvenile court judge that will ensure prompt notification and inform the placing agency that a copy of form JV-466 will be served on the agency and that one is currently available in the office of the juvenile court clerk.

(4) If form JV-466 has not been filed at the time the nonminor completes the voluntary reentry agreement described in section 11400(z), the placing agency must file form JV-466 on the nonminor's behalf within 15 court days of the date the voluntary reentry agreement was signed, unless the nonminor files form JV-466 prior to the expiration of the 15 court days.

(5) No filing fees are required for the filing of form JV-466 and, if filed, form JV-468. An endorsed, filed copy of each form filed must be provided at no cost to the nonminor or the placing agency that filed the request on the nonminor's behalf.

(Subd (c) amended effective September 1, 2022; adopted effective January 1, 2012; previously amended effective July 1, 2012, and January 1, 2016.)

(d) Determination of prima facie showing

(1) Within three court days of the filing of form JV-466 with the clerk of the juvenile court of general jurisdiction, a juvenile court judicial officer must review the form JV-466 and determine whether a prima facie showing has been made that the nonminor meets all of the criteria set forth below in (d)(1)(A)–(D) and enter an order as set forth in (d)(2) or (d)(3).

(A) The nonminor is eligible to seek assumption of dependency jurisdiction under the provisions of section 388.1(c), or the nonminor was previously under juvenile court jurisdiction subject to an order for foster care placement on the date the nonminor attained 18 years of age, including a nonminor whose adjudication was vacated under Penal Code section 236.14;

(B) The nonminor has not attained 21 years of age;

(C) The nonminor wants assistance to maintain or secure an appropriate, supervised placement or is in need of immediate placement and agrees to a supervised placement under a voluntary reentry agreement; and

(D) The nonminor intends to satisfy at least one of the eligibility criteria in section 11403(b).

(2) If the court determines that a prima facie showing has not been made, the court must enter a written order denying the request, listing the issues that resulted in the denial and informing the nonminor that a new form JV-466 may be filed when those issues are resolved.

(A) The court clerk must serve on the nonminor:

(i) A copy of the written order;

(ii) A blank copy of *Request to Return to Juvenile Court Jurisdiction and Foster Care* (form JV-466) and *Confidential Information—Request to Return to Juvenile Court Jurisdiction and Foster Care* (form JV-468);

(iii) A copy of *How to Ask to Return to Juvenile Court Jurisdiction and Foster Care* (form JV-464-INFO); and

(iv) The names and contact information for those attorneys approved by the court to represent children in juvenile court proceedings who have agreed to provide a consultation to any nonminor whose request was denied due to the failure to make a prima facie showing.

(B) The court clerk must serve on the placing agency a copy of the written order.

(C) Service must be by personal service, by first-class mail, or by electronic service in accordance with section 212.5 within two court days of the issuance of the order.

(D) A proof of service must be filed.

(3) If the judicial officer determines that a prima facie showing has been made, the judicial officer must issue a written order:

(A) Directing the court clerk to set the matter for a hearing; and

(B) Appointing an attorney to represent the nonminor solely for the hearing on the request.

(Subd (d) amended effective September 1, 2022; adopted effective January 1, 2012; previously amended effective July 1, 2012, January 1, 2014, January 1, 2016, and January 1, 2019.)

(e) Appointment of attorney

(1) If the nonminor included on the form JV-466 a request for the appointment of the court-appointed attorney who represented the nonminor during the period of time the nonminor was a ward or dependent or nonminor dependent, the judicial officer must appoint that attorney solely for the hearing on the request, if the attorney is available to accept such an appointment.

(2) If the nonminor did not request the appointment of the nonminor's former court-appointed attorney, the judicial officer must appoint an attorney to represent the nonminor solely for the hearing on the request. The attorney must be selected from the panel or organization of attorneys approved by the court to represent children in juvenile court proceedings.

(3) In addition to complying with the requirements in (g)(1) for service of notice of the hearing, the juvenile court clerk must notify the attorney of the appointment as soon as possible, but no later than one court day from the date the order of appointment was issued under (d)(3). This notification must be made by telephone, fax, e-mail, or other method approved by the presiding juvenile court judge that will ensure prompt notification. The notice must also include the nonminor's contact information and inform the attorney that a copy of the form JV-466 will be served on the attorney and that one is currently available in the office of the juvenile court clerk.

(4) If the request is granted, the court must continue the attorney's appointment to represent the nonminor regarding matters related to the nonminor's status as a nonminor dependent until the jurisdiction of the juvenile court is terminated, unless the court finds that the nonminor would not benefit from the appointment of an attorney.

(A) In order to find that a nonminor would not benefit from the appointment of an attorney, the court must find all of the following:

(i) The nonminor understands the nature of the proceedings;

(ii) The nonminor is able to communicate and advocate effectively with the court, other attorneys, and other parties, including social workers, probation officers, and other professionals involved in the case; and

(iii) Under the circumstances of the case, the nonminor would not gain any benefit from representation by an attorney.

(B) If the court finds that the nonminor would not benefit from representation by an attorney, the court must make a finding on the record as to each of the criteria in (e)(4)(A) and state the reasons for each finding.

(5) Representation of the nonminor by the court-appointed attorney for the hearing on the request to return to juvenile court jurisdiction and for matters related to the nonminor's status as a nonminor dependent must be at no cost to the nonminor.

(6) If the nonminor chooses to be represented by an attorney other than a court-appointed attorney, the fees for an attorney retained by the nonminor are the nonminor's responsibility.

(Subd (e) amended effective September 1, 2022; adopted effective January 1, 2012; previously amended effective July 1, 2012.)

(f) Setting the hearing

(1) Within two court days of the issuance of the order directing the court clerk to do so, the court clerk must set a hearing on the juvenile court's calendar within 15 court days from the date the form JV-466 was filed with the court of general jurisdiction.

(2) The hearing must be placed on the appearance calendar, heard before a juvenile court judicial officer, and recorded by a court reporter.

(Subd (f) amended effective July 1, 2012; adopted effective January 1, 2012.)

(g) Notice of hearing

(1) The juvenile court clerk must serve notice as soon as possible, but no later than five court days before the date the hearing is set, as follows:

(A) The notice of the date, time, place, and purpose of the hearing and a copy of the form JV-466 must be served on the nonminor, the nonminor's attorney, the child welfare services agency, the probation department, or the Indian tribal agency that was supervising the nonminor when the juvenile court terminated its delinquency, dependency, or transition jurisdiction over the nonminor, and the attorney for the child welfare services agency, the probation department, or the Indian tribe. Notice must not be served on the prosecuting attorney if delinquency jurisdiction has been dismissed, and the nonminor's petition is for the court to assume or resume transition jurisdiction under Welfare and Institutions Code section 450.

(B) The notice of the date, time, place, and purpose of the hearing must be served on the nonminor's parents only if the nonminor included in the form JV-466 a request that notice be provided to the nonminor's parents.

(C) The notice of the date, time, place, and purpose of the hearing must be served on the nonminor's tribal representative if the nonminor is an Indian child and indicated on the form JV-466 the nonminor's choice to have the Indian Child Welfare Act apply to the nonminor as a nonminor dependent.

(D) The notice of the date, time, place, and purpose of the hearing must be served on the local CASA office if the nonminor had a CASA and included on the form JV-466 a request that notice be provided to the nonminor's former CASA.

(2) The written notice served on the nonminor dependent must include:

(A) A statement that the nonminor may appear for the hearing by telephone; and

(B) Instructions regarding the local juvenile court procedures for arranging to appear and appearing at the hearing by telephone.

(3) Service of the notice must be by personal service, by first-class mail, or by electronic service in accordance with section 212.5.

(4) Proof of service of notice must be filed by the juvenile court clerk at least two court days prior to the hearing.

(Subd (g) amended effective September 1, 2022; adopted effective January 1, 2012; previously amended effective July 1, 2012, and January 1, 2019.)

(h) Reports

(1) The social worker, probation officer, or Indian tribal agency case worker (tribal case worker) must submit a report to the court that includes:

(A) Confirmation that the nonminor was previously under juvenile court jurisdiction subject to an order for foster care placement when the nonminor attained 18 years of age and that the nonminor has not attained 21 years of age, or is eligible to petition the court to assume jurisdiction over the nonminor pursuant to section 388.1;

(B) The condition or conditions under section 11403(b) that the nonminor intends to satisfy;

(C) The social worker, probation officer, or tribal case worker's opinion as to whether continuing in a foster care placement is in the nonminor's best interests and recommendation about the assumption or resumption of juvenile court jurisdiction over the nonminor as a nonminor dependent;

(D) Whether the nonminor and the placing agency have entered into a reentry agreement for placement in a supervised setting under the placement and care responsibility of the placing agency;

(E) The type of placement recommended if the request to return to juvenile court jurisdiction and foster care is granted;

(F) If the type of placement recommended is a placement in a setting where minor dependents also reside, the results of the background check of the nonminor under section 16504.5.

(i) The background check under section 16504.5 is required only if a minor dependent resides in the placement under consideration for the nonminor.

(ii) A criminal conviction is not a bar to a return to foster care and the resumption of juvenile court jurisdiction over the nonminor as a nonminor dependent.

(2) At least two court days before the hearing, the social worker, probation officer, or tribal case worker must file the report and any supporting documentation with the court and provide a copy to the nonminor and to the nonminor's attorney of record; and

(3) If the court determines that the report and other documentation submitted by the social worker, probation officer, or tribal case worker does not provide the information required by (h)(1) and the court is unable to make the findings and orders required by (i), the hearing must be continued for no more than five court days for the social worker, probation officer, tribal case worker, or nonminor to submit additional information as ordered by the court.

(*Subd (h) amended effective September 1, 2022; adopted effective January 1, 2012; previously amended effective July 1, 2012, January 1, 2014, and January 1, 2016.*)

(i) Findings and orders

The court must read and consider, and state on the record that it has read and considered, the report; the supporting documentation submitted by the social worker, probation officer, or tribal caseworker; the evidence submitted by the nonminor; and any other evidence. The following judicial findings and orders must be made and included in the written court documentation of the hearing:

(1) *Findings*

(A) Whether notice was given as required by law;

(B) Whether the nonminor was previously under juvenile court jurisdiction subject to an order for foster care placement when the nonminor attained 18 years of age, or meets the requirements of subparagraph (5) of subdivision (c) of section 388.1;

(C) Whether the nonminor has attained 21 years of age;

(D) Whether the nonminor intends to satisfy a condition or conditions under section 11403(b);

(E) The condition or conditions under section 11403(b) that the nonminor intends to satisfy;

(F) Whether continuing or reentering and remaining in a foster care placement is in the nonminor's best interests;

(G) Whether the nonminor and the placing agency have entered into a reentry agreement for placement in a supervised setting under the placement and care responsibility of the placing agency; and

(H) Whether a nonminor who is an Indian child chooses to have the Indian Child Welfare Act apply to the nonminor as a nonminor dependent.

(2) *Orders*

(A) If the court finds that the nonminor has not attained 21 years of age, that the nonminor intends to satisfy at least one condition under section 11403(b), and that the nonminor and placing agency have entered into a reentry agreement, the court must:

(i) Grant the request and enter an order assuming or resuming juvenile court jurisdiction over the nonminor as a nonminor dependent and vesting responsibility for the nonminor's placement and care with the placing agency;

(ii) Order the social worker, probation officer, or tribal case worker to develop with the nonminor and file with the court within 60 days a new Transitional Independent Living Case Plan;

(iii) Order the social worker or probation officer to consult with the tribal representative regarding a new Transitional Independent Living Case Plan for the nonminor who chooses to have the Indian Child Welfare Act apply to the nonminor as a nonminor dependent and who is not under the supervision of a tribal case worker;

(iv) Set a nonminor dependent status review hearing under rule 5.903 within the next six months; and

(v) Make the findings and enter the appropriate orders under (e)(4) regarding appointment of an attorney for the nonminor.

(B) If the court finds that the nonminor has not attained 21 years of age, but the nonminor does not intend to satisfy at least one of the conditions under section 11403(b) and/or the nonminor and placing agency have not entered into a reentry agreement, the court must:

(i) Enter an order denying the request, listing the reasons for the denial, and informing the nonminor that a new form JV-466 may be filed when those circumstances change;

(ii) Enter an order terminating the appointment of the attorney appointed by the court to represent the nonminor, effective seven calendar days after the hearing; and

(iii) In addition to the service of a copy of the written order as required in (i)(3), the juvenile court clerk must cause to be served on the nonminor a blank copy of the *Request to Return to Juvenile Court Jurisdiction and Foster Care* (form JV-466) and *Confidential Information—Request to Return to Juvenile Court Jurisdiction and Foster Care* (form JV-468), and a copy of *How to Ask to Return to Juvenile Court Jurisdiction and Foster Care* (form JV-464-INFO).

(C) If the court finds that the nonminor is over 21 years of age, the court must:

(i) Enter an order denying the request to have juvenile court jurisdiction resumed; and

(ii) Enter an order terminating the appointment of the attorney appointed by the court to represent the nonminor, effective seven calendar days after the hearing.

(3) *Findings and order: service*

(A) The written findings and order must be served by the juvenile court clerk on all persons provided with notice of the hearing under (g)(1).

(B) Service must be by personal service, by first-class mail, or by electronic service in accordance with section 212.5 within three court days of the issuance of the order.

(C) A proof of service must be filed.

(*Subd (i) amended effective September 1, 2022; adopted effective January 1, 2012; previously amended effective July 1, 2012, January 1, 2014, January 1, 2016, and January 1, 2019.*)

Rule 5.906 amended effective September 1, 2022; adopted effective January 1, 2012; previously amended effective July 1, 2012, January 1, 2014, January 1, 2016, and January 1, 2019.

Advisory Committee Comment

Assembly Bill 12 (Beall; Stats. 2010, ch. 559), known as the California Fostering Connections to Success Act, as amended by Assembly Bill 212 (Beall; Stats. 2011, ch. 459), implement the federal Fostering Connections to Success and Increasing Adoptions Act, Pub.L. No. 110-351, which provides funding resources to extend the support of the foster care system to children who are still in a foster care placement on their 18th birthday. Every effort was made in the development of the rules and forms to provide an efficient framework for the implementation of this important and complex legislation.

TITLE 6
[Reserved]

TITLE 7
Probate and Mental Health Rules

Division 1. Probate Rules. Rules 7.1–7.1105.
Division 2. Mental Health Rules. Rules 7.2201–7.2303.

Division 1
Probate Rules

Chap. 1.   General Provisions. Rules 7.1–7.10.
Chap. 2.   Notices, Publication, and Service. Rules 7.50–7.55.
Chap. 3.   Pleadings. Rules 7.101–7.104.
Chap. 4.   Appointment of Executors and Administrators. Rule 7.150.
Chap. 5.   Bonding of Personal Representatives, Guardians, Conservators, and Trustees. Rules 7.201–7.207.
Chap. 6.   Independent Administration of Estates. Rule 7.250.
Chap. 7.   Spousal or Domestic Partner Property Petitions. Rule 7.301.
Chap. 8.   Petitions for Instructions [Reserved].
Chap. 9.   Creditors' Claims. Rules 7.401–7.403.
Chap. 10. Sales of Real and Personal Property. Rules 7.451–7.454.
Chap. 11. Inventory and Appraisal. Rule 7.501.
Chap. 12. Accounts and Reports of Executors, Administrators, Conservators, and Guardians. Rules 7.550–7.576.
Chap. 13. Taxes [Reserved].
Chap. 14. Preliminary and Final Distributions. Rules 7.650–7.652.
Chap. 15. Compensation of Personal Representatives and Attorneys. Rules 7.700–7.707.
Chap. 16. Compensation in All Matters Other Than Decedents' Estates. Rules 7.750–7.776.
Chap. 17. Contested Hearings and Trials. Rules 7.801, 7.802.
Chap. 18. Discovery [Reserved].
Chap. 19. Trusts. Rules 7.901–7.903.
Chap. 20. Claims of Minors and Persons With Disabilities. Rules 7.950–7.955.
Chap. 21. Guardianships. Rules 7.1001–7.1020.
Chap. 22. Conservatorships. Rules 7.1050–7.1063.
Chap. 23. Appointed Counsel. Rules 7.1101–7.1105.

Chapter 1
General Provisions

Rule 7.1. Probate Rules
Rule 7.2. Preliminary provisions
Rule 7.3. Definitions and use of terms
Rule 7.4. Waiver of rules in probate proceedings
Rule 7.5. Waivers of court fees in decedents' estates, conservatorships, and guardianships
Rule 7.10. Ex parte communications in proceedings under the Probate Code and certain other proceedings

Rule 7.1.   Probate Rules
The rules in this title may be referred to as the Probate Rules.
Rule 7.1 adopted effective January 1, 2007.

Rule 7.2.   Preliminary provisions
(a) Application of rules
The rules in this title apply to every action and proceeding to which the Probate Code applies and, unless they are elsewhere explicitly made applicable, do not apply to any other action or proceeding.
(Subd (a) amended effective January 1, 2007.)
(b) Purpose of rules
The rules in this title are designed to implement the purposes of the probate law by promoting uniformity in practice and procedure.
(Subd (b) amended effective January 1, 2007.)
(c) Rules of construction
Unless the context otherwise requires, these preliminary provisions and the following rules of construction govern the construction of the rules in this title:
(1) To the extent that the rules in this title are substantially the same as existing statutory provisions relating to the same subject matter, they must be construed as a restatement and a continuation of those statutes; and
(2) To the extent that the rules in this title may add to existing statutory provisions relating to the same subject matter, they must be construed so as to implement the purposes of the probate law.

(Subd (c) amended effective January 1, 2007; previously amended effective January 1, 2003.)
(d) Jurisdiction
The rules in this title are not intended to expand, limit, or restrict the jurisdiction of the court in proceedings under the Probate Code.
(Subd (d) adopted effective January 1, 2003.)
Rule 7.2 amended and renumbered effective January 1, 2007; adopted as rule 7.1 effective January 1, 2000; previously amended effective January 1, 2003.

Rule 7.3.   Definitions and use of terms
As used in the rules in this title, unless the context or subject matter otherwise requires:
(1) The definitions in division 1, part 2 of the Probate Code apply.
(2) "Pleading" means a contest, answer, petition, application, objection, response, statement of interest, report, or account filed in proceedings under the Probate Code.
(3) "Amended pleading" means a pleading that completely restates and supersedes the pleading it amends for all purposes.
(4) "Amendment to a pleading" means a pleading that modifies another pleading and alleges facts or requests relief materially different from the facts alleged or the relief requested in the modified pleading. An amendment to a pleading does not restate or supersede the modified pleading but must be read together with that pleading.
(5) "Supplement to a pleading" and "supplement" mean a pleading that modifies another pleading but does not allege facts or request relief materially different from the facts alleged or the relief requested in the supplemented pleading. A supplement to a pleading may add information to or may correct omissions in the modified pleading.
Rule 7.3 amended and renumbered effective January 1, 2007; adopted as rule 7.2 effective January 1, 2000; previously amended effective January 1, 2002, and January 1, 2003.

Rule 7.4.   Waiver of rules in probate proceedings
The court for good cause may waive the application of the rules in this title in an individual case.
Rule 7.4 renumbered effective January 1, 2007; adopted as rule 7.3 effective January 1, 2000; previously amended effective January 1, 2003.

Rule 7.5.   Waivers of court fees in decedents' estates, conservatorships, and guardianships
(a) Scope of rule
This rule governs initial fee waivers, as defined in rule 3.50(b), that are requested by petitioners for the appointment of fiduciaries, or by fiduciaries after their appointment, in decedents' estates, conservatorships, and guardianships under the Probate Code. The rule also governs initial fee waivers in other civil actions or proceedings in which conservators or guardians are parties representing the interests of their conservatees or wards.
(Subd (a) adopted effective September 1, 2015.)
(b) Court fee waiver requested by a petitioner for the appointment of a conservator or guardian of the person, estate, or person and estate of a conservatee or ward
A petitioner for the appointment of a conservator or guardian of the person, estate, or person and estate of a conservatee or ward must base an application for an initial fee waiver on the personal financial condition of the proposed conservatee or ward.
(Subd (b) adopted effective September 1, 2015.)
(c) Court fee waiver requested by a petitioner for the appointment of a personal representative of a decedent's estate
A petitioner for the appointment of a personal representative of a decedent's estate must base an application for an initial fee waiver on the petitioner's personal financial condition.
(Subd (c) adopted effective September 1, 2015.)
(d) Effect of appointment of a personal representative of a decedent's estate on a court fee waiver
The appointment of a personal representative of a decedent's estate may be a change of financial condition for fee waiver purposes under Government Code section 68636 in accordance with the following:

(1) If the successful petitioner is an appointed personal representative:

(A) The petitioner's continued eligibility for an initial fee waiver must be based on the combined financial condition of the petitioner and the decedent's estate.

(B) Upon marshaling or collecting assets of the decedent's estate following the petitioner's appointment and qualification as personal representative, the petitioner must notify the court of a change in financial condition under Government Code section 68636(a) that may affect his or her ability to pay all or a portion of the waived court fees and costs.

(C) The court may make a preliminary determination under Government Code section 68636(b) that the petitioner's appointment as fiduciary is a change of financial condition that makes the petitioner no longer eligible for an initial fee waiver based, in whole or in part, on the estimates of estate value and income contained in the petitioner's *Petition for Probate*. In that event, the court must give notice and conduct the hearing required by section 68636(b).

(2) If the successful petitioner is not an appointed personal representative:

(A) An initial fee waiver for that petitioner continues in effect according to its terms for subsequent fees incurred by that petitioner in the proceeding solely in his or her individual capacity.

(B) The appointed personal representative may apply for an initial fee waiver. The application must be based on the combined financial condition of the personal representative and the decedent's estate.

(Subd (d) adopted effective September 1, 2015.)

(e) Financial condition of the conservatee or ward

(1) The financial condition of the conservatee or ward for purposes of this rule includes:

(A) The financial condition—to the extent of the information known or reasonably available to the conservator or guardian, or the petitioner for the conservator's or guardian's appointment, upon reasonable inquiry—of any person who has a duty to support the conservatee or ward, including a spouse, registered domestic partner, or parent. A divorced spouse's or divorced registered domestic partner's duty to support a conservatee and a parent's duty to support a ward under this subparagraph is limited to the amount of support ordered by a court. Consideration of a support order as an element of the conservatee's or ward's financial condition under this rule is subject to the provisions of Government Code sections 68637(d) and (e), concerning the likelihood that the obligated person will pay all or any portion of the support ordered by the court;

(B) A conservatee's interest in community property that is outside the conservatorship estate and under the management or control of the conservatee's spouse or registered domestic partner; and

(C) The right to receive support, income, or other distributions from a trust or under a contract.

(2) Following the appointment of a conservator or guardian and the grant of an initial fee waiver based on the financial condition of the conservatee or ward, the conservator or guardian is the "person who received the initial fee waiver" for purposes of Government Code section 68636(a), whether or not he or she was the successful applicant for the initial waiver. The conservator or guardian must report to the court any changes in the financial condition of the conservatee or ward that affects his or her ability to pay all or a portion of the court fees and costs that were initially waived, including any changes in the financial condition of the persons or property mentioned in subparagraphs (1)(A) and (1)(B) of this subdivision of which the conservator or guardian becomes aware after reasonable investigation.

(Subd (e) adopted effective September 1, 2015.)

(f) Additional discretionary factors in the financial condition or circumstances of a decedent's, conservatee's, or ward's estate

(1) The financial condition of the decedent's, conservatee's, or ward's estate for purposes of this rule may, in the court's discretion, include consideration of:

(A) The estate's liquidity;

(B) Whether estate property or income is necessary for the support of a person entitled to a family allowance from the estate of a decedent, the conservatee or a person entitled to support from the conservatee, or the ward; or

(C) Whether property in a decedent's estate is specifically devised.

(2) If property of the estate is eliminated from consideration for initial court fee waiver purposes because of one or more of the factors listed in (1), the court may determine that the estate can pay a portion of court fees, can pay court fees over time, or can pay court fees at a later time, under an equitable arrangement within the meaning of Government Code sections 68632(c) and 68634(e)(5). An equitable arrangement under this paragraph may include establishment of a lien for initially waived court fees against property distributable from a decedent's estate or payable to the conservatee or ward or other successor in interest at the termination of a conservatorship or guardianship.

(Subd (f) adopted effective September 1, 2015.)

(g) Payment of previously waived court fees by a decedent's estate

If the financial condition of a decedent's estate is a change of financial condition of a fee waiver applicant under this rule that results in withdrawal of a previously granted initial waiver of fees in favor of a petitioner for the appointment of a personal representative, the estate must pay to the court, as an allowable expense of administration, the fees and costs previously waived.

(Subd (g) adopted effective September 1, 2015.)

(h) Termination or modification of previously granted initial fee waivers

(1) *Conservatorships and guardianships of the estate or person and estate*

Upon establishment of a conservatorship or guardianship of the estate or person and estate, the court may collect all or a portion of court fees previously waived from the estate of the conservatee or ward if the court finds that the estate has the ability to pay the fees, or a portion thereof, immediately, over a period of time, or under some other equitable agreement, without using moneys that normally would pay for the common necessaries of life for the conservatee or ward and his or her family. The court must comply with the notice and hearing requirements of the second paragraph of Government Code section 68634(e)(5) to make the findings authorized in this paragraph.

(2) *Conservatorships and guardianships of the person*

In a conservatorship or guardianship of the person, if the court seeks to reconsider or modify a court fee waiver previously granted based on collection, application, or consideration of support, assets, or income described in (e), it must proceed as provided in Government Code section 68636 and comply with the notice and hearing requirements of the second paragraph of Government Code section 68634(e)(5), including notice to the conservator or guardian, any support obligor, and any person in possession of the assets or income. The conservator or guardian must appear at the hearing on behalf of the conservatee or ward, and the court may also appoint counsel for the conservatee or ward under Probate Code section 1470.

(Subd (h) adopted effective September 1, 2015.)

(i) Civil actions in which a conservator or guardian is a party representing the interests of a conservatee or ward

In a civil action in which a conservator or guardian is a party representing the interests of a conservatee or ward against another party or parties, for purposes of Government Code sections 68631.5, 68636, and 68637:

(1) The conservator or guardian is the person with a duty to notify the court of a change of financial condition under section 68636(a) and the person the court may require to appear at a court hearing under sections 68636(b) and (c);

(2) The conservatee or ward and the persons identified in subparagraphs (1)(A) and (B) of subdivision (e) of this rule is the person or persons whose change of financial condition or circumstances of which the court is to be notified under section 68636(a); and

(3) The conservatee or ward is the person or party whose initial fees and costs were initially waived under sections 68636(c) and 68637.

(Subd (i) adopted effective September 1, 2015.)

(j) Advances of court fees and costs by legal counsel

(1) Government Code section 68633(g)—concerning agreements between applicants for initial court fee waivers and their legal counsel for counsel to advance court fees and costs and court hearings to determine the effect of the presence or absence of such agreements on the applications—applies to proceedings described in this rule.

(2) Conservators, guardians, and petitioners for their appointment applying for initial fee waivers under this rule represented by legal counsel, and their counsel, must complete the *Request to Waive Court Fees (Ward or Conservatee)* (form FW-001-GC), including items 2a and 2b, and, if a request to waive additional court fees is made, the *Request to Waive Additional Court Fees (Superior Court) (Ward or Conservatee)* (form FW-002-GC), including items 2a and 2b. The reference to "legal-aid type services" in these forms refers to legal services provided to an

applicant by counsel for or affiliated with a qualified legal services project defined in Business and Professions Code section 6213.

(Subd (j) adopted effective September 1, 2015.)

(k) Expiration of initial court fee waivers in decedents' estates, conservatorships, and guardianships

"Final disposition of the case" in decedent's estate, conservatorship, and guardianship proceedings for purposes of determining the expiration of fee waivers under Government Code section 68639 occurs on the later of the following events:

(1) Termination of the proceedings by order of court or under operation of law in conservatorships and guardianships of the person; or

(2) Discharge of personal representatives of decedents' estates and discharge of conservators or guardians of estates.

(Subd (k) adopted effective September 1, 2015.)
Rule 7.5 adopted effective September 1, 2015.

Rule 7.10. Ex parte communications in proceedings under the Probate Code and certain other proceedings

(a) Definitions

As used in this rule, the following terms have the meanings stated below:

(1) "Fiduciary" has the meaning specified in Probate Code section 39, and includes LPS conservators.

(2) "Person" has the meaning specified in Probate Code section 56.

(3) "Pleading" has the meaning specified in rule 7.3, but also includes petitions and objections or other opposition filed in LPS conservatorships. The term does not include creditors' claims and requests for special notice.

(4) A "party" is a fiduciary appointed in a proceeding under the Probate Code or an LPS conservatorship proceeding, and any other person who has filed a pleading in the proceeding concerning a matter then pending in the court.

(5) A "ward" is a minor subject to a guardianship under Division 4 of the Probate Code, including a proposed ward concerning whom a petition for appointment of a guardian has been filed.

(6) "Ex parte communication" is a communication between any party, attorney, or person in a proceeding under the Probate Code or an LPS conservatorship proceeding and the court outside the presence of all parties and attorneys, including written communications sent to the court without copies having been provided to other interested persons.

(7) "LPS Act" is the Lanterman-Petris-Short Act, part 1 of division 5 of the Welfare and Institutions Code, commencing with section 5000.

(8) "LPS Conservatorship" is a conservatorship proceeding under chapter 3 of the LPS Act, commencing with section 5350 of the Welfare and Institutions Code, for persons gravely disabled as the result of a mental disorder or impairment by chronic alcoholism.

(9) A "conservatee" is a person subject to a conservatorship under division 4 of the Probate Code or chapter 3 of the LPS Act, including a proposed conservatee concerning whom a petition for appointment of a conservator has been filed.

(10) A "matter then pending in the court" in proceedings under the Probate Code or in an LPS conservatorship proceeding refers to a request for relief or opposition in pleadings filed in the proceeding that has not yet been resolved by a decision of the court or an agreement of the parties.

(11) Concerning a proceeding under the Probate Code or an LPS conservatorship proceeding, the term "open proceeding" refers to a proceeding that has been commenced and has not been concluded by the final discharge of all fiduciaries or otherwise terminated as provided by law, whether or not there is a matter then pending in the court in the proceeding at any point in time.

(Subd (a) adopted effective January 1, 2008.)

(b) Ex parte communications by parties and attorneys prohibited

(1) Except under a stipulation of all parties to the contrary, no ex parte communications may be made by a party or an attorney for a party and the court concerning a matter then pending in the court in proceedings under the Probate Code or in an LPS conservatorship proceeding.

(2) Except as provided in (c)(1), the court must treat an ex parte communication to the court described in (1) in the same way that an ex parte communication from a party or attorney for a party must be treated in other civil actions or proceedings or in criminal actions.

(Subd (b) adopted effective January 1, 2008.)

(c) Ex parte communications received and considered

(1) Notwithstanding (b)(2), a judicial officer or court staff may receive an ex parte communication concerning an open proceeding under the Probate Code or an open LPS conservatorship proceeding for the limited purpose of ascertaining whether it is a communication described in (b) or a communication described in (c)(2).

(2) Subject to the requirements of (c)(3), a judicial officer may consider an ex parte communication from a person about a fiduciary's performance of his or her duties and responsibilities or regarding a conservatee or ward in an open proceeding under the Probate Code or an open LPS conservatorship proceeding. The court may decline to take further action on the communication, with or without replying to the person or returning any written communication received from the person. The court may also take appropriate action, consistent with due process and California law, including one or any combination of the following:

(A) Review the court file and take any action that is supported by the record, including ordering a status report or accounting if it appears that a status report or accounting should have been filed by a fiduciary but is delinquent.

(B) Refer the communication to a court investigator for further action, and receive, consider, and respond to any report from the investigator concerning it;

(C) If the communication discloses possible criminal activity, refer the matter to the appropriate law enforcement agency or prosecutor's office;

(D) If the communication discloses conduct that might subject a person or organization to disciplinary action on a license, refer the matter to the appropriate licensing agency;

(E) If the communication discloses possible elder or dependent adult abuse, or child abuse, refer the matter to appropriate state or local governmental agencies, including adult protective or child protective service departments; and

(F) Set a hearing regarding the communication, compel the fiduciary's attendance, and require a response from the fiduciary concerning the issues raised by the communication.

(3) The court must fully disclose communications described in (c)(2) and any response made by the court to the fiduciary and all other parties to any matter then pending in the court, and their attorneys, unless the court finds good cause to dispense with the disclosure if necessary to protect a conservatee or ward from harm. If the court dispenses with disclosure to any party or attorney, it must make written findings in support of its determination of good cause, and preserve the communication received and any response made by the court. The court may place its findings and the preserved communication under seal or otherwise secure their confidentiality.

(Subd (c) adopted effective January 1, 2008.)
Rule 7.10 adopted effective January 1, 2008.

Chapter 2
Notices, Publication, and Service

Rule 7.50. Description of pleading in notice of hearing
Rule 7.51. Service of notice of hearing
Rule 7.52. Service of notice when recipient's address unknown
Rule 7.53. Notice of hearing of amended or supplemented pleadings
Rule 7.54. Publication of Notice of Petition to Administer Estate
Rule 7.55. Ex parte application for order

Rule 7.50. Description of pleading in notice of hearing

The notice of hearing on a pleading filed in a proceeding under the Probate Code must state the complete title of the pleading to which the notice relates.

Rule 7.50 adopted effective January 1, 2003.

Rule 7.51. Service of notice of hearing

(a) Direct notice required

(1) Except as otherwise permitted in the Probate Code, a notice sent by mail under Probate Code section 1220 must be mailed individually and directly to the person entitled to notice.

(2) A notice mailed to a person in care of another person is insufficient unless the person entitled to notice is an adult and has directed the party giving notice in writing to send the notice in care of the second person.

(3) Notices mailed to more than one person in the same household must be sent separately to each person.

(b) Notice to attorney

If a notice is required or permitted to be given to a person who is represented by an attorney of record in the proceeding, the notice must be sent as required in Probate Code section 1214.

(c) Notice to guardian or conservator

(1) When a guardian or conservator has been appointed for a person entitled to notice, the notice must be sent to the guardian or conservator.

(2) A copy of the notice must also be sent to the ward or conservatee unless:

(A) The court dispenses with such notice; or

(B) Under Probate Code section 1210 in a decedent's estate proceeding, the notice is personally served on a California-resident guardian or conservator of the estate of the ward or conservatee.

(Subd (c) amended effective January 1, 2004.)

(d) Notice to minor

Except as permitted in Probate Code section 1460.1 for guardianships, conservatorships, and certain protective proceedings under division 4 of the Probate Code, notice to a minor must be sent directly to the minor. A separate copy of the notice must be sent to the person or persons having legal custody of the minor, with whom the minor resides.

(e) Notice required in a decedent's estate when a beneficiary has died

(1) *Notice when a beneficiary dies after the decedent*

Notice must be sent to the personal representative of a beneficiary who died after the decedent and survived for a period required by the decedent's will. If no personal representative has been appointed for the postdeceased beneficiary, notice must be sent to his or her beneficiaries or other persons entitled to succeed to his or her interest in the decedent's estate.

(2) *Notice when a beneficiary of the decedent's will dies before the decedent*

When a beneficiary under the will of the decedent died before the decedent or fails to survive the decedent for a period required by the decedent's will, notice must be sent to the persons named in the decedent's will as substitute beneficiaries of the gift to the predeceased beneficiary. If the decedent's will does not make a substitute disposition of that gift, notice must be sent as follows:

(A) If the predeceased beneficiary is a "transferee" under Probate Code section 21110(c), to the issue of the predeceased beneficiary determined under Probate Code section 240 and to the residuary beneficiaries of the decedent or to the decedent's heirs if decedent's will does not provide for distribution of the residue of the estate.

(B) If the predeceased beneficiary is not a "transferee" under Probate Code section 21110(c), to the residuary beneficiaries of the decedent or to the decedent's heirs if decedent's will does not provide for distribution of the residue of the estate.

(f) Notice when Indian Child Welfare Act may apply

If the court or the petitioner knows or has reason to know, as described in section 224.2(d) of the Welfare and Institutions Code, that an Indian child is the subject of a guardianship or specified conservatorship proceeding, notice must be given as prescribed in rule 7.1015(e).

(Subd (f) adopted effective January 1, 2022.)

Rule 7.51 amended effective January 1, 2022; adopted effective January 1, 2003; previously amended effective January 1, 2004.

Rule 7.52. Service of notice when recipient's address unknown

(a) Declaration of diligent search

Petitioner must file a declaration describing efforts made to locate a person entitled to notice in a proceeding under the Probate Code, but whose address is unknown, before the court will prescribe an alternate form of notice or dispense with notice under (c). The declaration must state the name of the person whose address is unknown, the last known address of the person, the approximate date when the person was last known to reside there, the efforts made to locate the person, and any facts that explain why the person's address cannot be obtained. The declaration must include a description of the attempts to learn of the person's business and residence addresses by:

(1) Inquiry of the relatives, friends, acquaintances, and employers of the person entitled to notice and of the person who is the subject of the proceeding;

(2) Review of appropriate city telephone directories and directory assistance; and

(3) Search of the real and personal property indexes in the recorder's and assessor's offices for the county where the person was last known or believed to reside.

(b) Mailed notice to county seat

Mailing notice to a person at a county seat is not a manner of giving notice reasonably calculated to give actual notice.

(c) The court may prescribe or dispense with notice

If a person entitled to notice cannot be located after diligent search, the court may prescribe the manner of giving notice to that person or may dispense with notice to that person.

Rule 7.52 adopted effective January 1, 2003.

Rule 7.53. Notice of hearing of amended or supplemented pleadings

(a) Amended pleading and amendment to a pleading

An amended pleading or an amendment to a pleading requires the same notice of hearing (including publication) as the pleading it amends.

(b) Supplement to a pleading

A supplement to a pleading does not require additional notice of hearing, but a copy of a supplement to a pleading must be served if service of a copy of the pleading was required, unless waived by the court.

Rule 7.53 adopted effective January 1, 2003.

Rule 7.54. Publication of Notice of Petition to Administer Estate

Publication and service of a *Notice of Petition to Administer Estate* (form DE-121) under Probate Code sections 8110–8125 is sufficient notice of any instrument offered for probate that is filed with, and specifically referred to in, the petition for which notice is given. Any other instrument must be presented in an amended petition, and a new notice must be published and served.

Rule 7.54 amended effective January 1, 2007; adopted effective January 1, 2003.

Rule 7.55. Ex parte application for order

(a) Special notice allegation

An ex parte application for an order must allege whether special notice has been requested.

(Subd (a) amended effective January 1, 2007.)

(b) Allegation if special notice requested

If special notice has been requested, the application must identify each person who has requested special notice and must allege that special notice has been given to or waived by each person who has requested it.

(Subd (b) amended effective January 1, 2007.)

(c) Proof of service or waiver of special notice

Proofs of service of special notice or written waivers of special notice must be filed with the application.

(Subd (c) amended effective January 1, 2007.)

Rule 7.55 amended effective January 1, 2007; adopted effective January 1, 2003.

Chapter 3
Pleadings

Rule 7.101. Use of Judicial Council forms
Rule 7.102. Titles of pleadings and orders
Rule 7.103. Signature and verification of pleadings
Rule 7.104. Execution and verification of amended pleadings, amendments to pleadings, and supplements to pleadings; use of Judicial Council forms

Rule 7.101. Use of Judicial Council forms

(a) Use of mandatory forms

If a petition, an order, or another document to be submitted to the court is one for which the Judicial Council has adopted a mandatory form, that form must be used. Except as provided in this rule, if the Judicial Council has adopted a mandatory form in more than one alternative version, one of the alternative versions must be used. If that form is inadequate in a particular situation, an addendum may be attached to it.

(Subd (a) amended and lettered effective January 1, 2007; adopted as untitled subd effective January 1, 2001.)

(b) Alternative mandatory forms

The following forms have been adopted by the Judicial Council as alternative mandatory forms for use in probate proceedings or other proceedings governed by provisions of the Probate Code:

(1) *Petition for Appointment of Guardian of Minor* (form GC-210) and *Petition for Appointment of Guardian of the Person* (form GC-210(P));

(2) *Petition for Appointment of Temporary Guardian* (form GC-110) and *Petition for Appointment of Temporary Guardian of the Person* (form GC-110(P));

(3) *Petition for Approval of Compromise of Claim or Action or Disposition of Proceeds of Judgment for Minor or Person With a Disability* (form MC-350) and *Petition for Expedited Approval of Compromise of Claim or Action or Disposition of Proceeds of Judgment for Minor or Person With a Disability* (form MC-350EX).

(Subd (b) amended effective January 1, 2021; adopted effective January 1, 2007; previously amended effective January 1, 2010, and January 1, 2014.)

(c) Use of guardianship petitions

Notwithstanding any other provision of this rule, a party petitioning for appointment of a temporary guardian of the person of a minor may file either form GC-110 or form GC-110(P). A party petitioning for appointment of a general guardian of the person of a minor may file either form GC-210 or form GC-210(P). A party petitioning for appointment of a temporary guardian of the estate or the person and estate of a minor must file form GC-110. A party petitioning for appointment of a general guardian of the estate or the person and estate of a minor must file form GC-210.

(Subd (c) adopted effective January 1, 2007.)

Rule 7.101 amended effective January 1, 2021; adopted effective January 1, 2001; previously amended effective January 1, 2002, January 1, 2007, January 1, 2010, and January 1, 2014.

Rule 7.101.5. Electronic generation of mandatory Judicial Council form orders [Repealed]

Rule 7.101.5 repealed effective January 1, 2012; adopted effective January 1, 2007.

Rule 7.102. Titles of pleadings and orders

The title of each pleading and of each proposed order must clearly and completely identify the nature of the relief sought or granted.

Rule 7.102 amended effective January 1, 2003; adopted effective January 1, 2001; previously amended effective January 1, 2002.

Rule 7.103. Signature and verification of pleadings

(a) Signature of parties

A pleading must be in writing and must be signed by all persons joining in it.

(b) Verification by parties

All pleadings filed in proceedings under the Probate Code must be verified. If two or more persons join in a pleading, it may be verified by any of them.

(c) Signature and verification by attorney

If a person is absent from the county where his or her attorney's office is located, or for some other cause is unable to sign or verify a pleading, the attorney may sign or verify it, unless the person is, or is seeking to become, a fiduciary appointed in the proceeding.

Rule 7.103 adopted effective January 1, 2003.

Rule 7.104. Execution and verification of amended pleadings, amendments to pleadings, and supplements to pleadings; use of Judicial Council forms

(a) Amended pleading and amendment to a pleading

(1) All persons required to sign a pleading must sign an amended pleading. One of the persons required to verify a pleading must verify an amended pleading.

(2) All persons required to sign a pleading must sign an amendment to that pleading. One of the persons required to verify a pleading must verify an amendment to that pleading.

(3) A Judicial Council form must be used for an amended pleading, with the word "Amended" added to its caption, if the form was used for the pleading that is amended. A Judicial Council form must not be used for an amendment to a pleading.

(b) Supplement to a pleading

(1) A supplement to a pleading must be signed and verified by one of the persons who were required to sign and verify the pleading that is supplemented. However, the court may, in the exercise of its discretion, accept for filing and consider a supplement to a pleading signed under penalty of perjury by an attorney for the party offering it, where the information contained in the supplement is particularly within the knowledge of the attorney.

(2) A Judicial Council form must not be used for a supplement to a pleading.

Rule 7.104 adopted effective January 1, 2003.

Chapter 4
Appointment of Executors and Administrators

Rule 7.150. Acknowledgment of receipt of statement of duties and liabilities of personal representative

Before the court issues letters, each personal representative of a decedent's estate (other than a company authorized to conduct a trust business in California) must execute and file an acknowledgment of receipt of *Duties and Liabilities of Personal Representative* (form DE-147).

Rule 7.150 amended effective January 1, 2007; adopted effective January 1, 2000; previously amended effective January 1, 2002.

Rule 7.151. Reimbursement of graduated filing fee by successful subsequent petitioner [Repealed]

Rule 7.151 repealed effective January 1, 2020; adopted effective January 1, 2004; previously amended effective January 1, 2007, and March 1, 2008.

Chapter 5
Bonding of Personal Representatives, Guardians, Conservators, and Trustees

Rule 7.201. Waiver of bond in will
Rule 7.202. Two or more personal representatives
Rule 7.203. Separate bonds for individuals
Rule 7.204. Duty to apply for order increasing bond
Rule 7.205. Independent power to sell real property
Rule 7.206. Bond upon sale of real property
Rule 7.207. Bonds of conservators and guardians

Rule 7.201. Waiver of bond in will

(a) Statement of waiver in petition

If the will waives bond, the Petition for Probate must so state.

(Subd (a) amended effective January 1, 2007; previously amended effective January 1, 2001, and January 1, 2002.)

(b) Court's discretion to require bond

The court may require bond if the proposed personal representative resides outside California or for other good cause, even if the will waives bond.

(Subd (b) amended effective January 1, 2001.)

Rule 7.201 amended effective January 1, 2007; adopted effective January 1, 2000; previously amended effective January 1, 2001, and January 1, 2002.

Rule 7.202. Two or more personal representatives

If a will admitted to probate names two or more persons to serve as executors but not all serve and the will does not expressly waive bond if fewer than all of the named persons serve, the court must require each executor to give a bond unless the court waives this requirement under Probate Code section 8481(a)(2).

Rule 7.202 amended effective January 1, 2002; adopted effective January 1, 2000.

Rule 7.203. Separate bonds for individuals

Because a corporate fiduciary (whether personal representative, guardian, conservator, or trustee) cannot assume responsibility for the acts of an individual cofiduciary, an individual cofiduciary who is required to give a bond must provide a separate bond, except to the extent that the court orders the assets to be held solely by the corporate cofiduciary.

Rule 7.203 amended effective January 1, 2002; adopted effective January 1, 2000.

Rule 7.204. Duty to apply for order increasing bond

(a) Ex parte application for order

Immediately upon the occurrence of facts making it necessary or appropriate to increase the amount of the bond, the personal representative, or the guardian or conservator of the estate, must make an ex parte application for an order increasing the bond.

(Subd (a) amended effective January 1, 2003; previously amended effective January 1, 2002.)

(b) Attorney's duty

If the personal representative, or the guardian or conservator of the estate, has not already made application under (a), the attorney for the personal representative, or the attorney for the guardian or conservator of the estate, must make the ex parte application immediately upon becoming aware of the need to increase bond.

(Subd (b) amended effective January 1, 2003; previously amended effective January 1, 2002.)

(c) Amount

(1) The application by a personal representative under (a) or by the attorney for a personal representative under (b) must show the value of the estate's personal property and the probable annual gross income of the estate.

(2) The application by a guardian or conservator of the estate under (a) or by the attorney for a guardian or conservator of the estate under (b) must show the value of the estate's personal property, the probable annual gross income of all of the property of the estate, and the sum of the

probable annual gross payments of the public benefits of the ward or conservatee identified in Probate Code section 2320(c)(3).

(3) If the personal representative has full Independent Administration of Estates Act (IAEA) authority or the guardian or conservator of the estate has authority to sell estate real property without court confirmation, the application must also show the amount of the equity in estate real property.

(Subd (c) amended effective January 1, 2003; previously amended effective January 1, 2002.)

Rule 7.204 amended effective January 1, 2002; adopted effective January 1, 2000.

Rule 7.205. Independent power to sell real property

If the personal representative requests or has been granted an independent power to sell or hypothecate real estate or to lease it for a term of more than one year, the personal representative must state in the request to fix the amount of the bond the value of the real property less encumbrances.

Rule 7.205 amended effective January 1, 2002; adopted effective January 1, 2000.

Rule 7.206. Bond upon sale of real property

If a bond or additional bond is required in an order confirming sale of real estate, the court must not file the order until the additional bond is filed.

Rule 7.206 amended effective January 1, 2002; adopted effective January 1, 2000.

Rule 7.207. Bonds of conservators and guardians

(a) Bond includes reasonable amount for recovery on the bond

Except as otherwise provided by statute, every conservator or guardian of the estate must furnish a bond that includes an amount determined under (b) as a reasonable amount for the cost of recovery to collect on the bond under Probate Code section 2320(c)(4).

(Subd (a) amended effective January 1, 2010; adopted effective January 1, 2008.)

(b) Amount of bond for the cost of recovery on the bond

The reasonable amount of bond for the cost of recovery to collect on the bond, including attorney's fees and costs, under Probate Code section 2320(c)(4) is:

(1) Ten percent (10%) of the value up to and including $500,000 of the following:

(A) The value of personal property of the estate;

(B) The value, less encumbrances, of real property of the estate that the guardian or conservator has the independent power to sell without approval or confirmation of the court under Probate Code sections 2590 and 2591(d);

(C) The probable annual income from all assets of the estate; and

(D) The probable annual gross payments described in Probate Code section 2320(c)(3); and

(2) Twelve percent (12%) of the value above $500,000 up to and including $1,000,000 of the property, income, and payments described in (1); and

(3) Two percent (2%) of the value above $1,000,000 of the property, income, and payments described in (1).

(Subd (b) repealed, amended and relettered effective January 1, 2010; adopted as subd (c) effective January 1, 2008.)

Rule 7.207 amended effective January 1, 2010; adopted effective January 1, 2008.

Chapter 6
Independent Administration of Estates

Rule 7.250. Report of actions taken under the Independent Administration of Estates Act

(a) Report required

In any accounting, report, petition for preliminary distribution, or petition for final distribution, the petitioner must list and describe all actions taken without prior court approval under the Independent Administration of Estates Act (IAEA) if notice of the proposed action was required. The description of the action must include the following:

(1) The nature of the action;

(2) When the action was taken;

(3) A statement of when and to whom notice was given;

(4) Whether notice was waived, and if so, by whom; and

(5) Whether any objections were received.

(Subd (a) amended effective January 1, 2002.)

(b) Actions reported in previous reports

An action taken under the IAEA that was (1) properly listed and described in a prior accounting, report, or petition for distribution, and (2) approved by the court, need not be listed and described in a subsequent account, report, or petition for distribution.

(Subd (b) amended effective January 1, 2007.)

Rule 7.250 amended effective January 1, 2007; adopted effective January 1, 2000; previously amended effective January 1, 2002.

Chapter 7
Spousal or Domestic Partner Property Petitions

Rule 7.301. Spousal or domestic partner property petition filed with petition for probate

A petition for spousal or domestic partner property determination or confirmation must be filed separately from a petition for probate of will or for letters of administration, even if both petitions are filed at the same time. The two petitions must be filed under the same case number.

Rule 7.301 amended effective January 1, 2007; adopted effective January 1, 2000; previously amended effective January 1, 2002.

Chapter 8
Petitions for Instructions
[Reserved]

Chapter 9
Creditors' Claims

Rule 7.401. Personal representative's action on the claim
Rule 7.402. Court's action on the claim
Rule 7.403. Listing all claims in the final report

Rule 7.401. Personal representative's action on the claim

For each creditor's claim filed with the court, the personal representative (whether or not acting under the Independent Administration of Estates Act (IAEA)) must:

(1) Allow or reject in whole or in part the claim in writing;

(2) Serve a copy of the allowance or rejection on the creditor and the creditor's attorney; and

(3) File a copy of the allowance or rejection with proof of service with the court.

Rule 7.401 amended effective January 1, 2002; adopted effective January 1, 2000.

Rule 7.402. Court's action on the claim

Except as to claims of the personal representative or the attorney, if the personal representative has authority to act under the Independent Administration of Estates Act (IAEA), the court must not act on the personal representative's allowance or rejection of a creditor's claim unless good cause is shown.

Rule 7.402 amended effective January 1, 2002; adopted effective January 1, 2000.

Rule 7.403. Listing all claims in the final report

For each claim presented, the personal representative must state in the final report or petition for final distribution:

(1) The claimant's name;

(2) The date of filing of the claim;

(3) The nature of the claim;

(4) The amount claimed;

(5) The disposition of the claim; and

(6) If the claim was rejected, the date of service of the rejection and whether or not a lawsuit was filed.

Rule 7.403 amended effective January 1, 2002; adopted effective January 1, 2000.

Chapter 10
Sales of Real and Personal Property

Rule 7.451. Refusal to show property to prospective buyers
Rule 7.452. Petitioner or attorney required at hearing
Rule 7.453. Petition for exclusive listing
Rule 7.454. Ex parte application for order authorizing sale of securities or other personal property

Rule 7.451. Refusal to show property to prospective buyers

Upon a showing that the fiduciary has denied any bona fide prospective buyer or his or her broker a reasonable opportunity to inspect the property, the court must not confirm the sale but must continue the sale to allow inspection unless good cause is shown for the court to confirm the sale.

Rule 7.451 amended effective January 1, 2002; adopted effective January 1, 2000.

Rule 7.452. Petitioner or attorney required at hearing

The court must not proceed with the hearing on a petition to confirm a sale of property unless the petitioner's attorney or petitioner, if unrepresented, is present.

Rule 7.452 amended effective January 1, 2002; adopted effective January 1, 2000.

Rule 7.453. Petition for exclusive listing

A petition for approval of an exclusive listing under Probate Code section 10150(c) must state the following:

(1) A description of the property to be sold;

(2) The name of the broker to be employed;

(3) A summary of the terms of the exclusive listing agreement or include a copy of the listing agreement; and

(4) A detailed statement of the facts supporting the "necessity and the advantage" to the estate of having the exclusive listing.

Rule 7.453 amended effective January 1, 2002; adopted effective January 1, 2000.

Rule 7.454. Ex parte application for order authorizing sale of securities or other personal property

An ex parte application for authority to sell or to surrender tangible or intangible personal property must state whether or not the property is specifically devised. If it is specifically devised, the written consent of the specific devisee to the sale or surrender must be filed.

Rule 7.454 adopted effective January 1, 2003.

Chapter 11
Inventory and Appraisal

Rule 7.501. Inventory and Appraisal to show sufficiency of bond

(a) Statement required

Every Inventory and Appraisal must contain one of the following statements:

(1) "Bond is waived";

(2) "Bond has been filed in the amount of $ *(specify amount)* and is insufficient"; or

(3) "Bond has been filed in the amount of $ *(specify amount)* and is sufficient."

(Subd (a) amended effective January 1, 2007; previously amended effective January 1, 2002.)

(b) Insufficient bond

If the bond is insufficient, the fiduciary (the personal representative, or the guardian or conservator of the estate), or the attorney for the fiduciary, must immediately make ex parte application as provided in rule 7.204 for an order increasing the amount of the bond.

(Subd (b) amended effective January 1, 2003; previously amended effective January 1, 2002.)

(c) Statement signed by attorney

The statement required by (a) must be signed by the attorney of record for each fiduciary who has an attorney of record and by each fiduciary who does not.

(Subd (c) amended effective January 1, 2003; previously amended effective January 1, 2002.)

Rule 7.501 amended effective January 1, 2007; adopted effective January 1, 2000; previously amended effective January 1, 2002, and January 1, 2003.

Chapter 12
Accounts and Reports of Executors, Administrators, Conservators, and Guardians

Chapter 12 amended effective January 1, 2008.

Rule 7.550. Effect of waiver of account
Rule 7.575. Accounts of conservators and guardians
Rule 7.576. Final account of conservator of the estate

Rule 7.550. Effect of waiver of account

(a) Waiver of account

Except as provided in (b), if an accounting is waived under Probate Code section 10954, the details of receipts and disbursements need not be listed in the report required under section 10954(c)(1).

(Subd (a) amended effective January 1, 2007; adopted as part of unlettered subdivision effective January 1, 2003; previously amended effective January 1, 2004.)

(b) Information required in report on waiver of account

The report required when an account has been waived must list the information required by law, including information as to:

(1) Creditors' claims;

(2) Sales, purchases, or exchanges of assets;

(3) Changes in the form of assets;

(4) Assets on hand;

(5) Whether the estate is solvent;

(6) Detailed schedules of receipts and gains or losses on sale (where an amount other than the amount of the Inventory and Appraisal is used as a basis for calculating fees or commissions);

(7) Costs of administration (if reimbursement of these costs is requested);

(8) The amount of any fees or commissions paid or to be paid;

(9) The calculation of such fees or commissions as described in rule 7.705.

(Subd (b) amended effective January 1, 2020; adopted as part of unlettered subdivision effective January 1, 2003; previously amended effective January 1, 2004, and January 1, 2007.)

Rule 7.550 amended effective January 1, 2020; adopted effective January 1, 2003; previously amended effective January 1, 2004, and January 1, 2007.

Rule 7.551. Final accounts or reports in estates with nonresident beneficiaries [Repealed]

Rule 7.551 repealed effective January 1, 2015; adopted effective January 1, 2004.

Rule 7.552. Graduated filing fee adjustments for estates commenced on or after August 18, 2003, and before January 1, 2008 [Repealed]

Rule 7.552 repealed effective January 1, 2015; adopted effective January 1, 2004; previously amended effective January 1, 2007, and March 1, 2008.

Rule 7.553. Graduated filing fee statements for decedents' estates commenced on or after January 1, 2008 [Repealed]

Rule 7.553 repealed effective January 1, 2015; adopted effective March 1, 2008.

Rule 7.575. Accountings of conservators and guardians

Unless waived by the court under Probate Code section 2628, a conservator or guardian of the estate must file accountings in the frequency, manner, and circumstances specified in Probate Code section 2620. The court may order accountings to be filed more frequently than required by the statute. An accounting must be filed as a standard accounting unless this rule authorizes filing a simplified accounting.

(a) Information required in all accountings

Notwithstanding any other provision of this rule or the Judicial Council accounting forms, each accounting filed with the court must include:

(1) All information required by Probate Code section 1061 in the *Summary of Account—Standard and Simplified Accounts* (form GC-400(SUM)/GC-405(SUM));

(2) All information required by Probate Code sections 1062–1063 in the supporting schedules; and

(3) All information required by Probate Code section 1064 in the petition for approval of the accounting or the report accompanying the petition.

(Subd (a) amended effective January 1, 2020; adopted effective January 1, 2008.)

(b) Supporting documents

Each accounting filed with the court must include the supporting documents, including all account statements, specified in Probate Code section 2620(c).

(1) An account statement includes:

(A) An original account statement; or

(B) A verified electronic statement.

(2) A court may also accept a computer-generated printout of an original verified electronic statement if the fiduciary verifies that the statement was received in electronic form and printed without alteration.

(3) A verification under this subdivision must be executed by the fiduciary as required by Code of Civil Procedure section 2015.5.

(Subd (b) amended effective January 1, 2023; adopted effective January 1, 2020.)

(c) Standard accounting

A "standard accounting" reports receipts and disbursements in subject-matter categories, with each category subtotaled on a separate form. A conservator, guardian, or trustee must file each accounting as a standard accounting unless a simplified accounting is authorized in (d)(1).

(Subd (c) relettered and amended effective January 1, 2020; adopted as subd (b) effective January 1, 2008.)

(d) Simplified accounting

A "simplified accounting" reports individual receipts and disbursements chronologically, by receipt or payment date, without separating them into subject matter categories.

(1) A conservator, guardian, or trustee may file a simplified accounting only if all the following requirements are met:

(A) The estate or trust contains no income-generating real property;

(B) The estate or trust contains neither a whole nor a partial interest in a trade or business;

(C) The appraised value of the estate or trust, excluding the value of the conservatee's or ward's personal residence, is less than $500,000; and

(D) The court has not directed the fiduciary to file a standard accounting.

(2) If the requirements in (1) are met, but either *Schedule A, Receipts—Simplified Account* (form GC-405(A)) or *Schedule C, Disbursements—Simplified Account* (form GC-405(C)) would be longer than five pages, the fiduciary must use the standard receipt forms—forms GC-400(A)(1)–(6)—or the standard disbursement forms—forms GC-400(C)(1)–(11)—as applicable, but may otherwise file a simplified accounting.

(Subd (d) relettered and amended effective January 1, 2020; adopted as subd (c) effective January 1, 2008.)

(e) Judicial Council forms

The Judicial Council has approved two overlapping sets of forms for accountings in conservatorships and guardianships.

(1) Forms intended for use in standard accountings are numbered GC-400.

(2) Forms intended for use in simplified accountings are numbered GC-405.

(3) Forms intended for use in both accounting formats bear both numbers.

(4) Each form number is followed by a suffix—for example, GC-405(A)—to specify that form's intended use. The suffix indicates either the letter or the subject matter of the form's schedule.

(5) The *Summary of Account—Standard and Simplified Accounts* (form GC-400(SUM)/GC-405(SUM)) must be used in all accountings.

(6) Except for the *Summary of Account*, all standard accounting forms are optional. A fiduciary who files a standard accounting and elects not to use the Judicial Council forms must:

(A) Report receipts and disbursements in the subject-matter categories specified on the Judicial Council standard accounting forms for receipts and disbursements schedules;

(B) Provide the same information about any asset, property, transaction, receipt, disbursement, or other matter that is required on the applicable Judicial Council standard accounting form; and

(C) Provide the information in the same general format as that of the applicable Judicial Council standard accounting form, except that instructional material and material contained or requested in the form's header and footer may be omitted.

(7) *Schedule A, Receipts—Simplified Account* (form GC-405(A)) and *Schedule C, Disbursements—Simplified Account* (form GC-405(C)) must be used in all simplified accountings unless (d)(2) requires use of the standard forms for Schedule A or Schedule C.

(8) A fiduciary filing a simplified accounting must use the appropriate form in the GC-405 series whenever the accounting covers an asset, a transaction, or an event to which that form applies.

(Subd (e) amended effective January 1, 2023; adopted as subd (d) effective January 1, 2008; previously relettered and amended effective January 1, 2020.)

(f) Order waiving an accounting

The court may make an order waiving an otherwise required accounting if all the conditions in Probate Code section 2628(a) are met. If the conservatee or ward owns a personal residence, the request for an order waiving the accounting must include, in addition to the information needed to verify that all the conditions in section 2628(a) are met, the following information and documents regarding the personal residence:

(1) The street address of the residence;

(2) A true copy of the most recent residential property tax bill;

(3) A true copy of the declarations page from the homeowner's insurance policy covering the residence;

(4) A true copy of the most recent statement for any mortgage or loan secured by the residence; and

(5) A true copy of the most recent fee or dues statement for any homeowners' association or similar association.

(Subd (f) repealed and adopted effective January 1, 2020.)

Rule 7.575 amended effective January 1, 2023; adopted effective January 1, 2008; previously amended effective January 1, 2020.

Rule 7.576. Final account of conservator of the estate

(a) Filing and approval of final account

A conservator of the estate whose administration is terminated for any reason, including removal, resignation, or termination of the conservatorship, must file and obtain the court's approval of a final account of the administration.

(Subd (a) adopted effective January 1, 2023.)

(b) Delivery of final account of removed or resigned conservator

A conservator of the estate who has resigned or been removed must deliver a copy of the conservator's final account and the petition for its settlement with the notice of hearing required by Probate Code section 1460(b)(1) to the successor conservator of the estate in any manner permitted by Probate Code section 1215, unless the court dispenses with that notice.

(Subd (b) adopted effective January 1, 2023.)

(c) Delivery of final account after termination of conservatorship

After termination of a conservatorship, a conservator of the estate must deliver a copy of the conservator's final account and the petition for its settlement with the notice of hearing required by Probate Code section 1460(b)(2)–(3) to both the former conservatee and the spouse or domestic partner of the former conservatee in any manner permitted by Probate Code section 1215, unless the court dispenses with that notice.

(Subd (c) adopted effective January 1, 2023.)

Rule 7.576 adopted effective January 1, 2023.

Chapter 13
Taxes
[Reserved]

Chapter 14
Preliminary and Final Distributions

Rule 7.650. Decree of distribution establishing testamentary trusts
Rule 7.651. Description of property in petition for distribution
Rule 7.652. Allegations in petition for distribution concerning character of property

Rule 7.650. Decree of distribution establishing testamentary trusts

(a) Determining the trust

Upon distribution, the court must:

(1) Determine whether or not a valid trust has been created by the will;

(2) Determine the terms of the trust; and

(3) Order distribution of the trust property to the trustee.

(Subd (a) amended effective January 1, 2002.)

(b) Terms of the trust

The order for distribution must incorporate the terms of the trust so as to give effect to the conditions existing at the time distribution is ordered. The pertinent provisions must be stated in the present tense and in the third person instead of quoting the will verbatim.

(Subd (b) amended effective January 1, 2002.)

Rule 7.650 amended effective January 1, 2002; adopted effective January 1, 2000.

Rule 7.651. Description of property in petition for distribution

(a) Property description

A petition for distribution must list and describe in detail the property to be distributed, in the body of the petition or in an attachment that is incorporated in the petition by reference. If an account is filed with the petition, the description must be included in a schedule in the account.

(b) Specific description requirements

The description under (a) must:

(1) Include the amount of cash on hand;

(2) Indicate whether promissory notes are secured or unsecured, and describe in detail the security interest of any secured notes;

(3) Include the complete legal description, street address (if any), and assessor's parcel number (if any) of real property; and

(4) Include the complete description of each individual security held in "street name" in security brokers' accounts.

Rule 7.651 adopted effective January 1, 2004.

Rule 7.652. Allegations in petition for distribution concerning character of property

(a) Required allegations

If the character of property to be distributed may affect the distribution, a petition for distribution must allege:

(1) The character of the property to be distributed, whether separate, community, or quasi-community; and

(2) That the community or quasi-community property to be distributed is either the decedent's one-half interest only, or the entire interest of the decedent and the decedent's spouse.

(b) Compliance with Probate Code section 13502
If any property is to be distributed outright to the surviving spouse, a written election by the surviving spouse that complies with Probate Code section 13502 must have been filed, and the petition must show the filing date of the election.

Rule 7.652 adopted effective January 1, 2004.

Chapter 15
Compensation of Personal Representatives and Attorneys

Rule 7.700. Compensation paid in advance
Rule 7.701. Allowance on account of statutory compensation
Rule 7.702. Petition for extraordinary compensation
Rule 7.703. Extraordinary compensation
Rule 7.704. Apportionment of statutory compensation
Rule 7.705. Calculation of statutory compensation
Rule 7.706. Compensation when personal representative is an attorney
Rule 7.707. Application of compensation provisions

Rule 7.700. Compensation paid in advance

(a) No compensation in advance of court order
The personal representative must neither pay nor receive, and the attorney for the personal representative must not receive, statutory commissions or fees or fees for extraordinary services in advance of an order of the court authorizing their payment.

(b) Surcharge for payment or receipt of advance compensation
In addition to removing the personal representative and imposing any other sanctions authorized by law against the personal representative or the attorney for the personal representative, the court may surcharge the personal representative for payment or receipt of statutory commissions or fees or fees for extraordinary services in advance of an order of the court authorizing their payment. The surcharge may include interest at the legal rate from the date of payment.

Rule 7.700 adopted effective January 1, 2003.

Rule 7.701. Allowance on account of statutory compensation
The court may authorize an allowance of statutory fees or commissions on account before approval of the final account and the decree of final distribution. Any allowance made before settlement of the final account must be low enough to avoid the possibility of overpayment. The allowance:

(1) Must be based on the estimated amount of statutory compensation payable on the estate determined as of the date of the petition for allowance;

(2) Must be in proportion to the work actually performed; and

(3) Must be based upon a detailed description of the ordinary services performed and remaining to be performed.

Rule 7.701 adopted effective January 1, 2003.

Rule 7.702. Petition for extraordinary compensation
A petition for extraordinary compensation must include, or be accompanied by, a statement of the facts upon which the petition is based. The statement of facts must:

(1) Show the nature and difficulty of the tasks performed;

(2) Show the results achieved;

(3) Show the benefit of the services to the estate;

(4) Specify the amount requested for each category of service performed;

(5) State the hourly rate of each person who performed services and the hours spent by each of them;

(6) Describe the services rendered in sufficient detail to demonstrate the productivity of the time spent; and

(7) State the estimated amount of statutory compensation to be paid by the estate, if the petition is not part of a final account or report.

Rule 7.702 adopted effective January 1, 2003.

Rule 7.703. Extraordinary compensation

(a) Discretion of the court
An award of extraordinary compensation to the personal representative or to the attorney for the personal representative is within the discretion of the court. The court may consider the amount of statutory compensation when determining compensation for extraordinary services.

(b) Examples of extraordinary services by personal representative
The following is a nonexclusive list of activities for which extraordinary compensation may be awarded to the personal representative:

(1) Selling, leasing, exchanging, financing, or foreclosing real or personal property;

(2) Carrying on decedent's business if necessary to preserve the estate or under court order;

(3) Preparing tax returns; and

(4) Handling audits or litigation connected with tax liabilities of the decedent or of the estate.

(c) Examples of extraordinary services by attorney
The following is a nonexclusive list of activities for which extraordinary compensation may be awarded to the attorney for the personal representative:

(1) Legal services in connection with the sale of property held in the estate;

(2) Services to secure a loan to pay estate debts;

(3) Litigation undertaken to benefit the estate or to protect its interests;

(4) Defense of the personal representative's account;

(5) Defense of a will contested after its admission to probate;

(6) Successful defense of a will contested before its admission to probate;

(7) Successful defense of a personal representative in a removal proceeding;

(8) Extraordinary efforts to locate estate assets;

(9) Litigation in support of attorney's request for extraordinary compensation, where prior compensation awards are not adequate compensation under all the circumstances;

(10) Coordination of ancillary administration; and

(11) Accounting for a deceased, incapacitated, or absconded personal representative under Probate Code section 10953.

(d) Contingency fee agreement for extraordinary legal services
An attorney may agree to perform extraordinary services for a personal representative on a contingent-fee basis on the following conditions:

(1) The agreement must be in writing and must comply with section 6147 of the Business and Professions Code;

(2) The court must approve the agreement in the manner provided in Probate Code section 10811(c), based on findings that the compensation under the agreement is just and reasonable, that the agreement is to the advantage of the estate, and that the agreement is in the best interest of the persons interested in the estate; and

(3) In the absence of an emergency or other unusual circumstances, the personal representative must obtain the court's approval of the contingency fee agreement before services are performed under it.

(Subd (d) amended effective January 1, 2007.)

(e) Use of paralegals in the performance of extraordinary services
Extraordinary legal services may include the services of a paralegal as defined in Business and Professions Code section 6450(a) only if the request for extraordinary legal fees for the paralegal's services:

(1) Describes the qualifications of the paralegal (including education, certification, continuing education, and experience). The description must state that the paralegal:

(A) Acted under the direction and supervision of an attorney;

(B) Satisfies one or more of the minimum qualifications specified in Business and Professions Code section 6450(c); and

(C) Has completed mandatory continuing education required by Business and Professions Code section 6450(d) for the last two-year certification period ending before the year during which any part of the paralegal's services were performed.

(2) States the hours spent by the paralegal and the hourly rate requested for the paralegal's services;

(3) Describes the services performed by the paralegal;

(4) States why it was appropriate to use the paralegal's services in the particular case; and

(5) Demonstrates that the total amount requested for the extraordinary services of the attorney and the paralegal does not exceed the amount appropriate if the attorney had performed the services without the paralegal's assistance.

(Subd (e) amended effective July 1, 2010.)

Rule 7.703 amended effective July 1, 2010; adopted effective January 1, 2003; previously amended effective January 1, 2007.

Rule 7.704. Apportionment of statutory compensation

(a) One statutory commission and fee
There is one statutory commission for ordinary services by the personal representative of the estate and one statutory attorney fee for ordinary legal services to the personal representative, regardless of the

number of personal representatives or attorneys performing the services. The court may apportion statutory commissions and fees among multiple, successive, and concurrent personal representatives or attorneys. The apportionment must be based on the agreement of the multiple personal representatives or attorneys or, if there is no agreement, according to the services actually rendered by each of them.

(b) Notice of hearing

If there has been a change of personal representative or a substitution of attorneys for the personal representative, notice of hearing of any interim or final petition seeking or waiving an award of statutory compensation must be given to all prior personal representatives or attorneys unless:

(1) A waiver of notice executed by all prior personal representatives or attorneys is on file or is filed with the petition;

(2) A written, signed agreement on the allocation of statutory commissions or fees between the present personal representative or attorney and all prior personal representatives or attorneys is on file or is included in or filed with the petition; or

(3) The court's file and the petition demonstrate that the commissions or fees of the prior personal representatives or attorneys have been previously provided for and allowed by the court.

Rule 7.704 adopted effective January 1, 2003.

Rule 7.705. Calculation of statutory compensation

(a) Account filed

A petition for statutory commissions or attorney fees must state the amount of statutory compensation payable and set forth the estate accounted for and the calculation of statutory compensation. The calculation must be stated in the petition in substantially the following form:

COMMISSION OR FEE BASE

Inventory and Appraisal	$____
Receipts, Excluding Principal	$____
Gains on Sales	$____
Losses on Sales	$(____)
TOTAL COMMISSION OR FEE BASE	$____

COMMISSION OR FEE COMPUTATION

4% on first $100,000	($___)[1]	$___[2]
3% on next $100,000	($___)	$___
2% on next $800,000	($___)	$___
1% on next $9,000,000	($___)	$___
½ of 1% on next $15,000,000	($___)	$___
Amount requested from the court for estates above $25,000,000	($___)	$___
TOTAL COMMISSION OR FEE		$___[3]

1. Enter in this column the amount of the estate accounted for in each category. The sum of the entries in this column would equal the total commission or fee base.
2. Enter in this column the product of the amount of the estate accounted for in each category multiplied by the percentage for that category.
3. Enter here the sum of the products entered in this column.

(b) Account waived

When an account has been waived, the report must contain the information required by rule 7.550. If the report is accompanied by a request for statutory commissions or fees, the basis for their computation must be included in the petition substantially in the form provided in (a). Notwithstanding the waiver of account, if the petition and report requests statutory commissions or fees based on any amount other than the amount of the Inventory and Appraisal, detailed schedules of receipts and gains and losses on sales must be included.

Rule 7.705 adopted effective January 1, 2003.

Rule 7.706. Compensation when personal representative is an attorney

(a) Personal representative's compensation only

Notwithstanding the provisions of the decedent's will, a personal representative who is an attorney may receive the personal representative's compensation but may not receive compensation for legal services as the attorney for the personal representative unless the court approves the right to compensation for legal services in advance and finds the arrangement is to the advantage, benefit, and best interest of the decedent's estate.

(b) Agreement not to participate in compensation

A law firm of which the personal representative is a partner or shareholder may request compensation for legal services in addition to the personal representative's compensation if a written agreement not to participate in each other's compensation, signed by the personal representative and by authorized representatives of the law firm, has been filed in the estate proceeding.

Rule 7.706 adopted effective January 1, 2003.

Rule 7.707. Application of compensation provisions

For proceedings commenced after June 30, 1991, the law in effect on the date of the court's order awarding statutory compensation determines the amount of such compensation.

Rule 7.707 adopted effective January 1, 2003.

Chapter 16
Compensation in All Matters Other Than Decedents' Estates

Rule 7.750. Application of rules to guardianships and conservatorships
Rule 7.751. Petitions for orders allowing compensation for guardians or conservators and their attorneys
Rule 7.752. Court may order accounting before allowing compensation
Rule 7.753. Contingency fee agreements in guardianships and conservatorships
Rule 7.754. Use of paralegals in the performance of legal services for the guardian or conservator
Rule 7.755. Advance payments and periodic payments to guardians, conservators, and to their attorneys on account for future services
Rule 7.756. Compensation of conservators and guardians
Rule 7.776. Compensation of trustees

Rule 7.750. Application of rules to guardianships and conservatorships

The rules in this chapter apply to guardianships and conservatorships under division 4 of the Probate Code (Prob. Code, § 1400 et seq.) and to conservatorships under the Lanterman-Petris-Short Act (Welf. & Inst. Code, §§ 5350–5371). They do not apply to guardianships under chapter 2 of division 2 of the Welfare and Institutions Code (Welf. & Inst. Code, § 200 et seq.). Under Probate Code section 2646, the rules in this chapter applicable to guardianships and conservatorships apply only to compensation payable from the estate of the ward or conservatee or from money or property recovered or collected for the estate of the ward or conservatee.

Rule 7.750 adopted effective January 1, 2003.

Rule 7.751. Petitions for orders allowing compensation for guardians or conservators and their attorneys

(a) Petition for allowance of compensation for services performed before appointment of guardian or conservator

A petition for allowance of compensation to a guardian or conservator or to the attorney for a guardian or conservator may include a request for compensation for services rendered before an order appointing a guardian or conservator. The petition must show facts demonstrating the necessity for preappointment services.

(Subd (a) amended effective January 1, 2007.)

(b) Required showing in petition for allowance of compensation

All petitions for orders fixing and allowing compensation must comply with the requirements of rule 7.702 concerning petitions for extraordinary compensation in decedents' estates, to the extent applicable to guardianships and conservatorships, except that the best interest of the ward or conservatee is to be considered instead of the interest of beneficiaries of the estate.

Rule 7.751 amended effective January 1, 2007; adopted effective January 1, 2003.

Rule 7.752. Court may order accounting before allowing compensation

Notwithstanding the time period after which a petition may be filed for an allowance of compensation to a guardian, conservator, or an attorney for a guardian or conservator, the court may order the guardian or conservator to file an accounting before or at the time a petition for an allowance of compensation is filed or heard.

Rule 7.752 adopted effective January 1, 2003.

Rule 7.753. Contingency fee agreements in guardianships and conservatorships

A guardian or conservator of the estate may contract with an attorney for a contingency fee for the attorney's services on behalf of the ward or

conservatee, or the estate, in connection with a matter that is of a type customarily the subject of a contingency fee agreement, if the court has authorized the guardian or conservator to do so, or if the agreement has been approved by the court under Probate Code section 2644. The agreement must also satisfy the requirements of rule 7.703(d)(1).
Rule 7.753 adopted effective January 1, 2003.

Rule 7.754. Use of paralegals in the performance of legal services for the guardian or conservator

An attorney for a guardian or conservator may use the services of a paralegal acting under the direction and supervision of the attorney. A request for an allowance of compensation for the services of a paralegal must satisfy the requirements of rule 7.703(e).
Rule 7.754 adopted effective January 1, 2003.

Rule 7.755. Advance payments and periodic payments to guardians, conservators, and to their attorneys on account for future services

(a) No advance payments

A guardian or conservator must neither pay nor receive, and the attorney for a guardian or conservator must not receive, any payment from the estate of the ward or conservatee for services rendered in advance of an order of the court authorizing the payment. If an advance payment is made or received, the court may surcharge the guardian or conservator in the manner provided in rule 7.700(b), in addition to removing the guardian or conservator or imposing any other sanction authorized by law on the guardian or conservator or on the attorney.

(b) Periodic payments to attorneys on account

A guardian or conservator may request the court to authorize periodic payment of attorney fees on account of future services under Probate Code section 2643 on a showing of an ongoing need for legal services.
Rule 7.755 adopted effective January 1, 2003.

Rule 7.756. Compensation of conservators and guardians

(a) Standards for determining just and reasonable compensation

The court may consider the following nonexclusive factors in determining just and reasonable compensation for a conservator from the estate of the conservatee or a guardian from the estate of the ward for services rendered in the best interest of the conservatee or ward up to that time:

(1) The size and nature of the conservatee's or ward's estate;
(2) The benefit to the conservatee or ward, or his or her estate, of the conservator's or guardian's services;
(3) The necessity for the services performed;
(4) The conservatee's or ward's anticipated future needs and income;
(5) The time spent by the conservator or guardian in the performance of services;
(6) Whether the services performed were routine or required more than ordinary skill or judgment;
(7) Any unusual skill, expertise, or experience brought to the performance of services;
(8) The conservator's or guardian's estimate of the value of the services performed; and
(9) The compensation customarily allowed by the court in the community where the court is located for the management of conservatorships or guardianships of similar size and complexity.

(Subd (a) amended effective January 1, 2023; adopted effective January 1, 2008.)

(b) No single factor determinative

No single factor listed in (a) should be the exclusive basis for the court's determination of just and reasonable compensation for services rendered in the best interest of the conservatee or ward.

(Subd (b) amended effective January 1, 2023; adopted effective January 1, 2008.)

(c) No inflexible maximum or minimum compensation or maximum approved hourly rate

This rule is not authority for a court to set an inflexible maximum or minimum compensation or a maximum approved hourly rate for compensation.

(Subd (c) adopted effective January 1, 2008.)
Rule 7.756 amended effective January 1, 2023; adopted effective January 1, 2008.

Rule 7.776. Compensation of trustees

In determining or approving compensation of a trustee, the court may consider, among other factors, the following:

(1) The gross income of the trust estate;
(2) The success or failure of the trustee's administration;
(3) Any unusual skill, expertise, or experience brought to the trustee's work;
(4) The fidelity or disloyalty shown by the trustee;
(5) The amount of risk and responsibility assumed by the trustee;
(6) The time spent in the performance of the trustee's duties;
(7) The custom in the community where the court is located regarding compensation authorized by settlors, compensation allowed by the court, or charges of corporate trustees for trusts of similar size and complexity; and
(8) Whether the work performed was routine, or required more than ordinary skill or judgment.

Rule 7.776 renumbered effective January 1, 2008; adopted as rule 7.756 effective January 1, 2003; previously amended effective January 1, 2007.

Chapter 17
Contested Hearings and Trials

Rule 7.801. Objections and responses
Rule 7.802. Electronic filing and service in contested probate proceedings

Rule 7.801. Objections and responses

If the court continues a matter to allow a written objection or response to be made, and the responding or objecting party fails to serve and file a timely objection or response, the court may deem the objections or responses waived.
Rule 7.801 adopted effective January 1, 2000.

Rule 7.802. Electronic filing and service in contested probate proceedings

The provisions of Code of Civil Procedure section 1010.6 and rules 2.250–2.261 of the California Rules of Court concerning filing and service by electronic means apply to contested proceedings under the Probate Code and the Probate Rules to the same extent as they apply to other contested civil proceedings in each superior court in this state.
Rule 7.802 adopted effective January 1, 2016.

Chapter 18
Discovery
[Reserved]

Chapter 19
Trusts

Rule 7.901. Trustee's accounts
Rule 7.902. Beneficiaries to be listed in petitions and accounts
Rule 7.903. Trusts funded by court order

Rule 7.901. Trustee's accounts

(a) Period covered

A trustee's account must state the period covered by the account.

(Subd (a) amended effective January 1, 2002.)

(b) First account

The first account in a testamentary trust must reconcile the initial assets on hand with the decree of distribution of the estate.

(Subd (b) amended effective January 1, 2002.)

(c) Principal and income

All trustee's accounts in a trust that distributes income to a beneficiary must allocate receipts and disbursements between (1) principal receipts and disbursements, and (2) income receipts and disbursements.

(Subd (c) amended effective January 1, 2002.)
Rule 7.901 amended effective January 1, 2002; adopted effective January 1, 2001.

Rule 7.902. Beneficiaries to be listed in petitions and accounts

A petition and account involving a trust must state the names and last known addresses of all vested or contingent beneficiaries, including all persons in being who may or will receive income or corpus of the trust, provided, however, that (1) during the time that the trust is revocable and the person holding the power to revoke the trust is competent, the names and last known addresses of beneficiaries who do not hold the power to revoke do not need to be stated, and (2) the petition or account does not need to state the name and last known address of any beneficiary who need not be given notice under Probate Code section 15804.
Rule 7.902 amended effective January 1, 2007; adopted effective January 1, 2002.

Rule 7.903. Trusts funded by court order

(a) Definitions

(1) "Trust funded by court order" under this rule means and refers to a trust that will receive funds under Probate Code section 2580 et seq. (substituted judgment); section 3100 et seq. (proceedings for particular transactions involving disabled spouses or registered domestic partners); or section 3600 et seq. (settlement of claims or actions or disposition of judgments involving minors or persons with disabilities).

(2) "Continuing jurisdiction of the court" under (b) means and refers to the court's continuing subject matter jurisdiction over trust proceedings under division 9 of the Probate Code (Prob. Code, § 15000 et seq.).

(3) "Court supervision under the Probate Code" under (b) means and refers to the court's authority to require prior court approval or subsequent confirmation of the actions of the trustee as for the actions of a guardian or conservator of the estate under division 4 of the Probate Code (Prob. Code, § 1400 et seq.).

(b) Continuing jurisdiction and court supervision

The order creating or approving the funding of a trust funded by court order must provide that the trust is subject to the continuing jurisdiction of the court and may provide that the trust is to be subject to court supervision under the Probate Code.

(c) Required provisions in trust instruments

Except as provided in (d), unless the court otherwise orders for good cause shown, trust instruments for trusts funded by court order must:

(1) Not contain "no-contest" provisions;

(2) Prohibit modification or revocation without court approval;

(3) Clearly identify the trustee and any other person with authority to direct the trustee to make disbursements;

(4) Prohibit investments by the trustee other than those permitted under Probate Code section 2574;

(5) Require persons identified in (3) to post bond in the amount required under Probate Code section 2320 et seq.;

(6) Require the trustee to file accounts and reports for court approval in the manner and frequency required by Probate Code sections 1060 et seq. and 2620 et seq.;

(7) Require court approval of changes in trustees and a court order appointing any successor trustee; and

(8) Require compensation of the trustee, the members of any advisory committee, or the attorney for the trustee, to be in just and reasonable amounts that must be fixed and allowed by the court. The instrument may provide for periodic payments of compensation on account, subject to the requirements of Probate Code section 2643 and rule 7.755.

(Subd (c) amended effective January 1, 2007; previously amended effective July 1, 2005.)

(d) Trust instruments for smaller trusts

Unless the court otherwise orders for good cause shown, the requirements of (c)(5)–(8) of this rule do not apply to trust instruments for trusts that will have total assets of $20,000 or less after receipt of the property ordered by the court.

Rule 7.903 amended effective January 1, 2007; adopted effective January 1, 2005; previously amended effective July 1, 2005.

Advisory Committee Comment

Subdivision (a) of this rule defines a court-funded trust as a product of three court proceedings. Two of these—a petition for substituted judgment in a probate conservatorship (Prob. Code, § 2580) and a proceeding for a particular transaction in the property of an impaired spouse or domestic partner without a conservator (Prob. Code, § 3100; Fam. Code, § 297.5)—are regularly heard in the probate department of the court. The third proceeding, an application for an order approving the settlement of a minor's claim or a pending action involving a minor or person with a disability or approving the disposition of the proceeds of a judgment in favor of a minor or person with a disability (Prob. Code, § 3600), may be heard in either a probate or a civil department.

The Judicial Council has adopted standard 7.10 of the Standards of Judicial Administration to address proceedings under Probate Code section 3600 that involve court-funded trusts and are heard in civil departments. The standard makes two recommendations concerning the expertise of judicial officers who hear these proceedings on trust issues. The recommendations are to develop practices and procedures that (1) provide for determination of the trust issues in these matters by the probate department of the court or by a judicial officer who regularly hears probate proceedings or (2) ensure that judicial officers who hear these matters have experience or receive training in substantive and technical issues involving trusts, including special needs trusts.

Chapter 20
Claims of Minors and Persons With Disabilities

Rule 7.950. Petition for approval of compromise of claim or action or disposition of proceeds of judgment for minor or person with a disability
Rule 7.950.5. Petition for expedited approval of compromise of claim or action or disposition of proceeds of judgment for minor or person with a disability
Rule 7.951. Disclosure of attorney's interest in petition for approval of compromise of claim
Rule 7.952. Attendance at hearing on petition for approval of compromise of claim
Rule 7.953. Order for the deposit of funds of a minor or a person with a disability
Rule 7.954. Petition for the withdrawal of funds deposited for a minor or a person with a disability
Rule 7.955. Attorney's fees for services to minor or person with a disability

Rule 7.950. Petition for approval of compromise of claim or action or disposition of proceeds of judgment for minor or person with a disability

A petition for court approval of a compromise of, or a covenant not to sue or enforce judgment on, a minor's disputed claim; a compromise or settlement of a pending action or proceeding to which a minor or person with a disability is a party; or the disposition of the proceeds of a judgment for a minor or person with a disability under Probate Code sections 3500 and 3600–3613 or Code of Civil Procedure section 372 must be verified by the petitioner and must contain a full disclosure of all information that has any bearing on the reasonableness of the compromise, covenant, settlement, or disposition. Except as provided in rule 7.950.5, the petition must be submitted on a completed *Petition for Approval of Compromise of Claim or Action or Disposition of Proceeds of Judgment for Minor or Person With a Disability* (form MC-350).

Rule 7.950 amended effective January 1, 2021; adopted effective January 1, 2002; previously amended effective January 1, 2007, and January 1, 2010.

Rule 7.950.5. Petition for expedited approval of compromise of claim or action or disposition of proceeds of judgment for minor or person with a disability

(a) Authorized use of petition for expedited approval

If all the circumstances specified in paragraphs (1) through (9) of this rule exist, a petitioner for court approval of a compromise of, or a covenant not to sue or enforce judgment on, a minor's disputed claim; a compromise or settlement of a pending action or proceeding to which a minor or person with a disability is a party; or the disposition of the proceeds of a judgment for a minor or person with a disability under Probate Code sections 3500 and 3600–3613 or Code of Civil Procedure section 372 may satisfy the disclosure requirements of rule 7.950 by submitting the petition on a completed *Petition for Expedited Approval of Compromise of Claim or Action or Disposition of Proceeds of Judgment for Minor or Person With a Disability* (form MC-350EX).

(1) The petitioner is represented by an attorney authorized to practice in the courts of this state;

(2) The claim is not for damages for the wrongful death of a person;

(3) No portion of the net proceeds of the compromise, settlement, or judgment in favor of the minor or disabled claimant is to be placed in a trust;

(4) There are no unresolved disputes concerning liens to be satisfied from the proceeds of the compromise, settlement, or judgment;

(5) The petitioner's attorney did not become involved in the matter at the direct or indirect request of a person against whom the claim is asserted or an insurance carrier for that person;

(6) The petitioner's attorney is neither employed by nor associated with a defendant or insurance carrier in connection with the petition;

(7) If an action has been filed on the claim:

(A) All defendants that have appeared in the action are participating in the compromise; or

(B) The court has finally determined that the settling parties entered into the settlement in good faith;

(8) The judgment for the minor or claimant with a disability (exclusive of interest and costs) or the total amount payable to the minor or claimant with a disability and all other parties under the proposed compromise or settlement is $50,000 or less or, if greater:

(A) The total amount payable to the minor or claimant with a disability represents payment of the individual-person policy limits of all liability insurance policies covering all proposed contributing parties; and

(B) All proposed contributing parties would be substantially unable to discharge an adverse judgment on the claim from assets other than the proceeds of their liability insurance policies; and

(9) The court does not otherwise order.

(Subd (a) amended effective January 1, 2021; adopted effective January 1, 2010.)

(b) Determination of petition

A petition for expedited approval must be determined by the court not more than 35 days after it is filed, unless a hearing is requested, required, or scheduled under (c), or the time for determination is extended for good cause by order of the court.

(Subd (b) amended effective January 1, 2021; adopted effective January 1, 2010.)

(c) Hearing on petition

(1) The petition for expedited approval must be determined by the court without a hearing unless:

(A) A hearing is requested by the petitioner at the time the petition is filed;

(B) An objection or other opposition to the petition is filed by an interested party; or

(C) A hearing is scheduled by the court under (2) or (3).

(2) The court may, on its own motion, elect to schedule and conduct a hearing on a petition for expedited approval. The court must make its election to schedule the hearing and must give notice of its election and the date, time, and place of the hearing to the petitioner and all other interested parties not more than 25 days after the date the petition is filed.

(3) If the court decides not to grant a petition for expedited approval in full as requested, it must schedule a hearing and give notice of its intended ruling and the date, time, and place of the hearing to the petitioner and all other interested parties within the time provided in (2).

(Subd (c) amended effective January 1, 2021; adopted effective January 1, 2010.)

Rule 7.950.5 amended effective January 1, 2021; adopted effective January 1, 2010.

Rule 7.951. Disclosure of attorney's interest in petition for approval of compromise of claim

If the petitioner has been represented or assisted by an attorney in preparing the petition for approval of the compromise of the claim or in any other respect with regard to the claim, the petition must disclose the following information:

(1) The name, state bar number, law firm, if any, and business address of the attorney;

(2) Whether the attorney became involved with the petition, directly or indirectly, at the instance of any party against whom the claim is asserted or of any party's insurance carrier;

(3) Whether the attorney represents or is employed by any other party or any insurance carrier involved in the matter;

(4) Whether the attorney has received any attorney's fees or other compensation for services provided in connection with the claim giving rise to the petition or with the preparation of the petition, and, if so, the amounts and the identity of the person who paid the fees or other compensation;

(5) If the attorney has not received any attorney's fees or other compensation for services provided in connection with the claim giving rise to the petition or with the preparation of the petition, whether the attorney expects to receive any fees or other compensation for these services, and, if so, the amounts and the identity of the person who is expected to pay the fees or other compensation; and

(6) The terms of any agreement between the petitioner and the attorney.

Rule 7.951 amended effective January 1, 2021; adopted effective January 1, 2002.

Rule 7.952. Attendance at hearing on petition for approval of compromise of claim

(a) Attendance of petitioner and claimant

The person petitioning for approval of the compromise of the claim on behalf of the minor or person with a disability and the minor or person with a disability must attend the hearing on the petition unless the court for good cause dispenses with their personal appearance.

(Subd (a) amended effective January 1, 2021; previously amended effective January 1, 2007.)

(b) Attendance of physician and other witnesses

The court may require the presence and testimony of witnesses, including the attending or examining physician, at the hearing.

(Subd (b) amended effective January 1, 2021.)

Rule 7.952 amended effective January 1, 2021; adopted effective January 1, 2002; previously amended effective January 1, 2007.

Rule 7.953. Order for the deposit of funds of a minor or a person with a disability

(a) Acknowledgment of receipt by financial institution

In any case in which the court orders that funds to be received by a minor or a person with a disability must be deposited in a financial institution and not disbursed without further order of the court, the order must include a provision that a certified or filed endorsed copy of the order must be delivered to a manager at the financial institution where the funds are to be deposited, and that a receipt from the financial institution must be promptly filed with the court, acknowledging receipt of both the funds deposited and the order for deposit of funds.

(Subd (a) amended effective January 1, 2007.)

(b) Order permitting the withdrawal of funds by a former minor

If, in the order approving the compromise of a minor's claim, there is a finding that the minor will attain the age of majority on a definite date, the order for deposit may require that the depository permit the withdrawal of funds by the former minor after that date, without further order of the court.

Rule 7.953 amended effective January 1, 2007; adopted effective January 1, 2002.

Rule 7.954. Petition for the withdrawal of funds deposited for a minor or a person with a disability

(a) Verified petition required

A petition for the withdrawal of funds deposited for a minor or a person with a disability must be verified and must include the identity of the depository, a showing of the amounts previously withdrawn, a statement of the balance on deposit at the time of the filing of the petition, and a justification for the withdrawal.

(Subd (a) amended effective January 1, 2007.)

(b) Ex parte or noticed hearing

A petition for the withdrawal of funds may be considered ex parte or set for a hearing at the discretion of the court.

Rule 7.954 amended effective January 1, 2007; adopted effective January 1, 2002.

Rule 7.955. Attorney's fees for services to minor or person with a disability

(a) Reasonable attorney's fees

(1) In all cases under Code of Civil Procedure section 372 or Probate Code sections 3600–3601, unless the court has approved the fee agreement in advance, the court must use a reasonable fee standard when approving and allowing the amount of attorney's fees payable from money or property paid or to be paid for the benefit of a minor or a person with a disability.

(2) The court must give consideration to the terms of any representation agreement made between the attorney and the representative of the minor or person with a disability and must evaluate the agreement based on the facts and circumstances existing at the time the agreement was made, except where the attorney and the representative of the minor or person with a disability contemplated that the attorney's fee would be affected by later events.

(Subd (a) amended and lettered effective January 1, 2010; adopted as unlettered subd effective January 1, 2003.)

(b) Factors the court may consider in determining a reasonable attorney's fee

In determining a reasonable attorney's fee, the court may consider the following nonexclusive factors:

(1) The fact that a minor or person with a disability is involved and the circumstances of that minor or person with a disability.

(2) The amount of the fee in proportion to the value of the services performed.

(3) The novelty and difficulty of the questions involved and the skill required to perform the legal services properly.

(4) The amount involved and the results obtained.

(5) The time limitations or constraints imposed by the representative of the minor or person with a disability or by the circumstances.

(6) The nature and length of the professional relationship between the attorney and the representative of the minor or person with a disability.

(7) The experience, reputation, and ability of the attorney or attorneys performing the legal services.

(8) The time and labor required.

(9) The informed consent of the representative of the minor or person with a disability to the fee.

(10) The relative sophistication of the attorney and the representative of the minor or person with a disability.

(11) The likelihood, if apparent to the representative of the minor or person with a disability when the representation agreement was made, that the attorney's acceptance of the particular employment would preclude other employment.

(12) Whether the fee is fixed, hourly, or contingent.

(13) If the fee is contingent:

(A) The risk of loss borne by the attorney;

(B) The amount of costs advanced by the attorney; and

(C) The delay in payment of fees and reimbursement of costs paid by the attorney.

(14) Statutory requirements for representation agreements applicable to particular cases or claims.

(Subd (b) adopted effective January 1, 2010.)

(c) Attorney's declaration

A petition requesting court approval and allowance of an attorney's fee under (a) must include a declaration from the attorney that addresses the factors listed in (b) that are applicable to the matter before the court.

(Subd (c) adopted effective January 1, 2010.)

(d) Preemption

The Judicial Council has preempted all local rules relating to the determination of reasonable attorney's fees to be awarded from the proceeds of a compromise, settlement, or judgment under Probate Code sections 3600–3601. No trial court, or any division or branch of a trial court, may enact or enforce any local rule concerning this field, except a rule pertaining to the assignment or scheduling of a hearing on a petition or application for court approval or allowance of attorney's fees under sections 3600–3601. All local rules concerning this field are null and void unless otherwise permitted by a statute or a rule in the California Rules of Court.

(Subd (d) adopted effective January 1, 2010.)

Rule 7.955 amended effective January 1, 2021; adopted effective January 1, 2003; previously amended effective January 1, 2007, and January 1, 2010.

Advisory Committee Comment

This rule requires the court to approve and allow attorney's fees in an amount that is reasonable under all the facts and circumstances, under Probate Code section 3601. The rule is declaratory of existing law concerning attorney's fees under a contingency fee agreement when the fees must be approved by the court. The facts and circumstances that the court may consider are discussed in a large body of decisional law under section 3601 and under other statutes that require the court to determine reasonable attorney's fees. The factors listed in rule 7.955(b) are modeled in part after those provided in rule 1.5 of the Rules of Professional Conduct of the State Bar of California concerning an unconscionable attorney's fee, but the advisory committee does not intend to suggest or imply that an attorney's fee must be found to be unconscionable under rule 1.5 to be determined to be unreasonable under this rule.

The rule permits, but does not require, the court to allow attorney's fees in an amount specified in a contingency fee agreement. The amount of attorney's fees allowed by the court must meet the reasonableness standard of section 3601 no matter how they are determined.

Chapter 21
Guardianships

Rule 7.1001. Guardian screening form
Rule 7.1002. Acknowledgment of receipt of *Duties of Guardian*
Rule 7.1002.5. Guardianship of ward 18 to 20 years of age
Rule 7.1003. Confidential guardianship status report (Prob. Code, § 1513.2)
Rule 7.1004. Termination of guardianship
Rule 7.1005. Service of copy of final account or report after resignation or removal of guardian
Rule 7.1006. Service of copy of final account on termination of guardianship
Rule 7.1007. Settlement of accounts and release by former minor
Rule 7.1008. Visitation by former guardian after termination of guardianship
Rule 7.1009. Standards of conduct for the guardian of the estate
Rule 7.1011. Taking possession of an asset of the ward at an institution or opening or changing ownership of an account or safe-deposit box in a financial institution
Rule 7.1012. The good cause exception to notice of the hearing on a petition for appointment of a temporary guardian
Rule 7.1013. Change of ward's residence
Rule 7.1014. Communications between courts in different California counties concerning guardianship venue
Rule 7.1015. Guardianship and certain conservatorship proceedings involving Indian children (Prob. Code, §§ 1449, 1459, 1459.5, 1460.2, 1511(b), (i); Welf. & Inst. Code, §§ 224–224.6; 25 U.S.C. §§ 1901–1963; 25 C.F.R. §§ 23.1–23.144)
Rule 7.1016. Participation and testimony of wards in guardianship proceedings
Rule 7.1020. Special Immigrant Juvenile findings in guardianship proceedings

Rule 7.1001. Guardian screening form

(a) Screening form to be submitted with petition

Each proposed probate guardian, except a public guardian, or a bank or other entity entitled to conduct the business of a trust company, must submit to the court with the petition for appointment of guardian a completed *Confidential Guardian Screening Form* (form GC-212).

(Subd (a) amended effective January 1, 2002.)

(b) Use of form

The information on the *Confidential Guardian Screening Form* is used by the court and by persons or agencies designated by the court to assist the court in determining whether a proposed guardian should be appointed.

(Subd (b) amended effective January 1, 2002.)

(c) Form to be confidential

The *Confidential Guardian Screening Form* and the information contained on the form are confidential. The clerk must maintain these forms in a manner that will protect and preserve their confidentiality.

(Subd (c) amended effective January 1, 2007; previously amended effective January 1, 2002.)

Rule 7.1001 amended effective January 1, 2007; adopted effective January 1, 2001; previously amended effective January 1, 2002.

Rule 7.1002. Acknowledgment of receipt of *Duties of Guardian*

Before the court issues letters, each guardian must execute and file an acknowledgment of receipt of the *Duties of Guardian* (form GC-248).

Rule 7.1002 amended effective July 1, 2016; adopted effective January 1, 2001; previously amended effective January 1, 2002, and January 1, 2007.

Rule 7.1002.5. Guardianship of ward 18 to 20 years of age

(a) Authority

The court may extend an existing guardianship of the person past a ward's 18th birthday or appoint a new guardian of the person for a ward who is at least 18 but not yet 21 years of age if the ward is the petitioner or has given consent as provided in section 1510.1 of the Probate Code and this rule.

(Subd (a) adopted effective July 1, 2016.)

(b) Consent to appointment of guardian of the person

The court may appoint a new guardian of the person under this rule only if the ward has given consent, both to the appointment and to the guardian's performance of the duties of a guardian, by signing the petition.

(Subd (b) adopted effective July 1, 2016.)

(c) Consent to extension of guardianship of the person

The court may extend a guardianship of the person under this rule only if the ward has given consent, both to the extension and to the guardian's continued performance of the duties of a guardian, by signing the *Petition to Extend Guardianship of the Person* (form GC-210(PE)).

(Subd (c) adopted effective July 1, 2016.)

(d) Dispute

In the event of a dispute over the guardian's intended action, the guardian may not act against the ward's desires without the ward's express consent unless failure to act as intended would breach the guardian's fiduciary duties to the ward.

(Subd (d) adopted effective July 1, 2016.)

(e) Modification of consent

(1) A ward may withdraw his or her consent to the establishment or extension of a guardianship under this rule by filing a petition to terminate the guardianship under rule 7.1004(b)(2)(B).

(2) In addition to any other petition authorized by section 2359(a), the ward may file a petition at any time during a guardianship established or extended under this rule to withdraw or modify his or her consent to the guardian's performance of a specific duty or duties.

(Subd (e) adopted effective July 1, 2016.)

Rule 7.1002.5 adopted effective July 1, 2016.

Rule 7.1003. Confidential guardianship status report (Prob. Code, § 1513.2)

(a) Due date of status report

Each guardian required by the court to complete, sign, and file the status report authorized by Probate Code section 1513.2 must file the completed and signed report no later than one month after the anniversary of the date of the order appointing him or her as guardian. Co-guardians may sign and file their reports jointly.

(b) Court clerk's duties

The clerk of each court that requires guardians to file the status report authorized by Probate Code section 1513.2 must:

(1) Determine the annual due date for the completed report from each appointed guardian required to file the report;

(2) Fill in the due date for the completed report, in the space provided in the form for that purpose, on each blank copy of the form that must be mailed to appointed guardians under (3); and

(3) Mail by first class mail to each appointed guardian no later than one month prior to the date the status report is due under (a) a blank copy of *Confidential Guardianship Status Report* (form GC-251) for each child under guardianship under the same case number.

(Subd (b) amended effective January 1, 2007.)

(c) Access to status report

(1) Except as provided in paragraph (2), the clerk must make a status report submitted under Probate Code section 1513.2 available only to persons served in the guardianship proceedings or their attorneys.

(2) If the ward is an Indian child and the child's tribe has intervened in the proceeding, the clerk must also make the status report available to the representative designated by the child's tribe.

(3) Paragraphs (1) and (2) are not intended to preclude an interested person or an Indian child's tribe that has not intervened from filing a petition for a court order directing the clerk to make the status report available to that person or tribe.

(Subd (c) adopted effective January 1, 2022.)

Rule 7.1003 amended effective January 1, 2022; adopted effective January 1, 2004; previously amended effective January 1, 2007.

Rule 7.1004. Termination of guardianship

(a) Operation of law or court order

A guardianship of the person or estate of a minor may terminate by operation of law or may be terminated by court order where the court determines that it would be in the ward's best interest to terminate the guardianship.

(b) Guardian of the person

(1) Under Probate Code section 1600 a guardianship of the person terminates by operation of law, and the guardian of the person need not file a petition for its termination, when the ward attains majority except as provided in (2), dies, is adopted, or is emancipated.

(2) If the court has appointed a guardian of the person for a ward 18 years of age or older or extended a guardianship of the person past the ward's 18th birthday, the guardianship terminates:

(A) By operation of law when the ward attains 21 years of age, marries, or dies; or

(B) By order of the court when the ward files a petition under Probate Code section 1601.

(Subd (b) amended effective July 1, 2016.)

(c) Duty of guardian of estate on termination

A guardian of the estate whose administration is terminated by operation of law or court order must file and obtain the court's approval of a final account or report of the administration.

Rule 7.1004 amended effective July 1, 2016; adopted effective January 1, 2004.

Rule 7.1005. Service of copy of final account or report after resignation or removal of guardian

A resigned or removed guardian of the estate must serve a copy of the guardian's final account or report and the petition for its settlement, with the notice of hearing that must be served on the successor guardian of the estate under Probate Code section 1460(b)(1), unless the court dispenses with such service.

Rule 7.1005 adopted effective January 1, 2004.

Rule 7.1006. Service of copy of final account on termination of guardianship

(a) Minor living

In addition to service of notices of hearing required under Probate Code section 1460(b), on termination of the guardianship the guardian of the estate must serve a copy of the guardian's final account and petition for its settlement on the minor, unless the court dispenses with such service.

(b) Personal representative of deceased minor

If the minor is deceased, in addition to service of notices of hearing required under Probate Code section 1460(b), on termination of the guardianship the guardian of the estate must serve a notice of hearing and a copy of the guardian's final account and petition for its settlement on the personal representative of the deceased minor's estate, unless the court dispenses with such service.

(c) Successors in interest to deceased minor

If the minor is deceased and no personal representative of the minor's estate has been appointed or qualified or if the personal representative of the minor's estate is also the guardian, on termination of the guardianship, in addition to the notices of hearing required under Probate Code section 1460(b), the guardian of the estate must serve a notice of hearing and a copy of the guardian's final account and petition for its settlement on the persons entitled to succeed to the deceased minor's estate, unless the court dispenses with such service.

Rule 7.1006 adopted effective January 1, 2004.

Rule 7.1007. Settlement of accounts and release by former minor

(a) Release of guardian of estate by ward after majority

A ward who has attained majority may settle accounts with his or her guardian of the estate and may give a valid release to the guardian if the court determines, at the time of the hearing on the final account, or on the final report and petition for termination on waiver of account, that the release has been obtained fairly and without undue influence. The release is not effective to discharge the guardian until one year after the ward has attained majority.

(b) Appearance of ward

The court may require the personal appearance of the ward at the hearing on the final account or report of the guardian of the estate after termination of the guardianship.

Rule 7.1007 adopted effective January 1, 2004.

Rule 7.1008. Visitation by former guardian after termination of guardianship

(a) Visitation order at time of termination of guardianship

Subject to the provisions of Welfare and Institutions Code section 304, a guardian may request the court to order visitation with the child under guardianship at the time of termination of the guardianship either in the guardian's petition for termination or in the guardian's objections or other pleading filed in response to the petition of another party for termination. The court may then order visitation if it is in the best interest of the child.

(b) Request for visitation after termination of guardianship

If no order was entered under (a) concerning visitation between the former guardian and the former ward at termination of the guardianship and no dependency proceedings for the child are pending, the former guardian may request the court to order visitation with the former ward after termination of the guardianship as provided in Family Code section 3105, Probate Code section 1602, rule 5.475, and this rule, as follows:

(1) If either parent of the former ward is living, in an independent action for visitation under the Family Code; or

(2) If neither parent of the former ward is living, in a guardianship proceeding under the Probate Code, including a proceeding commenced for that purpose.

(c) Declaration under UCCJEA

A guardian or former guardian requesting visitation under this rule must file a *Declaration Under Uniform Child Custody Jurisdiction and Enforcement Act (UCCJEA)* (form FL-105/GC-120) with his or her request for visitation.

(Subd (c) amended effective January 1, 2007.)

(d) Transmission of visitation order

Following the termination of the guardianship the clerk of the superior court issuing the visitation order concerning the guardian or former guardian and the ward or former ward must promptly transmit an endorsed filed copy of the order to the superior court of the county where a custody proceeding under the Family Code is pending or, if none, to the superior court of the county in which the custodial parent resides. An order transmitted to the court in the county where the custodial parent resides may be sent to the receiving court's Court Operations Manager, Family Division, or similar senior manager or clerk responsible for the

Rule 7.1009. Standards of conduct for the guardian of the estate

Except as otherwise required by statute, in the exercise of ordinary care and diligence in managing and controlling the estates of the ward, the guardian of the estate is to be guided by the following principles:

(a) Avoidance of actual and apparent conflicts of interest with the ward

The guardian must avoid actual conflicts of interest and, consistent with his or her fiduciary duty to the ward, the appearance of conflicts of interest. The guardian must avoid any personal, business, or professional interest or relationship that is or reasonably could be perceived as being self-serving or adverse to the best interest of the ward. In particular:

(1) Except as appropriate for guardians who are not professional fiduciaries with full disclosure to the court, the guardian should not personally provide medical or legal services to the ward;

(2) The guardian must be independent from all service providers, except when (a) no other guardian or service providers are reasonably available, (b) the exception is in the best interest of the ward, (c) the circumstances are fully disclosed to the court, and (d) prior court approval has been obtained;

(3) The guardian must neither solicit nor accept incentives from service providers; and

(4) The guardian must not engage his or her family members to provide services to the ward for a profit or fee when other alternatives are reasonably available. Where family members do provide such services, their relationship to the guardian must be fully disclosed to the court, the terms of engagement must be in the best interest of the ward compared to the terms available from independent service providers, the services must be competently performed, and the guardian must be able to exercise appropriate control and supervision.

A guardian's employees, including family members, are not service providers and are not providing services to the ward for a profit or fee within the meaning of this rule if their compensation is paid by the guardian and their services are either included in the guardian's petition for allowance of the guardian's compensation or are not paid from the ward's estate.

(Subd (a) adopted effective January 1, 2008.)

(b) Guardianship estate management

In addition to complying with applicable standards of estate management specified in rule 7.1059(b), the guardian of the estate must:

(1) Manage the estate primarily for the ward's long-term benefit if the ward has a parent available who can provide sufficient support;

(2) If it would be in the best interest of the ward and the estate, consider requesting court authority to support the ward from the estate if the ward does not have a parent available who can provide sufficient support.

(Subd (b) adopted effective January 1, 2008.)
Rule 7.1009 adopted effective January 1, 2008.

Advisory Committee Comment

The Probate and Mental Health Advisory Committee consulted with several organizations in the development of rule 7.1009, including the National Guardianship Association, a nationwide voluntary association of professional and family fiduciaries, guardians, and allied professionals. In developing this rule, the Probate and Mental Health Advisory Committee considered the National Guardianship Association's Standards of Practice. Some of these standards have been incorporated into the rule.

Rule 7.1010. Qualifications and continuing education requirements for private professional guardians [Repealed]

Rule 7.1010 repealed effective July 1, 2008; amended effective January 1, 2007; adopted effective January 1, 2006; previously amended effective July 1, 2006.

Rule 7.1011. Taking possession of an asset of the ward at an institution or opening or changing ownership of an account or safe-deposit box in a financial institution

(a) Definitions

As used in this rule, the following terms have the meanings stated below:

(1) An "institution" is an insurance company, insurance broker, insurance agent, investment company, investment bank, securities broker-dealer, investment advisor, financial planner, financial advisor, or any other person who takes, holds, or controls an asset subject to a guardianship that is not a "financial institution" within the meaning of this rule;

(2) A "financial institution" is a bank, trust (except as provided in (d)), savings and loan association, savings bank, industrial bank, or credit union; and

(3) "Taking possession" or "taking control" of an asset held or controlled by an institution includes changing title to the asset, withdrawing all or any portion of the asset, or transferring all or any portion of the asset from the institution.

(Subd (a) adopted effective January 1, 2009.)

(b) Responsibilities of the guardian when taking possession or control of an asset of the ward at an institution

When taking possession or control of an asset held by an institution in the name of the ward, the temporary or general guardian of the estate must provide the following to the institution:

(1) A certified copy of the guardian's *Letters of Temporary Guardianship or Conservatorship* (form GC-150) or *Letters of Guardianship* (form GC-250) containing the Notice to Institutions and Financial Institutions on the second page; and

(2) A blank copy of a *Notice of Taking Possession or Control of an Asset of Minor or Conservatee* (form GC-050).

(Subd (b) adopted effective January 1, 2009.)

(c) Responsibilities of the guardian when opening or changing the name on an account or a safe-deposit box in a financial institution

When opening or changing the name on an account or a safe-deposit box in a financial institution, the temporary or general guardian of the estate must provide the following to the financial institution:

(1) A certified copy of the guardian's *Letters of Temporary Guardianship or Conservatorship* (form GC-150) or *Letters of Guardianship* (form GC-250) containing the Notice to Institutions and Financial Institutions on the second page; and

(2) A blank copy of a *Notice of Opening or Changing a Guardianship or Conservatorship Account or Safe-Deposit Box* (form GC-051).

(Subd (c) adopted effective January 1, 2009.)

(d) Application of this rule to trust arrangements

This rule applies to Totten trust accounts but does not apply to any other trust arrangement described in Probate Code section 82(b).

(Subd (d) adopted effective January 1, 2009.)
Rule 7.1011 adopted effective January 1, 2009.

Rule 7.1012. The good cause exception to notice of the hearing on a petition for appointment of a temporary guardian

(a) Purpose

The purpose of this rule is to establish uniform standards for the good cause exception to the notice of the hearing required on a petition for appointment of a temporary guardian under Probate Code section 2250(e).

(Subd (a) amended effective January 1, 2009; adopted effective January 1, 2008.)

(b) Good cause for exceptions to notice limited

Good cause for an exception to the notice required by section 2250(e) must be based on a showing that the exception is necessary to protect the proposed ward or his or her estate from immediate and substantial harm.

(Subd (b) amended effective January 1, 2009; adopted effective January 1, 2008.)

(c) Court may waive or change the time or manner of giving notice

An exception to the notice requirement of section 2250(e) may include one or any combination of the following:

(1) Waiving notice to one, more than one, or all persons entitled to notice;

(2) Requiring a different period of notice; and

(3) Changing the required manner of giving notice, including requiring notice by telephone, fax, e-mail, or a combination of these methods, instead of notice by personal delivery to the proposed ward's parents or to a person with a visitation order.

(Subd (c) amended effective January 1, 2009; adopted effective January 1, 2008.)

(d) Good cause exceptions to notice

Good cause for an exception to the notice requirement of section 2250(e) may include a showing of:

(1) Harm caused by the passage of time. The showing must demonstrate the immediate and substantial harm to the ward or the ward's estate that could occur during the notice period.

(2) Harm that one or more persons entitled to notice might do to the proposed ward, including abduction; or harm to the proposed ward's estate if notice to those persons is given. Such a showing would not support an exception to the requirement to give notice to any other person entitled to notice unless it also demonstrates that notice cannot reasonably be given to the other person without also giving notice to the persons who might cause harm.

(3) The death or incapacity of the proposed ward's custodial parent and the petitioner's status as the custodial parent's nominee.

(4) Medical emergency. The emergency must be immediate and substantial and treatment (1) must be reasonably unavailable unless a temporary guardian is appointed and (2) cannot be deferred for the notice period because of the proposed ward's pain or extreme discomfort or a significant risk of harm.

(5) Financial emergency. The emergency must be immediate and substantial and other means shown likely to be ineffective to prevent loss or further loss to the proposed ward's estate or loss of support for the proposed ward during the notice period.

(Subd (d) amended effective January 1, 2009; adopted effective January 1, 2008.)

(e) Contents of request for good cause exception to notice

(1) When the temporary guardianship petition is prepared on the *Petition for Appointment of Temporary Guardian* (form GC-110), a request for a good cause exception to the notice requirement of section 2250(e) must be in writing, separate from the petition for appointment of a temporary guardian, and must include:

(A) An application containing the case caption and stating the relief requested;

(B) An affirmative factual showing in support of the application in a declaration under penalty of perjury containing competent testimony based on personal knowledge;

(C) A declaration under penalty of perjury based on personal knowledge containing the information required for an ex parte application under rule 3.1204(b); and

(D) A proposed order.

(2) When the temporary guardianship petition is prepared on the *Petition for Appointment of Temporary Guardian of the Person* (form GC-110(P)), a request for a good cause exception to the notice requirement of section 2250(e) may be included in the petition.

(Subd (e) amended effective January 1, 2009; adopted effective January 1, 2008.)

Rule 7.1012 amended effective January 1, 2009; adopted effective January 1, 2008.

Rule 7.1013. Change of ward's residence

(a) Pre-move notice of change of personal residence required

Unless an emergency requires a shorter period of notice, the guardian of the person must mail copies of a notice of an intended change of the ward's personal residence to the persons listed below at least 15 days before the date of the proposed change and file the original notice with proof of mailing with the court. Copies of the notice must be mailed to:

(1) The ward if he or she is 12 years of age or older;

(2) The attorney of record for the ward;

(3) The ward's parents and any former Indian custodian;

(4) Any person who had legal custody of the ward when the first petition for appointment of a guardian was filed in the proceeding;

(5) A guardian of the ward's estate;

(6) Any person who was nominated as guardian of the ward but was not appointed guardian in the proceeding; and

(7) The ward's tribe, if the ward is an Indian child and the ward's tribe has intervened in the proceeding.

(Subd (a) amended effective January 1, 2022; adopted effective January 1, 2008.)

(b) Ward's personal residence

The "ward's personal residence" under (a) is the ward's residence when the first petition for appointment of a guardian was filed in the proceeding.

(Subd (b) adopted effective January 1, 2008.)

(c) Post-move notice of a change of residence required

The guardian of the person of a minor must file a notice of a change of the ward's residence with the court within 30 days of the date of any change. Unless waived by the court for good cause to prevent harm to the ward, the guardian, the guardian's attorney, or an employee of the guardian's attorney must also mail a copy of the notice to the persons listed below and file a proof of mailing with the original notice. Unless waived, copies of the notice must be mailed to:

(1) The ward's attorney of record;

(2) The ward's parents and any former Indian custodian;

(3) Any person who had legal custody of the ward when the first petition for appointment of a guardian was filed in the proceeding;

(4) A guardian of the ward's estate;

(5) Any person who was nominated as guardian of the ward but was not appointed guardian in the proceeding; and

(6) The ward's tribe, if the ward is an Indian child and the ward's tribe has intervened in the proceeding.

(Subd (c) amended effective January 1, 2022; adopted effective January 1, 2008.)

(d) Ward's residence

The "ward's residence" under (c) is the ward's residence at any time after appointment of a guardian.

(Subd (d) adopted effective January 1, 2008.)

(e) Use of Judicial Council forms GC-079 and GC-080

(1) The *Pre-Move Notice of Proposed Change of Personal Residence of Conservatee or Ward* (form GC-079) must be used for the pre-move notice required under (a) and Probate Code section 2352(e)(3). The guardian, the guardian's attorney, or an employee of the attorney may complete the mailing and sign the proof of mailing on page 2 of the form. If the notice is mailed less than 15 days before the date of the move because an emergency requires a shorter period of notice, the basis for the emergency must be stated in the notice.

(2) The *Post-Move Notice of Change of Residence of Conservatee or Ward* (form GC-080) must be used for the post-move notice required under (c) and Probate Code section 2352(e)(1) and (2). The guardian, the guardian's attorney, or an employee of the attorney may complete the mailing and sign the proof of mailing on page 2 of the form.

(Subd (e) adopted effective January 1, 2008.)

(f) Prior court approval required to establish ward's residence outside California

Notwithstanding any other provision of this rule, prior court approval is required before a ward's residence may be established outside the state of California.

(Subd (f) adopted effective January 1, 2008.)

(g) Wards 18 to 20 years of age

For a ward who is at least 18 but not yet 21 years of age, a copy of any notice under this rule must be mailed only to the ward and the ward's attorney of record.

(Subd (g) adopted effective July 1, 2016.)

Rule 7.1013 amended effective January 1, 2022; adopted effective January 1, 2008; previously amended effective July 1, 2016.

Rule 7.1014. Communications between courts in different California counties concerning guardianship venue

(a) Purpose of rule

This rule addresses the communications between courts concerning guardianship venue required by Probate Code section 2204(b). These communications are between the superior court in one California county where a guardianship proceeding has been filed (referred to in this rule as the guardianship court) and one or more superior courts in one or more other California counties where custody or visitation proceedings under the Family Code involving the ward or proposed ward were previously filed (referred to in this rule as the family court or courts, or the other court or courts).

(Subd (a) adopted effective January 1, 2013.)

(b) Substantive communications between judicial officers

Before making a venue decision on a petition for appointment of a general guardian in a guardianship proceeding described in (a), or a decision on a petition to transfer under Probate Code section 2212 filed in the proceeding before the appointment of a guardian or temporary guardian, the judicial officer responsible for the proceeding in the guardianship court must communicate with the judicial officer or officers responsible for the custody proceeding or proceedings in the family court or courts concerning which county provides the venue for the guardianship proceeding that is in the best interests of the ward or the proposed ward.

(1) If the currently responsible judicial officer in the family court or courts cannot be identified, communication must be made with the managing or supervising judicial officer of the family departments of the

other court or courts, if any, or his or her designee, or with the presiding judge of the other court or courts or his or her designee.

(2) If courts in more than two counties are involved, simultaneous communications among judicial officers of all of the courts are recommended, if reasonably practicable. If communications occur between some but not all involved courts, the record of these communications must be made available to those judicial officers of the courts who were not included at or before the time the judicial officer of the guardianship court communicates with them.

(3) A record must be made of all communications between judicial officers under this subdivision.

(4) The parties to the guardianship proceeding, including a petitioner for transfer; all persons entitled to notice of the hearing on the petition for appointment of a guardian; and any additional persons ordered by the guardianship court must promptly be informed of the communications and given access to the record of the communications.

(5) The provisions of Family Code section 3410(b) apply to communications between judicial officers under this subdivision, except that the term "jurisdiction" in that section corresponds to "venue" in this context, and the term "parties" in that section identifies the persons listed in (4).

(Subd (b) adopted effective January 1, 2013.)

(c) Preliminary communications

To assist the judicial officer in making the communication required in (b), the guardianship court may have preliminary communications with each family court to collect information about the proceeding in that court or for other routine matters, including calendar management, and scheduling.

(1) The guardianship court should attempt to collect, and each family court is encouraged to provide, as much of the following information about the proceeding in the family court as is reasonable under the circumstances:

(A) The case number or numbers and the nature of each family court proceeding;

(B) The names of the parties to each family court proceeding, including contact information for self-represented parties; their relationship or other connection to the ward or proposed ward in the guardianship proceeding, and the names and contact information of counsel for any parties represented by counsel;

(C) The current status (active or inactive) of each family court proceeding, whether any future hearings are set in each proceeding, and if so, their dates and times, locations, and nature;

(D) The contents and dates filed of orders in the each family court proceeding that decide or resolve custody or visitation issues concerning the ward or proposed ward in the guardianship proceeding;

(E) Whether any orders of each family court are final, were appealed from, or were the subject of extraordinary writ proceedings, and the current status of any such appeal or proceeding;

(F) The court branch and department where each family court proceeding was assigned and where the proceeding is currently assigned or pending;

(G) The identity of the judicial officer currently assigned to or otherwise responsible for each family court proceeding; and

(H) Other information about each family court proceeding requested by the judicial officer of the guardianship court.

(2) In the discretion of the judicial officer of the guardianship court, preliminary communications under this rule may be between judicial officers of the courts involved or between staff of the guardianship court and judicial officers or court staff of each other court.

(3) Family Code section 3410(c) applies to preliminary communications under this rule.

(Subd (c) adopted effective January 1, 2013.)

(d) Applicability of this rule to petitions to transfer filed after the appointment of a guardian or temporary guardian

Subdivisions (b) and (c) of this rule may, in the discretion of the guardianship court, apply to petitions for transfer described in Probate Code section 2204(b)(2).

(Subd (d) adopted effective January 1, 2013.)

(e) "Record" under this rule

"Record" under this rule has the meaning provided in Family Code section 3410(e).

(Subd (e) adopted effective January 1, 2013.)

Rule 7.1014 adopted effective January 1, 2013.

Rule 7.1015. Guardianship and certain conservatorship proceedings involving Indian children (Prob. Code, §§ 1449, 1459, 1459.5, 1460.2, 1511(b), (i); Welf. & Inst. Code, §§ 224–224.6; 25 U.S.C. §§ 1901–1963; 25 C.F.R. §§ 23.1–23.144)

(a) Definitions

As used in this rule, unless the context or subject matter otherwise requires:

(1) "Act" means the federal Indian Child Welfare Act (25 U.S.C. §§ 1901–1963).

(2) "Petitioner" refers to:

(A) A petitioner for the appointment of a guardian of the person of a minor child; or

(B) A petitioner for the appointment of a conservator of the person of a formerly married minor child whose marriage has been dissolved.

(Subd (a) amended effective January 1, 2022; adopted effective January 1, 2008.)

(b) Applicability of this rule and rules 5.480 through 5.488

(1) This rule applies to the following proceedings under division 4 of the Probate Code:

(A) A guardianship of the person or of the person and estate, including a temporary guardianship, in which the proposed guardian of the person is not the proposed ward's biological parent or Indian custodian;

(B) A conservatorship or limited conservatorship of the person or of the person and estate, including a temporary conservatorship, of a formerly married minor whose marriage has been dissolved in which the proposed conservator of the person is not the proposed conservatee's biological parent or Indian custodian and is seeking physical custody of the proposed conservatee.

(2) Unless the context requires otherwise, rules 5.480 through 5.488 apply to the proceedings listed in (1).

(3) When applied to the proceedings listed in (1), references in rules 5.480 through 5.488 to social workers, probation officers, county probation departments, or county social welfare departments are references to the petitioner or petitioners for the appointment of a guardian or conservator of the person and to the appointed temporary or general guardian or conservator of the person.

(4) If the court appoints a guardian or conservator of the person of a child in a proceeding listed in (1), the duties and responsibilities of a petitioner under the Act and this rule become the duties and responsibilities of the appointed guardian or conservator. The petitioner must cooperate with and provide any information the petitioner knows or possesses concerning the child to the appointed guardian or conservator.

(Subd (b) amended effective January 1, 2022; adopted effective January 1, 2008.)

(c) Duty of inquiry

(1) The court, the court investigator or county officer appointed to conduct an investigation under Probate Code section 1513 or 1826, and each petitioner have an affirmative and continuing duty to inquire whether each child who is the subject of a proceeding identified in (b)(1) is or may be an Indian child.

(2) Before filing a petition for appointment of a guardian or conservator of the person, the petitioner must ask the child who is the subject of the proceeding, if the child is old enough, the parents, any Indian custodian or previously appointed guardian of the person, and available extended family members, as defined in 25 U.S.C. § 1903(2), or other persons having an interest in the child whether the child is or may be an Indian child, complete *Indian Child Inquiry Attachment* (form ICWA-010(A)), and attach that form to the petition.

(3) At the beginning of any proceeding identified in (b)(1) and at any hearing in such a proceeding that may result in the appointment of a guardian or conservator, the court must:

(A) Ask each participant present whether the participant knows or has reason to know that the child is an Indian child;

(B) Instruct the parties to inform the court if they subsequently receive information that provides reason to know that the child is an Indian child; and

(C) Order the parent, Indian custodian, or existing guardian, if available, to complete *Parental Notification of Indian Status* (form ICWA-020).

(4) If the parent, Indian custodian, or guardian is not available at the beginning of a proceeding identified in (b)(1), the court must order the

petitioner to use reasonable diligence to find and inform the parent, Indian custodian, or guardian that the court has ordered that person to complete and deliver to the petitioner a *Parental Notification of Indian Status* (form ICWA-020).

(5) If the court or county investigator, the petitioner, or the attorney for the petitioner knows or has reason to know or believe that an Indian child is the subject of the proceeding but has not conclusively determined that the child is an Indian child, that person must, as soon as practicable, conduct further inquiry by:

(A) Interviewing the parents, Indian custodian, and extended family members to gather the information listed in Welfare and Institutions Code section 224.3(a)(5);

(B) Contacting the federal Bureau of Indian Affairs and the California Department of Social Services for assistance in identifying the names and contact information of the tribes of which the child may be a member or eligible for membership;

(C) Contacting the tribes and any other persons who reasonably can be expected to have information regarding the child's tribal membership or eligibility for membership. These contacts must at a minimum use the methods and share the information listed in Welfare and Institutions Code section 224.2(e)(2)(C); and

(D) Filing with the court documentation of that further inquiry, including, at a minimum:

(i) The names of all persons contacted and interviewed or attempted to be interviewed under subparagraph (A), the dates of those contacts and interviews, and any information gathered from them; and

(ii) The dates and methods of contact with the agencies listed in subparagraph (B) and the tribes and persons in subparagraph (C) and any information gathered as a result of those contacts.

(6) If the court knows or has reason to know or believe that an Indian child is involved in the proceeding but does not have sufficient evidence to determine that the child is an Indian child, and the further inquiry conducted in (5) has not been conducted, the court must order one or more of the persons named in (5) to conduct the inquiry and submit the documentation described in that paragraph.

(7) The circumstances that may provide reason to believe the child may be an Indian child are those set forth in Welfare and Institutions Code section 224.2(e)(1). The circumstances that may provide reason to know the child is an Indian child are those set forth in Welfare and Institutions Code section 224.2(d) and rule 5.481(b).

(Subd (c) amended and relettered effective January 1, 2022; adopted as subd (d) effective January 1, 2008; previously amended effective July 1, 2012.)

(d) Temporary guardianships and conservatorships of an Indian child

In addition to the applicable requirements in Probate Code sections 2250–2257 and California Rules of Court, rules 7.1012 and 7.1062, the following requirements apply to temporary guardianship and conservatorship proceedings if the court knows or has reason to know that the proposed ward is an Indian child:

(1) Before appointing a temporary guardian or conservator of the person for an Indian child over the objection of a parent, tribe, or Indian custodian, the court must:

(A) Advise the parent or Indian custodian that if they cannot afford counsel, the court will appoint counsel for them under section 1912(b) of the Indian Child Welfare Act; and

(B) Find, in addition to facts in the petition establishing good cause for the appointment and any other showing the court may require under Probate Code section 2250(b), that the appointment is necessary to prevent imminent physical damage or harm to the child.

(2) At a hearing under Probate Code section 2250(f) or on a petition, including an ex parte petition, to terminate a temporary guardianship or conservatorship of an Indian child, the court must determine whether the temporary guardianship or conservatorship is still necessary to prevent imminent physical damage or harm to the child. If the court determines that the temporary guardianship or conservatorship is no longer necessary, the court must terminate the temporary guardianship or conservatorship and, if a parent or Indian custodian is available, order the child returned to the physical custody of the parent or Indian custodian.

(3) Before extending a temporary guardianship or conservatorship of an Indian child, under Probate Code section 2257(b), more than 30 days from the date of its establishment, the court must, in addition to finding good cause for the extension, determine that:

(A) Terminating the temporary guardianship or conservatorship would subject the child to imminent physical damage or harm;

(B) The court has been unable to transfer the proceeding to the jurisdiction of the appropriate Indian tribe; and

(C) It has not been possible to hold a hearing on the petition to appoint a guardian that complies with the substantive requirements of the Act for a foster care placement proceeding.

(Subd (d) adopted effective January 1, 2022.)

(e) Notice

If, at any time after the filing of a petition for appointment of a guardian or conservator for a minor child, the court or petitioner knows or has reason to know, within the meaning of Welfare and Institutions Code section 224.2(d) and rule 5.481(b), that an Indian child is the subject of the proceeding, the petitioner and the court must give notice of the proceeding and the right of the child's tribe to intervene in the manner prescribed by Welfare and Institutions Code section 224.3(a) and rule 5.481(c) to the child's parents, the child's Indian custodian or previously appointed guardian of the person, if any, and the child's tribe or, if the child's tribe has not been determined, all tribes of which the child may be a member or eligible for membership.

(Subd (e) amended and relettered effective January 1, 2022; adopted as subd (c) effective January 1, 2008.)

Rule 7.1015 amended effective January 1, 2022; adopted effective January 1, 2008; previously amended effective July 1, 2012.

Rule 7.1016. Participation and testimony of wards in guardianship proceedings

(a) Definitions

As used in this rule, the following terms have the meanings specified:

(1) "Ward" includes "proposed ward."

(2) A "proceeding" is a matter before the court for decision in a probate guardianship of the person that concerns appointment or removal of a guardian, visitation, determination of the ward's place of residence, or termination of the guardianship by court order.

(3) "Party," as used in this rule to refer to the ward, means a ward who has filed a petition or opposition to a petition concerning a proceeding or other matter subject to this rule.

(Subd (a) adopted effective January 1, 2013.)

(b) Purpose and scope of rule

(1) This rule applies Family Code section 3042 to the participation and testimony of the ward in a proceeding in a probate guardianship of the person. The testimony of other minors in a guardianship case is governed by Evidence Code sections 765(b) and 767(b).

(2) The court in its discretion may apply this rule, in whole or in part, to the participation and testimony of a ward in a guardianship of the estate or in a matter before the court in a guardianship of the person that is not a proceeding within the meaning of this rule. The phrase "or other matter subject to this rule" following the term "proceeding" is a reference to the matters described in this paragraph.

(3) No statutory mandate, rule, or practice requires a ward who is not a party to the proceeding or other matter subject to this rule to participate in court or prohibits him or her from doing so. When a ward desires to participate but is not a party to the proceeding or other matter subject to this rule, the court must balance the protection of the ward, the statutory duty to consider the wishes of and input from the ward, and the probative value of the ward's input while ensuring all parties' due process rights to challenge evidence relied on by the court in making decisions affecting the ward in matters covered by the rule.

(4) This rule rather than rule 5.250, on children's participation and testimony in family court proceedings, applies in probate guardianship proceedings.

(Subd (b) adopted effective January 1, 2013.)

(c) Determining whether the nonparty ward wishes to address the court

(1) The following persons must inform the court if they have information indicating that a ward who is not a party wishes to address the court in a proceeding or other matter subject to this rule:

(A) The ward's counsel;

(B) A court or county guardianship investigator;

(C) A child custody recommending counselor who provides recommendations to the judicial officer under Family Code section 3183;

(D) An expert appointed by the court under Evidence Code section 730 to assist the court in the matter; or

(E) The ward's guardian ad litem.

(2) The following persons may inform the court if they have information indicating that a ward who is not a party wishes to address the court in a proceeding or other matter subject to this rule:

(A) A party in the guardianship case; and

(B) An attorney for a party in the guardianship case.

(3) In the absence of information indicating that a ward who is not a party wishes to address the court in a proceeding or other matter subject to this rule, the judicial officer may inquire whether the ward wishes to do so.

(Subd (c) adopted effective January 1, 2013.)

(d) Guidelines for determining whether addressing the court is in the nonparty ward's best interest

(1) When a ward who is not a party indicates that he or she wishes to address the court, the judicial officer must consider whether involving the ward in the proceeding or other matter subject to this rule is in the ward's best interest.

(2) If the ward is 12 years old or older, the judicial officer must hear from the ward unless the court makes a finding that addressing the court is not in the ward's best interest and states the reasons on the record.

(3) In determining whether addressing the court is in the ward's best interest, the judicial officer should consider the following:

(A) Whether the ward is of sufficient age and capacity to form an intelligent preference as to the matter to be decided;

(B) Whether the ward is of sufficient age and capacity to understand the nature of testimony;

(C) Whether information has been presented indicating that the ward may be at risk emotionally if he or she is permitted or denied the opportunity to address the court or that the ward may benefit from addressing the court;

(D) Whether the subject areas about which the ward is anticipated to address the court are relevant to the decision the court must make;

(E) Whether the appointment of counsel under Probate Code section 1470 or a guardian ad litem for the ward would be helpful to the determination or would be necessary to protect the ward's interests; and

(F) Whether any other factors weigh in favor of or against having the ward address the court, taking into consideration the ward's desire to do so.

(Subd (d) adopted effective January 1, 2013.)

(e) Guidelines for receiving testimony and other input from the nonparty ward

(1) No testimony of a ward may be received without such testimony being heard on the record or in the presence of the parties. This requirement may not be waived.

(2) On deciding to take the testimony of a ward who is not a party in a proceeding or other matter subject to this rule, the judicial officer should balance the necessity of taking the ward's testimony in the courtroom with parents, the guardian or proposed guardian, other parties, and attorneys present with the need to create an environment in which the ward can be open and honest. In each case in which a ward's testimony will be taken, the judicial officer should consider:

(A) Where the testimony will be taken;

(B) Who should be present when the testimony is taken;

(C) How the ward will be questioned; and

(D) Whether a court reporter is available in all instances, but especially when the ward's testimony may be taken outside the presence of the parties and their attorneys. If the court reporter will not be available, whether there are other means to collect, preserve, transcribe, and make the ward's testimony available to parties and their attorneys.

(3) In taking testimony from a ward who is not a party to the proceeding or other matter subject to this rule, the court must take the special care required by Evidence Code section 765(b). If the ward is not represented by an attorney, the court must inform the ward in an age-appropriate manner about the limitations on confidentiality of testimony and that the information provided to the court will be on the record and provided to the parties in the case.

(4) In the process of listening to and inviting the ward's input, the court must allow but not require the ward to state a preference regarding the matter to be decided in the proceeding or other matter subject to this rule and should provide information in an age-appropriate manner about the process by which the court will make a decision.

(5) In any case in which a ward who is not a party to the proceeding or other matter subject to this rule will be called to testify, the court must consider the appointment of counsel for the ward under Probate Code section 1470 and may consider the appointment of a guardian ad litem for the ward. In addition to satisfying the requirements for minor's counsel under rule 7.1101, minor's counsel must:

(A) Provide information to the ward in an age-appropriate manner about the limitations on the confidentiality of testimony and indicate to the ward the possibility that information provided to the court will be on the record and provided to the parties in the case;

(B) Allow but not require the ward to state a preference regarding the issues to be decided in the proceeding or other matter subject to this rule, and provide information in an age-appropriate manner about the process by which the court will make a decision;

(C) If appropriate, provide the ward with an orientation to the courtroom or other place where the ward will testify; and

(D) Inform the parties and the court about the ward's desire to provide input.

(6) If the court precludes the calling of a ward who is not a party as a witness in a proceeding or other matter subject to this rule, alternatives for the court to obtain information or other input from the ward may include:

(A) A court or county guardianship investigator participating in the case under Probate Code section 1513 or 1513.2;

(B) Appointment of a child custody evaluator or investigator under Evidence Code section 730;

(C) Appointment of counsel or a guardian ad litem for the ward;

(D) Admissible evidence provided by the ward's parents, parties, or witnesses in the proceeding or other matter subject to this rule;

(E) Information provided by a child custody recommending counselor authorized under Family Code section 3183 to make a recommendation to the court; and

(F) Information provided from a child interview center or professional to avoid unnecessary multiple interviews.

(7) If the court precludes the calling of a ward who is not a party as a witness in a proceeding or other matter subject to this rule and specifies one of the other alternatives, the court must require that the information or evidence obtained by alternative means and provided by a professional (other than counsel for the ward or counsel for any party) or a nonparty:

(A) Be in writing and fully document the ward's views on the matters on which he or she wished to express an opinion;

(B) Describe the ward's input in sufficient detail to assist the court in making its decision;

(C) Be provided to the court and to the parties by a person who will be available for testimony and cross-examination; and

(D) Be filed in the confidential portion of the case file.

(Subd (e) adopted effective January 1, 2013.)

(f) Responsibilities of court-connected or appointed professionals—all wards

A child custody evaluator, an expert witness appointed under Evidence Code section 730, an investigator, a child custody recommending counselor or other custody mediator appointed or assigned to meet with a ward must:

(1) Provide information to the ward in an age-appropriate manner about the limitations on confidentiality of testimony and the possibility that information provided to the professional may be shared with the court on the record and provided to the parties in the case;

(2) Allow but not require the ward to state a preference regarding the issues to be decided in the proceeding or other matter subject to this rule, and provide information in an age-appropriate manner about the process by which the court will make a decision; and

(3) Provide to the other parties in the case information about how best to support the interest of the ward during the court process.

(Subd (f) adopted effective January 1, 2013.)

(g) Methods of providing information to parties and supporting nonparty wards

Courts should provide information to the parties and the ward who is not a party to the proceeding or other matter subject to this rule when the ward wants to participate or testify. Methods of providing information may include:

(1) Having court or county guardianship investigators and experts appointed under Evidence Code section 730 meet jointly or separately with the parties and their attorneys to discuss alternatives to having the ward provide direct testimony;

(2) Providing an orientation for the ward about the court process and the role of the judicial officer in making decisions, how the courtroom or chambers will be set up, and what participating or testifying will entail;

(3) Providing information to parties before the ward participates or testifies so that they can consider the possible effect on the ward of participating or not participating in the proceeding or other matter subject to this rule;

(4) Appointing counsel under Probate Code section 1470 or a guardian ad litem for the ward to assist in the provision of information to the ward concerning his or her decision to participate in the proceeding or testify;

(5) Including information in guardianship orientation presentations and publications about the options available to a ward who is not a party to the proceeding or other matter subject to this rule to participate or testify or not to do so, and the consequences of a ward's decision whether to become a party to the proceeding or other matter subject to this rule; and

(6) Providing an interpreter for the ward.

(Subd (g) adopted effective January 1, 2013.)

(h) If the ward is a party to the proceeding

(1) A ward who is a party to the proceeding or other matter subject to this rule is subject to the law of discovery applied to parties in civil actions and may be called as a witness by any other party unless the court makes a finding that providing information in response to discovery requests or testifying as a witness is not in the ward's best interest and states the reasons on the record.

(2) The court must consider appointing counsel under Probate Code section 1470 or a guardian ad litem for a ward who is a party to the proceeding or other matter subject to this rule if the ward is not represented by counsel.

(3) In determining whether providing information in response to discovery requests or testifying as a witness is in the ward's best interest, the judicial officer should consider the following:

(A) Whether information has been presented indicating that the ward may be at risk emotionally if he or she is permitted or denied the opportunity to provide information in response to discovery requests or by testimony;

(B) Whether the subject areas about which the ward is anticipated to provide information in response to discovery requests or by testimony are relevant to the decision the court must make; and

(C) Whether any other factors weigh in favor of or against having the ward provide information in response to discovery requests or by testimony.

(4) In taking testimony from a ward who is a party to the proceeding or other matter subject to this rule, the court must take the special care required by Evidence Code section 765(b). If the ward is not represented by an attorney, the court must inform the ward in an age-appropriate manner about the limitations on confidentiality of testimony and that the information provided to the court will be on the record and provided to the parties in the case.

(Subd (h) adopted effective January 1, 2013.)

(i) Education and training of judicial officers and court staff

Education and training content for court staff and judicial officers should include information on wards' participation in proceedings or other matters subject to this rule, methods other than direct testimony for receiving input from a ward, procedures for taking a ward's testimony, and differences in the application of this rule to wards who are and are not parties to the proceeding or other matters subject to this rule.

(Subd (i) adopted effective January 1, 2013.)

Rule 7.1016 adopted effective January 1, 2013.

Rule 7.1020. Special Immigrant Juvenile findings in guardianship proceedings

(a) Application

This rule applies to a request by or on behalf of a minor who is a ward or a proposed ward in a probate guardianship proceeding for judicial findings needed as a basis for filing a petition for classification as a Special Immigrant Juvenile (SIJ) under federal immigration law. The term "request under this rule" as used in this rule refers exclusively to such a request. This rule also applies to any opposition to a request under this rule, any hearing on such a request and opposition, and any findings of the court in response to such a request.

(Subd (a) adopted effective January 1, 2016.)

(b) Request for findings

(1) *Who may file request*

Any person or entity authorized under Probate Code section 1510 or 1510.1 to petition for the appointment of a guardian of the person of a minor, including the ward or proposed ward if 12 years of age or older, may file a request for findings regarding the minor under this rule.

(A) If there is more than one ward or proposed ward in the proceeding, a minor eligible to file a request for findings under this rule may do so only for himself or herself.

(B) The court may appoint an attorney under Probate Code section 1470 or a guardian ad litem under Probate Code sections 1003 and 1003.5 to file and present a request for findings under this rule for a minor or to represent the interests of a minor in a proceeding to decide a request filed on the minor's behalf by another.

(2) *Form of request*

(A) A request for findings under this rule must be made by verified petition. A separate request must be filed for each minor seeking SIJ findings.

(B) A request for findings under this rule by or on behalf of a minor filed concurrently with a petition for the appointment of a guardian of the person or for extension of a guardianship of the person past the 18th birthday of the minor must be prepared and filed as a separate petition, not as an attachment to the petition for appointment.

(Subd (b) amended effective July 1, 2016; adopted effective January 1, 2016.)

(c) Notice of hearing

Notice of a hearing of a request for findings under this rule, and a copy of the request, must be sent to the minor's parents and the persons listed in section 1460(b) of the Probate Code, in the manner and within the time provided in that section, subject to the provisions of subdivision (e) of that section and sections 1202 and 1460.1 of that code.

(Subd (c) adopted effective January 1, 2016.)

(d) Opposition to request

Any of the persons who must be given notice of hearing of a request for findings under this rule may file an objection or other opposition to the request.

(Subd (d) adopted effective January 1, 2016.)

(e) Hearing on request

(1) If filed concurrently, a request for findings under this rule by or on behalf of a minor and a petition for appointment of a guardian of the person or extension of a guardianship of the person past the 18th birthday of that minor may be heard and determined together.

(2) Hearings on separate requests for findings under this rule by or on behalf of more than one ward or proposed ward in the same guardianship proceeding may be consolidated on the motion of any party or on the court's own motion.

(3) Hearings on requests for findings under this rule by or on behalf of minors who are siblings or half-siblings and are wards or proposed wards in separate guardianship proceedings may be consolidated on the motion of any party in either proceeding or on the motion of the court in either proceeding. If multiple departments of a single court or courts in more than one county are involved, they may communicate with each other on consolidation issues in the manner provided for inter-court communications on venue issues in guardianship and family law matters under section 2204 of the Probate Code and rule 7.1014.

(4) Hearings on contested requests for findings under this rule must be conducted in the same manner as hearings on other contested petitions under the Probate Code.

(5) Probate Code section 1022 applies to uncontested requests for findings under this rule.

(Subd (e) amended effective July 1, 2016; adopted effective January 1, 2016.)

(f) Separate findings in multi-ward cases under this rule

The court must issue separate findings for each minor in a guardianship proceeding in which more than one minor is the subject of a request under this rule.

(Subd (f) adopted effective January 1, 2016.)

Rule 7.1020 amended effective July 1, 2016; adopted effective January 1, 2016.

Chapter 22
Conservatorships

Rule 7.1050. Conservator forms
Rule 7.1051. Acknowledgment of receipt of Duties of Conservator
Rule 7.1059. Standards of conduct for the conservator of the estate
Rule 7.1060. Investigations and reports by court investigators
Rule 7.1061. Taking possession of an asset of the conservatee at an institution or opening or changing ownership of an account or safe-deposit box in a financial institution
Rule 7.1062. The good cause exception to notice of the hearing on a petition for appointment of a temporary conservator

Rule 7.1063. Change of conservatee's residence

Rule 7.1050. Conservator forms

(a) Forms to be submitted with petition

Each petitioner, unless the petitioner is a bank or other entity entitled to conduct the business of a trust company, must submit to the court with the petition for appointment of conservator a completed *Confidential Supplemental Information* statement (form GC-312). In addition, each proposed conservator, except a bank or other entity entitled to conduct the business of a trust company, or a public guardian, must submit a completed *Confidential Conservator Screening Form* (form GC-314).

(Subd (a) amended effective January 1, 2007; previously amended effective January 1, 2002.)

(b) Use of form

The information on the *Confidential Conservator Screening Form* is used by the court and by persons or agencies designated by the court to assist the court in determining whether a proposed conservator should be appointed.

(Subd (b) amended effective January 1, 2002.)

(c) Forms to be confidential

The *Confidential Conservator Screening Form*, the *Confidential Supplemental Information* statement, and the information contained on these forms are confidential. The clerk must maintain these forms in a manner that will protect and preserve their confidentiality.

(Subd (c) amended effective January 1, 2007; previously amended effective January 1, 2002.)

Rule 7.1050 amended effective January 1, 2007; adopted effective January 1, 2001; previously amended effective January 1, 2002.

Rule 7.1051. Acknowledgment of receipt of Duties of Conservator

Before the court issues letters, each conservator must execute and file an acknowledgment of receipt of the *Duties of Conservator and Acknowledgment of Receipt of Handbook* (form GC-348).

Rule 7.1051 amended effective January 1, 2002; adopted effective January 1, 2001.

Rule 7.1052. Termination of conservatorship [Repealed]

Rule 7.1052 repealed effective January 1, 2023; adopted effective January 1, 2004.

Rule 7.1053. Service of final account of removed or resigned conservator [Repealed]

Rule 7.1053 repealed effective January 1, 2023; adopted effective January 1, 2004.

Rule 7.1054. Service of final account after termination of conservatorship [Repealed]

Rule 7.1054 repealed effective January 1, 2023; adopted effective January 1, 2004.

Rule 7.1059. Standards of conduct for the conservator of the estate

Except as otherwise required by statute, in the exercise of ordinary care and diligence in managing and controlling the estate of the conservatee, the conservator of the estate is to be guided by the following principles:

(a) Avoidance of actual and apparent conflicts of interest with the conservatee

The conservator must avoid actual conflicts of interest and, consistent with his or her fiduciary duty to the conservatee, the appearance of conflicts of interest. The conservator must avoid any personal, business, or professional interest or relationship that is or reasonably could be perceived as being self-serving or adverse to the best interest of the conservatee. In particular:

(1) Except as appropriate for conservators who are not professional fiduciaries with full disclosure to the court, the conservator should not personally provide housing, medical, or legal services to the conservatee;

(2) The conservator must be independent from all service providers, except when (a) no other conservator or service providers are reasonably available, (b) the exception is in the best interest of the conservatee, (c) the circumstances are fully disclosed to the court, and (d) prior court approval has been obtained;

(3) The conservator must neither solicit nor accept incentives from service providers; and

(4) The conservator must not engage his or her family members to provide services to the conservatee for a profit or fee when other alternatives are reasonably available. Where family members do provide such services, their relationship to the conservator must be fully disclosed to the court, the terms of engagement must be in the best interest of the conservatee compared to the terms available from independent service providers, the services must be competently performed, and the conservator must be able to exercise appropriate control and supervision.

A conservator's employees, including family members, are not service providers and are not providing services to the conservatee for a profit or fee within the meaning of this rule if their compensation is paid by the conservator and their services are either included in the conservator's petition for allowance of the conservator's compensation or are not paid from the conservatee's estate.

(Subd (a) adopted effective January 1, 2008.)

(b) Conservatorship estate management

The conservator of the estate must:

(1) Provide competent management of the conservatee's property, with the care of a prudent person dealing with someone else's property;

(2) Refrain from unreasonably risky investments;

(3) Refrain from making loans or gifts of estate property, except as authorized by the court after full disclosure;

(4) Manage the estate for the benefit of the conservatee;

(5) Subject to the duty of full disclosure to the court and persons entitled under law to receive it, closely guard against unnecessary or inappropriate disclosure of the conservatee's financial information;

(6) Keep the money and property of the estate separate from the conservator's or any other person's money or property, except as may be permitted under statutes authorizing public guardians or public conservators and certain regulated private fiduciaries to maintain common trust funds or similar common investments;

(7) Hold title reflecting the conservatorship in individual securities, mutual funds, securities broker accounts, and accounts with financial institutions;

(8) Keep accurate records of all transactions. Professional fiduciaries must maintain prudent accounting systems and procedures designed to protect against embezzlement and other cash-asset mismanagement;

(9) Undertake as soon as possible after appointment and qualification to locate and safeguard the conservatee's estate planning documents, including wills, living trusts, powers of attorney for health care and finances, life insurance policies, and pension records;

(10) Undertake as soon as possible after appointment and qualification to secure the real and personal property of the estate, insuring it at appropriate levels, and protecting it against damage, destruction, or loss;

(11) Make reasonable efforts to preserve property identified in the conservatee's estate planning documents;

(12) Communicate as necessary and appropriate with the conservator of the person of the conservatee, if any, and with the trustee of any trust of which the conservatee is a beneficiary;

(13) Pursue claims against others on behalf of the estate when it would be in the best interest of the conservatee or the estate to do so. Consider requesting prior court authority to pursue or compromise large or complex claims, particularly those that might require litigation and the assistance of counsel and those that might result in an award of attorneys' fees for the other party against the estate if unsuccessful, and request such approval before entering into a contingent fee agreement with counsel;

(14) Defend against actions or claims against the estate when it would be in the best interest of the conservatee or the estate to do so. Consider requesting court approval or instructions concerning the defense or compromise of litigation against the estate;

(15) Collect all public and insurance benefits for which the conservatee is eligible;

(16) Evaluate the conservatee's ability to manage cash or other assets and take appropriate action, including obtaining prior court approval when necessary or appropriate, to enable the conservatee to do so to the level of his or her ability;

(17) When disposing of the conservatee's tangible personal property, inform the conservatee's family members in advance and give them an opportunity to acquire the property, with approval or confirmation of the court; and

(18) In deciding whether it is in the best interest of the conservatee to dispose of property of the estate, consider the following factors, among others, as appropriate in the circumstances:

(A) The likely benefit or improvement of the conservatee's life that disposing of the property would bring;

(B) The likelihood that the conservatee would need or benefit from the property in the future;

(C) Subject to the factors specified in Probate Code section 2113, the previously expressed or current desires of the conservatee concerning the property;

(D) The provisions of the conservatee's estate plan concerning the property;

(E) The tax consequences of the disposition transaction;

(F) The impact of the disposition transaction on the conservatee's entitlement to public benefits;

(G) The condition of the entire estate;

(H) Alternatives to disposition of the property;

(I) The likelihood that the property will deteriorate or be subject to waste if retained in the estate; and

(J) The benefit versus the cost or liability of maintaining the property in the estate.

(Subd (b) adopted effective January 1, 2008.)

Rule 7.1059 adopted effective January 1, 2008.

Advisory Committee Comment

The Probate and Mental Health Advisory Committee consulted with several organizations in the development of rule 7.1059, including the National Guardianship Association, a nationwide voluntary association of professional and family fiduciaries, guardians, and allied professionals. In developing this rule, the Probate and Mental Health Advisory Committee considered the National Guardianship Association's Standards of Practice. Some of these standards have been incorporated into the rules.

Rule 7.1060. Investigations and reports by court investigators

(a) Order Appointing Court Investigator (form GC-330)

Order Appointing Court Investigator (form GC-330) is an optional form within the meaning of rule 1.35 of these rules, except as follows:

(1) A court may, by local rule, require that form GC-330 be used for orders appointing court investigators and directing them to conduct all or any of the investigations described in the form and to prepare, file, and deliver copies of reports concerning those investigations. Form GC-330 must be prepared only by the court.

(2) A court may, by local rule, require that a general order, a court-prepared order, or a local form order instead of form GC-330 be used to appoint and direct the actions of court investigators concerning all or any of the investigations and reports described in form GC-330.

(Subd (a) amended effective January 1, 2023; adopted effective January 1, 2011.)

(b) Order Appointing Court Investigator (Review and Successor Conservator Investigations) (form GC-331)

Order Appointing Court Investigator (Review and Successor Conservator Investigations) (form GC-331) is an optional form within the meaning of rule 1.35 of these rules, except as follows:

(1) A court may, by local rule, require that form GC-331 be used for orders appointing court investigators and directing them to conduct all or any of the review investigations under Probate Code sections 1850 or 1850.5 and 1851 or investigations concerning the appointment of successor conservators under Probate Code sections 2684 and 2686 described in the form and to prepare, file, and deliver copies of reports concerning those investigations. Form GC-331 must be prepared only by the court.

(2) A court may, by local rule, require that a general order, a court-prepared order, or a local form order instead of form GC-331 be used to appoint and direct the actions of court investigators concerning all or any of the investigations and reports described in form GC-331.

(Subd (b) amended effective January 1, 2023; adopted effective January 1, 2011.)

Rule 7.1060 amended effective January 1, 2023; adopted effective January 1, 2011.

Rule 7.1061. Taking possession of an asset of the conservatee at an institution or opening or changing ownership of an account or safe-deposit box in a financial institution

(a) Definitions

As used in this rule, the following terms have the meanings stated below:

(1) An "institution" is an insurance company, insurance broker, insurance agent, investment company, investment bank, securities broker-dealer, investment advisor, financial planner, financial advisor, or any other person who takes, holds, or controls an asset subject to a guardianship that is not a "financial institution" within the meaning of this rule;

(2) A "financial institution" is a bank, trust (except as provided in (d)), savings and loan association, savings bank, industrial bank, or credit union; and

(3) "Taking possession" or "taking control" of an asset held or controlled by an institution includes changing title to the asset, withdrawing all or any portion of the asset, or transferring all or any portion of the asset from the institution.

(Subd (a) adopted effective January 1, 2009.)

(b) Responsibilities of the conservator when taking possession or control of an asset of the conservatee at an institution

When taking possession or control of an asset held by an institution in the name of the conservatee, the temporary, general, or limited conservator of the estate must provide the following to the institution:

(1) A certified copy of the conservator's *Letters of Temporary Guardianship or Conservatorship* (form GC-150) or *Letters of Conservatorship* (form GC-350) containing the Notice to Institutions and Financial Institutions on the second page; and

(2) A blank copy of a *Notice of Taking Possession or Control of an Asset of Minor or Conservatee* (form GC-050).

(Subd (b) adopted effective January 1, 2009.)

(c) Responsibilities of the conservator when opening or changing the name on an account or a safe-deposit box at a financial institution

When opening or changing the name on an account or a safe-deposit box in a financial institution, the temporary, general, or limited conservator of the estate must provide the following to the financial institution:

(1) A certified copy of the guardian's *Letters of Temporary Guardianship or Conservatorship* (form GC-150) or *Letters of Conservatorship* (form GC-350) containing the Notice to Institutions and Financial Institutions on the second page; and

(2) A blank copy of a *Notice of Opening or Changing a Guardianship or Conservatorship Account or Safe-Deposit Box* (form GC-051).

(Subd (c) adopted effective January 1, 2009.)

(d) Application of this rule to Totten trust accounts

This rule applies to Totten trust accounts but does not apply to any other trust arrangement described in Probate Code section 82(b).

(Subd (d) adopted effective January 1, 2009.)

Rule 7.1061 adopted effective January 1, 2009.

Rule 7.1062. The good cause exception to notice of the hearing on a petition for appointment of a temporary conservator

(a) Purpose

The purpose of this rule is to establish uniform standards for the good cause exception to the notice of the hearing required on a petition for appointment of a temporary conservator under Probate Code section 2250(e).

(Subd (a) amended effective January 1, 2009; adopted effective January 1, 2008.)

(b) Good cause for exceptions to notice limited

Good cause for an exception to the notice required by section 2250(e) must be based on a showing that the exception is necessary to protect the proposed conservatee or his or her estate from immediate and substantial harm.

(Subd (b) amended effective January 1, 2009; adopted effective January 1, 2008.)

(c) Court may change the time or manner of giving notice

An exception to the notice requirement of section 2250(e) may include one or any combination of the following:

(1) Waiving notice to one, more than one, or all persons entitled to notice;

(2) Requiring a different period of notice; and

(3) Changing the required manner of giving notice, including requiring notice by telephone, fax, e-mail, or personal delivery, or a combination of these methods, instead of or in addition to notice by mail to the proposed conservatee's spouse or registered domestic partner and relatives.

(Subd (c) amended effective July 1, 2008; adopted effective January 1, 2008.)

(d) Good cause exceptions to notice

Good cause for an exception to the notice requirement of section 2250(e) may include a showing of:

(1) Harm caused by the passage of time. The showing must demonstrate the immediate and substantial harm to the conservatee or the conservatee's estate that could occur during the notice period.

(2) Harm that one or more persons entitled to notice might do to the proposed conservatee or the proposed conservatee's estate if notice is given. Such a showing would not support an exception to the requirement to give notice to any other person entitled to notice unless it also

demonstrates that notice cannot reasonably be given to the other person without also giving notice to the persons who might cause harm.

(3) *Medical emergency.* The emergency must be immediate and substantial and treatment (1) must be reasonably unavailable unless a temporary conservator is appointed and (2) cannot be deferred for the notice period because of the proposed conservatee's pain or extreme discomfort or a significant risk of harm.

(4) *Financial emergency.* The emergency must be immediate and substantial and other means shown likely to be ineffective to prevent loss or further loss to the proposed conservatee's estate during the notice period.

(Subd (d) amended effective January 1, 2009; adopted effective January 1, 2008.)

(e) Contents of request for good cause exception to notice

A request for a good cause exception to the notice requirement of section 2250(e) must be in writing, separate from the petition for appointment of a temporary conservator, and must include:

(1) An application containing the case caption and stating the relief requested;

(2) An affirmative factual showing in support of the application in a declaration under penalty of perjury containing competent testimony based on personal knowledge;

(3) A declaration under penalty of perjury based on personal knowledge containing the information required for an ex parte application under rule 3.1204(b); and

(4) A proposed order.

(Subd (e) amended effective January 1, 2009; adopted effective January 1, 2008.)

Rule 7.1062 amended effective January 1, 2009; adopted effective January 1, 2008; previously amended effective July 1, 2008.

Rule 7.1063. Change of conservatee's residence

(a) Pre-move notice of change of personal residence required

Unless an emergency requires a shorter period of notice, the conservator of the person must mail copies of a notice of an intended change of the conservatee's personal residence to the persons listed below at least 15 days before the date of the proposed change, and file the original notice with proof of mailing with the court. Copies of the notice must be mailed to:

(1) The conservatee;

(2) The conservatee's attorney of record;

(3) The conservatee's spouse or registered domestic partner; and

(4) The conservatee's relatives named in the *Petition for Appointment of Probate Conservator* (form GC-310), including the conservatee's "deemed relatives" under Probate Code section 1821(b)(1)–(4) if the conservatee has no spouse or registered domestic partner and no second-degree relatives.

(Subd (a) adopted effective January 1, 2008.)

(b) Conservatee's personal residence

(1) The "conservatee's personal residence" under (a) is the residence the conservatee understands or believes, or reasonably appears to understand or believe, to be his or her permanent residence on the date the first petition for appointment of a conservator was filed in the proceeding, whether or not the conservatee is living in that residence on that date. A residential care facility, including a board and care, intermediate care, skilled nursing, or secured perimeter facility, may be the conservatee's personal residence under this rule.

(2) If the conservatee cannot form or communicate an understanding or belief concerning his or her permanent residence on the date the first petition for appointment of a conservator was filed in the proceeding, his or her personal residence under this rule is the residence he or she last previously understood or believed, or appeared to understand or believe, to be his or her permanent residence.

(3) For purposes of this rule, the following changes of residence are or are not changes of the conservatee's personal residence, as indicated:

(A) A move from the conservatee's personal residence under this rule to a residential care facility or other residence is a change of the conservatee's personal residence under (a).

(B) A move from a residential care facility or other residence to another residence that is not the conservatee's personal residence under this rule is a change of the conservatee's personal residence under (a).

(C) A move from a residential care facility or other residence to the conservatee's personal residence under this rule is not a change of the conservatee's personal residence under (a).

(Subd (b) adopted effective January 1, 2008.)

(c) Post-move notice of a change of residence required

The conservator of the person must file a notice of a change of the conservatee's residence with the court within 30 days of the date of the change. Unless waived by the court for good cause to prevent harm to the conservatee, the conservator must mail a copy of the notice to the persons named below and file a proof of mailing with the original notice filed with the court. Unless waived, the notice must be mailed to:

(1) The conservatee's attorney of record;

(2) The conservatee's spouse or registered domestic partner; and

(3) The conservatee's relatives named in the *Petition for Appointment of Probate Conservator* (form GC-310), including the conservatee's "deemed relatives" under Probate Code section 1821(b)(1)–(4) if the conservatee has no spouse or registered domestic partner and no second-degree relatives.

(Subd (c) adopted effective January 1, 2008.)

(d) Conservatee's residence

The "conservatee's residence" under (c) is the conservatee's residence at any time after appointment of a conservator.

(Subd (d) adopted effective January 1, 2008.)

(e) Use of Judicial Council forms GC-079 and GC-080

(1) The *Pre-Move Notice of Proposed Change of Personal Residence of Conservatee or Ward* (form GC-079) must be used for the pre-move notice required under (a) and Probate Code section 2352(e)(3). The conservator, the conservator's attorney, or an employee of the attorney may complete the mailing and sign the Proof of Mailing on page 2 of the form. If the notice is mailed less than 15 days before the date of the move because an emergency requires a shorter period of notice, the basis for the emergency must be stated in the notice.

(2) The *Post-Move Notice of Change of Residence of Conservatee or Ward* (form GC-080) must be used for the post-move notice required under (c) and Probate Code section 2352(e)(1) and (2). The conservator, the conservator's attorney, or an employee of the attorney may complete the mailing and sign the Proof of Mailing on page 2 of the form.

(Subd (e) adopted effective January 1, 2008.)

(f) Prior court approval required to establish conservatee's residence outside California

Notwithstanding any other provision of this rule, prior court approval is required before a conservatee's residence may be established outside the state of California.

(Subd (f) adopted effective January 1, 2008.)

Rule 7.1063 adopted effective January 1, 2008.

Chapter 23
Appointed Counsel

Chapter 23 amended effective January 1, 2020; adopted effective January 1, 2008.

Rule 7.1101. Scope, definitions, and general qualifications
Rule 7.1102. Qualifications and annual education required for counsel appointed to represent a ward or proposed ward (Prob. Code, §§ 1456, 1470(a))
Rule 7.1103. Qualifications and annual education required for counsel appointed to represent a conservatee, proposed conservatee, or person alleged to lack legal capacity (Prob. Code, §§ 1456, 1470(a), 1471)
Rule 7.1104. Local administration
Rule 7.1105. Certification of attorney qualifications

Rule 7.1101. Scope, definitions, and general qualifications

(a) Scope (Prob. Code, §§ 1456, 1470–1471)

The rules in this chapter establish minimum qualifications, annual education requirements, and certification requirements that an attorney must meet as conditions of court appointment as counsel under Probate Code section 1470 or 1471 in a proceeding under division 4 of that code.

(1) The rules in this chapter apply to an appointed attorney regardless of whether the attorney is a sole practitioner or works for a private law firm, a legal services organization, or a public defender's office.

(2) The rules in this chapter do not apply to:

(A) Retained counsel;

(B) Counsel appointed under the authority of any law other than Probate Code section 1470 or 1471.

(Subd (a) adopted effective January 1, 2020.)

(b) Definitions

For purposes of this chapter, the following terms are used as defined below:

(1) "Appointed counsel" or "appointed attorney" means an attorney appointed by the court under Probate Code section 1470 or 1471 who

assumes direct personal responsibility for representing a ward or proposed ward, a conservatee or proposed conservatee, or a person alleged to lack legal capacity in a proceeding under division 4 of the Probate Code.

(2) "Probate guardianship" means any proceeding related to a general or temporary guardianship under division 4 of the Probate Code.

(3) "Probate conservatorship" means any proceeding related to a conservatorship or limited conservatorship, general or temporary, under division 4 of the Probate Code.

(4) "LPS Act" refers to the Lanterman-Petris-Short Act (Welf. & Inst. Code, §§ 5000–5556), which provides for involuntary mental health treatment and conservatorship for persons who are gravely disabled as the result of a mental health disorder.

(5) A "contested matter" is a matter that requires a noticed hearing and in which an objection is filed in writing or made orally in open court by any person entitled to appear at the hearing and support or oppose the petition.

(6) "Trial" means the determination of one or more disputed issues of fact by means of an evidentiary hearing.

(Subd (b) adopted effective January 1, 2020.)

(c) General qualifications

To qualify for any appointment under Probate Code section 1470 or 1471, an attorney must:

(1) Be an active member in good standing of the State Bar of California or a registered legal aid attorney qualified to practice law in California under rule 9.45;

(2) Have had no professional discipline imposed in the 12 months immediately preceding the date of submitting any initial or annual certification of compliance; and

(3) Have demonstrated to the court that the attorney or the attorney's firm or employer:

(A) Is covered by professional liability insurance with coverage limits no less than $100,000 per claim and $300,000 per year; or

(B) Is covered for professional liability at an equivalent level through a self-insurance program;

(4) Have met the applicable qualifications and annual education requirements in this chapter and have a current certification on file with the appointing court; and

(5) Have satisfied any additional requirements established by local rule.

(Subd (c) adopted effective January 1, 2020.)

(d) Local rules

The rules in this chapter establish minimum qualifications and requirements. Nothing in this chapter prohibits a court from establishing, by local rule adopted under rule 10.613, additional or more rigorous qualifications or requirements.

(Subd (d) adopted effective January 1, 2020.)

(e) Retroactivity

The amendments to this chapter adopted effective January 1, 2020, are not retroactive. They do not require an attorney who submitted an initial certification of qualifications under this chapter as it read on or before December 31, 2019, to submit a new initial certification.

(Subd (e) adopted effective January 1, 2020.)

Rule 7.1101 adopted effective January 1, 2020.

Rule 7.1102. Qualifications and annual education required for counsel appointed to represent a ward or proposed ward (Prob. Code, §§ 1456, 1470(a))

Except as provided in rule 7.1104(b), an attorney appointed for a ward or proposed ward must have met the qualifications in either (a) or (b) and, in every calendar year after first availability for appointment, must meet the annual education requirements in (c).

(a) Experience-based qualifications

An attorney is qualified for appointment if the attorney has met the experience requirements described in either (1) or (2).

(1) Within the five years immediately before first availability for appointment, the attorney has personally represented a petitioner, an objector, a respondent, a minor child, or a nonminor dependent in at least three of any combination of the following proceedings, at least one of which must have been a contested matter or trial:

(A) A probate guardianship proceeding;

(B) A juvenile court child welfare proceeding; or

(C) A family law child custody proceeding.

(2) At the time of first availability for appointment, the attorney meets the experience requirements:

(A) In rule 5.660(d) and any applicable local rules for appointment to represent a minor child or nonminor dependent in a juvenile court child welfare proceeding; or

(B) In rule 5.242(f) for appointment to represent a minor child in a family law child custody proceeding.

(Subd (a) adopted effective January 1, 2020.)

(b) Alternative qualifications

An attorney who does not yet meet the experience-based qualifications in (a) may, until the attorney has gained the necessary experience, qualify for appointment if the attorney meets the requirements in (1) or (2).

(1) At the time of appointment, the attorney works for an attorney, a private law firm, or a legal services organization approved by the court for appointment under Probate Code section 1470 to represent wards or proposed wards, and the attorney is supervised by or working in close professional consultation with a qualified attorney who has satisfied the experience requirements in (a); or

(2) In the 12 months immediately before first availability for appointment, the attorney has completed at least three hours of professional education approved by the State Bar of California for Minimum Continuing Legal Education (MCLE) credit in the subjects listed in (d) and, at the time of appointment, the attorney is working in close professional consultation with a qualified attorney who has satisfied the experience requirements in (a).

(Subd (b) adopted effective January 1, 2020.)

(c) Annual education

Each calendar year after first availability for appointment, an attorney appointed by the court to represent a ward or proposed ward must complete at least three hours of professional education approved by the State Bar for MCLE credit in the subjects listed in (d).

(Subd (c) adopted effective January 1, 2020.)

(d) Subject matter and delivery of education

Education in the following subjects—delivered in person or by any State Bar–approved method of distance learning—may be used to satisfy this rule's education requirements:

(1) State and federal statutes—including the federal Indian Child Welfare Act of 1978 (25 U.S.C. §§ 1901–1963)—rules of court, and case law governing probate guardianship proceedings and the legal rights of parents and children;

(2) Child development, including techniques for communicating with a child client; and

(3) Risk factors for child abuse and neglect and family violence.

(Subd (d) adopted effective January 1, 2020.)

Rule 7.1102 adopted effective January 1, 2020.

Rule 7.1103. Qualifications and annual education required for counsel appointed to represent a conservatee, proposed conservatee, or person alleged to lack legal capacity (Prob. Code, §§ 1456, 1470(a), 1471)

Except as provided in rule 7.1104(b), an attorney appointed to represent the interests of a conservatee, proposed conservatee, or person alleged to lack legal capacity must have met the qualifications in (a) or (b) and, in every calendar year after first availability for appointment, must meet the annual education requirements in (c).

(a) Experience-based qualifications

An attorney is qualified for appointment if, within the five years immediately preceding first availability for appointment, the attorney has personally represented a petitioner, an objector, a conservatee or proposed conservatee, or a person alleged to lack legal capacity or be gravely disabled in at least three separate proceedings under either division 4 of the Probate Code or the LPS Act, including at least one contested matter or trial.

(Subd (a) adopted effective January 1, 2020.)

(b) Alternative qualifications

An attorney who does not yet meet the experience-based qualifications in (a) may, until the attorney has gained the necessary experience, qualify for appointment if the attorney meets the requirements in (1) or (2).

(1) At the time of appointment, the attorney works for an attorney, a private law firm, a public defender's office, or a legal services organization (including the organization designated by the Governor as the state protection and advocacy agency, as defined in section 4900(i) of the Welfare and Institutions Code) approved by the court for appointment to represent conservatees, proposed conservatees, and persons alleged to lack legal capacity, and the attorney is supervised by or working in close

professional consultation with a qualified attorney who has satisfied the experience requirements in (a); or

(2) In the 12 months immediately before first availability for appointment, the attorney has completed at least three hours of professional education approved by the State Bar of California for Minimum Continuing Legal Education (MCLE) credit in the subjects listed in (d), and, at the time of appointment, the attorney is working in close professional consultation with a qualified attorney who has satisfied the experience requirements in (a).

(Subd (b) adopted effective January 1, 2020.)

(c) Annual education

(1) Each calendar year after first availability for appointment, an attorney appointed by the court to represent a conservatee, proposed conservatee, or person alleged to lack legal capacity must complete at least three hours of professional education approved by the State Bar for MCLE credit in the subjects listed in (d).

(2) The annual education in (1) must include at least one hour of instruction on less restrictive alternatives to conservatorship, as specified in (d)(4).

(Subd (c) amended effective January 1, 2024; adopted effective January 1, 2020.)

(d) Subject matter and delivery of education

Education in the following subjects—delivered in person or by any State Bar–approved method of distance learning—may be used to satisfy this rule's education requirements:

(1) State and federal statutes—including the federal Americans with Disabilities Act (42 U.S.C. §§ 12101–12213)—rules of court, and case law governing probate conservatorship proceedings, capacity determinations, and the legal rights of conservatees, persons alleged to lack legal capacity, and persons with disabilities;

(2) The attorney-client relationship and lawyer's ethical duties to a client under the California Rules of Professional Conduct and other applicable law; and

(3) Special considerations for representing an older adult or a person with a disability, including:

(A) Communicating with an older client or a client with a disability;

(B) Vulnerability of older adults and persons with disabilities to undue influence, physical and financial abuse, and neglect; and

(C) Effects of aging, major neurocognitive disorders (including dementia), and intellectual and developmental disabilities on a person's ability to perform the activities of daily living.

(4) The less restrictive alternatives to conservatorship, including supported decisionmaking, stated in Probate Code section 1800.3.

(Subd (d) amended effective January 1, 2024; adopted effective January 1, 2020.)

Rule 7.1103 amended effective January 1, 2024; adopted effective January 1, 2020.

Rule 7.1104. Local administration

(a) Procedures

(1) A local court may create and maintain lists or panels of certified attorneys or approve the public defender's office and one or more legal services organizations to provide qualified attorneys for appointment under Probate Code sections 1470 and 1471 to represent specific categories of persons in proceedings under division 4 of that code.

(2) A court may establish, by local rule adopted under rule 10.613, procedural requirements, including submission of an application, as conditions for approval for appointment or placement on a list or panel.

(Subd (a) adopted effective January 1, 2020.)

(b) Exception to qualifications

A court may appoint an attorney who is not qualified under rule 7.1102 or 7.1103 on an express finding, on the record or in writing, of circumstances that make such an appointment necessary. These circumstances may include, but are not limited to, when:

(1) No qualified attorney is available for appointment; or

(2) The needs or interests of the person to be represented cannot be served without the appointment of an attorney who has other specific knowledge, skills, or experience.

(Subd (b) adopted effective January 1, 2020.)

Rule 7.1104 adopted effective January 1, 2020.

Rule 7.1105. Certification of attorney qualifications

(a) Initial certification

Before first availability for appointment under Probate Code section 1470 or 1471, an attorney must certify to the court that the attorney:

(1) Meets the licensing, disciplinary status, and insurance requirements in rule 7.1101(c)(1)–(3); and

(2) Meets the qualifications in rule 7.1102 for appointment to represent wards or the qualifications in rule 7.1103 for appointment to represent conservatees, or both, depending on the appointments the attorney wishes to be available for.

(Subd (a) adopted effective January 1, 2020.)

(b) Annual certification

To remain eligible for appointment under Probate Code section 1470 or 1471, an attorney who has submitted an initial certification must certify to the court, no later than March 31 of each following year, that:

(1) The attorney meets the licensing, disciplinary status, and insurance requirements in rule 7.1101(c)(1)–(3); and

(2) The attorney has completed the applicable annual education—in rule 7.1102, 7.1103, or both—required for the previous calendar year.

(Subd (b) adopted effective January 1, 2020.)

(c) Notification of disciplinary action

An appointed attorney must notify the court in writing within five court days of any disciplinary action taken against the attorney by the State Bar of California. The notification must describe the charges, disposition, and terms of any reproof, probation, or suspension.

(Subd (c) adopted effective January 1, 2020.)

(d) Documentation

A court to which an attorney has submitted a certification under this rule may require the attorney to submit documentation or other information in support of any statement in the certification.

(Subd (d) adopted effective January 1, 2020.)

(e) Confidentiality

The certifications required by this rule and any supporting documentation or information submitted to the court must be maintained confidentially by the court. They must not be filed or lodged in a case file.

(Subd (e) adopted effective January 1, 2020.)

Rule 7.1105 adopted effective January 1, 2020.

Division 2
Mental Health Rules

Chap. 1. [Reserved]
Chap. 2. CARE Act Rules. Rules 7.2201–7.2303.

Chapter 1
[Reserved]

Chapter 2
CARE Act Rules

Art. 1. Preliminary Provisions. Rules 7.2201–7.2210.
Art. 2. Commencement of Proceedings. Rules 7.2221–7.2230.
Art. 3. Notice and Joinder. Rules 7.2235, 7.2240.
Art. 4. Accountability. Rules 7.2301, 7.2303.

Article 1
Preliminary Provisions

Rule 7.2201. Title and purpose
Rule 7.2205. Definitions
Rule 7.2210. General provisions

Rule 7.2201. Title and purpose

The rules in this chapter may be referred to as the CARE Act rules. These rules are intended to implement the policies and provisions governing judicial proceedings under the CARE Act.

Rule 7.2201 adopted effective September 1, 2023.

Rule 7.2205. Definitions

As used in this chapter, the terms defined in Welfare and Institutions Code section 5971 have the meaning stated in that section. In addition, as used in this chapter:

(1) "CARE Act" refers to the Community Assistance, Recovery, and Empowerment Act, as codified at Welfare and Institutions Code sections 5970–5987.

(2) "Intensive treatment" is involuntary mental health treatment authorized under section 5250.

(3) A "section" is a section of the Welfare and Institutions Code unless otherwise specified.

Rule 7.2205 adopted effective September 1, 2023.

Rule 7.2210. General provisions

(a) Local rules

A superior court may, subject to the limits in the CARE Act and these rules, adopt local rules to govern CARE Act proceedings.

(Subd (a) adopted effective September 1, 2023.)

(b) Access to records (§ 5977.4(a))

All documents filed and all evaluations, reports, and other documents submitted to the court in CARE Act proceedings are confidential, notwithstanding disclosure of their contents during a CARE Act hearing. No person other than the respondent, the respondent's counsel, the county behavioral health director or the director's designee, counsel for the director or the director's designee, and, with the respondent's express consent given in writing or orally in court, the respondent's supporter may inspect **or copy** the case records without a court order.

(Subd (b) amended effective September 1, 2024; adopted effective September 1, 2023.)

(c) Sealing of records (§ 5976.5(e))

(1) A motion to seal records under section 5976.5(e) must specify the records to which it applies.

(2) The respondent must serve the motion to seal on the other parties not later than the close of the next court day after the motion is filed.

(3) Any opposition to the motion must be filed within 10 court days of the date of service in (2).

(4) The extensions of time in Code of Civil Procedure sections 1010.6 and 1013 apply to motions under section 5976.5(e).

(5) The court may grant the motion without a hearing or, if timely opposition is filed, set a hearing on the motion, and provide at least five court days' notice to all parties.

(6) *Order*

(A) If the court grants the motion and the sealed record is in paper format, the clerk must place on the envelope or container of the record a label prominently stating "SEALED BY ORDER OF THE COURT ON (DATE)." If the sealed record is in electronic form, the clerk must file the court's order, maintain the record ordered sealed in a secure manner, and clearly identify the record as sealed by court order on a specified date.

(B) The order must state whether any person other than the court is authorized to inspect the sealed record.

(7) Rules 2.550 and 2.551 do not apply to motions to seal records under section 5976.5(e).

(Subd (c) adopted effective September 1, 2024.)

(d) Respondent within juvenile court jurisdiction (§ 5977.4(c))

(1) *Informing the juvenile court*

Upon learning that a respondent is within a juvenile court's dependency, delinquency, or transition jurisdiction, the CARE Act court must inform the juvenile court that a CARE Act petition has been filed on behalf of that respondent. The court may communicate this information in any suitable manner.

(2) *Concurrent jurisdiction with juvenile court*

The CARE Act court is not precluded by statute from exercising jurisdiction over a respondent who is within a juvenile court's dependency, delinquency, or transition jurisdiction. The CARE Act court and the juvenile court may, therefore, exercise concurrent jurisdiction over such a respondent.

(Subd (d) adopted effective September 1, 2024.)

(e) Notification of respondent's attorney in related proceedings (§ 5977.4(c))

If the CARE Act court learns that the respondent has been referred from a proceeding identified in section 5978 or that the respondent is within a juvenile court's dependency, delinquency, or transition jurisdiction, the court must order the county agency to:

(1) Notify the respondent's attorney, if any, in the related case that a CARE Act petition has been filed on behalf of the respondent; and

(2) Provide the attorney with the contact information of the respondent's CARE Act attorney, if known.

(Subd (e) adopted effective September 1, 2024.)

(f) No communication of further information (§ 5976.5)

Subdivisions (d) and (e) of this rule do not authorize the communication of information other than that identified in those subdivisions absent an express waiver by the respondent.

(Subd (f) adopted effective September 1, 2024.)

Rule 7.2210 amended effective September 1, 2024; adopted September 1, 2023.

Advisory Committee Comment

Subdivisions (d) and (e). As used in these subdivisions, the phrase "within a juvenile court's dependency, delinquency, or transition jurisdiction" refers to a respondent whom a juvenile court has found to be described by Welfare and Institutions Code section 300, 450, 601, or 602 and who is currently within the juvenile court's jurisdiction based on one of those descriptions. The term does not refer to any other party to a juvenile court proceeding.

Subdivision (d)(2). The subdivision is intended to describe the effect of existing law. Neither the juvenile court law (Welf. & Inst. Code, §§ 200–987) nor the CARE Act precludes concurrent jurisdiction or, conversely, confers exclusive jurisdiction on either court over matters relating to the mental health treatment of persons who meet the statutory jurisdictional criteria of both.

Article 2
Commencement of Proceedings

Rule 7.2221. Papers to be filed (§ 5975)
Rule 7.2223. Venue and transfer (§ 5973)
Rule 7.2225. Persons who may file petition (§§ 5974, 5978)
Rule 7.2230. Counsel for respondent (§§ 5976(c), 5977(a)(3)(A), (a)(5)(C) & (b)(1))

Rule 7.2221. Papers to be filed *(§ 5975)*

[1] A petition to commence CARE Act proceedings must be made on *Petition to Commence CARE Act Proceedings* (form CARE-100). The petition must include either:

(1) A completed *Mental Health Declaration—CARE Act Proceedings* (form CARE-101); or

(2) The evidence described in section 5975(d)(2).

(Subd (a) amended effective September 1, 2024; adopted effective September 1, 2023.)

[2]

Rule 7.2221 amended effective September 1, 2024; adopted effective September 1, 2023.

Rule 7.2221 2024 Deletes. [1] (a) Petition packet (§ 5975) [2] (b) Acceptance of papers for filing

On receipt of a petition, the clerk must file the petition packet, assign a case number, and place the packet in a confidential file.

Rule 7.2223. Venue and transfer (§ 5973)

(a) Filing

A petition to commence CARE Act proceedings may be filed in the superior court of:

(1) The county where the respondent resides at the time of filing;

(2) The county where the respondent is found at the time of filing; or

(3) A county where the respondent is a defendant or respondent in a pending criminal or civil action or proceeding.

(Subd (a) adopted effective September 1, 2023.)

(b) Transfer

If the court orders the proceeding transferred to the superior court of the respondent's county of residence, the courts must proceed as follows:

(1) The clerk of the transferring court must mail notice and a copy of the order to:

(A) The petitioner and petitioner's counsel, if any;

(B) A former petitioner to whom the court has assigned notice rights under section 5977(b)(7)(B)(ii), if any;

(C) The respondent, the respondent's counsel, if any, and, with the respondent's express consent given in writing or orally in court, the respondent's supporter, if any;

(D) The county behavioral health agency of the county in which the petition was filed and the agency's counsel, if the agency is not the petitioner;

(E) The county agency preparing a report ordered under section 5977(a)(3)(B) and the agency's counsel; and

(F) The county behavioral health agency in the respondent's county of residence and the agency's counsel.

(2) The clerk of the transferring court must transmit to the clerk of the receiving court a certified copy of the order and all papers on file in the proceeding.

(3) When a court receives the case file of a transferred proceeding, the receiving court must send written notification of receipt to the transferring court.

(4) If the transferring court has not received a notification of receipt within 60 days of the transfer order, it must make a reasonable inquiry into the status of the transferred proceeding.

(Subd (b) adopted effective September 1, 2023.)

Rule 7.2223 adopted effective September 1, 2023.

Rule 7.2225. [1] *Persons who may file petition* (§§ 5974, 5978)

[2] Any person identified in section 5974 may file a petition to begin CARE Act proceedings. If a petition is based on a referral authorized by section 5978, only the person designated in that section may file the petition.

(Subd (a) amended effective September 1, 2024; adopted effective September 1, 2023.)

[3]

Rule 7.2225 amended effective September 1, 2024; adopted effective September 1, 2023.

Rule 7.2225   2024 Deletes. [1] Petitioner **[2]** (a) Persons who may file petition
A petition to commence proceedings under the CARE Act may be filed by any of the persons identified in section 5974 or, in the circumstances specified therein, section 5978. **[3]** (b) Petitioner on referral under Penal Code section 1370.01
On referral by a court under Penal Code section 1370.01, an agency designated by the county will be the petitioner.

Rule 7.2230.   Counsel for respondent (§§ 5976(c), 5977(a)(3)(A), (a)(5)(C) & (b)(1))

(a) Appointment

If the court finds that the petitioner has made a prima facie showing that the respondent is or may be a person described by section 5972, the court must **[1]**:

(1) Appoint a qualified legal services project as counsel to represent the respondent; or

(2) If no qualified legal services project has agreed to accept CARE Act appointments from the court, appoint a public defender or an attorney acting in that capacity to represent the respondent.

(Subd (a) amended effective September 1, 2024; adopted effective September 1, 2023.)

Rule 7.2230(a)   2024 Deletes. [1], in accordance with procedures established by local rule

(b) Copy of petition

On appointment, the court must provide a copy of the petition packet to appointed counsel.

(Subd (b) adopted effective September 1, 2023.)

(c) Substitution (§ 5977(b)(1))

(1) The court may relieve appointed counsel:

(A) At the request of counsel or the respondent, on substitution of the respondent's own chosen counsel or appointment of substitute counsel; or

(B) For cause, on appointment of substitute counsel.

(2) The respondent must make arrangements for the compensation, if any, of chosen counsel.

(Subd (c) adopted effective September 1, 2023.)

Rule 7.2230 amended effective September 1, 2024; adopted effective September 1, 2023.

Article 3
Notice and Joinder

Rule 7.2235. Notice of proceedings (§§ 5977–5977.3, 5979)
Rule 7.2240. Joinder of local government entity (§ 5977.1(d)(4))

Rule 7.2235.   Notice of proceedings (§§ 5977–5977.3, 5979)

(a) Notice of order for report to augment petition (§ 5977(a)(3) & (4))

(1) Before engaging the respondent and preparing a report ordered under section 5977(a)(3)(B), the county agency ordered to file the report and serve notice of that order must give written notice to the respondent by serving the respondent personally or, if personal service is not practicable, by any method reasonably calculated to give the respondent actual notice. Proof of service on the respondent by any method other than personal service must include an explanation why personal service is impracticable and why the alternative method of service used is reasonably calculated to give the respondent actual notice.

(2) The county agency must give notice to the respondent's counsel and the petitioner as provided in (d).

(3) Notice must be given on *Notice of Order for CARE Act Report* (form CARE-106) and must include a copy of *Order for CARE Act Report* (form CARE-105) issued by the court.

(4) Notice to the respondent and the respondent's counsel must also include a copy of the petition packet filed to begin the proceedings and *Information for Respondents—About the CARE Act* (form CARE-060-INFO).

(5) If the court grants the county agency additional time to engage the respondent in voluntary treatment and services before filing the report, the county agency must, within five calendar days of the order, serve written notice of the extended report deadline on the respondent, the respondent's counsel, and the petitioner on form CARE-106 as provided in (d).

(Subd (a) adopted effective September 1, 2023.)

(b) Notice of initial appearance (§ 5977(a)(3)(A), (a)(5)(C))

(1) The county must give at least five court days' notice of the date, time, and location of the initial appearance under section 5977(b) to the respondent and the respondent's counsel, the petitioner and the petitioner's counsel unless the county behavioral health agency is the petitioner, and, if the respondent does not reside in the county where the petition is filed, the county behavioral health agency in the respondent's county of residence and the agency's counsel.

(2) Notice must be given on *Notice of Initial Appearance—CARE Act Proceedings* (form CARE-110).

(3) *Notice to respondent*

(A) Notice must be served personally on the respondent or, if personal service is not practicable, by any method reasonably calculated to give the respondent actual notice. Proof of service on the respondent by any method other than personal service must include an explanation why personal service is impracticable and why the alternative method of service used is reasonably calculated to give the respondent actual notice.

(B) Notice to the respondent must include copies of the following:

(i) The petition packet filed to begin the proceedings;

(ii) Any report ordered and filed under section 5977(a)(3);

(iii) *Notice of Respondent's Rights—CARE Act Proceedings* (form CARE-113); and

(iv) *Information for Respondents—About the CARE Act* (form CARE-060-INFO).

(4) *Notice to respondent's counsel*

(A) Notice must be served on the respondent's counsel by any method provided in (d).

(B) Notice to the respondent's counsel must include copies of the following:

(i) The petition packet filed to begin the proceedings; and

(ii) Any report ordered under section 5977(a)(3).

(5) *Notice to other persons*

Notice must be served on all other persons entitled to receive notice by any method provided in (d).

(Subd (b) adopted effective September 1, 2023.)

(c) Notice of other hearings (§§ 5977–5977.3, 5979)

(1) The county must give at least five court days' notice of any hearing after the initial appearance to the respondent, the respondent's counsel, any local government entity the court has joined as a party to the proceedings, and, with the respondent's express consent given in writing or orally in court, the respondent's supporter.

(2) Notice must be given on *Notice of Hearing—CARE Act Proceedings* (form CARE-115) and, except as provided in (3), served as provided in (d).

(3) Notice to the respondent must be served personally or, if personal service is not practicable, by any method reasonably calculated to give the respondent actual notice and include a copy of *Notice of Respondent's Rights—CARE Act Proceedings* (form CARE-113). Proof of service on the respondent by any method other than personal service must include an explanation why personal service is impracticable and why the alternative method of service used is reasonably calculated to give the respondent actual notice.

(4) Notice to the respondent and the respondent's counsel of a clinical evaluation hearing under section 5977.1(c) must include a copy of the evaluation ordered under section 5977.1(b).

(5) Notice to the respondent and the respondent's counsel of a status review hearing under section 5977.2(a)(1) must include a copy of the report required by that section.

(6) Notice to the respondent and the respondent's counsel of a one-year status hearing under section 5977.3(a)(1) must include a copy of the report required by that section.

(Subd (c) adopted effective September 1, 2023.)

(d) Method of service

Unless personal service is required, any notice or other document required by this rule to be served may be served as follows:

(1) Personally or by first-class mail, express mail, or overnight delivery on any person;

(2) By fax transmission as provided in rule 2.306; or

(3) Electronically as provided in Code of Civil Procedure section 1010.6 and rule 2.251.

(Subd (d) adopted effective September 1, 2023.)

Rule 7.2235 adopted effective September 1, 2023.

Rule 7.2240. Joinder of local government entity (§ 5977.1(d)(4))

(a) Order to show cause

Before granting a motion or request to join as a party to the proceedings another local government entity that would be required to provide a service or support under a proposed CARE plan, the court must:

(1) Order the local government entity and all parties to show cause why the entity should not be joined as a party to the CARE Act proceedings and ordered to provide the service or support; and

(2) Set the hearing on the order to show cause no fewer than 15 calendar days after the date of the order's issuance.

(Subd (a) adopted effective September 1, 2023.)

(b) Manner of service

The moving party must serve the order to show cause on the local government entity in the manner of a summons as provided in Code of Civil Procedure sections 415.10 and 416.50.

(Subd (b) adopted effective September 1, 2023.)

Rule 7.2240 adopted effective September 1, 2023.

Article 4
Accountability

Rule 7.2301. Order to show cause (§ 5979(b))
Rule 7.2303. Participation in accountability hearings (§ 5979)

Rule 7.2301. Order to show cause (§ 5979(b))

When a presiding judge or the presiding judge's designee issues an order to show cause why the county or other local government entity should not be fined for not complying with court orders, as provided in section 5979(b)(2)(A), the clerk must serve the order to show cause on the county or other local government entity and the parties and their counsel no fewer than 15 calendar days before the date set for hearing.

Rule 7.2301 adopted effective September 1, 2023.

Rule 7.2303. Participation in accountability hearings (§ 5979)

The respondent and the respondent's counsel are entitled to be present at and participate in all proceedings under section 5979(a) and (b).

Rule 7.2303 adopted effective September 1, 2023.

TITLE 8
Appellate Rules

Division 1. Rules Relating to the Supreme Court and Courts of Appeal. Rules 8.1–8.552.
Division 2. Rules Relating to Death Penalty Appeals and Habeas Corpus Proceedings. Rules 8.601–8.652.
Division 3. Rules Relating to Miscellaneous Appeals and Writ Proceedings. Rules 8.700–8.730.
Division 4. Rules Relating to the Superior Court Appellate Division. Rules 8.800–8.936.
Division 5. Rules Relating to Appeals and Writs in Small Claims Cases. Rules 8.950–8.977.
Division 6. Transfer of Appellate Division Cases to the Court of Appeal. Rules 8.1000–8.1018.
Division 7. Publication of Appellate Opinions. Rules 8.1100–8.1125.

Division 1
Rules Relating to the Supreme Court and Courts of Appeal

Chap. 1. General Provisions. Rules 8.1–8.90.
Chap. 2. Civil Appeals. Rules 8.100–8.278.
Chap. 3. Criminal Appeals. Rules 8.300–8.368.
Chap. 4. Habeas Corpus Appeals and Writs. Rules 8.380–8.398.
Chap. 5. Juvenile Appeals and Writs. Rules 8.400–8.474.
Chap. 6. Conservatorship and Civil Commitment Appeals. Rules 8.480–8.483.
Chap. 7. Writs of Mandate, Certiorari, and Prohibition in the Supreme Court and Court of Appeal. Rules 8.485–8.493.
Chap. 8. [Reserved].
Chap. 9. Proceedings in the Supreme Court. Rules 8.500–8.552.

Chapter 1
General Provisions

Art. 1. In General. Rules 8.1–8.23.
Art. 2. Service, Filing, Filing Fees, Form, and Privacy. Rules 8.25–8.44.
Art. 3. Sealed and Confidential Records. Rules 8.45–8.47.
Art. 4. Applications and Motions; Extending and Shortening Time. Rules 8.50–8.68.
Art. 5. E-filing. Rules 8.70–8.79.
Art. 6. Public Access to Electronic Appellate Court Records. Rules 8.80–8.85.
Art. 7. Privacy. Rule 8.90.

Article 1
In General

Rule 8.1. Title
Rule 8.4. Application of division
Rule 8.7. Construction
Rule 8.10. Definitions and use of terms
Rule 8.11. Scope of rules
Rule 8.13. Amendments to rules
Rule 8.16. Amendments to statutes
Rule 8.18. Documents violating rules not to be filed
Rule 8.20. California Rules of Court prevail
Rule 8.23. Sanctions to compel compliance

Rule 8.1. Title

The rules in this title may be referred to as the Appellate Rules. All references in this title to "these rules" are to the Appellate Rules.
Rule 8.1 adopted effective January 1, 2007.

Rule 8.4. Application of division

The rules in this division apply to:
(1) Appeals from the superior courts, except appeals to the appellate divisions of the superior courts;
(2) Original proceedings, motions, applications, and petitions in the Courts of Appeal and the Supreme Court; and
(3) Proceedings for transferring cases within the appellate jurisdiction of the superior court to the Court of Appeal for review, unless rules 8.1000–8.1018 provide otherwise.
Rule 8.4 amended and renumbered effective January 1, 2007; repealed and adopted as rule 53 effective January 1, 2005.

Rule 8.7. Construction

The rules of construction stated in rule 1.5 apply to these rules. In addition, in these rules the headings of divisions, chapters, articles, rules, and subdivisions are substantive.
Rule 8.7 adopted effective January 1, 2007.

Rule 8.10. Definitions and use of terms

Unless the context or subject matter requires otherwise, the definitions and use of terms in rule 1.6 apply to these rules. In addition, the following apply:
(1) "Appellant" means the appealing party.
(2) "Respondent" means the adverse party.
(3) "Party" includes any attorney of record for that party.
(4) "Judgment" includes any judgment or order that may be appealed.
(5) "Superior court" means the court from which an appeal is taken.
(6) "Reviewing court" means the Supreme Court or the Court of Appeal to which an appeal is taken, in which an original proceeding is begun, or to which an appeal or original proceeding is transferred.
(7) The word "briefs" includes petitions for rehearing, petitions for review, and answers thereto. It does not include petitions for extraordinary relief in original proceedings.
(8) "Attach" or "attachment" may refer to either physical attachment or electronic attachment, as appropriate.
(9) "Copy" or "copies" may refer to electronic copies, as appropriate.
(10) "Cover" includes the cover page of a document filed electronically.
(11) "Written" and "writing" include electronically created written materials, whether or not those materials are printed on paper.
Rule 8.10 amended effective January 1, 2016; repealed and adopted as rule 40 effective January 1, 2005; previously amended and renumbered as rule 8.10 effective January 1, 2007.

Rule 8.11. Scope of rules

These rules apply to documents filed and served electronically as well as in paper form, unless otherwise provided.
Rule 8.11 adopted effective January 1, 2016.

Rule 8.13. Amendments to rules

Only the Judicial Council may amend these rules, except the rules in division 7, which may be amended only by the Supreme Court. An amendment by the Judicial Council must be published in the advance pamphlets of the Official Reports and takes effect on the date ordered by the Judicial Council.
Rule 8.13 amended effective January 1, 2024; repealed and adopted as rule 54 effective January 1, 2005; previously amended and renumbered effective January 1, 2007.

Rule 8.16. Amendments to statutes

In these rules, a reference to a statute includes any subsequent amendment to the statute.
Rule 8.16 adopted effective January 1, 2007.

Rule 8.18. Documents violating rules not to be filed

Except as these rules provide otherwise, the reviewing court clerk must not file any record or other document that does not conform to these rules.
Rule 8.18 amended effective January 1, 2009; repealed and adopted as rule 46 effective January 1, 2005; previously amended and renumbered effective January 1, 2007.

Advisory Committee Comment

The exception in this rule acknowledges that there are different rules that apply to certain non-conforming documents. For example, this rule does not apply to nonconforming or late briefs, which are addressed by rules 8.204(e) and 8.220(a), respectively, or to nonconforming supporting documents accompanying a writ petition under chapter 7, which are addressed by rule 8.486(c)(2).

Rule 8.20. California Rules of Court prevail

A Court of Appeal must accept for filing a record, brief, or other document that complies with the California Rules of Court despite any local rule imposing other requirements.

Rule 8.20 amended and renumbered effective January 1, 2007; repealed and adopted as rule 80 effective January 1, 2005.

Rule 8.23. Sanctions to compel compliance

The failure of a court reporter or clerk to perform any duty imposed by statute or these rules that delays the filing of the appellate record is an unlawful interference with the reviewing court's proceedings. It may be treated as an interference in addition to or instead of any other sanction that may be imposed by law for the same breach of duty. This rule does not limit the reviewing court's power to define and remedy any other interference with its proceedings.

Rule 8.23 renumbered effective January 1, 2007; repealed and adopted as rule 46.5 effective January 1, 2005.

Article 2
Service, Filing, Filing Fees, Form, and Privacy

Title 8, Appellate Rules—Division 1, Rules Relating to the Supreme Court and Courts of Appeal—Chapter 1, General Provisions—Article 2, Service, Filing Fees, Form, and Privacy; amended effective January 1, 2017; previously amended effective October 28, 2011.

Rule 8.25. Service, filing, and filing fees
Rule 8.26. Waiver of fees and costs
Rule 8.29. Service on nonparty public officer or agency
Rule 8.32. Address and other contact information of record; notice of change
Rule 8.36. Substituting parties; substituting or withdrawing attorneys
Rule 8.40. Cover requirements for documents filed in paper form
Rule 8.41. Protection of privacy in documents and records
Rule 8.42. Requirements for signatures of multiple parties on filed documents
Rule 8.44. Number of copies of filed documents

Rule 8.25. Service, filing, and filing fees

(a) Service

(1) Before filing any document, a party must serve one copy of the document on the attorney for each party separately represented, on each unrepresented party, and on any other person or entity when required by statute or rule.

(2) The party must attach to the document presented for filing a proof of service showing service on each person or entity required to be served under (1), or, if using an electronic filing service provider's automatic electronic document service, the party may have the electronic filing service provider generate a proof of service. The proof must name each party represented by each attorney served.

(Subd (a) amended effective January 1, 2021; previously amended effective January 1, 2007.)

(b) Filing

(1) A document is deemed filed on the date the clerk receives it.

(2) Unless otherwise provided by these rules or other law, a filing is not timely unless the clerk receives the document before the time to file it expires.

(3) A brief, an application to file an amicus curiae brief, an answer to an amicus curiae brief, a petition for rehearing, an answer to a petition for rehearing, a petition for transfer of an appellate division case to the Court of Appeal, an answer to such a petition for transfer, a petition for review, an answer to a petition for review, or a reply to an answer to a petition for review is timely if the time to file it has not expired on the date of:

(A) Its mailing by priority or express mail as shown on the postmark or the postal receipt; or

(B) Its delivery to a common carrier promising overnight delivery as shown on the carrier's receipt.

(4) The provisions of (3) do not apply to original proceedings.

(5) If the clerk receives a document by mail from an inmate or a patient in a custodial institution after the period for filing the document has expired but the envelope shows that the document was mailed or delivered to custodial officials for mailing within the period for filing the document, the document is deemed timely. The clerk must retain in the case file the envelope in which the document was received.

(Subd (b) amended effective July 1, 2012; previously amended effective January 1, 2007, January 1, 2009, July 1, 2010, and January 1, 2011.)

(c) Filing fees

(1) Unless otherwise provided by law, any document for which a filing fee is required under Government Code sections 68926 or 68927 must be accompanied at the time of filing by the required fee or an application for a waiver of court fees under rule 8.26.

(2) Documents for which a filing fee may be required under Government Code sections 68926 or 68927 include:

(A) A notice of appeal in a civil case. For purposes of this rule, "notice of appeal" includes a notice of cross-appeal;

(B) A petition for a writ within the original civil jurisdiction of the Supreme Court or Court of Appeal;

(C) A petition for review in a civil case in the Supreme Court;

(D) The following where the document is the first document filed in the Court of Appeal or Supreme Court by a party other than the appellant or petitioner in a civil case. For purposes of this rule, a "party other than the appellant" does not include a respondent who files a notice of cross-appeal.

(i) An application or an opposition or other response to an application;

(ii) A motion or an opposition or other response to a motion;

(iii) A respondent's brief;

(iv) A preliminary opposition to a petition for a writ, excluding a preliminary opposition requested by the court unless the court has notified the parties that it is considering issuing a peremptory writ in the first instance;

(v) A return (by demurrer, verified answer, or both) after the court issues an alternative writ or order to show cause;

(vi) Any answer to a petition for review in the Supreme Court; and

(vii) Any brief filed in the Supreme Court after the Court grants review.

(3) If a document other than the notice of appeal or a petition for a writ is not accompanied by the filing fee or an application for a waiver of court fees under rule 8.26, the clerk must file the document and must promptly notify the filing party in writing that the court may strike the document unless, within the stated time of not less than 5 court days after the notice is sent, the filing party either:

(A) Pays the filing fee; or

(B) Files an application for a waiver under rule 8.26 if the party has not previously filed such an application.

(4) If the party fails to take the action specified in a notice given under (3), the reviewing court may strike the document, but may vacate the striking of the document for good cause.

(Subd (c) amended effective January 1, 2018; adopted effective October 28, 2011.)

Rule 8.25 amended effective January 1, 2021; adopted as rule 40.1 effective January 1, 2005; previously amended and renumbered effective January 1, 2007; previously amended effective January 1, 2009, July 1, 2010, January 1, 2011, October 28, 2011, July 1, 2012, and January 1, 2018.

Advisory Committee Comment

Subdivision (a). Code of Civil Procedure sections 1010.6–1013a describe generally permissible methods of service. *Information Sheet for Proof of Service (Court of Appeal)* (form APP-009-INFO) provides additional information about how to serve documents and how to provide proof of service. In the Supreme Court and the Courts of Appeal, registration with the court's electronic filing service provider is deemed to show agreement to accept service electronically at the email address provided, unless a party affirmatively opts out of electronic service under rule 8.78(a)(2)(B). This procedure differs from the procedure for electronic service in the superior courts, including their appellate divisions. See rules 2.250–2.261.

Subdivision (b). In general, to be filed on time, a document must be received by the clerk before the time for filing that document expires. There are, however, some limited exceptions to this general rule. For example, (5) provides that if the clerk receives a document by mail from a custodial institution after the deadline for filing the document has expired but the envelope shows that the document was mailed or delivered to custodial officials for mailing before the deadline expired, the document is deemed timely. This provision applies to notices of appeal as well as to other documents mailed from a custodial institution and reflects the "prison-delivery" exception articulated by the California Supreme Court in *In re Jordan* (1992) 4 Cal.4th 116 and *Silverbrand v. County of Los Angeles* (2009) 46 Cal.4th 106.

Note that if a deadline runs from the date of filing, it runs from the date that the document is actually received and deemed filed under (b)(1); neither (b)(3) nor (b)(5) changes that date. Nor do these provisions extend the date of finality of an appellate opinion or any other deadline that is based on finality, such as the deadline for the court to modify its opinion or order rehearing. Subdivision (b)(5) is also not intended to limit a criminal defendant's appeal rights under the case law of constructive filing. (See, e.g., *In re Benoit* (1973) 10 Cal.3d 72.)

Subdivision (b)(3). This rule includes applications to file amicus curiae briefs because, under rules 8.200(c)(4) and 8.520(f)(5), a proposed amicus curiae brief must accompany the application to file the brief.

Subdivision (c). Government Code section 68926 establishes fees in civil cases for filing a notice of appeal, filing a petition a for a writ within the original civil jurisdiction of the Supreme Court or a Court of Appeal, and for a party other than appellant or petitioner filing its first document in such an appeal or writ proceeding in the Supreme Court or a Court of Appeal. Government Code section 68927 establishes fees for filing a petition for review in a civil case in the Supreme Court and for a party other than the petitioner filing its first document in a civil case in the Supreme Court. These statutes provide that fees may not be charged in appeals from, petitions for writs involving, or petitions for review from decisions in juvenile cases or proceedings to declare a minor free from parental custody or control, or proceedings under the Lanterman-Petris-Short Act (Part 1 (commencing with Section 5000) of Division 5 of the Welfare and Institutions Code).

Subdivision (c)(2)(A) and (D). Under rule 8.100(f), "notice of appeal" includes a notice of a cross-appeal and a respondent who files a notice of cross-appeal in a civil appeal is considered an appellant and is required to pay the fee for filing a notice of appeal under Government Code section 68926.

A person who files an application to file an amicus brief is not a "party" and therefore is not subject to the fees applicable to a party other than the appellant or petitioner.

Subdivision (c)(3). Rule 8.100 establishes the procedures applicable when an appellant in a civil appeal fails to pay the fee for filing a notice of appeal or the deposit for the clerk's transcript that must also be paid at that time.

Rule 8.26. Waiver of fees and costs

(a) Application form

An application for initial waiver of court fees and costs in the Supreme Court or Court of Appeal must be made on *Request to Waive Court Fees* (form FW-001) or, if the application is made for the benefit of a (proposed) ward or conservatee, on *Request to Waive Court Fees (Ward or Conservatee)* (form FW-001-GC). The clerk must provide *Request to Waive Court Fees* (form FW-001) or *Request to Waive Court Fees (Ward or Conservatee)* (form FW-001-GC) and the *Information Sheet on Waiver of Fees and Costs (Supreme Court, Court of Appeal, or Appellate Division)* (form APP-015/FW-015-INFO) without charge to any person who requests any fee waiver application or states that he or she is unable to pay any court fee or cost.

(Subd (a) amended effective September 1, 2015; adopted effective July 1, 2009.)

(b) Filing the application

(1) Appeals

(A) The appellant should submit any application for initial waiver of court fees and costs for an appeal with the notice of appeal in the superior court that issued the judgment or order being appealed. For purposes of this rule, a respondent who files a notice of cross-appeal is an "appellant."

(B) A party other than the appellant should submit any application for initial waiver of the court fees and costs for an appeal at the time the fees are to be paid to the court.

(2) Writ proceedings

(A) The petitioner should submit the application for waiver of the court fees and costs for a writ proceeding with the writ petition.

(B) A party other than the petitioner should submit any application for initial waiver of the court fees and costs at the time the fees for filing its first document in the writ proceeding are to be paid to the reviewing court.

(3) Petitions for review

(A) The petitioner should submit the application for waiver of the court fees and costs for a petition for review in the Supreme Court with the petition.

(B) A party other than the petitioner should submit any application for initial waiver of the court fees and costs at the time the fees for filing its first document in the proceeding are to be paid to the Supreme Court.

(Subd (b) amended effective October 28, 2011; adopted effective July 1, 2009.)

(c) Procedure for determining application

The application must be considered and determined as required by Government Code section 68634.5. An order from the Supreme Court or Court of Appeal determining the application for initial fee waiver or setting a hearing on the application in the Supreme Court or Court of Appeal may be made on *Order on Court Fee Waiver (Court of Appeal or Supreme Court)* (form APP-016/FW-016) or, if the application is made for the benefit of a (proposed) ward or conservatee, on *Order on Court Fee Waiver (Court of Appeal or Supreme Court) (Ward or Conservatee)* (form APP-016-GC/FW-016-GC).

(Subd (c) amended effective September 1, 2015; adopted effective July 1, 2009.)

(d) Application granted unless acted on by the court

The application for initial fee waiver is deemed granted unless the court gives notice of action on the application within five court days after the application is filed.

(Subd (d) adopted effective July 1, 2009.)

(e) Court fees and costs waived

Court fees and costs that must be waived on granting an application for initial waiver of court fees and costs in the Supreme Court or Court of Appeal include:

(1) The fee for filing the notice of appeal and the fee required for a party other than the appellant filing its first document under Government Code section 68926;

(2) The fee for filing an original proceeding and the fee required for a party other than the petitioner filing its first document under Government Code section 68926;

(3) The fee for filing a petition for review and the fee required for a party other than the petitioner filing its first document under Government Code section 68927; and

(4) Any court fee for telephonic oral argument.

(Subd (e) amended effective October 28, 2011; adopted effective July 1, 2009.)

(f) Denial of the application

If an application is denied, the applicant must pay the court fees and costs or submit the new application or additional information requested by the court within 10 days after the clerk gives notice of the denial.

(Subd (f) adopted effective July 1, 2009.)

(g) Confidential records

(1) No person may have access to an application for an initial fee waiver submitted to the court except the court and authorized court personnel, any persons authorized by the applicant, and any persons authorized by order of the court. No person may reveal any information contained in the application except as authorized by law or order of the court. An order granting access to an application or financial information may include limitations on who may access the information and on the use of the information after it has been released.

(2) Any person seeking access to an application or financial information provided to the court by an applicant must make the request by motion, supported by a declaration showing good cause as to why the confidential information should be released.

(Subd (g) adopted effective July 1, 2009.)

Rule 8.26 amended effective September 1, 2015; adopted effective July 1, 2009; previously amended effective October 28, 2011.

Advisory Committee Comment

Subdivision (a). The waiver of court fees and costs is called an "initial" waiver because, under Government Code section 68630 and following, any such waiver may later be modified, terminated, or retroactively withdrawn if the court determines that the applicant was not or is no longer eligible for a waiver. The court may, at a later time, order that the previously waived fees be paid.

Subdivision (b)(1). If an applicant is requesting waiver of both Court of Appeal fees, such as the fee for filing the notice of appeal, and superior court fees, such as the fee for preparing, certifying, copying, and transmitting the clerk's transcript, the clerk of the superior court may ask the applicant to provide two signed copies of *Request to Waive Court Fees* (form FW-001).

Subdivision (e). The parties in an appeal may also ask the superior court to waive the deposit required under Government Code section 68926.1 and the fees under rule 8.122 for preparing, certifying, copying, and transmitting the clerk's transcript to the reviewing court and to the requesting party.

Rule 8.29. Service on nonparty public officer or agency

(a) Proof of service

When a statute or this rule requires a party to serve any document on a nonparty public officer or agency, the party must file proof of such service with the document unless a statute permits service after the document is filed, in which case the proof of service must be filed immediately after the document is served on the public officer or agency.

(Subd (a) relettered effective January 1, 2007; adopted as subd (b) effective January 1, 2004.)

(b) Identification on cover

When a statute or this rule requires a party to serve any document on a nonparty public officer or agency, the cover of the document must contain a statement that identifies the statute or rule requiring service of the document on the public officer or agency in substantially the following form: "Service on [insert name of the officer or agency] required by [insert citation to the statute or rule]."

(Subd (b) relettered effective January 1, 2007; adopted as subd (c) effective January 1, 2004.)

(c) Service on the Attorney General

In addition to any statutory requirements for service of briefs on public officers or agencies, a party must serve its brief or petition on the Attorney General if the brief or petition:

(1) Questions the constitutionality of a state statute; or

(2) Is filed on behalf of the State of California, a county, or an officer whom the Attorney General may lawfully represent in:

(A) A criminal case;

(B) A case in which the state or a state officer in his or her official capacity is a party; or

(C) A case in which a county is a party, unless the county's interest conflicts with that of the state or a state officer in his or her official capacity.

(Subd (c) adopted effective January 1, 2007.)

Rule 8.29 amended and renumbered effective January 1, 2007; adopted as rule 44.5 effective January 1, 2004; previously amended effective July 1, 2004.

Advisory Committee Comment

Rule 8.29 refers to statutes that require a party to serve documents on a nonparty public officer or agency. For a list of examples of such statutory requirements, please see the *Civil Case Information Statement* (form APP-004).

Rule 8.32. Address and other contact information of record; notice of change

(a) Address and other contact information of record

In any case pending before the court, the court will use the mailing address, telephone number, fax number, and e-mail address that an attorney or unrepresented party provides on the first document filed in that case as the mailing address, telephone number, fax number, and e-mail address of record unless the attorney or unrepresented party files a notice under (b).

(Subd (a) amended effective January 1, 2013; adopted effective January 1, 2007.)

(b) Notice of change

(1) An attorney or unrepresented party whose mailing address, telephone number, fax number, or e-mail address changes while a case is pending must promptly serve and file a written notice of the change in the reviewing court in which the case is pending.

(2) The notice must specify the title and number of the case or cases to which it applies. If an attorney gives the notice, the notice must include the attorney's California State Bar number.

(Subd (b) amended effective January 1, 2013; adopted as subd (a) effective January 1, 2005; previously amended and relettered effective January 1, 2007; previously amended effective July 1, 2008.)

(c) Multiple addresses or other contact information

If an attorney or an unrepresented party has more than one mailing address, telephone number, fax number, or e-mail address, only one mailing address, telephone number, fax number, or e-mail address for that attorney or unrepresented party may be used in a given case.

(Subd (c) repealed, amended and relettered effective January 1, 2013; adopted as subd (c) effective January 1, 2005; previously amended and relettered as subd (d) effective January 1, 2007; previously amended effective January 1, 2008, and July 1, 2008.)

Rule 8.32 amended effective January 1, 2013; repealed and adopted as rule 40.5 effective January 1, 2005; previously amended and renumbered effective January 1, 2007; previously amended effective January 1, 2008, and July 1, 2008.

Rule 8.36. Substituting parties; substituting or withdrawing attorneys

(a) Substituting parties

Substitution of parties in an appeal or original proceeding must be made by serving and filing a motion in the reviewing court. The clerk of that court must notify the superior court of any ruling on the motion.

(b) Substituting attorneys

A party may substitute attorneys by serving and filing in the reviewing court a substitution signed by the party represented and the new attorney. In all appeals and in original proceedings related to a superior court proceeding, the party must also serve the superior court.

(c) Withdrawing attorney

(1) An attorney may request withdrawal by filing a motion to withdraw. Unless the court orders otherwise, the motion need be served only on the party represented and the attorneys directly affected.

(2) The proof of service need not include the address of the party represented. But if the court grants the motion, the withdrawing attorney must promptly provide the court and the opposing party with the party's current or last known address and telephone number.

(3) In all appeals and in original proceedings related to a superior court proceeding, the reviewing court clerk must notify the superior court of any ruling on the motion.

(4) If the motion is filed in any proceeding pending in the Supreme Court after grant of review, the clerk/executive officer of the Supreme Court must also notify the Court of Appeal of any ruling on the motion.

(Subd (c) amended effective January 1, 2018.)

Rule 8.36 amended effective January 1, 2018; repealed and adopted as rule 48 effective January 1, 2005; previously renumbered effective January 1, 2007.

Rule 8.40. Cover requirements for documents filed in paper form

(a) Cover color

(1) As far as practicable, the covers of briefs and petitions filed in paper form must be in the following colors:

Appellant's opening brief or appendix	green
Respondent's brief or appendix	yellow
Appellant's reply brief or appendix	tan
Joint appendix	white
Amicus curiae brief	gray
Answer to amicus curiae brief	blue
Petition for rehearing	orange
Answer to petition for rehearing	blue
Petition for original writ	red
Answer (or opposition) to petition for original writ	red
Reply to answer (or opposition) to petition for original writ	red
Petition for transfer of appellate division case to Court of Appeal	white
Answer to petition for transfer of appellate division case to Court of Appeal	blue
Petition for review	white
Answer to petition for review	blue
Reply to answer to petition for review	white
Opening brief on the merits	white
Answer brief on the merits	blue
Reply brief on the merits	white

(2) In appeals under rule 8.216, the cover of a combined respondent's brief and appellant's opening brief filed in paper form must be yellow, and the cover of a combined reply brief and respondent's brief filed in paper form must be tan.

(3) A paper brief or petition not conforming to (1) or (2) must be accepted for filing, but in case of repeated violations by an attorney or party, the court may proceed as provided in rule 8.204(e)(2).

(Subd (a) repealed, amended and relettered effective January 1, 2020; adopted as subd (c) effective January 1, 2005; previously amended and relettered effective January 1, 2007; previously amended effective January 1, 2011, and January 1, 2016.)

(b) Cover information

(1) Except as provided in (2), the cover—or first page if there is no cover—of every document filed in a reviewing court must include the name, mailing address, telephone number, fax number (if available), e-mail address (if available), and California State Bar number of each attorney filing or joining in the document, or of the party if he or she is unrepresented. The inclusion of a fax number or e-mail address on any document does not constitute consent to service by fax or e-mail unless otherwise provided by law.

(2) If more than one attorney from a law firm, corporation, or public law office is representing one party and is joining in the document, the name and State Bar number of each attorney joining in the document must be provided on the cover. The law firm, corporation, or public law office representing each party must designate one attorney to receive notices and other communication in the case from the court by placing an asterisk before that attorney's name on the cover and must provide the contact information specified under (1) for that attorney. Contact information for the other attorneys from the same law firm, corporation, or public law office is not required but may be provided.

(Subd (b) relettered effective January 1, 2020; adopted as subd (d) effective January 1, 2005; previously amended and relettered effective January 1, 2007; previously amended effective January 1, 2013.)

Rule 8.40 amended effective January 1, 2020; repealed and adopted as rule 44 effective January 1, 2005; previously amended and renumbered as rule 8.40 effective January 1, 2007; previously amended effective January 1, 2006, January 1, 2011, January 1, 2013, and January 1, 2016.

Rule 8.41. Protection of privacy in documents and records

The provisions on protection of privacy in rule 1.201 apply to documents and records under these rules.

Rule 8.41 adopted effective January 1, 2017.

Rule 8.42. Requirements for signatures of multiple parties on filed documents

When a document to be filed in paper form, such as a stipulation, requires the signatures of multiple parties, the original signature of at least one party must appear on the document filed in the reviewing court; the other signatures may be in the form of copies of the signed signature page of the document. Electronically filed documents must comply with the relevant provisions of rule 8.77.

Rule 8.42 amended effective January 1, 2016; adopted effective January 1, 2014.

Rule 8.44. Number of copies of filed documents

(a) Documents filed in the Supreme Court

Except as these rules provide otherwise, the number of copies of every brief, petition, motion, application, or other document that must be filed in the Supreme Court and that is filed in paper form is as follows:

(1) An original of a petition for review, an answer, a reply, a brief on the merits, an amicus curiae brief, an answer to an amicus curiae brief, a petition for rehearing, or an answer to a petition for rehearing and either

(A) 13 paper copies; or

(B) 8 paper copies and one electronic copy;

(2) Unless the court orders otherwise, an original of a petition for a writ within the court's original jurisdiction, an opposition or other response to the petition, or a reply; and either:

(A) 10 paper copies; or

(B) 8 paper copies and one electronic copy;

(3) Unless the court orders otherwise, an original and 2 copies of any supporting document accompanying a petition for writ of habeas corpus, an opposition or other response to the petition, or a reply;

(4) An original and 8 copies of a petition for review to exhaust state remedies under rule 8.508, an answer, or a reply, or an amicus curiae letter under rule 8.500(g);

(5) An original and 8 copies of a motion or an opposition or other response to a motion; and

(6) An original and 1 copy of an application, including an application to extend time, or any other document.

(Subd (a) amended effective January 1, 2016; previously amended effective January 1, 2014.)

(b) Documents filed in a Court of Appeal

Except as these rules provide otherwise, the number of copies of every brief, petition, motion, application, or other document that must be filed in a Court of Appeal and that is filed in paper form is as follows:

(1) An original and 4 paper copies of a brief, an amicus curiae brief, or an answer to an amicus curiae brief. In civil appeals, for briefs other than petitions for rehearing or answers thereto, 1 electronic copy or, in case of undue hardship, proof of delivery of 4 paper copies to the Supreme Court, as provided in rule 8.212(c) is also required;

(2) An original of a petition for writ of habeas corpus filed under rule 8.380 by a person who is not represented by an attorney and 1 set of any supporting documents;

(3) An original and 4 copies of any other petition, an answer, opposition or other response to a petition, or a reply;

(4) Unless the court orders otherwise, an original and 1 copy of a motion or an opposition or other response to a motion;

(5) Unless the court provides otherwise by local rule or order, 1 set of any separately bound supporting documents accompanying a document filed under (3) or (4);

(6) An original and 1 copy of an application, other than an application to extend time, or any other document; and

(7) An original and 1 copy of an application to extend time. In addition, 1 copy for each separately represented and unrepresented party must be provided to the court.

(Subd (b) amended effective January 1, 2016; previously amended effective January 1, 2011, January 1, 2013, and January 1, 2014.)

(c) Electronic copies of paper documents

Even when filing a paper document is permissible, a court may provide by local rule for the submission of an electronic copy of the paper document either in addition to the copies of a document required to be filed under (a) or (b) or as a substitute for one or more of these copies. The local rule must provide for an exception if it would cause undue hardship for a party to submit an electronic copy.

(Subd (c) amended effective January 1, 2020; adopted effective January 1, 2014; previously amended effective January 1, 2016.)

Rule 8.44 amended effective January 1, 2020; adopted effective January 1, 2007; previously amended effective January 1, 2007, January 1, 2011, January 1, 2013, January 1, 2014, and January 1, 2016.

Advisory Committee Comment

The initial sentence of this rule acknowledges that there are exceptions to this rule's requirements concerning the number of copies. See, for example, rule 8.150, which specifies the number of copies of the record that must be filed.

Information about electronic submission of copies of documents can be found on the web page for the Supreme Court at: *www.courts.ca.gov/appellatebriefs* or for the Court of Appeal District in which the brief is being filed at: *www.courts.ca.gov/courtsofappeal.*

Note that submitting an electronic copy of a document under this rule or under a local rule adopted pursuant to subdivision (c) does not constitute filing a document electronically under rules 8.70–8.79 and thus does not substitute for the filing of the original document with the court in paper format.

Article 3
Sealed and Confidential Records

Division 1, Rules Relating to the Supreme Court and Courts of Appeal—Chapter 1, General Provisions—Article 3, Sealed and Confidential Records; adopted effective January 1, 2014.

Rule 8.45. General provisions
Rule 8.46. Sealed records
Rule 8.47. Confidential records

Rule 8.45. General provisions

(a) Application

The rules in this article establish general requirements regarding sealed and confidential records in appeals and original proceedings in the Supreme Court and Courts of Appeal. Where other laws establish specific requirements for particular types of sealed or confidential records that differ from the requirements in this article, those specific requirements supersede the requirements in this article.

(Subd (a) adopted effective January 1, 2014.)

(b) Definitions

As used in this article:

(1) "Record" means all or part of a document, paper, exhibit, transcript, or other thing filed or lodged with the court by electronic means or otherwise.

(2) A "lodged" record is a record temporarily deposited with the court but not filed.

(3) A "sealed" record is a record that is closed to inspection by the public or a party by order of a court under rules 2.550–2.551 or rule 8.46.

(4) A "conditionally sealed" record is a record that is filed or lodged subject to a pending application or motion to file it under seal.

(5) A "confidential" record is a record that, in court proceedings, is required by statute, rule of court, or other authority except a court order under rules 2.550–2.551 or rule 8.46 to be closed to inspection by the public or a party.

(6) A "redacted version" is a version of a filing from which all portions that disclose material contained in a sealed, conditionally sealed, or confidential record have been removed.

(7) An "unredacted version" is a version of a filing or a portion of a filing that discloses material contained in a sealed, conditionally sealed, or confidential record.

(Subd (b) amended effective January 1, 2016; adopted effective January 1, 2014.)

(c) Format of sealed and confidential records

(1) Unless otherwise provided by law or court order, sealed or confidential records that are part of the record on appeal or the supporting documents or other records accompanying a motion, petition for a writ of habeas corpus, other writ petition, or other filing in the reviewing court must be kept separate from the rest of a clerk's or reporter's transcript, appendix, supporting documents, or other records sent to the reviewing court and in a secure manner that preserves their confidentiality.

(A) If the records are in paper format, they must be placed in a sealed envelope or other appropriate sealed container. This requirement does not apply to a juvenile case file but does apply to any record contained within a juvenile case file that is sealed or confidential under authority other than Welfare and Institutions Code section 827 et seq.

(B) Sealed records, and if applicable the envelope or other container, must be marked as "Sealed by Order of the Court on *(Date)*."

(C) Confidential records, and if applicable the envelope or other container, must be marked as "Confidential *(Basis)*—May Not Be Examined Without Court Order." The basis must be a citation to or other brief description of the statute, rule of court, case, or other authority that establishes that the record must be closed to inspection in the court proceeding.

(D) The superior court clerk or party transmitting sealed or confidential records to the reviewing court must prepare a sealed or confidential index of these materials. If the records include a transcript of any in-camera proceeding, the index must list the date and the names of all parties present at the hearing and their counsel. This index must be transmitted and kept with the sealed or confidential records.

(2) Except as provided in (3) or by court order, the alphabetical and chronological indexes to a clerk's or reporter's transcript, appendix, supporting documents, or other records sent to the reviewing court that are available to the public must list each sealed or confidential record by title, not disclosing the substance of the record, and must identify it as "Sealed" or "Confidential"—May Not Be Examined Without Court Order."

(3) Records relating to a request for funds under Penal Code section 987.9 or other proceedings the occurrence of which is not to be disclosed under the court order or applicable law must not be bound together with, or electronically transmitted as a single document with, other sealed or confidential records and must not be listed in the index required under (1)(D) or the alphabetical or chronological indexes to a clerk's or reporter's transcript, appendix, supporting documents to a petition, or other records sent to the reviewing court.

(Subd (c) amended effective January 1, 2016; adopted effective January 1, 2014.)

(d) Transmission of and access to sealed and confidential records

(1) A sealed or confidential record must be transmitted in a secure manner that preserves the confidentiality of the record.

(2) Unless otherwise provided by (3)–(5) or other law or court order, a sealed or confidential record that is part of the record on appeal or the supporting documents or other records accompanying a motion, petition for a writ of habeas corpus, other writ petition, or other filing in the reviewing court must be transmitted only to the reviewing court and the party or parties who had access to the record in the trial court or other proceedings under review and may be examined only by the reviewing court and that party or parties. If a party's attorney but not the party had access to the record in the trial court or other proceedings under review, only the party's attorney may examine the record.

(3) Except as provided in (4), if the record is a reporter's transcript or any document related to any in-camera hearing from which a party was excluded in the trial court, the record must be transmitted to and examined by only the reviewing court and the party or parties who participated in the in-camera hearing.

(4) A reporter's transcript or any document related to an in-camera hearing concerning a confidential informant under Evidence Code sections 1041–1042 must be transmitted only to the reviewing court.

(5) A probation report must be transmitted only to the reviewing court and to appellate counsel for the People and the defendant who was the subject of the report.

(Subd (d) amended effective January 1, 2019; adopted effective January 1, 2014.)

Rule 8.45 amended effective January 1, 2019; adopted effective January 1, 2014; previously amended effective January 1, 2016.

Advisory Committee Comment

Subdivision (a). Many laws address sealed and confidential records. These laws differ from each other in a variety of respects, including what information is closed to inspection, from whom it is closed, under what circumstances it is closed, and what procedures apply to closing or opening it to inspection. It is very important to determine if any such law applies with respect to a particular record because where other laws establish specific requirements that differ from the requirements in this article, those specific requirements supersede the requirements in this article.

Subdivision (b)(5). Examples of confidential records are records in juvenile proceedings (Welf. & Inst. Code, § 827 and California Rules of Court, rule 8.401), records of the family conciliation court (Fam. Code, § 1818(b)), fee waiver applications (Gov. Code, § 68633(f)), and court-ordered diagnostic reports (Penal Code, § 1203.03). This term also encompasses records closed to inspection by a court order other than an order under rules 2.550–2.551 or 8.46, such as situations in which case law, statute, or rule has established a category of records that must be closed to inspection and a court has found that a particular record falls within that category and has ordered that it be closed to inspection. Examples include discovery material subject to a protective order under Code of Civil Procedure sections 2030.090, 2032.060, or 2033.080 and records closed to inspection by court order under *People v. Marsden* (1970) 2 Cal.3d 118 or *Pitchess v. Superior Court* (1974) 11 Cal.3d 531. For more examples of confidential records, please see appendix 1 of the *Trial Court Records Manual* at www.courts.ca.gov/documents/trial-court-records-manual.pdf.

Subdivisions (c) and (d). The requirements in this rule for format and transmission of and access to sealed and confidential records apply only unless otherwise provided by law. Special requirements that govern transmission of and/or access to particular types of records may supersede the requirements in this rule. For example, rules 8.619(g) and 8.622(e) require copies of reporters' transcripts in capital cases to be sent to the Habeas Corpus Resource Center and the California Appellate Project in San Francisco, and under rules 8.336(g)(2) and 8.409(e)(2), in non-capital felony appeals, if the defendant—or in juvenile appeals, if the appellant or the respondent—is not represented by appellate counsel when the clerk's and reporter's transcripts are certified as correct, the clerk must send that counsel's copy of the transcripts to the district appellate project.

Subdivision (c)(1)(C). For example, for juvenile records, this mark could state "Confidential—Welf. & Inst. Code, § 827" or "Confidential—Juvenile Case File"; for a fee waiver application, this mark could state "Confidential—Gov. Code, § 68633(f)" or "Confidential—Fee Waiver Application"; and for a transcript of an in-camera hearing under *People v. Marsden* (1970) 2 Cal.3d 118, this mark could say "Confidential—*Marsden* Hearing."

Subdivision (c)(2). Subdivision (c)(2) requires that, with certain exceptions, the alphabetical and chronological indexes to the clerk's and reporter's transcripts, appendixes, and supporting documents must list any sealed and confidential records but identify them as sealed or confidential. The purpose of this provision is to assist the parties in making—and the court in adjudicating—motions to unseal sealed records or to provide confidential records to a party. To protect sealed and confidential records from disclosure until the court issues an order, however, each index must identify sealed and confidential records without disclosing their substance.

Subdivision (c)(3). Under certain circumstances, the Attorney General has a statutory right to request copies of documents filed under Penal Code section 987.9(d). To facilitate compliance with such requests, this subdivision requires that such documents not be bound with other confidential documents.

Subdivision (d). See rule 8.47(b) for special requirements concerning access to certain confidential records.

Subdivision (d)(2) and (3). Because the term "party" includes any attorney of record for that party, under rule 8.10(3), when a party who had access to a record in the trial court or other proceedings under review or who participated in an in-camera hearing—such as a *Marsden* hearing in a criminal or juvenile proceeding—is represented by appellate counsel, the confidential record or transcript must be transmitted to that party's appellate counsel. Under rules 8.336(g)(2) and 8.409(e)(2), in non-capital felony appeals, if the defendant—or in juvenile appeals, if the appellant or the respondent—is not represented by appellate counsel when the clerk's and reporter's transcripts are certified as correct, the clerk must send the copy of the transcripts that would go to appellate counsel, including confidential records such as transcripts of *Marsden* hearings, to the district appellate project.

Subdivision (d)(5). This rule limits to whom a copy of a probation report is transmitted based on the provisions of Penal Code section 1203.05, which limit who may inspect or copy probation reports.

Rule 8.46. Sealed records

(a) Application

This rule applies to sealed records and records proposed to be sealed on appeal and in original proceedings, but does not apply to confidential records.

(Subd (a) amended effective January 1, 2014; previously amended effective January 1, 2006, and January 1, 2007.)

(b) Record sealed by the trial court

If a record sealed by order of the trial court is part of the record on appeal or the supporting documents or other records accompanying a motion, petition for a writ of habeas corpus, other writ petition, or other filing in the reviewing court:

(1) The sealed record must remain sealed unless the reviewing court orders otherwise under (e). Rule 8.45 governs the form and transmission of and access to sealed records.

(2) The record on appeal or supporting documents filed in the reviewing court must also include:

(A) The motion or application to seal filed in the trial court;

(B) All documents filed in the trial court supporting or opposing the motion or application; and

(C) The trial court order sealing the record.

(Subd (b) repealed, amended and relettered effective January 1, 2014; adopted as subd (c); previously amended effective January 1, 2004, and January 1, 2007.)

(c) Record not sealed by the trial court

A record filed or lodged publicly in the trial court and not ordered sealed by that court must not be filed under seal in the reviewing court.

(Subd (c) relettered effective January 1, 2014; adopted as subd (d).)

(d) Record not filed in the trial court; motion or application to file under seal

(1) A record not filed in the trial court may be filed under seal in the reviewing court only by order of the reviewing court; it must not be filed under seal solely by stipulation or agreement of the parties.

(2) To obtain an order under (1), a party must serve and file a motion or application in the reviewing court, accompanied by a declaration containing facts sufficient to justify the sealing. At the same time, the party must lodge the record under (3), unless good cause is shown not to lodge it.

(3) To lodge a record, the party must transmit the record to the court in a secure manner that preserves the confidentiality of the record to be lodged. The record must be transmitted separately from the rest of a clerk's or reporter's transcript, appendix, supporting documents, or other records sent to the reviewing court with a cover sheet that complies with rule 8.40(b) if the record is in paper form or rule 8.74(a)(9) if the record is in electronic form, and that labels the contents as "CONDITIONALLY UNDER SEAL." If the record is in paper form, it must be placed in a sealed envelope or other appropriate sealed container.

(4) If necessary to prevent disclosure of material contained in a conditionally sealed record, any motion or application, any opposition, and any supporting documents must be filed in a redacted version and lodged in a complete unredacted version conditionally under seal. The cover of the redacted version must identify it as "Public—Redacts material from conditionally sealed record." In juvenile cases, the cover of the redacted version must identify it as "Redacted version—Redacts material from conditionally sealed record." The cover of the unredacted version must identify it as "May Not Be Examined Without Court Order—Contains material from conditionally sealed record." Unless the court orders otherwise, any party that had access to the record in the trial court or other proceedings under review must be served with a complete, unredacted version of all papers as well as a redacted version.

(5) On receiving a lodged record, the clerk must note the date of receipt on the cover sheet and retain but not file the record. The record must remain conditionally under seal pending determination of the motion or application.

(6) The court may order a record filed under seal only if it makes the findings required by rule 2.550(d)–(e).

(7) If the court denies the motion or application to seal the record, the lodging party may notify the court that the lodged record is to be filed unsealed. This notification must be received within 10 days of the order denying the motion or application to seal, unless otherwise ordered by the court. On receipt of this notification, the clerk must unseal and file the record. If the lodging party does not notify the court within 10 days of the order, the clerk must (1) return the lodged record to the lodging party if it is in paper form, or (2) permanently delete the lodged record if it is in electronic form.

(8) An order sealing the record must direct the sealing of only those documents and pages or, if reasonably practical, portions of those documents and pages, that contain the material that needs to be placed under seal. All other portions of each document or page must be included in the public file.

(9) Unless the sealing order provides otherwise, it prohibits the parties from disclosing the contents of any materials that have been sealed in anything that is subsequently publicly filed.

(Subd (d) amended effective January 1, 2020; adopted as subd (e); previously amended effective July 1, 2002, January 1, 2004, January 1, 2007, January 1, 2016, and January 1, 2019; previously amended and relettered as subd (d) effective January 1, 2014.)

(e) Challenge to an order denying a motion or application to seal a record

Notwithstanding the provisions in (d)(1)–(2), when an appeal or original proceeding challenges an order denying a motion or application to seal a record, the appellant or petitioner must lodge the subject record labeled as conditionally under seal in the reviewing court as provided in (d)(3)–(5), and the reviewing court must maintain the record conditionally under seal during the pendency of the appeal or original proceeding. Once the reviewing court's decision on the appeal or original proceeding becomes final, the clerk must (1) return the lodged record to the lodging party if it is in paper form, or (2) permanently delete the lodged record if it is in electronic form.

(Subd (e) adopted effective January 1, 2019.)

(f) Unsealing a record in the reviewing court

(1) A sealed record must not be unsealed except on order of the reviewing court.

(2) Any person or entity may serve and file a motion, application, or petition in the reviewing court to unseal a record.

(3) If the reviewing court proposes to order a record unsealed on its own motion, the court must send notice to the parties stating the reason for unsealing the record. Unless otherwise ordered by the court, any party may serve and file an opposition within 10 days after the notice is sent, and any other party may serve and file a response within 5 days after an opposition is filed.

(4) If necessary to prevent disclosure of material contained in a sealed record, the motion, application, or petition under (2) and any opposition, response, and supporting documents under (2) or (3) must be filed in both a redacted version and a complete unredacted version. The cover of the redacted version must identify it as "Public—Redacts material from sealed record." In juvenile cases, the cover of the redacted version must identify it as "Redacted version—Redacts material from sealed record." The cover of the unredacted version must identify it as "May Not Be Examined Without Court Order—Contains material from sealed record." Unless the court orders otherwise, any party that had access to the sealed record in the trial court or other proceedings under review must be served with a complete, unredacted version of all papers as well as a redacted version. If a party's attorney but not the party had access to the record in the trial court or other proceedings under review, only the party's attorney may be served with the complete, unredacted version.

(5) In determining whether to unseal a record, the court must consider the matters addressed in rule 2.550(c)–(e).

(6) The order unsealing a record must state whether the record is unsealed entirely or in part. If the order unseals only part of the record or unseals the record only as to certain persons, the order must specify the particular records that are unsealed, the particular persons who may have access to the record, or both.

(7) If, in addition to the record that is the subject of the sealing order, a court has previously ordered the sealing order itself, the register of actions, or any other court records relating to the case to be sealed, the unsealing order must state whether these additional records are unsealed.

(Subd (f) amended and relettered effective January 1, 2019; adopted as subd (f); previously amended effective January 1, 2004, January 1, 2007, and January 1, 2016; previously amended and relettered as subd (e) effective January 1, 2014.)

(g) Disclosure of nonpublic material in public filings prohibited

(1) Nothing filed publicly in the reviewing court—including any application, brief, petition, or memorandum—may disclose material contained in a record that is sealed, lodged conditionally under seal, or otherwise subject to a pending motion to file under seal.

(2) If it is necessary to disclose material contained in a sealed record in a filing in the reviewing court, two versions must be filed:

(A) A public redacted version. The cover of this version must identify it as "Public—Redacts material from sealed record." In juvenile cases, the cover of the redacted version must identify it as "Redacted Version—Redacts material from sealed record."

(B) An unredacted version. If this version is in paper format, it must be placed in a sealed envelope or other appropriate sealed container. The cover of this version, and if applicable the envelope or other container, must identify it as "May Not Be Examined Without Court Order—Contains material from sealed record." Sealed material disclosed in this version must be identified as such in the filing and accompanied by a citation to the court order sealing that material.

(C) Unless the court orders otherwise, any party who had access to the sealed record in the trial court or other proceedings under review must be served with both the unredacted version of all papers as well as the redacted version. Other parties must be served with only the public redacted version. If a party's attorney but not the party had access to the record in the trial court or other proceedings under review, only the party's attorney may be served with the unredacted version.

(3) If it is necessary to disclose material contained in a conditionally sealed record in a filing in the reviewing court:

(A) A public redacted version must be filed. The cover of this version must identify it as "Public—Redacts material from conditionally sealed record." In juvenile cases, the cover of the redacted version must identify it as "Redacted version—Redacts material from conditionally sealed record."

(B) An unredacted version must be lodged. The filing must be transmitted in a secure manner that preserves the confidentiality of the filing being lodged. If this version is in paper format, it must be placed in a sealed envelope or other appropriate sealed container. The cover of this version, and if applicable the envelope or other container, must identify it as "May Not Be Examined Without Court Order—Contains material from conditionally sealed record." Conditionally sealed material disclosed in this version must be identified as such in the filing.

(C) Unless the court orders otherwise, any party who had access to the conditionally sealed record in the trial court or other proceedings under review must be served with both the unredacted version of all papers as well as the redacted version. Other parties must be served with only the public redacted version.

(D) If the court denies the motion or application to seal the record, the party who filed the motion or application may notify the court that the unredacted version lodged under (B) is to be filed unsealed. This notification must be received within 10 days of the order denying the motion or application to seal, unless otherwise ordered by the court. On receipt of this notification, the clerk must unseal and file the lodged unredacted version. If the party who filed the motion or application does not notify the court within 10 days of the order, the clerk must (1) return the lodged unredacted version to the lodging party if it is in paper form, or (2) permanently delete the lodged unredacted version if it is in electronic form.

(Subd (g) amended and relettered effective January 1, 2019; adopted as subd (g); previously amended effective January 1, 2007; previously amended and relettered as subd (f) effective January 1, 2014.)

Rule 8.46 amended effective January 1, 2020; repealed and adopted as rule 12.5 effective January 1, 2002; previously amended and renumbered as rule 8.160 effective January 1, 2007; previously renumbered as rule 8.46 effective January 1, 2010; previously amended effective July 1, 2002, January 1, 2004, January 1, 2006, January 1, 2014, January 1, 2016, and January 1, 2019.

Advisory Committee Comment

This rule and rules 2.550–2.551 for the trial courts provide a standard and procedures for courts to use when a request is made to seal a record. The standard is based on *NBC Subsidiary (KNBC-TV), Inc. v. Superior Court* (1999) 20 Cal.4th 1178. The sealed records rules apply to civil and criminal cases. They recognize the First Amendment right of access to documents used at trial or as a basis of adjudication. Except as otherwise expressly provided in this rule, motions in a reviewing court relating to the sealing or unsealing of a record must follow rule 8.54.

Subdivision (e). This subdivision is not intended to expand the availability of existing appellate review for any person aggrieved by a court's denial of a motion or application to seal a record.

Rule 8.47. Confidential records

(a) Application

This rule applies to confidential records but does not apply to records sealed by court order under rules 2.550–2.551 or rule 8.46 or to conditionally sealed records under rule 8.46. Unless otherwise provided by this rule or other law, rule 8.45 governs the form and transmission of and access to confidential records.

(Subd (a) adopted effective January 1, 2014.)

(b) Records of *Marsden* hearings and other in-camera proceedings

(1) This subdivision applies to reporter's transcripts of and documents filed or lodged by a defendant in connection with:

(A) An in-camera hearing conducted by the superior court under *People v. Marsden* (1970) 2 Cal.3d 118; or

(B) Another in-camera hearing at which the defendant was present but from which the People were excluded in order to prevent disclosure of information about defense strategy or other information to which the prosecution was not allowed access at the time of the hearing.

(2) Except as provided in (3), if the defendant raises a *Marsden* issue or an issue related to another in-camera hearing covered by this rule in a brief, petition, or other filing in the reviewing court, the following procedures apply:

(A) The brief, including any portion that discloses matters contained in the transcript of the in-camera hearing, and other documents filed or lodged in connection with the hearing, must be filed publicly. The requirement to publicly file this brief does not apply in juvenile cases; rule 8.401 governs the format of and access to such briefs in juvenile cases.

(B) The People may serve and file an application requesting a copy of the reporter's transcript of, and documents filed or lodged by a defendant in connection with, the in-camera hearing.

(C) Within 10 days after the application is filed, the defendant may serve and file opposition to this application on the basis that the transcript or documents contain confidential material not relevant to the issues raised by the defendant in the reviewing court. Any such opposition must identify the page and line numbers of the transcript or documents containing this irrelevant material.

(D) If the defendant does not timely serve and file opposition to the application, the reviewing court clerk must send to the People a copy of the reporter's transcript of, and documents filed or lodged by a defendant in connection with, the in-camera hearing.

(3) A defendant may serve and file a motion or application in the reviewing court requesting permission to file under seal a brief, petition, or other filing that raises a *Marsden* issue or an issue related to another in-camera hearing covered by this subdivision, and requesting an order maintaining the confidentiality of the relevant material from the reporter's transcript of, or documents filed or lodged in connection with, the in-camera hearing.

(A) Except as otherwise provided in this rule, rule 8.46(d) governs a motion or application under this subdivision.

(B) The declaration accompanying the motion or application must contain facts sufficient to justify an order maintaining the confidentiality of the relevant material from the reporter's transcript of, or documents filed or lodged in connection with, the in-camera hearing and sealing of the brief, petition, or other filing.

(C) At the time the motion or application is filed, the defendant must:

(i) File a public redacted version of the brief, petition, or other filing that he or she is requesting be filed under seal. The cover of this version must identify it as "Public—Redacts material from conditionally sealed record." The requirement to publicly file the redacted version does not apply in juvenile cases; rule 8.401 generally governs access to filings in juvenile cases. In juvenile cases, the cover of the redacted version must identify it as "Redacted version—Redacts material from conditionally sealed record."

(ii) Lodge an unredacted version of the brief, petition, or other filing that he or she is requesting be filed under seal. The filing must be transmitted in a secure manner that preserves the confidentiality of the filing being lodged. If this version is in paper format, it must be placed in a sealed envelope or other appropriate sealed container. The cover of the unredacted version of the document, and if applicable the envelope or other container, must identify it as "May Not Be Examined Without Court Order—Contains material from conditionally sealed record." Conditionally sealed material disclosed in this version must be identified as such in the filing.

(D) If the court denies the motion or application to file the brief, petition, or other filing under seal, the defendant may notify the court that the unredacted brief, petition, or other filing lodged under (C)(ii) is to be filed unsealed. This notification must be received within 10 days of the order denying the motion or application to file the brief, petition, or other filing under seal, unless otherwise ordered by the court. On receipt of this notification, the clerk must unseal and file the lodged unredacted brief, petition, or other filing. If the defendant does not notify the court within 10 days of the order, the clerk must (1) return the lodged unredacted brief, petition, or other filing to the defendant if it is in paper form, or (2) permanently delete the lodged unredacted brief, petition, or other filing if it is in electronic form.

(Subd (b) amended effective January 1, 2019; adopted effective January 1, 2014; previously amended effective January 1, 2016.)

(c) Other confidential records

Except as otherwise provided by law or order of the reviewing court:

(1) Nothing filed publicly in the reviewing court—including any application, brief, petition, or memorandum—may disclose material contained in a confidential record, including a record that, by law, a party may choose be kept confidential in reviewing court proceedings and that the party has chosen to keep confidential.

(2) To maintain the confidentiality of material contained in a confidential record, if it is necessary to disclose such material in a filing in the reviewing court, a party may serve and file a motion or application in the reviewing court requesting permission for the filing to be under seal.

(A) Except as otherwise provided in this rule, rule 8.46(d) governs a motion or application under this subdivision.

(B) The declaration accompanying the motion or application must contain facts sufficient to establish that the record is required by law to be closed to inspection in the reviewing court and to justify sealing of the brief, petition, or other filing.

(C) At the time the motion or application is filed, the party must:

(i) File a redacted version of the brief, petition, or other filing that he or she is requesting be filed under seal. The cover of this version must identify it as "Public—Redacts material from conditionally sealed record." In juvenile cases, the cover of this version must identify it as "Redacted version—Redacts material from conditionally sealed record."

(ii) Lodge an unredacted version of the brief, petition, or other filing that he or she is requesting be filed under seal. The filing must be transmitted in a secure manner that preserves the confidentiality of the filing being lodged. If this version is in paper format, it must be placed in a sealed envelope or other appropriate sealed container. The cover of the unredacted version of the document, and if applicable the envelope or other container, must identify it as "May Not Be Examined Without Court Order—Contains material from conditionally sealed record." Material from a confidential record disclosed in this version must be identified and accompanied by a citation to the statute, rule of court, case, or other authority establishing that the record is required by law to be closed to inspection in the reviewing court.

(D) If the court denies the motion or application to file the brief, petition, or other filing under seal, the party who filed the motion or application may notify the court that the unredacted brief, petition, or other filing lodged under (C)(ii) is to be filed unsealed. This notification must be received within 10 days of the order denying the motion or application to file the brief, petition, or other filing under seal, unless otherwise ordered by the court. On receipt of this notification, the clerk must unseal and file the lodged unredacted brief, petition, or other filing. If the party who filed the motion or application does not notify the court within 10 days of the order, the clerk must (1) return the lodged unredacted brief, petition, or other filing to the lodging party if it is in paper form, or (2) permanently delete the lodged unredacted brief, petition, or other filing if it is in electronic form.

(Subd (c) amended effective January 1, 2019; adopted effective January 1, 2014; previously amended effective January 1, 2016.)

Rule 8.47 amended effective January 1, 2019; adopted effective January 1, 2014; previously amended effective January 1, 2016.

Advisory Committee Comment

Subdivisions (a) and (c). Note that there are many laws that address the confidentiality of various records. These laws differ from each other in a variety of respects, including what information is closed to inspection, from whom it is closed, under what circumstances it is closed, and what procedures apply to closing or opening it to inspection. It is very important to determine if any such law applies with respect to a particular record because this rule applies only to confidential records as defined in rule 8.45, and the procedures in this rule apply only "unless otherwise provided by law." Thus, where other laws establish specific requirements that differ from the requirements in this rule, those specific requirements supersede the requirements in this rule. For example, although Penal Code section 1203.05 limits who may inspect or copy probation reports, much of the material contained in such reports—such as the factual summary of the offense(s); the evaluations, analyses, calculations, and recommendations of the probation officer; and other nonpersonal information—is not considered confidential under that statute and is routinely discussed in openly filed appellate briefs (see *People v. Connor* (2004) 115 Cal.App.4th 669, 695–696). In addition, this rule does not alter any existing authority for a court to open a confidential record to inspection by the public or another party to a proceeding.

Subdivision (c)(1). The reference in this provision to records that a party may choose be kept confidential in reviewing court proceedings is intended to encompass situations in which a record may be subject to a privilege that a party may choose to maintain or choose to waive.

Subdivision (c)(2). Note that when a record has been sealed by court order, rule 8.46(g)(2) requires a party to file redacted (public) and unredacted (sealed) versions of any filing that discloses material from the sealed record; it does not require the party to make a motion or application for permission to do so. By contrast, this rule requires court permission before redacted (public) and unredacted (sealed) filings may be made to prevent disclosure of material from confidential records.

Article 4
Applications and Motions; Extending and Shortening Time

Division 1, Rules Relating to the Supreme Court and Courts of Appeal—Chapter 1, General Provisions—Article 4, Applications and Motions; Extending and Shortening Time; renumbered effective January 1, 2014; adopted as Article 3.

Rule 8.50. Applications
Rule 8.54. Motions
Rule 8.57. Motions before the record is filed
Rule 8.60. Extending time
Rule 8.63. Policies and factors governing extensions of time
Rule 8.66. Tolling or extending time because of public emergency
Rule 8.68. Shortening time

Rule 8.50. Applications
(a) Service and filing

Except as these rules provide otherwise, parties must serve and file all applications in the reviewing court, including applications to extend the time to file records, briefs, or other documents, and applications to shorten time. For good cause, the Chief Justice or presiding justice may excuse advance service.

(Subd (a) amended effective January 1, 2007.)

(b) Contents

The application must state facts showing good cause—or making an exceptional showing of good cause, when required by these rules—for granting the application and must identify any previous application filed by any party.

(Subd (b) amended effective January 1, 2023; previously amended effective January 1, 2007.)

(c) Disposition

Unless the court determines otherwise, the Chief Justice or presiding justice may rule on the application.

(Subd (c) relettered effective January 1, 2016; adopted as subd (d).)

Rule 8.50 amended effective January 1, 2023; repealed and adopted as rule 43 effective January 1, 2005; previously amended and renumbered as rule 8.50 effective January 1, 2007; previously amended effective January 1, 2016.

Advisory Committee Comment

Rule 8.50 addresses applications generally. Rules 8.60, 8.63, and 8.68 address applications to extend or shorten time.

Subdivision (a). A party other than the appellant or petitioner who files an application or opposition to an application may be required to pay a filing fee under Government Code sections 68926 or 68927 if the application or opposition is the first document filed in the appeal or writ proceeding in the reviewing court by that party. See rule 8.25(c).

Subdivision (b). An exceptional showing of good cause is required in applications in certain juvenile proceedings under rules 8.416, 8.417, 8.450, 8.452, and 8.454.

Rule 8.54. Motions
(a) Motion and opposition

(1) Except as these rules provide otherwise, a party wanting to make a motion in a reviewing court must serve and file a written motion stating the grounds and the relief requested and identifying any documents on which the motion is based.

(2) A motion must be accompanied by a memorandum and, if it is based on matters outside the record, by declarations or other supporting evidence.

(3) Any opposition must be served and filed within 15 days after the motion is filed.

(Subd (a) amended effective January 1, 2007.)

(b) Disposition

(1) The court may rule on a motion at any time after an opposition or other response is filed or the time to oppose has expired.

(2) On a party's request or its own motion, the court may place a motion on calendar for a hearing. The clerk must promptly send each party a notice of the date and time of the hearing.

(c) Failure to oppose motion

A failure to oppose a motion may be deemed a consent to the granting of the motion.

Rule 8.54 amended and renumbered effective January 1, 2007; repealed and adopted as rule 41 effective January 1, 2005.

Advisory Committee Comment

Subdivision (a). A party other than the appellant or petitioner who files a motion or opposition to a motion may be required to pay a filing fee under Government Code sections 68926 or 68927 if the motion or opposition is the first document filed in the appeal or writ proceeding in the reviewing court by that party. See rule 8.25(c).

Subdivision (c). Subdivision (c) provides that a "failure to oppose a motion" may be deemed a consent to the granting of the motion. The provision is not intended to indicate a position on the question whether there is an implied right to a hearing to oppose a motion to dismiss an appeal.

Rule 8.57. Motions before the record is filed
(a) Motion to dismiss appeal

A motion to dismiss an appeal before the record is filed in the reviewing court must be accompanied by a certificate of the superior court clerk, a declaration, or both, stating:

(1) The nature of the action and the relief sought by the complaint and any cross-complaint or complaint in intervention;

(2) The names, addresses, and telephone numbers of all attorneys of record—stating whom each represents—and unrepresented parties;

(3) A description of the judgment or order appealed from, its entry date, and the service date of any written notice of its entry;

(4) The factual basis of any extension of the time to appeal under rule 8.108;

(5) The filing dates of all notices of appeal and the courts in which they were filed;

(6) The filing date of any document necessary to procure the record on appeal; and

(7) The status of the record preparation process, including any order extending time to prepare the record.

(Subd (a) amended effective January 1, 2007.)

(b) Other motions

Any other motion filed before the record is filed in the reviewing court must be accompanied by a declaration or other evidence necessary to advise the court of the facts relevant to the relief requested.

Rule 8.57 amended and renumbered effective January 1, 2007; repealed and adopted as rule 42 effective January 1, 2005.

Rule 8.60. Extending time

(a) Computing time

The Code of Civil Procedure governs computing and extending the time to do any act required or permitted under these rules.

(b) Extending time

Except as these rules provide otherwise, for good cause—or on an exceptional showing of good cause, when required by these rules—the Chief Justice or presiding justice may extend the time to do any act required or permitted under these rules.

(Subd (b) amended effective January 1, 2023; previously amended effective January 1, 2007.)

(c) Application for extension

(1) An application to extend time must include a declaration stating facts, not mere conclusions, and must be served on all parties. For good cause, the Chief Justice or presiding justice may excuse advance service.

(2) The application must state:

(A) The due date of the document to be filed;

(B) The length of the extension requested;

(C) Whether any earlier extensions have been granted and, if so, their lengths and whether granted by stipulation or by the court; and

(D) Good cause—or an exceptional showing of good cause, when required by these rules—for granting the extension, consistent with the factors in rule 8.63(b).

(Subd (c) amended effective January 1, 2023; adopted as subd (d) effective January 1, 2005; previously amended and relettered effective January 1, 2007.)

(d) Relief from default

For good cause, a reviewing court may relieve a party from default for any failure to comply with these rules except the failure to file a timely notice of appeal or a timely statement of reasonable grounds in support of a certificate of probable cause.

(Subd (d) relettered effective January 1, 2007; adopted as subd (e) effective January 1, 2005.)

(e) No extension by superior court

Except as these rules provide otherwise, a superior court may not extend the time to do any act to prepare the appellate record.

(Subd (e) relettered effective January 1, 2007; adopted as subd (f) effective January 1, 2005.)

(f) Notice to party

(1) In a civil case, counsel must deliver to his or her client or clients a copy of any stipulation or application to extend time that counsel files. Counsel must attach evidence of such delivery to the stipulation or application, or certify in the stipulation or application that the copy has been delivered.

(2) In a class action, the copy required under (1) need be delivered to only one represented party.

(3) The evidence or certification of delivery under (1) need not include the address of the party notified.

(Subd (f) amended and relettered effective January 1, 2007; adopted as subd (g) effective January 1, 2005.)

Rule 8.60 amended effective January 1, 2023; repealed and adopted as rule 45 effective January 1, 2005; previously amended and renumbered as rule 8.60 effective January 1, 2007.

Advisory Committee Comment

Subdivisions (b) and (c). An exceptional showing of good cause is required in applications in certain juvenile proceedings under rules 8.416, 8.417, 8.450, 8.452, and 8.454.

Rule 8.63. Policies and factors governing extensions of time

(a) Policies

(1) The time limits prescribed by these rules should generally be met to ensure expeditious conduct of appellate business and public confidence in the efficient administration of appellate justice.

(2) The effective assistance of counsel to which a party is entitled includes adequate time for counsel to prepare briefs or other documents that fully advance the party's interests. Adequate time also allows the preparation of accurate, clear, concise, and complete submissions that assist the courts.

(3) For a variety of legitimate reasons, counsel may not always be able to prepare briefs or other documents within the time specified in the rules of court. To balance the competing policies stated in (1) and (2), applications to extend time in the reviewing courts must demonstrate good cause—or an exceptional showing of good cause, when required by these rules—under (b). If good cause is shown, the court must extend the time.

(Subd (a) amended effective January 1, 2023; previously amended effective January 1, 2007.)

(b) Factors considered

In determining good cause—or an exceptional showing of good cause, when required by these rules—the court must consider the following factors when applicable:

(1) The degree of prejudice, if any, to any party from a grant or denial of the extension. A party claiming prejudice must support the claim in detail.

(2) In a civil case, the positions of the client and any opponent with regard to the extension.

(3) The length of the record, including the number of relevant trial exhibits. A party relying on this factor must specify the length of the record. In a civil case, a record containing one volume of clerk's transcript or appendix and two volumes of reporter's transcript is considered an average-length record.

(4) The number and complexity of the issues raised. A party relying on this factor must specify the issues.

(5) Whether there are settlement negotiations and, if so, how far they have progressed and when they might be completed.

(6) Whether the case is entitled to priority.

(7) Whether counsel responsible for preparing the document is new to the case.

(8) Whether other counsel or the client needs additional time to review the document.

(9) Whether counsel responsible for preparing the document has other time-limited commitments that prevent timely filing of the document. Mere conclusory statements that more time is needed because of other pressing business will not suffice. Good cause requires a specific showing of other obligations of counsel that:

(A) Have deadlines that as a practical matter preclude filing the document by the due date without impairing its quality; or

(B) Arise from cases entitled to priority.

(10) Illness of counsel, a personal emergency, or a planned vacation that counsel did not reasonably expect to conflict with the due date and cannot reasonably rearrange.

(11) Any other factor that constitutes good cause in the context of the case.

(Subd (b) amended effective January 1, 2023; previously amended effective January 1, 2007.)

Rule 8.63 amended effective January 1, 2023; repealed and adopted as rule 45.5 effective January 1, 2005; previously amended and renumbered effective January 1, 2007.

Advisory Committee Comment

An exceptional showing of good cause is required in applications in certain juvenile proceedings under rules 8.416, 8.417, 8.450, 8.452, and 8.454.

Rule 8.66. Tolling or extending time because of public emergency

(a) Emergency tolling or extensions of time

If made necessary by the occurrence or danger of an earthquake, fire, public health crisis, or other public emergency, or by the destruction of or danger to a building housing a reviewing court, the Chair of the Judicial Council, notwithstanding any other rule in this title, may:

(1) Toll for up to 30 days or extend by no more than 30 days any time periods specified by these rules; or

(2) Authorize specified courts to toll for up to 30 days or extend by no more than 30 days any time periods specified by these rules.

(Subd (a) amended effective April 4, 2020; previously amended effective January 1, 2007.)

(b) Applicability of order

(1) An order under (a)(1) must specify the length of the tolling or extension and whether the order applies throughout the state, only to specified courts, or only to courts or attorneys in specified geographic areas, or applies in some other manner.

(2) An order under (a)(2) must specify the length of the authorized tolling or extension.

(Subd (b) amended effective April 4, 2020.)

(c) Renewed orders

If made necessary by the nature or extent of the public emergency, with or without a request, the Chair of the Judicial Council may renew an order issued under this rule prior to its expiration. An order may be renewed for additional periods not to exceed 30 days per renewal.

(Subd (c) amended effective April 4, 2020; previously amended effective January 1, 2007.)

Rule 8.66 amended effective April 4, 2020; previously amended and renumbered effective January 1, 2007; repealed and adopted as rule 45.1 effective January 1, 2005.

Advisory Committee Comment

The Chief Justice of California is the Chair of the Judicial Council (see rule 10.2).

Any tolling ordered under this rule is excluded from the time period specified by the rules. (See *Woods v. Young* (1991) 53 Cal.3d 315, 326, fn. 3 ["Tolling may be analogized to a clock that is stopped and then restarted. Whatever period of time that remained when the clock is stopped is available when the clock is restarted, that is, when the tolling period has ended."].)

The tolling and extension of time authorized under this rule include and apply to all rules of court that govern finality in both the Supreme Court and the Courts of Appeal.

Rule 8.68. Shortening time

For good cause and except as these rules provide otherwise, the Chief Justice or presiding justice may shorten the time to do any act required or permitted under these rules.

Rule 8.68 adopted effective January 1, 2007.

Article 5
E-filing

Division 1, Rules Relating to the Supreme Court and Courts of Appeal—Chapter 1, General Provisions—Article 5, E-filing; renumbered effective January 1, 2014; adopted as Article 4; previously amended effective January 1, 2012.

Rule 8.70. Application, construction, and definitions
Rule 8.71. Electronic filing
Rule 8.72. Responsibilities of court and electronic filer
Rule 8.73. Contracts with electronic filing service providers
Rule 8.74. Format of electronic documents
Rule 8.75. Requirements for signatures on documents
Rule 8.76. Payment of filing fees
Rule 8.77. Actions by court on receipt of electronically submitted document; date and time of filing
Rule 8.78. Electronic service
Rule 8.79. Court order requiring electronic service

Rule 8.70. Application, construction, and definitions

(a) Application

Notwithstanding any other rules to the contrary, the rules in this article govern filing and service by electronic means in the Supreme Court and the Courts of Appeal.

(Subd (a) amended and relettered effective January 1, 2017; adopted as subd (b) effective July 1, 2010; previously amended effective January 1, 2012.)

(b) Construction

The rules in this article must be construed to authorize and permit filing and service by electronic means to the extent feasible.

(Subd (b) relettered effective January 1, 2017; adopted as subd (c) effective July 1, 2010.)

(c) Definitions

As used in this article, unless the context otherwise requires:

(1) "The court" means the Supreme Court or a Court of Appeal.

(2) A "document" is any writing submitted to the reviewing court by a party or other person, including a brief, a petition, an appendix, or a motion. A document is also any writing transmitted by a trial court to the reviewing court, including a notice or a clerk's or reporter's transcript, and any writing prepared by the reviewing court, including an opinion, an order, or a notice. A document may be in paper or electronic form.

(3) "Electronic service" is service of a document on a party or other person by either electronic transmission or electronic notification. Electronic service may be performed directly by a party or other person, by an agent of a party or other person including the party or other person's attorney, through an electronic filing service provider, or by a court.

(4) "Electronic transmission" means the sending of a document by electronic means to the electronic service address at or through which a party or other person has authorized electronic service.

(5) "Electronic notification" means the notification of a party or other person that a document is served by sending an electronic message to the electronic service address at or through which the party or other person has authorized electronic service, specifying the exact name of the document served and providing a hyperlink at which the served document can be viewed and downloaded.

(6) "Electronic service address" of a party means the electronic address at or through which the party has authorized electronic service.

(7) An "electronic filer" is a person filing a document in electronic form directly with the court, by an agent, or through an electronic filing service provider.

(8) "Electronic filing" is the electronic transmission to a court of a document in electronic form for filing. Electronic filing refers to the activity of filing by the electronic filer and does not include the court's actions upon receipt of the document for filing, including processing and review of the document and its entry into the court's records.

(9) An "electronic filing service provider" is a person or entity that receives an electronic filing from a party for retransmission to the court or for electronic service on other parties, or both. In submission of filings, the electronic filing service provider does so on behalf of the electronic filer and not as an agent of the court.

(10) An "electronic signature" is an electronic sound, symbol, or process attached to or logically associated with an electronic record and executed or adopted by a person with the intent to sign a document or record created, generated, sent, communicated, received, or stored by electronic means.

(11) A "secure electronic signature" is a type of electronic signature that is unique to the person using it, capable of verification, under the sole control of the person using it, and linked to data in such a manner that if the data are changed, the electronic signature is invalidated.

(Subd (c) amended effective January 1, 2022; adopted as subd (d) effective January 1, 2011; previously amended effective January 1, 2012; previously amended and relettered effective January 1, 2017.)

Rule 8.70 amended effective January 1, 2022; adopted effective July 1, 2010; previously amended effective January 1, 2011, January 1, 2012, and January 1, 2017.

Advisory Committee Comment

Subdivision (c)(3). The definition of "electronic service" has been amended to provide that a party may effectuate service not only by the electronic transmission of a document, but also by providing electronic notification of where a document served electronically may be located and downloaded. This amendment is intended to expressly authorize electronic notification as an alternative means of service. This amendment is consistent with the amendment of Code of Civil Procedure section 1010.6, effective January 1, 2011, to authorize service by electronic notification. (See Stats. 2010, ch. 156 (Sen. Bill 1274).) The amendments change the law on electronic service as understood by the appellate court in *Insyst, Ltd. v. Applied Materials, Inc.* (2009) 170 Cal.App.4th 1129, which interpreted the rules as authorizing only electronic transmission as an effective means of electronic service.

Subdivision (c)(10). The definition of electronic signature is based on the definition in the Uniform Electronic Transactions Act, Civil Code section 1633.2.

Subdivision (c)(11). The definition of secure electronic signature is based on the first four requirements of a "digital signature" set forth in Government Code section 16.5(a), specifically the requirements stated in section 16.5(a)(1)–(4). The section 16.5(a)(5) requirement of conformance to regulations adopted by the Secretary of State does not apply to secure electronic signatures.

Rule 8.71. Electronic filing

(a) Mandatory electronic filing

Except as otherwise provided by these rules, the *Supreme Court Rules Regarding Electronic Filing*, or court order, all parties are required to file all documents electronically in the reviewing court.

(Subd (a) amended effective January 1, 2020; adopted effective January 1, 2017.)

(b) Self-represented parties

(1) Self-represented parties are exempt from the requirement to file documents electronically.

(2) A self-represented party may agree to file documents electronically. By electronically filing any document with the court, a self-represented party agrees to file documents electronically.

(3) In cases involving both represented and self-represented parties, represented parties are required to file documents electronically; however, in these cases, each self-represented party may file documents in paper form.

(Subd (b) adopted effective January 1, 2017.)

(c) Trial courts

Trial courts are exempt from the requirement to file documents electronically, but are permitted to file documents electronically.

(Subd (c) adopted effective January 1, 2017.)

(d) Excuse for undue hardship or significant prejudice

A party must be excused from the requirement to file documents electronically if the party shows undue hardship or significant prejudice. A court must have a process for parties, including represented parties, to apply for relief and a procedure for parties excused from filing documents electronically to file them in paper form.

(Subd (d) adopted effective January 1, 2017.)

(e) Applications for fee waivers

The court may permit electronic filing of an application for waiver of court fees and costs in any proceeding in which the court accepts electronic filings.

(Subd (e) adopted effective January 1, 2017.)

(f) Effect of document filed electronically

(1) A document that the court, a party, or a trial court files electronically under the rules in this article has the same legal effect as a document in paper form.

(2) Filing a document electronically does not alter any filing deadline.

(Subd (f) adopted effective January 1, 2017.)

(g) Paper documents

When it is not feasible for a party to convert a document to electronic form by scanning, imaging, or another means, the court may allow that party to file the document in paper form.

(Subd (g) adopted effective January 1, 2017.)

Rule 8.71 amended effective January 1, 2020; adopted January 1, 2017.

Rule 8.72. Responsibilities of court and electronic filer

(a) Responsibilities of court

(1) The court will publish, in both electronic form and print form, the court's electronic filing requirements.

(2) If the court is aware of a problem that impedes or precludes electronic filing, it must promptly take reasonable steps to provide notice of the problem.

(Subd (a) amended effective January 1, 2020; adopted effective July 1, 2010; previously amended effective January 1, 2017.)

(b) Responsibilities of electronic filer

Each electronic filer must:

(1) Take all reasonable steps to ensure that the filing does not contain computer code, including viruses, that might be harmful to the court's electronic filing system and to other users of that system;

(2) Furnish one or more electronic service addresses, in the manner specified by the court, at which the electronic filer agrees to accept receipt and filing confirmations under rule 8.77 and, if applicable, at which the electronic filer agrees to receive electronic service; and

(3) Immediately provide the court and all parties with any change to the electronic filer's electronic service address.

(Subd (b) amended effective January 1, 2021; adopted effective January 1, 2020.)

Rule 8.72 amended effective January 1, 2021; adopted as rule 8.74 effective July 1, 2010; previously amended and renumbered effective January 1, 2017; previously amended effective January 1, 2020.

Advisory Committee Comment

Subdivision (b)(1). One example of a reasonable step an electronic filer may take is to use a commercial virus scanning program. Compliance with this subdivision requires more than an absence of intent to harm the court's electronic filing system or other users' systems.

Rule 8.73. Contracts with electronic filing service providers

(a) Right to contract

(1) The court may contract with one or more electronic filing service providers to furnish and maintain an electronic filing system for the court.

(2) If the court contracts with an electronic filing service provider, the court may require electronic filers to transmit the documents to the provider.

(3) If the court contracts with an electronic service provider or the court has an in-house system, the provider or system must accept filing from other electronic filing service providers to the extent the provider or system is compatible with them.

(Subd (a) amended effective January 1, 2011; adopted effective July 1, 2010.)

(b) Provisions of contract

The court's contract with an electronic filing service provider may allow the provider to charge electronic filers a reasonable fee in addition to the court's filing fee. Whenever possible, the contract should require that the electronic filing service provider agree to waive a fee that normally would be charged to a party when the court orders that the fee be waived for that party. The contract may also allow the electronic filing service provider to make other reasonable requirements for use of the electronic filing system.

(Subd (b) amended effective January 1, 2017; adopted effective July 1, 2010.)

(c) Transmission of filing to court

An electronic filing service provider must promptly transmit any electronic filing and any applicable filing fee to the court.

(Subd (c) amended effective January 1, 2011; adopted effective July 1, 2010.)

(d) Confirmation of receipt and filing of document

(1) An electronic filing service provider must promptly send to an electronic filer its confirmation of the receipt of any document that the filer has transmitted to the provider for filing with the court.

(2) The electronic filing service provider must send its confirmation to the filer's electronic service address and must indicate the date and time of receipt, in accordance with rule 8.77.

(3) After reviewing the documents, the court must arrange to promptly transmit confirmation of filing or notice of rejection to the electronic filer in accordance with rule 8.77.

(Subd (d) amended effective January 1, 2017; adopted effective July 1, 2010; previously amended effective January 1, 2011.)

(e) Ownership of information

All contracts between the court and electronic filing service providers must acknowledge that the court is the owner of the contents of the filing system and has the exclusive right to control the system's use.

(Subd (e) adopted effective July 1, 2010.)

Rule 8.73 amended and renumbered effective January 1, 2017; adopted as rule 8.75 effective July 1, 2010; previously amended effective January 1, 2011.

Rule 8.74. Format of electronic documents

(a) Formatting requirements applicable to all electronic documents

(1) *Text-searchable portable document format:* Electronic documents must be in text-searchable portable document format (PDF) while maintaining the original document formatting. In the limited circumstances in which a document cannot practicably be converted to a text-searchable PDF, the document may be scanned or converted to non-text-searchable PDF. An electronic filer is not required to use a specific vendor, technology, or software for creation of a searchable-format document, unless the electronic filer agrees to such use. The software for creating and reading electronic documents must be in the public domain or generally available at a reasonable cost. The printing of an electronic document must not result in the loss of document text, formatting, or appearance. The electronic filer is responsible for ensuring that any document filed is complete and readable.

(2) *Pagination:* The electronic page counter for the electronic document must match the page number for each page of the document. The page numbering of a document filed electronically must begin with the first page or cover page as page 1 and thereafter be paginated consecutively using only arabic numerals (e.g., 1, 2, 3). The page number for the cover page may be suppressed and need not appear on the cover page. When a document is filed in both paper form and electronic form, the pagination in both versions must comply with this paragraph.

(3) *Bookmarking:* An electronic bookmark is a descriptive text link that appears in the bookmarks panel of an electronic document. Each electronic document must include an electronic bookmark to each heading, subheading, and the first page of any component of the document, including any table of contents, table of authorities, petition, verification, memorandum, declaration, certificate of word count, certificate of interested entities or persons, proof of service, exhibit, or attachment. Each electronic bookmark must briefly describe the item to which it is linked. For example, an electronic bookmark to a heading must provide the text of the heading, and an electronic bookmark to an exhibit or attachment must include the letter or number of the exhibit or attachment and a brief description of the exhibit or attachment. An electronic appendix must have bookmarks to the indexes and to the first page of each separate exhibit or attachment. Exhibits or attachments within an exhibit or attachment must be bookmarked. All bookmarks must be set to retain the reader's selected zoom setting.

(4) *Protection of sensitive information:* Electronic filers must comply with rules 1.201, 8.45, 8.46, 8.47, and 8.401 regarding the protection of

sensitive information, except for those requirements exclusively applicable to paper form.

(5) *Size and multiple files:* An electronic filing may not be larger than 25 megabytes. This rule does not change the limitations on word count or number of pages otherwise established by the California Rules of Court for documents filed in the court. Although certain provisions in the California Rules of Court require volumes of no more than 300 pages (see, e.g., rules 8.124(d)(1), 8.144(b)(6), 8.144(g)), an electronic filing may exceed 300 pages so long as its individual components comply with the 300-page volume requirement and the electronic filing does not exceed 25 megabytes. If a document exceeds the 25-megabyte file-size limitation, the electronic filer must submit the document in more than one file, with each file 25 megabytes or less. The first file must include a master chronological and alphabetical index stating the contents for all files. Each file must have a cover page stating (a) the file number for that file and the total number of files for that document, (b) the volumes contained in that file, and (c) the page numbers contained in that file. (For example: File 2 of 4, Volumes 3–4, pp. 301–499.) In addition, each file must be paginated consecutively across all files in the document, including the cover pages for each file. (For example, if the first file ends on page 300, the cover of the second file must be page 301.) If a multiple-file document is submitted to the court in both electronic form and paper form, the cover pages for each file must be included in the paper documents.

(6) *Manual Filing:*

(A) When an electronic filer seeks to file an electronic document consisting of more than 10 files, or when the document cannot or should not be electronically filed in multiple files, or when electronically filing the document would cause undue hardship, the document must not be electronically filed but must be manually filed with the court on an electronic medium such as a flash drive, DVD, or compact disc (CD). When an electronic filer files with the court one or more documents on an electronic medium, the electronic filer must electronically file, on the same day, a "manual filing notification" notifying the court and the parties that one or more documents have been filed on electronic media, explaining the reason for the manual filing. The electronic media must be served on the parties in accordance with the requirements for service of paper documents. To the extent practicable, each document or file on electronic media must comply with the format requirements of this rule.

(B) Electronic media files such as audio or video must be manually filed. Audio files must be filed in .wav or mp3 format. Video files must be filed in .avi or mp4 format.

(C) If manually filed, photographs must be filed in .jpg, .png, .tif, or .pdf format.

(D) If an original electronic media file is converted to a required format for manual filing, the electronic filer must retain the original.

(7) *Page size:* All documents must have a page size of 8-1/2 by 11 inches.

(8) *Color:* An electronic document with a color component may be electronically filed or manually filed on electronic media, depending on its file size. An electronic document must not have a color cover.

(9) *Cover or first-page information:*

(A) Except as provided in (B), the cover—or first page, if there is no cover—of every electronic document filed in a reviewing court must include the name, mailing address, telephone number, fax number (if available), email address (if available), and California State Bar number of each attorney filing or joining in the document, or of the party if he or she is unrepresented. The inclusion of a fax number or email address on any electronic document does not constitute consent to service by fax or email unless otherwise provided by law.

(B) If more than one attorney from a law firm, corporation, or public law office is representing one party and is joining in the document, the name and State Bar number of each attorney joining in the electronic document must be provided on the cover. The law firm, corporation, or public law office representing each party must designate one attorney to receive notices and other communication in the case from the court by placing an asterisk before that attorney's name on the cover and must provide the contact information specified under (A) for that attorney. Contact information for the other attorneys from the same law firm, corporation, or public law office is not required but may be provided.

(Subd (a) amended effective January 1, 2020; adopted effective July 1, 2010; previously amended effective January 1, 2011.)

(b) Additional formatting requirements applicable to documents prepared for electronic filing in the first instance in a reviewing court

(1) *Font:* The font style must be a proportionally spaced serif face. Century Schoolbook is preferred. A sans-serif face may be used for headings, subheadings, and captions. Font size must be 13-points, including in footnotes. Case names must be italicized or underscored. For emphasis, italics or boldface may be used or the text may be underscored. Do not use all capitals (i.e., ALL CAPS) for emphasis.

(2) *Spacing:* Lines of text must be 1.5 spaced. Footnotes, headings, subheadings, and quotations may be single-spaced. The lines of text must be unnumbered.

(3) *Margins:* The margins must be set at 1-1/2 inches on the left and right and 1 inch on the top and bottom. Quotations may be block-indented.

(4) *Alignment:* Paragraphs must be left-aligned, not justified.

(5) *Hyperlinks:* Hyperlinks to legal authorities and appendixes or exhibits are encouraged but not required. However, if an electronic filer elects to include hyperlinks in a document, the hyperlink must be active as of the date of filing, and if the hyperlink is to a legal authority, it should be formatted to standard citation format as provided in the California Rules of Court.

(Subd (b) adopted effective January 1, 2020.)

(c) Additional formatting requirements for certain electronic documents

(1) *Brief:* In addition to compliance with this rule, an electronic brief must also comply with the contents and length requirements stated in rule 8.204(a) and (c). The brief need not be signed. The cover must state:

(A) The title of the brief;

(B) The title, trial court number, and Court of Appeal number of the case;

(C) The names of the trial court and each participating trial judge; and

(D) The name of the party that each attorney on the brief represents.

(2) *Request for judicial notice or request, application, or motion supported by documents:* When seeking judicial notice of matter not already in the appellate record, or when a request, application, or motion is supported by matter not already in the appellate record, the electronic filer must attach a copy of the matter to the request, application, or motion, or an explanation of why it is not practicable to do so. The request, application, or motion and its attachments must comply with this rule.

(3) *Appendix:* The format of an appendix must comply with this rule and rule 8.144 pertaining to clerks' transcripts.

(4) *Agreed statement and settled statement:* The format for an agreed statement or a settled statement must comply with this rule and rule 8.144.

(5) *Reporter's transcript and clerk's transcript:* The format for an electronic reporter's transcript must comply with Code of Civil Procedure section 271 and rule 8.144. The format for an electronic clerk's transcript must comply with this rule and rule 8.144.

(6) *Exhibits:* Electronic exhibits must be submitted in files no larger than 25 megabytes, rather than as individual documents.

(7) *Sealed and confidential records:* Under rule 8.45(c)(1), electronic records that are sealed or confidential must be filed separately from publicly filed records. If one or more pages are omitted from a record and filed separately as a sealed or confidential record, an omission page or pages must be inserted in the publicly filed record at the location of the omitted page or pages. The omission page or pages must identify the type of page or pages omitted. Each omission page must be paginated consecutively with the rest of the publicly filed record. Each single omission page or the first omission page in a range of omission pages must be bookmarked and must be listed in any indexes included in the publicly filed record. The PDF counter for each omission page must match the page number of the page omitted from the publicly filed record. Separately-filed sealed or confidential records must comply with this rule and rules 8.45, 8.46, and 8.47.

(Subd (c) adopted effective January 1, 2020.)

(d) Other formatting rules

This rule prevails over other formatting rules.

(Subd (d) adopted effective January 1, 2020.)

Rule 8.74 amended effective January 1, 2020; adopted as rule 8.76 effective July 1, 2010; previously amended effective January 1, 2011; previously amended and renumbered effective January 1, 2017.

Advisory Committee Comment

Subdivision (a)(1). If an electronic filer must file a document that the electronic filer possesses only in paper form, use of a scanned image is a permitted means of conversion to PDF, but optical character recognition must be used, if possible. If a document cannot practicably be converted to a text-searchable PDF (e.g., if the document is entirely or substantially handwritten, a photograph, or a graphic such as a chart or diagram that is not primarily text based), the document may be converted to a non-text-searchable PDF file.

Subdivision (a)(3). An electronic bookmark's brief description of the item to which it is linked should enable the reader to easily identify the item. For example, if a declaration is attached to a document, the bookmark to the declaration might say "Robert Smith Declaration," and if a complaint is attached to a declaration as an exhibit, the bookmark to the complaint might say "Exhibit A, First Amended Complaint filed 8/12/17."

Subdivision (b). Subdivision (b) governs documents prepared for electronic filing in the first instance in a reviewing court and does not apply to previously created documents (such as exhibits), whose formatting cannot or should not be altered.

Subdivision (c)(7). In identifying the type of pages omitted, the omission page might say, for example, "probation report" or "*Marsden* hearing transcript."

Rule 8.75. Requirements for signatures on documents

(a) Documents signed under penalty of perjury

When a document must be signed under penalty of perjury, the document is deemed to have been signed by the declarant if filed electronically, provided that either of the following conditions is satisfied:

(1) The declarant has signed the document using an electronic signature (or a secure electronic signature if the declarant is not the electronic filer) and declares under penalty of perjury under the laws of the State of California that the information submitted is true and correct; or

(2) The declarant, before filing, has physically signed a printed form of the document. By electronically filing the document, the electronic filer certifies that the original signed document is available for inspection and copying at the request of the court or any other party. In the event this second method of submitting documents electronically under penalty of perjury is used, the following conditions apply:

(A) At any time after the electronic version of the document is filed, any other party may serve a demand for production of the original signed document. The demand must be served on all other parties but need not be filed with the court.

(B) Within five days of service of the demand under (A), the party or other person on whom the demand is made must make the original signed document available for inspection and copying by all other parties.

(C) At any time after the electronic version of the document is filed, the court may order the electronic filer to produce the original signed document for inspection and copying by the court. The order must specify the date, time, and place for the production and must be served on all parties.

(Subd (a) amended effective January 1, 2022; adopted effective July 1, 2010; previously amended effective January 1, 2014.)

(b) Documents not signed under penalty of perjury

(1) If a document does not require a signature under penalty of perjury, the document is deemed signed by the electronic filer.

(2) When a document to be filed electronically, such as a stipulation, requires the signatures of multiple persons, the document is deemed to have been signed by those persons if filed electronically, provided that either of the following procedures is satisfied:

(A) The parties or other persons have signed the document using a secure electronic signature; or

(B) The electronic filer has obtained all the signatures either in the form of an original signature on a printed form of the document or in the form of a copy of the signed signature page of the document. The electronic filer must maintain the original signed document and any copies of signed signature pages and must make them available for inspection and copying as provided in (a)(2)(B). The court and any party may demand production of the original signed document and any copies of the signed signature pages as provided in (a)(2)(A)–(C). By electronically filing the document, the electronic filer indicates that all persons whose signatures appear on it have signed the document and that the filer has possession of the signatures of all those persons in a form permitted by this rule.

(Subd (b) amended effective January 1, 2022; adopted effective July 1, 2010.)

(c) Judicial signatures

If a document requires a signature by a court or a judicial officer, the document may be electronically signed in any manner permitted by law.

(Subd (c) amended and relettered effective January 1, 2022; adopted as subd (e) effective July 1, 2010.)

Rule 8.75 amended effective January 1, 2022; adopted as rule 8.77 effective July 1, 2010; previously amended effective January 1, 2014; previously renumbered effective January 1, 2017.

Advisory Committee Comment

The requirements for electronic signatures that are compliant with the rule do not impair the power of the courts to resolve disputes about the validity of a signature.

Rule 8.76. Payment of filing fees

(a) Use of credit cards and other methods

The court may permit the use of credit cards, debit cards, electronic fund transfers, or debit accounts for the payment of filing fees associated with electronic filing, as provided in Government Code section 6159 and other applicable law. The court may also authorize other methods of payment.

(Subd (a) adopted effective July 1, 2010.)

(b) Fee waivers

Eligible persons may seek a waiver of court fees and costs, as provided in Government Code section 68634.5 and rule 8.26.

(Subd (b) adopted effective July 1, 2010.)

Rule 8.76 renumbered effective January 1, 2017; adopted as rule 8.78 effective July 1, 2010.

Advisory Committee Comment

Subdivision (b). A fee charged by an electronic filing service provider under rule 8.73(b) is not a court fee that can be waived under Government Code section 68634.5 and rule 8.26.

Rule 8.77. Actions by court on receipt of electronically submitted document; date and time of filing

(a) Confirmation of receipt and filing of document

(1) *Confirmation of receipt*

When the court receives an electronically submitted document, the court must arrange to promptly send the electronic filer confirmation of the court's receipt of the document, indicating the date and time of receipt by the court.

(2) *Filing*

If the electronically submitted document received by the court complies with filing requirements, the document is deemed filed on the date and time it was received by the court as stated in the confirmation of receipt.

(3) *Confirmation of filing*

When the court files an electronically submitted document, the court must arrange to promptly send the electronic filer confirmation that the document has been filed. The filing confirmation must indicate the date and time of filing as specified in the confirmation of receipt, and must also specify:

(A) Any transaction number associated with the filing; and

(B) The titles of the documents as filed by the court.

(4) *Transmission of confirmations*

The court must arrange to send receipt and filing confirmation to the electronic filer at the electronic service address that the filer furnished to the court under rule 8.72(b)(2). The court or the electronic filing service provider must maintain a record of all receipt and filing confirmations.

(5) *Filer responsible for verification*

In the absence of confirmation of receipt and filing, there is no presumption that the court received and filed the document. The electronic filer is responsible for verifying that the court received and filed any document that the electronic filer submitted to the court electronically.

(Subd (a) amended effective January 1, 2021; adopted effective July 1, 2010; previously amended effective January 1, 2011, January 1, 2017, and January 1, 2020.)

(b) Notice of rejection of document for filing

If the clerk does not file a document because it does not comply with applicable filing requirements, the court must arrange to promptly send notice of the rejection of the document for filing to the electronic filer. The notice must state the reasons that the document was rejected for filing.

(Subd (b) amended effective January 1, 2017; adopted effective July 1, 2010.)

(c) Document received after close of business

A document that is received electronically by the court after 11:59 p.m. is deemed to have been received on the next court day.

(Subd (c) amended effective January 1, 2011; adopted effective July 1, 2010.)

(d) Delayed delivery

If a filer fails to meet a filing deadline imposed by court order, rule, or statute because of a failure at any point in the electronic transmission and receipt of a document, the filer may file the document on paper or electronically as soon thereafter as practicable and accompany the filing with a motion to accept the document as timely filed. For good cause shown, the court may enter an order permitting the document to be filed nunc pro tunc to the date the filer originally sought to transmit the document electronically.

(Subd (d) amended effective January 1, 2017; adopted effective July 1, 2010.)

(e) Endorsement

(1) The court's endorsement of a document electronically filed must contain the following: "Electronically filed by [Name of Court], on _____ (date)," followed by the name of the court clerk.

(2) The endorsement required under (1) has the same force and effect as a manually affixed endorsement stamp with the signature and initials of the court clerk.

(3) A record on appeal, brief, or petition in an appeal or original proceeding that is filed and endorsed electronically may be printed and served on the appellant or respondent in the same manner as if it had been filed in paper form.

(Subd (e) amended effective January 1, 2012; adopted effective July 1, 2010.)
Rule 8.77 amended effective January 1, 2021; adopted as rule 8.79 effective July 1, 2010; previously amended effective January 1, 2011, January 1, 2012, and January 1, 2020; previously amended and renumbered effective January 1, 2017.

Rule 8.78. Electronic service

(a) Authorization for electronic service; exceptions

(1) A document may be electronically served under these rules:

(A) If electronic service is provided for by law or court order; or

(B) If the recipient agrees to accept electronic services as provided by these rules and the document is otherwise authorized to be served by mail, express mail, overnight delivery, or fax transmission.

(2) A party indicates that the party agrees to accept electronic service by:

(A) Serving a notice on all parties that the party accepts electronic service and filing the notice with the court. The notice must include the electronic service address at which the party agrees to accept service; or

(B) Registering with the court's electronic filing service provider and providing the party's electronic service address. Registration with the court's electronic filing service provider is deemed to show that the party agrees to accept service at the electronic service address that the party has provided, unless the party serves a notice on all parties and files the notice with the court that the party does not accept electronic service and chooses instead to be served paper copies at an address specified in the notice.

(3) A document may be electronically served on a nonparty if the nonparty consents to electronic service or electronic service is otherwise provided for by law or court order. All provisions of this rule that apply or relate to a party also apply to any nonparty who has agreed to or is otherwise required by law or court order to accept electronic service or to electronically serve documents.

(Subd (a) amended effective January 1, 2021; adopted effective July 1, 2010; previously amended effective January 1, 2011, January 1, 2016, January 1, 2017, and January 1, 2020.)

(b) Maintenance of electronic service lists

When the court orders or permits electronic service in a case, it must maintain and make available electronically to the parties an electronic service list that contains the parties' current electronic service addresses as provided by the parties that have been ordered to or have consented to electronic service in the case.

(Subd (b) amended effective January 1, 2017; adopted effective July 1, 2010; previously amended effective January 1, 2011.)

(c) Service by the parties

Notwithstanding (b), parties are responsible for electronic service on all other parties in the case. A party may serve documents electronically directly, by an agent, or through a designated electronic filing service provider.

(Subd (c) amended effective January 1, 2016; adopted effective July 1, 2010, and January 1, 2011.)

(d) Change of electronic service address

(1) A party whose electronic service address changes while the appeal or original proceeding is pending must promptly file a notice of change of address electronically with the court and must serve this notice electronically on all other parties.

(2) A party's election to contract with an electronic filing service provider to electronically file and serve documents or to receive electronic service of documents on the party's behalf does not relieve the party of its duties under (1).

(Subd (d) amended effective January 1, 2017; adopted effective July 1, 2010; previously amended effective January 1, 2011.)

(e) Reliability and integrity of documents served by electronic notification

A party that serves a document by means of electronic notification must:

(1) Ensure that the documents served can be viewed and downloaded using the hyperlink provided;

(2) Preserve the document served without any change, alteration, or modification from the time the document is posted until the time the hyperlink is terminated; and

(3) Maintain the hyperlink until the case is final.

(Subd (e) repealed and adopted effective January 1, 2011.)

(f) Proof of service

(1) Proof of electronic service may be by any of the methods provided in Code of Civil Procedure section 1013a, with the following exceptions:

(A) The proof of electronic service does not need to state that the person making the service is not a party to the case.

(B) The proof of electronic service must state:

(i) The electronic service address of the person making the service, in addition to that person's residence or business address;

(ii) The date of the electronic service, instead of the date and place of deposit in the mail;

(iii) The name and electronic service address of the person served, in place of that person's name and address as shown on the envelope; and

(iv) That the document was served electronically, in place of the statement that the envelope was sealed and deposited in the mail with postage fully prepaid.

(2) Proof of electronic service may be in electronic form and may be filed electronically with the court.

(3) The party filing the proof of electronic service must maintain the printed form of the document bearing the declarant's original signature and must make the document available for inspection and copying on the request of the court or any party to the action or proceeding in which it is filed, in the manner provided in rule 8.75.

(Subd (f) amended effective January 1, 2017; adopted effective July 1, 2010; previously amended effective January 1, 2011.)

(g) Electronic delivery by court and electronic service on court

(1) The court may deliver any notice, order, opinion, or other document issued by the court by electronic means.

(2) A document may be electronically served on a court if the court consents to electronic service or electronic service is otherwise provided for by law or court order. A court indicates that it agrees to accept electronic service by:

(A) Serving a notice on all parties that the court accepts electronic service. The notice must include the electronic service address at which the court agrees to accept service; or

(B) Adopting a local rule stating that the court accepts electronic service. The rule must indicate where to obtain the electronic service address at which the court agrees to accept service.

(Subd (g) amended effective January 1, 2021; adopted effective July 1, 2010; previously amended effective January 1, 2016.)
Rule 8.78 amended effective January 1, 2021; adopted as rule 8.80 effective July 1, 2010; previously amended and renumbered as rule 8.71 effective January 1, 2011, and amended and renumbered as rule 8.78 effective January 1, 2017; previously amended effective January 1, 2016, and January 1, 2020.

Advisory Committee Comment

In the Supreme Court and the Courts of Appeal, registration with the court's electronic filing service provider is deemed to show agreement to accept service electronically at the email address provided, unless a party affirmatively opts out of electronic service under rule 8.78(a)(2)(B). This procedure differs from the procedure for electronic service in the superior courts, including their appellate divisions. See rules 2.250–2.261.

Rule 8.79. Court order requiring electronic service

(a) Court order

(1) The court may, on the motion of any party or on its own motion, provided that the order would not cause undue hardship or significant prejudice to any party, order some or all parties to do either or both of the following:

(A) Serve all documents electronically, except when personal service is required by statute or rule; or

(B) Accept electronic service of documents.

(2) The court will not:

(A) Order a self-represented party to electronically serve or accept electronic service of documents; or

(B) Order a trial court to electronically serve documents.

(3) If the reviewing court proposes to make an order under (1) on its own motion, the court must mail notice to the parties. Any party may serve and file an opposition within 10 days after the notice is mailed or as the court specifies.

(Subd (a) amended effective January 1, 2017; adopted effective July 1, 2010; previously amended effective January 1, 2011.)

(b) Serving in paper form

When it is not feasible for a party to convert a document to electronic form by scanning, imaging, or another means, the court may allow that party to serve the document in paper form.

(Subd (b) amended and relettered effective January 1, 2017; adopted as subd (c) effective July 1, 2010.)

Rule 8.79 amended and renumbered effective January 1, 2017; adopted as rule 8.73 effective July 1, 2010; previously amended effective January 1, 2011.

Article 6
Public Access to Electronic Appellate Court Records

Title 8, Appellate Rules—Division 1, Rules Relating to the Supreme Court and Courts of Appeal—Chapter 1, General Provisions—Article 6, Public Access to Electronic Appellate Court Records; adopted effective January 1, 2016.

Rule 8.80. Statement of purpose
Rule 8.81. Application and scope
Rule 8.82. Definitions
Rule 8.83. Public access
Rule 8.84. Limitations and conditions
Rule 8.85. Fees for copies of electronic records

Rule 8.80. Statement of purpose

(a) Intent

The rules in this article are intended to provide the public with reasonable access to appellate court records that are maintained in electronic form, while protecting privacy interests.

(Subd (a) adopted effective January 1, 2016.)

(b) Benefits of electronic access

Improved technologies provide courts with many alternatives to the historical paper-based record receipt and retention process, including the creation and use of court records maintained in electronic form. Providing public access to appellate court records that are maintained in electronic form may save the courts and the public time, money, and effort and encourage courts to be more efficient in their operations. Improved access to appellate court records may also foster in the public a more comprehensive understanding of the appellate court system.

(Subd (b) adopted effective January 1, 2016.)

(c) No creation of rights

The rules in this article are not intended to give the public a right of access to any record that they are not otherwise entitled to access. The rules do not create any right of access to sealed or confidential records.

(Subd (c) adopted effective January 1, 2016.)

Rule 8.80 adopted effective January 1, 2016.

Advisory Committee Comment

The rules in this article acknowledge the benefits that electronic court records provide but attempt to limit the potential for unjustified intrusions into the privacy of individuals involved in litigation that can occur as a result of remote access to electronic court records. The proposed rules take into account the limited resources currently available in the appellate courts. It is contemplated that the rules may be modified to provide greater electronic access as the courts' technical capabilities improve and with the knowledge gained from the experience of the courts in providing electronic access under these rules.

Subdivision (c). Rules 8.45–8.47 govern sealed and confidential records in the appellate courts.

Rule 8.81. Application and scope

(a) Application

The rules in this article apply only to records of the Supreme Court and Courts of Appeal.

(Subd (a) adopted effective January 1, 2016.)

(b) Access by parties and attorneys

The rules in this article apply only to access to court records by the public. They do not limit access to court records by a party to an action or proceeding, by the attorney of a party, or by other persons or entities that are entitled to access by statute or rule.

(Subd (b) adopted effective January 1, 2016.)

Rule 8.81 adopted effective January 1, 2016.

Rule 8.82. Definitions

As used in this article, the following definitions apply:

(1) "Court record" is any document, paper, exhibit, transcript, or other thing filed in an action or proceeding; any order, judgment, or opinion of the court; and any court minutes, index, register of actions, or docket. The term does not include the personal notes or preliminary memoranda of justices, judges, or other judicial branch personnel.

(2) "Electronic record" is a court record that requires the use of an electronic device to access. The term includes both a record that has been filed electronically and an electronic copy or version of a record that was filed in paper form.

(3) "The public" means an individual, a group, or an entity, including print or electronic media, or the representative of an individual, a group, or an entity.

(4) "Electronic access" means computer access to court records available to the public through both public terminals at the courthouse and remotely, unless otherwise specified in the rules in this article.

(5) Providing electronic access to electronic records "to the extent it is feasible to do so" means that electronic access must be provided to the extent the court determines it has the resources and technical capacity to do so.

(6) "Bulk distribution" means distribution of multiple electronic records that is not done on a case-by-case basis.

Rule 8.82 adopted effective January 1, 2016.

Rule 8.83. Public access

(a) General right of access

All electronic records must be made reasonably available to the public in some form, whether in electronic or in paper form, except sealed or confidential records.

(Subd (a) adopted effective January 1, 2016.)

(b) Electronic access required to extent feasible

(1) Electronic access, both remote and at the courthouse, will be provided to the following court records, except sealed or confidential records, to the extent it is feasible to do so:

(A) Dockets or registers of actions;

(B) Calendars;

(C) Opinions; and

(D) The following Supreme Court records:

i. Results from the most recent Supreme Court weekly conference;

ii. Party briefs in cases argued in the Supreme Court for at least the preceding three years;

iii. Supreme Court minutes from at least the preceding three years.

(2) If a court maintains records in civil cases in addition to those listed in (1) in electronic form, electronic access to these records, except those listed in (c), must be provided both remotely and at the courthouse, to the extent it is feasible to do so.

(Subd (b) adopted effective January 1, 2016.)

(c) Courthouse electronic access only

If a court maintains the following records in electronic form, electronic access to these records must be provided at the courthouse, to the extent it is feasible to do so, but remote electronic access may not be provided to these records:

(1) Any reporter's transcript for which the reporter is entitled to receive a fee; and

(2) Records other than those listed in (b)(1) in the following proceedings:

(A) Proceedings under the Family Code, including proceedings for dissolution, legal separation, and nullity of marriage; child and spousal support proceedings; child custody proceedings; and domestic violence prevention proceedings;

(B) Juvenile court proceedings;

(C) Guardianship or conservatorship proceedings;

(D) Mental health proceedings;

(E) Criminal proceedings;

(F) Civil harassment proceedings under Code of Civil Procedure section 527.6;

(G) Workplace violence prevention proceedings under Code of Civil Procedure section 527.8;

(H) Private postsecondary school violence prevention proceedings under Code of Civil Procedure section 527.85;

(I) Elder or dependent adult abuse prevention proceedings under Welfare and Institutions Code section 15657.03; and

(J) Proceedings to compromise the claims of a minor or a person with a disability.

(d) Remote electronic access allowed in extraordinary cases

Notwithstanding (c)(2), the presiding justice of the court, or a justice assigned by the presiding justice, may exercise discretion, subject to (d)(1), to permit remote electronic access by the public to all or a portion of the public court records in an individual case if (1) the number of requests for access to documents in the case is extraordinarily high and (2) responding to those requests would significantly burden the operations of the court. An individualized determination must be made in each case in which such remote electronic access is provided.

(1) In exercising discretion under (d), the justice should consider the relevant factors, such as:

(A) The privacy interests of parties, victims, witnesses, and court personnel, and the ability of the court to redact sensitive personal information;

(B) The benefits to and burdens on the parties in allowing remote electronic access; and

(C) The burdens on the court in responding to an extraordinarily high number of requests for access to documents.

(2) The following information must be redacted from records to which the court allows remote access under (d): driver's license numbers; dates of birth; social security numbers; Criminal Identification and Information and National Crime Information numbers; addresses, e-mail addresses, and phone numbers of parties, victims, witnesses, and court personnel; medical or psychiatric information; financial information; account numbers; and other personal identifying information. The court may order any party who files a document containing such information to provide the court with both an original unredacted version of the document for filing in the court file and a redacted version of the document for remote electronic access. No juror names or other juror identifying information may be provided by remote electronic access. Subdivision (d)(2) does not apply to any document in the original court file; it applies only to documents that are made available by remote electronic access.

(3) Five days' notice must be provided to the parties and the public before the court makes a determination to provide remote electronic access under this rule. Notice to the public may be accomplished by posting notice on the court's website. Any person may file comments with the court for consideration, but no hearing is required.

(4) The court's order permitting remote electronic access must specify which court records will be available by remote electronic access and what categories of information are to be redacted. The court is not required to make findings of fact. The court's order must be posted on the court's website and a copy sent to the Judicial Council.

(Subd (d) adopted effective January 1, 2016.)

(e) Access only on a case-by-case basis

With the exception of the records covered by (b)(1), electronic access to an electronic record may be granted only when the record is identified by the number of the case, the caption of the case, the name of a party, the name of the attorney, or the date of oral argument, and only on a case-by-case basis.

(Subd (e) adopted effective January 1, 2016.)

(f) Bulk distribution

Bulk distribution may be provided only of the records covered by (b)(1).

(Subd (f) adopted effective January 1, 2016.)

(g) Records that become inaccessible

If an electronic record to which electronic access has been provided is made inaccessible to the public by court order or by operation of law, the court is not required to take action with respect to any copy of the record that was made by a member of the public before the record became inaccessible.

(Subd (g) adopted effective January 1, 2016.)

Rule 8.83 adopted effective January 1, 2016.

Advisory Committee Comment

The rule allows a level of access by the public to all electronic records that is at least equivalent to the access that is available for paper records and, for some types of records, is much greater. At the same time, it seeks to protect legitimate privacy concerns.

Subdivision (b). Courts should encourage availability of electronic access to court records at public off-site locations.

Subdivision (c). This subdivision excludes certain records (those other than the register, calendar, opinions, and certain Supreme Court records) in specified types of cases (notably criminal, juvenile, and family court matters) from remote electronic access. The committees recognized that while these case records are public records and should remain available at the courthouse, either in paper or electronic form, they often contain sensitive personal information. The court should not publish that information over the Internet. However, the committees also recognized that the use of the Internet may be appropriate in certain individual cases of extraordinary public interest where information regarding a case will be widely disseminated through the media. In such cases, posting of selected nonconfidential court records, redacted where necessary to protect the privacy of the participants, may provide more timely and accurate information regarding the court proceedings, and may relieve substantial burdens on court staff in responding to individual requests for documents and information. Thus, under subdivision (d), if the presiding justice makes individualized determinations in a specific case, certain records in individual cases may be made available over the Internet.

Subdivision (d). Courts must send a copy of the order permitting remote electronic access in extraordinary cases to: Legal Services, Judicial Council of California, 455 Golden Gate Avenue, San Francisco, CA 94102-3688.

Subdivisions (e) and (f). These subdivisions limit electronic access to records (other than the register, calendars, opinions, and certain Supreme Court records) to a case-by-case basis and prohibit bulk distribution of those records. These limitations are based on the qualitative difference between obtaining information from a specific case file and obtaining bulk information that may be manipulated to compile personal information culled from any document, paper, or exhibit filed in a lawsuit. This type of aggregate information may be exploited for commercial or other purposes unrelated to the operations of the courts, at the expense of privacy rights of individuals.

Rule 8.84. Limitations and conditions

(a) Means of access

Electronic access to records required under this article must be provided by means of a network or software that is based on industry standards or is in the public domain.

(Subd (a) adopted effective January 1, 2016.)

(b) Official record

Unless electronically certified by the court, a court record available by electronic access is not the official record of the court.

(Subd (b) adopted effective January 1, 2016.)

(c) Conditions of use by persons accessing records

Electronic access to court records may be conditioned on:

(1) The user's consent to access the records only as instructed; and

(2) The user's consent to monitoring of access to its records.

The court must give notice of these conditions, in any manner it deems appropriate. Access may be denied to a member of the public for failure to comply with either of these conditions of use.

(Subd (c) adopted effective January 1, 2016.)

(d) Notices to persons accessing records

The court must give notice of the following information to members of the public accessing its records electronically, in any manner it deems appropriate:

(1) The identity of the court staff member to be contacted about the requirements for accessing the court's records electronically.

(2) That copyright and other proprietary rights may apply to information in a case file, absent an express grant of additional rights by the holder of the copyright or other proprietary right. This notice must advise the public that:

(A) Use of such information in a case file is permissible only to the extent permitted by law or court order; and

(B) Any use inconsistent with proprietary rights is prohibited.

(3) Whether electronic records are the official records of the court. The notice must describe the procedure and any fee required for obtaining a certified copy of an official record of the court.

(4) That any person who willfully destroys or alters any court record maintained in electronic form is subject to the penalties imposed by Government Code section 6201.

(Subd (d) adopted effective January 1, 2016.)

(e) Access policy

A privacy policy must be posted on the California Courts public-access website to inform members of the public accessing its electronic records of the information collected regarding access transactions and the uses that may be made of the collected information.

(Subd (e) adopted effective January 1, 2016.)

Rule 8.84 adopted effective January 1, 2016.

Rule 8.85. Fees for copies of electronic records

The court may impose fees for the costs of providing copies of its electronic records, under Government Code section 68928.

Rule 8.85 adopted effective January 1, 2016.

Article 7
Privacy

Title 8, Appellate Rules—Division 1, Rules Relating to the Supreme Court and Courts of Appeal—Chapter 1, General Provisions—Article 7, Privacy; adopted effective January 1, 2017.

Rule 8.90. Privacy in opinions

(a) Application

(1) This rule provides guidance on the use of names in appellate court opinions.

(2) Reference to juveniles in juvenile court proceedings is governed by rule 8.401(a).

(3) Where other laws establish specific privacy-protection requirements that differ from the provisions in this rule, those specific requirements supersede the provisions in this rule.

(Subd (a) adopted effective January 1, 2017.)

(b) Persons protected

To protect personal privacy interests, in all opinions, the reviewing court should consider referring to the following people by first name and last initial or, if the first name is unusual or other circumstances would defeat the objective of anonymity, by initials only:

(1) Children in all proceedings under the Family Code and protected persons in domestic violence-prevention proceedings;

(2) Wards in guardianship proceedings and conservatees in conservatorship proceedings;

(3) Patients in mental health proceedings;

(4) Victims in criminal proceedings;

(5) Protected persons in civil harassment proceedings under Code of Civil Procedure section 527.6;

(6) Protected persons in workplace violence-prevention proceedings under Code of Civil Procedure section 527.8;

(7) Protected persons in private postsecondary school violence-prevention proceedings under Code of Civil Procedure section 527.85;

(8) Protected persons in elder or dependent adult abuse-prevention proceedings under Welfare and Institutions Code section 15657.03;

(9) Minors or persons with disabilities in proceedings to compromise the claims of a minor or a person with a disability;

(10) Persons in other circumstances in which personal privacy interests support not using the person's name; and

(11) Persons in other circumstances in which use of that person's full name would defeat the objective of anonymity for a person identified in (1)–(10).

(Subd (b) adopted effective January 1, 2017.)
Rule 8.90 adopted effective January 1, 2017.

Advisory Committee Comment

Subdivision (b)(1)–(9) lists people in proceedings under rule 8.83 for which remote electronic access to records—except dockets or registers of actions, calendars, opinions, and certain Supreme Court records—may not be provided. If the court maintains these records in electronic form, electronic access must be provided at the courthouse only, to the extent it is feasible to do so. (Cal. Rules of Court, rule 8.83(c).) Subdivision (b)(1)–(9) recognize the privacy considerations of certain persons subject to the proceedings listed in rule 8.83(c). Subdivision (b)(10) recognizes people in circumstances other than the listed proceedings, such as witnesses, in which the court should consider referring to a person by first name and last initial, or, if the first name is unusual or other circumstances would defeat the objective of protecting personal privacy interests, by initials. Subdivision (b)(11) recognizes people in circumstances other than the listed proceedings, such as relatives, in which the court should consider referring to a person by first name and last initial or by initials if the use of that person's full name would identify another person whose personal privacy interests support remaining anonymous.

Chapter 2
Civil Appeals

Art. 1. Taking the Appeal. Rules 8.100–8.116.
Art. 2. Record on Appeal. Rules 8.120–8.163.
Art. 3. Briefs in the Court of Appeal. Rules 8.200–8.224.
Art. 4. Hearing and Decision in the Court of Appeal. Rules 8.240–8.278.

Article 1
Taking the Appeal

Rule 8.100. Filing the appeal
Rule 8.104. Time to appeal
Rule 8.108. Extending the time to appeal
Rule 8.112. Petition for writ of supersedeas
Rule 8.116. Request for writ of supersedeas or temporary stay

Rule 8.100. Filing the appeal

(a) Notice of appeal

(1) To appeal from a superior court judgment or an appealable order of a superior court, other than in a limited civil case, an appellant must serve and file a notice of appeal in that superior court. The appellant or the appellant's attorney must sign the notice.

(2) The notice of appeal must be liberally construed. The notice is sufficient if it identifies the particular judgment or order being appealed. The notice need not specify the court to which the appeal is taken; the appeal will be treated as taken to the Court of Appeal for the district in which the superior court is located.

(3) Failure to serve the notice of appeal neither prevents its filing nor affects its validity, but the appellant may be required to remedy the failure.

(b) Fee and deposit

(1) Unless otherwise provided by law, the notice of appeal must be accompanied by the $775 filing fee under Government Code sections 68926 and 68926.1(b), an application for a waiver of court fees and costs on appeal under rule 8.26, or an order granting such an application. The fee may be paid by check or money order payable to "Clerk/Executive Officer, Court of Appeal"; if the fee is paid in cash, the clerk must give a receipt. The fee may also be paid by any method permitted by the court pursuant to rules 2.258 and 8.78.

(2) The appellant must also deposit $100 with the superior court clerk as required under Government Code section 68926.1, unless otherwise provided by law or the superior court waives the deposit.

(3) The clerk must file the notice of appeal even if the appellant does not present the filing fee, the deposit, or an application for, or order granting, a waiver of fees and costs.

(Subd (b) amended effective January 1, 2018; previously amended effective August 17, 2003, January 1, 2007, July 1, 2009, July 27, 2012, and January 1, 2016.)

(c) Failure to pay filing fee

(1) The reviewing court clerk must promptly notify the appellant in writing if:

(A) The reviewing court receives a notice of appeal without the filing fee required by (b)(1), a certificate of cash payment under (e)(5), or an application for, or order granting, a fee waiver under rule 8.26;

(B) A check for the filing fee is dishonored; or

(C) An application for a waiver under rule 8.26 is denied.

(2) A clerk's notice under (1)(A) or (B) must state that the court may dismiss the appeal unless, within 15 days after the notice is sent, the appellant either:

(A) Pays the fee; or

(B) Files an application for a waiver under rule 8.26 if the appellant has not previously filed such an application.

(3) If the appellant fails to take the action specified in a notice given under (2), the reviewing court may dismiss the appeal, but may vacate the dismissal for good cause.

(Subd (c) amended effective July 1, 2009; previously amended effective January 1, 2007, and January 1, 2008.)

(d) Failure to pay deposit

(1) If the appellant fails to pay the deposit to the superior court required under (b)(2), the superior court clerk must promptly notify the appellant in writing that the reviewing court may dismiss the appeal unless, within 15 days after the notice is sent, the appellant either:

(A) Makes the deposit; or

(B) Files an application in the superior court for a waiver of fees and costs if the appellant has not previously filed such an application or an order granting such an application.

(2) If the appellant fails to take the action specified in a notice given under (1), the superior court clerk must notify the reviewing court of the default.

(3) If the superior court clerk notifies the reviewing court of a default under (2), the reviewing court may dismiss the appeal, but may vacate the dismissal for good cause.

(Subd (d) amended effective July 1, 2009; adopted effective January 1, 2008.)

(e) Superior court clerk's duties

(1) The superior court clerk must promptly send a notification of the filing of the notice of appeal to the attorney of record for each party, to any unrepresented party, and to the reviewing court clerk.

(2) The notification must show the date it was sent and must state the number and title of the case and the date the notice of appeal was filed. If the information is available, the notification must include:

(A) The name, address, telephone number, e-mail address, and California State Bar number of each attorney of record in the case;

(B) The name of the party each attorney represented in the superior court; and

(C) The name, address, telephone number and e-mail address of any unrepresented party.

(3) A copy of the notice of appeal is sufficient notification under (1) if the required information is on the copy or is added by the superior court clerk.

(4) The sending of a notification under (1) is a sufficient performance of the clerk's duty despite the death of the party or the discharge, disqualification, suspension, disbarment, or death of the attorney.

(5) With the notification of the appeal, the superior court clerk must send the reviewing court the filing fee or an application for, or order granting, a waiver of that fee. If the fee was paid in cash, the clerk must send the reviewing court a certificate of payment and thereafter a check for the amount of the fee.

(6) Failure to comply with any provision of this subdivision does not affect the validity of the notice of appeal.

(Subd (e) amended effective January 1, 2016; adopted as subd (d) effective January 1, 2002; previously amended effective January 1, 2007; relettered effective January 1, 2008.)

(f) Notice of cross-appeal

As used in this rule, "notice of appeal" includes a notice of cross-appeal and "appellant" includes a respondent filing a notice of cross-appeal.

(Subd (f) relettered effective January 1, 2008; adopted as subd (e) effective January 1, 2002.)

(g) Civil case information statement

(1) Within 15 days after the superior court clerk sends the notification of the filing of the notice of appeal required by (e)(1), the appellant must serve and file in the reviewing court a completed *Civil Case Information Statement* (form APP-004), attaching a copy of the judgment or appealed order that shows the date it was entered.

(2) If the appellant fails to timely file a case information statement under (1), the reviewing court clerk must notify the appellant in writing that the appellant must file the statement within 15 days after the clerk's notice is sent and that if the appellant fails to comply, the court may either impose monetary sanctions or dismiss the appeal. If the appellant fails to file the statement as specified in the notice, the court may impose the sanctions specified in the notice.

(Subd (g) amended effective January 1, 2016; adopted as subd (f) effective January 1, 2003; previously amended and relettered as subd (g) effective January 1, 2008; previously amended effective January 1, 2007, and January 1, 2014.)

Rule 8.100 amended effective January 1, 2018; repealed and adopted as rule 1 effective January 1, 2002; previously amended and renumbered as rule 8.100 effective January 1, 2007; previously amended effective January 1, 2003, August 17, 2003, January 1, 2008, July 1, 2009, July 27, 2012, January 1, 2014, and January 1, 2016.)

Advisory Committee Comment

Subdivision (a). In subdivision (a)(1), the reference to "judgment" is intended to include part of a judgment. Subdivision (a)(1) includes an explicit reference to "appealable order" to ensure that litigants do not overlook the applicability of this rule to such orders.

Subdivision (c)(2). This subdivision addresses the content of a clerk's notice that a check for the filing fee has been dishonored or that the reviewing court has received a notice of appeal without the filing fee, a certificate of cash payment, or an application for, or order granting, a fee waiver. Rule 8.26(f) addresses what an appellant must do when a fee waiver application is denied.

Subdivision (e). Under subdivision (e)(2), a notification of the filing of a notice of appeal must show the date that the clerk sent the document. This provision is intended to establish the date when the 20-day extension of the time to file a cross-appeal under rule 8.108(e) begins to run.

Subdivision (e)(1) requires the clerk to send a notification of the filing of the notice of appeal to the appellant's attorney or to the appellant if unrepresented. Knowledge of the date of that notification allows the appellant's attorney or the appellant to track the running of the 20-day extension of time to file a cross-appeal under rule 8.108(e).

Rule 8.104. Time to appeal

(a) Normal time

(1) Unless a statute or rules 8.108, 8.702, or 8.712 provide otherwise, a notice of appeal must be filed on or before the earliest of:

(A) 60 days after the superior court clerk serves on the party filing the notice of appeal a document entitled "Notice of Entry" of judgment or a filed-endorsed copy of the judgment, showing the date either was served;

(B) 60 days after the party filing the notice of appeal serves or is served by a party with a document entitled "Notice of Entry" of judgment or a filed-endorsed copy of the judgment, accompanied by proof of service; or

(C) 180 days after entry of judgment.

(2) Service under (1)(A) and (B) may be by any method permitted by the Code of Civil Procedure, including electronic service when permitted under Code of Civil Procedure section 1010.6 and rules 2.250–2.261.

(3) If the parties stipulated in the trial court under Code of Civil Procedure section 1019.5 to waive notice of the court order being appealed, the time to appeal under (1)(C) applies unless the court or a party serves notice of entry of judgment or a filed-endorsed copy of the judgment to start the time period under (1)(A) or (B).

(Subd (a) amended effective July 1, 2017; previously amended effective January 1, 2007, January 1, 2010, July 1, 2012, July 1, 2014, and January 1, 2016.)

(b) No extension of time; late notice of appeal

Except as provided in rule 8.66, no court may extend the time to file a notice of appeal. If a notice of appeal is filed late, the reviewing court must dismiss the appeal.

(Subd (b) amended effective January 1, 2007; adopted effective January 1, 2005.)

(c) What constitutes entry

For purposes of this rule:

(1) The entry date of a judgment is the date the judgment is filed under Code of Civil Procedure section 668.5, or the date it is entered in the judgment book.

(2) The entry date of an appealable order that is entered in the minutes is the date it is entered in the permanent minutes. But if the minute order directs that a written order be prepared, the entry date is the date the signed order is filed; a written order prepared under rule 3.1312 or similar local rule is not such an order prepared by direction of a minute order.

(3) The entry date of an appealable order that is not entered in the minutes is the date the signed order is filed.

(4) The entry date of a decree of distribution in a probate proceeding is the date it is entered at length in the judgment book or other permanent court record.

(5) An order signed electronically has the same effect as an order signed on paper.

(Subd (c) amended effective January 1, 2017; adopted as subd (c) effective January 1, 2002; relettered as subd (d) effective January 1, 2005; previously amended effective January 1, 2007; previously repealed and relettered as subd (c) effective January 1, 2011.)

(d) Premature notice of appeal

(1) A notice of appeal filed after judgment is rendered but before it is entered is valid and is treated as filed immediately after entry of judgment.

(2) The reviewing court may treat a notice of appeal filed after the superior court has announced its intended ruling, but before it has rendered judgment, as filed immediately after entry of judgment.

(Subd (d) relettered effective January 1, 2011; adopted as subd (d) effective January 1, 2002; previously relettered as subd (e) effective January 1, 2005.)

(e) Appealable order

As used in (a) and (d), "judgment" includes an appealable order if the appeal is from an appealable order.

(Subd (e) amended effective July 1, 2011; adopted as subd (f); previously amended effective January 1, 2005; previously relettered effective January 1, 2011.)

Rule 8.104 amended effective July 1, 2017; repealed and adopted as rule 2 effective January 1, 2002; previously amended and renumbered as rule 8.104 effective January 1, 2007; previously amended effective January 1, 2005, January 1, 2010, January 1, 2011, July 1, 2011, July 1, 2012, July 1, 2014, January 1, 2016, and January 1, 2017.

Advisory Committee Comment

Subdivision (a). This subdivision establishes the standard time for filing a notice of appeal and identifies rules that establish very limited exceptions to this standard time period for cases involving certain postjudgment motions and cross-appeals (rule 8.108), certain expedited appeals under the California Environmental Quality Act (rule 8.702), and appeals under Code of Civil Procedure section 1294.4 of an order dismissing or denying a petition to compel arbitration (rule 8.712).

Under subdivision (a)(1)(A), a notice of entry of judgment (or a copy of the judgment) must show the date on which the clerk served the document. The proof of service establishes the date that the 60-day period under subdivision (a)(1)(A) begins to run.

Subdivision (a)(1)(B) requires that a notice of entry of judgment (or a copy of the judgment) served by or on a party be accompanied by proof of service. The proof of service establishes the date that the 60-day period under subdivision (a)(1)(B) begins to run. Although the general rule on service (rule 8.25(a)) requires proof of service for all documents served by parties, the requirement is reiterated here because of the serious consequence of a failure to file a timely notice of appeal (see subd. (e)).

Subdivision (b). See rule 8.25(b)(5) for provisions concerning the timeliness of documents mailed by inmates and patients from custodial institutions. Subdivision (b) is declarative of the case law, which holds that the reviewing court lacks jurisdiction to excuse a late-filed notice of appeal. (*Hollister Convalescent Hosp., Inc. v. Rico* (1975) 15 Cal.3d 660, 666–674; *Estate of Hanley* (1943) 23 Cal.2d 120, 122–124.)

In criminal cases, the time for filing a notice of appeal is governed by rule 8.308 and by the case law of "constructive filing." (See, e.g., *In re Benoit* (1973) 10 Cal.3d 72.)

Rule 8.108. Extending the time to appeal

(a) Extension of time

This rule operates only to extend the time to appeal otherwise prescribed in rule 8.104(a); it does not shorten the time to appeal. If the normal time to appeal stated in rule 8.104(a) is longer than the time provided in this rule, the time to appeal stated in rule 8.104(a) governs.

(Subd (a) adopted effective January 1, 2008.)

(b) Motion for new trial

If any party serves and files a valid notice of intention to move for a new trial, the following extensions of time apply:

(1) If the motion for a new trial is denied, the time to appeal from the judgment is extended for all parties until the earliest of:

(A) 30 days after the superior court clerk or a party serves an order denying the motion or a notice of entry of that order;

(B) 30 days after denial of the motion by operation of law; or

(C) 180 days after entry of judgment.

(2) If the trial court makes a finding of excessive or inadequate damages and grants the motion for a new trial subject to the condition that the motion is denied if a party consents to the additur or remittitur of damages, the time to appeal is extended as follows:

(A) If a party serves an acceptance of the additur or remittitur within the time for accepting the additur or remittitur, the time to appeal from the judgment is extended for all parties until 30 days after the date the party serves the acceptance.

(B) If a party serves a rejection of the additur or remittitur within the time for accepting the additur or remittitur or if the time for accepting the additur or remittitur expires, the time to appeal from the new trial order is extended for all parties until the earliest of 30 days after the date the party serves the rejection or 30 days after the date on which the time for accepting the additur or remittitur expired.

(Subd (b) amended effective July 1, 2012; adopted as subd (a) effective January 1, 2002; previously amended and relettered effective January 1, 2008; previously amended effective January 1, 2011.)

(c) Motion to vacate judgment

If, within the time prescribed by rule 8.104 to appeal from the judgment, any party serves and files a valid notice of intention to move—or a valid motion—to vacate the judgment, the time to appeal from the judgment is extended for all parties until the earliest of:

(1) 30 days after the superior court clerk or a party serves an order denying the motion or a notice of entry of that order;

(2) 90 days after the first notice of intention to move—or motion—is filed; or

(3) 180 days after entry of judgment.

(Subd (c) amended effective January 1, 2011; adopted as subd (b) effective January 1, 2002; previously amended effective January 1, 2007; previously relettered effective January 1, 2008.)

(d) Motion for judgment notwithstanding the verdict

(1) If any party serves and files a valid motion for judgment notwithstanding the verdict and the motion is denied, the time to appeal from the judgment is extended for all parties until the earliest of:

(A) 30 days after the superior court clerk or a party serves an order denying the motion or a notice of entry of that order;

(B) 30 days after denial of the motion by operation of law; or

(C) 180 days after entry of judgment.

(2) Unless extended by (g)(2), the time to appeal from an order denying a motion for judgment notwithstanding the verdict is governed by rule 8.104.

(Subd (d) amended effective January 1, 2015; adopted as subd (c) effective January 1, 2002; previously relettered as subd (d) effective January 1, 2008; previously amended effective January 1, 2007, and January 1, 2011.)

(e) Motion to reconsider appealable order

If any party serves and files a valid motion to reconsider an appealable order under Code of Civil Procedure section 1008, subdivision (a), the time to appeal from that order is extended for all parties until the earliest of:

(1) 30 days after the superior court clerk or a party serves an order denying the motion or a notice of entry of that order;

(2) 90 days after the first motion to reconsider is filed; or

(3) 180 days after entry of the appealable order.

(Subd (e) amended effective January 1, 2011; adopted as subd (d) effective January 1, 2002; previously relettered effective January 1, 2008.)

(f) Public entity actions under Government Code section 962, 984, or 985

If a public entity defendant serves and files a valid request for a mandatory settlement conference on methods of satisfying a judgment under Government Code section 962, an election to pay a judgment in periodic payments under Government Code section 984 and rule 3.1804, or a motion for a posttrial hearing on reducing a judgment under Government Code section 985, the time to appeal from the judgment is extended for all parties until the earliest of:

(1) 90 days after the superior court clerk serves the party filing the notice of appeal with a document entitled "Notice of Entry" of judgment, or a filed-endorsed copy of the judgment, showing the date either was served;

(2) 90 days after the party filing the notice of appeal serves or is served by a party with a document entitled "Notice of Entry" of judgment or a filed-endorsed copy of the judgment, accompanied by proof of service; or

(3) 180 days after entry of judgment.

(Subd (f) amended effective January 1, 2016; adopted effective January 1, 2011.)

(g) Cross-appeal

(1) If an appellant timely appeals from a judgment or appealable order, the time for any other party to appeal from the same judgment or order is extended until 20 days after the superior court clerk serves notification of the first appeal.

(2) If an appellant timely appeals from an order granting a motion for new trial, an order granting—within 150 days after entry of judgment—a motion to vacate the judgment, or a judgment notwithstanding the verdict, the time for any other party to appeal from the original judgment or from an order denying a motion for judgment notwithstanding the verdict is extended until 20 days after the clerk serves notification of the first appeal.

(Subd (g) amended and relettered effective January 1, 2011; adopted as subd (e) effective January 1, 2002; previously relettered as subd (f) effective January 1, 2008.)

(h) Service; proof of service

Service under this rule may be by any method permitted by the Code of Civil Procedure, including electronic service when permitted under Code of Civil Procedure section 1010.6 and rules 2.250–2.261. An order or notice that is served must be accompanied by proof of service.

(Subd (h) amended and relettered effective January 1, 2011; adopted as subd (f) effective January 1, 2002; previously relettered as subd (g) effective January 1, 2008.)

Rule 8.108 amended effective January 1, 2016; repealed and adopted as rule 3 effective January 1, 2002; previously amended and renumbered as rule 8.108 effective January 1, 2007; previously amended effective January 1, 2008, January 1, 2011, July 1, 2012, and January 1, 2015.

Advisory Committee Comment

Subdivisions (b)–(f) operate only when a party serves and files a "valid" motion, election, request, or notice of intent to move for the relief in question. As used in these provisions, the word "valid" means only that the motion, election, request, or notice complies with all procedural requirements; it does not mean that the motion, election, request, or notice must also be substantively meritorious. For example, under the rule a timely new trial motion on the ground of excessive damages (Code Civ. Proc., § 657) extends the time to appeal from the judgment even if the trial court ultimately determines the damages were not excessive. Similarly, a timely motion to reconsider (*id.*, § 1008) extends the time to appeal from an appealable order for which reconsideration was sought even if the trial court ultimately determines the motion was not "based upon new or different facts, circumstances, or law," as subdivision (a) of section 1008 requires.

Subdivision (b). Subdivision (b)(1) provides that the denial of a motion for new trial triggers a 30-day extension of the time to appeal from the judgment beginning on the date that the superior court clerk or a party serves either the order denial or a notice of entry of that order. This provision is intended to eliminate a trap for litigants and to make the rule consistent with the primary rule on the time to appeal from the judgment (rule 8.104(a)).

Subdivision (c). The Code of Civil Procedure provides two distinct statutory motions to vacate a judgment: (1) a motion to vacate a judgment and enter "another and different judgment" because of judicial error (*id.*, § 663), which requires a notice of intention to move to vacate (*id.*, § 663a); and (2) a motion to vacate a judgment because of mistake, inadvertence, surprise, or neglect, which requires a motion to vacate but not a notice of intention to so move (*id.*, § 473, subd. (b)). The courts also recognize certain nonstatutory motions to vacate a judgment, e.g., when the judgment is void on the face of the record or was obtained by extrinsic fraud. (See 8 Witkin, Cal. Procedure (4th ed. 1997) Attack on Judgment in Trial Court, §§ 222–236, pp. 726–750.) Subdivision (c) is intended to apply to all such motions.

In subdivision (c) the phrase "within the time prescribed by rule 8.104 to appeal from the judgment" is intended to incorporate in full the provisions of rule 8.104(a).

Under subdivision (c)(1), the 30-day extension of the time to appeal from the judgment begins when the superior court clerk or a party serves the order denying the motion or notice of entry of that order. This provision is discussed further under subdivision (b) of this comment.

Subdivision (d). Subdivision (d)(1) provides an extension of time after an order denying a motion for judgment notwithstanding the verdict regardless of whether the moving party also moved unsuccessfully for a new trial.

Subdivision (d) further specifies the times to appeal when, as often occurs, a motion for judgment notwithstanding the verdict is joined with a motion for new trial and both motions are denied. Under subdivision (b), the appellant has 30 days after notice of the denial of the new trial motion to appeal from the judgment. Subdivision (d) allows the appellant the longer time provided by rule 8.104 to appeal from the order denying the motion for judgment notwithstanding the verdict, subject to that time being further extended in the circumstances covered by subdivision (g)(2).

Under subdivision (d)(1)(A), the 30-day extension of the time to appeal from the judgment begins when the superior court clerk or a party serves the order denying the motion or notice of entry of that order. This provision is discussed further under subdivision (b) of this comment.

Subdivision (e). The scope of subdivision (e) is specific. It applies to any "appealable order," whether made before or after judgment (see Code Civ. Proc., § 904.1, subd. (a)(2)–(12)), but it extends only the time to appeal "from that order." The subdivision thus takes no position on whether a judgment is subject to a motion to reconsider (see, e.g., *Ramon v. Aerospace Corp.* (1996) 50 Cal.App.4th 1233, 1236–1238 [postjudgment motion to reconsider order granting summary judgment did not extend time to appeal from judgment because trial court had no power to rule on such motion after entry of judgment]), or whether an order denying a motion to reconsider is itself appealable (compare *Santee v. Santa Clara County Office of Education* (1990) 220 Cal.App.3d 702, 710–711 [order appealable if motion based on new facts] with *Rojes v. Riverside General Hospital* (1988) 203 Cal.App.3d 1151, 1160–1161 [order not appealable under any circumstances]). Both these issues are legislative matters.

Subdivision (e) applies only when a "party" makes a valid motion to "reconsider" an appealable order under subdivision (a) of Code of Civil Procedure section 1008; it therefore does not apply when a court reconsiders an order on its own motion (*id.*, subd. (d)) or when a party makes "a subsequent application for the same order" (*id.*, subd. (c)). The statute provides no time limits within which either of the latter events must occur.

Under subdivision (e)(1), the 30-day extension of the time to appeal from the order begins when the superior court clerk or a party serves the order denying the motion or notice of entry of that order. The purpose of this provision is discussed further under subdivision (b) of this comment.

Among its alternative periods of extension of the time to appeal, subdivision (e) provides in paragraph (2) for a 90-day period beginning on the filing of the motion to reconsider or, if there is more than one such motion, the filing of the first such motion. The provision is consistent with subdivision (c)(2), governing motions to vacate judgment; as in the case of those motions, there is no time limit for a ruling on a motion to reconsider.

Subdivision (g). Consistent with case law, subdivision (g)(1) extends the time to appeal after another party appeals only if the later appeal is taken "from the same order or judgment as the first appeal." (*Commercial & Farmers Nat. Bank v. Edwards* (1979) 91 Cal.App.3d 699, 704.)

The former rule (former rule 3(c), second sentence) provided an extension of time for filing a protective cross-appeal from the judgment when the trial court granted a motion for new trial or a motion to vacate the judgment, but did not provide the same extension when the trial court granted a motion for judgment notwithstanding the verdict. One case declined to infer that the omission was unintentional, but suggested that the Judicial Council might consider amending the rule to fill the gap. (*Lippert v. AVCO Community Developers, Inc.* (1976) 60 Cal.App.3d 775, 778 & fn. 3.) Rule 8.108(e)(2) fills the gap thus identified.

Subdivision (h). Under subdivision (h), an order or notice that is served under this rule must be accompanied by proof of service. The date of the proof of service establishes the date when an extension of the time to appeal begins to run after service of such an order or notice.

Rule 8.112. Petition for writ of supersedeas

(a) Petition

(1) A party seeking a stay of the enforcement of a judgment or order pending appeal may serve and file a petition for writ of supersedeas in the reviewing court.

(2) The petition must bear the same title as the appeal and, if known, the appeal's docket number.

(3) The petition must explain the necessity for the writ and include a memorandum.

(4) If the record has not been filed in the reviewing court:

(A) The petition must include a statement of the case sufficient to show that the petitioner will raise substantial issues on appeal, including a fair summary of the material facts and the issues that are likely to be raised on appeal.

(B) The petitioner must file the following documents with the petition:

(i) The judgment or order, showing its date of entry;

(ii) The notice of appeal, showing its date of filing;

(iii) A reporter's transcript of any oral statement by the court supporting its rulings related to the issues that are likely to be raised on appeal, or, if a transcript is unavailable, a declaration fairly summarizing any such statements;

(iv) Any application for a stay filed in the trial court, any opposition to that application, and a reporter's transcript of the oral proceedings concerning the stay or, if a transcript is unavailable, a declaration fairly summarizing the proceedings, including the parties' arguments and any statement by the court supporting its ruling; and

(v) Any other document from the trial court proceeding that is necessary for proper consideration of the petition.

(C) The documents listed in (B) must comply with the following requirements:

(i) If filed in paper form, they must be bound together at the end of the petition or in separate volumes not exceeding 300 pages each. The pages must be consecutively numbered;

(ii) If filed in paper form, they must be index-tabbed by number or letter, and

(iii) They must begin with a table of contents listing each document by its title and its index number or letter.

(5) The petition must be verified.

(*Subd (a) amended effective January 1, 2016; previously amended effective January 1, 2007, January 1, 2008, January 1, 2010, and July 1, 2013.*)

(b) Opposition

(1) Unless otherwise ordered, any opposition must be served and filed within 15 days after the petition is filed.

(2) An opposition must state any material facts not included in the petition and include a memorandum.

(3) The court may not issue a writ of supersedeas until the respondent has had the opportunity to file an opposition.

(*Subd (b) amended effective January 1, 2007.*)

(c) Temporary stay

(1) The petition may include a request for a temporary stay under rule 8.116 pending the ruling on the petition.

(2) A separately filed request for a temporary stay must be served on the respondent. For good cause, the Chief Justice or presiding justice may excuse advance service.

(*Subd (c) amended effective January 1, 2007.*)

(d) Issuing the writ

(1) The court may issue the writ on any conditions it deems just.

(2) The court must hold a hearing before it may issue a writ staying an order that awards or changes the custody of a minor.

(3) The court must notify the superior court, under rule 8.489, of any writ or temporary stay that it issues.

(*Subd (d) amended effective January 1, 2009; previously amended effective January 1, 2007, and January 1, 2008.*)

Rule 8.112 amended effective January 1, 2016; repealed and adopted as rule 49 effective January 1, 2005; previously amended and renumbered as rule 8.112 effective January 1, 2007; previously amended effective January 1, 2008, January 1, 2009, January 1, 2010, and July 1, 2013.

Advisory Committee Comment

Subdivision (a). If the preparation of a reporter's transcript has not yet been completed at that time a petition for a writ of supersedeas is filed, that transcript is "unavailable" within the meaning of (a)(4)(B).

Rule 8.116. Request for writ of supersedeas or temporary stay

(a) Information on cover

If a petition for original writ, petition for review, or any other document requests a writ of supersedeas or temporary stay from a reviewing court, the cover of the document must:

(1) Prominently display the notice "STAY REQUESTED"; and

(2) Identify the nature and date of the proceeding or act sought to be stayed.

(Subd (a) amended effective January 1, 2007.)

(b) Additional information

The following information must appear either on the cover or at the beginning of the text:

(1) The trial court and department involved; and

(2) The name and telephone number of the trial judge whose order the request seeks to stay.

(Subd (b) amended effective January 1, 2007.)

(c) Sanction

If the document does not comply with (a) and (b), the reviewing court may decline to consider the request for writ of supersedeas or temporary stay.

Rule 8.116 amended and renumbered effective January 1, 2007; repealed and adopted as rule 49.5 effective January 1, 2005.

Article 2
Record on Appeal

Rule 8.120. Record on appeal
Rule 8.121. Notice designating the record on appeal
Rule 8.122. Clerk's transcript
Rule 8.123. Record of administrative proceedings
Rule 8.124. Appendixes
Rule 8.128. Superior court file instead of clerk's transcript
Rule 8.130. Reporter's transcript
Rule 8.134. Agreed statement
Rule 8.137. Settled statement
Rule 8.140. Failure to procure the record
Rule 8.144. Form of the record
Rule 8.147. Record in multiple or later appeals in same case
Rule 8.149. When the record is complete
Rule 8.150. Filing the record
Rule 8.153. Lending the record
Rule 8.155. Augmenting and correcting the record
Rule 8.163. Presumption from the record

Rule 8.120. Record on appeal

Except as otherwise provided in this chapter, the record on an appeal in a civil case must contain the records specified in (a) and (b), which constitute the normal record on appeal.

(a) Record of written documents

(1) A record of the written documents from the superior court proceedings in the form of one of the following:

(A) A clerk's transcript under rule 8.122;

(B) An appendix under rule 8.124;

(C) The original superior court file under rule 8.128, if a local rule of the reviewing court permits this form of the record;

(D) An agreed statement under rule 8.134(a)(2); or

(E) A settled statement under rule 8.137.

(2) If an appellant intends to raise any issue that requires consideration of the record of an administrative proceeding that was admitted in evidence, refused, or lodged in the superior court, the record on appeal must include that administrative record, transmitted under rule 8.123.

(Subd (a) adopted effective January 1, 2008.)

(b) Record of the oral proceedings

If an appellant intends to raise any issue that requires consideration of the oral proceedings in the superior court, the record on appeal must include a record of these oral proceedings in the form of one of the following:

(1) A reporter's transcript under rule 8.130;

(2) An agreed statement under rule 8.134; or

(3) A settled statement under rule 8.137.

(Subd (b) adopted effective January 1, 2008.)
Rule 8.120 adopted effective January 1, 2008.

Advisory Committee Comment

Rules 8.45–8.47 address the appropriate handling of sealed and confidential records that are included in the record on appeal. Examples of confidential records include records of the family conciliation court (Fam. Code, § 1818 (b)) and fee waiver applications (Gov. Code, § 68633(f)).

Rule 8.121. Notice designating the record on appeal

(a) Time to file

Within 10 days after filing the notice of appeal, an appellant must serve and file a notice in the superior court designating the record on appeal. The appellant may combine its notice designating the record with its notice of appeal.

(Subd (a) adopted effective January 1, 2008.)

(b) Contents

(1) The notice must:

(A) Specify the date the notice of appeal was filed.

(B) Specify which form of the record of the written documents from the superior court proceedings listed in rule 8.120(a)(1) the appellant elects to use. If the appellant elects to use a clerk's transcript, the notice must also designate the documents to be included in the clerk's transcript as required under rule 8.122(b)(1).

(C) Specify whether the appellant elects to proceed with or without a record of the oral proceedings in the trial court. If the appellant elects to proceed with a record of the oral proceedings in the trial court, the notice must specify which form of the record listed in rule 8.120(b) the appellant elects to use. If the appellant elects to use a reporter's transcript, the notice must designate the proceedings to be included in the transcript as required under rule 8.130.

(2) If an appellant intends to raise any issue that requires consideration of the record of an administrative proceeding that was admitted in evidence, refused, or lodged in the superior court, the notice must also request that this administrative record be transmitted to the reviewing court under rule 8.123.

(Subd (b) adopted effective January 1, 2008.)

(c) Copy to the reviewing court

The clerk must promptly send the reviewing court a copy of any notice filed under this rule.

(Subd (c) adopted effective January 1, 2008.)
Rule 8.121 adopted effective January 1, 2008.

Advisory Committee Comment

The Judicial Council has adopted an optional form—*Appellant's Notice Designating Record on Appeal* (form APP-003)—that can be used to provide the notice required by this rule.

This rule makes the filing of a notice designating the record an "act required to procure the record" within the meaning of rule 8.140(a). Under that rule, a failure to file such a notice triggers the clerk's duty to issue a 15-day notice of default and thereby allows the appellant to cure the default in superior court.

Rule 8.122. Clerk's transcript

(a) Designation

(1) A notice designating documents to be included in a clerk's transcript must identify each designated document by its title and filing date or, if the filing date is not available, the date it was signed. The notice may specify portions of designated documents that are not to be included in the transcript. For minute orders or instructions, it is sufficient to collectively designate all minute orders or all minute orders entered between specified dates, or all written jury instructions given, refused, or withdrawn.

(2) Within 10 days after the appellant serves its notice designating a clerk's transcript, the respondent may serve and file a notice in superior court designating any additional documents the respondent wants included in the transcript.

(3) Except as provided in (b)(4), all exhibits admitted in evidence, refused, or lodged are deemed part of the record, but a party wanting a copy of an exhibit included in the transcript must specify that exhibit by number or letter in its notice of designation. If the superior court has returned a designated exhibit to a party, the party in possession of the exhibit must deliver it to the superior court clerk within 10 days after the notice designating the exhibit is served.

(Subd (a) amended effective January 1, 2010; previously amended effective January 1, 2005, January 1, 2007, and January 1, 2008.)

(b) Contents of transcript

(1) The transcript must contain:

(A) The notice of appeal;

(B) Any judgment appealed from and any notice of its entry;

(C) Any order appealed from and any notice of its entry;

(D) Any notice of intention to move for a new trial or motion to vacate the judgment, for judgment notwithstanding the verdict, or for reconsideration of an appealed order, and any order on such motion and any notice of its entry;

(E) Any notices or stipulations to prepare clerk's or reporter's transcripts or to proceed by agreed or settled statement; and

(F) The register of actions, if any.

(2) Each document listed in (1)(A), (B), (C), and (D) must show the date necessary to determine the timeliness of the appeal under rule 8.104 or 8.108.

(3) Except as provided in (4), if designated by any party, the transcript must also contain:

(A) Any other document filed or lodged in the case in superior court;

(B) Any exhibit admitted in evidence, refused, or lodged; and

(C) Any jury instruction that any party submitted in writing and the cover page required by rule 2.1055(b)(2) indicating the party requesting it, and any written jury instructions given by the court.

(4) Unless the reviewing court orders or the parties stipulate otherwise:

(A) The clerk must not copy or transmit to the reviewing court the original of a deposition except those portions of a deposition presented or offered into evidence under rule 2.1040.

(B) The clerk must not include in the transcript the record of an administrative proceeding that was admitted in evidence, refused, or lodged in the trial court. Any such administrative record must be transmitted to the reviewing court as specified in rule 8.123.

(Subd (b) amended effective July 1, 2011; previously amended effective January 1, 2007, January 1, 2008, and January 1, 2011.)

(c) Deposit for cost of transcript

(1) Within 30 days after the respondent files a designation under (a)(2) or the time for filing it expires, whichever first occurs, the superior court clerk must send:

(A) To the appellant, notice of the estimated cost to prepare an original and one copy of the clerk's transcript; and

(B) To each party other than the appellant, notice of the estimated cost to prepare a copy of the clerk's transcript for that party's use.

(2) A notice under (1) must show the date it was sent.

(3) Unless otherwise provided by law, within 10 days after the clerk sends a notice under (1), the appellant and any party wanting to purchase a copy of the clerk's transcript must either deposit the estimated cost specified in the notice under (1) with the clerk or submit an application for, or an order granting, a waiver of the cost.

(4) If the appellant does not submit a required deposit or an application for, or an order granting, a waiver of the cost within the required period, the clerk must promptly issue a notice of default under rule 8.140.

(Subd (c) amended effective January 1, 2014; previously amended effective January 1, 2007, January 1, 2008, and July 1, 2009.)

(d) Preparation of transcript

(1) Within the time specified in (2), the clerk must:

(A) Prepare and certify the original transcript;

(B) Prepare one copy of the transcript for the appellant; and

(C) Prepare additional copies for parties that have requested a copy of the clerk's transcript and have made deposits as provided in (c)(3) or received an order waiving the cost.

(2) Except as provided in (3), the clerk must complete preparation of the transcripts required under (1) within 30 days after either:

(A) The appellant deposits either the estimated cost of the clerk's transcript or a preexisting order granting a waiver of that cost; or

(B) The court grants an application submitted under (c)(3) to waive that cost.

(3) If the appellant elects under rule 8.121 to proceed with a reporter's transcript, the clerk need not complete preparation of the transcripts required under (1) until 30 days after the appellant deposits the estimated cost of the reporter's transcript or one of the substitutes under rule 8.130(b).

(4) If the appeal is abandoned or dismissed before the clerk has completed preparation of the transcript, the clerk must refund any portion of the deposit under (c) exceeding the preparation cost actually incurred.

(Subd (d) amended effective January 1, 2014; previously amended effective January 1, 2003, and January 1, 2007.)

Rule 8.122 amended effective January 1, 2014; repealed and adopted as rule 5 effective January 1, 2002; previously amended effective January 1, 2003, January 1, 2005; previously amended and renumbered as rule 8.120 effective January 1, 2007, and as rule 8.122 effective January 1, 2008; previously amended effective July 1, 2009, January 1, 2010, January 1, 2011, and July 1, 2011.

Advisory Committee Comment

Subdivision (a). Subdivision (a)(1) allows a party designating documents for inclusion in the clerk's transcript to specify *portions* of such documents that are not to be included, e.g., because they are duplicates of other designated documents or are not necessary for proper consideration of the issues raised in the appeal. The notice of designation should identify any portion to be omitted by means of a descriptive reference, e.g., by specific page or exhibit numbers. This provision is intended to simplify and therefore expedite the preparation of the clerk's transcript, to reduce its cost to the parties, and to relieve the courts of the burden of reviewing a record containing redundant, irrelevant, or immaterial documents.

Subdivision (b). The supporting and opposing memoranda and attachments to any motion to vacate the judgment, for judgment notwithstanding the verdict, or for reconsideration of an appealed order are not required to be included in the clerk's transcript under subdivision (b)(1)(D) but may be included by designation of a party under (b)(3) or on motion of a party or the reviewing court under rule 8.155.

Subdivision (b)(1)(F) requires the clerk's transcript to include the register of actions, if any. This provision is intended to assist the reviewing court in determining the accuracy of the clerk's transcript.

Subdivision (c). Under subdivision (c)(2), a clerk who sends a notice under subdivision (c)(1) must include a certificate stating the date on which the clerk sent it. This provision is intended to establish the date when the 10-day period for depositing the cost of the clerk's transcript under this rule begins to run.

The Superior Court will make the determination on any application to waive the fees for preparing, certifying, copying, and transmitting the clerk's transcript.

Subdivision (d). The different timelines for preparing a clerk's transcript under subdivision (d)(2)(A) and (B) recognize that an appellant may apply for and receive a waiver of fees at different points during the appellate process. Some appellants may have applied for and obtained an order waiving fees before receiving the estimate of the cost of the clerk's transcript and thus may be able to provide that order to the court in lieu of making a deposit for the clerk's transcript. Other appellants may not apply for a waiver until after they receive the estimate of the cost for the clerk's transcript, in which case the time for preparing the transcript runs from the granting of that waiver.

In cases in which a reporter's transcript has been designated, subdivision (d)(3) gives the clerk the option of waiting until the deposit for the reporter's transcript has been made before beginning preparation of the clerk's transcript.

Rule 8.123. Record of administrative proceedings

(a) Application

This rule applies if the record of an administrative proceeding was admitted in evidence, refused, or lodged in the superior court.

(Subd (a) adopted effective January 1, 2008.)

(b) Designation

(1) An appellant's notice designating the record on appeal under rule 8.121 that requests a record of an administrative proceeding be transmitted to the reviewing court must identify the administrative record by the title and date or dates of the administrative proceedings.

(2) If an appellant does not request that an administrative record admitted in evidence, refused, or lodged in the superior court be transmitted to the reviewing court, the respondent, within 10 days after the appellant serves its notice designating the record on appeal, may serve and file in the superior court a notice requesting that this administrative record be transmitted to the reviewing court.

(Subd (b) adopted effective January 1, 2008.)

(c) Transmittal to the reviewing court

Except as provided in (d), if any administrative record is designated by a party, the superior court clerk must transmit the original administrative record, or electronic administrative record, with any clerk's or reporter's transcript sent to the reviewing court under rule 8.150. If the appellant has elected under rule 8.121 to use neither a clerk's transcript nor a reporter's transcript, the superior court clerk must transmit any administrative record designated by a party to the reviewing court no later than 45 days after the respondent files a designation under (b)(2) or the time for filing it expires, whichever first occurs.

(Subd (c) amended effective January 1, 2016; adopted as subd (d) effective January 1, 2008; previously amended and relettered as subd (c) effective January 1, 2013.)

(d) Administrative records returned to parties

(1) If the superior court has returned a designated administrative record to a party, the party in possession of the administrative record must make that record available to the other parties in the case for copying within 15 days after the notice designating the record on appeal is served and lodge the record with the clerk of the reviewing court at the time the last respondent's brief is due.

(2) A party seeking an administrative record that was returned to another party must first ask the possessing party to provide a copy or lend it for copying. The possessing party should reasonably cooperate with such requests.

(3) If the request under (2) is unsuccessful, the requesting party may serve and file in the reviewing court a notice identifying the administrative record and requesting that the possessing party deliver the administrative record to the requesting party or, if the possessing party prefers, to the

reviewing court. The possessing party must comply with the request within 10 days after the notice was served.

(4) If the possessing party sends the administrative record to the requesting party, that party must copy and return it to the possessing party within 10 days after receiving it.

(5) If the possessing party sends the administrative record to the reviewing court, that party must:

(A) Include with the administrative record a copy of the notice served by the requesting party; and

(B) Immediately notify the requesting party that it has sent the administrative record to the reviewing court.

(Subd (d) amended and relettered effective January 1, 2013; adopted as subd (c) effective January 1, 2008.)

(e) Return by reviewing court

On request, the reviewing court may return an administrative record to the superior court or, if the record was lodged by a party under (d), to the lodging party. When the remittitur issues, the reviewing court must return any administrative record to the superior court or, if the record was lodged by a party under (d), to the lodging party.

(Subd (e) amended effective January 1, 2013; adopted effective January 1, 2008.)

Rule 8.123 amended effective January 1, 2016; adopted effective January 1, 2008; previously amended effective January 1, 2013.

Rule 8.124. Appendixes

(a) Notice of election

(1) Unless the superior court orders otherwise on a motion served and filed within 10 days after the notice of election is served, this rule governs if:

(A) The appellant elects to use an appendix under this rule in the notice designating the record on appeal under rule 8.121; or

(B) The respondent serves and files a notice in the superior court electing to use an appendix under this rule within 10 days after the appellant's notice designating the record on appeal is filed and no waiver of the fee for a clerk's transcript is granted to the appellant. If the appellant has a fee waiver, the respondent cannot elect an appendix instead of a clerk's transcript.

(2) When a party files a notice electing to use an appendix under this rule, the superior court clerk must promptly send a copy of the register of actions, if any, to the attorney of record for each party and to any unrepresented party.

(3) The parties may prepare separate appendixes or they may stipulate to a joint appendix.

(Subd (a) amended effective January 1, 2024; previously amended effective January 1, 2005, January 1, 2007, January 1, 2008, January 1, 2010, and January 1, 2016.)

(b) Contents of appendix

(1) A joint appendix or an appellant's appendix must contain:

(A) All items required by rule 8.122(b)(1), showing the dates required by rule 8.122(b)(2);

(B) Any item listed in rule 8.122(b)(3) that is necessary for proper consideration of the issues, including, for an appellant's appendix, any item that the appellant should reasonably assume the respondent will rely on;

(C) The notice of election; and

(D) For a joint appendix, the stipulation designating its contents.

(2) An appendix may incorporate by reference all or part of the record on appeal in another case pending in the reviewing court or in a prior appeal in the same case.

(A) The other appeal must be identified by its case name and number. If only part of a record is being incorporated by reference, that part must be identified by citation to the volume and page numbers of the record where it appears and either the title of the document or documents or the date of the oral proceedings to be incorporated. The parts of any record incorporated by reference must be identified both in the body of the appendix and in a separate section at the end of the index.

(B) If the appendix incorporates by reference any such record, the cover of the appendix must prominently display the notice "Record in case number: _____ incorporated by reference," identifying the number of the case from which the record is incorporated.

(C) On request of the reviewing court or any party, the designating party must provide a copy of the materials incorporated by reference to the court or another party or lend them for copying as provided in (c).

(3) An appendix must not:

(A) Contain documents or portions of documents filed in superior court that are unnecessary for proper consideration of the issues.

(B) Contain transcripts of oral proceedings that may be designated under rule 8.130.

(C) Contain the record of an administrative proceeding that was admitted in evidence, refused, or lodged in the trial court. Any such administrative record must be transmitted to the reviewing court as specified in rule 8.123.

(D) Incorporate any document by reference except as provided in (2).

(4) All exhibits admitted in evidence, refused, or lodged are deemed part of the record, whether or not the appendix contains copies of them.

(5) A respondent's appendix may contain any document that could have been included in the appellant's appendix or a joint appendix.

(6) An appellant's reply appendix may contain any document that could have been included in the respondent's appendix.

(Subd (b) amended effective January 1, 2010; previously amended effective January 1, 2007, and January 1, 2008.)

(c) Document or exhibit held by other party

If a party preparing an appendix wants it to contain a copy of a document or an exhibit in the possession of another party:

(1) The party must first ask the party possessing the document or exhibit to provide a copy or lend it for copying. All parties should reasonably cooperate with such requests.

(2) If the attempt under (1) is unsuccessful, the party may serve and file in the reviewing court a notice identifying the document or specifying the exhibit's trial court designation and requesting the party possessing the document or exhibit to deliver it to the requesting party or, if the possessing party prefers, to the reviewing court. The possessing party must comply with the request within 10 days after the notice was served.

(3) If the party possessing the document or exhibit sends it to the requesting party non-electronically, that party must copy and return it to the possessing party within 10 days after receiving it.

(4) If the party possessing the document or exhibit sends it to the reviewing court, that party must:

(A) Accompany the document or exhibit with a copy of the notice served by the requesting party; and

(B) Immediately notify the requesting party that it has sent the document or exhibit to the reviewing court.

(5) On request, the reviewing court may return a document or an exhibit to the party that sent it non-electronically. When the remittitur issues, the reviewing court must return all documents or exhibits to the party that sent them, if they were sent non-electronically.

(Subd (c) amended effective January 1, 2016; adopted effective January 1, 2005, previously amended effective January 1, 2007, and January 1, 2010.)

(d) Form of appendix

(1) An appendix must comply with the requirements of rule 8.144 for a clerk's transcript.

(2) In addition to the information required on the cover of a brief by rule 8.204(b)(10), the cover of an appendix must prominently display the title "Joint Appendix" or "Appellant's Appendix" or "Respondent's Appendix" or "Appellant's Reply Appendix."

(3) An appendix must not be bound or transmitted electronically as one document with a brief.

(Subd (d) amended effective January 1, 2018; adopted as subd (c) effective January 1, 2002; relettered as subd (d) effective January 1, 2005; previously amended effective January 1, 2007, January 1, 2016, and January 1, 2017.)

(e) Service and filing

(1) A party preparing an appendix must:

(A) Serve the appendix on each party, unless otherwise agreed by the parties or ordered by the reviewing court; and

(B) File the appendix in the reviewing court.

(2) A joint appendix or an appellant's appendix must be served and filed before or together with the appellant's opening brief.

(3) A respondent's appendix, if any, must be served and filed with the respondent's brief.

(4) An appellant's reply appendix, if any, must be served and filed with the appellant's reply brief.

(Subd (e) amended effective January 1, 2024; adopted as subd (d) effective January 1, 2002; relettered effective January 1, 2005; previously amended effective January 1, 2007.)

(f) Cost of appendix

(1) Each party must pay for its own appendix.

(2) The cost of a joint appendix must be paid:

(A) By the appellant;

(B) If there is more than one appellant, by the appellants equally; or
(C) As the parties may agree.

(Subd (f) amended effective January 1, 2007; adopted as subd (e) effective January 1, 2002; relettered effective January 1, 2005.)

(g) Inaccurate or noncomplying appendix

Filing an appendix constitutes a representation that the appendix consists of accurate copies of documents in the superior court file. The reviewing court may impose monetary or other sanctions for filing an appendix that contains inaccurate copies or otherwise violates this rule.

(Subd (g) adopted as subd (f) effective January 1, 2002; relettered effective January 1, 2005.)

Rule 8.124 amended effective January 1, 2024; repealed and adopted as rule 5.1 effective January 1, 2002; previously amended and renumbered as rule 8.124 effective January 1, 2007; previously amended effective January 1, 2005, January 1, 2008, January 1, 2010, January 1, 2016, January 1, 2017, and January 1, 2018.

Advisory Committee Comment

Subdivision (a). Under this provision either party may elect to have the appeal proceed by way of an appendix. If the appellant's fees for a clerk's transcript are not waived and the respondent timely elects to use an appendix, that election will govern unless the superior court orders otherwise. This election procedure differs from all other appellate rules governing designation of a record on appeal. In those rules, the appellant's designation, or the stipulation of the parties, determines the type of record on appeal. Before making this election, respondents should check whether the appellant has been granted a fee waiver that is still in effect. If the trial court has granted appellant a fee waiver for the clerk's transcript, or grants such a waiver after the notice of appeal is filed, respondent cannot elect to proceed by way of an appendix.

Subdivision (a)(2) is intended to assist appellate counsel in preparing an appendix by providing them with the list of pleadings and other filings found in the register of actions or "docket sheet" in those counties that maintain such registers. (See Gov. Code, § 69845.) The provision is derived from rule 10-1 of the United States Circuit Rules (9th Cir.).

Subdivision (b). Under subdivision (b)(1)(A), a joint appendix or an appellant's appendix must contain any register of actions that the clerk sent to the parties under subdivision (a)(2). This provision is intended to assist the reviewing court in determining the accuracy of the appendix. The provision is derived from rule 30-1.3(a)(ii) of the United States Circuit Rules (9th Cir.).

In support of or opposition to pleadings or motions, the parties may have filed a number of lengthy documents in the proceedings in superior court, including, for example, declarations, memorandums, trial briefs, documentary exhibits (e.g., insurance policies, contracts, deeds), and photocopies of judicial opinions or other publications. Subdivision (b)(3)(A) prohibits the inclusion of such documents in an appendix when they are not necessary for proper consideration of the issues raised in the appeal. Even if a document is otherwise includable in an appendix, the rule prohibits the inclusion of any substantial *portion* of the document that is not necessary for proper consideration of the issues raised in the appeal. The prohibition is intended to simplify and therefore expedite the preparation of the appendix, to reduce its cost to the parties, and to relieve the courts of the burden of reviewing a record containing redundant, irrelevant, or immaterial documents. The provision is adapted from rule 30-1.4 of the United States Circuit Rules (9th Cir.).

Subdivision (b)(3)(B) prohibits the inclusion in an appendix of transcripts of oral proceedings that may be made part of a reporter's transcript. (Compare rule 8.130(e)(3) [the reporter must not copy into the reporter's transcript any document includable in the clerk's transcript under rule 8.122].) The prohibition is intended to prevent a party filing an appendix from evading the requirements and safeguards imposed by rule 8.130 on the process of designating and preparing a reporter's transcript, or the requirements imposed by rule 8.144(e) on the use of daily or other transcripts instead of a reporter's transcript (i.e., renumbered pages, required indexes). In addition, if an appellant were to include in its appendix a transcript of less than all the proceedings, the respondent would not learn of any need to designate additional proceedings (under rule 8.130(a)(3)) until the appellant had served its appendix with its brief, when it would be too late to designate them. Note also that a party may file a certified transcript of designated proceedings instead of a deposit for the reporter's fee (rule 8.130(b)(3)).

Subdivision (d). In current practice, served copies of filed documents often bear no clerk's date stamp and are not conformed by the parties serving them. Consistently with this practice, subdivision (d) does not require such documents to be conformed. The provision thereby relieves the parties of the burden of obtaining conformed copies at the cost of considerable time and expense and expedites the preparation of the appendix and the processing of the appeal. It is to be noted, however, that under subdivision (b)(1)(A) each document necessary to determine the timeliness of the appeal must show the date required under rule 8.104 or 8.108. Note also that subdivision (g) of rule 8.124 provides that a party filing an appendix represents under penalty of sanctions that its copies of documents are accurate.

Subdivision (e). Subdivision (e)(2) requires a joint appendix to be filed with the appellant's opening brief or before the filing of the appellant's opening brief. The provision is intended to improve the briefing process by enabling the appellant's opening brief to include citations to the record and, by allowing earlier filing of the appendix, to assist courts in considering petitions for supersedeas. To provide for the case in which a respondent concludes in light of the appellant's opening brief that the joint appendix should have included additional documents, subdivision (b)(5) permits such a respondent to present in an appendix filed with its respondent's brief (see subd. (e)(3)) any document that could have been included in the joint appendix.

Under subdivision (e)(2)–(4) an appendix is required to be filed, at the latest, "with" the associated brief. This provision is intended to clarify that an extension of a briefing period ipso facto extends the filing period of an appendix associated with the brief.

Subdivision (g). Under subdivision (g), sanctions do not depend on the degree of culpability of the filing party—i.e., on whether the party's conduct was willful or negligent—but on the nature of the inaccuracies and the importance of the documents they affect.

Rule 8.128. Superior court file instead of clerk's transcript

(a) Stipulation; time to file

(1) If a local rule of the reviewing court permits, the parties may stipulate to use the original superior court file instead of a clerk's transcript under rule 8.122. This rule and any supplemental provisions of the local rule then govern unless the superior court orders otherwise after notice to the parties.

(2) Parties intending to proceed under this rule must file their stipulation in superior court with the appellant's notice designating the record on appeal under rule 8.121. The parties must serve the reviewing court with a copy of the stipulation.

(Subd (a) amended effective January 1, 2008; previously amended effective January 1, 2007.)

(b) Cost estimate; preparation of file; transmittal

(1) Within 10 days after a stipulation under (a) is filed, the superior court clerk must send the appellant an estimate of the cost to prepare the file, including the cost of sending the index under (3). The appellant must deposit the cost or file an application for, or an order granting, a waiver of the cost within 10 days after the clerk sends the estimate.

(2) Within 10 days after the appellant deposits the cost or the court files an order waiving that cost, the superior court clerk must put the superior court file in chronological order, number the pages, and attach a chronological index and a list of all attorneys of record, the parties they represent, and any unrepresented parties.

(3) The clerk must send copies of the index to all attorneys of record and any unrepresented parties for their use in paginating their copies of the file to conform to the index.

(4) The clerk must send the prepared file to the reviewing court with the reporter's transcript. If the appellant elected to proceed without a reporter's transcript, the clerk must immediately send the prepared file to the reviewing court.

(Subd (b) amended effective January 1, 2016; previously amended effective July 1, 2009.)

Rule 8.128 amended effective January 1, 2016; repealed and adopted as rule 5.2 effective January 1, 2002; previously amended and renumbered as rule 8.128 effective January 1, 2007; previously amended effective January 1, 2008, and July 1, 2009.

Advisory Committee Comment

Subdivision (b). The Superior Court will make the determination on any application to waive the fees for preparing and transmitting the trial court file.

Rule 8.130. Reporter's transcript

(a) Notice

(1) A notice under rule 8.121 designating a reporter's transcript must specify the date of each proceeding to be included in the transcript and may specify portions of designated proceedings that are not to be included. The notice must identify any proceeding for which a certified transcript has previously been prepared by checking the appropriate box on *Appellant's Notice Designating Record on Appeal (Unlimited Civil)* (form APP-003) or, if that form is not used, placing an asterisk before that proceeding in the notice.

(2) If the appellant designates less than all the testimony, the notice must state the points to be raised on appeal; the appeal is then limited to those points unless, on motion, the reviewing court permits otherwise.

(3) If the appellant serves and files a notice designating a reporter's transcript, the respondent may, within 10 days after such service, serve and file a notice in superior court designating any additional proceedings the respondent wants included in the transcript. The notice must identify any proceeding for which a certified transcript has previously been prepared by checking the appropriate box on *Respondent's Notice Designating Record on Appeal (Unlimited Civil Case)* (form APP-010) or,

if that form is not used, placing an asterisk before that proceeding in the notice.

(4) If the appellant elects to proceed without a reporter's transcript, the respondent cannot require that a reporter's transcript be prepared. But the reviewing court, on its own or the respondent's motion, may order the record augmented under rule 8.155 to prevent a miscarriage of justice. Unless the court orders otherwise, the appellant is responsible for the cost of any reporter's transcript the court may order under this subdivision.

(5) Except when a party submits a certified transcript that contains all the designated proceedings under (b)(3)(C) with the notice of designation, the notice of designation must be served on each known reporter of the designated proceedings.

(Subd (a) amended effective January 1, 2014; previously amended effective January 1, 2005, January 1, 2007, and January 1, 2008.)

(b) Deposit or substitute for cost of transcript

(1) With its notice of designation, a party must deposit with the superior court clerk the approximate cost of transcribing the proceedings it designates and a fee of $50 for the superior court to hold this deposit in trust. The deposit must be either:

(A) The amount specified in the reporter's written estimate; or

(B) An amount calculated as follows:

(i) For proceedings that have not previously been transcribed: $325 per fraction of the day's proceedings that did not exceed three hours, or $650 per day or fraction that exceeded three hours.

(ii) For proceedings that have previously been transcribed: $80 per fraction of the day's proceedings that did not exceed three hours, or $160 per day or fraction that exceeded three hours.

(2) If the reporter believes the deposit is inadequate, within 15 days after the clerk sends the notice under (d)(1) the reporter may file with the clerk and send to the designating party an estimate of the transcript's total cost at the statutory rate, showing the additional deposit required. The party must deposit the additional sum within 10 days after the reporter sends the estimate.

(3) Instead of a deposit under (1), the party may substitute:

(A) The reporter's written waiver of a deposit. A reporter may waive the deposit for a part of the designated proceedings, but such a waiver replaces the deposit for only that part.

(B) A copy of a Transcript Reimbursement Fund application filed under (c)(1).

(C) A certified transcript of all of the proceedings designated by the party. The transcript submitted by the party must not be accepted as a substitute for a deposit under (1) unless it complies with the format requirements of rule 8.144.

(Subd (b) amended effective January 1, 2024; previously amended effective January 1, 2007, January 1, 2010, January 1, 2014, and January 1, 2016.)

(c) Transcript Reimbursement Fund application

(1) With its notice of designation, a party may serve and file a copy of its application to the Court Reporters Board for payment or reimbursement from the Transcript Reimbursement Fund under Business and Professions Code section 8030.2 et seq.

(2) Within 90 days after the appellant serves and files a copy of its application to the Court Reporters Board, the appellant must either file with the superior court a copy of the Court Reporters Board's provisional approval of the application or take one of the following actions:

(A) Deposit the amount required under (b) or the reporter's written waiver of this deposit;

(B) File an agreed statement or a stipulation that the parties are attempting to agree on a statement under rule 8.134;

(C) File a motion to use a settled statement instead of a reporter's transcript under rule 8.137;

(D) Notify the superior court clerk that it elects to proceed without a record of the oral proceedings; or

(E) Serve and file an abandonment under rule 8.244.

(3) Within 90 days after the respondent serves and files a copy of its application to the Court Reporters Board, the respondent must either file with the superior court a copy of the Court Reporters Board's provisional approval of the application or take one of the following actions:

(A) Deposit the amount required under (b) or the reporter's written waiver of this deposit; or

(B) Notify the superior court clerk that it no longer wants the additional proceedings it designated for inclusion in the reporter's transcript.

(4) If the appellant fails to timely take one of the actions specified in (2) or the respondent fails to timely make the deposit or send the notice under (3), the superior court clerk must promptly issue a notice of default under rule 8.140.

(5) If the Court Reporters Board provisionally approves the application, the reporter's time to prepare the transcript under (f)(1) begins when the reporter receives notice of the provisional approval from the clerk under (d)(2).

(Subd (c) amended effective January 1, 2014; previously amended effective January 1, 2007.)

(d) Superior court clerk's duties

(1) The clerk must file a party's notice of designation even if the party does not present the required deposit under (b)(1) or a substitute under (b)(3) with its notice of designation.

(2) The clerk must promptly send the reporter notice of the designation and of the deposit or substitute and notice to prepare the transcript, showing the date the notice was sent to the reporter, when the court receives:

(A) The required deposit under (b)(1);

(B) A reporter's written waiver of a deposit under (b)(3); or

(C) A copy of the Court Reporters Board's provisional approval of the party's application for payment from the Transcript Reimbursement Fund under (c).

(3) If the appellant does not present the deposit under (b)(1) or a substitute under (b)(3) with its notice of designation or does not present an additional deposit required under (b)(2):

(A) The clerk must promptly notify the appellant in writing that, within 15 days after the notice is sent, the appellant must take one of the following actions or the court may dismiss the appeal:

(i) Deposit the amount required or a substitute permitted under (b);

(ii) File an agreed statement or a stipulation that the parties are attempting to agree on a statement under rule 8.134;

(iii) File a motion to use a settled statement instead of a reporter's transcript under rule 8.137;

(iv) Notify the superior court clerk that it elects to proceed without a record of the oral proceedings; or

(v) Serve and file an abandonment under rule 8.244.

(B) If the appellant elects to use a reporter's transcript and fails to take one of the actions specified in the notice under (A), rule 8.140(b) and (c) apply.

(4) If the respondent does not present the deposit under (b)(1) or a substitute under (b)(3) with its notice of designation or does not present an additional deposit required under (b)(2), the clerk must file the notice of designation and promptly issue a notice of default under rule 8.140.

(5) The clerk must promptly notify the reporter if a check for a deposit is dishonored or an appeal is abandoned or is dismissed before the reporter has filed the transcript.

(Subd (d) amended effective January 1, 2016; previously amended effective January 1, 2007, January 1, 2008, and January 1, 2014.)

(e) Contents of transcript

(1) Except when a party deposits a certified transcript of all the designated proceedings under (b)(3)(C), the reporter must transcribe all designated proceedings that have not previously been transcribed and include in the transcript a copy of all designated proceedings that have previously been transcribed. The reporter must note in the transcript where any proceedings were omitted and the nature of those proceedings. The reporter must also note where any exhibit was marked for identification and where it was admitted or refused, identifying such exhibits by number or letter.

(2) If a party designates a portion of a witness's testimony to be transcribed, the reporter must transcribe the witness's entire testimony unless the parties stipulate otherwise.

(3) The reporter must not copy any document includable in the clerk's transcript under rule 8.122.

(Subd (e) amended effective January 1, 2014; previously amended effective January 1, 2007, and January 1, 2008.)

(f) Filing the transcript; copies; payment

(1) Within 30 days after notice is sent under (d)(2), the reporter must prepare and certify an original of the transcript and file it in superior court. The reporter must also file one copy of the original transcript, or more than one copy if multiple appellants equally share the cost of preparing the record (see rule 8.147(a)(2)). Only the reviewing court can extend the time to prepare the reporter's transcript (see rule 8.60).

(2) When the transcript is completed, the reporter must notify all parties to the appeal that the transcript is complete, bill each designating party at the statutory rate, and send a copy of the bill to the superior court clerk. The clerk must pay the reporter from that party's deposited funds and refund any excess deposit or notify the party of any additional funds needed. In a multiple reporter case, the clerk must pay each reporter who certifies under penalty of perjury that his or her transcript portion is completed.

(3) If the appeal is abandoned or is dismissed before the reporter has filed the transcript, the reporter must inform the superior court clerk of the cost of the portion of the transcript that the reporter has completed. The clerk must pay that amount to the reporter from the appellant's deposited funds and refund any excess deposit.

(Subd (f) amended effective January 1, 2018; previously amended effective January 1, 2007, July 1, 2008, January 1, 2014, January 1, 2016, and January 1, 2017.)

(g) Disputes over transcript costs

Notwithstanding any dispute that may arise over the estimated or billed costs of a reporter's transcript, a designating party must timely comply with the requirements under this rule regarding deposits for transcripts. If a designating party believes that a reporter's estimate or bill is excessive, the designating party may file a complaint with the Court Reporters Board.

(Subd (g) adopted effective January 1, 2014.)

(h) Agreed or settled statement when proceedings cannot be transcribed

(1) If any portion of the designated proceedings cannot be transcribed, the superior court clerk must so notify the designating party in writing; the notice must show the date it was sent. The party may then substitute an agreed or settled statement for that portion of the designated proceedings by complying with either (A) or (B):

(A) Within 10 days after the notice is sent, the party may file in superior court, under rule 8.134, an agreed statement or a stipulation that the parties are attempting to agree on a statement. If the party files a stipulation, within 30 days thereafter the party must file the agreed statement, move to use a settled statement under rule 8.137, or proceed without such a statement; or

(B) Within 10 days after the notice is sent, the party may move in superior court to use a settled statement. If the court grants the motion, the statement must be served, filed, and settled as rule 8.137 provides, but the order granting the motion must fix the times for doing so.

(2) If the agreed or settled statement contains all the oral proceedings, it will substitute for the reporter's transcript; if it contains a portion of the proceedings, it will be incorporated into that transcript.

(3) This remedy supplements any other available remedies.

(Subd (h) amended effective January 1, 2016; adopted as subd (g); previously amended effective January 1, 2007; previously relettered as subd (h) effective January 1, 2014.)

Rule 8.130 amended effective January 1, 2024; repealed and adopted as rule 4 effective January 1, 2002; previously amended and renumbered as rule 8.130 effective January 1, 2007; previously amended effective January 1, 2005, January 1, 2008, July 1, 2008, January 1, 2010, January 1, 2014, January 1, 2016, January 1, 2017, and January 1, 2018.

Advisory Committee Comment

Subdivision (a). Subdivision (a)(1) requires that every notice designating a reporter's transcript identify which proceedings are to be included, and that it do so by specifying the date or dates on which those proceedings took place. Those proceedings for which a certified transcript has previously been prepared must be identified in the party's designation. If the appellant does not want a portion of the proceedings on a given date to be included, the notice should identify that portion by means of a descriptive reference (e.g., "August 3, 2004, but not the proceedings on defendant's motion to tax costs").

As used in subdivision (a)(1), the phrase "proceedings" includes all instructions that the court gives, whether or not submitted in writing, and any instructions that counsel orally propose but the court refuses; all such instructions are included in the reporter's transcript if designated under this rule. All instructions that counsel submit in writing, whether or not given to the jury, are lodged with the superior court clerk and are included in the clerk's transcript if designated under rule 8.122.

Under subdivision (a), portions of depositions read in open court but not reported, or not read but lodged with the superior court clerk, are included in the clerk's transcript if designated under rule 8.122.

Subdivision (b). Where a certified transcript has been previously prepared, subdivision (b) makes clear that the certified transcript may be filed in lieu of a deposit for the transcript only where the certified transcript contains all of the proceedings identified in the notice of designation and the transcript complies with the format requirements of rule 8.144 (e.g., cover information, renumbered pages, required indexes). Parties using this alternative to a deposit are responsible for ensuring that such transcripts are in the proper format. Parties may arrange with a court reporter to do the necessary formatting of the transcript or may do the formatting themselves. Otherwise, where a certified transcript has been previously prepared for only some of the designated proceedings, subdivision (b)(1) authorizes a reduced fee to be deposited for those proceedings. This reduced deposit amount was established in recognition of the holding in *Hendrix v. Superior Court of San Bernardino County* (2011) 191 Cal.App.4th 889 that the statutory rate for an original transcript only applies to the first transcription of the reporter's notes. The amount of the deposit is based on the rate established by Government Code section 69950(b) for a first copy of a reporter's transcript purchased by any court, party, or other person who does not simultaneously purchase the original.

To eliminate any ambiguity, subdivision (b)(3) recognizes, first, that a party may substitute a court reporter's written waiver of a deposit for part of the designated proceedings and, second, that in such event the waiver replaces the deposit for only that part.

Subdivision (b) and subdivision (f) refer to the "statutory rate" for reporter's transcripts. The fees for reporter's transcripts are established by Government Code sections 69950 and 69554.

Subdivision (c). Under subdivision (c), an application to the Court Reporters Board for payment or reimbursement of the cost of the reporter's transcript from the Transcript Reimbursement Fund (Bus. & Prof. Code, §8030.8) is a permissible substitute for the required deposit of the reporter's fee (subd. (b)(3)) and thereby prevents issuance of a notice of default. (subd. (d)(5)).

Business and Professions Code sections 8030.6 and 8030.8 use the term "reimbursement" to mean not only a true reimbursement, i.e., repaying a party who has previously paid the reporter out of the party's own funds (see *id.*, §8030.8, subd. (d)), but also a direct payment to a reporter who has not been previously paid by the party (see *id.*, §8030.6, subds. (b) and (d)). Subdivision (f) recognizes this special dual meaning by consistently using the compound phrase "payment or reimbursement."

Subdivision (d). Under subdivision (d)(2), the clerk's notice to the reporter must show the date on which the clerk sent the notice. This provision is intended to establish the date when the period for preparing the reporter's transcript under subdivision (f)(1) begins to run.

Subdivision (e). Subdivision (e)(1) clarifies that: (1) when a certified transcript containing all of the proceedings identified in the notice of designation is submitted in lieu of a deposit, the court reporter will not prepare a reporter's transcript; and (2) that the court reporter will only transcribe those proceedings that have not previously been transcribed and will include a copy of those proceedings that have previously been transcribed in the reporter's transcript. Under rule 8.144, the full transcript, including the previously transcribed material, must meet the format requirements for a reporter's transcript.

Subdivision (e)(3) is not intended to relieve the reporter of the duty to report all oral proceedings, including the reading of instructions or other documents.

Subdivision (f). Subdivision (f)(1) requires the reporter to prepare and file additional copies of the record "if multiple appellants equally share the cost of preparing the record ...." The reason for the requirement is explained in the comment to rule 8.147(a)(2).

Rule 8.134. Agreed statement

(a) Contents of statement

(1) The record on appeal may consist wholly or partly of an agreed statement. The statement must explain the nature of the action, the basis of the reviewing court's jurisdiction, and how the superior court decided the points to be raised on appeal. The statement should recite only those facts needed to decide the appeal and must be signed by the parties.

(2) If the agreed statement replaces a clerk's transcript, the statement must be accompanied by copies of all items required by rule 8.122(b)(1), showing the dates required by rule 8.122(b)(2).

(3) The statement may be accompanied by copies of any document includable in the clerk's transcript under rule 8.122(b)(3) and (4).

(Subd (a) amended effective January 1, 2008; previously amended effective January 1, 2007.)

(b) Time to file; extension of time

(1) An appellant intending to proceed under this rule must file either an agreed statement or a stipulation that the parties are attempting to agree on a statement in superior court with its notice designating the record on appeal under rule 8.121.

(2) If the appellant files the stipulation and the parties can agree on the statement, the appellant must file the statement within 40 days after filing the notice of appeal.

(3) If the appellant files the stipulation and the parties cannot agree on the statement, the appellant must file a new notice designating the record on appeal under rule 8.121 within 50 days after filing the notice of appeal.

(Subd (b) amended effective January 1, 2008; previously amended effective January 1, 2007.)

Rule 8.134 amended effective January 1, 2008; repealed and adopted as rule 6 effective January 1, 2002; previously amended and renumbered effective January 1, 2007.

Advisory Committee Comment

Subdivision (b). Subdivision (b)(1) requires the appellant to file, with the appellant's notice designating the record under rule 8.121, either an agreed statement or a stipulation that the parties are attempting to agree on a statement. The provision is intended to prevent issuance of a notice of default while the parties are preparing an agreed statement.

Rule 8.137. Settled statement

(a) Description

A settled statement is a summary of the superior court proceedings approved by the superior court. An appellant may either elect under (b)(1) or move under (b)(2) to use a settled statement as the record of the oral proceedings in the superior court, instead of a reporter's transcript.

(Subd (a) adopted effective January 1, 2018.)

(b) When a settled statement may be used

(1) An appellant may elect in his or her notice designating the record on appeal under rule 8.121 to use a settled statement as the record of the oral proceedings in the superior court without filing a motion under (2) if:

(A) The designated oral proceedings in the superior court were not reported by a court reporter; or

(B) The appellant has an order waiving his or her court fees and costs.

(2) An appellant intending to proceed under this rule for reasons other than those listed in (1) must serve and file in superior court with its notice designating the record on appeal under rule 8.121 a motion to use a settled statement instead of a reporter's transcript.

(A) The motion must be supported by a showing that:

(i) A substantial cost saving will result and the statement can be settled without significantly burdening opposing parties or the court;

(ii) The designated oral proceedings cannot be transcribed; or

(iii) Although the appellant does not have a fee waiver, he or she is unable to pay for a reporter's transcript and funds are not available from the Transcript Reimbursement Fund (see rule 8.130(c)).

(B) If the court denies the motion, the appellant must file a new notice designating the record on appeal under rule 8.121 within 10 days after the superior court clerk sends, or a party serves, the order of denial.

(3) An appellant's notice under (1) or motion under (2) must:

(A) Specify the date of each oral proceeding to be included in the settled statement;

(B) Identify whether each proceeding designated under (A) was reported by a court reporter and, if so, for each such proceeding:

(i) Provide the name of the court reporter, if known; and

(ii) Identify whether a certified transcript has previously been prepared by checking the appropriate box on *Appellant's Notice Designating Record on Appeal (Unlimited Civil Case)* (form APP-003) or, if that form is not used, placing an asterisk before that proceeding in the notice.

(4) If the designated oral proceedings in the superior court were reported by a court reporter:

(A) Within 10 days after the appellant serves either a notice under (1) or a motion under (2), the respondent may serve and file a notice indicating that he or she is electing to provide a reporter's transcript in lieu of proceeding with a settled statement. The respondent must also either:

(i) Deposit a certified transcript of all of the proceedings designated by the appellant under (3) and any additional proceedings designated by the respondent under rule 8.130(b)(3)(C); or

(ii) Serve and file a notice that the respondent is requesting preparation, at the respondent's expense, of a reporter's transcript of all proceedings designated by the appellant under (3) and any additional proceedings designated by the respondent. This notice must be accompanied by either the required deposit for the reporter's transcript under rule 8.130(b)(1) or the reporter's written waiver of the deposit in lieu of all or a portion of the deposit under rule 8.130(b)(3)(A).

(B) If the respondent timely deposits the certified transcript as required under (i), the appellant's motion to use a settled statement will be dismissed. If the respondent timely files the notice and makes the deposit or files the waiver as provided under (ii), the appellant's motion to use a settled statement will be dismissed and the clerk must promptly send the reporter notice of the designation and of the deposit, waiver, or both—and notice to prepare the transcript—as provided under rule 8.130(d).

(Subd (b) relettered and amended effective January 1, 2018; previously amended effective January 1, 2007, January 1, 2008, and January 1, 2016.)

(c) Time to file proposed statement

(1) If the respondent does not file a notice under (b)(4)(A) electing to provide a reporter's transcript in lieu of proceeding with a settled statement, the appellant must serve and file a proposed statement in superior court within 30 days after filing its notice under (b)(1) or within 30 days after the superior court clerk sends, or a party serves, an order granting a motion under (b)(2).

(2) Appellants who are not represented by an attorney are encouraged to file their proposed statement on *Proposed Statement on Appeal (Unlimited Civil Case)* (form APP-014). The court may order an appellant to use form APP-014.

(Subd (c) relettered and amended effective January 1, 2018; adopted as subd (b); previously amended effective January 1, 2007, January 1, 2008, and January 1, 2016.)

(d) Contents of proposed statement

The proposed statement must:

(1) Contain a statement of the points the appellant is raising on appeal. If the condensed narrative under (2) covers only a portion of the oral proceedings, the appeal is then limited to the points identified in the statement unless the reviewing court determines that the record permits the full consideration of another point or, on motion, the reviewing court permits otherwise.

(2) Contain a condensed narrative of the oral proceedings that the appellant specified under (b)(3).

(A) The condensed narrative must include a concise factual summary of the evidence and the testimony of each witness relevant to the points that the appellant states under (1) are being raised on appeal. Subject to the court's approval in settling the statement, the appellant may present some or all of the evidence by question and answer. Any evidence or portion of a proceeding not included will be presumed to support the judgment or order appealed from.

(B) If one of the points that the appellant states will be raised on appeal is a challenge to the giving, refusal, or modification of a jury instruction, the condensed narrative must include any instructions submitted orally and not in writing and must identify the party that requested the instruction and any modification.

(3) Have attached to it a copy of the judgment or order being appealed.

(Subd (d) adopted effective January 1, 2018.)

(e) Respondent's response to proposed statement

Within 20 days after the appellant serves the proposed statement, the respondent may serve and file either:

(1) Proposed amendments to the proposed statement; or

(2) A notice indicating that he or she is electing to provide a reporter's transcript in lieu of proceeding with a settled statement. The respondent must also either:

(A) Deposit a certified transcript of all the proceedings specified by the appellant under (b)(3) of this rule and any additional proceedings designated by the respondent under rule 8.130(b)(3)(C); or

(B) Serve and file a notice that the respondent is requesting preparation, at the respondent's expense, of a reporter's transcript of all proceedings specified by the appellant under (b)(3) of this rule and any additional proceedings designated by the respondent. This notice must be accompanied by either the required deposit for the reporter's transcript under rule 8.130(b)(1) or the reporter's written waiver of the deposit in lieu of all or a portion of the deposit under rule 8.130(b)(3)(A).

(Subd (e) adopted effective January 1, 2018.)

(f) Review of appellant's proposed statement

(1) No later than 10 days after the respondent files proposed amendments or the time to do so expires, whichever is earlier, a party may request a hearing to review and correct the proposed statement. No hearing will be held unless ordered by the trial court judge, and the judge will not ordinarily order a hearing unless there is a factual dispute about a material aspect of the trial court proceedings.

(2) The trial court judge may order that a transcript be prepared as the record of the oral proceedings instead of correcting a proposed statement on appeal if the trial court proceedings were reported by a court reporter, the trial court judge determines that doing so would save court time and resources, and the court has a local rule permitting such an order. The court will pay for any transcript ordered under this subdivision.

(3) Except as provided in (2), if no hearing is ordered, no later than 10 days after the time for requesting a hearing expires, the trial court judge must review the proposed statement and any proposed amendments filed by the respondent and take one of the following actions:

(A) If the proposed statement does not contain material required under (d), the trial court judge may order the appellant to prepare a new proposed statement. The order must identify the additional material that must be included in the statement to comply with (d) and the date by which the new proposed statement must be served and filed. If the appellant does not serve and file a new proposed statement as directed, the appellant will be deemed to be in default, and rule 8.140 will apply.

(B) If the trial court judge does not issue an order under (A), the judge must either:

(i) Make any corrections or modifications to the statement necessary to ensure that it is an accurate summary of the evidence and the testimony of each witness relevant to the points that the appellant states under (d)(1) are being raised on appeal; or

(ii) Identify the necessary corrections and modifications, and order the appellant to prepare a statement incorporating these corrections and modifications.

(4) If a hearing is ordered, the court must promptly set the hearing date and provide the parties with at least 5 days' written notice of the hearing date. No later than 10 days after the hearing, the trial court judge must either:

(A) Make any corrections or modifications to the statement necessary to ensure that it is an accurate summary of the evidence and the testimony of each witness relevant to the points that the appellant states under (d)(1) are being raised on appeal; or

(B) Identify the necessary corrections and modifications and order the appellant to prepare a statement incorporating these corrections and modifications.

(5) The trial court judge must not eliminate the appellant's specification of grounds of appeal from the proposed statement.

(Subd (f) relettered and amended effective January 1, 2018; adopted as subd (c).)

(g) Review of the corrected statement

(1) If the trial court judge makes any corrections or modifications to the proposed statement under (f), the clerk must serve copies of the corrected or modified statement on the parties. If under (f) the trial court judge orders the appellant to prepare a statement incorporating corrections and modifications, the appellant must serve and file the corrected or modified statement within the time ordered by the court. If the appellant does not serve and file a corrected or modified statement as directed, the appellant will be deemed to be in default and rule 8.140 will apply.

(2) Within 10 days after the corrected or modified statement is served on the parties, any party may serve and file proposed modifications or objections to the statement.

(3) Within 10 days after the time for filing proposed modifications or objections under (2) has expired, the trial court judge must review the corrected or modified statement and any proposed modifications or objections to the statement filed by the parties. The procedures in (f)(2) or (f)(3) apply if the trial court judge determines that further corrections or modifications are necessary to ensure that the statement is an accurate summary of the evidence and the testimony of each witness relevant to the points that the appellant states under (d)(1) are being raised on appeal.

(Subd (g) amended effective April 1, 2023; adopted effective January 1, 2018.)

(h) Certification of the statement on appeal

(1) If the trial court judge does not order the preparation of a transcript under (f)(2) in lieu of correcting the proposed statement or order any corrections or modifications to the proposed statement under (f)(3), (f)(4), or (g)(3), the judge must promptly certify the statement.

(2) The parties may serve and file a stipulation that the statement as originally served under (c) or as corrected or modified under (f)(3), (f)(4), or (g)(3) is correct. Such a stipulation is equivalent to the judge's certification of the statement.

(3) Upon certification of the statement under (1) or receipt of a stipulation under (2), the certified statement must immediately be transmitted to the clerk for filing of the record under rule 8.150.

(Subd (h) adopted effective January 1, 2018.)

Rule 8.137 amended effective April 1, 2023; repealed and adopted as rule 7 effective January 1, 2002; previously amended and renumbered as rule 8.137 effective January 1, 2007; previously amended January 1, 2008, January 1, 2016, and January 1, 2018.

Advisory Committee Comment

Subdivision (b). This rule requires the appellant to file only one copy of the settled statement, i.e., for the use of the reviewing court. Because all parties participate in preparing the settled statement, it may be assumed that each will retain a copy for its own use.

Rule 8.140. Failure to procure the record

(a) Notice of default

Except as otherwise provided by these rules, if a party fails to timely do an act required to procure the record, the superior court clerk must promptly notify the party in writing that it must do the act specified in the notice within 15 days after the notice is sent, and that if it fails to comply, the reviewing court may impose one of the following sanctions:

(1) If the defaulting party is the appellant, the court may dismiss the appeal; or

(2) If the defaulting party is the respondent, the court may proceed with the appeal on the record designated by the appellant.

(Subd (a) amended effective January 1, 2016; previously amended effective January 1, 2007, January 1, 2008, and January 1, 2014.)

(b) Sanctions

If a party fails to take the action specified in a notice given under (a), the superior court clerk must promptly notify the reviewing court of the default, and the reviewing court may impose one of the following sanctions:

(1) If the defaulting party is the appellant, the reviewing court may dismiss the appeal. If the appeal is dismissed, the reviewing court must promptly notify the superior court. The reviewing court may vacate the dismissal for good cause.

(2) If the defaulting party is the respondent, the reviewing court may order the appeal to proceed on the record designated by the appellant, but the respondent may obtain relief from default under rule 8.60(d).

(Subd (b) amended effective January 1, 2014; previously amended effective January 1, 2007, and January 1, 2008.)

(c) Motion for sanctions

If the superior court clerk fails to give a notice required by (a), a party may serve and file a motion for sanctions under (b) in the reviewing court, but the motion must be denied if the defaulting party cures the default within 15 days after the motion is served.

Rule 8.140 amended effective January 1, 2016; adopted as rule 8 effective January 1, 2002; previously amended and renumbered as rule 8.140 effective January 1, 2007; previously amended effective January 1, 2008, and January 1, 2014.

Advisory Committee Comment

Subdivision (a). In subdivision (a), the reference to a failure to "timely" do a required act is intended to include any valid extension of that time.

Rule 8.144. Form of the record

(a) The provisions of this rule must be applied in a manner consistent with Code of Civil Procedure section 271.

(Subd (a) adopted effective January 1, 2018.)

(b) Format

(1) *Application to electronic and paper clerks' and reporters' transcripts*

The requirements for clerks' and reporters' transcripts in this subdivision apply to clerks' and reporters' transcripts delivered in electronic form and in paper form.

(2) *General*

In the clerk's and reporter's transcripts:

(A) All documents filed must have a page size of 8½ by 11 inches;

(B) The text must be reproduced as legibly as printed matter;

(C) The contents must be arranged chronologically;

(D) The pages must be consecutively numbered, except as provided in (f), beginning with volume one's cover as page 1 and continuing throughout the transcript, including the indexes, certificates, and cover pages for subsequent volumes, and using only Arabic numerals (i.e., 1, 2, 3); and

(E) The margin must be at least 1¼ inches from the left edge.

(3) *Line numbering*

In the reporter's transcript the lines on each page must be consecutively numbered, and must be double-spaced or one-and-a-half-spaced; double-spaced means three lines to a vertical inch.

(4) *Sealed and confidential records*

The clerk's and reporter's transcripts must comply with rules 8.45–8.47 relating to sealed and confidential records.

(5) *Indexes*

Except as provided in rule 8.45:

(A) The clerk's transcript must contain, at the beginning of the first volume, alphabetical and chronological indexes listing each document and the volume, where applicable, and page where it first appears;

(B) The reporter's transcript must contain:

(i) Alphabetical and chronological indexes listing the volume, where applicable, and page where each witness's direct, cross, and any other examination begins; and

(ii) An index listing the volume, where applicable, and page where any exhibit is marked for identification and where it is admitted or refused. The index must identify each exhibit by number or letter and a brief description of the exhibit.

(C) Each index prepared under this paragraph must begin on a separate page.

(6) *Volumes*

(A) **Except as provided in (B),** clerks' and reporters' transcripts must be produced in volumes of no more than 300 pages.

(B) **If a clerk's or reporter's transcript is being delivered in electronic form to all courts, parties, and persons entitled to the transcript, it may be produced in a single volume but must comply with the requirements of rule 8.74(a)(5).**

(7) *Cover*

(A) The cover of each volume of the clerk's and reporter's transcripts must state the title and trial court number of the case, the names of the trial court and each participating trial judge, the names and addresses of appellate counsel for each party, the volume number, the total number of volumes in the transcript, and the inclusive page numbers of that volume.

(B) In reporters' transcripts, in addition to the information required by (A), the cover of each volume must state the dates of the proceedings reported in that volume.

(Subd (b) amended effective January 1, 2024; previously amended effective January 1, 2007, January 1, 2014, January 1, 2016, January 1, 2017, and January 1, 2018.)

(c) Additional requirements for record in paper form

In addition to complying with (b), if the clerk's or reporter's transcript is filed in paper form:

(1) The paper must be white or unbleached and of at least 20-pound weight;

(2) In the clerk's transcript only one side of the paper may be used; in the reporter's transcript both sides may be used, but the margins must then be 1¼ inches on each edge; and

(3) Clerks' and reporters' transcripts must be bound on the left margin.

(Subd (c) adopted effective January 1, 2018.)

(d) Additional requirements for reporter's transcript delivered in electronic form

(1) *General*

In addition to complying with (b), a reporter's transcript delivered in electronic form must:

(A) Be generated electronically; it must not be created from a scanned document unless ordered by the court.

(B) Be in full text-searchable PDF (portable document format) or other searchable format approved by the court.

(C) Ensure that the electronic page counter in the PDF file viewer matches the transcript page numbering except as provided in (f)(2) or (3).

(D) Include an electronic bookmark to each heading and subheading; all sessions or hearings (date lines); all witness examinations where each witness's direct, cross, and any other examination begins; all indexes; and all exhibits where any exhibit is marked for identification and where it is admitted or refused. All bookmarks, when clicked, must retain the user's currently selected zoom settings.

(E) Be digitally and electronically signed by the court reporter, unless the court reporter lacks the technical ability to provide a digital signature, in which case only an electronic signature is required.

(F) Permit users to copy and paste, keeping the original formatting, but with headers, footers, line numbers, and page numbers excluded.

(G) Permit courts to electronically add filed/received stamps.

(2) *Multivolume or multireporter transcripts*

In addition to the requirements in (1), for multivolume or multireporter transcripts delivered in electronic form , each individual reporter must provide a digitally and electronically signed certificate with his or her respective portion of the transcript. If the court reporter lacks the technical ability to provide a digital signature, then only an electronic signature is required.

(3) *Additional functionality or enhancements*

Nothing in this rule prohibits courts from accepting additional functionality or enhancements in reporters' transcripts delivered in electronic form.

(Subd (d) amended effective January 1, 2024; adopted effective January 1, 2018.)

(e) Daily transcripts

Daily or other certified transcripts may be used for all or part of the reporter's transcript, but the pages must be renumbered consecutively and the required indexes and covers must be added.

(Subd (e) relettered effective January 1, 2018; adopted as subd (d).)

(f) Pagination in multiple reporter cases

(1) In a multiple reporter case, each reporter must promptly estimate the number of pages in each segment reported and inform the designated primary reporter of the estimate. The primary reporter must then assign beginning and ending page numbers for each segment.

(2) If a segment exceeds the assigned number of pages, the reporter must number the additional pages with the ending page number, a hyphen, and a new number, starting with 1 and continuing consecutively.

(3) If a segment has fewer than the assigned number of pages, on the last page of the segment, before the certificate page, the reporter must state in parentheses "(next volume and page number is _____)," and on the certificate page the reporter must add a hyphen to the last page number used, followed by the segment's assigned ending page number.

(Subd (f) amended effective January 1, 2024; adopted as subd (e); previously amended and relettered effective January 1, 2018.)

(g) Agreed or settled statements

Agreed or settled statements must conform with this rule insofar as practicable.

(Subd (g) relettered effective January 1, 2018; adopted as subd (f).)

Rule 8.144 amended effective January 1, 2024; repealed and adopted as rule 9 effective January 1, 2002; previously amended and renumbered as rule 8.144 effective January 1, 2007; previously amended effective January 1, 2008, January 1, 2014, January 1, 2016, January 1, 2017, and January 1, 2018.

Advisory Committee Comment

Subdivision (b). Paragraph (1) of subdivision (b) clarifies that the format requirements for reporters' transcripts, including the requirements for indexes, volumes, and covers, that previously applied to transcripts delivered in paper form now apply to transcripts delivered in both paper and electronic form.

Paragraphs (4) and (5) of subdivision (b) refer to special requirements concerning sealed and confidential records established by rules 8.45–8.47. Rule 8.45(c)(2) and (3) establishes special requirements regarding references to sealed and confidential records in the alphabetical and chronological indexes to clerks' and reporters' transcripts.

Rule 8.147. Record in multiple or later appeals in same case

(a) Multiple appeals

(1) If more than one appeal is taken from the same judgment or a related order, only one record need be prepared, which must be filed within the time allowed for filing the record in the latest appeal.

(2) If there is more than one separately represented appellant, they must equally share the cost of preparing the record, unless otherwise agreed by the appellants or ordered by the superior court. Appellants equally sharing the cost are each entitled to a copy of the record.

(b) Later appeal

In an appeal in which the parties are using either a clerk's transcript under rule 8.122 or a reporter's transcript under rule 8.130:

(1) A party wanting to incorporate by reference all or parts of a record in a prior appeal in the same case must specify those parts in its designation of the record.

(A) The prior appeal must be identified by its case name and number. If only part of a record is being incorporated by reference, that part must be identified by citation to the volume, where applicable, and page numbers of the record where it appears and either the title of the document or documents or the date of the oral proceedings to be incorporated. The parts of any record incorporated by reference must be identified in a separate section at the end of the designation of the record.

(B) If the transcript incorporates by reference any such record, the cover of the transcript must prominently display the notice "Record in case number: _____ incorporated by reference," identifying the number of the case from which the record is incorporated.

(C) On request of the reviewing court or any party, the designating party must provide a copy of the materials incorporated by reference to the reviewing court or another party or lend them as provided in rule 8.153.

(2) A party wanting any parts of a clerk's transcript or other record of the written documents from a prior appeal in the same case to be copied

into the clerk's transcript in a later appeal must specify those parts in its designation of the record as provided in (1). The estimated cost of copying these materials must be included in the clerk's estimate of the cost of preparing the transcript under rule 8.122(c)(1). On request of the trial court clerk, the designating party must provide a copy of or lend the materials to be copied to the clerk. The parts of any record from a prior appeal that are copied into a clerk's transcript under this rule must be placed in a separate section at the end of the transcript and identified in a separate section at the end of the indexes.

(Subd (b) amended effective January 1, 2016; previously amended effective January 1, 2007, January 1, 2008, and January 1, 2010.)

Rule 8.147 amended effective January 1, 2016; repealed and adopted as rule 10 effective January 1, 2002; previously amended and renumbered as rule 8.147 effective January 1, 2007; previously amended effective January 1, 2008, and January 1, 2010.

Advisory Committee Comment

Subdivision (a). Subdivision (a)(1) provides broadly for a single record whenever there are multiple appeals "from the same judgment or a related order." Multiple appeals from the *same judgment* include all cases in which opposing parties, or multiple parties on the same side of the case, appeal from the judgment. Multiple appeals from a judgment *and a related order* include all cases in which one party appeals from the judgment and another party appeals from any appealable order arising from or related to the judgment, i.e., not only orders contemplated by rule 8.108 (e.g., denying a motion for judgment notwithstanding the verdict) but also, for example, posttrial orders granting or denying attorney fees. The purpose is to encourage, when practicable, the preparation of a single record for all appeals taken in the same case. In specifying that "only one *record* need be prepared," of course, the rule does not depart from the basic requirement that an *original* and at least one *copy* of the record be prepared.

The second sentence of subdivision (a)(2) applies when multiple appellants equally share the cost of preparing the record and that cost includes the cost of a copy for each appellant. An appellant wanting the reporter to prepare an additional copy of the record—i.e., additional to the copy required by rule 8.130(f)(1)—must make a timely deposit adequate to cover the cost of that copy.

Rule 8.149. When the record is complete

(a) Record of written documents

If the appellant elected to proceed without a record of the oral proceedings in the trial court and the parties are not proceeding by appendix under rule 8.124, the record is complete:

(1) If a clerk's transcript will be used, when the clerk's transcript is certified under rule 8.122(d);

(2) If the original superior court file will be used instead of the clerk's transcript, when that original file is ready for transmission as provided under rule 8.128(b);

(3) If an agreed statement will be used instead of the clerk's transcript, when the appellant files the agreed statement under rule 8.134(b);

(4) If a settled statement will be used instead of the clerk's transcript, when the statement has been certified by the trial court under rule 8.137(c); or

(5) If any party requested that a record of an administrative proceeding held by the superior court be transmitted to the reviewing court, when that record of that administrative proceeding is ready for transmittal to the reviewing court and any clerk's transcript or other record of the documents from the trial court is complete as provided in (1)–(4).

(Subd (a) adopted effective January 1, 2014.)

(b) Record of the oral proceedings

(1) If the parties are not proceeding by appendix under rule 8.124 and the appellant elected to proceed with a record of the oral proceedings in the trial court, the record is complete when the clerk's transcript or other record of the documents from the trial court is complete as provided in (a) and:

(A) If the appellant elected to use a reporter's transcript, when the certified reporter's transcript is delivered to the court under rule 8.130;

(B) If an agreed statement will be used instead of the reporter's transcript, when the appellant files the agreed statement under rule 8.134(b); or

(C) If a settled statement will be used instead of the reporter's transcript, when the statement has been certified by the trial court under rule 8.137(c).

(2) If the parties are proceeding by appendix under rule 8.124 and the appellant elected to proceed with a record of the oral proceedings in the trial court, the record is complete when the record of the oral proceedings is complete—as provided in (1)(A), (B), or (C)—and the record of any administrative proceeding held by the superior court that a party requested be transmitted to the reviewing court is ready for transmittal to the reviewing court.

(Subd (b) adopted effective January 1, 2014.)

Rule 8.149 adopted effective January 1, 2014.

Rule 8.150. Filing the record

(a) Superior court clerk's duties

When the record is complete, the superior court clerk must promptly send the original to the reviewing court and the copy to the appellant.

(Subd (a) amended effective January 1, 2007.)

(b) Reviewing court clerk's duties

On receiving the record, the reviewing court clerk must promptly file the original and send notice of the filing date to the parties.

(Subd (b) amended effective January 1, 2016; adopted as part of subd (a) effective January 1, 2002; previously amended and lettered as subd (b) effective January 1, 2007.)

Rule 8.150 amended effective January 1, 2016; repealed and adopted as rule 11 effective January 1, 2002; previously amended and renumbered as rule 8.150 effective January 1, 2007.

Advisory Committee Comment

Subdivision (a). Under rule 8.71(c), the superior court clerk may send the record to the reviewing court in electronic form.

Rule 8.153. Lending the record

(a) Request

Within 20 days after the record is filed in the reviewing court, a party that has not purchased its own copy of the record may request another party, in writing, to lend it that party's copy of the record. The other party must then lend its copy of the record when it serves its brief.

(b) Time to return

The borrowing party must return the copy of the record when it serves its brief or the time to file its brief has expired.

(c) Cost

The borrowing party must bear the cost of sending the copy of the record to and from the borrowing party.

Rule 8.153 adopted effective January 1, 2007.

Rule 8.155. Augmenting and correcting the record

(a) Augmentation

(1) At any time, on motion of a party or its own motion, the reviewing court may order the record augmented to include:

(A) Any document filed or lodged in the case in superior court; or

(B) A certified transcript—or agreed or settled statement—of oral proceedings not designated under rule 8.130. Unless the court orders otherwise, the appellant is responsible for the cost of any additional transcript the court may order under this subdivision.

(2) A party must attach to its motion a copy, if available, of any document or transcript that it wants added to the record. The pages of the attachments must be consecutively numbered, beginning with the number one. If the reviewing court grants the motion it may augment the record with the copy.

(3) If the party cannot attach a copy of the matter to be added, the party must identify it as required under rules 8.122 and 8.130.

(Subd (a) amended effective January 1, 2008; previously amended effective January 1, 2007.)

(b) Omissions

(1) If a clerk or reporter omits a required or designated portion of the record, a party may serve and file a notice in superior court specifying the omitted portion and requesting that it be prepared, certified, and sent to the reviewing court. The party must serve a copy of the notice on the reviewing court.

(2) The clerk or reporter must comply with a notice under (1) within 10 days after it is filed. If the clerk or reporter fails to comply, the party may serve and file a motion to augment under (a), attaching a copy of the notice.

(c) Corrections

(1) On motion of a party, on stipulation, or on its own motion, the reviewing court may order the correction or certification of any part of the record.

(2) The reviewing court may order the superior court to settle disputes about omissions or errors in the record.

(d) Notice

The reviewing court clerk must send all parties notice of the receipt and filing of any matter under this rule.

Rule 8.155 amended effective January 1, 2008; repealed and adopted as rule 12 effective January 1, 2002; previously amended and renumbered effective January 1, 2007.

Advisory Committee Comment

Subdivision (a). Subdivision (a)(1) makes it clear that a party may apply for—and the reviewing court may order—augmentation of the record at any time. Whether the motion is made within a reasonable time and is not for the purpose of delay, however, are among the factors the reviewing court may consider in ruling on such a motion.

Rule 8.160. Sealed records [Renumbered]

Rule 8.160 renumbered to rule 8.46 effective January 1, 2010; repealed and adopted as rule 12.5 effective January 1, 2002; previously amended and renumbered as rule 8.160 effective January 1, 2007; previously amended effective July 1, 2002, January 1, 2004, and January 1, 2006.

Rule 8.163. Presumption from the record

The reviewing court will presume that the record in an appeal includes all matters material to deciding the issues raised. If the appeal proceeds without a reporter's transcript, this presumption applies only if the claimed error appears on the face of the record.

Rule 8.163 amended and renumbered effective January 1, 2007; repealed and adopted as rule 52 effective January 1, 2005.

Advisory Committee Comment

The intent of rule 8.163 is explained in the case law. (See, e.g., *Dumas v. Stark* (1961) 56 Cal.2d 673, 674.)

Article 3
Briefs in the Court of Appeal

Rule 8.200. Briefs by parties and amici curiae
Rule 8.204. Contents and format of briefs
Rule 8.208. Certificate of Interested Entities or Persons
Rule 8.212. Service and filing of briefs
Rule 8.216. Appeals in which a party is both appellant and respondent
Rule 8.220. Failure to file a brief
Rule 8.224. Transmitting exhibits

Rule 8.200. Briefs by parties and amici curiae

(a) Parties' briefs

(1) Each appellant must serve and file an appellant's opening brief.

(2) Each respondent must serve and file a respondent's brief.

(3) Each appellant may serve and file a reply brief.

(4) No other brief may be filed except with the permission of the presiding justice, unless it qualifies under (b) or (c)(7).

(5) Instead of filing a brief, or as part of its brief, a party may join in or adopt by reference all or part of a brief in the same or a related appeal.

(Subd (a) amended effective January 1, 2017; previously amended effective January 1, 2003.)

(b) Supplemental briefs after remand or transfer from Supreme Court

(1) Within 15 days after finality of a Supreme Court decision remanding or order transferring a cause to a Court of Appeal for further proceedings, any party may serve and file a supplemental opening brief in the Court of Appeal. Within 15 days after such a brief is filed, any opposing party may serve and file a supplemental responding brief.

(2) Supplemental briefs must be limited to matters arising after the previous Court of Appeal decision in the cause, unless the presiding justice permits briefing on other matters.

(3) Supplemental briefs may not be filed if the previous decision of the Court of Appeal was a denial of a petition for a writ within its original jurisdiction without issuance of an alternative writ or order to show cause.

(Subd (b) adopted effective January 1, 2003.)

(c) Amicus curiae briefs

(1) Within 14 days after the last appellant's reply brief is filed or could have been filed under rule 8.212, whichever is earlier, any person or entity may serve and file an application for permission of the presiding justice to file an amicus curiae brief. For good cause, the presiding justice may allow later filing.

(2) The application must state the applicant's interest and explain how the proposed amicus curiae brief will assist the court in deciding the matter.

(3) The application must also identify:

(A) Any party or any counsel for a party in the pending appeal who:

(i) Authored the proposed amicus brief in whole or in part; or

(ii) Made a monetary contribution intended to fund the preparation or submission of the brief; and

(B) Every person or entity who made a monetary contribution intended to fund the preparation or submission of the brief, other than the amicus curiae, its members, or its counsel in the pending appeal.

(4) The proposed brief must be served and must accompany the application, and may be combined with it.

(5) The covers of the application and proposed brief must identify the party the applicant supports, if any.

(6) If the court grants the application, any party may file an answer within the time the court specifies. The answer must be served on all parties and the amicus curiae.

(7) The Attorney General may file an amicus curiae brief without the presiding justice's permission, unless the brief is submitted on behalf of another state officer or agency. The Attorney General must serve and file the brief within 14 days after the last appellant's reply brief is filed or could have been filed under rule 8.212, whichever is earlier, and must provide the information required by (2) and comply with (5). Any party may serve and file an answer within 14 days after the brief is filed.

(Subd (c) amended effective January 1, 2009; adopted as subd (b) effective January 1, 2002; previously relettered effective January 1, 2003; previously amended effective January 1, 2007, and January 1, 2008.)

Rule 8.200 amended effective January 1, 2017; repealed and adopted as rule 13 effective January 1, 2002; previously amended and renumbered effective January 1, 2007; previously amended effective January 1, 2003, January 1, 2008, and January 1, 2009.

Advisory Committee Comment

Subdivision (a)(2). A respondent, other than a respondent who has filed a notice of cross-appeal, who files a respondent's brief may be required to pay a filing fee under Government Code sections 68926 if the respondent's brief is the first document filed in the appellate proceeding in the Court of Appeal by that party. See rule 8.25(c).

Subdivision (b). After the Supreme Court remands or transfers a cause to the Court of Appeal for further proceedings (i.e., under rules 8.528(c)–(e) or 10.1000(a)(1)(B)), the parties are permitted to file supplemental briefs. The first 15-day briefing period begins on the day of *finality* (under rule 8.532) of the Supreme Court decision remanding or order transferring the cause to the Court of Appeal. The rule specifies that "any party" may file a supplemental opening brief, and if such a brief is filed, "any opposing party" may file a supplemental responding brief. In this context the phrase "any party" is intended to mean any *or all* parties. Such a decision or order of transfer to the Court of Appeal thus triggers, first, a 15-day period in which any or all parties may file supplemental opening briefs and, second—if any party files such a brief—an additional 15-day period in which any opposing party may file a supplemental responding brief.

Subdivision (c)(1). The time within which a reply brief "could have been filed under rule 8.212" includes any authorized extension of the deadline specified in rule 8.212.

Rule 8.204. Contents and format of briefs

(a) Contents

(1) Each brief must:

(A) Begin with a table of contents and a table of authorities separately listing cases, constitutions, statutes, court rules, and other authorities cited;

(B) State each point under a separate heading or subheading summarizing the point, and support each point by argument and, if possible, by citation of authority; and

(C) Support any reference to a matter in the record by a citation to the volume and page number of the record where the matter appears. If any part of the record is submitted in an electronic form, citations to that part must identify, with the same specificity required for the printed record, the place in the record where the matter appears.

(2) An appellant's opening brief must:

(A) State the nature of the action, the relief sought in the trial court, and the judgment or order appealed from;

(B) State that the judgment appealed from is final, or explain why the order appealed from is appealable; and

(C) Provide a summary of the significant facts limited to matters in the record.

(Subd (a) amended effective January 1, 2024; previously amended effective January 1, 2006.)

(b) Format of briefs filed in paper form

(1) A brief may be reproduced by any process that produces a clear, black image of letter quality. All documents filed must have a page size of 8½ by 11 inches. If filed in paper form, the paper must be white or unbleached and of at least 20-pound weight.

(2) Any conventional font may be used. The font may be either proportionally spaced or monospaced.

(3) The font style must be roman; but for emphasis, italics or boldface may be used or the text may be underscored. Case names must be italicized or underscored. Headings may be in uppercase letters.

(4) Except as provided in (11), the font size, including footnotes, must not be smaller than 13-point, and both sides of the paper may be used.

(5) The lines of text must be unnumbered and at least one-and-a-half-spaced. Headings and footnotes may be single-spaced. Quotations may be block-indented and single-spaced. Single-spaced means six lines to a vertical inch.

(6) The margins must be at least 1½ inches on the left and right and 1 inch on the top and bottom.

(7) The pages must be consecutively numbered. The page numbering must begin with the cover page as page 1 and use only Arabic numerals (e.g., 1, 2, 3). The page number may be suppressed and need not appear on the cover page.

(8) If filed in paper form, the brief must be filed unbound unless otherwise provided by local rule or court order.

(9) The brief need not be signed.

(10) If filed in paper form, the cover must be in the color prescribed by rule 8.40(a). In addition to providing the cover information required by rule 8.40(b), the cover must state:

(A) The title of the brief;

(B) The title, trial court number, and Court of Appeal number of the case;

(C) The names of the trial court and each participating trial judge; and

(D) The name of the party that each attorney on the brief represents.

(11) If the brief is produced on a typewriter:

(A) A typewritten original and carbon copies may be filed only with the presiding justice's permission, which will ordinarily be given only to unrepresented parties proceeding in forma pauperis. All other typewritten briefs must be filed as photocopies.

(B) Both sides of the paper may be used if a photocopy is filed; only one side may be used if a typewritten original and carbon copies are filed.

(C) The type size, including footnotes, must not be smaller than standard pica, 10 characters per inch. Unrepresented incarcerated litigants may use elite type, 12 characters per inch, if they lack access to a typewriter with larger characters.

(Subd (b) amended effective January 1, 2020; previously amended effective January 1, 2004, July 1, 2004, January 1, 2006, January 1, 2007, January 1, 2013, January 1, 2014, January 1, 2016, and January 1, 2017.)

(c) Length

(1) Except as provided in (5), a brief produced on a computer must not exceed 14,000 words, including footnotes. Such a brief must include a certificate by appellate counsel or an unrepresented party stating the number of words in the brief. The person certifying may rely on the word count of the computer program used to prepare the brief.

(2) Except as provided in (5), a brief produced on a typewriter must not exceed 50 pages.

(3) The tables required under (a)(1), the cover information required under (b)(10), the Certificate of Interested Entities or Persons required under rule 8.208, a certificate under (1), any signature block, and any attachment under (d) are excluded from the limits stated in (1) or (2).

(4) A combined brief in an appeal governed by rule 8.216 must not exceed double the limits stated in (1) or (2).

(5) A petition for rehearing or an answer to a petition for rehearing produced on a computer must not exceed 7,000 words, including footnotes. A petition or answer produced on a typewriter must not exceed 25 pages.

(6) On application, the presiding justice may permit a longer brief for good cause.

(Subd (c) amended effective January 1, 2020; previously amended effective January 1, 2007, and January 1, 2011.)

(d) Attachments to briefs

A party filing a brief may attach copies of exhibits or other materials in the appellate record or copies of relevant local, state, or federal regulations or rules, out-of-state statutes, or other similar citable materials that are not readily accessible. These attachments must not exceed a combined total of 10 pages, but on application the presiding justice may permit additional pages of attachments for good cause. A copy of an opinion required to be attached to the brief under rule 8.1115(c) does not count toward this 10-page limit.

(Subd (d) amended effective January 1, 2007.)

(e) Noncomplying briefs

If a brief does not comply with this rule:

(1) The reviewing court clerk may decline to file it, but must mark it "received but not filed" and return it to the party; or

(2) If the brief is filed, the reviewing court may, on its own or a party's motion, with or without notice:

(A) Order the brief returned for corrections and refiling within a specified time;

(B) Strike the brief with leave to file a new brief within a specified time; or

(C) Disregard the noncompliance.

(Subd (e) amended effective January 1, 2006.)

Rule 8.204 amended effective January 1, 2024; repealed and adopted as rule 14 effective January 1, 2002; previously amended and renumbered as rule 8.204 effective January 1, 2007; previously amended effective January 1, 2004, July 1, 2004, January 1, 2006, January 1, 2011, January 1, 2013, January 1, 2014, January 1, 2016, January 1, 2017, and January 1, 2020.

Advisory Committee Comment

Subdivision (b). The first sentence of subdivision (b)(1) confirms that any method of reproduction is acceptable provided it results in a clear black image of letter quality. The provision is derived from subdivision (a)(1) of rule 32 of the Federal Rules of Appellate Procedure (28 U.S.C.) (FRAP 32).

Paragraphs (2), (3), and (4) of subdivision (b) state requirements of *font, font style*, and *font size* (see also subd. (b)(11)(C)).

Subdivision (b)(2) allows the use of any conventional font—e.g., Times New Roman, Courier, Arial, Helvetica, etc.—and permits the font to be either proportionally spaced or monospaced.

Subdivision (b)(3) requires the font style to be roman, but permits the use of italics, boldface, or underscoring for emphasis; it also requires case names to be italicized or underscored. These provisions are derived from FRAP 32(a)(6).

Subdivision (b)(5) allows headings to be single-spaced; it is derived from FRAP 32(a)(4). The provision also permits quotations of any length to be block-indented and single-spaced at the discretion of the brief writer.

See also rule 1.200 concerning the format of citations. Brief writers are encouraged to follow the citation form of the *California Style Manual* (4th ed., 2000).

Subdivision (c). Subdivision (c) governs the maximum permissible length of a brief. It is derived from the federal procedure of measuring the length of a brief produced on a computer by the number of words in the brief. (FRAP 32(a)(7).) Subdivision (c)(1), like FRAP 32(a)(7)(B)(i), imposes a limit of 14,000 words if the brief is produced on a computer. Subdivision (c)(1) implements this provision by requiring the writer of a brief produced on a computer to include a certificate stating the number of words in the brief, but allows the writer to rely on the word count of the computer program used to prepare the brief. This requirement, too, is adapted from the federal rule. (FRAP 32(a)(7)(C).) For purposes of this rule, a "brief produced on a computer" includes a commercially printed brief.

Subdivision (c)(3) specifies certain items that are not counted toward the maximum brief length. Signature blocks, as referenced in this provision, include not only the signatures, but also the printed names, titles, and affiliations of any attorneys filing or joining in the brief, which may accompany the signature.

Subdivision (c)(5) clarifies that a party seeking permission to exceed the page or word limits stated in subdivision (c)(1) and (2) must proceed by application under rule 8.50 rather than by motion under rule 8.54, and must show good cause.

Subdivision (d). Subdivision (d) permits a party filing a brief to attach copies of exhibits or other materials, provided they are part of the record on appeal and do not exceed a total of 10 pages. If the brief writer attaches, under rule 8.1115(c), a copy of an unpublished opinion or an opinion available only in computerized form, that opinion does not count toward the 10-page limit stated in rule 8.204(d).

Subdivision (e). Subdivision (e) states the consequences of submitting briefs that do not comply with this rule: (e)(1) recognizes the power of the reviewing court clerk to decline to file such a brief, and (e)(2) recognizes steps the reviewing court may take to obtain a brief that does comply with the rule. Subdivision (e)(2) does not purport to limit the inherent power of the reviewing court to fashion other sanctions for such noncompliance.

Rule 8.208. Certificate of Interested Entities or Persons

(a) Purpose and intent

The California Code of Judicial Ethics states the circumstances under which an appellate justice must disqualify himself or herself from a proceeding. The purpose of this rule is to provide justices of the Courts of Appeal with additional information to help them determine whether to disqualify themselves from a proceeding.

(b) Application

This rule applies in appeals in civil cases other than family, juvenile, guardianship, and conservatorship cases.

(Subd (b) adopted effective January 1, 2008.)

(c) Definitions

For purposes of this rule:

(1) "Certificate" means a Certificate of Interested Entities or Persons signed by appellate counsel or an unrepresented party.

(2) "Entity" means a corporation, a partnership, a firm, or any other association, but does not include a governmental entity or its agencies or a natural person.

(Subd (c) relettered effective January 1, 2008; adopted as subd (b) effective July 1, 2006.)

(d) Serving and filing a certificate

(1) Except as otherwise provided in this rule, if a party files a motion, an application, or an opposition to such motion or application in the Court of Appeal before filing its principal brief, the party must serve and file its certificate at the time it files the first such motion, application, or opposition and must include a copy of this certificate in the party's principal brief. If no motion, application, or opposition to such motion or application is filed before the parties file their principal briefs, each party must include its certificate in its principal brief. The certificate must appear after the cover and before the tables.

(2) If the identity of any party or any entity or person subject to disclosure under this rule has not been publicly disclosed in the proceedings and a party wants to keep that identity confidential, the party may serve and file an application for permission to file its certificate under seal separately from its principal brief, motion, application, or opposition. If the application is granted, the party must file the certificate under seal and without service within 10 days of the court's order granting the application.

(3) If a party fails to file a certificate as required under (1), the clerk must notify the party in writing that the party must file the certificate within 15 days after the clerk's notice is sent and that if the party fails to comply, the court may impose one of the following sanctions:

(A) If the party is the appellant, the court may strike the document or dismiss the appeal; or

(B) If the party is the respondent, the court may strike the document or decide the appeal on the record, the opening brief, and any oral argument by the appellant.

(4) If the party fails to file the certificate as specified in the notice under (2), the court may impose the sanctions specified in the notice.

(Subd (d) amended effective January 1, 2016; adopted as subd (c) effective July 1, 2006; previously amended and relettered effective January 1, 2008; previously amended effective January 1, 2009.)

(e) Contents of certificate

(1) If an entity is a party, that party's certificate must list any other entity or person that the party knows has an ownership interest of 10 percent or more in the party.

(2) If a party knows of any person or entity, other than the parties themselves, that has a financial or other interest in the outcome of the proceeding that the party reasonably believes the justices should consider in determining whether to disqualify themselves under canon 3E of the Code of Judicial Ethics, the party's certificate must list that entity or person and identify the nature of the interest of the person or entity. For purposes of this subdivision:

(A) A mutual or common investment fund's ownership of securities or bonds issued by an entity does not constitute a financial interest in that entity.

(B) An interest in the outcome of the proceeding does not arise solely because the entity or person is in the same industry, field of business, or regulatory category as a party and the case might establish a precedent that would affect that industry, field of business, or regulatory category.

(C) A party's insurer does not have a financial interest in the outcome of the proceeding solely on the basis of its status as insurer for that party.

(3) If the party knows of no entity or person that must be listed under (1) or (2), the party must so state in the certificate.

(Subd (e) amended effective January 1, 2009; adopted as subd (d) effective July 1, 2006; previously amended effective January 1, 2007; previously relettered effective January 1, 2008.)

(f) Supplemental information

A party that learns of changed or additional information that must be disclosed under (e) must promptly serve and file a supplemental certificate in the reviewing court.

(Subd (f) amended and relettered effective January 1, 2008; adopted as subd (e) effective July 1, 2006.)

Rule 8.208 amended effective January 1, 2016; adopted as rule 14.5 effective July 1, 2006; previously amended and renumbered as rule 8.208 effective January 1, 2007; previously amended effective January 1, 2008, and January 1, 2009.

Advisory Committee Comment

The Judicial Council has adopted an optional form, *Certificate of Interested Entities or Persons* (form APP-008), that can be used to file the certificate required by this rule.

Subdivision (e). This subdivision requires a party to list on its certificate entities or persons that the party *knows* have specified interests. This subdivision does not impose a duty on a party to gather information not already known by that party.

Rule 8.212. Service and filing of briefs

(a) Time to file

(1) An appellant must serve and file its opening brief within:

(A) 40 days after the record—or the reporter's transcript, after a rule 8.124 election—is filed in the reviewing court; or

(B) 70 days after the filing of a rule 8.124 election, if the appeal proceeds without a reporter's transcript.

(2) A respondent must serve and file its brief within 30 days after the appellant files its opening brief.

(3) An appellant must serve and file its reply brief, if any, within 20 days after the respondent files its brief.

(Subd (a) amended effective January 1, 2010; previously amended effective January 1, 2007.)

(b) Extensions of time

(1) Except as otherwise provided by statute or when the time to file the brief has previously been extended under (3) or rule 8.220(d), the parties may extend each period under (a) by up to 60 days by filing one or more stipulations in the reviewing court before the brief is due. Stipulations must be signed by and served on all parties.

(2) A stipulation under (1) is effective on filing. The reviewing court may not shorten a stipulated extension.

(3) Before the brief is due, a party may apply to the presiding justice for an extension of each period under (a), or under rule 8.200(c)(6) or (7), on a showing that there is good cause and that:

(A) The applicant was unable to obtain—or it would have been futile to seek—the extension by stipulation; or

(B) The parties have stipulated to the maximum extension permitted under (1) and the applicant seeks a further extension.

(4) A party need not apply for an extension or relief from default if it can file its brief within the time prescribed by rule 8.220(a). The clerk must file a brief submitted within that time if it otherwise complies with these rules.

(Subd (b) amended effective January 1, 2015; previously amended effective January 1, 2003, July 1, 2005, January 1, 2007, January 1, 2010, January 1, 2011, January 1, 2013, and January 1, 2014.)

(c) Service

(1) One copy of each brief must be served on the superior court clerk for delivery to the trial judge.

(2) If a brief is not filed electronically under rules 8.70–8.79, one electronic copy of each brief must be submitted to the Court of Appeal. For purposes of this requirement, the term "brief" does not include a petition for rehearing or an answer thereto.

(A) The copy must be a single computer file in text-searchable Portable Document Format (PDF), and it must exactly duplicate the appearance of the paper copy, including the order and pagination of all of the brief's components. By electronically submitting the copy, the filer certifies that the copy complies with these requirements and that all reasonable steps have been taken to ensure that the copy does not contain computer code, including viruses, that might be harmful to the court's system for receipt of electronic copies or to other users of that system.

(B) If the brief discloses material contained in a sealed or conditionally sealed record, the party serving the brief must comply with rule 8.46(f) and include as the first page in the PDF document a cover sheet that contains the information required by rule 8.204(b)(10).

(C) If it would cause undue hardship for the party filing the brief to submit an electronic copy of the brief to the Court of Appeal, the party may instead serve four paper copies of the brief on the Supreme Court. If the brief discloses material contained in a sealed or conditionally sealed record, the party serving the brief must comply with rule 8.46(f) and attach a cover sheet that contains the information required by rule 8.204(b)(10). The clerk/executive officer of the Court of Appeal must promptly notify the Supreme Court of any court order unsealing the brief. In the absence of such notice, the clerk/executive officer of the Supreme Court must keep all copies of the unredacted brief under seal.

(3) One copy of each brief must be served on a public officer or agency when required by rule 8.29.

(Subd (c) amended effective January 1, 2018; previously amended effective January 1, 2004, January 1, 2005, January 1, 2007, January 1, 2008, January 1, 2013, January 1, 2014, and January 1, 2015.)

Rule 8.212 amended effective January 1, 2018; repealed and adopted as rule 15 effective January 1, 2002; previously amended and renumbered effective January 1, 2007; previously amended effective January 1, 2003, January 1, 2004, January 1, 2005, July 1, 2005, January 1, 2008, January 1, 2010, January 1, 2011, January 1, 2013, January 1, 2014, and January 1, 2015.

Advisory Committee Comment

Subdivision (a). Note that the sequence and timing of briefing in appeals in which a party is both appellant and respondent (cross-appeals) are governed by rule 8.216. Typically, a cross-appellant's combined respondent's brief and opening brief must be filed within the time specified in (a)(2) for the respondent's brief.

Subdivision (b). Extensions of briefing time are limited by statute in some cases. For example, under Public Resources Code section 21167.6(h) in cases under section 21167, extensions are limited to one 30-day extension for the opening brief and one 30-day extension for "preparation of responding brief."

Under rule 8.42, the original signature of only one party is required on the stipulation filed with the court; the signatures of the other parties may be in the form of copies of the signed signature page of the document. Signatures on electronically filed documents are subject to the requirements of rule 8.77.

Subdivision (b)(2) clarifies that a party seeking an extension of time from the presiding justice must proceed by application under rule 8.50 rather than by motion under rule 8.54.

Subdivision (c). In subdivision (c)(2) the word "brief" means only (1) an appellant's opening brief, (2) a respondent's brief, (3) an appellant's reply brief, (4) an amicus curiae brief, or (5) an answer thereto. It follows that no other documents or papers filed in the Court of Appeal, whatever their nature, should be served on the Supreme Court. Further, only briefs filed in the Court of Appeal "in a civil appeal" must be served on the Supreme Court. It follows that no briefs filed in the Court of Appeal in criminal appeals or in original proceedings should be served on the Supreme Court.

Information about electronic submission of copies of briefs to the Court of Appeal can be found on the web page for the Court of Appeal district in which the brief is being filed on the California Courts website at *www.courts.ca.gov/ courtsofappeal*.

Examples of "undue hardship" under (2)(C) include but are not limited to when a party does not have access to a computer or the software necessary to prepare an electronic copy of a brief or does not have e-mail access to electronically submit a brief to the Court of Appeal.

Rule 8.216. Appeals in which a party is both appellant and respondent

(a) Briefing sequence and time to file briefs

In an appeal in which any party is both an appellant and a respondent:

(1) The parties must jointly—or separately if unable to agree—submit a proposed briefing sequence to the reviewing court within 20 days after the second notice of appeal is filed.

(2) After receiving the proposal, the reviewing court must order a briefing sequence and prescribe briefing periods consistent with rule 8.212(a).

(3) Extensions of time are governed by rule 8.212(b).

(Subd (a) amended effective January 1, 2007.)

(b) Contents of briefs

(1) A party that is both an appellant and a respondent must combine its respondent's brief with its appellant's opening brief or its reply brief, if any, whichever is appropriate under the briefing sequence that the reviewing court orders.

(2) A combined brief must address the points raised in each appeal separately but may include a single summary of the significant facts.

(3) A party must confine a reply brief, or the reply portion of a combined brief, to points raised in its appeal.

(Subd (b) amended effective January 1, 2009; previously amended effective January 1, 2007.)

Rule 8.216 amended effective January 1, 2009; repealed and adopted as rule 16 effective January 1, 2002; previously amended and renumbered effective January 1, 2007.

Advisory Committee Comment

Rule 8.216 applies, first, to all cases in which opposing parties both appeal from the judgment. In addition, it applies to all cases in which one party appeals from the judgment and another party appeals from any appealable order arising from or related to the judgment, i.e., not only orders contemplated by rule 8.108 (denying a motion for judgment notwithstanding the verdict) but also, for example, posttrial orders granting or denying attorney fees. The purpose of the rule is to provide, in all such appeals, a single unified procedure for resolving uncertainties as to the order in which the parties must file their briefs.

As used in this rule, "appellant" includes cross-appellant and "respondent" includes cross-respondent. (Compare rule 8.100(e).)

Subdivision (a). Subdivision (a) implements the above-stated purpose by providing a procedure for determining both the briefing *sequence*—i.e., the order in which the parties must file their briefs—and the briefing *periods*—i.e., the periods of time (e.g., 30 days or 70 days, etc.) within which the briefs must be filed. Subdivision (a)(1) places the burden on the parties in the first instance to propose a briefing sequence, jointly if possible but separately if not. The purpose of this requirement is to assist the reviewing court by giving it the benefit of the parties' views on what is the most efficient briefing sequence in the circumstances of the case. Subdivision (a)(2) then prescribes the role of the reviewing court: after considering the parties' proposal, the court will decide on the briefing sequence, prescribe the briefing periods, and notify the parties of both. The reviewing court, of course, may thereafter modify its order just as it may do in a single-appeal case. Extensions of time are governed by rule 8.212(b).

Subdivision (b). The purpose of subdivision (b)(3) is to ensure that in its reply brief a party addresses only issues germane to its own appeal. For example, a cross-appellant may not use its *cross-appellant's* reply brief to answer points raised in the *appellant's* reply brief.

Rule 8.220. Failure to file a brief

(a) Notice to file

If a party fails to timely file an appellant's opening brief or a respondent's brief, the reviewing court clerk must promptly notify the party in writing that the brief must be filed within 15 days after the notice is sent and that if the party fails to comply, the court may impose one of the following sanctions:

(1) If the brief is an appellant's opening brief, the court may dismiss the appeal;

(2) If the brief is a respondent's brief, the court may decide the appeal on the record, the opening brief, and any oral argument by the appellant.

(Subd (a) amended effective January 1, 2016; previously amended effective January 1, 2007, and January 1, 2008.)

(b) Combined brief

A party that is both an appellant and a respondent under rule 8.216 may file its combined respondent's brief and appellant's reply brief within the period specified in the notice under (a).

(Subd (b) amended effective January 1, 2007.)

(c) Sanction

If a party fails to file the brief as specified in a notice under (a), the court may impose the sanction specified in the notice.

(Subd (c) amended effective January 1, 2008.)

(d) Extension of time

Within the period specified in the notice under (a), a party may apply to the presiding justice for an extension of that period for good cause. If the extension is granted and the brief is not filed within the extended period, the court may impose the sanction under (c) without further notice.

Rule 8.220 amended effective January 1, 2016; repealed and adopted as rule 17 effective January 1, 2002; previously amended and renumbered as rule 8.220 effective January 1, 2007; previously amended effective January 1, 2008.

Advisory Committee Comment

Subdivision (a). Subdivision (a) applies to all appellant's opening briefs and respondent's briefs, but does not apply to reply briefs.

A brief is "timely" under subdivision (a) if it is filed within the normal rule time prescribed for that brief or any extension of that time.

A party that fails to timely file a required brief need not make a formal motion to permit a late filing (e.g., under rule 8.60(d)); it is sufficient to file the brief within the 15-day grace period specified in the notice under subdivision (a).

Subdivision (d). Subdivision (d) clarifies that a party seeking an extension of time from the presiding justice must proceed by application under rule 8.50 rather than by motion under rule 8.54. In conformity with current practice, the subdivision also clarifies that if a brief is not filed within an extension granted by the court, the court may impose sanctions without further notice.

Rule 8.224. Transmitting exhibits

(a) Notice of designation

(1) Within 10 days after the last respondent's brief is filed or could be filed under rule 8.220, a party wanting the reviewing court to consider any original exhibits that were admitted in evidence, refused, or lodged but that were not copied in the clerk's transcript under rule 8.122 or the appendix under rule 8.124 must serve and file a notice in superior court designating such exhibits.

(2) Within 10 days after a notice under (1) is served, any other party wanting the reviewing court to consider additional exhibits must serve and file a notice in superior court designating such exhibits.

(3) A party filing a notice under (1) or (2) must serve a copy on the reviewing court.

(Subd (a) amended effective January 1, 2008; previously amended effective January 1, 2007.)

(b) Transmittal

Unless the reviewing court orders otherwise, within 20 days after the first notice under (a) is filed:

(1) The superior court clerk must put any designated exhibits in the clerk's possession into numerical or alphabetical order and send them to the reviewing court. The superior court clerk must also send a list of the exhibits sent. If the exhibits are not transmitted electronically, the superior court clerk must send two copies of the list. If the reviewing court clerk finds the list correct, the clerk must sign and return a copy to the superior court clerk.

(2) Any party in possession of designated exhibits returned by the superior court must put them into numerical or alphabetical order and send them to the reviewing court. The party must also send a list of the exhibits sent. If the exhibits are not transmitted electronically, the party must send two copies of the list. If the reviewing court clerk finds the list correct, the clerk must sign and return a copy to the party.

(Subd (b) amended effective January 1, 2016.)

(c) Application for later transmittal

After the periods specified in (a) have expired, a party may apply to the reviewing court for permission to send an exhibit to that court.

(d) Request and return by reviewing court

At any time the reviewing court may direct the superior court or a party to send it an exhibit. On request, the reviewing court may return an exhibit to the superior court or to the party that sent it. When the remittitur issues, the reviewing court must return all exhibits not transmitted electronically to the superior court or to the party that sent them.

(Subd (d) amended effective January 1, 2016.)

Rule 8.224 amended effective January 1, 2016; repealed and adopted as rule 18 effective January 1, 2002; previously amended and renumbered as rule 8.224 effective January 1, 2007; previously amended effective January 1, 2008.

Advisory Committee Comment

Subdivision (b). Subdivision (b)(2) provides a procedure by which parties send designated exhibits directly to the reviewing court in cases in which the superior court has returned the exhibits to the parties under Code of Civil Procedure section 1952 or other provision. (See also rule 8.122(a)(3).)

Subdivision (c). Subdivision (c) addresses the case in which a party's need to designate a certain exhibit does not arise until after the period specified in subdivision (a) has expired—for example, when the appellant makes a point in its reply brief that the respondent reasonably believes justifies the reviewing court's consideration of an exhibit it had not previously designated. In that event, the subdivision authorizes the party to apply to the reviewing court for permission to send the exhibit on a showing of good cause.

Article 4
Hearing and Decision in the Court of Appeal

Rule 8.240. Calendar preference
Rule 8.244. Settlement, abandonment, voluntary dismissal, and compromise
Rule 8.248. Prehearing conference
Rule 8.252. Judicial notice; findings and evidence on appeal
Rule 8.254. New Authorities
Rule 8.256. Oral argument and submission of the cause
Rule 8.260. Opinions [Reserved]
Rule 8.264. Filing, finality, and modification of decision
Rule 8.268. Rehearing
Rule 8.272. Remittitur
Rule 8.276. Sanctions
Rule 8.278. Costs on appeal

Rule 8.240. Calendar preference

A party seeking calendar preference must promptly serve and file a motion for preference in the reviewing court. As used in this rule, "calendar preference" means an expedited appeal schedule, which may include expedited briefing and preference in setting the date of oral argument.

Rule 8.240 amended and renumbered effective January 1, 2007; repealed and adopted as rule 19 effective January 1, 2003.

Advisory Committee Comment

Rule 8.240 requires a party claiming preference to file a motion for preference in the reviewing court. The motion requirement relieves the reviewing court of the burden of searching the record to determine if preference should be ordered. The requirement is not intended to bar the court from ordering preference without a motion when the ground is apparent on the face of the appeal, e.g., in appeals from judgments of dependency (Welf. & Inst. Code, §395).

The rule is broad in scope: it includes motions for preference on the grounds (1) that a statute provides for preference in the reviewing court (e.g., Code Civ. Proc., §§44 [probate proceedings, contested elections, libel by public official], 45 [judgment freeing minor from parental custody]); (2) that the reviewing court should exercise its discretion to grant preference when a statute provides for trial preference (e.g., *id.*, §§35 [certain election matters], 36 [party over 70 and in poor health; party with terminal illness; minor in wrongful death action]; see *Warren v. Schecter* (1997) 57 Cal.App.4th 1189, 1198–1199); and (3) that the reviewing court should exercise its discretion to grant preference on a nonstatutory ground (e.g., economic hardship).

Because valid grounds for preference could arise after the filing of the reply brief, e.g., a diagnosis of terminal illness, the rule requires the motion to be filed "promptly," i.e., as soon as the ground for preference arises.

Rule 8.244. Settlement, abandonment, voluntary dismissal, and compromise

(a) Notice of settlement

(1) If a civil case settles after a notice of appeal has been filed either as a whole or as to any party, the appellant who has settled must immediately serve and file a notice of settlement in the Court of Appeal. If the parties have designated a clerk's or a reporter's transcript and the record has not been filed in the Court of Appeal, the appellant must also immediately serve a copy of the notice on the superior court clerk.

(2) If the case settles after the appellant receives a notice setting oral argument or a prehearing conference, the appellant must also immediately notify the Court of Appeal of the settlement by telephone or other expeditious method.

(3) Within 45 days after filing a notice of settlement—unless the court has ordered a longer time period on a showing of good cause—the appellant who filed the notice of settlement must file either an abandonment under (b), if the record has not yet been filed in the Court of Appeal, or a request to dismiss under (c), if the record has already been filed in the Court of Appeal.

(4) If the appellant does not file an abandonment, a request to dismiss, or a letter stating good cause why the appeal should not be dismissed within the time period specified under (3), the court may dismiss the appeal as to that appellant and order each side to bear its own costs on appeal.

(5) This subdivision does not apply to settlements requiring findings to be made by the Court of Appeal under Code of Civil Procedure section 128(a)(8).

(Subd (a) amended effective January 1, 2007; previously amended effective January 1, 2006.)

(b) Abandonment

(1) Before the record is filed in the Court of Appeal, the appellant may serve and file in superior court an abandonment of the appeal or a stipulation to abandon the appeal. The filing effects a dismissal of the appeal and restores the superior court's jurisdiction.

(2) The superior court clerk must promptly notify the Court of Appeal and the parties of the abandonment or stipulation.

(c) Request to dismiss

(1) After the record is filed in the Court of Appeal, the appellant may serve and file in that court a request or a stipulation to dismiss the appeal.

(2) On receipt of a request or stipulation to dismiss, the court may dismiss the appeal and direct immediate issuance of the remittitur.

(d) Approval of compromise

If a guardian or conservator seeks approval of a proposed compromise of a pending appeal, the Court of Appeal may, before ruling on the compromise, direct the trial court to determine whether the compromise is in the minor's or the conservatee's best interests and to report its findings.

Rule 8.244 amended and renumbered effective January 1, 2007; repealed and adopted as rule 20 effective January 1, 2003; previously amended effective January 1, 2006.

Rule 8.248. Prehearing conference

(a) Statement and conference

After the notice of appeal is filed in a civil case, the presiding justice may:

(1) Order one or more parties to serve and file a concise statement describing the nature of the case and the issues presented; and

(2) Order all necessary persons to attend a conference to consider case management issues, settlement, and other relevant matters.

(Subd (a) amended effective January 1, 2016; previously amended effective January 1, 2007.)

(b) Agreement

An agreement reached in a conference must be signed by the parties and filed. Unless the Court of Appeal orders otherwise, the agreement governs the appeal.

(c) Proceedings after conference

(1) Unless allowed by a filed agreement, no matter recited in a statement under (a)(1) or discussed in a conference under (a)(2) may be considered in any subsequent proceeding in the appeal other than in another conference.

(2) If settlement is addressed at the conference, other than an inquiry solely about the parties' interest in settlement, neither the presiding officer nor any court personnel present at the conference may participate in or influence the determination of the appeal.

(Subd (c) amended effective January 1, 2016.)

(d) Time to file brief

The time to file a party's brief under rule 8.212(a) is tolled from the date the Court of Appeal sends notice of the conference until the date it sends notice that the conference is concluded.

(Subd (d) amended effective January 1, 2016; previously amended effective January 1, 2007.)

Rule 8.248 amended effective January 1, 2016; repealed and adopted as rule 21 effective January 1, 2003; previously amended and renumbered as rule 8.248 effective January 1, 2007.

Advisory Committee Comment

Subdivision (a). Subdivision (a)(1) requires each party to *serve* any statement it files. (Cf. rule 3.1380(c) [pretrial settlement conference statement must be served on each party].) The service requirement is not intended to prohibit the presiding justice from ordering the parties to submit additional, confidential material in appropriate cases.

Subdivision (d). If a prehearing conference is ordered before the due date of the appellant's opening brief, the time to file the brief is not *extended* but *tolled*, in order to avoid unwarranted lengthening of the briefing process. For example, if the conference is ordered 15 days after the start of the normal 30-day briefing period, the rule simply *suspends* the running of that period; when the period resumes, the party will not receive an automatic extension of a full 30 days but rather the remaining 15 days of the original briefing period, unless the period is otherwise extended.

Under subdivision (d) the tolling period continues "until the date [the Court of Appeal] sends notice that the conference is *concluded*" (italics added). This provision is intended to accommodate the possibility that the conference may not conclude on the date it begins.

Whether or not the conference concludes on the date it begins, subdivision (d) requires the clerk/executive officer of the Court of Appeal to send the parties a notice that the conference is concluded. This provision is intended to facilitate the calculation of the new briefing due dates.

Rule 8.252. Judicial notice; findings and evidence on appeal

(a) Judicial notice

(1) To obtain judicial notice by a reviewing court under Evidence Code section 459, a party must serve and file a separate motion with a proposed order.

(2) The motion must state:

(A) Why the matter to be noticed is relevant to the appeal;

(B) Whether the matter to be noticed was presented to the trial court and, if so, whether judicial notice was taken by that court;

(C) If judicial notice of the matter was not taken by the trial court, why the matter is subject to judicial notice under Evidence Code section 451, 452, or 453; and

(D) Whether the matter to be noticed relates to proceedings occurring after the order or judgment that is the subject of the appeal.

(3) If the matter to be noticed is not in the record, the party must attach to the motion a copy of the matter to be noticed or an explanation of why it is not practicable to do so. The motion with attachments must comply with rule 8.74 if filed in electronic form.

(Subd (a) amended effective January 1, 2020; previously amended effective January 1, 2009, January 1, 2013, and January 1, 2015.)

(b) Findings on appeal

A party may move that the reviewing court make findings under Code of Civil Procedure section 909. The motion must include proposed findings.

(c) Evidence on appeal

(1) A party may move that the reviewing court take evidence.

(2) An order granting the motion must:

(A) State the issues on which evidence will be taken;

(B) Specify whether the court, a justice, or a special master or referee will take the evidence; and

(C) Give notice of the time and place for taking the evidence.

(3) For documentary evidence, a party may offer an electronic copy, or if filed in paper form, the original, a certified copy, or a photocopy. The court may admit the document in evidence without a hearing.

(Subd (c) amended effective January 1, 2020; previously amended effective January 1, 2007, and January 1, 2016.)

Rule 8.252 amended effective January 1, 2020; repealed and adopted as rule 22 effective January 1, 2003; previously amended and renumbered as rule 8.252 effective January 1, 2007; previously amended effective January 1, 2009, January 1, 2013, January 1, 2015, and January 1, 2016.

Advisory Committee Comment

Subdivisions (b) and (c). Although appellate courts are authorized to take evidence and make findings of fact on appeal by Code of Civil Procedure section 909 and this rule, this authority should be exercised sparingly. (See *In re Zeth S.* (2003) 31 Cal.4th 396.)

Rule 8.254. New Authorities

(a) Letter to court

If a party learns of significant new authority, including new legislation, that was not available in time to be included in the last brief that the party filed or could have filed, the party may inform the Court of Appeal of this authority by letter.

(Subd (a) adopted effective July 1, 2012.)

(b) Form and content

The letter may provide only a citation to the new authority and identify, by citation to a page or pages in a brief on file, the issue on appeal to which the new authority is relevant. No argument or other discussion of the authority is permitted in the letter.

(Subd (b) adopted effective July 1, 2012.)

(c) Service and filing

The letter must be served and filed before the court files its opinion and as soon as possible after the party learns of the new authority. If the letter is served and filed after oral argument is heard, it may address only new authority that was not available in time to be addressed at oral argument.

(Subd (c) adopted effective July 1, 2012.)

Rule 8.254 adopted effective July 1, 2012.

Advisory Committee Comment

This rule does not preclude a party from asking the presiding justice for permission to file supplemental briefing under rule 8.200(a)(4). A letter filed under this rule does not change the date of submission under rule 8.256.

Rule 8.256. Oral argument and submission of the cause

(a) Frequency and location of argument

(1) Each Court of Appeal and division must hold a session at least once each quarter.

(2) A Court of Appeal may hold sessions at places in its district other than the court's permanent location.

(3) Subject to approval by the Chair of the Judicial Council, a Court of Appeal may hold a session in another district to hear a cause transferred to it from that district.

(b) Notice of argument

The clerk/executive officer of the Court of Appeal must send a notice of the time and place of oral argument to all parties at least 20 days before the argument date. The presiding justice may shorten the notice period for good cause; in that event, the clerk/executive officer must immediately notify the parties by telephone or other expeditious method.

(Subd (b) amended effective January 1, 2018.)

(c) Conduct of argument

Unless the court provides otherwise by local rule or order:

(1) The appellant, petitioner, or moving party has the right to open and close. If there are two or more such parties, the court must set the sequence of argument.

(2) Each side is allowed 30 minutes for argument. If multiple parties are represented by separate counsel, or if an amicus curiae—on written request—is granted permission to argue, the court may apportion or expand the time.

(3) Only one counsel may argue for each separately represented party.

(d) When the cause is submitted

(1) A cause is submitted when the court has heard oral argument or approved its waiver and the time has expired to file all briefs and papers, including any supplemental brief permitted by the court.

(2) If the Supreme Court transfers a cause to the Court of Appeal and supplemental briefs may be filed under rule 8.200(b), the cause is

submitted when the last such brief is or could be timely filed. The Court of Appeal may order the cause submitted at an earlier time if the parties so stipulate.

(Subd (d) amended effective January 1, 2007.)

(e) Vacating submission

(1) Except as provided in (2), the court may vacate submission only by an order stating its reasons and setting a timetable for resubmission.

(2) If a cause is submitted under (d)(2), an order setting oral argument vacates submission and the cause is resubmitted when the court has heard oral argument or approved its waiver.

(Subd (e) amended effective January 1, 2007.)

Rule 8.256 amended effective January 1, 2018; repealed and adopted as rule 23 effective January 1, 2003; previously amended and renumbered effective January 1, 2007.

Rule 8.260. Opinions [Reserved]

Rule 8.260 adopted effective January 1, 2007.

Rule 8.264. Filing, finality, and modification of decision

(a) Filing the decision

(1) The clerk/executive officer of the Court of Appeal must promptly file all opinions and orders of the court and promptly send copies showing the filing date to the parties and, when relevant, to the lower court or tribunal.

(2) A decision by opinion must identify the participating justices, including the author of the majority opinion and of any concurring or dissenting opinion, or the justices participating in a "by the court" opinion.

(Subd (a) amended effective January 1, 2018.)

(b) Finality of decision

(1) Except as otherwise provided in this rule, a Court of Appeal decision in a civil appeal, including an order dismissing an appeal involuntarily, is final in that court 30 days after filing.

(2) The following Court of Appeal decisions are final in that court on filing:

(A) The denial of a petition for writ of supersedeas; and

(B) The dismissal of an appeal on request or stipulation.

(3) If a Court of Appeal certifies its opinion for publication or partial publication after filing its decision and before its decision becomes final in that court, the finality period runs from the filing date of the order for publication.

(Subd (b) amended effective January 1, 2009; previously amended effective January 1, 2007.)

(c) Modification of decision

(1) A reviewing court may modify a decision until the decision is final in that court. If the office of the clerk/executive officer is closed on the date of finality, the court may modify the decision on the next day the office is open.

(2) An order modifying an opinion must state whether it changes the appellate judgment. A modification that does not change the appellate judgment does not extend the finality date of the decision. If a modification changes the appellate judgment, the finality period runs from the filing date of the modification order.

(Subd (c) amended effective January 1, 2018.)

(d) Consent to increase or decrease in amount of judgment

If a Court of Appeal decision conditions the affirmance of a money judgment on a party's consent to an increase or decrease in the amount, the judgment is reversed unless, before the decision is final under (b), the party serves and files a copy of a consent in the Court of Appeal. If a consent is filed, the finality period runs from the filing date of the consent. The clerk/executive officer must send one filed-endorsed copy of the consent to the superior court with the remittitur.

(Subd (d) amended effective January 1, 2018; previously amended effective January 1, 2016.)

Rule 8.264 amended effective January 1, 2018; repealed and adopted as rule 24 effective January 1, 2003; previously amended and renumbered as rule 8.264 effective January 1, 2007; previously amended effective January 1, 2009, and January 1, 2016.

Advisory Committee Comment

Subdivision (b). As used in subdivision (b)(1), "decision" includes all interlocutory orders of the Court of Appeal. (See Advisory Committee Comment to rule 8.500(a) and (e).) This provision addresses the finality of decisions in civil appeals and, through a cross-reference in rule 8.470, in juvenile appeals. See rule 8.366 for provisions addressing the finality of decisions in proceedings under chapter 3, relating to criminal appeals; rule 8.387 for provisions addressing finality of decisions under chapter 4, relating to habeas corpus proceedings; and rule 8.490 for provisions addressing the finality of decisions in proceedings under chapter 7, relating to writs of mandate, certiorari, and prohibition.

Subdivision (b)(3) provides that a postfiling decision of the Court of Appeal to publish its opinion in whole under rule 8.1105(c) or in part under rule 8.1100(a) restarts the 30-day finality period. This provision is based on rule 40-2 of the United States Circuit Rules (9th Cir.). It is intended to allow parties sufficient time to petition the Court of Appeal for rehearing and/or the Supreme Court for review—and to allow potential amici curiae sufficient time to express their views—when the Court of Appeal changes the publication status of an opinion. The rule thus recognizes that the publication status of an opinion may affect a party's decision whether to file a petition for rehearing and/or a petition for review.

Rule 8.268. Rehearing

(a) Power to order rehearing

(1) On petition of a party or on its own motion, a reviewing court may order rehearing of any decision that is not final in that court on filing.

(2) An order for rehearing must be filed before the decision is final. If the clerk's office is closed on the date of finality, the court may file the order on the next day the clerk's office is open.

(b) Petition and answer

(1) A party may serve and file a petition for rehearing within 15 days after:

(A) The filing of the decision;

(B) A publication order restarting the finality period under rule 8.264(b)(3), if the party has not already filed a petition for rehearing;

(C) A modification order changing the appellate judgment under rule 8.264(c)(2); or

(D) The filing of a consent under rule 8.264(d).

(2) A party must not file an answer to a petition for rehearing unless the court requests an answer. The clerk must promptly send to the parties copies of any order requesting an answer and immediately notify the parties by telephone or another expeditious method. Any answer must be served and filed within 8 days after the order is filed unless the court orders otherwise. A petition for rehearing normally will not be granted unless the court has requested an answer.

(3) The petition and answer must comply with the relevant provisions of rule 8.204, including the length provisions in subdivision (c)(5).

(4) Before the decision is final and for good cause, the presiding justice may relieve a party from a failure to file a timely petition or answer.

(Subd (b) amended effective January 1, 2020; previously amended effective January 1, 2004, January 1, 2007, and January 1, 2009.)

(c) No extension of time

The time for granting or denying a petition for rehearing in the Court of Appeal may not be extended. If the court does not rule on the petition before the decision is final, the petition is deemed denied.

(d) Effect of granting rehearing

An order granting a rehearing vacates the decision and any opinion filed in the case and sets the cause at large in the Court of Appeal.

Rule 8.268 amended effective January 1, 2020; repealed and adopted as rule 25 effective January 1, 2003; previously amended effective January 1, 2004, and January 1, 2009; previously amended and renumbered effective January 1, 2007.

Rule 8.272. Remittitur

(a) Issuance of remittitur

A Court of Appeal must issue a remittitur after a decision in an appeal.

(Subd (a) amended effective January 1, 2008; previously amended effective January 1, 2007.)

(b) Clerk's duties

(1) If a Court of Appeal decision is not reviewed by the Supreme Court:

(A) The clerk/executive officer of the Court of Appeal must issue a remittitur immediately after the Supreme Court denies review, or the period for granting review expires, or the court dismisses review under rule 8.528(b); and

(B) The clerk/executive officer must send the lower court or tribunal the Court of Appeal remittitur and a filed-endorsed copy of the opinion or order.

(2) After Supreme Court review of a Court of Appeal decision:

(A) On receiving the Supreme Court remittitur, the clerk/executive officer of the Court of Appeal must issue a remittitur immediately if there will be no further proceedings in the Court of Appeal; and

(B) The clerk must send the lower court or tribunal the Court of Appeal remittitur, a copy of the Supreme Court remittitur, and a filed-endorsed copy of the Supreme Court opinion or order.

(Subd (b) amended effective January 1, 2018; previously amended effective January 1, 2007, and January 1, 2016.)

(c) Immediate issuance, stay, and recall

(1) A Court of Appeal may direct immediate issuance of a remittitur only on the parties' stipulation or on dismissal of the appeal under rule 8.244(c)(2).

(2) On a party's or its own motion or on stipulation, and for good cause, the court may stay a remittitur's issuance for a reasonable period or order its recall.

(3) An order recalling a remittitur issued after a decision by opinion does not supersede the opinion or affect its publication status.

(Subd (c) amended effective January 1, 2007.)

(d) Notice

(1) The remittitur is deemed issued when the clerk/executive officer enters it in the record. The clerk/executive officer must immediately send the parties notice of issuance of the remittitur, showing the date of entry.

(2) If, without requiring further proceedings in the trial court, the decision changes the length of a state prison sentence, applicable credits, or the maximum permissible confinement to the Department of Corrections and Rehabilitation, Division of Juvenile Justice, the clerk/executive officer must send a copy of the remittitur and opinion or order to either the Department of Corrections and Rehabilitation or the Division of Juvenile Justice.

(Subd (d) amended effective January 1, 2018; previously amended effective January 1, 2007.)

Rule 8.272 amended effective January 1, 2018; repealed and adopted as rule 26 effective January 1, 2003; previously amended effective January 1, 2007, January 1, 2008, and January 1, 2016.

Advisory Committee Comment

See rule 8.386 for provisions addressing remittitur in habeas corpus proceedings and rule 8.490 for provisions addressing remittitur in other writ proceedings.

Rule 8.276. Sanctions

(a) Grounds for sanctions

On motion of a party or its own motion, a Court of Appeal may impose sanctions, including the award or denial of costs under rule 8.278, on a party or an attorney for:

(1) Taking a frivolous appeal or appealing solely to cause delay;

(2) Including in the record any matter not reasonably material to the appeal's determination;

(3) Filing a frivolous motion; or

(4) Committing any other unreasonable violation of these rules.

(Subd (a) amended and relettered effective January 1, 2008; adopted as subd (e) effective January 1, 2003; previously amended effective January 1, 2007.)

(b) Motions for sanctions

(1) A party's motion under (a) must include a declaration supporting the amount of any monetary sanction sought and must be served and filed before any order dismissing the appeal but no later than 10 days after the appellant's reply brief is due.

(2) If a party files a motion for sanctions with a motion to dismiss the appeal and the motion to dismiss is not granted, the party may file a new motion for sanctions within 10 days after the appellant's reply brief is due.

(Subd (b) amended and lettered effective January 1, 2008; adopted as part of subd (e) effective January 1, 2003; previously amended effective January 1, 2007.)

(c) Notice

The court must give notice in writing if it is considering imposing sanctions.

(Subd (c) amended and lettered effective January 1, 2008; adopted as part of subd (e) effective January 1, 2003; previously amended effective January 1, 2007.)

(d) Opposition

Within 10 days after the court sends such notice, a party or attorney may serve and file an opposition, but failure to do so will not be deemed consent. An opposition may not be filed unless the court sends such notice.

(Subd (d) amended and lettered effective January 1, 2008; adopted as part of subd (e) effective January 1, 2003; previously amended effective January 1, 2007.)

(e) Oral argument

Unless otherwise ordered, oral argument on the issue of sanctions must be combined with oral argument on the merits of the appeal.

(Subd (e) amended and lettered effective January 1, 2008; adopted as part of subd (e) effective January 1, 2003; previously amended effective January 1, 2007.)

Rule 8.276 amended effective January 1, 2008; repealed and adopted as rule 27 effective January 1, 2003; previously amended and renumbered effective January 1, 2007.

Rule 8.278. Costs on appeal

(a) Award of costs

(1) Except as provided in this rule, the party prevailing in the Court of Appeal in a civil case other than a juvenile case is entitled to costs on appeal.

(2) The prevailing party is the respondent if the Court of Appeal affirms the judgment without modification or dismisses the appeal. The prevailing party is the appellant if the court reverses the judgment in its entirety.

(3) If the Court of Appeal reverses the judgment in part or modifies it, or if there is more than one notice of appeal, the opinion must specify the award or denial of costs.

(4) In probate cases, the prevailing party must be awarded costs unless the Court of Appeal orders otherwise, but the superior court must decide who will pay the award.

(5) In the interests of justice, the Court of Appeal may also award or deny costs as it deems proper.

(Subd (a) adopted effective January 1, 2008.)

(b) Judgment for costs

(1) The clerk/executive officer of the Court of Appeal must enter on the record, and insert in the remittitur, a judgment awarding costs to the prevailing party under (a)(2) or as directed by the court under (a)(3), (a)(4), or (a)(5).

(2) If the clerk/executive officer fails to enter judgment for costs, the court may recall the remittitur for correction on its own motion, or on a party's motion made not later than 30 days after the remittitur issues.

(Subd (b) amended effective January 1, 2018; adopted effective January 1, 2008.)

(c) Procedure for claiming or opposing costs

(1) Within 40 days after issuance of the remittitur, a party claiming costs awarded by a reviewing court must serve and file in the superior court a verified memorandum of costs under rule 3.1700.

(2) A party may serve and file a motion in the superior court to strike or tax costs claimed under (1) in the manner required by rule 3.1700.

(3) An award of costs is enforceable as a money judgment.

(Subd (c) amended effective January 1, 2016; adopted effective January 1, 2008.)

(d) Recoverable costs

(1) A party may recover only the following costs, if reasonable:

(A) Filing fees;

(B) The amount the party paid for any portion of the record, whether an original or a copy or both. The cost to copy parts of a prior record under rule 8.147(b)(2) is not recoverable unless the Court of Appeal ordered the copying;

(C) The cost to produce additional evidence on appeal;

(D) The costs to notarize, serve, mail, and file the record, briefs, and other papers;

(E) The cost to print and reproduce any brief, including any petition for rehearing or review, answer, or reply;

(F) The cost to procure a surety bond, including the premium, the cost to obtain a letter of credit as collateral, and the fees and net interest expenses incurred to borrow funds to provide security for the bond or to obtain a letter of credit, unless the trial court determines the bond was unnecessary; and

(G) The fees and net interest expenses incurred to borrow funds to deposit with the superior court in lieu of a bond or undertaking, unless the trial court determines the deposit was unnecessary.

(2) Unless the court orders otherwise, an award of costs neither includes attorney's fees on appeal nor precludes a party from seeking them under rule 3.1702.

(Subd (d) amended effective January 1, 2013; adopted effective January 1, 2008.)

Rule 8.278 amended effective January 1, 2018; adopted effective January 1, 2008; previously amended effective January 1, 2009, January 1, 2013, and January 1, 2016.

Advisory Committee Comment

This rule is not intended to expand the categories of appeals subject to the award of costs. See rule 8.493 for provisions addressing costs in writ proceedings.

Subdivision (c). Subdivision (c)(2) provides the procedure for a party to move in the trial court to strike or tax costs that another party has claimed under subdivision (c)(1). It is not intended that the trial court's authority to strike or tax unreasonable costs be limited by any failure of the moving party to move for sanctions in the Court of Appeal under rule 8.276; a party may seek to strike or tax costs on the ground that an opponent included unnecessary materials in the record even if the party did not move the Court of Appeal to sanction the opponent under that rule.

Subdivision (d). Subdivision (d)(1)(B) is intended to refer not only to a normal record prepared by the clerk and the reporter under rules 8.122 and 8.130 but also, for example, to an appendix prepared by a party under rule 8.124 and to a superior court file to which the parties stipulate under rule 8.128.

Subdivision (d)(1)(D), allowing recovery of the "costs to notarize, serve, mail, and file the record, briefs, and other papers," is intended to include fees charged by electronic filing service providers for electronic filing and service of documents.

"Net interest expenses" in subdivisions (d)(1)(F) and (G) means the interest expenses incurred to borrow the funds that are deposited minus any interest earned by the borrower on those funds while they are on deposit.

Chapter 3
Criminal Appeals

Art. 1. Taking the Appeal. Rules 8.300–8.316.
Art. 2. Record on Appeal. Rules 8.320–8.346.
Art. 3. Briefs, Hearing, and Decision. Rules 8.360–8.368.

Article 1
Taking the Appeal

Rule 8.300. Appointment of appellate counsel by the Court of Appeal
Rule 8.304. Filing the appeal; certificate of probable cause
Rule 8.308. Time to appeal
Rule 8.312. Stay of execution and release on appeal
Rule 8.316. Abandoning the appeal

Rule 8.300. Appointment of appellate counsel by the Court of Appeal

(a) Procedures

(1) Each Court of Appeal must adopt procedures for appointing appellate counsel for indigents not represented by the State Public Defender in all cases in which indigents are entitled to appointed counsel.

(2) The procedures must require each attorney seeking appointment to complete a questionnaire showing the attorney's California State Bar number, date of admission, qualifications, and experience.

(b) List of qualified attorneys

(1) The Court of Appeal must evaluate the attorney's qualifications for appointment and, if the attorney is qualified, place the attorney's name on a list to receive appointments in appropriate cases.

(2) Each court's appointments must be based on criteria approved by the Judicial Council or its designated oversight committee.

(Subd (b) amended effective January 1, 2007.)

(c) Demands of the case

In matching counsel with the demands of the case, the Court of Appeal should consider:

(1) The length of the sentence;
(2) The complexity or novelty of the issues;
(3) The length of the trial and of the reporter's transcript; and
(4) Any questions concerning the competence of trial counsel.

(Subd (c) amended effective January 1, 2007.)

(d) Evaluation

The court must review and evaluate the performance of each appointed counsel to determine whether counsel's name should remain on the list at the same level, be placed on a different level, or be deleted from the list.

(e) Contracts to perform administrative functions

(1) The court may contract with an administrator having substantial experience in handling appellate court appointments to perform any of the duties prescribed by this rule.

(2) The court must provide the administrator with the information needed to fulfill the administrator's duties.

Rule 8.300 amended and renumbered effective January 1, 2007; repealed and adopted as rule 76.5 effective January 1, 2005.

Advisory Committee Comment

Subdivision (b). The "designated oversight committee" referred to in subdivision (b)(2) is currently the Appellate Indigent Defense Oversight Advisory Committee. The criteria approved by this committee can be found on the judicial branch's public website at *www.courts.ca.gov/4206.htm*.

Rule 8.304. Filing the appeal; certificate of probable cause

(a) Notice of appeal

(1) To appeal from a judgment or an appealable order of the superior court in a felony case—other than a judgment imposing a sentence of death—the defendant or the People must file a notice of appeal in that superior court. To appeal after a plea of guilty or nolo contendere or after an admission of probation violation, the defendant must also comply with (b).

(2) As used in (1), "felony case" means any criminal action in which a felony is charged, regardless of the outcome. A felony is "charged" when an information or indictment accusing the defendant of a felony is filed or a complaint accusing the defendant of a felony is certified to the superior court under Penal Code section 859a. A felony case includes an action in which the defendant is charged with:

(A) A felony and a misdemeanor or infraction, but is convicted of only the misdemeanor or infraction;

(B) A felony, but is convicted of only a lesser offense; or

(C) An offense filed as a felony but punishable as either a felony or a misdemeanor, and the offense is thereafter deemed a misdemeanor under Penal Code section 17(b).

(3) If the defendant appeals, the defendant or the defendant's attorney must sign the notice of appeal. If the People appeal, the attorney for the People must sign the notice.

(4) The notice of appeal must be liberally construed. Except as provided in (b), the notice is sufficient if it identifies the particular judgment or order being appealed. The notice need not specify the court to which the appeal is taken; the appeal will be treated as taken to the Court of Appeal for the district in which the superior court is located.

(Subd (a) amended effective January 1, 2007.)

(b) Appeal from a judgment of conviction after plea of guilty or nolo contendere or after admission of probation violation

(1) Appeal requiring a certificate of probable cause

(A) To appeal from a superior court judgment after a plea of guilty or nolo contendere or after an admission of probation violation on grounds that affect the validity of the plea or admission, the defendant must file in that superior court—with the notice of appeal required by (a)—the written statement required by Penal Code section 1237.5 for issuance of a certificate of probable cause.

(B) Within 20 days after the defendant files a written statement under Penal Code section 1237.5, the superior court must sign and file either a certificate of probable cause or an order denying the certificate.

(2) Appeal not requiring a certificate of probable cause

To appeal from a superior court judgment after a plea of guilty or nolo contendere or after an admission of probation violation on grounds that do not affect the validity of the plea or admission, the defendant need not file the written statement required by Penal Code section 1237.5 for issuance of a certificate of probable cause. No certificate of probable cause is required for an appeal based on or from:

(A) The denial of a motion to suppress evidence under Penal Code section 1538.5;

(B) The sentence or other matters occurring after the plea or admission that do not affect the validity of the plea or admission; or

(C) An appealable order for which, by law, no certificate of probable cause is required.

(3) Appeal without a certificate of probable cause

If the defendant does not file the written statement required by Penal Code section 1237.5 or the superior court denies a certificate of probable cause, the appeal will be limited to issues that do not require a certificate of probable cause.

(Subd (b) amended effective January 1, 2022; previously amended effective January 1, 2007, and July 1, 2007.)

(c) Notification of the appeal

(1) When a notice of appeal is filed, the superior court clerk must promptly send a notification of the filing to the attorney of record for each party, any unrepresented defendant, the district appellate project, to the reviewing court clerk, each court reporter, and any primary reporter or reporting supervisor. The notification must specify whether the defendant filed a statement under (b)(1)(A) and, if so, whether the superior court filed a certificate or an order denying a certificate under (b)(1)(B).

(2) The notification must show the date it was sent, the number and title of the case, and the dates that the notice of appeal and any certificate or order denying a certificate under (b)(1)(B) were filed. If the information is available, the notification must also include:

(A) The name, address, telephone number, e-mail address, and California State Bar number of each attorney of record in the case;

(B) The name of the party each attorney represented in the superior court; and

(C) The name, address, telephone number and e-mail address of any unrepresented defendant.

(3) The notification to the reviewing court clerk must also include a copy of the notice of appeal, any certificate filed under (b)(1), and the sequential list of reporters made under rule 2.950.

(4) A copy of the notice of appeal is sufficient notification under (1) if the required information is on the copy or is added by the superior court clerk.

(5) The sending of a notification under (1) is a sufficient performance of the clerk's duty despite the discharge, disqualification, suspension, disbarment, or death of the attorney.

(6) Failure to comply with any provision of this subdivision does not affect the validity of the notice of appeal.

(Subd (c) amended effective January 1, 2022; previously amended effective January 1, 2007, and January 1, 2016.)

Rule 8.304 amended effective January 1, 2022; repealed and adopted as rule 30 effective January 1, 2004; previously amended and renumbered as rule 8.304 effective January 1, 2007; previously amended effective July 1, 2007, and January 1, 2016.

Advisory Committee Comment

Subdivision (a). Penal Code section 1235(b) provides that an appeal from a judgment or appealable order in a "felony case" is taken to the Court of Appeal, and Penal Code section 691(f) defines "felony case" to mean "a criminal action in which a felony is charged." Rule 8.304(a)(2) makes it clear that a "felony case" is an action in which a felony is charged *regardless of the outcome of the action*. Thus the question whether to file a notice of appeal under this rule or under the rules governing appeals to the appellate division of the superior court (rule 8.800 et seq.) is answered simply by examining the accusatory pleading: if that document charged the defendant with at least one count of felony (as defined in Pen. Code, § 17(a)), the Court of Appeal has appellate jurisdiction and the appeal must be taken under this rule *even if the prosecution did not result in a punishment of imprisonment in a state prison*.

It is settled case law that an appeal is taken to the Court of Appeal not only when the defendant is charged with and convicted of a felony, but also when the defendant is charged with both a felony and a misdemeanor (Pen. Code, § 691(f)) but is convicted of only the misdemeanor (e.g., *People v. Brown* (1970) 10 Cal.App.3d 169); when the defendant is charged with a felony but is convicted of only a lesser offense (Pen. Code, § 1159; e.g., *People v. Spreckels* (1954) 125 Cal.App.2d 507); and when the defendant is charged with an offense filed as a felony but punishable as either a felony or a misdemeanor, and the offense is thereafter deemed a misdemeanor under Penal Code section 17(b) (e.g., *People v. Douglas* (1999) 20 Cal.4th 85; *People v. Clark* (1971) 17 Cal.App.3d 890).

Trial court unification did not change this rule: after as before unification, "Appeals in felony cases lie to the [C]ourt of [A]ppeal, regardless of whether the appeal is from the superior court, the municipal court, or the action of a magistrate. *Cf.* Cal. Const. art. VI, § 11(a) [except in death penalty cases, Courts of Appeal have appellate jurisdiction when superior courts have original jurisdiction 'in causes of a type within the appellate jurisdiction of the [C]ourts of [A]ppeal on June 30, 1995.']." (*Recommendation on Trial Court Unification: Revision of Codes* (July 1998) 28 Cal. Law Revision Com. Rep. (1998) pp. 455–456.)

Subdivision (b). Subdivision (b)(1) reiterates the requirement stated in Penal Code section 1237.5(a) that to challenge the validity of a plea or the admission of a probation violation on appeal under Penal Code section 1237(a), the defendant must file both a notice of appeal and the written statement required by section 1237.5(a) for the issuance of a certificate of probable cause. (See *People v. Mendez* (1999) 19 Cal.4th 1084, 1098 [probable cause certificate requirement is to be applied strictly].)

Subdivision (b)(2) identifies exceptions to the certificate-of-probable-cause requirement, including an appeal that challenges the denial of a motion to suppress evidence under Penal Code section 1538.5 (see *People v. Stamps* (2020) 9 Cal.5th 685, 694) and an appeal that does not challenge the validity of the plea or the admission of a probation violation (see, e.g., *id.* at pp. 694–698 [appeal based on a postplea change in the law]; *People v. Arriaga* (2014) 58 Cal.4th 950, 958–960 [appeal from the denial of a motion to vacate a conviction based on inadequate advisement of potential immigration consequences under Penal Code section 1016.5]; and *People v. French* (2008) 43 Cal.4th 36, 45–46 [appeal that challenges a postplea sentencing issue that was not resolved by, and as a part of, the negotiated disposition]).

Subdivision (b)(2)(C) clarifies that no certificate of probable cause is required for an appeal from an order that, by law, is appealable without a certificate. (See, e.g., Pen. Code, § 1473.7.)

Subdivision (b)(3) makes clear that if a defendant raises on appeal an issue that requires a certificate of probable cause, but the defendant does not file the written statement required by Penal Code section 1237.5 or the superior court denies the certificate, then the appeal is limited to issues, such as those identified in subdivision (b)(2), that do not require a certificate of probable cause. (See *Mendez, supra* 19 Cal.4th at pp. 1088–1089.)

Rule 8.308. Time to appeal

(a) Normal time

Except as provided in (b) or as otherwise provided by law, a notice of appeal and any statement required by Penal Code section 1237.5 must be filed within 60 days after the rendition of the judgment or the making of the order being appealed. Except as provided in rule 8.66, no court may extend the time to file a notice of appeal.

(Subd (a) amended effective July 1, 2007; previously amended effective January 1, 2005, and January 1, 2007.)

(b) Cross-appeal

If the defendant or the People timely appeals from a judgment or appealable order, the time for any other party to appeal from the same judgment or order is either the time specified in (a) or 30 days after the superior court clerk sends notification of the first appeal, whichever is later.

(Subd (b) amended effective January 1, 2016; adopted effective January 1, 2007; previously amended effective January 1, 2008.)

(c) Premature notice of appeal

A notice of appeal filed before the judgment is rendered or the order is made is premature, but the reviewing court may treat the notice as filed immediately after the rendition of judgment or the making of the order.

(Subd (c) relettered effective January 1, 2007; adopted as subd (b) effective January 1, 2004.)

(d) Late notice of appeal

The superior court clerk must mark a late notice of appeal "Received [date] but not filed," notify the party that the notice was not filed because it was late, and send a copy of the marked notice of appeal to the district appellate project.

(Subd (d) relettered effective January 1, 2007; adopted as subd (c) effective January 1, 2004.)

Rule 8.308 amended effective January 1, 2016; adopted as rule 30.1 effective January 1, 2004; previously amended and renumbered as rule 8.308 effective January 1, 2007; previously amended effective January 1, 2005, July 1, 2007, January 1, 2008, and July 1, 2010.

Advisory Committee Comment

Subdivision (c). The subdivision requires the clerk to send a copy of a late notice of appeal, marked with the date it was received but not filed, to the appellate project for the district; that entity is charged with the duty, among others, of dealing with indigent criminal appeals that suffer from procedural defect, but it can do so efficiently only if it is promptly notified of such cases.

Subdivision (d). See rule 8.25(b)(5) for provisions concerning the timeliness of documents mailed by inmates or patients from custodial institutions.

Rule 8.312. Stay of execution and release on appeal

(a) Application

Pending appeal, the defendant may apply to the reviewing court:

(1) For a stay of execution after a judgment of conviction or an order granting probation; or

(2) For bail, to reduce bail, or for release on other conditions.

(Subd (a) amended effective January 1, 2007.)

(b) Showing

The application must include a showing that the defendant sought relief in the superior court and that the court unjustifiably denied the application.

(c) Service

The application must be served on the district attorney and on the Attorney General.

(d) Interim relief

Pending its ruling on the application, the reviewing court may grant the relief requested. The reviewing court must notify the superior court under rule 8.489 of any stay that it grants.

(Subd (d) amended effective January 1, 2009; previously amended effective January 1, 2007.)

Rule 8.312 amended effective January 1, 2009; adopted as rule 30.2 effective January 1, 2004; previously amended and renumbered effective January 1, 2007.

Advisory Committee Comment

Subdivision (a). The remedy of an application for bail under (a)(2) is separate from but consistent with the statutory remedy of a petition for habeas corpus under Penal Code section 1490. (*In re Brumback* (1956) 46 Cal.2d 810, 815, fn. 3.)

An order of the Court of Appeal denying bail or reduction of bail, or for release on other conditions, is final on filing. (See rule 8.366(b)(2)(A).)

Subdivision (d). The first sentence of (d) recognizes the case law holding that a reviewing court may grant bail or reduce bail, or release the defendant on other conditions, pending its ruling on an application for that relief. (See, e.g., *In re Fishman* (1952) 109 Cal.App.2d 632, 633; *In re Keddy* (1951) 105 Cal.App.2d 215, 217.) The second sentence of the subdivision requires the reviewing court to notify the superior court under rule 8.489 when it grants either (1) a stay to preserve the status quo pending its ruling on a stay application or (2) the stay requested by that application.

Rule 8.316. Abandoning the appeal

(a) How to abandon

An appellant may abandon the appeal at any time by filing an abandonment of the appeal signed by the appellant or the appellant's attorney of record.

(b) Where to file; effect of filing

(1) If the record has not been filed in the reviewing court, the appellant must file the abandonment in the superior court. The filing effects a dismissal of the appeal and restores the superior court's jurisdiction.

(2) If the record has been filed in the reviewing court, the appellant must file the abandonment in that court. The reviewing court may dismiss the appeal and direct immediate issuance of the remittitur.

(c) Clerk's duties

(1) The clerk of the court in which the appellant files the abandonment must immediately notify the adverse party of the filing or of the order of dismissal. If the defendant abandons the appeal, the clerk must notify both the district attorney and the Attorney General.

(2) If the appellant files the abandonment in the superior court, the clerk must immediately notify the reviewing court.

(3) The clerk must immediately notify the reporter if the appeal is abandoned before the reporter has filed the transcript.

Rule 8.316 renumbered effective January 1, 2007; adopted as rule 30.3 effective January 1, 2004.

Article 2
Record on Appeal

Rule 8.320. Normal record; exhibits
Rule 8.324. Application in superior court for addition to normal record
Rule 8.332. Juror-identifying information
Rule 8.336. Preparing, certifying, and sending the record
Rule 8.340. Augmenting or correcting the record in the Court of Appeal
Rule 8.344. Agreed statement
Rule 8.346. Settled statement

Rule 8.320. Normal record; exhibits

(a) Contents

If the defendant appeals from a judgment of conviction, or if the People appeal from an order granting a new trial, the record must contain a clerk's transcript and a reporter's transcript, which together constitute the normal record.

(b) Clerk's transcript

The clerk's transcript must contain:

(1) The accusatory pleading and any amendment;

(2) Any demurrer or other plea;

(3) All court minutes;

(4) All jury instructions that any party submitted in writing and the cover page required by rule 2.1055(b)(2) indicating the party requesting each instruction, and any written jury instructions given by the court;

(5) Any written communication between the court and the jury or any individual juror;

(6) Any verdict;

(7) Any written opinion of the court;

(8) The judgment or order appealed from and any abstract of judgment or commitment;

(9) Any motion for new trial, with supporting and opposing memoranda and attachments;

(10) The notice of appeal and any certificate of probable cause filed under rule 8.304(b);

(11) Any transcript of a sound or sound-and-video recording furnished to the jury or tendered to the court under rule 2.1040;

(12) Any application for additional record and any order on the application;

(13) And, if the appellant is the defendant:

(A) Any written defense motion denied in whole or in part, with supporting and opposing memoranda and attachments;

(B) If related to a motion under (A), any search warrant and return and the reporter's transcript of any preliminary examination or grand jury hearing;

(C) Any document admitted in evidence to prove a prior juvenile adjudication, criminal conviction, or prison term;

(D) The probation officer's report; and

(E) Any court-ordered diagnostic or psychological report required under Penal Code section 1203.03(b) or 1369.

(Subd (b) amended effective January 1, 2014; previously amended effective January 1, 2005, January 1, 2007, January 1, 2008, and January 1, 2010.)

(c) Reporter's transcript

The reporter's transcript must contain:

(1) The oral proceedings on the entry of any plea other than a not guilty plea;

(2) The oral proceedings on any motion in limine;

(3) The oral proceedings at trial, but excluding the voir dire examination of jurors and any opening statement;

(4) All instructions given orally;

(5) Any oral communication between the court and the jury or any individual juror;

(6) Any oral opinion of the court;

(7) The oral proceedings on any motion for new trial;

(8) The oral proceedings at sentencing, granting or denying of probation, or other dispositional hearing;

(9) And, if the appellant is the defendant:

(A) The oral proceedings on any defense motion denied in whole or in part except motions for disqualification of a judge and motions under Penal Code section 995;

(B) The closing arguments; and

(C) Any comment on the evidence by the court to the jury.

(Subd (c) amended effective January 1, 2007.)

(d) Limited normal record in certain appeals

If the People appeal from a judgment on a demurrer to the accusatory pleading, or if the defendant or the People appeal from an appealable order other than a ruling on a motion for new trial, the normal record is composed of:

(1) *Clerk's transcript*

A clerk's transcript containing:

(A) The accusatory pleading and any amendment;

(B) Any demurrer or other plea;

(C) Any written motion or notice of motion granted or denied by the order appealed from, with supporting and opposing memoranda and attachments;

(D) The judgment or order appealed from and any abstract of judgment or commitment;

(E) Any court minutes relating to the judgment or order appealed from and:

(i) If there was a trial in the case, any court minutes of proceedings at the time the original verdict is rendered and any subsequent proceedings; or

(ii) If the original judgment of conviction is based on a guilty plea or nolo contendere plea, any court minutes of the proceedings at the time of entry of such plea and any subsequent proceedings;

(F) The notice of appeal; and

(G) If the appellant is the defendant, all probation officer reports and any court-ordered diagnostic report required under Penal Code section 1203.03(b).

(2) *Reporter's transcript*

(A) A reporter's transcript of any oral proceedings incident to the judgment or order being appealed; and

(B) If the appeal is from an order after judgment, a reporter's transcript of:

(i) The original sentencing proceeding; and

(ii) If the original judgment of conviction is based on a guilty plea or nolo contendere plea, the proceedings at the time of entry of such plea.

(Subd (d) amended effective January 1, 2013; previously amended effective January 1, 2007.)

(e) Exhibits

Exhibits admitted in evidence, refused, or lodged are deemed part of the record, but may be transmitted to the reviewing court only as provided in rule 8.224.

(Subd (e) amended effective January 1, 2007.)

(f) Stipulation for partial transcript

If counsel for the defendant and the People stipulate in writing before the record is certified that any part of the record is not required for proper determination of the appeal, that part must not be prepared or sent to the reviewing court.

Rule 8.320 amended effective January 1, 2014; repealed and adopted as rule 31 effective January 1, 2004; previously amended and renumbered effective January

1, 2007; previously amended effective January 1, 2005, January 1, 2008, January 1, 2010, and January 1, 2013.

Advisory Committee Comment

Rules 8.45–8.46 address the appropriate handling of sealed and confidential records that must be included in the record on appeal. Examples of confidential records include Penal Code section 1203.03 diagnostic reports, records closed to inspection by court order under *People v. Marsden* (1970) 2 Cal.3d 118 or *Pitchess v. Superior Court* (1974) 11 Cal.3d 531, in-camera proceedings on a confidential informant, and defense expert funding requests (Pen. Code, § 987.9; *Keenan v. Superior Court* (1982) 31 Cal.3d 424, 430).

Subdivision (d)(1)(E). This rule identifies the minutes that must be included in the record. The trial court clerk may include additional minutes beyond those identified in this rule if that would be more cost-effective.

Rule 8.483 governs the normal record and exhibits in civil commitment appeals.

Rule 8.324. Application in superior court for addition to normal record

(a) Appeal by the People

The People, as appellant, may apply to the superior court for inclusion in the record of any item that would be part of the normal record in a defendant's appeal.

(b) Application by either party

Either the People or the defendant may apply to the superior court for inclusion in the record of any of the following items:

(1) In the clerk's transcript: any written defense motion granted in whole or in part or any written motion by the People, with supporting and opposing memoranda and attachments;

(2) In the reporter's transcript:

(A) The voir dire examination of jurors;

(B) Any opening statement; and

(C) The oral proceedings on motions other than those listed in rule 8.320(c).

(Subd (b) amended effective January 1, 2007.)

(c) Application

(1) An application for additional record must describe the material to be included and explain how it may be useful in the appeal.

(2) The application must be filed in the superior court with the notice of appeal or as soon thereafter as possible, and will be treated as denied if it is filed after the record is sent to the reviewing court.

(3) The clerk must immediately present the application to the trial judge.

(d) Order

(1) Within five days after the application is filed, the judge must order that the record include as much of the additional material as the judge finds proper to fully present the points raised by the applicant. Denial of the application does not preclude a motion in the reviewing court for augmentation under rule 8.155.

(2) If the judge does not rule on the application within the time prescribed by (1), the requested material—other than exhibits—must be included in the clerk's transcript or the reporter's transcript without a court order.

(3) The clerk must immediately notify the reporter if additions to the reporter's transcript are required under (1) or (2).

(Subd (d) amended effective January 1, 2007.)

Rule 8.324 amended and renumbered effective January 1, 2007; adopted as rule 31.1 effective January 1, 2004.

Rule 8.328. Confidential records [Repealed]

Rule 8.328 repealed effective January 1, 2014; adopted as rule 31.2 effective January 1, 2004; previously amended effective January 1, 2005, and January 1, 2011; previously amended and renumbered effective January 1, 2007.

Rule 8.332. Juror-identifying information

(a) Application

A clerk's transcript, a reporter's transcript, or any other document in the record that contains juror-identifying information must comply with this rule.

(Subd (a) amended effective January 1, 2007.)

(b) Juror names, addresses, and telephone numbers

(1) The name of each trial juror or alternate sworn to hear the case must be replaced with an identifying number wherever it appears in any document. The superior court clerk must prepare and keep under seal in the case file a table correlating the jurors' names with their identifying numbers. The clerk and the reporter must use the table in preparing all transcripts or other documents.

(2) The addresses and telephone numbers of trial jurors and alternates sworn to hear the case must be deleted from all documents.

(c) Potential jurors

Information identifying potential jurors called but not sworn as trial jurors or alternates must not be sealed unless otherwise ordered under Code of Civil Procedure section 237(a)(1).

Rule 8.332 amended and renumbered effective January 1, 2007; adopted as rule 31.3 effective January 1, 2004.

Advisory Committee Comment

Rule 8.332 implements Code of Civil Procedure section 237.

Rule 8.336. Preparing, certifying, and sending the record

(a) Immediate preparation when appeal is likely

(1) The reporter and the clerk must begin preparing the record immediately after a verdict or finding of guilt of a felony is announced following a trial on the merits, unless the judge determines that an appeal is unlikely under (2).

(2) In determining the likelihood of an appeal, the judge must consider the facts of the case and the fact that an appeal is likely if the defendant has been convicted of a crime for which probation is prohibited or is prohibited except in unusual cases, or if the trial involved a contested question of law important to the outcome.

(3) A determination under (2) is an administrative decision intended to further the efficient operation of the court and not intended to affect any substantive or procedural right of the defendant or the People. The determination cannot be cited to prove or disprove any legal or factual issue in the case and is not reviewable by appeal or writ.

(b) Appeal after plea of guilty or nolo contendere or after admission of probation violation

In an appeal under rule 8.304(b)(1), the time to prepare, certify, and file the record begins when the court files a certificate of probable cause under rule 8.304(b)(2).

(Subd (b) amended effective January 1, 2007.)

(c) Clerk's transcript

(1) Except as provided in (a) or (b), the clerk must begin preparing the clerk's transcript immediately after the notice of appeal is filed.

(2) Within 20 days after the notice of appeal is filed, the clerk must complete preparation of an original and two copies of the clerk's transcript, one for defendant's counsel and one for the Attorney General or the district attorney, whichever is the counsel for the People on appeal.

(3) On request, the clerk must prepare an extra copy for the district attorney or the Attorney General, whichever is not counsel for the People on appeal.

(4) If there is more than one appealing defendant, the clerk must prepare an extra copy for each additional appealing defendant represented by separate counsel.

(5) The clerk must certify as correct the original and all copies of the clerk's transcript.

(Subd (c) amended effective January 1, 2007.)

(d) Reporter's transcript

(1) Except as provided in (a) or (b), the reporter must begin preparing the reporter's transcript immediately on being notified by the clerk under rule 8.304(c)(1) that the notice of appeal has been filed.

(2) The reporter must prepare an original and the same number of copies of the reporter's transcript as (c) requires of the clerk's transcript, and must certify each as correct.

(3) The reporter must deliver the original and all copies to the superior court clerk as soon as they are certified, but no later than 20 days after the notice of appeal is filed.

(4) Any portion of the transcript transcribed during trial must not be retyped unless necessary to correct errors, but must be repaginated and combined with any portion of the transcript not previously transcribed. Any additional copies needed must not be retyped but, if the transcript is in paper form, must be prepared by photocopying or an equivalent process.

(5) In a multireporter case, the clerk must accept any completed portion of the transcript from the primary reporter one week after the time prescribed by (3) even if other portions are uncompleted. The clerk must promptly pay each reporter who certifies that all portions of the transcript assigned to that reporter are completed.

(Subd (d) amended effective January 1, 2018; previously amended effective January 1, 2007, January 1, 2014, January 1, 2016, and January 1, 2017.)

(e) Extension of time

(1) The superior court may not extend the time for preparing the record.

(2) The reviewing court may order one or more extensions of time for preparing the record, including a reporter's transcript, not exceeding a total of 60 days, on receipt of:

(A) A declaration showing good cause; and

(B) In the case of a reporter's transcript, certification by the superior court presiding judge, or a court administrator designated by the presiding judge, that an extension is reasonable and necessary in light of the workload of all reporters in the court.

(Subd (e) amended effective January 1, 2014; previously amended effective January 1, 2007.)

(f) Form of record

The clerk's and reporter's transcripts must comply with rules 8.45–8.47, relating to sealed and confidential records, and rule 8.144.

(Subd (f) adopted effective January 1, 2014.)

(g) Sending the transcripts

(1) When the clerk and reporter's transcripts are certified as correct, the clerk must promptly send:

(A) The original transcripts to the reviewing court, noting the sending date on each original;

(B) One copy of each transcript to appellate counsel for each defendant represented by separate counsel and to the Attorney General or the district attorney, whichever is counsel for the People on appeal; and

(C) One copy of each transcript to the district attorney or Attorney General if requested under (c)(3).

(2) If the defendant is not represented by appellate counsel when the transcripts are certified as correct, the clerk must send that defendant's counsel's copy of the transcripts to the district appellate project.

(Subd (g) repealed and relettered effective January 1, 2014; previously amended as subd (f) effective January 1, 2007.)

(h) Supervision of preparation of record

Each clerk/executive officer of the Court of Appeal, under the supervision of the administrative presiding justice or the presiding justice, must take all appropriate steps to ensure that superior court clerks and reporters promptly perform their duties under this rule. This provision does not affect the superior courts' responsibility for the prompt preparation of appellate records.

(Subd (h) amended effective January 1, 2018.)

Rule 8.336 amended effective January 1, 2018; repealed and adopted as rule 32 effective January 1, 2004; previously amended and renumbered as rule 8.336 effective January 1, 2007; previously amended effective January 1, 2010, January 1, 2014, January 1, 2016, January 1, 2017, and January 1, 2018.

Advisory Committee Comment

Subdivision (a). Subdivision (a) implements Code of Civil Procedure section 269(b).

Subdivision (f). Examples of confidential records include Penal Code section 1203.03 diagnostic reports, records closed to inspection by court order under *People v. Marsden* (1970) 2 Cal.3d 118 or *Pitchess v. Superior Court* (1974) 11 Cal.3d 531, in-camera proceedings on a confidential informant, and defense expert funding requests (Pen. Code, § 987.9; *Keenan v. Superior Court* (1982) 31 Cal.3d 424, 430).

Subdivision (g). Under rule 8.71(c), the superior court clerk may send the record to the reviewing court in electronic form.

Rule 8.340. Augmenting or correcting the record in the Court of Appeal

(a) Subsequent trial court orders

(1) If, after the record is certified, the trial court amends or recalls the judgment or makes any other order in the case, including an order affecting the sentence or probation, the clerk must promptly certify and send a copy of the amended abstract of judgment or other order—as an augmentation of the record—to:

(A) The reviewing court, the probation officer, the defendant,

(B) The defendant's appellate counsel for each defendant represented by separate counsel, and the Attorney General or the district attorney, whichever is counsel for the People on appeal; and

(C) The district attorney or Attorney General, whichever is not counsel for the People on appeal, if he or she requested a copy of the clerk's transcript under 8.336(c)(3).

(2) If there is any additional document or transcript related to the amended judgment or new order that any rule or order requires be included in the record, the clerk must send this document or transcript with the amended abstract of judgment or other order. The clerk must promptly copy and certify any such document, and the reporter must promptly prepare and certify any such transcript.

(Subd (a) amended effective January 1, 2007.)

(b) Omissions

(1) If, after the record is certified, the superior court clerk or the reporter learns that the record omits a document or transcript that any rule or order requires to be included, the clerk must promptly copy and certify the document or the reporter must promptly prepare and certify the transcript. Without the need for a court order, the clerk must promptly send the document or transcript—as an augmentation of the record—to all those who are listed under (a)(1).

(Subd (b) amended effective January 1, 2007.)

(c) Augmentation or correction by the reviewing court

At any time, on motion of a party or on its own motion, the reviewing court may order the record augmented or corrected as provided in rule 8.155. The clerk must send any document or transcript added to the record to all those who are listed under (a)(1).

(Subd (c) amended and relettered effective January 1, 2007; adopted as subd (d) effective January 1, 2004.)

(d) Defendant not yet represented

If the defendant is not represented by appellate counsel when the record is augmented or corrected, the clerk must send that defendant's counsel's copy of the augmentations or corrections to the district appellate project.

(Subd (d) adopted effective January 1, 2007.)

Rule 8.340 amended and renumbered effective January 1, 2007; adopted as rule 32.1 effective January 1, 2004.

Advisory Committee Comment

Subdivision (b). The words "or order" in the first sentence of (b) are intended to refer to any court order to include additional material in the record, e.g., an order of the superior court under rule 8.324(d)(1).

Rule 8.344. Agreed statement

If the parties present the appeal on an agreed statement, they must comply with the relevant provisions of rule 8.134, but the appellant must file an original and, if the statement is filed in paper form, three copies of the statement in superior court within 25 days after filing the notice of appeal.

Rule 8.344 amended effective January 1, 2016; adopted as rule 32.2 effective January 1, 2004; amended and renumbered as rule 8.344 effective January 1, 2007.

Rule 8.346. Settled statement

(a) Application

As soon as a party learns that any portion of the oral proceedings cannot be transcribed, the party may serve and file in superior court an application for permission to prepare a settled statement. The application must explain why the oral proceedings cannot be transcribed.

(b) Order and proposed statement

The judge must rule on the application within five days after it is filed. If the judge grants the application, the parties must comply with the relevant provisions of rule 8.137, but the applicant must deliver a proposed statement to the judge for settlement within 30 days after it is ordered, unless the reviewing court extends the time.

(Subd (b) amended effective January 1, 2007.)

(c) Serving and filing the settled statement

The applicant must prepare, serve, and file in superior court an original and, if the statement is filed in paper form, three copies of the settled statement.

(Subd (c) amended effective January 1, 2016.)

Rule 8.346 amended effective January 1, 2016; adopted as rule 32.3 effective January 1, 2004; amended and renumbered as rule 8.346 effective January 1, 2007.

Article 3
Briefs, Hearing, and Decision

Rule 8.360. Briefs by parties and amici curiae
Rule 8.361. Certificate of interested entities or persons
Rule 8.366. Hearing and decision in the Court of Appeal
Rule 8.368. Hearing and decision in the Supreme Court

Rule 8.360. Briefs by parties and amici curiae

(a) Contents and form

Except as provided in this rule, briefs in criminal appeals must comply as nearly as possible with rules 8.200 and 8.204.

(Subd (a) amended effective January 1, 2007.)

(b) Length

(1) A brief produced on a computer must not exceed 25,500 words, including footnotes. Such a brief must include a certificate by appellate counsel or an unrepresented defendant stating the number of words in the brief; the person certifying may rely on the word count of the computer program used to prepare the brief.

(2) A typewritten brief must not exceed 75 pages.

(3) The tables required under rule 8.204(a)(1), the cover information required under rule 8.204(b)(10), any Certificate of Interested Entities or Persons required under rule 8.361, a certificate under (1), any signature block, and any attachment permitted under rule 8.204(d) are excluded from the limits stated in (1) or (2).

(4) A combined brief in an appeal governed by (e) must not exceed double the limit stated in (1) or (2).

(5) On application, the presiding justice may permit a longer brief for good cause.

(Subd (b) amended effective January 1, 2011; previously amended effective January 1, 2007.)

(c) Time to file

(1) The appellant's opening brief must be served and filed within 40 days after the record is filed in the reviewing court.

(2) The respondent's brief must be served and filed within 30 days after the appellant's opening brief is filed.

(3) The appellant must serve and file a reply brief, if any, within 20 days after the respondent files its brief.

(4) The time to serve and file a brief may not be extended by stipulation, but only by order of the presiding justice under rule 8.60.

(5) If a party fails to timely file an appellant's opening brief or a respondent's brief, the reviewing court clerk must promptly notify the party in writing that the brief must be filed within 30 days after the notice is sent, and that failure to comply may result in one of the following sanctions:

(A) If the brief is an appellant's opening brief:

(i) If the appellant is the People, the court will dismiss the appeal;

(ii) If the appellant is the defendant and is represented by appointed counsel on appeal, the court will relieve that appointed counsel and appoint new counsel;

(iii) If the appellant is the defendant and is not represented by appointed counsel, the court will dismiss the appeal; or

(B) If the brief is a respondent's brief, the court will decide the appeal on the record, the opening brief, and any oral argument by the appellant.

(6) If a party fails to comply with a notice under (5), the court may impose the sanction specified in the notice.

(Subd (c) amended effective January 1, 2016; previously amended effective January 1, 2007.)

(d) Service

(1) Defendant's appellate counsel must serve each brief for the defendant on the People and the district attorney, and must send a copy of each to the defendant personally unless the defendant requests otherwise.

(2) The proof of service under (1) must state that a copy of the defendant's brief was sent to the defendant, or counsel must file a signed statement that the defendant requested in writing that no copy be sent.

(3) The People must serve two copies of their briefs on the appellate counsel for each defendant who is a party to the appeal and one copy on the district appellate project. If the district attorney is representing the People, one copy of the district attorney's brief must be served on the Attorney General.

(4) A copy of each brief must be served on the superior court clerk for delivery to the trial judge.

(Subd (d) amended effective January 1, 2013.)

(e) When a defendant and the People appeal

When both a defendant and the People appeal, the defendant must file the first opening brief unless the reviewing court orders otherwise, and rule 8.216(b) governs the contents of the briefs.

(Subd (e) amended effective January 1, 2007.)

(f) Amicus curiae briefs

Amicus curiae briefs may be filed as provided in rule 8.200(c).

(Subd (f) amended effective January 1, 2007.)

Rule 8.360 amended effective January 1, 2016; repealed and adopted as rule 33 effective January 1, 2004; previously amended and renumbered as rule 8.360 effective January 1, 2007; previously amended effective January 1, 2011, and January 1, 2013.

Advisory Committee Comment

Subdivision (b). Subdivision (b)(1) states the maximum permissible length of a brief produced on a computer in terms of word count rather than page count. This provision tracks a provision in rule 8.204(c) governing Court of Appeal briefs and is explained in the comment to that provision. The word count assumes a brief using one-and-one-half spaced lines of text, as permitted by rule 8.204(b)(5). Subdivision (b)(3) specifies certain items that are not counted toward the maximum brief length. Signature blocks as referenced in this provision, include not only the signatures, but also the printed names, titles, and affiliations of any attorneys filing or joining in the brief, which may accompany the signature.

The maximum permissible length of briefs in death penalty appeals is prescribed in rule 8.630.

Rule 8.361. Certificate of interested entities or persons

In criminal cases in which an entity is a defendant, that defendant must comply with the requirements of rule 8.208 concerning serving and filing a certificate of interested entities or persons.

Rule 8.361 adopted effective January 1, 2009.

Advisory Committee Comment

Under rule 8.208(c), for purposes of certificates of interested entities or persons, an "entity" means a corporation, a partnership, a firm, or any other association but does not include a governmental entity or its agencies or a natural person.

Rule 8.366. Hearing and decision in the Court of Appeal

(a) General application of rules 8.252–8.272

Except as provided in this rule, rules 8.252–8.272 govern the hearing and decision in the Court of Appeal of an appeal in a criminal case.

(Subd (a) amended and lettered effective January 1, 2009; adopted as unlettered subd effective January 1, 2004.)

(b) Finality

(1) Except as otherwise provided in this rule, a Court of Appeal decision in a proceeding under this chapter, including an order dismissing an appeal involuntarily, is final in that court 30 days after filing.

(2) The following Court of Appeal decisions are final in that court on filing:

(A) The denial of an application for bail or to reduce bail pending appeal; and

(B) The dismissal of an appeal on request or stipulation.

(3) If a Court of Appeal certifies its opinion for publication or partial publication after filing its decision and before its decision becomes final in that court, the finality period runs from the filing date of the order for publication.

(4) If an order modifying an opinion changes the appellate judgment, the finality period runs from the filing date of the modification order.

(Subd (b) adopted effective January 1, 2009.)

(c) Sanctions

Except for (a)(1), rule 8.276 applies in criminal appeals.

(Subd (c) amended and lettered effective January 1, 2009; adopted as unlettered subd effective January 1, 2004.)

Rule 8.366 amended effective January 1, 2009; adopted as rule 33.1 effective January 1, 2004; previously amended and renumbered effective January 1, 2007; previously amended effective January 1, 2008.

Advisory Committee Comment

Subdivision (b). As used in subdivision (b)(1), "decision" includes all interlocutory orders of the Court of Appeal. (See Advisory Committee Comment to rule 8.500(a) and (e).) This provision addresses the finality of decisions in criminal appeals. See rule 8.264(b) for provisions addressing the finality of decisions in proceedings under chapter 2, relating to civil appeals, and rule 8.490 for provisions addressing the finality of proceedings under chapter 7, relating to writs of mandate, certiorari, and prohibition.

Rule 8.368. Hearing and decision in the Supreme Court

Rules 8.500 through 8.552 govern the hearing and decision in the Supreme Court of an appeal in a criminal case.

Rule 8.368 amended and renumbered effective January 1, 2007; adopted as rule 33.2 effective January 1, 2004.

Chapter 4
Habeas Corpus Appeals and Writs

Art. 1. Habeas Corpus Proceedings Not Related to Judgment of Death. Rules 8.380–8.388.

Art. 2. Appeals From Superior Court Decisions in Death Penalty–Related Habeas Corpus Proceedings. Rules 8.390–8.398.

Article 1
Habeas Corpus Proceedings Not Related to Judgment of Death

Title 8, Appellate Rules—Division 1, Rules Relating to the Supreme Court and Courts of Appeal—Chapter 4, Habeas Corpus Appeals and Writs—Article 1,

Habeas Corpus Proceedings Not Related to Judgment of Death adopted effective April 25, 2019.

Rule 8.380. Petition for writ of habeas corpus filed by petitioner not represented by an attorney
Rule 8.384. Petition for writ of habeas corpus filed by an attorney for a party
Rule 8.385. Proceedings after the petition is filed
Rule 8.386. Proceedings if the return is ordered to be filed in the reviewing court
Rule 8.387. Decision in habeas corpus proceedings
Rule 8.388. Appeal from order granting relief by writ of habeas corpus

Rule 8.380. Petition for writ of habeas corpus filed by petitioner not represented by an attorney

(a) Required Judicial Council form

A person who is not represented by an attorney and who petitions a reviewing court for writ of habeas corpus seeking release from, or modification of the conditions of, custody of a person confined in a state or local penal institution, hospital, narcotics treatment facility, or other institution must file the petition on *Petition for Writ of Habeas Corpus* (form HC-001). For good cause the court may permit the filing of a petition that is not on that form, but the petition must be verified.

(Subd (a) amended effective January 1, 2020; previously amended effective January 1, 2006, January 1, 2007, January 1, 2009, and January 1, 2018.)

(b) Form and content

A petition filed under (a) need not comply with the provisions of rules 8.40, 8.204, or 8.486 that prescribe the form and content of a petition and require the petition to be accompanied by a memorandum. If any supporting documents accompanying the petition are sealed or confidential records, rules 8.45–8.47 govern these documents.

(Subd (b) amended effective January 1, 2014; adopted as part of subd (a) effective January 1, 2005; previously repealed, amended and lettered effective January 1, 2009.)

(c) Number of copies

In the Court of Appeal, the petitioner must file the original of the petition under (a) and one set of any supporting documents. In the Supreme Court, the petitioner must file an original and, if the petition is filed in paper form, 10 copies of the petition and an original and, if the document is filed in paper form, 2 copies of any supporting document accompanying the petition unless the court orders otherwise.

(Subd (c) amended effective January 1, 2016; adopted as part of subd (a) effective January 1, 2005; previously repealed, amended, and lettered as subd (c) effective January 1, 2009.)

Rule 8.380 amended effective January 1, 2020; repealed and adopted as rule 60 effective January 1, 2005; previously amended and renumbered as rule 8.380 effective January 1, 2007; previously amended effective January 1, 2006, January 1, 2009, January 1, 2014, January 1, 2016, and January 1, 2018.

Advisory Committee Comment

Subdivision (b). Examples of confidential records include Penal Code section 1203.03 diagnostic reports, records closed to inspection by court order under *People v. Marsden* (1970) 2 Cal.3d 118 or *Pitchess v. Superior Court* (1974) 11 Cal.3d 531, in-camera proceedings on a confidential informant, and defense expert funding requests (Pen. Code, § 987.9; *Keenan v. Superior Court* (1982) 31 Cal.3d 424, 430).

Rule 8.384. Petition for writ of habeas corpus filed by an attorney for a party

(a) Form and content of petition and memorandum

(1) A petition for habeas corpus filed by an attorney need not be filed on *Petition for Writ of Habeas Corpus* (form HC-001), but must contain the information requested in that form and must be verified. All petitions filed by attorneys, whether or not on form HC-001, must be either typewritten or produced on a computer, and must comply with this rule and rule 8.40(b)–(c) relating to document covers and rule 8.204(a)(1)(A) relating to tables of contents and authorities. A petition that is not on form HC-001 must also comply with the remainder of rule 8.204(a)–(b).

(2) Any memorandum accompanying the petition must comply with rule 8.204(a)–(b). Except in habeas corpus proceedings related to sentences of death, any memorandum must also comply with the length limits in rule 8.204(c).

(3) The petition and any memorandum must support any reference to a matter in the supporting documents by a citation to its index number or letter and page.

(Subd (a) amended effective January 1, 2020; adopted as part of subd (b) effective January 1, 2006; previously repealed, amended, and lettered as subd (a) effective January 1, 2009; previously amended effective January 1, 2016, and January 1, 2018.)

(b) Supporting documents

(1) The petition must be accompanied by a copy of any petition—excluding exhibits—pertaining to the same judgment and petitioner that was previously filed in any state court or any federal court. If such documents have previously been filed in the same Court of Appeal where the petition is filed or in the Supreme Court and the petition so states and identifies the documents by case name and number, copies of these documents need not be included in the supporting documents.

(2) If the petition asserts a claim that was the subject of an evidentiary hearing, the petition must be accompanied by a certified transcript of that hearing.

(3) Rule 8.486(c)(1) and (2) govern the form of any supporting documents accompanying the petition.

(4) If any supporting documents accompanying the petition are sealed or confidential records, rules 8.45–8.47 govern these documents.

(Subd (b) amended effective January 1, 2014; previously amended effective January 1, 2007, and January 1, 2009.)

(c) Number of copies

If the petition is filed in the Supreme Court, the attorney must file the number of copies of the petition and supporting documents required by rule 8.44(a). If the petition is filed in the Court of Appeal, the attorney must file the number of copies of the petition and supporting documents required by rule 8.44(b).

(Subd (c) amended and lettered effective January 1, 2009; adopted as part of subd (b) effective January 1, 2006.)

(d) Noncomplying petitions

The clerk must file an attorney's petition not complying with (a)–(c) if it otherwise complies with the rules of court, but the court may notify the attorney that it may strike the petition or impose a lesser sanction if the petition is not brought into compliance within a stated reasonable time of not less than five days.

(Subd (d) amended and lettered effective January 1, 2009; adopted as part of subd (b) effective January 1, 2006.)

Rule 8.384 amended effective January 1, 2020; adopted as rule 60.5 effective January 1, 2006; previously amended and renumbered as rule 8.384 effective January 1, 2007; previously amended effective January 1, 2009, January 1, 2014, January 1, 2016, and January 1, 2018.

Advisory Committee Comment

Subdivision (b)(4). Examples of confidential records include Penal Code section 1203.03 diagnostic reports, records closed to inspection by court order under *People v. Marsden* (1970) 2 Cal.3d 118 or *Pitchess v. Superior Court* (1974) 11 Cal.3d 531, in-camera proceedings on a confidential informant, and defense expert funding requests (Pen. Code, § 987.9; *Keenan v. Superior Court* (1982) 31 Cal.3d 424, 430).

Rule 8.385. Proceedings after the petition is filed

(a) Production of record

Before ruling on the petition, the court may order the custodian of any relevant record to produce the record or a certified copy to be filed with the court. Sealed and confidential records are governed by rules 8.45–8.47.

(Subd (a) amended effective January 1, 2014; adopted effective January 1, 2009.)

(b) Informal response

(1) Before ruling on the petition, the court may request an informal written response from the respondent, the real party in interest, or an interested person. The court must send a copy of any request to the petitioner.

(2) The response must be served and filed within 15 days or as the court specifies. If the petitioner is not represented by counsel in the habeas corpus proceeding, one copy of the informal response and any supporting documents must be served on the petitioner. If the petitioner is represented by counsel in the habeas corpus proceeding, the response must be served on the petitioner's counsel. If the response is served in paper form, two copies must be served on the petitioner's counsel. If the petitioner is represented by court-appointed counsel other than the State Public Defender's Office or Habeas Corpus Resource Center, one copy must also be served on the applicable appellate project.

(3) If a response is filed, the court must notify the petitioner that a reply may be served and filed within 15 days or as the court specifies. The court may not deny the petition until that time has expired.

(Subd (b) amended effective January 1, 2016; adopted effective January 1, 2009; previously amended effective January 1, 2014.)

(c) Petition filed in an inappropriate court

(1) A Court of Appeal may deny without prejudice a petition for writ of habeas corpus that is based primarily on facts occurring outside the court's appellate district, including petitions that question:

(A) The validity of judgments or orders of trial courts located outside the district; or

(B) The conditions of confinement or the conduct of correctional officials outside the district.

(2) A Court of Appeal should deny without prejudice a petition for writ of habeas corpus that challenges the denial of parole or the petitioner's suitability for parole if the issue was not first adjudicated by the trial court that rendered the underlying judgment.

(3) If the court denies a petition solely under (1), the order must state the basis of the denial and must identify the appropriate court in which to file the petition.

(Subd (c) amended effective January 1, 2012; adopted effective January 1, 2009.)

(d) Order to show cause

If the petitioner has made the required prima facie showing that he or she is entitled to relief, the court must issue an order to show cause. An order to show cause does not grant the relief sought in the petition.

(Subd (d) adopted effective January 1, 2009.)

(e) Return to the superior court

The reviewing court may order the respondent to file a return in the superior court. The order vests jurisdiction over the cause in the superior court, which must proceed under rule 4.551.

(Subd (e) adopted effective January 1, 2009.)

(f) Return to the reviewing court

If the return is ordered to be filed in the Supreme Court or the Court of Appeal, rule 8.386 applies [1].

(Subd (f) amended effective September 1, 2024; adopted effective January 1, 2009.)

Rule 8.385(f) 2024 Deletes. [1] and the court in which the return is ordered filed must appoint counsel for any unrepresented petitioner who desires but cannot afford counsel

(g) Appointment of counsel

(1) If the return is ordered to be filed in the Supreme Court or the Court of Appeal, the court in which the return is ordered filed must appoint counsel for any unrepresented petitioner who desires but cannot afford counsel.

(2) When a petition raises a claim under Penal Code section 745(a) and requests appointment of counsel, the court must appoint counsel if the petitioner cannot afford counsel and either the petition alleges facts that would establish a violation of section 745(a) or the State Public Defender requests that counsel be appointed. Newly appointed counsel may amend a petition filed before their appointment.

(Subd (g) was adopted effective September 1, 2024.)

Rule 8.385 amended effective September 1, 2024; adopted effective January 1, 2009; previously amended effective January 1, 2012, January 1, 2014, and January 1, 2016.

Advisory Committee Comment

Subdivision (a). Examples of confidential records include Penal Code section 1203.03 diagnostic reports, records closed to inspection by court order under *People v. Marsden* (1970) 2 Cal.3d 118 or *Pitchess v. Superior Court* (1974) 11 Cal.3d 531, in-camera proceedings on a confidential informant, and defense expert funding requests (Pen. Code, § 987.9; *Keenan v. Superior Court* (1982) 31 Cal.3d 424, 430).

Subdivision (c). Except for subdivision (c)(2), rule 8.385(c) restates former section 6.5 of the Standards of Judicial Administration. Subdivision (c)(2) is based on the California Supreme Court decision in *In re Roberts* (2005) 36 Cal.4th 575, which provides that petitions for writ of habeas corpus challenging denial or suitability for parole should first be adjudicated in the trial court that rendered the underlying judgment. The committee notes, however, that courts of appeal have original jurisdiction in writ proceedings and may, under appropriate circumstances, adjudicate a petition that challenges the denial or suitability of parole even if the petition was not first adjudicated by the trial court that rendered the underlying judgment. (*In re Kler* (2010) 188 Cal.App.4th 1399.) A court of appeal may, for example, adjudicate a petition that follows the court's prior reversal of a denial of parole by the Board of Parole Hearings where the issues presented by the petition directly flow from the court of appeal's prior decision and the limited hearing conducted. (*Id.* at 1404–05.)

Subdivision (d). Case law establishes the specificity of the factual allegations and support for these allegations required in a petition for a writ of habeas corpus (see, e.g., *People v. Duvall* (1995) 9 Cal.4th 464, 474–475, and *Ex parte Swain* (1949) 34 Cal.2d 300, 303–304. A court evaluating whether a petition meeting these requirements makes a prima facie showing asks whether, assuming the petition's factual allegations are true, the petitioner would be entitled to relief (*People v. Duvall*, supra).

Issuing an order to show cause is just one of the actions a court might take on a petition for a writ of habeas corpus. Examples of other actions that a court might take include denying the petition summarily, requesting an informal response from the respondent under (b), or denying the petition without prejudice under (c) because it is filed in an inappropriate court.

Rule 8.386. Proceedings if the return is ordered to be filed in the reviewing court

(a) Application

This rule applies if the Supreme Court orders the return to be filed in the Supreme Court or the Court of Appeal or if the Court of Appeal orders the return to be filed in the Court of Appeal.

(Subd (a) adopted effective January 1, 2009.)

(b) Serving and filing return

(1) Unless the court orders otherwise, any return must be served and filed within 30 days after the court issues the order to show cause.

(2) If the return is filed in the Supreme Court, the respondent must file the number of copies of the return and any supporting documents required by rule 8.44(a). If the return is filed in the Court of Appeal, the respondent must file the number of copies of the return and any supporting documents required by rule 8.44(b).

(3) The return and any supporting documents must be served on the petitioner's counsel. If the return is served in paper form, two copies must be served on the petitioner's counsel. If the petitioner is represented for the habeas corpus proceeding by court-appointed counsel other than the State Public Defender's Office or Habeas Corpus Resource Center, one copy must be served on the applicable appellate project.

(Subd (b) amended effective January 1, 2016; adopted effective January 1, 2009; previously amended effective January 1, 2014.)

(c) Form and content of return

(1) The return must be either typewritten or produced on a computer and must comply with Penal Code section 1480 and rules 8.40(b)–(c) and 8.204(a)–(b). Except in habeas corpus proceedings related to sentences of death, any memorandum accompanying a return must also comply with the length limits in rule 8.204(c).

(2) Rule 8.486(c)(1) and (2) govern the form of any supporting documents accompanying the return. The return must support any reference to a matter in the supporting documents by a citation to its index number or letter and page.

(3) Any material allegation of the petition not controverted by the return is deemed admitted for purposes of the proceeding.

(Subd (c) amended effective January 1, 2016; adopted effective January 1, 2009; previously amended effective January 1, 2014.)

(d) Traverse

(1) Unless the court orders otherwise, within 30 days after the respondent files a return, the petitioner may serve and file a traverse.

(2) Any traverse must be either typewritten or produced on a computer and must comply with Penal Code section 1484 and rules 8.40(b)–(c) and 8.204(a)–(b). Except in habeas corpus proceedings related to sentences of death, any memorandum accompanying a traverse must also comply with the length limits in rule 8.204(c).

(3) Rule 8.486(c)(1) and (2) govern the form of any supporting documents accompanying the traverse.

(4) Any material allegation of the return not denied in the traverse is deemed admitted for purposes of the proceeding.

(5) If the return is filed in the Supreme Court, the attorney must file the number of copies of the traverse required by rule 8.44(a). If the return is filed in the Court of Appeal, the attorney must file the number of copies of the traverse required by rule 8.44(b).

(Subd (d) amended effective January 1, 2014; adopted effective January 1, 2009.)

(e) Judicial notice

Rule 8.252(a) governs judicial notice in the reviewing court.

(Subd (e) adopted effective January 1, 2009.)

(f) Evidentiary hearing ordered by the reviewing court

(1) An evidentiary hearing is required if, after considering the verified petition, the return, any traverse, any affidavits or declarations under penalty of perjury, and matters of which judicial notice may be taken, the court finds there is a reasonable likelihood that the petitioner may be entitled to relief and the petitioner's entitlement to relief depends on the resolution of an issue of fact.

(2) If the court issues an order to show cause on a claim raised under Penal Code section 745(a), the court must hold an evidentiary

hearing unless the state declines to show cause. The defendant may appear remotely, and the court may conduct the hearing with remote technology, unless counsel indicates the defendant's presence in court is needed.

[1] **(3)** The court may appoint a referee to conduct the hearing and make recommended findings of fact.

(Subd (f) amended effective September 1, 2024; adopted effective January 1, 2009.)

Rule 8.386(f)   2024 Deletes. [1] (2)

(g) Oral argument and submission of the cause

Unless the court orders otherwise:

(1) Rule 8.256 governs oral argument and submission of the cause in the Court of Appeal.

(2) Rule 8.524 governs oral argument and submission of the cause in the Supreme Court.

(Subd (g) adopted effective January 1, 2009.)

Rule 8.386 amended effective September 1, 2024; adopted effective January 1, 2009; previously amended effective January 1, 2014, and January 1, 2016.

Rule 8.387.   Decision in habeas corpus proceedings

(a) Filing the decision

(1) Rule 8.264(a) governs the filing of the decision in the Court of Appeal.

(2) Rule 8.532(a) governs the filing of the decision in the Supreme Court.

(Subd (a) adopted effective January 1, 2009.)

(b) Finality of decision in the Court of Appeal

(1) *General finality period*

Except as otherwise provided in this rule, a Court of Appeal decision in a habeas corpus proceeding is final in that court 30 days after filing.

(2) *Denial of a petition for writ of habeas corpus without issuance of an order to show cause*

(A) Except as provided in (B), a Court of Appeal decision denying a petition for writ of habeas corpus without issuance of an order to show cause is final in the Court of Appeal upon filing.

(B) A Court of Appeal decision denying a petition for writ of habeas corpus without issuing an order to show cause is final in that court on the same day that its decision in a related appeal is final if the two decisions are filed on the same day. If the Court of Appeal orders rehearing of the decision in the appeal, its decision denying the petition for writ of habeas corpus is final when its decision on rehearing is final.

(3) *Decision in a habeas corpus proceeding after issuance of an order to show cause*

(A) If necessary to prevent mootness or frustration of the relief granted or to otherwise promote the interests of justice, a Court of Appeal may order early finality in that court of a decision in a habeas corpus proceeding after issuing an order to show cause. The decision may provide for finality in that court on filing or within a stated period of less than 30 days.

(B) If a Court of Appeal certifies its opinion for publication or partial publication after filing its decision and before its decision becomes final in that court, the finality period runs from the filing date of the order for publication.

(Subd (b) adopted effective January 1, 2009.)

(c) Finality of decision in the Supreme Court

Rule 8.532(b) governs finality of a decision in the Supreme Court.

(Subd (c) adopted effective January 1, 2009.)

(d) Modification of decision

(1) A reviewing court may modify a decision until the decision is final in that court. If the clerk's office is closed on the date of finality, the court may modify the decision on the next day the clerk's office is open.

(2) An order modifying an opinion must state whether it changes the appellate judgment. A modification that does not change the appellate judgment does not extend the finality date of the decision. If a modification changes the appellate judgment, the finality period runs from the filing date of the modification order.

(Subd (d) adopted effective January 1, 2009.)

(e) Rehearing

(1) Rule 8.268 governs rehearing in the Court of Appeal.

(2) Rule 8.536 governs rehearing in the Supreme Court.

(Subd (e) adopted effective January 1, 2009.)

(f) Remittitur

(1) A Court of Appeal must issue a remittitur in a habeas corpus proceeding under this chapter except when the court denies the petition without issuing an order to show cause or orders the return filed in the superior court.

(2) A Court of Appeal must also issue a remittitur if the Supreme Court issues a remittitur to the Court of Appeal.

(3) Rule 8.272(b)–(d) governs issuance of a remittitur by a Court of Appeal in habeas corpus proceedings, including the clerk's duties; immediate issuance, stay, and recall of remittitur; and notice of issuance.

(Subd (f) amended effective January 1, 2014; adopted as unlettered subd effective January 1, 2008; previously amended and lettered effective January 1, 2009.)

Rule 8.387 amended effective January 1, 2014; adopted as rule 8.386 effective January 1, 2008; previously amended and renumbered effective January 1, 2009.

Advisory Committee Comment

A party may seek review of a Court of Appeal decision in a habeas corpus proceeding by way of a petition for review in the Supreme Court under rule 8.500.

Subdivision (f). Under this rule, a remittitur serves as notice that the habeas corpus proceedings have concluded.

Rule 8.388.   Appeal from order granting relief by writ of habeas corpus

(a) Application

Except as otherwise provided in this rule, rules 8.304–8.368 and 8.508 govern appeals under Penal Code section 1506 or 1507 from orders granting all or part of the relief sought in a petition for writ of habeas corpus. This rule does not apply to appeals under Penal Code section 1509.1 from superior court decisions in death penalty–related habeas corpus proceedings.

(Subd (a) amended effective April 25, 2019; previously amended effective January 1, 2007.)

(b) Contents of record

In an appeal under this rule, the record must contain:

(1) The petition, the return, and the traverse;

(2) The order to show cause;

(3) All court minutes;

(4) All documents and exhibits submitted to the court;

(5) The reporter's transcript of any oral proceedings;

(6) Any written opinion of the court;

(7) The order appealed from; and

(8) The notice of appeal.

(Subd (b) amended effective January 1, 2007.)

Rule 8.388 amended effective April 25, 2019; repealed and adopted as rule 39.2 effective January 1, 2005; previously amended and renumbered as rule 8.388 effective January 1, 2007.

Article 2
Appeals From Superior Court Decisions in Death Penalty–Related Habeas Corpus Proceedings

Title 8, Appellate Rules—Division 1, Rules Relating to the Supreme Court and Courts of Appeal—Chapter 4, Habeas Corpus Appeals and Writs—Article 2, Appeals From Superior Court Decisions in Death Penalty–Related Habeas Corpus Proceedings adopted effective April 25, 2019.

Rule 8.390. Application
Rule 8.391. Qualifications and appointment of counsel by the Court of Appeal
Rule 8.392. Filing the appeal; certificate of appealability
Rule 8.393. Time to appeal
Rule 8.394. Stay of execution on appeal
Rule 8.395. Record on appeal
Rule 8.396. Briefs by parties and amici curiae
Rule 8.397. Claim of ineffective assistance of trial counsel not raised in the superior court
Rule 8.398. Finality

Rule 8.390.   Application

(a) Application

The rules in this article apply only to appeals under Penal Code section 1509.1 from superior court decisions in death penalty–related habeas corpus proceedings.

(Subd (a) adopted effective April 25, 2019.)

(b) General application of rules for criminal appeals

Except as otherwise provided in this article, rules 8.300, 8.316, 8.332, 8.340–8.346, and 8.366–8.368 govern appeals subject to the rules in this article.

(Subd (b) adopted effective April 25, 2019.)

Rule 8.390 adopted effective April 25, 2019.

Rule 8.391. Qualifications and appointment of counsel by the Court of Appeal

(a) Qualifications

To be appointed by the Court of Appeal to represent an indigent petitioner not represented by the State Public Defender in an appeal under this article, an attorney must:

(1) Meet the minimum qualifications established by rule 8.652 for attorneys to be appointed to represent a person in a death penalty–related habeas corpus proceeding, including being willing to cooperate with an assisting counsel or entity that the court may designate;

(2) Be familiar with appellate practices and procedures in the California courts, including those related to death penalty appeals; and

(3) Not have represented the petitioner in the habeas corpus proceedings that are the subject of the appeal unless the petitioner and counsel expressly request, in writing, continued representation.

(Subd (a) adopted effective April 25, 2019.)

(b) Designation of assisting entity or counsel

Either before or at the time it appoints counsel, the court must designate an assisting entity or counsel.

(Subd (b) adopted effective April 25, 2019.)

Rule 8.391 adopted effective April 25, 2019.

Rule 8.392. Filing the appeal; certificate of appealability

(a) Notice of appeal

(1) To appeal from a superior court decision in a death penalty–related habeas corpus proceeding, the petitioner or the People must serve and file a notice of appeal in that superior court. To appeal a decision denying relief on a successive habeas corpus petition, the petitioner must also comply with (b).

(2) If the petitioner appeals, petitioner's counsel, or, in the absence of counsel, the petitioner, is responsible for signing the notice of appeal. If the People appeal, the attorney for the People must sign the notice.

(Subd (a) adopted effective April 25, 2019.)

(b) Appeal of decision denying relief on a successive habeas corpus petition

(1) The petitioner may appeal the decision of the superior court denying relief on a successive death penalty–related habeas corpus petition only if the superior court or the Court of Appeal grants a certificate of appealability under Penal Code section 1509.1(c).

(2) The petitioner must identify in the notice of appeal that the appeal is from a superior court decision denying relief on a successive petition and indicate whether the superior court granted or denied a certificate of appealability.

(3) If the superior court denied a certificate of appealability, the petitioner must attach to the notice of appeal a request to the Court of Appeal for a certificate of appealability. The request must identify the petitioner's claim or claims for relief and explain how the requirements of Penal Code section 1509(d) have been met.

(4) On receiving the request for a certificate of appealability, the Court of Appeal clerk must promptly file the request and send notice of the filing date to the parties.

(5) The People need not file an answer to a request for a certificate of appealability unless the court requests an answer. The clerk must promptly send to the parties and the assisting entity or counsel copies of any order requesting an answer and immediately notify the parties by telephone or another expeditious method. Any answer must be served on the parties and the assisting entity or counsel and filed within five days after the order is filed unless the court orders otherwise.

(6) The Court of Appeal must grant or deny the request for a certificate of appealability within 10 days of the filing of the request in that court. If the Court of Appeal grants a certificate of appealability, the certificate must identify the substantial claim or claims for relief shown by the petitioner. The clerk must send a copy of the certificate or its order denying the request for a certificate to:

(A) The attorney for the petitioner or, if unrepresented, to the petitioner;

(B) The district appellate project and, if designated, any assisting entity or counsel other than the district appellate project;

(C) The Attorney General;

(D) The district attorney;

(E) The superior court clerk; and

(F) The clerk/executive officer of the Supreme Court.

(7) If both the superior court and the Court of Appeal deny a certificate of appealability, the clerk/executive officer of the Court of Appeal must mark the notice of appeal "Inoperative," notify the petitioner, and send a copy of the marked notice of appeal to the superior court clerk, the clerk/executive officer of the Supreme Court, the district appellate project, and, if designated, any assisting entity or counsel other than the district appellate project.

(Subd (b) adopted effective April 25, 2019.)

(c) Notification of the appeal

(1) Except as provided in (2), when a notice of appeal is filed, the superior court clerk must promptly—and no later than five days after the notice of appeal is filed—send a notification of the filing to:

(A) The attorney for the petitioner or, if unrepresented, to the petitioner;

(B) The district appellate project and, if designated, any assisting entity or counsel other than the district appellate project;

(C) The Attorney General;

(D) The district attorney;

(E) The clerk/executive officer of the Court of Appeal;

(F) The clerk/executive officer of the Supreme Court;

(G) Each court reporter; and

(H) Any primary reporter or reporting supervisor.

(2) If the petitioner is appealing from a superior court decision denying relief on a successive petition and the superior court did not issue a certificate of appealability, the clerk must not send the notification of the filing of a notice of appeal to the court reporter or reporters unless the clerk receives a copy of a certificate of appealability issued by the Court of Appeal under (b)(6). The clerk must send the notification no later than five days after the superior court receives the copy of the certificate of appealability.

(3) The notification must show the date it was sent, the number and title of the case, and the dates the notice of appeal was filed and any certificate of appealability was issued. If the information is available, the notification must also include:

(A) The name, address, telephone number, e-mail address, and California State Bar number of each attorney of record in the case; and

(B) The name of the party each attorney represented in the superior court.

(4) The notification to the clerk/executive officer of the Court of Appeal must also include a copy of the notice of appeal, any certificate of appealability or denial of a certificate of appealability issued by the superior court, and the sequential list of reporters made under rule 2.950.

(5) A copy of the notice of appeal is sufficient notification under (1) if the required information is on the copy or is added by the superior court clerk.

(6) The sending of a notification under (1) is a sufficient performance of the clerk's duty despite the discharge, disqualification, suspension, disbarment, or death of the attorney.

(7) Failure to comply with any provision of this subdivision does not affect the validity of the notice of appeal.

(Subd (c) adopted effective April 25, 2019.)

Rule 8.392 adopted effective April 25, 2019.

Advisory Committee Comment

Subdivision (b). This subdivision addresses issuance of a certificate of appealability by the Court of Appeal. Rule 4.576(b) addresses issuance of a certificate of appealability by the superior court.

Rule 8.393. Time to appeal

A notice of appeal under this article must be filed within 30 days after the rendition of the judgment or the making of the order being appealed.

Rule 8.393 adopted effective April 25, 2019.

Rule 8.394. Stay of execution on appeal

(a) Application

Pending appeal under this article, the petitioner may apply to the reviewing court for a stay of execution of the death penalty. The application must be served on the People.

(Subd (a) adopted effective April 25, 2019.)

(b) Interim relief

Pending its ruling on the application, the reviewing court may grant the relief requested. The reviewing court must notify the superior court under rule 8.489 of any stay that it grants. Notification must also be sent to the clerk/executive officer of the Supreme Court.

(Subd (b) adopted effective April 25, 2019.)

Rule 8.394 adopted effective April 25, 2019.

Rule 8.395. Record on appeal

(a) Contents

In an appeal under this article, the record must contain:

(1) A clerk's transcript containing:

(A) The petition;

(B) Any informal response to the petition and any reply to the informal response;

(C) Any order to show cause;

(D) Any reply, return, answer, denial, or traverse;

(E) All supporting documents under rule 4.571, including the record prepared for the automatic appeal and all briefs, rulings, and other documents filed in the automatic appeal;

(F) Any other documents and exhibits submitted to the court, including any transcript of a sound or sound-and-video recording tendered to the court under rule 2.1040 and any visual aids submitted to the court;

(G) Any written communication between the court and the parties, including printouts of any e-mail messages and their attachments;

(H) All court minutes;

(I) Any statement of decision required by Penal Code section 1509(f) and any other written decision of the court;

(J) The order appealed from;

(K) The notice of appeal; and

(L) Any certificate of appealability issued by the superior court or the Court of Appeal.

(2) A reporter's transcript of any oral proceedings.

(Subd (a) adopted effective April 25, 2019.)

(b) Stipulation for partial transcript

If counsel for the petitioner and the People stipulate in writing before the record is certified that any part of the record is not required for proper determination of the appeal, that part need not be prepared or sent to the reviewing court.

(Subd (b) adopted effective April 25, 2019.)

(c) Preparation of record

(1) The reporter and the clerk must begin preparing the record immediately after the superior court issues the decision on an initial petition under Penal Code section 1509.

(2) If either party appeals from a superior court decision on a successive petition under Penal Code section 1509.1(c):

(A) The clerk must begin preparing the clerk's transcript immediately after the filing of the notice of appeal or, if one is required, the superior court's issuance of a certificate of appealability or the clerk's receipt of a copy of a certificate of appealability issued by the Court of Appeal under rule 8.391(b)(5), whichever is later. If a certificate of appealability is required to appeal the decision of the superior court, the clerk must not begin preparing the clerk's transcript until a certificate of appealability has issued.

(B) The reporter must begin preparing the reporter's transcript immediately on being notified by the clerk under rule 8.392(c) that the notice of appeal has been filed.

(Subd (c) adopted effective April 25, 2019.)

(d) Clerk's transcript

(1) Within 30 days after the clerk is required to begin preparing the transcript, the clerk must complete preparation of an original and four copies of the clerk's transcript.

(2) On request, the clerk must prepare an extra copy for the district attorney or the Attorney General, whichever is not counsel for the People on appeal.

(3) The clerk must certify as correct the original and all copies of the clerk's transcript.

(Subd (d) adopted effective April 25, 2019.)

(e) Reporter's transcript

(1) The reporter must prepare an original and the same number of copies of the reporter's transcript as (d) requires of the clerk's transcript, and must certify each as correct.

(2) As soon as the transcripts are certified, but no later than 30 days after the reporter is required to begin preparing the transcript, the reporter must deliver the original and all copies to the superior court clerk.

(3) Any portion of the transcript transcribed during superior court habeas corpus proceedings must not be retyped unless necessary to correct errors, but must be repaginated and combined with any portion of the transcript not previously transcribed. Any additional copies needed must not be retyped but, if the transcript is in paper form, must be prepared by photocopying or an equivalent process.

(4) In a multireporter case, the clerk must accept any completed portion of the transcript from the primary reporter one week after the time prescribed by (2) even if other portions are uncompleted. The clerk must promptly pay each reporter who certifies that all portions of the transcript assigned to that reporter are completed.

(Subd (e) adopted effective April 25, 2019.)

(f) Extension of time

(1) Except as provided in this rule, rules 8.60 and 8.63 govern requests for extension of time to prepare the record.

(2) On request of the clerk or a reporter showing good cause, the superior court may extend the time prescribed in (d) or (e) for preparing the clerk's or reporter's transcript for no more than 30 days. If the superior court orders an extension, the order must specify the reason justifying the extension. The clerk must promptly send a copy of the order to the reviewing court.

(3) For any further extension, the clerk or reporter must file a request in the reviewing court showing good cause.

(4) A request under (2) or (3) must be supported by:

(A) A declaration showing good cause. The court may presume good cause if the clerk's and reporter's transcripts combined will likely exceed 10,000 pages, not including the supporting documents submitted with the petition, any informal response, reply to the informal response, return, answer, or traverse; and

(B) In the case of a reporter's transcript, certification by the superior court presiding judge or a court administrator designated by the presiding judge that an extension is reasonable and necessary in light of the workload of all reporters in the court.

(Subd (f) adopted effective April 25, 2019.)

(g) Form of record

(1) The reporter's transcript must be in electronic form. The clerk is encouraged to send the clerk's transcript in electronic form if the court is able to do so.

(2) The clerk's and reporter's transcripts must comply with rules 8.45–8.47, relating to sealed and confidential records, and rule 8.144.

(Subd (g) adopted effective April 25, 2019.)

(h) Sending the transcripts

(1) When the clerk's and reporter's transcripts are certified as correct, the clerk must promptly send:

(A) The original transcripts to the reviewing court, noting the sending date on each original; and

(B) One copy of each transcript to:

(i) Appellate counsel for the petitioner;

(ii) The assisting entity or counsel, if designated, or the district appellate project;

(iii) The Attorney General or the district attorney, whichever is counsel for the People on appeal;

(iv) The district attorney or Attorney General if requested under (d)(2); and

(v) The Governor.

(2) If the petitioner is not represented by appellate counsel when the transcripts are certified as correct, the clerk must send that copy of the transcripts to the assisting entity or counsel, if designated, or the district appellate project.

(Subd (h) adopted effective April 25, 2019.)

(i) Supervision of preparation of record

The clerk/executive officer of the Court of Appeal, under the supervision of the administrative presiding justice or the presiding justice, must take all appropriate steps to ensure that superior court clerks and reporters promptly perform their duties under this rule. This provision does not affect the responsibility of the superior courts for the prompt preparation of appellate records.

(Subd (i) adopted effective April 25, 2019.)

(j) Augmenting or correcting the record in the Court of Appeal

Rule 8.340 governs augmenting or correcting the record in the Court of Appeal, except that copies of augmented or corrected records must be sent to those listed in (h).

(Subd (j) adopted effective April 25, 2019.)

(k) Judicial notice

Rule 8.252(a) governs judicial notice in the reviewing court.

(Subd (k) adopted effective April 25, 2019.)

Rule 8.395 adopted effective April 25, 2019.

Rule 8.396. Briefs by parties and amici curiae

(a) Contents and form

(1) Except as provided in this rule, briefs in appeals governed by the rules in this article must comply as nearly as possible with rules 8.200 and 8.204.

(2) If, as permitted by Penal Code section 1509.1(b), the petitioner wishes to raise a claim in the appeal of ineffective assistance of trial counsel that was not raised in the superior court habeas corpus proceedings, that claim must be raised in the first brief filed by the petitioner. A brief containing such a claim must comply with the additional requirements in rule 8.397.

(3) If the petitioner is appealing from a decision of the superior court denying relief on a successive death penalty–related habeas corpus petition, the petitioner may only raise claims in the briefs that were identified in the certificate of appealability that was issued and any additional claims added by the Court of Appeal as provided in Penal Code section 1509.1(c).

(Subd (a) adopted effective April 25, 2019.)

(b) Length

(1) A brief produced on a computer must not exceed the following limits, including footnotes, except that if the presiding justice permits the appellant to file an opening brief that exceeds the limit set in (1)(A) or (3)(A), the respondent's brief may not exceed the same length:

(A) Appellant's opening brief: 102,000 words.

(B) Respondent's brief: 102,000 words.

(C) Reply brief: 47,600 words.

(2) A brief under (1) must include a certificate by appellate counsel stating the number of words in the brief; counsel may rely on the word count of the computer program used to prepare the brief.

(3) A typewritten brief must not exceed the following limits, except that if the presiding justice permits the appellant to file an opening brief that exceeds the limit set in (1)(A) or (3)(A), the respondent's brief may not exceed the same length:

(A) Appellant's opening brief: 300 pages.

(B) Respondent's brief: 300 pages.

(C) Reply brief: 140 pages.

(4) The tables required under rule 8.204(a)(1), the cover information required under rule 8.204(b)(10), a certificate under (2), any signature block, and any attachment permitted under rule 8.204(d) are excluded from the limits stated in (1) and (3).

(5) A combined brief in an appeal governed by (e) must not exceed double the limit stated in (1) or (3).

(6) On application, the presiding justice may permit a longer brief for good cause.

(Subd (b) adopted effective April 25, 2019.)

(c) Time to file

(1) The appellant's opening brief must be served and filed within 210 days after either the record is filed or appellate counsel is appointed, whichever is later.

(2) The respondent's brief must be served and filed within 120 days after the appellant's opening brief is filed.

(3) The appellant must serve and file a reply brief, if any, within 60 days after the filing of respondent's brief.

(4) If the clerk's and reporter's transcripts combined exceed 10,000 pages, the time limits stated in (1) and (2) are extended by 15 days for each 1,000 pages of combined transcript over 10,000 pages, up to 20,000 pages. The time limits in (1) and (2) may be extended further by order of the presiding justice under rule 8.60.

(5) The time to serve and file a brief may not be extended by stipulation, but only by order of the presiding justice under rule 8.60.

(6) If a party fails to timely file an appellant's opening brief or a respondent's brief, the clerk/executive officer of the Court of Appeal must promptly notify the party in writing that the brief must be filed within 30 days after the notice is sent, and that failure to comply may result in sanctions specified in the notice.

(Subd (c) adopted effective April 25, 2019.)

(d) Service

(1) The petitioner's appellate counsel must serve each brief for the petitioner on the assisting entity or counsel, the Attorney General, and the district attorney, and must deliver a copy of each to the petitioner unless the petitioner requests otherwise.

(2) The proof of service must state that a copy of the petitioner's brief was delivered to the petitioner or will be delivered in person to the petitioner within 30 days after the filing of the brief, or counsel must file a signed statement that the petitioner requested in writing that no copy be delivered.

(3) The People must serve each of their briefs on the appellate counsel for the petitioner, the assisting entity or counsel, and either the district attorney or the Attorney General, whichever is not representing the People on appeal.

(4) A copy of each brief must be served on the superior court clerk for delivery to the superior court judge who issued the order being appealed.

(Subd (d) adopted effective April 25, 2019.)

(e) When the petitioner and the People appeal

When both the petitioner and the People appeal, the petitioner must file the first opening brief unless the reviewing court orders otherwise, and rule 8.216(b) governs the contents of the briefs.

(Subd (e) adopted effective April 25, 2019.)

(f) Amicus curiae briefs

Amicus curiae briefs may be filed as provided in rule 8.200(c), except that an application for permission of the presiding justice to file an amicus curiae brief must be filed within 14 days after the last appellant's reply brief is filed or could have been filed under (c), whichever is earlier.

(Subd (f) adopted effective April 25, 2019.)

Rule 8.396 adopted effective April 25, 2019.

Advisory Committee Comment

Subdivision (a)(3). This subdivision is intended to implement the sentence in Penal Code section 1509.1(c) providing that "[t]he jurisdiction of the court of appeal is limited to the claims identified in the certificate [of appealability] and any additional claims added by the court of appeal within 60 days of the notice of appeal."

Subdivision (b)(4). This subdivision specifies certain items that are not counted toward the maximum brief length. Signature blocks referred to in this provision include not only the signatures, but also the printed names, titles, and affiliations of any attorneys filing or joining in the brief, which may accompany the signature.

Rule 8.397. Claim of ineffective assistance of trial counsel not raised in the superior court

(a) Application

This rule governs claims under Penal Code section 1509.1(b) of ineffective assistance of trial counsel not raised in the superior court habeas corpus proceeding giving rise to an appeal under this article.

(Subd (a) adopted effective April 25, 2019.)

(b) Discussion of claim in briefs

(1) A claim subject to this rule must be raised in the first brief filed by the petitioner.

(2) All discussion of claims subject to this rule must be addressed in a separate part of the brief under a heading identifying this part as addressing claims of ineffective assistance of trial counsel that were not raised in a superior court habeas corpus proceeding.

(3) Discussion of each claim within this part of the brief must be under a separate subheading identifying the claim. Petitioner's brief must include a summary of the claim under the subheading, and each claim must be supported by argument and, if possible, by citation of authority.

(4) This part of the brief may include references to matters:

(A) In the record on appeal prepared under rule 8.395. Any reference to a matter in the record must be supported by a citation to the volume and page number of the record where the matter appears.

(B) Of which the court has taken judicial notice.

(C) In a proffer required under (c). Any reference to a matter in a proffer must be supported by a citation to its index number or letter and page.

(Subd (b) adopted effective April 25, 2019.)

(c) Proffer

(1) A brief raising a claim under Penal Code section 1509.1(b) of ineffective assistance of trial counsel not raised in a superior court habeas corpus proceeding must be accompanied by a proffer of any reasonably available documentary evidence supporting the claim that is not in either the record on appeal prepared under rule 8.395 or matters of which the court has taken judicial notice. A brief responding to such a claim must be accompanied by a proffer of any reasonably available documentary evidence the People are relying on that is not in the petitioner's proffer, the record on appeal prepared under rule 8.395, or matters of which the court has taken judicial notice.

(A) If a brief raises a claim that was the subject of an evidentiary hearing, the proffer must include a certified transcript of that hearing.

(B) Evidence may be in the form of affidavits or declarations under penalty of perjury.

(2) The proffer must comply with the following formatting requirements:

(A) The pages must be consecutively numbered.

(B) It must begin with a table of contents listing each document by its title and its index number or letter. If a document has attachments, the table of contents must give the title of each attachment and a brief description of its contents.

(C) If submitted in paper form:

(i) It must be bound together at the end of the brief or in separate volumes not exceeding 300 pages each.

(ii) It must be index-tabbed by number or letter.

(3) The clerk must file any proffer not complying with (2), but the court may notify the filer that it may strike the proffer and the portions of the brief referring to the proffer if the documents are not brought into compliance within a stated reasonable time of not less than five court days.

(4) If any documents in the proffer are sealed or confidential records, rules 8.45–8.47 govern these documents.

(Subd (c) adopted effective April 25, 2019.)

(d) Evidentiary hearing

An evidentiary hearing is required if, after considering the briefs, the proffer, and matters of which judicial notice may be taken, the court finds there is a reasonable likelihood that the petitioner may be entitled to relief and the petitioner's entitlement to relief depends on the resolution of an issue of fact. The reviewing court may take one of the following actions:

(1) Order a limited remand to the superior court to consider the claim under Penal Code section 1509.1(b). The order for limited remand vests jurisdiction over the claim in the superior court, which must proceed under rule 4.574(d)(2)–(3) and (e)–(g) and rule 4.575 for death penalty–related habeas corpus proceedings in the superior court. The clerk/executive officer of the Court of Appeal must send a copy of any such order to the clerk/executive officer of the Supreme Court.

(2) Appoint a referee to conduct the hearing and make recommended findings of fact.

(3) Conduct the hearing itself or designate a justice of the court to conduct the hearing.

(Subd (d) adopted effective April 25, 2019.)

(e) Procedures following limited remand

(1) If the reviewing court orders a limited remand to the superior court to consider a claim under Penal Code section 1509.1(b), it may stay the proceedings on the remainder of the appeal pending the decision of the superior court on remand. The clerk/executive officer of the Court of Appeal must send a copy of any such stay to the clerk/executive officer of the Supreme Court.

(2) If any party wishes to appeal from the superior court decision on remand, the party must file a notice of appeal as provided in rule 8.392.

(3) If an appeal is filed from the superior court decision on remand, the reviewing court may consolidate this appeal with any pending appeal under Penal Code section 1509.1 from the superior court's decisions in the same habeas corpus proceeding. A copy of any consolidation order must be promptly sent to the superior court clerk. The superior court clerk must then augment the record on appeal to include all items listed in rule 8.395(a) from the remanded proceedings.

(Subd (e) adopted effective April 25, 2019.)
Rule 8.397 adopted effective April 25, 2019.

Advisory Committee Comment

Penal Code section 1509.1(b) states when a claim of ineffective assistance of trial counsel not raised in the superior court habeas corpus proceeding may be raised in an appeal under this article.

Rule 8.398. Finality

(a) General rule

Except as otherwise provided in this rule, rule 8.366(b) governs the finality of a Court of Appeal decision in a proceeding under this article.

(Subd (a) adopted effective April 25, 2019.)

(b) Denial of certificate of appealability

The Court of Appeal's denial of an application for a certificate of appealability in a proceeding under this article is final in that court on filing.

(Subd (b) adopted effective April 25, 2019.)
Rule 8.398 adopted effective April 25, 2019.

Chapter 5
Juvenile Appeals and Writs

Art. 1. General Provisions. Rules 8.400, 8.401.
Art. 2. Appeals. Rules 8.403–8.417.
Art. 3. Writs. Rules 8.450–8.456.
Art. 4. Hearing and Decision. Rules 8.470–8.474.

Article 1
General Provisions

Title 8, Appellate Rules—Division 1, Rules Relating to the Supreme Court and Courts of Appeal—Chapter 5, Juvenile Appeals and Writs—Article 1, General Provisions; adopted effective July 1, 2010.

Rule 8.400. Application
Rule 8.401. Confidentiality

Rule 8.400. Application

The rules in this chapter govern:

(1) Appeals from judgments or appealable orders in:

(A) Cases under Welfare and Institutions Code sections 300, 601, and 602; and

(B) Actions to free a child from parental custody and control under Family Code section 7800 et seq. and Probate Code section 1516.5;

(2) Appeals of orders requiring or dispensing with an alleged father's consent for the adoption of a child under Family Code section 7662 et seq.; and

(3) Writ petitions under Welfare and Institutions Code sections 366.26 and 366.28.

Rule 8.400 amended effective January 1, 2017; adopted as rule 37 effective January 1, 2005; previously amended effective January 1, 2006, January 1, 2008, and July 1, 2010; previously amended and renumbered effective January 1, 2007.

Rule 8.401. Confidentiality

(a) References to juveniles or relatives in documents

To protect the anonymity of juveniles involved in juvenile court proceedings:

(1) In all documents filed by the parties in proceedings under this chapter, a juvenile must be referred to by first name and last initial; but if the first name is unusual or other circumstances would defeat the objective of anonymity, the initials of the juvenile may be used.

(2) In opinions that are not certified for publication and in court orders, a juvenile may be referred to either by first name and last initial or by his or her initials. In opinions that are certified for publication in proceedings under this chapter, a juvenile must be referred to by first name and last initial; but if the first name is unusual or other circumstances would defeat the objective of anonymity, the initials of the juvenile may be used.

(3) In all documents filed by the parties and in all court orders and opinions in proceedings under this chapter, if use of the full name of a juvenile's relative would defeat the objective of anonymity for the juvenile, the relative must be referred to by first name and last initial; but if the first name is unusual or other circumstances would defeat the objective of anonymity for the juvenile, the initials of the relative may be used.

(Subd (a) adopted effective January 1, 2012.)

(b) Access to filed documents and records

For the purposes of this rule, "filed document" means a brief, petition, motion, application, or other thing filed by the parties in the reviewing court in a proceeding under this chapter; "record on appeal" means the documents referenced in rule 8.407; "record on a writ petition" means the documents referenced in rules 8.450 and 8.454; and "records in the juvenile case file" means all or part of a document, paper, exhibit, transcript, opinion, order, or other thing filed or lodged in the juvenile court.

(1) Except as provided in (2)–(4), a filed document, the record on appeal, or the record on a writ petition may be inspected only by the reviewing court, appellate project personnel, the parties, attorneys for the parties, or other persons the reviewing court may designate.

(2) Access to records in the juvenile case file, including any such records made part of the record on appeal or the record on a writ petition, is governed by Welfare and Institutions Code section 827. A person who is not described in section 827(a)(1)(A)–(P) may not access records in the juvenile case file, including any such records made part of the record on appeal or the record on a writ petition, unless that person petitioned the juvenile court under section 827(a)(1)(Q) and was granted access by order of the juvenile court.

(3) A filed document that protects anonymity as required by (a) may be inspected by any person or entity that is considering filing an amicus curiae brief.

(4) Access to a filed document or items in the record on appeal or the record on a writ petition that are sealed or confidential under authority other than Welfare and Institutions Code section 827 is governed by rules 8.45–8.47 and the applicable statute, rule, sealing order, or other authority.

(Subd (b) amended effective September 1, 2020; adopted as subd (a) effective July 1, 2010; previously amended and relettered effective January 1, 2012; previously amended effective January 1, 2014.)

(c) Access to oral argument

The court may limit or prohibit public admittance to oral argument.

(Subd (c) relettered effective January 1, 2012; adopted as subd (b) effective July 1, 2010.)

Rule 8.401 amended effective September 1, 2020; adopted effective July 1, 2010; previously amended effective January 1, 2012, and January 1, 2014.

Advisory Committee Comment

Subdivision (b)(2). Welfare and Institutions Code section 827(a)(1)(Q) authorizes a petition by which a person may request access to records in the juvenile case file. The petition process is stated in rule 5.552. The Judicial Council has adopted a mandatory form—*Petition for Access to Juvenile Case File* (form JV-570)—that must be filed in the juvenile court to make the request. This form is available at any courthouse or county law library or online at www.courts.ca.gov/forms.

Article 2
Appeals

Title 8, Appellate Rules—Division 1, Rules Relating to the Supreme Court and Courts of Appeal—Chapter 5, Juvenile Appeals and Writs—Article 2, Appeals; renumbered effective July 1, 2010; adopted as article 1 effective January 1, 2007.

Rule 8.403. Right to appointment of appellate counsel and prerequisites for appeal
Rule 8.404. Stay pending appeal
Rule 8.405. Filing the appeal
Rule 8.406. Time to appeal
Rule 8.407. Record on appeal
Rule 8.408. Record in multiple appeals in the same case
Rule 8.409. Preparing and sending the record
Rule 8.410. Augmenting and correcting the record in the reviewing court
Rule 8.411. Abandoning the appeal
Rule 8.412. Briefs by parties and amici curiae
Rule 8.416. Appeals from all terminations of parental rights; dependency appeals in Orange, Imperial, and San Diego Counties and in other counties by local rule
Rule 8.417. Appeals from orders transferring a minor from juvenile court to a court of criminal jurisdiction

Rule 8.403. Right to appointment of appellate counsel and prerequisites for appeal

(a) Welfare and Institutions Code section 601 or 602 proceedings

In appeals of proceedings under Welfare and Institutions Code section 601 or 602, the child is entitled to court-appointed counsel.

(Subd (a) amended effective January 1, 2013; adopted effective July 1, 2010.)

(b) Welfare and Institutions Code section 300 proceedings

(1) Any judgment, order, or decree setting a hearing under Welfare and Institutions Code section 366.26 may be reviewed on appeal following the order at the Welfare and Institutions Code section 366.26 hearing only if:

(A) The procedures in rules 8.450 and 8.452 regarding writ petitions in these cases have been followed; and

(B) The petition for an extraordinary writ was summarily denied or otherwise not decided on the merits.

(2) The reviewing court may appoint counsel to represent an indigent child, parent, or guardian.

(3) Rule 5.661 governs the responsibilities of trial counsel in Welfare and Institutions Code section 300 proceedings with regard to appellate representation of the child.

(Subd (b) adopted effective July 1, 2010.)

Rule 8.403 amended effective January 1, 2013; adopted effective July 1, 2010.

Advisory Committee Comment

The right to appeal in Welfare and Institutions Code section 601 or 602 (juvenile delinquency) cases is established by Welfare and Institutions Code section 800 and case law (see, for example, *In re Michael S.* (2007) 147 Cal.App.4th 1443, *In re Jeffrey M.* (2006) 141 Cal.App.4th 1017 and *In re Sean R.* (1989) 214 Cal.App.3d 662). The right to appeal in Welfare and Institutions Code section 300 (juvenile dependency) cases is established by Welfare and Institutions Code section 395 and case law (see, for example, *In re Aaron R.* (2005) 130 Cal.App.4th 697, and *In re Merrick V.* (2004) 122 Cal.App.4th 235).

Subdivision (b)(1). Welfare and Institutions Code section 366.26(*l*) establishes important limitations on appeals of judgments, orders, or decrees setting a hearing under section 366.26, including requirements for the filing of a petition for an extraordinary writ and limitations on the issues that can be raised on appeal.

Rule 8.404. Stay pending appeal

The court must not stay an order or judgment pending an appeal unless suitable provision is made for the maintenance, care, and custody of the child.

Rule 8.404 adopted effective July 1, 2010.

Advisory Committee Comment

This rule does not apply to a court's order under rule 5.770(e)(2) staying the criminal court proceedings during the pendency of an appeal of an order transferring the minor from juvenile court to a court of criminal jurisdiction.

Rule 8.405. Filing the appeal

(a) Notice of appeal

(1) To appeal from a judgment or appealable order under these rules, the appellant must file a notice of appeal in the superior court. Any notice of appeal on behalf of the child in a Welfare and Institutions Code section 300 proceeding must be authorized by the child or the child's CAPTA guardian ad litem.

(2) The appellant or the appellant's attorney must sign the notice of appeal.

(3) The notice of appeal must be liberally construed, and is sufficient if it identifies the particular judgment or order being appealed. The notice need not specify the court to which the appeal is taken; the appeal will be treated as taken to the Court of Appeal for the district in which the superior court is located.

(Subd (a) adopted effective July 1, 2010.)

(b) Superior court clerk's duties

(1) When a notice of appeal is filed, the superior court clerk must immediately:

(A) Send a notification of the filing to:

(i) Each party other than the appellant, including the child if the child is 10 years of age or older;

(ii) The attorney of record for each party;

(iii) Any person currently awarded by the juvenile court the status of the child's de facto parent;

(iv) Any Court Appointed Special Advocate (CASA) volunteer;

(v) If the court knows or has reason to know that an Indian child is involved, the Indian custodian, if any, and tribe of the child or the Bureau of Indian Affairs, as required under Welfare and Institutions Code section 224.2; and

(vi) The reviewing court clerk; and

(B) Notify the reporter, in a manner providing immediate notice, to prepare a reporter's transcript and deliver it to the clerk within 20 days after the notice of appeal is filed.

(2) The notification must show the name of the appellant, the date it was sent, the number and title of the case, and the date the notice of appeal was filed. If the information is available, the notification must also include:

(A) The name, address, telephone number, e-mail address, and California State Bar number of each attorney of record in the case;

(B) The name of the party that each attorney represented in the superior court; and

(C) The name, address, telephone number and e-mail address of any unrepresented party.

(3) The notification to the reviewing court clerk must also include a copy of the notice of appeal and any sequential list of reporters made under rule 2.950.

(4) A copy of the notice of appeal is sufficient notification if the required information is on the copy or is added by the superior court clerk.

(5) The sending of a notification is a sufficient performance of the clerk's duty despite the discharge, disqualification, suspension, disbarment, or death of the attorney.

(6) Failure to comply with any provision of this subdivision does not affect the validity of the notice of appeal.

(Subd (b) amended effective January 1, 2021; adopted effective July 1, 2010; previously amended effective January 1, 2016.)

Rule 8.405 amended effective January 1, 2021; adopted effective July 1, 2010; previously amended effective January 1, 2016.

Advisory Committee Comment

Subdivision (a). *Notice of Appeal—Juvenile (California Rules of Court, Rule 8.400)* (form JV-800) may be used to file the notice of appeal required under this rule. This form is available at any courthouse or county law library or online at www.courts.ca.gov/forms.

Rule 8.406. Time to appeal
(a) Normal time
(1) Except as provided in (A), (B), and (2), a notice of appeal must be filed within 60 days after the rendition of the judgment or the making of the order being appealed.

(A) In matters heard by a referee not acting as a temporary judge, a notice of appeal must be filed within 60 days after the referee's order becomes final under rule 5.540(c).

(B) When an application for rehearing of an order of a referee not acting as a temporary judge is denied under rule 5.542, a notice of appeal from the referee's order must be filed within 60 days after that order is served under rule 5.538(b)(3) or 30 days after entry of the order denying rehearing, whichever is later.

(2) To appeal from an order transferring a minor to a court of criminal jurisdiction:

(A) Except as provided in (B) and (C), a notice of appeal must be filed within 30 days of the making of the order.

(B) If the matter is heard by a referee not acting as a temporary judge, a notice of appeal must be filed within 30 days after the referee's order becomes final under rule 5.540(c).

(C) When an application for rehearing of an order of a referee not acting as a temporary judge is denied under rule 5.542, a notice of appeal from the referee's order must be filed within 30 days after entry of the order denying rehearing.

(Subd (a) amended effective April 1, 2023; adopted effective July 1, 2010; previously amended effective January 1, 2023.)

(b) Cross-appeal
If an appellant timely appeals from a judgment or appealable order, the time for any other party to appeal from the same judgment or order is either the time specified in (a) or 20 days after the superior court clerk sends notification of the first appeal, whichever is later.

(Subd (b) amended effective January 1, 2016; adopted effective July 1, 2010.)

(c) No extension of time; late notice of appeal
Except as provided in rule 8.66, no court may extend the time to file a notice of appeal. The superior court clerk must mark a late notice of appeal "Received [date] but not filed," notify the party that the notice was not filed because it was late, and send a copy of the marked notice of appeal to the district appellate project.

(Subd (c) repealed and relettered effective July 1, 2010; adopted as subd (d) effective July 1, 2010.)

(d) Premature notice of appeal
A notice of appeal is premature if filed before the judgment is rendered or the order is made, but the reviewing court may treat the notice as filed immediately after the rendition of judgment or the making of the order.

(Subd (d) relettered effective July 1, 2010; adopted as subd (e) effective July 1, 2010.)

Rule 8.406 amended effective April 1, 2023; adopted effective July 1, 2010; previously amended effective July 1, 2010, January 1, 2016, and January 1, 2023.

Advisory Committee Comment
Subdivision (c). See rule 8.25(b)(5) for provisions concerning the timeliness of documents mailed by inmates or patients from custodial institutions.

Rule 8.407. Record on appeal
(a) Normal record: clerk's transcript
The clerk's transcript must contain:
(1) The petition;
(2) Any notice of hearing;
(3) All court minutes;
(4) Any report or other document submitted to the court;
(5) The jurisdictional and dispositional findings and orders;
(6) The judgment or order appealed from;
(7) Any application for rehearing;
(8) The notice of appeal and any order pursuant to the notice;
(9) Any transcript of a sound or sound-and-video recording tendered to the court under rule 2.1040;
(10) Any application for additional record and any order on the application;
(11) Any opinion or dispositive order of a reviewing court in the same case; and
(12) Any written motion or notice of motion by any party, with supporting and opposing memoranda and attachments, and any written opinion of the court.

(Subd (a) amended effective January 1, 2017; previously amended effective January 1, 2007, and July 1, 2010.)

(b) Normal record: reporter's transcript
The reporter's transcript must contain any oral opinion of the court and:

(1) In appeals from disposition orders, the oral proceedings at hearings on:
(A) Jurisdiction;
(B) Disposition;
(C) Any motion by the appellant that was denied in whole or in part; and
(D) In cases under Welfare and Institutions Code section 300 et seq., hearings:
(i) On detention; and
(ii) At which a parent of the child made his or her initial appearance.

(2) In appeals from an order terminating parental rights under Welfare and Institutions Code section 300 et seq., the oral proceedings at all section 366.26 hearings.

(3) In all other appeals, the oral proceedings at any hearing that resulted in the order or judgment being appealed.

(Subd (b) amended effective January 1, 2017; previously amended effective January 1, 2007.)

(c) Application in superior court for addition to normal record
(1) Any party or Indian tribe that has intervened in the proceedings may apply to the superior court for inclusion of any oral proceedings in the reporter's transcript.

(2) An application for additional record must describe the material to be included and explain how it may be useful in the appeal.

(3) The application must be filed in the superior court with the notice of appeal or as soon thereafter as possible, and will be treated as denied if it is filed after the record is sent to the reviewing court.

(4) The clerk must immediately present the application to the trial judge.

(5) Within five days after the application if filed, the judge must order that the record include as much of the additional material as the judge finds proper to fully present the points raised by the applicant. Denial of the application does not preclude a motion in the reviewing court for augmentation under rule 8.155.

(6) If the judge does not rule on the application within the time prescribed by (5), the requested material–other than exhibits–must be included in the clerk's transcript or the reporter's transcript without a court order.

(7) The clerk must immediately notify the reporter if additions to the reporter's transcript are required under (5) or (6).

(Subd (c) amended effective July 1, 2010; previously amended effective January 1, 2007.)

(d) Agreed or settled statement
To proceed by agreed or settled statement, the parties must comply with rule 8.344 or 8.346, as applicable.

(Subd (d) amended effective January 1, 2007.)

(e) Transmitting exhibits
Exhibits that were admitted in evidence, refused, or lodged may be transmitted to the reviewing court as provided in rule 8.224.

(Subd (e) repealed and relettered effective January 1, 2014; previously amended as subd (f) effective January 1, 2007.)

Rule 8.407 amended effective January 1, 2017; adopted as rule 37.1 effective January 1, 2005; previously amended and renumbered as rule 8.404 effective January 1, 2007, and July 1, 2010; previously amended effective January 1, 2014.

Advisory Committee Comment
Rules 8.45–8.47 address the appropriate handling of sealed or confidential records that must be included in the record on appeal. Examples of confidential records include records of proceedings closed to inspection by court order under *People v. Marsden* (1970) 2 Cal.3d 118 and in-camera proceedings on a confidential informant.

Subdivision (a)(4). Examples of the documents that must be included in the clerk's transcript under this provision include all documents filed with the court relating to the Indian Child Welfare Act, including but not limited to all inquiries regarding a child under the Indian Child Welfare Act (*Indian Child Inquiry Attachment* [form ICWA-010(A)]), any *Parental Notification of Indian Status* (form ICWA-020), any *Notice of Child Custody Proceeding for Indian Child* (form ICWA-030) sent, any signed return receipts for the mailing of form ICWA-030, and any responses received to form ICWA-030.

Subdivision (b). Subdivision (b)(1) provides that only the reporter's transcript of a hearing that resulted in the order being appealed must be included in the normal record. This provision is intended to achieve consistent record requirements in all appeals of cases under Welfare and Institutions Code section 300, 601, or 602 and to reduce the delays and expense caused by transcribing proceedings not necessary to the appeal.

Subdivision (b)(1)(A) recognizes that findings made in a jurisdictional hearing are not separately appealable and can be challenged only in an appeal from the ensuing disposition order. The rule therefore specifically provides that a reporter's transcript of jurisdictional proceedings must be included in the normal record on appeal from a disposition order.

Subdivision (b)(1)(C) specifies that the oral proceedings on any motion by the appellant that was denied in whole or in part must be included in the normal record on appeal from a disposition order. Rulings on such motions usually have some impact on either the jurisdictional findings or the subsequent disposition order. Routine inclusion of these proceedings in the record will promote expeditious resolution of appeals of cases under Welfare and Institutions Code section 300, 601, or 602.

Rule 8.408. Record in multiple appeals in the same case

If more than one appeal is taken from the same judgment or related order, only one appellate record need be prepared, which must be filed within the time allowed for filing the record in the latest appeal.

Rule 8.408 renumbered effective July 1, 2010; adopted as rule 8.406 effective January 1, 2007.

Rule 8.409. Preparing and sending the record

(a) Application

This rule applies to appeals in juvenile cases except cases governed by rules 8.416 and 8.417.

(Subd (a) amended effective January 1, 2023; previously amended effective January 1, 2007, July 1, 2010, and January 1, 2015.)

(b) Form of record

The clerk's and reporter's transcripts must comply with rules 8.45–8.47, relating to sealed and confidential records, and with rule 8.144.

(Subd (b) amended effective January 1, 2015; adopted effective January 1, 2014.)

(c) Preparing and certifying the transcripts

Except in cases governed by rule 8.417, within 20 days after the notice of appeal is filed:

(1) The clerk must prepare and certify as correct an original of the clerk's transcript and one copy each for the appellant, the respondent, the child's Indian tribe if the tribe has intervened, and the child if the child is represented by counsel on appeal or if a recommendation has been made to the Court of Appeal for appointment of counsel for the child under rule 8.403(b)(2) and that recommendation is either pending with or has been approved by the Court of Appeal but counsel has not yet been appointed; and

(2) The reporter must prepare, certify as correct, and deliver to the clerk an original of the reporter's transcript and the same number of copies as (1) requires of the clerk's transcript.

(Subd (c) amended effective January 1, 2023; adopted as subd (b); previously amended and relettered as subd (c) effective January 1, 2014; previously amended effective January 1, 2007, January 1, 2015, January 1, 2017, and January 1, 2018.)

(d) Extension of time

(1) The superior court may not extend the time to prepare the record.

(2) The reviewing court may order one or more extensions of time for preparing the record, including a reporter's transcript, not exceeding a total of 60 days, on receipt of:

(A) A declaration showing good cause; and

(B) In the case of a reporter's transcript, certification by the superior court presiding judge, or a court administrator designated by the presiding judge, that an extension is reasonable and necessary in light of the workload of all reporters in the court.

(Subd (d) amended and relettered effective January 1, 2014; previously amended as subd (c) effective January 1, 2007.)

(e) Sending the record

(1) When the transcripts are certified as correct, the court clerk must immediately send:

(A) The original transcripts to the reviewing court, noting the sending date on each original; and

(B) One copy of each transcript to the appellate counsel for the following, if they have appellate counsel:

(i) The appellant;

(ii) The respondent;

(iii) The child's Indian tribe if the tribe has intervened; and

(iv) The child.

(2) If appellate counsel has not yet been retained or appointed for the appellant or the respondent, or if a recommendation has been made to the Court of Appeal for appointment of counsel for the child under rule 8.403(b)(2) and that recommendation is either pending with or has been approved by the Court of Appeal but counsel has not yet been appointed, when the transcripts are certified as correct, the clerk must send that counsel's copy of the transcripts to the district appellate project. If a tribe that has intervened is not represented by counsel when the transcripts are certified as correct, the clerk must send that counsel's copy of the transcripts to the tribe.

(3) The clerk must not send a copy of the transcripts to the Attorney General or the district attorney unless that office represents a party.

(Subd (e) amended effective January 1, 2015; adopted as subd (d); previously amended effective January 1, 2007, and January 1, 2013; previously relettered as subd (e) effective January 1, 2014.)

Rule 8.409 amended effective January 1, 2023; adopted as rule 37.2 effective January 1, 2005; previously amended and renumbered as rule 8.408 effective January 1, 2007, and as rule 8.409 effective July 1, 2010; previously amended effective January 1, 2013, January 1, 2014, January 1, 2015, January 1, 2017, and January 1, 2018.

Advisory Committee Comment

Subdivision (a). Subdivision (a) calls litigants' attention to the fact that different rules govern the record in appeals from judgments or orders terminating parental rights and in dependency appeals in certain counties (rule 8.416), and in appeals from orders granting a motion to transfer a minor from juvenile court to a court of criminal jurisdiction (rule 8.417).

Subdivision (b). Examples of confidential records include records closed to inspection by court order under *People v. Marsden* (1970) 2 Cal.3d 118 and in-camera proceedings on a confidential informant.

Subdivision (c). Subdivision (c) calls litigants' attention to the fact that a different rule (rule 8.417) governs the record in appeals from orders granting a motion to transfer a minor from juvenile court to a court of criminal jurisdiction.

Subdivision (e). Under rule 8.71(c), the superior court clerk may send the record to the reviewing court in electronic form. Subsection (1)(B) clarifies that when a child's Indian tribe has intervened in the proceedings, the tribe is a party who must receive a copy of the appellate record. The statutes that require notices to be sent to a tribe by registered or certified mail return receipt requested and generally be addressed to the tribal chairperson (25 U.S.C. § 1912(a), 25 C.F.R. § 23.11, and Welf. & Inst. Code, § 224.2) do not apply to the sending of the appellate record.

Rule 8.410. Augmenting and correcting the record in the reviewing court

(a) Omissions

If, after the record is certified, the superior court clerk or the reporter learns that the record omits a document or transcript that any rule or order requires to be included, without the need for a motion or court order, the clerk must promptly copy and certify the document or the reporter must promptly prepare and certify the transcript and the clerk must promptly send the document or transcript—as an augmentation of the record—to all those who are listed under 8.409(e).

(Subd (a) amended effective January 1, 2015; adopted effective July 1, 2010.)

(b) Augmentation or correction by the reviewing court

(1) On motion of a party or on its own motion, the reviewing court may order the record augmented or corrected as provided in rule 8.155(a) and (c).

(2) If, after the record is certified, the trial court amends or recalls the judgment or makes any other order in the case, the trial court clerk must notify each entity and person to whom the record is sent under rule 8.409(e).

(Subd (b) amended effective January 1, 2015; adopted effective July 1, 2010.)

Rule 8.410 amended effective January 1, 2015; adopted effective July 1, 2010.

Rule 8.411. Abandoning the appeal

(a) How to abandon

An appellant may abandon the appeal at any time by filing an abandonment of the appeal. The abandonment must be authorized by the appellant and signed by either the appellant or the appellant's attorney of record. In a Welfare and Institutions Code section 300 proceeding in which the child is the appellant, the abandonment must be authorized by the child or, if the child is not capable of giving authorization, by the child's CAPTA guardian ad litem.

(Subd (a) adopted effective July 1, 2010.)

(b) Where to file; effect of filing

(1) If the record has not been filed in the reviewing court, the appellant must file the abandonment in the superior court. The filing effects a dismissal of the appeal and restores the superior court's jurisdiction.

(2) If the record has been filed in the reviewing court, the appellant must file the abandonment in that court. The reviewing court may dismiss the appeal and direct immediate issuance of the remittitur.

(Subd (b) adopted effective July 1, 2010.)

(c) Clerk's duties

(1) If the abandonment is filed in the superior court, the clerk must immediately send a notification of the abandonment to:

(A) Every other party;

(B) The reviewing court; and

(C) The reporter if the appeal is abandoned before the reporter has filed the transcript.

(2) If the abandonment is filed in the reviewing court and the reviewing court orders the appeal dismissed, the clerk must immediately send a notification of the order of dismissal to every party.

(Subd (c) amended effective January 1, 2016; adopted effective July 1, 2010.)
Rule 8.411 amended January 1, 2016; adopted effective July 1, 2010.

Advisory Committee Comment

The Supreme Court has held that appellate counsel for an appealing minor has the power to move to dismiss a dependency appeal based on counsel's assessment of the child's best interests, but that the motion to dismiss requires the authorization of the child or, if the child is incapable of giving authorization, the authorization of the child's CAPTA guardian ad litem (*In re Josiah Z.* (2005) 36 Cal.4th 664).

Rule 8.412. Briefs by parties and amici curiae

(a) Contents, form, and length

(1) Rule 8.200 governs the briefs that may be filed by parties and amici curiae.

(2) Except as provided in (3), rule 8.204 governs the form and contents of briefs. Rule 8.216 also applies in appeals in which a party is both appellant and respondent.

(3) Rule 8.360(b) governs the length of briefs.

(Subd (a) amended effective July 1, 2010; previously amended effective January 1, 2007.)

(b) Time to file

(1) Except in appeals governed by rules 8.416 and 8.417, the appellant must serve and file the appellant's opening brief within 40 days after the record is filed in the reviewing court.

(2) The respondent must serve and file the respondent's brief within 30 days after the appellant's opening brief is filed.

(3) The appellant must serve and file any reply brief within 20 days after the respondent's brief is filed.

(4) In dependency cases in which the child is not an appellant but has appellate counsel, the child must serve and file any brief within 10 days after the respondent's brief is filed.

(5) Rule 8.220 applies if a party fails to timely file an appellant's opening brief or a respondent's brief, but the period specified in the notice required by that rule must be 30 days.

(Subd (b) amended effective January 1, 2023; previously amended effective January 1, 2007, and July 1, 2010.)

(c) Extensions of time

The superior court may not order any extensions of time to file briefs. Except in appeals governed by rules 8.416 and 8.417, the reviewing court may order extensions of time for good cause.

(Subd (c) amended effective January 1, 2023; previously amended effective January 1, 2007, and July 1, 2010.)

(d) Failure to file a brief

(1) Except in appeals governed by rules 8.416 and 8.417, if a party fails to timely file an appellant's opening brief or a respondent's brief, the reviewing court clerk must promptly notify the party's counsel or the party, if not represented, in writing that the brief must be filed within 30 days after the notice is sent and that failure to comply may result in one of the following sanctions:

(A) If the brief is an appellant's opening brief:

(i) If the appellant is the county, the court will dismiss the appeal;

(ii) If the appellant is other than the county and is represented by appointed counsel on appeal, the court will relieve that appointed counsel and appoint new counsel;

(iii) If the appellant is other than the county and is not represented by appointed counsel, the court will dismiss the appeal.

(B) If the brief is a respondent's brief, the court will decide the appeal on the record, the opening brief, and any oral argument by the appellant.

(2) If a party fails to comply with a notice under (1), the court may impose the sanction specified in the notice.

(3) Within the period specified in the notice under (1), a party may apply to the presiding justice for an extension of that period for good cause. If an extension is granted beyond the 30-day period and the brief is not filed within the extended period, the court may impose the sanction under (2) without further notice.

(Subd (d) amended effective January 1, 2023; adopted effective January 1, 2007; previously amended effective July 1, 2010, and January 1, 2016.)

(e) Additional service requirements

(1) A copy of each brief must be served on the superior court clerk for delivery to the superior court judge.

(2) A copy of each brief must be served on the child's trial counsel, or, if the child is not represented by trial counsel, on the child's guardian ad litem appointed under rule 5.662.

(3) If the Court of Appeal has appointed counsel for any party:

(A) The county child welfare department and the People must serve two copies of their briefs on that counsel; and

(B) Each party must serve a copy of its brief on the district appellate project.

(4) In delinquency cases the parties must serve copies of their briefs on the Attorney General and the district attorney. In all other cases the parties must not serve copies of their briefs on the Attorney General or the district attorney unless that office represents a party.

(5) The parties must not serve copies of their briefs on the Supreme Court under rule 8.44(b)(1).

(Subd (e) amended effective July 1, 2007; adopted as subd (d) effective January 1, 2005; previously amended and relettered effective January 1, 2007.)
Rule 8.412 amended effective January 1, 2023; adopted as rule 37.3 effective January 1, 2005; previously amended and renumbered as rule 8.412 effective January 1, 2007; previously amended effective July 1, 2007, July 1, 2010, and January 1, 2016.

Advisory Committee Comment

Subdivision (b). Subdivision (b)(1) calls litigants' attention to the fact that different rules govern the time to file an appellant's opening brief in appeals from judgments or orders terminating parental rights and in dependency appeals in certain counties (rule 8.416(e)), and in appeals from orders granting a motion to transfer a minor from juvenile court to a court of criminal jurisdiction (rule 8.417(f)).

Subdivision (c). Subdivision (c) calls litigants' attention to the fact that different rules govern the showing required for extensions of time to file briefs in appeals from judgments or orders terminating parental rights and in dependency appeals in certain counties (rule 8.416(f)), and in appeals from orders granting a motion to transfer a minor from juvenile court to a court of criminal jurisdiction (rule 8.417(g)).

Subdivision (d). Subdivision (d) calls litigants' attention to the fact that different rules govern the time period specified in the notice of failure to timely file an appellant's opening brief or a respondent's brief in appeals from judgments or orders terminating parental rights, in dependency appeals in certain counties (rule 8.416(g)), and in appeals from orders granting a motion to transfer a minor from juvenile court to a court of criminal jurisdiction (rule 8.417(h)).

Rule 8.416. Appeals from all terminations of parental rights; dependency appeals in Orange, Imperial, and San Diego Counties and in other counties by local rule

(a) Application

(1) This rule governs:

(A) Appeals from judgments or appealable orders of all superior courts terminating parental rights under Welfare and Institutions Code section 366.26 or freeing a child from parental custody and control under Family Code section 7800 et seq.; and

(B) Appeals from judgments or appealable orders in all juvenile dependency cases of:

(i) The Superior Courts of Orange, Imperial, and San Diego Counties; and

(ii) Other superior courts when the superior court and the District Court of Appeal with jurisdiction to hear appeals from that superior court have agreed and have adopted local rules providing that this rule will govern appeals from that superior court.

(2) In all respects not provided for in this rule, rules 8.403–8.412 apply.

(Subd (a) amended effective July 1, 2010; previously amended effective January 1, 2007.)

(b) Form of record

(1) The clerk's and reporter's transcripts must comply with rules 8.45–8.47, relating to sealed and confidential records, and, except as provided in (2) and (3), with rule 8.144.

(2) In appeals under (a)(1)(A), the cover of the record must prominently display the title "Appeal From [Judgment or Order] Terminating

Parental Rights Under [Welfare and Institutions Code Section 366.26 or Family Code Section 7800 et seq.]," whichever is appropriate.

(3) In appeals under (a)(1)(B), the cover of the record must prominently display the title "Appeal From [Judgment or Order] Under [Welfare and Institutions Code Section 300 et seq. or Family Code Section 7800 et seq.]," whichever is appropriate.

(Subd (b) amended effective April 1, 2023; previously amended effective July 1, 2010, and January 1, 2015.)

(c) Preparing, certifying, and sending the record

(1) Within 20 days after the notice of appeal is filed:

(A) The clerk must prepare and certify as correct an original of the clerk's transcript and one copy each for the appellant, the respondent, the district appellate project, the child's Indian tribe if the tribe has intervened, and the child if the child is represented by counsel on appeal or if a recommendation has been made to the Court of Appeal for appointment of counsel for the child under rule 8.403(b)(2) and that recommendation is either pending with or has been approved by the Court of Appeal but counsel has not yet been appointed; and

(B) The reporter must prepare, certify as correct, and deliver to the clerk an original of the reporter's transcript and the same number of copies as (A) requires of the clerk's transcript.

(2) When the clerk's and reporter's transcripts are certified as correct, the clerk must immediately send:

(A) The original transcripts to the reviewing court by the most expeditious method, noting the sending date on each original; and

(B) One copy of each transcript to the district appellate project and to the appellate counsel for the following, if they have appellate counsel, by any method as fast as United States Postal Service express mail:

(i) The appellant;

(ii) The respondent;

(iii) The child's Indian tribe if the tribe has intervened; and

(iv) The child.

(3) If appellate counsel has not yet been retained or appointed for the appellant or the respondent or if a recommendation has been made to the Court of Appeal for appointment of counsel for the child under rule 8.403(b)(2) and that recommendation is either pending with or has been approved by the Court of Appeal but counsel has not yet been appointed, when the transcripts are certified as correct, the clerk must send that counsel's copies of the transcripts to the district appellate project. If a tribe that has intervened is not represented by counsel when the transcripts are certified as correct, the clerk must send that counsel's copy of the transcripts to the tribe.

(Subd (c) amended effective January 1, 2018; previously amended effective January 1, 2007, July 1, 2010, January 1, 2015, and January 1, 2017.)

(d) Augmenting or correcting the record

(1) Except as provided in (2) and (3), rule 8.410 governs any augmentation or correction of the record.

(2) An appellant must serve and file any motion for augmentation or correction within 15 days after receiving the record. A respondent must serve and file any such motion within 15 days after the appellant's opening brief is filed.

(3) The clerk and the reporter must prepare any supplemental transcripts within 20 days, giving them the highest priority.

(4) The clerk must certify and send any supplemental transcripts as required by (c).

(Subd (d) amended effective July 1, 2010; previously amended effective January 1, 2007.)

(e) Time to file briefs

(1) To permit determination of the appeal within 250 days after the notice of appeal is filed, the appellant must serve and file the appellant's opening brief within 30 days after the record is filed in the reviewing court.

(2) Rule 8.412(b) governs the time for filing other briefs.

(Subd (e) amended effective July 1, 2010.)

(f) Extensions of time

The superior court may not order any extensions of time to prepare the record or to file briefs; the reviewing court may order extensions of time, but must require an exceptional showing of good cause.

(g) Failure to file a brief

Rule 8.412(d) applies if a party fails to timely file an appellant's opening brief or a respondent's brief, but the period specified in the notice required by that rule must be 15 days.

(Subd (g) amended effective July 1, 2010; adopted effective January 1, 2007.)

(h) Oral argument and submission of the cause

(1) Unless the reviewing court orders otherwise, counsel must serve and file any request for oral argument no later than 15 days after the appellant's reply brief is filed or due to be filed. Failure to file a timely request will be deemed a waiver.

(2) The court must hear oral argument within 60 days after the appellant's last reply brief is filed or due to be filed, unless the court extends the time for good cause or counsel waive argument.

(3) If counsel waive argument, the cause is deemed submitted no later than 60 days after the appellant's reply brief is filed or due to be filed.

(Subd (h) relettered effective January 1, 2007; adopted as subd (g) effective January 1, 2005.)

Rule 8.416 amended effective April 1, 2023; adopted as rule 37.4 effective January 1, 2005; previously amended and renumbered effective January 1, 2007; previously amended effective July 1, 2010, January 1, 2015, January 1, 2017, and January 1, 2018.

Advisory Committee Comment

Subdivision (c). Under rule 8.71(c), the superior court clerk may send the record to the reviewing court in electronic form.

Subdivision (g). Effective January 1, 2007, revised rule 8.416 incorporates a new subdivision (g) to address a failure to timely file a brief in all termination of parental rights cases and in dependency appeals in Orange, Imperial, and San Diego Counties. Under the new subdivision, appellants would not have the full 30-day grace period given in rule 8.412(d) in which to file a late brief, but instead would have the standard 15-day grace period that is given in civil cases. The intent of this revision is to balance the need to determine the appeal within 250 days with the need to protect appellants' rights in this most serious of appeals.

Subdivision (h). Subdivision (h)(1) recognizes certain reviewing courts' practice of requiring counsel to file any request for oral argument within a time period other than 15 days after the appellant's reply brief is filed or due to be filed. The reviewing court is still expected to determine the appeal "within 250 days after the notice of appeal is filed." (Subdivision (e).)

Rule 8.417. Appeals from orders transferring a minor from juvenile court to a court of criminal jurisdiction

(a) Application

This rule governs appeals from orders of the juvenile court granting a motion to transfer a minor from juvenile court to a court of criminal jurisdiction.

(Subd (a) adopted effective January 1, 2023.)

(b) Form of record

(1) The clerk's and reporter's transcripts must comply with rules 8.45–8.47, relating to sealed and confidential records, and, except as provided in (2), with rule 8.144.

(2) The cover of the record must prominently display the title "Appeal from Order Transferring a Minor from Juvenile Court to a Court of Criminal Jurisdiction Under Welfare and Institutions Code Section 801."

(Subd (b) adopted effective January 1, 2023.)

(c) Record on appeal

(1) In addition to the items listed in rule 8.407(a), the clerk's transcript must contain:

(A) Any report by the probation officer on the behavioral patterns and social history of the minor, including any oral or written statement offered by the victim under Welfare and Institutions Code section 656.2;

(B) Any other probation report or document filed with the court on the petition under Welfare and Institutions Code section 602; and

(C) Any document in written or electronic form submitted to the court in connection with the prima facie showing under rule 5.766(c) or the motion to transfer jurisdiction.

(2) In addition to the items listed in rule 8.407(b), any reporter's transcript must contain the oral proceedings at any hearings on the prima facie showing under rule 5.766(c) and the motion to transfer jurisdiction.

(Subd (c) adopted effective January 1, 2023.)

(d) Preparing, certifying, and sending the record

(1) Within 20 court days after the notice of appeal is filed:

(A) The clerk must prepare and certify as correct an original of the clerk's transcript and one copy each for the appellant, the respondent, and the district appellate project; and

(B) The reporter must prepare, certify as correct, and deliver to the clerk an original of the reporter's transcript and the same number of copies as (A) requires of the clerk's transcript.

(2) When the clerk's and reporter's transcripts are certified as correct, the clerk must immediately send:

(A) The original transcripts to the reviewing court by the most expeditious method, noting the sending date on each original; and

(B) One copy of each transcript to the district appellate project and to the appellate counsel for the following, if they have appellate counsel, by any method as fast as United States Postal Service express mail:

(i) The appellant; and

(ii) The respondent.

(3) If appellate counsel has not yet been retained or appointed for the minor, when the transcripts are certified as correct, the clerk must send that counsel's copies of the transcripts to the district appellate project.

(Subd (d) adopted effective January 1, 2023.)

(e) Augmenting or correcting the record

(1) Except as provided in (2) and (3), rule 8.410 governs any augmentation or correction of the record.

(2) An appellant must serve and file any motion for augmentation or correction within 15 days after receiving the record. A respondent must serve and file any such motion within 15 days after the appellant's opening brief is filed.

(3) The clerk and the reporter must prepare any supplemental transcripts within 20 days, giving them the highest priority.

(4) The clerk must certify and send any supplemental transcripts as required by (d).

(Subd (e) adopted effective January 1, 2023.)

(f) Time to file briefs

(1) The appellant must serve and file the appellant's opening brief within 30 days after the record is filed in the reviewing court.

(2) Rule 8.412(b) governs the time for filing other briefs.

(Subd (f) adopted effective January 1, 2023.)

(g) Extensions of time

The superior court may not order any extensions of time to prepare the record or to file briefs; the reviewing court may order extensions of time but must require an exceptional showing of good cause.

(Subd (g) adopted effective January 1, 2023.)

(h) Failure to file a brief

Rule 8.412(d) applies if a party fails to timely file an appellant's opening brief or a respondent's brief, but the period specified in the notice required by that rule must be 15 days.

(Subd (h) adopted effective January 1, 2023.)

(i) Oral argument and submission of the cause

(1) Unless the reviewing court orders otherwise, counsel must serve and file any request for oral argument no later than 15 days after the appellant's reply brief is filed or due to be filed. Failure to file a timely request will be deemed a waiver.

(2) The court must hear oral argument within 60 days after the appellant's last reply brief is filed or due to be filed, unless the court extends the time for good cause or counsel waive argument.

(3) If counsel waive argument, the cause is deemed submitted no later than 60 days after the appellant's reply brief is filed or due to be filed.

(Subd (i) adopted effective January 1, 2023.)

Rule 8.417 adopted effective January 1, 2023.

Advisory Committee Comment

Subdivision (d). Under rule 8.71(c), the superior court clerk may send the record to the reviewing court in electronic form.

Article 3
Writs

Title 8, Appellate Rules—Division 1, Rules Relating to the Supreme Court and Courts of Appeal—Chapter 5, Juvenile Appeals and Writs—Article 3, Writs; renumbered effective July 1, 2010; adopted as article 2 effective January 1, 2007.

Rule 8.450. Notice of intent to file writ petition to review order setting hearing under Welfare and Institutions Code section 366.26

Rule 8.452. Writ petition to review order setting hearing under Welfare and Institutions Code section 366.26

Rule 8.454. Notice of intent to file writ petition under Welfare and Institutions Code section 366.28 to review order designating specific placement of a dependent child after termination of parental rights

Rule 8.456. Writ petition under Welfare and Institutions Code section 366.28 to review order designating or denying specific placement of a dependent child after termination of parental rights

Rule 8.450. Notice of intent to file writ petition to review order setting hearing under Welfare and Institutions Code section 366.26

(a) Application

Rules 8.450–8.452 and 8.490 govern writ petitions to review orders setting a hearing under Welfare and Institutions Code section 366.26.

(Subd (a) amended effective July 1, 2010; previously amended effective January 1, 2006, July 1, 2006, January 1, 2007, and January 1, 2009.)

(b) Purpose

Rules 8.450–8.452 are intended to encourage and assist the reviewing courts to determine on their merits all writ petitions filed under these rules within the 120-day period for holding a hearing under Welfare and Institutions Code section 366.26.

(Subd (b) amended effective January 1, 2007.)

(c) Who may file

The petitioner's trial counsel, or, in the absence of trial counsel, the party, is responsible for filing any notice of intent and writ petition under rules 8.450–8.452. Trial counsel is encouraged to seek assistance from or consult with attorneys experienced in writ procedure.

(Subd (c) amended effective January 1, 2008; previously amended effective January 1, 2007.)

(d) Extensions of time

The superior court may not extend any time period prescribed by rules 8.450–8.452. The reviewing court may extend any time period but must require an exceptional showing of good cause.

(Subd (d) amended effective January 1, 2013; previously amended effective January 1, 2007, and July 1, 2010.)

(e) Notice of intent

(1) A party seeking writ review under rules 8.450–8.452 must file in the superior court a notice of intent to file a writ petition and a request for the record.

(2) The notice must include all known dates of the hearing that resulted in the order under review.

(3) The notice must be authorized by the party intending to file the petition and must be signed by that party or by the attorney of record for that party.

(4) The date of the order setting the hearing is the date on which the court states the order on the record orally, or issues an order in writing, whichever occurs first. The notice of intent must be filed according to the following timeline requirements:

(A) If the party was present at the hearing when the court ordered a hearing under Welfare and Institutions Code section 366.26, the notice of intent must be filed within 7 days after the date of the order setting the hearing.

(B) If the party was notified of the order setting the hearing only by mail, the notice of intent must be filed within 12 days after the date the clerk mailed the notification.

(C) If the party was notified of the order setting the hearing by mail, and the notice was mailed to an address outside California but within the United States, the notice of intent must be filed within 17 days after the date the clerk mailed the notification.

(D) If the party was notified of the order setting the hearing by mail, and the notice was mailed to an address outside the United States, the notice of intent must be filed within 27 days after the date the clerk mailed the notification.

(E) If the order was made by a referee not acting as a temporary judge, the party has an additional 10 days to file the notice of intent as provided in rule 5.540(c).

(Subd (e) amended effective July 1, 2010; previously amended effective January 1, 2007, and July 1, 2010.)

(f) Premature or late notice of intent to file writ petition

(1) A notice of intent to file a writ petition under Welfare and Institutions Code section 366.26 is premature if filed before an order setting a hearing under Welfare and Institutions Code section 366.26 has been made.

(2) If a notice of intent is premature or late, the superior court clerk must promptly:

(A) Mark the notice of intent "Received [date] but not filed;"

(B) Return the marked notice of intent to the party with a notice stating that:

(i) The notice of intent was not filed either because it is premature, as no order setting a hearing under Welfare and Institutions Code section 366.26 has been made, or because it was late; and

(ii) The party should contact his or her attorney as soon as possible to discuss this notice, because the time available to take appropriate steps to protect the party's interests may be short; and

(C) Send a copy of the marked notice of intent and clerk's notice to the party's counsel of record, if applicable.

(Subd (f) adopted effective January 1, 2013.)

(g) Sending the notice of intent

(1) When the notice of intent is filed, the superior court clerk must immediately send a copy of the notice to:

(A) The attorney of record for each party;

(B) Each party, including the child if the child is 10 years of age or older;

(C) Any known sibling of the child who is the subject of the hearing if that sibling either is the subject of a dependency proceeding or has been adjudged to be a dependent child of the juvenile court as follows:

(i) If the sibling is under 10 years of age, on the sibling's attorney; or

(ii) If the sibling is 10 years of age or over, on the sibling and the sibling's attorney;

(D) The mother, the father, and any presumed and alleged parents;

(E) The child's legal guardian, if any;

(F) Any person currently awarded by the juvenile court the status of the child's de facto parent;

(G) The probation officer or social worker;

(H) Any Court Appointed Special Advocate (CASA) volunteer;

(I) The grandparents of the child, if their address is known and if the parents' whereabouts are unknown; and

(J) If the court knows or has reason to know that an Indian child is involved, the Indian custodian, if any, and tribe of the child or the Bureau of Indian Affairs, as required under Welfare and Institutions Code section 224.2.

(2) The clerk must promptly send by first-class mail, e-mail, or fax a copy of the notice of intent and a list of those to whom the notice of intent was sent to:

(A) The reviewing court; and

(B) The petitioner if the clerk sent the notice of intent to the Indian custodian, tribe of the child, or the Bureau of Indian Affairs.

(3) If the party was notified of the order setting the hearing only by mail, the clerk must include the date that the notification was mailed.

(Subd (g) amended effective January 1, 2017; previously amended effective January 1, 2006, July 1, 2006, January 1, 2007, and July 1, 2010; previously amended and relettered effective January 1, 2013.)

(h) Preparing the record

When the notice of intent is filed, the superior court clerk must:

(1) Immediately notify each court reporter, in a manner providing immediate notice, to prepare a reporter's transcript of the oral proceedings at each session of the hearing that resulted in the order under review and deliver the transcript to the clerk within 12 calendar days after the notice of intent is filed; and

(2) Within 20 days after the notice of intent is filed, prepare a clerk's transcript that includes the notice of intent, proof of service, and all items listed in rule 8.407(a).

(Subd (h) amended effective January 1, 2021; adopted as subd (g); previously amended effective January 1, 2006, January 1, 2007, January 1, 2008, and July 1, 2010; previously amended and relettered as subd (h) effective January 1, 2013.)

(i) Sending the record

When the transcripts are certified as correct, the superior court clerk must immediately send:

(1) The original transcripts to the reviewing court by the most expeditious method, noting the sending date on each original, and

(2) One copy of each transcript to each counsel of record and any unrepresented party by any means as fast as United States Postal Service express mail.

(Subd (i) relettered effective January 1, 2013; previously amended as subd (h) effective January 1, 2007.)

(j) Reviewing court clerk's duties

(1) The reviewing court clerk must immediately lodge the notice of intent. When the notice is lodged, the reviewing court has jurisdiction of the writ proceedings.

(2) When the record is filed in the reviewing court, that court's clerk must immediately notify the parties, stating the date on which the 10-day period for filing the writ petition under rule 8.452(c)(1) will expire.

(Subd (j) relettered effective January 1, 2013; previously amended as subd (i) effective January 1, 2007.)

Rule 8.450 amended effective January 1, 2021; adopted as rule 38 effective January 1, 2005; previously amended and renumbered effective January 1, 2007; previously amended effective January 1, 2006, July 1, 2006, January 1, 2008, January 1, 2009, July 1, 2010, January 1, 2013, and January 1, 2017.

Advisory Committee Comment

Subdivision (d). The case law generally recognizes that the reviewing courts may grant extensions of time under these rules for exceptional good cause. (See, e.g., *Jonathan M. v. Superior Court* (1995) 39 Cal.App.4th 1826, and *In re Cathina W.* (1998) 68 Cal.App.4th 716 [recognizing that a late notice of intent may be filed on a showing of exceptional circumstances not under the petitioner's control].) It may constitute exceptional good cause for an extension of the time to file a notice of intent if a premature notice of intent is returned to a party shortly before the issuance of an order setting a hearing under Welfare and Institutions Code section 366.26.

Subdivision (e)(4). See rule 8.25(b)(5) for provisions concerning the timeliness of documents mailed by inmates or patients from custodial institutions.

Subdivision (f)(1). A party who prematurely attempts to file a notice of intent to file a writ petition under Welfare and Institutions Code section 366.26 is not precluded from later filing such a notice after the issuance of an order setting a hearing under Welfare and Institutions Code section 366.26.

Subdivision (i). Under rule 8.71(c), the superior court clerk may send the record to the reviewing court in electronic form.

Rule 8.452. Writ petition to review order setting hearing under Welfare and Institutions Code section 366.26

(a) Petition

(1) The petition must be liberally construed and must include:

(A) The identities of the parties;

(B) The date on which the superior court made the order setting the hearing;

(C) The date on which the hearing is scheduled to be held;

(D) A summary of the grounds of the petition; and

(E) The relief requested.

(2) The petition must be verified.

(3) The petition must be accompanied by a memorandum.

(Subd (a) amended effective January 1, 2018; previously amended effective January 1, 2007, and July 1, 2010.)

(b) Contents of the memorandum

(1) The memorandum must provide a summary of the significant facts, limited to matters in the record.

(2) The memorandum must state each point under a separate heading or subheading summarizing the point and support each point by argument and citation of authority.

(3) The memorandum must support any reference to a matter in the record by a citation to the record. The memorandum should explain the significance of any cited portion of the record and note any disputed aspects of the record.

(Subd (b) amended effective January 1, 2007.)

(c) Serving and filing the petition and response

(1) The petition must be served and filed within 10 days after the record is filed in the reviewing court. The petitioner must serve a copy of the petition on:

(A) Each attorney of record;

(B) Any unrepresented party, including the child if the child is 10 years of age or older;

(C) Any known sibling of the child who is the subject of the hearing if that sibling either is the subject of a dependency proceeding or has been adjudged to be a dependent child of the juvenile court as follows:

(i) If the sibling is under 10 years of age, on the sibling's attorney;

(ii) If the sibling is 10 years of age or over, on the sibling and the sibling's attorney;

(D) The child's Court Appointed Special Advocate (CASA) volunteer;

(E) Any person currently awarded by the juvenile court the status of the child's de facto parent; and

(F) If the court sent the notice of intent to file the writ petition to an Indian custodian, tribe, or Bureau of Indian Affairs, then to that Indian custodian, tribe of the child, or the Bureau of Indian Affairs as required under Welfare and Institutions Code section 224.2.

(2) Any response must be served on each of the people and entities listed above and filed:

(A) Within 10 days—or, if the petition was served by mail, within 15 days—after the petition is filed; or

(B) Within 10 days after a respondent receives a request from the reviewing court for a response, unless the court specifies a shorter time.

(Subd (c) amended effective July 1, 2010; previously amended effective January 1, 2007.)

(d) Order to show cause or alternative writ

If the court intends to determine the petition on the merits, it must issue an order to show cause or alternative writ.

(Subd (d) repealed and relettered effective July 1, 2010; adopted as subd (d) effective January 1, 2006; previously relettered as subd (e) effective January 1, 2006.)

(e) Augmenting or correcting the record in the reviewing court

(1) Except as provided in (2) and (3), rule 8.410 governs any augmentation or correction of the record.

(2) The petitioner must serve and file any request for augmentation or correction within 5 days—or, if the record exceeds 300 pages, within 7 days; or, if the record exceeds 600 pages, within 10 days—after receiving the record. A respondent must serve and file any such request within 5 days after the petition is filed or an order to show cause has issued, whichever is later.

(3) A party must attach to its motion a copy, if available, of any document or transcript that the party wants added to the record. Except as provided in rule 8.144(f) for reporters' transcripts in multiple reporter cases, the pages of the attachment must be consecutively numbered, beginning with the number one. If the reviewing court grants the motion, it may augment the record with the copy.

(4) If the party cannot attach a copy of the matter to be added, the party must identify it as required under rules 8.122(a)(1) and 8.130(a)(1).

(5) An order augmenting or correcting the record may grant no more than 15 days for compliance. The clerk and the reporter must give the order the highest priority.

(6) The clerk must certify and send any supplemental transcripts as required by rule 8.450(h). If the augmentation or correction is ordered, the time to file any petition or response is extended by the number of additional days granted to augment or correct the record.

(Subd (e) amended effective January 1, 2024; adopted as subd (e) effective January 1, 2005; previously relettered as subd (f) effective January 1, 2006; previously amended effective January 1, 2007; previously amended and relettered effective July 1, 2010.)

(f) Stay

The reviewing court may stay the hearing set under Welfare and Institutions Code section 366.26, but must require an exceptional showing of good cause.

(Subd (f) relettered effective July 1, 2010; adopted as subd (f) effective January 1, 2005; previously relettered as subd (g) effective January 1, 2006.)

(g) Oral argument

(1) The reviewing court must hear oral argument within 30 days after the response is filed or due to be filed, unless the court extends the time for good cause or counsel waive argument.

(2) If argument is waived, the cause is deemed submitted not later than 30 days after the response is filed or due to be filed.

(Subd (g) relettered effective July 1, 2010; adopted as subd (g) effective January 1, 2005; previously relettered as subd (h) effective January 1, 2006.)

(h) Decision

(1) Absent exceptional circumstances, the reviewing court must decide the petition on the merits by written opinion.

(2) The reviewing court clerk must promptly notify the parties of any decision and must promptly send a certified copy of any writ or order to the court named as respondent.

(3) If the writ or order stays or prohibits proceedings set to occur within 7 days or requires action within 7 days—or in any other urgent situation—the reviewing court clerk must make a reasonable effort to notify the clerk of the respondent court by telephone or e-mail. The clerk of the respondent court must then notify the judge or officer most directly concerned.

(4) The reviewing court clerk need not give telephonic or e-mail notice of the summary denial of a writ, unless a stay previously issued will be dissolved.

(Subd (h) amended effective January 1, 2017; adopted as subd (h) effective January 1, 2005; previously relettered as subd (i) effective January 1, 2006, and subd (h) effective July 1, 2010; previously amended effective January 1, 2007.)

(i) Filing, modification, finality of decision, and remittitur

Rule 8.490 governs the filing, modification, finality of decisions, and remittitur in writ proceedings under this rule.

(Subd (i) adopted effective July 1, 2010.)

Rule 8.452 amended effective January 1, 2024; adopted as rule 38.1 effective January 1, 2005; previously amended and renumbered effective January 1, 2007; previously amended effective January 1, 2006, July 1, 2010, January 1, 2017, and January 1, 2018.

Advisory Committee Comment

Subdivision (d). Subdivision (d) tracks the second sentence of former rule 39.1B(*l*). (But see *Maribel M. v. Superior Court* (1998) 61 Cal.App.4th 1469, 1471–1476.)

Subdivision (h). Subdivision (h)(1) tracks former rule 39.1B(o). (But see *Maribel M. v. Superior Court* (1998) 61 Cal.App.4th 1469, 1471–1476.)

Rule 8.454. Notice of intent to file writ petition under Welfare and Institutions Code section 366.28 to review order designating specific placement of a dependent child after termination of parental rights

(a) Application

Rules 8.454–8.456 and 8.490 govern writ petitions to review placement orders following termination of parental rights entered on or after January 1, 2005. "Posttermination placement order" as used in this rule and rule 8.456 refers to orders following termination of parental rights.

(Subd (a) amended effective July 1, 2010; previously amended effective January 1, 2007, and January 1, 2009.)

(b) Purpose

The purpose of this rule is to facilitate and implement Welfare and Institutions Code section 366.28. Delays caused by appeals from court orders designating the specific placement of a dependent child after parental rights have been terminated may cause a substantial detriment to the child.

(c) Who may file

The petitioner's trial counsel, or, in the absence of trial counsel, the party, is responsible for filing any notice of intent and writ petition under rules 8.454–8.456. Trial counsel is encouraged to seek assistance from, or consult with, attorneys experienced in writ procedure.

(Subd (c) amended effective January 1, 2008; previously amended effective January 1, 2007.)

(d) Extensions of time

The superior court may not extend any time period prescribed by rules 8.454–8.456. The reviewing court may extend any time period, but must require an exceptional showing of good cause.

(Subd (d) amended effective January 1, 2007.)

(e) Notice of intent

(1) A party seeking writ review under rules 8.454–8.456 must file in the superior court a notice of intent to file a writ petition and a request for the record.

(2) The notice must include all known dates of the hearing that resulted in the order under review.

(3) The notice must be authorized by the party intending to file the petition and signed by the party or by the attorney of record for that party.

(4) The notice must be served and filed within 7 days after the date of the posttermination placement order or, if the order was made by a referee not acting as a temporary judge, within 7 days after the referee's order becomes final under rule 5.540(c). The date of the posttermination placement order is the date on which the court states the order on the record orally or in writing, whichever first occurs.

(5) If the party was notified of the posttermination placement order only by mail, the notice of intent must be filed within 12 days after the date that the clerk mailed the notification.

(Subd (e) amended effective July 1, 2010; previously amended effective January 1, 2007.)

(f) Premature or late notice of intent to file writ petition

(1) A notice of intent to file a writ petition under Welfare and Institutions Code section 366.28 is premature if filed before a date for a posttermination placement order has been made. The reviewing court may treat the notice as filed immediately after the posttermination order has been made.

(2) The superior court clerk must mark a late notice of intent to file a writ petition under section 366.28 "Received [date] but not filed," notify the party that the notice was not filed because it was late, and send a copy of the marked notice to the party's counsel of record, if applicable.

(Subd (f) amended effective July 1, 2013; adopted effective January 1, 2006; previously amended effective January 1, 2007.)

(g) Sending the notice of intent

(1) When the notice of intent is filed, the superior court clerk must immediately send a copy of the notice to:

(A) The attorney of record for each party;

(B) Each party, including the child if the child is 10 years of age or older;

(C) Any known sibling of the child who is the subject of the hearing if that sibling either is the subject of a dependency proceeding or has been adjudged to be a dependent child of the juvenile court as follows:

(i) If the sibling is under 10 years of age, on the sibling's attorney;

(ii) If the sibling is 10 years of age or over, on the sibling and the sibling's attorney;

(D) Any prospective adoptive parent;

(E) The child's legal guardian if any;

(F) Any person currently awarded by the juvenile court the status of the child's de facto parent;

(G) The probation officer or social worker;

(H) The child's Court Appointed Special Advocate (CASA) volunteer, if any; and

(I) If the court knows or has reason to know that an Indian child is involved, the Indian custodian, if any, and tribe of the child or the Bureau of Indian Affairs as required under Welfare and Institutions Code section 224.2.

(2) The clerk must promptly send by first-class mail, e-mail, or fax a copy of the notice of intent and a list of those to whom the notice of intent was sent to:

(A) The reviewing court; and

(B) The petitioner if the clerk sent a copy of the notice of intent to the Indian custodian, tribe of the child, or the Bureau of Indian Affairs.

(3) If the party was notified of the posttermination placement order only by mail, the clerk must include the date that the notification was mailed.

(Subd (g) amended effective January 1, 2017; adopted as subd (f) effective January 1, 2005; relettered effective January 1, 2006; previously amended effective January 1, 2007, and July 1, 2010.)

(h) Preparing the record

When the notice of intent is filed, the superior court clerk must:

(1) Immediately notify each court reporter, in a manner providing immediate notice, to prepare a reporter's transcript of the oral proceedings at each session of the hearing that resulted in the order under review and to deliver the transcript to the clerk within 12 calendar days after the notice of intent is filed; and

(2) Within 20 days after the notice of intent is filed, prepare a clerk's transcript that includes the notice of intent, proof of service, and all items listed in rule 8.407(a).

(Subd (h) amended effective January 1, 2021; adopted as subd (g) effective January 1, 2005; previously amended and relettered effective January 1, 2006; previously amended effective July 1, 2006, January 1, 2007, January 1, 2008, July 1, 2010, and July 1, 2013.)

(i) Sending the record

When the transcripts are certified as correct, the superior court clerk must immediately send:

(1) The original transcripts to the reviewing court by the most expeditious method, noting the sending date on each original; and

(2) One copy of each transcript to each counsel of record and any unrepresented party and unrepresented custodian of the dependent child by any means as fast as United States Postal Service express mail.

(Subd (i) amended effective January 1, 2007; adopted as subd (h) effective January 1, 2005; relettered effective January 1, 2006.)

(j) Reviewing court clerk's duties

(1) The reviewing court clerk must promptly lodge the notice of intent. When the notice is lodged, the reviewing court has jurisdiction over the writ proceedings.

(2) When the record is filed in the reviewing court, that court's clerk must immediately notify the parties, stating the date on which the 10-day period for filing the writ petition under rule 8.456(c)(1) will expire.

(Subd (j) amended effective January 1, 2007; adopted as subd (i) effective January 1, 2005; relettered effective January 1, 2006.)

Rule 8.454 amended effective January 1, 2021; adopted as rule 38.2 effective January 1, 2005; previously amended and renumbered effective January 1, 2007; previously amended effective January 1, 2006, July 1, 2006, January 1, 2008, January 1, 2009, July 1, 2010, July 1, 2013, and January 1, 2017.

Advisory Committee Comment

Subdivision (f)(2). See rule 8.25(b)(5) for provisions concerning the timeliness of documents mailed by inmates or patients from custodial institutions.

Subdivision (i). Under rule 8.71(c), the superior court clerk may send the record to the reviewing court in electronic form.

Rule 8.456. Writ petition under Welfare and Institutions Code section 366.28 to review order designating or denying specific placement of a dependent child after termination of parental rights

(a) Petition

(1) The petition must be liberally construed and must include:

(A) The identities of the parties;

(B) The date on which the superior court made the posttermination placement order;

(C) A summary of the grounds of the petition; and

(D) The relief requested.

(2) The petition must be verified.

(3) The petition must be accompanied by a memorandum.

(Subd (a) amended effective January 1, 2018; previously amended effective January 1, 2007, and July 1, 2010.)

(b) Contents of memorandum

(1) The memorandum must provide a summary of the significant facts, limited to matters in the record.

(2) The memorandum must state each point under a separate heading or subheading summarizing the point and support each point by argument and citation of authority.

(3) The memorandum must support any reference to a matter in the record by a citation to the record. The memorandum should explain the significance of any cited portion of the record and note any disputed aspects of the record.

(Subd (b) amended effective January 1, 2007.)

(c) Serving and filing the petition and response

(1) The petition must be served and filed within 10 days after the record is filed in the reviewing court. The petitioner must serve petition on:

(A) Each attorney of record;

(B) Any unrepresented party, including the child if the child is 10 years of age or older;

(C) Any known sibling of the child who is the subject of the hearing if that sibling either is the subject of a dependency proceeding or has been adjudged to be a dependent child of the juvenile court as follows:

(i) If the sibling is under 10 years of age, on the sibling's attorney;

(ii) If the sibling is 10 years of age or over, on the sibling and the sibling's attorney;

(D) Any prospective adoptive parent;

(E) The child's Court Appointed Special Advocate (CASA) volunteer;

(F) Any person currently awarded by the juvenile court the status of the child's de facto parent; and

(G) If the court sent the notice of intent to file the writ petition to an Indian custodian, tribe, or Bureau of Indian Affairs, then to that Indian custodian, tribe, or the Bureau of Indian Affairs as required under Welfare and Institutions Code section 224.2.

(2) Any response must be served on each of the people and entities listed in (1) and filed:

(A) Within 10 days—or, if the petition was served by mail, within 15 days—after the petition is filed; or

(B) Within 10 days after a respondent receives a request from the reviewing court for a response, unless the court specifies a shorter time.

(Subd (c) amended effective July 1, 2010; previously amended effective January 1, 2006, and January 1, 2007.)

(d) Order to show cause or alternative writ

If the court intends to determine the petition on the merits, it must issue an order to show cause or alternative writ.

(Subd (d) repealed and relettered effective July 1, 2010; adopted as subd (d) effective January 1, 2005; previously relettered as subd (e) effective January 1, 2006.)

(e) Augmenting or correcting the record in the reviewing court

(1) Except as provided in (2) and (3), rule 8.410 governs augmentation or correction of the record.

(2) The petitioner must serve and file any request for augmentation or correction within 5 days—or, if the record exceeds 300 pages, within 7 days; or, if the record exceeds 600 pages, within 10 days—after receiving the record. A respondent must serve and file any such request within 5 days after the petition is filed or an order to show cause has issued, whichever is later.

(3) A party must attach to its motion a copy, if available, of any document or transcript that it wants added to the record. Except as provided in rule 8.144(f) for reporters' transcripts in multiple reporter cases, the pages of the attachment must be consecutively numbered, beginning with the number one. If the reviewing court grants the motion, it may augment the record with the copy.

(4) If the party cannot attach a copy of the matter to be added, the party must identify it as required under rules 8.122(a)(1) and 8.130(a)(1).

(5) An order augmenting or correcting the record may grant no more than 15 days for compliance. The clerk and the reporter must give the order the highest priority.

(6) The clerk must certify and send any supplemental transcripts as required by rule 8.454(i). If the augmentation or correction is ordered, the

time to file any petition or response is extended by the number of additional days granted to augment or correct the record.

(Subd (e) amended effective January 1, 2024; adopted as subd (e) effective January 1, 2005; previously relettered as subd (f) effective January 1, 2006; previously amended effective January 1, 2007; previously amended and relettered effective July 1, 2010.)

(f) Stay

A request by petitioner for a stay of the posttermination placement order will not be granted unless the writ petition shows that implementation of the superior court's placement order pending the reviewing court's decision is likely to cause detriment to the child if the order is ultimately reversed.

(Subd (f) relettered effective July 1, 2010; adopted as subd (f) effective January 1, 2005; previously relettered as subd (g) effective January 1, 2006; previously amended effective February 24, 2006.)

(g) Oral argument

(1) The reviewing court must hear oral argument within 30 days after the response is filed or due to be filed, unless the court extends the time for good cause or counsel waive argument.

(2) If argument is waived, the cause is deemed submitted not later than 30 days after the response is filed or due to be filed.

(Subd (g) relettered effective July 1, 2010; adopted as subd (g) effective January 1, 2005; previously relettered as subd (h) effective January 1, 2006; previously amended effective January 1, 2007.)

(h) Decision

(1) Absent exceptional circumstances, the reviewing court must review the petition and decide it on the merits by written opinion.

(2) The reviewing court clerk must promptly notify the parties of any decision and must promptly send a certified copy of any writ or order to the court named as respondent.

(3) If the writ or order stays or requires action within 7 days—or in any other urgent situation—the reviewing court clerk must make a reasonable effort to notify the clerk of the respondent court by telephone or e-mail. The clerk of the respondent court must then notify the judge or officer most directly concerned.

(4) The reviewing court clerk need not give telephonic or e-mail notice of the summary denial of a writ, unless a stay previously issued and will be dissolved.

(5) Rule 8.490 governs the filing, modification, finality of decisions, and remittitur in writ proceedings under this rule.

(Subd (h) amended effective January 1, 2017; adopted as subd (h) effective January 1, 2005; previously relettered as subd (i) effective January 1, 2006; previously amended and relettered as subd (h) effective July 1, 2010.)

(i) Right to appeal other orders

This section does not affect the right of a parent, a legal guardian, or the child to appeal any order that is otherwise appealable and that is issued at a hearing held under Welfare and Institutions Code section 366.26.

(Subd (i) relettered effective July 1, 2010; adopted as subd (i) effective January 1, 2005; previously relettered as subd (j) effective January 1, 2006; previously amended effective January 1, 2007.)

Rule 8.456 amended effective January 1, 2024; adopted as rule 38.3 effective January 1, 2005; previously amended and renumbered effective January 1, 2007; previously amended effective January 1, 2006, February 24, 2006, July 1, 2010, January 1, 2017, and January 1, 2018.

Article 4
Hearing and Decision

Division 1, Rules Relating to the Supreme Court and Courts of Appeal—Chapter 5, Juvenile Appeals and Writs—Article 4, Hearing and Decision, renumbered effective January 1, 2011.

Rule 8.470. Hearing and decision in the Court of Appeal
Rule 8.472. Hearing and decision in the Supreme Court
Rule 8.474. Procedures and data

Rule 8.470. Hearing and decision in the Court of Appeal

Except as provided in rules 8.400–8.456, rules 8.252–8.272 govern hearing and decision in the Court of Appeal in juvenile cases.

Rule 8.470 amended and renumbered effective January 1, 2007; adopted as rule 38.4 effective January 1, 2005; previously amended effective July 1, 2005.

Rule 8.472. Hearing and decision in the Supreme Court

Rules 8.500–8.552 govern hearing and decision in the Supreme Court in juvenile cases.

Rule 8.472 amended and renumbered effective January 1, 2007; adopted as rule 38.5 effective January 1, 2005; previously amended effective July 1, 2005.

Rule 8.474. Procedures and data

(a) Procedures

The judges and clerks of the superior courts and the reviewing courts must adopt procedures to identify the records and expedite the processing of all appeals and writs in juvenile cases.

(b) Data

The clerks of the superior courts and the reviewing courts must provide the data required to assist the Judicial Council in evaluating the effectiveness of the rules governing appeals and writs in juvenile cases.

(Subd (b) amended effective January 1, 2016.)

Rule 8.474 amended effective January 1, 2016; adopted as rule 38.6 effective January 1, 2005; previously renumbered as rule 8.474 effective January 1, 2007.

Chapter 6
Conservatorship and Civil Commitment Appeals

Title 8, Appellate Rules—Division 1, Rules Relating to the Supreme Court and Courts of Appeal—Chapter 6, Conservatorship and Civil Commitment Appeals amended effective January 1, 2020.

Rule 8.480. Appeal from order establishing conservatorship
Rule 8.482. Appeal from judgment authorizing conservator to consent to sterilization of conservatee
Rule 8.483. Appeal from order of civil commitment

Rule 8.480. Appeal from order establishing conservatorship

(a) Application

Except as otherwise provided in this rule, rules 8.304–8.368 and 8.508 govern appeals from orders establishing conservatorships under Welfare and Institutions Code section 5350 et seq.

(Subd (a) amended effective January 1, 2007.)

(b) Clerk's transcript

The clerk's transcript must contain:

(1) The petition;

(2) Any demurrer or other plea;

(3) Any written motion with supporting and opposing memoranda and attachments;

(4) Any filed medical or social worker reports;

(5) All court minutes;

(6) All instructions submitted in writing, each noting the party requesting it;

(7) Any verdict;

(8) Any written opinion of the court;

(9) The judgment or order appealed from;

(10) The notice of appeal; and

(11) Any application for additional record and any order on the application.

(Subd (b) amended effective January 1, 2007.)

(c) Reporter's transcript

The reporter's transcript must contain all oral proceedings, excluding the voir dire examination of jurors and any opening statement.

(d) Sending the record

The clerk must not send a copy of the record to the Attorney General or the district attorney unless that office represents a party.

(e) Briefs

The parties must not serve copies of their briefs:

(1) On the Attorney General or the district attorney, unless that office represents a party; or

(2) On the Supreme Court under rule 8.44(b)(1).

(Subd (e) amended effective January 1, 2007.)

Rule 8.480 amended and renumbered effective January 1, 2007; repealed and adopted as rule 39 effective January 1, 2005.

Advisory Committee Comment

Subdivision (a). Under rule 8.71(c), the superior court clerk may send the record to the reviewing court in electronic form.

Rule 8.482. Appeal from judgment authorizing conservator to consent to sterilization of conservatee

(a) Application

Except as otherwise provided in this rule, rules 8.304–8.368 and 8.508 govern appeals from judgments authorizing a conservator to consent to the sterilization of an adult conservatee with a developmental disability.

(Subd (a) amended effective January 1, 2023; previously amended effective January 1, 2007.)

(b) When appeal is taken automatically

An appeal from a judgment authorizing a conservator to consent to the sterilization of an adult conservatee with a developmental disability is taken automatically, without any action by the conservatee, when the judgment is rendered.

(Subd (b) amended effective January 1, 2023.)

(c) Superior court clerk's duties

After entering the judgment, the clerk must immediately:

(1) Begin preparing a clerk's transcript and notify the reporter to prepare a reporter's transcript; and

(2) Send certified copies of the judgment to the Court of Appeal and the Attorney General.

(Subd (c) amended effective January 1, 2016; previously amended effective January 1, 2007.)

(d) Clerk's transcript

The clerk's transcript must contain:

(1) The petition and notice of hearing;

(2) All court minutes;

(3) Any application, motion, or notice of motion, with supporting and opposing memoranda and attachments;

(4) Any report or other document submitted to the court;

(5) Any transcript of a proceeding pertaining to the case;

(6) The statement of decision; and

(7) The judgment or order appealed from.

(Subd (d) amended effective January 1, 2007.)

(e) Reporter's transcript

The reporter's transcript must contain all oral proceedings, including:

(1) All proceedings at the hearing on the petition, with opening statements and closing arguments;

(2) All proceedings on motions;

(3) Any comments on the evidence by the court; and

(4) Any oral opinion or oral statement of decision.

(Subd (e) amended effective January 1, 2007.)

(f) Preparing and sending transcripts

(1) The clerk and the reporter must prepare and send an original and two copies of each of the transcripts as provided in rule 8.336.

(2) Probate Code section 1963 governs the cost of preparing the record on appeal.

(Subd (f) amended effective January 1, 2007.)

(g) Confidential material

(1) Written reports of physicians, psychologists, and clinical social workers, and any other matter marked confidential by the court, may be inspected only by court personnel, the parties and their counsel, the district appellate project, and other persons designated by the court.

(2) Material under (1) must be sent to the reviewing court in a secure manner that preserves its confidentiality. If the material is in paper format, it must be sent to the reviewing court in a sealed envelope marked "CONFIDENTIAL—MAY NOT BE EXAMINED WITHOUT COURT ORDER."

(Subd (g) amended effective January 1, 2016.)

(h) Trial counsel's continuing representation

To expedite preparation and certification of the record, the conservatee's trial counsel must continue to represent the conservatee until appellate counsel is retained or appointed.

(i) Appointment of appellate counsel

If appellate counsel has not been retained for the conservatee, the reviewing court must appoint such counsel.

Rule 8.482 amended effective January 1, 2023; repealed and adopted as rule 39.1 effective January 1, 2005; previously amended and renumbered as rule 8.482 effective January 1, 2007; previously amended effective January 1, 2016.

Advisory Committee Comment

Subdivision (a). Under rule 8.71(c), the superior court clerk may send the record to the reviewing court in electronic form.

Rule 8.483. Appeal from order of civil commitment

(a) Application and contents

(1) *Application*

Except as otherwise provided in this rule, rules 8.300–8.368 and 8.508 govern appeals from civil commitment orders under Penal Code sections 1026 et seq. (not guilty by reason of insanity), 1370 et seq. (incompetent to stand trial), 1600 et seq. (outpatient placement and revocation), and 2962 et seq. (offenders with mental health disorders); Welfare and Institutions Code sections 1800 et seq. (extended detention of dangerous persons), 6500 et seq. (dangerous persons with developmental disabilities), and 6600 et seq. (sexually violent predators); and former Welfare and Institutions Code section 6300 et seq. (mentally disordered sex offenders).

(2) *Contents*

In an appeal from a civil commitment order, the record must contain a clerk's transcript and a reporter's transcript, which together constitute the normal record.

(Subd (a) amended effective January 1, 2023; adopted effective January 1, 2020.)

(b) Clerk's transcript

The clerk's transcript must contain:

(1) The petition and any supporting documents filed along with the petition;

(2) Any demurrer or other plea, admission, or denial;

(3) All court minutes;

(4) All jury instructions that any party submitted in writing and the cover page required by rule 2.1055(b)(2) indicating the party requesting each instruction, and any written jury instructions given by the court;

(5) Any written communication between the court and the jury or any individual juror;

(6) Any verdict;

(7) Any written opinion of the court;

(8) The commitment order and any judgment or other order appealed from;

(9) Any motion for new trial, with supporting and opposing memoranda and attachments;

(10) The notice of appeal;

(11) Any transcript of a sound or sound-and-video recording furnished to the jury or tendered to the court under rule 2.1040;

(12) Any application for additional record and any order on the application;

(13) Any diagnostic or psychological reports submitted to the court, including at the trial or probable cause hearing;

(14) Any written waiver of the right to a jury trial or the right to be present; and

(15) If the appellant is the person subject to the civil commitment order:

(A) Any written defense motion denied in whole or in part, with supporting and opposing memoranda and attachments; and

(B) Any document admitted in evidence to prove a juvenile adjudication, criminal conviction, or prison term.

(Subd (b) adopted effective January 1, 2020.)

(c) Reporter's transcript

The reporter's transcript must contain:

(1) The oral proceedings on the entry of any admission or submission to the commitment petition;

(2) The oral proceedings on any motion in limine;

(3) The oral proceedings at trial, excluding the voir dire examination of jurors and any opening statement;

(4) All instructions given orally;

(5) Any oral communication between the court and the jury or any individual juror;

(6) Any oral opinion of the court;

(7) The oral proceedings on any motion for new trial;

(8) The oral proceedings of the commitment hearing or other dispositional hearing, including any probable cause hearing;

(9) Any oral waiver of the right to a jury trial or the right to be present; and

(10) If the appellant is the person subject to the civil commitment order:

(A) The oral proceedings on any defense motion denied in whole or in part except motions for disqualification of a judge;

(B) The closing arguments; and

(C) Any comment on the evidence by the court to the jury.

(Subd (c) adopted effective January 1, 2020.)

(d) Exhibits

Exhibits admitted in evidence, refused, or lodged are deemed part of the record, but may be transmitted to the reviewing court only as provided in rule 8.224.

(Subd (d) adopted effective January 1, 2020.)

(e) Stipulation for partial transcript

If counsel for the person subject to the civil commitment order and the People stipulate in writing before the record is certified that any part of the record is not required for proper determination of the appeal, that part must not be prepared or sent to the reviewing court.

(Subd (e) adopted effective January 1, 2020.)

Rule 8.483 amended effective January 1, 2023; adopted effective January 1, 2020.

Advisory Committee Comment

The record on appeal of orders establishing conservatorships under Welfare and Institutions Code section 5350 et seq., including Murphy conservatorships for persons who are gravely disabled as defined in Welfare and Institutions Code section 5008(h)(1)(B), is governed by rule 8.480.

Chapter 7
Writs of Mandate, Certiorari, and Prohibition in the Supreme Court and Court of Appeal

Title 8, Appellate Rules—Division 1, Rules Relating to the Supreme Court and Courts of Appeal—Chapter 7, Writs of Mandate, Certiorari, and Prohibition in the Supreme Court and Court of Appeal adopted effective January 1, 2009.

Rule 8.485. Application
Rule 8.486. Petitions
Rule 8.487. Opposition and amicus curiae briefs
Rule 8.488. Certificate of Interested Entities or Persons
Rule 8.489. Notice to trial court
Rule 8.490. Filing, finality, and modification of decisions; rehearing; remittitur
Rule 8.491. Responsive pleading under Code of Civil Procedure section 418.10
Rule 8.492. Sanctions
Rule 8.493. Costs

Rule 8.485. Application

(a) Writ proceedings governed

Except as provided in (b), the rules in this chapter govern petitions to the Supreme Court and Court of Appeal for writs of mandate, certiorari, or prohibition, or other writs within the original jurisdiction of these courts. In all respects not provided for in these rules, rule 8.204 governs the form and content of documents in the proceedings governed by this chapter.

(Subd (a) adopted effective January 1, 2009.)

(b) Writ proceedings not governed

These rules do not apply to proceedings for writs of mandate, certiorari, or prohibition in the appellate division of the superior court under rules 8.930–8.936, writs of supersedeas under rule 8.116, writs of habeas corpus except as provided in rule 8.384, writs to review orders setting a hearing under Welfare and Institutions Code section 366.26, writs under Welfare and Institutions Code section 366.28 to review orders designating or denying a specific placement of a dependent child after termination of parental rights, and writs under rules 8.450–8.456 except as provided in rules 8.452 and 8.456, or writs under rules 8.495–8.498.

(Subd (b) amended effective January 1, 2014; adopted effective January 1, 2009; previously amended effective July 1, 2012.)

Rule 8.485 amended effective January 1, 2014; adopted effective January 1, 2009; previously amended effective July 1, 2012.

Rule 8.486. Petitions

(a) Contents of petition

(1) If the petition could have been filed first in a lower court, it must explain why the reviewing court should issue the writ as an original matter.

(2) If the petition names as respondent a judge, court, board, or other officer acting in a public capacity, it must disclose the name of any real party in interest.

(3) If the petition seeks review of trial court proceedings that are also the subject of a pending appeal, the notice "Related Appeal Pending" must appear on the cover of the petition and the first paragraph of the petition must state:

(A) The appeal's title, trial court docket number, and any reviewing court docket number; and

(B) If the petition is filed under Penal Code section 1238.5, the date the notice of appeal was filed.

(4) The petition must be verified.

(5) The petition must be accompanied by a memorandum, which need not repeat facts alleged in the petition.

(6) Rule 8.204(c) governs the length of the petition and memorandum, but, in addition to the exclusions provided in that rule, the verification and any supporting documents are excluded from the limits stated in rule 8.204(c)(1) and (2).

(7) If the petition requests a temporary stay, it must comply with the following or the reviewing court may decline to consider the request for a temporary stay:

(A) The petition must explain the urgency.

(B) The cover of the petition must prominently display the notice "STAY REQUESTED" and identify the nature and date of the proceeding or act sought to be stayed.

(C) The trial court and department involved and the name and telephone number of the trial judge whose order the request seeks to stay must appear either on the cover or at the beginning of the text.

(Subd (a) amended effective January 1, 2011; adopted as subd (b) effective January 1, 2005; previously amended effective January 1, 2006, and January 1, 2007; previously repealed, amended and relettered effective January 1, 2009.)

(b) Contents of supporting documents

(1) A petition that seeks review of a trial court ruling must be accompanied by an adequate record, including copies of:

(A) The ruling from which the petition seeks relief;

(B) All documents and exhibits submitted to the trial court supporting and opposing the petitioner's position;

(C) Any other documents or portions of documents submitted to the trial court that are necessary for a complete understanding of the case and the ruling under review; and

(D) A reporter's transcript of the oral proceedings that resulted in the ruling under review.

(2) In exigent circumstances, the petition may be filed without the documents required by (1)(A)–(C) but must include a declaration that explains the urgency and the circumstances making the documents unavailable and fairly summarizes their substance.

(3) If a transcript under (1)(D) is unavailable, the record must include a declaration:

(A) Explaining why the transcript is unavailable and fairly summarizing the proceedings, including the parties' arguments and any statement by the court supporting its ruling. This declaration may omit a full summary of the proceedings if part of the relief sought is an order to prepare a transcript for use by an indigent criminal defendant in support of the petition and if the declaration demonstrates the need for and entitlement to the transcript; or

(B) Stating that the transcript has been ordered, the date it was ordered, and the date it is expected to be filed, which must be a date before any action requested of the reviewing court other than issuance of a temporary stay supported by other parts of the record.

(4) If the petition does not include the required record or explanations or does not present facts sufficient to excuse the failure to submit them, the court may summarily deny a stay request, the petition, or both.

(Subd (b) amended effective January 1, 2014; adopted as subd (c) effective January 1, 2005; previously amended effective January 1, 2006, July 1, 2006, January 1, 2007, and July 1, 2009; previously amended and relettered effective January 1, 2009.)

(c) Form of supporting documents

(1) Documents submitted under (b) must comply with the following requirements:

(A) If submitted in paper form, they must be bound together at the end of the petition or in separate volumes not exceeding 300 pages each. The pages must be consecutively numbered.

(B) If submitted in paper form, they must be index-tabbed by number or letter.

(C) They must begin with a table of contents listing each document by its title and its index number or letter. If a document has attachments, the table of contents must give the title of each attachment and a brief description of its contents.

(2) The clerk must file any supporting documents not complying with (1), but the court may notify the petitioner that it may strike or summarily deny the petition if the documents are not brought into compliance within a stated reasonable time of not less than 5 days.

(3) Rule 8.44(a) governs the number of copies of supporting documents to be filed in the Supreme Court. Rule 8.44(b) governs the number of supporting documents to be filed in the Court of Appeal.

(Subd (c) amended effective January 1, 2016; adopted as subd (d) effective January 1, 2005; previously amended effective January 1, 2006, and January 1, 2007; previously amended and relettered as subd (c) effective January 1, 2009.)

(d) Sealed and confidential records

Rules 8.45–8.47 govern sealed and confidential records in proceedings under this chapter.

(Subd (d) amended effective January 1, 2014; adopted as subd (e) effective January 1, 2005; previously amended effective January 1, 2007, and January 1, 2011; previously relettered effective January 1, 2009.)

(e) Service

(1) If the respondent is the superior court or a judge of that court, the petition and one set of supporting documents must be served on any named real party in interest, but only the petition must be served on the respondent.

(2) If the respondent is not the superior court or a judge of that court, both the petition and one set of supporting documents must be served on the respondent and on any named real party in interest.

(3) In addition to complying with the requirements of rule 8.25, the proof of service must give the telephone number of each attorney served.

(4) The petition must be served on a public officer or agency when required by statute or rule 8.29.

(5) The clerk must file the petition even if its proof of service is defective, but if the petitioner fails to file a corrected proof of service within 5 days after the clerk gives notice of the defect the court may strike the petition or impose a lesser sanction.

(6) The court may allow the petition to be filed without proof of service.

(Subd (e) relettered effective January 1, 2009; adopted as subd (f) effective January 1, 2005; previously amended effective January 1, 2007.)

Rule 8.486 amended effective January 1, 2016; repealed and adopted as rule 56 effective January 1, 2005; previously amended and renumbered as rule 8.490 effective January 1, 2007, and as rule 8.486 effective January 1, 2009; previously amended effective July 1, 2005, January 1, 2006, July 1, 2006, January 1, 2008, July 1, 2009, January 1, 2011, and January 1, 2014.)

Advisory Committee Comment

Subdivision (a). Because of the importance of the point, rule 8.486(a)(6) explicitly states that the provisions of rule 8.204(c)—and hence the word-count limits imposed by that rule—apply to a petition for original writ.

Subdivision (d). Examples of confidential records include records of the family conciliation court (Fam. Code, § 1818 (b)) and fee waiver applications (Gov. Code, § 68633(f)).

Subdivision (e). Rule 8.25, which generally governs service and filing in reviewing courts, also applies to the original proceedings covered by this rule.

Rule 8.487. Opposition and amicus curiae briefs

(a) Preliminary opposition

(1) Within 10 days after the petition is filed, the respondent or any real party in interest, separately or jointly, may serve and file a preliminary opposition.

(2) A preliminary opposition must contain a memorandum and a statement of any material fact not included in the petition.

(3) Within 10 days after a preliminary opposition is filed, the petitioner may serve and file a reply.

(4) Without requesting preliminary opposition or waiting for a reply, the court may grant or deny a request for temporary stay, deny the petition, issue an alternative writ or order to show cause, or notify the parties that it is considering issuing a peremptory writ in the first instance.

(Subd (a) adopted effective January 1, 2009.)

(b) Return or opposition; reply

(1) If the court issues an alternative writ or order to show cause, the respondent or any real party in interest, separately or jointly, may serve and file a return by demurrer, verified answer, or both. If the court notifies the parties that it is considering issuing a peremptory writ in the first instance, the respondent or any real party in interest may serve and file an opposition.

(2) Unless the court orders otherwise, the return or opposition must be served and filed within 30 days after the court issues the alternative writ or order to show cause or notifies the parties that it is considering issuing a peremptory writ in the first instance.

(3) Unless the court orders otherwise, the petitioner may serve and file a reply within 15 days after the return or opposition is filed.

(4) If the return is by demurrer alone and the demurrer is not sustained, the court may issue the peremptory writ without granting leave to answer.

(Subd (b) adopted effective January 1, 2009.)

(c) Supporting documents

Any supporting documents accompanying a preliminary opposition, return or opposition, or reply must comply with rule 8.486(c)–(d).

(Subd (c) adopted effective January 1, 2014.)

(d) Attorney General's amicus curiae brief

(1) If the court issues an alternative writ or order to show cause, the Attorney General may file an amicus curiae brief without the permission of the Chief Justice or presiding justice, unless the brief is submitted on behalf of another state officer or agency.

(2) The Attorney General must serve and file the brief within 14 days after the return is filed or, if no return is filed, within 14 days after the date it was due. For good cause, the Chief Justice or presiding justice may allow later filing.

(3) The brief must provide the information required by rule 8.200(c)(2) and comply with rule 8.200(c)(5).

(4) Any party may serve and file an answer within 14 days after the brief is filed.

(Subd (d) amended effective January 1, 2017; adopted as subd (c) effective January 1, 2009; previously relettered as subd (d) effective January 1, 2014.)

(e) Other amicus curiae briefs

(1) This subdivision governs amicus curiae briefs when the court issues an alternative writ or order to show cause.

(2) Any person or entity may serve and file an application for permission of the Chief Justice or presiding justice to file an amicus curiae brief.

(3) The application must be filed no later than 14 days after the return is filed or, if no return is filed, within 14 days after the date it was due. For good cause, the Chief Justice or presiding justice may allow later filing.

(4) The proposed brief must be served on all parties. It must accompany the application and may be combined with it.

(5) The proposed brief must provide the information required by rule 8.200(c)(2) and (3) and comply with rule 8.200(c)(5).

(6) If the court grants the application, any party may file either an answer to the individual amicus curiae brief or a consolidated answer to multiple amicus curiae briefs filed in the case. If the court does not specify a due date, the answer must be filed within 14 days after either the court rules on the last timely filed application to file an amicus curiae brief or the time for filing applications to file an amicus curiae brief expires, whichever is later. The answer must be served on all parties and the amicus curiae.

(Subd (e) adopted effective January 1, 2017.)

Rule 8.487 amended effective January 1, 2017; adopted effective January 1, 2009; previously amended effective January 1, 2014.

Advisory Committee Comment

A party other than the petitioner who files a preliminary opposition under (a) or a return or opposition under (b) may be required to pay a filing fee under Government Code section 68926 if the preliminary opposition, return, or opposition is the first document filed in the writ proceeding in the reviewing court by that party. See rule 8.25(c).

Subdivision (a). Consistent with practice, rule 8.487 draws a distinction between a "preliminary opposition," which the respondent or a real party in interest may file before the court takes any action on the petition ((a)(1)), and a more formal "opposition," which the respondent or a real party in interest may file if the court notifies the parties that it is considering issuing a peremptory writ in the first instance ((b)(1)).

Subdivision (a)(1) allows the respondent or any real party in interest to serve and file a preliminary opposition within 10 days after the petition is filed. The reviewing court retains the power to act in any case without obtaining preliminary opposition ((a)(4)).

Subdivision (a)(3) allows a petitioner to serve and file a reply within 10 days after a preliminary opposition is filed. To permit prompt action in urgent cases, however, the provision recognizes that the reviewing court may act on the petition without waiting for a reply.

Subdivision (a)(4) recognizes that the reviewing court may "grant or deny a request for temporary stay" without requesting preliminary opposition or waiting for a reply.

The several references in rule 8.487 to the power of the court to issue a peremptory writ in the first instance after notifying the parties that it is considering doing so ((a)–(b)) implement the rule of *Palma v. U.S. Industrial Fasteners, Inc.* (1984) 36 Cal.3d 171.

Subdivision (b). Subdivision (b)(2) requires that the return or opposition be served and filed within 30 days after the court issues the alternative writ or order to show cause or notifies the parties that it is considering issuing a peremptory writ in the first instance. To permit prompt action in urgent cases, however, the provision recognizes that the reviewing court may order otherwise.

Subdivision (b)(3) formalizes the common practice of permitting petitioners to file replies to returns and specifies that such a reply must be served and filed within 15 days after the return is filed. To permit prompt action in urgent cases, however, the provision recognizes that the reviewing court may order otherwise.

Subdivision (c). Examples of confidential records include records of the family conciliation court (Fam. Code, § 1818 (b)) and fee waiver applications (Gov. Code, § 68633(f)).

Subdivisions (d) and (e). These provisions do not alter the court's authority to request or permit the filing of amicus briefs or amicus letters in writ proceedings in circumstances not covered by these subdivisions, such as before the court has determined whether to issue an alternative writ or order to show cause or when it notifies the parties that it is considering issuing a peremptory writ in the first instance.

Rule 8.488. Certificate of Interested Entities or Persons

(a) Application

This rule applies in writ proceedings in criminal cases in which an entity is the defendant and in civil cases other than family, juvenile, guardianship, and conservatorship cases.

(Subd (a) adopted effective January 1, 2009.)

(b) Compliance with rule 8.208

Each party in a civil case and any entity that is a defendant in a criminal case must comply with the requirements of rule 8.208 concerning serving and filing a certificate of interested entities or persons.

(Subd (b) adopted effective January 1, 2009.)

(c) Placement of certificates

(1) The petitioner's certificate must be included in the petition.

(2) The certificates of the respondent and real party in interest must be included in their preliminary opposition or, if no such opposition is filed, in their return, if any.

(3) The certificate must appear after the cover and before the tables.

(4) If the identity of any party has not been publicly disclosed in the proceedings, the party may file an application for permission to file its certificate under seal separately from the petition, preliminary opposition, or return.

(Subd (c) adopted effective January 1, 2009.)

(d) Failure to file a certificate

(1) If a party fails to file a certificate as required under (b) and (c), the clerk must notify the party in writing that the party must file the certificate within 10 days after the clerk's notice is sent and that if the party fails to comply, the court may impose one of the following sanctions:

(A) If the party is the petitioner, the court may strike the petition; or

(B) If the party is the respondent or the real party in interest, the court may strike that party's document.

(2) If the party fails to file the certificate as specified in the notice under (1), the court may impose the sanctions specified in the notice.

(Subd (d) amended effective January 1, 2016; adopted effective January 1, 2009.)

Rule 8.488 amended effective January 1, 2016; adopted effective January 1, 2009.

Advisory Committee Comment

The Judicial Council has adopted an optional form, *Certificate of Interested Entities or Persons* (form APP-008), that can be used to file the certificate required by this provision.

Subdivision (a). Under rule 8.208(c), for purposes of certificates of interested entities or persons, an "entity" means a corporation, a partnership, a firm, or any other association, but does not include a governmental entity or its agencies or a natural person.

Rule 8.489. Notice to trial court

(a) Notice if writ issues

If a writ or order issues directed to any judge, court, board, or other officer, the reviewing court clerk must promptly send a certified copy of the writ or order to the person or entity to whom it is addressed.

(Subd (a) adopted effective January 1, 2009.)

(b) Notice by telephone

(1) If the writ or order stays or prohibits proceedings set to occur within 7 days or requires action within 7 days—or in any other urgent situation—the reviewing court clerk must make a reasonable effort to notify the clerk of the respondent court by telephone or e-mail. The clerk of the respondent court must then notify the judge or officer most directly concerned.

(2) The clerk need not give telephonic or e-mail notice of the summary denial of a writ, whether or not a stay previously issued.

(Subd (b) amended effective January 1, 2017; adopted effective January 1, 2009.)

Rule 8.489 amended effective January 1, 2017; adopted effective January 1, 2009.

Rule 8.490. Filing, finality, and modification of decisions; rehearing; remittitur

(a) Filing and modification of decisions

Rule 8.264(a) and (c) govern the filing and modification of decisions in writ proceedings.

(Subd (a) adopted effective January 1, 2009.)

(b) Finality of decision

(1) Except as otherwise ordered by the court, the following decisions regarding petitions for writs within the court's original jurisdiction are final in the issuing court when filed:

(A) An order denying or dismissing such a petition without issuance of an alternative writ, order to show cause, or writ of review; and

(B) An order denying or dismissing such a petition as moot after issuance of an alternative writ, order to show cause, or writ of review.

(2) All other decisions in a writ proceeding are final 30 days after the decision is filed, except as follows:

(A) If necessary to prevent mootness or frustration of the relief granted or to otherwise promote the interests of justice, the court may order early finality in that court of a decision granting a petition for a writ within its original jurisdiction or denying such a petition after issuing an alternative writ, order to show cause, or writ of review. The decision may provide for finality in that court on filing or within a stated period of less than 30 days.

(B) If a Court of Appeal certifies its opinion for publication or partial publication after filing its decision and before the decision becomes final in that court, the 30 days or other finality period ordered under (A) runs from the filing date of the order for publication.

(C) If an order modifying a decision changes the appellate judgment, the 30 days or other finality period ordered under (A) runs from the filing date of the modification order.

(Subd (b) amended effective January 1, 2014; adopted effective January 1, 2009.)

(c) Rehearing

(1) Rule 8.268 governs rehearing in the Courts of Appeal.

(2) Rule 8.536 governs rehearing in the Supreme Court.

(Subd (c) adopted effective January 1, 2014.)

(d) Remittitur

A Court of Appeal must issue a remittitur in a writ proceeding under this chapter except when the court issues one of the orders listed in (b)(1). Rule 8.272(b)–(d) governs issuance of a remittitur by a Court of Appeal in writ proceedings under this chapter.

(Subd (d) amended and relettered effective January 1, 2014; adopted as subd (c) effective January 1, 2009.)

Rule 8.490 amended effective January 1, 2014; adopted effective January 1, 2009.

Advisory Committee Comment

Subdivision (b). This provision addresses the finality of decisions in proceedings relating to writs of mandate, certiorari, and prohibition. See rule 8.264(b) for provisions addressing the finality of decisions in proceedings under chapter 2, relating to civil appeals, and rule 8.366 for provisions addressing the finality of decisions in proceedings under chapter 3, relating to criminal appeals.

Subdivision (b)(1). Examples of situations in which the court may issue an order dismissing a writ petition include when the petitioner fails to comply with an order of the court, when the court recalls the alternative writ, order to show cause, or writ of review as improvidently granted, or when the petition becomes moot.

Subdivision (d). Under this rule, a remittitur serves as notice that the writ proceedings have concluded.

Rule 8.491. Responsive pleading under Code of Civil Procedure section 418.10

If the Court of Appeal denies a petition for writ of mandate brought under Code of Civil Procedure section 418.10(c) and the Supreme Court denies review of the Court of Appeal's decision, the time to file a responsive pleading in the trial court is extended until 10 days after the Supreme Court files its order denying review.

Rule 8.491 adopted effective January 1, 2009.

Rule 8.492. Sanctions

(a) Grounds for sanctions

On motion of a party or its own motion, a Court of Appeal may impose sanctions, including the award or denial of costs under rule 8.493, on a party or an attorney for:

(1) Filing a frivolous petition or filing a petition solely to cause delay; or

(2) Committing any other unreasonable violation of these rules.

(Subd (a) adopted effective January 1, 2009.)

(b) Notice

The court must give notice in writing if it is considering imposing sanctions.

(Subd (b) adopted effective January 1, 2009.)

(c) Opposition

Within 10 days after the court sends such notice, a party or attorney may serve and file an opposition, but failure to do so will not be deemed consent. An opposition may not be filed unless the court sends such notice.

(Subd (c) adopted effective January 1, 2009.)

(d) Oral argument

Unless otherwise ordered, oral argument on the issue of sanctions must be combined with any oral argument on the merits of the petition.

(Subd (d) adopted effective January 1, 2009.)
Rule 8.492 adopted effective January 1, 2009.

Rule 8.493. Costs

(a) Award of costs

(1) Except in a criminal or juvenile or other proceeding in which a party is entitled to court-appointed counsel:

(A) Unless otherwise ordered by the court under (B), the prevailing party in an original proceeding is entitled to costs if the court resolves the proceeding by written opinion after issuing an alternative writ, an order to show cause, or a peremptory writ in the first instance.

(B) In the interests of justice, the court may also award or deny costs as it deems proper in the proceedings listed in (A) and in other circumstances.

(2) The opinion or order resolving the proceeding must specify the award or denial of costs.

(Subd (a) adopted effective January 1, 2009.)

(b) Procedures for recovering costs

Rule 8.278(b)–(d) governs the procedure for recovering costs under this rule.

(Subd (b) adopted effective January 1, 2009.)
Rule 8.493 adopted effective January 1, 2009.

Rule 8.494. Review of Workers' Compensation Appeals Board cases [Renumbered]

Rule 8.494 renumbered to rule 8.495 effective January 1, 2009; repealed and adopted as rule 57 effective January 1, 2005; previously amended effective July 1, 2006; previously amended and renumbered effective January 1, 2007.

Chapter 8
[Reserved]

Title 8, Appellate Rules—Division 1, Rules Relating to the Supreme Court and Courts of Appeal—Chapter 8, [Reserved] amended effective April 25, 2019; adopted as chapter 7 effective January 1, 2007; amended and renumbered effective January 1, 2009; previously amended effective July 1, 2012.

Rule 8.495. Review of Workers' Compensation Appeals Board cases [Renumbered]

Rule 8.495 renumbered as rule 8.720 effective April 25, 2019; repealed and adopted as rule 57 effective January 1, 2005; previously amended effective July 1, 2006, January 1, 2016, and January 1, 2018; previously amended and renumbered as rule 8.494 effective January 1, 2007; previously renumbered as rule 8.495 effective January 1, 2009.

Rule 8.496. Review of Public Utilities Commission cases [Renumbered]

Rule 8.496 renumbered as rule 8.724 effective April 25, 2019; repealed and adopted as rule 58 effective January 1, 2005; previously amended effective July 1, 2006, and January 1, 2016; previously amended and renumbered as rule 8.496 effective January 1, 2007.

Rule 8.497. Review of California Environmental Quality Act cases under Public Resources Code sections 21178–21189.3 [Repealed]

Rule 8.497 repealed effective July 1, 2014; adopted effective July 1, 2012.

Rule 8.498. Review of Agricultural Labor Relations Board and Public Employment Relations Board cases [Renumbered]

Rule 8.498 renumbered as rule 8.728 effective April 25, 2019; repealed and adopted as rule 59 effective January 1, 2005; previously amended effective July 1, 2006, and January 1, 2016; previously amended and renumbered as rule 8.498 effective January 1, 2007.

Rule 8.499. Filing, modification, and finality of decision; remittitur [Renumbered]

Rule 8.499 renumbered as rule 8.730 effective April 25, 2019; adopted effective January 1, 2008; previously amended effective January 1, 2011, and July 1, 2012.

Chapter 9
Proceedings in the Supreme Court

Title 8, Appellate Rules—Division 1, Rules Relating to the Supreme Court and Courts of Appeal—Chapter 9, Proceedings in the Supreme Court renumbered effective January 1, 2009; adopted as chapter 8 effective January 1, 2007.

Rule 8.500. Petition for review
Rule 8.504. Form and contents of petition, answer, and reply
Rule 8.508. Petition for review to exhaust state remedies
Rule 8.512. Ordering review
Rule 8.516. Issues on review
Rule 8.520. Briefs by parties and amici curiae; judicial notice
Rule 8.524. Oral argument and submission of the cause
Rule 8.528. Disposition
Rule 8.532. Filing, finality, and modification of decision
Rule 8.536. Rehearing
Rule 8.540. Remittitur
Rule 8.544. Costs and sanctions
Rule 8.548. Decision on request of a court of another jurisdiction
Rule 8.552. Transfer for decision

Rule 8.500. Petition for review

(a) Right to file a petition, answer, or reply

(1) A party may file a petition in the Supreme Court for review of any decision of the Court of Appeal, including any interlocutory order, except the denial of a transfer of a case within the appellate jurisdiction of the superior court.

(2) A party may file an answer responding to the issues raised in the petition. In the answer, the party may ask the court to address additional issues if it grants review.

(3) The petitioner may file a reply to the answer.

(Subd (a) amended effective January 1, 2004.)

(b) Grounds for review

The Supreme Court may order review of a Court of Appeal decision:

(1) When necessary to secure uniformity of decision or to settle an important question of law;

(2) When the Court of Appeal lacked jurisdiction;

(3) When the Court of Appeal decision lacked the concurrence of sufficient qualified justices; or

(4) For the purpose of transferring the matter to the Court of Appeal for such proceedings as the Supreme Court may order.

(Subd (b) amended effective January 1, 2007.)

(c) Limits of review

(1) As a policy matter, on petition for review the Supreme Court normally will not consider an issue that the petitioner failed to timely raise in the Court of Appeal.

(2) A party may petition for review without petitioning for rehearing in the Court of Appeal, but as a policy matter the Supreme Court normally will accept the Court of Appeal opinion's statement of the issues and facts unless the party has called the Court of Appeal's attention to any alleged omission or misstatement of an issue or fact in a petition for rehearing.

(d) Petitions in nonconsolidated proceedings

If the Court of Appeal decides an appeal and denies a related petition for writ of habeas corpus without issuing an order to show cause and without formally consolidating the two proceedings, a party seeking review of both decisions must file a separate petition for review in each proceeding.

(e) Time to serve and file

(1) A petition for review must be served and filed within 10 days after the Court of Appeal decision is final in that court. For purposes of this rule, the date of finality is not extended if it falls on a day on which the office of the clerk/executive officer is closed.

(2) The time to file a petition for review may not be extended, but the Chief Justice may relieve a party from a failure to file a timely petition for review if the time for the court to order review on its own motion has not expired.

(3) If a petition for review is presented for filing before the Court of Appeal decision is final in that court, the clerk/executive officer of the Supreme Court must accept it and file it on the day after finality.

(4) Any answer to the petition must be served and filed within 20 days after the petition is filed.

(5) Any reply to the answer must be served and filed within 10 days after the answer is filed.

(Subd (e) amended effective January 1, 2018; previously amended effective January 1, 2007, and January 1, 2009.)

(f) Additional requirements

(1) The petition must also be served on the superior court clerk and, if filed in paper format, the clerk/executive officer of the Court of Appeal. Electronic filing of a petition constitutes service of the petition on the clerk/executive officer of the Court of Appeal.

(2) A copy of each brief must be served on a public officer or agency when required by statute or by rule 8.29.

(3) The clerk/executive officer of the Supreme Court must file the petition even if its proof of service is defective, but if the petitioner fails to file a corrected proof of service within 5 days after the clerk gives notice of the defect the court may strike the petition or impose a lesser sanction.

(Subd (f) amended effective January 1, 2020; previously amended effective January 1, 2004, January 1, 2007, and January 1, 2018.)

(g) Amicus curiae letters

(1) Any person or entity wanting to support or oppose a petition for review or for an original writ must serve on all parties and send to the Supreme Court an amicus curiae letter rather than a brief.

(2) The letter must describe the interest of the amicus curiae. Any matter attached to the letter or incorporated by reference must comply with rule 8.504(e).

(3) Receipt of the letter does not constitute leave to file an amicus curiae brief on the merits under rule 8.520(f).

(Subd (g) amended effective January 1, 2007; previously amended effective July 1, 2004.)

Rule 8.500 amended effective January 1, 2020; repealed and adopted as rule 28 effective January 1, 2003; previously amended effective January 1, 2004, July 1, 2004, January 1, 2009, and January 1, 2018; previously amended and renumbered effective January 1, 2007.

Advisory Committee Comment

Subdivision (a). A party other than the petitioner who files an answer may be required to pay a filing fee under Government Code section 68927 if the answer is the first document filed in the proceeding in the Supreme Court by that party. See rule 8.25(c).

Subdivision (a)(1) makes it clear that any interlocutory order of the Court of Appeal—such as an order denying an application to appoint counsel, to augment the record, or to allow oral argument—is a "decision" that may be challenged by petition for review.

Subdivision (e). Subdivision (e)(1) provides that a petition for review must be served and filed within 10 days after the Court of Appeal decision is *final in that court*. Finality in the Court of Appeal is generally governed by rules 8.264(b) (civil appeals), 8.366(b) (criminal appeals), 8.387(b) (habeas corpus proceedings), and 8.490(b) (proceedings for writs of mandate, certiorari, and prohibition). These rules declare the general rule that a Court of Appeal decision is final in that court 30 days after filing. They then carve out specific exceptions—decisions that they declare to be final immediately on filing (see rules 8.264(b)(2), 8.366(b)(2), and 8.490(b)(1)). The plain implication is that all other Court of Appeal orders—specifically, interlocutory orders that may be the subject of a petition for review—are *not* final on filing. This implication is confirmed by current practice, in which parties may be allowed to apply for—and the Courts of Appeal may grant—reconsideration of such interlocutory orders; reconsideration, of course, would be impermissible if the orders were in fact final on filing.

Contrary to paragraph (2) of subdivision (e), paragraphs (4) and (5) do not prohibit extending the time to file an answer or reply; because the subdivision thus expressly forbids an extension of time only with respect to the petition for review, by clear negative implication it permits an application to extend the time to file an answer or reply under rule 8.50.

See rule 8.25(b)(5) for provisions concerning the timeliness of documents mailed by inmates or patients from custodial institutions.

Subdivision (f). The general requirements relating to service of documents in the appellate courts are established by rule 8.25. Subdivision (f)(1) requires that the petition (but not an answer or reply) be served on the clerk/executive officer of the Court of Appeal. To assist litigants, (f)(1) also states explicitly what is impliedly required by rule 8.212(c), i.e., that the petition must also be served on the superior court clerk (for delivery to the trial judge).

Rule 8.504. Form and contents of petition, answer, and reply

(a) In general

Except as provided in this rule, a petition for review, answer, and reply must comply with the relevant provisions of rule 8.204.

(Subd (a) amended effective January 1, 2007.)

(b) Contents of a petition

(1) The body of the petition must begin with a concise, nonargumentative statement of the issues presented for review, framing them in terms of the facts of the case but without unnecessary detail.

(2) The petition must explain how the case presents a ground for review under rule 8.500(b).

(3) If a petition for rehearing could have been filed in the Court of Appeal, the petition for review must state whether it was filed and, if so, how the court ruled.

(4) If the petition seeks review of a Court of Appeal opinion, a copy of the opinion showing its filing date and a copy of any order modifying the opinion or directing its publication must be bound at the back of the original petition and each copy filed in the Supreme Court or, if the petition is not filed in paper form, attached.

(5) If the petition seeks review of a Court of Appeal order, a copy of the order showing the date it was entered must be bound at the back of the original petition and each copy filed in the Supreme Court or, if the petition is not filed in paper form, attached.

(6) If the petition seeks review of a Court of Appeal order summarily denying a writ petition, a copy of the underlying trial court order that was the subject of the writ proceeding in the Court of Appeal showing the date it was entered must be bound at the back of the original petition and each copy filed in the Supreme Court or, if the petition is not filed in paper form, attached.

(7) The title of the case and designation of the parties on the cover of the petition must be identical to the title and designation in the Court of Appeal opinion or order that is the subject of the petition.

(8) Rule 8.508 governs the form and content of a petition for review filed by the defendant in a criminal case for the sole purpose of exhausting state remedies before seeking federal habeas corpus review.

(Subd (b) amended effective January 1, 2024; previously amended effective January 1, 2004, January 1, 2007, January 1, 2009, and January 1, 2016.)

(c) Contents of an answer

An answer that raises additional issues for review must contain a concise, nonargumentative statement of those issues, framing them in terms of the facts of the case but without unnecessary detail.

(d) Length

(1) If produced on a computer, a petition or answer must not exceed 8,400 words, including footnotes, and a reply must not exceed 4,200 words, including footnotes. Each petition, answer, or reply must include a certificate by appellate counsel or an unrepresented party stating the number of words in the document. The person certifying may rely on the word count of the computer program used to prepare the document.

(2) If typewritten, a petition or answer must not exceed 30 pages and a reply must not exceed 15 pages.

(3) The tables, the cover information required under rule 8.204(b)(10), the Court of Appeal opinion, a certificate under (1), any signature block, and any attachment under (e)(1) are excluded from the limits stated in (1) and (2).

(4) On application and for good cause, the Chief Justice may permit a longer petition, answer, reply, or attachment.

(Subd (d) amended effective January 1, 2011; adopted as subd (e) effective January 1, 2003; previously relettered effective January 1, 2004; previously amended effective January 1, 2007.)

(e) Attachments and incorporation by reference

(1) No attachments are permitted except:

(A) An opinion or order required to be attached under (b)(4)–(6);

(B) Exhibits or orders of a trial court or Court of Appeal that the party considers unusually significant;

(C) Copies of relevant local, state, or federal regulations or rules, out-of-state statutes, or other similar citable materials that are not readily accessible; and

(D) An opinion required to be attached under rule 8.1115(c).

(2) The attachments under (1)(B) and (C) must not exceed a combined total of 10 pages.

(3) No incorporation by reference is permitted except a reference to a petition, an answer, or a reply filed by another party in the same case or filed in a case that raises the same or similar issues and in which a petition for review is pending or has been granted.

(Subd (e) amended effective January 1, 2024; adopted as subd (f) effective January 1, 2003; previously relettered effective January 1, 2004; previously amended effective January 1, 2007, and January 1, 2009.)

Rule 8.504 amended effective January 1, 2024; adopted as rule 28.1 effective January 1, 2003; previously amended and renumbered as rule 8.504 effective January 1, 2007; previously amended effective January 1, 2004, January 1, 2009, January 1, 2011, and January 1, 2016.

Advisory Committee Comment

Subdivision (d). Subdivision (d) states in terms of word counts rather than page counts the maximum permissible lengths of a petition for review, answer, or reply produced on a computer. This provision tracks a provision in rule 8.204(c) governing Court of Appeal briefs and is explained in the advisory committee comment to that provision. Subdivision (d)(3) specifies certain items that are not counted toward the maximum length of a petition, answer, or reply. Signature blocks, as referenced in this provision include not only the signatures, but also the printed names, titles, and affiliations of any attorneys filing or joining in the petition, answer, or reply, which may accompany the signature.

Rule 8.508. Petition for review to exhaust state remedies

(a) Purpose

After decision by the Court of Appeal in a criminal case, a defendant may file an abbreviated petition for review in the Supreme Court for the sole purpose of exhausting state remedies before presenting a claim for federal habeas corpus relief.

(b) Form and contents

(1) The words "Petition for Review to Exhaust State Remedies" must appear prominently on the cover of the petition.

(2) Except as provided in (3), the petition must comply with rule 8.504.

(3) The petition need not comply with rule 8.504(b)(1)–(2) but must include:

(A) A statement that the case presents no grounds for review under rule 8.500(b) and the petition is filed solely to exhaust state remedies for federal habeas corpus purposes;

(B) A brief statement of the underlying proceedings, including the nature of the conviction and the punishment imposed; and

(C) A brief statement of the factual and legal bases of the claim.

(Subd (b) amended effective January 1, 2007.)

(c) Service

The petition must be served on the clerk/executive officer of the Court of Appeal but need not be served on the superior court clerk.

(Subd (c) amended effective January 1, 2018.)

Rule 8.508 amended effective January 1, 2018; adopted as rule 33.3 effective January 1, 2004; previously amended and renumbered effective January 1, 2007.

Advisory Committee Comment

Subdivision (b). Although a petition under this rule must state that "the case presents no grounds for review under rule 8.500(b)" (see (b)(3)(A)), this does not mean the Supreme Court cannot order review if it determines the case warrants review. The list of grounds for granting review in rule 8.500(b) is not intended to be exclusive, and from time to time the Supreme Court has exercised its discretion to order review in a case that does not present one of the listed grounds. (Compare U.S. Supreme Court Rule 10 [the listed grounds for granting certiorari, "although neither controlling nor fully measuring the Court's discretion, indicate the character of the reasons the Court considers"].)

Subdivision (b)(3)(C) requires the petition to include a statement of the factual and legal bases of the claim. This showing is required by federal law: "for purposes of exhausting state remedies, a claim for relief [in state court] ... must include reference to a specific federal constitutional guarantee, as well as a statement of the facts that entitle the petitioner to relief." (*Gray v. Netherland* (1996) 518 U.S. 152, 162–163, citing *Picard v. Connor* (1971) 404 U.S. 270.) The federal courts will decide whether a petition filed in compliance with this rule satisfies federal exhaustion requirements, and practitioners should consult federal law to determine whether the petition's statement of the factual and legal bases for the claim is sufficient for that purpose.

Rule 8.512. Ordering review

(a) Transmittal of record

On receiving a copy of a petition for review or on request of the Supreme Court, whichever is earlier, the clerk/executive officer of the Court of Appeal must promptly send the record to the Supreme Court. If the petition is denied, the clerk/executive officer of the Supreme Court must promptly return the record to the Court of Appeal if the record was transmitted in paper form.

(Subd (a) amended effective January 1, 2018; previously amended effective January 1, 2016.)

(b) Determination of petition

(1) The court may order review within 60 days after the last petition for review is filed. Before the 60-day period or any extension expires, the court may order one or more extensions to a date not later than 90 days after the last petition is filed.

(2) If the court does not rule on the petition within the time allowed by (1), the petition is deemed denied.

(Subd (b) amended effective January 1, 2004.)

(c) Review on the court's own motion

(1) If no petition for review is filed, the Supreme Court may, on its own motion, order review of a Court of Appeal decision within 30 days after the decision is final in that court. Before the 30-day period or any extension expires, the Supreme Court may order one or more extensions to a date not later than 90 days after the decision is final in the Court of Appeal. If any such period ends on a day on which the office of the clerk/executive officer is closed, the court may order review on its own motion on the next day the office is open.

(2) If a petition for review is filed, the Supreme Court may deny the petition but order review on its own motion within the periods prescribed in (b)(1).

(Subd (c) amended effective January 1, 2018; adopted as subd (d) effective January 1, 2003; previously amended and relettered effective January 1, 2004.)

(d) Order; grant and hold

(1) An order granting review must be signed by at least four justices; an order denying review may be signed by the Chief Justice alone.

(2) On or after granting review, the court may order action in the matter deferred until the court disposes of another matter or pending further order of the court.

(Subd (d) adopted effective January 1, 2004.)

Rule 8.512 amended effective January 1, 2018; adopted as rule 28.2 effective January 1, 2003; previously amended effective January 1, 2004, and January 1, 2016; previously renumbered as rule 8.512 effective January 1, 2007.

Advisory Committee Comment

Subdivision (b). The Supreme Court deems the 60-day period within which it may grant review to begin on the filing date of the last petition for review that either (1) is timely in the sense that it is filed within the rule time for such petitions (i.e., 10 days after finality of the Court of Appeal decision) or (2) is treated as timely—although presented for filing after expiration of the rule time—in the sense that it is filed with permission of the Chief Justice on a showing of good cause for relief from default. In each circumstance it is the filing of the petition that triggers the 60-day period.

Rule 8.516. Issues on review

(a) Issues to be briefed and argued

(1) On or after ordering review, the Supreme Court may specify the issues to be briefed and argued. Unless the court orders otherwise, the parties must limit their briefs and arguments to those issues and any issues fairly included in them.

(2) Notwithstanding an order specifying issues under (1), the court may, on reasonable notice, order oral argument on fewer or additional issues or on the entire cause.

(b) Issues to be decided

(1) The Supreme Court may decide any issues that are raised or fairly included in the petition or answer.

(2) The court may decide an issue that is neither raised nor fairly included in the petition or answer if the case presents the issue and the court has given the parties reasonable notice and opportunity to brief and argue it.

(3) The court need not decide every issue the parties raise or the court specifies.

Rule 8.516 renumbered effective January 1, 2007; repealed and adopted as rule 29 effective January 1, 2003.

Rule 8.520. Briefs by parties and amici curiae; judicial notice

(a) Parties' briefs; time to file

(1) Within 30 days after the Supreme Court files the order of review, the petitioner must serve and file in that court either an opening brief on the merits or the brief it filed in the Court of Appeal.

(2) Within 30 days after the petitioner files its brief or the time to do so expires, the opposing party must serve and file either an answer brief on the merits or the brief it filed in the Court of Appeal.

(3) The petitioner may file a reply brief on the merits or the reply brief it filed in the Court of Appeal. A reply brief must be served and filed within 20 days after the opposing party files its brief.

(4) A party filing a brief it filed in the Court of Appeal must attach to the cover a notice of its intent to rely on the brief in the Supreme Court.

(5) The time to serve and file a brief may not be extended by stipulation but only by order of the Chief Justice under rule 8.60.

(6) The court may designate which party is deemed the petitioner or otherwise direct the sequence in which the parties must file their briefs.

(Subd (a) amended effective January 1, 2007.)

(b) Form and content

(1) Briefs filed under this rule must comply with the relevant provisions of rule 8.204.

(2) The body of the petitioner's brief on the merits must begin by quoting either:

(A) Any order specifying the issues to be briefed; or, if none,

(B) The statement of issues in the petition for review and, if any, in the answer.

(3) Unless the court orders otherwise, briefs on the merits must be limited to the issues stated in (2) and any issues fairly included in them.

(Subd (b) amended effective January 1, 2007.)

(c) Length

(1) If produced on a computer, an opening or answering brief on the merits must not exceed 14,000 words, including footnotes, and a reply brief on the merits must not exceed 8,400 words, including footnotes. Each brief must include a certificate by appellate counsel or an unrepresented party stating the number of words in the brief. The person certifying may rely on the word count of the computer program used to prepare the brief.

(2) If typewritten, an opening or answering brief on the merits must not exceed 50 pages and a reply brief on the merits must not exceed 30 pages.

(3) The tables required under rule 8.204(a)(1), the cover information required under rule 8.204(b)(10), a certificate under (1), any signature block, any attachment under (h), and any quotation of issues required by (b)(2) are excluded from the limits stated in (1) and (2).

(4) On application and for good cause, the Chief Justice may permit a longer brief.

(Subd (c) amended effective January 1, 2011; previously amended effective January 1, 2007, and January 1, 2009.)

(d) Supplemental briefs

(1) A party may file a supplemental brief limited to new authorities, new legislation, or other matters that were not available in time to be included in the party's brief on the merits.

(2) A supplemental brief must not exceed 2,800 words, including footnotes, if produced on a computer or 10 pages if typewritten, and must be served and filed no later than 10 days before oral argument.

(Subd (d) amended effective January 1, 2007.)

(e) Briefs on the court's request

The court may request additional briefs on any or all issues, whether or not the parties have filed briefs on the merits.

(f) Amicus curiae briefs

(1) After the court orders review, any person or entity may serve and file an application for permission of the Chief Justice to file an amicus curiae brief.

(2) The application must be filed no later than 30 days after all briefs that the parties may file under this rule—other than supplemental briefs—have been filed or were required to be filed. For good cause, the Chief Justice may allow later filing.

(3) The application must state the applicant's interest and explain how the proposed amicus curiae brief will assist the court in deciding the matter.

(4) The application must also identify:

(A) Any party or any counsel for a party in the pending appeal who:

(i) Authored the proposed amicus brief in whole or in part; or

(ii) Made a monetary contribution intended to fund the preparation or submission of the brief; and

(B) Every person or entity who made a monetary contribution intended to fund the preparation or submission of the brief, other than the amicus curiae, its members, or its counsel in the pending appeal.

(5) The proposed brief must be served. It must accompany the application and may be combined with it.

(6) The covers of the application and proposed brief must identify the party the applicant supports, if any.

(7) If the court grants the application, any party may file either an answer to the individual amicus curiae brief or a consolidated answer to multiple amicus curiae briefs filed in the case. The answer must be filed within 30 days after either the court rules on the last timely filed application to file an amicus curiae brief or the time for filing applications to file an amicus curiae brief expires, whichever is later. The answer must be served on all parties and the amicus curiae.

(8) The Attorney General may file an amicus curiae brief without the Chief Justice's permission unless the brief is submitted on behalf of another state officer or agency. The Attorney General must serve and file the brief within the time specified in (2) and must provide the information required by (3) and comply with (6). Any answer must comply with (7).

(Subd (f) amended effective January 1, 2011; previously amended effective January 1, 2008, and January 1, 2009.)

(g) Judicial notice

To obtain judicial notice by the Supreme Court under Evidence Code section 459, a party must comply with rule 8.252(a).

(Subd (g) amended effective January 1, 2007.)

(h) Attachments

A party filing a brief may attach copies of relevant local, state, or federal regulations or rules, out-of-state statutes, or other similar citable materials that are not readily accessible. These attachments must not exceed a combined total of 10 pages. A copy of an opinion required to be attached to the brief under rule 8.1115(c) does not count toward this 10-page limit.

(Subd (h) adopted effective January 1, 2007.)

Rule 8.520 amended effective January 1, 2011; adopted as rule 29.1 effective January 1, 2003; previously amended and renumbered effective January 1, 2007; previously amended effective January 1, 2008, and January 1, 2009.

Advisory Committee Comment

Subdivision (a). A party other than the petitioner who files a brief may be required to pay a filing fee under Government Code section 68927 if the brief is the first document filed in the proceeding in the Supreme Court by that party. See rule 8.25(c).

Subdivisions (c) and (d). Subdivisions (c) and (d) state in terms of word count rather than page count the maximum permissible lengths of Supreme Court briefs produced on a computer. This provision tracks an identical provision in rule 8.204(c) governing Court of Appeal briefs and is explained in the advisory committee comment to that provision. Subdivision (c)(3) specifies certain items that are not counted toward the maximum brief length. The signature block referenced in this provision includes not only the signatures, but also the printed names, titles, and affiliations of any attorneys filing or joining in the brief, which may accompany the signature.

Rule 8.524. Oral argument and submission of the cause

(a) Application

This rule governs oral argument in the Supreme Court unless the court provides otherwise in its Internal Operating Practices and Procedures or by order.

(b) Place of argument

The Supreme Court holds regular sessions in San Francisco, Los Angeles, and Sacramento on a schedule fixed by the court, and may hold special sessions elsewhere.

(c) Notice of argument

The Supreme Court clerk must send notice of the time and place of oral argument to all parties at least 20 days before the argument date. The Chief Justice may shorten the notice period for good cause; in that event, the clerk must immediately notify the parties by telephone or other expeditious method.

(d) Sequence of argument

The petitioner for Supreme Court relief has the right to open and close. If there are two or more petitioners—or none—the court must set the sequence of argument.

(e) Time for argument

Each side is allowed 30 minutes for argument.

(f) Number of counsel

(1) Only one counsel on each side may argue—regardless of the number of parties on the side—unless the court orders otherwise on request.

(2) Requests to divide oral argument among multiple counsel must be filed within 10 days after the date of the order setting the case for argument.

(3) Multiple counsel must not divide their argument into segments of less than 10 minutes per person, except that one counsel for the opening side—or more, if authorized by the Chief Justice on request—may reserve any portion of that counsel's time for rebuttal.

(g) Argument by amicus curiae

An amicus curiae is not entitled to argument time but may ask a party for permission to use a portion or all of the party's time, subject to the 10-minute minimum prescribed in (f)(3). If permission is granted, counsel must file a request under (f)(2).

(h) Submission of the cause

(1) A cause is submitted when the court has heard oral argument or approved its waiver and the time has expired to file all briefs and papers, including any supplemental brief permitted by the court.

(2) The court may vacate submission only by an order stating the court's reasons and setting a timetable for resubmission.

Rule 8.524 renumbered effective January 1, 2007; repealed and adopted as rule 29.2 effective January 1, 2003.

Advisory Committee Comment

Subdivision (d). In subdivision (d), "The petitioner for Supreme Court relief" can be a petitioner for review, a petitioner for transfer (rule 8.552), a petitioner in an original proceeding in the Supreme Court, or a party designated as petitioner in a proceeding on request of a court of another jurisdiction (rule 8.548(b)(1)).

The number of petitioners is "none" when the court grants review on its own motion or transfers a cause to itself on its own motion.

Subdivision (e). The time allowed for argument in death penalty appeals is prescribed in rule 8.638.

Subdivision (f). The number of counsel allowed to argue on each side in death penalty appeals is prescribed in rule 8.638.

Rule 8.528. Disposition

(a) Normal disposition

After review, the Supreme Court normally will affirm, reverse, or modify the judgment of the Court of Appeal, but may order another disposition.

(b) Dismissal of review

(1) The Supreme Court may dismiss review. The clerk/executive officer of the Supreme Court must promptly send an order dismissing review to all parties and the Court of Appeal.

(2) When the Court of Appeal receives an order dismissing review, the decision of that court is final and its clerk/executive officer must promptly issue a remittitur or take other appropriate action.

(3) An order dismissing review does not affect the publication status of the Court of Appeal opinion unless the Supreme Court orders otherwise.

(Subd (b) amended effective January 1, 2018; previously amended effective January 1, 2017.)

(c) Remand for decision on remaining issues

If it decides fewer than all the issues presented by the case, the Supreme Court may remand the cause to a Court of Appeal for decision on any remaining issues.

(d) Transfer without decision

After ordering review, the Supreme Court may transfer the cause to a Court of Appeal without decision but with instructions to conduct such proceedings as the Supreme Court orders.

(e) Retransfer without decision

After transferring to itself, before decision, a cause pending in the Court of Appeal, the Supreme Court may retransfer the cause to a Court of Appeal without decision.

(f) Court of Appeal briefs after remand or transfer

Any supplemental briefing in the Court of Appeal after remand or transfer from the Supreme Court is governed by rule 8.200(b).

(Subd (f) amended effective January 1, 2007.)

Rule 8.528 amended effective January 1, 2018; repealed and adopted as rule 29.3 effective January 1, 2003; previously amended and renumbered effective January 1, 2007; previously amended effective January 1, 2017.

Advisory Committee Comment

Subdivision (a). Subdivision (a) serves two purposes. First, it declares that the Supreme Court's normal disposition of a cause after completing its review is to affirm, reverse, or modify *the judgment of the Court of Appeal.* Second, the subdivision recognizes that, when necessary, the Supreme Court may order "another disposition" appropriate to the circumstances. Subdivisions (b)–(e) provide examples of such "other dispositions," but the list is not intended to be exclusive.

As used in subdivision (a), "the judgment of the Court of Appeal" includes a decision of that court denying a petition for original writ without issuing an alternative writ or order to show cause. The Supreme Court's method of disposition after reviewing such a decision, however, has evolved. In earlier cases the Supreme Court itself denied or granted the requested writ, in effect treating the matter as if it were an original proceeding in the Supreme Court. (E.g., *City of San Jose v. Superior Court* (1993) 5 Cal.4th 47, 58 ["The alternative writ of mandate is discharged and the petition for a peremptory writ of mandate is denied."].) By contrast, current Supreme Court practice is to affirm or reverse the judgment of the Court of Appeal summarily denying the writ petition. (E.g., *People v. Superior Court (Laff)* (2001) 25 Cal.4th 703, 742–743 ["The judgment of the Court of Appeal is reversed with directions to vacate its order denying the petition, and to issue a writ of mandate...."]; *State Comp. Ins. Fund v. Superior Court* (2001) 24 Cal.4th 930, 944 ["The judgment of the Court of Appeal summarily denying the petition for writ of mandate is affirmed and the order to show cause ... is discharged."].) As the cited cases illustrate, if the Supreme Court affirms such a judgment it will normally discharge any alternative writ or order to show cause it issued when granting review; if the court reverses the judgment it will normally include a direction to the Court of Appeal, e.g., to issue the requested writ or to reconsider the petition.

Subdivision (b). An earlier version of this rule purported to limit Supreme Court *dismissals of review* to cases in which the court had "improvidently" granted review. In practice, however, the court may dismiss review for a variety of other reasons. For example, after the court decides a "lead" case, its current practice is to dismiss review in any pending companion case (i.e., a "grant and hold" matter under rule 8.512(c)) that appears correctly decided in light of the lead case and presents no additional issue requiring resolution by the Supreme Court or the Court of Appeal. The Supreme Court may also dismiss review when a supervening event renders the case moot for any reason, e.g., when the parties reach a settlement, when a party seeking personal relief dies, or when the court orders review to construe a statute that is then repealed before the court can act. Reflecting this practice, the Supreme Court now dismisses review—even in the rare case in which the grant of review was arguably "improvident"—by an order that says simply that "review is dismissed."

An order of review ipso facto transfers jurisdiction of the cause to the Supreme Court. By the same token, an order dismissing review ipso facto retransfers jurisdiction to the Court of Appeal. The Court of Appeal has no discretion to exercise after the Supreme Court dismisses review: the clerk/executive officer of the Supreme Court must promptly send the dismissal order to the Court of Appeal; when the clerk/executive officer of the Court of Appeal files that order, the Court of Appeal decision immediately becomes final.

If the decision of the Court of Appeal made final by (b)(2) requires issuance of a remittitur under rule 8.272(a), the clerk/executive officer must issue the remittitur; if the decision does not require issuance of a remittitur—e.g., if the decision is an interlocutory order (see rule 8.500(a)(1))—the clerk/executive officer must take whatever action is appropriate in the circumstances.

Subdivision (d). Subdivision (d) is intended to apply primarily to two types of cases: (1) those in which the court granted review "for the purpose of transferring the matter to the Court of Appeal for such proceedings as the Supreme Court may order" (rule 8.500(b)(4)) and (2) those in which the court, after deciding a "lead case," determines that a companion "grant and hold" case (rule 8.512(c)) should be reconsidered by the Court of Appeal in light of the lead case or presents an additional issue or issues that require resolution by the Court of Appeal.

Subdivision (e). Subdivision (e) is intended to apply to cases in which the Supreme Court, after *transferring* to itself before decision a cause pending in the Court of Appeal, *retransfers* the matter to that court without decision and with or without instructions.

Rule 8.532. Filing, finality, and modification of decision

(a) Filing the decision

The clerk/executive officer of the Supreme Court must promptly file all opinions and orders issued by the court and promptly send copies showing the filing date to the parties and, when relevant, to the lower court or tribunal.

(Subd (a) amended effective January 1, 2018.)

(b) Finality of decision

(1) Except as provided in (2), a Supreme Court decision is final 30 days after filing unless:

(A) The court orders a shorter period; or

(B) Before the 30-day period or any extension expires the court orders one or more extensions, not to exceed a total of 60 additional days.

(2) The following Supreme Court decisions are final on filing:

(A) The denial of a petition for review of a Court of Appeal decision;

(B) A disposition ordered under rule 8.528(b), (d), or (e);

(C) The denial of a petition for a writ within the court's original jurisdiction without issuance of an alternative writ or order to show cause; and

(D) The denial of a petition for writ of supersedeas.

(Subd (b) amended effective January 1, 2007.)

(c) Modification of decision

The Supreme Court may modify a decision as provided in rule 8.264(c).

(Subd (c) amended effective January 1, 2007.)

Rule 8.532 amended effective January 1, 2018; repealed and adopted as rule 29.4 effective January 1, 2003; previously amended and renumbered effective January 1, 2007.

Advisory Committee Comment

Subdivision (b). Subdivision (b)(2)(A) recognizes the general rule that the denial of a petition for review of a Court of Appeal decision is final on filing. Subdivision (b)(2)(B)–(D) recognizes several additional types of Supreme Court decisions that are final on filing. Thus (b)(2)(B) recognizes that a dismissal, a transfer, and a retransfer under (b), (d), and (e), respectively, of rule 8.528 are decisions final on filing. A remand under rule 8.528(c) is not a decision final on filing because it is not a separately filed order; rather, as part of its appellate judgment at the end of its opinion in such cases the Supreme Court simply orders the cause remanded to the Court of Appeal for disposition of the remaining issues in the appeal.

Subdivision (b)(2)(C) recognizes that an order denying a petition for a writ within the court's original jurisdiction without issuance of an alternative writ or order to show cause is final on filing. The provision reflects the settled Supreme Court practice, since at least 1989, of declining to file petitions for rehearing in such matters. (See, e.g., *In re Hayes* (S004421) Minutes, Cal. Supreme Ct., July 28, 1989

["The motion to vacate this court's order of May 18, 1989 [denying a petition for habeas corpus without opinion] is denied. Because the California Rules of Court do not authorize the filing of a petition for rehearing of such an order, the alternate request to consider the matter as a petition for rehearing is denied."].)

Subdivision (b)(2)(D) recognizes that an order denying a petition for writ of supersedeas is final on filing.

Rule 8.536. Rehearing
(a) Power to order rehearing
The Supreme Court may order rehearing as provided in rule 8.268(a).
(Subd (a) amended effective January 1, 2007.)

(b) Petition and answer
A petition for rehearing and any answer must comply with rule 8.268(b)(1) and (3). Any answer to the petition must be served and filed within eight days after the petition is filed. Before the Supreme Court decision is final and for good cause, the Chief Justice may relieve a party from a failure to file a timely petition or answer.
(Subd (b) amended effective January 1, 2007; previously amended effective January 1, 2004.)

(c) Extension of time
The time for granting or denying a petition for rehearing in the Supreme Court may be extended under rule 8.532(b)(1)(B). If the court does not rule on the petition before the decision is final, the petition is deemed denied.
(Subd (c) amended effective January 1, 2007.)

(d) Determination of petition
An order granting a rehearing must be signed by at least four justices; an order denying rehearing may be signed by the Chief Justice alone.

(e) Effect of granting rehearing
An order granting a rehearing vacates the decision and any opinion filed in the case and sets the cause at large in the Supreme Court.

Rule 8.536 amended and renumbered effective January 1, 2007; repealed and adopted as rule 29.5 effective January 1, 2003; previously amended effective January 1, 2004.

Rule 8.540. Remittitur
(a) Proceedings requiring issuance of remittitur
The Supreme Court must issue a remittitur after a decision in:
(1) A review of a Court of Appeal decision; or
(2) An appeal from a judgment of death or in a cause transferred to the court under rule 8.552.
(Subd (a) amended effective January 1, 2007.)

(b) Clerk's duties
(1) The clerk must issue a remittitur when a decision of the court is final. The remittitur is deemed issued when the clerk enters it in the record.

(2) After review of a Court of Appeal decision, the clerk/executive officer of the Supreme Court must address the remittitur to the Court of Appeal and send that court a copy of the remittitur and a filed-endorsed copy of the Supreme Court opinion or order. The clerk must send two copies of any document sent in paper form.

(3) After a decision in an appeal from a judgment of death or in a cause transferred to the court under rule 8.552, the clerk must send the remittitur and a filed-endorsed copy of the Supreme Court opinion or order to the lower court or tribunal.

(4) The clerk must comply with the requirements of rule 8.272(d).

(Subd (b) amended effective January 1, 2018; previously amended effective January 1, 2007, and January 1, 2016.)

(c) Immediate issuance, stay, and recall
(1) The Supreme Court may direct immediate issuance of a remittitur on the parties' stipulation or for good cause.

(2) On a party's or its own motion and for good cause, the court may stay a remittitur's issuance for a reasonable period or order its recall.

(3) An order recalling a remittitur issued after a decision by opinion does not supersede the opinion or affect its publication status.

Rule 8.540 amended effective January 1, 2018; repealed and adopted as rule 29.6 effective January 1, 2003; previously amended and renumbered as rule 8.540 effective January 1, 2007; previously amended effective January 1, 2016.

Rule 8.544. Costs and sanctions
In a civil case, the Supreme Court may direct the Court of Appeal to award costs, if any; or may order the parties to bear their own costs; or may make any other award of costs the Supreme Court deems proper. The Supreme Court may impose sanctions on a party or an attorney under rule 8.276 for committing any unreasonable violation of these rules.

Rule 8.544 amended effective July 1, 2008; adopted as rule 29.7 effective January 1, 2003; previously amended and renumbered effective January 1, 2007.

Advisory Committee Comment
If the Supreme Court makes an award of costs, the party claiming such costs must proceed under rule 8.278(c).

Rule 8.548. Decision on request of a court of another jurisdiction
(a) Request for decision
On request of the United States Supreme Court, a United States Court of Appeals, or the court of last resort of any state, territory, or commonwealth, the Supreme Court may decide a question of California law if:
(1) The decision could determine the outcome of a matter pending in the requesting court; and
(2) There is no controlling precedent.
(Subd (a) amended effective January 1, 2007.)

(b) Form and contents of request
The request must take the form of an order of the requesting court containing:
(1) The title and number of the case, the names and addresses of counsel and any unrepresented party, and a designation of the party to be deemed the petitioner if the request is granted;
(2) The question to be decided, with a statement that the requesting court will accept the decision;
(3) A statement of the relevant facts prepared by the requesting court or by the parties and approved by the court; and
(4) An explanation of how the request satisfies the requirements of (a).
(Subd (b) amended effective January 1, 2007.)

(c) Supporting materials
Copies of all relevant briefs must accompany the request. At any time, the Supreme Court may ask the requesting court to furnish additional record materials, including transcripts and exhibits.

(d) Serving and filing the request
The requesting court clerk must file an original, and if the request is filed in paper form, 10 copies, of the request in the Supreme Court with a certificate of service on the parties.
(Subd (d) amended effective January 1, 2016.)

(e) Letters in support or opposition
(1) Within 20 days after the request is filed, any party or other person or entity wanting to support or oppose the request must send a letter to the Supreme Court, with service on the parties and on the requesting court.

(2) Within 10 days after service of a letter under (1), any party may send a reply letter to the Supreme Court, with service on the other parties and the requesting court.

(3) A letter or reply asking the court to restate the question under (f)(5) must propose new wording.

(f) Proceedings in the Supreme Court
(1) In exercising its discretion to grant or deny the request, the Supreme Court may consider whether resolution of the question is necessary to secure uniformity of decision or to settle an important question of law, and any other factor the court deems appropriate.

(2) An order granting the request must be signed by at least four justices; an order denying the request may be signed by the Chief Justice alone.

(3) If the court grants the request, the rules on review and decision in the Supreme Court govern further proceedings in that court.

(4) If, after granting the request, the court determines that a decision on the question may require an interpretation of the California Constitution or a decision on the validity or meaning of a California law affecting the public interest, the court must direct the clerk to send to the Attorney General—unless the Attorney General represents a party to the litigation—a copy of the request and the order granting it.

(5) At any time, the Supreme Court may restate the question or ask the requesting court to clarify the question.

(6) After filing the opinion, the clerk must promptly send filed-endorsed copies to the requesting court and the parties and must notify that court and the parties when the decision is final.

(7) Supreme Court decisions pursuant to this rule are published in the Official Reports and have the same precedential effect as the court's other decisions.

(Subd (f) amended effective January 1, 2016; previously amended effective January 1, 2007.)

Rule 8.548 amended effective January 1, 2016; adopted as rule 29.8 effective January 1, 2003; previously amended and renumbered as rule 8.548 effective January 1, 2007.

Rule 8.552. Transfer for decision

(a) Time of transfer

On a party's petition or its own motion, the Supreme Court may transfer to itself, for decision, a cause pending in a Court of Appeal.

(b) When a cause is pending

For purposes of this rule, a cause within the appellate jurisdiction of the superior court is not pending in the Court of Appeal until that court orders it transferred under rule 8.1002. Any cause pending in the Court of Appeal remains pending until the decision of the Court of Appeal is final in that court.

(Subd (b) amended effective January 1, 2009; previously amended effective January 1, 2007.)

(c) Grounds

The Supreme Court will not order transfer under this rule unless the cause presents an issue of great public importance that the Supreme Court must promptly resolve.

(d) Petition and answer

A party seeking transfer under this rule must promptly serve and file in the Supreme Court a petition explaining how the cause satisfies the requirements of (c). Within 20 days after the petition is filed, any party may serve and file an answer. The petition and any answer must conform to the relevant provisions of rule 8.504.

(Subd (d) amended effective January 1, 2007.)

(e) Order

Transfer under this rule requires a Supreme Court order signed by at least four justices; an order denying transfer may be signed by the Chief Justice alone.

Rule 8.552 amended effective January 1, 2009; repealed and adopted as rule 29.9 effective January 1, 2003; previously amended and renumbered effective January 1, 2007.

Advisory Committee Comment

Rule 8.552 applies only to causes that the Supreme Court transfers to itself for the purpose of reaching a decision on the merits. The rule implements a portion of article VI, section 12(a) of the Constitution. As used in article VI, section 12(a) and the rule, the term "cause" is broadly construed to include " 'all cases, matters, and proceedings of every description' " adjudicated by the Courts of Appeal and the Supreme Court. (*In re Rose* (2000) 22 Cal.4th 430, 540, quoting *In re Wells* (1917) 174 Cal. 467, 471.)

Subdivision (b). For provisions addressing the finality of Court of Appeal decisions, see rules 8.264(b) (civil appeals), 8.366(b) (criminal appeals), 8.490 (proceedings for writs of mandate, certiorari, and prohibition), and 8.1018(a) (transfer of appellate division cases).

Division 2
Rules Relating to Death Penalty Appeals and Habeas Corpus Proceedings

Title 8, Appellate Rules—Division 2, Rules Relating to Death Penalty Appeals and Habeas Corpus Proceedings adopted effective April 25, 2019.

Chap. 1. General Provisions. Rule 8.601.
Chap. 2. Automatic Appeals From Judgments of Death. Rules 8.603–8.642.
Chap. 3. Death Penalty–Related Habeas Corpus Proceedings. Rule 8.652.

Chapter 1
General Provisions

Title 8, Appellate Rules—Division 2, Rules Relating to Death Penalty Appeals and Habeas Corpus Proceedings—Chapter 1, General Provisions adopted effective April 25, 2019.

Rule 8.600. In general [Renumbered]

Rule 8.600 renumbered as rule 8.603 effective April 25, 2019; repealed and adopted as rule 34 effective January 1, 2004; previously amended and renumbered effective January 1, 2007; previously amended effective January 1, 2018.

Rule 8.601. Definitions

For purposes of this division:

(1) "Appointed counsel" or "appointed attorney" means an attorney appointed to represent a person in a death penalty appeal, death penalty–related habeas corpus proceedings, or an appeal of a decision in death penalty–related habeas corpus proceedings. Appointed counsel may be either lead counsel or associate counsel.

(2) "Lead counsel" means an appointed attorney or an attorney in the Office of the State Public Defender, the Habeas Corpus Resource Center, the California Appellate Project–San Francisco, or a Court of Appeal district appellate project who is responsible for the overall conduct of the case and for supervising the work of associate and supervised counsel. If two or more attorneys are appointed to represent a person jointly in a death penalty appeal, in death penalty–related habeas corpus proceedings, or in both classes of proceedings together, one such attorney will be designated as lead counsel.

(3) "Associate counsel" means an appointed attorney who does not have the primary responsibility for the case but nevertheless has casewide responsibility. Associate counsel must meet the same minimum qualifications as lead counsel.

(4) "Supervised counsel" means an attorney who works under the immediate supervision and direction of lead or associate counsel but is not appointed by the court. Supervised counsel must be an active member of the State Bar of California.

(5) "Assisting counsel or entity" means an attorney or entity designated by the appointing court to provide appointed counsel with consultation and resource assistance. An assisting counsel must be an experienced capital appellate counsel or habeas corpus practitioner, as appropriate. An assisting counsel in an automatic appeal must, at a minimum, meet the qualifications for appointed appellate counsel, including the case experience requirements in rule 8.605(c)(2). An assisting counsel in a habeas corpus proceeding must, at a minimum, meet the qualifications for appointed habeas corpus counsel, including the case experience requirements in rule 8.652(c)(2)(A). Entities that may be designated include the Office of the State Public Defender, the Habeas Corpus Resource Center, the California Appellate Project–San Francisco, and a Court of Appeal district appellate project.

(6) "Trial counsel" means both the defendant's trial counsel and the prosecuting attorney.

(7) "Panel" means a panel of attorneys from which superior courts may appoint counsel in death penalty–related habeas corpus proceedings.

(8) "Committee" means a death penalty–related habeas corpus panel committee that accepts and reviews attorney applications to determine whether applicants are qualified for inclusion on a panel.

Rule 8.601 adopted effective April 25, 2019.

Advisory Committee Comment

Number (3). The definition of "associate counsel" in (3) is intended to make it clear that, although appointed lead counsel has overall and supervisory responsibility in a capital case, appointed associate counsel also has casewide responsibility.

Chapter 2
Automatic Appeals From Judgments of Death

Title 8, Appellate Rules—Division 2, Rules Relating to Death Penalty Appeals and Habeas Corpus Proceedings—Chapter 2, Automatic Appeals From Judgments of Death; amended and renumbered effective April 25, 2019; adopted as chapter 9 effective January 1, 2007; previously amended and renumbered as chapter 10 effective January 1, 2009.

Art. 1. General Provisions. Rules 8.603, 8.605.
Art. 2. Record on Appeal. Rules 8.608–8.622.
Art. 3. Briefs, Hearing, and Decision. Rules 8.630–8.642.

Article 1
General Provisions

Rule 8.603. In general
Rule 8.605. Qualifications of counsel in death penalty appeals

Rule 8.603. In general

(a) Automatic appeal to Supreme Court

If a judgment imposes a sentence of death, an appeal by the defendant is automatically taken to the Supreme Court.

(b) Copies of judgment

When a judgment of death is rendered, the superior court clerk must immediately send certified copies of the commitment to the Supreme Court, the Attorney General, the Governor, the Habeas Corpus Resource Center, and the California Appellate Project–San Francisco.

(Subd (b) amended effective April 25, 2019.)

Rule 8.603 amended and renumbered effective April 25, 2019; repealed and adopted as rule 34 effective January 1, 2004; previously amended and renumbered as rule 8.600 effective January 1, 2007; previously amended effective January 1, 2018.

Rule 8.605. Qualifications of counsel in death penalty appeals

(a) Purpose

This rule defines the minimum qualifications for attorneys appointed by the Supreme Court in death penalty appeals. These minimum qualifications are designed to promote competent representation and to avoid unnecessary delay and expense by assisting the court in appointing qualified counsel. Nothing in this rule is intended to be used as a standard by which to measure whether the defendant received effective assistance of counsel. An attorney is not entitled to appointment simply because the attorney meets these minimum qualifications.

(Subd (a) amended effective April 25, 2019.)

(b) General qualifications

The Supreme Court may appoint an attorney only if it has determined, after reviewing the attorney's experience, writing samples, references, and evaluations under (c) and (d), that the attorney has demonstrated the commitment, knowledge, and skills necessary to competently represent the defendant. An appointed attorney must be willing to cooperate with an assisting counsel or entity that the court may designate.

(Subd (b) amended effective April 25, 2019.)

(c) Qualifications for appointed appellate counsel

Except as provided in (d), an attorney appointed as lead or associate counsel in a death penalty appeal must satisfy the following minimum qualifications and experience:

(1) *California legal experience*

Active practice of law in California for at least four years.

(2) *Criminal appellate experience*

Either:

(A) Service as counsel of record for either party in seven completed felony appeals, including as counsel of record for a defendant in at least four felony appeals, one of which was a murder case; or

(B) Service as:

(i) Counsel of record for either party in five completed felony appeals, including as counsel of record for a defendant in at least three of these appeals; and

(ii) Supervised counsel for a defendant in two death penalty appeals in which the opening brief has been filed. Service as supervised counsel in a death penalty appeal will apply toward this qualification only if lead or associate counsel in that appeal attests that the supervised attorney performed substantial work on the case and recommends the attorney for appointment.

(3) *Knowledge*

Familiarity with Supreme Court practices and procedures, including those related to death penalty appeals.

(4) *Training*

(A) Within three years before appointment, completion of at least nine hours of Supreme Court–approved appellate criminal defense training, continuing education, or course of study, at least six hours of which involve death penalty appeals. Counsel who serves as an instructor in a course that satisfies the requirements of this rule may receive course participation credit for instruction, on request to and approval by the Supreme Court, in an amount to be determined by the Supreme Court.

(B) If the Supreme Court has previously appointed counsel to represent a person in a death penalty appeal or a related habeas corpus proceeding, and counsel has provided active representation within three years before the request for a new appointment, the court, after reviewing counsel's previous work, may find that such representation constitutes compliance with some or all of this requirement.

(5) *Skills*

Proficiency in issue identification, research, analysis, writing, and advocacy, taking into consideration all of the following:

(A) Two writing samples—ordinarily appellate briefs—written by the attorney and presenting an analysis of complex legal issues;

(B) If the attorney has previously been appointed in a death penalty appeal or death penalty–related habeas corpus proceeding, the evaluation of the assisting counsel or entity in that proceeding;

(C) Recommendations from two attorneys familiar with the attorney's qualifications and performance; and

(D) If the attorney is on a panel of attorneys eligible for appointments to represent indigents in the Court of Appeal, the evaluation of the administrator responsible for those appointments.

(Subd (c) repealed, amended and relettered effective April 25, 2019; adopted as subd (d) effective January 1, 2005; previously amended effective January 1, 2007.)

(d) Alternative qualifications

The Supreme Court may appoint an attorney who does not meet the California law practice requirement of (c)(1) or the criminal appellate experience requirements of (c)(2) if the attorney has the qualifications described in (c)(3)–(5) and:

(1) The court finds that the attorney has extensive experience in another jurisdiction or a different type of practice (such as civil trials or appeals, academic work, or work for a court or prosecutor) for at least four years, providing the attorney with experience in complex cases substantially equivalent to that of an attorney qualified under (c).

(2) Ongoing consultation is available to the attorney from an assisting counsel or entity designated by the court.

(3) Within two years before appointment, the attorney has completed at least 18 hours of Supreme Court–approved appellate criminal defense or habeas corpus defense training, continuing education, or course of study, at least nine hours of which involve death penalty appellate or habeas corpus proceedings. The Supreme Court will determine in each case whether the training, education, or course of study completed by a particular attorney satisfies the requirements of this subdivision in light of the attorney's individual background and experience. If the Supreme Court has previously appointed counsel to represent a person in a death penalty appeal or a related habeas corpus proceeding, and counsel has provided active representation within three years before the request for a new appointment, the court, after reviewing counsel's previous work, may find that such representation constitutes compliance with some or all of this requirement.

(Subd (d) repealed, amended and relettered effective April 25, 2019; adopted as subd (f) effective January 1, 2005.)

(e) Use of supervised counsel

An attorney who does not meet the qualifications described in (c) or (d) may assist lead or associate counsel, but must work under the immediate supervision and direction of lead or associate counsel.

(Subd (e) repealed, amended and relettered effective April 25, 2019; adopted as subd (h) effective January 1, 2005.)

(f) Appellate and habeas corpus appointment

(1) An attorney appointed to represent a person in both a death penalty appeal and death penalty–related habeas corpus proceedings must meet the minimum qualifications of both (c) or (d) and rule 8.652.

(2) Notwithstanding (1), two attorneys together may be eligible for appointment to represent a person jointly in both a death penalty appeal and death penalty–related habeas corpus proceedings if the Supreme Court finds that one attorney satisfies the minimum qualifications set forth in (c) or (d), and the other attorney satisfies the minimum qualifications set forth in rule 8.652.

(Subd (f) repealed, amended and relettered effective April 25, 2019; adopted as subd (i) effective January 1, 2005.)

(g) Designated entities as appointed counsel

(1) Notwithstanding any other provision of this rule, both the State Public Defender and the California Appellate Project–San Francisco are qualified to serve as appointed counsel in death penalty appeals

(2) When serving as appointed counsel in a death penalty appeal, the State Public Defender or the California Appellate Project–San Francisco must not assign any attorney as lead counsel unless it finds the attorney qualified under (c)(1)–(5) or the Supreme Court finds the attorney qualified under (d).

(Subd (g) repealed, amended and relettered effective April 25, 2019; adopted as subd (j) effective January 1, 2005.)

Rule 8.605 amended effective April 25, 2019; repealed and adopted as rule 76.6 effective January 1, 2005; previously amended and renumbered effective January 1, 2007.

Article 2
Record on Appeal

Rule 8.608. General provisions
Rule 8.610. Contents and form of the record
Rule 8.611. Juror-identifying information
Rule 8.613. Preparing and certifying the record of preliminary proceedings
Rule 8.616. Preparing the trial record
Rule 8.619. Certifying the trial record for completeness
Rule 8.622. Certifying the trial record for accuracy

Rule 8.608. General provisions

(a) Supervising preparation of record

The clerk/executive officer of the Supreme Court, under the supervision of the Chief Justice, must take all appropriate steps to ensure that superior court clerks and reporters promptly perform their duties under the rules in this article. This provision does not affect the superior courts' responsibility for the prompt preparation of appellate records in capital cases.

(Subd (a) adopted effective April 25, 2019.)

(b) Extensions of time

When a rule in this article authorizes a trial court to grant an extension of a specified time period, the court must consider the relevant policies and factors stated in rule 8.63.

(Subd (b) adopted effective April 25, 2019.)

(c) Delivery date

The delivery date of a transcript sent by mail is the mailing date plus five days.

(Subd (c) adopted effective April 25, 2019.)
Rule 8.608 adopted effective April 25, 2019.

Rule 8.610. Contents and form of the record

(a) Contents of the record

(1) The record must include a clerk's transcript containing:

(A) The accusatory pleading and any amendment;

(B) Any demurrer or other plea;

(C) All court minutes;

(D) All instructions submitted in writing, the cover page required by rule 2.1055(b)(2) indicating the party requesting each instruction, and any written jury instructions given by the court;

(E) Any written communication, including printouts of any e-mail or text messages and their attachments, between the court and the parties, the jury or any individual juror or prospective juror;

(F) Any verdict;

(G) Any written opinion of the court;

(H) The judgment or order appealed from and any abstract of judgment or commitment;

(I) Any motion for new trial, with supporting and opposing memoranda and attachments;

(J) Any transcript of a sound or sound-and-video recording furnished to the jury or tendered to the court under rule 2.1040, including witness statements;

(K) Any application for additional record and any order on the application;

(L) Any written defense motion or any written motion by the People, with supporting and opposing memoranda and attachments;

(M) If related to a motion under (L), any search warrant and return and the reporter's transcript of any preliminary examination or grand jury hearing;

(N) Any document admitted in evidence to prove a prior juvenile adjudication, criminal conviction, or prison term;

(O) The probation officer's report;

(P) Any court-ordered diagnostic or psychological report required under Penal Code section 1369;

(Q) Any copies of visual aids provided to the clerk under rule 4.230(f). If a visual aid is oversized, a photograph of that visual aid must be included in place of the original. For digital or electronic presentations, printouts showing the full text of each slide or image must be included;

(R) Each juror questionnaire, whether or not the juror was selected;

(S) The table correlating the jurors' names with their identifying numbers required by rule 8.611;

(T) The register of actions;

(U) All documents filed under Penal Code section 987.2 or 987.9; and

(V) Any other document filed or lodged in the case.

(2) The record must include a reporter's transcript containing:

(A) The oral proceedings on the entry of any plea other than a not guilty plea;

(B) The oral proceedings on any motion in limine;

(C) The voir dire examination of jurors;

(D) Any opening statement;

(E) The oral proceedings at trial;

(F) All instructions given orally;

(G) Any oral communication between the court and the jury or any individual juror;

(H) Any oral opinion of the court;

(I) The oral proceedings on any motion for new trial;

(J) The oral proceedings at sentencing, granting or denying of probation, or other dispositional hearing;

(K) The oral proceedings on any motion under Penal Code section 1538.5 denied in whole or in part;

(L) The closing arguments;

(M) Any comment on the evidence by the court to the jury;

(N) The oral proceedings on motions in addition to those listed above; and

(O) Any other oral proceedings in the case, including any proceedings that did not result in a verdict or sentence of death because the court ordered a mistrial or a new trial.

(3) All exhibits admitted in evidence, refused, or lodged are deemed part of the record, but, except as provided in rule 8.622, may be transmitted to the reviewing court only as provided in rule 8.634.

(4) The superior court or the Supreme Court may order that the record include additional material.

(Subd (a) amended effective April 25, 2019; previously amended effective January 1, 2007.)

(b) Sealed and confidential records

Rules 8.45–8.47 govern sealed and confidential records in appeals under this chapter.

(Subd (b) amended effective April 25, 2019; previously amended effective January 1, 2007, and January 1, 2014.)

(c) Juror-identifying information

Any document in the record containing juror-identifying information must be edited in compliance with rule 8.611. Unedited copies of all such documents and a copy of the table required by the rule, under seal and bound together if filed in paper form, must be included in the record sent to the Supreme Court.

(Subd (c) amended effective April 25, 2019; previously amended effective January 1, 2007, and January 1, 2016.)

(d) Form of record

The clerk's transcript and the reporter's transcript must comply with rules 8.45–8.47, relating to sealed and confidential records, and rule 8.144.

(Subd (d) amended effective January 1, 2014; previously amended effective January 1, 2005, and January 1, 2007.)

Rule 8.610 amended effective April 25, 2019; adopted as rule 34.1 effective January 1, 2004; previously amended and renumbered as rule 8.610 effective January 1, 2007; previously amended effective January 1, 2005, January 1, 2014, and January 1, 2016.

Advisory Committee Comment

Subdivision (a). Subdivision (a) implements Penal Code section 190.7(a).

Subdivision (b). The clerk's and reporter's transcripts may contain records that are sealed or confidential. Rules 8.45–8.47 address the handling of such records, including requirements for the format, labeling, and transmission of and access to such records. Examples of confidential records include Penal Code section 1203.03 diagnostic reports, records closed to inspection by court order under *People v. Marsden* (1970) 2 Cal.3d 118 or *Pitchess v. Superior Court* (1974) 11 Cal.3d 531, in-camera proceedings on a confidential informant, and defense investigation and expert funding requests (Pen. Code, §§ 987.2 and 987.9; *Puett v. Superior Court* (1979) 96 Cal.App.3d 936, 940, fn. 2; *Keenan v. Superior Court* (1982) 31 Cal.3d 424, 430).

Rule 8.611. Juror-identifying information

(a) Application

A clerk's transcript, a reporter's transcript, or any other document in the record that contains juror-identifying information must comply with this rule.

(Subd (a) adopted effective April 25, 2019.)

(b) Juror names, addresses, and telephone numbers

(1) The name of each trial juror or alternate sworn to hear the case must be replaced with an identifying number wherever it appears in any document. The superior court clerk must prepare and keep under seal in the case file a table correlating the jurors' names with their identifying numbers. The clerk and the reporter must use the table in preparing all transcripts or other documents.

(2) The addresses and telephone numbers of trial jurors and alternates sworn to hear the case must be deleted from all documents.

(Subd (b) adopted effective April 25, 2019.)

(c) Potential jurors

Information identifying potential jurors called but not sworn as trial jurors or alternates must not be sealed unless otherwise ordered under Code of Civil Procedure section 237(a)(1).

(Subd (c) adopted effective April 25, 2019.)
Rule 8.611 adopted effective April 25, 2019.

Advisory Committee Comment

Rule 8.611 implements Code of Civil Procedure section 237.

Rule 8.613. Preparing and certifying the record of preliminary proceedings

(a) Definitions
For purposes of this rule:

(1) The "preliminary proceedings" are all proceedings held before and including the filing of the information or indictment, whether in open court or otherwise, and include the preliminary examination or grand jury proceeding;

(2) The "record of the preliminary proceedings" is the court file and the reporter's transcript of the preliminary proceedings;

(3) The "responsible judge" is the judge assigned to try the case or, if none is assigned, the presiding superior court judge or designee of the presiding judge; and

(4) The "designated judge" is the judge designated by the presiding judge to supervise preparation of the record of preliminary proceedings.

(Subd (a) amended effective January 1, 2007.)

(b) Notice of intent to seek death penalty
In any case in which the death penalty may be imposed:

(1) If the prosecution notifies the responsible judge that it intends to seek the death penalty, the judge must notify the presiding judge and the clerk. The clerk must promptly enter the information in the court file.

(2) If the prosecution does not give notice under (1)—and does not give notice to the contrary—the clerk must notify the responsible judge 60 days before the first date set for trial that the prosecution is presumed to seek the death penalty. The judge must notify the presiding judge, and the clerk must promptly enter the information in the court file.

(c) Assignment of judge designated to supervise preparation of record of preliminary proceedings

(1) Within five days after receiving notice under (b), the presiding judge must designate a judge to supervise preparation of the record of the preliminary proceedings.

(2) If there was a preliminary examination, the designated judge must be the judge who conducted it.

(d) Notice to prepare transcript and lists
Within five days after receiving notice under (b)(1) or notifying the judge under (b)(2), the clerk must do the following:

(1) Notify each reporter who reported a preliminary proceeding to prepare a transcript of the proceeding. If there is more than one reporter, the designated judge may assign a reporter or another designee to perform the functions of the primary reporter.

(2) Notify trial counsel to submit the lists of appearances, exhibits, and motions required by rule 4.119.

(Subd (d) amended effective April 25, 2019.)

(e) Reporter's duties

(1) The reporter must prepare an original and five copies of the reporter's transcript in electronic form and two additional copies in electronic form for each codefendant against whom the death penalty is sought. The transcript must include the preliminary examination or grand jury proceeding unless a transcript of that examination or proceeding has already been filed in superior court for inclusion in the clerk's transcript.

(2) The reporter must certify the original and all copies of the reporter's transcript as correct.

(3) Within 20 days after receiving the notice to prepare the reporter's transcript, the reporter must deliver the original and all copies of the transcript to the clerk.

(Subd (e) amended effective April 25, 2019.)

(f) Review by counsel

(1) Within five days after the reporter delivers the transcript, the clerk must deliver the original transcript and the lists of appearances, exhibits, and motions required by rule 4.119 to the designated judge and one copy of the transcript and each list required by rule 4.119 that is not required to be sealed to each trial counsel. If a different attorney represented the defendant or the People in the preliminary proceedings, both attorneys must perform the tasks required by (2).

(2) Each trial counsel must promptly:

(A) Review the reporter's transcript and the lists of appearances, exhibits, and motions to identify any errors or omissions in the transcript;

(B) Review the docket sheets and minute orders to determine whether all preliminary proceedings have been transcribed; and

(C) Review the court file to determine whether it is complete.

(3) Within 21 days after the clerk delivers the transcript and lists under (1), trial counsel must confer regarding any errors or omissions in the reporter's transcript or court file identified by trial counsel during the review required under (2) and determine whether any other proceedings or discussions should have been transcribed.

(Subd (f) amended effective April 25, 2019; previously amended effective January 1, 2007.)

(g) Declaration and request for corrections or additions

(1) Within 30 days after the clerk delivers the reporter's transcript and lists, each trial counsel must serve and file:

(A) A declaration stating that counsel or another person under counsel's supervision has performed the tasks required by (f), including conferring with opposing counsel; and

(B) Either:

(i) A request for corrections or additions to the reporter's transcript or court file. Immaterial typographical errors that cannot conceivably cause confusion are not required to be brought to the court's attention; or

(ii) A statement that counsel does not request any corrections or additions.

(C) The requirements of (B) may be satisfied by a joint statement or request filed by counsel for all parties.

(2) If a different attorney represented the defendant in the preliminary proceedings, that attorney must also file the declaration required by (1).

(3) A request for additions to the reporter's transcript must state the nature and date of the proceedings and, if known, the identity of the reporter who reported them.

(4) If any counsel fails to timely file a declaration under (1), the designated judge must not certify the record and must set the matter for hearing, require a showing of good cause why counsel has not complied, and fix a date for compliance.

(Subd (g) amended effective April 25, 2019; previously amended effective January 1, 2007.)

(h) Corrections or additions to the record of preliminary proceedings
If any counsel files a request for corrections or additions:

(1) Within 15 days after the last request is filed, the designated judge must hold a hearing and order any necessary corrections or additions.

(2) If any portion of the proceedings cannot be transcribed, the judge may order preparation of a settled statement under rule 8.346.

(3) Within 20 days after the hearing under (1), the original reporter's transcript and court file must be corrected or augmented to reflect all corrections or additions ordered. The clerk must promptly send copies of the corrected or additional pages to trial counsel.

(4) The judge may order any further proceedings to correct or complete the record of the preliminary proceedings.

(5) When the judge is satisfied that all corrections and additions ordered have been made and copies of all corrected or additional pages have been sent to the parties, the judge must certify the record of the preliminary proceedings as complete and accurate.

(6) The record of the preliminary proceedings must be certified as complete and accurate within 120 days after the presiding judge orders preparation of the record.

(Subd (h) amended effective January 1, 2007.)

(i) Transcript delivered in electronic form

(1) When the record of the preliminary proceedings is certified as complete and accurate, the clerk must promptly notify the reporter to prepare five copies of the transcript in electronic form and two additional copies in electronic form for each codefendant against whom the death penalty is sought.

(2) Each transcript delivered in electronic form must comply with the applicable requirements of rule 8.144 and any additional requirements prescribed by the Supreme Court, and must be further labeled to show the date it was made.

(3) A copy of a sealed or confidential transcript delivered in electronic form must be separated from any other transcripts and labeled as required by rule 8.45.

(4) The reporter is to be compensated for copies delivered in electronic form as provided in Government Code section 69954(b).

(5) Within 20 days after the clerk notifies the reporter under (1), the reporter must deliver the copies in electronic form to the clerk.

(Subd (i) amended effective April 25, 2019; previously amended effective January 1, 2007, January 1, 2017, and January 1, 2018.)

(j) Delivery to the superior court
Within five days after the reporter delivers the copies in electronic form, the clerk must deliver to the responsible judge, for inclusion in the record:

(1) The certified original reporter's transcript of the preliminary proceedings and the copies that have not been distributed to counsel; and

(2) The complete court file of the preliminary proceedings or a certified copy of that file.

(Subd (j) amended effective April 25, 2019; previously amended effective January 1, 2007, and January 1, 2018.)

(k) Extension of time

(1) Except as provided in (2), the designated judge may extend for good cause any of the periods specified in this rule.

(2) The period specified in (h)(6) may be extended only as follows:

(A) The designated judge may request an extension of the period by presenting a declaration to the responsible judge explaining why the time limit cannot be met; and

(B) The responsible judge may order an extension not exceeding 90 additional days; in an exceptional case the judge may order an extension exceeding 90 days, but must state on the record the specific reason for the greater extension.

(Subd (k) amended effective January 1, 2007.)

(l) Notice that the death penalty is no longer sought

After the clerk has notified the court reporter to prepare the pretrial record, if the death penalty is no longer sought, the clerk must promptly notify the reporter that this rule does not apply.

(Subd (l) amended effective April 25, 2019; previously amended effective January 1, 2007.)

Rule 8.613 amended effective April 25, 2019; adopted as rule 34.2 effective January 1, 2004; previously amended and renumbered as rule 8.613 effective January 1, 2007; previously amended effective January 1, 2017, and January 1, 2018.

Advisory Committee Comment

Rule 8.613 implements Penal Code section 190.9(a). Rules 8.613–8.622 govern the process of preparing and certifying the record in any appeal from a judgment of death; specifically, rule 8.613 provides for the record of the preliminary proceedings in such an appeal.

Subdivision (f). As used in subdivision (f)—as in all rules in this chapter—trial counsel "means both the defendant's trial counsel and the prosecuting attorney." (Rule 8.600(e)(2).)

Subdivision (i). Subdivision (i)(4) restates a provision of former rule 35(b), second paragraph, as it was in effect on December 31, 2003.

Rule 8.616. Preparing the trial record

(a) Clerk's duties

(1) The clerk must promptly—and no later than five days after the judgment of death is rendered:

(A) Notify the reporter to prepare the reporter's transcript; and

(B) Notify trial counsel to submit the lists of appearances, exhibits, and motions required by rule 4.230.

(2) The clerk must prepare an original and eight copies of the clerk's transcript and two additional copies for each codefendant sentenced to death. The clerk is encouraged to send the clerk's transcript in electronic form if the court is able to do so.

(3) The clerk must certify the original and all copies of the clerk's transcript as correct.

(Subd (a) amended effective April 25, 2019.)

(b) Reporter's duties

(1) The reporter must prepare an original and five copies of the reporter's transcript in electronic form and two additional copies in electronic form for each codefendant sentenced to death.

(2) Any portion of the transcript transcribed during trial must not be retyped unless necessary to correct errors, but must be repaginated and combined with any portion of the transcript not previously transcribed. Any additional copies needed must not be retyped but, if the transcript is in paper form, must be prepared by photocopying or an equivalent process.

(3) The reporter must certify the original and all copies of the reporter's transcript as correct and deliver them to the clerk.

(Subd (b) amended effective April 25, 2019; previously amended effective January 1, 2016.)

(c) Sending the record to trial counsel

Within 30 days after the judgment of death is rendered, the clerk must deliver one copy of the clerk's and reporter's transcripts and one copy of each list of appearances, exhibits, and motions required by rule 4.230 that is not required to be sealed to each trial counsel. The clerk must retain the original transcripts and any remaining copies. If counsel does not receive the transcripts within that period, counsel must promptly notify the superior court.

(Subd (c) amended effective April 25, 2019.)

(d) Extension of time

(1) On request of the clerk or a reporter and for good cause, the superior court may extend the period prescribed in (c) for no more than 30 days. For any further extension the clerk or reporter must file a request in the Supreme Court, showing good cause.

(2) A request under (1) must be supported by a declaration explaining why the extension is necessary. The court may presume good cause if the clerk's and reporter's transcripts combined will likely exceed 10,000 pages.

(3) If the superior court orders an extension under (1), the order must specify the reason justifying the extension. The clerk must promptly send a copy of the order to the Supreme Court.

Rule 8.616 amended effective April 25, 2019; repealed and adopted as rule 35 effective January 1, 2004; previously renumbered as rule 8.606 effective January 1, 2007; previously amended effective January 1, 2016.

Advisory Committee Comment

Rule 8.616 implements Penal Code section 190.8(b).

Rule 8.619. Certifying the trial record for completeness

(a) Review by counsel after trial

(1) When the clerk delivers the clerk's and reporter's transcripts and the lists of appearances, exhibits, motions, and jury instructions required by rule 4.230 to trial counsel, each counsel must promptly:

(A) Review the docket sheets, minute orders, and the lists of appearances, exhibits, motions, and jury instructions to determine whether the reporter's transcript is complete; and

(B) Review the court file to determine whether the clerk's transcript is complete.

(2) Within 21 days after the clerk delivers the transcripts and lists under (1), trial counsel must confer regarding any errors or omissions in the reporter's transcript or clerk's transcript identified by trial counsel during the review required under (1).

(Subd (a) repealed, amended and relettered effective April 25, 2019; adopted as subd (b); previously amended effective January 1, 2007.)

(b) Declaration and request for additions or corrections

(1) Within 30 days after the clerk delivers the transcripts, each trial counsel must serve and file:

(A) A declaration stating that counsel or another person under counsel's supervision has performed the tasks required by (a), including conferring with opposing counsel; and

(B) Either:

(i) A request to include additional materials in the record or to correct errors that have come to counsel's attention. Immaterial typographical errors that cannot conceivably cause confusion are not required to be brought to the court's attention; or

(ii) A statement that counsel does not request any additions or corrections.

(2) The requirements of (1)(B) may be satisfied by a joint statement or request filed by counsel for all parties.

(3) If the clerk's and reporter's transcripts combined exceed 10,000 pages, the time limits stated in (a)(2) and (b)(1) are extended by three days for each 1,000 pages of combined transcript over 10,000 pages.

(4) A request for additions to the reporter's transcript must state the nature and date of the proceedings and, if known, the identity of the reporter who reported them.

(5) If any counsel fails to timely file a declaration under (1), the judge must not certify the record and must set the matter for hearing, require a showing of good cause why counsel has not complied, and fix a date for compliance.

(Subd (b) amended and relettered effective April 25, 2019; adopted as subd (c); previously amended effective January 1, 2007.)

(c) Completion of the record

If any counsel files a request for additions or corrections:

(1) The clerk must promptly deliver the original transcripts to the judge who presided at the trial.

(2) Within 15 days after the last request is filed, the judge must hold a hearing and order any necessary additions or corrections. The order must require that any additions or corrections be made within 10 days of its date.

(3) The clerk must promptly—and in any event within five days—notify the reporter of an order under (2). If any portion of the proceedings cannot be transcribed, the judge may order preparation of a settled statement under rule 8.346.

(4) The original transcripts must be augmented or corrected to reflect all additions or corrections ordered. The clerk must promptly send copies of the additional or corrected pages to trial counsel.

(5) Within five days after the augmented or corrected transcripts are filed, the judge must set another hearing to determine whether the record has been completed or corrected as ordered. The judge may order further proceedings to complete or correct the record.

(6) When the judge is satisfied that all additions or corrections ordered have been made and copies of all additional or corrected pages have been sent to trial counsel, the judge must certify the record as complete and redeliver the original transcripts to the clerk.

(7) The judge must certify the record as complete within 30 days after the last request to include additional materials or make corrections is filed or, if no such request is filed, after the last statement that counsel does not request any additions or corrections is filed.

(Subd (c) amended and relettered effective April 25, 2019; adopted as subd (d); previously amended effective January 1, 2007.)

(d) Transcript delivered in electronic form

(1) When the record is certified as complete, the clerk must promptly notify the reporter to prepare five copies of the transcript in electronic form and two additional copies in electronic form for each codefendant sentenced to death.

(2) Each copy delivered in electronic form must comply with the applicable requirements of rule 8.144 and any additional requirements prescribed by the Supreme Court, and must be further labeled to show the date it was made.

(3) A copy of a sealed or confidential transcript delivered in electronic form must be separated from any other transcripts and labeled as required by rule 8.45.

(4) The reporter is to be compensated for copies delivered in electronic form as provided in Government Code section 69954(b).

(5) Within 10 days after the clerk notifies the reporter under (1), the reporter must deliver the copies in electronic form to the clerk.

(Subd (d) amended and relettered effective April 25, 2019; adopted as subd (e); previously amended effective January 1, 2017, and January 1, 2018.)

(e) Extension of time

(1) The court may extend for good cause any of the periods specified in this rule.

(2) An application to extend the period to review the record under (a) or the period to file a declaration under (b) must be served and filed within the relevant period.

(3) If the court orders an extension of time, the order must specify the justification for the extension. The clerk must promptly send a copy of the order to the Supreme Court.

(Subd (e) amended and relettered effective April 25, 2019; adopted as subd (f).)

(f) Sending the certified record

(1) When the record is certified as complete, the clerk must promptly send one copy of the clerk's transcript and one copy of the reporter's transcript:

(A) To each defendant's appellate counsel and each defendant's habeas corpus counsel. If either counsel has not been retained or appointed, the clerk must keep that counsel's copies until counsel is retained or appointed.

(B) To the Attorney General, the Habeas Corpus Resource Center, and the California Appellate Project in San Francisco.

(2) The reporter's transcript must be in electronic form. The clerk is encouraged to send the clerk's transcript in electronic form if the court is able to do so.

(Subd (f) amended and relettered effective April 25, 2019; adopted as subd (g); previously amended effective January 1, 2018.)

(g) Notice of delivery

When the clerk sends the record to the defendant's appellate counsel, the clerk must serve a notice of delivery on the clerk/executive officer of the Supreme Court.

(Subd (g) amended and relettered effective April 25, 2019; adopted as subd (h); previously amended effective January 1, 2018.)

Rule 8.619 amended effective April 25, 2019; adopted as rule 35.1 effective January 1, 2004; previously amended and renumbered as rule 8.619 effective January 1, 2007; previously amended effective January 1, 2017, and January 1, 2018.

Advisory Committee Comment

Rule 8.619 implements Penal Code section 190.8(c)–(e).

Subdivision (d)(4) restates a provision of former rule 35(b), second paragraph, as it was in effect on December 31, 2003.

Rule 8.622. Certifying the trial record for accuracy

(a) Request for corrections or additions

(1) Within 90 days after the clerk delivers the record to defendant's appellate counsel:

(A) Any party may serve and file a request for corrections or additions to the record. Immaterial typographical errors that cannot conceivably cause confusion are not required to be brought to the court's attention. Items that a party may request to be added to the clerk's transcript include a copy of any exhibit admitted in evidence, refused, or lodged that is a document in paper or electronic form. The requesting party must state the reason that the exhibit needs to be included in the clerk's transcript. Parties may file a joint request for corrections or additions.

(B) Appellate counsel must review all sealed records that they are entitled to access under rule 8.45 and file an application to unseal any such records that counsel determines no longer meet the criteria for sealing specified in rule 2.550(d). Notwithstanding rule 8.46(e), this application must be filed in the trial court and these records may be unsealed on order of the trial court.

(2) A request for additions to the reporter's transcript must state the nature and date of the proceedings and, if known, the identity of the reporter who reported them. A request for an exhibit to be included in the clerk's transcript must specify that exhibit by number or letter.

(3) Unless otherwise ordered by the court, within 10 days after a party serves and files a request for corrections or additions to the record, defendant's appellate counsel and the trial counsel from the prosecutor's office must confer regarding the request and any application to unseal records served on the prosecutor's office.

(4) If the clerk's and reporter's transcripts combined exceed 10,000 pages, the time limits stated in (1), (3), and (b)(4) are extended by 15 days for each 1,000 pages of combined transcript over 10,000 pages.

(Subd (a) amended effective January 1, 2024; previously amended effective April 25, 2019.)

(b) Correction of the record

(1) If any counsel files a request for corrections or additions, the procedures and time limits of rule 8.619(c)(1)–(5) must be followed.

(2) If any application to unseal a record is filed, the judge must grant or deny the application before certifying the record as accurate.

(3) When the judge is satisfied that all corrections or additions ordered have been made, the judge must certify the record as accurate and redeliver the record to the clerk.

(4) The judge must certify the record as accurate within 30 days after the last request to include additional materials or make corrections is filed.

(Subd (b) amended effective April 25, 2019; previously amended effective January 1, 2007.)

(c) Copies of the record

(1) When the record is certified as accurate, the clerk must promptly notify the reporter to prepare six copies of the reporter's transcript in electronic form and two additional copies in electronic form for each codefendant sentenced to death.

(2) In preparing the copies, the procedures and time limits of rule 8.619(d)(2)–(5) must be followed.

(Subd (c) amended effective April 25, 2019; previously amended effective January 1, 2007, and January 1, 2018.)

(d) Extension of time

(1) The court may extend for good cause any of the periods specified in this rule.

(2) An application to extend the period to request corrections or additions under (a) must be served and filed within that period.

(3) If the court orders an extension of time, the order must specify the justification for the extension. The clerk must promptly send a copy of the order to the Supreme Court.

(4) If the court orders an extension of time, the court may conduct a status conference or require the counsel who requested the extension to file a status report on counsel's progress in reviewing the record.

(Subd (d) amended effective April 25, 2019.)

(e) Sending the certified record

When the record is certified as accurate, the clerk must promptly send:

(1) To the Supreme Court: the corrected original record, including the judge's certificate of accuracy. The reporter's transcript must be in electronic form. The clerk is encouraged to send the clerk's transcript in electronic form if the court is able to do so.

(2) To each defendant's appellate counsel, each defendant's habeas corpus counsel, the Attorney General, the Habeas Corpus Resource Center, and the California Appellate Project in San Francisco: a copy of the order certifying the record and a copy of the reporter's transcript in electronic form.

(3) To the Governor: the copies of the transcripts required by Penal Code section 1218, with copies of any corrected or augmented pages inserted.

(Subd (e) amended effective April 25, 2019; previously amended effective January 1, 2018.)

Rule 8.622 amended effective January 1, 2024; adopted as rule 35.2 effective January 1, 2004; previously amended and renumbered as rule 8.622 effective January 1, 2007; previously amended effective January 1, 2018, and April 25, 2019.

Advisory Committee Comment

Rule 8.622 implements Penal Code section 190.8(g).

Rule 8.625. Certifying the record in pre-1997 trials [Repealed]

Rule 8.625 repealed effective April 25, 2019; adopted as rule 35.3 effective January 1, 2004; previously amended and renumbered as rule 8.625 effective January 1, 2007; previously amended effective January 1, 2017, and January 1, 2018.

Article 3
Briefs, Hearing, and Decision

Rule 8.630. Briefs by parties and amicus curiae
Rule 8.631. Applications to file overlength briefs in appeals from a judgment of death
Rule 8.634. Transmitting exhibits; augmenting the record in the Supreme Court
Rule 8.638. Oral argument and submission of the cause
Rule 8.642. Filing, finality, and modification of decision; rehearing; remittitur

Rule 8.630. Briefs by parties and amicus curiae

(a) Contents and form

Except as provided in this rule, briefs in appeals from judgments of death must comply as nearly as possible with rules 8.200 and 8.204.

(Subd (a) amended effective January 1, 2007.)

(b) Length

(1) A brief produced on a computer must not exceed the following limits, including footnotes:

(A) Appellant's opening brief: 102,000 words.

(B) Respondent's brief: 102,000 words. If the Chief Justice permits the appellant to file an opening brief that exceeds the limit set in (1)(A) or (3)(A), respondent's brief may not exceed the length of appellant's opening brief approved by the Chief Justice.

(C) Reply brief: 47,600 words.

(D) Petition for rehearing and answer: 23,800 words each.

(2) A brief under (1) must include a certificate by appellate counsel stating the number of words in the brief; counsel may rely on the word count of the computer program used to prepare the brief.

(3) A typewritten brief must not exceed the following limits:

(A) Appellant's opening brief: 300 pages.

(B) Respondent's brief: 300 pages. If the Chief Justice permits the appellant to file an opening brief that exceeds the limit set in (1)(A) or (3)(A), respondent's brief may not exceed the length of appellant's opening brief approved by the Chief Justice.

(C) Reply brief: 140 pages.

(D) Petition for rehearing and answer: 70 pages each.

(4) The tables required under rule 8.204(a)(1), the cover information required under rule 8.204(b)(10), a certificate under (2), any signature block, and any attachment permitted under rule 8.204(d) are excluded from the limits stated in (1) and (3).

(5) On application, the Chief Justice may permit a longer brief for good cause. An application in any case in which the certified record is filed in the California Supreme Court on or after January 1, 2008, must comply with rule 8.631.

(Subd (b) amended effective January 1, 2011; previously amended effective January 1, 2007, and January 1, 2008.)

(c) Time to file

(1) Except as provided in (2), the times to file briefs in an appeal from a judgment of death are as follows:

(A) The appellant's opening brief must be served and filed within 210 days after the record is certified as complete or the superior court clerk delivers the completed record to the defendant's appellate counsel, whichever is later. The clerk/executive officer of the Supreme Court must promptly notify the defendant's appellate counsel and the Attorney General of the due date for the appellant's opening brief.

(B) The respondent's brief must be served and filed within 120 days after the appellant's opening brief is filed. The clerk/executive officer of the Supreme Court must promptly notify the defendant's appellate counsel and the Attorney General of the due date for the respondent's brief.

(C) If the clerk's and reporter's transcripts combined exceed 10,000 pages, the time limits stated in (A) and (B) are extended by 15 days for each 1,000 pages of combined transcript over 10,000 pages.

(D) The appellant must serve and file a reply brief, if any, within 60 days after the respondent files its brief.

(2) In any appeal from a judgment of death imposed after a trial that began before January 1, 1997, the time to file briefs is governed by rule 8.360(c).

(3) The Chief Justice may extend the time to serve and file a brief for good cause.

(Subd (c) amended effective January 1, 2018; previously amended effective January 1, 2007.)

(d) Supplemental briefs

Supplemental briefs may be filed as provided in rule 8.520(d).

(Subd (d) amended effective January 1, 2007.)

(e) Amicus curiae briefs

Amicus curiae briefs may be filed as provided in rule 8.520(f).

(Subd (e) amended effective January 1, 2007.)

(f) Briefs on the court's request

The court may request additional briefs on any or all issues.

(g) Service

(1) The Supreme Court Policy on Service of Process by Counsel for Defendant governs service of the defendant's briefs.

(2) The Attorney General must serve two paper copies or one electronic copy of the respondent's brief on each defendant's appellate counsel and, for each defendant sentenced to death, one copy on the California Appellate Project in San Francisco.

(3) A copy of each brief must be served on the superior court clerk for delivery to the trial judge.

(Subd (g) amended effective January 1, 2016.)

(h) Judicial notice

To obtain judicial notice by the Supreme Court under Evidence Code section 459, a party must comply with rule 8.252(a).

(Subd (h) amended effective January 1, 2007.)

Rule 8.630 amended effective January 1, 2018; repealed and adopted as rule 36 effective January 1, 2004; previously amended and renumbered as rule 8.630 effective January 1, 2007; previously amended effective January 1, 2008, January 1, 2011, and January 1, 2016.

Advisory Committee Comment

Subdivision (b). Subdivision (b)(1) states the maximum permissible lengths of briefs produced on a computer in terms of word count rather than page count. This provision tracks a provision in rule 8.204(c) governing Court of Appeal briefs and is explained in the comment to that provision. Each word count assumes a brief using one-and-one-half spaced lines of text, as permitted by rule 8.204(b)(5).

Subdivision (b)(4) specifies certain items that are not counted toward the maximum brief length. Signature blocks, as referenced in this provision includes not only the signatures, but also the printed names, titles, and affiliations of any attorneys filing or joining in the brief, which may accompany the signature.

Subdivision (g). Subdivision (g)(1) is a cross-reference to Policy 4 of the Supreme Court Policies Regarding Cases Arising From Judgments of Death.

Rule 8.631. Applications to file overlength briefs in appeals from a judgment of death

(a) Cases in which this rule applies

This rule applies in appeals from a judgment of death in which the certified record is filed in the California Supreme Court on or after January 1, 2008.

(Subd (a) adopted effective January 1, 2008.)

(b) Policies

(1) The brief limits set by rule 8.630 are substantially higher than for other appellate briefs in recognition of the number, significance, and complexity of the issues generally presented in appeals from judgments of death and are designed to be sufficient to allow counsel to prepare adequate briefs in the majority of such appeals.

(2) In a small proportion of such appeals, counsel may not be able to prepare adequate briefs within the limits set by rule 8.630. In those cases, necessary additional briefing will be permitted.

(3) A party may not file a brief that exceeds the limit set by rule 8.630 unless the court finds that good cause has been shown in an application filed within the time limits set in (d).

(Subd (b) adopted effective January 1, 2008.)

(c) Factors considered

The court will consider the following factors in determining whether good cause exists to grant an application to file a brief that exceeds the limit set by rule 8.630:

(1) The unusual length of the record. A party relying on this factor must specify the length of each of the following components of the record:

(A) The reporter's transcript;

(B) The clerk's transcript; and

(C) The portion of the clerk's transcript that is made up of juror questionnaires.

(2) The number of codefendants in the case and whether they were tried separately from the appellant;

(3) The number of homicide victims in the case and whether the homicides occurred in more than one incident;

(4) The number of other crimes in the case and whether they occurred in more than one incident;

(5) The number of rulings by the trial court on unusual, factually intensive, or legally complex motions that the party may assert are erroneous and prejudicial. A party relying on this factor must briefly describe the nature of these motions;

(6) The number of rulings on objections by the trial court that the party may assert are erroneous and prejudicial;

(7) The number and nature of unusual, factually intensive, or legally complex hearings held in the trial court that the party may assert raise issues on appeal; and

(8) Any other factor that is likely to contribute to an unusually high number of issues or unusually complex issues on appeal. A party relying on this factor must briefly specify those issues.

(Subd (c) adopted effective January 1, 2008.)

(d) Time to file and contents of application

(1) An application to file a brief that exceeds the limits set by rule 8.630 must be served and filed as follows:

(A) For an appellant's opening brief or respondent's brief:

(i) If counsel has not filed an application requesting an extension of time to file the brief, no later than 45 days before the brief is due.

(ii) If counsel has filed an application requesting an extension of time to file the brief, within the time specified by the court in its order regarding the extension of time.

(B) For an appellant's reply brief:

(i) If counsel has not filed an application requesting an extension of time to file the brief, no later than 30 days before the brief is due.

(ii) If counsel has filed an application requesting an extension of time to file the brief, within the time specified by the court in its order regarding the extension of time.

(2) After the time specified in (1), an application to file a brief that exceeds the applicable limit may be filed only under the following circumstances:

(A) New authority substantially affects the issues presented in the case and cannot be adequately addressed without exceeding the applicable limit. Such an application must be filed within 30 days of finality of the new authority; or

(B) Replacement counsel has been appointed to represent the appellant and has determined that it is necessary to file a brief that exceeds the applicable limit. Such an application must be filed within the time specified by the court in its order setting the deadline for replacement counsel to file the appellant's brief.

(3) The application must:

(A) State the number of additional words or typewritten pages requested.

(B) State good cause for granting the additional words or pages requested, consistent with the factors in (c). The number of additional words or pages requested must be commensurate with the good cause shown. The application must explain why the factors identified demonstrate good cause in the particular case. The application must not state mere conclusions or make legal arguments regarding the merits of the issues on appeal.

(C) Not exceed 5,100 words if produced on a computer or 15 pages if typewritten.

(Subd (d) adopted effective January 1, 2008.)

Rule 8.631 adopted effective January 1, 2008.

Advisory Committee Comment

Subdivision (a). In all cases in which a judgment of death was imposed after a trial that began after January 1, 1997, the record filed with the Supreme Court will be the record that has been certified for accuracy under rule 8.622. In cases in which a judgment of death was imposed after a trial that began before January 1, 1997, the record filed with the Supreme Court will be the certified record under rule 8.625.

Subdivision (c)(1). As in guideline 8 of the Supreme Court's Guidelines for Fixed Fee Appointments, juror questionnaires generally will not be taken into account in considering whether the length of the record is unusual unless these questionnaires are relevant to an issue on appeal. A record of 10,000 pages or less, excluding juror questionnaires, is not considered a record of unusual length; 70 percent of the records in capital appeals filed between 2001 and 2004 were 10,000 pages or less, excluding juror questionnaires.

Subdivision (c)(5). Examples of unusual, factually intensive, or legally complex motions include motions to change venue, admit scientific evidence, or determine competency.

Subdivisions (c)(5)–(8). Because an application must be filed before briefing is completed, the issues identified in the application will be those that the party anticipates *may* be raised on appeal. If the party does not ultimately raise all of these issues on appeal, the party is expected to have reduced the length of the brief accordingly.

Subdivision (c)(7). Examples of unusual, factually intensive, or legally complex hearings include jury composition proceedings and hearings to determine the defendant's competency or sanity, whether the defendant has an intellectual disability, and whether the defendant may be self-represented.

Subdivision (d)(1)(A)(ii). To allow the deadline for an application to file an overlength brief to be appropriately tied to the deadline for filing that brief, if counsel requests an extension of time to file a brief, the court will specify in its order regarding the request to extend the time to file the brief, when any application to file an overlength brief is due. Although the order will specify the deadline by which an application must be filed, counsel are encouraged to file such applications sooner, if possible.

Subdivision (d)(3). These requirements apply to applications filed under either (d)(1) or (d)(2).

Rule 8.634. Transmitting exhibits; augmenting the record in the Supreme Court

(a) Application

Except as provided in (b), rule 8.224 governs the transmission of exhibits to the Supreme Court.

(Subd (a) amended effective January 1, 2007; previously amended effective January 1, 2004.)

(b) Time to file notice of designation

No party may file a notice designating exhibits under rule 8.224(a) until the clerk/executive officer of the Supreme Court notifies the parties of the time and place of oral argument.

(Subd (b) amended effective January 1, 2018; previously amended effective January 1, 2007.)

(c) Augmenting the record in the Supreme Court

At any time, on motion of a party or on its own motion, the Supreme Court may order the record augmented or corrected as provided in rule 8.155.

(Subd (c) amended effective January 1, 2007; adopted effective January 1, 2004.)

Rule 8.634 amended effective January 1, 2018; adopted as rule 36.1 effective January 1, 2003; previously amended effective January 1, 2004; previously amended and renumbered effective January 1, 2007.

Rule 8.638. Oral argument and submission of the cause

(a) Application

Except as provided in (b), rule 8.524 governs oral argument and submission of the cause in the Supreme Court unless the court provides otherwise in its Internal Operating Practices and Procedures or by order.

(Subd (a) amended effective January 1, 2007; previously amended effective January 1, 2004.)

(b) Procedure

(1) The appellant has the right to open and close.

(2) Each side is allowed 45 minutes for argument.

(3) Two counsel may argue on each side if, within 10 days after the date of the order setting the case for argument, they notify the court that the case requires it.

(Subd (b) amended effective January 1, 2004.)

Rule 8.638 amended and renumbered effective January 1, 2007; adopted as rule 36.2 effective January 1, 2003; previously amended effective January 1, 2004.

Rule 8.642. Filing, finality, and modification of decision; rehearing; remittitur

Rules 8.532 through 8.540 govern the filing, finality, and modification of decision, rehearing, and issuance of remittitur by the Supreme Court in an appeal from a judgment of death.

Rule 8.642 amended and renumbered effective January 1, 2007; adopted as rule 36.3 effective January 1, 2004.

Chapter 3
Death Penalty–Related Habeas Corpus Proceedings

Title 8, Appellate Rules—Division 2, Rules Relating to Death Penalty Appeals and Habeas Corpus Proceedings—Chapter 3, Death Penalty–Related Habeas Corpus Proceedings adopted effective April 25, 2019.

Rule 8.652. Qualifications of counsel in death penalty–related habeas corpus proceedings

Rule 8.652. Qualifications of counsel in death penalty–related habeas corpus proceedings

(a) Purpose

This rule defines the minimum qualifications for attorneys to be appointed by a court to represent a person in a habeas corpus proceeding related to a sentence of death. These minimum qualifications are designed to promote competent representation in habeas corpus proceedings related to sentences of death and to avoid unnecessary delay and expense by assisting the courts in appointing qualified counsel. Nothing in this rule is intended to be used as a standard by which to measure whether a person received effective assistance of counsel. An attorney is not entitled to appointment simply because the attorney meets these minimum qualifications.

(Subd (a) adopted effective April 25, 2019.)

(b) General qualifications

An attorney may be included on a panel, appointed by the Supreme Court, or appointed by a court under a local rule as provided in rule 4.562, only if it is determined, after reviewing the attorney's experience, training, writing samples, references, and evaluations, that the attorney meets the minimum qualifications in this rule and has demonstrated the commitment, knowledge, and skills necessary to competently represent a person in a habeas corpus proceeding related to a sentence of death. An appointed attorney must be willing to cooperate with an assisting counsel or entity that the appointing court designates.

(Subd (b) adopted effective April 25, 2019.)

(c) Qualifications for appointed habeas corpus counsel

An attorney included on a panel, appointed by the Supreme Court, or appointed by a court under a local rule as provided in rule 4.562, must satisfy the following minimum qualifications:

(1) *California legal experience*

Active practice of law in California for at least five years.

(2) *Case experience*

The case experience identified in (A), (B), or (C).

(A) Service as counsel of record for a petitioner in a death penalty–related habeas corpus proceeding in which the petition has been filed in the California Supreme Court, a Court of Appeal, or a superior court.

(B) Service as:

(i) Supervised counsel in two death penalty–related habeas corpus proceedings in which the petition has been filed. Service as supervised counsel in a death penalty–related habeas corpus proceeding will apply toward this qualification only if lead or associate counsel in that proceeding attests that the attorney performed substantial work on the case and recommends the attorney for appointment; and

(ii) Counsel of record for either party in a combination of at least five completed appeals, habeas corpus proceedings, or jury trials in felony cases, including as counsel of record for a petitioner in at least two habeas corpus proceedings, each involving a serious felony in which the petition has been filed. Service as counsel of record in an appeal where counsel did not file a brief, or in a habeas corpus proceeding where counsel did not file a petition, informal response, or a return, does not satisfy any part of this combined case experience. The combined case experience must be sufficient to demonstrate proficiency in investigation, issue identification, and writing.

(C) Service as counsel of record for either party in a combination of at least eight completed appeals, habeas corpus proceedings, or jury trials in felony cases, including as counsel of record for a petitioner in at least two habeas corpus proceedings, each involving a serious felony in which the petition has been filed. Service as counsel of record in an appeal where counsel did not file a brief, or in a habeas corpus proceeding where counsel did not file a petition, informal response, or a return, does not satisfy any part of this combined case experience. The combined case experience must be sufficient to demonstrate proficiency in investigation, issue identification, and writing.

(3) *Knowledge*

Familiarity with the practices and procedures of the California courts and the federal courts in death penalty–related habeas corpus proceedings.

(4) *Training*

(A) Within three years before being included on a panel, appointed by the Supreme Court, or appointed by a court under a local rule as provided in rule 4.562, completion of at least 15 hours of appellate criminal defense or habeas corpus defense training approved for Minimum Continuing Legal Education credit by the State Bar of California, at least 10 hours of which address death penalty–related habeas corpus proceedings.

(B) Counsel who serves as an instructor in a course that satisfies the requirements of this rule may receive course participation credit for instruction, on request to and approval by the committee, the Supreme Court, or a court appointing counsel under a local rule as provided in rule 4.562, in an amount to be determined by the approving entity.

(C) If the attorney has previously represented a petitioner in a death penalty–related habeas corpus proceeding, the committee, the Supreme Court, or the court appointing counsel under a local rule as provided in rule 4.562, after reviewing counsel's previous work, may find that such representation constitutes compliance with some or all of this requirement.

(5) *Skills*

Demonstrated proficiency in issue identification, research, analysis, writing, investigation, and advocacy. To enable an assessment of the attorney's skills:

(A) The attorney must submit:

(i) Three writing samples written by the attorney and presenting analyses of complex legal issues. If the attorney has previously served as lead counsel of record for a petitioner in a death penalty–related habeas corpus proceeding, these writing samples must include one or more habeas corpus petitions filed by the attorney in that capacity. If the attorney has previously served as associate or supervised counsel for a petitioner in a death penalty–related habeas corpus proceeding, these writing samples must include the portion of the habeas corpus petition prepared by the attorney in that capacity. If the attorney has not served as lead counsel of record for a petitioner in a death penalty–related habeas corpus proceeding, these writing samples must include two or more habeas corpus petitions filed by the attorney as counsel of record for a petitioner in a habeas corpus proceeding involving a serious felony; and

(ii) Recommendations from two attorneys familiar with the attorney's qualifications and performance.

(B) The committee, the Supreme Court, or the court appointing counsel under a local rule as provided in rule 4.562, must obtain and review:

(i) If the attorney has previously been appointed in a death penalty appeal or death penalty–related habeas corpus proceeding, the evaluation of the assisting counsel or entity in those proceedings; and

(ii) If the attorney is on a panel of attorneys eligible for appointments to represent indigent appellants in the Court of Appeal, the evaluation of the administrator responsible for those appointments.

(Subd (c) adopted effective April 25, 2019.)

(d) Alternative experience

An attorney who does not meet the experience requirements of (c)(1) and (2) may be included on a panel or appointed by the Supreme Court if the attorney meets the qualifications described in (c)(3) and (5), excluding the writing samples described in (c)(5)(A)(i), and:

(1) The committee or the Supreme Court finds that the attorney has:

(A) Extensive experience as an attorney at the Habeas Corpus Resource Center or the California Appellate Project–San Francisco, or in another jurisdiction or a different type of practice (such as civil trials or appeals, academic work, or work for a court or as a prosecutor), for at least five years, providing the attorney with experience in complex cases substantially equivalent to that of an attorney qualified under (c)(1) and (2); and

(B) Demonstrated proficiency in issue identification, research, analysis, writing, investigation, and advocacy. To enable an assessment of the attorney's skills, the attorney must submit three writing samples written by the attorney and presenting analyses of complex legal issues, including habeas corpus petitions filed by the attorney, if any.

(2) Ongoing consultation is available to the attorney from an assisting counsel or entity designated by the court.

(3) Within two years before being included on a panel or appointed by the Supreme Court, the attorney has completed at least 18 hours of appellate criminal defense or habeas corpus defense training approved for Minimum Continuing Legal Education credit by the State Bar of California, at least 10 hours of which involve death penalty–related habeas corpus proceedings. The committee or the Supreme Court will determine whether the training completed by an attorney satisfies the requirements of this subdivision in light of the attorney's individual background and experience.

(Subd (d) adopted effective April 25, 2019.)

(e) Attorneys without trial experience

If an evidentiary hearing is ordered in a death penalty–related habeas corpus proceeding and an attorney appointed under (c) or (d) to represent a person in that proceeding lacks experience in conducting trials or evidentiary hearings, the attorney must associate with an attorney who has such experience.

(Subd (e) adopted effective April 25, 2019.)

(f) Use of supervised counsel

An attorney who does not meet the qualifications described in (c) or (d) may assist lead or associate counsel, but must work under the immediate supervision and direction of lead or associate counsel.

(Subd (f) adopted effective April 25, 2019.)

(g) Appellate and habeas corpus appointment

(1) An attorney appointed to represent a person in both a death penalty appeal and death penalty–related habeas corpus proceedings must meet the minimum qualifications of both (c) or (d) and rule 8.605.

(2) Notwithstanding (1), two attorneys together may be eligible for appointment to represent a person jointly in both a death penalty appeal and death penalty–related habeas corpus proceedings if it is determined that one attorney satisfies the minimum qualifications stated in (c) or (d) and the other attorney satisfies the minimum qualifications stated in rule 8.605.

(Subd (g) adopted effective April 25, 2019.)

(h) Entities as appointed counsel

(1) Notwithstanding any other provision of this rule, the Habeas Corpus Resource Center and the California Appellate Project–San Francisco are qualified to serve as appointed counsel in death penalty–related habeas corpus proceedings.

(2) When serving as appointed counsel in a death penalty–related habeas corpus proceeding, the Habeas Corpus Resource Center or the California Appellate Project–San Francisco must not assign any attorney as lead counsel unless it finds the attorney is qualified under (c) or (d).

(Subd (h) adopted effective April 25, 2019.)

(i) Attorney appointed by federal court

Notwithstanding any other provision of this rule, a court may appoint an attorney who is under appointment by a federal court in a death penalty–related habeas corpus proceeding for the purpose of exhausting state remedies in the California courts if the court finds that the attorney has the commitment, proficiency, and knowledge necessary to represent the person competently in state proceedings. Counsel under appointment by a federal court is not required to also be appointed by a state court in order to appear in a state court proceeding.

(Subd (i) adopted effective April 25, 2019.)
Rule 8.652 adopted effective April 25, 2019.

Division 3
Rules Relating to Miscellaneous Appeals and Writ Proceedings

Title 8, Appellate Rules—Division 3, Rules Relating to Miscellaneous Appeals and Writ Proceedings adopted effective April 25, 2019.

Chap. 1. Review of California Environmental Quality Act Cases Involving Streamlined CEQA Projects. Rules 8.700–8.705.

Chap. 2. Appeals Under Code of Civil Procedure Section 1294.4 From an Order Dismissing or Denying a Petition to Compel Arbitration. Rules 8.710–8.717.

Chap. 3. Miscellaneous Writs. Rules 8.720–8.730.

Chapter 1
Review of California Environmental Quality Act Cases Involving Streamlined CEQA Projects

Title 8, Appellate Rules—Division 3, Rules Relating to Miscellaneous Appeals and Writ Proceedings—Chapter 1, Review of California Environmental Quality Act Cases Involving Streamlined CEQA Projects amended effective March 11, 2022; adopted effective July 1, 2014; previously amended effective January 1, 2017; previously renumbered from chapter 11 effective April 25, 2019.

Rule 8.700. Definitions and application
Rule 8.701. Filing and service
Rule 8.702. Appeals
Rule 8.703. Writ proceedings
Rule 8.705. Court of Appeal costs in certain streamlined CEQA projects

Rule 8.700. Definitions and application

(a) Definitions

As used in this chapter:

(1) A "streamlined CEQA project" means any project within the definitions stated in (2) through (8).

(2) An "environmental leadership development project" or "leadership project" means a project certified by the Governor under Public Resources Code sections 21182–21184.

(3) The "Sacramento entertainment and sports center project" or "Sacramento arena project" means an entertainment and sports center project as defined by Public Resources Code section 21168.6.6, for which the proponent provided notice of election to proceed under that statute described in section 21168.6.6(j)(1).

(4) An "Oakland sports and mixed-use project" or "Oakland ballpark project" means a project as defined in Public Resources Code section 21168.6.7 and certified by the Governor under that section.

(5) An "Inglewood arena project" means a project as defined in Public Resources Code section 21168.6.8 and certified by the Governor under that section.

(6) An "expanded capitol building annex project" means a state capitol building annex project, annex project-related work, or state office building project as defined by Public Resources Code section 21189.50.

(7) An "Old Town Center transit and transportation facilities project" or "Old Town Center project" means a project as defined in Public Resources Code section 21189.70.

(8) An "environmental leadership transit project" means a project as defined in Public Resources Code section 21168.6.9.

(Subd (a) amended effective January 1, 2023; adopted effective July 1, 2014; previously amended effective January 1, 2017, and March 11, 2022.)

(b) Proceedings governed

The rules in this chapter govern appeals and writ proceedings in the Court of Appeal to review a superior court judgment or order in an action or proceeding brought to attack, review, set aside, void, or annul the certification of the environmental impact report or the granting of any project approvals for a streamlined CEQA project.

(Subd (b) amended effective March 11, 2022; adopted effective July 1, 2014; previously amended effective January 1, 2017.)

Rule 8.700 amended effective January 1, 2023; adopted effective July 1, 2014; previously amended effective January 1, 2017, and March 11, 2022.

Rule 8.701. Filing and service

(a) Service

Except when the court orders otherwise under (b) or as otherwise provided by law, all documents that the rules in this chapter require be served on the parties must be served by personal delivery, electronic service, express mail, or other means consistent with Code of Civil Procedure sections 1010, 1011, 1012, and 1013 and reasonably calculated to ensure delivery of the document to the parties not later than the close of the business day after the document is filed or lodged with the court.

(Subd (a) adopted effective July 1, 2014.)

(b) Electronic filing and service

(1) In accordance with rule 8.71, all parties except self-represented parties are required to file all documents electronically except as otherwise provided by these rules, the local rules of the reviewing court, or court order. Notwithstanding rule 8.71(b), a court may order a self-represented party to file documents electronically.

(2) All documents must be served electronically on parties who have consented to electronic service or who are otherwise required by law or court order to accept electronic service. All parties represented by counsel are deemed to have consented to electronic service. All self-represented parties may so consent.

(Subd (b) amended effective January 1, 2017; adopted effective July 1, 2014.)

(c) Exemption from extension of time

The extension of time provided in Code of Civil Procedure section 1010.6 for service completed by electronic means does not apply to any service in actions governed by these rules.

(Subd (c) adopted effective July 1, 2014.)

Rule 8.701 amended effective January 1, 2017; adopted effective July 1, 2014.

Rule 8.702. Appeals

(a) Application of general rules for civil appeals

Except as otherwise provided by the rules in this chapter, rules 8.100–8.278, relating to civil appeals, apply to appeals under this chapter.

(Subd (a) adopted effective July 1, 2014.)

(b) Notice of appeal

(1) *Time to appeal*

The notice of appeal must be served and filed on or before the earlier of:

(A) Five court days after the superior court clerk serves on the party filing the notice of appeal a document entitled "Notice of Entry" of judgment or a filed-endorsed copy of the judgment, showing the date either was served; or

(B) Five court days after the party filing the notice of appeal serves or is served by a party with a document entitled "Notice of Entry" of judgment or a filed-endorsed copy of the judgment, accompanied by proof of service.

(2) *Contents of notice of appeal*

The notice of appeal must:

(A) State that the superior court judgment or order being appealed is governed by the rules in this chapter;

(B) Indicate whether the judgment or order pertains to a streamlined CEQA project;

(C) If the judgment or order being appealed pertains to an environmental leadership development project, an Oakland ballpark project, or an Inglewood arena project, provide notice that the person or entity that applied for certification or approval of the project as such a project must make the payments required by rule 8.705; and

(D) If the judgment or order being appealed pertains to an environmental leadership transit project, provide notice that the project applicant must make the payments required by rule 8.705.

(Subd (b) amended effective January 1, 2023; adopted effective July 1, 2014; previously amended effective January 1, 2016, January 1, 2017, and March 11, 2022.)

(c) Extending the time to appeal

(1) *Motion for new trial*

If any party serves and files a valid notice of intention to move for a new trial or, under rule 3.2237, a valid motion for a new trial and that motion is denied, the time to appeal from the judgment is extended for all parties until the earlier of:

(A) Five court days after the superior court clerk or a party serves an order denying the motion or a notice of entry of that order; or

(B) Five court days after denial of the motion by operation of law.

(2) *Motion to vacate judgment*

If, within the time prescribed by subdivision (b) to appeal from the judgment, any party serves and files a valid notice of intention to move—or a valid motion—to vacate the judgment and that motion is denied, the time to appeal from the judgment is extended for all parties until five court days after the superior court clerk or a party serves an order denying the motion or a notice of entry of that order.

(3) *Motion to reconsider appealable order*

If any party serves and files a valid motion to reconsider an appealable order under Code of Civil Procedure section 1008, subdivision (a), the time to appeal from that order is extended for all parties until five court days after the superior court clerk or a party serves an order denying the motion or a notice of entry of that order.

(4) *Cross-appeal*

If an appellant timely appeals from a judgment or appealable order, the time for any other party to appeal from the same judgment or order is extended until five court days after the superior court clerk serves notification of the first appeal.

(Subd (c) adopted effective July 1, 2014.)

(d) Record on appeal

(1) *Record of written documents*

The record of the written documents from the superior court proceedings other than the administrative record must be in the form of a joint appendix or separate appellant's and respondent's appendixes under rule 8.124.

(2) *Record of the oral proceedings*

(A) The appellant must serve and file with its notice of appeal a notice designating the record under rule 8.121 specifying whether the appellant elects to proceed with or without a record of the oral proceedings in the trial court. If the appellant elects to proceed with a record of the oral proceedings in the trial court, the notice must designate a reporter's transcript.

(B) Any party that submits a copy of a Transcript Reimbursement Fund application in lieu of a deposit under rule 8.130(b)(3) must serve all other parties with notice of this submission when the party serves its notice of designation of the record. Within five days after service of this notice, any other party may submit to the trial court the required deposit for the reporter's transcript under rule 8.130(b)(1), the reporter's written waiver of the deposit under rule 8.130(b)(3)(A), or a certified transcript of all of the proceedings designated by the party under rule 8.130(b)(3)(C).

(C) Within 10 days after the superior court notifies the court reporter to prepare the transcript under rule 8.130(d)(2), the reporter must prepare and certify an original of the transcript and file the original and required number of copies in superior court.

(D) If the appellant does not present its notice of designation as required under (A) or if any designating party does not submit the required deposit for the reporter's transcript under rule 8.130(b)(1) or a permissible substitute under rule 8.130(b)(3) with its notice of designation or otherwise fails to timely do another act required to procure the record, the superior court clerk must serve the defaulting party with a notice indicating that the party must do the required act within two court days of service of the clerk's notice or the reviewing court may impose one of the following sanctions:

(i) If the defaulting party is the appellant, the court may dismiss the appeal; or

(ii) If the defaulting party is the respondent, the court may proceed with the appeal on the record designated by the appellant.

(Subd (d) adopted effective July 1, 2014.)

(e) Superior court clerk duties

Within five court days following the filing of a notice of appeal under this rule, the superior court clerk must:

(1) Serve the following on each party:

(A) Notification of the filing of the notice of appeal; and

(B) A copy of the register of actions, if any.

(2) Transmit the following to the reviewing court clerk:

(A) A copy of the notice of appeal;

(B) A copy of the appellant's notice designating the record; and

(C) An electronic copy of the administrative record.

(Subd (e) adopted effective July 1, 2014.)

(f) Briefing

(1) *Electronic filing*

Unless otherwise ordered by the reviewing court, all briefs must be electronically filed.

(2) *Time to serve and file briefs*

Unless otherwise ordered by the reviewing court:

(A) An appellant must serve and file its opening brief within 25 days after the notice of appeal is served and filed.

(B) A respondent must serve and file its brief within 25 days after the appellant files its opening brief.

(C) An appellant must serve and file its reply brief, if any, within 15 days after the respondent files its brief.

(3) *Contents and form of briefs*

(A) The briefs must comply as nearly as possible with rule 8.204.

(B) If a designated reporter's transcript has not been filed at least 5 days before the date by which a brief must be filed, an initial version of the brief may be served and filed in which references to a matter in the reporter's transcript are not supported by a citation to the volume and page number of the reporter's transcript where the matter appears. Within 10 days after the reporter's transcript is filed, a revised version of the brief must be served and filed in which all references to a matter in the reporter's transcript must be supported by a citation to the volume and page number of the reporter's transcript where the matter appears.

(C) Unless otherwise ordered by the court, within 5 days after filing its brief, each party must submit an electronic version of the brief that contains hyperlinks to material cited in the brief, including electronically searchable copies of the record on appeal, cited decisions, and the parties' other briefs. Such briefs must comply with any local requirements of the reviewing court relating to e-briefs.

(4) *Extensions of time to file briefs*

If the parties stipulate to extend the time to file a brief under rule 8.212(b), they are deemed to have agreed that the statutorily prescribed time for resolving the action may be extended by the stipulated number of days of the extension for filing the brief and, to that extent, to have waived any objection to noncompliance with the deadlines for completing review stated in Public Resources Code sections 21168.6.6–21168.6.9, 21185, 21189.51, and 21189.70.3 for the duration of the stipulated extension.

(5) *Failure to file brief*

If a party fails to timely file an appellant's opening brief or a respondent's brief, the reviewing court clerk must serve the party with a notice indicating that if the required brief is not filed within two court days of service of the clerk's notice, the court may impose one of the following sanctions:

(A) If the brief is an appellant's opening brief, the court may dismiss the appeal;

(B) If the brief is a respondent's brief, the court may decide the appeal on the record, the opening brief, and any oral argument by the appellant; or

(C) Any other sanction that the court finds appropriate.

(Subd (f) amended effective January 1, 2023; adopted effective July 1, 2014; previously amended effective January 1, 2017, and March 11, 2022.)

(g) Oral argument

Unless otherwise ordered by the reviewing court, oral argument will be held within 45 days after the last reply brief is filed. The reviewing court clerk must send a notice of the time and place of oral argument to all parties at least 15 days before the argument date. The presiding justice may shorten the notice period for good cause; in that event, the clerk must immediately notify the parties by telephone or other expeditious method.

(Subd (g) adopted effective July 1, 2014.)

Rule 8.702 amended effective January 1, 2023; adopted effective July 1, 2014; previously amended effective January 1, 2016, January 1, 2017, and March 11, 2022.

Advisory Committee Comment

Subdivision (b). It is very important to note that the time period to file a notice of appeal under this rule is the same time period for filing most postjudgment motions in a case regarding the Sacramento arena project, and in a case regarding any other streamlined CEQA project, the deadline for filing a notice of appeal may be earlier than the deadline for filing a motion for a new trial, a motion for reconsideration, or a motion to vacate the judgment.

Rule 8.703. Writ proceedings

(a) Application of general rules for writ proceedings

Except as otherwise provided by the rules in this chapter, rules 8.485–8.493—relating to writs of mandate, certiorari, and prohibition in the Supreme Court and Court of Appeal—apply to writ proceedings under this chapter.

(Subd (a) adopted effective July 1, 2014.)

(b) Petition

(1) *Time for filing petition*

A petition for a writ challenging a superior court judgment or order governed by the rules in this chapter must be served and filed on or before the earliest of:

(A) Thirty days after the superior court clerk serves on the party filing the petition a document entitled "Notice of Entry" of judgment or order, or a filed-endorsed copy of the judgment or order, showing the date either was served; or

(B) Thirty days after the party filing the petition serves or is served by a party with a document entitled "Notice of Entry" of judgment or order, or a filed-endorsed copy of the judgment or order, accompanied by proof of service.

(2) *Contents of petition*

In addition to any other applicable requirements, the petition must:

(A) State that the superior court judgment or order being challenged is governed by the rules in this chapter;

(B) Indicate whether the judgment or order pertains to a streamlined CEQA project;

(C) If the judgment or order pertains to an environmental leadership development project, an Oakland ballpark project, or an Inglewood arena project, provide notice that the person or entity that applied for certification of the project as such a project must make the payments required by rule 8.705; and

(D) If the judgment or order pertains to an environmental leadership transit project, provide notice that the project applicant must make the payments required by rule 8.705.

(Subd (b) amended effective January 1, 2023; adopted effective July 1, 2014; previously amended effective January 1, 2016, January 1, 2017, and March 11, 2022.)

Rule 8.703 amended effective January 1, 2023; adopted effective July 1, 2014; previously amended effective January 1, 2016, January 1, 2017, and March 11, 2022.

Rule 8.705. Court of Appeal costs in certain streamlined CEQA projects

In fulfillment of the provisions in Public Resources Code sections 21168.6.7, 21168.6.8, 21168.6.9, and 21183 regarding payment of the Court of Appeal's costs with respect to cases concerning environmental leadership development, environmental leadership transit, Oakland ballpark, and Inglewood arena projects:

(1) Within 10 days after service of the notice of appeal or petition in a case concerning an environmental leadership development project, the person or entity that applied for certification of the project as an environmental leadership development project must pay a fee of $215,000 to the Court of Appeal.

(2) Within 10 days after service of the notice of appeal or petition in a case concerning an environmental leadership transit project, the project applicant must pay a fee of $215,000 to the Court of Appeal.

(3) Within 10 days after service of the notice of appeal or petition in a case concerning an Oakland ballpark project or Inglewood arena project, the person or entity that applied for certification of the project as an Oakland ballpark project or Inglewood arena project must pay a fee of $140,000 to the Court of Appeal.

(4) If the Court of Appeal incurs the costs of any special master appointed by the Court of Appeal in the case or of any contract personnel retained by the Court of Appeal to work on the case, the person or entity that applied for certification of the project or the project applicant must also pay, within 10 days of being ordered by the court, those incurred or estimated costs.

(5) If the party fails to timely pay the fee or costs specified in this rule, the court may impose sanctions that the court finds appropriate after notifying the party and providing the party with an opportunity to pay the required fee or costs.

(6) Any fee or cost paid under this rule is not a recoverable cost.

Rule 8.705 amended effective January 1, 2023; adopted effective July 1, 2014; previously amended effective March 11, 2022.

Chapter 2
Appeals Under Code of Civil Procedure Section 1294.4 From an Order Dismissing or Denying a Petition to Compel Arbitration

Title 8, Appellate Rules—Division 3, Rules Relating to Miscellaneous Appeals and Writ Proceedings—Chapter 2, Appeals Under Code of Civil Procedure Section 1294.4 From an Order Dismissing or Denying a Petition to Compel Arbitration renumbered from chapter 12 effective April 25, 2019; adopted effective July 1, 2017.

Rule 8.710. Application
Rule 8.711. Filing and service
Rule 8.712. Notice of appeal
Rule 8.713. Record on appeal
Rule 8.714. Superior court clerk duties
Rule 8.715. Briefing
Rule 8.716. Oral argument
Rule 8.717. Extensions of time

Rule 8.710. Application

(a) Application of the rules in this chapter

The rules in this chapter govern appeals under Code of Civil Procedure section 1294.4 from a superior court order dismissing or denying a petition to compel arbitration.

(Subd (a) adopted effective July 1, 2017.)

(b) Application of general rules for civil appeals

Except as otherwise provided by the rules in this chapter, rules 8.100–8.278, relating to civil appeals, apply to appeals under this chapter.

(Subd (b) adopted effective July 1, 2017.)

Rule 8.710 adopted effective July 1, 2017.

Rule 8.711. Filing and service

(a) Method of service

Except as otherwise provided by law:

(1) All documents must be served electronically on parties who have consented to electronic service or who are otherwise required by law or court order to accept electronic service. All parties represented by counsel are deemed to have consented to electronic service. All self-represented parties may so consent.

(2) All documents that the rules in this chapter require be served on the parties that are not served electronically must be served by personal delivery, express mail, or other means consistent with Code of Civil Procedure sections 1010, 1011, 1012, and 1013, and reasonably calculated to ensure delivery of the document to the parties not later than the close of the business day after the document is filed or lodged with the court.

(Subd (a) adopted effective July 1, 2017.)

(b) Electronic filing

In accordance with rule 8.71, all parties except self-represented parties are required to file all documents electronically except as otherwise provided by these rules, the local rules of the reviewing court, or court order. Notwithstanding rule 8.71(b), in appeals governed by this chapter, a court may order a self-represented party to file documents electronically.

(Subd (b) adopted effective July 1, 2017.)

(c) Exemption from extension of time

The extension of time provided in Code of Civil Procedure section 1010.6 for service completed by electronic means does not apply to any service in actions governed by these rules.

(Subd (c) adopted effective July 1, 2017.)

Rule 8.711 adopted effective July 1, 2017.

Rule 8.712. Notice of appeal

(a) Contents of notice of appeal

(1) The notice of appeal must state that the superior court order being appealed is governed by the rules in this chapter.

(2) Copies of the order being appealed and the order granting preference under Code of Civil Procedure section 36 must be attached to the notice of appeal.

(Subd (a) adopted effective July 1, 2017.)

(b) Time to appeal

The notice of appeal must be served and filed on or before the earlier of:

(1) Twenty days after the superior court clerk serves on the party filing the notice of appeal a document entitled "Notice of Entry" of the order dismissing or denying a petition to compel arbitration or a filed-endorsed copy of the order, showing the date either was served; or

(2) Twenty days after the party filing the notice of appeal serves or is served by a party with a document entitled "Notice of Entry" of the order dismissing or denying a petition to compel arbitration or a filed-endorsed copy of the order, accompanied by proof of service.

(Subd (b) adopted effective July 1, 2017.)

(c) Extending the time to appeal

(1) *Motion to reconsider appealable order*

If any party serves and files a valid motion under subdivision (a) of Code of Civil Procedure section 1008 to reconsider the order dismissing or denying a petition to compel arbitration, the time to appeal from that order is extended for all parties until five court days after the superior court clerk or a party serves an order denying the motion or a notice of entry of that order.

(2) *Cross-appeal*

If an appellant timely appeals from the order dismissing or denying a petition to compel arbitration, the time for any other party to appeal from the same order is extended until five court days after the superior court clerk serves notification of the first appeal.

(Subd (c) adopted effective July 1, 2017.)

Rule 8.712 adopted effective July 1, 2017.

Rule 8.713. Record on appeal

(a) Record of written documents

The record of the written documents from the superior court proceedings must be in the form of a joint appendix or separate appellant's and respondent's appendixes under rule 8.124.

(Subd (a) adopted effective July 1, 2017.)

(b) Record of the oral proceedings

(1) The appellant must serve and file with its notice of appeal a notice designating the record under rule 8.121, specifying whether the appellant elects to proceed with or without a record of the oral proceedings in the trial court. If the appellant elects to proceed with a record of the oral proceedings in the trial court, the notice must designate a reporter's transcript.

(2) Within 10 days after the superior court notifies the court reporter to prepare the transcript under rule 8.130(d)(2), the reporter must prepare and certify an original of the transcript and file the original and required number of copies in superior court.

(3) If the appellant does not present its notice of designation as required under (1) or if any designating party does not submit the required deposit for the reporter's transcript under rule 8.130(b)(1) or a permissible substitute under rule 8.130(b)(3) with its notice of designation or otherwise fails to timely do another act required to procure the record, the superior court clerk must serve the defaulting party with a notice indicating that the party must do the required act within two court days of service of the clerk's notice or the reviewing court may impose one of the following sanctions:

(A) If the defaulting party is the appellant, the court may dismiss the appeal; or

(B) If the defaulting party is the respondent, the court may proceed with the appeal on the record designated by the appellant.

(4) Within 10 days after the record is filed in the reviewing court, a party that has not purchased its own copy of the record may request the appellant, in writing, to lend it the appellant's copy of the record at the time that the appellant serves its final opening brief under rule 8.715(b)(2). The borrowing party must return the copy of the record when it serves its brief or the time to file its brief has expired. The cost of sending the copy of the record to and from the borrowing party shall be treated as a cost on appeal under rule 8.891(d)(1)(B).

(Subd (b) adopted effective July 1, 2017.)

Rule 8.713 adopted effective July 1, 2017.

Rule 8.714. Superior court clerk duties

Within five court days following the filing of a notice of appeal under this rule, the superior court clerk must:

(1) Serve the following on each party:

(A) Notification of the filing of the notice of appeal; and

(B) A copy of the register of actions, if any.

(2) Transmit the following to the reviewing court clerk:

(A) A copy of the notice of appeal, with the copies of the order being appealed and the order granting preference under Code of Civil Procedure section 36 attached; and

(B) A copy of the appellant's notice designating the record.

Rule 8.714 adopted effective July 1, 2017.

Rule 8.715. Briefing

(a) Time to serve and file briefs

Unless otherwise ordered by the reviewing court:

(1) An appellant must serve and file its opening brief within 10 days after the notice of appeal is served and filed;

(2) A respondent must serve and file its brief within 25 days after the appellant files its opening brief; and

(3) An appellant must serve and file its reply brief, if any, within 15 days after the respondent files its brief.

(Subd (a) adopted effective July 1, 2017.)

(b) Contents and form of briefs

(1) The briefs must comply as nearly as possible with rule 8.204.

(2) If a designated reporter's transcript has not been filed at least 5 days before the date by which a brief must be filed, an initial version of the brief may be served and filed in which references to a matter in the reporter's transcript are not supported by a citation to the volume and page number of the reporter's transcript where the matter appears. Within 10 days after the reporter's transcript is filed, a revised version of the brief must be served and filed in which all references to a matter in the reporter's transcript must be supported by a citation to the volume and page number of the reporter's transcript where the matter appears. No other changes to the initial version of the brief are permitted.

(Subd (b) adopted effective July 1, 2017.)

(c) Stipulated extensions of time to file briefs

If the parties stipulate to extend the time to file a brief under rule 8.212(b), they are deemed to have agreed that such an extension will promote the interests of justice, that the time for resolving the action may be extended beyond 100 days by the number of days by which the parties stipulated to extend the time for filing the brief, and that to that extent, they have waived any objection to noncompliance with the deadlines for completing review stated in Code of Civil Procedure section 1294.4 for the duration of the stipulated extension.

(Subd (c) adopted effective July 1, 2017.)

(d) Failure to file brief

If a party fails to timely file an appellant's opening brief or a respondent's brief, the reviewing court clerk must serve the party with a notice indicating that if the required brief is not filed within two court days of service of the clerk's notice, the court may impose one of the following sanctions:

(1) If the brief is an appellant's opening brief, the court may dismiss the appeal;

(2) If the brief is a respondent's brief, the court may decide the appeal on the record, the opening brief, and any oral argument by the appellant; or

(3) Any other sanction that the court finds appropriate.

(Subd (d) adopted effective July 1, 2017.)

Rule 8.715 adopted effective July 1, 2017.

Rule 8.716. Oral argument

The reviewing court clerk must send a notice of the time and place of oral argument to all parties at least 10 days before the argument date. The presiding justice may shorten the notice period for good cause; in that event, the clerk must immediately notify the parties by telephone or other expeditious method.

Rule 8.716 adopted effective July 1, 2017.

Rule 8.717. Extensions of time

The Court of Appeal may grant an extension of the time in appeals governed by this chapter only if good cause is shown and the extension will promote the interests of justice.

Rule 8.717 adopted effective July 1, 2017.

Chapter 3
Miscellaneous Writs

Title 8, Appellate Rules—Division 3, Rules Relating to Miscellaneous Appeals and Writ Proceedings—Chapter 3, Miscellaneous Writs amended and renumbered as chapter 3 effective April 25, 2019; adopted as chapter 7 effective January 1, 2007; amended and renumbered as chapter 8 effective January 1, 2009; previously amended effective July 1, 2012.

Rule 8.720. Review of Workers' Compensation Appeals Board cases
Rule 8.724. Review of Public Utilities Commission cases
Rule 8.728. Review of Agricultural Labor Relations Board and Public Employment Relations Board cases
Rule 8.730. Filing, modification, and finality of decision; remittitur

Rule 8.720. Review of Workers' Compensation Appeals Board cases

(a) Petition

(1) A petition to review an order, award, or decision of the Workers' Compensation Appeals Board must include:

(A) The order, award, or decision to be reviewed; and

(B) The workers' compensation judge's minutes of hearing and summary of evidence, findings and opinion on decision, and report and recommendation on the petition for reconsideration.

(2) If the petition claims that the board's ruling is not supported by substantial evidence, it must fairly state and attach copies of all the relevant material evidence.

(3) The petition must be verified.

(4) The petition must be accompanied by proof of service of a copy of the petition on the Secretary of the Workers' Compensation Appeals Board in San Francisco, or two copies if the petition is served in paper form, and one copy on each party who appeared in the action and whose interest is adverse to the petitioner. Service on the board's local district office is not required.

(Subd (a) amended effective January 1, 2018; previously amended effective January 1, 2007, and January 1, 2016.)

(b) Answer and reply

(1) Within 25 days after the petition is filed, the board or any real party in interest may serve and file an answer and any relevant exhibits not included in the petition.

(2) Within 15 days after an answer is filed, the petitioner may serve and file a reply.

(c) Certificate of Interested Entities or Persons

(1) Each party other than the board must comply with the requirements of rule 8.208 concerning serving and filing a Certificate of Interested Entities or Persons.

(2) The petitioner's certificate must be included in the petition and the real party in interest's certificate must be included in the answer. The certificate must appear after the cover and before the tables.

(3) If a party fails to file a certificate as required under (1) and (2), the clerk must notify the party in writing that the party must file the certificate within 10 days after the clerk's notice is sent and that failure to comply will result in one of the following sanctions:

(A) If the party is the petitioner, the court will strike the petition; or

(B) If the party is the real party in interest, the court will strike the document.

(4) If the party fails to comply with the notice under (3), the court may impose the sanctions specified in the notice.

(Subd (c) amended effective January 1, 2016; adopted effective July 1, 2006; previously amended effective January 1, 2007.)

Rule 8.720 renumbered effective April 25, 2019; repealed and adopted as rule 57 effective January 1, 2005; previously amended effective July 1, 2006, January 1, 2016, and January 1, 2018; previously amended and renumbered as rule 8.494 effective January 1, 2007; previously renumbered as rule 8.495 effective January 1, 2009.

Advisory Committee Comment

Subdivision (a). Subdivision (a)(3) specifies that the petition must be served on the Secretary of the Workers' Compensation Appeals Board in San Francisco. Neither the petition nor a courtesy copy should be served on the local district office of the board.

Subdivision (b). To clarify that a respondent may rely on exhibits filed with the petition without duplicating them in the answer, (b)(1) specifies that exhibits filed with an answer must be limited to exhibits "not included in the petition."

Rule 8.724. Review of Public Utilities Commission cases

(a) Petition

(1) A petition to review an order or decision of the Public Utilities Commission must be verified and must be served on the executive director and general counsel of the commission and any real parties in interest.

(2) A real party in interest is one who was a party of record to the proceeding and took a position adverse to the petitioner.

(b) Answer and reply

(1) Within 35 days after the petition is filed, the commission or any real party in interest may serve and file an answer.

(2) Within 25 days after an answer is filed, the petitioner may serve and file a reply.

(c) Certificate of Interested Entities or Persons

(1) Each party other than the commission must comply with the requirements of rule 8.208 concerning serving and filing a Certificate of Interested Entities or Persons.

(2) The petitioner's certificate must be included in the petition and the real party in interest's certificate must be included in the answer. The certificate must appear after the cover and before the tables.

(3) If a party fails to file a certificate as required under (1) and (2), the clerk must notify the party in writing that the party must file the certificate within 10 days after the clerk's notice is sent and that failure to comply will result in one of the following sanctions:

(A) If the party is the petitioner, the court will strike the petition; or

(B) If the party is the real party in interest, the court will strike the document.

(4) If the party fails to comply with the notice under (3), the court may impose the sanctions specified in the notice.

(Subd (c) amended effective January 1, 2016; adopted effective July 1, 2006; previously amended effective January 1, 2007.)

Rule 8.724 renumbered effective April 25, 2019; repealed and adopted as rule 58 effective January 1, 2005; previously amended effective July 1, 2006, and January 1, 2016; previously amended and renumbered as rule 8.496 effective January 1, 2007.

Advisory Committee Comment

Subdivision (b). A party other than the petitioner who files an answer may be required to pay a filing fee under Government Code section 68926 if the answer is the first document filed in the writ proceeding in the reviewing court by that party. See rule 8.25(c).

Rule 8.728. Review of Agricultural Labor Relations Board and Public Employment Relations Board cases

(a) Petition

(1) A petition to review an order or decision of the Agricultural Labor Relations Board or the Public Employment Relations Board must be filed in the Court of Appeal and served on the executive secretary of the Agricultural Labor Relations Board or the general counsel of the Public Employment Relations Board in Sacramento and on any real parties in interest.

(2) A real party in interest is a party of record to the proceeding.

(3) The petition must be verified.

(b) Record

Within the time permitted by statute, the board must file the certified record of the proceedings and simultaneously file and serve on all parties an index to that record.

(c) Briefs

(1) The petitioner must serve and file its brief within 35 days after the index is filed.

(2) Within 35 days after the petitioner's brief is filed, the board must—and any real party in interest may—serve and file a respondent's brief.

(3) Within 25 days after the respondent's brief is filed, the petitioner may serve and file a reply brief.

(d) Certificate of Interested Entities or Persons

(1) Each party other than the board must comply with the requirements of rule 8.208 concerning serving and filing a Certificate of Interested Entities or Persons.

(2) The petitioner's certificate must be included in the petition and the real party in interest's certificate must be included in the answer. The certificate must appear after the cover and before the tables.

(3) If a party fails to file a certificate as required under (1) and (2), the clerk must notify the party in writing that the party must file the certificate within 10 days after the clerk's notice is sent and that failure to comply will result in one of the following sanctions:

(A) If the party is the petitioner, the court will strike the petition; or

(B) If the party is the real party in interest, the court will strike the document.

(4) If the party fails to comply with the notice under (3), the court may impose the sanctions specified in the notice.

(Subd (d) amended effective January 1, 2016; adopted effective July 1, 2006; previously amended effective January 1, 2007.)

Rule 8.728 renumbered effective April 25, 2019; repealed and adopted as rule 59 effective January 1, 2005; previously amended effective July 1, 2006, and January 1, 2016; previously amended and renumbered as rule 8.498 effective January 1, 2007.

Advisory Committee Comment

A party other than the petitioner who files an answer or brief may be required to pay a filing fee under Government Code section 68926 if the answer or brief is the first document filed in the writ proceeding in the reviewing court by that party. See rule 8.25(c).

Rule 8.730. Filing, modification, and finality of decision; remittitur

(a) Filing of decisions

Rule 8.264(a) governs the filing of decisions in writ proceedings under this chapter in the Court of Appeal and rule 8.532(a) governs the filing of decisions in the Supreme Court.

(Subd (a) adopted effective January 1, 2011.)

(b) Modification of decisions

Rule 8.264(c) governs the modification of decisions in writ proceedings under this chapter.

(Subd (b) adopted effective January 1, 2011.)

(c) Finality of decision

(1) A court's denial of a petition for a writ under rule 8.720, 8.724, or 8.728 without issuance of a writ of review is final in that court when filed.

(2) Except as otherwise provided in this rule, a decision in a writ proceeding under this chapter is final in that court 30 days after the decision is filed.

(3) If necessary to prevent mootness or frustration of the relief granted or to otherwise promote the interests of justice, the court may order early finality in that court of a decision granting a petition for a writ under this chapter or, except as provided in (1), a decision denying such a petition. The decision may provide for finality in that court on filing or within a stated period of less than 30 days.

(4) If a Court of Appeal certifies its opinion for publication or partial publication after filing its decision and before its decision becomes final in that court, the finality period runs from the filing date of the order for publication.

(5) If an order modifying an opinion changes the appellate judgment, the finality period runs from the filing date of the modification order.

(Subd (c) amended effective April 1, 2023; adopted effective January 1, 2011; previously amended effective July 1, 2012.)

(d) Remittitur

A Court of Appeal must issue a remittitur in a writ proceeding under this chapter except when the court denies the petition under rule 8.720, 8.724, or 8.728 without issuing a writ of review. Rule 8.272(b)–(d) governs issuance of a remittitur in writ proceedings under this chapter.

(Subd (d) amended effective April 1, 2023; adopted as unlettered subd effective January 1, 2008; previously lettered and amended effective January 1, 2011; previously amended effective July 1, 2012.)

Rule 8.730 amended effective April 1, 2023; adopted as rule 8.499 effective January 1, 2008; previously amended effective January 1, 2011, and July 1, 2012; previously renumbered effective April 25, 2019.

Division 4
Rules Relating to the Superior Court Appellate Division

Title 8, Appellate Rules—Division 4, Rules Relating to the Superior Court Appellate Division renumbered from Division 2 effective April 25, 2019; adopted as Division 2 effective January 1, 2009.

Advisory Committee Comment

Division 4. The rules relating to the superior court appellate division begin with Chapter 1, which contains general rules applicable to appeals in all three types of cases within the jurisdiction of the appellate division—limited civil, misdemeanor, and infraction. Because the procedures relating to taking appeals and preparing the record in limited civil, misdemeanor, and infraction appeals differ, there are separate chapters addressing these topics: Chapter 2 addresses taking appeals and record preparation in limited civil cases, and Chapter 3 addresses taking appeals and record preparation in misdemeanor cases. Because the procedures for briefing and rendering decisions are generally the same in limited civil and misdemeanor appeals, Chapter 4 addresses these procedures in appeals of both types of cases. To make the distinct procedures for appeals in infraction proceedings easier to find and understand, these procedures are located in a separate chapter—Chapter 5. Chapter 6 addresses writ proceedings in the appellate division.

Chap. 1. General Rules Applicable to Appellate Division Proceedings. Rules 8.800–8.819.

Chap. 2. Appeals and Records in Limited Civil Cases. Rules 8.820–8.845.

Chap. 3. Appeals and Records in Misdemeanor Cases. Rules 8.850–8.874.

Chap. 4. Briefs, Hearing, and Decision in Limited Civil and Misdemeanor Appeals. Rules 8.880–8.891.

Chap. 5. Appeals in Infraction Cases. Rules 8.900–8.929.

Chap. 6. Writ Proceedings. Rules 8.930–8.936.

Chapter 1
General Rules Applicable to Appellate Division Proceedings

Chapter 1 adopted effective January 1, 2009.

Rule 8.800. Application of division and scope of rules
Rule 8.802. Construction
Rule 8.803. Definitions
Rule 8.804. Requirements for signatures on documents
Rule 8.805. Amendments to rules and statutes
Rule 8.806. Applications
Rule 8.808. Motions
Rule 8.809. Judicial notice
Rule 8.810. Extending time
Rule 8.811. Policies and factors governing extensions of time
Rule 8.812. Relief from default
Rule 8.813. Shortening time
Rule 8.814. Substituting parties; substituting or withdrawing attorneys
Rule 8.815. Form of filed documents
Rule 8.816. Address and other contact information of record; notice of change
Rule 8.817. Service and filing
Rule 8.818. Waiver of fees and costs
Rule 8.819. Sealed records

Rule 8.800. Application of division and scope of rules

(a) Application

The rules in this division apply to:

(1) Appeals in the appellate division of the superior court; and

(2) Writ proceedings, motions, applications, and petitions in the appellate division of the superior court.

(Subd (a) amended and lettered effective January 1, 2016; adopted as unlettered subdivision.)

(b) Scope of rules

The rules in this division apply to documents filed and served electronically as well as in paper form, unless otherwise provided.

(Subd (b) adopted effective January 1, 2016.)

Rule 8.800 amended effective January 1, 2016; adopted effective January 1, 2009.

Rule 8.802. Construction

(a) Construction

The rules in this division must be construed to ensure that the proceedings they govern will be justly and speedily determined.

(Subd (a) adopted effective January 1, 2009.)

(b) Terminology

As used in this division:

(1) "Must" is mandatory;

(2) "May" is permissive;

(3) "May not" means is not permitted to;

(4) "Will" expresses a future contingency or predicts action by a court or person in the ordinary course of events, but does not signify a mandatory duty; and

(5) "Should" expresses a preference or a nonbinding recommendation.

(Subd (b) adopted effective January 1, 2009.)

(c) Construction of additional terms

In the rules:

(1) Each tense (past, present, or future) includes the others;

(2) Each gender (masculine, feminine, or neuter) includes the others;

(3) Each number (singular or plural) includes the other; and

(4) The headings of divisions, chapters, articles, rules, and subdivisions are substantive.

(Subd (c) adopted effective January 1, 2009.)

Rule 8.802 adopted effective January 1, 2009.

Rule 8.803. Definitions

As used in this division, unless the context or subject matter otherwise requires:

(1) "Action" includes special proceeding.

(2) "Case" includes action or proceeding.

(3) "Civil case" means a case prosecuted by one party against another for the declaration, enforcement, or protection of a right or the redress or prevention of a wrong. Civil cases include all cases except criminal cases.

(4) "Unlimited civil cases" and "limited civil cases" are defined in Code of Civil Procedure section 85 et seq.

(5) "Criminal case" means a proceeding by which a party charged with a public offense is accused and brought to trial and punishment.

(6) "Rule" means a rule of the California Rules of Court.

(7) "Local rule" means every rule, regulation, order, policy, form, or standard of general application adopted by a court to govern practice and procedure in that court or by a judge of the court to govern practice or procedure in that judge's courtroom.

(8) "Presiding judge" includes the acting presiding judge or the judge designated by the presiding judge.

(9) "Judge" includes, as applicable, a judge of the superior court, a commissioner, or a temporary judge.

(10) "Person" includes a corporation or other legal entity as well as a natural person.

(11) "Appellant" means the appealing party.

(12) "Respondent" means the adverse party.

(13) "Party" is a person appearing in an action. Parties include both self-represented persons and persons represented by an attorney of record. "Party," "applicant," "petitioner," or any other designation of a party includes the party's attorney of record.

(14) "Attorney" means a member of the State Bar of California.

(15) "Counsel" means an attorney.

(16) "Prosecuting attorney" means the city attorney, county counsel, or district attorney prosecuting an infraction or misdemeanor case.

(17) "Complaint" includes a citation.

(18) "Service" means service in the manner prescribed by a statute or rule.

(19) "Declaration" includes "affidavit."

(20) "Trial court" means the superior court from which an appeal is taken.

(21) "Reviewing court" means the appellate division of the superior court.

(22) "Judgment" includes any judgment or order that may be appealed.

(23) "Attach" or "attachment" may refer to either physical attachment or electronic attachment, as appropriate.

(24) "Copy" or "copies" may refer to electronic copies, as appropriate.

(25) "Cover" includes the cover page of a document filed electronically.

(26) "Written" and "writing" include electronically created written materials, whether or not those materials are printed on paper.

Rule 8.803 amended and renumbered effective January 1, 2016; adopted as rule 8.804 effective January 1, 2009; previously amended effective January 1, 2014.

Advisory Committee Comment

Item (18). See rule 1.21 for general requirements relating to service, including proof of service.

Rule 8.804. Requirements for signatures on documents

Except as otherwise provided, or required by order of the court, signatures on electronically filed documents must comply with the requirements of rule 8.77.

Rule 8.804 adopted effective January 1, 2016.

Rule 8.805. Amendments to rules and statutes

(a) Amendments to rules

Only the Judicial Council may amend these rules, except the rules in division 7, which may be amended only by the Supreme Court. An amendment by the Judicial Council must be published in the advance pamphlets of the Official Reports and takes effect on the date ordered by the Judicial Council.

(Subd (a) amended effective April 1, 2023; adopted effective January 1, 2009.)

(b) Amendments to statutes

In these rules, a reference to a statute includes any subsequent amendment to the statute.

(Subd (b) adopted effective January 1, 2009.)

Rule 8.805 amended effective April 1, 2023; adopted effective January 1, 2009.

Rule 8.806. Applications

(a) Service and filing

Except as these rules provide otherwise, parties must serve and file all applications, including applications to extend time to file records, briefs, or other documents and applications to shorten time. Applications to extend the time to prepare the record on appeal may be filed in either the trial court or the appellate division. All other applications must be filed in the appellate division. For good cause, the presiding judge of the court where the application was filed, or his or her designee, may excuse advance service.

(Subd (a) adopted effective January 1, 2009.)

(b) Contents

The application must:

(1) State facts showing good cause to grant the application; and

(2) Identify any previous applications relating to the same subject filed by any party in the same appeal or writ proceeding.

(Subd (b) adopted effective January 1, 2009.)

(c) Envelopes

If any party or parties in the case are served in paper form, an application must be accompanied by addressed, postage-prepaid envelopes for the clerk's use in mailing copies of the order on the application to those parties.

(Subd (c) amended effective January 1, 2016; adopted effective January 1, 2009.)

(d) Disposition

Unless the court determines otherwise, the presiding judge of the court in which the application was filed, or his or her designee, may rule on the application.

(Subd (d) adopted effective January 1, 2009.)

Rule 8.806 amended effective January 1, 2016; adopted effective January 1, 2009.

Advisory Committee Comment

Subdivision (a). See rule 1.21 for the meaning of "serve and file," including the requirements for proof of service.

Subdivisions (a) and (d). These provisions permit the presiding judge to designate another judge, such as the trial judge, to handle applications.

Rule 8.808. Motions

(a) Motion and opposition

(1) Except as these rules provide otherwise, to make a motion in the appellate division a party must serve and file a written motion, stating the grounds and the relief requested and identifying any documents on which it is based.

(2) A motion must be accompanied by a memorandum and, if it is based on matters outside the record, by declarations or other supporting evidence.

(3) Any opposition to the motion must be served and filed within 15 days after the motion is filed.

(Subd (a) adopted effective January 1, 2009.)

(b) Disposition

(1) The court may rule on a motion at any time after an opposition or other response is filed or the time to oppose has expired.

(2) On a party's request or its own motion, the appellate division may place a motion on calendar for a hearing. The clerk must promptly send each party a notice of the date and time of the hearing.

(Subd (b) adopted effective January 1, 2009.)
Rule 8.808 adopted effective January 1, 2009.

Advisory Committee Comment

Subdivision (a)(1). See rule 1.21 for the meaning of "serve and file," including the requirements for proof of service.

Subdivision (b). Although a party may request a hearing on a motion, a hearing will be held only if the court determines that one is needed.

Rule 8.809. Judicial notice

(a) Motion required

(1) To obtain judicial notice by a reviewing court under Evidence Code section 459, a party must serve and file a separate motion with a proposed order.

(2) The motion must state:

(A) Why the matter to be noticed is relevant to the appeal;

(B) Whether the matter to be noticed was presented to the trial court and, if so, whether judicial notice was taken by that court;

(C) If judicial notice of the matter was not taken by the trial court, why the matter is subject to judicial notice under Evidence Code section 451, 452, or 453; and

(D) Whether the matter to be noticed relates to proceedings occurring after the order or judgment that is the subject of the appeal.

(Subd (a) amended effective January 1, 2013; adopted effective January 1, 2011.)

(b) Copy of matter to be judicially noticed

If the matter to be noticed is not in the record, the party must serve and file a copy with the motion or explain why it is not practicable to do so. The pages of the copy of the matter or matters to be judicially noticed must be consecutively numbered, beginning with the number 1.

(Subd (b) amended effective January 1, 2015; adopted effective January 1, 2011.)

Rule 8.809 amended effective January 1, 2015; adopted effective January 1, 2011; previously amended effective January 1, 2013.

Rule 8.810. Extending time

(a) Computing time

The Code of Civil Procedure governs computing and extending the time to do any act required or permitted under these rules.

(Subd (a) adopted effective January 1, 2009.)

(b) Extension by trial court

(1) For good cause and except as these rules provide otherwise, the presiding judge of the trial court, or his or her designee, may extend the time to do any act to prepare the record on appeal.

(2) The trial court may not extend:

(A) The time to do an act if that time—including any valid extension—has expired; or

(B) The time for a court reporter to prepare a transcript.

(3) Notwithstanding anything in these rules to the contrary, the trial court may grant an initial extension to any party to do any act to prepare the record on appeal on an ex parte basis.

(Subd (b) amended effective March 1, 2014; adopted effective January 1, 2009.)

(c) Extension by appellate division

For good cause and except as these rules provide otherwise, the presiding judge of the appellate division, or his or her designee, may extend the time to do any act required or permitted under these rules, except the time to file a notice of appeal.

(Subd (c) adopted effective January 1, 2009.)

(d) Application for extension

(1) An application to extend time, including an application requesting an extension of time to prepare a transcript from either a court reporter or a person preparing a transcript of an official electronic recording, must be served on all parties. For good cause, the presiding judge of the appellate division, or his or her designee, may excuse advance service.

(2) The application must include a declaration stating facts, not mere conclusions, that establish good cause for granting the extension. For applications filed by counsel or self-represented litigants, the facts provided to establish good cause must be consistent with the policies and factors stated in rule 8.811.

(3) The application must state:

(A) The due date of the document to be filed;

(B) The length of the extension requested; and

(C) Whether any earlier extensions have been granted and, if so, their lengths.

(Subd (d) amended effective March 1, 2014; adopted effective January 1, 2009.)

(e) Notice to party

(1) In a civil case, counsel must deliver to his or her client or clients a copy of any stipulation or application to extend time that counsel files. Counsel must attach evidence of such delivery to the stipulation or application or certify in the stipulation or application that the copy has been delivered.

(2) The evidence or certification of delivery under (1) need not include the address of the party notified.

(Subd (e) adopted effective January 1, 2009.)

Rule 8.810 amended effective March 1, 2014; adopted effective January 1, 2009.

Advisory Committee Comment

Subdivision (b)(1). This provision permits the presiding judge to designate another judge, such as the trial judge, to handle applications to extend time.

Rule 8.811. Policies and factors governing extensions of time

(a) Policies

(1) The time limits prescribed by these rules should generally be met to ensure expeditious conduct of appellate business and public confidence in the efficient administration of appellate justice.

(2) The effective assistance of counsel to which a party is entitled includes adequate time for counsel to prepare briefs or other documents that fully advance the party's interests. Adequate time also allows the preparation of accurate, clear, concise, and complete submissions that assist the courts.

(3) For a variety of legitimate reasons, counsel or self-represented litigants may not always be able to prepare briefs or other documents within the time specified in the rules of court. To balance the competing policies stated in (1) and (2), applications to extend time in the appellate division must demonstrate good cause under (b). If good cause is shown, the court must extend the time.

(Subd (a) adopted effective January 1, 2009.)

(b) Factors considered

In determining good cause, the court must consider the following factors when applicable:

(1) The degree of prejudice, if any, to any party from a grant or denial of the extension. A party claiming prejudice must support the claim in detail.

(2) In a civil case, the positions of the client and any opponent with regard to the extension.

(3) The length of the record, including the number of relevant trial exhibits. A party relying on this factor must specify the length of the record.

(4) The number and complexity of the issues raised. A party relying on this factor must specify the issues.

(5) Whether there are settlement negotiations and, if so, how far they have progressed and when they might be completed.

(6) Whether the case is entitled to priority.

(7) Whether counsel responsible for preparing the document is new to the case.

(8) Whether other counsel or the client needs additional time to review the document.

(9) Whether counsel or a self-represented party responsible for preparing the document has other time-limited commitments that prevent timely filing of the document. Mere conclusory statements that more time is needed because of other pressing business will not suffice. Good cause

requires a specific showing of other obligations of counsel or a self-represented party that:

(A) Have deadlines that as a practical matter preclude filing the document by the due date without impairing its quality; or

(B) Arise from cases entitled to priority.

(10) Illness of counsel or a self-represented party, a personal emergency, or a planned vacation that counsel or a self-represented party did not reasonably expect to conflict with the due date and cannot reasonably rearrange.

(11) Any other factor that constitutes good cause in the context of the case.

(Subd (b) adopted effective January 1, 2009.)
Rule 8.811 adopted effective January 1, 2009.

Rule 8.812. Relief from default

For good cause, the presiding judge of the appellate division, or his or her designee, may relieve a party from a default for any failure to comply with these rules, except the failure to file a timely notice of appeal.
Rule 8.812 adopted effective January 1, 2009.

Rule 8.813. Shortening time

For good cause and except as these rules provide otherwise, the presiding judge of the appellate division, or his or her designee, may shorten the time to do any act required or permitted under these rules.
Rule 8.813 adopted effective January 1, 2009.

Rule 8.814. Substituting parties; substituting or withdrawing attorneys

(a) Substituting parties

Substitution of parties in an appeal or original proceeding must be made by serving and filing a motion in the appellate division. The clerk of the appellate division must notify the trial court of any ruling on the motion.

(Subd (a) adopted effective January 1, 2009.)

(b) Substituting attorneys

A party may substitute attorneys by serving and filing in the appellate division a stipulation signed by the party represented and the new attorney.

(Subd (b) adopted effective January 1, 2009.)

(c) Withdrawing attorney

(1) An attorney may request withdrawal by filing a motion to withdraw. Unless the court orders otherwise, the motion need be served only on the party represented and the attorneys directly affected.

(2) The proof of service need not include the address of the party represented. But if the court grants the motion, the withdrawing attorney must promptly provide the court and the opposing party with the party's current or last known address, e-mail address, and telephone number.

(3) In all appeals and in original proceedings related to a trial court proceeding, the appellate division clerk must notify the trial court of any ruling on the motion.

(Subd (c) amended effective January 1, 2016; adopted effective January 1, 2009.)
Rule 8.814 amended effective January 1, 2016; adopted effective January 1, 2009.

Rule 8.815. Form of filed documents

Except as these rules provide otherwise, documents filed in the appellate division may be either produced on a computer or typewritten and must comply with the relevant provisions of rule 8.883(c).
Rule 8.815 adopted effective January 1, 2020.

Rule 8.816. Address and other contact information of record; notice of change

(a) Address and other contact information of record

(1) Except as provided in (2), the cover—or first page if there is no cover—of every document filed in the appellate division must include the name, mailing address, telephone number, fax number (if available), e-mail address (if available), and California State Bar number of each attorney filing or joining in the document, or of the party if he or she is unrepresented. The inclusion of a fax number or e-mail address on any document does not constitute consent to service by fax or e-mail unless otherwise provided by law.

(2) If more than one attorney from a law firm, corporation, or public law office is representing one party and is joining in the document, the name and State Bar number of each attorney joining in the document must be provided on the cover. The law firm, corporation, or public law office representing each party must designate one attorney to receive notices and other communication in the case from the court by placing an asterisk before that attorney's name on the cover and must provide the contact information specified under (1) for that attorney. Contact information for the other attorneys from the same law firm, corporation, or public law office is not required but may be provided.

(3) In any case pending before the appellate division, the appellate division will use the mailing address, telephone number, fax number, and e-mail address that an attorney or unrepresented party provides on the first document filed in that case as the mailing address, telephone number, fax number, and e-mail address of record unless the attorney or unrepresented party files a notice under (b).

(Subd (a) amended effective January 1, 2013; adopted effective January 1, 2009.)

(b) Notice of change

(1) An attorney or unrepresented party whose mailing address, telephone number, fax number, or e-mail address changes while a case is pending must promptly serve and file a written notice of the change in the appellate division in which the case is pending.

(2) The notice must specify the title and number of the case or cases to which it applies. If an attorney gives the notice, the notice must include the attorney's California State Bar number.

(Subd (b) amended effective January 1, 2013; adopted effective January 1, 2009.)

(c) Multiple addresses or other contact information

If an attorney or unrepresented party has more than one mailing address, telephone number, fax number, or e-mail address, only one mailing address, telephone number, fax number, and e-mail address may be used in a given case.

(Subd (c) repealed, relettered and amended effective January 1, 2013; adopted as subd (d) effective January 1, 2009.)
Rule 8.816 amended effective January 1, 2013; adopted effective January 1, 2009.

Rule 8.817. Service and filing

(a) Service

(1) Before filing any document, a party must serve, by any method permitted by the Code of Civil Procedure, one copy of the document on the attorney for each party separately represented, on each unrepresented party, and on any other person or entity when required by statute or rule.

(2) The party must attach to the document presented for filing a proof of service showing service on each person or entity required to be served under (1). The proof must name each party represented by each attorney served.

(Subd (a) adopted effective January 1, 2009.)

(b) Filing

(1) A document is deemed filed on the date the clerk receives it.

(2) Unless otherwise provided by these rules or other law, a filing is not timely unless the clerk receives the document before the time to file it expires.

(3) A brief, a petition for rehearing, or an answer to a petition for rehearing is timely if the time to file it has not expired on the date of:

(A) Its mailing by priority or express mail as shown on the postmark or the postal receipt; or

(B) Its delivery to a common carrier promising overnight delivery as shown on the carrier's receipt.

(4) The provisions of (3) do not apply to original proceedings.

(5) If the clerk receives a document by mail from an inmate or a patient in a custodial institution after the period for filing the document has expired but the envelope shows that the document was mailed or delivered to custodial officials for mailing within the period for filing the document, the document is deemed timely. The clerk must retain in the case file the envelope in which the document was received.

(Subd (b) amended effective July 1, 2010; adopted effective January 1, 2009.)
Rule 8.817 amended effective July 1, 2010; adopted effective January 1, 2009.

Advisory Committee Comment

Subdivision (a). Subdivision (a)(1) requires service "by any method permitted by the Code of Civil Procedure." The reference is to the several permissible methods of service provided in Code of Civil Procedure sections 1010–1020. *What Is Proof of Service?* (form APP-109-INFO) provides additional information about how to serve documents and how to provide proof of service.

Subdivision (b). In general, to be filed on time, a document must be received by the clerk before the time for filing that document expires. There are, however, some limited exceptions to this general rule. For example, (5) provides that if the superior court clerk receives a document by mail from a custodial institution after the deadline for filing the document has expired but the envelope shows that the document was mailed or delivered to custodial officials for mailing before the deadline expired, the document is deemed timely. This provision reflects the "prison-delivery" exception articulated by the California Supreme Court in *In re Jordan* (1992) 4 Cal.4th 116 and *Silverbrand v. County of Los Angeles* (2009) 46 Cal.4th 106.

Note that if a deadline runs from the date of filing, it runs from the date that the document is actually received and deemed filed under (b)(1); neither (b)(3) nor (b)(5) changes that date. Nor do these provisions extend the date of finality of an appellate opinion or any other deadline that is based on finality, such as the deadline for the court to modify its opinion or order rehearing. Subdivision (b)(5) is also not intended to limit a criminal defendant's appeal rights under the case law of constructive filing. (See, e.g., *In re Benoit* (1973) 10 Cal.3d 72.)

Rule 8.818. Waiver of fees and costs

(a) Applications for waiver of fees and costs

(1) *Appeals*

(A) If the trial court previously issued an order granting a party's request to waive court fees and costs in a case, and that fee waiver is still in effect, all of the court fees for an appeal to the appellate division in that case that are listed in (d) are waived by that order, and the party is not required to file a new application for waiver of court fees and costs for an appeal to the appellate division in that case.

(B) If the trial court did not previously issue an order granting a party's request to waive court fees and costs in a case or an order that was previously issued is no longer in effect, an application for initial waiver of court fees and costs for an appeal must be made on *Request to Waive Court Fees* (form FW-001). The appellant should file the application with the notice of appeal in the trial court that issued the judgment or order being appealed. The respondent should file any application at the time the fees are to be paid to the court.

(2) *Writ Proceedings*

To request the waiver of fees and costs in a writ proceeding, the petitioner must complete *Request to Waive Court Fees* (form FW-001). The petitioner should file the application with the writ petition.

(3) *Forms*

The clerk must provide *Request to Waive Court Fees* (form FW-001) and *Information Sheet on Waiver of Fees and Costs (Supreme Court, Court of Appeal, Appellate Division)* (form APP-015/FW-015-INFO) without charge to any person who requests any fee waiver application or states that he or she is unable to pay any court fee or cost.

(Subd (a) adopted effective July 1, 2009.)

(b) Procedure for determining application

The application must be considered and determined as required by Government Code section 68634.5. An order determining the application for initial fee waiver or setting a hearing on the application may be made on *Order on Court Fee Waiver (Superior Court)* (form FW-003).

(Subd (b) adopted effective July 1, 2009.)

(c) Application granted unless acted on by the court

The application for initial fee waiver is deemed granted unless the court gives notice of action on the application within five court days after the application is filed.

(Subd (c) adopted effective July 1, 2009.)

(d) Court fees and costs waived

Court fees and costs that must be waived upon granting an application for initial waiver of court fees and costs are listed in rule 3.55. The court may waive other necessary court fees and costs itemized in the application upon granting the application, either at the outset or upon later application.

(Subd (d) amended effective July 1, 2015; adopted effective July 1, 2009.)

(e) Denial of the application

If an application is denied, the applicant must pay the court fees and costs or submit the new application or additional information requested by the court within 10 days after the clerk gives notice of the denial.

(Subd (e) adopted effective July 1, 2009.)

(f) Confidential Records

(1) No person may have access to an application for an initial fee waiver submitted to the court except the court and authorized court personnel, any person authorized by the applicant, and any persons authorized by order of the court. No person may reveal any information contained in the application except as authorized by law or order of the court. An order granting access to an application or financial information may include limitations on who may access the information and on the use of the information after it has been released.

(2) Any person seeking access to an application or financial information provided to the court by an applicant must make the request by motion, supported by a declaration showing good cause as to why the confidential information should be released.

(Subd (f) adopted effective July 1, 2009.)

Rule 8.818 amended effective July 1, 2015; adopted effective July 1, 2009.

Advisory Committee Comment

Subdivision (a)(1)(B). The waiver of court fees and costs is called an "initial" waiver because, under Government Code section 68630 and following, any such waiver may later be modified, ended, or retroactively withdrawn if the court determines that the applicant was not or is no longer eligible for a waiver. The court may, at a later time, order that the previously waived fees be paid.

Rule 8.819. Sealed records

Rule 8.46 governs records sealed by court order under rules 2.550–2.551 and records proposed to be sealed in the appellate division.

Rule 8.819 adopted effective January 1, 2010.

Chapter 2
Appeals and Records in Limited Civil Cases

Chapter 2 adopted effective January 1, 2009.

Art. 1. Taking Civil Appeals. Rules 8.820–8.825.
Art. 2. Record in Civil Appeals. Rules 8.830–8.845.

Article 1
Taking Civil Appeals

Article 1 adopted effective January 1, 2009.

Rule 8.820. Application of chapter
Rule 8.821. Notice of appeal
Rule 8.822. Time to appeal
Rule 8.823. Extending the time to appeal
Rule 8.824. Writ of supersedeas
Rule 8.825. Abandonment, voluntary dismissal, and compromise

Rule 8.820. Application of chapter

The rules in this chapter apply to appeals in limited civil cases, except small claims cases.

Rule 8.820 adopted effective January 1, 2009.

Advisory Committee Comment

Chapters 1 and 4 of this division also apply in appeals in limited civil cases.

Rule 8.821. Notice of appeal

(a) Notice of appeal

(1) To appeal from a judgment or appealable order in a limited civil case, except a small claims case, an appellant must serve and file a notice of appeal in the superior court that issued the judgment or order being appealed. The appellant or the appellant's attorney must sign the notice.

(2) The notice of appeal must be liberally construed and is sufficient if it identifies the particular limited civil case judgment or order being appealed.

(3) Failure to serve the notice of appeal neither prevents its filing nor affects its validity, but the appellant may be required to remedy the failure.

(Subd (a) adopted effective January 1, 2009.)

(b) Filing fee

(1) Unless otherwise provided by law, the notice of appeal must be accompanied by the filing fee required under Government Code sections 70621 and 70602.5, an application for a waiver of court fees and costs on appeal under rule 8.818, or an order granting an application for a waiver of court fees and costs. The filing fee is nonrefundable.

(2) The clerk must file the notice of appeal even if the appellant does not present the filing fee or an application for, or order granting, a waiver of court fees and costs.

(Subd (b) amended effective January 1, 2013; adopted effective January 1, 2009; previously amended effective July 1, 2009.)

(c) Failure to pay filing fee

(1) The clerk must promptly notify the appellant in writing if:

(A) The court receives a notice of appeal without the filing fee required by (b) or an application for, or order granting, a waiver of court fees and costs;

(B) A check for the filing fee is dishonored; or

(C) An application for a waiver under rule 8.818 is denied.

(2) A clerk's notice under (1)(A) or (B) must state that the court may dismiss the appeal unless, within 15 days after the notice is sent, the appellant either:

(A) Pays the fee; or

(B) Files an application for a waiver under rule 8.818 if the appellant has not previously filed such an application or an order granting such an application.

(3) If the appellant fails to take the action specified in the notice given under (2), the appellate division may dismiss the appeal, but may vacate the dismissal for good cause.

(Subd (c) amended effective July 1, 2009; adopted effective January 1, 2009.)

(d) Notification of the appeal

(1) When the notice of appeal is filed, the trial court clerk must promptly send a notification of the filing of the notice of appeal to the attorney of record for each party and to any unrepresented party. The clerk must also send or deliver this notification to the appellate division clerk.

(2) The notification must show the date it was sent and must state the number and title of the case and the date the notice of appeal was filed.

(3) A copy of the notice of appeal is sufficient notification under (1) if the required information is on the copy or is added by the trial court clerk.

(4) The sending of a notification under (1) is a sufficient performance of the clerk's duty despite the death of the party or the discharge, disqualification, suspension, disbarment, or death of the attorney.

(5) Failure to comply with any provision of this subdivision does not affect the validity of the notice of appeal.

(Subd (d) amended effective January 1, 2016; adopted effective January 1, 2009.)

(e) Notice of cross-appeal

As used in this rule, "notice of appeal" includes a notice of cross-appeal and "appellant" includes a respondent filing a notice of cross-appeal.

(Subd (e) adopted effective January 1, 2009.)

Rule 8.821 amended effective January 1, 2016; adopted effective January 1, 2009; previously amended effective July 1, 2009, and January 1, 2013.

Advisory Committee Comment

Subdivision (a). *Notice of Appeal/Cross-Appeal (Limited Civil Case)* (form APP-102) may be used to file the notice of appeal required under this rule. This form is available at any courthouse or county law library or online at *www.courts.ca.gov/forms.htm.*

Subdivision (b). For information about the amount of the filing fee, see the current Statewide Civil Fee Schedule linked at *www.courts.ca.gov/7646.htm* (note that the "Appeal and Writ Related Fees" section appears near the end of the schedule and that there are different fees for limited civil cases depending on the amount demanded in the case.)

Subdivision (c)(2). This subdivision addresses the content of a clerk's notice that a check for the filing fee has been dishonored or that the reviewing court has received a notice of appeal without the filing fee, a certificate of cash payment, or an application for, or order granting, a fee waiver. Rule 8.818(e) addresses what an appellant must do when a fee waiver application is denied.

Rule 8.822. Time to appeal

(a) Normal time

(1) Unless a statute or rule 8.823 provides otherwise, a notice of appeal must be filed on or before the earliest of:

(A) 30 days after the trial court clerk serves the party filing the notice of appeal a document entitled "Notice of Entry" of judgment or a filed-endorsed copy of the judgment, showing the date it was served;

(B) 30 days after the party filing the notice of appeal serves or is served by a party with a document entitled "Notice of Entry" of judgment or a filed-endorsed copy of the judgment, accompanied by proof of service; or

(C) 90 days after the entry of judgment.

(2) Service under (1)(A) and (B) may be by any method permitted by the Code of Civil Procedure, including electronic service when permitted under Code of Civil Procedure section 1010.6 and rules 2.250–2.261.

(3) If the parties stipulated in the trial court under Code of Civil Procedure section 1019.5 to waive notice of the court order being appealed, the time to appeal under (1)(C) applies unless the court or a party serves notice of entry of judgment or a filed-endorsed copy of the judgment to start the time period under (1)(A) or (B).

(Subd (a) amended effective January 1, 2016; adopted effective January 1, 2009; previously amended effective January 1, 2011, July 1, 2012, and March 1, 2014.)

(b) What constitutes entry

For purposes of this rule:

(1) The entry date of a judgment is the date the judgment is filed under Code of Civil Procedure section 668.5 or the date it is entered in the judgment book.

(2) The date of entry of an appealable order that is entered in the minutes is the date it is entered in the permanent minutes. But if the minute order directs that a written order be prepared, the entry date is the date the signed order is filed; a written order prepared under rule 3.1312 or similar local rule is not such an order prepared by direction of a minute order.

(3) The entry date of an order that is not entered in the minutes is the date the signed order is filed.

(Subd (b) adopted effective January 1, 2009.)

(c) Premature notice of appeal

(1) A notice of appeal filed after judgment is rendered but before it is entered is valid and is treated as filed immediately after entry of judgment.

(2) The appellate division may treat a notice of appeal filed after the trial court has announced its intended ruling, but before it has rendered judgment, as filed immediately after entry of judgment.

(Subd (c) adopted effective January 1, 2009.)

(d) Late notice of appeal

If a notice of appeal is filed late, the appellate division must dismiss the appeal.

(Subd (d) adopted effective January 1, 2009.)

Rule 8.822 amended effective January 1, 2016; adopted effective January 1, 2009; previously amended effective January 1, 2011, July 1, 2012, and March 1, 2014.

Advisory Committee Comment

Under rule 8.804(23), the term "judgment" includes any order that may be appealed.

Subdivision (d). See rule 8.817(b)(5) for provisions concerning the timeliness of documents mailed by inmates or patients from custodial institutions.

Rule 8.823. Extending the time to appeal

(a) Extension of time

This rule operates only to increase the time to appeal otherwise prescribed in rule 8.822(a); it does not shorten the time to appeal. If the normal time to appeal stated in rule 8.822(a) would be longer than the time provided in this rule, the time to appeal stated in rule 8.822(a) governs.

(Subd (a) adopted effective January 1, 2009.)

(b) Motion for a new trial

If any party serves and files a valid notice of intention to move for a new trial, the following extensions of time apply:

(1) If the motion is denied, the time to appeal from the judgment is extended for all parties until the earliest of:

(A) 15 days after the trial court clerk or a party serves an order denying the motion or a notice of entry of that order;

(B) 15 days after denial of the motion by operation of law; or

(C) 90 days after entry of judgment; or

(2) If the trial court makes a finding of excessive or inadequate damages and grants the motion for a new trial subject to the condition that the motion is denied if a party consents to the additur or remittitur of damages:

(A) If a party serves an acceptance of the additur or remittitur within the time for accepting the additur or remittitur, the time to appeal from the judgment is extended for all parties until 15 days after the date the party serves the acceptance.

(B) If a party serves a rejection of the additur or remittitur within the time for accepting the additur or remittitur or if the time for accepting the additur or remittitur expires, the time to appeal from the new trial order is extended for all parties until the earliest of 30 days after the date the party serves the rejection or 30 days after the date on which the time for accepting the additur or remittitur expired.

(Subd (b) amended effective March 1, 2014; adopted effective January 1, 2009; previously amended effective July 1, 2012.)

(c) Motion to vacate judgment

If, within the time prescribed by rule 8.822 to appeal from the judgment, any party serves and files a valid notice of intention to move to vacate the judgment or a valid motion to vacate the judgment, the time to appeal from the judgment is extended for all parties until the earliest of:

(1) 15 days after the trial court clerk or a party serves an order denying the motion or a notice of entry of that order;

(2) 45 days after the first notice of intention to move or motion is filed; or

(3) 90 days after entry of judgment.

(Subd (c) amended effective March 1, 2014; adopted effective January 1, 2009.)

(d) Motion for judgment notwithstanding the verdict

(1) If any party serves and files a valid motion for judgment notwithstanding the verdict and the motion is denied, the time to appeal from the judgment is extended for all parties until the earliest of:

(A) 15 days after the trial court clerk or a party serves an order denying the motion or a notice of entry of that order;

(B) 15 days after denial of the motion by operation of law; or

(C) 90 days after entry of judgment.

(2) Unless extended by (e)(2), the time to appeal from an order denying a motion for judgment notwithstanding the verdict is governed by rule 8.822.

(Subd (d) amended effective March 1, 2014; adopted effective January 1, 2009.)

(e) Motion to reconsider appealable order

If any party serves and files a valid motion to reconsider an appealable order under Code of Civil Procedure section 1008(a), the time to appeal from that order is extended for all parties until the earliest of:

(1) 15 days after the superior court clerk or a party serves an order denying the motion or a notice of entry of that order;

(2) 45 days after the first motion to reconsider is filed; or

(3) 90 days after entry of the appealable order.

(Subd (e) amended effective March 1, 2014; adopted effective January 1, 2009.)

(f) Public entity actions under Government Code section 962, 984, or 985

If a public entity defendant serves and files a valid request for a mandatory settlement conference on methods of satisfying a judgment under Government Code section 962, an election to pay a judgment in periodic payments under Government Code section 984 and rule 3.1804, or a motion for a posttrial hearing on reducing a judgment under Government Code section 985, the time to appeal from the judgment is extended for all parties until the earliest of:

(1) 60 days after the superior court clerk serves the party filing the notice of appeal with a document entitled "Notice of Entry" of judgment or a filed-endorsed copy of the judgment, showing the date either was served;

(2) 60 days after the party filing the notice of appeal serves or is served by a party with a document entitled "Notice of Entry" of judgment or a filed-endorsed copy of the judgment, accompanied by proof of service; or

(3) 90 days after entry of judgment.

(Subd (f) amended effective January 1, 2016; adopted effective January 1, 2011.)

(g) Cross-appeal

(1) If an appellant timely appeals from a judgment or appealable order, the time for any other party to appeal from the same judgment or order is extended until 10 days after the trial court clerk serves notification of the first appeal.

(2) If an appellant timely appeals from an order granting a motion for a new trial, an order granting—within 75 days after entry of judgment—a motion to vacate the judgment, or a judgment notwithstanding the verdict, the time for any other party to appeal from the original judgment or from an order denying a motion for judgment notwithstanding the verdict is extended until 10 days after the clerk serves notification of the first appeal.

(Subd (g) amended effective March 1, 2014; adopted as subd (f) effective January 1, 2009; previously relettered as subd (g) effective January 1, 2011.)

(h) Proof of service

Service under this rule may be by any method permitted by the Code of Civil Procedure, including electronic service when permitted under Code of Civil Procedure section 1010.6 and rules 2.250–2.261. An order or notice that is served must be accompanied by proof of service.

(Subd (h) amended effective March 1, 2014; adopted as subd (g) effective January 1, 2009; previously amended and relettered as subd (h) effective January 1, 2011.)

Rule 8.823 amended effective January 1, 2016; adopted effective January 1, 2009; previously amended effective January 1, 2011, July 1, 2012, and March 1, 2014.

Rule 8.824. Writ of supersedeas

(a) Petition

(1) A party seeking a stay of the enforcement of a judgment or order pending appeal may serve and file a petition for writ of supersedeas in the appellate division.

(2) The petition must bear the same title as the appeal.

(3) The petition must explain the necessity for the writ and include a memorandum.

(4) If the record has not been filed in the reviewing court:

(A) The petition must include a statement of the case sufficient to show that the petitioner will raise substantial issues on appeal, including a fair summary of the material facts and the issues that are likely to be raised on appeal.

(B) The petitioner must file the following documents with the petition:

(i) The judgment or order, showing its date of entry;

(ii) The notice of appeal, showing its date of filing;

(iii) A reporter's transcript of any oral statement by the court supporting its rulings related to the issues that are likely to be raised on appeal, or, if a transcript is unavailable, a declaration fairly summarizing any such statements;

(iv) Any application for a stay filed in the trial court, any opposition to that application, and a reporter's transcript of the oral proceedings concerning the stay or, if a transcript is unavailable, a declaration fairly summarizing the proceedings, including the parties' arguments and any statement by the court supporting its ruling; and

(v) Any other document from the trial court proceeding that is necessary for proper consideration of the petition.

(C) The documents listed in (B) must comply with the following requirements:

(i) If filed in paper form, they must be bound together at the end of the petition or in separate volumes not exceeding 300 pages each. The pages must be consecutively numbered;

(ii) If filed in paper form, they must be index-tabbed by number or letter; and

(iii) They must begin with a table of contents listing each document by its title and its index number or letter.

(5) The petition must be verified.

(Subd (a) amended effective January 1, 2016; adopted effective January 1, 2009; previously amended effective January 1, 2010.)

(b) Opposition

(1) Unless otherwise ordered, any opposition must be served and filed within 15 days after the petition is filed.

(2) An opposition must state any material facts not included in the petition and include a memorandum.

(3) The court may not issue a writ of supersedeas until the respondent has had the opportunity to file an opposition.

(Subd (b) adopted effective January 1, 2009.)

(c) Temporary stay

(1) The petition may include a request for a temporary stay pending the ruling on the petition.

(2) A separately filed request for a temporary stay must be served on the respondent. For good cause, the presiding judge may excuse advance service.

(Subd (c) adopted effective January 1, 2009.)

(d) Issuing the writ

(1) The court may issue the writ on any conditions it deems just.

(2) The court must notify the trial court, under rule 8.904, of any writ or stay that it issues.

(Subd (d) adopted effective January 1, 2009.)

Rule 8.824 amended effective January 1, 2016; adopted effective January 1, 2009; previously amended effective January 1, 2010.

Advisory Committee Comment

Subdivision (a). If the preparation of a reporter's transcript has not yet been completed at that time a petition for a writ of supersedeas is filed, that transcript is "unavailable" within the meaning of (a)(4)(B).

Rule 8.825. Abandonment, voluntary dismissal, and compromise

(a) Notice of settlement

(1) If a civil case settles after a notice of appeal has been filed, either as a whole or as to any party, the appellant who has settled must immediately serve and file a notice of settlement in the appellate division. If the parties have designated a clerk's or a reporter's transcript and the record has not been filed in the appellate division, the appellant must also immediately serve a copy of the notice on the trial court clerk.

(2) If the case settles after the appellant receives a notice setting oral argument, the appellant must also immediately notify the appellate division of the settlement by telephone or other expeditious method.

(3) Within 45 days after filing a notice of settlement—unless the court has ordered a longer time period on a showing of good cause—the appellant who filed the notice of settlement must file an abandonment under (b).

(4) If the appellant does not file an abandonment or a letter stating good cause why the appeal should not be dismissed within the time period specified under (3), the court may dismiss the appeal as to that appellant and order each side to bear its own costs on appeal.

(5) Subdivision (a) does not apply to settlements requiring findings to be made by the Court of Appeal under Code of Civil Procedure section 128(a)(8).

(Subd (a) adopted effective January 1, 2009.)

(b) Abandonment

(1) The appellant may serve and file an abandonment of the appeal or a stipulation to abandon the appeal in the appellate division.

(2) If the record has not been filed in the appellate division, the filing of an abandonment effects a dismissal of the appeal and restores the trial court's jurisdiction. If the record has been filed in the appellate division, the appellate division may dismiss the appeal and direct immediate issuance of the remittitur.

(3) The clerk must promptly notify the adverse party of an abandonment. If the record has not been filed in the appellate division, the clerk must also immediately notify the trial court.

(4) If the appeal is abandoned before the clerk has completed preparation of the transcript, the clerk must refund any portion of a deposit exceeding the preparation cost actually incurred.

(5) If the appeal is abandoned before the reporter has filed the transcript, the reporter must inform the trial court clerk of the cost of the portion of the transcript that the reporter has completed. The clerk must pay that amount to the reporter from the appellant's deposited funds and refund any excess deposit.

(Subd (b) adopted effective January 1, 2009.)

(c) Approval of compromise

If a guardian or conservator seeks approval of a proposed compromise of a pending appeal, the appellate division may, before ruling on the compromise, direct the trial court to determine whether the compromise is in the minor's or the conservatee's best interest and to report its findings.

(Subd (c) adopted effective January 1, 2009.)
Rule 8.825 adopted effective January 1, 2009.

Advisory Committee Comment

Abandonment of Appeal (Limited Civil Case) (form APP-107) may be used to file an abandonment under this rule. This form is available at any courthouse or county law library or online at *www.courts.ca.gov/forms*.

Article 2
Record in Civil Appeals

Article 2 adopted effective January 1, 2009.

Rule 8.830. Record on appeal
Rule 8.831. Notice designating the record on appeal
Rule 8.832. Clerk's transcript
Rule 8.833. Trial court file instead of clerk's transcript
Rule 8.834. Reporter's transcript
Rule 8.835. Record when trial proceedings were officially electronically recorded
Rule 8.836. Agreed statement
Rule 8.837. Statement on appeal
Rule 8.838. Form of the record
Rule 8.839. Record in multiple appeals
Rule 8.840. Completion and filing of the record
Rule 8.841. Augmenting and correcting the record in the appellate division
Rule 8.842. Failure to procure the record
Rule 8.843. Transmitting exhibits
Rule 8.845. Appendixes

Rule 8.830. Record on appeal

(a) Normal record

Except as otherwise provided in this chapter, the record on an appeal to the appellate division in a civil case must contain the following, which constitute the normal record on appeal:

(1) A record of the written documents from the trial court proceedings in the form of one of the following:

(A) A clerk's transcript under rule 8.832;

(B) An appendix under rule 8.845;

(C) If the court has a local rule for the appellate division electing to use this form of the record, the original trial court file under rule 8.833; or

(D) An agreed statement under rule 8.836.

(2) If an appellant wants to raise any issue that requires consideration of the oral proceedings in the trial court, the record on appeal must include a record of these oral proceedings in the form of one of the following:

(A) A reporter's transcript under rule 8.834 or a transcript prepared from an official electronic recording under rule 8.835;

(B) If the court has a local rule for the appellate division permitting this form of the record, an official electronic recording of the proceedings under rule 8.835;

(C) An agreed statement under rule 8.836; or

(D) A statement on appeal under rule 8.837.

(Subd (a) amended effective January 1, 2021; adopted effective January 1, 2009.)

(b) Presumption from the record

The appellate division will presume that the record in an appeal includes all matters material to deciding the issues raised. If the appeal proceeds without a reporter's transcript, this presumption applies only if the claimed error appears on the face of the record.

(Subd (b) adopted effective January 1, 2009.)
Rule 8.830 amended effective January 1, 2021; adopted effective January 1, 2009.

Advisory Committee Comment

Subdivision (a). The options of using the original trial court file instead of a clerk's transcript under (1)(C) or an electronic recording itself, rather than a transcript, under (2)(B) are available only if the court has local rules for the appellate division authorizing these options.

Rule 8.831. Notice designating the record on appeal

(a) Time to file

Within 10 days after filing the notice of appeal, an appellant must serve and file a notice in the trial court designating the record on appeal. The appellant may combine its notice designating the record with its notice of appeal.

(Subd (a) adopted effective January 1, 2009.)

(b) Contents

The notice must specify:

(1) The date the notice of appeal was filed;

(2) Which form of the record of the written documents from the trial court proceedings listed in rule 8.830(a)(1) the appellant elects to use. If the appellant elects to use a clerk's transcript, the notice must also:

(A) Provide the filing date of each document that is required to be included in the clerk's transcript under 8.832(a)(1) or, if the filing date is not available, the date it was signed; and

(B) Designate, as provided under 8.832(b), any documents in addition to those required under 8.832(a)(1) that the appellant wants included in the clerk's transcript;

(3) Whether the appellant elects to proceed with or without a record of the oral proceedings in the trial court;

(4) If the appellant elects to proceed with a record of the oral proceedings in the trial court, the notice must specify which form of the record listed in rule 8.830(a)(2) the appellant elects to use;

(5) If the appellant elects to use a reporter's transcript, the notice must designate the proceedings to be included in the transcript as required under rule 8.834;

(6) If the appellant elects to use an official electronic recording, the appellant must attach a copy of the stipulation required under rule 8.835(c); and

(7) If the appellant elects to use an agreed statement, the appellant must attach to the notice either the agreed statement or stipulation as required under rule 8.836(c)(1).

(Subd (b) adopted effective January 1, 2009.)
Rule 8.831 adopted effective January 1, 2009.

Advisory Committee Comment

Appellant's Notice Designating Record on Appeal (Limited Civil Case) (form APP-103) may be used to file the designation required under this rule. This form is available at any courthouse or county law library or online at *www.courts.ca.gov/forms*. To assist parties in making appropriate choices, courts are encouraged to include information about whether the proceedings were recorded by a court reporter or officially electronically recorded in any information that the court provides to parties concerning their appellate rights.

If the appellant designates a clerk's transcript or reporter's transcript under this rule, the respondent will have an opportunity to designate additional documents to be included in the clerk's transcript under rule 8.832(b)(2) or additional proceedings to be included in the reporter's transcript under rule 8.834(a)(3).

Rule 8.832. Clerk's transcript

(a) Contents of clerk's transcript

(1) The clerk's transcript must contain:

(A) The notice of appeal;

(B) Any judgment appealed from and any notice of its entry;

(C) Any order appealed from and any notice of its entry;

(D) Any notice of intention to move for a new trial or motion to vacate the judgment, for judgment notwithstanding the verdict, or for reconsideration of an appealed order, and any order on such motion and any notice of its entry;

(E) The notice designating the record on appeal; and

(F) The register of actions, if any.

(2) Each document listed in (1)(A), (B), (C), and (D) must show the date necessary to determine the timeliness of the appeal under rule 8.822 or 8.823.

(3) If designated by any party, the clerk's transcript must also contain:

(A) Any other document filed or lodged in the case in the trial court;

(B) Any exhibit admitted in evidence, refused, or lodged; and

(C) Any jury instructions that any party submitted in writing, the cover page required by rule 2.1055(b)(2), and any written jury instructions given by the court.

(Subd (a) amended effective January 1, 2011; adopted effective January 1, 2009.)

(b) Notice of designation

(1) Within 10 days after the appellant serves a notice under rule 8.831 indicating that the appellant elects to use a clerk's transcript, the respondent may serve and file a notice in the trial court designating any additional documents the respondent wants included in the clerk's transcript.

(2) A notice designating documents to be included in a clerk's transcript must identify each designated document by its title and filing date or, if the filing date is not available, the date it was signed. A notice designating documents in addition to those listed in (a)(1) may specify portions of designated documents that are not to be included in the clerk's transcript. For minute orders or jury instructions, it is sufficient to collectively designate all minute orders or all minute orders entered between specified dates, or all written instructions given, refused, or withdrawn.

(3) All exhibits admitted in evidence, refused, or lodged are deemed part of the record, but a party wanting an exhibit included in the transcript must specify that exhibit by number or letter in its designation. If the trial court has returned a designated exhibit to a party, the party in possession of the exhibit must deliver it to the trial court clerk within 10 days after the notice designating the exhibit is served.

(Subd (b) amended effective January 1, 2010; adopted effective January 1, 2009.)

(c) Deposit for cost of clerk's transcript

(1) Within 30 days after the respondent files a designation under (b)(1) or the time to file it expires, whichever first occurs, the trial court clerk must send:

(A) To the appellant, notice of the estimated cost to prepare an original and one copy of the clerk's transcript; and

(B) To each party other than the appellant, notice of the estimated cost to prepare a copy of the clerk's transcript for that party's use.

(2) A notice under (1) must show the date it was sent.

(3) Unless otherwise provided by law, within 10 days after the clerk sends a notice under (1), the appellant and any party wanting to purchase a copy of the clerk's transcript must either deposit the estimated cost specified in the notice under (1) with the clerk or submit an application for a waiver of the cost under rule 8.818 or an order granting a waiver of this cost.

(4) If the appellant does not submit a required deposit or an application for, or an order granting a waiver of the cost within the required period, the clerk must promptly issue a notice of default under rule 8.842.

(Subd (c) amended effective January 1, 2014; adopted effective January 1, 2009; previously amended effective July 1, 2009.)

(d) Preparing the clerk's transcript

(1) The clerk must:

(A) Prepare and certify the original transcript;

(B) Prepare one copy of the transcript for the appellant; and

(C) Prepare any additional copies for parties that have requested a copy of the clerk's transcript and have made deposits as provided in (c)(3) or received an order waiving the cost.

(2) Except as provided in (3), the clerk must complete preparation of the transcripts required under (1) within 30 days after either:

(A) The appellant deposits either the estimated cost of the clerk's transcript or a preexisting order granting a waiver of that cost; or

(B) The court grants an application submitted under (c)(3) to waive that cost.

(3) If the appellant elects under rule 8.831 to proceed with a reporter's transcript, the clerk need not complete preparation of the transcripts required under (1) until 30 days after the appellant deposits the estimated cost of the reporter's transcript or one of the substitutes under rule 8.834(b).

(4) If the appeal is abandoned or dismissed before the clerk has completed preparation of the transcript, the clerk must refund any portion of the deposit under (c)(3) exceeding the preparation cost actually incurred.

(Subd (d) amended effective January 1, 2014; adopted effective January 1, 2009.)

Rule 8.832 amended effective January 1, 2014; adopted effective January 1, 2009; previously amended effective July 1, 2009, January 1, 2010, and January 1, 2011.

Advisory Committee Comment

Subdivision (a). The supporting and opposing memoranda and attachments to any motion to vacate the judgment, for judgment notwithstanding the verdict, or for reconsideration of an appealed order are not required to be included in the clerk's transcript under subdivision (a)(1)(D) but may be included by designation of a party under (a)(3) or on motion of a party or the reviewing court under rule 8.841.

Subdivision (d). The different timelines for preparing a clerk's transcript under subdivision (d)(2)(A) and (B) recognize that an appellant may apply for and receive a waiver of fees at different points during the appellate process. Some appellants may have applied for and obtained an order waiving fees before receiving the estimate of the cost of the clerk's transcript and thus may be able to provide that order to the court in lieu of making a deposit for the clerk's transcript. Other appellants may not apply for a waiver until after they receive the estimate of the cost for the clerk's transcript, in which case the time for preparing the transcript runs from the granting of that waiver.

In cases in which a reporter's transcript has been designated, subdivision (d)(3) gives the clerk the option of waiting until the deposit for the reporter's transcript has been made before beginning preparation of the clerk's transcript.

Rule 8.833. Trial court file instead of clerk's transcript

(a) Application

If the court has a local rule for the appellate division electing to use this form of the record, the original trial court file may be used instead of a clerk's transcript. This rule and any supplemental provisions of the local rule then govern unless the trial court orders otherwise after notice to the parties.

(Subd (a) adopted effective January 1, 2009.)

(b) Cost estimate; preparation of file; transmittal

(1) Within 10 days after the appellant serves a notice under rule 8.831 indicating that the appellant elects to use a clerk's transcript, the trial court clerk may send the appellant a notice indicating that the appellate division for that court has elected by local court rule to use the original trial court file instead of a clerk's transcript and providing the appellant with an estimate of the cost to prepare the file, including the cost of sending the index under (4).

(2) Within 10 days after the clerk sends the estimate under (1), the appellant must deposit the estimated cost with the clerk, unless otherwise provided by law or the party submits an application for a waiver of the cost under rule 8.818 or an order granting a waiver of this cost.

(3) Within 10 days after the appellant deposits the cost or the court files an order waiving that cost, the trial court clerk must put the trial court file in chronological order, number the pages, and attach a chronological index and a list of all attorneys of record, the parties they represent, and any unrepresented parties.

(4) The clerk must send copies of the index to all attorneys of record and any unrepresented parties for their use in paginating their copies of the file to conform to the index.

(5) If the appellant elected to proceed with a reporter's transcript, the clerk must send the prepared file to the appellate division with the reporter's transcript. If the appellant elected to proceed without a reporter's transcript, the clerk must immediately send the prepared file to the appellate division.

(Subd (b) amended effective January 1, 2016; adopted effective January 1, 2009; previously amended effective July 1, 2009.)

Rule 8.833 amended effective January 1, 2016; adopted effective January 1, 2009; previously amended effective July 1, 2009.

Rule 8.834. Reporter's transcript

(a) Notice

(1) A notice designating a reporter's transcript under rule 8.831 must specify the date of each proceeding to be included in the transcript and may specify portions of the designated proceedings that are not to be included. The notice must identify any proceeding for which a certified transcript has previously been prepared by checking the appropriate box on *Appellant's Notice Designating Record on Appeal (Limited Civil Case)* (form APP-103) or, if that form is not used, placing an asterisk before that proceeding.

(2) If the appellant designates less than all the testimony, the notice must state the points to be raised on the appeal; the appeal is then limited to those points unless, on motion, the appellate division permits otherwise.

(3) If the appellant serves and files a notice under rule 8.831 designating a reporter's transcript, the respondent may, within 10 days after such service, serve and file a notice in the trial court designating any additional proceedings the respondent wants included in the reporter's transcript. The notice must identify any proceeding for which a certified transcript has previously been prepared by checking the appropriate box on *Respondent's Notice Designating Record on Appeal (Limited Civil Case)* (form APP-110) or, if that form is not used, placing an asterisk before that proceeding.

(4) Except when a party deposits a certified transcript of all the designated proceedings under (b)(2)(D) with the notice of designation, the clerk must promptly send a copy of each notice to the reporter. The copy must show the date it was sent.

(Subd (a) amended effective January 1, 2016; adopted effective January 1, 2009; previously amended effective January 1, 2014.)

(b) Deposit or substitute for cost of transcript

(1) Within 10 days after the clerk sends a notice under (a)(4), the reporter must file the estimate with the clerk—or notify the clerk in writing of the date that he or she notified the appellant directly—of the estimated cost of preparing the reporter's transcript at the statutory rate.

(2) Within 10 days after the clerk notifies the appellant of the estimated cost of preparing the reporter's transcript or within 10 days after the reporter notifies the appellant directly—the appellant must do one of the following:

(A) Deposit with the clerk an amount equal to the estimated cost and a fee of $50 for the superior court to hold this deposit in trust;

(B) File with the clerk a written waiver of the deposit signed by the reporter;

(C) File a copy of a Transcript Reimbursement Fund application filed under (3);

(D) File a certified transcript of all of the designated proceedings. The transcript submitted by the party must not be accepted as a substitute for a deposit under (A) unless it complies with the format requirements of rule 8.838; or

(E) Notify the clerk that:

(i) He or she now elects to use a statement on appeal instead of a reporter's transcript. The appellant must prepare, serve, and file a proposed statement on appeal within 20 days after serving and filing the notice and must otherwise comply with the requirements for statements on appeal under rule 8.837;

(ii) He or she now elects to proceed without a record of the oral proceedings in the trial court; or

(iii) He or she is abandoning the appeal by filing an abandonment in the reviewing court under rule 8.825.

(3) With its notice of designation, a party may serve and file a copy of its application to the Court Reporters Board for payment or reimbursement from the Transcript Reimbursement Fund under Business and Professions Code section 8030.2 et seq.

(A) Within 90 days after the appellant serves and files a copy of its application to the Court Reporters Board, the appellant must either file with the court a copy of the Court Reporters Board's provisional approval of the application or take one of the following actions:

(i) Deposit the amount required under (2) or the reporter's written waiver of this deposit;

(ii) Notify the superior court that he or she now elects to use a statement on appeal instead of a reporter's transcript. The appellant must prepare, serve, and file a proposed statement on appeal within 20 days after serving and filing the notice and must otherwise comply with the requirements for statements on appeal under rule 8.837;

(iii) Notify the superior court that that he or she elects to proceed without a record of the oral proceedings; or

(iv) Notify the superior court that he or she is abandoning the appeal by filing an abandonment in the reviewing court under rule 8.825.

(B) Within 90 days after the respondent serves and files a copy of its application to the Court Reporters Board, the respondent must either file with the court a copy of the Court Reporters Board's provisional approval of the application or take one of the following actions:

(i) Deposit the amount required under (2) or the reporter's written waiver of this deposit; or

(ii) Notify the superior court that the respondent no longer wants the additional proceedings it designated for inclusion in the reporter's transcript.

(C) If the appellant fails to timely take one of the actions specified in (A) or the respondent fails to timely make the deposit or send the notice under (B), the clerk must promptly issue a notice of default under rule 8.842.

(D) If the Court Reporters Board provisionally approves the application, the reporter's time to prepare the transcript under (d)(1) begins when the clerk sends notice of the provisional approval under (4).

(4) The clerk must promptly notify the reporter to prepare the transcript when the court receives:

(A) The required deposit under (2)(A);

(B) A waiver of the deposit signed by the reporter under (2)(B); or

(C) A copy of the Court Reporters Board's provisional approval of the party's application for payment from the Transcript Reimbursement Fund under (3).

(Subd (b) amended effective January 1, 2024; adopted effective January 1, 2009; previously amended effective January 1, 2014, and January 1, 2016.)

(c) Contents of reporter's transcript

(1) Except when a party deposits a certified transcript of all the designated proceedings under (b)(2)(D), the reporter must transcribe all designated proceedings that have not previously been transcribed and provide a copy of all designated proceedings that have previously been transcribed. The reporter must note in the transcript where any proceedings were omitted and the nature of those proceedings. The reporter must also note where any exhibit was marked for identification and where it was admitted or refused, identifying such exhibits by number or letter.

(2) The reporter must not transcribe the voir dire examination of jurors, any opening statement, or the proceedings on a motion for new trial, unless they are designated.

(3) If a party designates a portion of a witness's testimony to be transcribed, the reporter must transcribe the witness's entire testimony unless the parties stipulate otherwise.

(4) The reporter must not copy any document includable in the clerk's transcript under rule 8.832.

(Subd (c) amended effective January 1, 2014; adopted effective January 1, 2009.)

(d) Filing the reporter's transcript; copies; payment

(1) Within 20 days after the clerk notifies the reporter to prepare the transcript under (b)(2), the reporter must prepare and certify an original of the reporter's transcript and file it in the trial court. The reporter must also file one copy of the original transcript or more than one copy if multiple appellants equally share the cost of preparing the record. Only the presiding judge of the appellate division, or his or her designee, may extend the time to prepare the reporter's transcript (see rule 8.810).

(2) When the transcript is completed, the reporter must notify all parties to the appeal that the transcript is complete, bill each designating party at the statutory rate, and send a copy of the bill to the clerk. The clerk must pay the reporter from that party's deposited funds and refund any excess deposit or notify the party of any additional funds needed. In a multiple reporter case, the clerk must pay each reporter who certifies under penalty of perjury that his or her transcript portion is completed.

(3) If the appeal is abandoned or is dismissed before the reporter has filed the transcript, the reporter must inform the clerk of the cost of the portion of the transcript that the reporter has completed. The clerk must pay that amount to the reporter from the appellant's deposited funds and refund any excess deposit.

(Subd (d) amended effective January 1, 2018; adopted effective January 1, 2009; previously amended effective January 1, 2014, March 1, 2014, and January 1, 2017.)

(e) Disputes over transcript costs

Notwithstanding any dispute that may arise over the estimated or billed costs of a reporter's transcript, a designating party must timely comply with the requirements under this rule regarding deposits for transcripts. If a designating party believes that a reporter's estimate or bill is excessive, the designating party may file a complaint with the Court Reporters Board.

(Subd (e) adopted effective January 1, 2014.)

(f) Notice when proceedings cannot be transcribed

(1) If any portion of the designated proceedings were not reported or cannot be transcribed, the trial court clerk must so notify the designating party in writing; the notice must:

(A) Indicate whether the identified proceedings were officially electronically recorded under Government Code section 69957; and

(B) Show the date it was sent.

(2) Within 10 days after the notice under (1) is sent, the designating party must file a new election notifying the court whether the party elects to proceed with or without a record of the identified oral proceedings. If the party elects to proceed with a record of these oral proceedings, the notice must specify which form of the record listed in rule 8.830(a)(2) the party elects to use.

(A) The party may not elect to use a reporter's transcript.

(B) The party may not elect to use an official electronic recording or a transcript prepared from an official electronic recording under rule 8.835 unless the clerk's notice under (1) indicates that proceedings were officially electronically recorded under Government Code section 69957.

(C) The party must comply with the requirements applicable to the form of the record elected.

(3) This remedy supplements any other available remedies.

(Subd (f) amended effective January 1, 2016; adopted as subd (e) effective January 1, 2009; previously relettered as subd (f) effective January 1, 2014; previously amended effective March 1, 2014.)

Rule 8.834 amended effective January 1, 2024; adopted effective January 1, 2009; previously amended effective January 1, 2014, March 1, 2014, January 1, 2016, January 1, 2017, and January 1, 2018.

Advisory Committee Comment

Subdivision (b). Sometimes a party in a trial court proceeding will purchase a reporter's transcript of all or part of the proceedings before any appeal is filed. In recognition of the fact that such transcripts may already have been purchased, this rule allows an appellant, in lieu of depositing funds for a reporter's transcript, to deposit with the trial court a certified transcript of the proceedings necessary for the appeal. Subdivision (b)(2)(D) makes clear that the certified transcript may be filed in lieu of a deposit for a reporter's transcript only where the certified transcript contains all of the proceedings designated, and the transcript complies with the format requirements of rule 8.838 (e.g., cover information, renumbered pages, required indexes). Parties using this alternative to a deposit are responsible for ensuring that such transcripts are in the proper format. Parties may arrange with a court reporter to do the necessary formatting of the transcript or may do the formatting themselves.

Rule 8.835. Record when trial proceedings were officially electronically recorded

(a) Application

This rule applies only if:

(1) The trial court proceedings were officially recorded electronically under Government Code section 69957; and

(2) The electronic recording was prepared in compliance with applicable rules regarding electronic recording of court proceedings.

(Subd (a) adopted effective January 1, 2009.)

(b) Transcripts from official electronic recording

Written transcripts of official electronic recordings may be prepared under rule 2.952. A transcript prepared and certified as provided in that rule is prima facie a true and complete record of the oral proceedings it purports to cover and satisfies any requirement in these rules or in any statute for a reporter's transcript of oral proceedings.

(Subd (b) adopted effective January 1, 2009.)

(c) Use of official recording as record of oral proceedings

If the court has a local rule for the appellate division permitting this, on stipulation of the parties or on order of the trial court under rule 8.837(d)(6), the original of an official electronic recording of the trial court proceedings, or a copy made by the court, may be transmitted as the record of these oral proceedings without being transcribed. Such an official electronic recording satisfies any requirement in these rules or in any statute for a reporter's transcript of these proceedings.

(Subd (c) amended effective July 1, 2010; adopted effective January 1, 2009.)

(d) Notice when proceedings were not officially electronically recorded or cannot be transcribed

(1) If the appellant elects under rule 8.831 to use a transcript prepared from an official electronic recording or the recording itself, the trial court clerk must notify the appellant in writing if any portion of the designated proceedings was not officially electronically recorded or cannot be transcribed. The notice must:

(A) Indicate whether the identified proceedings were reported by a court reporter; and

(B) Show the date it was sent.

(2) Within 10 days after the notice under (1) is sent, the appellant must file a new election notifying the court whether the appellant elects to proceed with or without a record of the oral proceedings that were not recorded or cannot be transcribed. If the appellant elects to proceed with a record of these oral proceedings, the notice must specify which form of the record listed in rule 8.830(a)(2) the appellant elects to use.

(A) The appellant may not elect to use an official electronic recording or a transcript prepared from an official electronic recording.

(B) The appellant may not elect to use a reporter's transcript unless the clerk's notice under (1) indicates that proceedings were reported by a court reporter.

(C) The appellant must comply with the requirements applicable to the form of the record elected.

(Subd (d) amended effective January 1, 2016; adopted effective January 1, 2009; previously amended effective March 1, 2014.)

Rule 8.835 amended effective January 1, 2016; adopted effective January 1, 2009; previously amended effective July 1, 2010, and March 1, 2014.

Rule 8.836. Agreed statement

(a) What is an agreed statement

An agreed statement is a summary of the trial court proceedings that is agreed to by the parties. If the parties have prepared an agreed statement or stipulated to prepare one, the appellant can elect under rule 8.831 to use an agreed statement as the record of the documents filed in the trial court, replacing the clerk's transcript, and as the record of the oral proceedings in the trial court, replacing the reporter's transcript.

(Subd (a) adopted effective January 1, 2009.)

(b) Contents of an agreed statement

(1) The agreed statement must explain the nature of the action, the basis of the appellate division's jurisdiction, and the rulings of the trial court relating to the points to be raised on appeal. The statement should recite only those facts that a party considers relevant to decide the appeal and must be signed by the parties.

(2) If the agreed statement replaces a clerk's transcript, the statement must be accompanied by copies of all items required by rule 8.832(a)(1), showing the dates required by rule 8.832(a)(2).

(3) The statement may be accompanied by copies of any document includable in the clerk's transcript under rule 8.832(a)(3).

(Subd (b) adopted effective January 1, 2009.)

(c) Time to file; extension of time

(1) If an appellant indicates on its notice designating the record under rule 8.831 that it elects to use an agreed statement under this rule, the appellant must file with the notice designating the record either the agreed statement or a stipulation that the parties are attempting to agree on a statement.

(2) If the appellant files a stipulation under (1), within 30 days after filing the notice of designation under rule 8.831, the appellant must either:

(A) File the statement if the parties were able to agree on the statement; or

(B) File both a notice stating that the parties were not able to agree on the statement and a new notice designating the record under rule 8.831. In the new notice designating the record, the appellant may not elect to use an agreed statement.

(Subd (c) adopted effective January 1, 2009.)

Rule 8.836 adopted effective January 1, 2009.

Rule 8.837. Statement on appeal

(a) Description

A statement on appeal is a summary of the trial court proceedings that is approved by the trial court. An appellant can elect under rule 8.831 to use a statement on appeal as the record of the oral proceedings in the trial court, replacing the reporter's transcript.

(Subd (a) adopted effective January 1, 2009.)

(b) Preparing the proposed statement

(1) If the appellant elects in its notice designating the record under rule 8.831 to use a statement on appeal, the appellant must serve and file a proposed statement within 20 days after filing the notice under rule 8.831. If the appellant does not serve and file a proposed statement within this time, rule 8.842 applies.

(2) Appellants who are not represented by an attorney must file their proposed statement on *Statement on Appeal (Limited Civil Case)* (form APP-104). For good cause, the court may permit the filing of a statement that is not on form APP-104.

(Subd (b) amended effective March 1, 2014; adopted effective January 1, 2009.)

(c) Contents of the proposed statement

The proposed statement must contain:

(1) A statement of the points the appellant is raising on appeal. If the condensed narrative under (3) covers only a portion of the oral proceedings, then the appeal is limited to the points identified in the statement unless the appellate division determines that the record permits the full consideration of another point or, on motion, the appellate division permits otherwise.

(A) The statement must specify the intended grounds of appeal by clearly stating each point to be raised but need not identify each particular ruling or matter to be challenged.

(B) If one of the grounds of appeal is insufficiency of the evidence, the statement must specify how it is insufficient.

(2) A summary of the trial court's rulings and judgment.

(3) A condensed narrative of the oral proceedings that the appellant believes necessary for the appeal.

(A) The condensed narrative must include a concise factual summary of the evidence and the testimony of each witness that is relevant to the points which the appellant states under (1) are being raised on appeal. Any evidence or portion of a proceeding not included will be presumed to support the judgment or order appealed from.

(B) If one of the points which the appellant states under (1) is being raised on appeal is a challenge to the giving, refusal, or modification of a jury instruction, the condensed narrative must include any instructions submitted orally and not in writing and must identify the party that requested the instruction and any modification.

(Subd (c) amended effective March 1, 2014; adopted effective January 1, 2009.)

(d) Review of the appellant's proposed statement

(1) Within 10 days after the appellant files the proposed statement, the respondent may serve and file proposed amendments to that statement.

(2) No later than 10 days after the respondent files proposed amendments or the time to do so expires, a party may request a hearing to review and correct the proposed statement. No hearing will be held unless ordered by the trial court judge, and the judge will not ordinarily order a hearing unless there is a factual dispute about a material aspect of the trial court proceedings.

(3) Except as provided in (6), if no hearing is ordered, no later than 10 days after the time for requesting a hearing expires, the trial court judge must review the proposed statement and any proposed amendments filed by the respondent and take one of the following actions:

(A) If the proposed statement does not contain material required under (c), the trial judge may order the appellant to prepare a new proposed statement. The order must identify the additional material that must be included in the statement to comply with (c) and the date by which the new proposed statement must be served and filed. If the appellant does not serve and file a new proposed statement as directed, rule 8.842 applies.

(B) If the trial judge does not issue an order under (A), the trial judge must either:

(i) Make any corrections or modifications to the statement necessary to ensure that it is an accurate summary of the evidence and the testimony of each witness that is relevant to the points which the appellant states under (c)(1) are being raised on appeal; or

(ii) Identify the necessary corrections and modifications and order the appellant to prepare a statement incorporating these corrections and modifications.

(4) If a hearing is ordered, the court must promptly set the hearing date and provide the parties with at least 5 days' written notice of the hearing date. No later than 10 days after the hearing, the trial court judge must either:

(A) Make any corrections or modifications to the statement necessary to ensure that it is an accurate summary of the evidence and the testimony of each witness that is relevant to the points which the appellant states under (c)(1) are being raised on appeal; or

(B) Identify the necessary corrections and modifications and order the appellant to prepare a statement incorporating these corrections and modifications.

(5) The trial court judge must not eliminate the appellant's specification of grounds of appeal from the proposed statement.

(6) If the trial court proceedings were reported by a court reporter or officially electronically recorded under Government Code section 69957 and the trial court judge determines that it would save court time and resources, instead of correcting a proposed statement on appeal:

(A) If the court has a local rule for the appellate division permitting the use of an official electronic recording as the record of the oral proceedings, the trial court judge may order that the original of an official electronic recording of the trial court proceedings, or a copy made by the court, be transmitted as the record of these oral proceedings without being transcribed. The court will pay for any copy of the official electronic recording ordered under this subdivision; or

(B) If the court has a local rule permitting this, the trial court judge may order that a transcript be prepared as the record of the oral proceedings. The court will pay for any transcript ordered under this subdivision.

(Subd (d) amended effective March 1, 2014; adopted effective January 1, 2009.)

(e) Review of the corrected statement

(1) If the trial court judge makes any corrections or modifications to the proposed statement under (d), the clerk must serve copies of the corrected or modified statement on the parties. If under (d) the trial court judge orders the appellant to prepare a statement incorporating corrections and modifications, the appellant must serve and file the corrected or modified statement within the time ordered by the court. If the appellant does not serve and file a corrected or modified statement as directed, rule 8.842 applies.

(2) Within 10 days after the corrected or modified statement is served on the parties, any party may serve and file proposed modifications or objections to the statement.

(3) Within 10 days after the time for filing proposed modifications or objections under (2) has expired, the judge must review the corrected or modified statement and any proposed modifications or objections to the statement filed by the parties. The procedures in (d)(3) or (d)(4) apply if the judge determines that further corrections or modifications are necessary to ensure that the statement is an accurate summary of the evidence and the testimony of each witness relevant to the points which the appellant states under (c)(1) are being raised on appeal.

(Subd (e) amended effective April 1, 2023; adopted effective January 1, 2009; previously amended effective March 1, 2014.)

(f) Certification of the statement on appeal

If the trial court judge does not make or order any corrections or modifications to the proposed statement under (d)(3), (d)(4), or (e)(3) and does not order either the use of an official electronic recording or the preparation of a transcript in lieu of correcting the proposed statement under (d)(6), the judge must promptly certify the statement.

(Subd (f) amended effective March 1, 2014; adopted effective January 1, 2009.)
Rule 8.837 amended effective April 1, 2023; adopted effective January 1, 2009; previously amended effective March 1, 2014.

Advisory Committee Comment

Subdivision (b)(2). *Proposed Statement on Appeal (Limited Civil Case)* (form APP-104) is available at any courthouse or county law library or online at www.courts.ca.gov/forms.

Subdivision (d). Under rule 8.804, the term "judge" includes a commissioner or a temporary judge.

Subdivisions (d)(3)(B), (d)(4), and (f). The judge need not ensure that the statement as modified or corrected is complete, but only that it is an accurate summary of the evidence and testimony relevant to the issues identified by the appellant.

Rule 8.838. Form of the record

(a) Paper and format

Except as otherwise provided in this rule, clerks' and reporters' transcripts must comply with the requirements of rule 8.144(a), (b)(1)–(4) and (6), (c), and (d).

(Subd (a) amended effective January 1, 2024; adopted effective January 1, 2009; previously amended effective January 1, 2018.)

(b) Indexes

At the beginning of the first volume of each:

(1) The clerk's transcript must contain alphabetical and chronological indexes listing each document and the volume, where applicable, and page where it first appears;

(2) The reporter's transcript must contain alphabetical and chronological indexes listing the volume, where applicable, and page where each witness's direct, cross, and any other examination, begins; and

(3) The reporter's transcript must contain an index listing the volume, where applicable, and page where any exhibit is marked for identification and where it is admitted or refused.

(Subd (b) amended effective January 1, 2016; adopted effective January 1, 2009.)

(c) Binding and cover

(1) If filed in paper form, clerks' and reporters' transcripts must be bound on the left margin, except that transcripts may be bound at the top if required by a local rule of the appellate division.

(2) Each volume's cover must state the title and trial court number of the case, the names of the trial court and each participating trial judge, the names and addresses of appellate counsel for each party, the volume number, and the inclusive page numbers of that volume.

(3) In addition to the information required by (2), the cover of each volume of the reporter's transcript must state the dates of the proceedings reported in that volume.

(Subd (c) amended effective January 1, 2024; adopted effective January 1, 2009; previously amended effective January 1, 2014, and January 1, 2016.)

Rule 8.838 amended effective January 1, 2024; adopted effective January 1, 2009; previously amended effective January 1, 2014, January 1, 2016, and January 1, 2018.

Rule 8.839. Record in multiple appeals

(a) Single record

If more than one appeal is taken from the same judgment or a related order, only one record need be prepared, which must be filed within the time allowed for filing the record in the latest appeal.

(Subd (a) adopted effective January 1, 2009.)

(b) Cost

If there is more than one separately represented appellant, they must equally share the cost of preparing the record, unless otherwise agreed by the appellants or ordered by the trial court. Appellants equally sharing the cost are each entitled to a copy of the record.

(Subd (b) adopted effective January 1, 2009.)

Rule 8.839 adopted effective January 1, 2009.

Rule 8.840. Completion and filing of the record

(a) When the record is complete

(1) If the appellant elected under rule 8.831 or 8.834(b) to proceed without a record of the oral proceedings in the trial court and the parties are not proceeding by appendix under rule 8.845, the record is complete:

(A) If a clerk's transcript will be used, when the clerk's transcript is certified under rule 8.832(d);

(B) If the original trial court file will be used instead of the clerk's transcript, when that original file is ready for transmission as provided under rule 8.833(b); or

(C) If an agreed statement will be used instead of the clerk's transcript, when the appellant files the agreed statement under rule 8.836(b).

(2) If the parties are not proceeding by appendix under rule 8.845 and the appellant elected under rule 8.831 to proceed with a record of the oral proceedings in the trial court, the record is complete when the clerk's transcript or other record of the documents from the trial court is complete as provided in (1) and:

(A) If the appellant elected to use a reporter's transcript, when the certified reporter's transcript is delivered to the court under rule 8.834(d);

(B) If the appellant elected to use a transcript prepared from an official electronic recording, when the transcript has been prepared under rule 8.835;

(C) If the parties stipulated to the use of an official electronic recording of the proceedings, when the electronic recording has been prepared under rule 8.835; or

(D) If the appellant elected to use a statement on appeal, when the statement on appeal has been certified by the trial court or a transcript or an official electronic recording has been prepared under rule 8.837(d)(6).

(3) If the parties are proceeding by appendix under rule 8.845 and the appellant elected under rule 8.831 to proceed with a record of the oral proceedings in the trial court, the record is complete when the record of the oral proceedings is complete as provided in (2)(A), (B), (C), or (D).

(Subd (a) amended effective January 1, 2021; adopted effective January 1, 2014.)

(b) Filing the record

When the record is complete, the trial court clerk must promptly send the original to the appellate division and send to the appellant and respondent copies of any certified statement on appeal and any copies of transcripts or official electronic recordings that they have purchased. The appellate division clerk must promptly file the original and send notice of the filing date to the parties.

(Subd (b) amended effective January 1, 2016; adopted as unlettered subd effective January 1, 2009; previously amended and lettered as subd (b) effective January 1, 2014.)

Rule 8.840 amended effective January 1, 2021; adopted effective January 1, 2009; previously amended effective January 1, 2014, and January 1, 2016.

Rule 8.841. Augmenting and correcting the record in the appellate division

(a) Augmentation

(1) At any time, on motion of a party or its own motion, the appellate division may order the record augmented to include:

(A) Any document filed or lodged in the case in the trial court; or

(B) A certified transcript—or agreed statement or a statement on appeal—of oral proceedings not designated under rule 8.831.

(2) A party must attach to its motion a copy, if available, of any document or transcript that it wants added to the record. The pages of the attachments must be consecutively numbered, beginning with the number 1. If the appellate division grants the motion, it may augment the record with the copy.

(3) If the party cannot attach a copy of the matter to be added, the party must identify it as required under rules 8.831.

(Subd (a) adopted effective January 1, 2009.)

(b) Correction

(1) On agreement of the parties, motion of a party, or on its own motion, the appellate division may order the correction or certification of any part of the record.

(2) The appellate division may order the trial court to settle disputes about omissions or errors in the record or to make corrections pursuant to stipulation filed by the parties in that court.

(Subd (b) adopted effective January 1, 2009.)

(c) Omissions

(1) If a clerk or reporter omits a required or designated portion of the record, a party may serve and file a notice in the trial court specifying the omitted portion and requesting that it be prepared, certified, and sent to the appellate division. The party must serve a copy of the notice on the appellate division.

(2) The clerk or reporter must comply with a notice under (1) within 10 days after it is filed. If the clerk or reporter fails to comply, the party may serve and file a motion to augment under (a), attaching a copy of the notice.

(Subd (c) adopted effective January 1, 2009.)

(d) Notice

The appellate division clerk must send all parties notice of the receipt and filing of any matter under this rule.

(Subd (d) adopted effective January 1, 2009.)

Rule 8.841 adopted effective January 1, 2009.

Rule 8.842. Failure to procure the record

(a) Notice of default

Except as otherwise provided by these rules, if a party fails to do any act required to procure the record, the trial court clerk must promptly notify that party in writing that it must do the act specified in the notice within 15 days after the notice is sent and that, if it fails to comply, the reviewing court may impose the following sanctions:

(1) If the defaulting party is the appellant, the court may dismiss the appeal; or

(2) If the defaulting party is the respondent, the court may proceed with the appeal on the record designated by the appellant.

(Subd (a) amended effective January 1, 2016; adopted effective January 1, 2009; previously amended effective January 1, 2014.)

(b) Sanctions

If the party fails to take the action specified in a notice given under (a), the trial court clerk must promptly notify the appellate division of the default, and the appellate division may impose one of the following sanctions:

(1) If the defaulting party is the appellant, the reviewing court may dismiss the appeal. If the appeal is dismissed, the reviewing court must promptly notify the superior court. The reviewing court may vacate the dismissal for good cause.

(2) If the defaulting party is the respondent, the reviewing court may order the appeal to proceed on the record designated by the appellant, but the respondent may obtain relief from default under rule 8.812.

(Subd (b) amended effective January 1, 2014; adopted effective January 1, 2009; previously amended effective January 1, 2011.)

Rule 8.842 amended effective January 1, 2016; adopted effective January 1, 2009; previously amended effective January 1, 2011, and January 1, 2014.

Rule 8.843. Transmitting exhibits

(a) Notice of designation

(1) If a party wants the appellate division to consider any original exhibits that were admitted in evidence, refused, or lodged but that were

not copied in the clerk's transcript under rule 8.832 or the appendix under rule 8.845 or included in the original file under rule 8.833, within 10 days after the last respondent's brief is filed or could be filed under rule 8.882 the party must serve and file a notice in the trial court designating such exhibits.

(2) Within 10 days after a notice under (1) is served, any other party wanting the appellate division to consider additional exhibits must serve and file a notice in the trial court designating such exhibits.

(3) A party filing a notice under (1) or (2) must serve a copy on the appellate division.

(Subd (a) amended effective January 1, 2021; adopted effective January 1, 2009.)

(b) Application for later transmittal

After the periods specified in (a) have expired, a party may apply to the appellate division for permission to send an exhibit to that court.

(Subd (b) adopted effective January 1, 2009.)

(c) Request by appellate division

At any time the appellate division may direct the trial court or a party to send it an exhibit.

(Subd (c) adopted effective January 1, 2009.)

(d) Transmittal

Unless the appellate division orders otherwise, within 20 days after notice under (a) is filed or after the appellate division directs that an exhibit be sent:

(1) The trial court clerk must put any designated exhibits in the clerk's possession into numerical or alphabetical order and send them to the appellate division. The trial court clerk must also send a list of the exhibits sent. If the exhibits are not transmitted electronically, the trial court clerk must send two copies of the list. If the appellate division clerk finds the list correct, the clerk must sign and return a copy to the trial court clerk.

(2) Any party in possession of designated exhibits returned by the trial court must put them into numerical or alphabetical order and send them to the appellate division. The party must also send a list of the exhibits sent. If the exhibits are not transmitted electronically, the party must send two copies of the list. If the appellate division clerk finds the list correct, the clerk must sign and return a copy to the party.

(Subd (d) amended effective January 1, 2016; adopted effective January 1, 2009.)

(e) Return by appellate division

On request, the appellate division may return an exhibit to the trial court or to the party that sent it. When the remittitur issues, the appellate division must return all exhibits not transmitted electronically to the trial court or to the party that sent them.

(Subd (e) amended effective January 1, 2016; adopted effective January 1, 2009.)

Rule 8.843 amended effective January 1, 2021; adopted effective January 1, 2009; previously amended effective January 1, 2016.

Rule 8.845. Appendixes

(a) Notice of election

(1) Unless the superior court orders otherwise on a motion served and filed within 10 days after the notice of election is served, this rule governs if:

(A) The appellant elects to use an appendix under this rule in the notice designating the record on appeal under rule 8.831; or

(B) The respondent serves and files a notice in the superior court electing to use an appendix under this rule within 10 days after the appellant's notice designating the record on appeal is filed, and no waiver of the fee for a clerk's transcript is granted to the appellant. If the appellant has a fee waiver, the respondent cannot elect an appendix instead of a clerk's transcript.

(2) When a party files a notice electing to use an appendix under this rule, the superior court clerk must promptly send a copy of the register of actions, if any, to the attorney of record for each party and to any unrepresented party.

(3) The parties may prepare separate appendixes or they may stipulate to a joint appendix.

(Subd (a) amended effective January 1, 2024; adopted effective January 1, 2021.)

(b) Contents of appendix

(1) A joint appendix or an appellant's appendix must contain:

(A) All items required by rule 8.832(a)(1), showing the dates required by rule 8.832(a)(2);

(B) Any item listed in rule 8.832(a)(3) that is necessary for proper consideration of the issues, including, for an appellant's appendix, any item that the appellant should reasonably assume the respondent will rely on;

(C) The notice of election; and

(D) For a joint appendix, the stipulation designating its contents.

(2) An appendix may incorporate by reference all or part of the record on appeal in another case pending in the reviewing court or in a prior appeal in the same case.

(A) The other appeal must be identified by its case name and number. If only part of a record is being incorporated by reference, that part must be identified by citation to the volume and page numbers of the record where it appears and either the title of the document or documents or the date of the oral proceedings to be incorporated. The parts of any record incorporated by reference must be identified both in the body of the appendix and in a separate section at the end of the index.

(B) If the appendix incorporates by reference any such record, the cover of the appendix must prominently display the notice "Record in case number: _____ incorporated by reference," identifying the number of the case from which the record is incorporated.

(C) On request of the reviewing court or any party, the designating party must provide a copy of the materials incorporated by reference to the court or another party or lend them for copying as provided in (c).

(3) An appendix must not:

(A) Contain documents or portions of documents filed in superior court that are unnecessary for proper consideration of the issues.

(B) Contain transcripts of oral proceedings that may be designated under rule 8.834.

(C) Incorporate any document by reference except as provided in (2).

(4) All exhibits admitted in evidence, refused, or lodged are deemed part of the record, whether or not the appendix contains copies of them.

(5) A respondent's appendix may contain any document that could have been included in the appellant's appendix or a joint appendix.

(6) An appellant's reply appendix may contain any document that could have been included in the respondent's appendix.

(Subd (b) adopted effective January 1, 2021.)

(c) Document or exhibit held by other party

If a party preparing an appendix wants it to contain a copy of a document or an exhibit in the possession of another party:

(1) The party must first ask the party possessing the document or exhibit to provide a copy or lend it for copying. All parties should reasonably cooperate with such requests.

(2) If the request under (1) is unsuccessful, the party may serve and file in the reviewing court a notice identifying the document or specifying the exhibit's trial court designation and requesting the party possessing the document or exhibit to deliver it to the requesting party or, if the possessing party prefers, to the reviewing court. The possessing party must comply with the request within 10 days after the notice was served.

(3) If the party possessing the document or exhibit sends it to the requesting party nonelectronically, that party must copy and return it to the possessing party within 10 days after receiving it.

(4) If the party possessing the document or exhibit sends it to the reviewing court, that party must:

(A) Accompany the document or exhibit with a copy of the notice served by the requesting party; and

(B) Immediately notify the requesting party that it has sent the document or exhibit to the reviewing court.

(5) On request, the reviewing court may return a document or an exhibit to the party that sent it nonelectronically. When the remittitur issues, the reviewing court must return all documents or exhibits to the party that sent them, if they were sent nonelectronically.

(Subd (c) adopted effective January 1, 2021.)

(d) Form of appendix

(1) An appendix must comply with the requirements of rule 8.838 for a clerk's transcript.

(2) In addition to the information required on the cover of a brief by rule 8.883(c)(8), the cover of an appendix must prominently display the title "Joint Appendix" or "Appellant's Appendix" or "Respondent's Appendix" or "Appellant's Reply Appendix."

(3) An appendix must not be bound with or transmitted electronically with a brief as one document.

(Subd (d) adopted effective January 1, 2021.)

(e) Service and filing

(1) A party preparing an appendix must:

(A) Serve the appendix on each party, unless otherwise agreed by the parties or ordered by the reviewing court; and

(B) File the appendix in the reviewing court.

(2) A joint appendix or an appellant's appendix must be served and filed before or together with the appellant's opening brief.

(3) A respondent's appendix, if any, must be served and filed with the respondent's brief.

(4) An appellant's reply appendix, if any, must be served and filed with the appellant's reply brief.

(Subd (e) amended effective January 1, 2024; adopted effective January 1, 2021.)

(f) Cost of appendix

(1) Each party must pay for its own appendix.

(2) The cost of a joint appendix must be paid:

(A) By the appellant;

(B) If there is more than one appellant, by the appellants equally; or

(C) As the parties may agree.

(Subd (f) adopted effective January 1, 2021.)

(g) Inaccurate or noncomplying appendix

Filing an appendix constitutes a representation that the appendix consists of accurate copies of documents in the superior court file. The reviewing court may impose monetary or other sanctions for filing an appendix that contains inaccurate copies or otherwise violates this rule.

(Subd (g) adopted effective January 1, 2021.)

Rule 8.845 amended effective January 1, 2024; adopted effective January 1, 2021.

Advisory Committee Comment

Subdivision (a). Under this provision, either party may elect to have the appeal proceed by way of an appendix. If the appellant's fees for a clerk's transcript are not waived and the respondent timely elects to use an appendix, that election will govern unless the superior court orders otherwise. This election procedure differs from all other appellate rules governing designation of a record on appeal. In those rules, the appellant's designation, or the stipulation of the parties, determines the type of record on appeal. Before making this election, respondents should check whether the appellant has been granted a fee waiver that is still in effect. If the trial court has granted the appellant a fee waiver for the clerk's transcript, or grants such a waiver after the notice of appeal is filed, the respondent cannot elect to proceed by way of an appendix.

Subdivision (a)(2) is intended to assist appellate counsel in preparing an appendix by providing counsel with the list of pleadings and other filings found in the register of actions or "docket sheet" in those counties that maintain such registers. (See Gov. Code, § 69845.) The provision is derived from rule 10-1 of the United States Circuit Rules (9th Cir.).

Subdivision (b). Under subdivision (b)(1)(A), a joint appendix or an appellant's appendix must contain any register of actions that the clerk sent to the parties under subdivision (a)(2). This provision is intended to assist the reviewing court in determining the accuracy of the appendix. The provision is derived from rule 30-1.3(a)(ii) of the United States Circuit Rules (9th Cir.).

In support of or opposition to pleadings or motions, the parties may have filed a number of lengthy documents in the proceedings in superior court, including, for example, declarations, memorandums, trial briefs, documentary exhibits (e.g., insurance policies, contracts, deeds), and photocopies of judicial opinions or other publications. Subdivision (b)(3)(A) prohibits the inclusion of such documents in an appendix when they are not necessary for proper consideration of the issues raised in the appeal. Even if a document is otherwise includable in an appendix, the rule prohibits the inclusion of any substantial *portion* of the document that is not necessary for proper consideration of the issues raised in the appeal. The prohibition is intended to simplify and therefore expedite the preparation of the appendix, to reduce its cost to the parties, and to relieve the courts of the burden of reviewing a record containing redundant, irrelevant, or immaterial documents. The provision is adapted from rule 30-1.4 of the United States Circuit Rules (9th Cir.).

Subdivision (b)(3)(B) prohibits the inclusion in an appendix of transcripts of oral proceedings that may be made part of a reporter's transcript. (Compare rule 8.834(c)(4) [the reporter must not copy into the reporter's transcript any document includable in the clerk's transcript under rule 8.832].) The prohibition is intended to prevent a party filing an appendix from evading the requirements and safeguards imposed by rule 8.834 on the process of designating and preparing a reporter's transcript. In addition, if an appellant were to include in its appendix a transcript of less than all the proceedings, the respondent would not learn of any need to designate additional proceedings (under rule 8.834(a)(3)) until the appellant had served its appendix with its brief, when it would be too late to designate them. Note also that a party may file a certified transcript of designated proceedings instead of a deposit for the reporter's fee (Cal. Rules of Court, rule 8.834(b)(2)(D)).

Subdivision (d). In current practice, served copies of filed documents often bear no clerk's date stamp and are not conformed by the parties serving them. Consistent with this practice, subdivision (d) does not require such documents to be conformed. The provision thereby relieves the parties of the burden of obtaining conformed copies at the cost of considerable time and expense, and expedites the preparation of the appendix and the processing of the appeal. It is to be noted, however, that under subdivision (b)(1)(A) each document necessary to determine the timeliness of the appeal must show the date required under rule 8.822 or 8.823. Note also that subdivision (g) of rule 8.845 provides that a party filing an appendix represents under penalty of sanctions that its copies of documents are accurate.

Subdivision (e). Subdivision (e)(2) requires a joint appendix to be filed with the appellant's opening brief or before the filing of the appellant's opening brief. The provision is intended to improve the briefing process by enabling the appellant's opening brief to include citations to the record and, by allowing earlier filing of the appendix, to assist courts in considering petitions for supersedeas. To provide for the case in which a respondent concludes in light of the appellant's opening brief that the joint appendix should have included additional documents, subdivision (b)(5) permits such a respondent to present in an appendix filed with its respondent's brief (see subd. (e)(3)) any document that could have been included in the joint appendix.

Under subdivision (e)(2)–(4), an appendix is required to be filed, at the latest, "with" the associated brief. This provision is intended to clarify that an extension of a briefing period ipso facto extends the filing period of an appendix associated with the brief.

Subdivision (g). Under subdivision (g), sanctions do not depend on the degree of culpability of the filing party—i.e., on whether the party's conduct was willful or negligent—but on the nature of the inaccuracies and the importance of the documents they affect.

Chapter 3
Appeals and Records in Misdemeanor Cases

Chapter 3 adopted effective January 1, 2009.

Art. 1: Taking Appeals in Misdemeanor Cases. Rules 8.850–8.855.
Art. 2: Record in Misdemeanor Appeals. Rules 8.860–8.874.

Article 1
Taking Appeals in Misdemeanor Cases

Article 1 adopted effective January 1, 2009.

Rule 8.850. Application of chapter
Rule 8.851. Appointment of appellate counsel
Rule 8.852. Notice of appeal
Rule 8.853. Time to appeal
Rule 8.854. Stay of execution and release on appeal
Rule 8.855. Abandoning the appeal

Rule 8.850. Application of chapter

The rules in this chapter apply only to appeals in misdemeanor cases. In postconviction appeals, misdemeanor cases are cases in which the defendant was convicted of a misdemeanor and was not charged with any felony. In preconviction appeals, misdemeanor cases are cases in which the defendant was charged with a misdemeanor but was not charged with any felony. A felony is "charged" when an information or indictment accusing the defendant of a felony is filed or a complaint accusing the defendant of a felony is certified to the superior court under Penal Code section 859a.

Rule 8.850 adopted effective January 1, 2009.

Advisory Committee Comment

Chapters 1 and 4 of this division also apply in appeals from misdemeanor cases. The rules that apply in appeals in felony cases are located in chapter 3 of division 1 of this title.

Penal Code section 1466 provides that an appeal in a "misdemeanor or infraction case" is to the appellate division of the superior court, and Penal Code section 1235(b), in turn, provides that an appeal in a "felony case" is to the Court of Appeal. Penal Code section 691(g) defines "misdemeanor or infraction case" to mean "a criminal action in which a misdemeanor or infraction is charged *and does not include a criminal action in which a felony is charged* in conjunction with a misdemeanor or infraction" (emphasis added), and section 691(f) defines "felony case" to mean "a criminal action in which a felony is charged *and includes a criminal action in which a misdemeanor or infraction is charged in conjunction with a felony*" (emphasis added).

As rule 8.304 from the rules on felony appeals provides, the following types of cases are felony cases, not misdemeanor cases: (1) an action in which the defendant is charged with a felony and a misdemeanor, but is convicted of only the misdemeanor; (2) an action in which the defendant is charged with felony, but is convicted of only a lesser offense; or (3) an action in which the defendant is charged with an offense filed as a felony but punishable as either a felony or a misdemeanor, and the offense is thereafter deemed a misdemeanor under Penal Code section 17(b). Rule 8.304 makes it clear that a "felony case" is an action in which a felony is charged *regardless of the outcome of the action*. Thus the question of which rules apply—these rules governing appeals in misdemeanor cases or the rules governing appeals in felony cases—is answered simply by examining the accusatory pleading: if that document charged the defendant with at least one count of felony (as defined in Penal Code, section 17(a)), the Court of Appeal has appellate jurisdiction and the appeal must be taken under the rules on felony appeals *even if the prosecution did not result in a punishment of imprisonment in a state prison.*

It is settled case law that an appeal is taken to the Court of Appeal not only when the defendant is charged with and convicted of a felony, but also when the defendant is charged with both a felony and a misdemeanor (Pen. Code, § 691(f)) but is convicted of only the misdemeanor (e.g., *People v. Brown* (1970) 10 Cal.App.3d 169); when the defendant is charged with a felony but is convicted of only a lesser offense (Pen. Code, § 1159; e.g., *People v. Spreckels* (1954) 125 Cal.App.2d 507); and when the defendant is charged with an offense filed as a felony but punishable as either a felony or a misdemeanor, and the offense is thereafter deemed a misdemeanor under Penal Code section 17(b) (e.g., *People v. Douglas* (1999) 20 Cal.4th 85; *People v. Clark* (1971) 17 Cal.App.3d 890).

Trial court unification did not change this rule: after as before unification, "Appeals in felony cases lie to the [C]ourt of [A]ppeal, regardless of whether the appeal is from the superior court, the municipal court, or the action of a magistrate. *Cf.* Cal. Const. art. VI, § 11(a) [except in death penalty cases, Courts of Appeal have appellate jurisdiction when superior courts have original jurisdiction 'in causes of a type within the appellate jurisdiction of the [C]ourts of [A]ppeal on June 30, 1995....']." ("Recommendation on Trial Court Unification" (July 1998) 28 *Cal. Law Revision Com. Rep.* 455–56.)

Rule 8.851. Appointment of appellate counsel

(a) Standards for appointment

(1) On application, the appellate division must appoint appellate counsel for a defendant who was represented by appointed counsel in the trial court or establishes indigency and who:

(A) Was convicted of a misdemeanor and is subject to incarceration or a fine of more than $500 (including penalty and other assessments), or who is likely to suffer significant adverse collateral consequences as a result of the conviction; or

(B) Is charged with a misdemeanor and the appeal is a critical stage of the criminal process.

(2) On application, the appellate division may appoint counsel for any other indigent defendant charged with or convicted of a misdemeanor.

(3) For applications under (1)(A), a defendant is subject to incarceration or a fine if the incarceration or fine is in a sentence, is a condition of probation, or may be ordered if the defendant violates probation.

(Subd (a) amended effective September 1, 2020; adopted effective January 1, 2009.)

(b) Application; duties of trial counsel and clerk

(1) If defense trial counsel has reason to believe that the client is indigent and will file an appeal or is a party in an appeal described in (a)(1)(B), counsel must prepare and file in the trial court an application to the appellate division for appointment of counsel.

(2) If the defendant was represented by appointed counsel in the trial court, the application must include trial counsel's declaration to that effect. If the defendant was not represented by appointed counsel in the trial court, the application must include a declaration of indigency in the form required by the Judicial Council.

(3) Within 15 court days after an application is filed in the trial court, the clerk must send it to the appellate division. A defendant may, however, apply directly to the appellate division for appointment of counsel at any time after the notice of appeal is filed.

(4) The appellate division must grant or deny a defendant's application for appointment of counsel within 30 days after the application is filed.

(Subd (b) amended effective September 1, 2020; adopted effective January 1, 2009; previously amended effective March 1, 2014.)

(c) Defendant found able to pay in trial court

(1) If a defendant was represented by appointed counsel in the trial court and was found able to pay all or part of the cost of counsel in proceedings under Penal Code section 987.8 or 987.81, the findings in those proceedings must be included in the record or, if the findings were made after the record is sent to the appellate division, must be sent as an augmentation of the record.

(2) In cases under (1), the appellate division may determine the defendant's ability to pay all or part of the cost of counsel on appeal, and if it finds the defendant able, may order the defendant to pay all or part of that cost.

(Subd (c) adopted effective January 1, 2009.)

Rule 8.851 amended effective September 1, 2020; adopted effective January 1, 2009; previously amended March 1, 2014.

Advisory Committee Comment

Request for Court-Appointed Lawyer in Misdemeanor Appeal (form CR-133) may be used to request that appellate counsel be appointed in a misdemeanor case. If the defendant was not represented by the public defender or other appointed counsel in the trial court, the defendant must use *Defendant's Financial Statement on Eligibility for Appointment of Counsel and Reimbursement and Record on Appeal at Public Expense* (form CR-105) to show indigency. These forms are available at any courthouse or county law library or online at *www.courts.ca.gov/forms.*

Subdivision (a)(1)(B). In *Gardner v. Appellate Division of Superior Court* (2019) 6 Cal.5th 998, the California Supreme Court addressed what constitutes a critical stage of the criminal process. The court provided the analysis for determining whether a defendant has a right to counsel in confrontational proceedings other than trial, and held that the pretrial prosecution appeal of an order granting the defendant's motion to suppress evidence was a critical stage of the process at which the defendant, who was represented by appointed counsel in the trial court, had a right to appointed counsel as a matter of state constitutional law.

Rule 8.852. Notice of appeal

(a) Notice of appeal

(1) To appeal from a judgment or an appealable order of the trial court in a misdemeanor case, the defendant or the People must file a notice of appeal in the trial court. The notice must specify the judgment or order—or part of it—being appealed.

(2) If the defendant appeals, the defendant or the defendant's attorney must sign the notice of appeal. If the People appeal, the attorney for the People must sign the notice.

(3) The notice of appeal must be liberally construed in favor of its sufficiency.

(Subd (a) adopted effective January 1, 2009.)

(b) Notification of the appeal

(1) When a notice of appeal is filed, the trial court clerk must promptly send a notification of the filing to the attorney of record for each party and to any unrepresented defendant. The clerk must also send or deliver this notification to the appellate division clerk.

(2) The notification must show the date it was sent or delivered, the number and title of the case, the date the notice of appeal was filed, and whether the defendant was represented by appointed counsel.

(3) The notification to the appellate division clerk must also include a copy of the notice of appeal.

(4) A copy of the notice of appeal is sufficient notification under (1) if the required information is on the copy or is added by the trial court clerk.

(5) The sending of a notification under (1) is a sufficient performance of the clerk's duty despite the discharge, disqualification, suspension, disbarment, or death of the attorney.

(6) Failure to comply with any provision of this subdivision does not affect the validity of the notice of appeal.

(Subd (b) amended effective January 1, 2016; adopted effective January 1, 2009.)

Rule 8.852 amended effective January 1, 2016; adopted effective January 1, 2009.

Advisory Committee Comment

Notice of Appeal (Misdemeanor) (form CR-132) may be used to file the notice of appeal required under this rule. This form is available at any courthouse or county law library or online at *www.courts.ca.gov/forms.*

Subdivision (a). The only orders that a defendant can appeal in a misdemeanor case are (1) orders granting or denying a motion to suppress evidence (Penal Code section 1538.5(j)); and (2) orders made after the final judgment that affects the substantial rights of the defendant (Penal Code section 1466).

Rule 8.853. Time to appeal

(a) Normal time

A notice of appeal must be filed within 30 days after the rendition of the judgment or the making of the order being appealed. If the defendant is committed before final judgment for insanity or narcotics addiction, the notice of appeal must be filed within 30 days after the commitment.

(Subd (a) adopted effective January 1, 2009.)

(b) Cross-appeal

If the defendant or the People timely appeal from a judgment or appealable order, the time for any other party to appeal from the same judgment or order is either the time specified in (a) or 15 days after the trial court clerk sends notification of the first appeal, whichever is later.

(Subd (b) amended effective January 1, 2016; adopted effective January 1, 2009.)

(c) Premature notice of appeal

A notice of appeal filed before the judgment is rendered or the order is made is premature, but the appellate division may treat the notice as filed immediately after the rendition of the judgment or the making of the order.

(Subd (c) adopted effective January 1, 2009.)

(d) Late notice of appeal

The trial court clerk must mark a late notice of appeal "Received [date] but not filed" and notify the party that the notice was not filed because it was late.

(Subd (d) adopted effective January 1, 2009.)

Rule 8.853 amended effective January 1, 2016; adopted effective January 1, 2009; previously amended effective July 1, 2010.

Advisory Committee Comment

Subdivision (d). See rule 8.817(b)(5) for provisions concerning the timeliness of documents mailed by inmates or patients from custodial institutions.

Rule 8.854. Stay of execution and release on appeal

(a) Application

Pending appeal, the defendant may apply to the appellate division:

(1) For a stay of execution after a judgment of conviction or an order granting probation; or

(2) For bail for release from custody, to reduce bail for release from custody, or for release on other conditions.

(Subd (a) adopted effective January 1, 2009.)

(b) Showing

The application must include a showing that the defendant sought relief in the trial court and that the court unjustifiably denied the application.

(Subd (b) adopted effective January 1, 2009.)

(c) Service

The application must be served on the prosecuting attorney.

(Subd (c) adopted effective January 1, 2009.)

(d) Interim relief

Pending its ruling on the application, the appellate division may grant the relief requested. The appellate division must notify the trial court of any stay that it grants.

(Subd (d) adopted effective January 1, 2009.)

Rule 8.854 adopted effective January 1, 2009.

Advisory Committee Comment

Subdivision (c). As defined in rule 8.804, the "prosecuting attorney" may be the city attorney, county counsel, district attorney, or state Attorney General, depending on what government agency filed the criminal charges.

Rule 8.855. Abandoning the appeal

(a) How to abandon

An appellant may abandon the appeal at any time by filing an abandonment of the appeal signed by the appellant or the appellant's attorney of record.

(Subd (a) adopted effective January 1, 2009.)

(b) Where to file; effect of filing

(1) The appellant must file the abandonment in the appellate division.

(2) If the record has not been filed in the appellate division, the filing of an abandonment effects a dismissal of the appeal and restores the trial court's jurisdiction.

(3) If the record has been filed in the appellate division, the appellate division may dismiss the appeal and direct immediate issuance of the remittitur.

(Subd (b) adopted effective January 1, 2009.)

(c) Clerk's duties

(1) The appellate division clerk must immediately notify the adverse party of the filing or of the order of dismissal.

(2) If the record has not been filed in the appellate division, the clerk must immediately notify the trial court.

(3) If a reporter's transcript has been requested, the clerk must immediately notify the reporter if the appeal is abandoned before the reporter has filed the transcript.

(Subd (c) adopted effective January 1, 2009.)

Rule 8.855 adopted effective January 1, 2009.

Advisory Committee Comment

Abandonment of Appeal (Misdemeanor) (form CR-137) may be used to file an abandonment under this rule. This form is available at any courthouse or county law library or online at *www.courtinfo.ca.gov/forms*.

Article 2
Record in Misdemeanor Appeals

Article 2 adopted effective January 1, 2009.

Rule 8.860. Normal record on appeal
Rule 8.861. Contents of clerk's transcript
Rule 8.862. Preparation of clerk's transcript
Rule 8.863. Trial court file instead of clerk's transcript
Rule 8.864. Record of oral proceedings
Rule 8.865. Contents of reporter's transcript
Rule 8.866. Preparation of reporter's transcript
Rule 8.867. Limited normal record in certain appeals
Rule 8.868. Record when trial proceedings were officially electronically recorded
Rule 8.869. Statement on appeal
Rule 8.870. Exhibits
Rule 8.871. Juror-identifying information
Rule 8.872. Sending and filing the record in the appellate division
Rule 8.873. Augmenting or correcting the record in the appellate division
Rule 8.874. Failure to procure the record

Rule 8.860. Normal record on appeal

(a) Contents

Except as otherwise provided in this chapter, the record on an appeal to a superior court appellate division in a misdemeanor criminal case must contain the following, which constitute the normal record on appeal:

(1) A record of the written documents from the trial court proceedings in the form of one of the following:

(A) A clerk's transcript under rule 8.861 or 8.867; or

(B) If the court has a local rule for the appellate division electing to use this form of the record, the original trial court file under rule 8.863.

(2) If an appellant wants to raise any issue that requires consideration of the oral proceedings in the trial court, the record on appeal must include a record of the oral proceedings in the form of one of the following:

(A) A reporter's transcript under rules 8.865–8.867 or a transcript prepared from an official electronic recording under rule 8.868;

(B) If the court has a local rule for the appellate division permitting this form of the record, an official electronic recording of the proceedings under rule 8.868; or

(C) A statement on appeal under rule 8.869.

(Subd (a) adopted effective January 1, 2009.)

(b) Stipulation for limited record

If, before the record is certified, the appellant and the respondent stipulate in writing that any part of the record is not required for proper determination of the appeal and file that stipulation in the trial court, that part of the record must not be prepared or sent to the appellate division.

(Subd (b) amended effective July 1, 2009; adopted effective January 1, 2009.)

Rule 8.860 amended effective July 1, 2009; adopted effective January 1, 2009.

Rule 8.861. Contents of clerk's transcript

Except in appeals covered by rule 8.867 or when the parties have filed a stipulation under rule 8.860(b) that any of these items is not required for proper determination of the appeal, the clerk's transcript must contain:

(1) The complaint, including any notice to appear, and any amendment;

(2) Any demurrer or other plea;

(3) All court minutes;

(4) Any jury instructions that any party submitted in writing, the cover page required by rule 2.1055(b)(2), and any written jury instructions given by the court;

(5) Any written communication between the court and the jury or any individual juror;

(6) Any verdict;

(7) Any written findings or opinion of the court;

(8) The judgment or order appealed from;

(9) Any motion or notice of motion for new trial, in arrest of judgment, or to dismiss the action, with supporting and opposing memoranda and attachments;

(10) Any transcript of a sound or sound-and-video recording furnished to the jury or tendered to the court under rule 2.1040; and

(11) The notice of appeal; and

(12) If the appellant is the defendant:

(A) Any written defense motion denied in whole or in part, with supporting and opposing memoranda and attachments;

(B) If related to a motion under (A), any search warrant and return;

(C) Any document admitted in evidence to prove a prior juvenile adjudication, criminal conviction, or prison term. If a record was closed to public inspection in the trial court because it is required to be kept confidential by law, it must remain closed to public inspection in the appellate division unless that court orders otherwise;

(D) The probation officer's report; and

(E) Any court-ordered psychological report required under Penal Code section 1369.

Rule 8.861 amended effective January 1, 2010; adopted effective January 1, 2009.

Advisory Committee Comment

Rule 8.862(c) addresses the appropriate handling of probation officers' reports that must be included in the clerk's transcript under (12)(D).

Rule 8.862. Preparation of clerk's transcript

(a) When preparation begins

Unless the original court file will be used in place of a clerk's transcript under rule 8.863, the clerk must begin preparing the clerk's transcript immediately after the notice of appeal is filed.

(Subd (a) adopted effective January 1, 2009.)

(b) Format of transcript

The clerk's transcript must comply with rule 8.144.

(Subd (b) adopted effective January 1, 2009.)

(c) Probation officer's reports

A probation officer's report included in the clerk's transcript under rule 8.861(12)(D) must appear in only the copies of the appellate record that are sent to the reviewing court, to appellate counsel for the People, and to appellate counsel for the defendant who was the subject of the report or to the defendant if he or she is self-represented. If the report is in paper form, it must be placed in a sealed envelope. The reviewing court's copy of the report, and if applicable, the envelope, must be marked "CONFIDENTIAL—MAY NOT BE EXAMINED WITHOUT COURT ORDER—PROBATION OFFICER REPORT."

(Subd (c) amended effective January 1, 2016; adopted effective January 1, 2010.)

(d) When preparation must be completed

Within 20 days after the notice of appeal is filed, the clerk must complete preparation of an original clerk's transcript for the appellate division, one copy for the appellant, and one copy for the respondent. If there is more than one appellant, the clerk must prepare an extra copy for each additional appellant who is represented by separate counsel or self-represented.

(Subd (d) relettered effective January 1, 2010; adopted as subd (c) effective January 1, 2009; previously amended effective July 1, 2009.)

(e) Certification

The clerk must certify as correct the original and all copies of the clerk's transcript.

(Subd (e) relettered effective January 1, 2010; adopted as subd (d) effective January 1, 2009.)

Rule 8.862 amended effective January 1, 2016; adopted effective January 1, 2009; previously amended effective July 1, 2009, and January 1, 2010.

Advisory Committee Comment

Rule 8.872 addresses when the clerk's transcript is sent to the appellate division in misdemeanor appeals.

Rule 8.863. Trial court file instead of clerk's transcript

(a) Application

If the court has a local rule for the appellate division electing to use this form of the record, the original trial court file may be used instead of a clerk's transcript. This rule and any supplemental provisions of the local rule then govern unless the trial court orders otherwise after notice to the parties.

(Subd (a) adopted effective January 1, 2009.)

(b) When original file must be prepared

Within 20 days after the filing of the notice of appeal, the trial court clerk must put the trial court file in chronological order, number the pages, and attach a chronological index and a list of all attorneys of record, the parties they represent, and any unrepresented parties.

(Subd (b) adopted effective January 1, 2009.)

(c) Copies

The clerk must send a copy of the index to the appellant and the respondent for use in paginating their copies of the file to conform to the index. If there is more than one appellant, the clerk must prepare an extra copy of the index for each additional appellant who is represented by separate counsel or self-represented.

(Subd (c) amended effective July 1, 2009; adopted effective January 1, 2009.)

Rule 8.863 amended effective July 1, 2009; adopted effective January 1, 2009.

Advisory Committee Comment

Rule 8.872 addresses when the original file is sent to the appellate division in misdemeanor appeals.

Rule 8.864. Record of oral proceedings

(a) Appellant's election

The appellant must notify the trial court whether he or she elects to proceed with or without a record of the oral proceedings in the trial court. If the appellant elects to proceed with a record of the oral proceedings in the trial court, the notice must specify which form of the record of the oral proceedings in the trial court the appellant elects to use:

(1) A reporter's transcript under rules 8.865–8.867 or a transcript prepared from an official electronic recording of the proceedings under rule 8.868(b). If the appellant elects to use a reporter's transcript, the clerk must promptly send a copy of appellant's notice making this election and the notice of appeal to each court reporter;

(2) An official electronic recording of the proceedings under rule 8.868(c). If the appellant elects to use the official electronic recording itself, rather than a transcript prepared from that recording, the appellant must attach a copy of the stipulation required under rule 8.868(c); or

(3) A statement on appeal under rule 8.869.

(Subd (a) amended effective January 1, 2016; adopted effective January 1, 2009.)

(b) Time for filing election

The notice of election required under (a) must be filed no later than the following:

(1) If no application for appointment of counsel is filed, 20 days after the notice of appeal is filed; or

(2) If an application for appointment of counsel is filed before the period under (A) expires, either 10 days after the court appoints counsel to represent the defendant on appeal or denies the application for appointment of counsel or 20 days after the notice of appeal is filed, whichever is later.

(Subd (b) adopted effective January 1, 2009.)

(c) Failure to file election

If the appellant does not file an election within the time specified in (b), rule 8.874 applies.

(Subd (c) amended effective March 1, 2014; adopted effective January 1, 2010.)

Rule 8.864 amended effective January 1, 2016; adopted effective January 1, 2009; previously amended effective January 1, 2010, and March 1, 2014.

Advisory Committee Comment

Notice Regarding Record of Oral Proceedings (Misdemeanor) (form CR-134) may be used to file the election required under this rule. This form is available at any courthouse or county law library or online at *www.courtinfo.ca.gov/forms*. To assist parties in making an appropriate election, courts are encouraged to include information about whether the proceedings were recorded by a court reporter or officially electronically recorded in any information that the court provides to parties concerning their appellate rights.

Rule 8.865. Contents of reporter's transcript

(a) Normal contents

Except in appeals covered by rule 8.867, when the parties have filed a stipulation under rule 8.860(b), or when, under a procedure established by a local rule adopted pursuant to (b), the trial court has ordered that any of these items is not required for proper determination of the appeal, the reporter's transcript must contain:

(1) The oral proceedings on the entry of any plea other than a not guilty plea;

(2) The oral proceedings on any motion in limine;

(3) The oral proceedings at trial, but excluding the voir dire examination of jurors and any opening statement;

(4) Any jury instructions given orally;

(5) Any oral communication between the court and the jury or any individual juror;

(6) Any oral opinion of the court;

(7) The oral proceedings on any motion for new trial;

(8) The oral proceedings at sentencing, granting or denying probation, or other dispositional hearing;

(9) If the appellant is the defendant, the reporter's transcript must also contain:

(A) The oral proceedings on any defense motion denied in whole or in part except motions for disqualification of a judge;

(B) Any closing arguments; and

(C) Any comment on the evidence by the court to the jury.

(Subd (a) lettered and amended effective March 1, 2014; adopted effective January 1, 2009.)

(b) Local procedure for determining contents

A court may adopt a local rule that establishes procedures for determining whether any of the items listed in (a) is not required for proper determination of the appeal or whether a form of the record other than a reporter's transcript constitutes a record of sufficient completeness for proper determination of the appeal.

(Subd (b) adopted effective March 1, 2014.)

Rule 8.865 amended effective March 1, 2014; adopted effective January 1, 2009.

Advisory Committee Comment

Subdivision (b). Both the United States Supreme Court and the California Supreme Court have held that, where the State has established a right to appeal, an indigent defendant convicted of a criminal offense has a constitutional right to a "'record of sufficient completeness' to permit proper consideration of [his] claims." (*Mayer v. Chicago* (1971) 404 U.S. 189, 193–194; *March v. Municipal Court* (1972) 7 Cal.3d 422, 427–428.) The California Supreme Court has also held that an indigent appellant is denied his or her right under the Fourteenth Amendment to the competent assistance of counsel on appeal if counsel fails to obtain an appellate record adequate for consideration of appellant's claims of errors (*People v. Barton* (1978) 21 Cal.3d 513, 518–520).

The *Mayer* and *March* decisions make clear, however, that the constitutionally required "record of sufficient completeness" does not necessarily mean a complete verbatim transcript; other forms of the record, such as a statement on appeal, or a partial transcript may be sufficient. The record that is necessary depends on the grounds for the appeal in the particular case. Under these decisions, where the grounds of appeal make out a colorable need for a complete transcript, the burden is on the State to show that only a portion of the transcript or an alternative form of the record will suffice for an effective appeal on those grounds. The burden of overcoming the need for a verbatim reporter's transcript appears to be met where a verbatim recording of the proceedings is provided. (*Mayer, supra,* 404 U.S. at p. 195; cf. *Eyrich v. Mun. Court* (1985) 165 Cal.App.3d 1138, 1140 ["Although use of a court reporter is one way of obtaining a verbatim record, it may also be acquired through an electronic recording when no court reporter is available"].)

Some courts have adopted local rules that establish procedures for determining whether only a portion of a verbatim transcript or an alternative form of the record will be sufficient for an effective appeal, including (1) requiring the appellant to specify the points the appellant is raising on appeal; (2) requiring the appellant and respondent to meet and confer about the content and form of the record; and (3) holding a hearing on the content and form of the record. Local procedures can be tailored to reflect the methods available in a particular court for making a record of the trial court proceedings that is sufficient for an effective appeal.

Rule 8.866. Preparation of reporter's transcript

(a) When preparation begins

(1) Unless the court has adopted a local rule under rule 8.865(b) that provides otherwise, the reporter must immediately begin preparing the reporter's transcript if the notice sent to the reporter by the clerk under rule 8.864(a)(1) indicates either:

(A) That the defendant was represented by appointed counsel at trial; or

(B) That the appellant is the People.

(2) If the notice sent to the reporter by the clerk under rule 8.864(a)(1) indicates that the appellant is the defendant and that the defendant was not represented by appointed counsel at trial:

(A) Within 10 days after the date the clerk sent the notice under rule 8.864(a)(1), the reporter must file with the clerk the estimated cost of preparing the reporter's transcript.

(B) The clerk must promptly notify the appellant and his or her counsel of the estimated cost of preparing the reporter's transcript. The notification must show the date it was sent.

(C) Within 10 days after the date the clerk sent the notice under (B), the appellant must do one of the following:

(i) Deposit with the clerk an amount equal to the estimated cost of preparing the transcript;

(ii) File a waiver of the deposit signed by the reporter;

(iii) File a declaration of indigency supported by evidence in the form required by the Judicial Council;

(iv) File a certified transcript of all of the proceedings required to be included in the reporter's transcript under rule 8.865. The transcript submitted by the appellant must not be accepted as a substitute for a deposit under (i) unless it complies with the format requirements of rule 8.838;

(v) Notify the clerk by filing a new election that he or she will be using a statement on appeal instead of a reporter's transcript. The appellant must prepare, serve, and file a proposed statement on appeal within 20 days after serving and filing the notice and must otherwise comply with the requirements for statements on appeal under rule 8.869; or

(vi) Notify the clerk by filing a new election that he or she now elects to proceed without a record of the oral proceedings in the trial court; or

(vii) Notify the clerk that he or she is abandoning the appeal by filing an abandonment in the reviewing court under rule 8.855.

(D) If the trial court determines that the appellant is not indigent, within 10 days after the date the clerk sends notice of this determination to the appellant, the appellant must do one of the following:

(i) Deposit with the clerk an amount equal to the estimated cost of preparing the transcript;

(ii) File with the clerk a waiver of the deposit signed by the reporter;

(iii) File a certified transcript of all of the proceedings required to be included in the reporter's transcript under rule 8.865. The transcript submitted by the appellant must not be accepted as a substitute for a deposit under (i) unless it complies with the format requirements of rule 8.838;

(iv) Notify the clerk by filing a new election that he or she will be using a statement on appeal instead of a reporter's transcript. The appellant must prepare, serve, and file a proposed statement on appeal within 20 days after serving and filing the notice and must otherwise comply with the requirements for statements on appeal under rule 8.869;

(v) Notify the clerk by filing a new election that he or she now elects to proceed without a record of the oral proceedings in the trial court; or

(vi) Notify the clerk that he or she is abandoning the appeal by filing an abandonment in the reviewing court under rule 8.855.

(E) The clerk must promptly notify the reporter to begin preparing the transcript when:

(i) The clerk receives the required deposit under (C)(i) or (D)(i);

(ii) The clerk receives a waiver of the deposit signed by the reporter under (C)(ii) or (D)(ii); or

(iii) The trial court determines that the appellant is indigent and orders that the appellant receive the transcript without cost.

(Subd (a) amended effective January 1, 2024; adopted effective January 1, 2009; previously amended effective March 1, 2014, and January 1, 2016.)

(b) Format of transcript

The reporter's transcript must comply with rule 8.838.

(Subd (b) amended effective January 1, 2024; adopted effective January 1, 2009.)

(c) Copies and certification

The reporter must prepare an original and the same number of copies of the reporter's transcript as rule 8.862 requires of the clerk's transcript and must certify each as correct.

(Subd (c) adopted effective January 1, 2009.)

(d) When preparation must be completed

(1) The reporter must deliver the original and all copies to the trial court clerk as soon as they are certified but no later than 20 days after the reporter is required to begin preparing the transcript under (a). Only the presiding judge of the appellate division or his or her designee may extend the time to prepare the reporter's transcript (see rule 8.810).

(2) If the appellant deposited with the clerk an amount equal to the estimated cost of preparing the transcript and the appeal is abandoned or dismissed before the reporter has filed the transcript, the reporter must inform the clerk of the cost of the portion of the transcript that the reporter has completed. The clerk must pay that amount to the reporter from the appellant's deposited funds and refund any excess deposit to the appellant.

(Subd (d) amended effective March 5, 2018; adopted effective January 1, 2009; previously amended effective March 1, 2014, January 1, 2017, and January 1, 2018.)

(e) Multi-reporter cases

In a multi-reporter case, the clerk must accept any completed portion of the transcript from the primary reporter one week after the time prescribed by (d) even if other portions are uncompleted. The clerk must promptly pay each reporter who certifies that all portions of the transcript assigned to that reporter are completed.

(Subd (e) adopted effective January 1, 2009.)

(f) Notice when proceedings were not reported or cannot be transcribed

(1) If any portion of the oral proceedings to be included in the reporter's transcript was not reported or cannot be transcribed, the trial court clerk must so notify the parties in writing. The notice must:

(A) Indicate whether the identified proceedings were officially electronically recorded under Government Code section 69957; and

(B) Show the date it was sent.

(2) Within 15 days after this notice is sent by the clerk, the appellant must serve and file a notice with the court stating whether the appellant

elects to proceed with or without a record of the identified proceedings. When the party elects to proceed with a record of these oral proceedings:

(A) If the clerk's notice under (1) indicates that the proceedings were officially electronically recorded under Government Code section 69957, the appellant's notice must specify which form of the record listed in rule 8.864(a) other than a reporter's transcript the appellant elects to use. The appellant must comply with the requirements applicable to the form of the record elected.

(B) If the clerk's notice under (1) indicates that the proceedings were not officially electronically recorded under Government Code section 69957, the appellant must prepare, serve, and file a proposed statement on appeal within 20 days after serving and filing the notice.

(Subd (f) amended effective January 1, 2016; adopted effective March 1, 2014.)
Rule 8.866 amended effective January 1, 2024; adopted effective January 1, 2009; previously amended effective March 1, 2014, January 1, 2016, January 1, 2017, January 1, 2018, and March 5, 2018.

Advisory Committee Comment

Subdivision (a). If the appellant was not represented by the public defender or other appointed counsel in the trial court, the appellant must use *Defendant's Financial Statement on Eligibility for Appointment of Counsel and Reimbursement and Record on Appeal at Public Expense* (form CR-105) to show indigency. This form is available at any courthouse or county law library or online at *www.courts.ca.gov/forms.*

Subdivisions (a)(2)(C)(iv) and (a)(2)(D)(iii). Sometimes a party in a trial court proceeding will purchase a reporter's transcript of all or part of the proceedings before any appeal is filed. In recognition of the fact that such transcripts may already have been purchased, this rule allows an appellant, in lieu of depositing funds for a reporter's transcript, to deposit with the trial court a certified transcript of the proceedings necessary for the appeal. Subdivisions (a)(2)(C)(iv) and (a)(2)(D)(iii) make clear that the certified transcript may be filed in lieu of a deposit for a reporter's transcript only where the certified transcript contains all of the proceedings required under rule 8.865 and the transcript complies with the format requirements of rule 8.838 (e.g., cover information, renumbered pages, required indexes). Parties using this alternative to a deposit are responsible for ensuring that such transcripts are in the proper format. Parties may arrange with a court reporter to do the necessary formatting of the transcript or may do the formatting themselves.

Rule 8.867. Limited normal record in certain appeals

(a) Application and additions

This rule establishes a limited normal record for certain appeals. This rule does not alter the parties' right to request that exhibits be transmitted to the reviewing court under rule 8.870 nor preclude either an application in the superior court under (e) for additions to the limited normal record or a motion in the reviewing court for augmentation under rule 8.841.

(Subd (a) adopted effective March 1, 2014.)

(b) Pretrial appeals of rulings on motions under Penal Code section 1538.5

If before trial either the defendant or the People appeal a ruling on a motion under Penal Code section 1538.5 for the return of property or the suppression of evidence, the normal record is composed of:

(1) *Record of the documents filed in the trial court*

A clerk's transcript or original trial court file containing:

(A) The complaint, including any notice to appear, and any amendment;

(B) The motion under Penal Code section 1538.5, with supporting and opposing memoranda, and attachments;

(C) The order on the motion under Penal Code section 1538.5;

(D) Any court minutes relating to the order; and

(E) The notice of appeal.

(2) *Record of the oral proceedings in the trial court*

If an appellant wants to raise any issue that requires consideration of the oral proceedings in the trial court, a reporter's transcript, a transcript prepared under rule 8.868, an official electronic recording under rule 8.868, or a statement on appeal under rule 8.869 summarizing any oral proceedings incident to the order on the motion under Penal Code section 1538.5.

(Subd (b) adopted effective March 1, 2014.)

(c) Appeals from judgments on demurrers or certain appealable orders

If the People appeal from a judgment on a demurrer to the complaint, including any notice to appear, or if the defendant or the People appeal from an appealable order other than a ruling on a motion for new trial or a ruling covered by (a), the normal record is composed of:

(1) *Record of the documents filed in the trial court*

A clerk's transcript or original trial court file containing:

(A) The complaint, including any notice to appear, and any amendment;

(B) Any demurrer or other plea;

(C) Any motion or notice of motion granted or denied by the order appealed from, with supporting and opposing memoranda and attachments;

(D) The judgment or order appealed from and any abstract of judgment or commitment;

(E) Any court minutes relating to the judgment or order appealed from and

(i) If there was a trial in the case, any court minutes of proceedings at the time the original verdict is rendered and any subsequent proceedings; or

(ii) If the original judgment of conviction is based on a guilty plea or nolo contendere plea, any court minutes of the proceedings at the time of entry of such plea and any subsequent proceedings;

(F) The notice of appeal; and

(G) If the appellant is the defendant, all probation officer reports.

(2) *Record of the oral proceedings in the trial court*

If an appellant wants to raise any issue which requires consideration of the oral proceedings in the trial court:

(A) A reporter's transcript, a transcript prepared under rule 8.868, an official electronic recording under rule 8.868, or a statement on appeal under rule 8.869 summarizing any oral proceedings incident to the judgment or order being appealed.

(B) If the appeal is from an order after judgment, a reporter's transcript, a transcript prepared under rule 8.868, an official electronic recording under rule 8.868, or a statement on appeal under rule 8.869 summarizing any oral proceedings from:

(i) The original sentencing proceeding; and

(ii) If the original judgment of conviction is based on a guilty plea or nolo contendere plea, the proceedings at the time of entry of such plea.

(Subd (c) amended and lettered effective March 1, 2014; adopted effective January 1, 2009; previously amended effective January 1, 2013.)

(d) Appeals of the conditions of probation

If a defendant's appeal of the judgment contests only the conditions of probation, the normal record is composed of:

(1) *Record of the documents filed in the trial court*

A clerk's transcript or original trial court file containing:

(A) The complaint, including any notice to appear, and any amendment;

(B) The judgment or order appealed from and any abstract of judgment or commitment;

(C) Any court minutes relating to the judgment or order appealed from and:

(i) If there was a trial in the case, any court minutes of proceedings at the time the original verdict is rendered and any subsequent proceedings; or

(ii) If the original judgment of conviction is based on a guilty plea or nolo contendere plea, any court minutes of the proceedings at the time of entry of such plea and any subsequent proceedings;

(D) The notice of appeal; and

(E) All probation officer reports.

(2) *Record of the oral proceedings in the trial court*

If an appellant wants to raise any issue that requires consideration of the oral proceedings in the trial court, a reporter's transcript, a transcript prepared under rule 8.868, an official electronic recording under rule 8.868, or a statement on appeal under rule 8.869 summarizing any oral proceedings from:

(A) The sentencing proceeding; and

(B) If the judgment of conviction is based on a guilty plea or nolo contendere plea, the proceedings at the time of entry of such plea.

(Subd (d) adopted effective March 1, 2014.)

(e) Additions to the record

Either the People or the defendant may apply to the superior court for inclusion in the record under (b), (c), or (d) of any item that would ordinarily be included in the clerk's transcript under rule 8.861 or a reporter's transcript under rule 8.865.

(1) An application for additional record must describe the material to be included and explain how it may be useful in the appeal.

(2) The application must be filed in the superior court with the notice of appeal or as soon thereafter as possible, and will be treated as denied if it is filed after the record is sent to the reviewing court.

(3) The clerk must immediately present the application to the trial judge.

(4) Within five days after the application is filed, the judge must order that the record include as much of the additional material as the judge finds proper to fully present the points raised by the applicant. Denial of the application does not preclude a motion in the reviewing court for augmentation under rule 8.841.

(5) If the judge does not rule on the application within the time prescribed by (4), the requested material—other than exhibits—must be included in the clerk's transcript or the reporter's transcript without a court order.

(6) The clerk must immediately notify the reporter if additions to the reporter's transcript are required under (4) or (5).

(Subd (e) adopted effective March 1, 2014.)

Rule 8.867 amended effective March 1, 2014; adopted effective January 1, 2009; previously amended effective January 1, 2013.

Advisory Committee Comment

Subdivisions (b)(1)(D), (c)(1)(E), and (d)(1)(C). These provisions identify the minutes that must be included in the record. The trial court clerk may include additional minutes beyond those identified in these subdivisions if that would be more cost-effective.

Subdivisions (c)(1)(G) and (d)(1)(E). Rule 8.862(c) addresses the appropriate handling of probation officers' reports that must be included in the clerk's transcript.

Rule 8.868. Record when trial proceedings were officially electronically recorded

(a) Application

This rule applies only if:

(1) The trial court proceedings were officially recorded electronically under Government Code section 69957; and

(2) The electronic recording was prepared in compliance with applicable rules regarding electronic recording of court proceedings.

(Subd (a) adopted effective January 1, 2009.)

(b) Transcripts from official electronic recording

Written transcripts of an official electronic recording may be prepared under rule 2.952. A transcript prepared and certified as provided in that rule is prima facie a true and complete record of the oral proceedings it purports to cover, and satisfies any requirement in these rules or in any statute for a reporter's transcript of oral proceedings.

(Subd (b) adopted effective January 1, 2009.)

(c) Use of official recording as record of oral proceedings

If the court has a local rule for the appellate division permitting this, on stipulation of the parties or on order of the trial court under rule 8.869(d)(6), the original of an official electronic recording of the trial court proceedings, or a copy made by the court, may be transmitted as the record of these oral proceedings without being transcribed. Such an electronic recording satisfies any requirement in these rules or in any statute for a reporter's transcript of these proceedings.

(Subd (c) amended effective July 1, 2010; adopted effective January 1, 2009.)

(d) Contents

Except in appeals when either the parties have filed a stipulation under rule 8.860(b) or the trial court has ordered that any of these items is not required for proper determination of the appeal, rules 8.865 and 8.867 govern the contents of a transcript of an official electronic recording.

(Subd (d) adopted effective March 1, 2014.)

(e) When preparation begins

(1) If the appellant files an election under rule 8.864 to use a transcript of an official electronic recording or a copy of the official electronic recording as the record of the oral proceedings, unless the trial court has a local rule providing otherwise, preparation of a transcript or a copy of the recording must begin immediately if either:

(A) The defendant was represented by appointed counsel at trial; or

(B) The appellant is the People.

(2) If the appellant is the defendant and the defendant was not represented by appointed counsel at trial:

(A) Within 10 days after the date the defendant files the election under rule 8.864(a)(1), the clerk must notify the appellant and his or her counsel of the estimated cost of preparing the transcript or the copy of the recording. The notification must show the date it was sent.

(B) Within 10 days after the date the clerk sent the notice under (A), the appellant must do one of the following:

(i) Deposit with the clerk an amount equal to the estimated cost of preparing the transcript or the copy of the recording;

(ii) File a declaration of indigency supported by evidence in the form required by the Judicial Council;

(iii) Notify the clerk by filing a new election that he or she will be using a statement on appeal instead of a transcript or copy of the recording. The appellant must prepare, serve, and file a proposed statement on appeal within 20 days after serving and filing the notice and must otherwise comply with the requirements for statements on appeal under rule 8.869;

(iv) Notify the clerk by filing a new election that he or she now elects to proceed without a record of the oral proceedings in the trial court; or

(v) Notify the clerk that he or she is abandoning the appeal by filing an abandonment in the reviewing court under rule 8.855.

(C) If the trial court determines that the appellant is not indigent, within 10 days after the date the clerk sends notice of this determination to the appellant, the appellant must do one of the following:

(i) Deposit with the clerk an amount equal to the estimated cost of preparing the transcript or the copy of the recording;

(ii) Notify the clerk by filing a new election that he or she will be using a statement on appeal instead of a reporter's transcript. The appellant must prepare, serve, and file a proposed statement on appeal within 20 days after serving and filing the notice and must otherwise comply with the requirements for statements on appeal under rule 8.869;

(iii) Notify the clerk by filing a new election that he or she now elects to proceed without a record of the oral proceedings in the trial court; or

(iv) Notify the clerk that he or she is abandoning the appeal by filing an abandonment in the reviewing court under rule 8.855.

(D) Preparation of the transcript or the copy of the recording must begin when:

(i) The clerk receives the required deposit under (B)(i) or (C)(i); or

(ii) The trial court determines that the defendant is indigent and orders that the defendant receive the transcript or the copy of the recording without cost.

(Subd (e) amended effective January 1, 2016; adopted as subd (d) effective January 1, 2009; previously amended and relettered as subd (e) effective March 1, 2014.)

(f) Notice when proceedings were not officially electronically recorded or cannot be transcribed

(1) If any portion of the oral proceedings to be included in the transcript was not officially electronically recorded under Government Code section 69957 or cannot be transcribed, the trial court clerk must so notify the parties in writing. The notice must:

(A) Indicate whether the identified proceedings were reported by a court reporter; and

(B) Show the date it was sent.

(2) Within 15 days after this notice is sent by the clerk, the appellant must serve and file a notice with the court stating whether the appellant elects to proceed with or without a record of the identified oral proceedings. When the party elects to proceed with a record of these oral proceedings:

(A) If the clerk's notice under (1) indicates that the proceedings were reported by a court reporter, the appellant's notice must specify which form of the record listed in rule 8.864(a) other than an official electronic recording or a transcript prepared from an official electronic recording the appellant elects to use. The appellant must comply with the requirements applicable to the form of the record elected.

(B) If the clerk's notice under (1) indicates that the proceedings were not reported by a court reporter, the appellant must prepare, serve, and file a proposed statement on appeal within 20 days after serving and filing the notice.

(Subd (f) amended effective January 1, 2016; adopted effective March 1, 2014.)

Rule 8.868 amended effective January 1, 2016; adopted effective January 1, 2009; previously amended effective July 1, 2010, and March 1, 2014.

Advisory Committee Comment

Subdivision (d). If the appellant was not represented by the public defender or other appointed counsel in the trial court, the appellant must use *Defendant's Financial Statement on Eligibility for Appointment of Counsel and Reimbursement and Record on Appeal at Public Expense* (form CR-105) to show indigency. This form is available at any courthouse or county law library or online at www.courtinfo.ca.gov/forms.

Rule 8.869. Statement on appeal

(a) Description

A statement on appeal is a summary of the trial court proceedings that is approved by the trial court. An appellant can elect under rule 8.864 to use a statement on appeal as the record of the oral proceedings in the trial court, replacing the reporter's transcript.

(Subd (a) adopted effective January 1, 2009.)

(b) Preparing the proposed statement

(1) If the appellant elects under rule 8.864 to use a statement on appeal, the appellant must prepare, serve, and file a proposed statement within 20 days after filing the record preparation election.

(2) Appellants who are not represented by an attorney must file their proposed statement on *Proposed Statement on Appeal (Misdemeanor)* (form CR-135). For good cause, the court may permit the filing of a statement that is not on form CR-135.

(3) If the appellant does not serve and file a proposed statement within the time specified in (1), rule 8.874 applies.

(Subd (b) amended effective March 1, 2014; adopted effective January 1, 2009.)

(c) Contents of the proposed statement on appeal

A proposed statement prepared by the appellant must contain:

(1) A statement of the points the appellant is raising on appeal. The appeal is then limited to those points unless the appellate division determines that the record permits the full consideration of another point.

(A) The statement must specify the intended grounds of appeal by clearly stating each point to be raised but need not identify each particular ruling or matter to be challenged.

(B) If one of the grounds of appeal is insufficiency of the evidence, the statement must specify how it is insufficient.

(2) A summary of the trial court's rulings and the sentence imposed on the defendant.

(3) A condensed narrative of the oral proceedings that the appellant believes necessary for the appeal.

(A) The condensed narrative must include a concise factual summary of the evidence and the testimony of each witness that is relevant to the points which the appellant states under (1) are being raised on appeal. Any evidence or portion of a proceeding not included will be presumed to support the judgment or order appealed from.

(B) If one of the points which the appellant states under (1) is being raised on appeal is a challenge to the giving, refusal, or modification of a jury instruction, the condensed narrative must include any instructions submitted orally and not in writing and must identify the party that requested the instruction and any modification.

(Subd (c) amended effective March 1, 2014; adopted effective January 1, 2009; previously amended effective July 1, 2009.)

(d) Review of the appellant's proposed statement

(1) Within 10 days after the appellant files the proposed statement, the respondent may serve and file proposed amendments to that statement.

(2) No later than 10 days after either the respondent files proposed amendments or the time to do so expires, a party may request a hearing to review and correct the proposed statement. No hearing will be held unless ordered by the trial court judge, and the judge will not ordinarily order a hearing unless there is a factual dispute about a material aspect of the trial court proceedings.

(3) Except as provided in (6), if no hearing is ordered, no later than 10 days after the time for requesting a hearing expires, the trial court judge must review the proposed statement and any proposed amendments filed by the respondent and take one of the following actions:

(A) If the proposed statement does not contain material required under (c), the trial court judge may order the appellant to prepare a new proposed statement. The order must identify the additional material that must be included in the statement to comply with (c) and the date by which the new proposed statement must be served and filed. If the appellant does not serve and file a new proposed statement as directed, rule 8.874 applies.

(B) If the trial court judge does not issue an order under (A), the trial court judge must either:

(i) Make any corrections or modifications to the statement necessary to ensure that it is an accurate summary of the evidence and the testimony of each witness that is relevant to the points which the appellant states under (c)(1) are being raised on appeal; or

(ii) Identify the necessary corrections and modifications and order the appellant to prepare a statement incorporating these corrections and modifications.

(4) If a hearing is ordered, the court must promptly set the hearing date and provide the parties with at least 5 days' written notice of the hearing date. No later than 10 days after the hearing, the trial court judge must either:

(A) Make any corrections or modifications to the statement necessary to ensure that it is an accurate summary of the evidence and the testimony of each witness that is relevant to the points which the appellant states under (c)(1) are being raised on appeal; or

(B) Identify the necessary corrections and modifications and order the appellant to prepare a statement incorporating these corrections and modifications.

(5) The trial court judge must not eliminate the appellant's specification of grounds of appeal from the proposed statement.

(6) If the trial court proceedings were reported by a court reporter or officially recorded electronically under Government Code section 69957 and the trial court judge determines that it would save court time and resources, instead of correcting a proposed statement on appeal:

(A) If the court has a local rule for the appellate division permitting the use of an official electronic recording as the record of the oral proceedings, the trial court judge may order that the original of an official electronic recording of the trial court proceedings, or a copy made by the court, be transmitted as the record of these oral proceedings without being transcribed. The court will pay for any copy of the official electronic recording ordered under this subdivision; or

(B) If the court has a local rule permitting this, the trial court judge may order that a transcript be prepared as the record of the oral proceedings. The court will pay for any transcript ordered under this subdivision.

(Subd (d) amended effective March 1, 2014; adopted effective January 1, 2009.)

(e) Review of the corrected or modified statement

(1) If the trial court judge makes any corrections or modifications to the proposed statement under (d), the clerk must serve copies of the corrected or modified statement on the parties. If under (d) the trial court judge orders the appellant to prepare a statement incorporating corrections and modifications, the appellant must serve and file the corrected or modified statement within the time ordered by the court. If the appellant does not serve and file a corrected or modified statement as directed, rule 8.874 applies.

(2) Within 10 days after the corrected or modified statement is served on the parties, any party may serve and file proposed modifications or objections to the statement.

(3) Within 10 days after the time for filing proposed modifications or objections under (2) has expired, the judge must review the corrected or modified statement and any proposed modifications or objections to the statement filed by the parties. The procedures in (d)(3) or (4) apply if the judge determines that further corrections or modifications are necessary to ensure that the statement is an accurate summary of the evidence and the testimony of each witness relevant to the points which the appellant states under (c)(1) are being raised on appeal.

(Subd (e) amended effective March 1, 2014; adopted effective January 1, 2009.)

(f) Certification of the statement on appeal

If the trial court judge does not make or order any corrections or modifications to the proposed statement under (d)(3), (d)(4), or (e)(3) and does not order either the use of an official electronic recording or preparation of a transcript in lieu of correcting the proposed statement under (d)(6), the judge must promptly certify the statement.

(Subd (f) amended effective March 1, 2014; adopted effective January 1, 2009.)

(g) Extensions of time

For good cause, the trial court may grant an extension of not more than 15 days to do any act required or permitted under this rule.

(Subd (g) adopted effective January 1, 2009.)

Rule 8.869 amended effective March 1, 2014; adopted effective January 1, 2009; previously amended effective July 1, 2009.

Advisory Committee Comment

Rules 8.806, 8.810, and 8.812 address applications for extensions of time and relief from default.

Subdivision (b)(2). *Proposed Statement on Appeal (Misdemeanor)* (form CR-135) is available at any courthouse or county law library or online at *www.courts.ca.gov/forms*.

Subdivision (d). Under rule 8.804, the term "judge" includes a commissioner or a temporary judge.

Subdivisions (d)(3)(B), (d)(4), and (f). The judge need not ensure that the statement as modified or corrected is complete, but only that it is an accurate summary of the evidence and testimony relevant to the issues identified by the appellant.

Rule 8.870. Exhibits

(a) Exhibits deemed part of record
Exhibits admitted in evidence, refused, or lodged are deemed part of the record, but may be transmitted to the appellate division only as provided in this rule.
(Subd (a) adopted effective January 1, 2009.)

(b) Notice of designation
(1) Within 10 days after the last respondent's brief is filed or could be filed under rule 8.882, if the appellant wants the appellate division to consider any original exhibits that were admitted in evidence, refused, or lodged, the appellant must serve and file a notice in the trial court designating such exhibits.

(2) Within 10 days after a notice under (1) is served, any other party wanting the appellate division to consider additional exhibits must serve and file a notice in trial court designating such exhibits.

(3) A party filing a notice under (1) or (2) must serve a copy on the appellate division.
(Subd (b) adopted effective January 1, 2009.)

(c) Request by appellate division
At any time, the appellate division may direct the trial court or a party to send it an exhibit.
(Subd (c) adopted effective January 1, 2009.)

(d) Transmittal
Unless the appellate division orders otherwise, within 20 days after the first notice under (b) is filed or after the appellate division directs that an exhibit be sent:

(1) The trial court clerk must put any designated exhibits in the clerk's possession into numerical or alphabetical order and send them to the appellate division. The trial court clerk must also send a list of the exhibits sent. If the exhibits are not transmitted electronically, the trial court clerk must send two copies of the list. If the appellate division clerk finds the list correct, the clerk must sign and return a copy to the trial court clerk.

(2) Any party in possession of designated exhibits returned by the trial court must put them into numerical or alphabetical order and send them to the appellate division. The party must also send a list of the exhibits sent. If the exhibits are not transmitted electronically, the party must send two copies of the list. If the appellate division clerk finds the list correct, the clerk must sign and return a copy to the party.
(Subd (d) amended effective January 1, 2016; adopted effective January 1, 2009.)

(e) Return by appellate division
On request, the appellate division may return an exhibit to the trial court or to the party that sent it. When the remittitur issues, the appellate division must return all exhibits not transmitted electronically to the trial court or to the party that sent them.
(Subd (e) amended effective January 1, 2016; adopted effective January 1, 2009.)

Rule 8.870 amended effective January 1, 2016; adopted effective January 1, 2009.

Rule 8.871. Juror-identifying information

(a) Applicability
In a criminal case, a clerk's transcript, a reporter's transcript, or any other document in the record that contains juror-identifying information must comply with this rule.
(Subd (a) adopted effective January 1, 2009.)

(b) Juror names, addresses, and telephone numbers
(1) The name of each trial juror or alternate sworn to hear the case must be replaced with an identifying number wherever it appears in any document. The trial court clerk must prepare and keep under seal in the case file a table correlating the jurors' names with their identifying numbers. The clerk and the reporter must use the table in preparing all transcripts or other documents.

(2) The addresses and telephone numbers of trial jurors and alternates sworn to hear the case must be deleted from all documents.
(Subd (b) adopted effective January 1, 2009.)

(c) Potential jurors
Information identifying potential jurors called but not sworn as trial jurors or alternates must not be sealed unless otherwise ordered under Code of Civil Procedure section 237(a)(1).
(Subd (c) adopted effective January 1, 2009.)

Rule 8.871 adopted effective January 1, 2009.

Advisory Committee Comment

This rule implements Code of Civil Procedure section 237.

Rule 8.872. Sending and filing the record in the appellate division

(a) When the record is complete
(1) If the appellant elected under rule 8.864 to proceed without a record of the oral proceedings in the trial court, the record is complete when the clerk's transcript is certified as correct or, if the original trial court file will be used instead of the clerk's transcript, when that original file is ready for transmission as provided under rule 8.863(b).

(2) If the appellant elected under rule 8.864 to proceed with a record of the oral proceedings in the trial court, the record is complete when the clerk's transcript is certified as correct or the original file is ready for transmission as provided in (1) and:

(A) If the appellant elected to use a reporter's transcript, the certified reporter's transcript is delivered to the court under rule 8.866;

(B) If the appellant elected to use a transcript prepared from an official electronic recording, the transcript has been prepared under rule 8.868;

(C) If the parties stipulated to the use of an official electronic recording of the proceedings, the electronic recording has been prepared under rule 8.868; or

(D) If the appellant elected to use a statement on appeal, the statement on appeal has been certified by the trial court or a transcript or an official electronic recording has been prepared under rule 8.869(d)(6).
(Subd (a) adopted effective January 1, 2009.)

(b) Sending the record
When the record is complete, the clerk must promptly send:

(1) The original record to the appellate division;

(2) One copy of the clerk's transcript or index to the original court file and one copy of any record of the oral proceedings to each appellant who is represented by separate counsel or is self-represented; and

(3) One copy of the clerk's transcript or index to the original court file and one copy of any record of the oral proceedings to the respondent.
(Subd (b) adopted effective January 1, 2009.)

(c) Filing the record
On receipt, the appellate division clerk must promptly file the original record and send notice of the filing date to the parties.
(Subd (c) amended effective January 1, 2016; adopted effective January 1, 2009.)

Rule 8.872 amended effective January 1, 2016; adopted effective January 1, 2009.

Rule 8.873. Augmenting or correcting the record in the appellate division

(a) Subsequent trial court orders
If, after the record is certified, the trial court amends or recalls the judgment or makes any other order in the case, including an order affecting the sentence or probation, the clerk must promptly certify and send a copy of the amended abstract of judgment or other order as an augmentation of the record to all those who received the record under rule 8.872(b). If there is any additional document or transcript related to the amended judgment or new order that any rule or order requires be included in the record, the clerk must send these documents or transcripts with the amended abstract of judgment or other order. The clerk must promptly copy and certify any such document and the reporter must promptly prepare and certify any such transcript.
(Subd (a) adopted effective January 1, 2009.)

(b) Omissions
If, after the record is certified, the trial court clerk or the reporter learns that the record omits a document or transcript that any rule or order requires to be included, the clerk must promptly copy and certify the document or the reporter must promptly prepare and certify the transcript. Without the need for a court order, the clerk must promptly send the document or transcript as an augmentation of the record to all those who received the record under rule 8.872(b).
(Subd (b) adopted effective January 1, 2009.)

(c) Augmentation or correction by the appellate division
At any time, on motion of a party or on its own motion, the appellate division may order the record augmented or corrected as provided in rule 8.841.
(Subd (c) adopted effective January 1, 2009.)

Rule 8.873 adopted effective January 1, 2009.

Rule 8.874. Failure to procure the record

(a) Notice of default
If a party fails to do any act required to procure the record, the trial court clerk must promptly notify that party in writing that it must do the

act specified in the notice within 15 days after the notice is sent and that, if it fails to comply, the appellate division may impose the following sanctions:

(1) When the defaulting party is the appellant:

(A) If the appellant is the defendant and is represented by appointed counsel on appeal, the appellate division may relieve that appointed counsel and appoint new counsel; or

(B) If the appellant is the People or the appellant is the defendant and is not represented by appointed counsel, the appellate division may dismiss the appeal.

(2) When the defaulting party is the respondent:

(A) If the respondent is the defendant and is represented by appointed counsel on appeal, the appellate division may relieve that appointed counsel and appoint new counsel; or

(B) If the respondent is the People or the respondent is the defendant and is not represented by appointed counsel, the appellate division may proceed with the appeal on the record designated by the appellant.

(Subd (a) amended effective January 1, 2016; adopted effective March 1, 2014.)

(b) Sanctions

If the party fails to take the action specified in a notice given under (a), the trial court clerk must promptly notify the appellate division of the default and the appellate division may impose the sanction specified in the notice. If the appellate division dismisses the appeal, it may vacate the dismissal for good cause. If the appellate division orders the appeal to proceed on the record designated by the appellant, the respondent may obtain relief from default under rule 8.812.

(Subd (b) adopted effective March 1, 2014.)

Rule 8.874 amended effective January 1, 2016; adopted effective March 1, 2014.

Chapter 4
Briefs, Hearing, and Decision in Limited Civil and Misdemeanor Appeals

Chapter 4 adopted effective January 1, 2009.

Rule 8.880. Application
Rule 8.881. Notice of briefing schedule
Rule 8.882. Briefs by parties and amici curiae
Rule 8.883. Contents and form of briefs
Rule 8.884. Appeals in which a party is both appellant and respondent
Rule 8.885. Oral argument
Rule 8.886. Submission of the cause
Rule 8.887. Decisions
Rule 8.888. Finality and modification of decision
Rule 8.889. Rehearing
Rule 8.890. Remittitur
Rule 8.891. Costs and sanctions in civil appeals

Rule 8.880. Application

Except as otherwise provided, the rules in this chapter apply to both civil and misdemeanor appeals in the appellate division.

Rule 8.880 adopted effective January 1, 2009.

Rule 8.881. Notice of briefing schedule

When the record is filed, the clerk of the appellate division must promptly send a notice to each appellate counsel or unrepresented party giving the dates the briefs are due.

Rule 8.881 amended effective January 1, 2016; adopted effective January 1, 2009.

Rule 8.882. Briefs by parties and amici curiae

(a) Briefs by parties

(1) The appellant must serve and file an appellant's opening brief within:

(A) 30 days after the record—or the reporter's transcript, after a rule 8.845 election in a civil case—is filed in the appellate division; or

(B) 60 days after the filing of a rule 8.845 election in a civil case, if the appeal proceeds without a reporter's transcript.

(2) Any respondent's brief must be served and filed within 30 days after the appellant files its opening brief.

(3) Any appellant's reply brief must be served and filed within 20 days after the respondent files its brief.

(4) No other brief may be filed except with the permission of the presiding judge.

(5) Instead of filing a brief, or as part of its brief, a party may join in a brief or adopt by reference all or part of a brief in the same or a related appeal.

(Subd (a) amended effective January 1, 2021; adopted effective January 1, 2009.)

(b) Extensions of time

(1) Except as otherwise provided by statute, in a civil case, the parties may extend each period under (a) by up to 30 days by filing one or more stipulations in the appellate division before the brief is due. Stipulations must be signed by and served on all parties. If the stipulation is filed in paper form, the original signature of at least one party must appear on the stipulation filed in the appellate division; the signatures of the other parties may be in the form of fax copies of the signed signature page of the stipulation. If the stipulation is electronically filed, the signatures must comply with the requirements of rule 8.77.

(2) A stipulation under (1) is effective on filing. The appellate division may not shorten such a stipulated extension.

(3) Before the brief is due, a party may apply to the presiding judge of the appellate division for an extension of the time period for filing a brief under (a). The application must show that there is good cause to grant an extension under rule 8.811(b). In civil appeals, the application must also show that:

(A) The applicant was unable to obtain—or it would have been futile to seek—the extension by stipulation; or

(B) The parties have stipulated to the maximum extension permitted under (1) and the applicant seeks a further extension.

(4) A party need not apply for an extension or relief from default if it can file its brief within the time prescribed by (c). The clerk must file a brief submitted within that time if it otherwise complies with these rules.

(Subd (b) amended effective January 1, 2016; adopted effective January 1, 2009; previously amended effective January 1, 2010, and January 1, 2013.)

(c) Failure to file a brief

(1) If a party in a civil appeal fails to timely file an appellant's opening brief or a respondent's brief, the appellate division clerk must promptly notify the party in writing that the brief must be filed within 15 days after the notice is sent and that if the party fails to comply, the court may impose one of the following sanctions:

(A) If the brief is an appellant's opening brief, the court may dismiss the appeal; or

(B) If the brief is a respondent's brief, the court may decide the appeal on the record, the appellant's opening brief, and any oral argument by the appellant.

(2) If the appellant in a misdemeanor appeal fails to timely file an opening brief, the appellate division clerk must promptly notify the appellant in writing that the brief must be filed within 30 days after the notice is sent and that if the appellant fails to comply, the court may impose one of the following sanctions:

(A) If the appellant is the defendant and is represented by appointed counsel on appeal, the court may relieve that appointed counsel and appoint new counsel; or

(B) In all other cases, the court may dismiss the appeal.

(3) If the respondent in a misdemeanor appeal fails to timely file a brief, the appellate division clerk must promptly notify the respondent in writing that the brief must be filed within 30 days after the notice is sent and that if the respondent fails to comply, the court may impose one of the following sanctions:

(A) If the respondent is the defendant and is represented by appointed counsel on appeal, the court may relieve that appointed counsel and appoint new counsel; or

(B) In all other cases, the court may decide the appeal on the record, the appellant's opening brief, and any oral argument by the appellant.

(4) If a party fails to comply with a notice under (1), (2), or (3), the court may impose the sanction specified in the notice.

(Subd (c) amended effective January 1, 2016; adopted as subd (b) effective January 1, 2009; previously relettered as subd (c) effective January 1, 2009; previously amended effective March 1, 2014.)

(d) Amicus curiae briefs

(1) Within 14 days after the appellant's reply brief is filed or was required to be filed, whichever is earlier, any person or entity may serve and file an application for permission of the presiding judge to file an amicus curiae brief. For good cause, the presiding judge may allow later filing.

(2) The application must state the applicant's interest and explain how the proposed amicus curiae brief will assist the court in deciding the matter.

(3) The application must also identify:

(A) Any party or any counsel for a party in the pending appeal who:

(i) Authored the proposed amicus brief in whole or in part; or

(ii) Made a monetary contribution intended to fund the preparation or submission of the brief; and

(B) Every person or entity who made a monetary contribution intended to fund the preparation or submission of the brief, other than the amicus curiae, its members, or its counsel in the pending appeal.

(4) The proposed brief must be served and must accompany the application and may be combined with it.

(5) The Attorney General may file an amicus curiae brief without the presiding judge's permission, unless the brief is submitted on behalf of another state officer or agency; but the presiding judge may prescribe reasonable conditions for filing and answering the brief.

(Subd (d) amended and relettered effective January 1, 2009; adopted as subd (c) effective January 1, 2009.)

(e) Service and filing

(1) Copies of each brief must be served as required by rule 8.817.

(2) Unless the court provides otherwise by local rule or order in the specific case, only the original brief, with proof of service, must be filed in the appellate division.

(3) A copy of each brief must be served on the trial court clerk for delivery to the judge who tried the case.

(4) A copy of each brief must be served on a public officer or agency when required by rule 8.817.

(5) In misdemeanor appeals:

(A) Defendant's appellate counsel must serve each brief for the defendant on the People and must send a copy of each brief to the defendant personally unless the defendant requests otherwise;

(B) The proof of service under (A) must state that a copy of the defendant's brief was sent to the defendant, or counsel must file a signed statement that the defendant requested in writing that no copy be sent; and

(C) The People must serve two copies of their briefs on the appellate counsel for each defendant who is a party to the appeal.

(Subd (e) amended effective January 1, 2018; adopted as subd (d) effective January 1, 2009; previously amended and relettered as subd (e) effective January 1, 2009.)

Rule 8.882 amended effective January 1, 2021; adopted effective January 1, 2009; previously amended effective January 1, 2009, January 1, 2010, January 1, 2013, March 1, 2014, January 1, 2016, and January 1, 2018.

Advisory Committee Comment

Subdivision (a). Note that the sequence and timing of briefing in appeals in which a party is both appellant and respondent (cross-appeals) are governed by rule 8.884. Typically, a cross-appellant's combined respondent's brief and opening brief must be filed within the time specified in (a)(2) for the respondent's brief.

Subdivision (b). Extensions of briefing time are limited by statute in some cases. For example, under Public Resources Code section 21167.6(h) in cases under section 21167 extensions are limited to one 30-day extension for the opening brief and one 30-day extension for "preparation of responding brief."

Rule 8.883. Contents and form of briefs

(a) Contents

(1) Each brief must:

(A) State each point under a separate heading or subheading summarizing the point and support each point by argument and, if possible, by citation of authority; and

(B) Support any reference to a matter in the record by a citation to the volume and page number of the record where the matter appears.

(2) An appellant's opening brief must:

(A) State the nature of the action, the relief sought in the trial court, and the judgment or order appealed from;

(B) State that the judgment appealed from is final or explain why the order appealed from is appealable; and

(C) Provide a summary of the significant facts limited to matters in the record.

(Subd (a) adopted effective January 1, 2009.)

(b) Length

(1) A brief produced on a computer must not exceed 6,800 words, including footnotes. Such a brief must include a certificate by appellate counsel or an unrepresented party stating the number of words in the brief. The person certifying may rely on the word count of the computer program used to prepare the brief.

(2) A brief produced on a typewriter must not exceed 20 pages.

(3) The information listed on the cover, any table of contents or table of authorities, the certificate under (1), and any signature block are excluded from the limits stated in (1) or (2).

(4) On application, the presiding judge may permit a longer brief for good cause. A lengthy record or numerous or complex issues on appeal will ordinarily constitute good cause. If the court grants an application to file a longer brief, it may order that the brief include a table of contents and a table of authorities.

(Subd (b) amended effective January 1, 2013; adopted effective January 1, 2009; previously amended effective January 1, 2011.)

(c) Form

(1) A brief may be reproduced by any process that produces a clear, black image of letter quality. All documents filed must have a page size of 8½ by 11 inches. If filed in paper form, the paper must be white or unbleached and of at least 20-pound weight. Both sides of the paper may be used if the brief is not bound at the top.

(2) Any conventional font may be used. The font may be either proportionally spaced or monospaced.

(3) The font style must be roman; but for emphasis, italics or boldface may be used or the text may be underscored. Case names must be italicized or underscored. Headings may be in uppercase letters.

(4) Except as provided in (11), the font size, including footnotes, must not be smaller than 13-point.

(5) The lines of text must be at least one-and-a-half-spaced. Headings and footnotes may be single-spaced. Quotations may be block-indented and single-spaced. Single-spaced means six lines to a vertical inch.

(6) The margins must be at least 1½ inches on the left and right and 1 inch on the top and bottom.

(7) The pages must be consecutively numbered.

(8) The cover—or first page if there is no cover—must include the information required by rule 8.816(a)(1).

(9) If filed in paper form, the brief must be bound on the left margin, except that briefs may be bound at the top if required by a local rule of the appellate division. If the brief is stapled, the bound edge and staples must be covered with tape.

(10) The brief need not be signed.

(11) If the brief is produced on a typewriter:

(A) A typewritten original and carbon copies may be filed only with the presiding judge's permission, which will ordinarily be given only to unrepresented parties proceeding in forma pauperis. All other typewritten briefs must be filed as photocopies.

(B) Both sides of the paper may be used if a photocopy is filed; only one side may be used if a typewritten original and carbon copies are filed.

(C) The type size, including footnotes, must not be smaller than standard pica, 10 characters per inch. Unrepresented incarcerated litigants may use elite type, 12 characters per inch, if they lack access to a typewriter with larger characters.

(Subd (c) amended effective January 1, 2016; adopted effective January 1, 2009; previously amended effective January 1, 2011, January 1, 2013, and January 1, 2014.)

(d) Noncomplying briefs

If a brief does not comply with this rule:

(1) The reviewing court clerk may decline to file it, but must mark it "received but not filed" and return it to the party; or

(2) If the brief is filed, the presiding judge may with or without notice:

(A) Order the brief returned for corrections and refiling within a specified time;

(B) Strike the brief with leave to file a new brief within a specified time; or

(C) Disregard the noncompliance.

(Subd (d) adopted effective January 1, 2009.)

Rule 8.883 amended effective January 1, 2016; adopted effective January 1, 2009; previously amended effective January 1, 2011, January 1, 2013, and January 1, 2014.

Advisory Committee Comment

Subdivision (b). Subdivision (b)(1) states the maximum permissible lengths of briefs produced on a computer in terms of word count rather than page count. This provision tracks a provision in rule 8.204(c) governing Court of Appeal briefs and is explained in the comment to that provision. Subdivision (b)(3) specifies certain items that are not counted toward the maximum brief length. Signature blocks, as referenced in this provision, include not only the signatures, but also the printed names, titles, and affiliations of any attorneys filing or joining in the brief, which may accompany the signature.

Rule 8.884. Appeals in which a party is both appellant and respondent

(a) Briefing sequence and time to file briefs

In an appeal in which any party is both an appellant and a respondent:

(1) The parties must jointly—or separately if unable to agree—submit a proposed briefing sequence to the appellate division within 20 days after the second notice of appeal is filed.

(2) After receiving the proposal, the appellate division must order a briefing sequence and prescribe briefing periods consistent with rule 8.882(a).

(Subd (a) adopted effective January 1, 2009.)

(b) Contents of briefs

(1) A party that is both an appellant and a respondent must combine its respondent's brief with its appellant's opening brief or its reply brief, if any, whichever is appropriate under the briefing sequence that the appellate division orders under (a).

(2) A party must confine a reply brief to points raised in its own appeal.

(3) A combined brief must address the points raised in each appeal separately but may include a single summary of the significant facts.

(Subd (b) amended effective January 1, 2009; adopted effective January 1, 2009.)

Rule 8.884 amended effective January 1, 2009; adopted effective January 1, 2009.

Rule 8.885. Oral argument

(a) Calendaring and sessions

(1) Unless otherwise ordered, and except as provided in (2), all appeals in which the last reply brief was filed or the time for filing this brief expired 45 or more days before the date of a regular appellate division session must be placed on the calendar for that session by the appellate division clerk. By order of the presiding judge or the division, any appeal may be placed on the calendar for oral argument at any session.

(2) Oral argument will not be set in appeals under *People v. Wende* (1979) 25 Cal.3d 436 where no arguable issue is raised.

(Subd (a) amended effective January 1, 2020; adopted effective January 1, 2009.)

(b) Oral argument by videoconference

(1) Oral argument may be conducted by videoconference if:

(A) It is ordered by the presiding judge of the appellate division or the presiding judge's designee on application of any party or on the court's own motion. An application from a party requesting that oral argument be conducted by videoconference must be filed within 10 days after the court sends notice of oral argument under (c)(1); or

(B) A local rule authorizes oral argument to be conducted by videoconference consistent with these rules.

(2) If oral argument is conducted by videoconference:

(A) Each judge of the appellate division panel assigned to the case must participate in the entire oral argument either in person at the superior court that issued the judgment or order that is being appealed or by videoconference from another court.

(B) Unless otherwise allowed by local rule or ordered by the presiding judge of the appellate division or the presiding judge's designee, all the parties must appear at oral argument in person at the superior court that issued the judgment or order that is being appealed.

(C) The oral argument must be open to the public at the superior court that issued the judgment or order that is being appealed. If provided by local rule or ordered by the presiding judge of the appellate division or the presiding judge's designee, oral argument may also be open to the public at any of the locations from which a judge of the appellate division is participating in oral argument.

(D) The appellate division must ensure that:

(i) During oral argument, the participants in oral argument are visible and their statements are audible to all other participants, court staff, and any members of the public attending the oral argument;

(ii) Participants are identified when they speak; and

(iii) Only persons who are authorized to participate in the proceedings speak.

(E) A party must not be charged any fee to participate in oral argument by videoconference if the party participates from the superior court that issued the judgment or order that is being appealed or from a location from which a judge of the appellate division panel is participating in oral argument.

(Subd (b) adopted effective January 1, 2010.)

(c) Notice of argument

(1) Except for appeals covered by (a)(2), as soon as all parties' briefs are filed or the time for filing these briefs has expired, the appellate division clerk must send a notice of the time and place of oral argument to all parties. The notice must be sent at least 20 days before the date for oral argument. The presiding judge may shorten the notice period for good cause; in that event, the clerk must immediately notify the parties by telephone or other expeditious method.

(2) If oral argument will be conducted by videoconference under (b), the clerk must specify, either in the notice required under (1) or in a supplemental notice sent to all parties at least 5 days before the date for oral argument, the location from which each judge of the appellate division panel assigned to the case will participate in oral argument.

(Subd (c) amended effective January 1, 2020; adopted as subd (b) effective January 1, 2009; previously amended and relettered as subd (c) effective January 1, 2010.)

(d) Waiver of argument

(1) Parties may waive oral argument in advance by filing a notice of waiver of oral argument within 7 days after the notice of oral argument is sent.

(2) The court may vacate oral argument if all parties waive oral argument.

(3) If the court vacates oral argument, the court must notify the parties that no oral argument will be held.

(4) If all parties do not waive oral argument, or if the court rejects a waiver request, the matter will remain on the oral argument calendar. Any party who previously filed a notice of waiver may participate in the oral argument.

(Subd (d) amended effective January 1, 2020; adopted as subd (c) effective January 1, 2009; previously relettered as subd (d) effective January 1, 2010.)

(e) Conduct of argument

Unless the court provides otherwise:

(1) The appellant, petitioner, or moving party has the right to open and close. If there are two or more such parties, the court must set the sequence of argument.

(2) Each side is allowed 10 minutes for argument. The appellant may reserve part of this time for reply argument. If multiple parties are represented by separate counsel, or if an amicus curiae—on written request—is granted permission to argue, the court may apportion or expand the time.

(3) Only one counsel may argue for each separately represented party.

(Subd (e) amended and relettered effective January 1, 2010; adopted as subd (d) effective January 1, 2009.)

Rule 8.885 amended effective January 1, 2020; adopted effective January 1, 2009; previously amended effective January 1, 2010.

Advisory Committee Comment

Subdivision (a). Under rule 10.1108, the appellate division must hold a session at least once each quarter, unless no matters are set for oral argument that quarter, but may choose to hold sessions more frequently.

Rule 8.886. Submission of the cause

(a) When the cause is submitted

(1) Except as provided in (2), a cause is submitted when the court has heard oral argument or approved its waiver and the time has expired to file all briefs and papers, including any supplemental brief permitted by the court. The appellate division may order the cause submitted at an earlier time if the parties so stipulate.

(2) For appeals that raise no arguable issues under *People v. Wende* (1979) 25 Cal.3d 436, the cause is submitted when the time has expired to file all briefs and papers, including any supplemental brief permitted by the court.

(Subd (a) amended effective January 1, 2020; adopted effective January 1, 2009.)

(b) Vacating submission

The court may vacate submission only by an order stating its reasons and setting a timetable for resubmission.

(Subd (b) adopted effective January 1, 2009.)

Rule 8.886 amended effective January 1, 2020; adopted effective January 1, 2009.

Rule 8.887. Decisions

(a) Written opinions

Appellate division judges are not required to prepare a written opinion in any case but may do so when they deem it advisable or in the public interest. A decision by opinion must identify the participating judges, including the author of the majority opinion and of any concurring or dissenting opinion, or the judges participating in a "by the court" opinion.

(Subd (a) adopted effective January 1, 2009.)

(b) Filing the decision

The appellate division clerk must promptly file all opinions and orders of the court and on the same day send copies (by e-mail where permissible under rule 2.251) showing the filing date to the parties and, when relevant, to the trial court.

(Subd (b) amended effective January 1, 2019; adopted effective January 1, 2009.)

(c) Opinions certified for publication

(1) Opinions certified for publication must comply to the extent practicable with the *California Style Manual*.

(2) When the opinion is certified for publication, the clerk must immediately send:

(A) Two paper copies and one electronic copy to the Reporter of Decisions in a format approved by the Reporter.

(B) One copy to the Court of Appeal for the district. The copy must bear the notation "This opinion has been certified for publication in the Official Reports. It is being sent to assist the Court of Appeal in deciding whether to order the case transferred to the court on the court's own motion under rules 8.1000–8.1018." The clerk/executive officer of the Court of Appeal must promptly file that copy or make a docket entry showing its receipt.

(Subd (c) amended effective January 1, 2018; adopted effective January 1, 2009; previously amended effective January 1, 2011, and March 1, 2014.)

Rule 8.887 amended effective January 1, 2019; adopted effective January 1, 2009; previously amended effective January 1, 2011, March 1, 2014, and January 1, 2018.

Rule 8.888. Finality and modification of decision

(a) Finality of decision

(1) Except as otherwise provided in this rule, an appellate division decision, including an order dismissing an appeal involuntarily, is final 30 days after the decision is sent by the court clerk to the parties.

(2) If the appellate division certifies a written opinion for publication or partial publication after its decision is filed and before its decision becomes final in that court, the finality period runs from the date the order for publication is sent by the court clerk to the parties.

(3) The following appellate division decisions are final in that court when filed:

(A) The denial of a petition for writ of supersedeas;

(B) The denial of an application for bail or to reduce bail pending appeal; and

(C) The dismissal of an appeal on request or stipulation.

(Subd (a) amended effective January 1, 2019; adopted effective January 1, 2009.)

(b) Modification of judgment

(1) The appellate division may modify its decision until the decision is final in that court. If the clerk's office is closed on the date of finality, the court may modify the decision on the next day the clerk's office is open.

(2) An order modifying a decision must state whether it changes the appellate judgment. A modification that does not change the appellate judgment does not extend the finality date of the decision. If a modification changes the appellate judgment, the finality period runs from the date the modification order is sent by the court clerk to the parties.

(Subd (b) amended effective January 1, 2019; adopted effective January 1, 2009.)

(c) Consent to increase or decrease in amount of judgment

If an appellate division decision conditions the affirmance of a money judgment on a party's consent to an increase or decrease in the amount, the judgment is reversed unless, before the decision is final under (a), the party serves and files a copy of a consent in the appellate division. If a consent is filed, the finality period runs from the filing date of the consent. The clerk must send one filed-endorsed copy of the consent to the trial court with the remittitur.

(Subd (c) amended effective January 1, 2016; adopted effective January 1, 2009.)

Rule 8.888 amended effective January 1, 2019; adopted effective January 1, 2009; previously amended effective January 1, 2016.

Rule 8.889. Rehearing

(a) Power to order rehearing

(1) On petition of a party or on its own motion, the appellate division may order rehearing of any decision that is not final in that court on filing.

(2) An order for rehearing must be filed before the decision is final. If the clerk's office is closed on the date of finality, the court may file the order on the next day the clerk's office is open.

(Subd (a) adopted effective January 1, 2009.)

(b) Petition and answer

(1) A party may serve and file a petition for rehearing within 15 days after the following, whichever is later:

(A) The decision is sent by the court clerk to the parties;

(B) A publication order restarting the finality period under rule 8.888(a)(2), if the party has not already filed a petition for rehearing, is sent by the court clerk to the parties;

(C) A modification order changing the appellate judgment under rule 8.888(b) is sent by the court clerk to the parties; or

(D) A consent is filed under rule 8.888(c).

(2) A party must not file an answer to a petition for rehearing unless the court requests an answer. The clerk must promptly send to the parties copies of any order requesting an answer and immediately notify the parties by telephone or another expeditious method. Any answer must be served and filed within 8 days after the order is filed unless the court orders otherwise. A petition for rehearing normally will not be granted unless the court has requested an answer.

(3) The petition and answer must comply with the relevant provisions of rule 8.883.

(4) Before the decision is final and for good cause, the presiding judge may relieve a party from a failure to file a timely petition or answer.

(Subd (b) amended effective January 1, 2019; adopted effective January 1, 2009.)

(c) No extensions of time

The time for granting or denying a petition for rehearing in the appellate division may not be extended. If the court does not rule on the petition before the decision is final, the petition is deemed denied.

(Subd (c) adopted effective January 1, 2009.)

(d) Effect of granting rehearing

An order granting a rehearing vacates the decision and any opinion filed in the case. If the appellate division orders rehearing, it may place the case on calendar for further argument or submit it for decision.

(Subd (d) adopted effective January 1, 2009.)

Rule 8.889 amended effective January 1, 2019; adopted effective January 1, 2009.

Rule 8.890. Remittitur

(a) Proceedings requiring issuance of remittitur

An appellate division must issue a remittitur after a decision in an appeal.

(Subd (a) adopted effective January 1, 2009.)

(b) Clerk's duties

(1) If an appellate division case is not transferred to the Court of Appeal under rule 8.1000 et seq., the appellate division clerk must:

(A) Issue a remittitur immediately after the Court of Appeal denies transfer or the period for granting transfer under rule 8.1008(a) expires if there will be no further proceedings in the appellate division;

(B) Send the remittitur to the trial court with a filed-endorsed copy of the opinion or order; and

(C) Return to the trial court with the remittitur all original records, exhibits, and documents sent nonelectronically to the appellate division in connection with the appeal, except any certification for transfer under rule 8.1005, the transcripts or statement on appeal, briefs, and the notice of appeal.

(2) If an appellate division case is transferred to a Court of Appeal under rule 8.1000 et seq., on receiving the Court of Appeal remittitur, the appellate division clerk must issue a remittitur and return documents to the trial court as provided in rule 8.1018.

(Subd (b) amended effective January 1, 2016; adopted effective January 1, 2009; previously amended effective January 1, 2011.)

(c) Immediate issuance, stay, and recall

(1) The appellate division may direct immediate issuance of a remittitur only on the parties' stipulation or on dismissal of the appeal on the request or stipulation of the parties under rule 8.825(b)(2).

(2) On a party's or its own motion or on stipulation, and for good cause, the court may stay a remittitur's issuance for a reasonable period or order its recall.

(3) An order recalling a remittitur issued after a decision by opinion does not supersede the opinion or affect its publication status.

(Subd (c) amended effective March 1, 2014; adopted effective January 1, 2009.)

(d) Notice

The remittitur is deemed issued when the clerk enters it in the record. The clerk must immediately send the parties notice of issuance of the remittitur, showing the date of entry.

(Subd (d) adopted effective January 1, 2009.)
Rule 8.890 amended effective January 1, 2016; adopted effective January 1, 2009; previously amended effective January 1, 2011, and March 1, 2014.

Rule 8.891. Costs and sanctions in civil appeals

(a) Right to costs

(1) Except as provided in this rule or by statute, the prevailing party in a civil appeal is entitled to costs on appeal.

(2) The prevailing party is the respondent if the appellate division affirms the judgment without modification or dismisses the appeal. The prevailing party is the appellant if the appellate division reverses the judgment in its entirety.

(3) If the appellate division reverses the judgment in part or modifies it, or if there is more than one notice of appeal, the appellate division must specify the award or denial of costs in its decision.

(4) In the interests of justice, the appellate division may also award or deny costs as it deems proper.

(Subd (a) amended effective September 1, 2023; adopted effective January 1, 2009.)

(b) Judgment for costs

(1) The appellate division clerk must enter on the record and insert in the remittitur judgment awarding costs to the prevailing party under (a).

(2) If the clerk fails to enter judgment for costs, the appellate division may recall the remittitur for correction on its own motion or on a party's motion made not later than 30 days after the remittitur issues.

(Subd (b) adopted effective January 1, 2009.)

(c) Procedure for claiming or opposing costs

(1) Within 30 days after the clerk sends notice of issuance of the remittitur, a party claiming costs awarded by the appellate division must serve and file in the trial court a verified memorandum of costs under rule 3.1700(a)(1).

(2) A party may serve and file a motion in the trial court to strike or tax costs claimed under (1) in the manner required by rule 3.1700.

(3) An award of costs is enforceable as a money judgment.

(Subd (c) amended effective January 1, 2011; adopted effective January 1, 2009.)

(d) Recoverable costs

(1) A party may recover only the costs of the following, if reasonable:
 (A) Filing fees;
 (B) The amount the party paid for any portion of the record, whether an original or a copy or both, subject to reduction by the appellate division under subdivision (e);
 (C) The cost to produce additional evidence on appeal;
 (D) The costs to notarize, serve, mail, and file the record, briefs, and other papers;
 (E) The cost to print and reproduce any brief, including any petition for rehearing or review, answer, or reply;
 (F) The cost to procure a surety bond, including the premium, the cost to obtain a letter of credit as collateral, and the fees and net interest expenses incurred to borrow funds to provide security for the bond or to obtain a letter of credit, unless the trial court determines the bond was unnecessary; and
 (G) The fees and net interest expenses incurred to borrow funds to deposit with the superior court in lieu of a bond or undertaking, unless the trial court determines the deposit was unnecessary.

(2) Unless the court orders otherwise, an award of costs neither includes attorney's fees on appeal nor precludes a party from seeking them under rule 3.1702.

(Subd (d) amended effective January 1, 2013; adopted effective January 1, 2009.)

(e) Sanctions

(1) On motion of a party or its own motion, the appellate division may impose sanctions, including the award or denial of costs, on a party or an attorney for:
 (A) Taking a frivolous appeal or appealing solely to cause delay; or
 (B) Committing any unreasonable violation of these rules.

(2) A party's motion under (1) must include a declaration supporting the amount of any monetary sanction sought and must be served and filed before any order dismissing the appeal but no later than 10 days after the appellant's reply brief is due. If a party files a motion for sanctions with a motion to dismiss the appeal and the motion to dismiss is not granted, the party may file a new motion for sanctions within 10 days after the appellant's reply brief is due.

(3) The court must give notice in writing if it is considering imposing sanctions. Within 10 days after the court sends such notice, a party or attorney may serve and file an opposition, but failure to do so will not be deemed consent. An opposition may not be filed unless the court sends such notice.

(4) Unless otherwise ordered, oral argument on the issue of sanctions must be combined with oral argument on the merits of the appeal.

(Subd (e) adopted effective January 1, 2009.)
Rule 8.891 amended effective September 1, 2023; adopted effective January 1, 2009; previously amended effective January 1, 2011, and January 1, 2013.

Advisory Committee Comment

Subdivision (a). The subdivision (a)(1) exception to the general rule of awarding costs to the prevailing party for statutes that require further analysis or findings reflects the holding of *Pollock v. Tri-Modal Distribution Services, Inc.* (2021) 11 Cal.5th 918 (regarding costs on appeal in an action under the California Fair Employment and Housing Act) and the constitutional mandate that rules of court "shall not be inconsistent with statute" (Cal. Const., art. VI, § 6(d)).

Subdivision (d). "Net interest expenses" in subdivisions (d)(1)(F) and (G) means the interest expenses incurred to borrow the funds that are deposited minus any interest earned by the borrower on those funds while they are on deposit.

Subdivision (d)(1)(D), allowing recovery of the "costs to notarize, serve, mail, and file the record, briefs, and other papers," is intended to include fees charged by electronic filing service providers for electronic filing and service of documents.

Chapter 5
Appeals in Infraction Cases

Chapter 5 adopted effective January 1, 2009.

Art. 1. Taking Appeals in Infraction Cases. Rules 8.900–8.904.
Art. 2. Record in Infraction Appeals. Rules 8.910–8.924.
Art. 3. Briefs, Hearing, and Decision in Infraction Appeals. Rules 8.925–8.929.

Article 1
Taking Appeals in Infraction Cases

Article 1 adopted effective January 1, 2009.

Rule 8.900. Application of chapter
Rule 8.901. Notice of appeal
Rule 8.902. Time to appeal
Rule 8.903. Stay of execution on appeal
Rule 8.904. Abandoning the appeal

Rule 8.900. Application of chapter

The rules in this chapter apply only to appeals in infraction cases. An infraction case is a case in which the defendant was convicted only of an infraction and was not charged with any felony. A felony is "charged" when an information or indictment accusing the defendant of a felony is filed or a complaint accusing the defendant of a felony is certified to the superior court under Penal Code section 859a.

Rule 8.900 adopted effective January 1, 2009.

Advisory Committee Comment

Chapter 1 of this division also applies in appeals from infraction cases. Chapters 3 and 4 of this division apply to appeals in misdemeanor cases. The rules that apply in appeals in felony cases are located in chapter 3 of division 1 of this title.

Penal Code section 1466 provides that an appeal in a "misdemeanor or infraction case" is to the appellate division of the superior court, and Penal Code section 1235(b), in turn, provides that an appeal in a "felony case" is to the Court of Appeal. Penal Code section 691(g) defines "misdemeanor or infraction case" to mean "a criminal action in which a misdemeanor or infraction is charged *and does not include a criminal action in which a felony is charged* in conjunction with a misdemeanor or infraction" (emphasis added), and section 691(f) defines "felony case" to mean "a criminal action in which a felony is charged *and includes a criminal action in which a misdemeanor or infraction is charged in conjunction with a felony*" (emphasis added).

As rule 8.304 from the rules on felony appeals makes clear, a "felony case" is an action in which a felony is charged *regardless of the outcome of the action*. Thus the question of which rules apply—these appellate division rules or the rules governing appeals in felony cases—is answered simply by examining the accusatory pleading: if that document charged the defendant with at least one count of felony (as defined in Penal Code, section 17(a)), the Court of Appeal has appellate jurisdiction and the appeal must be taken under the rules on felony appeals *even if the prosecution did not result in a punishment of imprisonment in a state prison*.

It is settled case law that an appeal is taken to the Court of Appeal not only when the defendant is charged with and convicted of a felony, but also when the defendant is charged with both a felony and a misdemeanor (Pen. Code, § 691(f)) but is convicted of only the misdemeanor (e.g., *People v. Brown* (1970) 10 Cal.App.3d 169); when the defendant is charged with a felony but is convicted of only a lesser offense (Pen. Code, § 1159; e.g., *People v. Spreckels* (1954) 125 Cal.App.2d 507); and when the defendant is charged with an offense filed as a felony but punishable as either a felony or a misdemeanor, and the offense is thereafter deemed a misdemeanor under Penal Code section 17(b) (e.g., *People v. Douglas* (1999) 20 Cal.4th 85; *People v. Clark* (1971) 17 Cal.App.3d 890).

Trial court unification did not change this rule: after as before unification, "Appeals in felony cases lie to the [C]ourt of [A]ppeal, regardless of whether the appeal is from the superior court, the municipal court, or the action of a magistrate. *Cf.* Cal. Const. art. VI, § 11(a) [except in death penalty cases, Courts of Appeal have appellate jurisdiction when superior courts have original jurisdiction 'in causes of a type within the appellate jurisdiction of the [C]ourts of [A]ppeal on June 30, 1995....']." ("Recommendation on Trial Court Unification" (July 1998) 28 *Cal. Law Revision Com. Rep.* 455–56.)

Rule 8.901. Notice of appeal

(a) Notice of appeal

(1) To appeal from a judgment or an appealable order in an infraction case, the defendant or the People must file a notice of appeal in the trial court that issued the judgment or order being appealed. The notice must specify the judgment or order—or part of it—being appealed.

(2) If the defendant appeals, the defendant or the defendant's attorney must sign the notice of appeal. If the People appeal, the attorney for the People must sign the notice.

(3) The notice of appeal must be liberally construed in favor of its sufficiency.

(Subd (a) adopted effective January 1, 2009.)

(b) Notification of the appeal

(1) When a notice of appeal is filed, the trial court clerk must promptly send a notification of the filing to the attorney of record for each party and to any unrepresented defendant. The clerk must also send or deliver this notification to the appellate division clerk.

(2) The notification must show the date it was sent or delivered, the number and title of the case, and the date the notice of appeal was filed.

(3) The notification to the appellate division clerk must also include a copy of the notice of appeal.

(4) A copy of the notice of appeal is sufficient notification under (1) if the required information is on the copy or is added by the trial court clerk.

(5) The sending of a notification under (1) is a sufficient performance of the clerk's duty despite the discharge, disqualification, suspension, disbarment, or death of the attorney.

(6) Failure to comply with any provision of this subdivision does not affect the validity of the notice of appeal.

(Subd (b) amended effective January 1, 2016; adopted effective January 1, 2009.)

Rule 8.901 amended effective January 1, 2016; adopted effective January 1, 2009.

Advisory Committee Comment

Notice of Appeal and Record on Appeal (Infraction) (form CR-142) may be used to file the notice of appeal required under this rule. This form is available at any courthouse or county law library or online at *www.courts.ca.gov/forms.*

Rule 8.902. Time to appeal

(a) Normal time

A notice of appeal must be filed within 30 days after the rendition of the judgment or the making of the order being appealed. If the defendant is committed before final judgment for insanity or narcotics addiction, the notice of appeal must be filed within 30 days after the commitment.

(Subd (a) adopted effective January 1, 2009.)

(b) Cross-appeal

If the defendant or the People timely appeals from a judgment or appealable order, the time for any other party to appeal from the same judgment or order is either the time specified in (a) or 30 days after the trial court clerk sends notification of the first appeal, whichever is later.

(Subd (b) amended effective January 1, 2016; adopted effective January 1, 2009.)

(c) Premature notice of appeal

A notice of appeal filed before the judgment is rendered or the order is made is premature, but the appellate division may treat the notice as filed immediately after the rendition of the judgment or the making of the order.

(Subd (c) adopted effective January 1, 2009.)

(d) Late notice of appeal

The trial court clerk must mark a late notice of appeal "Received [date] but not filed" and notify the party that the notice was not filed because it was late.

(Subd (d) adopted effective January 1, 2009.)

Rule 8.902 amended effective January 1, 2016; adopted effective January 1, 2009; previously amended effective July 1, 2010.

Advisory Committee Comment

Subdivision (d). See rule 8.817(b)(5) for provisions concerning the timeliness of documents mailed by inmates or patients from custodial institutions.

Rule 8.903. Stay of execution on appeal

(a) Application

Pending appeal, the defendant may apply to the appellate division for a stay of execution after a judgment of conviction.

(Subd (a) adopted effective January 1, 2009.)

(b) Showing

The application must include a showing that the defendant sought relief in the trial court and that the court unjustifiably denied the application.

(Subd (b) adopted effective January 1, 2009.)

(c) Service

The application must be served on the prosecuting attorney.

(Subd (c) adopted effective January 1, 2009.)

(d) Interim relief

Pending its ruling on the application, the appellate division may grant the relief requested. The appellate division must notify the trial court of any stay that it grants.

(Subd (d) adopted effective January 1, 2009.)

Rule 8.903 adopted effective January 1, 2009.

Advisory Committee Comment

Subdivision (c). Under rule 8.804, the prosecuting attorney means the city attorney, county counsel, or district attorney prosecuting the infraction.

Rule 8.904. Abandoning the appeal

(a) How to abandon

An appellant may abandon the appeal at any time by filing an abandonment of the appeal signed by the appellant or the appellant's attorney of record.

(Subd (a) adopted effective January 1, 2009.)

(b) Where to file; effect of filing

(1) The appellant must file the abandonment in the appellate division.

(2) If the record has not been filed in the appellate division, the filing of an abandonment effects a dismissal of the appeal and restores the trial court's jurisdiction.

(3) If the record has been filed in the appellate division, the appellate division may dismiss the appeal and direct immediate issuance of the remittitur.

(Subd (b) adopted effective January 1, 2009.)

(c) Clerk's duties

(1) The appellate division clerk must immediately notify the adverse party of the filing or of the order of dismissal.

(2) If the record has not been filed in the appellate division, the clerk must immediately notify the trial court.

(3) If a reporter's transcript has been requested, the clerk must immediately notify the reporter if the appeal is abandoned before the reporter has filed the transcript.

(Subd (c) adopted effective January 1, 2009.)

Rule 8.904 adopted effective January 1, 2009.

Advisory Committee Comment

Abandonment of Appeal (Infraction) (form CR-145) may be used to file an abandonment under this rule. This form is available at any courthouse or county law library or online at *www.courts.ca.gov/forms.*

Rule 8.907. Record on appeal [Renumbered]

Rule 8.907 renumbered to rule 8.957 effective January 1, 2009; adopted as rule 153 effective July 1, 1964; previously amended effective July 1, 1972, July 1, 1973, January 1, 1977, and January 1, 2005; previously amended and renumbered effective January 1, 2007.

Article 2
Record in Infraction Appeals

Article 2 adopted effective January 1, 2009.

Rule 8.910. Normal record on appeal
Rule 8.911. Prosecuting attorney's notice regarding the record
Rule 8.912. Contents of clerk's transcript
Rule 8.913. Preparation of clerk's transcript
Rule 8.914. Trial court file instead of clerk's transcript
Rule 8.915. Record of oral proceedings
Rule 8.916. Statement on appeal
Rule 8.917. Record when trial proceedings were officially electronically recorded
Rule 8.918. Contents of reporter's transcript

Rule 8.919. Preparation of reporter's transcript
Rule 8.920. Limited normal record in certain appeals
Rule 8.921. Exhibits
Rule 8.922. Sending and filing the record in the appellate division
Rule 8.923. Augmenting or correcting the record in the appellate division
Rule 8.924. Failure to procure the record

Rule 8.910. Normal record on appeal

(a) Contents

Except as otherwise provided in this chapter, the record on an appeal to a superior court appellate division in an infraction criminal case must contain the following, which constitute the normal record on appeal:

(1) A record of the written documents from the trial court proceedings in the form of one of the following:

(A) A clerk's transcript under rule 8.912 or 8.920; or

(B) If the court has a local rule for the appellate division electing to use this form of the record, the original trial court file under rule 8.914.

(2) If an appellant wants to raise any issue that requires consideration of the oral proceedings in the trial court, the record on appeal must include a record of the oral proceedings in the form of one of the following:

(A) A statement on appeal under rule 8.916;

(B) If the court has a local rule for the appellate division permitting this form of the record, an official electronic recording of the proceedings under rule 8.917; or

(C) A reporter's transcript under rules 8.918–8.920 or a transcript prepared from an official electronic recording under rule 8.917.

(Subd (a) adopted effective January 1, 2009.)

(b) Stipulation for limited record

If before the record is certified, the appellant and the respondent stipulate in writing that any part of the record is not required for proper determination of the appeal and file the stipulation in the trial court, that part of the record must not be prepared or sent to the appellate division.

(Subd (b) amended effective January 1, 2010; adopted effective January 1, 2009.)

Rule 8.910 amended effective January 1, 2010; adopted effective January 1, 2009.

Rule 8.911. Prosecuting attorney's notice regarding the record

If the prosecuting attorney does not want to receive a copy of the record on appeal, within 10 days after the notification of the appeal under rule 8.901(b) is sent to the prosecuting attorney, the prosecuting attorney must serve and file a notice indicating that he or she does not want to receive the record.

Rule 8.911 amended effective January 1, 2016; adopted effective January 1, 2009.

Rule 8.912. Contents of clerk's transcript

Except in appeals covered by rule 8.920 or when the parties have filed a stipulation under rule 8.910(b) that any of these items is not required for proper determination of the appeal, the clerk's transcript must contain:

(1) The complaint, including any notice to appear, and any amendment;

(2) Any demurrer or other plea;

(3) All court minutes;

(4) Any written findings or opinion of the court;

(5) The judgment or order appealed from;

(6) Any motion or notice of motion for new trial, in arrest of judgment, or to dismiss the action, with supporting and opposing memoranda and attachments;

(7) Any transcript of a sound or sound-and-video recording tendered to the court under rule 2.1040;

(8) The notice of appeal; and

(9) If the appellant is the defendant:

(A) Any written defense motion denied in whole or in part, with supporting and opposing memoranda and attachments; and

(B) If related to a motion under (A), any search warrant and return.

Rule 8.912 adopted effective January 1, 2009.

Rule 8.913. Preparation of clerk's transcript

(a) When preparation begins

Unless the original court file will be used in place of a clerk's transcript under rule 8.914, the clerk must begin preparing the clerk's transcript immediately after the notice of appeal is filed.

(Subd (a) adopted effective January 1, 2009.)

(b) Format of transcript

The clerk's transcript must comply with rule 8.144.

(Subd (b) adopted effective January 1, 2009.)

(c) When preparation must be completed

Within 20 days after the notice of appeal is filed, the clerk must complete preparation of an original clerk's transcript for the appellate division and one copy for the appellant. If there is more than one appellant, the clerk must prepare an extra copy for each additional appellant who is represented by separate counsel or self-represented. If the defendant is the appellant, a copy must also be prepared for the prosecuting attorney unless the prosecuting attorney has notified the court under rule 8.911 that he or she does not want to receive the record. If the People are the appellant, a copy must also be prepared for the respondent.

(Subd (c) adopted effective January 1, 2009.)

(d) Certification

The clerk must certify as correct the original and all copies of the clerk's transcript.

(Subd (d) adopted effective January 1, 2009.)

Rule 8.913 adopted effective January 1, 2009.

Advisory Committee Comment

Rule 8.922 addresses when the clerk's transcript is sent to the appellate division in infraction appeals.

Rule 8.914. Trial court file instead of clerk's transcript

(a) Application

If the court has a local rule for the appellate division electing to use this form of the record, the original trial court file may be used instead of a clerk's transcript. This rule and any supplemental provisions of the local rule then govern unless the trial court orders otherwise after notice to the parties.

(Subd (a) adopted effective January 1, 2009.)

(b) When original file must be prepared

Within 20 days after the filing of the notice of appeal, the trial court clerk must put the trial court file in chronological order, number the pages, and attach a chronological index and a list of all attorneys of record, the parties they represent, and any unrepresented parties.

(Subd (b) adopted effective January 1, 2009.)

(c) Copies

The clerk must send a copy of the index to the appellant for use in paginating his or her copy of the file to conform to the index. If there is more than one appellant, the clerk must prepare an extra copy of the index for each additional appellant who is represented by separate counsel or self-represented. If the defendant is the appellant, a copy must also be prepared for the prosecuting attorney unless the prosecuting attorney has notified the court under rule 8.911 that he or she does not want to receive the record. If the People are the appellant, a copy must also be prepared for the respondent.

(Subd (c) adopted effective January 1, 2009.)

Rule 8.914 adopted effective January 1, 2009.

Advisory Committee Comment

Rule 8.922 addresses when the original file is sent to the appellate division in infraction appeals.

Rule 8.915. Record of oral proceedings

(a) Appellant's election

The appellant must notify the trial court whether he or she elects to proceed with or without a record of the oral proceedings in the trial court. If the appellant elects to proceed with a record of the oral proceedings in the trial court, the notice must specify which form of the record of the oral proceedings in the trial court the appellant elects to use:

(1) A statement on appeal under rule 8.916;

(2) If the court has a local rule for the appellate division permitting this, an official electronic recording of the proceedings under rule 8.917(c). The appellant must attach to the notice a copy of the stipulation required under rule 8.917(c); or

(3) A reporter's transcript under rules 8.918–8.920 or a transcript prepared from an official electronic recording of the proceedings under rule 8.917(b). If the appellant elects to use a reporter's transcript, the clerk must promptly send a copy of appellant's notice making this election and the notice of appeal to each court reporter.

(Subd (a) amended effective January 1, 2016; adopted effective January 1, 2009.)

(b) Time for filing election

The notice of election required under (a) must be filed with the notice of appeal.

(Subd (b) adopted effective January 1, 2009.)

(c) Failure to file election

If the appellant does not file an election within the time specified in (b), rule 8.924 applies.

(Subd (c) amended effective March 1, 2014; adopted effective January 1, 2010.)
Rule 8.915 amended effective January 1, 2016; adopted effective January 1, 2009; previously amended effective January 1, 2010, and March 1, 2014.

Advisory Committee Comment

Notice of Appeal and Record of Oral Proceedings (Infraction) (form CR-142) may be used to file the election required under this rule. This form is available at any courthouse or county law library or online at *www.courtinfo.ca.gov/forms*. To assist appellants in making an appropriate election, courts are encouraged to include information about whether the proceedings were recorded by a court reporter or officially electronically recorded in any information that the court provides to parties concerning their appellate rights.

Rule 8.916. Statement on appeal

(a) Description

A statement on appeal is a summary of the trial court proceedings that is approved by the trial court.

(Subd (a) adopted effective January 1, 2009.)

(b) Preparing the proposed statement

(1) If the appellant elects under rule 8.915 to use a statement on appeal, the appellant must prepare and file a proposed statement within 20 days after filing the record preparation election. If the defendant is the appellant and the prosecuting attorney appeared in the case, the defendant must serve a copy of the proposed statement on the prosecuting attorney. If the People are the appellant, the prosecuting attorney must serve a copy of the proposed statement on the respondent.

(2) Appellants who are not represented by an attorney must file their proposed statements on *Proposed Statement on Appeal (Infraction)* (form CR-143). For good cause, the court may permit the filing of a statement that is not on form CR-143.

(3) If the appellant does not serve and file a proposed statement within the time specified in (1), rule 8.924 applies.

(Subd (b) amended effective March 1, 2014; adopted effective January 1, 2009.)

(c) Contents of the proposed statement on appeal

A proposed statement prepared by the appellant must contain:

(1) A statement of the points the appellant is raising on appeal. The appeal is then limited to those points unless the appellate division determines that the record permits the full consideration of another point.

(A) The statement must specify the intended grounds of appeal by clearly stating each point to be raised but need not identify each particular ruling or matter to be challenged.

(B) If one of the grounds of appeal is insufficiency of the evidence, the statement must specify how it is insufficient.

(2) A summary of the trial court's rulings and the sentence imposed on the defendant.

(3) A condensed narrative of the oral proceedings that the appellant believes necessary for the appeal. The condensed narrative must include a concise factual summary of the evidence and the testimony of each witness that is relevant to the points which the appellant states under (1) are being raised on appeal. Any evidence or portion of a proceeding not included will be presumed to support the judgment or order appealed from.

(Subd (c) amended effective March 1, 2014; adopted effective January 1, 2009; previously amended effective July 1, 2009.)

(d) Review of the appellant's proposed statement

(1) Within 10 days after the appellant files the proposed statement, the respondent may serve and file proposed amendments to that statement.

(2) No later than 10 days after the respondent files proposed amendments or the time to do so expires, a party may request a hearing to review and correct the proposed statement. No hearing will be held unless ordered by the trial court judge, and the judge will not ordinarily order a hearing unless there is a factual dispute about a material aspect of the trial court proceedings.

(3) Except as provided in (6), if no hearing is ordered, no later than 10 days after the time for requesting a hearing expires, the trial court judge must review the proposed statement and any proposed amendments filed by the respondent and take one of the following actions:

(A) If the proposed statement does not contain material required under (c), the trial court judge may order the appellant to prepare a new proposed statement. The order must identify the additional material that must be included in the statement to comply with (c) and the date by which the new proposed statement must be served and filed. If the appellant does not serve and file a new proposed statement as directed, rule 8.924 applies.

(B) If the trial court judge does not issue an order under (A), the trial court judge must either:

(i) Make any corrections or modifications to the statement necessary to ensure that it is an accurate summary of the evidence and the testimony of each witness that is relevant to the points which the appellant states under (c)(1) are being raised on appeal; or

(ii) Identify the necessary corrections and modifications and order the appellant to prepare a statement incorporating these corrections and modifications.

(4) If a hearing is ordered, the court must promptly set the hearing date and provide the parties with at least 5 days' written notice of the hearing date. No later than 10 days after the hearing, the trial court judge must either:

(A) Make any corrections or modifications to the statement necessary to ensure that it is an accurate summary of the evidence and the testimony of each witness that is relevant to the points which the appellant states under (c)(1) are being raised on appeal; or

(B) Identify the necessary corrections and modifications and order the appellant to prepare a statement incorporating these corrections and modifications.

(5) The trial court judge must not eliminate the appellant's specification of grounds of appeal from the proposed statement.

(6) If the trial court proceedings were reported by a court reporter or officially electronically recorded electronically under Government Code section 69957 and the trial court judge determines that it would save court time and resources, instead of correcting a proposed statement on appeal:

(A) If the court has a local rule for the appellate division permitting the use of an official electronic recording as the record of the oral proceedings, the trial court judge may order that the original of an official electronic recording of the trial court proceedings, or a copy made by the court, be transmitted as the record of these oral proceedings without being transcribed. The court will pay for any copy of the official electronic recording ordered under this subdivision; or

(B) If the court has a local rule permitting this, the trial court judge may order that a transcript be prepared as the record of the oral proceedings. The court will pay for any transcript ordered under this subdivision.

(Subd (d) amended effective March 1, 2014; adopted effective January 1, 2009.)

(e) Review of the corrected or modified statement

(1) If the trial court judge makes any corrections or modifications to the proposed statement under (d), the clerk must serve copies of the corrected or modified statement on the parties. If under (d) the trial court judge orders the appellant to prepare a statement incorporating corrections and modifications, the appellant must serve and file the corrected or modified statement within the time ordered by the court. If the prosecuting attorney did not appear at the trial, no copy of the statement is to be sent to or served on the prosecuting attorney. If the appellant does not serve and file a corrected or modified statement as directed, rule 8.924 applies.

(2) Within 10 days after the statement is served on the parties, any party may serve and file proposed modifications or objections to the statement.

(3) Within 10 days after the time for filing proposed modifications or objections under (2) has expired, the judge must review the corrected or modified statement and any proposed modifications or objections to the statement filed by the parties. The procedures in (d)(3) or (d)(4) apply if the judge determines that further corrections or modifications are necessary to ensure that the statement is an accurate summary of the evidence and the testimony of each witness relevant to the points which the appellant states under (c)(1) are being raised on appeal.

(Subd (e) amended effective March 1, 2014; adopted effective January 1, 2009.)

(f) Certification of the statement on appeal

If the trial court judge does not make or order any corrections or modifications to the proposed statement under (d)(3), (d)(4), or (e)(3) and does not direct the preparation of a transcript in lieu of correcting the proposed statement under (d)(6), the judge must promptly certify the statement.

(Subd (f) amended effective March 1, 2014; adopted effective January 1, 2009.)

(g) Extensions of time

For good cause, the trial court may grant an extension of not more than 15 days to do any act required or permitted under this rule.

(Subd (g) adopted effective January 1, 2009.)

Rule 8.916 amended effective March 1, 2014; adopted effective January 1, 2009; previously effective July 1, 2009.

Advisory Committee Comment

Rules 8.806, 8.810, and 8.812 address applications for extensions of time and relief from default.

Subdivision (b)(2). *Proposed Statement on Appeal (Infraction)* (form CR-143) is available at any courthouse or county law library or online at www.courts.ca.gov/forms.

Subdivision (d). Under rule 8.804, the term "judge" includes a commissioner or a temporary judge.

Subdivisions (d)(3)(B), (d)(4), and (f). The judge need not ensure that the statement as modified or corrected is complete, but only that it is an accurate summary of the evidence and testimony relevant to the issues identified by the appellant.

Rule 8.917. Record when trial proceedings were officially electronically recorded

(a) Application

This rule applies only if:

(1) The trial court proceedings were officially recorded electronically under Government Code section 69957; and

(2) The electronic recording was prepared in compliance with applicable rules regarding electronic recording of court proceedings.

(Subd (a) adopted effective January 1, 2009.)

(b) Transcripts from official electronic recording

Written transcripts of official electronic recordings may be prepared under rule 2.952. A transcript prepared and certified as provided in that rule is prima facie a true and complete record of the oral proceedings it purports to cover, and satisfies any requirement in these rules or in any statute for a reporter's transcript of oral proceedings.

(Subd (b) adopted effective January 1, 2009.)

(c) Use of official recording as record of oral proceedings

If the court has a local rule for the appellate division permitting this, on stipulation of the parties or on order of the trial court under rule 8.916(d)(6), the original of an official electronic recording of the trial court proceedings, or a copy made by the court, may be transmitted as the record of these oral proceedings without being transcribed. This official electronic recording satisfies any requirement in these rules or in any statute for a reporter's transcript of these proceedings.

(Subd (c) amended effective July 1, 2010; adopted effective January 1, 2009.)

(d) Contents

Except in appeals when either the parties have filed a stipulation under rule 8.910(b) or the trial court has ordered that any of these items is not required for proper determination of the appeal, rules 8.918 and 8.920 govern the contents of a transcript of an official electronic recording.

(Subd (d) adopted effective March 1, 2014.)

(e) When preparation begins

(1) If the appellant is the People, preparation of a transcript or a copy of the recording must begin immediately after the appellant files an election under rule 8.915(a) to use a transcript of an official electronic recording or a copy of the official electronic recording as the record of the oral proceedings.

(2) If the appellant is the defendant:

(A) Within 10 days after the date the appellant files the election under rule 8.915(a), the clerk must notify the appellant and his or her counsel of the estimated cost of preparing the transcript or the copy of the recording. The notification must show the date it was sent.

(B) Within 10 days after the date the clerk sent the notice under (A), the appellant must do one of the following:

(i) Deposit with the clerk an amount equal to the estimated cost of preparing the transcript or the copy of the recording;

(ii) File a declaration of indigency supported by evidence in the form required by the Judicial Council; or

(iii) Notify the clerk by filing a new election that he or she will be using a statement on appeal instead of a transcript or copy of the recording. The appellant must prepare, serve, and file a proposed statement on appeal within 20 days after serving and filing the notice and must otherwise comply with the requirements for statements on appeal under rule 8.869;

(iv) Notify the clerk by filing a new election that he or she now elects to proceed without a record of the oral proceedings in the trial court; or

(v) Notify the clerk that he or she is abandoning the appeal by filing an abandonment in the reviewing court under rule 8.904.

(C) If the trial court determines that the appellant is not indigent, within 10 days after the date the clerk sends notice of this determination to the appellant, the appellant must do one of the following:

(i) Deposit with the clerk an amount equal to the estimated cost of preparing the transcript or the copy of the recording;

(ii) Notify the clerk by filing a new election that he or she will be using a statement on appeal instead of a reporter's transcript. The appellant must prepare, serve, and file a proposed statement on appeal within 20 days after serving and filing the notice and must otherwise comply with the requirements for statements on appeal under rule 8.869;

(iii) Notify the clerk by filing a new election that he or she now elects to proceed without a record of the oral proceedings in the trial court; or

(iv) Notify the clerk that he or she is abandoning the appeal by filing an abandonment in the reviewing court under rule 8.904.

(D) Preparation of the transcript or the copy of the recording must begin when:

(i) The clerk receives the required deposit under (B)(i) or (C)(i); or

(ii) The trial court determines that the defendant is indigent and orders that the defendant receive the transcript or the copy of the recording without cost.

(Subd (e) amended effective January 1, 2016; adopted as subd (d) effective January 1, 2009; previously amended and relettered as subd (e) effective March 1, 2014.)

(f) Notice when proceedings were not officially electronically recorded or cannot be transcribed

(1) If any portion of the oral proceedings to be included in the transcript were not officially electronically recorded under Government Code section 69957 or cannot be transcribed, the trial court clerk must so notify the parties in writing. The notice must:

(A) Indicate whether the identified proceedings were reported by a court reporter; and

(B) Show the date it was sent.

(2) Within 15 days after this notice is sent by the clerk, the appellant must serve and file a notice with the court stating whether the appellant elects to proceed with or without a record of the identified proceedings. When the party elects to proceed with a record of these oral proceedings:

(A) If the clerk's notice under (1) indicates that the proceedings were reported by a court reporter, the appellant's notice must specify which form of the record listed in rule 8.915(a) other than an official electronic recording or a transcript prepared from an official electronic recording the appellant elects to use. The appellant must comply with the requirements applicable to the form of the record elected.

(B) If the clerk's notice under (1) indicates that the proceedings were not reported by a court reporter, the appellant must prepare, serve, and file a proposed statement on appeal within 20 days after serving and filing the notice.

(Subd (f) amended effective January 1, 2016; adopted March 1, 2014.)

Rule 8.917 amended effective January 1, 2016; adopted effective January 1, 2009; previously amended effective July 1, 2010, and March 1, 2014.

Advisory Committee Comment

Subdivision (d). The appellant must use *Defendant's Financial Statement on Eligibility for Appointment of Counsel and Reimbursement and Record on Appeal at Public Expense* (form CR-105) to show indigency. This form is available at any courthouse or county law library or online at www.courtinfo.ca.gov/forms.

Rule 8.918. Contents of reporter's transcript

(a) Normal contents

Except in appeals covered by rule 8.920, when the parties have filed a stipulation under rule 8.910(b), or when, under a procedure established by a local rule adopted pursuant to (b), the trial court has ordered that any of these items is not required for proper determination of the appeal, the reporter's transcript must contain:

(1) The oral proceedings on the entry of any plea other than a not guilty plea;

(2) The oral proceedings on any motion in limine;

(3) The oral proceedings at trial, but excluding any opening statement;

(4) Any oral opinion of the court;

(5) The oral proceedings on any motion for new trial;

(6) The oral proceedings at sentencing or other dispositional hearing;

(7) If the appellant is the defendant, the reporter's transcript must also contain:

(A) The oral proceedings on any defense motion denied in whole or in part except motions for disqualification of a judge; and

(B) The closing arguments.

(Subd (a) amended and lettered effective March 1, 2014; adopted effective January 1, 2009.)

(b) Local procedure for determining contents

A trial court may adopt a local rule that establishes procedures for determining whether any of the items listed in (a) is not required for proper determination of the appeal or whether a form of the record other than a reporter's transcript constitutes a record of sufficient completeness for proper determination of the appeal.

(Subd (b) adopted effective March 1, 2014.)
Rule 8.918 amended effective March 1, 2014; adopted effective January 1, 2009.

Advisory Committee Comment

Subdivision (b). Both the United States Supreme Court and the California Supreme Court have held that, where the State has established a right to appeal, an indigent defendant convicted of a criminal offense has a constitutional right to a "'record of sufficient completeness' to permit proper consideration of [his] claims." (*Mayer v. Chicago* (1971) 404 U.S. 189, 193–194; *March v. Municipal Court* (1972) 7 Cal.3d 422, 427–428.) The California Supreme Court has also held that an indigent appellant is denied his or her right under the Fourteenth Amendment to the competent assistance of counsel on appeal if counsel fails to obtain an appellate record adequate for consideration of appellant's claims of errors (*People v. Barton* (1978) 21 Cal.3d 513, 518–520).

The *Mayer* and *March* decisions make clear, however, that the constitutionally required "record of sufficient completeness" does not necessarily mean a complete verbatim transcript; other forms of the record, such as a statement on appeal or a partial transcript, may be sufficient. The record that is necessary depends on the grounds for the appeal in the particular case. Under these cases, where the grounds of appeal make out a colorable need for a complete transcript, the burden is on the State to show that only a portion of the transcript or an alternative form of the record will suffice for an effective appeal on those grounds. The burden of overcoming the need for a verbatim reporter's transcript appears to be met where a verbatim recording of the proceedings is provided. (*Mayer, supra*, 404 U.S. at p. 195; cf. *Eyrich v. Mun. Court* (1985) 165 Cal.App.3d 1138, 1140 ["Although use of a court reporter is one way of obtaining a verbatim record, it may also be acquired through an electronic recording when no court reporter is available"].)

Some courts have adopted local rules that establish procedures for determining whether only a portion of a verbatim transcript or an alternative form of the record will be sufficient for an effective appeal, including: (1) requiring the appellant to specify the points the appellant is raising on appeal; (2) requiring the appellant and respondent to meet and confer about the content and form of the record; and (3) holding a hearing on the content and form of the record. Local procedures can be tailored to reflect the methods available in a particular court for making a record of the trial court proceedings that is sufficient for an effective appeal.

Rule 8.919. Preparation of reporter's transcript

(a) When preparation begins

(1) Unless the court has adopted a local rule under rule 8.920(b) that provides otherwise, the reporter must immediately begin preparing the reporter's transcript if the notice sent to the reporter by the clerk under rule 8.915(a)(3) indicates that the appellant is the People.

(2) If the notice sent to the reporter by the clerk under rule 8.915(a)(3) indicates that the appellant is the defendant:

(A) Within 10 days after the date the clerk sent the notice under rule 8.915(a)(3), the reporter must file with the clerk the estimated cost of preparing the reporter's transcript; and

(B) The clerk must promptly notify the appellant and his or her counsel of the estimated cost of preparing the reporter's transcript. The notification must show the date it was sent.

(C) Within 10 days after the date the clerk sent the notice under (B), the appellant must do one of the following:

(i) Deposit with the clerk an amount equal to the estimated cost of preparing the transcript;

(ii) File a waiver of the deposit signed by the reporter;

(iii) File a declaration of indigency supported by evidence in the form required by the Judicial Council;

(iv) File a certified transcript of all of the proceedings required to be included in the reporter's transcript under rule 8.918. The transcript submitted by the appellant must not be accepted as a substitute for a deposit under (i) unless it complies with the format requirements of rule 8.838;

(v) Notify the clerk by filing a new election that he or she will be using a statement on appeal instead of a reporter's transcript. The appellant must prepare, serve, and file a proposed statement on appeal within 20 days after serving and filing the notice and must otherwise comply with the requirements for statements on appeal under rule 8.916;

(vi) Notify the clerk by filing a new election that he or she now elects to proceed without a record of the oral proceedings in the trial court; or

(vii) Notify the clerk that he or she is abandoning the appeal by filing an abandonment in the reviewing court under rule 8.904.

(D) If the trial court determines that the appellant is not indigent, within 10 days after the date the clerk sends notice of this determination to the appellant, the appellant must do one of the following:

(i) Deposit with the clerk an amount equal to the estimated cost of preparing the transcript;

(ii) File with the clerk a waiver of the deposit signed by the reporter;

(iii) File a certified transcript of all of the proceedings required to be included in the reporter's transcript under rule 8.918. The transcript submitted by the appellant must not be accepted as a substitute for a deposit under (i) unless it complies with the format requirements of rule 8.838;

(iv) Notify the clerk by filing a new election that he or she will be using a statement on appeal instead of a reporter's transcript. The appellant must prepare, serve, and file a proposed statement on appeal within 20 days after serving and filing the notice and must otherwise comply with the requirements for statements on appeal under rule 8.916;

(v) Notify the clerk by filing a new election that he or she now elects to proceed without a record of the oral proceedings in the trial court; or

(vi) Notify the clerk that he or she is abandoning the appeal by filing an abandonment in the reviewing court under rule 8.904.

(E) The clerk must promptly notify the reporter to begin preparing the transcript when:

(i) The clerk receives the required deposit under (C)(i) or (D)(i); or

(ii) The clerk receives a waiver of the deposit signed by the reporter under (C)(ii) or (D)(ii); or

(iii) The trial court determines that the defendant is indigent and orders that the defendant receive the transcript without cost.

(Subd (a) amended effective January 1, 2024; adopted effective January 1, 2009; previously amended effective March 1, 2014, and January 1, 2016.)

(b) Format of transcript

The reporter's transcript must comply with rule 8.838.

(Subd (b) amended effective January 1, 2024; adopted effective January 1, 2009.)

(c) Copies and certification

The reporter must prepare an original and the same number of copies of the reporter's transcript as rule 8.913(c) requires of the clerk's transcript and must certify each as correct.

(Subd (c) adopted effective January 1, 2009.)

(d) When preparation must be completed

The reporter must deliver the original and all copies to the trial court clerk as soon as they are certified but no later than 20 days after the reporter is required to begin preparing the transcript under (a). Only the presiding judge of the appellate division or his or her designee may extend the time to prepare the reporter's transcript (see rule 8.810).

(Subd (d) amended effective January 1, 2018; adopted effective January 1, 2009; previously amended effective March 1, 2014, January 1, 2017, and January 1, 2018.)

(e) Multi-reporter cases

In a multi-reporter case, the clerk must accept any completed portion of the transcript from the primary reporter one week after the time prescribed by (d) even if other portions are uncompleted. The clerk must promptly pay each reporter who certifies that all portions of the transcript assigned to that reporter are completed.

(Subd (e) adopted effective January 1, 2009.)

(f) Notice when proceedings cannot be transcribed

(1) If any portion of the oral proceedings to be included in the reporter's transcript was not reported or cannot be transcribed, the trial court clerk must so notify the parties in writing. The notice must:

(A) Indicate whether the identified proceedings were officially electronically recorded under Government Code section 69957; and

(B) Show the date it was sent.

(2) Within 15 days after this notice is sent by the clerk, the appellant must serve and file a notice with the court stating whether the appellant elects to proceed with or without a record of the identified proceedings. When the party elects to proceed with a record of these oral proceedings:

(A) If the clerk's notice under (1) indicates that the proceedings were officially electronically recorded under Government Code section 69957, the appellant's notice must specify which form of the record listed in rule 8.915(a) other than a reporter's transcript the appellant elects to use. The appellant must comply with the requirements applicable to the form of the record elected.

(B) If the clerk's notice under (1) indicates that the proceedings were not officially electronically recorded under Government Code section 69957, the appellant must prepare, serve, and file a proposed statement on appeal within 20 days after serving and filing the notice.

(Subd (f) amended effective January 1, 2016; adopted effective March 1, 2014.)
Rule 8.919 amended effective January 1, 2024; adopted effective January 1, 2009; previously amended effective March 1, 2014, January 1, 2016, January 1, 2017, January 1, 2018, and January 1, 2018.

Advisory Committee Comment

Subdivision (a). The appellant must use *Defendant's Financial Statement on Eligibility for Appointment of Counsel and Reimbursement and Record on Appeal at Public Expense* (form CR-105) to show indigency. This form is available at any courthouse or county law library or online at www.courts.ca.gov/forms.

Subdivisions (a)(2)(C)(iv) and (a)(2)(D)(iii). Sometimes a party in a trial court proceeding will purchase a reporter's transcript of all or part of the proceedings before any appeal is filed. In recognition of the fact that such transcripts may already have been purchased, this rule allows an appellant, in lieu of depositing funds for a reporter's transcript, to deposit with the trial court a certified transcript of the proceedings necessary for the appeal. Subdivisions (a)(2)(C)(iv) and (a)(2)(D)(iii) make clear that the certified transcript may be filed in lieu of a deposit for a reporter's transcript only where the certified transcript contains all of the proceedings required under rule 8.865 and the transcript complies with the format requirements of rule 8.838 (e.g., cover information, renumbered pages, required indexes). Parties using this alternative to a deposit are responsible for ensuring that such transcripts are in the proper format. Parties may arrange with a court reporter to do the necessary formatting of the transcript or may do the formatting themselves.

Rule 8.920. Limited normal record in certain appeals

If the People appeal from a judgment on a demurrer to the complaint, including any notice to appear, or if the defendant or the People appeal from an appealable order other than a ruling on a motion for new trial, the normal record is composed of:

(1) *Record of the documents filed in the trial court*

A clerk's transcript or original trial court file containing:

(A) The complaint, including any notice to appear, and any amendment;

(B) Any demurrer or other plea;

(C) Any motion or notice of motion granted or denied by the order appealed from, with supporting and opposing memoranda and attachments;

(D) The judgment or order appealed from and any abstract of judgment;

(E) Any court minutes relating to the judgment or order appealed from and

(i) If there was a trial in the case, any court minutes of proceedings at the time the original judgment is rendered and any subsequent proceedings; or

(ii) If the original judgment of conviction is based on a guilty plea or nolo contendere plea, any court minutes of the proceedings at the time of entry of such plea and any subsequent proceedings; and

(F) The notice of appeal.

(2) *Record of the oral proceedings in the trial court*

If an appellant wants to raise any issue that requires consideration of the oral proceedings in the trial court:

(A) A reporter's transcript, a transcript prepared under rule 8.917, an official electronic recording under rule 8.917, or a statement on appeal under rule 8.916 summarizing any oral proceedings incident to the judgment or order being appealed.

(B) If the appeal is from an order after judgment, a reporter's transcript, a transcript prepared under rule 8.917, an official electronic recording under rule 8.917, or a statement on appeal under rule 8.916 summarizing any oral proceedings from:

(i) The original sentencing proceeding; and

(ii) If the original judgment of conviction is based on a guilty plea or nolo contendere plea, the proceedings at the time of entry of such plea.

Rule 8.920 amended effective January 1, 2013; adopted effective January 1, 2009.

Advisory Committee Comment

Subdivision (1)(E). This rule identifies the minutes that must be included in the record. The trial court clerk may include additional minutes beyond those identified in this rule if that would be more cost-effective.

Rule 8.921. Exhibits

(a) Exhibits deemed part of record

Exhibits admitted in evidence, refused, or lodged are deemed part of the record but may be transmitted to the appellate division only as provided in this rule.

(Subd (a) adopted effective January 1, 2009.)

(b) Notice of designation

(1) Within 10 days after the last respondent's brief is filed or could be filed under rule 8.927, if the appellant wants the appellate division to consider any original exhibits that were admitted in evidence, refused, or lodged, the appellant must serve and file a notice in the trial court designating such exhibits.

(2) Within 10 days after a notice under (1) is served, any other party wanting the appellate division to consider additional exhibits must serve and file a notice in trial court designating such exhibits.

(3) A party filing a notice under (1) or (2) must serve a copy on the appellate division.

(Subd (b) adopted effective January 1, 2009.)

(c) Request by appellate division

At any time the appellate division may direct the trial court or a party to send it an exhibit.

(Subd (c) adopted effective January 1, 2009.)

(d) Transmittal

Unless the appellate division orders otherwise, within 20 days after notice under (b) is filed or after the appellate division directs that an exhibit be sent:

(1) The trial court clerk must put any designated exhibits in the clerk's possession into numerical or alphabetical order and send them to the appellate division. The trial court clerk must also send a list of the exhibits sent. If the exhibits are not transmitted electronically, the trial court clerk must send two copies of the list. If the appellate division clerk finds the list correct, the clerk must sign and return a copy to the trial court clerk.

(2) Any party in possession of designated exhibits returned by the trial court must put them into numerical or alphabetical order and send them to the appellate division. The party must also send a list of the exhibits sent. If the exhibits are not transmitted electronically, the party must send two copies of the list. If the appellate division clerk finds the list correct, the clerk must sign and return a copy to the party.

(Subd (d) amended effective January 1, 2016; adopted effective January 1, 2009.)

(e) Return by appellate division

On request, the appellate division may return an exhibit to the trial court or to the party that sent it. When the remittitur issues, the appellate division must return all exhibits not transmitted electronically to the trial court or to the party that sent them.

(Subd (e) amended effective January 1, 2016; adopted effective January 1, 2009.)

Rule 8.921 amended effective January 1, 2016; adopted effective January 1, 2009.

Rule 8.922. Sending and filing the record in the appellate division

(a) When the record is complete

(1) If the appellant elected under rule 8.915 to proceed without a record of the oral proceedings in the trial court, the record is complete when the clerk's transcript is certified as correct or, if the original trial court file will be used instead of the clerk's transcript, when that original file is ready for transmission as provided under rule 8.914(b).

(2) If the appellant elected under rule 8.915 to proceed with a record of the oral proceedings in the trial court, the record is complete when the clerk's transcript is certified as correct or the original file is ready for transmission as provided in (1) and:

(A) If the appellant elected to use a reporter's transcript, the certified reporter's transcript is delivered to the court under rule 8.919;

(B) If the appellant elected to use a transcript prepared from an official electronic recording, the transcript has been prepared under rule 8.917;

(C) If the parties stipulated to the use of an official electronic recording of the proceedings, the electronic recording has been prepared under rule 8.917; or

(D) If the appellant elected to use a statement on appeal, the statement on appeal has been certified by the trial court or a transcript or copy of an official electronic recording has been prepared under rule 8.916(d)(6).

(Subd (a) adopted effective January 1, 2009.)

(b) Sending the record

When the record is complete, the clerk must promptly send:

(1) The original record to the appellate division;

(2) One copy of the clerk's transcript or index to the original court file and one copy of any record of the oral proceedings to each appellant who is represented by separate counsel or is self-represented;

(3) If the defendant is the appellant, one copy of the clerk's transcript or index to the original court file and one copy of any record of the oral proceedings to the prosecuting attorney unless the prosecuting attorney has notified the court under rule 8.911 that he or she does not want to receive the record; and

(4) If the People are the appellant, a copy of the clerk's transcript or index to the original court file and one copy of any record of the oral proceedings to the respondent.

(Subd (b) adopted effective January 1, 2009.)

(c) Filing the record

On receipt, the appellate division clerk must promptly file the original record and send notice of the filing date to the parties.

(Subd (c) amended effective January 1, 2016; adopted effective January 1, 2009.)

Rule 8.922 amended effective January 1, 2016; adopted effective January 1, 2009.

Rule 8.923. Augmenting or correcting the record in the appellate division

(a) Subsequent trial court orders

If, after the record is certified, the trial court amends or recalls the judgment or makes any other order in the case, including an order affecting the sentence or probation, the clerk must promptly certify and send a copy of the amended abstract of judgment or other order as an augmentation of the record to all those who received the record under rule 8.872(b). If there is any additional document or transcript related to the amended judgment or new order that any rule or order requires be included in the record, the clerk must send these documents or transcripts with the amended abstract of judgment or other order. The clerk must promptly copy and certify any such document and the reporter must promptly prepare and certify any such transcript.

(Subd (a) adopted effective January 1, 2009.)

(b) Omissions

If, after the record is certified, the trial court clerk or the reporter learns that the record omits a document or transcript that any rule or order requires to be included, the clerk must promptly copy and certify the document or the reporter must promptly prepare and certify the transcript. Without the need for a court order, the clerk must promptly send the document or transcript as an augmentation of the record to all those who received the record under rule 8.922(b).

(Subd (b) adopted effective January 1, 2009.)

(c) Augmentation or correction by the appellate division

At any time, on motion of a party or on its own motion, the appellate division may order the record augmented or corrected as provided in rule 8.841.

(Subd (c) adopted effective January 1, 2009.)

Rule 8.923 adopted effective January 1, 2009.

Rule 8.924. Failure to procure the record

(a) Notice of default

If a party fails to do any act required to procure the record, the trial court clerk must promptly notify that party in writing that it must do the act specified in the notice within 15 days after the notice is sent and that, if it fails to comply, the reviewing court may impose the following sanctions:

(1) If the defaulting party is the appellant, the court may dismiss the appeal or, if the default relates only to procurement of the record of the oral proceedings, may proceed on the clerk's transcript or other record of the written documents from the trial court proceedings; or

(2) If the defaulting party is the respondent, the court may proceed with the appeal on the record designated by the appellant.

(Subd (a) amended effective January 1, 2016; adopted effective March 1, 2014.)

(b) Sanctions

If the party fails to take the action specified in a notice given under (a), the trial court clerk must promptly notify the appellate division of the default and the appellate division may impose the sanction specified in the notice. If the appellate division dismisses the appeal, it may vacate the dismissal for good cause. If the appellate division orders the appeal to proceed on the record designated by the appellant, the respondent may obtain relief from default under rule 8.812.

(Subd (b) adopted effective March 1, 2014.)

Rule 8.924 amended effective January 1, 2016; adopted effective March 1, 2014.

Article 3
Briefs, Hearing, and Decision in Infraction Appeals

Article 3 adopted effective January 1, 2009.

Rule 8.925. General application of chapter 4
Rule 8.926. Notice of briefing schedule
Rule 8.927. Briefs
Rule 8.928. Contents and form of briefs
Rule 8.929. Oral argument

Rule 8.925. General application of chapter 4

Except as provided in this article, rules 8.880–8.890 govern briefs, hearing, and decision in the appellate division in infraction cases.

Rule 8.925 adopted effective January 1, 2009.

Rule 8.926. Notice of briefing schedule

When the record is filed, the clerk of the appellate division must promptly send, to each appellate counsel or unrepresented party, a notice giving the dates the briefs are due.

Rule 8.926 amended effective January 1, 2016; adopted effective January 1, 2009.

Rule 8.927. Briefs

(a) Time to file briefs

(1) The appellant must serve and file an appellant's opening brief within 30 days after the record is filed in the appellate division.

(2) Any respondent's brief must be served and filed within 30 days after the appellant files its opening brief.

(3) Any appellant's reply brief must be served and filed within 20 days after the respondent files its brief.

(4) No other brief may be filed except with the permission of the presiding judge.

(5) Instead of filing a brief, or as part of its brief, a party may join in a brief or adopt by reference all or part of a brief in the same or a related appeal.

(Subd (a) adopted effective January 1, 2009.)

(b) Failure to file a brief

(1) If the appellant fails to timely file an opening brief, the appellate division clerk must promptly notify the appellant in writing that the brief must be filed within 20 days after the notice is sent and that if the appellant fails to comply, the court may dismiss the appeal.

(2) If the respondent fails to timely file a brief, the appellate division clerk must promptly notify the respondent in writing that the brief must be filed within 20 days after the notice is sent and that if the respondent fails to comply, the court will decide the appeal on the record, the appellant's opening brief, and any oral argument by the appellant.

(3) If a party fails to comply with a notice under (1) or (2), the court may impose the sanction specified in the notice.

(Subd (b) amended effective January 1, 2016; adopted effective January 1, 2009; previously amended effective March 1, 2014.)

(c) Service and filing

(1) Copies of each brief must be served as required by rule 8.25.

(2) Unless the appellate division provides otherwise by local rule or order in the specific case, only the original brief, with proof of service, must be filed in the appellate division.

(3) A copy of each brief must be served on the trial court clerk for delivery to the judge who tried the case.

(4) A copy of each brief must be served on a public officer or agency when required by rule 8.29.

(Subd (c) adopted effective January 1, 2009.)

Rule 8.927 amended effective January 1, 2016; adopted effective January 1, 2009; previously amended effective March 1, 2014.

Rule 8.928. Contents and form of briefs

(a) Contents

(1) Each brief must:

(A) State each point under a separate heading or subheading summarizing the point and support each point by argument and, if possible, by citation of authority; and

(B) Support any reference to a matter in the record by a citation to the volume and page number of the record where the matter appears.

(2) An appellant's opening brief must:

(A) State the nature of the action, the relief sought in the trial court, and the judgment or order appealed from;

(B) State that the judgment appealed from is final or explain why the order appealed from is appealable; and

(C) Provide a summary of the significant facts limited to matters in the record.

(Subd (a) adopted effective January 1, 2009.)

(b) Length

(1) A brief produced on a computer must not exceed 5,100 words, including footnotes. Such a brief must include a certificate by appellate counsel or an unrepresented party stating the number of words in the brief. The person certifying may rely on the word count of the computer program used to prepare the brief.

(2) A brief produced on a typewriter must not exceed 15 pages.

(3) The information listed on the cover, any table of contents or table of authorities, the certificate under (1), and any signature block are excluded from the limits stated in (1) or (2).

(4) On application, the presiding judge may permit a longer brief for good cause. A lengthy record or numerous or complex issues on appeal will ordinarily constitute good cause.

(Subd (b) amended effective January 1, 2013; adopted effective January 1, 2009; previously amended effective January 1, 2011.)

(c) Form

(1) A brief may be reproduced by any process that produces a clear, black image of letter quality. All documents filed must have a page size of 8½ by 11 inches. If filed in paper form, the paper must be white or unbleached and of at least 20-pound weight. Both sides of the paper may be used if the brief is not bound at the top.

(2) Any conventional font may be used. The font may be either proportionally spaced or monospaced.

(3) The font style must be roman; but for emphasis, italics or boldface may be used or the text may be underscored. Case names must be italicized or underscored. Headings may be in uppercase letters.

(4) Except as provided in (11), the font size, including footnotes, must not be smaller than 13-point.

(5) The lines of text must be unnumbered and at least one-and-a-half-spaced. Headings and footnotes may be single-spaced. Quotations may be block-indented and single-spaced. Single-spaced means six lines to a vertical inch.

(6) The margins must be at least 1½ inches on the left and right and 1 inch on the top and bottom.

(7) The pages must be consecutively numbered.

(8) The cover—or first page if there is no cover—must include the information required by rule 8.816(a)(1).

(9) If filed in paper form, the brief must be bound on the left margin, except that briefs may be bound at the top if required by a local rule of the appellate division. If the brief is stapled, the bound edge and staples must be covered with tape.

(10) The brief need not be signed.

(11) If the brief is produced on a typewriter:

(A) A typewritten original and carbon copies may be filed only with the presiding justice's permission, which will ordinarily be given only to unrepresented parties proceeding in forma pauperis. All other typewritten briefs must be filed as photocopies.

(B) Both sides of the paper may be used if a photocopy is filed; only one side may be used if a typewritten original and carbon copies are filed.

(C) The type size, including footnotes, must not be smaller than standard pica, 10 characters per inch. Unrepresented incarcerated litigants may use elite type, 12 characters per inch, if they lack access to a typewriter with larger characters.

(Subd (c) amended effective January 1, 2016; adopted effective January 1, 2009; previously amended effective January 1, 2013, and March 1, 2014.)

(d) Noncomplying briefs

If a brief does not comply with this rule:

(1) The reviewing court clerk may decline to file it, but must mark it "received but not filed" and return it to the party; or

(2) If the brief is filed, the presiding judge may with or without notice:

(A) Order the brief returned for corrections and refiling within a specified time;

(B) Strike the brief with leave to file a new brief within a specified time; or

(C) Disregard the noncompliance.

(Subd (d) adopted effective January 1, 2009.)

Rule 8.928 amended effective January 1, 2016; adopted effective January 1, 2009; previously amended effective January 1, 2011, January 1, 2013, and March 1, 2014.

Advisory Committee Comment

Subdivision (b). Subdivision (b)(1) states the maximum permissible lengths of briefs produced on a computer in terms of word count rather than page count. This provision tracks a provision in rule 8.204(c) governing Court of Appeal briefs and is explained in the comment to that provision. Subdivision (b)(3) specifies certain items that are not counted toward the maximum brief length. Signature blocks, as referenced in this provision include not only the signatures, but also the printed names, titles, and affiliations of any attorneys filing or joining in the brief, which may accompany the signature.

Rule 8.929. Oral argument

(a) Calendaring and sessions

Unless otherwise ordered, all appeals in which the last reply brief was filed or the time for filing this brief expired 45 or more days before the date of a regular appellate division session must be placed on the calendar for that session by the appellate division clerk. By order of the presiding judge or the appellate division, any appeal may be placed on the calendar for oral argument at any session.

(Subd (a) adopted effective January 1, 2009.)

(b) Oral argument by videoconference

(1) Oral argument may be conducted by videoconference if:

(A) It is ordered by the presiding judge of the appellate division or the presiding judge's designee on application of any party or on the court's own motion. An application from a party requesting that oral argument be conducted by videoconference must be filed within 10 days after the court sends notice of oral argument under (c)(1); or

(B) A local rule authorizes oral argument to be conducted by videoconference consistent with these rules.

(2) If oral argument is conducted by videoconference:

(A) Each judge of the appellate division panel assigned to the case must participate in the entire oral argument either in person at the superior court that issued the judgment or order that is being appealed or by videoconference from another court.

(B) Unless otherwise allowed by local rule or ordered by the presiding judge of the appellate division or the presiding judge's designee, all of the parties must appear at oral argument in person at the superior court that issued the judgment or order that is being appealed.

(C) The oral argument must be open to the public at the superior court that issued the judgment or order that is being appealed. If provided by local rule or ordered by the presiding judge of the appellate division or the presiding judge's designee, oral argument may also be open to the public at any of the locations from which a judge of the appellate division is participating in oral argument.

(D) The appellate division must ensure that:

(i) During oral argument, the participants in oral argument are visible and their statements are audible to all other participants, court staff, and any members of the public attending the oral argument;

(ii) Participants are identified when they speak; and

(iii) Only persons who are authorized to participate in the proceedings speak.

(E) A party must not be charged any fee to participate in oral argument by videoconference if the party participates from the superior court that issued the judgment or order that is being appealed or from a location from which a judge of the appellate division panel is participating in oral argument.

(Subd (b) adopted effective January 1, 2010.)

(c) Notice of argument

(1) As soon as all parties' briefs are filed or the time for filing these briefs has expired, the appellate division clerk must send a notice of the time and place of oral argument to all parties. The notice must be sent at least 20 days before the date for oral argument. The presiding judge may shorten the notice period for good cause; in that event, the clerk must immediately notify the parties by telephone or other expeditious method.

(2) If oral argument will be conducted by videoconference under (b), the clerk must specify, either in the notice required under (1) or in a supplemental notice sent to all parties at least 5 days before the date for oral argument, the location from which each judge of the appellate division panel assigned to the case will participate in oral argument.

(Subd (c) amended and relettered effective January 1, 2010; adopted as subd (b) effective January 1, 2009.)

(d) Waiver of argument

Parties may waive oral argument.

(Subd (d) relettered effective January 1, 2010; adopted as subd (c) effective January 1, 2009.)

(e) Conduct of argument

Unless the court provides otherwise:

(1) The appellant, petitioner, or moving party has the right to open and close. If there are two or more such parties, the court must set the sequence of argument.

(2) Each side is allowed 5 minutes for argument. The appellant may reserve part of this time for reply argument. If multiple parties are represented by separate counsel, or if an amicus curiae—on written request—is granted permission to argue, the court may apportion or expand the time.

(3) Only one counsel may argue for each separately represented party.
(Subd (e) amended and relettered effective January 1, 2010; adopted as subd (d) effective January 1, 2009.)

Rule 8.929 amended effective January 1, 2010; adopted effective January 1, 2009.

Advisory Committee Comment

Subdivision (a). Under rule 10.1108, the appellate division must hold a session at least once each quarter, unless no matters are set for oral argument that quarter, but may choose to hold sessions more frequently.

Chapter 6
Writ Proceedings

Chapter 6 adopted effective January 1, 2009.

Rule 8.930. Application
Rule 8.931. Petitions filed by persons not represented by an attorney
Rule 8.932. Petitions filed by an attorney for a party
Rule 8.933. Opposition
Rule 8.934. Notice to trial court
Rule 8.935. Filing, finality, and modification of decisions; rehearing; remittitur
Rule 8.936. Costs

Rule 8.930. Application

(a) Writ proceedings governed

Except as provided in (b), the rules in this chapter govern proceedings in the appellate division for writs of mandate, certiorari, or prohibition, or other writs within the original jurisdiction of the appellate division, including writs relating to a postjudgment enforcement order of the small claims division. In all respects not provided for in this chapter, rule 8.883, regarding the form and content of briefs, applies.

(Subd (a) amended effective January 1, 2016; adopted effective January 1, 2009.)

(b) Writ proceedings not governed

The rules in this chapter do not apply to:

(1) Petitions for writs of supersedeas under rule 8.824;

(2) Petitions for writs relating to acts of the small claims division other than a postjudgment enforcement order; or

(3) Petitions for writs not within the original jurisdiction of the appellate division.

(Subd (b) amended effective January 1, 2016; adopted effective January 1, 2009.)

Rule 8.930 amended effective January 1, 2016; adopted effective January 1, 2009.

Advisory Committee Comment

Information on Writ Proceedings in Misdemeanor, Infraction, and Limited Civil Cases (form APP-150-INFO) provides additional information about proceedings for writs in the appellate division of the superior court. This form is available at any courthouse or county law library or online at *www.courts.ca.gov/forms*.

Subdivision (b)(1). The superior courts, not the appellate divisions, have original jurisdiction in habeas corpus proceedings (see Cal. Const., art. VI, § 10). Habeas corpus proceedings in the superior courts are governed by rules 4.550 et seq.

Subdivision (b)(2). A petition that seeks a writ relating to an act of the small claims division other than a postjudgment enforcement order is heard by a single judge of the appellate division (see Code Civ. Proc. § 116.798(a)) and is governed by rules 8.970 et seq.

Rule 8.931. Petitions filed by persons not represented by an attorney

(a) Petitions

A person who is not represented by an attorney and who petitions the appellate division for a writ under this chapter must file the petition on *Petition for Writ (Misdemeanor, Infraction, or Limited Civil Case)* (form APP-151). For good cause the court may permit an unrepresented party to file a petition that is not on form APP-151, but the petition must be verified.

(Subd (a) amended effective January 1, 2018; adopted effective January 1, 2009.)

(b) Contents of supporting documents

(1) The petition must be accompanied by an adequate record, including copies of:

(A) The ruling from which the petition seeks relief;

(B) All documents and exhibits submitted to the trial court supporting and opposing the petitioner's position;

(C) Any other documents or portions of documents submitted to the trial court that are necessary for a complete understanding of the case and the ruling under review; and

(D) A reporter's transcript, a transcript of an electronic recording or, if the court has a local rule permitting this, an electronic recording of the oral proceedings that resulted in the ruling under review.

(2) In extraordinary circumstances, the petition may be filed without the documents required by (1)(A)–(C) but must include a declaration that explains the urgency and the circumstances making the documents unavailable and fairly summarizes their substance.

(3) If a transcript or electronic recording under (1)(D) is unavailable, the record must include a declaration:

(A) Explaining why the transcript or electronic recording is unavailable and fairly summarizing the proceedings, including the parties' arguments and any statement by the court supporting its ruling. This declaration may omit a full summary of the proceedings if part of the relief sought is an order to prepare a transcript for use by an indigent criminal defendant in support of the petition and if the declaration demonstrates the need for and entitlement to the transcript; or

(B) Stating that the transcript or electronic recording has been ordered, the date it was ordered, and the date it is expected to be filed, which must be a date before any action requested of the appellate division other than issuance of a temporary stay supported by other parts of the record.

(4) If the petition does not include the required record or explanations or does not present facts sufficient to excuse the failure to submit them, the court may summarily deny a stay request, the petition, or both.

(Subd (b) amended effective January 1, 2014; adopted effective January 1, 2009; previously amended effective January 1, 2009.)

(c) Form of supporting documents

(1) Documents submitted under (b) must comply with the following requirements:

(A) If submitted in paper form, they must be bound together at the end of the petition or in separate volumes not exceeding 300 pages each. The pages must be consecutively numbered.

(B) If submitted in paper form, they must be index-tabbed by number or letter.

(C) They must begin with a table of contents listing each document by its title and its index number or letter. If a document has attachments, the table of contents must give the title of each attachment and a brief description of its contents.

(2) The clerk must file any supporting documents not complying with (1), but the court may notify the petitioner that it may strike or summarily deny the petition if the documents are not brought into compliance within a stated reasonable time of not less than five days.

(3) Unless the court provides otherwise by local rule or order, only one set of the supporting documents needs to be filed in support of a petition, an answer, an opposition, or a reply.

(Subd (c) amended effective January 1, 2016; adopted effective January 1, 2009; previously amended effective January 1, 2011.)

(d) Service

(1) The petition and one set of supporting documents must be served on any named real party in interest, but only the petition must be served on the respondent.

(2) The proof of service must give the telephone number of each attorney or unrepresented party served.

(3) The petition must be served on a public officer or agency when required by statute or rule 8.29.

(4) The clerk must file the petition even if its proof of service is defective, but if the petitioner fails to file a corrected proof of service within five days after the clerk gives notice of the defect the court may strike the petition or impose a lesser sanction.

(5) The court may allow the petition to be filed without proof of service.

(Subd (d) adopted effective January 1, 2009.)

Rule 8.931 amended effective January 1, 2018; adopted effective January 1, 2009; previously amended effective January 1, 2009, January 1, 2011, January 1, 2014, and January 1, 2016.

Advisory Committee Comment

Subdivision (a). *Petition for Writ (Misdemeanor, Infraction, or Limited Civil Case)* (form APP-151) is available at any courthouse or county law library or online at *www.courts.ca.gov/forms*.

Subdivision (b). Rule 2.952 addresses the use of electronic recordings and transcripts of such recordings as the official record of proceedings.

Subdivision (d). Rule 8.25, which generally governs service and filing in appellate divisions, also applies to the original proceedings covered by this rule.

Rule 8.932. Petitions filed by an attorney for a party

(a) General application of rule 8.931

Except as provided in this rule, rule 8.931 applies to any petition for an extraordinary writ filed by an attorney.

(Subd (a) adopted effective January 1, 2009.)

(b) Form and content of petition

(1) A petition for an extraordinary writ filed by an attorney may, but is not required to be, filed on *Petition for Writ (Misdemeanor, Infraction, or Limited Civil Case)* (form APP-151).

(2) The petition must disclose the name of any real party in interest.

(3) If the petition seeks review of trial court proceedings that are also the subject of a pending appeal, the notice "Related Appeal Pending" must appear on the cover of the petition, and the first paragraph of the petition must state the appeal's title and any appellate division docket number.

(4) The petition must be verified.

(5) The petition must be accompanied by a memorandum, which need not repeat facts alleged in the petition.

(6) Rule 8.883(b) governs the length of the petition and memorandum, but the verification and any supporting documents are excluded from the limits stated in rule 8.883(b)(1) and (2).

(7) If the petition requests a temporary stay, it must explain the urgency.

(Subd (b) adopted effective January 1, 2009.)
Rule 8.932 adopted effective January 1, 2009.

Rule 8.933. Opposition

(a) Preliminary opposition

(1) Within 10 days after the petition is filed, the respondent or any real party in interest, separately or jointly, may serve and file a preliminary opposition.

(2) An opposition must contain a memorandum and a statement of any material fact not included in the petition.

(3) Within 10 days after an opposition is filed, the petitioner may serve and file a reply.

(4) Without requesting opposition or waiting for a reply, the court may grant or deny a request for temporary stay, deny the petition, issue an alternative writ or order to show cause, or notify the parties that it is considering issuing a peremptory writ in the first instance.

(Subd (a) adopted effective January 1, 2009.)

(b) Return or opposition; reply

(1) If the court issues an alternative writ or order to show cause, the respondent or any real party in interest, separately or jointly, may serve and file a return by demurrer, verified answer, or both. If the court notifies the parties that it is considering issuing a peremptory writ in the first instance, the respondent or any real party in interest may serve and file an opposition.

(2) Unless the court orders otherwise, the return or opposition must be served and filed within 30 days after the court issues the alternative writ or order to show cause or notifies the parties that it is considering issuing a peremptory writ in the first instance.

(3) Unless the court orders otherwise, the petitioner may serve and file a reply within 15 days after the return or opposition is filed.

(4) If the return is by demurrer alone and the demurrer is not sustained, the court may issue the peremptory writ without granting leave to answer.

(Subd (b) adopted effective January 1, 2009.)

(c) Form of preliminary opposition, return, or opposition

Any preliminary opposition, return, or opposition must comply with rule 8.931(c). If it is filed by an attorney, it must also comply with rule 8.932(b)(3)–(7).

(Subd (c) adopted effective January 1, 2014.)
Rule 8.933 amended effective January 1, 2014; adopted effective January 1, 2009.

Rule 8.934. Notice to trial court

(a) Notice if writ issues

If a writ or order issues directed to any judge, court, or other officer, the appellate division clerk must promptly send a certified copy of the writ or order to the person or entity to whom it is directed.

(Subd (a) adopted effective January 1, 2009.)

(b) Notice by telephone

(1) If the writ or order stays or prohibits proceedings set to occur within seven days or requires action within seven days—or in any other urgent situation—the appellate division clerk must make a reasonable effort to notify the clerk of the respondent court by telephone. The clerk of the respondent court must then notify the judge or officer most directly concerned.

(2) The clerk need not give notice by telephone of the summary denial of a writ, whether or not a stay previously issued.

(Subd (b) adopted effective January 1, 2009.)
Rule 8.934 adopted effective January 1, 2009.

Rule 8.935. Filing, finality, and modification of decisions; rehearing; remittitur

(a) Filing of decision

(1) The appellate division clerk must promptly file all opinions and orders of the court and on the same day send copies (by e-mail where permissible under rule 2.251) showing the filing date to the parties and, when relevant, to the trial court.

(2) A decision must identify the participating judges, including the author of any majority opinion and of any concurring or dissenting opinion, or the judges participating in a "by the court" decision.

(Subd (a) amended effective January 1, 2019; adopted effective January 1, 2014.)

(b) Finality of decision

(1) Except as otherwise ordered by the court, the following appellate division decisions regarding petitions for writs within the court's original jurisdiction are final in the issuing court when filed:

(A) An order denying or dismissing such a petition without issuance of an alternative writ, order to show cause, or writ of review; and

(B) An order denying or dismissing such a petition as moot after issuance of an alternative writ, order to show cause, or writ of review.

(2) Except as otherwise provided in (3), all other appellate division decisions in a writ proceeding are final 30 days after the decision is sent by the court clerk to the parties.

(3) If necessary to prevent mootness or frustration of the relief granted or to otherwise promote the interests of justice, an appellate division may order early finality in that court of a decision granting a petition for a writ within its original jurisdiction or denying such a petition after issuing an alternative writ, order to show cause, or writ of review. The decision may provide for finality in that court on filing or within a stated period of less than 30 days.

(Subd (b) amended effective January 1, 2019; adopted as subd (a) effective January 1, 2009; previously amended and relettered effective January 1, 2014.)

(c) Modification of decisions

Rule 8.888(b) governs the modification of appellate division decisions in writ proceedings.

(Subd (c) adopted effective January 1, 2014.)

(d) Rehearing

Rule 8.889 governs rehearing in writ proceedings in the appellate division.

(Subd (d) adopted effective January 1, 2014.)

(e) Remittitur

Except as provided in rule 8.1018 for cases transferred to the Court of Appeal, the appellate division must issue a remittitur after the court issues a decision in a writ proceeding except when the court issues one of the orders listed in (b)(1). Rule 8.890(b)–(d) govern issuance of a remittitur in these proceedings, including the clerk's duties, immediate issuance, stay, and recall of remittitur, and notice of issuance.

(Subd (e) amended and relettered effective January 1, 2014; adopted as subd (b) effective January 1, 2009.)
Rule 8.935 amended effective January 1, 2019; adopted effective January 1, 2009; previously amended effective January 1, 2014.

Advisory Committee Comment

Subdivision (b). This provision addresses the finality of decisions in proceedings relating to writs of mandate, certiorari, and prohibition. See rule 8.888(a) for provisions addressing the finality of decisions in appeals.

Subdivision (b)(1). Examples of situations in which the appellate division may issue an order dismissing a writ petition include when the petitioner fails to comply with an order of the court, when the court recalls the alternative writ, order to show cause, or writ of review as improvidently granted, or when the petition becomes moot.

Subdivision (d). Under this rule, a remittitur serves as notice that the writ proceedings have concluded.

Rule 8.936. Costs

(a) Entitlement to costs

Except in a criminal proceeding or other proceeding in which a party is entitled to court-appointed counsel, the prevailing party in an original proceeding is entitled to costs if the court resolves the proceeding after issuing an alternative writ, an order to show cause, or a peremptory writ in the first instance.

(Subd (a) adopted effective January 1, 2009.)

(b) Award of costs

(1) In the interests of justice, the court may award or deny costs as it deems proper.

(2) The opinion or order resolving the proceeding must specify the award or denial of costs.

(3) Rule 8.891(b)–(d) governs the procedure for recovering costs under this rule.

(Subd (b) adopted effective January 1, 2009.)
Rule 8.936 adopted effective January 1, 2009.

Division 5
Rules Relating to Appeals and Writs in Small Claims Cases

Title 8, Appellate Rules—Division 5, Rules Relating to Appeals and Writs in Small Claims renumbered from Division 3 effective April 25, 2019; amended effective January 1, 2016.

Chap. 1. Trial of Small Claims Cases on Appeals. Rules 8.950–8.966.
Chap. 2. Writ Petitions. Rules 8.970–8.977.

Chapter 1
Trial of Small Claims Cases on Appeal

Title 8, Appellate Rules—Division 3, Rules Relating to Appeals and Writs in Small Claims—Chapter 1, Trial of Small Claims Cases on Appeal; adopted effective January 1, 2016.

Rule 8.950. Application
Rule 8.952. Definitions
Rule 8.954. Filing the appeal
Rule 8.957. Record on appeal
Rule 8.960. Continuances
Rule 8.963. Abandonment, dismissal, and judgment for failure to bring to trial
Rule 8.966. Examination of witnesses

Rule 8.950. Application

The rules in this chapter supplement article 7 of the Small Claims Act, Code of Civil Procedure sections 116.710 et seq., providing for new trials of small claims cases on appeal, and must be read in conjunction with those statutes.

Rule 8.950 amended effective January 1, 2016; adopted as rule 151 effective July 1, 1964; previously amended effective January 1, 1977, and January 1, 2005; previously amended and renumbered as rule 8.900 effective January 1, 2007; previously renumbered as rule 8.950 effective January 1, 2009.

Rule 8.952. Definitions

The definitions in rule 1.6 apply to these rules unless the context or subject matter requires otherwise. In addition, the following definitions apply to these rules:

(1) "Small claims court" means the trial court from which the appeal is taken.

(2) "Appeal" means a new trial before a different judge on all claims, whether or not appealed.

(3) "Appellant" means the party appealing; "respondent" means the adverse party. "Plaintiff" and "defendant" refer to the parties as they were designated in the small claims court.

Rule 8.952 renumbered effective January 1, 2009; adopted as rule 158 effective July 1, 1964; previously amended and renumbered as rule 156 effective July 1, 1991; previously amended effective January 1, 2005; previously amended and renumbered as rule 8.902 effective January 1, 2007.

Rule 8.954. Filing the appeal

(a) Notice of appeal

To appeal from a judgment in a small claims case, an appellant must file a notice of appeal in the small claims court. The appellant or the appellant's attorney must sign the notice. The notice is sufficient if it states in substance that the appellant appeals from a specified judgment or, in the case of a defaulting defendant, from the denial of a motion to vacate the judgment. A notice of appeal must be liberally construed.

(Subd (a) amended effective January 1, 2007; previously amended effective July 1, 1973, January 1, 1977, January 1, 1979, January 1, 1984, July 1, 1991, and January 1, 2005.)

(b) Notification by clerk

(1) The clerk of the small claims court must promptly mail a notification of the filing of the notice of appeal to each other party at the party's last known address.

(2) The notification must state the number and title of the case and the date the notice of appeal was filed. If a party dies before the clerk mails the notification, the mailing is a sufficient performance of the clerk's duty.

(3) A failure of the clerk to give notice of the judgment or notification of the filing of the notice of appeal does not extend the time for filing the notice of appeal or affect the validity of the appeal.

(Subd (b) amended effective January 1, 2007; previously amended and relettered effective January 1, 1977; previously amended effective July 1, 1991, and January 1, 2005.)

(c) Premature notice of appeal

A notice of appeal filed after judgment is rendered but before it is entered is valid and is treated as filed immediately after entry. A notice of appeal filed after the judge has announced an intended ruling but before judgment is rendered may, in the discretion of the reviewing court be treated as filed immediately after entry of the judgment.

(Subd (c) amended effective January 1, 2007; adopted as subd (d) effective July 1, 1964; relettered effective January 1, 1977; previously amended effective July 1, 1991, and January 1, 2005.)

Rule 8.954 renumbered effective January 1, 2009; adopted as rule 152 effective July 1, 1964; previously amended effective July 1, 1973, January 1, 1977, January 1, 1979, January 1, 1984, July 1, 1991, and January 1, 2005; previously amended and renumbered as rule 8.904 effective January 1, 2007.

Rule 8.957. Record on appeal

Within five days after the filing of the notice of appeal and the payment of any fees required by law, the clerk of the small claims court must transmit the file and all related papers, including the notice of appeal, to the clerk of the court assigned to hear the appeal.

Rule 8.957 renumbered effective January 1, 2009; adopted as rule 153 effective July 1, 1964; previously amended effective July 1, 1972, July 1, 1973, January 1, 1977, and January 1, 2005; previously amended and renumbered as rule 8.907 effective January 1, 2007.

Rule 8.960. Continuances

For good cause, the court assigned to hear the appeal may continue the trial. A request for a continuance may be presented by one party or by stipulation. The court may grant a continuance not to exceed 30 days, but in a case of extreme hardship the court may grant a continuance exceeding 30 days.

Rule 8.960 renumbered effective January 1, 2009; adopted as rule 154 effective July 1, 1964; previously amended effective January 1, 1977, July 1, 1991, and January 1, 2005; previously renumbered as rule 8.910 effective January 1, 2007.

Rule 8.963. Abandonment, dismissal, and judgment for failure to bring to trial

(a) Before the record is filed

Before the record has been transmitted to the court assigned to hear the appeal, the appellant may file in the small claims court an abandonment of the appeal or a stipulation to abandon the appeal. Either filing operates to dismiss the appeal and return the case to the small claims court.

(Subd (a) amended effective January 1, 2007; previously amended effective July 1, 1972, January 1, 1977, and January 1, 2005.)

(b) After the record is filed

After the record has been transmitted to the court assigned to hear the appeal, the court may dismiss the appeal on the appellant's written request or the parties' stipulation filed in that court.

(Subd (b) amended effective January 1, 2007; previously amended effective January 1, 2005.)

(c) Dismissal or judgment by the court

(1) The court must dismiss the appeal if the case is not brought to trial within one year after the date of filing the appeal. If a new trial is ordered, the court must dismiss the appeal if the case is not brought to trial within one year after the entry date of the new trial order.

(2) Notwithstanding (1), the court must not order dismissal or enter judgment if there was in effect a written stipulation extending the time for trial or on a showing that the appellant exercised reasonable diligence to bring the case to trial.

(3) Notwithstanding (1) and (2), the court must dismiss the appeal if the case is not brought to trial within three years after either the notice of

appeal is filed or the most recent new trial order is entered in the court assigned to hear the appeal.

(Subd (c) amended effective January 1, 2007; previously amended effective January 1, 1977, July 1, 1991, and January 1, 2005.)

(d) Notification by clerk

If an appellant files an abandonment, the clerk of the court in which it is filed must immediately notify the adverse party of the filing. The clerk of the court assigned to hear the appeal must immediately notify the parties of any order of dismissal or any judgment for defendant made by the court under (c).

(Subd (d) amended effective January 1, 2007; previously amended effective January 1, 2005.)

(e) Return of papers

If an appeal is dismissed, the clerk of the court assigned to hear the appeal must promptly transmit to the small claims court a copy of the dismissal order and all original papers and exhibits sent to the court assigned to hear the appeal. The small claims court must then proceed with the case as if no appeal had been taken.

(Subd (e) amended effective January 1, 2007; previously amended effective January 1, 2005.)

(f) Approval of compromise

If a guardian or conservator seeks approval of a proposed compromise of a pending appeal in which a new trial has been ordered, the court assigned to hear the appeal may, before ruling on the compromise, hear and determine whether the proposed compromise is for the best interest of the ward or conservatee.

(Subd (f) amended effective January 1, 2007; previously amended effective January 1, 2005.)

Rule 8.963 renumbered effective January 1, 2009; adopted as rule 157 effective July 1, 1964; amended and renumbered as rule 155 effective July 1, 1991; previously amended effective January 1, 1972, July 1, 1972, and January 1, 2005; previously amended and renumbered as rule 8.913 effective January 1, 2007.

Rule 8.966. Examination of witnesses

The court may allow parties or attorneys representing parties to the appeal to conduct direct and cross-examination, subject to the court's discretion to control the manner, mode, and duration of examination in keeping with informality and the circumstances.

Rule 8.966 renumbered effective January 1, 2009; adopted as rule 157 effective July 1, 1999; previously amended and renumbered as rule 8.916 effective January 1, 2007.

Chapter 2
Writ Petitions

Title 8, Appellate Rules—Division 3, Rules Relating to Appeals and Writs in Small Claims Cases—Chapter 2, Writ Petitions; adopted effective January 1, 2016.

Rule 8.970. Application
Rule 8.971. Definitions
Rule 8.972. Petitions filed by persons not represented by an attorney
Rule 8.973. Petitions filed by an attorney for a party
Rule 8.974. Opposition
Rule 8.975. Notice to small claims court
Rule 8.976. Filing, finality, and modification of decisions; remittitur
Rule 8.977. Costs

Rule 8.970. Application

(a) Writ proceedings governed

Except as provided in (b), the rules in this chapter govern proceedings under Code of Civil Procedure section 116.798(a) for writs of mandate, certiorari, or prohibition, relating to an act of the small claims division, other than a postjudgment enforcement order. In all respects not provided for in this chapter, rule 8.883, regarding the form and content of briefs, applies.

(Subd (a) adopted effective January 1, 2016.)

(b) Writ proceedings not governed

The rules in this chapter do not apply to:

(1) Proceedings under Code of Civil Procedure section 116.798(c) for writs relating to a postjudgment enforcement order of the small claims division, which are governed by rules 8.930–8.936.

(2) Proceedings under Code of Civil Procedure section 116.798(b) for writs relating to an act of a superior court in a small claims appeal, which are governed by rules 8.485–8.493.

(Subd (b) adopted effective January 1, 2016.)

Rule 8.970 adopted effective January 1, 2016.

Advisory Committee Comment

Code of Civil Procedure section 116.798 provides where writs in small claims actions may be heard.

The Judicial Council form *Information on Writ Proceedings in Small Claims Actions* (form SC-300-INFO) provides additional information about proceedings for writs in small claims actions in the appellate division of the superior court. This form is available at any courthouse or county law library or online at *www.courts.ca.gov/forms*.

Rule 8.971. Definitions

The definitions in rule 1.6 apply to these rules unless the context or subject matter requires otherwise. In addition, the following definitions apply to these rules:

(1) "Writ" means an order telling the small claims court to do something that the law says it must do, or not do something the law says it must not do. The various types of writs covered by this chapter are described in statutes beginning at section 1067 of the Code of Civil Procedure.

(2) "Petition" means a request for a writ.

(3) "Petitioner" means the person asking for the writ.

(4) "Respondent" and "small claims court" mean the court against which the writ is sought.

(5) "Real party in interest" means any other party in the small claims court case who would be affected by a ruling regarding the request for a writ.

Rule 8.971 adopted effective January 1, 2016.

Rule 8.972. Petitions filed by persons not represented by an attorney

(a) Petitions

(1) A person who is not represented by an attorney and who requests a writ under this chapter must file the petition on a *Petition for Writ (Small Claims)* (form SC-300). For good cause the court may permit an unrepresented party to file a petition that is not on that form, but the petition must be verified.

(2) If the petition raises any issue that would require the appellate division judge considering it to understand what was said in the small claims court, it must include a statement that fairly summarizes the proceedings, including the parties' arguments and any statement by the small claims court supporting its ruling.

(3) The clerk must file the petition even if it is not verified but if the party asking for the writ fails to file a verification within five days after the clerk gives notice of the defect, the court may strike the petition.

(Subd (a) amended effective January 1, 2018; adopted effective January 1, 2016.)

(b) Contents of supporting documents

(1) The petition must be accompanied by copies of the following:

(A) The small claims court ruling from which the petition seeks relief;

(B) All documents and exhibits submitted to the small claims court supporting and opposing the petitioner's position; and

(C) Any other documents or portions of documents submitted to the small claims court that are necessary for a complete understanding of the case and the ruling under review.

(2) If the petition does not include the required documents or does not present facts sufficient to excuse the failure to submit them, the appellate division judge may summarily deny a stay request, the petition, or both.

(Subd (b) adopted effective January 1, 2016.)

(c) Form of supporting documents

(1) Documents submitted under (b) must comply with the following requirements:

(A) They must be attached to the petition. The pages must be consecutively numbered.

(B) They must each be given a number or letter.

(2) The clerk must file any supporting documents not complying with (1), but the court may notify the petitioner that it may strike or summarily deny the petition if the documents are not brought into compliance within a stated reasonable time of not less than five days.

(Subd (c) adopted effective January 1, 2016.)

(d) Service

(1) The petition and all its attachments, and a copy of *Information on Writ Proceedings in Small Claims Cases* (form SC-300-INFO) must be served personally or by mail on all the parties in the case, and the petition must be served on the small claims court.

(2) The petitioner must file a proof of service at the same time the petition is filed.

(3) The clerk must file the petition even if its proof of service is defective but if the party asking for the writ fails to file a corrected proof of service within five days after the clerk gives notice of the defect, the

court may strike the petition or allow additional time to file a corrected proof of service.

(4) The court may allow the petition to be filed without proof of service.

(Subd (d) adopted effective January 1, 2016.)

Rule 8.972 amended effective January 1, 2018; adopted effective January 1, 2016.

Advisory Committee Comment

Subdivision (a). *Petition for Writ (Small Claims)* (form SC-300) and *Information on Writ Proceedings in Small Claims Actions* (form SC-300-INFO) are available at any courthouse or county law library or online at *www.courts.ca.gov/forms*.

Rule 8.973. Petitions filed by an attorney for a party

(a) General application of rule 8.972

Except as provided in this rule, rule 8.972 applies to any petition for an extraordinary writ filed by an attorney under this chapter.

(Subd (a) adopted effective January 1, 2016.)

(b) Form and content of petition

(1) A petition for an extraordinary writ filed by an attorney may, but is not required to be, filed on *Petition for Writ (Small Claims)* (form SC-300). It must contain all the information requested in that form.

(2) The petition must disclose the name of any real party in interest.

(3) If the petition seeks review of small claims court proceedings that are also the subject of a pending appeal, the notice "Related Appeal Pending" must appear on the cover of the petition, and the first paragraph of the petition must state the appeal's title and any appellate division docket number.

(4) The petition must be verified.

(5) The petition must be accompanied by a memorandum, which need not repeat facts alleged in the petition.

(6) Rule 8.883(b) governs the length of the petition and memorandum, but the verification and any supporting documents are excluded from the limits stated in rule 8.883(b)(1) and (2).

(7) If the petition requests a temporary stay, it must explain the urgency.

(Subd (b) adopted effective January 1, 2016.)

Rule 8.973 adopted effective January 1, 2016.

Rule 8.974. Opposition

(a) Preliminary opposition

(1) The respondent and real party in interest are not required to file any opposition to the petition unless asked to do so by the appellate division judge.

(2) Within 10 days after the petition is filed, the respondent or any real party in interest may serve and file a preliminary opposition.

(3) A preliminary opposition should contain any legal arguments the party wants to make as to why the appellate division judge should not issue a writ and a statement of any material facts not included in the petition.

(4) Without requesting opposition, the appellate division judge may grant or deny a request for temporary stay, deny the petition, issue an alternative writ or order to show cause, or notify the parties that the judge is considering issuing a peremptory writ in the first instance.

(Subd (a) adopted effective January 1, 2016.)

(b) Return or opposition; reply

(1) If the appellate division judge issues an alternative writ or order to show cause, the respondent or any real party in interest, individually or jointly, may serve and file a return (which is a response to the petition) by demurrer, verified answer, or both. If the appellate division judge notifies the parties that he or she is considering issuing a peremptory writ in the first instance, the respondent or any real party in interest may serve and file an opposition.

(2) Unless the appellate division judge orders otherwise, the return or opposition must be served and filed within 30 days after the appellate division judge issues the alternative writ or order to show cause or notifies the parties that it is considering issuing a peremptory writ in the first instance.

(3) Unless the appellate division judge orders otherwise, the petitioner may serve and file a reply within 15 days after the return or opposition is filed.

(4) If the return is by demurrer alone and the demurrer is not sustained, the appellate division judge may issue the peremptory writ without granting leave to answer.

(Subd (b) adopted effective January 1, 2016.)

(c) Form of preliminary opposition, return, or opposition

Any preliminary opposition, return, or opposition must comply with rule 8.931(c). If it is filed by an attorney, it must also comply with rule 8.932(b)(3)–(7).

(Subd (c) adopted effective January 1, 2016.)

Rule 8.974 adopted effective January 1, 2016.

Rule 8.975. Notice to small claims court

(a) Notice if writ issues

If a writ or order issues directed to any judge, court, or other officer, the appellate division clerk must promptly send a certified copy of the writ or order to the person or entity to whom it is directed.

(Subd (a) adopted effective January 1, 2016.)

(b) Notice by telephone

(1) If the writ or order stays or prohibits proceedings set to occur within seven days or requires action within seven days—or in any other urgent situation—the appellate division clerk must make a reasonable effort to notify the clerk of the respondent small claims court by telephone. The clerk of the respondent small claims court must then notify the judge or officer most directly concerned.

(2) The appellate division clerk need not give notice by telephone of the summary denial of a writ, whether or not a stay was previously issued.

(Subd (b) adopted effective January 1, 2016.)

Rule 8.975 adopted effective January 1, 2016.

Rule 8.976. Filing, finality, and modification of decisions; remittitur

(a) Filing of decision

The appellate division clerk must promptly file all opinions and orders in proceedings under this chapter and on the same day send copies (by e-mail where permissible under rule 2.251) showing the filing date to the parties and, when relevant, to the small claims court.

(Subd (a) amended effective January 1, 2019; adopted effective January 1, 2016.)

(b) Finality of decision

(1) Except as otherwise ordered by the appellate division judge, the following decisions regarding petitions for writs under this chapter are final in the issuing court when filed:

(A) An order denying or dismissing such a petition without issuance of an alternative writ, order to show cause, or writ of review; and

(B) An order denying or dismissing such a petition as moot after issuance of an alternative writ, order to show cause, or writ of review.

(2) Except as otherwise provided in (3), all other decisions in a writ proceeding under this chapter are final 30 days after the decision is sent by the court clerk to the parties.

(3) If necessary to prevent mootness or frustration of the relief granted or to otherwise promote the interests of justice, a judge in the appellate division may order early finality of a decision granting a petition for a writ under this chapter or denying such a petition after issuing an alternative writ, order to show cause, or writ of review. The decision may provide for finality on filing or within a stated period of less than 30 days.

(Subd (b) amended effective January 1, 2019; adopted effective January 1, 2016.)

(c) Modification of decisions

Rule 8.888(b) governs the modification of decisions in writ proceedings under this chapter.

(Subd (c) adopted effective January 1, 2016.)

(d) Remittitur

The appellate division must issue a remittitur after the judge issues a decision in a writ proceeding under this chapter except when the judge issues one of the orders listed in (b)(1). The remittitur is deemed issued when the clerk enters it in the record. The clerk must immediately send the parties notice of issuance of the remittitur, showing the date of entry.

(Subd (d) adopted effective January 1, 2016.)

Rule 8.976 amended effective January 1, 2019; adopted effective January 1, 2016.

Advisory Committee Comment

Subdivision (b)(1). Examples of situations in which the appellate division judge may issue an order dismissing a writ petition include when the petitioner fails to comply with an order, when the judge recalls the alternative writ, order to show cause, or writ of review as improvidently granted, or when the petition becomes moot.

Rule 8.977. Costs

(a) Entitlement to costs

The prevailing party in an original proceeding is entitled to costs if the appellate division judge resolves the proceeding after issuing an alternative writ, an order to show cause, or a peremptory writ in the first instance.

(Subd (a) adopted effective January 1, 2016.)

(b) Award of costs

(1) In the interests of justice, the appellate division judge may award or deny costs as the court deems proper.

(2) The opinion or order resolving the proceeding must specify the award or denial of costs.

(3) Rule 8.891(b)–(d) governs the procedure for recovering costs under this rule.

(Subd (b) adopted effective January 1, 2016.)
Rule 8.977 adopted effective January 1, 2016.

Division 6
Transfer of Appellate Division Cases to the Court of Appeal

Title 8, Appellate Rules—Division 6, Transfer of Appellate Division Cases to the Court of Appeal renumbered from Division 4 effective April 25, 2019.

Rule 8.1000. Application
Rule 8.1002. Transfer authority
Rule 8.1005. Certification for transfer by the appellate division
Rule 8.1006. Petition for transfer
Rule 8.1007. Transmitting record to Court of Appeal
Rule 8.1008. Order for transfer
Rule 8.1012. Briefs and argument
Rule 8.1014. Proceedings in the appellate division after certification or transfer
Rule 8.1016. Disposition of transferred case
Rule 8.1018. Finality and remittitur

Rule 8.1000. Application

Rules 8.1000–8.1018 govern the transfer of cases within the appellate jurisdiction of the superior court—other than appeals in small claims cases—to the Court of Appeal. Unless the context requires otherwise, the term "case" as used in these rules means cases within that jurisdiction.

Rule 8.1000 amended effective January 1, 2011; repealed and adopted as rule 61 effective January 1, 2003; previously amended and renumbered effective January 1, 2007.

Advisory Committee Comment

The rules in this division implement the authority of the Court of Appeal under Code of Civil Procedure section 911 and Penal Code section 1471 to order any case on appeal to a superior court in its district transferred to the Court of Appeal if it determines that transfer is necessary to secure uniformity of decision or to settle important questions of law.

Rule 8.1002. Transfer authority

A Court of Appeal may order a case transferred to it for hearing and decision if it determines that transfer is necessary to secure uniformity of decision or to settle an important question of law. Transfer may be ordered on:

(1) Certification of the case for transfer by the superior court appellate division under rule 8.1005;

(2) Petition for transfer under rule 8.1006; or

(3) The Court of Appeal's own motion.

Rule 8.1002 amended effective January 1, 2011; repealed and adopted as rule 62 effective January 1, 2003; previously amended and renumbered effective January 1, 2007.

Rule 8.1005. Certification for transfer by the appellate division

(a) Authority to certify

(1) The appellate division may certify a case for transfer to the Court of Appeal on its own motion or on a party's application if it determines that transfer is necessary to secure uniformity of decision or to settle an important question of law.

(2) Except as provided in (3), a case may be certified for transfer by a majority of the appellate division judges to whom the case has been assigned or who decided the appeal or, if the case has not yet been assigned, by any two appellate division judges.

(3) If an appeal from a conviction of a traffic infraction is assigned to a single appellate division judge under Code of Civil Procedure section 77, the case may be certified for transfer by that judge.

(4) If an assigned or deciding judge is unable to act on the certification for transfer, a judge designated or assigned to the appellate division by the chair of the Judicial Council may act in that judge's place.

(Subd (a) amended effective January 1, 2011; previously amended effective January 1, 2007.)

(b) Application for certification

(1) A party may serve and file an application asking the appellate division to certify a case for transfer at any time after the record on appeal is filed in the appellate division but no later than 15 days after:

(A) The decision is sent by the court clerk to the parties;

(B) A publication order restarting the finality period under rule 8.888(a)(2) is sent by the court clerk to the parties;

(C) A modification order changing the appellate judgment under rule 8.888(b) is sent by the court clerk to the parties; or

(D) A consent is filed under rule 8.888(c).

(2) The party may include the application in a petition for rehearing.

(3) The application must explain why transfer is necessary to secure uniformity of decision or to settle an important question of law.

(4) Within five days after the application is filed, any other party may serve and file an answer.

(5) No hearing will be held on the application. Failure to certify the case within the time specified in (c) is deemed a denial of the application.

(Subd (b) amended effective January 1, 2019; previously amended effective January 1, 2011.)

(c) Time to certify

The appellate division may certify a case for transfer at any time after the record on appeal is filed in the appellate division and before the appellate division decision is final in that court.

(Subd (c) repealed, amended and relettered effective January 1, 2011; adopted as subd (d).)

(d) Contents of order certifying case for transfer

An order certifying a case for transfer must:

(1) Clearly state that the appellate division is certifying the case for transfer to the Court of Appeal;

(2) Briefly describe why transfer is necessary to secure uniformity of decision or to settle an important question of law; and

(3) State whether there was a decision on appeal and, if so, its date and disposition.

(Subd (d) amended and relettered effective January 1, 2011; adopted as subd (e); previously amended effective January 1, 2007.)

(e) Superior court clerk's duties

(1) If the appellate division orders a case certified for transfer, the clerk must promptly send a copy of the certification order to the clerk/executive officer of the Court of Appeal, the parties, and, in a criminal case, the Attorney General.

(2) If the appellate division denies a certification application by order, the clerk must promptly send a copy of the order to the parties.

(Subd (e) amended effective January 1, 2018; adopted as subd (f); previously amended and relettered effective January 1, 2011.)

Rule 8.1005 amended effective January 1, 2019; repealed and adopted as rule 63 effective January 1, 2003; previously amended and renumbered effective January 1, 2007; previously amended effective January 1, 2010, January 1, 2011, and January 1, 2018.

Rule 8.1006. Petition for transfer

(a) Right to file petition

A party may file a petition in the Court of Appeal asking for an appellate division case to be transferred to that court only if an application for certification for transfer was first filed in the appellate division and denied.

(Subd (a) adopted effective January 1, 2011.)

(b) Time to file petition

(1) The petition must be served and filed in the Court of Appeal after the appellate division issues its decision in the case but no later than 15 days after the decision is final in that court. A copy of the petition must also be served on the appellate division.

(2) The time to file a petition for transfer may not be extended, but the presiding justice may relieve a party from a failure to file a timely petition for transfer if the time for the Court of Appeal to order transfer on its own motion has not expired.

(Subd (b) adopted effective January 1, 2011.)

(c) Form and contents of petition

(1) Except as provided in this rule, a petition must comply with the form and contents requirements of rule 8.204(a)(1), (b), and (d).

(2) The body of the petition must begin with a concise, nonargumentative statement of the issues presented for review, framing them in terms of the facts of the case but without unnecessary detail.

(3) The petition must explain why transfer is necessary to secure uniformity of decision or to settle an important question of law.

(4) The petition must not exceed 5,600 words, including footnotes, if produced on a computer, and 20 pages if typewritten. A petition produced

on a computer must include a certificate by counsel or an unrepresented party stating the number of words in the document. The person certifying may rely on the word count of the computer program used to prepare the document. A certificate stating the number of words, the tables required by rule 8.204(a)(1), the cover information required under rule 8.204(b)(10), any signature block, and any attachment permitted under rule 8.204(d) are excluded from these length limits.

(Subd (c) adopted effective January 1, 2011.)

(d) Answer to petition

(1) Any answer must be served and filed within 10 days after the petition is filed unless the court orders otherwise.

(2) Except as provided in this rule, any answer must comply with the form and contents requirements of rule 8.204(a)(1), (b), and (d).

(3) An answer must comply with the length requirements of (c)(4).

(Subd (d) adopted effective January 1, 2011.)

Rule 8.1006 adopted effective January 1, 2011.

Advisory Committee Comment

See rule 8.40 for requirements regarding the covers of documents filed in the appellate courts and rule 8.44(b) for the number of copies of documents that must be provided to the Court of Appeal.

Rule 8.1007. Transmitting record to Court of Appeal

(a) Clerks' duties

(1) To assist the Court of Appeal in determining whether to order transfer, the superior court clerk must send the record specified in (b) to the Court of Appeal within five days after:

(A) The appellate division certifies a case for transfer under rule 8.1005;

(B) The superior court clerk sends a copy of an appellate division opinion certified for publication to the Court of Appeal under rule 8.887;

(C) The superior court clerk receives a copy of a petition for transfer under rule 8.1006; or

(D) The superior court receives a request for the record from the Court of Appeal.

(2) The clerk/executive officer of the Court of Appeal must promptly notify the parties when the clerk files the record.

(Subd (a) amended effective January 1, 2018; adopted as subd (b); previously amended effective January 1, 2007, and July 1, 2009; previously amended and relettered effective January 1, 2011.)

(b) Contents

The record sent to the Court of Appeal under (a) must contain:

(1) The original record on appeal prepared under rules 8.830–8.843, 8.860–8.873, or 8.910–8.923;

(2) Any briefs filed in the appellate division;

(3) The decision of the appellate division; and

(4) Any application for certification for transfer, any answer to that application, and the appellate division's order on the application.

(Subd (b) amended and relettered effective January 1, 2011; adopted as subd (a); previously amended effective January 1, 2007, and July 1, 2009.)

Rule 8.1007 amended effective January 1, 2018; repealed and adopted as rule 65 effective January 1, 2003; previously amended and renumbered as rule 8.1010 effective January 1, 2007, and as rule 8.1007 effective January 1, 2011; previously amended effective July 1, 2009.

Advisory Committee Comment

Under rule 8.71(c), the superior court clerk may send the record to the reviewing court in electronic form.

Rule 8.1008. Order for transfer

(a) Time to transfer

(1) The Court of Appeal may order transfer

(A) After the appellate division certifies the case for transfer or on petition for transfer, within 20 days after the record sent under rule 8.1007 is filed in the Court of Appeal; or

(B) On its own motion, within 30 days after the appellate division decision is final in that court.

(2) Within either period specified in (1), the Court of Appeal may order an extension not exceeding 20 days.

(3) If the Court of Appeal does not timely order transfer, transfer is deemed denied.

(Subd (a) repealed, amended and relettered effective January 1, 2011; adopted as subd (c); previously amended effective January 1, 2007.)

(b) Court of Appeal clerk's duties

(1) When a transfer order is filed, the clerk must promptly send a copy of the order to the superior court clerk, the parties, and, in a criminal case, the Attorney General.

(2) With the copy of the transfer order sent to the parties and the Attorney General, the clerk must send notice of the time to serve and file any briefs ordered under rule 8.1012 and, if specified by the Court of Appeal, the issues to be briefed and argued.

(3) If the court denies transfer after the appellate division certifies a case for transfer or after a party files a petition for transfer, the clerk must promptly send notice of the denial to the parties, the appellate division, and, in a criminal case, the Attorney General.

(4) Failure to send any order or notice under this subdivision does not affect the jurisdiction of the Court of Appeal.

(Subd (b) repealed, amended and relettered effective January 1, 2011; adopted as subd (f); previously amended effective January 1, 2007.)

Rule 8.1008 amended effective January 1, 2011; repealed and adopted as rule 64 effective January 1, 2003; previously amended and renumbered effective January 1, 2007; previously amended effective July 1, 2003, and January 1, 2008.

Rule 8.1010. Record on transfer [Renumbered]

Rule 8.1010 renumbered as rule 8.1007 effective January 1, 2011.

Rule 8.1012. Briefs and argument

(a) When briefs permitted

(1) After the Court of Appeal orders transfer, the parties may file briefs in the Court of Appeal only if ordered by the court. The court may order briefs either on a party's application or the court's own motion. The court must prescribe the briefing sequence in any briefing order.

(2) Instead of filing a brief, or as part of its brief, a party may join in or adopt by reference all or part of a brief filed in the Court of Appeal in the same or a related case.

(Subd (a) amended effective January 1, 2011.)

(b) Time to file briefs

Unless otherwise provided in the court's order under (a):

(1) The opening brief must be served and filed within 20 days after entry of the briefing order.

(2) The responding brief must be served and filed within 20 days after the opening brief is filed.

(3) Any reply brief must be served and filed within 10 days after the responding brief is filed.

(Subd (b) amended effective January 1, 2011.)

(c) Additional service requirements

(1) Any brief of a defendant in a criminal case must be served on the prosecuting attorney and the Attorney General.

(2) Every brief must be served on the appellate division from which the case was transferred.

(Subd (c) amended effective January 1, 2011.)

(d) Form and contents of briefs

(1) Except as provided in this rule, briefs must comply with the form and contents requirements of rule 8.204(a)(1), (b), and (d).

(2) No brief may exceed 5,600 words if produced on a computer or 20 pages if typewritten. The person certifying may rely on the word count of the computer program used to prepare the document. A certificate stating the number of words, the tables required by rule 8.204(a)(1), the cover information required under rule 8.204(b)(10), any signature block, and any attachment permitted under rule 8.204(d) are excluded from these length limits.

(Subd (d) amended effective January 1, 2011; previously amended effective January 1, 2007.)

(e) Limitation of issues

(1) On or after ordering transfer, the Court of Appeal may specify the issues to be briefed and argued. Unless the court orders otherwise, the parties must limit their briefs and arguments to those issues and any issues fairly included in those issues.

(2) Notwithstanding an order specifying issues under (1), the court may, on reasonable notice, order oral argument on fewer or additional issues or on the entire case.

(Subd (e) adopted effective January 1, 2011.)

Rule 8.1012 amended effective January 1, 2011; repealed and adopted as rule 66 effective January 1, 2003; previously amended and renumbered effective January 1, 2007.

Rule 8.1014. Proceedings in the appellate division after certification or transfer

When the appellate division certifies a case for transfer or the Court of Appeal orders transfer, further action by the appellate division is limited to preparing and sending the record under rule 8.1007 until termination of the proceedings in the Court of Appeal.

Rule 8.1016. Disposition of transferred case

(a) Decision on limited issues

The Court of Appeal may decide fewer than all the issues raised and may retransfer the case to the appellate division for decision on any remaining issues.

(b) Retransfer without decision

The Court of Appeal may vacate a transfer order without decision and retransfer the case to the appellate division with or without directions to conduct further proceedings.

(Subd (b) amended effective January 1, 2011; previously amended effective January 1, 2007.)

Rule 8.1016 amended effective January 1, 2011; repealed and adopted as rule 68 effective January 1, 2003; previously amended and renumbered effective January 1, 2007.

Rule 8.1018. Finality and remittitur

(a) When transfer is denied

If the Court of Appeal denies transfer of a case from the appellate division of the superior court after the appellate division certifies the case for transfer or after a party files a petition for transfer, the denial is final immediately. On receiving notice under rule 8.1008(b) that the Court of Appeal has denied transfer or if the period for ordering transfer under rule 8.1008(a) expires, the appellate division clerk must promptly issue a remittitur if there will be no further proceedings in that court.

(Subd (a) amended effective January 1, 2011; adopted effective January 1, 2009.)

(b) When transfer order is vacated

If the appellate division issued a decision before transfer and the Court of Appeal vacates its transfer order under rule 8.1016(b) and retransfers the case without directing further proceedings, the appellate division's decision is final when the appellate division receives the order vacating transfer. The appellate division clerk must promptly issue a remittitur.

(Subd (b) adopted effective January 1, 2011.)

(c) When the Court of Appeal issues a decision

If the Court of Appeal issues a decision on a case it has ordered transferred from the appellate division of the superior court, filing, finality, and modification of that decision are governed by rule 8.264 and remittitur is governed by rule 8.272, except that the clerk/executive officer must address the remittitur to the appellate division and send that court a copy of the remittitur and a filed-endorsed copy of the Court of Appeal opinion or order. If the remittitur and opinion are sent in paper format, two copies must be sent. On receipt of the Court of Appeal remittitur, the appellate division clerk must promptly issue a remittitur if there will be no further proceedings in that court.

(Subd (c) amended effective January 1, 2018; adopted as subd (a); previously relettered as subd (b) effective January 1, 2009; previously repealed, amended and relettered as subd (c) effective January 1, 2011; previously amended effective January 1, 2016.)

(d) Documents to be returned

When the Court of Appeal denies or vacates transfer or issues a remittitur under (c), the clerk/executive officer must return to the appellate division any part of the record sent nonelectronically to the Court of Appeal under rule 8.1007 and any exhibits that were sent nonelectronically.

(Subd (d) amended effective January 1, 2018; adopted as subd (c) effective January 1, 2003; previously relettered subd (d) effective January 1, 2009; previously amended effective January 1, 2011, and January 1, 2016.)

Rule 8.1018 amended effective January 1, 2018; repealed and adopted as rule 69 effective January 1, 2003; previously renumbered as rule 8.1018 effective January 1, 2007; previously amended effective January 1, 2009, January 1, 2011, and January 1, 2016.

Advisory Committee Comment

Subdivision (a). The finality of Court of Appeal decisions in appeals is generally addressed in rules 8.264 (civil appeals) and 8.366 (criminal appeals).

Division 7
Publication of Appellate Opinions

Title 8, Appellate Rules—Division 7, Publication of Appellate Opinions renumbered from Division 5 effective April 25, 2019.

Rule 8.1100. Authority
Rule 8.1105. Publication of appellate opinions
Rule 8.1110. Partial publication
Rule 8.1115. Citation of opinions
Rule 8.1120. Requesting publication of unpublished opinions
Rule 8.1125. Requesting depublication of published opinions

Rule 8.1100. Authority

The rules governing the publication of appellate opinions are adopted by the Supreme Court under section 14 of article VI of the California Constitution and published in the California Rules of Court at the direction of the Judicial Council.

Rule 8.1100 adopted effective January 1, 2007.

Rule 8.1105. Publication of appellate opinions

(a) Supreme Court

All opinions of the Supreme Court are published in the Official Reports.

(b) Courts of Appeal and appellate divisions

Except as provided in (e), an opinion of a Court of Appeal or a superior court appellate division is published in the Official Reports if a majority of the rendering court certifies the opinion for publication before the decision is final in that court.

(Subd (b) amended effective July 23, 2008; adopted effective April 1, 2007.)

(c) Standards for certification

An opinion of a Court of Appeal or a superior court appellate division — whether it affirms or reverses a trial court order or judgment — should be certified for publication in the Official Reports if the opinion:

(1) Establishes a new rule of law;

(2) Applies an existing rule of law to a set of facts significantly different from those stated in published opinions;

(3) Modifies, explains, or criticizes with reasons given, an existing rule of law;

(4) Advances a new interpretation, clarification, criticism, or construction of a provision of a constitution, statute, ordinance, or court rule;

(5) Addresses or creates an apparent conflict in the law;

(6) Involves a legal issue of continuing public interest;

(7) Makes a significant contribution to legal literature by reviewing either the development of a common law rule or the legislative or judicial history of a provision of a constitution, statute, or other written law;

(8) Invokes a previously overlooked rule of law, or reaffirms a principle of law not applied in a recently reported decision; or

(9) Is accompanied by a separate opinion concurring or dissenting on a legal issue, and publication of the majority and separate opinions would make a significant contribution to the development of the law.

(Subd (c) amended effective April 1, 2007; previously amended effective January 1, 2007.)

(d) Factors not to be considered

Factors such as the workload of the court, or the potential embarrassment of a litigant, lawyer, judge, or other person should not affect the determination of whether to publish an opinion.

(Subd (d) adopted effective April 1, 2007.)

(e) Changes in publication status

(1) Unless otherwise ordered under (2):

(A) An opinion is no longer considered published if the rendering court grants rehearing.

(B) Grant of review by the Supreme Court of a decision by the Court of Appeal does not affect the appellate court's certification of the opinion for full or partial publication under rule 8.1105(b) or rule 8.1110, but any such Court of Appeal opinion, whether officially published in hard copy or electronically, must be accompanied by a prominent notation advising that review by the Supreme Court has been granted.

(2) The Supreme Court may order that an opinion certified for publication is not to be published or that an opinion not certified is to be published. The Supreme Court may also order depublication of part of an opinion at any time after granting review.

(Subd (e) amended effective July 1, 2016; adopted as subd (d) effective January 1, 2005; previously relettered as subd (e) effective April 1, 2007.)

(f) Editing

(1) Computer versions of all opinions of the Supreme Court and Courts of Appeal must be provided to the Reporter of Decisions on the day of filing. Opinions of superior court appellate divisions certified for publication must be provided as prescribed in rule 8.887.

(2) The Reporter of Decisions must edit opinions for publication as directed by the Supreme Court. The Reporter of Decisions must submit edited opinions to the courts for examination, correction, and approval before finalization for the Official Reports.

(Subd (f) amended effective July 1, 2009; adopted as subd (e) effective January 1, 2005; previously amended effective January 1, 2007; previously relettered effective April 1, 2007.)

Rule 8.1105 amended effective July 1, 2016; repealed and adopted as rule 976 effective January 1, 2005; previously amended and renumbered effective January 1, 2007; previously amended effective April 1, 2007, July 23, 2008, and July 1, 2009.

Comment

Subdivision (e)(2). This subdivision allows the Supreme Court to order depublication of an opinion that is under review by that court.

Rule 8.1110. Partial publication

(a) Order for partial publication

A majority of the rendering court may certify for publication any part of an opinion meeting a standard for publication under rule 8.1105.

(Subd (a) amended effective January 1, 2007.)

(b) Opinion contents

The published part of the opinion must specify the part or parts not certified for publication. All material, factual and legal, including the disposition, that aids in the application or interpretation of the published part must be published.

(c) Construction

For purposes of rules 8.1105, 8.1115, and 8.1120, the published part of the opinion is treated as a published opinion and the unpublished part as an unpublished opinion.

(Subd (c) amended effective January 1, 2007.)

Rule 8.1110 amended and renumbered effective January 1, 2007; repealed and adopted as rule 976.1 effective January 1, 2005.

Rule 8.1115. Citation of opinions

(a) Unpublished opinion

Except as provided in (b), an opinion of a California Court of Appeal or superior court appellate division that is not certified for publication or ordered published must not be cited or relied on by a court or a party in any other action.

(b) Exceptions

An unpublished opinion may be cited or relied on:

(1) When the opinion is relevant under the doctrines of law of the case, res judicata, or collateral estoppel; or

(2) When the opinion is relevant to a criminal or disciplinary action because it states reasons for a decision affecting the same defendant or respondent in another such action.

(Subd (b) amended effective January 1, 2007.)

(c) Citation procedure

On request of the court or a party, a copy of an opinion citable under (b) must be promptly furnished to the court or the requesting party.

(Subd (c) amended effective July 1, 2016.)

(d) When a published opinion may be cited

A published California opinion may be cited or relied on as soon as it is certified for publication or ordered published.

(e) When review of published opinion has been granted

(1) *While review is pending*

Pending review and filing of the Supreme Court's opinion, unless otherwise ordered by the Supreme Court under (3), a published opinion of a Court of Appeal in the matter has no binding or precedential effect, and may be cited for potentially persuasive value only. Any citation to the Court of Appeal opinion must also note the grant of review and any subsequent action by the Supreme Court.

(2) *After decision on review*

After decision on review by the Supreme Court, unless otherwise ordered by the Supreme Court under (3), a published opinion of a Court of Appeal in the matter, and any published opinion of a Court of Appeal in a matter in which the Supreme Court has ordered review and deferred action pending the decision, is citable and has binding or precedential effect, except to the extent it is inconsistent with the decision of the Supreme Court or is disapproved by that court.

(3) *Supreme Court order*

At any time after granting review or after decision on review, the Supreme Court may order that all or part of an opinion covered by (1) or (2) is not citable or has a binding or precedential effect different from that specified in (1) or (2).

(Subd (e) adopted effective July 1, 2016.)

Rule 8.1115 amended effective July 1, 2016; repealed and adopted as rule 977 effective January 1, 2005; previously amended and renumbered as rule 8.115 effective January 1, 2007.

Comment

Subdivision (e)(1). The practice and rule in effect before July 1, 2016, automatically depublished the Court of Appeal decision under review, rendering it uncitable. Under subdivision (e)(1) of this rule, if the Supreme Court grants review of a published Court of Appeal decision, that decision now remains published and citable for its potentially persuasive value while review is pending unless the Supreme Court orders otherwise.

Under the authority recognized by subdivision (e)(3) of this rule, and as explained in the second paragraph of the comment to that subdivision, by standing administrative order of the Supreme Court, superior courts may choose to be bound by parts of a published Court of Appeal decision under review when those parts conflict with another published appellate court decision. (See *Auto Equity Sales, Inc. v. Superior Court* (1962) 57 Cal.2d 450, 456 (*Auto Equity*) ["where there is more than one appellate court decision, and such appellate decisions are in conflict[,] … the court exercising inferior jurisdiction can and must make a choice between the conflicting decisions"].)

Finally, it has long been the rule that no published Court of Appeal decision has *binding* effect on any other Court of Appeal (e.g., *In re Marriage of Hayden* (1981) 124 Cal.App.3d 72, 77, fn. 1; *Froyd v. Cook* (E.D.Cal. 1988) 681 F.Supp. 669, 672, fn. 9, and cases cited) or on the Supreme Court. Under prior practice and the former rule, a grant of review automatically depublished the decision under review. For this reason, the Court of Appeal was not allowed to cite or quote that review-granted decision concerning any substantive point. Under this subdivision, a published Court of Appeal decision as to which review has been granted remains published and is citable, while review is pending, for any potentially persuasive value.

Subdivision (e)(2). The fact that a Supreme Court decision does not discuss an issue addressed in the prior Court of Appeal decision does not constitute an expression of the Supreme Court's opinion concerning the correctness of the decision on that issue or of any law stated in the Court of Appeal decision with respect to any such issue.

Subdivision (e)(3). This subdivision specifically provides that the Supreme Court can order that an opinion under review by that court, or after decision on review by that court, have an effect other than the effect otherwise specified under this rule. For example, the court could order that, while review is pending, specified parts of the published Court of Appeal opinion have binding or precedential effect, rather than only potentially persuasive value. For purposes of subdivision (e)(2) and (3), a "decision on review" includes any order by the Supreme Court dismissing review. (See rules 8.528(b) [addressing an "order dismissing review"] & 8.532(b)(2)(B) [listing, among "decisions final on filing," an order filed under rule 8.528(b)].) Accordingly, upon dismissal of review, any published Court of Appeal opinion regains binding or precedential effect under rule 8.1115(e)(2) unless the court orders otherwise under that rule's subdivision (e)(3).

As provided in *Standing Order Exercising Authority Under California Rules of Court, Rule 8.1115(e)(3), Upon Grant of Review or Transfer of a Matter with an Underlying Published Court of Appeal Opinion,* Administrative Order 2021 04 21, under this subdivision, when the Supreme Court grants review of a published Court of Appeal opinion, the opinion may be cited, not only for its persuasive value, but also for the limited purpose of establishing the existence of a conflict in authority that would in turn allow *superior courts* to exercise discretion under *Auto Equity, supra,* 57 Cal.2d at page 456, to choose between sides of any such conflict. Superior courts may, in the exercise of their discretion, choose to follow a published review-granted Court of Appeal opinion, even if that opinion conflicts with a published, precedential Court of Appeal opinion. Such a review-granted Court of Appeal opinion has only this limited and potential precedential effect, however; superior courts are not *required* to follow that opinion's holding on the issue in conflict. Nor does such a Court of Appeal opinion, during the time when review is pending, have *any* precedential effect regarding any aspect or holding of the Court of Appeal opinion outside the part(s) or holding(s) in conflict. Instead it remains, in all other respects, "potentially persuasive only." This means, for example, that if a published Court of Appeal opinion as to which review has been granted addresses "conflict issue A," as well as another issue as to which there is no present conflict—"issue B"—the Court of Appeal's discussion of "issue B" remains "potentially persuasive" only, unless and until a published Court of Appeal opinion creates a conflict as to that issue. This paragraph of this comment applies with respect to all published Court of Appeal opinions giving rise to a grant of review by the Supreme Court on or after April 21, 2021.

Finally, as also provided in the administrative order, *supra,* under this subdivision, unless the Supreme Court specifies otherwise, an order transferring a matter to the Court of Appeal with directions to vacate its published opinion and reconsider the matter has the following effect: (1) If the Court of Appeal opinion has not yet been published in the bound volumes of the Official Appellate Reports, the opinion is deemed to be depublished (that is, the Reporter of Decisions is directed not to publish it in the Official Appellate Reports); or (2) If the underlying Court of Appeal opinion has already been published in the bound volumes of the Official Appellate Reports (or publication is imminent and hence as a practical matter the volume cannot be revised to eliminate the opinion), the underlying Court of Appeal opinion is deemed to be "not citable"—meaning it has neither precedential nor even potentially persuasive value, even though it will not be removed from the Official Appellate Reports. This paragraph of this comment applies only to such transfers occurring on and after April 21, 2021.

Rule 8.1120. Requesting publication of unpublished opinions

(a) Request

(1) Any person may request that an unpublished opinion be ordered published.

(2) The request must be made by a letter to the court that rendered the opinion, concisely stating the person's interest and the reason why the opinion meets a standard for publication.

(3) The request must be delivered to the rendering court within 20 days after the opinion is filed.

(4) The request must be served on all parties.

(b) Action by rendering court

(1) If the rendering court does not or cannot grant the request before the decision is final in that court, it must forward the request to the Supreme Court with a copy of its opinion, its recommendation for disposition, and a brief statement of its reasons. The rendering court must forward these materials within 15 days after the decision is final in that court.

(2) The rendering court must also send a copy of its recommendation and reasons to all parties and any person who requested publication.

(c) Action by Supreme Court

The Supreme Court may order the opinion published or deny the request. The court must send notice of its action to the rendering court, all parties, and any person who requested publication.

(d) Effect of Supreme Court order to publish

A Supreme Court order to publish is not an expression of the court's opinion of the correctness of the result of the decision or of any law stated in the opinion.

Rule 8.1120 renumbered effective January 1, 2007; repealed and adopted as rule 978 effective January 1, 2005.

Advisory Committee Comment

Subdivision (a). This rule previously required generally that a publication request be made "promptly," but in practice the term proved so vague that requests were often made after the Court of Appeal had lost jurisdiction. To assist persons intending to request publication and to give the Court of Appeal adequate time to act, this rule was revised to specify that the request must be made within 20 days after the opinion is filed. The change is substantive.

Subdivision (b). This rule previously did not specify the time within which the Court of Appeal was required to forward to the Supreme Court a publication request that it had not or could not have granted. In practice, however, it was not uncommon for the court to forward such a request after the Supreme Court had denied a petition for review in the same case or, if there was no such petition, had lost jurisdiction to grant review on its own motion. To assist the Supreme Court in timely processing publication requests, therefore, this rule was revised to require the Court of Appeal to forward the request within 15 days after the decision is final in that court. The change is substantive.

Rule 8.1125. Requesting depublication of published opinions

(a) Request

(1) Any person may request the Supreme Court to order that an opinion certified for publication not be published.

(2) The request must not be made as part of a petition for review, but by a separate letter to the Supreme Court not exceeding 10 pages.

(3) The request must concisely state the person's interest and the reason why the opinion should not be published.

(4) The request must be delivered to the Supreme Court within 30 days after the decision is final in the Court of Appeal.

(5) The request must be served on the rendering court and all parties.

(b) Response

(1) Within 10 days after the Supreme Court receives a request under (a), the rendering court or any person may submit a response supporting or opposing the request. A response submitted by anyone other than the rendering court must state the person's interest.

(2) A response must not exceed 10 pages and must be served on the rendering court, all parties, and any person who requested depublication.

(c) Action by Supreme Court

(1) The Supreme Court may order the opinion depublished or deny the request. It must send notice of its action to the rendering court, all parties, and any person who requested depublication.

(2) The Supreme Court may order an opinion depublished on its own motion, notifying the rendering court of its action.

(d) Effect of Supreme Court order to depublish

A Supreme Court order to depublish is not an expression of the court's opinion of the correctness of the result of the decision or of any law stated in the opinion.

Rule 8.1125 renumbered effective January 1, 2007; repealed and adopted as rule 979 effective January 1, 2005.

Advisory Committee Comment

Subdivision (a). This subdivision previously required depublication requests to be made "by letter to the Supreme Court," but in practice many were incorporated in petitions for review. To clarify and emphasize the requirement, the subdivision was revised specifically to state that the request "must not be made as part of a petition for review, but by a separate letter to the Supreme Court not exceeding 10 pages." The change is not substantive.

TITLE 9
Rules on Law Practice, Attorneys, and Judges

Division 1. General Provisions. Rule 9.0.
Division 2. Attorney Admission and Disciplinary Proceedings and Review of State Bar Proceedings. Rules 9.1–9.31.
Division 3. Legal Specialists. Rule 9.35.
Division 4. Appearances and Practice by Individuals Who Are Not Licensees of the State Bar of California. Rules 9.40–9.49.1.
Division 5. Censure, Removal, Retirement, or Private or Public Admonishment of Judges. Rules 9.60, 9.61.
Division 6. Judicial Ethics Opinions. Rule 9.80.
Division 7. State Bar Trustees. Rule 9.90.

Division 1
General Provisions

Rule 9.0. Title and source

(a) Title

The rules in this title may be referred to as the Rules on Law Practice, Attorneys, and Judges.

(b) Source

The rules in this title were adopted by the Supreme Court under its inherent authority over the admission and discipline of attorneys and under subdivisions (d) and (f) of section 18 of article VI of the Constitution of the State of California.

Rule 9.0 amended and renumbered effective January 1, 2018; adopted as rules 9.1 and 9.2 effective January 1, 2007.

Division 2
Attorney Admission and Disciplinary Proceedings and Review of State Bar Proceedings

Chap. 1. General Provisions. Rules 9.1, 9.2.
Chap. 2. Attorney Admissions. Rules 9.3–9.9.5.
Chap. 3. Attorney Disciplinary Proceedings. Rules 9.10–9.23.
Chap. 4. Legal Education. Rules 9.30, 9.31.

Chapter 1
General Provisions

Rule 9.1. Definitions
Rule 9.2. Interim Special Regulatory Assessment for Attorney Discipline

Rule 9.1. Definitions

As used in this division, unless the context otherwise requires:

(1) "Licensee" means a person licensed by the State Bar to practice law in this state.

(2) "State Bar Court" means the Hearing Department or the Review Department established under Business and Professions Code sections 6079.1 and 6086.65.

(3) "Review Department" means the Review Department of the State Bar Court established under Business and Professions Code section 6086.65.

(4) "General Counsel" means the general counsel of the State Bar of California.

(5) "Chief Trial Counsel" means the chief trial counsel of the State Bar of California appointed under Business and Professions Code section 6079.5.

Rule 9.1 amended effective January 1, 2019; adopted as rule 950 effective December 1, 1990; previously amended and renumbered as rule 9.5 effective January 1, 2007; previously renumbered as rule 9.1 effective January 1, 2018.

Rule 9.2. Interim Special Regulatory Assessment for Attorney Discipline

(a) This rule is adopted by the Supreme Court solely as an emergency interim measure to protect the public, the courts, and the legal profession from the harm that may be caused by the absence of an adequately functioning attorney disciplinary system. The Supreme Court contemplates that the rule may be modified or repealed once legislation designed to fund an adequate attorney disciplinary system is enacted and becomes effective.

(b)(1) Each active licensee shall pay a mandatory regulatory assessment of two hundred ninety-seven dollars ($297) to the State Bar of California. This assessment is calculated as the sum of the following amounts:

(A) Two hundred eighty-three dollars ($283) to support the following departments and activities:
Office of Chief Trial Counsel
Office of Probation
State Bar Court
Mandatory Fee Arbitration program
Office of Professional Competence
Office of General Counsel
Office of Licensee Records and Compliance
Licensee Billing
Office of Communications (support of discipline only)
California Young Lawyers Association (discipline-related only).

(B) Nine dollars ($9) to fund implementation of the workforce plan recommendations from the National Center for State Courts.

(C) Five dollars ($5) to make up for revenue the State Bar will forgo because of assessment scaling and assessment waivers, as provided for under this rule.

(2) The $297 assessment specifically excludes any funding for the State Bar's legislative lobbying, elimination of bias, and bar relations programs.

(3) Payment of this assessment is due by March 1, 2017. Late payment or nonpayment of the assessment shall subject a licensee to the same penalties and/or sanctions applicable to mandatory fees authorized by statute.

(4) The provisions regarding fee scaling, fee waivers, and penalty waivers contained in Business and Professions Code section 6141.1 and rules 2.15 and 2.16 of the Rules of the State Bar of California shall apply to requests for relief from payment of the assessment or any penalty under this rule. Applications for relief from payment shall be made to the State Bar, which may grant or deny waivers in conformance with its existing rules and regulations. The State Bar shall keep a record of all fee scaling and fee waivers approved and the amount of fees affected.

(Subd (b) amended effective January 1, 2019.)

(c) A special master appointed by the Supreme Court shall establish the Special Master's Attorney Discipline Fund, into which all money collected pursuant to this rule shall be deposited. The special master shall oversee the disbursement and allocation of funds from the Special Master's Attorney Discipline Fund for the limited purpose of maintaining, operating, and supporting an attorney disciplinary system, including payment of the reasonable costs and expenses of the special master as ordered by the Supreme Court. The special master shall exercise authority pursuant to the charge of the Supreme Court and shall submit quarterly reports and recommendations to the Supreme Court regarding the supervision and use of these funds. The State Bar shall respond in timely and accurate fashion to the special master's requests for information and reports.

Should any funds collected pursuant to this rule not be used for the limited purpose set forth in the rule, the Supreme Court may order the refund of an appropriate amount to licensees or take any other action that it deems appropriate.

(Subd (c) amended effective January 1, 2019.)

Rule 9.2 amended effective January 1, 2019; adopted as rule 9.9 effective November 16, 2016; previously renumbered effective January 1, 2018.

Chapter 2
Attorney Admissions

Admission and Disciplinary Proceedings and Review of State Bar Proceedings—Chapter 2, Attorney Admissions; adopted effective January 1, 2018.

Rule 9.3. Inherent power of Supreme Court
Rule 9.4. Nomination and appointment of Members to Committee of Bar Examiners
Rule 9.5. Supreme Court approval of admissions rules
Rule 9.6. Supreme Court approval of bar examination
Rule 9.7. Oath required when admitted to practice law
Rule 9.8. Roll of attorneys admitted to practice
Rule 9.8.5. State Bar Client Trust Account Protection Program
Rule 9.9. Online reporting by attorneys
Rule 9.9.5. Attorney Fingerprinting

Rule 9.3. Inherent power of Supreme Court

(a) Inherent power over admissions

The Supreme Court has the inherent power to admit persons to practice law in California. The State Bar serves as the administrative arm of the Supreme Court for admissions matters and in that capacity acts under the authority and at the direction of the Supreme Court. The Committee of Bar Examiners, acting under authority delegated to it by the State Bar Board of Trustees, is authorized to administer the requirements for admission to practice law, to examine all applicants for admission, and to certify to the Supreme Court for admission those applicants who fulfill the admission requirements.

(Subd (a) amended effective January 1, 2019; adopted effective January 1, 2018.)

(b) Inherent jurisdiction over practice of law

Nothing in this chapter may be construed as affecting the power of the Supreme Court to exercise its inherent jurisdiction over the practice of law in this state.

(Subd (b) adopted effective January 1, 2018.)

Rule 9.3 amended effective January 1, 2019; adopted effective January 1, 2018.

Rule 9.4. Nomination and appointment of members to the Committee of Bar Examiners

(a) Appointments

The Supreme Court is responsible for appointing ten examiners to the Committee of Bar Examiners, each for a four-year term. At least one of the ten examiners must be a judicial officer in this state, and the balance must be licensees of the State Bar. At least one of the attorney examiners shall have been admitted to practice law in California within three years from the date of his or her appointment. The court may reappoint an attorney or judicial officer examiner to serve no more than three additional full terms, and may fill any vacancy in the term of any appointed attorney or judicial officer examiner.

(Subd (a) amended effective January 1, 2019; adopted effective January 1, 2018.)

(b) Nominations

The Supreme Court must make its appointments from a list of candidates nominated by the Board of Trustees of the State Bar pursuant to a procedure approved by the court.

(Subd (b) adopted effective January 1, 2018.)

Rule 9.4 amended effective January 1, 2019; adopted effective January 1, 2018.

Rule 9.5. Supreme Court approval of admissions rules

All State Bar rules adopted by the State Bar Committee of Bar Examiners pertaining to the admission to practice law must be approved by the Board of Trustees and then submitted to the Supreme Court for its review and approval.

Rule 9.5 amended effective January 1, 2019; adopted effective January 1, 2018.

Rule 9.6. Supreme Court approval of bar examination

(a) Bar examination

The Committee of Bar Examiners, pursuant to the authority delegated to it by the Board of Trustees, is responsible for determining the bar examination's format, scope, topics, content, questions, and grading process, subject to review and approval by the Supreme Court. The Supreme Court must set the passing score of the examination.

(Subd (a) amended effective January 1, 2019; adopted effective January 1, 2018.)

(b) Analysis of validity

The State Bar must conduct an analysis of the validity of the bar examination at least once every seven years, or whenever directed by the Supreme Court. The State Bar must prepare and submit a report summarizing its findings and recommendations, if any, to the Supreme Court. Any recommendations proposing significant changes to the bar examination, and any recommended change to the passing score, must be submitted to the Supreme Court for its review and approval.

(Subd (b) amended effective January 1, 2019; adopted effective January 1, 2018.)

(c) Report on examination

The State Bar must provide the Supreme Court a report on each administration of the bar examination in a timely manner.

(Subd (c) adopted effective January 1, 2018.)

Rule 9.6 amended effective January 1, 2019; adopted effective January 1, 2018.

Rule 9.7. Oath required when admitted to practice law

In addition to the language required by Business and Professions Code section 6067, the oath to be taken by every person on admission to practice law is to conclude with the following: "As an officer of the court, I will strive to conduct myself at all times with dignity, courtesy and integrity."

Rule 9.7 renumbered effective January 1, 2018; adopted as rule 9.4 effective May 27, 2014.

Rule 9.8. Roll of attorneys admitted to practice

(a) State Bar to maintain the roll of attorneys

The State Bar must maintain, as part of the official records of the State Bar, a roll of attorneys, which is a list of all persons admitted to practice in this state. Such records must include the information specified in Business and Professions Code section 6002.1 and 6064 and other information as directed by the Supreme Court.

(Subd (a) amended effective January 1, 2019; adopted as unlettered subdivision effective May 1, 1996; previously amended effective January 1, 2007; previously lettered effective June 1, 2007.)

(b) Annual State Bar recommendation for one-time expungement of suspension for nonpayment of license fees

The State Bar is authorized to transmit to the Supreme Court on an annual basis the names of those licensees who meet all of the following criteria, along with a recommendation that their public record of suspension for nonpayment of license fees be expunged:

(1) The licensee has not on any previous occasion obtained an expungement under the terms of this rule or rule 9.31;

(2) The suspension was for 90 days or less;

(3) The suspension ended at least seven years before the date of the submission of the licensee's name to the Supreme Court;

(4) The licensee has no other record of suspension or involuntary inactive enrollment for discipline or otherwise.

(Subd (b) amended effective January 1, 2019; adopted effective June 1, 2007; previously amended effective August 1, 2017.)

(c) Records to be maintained by State Bar

Upon order of the Supreme Court of expungement of a licensee's record under (b) of this rule, the State Bar will remove or delete the record of such suspension from the licensee's public record. Notwithstanding any other provision of this rule, the State Bar must maintain such internal records as are necessary to apply the terms of (b) of this rule and to report to the Commission on Judicial Nominees Evaluation or appropriate governmental entities involved in judicial elections the licensee's eligibility for a judgeship under the California Constitution, article VI, section 15.

(Subd (c) amended effective January 1, 2019; adopted effective June 1, 2007.)

(d) Duty of disclosure by licensee

Expungement of a licensee's suspension under (b) of this rule will not relieve the licensee of his or her duty to disclose the suspension for purpose of determining the licensee's eligibility for a judgeship under the California Constitution, article VI, section 15. For all other purposes the suspension expunged under (b) of this rule is deemed not to have occurred and the licensee may answer accordingly any question relating to his or her record.

(Subd (d) amended effective January 1, 2019; adopted effective June 1, 2007.)

(e) Authorization for the Board of Trustees of the State Bar to adopt rules and regulations

The Board of Trustees of the State Bar is authorized to adopt such rules and regulations as it deems necessary and appropriate in order to comply with this rule.

(Subd (e) amended effective August 1, 2017; adopted effective June 1, 2007.)

(f) Inherent power of Supreme Court

Nothing in this rule may be construed as affecting the power of the Supreme Court to exercise its inherent power to direct the State Bar to expunge its records.

(Subd (f) adopted effective June 1, 2007.)

Rule 9.8 amended effective January 1, 2019; adopted as rule 950.5 by the Supreme Court effective May 1, 1996; previously amended and renumbered as rule 9.6 effective January 1, 2007; previously amended effective June 1, 2007, and August 1, 2017; previously renumbered effective January 1, 2018.

Rule 9.8.5. State Bar Client Trust Account Protection Program

(a) Client trust account protection program requirements

The State Bar of California must establish and administer a Client Trust Account Protection Program for the protection of client funds held in trust by a licensee that facilitates the State Bar's detection and deterrence of client trust accounting misconduct.

(1) The State Bar must impose the following requirements under this program:

(A) Annual Trust Account Certification - All licensees must annually (1) report whether or not, at any time during the prior year, they were responsible for client funds and funds entrusted by others under the provisions of rule 1.15 of the Rules of Professional Conduct and (2) if they were responsible, certify that they are knowledgeable about, and in compliance with, applicable rules and statutes governing client trust accounts and the safekeeping of funds entrusted by clients and others; and

(B) Annual Trust Account Registration - All licensees who were responsible for client funds and funds entrusted by others under the provisions of rule 1.15 of the Rules of Professional Conduct must, annually, register each and every trust account in which the licensee held such funds at any time during the prior year by identifying account numbers and financial institutions in a manner prescribed by the State Bar for such reporting that will securely maintain the information submitted.

(2) Among the other requirements the State Bar may impose under this program are the following:

(A) Annual Self-Assessment - All licensees who were responsible, at any time during the prior year, for a client trust account under the provisions of rule 1.15 of the Rules of Professional Conduct must complete an annual self-assessment on client trust accounting duties and practices;

(B) Compliance Review - If selected by the State Bar, a licensee must complete and submit to the State Bar a client trust accounting compliance review to be conducted by a certified public accountant at the licensee's expense; and

(C) Additional Actions - If selected by the State Bar, an additional action or actions based on the results of a compliance review may include an investigative audit, a notice of mandatory corrective action, and a referral for disciplinary action.

(Subd (a) adopted effective April 1, 2023.)

(b) Authorization for the Board of Trustees of the State Bar to adopt rules and regulations

The Board of Trustees of the State Bar is authorized to formulate and adopt such rules and regulations as it deems necessary and appropriate to comply with this rule, including a rule or regulation that defines a licensee who is responsible for client funds and funds entrusted by others under the provisions of rule 1.15 of the Rules of Professional Conduct.

(Subd (b) adopted effective April 1, 2023.)

(c) Failure to comply with program

A licensee who fails to satisfy the requirements of this program must be enrolled as an inactive licensee of the State Bar under the rules to be adopted by the Board of Trustees of the State Bar. Inactive enrollment imposed for noncompliance with the requirements of this program is cumulative and does not preclude a disciplinary proceeding or other actions for violations of the State Bar Act, the Rules of Professional Conduct, or other applicable laws.

(Subd (c) adopted effective April 1, 2023.)

(d) Fees and penalties

The State Bar has the authority to set and collect appropriate fees and penalties.

(Subd (d) adopted effective April 1, 2023.)

Rule 9.8.5 adopted effective January 1, 2023.

Rule 9.9. Online reporting by attorneys

(a) Required information

To maintain the roll of attorneys required by rule 9.8 and to facilitate communications by the State Bar with its licensees, each licensee must use an online account on a secure system provided by the State Bar to report [1]:

(1) [2] **A current office** address and telephone number, or if none, an alternative address; [3]

(2) [4] **A current** e-mail address not to be disclosed on the State Bar's website or otherwise to the public without the licensee's consent [5];

(3) **The URL of the licensee's professional website, if one is maintained;**

(4) **The licensee's practice sector, if applicable;**

(5) **The number of attorneys employed by the licensee's law firm, agency, or other legal employer, if any;**

(6) **Information about the licensee's trust account or accounts, if any, as set out in the Rules of the State Bar of California, rule 2.5;**

(7) **Legal specialties in which the licensee is certified, if any;**

(8) **Any other jurisdictions in which the licensee is admitted and the date(s) of admission;**

(9) **The jurisdiction, and the nature and date of any discipline imposed by another jurisdiction, if any, including the terms and conditions of any probation imposed, and, if suspended or disbarred in another jurisdiction, the date of any reinstatement in that jurisdiction;**

(10) **Any other information as directed by the California Supreme Court;**

(11) **Any other information as may be required by agreement with, or by conditions of probation imposed by, any other government agency; and**

(12) **Any other information as required by law.**

(Subd (a) amended effective January 1, 2024; adopted effective February 1, 2010; previously amended January 1, 2019.)

Rule 9.9(a) 2024 Deletes. [1] a current [2] Office [3] and [4] An [5] .

(b) Optional information

A licensee may also use an online attorney records account to **provide**:

(1) [1] an e-mail address for disclosure to the public on the State Bar [2] **website**; and

(2) [3] additional information as authorized by statute, rule, or Supreme Court directive, or as requested by the State Bar.

(Subd (b) amended effective January 1, 2024; adopted effective February 1, 2010; previously amended January 1, 2019.)

Rule 9.9(b) 2024 Deletes. [1] Provide [2] Web site [3] Provide

(c) Exclusions

Unless otherwise permitted by law or the Supreme Court, the State Bar may not use e-mail as substitute means of providing a notice required to initiate a State Bar disciplinary or regulatory proceeding or to otherwise change a licensee's status involuntarily.

(Subd (c) amended effective January 1, 2019; adopted effective February 1, 2010.)

(d) Exemption

A licensee who does not have online access or an e-mail address may claim an exemption from the reporting requirements of this rule. The exemption must be requested in the manner prescribed by the State Bar.

(Subd (d) amended effective January 1, 2019; adopted effective February 1, 2010.)

(e) Failure to Comply

A licensee who fails to satisfy the requirements of this rule will be enrolled as an inactive licensee of the State Bar under the rules to be adopted by the Board of Trustees of the State Bar. Inactive enrollment imposed for noncompliance with the requirements of this rule is cumulative and does not preclude a disciplinary proceeding or other action for violation of the State Bar Act, the Rules of Professional Conduct, or other applicable laws.

(Subd (e) adopted effective January 1, 2024.)

(f) Fees and penalties

The State Bar has the authority to set and collect appropriate fees and penalties.

(Subd (f) adopted effective January 1, 2024.)

Rule 9.9 amended effective January 1, 2024; adopted as rule 9.7 effective February 1, 2010; previously renumbered effective January 1, 2018; previously amended effective January 1, 2019.

Rule 9.9.5. Attorney Fingerprinting

(a) Subsequent arrest notification

(1) The State Bar must enter into a contract with the California Department of Justice for subsequent arrest notification services for attorneys whose license is on active status with the State Bar ("active licensed attorneys") and attorneys permitted to practice in the State of California pursuant to rules 9.44, 9.45, and 9.46 of the California Rules of Court ("special admissions attorneys").

(2) The State Bar must consider those active licensed attorneys and special admissions attorneys for whom it is already receiving subsequent arrest notification services as having satisfied the fingerprinting requirement of this rule and thereby exempt. The State Bar must adopt a procedure for notification of all attorneys as to whether they have been deemed to have already satisfied the requirement.

(Subd (a) adopted effective June 1, 2018.)

(b) Active licensed attorneys

Each active licensed attorney, with the exception of those attorneys specifically exempt under (a)(2) of this rule, must, pursuant to the procedure identified by the State Bar, be fingerprinted for the purpose of obtaining criminal offender record information regarding state and federal level convictions and arrests from the Department of Justice and the Federal Bureau of Investigation. These fingerprints will be retained by the Department of Justice for the limited purpose of subsequent arrest notification.

(Subd (b) adopted effective June 1, 2018.)

(c) Inactive licensed attorneys

An attorney whose license is on inactive status with the State Bar ("inactive licensed attorneys"), with the exception of those attorneys specifically exempt under (a)(2) of this rule, must, pursuant to the procedure identified by the State Bar, be fingerprinted prior to being placed on active status for the purposes described in (b) of this rule.

(Subd (c) adopted effective June 1, 2018.)

(d) Active licensed attorneys in foreign countries

Active licensed attorneys who are residing outside the United States and required to submit fingerprints under this rule should have their fingerprints taken by a licensed fingerprinting service agency and submit the hard copy fingerprint card to the State Bar. If fingerprinting services are not provided in the jurisdiction where the attorney is physically located, or the attorney is able to provide evidence that he/she is unable to access or afford such services, the attorney must notify the State Bar pursuant to the procedure identified by the State Bar. The attorney will be exempt from providing fingerprints until he or she returns to the United States for a period of not less than 60 days.

(Subd (d) adopted effective June 1, 2018.)

(e) Special admissions attorneys

Attorneys permitted to practice in the State of California pursuant to rules 9.44, 9.45, and 9.46 of the California Rules of Court, with the exception of those attorneys specifically exempt under (a)(2) of this rule, must, pursuant to the procedure identified by the State Bar, be fingerprinted for the purpose of obtaining criminal offender record information regarding state and federal level convictions and arrests from the Department of Justice and the Federal Bureau of Investigation. These fingerprints will be retained by the Department of Justice for the limited purpose of subsequent arrest notification.

(Subd (e) adopted effective June 1, 2018.)

(f) Implementation schedule and penalty for noncompliance

(1) The State Bar must develop a schedule for implementation that requires all attorneys subject to fingerprinting under (b) of this rule to be fingerprinted by December 1, 2019. The State Bar must develop a schedule for implementation that requires all special admissions attorneys subject to fingerprinting under (e) of this rule to be fingerprinted by the renewal of their application to practice law in the State of California.

(2) The State Bar has ongoing authority to require submission of fingerprints after December 1, 2019 for attorneys for whom it is not receiving subsequent arrest notification services and for attorneys transferring to active status. Failure to be fingerprinted if required by this rule may result in involuntary inactive enrollment pursuant to Business and Professions Code section 6054(d).

(3) The State Bar has ongoing authority to require submission of fingerprints after December 1, 2019, for special admissions attorneys for whom it is not receiving subsequent arrest notification services. Failure to be fingerprinted if required may result in a State Bar determination that the attorney cease providing legal services in California.

(Subd (f) adopted effective June 1, 2018.)

(g) Information obtained by fingerprint submission; disclosure limitations

Any information obtained by the State Bar as a result of fingerprint submission under this rule must be kept confidential and used solely for State Bar licensing and regulatory purposes.

(Subd (g) adopted effective June 1, 2018.)

(h) Fingerprint submission and processing costs

(1) Except as described in (h)(2), all costs incurred for the processing of fingerprints for the State Bar, including print furnishing and encoding, as required by Business and Professions Code section 6054, must be borne by the licensed attorney or special admissions attorney.

(2) The State Bar must develop procedures for granting waivers of the processing costs of running Department of Justice and Federal Bureau of Investigation background checks for licensed attorneys with demonstrable financial hardship.

(Subd (h) adopted effective June 1, 2018.)

(i) Attorneys who are physically unable to be fingerprinted

(1) If the Department of Justice makes a determination pursuant to Penal Code section 11105.7 that any attorney required to be fingerprinted under this rule is presently unable to provide legible fingerprints, the attorney will be deemed to have complied with the fingerprinting requirements of this rule.

(2) Attorneys required to be fingerprinted under this rule may also submit notification to the State Bar that they are unable to submit fingerprints due to disability, illness, accident, or other circumstances beyond their control. The State Bar must evaluate the notification and may require additional evidence. If the State Bar determines that the attorney is unable to submit fingerprints based on the information provided, the attorney will be deemed to have complied with the fingerprinting requirements of this rule.

(3) A determination of deemed compliance under (i)(1) and (i)(2) will apply only to those attorneys who are unable to supply legible fingerprints due to disability, illness, accident, or other circumstances beyond their control and will not apply to attorneys who are unable to provide fingerprints because of actions they have taken to avoid submitting their fingerprints.

(Subd (i) adopted effective June 1, 2018.)

Rule 9.9.5 adopted effective June 1, 2018.

Chapter 3
Attorney Disciplinary Proceedings

Title 9, Rules on Law Practice, Attorneys, and Judges—Division 2, Attorney Admission and Disciplinary Proceedings and Review of State Bar Proceedings—Chapter 3, Attorney Disciplinary Proceedings; renumbered from Chapter 2 effective January 1, 2018.

Rule 9.10. Authority of the State Bar Court
Rule 9.11. State Bar Court judges
Rule 9.12. Standard of review for State Bar Court Review Department
Rule 9.13. Review of State Bar Court decisions
Rule 9.14. Petitions for review by the Chief Trial Counsel
Rule 9.15. Petitions for review by State Bar; grounds for review; confidentiality
Rule 9.16. Grounds for review of State Bar Court decisions in the Supreme Court
Rule 9.17. Remand with instructions
Rule 9.18. Effective date of disciplinary orders and decisions
Rule 9.19. Conditions attached to reprovals
Rule 9.20. Duties of disbarred, resigned, or suspended attorneys
Rule 9.21. Resignations of licensees of the State Bar with disciplinary charges pending
Rule 9.22. Suspension of licensees of the State Bar for failure to comply with judgment or order for child or family support
Rule 9.23. Enforcement as money judgment disciplinary orders directing the payment of costs and disciplinary orders requiring reimbursement of the Client Security Fund

Rule 9.10. Authority of the State Bar Court

(a) Conviction proceedings

The State Bar Court exercises statutory powers under Business and Professions Code sections 6101 and 6102 with respect to the discipline of attorneys convicted of crimes. (See Bus. & Prof. Code §6087.) For purposes of this rule, a judgment of conviction is deemed final when the availability of appeal has been exhausted and the time for filing a petition for certiorari in the United States Supreme Court on direct review of the judgment of conviction has elapsed and no petition has been filed, or if filed the petition has been denied or the judgment of conviction has been affirmed. The State Bar Court must impose or recommend discipline in conviction matters as in other disciplinary proceedings. The power conferred upon the State Bar Court by this rule includes the power to place attorneys on interim suspension under subdivisions (a) and (b) of section 6102, and the power to vacate, delay the effective date of, and temporarily stay the effect of such orders.

(Subd (a) amended effective January 1, 2007.)

(b) Professional responsibility examination

The State Bar Court may:

(1) Extend the time within which a licensee of the State Bar must take and pass a professional responsibility examination;

(2) Suspend a licensee for failing to take and pass such examination; and

(3) Vacate licensee's suspension for failing to take and pass such examination.

(Subd (b) amended effective January 1, 2019; previously amended effective January 1, 2007.)

(c) Probation

The State Bar Court for good cause, may:

(1) Approve stipulations between the licensee and the Chief Trial Counsel for modification of the terms of a licensee's probation; and

(2) Make corrections and minor modifications to the terms of a licensee's disciplinary probation.

The order of the State Bar Court must be filed promptly with the Clerk of the Supreme Court.

(Subd (c) amended effective January 1, 2019; previously amended effective January 1, 2007.)

(d) Rule 9.20 compliance

The State Bar Court for good cause, may extend the time within which a licensee must comply with the provisions of rule 9.20 of the California Rules of Court.

(Subd (d) amended effective January 1, 2019; previously amended effective January 1, 2007.)

(e) Commencement of suspension

The State Bar Court for good cause, may delay temporarily the effective date of, or temporarily stay the effect of, an order for a licensee's disciplinary suspension from practice.

(Subd (e) amended effective January 1, 2019; previously amended effective January 1, 2007.)

(f) Readmission and reinstatement

Applications for readmission or reinstatement must, in the first instance, be filed and heard by the State Bar Court, except that no applicant who has been disbarred by the Supreme Court on two previous occasions may apply for readmission or reinstatement. Applicants for readmission or reinstatement must:

(1) Pass a professional responsibility examination;

(2) Establish their rehabilitation and present moral qualifications for readmission; and

(3) Establish present ability and learning in the general law. Applicants who resigned without charges pending more than five years before filing an application for reinstatement or readmission must establish present ability and learning in the general law by providing proof, at the time of filing the application, that they have taken and passed the Attorneys' Examination administered by the Committee of Bar Examiners pursuant to the authority delegated to it by the Board of Trustees within five years prior to the filing of the application for readmission or reinstatement. Applicants who resigned with charges pending or who were disbarred must establish present ability and learning in the general law by providing proof, at the time of filing the application for readmission or reinstatement, that they have taken and passed the Attorneys' Examination by State Bar within three years prior to the filing of the application for readmission or reinstatement.

(Subd (f) amended effective January 1, 2019; previously amended effective January 1, 2007, and January 1, 2010.)

(g) Inherent power of Supreme Court

Nothing in these rules may be construed as affecting the power of the Supreme Court to exercise its inherent jurisdiction over the lawyer discipline and admissions system.

(Subd (g) amended effective January 1, 2007.)

Rule 9.10 amended effective January 1, 2019; adopted as rule 951 effective December 1, 1990; previously amended by the Supreme Court effective April 1, 1996, and January 1, 2007; previously amended and renumbered effective January 1, 2010.

Rule 9.11. State Bar Court judges

(a) Applicant Evaluation and Nomination Committee

(1) In order to ensure that individuals appointed by the Supreme Court or by the executive or legislative branches have been evaluated objectively, the Supreme Court has established an independent Applicant Evaluation and Nomination Committee to solicit, receive, screen, and evaluate all applications for appointment or reappointment to any position of judge of the State Bar Court (hearing judge, presiding judge, and review department judge). The role of the committee is to determine whether appointees possess not only the statutorily enumerated qualifications, but also any qualifications that may be required by the Supreme Court to assist in the exercise of its ultimate authority over the discipline and admission of attorneys (see *Obrien v. Jones* (2000) 23 Cal.4th 40; *In re Attorney Discipline System* (1998) 19 Cal.4th 582; Cal. Const., art. VI, sec. 9).

(2) The committee serves at the pleasure of the Supreme Court. It shall consist of seven members appointed by the court of whom no more than four may be licensees of the State Bar in good standing, two must be retired or active judicial officers, and no more than three may be public members who have never been licensees of the State Bar or admitted to practice before any court in the United States. Two members of the committee must be present members of the Board of Trustees of the State Bar.

(3) The committee must adopt, and implement upon approval by the Supreme Court, procedures for:

(A) Timely notice to potential applicants of vacancies;

(B) Receipt of applications for appointments to those positions from both incumbents and other qualified persons;

(C) Solicitation and receipt of public comment;

(D) Evaluation and rating of applicants; and

(E) Transmittal of the materials specified in (b) of this rule to the Supreme Court and, as applicable, other appointing authorities.

The procedures adopted by the committee must include provisions to ensure confidentiality comparable to those followed by the Judicial Nominees Evaluation Commission established under Government Code section 12011.5.

(4) The Board of Trustees of the State Bar, in consultation with the Supreme Court if necessary, must provide facilities and support staff needed by the committee to carry out its obligations under this rule.

(Subd (a) amended effective July 1, 2022; previously amended effective February 15, 1995, July 1, 2000, January 1, 2007, January 1, 2009, and January 1, 2019.)

(b) Evaluations

(1) The committee must evaluate the qualifications of and rate all applicants for positions appointed by the Supreme Court and must submit to the Supreme Court the nominations of at least two candidates for each vacancy. Candidates shall be rated as "not recommended," "recommended," or "highly recommended." A rating of "not recommended" relates only to the position under consideration and does not indicate any lack of ability or expertise of the applicant generally. The committee must report in confidence to the Supreme Court its evaluation, rating and recommendation for applicants for appointment and the reasons therefore, including a succinct summary of their qualifications, at a time to be designated by the Supreme Court. The report must include written comments received by the committee, which must be transmitted to the Supreme Court together with the nominations.

(2) The committee must evaluate the qualifications of and rate all applicants for positions appointed by the Governor, the Senate Committee on Rules, or the Speaker of the Assembly, and must submit in confidence to the Supreme Court and, as applicable, to other appointing authorities, all applications for such positions together with the committee's evaluation, rating and recommendation for these applicants, including any written comments received by the committee, at a time to be designated by the Supreme Court.

(3) In determining the qualifications of an applicant for appointment or reappointment the committee must consider, among other appropriate factors, the following: industry, legal and judicial experience (including prior service as a judge of the State Bar Court), judicial temperament, honesty, objectivity, community respect, integrity, and ability. The committee must consider legal work experience broadly, including, but not limited to, litigation and non-litigation experience, legal work for a business or nonprofit entity, experience as a law professor or other academic position, legal work in any of the three branches of government, and legal work in dispute resolution.

The committee shall consider whether an applicant has demonstrated the ability to write cogently and to analyze legal provisions and principles. Among the issues the committee may also consider are (1) the applicant's demonstrated capacity to work independently and to set and meet performance goals, (2) the applicant's knowledge and experience relevant to issues that give rise to the majority of State Bar Court proceedings, including professional ethics and fiduciary obligations, (3) knowledge of practice and demeanor in the courtroom, and (4) whether the applicant has been in practice for 10 or more years. The committee shall accord weight to all experience that has provided the applicant with legal experience and exposure during which the individual has demonstrated the underlying skills necessary to serve as an effective State Bar Court judge. The committee shall apply the same criteria to candidates seeking appointment from all of the appointing authorities. Any evaluation or rating of an applicant and any recommendation for appointment or reappointment by the committee must be made in conformity with Business and Professions Code section 6079.1(b) and in light of the factors specified in Government Code section 12011.5(d), and those specified in this paragraph.

(4) Upon transmittal of its report to the Supreme Court, the committee must notify any incumbent who has applied for reappointment by the Supreme Court if he or she is or is not among the applicants recommended for appointment to the new term by the committee. The applicable appointing authority must notify as soon as possible an incumbent who has applied for reappointment but is not selected.

(Subd (b) amended effective July 1, 2022; adopted effective February 15, 1995; previously amended effective July 1, 2000, January 1, 2007, January 1, 2009, and January 1, 2019.)

(c) Appointments

Only applicants who are rated as recommended or highly recommended by the committee or by the Supreme Court may be appointed. At the request of the Governor, the Senate Committee on Rules, or the Speaker of the Assembly, the Supreme Court will reconsider a finding by the committee that a particular applicant is not recommended. The Supreme Court may make such orders as to the appointment of applicants as it deems appropriate, including extending the term of incumbent judges pending such order or providing for staggered terms.

(Subd (c) amended effective January 1, 2009; adopted effective February 15, 1995; previously amended effective July 1, 2000 and January 1, 2007.)

(d) Discipline for misconduct or disability

A judge of the State Bar Court is subject to discipline or retirement on the same grounds as a judge of a court of this state. Complaints concerning the conduct of a judge of the State Bar Court must be addressed to the Executive Director–Chief Counsel of the Commission on Judicial Performance, who is the Supreme Court's investigator for the purpose of evaluating those complaints, conducting any necessary further investigation, and determining whether formal proceedings should be instituted. If there is reasonable cause to institute formal proceedings, the investigator must notify the Supreme Court of that fact and must serve as or appoint the examiner and make other appointments and arrangements necessary for the hearing. The Supreme Court will then appoint one or more active or retired judges of superior courts or Courts of Appeal as its special master or masters to hear the complaint and the results of the investigation, and to report to the Supreme Court on the resulting findings, conclusions, and recommendations as to discipline. The procedures of the Commission on Judicial Performance must be followed by the investigator and special masters, to the extent feasible. The procedures in the Supreme Court after a discipline recommendation is filed will, to the extent feasible, be the same as the procedures followed when a determination of the Commission on Judicial Performance is filed.

(Subd (d) amended effective January 1, 2007; adopted as subd (b) effective December 1, 1990; relettered effective February 15, 1995; previously amended effective July 1, 2000.)

Rule 9.11 amended effective July 1, 2022; adopted as rule 961 effective December 1, 1990; previously amended February 15, 1995, July 1, 2000, January 1, 2009, and January 1, 2019; previously amended and renumbered effective January 1, 2007.

Rule 9.12. Standard of review for State Bar Court Review Department

In reviewing the decisions, orders, or rulings of a hearing judge under rule 301 of the Rules of Procedure of the State Bar of California or such other rule as may be adopted governing the review of any decisions, orders, or rulings by a hearing judge that fully disposes of an entire proceeding, the Review Department of the State Bar Court must independently review the record and may adopt findings, conclusions, and a decision or recommendation different from those of the hearing judge.

Rule 9.12 amended and renumbered effective January 1, 2007; adopted as rule 951.5 by the Supreme Court effective February 23, 2000.

Rule 9.13. Review of State Bar Court decisions

(a) Review of recommendation of disbarment or suspension

A petition to the Supreme Court by a licensee to review a decision of the State Bar Court recommending his or her disbarment or suspension from practice must be served and filed within 60 days after a certified copy of the decision complained of is filed with the Clerk of the Supreme Court. The State Bar may serve and file an answer to the petition within 15 days after filing of the petition. Within 5 days after filing of the answer, the petitioner may serve and file a reply. If review is ordered by the Supreme Court, the State Bar must serve and file a supplemental brief within 45 days after the order is filed. Within 15 days after filing of the supplemental brief, the petitioner may serve and file a reply brief.

(Subd (a) amended effective January 1, 2019; previously relettered and amended effective October 1, 1973; previously amended effective July 1, 1968, December 1, 1990, and January 1, 2007.)

(b) Review of recommendation to set aside stay of suspension or modify probation

A petition to the Supreme Court by a licensee to review a recommendation of the State Bar Court that a stay of an order of suspension be set aside or that the duration or conditions of probation be modified on account of a violation of probation must be served and filed within 15 days after a certified copy of the recommendation complained of is filed with the Clerk of the Supreme Court. Within 15 days after filing of the petition, the State Bar may serve and file an answer. Within 5 days after filing of the answer, the petitioner may serve and file a reply.

(Subd (b) amended effective January 1, 2019; adopted effective October 1, 1973; previously amended effective December 1, 1990, and January 1, 2007.)

(c) Review of interim decisions

A petition to the Supreme Court by a licensee to review a decision of the State Bar Court regarding interim suspension, the exercise of powers delegated by rule 9.10(b)–(e), or another interlocutory matter must be served and filed within 15 days after written notice of the adverse decision of the State Bar Court is mailed by the State Bar to the petitioner and to his or her counsel of record, if any, at their respective addresses under section 6002.1. Within 15 days after filing of the petition, the State Bar may serve and file an answer. Within 5 days after filing of the answer, the petitioner may serve and file a reply.

(Subd (c) amended effective January 1, 2019; adopted effective December 1, 1990; previously amended effective January 1, 2007.)

(d) Review of other decisions

A petition to the Supreme Court to review any other decision of the State Bar Court or action of the Board of Trustees of the State Bar, or of any board or committee appointed by it and authorized to make a determination under the provisions of the State Bar Act, or of the chief executive officer of the State Bar or the designee of the chief executive officer authorized to make a determination under article 10 of the State Bar Act or these rules of court, must be served and filed within 60 days after written notice of the action complained of is mailed to the petitioner and to his or her counsel of record, if any, at their respective addresses under Business and Professions Code section 6002.1. Within 15 days after filing of the petition, the State Bar may serve and file an answer and brief. Within 5 days after filing of the answer and brief, the petitioner may serve and file a reply. If review is ordered by the Supreme Court, the State Bar, within 45 days after filing of the order, may serve and file a supplemental brief. Within 15 days after filing of the supplemental brief, the petitioner may serve and file a reply brief.

(Subd (d) amended effective January 1, 2019; previously amended effective July 1, 1968, May 1, 1986, April 2, 1987, and January 1, 2007; previously relettered and amended effective October 1, 1973, and December 1, 1990.)

(e) Contents of petition

(1) A petition to the Supreme Court filed under (a) or (b) of this rule must be verified, must specify the grounds relied upon, must show that review within the State Bar Court has been exhausted, must address why review is appropriate under one or more of the grounds specified in rule 9.16, and must have attached a copy of the State Bar Court decision from which relief is sought.

(2) When review is sought under (c) or (d) of this rule, the petition must also be accompanied by a record adequate to permit review of the ruling, including:

(A) Legible copies of all documents and exhibits submitted to the State Bar Court or the State Bar supporting and opposing petitioner's position;

(B) Legible copies of all other documents submitted to the State Bar Court or the State Bar that are necessary for a complete understanding of the case and the ruling; and

(C) A transcript of the proceedings in the State Bar Court leading to the decision or, if a transcript is unavailable, a declaration by counsel explaining why a transcript is unavailable and fairly summarizing the proceedings, including arguments by counsel and the basis of the State Bar Court's decision, if stated; or a declaration by counsel stating that the transcript has been ordered, the date it was ordered, and the date it is expected to be filed, which must be a date before any action is requested from the Supreme Court other than issuance of a stay supported by other parts of the record.

(3) A petitioner who requests an immediate stay must explain in the petition the reasons for the urgency and set forth all relevant time constraints.

(4) If a petitioner does not submit the required record, the court may summarily deny the stay request, the petition, or both.

(Subd (e) amended effective January 1, 2019; previously repealed and adopted by the Supreme Court effective December 1, 1990, and February 1, 1991; previously repealed and adopted effective March 15, 1991; previously amended effective January 1, 2007.)

(f) Service

All petitions, briefs, reply briefs, and other pleadings filed by a petitioner under this rule must be accompanied by proof of service of three copies on the General Counsel of the State Bar at the San Francisco office of the State Bar, and of one copy on the Clerk of the State Bar Court at the Los Angeles office of the State Bar Court. The State Bar must serve the licensee at his or her address under Business and Professions Code section 6002.1, and his or her counsel of record, if any.

(Subd (f) amended effective January 1, 2019; adopted by the Supreme Court effective December 1, 1990; previously amended by the Supreme Court effective February 1, 1991; previously amended effective March 15, 1991, and January 1, 2007.)

Rule 9.13 amended effective January 1, 2019; adopted as rule 59 by the Supreme Court effective April 20, 1943, and by the Judicial Council effective July 1, 1943; previously amended and renumbered as rule 952 effective October 1, 1973, and as rule 9.13 effective January 1, 2007; previously amended effective July 1, 1976, May 1, 1986, April 2, 1987, December 1, 1990, February 1, 1991, and March 15, 1991.

Rule 9.14. Petitions for review by the Chief Trial Counsel

(a) Time for filing

The Chief Trial Counsel may petition for review of recommendations and decisions of the State Bar Court as follows:

(1) From recommendations that a licensee be suspended, within 60 days of the date the recommendation is filed with the Supreme Court.

(2) From recommendations that the duration or conditions of probation be modified, or a reinstatement application be granted, within 15 days of the date the recommendation is filed with the Supreme Court.

(3) From decisions not to place an eligible licensee on interim suspension, or vacating interim suspension, or a denial of a petition brought under Business and Professions Code section 6007(c), within 15 days of notice under the rules adopted by the State Bar.

(4) From decisions dismissing disciplinary proceedings or recommending approval, within 60 days of notice under the rules adopted by the State Bar.

(Subd (a) amended effective January 1, 2019; adopted effective March 15, 1991; previously adopted by the Supreme Court effective December 10, 1990; previously amended effective January 1, 2007.)

(b) Procedures

Proceedings under this rule with regard to briefing, service of process, and applicable time periods therefor must correspond to proceedings brought under rule 9.13, except that the rights and duties of the licensee and the State Bar under that rule are reversed.

(Subd (b) amended effective January 1, 2019; adopted as part of subd (d) effective March 15, 1991; previously adopted by the Supreme Court effective December 10, 1991; previously amended and relettered effective January 1, 2007.)

Rule 9.14 amended effective January 1, 2019; adopted as rule 952.5 effective March 15, 1991; previously amended and renumbered effective January 1, 2007.

Rule 9.15. Petitions for review by State Bar; grounds for review; confidentiality

(a) Petition for review by the State Bar

The State Bar may petition for review of the decision of the Review Department of the State Bar Court in moral character proceedings. All petitions under this rule must be served and filed with the Clerk of the Supreme Court within 60 days after the State Bar Court decision is filed and served on the General Counsel of the State Bar at the San Francisco office of the State Bar. The applicant may file and serve an answer within 15 days after filing of the petition. Within 5 days after filing of the answer the State Bar may serve and file a reply. If review is ordered by the Supreme Court, within 45 days after filing and service of the order, the applicant may serve and file a supplemental brief. Within 15 days after filing of the supplemental brief, the petitioner may serve and file a reply brief.

(Subd (a) amended effective January 1, 2019; previously amended effective January 1, 2007.)

(b) Contents of petition

A petition to the Supreme Court filed under this rule must show that review within the State Bar Court has been exhausted, must address why review is appropriate under one or more of the grounds specified in rule 9.16, and must have attached a copy of the State Bar Court decision for which review is sought.

(Subd (b) amended effective January 1, 2007.)

(c) Service

All petitions, briefs, reply briefs, and other pleadings filed by the State Bar must include a proof of service by mail to the applicant's last address provided to the State Bar or the applicant's attorney of record, if any. Filings by the applicant must include a proof of service of three copies on the General Counsel of the State Bar at the San Francisco office of the State Bar and one copy on the Clerk of the State Bar Court at the Los Angeles office of the State Bar Court.

(Subd (c) amended effective January 1, 2019; previously amended effective April 20, 1998, and January 1, 2007.)

(d) Confidentiality

All filings under this rule are confidential unless: (1) the applicant waives confidentiality in writing; or (2) the Supreme Court grants review. Once the Supreme Court grants review, filings under this rule are open to the public; however, if good cause exists, the Supreme Court may order portions of the record or the identity of witnesses or other third parties to the proceedings to remain confidential.

(Subd (d) amended effective January 1, 2007; adopted effective April 20, 1998.)

Rule 9.15 amended effective January 1, 2019; adopted as rule 952.6 by the Supreme Court effective July 1, 1993, and by the Judicial Council May 6, 1998; previously amended by the Supreme Court effective April 20, 1998; previously amended and renumbered effective January 1, 2007.

Rule 9.16. Grounds for review of State Bar Court decisions in the Supreme Court

(a) Grounds

The Supreme Court will order review of a decision of the State Bar Court recommending disbarment or suspension from practice when it appears:

(1) Necessary to settle important questions of law;

(2) The State Bar Court has acted without or in excess of jurisdiction;

(3) Petitioner did not receive a fair hearing;

(4) The decision is not supported by the weight of the evidence; or

(5) The recommended discipline is not appropriate in light of the record as a whole.

(Subd (a) amended effective January 1, 2007; adopted by the Supreme Court effective February 1, 1991.)

(b) Denial of review

Denial of review of a decision of the State Bar Court is a final judicial determination on the merits and the recommendation of the State Bar Court will be filed as an order of the Supreme Court.

(Subd (b) amended effective January 1, 2007; adopted by the Supreme Court effective February 1, 1991.)

Rule 9.16 amended and renumbered effective January 1, 2007; adopted as rule 954 effective February 1, 1991.

Rule 9.17. Remand with instructions

The Supreme Court may at any time remand a matter filed under this chapter to the State Bar Court or the State Bar with instructions to take such further actions or conduct such further proceedings as the Supreme Court deems necessary.

Rule 9.17 amended effective January 1, 2019; adopted as rule 953.5 effective February 1, 1991; previously amended and renumbered effective January 1, 2007.

Rule 9.18. Effective date of disciplinary orders and decisions

(a) Effective date of Supreme Court orders

Unless otherwise ordered, all orders of the Supreme Court imposing discipline or opinions deciding causes involving the State Bar become final 30 days after filing. The Supreme Court may grant a rehearing at any time before the decision or order becomes final. Petitions for rehearing must be served and filed within 15 days after the date the decision or order was filed. Unless otherwise ordered, when petitions for review under rules 9.13(c) and 9.14(a)(3) are acted upon summarily, the orders of the

Supreme Court are final forthwith and do not have law-of-the-case effect in subsequent proceedings in the Supreme Court.

(Subd (a) amended effective January 1, 2019; adopted effective March 15, 1991; previously adopted by the Supreme Court effective December 1, 1990; previously amended effective January 1, 2007.)

(b) Effect of State Bar Court orders when no review sought

Unless otherwise ordered, if no petition for review is filed within the time allowed by rule 9.13 (a), (b), and (d), or rule 9.14 (a)(1) and (2), as to a recommendation of the State Bar Court for the disbarment, suspension, or reinstatement of a licensee, the vacation of a stay, or modification of the duration or conditions of a probation, the recommendation of the State Bar Court will be filed as an order of the Supreme Court following the expiration of the time for filing a timely petition. The Clerk of the Supreme Court will mail notice of this effect to the licensee and his or her attorney of record, if any, at their respective addresses under Business and Professions Code section 6002.1 and to the State Bar.

(Subd (b) amended effective January 1, 2019; adopted effective March 15, 1991; previously adopted by the Supreme Court effective December 1, 1990; previously amended effective January 1, 2007.)

(c) Effect of State Bar Court orders in moral character proceedings when no review sought

Unless otherwise ordered, if no petition for review is filed within the time allowed by rule 9.15(a), as to a recommendation of the State Bar Court in moral character proceedings, the recommendation of the State Bar Court will be filed as an order of the Supreme Court following the expiration of the time for filing a timely petition. The Clerk of the Supreme Court will mail notice of this effect to the applicant's last address provided to the State Bar or to the applicant's attorney of record, if any, and to the State Bar.

(Subd (c) amended effective January 1, 2007.)

Rule 9.18 amended effective January 1, 2019; adopted as rule 953 effective March 15, 1991; previously amended effective February 1, 1996; previously amended and renumbered effective January 1, 2007.

Rule 9.19. Conditions attached to reprovals

(a) Attachment of conditions to reprovals

The State Bar may attach conditions, effective for a reasonable time, to a public or private reproval administered upon a licensee of the State Bar. Conditions so attached must be based on a finding by the State Bar that protection of the public and the interests of the licensee will be served thereby. The State Bar when administering the reproval must give notice to the licensee that failure to comply with the conditions may be punishable.

(Subd (a) amended effective January 1, 2019; previously amended effective January 1, 2007.)

(b) Sanctions for failure to comply

A licensee's failure to comply with conditions attached to a public or private reproval may be cause for a separate proceeding for willful breach of 8.1.1 of the Rules of Professional Conduct.

(Subd (b) amended effective January 1, 2019; previously amended effective January 1, 2007.)

Rule 9.19 amended effective January 1, 2019; adopted as rule 956 effective November 18, 1983; previously amended and renumbered effective January 1, 2007.

Rule 9.20. Duties of disbarred, resigned, or suspended attorneys

(a) Disbarment, suspension, and resignation orders

The Supreme Court may include in an order disbarring or suspending a licensee of the State Bar, or accepting his or her resignation, a direction that the licensee must, within such time limits as the Supreme Court may prescribe:

(1) Notify all clients being represented in pending matters and any co-counsel of his or her disbarment, suspension, or resignation and his or her consequent disqualification to act as an attorney after the effective date of the disbarment, suspension, or resignation, and, in the absence of co-counsel, also notify the clients to seek legal advice elsewhere, calling attention to any urgency in seeking the substitution of another attorney or attorneys;

(2) Deliver to all clients being represented in pending matters any papers or other property to which the clients are entitled, or notify the clients and any co-counsel of a suitable time and place where the papers and other property may be obtained, calling attention to any urgency for obtaining the papers or other property;

(3) Refund any part of fees paid that have not been earned; and

(4) Notify opposing counsel in pending litigation or, in the absence of counsel, the adverse parties of the disbarment, suspension, or resignation and consequent disqualification to act as an attorney after the effective date of the disbarment, suspension, or resignation, and file a copy of the notice with the court, agency, or tribunal before which the litigation is pending for inclusion in the respective file or files.

(Subd (a) amended effective January 1, 2019; previously amended effective December 1, 1990, and January 1, 2007.)

(b) Notices to clients, co-counsel, opposing counsel, and adverse parties

All notices required by an order of the Supreme Court or the State Bar Court under this rule must be given by registered or certified mail, return receipt requested, and must contain an address where communications may be directed to the disbarred, suspended, or resigned licensee.

(Subd (b) amended effective January 1, 2019; previously amended effective December 1, 1990, and January 1, 2007.)

(c) Filing proof of compliance

Within such time as the order may prescribe after the effective date of the licensee's disbarment, suspension, or resignation, the licensee must file with the Clerk of the State Bar Court an affidavit showing that he or she has fully complied with those provisions of the order entered under this rule. The affidavit must also specify an address where communications may be directed to the disbarred, suspended, or resigned licensee.

(Subd (c) amended effective January 1, 2019; previously amended effective December 1, 1990, and January 1, 2007.)

(d) Sanctions for failure to comply

A disbarred or resigned licensee's willful failure to comply with the provisions of this rule is a ground for denying his or her application for reinstatement or readmission. A suspended licensee's willful failure to comply with the provisions of this rule is a cause for disbarment or suspension and for revocation of any pending probation. Additionally, such failure may be punished as a contempt or a crime.

(Subd (d) amended effective January 1, 2019; previously relettered and amended effective December 1, 1990; previously amended effective January 1, 2007.)

Rule 9.20 amended effective January 1, 2019; adopted as rule 955 effective April 4, 1973; previously amended effective December 1, 1990; previously amended and renumbered effective January 1, 2007.

Rule 9.21. Resignations of licensees of the State Bar with disciplinary charges pending

(a) General provisions

A licensee of the State Bar against whom disciplinary charges are pending may tender a written resignation from the State Bar and relinquishment of the right to practice law. The written resignation must be signed and dated by the licensee at the time it is tendered and must be tendered to the Office of the Clerk, State Bar Court, 845 S. Figueroa Street, Los Angeles, California 90017. The resignation must be substantially in the form specified in (b) of this rule. In submitting a resignation under this rule, a licensee of the State Bar agrees to be transferred to inactive status in the State Bar effective on the filing of the resignation by the State Bar. Within 30 days after filing of the resignation, the licensee must perform the acts specified in rule 9.20(a)(1)–(4) and (b) and within 40 days after filing of the resignation, the licensee must file with the Office of the Clerk, State Bar Court, at the above address, the proof of compliance specified in rule 9.20(c). No resignation is effective unless and until it is accepted by the Supreme Court after consideration and recommendation by the State Bar Court.

(Subd (a) amended effective January 1, 2021; previously amended effective January 1, 2007, January 1, 2010, and January 1, 2019.)

(b) Form of resignation

The licensee's written resignation must be in substantially the following form:

"I, [name of licensee,] against whom charges are pending, hereby resign from the State Bar of California and relinquish all right to practice law in the State of California. I agree that, in the event that this resignation is accepted and I later file a petition for reinstatement, the State Bar will consider in connection therewith all disciplinary matters and proceedings against me at the time this resignation is accepted, in addition to other appropriate matters. I also agree that the Supreme Court may decline to accept my resignation unless I reach agreement with the Chief Trial Counsel on a written stipulation as to facts and conclusions of law regarding the disciplinary matters and proceedings that were pending against me at the time of my resignation. I further agree that, on the filing of this resignation by the Office of the Clerk, State Bar Court, I will be transferred to inactive status with the State Bar. On such transfer, I acknowledge that I will be ineligible to practice law or to advertise or hold myself out as practicing or as entitled to practice law. I further acknowledge that in the event the Supreme Court does not accept my resignation, I will remain an inactive licensee of the State Bar, pending any further order of the Supreme Court or the State Bar Court. I further agree that, within 30 days of the filing of the resignation by the Office of the Clerk, State Bar Court, I will perform the acts specified in rule 9.20(a)–(b) of the California Rules of Court, and within 40 days of the date of filing of this resignation by the Office of the Clerk, State Bar Court, I will notify that office as specified in rule 9.20(c) of the California Rules of Court."

(Subd (b) amended effective January 1, 2019; previously amended effective January 1, 2007, January 1, 2010, and January 1, 2014.)

(c) Consideration of resignation by State Bar Court and Supreme Court

When the Office of the Clerk of the State Bar Court receives a licensee's resignation tendered in conformity with this rule, it must promptly file the resignation. The State Bar Court must thereafter consider the licensee's resignation and the stipulated facts and conclusions of law, if any, agreed upon between the licensee and the Chief Trial Counsel, and must recommend to the Supreme Court whether the resignation should be accepted. The State Bars Court's recommendation must be made in light of the grounds set forth in (d) of this rule and, if the State Bar Court recommends acceptance of the resignation notwithstanding the existence of one or more of the grounds set forth in subsection (d), the State Bar Court's recommendation must include an explanation of the reasons for the recommendation that the resignation be accepted. The Office of the Clerk of the State Bar Court must transmit to the Clerk of the Supreme Court, three certified copies of the State Bar Court's recommendation together with the licensee's resignation, when, by the terms of the State Bar Court's recommendation, the resignation should be transmitted to the Supreme Court.

(Subd (c) amended effective January 1, 2019; previously amended effective January 1, 2007, and January 1, 2010.)

(d) Grounds for rejection of resignation by the Supreme Court

The Supreme Court will make such orders concerning the licensee's resignation as it deems appropriate. The Supreme Court may decline to accept the resignation based on a report by the State Bar Court that:

(1) Preservation of necessary testimony is not complete;

(2) After transfer to inactive status, the licensee has practiced law or has advertised or held himself or herself out as entitled to practice law;

(3) The licensee has failed to perform the acts specified by rule 9.20(a)–(b);

(4) The licensee has failed to provide proof of compliance as specified in rule 9.20(c);

(5) The Supreme Court has filed an order of disbarment as to the licensee;

(6) The State Bar Court has filed a decision or opinion recommending the licensee's disbarment;

(7) The licensee has previously resigned or has been disbarred and reinstated to the practice of law;

(8) The licensee and the Chief Trial Counsel have not reached agreement on a written stipulation as to facts and conclusions of law regarding the disciplinary matters and proceedings that were pending against the licensee at the time the resignation was tendered; or

(9) Acceptance of the resignation of the licensee will reasonably be inconsistent with the need to protect the public, the courts, or the legal profession.

(Subd (d) amended effective January 1, 2019; adopted as part of subd (c) effective December 14, 1984; previously amended and relettered effective January 1, 2007; previously amended effective January 1, 2010.)

(e) Rejection of resignation by the Supreme Court

A licensee whose resignation with charges pending is not accepted by the Supreme Court will remain an inactive licensee of the State Bar. The licensee may move the Review Department of the State Bar Court to be restored to active status, at which time the Office of the Chief Trial Counsel may demonstrate any basis for the licensee's continued ineligibility to practice law. The Review Department will expedite a motion to be restored to active status. Any return to active status will be conditioned on the licensee's payment of any due, penalty payments, and restitution owed by the licensee.

(Subd (e) amended effective January 1, 2019; adopted effective January 1, 2014.)

Rule 9.21 amended effective January 1, 2021; adopted as rule 960 by the Supreme Court effective December 14, 1984; previously amended and renumbered effective January 1, 2007; previously amended effective January 1, 2010, January 1, 2014, and January 1, 2019.

Rule 9.22. Suspension of licensees of the State Bar for failure to comply with judgment or order for child or family support

(a) State Bar recommendation for suspension of delinquent licensees

Under Family Code section 17520, the State Bar is authorized to transmit to the Supreme Court twice a year the names of those licensees listed by the State Department of Child Support Services as delinquent in their payments of court-ordered child or family support with a recommendation for their suspension from the practice of law.

(Subd (a) amended effective October 20, 2023; previously amended effective January 1, 2007, and January 1, 2019.)

(b) Conditions for reinstatement of a suspended licensee

The Supreme Court may reinstate a licensee suspended under this rule only after receipt of notification from the State Bar that the licensee's name has been removed from the State Department of Child Support Services list as provided in Family Code section 17520(h) and that the licensee has submitted a declaration under penalty of perjury stating whether the licensee practiced law during the suspension.

(Subd (b) amended effective October 20, 2023; adopted as part of subd (a) effective January 31, 1993; previously amended and lettered effective January 1, 2007; previously amended effective January 1, 2019.)

(c) Subsequent recommendation for suspension by the State Bar

Under Family Code section 17520(*l*), the State Bar is further authorized to promptly transmit to the Supreme Court with a recommendation for suspension from the practice of law the name of any licensee previously listed by the State Department of Child Support Services as delinquent in the payment of court-ordered child or family support, who has been reinstated under (b) of this rule, and who has subsequently been identified by the Department of Child Support Services as being delinquent.

(Subd (c) amended effective October 20, 2023; adopted as part of subd (a) effective January 31, 1993; previously amended and lettered effective January 1, 2007; previously amended effective January 1, 2019.)

(d) Compliance with Rule 9.20(a)–(c)

A licensee suspended under this rule must comply with the requirements of rule 9.20 in connection with an initial suspension under (a) of this rule and any subsequent suspension under (c) of this rule.

(Subd (d) adopted effective October 20, 2023.)

(e) Authorization for the Board of Trustees of the State Bar to adopt rules

The Board of Trustees of the State Bar is authorized to adopt such rules as it deems necessary and appropriate in order to comply with this rule. The rules of the State Bar must contain procedures governing the notification, suspension, and reinstatement of licensees of the State Bar in a manner not inconsistent with Family Code section 17520.

(Subd (e) amended and relettered effective October 20, 2023; adopted as subd (b) effective January 31, 1993; previously amended and relettered as subd (d) effective January 1, 2007; previously amended effective January 1, 2019.)

Rule 9.22 amended effective October 20, 2023; adopted as rule 962 effective January 31, 1993; previously amended by the Supreme Court effective April 1, 1996, and January 1, 2019; previously amended and renumbered effective January 1, 2007.

Rule 9.23. Enforcement as money judgment disciplinary orders directing the payment of costs and disciplinary orders requiring reimbursement of the Client Security Fund

(a) Authority to obtain money judgment

Under Business and Professions Code section 6086.10(a) the State Bar is authorized to enforce as a money judgment any disciplinary order assessing costs. Under Business and Professions Code section 6140.5(d) the State Bar is authorized to enforce as a money judgment any disciplinary order requiring reimbursement of the State Bar Client Security Fund.

(Subd (a) adopted by the Supreme Court effective April 1, 2007.)

(b) Duty of clerk of the superior court

The State Bar may file a certified copy of a final disciplinary order assessing costs or requiring reimbursement to the Client Security Fund, along with a certified copy of the certificate of costs and any record of Client Security Fund payments and costs, with the clerk of the superior court of any county. The clerk must immediately enter judgment in conformity with the order.

(Subd (b) amended effective January 1, 2019; adopted by the Supreme Court effective April 1, 2007.)

(c) Compromise of judgment

Motions for the compromise of any judgment entered under this rule must, in the first instance, be filed and heard by the State Bar Court.

(Subd (c) adopted by the Supreme Court effective April 1, 2007.)

(d) Power of the Supreme Court

Nothing in this rule may be construed as affecting the power of the Supreme Court to alter the amounts owed.

(Subd (d) adopted by the Supreme Court effective April 1, 2007.)

Rule 9.23 amended effective January 1, 2019; adopted by the Supreme Court effective April 1, 2007.

Chapter 4
Legal Education

Title 9, Rules on Law Practice, Attorneys, and Judges—Division 2, Attorney Admission and Disciplinary Proceedings and Review of State Bar Proceedings—Chapter 4, Legal Education; renumbered from Chapter 3 effective January 1, 2018.

Rule 9.30. Law school study in schools other than those accredited by the examining committee
Rule 9.31. Minimum continuing legal education
Rule 9.32. New Attorney Training

Rule 9.30. Law school study in schools other than those accredited by the examining committee

(a) Receipt of credit

A person who seeks to be certified to the Supreme Court for admission in and licensed to practice law under section 6060(e)(2) of the Business and Professions Code may receive credit for:

(1) Study in a law school in the United States other than one accredited by the examining committee established by the Board of Trustees of the State Bar under Business and Professions Code section 6046 only if the law school satisfies the requirements of (b) or (c) of this rule; or

(2) Instruction in law from a correspondence school only if the correspondence school requires 864 hours of preparation and study per year for four years and satisfies the requirements of (d) of this rule; or

(3) Study in a law school outside the United States other than one accredited by the examining committee established by the Board of Trustees of the State Bar under Business and Professions Code section 6046 only if the examining committee is satisfied that the academic program of such law school is substantially equivalent to that of a law school qualified under (b) of this rule.

(Subd (a) amended effective January 1, 2019; previously amended effective April 2, 1984, and January 1, 2007.)

(b) Requirements for unaccredited law schools in state

A law school in this state that is not accredited by the examining committee must:

(1) Be authorized to confer professional degrees by the laws of this state;

(2) Maintain a regular course of instruction in law, with a specified curriculum and regularly scheduled class sessions;

(3) Require classroom attendance of its students for a minimum of 270 hours a year for at least four years, and further require regular attendance of each student at not less than 80 percent of the regularly scheduled class hours in each course in which such student was enrolled and maintain attendance records adequate to determine each student's compliance with these requirements;

(4) Maintain, in a fixed location, physical facilities capable of accommodating the classes scheduled for that location;

(5) Have an adequate faculty of instructors in law. The faculty will prima facie be deemed adequate if at least 80 percent of the instruction in each academic period is by persons who possess one or more of the following qualifications:

(A) Admission to the general practice of the law in any jurisdiction in the United States;

(B) Judge of a United States court or a court of record in any jurisdiction in the United States; or

(C) Graduation from a law school accredited by the examining committee.

(6) Own and maintain a library consisting of not less than the following sets of books, all of which must be current and complete:

(A) The published reports of the decisions of California courts, with advance sheets and citator;

(B) A digest or encyclopedia of California law;

(C) An annotated set of the California codes; and

(D) A current, standard text or treatise for each course or subject in the curriculum of the school for which such a text or treatise is available.

(7) Establish and maintain standards for academic achievement, advancement in good standing and graduation, and provide for periodic testing of all students to determine the quality of their performance in relation to such standards; and

(8) Register with the examining committee, and maintain such records (available for inspection by the examining committee) and file with the examining committee such reports, notices, and certifications as may be required by the rules of the examining committee.

(Subd (b) amended effective January 1, 2007; previously amended effective April 2, 1984.)

(c) Requirements for unaccredited law schools outside the state

A law school in the United States that is outside the state of California and is not accredited by the examining committee must:

(1) Be authorized to confer professional degrees by the law of the state in which it is located;

(2) Comply with (b)(2), (3), (4), (5), (7), and (8) of this rule; and

(3) Own and maintain a library that is comparable in content to that specified in (b)(6) of this rule.

(Subd (c) amended effective January 1, 2007; previously amended effective April 2, 1984.)

(d) Registration and reports

A correspondence law school must register with the examining committee and file such reports, notices, and certifications as may be required by the rules of the examining committee concerning any person whose mailing address is in the state of California or whose application to, contract with, or correspondence with or from the law school indicates that the instruction by correspondence is for the purpose or with the intent of qualifying that person for admission to practice law in California.

(Subd (d) amended effective January 1, 2007.)

(e) Inspections

The examining committee may make such inspection of law schools not accredited by the committee or correspondence schools as may be necessary or proper to give effect to the provisions of Business and Professions Code section 6060, this rule, and the rules of the examining committee.

(Subd (e) amended effective January 1, 2007.)

(f) Application

This rule does not apply to any person who, on the effective date of the rule, had commenced the study of law in a manner authorized by Business and Professions Code section 6060(e) and registered as a law student before January 1, 1976 (as provided in Business and Professions Code section 6060(d) and otherwise satisfies the requirements of Business and Professions Code section 6060(e), provided that after January 1, 1976, credit will be given such person for any study in an unaccredited law school or by correspondence only if the school complies with the requirements of (b)(8) or (d) of this rule, whichever is applicable, and permits inspection under (e) of this rule.

(Subd (f) amended effective January 1, 2007.)

Rule 9.30 amended effective January 1, 2019; adopted as rule 957 by the Supreme Court effective October 8, 1975; previously amended effective April 2, 1984; previously amended and renumbered effective January 1, 2007.

Rule 9.31. Minimum continuing legal education

(a) Statutory authorization

This rule is adopted under Business and Professions Code section 6070.

(Subd (a) amended effective January 1, 2007.)

(b) State Bar minimum continuing legal education program

The State Bar must establish and administer a minimum continuing legal education program under rules adopted by the Board of Trustees of the State Bar. These rules may provide for carryforward of excess credit hours, staggering of the education requirement for implementation purposes, and retroactive credit for legal education.

(Subd (b) amended effective August 1, 2017; previously amended effective September 27, 2000, and January 1, 2007.)

(c) Minimum continuing legal education requirements

Each active licensee of the State Bar (1) not exempt under Business and Professions Code section 6070, (2) not a full-time employee of the

United States Government, its departments, agencies, and public corporations, acting within the scope of his or her employment, and (3) not otherwise exempt under rules adopted by the Board of Trustees of the State Bar, must, within 36-month periods designated by the State Bar, complete at least 25 hours of legal education approved by the State Bar or offered by a State Bar-approved provider. Four of those hours must address legal ethics. Licensees may be required to complete legal education in other specified areas within the 25-hour requirement under rules adopted by the State Bar. Each active licensee must report his or her compliance to the State Bar under rules adopted by the Board of Trustees of the State Bar.

(Subd (c) amended effective January 1, 2019; previously amended effective September 27, 2000, January 1, 2007, and August 1, 2017.)

(d) Failure to comply with program

A licensee of the State Bar who fails to satisfy the requirements of the State Bar's minimum continuing legal education program must be enrolled as an inactive licensee of the State Bar under rules adopted by the Board of Trustees of the State Bar.

(Subd (d) amended effective January 1, 2019; previously amended effective January 1, 2007, and August 1, 2017.)

(e) Fees and penalties

The State Bar has the authority to set and collect appropriate fees and penalties.

(Subd (e) amended effective January 1, 2007.)

(f) One-time expungement of a record of inactive enrollment for failure to comply with program

The State Bar is authorized to expunge a public record of a period of inactive enrollment for failure to comply with the minimum continuing legal education program for those licensees who meet all of the following criteria:

(1) The licensee has not on any previous occasion obtained an expungement under the terms of this rule or rule 9.6;

(2) The period of inactive enrollment was for 90 days or less;

(3) The period of inactive enrollment ended at least seven years before the date of expungement;

(4) The licensee has no other record of suspension or involuntary inactive enrollment for discipline or otherwise.

(Subd (f) amended effective January 1, 2019; adopted effective August 1, 2017.)

(g) Records to be maintained by State Bar

Under (f) of this rule, the State Bar will remove or delete the record of such period of inactive enrollment from the licensee's record. Notwithstanding any other provision of this rule, the State Bar must maintain such internal records as are necessary to apply the terms of (f) of this rule and to report to the Commission on Judicial Nominees Evaluation or appropriate governmental entities involved in judicial elections the licensee's eligibility for a judgeship under the California Constitution, article VI, section 15.

(Subd (g) amended effective January 1, 2019; adopted effective August 1, 2017.)

(h) Duty of disclosure by licensee

Expungement of the record of a licensee's period of inactive enrollment under (f) of this rule will not relieve the licensee of his or her duty to disclose the period of inactive enrollment for purpose of determining the licensee's eligibility for a judgeship under the California Constitution, article VI, section 15. For all other purposes, the record of inactive enrollment expunged under (f) of this rule is deemed not to have occurred and the licensee may answer accordingly any question relating to his or her record.

(Subd (h) amended effective January 1, 2019; adopted effective August 1, 2017.)
Rule 9.31 amended effective January 1, 2019; adopted as rule 958 effective December 6, 1990; previously amended effective December 25, 1992; previously amended by the Supreme Court effective September 27, 2000; previously amended and renumbered as rule 9.31 effective January 1, 2007; previously amended effective August 1, 2017.

Rule 9.32. New Attorney Training

(a) State Bar New Attorney Training

The State Bar must establish and administer a New Attorney Training program under rules adopted by the Board of Trustees of the State Bar, including Rules of the State Bar of California, Rules 2:140–2:144.

(Subd (a) adopted effective January 1, 2024.)

(b) State Bar New Attorney Training requirements

All new licensees of the State Bar must, by the last day of the month of their one year anniversary as a State Bar licensee, complete the New Attorney Training program and report having done so as provided in Rules of the State Bar of California, Rule 2:141.

(Subd (b) adopted effective January 1, 2024.)

(c) Failure to comply with program

A licensee of the State Bar who fails to satisfy the requirements of the State Bar New Attorney Training program will be enrolled as an inactive licensee of the State Bar under rules adopted by the Board of Trustees of the State Bar, including Rules of the State Bar of California, Rules 2:150–2:153.

(Subd (c) adopted effective January 1, 2024.)

(d) Fees and penalties

The State Bar has the authority to set and collect appropriate fees and penalties.

(Subd (d) adopted effective January 1, 2024.)
Rule 9.32 adopted effective January 1, 2024.

Division 3
Legal Specialists

Rule 9.35. Certified legal specialists

(a) Definition

A "certified specialist" is a California attorney who holds a current certificate as a specialist issued by the State Bar of California Board of Legal Specialization or any other entity approved by the State Bar to designate specialists.

(b) State Bar Legal Specialization Program

The State Bar must establish and administer a program for certifying legal specialists and may establish a program for certifying entities that certify legal specialists under rules adopted by the Board of Trustees of the State Bar.

(Subd (b) amended effective January 1, 2019; previously amended effective January 1, 2007.)

(c) Authority to practice law

No attorney may be required to obtain certification as a certified specialist as a prerequisite to practicing law in this state. Any attorney, alone or in association with any other attorney, has the right to practice in any field of law in this state and to act as counsel in every type of case, even though he or she is not certified as a specialist.

(Subd (c) amended effective January 1, 2007.)

(d) Failure to comply with program

A certified specialist who fails to comply with the requirements of the Legal Specialization Program of the State Bar will have her or his certification suspended or revoked under rules adopted by the Board of Trustees of the State Bar.

(Subd (d) amended effective January 1, 2019; previously amended effective January 1, 2007.)

(e) Fee and penalty

The State Bar has the authority to set and collect appropriate fees and penalties for this program.

(Subd (e) amended effective January 1, 2007.)

(f) Inherent power of Supreme Court

Nothing in these rules may be construed as affecting the power of the Supreme Court to exercise its inherent jurisdiction over the practice of law in California.

(Subd (f) amended effective January 1, 2007.)
Rule 9.35 amended effective January 1, 2019; adopted as rule 983.5 effective January 1, 1996; previously amended and renumbered effective January 1, 2007.

Division 4
Appearances and Practice by Individuals Who Are Not Licensees of the State Bar of California

Rule 9.40. Counsel *pro hac vice*
Rule 9.41. Appearances by military counsel
Rule 9.41.1. Registered military spouse attorney
Rule 9.42. Certified law students
Rule 9.43. Out-of-state attorney arbitration counsel
Rule 9.44. Registered foreign legal consultant
Rule 9.45. Registered legal aid attorneys
Rule 9.46. Registered in-house counsel
Rule 9.47. Attorneys practicing law temporarily in California as part of litigation

Rule 9.48. Nonlitigating attorneys temporarily in California to provide legal services

Rule 9.49. Provisional Licensure of 2020 Law School Graduates

Rule 9.49.1. Provisional Licensure with Pathway to Full Licensure for Certain Individuals

Rule 9.40. Counsel *pro hac vice*

(a) Eligibility

A person who is not a licensee of the State Bar of California but who is an attorney in good standing of and eligible to practice before the bar of any United States court or the highest court in any state, territory, or insular possession of the United States, and who has been retained to appear in a particular cause pending in a court of this state, may in the discretion of such court be permitted upon written application to appear as counsel *pro hac vice*, provided that an active licensee of the State Bar of California is associated as attorney of record. No person is eligible to appear as counsel *pro hac vice* under this rule if the person is:

(1) A resident of the State of California;

(2) Regularly employed in the State of California; or

(3) Regularly engaged in substantial business, professional, or other activities in the State of California.

(Subd (a) amended effective January 1, 2019; previously amended effective January 1, 2007.)

(b) Repeated appearances as a cause for denial

Absent special circumstances, repeated appearances by any person under this rule is a cause for denial of an application.

(Subd (b) lettered effective January 1, 2007; adopted as part of subd (a) effective September 13, 1972.)

(c) Application

(1) *Application in superior court*

A person desiring to appear as counsel *pro hac vice* in a superior court must file with the court a verified application together with proof of service by mail in accordance with Code of Civil Procedure section 1013a of a copy of the application and of the notice of hearing of the application on all parties who have appeared in the cause and on the State Bar of California at its San Francisco office. The notice of hearing must be given at the time prescribed in Code of Civil Procedure section 1005 unless the court has prescribed a shorter period.

(2) *Application in Supreme Court or Court of Appeal*

An application to appear as counsel *pro hac vice* in the Supreme Court or a Court of Appeal must be made as provided in rule 8.54, with proof of service on all parties who have appeared in the cause and on the State Bar of California at its San Francisco office.

(Subd (c) amended and relettered effective January 1, 2007; adopted as part of subd (b) effective September 13, 1972; subd (b) previously amended effective October 3, 1973, September 3, 1986, January 17, 1991, and March 15, 1991.)

(d) Contents of application

The application must state:

(1) The applicant's residence and office address;

(2) The courts to which the applicant has been admitted to practice and the dates of admission;

(3) That the applicant is a licensee in good standing in those courts;

(4) That the applicant is not currently suspended or disbarred in any court;

(5) The title of each court and cause in which the applicant has filed an application to appear as counsel *pro hac vice* in this state in the preceding two years, the date of each application, and whether or not it was granted; and

(6) The name, address, and telephone number of the active licensee of the State Bar of California who is attorney of record.

(Subd (d) amended effective January 1, 2019; adopted as part of subd (b) effective September 13, 1972; subd (b) previously amended effective October 3, 1973, September 3, 1986, January 17, 1991, and March 15, 1991; previously amended and lettered effective January 1, 2007.)

(e) Fee for application

[1] The State Bar of California may set an appropriate application fee to be paid by counsel *pro hac vice*.

(Subd (e) amended effective July 24, 2024; adopted as subd (c) effective September 3, 1986; previously amended and relettered effective January 1, 2007; previously amended effective January 1, 2019.)

Rule 9.40(e) 2024 Deletes. [1] An applicant for permission to appear as counsel *pro hac vice* under this rule must pay a reasonable fee not exceeding $50 to the State Bar of California with the copy of the application and the notice of hearing that is served on the State Bar. The Board of Trustees of the State Bar of California will fix the amount of the fee:

(1) To defray the expenses of administering the provisions of this rule that are applicable to the State Bar and the incidental consequences resulting from such provisions; and

(2) Partially to defray the expenses of administering the Board's other responsibilities to enforce the provisions of the State Bar Act relating to the competent delivery of legal services and the incidental consequences resulting therefrom.

(f) Counsel *pro hac vice* subject to jurisdiction of courts and State Bar

A person permitted to appear as counsel *pro hac vice* under this rule is subject to the jurisdiction of the courts of this state with respect to the law of this state governing the conduct of attorneys to the same extent as a licensee of the State Bar of California. The counsel *pro hac vice* must familiarize himself or herself and comply with the standards of professional conduct required of licensees of the State Bar of California and will be subject to the disciplinary jurisdiction of the State Bar **of California** with respect to any of his or her acts occurring in the course of such appearance. Article 5 of chapter 4, division 3 of the Business and Professions Code and the Rules of Procedure of the State Bar govern in any investigation or proceeding conducted by the State Bar **of California** under this rule.

(Subd (f) amended effective July 24, 2024; previously relettered as subd (d) effective September 3, 1986; previously amended and relettered effective January 1, 2007; previously amended effective January 1, 2019.)

(g) Representation in cases governed by the Indian Child Welfare Act (25 U.S.C. §1903 et seq.)

(1) The requirement in (a) that the applicant associate with an active licensee of the State Bar of California does not apply to an applicant seeking to appear in a California court to represent an Indian tribe in a child custody proceeding governed by the Indian Child Welfare Act; and

(2) An applicant seeking to appear in a California court to represent an Indian tribe in a child custody proceeding governed by the Indian Child Welfare Act constitutes a special circumstance for the purposes of the restriction in (b) that an application may be denied because of repeated appearances.

(Subd (g) adopted effective January 1, 2019.)

(h) Supreme Court and Court of Appeal not precluded from permitting argument in a particular case

This rule does not preclude the Supreme Court or a Court of Appeal from permitting argument in a particular case from a person who is not a licensee of the State Bar **of California**, but who is licensed to practice in another jurisdiction and who possesses special expertise in the particular field affecting the proceeding.

(Subd (h) amended effective July 24, 2024; previously relettered as subd (e) effective September 3, 1986; previously amended and relettered as subd (g) effective January 1, 2007; previously amended and relettered as subd (h) effective January 1, 2007.)

(i) Inherent Power of Supreme Court

Nothing in this rule may be construed as affecting the power of the Supreme Court to exercise its inherent jurisdiction over the practice of law in California.

(Subd (i) adopted effective July 24, 2024.)

Rule 9.40 amended effective July 24, 2024; adopted as rule 983 by the Supreme Court effective September 13, 1972; previously amended and renumbered effective January 1, 2007; previously amended effective October 3, 1973, September 3, 1986, January 17, 1991, March 15, 1991, and January 1, 2019.

Rule 9.41. Appearances by military counsel

(a) Permission to appear

A judge advocate (as that term is defined at 10 U.S.C. §801(13)) who is not a licensee of the State Bar of California but who is an attorney in good standing of and eligible to practice before the bar of any United States court or of the highest court in any state, territory, or insular possession of the United States may, in the discretion of a court of this state, be permitted to appear in that court to represent a person in the military service in a particular cause pending before that court, under the Servicemembers Civil Relief Act, 50 United States Code Appendix section 501 et seq., if:

(1) The judge advocate has been made available by the cognizant Judge Advocate General (as that term is defined at 10 United States Code section 801(1)) or a duly designated representative; and

(2) The court finds that retaining civilian counsel likely would cause substantial hardship for the person in military service or that person's family; and

(3) The court appoints a judge advocate as attorney to represent the person in military service under the Servicemembers Civil Relief Act.

Under no circumstances is the determination of availability of a judge advocate to be made by any court within this state, or reviewed by any court of this state. In determining the likelihood of substantial hardship as a result of the retention of civilian counsel, the court may take judicial notice of the prevailing pay scales for persons in the military service.

(Subd (a) amended effective January 1, 2019; previously amended effective January 1, 2007.)

(b) Notice to parties

The clerk of the court considering appointment of a judge advocate under this rule must provide written notice of that fact to all parties who have appeared in the cause. A copy of the notice, together with proof of service by mail in accordance with Code of Civil Procedure section 1013a, must be filed by the clerk of the court. Any party who has appeared in the matter may file a written objection to the appointment within 10 days of the date on which notice was given unless the court has prescribed a shorter period. If the court determines to hold a hearing in relation to the appointment, notice of the hearing must be given at least 10 days before the date designated for the hearing unless the court has prescribed a shorter period.

(Subd (b) amended effective January 1, 2007.)

(c) Appearing judge advocate subject to court and State Bar jurisdiction

A judge advocate permitted to appear under this rule is subject to the jurisdiction of the courts of this state with respect to the law of this state governing the conduct of attorneys to the same extent as a licensee of the State Bar of California. The judge advocate must become familiar with and comply with the standards of professional conduct required of licensees of the State Bar of California and is subject to the disciplinary jurisdiction of the State Bar of California. Division 3, chapter 4, article 5 of the Business and Professions Code and the Rules of Procedure of the State Bar of California govern any investigation or proceeding conducted by the State Bar under this rule.

(Subd (c) amended effective January 1, 2019; previously amended effective January 1, 2007.)

(d) Appearing judge advocate subject to rights and obligations of State Bar licensees concerning professional privileges

A judge advocate permitted to appear under this rule is subject to the rights and obligations with respect to attorney-client privilege, work-product privilege, and other professional privileges to the same extent as a licensee of the State Bar of California.

(Subd (d) amended effective January 1, 2019; previously amended effective January 1, 2007.)

Rule 9.41 amended effective January 1, 2019; adopted as rule 983.1 by the Supreme Court effective February 19, 1992; adopted by the Judicial Council effective February 21, 1992; previously amended and renumbered effective January 1, 2007.

Rule 9.41.1. Registered military spouse attorney

(a) Definitions

(1) "Military Spouse Attorney" means an active licensee in good standing of the bar of a United States state, jurisdiction, possession, territory, or dependency and who is married to, in a civil union with, or a registered domestic partner of, a Service Member.

(2) "Service Member" means an active duty member of the United States Uniformed Services who has been ordered stationed within California.

(3) "Active licensee in good standing of the bar of a United States state, jurisdiction, possession, territory, or dependency" means an attorney who:

(A) Is a licensee in good standing of the entity governing the practice of law in each jurisdiction in which the attorney is licensed to practice law, who has not been disbarred, has not resigned with charges pending, or is not suspended from practicing law for disciplinary misconduct in any other jurisdiction; and

(B) Remains an active licensee in good standing of the entity governing the practice of law in at least one United States state, jurisdiction, possession, territory, or dependency other than California while practicing law as a registered military spouse attorney in California.

(Subd (a) adopted effective March 1, 2019.)

(b) Scope of Practice

Subject to all applicable rules, regulations, and statutes, an attorney practicing law under this rule is permitted to practice law in California, under supervision, in all forms of legal practice that are permissible for a licensed attorney of the State Bar of California, including pro bono legal services.

(Subd (b) adopted effective March 1, 2019.)

(c) Requirements

For an attorney to qualify to practice law under this rule, the attorney must:

(1) Be an active licensee in good standing of the bar of a United States state, jurisdiction, possession, territory, or dependency;

(2) Be married to, be in a civil union with, or be a registered domestic partner of, a Service Member, except that the attorney may continue to practice as a registered military spouse attorney for one year after the termination of the marriage, civil union, or domestic partnership as provided in (i)(1)(G);

(3) Reside in California;

(4) Meet all of the requirements for admission to the State Bar of California, except that the attorney:

(A) Need not take the California bar examination or the Multistate Professional Responsibility Examination; and

(B) May practice law while awaiting the result of his or her Application for Determination of Moral Character from the State Bar of California.

(5) Comply with the rules adopted by the Board of Trustees relating to the State Bar Registered Military Spouse Attorney Program;

(6) Practice law under the supervision of an attorney who is an active licensee in good standing of the State Bar of California who has been admitted to the practice of law for two years or more;

(7) Abide by all of the laws and rules that govern licensees of the State Bar of California, including the Minimum Continuing Legal Education ("MCLE") requirements;

(8) Satisfy in his or her first year of practice under this rule all of the MCLE requirements, including ethics education, that licensees of the State Bar of California must complete every three years and, thereafter, satisfy the MCLE requirements for the registered military spouse attorney's compliance group as set forth in State Bar Rules 2.70 and 2.71. If the registered military spouse attorney's compliance group is required to report in less than thirty-six months, the MCLE requirements will be reduced proportionally ; and

(9) Not have taken and failed the California bar examination within five years immediately preceding initial application to register under this rule.

(Subd (c) adopted effective March 1, 2019.)

(d) Application

The attorney must comply with the following registration requirements:

(1) Register as an attorney applicant, file an Application for Determination of Moral Character with the Committee of Bar Examiners, and comply with Rules of Court, rule 9.9.5, governing attorney fingerprinting;

(2) Submit to the State Bar of California a declaration signed by the attorney agreeing that he or she will be subject to the disciplinary authority of the Supreme Court of California and the State Bar of California and attesting that he or she will not practice law in California other than under supervision of a California attorney during the time he or she practices law as a military spouse attorney in California; and

(3) Submit to the State Bar of California a declaration signed by a qualifying supervising attorney. The declaration must attest:

(A) that the applicant will be supervised as specified in this rule; and

(B) that the supervising attorney assumes professional responsibility for any work performed by the registered military spouse attorney under this rule.

(Subd (d) adopted effective March 1, 2019.)

(e) Application and Registration Fees

The State Bar of California may set appropriate application fees and initial and annual registration fees to be paid by registered military spouse attorney.

(Subd (e) adopted effective March 1, 2019.)

(f) State Bar Registered Military Spouse Attorney Program

The State Bar may establish and administer a program for registering registered military spouse attorneys under rules adopted by the Board of Trustees of the State Bar.

(Subd (f) adopted effective March 1, 2019.)

(g) Supervision

To meet the requirements of this rule, an attorney supervising a registered military spouse attorney:

(1) Must have practiced law as a full-time occupation for at least four years in any United States jurisdiction;

(2) Must have actively practiced law in California for at least two years immediately preceding the time of supervision and be a licensee in good standing of the State Bar of California;

(3) Must assume professional responsibility for any work that the registered military spouse attorney performs under the supervising attorney's supervision;

(4) Must assist, counsel, and provide direct supervision of the registered military spouse attorney in the activities authorized by this rule, approve in writing any appearance in court, deposition, arbitration or any proceeding by the registered military spouse attorney, and review such activities with the supervised military spouse attorney, to the extent required for the protection of the client or customer;

(5) Must read, approve, and personally sign any pleadings, briefs, or other similar documents prepared by the registered military spouse attorney before their filing, and must read and approve any documents prepared by the registered military spouse attorney before their submission to any other party;

(6) Must agree to assume control of the work of the registered military spouse attorney in the event the registration of the military spouse attorney is terminated, in accordance with applicable laws; and

(7) May, in his or her absence, designate another attorney meeting the requirements of (g)(1) through (g)(6) to provide the supervision required under this rule.

(Subd (g) adopted effective March 1, 2019.)

(h) Duration of Practice

A registered military spouse attorney must renew his or her registration annually and may practice for no more than a total of five years under this rule.

(Subd (h) adopted effective March 1, 2019.)

(i) Termination of Military Spouse Attorney Registration

(1) Registration as a registered military spouse attorney is terminated

(A) upon receipt of a determination by the Committee of Bar Examiners that the registered military spouse attorney is not of good moral character;

(B) for failure to annually register as a registered military spouse attorney and submit any related fee set by the State Bar;

(C) for failure to comply with the Minimum Continuing Legal Education requirements and to pay any related fee set by the State Bar;

(D) if the registered military spouse attorney no longer meets the requirements under (a)(3) of this section;

(E) upon the imposition of any discipline by the State Bar of California or any other professional or occupational licensing authority, including administrative or stayed suspension;

(F) for failure to otherwise comply with these rules or with the laws or standards of professional conduct applicable to a licensee of the State Bar of California;

(G) if the Service Member is no longer an active member of the United States Uniformed Services or is transferred to another state, jurisdiction, territory outside of California, except that if the Service Member has been assigned to an unaccompanied or remote assignment with no dependents authorized, the military spouse attorney may continue to practice pursuant to the provisions of this rule until the Service Member is assigned to a location with dependents authorized; or

(H) one year after the date of termination of the registered military spouse attorney's marriage, civil union, or registered domestic partnership.

(2) The supervising attorney of registered military spouse attorney suspended by these rules will assume the work of the registered military spouse attorney in accordance with applicable laws.

(Subd (i) adopted effective March 1, 2019.)

(j) Inherent Power of Supreme Court

Nothing in this rule may be construed as affecting the power of the Supreme Court of California to exercise its inherent jurisdiction over the practice of law in California.

(Subd (j) adopted effective March 1, 2019.)

(k) Effect of Rule on Multijurisdictional Practice

Nothing in this rule limits the scope of activities permissible under existing law by attorneys who are not licensees of the State Bar of California.

(Subd (k) adopted effective March 1, 2019.)

Rule 9.41.1 adopted by the Supreme Court effective March 1, 2019.

Rule 9.42. Certified law students

(a) Definitions

(1) A "certified law student" is a law student who has a currently effective certificate of registration as a certified law student from the State Bar.

(2) A "supervising attorney" is a licensee of the State Bar who agrees to supervise a certified law student under rules established by the State Bar and whose name appears on the application for certification.

(Subd (a) amended effective January 1, 2019; previously amended effective January 1, 2007.)

(b) State Bar certified law student program

The State Bar must establish and administer a program for registering law students under rules adopted by the Board of Trustees of the State Bar.

(Subd (b) amended effective January 1, 2019; previously amended effective January 1, 2007.)

(c) Eligibility for certification

To be eligible to become a certified law student, an applicant must:

(1) Have successfully completed one full year of studies (minimum of 270 hours) at a law school accredited by the American Bar Association or the State Bar of California, or both, or have passed the first year law students' examination;

(2) Have been accepted into, and be enrolled in, the second, third, or fourth year of law school in good academic standing or have graduated from law school, subject to the time period limitations specified in the rules adopted by the Board of Trustees of the State Bar; and

(3) Have either successfully completed or be currently enrolled in and attending academic courses in evidence and civil procedure.

(Subd (c) amended effective January 1, 2019.)

(d) Permitted activities

Subject to all applicable rules, regulations, and statutes, a certified law student may:

(1) Negotiate for and on behalf of the client subject to final approval thereof by the supervising attorney or give legal advice to the client, provided that the certified law student:

(A) Obtains the approval of the supervising attorney to engage in the activities;

(B) Obtains the approval of the supervising attorney regarding the legal advice to be given or plan of negotiation to be undertaken by the certified law student; and

(C) Performs the activities under the general supervision of the supervising attorney;

(2) Appear on behalf of the client in depositions, provided that the certified law student:

(A) Obtains the approval of the supervising attorney to engage in the activity;

(B) Performs the activity under the direct and immediate supervision and in the personal presence of the supervising attorney (or, exclusively in the case of government agencies, any deputy, assistant, or other staff attorney authorized and designated by the supervising attorney); and

(C) Obtains a signed consent form from the client on whose behalf the certified law student acts (or, exclusively in the case of government agencies, from the chief counsel or prosecuting attorney) approving the performance of such acts by such certified law student or generally by any certified law student;

(3) Appear on behalf of the client in any public trial, hearing, arbitration, or proceeding, or before any arbitrator, court, public agency, referee, magistrate, commissioner, or hearing officer, to the extent approved by such arbitrator, court, public agency, referee, magistrate, commissioner, or hearing officer, provided that the certified law student:

(A) Obtains the approval of the supervising attorney to engage in the activity;

(B) Performs the activity under the direct and immediate supervision and in the personal presence of the supervising attorney (or, exclusively in the case of government agencies, any deputy, assistant, or other staff attorney authorized and designated by the supervising attorney);

(C) Obtains a signed consent form from the client on whose behalf the certified law student acts (or, exclusively in the case of government agencies, from the chief counsel or prosecuting attorney) approving the performance of such acts by such certified law student or generally by any certified law student; and

(D) As a condition to such appearance, either presents a copy of the consent form to the arbitrator, court, public agency, referee, magistrate, commissioner, or hearing officer, or files a copy of the consent form in the court case file; and

(4) Appear on behalf of a government agency in the prosecution of criminal actions classified as infractions or other such minor criminal offenses with a maximum penalty or a fine equal to the maximum fine for infractions in California, including any public trial:

(A) Subject to approval by the court, commissioner, referee, hearing officer, or magistrate presiding at such public trial; and

(B) Without the personal appearance of the supervising attorney or any deputy, assistant, or other staff attorney authorized and designated by the supervising attorney, but only if the supervising attorney or the designated attorney has approved in writing the performance of such acts by the certified law student and is immediately available to attend the proceeding.

(Subd (d) amended effective January 1, 2007.)

(e) Failure to comply with program

A certified law student who fails to comply with the requirements of the State Bar certified law student program must have his or her certification withdrawn under rules adopted by the Board of Trustees of the State Bar.

(Subd (e) amended effective January 1, 2019; previously amended effective January 1, 2007.)

(f) Fee and penalty

The State Bar has the authority to set and collect appropriate fees and penalties for this program.

(Subd (f) amended effective January 1, 2007.)

(g) Inherent power of Supreme Court

Nothing in these rules may be construed as affecting the power of the Supreme Court to exercise its inherent jurisdiction over the practice of law in California.

(Subd (g) amended effective January 1, 2007.)

Rule 9.42 amended effective January 1, 2019; adopted as rule 983.2 by the Supreme Court effective December 29, 1993; previously amended and renumbered effective January 1, 2007.

Rule 9.43. Out-of-state attorney arbitration counsel

(a) Definition

An "out-of-state attorney arbitration counsel" is an attorney who is:

(1) Not a licensee of the State Bar of California but who is an attorney in good standing of and eligible to practice before the bar of any United States court or the highest court in any state, territory, or insular possession of the United States, and who has been retained to appear in the course of, or in connection with, an arbitration proceeding in this state;

(2) Has served a certificate in accordance with the requirements of Code of Civil Procedure section 1282.4 on the arbitrator, the arbitrators, or the arbitral forum, the State Bar of California, and all other parties and counsel in the arbitration whose addresses are known to the attorney; and

(3) Whose appearance has been approved by the arbitrator, the arbitrators, or the arbitral forum.

(Subd (a) amended effective January 1, 2019; previously amended effective January 1, 2007.)

(b) State Bar out-of-state attorney arbitration counsel program

The State Bar of California must establish and administer a program to implement the State Bar of California's responsibilities under Code of Civil Procedure section 1282.4. The State Bar of California's program may be operative only as long as the applicable provisions of Code of Civil Procedure section 1282.4 remain in effect.

(Subd (b) amended effective January 1, 2007.)

(c) Eligibility to appear as an out-of-state attorney arbitration counsel

To be eligible to appear as an out-of-state attorney arbitration counsel, an attorney must comply with all of the applicable provisions of Code of Civil Procedure section 1282.4 and the requirements of this rule and the related rules and regulations adopted by the State Bar of California.

(Subd (c) amended effective January 1, 2007.)

(d) Discipline

An out-of-state attorney arbitration counsel who files a certificate containing false information or who otherwise fails to comply with the standards of professional conduct required of licensees of the State Bar of California is subject to the disciplinary jurisdiction of the State Bar **of California** with respect to any of his or her acts occurring in the course of the arbitration.

(Subd (d) amended effective July 24, 2024; previously amended effective January 1, 2007; and January 1, 2019.)

(e) Disqualification

Failure to timely file and serve a certificate or, absent special circumstances, appearances in multiple separate arbitration matters are grounds for disqualification from serving in the arbitration in which the certificate was filed.

(Subd (e) amended effective January 1, 2007.)

(f) Fee

[1] The State Bar of California may set an appropriate application fee to be paid by the out-of-state attorney arbitration counsel.

(Subd (f) amended effective July 24, 2024; previously amended effective January 1, 2007.)

Rule 9.43(f) 2024 Deletes. [1] Out-of-state attorney arbitration counsel must pay a reasonable fee not exceeding $50 to the State Bar of California with the copy of the certificate that is served on the State Bar.

(g) Inherent power of Supreme Court

Nothing in [1] **this rule** may be construed as affecting the power of the Supreme Court to exercise its inherent jurisdiction over the practice of law in California.

(Subd (g) amended effective July 24, 2024; previously amended effective January 1, 2007.)

Rule 9.43(g) 2024 Deletes. [1] these rules

Rule 9.43 amended effective July 24, 2024; adopted as rule 983.4 by the Supreme Court effective July 1, 1999; previously amended and renumbered effective January 1, 2007; previously amended effective January 1, 2019.

Rule 9.44. Registered foreign legal consultant

(a) Definition

A "registered foreign legal consultant" is a person who:

(1) Is admitted to practice and is in good standing as an attorney or counselor-at-law or the equivalent in a foreign country; and

(2) Has a currently effective certificate of registration as a registered foreign legal consultant from the State Bar.

(Subd (a) amended effective January 1, 2007.)

(b) State Bar registered foreign legal consultant program

The State Bar must establish and administer a program for registering foreign attorneys or counselors-at-law or the equivalent under rules adopted by the Board of Trustees of the State Bar.

(Subd (b) amended effective January 1, 2019; previously amended effective January 1, 2007.)

(c) Eligibility for certification

To be eligible to become a registered foreign legal consultant, an applicant must:

(1) Present satisfactory proof that the applicant has been admitted to practice and has been in good standing as an attorney or counselor-at-law or the equivalent in a foreign country for at least four of the six years immediately preceding the application and, while so admitted, has actually practiced the law of that country;

(2) Present satisfactory proof that the applicant possesses the good moral character requisite for a person to be licensed as a licensee of the State Bar of California and proof of compliance with California Rules of Court, rule 9.9.5, governing attorney fingerprinting;

(3) Agree to comply with the provisions of the rules adopted by the Board of Trustees of the State Bar relating to security for claims against a foreign legal consultant by his or her clients;

(4) Agree to comply with the provisions of the rules adopted by the Board of Trustees of the State Bar relating to maintaining an address of record for State Bar purposes;

(5) Agree to notify the State Bar of any change in his or her status in any jurisdiction where he or she is admitted to practice or of any discipline with respect to such admission;

(6) Agree to be subject to the jurisdiction of the courts of this state with respect to the laws of the State of California governing the conduct of attorneys, to the same extent as a licensee of the State Bar of California;

(7) Agree to become familiar with and comply with the standards of professional conduct required of licensees of the State Bar of California;

(8) Agree to be subject to the disciplinary jurisdiction of the State Bar of California;

(9) Agree to be subject to the rights and obligations with respect to attorney client privilege, work-product privilege, and other professional privileges, to the same extent as attorneys admitted to practice law in California; and

(10) Agree to comply with the laws of the State of California, the rules and regulations of the State Bar of California, and these rules.

(Subd (c) amended effective January 1, 2019; previously amended effective January 1, 2007.)

(d) Authority to practice law

Subject to all applicable rules, regulations, and statutes, a registered foreign legal consultant may render legal services in California, except that he or she may not:

(1) Appear for a person other than himself or herself as attorney in any court, or before any magistrate or other judicial officer, in this state or prepare pleadings or any other papers or issue subpoenas in any action or proceeding brought in any court or before any judicial officer;

(2) Prepare any deed, mortgage, assignment, discharge, lease, or any other instrument affecting title to real estate located in the United States;

(3) Prepare any will or trust instrument affecting the disposition on death of any property located in the United States and owned by a resident or any instrument relating to the administration of a decedent's estate in the United States;

(4) Prepare any instrument in respect of the marital relations, rights, or duties of a resident of the United States, or the custody or care of the children of a resident; or

(5) Otherwise render professional legal advice on the law of the State of California, any other state of the United States, the District of Columbia, the United States, or of any jurisdiction other than the jurisdiction named in satisfying the requirements of (c) of this rule, whether rendered incident to preparation of legal instruments or otherwise.

(Subd (d) amended effective January 1, 2007.)

(e) Failure to comply with program

A registered foreign legal consultant who fails to comply with the requirements of the State Bar Registered Foreign Legal Consultant Program will have her or his certification suspended or revoked under rules adopted by the Board of Trustees of the State Bar.

(Subd (e) amended effective January 1, 2019; previously amended effective January 1, 2007.)

(f) Fee and penalty

The State Bar has the authority to set and collect appropriate fees and penalties for this program.

(Subd (f) amended effective January 1, 2007.)

(g) Inherent power of Supreme Court

Nothing in these rules may be construed as affecting the power of the Supreme Court to exercise its inherent jurisdiction over the practice of law in California.

(Subd (g) amended effective January 1, 2007.)

Rule 9.44 amended effective January 1, 2019; adopted as rule 988 effective December 1, 1993; previously amended and renumbered effective January 1, 2007.

Rule 9.45. Registered legal aid attorneys

(a) Definitions

The following definitions apply in this rule:

(1) "Eligible legal aid organization" means any of the following:

(A) A nonprofit entity in good standing in California and in the state in which it is incorporated, if other than California, that provides legal aid in civil matters, including family law and immigration law, to indigent and disenfranchised persons, especially underserved client groups, such as the elderly, persons with disabilities, people of color, juveniles, and limited English proficient persons; or

(B) A nonprofit law school approved by the American Bar Association located in California or accredited by the State Bar of California that provides legal aid as described above in subdivision (A).

(C) Entities that receive IOLTA funds pursuant to Business and Professions Code, section 6210, et seq., are deemed to be eligible legal aid organizations.

(2) "Active licensee in good standing of the bar of a United States state, jurisdiction, possession, territory, or dependency" means an attorney who:

(A) Is a licensee in good standing of the entity governing the practice of law in each jurisdiction in which the attorney is licensed to practice law, who has not been disbarred, has not resigned with charges pending, or is not suspended from practicing law for disciplinary misconduct in any other jurisdiction; and

(B) Remains an active licensee in good standing of the entity governing the practice of law in at least one United States state, jurisdiction, possession, territory, or dependency other than California while practicing law as a registered legal aid attorney in California.

(Subd (a) amended effective March 1, 2019; adopted as subd (j) effective November 15, 2004; previously relettered effective January 1, 2007; previously amended effective January 1, 2019.)

(b) Scope of practice

Subject to all applicable rules, regulations, and statutes, an attorney practicing law under this rule may practice law in California only while working, with or without pay, at an eligible legal aid organization, as defined in this rule, and, at that institution and only on behalf of its clients or customers, may engage, under supervision, in all forms of legal practice that are permissible for a licensee of the State Bar of California.

(Subd (b) amended effective March 1, 2019; adopted as subd (a) effective November 15, 2004; previously amended and relettered effective January 1, 2007; previously amended effective January 1, 2019.)

(c) Requirements

For an attorney to qualify to practice law under this rule, the attorney must:

(1) Be an active licensee in good standing of the bar of a United States state, jurisdiction, possession, territory, or dependency;

(2) Meet all of the requirements for admission to the State Bar of California, except that the attorney:

(A) Need not take the California bar examination or the Multistate Professional Responsibility Examination; and

(B) May practice law while awaiting the result of his or her Application for Determination of Moral Character;

(3) Comply with the rules adopted by the Board of Trustees relating to the State Bar Registered Legal Aid Attorney Program;

(4) Practice law under the supervision of an attorney who is employed by the eligible legal aid organization and who is a licensee in good standing of the State Bar of California;

(5) Abide by all of the laws and rules that govern licensees of the State Bar of California, including the Minimum Continuing Legal Education (MCLE) requirements;

(6) Satisfy in his or her first year of practice under this rule all of the MCLE requirements, including ethics education, that licensees of the State Bar of California must complete every three years and, thereafter, satisfy the MCLE requirements for the registered legal aid attorney's compliance group as set forth in State Bar Rules 2.70 and 2.71. If the registered legal aid attorney's compliance group is required to report in less than thirty-six months, the MCLE requirements will be reduced proportionally; and

(7) Not have taken and failed the California bar examination within five years immediately preceding initial application to register under this rule.

(Subd (c) amended and renumbered effective March 1, 2019; adopted as subd (b) effective November 15, 2004; previously relettered effective January 1, 2007; previously amended effective January 1, 2019.)

(d) Application

The attorney must comply with the following registration requirements:

(1) Register as a legal aid attorney; submit a separate application for each eligible legal aid organization; file an Application for Determination of Moral Character with the State Bar of California; and comply with Rules of Court, rule 9.9.5, governing attorney fingerprinting;

(2) Submit to the State Bar of California a declaration signed by the attorney agreeing that he or she will be subject to the disciplinary authority of the Supreme Court of California and the State Bar of California and attesting that he or she will not practice law in California other than under supervision of an attorney at an eligible legal aid organization during the time he or she practices law as a registered legal aid attorney in California; and

(3) Submit to the State Bar of California a declaration signed by a qualifying supervisor from each eligible legal aid organization in California. The declaration must attest:

(A) that the applicant will work, with or without pay, as an attorney for the organization;

(B) that the applicant will be supervised as specified in this rule;

(C) that the eligible legal aid organization and the supervising attorney assume professional responsibility for any work performed by the applicant under this rule;

(D) that the organization will notify the State Bar of California within 30 days of the cessation of the applicant's employment with that employer in California; and

(E) that the person signing the declaration believes, to the best of his or her knowledge after reasonable inquiry, that the applicant qualifies for registration under this rule and is an individual of good moral character.

(Subd (d) amended effective March 1, 2019; adopted as subd (c) effective November 15, 2004; previously relettered effective January 1, 2007.)

(e) Duration of practice

A registered legal aid attorney must renew his or her registration annually and may practice for no more than a total of five years under this rule.

(Subd (e) amended effective March 1, 2019; adopted as subd (d) effective November 15, 2004; previously relettered effective January 1, 2007.)

(f) Application and registration fees

The State Bar of California may set appropriate application fees and initial and annual registration fees to be paid by registered legal aid attorneys.

(Subd (f) amended effective March 1, 2019; adopted as subd (e) effective November 15, 2004; previously amended and relettered effective January 1, 2007.)

(g) State Bar Registered Legal Aid Attorney Program

The State Bar may establish and administer a program for registering California legal aid attorneys under rules adopted by the Board of Trustees of the State Bar.

(Subd (g) amended effective March 1, 2019; adopted as subd (f) effective November 15, 2004; previously relettered effective January 1, 2007; previously amended effective January 1, 2019.)

(h) Supervision

To meet the requirements of this rule, an attorney supervising a registered legal aid attorney:

(1) Must have practiced law as a full-time occupation for at least four years in any United States jurisdiction;

(2) Must have actively practiced law in California for at least two years immediately preceding the time of supervision and be a licensee in good standing of the State Bar of California;

(3) Must assume professional responsibility for any work that the registered legal aid attorney performs under the supervising attorney's supervision;

(4) Must assist, counsel, and provide direct supervision of the registered legal aid attorney in the activities authorized by this rule, approve in writing any appearance in court, deposition, arbitration or any proceeding by the registered legal aid attorney, and review such activities with the supervised registered legal aid attorney, to the extent required for the protection of the client or customer;

(5) Must read, approve, and personally sign any pleadings, briefs, or other similar documents prepared by the registered legal aid attorney before their filing, and must read and approve any documents prepared by the registered legal aid attorney before their submission; and

(6) May, in his or her absence, designate another attorney meeting the requirements of (1) through (5) to provide the supervision required under this rule.

(Subd (h) amended and renumbered effective March 1, 2019; adopted as subd (g) effective November 15, 2004; previously relettered effective January 1, 2007; previously amended effective January 1, 2019.)

(i) Inherent power of Supreme Court

Nothing in this rule may be construed as affecting the power of the Supreme Court of California to exercise its inherent jurisdiction over the practice of law in California.

(Subd (i) amended and relettered effective January 1, 2007; adopted as subd (h) effective November 15, 2004.)

(j) Effect of rule on multijurisdictional practice

Nothing in this rule limits the scope of activities permissible under existing law by attorneys who are not licensees of the State Bar of California.

(Subd (j) amended effective January 1, 2019; previously relettered effective January 1, 2007; adopted as subd (i) effective November 15, 2004.)

Rule 9.45 amended effective March 1, 2019; adopted as rule 964 by the Supreme Court effective November 15, 2004; previously amended and renumbered effective January 1, 2007; previously amended effective January 1, 2019.

Rule 9.46. Registered in-house counsel

(a) Definitions

The following definitions apply to terms used in this rule:

(1) "Qualifying institution" means a corporation, a partnership, an association, or other legal entity, including its subsidiaries and organizational affiliates, which has an office located in California. Neither a governmental entity nor an entity that provides legal services to others can be a qualifying institution for purposes of this rule. A qualifying institution must:

(A) Employ at least 5 full time employees; or

(B) Employ in California an attorney who is an active licensee in good standing of the State Bar of California.

(2) "Active licensee in good standing of the bar of a United States state, jurisdiction, possession, territory, or dependency" means an attorney who:

(A) Is a licensee in good standing of the entity governing the practice of law in each jurisdiction in which the attorney is licensed to practice law, who has not been disbarred, has not resigned with charges pending, or is not suspended from practicing law for disciplinary misconduct in any other jurisdiction; and

(B) Remains an active licensee in good standing of the entity governing the practice of law in at least one United States state, jurisdiction, possession, territory, or dependency, other than California, while practicing law as registered in-house counsel in California.

(Subd (a) amended effective March 1, 2019; adopted as subd (j) effective November 15, 2004; previously relettered effective January 1, 2007; previously amended effective January 1, 2019.)

(b) Scope of practice

Subject to all applicable rules, regulations, and statutes, an attorney practicing law under this rule is:

(1) Permitted to provide legal services in California to the qualifying institution that employs him or her;

(2) Permitted to provide *pro bono* legal services under supervision of a California attorney for either eligible legal aid organizations as defined by Rules of Court, rule 9.45(a)(1), or the qualifying institution that employs him or her;

(3) Not permitted to make court appearances in California state courts or to engage in any other activities for which *pro hac vice* admission is required if they are performed in California by an attorney who is not a licensee of the State Bar of California; and

(4) Not permitted to provide personal or individual representation to any customers, shareholders, owners, partners, officers, employees, servants, or agents of the qualifying institution, except as described in subdivision (b)(2).

(Subd (b) amended effective March 1, 2019; adopted as subd (a) effective November 15, 2004; previously amended and relettered effective January 1, 2007; previously amended effective January 1, 2019.)

(c) Requirements

For an attorney to qualify to practice law under this rule, the attorney must:

(1) Be an active licensee in good standing of the bar of a United States state, jurisdiction, possession, territory, or dependency;

(2) Meet all of the requirements for admission to the State Bar of California, except that the attorney:

(A) Need not take the California bar examination or the Multistate Professional Responsibility Examination; and

(B) May practice law while awaiting the result of his or her Application for Determination of Moral Character;

(3) Comply with the rules adopted by the Board of Trustees relating to the State Bar Registered In-House Counsel Program;

(4) Practice law exclusively for a single qualifying institution, except that, while practicing under this rule, the attorney may provide *pro bono* services through eligible legal aid organizations;

(5) Abide by all of the laws and rules that govern licensees of the State Bar of California, including the Minimum Continuing Legal Education (MCLE) requirements;

(6) Satisfy in his or her first year of practice under this rule all of the MCLE requirements, including ethics education, that licensees of the State Bar of California must complete every three years and, thereafter, satisfy the MCLE requirements for the registered in-house counsel's compliance group as set forth in State Bar Rules 2.70 and 2.71. If the registered in-house counsel's compliance group is required to report in less than thirty-six months, the MCLE requirement will be reduced proportionally; and

(7) Reside in California.

(Subd (c) amended effective March 1, 2019; adopted as subd (b) effective November 15, 2004; previously relettered effective January 1, 2007; previously amended effective January 1, 2019.)

(d) Application

The attorney must comply with the following registration requirements:

(1) Register as an in-house counsel; submit an application for the qualifying institution; file an Application for Determination of Moral

Character with the State Bar of California; and comply with Rules of Court, rule 9.9.5, governing attorney fingerprinting;

(2) Submit a supplemental form identifying the eligible legal aid organizations as defined by Rules of Court, rule 9.45(a)(1) and the supervising attorney, through which an in-house counsel intends to provide *pro bono* services, if applicable;

(3) Submit to the State Bar of California a declaration signed by the attorney agreeing that he or she will be subject to the disciplinary authority of the Supreme Court of California and the State Bar of California and attesting that he or she will not practice law in California other than on behalf of the qualifying institution during the time he or she is registered in-house counsel in California, except if supervised, a registered in-house counsel may provide *pro bono* services through an eligible legal aid organization; and

(4) Submit to the State Bar of California a declaration signed by an officer, a director, or a general counsel of the applicant's employer, on behalf of the applicant's employer. The declaration must attest:

(A) that the applicant is employed as an attorney for the employer;

(B) that the nature of the employment conforms to the requirements of this rule;

(C) that the employer will notify the State Bar of California within 30 days of the cessation of the applicant's employment in California; and

(D) that the person signing the declaration believes, to the best of his or her knowledge after reasonable inquiry, that the applicant qualifies for registration under this rule and is an individual of good moral character.

(Subd (d) amended effective March 1, 2019; adopted as subd (c) effective November 15, 2004; previously relettered effective January 1, 2007.)

(e) Duration of practice

A registered in-house counsel must renew his or her registration annually. There is no limitation on the number of years in-house counsel may register under this rule. Registered in-house counsel may practice law under this rule only for as long as he or she remains employed by the same qualifying institution that provided the declaration in support of his or her application. If an attorney practicing law as registered in-house counsel leaves the employment of his or her employer or changes employers, he or she must notify the State Bar of California within 30 days. If an attorney wishes to practice law under this rule for a new employer, he or she must first register as in-house counsel for that employer.

(Subd (e) amended and relettered effective January 1, 2007; adopted as subd (d) effective November 15, 2004.)

(f) Application and registration fees

The State Bar of California may set appropriate application fees and initial and annual registration fees to be paid by registered in-house counsel.

(Subd (f) relettered effective March 1, 2019; adopted as subd (f) effective November 15, 2004; previously amended and relettered as subd (g) effective January 1, 2007.)

(g) State Bar Registered In-House Counsel Program

The State Bar must establish and administer a program for registering California in-house counsel under rules adopted by the Board of Trustees.

(Subd (g) relettered effective March 1, 2019; adopted as subd (g) effective November 15, 2004; previously amended and relettered as subd (h) effective January 1, 2007; previously amended effective January 1, 2019.)

(h) Inherent power of Supreme Court

Nothing in this rule may be construed as affecting the power of the Supreme Court of California to exercise its inherent jurisdiction over the practice of law in California.

(Subd (h) relettered effective March 1, 2019; adopted as subd (h) effective November 15, 2004; previously amended and relettered as subd (i) effective January 1, 2007.)

(i) Effect of rule on multijurisdictional practice

Nothing in this rule limits the scope of activities permissible under existing law by attorneys who are not licensees of the State Bar of California.

(Subd (i) relettered effective March 1, 2019; adopted as subd (i) effective November 15, 2004; previously relettered as subd (j) effective January 1, 2007; previously amended effective January 1, 2019.)

Rule 9.46 amended effective March 1, 2019; adopted as rule 965 by the Supreme Court effective November 15, 2004; previously amended and renumbered effective January 1, 2007; previously amended effective January 1, 2019.

Rule 9.47. Attorneys practicing law temporarily in California as part of litigation

(a) Definitions

The following definitions apply to the terms used in this rule:

(1) "A formal legal proceeding" means litigation, arbitration, mediation, or a legal action before an administrative decision-maker.

(2) "Authorized to appear" means the attorney is permitted to appear in the proceeding by the rules of the jurisdiction in which the formal legal proceeding is taking place or will be taking place.

(3) "Active attorney in good standing of the bar of a United States state, jurisdiction, possession, territory, or dependency" means an attorney who meets all of the following criteria:

(A) Is a licensee in good standing of the entity governing the practice of law in each jurisdiction in which the attorney is licensed to practice law;

(B) Remains an active licensee in good standing of the entity governing the practice of law in at least one United States state, jurisdiction, possession, territory, or dependency while practicing law under this rule; and

(C) Has not been disbarred, has not resigned with charges pending, or is not suspended from practicing law in any other jurisdiction.

(Subd (a) amended effective January 1, 2019; adopted as subd (g) effective November 15, 2004; previously relettered effective January 1, 2007.)

(b) Requirements

For an attorney to practice law under this rule, the attorney must:

(1) Maintain an office in a United States jurisdiction other than California and in which the attorney is licensed to practice law;

(2) Already be retained by a client in the matter for which the attorney is providing legal services in California, except that the attorney may provide legal advice to a potential client, at the potential client's request, to assist the client in deciding whether to retain the attorney;

(3) Indicate on any Web site or other advertisement that is accessible in California either that the attorney is not a licensee of the State Bar of California or that the attorney is admitted to practice law only in the states listed; and

(4) Be an active attorney in good standing of the bar of a United States state, jurisdiction, possession, territory, or dependency.

(Subd (b) amended effective January 1, 2019; adopted as subd (a) effective November 15, 2004; previously relettered effective January 1, 2007.)

(c) Permissible activities

An attorney meeting the requirements of this rule, who complies with all applicable rules, regulations, and statutes, is not engaging in the unauthorized practice of law in California if the attorney's services are part of:

(1) A formal legal proceeding that is pending in another jurisdiction and in which the attorney is authorized to appear;

(2) A formal legal proceeding that is anticipated but is not yet pending in California and in which the attorney reasonably expects to be authorized to appear;

(3) A formal legal proceeding that is anticipated but is not yet pending in another jurisdiction and in which the attorney reasonably expects to be authorized to appear; or

(4) A formal legal proceeding that is anticipated or pending and in which the attorney's supervisor is authorized to appear or reasonably expects to be authorized to appear.

The attorney whose anticipated authorization to appear in a formal legal proceeding serves as the basis for practice under this rule must seek that authorization promptly after it becomes possible to do so. Failure to seek that authorization promptly, or denial of that authorization, ends eligibility to practice under this rule.

(Subd (c) relettered effective January 1, 2007; adopted as subd (b) effective November 15, 2004.)

(d) Restrictions

To qualify to practice law in California under this rule, an attorney must not:

(1) Hold out to the public or otherwise represent that he or she is admitted to practice law in California;

(2) Establish or maintain a resident office or other systematic or continuous presence in California for the practice of law;

(3) Be a resident of California;

(4) Be regularly employed in California;

(5) Regularly engage in substantial business or professional activities in California; or

(6) Have been disbarred, have resigned with charges pending, or be suspended from practicing law in any other jurisdiction.

(Subd (d) relettered effective January 1, 2007; adopted as subd (c) effective November 15, 2004.)

(e) Conditions

By practicing law in California under this rule, an attorney agrees that he or she is providing legal services in California subject to:

(1) The jurisdiction of the State Bar of California;

(2) The jurisdiction of the courts of this state to the same extent as is a licensee of the State Bar of California; and

(3) The laws of the State of California relating to the practice of law, the State Bar Rules of Professional Conduct, the rules and regulations of the State Bar of California, and these rules.

(Subd (e) amended effective January 1, 2019; adopted as subd (d) effective November 15, 2004; previously relettered effective January 1, 2007.)

(f) Inherent power of Supreme Court

Nothing in this rule may be construed as affecting the power of the Supreme Court of California to exercise its inherent jurisdiction over the practice of law in California.

(Subd (f) amended and relettered effective January 1, 2007; adopted as subd (e) effective November 15, 2004.)

(g) Effect of rule on multijurisdictional practice

Nothing in this rule limits the scope of activities permissible under existing law by attorneys who are not licensees of the State Bar of California.

(Subd (g) amended effective January 1, 2019; adopted as subd (f) effective November 15, 2004; previously relettered effective January 1, 2007.)

Rule 9.47 amended effective January 1, 2019; adopted as rule 966 by the Supreme Court effective November 15, 2004; previously amended and renumbered effective January 1, 2007.

Rule 9.48. Nonlitigating attorneys temporarily in California to provide legal services

(a) Definitions

The following definitions apply to terms used in this rule:

(1) "A transaction or other nonlitigation matter" includes any legal matter other than litigation, arbitration, mediation, or a legal action before an administrative decision-maker.

(2) "Active attorney in good standing of the bar of a United States state, jurisdiction, possession, territory, or dependency" means an attorney who meets all of the following criteria:

(A) Is a licensee in good standing of the entity governing the practice of law in each jurisdiction in which the attorney is licensed to practice law;

(B) Remains an active attorney in good standing of the entity governing the practice of law in at least one United States state, jurisdiction, possession, territory, or dependency other than California while practicing law under this rule; and

(C) Has not been disbarred, has not resigned with charges pending, or is not suspended from practicing law in any other jurisdiction.

(Subd (a) amended effective January 1, 2019; adopted as subd (h) effective November 15, 2004; previously relettered effective January 1, 2007.)

(b) Requirements

For an attorney to practice law under this rule, the attorney must:

(1) Maintain an office in a United States jurisdiction other than California and in which the attorney is licensed to practice law;

(2) Already be retained by a client in the matter for which the attorney is providing legal services in California, except that the attorney may provide legal advice to a potential client, at the potential client's request, to assist the client in deciding whether to retain the attorney;

(3) Indicate on any Web site or other advertisement that is accessible in California either that the attorney is not a licensee of the State Bar of California or that the attorney is admitted to practice law only in the states listed; and

(4) Be an active attorney in good standing of the bar of a United States state, jurisdiction, possession, territory, or dependency.

(Subd (b) amended effective January 1, 2019; adopted as subd (a) effective November 15, 2004; previously relettered effective January 1, 2007.)

(c) Permissible activities

An attorney who meets the requirements of this rule and who complies with all applicable rules, regulations, and statutes is not engaging in the unauthorized practice of law in California if the attorney:

(1) Provides legal assistance or legal advice in California to a client concerning a transaction or other nonlitigation matter, a material aspect of which is taking place in a jurisdiction other than California and in which the attorney is licensed to provide legal services;

(2) Provides legal assistance or legal advice in California on an issue of federal law or of the law of a jurisdiction other than California to attorneys licensed to practice law in California; or

(3) Is an employee of a client and provides legal assistance or legal advice in California to the client or to the client's subsidiaries or organizational affiliates.

(Subd (c) relettered effective January 1, 2007; adopted as subd (b) effective November 15, 2004.)

(d) Restrictions

To qualify to practice law in California under this rule, an attorney must not:

(1) Hold out to the public or otherwise represent that he or she is admitted to practice law in California;

(2) Establish or maintain a resident office or other systematic or continuous presence in California for the practice of law;

(3) Be a resident of California;

(4) Be regularly employed in California;

(5) Regularly engage in substantial business or professional activities in California; or

(6) Have been disbarred, have resigned with charges pending, or be suspended from practicing law in any other jurisdiction.

(Subd (d) amended and relettered effective January 1, 2007; adopted as subd (c) effective November 15, 2004.)

(e) Conditions

By practicing law in California under this rule, an attorney agrees that he or she is providing legal services in California subject to:

(1) The jurisdiction of the State Bar of California;

(2) The jurisdiction of the courts of this state to the same extent as is a licensee of the State Bar of California; and

(3) The laws of the State of California relating to the practice of law, the State Bar Rules of Professional Conduct, the rules and regulations of the State Bar of California, and these rules.

(Subd (e) amended effective January 1, 2019; adopted as subd (d) effective November 15, 2004; previously amended and relettered effective January 1, 2007.)

(f) Scope of practice

An attorney is permitted by this rule to provide legal assistance or legal services concerning only a transaction or other nonlitigation matter.

(Subd (f) relettered effective January 1, 2007; adopted as subd (e) effective November 15, 2004.)

(g) Inherent power of Supreme Court

Nothing in this rule may be construed as affecting the power of the Supreme Court of California to exercise its inherent jurisdiction over the practice of law in California.

(Subd (g) amended and relettered effective January 1, 2007; adopted as subd (f) effective November 15, 2004.)

(h) Effect of rule on multijurisdictional practice

Nothing in this rule limits the scope of activities permissible under existing law by attorneys who are not licensees of the State Bar of California.

(Subd (h) amended effective January 1, 2019; adopted as subd (g) effective November 15, 2004; previously relettered effective January 1, 2007.)

Rule 9.48 amended effective January 1, 2019; adopted as rule 967 by the Supreme Court effective November 15, 2004; previously amended and renumbered effective January 1, 2007.

Rule 9.49. Provisional Licensure of 2020 Law School Graduates

(a) State Bar Provisional Licensure Program

(1) The State Bar shall administer a program for provisionally licensing eligible 2020 Law School Graduates through December 31, 2022. The program shall be referred to as the "Provisional Licensure Program."

(2) The Provisional Licensure Program shall terminate on December 31, 2022, unless the California Supreme Court extends that date.

(3) Upon termination of the Provisional Licensure Program, no one who was provisionally licensed pursuant to this rule shall be permitted to continue to practice as a Provisionally Licensed Lawyer, nor shall they represent that they remain provisionally licensed or are otherwise authorized to practice law in the State of California unless they have been admitted to the practice of law in California after meeting all criteria for admission including passage of the California Bar Examination, or are otherwise authorized to practice law in this state other than under this rule. The temporary authorization to practice under supervision under the Provisional Licensure Program does not confer either a plenary license or any vested or implied right to be licensed.

(Subd (a) amended effective May 26, 2022; adopted effective November 9, 2020.)

(b) Definitions

(1) A "2020 Law School Graduate" means a person who became eligible to sit for the California Bar Examination under Business and Professions Code sections 6060 and 6061 between December 1, 2019 and December 31, 2020, either by graduating from a qualifying law school with a juris doctor (J.D.) or master of laws (LLM) degree during that time period, or by otherwise meeting the legal education requirements of Business and Professions Code sections 6060 and 6061 during that time period.

(2) For purposes of this rule, a "Provisionally Licensed Lawyer" means a 2020 Law School Graduate who meets the eligibility criteria of this rule and is granted provisional licensure by the State Bar.

(3) "Supervising Lawyer" means a lawyer who meets the eligibility criteria of this rule and who supervises one or more Provisionally Licensed Lawyers.

(4) "Firm" or "law firm" means a law partnership; a professional law corporation; a lawyer acting as a sole proprietorship; an association authorized to practice law; or lawyers employed in a legal services organization or in the legal department, division, or office of a corporation, of a governmental organization, or of another organization as defined by rule 1.01 of the Rules of Professional Conduct and the commentary thereto.

(Subd (b) amended effective February 1, 2021; adopted effective November 9, 2020.)

(c) Application Requirements

(1) To participate in the Provisional Licensure Program, an applicant must complete the following application requirements no later than June 1, 2022:

(A) Submit an Application for Provisional Licensure with the State Bar, along with a fee of $75, or $50 if the employer paying the fee receives State Bar Legal Services Trust Fund grants and is a qualified legal services project or qualified support center as defined by statute. There shall be no fee for applicants whose sole use of the Provisional License will be in an unpaid volunteer capacity under the direction of the Supervising Lawyer;

(B) Submit to the State Bar a declaration signed by the applicant agreeing that the applicant will be subject to the disciplinary authority of the Supreme Court of California and the State Bar with respect to the laws of the State of California and governing the conduct of lawyers, and attesting that the applicant will not practice California law other than under the supervision of a Supervising Lawyer during the time the applicant is provisionally licensed under this rule; and attesting that the applicant will not practice law in a jurisdiction where to do so would be in violation of laws of the profession in that jurisdiction; and

(C) Submit to the State Bar a declaration signed by a Supervising Lawyer who meets the requirements of this rule attesting that the applicant is employed by or volunteers at, or has a conditional offer to be employed by or volunteer with the firm where the Supervising Lawyer works and that the firm has an office located in California; that the nature of the employment conforms with the requirements of this rule; whether the employment is paid or unpaid; and that the Supervising Lawyer meets the eligibility requirements of and will comply with this rule. If an applicant works or volunteers for more than one firm concurrently as a Provisionally Licensed Lawyer, the applicant shall have a Supervising Lawyer at each firm and shall submit a declaration from each Supervising Lawyer.

(2) An Application for Provisional Licensure may be denied if:

(A) An applicant fails to comply with eligibility or application requirements;

(B) In connection with the Application for Provisional Licensure, an applicant makes a statement of material fact that the applicant knows to be false or makes the statement with reckless disregard as to its truth or falsity; or

(C) In connection with the Application for Provisional Licensure, an applicant fails to disclose a fact necessary to correct a statement known by the applicant to have created a material misapprehension in the matter, except that this rule does not authorize disclosure of information protected by Business and Professions Code section 6068, subdivision (e) or rule 1.6 of the California Rules of Professional Conduct.

(Subd (c) amended effective May 26, 2022; adopted effective November 9, 2020.)

(d) Eligibility Requirements

To qualify as a Provisionally Licensed Lawyer under this rule, the applicant must:

(1) Meet all of the requirements for admission to the State Bar with the following exceptions:

(A) The applicant need not have sat for or passed the California Bar Examination;

(B) The applicant need not have obtained a positive moral character determination, so long as the applicant submitted a complete Application for Determination of Moral Character to the State Bar prior to submission of an Application for Provisional Licensure and that application has not resulted in issuance of an adverse moral character determination by the State Bar; and

(C) The applicant need not have sat for or passed the Multistate Professional Responsibility Exam prior to submission of an Application for Provisional Licensure if the applicant attests they will complete the legal ethics components of the New Attorney Training, described under (e)(1) of this rule, within the first 30 days of licensure as a Provisionally Licensed Attorney. If the legal ethics components of the New Attorney Training is not made available to the applicant at the time of licensure, the 30 days shall run from the first day the training components are made available. The exemption set forth in (e)(1) of this rule does not apply to Provisionally Licensed Lawyers who must take the legal ethics components in lieu of passage of the MPRE.

(2) Comply with any rules or guidelines adopted by the State Bar relating to the State Bar's Provisional Licensure Program;

(3) Be employed by or volunteering with, or have a conditional offer of employment from or to volunteer with a firm that has an office located in California; and

(4) Practice law under a Supervising Lawyer who is an active licensee in good standing of the State Bar or is a current judge of a court of record within the California judicial branch, who satisfies the requirements for serving as a Supervising Lawyer under this rule.

(Subd (d) amended effective February 1, 2021; adopted effective November 9, 2020.)

(e) Responsibilities of Provisionally Licensed Lawyer

Provisionally Licensed Lawyer must comply with all of the following requirements. Failure to comply with these requirements shall result in immediate termination from the Provisional Licensure Program:

(1) Complete the State Bar New Attorney Training program, as described in State Bar Rule 2.53, during the first 12 months of licensure as a Provisionally Licensed Lawyer, unless they would otherwise be exempt from this requirement under the State Bar Rules if they were admitted to the State Bar as a lawyer;

(2) Expressly refer to themselves orally, including but not limited to, in conversations with clients or potential clients, and in writing, including but not limited to, in court pleadings or other papers filed in any court or tribunal, on letterhead, business cards, advertising, and signature blocks, as a Provisionally Licensed Lawyer and/or participant in the State Bar's Provisional Licensure Program, and not describe themselves as a fully-licensed lawyer, or imply in any way orally or in writing that they are a fully-licensed lawyer;

(3) Include on every document the Provisionally Licensed Lawyer files in court or with any other tribunal the following information about the Supervising Lawyer: name, mailing address, telephone number, and State Bar number;

(4) Maintain with the State Bar a current e-mail address and an address of record that is the current California office address of the Provisionally Licensed Lawyer's firm;

(5) Report to the State Bar immediately upon termination of supervision by the Supervising Lawyer for any reason;

(6) Report to the State Bar any information required of lawyers by the State Bar Act, such as that required by Business and Professions Code sections 6068(o) and 6068.8(c), or by other legal authority;

(7) If reassigned to a new Supervising Lawyer for the same firm, submit a declaration from the new Supervising Lawyer in compliance with (c)(1)(C) and obtain State Bar approval before the new Supervising Lawyer assumes supervisory responsibility over the Provisionally Licensed Lawyer.

(8) Submit a new Application for Provisional Licensure and obtain State Bar approval before beginning employment with a new firm;

(9) Abide by the laws of the State of California relating to the practice of law, the California Rules of Professional Conduct, and the rules and regulations of the State Bar.

(Subd (e) amended effective February 1, 2021; adopted effective November 9, 2020.)

(f) Prohibition on Accessing Client Trust Accounts

While practicing law under this rule, the Provisionally Licensed Lawyer must not open, maintain, withdraw funds from, deposit funds into, or attempt to open, maintain, or withdraw from or deposit into any client trust account.

(Subd (f) adopted effective November 9, 2020.)

(g) Permitted Activities

Subject to all applicable rules, regulations, and statutes, a Provisionally Licensed Lawyer may provide legal services to a client, including but not limited to appearing before a court or administrative tribunal, drafting legal documents, contracts or transactional documents, and pleadings, engaging in negotiations and settlement discussions, and providing other legal advice and counsel, provided that the work is performed under the supervision of a Supervising Lawyer.

(Subd (g) adopted effective November 9, 2020.)

(h) Communications and Work Product

For purposes of applying the privileges and doctrines relating to lawyer-client communications and lawyer work product, the Provisionally Licensed Lawyer shall be considered a subordinate of the Supervising Lawyer and thus communications and work product of the Provisionally Licensed Lawyer shall qualify for protection under such privileges and doctrines on the same basis.

(Subd (h) adopted effective November 9, 2020.)

(i) Supervision

(1) To meet the requirements of this rule, a Supervising Lawyer must:

(A) Work for the same firm by which the Provisionally Licensed Lawyer is or will be employed or at which the Provisionally Licensed Lawyer is or will be volunteering;

(B) Have practiced law for at least four years in any United States jurisdiction and have actively practiced law in California or taught law at a California Law School for at least two years immediately preceding the time of supervision, and be a licensee in good standing of the State Bar of California or be a current judge of a court of record within the California judicial branch;

(C) Exercise competence in any area of legal service authorized under California law in which the Supervising Lawyer is supervising the Provisionally Licensed Lawyer, consistent with the requirements of rule 1.1 of the Rules of Professional Conduct;

(D) With the exception of a current judge of a court of record within the California judicial branch, not be an inactive licensee in California, or ineligible to practice, actually suspended, under a stayed suspension order, or have resigned or been disbarred in any jurisdiction;

(E) Disclose in writing, via email or other means, at the outset of representation or before the Provisionally Licensed Lawyer begins to provide legal services, that a Provisionally Licensed Lawyer and/or participant in the State Bar's Provisional Licensure Program may provide legal services related to the client's matter;

(F) Be prepared to assume personal representation of the Provisionally Licensed Lawyer's clients if the Provisionally Licensed Lawyer becomes ineligible to practice under this rule or is otherwise unavailable to continue the representation;

(G) Agree to assume professional responsibility for any work that the Provisionally Licensed Lawyer performs under this rule; and

(H) Agree to notify the State Bar of California, in writing, within 10 calendar days if the Supervising Lawyer becomes aware or reasonably should have become aware that:

　i. The Provisionally Licensed Lawyer has terminated employment;

　ii. The Provisionally Licensed Lawyer is no longer eligible for participation in the Provisional Licensure Program;

　iii. The Supervising Lawyer no longer meets the requirements of this rule;

　iv. The Supervising Lawyer is no longer supervising the Provisionally Licensed Lawyer; or

　v. The Supervising Lawyer has changed offices or email addresses.

(2) A Supervising Lawyer may delegate some or all day-to-day supervisory responsibilities or supervisory responsibilities related to certain practice areas or assignments to another lawyer in the same organization who otherwise meets the requirements for Supervising Lawyers, without the need for those additional supervisors to file a declaration with the State Bar. The Supervising Lawyer's obligations under (i)(1)(G) are not affected by any such delegation.

(3) A Supervising Lawyer who is a current judge of a court of record within the California judicial branch and lawyers to whom the judge delegates day-to-day supervisory responsibilities pursuant to (2) shall not be subject to the requirements of (i)(D) through (G).

(Subd (i) amended effective May 26, 2022; adopted effective November 9, 2020; previously amended effective February 1, 2021.)

(j) Termination of Provisional Licensure

(1) A Provisionally Licensed Lawyer's provisional license terminates:

(A) Upon determination by the State Bar Court that the Provisionally Licensed Lawyer is culpable of conduct that would result in discipline if the Provisionally Licensed Lawyer were fully licensed by the State Bar of California, or upon imposition of any sanction for misconduct by any court or tribunal, or any professional or occupational licensing authority, including administrative or stayed suspension against the Provisionally Licensed Lawyer;

(B) Upon imposition of any discipline for misconduct by the State Bar of California, the Supreme Court, or any other bar, including administrative or stayed suspension, against the Supervising Lawyer, unless the Provisionally Licensed Lawyer has, within 15 calendar days of imposition of such discipline, obtained approval from the State Bar for a new Supervising Lawyer as required by this rule;

(C) Upon initial issuance of an adverse moral character determination by the State Bar. If the Provisionally Licensed Lawyer requests a review of the adverse determination under rule 4.47.1 of the Rules of the State Bar or appeals the adverse moral character determination of the Committee under rule 4.47 of the Rules of the State Bar, in lieu of termination the provisional license shall be suspended until final resolution of the review or appeal.

(D) Upon admission to the State Bar of California;

(E) Upon cessation of the Provisional Licensure Program;

(F) Upon request of the Provisionally Licensed Lawyer;

(G) For failure to complete the State Bar New Attorney Training Program consistent with (e)(1)(A) of this rule or failure to complete the legal ethics components under (d)(1)(C) of this rule;

(H) For failure to pay any fees required by the State Bar; or

(I) If the Provisionally Licensed Lawyer no longer meets the requirements of this rule.

(2) A notice of termination is effective ten calendar days from the date of receipt. Receipt is deemed to be five calendar days from the date of mailing to a California address or emailing to the provisional licensee's email address of record; ten calendar days from the date of mailing to an address elsewhere in the United States; and twenty calendar days from the date of mailing to an address outside the United States. Alternatively, receipt is when the State Bar delivers a document physically by personal service or otherwise.

(3) A Provisionally Licensed Lawyer whose provisional licensure terminated upon request or upon imposition of discipline against the Supervising Lawyer may be reinstated if they meet all eligibility and application requirements of this rule.

(Subd (j) amended effective May 26, 2022; adopted effective November 9, 2020.)

(k) Public Records

State Bar records for Provisionally Licensed Lawyers, including office address and discipline records, are public to the same extent as State Bar records related to fully-licensed lawyers.

(Subd (k) adopted effective November 9, 2020.)

(*l*) Inherent Power of Supreme Court

Nothing in these rules may be construed as affecting the power of the Supreme Court to exercise its inherent jurisdiction over the practice of law in California.

(Subd (l) adopted effective November 9, 2020.)

Rule 9.49 amended effective May 26, 2022; adopted effective November 9, 2020; previously amended effective February 1, 2021.

Rule 9.49.1. Provisional Licensure with Pathway to Full Licensure for Certain Individuals

(a) Expansion of the Provisional Licensure Program

The Provisional Licensure Program established pursuant to Rule 9.49 shall, no later than March 1, 2021, be expanded to include individuals who scored 1390 or higher on a California Bar Examination administered between July 2015 and February 2020, as determined by the first read score or final score, regardless of year of law school graduation or year satisfying the educational requirements to sit for the bar examination. The Provisional Licensure Program under this rule shall terminate on December 31, 2022, unless the California Supreme Court extends that date.

(Subd (a) amended effective May 26, 2022; adopted effective February 1, 2021.)

(b) Definitions

(1) The definitions of "Supervising Lawyer" and "Firm" or "Law Firm" as set forth in rule 9.49(b) shall apply to this rule.

(2) For purposes of this rule, "Provisionally Licensed Lawyer" means an individual who:

(A) Scored between 1390 and 1439 on any California Bar Examination administered between July 2015 and February 2020, as determined by the first read score or final score, regardless of year of law school graduation or year satisfying the educational requirements to sit for the bar examination; and

(B) Meets the eligibility criteria under (d) and is granted provisional licensure by the State Bar.

(3) For purposes of this rule, "legal practice" means the provision of permitted legal services to clients in compliance with rule 9.49(f) and (g).

(Subd (b) amended effective March 17, 2021; adopted effective February 1, 2021.)

(c) Application Requirements

All of the application requirements of rule 9.49(c) apply to applicants for provisional licensure under this rule. An application for provisional licensure under this rule must be submitted to the State Bar no later than May 31, 2021. Applications shall not be accepted after that date.

(Subd (c) adopted effective February 1, 2021.)

(d) Eligibility Requirements

With the exception of (d)(1)(A), all eligibility requirements of rule 9.49(d) apply to applicants for provisional licensure under this rule. However, an applicant who has previously received an adverse moral character determination is ineligible to apply under this rule unless more than two years has elapsed from the date of the final determination or after some other time set by the State Bar, for good cause shown, at the time of its adverse determination, within the meaning of State Bar Rule 4.49.

(Subd (d) amended effective March 17, 2021; adopted effective February 1, 2021.)

(e) Responsibilities of Provisionally Licensed Lawyer

All requirements of rule 9.49(e) and (f) apply to Provisionally Licensed Lawyers under this rule with the exception that the State Bar New Attorney Training program described in rule 9.49(e)(1) must be completed in order for a Provisionally Licensed Lawyer to qualify for admission to the State Bar of California under this rule.

(Subd (e) adopted effective February 1, 2021.)

(f) Permitted activities

All of the permitted activities set forth in rule 9.49(g) apply to Provisionally Licensed Lawyers under this rule.

(Subd (f) adopted effective February 1, 2021.)

(g) Communications and Work Product

For purposes of applying the privileges and doctrines relating to lawyer-client communications and lawyer work product, the Provisionally Licensed Lawyer under this rule shall be considered a subordinate of the Supervising Lawyer and thus communications and work product of the Provisionally Licensed Lawyer shall qualify for protection under such privileges and doctrines on the same basis.

(Subd (g) adopted effective February 1, 2021.)

(h) Termination of Provisional Licensure

The conditions for termination of a provisional license under rule 9.49(j) apply to Provisionally Licensed Lawyers under this rule.

(Subd (h) adopted effective February 1, 2021.)

(i) Admission to the State Bar of California

A Provisionally Licensed Lawyer, under this rule, shall be eligible for admission to the State Bar of California upon compliance with all of the following requirements.

(1) The Provisionally Licensed Lawyer shall complete 300 total hours of supervised legal practice in the Provisional Licensure Program;

(2) Provisionally Licensed Lawyers under rule 9.49 who also qualify for participation under this rule may receive credit for hours of supervised legal practice completed as a provisional licensee under rule 9.49 for purposes of meeting the hours requirement under (i)(1). Such individuals must comply with all of the application and eligibility requirements under this rule to qualify for admission to the State Bar of California.

(3) The Provisionally Licensed Lawyer shall submit, in the format developed by the State Bar of California, a record of the hours of supervised legal practice completed under supervision of the Supervising Lawyer(s).

(4) The Provisionally Licensed Lawyer must complete the required total number of hours of supervised legal practice, satisfy all eligibility requirements for admission not met at the time of application to the program, have an active positive moral character determination, submit a satisfactory evaluation(s) pursuant to (j)(2), and submit all other documentation of completion in the format required by the State Bar by December 31, 2022 to qualify for admission to the State Bar.

(5) A Provisionally Licensed Lawyer who satisfies the requirements of (i)(4), but has a disciplinary matter pending with the Office of Chief Trial Counsel or the State Bar Court shall, prior to the date the Provisional Licensure Program terminates under (a) and (h), be permitted to continue practicing as a Provisionally Licensed Lawyer if all other requirements of this rule have been met. If the disciplinary matter is pending as of the date the program terminates, the Provisionally Licensed Lawyer shall be placed in an abeyance status until the matter is resolved, and shall not continue to practice as Provisionally Licensed Lawyer.

(A) If the complaint is resolved with no disciplinary action, before or after the termination of the Provisional Licensure Program under (a) and (h), the Provisionally Licensed Lawyer shall qualify for admission to the State Bar as long as all other requirements for admission remain current and satisfied.

(B) If the complaint is resolved with a determination that the Provisionally Licensed Lawyer is culpable of conduct that would result in discipline if the Provisionally Licensed Lawyer were fully licensed by the State Bar of California, the Provisionally Licensed Lawyer shall not qualify for admission to the State Bar under this program and shall be terminated from the Provisional Licensure Program.

(6) The Provisionally Licensed Lawyer must comply with all the eligibility requirements for certification to the California Supreme Court for admission to the practice of law under Business and Professions Code section 6060 and rule 4.15 of the Rules of the State Bar of California. A Provisionally Licensed Lawyer who satisfies the requirements of (i)(4) shall be deemed to meet the requirement of Business and Professions Code section 6060, subdivision (g).

(Subd (i) amended effective May 26, 2022; adopted effective February 1, 2021; previously amended effective March 17, 2021.)

(j) Supervision and Evaluation of Provisionally Licensed Lawyer

(1) In addition to the requirements under (j)(2), all of the eligibility requirements, duties and responsibilities of a Supervising Lawyer set forth under rule 9.49(i) apply to Supervising Lawyers under this rule.

(2) Each Supervising Lawyer shall provide an evaluation of the Provisionally Licensed Lawyer in the format developed by the State Bar of California. The evaluation shall include the following:

(A) Verification of the number of hours of supervised legal practice completed;

(B) A general description of the types of supervised legal practice performed by the Provisionally Licensed Lawyer;

(C) Whether, in the opinion of the Supervising Lawyer, based on the supervised legal practice performed during the program, the Provisionally Licensed Lawyer possesses the minimum competence expected of an entry level attorney; and

(D) Other criteria established by the State Bar.

(3) If a Supervising Lawyer cannot attest that a Provisionally Licensed Lawyer possesses the minimum competence of an entry level attorney, the Provisionally Licensed Lawyer may not be admitted to the State Bar of California under this program without additional hours of supervised legal practice sufficient to establish to the Supervising Lawyer that the Provisionally Licensed Lawyer possesses the minimum competence of an entry level attorney, and submission of a satisfactory evaluation by that Supervising Lawyer before the termination of the program.

(Subd (j) adopted effective February 1, 2021.)

Rule 9.49.1 amended effective May 26, 2022; adopted effective February 1, 2021; previously amended effective March 17, 2021.

Division 5
Censure, Removal, Retirement, or Private or Public Admonishment of Judges

Rule 9.60. Review of determinations by the Commission on Judicial Performance

Rule 9.61. Proceedings involving private or public admonishment, censure, removal, retirement, or disqualification of a judge of the Supreme Court

Rule 9.60. Review of determinations by the Commission on Judicial Performance

(a) Time for petition for review to Supreme Court

A petition to the Supreme Court by a judge or former judge to review a determination by the Commission on Judicial Performance to retire, remove, censure, admonish, or disqualify the judge or former judge must be served and filed within 60 days after:

(1) The Commission, under its rules, notifies the judge or former judge that its determination has been filed or entered in its records; or

(2) The determination becomes final as to the Commission under its rules, whichever event is later.

(Subd (a) amended effective January 1, 2007.)

(b) Time for answer to petition for review and reply

Within 45 days after service of the petition, the Commission may serve and file an answer. Within 20 days after service of the answer, the judge or former judge may serve and file a reply. Each petition, answer, or reply submitted for filing must be accompanied by proof of service, including service on the Commission of three copies of any petition or reply filed by a judge or former judge. Extensions of time to file the petition, answer, or reply are disfavored and will be granted only upon a specific and affirmative showing of good cause. Good cause does not include ordinary press of business.

(Subd (b) lettered effective January 1, 2007; adopted as part of subd (a) effective December 1, 1996.)

(c) Contents and form

The petition, answer, and reply must address both the appropriateness of review and the merits of the Commission's determination, and they will serve as briefs on the merits in the event review is granted. Except as provided in these rules, the form of the petition, answer, and reply must, insofar as practicable, conform to rule 8.504 except that the lengths of the petition, answer, and reply must conform to the limits specified in rule 8.204(c). Each copy of the petition must contain:

(1) A copy of the Commission's determination;

(2) A copy of the notice of filing or entry of the determination in the records of the Commission;

(3) A copy of any findings of fact and conclusions of law; and

(4) A cover that bears the conspicuous notation "PETITION FOR REVIEW OF DETERMINATION BY COMMISSION ON JUDICIAL PERFORMANCE (RULE 9.60)" or words of like effect.

(Subd (c) amended and relettered effective January 1, 2007; adopted as subd (b) effective December 1, 1996.)

(d) Transmission of the record

Promptly upon the service and filing of the petition, the Commission must transmit to the Clerk of the Supreme Court the original record, including a transcript of the testimony, briefs, and all original papers and exhibits on file in the proceeding.

(Subd (d) amended and relettered effective January 1, 2007; adopted as subd (c) effective December 1, 1996.)

(e) Applicable rules on review

In the event review is granted, the rules adopted by the Judicial Council governing appeals from the superior court in civil cases, other than rule 8.272 relating to costs, apply to proceedings in the Supreme Court for review of a determination of the Commission except where express provision is made to the contrary or where such application would otherwise be clearly impracticable or inappropriate.

(Subd (e) amended and relettered effective January 1, 2007; adopted as subd (d) effective December 1, 1996.)

Rule 9.60 amended and renumbered effective January 1, 2007; adopted as rule 935 effective December 1, 1996.

Rule 9.61. Proceedings involving private or public admonishment, censure, removal, retirement, or disqualification of a judge of the Supreme Court

(a) Selection of appellate tribunal

Immediately on the filing of a petition to review a determination by the Commission on Judicial Performance to retire, remove, censure, admonish, or disqualify a justice of the Supreme Court, the Clerk of the Supreme Court must select, by lot, seven Court of Appeal justices who must elect one of their number presiding justice and perform the duties of the tribunal created under article VI, section 18(f) of the Constitution. This selection must be made upon notice to the Commission, the justice, and the counsel of record in a proceeding open to the public. No court of appeal justice who has served as a master or a member of the Commission in the particular proceeding or is otherwise disqualified may serve on the tribunal.

(Subd (a) amended effective January 1, 2007; previously amended effective December 1, 1996.)

(b) Clerk of Supreme Court as clerk of tribunal

The Clerk of the Supreme Court serves as the clerk of the tribunal.

(Subd (b) amended effective January 1, 2007.)

Rule 9.61 amended effective January 1, 2019; adopted as rule 921 effective November 13, 1976; previously amended and renumbered as rule 936 effective December 1, 1996, and as rule 9.61 effective January 1, 2007.

2019 Note: The amendment effective January 1, 2019, only amended the rule heading.

Division 6
Judicial Ethics Opinions

Rule 9.80. Committee on Judicial Ethics Opinions

(a) Purpose

The Supreme Court has established the Committee on Judicial Ethics Opinions to provide judicial ethics advisory opinions and advice to judicial officers and candidates for judicial office.

(Subd (a) adopted effective July 1, 2009.)

(b) Committee determinations

In providing its opinions and advice, the committee acts independently of the Supreme Court, the Commission on Judicial Performance, and all other entities. The committee must rely on the California Code of Judicial Ethics, the decisions of the Supreme Court and of the Commission on Judicial Performance, and may rely on other relevant sources in its opinions and advice.

(Subd (b) amended effective January 1, 2019; adopted effective July 1, 2009.)

(c) Membership

The committee consists of twelve members appointed by the Supreme Court, including at least one justice from a Court of Appeal and one member who is a subordinate judicial officer employed full-time by a superior court. The remaining members must be justices of a Court of Appeal or judges of a superior court, active or retired. No more than a total of two retired justices or judges may serve on the committee at one time, except that if an active justice or judge retires during his or her term, he or she will be permitted to complete his or her term. A retired justice or judge may only serve so long as he or she is not an active licensee of the State Bar of California and is not engaged in privately compensated dispute resolution activities.

(Subd (c) amended effective January 1, 2019; adopted effective July 1, 2009.)

(d) Terms

(1) Except as provided in subdivision (d)(2), all full terms are for four years. Appointments to fill a vacancy will be for the balance of the term vacated. A member may apply to be reappointed by the Supreme Court at the end of a four-year term and renewal of the term is not a presumption.

(2) To create staggered terms among the members of the committee, the Supreme Court appointed initial members of the committee as follows:

(A) Three members each to serve an initial term of five years. The court may reappoint these members to additional full terms.

(B) Three members each to serve an initial term of four years. The court may reappoint these members to additional full terms.

(C) Three members each to serve an initial term of three years. The court may reappoint these members to additional full terms.

(D) Three members each to serve an initial term of two years. The court may reappoint these members to additional full terms.

(3) Committee members may not simultaneously serve as members of the Commission on Judicial Performance or the California Judges Association's Judicial Ethics Committee. If a member of the committee accepts appointment to serve on one of these entities, that member will be deemed to have resigned from the committee and the Supreme Court will appoint a replacement.

(Subd (d) amended effective January 1, 2021; adopted effective July 1, 2009; previously amended effective January 1, 2016, and January 1, 2019.)

(e) Powers and duties

The committee is authorized to provide ethics advice to judicial officers and candidates for judicial office, including formal written opinions, informal written opinions, and expedited written opinions. Specifically, the committee is authorized to:

(1) Issue formal written opinions, informal written opinions, and expedited written opinions on proper judicial conduct under the California

Code of Judicial Ethics, the California Constitution, statutes, and any other authority deemed appropriate by the committee.

(2) Make recommendations to the Supreme Court for amending the Code of Judicial Ethics or these rules;

(3) Make recommendations regarding appropriate subjects for judicial education programs; and

(4) Make other recommendations to the Supreme Court as deemed appropriate by the committee or as requested by the court.

(Subd (e) amended effective January 1, 2021; adopted effective July 1, 2009.)

(f) Referrals to California Judges Association's Judicial Ethics Committee

The committee may adopt a revocable policy of referring requests for expedited advice, with conditions and exceptions as approved by the committee, to the California Judges Association's Judicial Ethics Committee.

(Subd (f) amended effective January 1, 2021; adopted effective July 1, 2009.)

(g) Chair and vice-chair

The Supreme Court will appoint a chair, and vice-chair from the members of the committee to serve a term of four years each. The chair and the vice-chair may be reappointed by the Supreme Court. When a member's term as chair or vice-chair ends and the member is not reappointed as chair or vice-chair, that member's committee membership term also ends unless the Supreme Court reappoints the member to the committee. The chair may call meetings as needed, and to otherwise coordinate the work of the committee.

(Subd (g) amended effective January 1, 2021; adopted effective July 1, 2009; previously amended effective January 1, 2016, and January 1, 2019.)

(h) Confidentiality

Communications to and from the committee are confidential except as described here. Encouraging judicial officers and candidates for judicial office to seek ethics opinions and advice from the committee will promote ethical conduct and the fair administration of justice. Establishing the confidentiality of committee proceedings and communications to and from the committee is critical to encourage judicial officers and candidates for judicial office to seek ethics opinions and advice from the committee. The necessity for preserving the confidentiality of these proceedings and communications to and from the committee outweighs the necessity for disclosure in the interest of justice. Therefore, to promote ethical conduct by judicial officers and candidates for judicial office and to encourage them to seek ethics opinions and advice from the committee, the following confidentiality requirements, and exceptions, apply to proceedings and other matters under this rule:

(1) Notwithstanding any other provision of law, and with the exception of formal opinions, informal opinions, expedited opinions, and comments from the public on draft formal opinions posted on the committee's website, all opinions, inquiries, replies, circulated drafts, records, documents, writings, files, communications with staff, work product of the committee or its staff, and deliberations and proceedings of the committee are confidential. All communications, written or verbal, from or to the person or entity requesting an opinion or advice are deemed to be official information within the meaning of the Evidence Code. In addition, all communications and documents regarding opinions or advice of the California Judges Association forwarded by the California Judges Association to the committee are deemed to be confidential information.

(2) Members of the committee and its staff may not disclose outside the committee or its staff any confidential information, including identifying information, obtained by the committee or its staff concerning an individual whose inquiry or conduct was the subject of any communication with the committee or its staff.

(3) A judicial officer or candidate for judicial office may waive confidentiality; any such waiver must be in writing. If the judicial officer or candidate making the request for an opinion or advice waives confidentiality or asserts reliance on an opinion or advice in judicial or attorney discipline proceedings, such opinion or advice no longer is confidential under these rules. Notwithstanding any waiver, committee deliberations and records are confidential.

(4) Members of the public and entities may submit comments on draft formal opinions for consideration by the committee members before deciding on whether to publish a final formal opinion. Such comments from the public are deemed not to be confidential communications and may be posted on the committee's website for public review at the committee's discretion.

(Subd (h) amended effective January 1, 2021; adopted effective January 1, 2019.)

(i) Opinion requests

(1) The committee may issue formal written opinions, informal written opinions, or expedited written opinions on any subject it deems appropriate. Any person or entity may suggest to the committee, in writing, topics to be addressed in a formal written opinion.

(2) Only judicial officers and candidates for judicial office may request informal written opinions and expedited written opinions.

(3) A judicial officer or candidate for judicial office requesting a written opinion, formal or informal, must submit the request in writing, including by electronic mail. The request must be in a form approved by the committee and must describe the facts and discuss the issues presented in the request. The identity, organizational affiliation, and geographic location of persons requesting opinions are confidential.

(4) A judicial officer or candidate for judicial office requesting an expedited written opinion may communicate in person, in writing, including by electronic mail, or by telephone to committee staff or any member of the committee.

(5) A judicial officer or candidate for judicial office requesting an opinion or advice must disclose to the committee whether the issue that is the subject of the inquiry is also the subject of pending litigation involving the inquiring judicial officer or candidate or a pending Commission on Judicial Performance or State Bar disciplinary proceeding involving the inquiring judicial officer or candidate.

(Subd (i) amended effective January 1, 2021; adopted effective July 1, 2009.)

(j) Consideration of requests

(1) The committee will determine whether a request for an opinion should be resolved with a formal written opinion, an informal written opinion, an expedited written opinion, or any combination or form of advice. The committee may decline to issue an opinion or advice.

(2) Eight members must vote affirmatively to adopt a formal written opinion. After the committee authorizes a formal written opinion and before it becomes final, it will be posted in draft form on the committee's website and made available for public comment for at least 45 days, unless the committee in its discretion decides such an opinion should be issued in final form in less time or with no prior notice. Public comments may be posted on the website following the public comment period at the committee's discretion. After the public comment period has expired, eight members must vote affirmatively to publish the opinion in its original form, or to modify or withdraw the formal written opinion.

(3) Informal written opinions and expedited written opinions must be approved by vote of the committee members. The committee must adopt procedures concerning the number of votes required to issue an informal written opinion or expedited written opinion.

(4) The committee must adopt procedures concerning the handling and determination of requests for opinions or advice.

(5) The committee will inform the inquiring judicial officer or candidate for judicial office that he or she must disclose all relevant information and that any opinion or advice issued by the committee is based on the premise that the inquiring judicial officer or candidate has disclosed all relevant information.

(6) The committee may confer in person, in writing, including by electronic mail, by telephone, or by videoconference as often as needed to conduct committee business and resolve pending requests.

(Subd (j) amended effective January 1, 2021; adopted effective July 1, 2009; previously amended effective January 1, 2019.)

(k) Opinion distribution

(1) The committee will, upon final approval of a formal written opinion, ensure distribution of the opinion, including to the person or entity who requested the opinion, all California judicial officers, and other interested persons.

(2) The committee's informal written opinions and expedited written opinions will, upon approval by the committee, be provided to the inquiring judicial officer or candidate for judicial office.

(3) The committee will post all formal written opinions on the committee's website. The committee may post its informal written opinions and expedited written opinions on the committee's website.

(4) The committee must maintain records of committee determinations and opinions at the committee's office.

(Subd (k) amended effective January 1, 2021; adopted effective July 1, 2009; previously amended effective January 1, 2019.)

***(l)* Withdrawn, modified, and superseding opinions**

The committee may withdraw, modify, or supersede an opinion or advice at any time.

(Subd (l) amended effective January 1, 2021; adopted effective July 1, 2009.)

(m) Internal operating rules

The committee must adopt procedures, subject to approval by the Supreme Court, to implement this rule.

(Subd (m) amended effective January 1, 2019; adopted effective July 1, 2009.)

(n) Website, e-mail address, and toll-free telephone number

The committee must maintain a website, e-mail address, and toll-free telephone number.

(Subd (n) amended effective January 1, 2019; adopted effective July 1, 2009.)
Rule 9.80 amended effective January 1, 2021; adopted effective July 1, 2009; previously amended effective January 1, 2016, and January 1, 2019.

Division 7
State Bar Trustees

Rule 9.90. Nominations and appointments of State Bar trustees

(a) State Bar Trustees Nominating Committee

(1) The Supreme Court appoints five attorneys to the State Bar Board of Trustees, each for a four-year term. The court may reappoint an attorney for one additional term. The court may also fill any vacancy in the term of, and make any reappointment of, any appointed attorney member. Each appointee must be an active licensee of the State Bar and have his or her principal office in California.

(2) In order to ensure that individuals appointed by the Supreme Court to the State Bar Board of Trustees have been evaluated objectively, the court has established an independent "State Bar Trustees Nominating Committee" to receive applications and screen and evaluate prospective appointees. The role of the committee is to determine whether applicants possess not only the statutorily enumerated qualifications, but also any other qualifications that may be required to carry out the duties of the Board of Trustees.

(3) The committee serves at the pleasure of the court. The committee will consist of seven members appointed by the court of whom five must be active licensees of the State Bar in good standing, and two must be active or retired judicial officers. A committee chair and vice-chair are designated by the court. The court will seek to create a broadly representative body to assist it in its considerations.

Except as provided below, all full terms are for three years. Members may not serve more than two consecutive full terms. Members will continue to serve until a successor is appointed. Appointments to fill a vacancy will be for the balance of the term vacated. Members who are appointed to fill a vacancy for the balance of a term are eligible to serve two full terms in addition to the remainder of the term for which they were appointed.

To create staggered terms among the members of the committee, the Supreme Court will appoint initial members of the committee as follows:

(A) Four members each to serve a term of three years. The court may reappoint these members to one full term.

(B) Three members each to serve a term of two years. The court may reappoint these members to one full term.

(4) The committee must adopt, and implement upon approval by the Supreme Court, procedures for:

(A) Receipt of applications and initial screening of applicants for appointments to fill the vacant positions, including adoption of a comprehensive application form;

(B) Receipt of evaluations concerning selected applicants;

(C) Evaluation and rating of applicants; and

(D) Transmittal of the materials specified in (b) of this rule to the Supreme Court.

The procedures adopted by the committee must include provisions to ensure the confidentiality of its evaluations.

(5) In recommending candidates, in order to provide for the appointment of trustees who bring to the board a variety of experiences, the committee should consider:

(A) Legal services attorneys, solo practitioners, attorneys with small firms, and attorneys with governmental entities;

(B) Historically underrepresented groups, such as those underrepresented because of race, ethnicity, gender, and sexual orientation;

(C) Legal academics;

(D) Geographic distribution;

(E) Years of practice;

(F) Attorneys who are in their first five years of practice;

(G) Participation in voluntary local or state bar activities;

(H) Participation in activities to benefit the public; and

(I) Other factors demonstrating a background that will help inform the work of the board.

(6) The State Bar must provide the support the committee requires to discharge its obligations under this rule.

(Subd (a) amended effective January 1, 2019; adopted effective January 23, 2013.)

(b) Evaluations

(1) The committee must evaluate the qualifications of and rate all applicants and must submit to the court the nominations of at least three qualified candidates for each vacancy. Candidates are to be rated as "not recommended," "recommended," and "highly recommended." A rating of "not recommended" relates only to the position under consideration and does not indicate any lack of ability or expertise of the applicant generally. The committee must report in confidence to the Supreme Court its evaluation, rating, and recommendation for applicants for appointment and the reasons therefore, including a succinct summary of their qualifications, at a time to be designated by the Supreme Court. The report must include written comments regarding the nominees received by the committee, which must be transmitted to the Supreme Court together with the nominations.

(2) In determining the qualifications of an applicant for appointment or reappointment the committee should, in addition to the factors cited in (a)(5), consider the following: focus on the public interest, public service, commitment to the administration of justice, objectivity, community respect, integrity, ability to work collaboratively, and balanced temperament.

(Subd (b) amended effective January 1, 2019; adopted effective January 23, 2013.)
Rule 9.90 amended effective January 1, 2019; adopted effective January 23, 2013.

TITLE 10
Judicial Administration Rules

Division 1. Judicial Council. Rules 10.1–10.81.
Division 2. Administration of the Judicial Branch. Rules 10.101–10.493.
Division 3. Judicial Administration Rules Applicable to All Courts. Rules 10.500–10.505.
Division 4. Trial Court Administration. Rules 10.601–10.970.
Division 5. Appellate Court Administration. Rules 10.1000–10.1108.

Division 1
Judicial Council

Chap. 1. The Judicial Council and Internal Committees. Rules 10.1–10.22.
Chap. 2. Judicial Council Advisory Committees and Task Forces. Rules 10.30–10.70.
Chap. 3. Judicial Council Advisory Body Meetings. Rule 10.75.
Chap. 4. Judicial Council staff. Rules 10.80, 10.81.

Chapter 1
The Judicial Council and Internal Committees

Rule 10.1. Authority, duties, and goals of the Judicial Council
Rule 10.2. Judicial Council membership and terms
Rule 10.3. Nonvoting members
Rule 10.4. Nominations and appointments to the Judicial Council
Rule 10.5. Notice and agenda of council meetings
Rule 10.6. Judicial Council meetings
Rule 10.10. Judicial Council internal committees
Rule 10.11. Executive and Planning Committee
Rule 10.12. Legislation Committee
Rule 10.13. Rules Committee
Rule 10.14. Litigation Management Committee
Rule 10.15. Judicial Branch Budget Committee
Rule 10.16. Technology Committee
Rule 10.20. Proposals for new or amended rules, standards, or forms; rule-making process in general
Rule 10.21. Proposals from members of the public for changes to rules, standards, or forms
Rule 10.22. Rule-making procedures

Rule 10.1. Authority, duties, and goals of the Judicial Council

(a) The Judicial Council

(1) The Judicial Council of California is a state entity established by the California Constitution and chaired by the Chief Justice of California. The Judicial Council sets the direction for improving the quality of justice and advancing the consistent, independent, impartial, and accessible administration of justice by the judicial branch for the benefit of the public.

(2) The council establishes policies and sets priorities for the judicial branch of government. The council may seek advice and recommendations from committees, task forces, and the public.

(3) The Judicial Council Governance Policies are located in Appendix D of these rules of court. The policies describe the council's:

(A) Purposes;
(B) Responsibilities;
(C) Policymaking role;
(D) Members and officers and their roles;
(E) Internal organization;
(F) Relationship with its advisory groups;
(G) Relationship with the Administrative Director and the Judicial Council staff that he or she directs; and
(H) Internal policies and procedures.

(Subd (a) amended effective July 29, 2014; previously amended effective January 1, 2007, and August 14, 2009.)

(b) Constitutional authority and duties

Article VI, section 6 of the California Constitution requires the council to improve the administration of justice by doing the following:

(1) Surveying judicial business;
(2) Making recommendations to the courts;
(3) Making annual recommendations to the Governor and the Legislature;
(4) Adopting rules for court administration and rules of practice and procedure that are not inconsistent with statute; and
(5) Performing other functions prescribed by statute.

(Subd (b) amended effective August 14, 2009.)

(c) Judicial branch goals

The Judicial Council develops judicial branch goals in its strategic and operational plans. At six-year intervals, the council develops and approves a long-range strategic plan. At three-year intervals, the council develops and approves an operational plan for the implementation of the strategic plan. Each plan is developed in consultation with branch stakeholders and justice system partners.

(Subd (c) amended effective August 14, 2009; previously amended effective January 1, 2007.)

(d) Judicial Council staff

The Judicial Council staff supports the council in performing its functions. The Administrative Director is the Secretary of the Judicial Council.

(Subd (d) amended effective July 29, 2014; adopted as subd (e) effective January 1, 1999; previously amended effective January 1, 2007; previously repealed and relettered as subd (d) effective August 14, 2009.)

Rule 10.1 amended effective July 29, 2014; adopted as rule 6.1 effective January 1, 1999; previously amended and renumbered effective January 1, 2007; previously amended effective August 14, 2009.

Rule 10.2. Judicial Council membership and terms

(a) Constitutional provision on membership and terms

(1) Under article VI, section 6 of the California Constitution, the Judicial Council consists of the Chief Justice and one other justice of the Supreme Court, 3 justices of Courts of Appeal, 10 judges of superior courts, 2 nonvoting court administrators, and such other nonvoting members as determined by the voting membership of the council, each appointed by the Chief Justice to three-year terms; 4 members of the State Bar appointed by its governing body to three-year terms; and 1 member of each house of the Legislature appointed as provided by the house.

(2) Council membership terminates if a member ceases to hold the position that qualified the member for appointment. A vacancy is filled by the appointing power for the remainder of the term.

(Subd (a) amended effective August 14, 2009; previously amended effective January 1, 2007.)

(b) Council officers and duties

(1) *Chair and vice-chair*

(A) The Chief Justice of California is the Chair of the Judicial Council and performs those functions prescribed by the Constitution and the laws of the State of California. The Chair is a voting member of the council. A reference to the Chair of the Judicial Council in the statutes or rules of this state means the Chief Justice of California.

(B) The Chief Justice appoints a vice-chair from among the judicial members of the council. When the chair is absent, unable to serve, or so directs, the vice-chair performs all of the duties of the chair.

(C) The Chief Justice appoints a Judicial Council member to serve as chair of the council in the event that both the Chief Justice and the council vice-chair are absent or unable to serve. The Chief Justice determines individuals to serve as chair from among the internal committee chairs and vice-chairs.

(2) *Chairs and vice-chairs of the internal committees*

The Judicial Council has five internal committees composed of Judicial Council members, as specified in rule 10.10. The Chief Justice appoints for a one-year term the chair and vice-chair of each of the council's internal committees. Chairs call meetings, as necessary, and provide reports to the council on the activities of the internal committees.

(3) *Officers*

The Judicial Council has eight officers: the chair, vice-chair, secretary, and the chairs of the council's five internal committees.

(4) Administrative Director

The Administrative Director is the secretary to the Judicial Council and performs administrative and policymaking functions as provided by the Constitution and the laws of the State of California and as delegated by the Judicial Council and the Chief Justice. The secretary is not a voting member of the council.

(Subd (b) amended effective January 1, 2016; previously amended effective August 14, 2009.)

(c) Role of members

(1) Council members are a governing body for California's judicial branch of government. In accepting appointment, they commit themselves to act in the best interest of the public and the judicial system for the purposes of maintaining and enhancing public access to the justice system, as well as preserving and enhancing impartial judicial decisionmaking and an independent judicial branch of government.

(2) Council members do not represent any particular constituency notwithstanding any of their other affiliations or roles.

(3) Council members communicate as representatives of the Judicial Council with the public, the courts, judicial officers, Judicial Council advisory bodies, other government entities, and justice system partners. They communicate about the council's processes, purposes, responsibilities, and issues and reasons for policy decisions, including those policy decisions where there is disagreement.

(Subd (c) amended effective August 14, 2009.)

(d) Terms

Council members are appointed to terms beginning September 15 and ending September 14. Terms for judge members are staggered. To the extent feasible, the State Bar and the Legislature should create staggered terms for their appointees.

(e) Restrictions on advisory committee membership

Unless otherwise provided by these rules or the Chief Justice waives this provision, neither council members nor nonvoting advisory council members may concurrently serve on a council advisory committee. This provision does not apply to members of the following advisory committees:

(1) Administrative Presiding Justices;

(2) Trial Court Presiding Judges; and

(3) Court Executives.

(Subd (e) amended effective January 1, 2015; previously amended effective January 1, 2007, and August 14, 2009.)

Rule 10.2 amended effective January 1, 2016; adopted as rule 6.2 effective January 1, 1999; previously amended and renumbered as rule 10.2 effective January 1, 2007; previously amended effective August 14, 2009, and January 1, 2015.

Rule 10.3. Nonvoting members

(a) Appointment

The Chief Justice appoints nonvoting advisory council members as specified in article VI, section 6 of the California Constitution or as approved by the Judicial Council.

(b) Voting

A nonvoting council member may make or second motions at a council meeting but may not vote. A nonvoting member may vote on an internal committee matter as specified in rule 10.10(e).

(Subd (b) amended effective September 1, 2017; previously amended January 1, 2007.)

Rule 10.3 amended effective September 1, 2017; adopted as rule 6.3 effective January 1, 1999; previously amended and renumbered effective January 1, 2007.

Rule 10.4. Nominations and appointments to the Judicial Council

(a) Nomination procedures

The Executive and Planning Committee assists the Chief Justice in selecting council members by submitting a list of nominees for each position. The committee uses the following procedures:

(1) The committee publicizes vacancies and solicits nominations. Nominations for advisory member positions are solicited from the Court Executives Advisory Committee, the Appellate Court Clerks Association, the California Court Commissioners Association, and other related bodies. The selected nominees should represent diverse backgrounds, experiences, and geographic locations.

(2) The committee submits a list of at least three nominees to the Chief Justice for each vacant position, except for the Supreme Court associate justice position. The committee gives added consideration to persons who have served on advisory committees or task forces.

(3) If the Chief Justice is a member of the Executive and Planning Committee, the Chief Justice does not participate in discussions relating to nominations.

(Subd (a) amended effective January 1, 2007.)

(b) Appointing order

The Chief Justice makes appointments to the council by order.

Rule 10.4 amended and renumbered effective January 1, 2007; adopted as rule 6.4 effective January 1, 1999.

Rule 10.5. Notice and agenda of council meetings

(a) Generally

The Judicial Council meets at the call of the Chief Justice no fewer than four times a year.

(Subd (a) amended effective January 1, 2004.)

(b) Meeting schedule

The Judicial Council must publish a regular annual schedule that states the planned date and location of each meeting. Additional meetings may be scheduled as necessary.

(Subd (b) amended effective January 1, 2016; previously amended effective January 1, 2004, and January 1, 2007.)

(c) Notice of business meetings

"Business meetings" are council meetings at which a majority of voting members are present to discuss and decide matters within the council's jurisdiction. The Judicial Council must give public notice of the date, location, and agenda of each business meeting at least seven days before the meeting. The notice must state whether the meeting is open or closed. If the meeting is partly closed, the notice must indicate which agenda items are closed. A meeting may be conducted without notice in case of an emergency requiring prompt action.

(Subd (c) amended effective January 1, 2016; previously amended effective January 1, 2004.)

(d) Budget meetings

A "budget meeting" is that portion of any business meeting at which trial court budgets are to be discussed. The Judicial Council must provide notice of a budget meeting in the same manner as any other business meeting. Budget meetings normally are scheduled as follows:

(1) A budget priority meeting, normally in February of each year, at which the Judicial Council adopts budget priorities for the trial courts for the budget year that begins July 1 of the next calendar year.

(2) A meeting at which the proposed budget is approved, normally in August of each year, at which the Judicial Council takes action on the following:

(A) Staff recommendations on trial court budget change requests for the next fiscal year;

(B) A total baseline budget for each trial court for the next fiscal year; and

(C) Any proposed changes in funding for a trial court.

(3) A budget allocation meeting, normally at the first council meeting after the state's budget is enacted, at which the Judicial Council approves the final budget allocations for each trial court, including approved budget adjustments.

(4) Other meetings following substantive changes to the trial court portion of the proposed State Budget made by the Governor in the proposed Governor's budget or by a committee or house of the Legislature, at which the Judicial Council will take appropriate action, if any.

(Subd (d) amended effective January 1, 2016; adopted effective January 1, 2004.)

(e) Form of notice

The notice and agenda for council meetings must be posted on the California Courts website (*www.courts.ca.gov*). In addition, the notice and agenda for budget meetings must be provided to designated employee representatives who have submitted a written request to the Judicial Council (attention Judicial Council Support).

(Subd (e) amended effective January 1, 2016; adopted as subd (d) effective January 1, 1999; previously amended and relettered as subd (e) effective January 1, 2004; previously amended effective January 1, 2007.)

(f) Contents of agenda

The agenda must contain a brief description of each item to be considered at the council meeting. All items are classified as discussion items, consent items, or informational items.

(1) *Consent items deemed approved*

All consent items are deemed approved without further action at the adjournment of each council meeting.

(2) *Moving consent items to discussion agenda*

A consent item must be moved to the discussion agenda if a council member so requests by giving 48 hours' advance notice to the Executive and Planning Committee, or if the Chief Justice moves the item to the discussion agenda.

(Subd (f) amended and relettered effective January 1, 2004; adopted as subd (e) effective January 1, 1999.)

(g) Meeting materials

(1) *General materials*

General meeting materials must be distributed to council members at least three business days before the date of the meeting, except in extraordinary circumstances. The Administrative Director may make copies of materials available to the media or attendees in advance of a business meeting and may specify that the materials are provided on agreement by the recipient that they will be kept confidential until the council has discussed or acted on specified items. The council may charge a fee to cover the costs of replicating and mailing these materials to members of the public.

(2) *Budget materials*

(A) *When available*

Materials involving trial court budgets must be made available at least five business days before the meeting if they have been distributed by that time to the members of the council. All other materials involving trial court budgets must be made available at the same time as the information is distributed to the council.

(B) *Distribution*

Materials must be made available by posting on the California Courts website and by distribution to designated employee representatives who have submitted a written request to the Judicial Council of California (attention Judicial Council Support).

(C) *Contents at the budget approval meeting*

Materials involving trial court budget proposals presented at the budget approval meeting must include proposed statewide requests for funding, existing trial court baseline budgets, adjustments proposed for any trial court baseline budget, and any court-specific budget change requests.

(Subd (g) amended effective January 1, 2016; adopted as subd (f) effective January 1, 1999; previously amended and relettered effective January 1, 2004; previously amended effective January 1, 2007.)

(h) Circulating orders

Between business meetings, the council may act by circulating order on urgent matters if the Chief Justice or the Administrative Director approves. Prior public notice of a proposed circulating order is not required. Each circulating order adopted by the council must be included on the agenda for the next business meeting as an information item.

(Subd (h) amended and relettered effective January 1, 2004; adopted as subd (g) effective January 1, 1999.)

Rule 10.5 amended effective January 1, 2016; adopted as rule 6.5 effective January 1, 1999; previously amended effective January 1, 2004; previously amended and renumbered as rule 10.5 effective January 1, 2007.

Rule 10.6. Judicial Council meetings

(a) Open meeting policy

Business meetings are open to the public unless they are closed under (b). Other meetings, such as orientation, planning, and educational meetings, may be made open to the public at the discretion of the Chief Justice. The Chief Justice may seek a recommendation from the Executive and Planning Committee on whether all or part of any meeting should be open or closed. Any discussion or decision of the full council at a business meeting regarding a trial court budget allocation must take place in an open meeting of the council, except for an executive session as provided in (b).

(Subd (a) amended effective January 1, 2007; previously amended effective January 1, 2004.)

(b) Closed sessions

The Chief Justice may close all or part of a business meeting because of the nature of the meeting or of matters to be discussed. The following matters will ordinarily be discussed in closed session:

(1) A personnel matter or a discussion of the character, competence, or physical or mental health of an individual;

(2) Claims or litigation in which the Judicial Council has an interest;

(3) Contract, labor, or legislative negotiations;

(4) The purchase, sale, or lease of real property;

(5) Security plans or procedures;

(6) Allegations of criminal or professional misconduct; and

(7) Discussions protected by the attorney-client privilege.

(c) Conduct at meeting

Members of the public who attend open meetings must remain orderly. The Chief Justice may order the removal of any disorderly persons.

(Subd (c) amended effective January 1, 2004.)

(d) Requests to speak—general

The Executive and Planning Committee, in its discretion, may allow a member of the public to speak at a business meeting. Unless the Chief Justice waives this requirement, any member of the public who wishes to speak at a business meeting must submit a request of no more than two pages to the chair of the Executive and Planning Committee by delivering it to the Judicial Council (attention Judicial Council Support) at least four business days before the meeting.

(1) *Contents of the request*

The request must include the following:

(A) A description of the agenda item to be addressed;

(B) A specific recitation of the proposed statement with an explanation of its relevance to the agenda item and the reasons it would be of benefit to the council in its deliberations;

(C) The name, residence, and occupation of the person asking to speak and, if applicable, the name, address, and purpose of the agency or organization that the speaker represents;

(D) If available, telephone and fax numbers and e-mail address of the person asking to speak and, if applicable and available, the telephone, fax numbers, and e-mail address of the agency or organization that the speaker represents;

(E) The words "Request to Speak at Judicial Council Meeting" displayed prominently in letters at least one-quarter-inch high on the envelope containing the request; and

(F) A copy of any written materials the speaker proposes to distribute at the meeting.

(2) *Notice of decision*

The Executive and Planning Committee must respond to the request at least two business days before the meeting. The committee may grant the request in part or whole, request additional information, circulate any written materials, or take other action it deems appropriate.

(Subd (d) amended effective January 1, 2016; previously amended effective January 1, 2004, and January 1, 2007.)

(e) Presentation of information on trial court budget matters

(1) *Presentation of written information*

Any designated employee representative has a right to provide written information on trial court budget allocations to the council.

(2) *Oral presentation*

Any designated employee representative who wishes to make an oral presentation to the Judicial Council must make a written request to the Judicial Council of California (attention Judicial Council Support) no later than 24 hours before the meeting unless the issue has arisen within the last five business days before the meeting, in which case the written request may be made on the day of the meeting.

(3) *Limit on number and time*

The Chief Justice or his or her designee may limit the number and time of speakers in order to avoid cumulative discussion.

(Subd (e) amended effective January 1, 2016; adopted effective January 1, 2004; previously amended effective January 1, 2007.)

(f) Video recording, photographing, and broadcasting at meeting

The Chief Justice may permit video recording, photographing, or broadcasting of a meeting. Any such video recording, photographing, or broadcasting is subject to regulations that ensure the meeting's security and dignity. A request to record, photograph, or broadcast a council meeting must be received by the Chief Justice at least two business days before the meeting.

(Subd (f) relettered effective January 1, 2004; adopted as subd (e) effective January 1, 1999.)

(g) Minutes as official records

The Secretary of the Judicial Council must prepare written minutes of each council meeting for approval at the next council meeting. When approved by the council, the minutes constitute the official record of the meeting.

(Subd (g) amended and relettered effective January 1, 2004; adopted as subd (f) effective January 1, 1999.)

Rule 10.6 amended effective January 1, 2016; adopted as rule 6.6 effective January 1, 1999; previously amended effective January 1, 2004; previously amended and renumbered as rule 10.6 effective January 1, 2007.

Rule 10.10. Judicial Council internal committees

(a) Judicial Council internal committees

The internal committees are:

(1) Executive and Planning Committee;
(2) Legislation Committee;
(3) Rules Committee;
(4) Litigation Management Committee;
(5) Technology Committee; and
(6) Judicial Branch Budget Committee.

(Subd (a) amended effective April 16, 2020; adopted effective August 14, 2009, previously amended effective February 20, 2014, and January 1, 2019.)

(b) Purpose of the internal committees

The internal committees of the Judicial Council assist the full membership of the council in its responsibilities by providing recommendations in their assigned areas, including rules for court administration, practice, and procedure, and by performing duties delegated by the council. Internal committees generally work at the same policy level as the council, focusing on the establishment of policies that emphasize long-term strategic leadership and that align with judicial branch goals.

(Subd (b) repealed and adopted effective August 14, 2009.)

(c) Membership and appointment

The Chief Justice appoints each council member and advisory council member to one or more internal committees for a one-year term.

(Subd (c) relettered effective August 14, 2009; adopted as subd (a) effective January 1, 1999; previously amended effective January 1, 2007.)

(d) Meetings

Each internal committee meets as often as necessary to perform its responsibilities. The Administrative Director, as secretary of the Judicial Council, may attend and participate in the meetings of each internal committee.

(Subd (d) amended effective January 1, 2016; adopted as subd (c) effective January 1, 1999; previously amended and relettered as subd (d) effective August 14, 2009.)

(e) Voting

An advisory council member may vote on any internal committee matter unless the committee is taking final action on behalf of the council.

(Subd (e) relettered effective August 14, 2009; adopted as subd (d) effective January 1, 1999.)

(f) Council review

The council may overrule or modify an action taken by an internal committee.

(Subd (f) relettered effective August 14, 2009; adopted as subd (e) effective January 1, 1999.)

(g) Reporting to the council

As often as necessary, each internal committee must report to the council on the committee's activities.

(Subd (g) relettered effective August 14, 2009; adopted as subd (f) effective January 1, 1999; previously amended effective January 1, 2007.)

(h) Oversight of advisory committees and other bodies

When an internal committee has been assigned by the Chief Justice with the responsibility for oversight over one or more advisory committees or other bodies, the internal committee ensures that the activities of each advisory body overseen by it are consistent with the council's goals and policies. To achieve these outcomes, the internal committee:

(1) Communicates the council's annual charge to each advisory body;

(2) Reviews the proposed annual agenda of each to determine whether the agenda is consistent with the advisory body's charge and with the priorities established by the council; and

(3) After review, approves the final annual agenda for each advisory body.

(Subd (h) adopted effective January 1, 2019.)

Rule 10.10 amended effective April 16, 2020; adopted as rule 6.10 effective January 1, 1999; previously amended and renumbered as rule 10.10 effective January 1, 2007; previously amended effective August 14, 2009, February 20, 2014, January 1, 2016, and January 1, 2019.

Rule 10.11. Executive and Planning Committee

(a) Actions on behalf of the Judicial Council

The Executive and Planning Committee may take action on behalf of the council between council meetings, except for:

(1) Adopting rules of court, standards of judicial administration, and forms;

(2) Making appointments that by statute must be made by the council; and

(3) Taking actions that are delegated to other council internal committees.

(Subd (a) adopted effective August 14, 2009.)

2009 Note: Subdivision (a) was derived from former subdivision (d).

(b) Planning

The committee oversees the council's strategic planning process.

(Subd (b) adopted effective August 14, 2009.)

2009 Note: Subdivision (b) was derived from former subdivision (e).

(c) Court facilities

The committee oversees the council's policies and procedures regarding court facilities, including development of policies, procedures, and guidelines for facilities; site selection; and capital appropriations.

(Subd (c) adopted effective August 14, 2009.)

(d) Agendas for council meetings

The committee establishes agendas for council meetings by determining:

(1) Whether items submitted for the council's agenda require the council's action and are presented in a form that provides the council with the information it needs to make well-informed decisions; and

(2) Whether each item should be on the consent, discussion, or information agenda; how much time should be allotted for discussion; what presenters should be invited to speak; and, when appropriate, which specific issues should be discussed.

(Subd (d) repealed and relettered effective January 1, 2019; adopted as subd (e) effective August 14, 2009.)

(e) Topics for making policy and receiving updates

The committee develops a schedule of topics that the council intends to consider for making policy and receives updates from the Administrative Director or Judicial Council staff.

(Subd (e) relettered effective January 1, 2019; adopted as subd (f) effective August 14, 2009; previously amended effective January 1, 2016.)

(f) Governance

The committee makes recommendations to the council regarding governance and oversees the council's review of its governance policies and principles.

(Subd (f) relettered effective January 1, 2019; adopted as subd (g) effective August 14, 2009.)

(g) Nominations

The committee recommends candidates to the Chief Justice for appointment to the Judicial Council and its advisory bodies.

(Subd (g) relettered effective January 1, 2019; adopted as subd (h) effective August 14, 2009.)

(h) Communications

The committee promotes effective policies for communications between the Judicial Council and the judicial branch.

(Subd (h) relettered effective January 1, 2019; adopted as subd (j) effective August 14, 2009.)

Rule 10.11 amended effective January 1, 2019; adopted as rule 6.11 effective January 1, 1999; previously amended and renumbered as rule 10.11 effective January 1, 2007; previously amended effective January 1, 2002, September 1, 2003, January 1, 2005, August 14, 2009, and January 1, 2016.

Rule 10.12. Legislation Committee

(a) Legislative activities

The Legislation Committee performs the following functions:

(1) Taking a position on behalf of the council on pending legislative bills, after evaluating input from the council advisory bodies and Judicial Council staff, and any other input received from the courts, provided that the position is consistent with the council's established policies and precedents;

(2) Making recommendations to the council on all proposals for council-sponsored legislation and on an annual legislative agenda after evaluating input from council advisory bodies and Judicial Council staff, and any other input received from the courts; and

(3) Representing the council's position before the Legislature and other bodies or agencies and acting as liaison with other governmental entities, the bar, the media, the judiciary, and the public regarding council-sponsored legislation, pending legislative bills, and the council's legislative positions and agendas.

(Subd (a) amended effective April 16, 2020; adopted as subd (b); previously amended effective September 1, 2003, and January 1, 2016; previously amended and relettered as subd (a) effective August 14, 2009.)

(b) Building consensus

The committee builds consensus on issues of importance to the judicial branch consistent with the council's strategic plan with entities and individuals outside of the branch.

(Subd (b) adopted effective August 14, 2009.)

(c) Coordination

The committee develops an annual plan for communication and interaction with other branches and levels of government, components of the justice system, the bar, the media, and the public.

(Subd (c) amended effective August 14, 2009; previously amended effective September 1, 2003.)

(d) Advisory committees

The committee may direct any advisory committee to provide it with analysis or recommendations on any pending or proposed legislation, and reviews all recommendations from advisory committees regarding pending or proposed legislation.

(Subd (d) amended effective January 1, 2007; adopted effective September 1, 2003.)

Rule 10.12 amended effective April 16, 2020; adopted as rule 6.12 effective January 1, 1999; previously amended and renumbered as rule 10.12 effective January 1, 2007; previously amended effective September 1, 2003, August 14, 2009, and January 1, 2016.

Rule 10.13. Rules Committee

(a) Rules, standards, and forms

The Rules Committee establishes and maintains a rule-making process that is understandable and accessible to justice system partners and the public. The committee:

(1) Identifies the need for new rules, standards, and forms;

(2) Establishes and publishes procedures for the proposal, adoption, and approval of rules of court, forms, and standards of judicial administration that ensure that relevant input from the public is solicited and considered;

(3) Reviews proposed rules, standards, and forms and circulates those proposals for public comment in accordance with its procedures and guidelines.

(4) Provides guidelines for the style and format of rules, forms, and standards and ensures that proposals are consistent with the guidelines;

(5) Ensures that proposals for new or amended rules, standards, and forms do not conflict with statutes or other rules; and

(6) Determines whether proposals for new or amended rules, standards, or forms have complied with its procedures.

(Subd (a) amended effective April 16, 2020; adopted effective August 14, 2009.)

(b) Jury instructions

The committee establishes and maintains a process for obtaining public comment on the jury instructions and assists the council in making informed decisions about jury instructions.

(Subd (b) adopted effective August 14, 2009.)

2009 Note: Subdivision (b) was derived from former subdivision (d).

(c) Recommendations

The Rules Committee assists the council in making informed decisions about rules of court, forms, standards of judicial administration, and jury instructions. The committee:

(1) Recommends whether the council should approve, modify, or reject each proposal;

(2) Recommends to the Executive and Planning Committee whether a proposal should be on the council's consent or discussion agenda and how much time should be allocated for discussion; and

(3) When appropriate, identifies issues for discussion.

If the Rules Committee recommends against approval, it states the reasons for its recommendation.

(Subd (c) amended effective April 16, 2020; adopted effective August 14, 2009.)

2009 Note: Subdivision (c) was derived from former subdivision (b).

(d) Circulating orders

The committee initiates circulating orders to allow the council to adopt rules, standards, and forms between council meetings, if necessary.

(Subd (d) adopted effective August 14, 2009.)

(e) Responsibility of the Administrative Director

The Administrative Director is responsible for ensuring that items submitted to the committee for circulation for comment and the council's agenda comply with the committee's procedures and its guidelines on format and style.

(Subd (e) repealed and relettered effective January 1, 2019; adopted as subd (f) effective August 14, 2009; previously amended January 1, 2016.)

Rule 10.13 amended effective April 16, 2020; adopted as rule 6.13 effective January 1, 1999; previously amended and renumbered as rule 10.13 effective January 1, 2007; previously amended effective September 1, 2003, August 14, 2009, January 1, 2016, and January 1, 2019.

Rule 10.14. Litigation Management Committee

(a) Litigation oversight

The Litigation Management Committee oversees litigation and claims against trial court judges, appellate court justices, the Judicial Council, its staff, the trial and appellate courts, and the employees of those bodies in which the likely monetary exposure is $100,000 or more or that raise issues of significance to the judicial branch by:

(1) Reviewing and approving any proposed settlement, stipulated judgment, or offer of judgment; and

(2) Consulting with the Administrative Director or Chief Counsel, on request, regarding important strategy issues.

(Subd (a) amended effective January 1, 2016; previously amended effective January 1, 2003, January 1, 2007, December 9, 2008, and August 14, 2009.)

(b) Recommendations

The committee makes recommendations to the Judicial Council for policies governing the management of litigation involving the courts.

(Subd (b) amended effective August 14, 2009.)

(c) Strategic decisions

The committee resolves written objections described in rule 10.202(d) presented by Legal Services.

(Subd (c) amended effective January 1, 2016; adopted effective January 1, 2003; previously amended effective January 1, 2007, and August 14, 2009.)

Rule 10.14 amended effective January 1, 2016; adopted as rule 6.14 effective January 1, 2001; previously amended and renumbered as rule 10.14 effective January 1, 2007; previously amended effective January 1, 2003, December 9, 2008, and August 14, 2009.

Rule 10.15. Judicial Branch Budget Committee

(a) Purpose

The Judicial Branch Budget Committee assists the council to exercise its responsibilities under rule 10.101 with respect to the branch budget.

(Subd (a) adopted effective January 1, 2019.)

(b) Budget responsibilities

In assisting the council on the branch budget, the committee:

(1) Ensures that proposed judicial branch budgets, allocation schedules, and related budgetary issues are brought to the Judicial Council in a timely manner and in a format that permits the council to establish funding priorities in the context of the council's annual program objectives, statewide policies, and long-range strategic and operational plans;

(2) Reviews and makes recommendations annually to the council on submitted budget change proposals for the judicial branch, coordinates these budget change proposals, and ensures that they are submitted to the council in a timely manner;

(3) Reviews and makes recommendations on the use of statewide emergency funding for the judicial branch;

(4) Reviews and makes recommendations on the funding of grants on programs assigned to the committee; and

(5) Acts on other assignments referred to it by the council.

(Subd (b) adopted effective January 1, 2019.)

Rule 10.15 adopted effective January 1, 2019.

Rule 10.16. Technology Committee

(a) Technology policies

The Technology Committee oversees the council's policies concerning information technology. The committee assists the council by providing technology recommendations focusing on the establishment of policies that emphasize long-term strategic leadership and that align with judicial branch goals. The committee is responsible for determining that council policies are complied with on specific projects approved and funded by the council and that those projects proceed on schedule and within scope and budget.

(Subd (a) amended effective September 1, 2015; adopted effective February 20, 2014.)

(b) Coordination

The committee coordinates the activities of the Administrative Director, council internal committees and advisory committees, the courts, justice partners, and stakeholders on matters relating to court information technology. The committee also, in collaboration or consultation with the Legislation Committee, coordinates with other branches of government on information technology issues.

(Subd (b) amended effective April 16, 2020; previously amended effective September 1, 2015, and January 1, 2016.)

(c) Reports

The committee seeks reports and recommendations from the Administrative Director, the courts, and stakeholders on information technology issues. It ensures that information technology reports to the council are clear, are comprehensive, and provide relevant options so that the council can make effective final information technology policy decisions.

(Subd (c) adopted effective February 20, 2014.)

(d) Strategic and tactical technology plans

(1) *Strategic technology plan*

The strategic technology plan describes the technology goals for the branch. With input from advisory committees and individual courts, the committee is responsible for developing and recommending a strategic technology plan for the branch and the courts.

(2) *Tactical technology plan*

The tactical technology plan outlines the technology initiatives and projects that provide a road map for achieving the goals in the strategic technology plan. The committee provides oversight approval and prioritization of the tactical technology plan, which is developed and recommended by advisory committees with input from the courts.

(Subd (d) adopted effective September 1, 2015.)

(e) Technology needs, standards, and systems

The committee will, in partnership with the courts, develop timelines and recommendations to the council for:

(1) Establishing an approach and vision for implementing information technology that serves the courts, litigants, attorneys, justice partners, and the public, while considering available resources and information technology needs;

(2) Improving judicial branch information technology governance to best serve the implementation of technological solutions;

(3) Reviewing and recommending information technology standards; and

(4) Encouraging the courts to leverage their collective economic purchasing power in acquiring technological systems.

(Subd (e) amended and relettered effective September 1, 2015; adopted as subd (d) effective February 20, 2014.)

(f) Sponsorship of branchwide technology initiatives

The committee may act as executive sponsor of branchwide technology initiatives under the workstream model in rule 10.53(c).

(Subd (f) adopted effective September 1, 2015.)

(g) Funding of branchwide technology initiatives and projects

The committee reviews, prioritizes, and recommends requests for the funding of branchwide technology initiatives and projects with input from advisory committees. Factors to be considered by the committee include overall return on investment, business risk, alignment with the technology goals approved by the council in the strategic technology plan, and the availability of sufficient funding from an identifiable funding source.

(Subd (g) adopted effective September 1, 2015.)

(h) Collaboration and consultation with the committee

Other committees and advisory bodies should collaborate or consult with the committee (1) before making decisions or recommendations on technology policies, standards, and projects, and (2) before recommending funding priorities or making recommendations to approve funding requests for branchwide technology initiatives and projects.

(Subd (h) adopted effective September 1, 2015.)

(i) Oversight of advisory committees and other bodies

In addition to performing its oversight responsibilities under rule 10.10(h), the Technology Committee oversees the branchwide technology initiatives sponsored by each advisory body for which it is responsible.

(Subd (i) amended effective January 1, 2019; adopted as subd (e) effective February 20, 2014; previously amended and relettered effective September 1, 2015.)

Rule 10.16 amended effective April 16, 2020; adopted effective February 20, 2014; previously amended effective September 1, 2015, January 1, 2016, and January 1, 2019.

Rule 10.20. Proposals for new or amended rules, standards, or forms; rule-making process in general

(a) Council meetings to consider proposals

The Judicial Council meets twice a year, generally in April and October, to consider proposals for the adoption, amendment, or repeal of California Rules of Court, California Standards of Judicial Administration, and Judicial Council forms.

(b) Proposals

The council will consider proposals that are submitted to it by an internal committee, an advisory committee, a task force, or Judicial Council staff, in accordance with rule 10.22 and any policies and procedures established by the Rules Committee.

(Subd (b) amended effective April 16, 2020; repealed and adopted effective January 1, 2002; previously amended effective January 1, 2007, and January 1, 2016.)

(c) Statewide uniformity

The council will establish uniform statewide practices and procedures where appropriate to achieve equal access to justice throughout California.

(Subd (c) relettered effective January 1, 2002; adopted as subd (g) effective January 1, 1999.)

Rule 10.20 amended effective April 16, 2020; adopted as rule 6.20 effective January 1, 1999; previously amended effective January 1, 2002, and January 1, 2016; previously amended and renumbered as rule 10.20 effective January 1, 2007.

Rule 10.21. Proposals from members of the public for changes to rules, standards, or forms

(a) Application

This rule applies to proposals for changes to rules, standards, or forms by a member of the public (any person or organization other than a Judicial Council internal committee, advisory committee, or task force, or Judicial Council staff).

(Subd (a) amended effective January 1, 2016.)

(b) Submission and content of proposals

Proposals must be submitted in writing to: Judicial Council of California, Attention: Chief Counsel. Proposals should include:

(1) The text of the proposed rule, standard, form, or amendment;

(2) A description of the problem to be addressed;

(3) The proposed solution and alternative solutions;

(4) Any likely implementation problems;

(5) Any need for urgent consideration;

(6) Known proponents and opponents;

(7) Any known fiscal impact; and

(8) If known, any previous action by the council or an advisory committee on the proposal.

(Subd (b) amended effective January 1, 2016.)

(c) Advisory committee's review of proposal

The Chief Counsel must refer each proposal from a member of the public to an appropriate advisory committee for consideration and recommendation, or, if no appropriate advisory committee exists, to the Rules Committee. A Judicial Council staff member may independently review the proposal and present an analysis and a recommendation to the committee. The committee may take one of the following actions:

(1) Accept the proposal, either as submitted or modified, and proceed under rule 10.22;

(2) Request further information or analysis; or

(3) Reject the proposal.

(Subd (c) amended effective April 16, 2020; previously amended effective January 1, 2007, and January 1, 2016.)

Rule 10.21 amended effective April 16, 2020; adopted as rule 6.21 effective January 1, 2002; previously amended and renumbered as rule 10.21 effective January 1, 2007; previously amended effective January 1, 2016.

Rule 10.22. Rule-making procedures

(a) Who may make proposals

A Judicial Council internal committee, advisory committee, task force, or Judicial Council staff may recommend that the council adopt, amend, or repeal a rule or standard or adopt, approve, revise, or revoke a form.

(Subd (a) amended effective January 1, 2016; previously amended effective January 1, 2007.)

(b) Legal and advisory committee review

The internal committee, advisory committee, task force, or Judicial Council staff (the proponent) must first submit its proposal to Legal Services for legal and drafting review. If the proponent is not an advisory committee, and an appropriate advisory committee exists, the proponent must also submit the proposal to that advisory committee for review.

(Subd (b) amended effective January 1, 2016; previously amended effective January 1, 2007.)

(c) Recommendation to Rules Committee

After the proposal has been reviewed by Legal Services and any appropriate advisory committee, the proponent must submit the proposal to the Rules Committee with a recommendation that it be (1) circulated for public comment or (2) submitted to the council for approval without public comment.

(Subd (c) amended effective April 16, 2020; previously amended effective January 1, 2016.)

(d) Review by Rules Committee

The Rules Committee must review the recommendation and may take one of the following actions:

(1) Circulate the proposal for public comment;

(2) If the proposal presents a nonsubstantive technical change or correction or a minor substantive change that is unlikely to create controversy, recommend that the council adopt it without circulating it for comment;

(3) Postpone circulation for comment and either request further information or analysis by the proponent or refer the matter to another council internal or advisory committee, the full council, or the Chief Justice; or

(4) Reject the proposal if it is contrary to statute, conflicts with other rules or standards, or is contrary to established council policy.

(Subd (d) amended April 16, 2020; previously amended effective January 1, 2007.)

(e) Review of comments

After a proposal is circulated, the proponent must review the comments and decide whether to reject the proposal or to recommend that the council adopt it, with or without modifications.

(f) Submission to council

If, after reviewing the comments, the proponent recommends that the council adopt the proposal, the matter will be placed on the council's agenda. The Rules Committee must review the recommendation and submit its own recommendation to the council. The council may adopt, modify, or reject the proposal.

(Subd (f) amended effective April 16, 2020.)

(g) Compelling circumstances

The procedures established in this rule must be followed unless the Rules Committee finds that compelling circumstances necessitate a different procedure. The committee's finding and a summary of the procedure used must be presented to the council with any recommendation to the council made under this subdivision.

(Subd (g) amended effective April 16, 2020.)

Rule 10.22 amended effective April 16, 2020; adopted as rule 6.22 effective January 1, 2002; previously amended and renumbered as rule 10.22 effective January 1, 2007; previously amended effective January 16, 2016.

Chapter 2
Judicial Council Advisory Committees and Task Forces

Rule 10.30. Judicial Council advisory bodies
Rule 10.31. Advisory committee membership and terms
Rule 10.32. Nominations and appointments to advisory committees
Rule 10.33. Advisory committee meetings
Rule 10.34. Duties and responsibilities of advisory committees
Rule 10.40. Appellate Advisory Committee
Rule 10.41. Civil and Small Claims Advisory Committee
Rule 10.42. Criminal Law Advisory Committee
Rule 10.43. Family and Juvenile Law Advisory Committee
Rule 10.44. Probate and Mental Health Advisory Committee
Rule 10.46. Trial Court Presiding Judges Advisory Committee
Rule 10.48. Court Executives Advisory Committee
Rule 10.50. Center for Judicial Education and Research Advisory Committee
Rule 10.51. Court Interpreters Advisory Panel
Rule 10.52. Administrative Presiding Justices Advisory Committee
Rule 10.53. Information Technology Advisory Committee
Rule 10.54. Traffic Advisory Committee
Rule 10.55. Advisory Committee on Providing Access and Fairness
Rule 10.56. Collaborative Justice Courts Advisory Committee
Rule 10.58. Advisory Committee on Civil Jury Instructions
Rule 10.59. Advisory Committee on Criminal Jury Instructions
Rule 10.60. Tribal Court–State Court Forum
Rule 10.61. Court Security Advisory Committee
Rule 10.62. Court Facilities Advisory Committee
Rule 10.63. Advisory Committee on Audits and Financial Accountability for the Judicial Branch
Rule 10.64. Trial Court Budget Advisory Committee
Rule 10.65. Trial Court Facility Modification Advisory Committee
Rule 10.66. Workload Assessment Advisory Committee
Rule 10.67. Judicial Branch Workers' Compensation Program Advisory Committee
Rule 10.68. Data Analytics Advisory Committee
Rule 10.70. Task forces, working groups, and other advisory bodies

Rule 10.30. Judicial Council advisory bodies

(a) Types of bodies

Judicial Council advisory bodies are typically advisory committees and task forces.

(Subd (a) adopted effective August 14, 2009.)

(b) Functions

The advisory bodies:

(1) Use the individual and collective experience, opinions, and wisdom of their members to provide policy recommendations and advice to the council on topics the Chief Justice or the council specifies;

(2) Work at the same policy level as the council, developing recommendations that focus on strategic goals and long-term impacts that align with judicial branch goals;

(3) Generally do not implement policy. The council may, however, assign policy-implementation and programmatic responsibilities to an advisory body and may request it make recommendations to the Administrative Director on implementation of council policy or programs;

(4) Do not speak or act for the council except when formally given such authority for specific and time-limited purposes; and

(5) Are responsible, through Judicial Council staff, for gathering stakeholder perspectives on policy recommendations they plan to present to the council.

(Subd (b) amended effective January 1, 2016; adopted effective August 14, 2009.)

2009 Note: Subdivision (b) was derived from former subdivision (b).

(c) Subcommittees

With the approval of the internal committee with oversight responsibility for the advisory body, an advisory body may form subcommittees, composed entirely of members, to carry out the body's duties, subject to available resources.

(Subd (c) amended effective February 20, 2014; adopted effective August 14, 2009.)

2009 Note: Subdivision (c) was derived from former subdivision (e).

(d) Oversight

The Chief Justice assigns oversight of each council advisory body to an internal committee. The council gives a general charge to each advisory body specifying the body's subject matter jurisdiction. The council and its internal committees provide direction to the advisory bodies.

(Subd (d) adopted effective August 14, 2009.)

(e) Preference for using existing advisory committees

Unless substantial reasons dictate otherwise, new projects requiring committee involvement must be assigned to existing advisory committees.

(Subd (e) adopted effective August 14, 2009.)

2009 Note: Subdivision (e) was derived from former subdivision (f).

(f) Role of the Administrative Director

The Administrative Director sits as an ex officio member of each advisory body.

(Subd (f) amended effective January 1, 2016; adopted effective August 14, 2009.)

(g) Creation

In addition to the advisory committees established by the rules in this division, the Chief Justice may create additional advisory bodies by order.

(Subd (g) adopted effective August 14, 2009.)

2009 Note: Subdivision (g) was derived from former subdivision (a).

Rule 10.30 amended effective January 1, 2016; adopted as rule 6.30 effective January 1, 1999; previously amended and renumbered as rule 10.30 effective January 1, 2007; previously amended effective September 1, 2003, August 14, 2009, and February 20, 2014.

Rule 10.31. Advisory committee membership and terms

(a) Membership

The categories of membership of each advisory committee are specified in the rules in this chapter. Each advisory committee consists of between 12 and 18 members, unless a different number is specified by the Chief Justice or required by these rules. Advisory committee members do not represent a specific constituency but must act in the best interests of the public and the entire court system.

(Subd (a) amended effective September 1, 2003.)

(b) Terms

The Chief Justice appoints advisory committee members to three-year terms unless another term is specified in these rules or in the order appointing a member. Terms are staggered so that an approximately equal number of each committee's members changes annually. Members may apply for reappointment but there is no presumption of reappointment. All appointments and reappointments are at the sole discretion of the Chief Justice.

(Subd (b) amended effective February 1, 2018; previously amended effective November 1, 2004, and January 1, 2007.)

(c) Chair and vice-chair

The Chief Justice appoints an advisory committee member to be a committee chair or vice-chair for a one-year term except for the chair and vice-chair of the Court Executives Advisory Committee, who may be appointed to two-year terms. Except for the Court Executives Advisory Committee, when a member's term as the chair of an advisory committee ends, that member's term on the committee also ends, unless the Chief Justice orders otherwise.

(Subd (c) amended effective February 1, 2018; previously amended effective September 1, 2000, January 1, 2004, and January 1, 2007.)

(d) Advisory members

On the request of the advisory committee, the Chief Justice may designate an advisory member to assist an advisory committee or a subcommittee. Advisory members are appointed for three-year terms unless another term is specified in the order appointing the advisory member. Advisory members may participate in discussions and make or second motions but cannot vote.

(Subd (d) amended effective February 1, 2018; previously amended effective January 1, 2007.)

(e) Termination of membership

Committee membership terminates if a member leaves the position that qualified the member for the advisory committee unless (g) applies or the Chief Justice determines that the individual may complete the current term.

(Subd (e) amended effective February 1, 2018.)

(f) Vacancies

Vacancies are filled as they occur according to the nomination procedures described in rule 10.32.

(Subd (f) amended effective January 1, 2007.)

(g) Retired judges

A judge's retirement does not cause a vacancy on the committee if the judge is eligible for assignment. A retired judge who is eligible for assignment may hold a committee position based on his or her last judicial position.

Rule 10.31 amended effective February 1, 2018; adopted as rule 6.31 effective January 1, 1999; previously amended and renumbered as rule 10.31 effective January 1, 2007; previously amended effective September 1, 2000, September 1, 2003, January 1, 2004, and November 1, 2004.

Rule 10.32. Nominations and appointments to advisory committees

(a) Nomination procedures

The Executive and Planning Committee assists the Chief Justice in selecting advisory committee members by submitting a list of nominees for each position. Unless otherwise specified in the rule applicable to a particular advisory committee, the nomination procedures are as follows:

(1) The Executive and Planning Committee must publicize vacancies and solicit nominations. If any group is designated to submit nominations for a position, the Executive and Planning Committee will request that the group submit at least three nominations for each advisory committee vacancy.

(2) The Executive and Planning Committee must submit at least three nominees for each advisory committee vacancy to the Chief Justice. The nominees should represent diverse backgrounds and experiences as well as geographic locations throughout California.

(Subd (a) amended effective September 1, 2003.)

(b) Court executive or administrator members

A court executive or administrator member may be a county clerk, a court administrator, or an executive officer if the member also serves as the clerk of the court.

(c) Judicial administrator member

A judicial administrator member may be any person experienced in court administration and is not required to be currently employed by a court.

(d) Judicial officer

A judicial officer member may be a judge of the superior court or a court commissioner or referee.

(Subd (d) amended effective September 1, 2003.)

(e) Appointing order

The Chief Justice appoints advisory committee members by order.

(Subd (e) amended effective September 1, 2003.)

Rule 10.32 amended and renumbered effective January 1, 2007; adopted as rule 6.32 effective January 1, 1999; previously amended effective September 1, 2003.

Rule 10.33. Advisory committee meetings

Each advisory committee may meet as often as its chair deems necessary, within available resources. Meetings may be in person or by teleconference.

Rule 10.33 renumbered effective January 1, 2007; adopted as rule 6.33 effective January 1, 1999; previously amended effective September 1, 2003.

Rule 10.34. Duties and responsibilities of advisory committees

(a) Role

Advisory committees are standing committees created by rule of court or the Chief Justice to make recommendations and offer policy alternatives to the Judicial Council for improving the administration of justice within their designated areas of focus by doing the following:

(1) Identifying issues and concerns affecting court administration and recommending solutions to the council;

(2) Proposing necessary changes to rules, standards, forms, and jury instructions;

(3) Reviewing pending legislation and making recommendations to the Legislation Committee on whether to support or oppose it;

(4) Recommending new legislation to the council;

(5) Recommending to the council pilot projects and other programs to evaluate new procedures or practices;

(6) Acting on assignments referred by the council or an internal committee; and

(7) Making other appropriate recommendations to the council.

(Subd (a) amended effective April 16, 2020; adopted effective August 14, 2009.)

2009 Note: Subdivision (a) was derived from former subdivision (a).

(b) Annual charges

(1) Advisory committees are assigned annual charges by the council or an internal committee specifying what should be achieved in a given year. The council or an internal committee may amend an advisory committee's annual charge at any time.

(2) Advisory committees have limited discretion to pursue matters in addition to those specified in each committee's annual charge, as long as the matters are consistent with a committee's general charge, within the limits of resources available to the committee, and within any other limits specified by the council, the designated internal committee, or the Administrative Director.

(Subd (b) amended effective January 1, 2016; adopted effective August 14, 2009.)

(c) Responsibilities of the chair

Advisory committee chairs are responsible, with the assistance of staff, to:

(1) Develop a realistic annual agenda for the advisory committee, consistent with the committee's annual charge by the Judicial Council or Judicial Council internal committee;

(2) Present the advisory committee's recommendations to the Judicial Council;

(3) Discuss with the Administrative Director or the Administrative Director's designee appropriate staffing and other resources for projects within the advisory committee's agenda; and

(4) Submit recommendations with respect to advisory committee membership.

(Subd (c) adopted effective August 14, 2009.)

(d) Role of the Administrative Director

(1) The Administrative Director determines whether projects undertaken by council advisory bodies in addition to those specified in the council's or internal committee's annual charge to the advisory body are consistent with the body's general charge, its approved annual agenda, and the Judicial Council's strategic plan. The Administrative Director also determines whether any additional matters are within the body's authorized budget and available resources.

(2) The Administrative Director is not bound by the recommendations of an advisory committee and may make alternative recommendations to the Judicial Council or recommend that an advisory committee's annual charge be amended.

(Subd (d) amended effective January 1, 2016; adopted effective August 14, 2009.)

(e) Role of staff

(1) Advisory committees are assisted by Judicial Council staff. The duties of staff members include drafting committee annual agendas, managing the committee's budget and resources, coordinating committee activities, providing legal and policy analysis to the committee, organizing and drafting reports, selecting and supervising consultants, providing technical assistance, and assisting committee chairs in presenting the committee's recommendations to the Judicial Council. Staff may provide independent legal or policy analysis of issues that is different from the committee's position, if authorized to do so by the Administrative Director.

(2) Staff report to the Administrative Director. The decisions or instructions of an advisory body or its chair are not binding on the staff except in instances when the council or the Administrative Director has specifically authorized such exercise of authority.

(Subd (e) amended effective January 1, 2016; adopted effective August 14, 2009.)

(f) Review of annual agendas

(1) Each committee must submit a proposed annual agenda that is reviewed by the internal committee with oversight responsibility, as designated by the Chief Justice. This subdivision does not apply to the Administrative Presiding Justices Advisory Committee.

(2) The internal committee that is responsible for oversight of the advisory committee reviews the proposed annual agenda and provides the advisory committee with an annual charge to ensure that its activities are consistent with the council's goals and priorities. The annual charge may:

(A) Approve or disapprove the annual agenda in whole or in part;

(B) Direct the committee to pursue specific projects on the annual agenda;

(C) Add or delete specific projects; and

(D) Reassign priorities.

(3) To pursue matters in addition to those specified in its annual charge, an advisory committee must have the approval of the internal committee with oversight responsibility for the advisory committee. The matters must be consistent with the advisory committee's general charge, as set forth in the rules of court, its approved annual agenda, and the council's long-range strategic plan. The additional matters must also be within the committee's authorized budget and available resources, as specified by the council or the Administrative Director.

(Subd (f) amended effective January 1, 2016; adopted effective August 14, 2009; previously amended effective February 20, 2014.)

2009 Note: Subdivision (f) was derived from former subdivision (d).

Rule 10.34 amended effective April 16, 2020; adopted as rule 6.34 effective January 1, 1999; previously amended and renumbered as rule 10.34 effective January 1, 2007; previously amended effective January 1, 2002, September 1, 2003, August 14, 2009, February 20, 2014, and January 16, 2016.

Rule 10.40. Appellate Advisory Committee

(a) Area of focus

The committee makes recommendations to the council for improving the administration of justice in appellate proceedings.

(Subd (a) amended effective January 1, 2007; previously amended effective January 1, 2002.)

(b) Additional duty

In addition to the duties described in rule 10.34 the committee makes proposals on training for justices and appellate support staff to the Governing Committee of the Center for Judicial Education and Research.

(Subd (b) amended effective January 1, 2007; previously amended effective January 1, 2002.)

(c) Membership

The committee must include at least one member from each of the following categories:

(1) Supreme Court justice;

(2) Court of Appeal justice;

(3) Trial court judicial officer with experience in the appellate division;

(4) Supreme Court clerk/executive officer;

(5) Appellate court clerk/executive officer;

(6) Trial court judicial administrator;

(7) Civil appellate lawyer;

(8) Criminal defense appellate lawyer;

(9) State Public Defender;

(10) Appellate lawyer of the Attorney General's Office; and

(11) Appellate lawyer of the Court of Appeal or Supreme Court.

(Subd (c) amended effective January 1, 2018; previously amended effective January 1, 2002, January 1, 2007, and July 1, 2014.)

Rule 10.40 amended effective January 1, 2018; adopted as rule 6.40 effective January 1, 1999; previously amended effective January 1, 2002, and July 1, 2014; previously amended and renumbered effective January 1, 2007.

Rule 10.41. Civil and Small Claims Advisory Committee

(a) Area of focus

The committee makes recommendations to the council for improving the administration of justice in civil and small claims proceedings.

(Subd (a) amended effective January 1, 2007.)

(b) Membership

The committee must include at least one member from each of the following categories:

(1) Appellate court justice;

(2) Trial court judicial officer;

(3) Judicial administrator;

(4) Lawyer whose primary area of practice is civil law;

(5) Legal secretary;

(6) Person knowledgeable about small claims law and procedure; and

(7) Person knowledgeable about court-connected alternative dispute resolution programs for civil and small claims cases.

(Subd (b) amended effective January 1, 2011; previously amended effective January 1, 2007.)

Rule 10.41 amended effective January 1, 2011; adopted as rule 6.41 effective January 1, 1999; previously amended and renumbered effective January 1, 2007.

Rule 10.42. Criminal Law Advisory Committee

(a) Area of focus

The committee makes recommendations to the council for improving the administration of justice in criminal proceedings.

(Subd (a) amended effective January 1, 2007.)

(b) Membership

The committee must include at least one member from each of the following categories:

(1) Appellate court justice;

(2) Trial court judicial officer;

(3) Judicial administrator;

(4) Prosecutor;

(5) Criminal defense lawyer;

(6) Probation officer; and

(7) Mental health professional with experience in criminal law issues.

(Subd (b) amended effective February 1, 2018; previously amended effective January 1, 2007, and January 1, 2011.)

Rule 10.42 amended effective February 1, 2018; adopted as rule 6.42 effective January 1, 1999; previously amended and renumbered as rule 10.42 effective January 1, 2007; previously amended effective January 1, 2011.

Rule 10.43. Family and Juvenile Law Advisory Committee

(a) Area of focus

The committee makes recommendations to the council for improving the administration of justice in all cases involving marriage, family, or children.

(Subd (a) amended effective January 1, 2007.)

(b) Membership

The committee must include at least one member from each of the following categories:

(1) Appellate court justice;

(2) Trial court judicial officer;

(3) Judicial administrator;

(4) Child custody mediator;

(5) Lawyer whose primary practice area is family law;

(6) Lawyer from a public or private defender's office whose primary practice area is juvenile law;

(7) Chief probation officer;

(8) Child welfare director;

(9) Court Appointed Special Advocate (CASA) director;

(10) County counsel assigned to juvenile dependency cases;

(11) Domestic violence prevention advocate;

(12) District attorney assigned to juvenile delinquency cases;

(13) Lawyer from the California Department of Child Support Services or a local child support agency;

(14) Public-interest children's rights lawyer; and

(15) Mental health professional with experience with family and children's issues.

(Subd (b) amended effective February 1, 2018; previously amended effective July 1, 2005, and January 1, 2007.)

Rule 10.43 amended effective February 1, 2018; adopted as rule 6.43 effective January 1, 1999; previously amended and renumbered as rule 10.43 effective January 1, 2007; previously amended effective July 1, 2005.

Rule 10.44. Probate and Mental Health Advisory Committee

(a) Area of focus

The committee makes recommendations to the council for improving the administration of justice in proceedings involving:

(1) Decedents' estates, trusts, conservatorships, guardianships, and other probate matters; and

(2) Mental health and developmental disabilities issues.

(Subd (a) amended effective January 1, 2007.)

(b) Additional duty

The committee must coordinate activities and work with the Family and Juvenile Law Advisory Committee in areas of common concern and interest.

(Subd (b) amended effective January 1, 2007.)

(c) Membership

The committee must include at least one member from each of the following categories:

(1) Judicial officer with experience in probate;

(2) Lawyer whose primary practice involves decedents' estates, trusts, guardianships, conservatorships, or elder abuse law;

(3) Lawyer or examiner who works for the court on probate or mental health matters;

(4) Lawyer working for a public interest organization or a court self-help center whose practice focuses on guardianships or conservatorships;

(5) Investigator who works for the court to investigate probate guardianships or conservatorships;

(6) Person knowledgeable in mental health or developmental disability law;

(7) Person knowledgeable in private management of probate matters in a fiduciary capacity; and

(8) County counsel, public guardian, or other similar public officer familiar with guardianship and conservatorship issues.

(Subd (c) amended effective February 1, 2018; previously amended effective January 1, 2007, and January 1, 2008.)

Rule 10.44 amended effective February 1, 2018; adopted as rule 6.44 effective July 1, 2000; previously amended and renumbered as rule 10.44 effective January 1, 2007; previously amended effective January 1, 2008.

Rule 10.45. Trial Court Budget Working Group [Renumbered]

Rule 10.45 renumbered as rule 10.107 effective August 14, 2009.

Rule 10.46. Trial Court Presiding Judges Advisory Committee

(a) Area of focus

The committee contributes to the statewide administration of justice by monitoring areas of significance to the justice system and making recommendations to the Judicial Council on policy issues affecting the trial courts.

(Subd (a) amended effective January 1, 2007; previously amended effective September 1, 2000, and April 18, 2003.)

(b) Additional duties

In addition to the duties specified in rule 10.34, the committee may:

(1) Recommend methods and policies within its area of focus to improve trial court presiding judges' access to and participation in council decision making, increase communication between the council and the trial courts, and provide for training programs for judicial and court support staff;

(2) Respond and provide input to the Judicial Council, appropriate advisory committees, or Judicial Council staff on pending policy proposals and offer new recommendations on policy initiatives in the areas of legislation, rules, forms, standards, studies, and recommendations concerning court administration; and

(3) Provide for liaison between the trial courts and the Judicial Council, its advisory committees, task forces, and working groups, and Judicial Council staff.

(Subd (b) amended effective January 1, 2016; previously amended effective September 1, 2000, April 18, 2003, and January 1, 2007.)

(c) Membership

The committee consists of the presiding judge of each superior court.

(Subd (c) amended effective January 1, 2007; previously amended effective September 1, 2000, and April 18, 2003.)

(d) Executive Committee

The advisory committee may establish an Executive Committee that, in addition to other powers provided by the advisory committee, may act on behalf of the full advisory committee between its meetings.

(Subd (d) amended effective April 18, 2003; adopted effective September 1, 2000.)

(e) Subcommittee membership

The committee has standing subcommittees on rules and legislation. The chair may create other subcommittees as he or she deems appropriate. The chair must strive for representation of courts of all sizes on subcommittees.

(Subd (e) repealed and adopted effective April 18, 2003.)

(f) Chair

The advisory committee must annually submit to the Chief Justice one nomination for the chair of the advisory committee. Any member of the advisory committee whose term as presiding judge would extend at least through the term of the advisory committee chair is eligible for nomination. The nomination must be made by a majority vote of the full advisory committee. In the event that no candidate receives a majority vote on the first ballot, subsequent ballots of the top two candidates will occur until a candidate receives a majority vote. The chair of the advisory committee serves as chair of any Executive Committee established under (d) and as an advisory member of the Judicial Council.

(Subd (f) amended effective July 1, 2013; adopted as subd (d) effective January 1, 1999; previously amended and relettered effective September 1, 2000; previously amended effective April 18, 2003, and January 1, 2007.)

Rule 10.46 amended effective January 1, 2016; adopted as rule 6.46 effective January 1, 1999; previously amended and renumbered as rule 10.46 effective January 1, 2007; previously amended effective September 1, 2000, April 18, 2003, and July 1, 2013.

Advisory Committee Comment

Subdivision (f): An advisory committee member may submit his or her own name, the name of another member of the advisory committee, or the name of an incoming member of the advisory committee to be considered for nomination. An incoming member of the advisory committee may be nominated by a current member of the advisory committee, but he or she may not participate in the voting process. Only current members of the advisory committee may vote. The successful candidate must receive 30 or more votes.

Rule 10.48. Court Executives Advisory Committee

(a) Area of focus

The committee makes recommendations to the council on policy issues affecting the trial courts.

(Subd (a) amended effective January 1, 2004.)

(b) Additional duties

In addition to the duties specified in rule 10.34, the committee must:

(1) Recommend methods and policies to improve trial court administrators' access to and participation in council decision making;

(2) Review and comment on legislation, rules, forms, standards, studies, and recommendations concerning court administration proposed to the council;

(3) Review and make proposals concerning the Judicial Branch Statistical Information System or other large-scope data collection efforts;

(4) Suggest methods and policies to increase communication between the council and the trial courts; and

(5) Meet periodically with the Judicial Council's executive team to enhance branch communications.

(Subd (b) amended effective January 1, 2016; previously amended effective January 1, 2004, January 1, 2007, and February 20, 2014.)

(c) Membership

The committee consists of the court executive officer of each superior court.

(Subd (c) repealed, relettered and amended effective February 20, 2014; adopted as subd (d) effective January 1, 1999; previously amended effective January 1, 2004, and January 1, 2007.)

(d) Executive Committee

The advisory committee may establish an Executive Committee that, in addition to other powers provided by the advisory committee, acts on behalf of the full advisory committee. To assist it in formulating proposals and making recommendations to the council, the Executive Committee may seek the advice of the advisory committee. The Executive Committee consists of the following members:

(1) The nine court executive officers or interim/acting court executive officers from the nine trial courts that have 48 or more judges;

(2) Four court executive officers from trial courts that have 16 to 47 judges;

(3) Two court executive officers from trial courts that have 6 to 15 judges;

(4) Two court executive officers from trial courts that have 2 to 5 judges; and

(5) One court executive officer from the trial courts as an at-large member appointed by the committee chair to a one-year term.

(Subd (d) adopted effective February 20, 2014.)

(e) Nominations

(1) The advisory committee must submit nominations for each vacancy on the Executive Committee. The Executive Committee will recommend three nominees for each Executive Committee vacancy from the nominations received and submit its recommendations to the Executive and Planning Committee of the Judicial Council. The list of nominees must enable the Chief Justice to appoint an Executive Committee that reflects a variety of experience, expertise, and locales (e.g., urban, suburban, and rural). Membership on the Executive Committee does not preclude appointment to any other advisory committee or task force.

(2) The Executive Committee must review and recommend to the Executive and Planning Committee of the Judicial Council the following:

(A) Members of the Executive Committee;

(B) Nonvoting court administrator members of the Judicial Council; and

(C) Members of other advisory committees who are court executives or judicial administrators.

(Subd (e) amended effective February 20, 2014; previously amended effective January 1, 2004, and January 1, 2007.)

(f) Chair and vice-chair

The Chief Justice may appoint the chair and vice-chair of the advisory committee for up to a two-year term from the current or incoming membership of the Executive Committee. The chair and vice-chair of the advisory committee serve as the chair and vice-chair of the Executive Committee established by subdivision (d).

(Subd (f) amended effective February 20, 2014; previously amended effective January 1, 2004, January 1, 2007, and January 1, 2008.)

(g) Meetings

The Executive Committee will meet approximately every two months, which includes the statewide meetings with the advisory committee. The advisory committee will meet during at least two statewide meetings per year.

(Subd (g) adopted effective February 20, 2014.)

Rule 10.48 amended effective January 1, 2016; adopted as rule 6.48 effective January 1, 1999; previously amended and renumbered as rule 10.48 effective January 1, 2007; previously amended effective January 1, 2004, January 1, 2008, and February 20, 2014.

Rule 10.49. Conference of Court Executives [Repealed]

Rule 10.49 repealed effective February 20, 2014; adopted as rule 6.49 effective January 1, 1999; previously amended effective January 1, 2004; previously amended and renumbered effective January 1, 2007.

Rule 10.50. Center for Judicial Education and Research Advisory Committee

(a) Establishment and purpose

In 1973, the Judicial Council of California and the California Judges Association created the Center for Judicial Education and Research (CJER). The oversight body then known as the Governing Committee of CJER was made an advisory committee to the council in 1993 through the adoption of former rule 1029. In 2001, the rule that specifies the duties of that advisory committee was made consistent with the rules pertaining to other Judicial Council advisory committees.

(Subd (a) amended effective January 1, 2019; adopted effective December 18, 2001; previously amended effective January 1, 2007, and January 1, 2016.)

(b) Area of focus

The committee makes recommendations to the council for improving the administration of justice through comprehensive and quality education and training for judicial officers and other judicial branch personnel.

(Subd (b) relettered and amended effective December 18, 2001; adopted as subd (a).)

(c) Additional duties

In addition to the duties described in rule 10.34, the committee must:

(1) Recommend rules, standards, policies, and procedures for judicial branch education;

(2) Recommend a strategic long-range plan for judicial branch education;

(3) Evaluate the effectiveness of judicial branch education, the quality of participation, the efficiency of delivery, and the impact on service to the public;

(4) Review and comment on proposals from other advisory committees and task forces that include education and training of judicial officers or court staff in order to ensure coordination, consistency, and collaboration in educational services;

(5) Establish educational priorities for implementation of curricula, programs, publications, and delivery systems;

(6) Identify the need for and recommend the appointment of education curriculum committees to implement the priorities, long-range plan, and programs and products of judicial branch education; create and adopt procedures for their operation; and review and approve their projects and products;

(7) Identify and foster collaborative opportunities with courts to promote and ensure the availability of training at the local court level;

(8) Identify, analyze, and implement systems to enhance the delivery of education and training statewide; and

(9) Identify and foster collaborative opportunities with internal and external partners to maximize the resources dedicated to education and training.

(Subd (c) amended effective May 21, 2021; adopted as subd (b) effective January 1, 1999; previously relettered and amended effective December 18, 2001; previously amended effective January 1, 2007.)

(d) Membership

The committee consists of at least the following members:

(1) Eleven sitting judicial officers, including at least one appellate court justice and one immediate past presiding judge;

(2) Three judicial administrators, including a supervisor or manager from a trial or appellate court;

(3) The Administrative Director as an advisory member;

(4) The president of the California Judges Association or his or her designee as an advisory member; and

(5) Other advisory members as the Chief Justice may appoint.

(Subd (d) amended effective January 1, 2015; adopted as subd (c); previously relettered and amended effective December 18, 2001.)

(e) Nominations

Nominations for vacant positions on the CJER Advisory Committee and its education curriculum committees will be solicited under the procedures described in rule 10.32. The president of the California Judges Association may submit nominations to the Executive and Planning Committee.

(Subd (e) amended effective May 21, 2021; previously amended effective December 18, 2001, January 1, 2007, and January 1, 2019.)

(f) Chair and vice-chair

The Chief Justice appoints the chair and vice-chair. The committee may make recommendations to the Chief Justice for these two positions.

(Subd (f) amended effective December 18, 2001.)

Rule 10.50 amended effective May 21, 2021; adopted as rule 6.50 effective January 1, 1999; previously amended and renumbered as rule 10.50 effective January 1, 2007; previously amended effective December 18, 2001, January 1, 2015, January 1, 2016, and January 1, 2019.

Rule 10.51. Court Interpreters Advisory Panel

(a) Area of focus

To assist the council in performing its duties under Government Code sections 68560 through 68566 and to promote access to spoken-language interpreters and interpreters for deaf and hearing-impaired persons, the advisory panel is charged with making recommendations to the council on:

(1) Interpreter use and need for interpreters in court proceedings; and

(2) Certification, registration, renewal of certification and registration, testing, recruiting, training, continuing education, and professional conduct of interpreters.

(Subd (a) amended effective October 1, 2004.)

(b) Additional duty

The advisory panel is charged with reviewing and making recommendations to the council on the findings of the study of language and interpreter use and need for interpreters in court proceedings that is conducted by the Judicial Council every five years under Government Code section 68563.

(Subd (b) amended effective January 1, 2016; previously amended effective October 1, 2004.)

(c) Membership

The advisory panel consists of 11 members. A majority of the members must be court interpreters. The advisory panel must include the specified numbers of members from the following categories:

(1) Four certified or registered court interpreters working as employees in trial courts, one from each of the four regions established by Government Code section 71807. For purposes of the appointment of members under this rule, the Superior Court of California, County of Ventura, is considered part of Region 1 as specified in section 71807, and the Superior Court of California, County of Solano, is considered part of Region 2 as specified in section 71807;

(2) Two interpreters certified or registered in a language other than Spanish, each working either in a trial court as an independent contractor or in an educational institution;

(3) One appellate court justice;

(4) Two trial court judges; and

(5) Two court administrators, including at least one trial court executive officer.

(Subd (c) amended effective October 1, 2004; previously amended effective July 1, 1999.)

(d) Advisors

The Chief Justice may also appoint nonmember advisors to assist the advisory panel.

(Subd (d) adopted effective October 1, 2004.)

Rule 10.51 amended effective January 1, 2016; adopted as rule 6.51 effective January 1, 1999; previously amended effective July 1, 1999, and October 1, 2004; previously renumbered as rule 10.51 effective January 1, 2007.

Rule 10.52. Administrative Presiding Justices Advisory Committee

(a) Area of focus

The committee makes recommendations to the council on policy issues affecting the administration and operation of the Courts of Appeal.

(Subd (a) amended effective January 1, 2007.)

(b) Additional duties

In addition to the duties described in rule 10.34, the committee must:

(1) Establish administrative policies that promote the quality of justice by advancing the efficient functioning of the appellate courts;

(2) Advise the council of the appellate courts' resource requirements and solicit the council's support in meeting budget, administrative, and staffing requirements;

(3) Make proposals on training for justices and appellate support staff to the Governing Committee of the Center for Judicial Education and Research; and

(4) Comment on and make recommendations to the council about appellate court operations, including:

(A) Initiatives to be pursued by the council or its staff; and

(B) The council's goals and strategies.

(Subd (b) amended effective January 1, 2016; previously amended effective January 1, 2007.)

(c) Membership

The committee consists of:

(1) The Chief Justice as chair; and

(2) The administrative presiding justices of the Courts of Appeal designated under rule 10.1004.

(Subd (c) amended effective January 1, 2007.)

(d) Funding

Each year, the committee must recommend budget change proposals to be submitted to the Chief Justice for legislative funding to operate the appellate courts. These proposals must be consistent with the budget management guidelines of the Judicial Council's Finance office.

(Subd (d) amended effective January 1, 2016; previously amended effective January 1, 2007.)

(e) Allocations

The committee allocates resources among the appellate courts and approves budget management guidelines based on the actual allocation made by the Chief Justice.

(Subd (e) amended effective January 1, 2007.)

(f) Administrative Director

The Administrative Director must meet regularly with the committee and must notify and, when appropriate, consult with the committee about appellate court personnel matters.

(Subd (f) amended effective January 1, 2016; previously amended effective January 1, 2007.)

Rule 10.52 amended effective January 1, 2016; adopted as rule 6.52 effective January 1, 1999; previously amended and renumbered as rule 10.52 effective January 1, 2007.

Rule 10.53. Information Technology Advisory Committee

(a) Areas of focus

The committee makes recommendations to the council for improving the administration of justice through the use of technology and for fostering cooperative endeavors to resolve common technological issues with other stakeholders in the justice system. The committee promotes, coordinates, and acts as executive sponsor for projects and initiatives that apply technology to the work of the courts.

(Subd (a) amended effective September 1, 2015; previously amended effective January 1, 2007.)

(b) Additional duties

In addition to the duties described in rule 10.34, the committee must:

(1) Oversee branchwide technology initiatives funded in whole or in part by the state;

(2) Recommend rules, standards, and legislation to ensure compatibility in information and communication technologies in the judicial branch;

(3) Provide input to the Judicial Council Technology Committee on the technology and business requirements of court technology projects and initiatives in funding requests;

(4) Review and recommend legislation, rules, or policies to balance the interests of privacy, access, and security in relation to court technology;

(5) Make proposals for technology education and training in the judicial branch;

(6) Assist courts in acquiring and developing useful technologies;

(7) Establish mechanisms to collect, preserve, and share best practices across the state;

(8) Maintain a long-range plan. Develop and recommend a tactical technology plan, described in rule 10.16, with input from the individual appellate and trial courts; and

(9) Develop and recommend the committee's annual agenda, identifying individual technology initiatives scheduled for the next year.

(Subd (b) amended effective September 1, 2015; previously amended effective January 1, 2007.)

(c) Sponsorship of branchwide technology initiatives

(1) *Oversight of branchwide technology initiatives*

The committee is responsible for overseeing branchwide technology initiatives that are approved as part of the committee's annual agenda. The committee may oversee these initiatives through a workstream model, a subcommittee model, or a hybrid of the two. Under the workstream model, committee members sponsor discrete technology initiatives executed by ad hoc teams of technology experts and experienced project and program managers from throughout the branch. Under the subcommittee model, committee members serve on subcommittees that carry out technology projects and develop and recommend policies and rules.

(2) *Technology workstreams*

Each technology workstream has a specific charge and duration that align with the objective and scope of the technology initiative assigned to the workstream. The individual tasks necessary to complete the initiative may be carried out by dividing the workstream into separate tracks. Technology workstreams are not advisory bodies for purposes of rule 10.75.

(3) *Executive sponsorship of technology workstreams*

The committee chair designates a member or two members of the committee to act as executive sponsors of each technology initiative monitored through the workstream model. The executive sponsor assumes overall executive responsibility for project deliverables and periodically provides high-level project status updates to the advisory committee and council. The executive sponsor is responsible for facilitating work plans for the initiative.

(4) *Responsibilities and composition of technology workstream teams*

A workstream team serves as staff on the initiative and is responsible for structuring, tracking, and managing the progress of individual tasks and milestones necessary to complete the initiative. The executive sponsor recommends, and the chair appoints, a workstream team of technology experts and experienced project and program managers from throughout the branch.

(Subd (c) adopted effective September 1, 2015.)

(d) Membership

The committee must include at least one member from each of the following categories:

(1) Appellate justice;
(2) Trial court judicial officer;
(3) Trial court judicial administrator;
(4) Appellate court judicial administrator;
(5) Trial court information technology officer;
(6) Member of the Senate;
(7) Member of the Assembly;
(8) Representative of the executive branch; and
(9) Lawyer.

(Subd (d) amended and relettered effective September 1, 2015; adopted as subd (c); previously amended effective January 1, 2007.)

(e) Member selection

The two legislative members are appointed by the respective houses. The executive member is appointed by the Governor. The lawyer member is appointed by the State Bar. In making all other appointments to the committee, factors to be considered include a candidate's technology expertise and experience, as well as an ability to act as lead executive sponsor for technology initiatives.

(Subd (e) amended and relettered effective September 1, 2015; adopted as subd (d).)

(f) Chair

The Chief Justice appoints a judicial officer to serve as chair.

(Subd (f) amended and relettered effective September 1, 2015; adopted as subd (e).)

Rule 10.53 amended effective September 1, 2015; adopted as rule 6.53 effective January 1, 1999; previously amended and renumbered effective January 1, 2007.

Rule 10.54. Traffic Advisory Committee

(a) Area of focus

The committee makes recommendations to the council for improving the administration of justice in the area of traffic procedure, practice, and case management and in other areas as stated in the fish and game, boating, forestry, public utilities, parks and recreation, and business licensing bail schedules.

(Subd (a) amended effective January 1, 2007.)

(b) Membership

The committee must include at least one member from each of the following categories:

(1) Trial court judicial officer;
(2) Judicial administrator;
(3) Juvenile hearing officer;
(4) Representative from the California Highway Patrol;
(5) Representative from the Department of Motor Vehicles;
(6) Representative from the Office of Traffic Safety; and
(7) Criminal defense lawyer.

(Subd (b) amended effective January 1, 2010; previously amended effective January 1, 2007.)

Rule 10.54 amended effective January 1, 2010; adopted as rule 6.54 effective January 1, 1999; previously amended and renumbered effective January 1, 2007.

Rule 10.55. Advisory Committee on Providing Access and Fairness

(a) Area of focus

The committee makes recommendations for improving access to the judicial system, fairness in the state courts, diversity in the judicial branch, and court services for self-represented parties.

(Subd (a) amended effective February 20, 2014; previously amended effective January 1, 2007.)

(b) Additional duties

In addition to the duties described in rule 10.34, the committee must recommend to the Governing Committee of the Center for Judicial Education and Research, proposals for the education and training of judicial officers and court staff.

(Subd (b) amended effective February 20, 2014; previously amended effective January 1, 2007.)

(c) Membership

The committee must include at least one member from each of the following categories:

(1) Appellate justice;
(2) Trial court judicial officer;
(3) Lawyer with expertise or interest in disability issues;
(4) Lawyer with expertise or interest in additional access, fairness, and diversity issues addressed by the committee;
(5) Lawyer from a trial court self-help center;
(6) Legal services lawyer;
(7) Court executive officer or trial court manager who has experience with self-represented litigants;
(8) County law librarian or other related professional;
(9) Judicial administrator; and
(10) Public member.

(Subd (c) amended effective February 20, 2014; previously amended effective January 1, 2007.)

(d) Cochairs

The Chief Justice appoints two advisory committee members to serve as cochairs. Each cochair is responsible for leading the advisory committee's work in the following areas:

(1) Physical, programmatic, and language access; fairness in the courts; and diversity in the judicial branch; and
(2) Issues confronted by self-represented litigants and those of limited or moderate income, including economic, education, and language challenges.

(Subd (d) adopted effective February 20, 2014.)

Rule 10.55 amended effective February 20, 2014; adopted as rule 6.55 effective January 1, 1999; previously amended and renumbered effective January 1, 2007.

Advisory Committee Comment

The advisory committee's area of focus includes assisting courts to improve access and fairness by recommending methods and tools to identify and address physical, programmatic, and language access; fairness in the courts; and diversity in the judicial branch, as well as addressing issues that affect the ability of litigants to access the courts including economic, education, and language challenges. An additional responsibility of the advisory committee to recommend to the council updated guidelines and procedures for court self-help centers, as needed, is stated in rule 10.960.

Rule 10.56. Collaborative Justice Courts Advisory Committee

(a) Area of focus

The committee makes recommendations to the Judicial Council on criteria for evaluating and improving adult and youth collaborative programs that incorporate judicial supervision, collaboration among justice system partners, or rehabilitative services. Collaborative programs include collaborative justice courts, diversion programs, and similar court-monitored programs that seek to improve outcomes and address problems facing court-involved and justice system-involved individuals and those at risk of becoming involved with the justice system, including, but not limited to, individuals with mental health issues, substance use disorders, or co-occurring disorders.

(Subd (a) amended effective January 1, 2022; previously amended effective January 1, 2007.)

(b) Additional duties

In addition to the duties described in rule 10.34, the committee must:

(1) Make recommendations to the council on best practices and guidelines for collaborative programs;
(2) Assess and measure the success programs, including assessing and recommending methods for collecting data to evaluate the effectiveness of these programs;
(3) Identify and disseminate to trial courts locally generated and nationally recognized best practices for collaborative programs, and training and program implementation activities that support collaborative programs;
(4) Recommend to the Center for Judicial Education and Research Advisory Committee minimum judicial education standards on collaborative programs, and educational activities to support those standards;
(5) Advise the council of potential funding sources, including those that may advance collaborative programs;
(6) Make allocation recommendations regarding Judicial Council-administered grant funding programs that support collaborative programs; and
(7) Identify and disseminate appropriate outreach activities needed to support collaborative programs, including but not limited to collaborations with educational institutions, professional associations, and community-based organizations.

(Subd (b) amended effective January 1, 2022; previously amended effective January 1, 2007, and January 1, 2016.)

(c) Membership

The committee must include the following:

(1) At least five judicial officers. Nominations for these appointments must be made in accordance with rule 10.32. The list of nominees should enable the Chair of the Judicial Council to appoint a committee with members from courts of varying sizes and locations and that reflects a variety of experience and expertise in different cases types.

(2) At least one member from each of the following categories:

(A) Judicial administrator;

(B) District attorney;

(C) Criminal defense attorney;

(D) Law enforcement (police/sheriff);

(E) Treatment provider or rehabilitation provider;

(F) Probation officer;

(G) Court-treatment coordinator;

(H) Treatment court graduate; and

(I) Public member.

(Subd (c) amended effective January 1, 2022; previously amended effective January 1, 2007.)

Rule 10.56 amended effective January 1, 2022; adopted as rule 6.56 effective January 1, 2000; previously amended effective January 1, 2002, and January 1, 2016; previously amended and renumbered as rule 10.56 effective January 1, 2007.

Rule 10.57. Judicial Service Advisory Committee [Repealed]

Rule 10.57 repealed effective October 25, 2013; adopted as rule 6.57 effective January 1, 2003; previously amended and renumbered effective January 1, 2007.

Rule 10.58. Advisory Committee on Civil Jury Instructions

(a) **Area of focus**

The committee regularly reviews case law and statutes affecting jury instructions and makes recommendations to the Judicial Council for updating, amending, and adding topics to the council's civil jury instructions.

(Subd (a) amended effective January 1, 2007.)

(b) **Membership**

The committee must include at least one member from each of the following categories, and a majority of the members must be judges:

(1) Appellate court justice;

(2) Trial court judge;

(3) Lawyer whose primary area of practice is civil law; and

(4) Law professor whose primary area of expertise is civil law.

Rule 10.58 amended and renumbered effective January 1, 2007; adopted as rule 6.58 effective September 1, 2003.

Rule 10.59. Advisory Committee on Criminal Jury Instructions

(a) **Area of focus**

The committee regularly reviews case law and statutes affecting jury instructions and makes recommendations to the Judicial Council for updating, amending, and adding topics to the council's criminal jury instructions.

(b) **Membership**

The committee must include at least one member from each of the following categories, and a majority of the members must be judges:

(1) Appellate court justice;

(2) Trial court judge;

(3) Lawyer whose primary area of practice is criminal defense;

(4) Deputy district attorney or other attorney who represents the People of the State of California in criminal matters; and

(5) Law professor whose primary area of expertise is criminal law.

Rule 10.59 renumbered effective January 1, 2007; adopted as rule 6.59 effective July 1, 2005.

Rule 10.60. Tribal Court–State Court Forum

(a) **Area of focus**

The forum makes recommendations to the council for improving the administration of justice in all proceedings in which the authority to exercise jurisdiction by the state judicial branch and the tribal justice systems overlaps.

(Subd (a) adopted effective October 25, 2013.)

(b) **Additional duties**

In addition to the duties described in rule 10.34, the forum must:

(1) Identify issues of mutual importance to tribal and state justice systems, including those concerning the working relationship between tribal and state courts in California;

(2) Make recommendations relating to the recognition and enforcement of court orders that cross jurisdictional lines, the determination of jurisdiction for cases that might appear in either court system, and the sharing of services between jurisdictions;

(3) Identify, develop, and share with tribal and state courts local rules of court, protocols, standing orders, and other agreements that promote tribal court–state court coordination and cooperation, the use of concurrent jurisdiction, and the transfer of cases between jurisdictions;

(4) Recommend appropriate activities needed to support local tribal court–state court collaborations; and

(5) Make proposals to the Governing Committee of the Center for Judicial Education and Research on educational publications and programming for judges and judicial support staff.

(Subd (b) adopted effective October 25, 2013.)

(c) **Membership**

The forum must include the following members:

(1) Tribal court judges or justices selected by tribes in California, as described in (d), but no more than one tribal court judge or justice from each tribe;

(2) At least three trial court judges from counties in which a tribal court is located;

(3) At least one appellate justice of the California Courts of Appeal;

(4) At least one member from each of the following committees: the Access and Fairness Advisory Committee, Civil and Small Claims Advisory Committee, Criminal Law Advisory Committee, Family and Juvenile Law Advisory Committee, Governing Committee of the Center for Judicial Education and Research, Probate and Mental Health Advisory Committee, and Traffic Advisory Committee; and

(5) At least one, but no more than three, California executive branch officials responsible for tribal-related work.

The composition of the forum must have an equal or a close-to-equal number of judges or justices from tribal courts and state courts.

(Subd (c) amended effective February 1, 2018; adopted effective October 25, 2013.)

(d) **Member Selection**

(1) The Chief Justice appoints all forum members, except tribal court judges and tribal court justices, who are appointed as described in (2).

(2) For each tribe in California with a tribal court, the tribal leadership will appoint the tribal court judge or justice member to the forum consistent with the following selection and appointment process.

(A) The forum cochairs will notify the tribal leadership of a vacancy for a tribal court judge or justice and request that they submit names of tribal court judges or justices to serve on the forum.

(B) A vacancy for a tribal court judge or justice will be filled as it occurs either on the expiration of a member's term or when the member has left the position that qualified the member for the forum.

(C) If there are more names of tribal court judges and justices submitted by the tribal leadership than vacancies, then the forum cochairs will confer and decide which tribal court judges or justices should be appointed. Their decision will be based on the diverse background and experience, as well as the geographic location, of the current membership.

(Subd (d) adopted effective October 25, 2013.)

(e) **Cochairs**

The Chief Justice appoints a state appellate justice or trial court judge and a tribal court appellate justice or judge to serve as cochairs, consistent with rule 10.31(c).

(Subd (e) adopted effective October 25, 2013.)

Rule 10.60 amended effective February 1, 2018; adopted effective October 25, 2013.

Judicial Council Comment

Tribes are recognized as distinct, independent political nations (see *Worcester v. Georgia* (1832) 31 U.S. 515, 559, and *Santa Clara Pueblo v. Martinez* (1978) 436 U.S. 49, 55, citing *Worcester*), which retain inherent authority to establish their own form of government, including tribal justice systems. (25 U.S.C.A. §3601(4).) Tribal justice systems are an essential part of tribal governments and serve to ensure the public health and safety and the political integrity of tribal governments. (25 U.S.C.A. §3601(5).) Traditional tribal justice practices are essential to the maintenance of the culture and identity of tribes. (25 U.S.C.A. §3601(7).)

The constitutional recognition of tribes as sovereigns in a government-to-government relationship with all other sovereigns is a well-established principle of federal Indian law. (See *Cohen's Handbook of Federal Indian Law* (2005) p.207.) In recognition of this sovereignty, the council's oversight of the forum, through an internal committee under rule 10.30(d), is limited to oversight of the forum's work and activities and does not include oversight of any tribe or tribal court.

Rule 10.61. Court Security Advisory Committee

(a) Area of Focus

The committee makes recommendations to the council for improving court security, including personal security and emergency response planning.

(Subd (a) adopted effective October 25, 2013.)

(b) Membership

The committee must include at least one member from each of the following categories:

(1) Appellate court justice;
(2) Appellate court administrator;
(3) Trial court judge;
(4) Trial court judicial administrator;
(5) Member of the Court Facilities Advisory Committee; and
(6) Member of the Trial Court Facility Modification Advisory Committee.

At least one member of the committee should be from a trial court that uses a marshal for court security services.

(Subd (b) adopted effective October 25, 2013.)

Rule 10.61 adopted effective October 25, 2013.

Rule 10.62. Court Facilities Advisory Committee

(a) Area of focus

The committee makes recommendations to the council concerning the judicial branch capital program for the trial and appellate courts.

(Subd (a) adopted effective February 20, 2014.)

(b) Membership

The committee must include at least one member from each of the following categories:

(1) Appellate court justice;
(2) Appellate court clerk/executive officer;
(3) Superior court judge;
(4) Court executive officer;
(5) Lawyer;
(6) Local government official or administrator; and
(7) Public member with expertise in real estate acquisition, construction, architecture, cost estimating, or facilities management and operations.

The committee also includes the chair and vice-chair of the Trial Court Facility Modification Advisory Committee, as non-voting members.

(Subd (b) amended effective January 1, 2018; adopted effective February 20, 2014.)

Rule 10.62 amended effective January 1, 2018; adopted effective February 20, 2014.

Rule 10.63. Advisory Committee on Audits and Financial Accountability for the Judicial Branch

(a) Purpose of the rule

One of the most important functions of government is to ensure that public funds are properly spent and accounted for. This committee is charged with advising and assisting the council in performing its responsibilities to ensure that the fiscal affairs of the judicial branch are managed efficiently, effectively, and transparently, and in performing its specific responsibilities relating to audits and contracting, as required by law and good public policy.

(Subd (a) adopted effective July 28, 2017.)

(b) Area of focus

The committee makes recommendations to the council on audits and practices that will promote financial accountability and efficiency in the judicial branch.

(Subd (b) amended and relettered effective July 28, 2017; adopted as subd (a) effective February 20, 2014.)

(c) Additional duties

In addition to the duties specified in rule 10.34, the committee must:

(1) Review and approve a yearly audit plan for the judicial branch that will ensure the adequacy and effectiveness of the judicial branch's accounting, financial reporting, compliance, and internal control system; review all audit reports of the judicial branch; recommend council action on audit reports that identify substantial issues; approve all other audit reports and have them posted publicly; and, where appropriate, make recommendations to the council on individual or systemic issues identified in audit reports;

(2) Advise and assist the council in performing its responsibilities and exercising its authority under Government Code sections 77009 and 77206 and under part 2.5 of the Public Contract Code (commencing with section 19201; the California Judicial Branch Contract Law);

(3) Review and recommend to the council proposed updates and revisions to the *Judicial Branch Contracting Manual*; and

(4) Make recommendations concerning any proposed changes to the annual compensation plan for Judicial Council staff.

(Subd (c) amended and relettered effective July 28, 2017; adopted as subd (b) effective February 20, 2014.)

(d) Membership

The committee may include members with experience in public or judicial branch finance and must include at least one member from each of the following categories:

(1) Justices of the Courts of Appeal;
(2) Judges of the superior courts;
(3) Clerk/executive officers of the Courts of Appeal; and
(4) Court executive officers of the superior courts.

The committee membership must also include at least one nonvoting advisory member who has significant governmental auditing experience.

The California Judges Association will recommend three nominees for a superior court judge position and submit its recommendations to the Executive and Planning Committee of the Judicial Council.

(Subd (d) amended and relettered effective July 28, 2017; adopted as subd (c) effective February 20, 2014.)

Rule 10.63 amended effective July 28, 2017; adopted effective February 20, 2014.

Advisory Committee Comment

The purpose of the Advisory Committee on Audits and Financial Accountability for the Judicial Branch is to advise and assist the council in performing its constitutional and statutory responsibilities relating to the fiscal affairs of the judicial branch. To improve the administration of the courts, article VI, section 6 of the California Constitution requires the council to survey judicial business and make recommendations. To ensure that the fiscal affairs of the courts are managed efficiently, effectively, and responsibly, Government Code section 77206 authorizes the council to regulate the fiscal management of the courts and provides for audits of the courts and Judicial Council staff by the council, its representatives, and other entities. Government Code section 77009(h) provides that the "Judicial Council or its representatives may perform audits, reviews, and investigations of superior court operations and records wherever they may be located." The Public Contract Code provides that the council shall publish a *Judicial Branch Contracting Manual* (Pub. Contract Code, §19206). It also provides that the California State Auditor, subject to appropriations, shall biennially identify and audit five or more judicial branch entities to assess the implementation of the California Judicial Branch Contract Law (JBCL) (Pub. Contract Code, §19210(a), (b)) and shall biennially conduct audits of Judicial Council staff to assess the implementation of, and compliance with, the JBCL (Pub. Contract Code, §19210(c)).

Rule 10.64. Trial Court Budget Advisory Committee

(a) Area of focus

The Trial Court Budget Advisory Committee makes recommendations to the council on the preparation, development, and implementation of the budget for the trial courts and provides input to the council on policy issues affecting trial court funding.

(Subd (a) adopted effective February 20, 2014.)

(b) Additional duties

In addition to the duties specified in rule 10.34, the committee may make recommendations to the council on:

(1) Trial court budget priorities to guide the development of the budget for the upcoming fiscal year;

(2) The allocation of trial court funding, including any changes to existing methodologies for allocating trial court budget augmentations and reductions; and

(3) Budget policies and procedures, as appropriate.

(Subd (b) adopted effective February 20, 2014.)

(c) Membership

(1) The advisory committee consists of an equal number of trial court presiding judges and court executive officers reflecting diverse aspects of state trial courts, including urban, suburban, and rural locales; the size and adequacy of budgets; and the number of authorized judgeships. For purposes of this rule, "presiding judge" means a current presiding judge or a judge who has served as a presiding judge within six years of the year of the appointment as a committee member. An existing presiding judge or past presiding judge member is eligible to be reappointed.

(2) No more than two members may be from the same court.

(3) The chairs of the Trial Court Presiding Judges Advisory Committee and the Court Executives Advisory Committee serve as ex officio voting members.

(4) Notwithstanding rule 10.31(e), a presiding judge is qualified to complete his or her term on the advisory committee even if his or her term as presiding judge of a trial court ends.

(5) The Judicial Council's chief administrative officer, and director of Budget Services serve as nonvoting members.

(Subd (c) amended effective January 1, 2019; adopted effective February 20, 2014; previously amended effective October 28, 2014.)

Rule 10.64 amended effective January 1, 2019; adopted effective February 20, 2014; previously amended effective October 28, 2014.

Rule 10.65. Trial Court Facility Modification Advisory Committee

(a) Area of focus

The committee makes recommendations to the council on facilities modifications, maintenance, and operations; environmental services; and utility management.

(Subd (a) adopted effective January 1, 2015.)

(b) Additional duties

In addition to the duties specified in rule 10.34, the committee:

(1) Makes recommendations to the council on policy issues, business practices, and budget monitoring and control for all facility-related matters in existing branch facilities.

(2) Makes recommendations to the council on funding and takes additional action in accordance with council policy, both for facility modifications and for operations and maintenance.

(3) Collaborates with the Court Facilities Advisory Committee in the development of the capital program, including providing input to design standards, prioritization of capital projects, and methods to reduce construction cost without impacting long-term operations and maintenance cost.

(4) Provides quarterly and annual reports on the facilities modification program in accordance with the council policy.

(Subd (b) adopted effective January 1, 2015.)

(c) Membership

The committee consists of members from the following categories:

(1) Trial court judges; and

(2) Court executive officers.

The committee includes the chair and vice-chair of the Court Facilities Advisory Committee, as nonvoting members.

(Subd (c) adopted effective January 1, 2015.)

Rule 10.65 adopted effective January 1, 2015.

Advisory Committee Comment

The Judicial Council policy referred to in the rule is contained in the *Trial Court Facility Modifications Policy* adopted by the council.

Rule 10.66. Workload Assessment Advisory Committee

(a) Area of focus

The committee makes recommendations to the council on judicial administration standards and measures that provide for the equitable allocation of resources across courts to promote the fair and efficient administration of justice.

(Subd (a) adopted effective January 1, 2015.)

(b) Additional duties

In addition to the duties specified in rule 10.34, the committee must recommend:

(1) Improvements to performance measures and implementation plans and any modifications to the Judicial Workload Assessment and the Resource Assessment Study Model;

(2) Processes, study design, and methodologies that should be used to measure and report on court administration; and

(3) Studies and analyses to update and amend case weights through time studies, focus groups, or other methods.

(Subd (b) adopted effective January 1, 2015.)

(c) Membership

(1) The advisory committee consists of an equal number of superior court judicial officers and court executive officers reflecting diverse aspects of state trial courts, including urban, suburban, and rural locales; size and adequacy of resources; number of authorized judgeships; and for judicial officers, diversity of case type experience.

(2) A judicial officer and court executive officer may be from the same court.

(Subd (c) adopted effective January 1, 2015.)

Rule 10.66 adopted effective January 1, 2015.

Rule 10.67. Judicial Branch Workers' Compensation Program Advisory Committee

(a) Area of focus

The committee makes recommendations to the council for improving the statewide administration of the Judicial Branch Workers' Compensation Program and on allocations to and from the Judicial Branch Workers' Compensation Fund established under Government Code section 68114.10.

(Subd (a) adopted effective January 1, 2015.)

(b) Additional duties

In addition to the duties specified in rule 10.34, the committee must review:

(1) The progress of the Judicial Branch Workers' Compensation Program;

(2) The annual actuarial report; and

(3) The annual allocation, including any changes to existing methodologies for allocating workers' compensation costs.

(Subd (b) adopted effective January 1, 2015.)

(c) Membership

The advisory committee consists of persons from trial courts and state judicial branch entities knowledgeable about workers' compensation matters, including court executive officers, appellate court clerks/executive officers, and human resources professionals.

(Subd (c) amended effective January 1, 2018; adopted effective January 1, 2015.)

Rule 10.67 amended effective January 1, 2018; adopted effective January 1, 2015; previously amended effective July 1, 2016.

Advisory Committee Comment

The Judicial Branch Workers' Compensation Program is administered by the Judicial Council staff under rule 10.350.

Rule 10.68. Data Analytics Advisory Committee

(a) Areas of focus

The committee makes recommendations to the Judicial Council regarding the collection, use, and sharing of judicial branch data and information to inform decision making, promote transparency, and improve the administration of justice while ensuring the security of nonpublic data and data sources.

(Subd (a) adopted effective March 11, 2022.)

(b) Additional duties

In addition to the duties described in rule 10.34, the committee must:

(1) Develop and recommend policies, or revisions to existing policies, concerning standards and measures to use in collecting, analyzing and sharing data and information that will advance the goals of increased access to justice, greater transparency and accountability, and enhanced delivery of services to the public.

(2) Develop and recommend performance measures, studies, and methodologies to measure and report on court administration, practices, and procedures, including workload assessments; and

(3) Identify, analyze, and report on emerging issues related to branch data and information, including usage of data and information to support branch projects and initiatives.

(Subd (b) adopted effective March 11, 2022.)

(c) Membership

The committee must include at least one member from each of the following categories:

(1) Appellate justice;

(2) Trial court judicial officer;

(3) Trial court or appellate court administrator; and

(4) Court staff with data and information management expertise.

(Subd (c) adopted effective March 11, 2022.)

(d) Member selection

Factors to be considered in making all appointments to the committee include a candidate's general expertise and experience in data, information, or technology governance and management.

(Subd (d) adopted effective March 11, 2022.)

Rule 10.68 adopted effective March 11, 2022.

Rule 10.70. Task forces, working groups, and other advisory bodies

(a) Established by Chief Justice or Judicial Council

The Chief Justice or the council may establish task forces and other advisory bodies to work on specific projects that cannot be addressed by the council's standing advisory committees. These task forces and other advisory bodies may be required to report to one of the internal committees, as designated in their charges.

(Subd (a) lettered and amended effective July 1, 2015; adopted as unlettered subd effective January 1, 1999.)

(b) Established by Administrative Director

The Administrative Director may establish working groups to work on specific projects identified by the Administrative Director that address areas and topics within the Administrative Director's purview.

(Subd (b) adopted effective July 1, 2015.)

Rule 10.70 amended effective July 1, 2015; adopted as rule 6.70 effective January 1, 1999; previously renumbered effective January 1, 2007; previously amended effective September 1, 2003, and August 14, 2009.

Rule 10.71. Court Facilities Transitional Task Force [Repealed]

Rule 10.71 repealed by its own provision effective June 30, 2007; adopted as rule 6.60 effective June 23, 2004; previously amended and renumbered effective January 1, 2007.

Chapter 3
Judicial Council Advisory Body Meetings

Title 10, Judicial Administration Rules—Division 1, Judicial Council—Chapter 3, Judicial Council Advisory Body Meetings; adopted effective July 1, 2014.

Rule 10.75. Meetings of advisory bodies

(a) Intent

The Judicial Council intends by this rule to supplement and expand on existing rules and procedures providing public access to the council and its advisory bodies. Existing rules and procedures provide for circulation of advisory body proposals regarding rules, forms, standards, and jury instructions for public comment, posting of written reports for the council on the California Courts website (*www.courts.ca.gov*), public attendance and comment during council meetings, real time audio casts of council meetings, and public posting of council meeting minutes. This rule expands public access to advisory body meetings.

(Subd (a) adopted effective July 1, 2014.)

(b) Advisory bodies and chairs

(1) "Advisory bodies," as used in this rule, means any multimember body created by the Judicial Council to review issues and report to the council. For purposes of this rule, subcommittees that are composed of less than a majority of the members of the advisory body are not advisory bodies. However, standing subcommittees that are charged with addressing a topic as a continuing matter are advisory bodies for purposes of this rule irrespective of their composition.

(2) "Chair," as used in this rule, includes a chair's designee.

(Subd (b) adopted effective July 1, 2014.)

(c) Open meetings

(1) *Meetings*

Advisory body meetings to review issues that the advisory body will report to the Judicial Council are open to the public, except as otherwise provided in this rule. A meeting open to the public includes a budget meeting, which is a meeting or portion of a meeting to discuss a proposed recommendation of the advisory body that the Judicial Council approve an allocation or direct an expenditure of public funds. A majority of advisory body members must not decide a matter included on a posted agenda for an upcoming meeting in advance of the meeting.

(2) *Exempt bodies*

The meetings of the following advisory bodies and their subcommittees are exempt from the requirements of this rule:

(A) Advisory Committee on Civil Jury Instructions;

(B) Advisory Committee on Criminal Jury Instructions; and

(C) Litigation Management Committee.

(3) *Rule committees*

With the exception of any budget meetings, the meetings of the rule committees listed in this subdivision and of their subcommittees are closed unless the chair concludes that a particular agenda item may be addressed in open session. Any budget meeting must be open to the public.

(A) Appellate Advisory Committee;

(B) Civil and Small Claims Advisory Committee;

(C) Criminal Law Advisory Committee;

(D) Family and Juvenile Law Advisory Committee;

(E) Probate and Mental Health Advisory Committee; and

(F) Traffic Advisory Committee.

(Subd (c) adopted effective July 1, 2014.)

(d) Closed sessions

The chair of an advisory body or an advisory body subcommittee may close a meeting, or portion of a meeting, to discuss any of the following:

(1) The appointment, qualifications, performance, or health of an individual, or other information that, if discussed in public, would constitute an unwarranted invasion of personal privacy;

(2) Claims, administrative claims, agency investigations, or pending or reasonably anticipated litigation naming, or reasonably anticipated to name, a judicial branch entity or a member, officer, or employee of such an entity;

(3) Negotiations concerning a contract, a labor issue, or legislation;

(4) The price and terms of payment for the purchase, sale, exchange, or lease of real property for a judicial branch facility before the property has been acquired or the relevant contracts have been executed;

(5) Security plans or procedures or other matters that if discussed in public would compromise the safety of the public or of judicial branch officers or personnel or the security of judicial branch facilities or equipment, including electronic data;

(6) Non-final audit reports or proposed responses to such reports;

(7) Trade secrets or privileged or confidential commercial and financial information;

(8) Development, modification, or approval of any licensing or other professional examination or examination procedure;

(9) Evaluation of individual grant applications; or

(10) Topics that judicial officers may not discuss in public without risking a violation of the California Code of Judicial Ethics, necessitating recusal, or encouraging disqualification motions or peremptory challenges against them, including proposed legislation, rules, forms, standards of judicial administration, or jury instructions.

(Subd (d) adopted effective July 1, 2014.)

(e) Notice of meetings

(1) *Regular meetings*

Public notice must be given of the date and agenda of each meeting that is subject to this rule, whether open or closed, at least five business days before the meeting.

(2) *Urgent circumstances*

A meeting that is subject to this rule may be conducted on 24-hours notice in case of urgent circumstances requiring prompt action. The minutes of such meetings must briefly state the facts creating the urgent circumstances requiring prompt action and the action taken.

(Subd (e) adopted effective July 1, 2014.)

(f) Form of notice

(1) The notice and agenda for a meeting subject to this rule, whether open or closed, must be posted on the California Courts website.

(2) The notice for meetings subject to this rule must state whether the meeting is open or closed. If a meeting is closed or partially closed, the notice must identify the closed agenda items and the specific subdivision of this rule authorizing the closure.

(3) For meetings that are open in part or in full, the notice must provide:

(A) The telephone number or other electronic means that a member of the public may use to attend the meeting;

(B) The time of the meeting, whether the public may attend in person, and, if so, the meeting location; and

(C) The e-mail address or other electronic means that the public may use to submit written comments regarding agenda items or requests to make an audio recording of a meeting.

(Subd (f) adopted effective July 1, 2014.)

(g) Contents of agenda

The agenda for a meeting subject to this rule, whether open or closed, must contain a brief description of each item to be considered during the meeting. If a meeting is closed or partially closed, the agenda must identify the specific subdivision of this rule authorizing the closure.

(Subd (g) adopted effective July 1, 2014.)

(h) Meeting materials

Materials for an open meeting must be posted on the California Courts website at least three business days before the date of the meeting, except in extraordinary circumstances.

(Subd (h) adopted effective July 1, 2014.)

(i) Public attendance

The public may attend open sessions of advisory body meetings by telephone or other available electronic means. If the members of an advisory body gather in person at a single location for a meeting, the public may attend in person at that location if the chair concludes security measures permit.

(Subd (i) adopted effective July 1, 2014.)

(j) Conduct at meeting

Members of the public who attend open meetings in person must remain orderly. The chair may order the removal of any disorderly person.

(Subd (j) adopted effective July 1, 2014.)

(k) Public comment

(1) *Written comment*

The public may submit written comments for any agenda item of a regularly noticed open meeting up to one complete business day before the meeting.

(2) *In-person comment*

If security measures permit public attendance at an open in-person advisory body meeting, the meeting must include an opportunity for public comment on each agenda item before the advisory body considers the item. Requests to comment on an agenda item must be submitted before the meeting begins, indicating the speaker's name, the name of the organization that the speaker represents, if any, and the agenda item that the public comment will address. The advisory body chair may grant a request to comment on an agenda item that is received after a meeting has begun.

(3) *Reasonable limits and timing*

The advisory body chair has discretion to establish reasonable limits on the length of time for each speaker and the total amount of time permitted for public comment. The chair may also decide whether public comments will be heard at the beginning of the meeting or in advance of the agenda items.

(Subd (k) adopted effective July 1, 2014.)

(l) Making an audio recording of a meeting

An advisory body chair may permit a member of the public to make an audio recording of an open meeting, or the open portion of a meeting, if a written request is submitted at least two business days before the meeting.

(Subd (l) adopted effective July 1, 2014.)

(m) Minutes as official records

Minutes of each meeting subject to this rule, whether open or closed, must be prepared for approval at a future meeting. When approved by the advisory body, the minutes constitute the official record of the meeting. Approved minutes for the open portion of a meeting must be posted on the California Courts website.

(Subd (m) adopted effective July 1, 2014.)

(n) Adjourned meetings

An advisory body chair may adjourn a meeting to reconvene at a specified time without issuing a new notice under (e)(1), provided that, if open agenda items remain for discussion, notice of the adjourned meeting is posted on the California Courts website 24 hours before the meeting reconvenes. The notice must identify any remaining open agenda items to be discussed, the time that the meeting will reconvene, the telephone number that the public may use to attend the meeting, and if the public may attend the reconvened meeting in person, the location. The advisory body may not consider new agenda items when the meeting reconvenes except as permitted under (e)(2).

(Subd (n) adopted effective July 1, 2014.)

(o) Action by e-mail between meetings

An advisory body may take action by e-mail between meetings in circumstances specified in this subdivision.

(1) *Circumstances*

An advisory body chair may distribute a proposal by e-mail to all advisory body members for action between meetings if:

(A) The advisory body discussed and considered the proposal at a previous meeting but concluded additional information was needed; or

(B) The chair concludes that prompt action is needed.

(2) *Notice*

If an e-mail proposal concerns a matter that otherwise must be discussed in an open meeting, the advisory body must provide public notice and allow one complete business day for public comment concerning the proposal before acting on the proposal. The notice must be posted on the California Courts website and must provide an e-mail address to which the public may submit written comments. The advisory body may forego public comment if the chair concludes that prompt action is required.

(3) *Communications*

If an e-mail proposal concerns a matter that otherwise must be discussed in an open meeting, after distribution of the proposal and until the advisory body has acted, advisory body members must restrict their communications with each other about the proposal to e-mail. This restriction only applies to proposals distributed under this subdivision.

(4) *Official record*

Written minutes describing the action taken on an e-mail proposal that otherwise must be discussed in an open meeting must be prepared for approval at a future meeting. The minutes must attach any public comments received. When approved by the advisory body, the minutes constitute the official record of the proposal. Approved minutes for such a proposal must be posted to the California Courts website. The e-mails exchanged concerning a proposal that otherwise would have been considered in a closed meeting will constitute the official record of the proposal.

(Subd (o) adopted effective July 1, 2014.)

(p) Review requirement

The Judicial Council will review the impact of this rule within one year of the rule's adoption and periodically thereafter to determine whether amendments are needed. In conducting its review, the council will consider, among other factors, the public interest in access to meetings of the council's advisory bodies, the obligation of the judiciary to comply with judicial ethics standards, and the public interest in the ability of advisory bodies to effectively assist the Judicial Council by offering policy recommendations and alternatives for improving the administration of justice.

(Subd (p) adopted effective July 1, 2014.)
Rule 10.75 adopted effective July 1, 2014.

Advisory Committee Comment

Subdivisions (a) and (c)(1). This rule expands public access to Judicial Council advisory bodies. The council recognizes the important public interest in access to those meetings and to information regarding administration and governance of the judicial branch. Meetings of the Judicial Council are open, and notice and materials for those meetings are provided to the public, under rules 10.5 and 10.6. Rules in Division 1 of Title 10 describe the council's advisory bodies and require that proposals for rules, standards, forms, and jury instructions be circulated for public comment. (See Cal. Rules of Court, rules 10.10–10.22, 10.30–10.70.) Reports to the council presenting proposals and recommendations are publicly posted on the California Courts website (*www.courts.ca.gov*). Internal committee chairs report at each council meeting regarding the activities of the internal committees in the period since the last council meeting, and internal committee meeting minutes also are posted on the California Courts website. This rule expands on those existing rules and procedures to increase public access by opening the meetings of advisory bodies to review issues that the advisory body will report to the council. The rule does not apply to meetings that do not involve review of issues to be reported to the council, such as meetings providing education and training of members, discussion of best practices, or sharing of information of general interest unrelated to advice or reports to the council. Those non-advisory matters are outside the scope of this rule.

Subdivision (b)(1). The definition provided in (b)(1) is intended exclusively for this rule and includes internal committees, advisory committees, task forces, and other similar multimember bodies that the council creates to review issues and report to it. (Cf. Cal. Rules of Court, rule 10.30(a) ["Judicial Council advisory bodies are typically advisory committees and task forces"].)

Subdivisions (c)(2), (c)(3), and (d)(10). The Code of Judicial Ethics governs the conduct of judges and is binding upon them. It establishes high standards of conduct that judges must personally observe, maintain, and enforce at all times to promote and protect public confidence in the integrity and impartiality of the judiciary. (See Code Judicial Ethics, Preamble, canon 1, canon 2A.) Among other things, compliance with these high ethical standards means avoiding conduct that could suggest a judge does not have an open mind in considering issues that may come before the judge. (*Id.*, canon 2A.) Judges also are prohibited from making public comments about a pending or impending proceeding (*id.*, canon 3B(9)), signifying that they may not publicly discuss case law that has not reached final disposition through the appellate process, or pending or anticipated litigation, conduct that would be required to participate in the work covered by the referenced subdivisions. Ethical standards also direct that they hear and decide all matters assigned to them, avoiding extrajudicial duties that would lead to their frequent disqualification. (*Id.*, canons 3B(1), 4A(4).)

The work of the three advisory bodies listed in subdivision (c)(2) exclusively involves discussion of topics that are uniquely difficult or impossible for judges to address while honoring the detailed ethical standards governing the judiciary. For example, as required by rule, the Litigation Management Committee discusses pending or anticipated claims and litigation against judicial officers, courts, and court employees. Jury instruction committees also may discuss decisions or rulings issued in cases that have not reached final resolution through the appellate process. Thus, opening the meetings of these three committees would result in precluding judges, who are specially learned in the law, from meaningful participation on those committees. Subdivision (c)(2) is added to avoid this result.

The work of the six rule committees listed in subdivision (c)(3) almost always will trigger similar issues. Those bodies focus primarily on developing, and providing input concerning, proposed legislation, rules, forms, and standards of judicial administration. That work necessarily entails a complex interchange of views, consideration of multiple perspectives, and the vetting of opposing legal arguments, which judges cannot undertake in public without risk that their comments will be misunderstood or used as a basis for disqualification or challenge. Service on the referenced committees, and public participation in discussing the referenced topics, may make it difficult for a judge to hear and decide all matters assigned to the judge and conceivably could lead to frequent disqualification of the judge, exposing the judge to risk of an ethical violation. This may create significant practical issues for courts related to judicial workloads, while also deterring individuals specially learned in the law from serving on advisory bodies, in turn depriving the public of the benefits of their training and experience in crafting procedures for the effective and efficient administration of justice. Subdivisions (c)(3) and (d)(10) are intended to prevent such deleterious results by clarifying that meetings of the six rule committees whose work almost entirely focuses on these topics ordinarily will be closed and that meetings of other bodies performing similar functions also will be closed as the chairs deem appropriate, with the exception that any budget meetings must be open.

Subdivision (d)(7). Definitions of the terms "trade secret," "privileged information," and "confidential commercial and financial information," are provided in rule 10.500(f)(10).

Subdivision (k)(1). Due to budget constraints, members' schedules, and the geographic diversity of most committees' membership, advisory body meetings typically are held via teleconference or other method not requiring the members' in person attendance. Because judicial officer and attorney members may have limited time for meetings (e.g., only a lunch hour), the volume of advisory body business to be accomplished in those periods may be considerable, and the costs of coordinating teleconferences that would accommodate spoken comments from the public would be significant in the aggregate, the rule only provides for public comment in writing. To ensure sufficient time for advisory body staff to gather and distribute written comments to members, and for members to review comments before the meeting, the rule requires that comments be submitted one complete business day before the meeting.

Chapter 4
Judicial Council staff

Title 10, Judicial Administration Rules—Division 1, Judicial Council—Chapter 4, Judicial Council staff; amended effective July 29, 2014; renumbered effective July 1, 2014.

Rule 10.80. Administrative Director of the Courts (Administrative Director)
Rule 10.81. Judicial Council staff

Rule 10.80. Administrative Director of the Courts (Administrative Director)

(a) Functions

The Administrative Director, appointed by the Judicial Council under article VI, section 6 of the Constitution, performs those functions prescribed by the Constitution and laws of the state, or delegated to the director by the Judicial Council or the Chief Justice.

(Subd (a) amended effective July 29, 2014; adopted as unlettered subd effective January 1, 1999; previously lettered subd (a) and amended effective August 14, 2009.)

(b) Accountability

The Administrative Director is accountable to the council and the Chief Justice for the performance of the Judicial Council staff. The Administrative Director's charge is to accomplish the council's goals and priorities.

(Subd (b) amended effective July 29, 2014; adopted effective August 14, 2009.)

(c) Interpretation of policies

The Administrative Director may use any reasonable interpretation of Judicial Council policies to achieve the council's goals, consistent with the limitations from the council and the Chief Justice.

(Subd (c) adopted effective August 14, 2009.)

(d) Responsibilities

In carrying out these duties, the Administrative Director is responsible for allocating the financial and other resources relating to the Judicial Council staff (including, for example, funding the operation of advisory bodies and other activities) to achieve the branch goals and policies adopted by the Judicial Council of California.

(Subd (d) amended effective July 29, 2014; adopted effective August 14, 2009.)

(e) Reports

The Administrative Director reports to the Judicial Council at least once annually on the progress made toward achieving the council's goals. When the council sets the direction on projects or programs that require more than one year to complete, the Administrative Director will report back to the council at regular intervals on their status and significant developments.

(Subd (e) adopted effective August 14, 2009.)

Rule 10.80 amended effective July 29, 2014; adopted as rule 6.80 effective January 1, 1999; previously amended and renumbered effective January 1, 2007; previously amended effective August 14, 2009.

Rule 10.81. Judicial Council staff

(a) Establishment

The Administrative Director, under the supervision of the Chief Justice, employs, organizes, and directs a staff that assists the council and its chair in carrying out their duties under the Constitution and laws of the state.

(Subd (a) amended effective July 29, 2014; previously amended effective January 1, 2007, and August 14, 2009.)

(b) References to "Administrative Office of the Courts"

The Judicial Council in the past referred to its staff as the "Administrative Office of the Courts". The following applies where the term "Administrative Office of the Courts" is used:

(1) *Rules of Court*

Throughout these rules of court and in all Judicial Council forms, all references to "Administrative Office of the Courts" or "AOC" are deemed to refer to the Judicial Council, the Administrative Director, or the Judicial Council staff, as appropriate.

(2) *Other Judicial Council materials and actions*

All references to "Administrative Office of the Courts" or "AOC" in any policy, procedure, manual, guideline, publication, or other material issued by the Judicial Council or its staff are deemed to refer to the Judicial Council, the Administrative Director, or the Judicial Council staff, as appropriate. Judicial Council staff will continue to be responsible for any active delegations or directives the Judicial Council made to the Administrative Office of the Court.

(3) *Statutes*

The Judicial Council, its staff, or the Administrative Director, as appropriate, will continue to perform all functions, duties, responsibilities, and other obligations imposed by statute or regulation on the Administrative Office of the Courts.

(4) *Agreements and proceedings*

The Judicial Council will continue to perform all duties, responsibilities, functions, or other obligations, and bear all liabilities, and exercise all rights, powers, authorities, benefits, and other privileges attributed to the "Administrative Office of the Courts" or "AOC" arising from contracts, memorandums of understanding, or other legal agreements, documents, proceedings, or transactions. The Judicial Council may be substituted for the "Administrative Office of the Courts" or "AOC" wherever necessary, with no prejudice to the substantive rights of any party.

(Subd (b) amended effective July 29, 2014; previously amended effective January 1, 2007.)

Rule 10.81 amended effective July 29, 2014; adopted as rule 6.81 effective January 1, 1999; previously amended and renumbered effective January 1, 2007; previously amended effective August 14, 2009.

Advisory Committee Comment

The Judicial Council in 1961 adopted a resolution that named its staff the "Administrative Office of the California Courts." In 1970, the council adopted a rule of court that renamed its staff the "Administrative Office of the Courts."

In recent years, the council became aware of recurring confusion about the relationship between the Administrative Office of the Courts and the Judicial Council. There was a common misperception that the Administrative Office of the Courts was a separate entity from the council having independent policymaking authority, when in fact, the members of the Judicial Council set policy, and staff, by whatever name, support the work of the council under the members' direction and oversight. The confusion about the role of the Administrative Office of the Courts impeded the council's ability to advance the interests of the judicial branch.

To allow the council to better achieve its mission, it decided in 2014 to retire the name "Administrative Office of the Courts." This adjustment underscored the unity of identity of the Judicial Council and its staff, and clarified that there has always been only a single entity. The retirement conformed the Judicial Council's practice with that of other state government entities, which do not assign a separate name to their staffs.

The 2014 amendments to this rule are intended to implement the retirement of the name "Administrative Office of the Courts" and clarify that in retiring the name no substantive legal change has occurred. The Judicial Council and its staff will continue to discharge any legal obligations and duties they may have, regardless of the discontinuance of the use of the name "Administrative Office of the Courts."

Division 2
Administration of the Judicial Branch

Chap. 1. Budget and Fiscal Management. Rules 10.101–10.106.
Chap. 2. Court Security. Rules 10.172–10.174.
Chap. 3. Court Facilities. Rules 10.180–10.184.
Chap. 4. Management of Claims and Litigation. Rules 10.201–10.203.
Chap. 5. Management of Human Resources. Rules 10.350–10.351.
Chap. 6. Court Technology, Information, and Automation. Rule 10.400.
Chap. 7. Minimum Education Requirements, Expectations, and Recommendations. Rules 10.451–10.493.

Chapter 1
Budget and Fiscal Management

Rule 10.101. Role of the Judicial Council
Rule 10.102. Acceptance of gifts
Rule 10.103. Limitation on intrabranch contracting
Rule 10.104. Limitation on contracting with former employees
Rule 10.105. Allocation of new fee, fine, and forfeiture revenue
Rule 10.106. Judicial branch travel expense reimbursement policy

Rule 10.101. Role of the Judicial Council

(a) Purpose

This rule specifies the responsibilities of the Judicial Council, the Chief Justice, the Administrative Director, and council staff with respect to the judicial branch budget.

(Subd (a) amended effective July 1, 2015; previously amended effective January 1, 2005, January 1, 2007, and August 14, 2009.)

(b) Duties of the Judicial Council

The Judicial Council must:

(1) Establish responsible fiscal priorities that best enable the judicial branch to achieve its goals and the Judicial Council to achieve its mission;

(2) Develop policies and procedures for the creation and implementation of a yearly budget for the judicial branch;

(3) Develop the budget of the judicial branch based on the priorities established and the needs of the courts;

(4) Communicate and advocate the budget of the judicial branch to the Governor and the Legislature;

(5) Allocate funds in a manner that ensures equal access to justice for all citizens of the state, ensures the ability of the courts to carry out their functions effectively, promotes implementation of statewide policies as established by statute and the Judicial Council, and promotes implementation of efficiencies and cost-saving measures;

(6) Resolve appeals on budget and allocation issues; and

(7) Ensure that the budget of the judicial branch remains within the limits of the appropriation set by the Legislature.

(Subd (b) amended effective July 1, 2015; previously amended effective January 1, 2007, and August 14, 2009.)

(c) Authority of the Chief Justice and Administrative Director

(1) The Chief Justice and the Administrative Director may take the following actions, on behalf of the Judicial Council, with regard to any of the Judicial Council's recommended budgets for the Supreme Court, the Courts of Appeal, the trial courts, the Judicial Council, the Habeas Corpus Resource Center, and council staff:

(A) Make technical changes to the proposed budget; and

(B) Make changes during their negotiations with the legislative and executive branches consistent with the goals and priorities adopted by the Judicial Council.

(2) The Chief Justice, on behalf of the Judicial Council, may allocate funding appropriated in the annual State Budget to the Supreme Court, the Courts of Appeal, the Judicial Council, the Habeas Corpus Resource Center, and council staff.

(3) After the end of each fiscal year, the Administrative Director must report to the Judicial Council on the actual expenditures from the budgets for the Supreme Court, the Courts of Appeal, the trial courts, the Judicial Council, the Habeas Corpus Resource Center, and council staff.

(Subd (c) amended effective July 1, 2015; adopted effective January 1, 2005; previously amended effective August 14, 2009.)

(d) Duties of the Administrative Director

The Administrative Director implements the directives of the Judicial Council and must:

(1) Present the judicial branch budget in negotiations with the Governor and the Legislature; and

(2) Allocate to the trial courts, on behalf of the Judicial Council, a portion of the prior fiscal year baseline allocation for the trial courts following approval of the State Budget and before the allocation of state trial court funding by the Judicial Council. The portion of the prior fiscal year baseline allocation that may be so allocated is limited to the amount estimated to be necessary for the operation of the courts pending action by the Judicial Council, and may not exceed 25 percent of the prior fiscal year baseline allocation for each trial court.

(Subd (d) amended effective July 1, 2015; adopted as subd (c) effective July 1, 1998; previously relettered effective January 1, 2005; previously amended effective January 1, 2001, January 1, 2007, and August 14, 2009.)

(e) Duties of the director of Finance

The director of Finance for the Judicial Council, under the direction of the Administrative Director, administers the budget policies and procedures developed and approved by the Judicial Council. The director of Finance must:

(1) Develop and administer a budget preparation process for the judicial branch, and ensure the submission of a final budget recommendation for the judicial branch to the Department of Finance by November 1 of each year;

(2) Develop, in consultation with the State Controller's Office and the Department of Finance, a manual of procedures for the budget request process, revenues, expenditures, allocations, and payments;

(3) Monitor all revenues and expenditures for the judicial branch;

(4) Develop recommendations for fiscal priorities and the allocation and reallocation of funds; and

(5) Assist all courts and the Administrative Director in preparing and managing budgets.

(Subd (e) amended effective July 1, 2015; adopted as subd (d) effective July 1, 1998; previously relettered effective January 1, 2005; previously amended effective January 1, 2007, and August 14, 2009.)

Rule 10.101 amended effective July 1, 2015; adopted as rule 2301 effective July 1, 1998; renumbered as rule 6.101 effective January 1, 1999; previously amended and renumbered effective January 1, 2007; previously amended effective January 1, 2001, January 1, 2005, and August 14, 2009.

Advisory Committee Comment

Subdivision (c)(1)(A). Examples of technical changes to the budget include calculation of fiscal need, translation of an approved concept to final fiscal need, and simple non-policy-related baseline adjustments such as health and retirement benefits, Pro Rata, and the Statewide Cost Allocation Plan.

Rule 10.102. Acceptance of gifts

(a) Administrative Director's authority to accept gifts

The Administrative Director may accept on behalf of any entity listed in (b) any gift of real or personal property if the gift and any terms and conditions are found to be in the best interest of the state. Any applicable standards used by the Director of Finance under Government Code section 11005.1 may be considered in accepting gifts.

(Subd (a) amended effective January 1, 2016; adopted as unlettered subd; previously amended and lettered as subd (a) effective January 1, 2004; previously amended effective January 1, 2007.)

(b) Delegation of authority

The Administrative Director may delegate the authority to accept gifts to the following, under any guidelines established by the Administrative Director:

(1) The executive officer of a superior court, for gifts to the superior court;

(2) The clerk/executive officer of a Court of Appeal, for gifts to that Court of Appeal;

(3) The clerk/executive officer of the Supreme Court, for gifts to the Supreme Court; and

(4) The Judicial Council's director of Finance, for gifts to the Judicial Council.

(Subd (b) amended effective January 1, 2018; previously adopted effective January 1, 2004; previously amended effective January 1, 2007, and January 1, 2016.)

Rule 10.102 amended effective January 1, 2018; adopted as rule 989.7 effective September 13, 1991; previously amended and renumbered as rule 6.102 effective January 1, 2004, and as rule 10.102 effective January 1, 2007; previously amended effective January 1, 2016.

Rule 10.103. Limitation on intrabranch contracting

(a) Definitions

For purposes of this rule, "judicial branch entity" includes a trial court, a Court of Appeal, the Supreme Court, and the Judicial Council.

(Subd (a) amended effective January 1, 2016.)

(b) Application

This rule is not applicable to:

(1) Part-time commissioners, with respect to services as a commissioner;

(2) Part-time court interpreters who are not subject to the cross-assignment system under Government Code section 71810, with respect to interpreter services provided to a court; and

(3) Court reporters, with respect to reporter services provided to a court.

(Subd (b) amended effective January 1, 2007.)

(c) Intrabranch limitations

An employee of a judicial branch entity must not:

(1) Engage in any employment, enterprise, or other activity from which he or she receives compensation or in which he or she has a financial interest and that is sponsored or funded by any judicial branch entity through or by a contract for goods or services for which compensation is paid, unless the activity is required as a condition of his or her regular judicial branch employment; or

(2) Contract with any judicial branch entity, on his or her own behalf, to provide goods or services for which compensation is paid.

(Subd (c) amended effective January 1, 2007.)

(d) Multiple employment

This rule does not prohibit any person from being employed by more than one judicial branch entity.

Rule 10.103 amended effective January 1, 2016; adopted as rule 6.103 effective January 1, 2004; previously amended and renumbered as rule 10.103 effective January 1, 2007.

Rule 10.104. Limitation on contracting with former employees

(a) Trial and appellate court contracts with former employees

A trial or appellate court may not enter into a contract for goods or services for which compensation is paid with a person previously employed by that court or by the Judicial Council:

(1) For a period of 12 months following the date of the former employee's retirement, dismissal, or separation from service, if he or she was employed in a policymaking position in the same general subject area as the proposed contract within the 12-month period before his or her retirement, dismissal, or separation; or

(2) For a period of 24 months following the date of the former employee's retirement, dismissal, or separation from service, if he or she engaged in any of the negotiations, transactions, planning, arrangements, or any part of the decision-making process relevant to the contract while employed in any capacity by the court or the Judicial Council.

(Subd (a) amended effective January 1, 2016.)

(b) Judicial Council contracts with former employees

The Judicial Council may not enter into a contract for goods or services for which compensation is paid with a person previously employed by it:

(1) For a period of 12 months following the date of the former employee's retirement, dismissal, or separation from service, if he or she was employed in a policymaking position at the Judicial Council in the same general subject area as the proposed contract within the 12-month period before his or her retirement, dismissal, or separation; or

(2) For a period of 24 months following the date of the former employee's retirement, dismissal, or separation from service, if he or she engaged in any of the negotiations, transactions, planning, arrangements, or any part of the decision-making process relevant to the contract while employed in any capacity by the Judicial Council.

(Subd (b) amended effective January 1, 2016; previously amended effective January 1, 2007.)

(c) Policymaking position

"Policymaking position" includes:

(1) In a trial court, the court's executive officer and any other position designated by the court as a policymaking position;

(2) In an appellate court, the clerk/executive officer and any other position designated by the court as a policymaking position; and

(3) In the Judicial Council, the Administrative Director, Chief of Staff, Chief Operating Officer, Chief Administrative Officer, any director, and any other position designated by the Administrative Director as a policymaking position.

(Subd (c) amended effective January 1, 2018; previously amended effective January 1, 2016.)

(d) Scope

This rule does not prohibit any court or the Judicial Council from (1) employing any person or (2) contracting with any former judge or justice.

(Subd (d) amended effective January 1, 2016.)

Rule 10.104 amended effective January 1, 2018; adopted as rule 6.104 effective January 1, 2004; previously amended and renumbered as rule 10.104 effective January 1, 2007; previously amended effective January 1, 2016.

Rule 10.105. Allocation of new fee, fine, and forfeiture revenue

(a) Allocation

The Judicial Council must annually allocate 80 percent of the amount of fee, fine, and forfeiture revenue deposited in the Trial Court Improvement Fund under Government Code section 77205(a) that exceeds the amount of fee, fine, and forfeiture revenue deposited in the Trial Court Improvement Fund in fiscal year 2002–2003 to one or more of the following:

(1) To the trial courts in the counties from which the increased amount is attributable;

(2) To other trial courts to support trial court operations; or

(3) For retention in the Trial Court Improvement Fund.

(Subd (a) amended effective January 1, 2007.)

(b) Methodology

The Judicial Council staff must recommend a methodology for the allocation and must recommend an allocation based on this methodology. On approval of a methodology by the Judicial Council, Judicial Council staff must issue a Finance Memo stating the methodology adopted by the Judicial Council.

(Subd (b) amended effective January 1, 2016; previously amended effective January 1, 2007.)

Rule 10.105 amended effective January 1, 2016; adopted as rule 6.105 effective December 10, 2004; previously amended and renumbered as rule 10.105 effective January 1, 2007.

Rule 10.106. Judicial branch travel expense reimbursement policy

(a) Adoption

The Judicial Council must adopt a fiscally responsible judicial branch travel expense reimbursement policy, under Government Code section 68506.5, that provides appropriate accountability for the use of public resources. Before adopting the initial policy, the Judicial Council must receive comments from the courts, court employee organizations, and other interested groups.

(Subd (a) adopted effective July 1, 2008.)

(b) Applicability

The judicial branch travel expense reimbursement policy applies to official state business travel by:

(1) Judicial officers and judicial officers sitting by assignment;

(2) Officers, employees, retired annuitants, and members of the Supreme Court, the Courts of Appeal, superior courts, the Judicial Council and its staff, the Habeas Corpus Resource Center, and the Commission on Judicial Performance; and

(3) Members of task forces, working groups, commissions, or similar bodies appointed by the Chief Justice, the Judicial Council, or the Administrative Director.

(Subd (b) amended effective January 1, 2016; adopted effective July 1, 2008.)

(c) Amendments

The Judicial Council delegates to the Administrative Director, under article VI, section 6(c) of the California Constitution and other applicable law, the authority to make technical changes and clarifications to the judicial branch travel expense reimbursement policy. The changes and clarifications must be fiscally responsible, provide for appropriate accountability, and be in general compliance with the policy initially adopted by the Judicial Council.

(Subd (c) amended effective January 1, 2016; adopted effective July 1, 2008.)

Rule 10.106 amended effective January 1, 2016; adopted effective July 1, 2008.

Rule 10.107. Trial Court Budget Working Group [Repealed]

Rule 10.107 repealed effective January 1, 2015; repealed and adopted as rule 6.45 effective January 1, 2005; previously renumbered as rule 10.45 effective January 1, 2007, and as rule 10.107 effective August 14, 2009.

Chapter 2
Court Security

Rule 10.172. Court security plans
Rule 10.173. Court security committees

Rule 10.174. Petition Regarding Disputes Related to Court Security Memoranda of Understanding

Rule 10.170. Working Group on Court Security [Repealed]

Rule 10.170 repealed effective October 25, 2013; adopted as rule 6.170 effective October 15, 2003; previously amended and renumbered effective January 1, 2007.

Rule 10.171. Working Group on Court Security Fiscal Guidelines [Repealed]

Rule 10.171 repealed effective October 25, 2013; adopted as rule 6.170 effective January 1, 2003; adopted as rule 6.171 effective October 15, 2003; previously amended and renumbered effective January 1, 2007.

Rule 10.172. Court security plans

(a) Responsibility

The presiding judge and the sheriff or marshal are responsible for developing an annual or multiyear comprehensive, countywide court security plan.

(Subd (a) adopted effective January 1, 2009.)

(b) Scope of security plan

(1) Each court security plan must, at a minimum, address the following general security subject areas:

(A) Composition and role of court security committees;

(B) Composition and role of executive team;

(C) Incident command system;

(D) Self-assessments and audits of court security;

(E) Mail handling security;

(F) Identification cards and access control;

(G) Courthouse landscaping security plan;

(H) Parking plan security;

(I) Interior and exterior lighting plan security;

(J) Intrusion and panic alarm systems;

(K) Fire detection and equipment;

(L) Emergency and auxiliary power;

(M) Use of private security contractors;

(N) Use of court attendants and employees;

(O) Administrative/clerk's office security;

(P) Jury personnel and jury room security;

(Q) Security for public demonstrations;

(R) Vital records storage security;

(S) Evacuation planning;

(T) Security for after-hours operations;

(U) Custodial services;

(V) Computer and data security;

(W) Workplace violence prevention; and

(X) Public access to court proceedings.

(2) Each court security plan must, at a minimum, address the following law enforcement subject areas:

(A) Security personnel and staffing;

(B) Perimeter and entry screening;

(C) Prisoner and inmate transport;

(D) Holding cells;

(E) Interior and public waiting area security;

(F) Courtroom security;

(G) Jury trial procedures;

(H) High-profile and high-risk trial security;

(I) Judicial protection;

(J) Incident reporting and recording;

(K) Security personnel training;

(L) Courthouse security communication;

(M) Hostage, escape, lockdown, and active shooter procedures;

(N) Firearms policies and procedures; and

(O) Restraint of defendants.

(3) Each court security plan should address additional security issues as needed.

(Subd (b) adopted effective January 1, 2009.)

(c) Court security assessment and assessment report

At least once every two years, the presiding judge and the sheriff or marshal are responsible for conducting an assessment of security with respect to all court operations. The assessment must include a comprehensive review of the court's physical security profile and security protocols and procedures. The assessment should identify security weaknesses, resource deficiencies, compliance with the court security plan, and any need for changes to the court security plan. The assessment must be summarized in a written assessment report.

(Subd (c) adopted effective January 1, 2009.)

(d) Submission of court security plan to the Judicial Council

On or before November 1, 2009, each superior court must submit a court security plan to the Judicial Council. On or before February 1, 2011, and each succeeding February 1, each superior court must give notice to the Judicial Council whether it has made any changes to the court security plan and, if so, identify each change made and provide copies of the current court security plan and current assessment report. In preparing any submission, a court may request technical assistance from Judicial Council staff.

(Subd (d) amended effective January 1, 2016; adopted effective January 1, 2009.)

(e) Plan review process

Judicial Council staff will evaluate for completeness submissions identified in (d). Annually, the submissions and evaluations will be provided to the Court Security Advisory Committee. Any submissions determined by the advisory committee to be incomplete or deficient must be returned to the submitting court for correction and completion.

(Subd (e) amended effective January 1, 2016; adopted effective January 1, 2009.)

(f) Delegation

The presiding judge may delegate any of the specific duties listed in this rule to another judge or, if the duty does not require the exercise of judicial authority, to the court executive officer or other court employee. The presiding judge remains responsible for all duties listed in this rule even if he or she has delegated particular tasks to someone else.

(Subd (f) adopted effective January 1, 2009.)

Rule 10.172 amended effective January 1, 2016; adopted effective January 1, 2009.

Advisory Committee Comment

This rule is adopted to comply with the mandate in Government Code section 69925, which requires the Judicial Council to provide for the areas to be addressed in a court security plan and to establish a process for the review of such plans.

Rule 10.173. Court security committees

(a) Establishment

Each superior court must establish a standing court security committee.

(Subd (a) adopted effective January 1, 2009.)

(b) Role of the court security committee

The court security committee and any subcommittees advise the presiding judge and sheriff or marshal on the preparation of court security plans and on the formulation and implementation of all other policies and procedures related to security for court operations and security for facilities where the court conducts its operations. The presiding judge and sheriff or marshal may delegate to a court security committee or subcommittee the responsibility for conducting the court security assessment and preparing the assessment report.

(Subd (b) adopted effective January 1, 2009.)

(c) Members

(1) The court security committee must be chaired by the presiding judge or a judge designated by the presiding judge.

(2) In addition to the chair, each court security committee must include at least one representative designated by the sheriff or marshal and either the court executive officer or other court administrator as designated by the presiding judge.

(3) The chair may appoint additional members as appropriate. Additional members may include representatives from other government agencies, including:

(A) The facilities management office of the government entity, or entities, that hold title to or are responsible for the facilities where the court conducts its operations;

(B) Local fire protection agencies;

(C) Agencies that occupy portions of a court facility; and

(D) Agencies other than the sheriff that manage local corrections or state prison facilities.

(Subd (c) adopted effective January 1, 2009.)

(d) Facility contact person

In those courts having more than one court facility, the chair of the court security committee must designate for each facility a single contact person to coordinate activities in the event of an emergency and to collaborate with the court security committee, at its request.

(Subd (d) adopted effective January 1, 2009.)

(e) Subcommittees

The chair of the court security committee may form subcommittees if appropriate, including a subcommittee for each court facility. The chair must determine the composition of each subcommittee based on the individual court's circumstances.

(Subd (e) adopted effective January 1, 2009.)

Rule 10.173 adopted effective January 1, 2009.

Rule 10.174. Petition Regarding Disputes Related to Court Security Memoranda of Understanding

(a) Application

This rule applies to petitions filed under Government Code section 69926(e).

(Subd (a) adopted effective November 1, 2012.)

(b) Request for assignment of Court of Appeal justice

(1) If a sheriff, county, or superior court is unable to resolve a dispute related to the memorandum of understanding required by Government Code section 69926(b), the sheriff, county, or superior court may file a petition for a writ of mandamus or writ of prohibition.

(2) On the first page, below the case number, the petition must include the following language in the statement of the character of the proceeding (see rule 2.111(6)): "Petition filed under Government Code section 69926(e): Assignment of Court of Appeal justice requested."

(3) On receipt of a petition, the superior court clerk must submit a request to the Chief Justice asking that he or she assign a Court of Appeal justice from an appellate district other than the one in which the county, the superior court, and the sheriff are located to hear and decide the petition.

(Subd (b) adopted effective November 1, 2012.)

(c) Superior court hearing

A petition filed under this rule must be heard and decided on an expedited basis and must be given priority over other matters to the extent permitted by law and the rules of court.

(Subd (c) adopted effective November 1, 2012.)

(d) Appeal

(1) Any notice of appeal of a decision under (c) must be filed in the same superior court in which the petition was initially filed and must include on the first page the following language, below the case number, in the statement of the character of the proceeding (see rule 2.111(6)): "Notice of Appeal Relating to Petition filed under Government Code section 69926(e): Transfer Requested."

(2) On receipt of the notice of appeal, the Court of Appeal must request that the Supreme Court transfer the appeal to an appellate district other than the one in which the county, the superior court, and the sheriff are located.

(Subd (d) adopted effective November 1, 2012.)

Rule 10.174 adopted effective November 1, 2012.

Chapter 3
Court Facilities

Rule 10.180. Court facilities standards
Rule 10.181. Court facilities policies, procedures, and standards
Rule 10.182. Operation and maintenance of court facilities
Rule 10.183. Decision making on transfer of responsibility for trial court facilities
Rule 10.184. Acquisition, space programming, construction, and design of court facilities

Rule 10.180. Court facilities standards

(a) Development of standards

Judicial Council staff is responsible for developing and maintaining standards for the alteration, remodeling, renovation, and expansion of existing court facilities and for the construction of new court facilities.

(Subd (a) amended effective January 1, 2016; previously amended effective April 21, 2006.)

(b) Adoption by the Judicial Council

The standards developed by Judicial Council staff must be submitted to the Judicial Council for review and adoption as the standards to be used for court facilities in the state. Nonsubstantive changes to the standards may be made by the Judicial Council staff; substantive changes must be submitted to the Judicial Council for review and adoption.

(Subd (b) amended effective January 1, 2016; previously amended effective April 21, 2006.)

(c) Use of standards

The Judicial Council and its staff, affected courts, and advisory groups on court facilities issues created under these rules must use the standards adopted under (b) in reviewing or recommending proposed alteration, remodeling, renovation, or expansion of an existing court facility or new construction. Courts and advisory groups must report deviations from the standards to Judicial Council staff through a process established for that purpose.

(Subd (c) amended effective January 1, 2016; previously amended effective June 23, 2004, and April 21, 2006.)

Rule 10.180 amended effective January 1, 2016; adopted as rule 6.150 effective July 1, 2002; previously amended effective June 23, 2004, and April 21, 2006; previously renumbered as rule 10.180 effective January 1, 2007.

Rule 10.181. Court facilities policies, procedures, and standards

(a) Responsibilities of Judicial Council staff

Judicial Council staff, after consultation with the Court Facilities Transitional Task Force, must prepare and present to the Judicial Council recommendations for policies, procedures, and standards concerning the operation, maintenance, alteration, remodeling, renovation, expansion, acquisition, space programming, design, and construction of appellate and trial court facilities under Government Code sections 69204(c) and 70391(e).

(Subd (a) amended effective January 1, 2016; adopted as part of unlettered subd; previously amended and lettered as subd (a) effective January 1, 2007.)

(b) Consultations with the affected court and with local governmental and community interests

The policies, procedures, and standards must ensure that decisions are made in consultation with the affected court, when appropriate, and that decisions concerning acquisition, design, and construction of court facilities are made in consultation with local governmental and community interests, when appropriate.

(Subd (b) lettered and amended effective January 1, 2007; adopted as part of unlettered subd.)

Rule 10.181 amended effective January 1, 2016; adopted as rule 6.180 effective June 23, 2004; previously amended effective April 21, 2006; previously amended and renumbered as rule 10.181 effective January 1, 2007.

Rule 10.182. Operation and maintenance of court facilities

(a) Intent

The intent of this rule is to allocate responsibility and decision making for the operation and maintenance of court facilities among the courts and Judicial Council staff.

(Subd (a) amended effective January 1, 2016.)

(b) Responsibilities of Judicial Council staff

(1) In addition to those matters expressly authorized by statute, Judicial Council staff are responsible for:

(A) Taking action on the operation of court facilities, including the day-to-day operation of a building and maintenance of a facility. Judicial Council staff must, in cooperation with the court, perform its responsibilities concerning operation of the court facility to effectively and efficiently support the day-to-day operation of the court system and services of the court. These actions include maintaining proper heating, ventilation, and air conditioning levels; providing functional electrical, fire safety, vertical transportation, mechanical, and plumbing systems through preventive maintenance and responsive repairs; and maintaining structural, nonstructural, security, and telecommunications infrastructures.

(B) Preparing and submitting budget allocation proposals to the Judicial Council, as part of the yearly judicial branch budget development cycle, specifying the amounts to be spent for the operation of court facilities as provided in (A).

(C) Developing policies, procedures, and guidelines concerning court facilities for submission to the Judicial Council.

(2) Judicial Council staff must consult with affected courts concerning the annual operations and maintenance needs assessment, development of annual priorities, and fiscal planning for the operational and maintenance needs of court facilities.

(3) Judicial Council staff may, when appropriate, delegate its responsibilities for ongoing operation and management to the court for some or all of the existing court facilities used by that court. Any delegation of responsibility must ensure that:

(A) The management of court facilities is consistent with the statewide goals and policies of the judicial branch;

(B) Access to all court facilities in California is promoted;

(C) Facilities decisions are made with consideration of operational costs and enhance economical, efficient, and effective court operations; and

(D) Courts have adequate and sufficient facilities and appropriate resources to undertake these delegated tasks.

(4) Judicial Council staff must, whenever feasible, seek review and recommendations from the Court Facilities Transitional Task Force before recommending action on appellate and trial court facilities issues to the Judicial Council.

(Subd (b) amended effective January 1, 2016; previously amended effective January 1, 2007.)

(c) Responsibilities of the courts

(1) The affected courts must consult with Judicial Council staff concerning the annual operations and maintenance needs assessment, development of annual priorities, and fiscal planning for the operational and maintenance needs of court facilities, including contingency planning for unforeseen facility maintenance needs.

(2) Each court to which responsibility is delegated under (b)(3) must report to Judicial Council staff quarterly or more often, as provided in the delegation. The report must include the activities and expenditures related to the delegation that are specified for reporting in the delegation. Each court must also account to Judicial Council staff for all expenditures related to the delegation. Judicial Council staff may conduct an internal audit of any receipts and expenditures.

(Subd (c) amended effective January 1, 2016; previously amended effective January 1, 2007.)

Rule 10.182 amended effective January 1, 2016; adopted as rule 6.181 effective June 23, 2004; previously amended and renumbered as rule 10.182 effective January 1, 2007.

Rule 10.183. Decision making on transfer of responsibility for trial court facilities

(a) Intent

The intent of this rule is to allocate among the Judicial Council, the trial courts, and Judicial Council staff, responsibility and decision making for the transfer of responsibility for trial court facilities from the counties to the Judicial Council.

(Subd (a) amended effective January 1, 2016.)

(b) Definitions

As used in this rule, the following terms have the same meaning as provided by Government Code section 70301:

(1) "Court facilities";

(2) "Maintenance";

(3) "Responsibility for facilities"; and

(4) "Shared use."

(Subd (b) amended effective January 1, 2007.)

(c) Responsibilities of the Judicial Council and the Executive and Planning Committee

The Judicial Council must determine the following issues concerning transfer of responsibility of court facilities, except in the case of a need for urgent action between meetings of the council, in which case the Executive and Planning Committee is authorized to act under rule 10.11(d).

(1) Rejection of transfer of responsibility for a building under Government Code section 70326; and

(2) A decision to dispose of a surplus court facility under Government Code section 70391(c).

(Subd (c) amended effective January 1, 2007.)

(d) Responsibilities of Judicial Council staff

Judicial Council staff are responsible for the following matters related to transfer of responsibility for court facilities, in addition to matters expressly authorized by statute:

(1) Keeping the courts informed and involved, as appropriate, in the negotiations with the counties for transfer of responsibility for court facilities;

(2) Except as provided in (c)(1), approving an agreement transferring responsibility for a court facility to the state;

(3) Administering a shared-use court facility, including:

(A) Making a decision to displace a minority county tenant under Government Code section 70344(b);

(B) Seeking a change in the amount of court space under Government Code section 70342; and

(C) Responding to a county seeking a change in the amount of county space under Government Code section 70342; and

(4) Auditing the collection of fees by trial courts under Government Code section 70391(d)(1) and the money in local courthouse construction funds under Government Code section 70391(d)(2).

(Subd (d) amended effective January 1, 2016; previously amended effective January 1, 2007.)

(e) Appeal of county facilities payment amount

The Administrative Director must obtain the approval of the Executive and Planning Committee before pursuing correction of a county facilities payment amount under Government Code section 70367. This provision does not preclude the Administrative Director from submitting a declaration as required by Government Code section 70367(a). The Administrative Director must report to the Executive and Planning Committee any decision not to appeal a county facilities payment amount.

(Subd (e) amended effective January 1, 2016.)

Rule 10.183 amended effective January 1, 2016; adopted as rule 6.182 effective June 23, 2004; previously amended and renumbered as rule 10.183 effective January 1, 2007.

Rule 10.184. Acquisition, space programming, construction, and design of court facilities

(a) Intent

The intent of this rule is to allocate responsibility and decision making for acquisition, space programming, construction, and design of court facilities among the courts, the Judicial Council, and its staff.

(Subd (a) amended effective January 1, 2016.)

(b) Responsibilities of Judicial Council staff

(1) In addition to those matters expressly provided by statute, Judicial Council staff are responsible for the acquisition, space programming, construction, and design of a court facility, consistent with the facilities policies and procedures adopted by the Judicial Council and the California Rules of Court.

(2) Judicial Council staff must prepare and submit to the Judicial Council separate annual capital outlay proposals for the appellate courts and the trial courts, as part of the yearly judicial branch budget development cycle, specifying the amounts to be spent for these purposes. The capital outlay proposal for the trial courts must specify the money that is proposed to be spent from the State Court Facilities Construction Fund and from other sources. The annual capital outlay proposals must be consistent with the Five-Year Capital Infrastructure Plan or must recommend appropriate changes in the Five-Year Capital Infrastructure Plan. Judicial Council staff must, whenever feasible, seek review and recommendations from the Court Facilities Transitional Task Force before recommending action to the Judicial Council on these issues.

(3) Judicial Council staff must consult with the affected courts concerning the annual capital needs of the courts.

(Subd (b) amended effective January 1, 2016; previously amended effective January 1, 2007.)

(c) Responsibilities of the courts

(1) Affected courts must consult with Judicial Council staff concerning the courts' annual capital needs.

(2) An affected court must work with the advisory group that is established for any court construction or major renovation project.

(Subd (c) amended effective January 1, 2016.)

(d) Advisory group for construction projects

Judicial Council staff, in consultation with the leadership of the affected court, must establish and work with an advisory group for each court construction or major renovation project. The advisory group consists of court judicial officers, other court personnel, and others affected by the court facility. The advisory group must work with Judicial Council staff on issues involved in the construction or renovation, from the selection of a space programmer and architect through occupancy of the facility.

(Subd (d) amended effective January 1, 2016.)

Rule 10.184 amended effective January 1, 2016; adopted as rule 6.183 effective June 23, 2004; previously amended and renumbered as rule 10.184 effective January 1, 2007.

Chapter 4
Management of Claims and Litigation

Rule 10.201. Claim and litigation procedure
Rule 10.202. Claims and litigation management
Rule 10.203. Contractual indemnification

Rule 10.201. Claim and litigation procedure

(a) Definitions

As used in this chapter:

(1) "Judicial branch entity" is as defined in Government Code section 900.3;

(2) "Judge" means a judge or justice of a judicial branch entity;

(3) "Legal Services" means the Judicial Council's Legal Services office; and

(4) "Litigation Management Committee" means the Litigation Management Committee of the Judicial Council.

(Subd (a) amended effective January 1, 2016; previously amended effective January 1, 2007.)

(b) Procedure for action on claims

To carry out the Judicial Council's responsibility under Government Code section 912.7 to act on a claim, claim amendment, or application for leave to present a late claim against a judicial branch entity or a judge, Legal Services, under the direction of the Administrative Director, must:

(1) On receipt of a claim, claim amendment, or application for leave to present a late claim forwarded by a judicial branch entity, promptly consult with a representative of that entity about the merits of the claim, claim amendment, or application for leave to present a late claim;

(2) Grant or deny an application for leave to present a late claim under Government Code section 911.6(b);

(3) If determined by Legal Services to be appropriate, refer a claim or claim amendment for further investigation to a claims adjuster or other investigator under contract with the Judicial Council;

(4) Reject a claim if it is not a proper charge against the judicial branch entity or judge;

(5) Allow a claim in the amount justly due as determined by Legal Services if it is a proper charge against the judicial branch entity and the amount is less than $100,000; and

(6) Make recommendations to the Litigation Management Committee regarding proposed settlements of claims requiring payments of $100,000 or more.

(Subd (b) amended effective January 1, 2016; previously amended effective January 1, 2007, and December 9, 2008.)

(c) Allowance and payment of claims

The following may allow and authorize payment of any claim arising out of the activities of a judicial branch entity or judge:

(1) Legal Services, under the direction of the Administrative Director, if the payment is less than $100,000; or

(2) The Litigation Management Committee, for any claim.

(Subd (c) amended effective January 1, 2016; previously amended effective December 9, 2008.)

(d) Settlement of lawsuits and payment of judgments

The following may settle lawsuits, after consultation with the affected entity and any judge or employee being defended by the Judicial Council, and authorize payment of judgments arising out of the activities of a judicial branch entity or judge:

(1) Legal Services, under the direction of the Administrative Director, if the payment is less than $100,000 and the lawsuit does not raise issues of significance to the judicial branch; or

(2) The Litigation Management Committee, for any settlement or judgment.

(Subd (d) amended effective January 1, 2016; previously amended effective December 9, 2008.)

Rule 10.201 amended effective January 1, 2016; adopted as rule 6.201 effective January 1, 2003; previously amended and renumbered as rule 10.201 effective January 1, 2007; previously amended effective December 9, 2008.

Rule 10.202. Claims and litigation management

(a) Intent

The intent of this rule is to:

(1) Ensure that the trial and appellate courts are provided with timely, quality legal assistance; and

(2) Promote the cost-effective, prompt, and fair resolution of actions, proceedings, and claims that affect the trial and appellate courts and involve justices of the Courts of Appeal or the Supreme Court, trial court judges, subordinate judicial officers, court executive officers or administrators, or employees of the trial and appellate courts.

(Subd (a) amended effective January 1, 2007; previously amended effective January 1, 2003.)

(b) Duties of Legal Services

To carry out the duty of the Judicial Council to provide for the representation, defense, and indemnification of justices of the Courts of Appeal or the Supreme Court, judges, subordinate judicial officers, court executive officers and administrators, and trial and appellate court employees under part 1 (commencing with section 810) to part 7 (commencing with section 995), inclusive, of the Government Code, Legal Services, under the direction of the Administrative Director and the Chief Counsel, must:

(1) Develop, manage, and administer a litigation management program for investigating and resolving all claims and lawsuits affecting the trial and appellate courts;

(2) Provide legal assistance to the trial or appellate court, and to any justice, judge, subordinate judicial officer, court executive officer or administrator, and trial or appellate court employee who is named as a defendant or responsible party, subject to the defense and indemnification provisions of part 1 (commencing with section 810) to part 7 (commencing with section 995), inclusive, of the Government Code, on receipt of notice of a claim or lawsuit affecting the trial or appellate court or of a dispute that is likely to result in a claim or lawsuit;

(3) Select and direct any counsel retained to represent any trial or appellate court, justice, judge, subordinate judicial officer, court executive officer or administrator, and trial or appellate court employee being provided legal representation under (2), after consultation with the trial or appellate court and any such individual defendant;

(4) Make settlement decisions in all claims and lawsuits other than those identified in (5), after consultation with the affected trial or appellate court, and any justice, judge, subordinate judicial officer, court executive officer or administrator, and trial or appellate court employee being provided legal representation under (2);

(5) Make recommendations to the Litigation Management Committee regarding proposed settlements of claims or lawsuits requiring payments of $100,000 or more or raising issues of significance to the judicial branch;

(6) Develop and implement risk avoidance programs for the trial and appellate courts;

(7) Provide an annual report to the Litigation Management Committee concerning the litigation management program; and

(8) Provide an annual report to each trial and appellate court concerning claims and lawsuits filed against that trial or appellate court.

(Subd (b) amended effective January 1, 2016; previously amended effective July 1, 2002, January 1, 2003, January 1, 2007, and December 9, 2008.)

(c) Duties of trial and appellate courts

The trial and appellate courts must:

(1) Notify Legal Services promptly on receipt of notice of a dispute that is likely to result in a claim or lawsuit, or of a claim or lawsuit filed, against the court, a justice, a judge or subordinate judicial officer, a court executive officer or administrator, or a court employee, and forward the claim and lawsuit to Legal Services for handling; and

(2) Consult with Legal Services regarding strategic and settlement decisions in claims and lawsuits.

(Subd (c) amended effective January 1, 2016; previously amended effective July 1, 2002, January 1, 2003, and January 1, 2007.)

(d) Disagreements about major strategic decisions

Following consultation with Legal Services, a presiding judge or administrative presiding justice may object to a proposed decision of Legal Services about major strategic decisions, such as retention of counsel and proposed settlements, by presenting to Legal Services a written statement of the objection. Legal Services must present the written objection to the Litigation Management Committee, which will resolve the objection.

(Subd (d) amended effective January 1, 2016; adopted effective January 1, 2003; previously amended effective January 1, 2007.)

Rule 10.202 amended effective January 1, 2016; adopted as rule 6.800 effective January 1, 2001; previously renumbered as rule 6.202 effective January 1, 2003; previously amended and renumbered as rule 10.202 effective January 1, 2007; previously amended effective July 1, 2002, and December 9, 2008.

Rule 10.203. Contractual indemnification

(a) Intent

The intent of this rule is to facilitate the use of contractual indemnities that allocate legal risk and liability to parties that contract with a superior court or Court of Appeal, the Supreme Court, or the Judicial Council (a "judicial branch entity" as defined in Gov. Code, § 900.3).

(Subd (a) amended effective January 1, 2016.)

(b) Defense and indemnification provisions

Notwithstanding rule 10.14, 10.201, or 10.202, a judicial branch entity may enter into a contract that requires the contractor or the contractor's insurer to indemnify, defend, and hold harmless the entity and its officers, agents, and employees against claims, demands, liability, damages, attorney fees, costs, expenses, or losses arising from the performance of the contract. Upon receipt of notice of a claim or lawsuit that may be subject to contractual indemnities, the judicial branch entity must notify

Legal Services, which will manage the claim or lawsuit to obtain the benefits of the contractual indemnities to the extent consistent with the interests of the public and the judicial branch.

(Subd (b) amended effective January 1, 2016; previously amended effective January 1, 2007.)

Rule 10.203 amended effective January 1, 2016; adopted as rule 6.203 effective October 15, 2003; previously amended and renumbered as rule 10.203 effective January 1, 2007.

Chapter 5
Ethics Training
[Repealed]

Title 10, Judicial Administration Rules—Division 2, Administration of the Judicial Branch—Chapter 5, Ethics Training; repealed effective January 1, 2013; adopted as Chapter 6.

Rule 10.301. Ethics training for Judicial Council members and judicial branch employees [Renumbered]

Rule 10.301 renumbered to rule 10.455 effective January 1, 2013; adopted as rule 6.301 effective January 1, 2004; previously amended and renumbered effective January 1, 2007.

Another Chapter 5 follows.

Chapter 5
Management of Human Resources

Title 10, Judicial Administration Rules—Division 2, Administration of the Judicial Branch—Chapter 5, Management of Human Resources; renumbered effective January 1, 2013; adopted as Chapter 6.

Rule 10.350. Workers' compensation program
Rule 10.351. Judicial branch policies on workplace conduct

Rule 10.350. Workers' compensation program

(a) Intent

The intent of this rule is to:

(1) Establish procedures for the Judicial Council's workers' compensation program for the trial courts; and

(2) Ensure that the trial courts' workers' compensation coverage complies with applicable law and is cost-efficient.

(Subd (a) amended effective January 1, 2016; previously amended effective January 1, 2007.)

(b) Duties of Judicial Council staff

To carry out the duty of the Judicial Council to establish a workers' compensation program for the trial courts, the council's Human Resources office must:

(1) Maintain a contract with a vendor to provide courts, on a voluntary basis, with a cost-efficient workers' compensation coverage program;

(2) Monitor the performance of the vendor with which it contracts to provide such services;

(3) Timely notify the trial courts concerning the terms of the workers' compensation coverage program;

(4) Timely inform the trial courts about the legal requirements with which a workers' compensation program must comply;

(5) Make personnel available by telephone to consult with trial courts regarding the cost and benefits of the plan being offered by the Judicial Council; and

(6) Review and approve or disapprove any other workers' compensation programs identified by a trial court for consideration as a vendor to provide workers' compensation benefits to its employees.

(Subd (b) amended effective January 1, 2016; previously amended effective January 1, 2007.)

(c) Duties of the trial courts

(1) Each trial court that elects to participate in the program made available through the Judicial Council must:

(A) Timely notify the Human Resources office of its decision to participate in the workers' compensation program being offered through the Judicial Council;

(B) Timely complete and return necessary paperwork to the Human Resources office; and

(C) Timely pay all costs associated with the program.

(2) Each trial court that elects not to participate in the workers' compensation program available through the Judicial Council must:

(A) Independently identify a workers' compensation benefits provider that fulfills all legal responsibilities to offer such benefits in California in a cost-efficient manner;

(B) Timely submit to the Human Resources office for its approval the information necessary to evaluate the workers' compensation program identified by the trial court to provide benefits for its employees; and

(C) Maintain a contract with a workers' compensation benefits provider that fulfills all legal responsibilities to offer such benefits in California in a cost-efficient manner.

(Subd (c) amended effective January 1, 2016; previously amended effective January 1, 2007.)

Rule 10.350 amended effective January 1, 2016; adopted as rule 6.302 effective January 1, 2005; previously amended and renumbered as rule 10.350 effective January 1, 2007.

Rule 10.351. Judicial branch policies on workplace conduct

The judicial branch is committed to providing a workplace free of harassment, discrimination, retaliation, and inappropriate workplace conduct based on a protected classification. Consistent with this commitment, each court must take reasonable steps to prevent and address such conduct, including adopting policies prohibiting harassment, discrimination, retaliation, and inappropriate workplace conduct based on a protected classification and establishing for such conduct complaint reporting and response procedures that satisfy the minimum requirements stated in this rule.

(a) Prohibition policies

Each court must ensure that its policies prohibiting harassment, discrimination, retaliation, and inappropriate workplace conduct based on a protected classification conform with the minimum requirements stated in this rule. These policies must contain:

(1) A prohibition against harassment, discrimination, retaliation, and inappropriate workplace conduct based on a protected classification by judicial officers, managers, supervisors, employees, other personnel, and other individuals with whom employees come into contact;

(2) A list of all protected classifications under applicable state and federal laws, including all protected classifications listed in Government Code section 12940(a);

(3) Definitions and a nonexhaustive list of examples of harassment, discrimination, retaliation, and inappropriate workplace conduct based on a protected classification;

(4) A clear prohibition of retaliation against anyone making a complaint or participating in an investigation of harassment, discrimination, retaliation, or inappropriate workplace conduct based on a protected classification; and

(5) Comprehensive complaint reporting, intake, investigatory, and follow-up processes.

(Subd (a) adopted effective January 17, 2020.)

(b) Complaint reporting process

Each court must adopt a process for employees to report complaints of harassment, discrimination, retaliation, and inappropriate workplace conduct based on a protected classification. These reporting processes must:

(1) Establish effective open-door policies and procedures for reporting complaints;

(2) Offer multiple avenues for raising complaints, either orally or in writing, and not require that the employee bring concerns to an immediate supervisor;

(3) Clearly identify individuals to whom complaints may be made regarding the conduct of administrative presiding justices, appellate court clerk/executive officers, presiding judges, court executive officers, judicial officers, and court management;

(4) Identify the Commission on Judicial Performance, California Department of Fair Employment and Housing, and U.S. Equal Employment Opportunity Commission as additional avenues for employees to lodge complaints, and provide contact information for those entities; and

(5) Instruct supervisors, managers, and directors with knowledge of harassment, discrimination, retaliation, or inappropriate workplace conduct based on a protected classification to report this information to the administrative presiding justice or an appellate court clerk/executive officer, a presiding judge, a court executive officer, human resources, or another appropriate judicial officer who is not involved with the conduct or named in the complaint.

(Subd (b) adopted effective January 17, 2020.)

(c) Court responsibility on receipt of complaint or knowledge of potential misconduct

Each court must develop processes to intake, investigate, and respond to complaints or known instances of harassment, discrimination, retaliation, or inappropriate workplace conduct based on a protected classification. These processes must provide for:

(1) Appropriate reassurances to complainants that their confidentiality in making a complaint will be preserved to the extent possible, including an explanation that disclosure of information will be limited to the extent consistent with conducting a fair, effective, and thorough investigation;

(2) Fair, timely, and thorough investigations of complaints that provide all parties with appropriate consideration and an opportunity to be heard. These investigations should be conducted by impartial, qualified investigators;

(3) Communication with complainants throughout the investigation process, including initial acknowledgment of complaints, follow-up communication as appropriate, and communication at the end of the process;

(4) Consideration of appropriate options for remedial action and resolution based on the evidence collected in the investigation; and

(5) Timely case closures.

(Subd (c) adopted effective January 17, 2020.)

(d) Implementation

All courts must implement the requirements of this rule by December 31, 2020, or as soon thereafter as possible, subject to any applicable obligations to meet and confer or consult with recognized employee organizations.

(Subd (d) amended effective April 16, 2020.)

Rule 10.351 amended effective April 16, 2020; adopted effective January 17, 2020.

Chapter 6
Court Technology, Information, and Automation

Title 10, Judicial Administration Rules—Division 2, Administration of the Judicial Branch—Chapter 6, Court Technology, Information, and Automation; renumbered effective January 1, 2013; adopted as Chapter 7.

Rule 10.400. Judicial Branch Statistical Information System (JBSIS)

(a) Purpose of rule

Consistent with article VI, section 6 of the California Constitution and Government Code section 68505, the Judicial Branch Statistical Information System (JBSIS) is established by the Judicial Council to provide accurate, consistent, and timely information for the judicial branch, the Legislature, and other state agencies that require information from the courts to fulfill their mandates.

(Subd (a) amended effective January 1, 2007.)

(b) Reporting required

Each trial court must collect and report to the Judicial Council information according to its capability and level of automation as prescribed by the *JBSIS Manual* adopted by the Judicial Council.

(Subd (b) amended effective January 1, 2007.)

(c) Automated JBSIS collection and reporting

By July 1, 1998, each trial court must develop a plan for meeting reporting requirements prescribed by the *JBSIS Manual*. By January 1, 2001, subject to adequate funding being made available, each trial court must develop, upgrade, replace, or procure automated case management systems needed to meet or exceed JBSIS data collection and reporting requirements prescribed by the *JBSIS Manual*.

(Subd (c) amended effective January 1, 2007; previously amended effective January 1, 2000.)

Rule 10.400 amended and renumbered effective January 1, 2007; adopted as rule 996 effective January 1, 1998; previously amended effective January 1, 2000.

Chapter 7
Minimum Education Requirements, Expectations, and Recommendations

Title 10, Judicial Administration Rules—Division 2, Administration of the Judicial Branch—Chapter 7, Minimum Education Requirements, Expectations, and Recommendations; renumbered effective January 1, 2013; adopted as Chapter 8.

Rule 10.451. Judicial branch education
Rule 10.452. Minimum education requirements, expectations, and recommendations
Rule 10.455. Ethics orientation for Judicial Council members and for judicial branch employees required to file a statement of economic interests
Rule 10.461. Minimum education requirements for Supreme Court and Court of Appeal justices
Rule 10.462. Minimum education requirements and expectations for trial court judges and subordinate judicial officers
Rule 10.463. Education requirements for family court judges and subordinate judicial officers
Rule 10.464. Education requirements and expectations for judges and subordinate judicial officers on domestic violence issues
Rule 10.468. Content-based and hours-based education for superior court judges and subordinate judicial officers regularly assigned to hear probate proceedings
Rule 10.469. Education recommendations for justices, judges, and subordinate judicial officers
Rule 10.471. Minimum education requirements for Supreme Court and Court of Appeal clerk/executive officers
Rule 10.472. Minimum education requirements for Supreme Court and Court of Appeal managing attorneys, supervisors, and other personnel
Rule 10.473. Minimum education requirements for trial court executive officers
Rule 10.474. Trial court managers, supervisors, and other personnel
Rule 10.478. Content-based and hours-based education for court investigators, probate attorneys, and probate examiners
Rule 10.479. Education recommendations for appellate and trial court personnel
Rule 10.481. Approved providers; approved course criteria
Rule 10.491. Minimum education requirements for Judicial Council employees
Rule 10.492. Temporary extension and pro rata reduction of judicial branch education requirements
Rule 10.493. Delivery methods defined

Rule 10.451. Judicial branch education

(a) Purpose

Judicial branch education for all justices, judges, subordinate judicial officers, and court personnel is essential to enhance the fair, effective, and efficient administration of justice. Participation in education activities is part of the official duties of judicial officers and court personnel. Judicial branch education is acknowledged as a vital component in achieving the goals of the Judicial Council's Long-Range Strategic Plan, which include access, fairness, and diversity; branch independence and accountability; modernization of management and administration; and quality of justice and service to the public. The responsibility for planning, conducting, and overseeing judicial branch education properly resides in the judicial branch.

(Subd (a) adopted effective January 1, 2007.)

(b) Education objectives

Justices, judges, subordinate judicial officers, court personnel, education committees, and others who plan and deliver education will endeavor to achieve the following objectives:

(1) To provide justices, judges, subordinate judicial officers, and court personnel with the knowledge, skills, and abilities required to perform their responsibilities competently, fairly, and efficiently;

(2) To ensure that education, including opportunities for orientation, continuing education, and professional development, is available to all justices, judges, subordinate judicial officers, and court personnel;

(3) To assist justices, judges, subordinate judicial officers, and court personnel in preserving the integrity and impartiality of the judicial system through their efforts to ensure that all members of the public have equal access to the courts and equal ability to participate in court proceedings and are treated in a fair and just manner;

(4) To promote the adherence of justices, judges, subordinate judicial officers, and court personnel to the highest ideals of personal and official conduct, as set forth in the California Code of Judicial Ethics and the Code of Ethics for the Court Employees of California;

(5) To improve the administration of justice, reduce court delay, and promote fair and efficient management of court proceedings;

(6) To promote standardized court practices and procedures; and

(7) To implement the recommendations adopted by the Judicial Council in the California Standards of Judicial Administration.

(Subd (b) adopted effective January 1, 2007.)

Rule 10.451 adopted effective January 1, 2007.

Rule 10.452. Minimum education requirements, expectations, and recommendations

(a) Purpose

Justices, judges, and subordinate judicial officers are entrusted by the public with the impartial and knowledgeable handling of proceedings that affect the freedom, livelihood, and happiness of the people involved. Court personnel assist justices, judges, and subordinate judicial officers in carrying out their responsibilities and must provide accurate and timely services to the public. Justices, judges, subordinate judicial officers, and court staff members are individually responsible for maintaining and improving their professional competence. To assist them in enhancing their professional competence, the judicial branch will develop and maintain a comprehensive and high-quality education program, including minimum education requirements, expectations, and recommendations, to provide educational opportunities for all justices, judges, subordinate judicial officers, and court personnel.

(Subd (a) amended effective January 1, 2023; adopted effective January 1, 2007; previously amended effective January 1, 2008.)

(b) Goals

The minimum education requirements, expectations, and recommendations stated in rules 10.461–10.479 are intended to achieve two complementary goals:

(1) To ensure that all justices, judges, subordinate judicial officers, and court personnel obtain education on the tasks, skills, abilities, and knowledge necessary to be successful in their new court assignments and roles; and

(2) To establish broad continuing education parameters based on multiyear education cycles for experienced individuals while preserving the ability of these individuals, working with the persons overseeing their work, to determine appropriate education content and providers.

(Subd (b) amended effective January 1, 2023; adopted effective January 1, 2007; previously amended effective January 1, 2008.)

(c) Relationship of minimum education requirements and expectations to education recommendations

The education requirements and expectations stated in rules 10.461, 10.462, and 10.471–10.474 are minimums. Justices, judges, and subordinate judicial officers should participate in more judicial education than is required and expected, related to each individual's responsibilities and judicial assignments and in accordance with the judicial education recommendations stated in rule 10.469. Additional education requirements related to specific responsibilities are stated in rule 10.463 (for those hearing family law matters), rule 10.464 (for those hearing domestic violence issues), and rule 10.468 (for those hearing probate proceedings).

(Subd (c) amended effective January 1, 2023; adopted effective January 1, 2007; previously amended effective January 1, 2008, and January 1, 2012.)

(d) Responsibilities of Chief Justice and administrative presiding justices

The Chief Justice and administrative presiding justices:

(1) Must grant sufficient leave to Supreme Court and Court of Appeal justices, the clerk/executive officer, and the managing attorney to complete the minimum education requirements stated in rules 10.461, 10.471, and 10.472, respectively;

(2) To the extent compatible with the efficient administration of justice, must grant to all justices, the clerk/executive officer, and the managing attorney sufficient leave to participate in education programs consistent with the education recommendations stated in rules 10.469 and 10.479. After a justice has completed any new justice education required under rule 10.461 or after a justice has completed the first year on the bench, the Chief Justice or the administrative presiding justice should grant each justice at least eight court days per calendar year to participate in continuing education relating to the justice's responsibilities;

(3) In addition to the educational leave required under (d)(1)–(2), should grant leave to a justice, clerk/executive officer, or managing attorney to serve on education committees and as a faculty member at education programs when the individual's services have been requested for judicial or legal education;

(4) Should establish an education plan for the court to facilitate the involvement of justices, the clerk/executive officer, and the managing attorney as both participants and faculty in education activities;

(5) Must ensure that justices, the clerk/executive officer, and the managing attorney are reimbursed by their court in accordance with the travel policies issued by the Judicial Council for travel expenses incurred in attending in-state education programs as a participant, except to the extent that: (i) certain expenses are covered by the Judicial Council; or (ii) the education provider or sponsor of the program pays the expenses. Provisions for these expenses must be part of every court's budget. The Chief Justice or the administrative presiding justice may approve reimbursement of travel expenses incurred by justices, the clerk/executive officer, and the managing attorney in attending out-of-state education programs as a participant; and

(6) Must retain the records and cumulative histories of participation provided by justices. These records and cumulative histories are subject to periodic audit by Judicial Council staff. The Chief Justice and the administrative presiding justices must report their courts' compliance with education requirements on an aggregate basis to the Judicial Council, on a form provided by the Judicial Council, within six months after the end of each three-year education cycle.

(Subd (d) amended effective January 1, 2023; adopted effective January 1, 2007; previously amended effective January 1, 2008, January 1, 2016, and January 1, 2018.)

(e) Responsibilities of presiding judges

Presiding judges:

(1) Must grant sufficient leave to their judges and subordinate judicial officers and to the court executive officer to enable them to complete the minimum education requirements and expectations stated in rules 10.462 and 10.473, respectively;

(2) To the extent compatible with the efficient administration of justice, must grant to their judges and subordinate judicial officers and to the court executive officer sufficient leave to participate in education programs consistent with the education recommendations stated in rules 10.469 and 10.479. After a judge or subordinate judicial officer has completed the new judge education required under rule 10.462, the presiding judge should grant each judge and subordinate judicial officer at least eight court days per calendar year to participate in continuing education relating to the judge's or subordinate judicial officer's responsibilities or current or future court assignment;

(3) In addition to the educational leave required or authorized under rule 10.603 or (e)(1)–(2), should grant leave to a judge or subordinate judicial officer or the executive officer to serve on education committees and as a faculty member at education programs when the judicial officer's or executive officer's services have been requested for judicial or legal education;

(4) Should establish an education plan for the court to facilitate the involvement of judges, subordinate judicial officers, and the executive officer as both participants and faculty in education activities and should consult with each judge, each subordinate judicial officer, and the executive officer regarding their education needs and requirements related to their current and future assignments;

(5) Should use their assignment powers to enable all judges and subordinate judicial officers to participate in educational activities;

(6) Must ensure that judges, subordinate judicial officers, and the court executive officer are reimbursed by their court in accordance with the Trial Court Financial Policies and Procedures Manual for travel expenses incurred in attending in-state education programs as a participant, except to the extent that: (i) certain expenses are covered by the Judicial Council; or (ii) the education provider or sponsor of the program pays the expenses. Provisions for these expenses must be part of every court's budget. The presiding judge may approve reimbursement of travel expenses incurred by judges, subordinate judicial officers, and the court executive officer in attending out-of-state education programs as a participant; and

(7) Must retain the records and cumulative histories of participation provided by judges. These records and cumulative histories are subject to periodic audit by Judicial Council staff. Presiding judges must report their courts' compliance with education requirements on an aggregate basis to the Judicial Council, on a form provided by the Judicial Council, within six months after the end of each three-year education cycle.

(Subd (e) amended effective January 1, 2023; adopted effective January 1, 2007; previously amended effective January 1, 2008, and January 1, 2016.)

(f) Responsibilities of Supreme Court and Court of Appeal justices, clerk/executive officers, managing attorneys, and supervisors

Justices, clerk/executive officers, managing attorneys, and supervisors:

(1) Must grant sufficient leave to all court personnel to enable them to complete the minimum education requirements stated in rule 10.472;

(2) To the extent compatible with the efficient administration of justice, must grant to all court personnel sufficient leave to participate in education programs consistent with the education recommendations stated in rule 10.479;

(3) Should allow and encourage court personnel, in addition to participating as students in educational activities, to serve on court personnel education committees and as faculty at court personnel education programs when an employee's services have been requested for these purposes;

(4) Should establish an education plan for their court to facilitate the involvement of court personnel as both participants and faculty in educational activities, and should consult with each court staff member regarding their education needs and requirements and professional development; and

(5) Must ensure that court personnel are reimbursed by their court in accordance with the travel policies issued by the Judicial Council for travel expenses incurred in attending in-state education programs as a participant, except to the extent that: (i) certain expenses are covered by the Judicial Council; or (ii) the education provider or sponsor of the program pays the expenses. Provisions for these expenses must be part of every court's budget. Reimbursement of travel expenses incurred by court personnel in attending out-of-state education programs as a participant may be approved by designated court administrators, as defined in local court policies.

(Subd (f) amended effective January 1, 2023; adopted effective January 1, 2008; previously amended effective January 1, 2016, and January 1, 2018.)

(g) Responsibilities of trial court executive officers, managers, and supervisors

Trial court executive officers, managers, and supervisors:

(1) Must grant sufficient leave to all court personnel to enable them to complete the minimum education requirements stated in rule 10.474;

(2) To the extent compatible with the efficient administration of justice, must grant to all court personnel sufficient leave to participate in education programs consistent with the education recommendations stated in rule 10.479;

(3) Should allow and encourage court personnel, in addition to participating as students in education activities, to serve on court personnel education committees and as faculty at court personnel education programs when an employee's services have been requested for these purposes;

(4) Should establish an education plan for their court to facilitate the involvement of court personnel as both participants and faculty in educational activities, and should consult with each court staff member regarding their education needs and requirements and professional development; and

(5) Must ensure that court personnel are reimbursed by their court in accordance with the *Trial Court Financial Policies and Procedures Manual* for travel expenses incurred in attending in-state education programs as a participant, except to the extent that: (i) certain expenses are covered by the Judicial Council; or (ii) the education provider or sponsor of the program pays the expenses. Provisions for these expenses must be part of every court's budget. The court executive officer may approve reimbursement of travel expenses incurred by court personnel in attending out-of-state education programs as a participant.

(Subd (g) amended effective January 1, 2023; adopted as subd (f) effective January 1, 2007; previously amended and relettered as subd (g) effective January 1, 2008; previously amended effective January 1, 2016.)

Rule 10.452 amended effective January 1, 2023; adopted effective January 1, 2007; previously amended effective January 1, 2008, January 1, 2012, January 1, 2016, and January 1, 2018.

Rule 10.455. Ethics orientation for Judicial Council members and for judicial branch employees required to file a statement of economic interests

(a) Authority

This rule is adopted under Government Code section 11146 et seq. and article VI, section 6 of the California Constitution.

(Subd (a) amended effective January 1, 2007.)

(b) Definitions

For purposes of this rule, "judicial branch employee" includes an employee of a trial or appellate court or the Judicial Council, but does not include court commissioners or referees.

(Subd (b) amended effective January 1, 2016.)

(c) Judicial Council members and judicial branch employees

(1) Judicial Council staff must provide an ethics orientation course for Judicial Council members and for judicial branch employees who are required to file a statement of economic interests.

(2) Judicial Council members must take the orientation course within six months of appointment. If a member is appointed to a subsequent term, he or she must take the course within six months of the reappointment.

(3) Judicial branch employees who are required to file a statement of economic interests must take the orientation course as follows:

(A) For employees who have taken the orientation course before the effective date of this rule, at least once during each consecutive two calendar years after the date of the last attendance.

(B) For new employees, within six months of becoming an employee and at least once during each consecutive two calendar years thereafter.

(C) For all other employees, within six months of the effective date of this rule and at least once during each consecutive two calendar years thereafter.

(Subd (c) amended effective January 1, 2016.)

Rule 10.455 amended effective January 1, 2016; adopted as rule 6.301 effective January 1, 2004; previously amended and renumbered as rule 10.301 effective January 1, 2007, and as rule 10.455 effective January 1, 2013.

2012 Note: In addition to renumbering the rule, the amendment, effective January 1, 2013, consisted of revising the heading.

Rule 10.461. Minimum education requirements for Supreme Court and Court of Appeal justices

(a) Applicability

All California Court of Appeal justices must complete the minimum judicial education requirements for new justices under (b), and all Supreme Court and Court of Appeal justices must complete minimum continuing education requirements as outlined under (c). All justices should participate in more judicial education than is required, related to each individual's responsibilities and in accordance with the judicial education recommendations set forth in rule 10.469.

(Subd (a) adopted effective January 1, 2008.)

(b) Content-based requirement

Each new Court of Appeal justice, within two years of confirmation of appointment, must attend a new appellate justice orientation program sponsored by a national provider of appellate orientation programs or by the Judicial Council's Center for Judicial Education and Research.

(Subd (b) amended effective January 1, 2016; adopted as unlettered subd effective January 1, 2007; previously amended and lettered as subd (b) effective January 1, 2008; previously amended effective January 1, 2012.)

(c) Hours-based continuing education

(1) Each justice must complete 30 hours of continuing judicial education every three years, beginning on the dates outlined:

(A) A new Supreme Court justice enters the three-year continuing education cycle on January 1 of the year following confirmation of appointment, and a new Court of Appeal justice enters the three-year continuing education cycle on January 1 of the year following the period provided for completion of the required new justice orientation program; continuing education requirements are prorated based on the number of years remaining in the three-year education cycle.

(B) For all other justices, the first continuing education cycle begins January 1, 2008.

(C) The first continuing education cycle for Supreme Court and Court of Appeal justices is for two years from January 1, 2008, through December 31, 2009, rather than three years. The continuing education requirements and limitations in (c) are consequently prorated for this two-year education cycle. The first three-year education cycle then begins January 1, 2010.

(2) The following education applies toward the required 30 hours of continuing judicial education:

(A) Any education offered by an approved provider under rule 10.481(a) and any other education approved by the Chief Justice or the administrative presiding justice as meeting the criteria listed in rule 10.481(b).

(B) Each hour of participation in education by an approved provider under rule 10.481, including education that is instructor-led (live remote or in-person), asynchronous (such as videos and e-learning), and self-directed study, counts toward the continuing education requirement on an hour-for-hour basis. Justices must complete at least half of their continuing education hours requirement as a participant in instructor-led (live remote or in-person) education. Justices may complete the balance of their education hours requirement through any other means with no limitation on any particular type of education.

(C) A justice who serves as faculty by teaching legal or judicial education to a legal or judicial audience may apply faculty service as continuing education hours. There is no restriction on the number or percentage of hours that a justice may claim as faculty service. Credit for faculty service counts toward the continuing education requirement on an hour-for-hour basis in the same manner as all other types of education.

(Subd (c) amended effective January 1, 2023; adopted effective January 1, 2008; previously amended effective January 1, 2012, and January 1, 2013.)

(d) Extension of time

(1) Upon request and for good cause, the Chief Justice or the administrative presiding justice may grant a justice a one-year extension of time to complete the continuing education requirement in this rule.

(2) If the Chief Justice or the administrative presiding justice grants a request for an extension of time, the Chief Justice or the administrative presiding justice and the justice should pursue interim means of obtaining relevant educational content.

(3) An extension of time to complete the hours-based continuing education requirement does not affect what is required in the next three-year education cycle.

(Subd (d) amended effective January 1, 2023; adopted effective January 1, 2008.)

(e) Records and summaries of participation for justices

Justices are responsible for:

(1) Tracking their own participation in education and keeping a record of participation for three years after each course or activity that is applied toward the requirements, on a form provided by the Chief Justice for the Supreme Court or by the administrative presiding justice for each appellate district of the Court of Appeal. The form must include the information regarding a justice's participation in education that is needed by the Chief Justice or the administrative presiding justice to complete the aggregate form required by rule 10.452(d)(6);

(2) At the end of each year, giving the Chief Justice or the administrative presiding justice a copy of their record of participation in education for that year, on the form provided by the Chief Justice or the administrative presiding justice; and

(3) At the end of each three-year education cycle, giving the Chief Justice or the administrative presiding justice a copy of their record of participation in education for that year and a cumulative history of participation for that three-year cycle, on the form provided by the Chief Justice or the administrative presiding justice.

(Subd (e) amended effective January 1, 2023; adopted effective January 1, 2008; previously amended effective August 15, 2008.)

Rule 10.461 amended effective January 1, 2023; adopted effective January 1, 2007; previously amended effective January 1, 2008, August 15, 2008, January 1, 2012, January 1, 2013, and January 1, 2016.

Advisory Committee Comment

The requirements formerly contained in subdivision (e)(2) of rule 970, which has been repealed, are carried forward without change in rule 10.461(b).

Judicial Council staff have developed an individual reporting form that justices may use in tracking their own participation in education as required by rule 10.461(e)(1). The form is available from the council's Center for Judicial Education and Research. The Chief Justice and the administrative presiding justices may determine which form should be used in their court and may provide the council-developed form or another appropriate form developed by their court or by another court.

Rule 10.462. Minimum education requirements and expectations for trial court judges and subordinate judicial officers

(a) Applicability

All California trial court judges must complete the minimum judicial education requirements for new judges under (c)(1) and are expected to participate in continuing education as outlined under (d). All subordinate judicial officers must complete the minimum education requirements for new subordinate judicial officers under (c)(1) and for continuing education as outlined under (d). All trial court judges and subordinate judicial officers who hear family law matters must complete additional education requirements set forth in rule 10.463. All trial court judges and subordinate judicial officers who hear certain types of matters must participate in education on domestic violence issues as provided in rule 10.464. All trial court judges and subordinate judicial officers regularly assigned to hear probate proceedings must complete additional education requirements set forth in rule 10.468. All trial court judges and subordinate judicial officers should participate in more judicial education than is required and expected, related to each individual's responsibilities and particular judicial assignment or assignments and in accordance with the judicial education recommendations set forth in rule 10.469.

(Subd (a) amended effective January 1, 2012; adopted effective January 1, 2007; previously amended effective January 1, 2008.)

(b) Definitions

Unless the context or subject matter otherwise requires, "subordinate judicial officers" as used in this rule means subordinate judicial officers as defined in rule 10.701.

(Subd (b) adopted effective January 1, 2007.)

(c) Content-based requirement

(1) New trial court judges and subordinate judicial officers must complete the "new judge education" curriculum provided by the Judicial Council's Center for Judicial Education and Research (CJER) as follows:

(A) The new judge orientation program within six months of taking the oath as a judge or subordinate judicial officer. For purposes of the new judge orientation program, a judge or subordinate judicial officer is considered "new" only once, and any judge or subordinate judicial officer who has completed the new judge orientation program, as required under this rule or under former rule 970, is not required to complete the program again. A judge or subordinate judicial officer who was appointed, elected, or hired before rule 970 was adopted on January 1, 1996, is not required to complete the program;

(B) An orientation course in their primary assignment (civil, criminal, family, juvenile justice or dependency, probate, or traffic) within one year of taking the oath as a judge or subordinate judicial officer; and

(C) The B. E. Witkin Judicial College of California within two years of taking the oath as a judge or subordinate judicial officer. If a new judge previously completed the Judicial College as a new subordinate judicial officer, then the presiding judge may determine whether the new judge must complete it again.

(2) Judges beginning a supervising judge role are expected to complete CJER's supervising judge orientation program within one year of beginning the supervising judge role, preferably before beginning the role. This expectation does not apply if they are returning to a similar supervising judge role after less than two years in another assignment or are beginning a supervising judge role less than two years after serving in the presiding judge role and completing CJER's presiding judge and court executive officer orientation program.

(3) Judges beginning a presiding judge role are expected to complete CJER's presiding judge and court executive officer orientation program within one year of beginning the presiding judge role, preferably before beginning the role. This expectation does not apply if they are returning to a presiding judge role after two years or less in another role or assignment.

(4) Judges are expected to and subordinate judicial officers must, if beginning a new primary assignment (unless they are returning to an assignment after less than two years in another assignment), complete a course on the new primary assignment, provided by CJER, the California Judges Association (CJA), or the local court, within one year of beginning the new assignment. CJER is responsible for identifying content for these courses and will share the identified content with CJA and the local courts.

(Subd (c) amended effective January 1, 2023; adopted effective January 1, 2007; previously amended effective January 1, 2008, July 1, 2008, January 1, 2012, and January 1, 2016.)

(d) Hours-based continuing education

(1) Each judge is expected to and each subordinate judicial officer must complete 30 hours of continuing judicial education every three years, beginning on the dates outlined:

(A) A new judge or new subordinate judicial officer enters the three-year continuing education cycle on January 1 of the year following the period provided for completion of the required new judge education; continuing education expectations for judges and requirements for subordinate judicial officers are prorated based on the number of years remaining in the three-year education cycle.

(B) For all other judges and subordinate judicial officers, the first three-year education cycle begins on January 1, 2007.

(2) The following education applies toward the expected or required 30 hours of continuing judicial education:

(A) The content-based courses under (c)(2), (3), and (4) for a new supervising judge, a new presiding judge, and a judge or subordinate judicial officer beginning a new primary assignment (the "new judge education" required under (c)(1) does not apply); and

(B) Any other education offered by an approved provider under rule 10.481(a) and any other education approved by the presiding judge as meeting the criteria listed in rule 10.481(b).

(3) Each hour of participation in education by an approved provider under rule 10.481, including education that is instructor-led (live remote or in-person), asynchronous (such as videos and e-learning), and self-

directed study, counts toward the continuing education expectation or requirement on an hour-for-hour basis. Judges and subordinate judicial officers must complete at least half of their continuing education hours expectation or requirement as a participant in instructor-led (live remote or in-person) education. Judges or subordinate judicial officers may complete the balance of their judicial education hours expectation or requirement through any other means with no limitation on any particular type of education.

(4) A judge or subordinate judicial officer who serves as faculty by teaching legal or judicial education for a legal or judicial audience may apply faculty service as continuing education hours. There is no restriction on the number or percentage of hours that a judge may claim as faculty service. Credit for faculty service counts toward the continuing education expectation or requirement on an hour-for-hour basis in the same manner as all other types of education.

(5) The presiding judge may require subordinate judicial officers to participate in specific courses or participate in education in a specific subject matter area as part of their continuing education.

(Subd (d) amended effective January 1, 2023; previously amended effective January 1, 2008, January 1, 2012, and January 1, 2013.)

(e) Extension of time

(1) Upon request and for good cause, a presiding judge may grant a judge or subordinate judicial officer an extension of time, up to one year, to complete the education expectations or requirements in this rule.

(2) If the presiding judge grants a request for an extension of time, the presiding judge and the judge or subordinate judicial officer should pursue interim means of obtaining relevant educational content.

(3) An extension of time to complete the hours-based continuing education expectation or requirement does not affect what is expected or required in the next three-year education cycle.

(Subd (e) amended effective January 1, 2023; adopted effective January 1, 2007.)

(f) Records and cumulative histories of participation for judges

Judges are responsible for:

(1) Tracking their own participation in education and keeping a record of participation for three years after each course or activity that is applied toward the requirements and expectations, on a form provided by the presiding judge. The form must include the information regarding a judge's participation in education that is needed by the presiding judge to complete the aggregate form required by rule 10.452(e)(7);

(2) At the end of each year, giving the presiding judge a copy of their record of participation in education for that year, on the form provided by the presiding judge; and

(3) At the end of each three-year education cycle, giving the presiding judge a copy of their record of participation in education for that year and a cumulative history of participation for that three-year education cycle, on the form provided by the presiding judge.

(Subd (f) amended effective January 1, 2023; adopted effective January 1, 2007; previously amended effective January 1, 2008, and August 15, 2008.)

(g) Records of participation for subordinate judicial officers

(1) Each court is responsible for tracking participation in education and for tracking completion of minimum education requirements for its subordinate judicial officers.

(2) Subordinate judicial officers must keep records of their own participation for three years after each course or activity that is applied toward the requirements.

(Subd (g) amended effective January 1, 2023; adopted effective January 1, 2007.)

Rule 10.462 amended effective January 1, 2023; adopted effective January 1, 2007; previously amended effective January 1, 2008, July 1, 2008, August 15, 2008, January 1, 2012, January 1, 2013, and January 1, 2016.

Advisory Committee Comment

The minimum judicial education requirements in rule 10.462 do not apply to retired judges seeking to sit on regular court assignment in the Temporary Assigned Judges Program. Retired judges who seek to serve in the Temporary Assigned Judges Program must comply with the education requirements included in the program's standards and guidelines established by the Chief Justice.

Judicial Council staff have developed an individual reporting form that judges may use in tracking their own participation in education as required by rule 10.462(f). The form is available from the council's Center for Judicial Education and Research. Presiding judges may determine which form should be used in their court and may provide the council-developed form or another appropriate form developed by their court or by another court.

Rule 10.463. Education requirements for family court judges and subordinate judicial officers

Each judge or subordinate judicial officer whose primary assignment is to hear family law matters, or who regularly hears family law matters regardless of their primary assignment, must complete the following education:

(a) Basic family law education

(1) Within one year of beginning a family law assignment, the judge or subordinate judicial officer must complete a basic educational program on California family law and procedure designed primarily for judicial officers. A judge or subordinate judicial officer who has completed the basic educational program need not complete the basic educational program again.

(2) All other judicial officers who regularly hear family law matters, including retired judges who sit on court assignment, must complete appropriate family law education.

(Subd (a) amended effective January 1, 2023; adopted as (1) effective January 1, 1992; previously amended and lettered effective January 1, 2003; previously amended effective January 1, 2008.)

(b) Continuing family law education

The judge or subordinate judicial officer must complete a periodic update on new developments in California family law and procedure at least once each education cycle.

(Subd (b) amended effective January 1, 2023; adopted as (2) effective January 1, 1992; previously amended and lettered effective January 1, 2003; previously amended effective January 1, 2008.)

(c) Other family law education

To the extent that judicial time and resources are available, the judge or subordinate judicial officer must complete additional educational programs on other aspects of family law including interdisciplinary subjects relating to the family.

(Subd (c) amended effective January 1, 2008; adopted as (3) effective January 1, 1992; previously amended and lettered effective January 1, 2003.)

Rule 10.463 amended effective January 1, 2023; adopted as rule 1200 effective January 1, 1992; previously amended and renumbered as rule 5.30 effective January 1, 2003, and as rule 10.463 effective January 1, 2008.

Advisory Committee Comment

In determining what constitutes "appropriate" education, judges and subordinate judicial officers should determine the number of hours of education on family law matters that is adequate for their assignment, taking into account the size of the court, the nature of their assignment, the mix of assignments, and other factors.

Rule 10.464. Education requirements and expectations for judges and subordinate judicial officers on domestic violence issues

(a) Judges and subordinate judicial officers hearing specified matters

Judges or subordinate judicial officers who hear criminal, family, juvenile justice, juvenile dependency, or probate matters must participate in appropriate education on domestic violence issues as part of their hours-based continuing education requirements and expectations under rule 10.462(d) each education cycle. Each judge or subordinate judicial officer whose primary assignment is in one of these areas also must participate in a periodic update on domestic violence as part of these requirements and expectations at least once each education cycle.

(Subd (a) amended effective January 1, 2023; adopted effective January 1, 2010.)

(b) Specified courses to include education on domestic violence issues

The education provider must include education on domestic violence issues at the Judicial College under rule 10.462(c)(1)(C) and in courses for primary assignments in criminal, family, juvenile justice, juvenile dependency, or probate under rule 10.462(c)(1)(B) or (c)(4).

(Subd (b) amended effective January 1, 2023; adopted effective January 1, 2010.)

Rule 10.464 amended effective January 1, 2023; adopted effective January 1, 2010.

Advisory Committee Comment

In determining what constitutes "appropriate" education, judges and subordinate judicial officers should determine the number of hours of education on domestic violence that is adequate for their assignment, taking into account the size of the court, the nature of their assignment, the mix of assignments, and other factors.

Rule 10.468. Content-based and hours-based education for superior court judges and subordinate judicial officers regularly assigned to hear probate proceedings

(a) Definitions

As used in this rule, the following terms have the meanings stated below:

(1) "Probate proceedings" are decedents' estates, guardianships and conservatorships under division 4 of the Probate Code, trust proceedings under division 9 of the Probate Code, and other matters governed by provisions of that code and by the rules in division 1 of title 7 of the California Rules of Court.

(2) A judicial officer "regularly assigned to hear probate proceedings" is a judge or subordinate judicial officer who is:

(A) Assigned to a dedicated probate department where probate proceedings are customarily heard on a full-time basis;

(B) Responsible for hearing most of the probate proceedings filed in a court that does not have a dedicated probate department; or

(C) Responsible for hearing probate proceedings on a regular basis in a department in a branch or other location remote from the main or central courthouse, whether or not the judicial officer also hears other kinds of matters in that department and whether or not there is a dedicated probate department in the main or central courthouse; or

(D) Designated by the presiding judge of a court with four or fewer authorized judges.

(Subd (a) amended effective January 1, 2024; adopted effective January 1, 2008; previously amended effective January 1, 2016, and January 1, 2023.)

(b) Content-based requirements

(1) Judicial officers beginning a regular assignment to hear probate proceedings after the effective date of this rule—unless they are returning to this assignment after less than two years in another assignment—must complete six hours of education on probate guardianships and conservatorships, including court-supervised fiduciary accounting and the less restrictive alternatives to conservatorship stated in Probate Code section 1800.3, within one year of starting the assignment.

(2) The education required in (1) may be applied toward satisfaction of the hours-based continuing education expected of judges and required of subordinate judicial officers under rule 10.462(d).

(3) The education required in (1) must be provided by the Center for Judicial Education and Research (CJER), an approved provider under rule 10.481(a), or education approved by the judicial officer's presiding judge as meeting the education criteria specified in rule 10.481(b).

(4) The education required in (1) may be instructor-led (live remote or in-person), asynchronous (such as videos and e-learning), or self-directed study.

(Subd (b) amended effective January 1, 2024; adopted effective January 1, 2008; previously amended effective January 1, 2023.)

(c) Hours-based continuing education

(1) In a court with five or more authorized judges, judicial officers regularly assigned to hear probate proceedings must complete 12 hours of continuing education every three-year education cycle on probate guardianships and conservatorships, including court-supervised fiduciary accounting and the less restrictive alternatives to conservatorship stated in Probate Code section 1800.3.

(2) In a court with four or fewer authorized judges, judicial officers regularly assigned to hear probate proceedings must complete nine hours of continuing education every three-year education cycle on probate guardianships and conservatorships, including court-supervised fiduciary accounting and the less restrictive alternatives to conservatorship stated in Probate Code section 1800.3.

(3) The three-year education cycle begins on and runs concurrently with the dates specified in rule 10.462(d)(1).

(4) The number of hours of education required in (1) or (2) may be reduced proportionately for judicial officers whose regular assignment to hear probate proceedings is for a period of less than three years.

(5) The education required in (1) or (2) may be applied toward satisfaction of the 30 hours of continuing education expected of judges or required of subordinate judicial officers under rule 10.462(d).

(6) Judicial officers may fulfill the education requirement in (1) or (2) through council-sponsored education, an approved provider under rule 10.481(a), or education approved by the judicial officer's presiding judge as meeting the education criteria specified in rule 10.481(b).

(7) The education required in (1) or (2) may be instructor-led (live remote or in-person), asynchronous (such as videos and e-learning), or self-directed study.

(Subd (c) amended effective January 1, 2024; adopted effective January 1, 2008; previously amended effective January 1, 2012, January 1, 2016, and January 1, 2023.)

(d) Extension of time

The provisions of rule 10.462(e) concerning extensions of time apply to the content-based and hours-based education required under (b) and (c) of this rule.

(Subd (d) adopted effective January 1, 2008.)

(e) Record keeping and reporting

(1) The provisions of rule 10.462(f) and (g) concerning, respectively, tracking participation, record keeping, and summarizing participation by judges and tracking participation by subordinate judicial officers, apply to the education required under this rule.

(2) Presiding judges' records of judicial officer participation in the education required by this rule are subject to audit by Judicial Council staff under rule 10.462. Judicial Council staff may require courts to report participation by judicial officers in the education required by this rule to ensure compliance with Probate Code section 1456.

(Subd (e) amended effective January 1, 2016; adopted effective January 1, 2008.)

Rule 10.468 amended effective January 1, 2024; adopted effective January 1, 2008; previously amended effective January 1, 2012, January 1, 2016, and January 1, 2023.

Rule 10.469. Education recommendations for justices, judges, and subordinate judicial officers

(a) Judicial education recommendations generally

Justices, judges, and subordinate judicial officers, as part of their continuing judicial education, should regularly participate in educational activities related to their responsibilities and particular judicial assignment or assignments. Minimum education requirements and expectations related to judicial responsibilities and assignments are stated in rules 10.461–10.462. Additional education requirements related to specific responsibilities are stated in rule 10.463 (for those hearing family law matters), rule 10.464 (for those hearing domestic violence issues), and rule 10.468 (for those hearing probate proceedings). The following recommendations illustrate for some specific responsibilities and assignments how justices, judges, and subordinate judicial officers should participate in more judicial education than is required and expected.

(Subd (a) amended effective January 1, 2023; adopted effective January 1, 2008; previously amended effective January 1, 2012.)

(b) Jury trial assignment

Judges or subordinate judicial officers assigned to jury trials should regularly refer to appropriate educational materials and should regularly complete appropriate educational programs devoted to the conduct of jury voir dire and the treatment of jurors.

(Subd (b) amended effective January 1, 2023; adopted effective January 1, 2008; previously amended effective January 1, 2012, and January 1, 2016.)

(c) Hearing of juvenile dependency matters

Judges or subordinate judicial officers who hear juvenile dependency matters, including retired judges who sit on court assignment, should regularly refer to appropriate educational materials and should annually complete appropriate education programs on juvenile dependency law and procedure, consistent with the requirements in Welfare and Institutions Code section 304.7.

(Subd (c) amended effective January 1, 2023; adopted effective January 1, 2008.)

(d) Capital case assignment

Judges assigned to hear a capital case should complete, before the commencement of the trial, a comprehensive education program on California law and procedure relevant to capital cases provided by the Center for Judicial Education and Research (CJER). A judge with a subsequent assignment to a capital case should complete a periodic update course within two years before the commencement of the trial. The periodic update may be provided through actual classroom instruction or through any other media as determined by CJER.

(Subd (d) amended effective January 1, 2023; adopted effective January 1, 2008.)

(e) Education on fairness and access, unconscious bias, and prevention of harassment, discrimination, retaliation, and inappropriate workplace conduct

(1) In order to achieve the objective of assisting judicial officers in preserving the integrity and impartiality of the judicial system through the prevention of bias, each justice, judge, and subordinate judicial officer should regularly participate in education on fairness and access. The

education should include the following subjects: race and ethnicity; gender; sexual orientation; persons with disabilities; persons with limited economic means; and persons without stable housing.

(2) Each justice, judge, and subordinate judicial officer must participate in education on unconscious bias, as well as the prevention of harassment, discrimination, retaliation, and inappropriate workplace conduct. This education must be taken at least once every three-year continuing education cycle as determined by rules 10.461(c)(1) and 10.462(d).

(Subd (e) amended effective January 1, 2023; adopted effective January 1, 2008; previously amended effective January 1, 2021.)

Rule 10.469 amended effective January 1, 2023; adopted effective January 1, 2008; previously amended effective January 1, 2012, January 1, 2016, and January 1, 2021.

Rule 10.471. Minimum education requirements for Supreme Court and Court of Appeal clerk/executive officers

(a) Applicability

All clerk/executive officers of the California Supreme Court and Courts of Appeal must complete these minimum education requirements. All clerk/executive officers should participate in more education than is required, related to each individual's responsibilities and in accordance with the education recommendations set forth in rule 10.479.

(Subd (a) amended effective January 1, 2023; adopted effective January 1, 2008; previously amended effective January 1, 2018.)

(b) Hours-based requirement

(1) Clerk/executive officers must complete 30 hours of continuing education every three years beginning on the following dates:

(A) For new clerk/executive officers, the first three-year cycle begins on January 1 of the year following their hire.

(B) For all other clerk/executive officers, the first three-year cycle begins on January 1, 2008.

(2) The following education applies toward the required 30 hours of continuing education:

(A) Any education offered by an approved provider under rule 10.481(a) and any other education, approved by the Chief Justice or the administrative presiding justice as meeting the criteria listed in rule 10.481(b).

(B) Each hour of participation in education by an approved provider under rule 10.481, including education that is instructor-led (live remote or in-person), asynchronous (such as videos and e-learning), and self-directed study, counts toward the continuing education requirement on an hour-for-hour basis. The Chief Justice or the administrative presiding justice has discretion to determine the number of hours, if any, of instructor-led (live remote or in-person) education required to meet the continuing education requirement.

(C) A clerk/executive officer who serves as faculty by teaching legal or judicial education to a legal or judicial audience may apply education hours as faculty service. There is no restriction on the number or percentage of hours that a clerk/executive officer may claim as faculty service. Credit for faculty service counts toward the continuing education requirement on an hour-for-hour basis in the same manner as all other types of education.

(Subd (b) amended effective January 1, 2023; adopted effective January 1, 2008; previously amended effective January 1, 2012, January 1, 2014, and January 1, 2018.)

(c) Extension of time

(1) Upon request and for good cause, the Chief Justice or the administrative presiding justice may grant a clerk/executive officer an extension of time, up to one year, to complete the education requirements in (b).

(2) If the Chief Justice or the administrative presiding justice grants a request for an extension of time, the Chief Justice or the administrative presiding justice and the clerk/executive officer must pursue interim means of obtaining relevant educational content.

(3) An extension of time to complete the hours-based requirement does not affect the timing of the clerk/executive officer's next three-year education cycle.

(Subd (c) amended effective January 1, 2023; adopted effective January 1, 2008; previously amended effective January 1, 2018.)

(d) Record of participation; statement of completion

Clerk/executive officers are responsible for:

(1) Tracking their own participation in education and keeping a record of participation for three years after each course or activity that is applied toward the requirements;

(2) At the end of each year, giving the Chief Justice or the administrative presiding justice a copy of their record of participation in education for that year; and

(3) At the end of each three-year education cycle, giving the Chief Justice or the administrative presiding justice a signed statement of completion for that three-year education cycle.

(Subd (d) amended effective January 1, 2023; adopted effective January 1, 2008; previously amended effective January 1, 2018.)

Rule 10.471 amended effective January 1, 2023; adopted effective January 1, 2008; previously amended effective January 1, 2012, January 1, 2014, and January 1, 2018.

Rule 10.472. Minimum education requirements for Supreme Court and Court of Appeal managing attorneys, supervisors, and other personnel

(a) Applicability

All California Supreme Court and Court of Appeal managing attorneys, supervisors, and other personnel must complete these minimum education requirements. All managing attorneys, supervisors, and other personnel should participate in more education than is required related to each individual's responsibilities and in accordance with the education recommendations set forth in rule 10.479.

(Subd (a) adopted effective January 1, 2008.)

(b) Content-based requirements

(1) Each new managing attorney or supervisor must complete orientation courses within one year of becoming a managing attorney or supervisor, unless the individual's supervisor determines that the new managing attorney or supervisor has already completed these orientation courses or courses covering equivalent content. The courses must include orientation about:

(A) The judicial branch of California;

(B) The local court; and

(C) Basic management and supervision.

(2) Each new court employee who is not a managing attorney or supervisor must complete orientation courses within one year of becoming a court employee, unless the employee's supervisor determines that the new court employee has already completed these orientation courses or courses covering equivalent content. The courses must include orientation about:

(A) The judicial branch of California;

(B) The local court;

(C) Basic employee issues, such as sexual harassment and safety; and

(D) The employee's specific job.

(3) The clerk/executive officer, the managing attorney, or the employee's supervisor may determine the appropriate content, delivery mechanism, and length of orientation based on the needs and role of each individual employee.

(Subd (b) amended effective January 1, 2023; adopted effective January 1, 2008; previously amended effective January 1, 2018.)

(c) Hours-based requirements

(1) Each managing attorney, supervisor, or appellate judicial attorney must complete 12 hours of continuing education every two years.

(2) Each court employee who is not a managing attorney, supervisor, or appellate judicial attorney must complete 8 hours of continuing education every two years, with the exception of employees who do not provide court administrative or operational services. Those employees are not subject to the continuing education hours-based requirement but must complete any education or training required by law and any other education required by the clerk/executive officer.

(3) The two-year education cycle for all managing attorneys, supervisors, and other personnel begins on January 1 of each even-numbered year. The orientation education required for new managing attorneys, supervisors, and other personnel under (b) applies toward the required hours of continuing education. New managing attorneys, supervisors, or employees enter the two-year continuing education cycle on their first day of employment and must complete a prorated number of continuing education hours for that two-year education cycle.

(4) Any education offered by an approved provider under rule 10.481(a) and any other education that is approved by the clerk/executive officer, the managing attorney, or the employee's supervisor as meeting the criteria listed in rule 10.481(b) applies toward the orientation education required under (b) and the continuing education required under (c)(1) and (2).

(5) Each hour of participation in education by an approved provider under rule 10.481, including education that is instructor-led (live remote

or in-person), asynchronous (such as videos and e-learning), and self-directed study approved in advance by the supervisor of the managing attorney, supervisor, appellate judicial attorney, or other employee, counts toward the continuing education requirement on an hour-for-hour basis. The administrative presiding justice or the clerk/executive officer has discretion to determine the number of hours, if any, of instructor-led (live remote or in-person) education required to meet the continuing education requirement.

(6) A managing attorney, supervisor, appellate judicial attorney, or other employee who serves as faculty by teaching legal or judicial education for a legal or judicial audience may apply education hours for the faculty service. There is no restriction on the number or percentage of hours that a managing attorney, supervisor, appellate judicial attorney, or other employee may claim as faculty service. Credit for faculty service counts toward the continuing education requirement on an hour-for-hour basis in the same manner as all other types of education.

(7) The administrative presiding justice or the clerk/executive officer may require supervisors and other court personnel to participate in specific courses or to participate in education in a specific subject matter area as part of their continuing education.

(Subd (c) amended effective January 1, 2023; adopted effective January 1, 2008; previously amended effective January 1, 2012, and January 1, 2018.)

(d) Extension of time

(1) Upon request and for good cause, the administrative presiding justice or the clerk/executive officer may grant an extension, up to one year, to complete the education requirements in this rule.

(2) If the administrative presiding justice or the clerk/executive officer grants a request for an extension of time, the administrative presiding justice or the clerk/executive officer and the managing attorney, supervisor, or employee who made the request must pursue interim means of obtaining relevant educational content.

(3) An extension of time to complete the hours-based requirement does not affect the timing of the next two-year education cycle.

(Subd (d) amended effective January 1, 2023; adopted effective January 1, 2008; previously amended effective January 1, 2018.)

(e) Records of participation

(1) Each court is responsible for tracking participation in education and for tracking completion of minimum education requirements for its managing attorneys, supervisors, and other personnel.

(2) Managing attorneys, supervisors, and employees must keep records of their own participation for two years after each course or activity that is applied toward the requirements.

(Subd (e) amended effective January 1, 2023; adopted effective January 1, 2008.)

Rule 10.472 amended effective January 1, 2023; adopted effective January 1, 2008; previously amended effective January 1, 2012, and January 1, 2018.

Rule 10.473. Minimum education requirements for trial court executive officers

(a) Applicability

All California trial court executive officers must complete these minimum education requirements. All executive officers should participate in more education than is required, related to each individual's responsibilities and in accordance with the education recommendations set forth in rule 10.479.

(Subd (a) amended effective January 1, 2008; adopted effective January 1, 2007.)

(b) Content-based requirement

(1) New executive officers must complete the presiding judge and court executive officer orientation program provided by the Judicial Council's Center for Judicial Education and Research (CJER) within one year of becoming an executive officer and should participate in additional education during the first year.

(2) Executive officers should participate in CJER's presiding judge and court executive officer orientation program each time a new presiding judge from their court participates in the course and each time the executive officer becomes the executive officer in a different court.

(Subd (b) amended effective January 1, 2023; adopted effective January 1, 2007; previously amended effective July 1, 2015.)

(c) Hours-based requirement

(1) Each executive officer must complete 30 hours of continuing education, including at least three hours of ethics education, every three years.

(2) For a new executive officer, the first three-year education cycle begins on January 1 of the year following the period provided for completion of the required education for new executive officers.

(3) The following education applies toward the required 30 hours of continuing education:

(A) Any education offered by an approved provider under rule 10.481(a) and any other education approved by the presiding judge as meeting the criteria listed in rule 10.481(b).

(B) Each hour of participation in education by an approved provider under rule 10.481, including education that is instructor-led (live remote or in-person), asynchronous (such as videos and e-learning), and self-directed study, counts toward the continuing education requirement on an hour-for-hour basis. The presiding judge has discretion to determine the number of hours, if any, of instructor-led (live remote or in-person) education required to meet the continuing education requirement.

(C) A court executive officer who serves as faculty by teaching legal or judicial education to a legal or judicial audience may apply education hours as faculty service. There is no restriction on the number or percentage of hours that a court executive officer may claim as faculty service. Credit for faculty service counts toward the continuing education requirement on an hour-for-hour basis in the same manner as all other types of education.

(Subd (c) amended effective January 1, 2023; previously amended effective January 1, 2008, January 1, 2011, January 1, 2012, January 1, 2013, and July 1, 2015.)

(d) Extension of time

(1) Upon request and for good cause, a presiding judge may grant an extension, up to one year, to complete the education requirements in this rule.

(2) If the presiding judge grants a request for an extension of time, the presiding judge and the executive officer must pursue interim means of obtaining relevant educational content.

(3) An extension of time to complete the hours-based requirement does not affect the timing of the executive officer's next three-year education cycle.

(Subd (d) amended effective January 1, 2023; adopted effective January 1, 2007.)

(e) Record of participation; statement of completion

Executive officers are responsible for:

(1) Tracking their own participation in education and keeping a record of participation for three years after each course or activity that is applied toward the requirements;

(2) At the end of each year, giving the presiding judge a copy of their record of participation in education for that year; and

(3) At the end of each three-year education cycle, giving the presiding judge a signed statement of completion for that three-year education cycle.

(Subd (e) amended effective January 1, 2023; adopted effective January 1, 2007; previously amended effective January 1, 2008.)

Rule 10.473 amended effective January 1, 2023; adopted as rule 10.463 effective January 1, 2007; previously amended and renumbered effective January 1, 2008; previously amended effective January 1, 2011, January 1, 2012, January 1, 2013, and July 1, 2015.

Rule 10.474. Trial court managers, supervisors, and other personnel

(a) Applicability

All California trial court managers, supervisors, and other personnel must complete these minimum education requirements. All managers, supervisors, and other personnel should participate in more education than is required, related to each individual's responsibilities and in accordance with the education recommendations set forth in rule 10.479.

(Subd (a) amended effective January 1, 2008; adopted effective January 1, 2007.)

(b) Content-based requirements

(1) Each new manager or supervisor must complete orientation courses within one year of becoming a manager or supervisor, unless the court's executive officer determines that the new manager or supervisor has already completed these orientation courses or courses covering equivalent content. The courses must include orientation about:

(A) The judicial branch of California;

(B) The local court; and

(C) Basic management and supervision.

(2) Each new court employee who is not a manager or supervisor must complete orientation courses within one year of becoming a court

employee, unless the employee's supervisor determines that the new court employee has already completed these orientation courses or courses covering equivalent content. The courses must include orientation about:

(A) The judicial branch of California;
(B) The local court;
(C) Basic employee issues, such as sexual harassment and safety; and
(D) The employee's specific job.

(3) The court executive officer may determine the appropriate content, delivery mechanism, and length of orientation based on the needs and role of each individual employee.

(Subd (b) amended effective January 1, 2023; adopted effective January 1, 2007; previously amended effective January 1, 2008.)

(c) Hours-based requirements

(1) Each court manager or supervisor must complete 12 hours of continuing education every two years.

(2) Each court employee who is not a manager or supervisor must complete 8 hours of continuing education every two years, with the exception of employees who do not provide court administrative or operational services. Those employees are not subject to the continuing education hours-based requirement but must complete any education or training required by law and any other education required by the court executive officer.

(3) The two-year continuing education cycle for all managers, supervisors, and other personnel begins on January 1 of each odd-numbered year. The orientation education required for new managers, supervisors, and other personnel under (b) applies toward the required hours of continuing education. New managers, supervisors, or employees enter the two-year continuing education cycle on their first day of employment and must complete a prorated number of continuing education hours for that two-year education cycle.

(4) Any education offered by an approved provider under rule 10.481(a) and any other education that is approved by the executive officer or the employee's supervisor as meeting the criteria listed in rule 10.481(b) applies toward the education required under this rule.

(5) Each hour of participation in education by an approved provider under rule 10.481, including education that is instructor-led (live remote or in-person), asynchronous (such as videos and e-learning), and self-directed study approved in advance by the direct supervisor of the manager, supervisor, or court employee, counts toward the continuing education requirement on an hour-for-hour basis. The court executive officer has discretion to determine the number of hours, if any, of instructor-led (live remote or in-person) education required to meet the continuing education requirement.

(6) A manager, supervisor, or employee who serves as faculty by teaching legal or judicial education to a legal or judicial audience may apply education hours as faculty service. There is no restriction on the number or percentage of hours that a manager, supervisor, or employee may claim as faculty service. Credit for faculty service counts toward the continuing education requirement on an hour-for-hour basis in the same manner as all other types of education.

(7) The court executive officer may require managers, supervisors, and other court personnel to participate in specific courses or to participate in education in a specific subject matter area as part of their continuing education.

(Subd (c) amended effective January 1, 2023; previously amended effective January 1, 2008, January 1, 2012, January 1, 2013, and January 1, 2015.)

(d) Extension of time

(1) Upon request and for good cause, the executive officer may grant an extension, up to one year, to complete the education requirements in this rule.

(2) If the executive officer grants a request for an extension of time, the executive officer and the manager, supervisor, or employee who made the request must pursue interim means of obtaining relevant educational content.

(3) An extension of time to complete the hours-based requirement does not affect the timing of the next two-year education cycle.

(Subd (d) amended effective January 1, 2023; adopted effective January 1, 2007; previously amended effective January 1, 2015.)

(e) Records of participation

(1) Each court is responsible for tracking participation in education and for tracking completion of minimum education requirements for its managers, supervisors, and other personnel.

(2) Managers, supervisors, and employees must keep records of their own participation for two years after each course or activity that is applied toward the requirements.

(Subd (e) amended January 1, 2023; adopted effective January 1, 2007.)

Rule 10.474 amended effective January 1, 2023; adopted as rule 10.464 effective January 1, 2007; previously amended and renumbered effective January 1, 2008; previously amended effective January 1, 2012, January 1, 2013, and January 1, 2015.

Advisory Committee Comment

The time frame for completion of compliance courses based on statutory or regulatory mandates is unaffected by the one-year extension in (d)(1).

Rule 10.478. Content-based and hours-based education for court investigators, probate attorneys, and probate examiners

(a) Definitions

As used in this rule, the following terms have the meanings specified below, unless the context or subject matter otherwise require:

(1) A "court investigator" is a person described in Probate Code section 1454(a) employed by or under contract with a court to provide the investigative services for the court required or authorized by law in guardianships, conservatorships, and other protective proceedings under division 4 of the Probate Code;

(2) A "probate attorney" is an active member of the State Bar of California who is employed by a court to perform the functions of a probate examiner and also to provide legal analysis, recommendations, advice, and other services to the court pertaining to probate proceedings;

(3) A "probate examiner" is a person employed by a court to review filings in probate proceedings in order to assist the court and the parties to get the filed matters properly ready for consideration by the court in accordance with the requirements of the Probate Code, the rules in division 1 of title 7 of the California Rules of Court, and the court's local rules; and

(4) "Probate proceedings" are decedents' estates, guardianships and conservatorships under division 4 of the Probate Code, trust proceedings under division 9 of the Probate Code, and other matters governed by provisions of that code and by the rules in division 1 of title 7 of the California Rules of Court.

(Subd (a) amended effective January 1, 2024; adopted effective January 1, 2008; previously amended effective January 1, 2016, and January 1, 2023.)

(b) Content-based requirements for court investigators

(1) Court investigators must complete 12 hours of education within one year of their start date after January 1, 2008. The education must include the following general topics:

(A) Court process and legal proceedings;
(B) Child abuse and neglect and the effect of domestic violence on children (guardianship investigators); elder and dependent adult abuse, including undue influence and other forms of financial abuse (conservatorship investigators);
(C) Medical issues;
(D) Access to and use of criminal-record information, confidentiality, ethics, conflicts of interest;
(E) Accessing and evaluating community resources for children and mentally impaired elderly or developmentally disabled adults;
(F) Interviewing children and persons with mental function or communication deficits; and
(G) The less restrictive alternatives to conservatorship stated in Probate Code section 1800.3.

(2) A court investigator may fulfill the education requirement in (1) through council-sponsored education, an approved provider (see rule 10.481(a)), or education approved by the court executive officer or the court investigator's supervisor as meeting the education criteria specified in rule 10.481(b).

(3) The education required in (1) may be applied to the specific-job portion of the orientation course required for all new court employees under rule 10.474(b)(2)(D) and the continuing education required for all nonmanagerial or non-supervisory court employees under rule 10.474(c)(2).

(4) Each hour of participation in education by an approved provider under rule 10.481, including education that is instructor-led (live remote or in-person), asynchronous (such as videos and e-learning), and self-directed study approved in advance by the court executive officer or the court investigator's supervisor, counts toward the continuing education requirement in (1) on an hour-for-hour basis.

(Subd (b) amended effective January 1, 2024; adopted effective January 1, 2008; previously amended effective January 1, 2012, January 1, 2016, and January 1, 2023.)

(c) Content-based education for probate attorneys

(1) Probate attorneys must complete 12 hours of education within six months of their start date after January 1, 2008, in probate-related topics, including guardianships, conservatorships, court-supervised fiduciary accounting, and the less restrictive alternatives to conservatorship stated in Probate Code section 1800.3.

(2) A probate attorney may fulfill the education requirement in (1) through council-sponsored education, an approved provider (see rule 10.481(a)), or education approved by the court executive officer or the probate attorney's supervisor as meeting the education criteria specified in rule 10.481(b).

(3) The education required in (1) may be applied to the specific-job portion of the orientation course required for all new court employees under rule 10.474(b)(2)(D) and the continuing education required for all nonmanagerial or non-supervisory court employees under rule 10.474(c)(2).

(4) Each hour of participation in education by an approved provider under rule 10.481, including education that is instructor-led (live remote or in-person), asynchronous (such as videos and e-learning), and self-directed study approved in advance by the court executive officer or the probate attorney's supervisor, counts toward the continuing education requirement in (1) on an hour-for-hour basis.

(Subd (c) amended effective January 1, 2024; adopted effective January 1, 2008; previously amended effective January 1, 2012, January 1, 2016, and January 1, 2023.)

(d) Content-based education for probate examiners

(1) Probate examiners must complete 20 hours of education within one year of their start date after January 1, 2008, in probate-related topics, of which 12 hours must be in guardianships and conservatorships, including court-appointed fiduciary accounting and the less restrictive alternatives to conservatorship stated in Probate Code section 1800.3.

(2) A probate examiner may fulfill the education requirement in (1) through council-sponsored education, an approved provider (see rule 10.481(a)), or education approved by the court executive officer or the probate examiner's supervisor as meeting the education criteria specified in rule 10.481(b).

(3) The education required in (1) may be applied to the specific-job portion of the orientation course required for all new court employees under rule 10.474(b)(2)(D) and the continuing education required for all nonmanagerial or non-supervisory court employees under rule 10.474(c)(2).

(4) Each hour of participation in education by an approved provider under rule 10.481, including education that is instructor-led (live remote or in-person), asynchronous (such as videos and e-learning), and self-directed study approved in advance by the court executive officer or the probate examiner's supervisor, counts toward the continuing education requirement in (1) on an hour-for-hour basis.

(Subd (d) amended effective January 1, 2024; adopted effective January 1, 2008; previously amended effective January 1, 2012, January 1, 2016, and January 1, 2023.)

(e) Hours-based education for court investigators

(1) Each court investigator must complete 12 hours of continuing education on some or all of the general topics listed in (b)(1) each two-year education cycle. The education cycle is determined in the same manner as in rule 10.474(c)(3).

(2) A court investigator may fulfill the education requirement in (1) through council-sponsored education, an approved provider (see rule 10.481(a)), or education approved by the court executive officer or the court investigator's supervisor as meeting the education criteria specified in rule 10.481(b).

(3) The education required in (1) may be applied to the continuing education required for all nonmanagerial or nonsupervisory court employees under rule 10.474(c)(2).

(4) Each hour of participation in education by an approved provider under rule 10.481, including education that is instructor-led (live remote or in-person), asynchronous (such as videos and e-learning), and self-directed study approved in advance by the court executive officer or the court investigator's supervisor, counts toward the continuing education requirement in (1) on an hour-for-hour basis.

(Subd (e) amended effective January 1, 2023; adopted effective January 1, 2008; previously amended effective January 1, 2012, and January 1, 2016.)

(f) Hours-based education for probate attorneys

(1) Probate attorneys must complete 12 hours of continuing education each two-year education cycle in probate-related subjects, of which six hours per year must be in guardianships and conservatorships, including court-supervised fiduciary accounting and the less restrictive alternatives to conservatorship stated in Probate Code section 1800.3. The education cycle is determined in the same manner as in rule 10.474(c)(3).

(2) A probate attorney may fulfill the education requirement in (1) through council-sponsored education, an approved provider (see rule 10.481(a)), or education approved by the court executive officer or the probate attorney's supervisor as meeting the education criteria specified in rule 10.481(b).

(3) The education required in (1) may be applied to the continuing education required for all nonmanagerial or nonsupervisory court employees under rule 10.474(c)(2).

(4) Each hour of participation in education by an approved provider under rule 10.481, including education that is instructor-led (live remote or in-person), asynchronous (such as videos and e-learning), and self-directed study approved in advance by the court executive officer or the probate attorney's supervisor, counts toward the continuing education requirement in (1) on an hour-for-hour basis.

(Subd (f) amended effective January 1, 2024; adopted effective January 1, 2008; previously amended effective January 1, 2012, January 1, 2016, and January 1, 2023.)

(g) Hours-based education for probate examiners

(1) Probate examiners must complete 12 hours of continuing education each two-year education cycle in probate-related subjects, of which six hours per year must be in guardianships and conservatorships, including court-appointed fiduciary accounting **and the less restrictive alternatives to conservatorship stated in Probate Code section 1800.3**. The education cycle is determined in the same manner as in rule 10.474(c)(3).

(2) A probate examiner may fulfill the education requirement in (1) through council-sponsored education, an approved provider (see rule 10.481(a)), or education approved by the court executive officer or the probate examiner's supervisor as meeting the education criteria specified in rule 10.481(b).

(3) The education required in (1) may be applied to the continuing education required for all nonmanagerial or nonsupervisory court employees under rule 10.474(c)(2).

(4) Each hour of participation in education by an approved provider under rule 10.481, including education that is instructor-led (live remote or in-person), asynchronous (such as videos and e-learning), and self-directed study approved in advance by the court executive officer or the probate examiner's supervisor, counts toward the continuing education requirement in (1) on an hour-for-hour basis.

(Subd (g) amended effective January 1, 2024; adopted effective January 1, 2008; previously amended effective January 1, 2012, January 1, 2016, and January 1, 2023.)

(h) Extension of time

The provisions of rule 10.474(d) concerning extensions of time apply to the content-based and hours-based education required under this rule.

(Subd (h) adopted effective January 1, 2008.)

(i) Record keeping and reporting

(1) The provisions of rule 10.474(e) concerning the responsibilities of courts and participating court employees to keep records and track the completion of educational requirements apply to the education required under this rule.

(2) Judicial Council staff may require courts to report participation by court investigators, probate attorneys, and probate examiners in the education required by this rule as necessary to ensure compliance with Probate Code section 1456.

(Subd (i) amended effective January 1, 2016; adopted effective January 1, 2008.)
Rule 10.478 amended effective January 1, 2024; adopted effective January 1, 2008; previously amended effective January 1, 2012, January 1, 2016, and January 1, 2023.

Rule 10.479. Education recommendations for appellate and trial court personnel

(a) Education recommendations generally

Appellate and trial court executive or administrative officers, managers, supervisors, and other employees, as part of their continuing education, should regularly participate in educational activities related to their responsibilities. Minimum education requirements for court personnel are stated in rules 10.471–10.474. The following recommendations illustrate how executive and administrative officers, managers, supervisors, and other personnel should participate in more education than is required for some specific responsibilities.

(Subd (a) amended effective January 1, 2023; adopted effective January 1, 2008.)

(b) Education on treatment of jurors

The presiding judge of each trial court should ensure that all court executives and all court employees who interact with jurors are properly trained in the appropriate treatment of jurors. Court executives and jury staff employees should regularly refer to appropriate educational materials and should regularly complete appropriate educational programs devoted to the treatment of jurors.

(Subd (b) amended effective January 1, 2023; adopted effective January 1, 2008.)

(c) Fairness and access education

In order to achieve the objective of assisting court employees in preserving the integrity and impartiality of the judicial system through the prevention of bias, all court executives and all court employees should regularly participate in education on fairness and access. The education should include instruction on the following subjects: race and ethnicity; gender; sexual orientation; persons with disabilities; sexual harassment; persons with limited economic means; and persons without stable housing.

(Subd (c) amended effective January 1, 2023; adopted effective January 1, 2008.)

(d) Education on quality service to court users

All court employees who regularly interact with members of the public should participate in education covering appropriate skills and conduct for working with court users.

(Subd (d) amended effective January 1, 2023; adopted effective January 1, 2008.)

Rule 10.479 amended effective January 1, 2023; adopted effective January 1, 2008.

Rule 10.481. Approved providers; approved course criteria

(a) Approved providers

The Judicial Council's Center for Judicial Education and Research (CJER) is responsible for maintaining a current list of approved providers. The list of approved providers must include the Judicial Council, the California Judges Association, and all California state courts. The list should also include other reputable national and state organizations that regularly offer education directed to justices, judges, and court personnel. The director of CJER may add or remove organizations from the list of approved providers as appropriate according to the criteria contained in (b). Any education program offered by any of the approved providers that is relevant to the work of the courts or enhances the participants' ability to perform their jobs may be applied toward the education requirements and expectations stated in rules 10.461–10.479, except for the requirements stated in the rules that require a specific provider or providers.

(Subd (a) amended effective January 1, 2023; adopted effective January 1, 2007; previously amended effective January 1, 2008, January 1, 2012, and January 1, 2016.)

(b) Approved education criteria

Education is not limited to the approved providers referred to in (a). Any education from another provider that is approved by the Chief Justice, the administrative presiding justice, or the presiding judge as meeting the criteria listed below may be applied toward the continuing education expectations and requirements for justices, judges, subordinate judicial officers, clerk/executive officers, or court executive officers. Similarly, any education from another provider that is approved by the clerk/executive officer, the court executive officer, or the employee's supervisor as meeting the criteria listed below may be applied toward the orientation or continuing education requirements for managers, supervisors, and other employees or the content-based or hours-based continuing education requirements for probate court investigators, probate attorneys, and probate examiners in rule 10.478.

(1) The education must meet the following two criteria:

(A) The subject matter is relevant to the work of the courts or the judicial branch; and

(B) Anticipated learning outcomes (how new knowledge, skills, or abilities will be applied, demonstrated, or used) are identified prior to the education work.

(2) The education must also meet at least two of the following five criteria:

(A) The learning environment is educationally sound (e.g., distractions are limited and the physical location is conducive to learning the subject matter);

(B) The participant receives or has access to all the reference tools and other materials and resources (such as handouts) that are required for learning and applying the content (such as job aids or scripts);

(C) The participant has an opportunity to practice using or applying the new information or skill (through direct experience, role-play, or case studies/hypothetical situations) as part of the learning experience;

(D) The participant has the opportunity to interact with knowledgeable faculty or other experts in the topical area to pose questions or clarify understanding;

(E) An assessment tool or activity (such as the development of an action plan to apply the newly gained knowledge or skill) enables the participants to determine whether the skills, abilities, or knowledge gained through the education can be used in the future in their work.

(Subd (b) amended effective January 1, 2023; adopted effective January 1, 2007; previously amended effective January 1, 2008, January 1, 2012, and January 1, 2018.)

Rule 10.481 amended effective January 1, 2023; adopted as rule 10.471 effective January 1, 2007; previously amended and renumbered as rule 10.481 effective January 1, 2008; previously amended effective January 1, 2008, January 1, 2012, January 1, 2016, and January 1, 2018.

Advisory Committee Comment

Subdivision (b). The director of CJER or their designee is available to assist those authorized to approve a request to apply education offered by a non-approved provider in determining whether the education meets the listed criteria.

Rule 10.491. Minimum education requirements for Judicial Council employees

(a) Applicability

Orientation and ongoing professional development for Judicial Council staff enables them to effectively provide service, leadership and expertise to the courts and to enhance trust and confidence in the judicial branch. All Judicial Council employees must complete minimum education requirements. These education requirements are included as a part of the employee performance evaluation process.

(Subd (a) amended effective January 1, 2017; adopted effective January 1, 2008; previously amended effective January 1, 2016.)

(b) Education requirements for new employees and new managers and supervisors

(1) Each new employee with supervisory or management responsibilities must complete the new manager/supervisor orientation within six months of being hired or appointed.

(2) Each new employee, including those with supervisory or management responsibilities, must complete the new employee orientation within six months of being hired.

(3) For good cause, the Administrative Director or the employee's office director may grant an extension, up to six months, to complete the education requirements in (1) and (2).

(4) Completion of the orientation courses counts toward the education hours requirement in (c).

(Subd (b) amended effective January 1, 2023; adopted effective January 1, 2008; previously amended effective January 1, 2016, and January 1, 2017.)

(c) Continuing education requirements

(1) Each employee must complete 20 hours of continuing education every two years, beginning on January 1, 2017.

(2) For new employees beginning employment after July 1 of any year, the education hours may be prorated for that year at the discretion of the employee's supervisor.

(3) The Administrative Director may require management or employees to complete specific compliance courses. This compliance education applies toward the continuing education requirement in (c)(1) on an hour-for-hour basis.

(4) Education offered by an approved provider described in rule 10.481(a), as well as education that is approved by the employee's supervisor as meeting the criteria listed in rule 10.481(b), applies toward the employee's continuing education requirement.

(5) Each hour of participation in education by an approved provider under rule 10.481, including education that is instructor-led (live remote or in-person), asynchronous (such as videos and e-learning), and self-directed study approved in advance by an employee's supervisor, counts toward the continuing education requirement on an hour-for-hour basis.

(6) Participation in education, whether as a learner or as faculty, counts toward an employee's continuing education requirement under this rule on an hour-for-hour basis.

(Subd (c) amended effective January 1, 2023; previously amended effective January 1, 2012, July 1, 2013, January 1, 2016, and January 1, 2017.)
Rule 10.491 amended effective January 1, 2023; adopted effective January 1, 2008; previously amended effective July 1, 2008, January 1, 2012, July 1, 2013, January 1, 2016, and January 1, 2017.

Rule 10.492. Temporary extension and pro rata reduction of judicial branch education requirements

(a) Application

This rule applies to the requirements and expectations in the California Rules of Court relating to judicial branch education, except rule 10.491 on minimum education requirements for Judicial Council employees.

(Subd (a) adopted effective January 1, 2021.)

(b) Definitions

As used in this rule:

(1) "Content-based education requirement" means a requirement or expectation of:

(A) Attendance at any specific program;

(B) A course of study on any specific topic or topics; or

(C) A course of study limited to a specific delivery method, such as traditional (live, face-to-face) education.

(2) "Hours-based education requirement" means a requirement or expectation of a specified number of hours of education to be completed within a specified time period.

(Subd (b) adopted effective January 1, 2021.)

(c) Content-based education requirement

(1) Notwithstanding any other rule, any deadline for completion of a content-based education requirement or expectation, except for the deadline for the B. E. Witkin Judicial College, is extended for 12 months from that deadline, even if the deadline has passed.

(2) The deadline for completion of the B. E. Witkin Judicial College is extended for 30 months from the deadline specified in rule 10.462(c)(1)(C), even if the deadline has passed.

(Subd (c) amended effective January 1, 2022; adopted effective January 1, 2021.)

(d) Hours-based education requirement

Notwithstanding any other rule, the months of April 2020 through March 2021 are excluded from the education cycles in which those months fall, and the number of hours of education to complete hours-based education requirements or expectations is prorated accordingly.

(Subd (d) adopted effective January 1, 2021.)

(e) Sunset

This rule remains in effect through December 31, 2024, or until amended or repealed.

(Subd (e) amended effective January 1, 2022; adopted effective January 1, 2021.)

Rule 10.492 amended effective January 1, 2022; adopted effective January 1, 2021.

Advisory Committee Comment

Various rules in title 10, chapter 7, of the California Rules of Court authorize, for good cause, the granting of an extension of time to complete content-based and hours-based education requirements and expectations. Nothing in this rule modifies that authority.

Nothing in this rule alters education requirements and expectations outside the California Rules of Court, including education requirements mandated by statute or regulation (e.g., Welf. & Inst. Code, § 304.7) or required by Judicial Council policy (e.g., the Qualifying Ethics Program and the Temporary Assigned Judges Program).

Subdivision (c). This subdivision applies to all rules of court containing content-based education requirements. Below are examples of this subdivision in practice.

Rule 10.462(c)(1) contains education requirements for new trial court judges and subordinate judicial officers. Based on the date on which individuals took their oath of office, rule 10.462(c)(1) allows judges six months within which to attend the New Judge Orientation (NJO) program, one year within which to attend an orientation course in their primary assignment, and two years within which to attend the B. E. Witkin Judicial College of California.

Under rule 10.462(c)(1), a judge who took the oath of office on January 1, 2020, is required to complete these programs by June 30, 2020 (NJO), December 31, 2020 (primary assignment orientation), and December 31, 2021 (judicial college), respectively. With the 12-month extension under rule 10.492(c), this same judge now has to complete these programs by June 30, 2021 (NJO), December 31, 2021 (primary assignment orientation), and December 31, 2022 (judicial college), respectively.

As another example of the 12-month extension under rule 10.492(c), a judge who took the oath of office on December 1, 2018, needs to complete NJO by April 30, 2020 (within 18 months), a primary assignment orientation by November 30, 2020 (within two years), and the judicial college by November 30, 2021 (within three years).

Using a different rule as an example, rule 10.478(b)(1) requires court investigators to complete 18 hours of education on specified topics within 1 year of their start date. Rule 10.492(c) allows a court investigator up to 2 years to complete this education.

Subdivision (d). This subdivision applies to all rules of court containing hours-based education requirements. Below are examples of this subdivision in practice.

Rule 10.461(c)(1) contains education requirements for Supreme Court and Court of Appeal justices. Each justice must complete 30 hours of judicial education every three years.

Under rule 10.492(d), a justice's hours requirements are prorated for the three-year education cycle that runs from January 1, 2019, through December 31, 2021. For example, justices who were confirmed for appointment before January 1, 2019, must complete 20 hours of education by December 31, 2021.

Education hours requirements for justices who were confirmed for appointment on or after January 1, 2019, would be prorated by rule 10.492(d) and prorated additionally based on the number of years remaining in the three-year educational cycle. For example, a justice confirmed for appointment on October 1, 2020, ordinarily has 10 hours of hours-based education to complete for the last year of the three-year cycle. Under rule 10.492(d), the months of January 2021 through March 2021 would be excluded, and the justice would have 7.5 hours rather than 10 hours of hours-based education to complete.

As an additional example, rule 10.474(c)(2) requires 8 hours of continuing education every two years for nonmanagement court staff. For a court employee hired on or before January 1, 2020, rule 10.492(d) prorates the number of hours of education required for the cycle that runs from January 1, 2020, through December 31, 2021. The number of hours required would be prorated for 4 quarters—April 1, 2020, through March 31, 2021—and would result in a reduced hours-based requirement of 4 hours.

Rule 10.493. Delivery methods defined

(1) "Asynchronous education" refers to training that learners participate in at their own pace outside the presence of an instructor or other learners. Asynchronous education includes viewing or listening to videos or audio files or participating in self-paced online courses.

(2) "E-learning" refers to any kind of instruction that is delivered through an electronic device using electronic media. E-learning can be either synchronous or asynchronous and either live or prerecorded, such as participating in live webinars, viewing or listening to videos or audio files, or participating in online courses.

(3) "Instructor-led training" means synchronous education, guided by faculty, that allows for real-time communication between faculty and participants. Live, synchronous education facilitated by an instructor may be delivered remotely via e-learning or in person. Examples of instructor-led training include in-person trainings in a classroom setting and live webinars.

(4) "Self-directed study" refers to education in which learners engage in a process where they take primary responsibility for planning, executing, and evaluating a course of study with or without guidance from a manager, supervisor, or peer. In self-directed learning, the individual learner assumes responsibility for the design and completion of a course of study. Prior approval to engage in self-directed study may be required to qualify for continuing education credit.

Rule 10.493 amended effective January 1, 2024; adopted effective January 1, 2021.

Division 3
Judicial Administration Rules Applicable to All Courts

Rule 10.500. Public access to judicial administrative records
Rule 10.501. Maintenance of budget and management information
Rule 10.502. Judicial sabbatical program
Rule 10.504. Smoking prohibited in all courts
Rule 10.505. Judicial robes

Rule 10.500. Public access to judicial administrative records

(a) Intent

(1) The Judicial Council intends by this rule to implement Government Code section 68106.2(g), added by Senate Bill X4 13 (Stats. 2009–10, 4th Ex. Sess. ch. 22), which requires adoption of rules of court that provide public access to nondeliberative and nonadjudicative court records, budget and management information.

(2) This rule clarifies and expands the public's right of access to judicial administrative records and must be broadly construed to further the public's right of access.

(Subd (a) adopted effective January 1, 2010.)

(b) Application

(1) This rule applies to public access to judicial administrative records, including records of budget and management information relating to the administration of the courts.

(2) This rule does not apply to, modify or otherwise affect existing law regarding public access to adjudicative records.

(3) This rule does not restrict the rights to disclosure of information otherwise granted by law to a recognized employee organization.

(4) This rule does not affect the rights of litigants, including parties to administrative proceedings, under the laws of discovery of this state, nor does it limit or impair any rights of discovery in a criminal case.

(5) This rule does not apply to electronic mail and text messages sent or received before the effective date of this rule.

(Subd (b) adopted effective January 1, 2010.)

(c) Definitions

As used in this rule:

(1) "Adjudicative record" means any writing prepared for or filed or used in a court proceeding, the judicial deliberation process, or the assignment or reassignment of cases and of justices, judges (including temporary and assigned judges), and subordinate judicial officers, or of counsel appointed or employed by the court.

(2) "Judicial administrative record" means any writing containing information relating to the conduct of the people's business that is prepared, owned, used, or retained by a judicial branch entity regardless of the writing's physical form or characteristics, except an adjudicative record. The term "judicial administrative record" does not include records of a personal nature that are not used in or do not relate to the people's business, such as personal notes, memoranda, electronic mail, calendar entries, and records of Internet use.

(3) "Judicial branch entity" means the Supreme Court, each Court of Appeal, each superior court, and the Judicial Council.

(4) "Judicial branch personnel" means justices, judges (including temporary and assigned judges), subordinate judicial officers, members of the Judicial Council and its advisory bodies, and directors, officers, employees, volunteers, and agents of a judicial branch entity.

(5) "Person" means any natural person, corporation, partnership, limited liability company, firm, or association.

(6) "Writing" means any handwriting, typewriting, printing, photographing, photocopying, electronic mail, fax, and every other means of recording on any tangible thing any form of communication or representation, including letters, words, pictures, sounds, symbols, or combinations, regardless of the manner in which the record has been stored.

(Subd (c) amended effective January 1, 2016; adopted effective January 1, 2010.)

(d) Construction of rule

(1) Unless otherwise indicated, the terms used in this rule have the same meaning as under the Legislative Open Records Act (Gov. Code, § 9070 et seq.) and the California Public Records Act (Gov. Code, § 6250 et seq.) and must be interpreted consistently with the interpretation applied to the terms under those acts.

(2) This rule does not require the disclosure of a record if the record is exempt from disclosure under this rule or is the type of record that would not be subject to disclosure under the Legislative Open Records Act or the California Public Records Act.

(Subd (d) adopted effective January 1, 2010.)

(e) Public access

(1) *Access*

(A) A judicial branch entity must allow inspection and copying of judicial administrative records unless the records are exempt from disclosure under this rule or by law.

(B) Nothing in this rule requires a judicial branch entity to create any record or to compile or assemble data in response to a request for judicial administrative records if the judicial branch entity does not compile or assemble the data in the requested form for its own use or for provision to other agencies. For purposes of this rule, selecting data from extractable fields in a single database using software already owned or licensed by the judicial branch entity does not constitute creating a record or compiling or assembling data.

(C) If a judicial administrative record contains information that is exempt from disclosure and the exempt portions are reasonably segregable, a judicial branch entity must allow inspection and copying of the record after deletion of the portions that are exempt from disclosure. A judicial branch entity is not required to allow inspection or copying of the portion of a writing that is a judicial administrative record unless that portion is reasonably segregable from the portion that constitutes an adjudicative record.

(D) If requested, a superior court must provide a copy of the certified judicial administrative record if the judicial administrative record requested has previously been certified by the superior court.

(2) *Examples*

Judicial administrative records subject to inspection and copying unless exempt from disclosure under subdivision (f) include, but are not limited to, the following:

(A) Budget information submitted to the Judicial Council after enactment of the annual Budget Act;

(B) Any other budget and expenditure document pertaining to the administrative operation of the courts, including quarterly financial statements and statements of revenue, expenditure, and reserves;

(C) Actual and budgeted employee salary and benefit information;

(D) Copies of executed contracts with outside vendors and payment information and policies concerning goods and services provided by outside vendors without an executed contract;

(E) Final audit reports; and

(F) Employment contracts between judicial branch entities and their employees.

(3) *Procedure for requesting records*

A judicial branch entity must make available on its public Web site or otherwise publicize the procedure to be followed to request a copy of or to inspect a judicial administrative record. At a minimum, the procedure must include the address to which requests are to be addressed, to whom requests are to be directed, and the office hours of the judicial branch entity.

(4) *Costs of duplication, search, and review*

(A) A judicial branch entity, on request, must provide a copy of a judicial administrative record not exempt from disclosure if the record is of a nature permitting copying, subject to payment of the fee specified in this rule or other applicable statutory fee. A judicial branch entity may require advance payment of any fee.

(B) A judicial branch entity may impose on all requests a fee reasonably calculated to cover the judicial branch entity's direct costs of duplication of a record or of production of a record in an electronic format under subdivision (i). The fee includes:

(i) A charge per page, per copy, or otherwise, as established and published by the Judicial Council, or as established by the judicial branch entity following a notice and comment procedure specified by the Judicial Council, representing the direct costs of equipment, supplies, and staff time required to duplicate or produce the requested record; and

(ii) Any other direct costs of duplication or production, including, but not limited to, the costs incurred by a judicial branch entity in retrieving the record from a remote storage facility or archive and the costs of mailing responsive records.

(C) In the case of requests for records for commercial use, a judicial branch entity may impose, in addition to the fee in (B), a fee reasonably calculated to cover the actual costs of staff search and review time, based on an hourly rate for salary and benefits of each employee involved.

(D) For purposes of this rule:

(i) "Commercial use" means a request for a use or purpose that furthers the commercial, trade, or profit interests of the requester or the person on whose behalf the request is being made. A request from a representative of the news media that supports its news-dissemination function is not a request for a commercial use.

(ii) "Representative of the news media" means a person who regularly gathers, prepares, collects, photographs, records, writes, edits, reports, or publishes news or information that concerns local, national, or international events or other matters of public interest for dissemination to the public for a substantial portion of the person's livelihood or for substantial financial gain.

(iii) "Search and review time" means actual time spent identifying and locating judicial administrative records, including material within documents, responsive to a request; determining whether any portions are exempt from disclosure; and performing all tasks necessary to prepare the records for disclosure, including redacting portions exempt from disclosure. "Search and review time" does not include time spent resolving general legal or policy issues regarding the applicability of particular exemptions.

(E) By January 1, 2012, the Judicial Council will review and evaluate the numbers of requests received, the time necessary to respond, and the fees imposed by judicial branch entities for access to records and information. The Judicial Council's review will consider the impact of this rule on both the public's access to records and information and on judicial branch entities' ability to carry out and fund core judicial operations.

(5) *Inspection*

A judicial branch entity must make judicial administrative records in its possession and not exempt from disclosure open to inspection at all times during the office hours of the judicial branch entity provided that the record is of a nature permitting inspection.

(6) *Time for determination of disclosable records*

A judicial branch entity, on a request that reasonably describes an identifiable record or records, must determine, within 10 calendar days from receipt of the request, whether the request, in whole or in part, seeks disclosable judicial administrative records in its possession and must promptly notify the requesting party of the determination and the reasons for the determination.

(7) *Response*

If a judicial branch entity determines that a request seeks disclosable judicial administrative records, the judicial branch entity must make the disclosable judicial administrative records available promptly. The judicial branch entity must include with the notice of the determination the estimated date and time when the records will be made available. If the judicial branch entity determines that the request, in whole or in part, seeks nondisclosable judicial administrative records, it must convey its determination in writing, include a contact name and telephone number to which inquiries may be directed, and state the express provision of this rule justifying the withholding of the records not disclosed.

(8) *Extension of time for determination of disclosable records*

In unusual circumstances, to the extent reasonably necessary to the proper processing of the particular request, a judicial branch entity may extend the time limit prescribed for its determination under (e)(6) by no more than 14 calendar days by written notice to the requesting party, stating the reasons for the extension and the date on which the judicial branch entity expects to make a determination. As used in this section, "unusual circumstances" means the following:

(A) The need to search for and collect the requested records from multiple locations or facilities that are separate from the office processing the request;

(B) The need to search for, collect, and appropriately examine a voluminous amount of records that are included in a single request; or

(C) The need for consultation, which must be conducted with all practicable speed, with another judicial branch entity or other governmental agency having substantial subject matter interest in the determination of the request, or with two or more components of the judicial branch entity having substantial subject matter interest in the determination of the request.

(9) *Reasonable efforts*

(A) On receipt of a request to inspect or obtain a copy of a judicial administrative record, a judicial branch entity, in order to assist the requester in making a focused and effective request that reasonably describes an identifiable judicial administrative record, must do all of the following to the extent reasonable under the circumstances:

(i) Assist the requester in identifying records and information responsive to the request or to the purpose of the request, if stated;

(ii) Describe the information technology and physical location in which the records exist; and

(iii) Provide suggestions for overcoming any practical basis for denying inspection or copying of the records or information sought.

(B) The requirements of (A) will be deemed to have been satisfied if the judicial branch entity is unable to identify the requested information after making a reasonable effort to elicit additional clarifying information from the requester that helps identify the record or records.

(C) The requirements of (A) do not apply to a request for judicial administrative records if the judicial branch entity makes the requested records available or determines that the requested records are exempt from disclosure under this rule.

(10) *No obstruction or delay*

Nothing in this rule may be construed to permit a judicial branch entity to delay or obstruct the inspection or copying of judicial administrative records that are not exempt from disclosure.

(11) *Greater access permitted*

Except as otherwise prohibited by law, a judicial branch entity may adopt requirements for itself that allow for faster, more efficient, or greater access to judicial administrative records than prescribed by the requirements of this rule.

(12) *Control of records*

A judicial branch entity must not sell, exchange, furnish, or otherwise provide a judicial administrative record subject to disclosure under this rule to a private entity in a manner that prevents a judicial branch entity from providing the record directly under this rule. A judicial branch entity must not allow a private entity to control the disclosure of information that is otherwise subject to disclosure under this rule.

(Subd (e) amended effective January 1, 2016; adopted effective January 1, 2010.)

(f) Exemptions

Nothing in this rule requires the disclosure of judicial administrative records that are any of the following:

(1) Preliminary writings, including drafts, notes, working papers, and inter-judicial branch entity or intra-judicial branch entity memoranda, that are not retained by the judicial branch entity in the ordinary course of business, if the public interest in withholding those records clearly outweighs the public interest in disclosure;

(2) Records pertaining to pending or anticipated claims or litigation to which a judicial branch entity is a party or judicial branch personnel are parties, until the pending litigation or claim has been finally adjudicated or otherwise resolved;

(3) Personnel, medical, or similar files, or other personal information whose disclosure would constitute an unwarranted invasion of personal privacy, including, but not limited to, records revealing home addresses, home telephone numbers, cellular telephone numbers, private electronic mail addresses, and social security numbers of judicial branch personnel and work electronic mail addresses and work telephone numbers of justices, judges (including temporary and assigned judges), subordinate judicial officers, and their staff attorneys;

(4) Test questions, scoring keys, and other examination data used to develop, administer, and score examinations for employment, certification, or qualification;

(5) Records whose disclosure is exempted or prohibited under state or federal law, including provisions of the California Evidence Code relating to privilege, or by court order in any court proceeding;

(6) Records whose disclosure would compromise the security of a judicial branch entity or the safety of judicial branch personnel, including but not limited to, court security plans, and security surveys, investigations, procedures, and assessments;

(7) Records related to evaluations of, complaints regarding, or investigations of justices, judges (including temporary and assigned judges), subordinate judicial officers, and applicants or candidates for judicial office. This exemption does not apply to any settlement agreement entered into on or after January 1, 2010 for which public funds were spent in payment of the settlement, including any settlement agreement arising from claims or complaints of sexual harassment or sexual discrimination. The names of judicial officers may not be redacted from any settlement agreement that is produced under this rule; however, the names of complainants or witnesses, and other information that would identify complainants or witnesses, may be redacted;

(8) The contents of real estate appraisals or engineering or feasibility estimates and evaluations made for or by the judicial branch entity related to the acquisition of property or to prospective public supply and construction contracts, until all of the property has been acquired or the relevant contracts have been executed. This provision does not affect the law of eminent domain;

(9) Records related to activities governed by Government Code sections 71600 et seq. and 71800 et seq. that reveal deliberative processes, impressions, evaluations, opinions, recommendations, meeting minutes, research, work products, theories, or strategy or that provide instruction, advice, or training to employees who are not represented by employee organizations under those sections. Nothing in this subdivision limits the disclosure duties of a judicial branch entity with respect to any other records relating to the activities governed by the employee relations acts referred to in this subdivision;

(10) Records that contain trade secrets or privileged or confidential commercial and financial information submitted in response to a judicial branch entity's solicitation for goods or services or in the course of a

judicial branch entity's contractual relationship with a commercial entity. For purposes of this rule:

(A) "Trade secret" means information, including a formula, pattern, compilation, program, device, method, technique, or process, that:

(i) Derives independent economic value, actual or potential, from not being generally known to the public or to other persons who can obtain economic value from its disclosure or use; and

(ii) Is the subject of efforts that are reasonable under the circumstances to maintain its secrecy;

(B) "Privileged information" means material that falls within recognized constitutional, statutory, or common law privileges;

(C) "Confidential commercial and financial information" means information whose disclosure would:

(i) Impair the judicial branch entity's ability to obtain necessary information in the future; or

(ii) Cause substantial harm to the competitive position of the person from whom the information was obtained.

(11) Records whose disclosure would disclose the judicial branch entity's or judicial branch personnel's decision-making process, provided that, on the facts of the specific request for records, the public interest served by nondisclosure clearly outweighs the public interest served by disclosure of the record; or

(12) If, on the facts of the specific request for records, the public interest served by nondisclosure of the record clearly outweighs the public interest served by disclosure of the record.

(Subd (f) amended effective June 1, 2018; adopted effective January 1, 2010.)

(g) Computer software; copyrighted materials

(1) Computer software developed by a judicial branch entity or used by a judicial branch entity for the storage or manipulation of data is not a judicial administrative record under this rule. For purposes of this rule "computer software" includes computer mapping systems, computer graphic systems, and computer programs, including the source, object, and other code in a computer program.

(2) This rule does not limit a judicial branch entity's ability to sell, lease, or license computer software for commercial or noncommercial use.

(3) This rule does not create an implied warranty on the part of any judicial branch entity for errors, omissions, or other defects in any computer software.

(4) This rule does not limit any copyright protection. A judicial branch entity is not required to duplicate records under this rule in violation of any copyright.

(5) Nothing in this subdivision is intended to affect the judicial administrative record status of information merely because the information is stored in a computer. Judicial administrative records stored in a computer will be disclosed as required in this rule.

(Subd (g) adopted effective January 1, 2010.)

(h) Waiver of exemptions

(1) Disclosure of a judicial administrative record that is exempt from disclosure under this rule or provision of law by a judicial branch entity or judicial branch personnel acting within the scope of their office or employment constitutes a waiver of the exemptions applicable to that particular record.

(2) This subdivision does not apply to disclosures:

(A) Made through discovery proceedings;

(B) Made through other legal proceedings or as otherwise required by law;

(C) Made to another judicial branch entity or judicial branch personnel for the purposes of judicial branch administration;

(D) Within the scope of a statute that limits disclosure of specified writings to certain purposes; or

(E) Made to any governmental agency or to another judicial branch entity or judicial branch personnel if the material will be treated confidentially.

(Subd (h) adopted effective January 1, 2010.)

(i) Availability in electronic format

(1) A judicial branch entity that has information that constitutes an identifiable judicial administrative record not exempt from disclosure under this rule and that is in an electronic format must, on request, produce that information in the electronic format requested, provided that:

(A) No law prohibits disclosure;

(B) The record already exists in the requested electronic format, or the judicial branch entity has previously produced the judicial administrative record in the requested format for its own use or for provision to other agencies;

(C) The requested electronic format is customary or standard for records of a similar type and is commercially available to private entity requesters; and

(D) The disclosure does not jeopardize or compromise the security or integrity of the original record or the computer software on which the original record is maintained.

(2) In addition to other fees imposed under this rule, the requester will bear the direct cost of producing a record if:

(A) In order to comply with (1), the judicial branch entity would be required to produce a record and the record is one that is produced only at otherwise regularly scheduled intervals or;

(B) Producing the requested record would require data compilation or extraction or any associated programming that the judicial branch entity is not required to perform under this rule but has agreed to perform in response to the request.

(3) Nothing in this subdivision shall be construed to require a judicial branch entity to reconstruct a record in an electronic format if the judicial branch entity no longer has the record available in an electronic format.

(Subd (i) adopted effective January 1, 2010.)

(j) Public access disputes

(1) Unless the petitioner elects to proceed under (2) below, disputes and appeals of decisions with respect to disputes with the Judicial Council or a superior court regarding access to budget and management information required to be maintained under rule 10.501 are subject to the process described in rule 10.803.

(2) Any person may institute proceedings for injunctive or declarative relief or writ of mandate in any court of competent jurisdiction to enforce his or her right to inspect or to receive a copy of any judicial administrative record under this rule.

(3) Whenever it is made to appear by verified petition that a judicial administrative record is being improperly withheld from disclosure, the court with jurisdiction will order the judicial branch entity to disclose the records or show cause why it should not do so. The court will decide the case after examining the record (in camera if appropriate), papers filed by the parties, and any oral argument and additional evidence as the court may allow.

(4) If the court finds that the judicial branch entity's decision to refuse disclosure is not justified under this rule, the court will order the judicial branch entity to make the record public. If the court finds that the judicial branch entity's decision was justified, the court will issue an order supporting the decision.

(5) An order of the court, either directing disclosure or supporting the decision of the judicial branch entity refusing disclosure, is not a final judgment or order within the meaning of Code of Civil Procedure section 904.1 from which an appeal may be taken, but will be immediately reviewable by petition to the appellate court for the issuance of an extraordinary writ. Upon entry of an order under this subdivision, a party must, in order to obtain review of the order, file a petition within 20 days after service of a written notice of entry of the order or within such further time not exceeding an additional 20 days as the court may for good cause allow. If the notice is served by mail, the period within which to file the petition will be extended by 5 days. A stay of an order or judgment will not be granted unless the petitioning party demonstrates it will otherwise sustain irreparable damage and probable success on the merits. Any person who fails to obey the order of the court will be cited to show cause why that is not in contempt of court.

(6) The court will award court costs and reasonable attorney fees to the plaintiff should the plaintiff prevail in litigation filed under this subdivision. The costs and fees will be paid by the judicial branch entity and will not become a personal liability of any individual. If the court finds that the plaintiff's case is clearly frivolous, it will award court costs and reasonable attorney fees to the judicial branch entity.

(Subd (j) amended effective January 1, 2016; adopted effective January 1, 2010.)
Rule 10.500 amended effective June 1, 2018; adopted effective January 1, 2010; previously amended effective January 1, 2016.

Advisory Committee Comment

Subdivision (a). By establishing a public access rule applicable to all judicial administrative records, the proposed rule would expand public access to these records. The Judicial Council recognizes the important public interest in access to records and information relating to the administration of the judicial branch. The Judicial Council also recognizes the importance of the privacy rights of individuals working in or doing business with judicial branch entities and the public's interest in an effective and independent judicial branch of state government. The report on this rule includes the Judicial Council's findings on the impact of this rule on these interests, and how these interests are protected by the rule.

Subdivisions (b)(1) and (b)(2). This rule does not apply to adjudicative records, and is not intended to modify existing law regarding public access to adjudicative records. California case law has established that, in general, subject to specific statutory exceptions, case records that accurately and officially reflect the work of the court are public records open to inspection. (*Estate of Hearst* (1977) 67 Cal.App.3d 777, 782–83.) However, documents prepared in the course of adjudicative work and not regarded as official case records, such as preliminary drafts, personal notes, and rough records of proceedings, are not subject to public access because the perceived harm to the judicial process by requiring this material to be available to the public is greater than the benefit the public might derive from its disclosure. (*Copley Press, Inc. v. Superior Court* (1992) 6 Cal.App.4th 106.)

Subdivision (c)(2). The application of this rule is intended to reflect existing case law under the California Public Records Act that exempts from the definition of "public record" certain types of personal records and information. The concept was first discussed in the California Assembly and establishes that if personal correspondence and information are "unrelated to the conduct of the people's business" they are therefore not public records. (*San Gabriel Tribune v. Superior Court* (1983) 143 Cal.App.3d 762, 774, citing Assembly Committee on Statewide Information Policy California Public Records Act of 1968, section B, page 9, Appendix to Assembly Journal (1970 Reg. Sess.).) Case law has further established that only records necessary or convenient to the discharge of official duty, or kept as necessary or convenient to the discharge of official duty, are public records for the purposes of the California Public Records Act and its predecessors. (*Braun v. City of Taft* (1984) 154 Cal.App.3d 332; *City Council of Santa Monica v. Superior Court* (1962) 204 Cal.App.2d 68.)

Subdivision (e)(4). The fees charged by a judicial branch entity under this rule are intended to allow the entity to recover an amount not to exceed the reasonable costs of responding to a request for records or information. In accordance with existing practice within the judicial branch and the other branches of government, the Judicial Council intends agencies and entities of the executive and legislative branches of the California state government to receive records or information requested from judicial branch entities for the agency's or entity's use free of charge. This subdivision is intended to provide, however, that requesters of records or information for the purpose of furthering the requester's commercial interests will be charged for costs incurred by the judicial branch entity in responding to the request, and that such costs will not be a charge against the budget of the judicial branch of the state General Fund.

Subdivision (f)(3). In addition to the types of records and information exempt from disclosure under the corresponding provision of the California Public Records Act, Government Code section 6254(c), this provision includes a further nonexclusive list of specific information that is exempt under this rule. The rule does not attempt to list each category of information that is specific to judicial branch entities and that may also be exempt under this rule. For example, although they are not specifically listed, this provision exempts from disclosure records maintained by any court or court-appointed counsel administrator for the purpose of evaluating attorneys seeking or being considered for appointment to cases.

Subdivision (f)(7). The 2018 amendments to (f)(7) clarify that settlement agreements are not exempt from disclosure. All judicial branch entities, including the Judicial Council, must disclose settlement agreements under a rule 10.500 request, given the public nature of these records. (See *Register Div. of Freedom Newspapers, Inc. v. County of Orange* (1984) 158 Cal.App.3d 893, 909.) By clarifying the public nature of settlement agreements and judicial branch entities' obligation to disclose them, the amended rule also clarifies that a judicial branch entity's disclosure of these agreements, whether maintained by the entity or its attorneys, would not implicate any ethical or legal obligations under Business and Professions Code section 6068(e)(1) or rule 3-100(A) of the State Bar Rules of Professional Conduct. The duty of a judicial branch entity to disclose public records of settlements is not constrained by which persons, division, or office within the entity maintains the records.

The 2018 amendments to rule 10.500 do not apply to records maintained by the Commission on Judicial Performance, an independent state entity established under article VI, section 18 of the California Constitution. Rule 10.500 is not applicable to the Commission on Judicial Performance which has separate rules that apply to its work and records.

Subdivision (f)(10). The definition of "trade secret" restates the definition in Civil Code section 3426.1.

Subdivision (f)(11). This subdivision is intended to reflect California law on the subject of the "deliberative process" exemption under the California Public Records Act, which is currently stated in the Supreme Court's decision in *Times Mirror Co. v. Superior Court* (1991) 53 Cal.3d 29 1325 and the later Court of Appeal decisions *California First Amendment Coalition v. Superior Court* (1998) 67 Cal.App.4th 159 and *Wilson v. Superior Court* (1996) 51 Cal.App.4th 1136.

Subdivision (j)(1). Under current rule 10.803 a petitioner may file a writ in a superior court regarding a dispute with a superior court or the Judicial Council with respect to disclosure of records and information required to be maintained under current rule 10.802. The writ petition must be heard on an expedited basis and includes a right to an appeal. The statutory authority for the hearing process set forth in current rule 10.803, Government Code section 71675(b), does not extend this procedure to other disputes with respect to public access. The rule provides that petitioners with a dispute with any other judicial branch entity, or with respect to records that are not required to be maintained under rule 10.802, may follow the procedure set forth in (j)(2) through (j)(6), which is equivalent to the dispute resolution procedure of the California Public Records Act. A petitioner eligible for the dispute resolution process set out in current rule 10.803 may also elect to proceed with his or her dispute under the procedure set forth in (j)(2) through (j)(6).

Rule 10.501. Maintenance of budget and management information

(a) Maintenance of information by the superior court

Each superior court must maintain for a period of three years from the close of the fiscal year to which the following relate:

(1) Official documents of the superior court pertaining to the approved superior court budget allocation adopted by the Judicial Council and actual final year-end superior court revenue and expenditure reports as required in budget procedures issued by Judicial Council staff to be maintained or reported to the council, including budget allocation, revenue, and expenditure reports;

(2) Records or other factual management information on matters that are within the scope of representation as defined in Government Code section 71634 unless distribution is otherwise precluded by law; and

(3) Records or other factual management information on other matters referred to in Government Code section 71634 unless distribution is otherwise precluded by law.

(Subd (a) amended effective January 1, 2016; adopted effective January 1, 2010.)

(b) Maintenance of information by Judicial Council staff

Judicial Council staff must maintain for a period of three years from the close of the fiscal year to which the following relate:

(1) Official approved budget allocations for each superior court;

(2) Actual final year-end superior court revenue and expenditure reports required by budget procedures issued by Judicial Council staff to be maintained or reported to the council that are received from the courts, including budget revenues and expenditures for each superior court;

(3) Budget priorities as adopted by the council; and

(4) Documents concerning superior court budgets considered or adopted by the council at council business meetings on court budgets.

(Subd (b) amended effective January 1, 2016; adopted effective January 1, 2010.)

Rule 10.501 amended effective January 1, 2016; adopted effective January 1, 2010.

Rule 10.502. Judicial sabbatical program

(a) Objective

Sabbatical leave is a privilege available to jurists by statute. The objective of sabbatical leave is to facilitate study that will benefit the administration of justice and enhance judges' performance of their duties.

(Subd (a) amended effective July 23, 2018.)

(b) Eligibility

Any judge is eligible to apply for an unpaid sabbatical under Government Code section 68554.

(Subd (b) amended effective July 23, 2018.)

(c) Application

(1) A judge may apply for a sabbatical by submitting a sabbatical proposal to the Administrative Director with a copy to the presiding judge or justice.

(2) The sabbatical proposal must include:

(A) The beginning and ending dates of the proposed sabbatical;

(B) A description of the sabbatical project, including an explanation of how the sabbatical will benefit the administration of justice and the judge's performance of his or her duties; and

(C) A statement from the presiding judge or justice of the affected court, indicating approval or disapproval of the sabbatical request and the reasons for such approval or disapproval, forwarded to the Executive and Planning Committee with a copy to the judge.

(Subd (c) amended effective July 23, 2018; previously amended effective January 1, 2007, and January 1, 2016.)

(d) Review of applications

The Executive and Planning Committee will make recommendations to the Judicial Council regarding sabbatical requests, with support from the council's human resources staff.

(Subd (d) amended effective July 23, 2018; previously amended effective January 1, 2007, and January 1, 2016.)

(e) Evaluation

(1) The Administrative Director must forward all sabbatical requests that comply with (c) to the Executive and Planning Committee.

(2) The Executive and Planning Committee must recommend granting or denying the sabbatical request after it considers the following factors:

(A) Whether the sabbatical will benefit the administration of justice in California and the judge's performance of his or her duties; and

(B) Whether the sabbatical leave will be detrimental to the affected court.

(Subd (e) amend effective July 23, 2018; previously amended effective January 1, 2016.)

(f) Length

A unpaid judicial sabbatical taken under Government Code section 68554 may not exceed one year.

(Subd (f) amended effective July 23, 2018.)

(g) Ethics and compensation

A judge on unpaid sabbatical leave is subject to the California Code of Judicial Ethics and may receive compensation and reimbursement for expenses for activities performed during that sabbatical leave as provided in canon 4H of the Code of Judicial Ethics.

(Subd (g) amended effective July 23, 2018.)

(h) Retirement and benefits

A judge on unpaid sabbatical leave under Government Code section 68554 receives no compensation, and the period of absence does not count as service toward retirement. The leave does not affect the term of office.

(Subd (h) amended and relettered effective July 23, 2018; adopted as subd (i) effective January 1, 2007.)

(i) Judge's report

On completion of a sabbatical leave, the judge must report in writing to the Judicial Council on how the leave benefited the administration of justice in California and on its effect on his or her official duties as a judicial officer.

(Subd (i) amended and relettered effective July 23, 2018; adopted as subd (h) effective January 1, 2007.)

Rule 10.502 amended effective July 23, 2018; adopted as rule 6.151 effective January 1, 2003; previously amended and renumbered as rule 10.502 effective January 1, 2007; previously amended effective January 1, 2016.

Rule 10.503. Use of recycled paper by all courts [Repealed]

Rule 10.503 repealed effective January 1, 2014; adopted as rule 989.1 effective January 1, 1994; previously amended and renumbered effective January 1, 2007.

Rule 10.504. Smoking prohibited in all courts

(a) Definition

"Court facilities" means courthouses and all areas of multipurpose buildings used for court operations.

(b) Smoking prohibited

Smoking is prohibited in all court facilities.

(Subd (b) amended effective January 1, 2007.)

(c) Signs

Conspicuous no-smoking signs must be placed in all court facilities.

(Subd (c) amended effective January 1, 2007.)

Rule 10.504 amended and renumbered effective January 1, 2007; adopted as rule 989.5 effective July 1, 1991.

Rule 10.505. Judicial robes

(a) Color and length

The judicial robe required by Government Code section 68110 must be black, must extend in front and back from the collar and shoulders to below the knees, and must have sleeves to the wrists.

(Subd (a) amended and lettered effective January 1, 2007; adopted as subd (e) effective September 24, 1959; relettered as subd (d) effective July 1, 1963; amended as an unlettered subd effective January 1, 2003.)

(b) Style

The judicial robe must conform to the style customarily worn in courts in the United States.

(Subd (b) amended and lettered effective January 1, 2007; adopted as subd (e) effective September 24, 1959; relettered as subd (d) effective July 1, 1963; amended as an unlettered subd effective January 1, 2003.)

Rule 10.505 amended and renumbered effective January 1, 2007; adopted as rule 249 effective January 1, 1949; previously amended effective September 24, 1959, and July 1, 1963; amended and renumbered as rule 299 effective January 1, 2003.

Division 4
Trial Court Administration

Chap. 1. General Rules on Trial Court Management. Rules 10.601–10.635.

Chap. 2. Trial Court Management of Human Resources. Rules 10.650–10.670.

Chap. 3. Subordinate Judicial Officers. Rules 10.700–10.703.

Chap. 4. Referees [Reserved].

Chap. 5. Temporary Judges. Rules 10.740–10.746.

Chap. 6. Court Interpreters. Rules 10.761, 10.762.

Chap. 7. Qualifications of Court Investigators, Probate Attorneys, and Probate Examiners. Rules 10.776, 10.777.

Chap. 8. Alternative Dispute Resolution Programs. Rules 10.780–10.783.

Chap. 9. Trial Court Budget and Fiscal Management. Rules 10.800–10.830.

Chap. 10. Trial Court Records Management. Rules 10.850–10.856.

Chap. 11. Trial Court Automation. Rule 10.870.

Chap. 12. Trial Court Management of Civil Cases. Rules 10.900–10.910.

Chap. 13. Trial Court Management of Criminal Cases. Rules 10.950–10.953.

Chap. 14. Management of Self-Help Centers. Rule 10.960.

Chap. 15. Elections Code Reports. Rule 10.970.

Chapter 1
General Rules on Trial Court Management

Rule 10.601. Superior court management
Rule 10.602. Selection and term of presiding judge
Rule 10.603. Authority and duties of presiding judge
Rule 10.605. Executive committee
Rule 10.608. Duties of all judges
Rule 10.609. Notification to State Bar of attorney misconduct
Rule 10.610. Duties of court executive officer
Rule 10.611. Nondiscrimination in court appointments
Rule 10.612. Use of gender-neutral language
Rule 10.613. Local court rules—adopting, filing, distributing, and maintaining
Rule 10.614. Local court forms
Rule 10.620. Public access to administrative decisions of trial courts
Rule 10.625. Certain demographic data relating to regular grand jurors
Rule 10.630. Reciprocal assignment orders
Rule 10.635. Limited situations in which a judicial officer may preside remotely from a location other than a courtroom

Rule 10.601. Superior court management

(a) Purpose

The rules in this division establish a system of trial court management that:

(1) Promotes equal access to the courts;

(2) Establishes decentralized management of trial court resources; and

(3) Enables the trial courts to operate in an efficient, effective, and accountable manner in serving the people of California.

(Subd (a) amended effective January 1, 2007.)

(b) Goals

The rules in this division are intended to ensure the authority and responsibility of the superior courts to do the following, consistent with statutes, rules of court, and standards of judicial administration:

(1) Manage their day-to-day operations with sufficient flexibility to meet the needs of those served by the courts;

(2) Establish the means of selecting presiding judges, assistant presiding judges, executive officers or court administrators, clerks of court, and jury commissioners;

(3) Manage their personnel systems, including the adoption of personnel policies;

(4) Manage their budget and fiscal operations, including allocating funding and moving funding between functions or line items;

(5) Provide input to the Judicial Council, the Trial Court Budget Advisory Committee, and Judicial Council on the trial court budget process; and

(6) Develop and implement processes and procedures to improve court operations and responsiveness to the public.

(Subd (b) amended effective January 1, 2016; previously amended effective January 1, 2002, and January 1, 2007.)

(c) Decentralized management

"Decentralized management" as used in the rules in this division refers to the administration of the trial courts on a countywide basis, unless an alternative structure has been approved by the Judicial Council, consistent with applicable statutes, rules, and standards of judicial administration.

(Subd (c) amended effective January 1, 2007.)

Rule 10.601 amended effective January 1, 2016; adopted as rule 2501 effective July 1, 1998; renumbered as rule 6.601 effective January 1, 1999; previously amended effective January 1, 2002; previously amended and renumbered as rule 10.601 effective January 1, 2007.

Rule 10.602. Selection and term of presiding judge

(a) Selection

(1) *Courts with three or more judges*

Each court that has three or more judges must select a presiding judge. Selection of the presiding judge may be by secret ballot. The court should establish an internal local rule or policy for the selection of the presiding judge and assistant presiding judge, if any.

(2) *Two-judge courts*

In a court having two judges, the selection of the presiding judge must conform to Government Code section 69508.5. If selection cannot be agreed on and neither judge has at least four years of experience, the senior judge must hold the office of presiding judge until both judges have at least four years of experience.

(Subd (a) amended effective January 1, 2007; previously amended effective January 1, 2005.)

(b) Requisite experience and waiver

A presiding judge must have at least four years of experience as a judge, unless this requirement is waived by a majority vote of the judges of the court. Nomination and selection of a presiding judge should take into consideration the judge's:

(1) Management and administrative ability;

(2) Interest in serving in the position;

(3) Experience and familiarity with a variety of trial court assignments;

(4) Ability to motivate and educate other judicial officers and court personnel;

(5) Ability to evaluate the strengths of the court's bench officers and make assignments based on those strengths as well as the best interests of the public and the court; and

(6) Other appropriate factors.

(Subd (b) amended effective January 1, 2007; previously amended effective January 1, 2005.)

(c) Term

A presiding judge in a court with two judges must be elected for a term of not less than one year. A presiding judge in a court with three or more judges must be elected for an initial term of not less than two years. The presiding judge may be elected for additional terms. The court may change the duration of the initial or additional term by local rule or policy so long as the initial term is not less than the duration specified in this rule. A presiding judge may be removed by a majority vote of the judges of the court.

(Subd (c) amended effective January 1, 2007; previously amended effective January 1, 2005.)

(d) Assistant presiding judge and acting presiding judge

(1) The court may elect an assistant presiding judge.

(2) If the court's internal local rule or policy does not provide for the designation of an acting presiding judge to serve if the presiding judge is absent or unable to act, the presiding judge must designate one.

(3) The court should provide the assistant presiding judge with training to foster an orderly succession to the office of presiding judge.

(Subd (d) amended effective January 1, 2007; previously amended effective January 1, 2005.)

(e) Caseload adjustment

To the extent possible, the judicial caseload should be adjusted to provide the presiding judge with sufficient time and resources to devote to the management and administrative duties of the office.

Rule 10.602 amended and renumbered effective January 1, 2007; adopted as rule 6.602 effective January 1, 2001; previously amended effective January 1, 2005.

Advisory Committee Comment

The internal local rule described in this rule relates only to the internal management of the court, and as such is exempt from the requirements in rule 10.613. (See rule 10.613(j).)

Rule 10.603. Authority and duties of presiding judge

(a) General responsibilities

The presiding judge is responsible, with the assistance of the court executive officer, for leading the court, establishing policies, and allocating resources in a manner that promotes access to justice for all members of the public, provides a forum for the fair and expeditious resolution of disputes, maximizes the use of judicial and other resources, increases efficiency in court operations, and enhances service to the public. The presiding judge is responsible for:

(1) Ensuring the effective management and administration of the court, consistent with any rules, policies, strategic plan, or budget adopted by the Judicial Council or the court;

(2) Ensuring that the duties of all judges specified under rule 10.608 are timely and orderly performed; and

(3) Ensuring that the court has adopted written policies and procedures allowing the presiding judge to perform efficiently the administrative duties of that office.

(Subd (a) amended effective January 1, 2007.)

(b) Authority

(1) The presiding judge is authorized to:

(A) Assign judges to departments and designate supervising judges for divisions, districts, or branch courts;

(B) Apportion the business of the court, including assigning and reassigning cases to departments;

(C) Call meetings of the judges;

(D) Appoint standing and special committees of judges;

(E) Act as the spokesperson for the court;

(F) Authorize and direct expenditures from the court's Trial Court Operations Fund; and

(G) Perform all acts necessary to accomplish the duties specified by the rules of court.

(2) No local rule or policy may limit the authority of the presiding judge as granted in the rules of court.

(Subd (b) amended effective January 1, 2007.)

(c) Duties

(1) *Assignments*

The presiding judge has ultimate authority to make judicial assignments. The presiding judge must:

(A) Designate a judge to preside in each department, including a master calendar judge when appropriate, and designate a presiding judge of the juvenile division and a supervising judge for each division, district, or branch court. In making judicial assignments, the presiding judge must take into account the following:

(i) The needs of the public and the court, as they relate to the efficient and effective management of the court's calendar;

(ii) The knowledge and abilities demanded by the assignment;

(iii) The judge's judicial and nonjudicial experience, including specialized training or education;

(iv) The judge's interests;

(v) The need for continuity in the assignment;

(vi) The desirability of exposing the judge to a particular type of assignment; and

(vii) Other appropriate factors. Judicial assignments must not be based solely or primarily on seniority;

(B) Assign to a master calendar judge any of the duties that may more appropriately be performed by that department;

(C) Supervise the court's calendar, apportion the business of the court among the several departments of the court as equally as possible, and publish for general distribution copies of a current calendar specifying the judicial assignments of the judges and the times and places assigned for hearings;

(D) Reassign cases between departments as convenience or necessity requires; and

(E) Designate a judge to act if by law or the rules of court a matter is required to be presented to or heard by a particular judge and that judge is absent, deceased, or unable to act.

(2) *Judicial schedules*

(A) The presiding judge must adopt a process for scheduling judges' vacations and absences from court for attendance at schools, conferences, workshops, and community outreach activities, and must prepare a plan for these vacations and absences from court.

(B) The plan should take into account [1] **rules 10.451, 10.452, and 10.462–10.469** (on judicial education) and standard 10.5 (on community activities) of the Standards of Judicial Administration.

(C) The presiding judge must review requests from judges for time absent from court and may approve any request that is consistent with the plan and with the orderly operation of the court.

(D) The presiding judge must allow each judge to take two days of personal leave per year. Personal leave may be taken at any time that is approved by the presiding judge.

(E) The presiding judge must allow the following number of days of vacation for each judge annually:

(i) 24 days for judges with less than 7 years of service as a California judge;

(ii) 27 days for judges with at least 7 but less than 14 years of service as a California judge; and

(iii) 30 days for judges with 14 or more years of service as a California judge.

(F) The presiding judge may authorize a judge to take more time off than is specified in (c)(2)(E) as justified by extraordinary circumstances, if the circumstances are documented and the authorization is in writing.

(G) The presiding judge, in his or her discretion, may allow a judge to take additional vacation days equal to the number of vacation days that the judge did not use in the previous year, up to a maximum of 30 such days. A court may, by local rule, establish a lower maximum number of such days. This paragraph applies only to vacation days accrued after January 1, 2001. It does not affect any unused vacation days that a judge may have accrued before January 1, 2001, which are governed by local court policy, nor does it create any right to compensation for unused vacation days.

(H) The court must, by local rule, define a day of vacation. Absence from court to attend an authorized education program, conference, or workshop for judges, or to participate in Judicial Council or other authorized committees or community outreach activities, is not vacation time if attendance is in accordance with the plan and has the prior approval of the presiding judge. Absence from court due to illness is not vacation time. This rule does not limit the time a judge may be absent from court when unable to work because of illness.

(I) To ensure compliance with the plan, the presiding judge must establish a system to monitor judges' absences from court and maintain records of those absences.

(3) *Submitted cases*

The presiding judge must supervise and monitor the number of causes under submission before the judges of the court and ensure that no cause under submission remains undecided and pending for longer than 90 days. As an aid in accomplishing this goal, the presiding judge must:

(A) Require each judge to report to the presiding judge all causes under submission for more than 30 days and, with respect to each cause, designate whether it has been under submission for 30 through 60 days, 61 through 90 days, or over 90 days;

(B) Compile a list of all causes under submission before judges of the court, designated as the submitted list, which must include the name of each judge, a list of causes under submission before that judge, and the length of time each cause has been under submission;

(C) Circulate monthly a complete copy of the submitted list to each judge of the court;

(D) Contact and alert each judge who has a cause under submission for over 30 days and discuss ways to ensure that the cause is timely decided;

(E) Consider providing assistance to a judge who has a cause under submission for over 60 days; and

(F) Consider requesting the services of Judicial Council staff to review the court's calendar management procedures and make recommendations whenever either of the following condition exists in the court for the most recent three months:

(i) More than 90 civil active cases are pending for each judicial position; or

(ii) More than 10 percent of the cases on the civil active list have been pending for one year or more.

(4) *Oversight of judicial officers*

The presiding judge must:

(A) *Judges*

Notify the Commission on Judicial Performance of:

(i) A judge's substantial failure to perform judicial duties, including any habitual neglect of duty, persistent refusal to carry out assignments as assigned by the presiding judge, or persistent refusal to carry out the directives of the presiding judge as authorized by the rules of court; or

(ii) Any absences caused by disability totaling more than 90 court days in a 12-month period, excluding absences authorized under (c)(2);

(B) *Notice*

Give the judge a copy of the notice to the commission under (A) if appropriate. If a copy is not given to the judge, the presiding judge must inform the commission of the reasons why so notifying the judge was deemed inappropriate;

(C) *Commissioners*

(i) Prepare and submit to the judges for consideration and adoption procedures for receiving, inquiring into, and resolving complaints lodged against subordinate judicial officers, consistent with rule 10.703; and

(ii) Notify the Commission on Judicial Performance if a subordinate judicial officer is disciplined or resigns, consistent with rule 10.703(j).

(D) *Temporary judges*

Be responsible for the recruitment, training, supervision, approval, and performance of temporary judges as provided in rules 2.810–2.819 and rules 10.740–10.746; and

(E) *Assigned judges*

For each assigned retired judge:

(i) Complete a confidential evaluation form;

(ii) Submit the form annually to the Administrative Director;

(iii) Direct complaints against the assigned judge to the Chief Justice, by forwarding them to the attention of the Administrative Director, and provide requested information in writing to the Administrative Director in a timely manner; and

(iv) Assist the Administrative Director in the process of investigating, evaluating, and making recommendations to the Chief Justice regarding complaints against retired judges who serve on assignment.

(5) *Personnel*

(A) The presiding judge must provide general direction to and supervision of the court executive officer, or, if the court has no executive officer, perform the duties of the court executive regarding personnel as specified in rule 10.610(c)(1).

(B) The presiding judge must approve, in writing, the total compensation package (salary and all benefits) offered to the court executive officer at the time of the executive officer's appointment and any subsequent changes to the executive officer's total compensation package.

(6) *Budget and fiscal management*

The presiding judge must:

(A) Establish a process for consulting with the judges of the court on budget requests, expenditure plans, and other budget or fiscal matters that the presiding judge deems appropriate;

(B) Establish responsible budget priorities and submit budget requests that will best enable the court to achieve its goals;

(C) Establish a documented process for setting and approving any changes to the court executive officer's total compensation package in a fiscally responsible manner consistent with the court's established budget; and

(D) Approve procurements, contracts, expenditures, and the allocation of funds in a manner that promotes the implementation of state and local budget priorities and that ensures equal access to justice and the ability of the court to carry out its functions effectively. In a court with an executive officer, the presiding judge may delegate these duties to the court executive officer, but the presiding judge must ensure that the court executive officer performs such delegated duties consistent with the court's established budget.

(7) *Meetings and committees*

The presiding judge must establish a process for consulting with the judges of the court and may call meetings of the judges as needed. The presiding judge may appoint standing and special committees of judges as needed to assist in the proper performance of the duties and functions of the court.

(8) *Liaison*

The presiding judge must:

(A) Provide for liaison between the court and the Judicial Council, Judicial Council staff, and other governmental and civic agencies;

(B) Meet with or designate a judge or judges to meet with any committee of the bench, bar, news media, or community to review problems and to promote understanding of the administration of justice, when appropriate; and

(C) Support and encourage the judges to actively engage in community outreach to increase public understanding of and involvement with the justice system and to obtain appropriate community input regarding the administration of justice, consistent with the California Code of Judicial Ethics and standard 10.5 of the Standards of Judicial Administration.

(9) *Planning*

The presiding judge must:

(A) Prepare, with the assistance of appropriate court committees and appropriate input from the community, a long-range strategic plan that is consistent with the plan and policies of the Judicial Council, for adoption in accordance with procedures established by local rules or policies; and

(B) Ensure that the court regularly and actively examines access issues, including any physical, language, or economic barriers that impede the fair administration of justice.

(10) *Appellate records*

The presiding judge is responsible for ensuring the timely preparation of records on appeal.

(A) The presiding judge ordinarily should delegate the following duties to the executive officer:

(i) Maintaining records of outstanding transcripts to be completed by each court reporter;

(ii) Reassigning court reporters as necessary to facilitate prompt completion of transcripts; and

(iii) Reviewing court reporters' requests for extensions of time to complete transcripts in appeals of criminal cases.

(B) After reasonable notice and hearing, the presiding judge must declare any reporter of the court who is delinquent in completing a transcript on appeal not competent to act as a reporter in court, under Government Code section 69944.

(11) *Local rules*

The presiding judge must prepare, with the assistance of appropriate court committees, proposed local rules to expedite and facilitate court business in accordance with Government Code section 68071 and rules 2.100, 3.20, and 10.613.

(Subd (c) amended effective September 1, 2024; previously amended effective January 1, 2001, January 1, 2002, January 1, 2006, July 1, 2006, January 1, 2007, July 1, 2010, and January 1, 2016.)

Rule 10.603(c) 2024 Deletes. [1] the principles contained in standards 10.11–10.13

(d) Delegation

The presiding judge may delegate any of the specific duties listed in this rule to another judge. Except for the duties listed in (c)(5)(B) and (c)(6)(C), the presiding judge may delegate to the court executive officer any of the duties listed in this rule that do not require the exercise of judicial authority. The presiding judge remains responsible for all duties listed in this rule even if he or she has delegated particular tasks to someone else.

(Subd (d) amended effective July 1, 2010; previously amended effective January 1, 2007.)

Rule 10.603 amended effective September 1, 2024; adopted as rule 6.603 effective January 1, 2001; previously amended and renumbered effective January 1, 2007; previously amended effective January 1, 2002, January 1, 2006, July 1, 2006, July 1, 2010, and January 1, 2016.

Rule 10.605. Executive committee

In accordance with the internal policies of the court, an executive committee may be established by the court to advise the presiding judge or to establish policies and procedures for the internal management of the court. An executive committee may be appointed by the presiding judge to advise the presiding judge.

Rule 10.605 renumbered effective January 1, 2007; adopted rule 6.605 effective January 1, 2001.

Rule 10.608. Duties of all judges

Each judge must:

(1) Hear all assigned matters unless:

(A) He or she is disqualified; or

(B) He or she has stated in writing the reasons for refusing to hear a cause assigned for trial, and the presiding judge, supervising judge, or master calendar judge has concurred;

(2) Immediately notify the master calendar judge or the presiding judge on the completion or continuation of a trial or any other matter assigned for hearing;

(3) Request approval of the presiding judge for any intended absence of one-half day or more, within a reasonable time before the intended absence;

(4) Follow the court's personnel plan in dealing with employees; and

(5) Follow directives of the presiding judge in matters of court management and administration, as authorized by the rules of court and the local rules and internal policies of the court.

Rule 10.608 amended and renumbered effective January 1, 2007; adopted as rule 6.608 effective January 1, 2001; previously amended effective January 1, 2006.

Rule 10.609. Notification to State Bar of attorney misconduct

(a) Notification by judge

When notification to the State Bar is required under Business and Professions Code section 6086.7, the judge issuing the order that triggers the notification requirement under section 6086.7 is responsible for notifying the State Bar. The judge may direct court staff to notify the State Bar.

(Subd (a) adopted effective January 1, 2014.)

(b) Contents of notice

The notice must include the State Bar member's full name and State Bar number, if known, and a copy of the order that triggered the notification requirement.

(Subd (b) adopted effective January 1, 2014.)

(c) Notification to attorney

If notification to the State Bar is made under this rule, the person who notified the State Bar must also inform the attorney who is the subject of the notification that the matter has been referred to the State Bar.

(Subd (c) adopted effective January 1, 2014.)

Rule 10.609 adopted effective January 1, 2014.

Advisory Committee Comment

Business and Professions Code section 6086.7 requires a court to notify the State Bar of any of the following: (1) a final order of contempt imposed on an attorney that may involve grounds warranting discipline under the State Bar Act; (2) a modification or reversal of a judgment in a judicial proceeding based in whole or in part on the misconduct, incompetent representation, or willful misrepresentation of an attorney; (3) the imposition of any judicial sanctions on an attorney of $1,000 or more, except sanctions for failure to make discovery; or (4) the imposition of any civil penalty on an attorney under Family Code section 8620. If the notification pertains to a final order of contempt, Business and Professions Code section 6086.7(a)(1) requires the court to transmit to the State Bar a copy of the relevant minutes, final order, and transcript, if one exists. This rule is intended to clarify who has the responsibility of notifying the State Bar under section 6086.7 and the required contents of the notice.

In addition to the requirements stated in Business and Professions Code section 6086.7, judges are subject to canon 3D(2) of the California Code of Judicial Ethics, which states: "Whenever a judge has personal knowledge, or concludes in a judicial decision, that a lawyer has committed misconduct or has violated any provision of the Rules of Professional Conduct, the judge shall take appropriate corrective action, which may include reporting the violation to the appropriate authority." The Advisory Committee Commentary states: "Appropriate corrective action could include direct communication with the judge or lawyer who has committed the violation, other direct action, such as a confidential referral to a judicial or lawyer assistance program, or a report of the violation to the presiding judge, appropriate authority, or other agency or body. Judges should note that in addition to the action required by Canon 3D(2), California law imposes mandatory additional reporting requirements on judges regarding lawyer misconduct. See Business and Professions Code section 6086.7."

Rule 10.610. Duties of court executive officer

(a) Selection

A court may employ an executive officer selected in accordance with procedures adopted by the court.

(b) General responsibilities

Acting under the direction of the presiding judge, the court executive officer is responsible for overseeing the management and administration of the nonjudicial operations of the court and allocating resources in a manner that promotes access to justice for all members of the public, provides a forum for the fair and expeditious resolution of disputes, maximizes the use of judicial and other resources, increases efficiency in court operations, and enhances service to the public.

(Subd (b) amended effective January 1, 2007.)

(c) Duties

Under the direction of the presiding judge and consistent with the law and rules of court, the court executive officer must perform the following duties, where they are not inconsistent with the authorized duties of the clerk of the court:

(1) *Personnel*

Provide general direction to and supervision of the employees of the court, and draft for court approval and administer a personnel plan for court employees that complies with rule 10.670. The court executive officer has the authority, consistent with the personnel plan, to hire, discipline, and terminate nonjudicial employees of the court.

(2) *Budget*

Make recommendations to the presiding judge on budget priorities; prepare and implement court budgets, including accounting, payroll, and financial controls; and employ sound budget and fiscal management practices and procedures to ensure that annual expenditures are within the court's budget.

(3) *Contracts*

Negotiate contracts on behalf of the court, in accordance with established contracting procedures and all applicable laws.

(4) *Calendar management*

Supervise and employ efficient calendar and case flow management systems, including analyzing and evaluating pending caseloads and recommending effective calendar management techniques.

(5) *Technology*

Analyze, evaluate, and implement technological and automated systems to assist the court.

(6) *Jury management*

Manage the jury system in the most efficient and effective way.

(7) *Facilities*

Plan physical space needs, and purchase and manage equipment and supplies.

(8) *Records*

Create and manage uniform record-keeping systems, collecting data on pending and completed judicial business and the internal operation of the court, as required by the court and the Judicial Council.

(9) *Recommendations*

Identify problems, recommending procedural and administrative changes to the court.

(10) *Public relations*

Provide a clearinghouse for news releases and other publications for the media and public.

(11) *Liaison*

Act as liaison to other governmental agencies.

(12) *Committees*

Provide staff for judicial committees.

(13) *Other*

Perform other duties as the presiding judge directs.

(Subd (c) amended effective January 1, 2007.)

Rule 10.610 amended and renumbered effective January 1, 2007; adopted as rule 6.610 effective January 1, 2001.

Rule 10.611. Nondiscrimination in court appointments

Each court should select attorneys, arbitrators, mediators, referees, masters, receivers, and other persons appointed by the court on the basis of merit. No court may discriminate in such selection on the basis of gender, race, ethnicity, disability, sexual orientation, or age.

Rule 10.611 amended and renumbered effective January 1, 2007; adopted as rule 989.2 effective January 1, 1999.

Rule 10.612. Use of gender-neutral language

Each court must use gender-neutral language in all new local rules, forms, and documents and must review and revise those now in use to ensure that they are written in gender-neutral language.

Rule 10.612 adopted effective January 1, 2007.

Rule 10.613. Local court rules—adopting, filing, distributing, and maintaining

(a) Definitions

As used in this rule:

(1) "Court" means a trial court; and

(2) "Local rule" means every rule, regulation, order, policy, form, or standard of general application adopted by a court to govern practice or procedure in that court or by a judge of the court to govern practice or procedure in that judge's courtroom.

(Subd (a) amended and relettered effective July 1, 1999; adopted as subd (b) and repealed effective July 1, 1991.)

(b) Local inspection and copying of rules

Each court must make its local rules available for inspection and copying in every location of the court that generally accepts filing of papers. The court may impose a reasonable charge for copying the rules and may impose a reasonable page limit on copying. The rules must be accompanied by a notice indicating where a full set of the rules may be purchased or otherwise obtained.

(Subd (b) amended effective January 1, 2003; adopted as subd (c) effective July 1, 1991; previously relettered effective July 1, 1999.)

(c) Publication of rules

(1) Each court executive officer must be the official publisher of the court's local rules unless the court, by a majority vote of the judges, appoints another public agency or a private company.

(2) The official publisher must have the local rules reproduced and make copies available for distribution to attorneys and litigants.

(3) The court must adopt rules in sufficient time to permit reproduction of the rules by the official publisher before the effective date of the changes.

(4) The official publisher may charge a reasonable fee.

(5) Within 30 days of selecting an official publisher or changing an official publisher, each court must notify the Judicial Council of the name, address, and telephone number of the official publisher. Within 30 days of a change in the cost of the rules, each court must notify the Judicial Council of the charge for the local rules. This information will be published annually by the Judicial Council.

(Subd (c) amended effective January 1, 2003; adopted as subd (d) effective July 1, 1991; amended and relettered effective July 1, 1999.)

(d) Filing rules with the Judicial Council

(1) Forty-five days before the effective date of January 1 or July 1, each court must file with the Judicial Council an electronic copy of rules and amendments to rules adopted by the court in a format authorized by the Judicial Council.

(2) The filing must be accompanied by a certificate from the presiding judge or court executive officer stating that:

(A) The court has complied with the applicable provisions of this rule;

(B) The court does or does not post local rules on the court's Web site; and

(C) The court does or does not provide assistance to members of the public in accessing the Internet or the court has delegated to and obtained the written consent of the county law librarian to provide public assistance under (e).

(3) Rules that do not comply with this rule will not be accepted for filing by the Judicial Council.

(Subd (d) amended effective January 1, 2009; adopted as subd (e) effective July 1, 1991; amended and relettered effective July 1, 1999; previously amended effective January 1, 2003, and January 1, 2007.)

(e) Deposit and maintenance of rules statewide for public inspection

(1) The Judicial Council must publish a list of courts that have filed rules and amendments to rules with the Judicial Council. The Judicial Council must deposit a paper copy of each rule and amendment in the office of the executive officer of each superior court that does not provide assistance to members of the public in accessing the Internet or has not obtained agreement from the county law librarian to provide assistance under this subdivision.

(2) The executive officer must make a complete current set of local rules and amendments available for public examination either in paper copy or through the Internet with public assistance. In a county maintaining an organized county law library, if the executive officer is satisfied that the rules and amendments will be maintained as required by this paragraph, the executive officer, with the approval of the superior court and the written consent of the county law librarian, may delegate the authority to the county law librarian to either receive and maintain paper copies of the rules and amendments, or make the rules and amendments available through the Internet with assistance to members of the public.

(3) On or before January 1 of each year, the executive officer of each court must notify the Judicial Council of the street address and room number of the place where the rules are maintained under this subdivision.

(Subd (e) amended effective January 1, 2007; adopted as subd (f) effective July 1, 1991; amended and relettered effective July 1, 1999; previously amended effective January 1, 2003.)

(f) Format of rules

(1) *Paper and electronic copies*

Paper copies may be typewritten or printed or produced by other process of duplication at the option of the court. Electronic rules must be prepared in a format authorized by the Judicial Council. All copies must be clear and legible.

(2) *Format of paper copies*

Paper copies must conform, as far as is practicable, to the requirements of chapter 1 of division 2 of title 2, except that both sides of the paper may be used, lines need not be numbered and may be single spaced, and the pages must not be permanently bound across the top but may be bound at the left side. ("Permanently bound" does not include binding with staples.) The left margin on the front and the right margin on the reverse must be at least one inch. The name of the court must be at the top of each page. The effective date of each rule and amended rule must be stated in parentheses following the text of the rule.

(3) *New pages and filing instructions*

New pages must be issued for added, repealed, or amended rules, with a list of currently effective rules and the date of adoption or of the latest amendment to each rule. Filing instructions must accompany each set of replacement pages.

(4) *Table of contents*

The rules must have a table of contents. The rules must list all local forms and indicate whether their use is mandatory or optional. If the total length of the court rules exceeds five pages, the rules must have an alphabetical subject matter index at the end of the rules. All courts must use any subject matter index the Judicial Council may have specified.

(Subd (f) amended effective January 1, 2007; adopted as subd (g) effective July 1, 1991; amended and relettered effective July 1, 1999; previously amended effective January 1, 2003.)

(g) Comment period for proposed rules

(1) *Timing*

Except for rules specifying the time of hearing and similar calendaring matters, the court must distribute each proposed rule for comment at least 45 days before it is adopted.

(2) *Organizations*

A proposed rule must be distributed for comment to the following organizations in each county located within a 100-mile radius of the county seat of the county in which the court is located:

(A) Civil rules to the county bar association in each county, the nearest office of the State Attorney General, and the county counsel in each county;

(B) Criminal rules to the county bar association in each county, the nearest office of the State Attorney General, the district attorney in each county, and the public defender in each county; and

(C) On request, any bar organization, newspaper, or other interested party.

(3) *Methods*

A court may distribute a proposed rule for comment by either of the following methods:

(A) Distributing a copy of the proposal to every organization listed in (g)(2); or

(B) Posting the proposal on the court's Web site and distributing to every organization listed in (g)(2) a notice that the proposed rule has been posted for comment and that a hard copy of the proposal is available on request.

(Subd (g) amended effective January 1, 2007; adopted as subd (h) effective July 1, 1991; relettered effective July 1, 1999; previously amended effective January 1, 2003.)

(h) Periodic review

Each court must periodically review its local rules and repeal rules that have become outdated, unnecessary, or inconsistent with statewide rules or statutes.

(Subd (h) amended effective January 1, 2007; adopted as subd (g) effective July 1, 1991; relettered effective July 1, 1999; previously amended effective January 1, 2003.)

(i) Alternative effective date

A court may adopt a rule to take effect on a date other than as provided by Government Code section 68071 if:

(1) The presiding judge submits to the Judicial Council the proposed rule and a statement of reasons constituting good cause for making the rule effective on the stated date;

(2) The Chair of the Judicial Council authorizes the rule to take effect on the date proposed; and

(3) The rule is made available for inspection as provided in (b) on or before the effective date.

(Subd (i) amended effective January 1, 2007; adopted as subd (j) effective January 1, 1993; relettered effective July 1, 1999; previously amended effective July 1, 2001.)

(j) Limitation

Except for (i), this rule does not apply to local rules that relate only to the internal management of the court.

(Subd (j) amended effective January 1, 2007; adopted effective July 1, 1999; previously amended effective July 1, 2001.)

Rule 10.613 amended effective January 1, 2009; adopted as rule 981 effective July 1, 1991; previously amended effective January 1, 1993, July 1, 1999, July 1, 2001, and January 1, 2003; previously amended and renumbered effective January 1, 2007.

Rule 10.614. Local court forms

Local forms must comply with the following:

(1) Each form must be on paper measuring no more than 8½ by 11 inches and no less than 8½ by 5 inches.

(2) The court must make copies of its forms available in the clerk's office. A court may, as an alternative, make its forms available in a booklet from which photocopies of the forms may be made. The court may charge for either copies of forms or the booklet of forms.

(3) The court must assign to each form a unique designator consisting of numbers or letters, or both. The designator must be positioned on the form in the same manner as the designator on a Judicial Council form.

(4) The effective date of each form must be placed on the form in the same manner as the effective date on a Judicial Council form, and each form must state whether it is a "Mandatory Form" or an "Optional Form" in the lower left corner of the first page.

(5) Each court must make available a current list of forms adopted or approved by that court. The list must include, for each form, its name, number, effective date, and whether the form is mandatory or optional. There must be two versions of the list, one organized by form number and one organized by form name. The court must modify its lists whenever it adopts, approves, revises, or repeals any form.

(6) Each form must be designed so that no typing is required on it within 1 inch of the top or within ½ inch of the bottom.

(7) All forms presented for filing must be firmly bound at the top and must contain two prepunched, normal-sized holes centered 2½ inches apart and ⅝ inch from the top of the form.

(8) If a form is longer than one page, the form may be filed on sheets printed on only one side even if the original form has two printed sides to a sheet. If a form is filed on a sheet printed on two sides, the reverse side must be rotated 180 degrees (printed head to foot).

Rule 10.614 amended effective January 1, 2014; adopted as rule 201.3 effective January 1, 2003; previously amended and renumbered effective January 1, 2007.

Rule 10.620. Public access to administrative decisions of trial courts

(a) Interpretation

The provisions of this rule concern public access to administrative decisions by trial courts as provided in this rule. This rule does not modify existing law regarding public access to the judicial deliberative process and does not apply to the adjudicative functions of the trial courts or the assignment of judges.

(b) Budget priorities

The Administrative Director may request, on 30 court days' notice, recommendations from the trial courts concerning judicial branch budget priorities. The notice must state that if a trial court is to make recommendations, the trial court must also give notice, as provided in (g), that interested members of the public may send input to the Judicial Council.

(Subd (b) amended effective January 1, 2016; previously amended effective January 1, 2005, and January 1, 2007.)

(c) Budget requests

Before making recommendations, if any, to the Judicial Council on items to be included in the judicial branch budget that is submitted annually to the Governor and the Legislature, a trial court must seek input from the public, as provided in (e), on what should be included in the recommendations.

(Subd (c) amended effective January 1, 2007.)

(d) Other decisions requiring public input

Each trial court must seek input from the public, as provided in (e), before making the following decisions:

(1) A request for permission from Judicial Council staff to reallocate budget funds from one program component to another in an amount greater than $400,000 or 10 percent of the total trial court budget, whichever is greater.

(2) The execution of a contract without competitive bidding in an amount greater than $400,000 or 10 percent of the total trial court budget, whichever is greater. This subdivision does not apply to a contract entered into between a court and a county that is provided for by statute.

(3) The cessation of any of the following services at a court location:

(A) The Family Law Facilitator; or

(B) The Family Law Information Center.

(Subd (d) amended effective January 1, 2016; previously amended effective January 1, 2007.)

(e) Manner of seeking public input

When a trial court is required to seek public input under this rule, it must provide public notice of the request at least 15 court days before the date on which the decision is to be made or the action is to be taken.

Notice must be given as provided in (g). Any interested person or entity who wishes to comment must send the comment to the court in writing or electronically unless the court requires that all public comment be sent either by e-mail or through a response system on the court's Web site. For good cause, in the event an urgent action is required, a trial court may take immediate action if it (1) gives notice of the action as provided in (f), (2) states the reasons for urgency, and (3) gives any public input received to the person or entity making the decision.

(Subd (e) amended effective January 1, 2007.)

(f) Information about other trial court administrative matters

A trial court must provide notice, not later than 15 court days after the event, of the following:

(1) Receipt of the annual allocation of the trial court budget from the Judicial Council after enactment of the Budget Act.

(2) The awarding of a grant to the trial court that exceeds the greater of $400,000 or 10 percent of the total trial court budget.

(3) The solicitation of proposals or the execution of a contract that exceeds the greater of $400,000 or 10 percent of the trial court budget.

(4) A significant permanent increase in the number of hours that a court location is open during any day for either court sessions or filing of papers. As used in this paragraph, a significant increase does not include an emergency or one-time need to increase hours.

(5) The action taken on any item for which input from the public was required under (d). The notice must show the person or persons who made the decision and a summary of the written and e-mail input received.

(Subd (f) amended effective January 1, 2016; previously amended effective January 1, 2007.)

(g) Notice

When notice is required to be given by this rule, it must be given in the following ways:

(1) Posted on the trial court's Web site, if any.

(2) Sent to any of the following persons or entities—subject to the requirements of (h)—who have requested in writing or by electronic mail to the court executive officer to receive such notice:

(A) A newspaper, radio station, and television station in the county;

(B) The president of a local or specialty bar association in the county;

(C) Representatives of a trial court employees organization;

(D) The district attorney, public defender, and county counsel;

(E) The county administrative officer; and

(F) If the court is sending notice electronically using the provisions of (h), any other person or entity that submits an electronic mail address to which the notice will be sent.

(3) Posted at all locations of the court that accept papers for filing.

(Subd (g) amended effective January 1, 2007.)

(h) Electronic notice

A trial court may require a person or entity that is otherwise entitled to receive notice under (g)(2) to submit an electronic mail address to which the notice will be sent.

(Subd (h) amended effective January 1, 2007.)

(i) Materials

When a trial court is required to seek public input under (b), (c), or (d), it must also provide for public viewing at one or more locations in the county of any written factual materials that have been specifically gathered or prepared for the review at the time of making the decision of the person or entity making the decision. This subdivision does not require the disclosure of materials that are otherwise exempt from disclosure or would be exempt from disclosure under the state Public Records Act (beginning with Government Code section 6250). The materials must be mailed or otherwise be made available not less than five court days before the decision is to be made except if the request is made within the five court days before the decision is to be made, the materials must be mailed or otherwise be made available the next court day after the request is made. A court must either (1) provide copies to a person or entity that requests copies of these materials in writing or by electronic mail to the executive officer of the court or other person designated by the executive office in the notice, if the requesting person or entity pays all mailing and copying costs as determined by any mailing and copy cost recovery policies established by the trial court, or (2) make all materials available electronically either on its Web site or by e-mail. This subdivision does not require the trial court to prepare reports. A person seeking documents may request the court to hold the material for pickup by that person instead of mailing.

(Subd (i) amended effective January 1, 2007.)

(j) Other requirements

This rule does not affect any other obligations of the trial court including any obligation to meet and confer with designated employee representatives. This rule does not change the procedures a court must otherwise follow in entering into a contract or change the types of matters for which a court may contract.

(Subd (j) amended effective January 1, 2007.)

(k) Enforcement

This rule may be enforced under Code of Civil Procedure section 1085.

Rule 10.620 amended effective January 1, 2016; adopted as rule 6.620 effective January 1, 2004; previously amended effective January 1, 2005; previously amended and renumbered as rule 10.620 effective January 1, 2007.

Advisory Committee Comment

The procedures required under this rule do not apply where statutes specify another procedure for giving public notice and allowing public input. (See, e.g., Gov. Code, § 68106 [notice of reduced court services]; *id.*, § 68511.7 [notice of proposed court budget plan].)

Rule 10.625. Certain demographic data relating to regular grand jurors

(a) Definitions

The following definitions apply under this rule:

(1) "Regular grand jury" means a body of citizens of a county selected by the court to investigate matters of civil concern in the county, whether or not that body has jurisdiction to return indictments.

(2) "Race or ethnicity" reflects the concept of race used by the United States Census Bureau and reflects self-identification by people according to the race or races with which they most closely identify. These categories are sociopolitical constructs and should not be interpreted as being scientific or anthropological in nature. The categories include both racial and national-origin groups.

(3) "Prospective regular grand juror" means those citizens who (a) respond in person to the jury summonses or questionnaires from the court for the purposes of grand jury service and are eligible to serve as regular grand jurors, or (b) either submit applications, are recruited, or are nominated by judicial officers and are eligible to serve as regular grand jurors.

(4) "Eligible to serve" means that the prospective regular grand juror meets each of the criteria set forth in Penal Code section 893(a) and is not disqualified by any factor set forth in section 893(b).

(Subd (a) adopted effective January 1, 2007.)

(b) Jury commissioner duties and responsibilities

(1) The jury commissioner or designee must create a method to capture the following data from prospective regular grand jurors:

(A) Age range, specifically:

(i) 18–25

(ii) 26–34

(iii) 35–44

(iv) 45–54

(v) 55–64

(vi) 65–74

(vii) 75 and over

(B) Gender; and

(C) Race or ethnicity from the following categories (candidates may select more than one category):

(i) American Indian or Alaska Native

(ii) Asian

(iii) Black or African American

(iv) Hispanic/Latino

(v) Native Hawaiian or other Pacific Islander

(vi) White

(vii) Other race or ethnicity (please state: _____)

(viii) Decline to answer

(2) Develop and maintain a database containing the following information regarding prospective regular grand jurors, the candidates who are ultimately selected by the court to serve as grand jurors, and any carry-over grand jurors: name, age range, occupation, gender, race or ethnicity, and the year(s) served on the regular grand jury. The database should indicate how the juror initially became a candidate (by random draw, application, or nomination).

(Subd (b) adopted effective January 1, 2007.)

(c) Annual summary

(1) The court must develop and maintain an annual summary of the information in the database maintained under (b)(2). The summary must

not include the names of the candidates and must be made available to the public.

(Subd (c) adopted effective January 1, 2007.)
Rule 10.625 adopted effective January 1, 2007.

Advisory Committee Comment

This rule is intended to facilitate the courts' continued efforts to achieve the goals stated in standard 10.50 [formerly section 17] of the Standards of Judicial Administration, which encourages courts to employ various methods of soliciting prospective candidates to serve on regular grand juries that reflect a representative cross-section of the community they serve. Those methods include obtaining recommendations for grand jurors who encompass a cross-section of the county's population base, solicited from a broad representation of community-based organizations, civic leaders, and superior court judges, referees, and commissioners subdivision (b)(2)); having the court consider carry-over grand jury selections under Penal Code section 901(b) to ensure broad-based representation (Subd (c)); and encouraging judges who nominate persons for grand jury service under Penal Code section 903.4 to select candidates from the list returned by the jury commissioner or otherwise employing a nomination procedure to ensure broad-based representation from the community.

This rule is also intended to assist the courts in establishing a formal mechanism whereby they can monitor the extent to which they achieve the goal of seating representative regular grand juries through a process comparable to that stated in Penal Code section 904.6(e), which requires that persons selected for the "criminal grand jury shall be selected at random from a source or sources reasonably representative of a cross section of the population which is eligible for jury service in the county."

Rule 10.630. Reciprocal assignment orders

A "reciprocal assignment order" is an order issued by the Chief Justice that permits judges in courts of different counties to serve in each other's courts.

Rule 10.630 amended effective July 1, 2015; adopted as rule 813 effective July 1, 1990; previously amended and renumbered effective January 1, 2007.

Rule 10.635. Limited situations in which a judicial officer may preside remotely from a location other than a courtroom

(a) Purpose

This rule prescribes when, in limited situations and in the interest of justice, a judicial officer may use remote technology to effectuate their own participation in a proceeding from a location other than a courtroom.

(b) Application

(1) This rule applies when a judicial officer presiding from a location other than a courtroom uses remote technology to effectuate their own participation in the proceeding.

(2) This rule does not apply when a judicial officer presides in person over a proceeding convened in a location other than a court facility, even if another participant appears remotely.

(3) This rule applies to all civil cases subject to Code of Civil Procedure section 367.75.

(4) Nothing in this rule limits a judicial officer from engaging in any other judicial functions, duties, or actions authorized by law to be performed in a location other than a courtroom.

(c) Definitions

As used in this rule:

(1) "Court facility" has the same meaning as that provided in Government Code section 70301(d).

(2) The following terms have the same meaning as those provided in rule 3.672(c):

(A) "Proceeding."
(B) "Remote proceeding."
(C) "Remote technology."

(d) Location of a judicial officer within a court facility

A judicial officer may preside remotely from a location within a court facility other than a courtroom only if doing so is in the interest of justice, the presiding judge approves, and either:

(1) No parties are appearing in person at the proceeding; or
(2) No courtrooms are available in the court facility.

(e) Location of a judicial officer outside a court facility

A judicial officer may not preside remotely from a location outside a court facility unless doing so is in the interest of justice, the presiding judge approves, and

(1) The judicial officer cannot safely access or preside from a court facility because of hazardous conditions, including those resulting from:

(A) Natural disaster;
(B) Severe weather;
(C) Public emergency;
(D) Facilities failure;
(E) Security threats; or
(F) Other extraordinary circumstances as determined by the presiding judge; or

(2) Presiding remotely in a matter is essential to prevent a significant delay that would substantially prejudice the litigants.

Rule 10.635 adopted effective July 1, 2024.

Chapter 2
Trial Court Management of Human Resources

Art. 1. Trial Court Employee Labor Relations. Rules 10.650–10.660.
Art. 2. Other Human Resources Rules. Rule 10.670.

Article 1
Trial Court Employee Labor Relations

Rule 10.650. Court Employee Labor Relations Rules
Rule 10.651. Purpose
Rule 10.652. Definitions
Rule 10.653. Right and obligation to meet and confer
Rule 10.654. Scope of representation
Rule 10.655. Governing court employee labor relations
Rule 10.656. Transition provisions
Rule 10.657. Construction
Rule 10.658. Interpretation
Rule 10.659. Other provisions
Rule 10.660. Enforcement of agreements—petitions (Gov. Code, §§ 71639.5, 71825.2)

Rule 10.650. Court Employee Labor Relations Rules

Rules 10.651–10.659 in this chapter are referred to as the Court Employee Labor Relations Rules.

Rule 10.650 adopted effective January 1, 2007.

Rule 10.651. Purpose

The purpose of the Court Employee Labor Relations Rules is to extend to trial court employees the right, and to require trial courts, to meet and confer in good faith over matters that the court, as opposed to the county, has authority to determine that are within the scope of representation, consistent with the procedures stated in this division.

The adoption of the Court Employee Labor Relations Rules is not intended to require changes in existing representation units, memoranda of agreements, statutes, or court rules relating to trial court employees, except as they would otherwise normally occur as provided for in this division.

Rule 10.651 amended and renumbered effective January 1, 2007; adopted as rule 2201 effective January 1, 1998, the effective date of Stats. 1997, ch. 850.

Rule 10.652. Definitions

As used in the Court Employee Labor Relations Rules:

(1) "Court" means a superior court.

(2) "Court employee" means any employee of a court, except those employees whose job classification confers safety retirement status.

(3) "Meet and confer in good faith" means that a court or such representatives as it may designate, and representatives of recognized employee organizations, have the mutual obligation personally to meet and confer promptly on request by either party and to continue for a reasonable period of time in order to exchange freely information, opinions, and proposals, and to endeavor to reach agreement on matters within the scope of representation. The process should include adequate time for the resolution of impasses where specific procedures for such resolution are contained in this division or a local rule, regulation, or ordinance, or when such procedures are used by mutual consent.

(4) "Recognized employee organization" means an employee organization that has been formally acknowledged by the county to represent court employees under the provisions of Government Code sections 3500–3510 or by the court under its rules or policies.

Rule 10.652 amended and renumbered effective January 1, 2007; adopted as rule 2202 effective January 1, 1998, the effective date of Stats. 1997, ch. 850.

Rule 10.653. Right and obligation to meet and confer

(a) Recognized employee organization

A recognized employee organization has the right to represent its court employee members in their employment relations with a court as to matters covered by the Court Employee Labor Relations Rules. Nothing in these rules prohibits any court employee from appearing in his or her own behalf regarding employment relations with a court.

(Subd (a) amended effective January 1, 2007.)

(b) Representatives of a court

Representatives of a court must meet and confer in good faith regarding matters within the scope of representation, as defined in the Court Employee Labor Relations Rules, with representatives of a recognized employee organization, and must consider fully such presentations as are made by the recognized employee organization on behalf of its members before arriving at a determination of policy or course of action. In meeting this obligation a court must also comply with the procedures and provisions stated in Government Code sections 3504.5, 3505.1, 3505.2, and 3505.3 applicable to a public agency.

(Subd (b) amended effective January 1, 2007.)

(c) Joint negotiations and designations

In fulfilling the provisions of (b), the court and the county must consult with each other, may negotiate jointly, and each may designate the other in writing as its agent on any matters within the scope of representation.

(Subd (c) amended effective January 1, 2007.)

(d) Intimidation

A court or a recognized employee organization must not interfere with, intimidate, restrain, coerce, or discriminate against court employees because of their exercise of any rights they may have under the Court Employee Labor Relations Rules or Government Code sections 3500–3510.

(Subd (d) amended effective January 1, 2007.)

Rule 10.653 amended and renumbered effective January 1, 2007; adopted as rule 2203 effective January 1, 1998, the effective date of Stats. 1997, ch. 850.

Rule 10.654. Scope of representation

(a) Matters included in the scope of representation

For purposes of the Court Employee Labor Relations Rules, the scope of representation includes all matters within the court's authority to determine relating to employment conditions and employer-employee relations, including, but not limited to, wages, hours, and terms and other conditions of employment, except, however, that the scope of representation does not include consideration of the merits, necessity, or organization of any service or activity provided by law or executive order.

(Subd (a) amended effective January 1, 2007.)

(b) Matters outside the scope of representation

In view of the unique and special responsibilities of the courts in the administration of justice, decisions regarding the following matters are not included within the scope of representation:

(1) The merits and administration of the court system;

(2) Coordination, consolidation, and merger of trial courts and support staff;

(3) Automation, including but not limited to fax filing, electronic recording, and implementation of information systems;

(4) Design, construction, and location of court facilities;

(5) Delivery of court services; and

(6) Hours of operation of the courts and court system.

(Subd (b) amended effective January 1, 2007.)

(c) Impact

Impact from such matters as in (b) must be included within the scope of representation as those matters affect wages, hours, terms, and conditions of employment of court employees, to the extent such matters are within the court's authority to determine.

(Subd (c) amended effective January 1, 2007.)

(d) Assignments and transfers

The superior court continues to have the right to determine assignments and transfers of court employees, provided that the process, procedures, and criteria for assignments and transfers are included within the scope of representation.

(Subd (d) amended effective January 1, 2007.)

Rule 10.654 amended and renumbered effective January 1, 2007; adopted as rule 2204 effective January 1, 1998, the effective date of Stats. 1997, ch. 850.

Rule 10.655. Governing court employee labor relations

(a) County rules and procedures

As they relate to court employees in their relations with the court, matters described in Government Code section 3507(a) through (d) are governed by any rules and administrative procedures and provisions adopted by the county under section 3507 that may apply to county employees generally, with the right of review by the appropriate Court of Appeal.

(Subd (a) amended effective January 1, 2007.)

(b) Court rules and policies

A court may adopt reasonable rules and policies after consultation in good faith with representatives of a recognized employee organization or organizations for the administration of employer-employee relations under this rule as to matters described in Government Code section 3507(e)–(i). The court and county jointly will establish procedures to determine the appropriateness of any bargaining unit of court employees. The court must consult with the county about any rules and policies that the court may adopt under this section. If the court does not adopt rules by January 1, 1998, the court is bound by existing county rules until the court adopts rules.

(Subd (b) amended effective January 1, 2007.)

Rule 10.655 amended and renumbered effective January 1, 2007; adopted as rule 2205 effective January 1, 1998, the effective date of Stats. 1997, ch. 850.

Rule 10.656. Transition provisions

(a) Court employee organization

On the effective date of the Court Employee Labor Relations Rules, the court must recognize the employee organization that represented its court employees at the time of adoption. The court and the recognized employee organization are bound by the terms of any memorandum of understanding or agreement to which the court is a party that is in effect as of the date of adoption of the Court Employee Labor Relations Rules for its duration, or until it expires or, before then, is replaced by a subsequent memorandum of understanding.

(Subd (a) amended effective January 1, 2007.)

(b) Court personnel rules and policies

A court's local rules governing court employees and a court's personnel rules, policies, and practices in effect at the time of adoption of the Court Employee Labor Relations Rules, to the extent they are not contrary to or inconsistent with the obligations and duties provided for in these rules, continue in effect until changed by the court. Before changing any rule, policy, or practice that affects any matter within the scope of representation as stated in these rules, the court must meet and confer in good faith with the recognized employee organization as provided for in these rules.

(Subd (b) amended effective January 1, 2007.)

(c) County employee representation units

Nothing contained in these rules is intended to preclude court employees from continuing to be included in representation units that contain county employees.

(Subd (c) amended effective January 1, 2007.)

Rule 10.656 amended and renumbered effective January 1, 2007; adopted as rule 2206 effective January 1, 1998, the effective date of Stats. 1997, ch. 850.

Rule 10.657. Construction

The enactment of the Court Employee Labor Relations Rules is not to be construed as making the provisions of Labor Code section 923 applicable to court employees.

Rule 10.657 amended and renumbered effective January 1, 2007; adopted as rule 2207 effective January 1, 1998, the effective date of Stats. 1997, ch. 850.

Rule 10.658. Interpretation

Where the language of the Court Employee Labor Relations Rules is the same or substantially the same as that contained in Government Code sections 3500 to 3510, it must be interpreted and applied in accordance with judicial interpretations of the same language.

Rule 10.658 amended and renumbered effective January 1, 2007; adopted as rule 2208 effective January 1, 1998, the effective date of Stats. 1997, ch. 850.

Rule 10.659. Other provisions

(a) Mediation

If, after a reasonable period of time, representatives of the court and the recognized employee organization fail to reach agreement, the court and the recognized employee organization or recognized employee organizations together may agree on the appointment of a mediator mutually agreeable to the parties. Costs of mediation are to be divided one-half to the court and one-half to the recognized employee organization or recognized employee organizations.

(Subd (a) amended effective January 1, 2007.)

(b) Submission for dispute resolution

In the absence of local procedures and provisions for resolving disputes on the appropriateness of a unit of representation, on the request of any of the parties, the dispute must be submitted to the Division of Conciliation of the Department of Industrial Relations for mediation or for recommendation for resolving the dispute.

(Subd (b) amended effective January 1, 2007.)

(c) Dues deduction

Nothing in the Court Employee Labor Relations Rules affects the right of a court employee to authorize a dues deduction from his or her salary or wages under Government Code sections 1157.1, 1157.2, 1157.3, 1157.4, 1157.5, or 1157.7.

(Subd (c) amended effective January 1, 2007.)

(d) Applicability of Government Code section 3502.5

The procedures and provisions stated in Government Code section 3502.5 are applicable to court employees.

(Subd (d) amended effective January 1, 2007.)

Rule 10.659 amended and renumbered effective January 1, 2007; adopted as rule 2209 effective January 1, 1998, the effective date of Stats. 1997, ch. 850.

Rule 10.660. Enforcement of agreements—petitions (Gov. Code, §§ 71639.5, 71825.2)

(a) Application

This rule applies to petitions filed under Government Code sections 71639.5 and 71825.2.

(Subd (a) amended effective October 24, 2008; previously amended effective December 10, 2004, and January 1, 2007.)

(b) Assignment of Court of Appeal justice to hear the petition

(1) The petition must state the following on the first page, below the case number, in the statement of the character of the proceeding (see rule 2.111(6)): "Petition filed under Government Code sections 71639.5 and 71825.2—Assignment of Court of Appeal justice required."

(2) When the petition is filed, the clerk of the court must immediately request of the Judicial Council's Assigned Judges Program the assignment of a hearing judge from the panel established under (e).

(3) The judge assigned to hear the petition in the superior court must be a justice from a Court of Appeal for a district other than the district for that superior court.

(Subd (b) amended effective January 1, 2016; previously amended effective December 10, 2004, and January 1, 2007.)

(c) Superior court hearing

(1) The superior court must hear and decide the petition on an expedited basis and must give the petition priority over other matters to the extent permitted by law and the rules of court.

(2) The petition must be heard by a judge assigned by the Chief Justice from the panel of hearing judges established under (e).

(Subd (c) amended effective January 1, 2007.)

(d) Appeal

An appeal of the superior court decision must be heard and decided on an expedited basis in the Court of Appeal for the district in which the petition was heard and must be given priority over other matters to the extent permitted by law and the rules of court. The notice of appeal must state the following on the first page, below the case number, in the statement of the character of the proceeding (see rule 2.111(6)): "Notice of Appeal on Petition filed under Government Code sections 71639.5 and 71825.2—Expedited Processing Requested."

(Subd (d) amended effective January 1, 2007; previously amended effective December 10, 2004.)

(e) Panel of hearing judges

The panel of judges who may hear the petitions in the superior court must consist of Court of Appeal justices selected by the Chief Justice as follows:

(1) The panel must include at least one justice from each district of the Court of Appeal.

(2) Each justice assigned to hear a petition under (c)(2) must have received training on hearing the petitions as specified by the Chief Justice.

Rule 10.660 amended effective January 1, 2016; adopted as rule 2211 effective January 1, 2001; previously amended and renumbered as rule 10.660 effective January 1, 2007; previously amended effective December 10, 2004, and October 24, 2008.

Article 2
Other Human Resources Rules

Rule 10.670. Trial court personnel plans

(a) Purpose

This rule establishes the authority and responsibility of the superior courts, on a countywide basis, to create and implement a system of personnel management designed to achieve lawful, uniform, and fair employment practices and procedures.

(Subd (a) amended effective January 1, 2007.)

(b) Countywide personnel plans

The superior court of each county must establish a single personnel plan on a countywide basis, consistent with applicable statutes, rules, and standards of judicial administration.

(Subd (b) amended effective January 1, 2007.)

(c) Provisions of a personnel plan

The personnel plan must ensure that treatment of employees complies with current law. The personnel plan should address the following issues:

(1) A salary-setting procedure;

(2) Regular review of job classifications and titles;

(3) An equal employment opportunity policy applying to all employees in accordance with applicable state and federal law;

(4) Recruitment, selection, and promotion policies;

(5) A sexual harassment prevention policy;

(6) A reasonable accommodation policy;

(7) Grievance or complaint procedures covering, but not limited to, sexual harassment, discrimination, and denial of reasonable accommodation;

(8) An employee benefits plan that includes health benefits, retirement benefits, workers' compensation benefits, disability leave, and paid and unpaid leave in compliance with state and federal law;

(9) Timekeeping and payroll policies and procedures that comply with applicable state and federal law;

(10) A records management policy, including confidentiality and retention of personnel records;

(11) Job-related training and continuing education programs for all personnel concerning at least the following:

(A) Sexual harassment awareness;

(B) Discrimination and bias; and

(C) Safety;

(12) A policy statement on professional behavior requiring that all employees conduct themselves in a professional manner at all times and refrain from offensive conduct or comments that reflect bias or harassment;

(13) A policy regarding conflicts of interest and incompatible activities;

(14) Procedures for discipline and discharge; and

(15) A labor policy consistent with rules 10.653–10.659.

(Subd (c) amended effective January 1, 2007.)

(d) Optional provisions

A personnel plan may contain additional provisions, including the following:

(1) Criteria and schedules for performance evaluations for all levels of employees;

(2) Job-related training and continuing education programs for all personnel as appropriate, with provisions for both paid and unpaid educational leave concerning:

(A) Career development, including basic and managerial skills; and

(B) Equal employment opportunity concepts and recruitment methods.

(3) An employee benefit plan that may include:

(A) Flex-time, part-time, job-sharing, and other alternative work schedules;

(B) Cafeteria options to use pretax dollars for dependent care and medical care and for sick leave for the care of dependents;

(C) An employee assistance program; and

(D) A deferred compensation plan.

(Subd (d) amended effective January 1, 2007.)

(e) Submission of personnel plans

The superior court of each county must submit to the Judicial Council a personnel plan in compliance with these provisions by March 1, 1999. The superior court of each county must submit to the Judicial Council any changes to this plan by March 1 of every following year. If requested by a superior court, Judicial Council staff must review the court's personnel plan and provide the court with technical assistance in preparing the plan.

(Subd (e) amended effective January 1, 2016; previously amended effective January 1, 2007.)

Rule 10.670 amended effective January 1, 2016; adopted as rule 2520 effective July 1, 1998; previously renumbered as rule 6.650 effective January 1, 1999; previously amended and renumbered as rule 10.670 effective January 1, 2007.

Chapter 3
Subordinate Judicial Officers

Rule 10.700. Role of subordinate judicial officers
Rule 10.701. Qualifications and education of subordinate judicial officers

Rule 10.702. Subordinate judicial officers: practice of law
Rule 10.703. Subordinate judicial officers: complaints and notice requirements

Rule 10.700. Role of subordinate judicial officers

(a) Application

This rule applies to all subordinate judicial officers except those acting as child support commissioners under Family Code section 4251.

(b) Role of subordinate judicial officers

The primary role of subordinate judicial officers is to perform subordinate judicial duties. However, a presiding judge may assign a subordinate judicial officer to sit as a temporary judge where lawful, if the presiding judge determines that, because of a shortage of judges, it is necessary for the effective administration of justice.

Rule 10.700 renumbered effective January 1, 2007; adopted as rule 6.609 effective July 1, 2002.

Rule 10.701. Qualifications and education of subordinate judicial officers

(a) Definition

For purposes of this rule, "subordinate judicial officer" means a person appointed by a court to perform subordinate judicial duties as authorized by article VI, section 22 of the California Constitution, including a commissioner, a referee, and a hearing officer.

(Subd (a) amended effective January 1, 2007.)

(b) Qualifications

Except as provided in (d), a person is ineligible to be a subordinate judicial officer unless the person is a member of the State Bar and:

(1) Has been admitted to practice law in California for at least 10 years or, on a finding of good cause by the presiding judge, for at least 5 years; or

(2) Is serving as a subordinate judicial officer in a trial court as of January 1, 2003.

(Subd (b) amended effective January 1, 2007.)

(c) Education

A subordinate judicial officer must comply with the education requirements of any position to which he or she is assigned, even if it is not his or her principal assignment. Such requirements include the following, as applicable: rules 5.30, 5.340, and 10.462 of the California Rules of Court, and Welfare and Institutions Code section 304.7.

(Subd (c) amended effective January 1, 2017; previously amended effective January 1, 2007.)

(d) Juvenile referees and hearing officers

A person appointed as a juvenile referee or as a hearing officer under Welfare and Institutions Code sections 255 or 5256.1 must meet the qualification requirements established by those sections. Such a person is ineligible to exercise the powers and perform the duties of another type of subordinate judicial officer unless he or she meets the qualifications established in (b).

(Subd (d) amended effective July 1, 2008; previously amended effective January 1, 2007.)

Rule 10.701 amended effective January 1, 2017; adopted as rule 6.660 effective January 1, 2003; previously amended and renumbered effective January 1, 2007; previously amended effective July 1, 2008.

Rule 10.702. Subordinate judicial officers: practice of law

A subordinate judicial officer may practice law only to the extent permitted by the Code of Judicial Ethics.

Rule 10.702 renumbered effective January 1, 2007; adopted as rule 6.665 effective January 1, 2003.

Rule 10.703. Subordinate judicial officers: complaints and notice requirements

(a) Intent

The procedures in this rule for processing complaints against subordinate judicial officers do not:

(1) Create a contract of employment;

(2) Change the existing employee-employer relationship between the subordinate judicial officer and the court;

(3) Change the status of a subordinate judicial officer from an employee terminable at will to an employee terminable only for cause; or

(4) Restrict the discretion of the presiding judge in taking appropriate corrective action.

(Subd (a) amended effective January 1, 2016; previously amended effective January 1, 2007.)

(b) Definitions

Unless the context requires otherwise, the following definitions apply to this rule:

(1) "Subordinate judicial officer" means an attorney employed by a court to serve as a commissioner, referee, or hearing officer, whether the attorney is acting as a commissioner, referee, hearing officer, or temporary judge. The term does not include any other attorney acting as a temporary judge.

(2) "Presiding judge" includes the person or group the presiding judge designates to perform any duty required by this rule to be performed by a presiding judge.

(3) "Commission" means the Commission on Judicial Performance. The commission exercises discretionary jurisdiction over the discipline of subordinate judicial officers under article VI, section 18.1 of the California Constitution.

(4) "Written reprimand" means written disciplinary action that is warranted either because of the seriousness of the misconduct or because previous corrective action has been ineffective.

(Subd (b) amended effective January 1, 2016.)

(c) Application

(1) A court that employs a subordinate judicial officer must use the procedures in this rule for processing complaints against the subordinate judicial officer if the complaint alleges conduct that if alleged against a judge would be within the jurisdiction of the commission under article VI, section 18 of the California Constitution.

(2) If a complaint against a subordinate judicial officer as described in (f) does not allege conduct that would be within the jurisdiction of the commission, the local procedures adopted under rule 10.603(c)(4)(C) apply. The local process may include any procedures from this rule for the court's adjudication of the complaint other than the provisions for referring the matter to the commission under (g) or giving notice of commission review under (k)(2)(B).

(3) A court may adopt additional policies and procedures for the adjudication of complaints against subordinate judicial officers not inconsistent with this rule.

(Subd (c) amended effective January 1, 2016; previously amended effective July 1, 2002, and January 1, 2007.)

(d) Promptness required

The presiding judge must ensure that the court processes each complaint promptly. To the extent reasonably possible, the court must complete action on each complaint within 90 days after the complaint is submitted.

(Subd (d) amended effective January 1, 2007.)

(e) Confidentiality

(1) All proceedings by a presiding judge under this rule must be conducted in a manner that is as confidential as is reasonably possible consistent with the need to conduct a thorough and complete investigation and the need for proper administration of the court.

(2) This rule does not prohibit access by the commission to any information relevant to the investigation of a complaint against a subordinate judicial officer.

(Subd (e) amended effective January 1, 2007.)

(f) Written complaints to presiding judge

(1) A complaint about the conduct of a subordinate judicial officer must be in writing and must be submitted to the presiding judge.

(2) Persons who are unable to file a written complaint because of a disability may present an oral complaint, which the presiding judge must commit to writing.

(3) The presiding judge has discretion to investigate complaints that are anonymous.

(4) The presiding judge must give written notice of receipt of the complaint to the complainant, if known.

(Subd (f) amended effective January 1, 2016; previously amended effective January 1, 2007.)

(g) Initial review of the complaint

(1) The presiding judge must review each complaint and determine if the complaint:

(A) May be closed after initial review;

(B) Requires investigation by the presiding judge; or

(C) Should be referred to the commission or to the presiding judge of another court for investigation or for investigation and adjudication.

(2) A presiding judge may request that the commission investigate and adjudicate the complaint if a local conflict of interest or disqualification prevents the court from acting on the complaint.

(3) In exceptional circumstances, a presiding judge may request the commission or the presiding judge of another court to investigate a complaint on behalf of the court and provide the results of the investigation to the court for adjudication.

(4) The court must maintain a file on every complaint received, containing the following:

(A) The complaint;

(B) The response of the subordinate judicial officer, if any;

(C) All evidence and reports produced by the investigation of the complaint, if any; and

(D) The final action taken on the complaint.

(Subd (g) amended effective January 1, 2016; previously amended effective January 1, 2007.)

(h) Closing a complaint after initial review

(1) After an initial review, the presiding judge may close without further action any complaint that:

(A) Relates to the permissible exercise of judicial or administrative discretion by the subordinate judicial officer; or

(B) Does not allege conduct that if alleged against a judge would be within the jurisdiction of the commission under article VI, section 18 of the California Constitution.

(2) If the presiding judge decides to close the complaint under (h)(1), the presiding judge must notify the complainant in writing of the decision to close the complaint. The notice must include the information required under (k).

(3) The presiding judge may, in his or her discretion, advise the subordinate judicial officer in writing of the decision to close the complaint.

(Subd (h) amended effective January 1, 2016; previously amended effective January 1, 2007.)

(i) Complaints requiring investigation

(1) If after an initial review of the complaint the presiding judge finds a basis for further inquiry, the presiding judge must conduct an investigation appropriate to the nature of the complaint.

(2) The investigation may include interviews of witnesses and a review of court records.

(3) The presiding judge may give the subordinate judicial officer a copy of the complaint or a summary of its allegations and allow him or her an opportunity to respond to the allegations during the investigation. The presiding judge must give the subordinate judicial officer a copy of the complaint or a summary of its allegations and allow the subordinate judicial officer an opportunity to respond to the allegations before the presiding judge decides to take any disciplinary action against the subordinate judicial officer.

(4) After completing the investigation, the presiding judge must, in his or her discretion:

(A) Close action on the complaint if the presiding judge finds the complaint lacks merit; or

(B) Impose discipline; or

(C) Take other appropriate corrective action, which may include, but is not limited to, oral counseling, oral reprimand, or warning of the subordinate judicial officer.

(5) If the presiding judge closes action on the complaint under (i)(4)(A) and the presiding judge is aware that the subordinate judicial officer knows of the complaint, the presiding judge must give the subordinate judicial officer written notice of the final action taken on the complaint.

(6) If the presiding judge decides to impose discipline or take other appropriate corrective action under (i)(4)(B) or (C), within 10 days after the completion of the investigation or as soon thereafter as is reasonably possible, the presiding judge must give the subordinate judicial officer the following in writing:

(A) Notice of the intended final action on the complaint; and

(B) The facts and other information forming the basis for the proposed action and the source of the facts and information.

(7) The notice of the intended final action on the complaint in (i)(6)(A) must include the following advice:

(A) The subordinate judicial officer may request an opportunity to respond to the intended final action within 10 days after service of the notice; and

(B) If the subordinate judicial officer does not request an opportunity to respond within 10 days after service of the notice, the proposed action will become final.

(8) If the subordinate judicial officer requests an opportunity to respond, the presiding judge must allow the subordinate judicial officer an opportunity to respond to the notice of the intended final action, either orally or in writing as specified by the presiding judge, in accordance with local rules.

(9) Within 10 days after the subordinate judicial officer has responded, the presiding judge must give the subordinate judicial officer written notice of the final action taken on the complaint.

(10) If the subordinate judicial officer does not request an opportunity to respond, the presiding judge must promptly give written notice of the final action to the complainant. The notice must include the information required under (k).

(Subd (i) amended effective January 1, 2016; previously amended effective January 1, 2006, and January 1, 2007.)

(j) Notice to the Commission on Judicial Performance

(1) If a court disciplines a subordinate judicial officer by written reprimand, suspension, or termination for conduct that, if alleged against a judge, would be within the jurisdiction of the commission under article VI, section 18 of the California Constitution, the presiding judge must promptly forward to the commission a copy of the portions of the court file that reasonably reflect the basis of the action taken by the court, including the complaint or allegations of misconduct and the subordinate judicial officer's response. This provision is applicable even when the disciplinary action does not result from a written complaint.

(2) If a subordinate judicial officer resigns (A) while an investigation under (i) is pending concerning conduct that, if alleged against a judge, would be within the jurisdiction of the commission under article VI, section 18 of the California Constitution, or (B) under circumstances that would lead a reasonable person to conclude that the resignation was due, at least in part, to a complaint or allegation of misconduct that, if alleged against a judge, would be within the jurisdiction of the commission under article VI, section 18 of the California Constitution, the presiding judge must, within 15 days of the resignation or as soon thereafter as is reasonably possible, forward to the commission the entire court file on any pending complaint about or allegation of misconduct committed by the subordinate judicial officer.

(3) On request by the commission, the presiding judge must forward to the commission any requested information regarding a complaint about or allegation of misconduct committed by a subordinate judicial officer.

(Subd (j) repealed, relettered and amended effective January 1, 2016; adopted as subd (k); previously amended effective January 1, 2007, and July 1, 2010.)

(k) Notice of final court action

(1) When the court has completed its action on a complaint, the presiding judge must promptly notify the complainant, if known, of the final court action.

(2) The notice to the complainant of the final court action must:

(A) Provide a general description of the action taken by the court consistent with any law limiting the disclosure of confidential employee information; and

(B) Include the following statement:

If you are dissatisfied with the court's action on your complaint, you have the right to request the Commission on Judicial Performance to review this matter under its discretionary jurisdiction to oversee the discipline of subordinate judicial officers. No further action will be taken on your complaint unless the commission receives your written request within 30 days after the date this notice was mailed. The commission's address is:

Commission on Judicial Performance
455 Golden Gate Avenue, Suite 14400
San Francisco, California 94102-3660

(Subd (k) relettered and amended effective January 1, 2016; adopted as subd (l); previously amended effective April 29, 1999, and January 1, 2007.)

Rule 10.703 amended effective January 1, 2016; adopted as rule 6.655 effective November 20, 1998; previously amended and renumbered effective January 1, 2007; previously amended effective April 29, 1999, July 1, 2002, January 1, 2006, and July 1, 2010.

Chapter 4
Referees
[Reserved]

Chapter 5
Temporary Judges

Rule 10.740. Responsibilities of the trial courts for temporary judge programs

Rule 10.741. Duties and authority of the presiding judge
Rule 10.742. Use of attorneys as court-appointed temporary judges
Rule 10.743. Administrator of temporary judges program
Rule 10.744. Application procedures to serve as a court-appointed temporary judge
Rule 10.745. Performance
Rule 10.746. Complaints

Rule 10.740. Responsibilities of the trial courts for temporary judge programs

Each trial court that uses temporary judges must develop, institute, and operate—by itself or in collaboration with another court or courts—a program to recruit, select, train, and evaluate attorneys qualified to serve as temporary judges.

Rule 10.740 amended and renumbered effective January 1, 2007; adopted as rule 6.740 effective July 1, 2006.

Rule 10.741. Duties and authority of the presiding judge

(a) General duties

The presiding judge is responsible for the recruitment, selection, training, appointment, supervision, assignment, performance, and evaluation of court-appointed temporary judges. In carrying out these responsibilities, the presiding judge is assisted by the Temporary Judge Administrator as provided in rule 10.743.

(Subd (a) amended effective January 1, 2007.)

(b) Publicizing the opportunity to serve as a temporary judge

(1) Except for those courts that have nine or fewer authorized judge positions or use only research attorneys as temporary judges, each trial court that uses court-appointed temporary judges must publicize the opportunity to serve as a temporary judge whenever the court seeks to add attorneys to its pool of temporary judges or within a reasonable time before conducting its mandatory training for temporary judges but, in any case, no less than once every three years.

(2) Courts must publicize this opportunity in a manner that maximizes the potential for a diverse applicant pool, which includes publicizing the opportunity to legal communities and organizations, including all local bar associations, in their geographical area. This publicity should encourage and must provide an equal opportunity for all eligible individuals to seek positions as court-appointed temporary judges and not exclude individuals based on their gender, race, ethnicity, disability, religion, sexual orientation, age, or other protected class.

(Subd (b) adopted effective July 1, 2012.)

(c) Nondiscrimination in application and selection procedure

Each trial court that uses court-appointed temporary judges must conduct an application and selection procedure for temporary judges that ensures the most qualified applicants for appointment are selected and must not reject applicants who otherwise meet the requirements for appointment based on their gender, race, ethnicity, disability, religion, sexual orientation, age, or other protected class. Among the qualifications to be considered in the selection procedure are the applicant's exposure to and experience with diverse populations and issues related to those populations.

(Subd (c) adopted effective July 1, 2012.)

(d) Authority to remove or discontinue

The presiding judge has the discretion to remove a court-appointed temporary judge or to discontinue using an attorney as a court-appointed temporary judge at any time.

(Subd (d) relettered effective July 1, 2012; adopted as subd (b) effective July 1, 2006.)

Rule 10.741 amended effective July 1, 2012; adopted as rule 6.741 effective July 1, 2006; previously amended and renumbered effective January 1, 2007.

Advisory Committee Comment

Subdivision (b). This subdivision is intended to offer all attorneys who satisfy the requirements for appointment under rule 2.812 the opportunity to serve as temporary judges and to expand the size and diversity of the pool of eligible candidates. Pursuant to the rule, courts that do not use temporary judges, that have nine or fewer authorized and funded judge positions, or that only use their research attorneys as temporary judges are exempt from the requirement to publicize the opportunity to serve as a temporary judge. Courts that use temporary judges may publicize the opportunity in a manner they determine to be most effective, given their individual circumstances. In attempting to broaden the diversity of the temporary judge applicant pool, courts also have the flexibility to widen the geographical areas in which they publicize the opportunity. Thus, courts are not limited to publicizing their temporary judge program through the local or state bar associations. However, they must include *all* local bar associations when they do so. Further, the method of publication is purposefully left to the court's discretion.

No-cost methods exist, such as email, use of the court's public website, and oral announcements at local bar association or legal organization events. Publicizing this opportunity no less than once every three years should increase the potential for greater diversity among the temporary judges who serve the courts.

Subdivision (c). This subdivision emphasizes that the selection and appointment process must be devoid of discrimination. These provisions are intended to discourage favoritism in the appointment process and permit the courts to consider, as an additional qualification, an attorney's exposure to and experience with the diverse populations and issues unique to that population in the county where they are seeking appointment. "Exposure to and experience with diverse populations" includes work, social interaction, educational experiences, or community involvement with individuals or groups from diverse communities that may appear in court.

Rule 10.742. Use of attorneys as court-appointed temporary judges

(a) Responsibility of the presiding judge

The presiding judge of the trial court is responsible for determining whether that court needs to use attorneys as temporary judges and, if so, the specific purposes for which attorneys are to be appointed as temporary judges.

(b) Conditions for the use of court-appointed temporary judges

The presiding judge may appoint an attorney as a court-appointed temporary judge only if all the following circumstances apply:

(1) The appointment of an attorney to serve as a temporary judge is necessary to fill a judicial need in that court;

(2) The attorney serving as a temporary judge has been approved by the court where the attorney will serve under rule 2.810 et seq.;

(3) The appointment of the attorney as a temporary judge does not result in any conflict of interest; and

(4) There is no appearance of impropriety resulting from the appointment of the attorney to serve as a temporary judge.

(Subd (b) amended effective January 1, 2007.)

Rule 10.742 amended effective January 1, 2017; adopted as rule 6.742 effective July 1, 2006; previously amended and renumbered as rule 10.742 effective January 1, 2007; previously amended effective January 1, 2016.

Advisory Committee Comment

Subdivisions (a)–(b). These subdivisions provide that the presiding judge in each court is responsible for determining whether court-appointed temporary judges need to be used in that court, and these subdivisions furnish the criteria for determining when their use is proper. Under (b)(1), the use and appointment of court-appointed temporary judges must be based on judicial needs. Under (b)(3), an attorney serving as a temporary judge would have a conflict of interest if the disqualifying factors in the Code of Judicial Ethics exist. Under (b)(4), the test for the appearance of impropriety is whether a person aware of the facts might entertain a doubt that the judge would be able to act with integrity, impartiality, and competence. In addition to the disqualifying factors listed in the Code of Judicial Ethics, an appearance of impropriety would be generated if any of the limitations in family law, unlawful detainer, and other cases identified in the Code of Judicial Ethics are present.

Rule 10.743. Administrator of temporary judges program

(a) Administrator

The presiding judge who appoints attorneys as temporary judges must designate a clerk, executive officer, or other court employee knowledgeable about temporary judges to serve as the Temporary Judge Administrator in that court.

(b) Duties of administrator

Under the supervision of the presiding judge, the Temporary Judge Administrator is responsible for the management of the temporary judges program in the court. The administrator's duties include:

(1) Receiving and processing applications from attorneys to serve as temporary judges with the court;

(2) Verifying the information on the applications;

(3) Assisting the presiding judge in the recruitment and selection of attorneys to serve as temporary judges, as provided in rule 10.741;

(4) Administering the court's program for the education and training of temporary judges;

(5) Maintaining records of attendance and completion of required courses by all attorneys serving as temporary judges in the court;

(6) Determining that attorneys have satisfied all the conditions required to be appointed as a temporary judge in that court, including continuing education requirements;

(7) Maintaining a list of attorneys currently appointed and qualified to serve as temporary judges in the court;

(8) Managing support services for temporary judges, such as providing mentoring programs and reference materials;

(9) Receiving and processing complaints and other information concerning the performance of attorneys serving as temporary judges;

(10) Assisting the presiding judge in identifying judicial needs that require the use of temporary judges and in addressing these needs; and

(11) Maintaining records, gathering statistics, and preparing and transmitting quarterly reports on the court's use of temporary judges as required under rule 10.742(c).

(Subd (b) amended effective July 1, 2012; previously amended effective January 1, 2007.)

Rule 10.743 amended effective July 1, 2012; adopted as rule 6.743 effective July 1, 2006; previously amended and renumbered effective January 1, 2007.

Advisory Committee Comment

The goal of this rule is to ensure the effective and efficient administration of the courts' use of temporary judges. The rule should be applied flexibly. In courts with large temporary judge programs, the court may want to designate a full-time administrator, and some of the administrator's duties may be delegated to other individuals. On the other hand, in courts that use only a few temporary judges, the Temporary Judge Administrator position may consume only part of the administrator's time and be combined with other duties. Also, courts that use only a small number of temporary judges may work with other courts, or may cooperate on a regional basis, to perform the functions and duties prescribed under this rule.

Rule 10.744. Application procedures to serve as a court-appointed temporary judge

(a) Application

Every attorney who applies for appointment as a temporary judge in a trial court must complete an application to serve as a temporary judge.

(b) Information required

The attorney must provide all applicable information requested on the application. This information must include:

(1) The attorney's name and contact information as required by the court;

(2) The attorney's State Bar number;

(3) The date of the attorney's admission to the State Bar of California and the dates of his or her admissions to practice in any other state;

(4) Length of membership in the State Bar of California and of practice in any other state;

(5) Whether the attorney is in good standing with the State Bar of California and in good standing as an attorney in any other state where the attorney has been admitted to practice;

(6) Whether the attorney has ever been disciplined, or is the subject of a pending disciplinary proceeding, by the State Bar of California or by any other state bar association or court of record; and, if so, an explanation of the circumstances;

(7) The areas of specialization for which the attorney has been certified in California or in any other state;

(8) The attorney's major area or areas of practice;

(9) Whether the attorney holds himself or herself out publicly as representing exclusively one side in any of the areas of litigation in which the attorney practices;

(10) Whether the attorney represents one side in more than 90 percent of all cases in any areas of litigation in which the attorney specializes or concentrates his or her practice;

(11) The location or locations in which the attorney principally practices;

(12) How often the attorney appears in the court where he or she is applying to serve as a temporary judge;

(13) A list of the attorney's previous service as a temporary judge in the court where the attorney is applying and in any other court;

(14) Whether the attorney has ever been removed as a temporary judge by any court;

(15) The types of cases on which the attorney is willing to serve as a temporary judge;

(16) Whether the attorney has ever been convicted of a felony or misdemeanor, or is a defendant in any pending felony or misdemeanor proceeding, and, if so, a statement about the conviction or pending proceeding;

(17) Whether the attorney has been a party in any legal proceeding and, if so, a brief description of the proceedings;

(18) Information concerning any circumstances or conditions that would adversely affect or limit the attorney's ability to serve as a temporary judge;

(19) Any facts concerning the attorney's background that may reflect positively or negatively on the attorney or that should be disclosed to the court; and

(20) Such additional information as the court may require.

(c) Continuing duty to disclose

An attorney appointed by a court to serve as a temporary judge has a continuing duty to disclose to the court any material changes in facts or circumstances that affect his or her ability to serve as a temporary judge. The attorney must disclose the changes to the court before the next time the attorney is assigned to serve as a temporary judge.

(d) Review of application

The presiding judge, assisted by the Temporary Judge Administrator, must review all applications and determine whether each applicant is qualified, has satisfied the requirements of rule 2.812, and should be appointed as a temporary judge. The presiding judge may delegate this task to another judge or a committee of judges, assisted by the Temporary Judge Administrator. In appointing attorneys as temporary judges, the presiding judge may go beyond the minimum qualifications and standards required under the California Rules of Court. The decision whether to appoint, use, retrain, remove, or discontinue using any particular attorney as a temporary judge is at the sole discretion of the presiding judge.

(Subd (d) amended effective January 1, 2007.)

Rule 10.744 amended and renumbered effective January 1, 2007; adopted as rule 6.744 effective July 1, 2006.

Rule 10.745. Performance

(a) Review required

The court must review on a regular basis the performance of temporary judges appointed by that court.

(b) Monitoring performance

In monitoring and reviewing the performance of court-appointed temporary judges, the court may use direct observation, audiotaping of hearings, reports by court staff, comments from mentor judges, and such other means as may be helpful.

Rule 10.745 renumbered effective January 1, 2007; adopted as rule 6.745 effective July 1, 2006.

Rule 10.746. Complaints

Each court must have procedures for receiving, investigating, and resolving complaints against court-appointed temporary judges.

Rule 10.746 renumbered effective January 1, 2007; adopted as rule 6.746 effective July 1, 2006.

Chapter 6
Court Interpreters

Rule 10.761. Regional Court Interpreter Employment Relations Committees
Rule 10.762. Cross-assignments for court interpreter employees

Rule 10.761. Regional Court Interpreter Employment Relations Committees

(a) Creation

Government Code sections 71807–71809 establish four Regional Court Interpreter Employment Relations Committees. Each committee has the authority, for spoken language court interpreters within its region as defined under Government Code section 71807(a), to:

(1) Set the terms and conditions of employment for court interpreters, subject to meet and confer in good faith, as authorized by Government Code section 71808;

(2) Adopt reasonable rules and regulations for the administration of employer-employee relations with recognized employee organizations, as authorized by Government Code section 71823(a); and

(3) Act as the representative of the superior courts within the region in bargaining with a recognized employee organization as authorized by Government Code section 71809.

(b) Membership

(1) Each Regional Court Interpreter Employment Committee consists of one representative from each superior court that has at least one interpreter employed as a court interpreter as defined by Government Code section 71806 and not excluded by section 71828(d).

(2) The following regions are established by Government Code section 71807:

(A) Region 1: Los Angeles, Santa Barbara, and San Luis Obispo Counties.

(B) Region 2: Counties of the First and Sixth Appellate Districts, except Solano County.

(C) Region 3: Counties of the Third and Fifth Appellate Districts.
(D) Region 4: Counties of the Fourth Appellate District.

(3) The court executive officer of each superior court may appoint the court's representative, under rule 10.610, which authorizes the court executive officer, acting under the direction of the presiding judge, to oversee the management and administration of the nonjudicial operations of the court.

(4) Each Regional Court Interpreter Employment Relations Committee may appoint a chief negotiator to bargain with recognized employee organizations. The chief negotiator may be Judicial Council staff.

(5) Any superior court that is not entitled to appoint a representative under this rule, including the superior courts of Ventura and Solano Counties, may appoint an advisory member to the committee for its region.

(Subd (b) amended effective January 1, 2016; previously amended effective January 1, 2006, and January 1, 2007.)

(c) Rules of procedure

Each Regional Court Interpreter Employment Relations Committee may adopt its own rules of procedure, including the procedure for selecting its chair, advisory members, and chief negotiator.

(d) Voting

(1) Each representative of a superior court has a number of votes equal to the number of court interpreter employees in that trial court as defined by Government Code section 71806 and not excluded by section 71828(d).

(2) On July 1, 2004, and annually thereafter each Regional Court Interpreter Employment Relations Committee must recalculate the number of votes of each representative of a superior court to equal the number of court interpreter employees in that court.

(Subd (d) amended effective January 1, 2006.)

(e) Judicial Council staff

Judicial Council staff will assist each Regional Court Interpreter Employment Relations Committee in performing its functions.

(Subd (e) amended effective January 1, 2016.)

Rule 10.761 amended effective January 1, 2016; adopted as rule 6.661 effective March 1, 2003; previously amended effective January 1, 2006; previously amended and renumbered as rule 10.761 effective January 1, 2007.

Rule 10.762. Cross-assignments for court interpreter employees

(a) Purpose

This rule implements a process for cross-assignment of a court interpreter employed by a superior court under Government Code section 71810(b).

(Subd (a) amended effective January 1, 2007.)

(b) Definitions

As used in this rule:

(1) "Home court" means the superior court in which the court interpreter is an employee. An employee's home court includes all locations of a superior court within a county.

(2) "Away court" means the superior court to which the court interpreter is temporarily cross-assigned.

(3) "Cross-assignment" means any assignment to perform spoken language interpretation for a superior court other than the interpreter's home court.

(4) "Regional court interpreter coordinator" means a Judicial Council employee whose duty it is to locate, assign, and schedule available court interpreter employees for courts within and across regions, which are described under Government Code section 71807(a).

(5) "Local court interpreter coordinator" means an employee of a superior court whose duty it is to locate, assign, and schedule available court interpreter employees for his or her court.

(Subd (b) amended effective January 1, 2016; previously amended effective January 1, 2007.)

(c) Procedure for cross-assignments

(1) Under Government Code section 71804.5(b) a court interpreter employed by a superior court is not permitted to be an employee of more than one superior court. A court interpreter employed by a superior court may not contract with another court, but may accept appointments to provide services to more than one court through cross-assignments.

(2) A superior court may attempt to fill an interpreting assignment with the employee of another court before hiring an independent contract court interpreter.

(3) If a superior court wants to fill an interpreting assignment with the employee of another court, the court must notify the regional court interpreter coordinator to locate an employee of a court within or across regions.

(4) Each local court interpreter coordinator must provide the schedule of each court interpreter employee available for cross-assignment to the regional court interpreter coordinator.

(5) A superior court may adopt additional internal procedures for cross-assigning a court interpreter employee that are not inconsistent with Government Code section 71810 and this rule.

(6) A Regional Court Interpreter Employment Relations Committee may approve alternative procedures for cross-assigning a court interpreter employee that permit the interpreter to directly arrange cross-assignments with an "away" court, provided that the procedures require notice to the regional coordinator.

(Subd (c) amended effective January 1, 2007.)

(d) Payment for cross-assignments

The home court must issue payment to the court interpreter for all cross-assignments, including per diem compensation and mileage reimbursement. Judicial Council staff will administer funding to the home court for payments associated with cross-assignments.

(Subd (d) amended effective January 1, 2016; previously amended effective January 1, 2007.)

(e) Duties of a court interpreter on cross-assignment

A court interpreter who accepts a cross-assignment is responsible for following the personnel rules of the home court while performing services for the away court.

(f) Superior courts of Ventura and Solano Counties

The superior courts of Ventura and Solano Counties may participate in the procedure for cross-assignments as follows:

(1) The Superior Court of Ventura County may accept or provide interpreters on cross-assignment under the procedures established in Region 1, as defined by Government Code section 71807.

(2) The Superior Court of Solano County may accept or provide interpreters on cross-assignment under the procedures established in Region 2, as defined by Government Code section 71807.

(Subd (f) amended effective January 1, 2007.)

Rule 10.762 amended effective January 1, 2016; adopted as rule 6.662 effective March 1, 2003; previously amended and renumbered as rule 10.672 effective January 1, 2007.

Chapter 7
Qualifications of Court Investigators, Probate Attorneys, and Probate Examiners

Chapter 7 adopted effective January 1, 2008.

Rule 10.776. Definitions
Rule 10.777. Qualifications of court investigators, probate attorneys, and probate examiners

Rule 10.776. Definitions

As used in the rules in this chapter, the following terms have the meanings stated below:

(1) A "court investigator" is a person described in Probate Code section 1454(a) employed by or under contract with a court to provide the investigative services for the court required or authorized by law in guardianships, conservatorships, and other protective proceedings under division 4 of the Probate Code;

(2) A "probate examiner" is a person employed by a court to review filings in probate proceedings in order to assist the court and the parties to get the filed matters ready for consideration by the court in accordance with the requirements of the Probate Code, title 7 of the California Rules of Court, and the court's local rules;

(3) A "probate attorney" is an active member of the State Bar of California who is employed by a court to perform the functions of a probate examiner and also to provide legal analysis, recommendations, advice, and other services to the court pertaining to probate proceedings;

(4) "Probate proceedings" are decedents' estates, guardianships and conservatorships under division 4 of the Probate Code, trust proceedings under division 9 of the Probate Code, and other matters governed by provisions of that code and the rules in title 7 of the California Rules of Court;

(5) An "accredited educational institution" is a college or university, including a community or junior college, accredited by a regional

accrediting organization recognized by the Council for Higher Education Accreditation.

Rule 10.776 amended effective January 1, 2016; adopted effective January 1, 2008.

Rule 10.777. Qualifications of court investigators, probate attorneys, and probate examiners

(a) Qualifications of court investigators

Except as otherwise provided in this rule, a person who begins employment with a court or enters into a contract to perform services with a court as a court investigator on or after January 1, 2008, must:

(1) Have a bachelor of arts or bachelor of science degree in a science, a social science, a behavioral science, liberal arts, or nursing from an accredited educational institution; and

(2) Have a minimum of two years' employment experience performing casework or investigations in a legal, financial, law enforcement, or social services setting.

(Subd (a) adopted effective January 1, 2008.)

(b) Qualifications of probate attorneys

Except as otherwise provided in this rule, a person who begins employment with a court as a probate attorney on or after January 1, 2008, must:

(1) Be an active member of the State Bar of California for:

(A) A minimum of five years; or

(B) A minimum of two years, plus a minimum of five years' current or former active membership in the equivalent organization of another state or eligibility to practice in the highest court of another state or in a court of the United States; and

(2) Have a minimum of two years' total experience, before or after admission as an active member of the State Bar of California, in one or more of the following positions:

(A) Court-employed staff attorney;

(B) Intern, court probate department (minimum six-month period);

(C) Court-employed probate examiner or court-employed or court-contracted court investigator;

(D) Attorney in a probate-related public or private legal practice;

(E) Deputy public guardian or conservator;

(F) Child protective services or adult protective services worker or juvenile probation officer; or

(G) Private professional fiduciary appointed by a court or employee of a private professional fiduciary or bank or trust company appointed by a court, with significant fiduciary responsibilities, including responsibility for court accountings.

(Subd (b) adopted effective January 1, 2008.)

(c) Qualifications of probate examiners

Except as otherwise provided in this rule, a person who begins employment with a court as a probate examiner on or after January 1, 2008, must have:

(1) A bachelor of arts or bachelor of science degree from an accredited educational institution and a minimum of two years' employment experience with one or more of the following employers:

(A) A court;

(B) A public or private law office; or

(C) A public administrator, public guardian, public conservator, or private professional fiduciary; or

(2) A paralegal certificate or an Associate of Arts degree from an accredited educational institution and a minimum of a total of four years' employment experience with one or more of the employers listed in (1); or

(3) A juris doctor degree from an educational institution approved by the American Bar Association or accredited by the Committee of Bar Examiners of the State Bar of California and a minimum of six months' employment experience with an employer listed in (1).

(Subd (c) adopted effective January 1, 2008.)

(d) Additional court-imposed qualifications and requirements

The qualifications in (a), (b), and (c) are minimums. A court may establish higher qualification standards for any position covered by this rule and may require applicants to comply with its customary hiring or personal-service contracting practices, including written applications, personal references, personal interviews, or entrance examinations.

(Subd (d) adopted effective January 1, 2008.)

(e) Exemption for smaller courts

The qualifications required under this rule may be waived by a court with eight or fewer authorized judges if it cannot find suitable qualified candidates for the positions covered by this rule or for other grounds of hardship. A court electing to waive a qualification under this subdivision must make express written findings showing the circumstances supporting the waiver and disclosing all alternatives considered, including those not selected.

(Subd (e) adopted effective January 1, 2008.)

(f) Record keeping and reporting

The Judicial Council may require courts to report on the qualifications of the court investigators, probate attorneys, or probate examiners hired or under contract under this rule, and on waivers made under (e), as necessary to ensure compliance with Probate Code section 1456.

(Subd (f) amended effective January 1, 2016; adopted effective January 1, 2008.)

Rule 10.777 amended effective January 1, 2016; adopted effective January 1, 2008.

Chapter 8
Alternative Dispute Resolution Programs

Chapter 8 renumbered effective January 1, 2008; adopted as Chapter 7 effective January 1, 2007.

Rule 10.780. Administration of alternative dispute resolution (ADR) programs
Rule 10.781. Court-related ADR neutrals
Rule 10.782. ADR program information
Rule 10.783. ADR program administration

Rule 10.780. Administration of alternative dispute resolution (ADR) programs

The rules in this chapter concern alternative dispute resolution (ADR) programs administered by the trial courts. General provisions concerning ADR are located in title 3, division 8.

Rule 10.780 amended effective January 1, 2008; adopted effective January 1, 2007.

Rule 10.781. Court-related ADR neutrals

(a) Qualifications of mediators for general civil cases

Each superior court that makes a list of mediators available to litigants in general civil cases or that recommends, selects, appoints, or compensates mediators to mediate any general civil case pending in the court must establish minimum qualifications for the mediators eligible to be included on the court's list or to be recommended, selected, appointed, or compensated by the court. A court that approves the parties' agreement to use a mediator who is selected by the parties and who is not on the court's list of mediators or that memorializes the parties' agreement in a court order has not thereby recommended, selected, or appointed that mediator within the meaning of this rule. In establishing these qualifications, courts are encouraged to consider the Model Qualification Standards for Mediators in Court-Connected Mediation Programs for General Civil Cases issued by the Judicial Council staff.

(Subd (a) amended effective January 1, 2016; adopted effective January 1, 2011.)

(b) Lists of neutrals

If a court makes available to litigants a list of ADR neutrals, the list must contain, at a minimum, the following information concerning each neutral listed:

(1) The types of ADR services available from the neutral;

(2) The neutral's résumé, including his or her general education and ADR training and experience; and

(3) The fees charged by the neutral for each type of service.

(Subd (b) amended and relettered effective January 1, 2011; adopted as subd (a); amended effective January 1, 2007.)

(c) Requirements to be on lists

In order to be included on a court list of ADR neutrals, an ADR neutral must sign a statement or certificate agreeing to:

(1) Comply with all applicable ethics requirements and rules of court; and

(2) Serve as an ADR neutral on a pro bono or modest-means basis in at least one case per year, not to exceed eight hours, if requested by the court. The court must establish the eligibility requirements for litigants to receive, and the application process for them to request, ADR services on a pro bono or modest-means basis.

(Subd (c) relettered effective January 1, 2011; adopted as subd (b); previously amended effective January 1, 2007.)

(d) Privilege to serve as a court-program neutral

Inclusion on a court list of ADR neutrals and eligibility to be recommended, appointed, or compensated by the court to serve as a neutral are privileges that are revocable and confer no vested right on the neutral.

(Subd (d) relettered effective January 1, 2011; adopted as subd (c) effective July 1, 2009.)

Rule 10.781 amended effective January 1, 2016; adopted as rule 1580.1 effective January 1, 2001; previously amended and renumbered as rule 10.781 effective January 1, 2007; previously amended effective July 1, 2009, and January 1, 2011.

Advisory Committee Comment

Subdivision (c). A court has absolute discretion to determine who may be included on a court list of ADR neutrals or is eligible to be recommended, selected, appointed, or compensated by the court to serve as a neutral (except as otherwise expressly provided by statute or rule of court).

Rule 10.782. ADR program information

(a) Report to Judicial Council

Each court must report information on its ADR programs to the Judicial Council, as requested by Judicial Council staff.

(Subd (a) amended effective January 1, 2016; previously amended effective January 1, 2007.)

(b) Parties and ADR neutrals to supply information

Subject to applicable limitations, including the confidentiality requirements in Evidence Code section 1115 et seq., courts must require parties and ADR neutrals, as appropriate, to supply pertinent information for the reports required under (a).

(Subd (b) amended effective January 1, 2007.)

Rule 10.782 amended effective January 1, 2016; adopted as rule 1580.2 effective January 1, 2001; previously amended and renumbered as rule 10.782 effective January 1, 2007.

Rule 10.783. ADR program administration

(a) ADR program administrator

The presiding judge in each trial court must designate the clerk or executive officer, or another court employee who is knowledgeable about ADR processes, to serve as ADR program administrator. The duties of the ADR program administrator must include:

(1) Developing informational material concerning the court's ADR programs;

(2) Educating attorneys and litigants about the court's ADR programs;

(3) Supervising the development and maintenance of any panels of ADR neutrals maintained by the court; and

(4) Gathering statistical and other evaluative information concerning the court's ADR programs.

(Subd (a) amended effective January 1, 2007; previously amended effective January 1, 2004.)

(b) ADR committee

(1) *Membership in courts with 18 or more authorized judges*

In each superior court that has 18 or more authorized judges, there must be an ADR committee. The members of the ADR committee must include, insofar as is practicable:

(A) The presiding judge or a judge designated by the presiding judge;

(B) One or more other judges designated by the presiding judge;

(C) The ADR program administrator;

(D) Two or more active members of the State Bar chosen by the presiding judge as representatives of those attorneys who regularly represent parties in general civil cases before the court, including an equal number of attorneys who represent plaintiffs and who represent defendants in these cases;

(E) One or more members of the court's panel of arbitrators chosen by the presiding judge; and

(F) If the court makes available to litigants a list of any ADR neutrals other than arbitrators, one or more neutrals chosen by the presiding judge from that list.

(2) *Additional members*

The ADR committee may include additional members selected by the presiding judge.

(3) *ADR committee in other courts*

Any other court may by rule establish an ADR committee as provided in (b)(1). Otherwise, the presiding judge or a judge designated by the presiding judge must perform the functions and have the powers of an ADR committee as provided in these rules.

(4) *Term of membership*

ADR committee membership is for a two-year term. The members of the ADR committee may be reappointed and may be removed by the presiding judge.

(5) *Responsibilities of ADR committee*

The ADR committee is responsible for overseeing the court's alternative dispute resolution programs for general civil cases, including those responsibilities relating to the court's judicial arbitration program specified in rule 3.813(b).

(Subd (b) amended effective January 1, 2007; previously adopted effective January 1, 2004.)

Rule 10.783 amended and renumbered effective January 1, 2007; adopted as rule 1580.3 effective January 1, 2001; previously amended effective January 1, 2004.

Chapter 9
Trial Court Budget and Fiscal Management

Chapter 9 renumbered effective January 1, 2008; adopted as Chapter 3 effective July 1, 1998; previously renumbered as Chapter 8 effective January 1, 2007.

Rule 10.800. Superior court budgeting
Rule 10.801. Superior court budget procedures
Rule 10.803. Information access disputes—writ petitions (Gov. Code, § 71675)
Rule 10.804. Superior court financial policies and procedures
Rule 10.805. Notice of change in court-county relationship
Rule 10.810. Court operations
Rule 10.811. Reimbursement of costs associated with homicide trials
Rule 10.815. Fees to be set by the court
Rule 10.820. Acceptance of credit cards by the superior courts
Rule 10.821. Acceptance of checks and other negotiable paper
Rule 10.830. Disposal of surplus court personal property

Rule 10.800. Superior court budgeting

(a) Purpose

This rule provides for local authority and accountability for development of budget requests and management of court operations within the authorized funding level. Superior courts must manage their budgets in a manner that is responsive to local needs, ensures equal access to justice, is consistent with Judicial Council policy and legislative direction, and does not exceed the total allocated budget.

(Subd (a) amended effective January 1, 2007; previously amended effective January 1, 2002.)

(b) Development of budget requests

Each superior court must prepare and submit to the Judicial Council a budget according to the schedule and procedures established by the council.

(Subd (b) amended effective January 1, 2016; previously amended effective January 1, 2002, and January 1, 2007.)

(c) Allocation of funding

(1) The funding allocation to each superior court is based on the amounts incorporated for that court in budget change proposals that have been funded through the Budget Act, except as otherwise ordered by the Judicial Council. The superior court of each county may distribute and periodically redistribute its annual allocation between programs, locations, and line items as needed, within the parameters of the *Trial Court Financial Policies and Procedures Manual* and consistent with council policy direction, to promote accessible justice and the effective, efficient, and accountable operation of the courts. The Judicial Council may make additional allocations as it deems appropriate.

(2) Each superior court is accountable for achieving the expected outcomes of the programs funded for that year. If a court is unable to do so, it must report the reasons to the Judicial Council.

(Subd (c) amended effective January 1, 2007; previously amended effective January 1, 2002.)

Rule 10.800 amended effective January 1, 2016; adopted as rule 2530 effective July 1, 1998; renumbered as rule 6.700 effective January 1, 1999; previously amended effective January 1, 2002; previously amended and renumbered as rule 10.800 effective January 1, 2007.

Rule 10.801. Superior court budget procedures

(a) Adoption of budget procedures by Judicial Council staff

Judicial Council staff must adopt superior court budget procedures to be included in the *Trial Court Financial Policies and Procedures Manual*, the annual Baseline Budget Development Package, and the annual *Budget Change Request Package*. These procedures include the following:

(1) Procedures permitting the superior courts to comment on the proposed budget procedures;

(2) Procedures for budget development, submission, and appeal;

(3) Procedures for budget implementation, including expenditure and revenue reporting;

(4) Reasonable time frames to comply with requirements or changes in the budget procedures;

(5) Procedures to ensure the reporting to the Judicial Council of relevant information on the implementation of programs funded;

(6) Procedures for providing timely management information to the Judicial Council on the baseline budget, revenues, and expenditures.

(7) An annual budget development and implementation calendar;

(8) Procedures for a superior court to follow if it projects that its budget will be exhausted before the end of the fiscal year, preventing the court from meeting its financial obligations or continuing operations; and

(9) Procedures governing the transfer of funds between individual programs and operations of expenditure.

(Subd (a) amended effective January 1, 2016; previously amended effective January 1, 2002, and January 1, 2007.)

(b) Technical assistance

Judicial Council staff, on request, provide technical assistance and ongoing training in budget development and implementation to the superior courts.

(Subd (b) amended effective January 1, 2016; previously amended effective January 1, 2002, and January 1, 2007.)

Rule 10.801 amended effective January 1, 2016; adopted as rule 2531 effective July 1, 1998; renumbered as rule 6.701 effective January 1, 1999; previously amended effective January 1, 2002; previously amended and renumbered as rule 10.801 effective January 1, 2007.

Rule 10.802. Maintenance of and public access to budget and management information [Repealed]

Rule 10.802 repealed effective January 1, 2010; adopted as rule 6.702 effective January 1, 2001; previously amended effective July 1, 2001, July 1, 2002, and January 1, 2004; previously amended and renumbered effective January 1, 2007.

Rule 10.803. Information access disputes—writ petitions (Gov. Code, § 71675)

(a) Availability

This rule applies to petitions filed under rule 10.500(j)(1) and Government Code section 71675(b).

(Subd (a) amended effective January 1, 2010; previously amended effective January 1, 2007.)

(b) Assignment of Court of Appeal justice to hear the petition

(1) The petition must state the following on the first page, below the case number, in the statement of the character of the proceeding (see rule 2.111(6)):

"Writ petition filed under rule 10.500(j)(1) and Government Code section 71675—Assignment of Court of Appeal justice required."

(2) When the petition is filed, the clerk of the court must immediately request of the Chief Justice the assignment of a hearing judge from the panel established under (e).

(3) If an assignment is made, the judge assigned to hear the petition in the superior court must be a justice from a Court of Appeal for a district other than the district for that superior court.

(Subd (b) amended effective January 1, 2010; previously amended effective January 1, 2007.)

(c) Superior court hearing

(1) The superior court must hear and decide the petition on an expedited basis and must give the petition priority over other matters to the extent permitted by law and the rules of court.

(2) The petition must be heard by a judge assigned by the Chief Justice from the panel of hearing judges established under (e).

(Subd (c) amended effective January 1, 2007.)

(d) Appeal

An appeal of the superior court decision must be heard and decided on an expedited basis in the Court of Appeal for the district in which the petition was heard and must be given priority over other matters to the extent permitted by law and rules of court. The notice of appeal must state the following on the first page, below the case number, in the statement of the character of the proceeding (see rule 2.111(6)):

"Notice of Appeal on Writ Petition filed under rule 10.500(j)(1) and Government Code section 71675—Expedited Processing Requested."

(Subd (d) amended effective January 1, 2010; previously amended effective January 1, 2007.)

(e) Panel of hearing judges

The panel of judges who may hear the petitions in the superior court must consist of Court of Appeal justices selected by the Chief Justice as follows:

(1) The panel must include at least one justice from each district of the Court of Appeal.

(2) Each justice assigned to hear a petition under (c)(2) must have received training on hearing the petitions as specified by the Chief Justice.

Rule 10.803 amended effective January 1, 2010; adopted as rule 6.710 effective October 15, 2004; previously amended and renumbered effective January 1, 2007.

Rule 10.804. Superior court financial policies and procedures

(a) Adoption

As part of its responsibility for regulating the budget and fiscal management of the trial courts, the Judicial Council adopts the *Trial Court Financial Policies and Procedures Manual*. The manual contains regulations establishing budget procedures, recordkeeping, accounting standards, and other financial guidelines for superior courts. The manual sets out a system of fundamental internal controls that will enable the trial courts to monitor their use of public funds, provide consistent and comparable financial statements, and demonstrate accountability.

(Subd (a) amended effective August 26, 2016; previously amended effective January 1, 2007, and July 1, 2015.)

(b) Amendments

(1) Before making any substantive amendments to the *Trial Court Financial Policies and Procedures Manual*, the Judicial Council must make the amendments available to the superior courts, the California Department of Finance, and the State Controller's Office for 30 days for comment.

(2) The Judicial Council delegates to the Administrative Director, under article VI, section 6 of the California Constitution and other applicable law, the authority to make technical changes and clarifications to the manual, provided the changes and clarifications are consistent with council policies.

(Subd (b) amended effective August 26, 2016; previously amended effective January 1, 2007, and July 1, 2015.)

(c) Date of adherence

Superior courts must adhere to the requirements contained in the *Trial Court Financial Policies and Procedures Manual*, except as otherwise provided in the manual. Superior courts must not be required to adhere to any substantive amendment to the manual sooner than 60 days after the amendment is adopted.

(Subd (c) amended effective August 26, 2016; previously amended January 1, 2007.)

Rule 10.804 amended effective August 26, 2016; adopted as rule 6.707 effective January 1, 2001; previously amended and renumbered effective January 1, 2007; previously amended effective July 1, 2015.

Advisory Committee Comment

Subdivision (a). Procurement and contracting policies and procedures for judicial branch entities, including superior courts, are addressed separately in the *Judicial Branch Contracting Manual*, which the Judicial Council adopted under Public Contract Code section 19206.

Subdivision (b)(2). Technical changes and clarifications include clarifying language that (1) does not change any substantive requirement imposed on courts; and (2) corrects typographical errors or citations, or makes reimbursement rate adjustments and other changes that result from changes in federal, state, or local rules, regulations or applicable law.

Rule 10.805. Notice of change in court-county relationship

If, under Government Code section 77212, the county gives notice to the superior court that the county will no longer provide a specific county service or the court gives notice to the county that the court will no longer use a specific county service, the court must, within 10 days of receiving or giving such notice, provide a copy of this notice to the Judicial Council's Finance office.

Rule 10.805 amended effective January 1, 2016; adopted as rule 6.705 effective January 1, 2000; previously amended and renumbered as rule 10.805 effective January 1, 2007.

Rule 10.810. Court operations

(a) Definition

Except as provided in subdivision (b) and subject to the requirements of subdivisions (c) and (d), "court operations" as defined in Government Code section 77003 includes the following costs:

(1) *(judicial salaries and benefits)* salaries, benefits, and public agency retirement contributions for superior and municipal court judges and for subordinate judicial officers;

(2) *(nonjudicial salaries and benefits)* salaries, benefits, and public agency retirement contributions for superior and municipal court staff whether permanent, temporary, full- or part-time, contract or per diem, including but not limited to all municipal court staff positions specifically prescribed by statute and county clerk positions directly supporting the superior courts;

(3) salaries and benefits for those sheriff, marshal, and constable employees as the court deems necessary for court operations in superior

and municipal courts and the supervisors of those sheriff, marshal, and constable employees who directly supervise the court security function;

(4) court-appointed counsel in juvenile dependency proceedings, and counsel appointed by the court to represent a minor as specified in Government Code section 77003;

(5) *(services and supplies)* operating expenses in support of judicial officers and court operations;

(6) *(collective bargaining)* collective bargaining with respect to court employees; and

(7) *(indirect costs)* a share of county general services as defined in subdivision (d), Function 11, and used by the superior and municipal courts.

(Subd (a) amended effective July 1, 1995; previously amended effective January 1, 1989, July 1, 1990, and July 1, 1991.)

(b) Exclusions

Excluded from the definition of "court operations" are the following:

(1) law library operations conducted by a trust pursuant to statute;

(2) courthouse construction and site acquisition, including space rental (for other than court records storage), alterations/remodeling, or relocating court facilities;

(3) district attorney services;

(4) probation services;

(5) indigent criminal and juvenile delinquency defense;

(6) civil and criminal grand jury expenses and operations (except for selection);

(7) pretrial release services;

(8) equipment and supplies for use by official reporters of the courts to prepare transcripts as specified by statute; and

(9) county costs as provided in subdivision (d) as unallowable.

(Subd (b) amended effective July 1, 1995; adopted effective July 1, 1988 as subd (c); previously amended effective January 1, 1989, and July 1, 1990.)

(c) Budget appropriations

Costs for court operations specified in subdivision (a) shall be appropriated in county budgets for superior and municipal courts, including contract services with county agencies or private providers except for the following:

(1) salaries, benefits, services, and supplies for sheriff, marshal, and constable employees as the court deems necessary for court operations in superior and municipal courts;

(2) salaries, benefits, services, and supplies for county clerk activities directly supporting the superior court; and

(3) costs for court-appointed counsel specified in Government Code section 77003.

Except as provided in this subdivision, costs not appropriated in the budgets of the courts are unallowable.

(Subd (c) amended effective July 1, 1995; adopted as subd (d) effective July 1, 1990.)

(d) Functional budget categories

Trial court budgets and financial reports shall identify all allowable court operations in the following eleven (11) functional budget categories. Costs for salary, wages, and benefits of court employees are to be shown in the appropriate functions provided the individual staff member works at least 25 percent time in that function. Individual staff members whose time spent in a function is less than 25 percent are reported in Function 10, All Other Court Operations. The functions and their respective costs are as follows:

Function 1. Judicial Officers

Costs reported in this function are
- Salaries and state benefits of
  - Judges
  - Full- or part-time court commissioners
  - Full- or part-time court referees
- Assigned judges' in-county travel expenses

Costs not reported in this function include
- County benefits of judicial officers (Function 10)
- Juvenile traffic hearing officers (Function 10)
- Mental health hearing officers (Function 10)
- Pro tem hearing officers (Function 10)
- Commissioner and referee positions specifically excluded by statute from state trial court funding (unallowable)
- Related data processing (Function 9)
- Any other related services, supplies, and equipment (Function 10)

Function 2. Jury Services

Costs reported in this function are
- Juror expenses of per diem fees and mileage
- Meals and lodging for sequestered jurors
- Salaries, wages, and benefits of jury commissioner and jury services staff (including selection of grand jury)
- Contractual jury services
- Jury-related office expenses (other than information technology)
- Jury-related communications, including "on call" services

Costs not reported in this function include
- Juror parking (unallowable)
- Civil and criminal grand jury costs (unallowable)
- Jury-related information systems (Function 9)

Function 3. Verbatim Reporting

Costs reported in this function are
- Salaries, wages, and benefits of court reporters who are court employees
- Salaries, wages, and benefits of electronic monitors and support staff
- Salaries, wages, and benefits of verbatim reporting coordinators and clerical support staff
- Contractual court reporters and monitors
- Transcripts for use by appellate or trial courts, or as otherwise required by law
- Related office expenses and equipment (purchased, leased, or rented) used to record court proceedings, except as specified in Government Code § 68073, e.g.,
  - notepaper, pens, and pencils
  - ER equipment and supplies

Costs not reported in this function include
- Office expenses and equipment for use by reporters to prepare transcripts (unallowable)

Expenses specified in Government Code § 69073 (unallowable)
Space use charges for court reporters (unallowable)

Function 4. Court Interpreters
Costs reported in this function are
    Salaries, wages, and benefits of courtroom interpreters and interpreter coordinators
    Per diem and contractual courtroom interpreters, including contractual transportation and travel allowances

Costs not reported in this function include
    Related data processing (Function 9)
    Any other related services, supplies, and equipment (Function 10)

Function 5. Collections Enhancement
Collections performed in the enforcement of court orders for fees, fines, forfeitures, restitutions, penalties, and assessments (beginning with the establishment of the accounts receivable record)

Costs reported in this function are
    Salaries, wages, and benefits of collection employees of the court, e.g.,
        financial hearing officers
        evaluation officers
        collection staff
    Contract collections costs
    County charges for collection services provided to the court by county agencies
    Related services, supplies, and equipment (except data processing, Function 9)

Costs not reported in this function include
    Staff whose principal involvement is in collecting "forthwith" payments, e.g.,
        counter clerks (Function 10)
        cashiers (Function 10)

Function 6. Dispute Resolution Programs
Costs reported in this function are
    Arbitrators' fees in mandatory judicial arbitration programs
    Salaries, wages, and benefits of court staff providing child custody and visitation mediation and related investigation services, e.g.,
        Director of Family Court Services
        mediators
        conciliators
        investigators
        clerical support staff
    Contract mediators providing child custody and visitation mediation services
    Salaries, wages, benefits, fees, and contract costs for other arbitration and mediation programs (programs not mandated by statute), e.g.,
        arbitration administrators
        clerical support staff
        arbitrators' fees and expenses

Costs not reported in this function include
    Related data processing (Function 9)
    Any other related services, supplies, and equipment (Function 10)

Function 7. Court-Appointed Counsel (Noncriminal)
Costs reported in this function are
    Expenses for court-appointed counsel as specified in Government Code § 77003

Function 8. Court Security
Court security services as deemed necessary by the court. Includes only the duties of
(a) courtroom bailiff,
(b) perimeter security (i.e., outside the courtroom but inside the court facility), and
(c) at least .25 FTE dedicated supervisors of these activities.

Costs reported in this function are
    Salary, wages, and benefits (including overtime) of sheriff, marshal, and constable employees who perform the court's security, i.e.,
        bailiffs
        weapons-screening personnel
    Salary, wages, and benefits (including overtime) of court staff performing court security, e.g.,
        court attendants
    Contractual security services
    Salary, wages, and benefits of supervisors of sheriff, marshal, and constable employees whose duties are greater than .25 FTE dedicated to this function
    Sheriff, marshal, and constable employee training
    Purchase of security equipment
    Maintenance of security equipment

Costs not reported in this function include
    Other sheriff, marshal, or constable employees (unallowable)

Court attendant training (Function 10)
Overhead costs attributable to the operation of the sheriff and marshal offices (unallowable)
Costs associated with the transportation and housing of detainees from the jail to the courthouse (unallowable)
Service of process in civil cases (unallowable)
Services and supplies, including data processing, not specified above as allowable
Supervisors of bailiffs and perimeter security personnel of the sheriff, marshal, or constable office who supervise these duties less than .25 FTE time (unallowable)

Function 9. Information Technology
Costs reported in this function are
    Salaries, wages, and benefits of court employees who plan, implement, and maintain court data processing and information technologies, e.g.,
        programmers
        analysts
    Contract and consulting services associated with court information/data processing needs and systems
    County Information Systems/Data Processing Department charges made to court for court systems, e.g.,
        jury-related systems
        court and case management, including courts' share of a criminal justice information system
        accounts receivable/collections systems
    Related services, supplies, and equipment, e.g.,
        software purchases and leases
        maintenance of automation equipment
        training associated with data processing systems' development
Costs not reported in this function include
    Information technology services not provided directly to the courts (i.e., services used by other budget units)
    Data processing for county general services, e.g., payroll, accounts payable (Function 11)

Function 10. All Other Court Operations
Costs reported in this function are
    Salaries, wages, and benefits (including any pay differentials and overtime) of court staff
        (a) not reported in Functions 2-9, or
        (b) whose time cannot be allocated to Functions 2-9 in increments of at least 25 percent time (.25 FTE);
    Judicial benefits, county-paid
    Allowable costs not reported in Functions 2-9.
    (Nonjudicial staff) Cost items may include, for example,
        juvenile traffic hearing officer
        mental health hearing officer
        court-appointed hearing officer (pro tem)
        executive officer
        court administrator
        clerk of the court
        administrative assistant
        personnel staff
        legal research personnel; staff attorney; planning and research staff
        secretary
        courtroom clerk
        clerical support staff
        calendar clerk
        deputy clerk
        accountant
        cashier
        counter clerk
        microfilming staff
        management analyst
        probate conservatorship and guardianship investigators
        probate examiner
        training staff employed by the court
    Personnel costs not reported in this function:
        Any of the above not employed by the court
    (Services and supplies) Cost items may include, for example,
        office supplies
        printing
        postage
        communications
        publications and legal notices, by the court
        miscellaneous departmental expenses
        books, publications, training fees, and materials for court personnel (judicial and nonjudicial)
        travel and transportation (judicial and nonjudicial)
        professional dues
        memberships and subscriptions
        statutory multidistrict judges' association expenses
        research, planning, and program coordination expenses
        small claims advisor program costs
        court-appointed expert witness fees (for the court's needs)
        court-ordered forensic evaluations and other professional services (for the court's own use)
        pro tem judges' expenses
        micrographics expenses
        public information services

vehicle use, including automobile insurance
equipment (leased, rented, or purchased) and furnishings, including interior painting, replacement/maintenance of flooring, and furniture repair
maintenance of office equipment
janitorial services
legal services for allowable court operations (County Counsel and contractual)
fidelity and faithful performance insurance (bonding and personal liability insurance on judges and court employees)
insurance on cash money and securities (hold-up and burglary)
general liability/comprehensive insurance for other than faulty maintenance or design of facility (e.g., "slip and fall," other injury, theft and damage of court equipment, slander, discrimination)
risk management services related to allowable insurance
space rental for court records
county records retention/destruction services
county messenger/mail service
court audits mandated under Government Code § 71383
Service and supply costs not reported in this function include
    Civic association dues (unallowable)
    Facility damages insurance (unallowable)
    County central service department charges not appropriated in the court budget (unallowable)

Function 11. County General Services ("Indirect Costs")

General county services are defined as all eligible accounting, payroll, budgeting, personnel, purchasing, and county administrator costs rendered in support of court operations. Costs for included services are allowable to the extent the service is provided to the court. The following costs, regardless of how characterized by the county or by which county department they are performed, are reported in this function only and are subject to the statutory maximum for indirect costs as specified in Government Code § 77003. To the extent costs are allowable under this rule, a county's approved Cost Plan may be used to determine the specific cost although the cost categories, or functions, may differ.

Cost items within the meaning of rule 10.810(a)(7) and the county departments often performing the service may include, for example,
County Administrator
    budget development and administration
    interdepartmental budget unit administration and operations
    personnel (labor) relations and administration
Auditor-Controller
    payroll
    financial audits
    warrant processing
    fixed asset accounting
    departmental accounting for courts, e.g., fines, fees, forfeitures, restitutions, penalties, and assessments; accounting for the Trial Court Special Revenue Fund
    accounts payable
    grant accounting
    management reporting
    banking
Personnel
    recruitment and examination of applicants
    maintenance and certification of eligible lists
    position classification
    salary surveys
    leave accounting
    employment physicals
    handling of appeals
Treasurer/Tax Collector
    warrant processing
    bank reconciliation
    retirement system administration
    receiving, safeguarding, investing, and disbursing court funds
Purchasing Agent
    process departmental requisitions
    issue and analyze bids
    make contracts and agreements for the purchase or rental of personal property
    store surplus property and facilitate public auctions
Unallowable costs
    Unallowable court-related costs are those
        (a) in support of county operations,
        (b) expressly prohibited by statute,
        (c) facility-related, or
        (d) exceptions of the nature referenced in Functions 1-11.
Unallowable cost items, including any related data processing costs, are not reported in Functions 1-11 and may include, for example,
Communications
    central communication control and maintenance for county emergency and general government radio equipment
Central Collections
    processing accounts receivable for county departments (not courts)
County Administrator
    legislative analysis and activities
    preparation and operation of general directives and operating procedures
    responses to questions from the Board, outside agencies, and the public executive functions: Board of Supervisors
    county advisory councils
Treasurer/Tax Collector
    property tax determination, collection, etc.

> General Services
> > rental and utilities support
> > coordinate county's emergency services
>
> Property Management
> > negotiations for the acquisition, sale, or lease of property, except for space rented for storage of court records
> > making appraisals
> > negotiating utility relocations
> > assisting County Counsel in condemnation actions
> > preparing deeds, leases, licenses, easements
> > collecting rents
> > building lease management services (except for storage of court records)
>
> Facility-related
> > construction services
> > right-of-way and easement services
> > purchase of land and buildings
> > construction
> > depreciation of buildings/use allowance
> > space rental/building rent (except for storage of court records)
> > building maintenance and repairs (except interior painting and to replace/repair flooring)
> > purchase, installation, and maintenance of H/V/A/C equipment
> > maintenance and repair of utilities
> > utility use charges (e.g., heat, light, water)
> > elevator purchase and maintenance
> > alterations/remodeling
> > landscaping and grounds maintenance services
> > exterior lighting and security
> > insurance on building damages (e.g., fire, earthquake, flood, boiler and machinery)
> > grounds' liability insurance
> > parking lot or facility maintenance
> > juror parking

(Subd (d) amended effective January 1, 2007; previously amended and relettered effective July 1, 1995.)

Rule 10.810 amended and renumbered effective January 1, 2007; adopted as rule 810 effective July 1, 1988; previously amended effective July 1, 1989, July 1, 1990, July 1, 1991, and July 1, 1995.

Advisory Committee Comment

Rule 10.810 is identical to former rule 810, except for the rule number. All references in statutes or rules to rule 810 apply to this rule.

Rule 10.811. Reimbursement of costs associated with homicide trials

(a) Intent

This rule permits courts that meet certain criteria to request reimbursement of extraordinary costs of homicide trials.

(Subd (a) amended effective January 1, 2007.)

(b) Criteria

A court that requests reimbursement of extraordinary costs of a homicide trial must meet all the following criteria:

(1) Be located in a county with a population of 300,000 or less;

(2) Have incurred extraordinary costs of a homicide trial; and

(3) Demonstrate an actual need for reimbursement.

(c) Submission

A request for reimbursement must be submitted by the court's presiding judge or executive officer to Judicial Council staff. All requests for reimbursement must comply with guidelines approved by the Judicial Council and include a completed *Request for Reimbursement of Extraordinary Homicide Trial Costs* form.

(Subd (c) amended effective January 1, 2016.)

Rule 10.811 amended effective January 1, 2016; adopted as rule 6.711 effective January 1, 2005; previously amended and renumbered as rule 10.811 effective January 1, 2007.

Rule 10.815. Fees to be set by the court

(a) Authority

Under Government Code section 70631, a superior court may charge a reasonable fee for a service or product not to exceed the costs of providing the service or product, if the Judicial Council approves the fee.

(b) Approved fees

The Judicial Council authorizes courts to charge a reasonable fee not to exceed costs for the following products and services unless courts are prohibited by law from charging a fee for, or providing, the product or service:

(1) Forms;

(2) Packages of forms;

(3) Information materials;

(4) Publications, including books, pamphlets, and local rules;

(5) Compact discs;

(6) DVDs;

(7) Audiotapes;

(8) Videotapes;

(9) Microfiches;

(10) Envelopes;

(11) Postage;

(12) Shipping;

(13) Off-site retrieval of documents;

(14) Direct fax filing under rule 2.304 (fee per page);

(15) Returning filed-stamped copies of documents by fax to persons who request that a faxed copy be sent to them;

(16) Training programs for attorneys who serve as court-appointed temporary judges, including the materials and food provided to the participants;

(17) Other training programs or events, including materials and food provided to the participants; and

(18) Telephone appearance services.

(Subd (b) amended effective January 1, 2023; previously amended effective July 1, 2006, and January 1, 2007.)

(c) Guidelines for determining costs

The fee charged for any product or service listed in (b) may not exceed the court's cost in providing the product or service. In determining the costs of a product or service, the court must:

(1) Identify the specific product or service; and

(2) Prepare an analysis of the direct and indirect costs on which the fee is based.

(d) Reasonableness

In deciding what specific fee or fees, if any, to charge for a product or service under (b), the court must determine that the fee charged is reasonable considering relevant factors such as the benefits to the court and the public from providing the product or service and the effects of charging the fee on public access to the court.

(e) Reporting requirement

Each court that charges a fee under this rule must provide Judicial Council staff with a description of the fee, how the amount of the fee was determined, and how the fee is applied.

(Subd (e) amended effective January 1, 2016.)

(f) Public notice

The court must notify the public of any fee that it charges under this rule by providing information concerning the fee in a conspicuous place such as the court's fee schedule.

(g) Procedure for adoption of fee

If a court proposes to change any fee authorized under (b) that it is already charging or to charge any new fee authorized under (b), the court must follow the procedures for adopting or amending a local rule under rule 10.613 of the California Rules of Court.

(Subd (g) amended effective January 1, 2007; previously amended effective July 1, 2006.)

Rule 10.815 amended effective January 1, 2023; adopted as rule 6.712 effective January 1, 2006; previously amended effective July 1, 2006, and January 1, 2016; amended and renumbered as rule 10.815 effective January 1, 2007.

Rule 10.820. Acceptance of credit cards by the superior courts

(a) Delegation of authority to Administrative Director

The Administrative Director is authorized, under rule 10.80, to approve on behalf of the Judicial Council requests from the superior courts to accept credit cards for the payment of court fees or to impose a charge for the use of credit cards. The authority is given to the Judicial Council by Government Code section 6159.

(Subd (a) amended effective January 1, 2016; previously amended effective January 1, 2007.)

(b) Standards for use of credit cards

The Administrative Director is authorized to approve requests under (a) for acceptance of credit cards if all of the following are true:

(1) The court (A) imposes a fee for the use of the credit card, or (B) demonstrates that the cost of acceptance of credit cards is not greater than the cost of acceptance of other means of payment of fees, or (C) demonstrates that it can absorb the cost of the acceptance of the credit card;

(2) The court has obtained a credit card acceptance contract that is competitive with other possible contracts the court could obtain; and

(3) The court provides alternative means for a person to pay court fees.

(Subd (b) amended effective January 1, 2016; previously amended effective January 1, 2007.)

(c) Standards for charge for the use of credit cards

The Administrative Director is authorized to approve requests under (a) for the imposition of a charge for the use of credit cards if both of the following are true:

(1) The proposed fee is not greater than the cost for acceptance of a credit card; and

(2) The proposed fee would not result in an undue hardship on people wishing to use credit cards for payment of fees.

(Subd (c) amended effective January 1, 2016; previously amended effective January 1, 2007.)

(d) Referral to Judicial Council

The Administrative Director may refer any request under (a) to the Judicial Council for its action.

(Subd (d) amended effective January 1, 2016; previously amended effective January 1, 2007.)

(e) Existing approvals ratified

The approval of any board of supervisors for any superior court to accept credit cards or charge a fee for the use of credit cards that was effective as of December 31, 1999, is ratified by the council as of January 1, 2000.

(Subd (e) amended effective January 1, 2009; previously amended effective January 1, 2007.)

Rule 10.820 amended effective January 1, 2016; adopted as rule 6.703 effective January 1, 2000; previously amended and renumbered as rule 10.820 effective January 1, 2007; previously amended effective January 1, 2009.

Rule 10.821. Acceptance of checks and other negotiable paper

(a) Conditions for acceptance

A personal check, bank cashier's check, money order, or traveler's check tendered in payment of any fee, fine, or bail deposit under Government Code section 71386 or Vehicle Code section 40510 or 40521 must be accepted by the court:

(1) If the personal check is drawn on a banking institution located in California by a person furnishing satisfactory proof of residence in California, is payable to the court without a second party endorsement, and is in an amount not exceeding the amount of the payment and is not postdated or staledated, unless the person drawing the check is known to have previously tendered worthless checks; or

(2) If the bank cashier's check or money order is drawn on a banking institution located in the United States and is in an amount not exceeding the amount of the payment; or

(3) If the person presenting the traveler's check shows satisfactory identification.

(Subd (a) amended effective January 1, 2007.)

(b) Requiring satisfactory proof of good credit

Except for checks tendered under the conditions specified in Vehicle Code section 40521(a), a court may require that a person drawing a personal check furnish satisfactory proof of good credit by showing a valid recognized credit card or by any other reasonable means.

(Subd (b) amended effective January 1, 2007.)

(c) Written policy for acceptance or rejection

A court may accept or reject any check or money order not meeting the requirements of this rule, under a written policy adopted by the court under Government Code section 71386(a).

(Subd (c) amended effective January 1, 2007.)

Rule 10.821 amended and renumbered effective January 1, 2007; adopted as rule 805 effective July 1, 1981.

Rule 10.830. Disposal of surplus court personal property

(a) Disposal of surplus property

Except as provided in (b), a superior court may:

(1) Sell, at fair market value, any personal property of the court that is no longer needed for court use;

(2) Trade or exchange any surplus personal property of the court, according to such terms and conditions as are agreed on, for personal property of another court, the state, a county, a city, a federal agency, a community redevelopment agency, a housing authority, a community development commission, a surplus property authority, a school district, or any irrigation, flood control, county board of education, or other special district, if the property to be acquired by the court is needed for court use;

(3) Donate, sell at less than fair market value, or otherwise transfer to another court, the state, a county, a city, a federal agency, a community redevelopment agency, a housing authority, a community development commission, a surplus property authority, a school district, or any irrigation, flood control, county board of education, or other special district, according to such terms and conditions as are agreed on, any personal property of the court that is no longer needed for court use; and

(4) Dispose of any personal property of the court that is no longer needed for court use, and that has negligible or no economic value, in any manner the court deems appropriate.

(Subd (a) amended effective January 1, 2007.)

(b) Exception for disposal of technology equipment acquired on or after July 1, 2000

A superior court that wishes to dispose of surplus technology equipment to which the court acquired title on or after July 1, 2000 must provide a written description of such technology equipment to the Administrative Director. If, within 60 days of receipt of the description, the Administrative Director determines that another court of record of the State of California is in need of the surplus technology equipment, the court holding title to the equipment must donate it to the court determined to be in need. If the Administrative Director determines that no other court needs the equipment or makes no determination within 60 days of receiving the written description of it, the court holding title to the equipment may dispose of it as provided in (a), (c), and (d). The Administrative Director must provide to the courts a definition of the term "technology equipment" as used in this rule and must provide 30 days' notice of any amendment to the definition.

(Subd (b) amended effective January 1, 2016; previously amended effective January 1, 2007.)

(c) Notice of disposal

Unless the property to be transferred under this rule is valued at $500 or less or the entity to which the property is to be transferred is another court of record of the State of California, the transferring superior court must, at least one week before the transfer, place a notice of its intended action:

(1) In three public places; or

(2) On the court's Web site; or

(3) In a newspaper of general circulation published in the county.

(Subd (c) amended effective January 1, 2007.)

(d) Proceeds of disposal

Any proceeds of a sale or other transfer under this rule must be deposited in the superior court's operations fund.

(Subd (d) amended effective January 1, 2007.)

Rule 10.830 amended effective January 1, 2016; adopted as rule 6.709 effective January 1, 2001; previously amended and renumbered as rule 10.830 effective January 1, 2007.

Chapter 10
Trial Court Records Management

Chapter 10 renumbered effective January 1, 2008; adopted as Chapter 4 effective January 1, 2001; previously amended and renumbered as Chapter 9 effective January 1, 2007.

Rule 10.850. Trial court records
Rule 10.851. Court indexes—automated maintenance
Rule 10.854. Standards and guidelines for trial court records
Rule 10.855. Superior court records sampling program
Rule 10.856. Notice of superior court records destruction

Rule 10.850. Trial court records

Unless otherwise provided, "court records" as used in this chapter consist of the records as defined in Government Code section 68151(a).
Rule 10.850 adopted effective January 1, 2011.

Rule 10.851. Court indexes—automated maintenance

(a) Authorized media

The clerk of each trial court may create, maintain, update, and make accessible the indexes required by law by photographic, microphotographic, photocopy, mechanical, magnetic, or electronic means. The clerk must make provision for preserving the information on a medium that will ensure its permanence and protect it from loss or damage arising from electronic failure or mechanical defect.

(Subd (a) amended effective January 1, 2007; adopted as unlettered subd; previously amended and relettered effective January 1, 2001.)

(b) Alphabetic index

A single alphabetic index may be maintained so long as the plaintiff-defendant distinction is retained.

(Subd (b) adopted effective January 1, 2001.)

(c) Public access

The indexes maintained under automated procedures must be accessible for public examination and use.

(Subd (c) amended effective January 1, 2007; adopted as part of unlettered subd; previously lettered and amended effective January 1, 2001.)

Rule 10.851 amended and renumbered effective January 1, 2007; adopted as rule 1010 effective January 1, 1975; renumbered as rule 999 effective January 1, 2003; amended and renumbered as rule 6.751 effective January 1, 2001.

Rule 10.854. Standards and guidelines for trial court records

(a) The standards and guidelines

Judicial Council staff, in collaboration with trial court presiding judges and court executives, must prepare, maintain, and distribute a manual providing standards and guidelines for the creation, maintenance, and retention of trial court records (the *Trial Court Records Manual*), consistent with the Government Code and the rules of court and policies adopted by the Judicial Council. The manual should assist the courts and the public to have complete, accurate, efficient, and accessible court records. Before the manual is issued, it must be made available for comment from the trial courts.

(Subd (a) amended effective January 1, 2016; adopted effective January 1, 2011.)

(b) Contents of the *Trial Court Records Manual*

The *Trial Court Records Manual* must provide standards and guidelines for the creation, maintenance, and retention of trial court records. These standards and guidelines must ensure that all court records subject to permanent retention are retained and made available to the public in perpetuity as legally required.

(Subd (b) adopted effective January 1, 2011.)

(c) Updating the manual

Judicial Council staff, in collaboration with trial court presiding judges and court executives, must periodically update the *Trial Court Records Manual* to reflect changes in technology that affect the creation, maintenance, and retention of court records. Except for technical changes, corrections, or minor substantive changes not likely to create controversy, proposed changes in the manual must be made available for comment from the courts before the manual is updated or changed. Courts must be notified of any changes in the standards or guidelines, including all those relating to the permanent retention of records.

(Subd (c) amended effective January 1, 2016; adopted effective January 1, 2011.)

(d) Adherence to standards and guidelines

Trial courts must adhere to the requirements contained in the *Trial Court Records Manual*, except as otherwise provided in the manual.

(Subd (d) adopted effective January 1, 2011.)
Rule 10.854 amended effective January 1, 2016; adopted effective January 1, 2011.

Rule 10.855. Superior court records sampling program

(a) Purpose

This rule establishes a program to preserve in perpetuity for study by historians and other researchers all superior court records filed before 1911 and a sample of superior court records filed after December 31, 1910, to document the progress and development of the judicial system, and to preserve evidence of significant events and social trends. This rule is not intended to restrict a court from preserving more records than the minimum required.

(Subd (a) amended effective January 1, 2007.)

(b) Scope

"Records" of the superior court, as used in this rule, does not include records of limited civil, small claims, misdemeanor, or infraction cases.

(Subd (b) adopted effective January 1, 2001.)

(c) Comprehensive and significant records

Each superior court must preserve forever comprehensive and significant court records as follows:

(1) All records filed before 1911;

(2) If practicable, all records filed after 1910 and before 1950;

(3) All case indexes; and

(4) All noncapital cases in which the California Supreme Court has issued a written opinion.

(Subd (c) amended effective July 1, 2016; adopted as subd (b) effective July 1, 1992; previously amended and relettered effective January 1, 2001; previously amended effective January 1, 2007.)

(d) Sample records

If a superior court destroys court records without preserving them in a medium described in (g), the court must preserve forever a sample of court records as provided by this rule of all cases, including sealed, expunged, and other confidential records to the extent permitted by law.

(Subd (d) amended effective July 1, 2016; adopted as subd (c) effective July 1, 1992; relettered effective January 1, 2001; previously amended effective January 1, 2007.)

(e) Court record defined

The "court record" under this rule consists of the following:

(1) All papers and documents in the case folder; but if no case folder is created by the court, all papers and documents that would have been in the case folder if one had been created; and

(2) The case folder, unless all information on the case folder is in papers and documents preserved in a medium described in (g); and

(3) If available, corresponding depositions, daily transcripts, and tapes of electronically recorded proceedings.

(Subd (e) amended effective July 1, 2016; adopted as subd (d) effective July 1, 1992; previously amended and relettered effective January 1, 2001; previously amended effective January 1, 2007.)

(f) Sampling technique

Three courts assigned in rotation by the Judicial Council must preserve the following:

(1) A random sample of 25 percent of their court records for a calendar year, with the exception of the Superior Court of Los Angeles County, which must preserve a random sample of 10 percent of its court records for a calendar year.

(2) All judgment books, minute books, and registers of action if maintained separately from the case files, for the calendar year.

(Subd (f) amended effective July 1, 2016; adopted as subd (e) effective July 1, 1992; repealed, amended, and relettered effective January 1, 2001; previously amended effective January 1, 2007.)

(g) Preservation medium

(1) Comprehensive and significant court records under (c) filed before 1911 must be preserved in their original paper form unless the paper is not available.

(2) Comprehensive and significant court records under (c) filed after 1910 and sample records under (d) must be retained permanently in accord with the requirements of the *Trial Court Records Manual*.

(Subd (g) amended and relettered effective July 1, 2016; adopted as subd (h); previously amended effective January 1, 2001, January 1, 2007, and January 1, 2011.)

(h) Access

The court must ensure the following:

(1) The comprehensive, significant, and sample court records are made reasonably available to all members of the public.

(2) Sealed and confidential records are made available to the public only as provided by law.

(3) If the records are preserved in a medium other than paper, equipment is provided to permit public viewing of the records.

(4) Reasonable provision is made for duplicating the records at cost.

(Subd (h) amended and relettered effective July 1, 2016; adopted as subd (j); previously amended effective January 1, 2007.)

(i) Storage

(1) Until statewide or regional archival facilities are established, each court is responsible for maintaining its comprehensive, significant, and sample court records in a secure and safe environment consistent with the archival significance of the records. The court may deposit the court records in a suitable California archival facility such as a university, college, library, historical society, museum, archive, or research institution whether publicly supported or privately endowed. The court must ensure that the records are kept and preserved according to commonly recognized archival principles and practices of preservation.

(2) If a local archival facility is maintaining the court records, the court may continue to use that facility's services if it meets the storage and access requirements under (h) and (i)(1). If the court solicits archival facilities interested in maintaining the comprehensive, significant, and sample court records, the court must follow the procedures specified under rule 10.856, except that the comprehensive, significant, and sample court records must not be destroyed. Courts may enter into agreements for long-term deposit of records subject to the storage and access provisions of this rule.

(Subd (i) amended and relettered effective July 1, 2016; adopted as subd (k); previously amended effective January 1, 1994, January 1, 2001, and January 1, 2007.)

(j) Application

The sampling program provided in this rule, as amended effective July 1, 2016, applies retroactively to all superior courts.

(Subd (j) repealed and relettered effective January 1, 2018; adopted effective July 1, 2016.)

Rule 10.855 amended effective January 1, 2018; adopted as rule 243.5 effective July 1, 1992; previously amended and renumbered as rule 6.755 effective January 1, 2001, and as rule 10.855 January 1, 2007; previously amended effective January 1, 1994, January 1, 1995, January 1, 2011, July 1, 2013, and July 1, 2016.

Advisory Committee Comment

Subdivision (c)(4). Capital cases are excluded under subdivision (c)(4) because these cases have an automatic right of appeal to the California Supreme Court, and trial court records are retained permanently under Government Code section 68152(c)(1) if the defendant is sentenced to death. Each year, the Judicial Council will make available to the superior courts a list of all noncapital cases in which the California Supreme Court has issued a written opinion.

Subdivision (j). Because the destruction of court records is discretionary, all courts may elect to apply the rule retroactively and destroy court records that are not required to be preserved under subdivisions (c), (d), and (f), but they are not required to do so.

Superior courts that destroyed court records under the prior sampling rule may have preserved only 10 percent of their records (formerly known as the "systematic sample") for the year that they are now assigned to preserve the sample defined in subdivision (f). Except for the Superior Court of Los Angeles County, these courts would not be able to meet the requirement in subdivision (f)(1). So long as these courts continue preserving the 10-percent sample for their assigned year, they will be deemed to have satisfied subdivision (f)(1).

Rule 10.856. Notice of superior court records destruction

(a) Scope

"Records" of the superior court, as used in this rule, do not include records of limited civil, small claims, misdemeanor, or infraction cases.

(Subd (a) adopted effective January 1, 2007.)

(b) Notice

The superior court must give 30 days' written notice of its intent to destroy court records open to public inspection to entities maintained on a master list by the Judicial Council and to any other entities that have informed the court directly that they wish to be notified.

(Subd (b) amended and relettered effective January 1, 2007; adopted as subd (a); previously amended effective January 1, 2001, and July 1, 2001.)

(c) Transfer to requesting entity

Records scheduled for destruction must be permanently transferred to the entity requesting possession of the records on written order of the presiding judge unless the request is denied for good cause shown. The cost of transferring the records must be paid by the requesting party.

(Subd (c) amended and relettered effective January 1, 2007; adopted as subd (b); previously amended effective January 1, 2001.)

(d) Request by two or more entities

If two or more entities request the same records, the presiding judge must order the transfer of those records to the entity that shows the greatest capability of caring for and preserving the records according to commonly recognized archival principles and practices of preservation and access, and that provides the greatest likelihood of making them available for historical or research purposes.

(Subd (d) amended and relettered effective January 1, 2007; adopted as subd (c); previously amended effective January 1, 2001.)

(e) Public access

No entity may receive the records unless the entity agrees to make the records reasonably available to all members of the public. Provision must be made for duplicating the records at cost.

(Subd (e) amended and relettered effective January 1, 2007; adopted as subd (d); previously amended effective January 1, 2001.)

(f) Destruction

If after 30 days no request for transfer of records scheduled for destruction has been received by the court, the clerk may destroy the records not designated for the historical and research program under rule 10.855, under a written order of the presiding judge of the court and in accordance with provisions of the Government Code.

(Subd (f) amended and relettered effective January 1, 2007; adopted as subd (e); previously amended effective January 1, 2001.)

(g) Extension of time

The time for retention of any of the court records specified in the notice may be extended by order of the court on its own motion, or on application of any interested member of the public for good cause shown and on such terms as are just. No fee may be charged for making the application.

(Subd (g) amended and relettered effective January 1, 2007; adopted as subd (f); previously amended effective January 1, 2001.)

(h) Forms

The court must use the following forms to implement the requirements of this rule:

(1) *Notice of Intent to Destroy Superior Court Records; Offer to Transfer Possession* (form REC-001(N), with a form on the reverse titled *Request for Transfer or Extension of Time for Retention of Superior Court Records* (form REC-001(R)), for optional use by the recipient of the notice; and

(2) *Notice of Hearing on Request for Transfer or Extension of Time for Retention of Superior Court Records; Court Order; Release and Receipt of Superior Court Records* (form REC-002(N)).

(Subd (h) amended effective July 1, 2010; adopted as subd (g); previously amended effective January 1, 2001; previously amended and relettered effective January 1, 2007.)

Rule 10.856 amended effective July 1, 2010; adopted as rule 243.6 effective January 1, 1994; previously amended effective July 1, 2001; previously amended and renumbered as rule 6.756 effective January 1, 2001, and as rule 10.856 effective January 1, 2007.

Chapter 11
Trial Court Automation

Chapter 11 renumbered effective January 1, 2008; adopted as Chapter 5 effective January 1, 2001; previously amended and renumbered as Chapter 10 effective January 1, 2007.

Rule 10.870. Trial court automation standards

Each superior court that acquires, develops, enhances, or maintains automated accounting or case management systems through funding provided under Government Code section 68090.8 must comply with the standards approved by the Judicial Council. The approved standards are stated in *Judicial Council Trial Court Automation Standards*.

Rule 10.870 amended effective January 1, 2016; adopted as rule 1011 effective March 1, 1992; renumbered as rule 999.1 effective July 1, 1993; previously amended and renumbered as rule 10.870 effective January 1, 2007.

Chapter 12
Trial Court Management of Civil Cases

Chapter 12 renumbered effective January 1, 2008; adopted as Chapter 11 effective January 1, 2007.

Rule 10.900. Case management and calendaring system
Rule 10.901. Internal management procedures
Rule 10.910. Assigned cases to be tried or dismissed—notification to presiding judge

Rule 10.900. Case management and calendaring system

Each superior court must adopt a case management and calendaring system for general civil cases that will advance the goals stated in standard 2.1 of the California Standards of Judicial Administration.

Rule 10.900 amended and renumbered effective January 1, 2007; adopted as rule 204.1 effective July 1, 2002.

Rule 10.901. Internal management procedures

Each court must:

(1) Maintain a calendar and caseflow management system that will ensure that a sufficient number of cases are set for trial, based on the court's experience, so that all departments will be occupied with judicial business;

(2) Adopt for judges and court personnel an internal operations manual of policies and procedures necessary for the efficient operation and management of the court;

(3) Maintain and periodically review for accuracy written local court procedures, policies, and operating practices not contained in local rules for quick, accurate, and complete reference; and

(4) Ensure that calendaring functions are performed as directed by the court and that personnel rendering direct and immediate service to the court are within its administrative control to the maximum extent consistent with the existing organizational structures.

Rule 10.901 amended and renumbered effective January 1, 2007; adopted as rule 208 effective January 1, 1985; previously amended and renumbered as rule 204.2 effective July 1, 2002.

Rule 10.910. Assigned cases to be tried or dismissed— notification to presiding judge

(a) Assignment of cases for trial

In a court employing the master calendar, each case transferred to a trial department must be tried, ordered off the calendar, or dismissed unless, for good cause arising after the commencement of the trial, the judge of the trial department continues the case for further hearing or, with the consent of the judge supervising the master calendar, reassigns the case to the judge supervising the master calendar for further disposition.

(Subd (a) amended effective January 1, 2007; adopted as untitled subd effective January 1, 1985; previously amended and lettered effective July 1, 2002.)

(b) Notification to presiding judge

A judge who has finished or continued the trial of a case or any special matter must immediately notify the judge supervising the master calendar. The judge to whose department a cause is assigned for trial or for hearing must accept the assignment unless disqualified or, for other good cause stated to the judge supervising the master calendar, the judge supervising the master calendar determines that in the interest of justice the cause should not be tried or heard before the judge. When the judge has refused a cause and is not disqualified, the judge must state the reasons in writing unless the judge supervising the master calendar has concurred.

(Subd (b) amended and lettered effective July 1, 2002; adopted as untitled subd effective January 1, 1985.)

Rule 10.910 amended and renumbered effective January 1, 2007; adopted as rule 226 effective January 1, 1985; previously amended effective July 1, 2002.

Chapter 13
Trial Court Management of Criminal Cases

Chapter 13 renumbered effective January 1, 2008; adopted as Chapter 12 effective January 1, 2007.

Rule 10.950. Role of presiding judge, supervising judge, criminal division, and master calendar department in courts having more than three judges
Rule 10.951. Duties of supervising judge of the criminal division
Rule 10.952. Meetings concerning the criminal court system
Rule 10.953. Procedures for disposition of cases before the preliminary hearing

Rule 10.950. Role of presiding judge, supervising judge, criminal division, and master calendar department in courts having more than three judges

The presiding judge of a court having more than three judges may designate one or more departments primarily to hear criminal cases. Two or more departments so designated must be the criminal division. The presiding judge may designate supervising judges for the criminal division, but retains final authority over all criminal and civil case assignments.

Rule 10.950 amended and renumbered effective January 1, 2007; adopted as rule 227.1 effective January 1, 1985.

Rule 10.951. Duties of supervising judge of the criminal division

(a) Duties

In addition to any other duties assigned by the presiding judge or imposed by these rules, a supervising judge of the criminal division must assign criminal matters requiring a hearing or cases requiring trial to a trial department.

(Subd (a) amended effective January 1, 2007.)

(b) Arraignments, pretrial motions, and readiness conferences

The presiding judge, supervising judge, or other designated judge must conduct arraignments, hear and determine any pretrial motions, preside over readiness conferences, and, where not inconsistent with law, assist in the disposition of cases without trial.

(Subd (b) amended effective January 1, 2008; previously amended effective January 1, 2007.)

(c) Mental health case protocols

The presiding judge, supervising judge, or other designated judge, in conjunction with the justice partners designated in rule 10.952, is encouraged to develop local protocols for cases involving offenders with mental illness or co-occurring disorders to ensure early identification of and appropriate treatment for offenders with mental illness or co-occurring disorders with the goals of reducing recidivism, responding to public safety concerns, and providing better outcomes for those offenders while using resources responsibly and reducing costs.

(Subd (c) adopted effective January 1, 2014.)

(d) Additional judges

To the extent that the business of the court requires, the presiding judge may designate additional judges under the direction of the supervising judge to perform the duties specified in this rule.

(Subd (d) relettered effective January 1, 2014; adopted as subd (c).)

(e) Courts without supervising judge

In a court having no supervising judge, the presiding judge performs the duties of a supervising judge.

(Subd (e) relettered effective January 1, 2014; previously amended as subd (d) effective January 1, 2007.)

Rule 10.951 amended effective January 1, 2014; adopted as rule 227.2 effective January 1, 1985; previously amended and renumbered effective January 1, 2007; previously amended effective January 1, 2008.

Rule 10.952. Meetings concerning the criminal court system

The supervising judge or, if none, the presiding judge must designate judges of the court to attend regular meetings to be held with the district attorney; public defender; representatives of the local bar, probation department, parole office, sheriff department, police departments, and Forensic Conditional Release Program (CONREP); county mental health director or his or her designee; county alcohol and drug programs director or his or her designee; court personnel; and other interested persons to identify and eliminate problems in the criminal court system and to discuss other problems of mutual concern.

Rule 10.952 amended effective January 1, 2015; adopted as rule 227.8 effective January 1, 1985; previously amended and renumbered effective January 1, 2007; previously amended effective January 1, 2014.

Rule 10.953. Procedures for disposition of cases before the preliminary hearing

(a) Disposition before preliminary hearing

Superior courts having more than three judges must, in cooperation with the district attorney and defense bar, adopt procedures to facilitate dispositions before the preliminary hearing and at all other stages of the proceedings. The procedures may include:

(1) Early, voluntary, informal discovery, consistent with part 2, title 6, chapter 10 of the Penal Code (commencing with section 1054); and

(2) The use of superior court judges as magistrates to conduct readiness conferences before the preliminary hearing and to assist, where not inconsistent with law, in the early disposition of cases.

(Subd (a) amended effective January 1, 2007; previously amended effective June 6, 1990, and January 1, 1991.)

(b) Case to be disposed of under rule 4.114

Pleas of guilty or no contest resulting from proceedings under (a) must be disposed of as provided in rule 4.114.

(Subd (b) amended effective January 1, 2007; previously amended effective July 1, 2001.)

Rule 10.953 amended and renumbered effective January 1, 2007; adopted as rule 227.10 effective January 1, 1985; previously amended effective June 6, 1990, January 1, 1991, and July 1, 2001.

Chapter 14
Management of Self-Help Centers

Chapter 14 adopted effective July 1, 2008.

Rule 10.960. Court self-help centers

(a) Scope and application

This rule applies to all court-based self-help centers whether the services provided by the center are managed by the court or by an entity other than the court.

(Subd (a) adopted effective January 1, 2008.)

(b) Purpose and core court function

Providing access to justice for self-represented litigants is a priority for California courts. The services provided by court self-help centers facilitate the timely and cost-effective processing of cases involving self-represented litigants and improve the delivery of justice to the public. Court programs, policies, and procedures designed to assist self-represented litigants and effectively manage cases involving self-represented litigants at all stages must be incorporated and budgeted as core court functions.

(Subd (b) adopted effective January 1, 2008.)

(c) Staffing

Court self-help centers provide assistance to self-represented litigants. A court self-help center must include an attorney and other qualified staff who provide information and education to self-represented litigants about the justice process, and who work within the court to provide for the effective management of cases involving self-represented litigants.

(Subd (c) adopted effective January 1, 2008.)

(d) Neutrality and availability

The information and education provided by court self-help centers must be neutral and unbiased, and services must be available to all sides of a case.

(Subd (d) adopted effective January 1, 2008.)

(e) Guidelines and procedures

The Advisory Committee on Providing Access and Fairness must recommend to the council updates to the *Guidelines for the Operation of Self-Help Centers in California Trial Courts* as needed. It should, in collaboration with judges, court executives, attorneys, and other parties with demonstrated interest in services to self-represented litigants, develop and disseminate guidelines, procedures and best practices for the operation of court self-help centers. The guidelines and procedures must address the following topics:

(1) Location and hours of operation;

(2) Scope of services;

(3) Attorney qualifications;

(4) Other staffing qualifications and supervision requirements;

(5) Language access;

(6) Contracts with entities other than the court that provide self-help services;

(7) Use of technology;

(8) Ethics;

(9) Efficiency of operation; and

(10) Security.

(Subd (e) amended effective January 1, 2015; adopted effective January 1, 2008; previously amended effective February 20, 2014.)

(f) Budget and funding

A court must include in its annual budget funding necessary for operation of its self-help center. In analyzing and making recommendations on the allocation of funding for a court self-help center, Judicial Council staff will consider the degree to which individual courts have been successful in meeting the guidelines and procedures for the operation of the self-help center.

(Subd (f) amended effective January 1, 2016; adopted effective January 1, 2008.)
Rule 10.960 amended effective January 1, 2016; adopted effective January 1, 2008; previously amended effective February 20, 2014, and January 1, 2015.

Chapter 15
Elections Code Reports

Chapter 15 adopted effective January 22, 2024.

Rule 10.970. Reports of findings and orders affecting voting rights (Elec. Code, § 2211.5)

(a) Application

This rule applies to the reports required by Elections Code section 2211.5 regarding findings and orders disqualifying a person from voting or restoring a person's right to register to vote under Elections Code sections 2208–2211.

(Subd (a) adopted effective January 1, 2024.)

(b) Forms

(1) The clerk must use *Confidential Report of Findings and Orders Affecting Voting Rights* (form MC-600) to submit each report under this rule.

(2) To report the information required by Elections Code section 2211.5(a)(1) and (b) for the period covered by each report, the clerk must attach to form MC-600 either:

(A) A completed *Attachment to Confidential Report of Findings and Orders Affecting Voting Rights* (form MC-600A) that includes the required information about each applicable determination made by the court in the period covered by the report; or

(B) A computer-generated report that presents the required information for the period covered by the report using the same clearly identified spaces as form MC-600A.

(Subd (b) adopted effective January 1, 2024.)
Rule 10.970 adopted effective January 1, 2024.

Division 5
Appellate Court Administration

Chap. 1. Rules Relating to the Supreme Court and Courts of Appeal. Rules 10.1000–10.1030.

Chap. 2. Rules Relating to the Superior Court Appellate Division. Rules 10.1100–10.1108.

Chapter 1
Rules Relating to the Supreme Court and Courts of Appeal

Rule 10.1000. Transfer of causes
Rule 10.1004. Court of Appeal administrative presiding justice
Rule 10.1008. Courts of Appeal with more than one division
Rule 10.1012. Supervising progress of appeals
Rule 10.1014. Oversight of administrative presiding justices and presiding justices
Rule 10.1016. Notice of failure to perform judicial duties
Rule 10.1017. Notification to State Bar of attorney misconduct
Rule 10.1020. Reviewing court clerk/executive officer
Rule 10.1024. Court of Appeal minutes
Rule 10.1028. Preservation and destruction of Court of Appeal records
Rule 10.1030. Local rules of Courts of Appeal

Rule 10.1000. Transfer of causes

(a) Transfer by Supreme Court

(1) The Supreme Court may transfer a cause:

(A) To itself from a Court of Appeal;

(B) From itself to a Court of Appeal;

(C) Between Courts of Appeal; or

(D) Between divisions of a Court of Appeal.

(2) The clerk of the transferee court must promptly send each party a copy of the transfer order with the new case number, if any.

(Subd (a) amended effective January 1, 2007.)

(b) Transfer by a Court of Appeal administrative presiding justice

(1) A Court of Appeal administrative presiding justice may transfer causes between divisions of that court as follows:

(A) If multiple appeals or writ petitions arise from the same trial court action or proceeding, the presiding justice may transfer the later appeals or petitions to the division assigned the first appeal or petition.

(B) If, because of recusals, a division does not have three justices qualified to decide a cause, the presiding justice may transfer it to a division randomly selected by the clerk.

(2) The clerk must promptly notify the parties of the division to which the cause was transferred.

Rule 10.1000 amended and renumbered effective January 1, 2007; adopted as rule 47.1 effective January 1, 2003.

Advisory Committee Comment

Subdivision (a). Subdivision (a)(1) implements article VI, section 12(a) of the Constitution. As used in article VI, section 12(a) and in the rule, the term "cause" is broadly construed to include " 'all cases, matters, and proceedings of every description' " adjudicated by the Courts of Appeal and the Supreme Court. (*In re Rose* (2000) 22 Cal.4th 430, 540, quoting *In re Wells* (1917) 174 Cal. 467, 471.)

Rule 10.1004. Court of Appeal administrative presiding justice

(a) Designation

(1) In a Court of Appeal with more than one division, the Chief Justice may designate a presiding justice to act as administrative presiding justice. The administrative presiding justice serves at the pleasure of the Chief Justice for the period specified in the designation order.

(2) The administrative presiding justice must designate another member of the court to serve as acting administrative presiding justice in the administrative presiding justice's absence. If the administrative presiding justice does not make that designation, the Chief Justice must do so.

(3) In a Court of Appeal with only one division, the presiding justice acts as the administrative presiding justice.

(Subd (a) amended effective January 1, 2007.)

(b) Responsibilities

The administrative presiding justice is responsible for leading the court, establishing policies, promoting access to justice for all members of the public, providing a forum for the fair and expeditious resolution of disputes, and maximizing the use of judicial and other resources.

(c) Duties

The administrative presiding justice must perform any duties delegated by a majority of the justices in the district with the Chief Justice's concurrence. In addition, the administrative presiding justice has responsibility for the following matters:

(1) *Personnel*

The administrative presiding justice has general direction and supervision of the clerk/executive officer and all court employees except those assigned to a particular justice or division;

(2) *Unassigned matters*

The administrative presiding justice has the authority of a presiding justice with respect to any matter that has not been assigned to a particular division;

(3) *Judicial Council*

The administrative presiding justice cooperates with the Chief Justice and any officer authorized to act for the Chief Justice in connection with the making of reports and the assignment of judges or retired judges under article VI, section 6 of the California Constitution;

(4) *Transfer of cases*

The administrative presiding justice cooperates with the Chief Justice in expediting judicial business and equalizing the work of judges by recommending, when appropriate, the transfer of cases by the Supreme Court under article VI, section 12 of the California Constitution;

(5) *Administration*

The administrative presiding justice supervises the administration of the court's day-to-day operations, including personnel matters, but must secure the approval of a majority of the justices in the district before implementing any change in court policies;

(6) *Budget*

The administrative presiding justice has sole authority in the district over the budget as allocated by the Chair of the Judicial Council, including budget transfers, execution of purchase orders, obligation of funds, and approval of payments; and

(7) *Facilities*

The administrative presiding justice, except as provided in (d), has sole authority in the district over the operation, maintenance, renovation, expansion, and assignment of all facilities used and occupied by the district.

(Subd (c) amended effective January 1, 2018; previously amended effective January 1, 2007.)

(d) Geographically separate divisions

Under the general oversight of the administrative presiding justice, the presiding justice of a geographically separate division:

(1) Generally directs and supervises all of the division's court employees not assigned to a particular justice;

(2) Has authority to act on behalf of the division regarding day-to-day operations;

(3) Administers the division budget for day-to-day operations, including expenses for maintenance of facilities and equipment; and

(4) Operates, maintains, and assigns space in all facilities used and occupied by the division.

(Subd (d) amended effective January 1, 2007.)

Rule 10.1004 amended effective January 1, 2018; repealed and adopted as rule 75 effective January 1, 2005; previously amended and renumbered effective January 1, 2007.

Rule 10.1008. Courts of Appeal with more than one division

Appeals and original proceedings filed in a Court of Appeal with more than one division, or transferred to such a court without designation of a division, may be assigned to divisions in a way that will equalize the distribution of business among them. The clerk/executive officer of the Court of Appeal must keep records showing the divisions in which cases and proceedings are pending.

Rule 10.1008 amended effective January 1, 2018; repealed and adopted as rule 47 effective January 1, 2005; previously amended and renumbered effective January 1, 2007.

Rule 10.1012. Supervising progress of appeals

(a) Duty to ensure prompt filing

The administrative presiding justices of Courts of Appeal with more than one division in the same city and the presiding justices of all other Courts of Appeal are generally responsible for ensuring that all appellate records and briefs are promptly filed. Staff must be provided for that purpose, to the extent that funds are appropriated and available.

(Subd (a) amended effective January 1, 2007.)

(b) Authority

Notwithstanding any other rule, the administrative presiding justices and presiding justices referred to in (a) may:

(1) Grant or deny applications to extend the time to file records, briefs, and other documents, except that a presiding justice may extend the time to file briefs in conjunction with an order to augment the record;

(2) Order the dismissal of an appeal or any other authorized sanction for noncompliance with these rules, if no application to extend time or for relief from default has been filed before the order is entered; and

(3) Grant relief from default or from a sanction other than dismissal imposed for the default.

(Subd (b) amended effective January 1, 2007.)

Rule 10.1012 amended and renumbered effective January 1, 2007; repealed and adopted as rule 77 effective January 1, 2005.

Rule 10.1014. Oversight of administrative presiding justices and presiding justices

(a) Purpose

Administrative presiding justices and presiding justices are accountable for the efficient, effective, and proper administration of the Courts of Appeal and each division of the Courts of Appeal. This rule is intended to advance that objective.

(Subd (a) adopted effective September 1, 2023.)

(b) Contention procedure

(1) Any person who contends that an administrative presiding justice or presiding justice has not properly addressed or managed an important matter related to the administration of a Court of Appeal or a division of a Court of Appeal may submit that contention to the administrative presiding justices collectively for their review, subject to (c)(1).

(2) Any administrative presiding justice or presiding justice who is the subject of a contention under this paragraph must cooperate with the administrative presiding justices responsible for reviewing that contention.

(3) Any administrative presiding justice who is the subject of a contention under this paragraph is recused from reviewing the contention.

(4) Following receipt and review of a contention, the administrative presiding justices collectively may take appropriate remedial or other lawful action to address the contention.

(5) Information on how to submit a contention will be posted on the judicial branch website.

(Subd (b) adopted effective September 1, 2023.)

(c) Presiding justices in districts with more than one division

(1) Before a person submits a contention under (b)(1) about a presiding justice of a district with more than one division, including the presiding justice of a geographically separate division, that person must first submit the contention to the administrative presiding justice of the district in which the division is located to provide an opportunity for the contention to be addressed by that administrative presiding justice.

(2) Presiding justices in districts with more than one division, including the presiding justice of a geographically separate division, must cooperate with the administrative presiding justice of the district in which the division is located when the administrative presiding justice is carrying out oversight responsibilities under this rule.

(Subd (c) adopted effective September 1, 2023.)

(d) Confidentiality

All procedures under this rule must be conducted in a manner that is as confidential as is reasonably possible, consistent with the need to conduct a thorough and complete investigation, the need for proper administration of the court, and resolution of the contention.

(1) This subdivision does not prohibit the person who submitted the contention or the justice who is the subject of the contention from making statements regarding the conduct underlying the contention.

(2) This subdivision does not preclude administrative presiding justices from communicating with the person who submitted the contention or the justice who is the subject of the contention about the conduct underlying the contention or the investigation, conclusion, or resolution of the contention.

(3) This subdivision does not preclude presiding justices from providing a notice to the Commission on Judicial Performance or forwarding to the commission any requested information.

(4) This subdivision does not preclude administrative presiding justices from making public, when appropriate, the conclusion or resolution of the contention.

(Subd (d) adopted effective September 1, 2023.)

Rule 10.1014 adopted effective September 1, 2023.

Advisory Committee Comment

Subdivision (b). Subdivision (b) provides a procedure by which any person may submit a contention to the administrative presiding justices regarding an administrative presiding justice or presiding justice related to the administration of a Court of Appeal or a division of a Court of Appeal.

Subdivision (b)(1). The term "any person" is intended to be construed broadly and would include a judicial officer, court employee, attorney, litigant, or member of the public.

The contentions that may be submitted to the administrative presiding justices under the procedures authorized by this rule are those that relate to the administration of a Court of Appeal district or a division of a Court of Appeal. Contentions related to the adjudication of a specific case or the decision in a specific case are not subject to the procedures in this rule. Personnel and employment matters are not subject to the procedures in this rule. Personnel matters, including complaints by or against employees, are already governed by employment laws and individual court personnel policies and procedures that vest responsibility for handling such matters with the clerk/executive officer. If an administrative presiding justice receives a submission and considers it outside the scope of the rule, it would be appropriate for the administrative presiding justice or their delegate to return the submission to the person who submitted it or to forward it to the appropriate official with responsibility for the contention, with a copy notifying the person who submitted it. For example, a personnel matter would be forwarded to the clerk/executive officer of the court.

Subdivision (b)(4). This paragraph authorizes the administrative presiding justices collectively to take appropriate remedial or other lawful action to address the contentions submitted under the procedures in this rule. Examples of actions that the administrative presiding justices may take include recommending amendments to the California Rules of Court or operational policies of the Courts of Appeal, referring a contention to the Commission on Judicial Performance, referring it to mediation, and conducting informal discussions with the person who submitted the contention and the justice who is the subject of the contention. This paragraph does not authorize administrative presiding justices to take actions that are within the sole purview of the Supreme Court or the Commission on Judicial Performance, for example, the removal, censure, or admonishment of a justice. Similarly, the rule does not authorize an administrative presiding justice to take personnel actions, as such actions are governed by other legal authorities and policies.

Subdivision (c). This subdivision is consistent with the governance structure provided in rule 10.1004, which gives administrative presiding justices responsibility for "leading the court, establishing policies, promoting access to justice for all members of the public, providing a forum for the fair and expeditious resolution of disputes, and maximizing the use of judicial and other resources" (Cal. Rules of Court, rule 10.1004(b)), along with more specific duties (Cal. Rules of Court, rule 10.1004(c)), and which also prescribes areas in which a presiding justice in a geographically separate division is given authority under the general oversight of the administrative presiding justice (Cal. Rules of Court rule 10.1004(d)).

Subdivision (d). Providing a process for persons to submit contentions under this rule for consideration and action by administrative presiding justices, either individually or collectively, will advance efficient, effective, and proper administration of the Courts of Appeal and each division of the Courts of Appeal. Establishing the confidentiality of this procedure is critical to encouraging persons to submit contentions with candor. The necessity for preserving the confidentiality of these procedures and of communications with administrative presiding justices outweighs the necessity for disclosure in the interest of justice.

Subdivision (d) is consistent with confidentiality provisions in other rules. Specifically, the text of subdivision (d) is modeled after provisions in California Rules of Court, rule 10.703(e), regarding the confidentiality of proceedings related to complaints about subordinate judicial officers in trial courts and authorizing certain notices regarding those proceedings, and in Rules of the Commission on Judicial Performance, rule 102. This subdivision is also consistent with maintaining the confidentiality of complaints against judges provided in California Rules of Court, rule 10.500(f)(7).

Rule 10.1016. Notice of failure to perform judicial duties

(a) Notice

(1) The Chief Justice or presiding justice must notify the Commission on Judicial Performance of a reviewing court justice's:

(A) Substantial failure to perform judicial duties, including any habitual neglect of duty; or

(B) Disability-caused absences totaling more than 90 court days in a 12-month period, excluding absences for authorized vacations and for attending schools, conferences, and judicial workshops.

(2) If the affected justice is a presiding justice, the administrative presiding justice must give the notice.

(Subd (a) amended effective January 1, 2007.)

(b) Copy to justice

The Chief Justice, administrative presiding justice, or presiding justice must give the affected justice a copy of any notice under (a).

Rule 10.1016 amended and renumbered effective January 1, 2007; repealed and adopted as rule 78 effective January 1, 2005.

Rule 10.1017. Notification to State Bar of attorney misconduct

(a) Notification by justice

When notification to the State Bar is required under Business and Professions Code section 6086.7, the senior justice issuing the order or the justice authoring the opinion that triggers the notification requirement under section 6086.7 is responsible for notifying the State Bar. The justice may direct the Clerk to notify the State Bar.

(Subd (a) adopted effective January 1, 2014.)

(b) Contents of notice

The notice must include the State Bar member's full name and State Bar number, if known, and a copy of the order or opinion that triggered the notification requirement.

(Subd (b) adopted effective January 1, 2014.)

(c) Notification to attorney

If notification to the State Bar is made under this rule, the person who notified the State Bar must also inform the attorney who is the subject of the notification that the matter has been referred to the State Bar.

(Subd (c) adopted effective January 1, 2014.)

Rule 10.1017 adopted effective January 1, 2014.

Advisory Committee Comment

Business and Professions Code section 6086.7 requires a court to notify the State Bar of any of the following: (1) a final order of contempt imposed on an attorney that may involve grounds warranting discipline under the State Bar Act; (2) a modification or reversal of a judgment in a judicial proceeding based in whole or in part on the misconduct, incompetent representation, or willful misrepresentation of an attorney; (3) the imposition of any judicial sanctions on an attorney of $1,000 or more, except sanctions for failure to make discovery; or (4) the imposition of any civil penalty on an attorney under Family Code section 8620. If the notification pertains to a final order of contempt, Business and Professions Code section 6086.7(a)(1) requires the court to transmit to the State Bar a copy of the relevant minutes, final order, and transcript, if one exists. This rule is intended to clarify which justice has the responsibility of notifying the State Bar under section 6086.7 and the required contents of the notice. In addition to the requirements stated in Business and Professions Code section 6086.7, judges are subject to canon 3D(2) of the California Code of Judicial Ethics, which states: "Whenever a judge has personal knowledge, or concludes in a judicial decision, that a lawyer has committed misconduct or has violated any provision of the Rules of Professional Conduct, the judge shall take appropriate corrective action, which may include reporting the violation to the appropriate authority." The Advisory Committee Commentary states: "Appropriate corrective action could include direct communication with the judge or lawyer who has committed the violation, other direct action, such as a confidential referral to a judicial or lawyer assistance program, or a report of the violation to the presiding judge, appropriate authority, or other agency or body. Judges should note that in addition to the action required by Canon 3D(2), California law imposes mandatory additional reporting requirements on judges regarding lawyer misconduct. See Business and Professions Code section 6068.7."

Rule 10.1020. Reviewing court clerk/executive officer

(a) Selection

A reviewing court may employ a clerk/executive officer selected in accordance with procedures adopted by the court.

(Subd (a) amended effective January 1, 2018.)

(b) Responsibilities

Acting under the general direction and supervision of the administrative presiding justice, the clerk/executive officer is responsible for planning, organizing, coordinating, and directing, with full authority and accountability, the management of the office of the clerk/executive officer and all nonjudicial support activities in a manner that promotes access to justice for all members of the public, provides a forum for the fair and expeditious resolution of disputes, and maximizes the use of judicial and other resources.

(Subd (b) amended effective January 1, 2018.)

(c) Duties

Under the direction of the administrative presiding justice, the clerk/executive officer has the following duties:

(1) *Personnel*

The clerk/executive officer directs and supervises all court employees assigned to the clerk/executive officer by the administrative presiding justice and ensures that the court receives a full range of human resources support;

(2) *Budget*

The clerk/executive officer develops, administers, and monitors the court budget and develops practices and procedures to ensure that annual expenditures are within the budget;

(3) *Contracts*

The clerk/executive officer negotiates contracts on the court's behalf in accord with established contracting procedures and applicable laws;

(4) *Calendar management*

The clerk/executive officer employs and supervises efficient calendar and caseflow management, including analyzing and evaluating pending caseloads and recommending effective calendar management techniques;

(5) *Technology*

The clerk/executive officer coordinates technological and automated systems activities to assist the court;

(6) *Facilities*

The clerk/executive officer coordinates facilities, space planning, court security, and business services support, including the purchase and management of equipment and supplies;

(7) *Records*

The clerk/executive officer creates and manages uniform recordkeeping systems, collecting data on pending and completed judicial business and the court's internal operation as the court and Judicial Council require;

(8) *Recommendations*

The clerk/executive officer identifies problems and recommends policy, procedural, and administrative changes to the court;

(9) *Public relations*

The clerk/executive officer represents the court to internal and external customers—including the other branches of government—on issues pertaining to the court;

(10) *Liaison*

The clerk/executive officer acts as liaison with other governmental agencies;

(11) *Committees*

The clerk/executive officer provides staff for judicial committees;

(12) *Administration*

The clerk/executive officer develops and implements administrative and operational programs and policies for the court and the office of the clerk/executive officer; and

(13) *Other*

The clerk/executive officer performs other duties as the administrative presiding justice directs.

(Subd (c) amended effective January 1, 2018; previously amended effective January 1, 2007.)

(d) Geographically separate divisions

Under the general oversight of the clerk/executive officer, an assistant clerk/executive officer of a geographically separate division has responsibility for the nonjudicial support activities of that division.

(Subd (d) amended effective January 1, 2018.)

Rule 10.1020 amended effective January 1, 2018; repealed and adopted as rule 76.1 effective January 1, 2005; previously amended and renumbered effective January 1, 2007.

Rule 10.1024. Court of Appeal minutes

(a) Purpose

Court of Appeal minutes should record the court's significant public acts and permit the public to follow the major events in the history of cases coming before the court.

(b) Required contents of minutes

The minutes must include:

(1) The filing date of each opinion, showing whether it was ordered published;

(2) Orders granting or denying rehearings or modifying opinions;

(3) Orders affecting an opinion's publication status, if issued after the opinion was filed;

(4) Summaries of all courtroom proceedings, showing at a minimum:

(A) The cases called for argument;

(B) The justices hearing argument;

(C) The name of the attorney arguing for each party; and

(D) Whether the case was submitted at the close of argument or the court requested further briefing;

(5) The date of submission, if other than the date of argument;

(6) Orders vacating submission, including the reason for vacating and the resubmission date;

(7) Orders dismissing appeals for lack of jurisdiction;

(8) Orders consolidating cases;

(9) Orders affecting a judgment or its finality date; and

(10) Orders changing or correcting any of the above.

(Subd (b) amended effective January 1, 2007.)

(c) Optional contents of minutes

At the court's discretion, the minutes may include such other matter as:

(1) Assignments of justices by the Chief Justice;

(2) Reports of the Commission on Judicial Appointments confirming justices; and

(3) Memorials.

(Subd (c) amended effective January 1, 2007.)

Rule 10.1024 amended and renumbered effective January 1, 2007; adopted as rule 71 effective January 1, 2005.

Rule 10.1028. Preservation and destruction of Court of Appeal records

(a) Form or forms in which records may be preserved

(1) Court of Appeal records may be created, maintained, and preserved in any form or forms of communication or representation, including paper or optical, electronic, magnetic, micrographic, or photographic media or other technology, if the form or forms of representation or communication satisfy the standards or guidelines for the creation, maintenance, reproduction, and preservation of court records established under rule 10.854.

(2) If records are preserved in a medium other than paper, the following provisions of Government Code section 68150 apply: subdivisions (c)–(l), excluding subdivision (i)(1).

(Subd (a) amended effective January 1, 2013.)

(b) Methods for signing, subscribing, or verifying documents

Any notice, order, ruling, decision, opinion, memorandum, certificate of service, or similar document issued by an appellate court or by a judicial officer of an appellate court may be signed, subscribed, or verified using a computer or other technology in accordance with procedures, standards, and guidelines established by the Judicial Council. Notwithstanding any other provision of law, all notices, orders, rulings, decisions, opinions, memoranda, certificates of service, or similar documents that are signed, subscribed, or verified by computer or other technological means under this subdivision shall have the same validity, and the same legal force and effect, as paper documents signed, subscribed, or verified by an appellate court or a judicial officer of the court.

(Subd (b) adopted effective January 1, 2013.)

(c) Permanent records

The clerk/executive officer of the Court of Appeal must permanently keep the court's minutes and a register of appeals and original proceedings.

(Subd (c) amended effective January 1, 2018; relettered from subd (b) effective January 1, 2013.)

(d) Time to keep other records

(1) Except as provided in (2) and (3), the clerk/executive officer may destroy all other records in a case 10 years after the decision becomes final, as ordered by the administrative presiding justice or, in a court with only one division, by the presiding justice.

(2) Except as provided in (3), in a criminal case in which the court affirms a judgment of conviction in whole or in part, the clerk/executive officer must keep the original reporter's transcript or, if the original is in paper, either the original or a true and correct electronic copy of the transcript, for 20 years after the decision becomes final.

(3) In a felony case in which the court affirms a judgment of conviction in whole or in part, the clerk/executive officer must keep the original reporter's transcript or, if the original is in paper, either the original or a true and correct electronic copy of the transcript, for 75 years after the decision becomes final.

(Subd (d) amended effective January 1, 2023; adopted as subd (c); previously relettered as subd (d) effective January 1, 2013; previously amended effective January 1, 2017, and January 1, 2018.)

Rule 10.1028 amended effective January 1, 2023; adopted as rule 70 effective January 1, 2005; previously renumbered effective January 1, 2007; previously amended effective January 1, 2013, January 1, 2017, and January 1, 2018.

Advisory Committee Comment

Subdivision (d). Subdivision (d) permits the Court of Appeal to keep an electronic copy of the reporter's transcript in lieu of keeping the original if the original transcript is in paper. Although subdivision (a) allows the Court of Appeal to maintain its records in any form that satisfies the otherwise applicable standards for maintenance of court records, including electronic forms, Code of Civil Procedure section 271 provides that an original reporter's transcript must be in electronic form unless a specified exception allows for an original paper transcript. Subdivision (d) therefore specifies that an electronic copy may be kept if the original transcript is in paper, to clarify that the paper original need not be kept by the court.

Rule 10.1030. Local rules of Courts of Appeal

(a) Publication

(1) A Court of Appeal must submit any local rule it adopts to the Reporter of Decisions for publication in the advance pamphlets of the Official Reports.

(2) As used in this rule, "publication" means printing in the manner in which amendments to the California Rules of Court are printed.

(Subd (a) relettered effective January 1, 2007.)

(b) Effective date

A local rule cannot take effect sooner than 45 days after the publication date of the advance pamphlet in which it is printed.

(Subd (b) relettered effective January 1, 2007.)

Rule 10.1030 amended and renumbered effective January 1, 2007; repealed and adopted as rule 80 effective January 1, 2005.

Chapter 2
Rules Relating to the Superior Court Appellate Division

Chapter 2 adopted effective January 1, 2009.

Rule 10.1100. Assignments to the appellate division
Rule 10.1104. Presiding judge
Rule 10.1108. Sessions

Rule 10.1100. Assignments to the appellate division

(a) Goal

In making assignments to the appellate division, the Chief Justice will consider the goal of promoting the independence and the quality of the appellate division.

(Subd (a) adopted effective January 1, 2009.)

(b) Factors considered

Factors considered in making the assignments may include:

(1) Length of service as a judge;

(2) Reputation in the judicial community;

(3) Degree of separateness of the appellate division work from the judge's regular assignments; and

(4) Any recommendation of the presiding judge.

(Subd (b) adopted effective January 1, 2009.)

(c) Who may be assigned

Judges assigned may include judges from another county, judges retired from the superior court or a court of higher jurisdiction, or a panel of judges from different superior courts who sit in turn in each of those superior courts.

(Subd (c) adopted effective January 1, 2009.)

(d) Terms of service

In specifying terms of service to the appellate division, the Chief Justice will consider the needs of the court.

(Subd (d) adopted effective January 1, 2009.)

Rule 10.1100 adopted effective January 1, 2009.

Advisory Committee Comment

The Chief Justice is responsible for assigning judges to the appellate division as provided in article VI, section 4 of the California Constitution and by statute.

Rule 10.1104. Presiding judge

(a) Designation of acting presiding judge

(1) The presiding judge of the appellate division must designate another member of the appellate division to serve as acting presiding judge in the absence of the presiding judge. If the presiding judge does not make that designation, the appellate division judge among those present who has the greatest seniority in the appellate division must act as presiding judge. When the judges are of equal seniority in the appellate division, the judge who is also senior in service in the superior court must act as presiding judge.

(2) As used in these rules, "presiding judge" includes acting presiding judge.

(Subd (a) adopted effective January 1, 2009.)

(b) Responsibilities

The presiding judge of the appellate division may convene the appellate division at any time and must supervise the business of the division.

(Subd (b) adopted effective January 1, 2009.)

Rule 10.1104 adopted effective January 1, 2009.

Advisory Committee Comment

Under Code of Civil Procedure section 77(a), the Chief Justice is responsible for designating one of the judges of each appellate division as the presiding judge.

Rule 10.1108. Sessions

The appellate division of each superior court must hold a session at least once each quarter unless there are no matters set for oral argument that quarter. The time and place of any session is determined by the presiding judge of the appellate division.

Rule 10.1108 adopted effective January 1, 2009.

Standards of Judicial Administration

Title 1. Standards for All Courts [Reserved].
Title 2. Standards for Proceedings in the Trial Courts. Standards 2.1–2.30.
Title 3. Standards for Civil Cases. Standards 3.1–3.25.
Title 4. Standards for Criminal Cases. Standards 4.10–4.42.
Title 5. Standards for Cases Involving Children and Families. Standards 5.20–5.45.
Title 6. [Reserved].
Title 7. Standards for Probate Proceedings. Standard 7.10.
Title 8. Standards for the Appellate Courts. Standard 8.1.
Title 9. Standards on Law Practice, Attorneys, and Judges [Reserved].
Title 10. Standards for Judicial Administration. Standards 10.5–10.80.

Title 1
Standards for All Courts
[Reserved]

STANDARDS OF JUDICIAL ADMINISTRATION
Title 2
Standards for Proceedings in the Trial Courts

STANDARDS OF JUDICIAL ADMINISTRATION

Standard 2.1. Case management and delay reduction—statement of general principles
Standard 2.2. Trial court case disposition time goals
Standard 2.10. Procedures for determining the need for an interpreter and a preappearance interview
Standard 2.11. Interpreted proceedings—instructing participants on procedure
Standard 2.20. Trial management standards
Standard 2.25. Uninterrupted jury selection
Standard 2.30. Judicial comment on verdict or mistrial

Standard 2.1.

Case management and delay reduction—statement of general principles

(a) Elimination of all unnecessary delays

Trial courts should be guided by the general principle that from the commencement of litigation to its resolution, whether by trial or settlement, any elapsed time other than reasonably required for pleadings, discovery, preparation, and court events is unacceptable and should be eliminated.

(Subd (a) amended and lettered effective January 1, 2004; adopted as part of unlettered subdivision effective July 1, 1987.)

(b) Court responsible for the pace of litigation

To enable the just and efficient resolution of cases, the court, not the lawyers or litigants, should control the pace of litigation. A strong judicial commitment is essential to reducing delay and, once achieved, maintaining a current docket.

(Subd (b) amended and lettered effective January 1, 2004; adopted as part of unlettered subdivision effective July 1, 1987.)

(c) Presiding judge's role

The presiding judge of each court should take an active role in advancing the goals of delay reduction and in formulating and implementing local rules and procedures to accomplish the following:

(1) The expeditious and timely resolution of cases, after full and careful consideration consistent with the ends of justice;

(2) The identification and elimination of local rules, forms, practices, and procedures that are obstacles to delay reduction, are inconsistent with statewide case management rules, or prevent the court from effectively managing its cases;

(3) The formulation and implementation of a system of tracking cases from filing to disposition; and

(4) The training of judges and nonjudicial administrative personnel in delay reduction rules and procedures adopted in the local jurisdiction.

(Subd (c) amended and lettered effective January 1, 2004; adopted as part of unlettered subdivision effective July 1, 1987.)

Standard 2.1 amended and renumbered effective January 1, 2007; adopted as sec. 2 effective July 1, 1987; previously amended effective January 1, 1994, and January 1, 2004.

Standard 2.2. Trial court case disposition time goals

(a) Trial Court Delay Reduction Act

The recommended goals for case disposition time in the trial courts in this standard are adopted under Government Code sections 68603 and 68620.

(Subd (a) amended effective January 1, 2007; adopted effective July 1, 1987; relettered effective January 1, 1989; previously amended effective January 1, 2004.)

(b) Statement of purpose

The recommended time goals are intended to guide the trial courts in applying the policies and principles of standard 2.1. They are administrative, justice-oriented guidelines to be used in the management of the courts. They are intended to improve the administration of justice by encouraging prompt disposition of all matters coming before the courts. The goals apply to all cases filed and are not meant to create deadlines for individual cases. Through its case management practices, a court may achieve or exceed the goals stated in this standard for the overall disposition of cases. The goals should be applied in a fair, practical, and flexible manner. They are not to be used as the basis for sanctions against any court or judge.

(Subd (b) amended effective January 1, 2007; adopted effective July 1, 1987, as (1); relettered effective January 1, 1989; previously amended effective January 1, 2004.)

(c) Definition

The definition of "general civil case" in rule 1.6 applies to this section. It includes both unlimited and limited civil cases.

(Subd (c) amended effective January 1, 2007; adopted effective January 1, 2004.)

(d) Civil cases—processing time goals

The goal of each trial court should be to process general civil cases so that all cases are disposed of within two years of filing.

(Subd (d) amended and relettered effective January 1, 2004; adopted effective July 1, 1987, as (2); previously amended effective July 1, 1988; amended and relettered as subd (c) effective January 1, 1989.)

(e) Civil cases—rate of disposition

Each trial court should dispose of at least as many civil cases as are filed each year and, if necessary to meet the case-processing goal in (d), dispose of more cases than are filed. As the court disposes of inactive cases, it should identify active cases that may require judicial attention.

(Subd (e) amended effective January 1, 2007; adopted effective July 1, 1987, as (3); previously amended effective July 1, 1988; previously amended and relettered as subd (d) effective January 1, 1989, and as subd (e) effective January 1, 2004.)

(f) General civil cases—case disposition time goals

The goal of each trial court should be to manage general civil cases, except those exempt under (g), so that they meet the following case disposition time goals:

(1) *Unlimited civil cases:*

The goal of each trial court should be to manage unlimited civil cases from filing so that:

(A) 75 percent are disposed of within 12 months;

(B) 85 percent are disposed of within 18 months; and

(C) 100 percent are disposed of within 24 months.

(2) *Limited civil cases:*

The goal of each trial court should be to manage limited civil cases from filing so that:

(A) 90 percent are disposed of within 12 months;
(B) 98 percent are disposed of within 18 months; and
(C) 100 percent are disposed of within 24 months.

(3) *Individualized case management*

The goals in (1) and (2) are guidelines for the court's disposition of all unlimited and limited civil cases filed in that court. In managing individual civil cases, the court must consider each case on its merits. To enable the fair and efficient resolution of civil cases, each case should be set for trial as soon as appropriate for that individual case consistent with rule 3.729.

(Subd (f) amended effective January 1, 2007; adopted as subd (g) effective July 1, 1987; relettered as subd (h) effective January 1, 1989; amended effective July 1, 1991; previously amended and relettered as subd (f) effective January 1, 2004.)

(g) Exceptional civil cases

A general civil case that meets the criteria in rules 3.715 and 3.400 and that involves exceptional circumstances or will require continuing review is exempt from the time goals in (d) and (f). Every exceptional case should be monitored to ensure its timely disposition consistent with the exceptional circumstances, with the goal of disposing of the case within three years.

(Subd (g) amended effective January 1, 2007; adopted effective January 1, 2004.)

(h) Small claims cases

The goals for small claims cases are:
(1) 90 percent disposed of within 75 days after filing; and
(2) 100 percent disposed of within 95 days after filing.

(Subd (h) adopted effective January 1, 2004.)

(i) Unlawful detainer cases

The goals for unlawful detainer cases are:
(1) 90 percent disposed of within 30 days after filing; and
(2) 100 percent disposed of within 45 days after filing.

(Subd (i) adopted effective January 1, 2004.)

(j) Felony cases—processing time goals

Except for capital cases, all felony cases disposed of should have a total elapsed processing time of no more than one year from the defendant's first arraignment to disposition.

(Subd (j) amended effective January 1, 2007; adopted effective January 1, 2004.)

(k) Misdemeanor cases

The goals for misdemeanor cases are:
(1) 90 percent disposed of within 30 days after the defendant's first arraignment on the complaint;
(2) 98 percent disposed of within 90 days after the defendant's first arraignment on the complaint; and
(3) 100 percent disposed of within 120 days after the defendant's first arraignment on the complaint.

(Subd (k) adopted effective January 1, 2004.)

(l) Felony preliminary examinations

The goal for felony cases at the time of the preliminary examination (excluding murder cases in which the prosecution seeks the death penalty) should be disposition by dismissal, by interim disposition by certified plea of guilty, or by finding of probable cause, so that:
(1) 90 percent of cases are disposed of within 30 days after the defendant's first arraignment on the complaint;
(2) 98 percent of cases are disposed of within 45 days after the defendant's first arraignment on the complaint; and
(3) 100 percent of cases are disposed of within 90 days after the defendant's first arraignment on the complaint.

(Subd (l) adopted effective January 1, 2004.)

(m) Cases removed from court's control excluded from computation of time

If a case is removed from the court's control, the period of time until the case is restored to court control should be excluded from the case disposition time goals. The matters that remove a case from the court's control for the purposes of this section include:

(1) Civil cases:
(A) The filing of a notice of conditional settlement under rule 3.1385;
(B) An automatic stay resulting from the filing of an action in a federal bankruptcy court;
(C) The removal of the case to federal court;
(D) An order of a federal court or higher state court staying the case;
(E) An order staying the case based on proceedings in a court of equal standing in another jurisdiction;
(F) The pendency of contractual arbitration under Code of Civil Procedure section 1281.4;
(G) The pendency of attorney fee arbitration under Business and Professions Code section 6201;
(H) A stay by the reporting court for active military duty or incarceration; and
(I) For 180 days, the exemption for uninsured motorist cases under rule 3.712(b).

(2) Felony or misdemeanor cases:
(A) Issuance of warrant;
(B) Imposition of a civil assessment under Penal Code section 1214.1;
(C) Pendency of completion of diversion under Penal Code section 1000 et seq.;
(D) Evaluation of mental competence under Penal Code section 1368;
(E) Evaluation as a narcotics addict under Welfare and Institutions Code sections 3050 and 3051;
(F) 90-day diagnostic and treatment program under Penal Code section 1203.3;
(G) 90-day evaluation period for a juvenile under Welfare and Institutions Code section 707.2;
(H) Stay by a higher court or by a federal court for proceedings in another jurisdiction;
(I) Stay by the reporting court for active military duty or incarceration; and
(J) Time granted by the court to secure counsel if the defendant is not represented at the first appearance.

(Subd (m) relettered effective January 1, 2024; adopted as subd (n) effective January 1, 2004; previously amended effective January 1, 2007.)

(n) Problems

A court that finds its ability to comply with these goals impeded by a rule of court or statute should notify the Judicial Council.

(Subd (n) relettered effective January 1, 2024; adopted as subd (o) effective January 1, 2004; previously amended effective January 1, 2007.)

Standard 2.2 amended effective January 1, 2024; adopted as sec. 2.1 effective July 1, 1987; previously amended effective January 1, 1988, July 1, 1988, January 1, 1989, January 1, 1990, July 1, 1991, and January 1, 2004; previously amended and renumbered effective January 1, 2007.

Standard 2.10. Procedures for determining the need for an interpreter and a preappearance interview

(a) When an interpreter is needed

An interpreter is needed if, after an examination of a party or witness, the court concludes that:
(1) The party cannot understand and speak English well enough to participate fully in the proceedings and to assist counsel; or
(2) The witness cannot speak English so as to be understood directly by counsel, court, and jury.

(Subd (a) amended effective January 1, 2007.)

(b) When an examination is required

The court should examine a party or witness on the record to determine whether an interpreter is needed if:
(1) A party or counsel requests such an examination; or
(2) It appears to the court that the party or witness may not understand and speak English well enough to participate fully in the proceedings.

(Subd (b) amended effective January 1, 2007.)

(c) Examination of party or witness

To determine if an interpreter is needed, the court should normally include questions on the following:
(1) Identification (for example: name, address, birthdate, age, place of birth);
(2) Active vocabulary in vernacular English (for example: "How did you come to the court today?" "What kind of work do you do?" "Where did you go to school?" "What was the highest grade you completed?" "Describe what you see in the courtroom." "What have you eaten today?"). Questions should be phrased to avoid "yes" or "no" replies;
(3) The court proceedings (for example: the nature of the charge or the type of case before the court, the purpose of the proceedings and function of the court, the rights of a party or criminal defendant, and the responsibilities of a witness).

(Subd (c) amended effective January 1, 2007.)

(d) Record of examination

After the examination, the court should state its conclusion on the record. The file in the case should be clearly marked and data entered electronically when appropriate by court personnel to ensure that an interpreter will be present when needed in any subsequent proceeding.

(Subd (d) amended effective January 1, 2007.)

(e) Good cause for preappearance interview

For good cause, the court should authorize a preappearance interview between the interpreter and the party or witness. Good cause exists if the interpreter needs clarification on any interpreting issues, including: colloquialisms, culturalisms, dialects, idioms, linguistic capabilities and traits, regionalisms, register, slang, speech patterns, or technical terms.

(Subd (e) amended effective January 1, 2007.)

Standard 2.10 amended and renumbered effective January 1, 2007; repealed and adopted as sec. 18 effective January 1, 1999.

Standard 2.11. Interpreted proceedings—instructing participants on procedure

(a) Instructions to interpreters

The court or the court's designee should give the following instructions to interpreters, either orally or in writing:

(1) Do not discuss the pending proceedings with a party or witness.

(2) Do not disclose communications between counsel and client.

(3) Do not give legal advice to a party or witness. Refer legal questions to the attorney or to the court.

(4) Inform the court if you are unable to interpret a word, expression, special terminology, or dialect, or have doubts about your linguistic expertise or ability to perform adequately in a particular case.

(5) Interpret all words, including slang, vulgarisms, and epithets, to convey the intended meaning.

(6) Use the first person when interpreting statements made in the first person. (For example, a statement or question should not be introduced with the words, "He says ….")

(7) Direct all inquiries or problems to the court and not to the witness or counsel. If necessary, you may request permission to approach the bench with counsel to discuss a problem.

(8) Position yourself near the witness or party without blocking the view of the judge, jury, or counsel.

(9) Inform the court if you become fatigued during the proceedings.

(10) When interpreting for a party at the counsel table, speak loudly enough to be heard by the party or counsel but not so loudly as to interfere with the proceedings.

(11) Interpret everything, including objections.

(12) If the court finds good cause under rule 2.893(e), hold a preappearance interview with the party or witness to become familiar with speech patterns and linguistic traits and to determine what technical or special terms may be used. Counsel may be present at the preappearance interview.

(13) During the preappearance interview with a non-English-speaking witness, give the witness the following instructions on the procedure to be followed when the witness is testifying:

(A) The witness must speak in a loud, clear voice so that the entire court and not just the interpreter can hear.

(B) The witness must direct all responses to the person asking the question, not to the interpreter.

(C) The witness must direct all questions to counsel or to the court and not to the interpreter. The witness may not seek advice from or engage in any discussion with the interpreter.

(14) During the preappearance interview with a non-English-speaking party, give the following instructions on the procedure to be used when the non-English-speaking party is not testifying:

(A) The interpreter will interpret all statements made in open court.

(B) The party must direct any questions to counsel. The interpreter will interpret all questions to counsel and the responses. The party may not seek advice from or engage in discussion with the interpreter.

(Subd (a) amended effective January 1, 2007.)

(b) Instructions to counsel

The court or the court's designee should give the following instructions to counsel, either orally or in writing:

(1) When examining a non-English-speaking witness, direct all questions to the witness and not to the interpreter. (For example, do not say to the interpreter, "Ask him if ….")

(2) If there is a disagreement with the interpretation, direct any objection to the court and not to the interpreter. Ask permission to approach the bench to discuss the problem.

(3) If you have a question regarding the qualifications of the interpreter, you may request permission to conduct a supplemental examination on the interpreter's qualifications.

Standard 2.11 amended and renumbered effective January 1, 2007; repealed and adopted as sec. 18.1 effective January 1, 1999.

Standard 2.20. Trial management standards

(a) General principles

The trial judge has the responsibility to manage the trial proceedings. The judge should take appropriate action to ensure that all parties are prepared to proceed, the trial commences as scheduled, all parties have a fair opportunity to present evidence, and the trial proceeds to conclusion without unnecessary interruption. When the trial involves a jury, the trial judge should manage proceedings with particular emphasis on the needs of the jury.

(Subd (a) amended effective January 1, 2007.)

(b) Techniques of trial management

The trial judge should employ the following trial management techniques:

(1) Participate with trial counsel in a trial management conference before trial.

(2) After consultation with counsel, set reasonable time limits.

(3) Arrange the court's docket to start trial as scheduled and inform parties of the number of hours set each day for the trial.

(4) Ensure that once trial has begun, momentum is maintained.

(5) Be receptive to using technology in managing the trial and the presentation of evidence.

(6) Attempt to maintain continuity in days of trial and hours of trial.

(7) Schedule arguments on legal issues at the beginning or end of the day so as not to interrupt the presentation of evidence.

(8) Permit sidebar conferences only when necessary, and keep them as short as possible.

(9) In longer trials, consider scheduling trial days to permit jurors time for personal business.

(Subd (b) amended effective January 1, 2007.)

Standard 2.20 amended and renumbered effective January 1, 2007; adopted as sec 8.9 effective July 1, 1997.

Standard 2.25. Uninterrupted jury selection

When practical, the trial judge, with the cooperation of the other judges of the court, should schedule court business to allow for jury selection uninterrupted by other court business.

Standard 2.25 amended and renumbered effective January 1, 2007; adopted as sec. 8.6 effective July 1, 1990.

Standard 2.30. Judicial comment on verdict or mistrial

At the conclusion of a trial, or on declaring a mistrial for failure of a jury to reach a verdict, it is appropriate for the trial judge to thank jurors for their public service, but the judge's comments should not include praise or criticism of the verdict or the failure to reach a verdict.

Standard 2.30 amended and renumbered effective January 1, 2007; adopted as sec. 14 effective January 1, 1976.

Title 3
Standards for Civil Cases

Standard 3.1. Appearance by telephone
Standard 3.10. Complex civil litigation
Standard 3.25. Examination of prospective jurors in civil cases

Standard 3.1. Appearance by telephone

(a) Recommended criteria for telephone equipment

Each court should have adequate telephone equipment for use in hearings at which counsel may appear by telephone. This equipment should:

(1) Permit each person participating in the hearing, whether in person or by telephone, to hear all other persons;

(2) Handle at least three incoming calls at one time and place those calls into a conference call in a simple and quick manner;

(3) Have a silent (visible) ringer;

(4) Be simple to learn and use;

(5) Be reasonable in cost; and

(6) Have full-duplex, simultaneous bidirectional speaker capability.

(Subd (a) amended effective January 1, 2007.)

(b) Optional features for telephone equipment

It is desirable if the telephone equipment can:

(1) Dial previously stored telephone numbers;

(2) Record conversations;

(3) Be moved easily from location to location; and

(4) Automatically queue incoming calls.

(Subd (b) amended effective January 1, 2007.)

(c) Award of attorney's fees

A court should consider, in awarding attorney's fees under any applicable provision of law, whether an attorney is claiming fees for appearing in person in a proceeding in which that attorney could have appeared by telephone.

(Subd (c) repealed and relettered effective January 1, 2008; adopted as subd (d) effective January 1, 1989; previously amended effective January 1, 2007.)

(d) Local procedures for telephone appearance

Each court should adopt a local rule or uniform local written policy specifying the following:

(1) Whether the court or the attorney initiates the telephone call for a telephone appearance;

(2) Whether the court sets a specified time for a telephone appearance or a time range; and

(3) How the parties are notified, in advance of the hearing, of the time or time range of the telephone appearance. In those courts using a tentative ruling recording system, that notice should be part of the tentative ruling recording.

(Subd (d) relettered effective January 1, 2008; adopted as subd (e) effective January 1, 1989; previously amended effective January 1, 2007.)

Standard 3.1 amended effective January 1, 2008; repealed and adopted as sec. 21 effective January 1, 1989; previously amended effective July 1, 1992, and January 1, 2007.

Standard 3.10. Complex civil litigation

(a) Judicial management

In complex litigation, judicial management should begin early and be applied continuously and actively, based on knowledge of the circumstances of each case.

(b) All-purpose assignment

Complex litigation should be assigned to one judge for all purposes. If such an assignment is not possible, a single judge should be assigned to hear law and motion matters and discovery matters.

(Subd (b) amended effective January 1, 2007; adopted as subd (d) effective July 1, 1982; previously relettered effective January 1, 2000.)

(c) Selection of judges for complex litigation assignments

In selecting judges for complex litigation assignments, the presiding judge should consider the needs of the court and the judge's ability, interest, training, experience (including experience with complex civil cases), and willingness to participate in educational programs related to the management of complex cases. Commissioners should not be employed in any phase of complex litigation, except under the judge's direct supervision to assist in the management of the case.

(Subd (c) amended and relettered effective January 1, 2000; adopted as subd (e) effective July 1, 1982.)

(d) Establishing time limits

Time limits should be regularly used to expedite major phases of complex litigation. Time limits should be established early, tailored to the circumstances of each case, firmly and fairly maintained, and accompanied by other methods of sound judicial management.

(Subd (d) relettered effective January 1, 2000; adopted as subd (f) effective July 1, 1982.)

(e) Preparation for trial

Litigants in complex litigation cases should be required to minimize evidentiary disputes and to organize efficiently their exhibits and other evidence before trial.

(Subd (e) amended and relettered effective January 1, 2007; adopted as subd (i) effective July 1, 1982; previously relettered as subd (g) effective January 1, 2000.)

(f) Dilatory tactics

Judges involved in complex litigation should be sensitive to dilatory or abusive litigation tactics and should be prepared to invoke disciplinary procedures for violations.

(Subd (f) relettered effective January 1, 2007; adopted as subd (j) effective July 1, 1982; previously relettered as subd (h) effective January 1, 2000.)

(g) Educational programs

Judges should be encouraged to attend educational programs on the management of complex litigation.

(Subd (g) relettered effective January 1, 2007; adopted as subd (k) effective July 1, 1982; previously amended and relettered as subd (i) effective January 1, 2000.)

(h) Staff assignment

Judges assigned to handle complex cases should be given research attorney and administrative staff assistance when possible.

(Subd (h) amended and relettered effective January 1, 2007; adopted as subd (j) effective January 1, 2000.)

Standard 3.10 amended and renumbered effective January 1, 2007; adopted as sec. 19 effective July 1, 1982; previously amended effective January 1, 1995, and January 1, 2000.

Standard 3.25. Examination of prospective jurors in civil cases

(a) In general

(1) *Methods and scope of examination*

The examination of prospective jurors in a civil case may be oral, by written questionnaire, or by both methods, and should include all questions necessary to ensure the selection of a fair and impartial jury. The *Juror Questionnaire for Civil Cases* (form MC-001) may be used. During any supplemental examination conducted by counsel for the parties, the trial judge should permit liberal and probing examination calculated to discover possible bias or prejudice with regard to the circumstances of the particular case.

(2) *Examination by counsel*

When counsel requests to be allowed to conduct a supplemental voir dire examination, the trial judge should permit counsel to conduct such examination without requiring prior submission of the questions to the judge unless a particular counsel has demonstrated unwillingness to avoid the type of examination proscribed in (f). In exercising his or her sound discretion as to the form and subject matter of voir dire questions, the trial judge should consider, among other criteria: (1) any unique or complex elements, legal or factual, in the case, and (2) the individual responses or conduct of jurors that may evince attitudes inconsistent with suitability to serve as a fair and impartial juror in the particular case. Questions regarding personal relationships of jurors should be relevant to the subject matter of the case.

(Subd (a) amended effective January 1, 2007; adopted effective January 1, 1972; previously amended effective January 1, 1974, July 1, 1993, and January 1, 2004.)

(b) Pre-voir dire conference

Before the examination the trial judge should, outside the prospective jurors' hearing and with a court reporter present, confer with counsel, at which time specific questions or areas of inquiry may be proposed that the judge in his or her discretion may inquire of the jurors. Thereafter, the judge should advise counsel of the questions or areas to be inquired into during the examination and voir dire procedure. The judge should also obtain from counsel the names of the witnesses whom counsel then plan to call at trial and a brief outline of the nature of the case, including any alleged injuries or damages and, in an eminent domain action, the respective contentions of the parties concerning the value of the property taken and any alleged severance damages and special benefits.

(Subd (b) amended effective January 1, 2007; adopted effective January 1, 1972; previously amended effective January 1, 1974.)

(c) Examination of jurors

Except as otherwise provided in (d), the trial judge's examination of prospective jurors should include the following areas of inquiry and any other matters affecting their qualifications to serve as jurors in the case:

(1) *To the entire jury panel after it has been sworn and seated:*

I am now going to question the prospective jurors who are seated in the jury box concerning their qualifications to serve as jurors in this case. All members of this jury panel, however, should pay close attention to my questions, making note of the answers you would give if these questions were put to you personally. If and when any other member of this panel is called to the jury box, the member will be asked to give his or her answers to these questions.

(2) In the trial of this case the parties are entitled to have a fair, unbiased, and unprejudiced jury. If there is any reason why any of you might be biased or prejudiced in any way, you must disclose such reason when you are asked to do so. It is your duty to make this disclosure.

(3) *In lengthy trials:*

This trial will likely take _____ days to complete, but it may take longer. Will any of you find it difficult or impossible to participate for this period of time?

(4) The nature of this case is as follows: *(Describe briefly, including any alleged injuries or damages and, in an eminent domain action, the name of the condemning agency, a description of the property being acquired, and the particular public project or purpose of the condemnation.)*

(5) The parties to this case and their respective attorneys are: *(Specify.)* Have you heard of or been acquainted with any of these parties or their attorneys?

(6) During the trial of this case, the following witnesses may be called to testify on behalf of the parties. These witnesses are: *(Do not identify the party on whose behalf the witnesses might be called.)* Have any of you heard of or been otherwise acquainted with any of the witnesses just named? The parties are not required and might not wish to call all of these witnesses, and they may later find it necessary to call other witnesses.

(7) Have any of you heard of, or have you any knowledge of, the facts or events in this case? Are any of you familiar with the places or property mentioned in this case?

(8) Do any of you believe that a case of this nature should not be brought into court for determination by a jury?

(9) Do any of you have any belief or feeling toward any of the parties, attorneys, or witnesses that might be regarded as a bias or prejudice for or against any of them? Do you have any interest, financial or otherwise, in the outcome of this case?

(10) Have any of you served as a juror or witness involving any of these parties, attorneys, or witnesses?

(11) Have any of you served as a juror in any other case? (If so, was it a civil or criminal case?) You must understand that there is a basic difference between a civil case and a criminal case. In a criminal case a defendant must be found guilty beyond a reasonable doubt; in a civil case such as this, you need only find that the evidence you accept as the basis of your decision is more convincing, and thus has the greater probability of truth, than the contrary evidence.

In the following questions I will be using the terms "family," "close friend," and "anyone with whom you have a significant personal relationship." The term "anyone with whom you have a significant personal relationship" means a domestic partner, life partner, former spouse, or anyone with whom you have an influential or intimate relationship that you would characterize as important.

(12) *If a corporation or "company" is a party:*

(A) Have you or, to your knowledge, has any member of your family, a close friend, or anyone with whom you have a significant personal relationship ever had any connection with, or any dealings with, the _____ corporation (or company)?

(B) Are any of you or them related to any officer, director, or employee of this corporation (or company) to your knowledge?

(C) Do you or they own any stock or other interest in this corporation (or company) to your knowledge?

(D) Have you or they ever done business as a corporation (or company)?

(E) The fact that a corporation (or company) is a party in this case must not affect your deliberations or your verdict. You may not discriminate between corporations (or companies) and natural individuals. Both are persons in the eyes of the law and both are entitled to have a fair and impartial trial based on the same legal standards. Do any of you have any belief or feeling for or against corporations (or companies) that might prevent you from being a completely fair and impartial juror in this case?

(13) Have you or, to your knowledge, has any member of your family, a close friend, or anyone with whom you have a significant personal relationship ever sued anyone, or presented a claim against anyone in connection with a matter similar to this case? (If so, did the matter terminate satisfactorily so far as you were concerned?)

(14) Has anyone ever sued you, or presented a claim against you or, to your knowledge, against any member of your family, a close friend, or anyone with whom you have a significant personal relationship, in connection with a matter similar to this case? (If so, did the matter terminate satisfactorily so far as you were concerned?)

(15) Are you or, to your knowledge, is any member of your family, a close friend, or anyone with whom you have a significant personal relationship presently involved in a lawsuit of any kind?

(16) *When appropriate:*

It may appear that one or more of the parties, witnesses, or attorneys come from a particular national, racial, or religious group (or may have a lifestyle different than your own). Would this in any way affect your judgment or the weight and credibility you would give to their testimony or to their contentions?

(17) Have you or, to your knowledge, has any member of your family, a close friend, or anyone with whom you have a significant personal relationship had any special training in: *(Describe briefly the fields of expertise involved in the case, such as law, medicine, nursing, or any other branch of the healing arts.)*

(18) *In personal injury or wrongful death cases:*

(A) You may be called on in this case to award damages for personal injury, pain, and suffering. Do any of you have any religious or other belief that pain and suffering are not real or any belief that would prevent you from awarding damages for pain and suffering if liability for them is established?

(B) Are there any of you who would not employ a medical doctor?

(C) Have you or, to your knowledge, has any member of your family, a close friend, or anyone with whom you have a significant personal relationship ever engaged in investigating or otherwise acting on claims for damages?

(D) Have you or they, to your knowledge, ever been in an accident with the result that a claim for personal injuries or for substantial property damage was made by someone involved in that accident, whether or not a lawsuit was filed?

(E) Have you or they, to your knowledge, ever been involved in an accident in which someone died or received serious personal injuries, whether or not a lawsuit was filed?

(F) Are there any of you who do not drive an automobile? (If so, have you ever driven an automobile, and if you have, give your reason for not presently driving.) Does your spouse or anyone with whom you have a significant personal relationship drive an automobile? (If that person does not drive but did so in the past, why did that person stop driving?)

(G) Plaintiff (or cross-complainant) _____ is claiming injuries. *(Describe briefly the general nature of the alleged injuries.)* Do you or, to your knowledge, does any member of your family, a close friend, or anyone with whom you have a significant personal relationship suffer from similar injuries? Have you or they, to your knowledge, suffered from similar injuries in the past? (If so, would that fact affect your point of view in this case to the extent that you might not be able to render a completely fair and impartial verdict?)

(19) It is important that I have your assurance that you will, without reservation, follow my instructions and rulings on the law and will apply that law to this case. To put it somewhat differently, whether you approve or disapprove of the court's rulings or instructions, it is your solemn duty to accept as correct these statements of the law. You may not substitute your own idea of what you think the law ought to be. Will all of you follow the law as given to you by me in this case?

(20) Each of you should now state your:

(A) Name;
(B) Children's ages and the number of children, if any;
(C) Occupation;
(D) Occupational history; and
(E) Present employer;

And for your spouse or anyone with whom you have a significant personal relationship, their:

(F) Names;
(G) Occupations;
(H) Occupational histories; and
(I) Present employers.

Please begin with juror number one.

(21) Do you know of any other reason, or has anything occurred during this question period, that might make you doubtful you would be a completely fair and impartial juror in this case? If there is, it is your duty to disclose the reason at this time.

(Subd (c) amended effective January 1, 2007; adopted effective January 1, 1972; previously amended effective January 1, 1974, and January 1, 2004.)

(d) Examination of jurors in eminent domain cases

In eminent domain cases, the trial judge's examination of prospective jurors should include, in the areas of inquiry in (c)(1) through (c)(12), the following matters, and any other matters affecting their qualifications to serve as jurors in the case:

(1) Have you or, to your knowledge, has any member of your family, a close friend, or anyone with whom you have a significant personal relationship ever had any connection with, or dealings with, the plaintiff agency? Are you or any of them related to any officer or employee of the plaintiff agency?

(2) Have you or, to your knowledge, has any member of your family, a close friend, or anyone with whom you have a significant personal relationship ever been involved in an eminent domain proceeding such as this or are you or they likely to become involved in such a proceeding in the future?

(3) To your knowledge, do you have relatives, close friends, or anyone with whom you have a significant personal relationship who has been or

will be affected by the proposed project or a similar public project? (If so, who and how affected?)

(4) Have you or, to your knowledge, has any member of your family, a close friend, or anyone with whom you have a significant personal relationship ever sold property to a public agency having the power of eminent domain?

(5) Are you or, to your knowledge, is any member of your family, a close friend, or anyone with whom you have a significant personal relationship presently involved in a lawsuit of any kind? (If so, does the lawsuit involve a public agency?)

(6) Have you or, to your knowledge, has any member of your family, a close friend, or anyone with whom you have a significant personal relationship ever been involved in a lawsuit involving a public agency?

(7) *When appropriate:*

It may appear that one or more of the parties, witnesses, or attorneys come from a particular national, racial, or religious group (or may have a lifestyle different from your own). Would this in any way affect your judgment or the weight and credibility you would give to their testimony or contentions?

(8) Have you or, to your knowledge, has any member of your family, a close friend, or anyone with whom you have a significant personal relationship had any special training in: *(Describe briefly the fields of expertise involved in the case, such as law, real estate, real estate appraising, engineering, surveying, geology, etc.)*

(9) Have you, has your spouse, or, to your knowledge, has any member of your family, a close friend, or anyone with whom you have a significant personal relationship ever been engaged in any phase of the real estate business including:

(A) Acting as a real estate agent, broker, or salesperson;
(B) Acting as a real estate appraiser;
(C) Dealing in trust deeds;
(D) Buying or selling real property as a business;
(E) Owning or managing income property; or
(F) Engaging in the construction business?

(10) Have you or, to your knowledge, has any member of your family, a close friend, or anyone with whom you have a significant personal relationship ever studied or engaged in: (State type of business, if any, conducted on subject property.)

(11) Have you or, to your knowledge, has any member of your family, a close friend, or anyone with whom you have a significant personal relationship ever been engaged in any work involving the acquisition of private property for public purposes? Or involving the zoning or planning of property?

(12) Under the law of this state, all private property is held subject to the necessary right of eminent domain, which is the right of the state or its authorized agencies to take private property for public use whenever the public interest so requires. The right of eminent domain is exercised through proceedings commonly called a condemnation action. This is a condemnation action.

(13) The Constitution of this state requires that a property owner be paid just compensation for the taking (or damaging) of his or her property for public use. It will be the duty of the jury ultimately selected in this case to determine the just compensation to be paid.

(14) *If no claim of severance damages:*

In order to find the amount of just compensation in this case, the jury will be called on to determine the fair market value of the real property being acquired.

(15) *If severance damages are claimed:*

In order to find the amount of just compensation in this case, the jury will be called on to determine the following:

(A) The fair market value of the real property being acquired.

(B) Severance damages, if any, to the defendant's remaining real property; that is, the depreciation in market value by reason of the severance of the part taken, or by the construction of the improvements in the manner proposed by the plaintiff, or both.

(C) *When applicable:* Special benefits, if any, to the defendant's remaining real property. *(The trial judge on request may advise the jury on the concept of special benefits.)*

(16) Just compensation is measured in terms of fair market value as of *(date)*, the date of value in this case.

(17) I will give you more specific instructions on the issues and determinations to be made in this case at the conclusion of all the evidence. However, I will now advise you of the definition of fair market value: *(See CACI 3501.)*

(18) *Private ownership of property:*

(A) Do you have any objection to the concept of private ownership of property?

(B) Do you have any objection to the right of the owner of private property to develop or use that property in whatever lawful way its owner sees fit?

(19) Do you have any objection to the plaintiff acquiring private property for a public use as long as just compensation is paid for the property?

(20) Do you have any objection to the defendant(s) seeking just compensation in these proceedings in the form of the fair market value of the subject property (and the damages that the defendant(s) contend will be caused to the remaining property)?

(21) Do you have any objection to the particular public project involved in this proceeding, previously referred to as the *(name of project)*?

(22) Are you or, to your knowledge, is any member of your family, a close friend, or anyone with whom you have a significant personal relationship a member of any organization that is opposed to such public projects?

(23) Do you have any objection to the concept that just compensation is measured by fair market value as I have defined that term for you earlier?

(24) Do you have any feeling that, because the plaintiff needs the property for public purposes, it should pay anything other than its fair market value?

(25) In these cases, the evidence of value is introduced for the most part by what the courts sometimes refer to as expert testimony. This expert testimony frequently is introduced through appraisers or real estate brokers. Do you have any prejudice against real estate brokers or appraisers, or that type of testimony?

(26) In a condemnation case the property owner produces all of his or her evidence of value first, then the government calls its witnesses. Having this in mind, will you keep your mind open throughout all the case and not determine the matter in your mind until all of the evidence is in?

(27) It is important that I have your assurance that you will, without reservation, follow my instructions and rulings on the law and will apply that law to this case. To put it somewhat differently, whether you approve or disapprove of the court's rulings or instructions, it is your solemn duty to accept as correct these statements of the law. You may not substitute your own idea of what you think the law ought to be. Will all of you follow the law as given to you by me in this case?

(28) Each of you should now state your:

(A) Name;
(B) Children's ages and number of children, if any;
(C) Occupation;
(D) Occupational history; and
(E) Present employer;

And for your spouse or anyone with whom you have a significant personal relationship, their:

(F) Names;
(G) Occupations;
(H) Occupational histories; and
(I) Present employers.

Please begin with juror number one.

(29) Each of you should now state whether you, your spouse, or anyone with whom you have a significant personal relationship owns or has an interest in any real property and, if so, whether its value or use is affected by the public project involved in this case.

We will again start with juror number one.

(30) Do you know of any other reason, or has anything occurred during this question period, that might make you doubtful you would be a completely fair and impartial juror in this case? If there is, it is your duty to disclose the reason at this time.

(Subd (d) amended effective January 1, 2007; adopted effective January 1, 1974; previously amended effective January 1, 1989, and January 1, 2004.)

(e) Subsequent conference and examination

On completion of the initial examination and on request of counsel for any party that the trial judge put additional questions to the jurors, the judge should, outside the jurors' hearing and with a court reporter present, confer with counsel, at which time additional questions or areas of inquiry may be proposed that the judge may inquire of the jurors.

(Subd (e) amended effective January 1, 2007; adopted effective January 1, 1972; previously amended effective January 1, 1974.)

(f) Improper questions

When any counsel examines the prospective jurors, the trial judge should not permit counsel to attempt to precondition the prospective jurors to a particular result or allow counsel to comment on the personal lives and families of the parties or their attorneys. Nor should the trial judge allow counsel to question the jurors concerning the pleadings, the applicable law, the meaning of particular words and phrases, or the comfort of the jurors, except in unusual circumstances, where, in the trial judge's sound discretion, such questions become necessary to insure the selection of a fair and impartial jury.

(Subd (f) amended effective January 1, 2007; adopted effective January 1, 1972; previously amended effective January 1, 1974.)

Standard 3.25 amended and renumbered effective January 1, 2007; adopted as sec. 8 effective January 1, 1972; previously amended effective January 1, 1974, January 1, 1989, July 1, 1993, and January 1, 2004.

Title 4
Standards for Criminal Cases

Standard 4.10. Guidelines for diversion drug court programs
Standard 4.15. Vacatur relief under Penal Code section 236.14
Standard 4.30. Examination of prospective jurors in criminal cases
Standard 4.35. Court use of risk/needs assessments at sentencing
Standard 4.40. Traffic infraction procedures
Standard 4.42. Traffic infraction trial scheduling

Standard 4.10. Guidelines for diversion drug court programs

(a) Minimum components

The components specified in this standard should be included as minimum requirements in any pre-plea diversion drug court program developed under Penal Code section 1000.5.

(Subd (a) amended effective January 1, 2007.)

(b) Early entry

Eligible participants should be identified early and enter into a supervision and treatment program promptly.

(1) A declaration of eligibility should be filed by the district attorney no later than the date of the defendant's first appearance in court.

(2) Participants designated as eligible by the district attorney should be ordered by the assigned drug court judge to report for assessment and treatment supervision within five days of the first court appearance.

(c) Treatment services

Participants should be given access to a continuum of treatment and rehabilitative services.

(1) The county drug program administrator should specify and certify appropriate drug treatment programs under Penal Code section 1211.

(2) The certified treatment programs should provide a minimum of two levels of treatment services to match participants to programs according to their needs for treatment, recognizing that some divertees may be at the stage of experimenting with illicit drugs while others may be further along in the addiction's progression.

(3) Each treatment level should be divided into phases in order to provide periodic reviews of treatment progress. Each phase may vary in length. It should be recognized that a participant is expected to progress in treatment but may relapse. Most participants, however, should be able to successfully complete the treatment program within 12 months.

(4) Each pre-plea diversion drug court program should have an assessment component to ensure that participants are initially screened and then periodically assessed by treatment personnel to ensure that appropriate treatment services are provided and to monitor the participants' progress through the phases.

(5) Treatment services should include educational and group outpatient treatment. Individual counseling, however, should be made available in special circumstances if an assessment based on acceptable professional standards indicates that individual counseling is the only appropriate form of treatment. Referrals should be made for educational and vocational counseling if it is determined to be appropriate by the judge.

(Subd (c) amended effective January 1, 2007.)

(d) Monitoring

Abstinence from and use of drugs should be monitored by frequent drug testing.

(1) Alcohol and other drug (AOD) testing is essential and should be mandatory in each pre-plea diversion drug court program to monitor participant compliance.

(2) Testing may be administered randomly or at scheduled intervals, but should occur no less frequently than one time per week during the first 90 days of treatment.

(3) The probation officer and court should be immediately notified when a participant has tested positive, has failed to submit to AOD testing, or has submitted an adulterated sample. In such cases, an interim hearing should be calendared and required as outlined in (e)(4).

(4) Participants should not be considered to have successfully completed the treatment program unless they have consistently had negative test results for a period of four months.

(Subd (d) amended effective January 1, 2007.)

(e) Judicial supervision

There should be early and frequent judicial supervision of each diversion drug court participant.

(1) Each participant should appear in court before a specifically assigned diversion drug court judge within 30 days after the first court appearance. At this time the participant should provide proof of registration, proof of completion of assessment, proof of entry into a specific treatment program, and initial drug test results.

(2) The second drug court appearance should be held no later than 30 days after the first drug court appearance. The third drug court appearance should be held no later than 60 days after the second drug court appearance.

(3) A final drug court appearance should be required no sooner than 12 months from entry into treatment unless continued treatment is found to be appropriate and necessary.

(4) Interim drug court appearances should be required within one week of the following: positive drug test results, failure to test, adulterated test, or failure to appear or participate in treatment.

(5) At each drug court appearance, the judge should receive a report of the participant's progress in treatment and drug test results and should review, monitor, and impose rewards and sanctions based on the participant's progress or lack of progress.

(f) Sanctions and incentives

The drug court responds directly to each participant's compliance or noncompliance with graduated sanctions or incentives.

(1) A clear regimen of incentives and sanctions should be established and implemented at each court hearing.

(2) The suggested range of incentives should be as follows:

(A) Encouragement;

(B) Advancement to next treatment phase;

(C) Reduction in diversion program fees (other than state-mandated fees);

(D) Completion of treatment and required court appearances and shortening of the term of diversion; and

(E) Other incentives the court may deem necessary or appropriate.

(3) The suggested range of sanctions should be as follows:

(A) Demotion to earlier treatment phase;

(B) Increased frequency of testing, supervision, or treatment requirements;

(C) Graduated length of incarceration for violating diversion order to abstain from use of illegal drugs and for nonparticipation in treatment; and

(D) Reinstatement of criminal proceedings.

(4) A participant should be terminated from the pre-plea diversion drug court, and criminal proceedings reinstated, if the drug court judge, after a hearing, makes a final and specific finding and determination at any time during the period of diversion that the participant has:

(A) Not performed satisfactorily in treatment;

(B) Failed to benefit from education, treatment, or rehabilitation;

(C) Been convicted of a misdemeanor that reflects the participant's propensity for violence; or

(D) Engaged in criminal conduct rendering him or her unsuitable for continued treatment.

(Subd (f) amended effective January 1, 2007.)

(g) National standards

In addition to meeting the minimum guidelines provided in this standard, courts are encouraged to look to the nationally accepted guidelines, *Defining Drug Courts: The Key Components*, developed by the National Association of Drug Court Professionals in cooperation with the Department of Justice, for further and detailed guidance in developing an effective diversion drug court program.

(Subd (g) amended effective January 1, 2007.)

Standard 4.10 amended and renumbered effective January 1, 2007; adopted as sec. 36 effective January 1, 1998.

Standard 4.15. Vacatur relief under Penal Code section 236.14

(a) Request to consolidate hearings for arrests and convictions that occurred in the same county

(1) The court should allow the filing of a single petition requesting vacatur relief under Penal Code section 236.14(a) for multiple arrests and convictions that occurred in the same county.

(2) The court should favor consolidating hearings for multiple arrests and convictions that occurred in the same county.

(3) The court may require the following documentation before granting a request to consolidate hearings:

(A) An agreement between the petitioner and all of the involved state or local prosecutorial agencies, as defined in Penal Code section 236.14(c), to consolidate the hearings;

(B) Documentation that states whether any of the involved state or local prosecutorial agencies, as defined in Penal Code section 236.14(c), intend to file an opposition to the petition; and

(C) Proof of service of the request to consolidate hearings on all of the involved state or local prosecutorial agencies, as defined in Penal Code section 236.14(c).

(4) The court should consider the following nonexclusive list of factors when deciding whether to consolidate hearings:

(A) The common questions of fact or law, if any;

(B) The convenience of parties, witnesses, and counsel;

(C) The efficient utilization of judicial facilities and staff resources;

(D) The calendar of the court; and

(E) The disadvantages of duplicative and inconsistent orders.

(Subd (a) adopted effective January 1, 2020.)

(b) Confidentiality

(1) The court should designate the petition and related filings and court records as confidential.

(2) At the hearing or any other proceeding accessible to the public, the court should consider implementing procedures consistent with Penal Code section 236.14(q), such as ordering the identity of the petitioner to be either "Jane Doe" or "John Doe."

(Subd (b) adopted effective January 1, 2020.)

(c) Initial court review and orders

(1) After 45 days from the filing of the petition, the court should conduct an initial review of the case. Concurrent with granting or denying a request to consolidate hearings, the court should:

(A) Grant relief without a hearing when the prosecuting agency files no opposition within 45 days from the date of service and the court finds that the petitioner meets the requirements for relief;

(B) Set a hearing date if an opposition is filed or a hearing is otherwise warranted; or

(C) Deny the petition without prejudice if the petitioner fails to provide the information required by Penal Code section 236.14(b).

(Subd (c) adopted effective January 1, 2020.)

(d) Notification

(1) The court should timely notify the petitioner and prosecuting agency of its decisions under subdivision (c)(1).

(2) The court should timely notify the relevant probation department of any decision to terminate probation.

(Subd (d) adopted effective January 1, 2020.)

(e) Additional relief

When granting the petition for vacatur relief under Penal Code section 236.14(a), the court should consider ordering the following additional relief, including, but not limited to:

(1) Sealing or destruction of probation or other postconviction supervision agency records related to the conviction;

(2) Expungement of DNA profiles and destruction of DNA samples, if they qualify under Penal Code section 299;

(3) Recall or return of court fines and fees, if paid;

(4) Sealing of the court file, if warranted under the factors in rule 2.550(d); and

(5) Additional relief that will carry out the purposes of Penal Code section 236.14.

(Subd (e) adopted effective January 1, 2020.)

Standard 4.15 adopted effective January 1, 2020.

Standard 4.30. Examination of prospective jurors in criminal cases

(a) In general

(1) This standard applies in all criminal cases.

(2) The examination of prospective jurors in a criminal case should include all questions necessary to insure the selection of a fair and impartial jury.

(3) The court may consider conducting sequestered voir dire on issues that are sensitive to prospective jurors, on questions concerning media reports of the case, and on any other issue that the court deems advisable.

(Subd (a) amended effective January 1, 2007; previously amended effective January 1, 1988, January 1, 1990, June 6, 1990, and January 1, 2006.)

(b) Examination of jurors

The trial judge's examination of prospective jurors in criminal cases should include the areas of inquiry listed below and any other matters affecting their qualifications to serve as jurors in the case. The trial judge may want to use the *Juror Questionnaire for Criminal Cases* (form JURY-002) to assist in the examination of prospective jurors. Form JURY-002 is an optional form and is not intended to constitute the complete examination of prospective jurors. Form JURY-002 is a tool for trial judges to use to make the initial examination of prospective jurors more efficient. If the court chooses to use form JURY-002, its use and any supplemental questions submitted by counsel must be discussed at the pre-voir dire conference required by rule 4.200. Excusing jurors based on questionnaire answers alone is generally not advisable.

(1) *Address to entire jury panel:*

Do any of you have any vision, hearing, or medical difficulties that may affect your jury service? *(Response.)*

(2) *In particular, for lengthy trials. Address to entire jury panel:*

This trial will likely take _____ days to complete, but it may take longer. *(State the days and times during the day when the trial will be in session.)*

Will any of you find it difficult or impossible to participate for this period of time? *(After the entire panel has been screened for time hardships, direct the excused jurors to return to the jury assembly room for possible reassignment to other courtrooms for voir dire.)*

(3) *At this point the court may wish to submit any juror questionnaire that has been developed to assist in voir dire. The court should remind panel members that their answers on the questionnaire are given under penalty of perjury. In addition, if a questionnaire is used, the court and counsel may wish to question individual prospective jurors further based on their responses to particular questions, and a procedure for doing so should be established at the pre-voir dire conference. Therefore, it may not be necessary to ask all of the prospective jurors questions 5 through 25 that follow, although the text may assist the court with following up with individual jurors about answers given on the questionnaire.*

To the entire jury panel:

I am now going to question the prospective jurors who are seated in the jury box concerning their qualifications to serve as jurors in this case. All the remaining members of this jury panel, however, should pay close attention to my questions, making note of the answers you would give if these questions were put to you personally. If and when any other member of this panel is called to the jury box, he or she will be asked to answer these questions.

(4) *To the prospective jurors seated in the jury box:*

In the trial of this case each side is entitled to have a fair, unbiased, and unprejudiced jury. If there is any fact or any reason why any of you might be biased or prejudiced in any way, you must disclose such reasons when you are asked to do so. It is your duty to make this disclosure.

(5) *To the prospective jurors seated in the jury box:*

Do any of you know anyone else on this jury panel? *(Response.)*

(6) Ladies and gentlemen of the jury: This is a criminal case entitled The People of the State of California v. _____. The (defendant is)(defendants are) seated _____.

(A) (Mr.)(Ms.)(defendant), please stand and face the prospective jurors in the jury box and in the audience seats. *(Defendant complies.)* Is there any member of the jury panel who is acquainted with the defendant or who may have heard (his)(her) name before today? If your answer is yes, please raise your hand.

(B) The defendant, _____, is represented by (his)(her) attorney, _____, who is seated _____. (Mr.)(Ms.)(defense attorney), would you please stand? Is there any member of the jury panel who knows or who has seen (Mr.)(Ms.) _____ before today?

(C) *(If there is more than one defendant, repeat (a) and (b) for each codefendant.)*

(7) The People are represented by _____, Deputy District Attorney, who is seated _____. (Mr.)(Ms.)(district attorney), would you please stand? Is there any member of the jury panel who knows or who has seen (Mr.)(Ms.) _____ before today?

(8) The defendant is charged by an (information)(indictment) filed by the district attorney with having committed the crime of _____, in violation of section _____ of the _____ Code, it being alleged that on or about _____ in the County of _____, the defendant did *(describe the offense)*. To (this charge)(these charges) the defendant has pleaded not guilty, and the jury will have to decide whether the defendant's guilt has been proved beyond a reasonable doubt. Having heard the charge(s) that (has)(have) been filed against the defendant, is there any member of the jury panel who feels that he or she cannot give this defendant a fair trial because of the nature of the charge(s) against (him)(her)?

(9) Have any of you heard of, or have you any prior knowledge of, the facts or events in this case?

(10) Do any of you have any ethical, religious, political, or other beliefs that would prevent you from serving as a juror in this case?

(11) During the trial of this case, the following persons may be called as witnesses to testify on behalf of the parties or their names may be mentioned in evidence: _____ *(Do not identify the side on whose behalf the witness might be called.)* Have any of you heard of or otherwise been acquainted with any of the witnesses just named? You should note that the parties are not required and might not wish to call all of these witnesses, and they may later find it necessary to call other witnesses.

(12) Do any of you have any financial or personal interest in the outcome of this case?

(13) How many of you have served previously as jurors in a criminal case?

To each person whose hand is raised:

(A) (Mr.)(Ms.)_____(or Juror ID number), you indicated you have been a juror in a criminal case. What were the charges in that case? *(Response.)*

(B) Do you feel you can put aside whatever you heard in that case and decide this case on the evidence to be presented and the law as I will state it to you? *(Response.)*

(14) May I see the hands of those jurors who have served on civil cases, but who have never served on a criminal case? *(Response.)* You must understand that there are substantial differences in the rules applicable to the trial of criminal cases from those applicable to the trial of civil cases. This is particularly true respecting the burden of proof that is placed on the People. In a civil case we say that the plaintiff must prove (his) (her) case by a preponderance of the evidence. In a criminal case, the defendant is presumed to be innocent, and before (he)(she) may be found guilty, the People must prove (his)(her) guilt beyond a reasonable doubt. If the jury has a reasonable doubt, the defendant must be acquitted. Will each of you be able to set aside the instructions that you received in your previous cases and try this case on the instructions given by me in this case?

(15) The fact that the defendant is in court for trial, or that charges have been made against (him)(her), is no evidence whatever of (his)(her) guilt. The jurors are to consider only evidence properly received in the courtroom in determining whether the defendant's guilt has been proved beyond a reasonable doubt. The defendant has entered a plea of "not guilty," which is a complete denial, making it necessary for the People, acting through the district attorney, to prove beyond a reasonable doubt the case against the defendant. If the evidence does not convince you of the truth of the charges beyond a reasonable doubt, the defendant is entitled to a verdict of not guilty.

In the following questions I will be using the terms "relative," "close friend," and "anyone with whom you have a significant personal relationship." The term "anyone with whom you have a significant personal relationship" means a domestic partner, life partner, former spouse, or anyone with whom you have an influential or intimate relationship that you would characterize as important.

(16) Have you or, to your knowledge, has any relative, close friend, or anyone with whom you have a significant personal relationship, ever been the victim of any crime? *(Response.)*

(17) Have you or, to your knowledge, has any relative, close friend, or anyone with whom you have a significant personal relationship, ever had any contact with law enforcement, including being: (a) stopped by the police? (b) accused of misconduct, whether or not it was a crime? (c) investigated as a suspect in a criminal case? (d) charged with a crime? or (e) a criminal defendant? *(Response.)*

(18) Have you or, to your knowledge, has any relative, close friend, or anyone with whom you have a significant personal relationship, had any law enforcement training or experience or been a member of or been employed by any law enforcement agency? By law enforcement agency, I include any police department, sheriff's office, highway patrol, district attorney's office, city attorney's office, attorney general's office, United States attorney's office, FBI, and others. *(If so, elicit the details of the experience or connection.)*

(19) Would you be able to listen to the testimony of a police or other peace officer and measure it the same way you would that of any other witness?

(20) *When appropriate:*

It may appear that one or more of the parties, attorneys, or witnesses come from a particular national, racial, or religious group (or may have a lifestyle different from your own). Would this in any way affect your judgment or the weight and credibility you would give to their testimony?

(21) It is important that I have your assurance that you will follow my instructions and rulings on the law and will apply that law to this case. To put it somewhat differently, whether you approve or disapprove of the court's rulings or instructions, it is your solemn duty to accept as correct these statements of the law. You must accept and follow my instructions even if you disagree with the law. You may not substitute your own idea of what you think the law ought to be. Will all of you follow the law as given to you by me in this case?

(22) Each of you should now state your:

(A) (Name)(or juror ID number);

(B) Children's ages and the number of children, if any;

(C) Occupation;

(D) Occupational history; and

(E) Present employer;

And for your spouse or anyone with whom you have a significant personal relationship, their:

(F) Occupations;

(G) Occupational histories; and

(H) Present employers;

And for your adult children, their:

(I) Occupations;

(J) Occupational histories; and

(K) Present employers.

Please begin with juror number one.

(23) Do you know of any other reason, or has anything occurred during this question period, that might make you doubtful you would be a completely fair and impartial juror in this case or why you should not be on this jury? If there is, it is your duty to disclose the reason at this time.

(24) *After the court conducts the initial examination, Code of Civil Procedure section 223 allows counsel to ask supplemental questions for the purposes of uncovering possible bias or prejudice relevant to challenges for cause. The court may, in the exercise of its discretion, limit the oral and direct questioning of prospective jurors by counsel. The court may specify the maximum amount of time that counsel for each party may question an individual juror, or may specify an aggregate amount of time for each party, which can then be allocated among the prospective jurors by counsel.*

(25) *After the conclusion of counsel questioning, the court asks each side to exercise any challenges for cause.*

(26) *After ruling on challenges for cause, if any, the court calls on each side, alternately, to exercise any preemptory challenges.*

(27) *If a new prospective juror is seated, the court should ask him or her:*

(A) Have you heard my questions to the other prospective jurors?

(B) Have any of the questions I have asked raised any doubt in your mind as to whether you could be a fair and impartial juror in this case?

(C) Can you think of any other reason why you might not be able to try this case fairly and impartially to both the prosecution and defendant, or why you should not be on this jury?

(D) Give us the personal information requested concerning your occupation, that of your spouse or anyone with whom you have a significant personal relationship, that of your adult children, and your prior jury experience.

(Thereupon, as to each new juror seated, the court must permit counsel to ask supplemental questions, and proceed with challenges as above.)

(Subd (b) amended effective January 1, 2023; adopted as subd (c) effective July 1, 1974; amended and relettered effective June 6, 1990; previously amended effective January 1, 1997, January 1, 2004, January 1, 2006, and January 1, 2007.)

(c) Improper questions

When any counsel examines the prospective jurors, the trial judge should not permit counsel to attempt to precondition the prospective jurors to a particular result or allow counsel to comment on the personal lives and families of the parties or their attorneys.

(Subd (c) amended effective January 1, 2006; adopted as subd (e) effective July 1, 1974; previously amended and relettered as subd (d) effective June 6, 1990; relettered as subd (c) effective January 1, 1997.)

Standard 4.30 amended effective January 1, 2023; adopted as sec. 8.5 July 1, 1974; previously amended effective January 1, 1988, January 1, 1990, June 6, 1990, January 1, 1997, January 1, 2004, and January 1, 2006; previously amended and renumbered as standard 4.30 effective January 1, 2007.

Standard 4.35. Court use of risk/needs assessments at sentencing

(a) Application and purpose

(1) This standard applies only to the use of the results of risk/needs assessments at sentencing.

(2) The use of the results of risk/needs assessments at sentencing is intended to:

(A) Prevent biases in sentencing;

(B) Reduce the risk of recidivism by focusing services and resources on medium- and high-risk offenders, who are most likely to reoffend;

(C) Reduce a defendant's risk of future recidivism by targeting that defendant's needs with appropriate intervention services through community supervision programs demonstrated to reduce recidivism; and

(D) Advance the legislative directive to improve public safety outcomes by routing offenders into community-based supervision informed by evidence-based practices.

(Subd (a) adopted effective January 1, 2018.)

(b) Definitions

(1) "Risk" refers to the likelihood that a person will reoffend without regard, unless otherwise specified, to the nature of the original offense or the nature of the reoffense.

(2) "Risk factors" refers to the "static" and "dynamic" factors that contribute to the risk score.

(3) "Static risk factors" refers to those risk factors that cannot be changed through treatment or intervention, such as age or prior criminal history.

(4) "Dynamic risk factors," also known as "needs," are factors that can be changed through treatment or intervention.

(5) "Results of a risk/needs assessment" refers to both a risk score and an assessment of a person's needs.

(6) A "risk score" refers to a descriptive evaluation of a person's risk level as a result of conducting an actuarial assessment with a validated risk/needs assessment instrument and may include such terms as "high," "medium," or "low" risk.

(7) "Amenability" or "suitability" refers to the likelihood that the person can be safely and effectively supervised in the community and benefit from supervision services that are informed by evidence-based practices that have been demonstrated to reduce recidivism.

(8) A "validated risk/needs assessment instrument" refers to a risk/needs assessment instrument demonstrated by scientific research to be accurate and reliable in assessing the risks and needs of the specific population on which it was validated.

(9) "Supervision" includes all forms of supervision referenced in Penal Code section 1203.2(a).

(Subd (b) adopted effective January 1, 2018.)

(c) Validation

The risk/needs assessment instrument should be validated.

(Subd (c) adopted effective January 1, 2018.)

(d) Proper uses of the results of a risk/needs assessment at sentencing

(1) The results of a risk/needs assessment should be considered only in context with all other information considered by the court at the time of sentencing, including the probation report, statements in mitigation and aggravation, evidence presented at a sentencing proceeding conducted under section 1204, and comments by counsel and any victim.

(2) The results of a risk/needs assessment should be one of many factors that may be considered and weighed at a sentencing hearing. Information generated by the risk/needs assessment should be used along with all other information presented in connection with the sentencing hearing to inform and facilitate the decision of the court. Risk/needs assessment information should not be used as a substitute for the sound independent judgment of the court.

(3) Although they may not be determinative, the results of a risk/needs assessment may be considered by the court as a relevant factor in assessing:

(A) Whether a defendant who is presumptively ineligible for probation has overcome the statutory limitation on probation;

(B) Whether an offender can be supervised safely and effectively in the community; and

(C) The appropriate terms and conditions of supervision and responses to violations of supervision.

(4) If a court uses the results of a risk/needs assessment, it should consider any limitations of the instrument that have been raised in the probation report or by counsel, including:

(A) That the instrument's risk scores are based on group data, such that the instrument is able to identify only groups of high-risk offenders, for example, not a particular high-risk individual;

(B) Whether the instrument's proprietary nature has been invoked to prevent the disclosure of information relating to how it weighs static and dynamic risk factors and how it determines risk scores;

(C) Whether any scientific research has raised questions that the instrument unfairly classifies offenders by gender, race, or ethnicity; and

(D) Whether the instrument has been validated on a relevant population.

(Subd (d) adopted effective January 1, 2018.)

(e) Improper uses of the results of a risk/needs assessment at sentencing

(1) The results of a risk/needs assessment should not be used to determine:

(A) Whether to incarcerate a defendant; or

(B) The severity of the sentence.

(2) The results of a risk/needs assessment should not be considered by the court for defendants statutorily ineligible for supervision.

(Subd (e) adopted effective January 1, 2018.)

(f) Amenability to or suitability for supervision

(1) A court should not interpret a "high" or "medium" risk score as necessarily indicating that a defendant is not amenable to or suitable for community-based supervision. Community-based supervision may be most effective for defendants with "high" and "medium" risk scores. A "low" risk score often, but not necessarily, indicates that a defendant is amenable to or suitable for community-based supervision. Risk scores must be interpreted in the context of all relevant sentencing information received by the court.

(2) Ordinarily a defendant's level of supervision should correspond to his or her level of risk of recidivism. In most cases, a court should order that a low-risk defendant receive less supervision and a high-risk defendant more.

(3) A court should order services that address the defendant's needs.

(Subd (f) adopted effective January 1, 2018.)

(g) Education regarding the nature, purpose, and limits of risk/needs assessment information is critical to the proper use of such information. Education should include all justice system partners.

(Subd (g) adopted effective January 1, 2018.)

Standard 4.35 adopted effective January 1, 2018.

Advisory Committee Comment

Subdivision (d)(1)–(2). Although the results of risk/needs assessments provide important information for use by the court at sentencing, they are not designed as a substitute for the exercise of judicial discretion and judgment. The information should not be used as the sole basis of the court's decision, but should be considered in the context of all of the information received in a sentencing proceeding. If justified by the circumstances of the case, it is appropriate for the court to impose a disposition not supported by the results of a risk/needs assessment. (See *State v. Loomis* (2016) 371 Wis.2d 235, 266 ["Just as corrections staff should disregard risk scores that are inconsistent with other factors, we expect that … courts will exercise discretion when assessing a … risk score with respect to each individual defendant"].)

Subdivision (d)(4). Court and justice partners should understand any limitations of the particular instrument used to generate the results of a risk/needs assessment. (See *State v. Loomis, supra,* 371 Wis.2d at p. 264 [requiring presentence investigation reports to state the limitations of the instrument used, including the proprietary nature of that instrument, any absence of a cross-validation study for relevant populations, and any questions raised in studies about whether the instrument disproportionately classifies minority offenders as having a higher risk of recidivism].) The Wisconsin court also required that all presentence investigation reports caution that risk/needs assessment tools must be constantly monitored and renormed for accuracy because of changing populations and subpopulations. (*Ibid.*) California courts should similarly consider any such limitations in the accuracy of the particular instrument employed in the case under review. (See *ibid.* ["Providing information to sentencing courts on the limitations and cautions attendant with the use of … risk assessments will enable courts to better assess the accuracy of the assessment and the appropriate weight to be given to the risk score"].)

Subdivision (d)(4)(D). Validating a risk/needs assessment instrument will increase its accuracy and reliability. Validation on a relevant population or subpopulation is recommended to account for differences in local policies, implementation practices, and offender populations. Ongoing monitoring and renorming of the instrument may be necessary to reflect changes in a population or subpopulation. Revalidation of the instrument is also necessary if any of its dynamic or static risk factors are modified.

Subdivision (e). When the court is considering whether to place a person on supervision at an original sentencing proceeding or after a violation of supervision, the results of a risk/needs assessment may assist the court in assessing the person's amenability to supervision and services in the community. But when the person is ineligible for supervision, or the court has otherwise decided not to grant or reinstate probation, the results of a risk/needs assessment should not be used in determining the period of incarceration to be imposed. (See *State v. Loomis, supra,* 371 Wis.2d at p. 256 [holding that risk/needs assessments should not be used to determine the severity of a sentence or whether a defendant is incarcerated]; *Malenchik v. State* (Ind. 2010) 928 N.E.2d 564, 573 ["It is clear that [risk/needs assessment instruments are neither intended] nor recommended to substitute for the judicial function of determining the length of sentence appropriate for each offender"].)

Subdivision (f). Risk/needs assessment instruments generally produce a numerical or descriptive "risk score" such as "high," "moderate," or "low" risk. It is critical that courts and justice partners understand the meaning and limitations of such designations. First, because risk assessments are based on group data, they are able to identify groups of high-risk offenders, not a particular high-risk individual. Second, in some assessment instruments, "risk" refers only to a generalized risk of committing a new offense, not to the seriousness of the subsequent offense (e.g., violent, sex, drug, or theft). Nor does "high risk" necessarily mean "highly dangerous." A high-risk drug offender, for example, may present a high risk that he or she will use drugs again, but does not necessarily present a high risk to commit a violent felony. Third, scientific research indicates that medium- and high-risk offenders may most benefit from evidence-based supervision and programs that address critical risk factors. Courts and probation departments should also consider how presentence investigation reports present risk assessment information. A report that merely refers to the defendant as "high risk" may incorrectly imply that the defendant presents a great danger to public safety and must therefore be incarcerated. Conversely, "low risk" does not necessarily mean "no risk."

Subdivision (g). An instrument's accuracy and reliability depend on its proper administration. Training and continuing education should be required for anyone who administers the instrument. Judges with sentencing assignments should receive appropriate training on the purpose, use, and limits of risk/needs assessments. (See Guiding Principle 4, Stakeholder Training, in Pamela M. Casey et al., *Using Offender Risk and Needs Assessment Information at Sentencing: Guidance for Courts from a National Working Group* (National Center for State Courts, 2011) pp. 21–22.)

Standard 4.40. Traffic infraction procedures

To insure the prompt and efficient disposition of traffic infraction cases, each court should:

(1) Authorize the clerk, within limits set by the court, to grant defendants extensions of time for the posting of bail and payment of fines.

(2) Authorize the clerk or other court official to accept offers of proof of correction or compliance in accordance with the bail schedule without the necessity of a court appearance.

Standard 4.40 amended and renumbered effective January 1, 2007; adopted as sec. 10.5 effective July 1, 1977.

Standard 4.41. Courtesy notice—traffic procedures [Repealed]

Standard 4.41 repealed effective January 1, 2017; adopted as sec. 10.6 effective January 1, 1987; previously amended and renumbered effective January 1, 2007.

Standard 4.42. Traffic infraction trial scheduling

(a) Review of procedures

Courts should adopt and periodically review procedures governing the scheduling of traffic infraction trials that minimize appearance time and costs for defendants, witnesses, and law enforcement officers.

(Subd (a) amended and lettered effective January 1, 2007; adopted as part of unlettered subdivision effective January 1, 1987.)

(b) Meetings

Courts should hold periodic meetings with representatives from local law enforcement agencies, the prosecution and defense bars, and other interested groups as appropriate in an effort to achieve this goal.

(Subd (b) amended and lettered effective January 1, 2007; adopted as part of unlettered subdivision effective January 1, 1987.)

Standard 4.42 amended and renumbered effective January 1, 2007; adopted as sec. 10.7 effective January 1, 1987.

Title 5
Standards for Cases Involving Children and Families

Standard 5.20. Uniform standards of practice for providers of supervised visitation
Standard 5.30. Family court matters
Standard 5.40. Juvenile court matters
Standard 5.45. Resource guidelines for child abuse and neglect cases

Standard 5.10. Guidelines for determining payment for costs of appointed counsel for children in family court [Repealed]

Standard 5.10 repealed effective January 1, 2008; adopted as sec. 20.6 effective January 1, 1992; previously amended effective January 1, 2005, and July 1, 2005; previously amended and renumbered effective January 1, 2007.

Standard 5.11. Guidelines for appointment of counsel for minors when time with or responsibility for the minor is disputed [Repealed]

Standard 5.11 repealed effective January 1, 2008; adopted as sec. 20.5 effective January 1, 1990; previously amended and renumbered effective January 1, 2007.

Standard 5.20. Uniform standards of practice for providers of supervised visitation

(a) Scope of service

This standard defines the standards of practice, including duties and obligations, for providers of supervised visitation under Family Code sections 3200 and 3200.5. Unless specified otherwise, the standards of practice are designed to apply to all providers of supervised visitation, whether the provider is a friend, relative, paid independent contractor, employee, intern, or volunteer operating independently or through a supervised visitation center or agency. The goal of these standards of practice is to assure the safety and welfare of the child, adults, and providers of supervised visitation. Once safety is assured, the best interest of the child is the paramount consideration at all stages and particularly in deciding the manner in which supervision is provided. Each court is encouraged to adopt local court rules necessary to implement these standards of practice.

(Subd (a) amended effective January 1, 2015; previously amended effective January 1, 2007.)

(b) Definitions

For purposes of this standard, the following definitions apply:

(1) A "nonprofessional provider," as defined in Family Code section 3200.5, is any person who is not paid for providing supervised visitation services.

(2) A "professional provider," as defined in Family Code section 3200.5, is any person who is paid for providing supervised visitation services, or an independent contractor, employee, intern, or volunteer operating independently or through a supervised visitation center or agency.

(3) A "provider," as defined in Family Code section 3200, includes any individual who functions as a visitation monitor, as well as supervised visitation centers.

(4) "Supervised visitation" is contact between a noncustodial party and one or more children in the presence of a neutral third person.

(5) A "TrustLine provider," is a professional supervised visitation provider who is registered on TrustLine, a database that is administered by the California Department of Social Services.

(Subd (b) amended effective January 1, 2021; previously amended effective January 1, 2007, and January 1, 2015.)

(c) Type of provider

Who provides the supervision and the manner in which supervision is provided depends on different factors, including local resources, the financial situation of the parties, and the degree of risk in each case. While the court makes the final decision as to the manner in which supervision is provided and any terms or conditions, the court may consider recommendations by the attorney for the child, the parties and their attorneys, Family Court Services staff, evaluators, and therapists. As specified in Family Code section 3200.5, in any case in which the court has determined that there is domestic violence or child abuse or neglect, as defined in section 11165.6 of the Penal Code, and the court determines supervision is necessary, the court must consider whether to use a professional or nonprofessional provider based on the child's best interest.

(Subd (c) amended effective January 1, 2015; previously amended effective January 1, 2007.)

(d) Qualifications of nonprofessional providers

(1) Unless otherwise ordered by the court or stipulated by the parties, the nonprofessional provider must:

(A) Have no record of a conviction for child molestation, child abuse, or other crimes against a person;

(B) Have proof of automobile insurance if transporting the child;

(C) Have no current or past court order in which the provider is the person being supervised; and

(D) Agree to adhere to and enforce the court order regarding supervised visitation.

(2) Unless otherwise ordered by the court or stipulated by the parties, the nonprofessional provider should:

(A) Be 21 years of age or older;

(B) Have no record of conviction for driving under the influence (DUI) within the last 5 years;

(C) Not have been on probation or parole for the last 10 years;

(D) Have no civil, criminal, or juvenile restraining orders within the last 10 years; and

(E) Not be financially dependent on the person being supervised.

(3) Sign a local court form or *Declaration of Supervised Visitation Provider (Nonprofessional)* (form FL-324(NP)) stating that all requirements to be a nonprofessional provider have been met.

(Subd (d) amended effective January 1, 2021; adopted as part of subd (c); previously relettered and amended effective January 1, 2015.)

(e) Qualifications of professional providers

The professional provider must:

(1) Be 21 years of age or older;

(2) Have no record of conviction for driving under the influence (DUI) within the last 5 years;

(3) Not have been on probation or parole for the last 10 years;

(4) Have no record of a conviction for child molestation, child abuse, or other crimes against a person;

(5) Have proof of automobile insurance if transporting the child;

(6) Have no civil, criminal, or juvenile restraining orders within the last 10 years;

(7) Have no current or past court order in which the provider is the person being supervised;

(8) Be able to speak the language of the party being supervised and of the child, or the provider must provide a neutral interpreter over the age of 18 who is able to do so;

(9) Agree to adhere to and enforce the court order regarding supervised visitation;

(10) Complete a Live Scan criminal background check, at the expense of the provider or the supervised visitation center or agency, before providing visitation services;

(11) Be registered as a TrustLine provider under chapter 3.35 (commencing with section 1596.60) of division 2 of the Health and Safety Code. Notwithstanding any other law, a person is ineligible to be a professional provider if the California Department of Social Services either:

(A) Denies that person's TrustLine registration under Health and Safety Code sections 1596.605 or 1596.607; or

(B) Revokes that person's TrustLine registration under Health and Safety Code section 1596.608;

(12) Meet the training requirements listed in (f);

(13) Sign a *Declaration of Supervised Visitation Provider (Professional)* (form FL-324(P)) stating that all requirements to be a professional provider have been met; and

(14) Sign a separate, updated form FL-324(P) each time the professional provider submits a report to the court.

(Subd (e) amended effective January 1, 2021; adopted as part of subd (c); previously relettered as subd (e) and amended effective January 1, 2015.)

(f) Training for professional providers

(1) Before providing services, professional providers must complete 24 hours of training, including at least 12 hours of classroom instruction in the following subjects:

(A) The role of a professional provider;

(B) Child abuse reporting laws;

(C) Record-keeping procedures;

(D) Screening, monitoring, and termination of visitation;

(E) Developmental needs of children;

(F) Legal responsibilities and obligations of a provider;

(G) Cultural sensitivity;

(H) Conflicts of interest, including the acceptance of gifts;

(I) Confidentiality;

(J) Issues relating to substance abuse, child abuse, sexual abuse, and domestic violence; and

(K) Basic knowledge of family and juvenile law.

(2) Of the 24 hours of training required in (1), the training must include at least:

(A) Three hours on the screening, monitoring, and termination of visitation;

(B) Three hours on the developmental needs of children;

(C) Three hours on issues relating to substance abuse, child abuse, sexual abuse, and domestic violence; and

(D) One hour on basic knowledge of family law.

(3) On or after January 1, 2021, to complete the required training in child abuse reporting laws under (1)(B), a professional provider must complete an online training required for mandated reporters that is provided by the California Department of Social Services. This mandatory online training is not intended to increase the total of 24 hours of training required in (1).

(Subd (f) amended effective January 1, 2021; adopted as subd (d) effective January 1, 2007; previously amended and relettered as subd (f) effective January 1, 2015.)

(g) Safety and security procedures

All providers must make every reasonable effort to assure the safety and welfare of the child and adults during the visitation. Professional providers should establish a written protocol, with the assistance of the local law enforcement agency, that describes the emergency assistance and responses that can be expected from the local law enforcement agency. In addition, the professional provider should:

(1) Establish and state in writing minimum security procedures and inform the parties of these procedures before the commencement of supervised visitation;

(2) Conduct comprehensive intake and screening to understand the nature and degree of risk for each case. The procedures for intake should include separate interviews with the parties before the first visit. During the interview, the provider should obtain identifying information and explain the reasons for temporary suspension or termination of a visit under this standard. If the child is of sufficient age and capacity, the provider should include the child in part of the intake or orientation process. Any discussion should be presented to the child in a manner appropriate to the child's developmental stage;

(3) Obtain during the intake process:

(A) Copies of any protective order;

(B) Current court orders;

(C) Any Judicial Council form relating to supervised visitation orders;

(D) A report of any written records of allegations of domestic violence or abuse; and

(E) An account of the child's health needs if the child has a chronic health condition; and

(4) Establish written procedures that must be followed in the event a child is abducted during supervised visitation.

(Subd (g) amended and relettered effective January 1, 2015; adopted as subd (d) effective January 1, 1998; previously amended and relettered as subd (e) effective January 1, 2007.)

(h) Ratio of children to provider

The ratio of children to a professional provider must be contingent on:

(1) The degree of risk factors present in each case;

(2) The nature of supervision required in each case;

(3) The number and ages of the children to be supervised during a visit;

(4) The number of people, as provided in the court order, visiting the child during the visit;

(5) The duration and location of the visit; and

(6) The experience of the provider.

(Subd (h) amended and relettered effective January 1, 2015; adopted as subd (e) effective January 1, 1998; previously amended and relettered as subd (f) effective January 1, 2007.)

(i) Conflict of interest

All providers should maintain neutrality by refusing to discuss the merits of the case or agree with or support one party over another. Any discussion between a provider and the parties should be for the purposes of arranging visitation and providing for the safety of the children. In order to avoid a conflict of interest, the professional provider should not:

(1) Be financially dependent on the person being supervised;

(2) Be an employee of the person being supervised;

(3) Be an employee of or affiliated with any superior court in the county in which the supervision is ordered unless specified in the employment contract; or

(4) Be in an intimate relationship with the person being supervised.

(Subd (i) amended and relettered effective January 1, 2015; adopted as subd (f) effective January 1, 1998; previously amended and relettered as subd (g) effective January 1, 2007.)

(j) Maintenance and disclosure of records for professional providers

(1) Professional providers must keep a record for each case, including the following:

(A) A written record of each contact and visit;

(B) Who attended the visit;

(C) Any failure to comply with the terms and conditions of the visitation; and

(D) Any incidence of abuse as required by law.

(2) Case recordings should be limited to facts, observations, and direct statements made by the parties, not personal conclusions, suggestions, or opinions of the provider. All contacts by the provider in person, in writing, or by telephone with either party, the children, the court, attorneys, mental health professionals, and referring agencies should be documented in the case file. All entries should be dated and signed by the person recording the entry.

(3) If ordered by the court or requested by either party or the attorney for either party or the attorney for the child, a report about the supervised visit must be produced. These reports should include facts, observations, and direct statements and not opinions or recommendations regarding future visitation. The original report must be sent to the court if so ordered, or to the requesting party or attorney, and copies should be sent to all parties, their attorneys, and the attorney for the child.

(4) Any identifying information about the parties and the child, including addresses, telephone numbers, places of employment, and schools, is confidential, should not be disclosed, and should be deleted from documents before releasing them to any court, attorney, attorney for the child, party, mediator, evaluator, mental health professional, social worker, or referring agency, except as required in reporting suspected child abuse.

(Subd (j) amended and relettered effective January 1, 2015; adopted as subd (g) effective January 1, 1998; previously amended and relettered as subd (h) effective January 1, 2007.)

(k) Confidentiality

Communications between parties and providers of supervised visitation are not protected by any privilege of confidentiality. Professional providers should, whenever possible, maintain confidentiality regarding the case except when:

(1) Ordered by the court;

(2) Subpoenaed to produce records or testify in court;

(3) Requested to provide information about the case by a mediator or evaluator in conjunction with a court-ordered mediation, investigation, or evaluation;

(4) Required to provide information about the case by Child Protective Services; or

(5) Requested to provide information about the case by law enforcement.

(Subd (k) amended and relettered effective January 1, 2015; adopted as subd (h) effective January 1, 1998; previously amended and relettered as subd (i) effective January 1, 2007.)

(*l*) Delineation of terms and conditions

The provider bears the sole responsibility for enforcement of all the terms and conditions of any supervised visitation. Unless otherwise ordered by the court, the provider should implement the following terms and conditions:

(1) Monitor conditions to assure the safety and welfare of the child;

(2) Enforce the frequency and duration of the visits as ordered by the court;

(3) Avoid any attempt to take sides with either party;

(4) Ensure that all contact between the child and the noncustodial party is within the provider's hearing and sight at all times, and that discussions are audible to the provider;

(5) Speak in a language spoken by the child and the noncustodial party;

(6) Allow no derogatory comments about the other parent, his or her family, caretaker, child, or child's siblings;

(7) Allow no discussion of the court case or possible future outcomes;

(8) Allow neither the provider nor the child to be used to gather information about the other party or caretaker or to transmit documents, information, or personal possessions;

(9) Allow no spanking, hitting, or threatening the child;

(10) Allow no visits to occur while the visiting party appears to be under the influence of alcohol or illegal drugs;

(11) Allow no emotional, verbal, physical, or sexual abuse;

(12) Allow no contact between the custodial and noncustodial parents unless ordered by the court; and

(13) Ensure that the parties follow any additional rules set forth by the provider or the court.

(Subd (l) amended and relettered effective January 1, 2015; adopted as subd (i) effective January 1, 1998; previously amended and relettered as subd (j) effective January 1, 2007.)

(m) Safety considerations for sexual abuse cases

In cases where there are allegations of sexual abuse, in addition to the requirements of (*l*), the provider should comply with the following terms and conditions, unless otherwise ordered by the court:

(1) Allow no exchanges of gifts, money, or cards;

(2) Allow no photographing, audiotaping, or videotaping of the child;

(3) Allow no physical contact with the child such as lap sitting, hair combing, stroking, hand holding, hugging, wrestling, tickling, horseplaying, changing diapers, or accompanying the child to the bathroom;

(4) Allow no whispering, passing notes, hand signals, or body signals; and

(5) Allow no supervised visitation in the location where the alleged sexual abuse occurred.

(Subd (m) amended and relettered effective January 1, 2015; adopted as subd (j) effective January 1, 1998; previously amended and relettered as subd (k) effective January 1, 2007.)

(n) Legal responsibilities and obligations of a provider

All nonprofessional providers of supervised visitation should, and all professional providers must:

(1) Advise the parties before commencement of supervised visitation that no confidential privilege exists;

(2) Report suspected child abuse to the appropriate agency, as provided by law, and inform the parties of the provider's obligation to make such reports; and

(3) Suspend or terminate visitation under (p).

(Subd (n) amended and relettered effective January 1, 2015; adopted as subd (k) effective January 1, 1998; previously amended and relettered as subd (l) effective January 1, 2007.)

(o) Additional legal responsibilities of professional providers

In addition to the legal responsibilities and obligations required in (n), professional providers must:

(1) Prepare a written contract to be signed by the parties before commencement of the supervised visitation. The contract should inform each party of the terms and conditions of supervised visitation; and

(2) Review custody and visitation orders relevant to the supervised visitation.

(Subd (o) amended and relettered effective January 1, 2015; adopted as subd (l) effective January 1, 1998; previously amended and relettered as subd (m) effective January 1, 2007.)

(p) Temporary suspension or termination of supervised visitation

(1) All providers must make every reasonable effort to provide a safe visit for the child and the noncustodial party.

(2) However, if a provider determines that the rules of the visit have been violated, the child has become acutely distressed, or the safety of the

child or the provider is at risk, the visit may be temporarily interrupted, rescheduled at a later date, or terminated.

(3) All interruptions or terminations of visits must be recorded in the case file.

(4) All providers must advise both parties of the reasons for interruption of a visit or termination.

(Subd (p) amended and relettered effective January 1, 2015; adopted as subd (m) effective January 1, 1998; previously amended and relettered as subd (n) effective January 1, 2007.)

(q) Additional requirements for professional providers

Professional providers must state the reasons for temporary suspension or termination of supervised visitation in writing and provide the written statement to both parties, their attorneys, the attorney for the child, and the court.

(Subd (q) amended and relettered effective January 1, 2015; adopted as subd (n) effective January 1, 1998; previously amended and relettered to subd (o) effective January 1, 2007.)

(r) Informational materials; procedures

(1) Each court is encouraged to make available to all providers informational materials about the role of a provider, the terms and conditions of supervised visitation, and the legal responsibilities and obligations of a provider under this standard.

(2) By January 1, 2022, each court must develop and adopt local rules that establish procedures for processing and maintaining:

(A) *Declaration of Supervised Visitation Provider (Professional)* (form FL-324(P)), along with the professional provider's original report required in (j)(3) of this standard; and

(B) The nonprofessional supervised visitation provider's declaration regarding qualifications, whether the provider uses the court's local form or *Declaration of Supervised Visitation Provider (Nonprofessional)* (form FL-324(NP)).

(Subd (r) adopted effective January 1, 2021.)

Standard 5.20 amended effective January 1, 2021; adopted as sec. 26.2 effective January 1, 1998; previously amended and renumbered effective January 1, 2007; previous amended effective January 1, 2015.

Standard 5.30. Family court matters

(a) Judicial assignments to family court

In a court with a separate family court, the presiding judge of the superior court should assign judges to the family court to serve for a minimum of three years. In selecting judges for family court assignments, the presiding judge should consider, in addition to rule 10.603(c)(1)(A) of the California Rules of Court, the judge's prior experience in family law litigation and mediation, as well as whether the judge prefers to serve in a family law department.

(Subd (a) adopted effective January 1, 2007.)

(b) Case assignment to same department

To the extent possible, family law actions related to the same family should be assigned to the same judicial officer for all purposes, so that all decisions that are made in a case through final judgment are issued by the same judicial officer.

(Subd (b) adopted effective January 1, 2007.)

(c) Importance of family court

The supervising judge in the family court, in consultation with the presiding judge of the superior court, should:

(1) Motivate and educate other judges regarding the significance of family court; and

(2) Work to ensure that sufficient judicial officers, court staff, family law facilitators, child custody mediators and evaluators, interpreters, financial resources, and adequate facilities are assigned to the family court to allow adequate time to hear and decide the matters before it.

(Subd (c) adopted effective January 1, 2007.)

(d) Compensation for court-appointed attorneys

The supervising judge of the family court should ensure that court-appointed attorneys in the family court are compensated at a level equivalent to attorneys appointed by the court in comparable types of cases.

(Subd (d) adopted effective January 1, 2007.)

(e) Training and education

Family court law is a specialized area of the law that requires dedication and study. The supervising judge of the family court has a responsibility to maintain high-quality services in family court. The quality of services provided by judicial officers and court staff depends, in significant part, on appropriate training and education, from the beginning of the family court assignment and on a continuing basis thereafter.

(1) Family court judicial officers, family law facilitators, child custody mediators and evaluators, interpreters, other court staff, and court-appointed attorneys should have sufficient training to perform their jobs competently.

(2) The supervising judge of the family court should promote access to printed, electronic, Internet, and other family law resources.

(Subd (e) adopted effective January 1, 2007.)

(f) Unique role of a family court

Under the direction of the presiding judge of the superior court, the family court, to the extent that it does not interfere with the adjudication process or violate any ethical constraints, is encouraged to:

(1) Provide active leadership within the community in determining the needs of, and obtaining and developing resources and services for children and families who participate in the family law court system;

(2) Investigate and determine the availability of specific prevention, intervention, and treatment services in the community for families who come before the family courts;

(3) Take an active role in helping the court develop rules and procedures that will result in the ordering of appropriate treatment and services for children and families;

(4) Exercise a leadership role in the development and maintenance of services for self-represented and financially disadvantaged litigants;

(5) Take an active part in the formation of a community-wide network to promote and coordinate private- and public-sector efforts to focus attention and resources on the needs of family law litigants;

(6) Educate the community and its institutions, including the media, concerning the role of the family court in meeting the complex needs of families;

(7) Encourage the development of community services and resources to assist families and children in the family court system, including self-help information; supervised visitation; substance abuse and drug prevention, intervention, and treatment; services for families with domestic violence issues; counseling; parenting education; vocational training; mediation; alternative dispute resolution options; and other resources to support families;

(8) Manage cases more efficiently and effectively to avoid conflicting orders;

(9) Take an active role in promoting completion of cases in a timely manner;

(10) Appoint counsel for children in appropriate family law custody cases; and

(11) Ensure that the best interest of children is served throughout the family court process.

(Subd (f) adopted effective January 1, 2007.)

(g) Appointment of attorneys and other persons

A court should follow the guidelines of standard 10.21 of the California Standards of Judicial Administration when appointing attorneys, arbitrators, mediators, referees, masters, receivers, and other persons.

(Subd (g) adopted effective January 1, 2007.)

Standard 5.30 adopted effective January 1, 2007.

Advisory Committee Comment

Standard 5.30. Family court matters include proceedings under the Family Code for dissolution of marriage, nullity of marriage, legal separation, custody and support of minor children; or actions under the Domestic Violence Prevention Act, the Uniform Parentage Act, the Uniform Child Custody Jurisdiction and Enforcement Act, Domestic Partner Registration Act, and the Uniform Interstate Family Support Act; local child support agency actions under the Family Code; and contempt proceedings relating to family law or local child support agency actions.

Subdivision (a). This subdivision implements the legislative mandate of Family Code section 2330.3(b) requiring the Judicial Council to adopt a standard of judicial administration prescribing a minimum length of a judge's family law assignment. Standard 5.30 sets a standard in family court that is similar to the juvenile court standards stated in standard 5.40, Juvenile Court Matters.

Family law is complex and constantly evolving. The laws concerning child custody, support, domestic violence, and property division are always changing. Not only does the family law judge have to understand family law and procedure but also issues that involve bankruptcy, estate planning, insurance, state and federal tax law, business, immigration, and criminal law, which can frequently arise in the context of a family law case. Because of the complexity and long-range impact of the judicial determinations, the presiding judge should strive to place experienced judges in family law assignments.

Considering the constantly evolving changes in the law, as well as the unique nature of the proceedings in family court, the family court judge should be willing to commit to a minimum tenure of three years. Not only does this tenure afford the judge the opportunity to become well acquainted with the complexity of the family court process, but it also provides continuity to a system that demands it.

Subdivision (b). This subdivision implements the legislative mandate of Family Code section 2330.3(a), which requires that dissolution actions, to the greatest extent possible, be assigned to the same superior court department for all purposes, so that all decisions in a case are made by the same judicial officer. This subdivision expands the Legislature's requirement by including other related family court matters, such as those filed under the Uniform Parentage Act, Domestic Violence Prevention Act, in recognition that the same families may enter the family court through a variety of actions.

The committee recognizes that having the same judicial officer hear all actions involving the same family may not be practical in all cases for reasons that include funding limitations, assignment rotations, illness, vacations, and retirements. In some courts, one judge does not hear all aspects of a family's legal problems because of multiple courthouse locations or specifically designated funding of certain issues (e.g., Title IV-D child support issues). However, the committee agrees with the legislative intent in enacting section 2330.3(a), which was to expedite and simplify the dissolution process, reduce the litigation expenses and costs, and encourage greater judicial supervision of cases involving dissolution of marriage. Family law actions often involve a succession of hearings to resolve the various issues that arise. A single judge's involvement over this period of time allows the judge to be more familiar with the particular actions and issues, which creates judicial efficiencies that expedite their handling. One judge hearing all actions involving a family also helps avoid conflicting orders, alleviates the need to hold multiple hearings on the same issue, improves the court process, promotes consistency, and enhances fairness in family proceedings.

Subdivision (c). The family court is an integral part of the justice system. Decisions made by family law judges can have significant and lasting impacts on the lives of the parties and their children. The work of the family court has a significant impact on the health of families and ultimately on the strength of the community. The parties deserve to have adequate time to present their cases, and the judges should have the resources they need to enable them to make informed decisions. It is only through the constant exertion of pressure to maintain resources and the continuous education of court-related personnel and administrators that the historic trend to give less priority and provide fewer resources to the family court can be changed.

Subdivision (d). Fees paid to court-appointed attorneys who represent children in family court are sometimes less than the fees paid attorneys doing other comparable legal work thereby demeaning the work of the family court and leading many to believe that such work is less important. It may also discourage attorneys from accepting these appointments. Compensation for legal work in the family court should reflect the importance of the work.

Subdivision (e)(2). A significant barrier to having well-trained attorneys and educated self-represented litigants is a lack of current educational materials relating to family court practice. Law libraries, law offices, and court systems traditionally have not devoted adequate resources to purchase such educational materials. With advances in technology, resources can be accessed, shared, developed, or made available through electronic/computer-based, online, and multimedia means, audiotape and videotape, DVD, CD, Web-based audiocasts and videocasts, and other media to supplement print materials.

Subdivision (f). In addition to the traditional role of fairly and efficiently resolving disputes before the court, a family court judge occupies a unique position within California's judiciary. California law empowers the family court judge not only to order relief related to the needs of families under its jurisdiction but also to enforce and review the compliance with such orders. This oversight function includes the obligation to understand and work with those public and private agencies that provide services for families. As such, the family court assignment requires a dramatic shift in emphasis from judging in the traditional sense. Active and public judicial support and encouragement of programs serving children and families in family court poses no conflict with traditional concepts of judicial ethics and is an important function of the family court judge. These efforts enhance the overall administration of justice for families.

Standard 5.40. Juvenile court matters

(a) Assignments to juvenile court

The presiding judge of the superior court should assign judges to the juvenile court to serve for a minimum of three years. Priority should be given to judges who have expressed an interest in the assignment.

(Subd (a) adopted effective July 1, 1989.)

(b) Importance of juvenile court

The presiding judge of the juvenile court, in consultation with the presiding judge of the superior court, should:

(1) Motivate and educate other judges regarding the significance of juvenile court.

(2) Work to ensure that sufficient judges and staff, facilities, and financial resources are assigned to the juvenile court to allow adequate time to hear and decide the matters before it.

(Subd (b) amended effective January 1, 2007; adopted effective July 1, 1989.)

(c) Standards of representation and compensation

The presiding judge of the juvenile court should:

(1) Encourage attorneys who practice in juvenile court, including all court-appointed and contract attorneys, to continue their practice in juvenile court for substantial periods of time. A substantial period of time is at least two years and preferably from three to five years.

(2) Confer with the county public defender, county district attorney, county counsel, and other public law office leaders and encourage them to raise the status of attorneys working in the juvenile courts as follows: hire attorneys who are interested in serving in the juvenile court for a substantial part of their careers; permit and encourage attorneys, based on interest and ability, to remain in juvenile court assignments for significant periods of time; and work to ensure that attorneys who have chosen to serve in the juvenile court have the same promotional and salary opportunities as attorneys practicing in other assignments within a law office.

(3) Establish minimum standards of practice to which all court-appointed and public office attorneys will be expected to conform. These standards should delineate the responsibilities of attorneys relative to investigation and evaluation of the case, preparation for and conduct of hearings, and advocacy for their respective clients.

(4) In conjunction with other leaders in the legal community, ensure that attorneys appointed in the juvenile court are compensated in a manner equivalent to attorneys appointed by the court in other types of cases.

(Subd (c) amended effective January 1, 2007; adopted effective July 1, 1992.)

(d) Training and orientation

The presiding judge of the juvenile court should:

(1) Establish relevant prerequisites for court-appointed attorneys and advocates in the juvenile court.

(2) Develop orientation and in-service training programs for judicial officers, attorneys, volunteers, law enforcement personnel, court personnel, and child advocates to ensure that all are adequately trained concerning all issues relating to special education rights and responsibilities, including the right of each child with exceptional needs to receive a free, appropriate public education and the right of each child with educational disabilities to receive accommodations.

(3) Promote the establishment of a library or other resource center in which information about juvenile court practice (including books, periodicals, videotapes, and other training materials) can be collected and made available to all participants in the juvenile system.

(4) Ensure that attorneys who appear in juvenile court have sufficient training to perform their jobs competently, as follows: require that all court-appointed attorneys meet minimum training and continuing legal education standards as a condition of their appointment to juvenile court matters; and encourage the leaders of public law offices that have responsibilities in juvenile court to require their attorneys who appear in juvenile court to have at least the same training and continuing legal education required of court-appointed attorneys.

(Subd (d) amended effective January 1, 2001; adopted effective July 1, 1989; previously amended and relettered effective July 1, 1992.)

(e) Unique role of a juvenile court judge

Judges of the juvenile court, in consultation with the presiding judge of the juvenile court and the presiding judge of the superior court, to the extent that it does not interfere with the adjudication process, are encouraged to:

(1) Provide active leadership within the community in determining the needs of and obtaining and developing resources and services for at-risk children and families. At-risk children include delinquents, dependents, and status offenders.

(2) Investigate and determine the availability of specific prevention, intervention, and treatment services in the community for at-risk children and their families.

(3) Exercise their authority by statute or rule to review, order, and enforce the delivery of specific services and treatment for at-risk children and their families.

(4) Exercise a leadership role in the development and maintenance of permanent programs of interagency cooperation and coordination among the court and the various public agencies that serve at-risk children and their families.

(5) Take an active part in the formation of a communitywide network to promote and unify private and public sector efforts to focus attention and resources for at-risk children and their families.

(6) Maintain close liaison with school authorities and encourage coordination of policies and programs.

(7) Educate the community and its institutions through every available means, including the media, concerning the role of the juvenile court in meeting the complex needs of at-risk children and their families.

(8) Evaluate the criteria established by child protection agencies for initial removal and reunification decisions and communicate the court's expectations of what constitutes "reasonable efforts" to prevent removal or hasten return of the child.

(9) Encourage the development of community services and resources to assist homeless, truant, runaway, and incorrigible children.

(10) Be familiar with all detention facilities, placements, and institutions used by the court.

(11) Act in all instances consistent with the public safety and welfare.

(Subd (e) amended effective January 1, 2007; adopted effective July 1, 1989; previously relettered effective July 1, 1992.)

(f) Appointment of attorneys and other persons

For the appointment of attorneys, arbitrators, mediators, referees, masters, receivers, and other persons, each court should follow rule 10.611 and the guidelines of standard 10.21.

(Subd (f) amended effective January 1, 2007; adopted effective January 1, 1999.)

(g) Educational rights of children in the juvenile court

The juvenile court should be guided by certain general principles:

(1) A significant number of children in the juvenile court process have exceptional needs that, if properly identified and assessed, would qualify such children to receive special education and related services under federal and state education law (a free, appropriate public education) (see Ed. Code, § 56000 et seq. and 20 U.S.C. § 1400 et seq.);

(2) Many children in the juvenile court process have disabilities that, if properly identified and assessed, would qualify such children to receive educational accommodations (see § 504 of the Rehabilitation Act of 1973 [29 U.S.C. § 794; 34 C.F.R. § 104.1 et seq.]);

(3) Unidentified and unremediated exceptional needs and unaccommodated disabilities have been found to correlate strongly with juvenile delinquency, substance abuse, mental health issues, teenage pregnancy, school failure and dropout, and adult unemployment and crime; and

(4) The cost of incarcerating children is substantially greater than the cost of providing special education and related services to exceptional needs children and providing educational accommodations to children with disabilities.

(Subd (g) adopted effective January 1, 2001.)

(h) Role of the juvenile court

The juvenile court should:

(1) Take responsibility, with the other juvenile court participants at every stage of the child's case, to ensure that the child's educational needs are met, regardless of whether the child is in the custody of a parent or is suitably placed in the custody of the child welfare agency or probation department and regardless of where the child is placed in school. Each child under the jurisdiction of the juvenile court with exceptional needs has the right to receive a free, appropriate public education, specially designed, at no cost to the parents, to meet the child's unique special education needs. (See Ed. Code, § 56031 and 20 U.S.C. § 1401(8).) Each child with disabilities under the jurisdiction of the juvenile court has the right to receive accommodations. (See § 504 of the Rehabilitation Act of 1973 [29 U.S.C. § 794; 34 C.F.R. § 104.1 et seq. (1980)].) The court should also ensure that each parent or guardian receives information and assistance concerning his or her child's educational entitlements as provided by law.

(2) Provide oversight of the social service and probation agencies to ensure that a child's educational rights are investigated, reported, and monitored. The court should work within the statutory framework to accommodate the sharing of information between agencies. A child who comes before the court and is suspected of having exceptional needs or other educational disabilities should be referred in writing for an assessment to the child's school principal or to the school district's special education office. (See Ed. Code, §§ 56320–56329.) The child's parent, teacher, or other service provider may make the required written referral for assessment. (See Ed. Code, § 56029.)

(3) Require that court reports, case plans, assessments, and permanency plans considered by the court address a child's educational entitlements and how those entitlements are being satisfied, and contain information to assist the court in deciding whether the right of the parent or guardian to make educational decisions for the child should be limited by the court under Welfare and Institutions Code section 361(a) or 726(b). Information concerning whether the school district has met its obligation to provide educational services to the child, including special educational services if the child has exceptional needs under Education Code section 56000 et seq., and to provide accommodations if the child has disabilities as defined in section 504 of the Rehabilitation Act of 1973 (29 U.S.C. § 794; 34 C.F.R. § 104.1 et seq. (1980)) should also be included, along with a recommendation for disposition.

(4) Facilitate coordination of services by joining the local educational agency as a party when it appears that an educational agency has failed to fulfill its legal obligations to provide special education and related services or accommodations to a child in the juvenile court who has been identified as having exceptional needs or educational disabilities. (See Welf. & Inst. Code, §§ 362(a), 727(a).)

(5) Make appropriate orders limiting the educational rights of a parent or guardian who cannot be located or identified, or who is unwilling or unable to be an active participant in ensuring that the child's educational needs are met, and appoint a responsible adult as educational representative for such a child or, if a representative cannot be identified and the child may be eligible for special education and related services or already has an individualized education program, use form JV-535 to refer the child to the local educational agency for special education and related services and prompt appointment of a surrogate parent. (Welf. & Inst. Code, §§ 361, 726; Ed. Code, § 56156.)

(6) Ensure that special education, related services, and accommodations to which the child is entitled are provided whenever the child's school placement changes. (See Ed. Code, § 56325.)

(Subd (h) amended effective January 1, 2007; adopted effective January 1, 2001; previously amended effective January 1, 2004.)

Standard 5.40 amended and renumbered effective January 1, 2007; adopted as sec. 24 effective January 1, 1989; previously amended effective July 1, 1992, January 1, 1999; January 1, 2001, and January 1, 2004.

Advisory Committee Comment

Subdivision (a). Considering the constantly evolving changes in the law, as well as the unique nature of the proceedings in juvenile court, the juvenile court judge should be willing to commit to a tenure of three years. Not only does this tenure afford the judge the opportunity to become well acquainted with the total juvenile justice complex, but it also provides continuity to a system that demands it.

Dependency cases under Welfare and Institutions Code section 300 for the most part last 18 months. The juvenile court judge has a responsibility to oversee these cases, and a single judge's involvement over this period of time is important to help ensure positive results. The ultimate goal should be to perfect a system that serves the needs of both recipients and providers. This can only be done over time and with constant application of effective energy.

Subdivision (b)(2). The juvenile court is an integral part of the justice system. It is only through the constant exertion of pressure to maintain resources and the continuous education of court-related personnel and administrators that the historic trend to minimize the juvenile court can be contained.

Subdivision (c)(4). The quality of justice in the juvenile court is in large part dependent on the quality of the attorneys who appear on behalf of the different parties before the court. The presiding judge of the juvenile court plays a significant role in ensuring that a sufficient number of attorneys of high quality are available to the parties appearing in juvenile court.

Juvenile court practice requires attorneys who have both a special interest in and a substantive understanding of the work of the court. Obtaining and retaining qualified attorneys for the juvenile court requires effective recruiting, training, and employment considerations.

The importance of juvenile court work must be stressed to ensure that juvenile court assignments have the same status and career enhancement opportunities as other assignments for public law office attorneys.

The presiding judge of the juvenile court should urge leaders of public law offices serving the juvenile court to assign experienced, interested, and capable attorneys to that court, and to establish hiring and promotional policies that will encourage the development of a division of the office dedicated to working in the juvenile court.

National commentators are in accord with these propositions: "Court-appointed and public attorneys representing children in abuse and neglect cases, as well as judges, should be specially trained or experienced. Juvenile and family courts should not be the 'training ground' for inexperienced attorneys or judges." (Metropolitan Court Judges Committee, National Council of Juvenile and Family Court Judges, *Deprived Children: A Judicial Response—73 Recommendations* (1986) p. 14.)

Fees paid to attorneys appearing in juvenile court are sometimes less than the fees paid attorneys doing other legal work. Such a payment scheme demeans the work of the juvenile court, leading many to believe that such work is less important. It may discourage attorneys from selecting juvenile court practice as a career option. The incarceration of a child in a detention facility or a child's permanent loss of his or her family through a termination of parental rights proceeding is at least as important as any other work in the legal system. Compensation for the legal work in the juvenile court should reflect the importance of this work.

Subdivision (d)(4). Juvenile court law is a specialized area of the law that requires dedication and study. The juvenile court judge has a responsibility to maintain high quality in the practice of law in the juvenile court. The quality of representation in the juvenile court depends in good part on the education of the lawyers who appear there. In order to make certain that all parties receive adequate representation, it is important that attorneys have adequate training before they begin practice in juvenile court and on a continuing basis thereafter. The presiding judge of the juvenile court should mandate such training for all court-appointed attorneys and urge leaders of public law offices to provide at least comparable training for attorneys assigned to juvenile court.

A minimum of six hours of continuing legal education is suggested; more hours are recommended. Education methods can include lectures and tapes that meet the legal education requirements.

In addition to basic legal training in juvenile dependency and delinquency law, evidentiary issues, and effective trial practice techniques, training should also include important related issues, including child development, alternative resources for families, effects and treatment of substance abuse, domestic violence, abuse, neglect, modification and enforcement of all court orders, dependency, delinquency, guardianships, conservatorships, interviewing children, and emancipation. Education may also include observational experience such as site visits to institutions and operations critical to the juvenile court.

A significant barrier to the establishment and maintenance of well-trained attorneys is a lack of educational materials relating to juvenile court practice. Law libraries, law offices, and court systems traditionally do not devote adequate resources to the purchase of such educational materials.

Effective January 1, 1993, guidelines and training material will be available from Judicial Council staff.

Subdivision (e)(11). A superior court judge assigned to the juvenile court occupies a unique position within California's judiciary. In addition to the traditional role of fairly and efficiently resolving disputes before the court, the juvenile court judge is statutorily required to discharge other duties. California law empowers the juvenile court judge not only to order services for children under its jurisdiction, but also to enforce and review the delivery of those services. This oversight function includes the obligation to understand and work with the public and private agencies, including school systems, that provide services and treatment programs for children and families. As such, the juvenile court assignment requires a dramatic shift in emphasis from judging in the traditional sense.

The legislative directive to juvenile court judges to "improve system performance in a vigorous and ongoing manner" (Welf. & Inst. Code, § 202) poses no conflict with traditional concepts of judicial ethics. Active and public judicial support and encouragement of programs serving children and families at risk are important functions of the juvenile court judge that enhance the overall administration of justice.

The standards in (e) are derived from statutory requirements in the following sections of the Welfare and Institutions Code as well as the supplementary material promulgated by the National Council of Juvenile and Family Court Judges and others: (1) Welfare and Institutions Code, sections 202, 209, 300, 317, 318, 319, 362, 600, 601, 654, 702, 727; (2) California Code of Judicial Conduct, canon 4; (3) Metropolitan Court Judges Committee, National Council of Juvenile and Family Court Judges, *Deprived Children: A Judicial Response—73 Recommendations* (1986), Recommendations 1–7, 14, 35, 40; and (4) National Council of Juvenile and Family Court Judges, Child Welfare League of America, Youth Law Center, and the National Center for Youth Law, *Making Reasonable Efforts: Steps for Keeping Families Together* pp. 43–59.

Standard 5.45. Resource guidelines for child abuse and neglect cases

(a) Guidelines

To improve the fair and efficient administration of child abuse and neglect cases in the California juvenile dependency system, judges and judicial officers assigned to the juvenile court, in consultation with the presiding judge of the juvenile court and the presiding judge of the superior or consolidated court, are encouraged to follow the resource guidelines of the National Council of Juvenile and Family Court Judges, titled "Resource Guidelines: Improving Court Practice in Child Abuse & Neglect Cases." The guidelines are meant to be goals to help courts achieve, among other objectives, the following:

(1) Adherence to statutory timelines;
(2) Effective calendar management;
(3) Effective representation by counsel;
(4) Child-friendly court facilities;
(5) Timely and thorough reports and services to ensure informed judicial decisions, including reasonable efforts findings; and
(6) Minimum time allocations for specified hearings.

(Subd (a) amended effective January 1, 2007.)

(b) Distribution of guidelines

Judicial Council staff will distribute a copy of the resource guidelines to each juvenile court and will provide individual copies to judicial officers and court administrators on written request.

(Subd (b) amended effective January 1, 2016; previously amended effective January 1, 2007.)

Standard 5.45 amended effective January 1, 2016; adopted as sec. 24.5 effective July 1, 1997; previously amended and renumbered as standard 5.45 effective January 1, 2007.

Advisory Committee Comment

Child abuse and neglect cases impose a special obligation on juvenile court judges to oversee case progress. Case oversight includes monitoring the agency's fulfillment of its responsibilities and parental cooperation with the case plan. Court involvement in child welfare cases occurs simultaneously with agency efforts to assist the family. Federal and state legal mandates assign to the juvenile court a series of interrelated and complex decisions that shape the course of state intervention and determine the future of the child and family.

Unlike almost all other types of cases in the court system, child abuse and neglect cases deal with an ongoing and changing situation. In a child welfare case, the court must focus on agency casework and parental behavior over an extended period of time. In making a decision, the court must take into account the agency's plan to help the family and anticipated changes in parental behavior. At the same time, the court must consider the evolving circumstances and needs of each child.

The purpose of these resource guidelines is to specify the essential elements of properly conducted court hearings. The guidelines describe the requirements of juvenile courts in fulfilling their oversight role under federal and state laws, and they specify the necessary elements of a fair, thorough, and speedy court process in child abuse and neglect cases. The guidelines cover all stages of the court process, from the initial removal hearing to the end of juvenile court involvement. These guidelines assume that the court will remain involved until after the child has been safely returned home, has been placed in another permanent home, or has reached adulthood.

Currently, juvenile courts in California operate under the same juvenile court law and rules, and yet the rules are implemented with considerable variation throughout the state. In part, this is due to the lack of resource guidelines. The adoption of the proposed resource guidelines will help encourage more consistent juvenile court procedures in the state.

The guidelines are meant to be goals, and, as such, some of them may appear out of reach because of fiscal constraints or lack of judicial and staff resources. The Judicial Council Family and Juvenile Law Advisory Committee and Judicial Council staff are committed to providing technical assistance to each juvenile court to aid in implementing these goals.

Title 6
[Reserved]

Title 7
Standards for Probate Proceedings

Standard 7.10. Settlements or judgments in certain civil cases involving minors or persons with disabilities

In matters assigned to or pending in civil departments of the court where court approval of trusts that will receive proceeds of settlements or judgments is required under Probate Code section 3600, each court should develop practices and procedures that:

(1) Provide for determination of the trust issues by the probate department of the court or, in a court that does not have a probate department, a judicial officer who regularly hears proceedings under the Probate Code; or

(2) Ensure that judicial officers who hear these matters are experienced or have received training in substantive and technical issues involving trusts (including special needs trusts).

Standard 7.10 amended and renumbered effective January 1, 2007; adopted as sec. 40 effective January 1, 2005.

Title 8
Standards for the Appellate Courts

Standard 8.1. Memorandum opinions

The Courts of Appeal should dispose of causes that raise no substantial issues of law or fact by memorandum or other abbreviated form of opinion. Such causes could include:

(1) An appeal that is determined by a controlling statute which is not challenged for unconstitutionality and does not present any substantial question of interpretation or application;

(2) An appeal that is determined by a controlling decision which does not require a reexamination or restatement of its principles or rules; or

(3) An appeal raising factual issues that are determined by the substantial evidence rule.

Standard 8.1 amended and renumbered effective January 1, 2007; adopted as sec. 6 effective July 1, 1970.

Title 9
Standards on Law Practice, Attorneys, and Judges
[Reserved]

Title 10
Standards for Judicial Administration

Standard 10.5. The role of the judiciary in the community
Standard 10.16. Model code of ethics for court employees
Standard 10.17. Trial court performance standards
Standard 10.20. Court's duty to prevent bias
Standard 10.21. Appointment of attorneys, arbitrators, mediators, referees, masters, receivers, and other persons
Standard 10.24. Children's waiting room
Standard 10.25. Reasonable accommodation for court personnel
Standard 10.31. Master jury list
Standard 10.41. Court sessions at or near state penal institutions
Standard 10.50. Selection of regular grand jury
Standard 10.51. Juror complaints
Standard 10.55. Local program on waste reduction and recycling
Standard 10.70. Implementation and coordination of mediation and other alternative dispute resolution (ADR) programs
Standard 10.71. Alternative dispute resolution (ADR) committees
Standard 10.72. ADR committees and criteria for referring cases to dispute resolution neutrals
Standard 10.80. Court records management standards

Standard 10.5. The role of the judiciary in the community

(a) **Community outreach an official judicial function**

Judicial participation in community outreach activities should be considered an official judicial function to promote public understanding of and confidence in the administration of justice. This function should be performed in a manner consistent with the California Code of Judicial Ethics.

(Subd (a) lettered effective January 1, 2007; adopted as part of unlettered subdivision effective April 1, 1999.)

(b) **Encouraged outreach activities**

The judiciary is encouraged to:

(1) Provide active leadership within the community in identifying and resolving issues of access to justice within the court system;

(2) Develop local education programs for the public designed to increase public understanding of the court system;

(3) Create local mechanisms for obtaining information from the public about how the court system may be more responsive to the public's needs;

(4) Serve as guest speakers, during or after normal court hours, to address local civic, educational, business, and charitable groups that have an interest in understanding the court system but do not espouse a particular political agenda with which it would be inappropriate for a judicial officer to be associated; and

(5) Take an active part in the life of the community where the participation of the judiciary will serve to increase public understanding and promote public confidence in the integrity of the court system.

(Subd (b) amended effective January 1, 2007.)

Standard 10.5 amended and renumbered effective January 1, 2007; adopted as sec. 39 effective April 1, 1999.

Standard 10.10. Judicial branch education [Repealed]

Standard 10.10 repealed effective January 1, 2008; adopted as sec. 25 effective January 1, 1999; previously amended and renumbered effective January 1, 2007.

Standard 10.11. General judicial education standards [Repealed]

Standard 10.11 repealed effective January 1, 2008; adopted as sec. 25 effective January 1, 1990; previously amended and renumbered as Sec. 25.1 effective January 1, 1999; previously amended and renumbered effective January 1, 2007.

Standard 10.12. Judicial education for judicial officers in particular judicial assignments [Repealed]

Standard 10.12 repealed effective January 1, 2008; adopted as sec. 25.2 effective January 1, 1999; previously amended and renumbered effective January 1, 2007.

Standard 10.13. Judicial education curricula provided in particular judicial assignments [Repealed]

Standard 10.13 repealed effective January 1, 2008; repealed and adopted as sec. 25.3 effective January 1, 1999; previously amended and renumbered effective January 1, 2007.

Standard 10.14. Judicial education for judges hearing capital cases [Repealed]

Standard 10.14 repealed effective January 1, 2008; adopted as sec. 25.4 effective January 1, 2004; previously amended and renumbered effective January 1, 2007.

Standard 10.15. General court employee education standards [Repealed]

Standard 10.15 repealed effective January 1, 2008; adopted as sec. 25.6 effective January 1, 1999; previously amended and renumbered effective January 1, 2007.

Standard 10.16. Model code of ethics for court employees

Each trial and appellate court should adopt a code of ethical behavior for its support staff, and in doing so should consider rule 10.670(c)(12) of the California Rules of Court, and the model Code of Ethics for the Court Employees of California approved by the Judicial Council on May 17, 1994, and any subsequent revisions. The approved model code is published by the Judicial Council.

Standard 10.16 amended effective January 1, 2016; adopted as sec. 35 effective July 1, 1994; previously amended and renumbered as standard 10.16 effective January 1, 2007; previously amended effective July 1, 2008.

Standard 10.17. Trial court performance standards

(a) **Purpose**

These standards are intended to be used by trial courts, in cooperation with the Judicial Council, for purposes of internal evaluation, self-assessment, and self-improvement. They are not intended as a basis for cross-court comparisons, nor are they intended as a basis for evaluating the performance of individual judges.

(Subd (a) lettered effective January 1, 2007; adopted as part of unlettered subdivision effective January 25, 1995.)

(b) **Standards**

The standards for trial court performance are as follows:

(1) *Access to justice*

(A) The court conducts its proceedings and other public business openly.

(B) Court facilities are safe, accessible, and convenient to use.

(C) All who appear before the court are given the opportunity to participate effectively without undue hardship or inconvenience.

(D) Judges and other trial court personnel are courteous and responsive to the public and accord respect to all with whom they come into contact.

(E) The costs of access to the trial court's proceedings and records—whether measured in terms of money, time, or the procedures that must be followed—are reasonable, fair, and affordable.

(2) *Expedition and timeliness*

(A) The trial court establishes and complies with recognized guidelines for timely case processing while, at the same time, keeping current with its incoming caseload.

(B) The trial court disburses funds promptly, provides reports and information according to required schedules, and responds to requests for information and other services on an established schedule that assures their effective use.

(C) The trial court promptly implements changes in law and procedure.

(3) *Equality, fairness, and integrity*

(A) Trial court procedures faithfully adhere to relevant laws, procedural rules, and established policies.

(B) Jury lists are representative of the jurisdiction from which they are drawn.

(C) Trial courts give individual attention to cases, deciding them without undue disparity among like cases and on legally relevant factors.

(D) Decisions of the trial court unambiguously address the issues presented to it and make clear how compliance can be achieved.

(E) The trial court takes appropriate responsibility for the enforcement of its orders.

(F) Records of all relevant court decisions and actions are accurate and properly preserved.

(4) *Independence and accountability*

(A) A trial court maintains its institutional integrity and observes the principle of comity in its governmental relations.

(B) The trial court responsibly seeks, uses, and accounts for its public resources.

(C) The trial court uses fair employment practices.

(D) The trial court informs the community of its programs.

(E) The trial court anticipates new conditions or emergent events and adjusts its operations as necessary.

(5) *Public trust and confidence*

(A) The trial court and the justice it delivers are perceived by the public as accessible.

(B) The public has trust and confidence that the basic trial court functions are conducted expeditiously and fairly and that its decisions have integrity.

(C) The trial court is perceived to be independent, not unduly influenced by other components of government, and accountable.

(Subd (b) lettered effective January 1, 2007; adopted as part of unlettered subdivision effective January 25, 1995.)

Standard 10.17 amended and renumbered effective January 1, 2007; adopted as sec. 30 effective January 25, 1995.

Standard 10.20. Court's duty to prevent bias

(a) Statement of purpose

The California judicial branch is committed to ensuring the integrity and impartiality of the judicial system and to court interactions free of bias and the appearance of bias. Consistent with this commitment, each court should work within its community to improve dialogue and engagement with members of various cultures, backgrounds, and groups to learn, understand, and appreciate the unique qualities and needs of each group.

(Subd (a) amended effective January 1, 2022; previously amended effective January 1, 1994, January 1, 1998, and January 1, 2007.)

(b) Duty to ensure integrity and impartiality of the judicial system

Each court, its judicial officers, and its employees have the duty to ensure the integrity and impartiality of the judicial system.

(1) *Refrain from and prevent biased conduct*

In all court interactions, each court, its judicial officers, and its employees should refrain from engaging in conduct and should take action to prevent others from engaging in conduct that exhibits bias, including but not limited to bias based on age, ancestry, color, ethnicity, gender, gender expression, gender identity, genetic information, marital status, medical condition, military or veteran status, national origin, physical or mental disability, political affiliation, race, religion, sex, sexual orientation, socioeconomic status, and any other classification protected by federal or state law, including Government Code section 12940(a) and Code of Judicial Ethics, canon 3(B)(5), whether that bias is directed toward counsel, court staff, witnesses, parties, jurors, or any other person. The court, judicial officers, and court employees may consider such classifications only if necessary or relevant to the proper exercise of their adjudicatory or administrative functions.

(2) *Ensure fairness*

Each judicial officer should ensure that courtroom interactions are conducted in a manner that is fair and impartial to all persons.

(3) *Ensure unbiased decisions*

Each judicial officer should ensure that all orders, rulings, and decisions are based on the sound exercise of judicial discretion and the balancing of competing rights and interests and are not influenced by stereotypes or biases.

(Subd (b) amended and relettered effective January 1, 2022; adopted as subd (a) effective January 1, 1987; previously amended effective January 1, 1994, January 1, 1998, and January 1, 2007.)

(c) Creation of local or regional committees on bias

To assist in providing court interactions free of bias and the appearance of bias, courts should collaborate with local bar associations to establish a local or regional committee. Trial courts may choose to form a regional committee. Appellate courts may choose to form separate or joint appellate court committees or join a trial court committee or regional committee formed by or composed of trial courts within the appellate courts' districts. Each committee should:

(1) Be composed of representative members of the court community, including but not limited to judicial officers, lawyers, court administrators, and individuals who interact with the court and reflect and represent the diverse and various needs and viewpoints of court users;

(2) Sponsor or support educational programs designed to eliminate unconscious and explicit biases within the court and legal communities. Education is critical to developing an awareness of the origins of bias and the impact of bias on individuals, culture, and society. Education should include:

(A) Information as to bias based on the protected classifications listed in (b)(1);

(B) Information regarding how unconscious and explicit biases based on these classifications develop, how to recognize unconscious and explicit biases, and how to address and eliminate unconscious and explicit biases; and

(C) Other topics on bias relevant to the local community informed by the committee's independent assessment of the unique educational needs in that community.

(3) Engage in regular outreach to the local community to learn about issues of importance to court users. Specifically, committee members should be encouraged to:

(A) Inform local community groups regarding the committee's activities; and

(B) Seek information from the local community regarding concerns as to bias in court interactions and how the court can address those concerns.

(Subd (c) amended and relettered effective January 1, 2022; adopted as subd (b) effective January 1, 1994; previously amended effective January 1, 1998, and January 1, 2007.)

(d) Providing information regarding complaint procedures

Each court should effectively communicate to its court users regarding existing procedures to submit complaints of bias in court interactions based on protected classifications, as listed in (b)(1). This should include information regarding how to submit complaints about court employees directly to the court and how to submit complaints about judicial officers either directly to the court or to the Commission on Judicial Performance. Possible methods of communication include providing this information on the court website, including the information in the court's local rules, displaying the information in courthouses, or any other similar method to ensure that courts are providing complaint procedure information to court users in a meaningful and accessible manner.

(Subd (d) amended and relettered effective January 1, 2022; adopted as subd (c) effective January 1, 1994; previously amended effective January 1, 2007.)

(e) Application of local rules

The existence of the local committee and its purpose should be memorialized in the applicable local rules of court.

(Subd (e) amended and relettered effective January 1, 2022; adopted as subd (d) effective January 1, 1994; previously amended effective January 1, 2007.)

(f) Implementation

All courts should implement the recommendations of this standard as soon as possible.

(Subd (f) adopted effective January 1, 2022.)

Standard 10.20 amended effective January 1, 2022; adopted as sec. 1 effective January 1, 1987; previously amended effective January 1, 1994, and January 1, 1998; previously amended and renumbered effective January 1, 2007.

Advisory Committee Comment

Subdivision (b). An earlier version of this standard referred to the "court's duty to prohibit bias." The word "prohibit" has been replaced with "prevent" in the title of the standard and in subdivision (b), such that the standard now asks courts, judicial officers, and court employees to take actions to prevent bias rather than prohibit bias. This change reflects a more comprehensive approach in how courts are to combat bias, focusing on understanding the many forms, causes, and impacts of bias rather than simply forbidding it. Preventing bias may include, for example, prohibiting bias; encouraging judicial officers, employees, and court users to report bias; being open to discussing and learning from real misunderstandings and instances of unconscious bias; and focusing on robust education regarding how unconscious and explicit biases develop, how to recognize them, and how to address and eliminate bias.

The judicial officer duties stated in this subdivision are consistent with the California Code of Judicial Ethics, which addresses judicial officer responsibilities for performing judicial duties without bias, prejudice, or harassment (canon 3(B)(5)); for requiring attorneys in proceedings before the judicial officer to refrain from manifesting bias, prejudice, or harassment (canon 3(B)(6)); for discharging judicial administrative duties without bias or prejudice (canon 3(C)(1)); and for requiring staff and court personnel under the judicial officer's control to refrain from manifesting bias, prejudice, or harassment in the performance of their duties (canon 3(C)(3)).

An earlier version of this standard applied solely to judges and referred to "courtroom proceedings." "Judge" has been expanded to "judicial officers," which includes all judges as defined by California Rules of Court, rule 1.6, and all appellate and Supreme Court justices. The expanded phrase broadly covers any judge, justice, subordinate judicial officer, or temporary judge who might conduct a courtroom proceeding. Additionally, in subdivision (b)(1), "courtroom proceedings" has been changed to "court interactions" to expand the scope of proceedings and actions covered by this standard to include not only proceedings occurring in courtrooms but also interactions in other areas of the court, including in the clerk's office and at public counters.

Subdivision (d). An earlier version of this standard encouraged local bias committees to create informal complaint procedures for court users and members of the public to submit complaints regarding bias in court proceedings. The recommendation that local bias committees create informal complaint procedures has been eliminated in large part because of the many existing and updated avenues for making complaints regarding bias in court interactions, and to avoid creating conflicts between those procedures. For example, the authority and procedures for addressing complaints concerning judicial officers and subordinate judicial officers are outlined in rules 10.603 and 10.703 of the California Rules of Court and canon 3(D) of the California Code of Judicial Ethics. Similarly, rules 10.351 and 10.610 of the California Rules of Court, as well as Government Code section 71650 et seq., include authority and complaint resolution processes for addressing complaints against court employees. In practice, courts have developed robust procedures for addressing such complaints against judicial officers, subordinate judicial officers, and court employees, and the Commission on Judicial Performance provides detailed information on its website at *cjp.ca.gov* about how to file complaints and the procedures it employs for addressing such complaints.

In addition to the concerns regarding duplicative and conflicting complaint procedures, the recommendation that local bias committees adopt informal complaint procedures created additional concerns. For example, the earlier version of the standard envisioned using informal complaint procedures to resolve incidents that do not warrant formal discipline; however, it is often difficult to determine at the outset if a complaint is disciplinary in nature or can be ameliorated by education. Other due process concerns were raised that local committees were not necessarily resourced to make these determinations, and may not have had the expertise to investigate and resolve these complaints. Additional concerns were raised that having local committees oversee complaints against judicial officers and court employees created privacy and confidentiality concerns for both complainants and respondents because any inquiry by a local bias committee would be known and resolved by a group of local attorneys, judicial officers, and other committee members who would necessarily need to know the particular facts of the complaint, thereby significantly expanding the number of local individuals who were aware of the existence or details of the complaint. Ethical concerns were also raised for judicial officers who were members of the local bias committees because judicial officers who become aware of complaints against other judicial officers may have ethical obligations that require them to take appropriate corrective action, which may include reporting the information to the presiding judge or justice or the Commission on Judicial Performance. Finally, there were concerns that local bias committee complaint procedures would conflict with existing personnel policies and labor relations agreements if the local committee attempted to resolve complaints against court employees outside of the procedures outlined in these policy documents.

This standard does not prevent courts and local or regional bias committees from choosing to create informal complaint resolution procedures. Some local bias committees have established effective informal complaint resolution procedures for resolving complaints against judicial officers, and each local court and local or regional bias committee should work to find solutions that work best for that local community. If so, they should fully consider how best to address the above concerns. Because of the specific labor and employment laws governing courts and court employees, including the direction provided in rule 10.351 of the California Rules of Court, and the fact that courts already have personnel policies and memorandums of understanding that govern complaints against court employees, having local or regional bias committees resolve complaints against court employees is not recommended.

Standard 10.21. Appointment of attorneys, arbitrators, mediators, referees, masters, receivers, and other persons

(a) Nondiscrimination in appointment lists

In establishing and maintaining lists of qualified attorneys, arbitrators, mediators, referees, masters, receivers, and other persons who are eligible for appointment, courts should ensure equal access for all applicants regardless of gender, race, ethnicity, disability, sexual orientation, or age.

(b) Nondiscrimination in recruitment

Each trial court should conduct a recruitment procedure for the appointment of attorneys, arbitrators, mediators, referees, masters, receivers, and other persons appointed by the court (the "appointment programs") by publicizing the existence of the appointment programs at least once annually through state and local bar associations, including specialty bar associations. This publicity should encourage and provide an opportunity for all eligible individuals, regardless of gender, race, ethnicity, disability, sexual orientation, or age, to seek positions on the rosters of the appointment programs. Each trial court also should use other methods of publicizing the appointment programs that maximize the opportunity for a diverse applicant pool.

(c) Nondiscrimination in application and selection procedure

Each trial court should conduct an application and selection procedure for the appointment programs that ensures that the most qualified applicants for an appointment are selected, regardless of gender, race, ethnicity, disability, sexual orientation, or age.

(Subd (c) amended effective January 1, 2007.)
Standard 10.21 amended and renumbered effective January 1, 2007; adopted as sec. 1.5 effective January 1, 1999.

Standard 10.24. Children's waiting room

Each court should endeavor to provide a children's waiting room located in the courthouse for the use of minors under the age of 16 who are present on court premises as participants or who accompany persons who are participants in court proceedings. The waiting room should be supervised and open during normal court hours. If a court does not have sufficient space in the courthouse for a children's waiting room, the court should create the necessary space when court facilities are reorganized or remodeled or when new facilities are constructed.

Standard 10.24 renumbered effective January 1, 2007; adopted as sec. 1.3 effective January 1, 1987.

Standard 10.25. Reasonable accommodation for court personnel

At least to the extent required by state and federal law, each court should evaluate existing facilities, programs, and services available to employees to ensure that no barriers exist to prevent otherwise-qualified employees with known disabilities from performing their jobs or participating fully in court programs or activities.

Standard 10.25 renumbered effective January 1, 2007; adopted as sec. 1.4 effective January 1, 1998.

Standard 10.31. Master jury list

The jury commissioner should use the National Change of Address System or other comparable means to update jury source lists and create as accurate a master jury list as reasonably practical.

Standard 10.31 amended and renumbered effective January 1, 2007; adopted as sec. 4.6 effective July 1, 1997.

Standard 10.40. Court security [Repealed]

Standard 10.40 repealed effective January 1, 2009; adopted as sec. 7 effective July 1, 1971; previously amended and renumbered effective January 1, 2007.

Standard 10.41. Court sessions at or near state penal institutions

(a) Provision of adequate protection

Facilities used regularly for judicial proceedings should not be located on the grounds of or immediately adjacent to a state penal institution unless the location, design, and setting of the court facility provide adequate protection against the possible adverse influence that the prison facilities and activities might have on the fairness of judicial proceedings.

(Subd (a) amended effective January 1, 2007.)

(b) Factors to be considered

In determining whether adequate protection is provided, the following factors should be considered:

(1) The physical and visual remoteness of the court facility from the facilities and activities of the prison;

(2) The location and appearance of the court facility with respect to the adjacent public areas through which jurors and witnesses would normally travel in going to and from the court;

(3) The accessibility of the facility to the press and the general public; and

(4) Any other factors that might affect the fairness of the judicial proceedings.

(Subd (b) lettered effective January 1, 2007; adopted as part of subd (a) effective July 1, 1975.)

(c) Compelling reasons of safety or court convenience

Unless the location, design, and setting of the facility for conducting court sessions meet the criteria in (a) and (b):

(1) Court sessions should not be conducted in or immediately adjacent to a state penal institution except for compelling reasons of safety or convenience of the court; and

(2) Court sessions should not be conducted at such a location when the trial is by jury or when the testimony of witnesses who are neither inmates nor employees of the institution will be required.

(Subd (c) amended and relettered effective January 1, 2007; adopted as subd (b) effective July 1, 1975.)
Standard 10.41 amended and renumbered effective January 1, 2007; adopted as sec. 7.5 effective July 1, 1975.

Standard 10.50. Selection of regular grand jury

(a) Definition

"Regular grand jury" means a body of citizens of a county selected by the court to investigate matters of civil concern in the county, whether or not that body has jurisdiction to return indictments.

(b) Regular grand jury list

The list of qualified candidates prepared by the jury commissioner to be considered for nomination to the regular grand jury should be obtained by one or more of the following methods:

(1) Names of members of the public obtained at random in the same manner as the list of trial jurors. However, the names obtained for nomination to the regular grand jury should be kept separate and distinct from the trial jury list, consistent with Penal Code section 899.

(2) Recommendations for grand jurors that encompass a cross-section of the county's population base, solicited from a broad representation of community-based organizations, civic leaders, and superior court judges, referees, and commissioners.

(3) Applications from interested citizens solicited through the media or a mass mailing.

(Subd (b) amended effective January 1, 2007.)

(c) Carryover grand jurors

The court is encouraged to consider carryover grand jury selections under Penal Code section 901(b) to ensure broad-based representation.

(d) Nomination of grand jurors

Judges who nominate persons for grand jury selection under Penal Code section 903.4 are encouraged to select candidates from the list returned by the jury commissioner or to otherwise employ a nomination procedure that will ensure broad-based representation from the community.

(Subd (d) amended effective January 1, 2007.)

(e) Disfavored nominations

Judges should not nominate to the grand jury a spouse or immediate family member (within the first degree of consanguinity) of any superior court judge, commissioner, or referee; elected official; or department head of any city, county, or governmental entity subject to grand jury scrutiny.

(Subd (e) amended effective January 1, 2007.)

Standard 10.50 amended and renumbered effective January 1, 2007; adopted as sec. 17 effective July 1, 1992.

Standard 10.51. Juror complaints

Each court should establish a reasonable mechanism for receiving and responding to juror complaints.

Standard 10.51 renumbered effective January 1, 2007; adopted as sec. 4.5 effective July 1, 1997.

Standard 10.55. Local program on waste reduction and recycling

Each court should adopt a program for waste reduction and recycling or participate in a county program.

Standard 10.55 amended and renumbered effective January 1, 2007; adopted as sec. 17.5 effective January 1, 1991.

Standard 10.70. Implementation and coordination of mediation and other alternative dispute resolution (ADR) programs

(a) Implementation of mediation programs for civil cases

Superior courts should implement mediation programs for civil cases as part of their core operations.

(Subd (a) adopted effective January 1, 2006.)

(b) Promotion of ADR programs

Superior courts should promote the development, implementation, maintenance, and expansion of successful mediation and other alternative dispute resolution (ADR) programs, through activities that include:

(1) Establishing appropriate criteria for determining which cases should be referred to ADR, and what ADR processes are appropriate for those cases. These criteria should include whether the parties are likely to benefit from the use of the ADR process;

(2) Developing, refining, and using lists of qualified ADR neutrals;

(3) Adopting appropriate criteria for referring cases to qualified ADR neutrals;

(4) Developing ADR information and providing educational programs for parties who are not represented by counsel; and

(5) Providing ADR education for judicial officers.

(Subd (b) amended effective January 1, 2007; adopted as unlettered subdivision effective July 1, 1992; lettered and amended effective January 1, 2006.)

(c) Coordination of ADR programs

Superior courts should coordinate ADR promotional activities and explore joint funding and administration of ADR programs with each other and with professional and community-based organizations.

(Subd (c) adopted effective January 1, 2006.)

Standard 10.70 amended and renumbered effective January 1, 2007; adopted as sec. 32 effective July 1, 1992; previously amended effective January 1, 2006.

Standard 10.71. Alternative dispute resolution (ADR) committees

Courts that are not required and that do not elect to have an ADR administrative committee as provided in rule 10.783 of the California Rules of Court should form committees of judges, attorneys, alternative dispute resolution (ADR) neutrals, and county ADR administrators, if any, to oversee the court's ADR programs and panels of neutrals for general civil cases.

Standard 10.71 amended and renumbered effective January 1, 2007; adopted as sec. 32.1 effective January 1, 2006.

Standard 10.72. ADR committees and criteria for referring cases to dispute resolution neutrals

(a) Training, experience, and skills

Courts should evaluate the ADR training, experience, and skills of potential ADR neutrals.

(Subd (a) amended effective January 1, 2006.)

(b) Additional considerations for continuing referrals

After a court has sufficient experience with an ADR neutral, the court should also consider indicators of client satisfaction, settlement rate, continuing ADR education, and adherence to applicable standards of conduct in determining whether to continue referrals to that neutral.

(Subd (b) amended effective January 1, 2006.)

Standard 10.72 amended and renumbered effective January 1, 2007; adopted as sec. 33 effective July 1, 1992; previously amended effective January 1, 2006.

Advisory Committee Comment

Although settlement rate is an important indicator of a neutral's effectiveness, it should be borne in mind that some disputes will not resolve, despite the best efforts of a skilled neutral. Neutrals should not feel pressure to achieve a high settlement rate through resolutions that may not be in the interest of one or more parties. Accordingly, settlement rate should be used with caution as a criterion for court referral of disputes to neutrals.

Standard 10.80. Court records management standards

Each court should develop records management practices consistent with the standards approved by the Judicial Council. The approved standards are specified in Judicial Council Court Records Management Standards, published by the Judicial Council.

Implementation of these standards, which cover creation, use, maintenance, and destruction of records, should lead to more efficient court administration, better protection and preservation of records, and improved public access to records.

Standard 10.80 amended effective January 1, 2016; adopted as sec. 34 effective January 1, 1993; previously amended and renumbered as standard 10.80 effective January 1, 2007.

Ethics Standards for Neutral Arbitrators in Contractual Arbitration

The Ethics Standards for Neutral Arbitrators in Contractual Arbitration *were adopted by the Judicial Council effective July, 2002, and further substantially amended and reorganized effective January 1, 2003.*

Standard 1. Purpose, intent, and construction.
Standard 2. Definitions.
Standard 3. Application and effective date.
Standard 4. Duration of duty.
Standard 5. General duty.
Standard 6. Duty to refuse appointment.
Standard 7. Disclosure.
Standard 8. **Additional disclosures in consumer arbitrations administered by a provider organization.**
Standard 9. **Arbitrators' duty to inform themselves about matters to be disclosed.**
Standard 10. Disqualification.
Standard 11. Duty to refuse gift, bequest, or favor.
Standard 12. **Duties and limitations regarding future professional relationships or employment.**
Standard 13. Conduct of proceeding.
Standard 14. Ex parte communications.
Standard 15. Confidentiality.
Standard 16. Compensation.
Standard 17. Marketing.

Standard 1. Purpose, intent, and construction.

(a) These standards are adopted under the authority of Code of Civil Procedure section 1281.85 and establish the minimum standards of conduct for neutral arbitrators who are subject to these standards. They are intended to guide the conduct of arbitrators, to inform and protect participants in arbitration, and to promote public confidence in the arbitration process.

(b) For arbitration to be effective there must be broad public confidence in the integrity and fairness of the process. Arbitrators are responsible to the parties, the other participants, and the public for conducting themselves in accordance with these standards so as to merit that confidence.

(c) These standards are to be construed and applied to further the purpose and intent expressed in subdivisions (a) and (b) and in conformance with all applicable law.

(d) These standards are not intended to affect any existing civil cause of action or create any new civil cause of action.

Comment to Standard 1

Code of Civil Procedure section 1281.85 provides that, beginning July 1, 2002, a person serving as a neutral arbitrator pursuant to an arbitration agreement shall comply with the ethics standards for arbitrators adopted by the Judicial Council pursuant to that section.

While the grounds for vacating an arbitration award are established by statute, not these standards, an arbitrator's violation of these standards may, under some circumstances, fall within one of those statutory grounds. (See Code Civ. Proc., §1286.2.) A failure to disclose within the time required for disclosure a ground for disqualification of which the arbitrator was then aware is a ground for vacatur of the arbitrator's award. (See Code Civ. Proc., §1286.2(a)(6)(A).) Violations of other obligations under these standards may also constitute grounds for vacating an arbitration award under section 1286.2(a)(3) if "the rights of the party were substantially prejudiced" by the violation.

While vacatur may be an available remedy for violation of these standards, these standards are not intended to affect any civil cause of action that may currently exist nor to create any new civil cause of action. These standards are also not intended to establish a ceiling on what is considered good practice in arbitration or to discourage efforts to educate arbitrators about best practices.

Standard 2. Definitions.

As used in these standards:

(a) **Arbitrator and neutral arbitrator**

(1) "Arbitrator" and "neutral arbitrator" mean any arbitrator who is subject to these standards and who is to serve impartially, whether selected or appointed:

(A) Jointly by the parties or by the arbitrators selected by the parties;

(B) By the court, when the parties or the arbitrators selected by the parties fail to select an arbitrator who was to be selected jointly by them; or

(C) By a dispute resolution provider organization, under an agreement of the parties.

(2) Where the context includes events or acts occurring before an appointment is final, "arbitrator" and "neutral arbitrator" include a person who has been served with notice of a proposed nomination or appointment. For purposes of these standards, "proposed nomination" does not include nomination of persons by a court under Code of Civil Procedure section 1281.6 to be considered for possible selection as an arbitrator by the parties or appointment as an arbitrator by the court.

(Subd (a) amended effective July 1, 2014.)

(b) "Applicable law" means constitutional provisions, statutes, decisional law, California Rules of Court, and other statewide rules or regulations that apply to arbitrators who are subject to these standards.

(c) "Conclusion of the arbitration" means the following:

(1) When the arbitrator is disqualified or withdraws or the case is settled or dismissed before the arbitrator makes an award, the date on which the arbitrator's appointment is terminated;

(2) When the arbitrator makes an award and no party makes a timely application to the arbitrator to correct the award, the final date for making an application to the arbitrator for correction; or

(3) When a party makes a timely application to the arbitrator to correct the award, the date on which the arbitrator serves a corrected award or a denial on each party, or the date on which denial occurs by operation of law.

(d) "Consumer arbitration" means an arbitration conducted under a predispute arbitration provision contained in a contract that meets the criteria listed in paragraphs (1) through (3) below. "Consumer arbitration" excludes arbitration proceedings conducted under or arising out of public or private sector labor-relations laws, regulations, charter provisions, ordinances, statutes, or agreements.

(1) The contract is with a consumer party, as defined in these standards;

(2) The contract was drafted by or on behalf of the nonconsumer party; and

(3) The consumer party was required to accept the arbitration provision in the contract.

(e) "Consumer party" is a party to an arbitration agreement who, in the context of that arbitration agreement, is any of the following:

(1) An individual who seeks or acquires, including by lease, any goods or services primarily for personal, family, or household purposes including, but not limited to, financial services, insurance, and other goods and services as defined in section 1761 of the Civil Code;

(2) An individual who is an enrollee, a subscriber, or insured in a health-care service plan within the meaning of section 1345 of the Health and Safety Code or health-care insurance plan within the meaning of section 106 of the Insurance Code;

(3) An individual with a medical malpractice claim that is subject to the arbitration agreement; or

(4) An employee or an applicant for employment in a dispute arising out of or relating to the employee's employment or the applicant's prospective employment that is subject to the arbitration agreement.

(f) "Dispute resolution neutral" means a temporary judge appointed under article VI, section 21 of the California Constitution, a referee appointed under Code of Civil Procedure section 638 or 639, an arbitrator, a neutral evaluator, a special master, a mediator, a settlement officer, or a settlement facilitator.

(g) "Dispute resolution provider organization" and "provider organization" mean any nongovernmental entity that, or individual who, coordinates, administers, or provides the services of two or more dispute resolution neutrals.

(h) "Domestic partner" means a domestic partner as defined in Family Code section 297.

(i) "Financial interest" means a financial interest within the meaning of Code of Civil Procedure section 170.5.

(j) "Gift" means a gift as defined in Code of Civil Procedure section 170.9(*l*).

(k) "Honoraria" means honoraria as defined in Code of Civil Procedure section 170.9(h) and (i).

(*l*) "Lawyer in the arbitration" means the lawyer hired to represent a party in the arbitration.

(m) "Lawyer for a party" means the lawyer hired to represent a party in the arbitration and any lawyer or law firm currently associated in the practice of law with the lawyer hired to represent a party in the arbitration.

(n) "Member of the arbitrator's immediate family" means the arbitrator's spouse or domestic partner and any minor child living in the arbitrator's household.

(o) "Member of the arbitrator's extended family" means the parents, grandparents, great-grandparents, children, grandchildren, great-grandchildren, siblings, uncles, aunts, nephews, and nieces of the arbitrator or the arbitrator's spouse or domestic partner or the spouse or domestic partner of such person.

(Subd (o) amended effective July 1, 2014.)

(p) Party

(1) "Party" means a party to the arbitration agreement:

(A) Who seeks to arbitrate a controversy pursuant to the agreement;

(B) Against whom such arbitration is sought; or

(C) Who is made a party to such arbitration by order of a court or the arbitrator upon such party's application, upon the application of any other party to the arbitration, or upon the arbitrator's own determination.

(2) "Party" includes the representative of a party, unless the context requires a different meaning.

(q) "Party-arbitrator" means an arbitrator selected unilaterally by a party.

(r) "Private practice of law" means private practice of law as defined in Code of Civil Procedure section 170.5.

(s) "Significant personal relationship" includes a close personal friendship.

Standard 2 amended effective July 1, 2014.

Comment to Standard 2

Subdivision (a). The definition of "arbitrator" and "neutral arbitrator" in this standard is intended to include all arbitrators who are to serve in a neutral and impartial manner and to exclude unilaterally selected arbitrators.

Subdivisions (l) and (m). Arbitrators should take special care to note that there are two different terms used in these standards to refer to lawyers who represent parties in the arbitration. In particular, arbitrators should note that the term "lawyer for a party" includes any lawyer or law firm currently associated in the practice of law with the lawyer hired to represent a party in the arbitration.

Subdivision (p)(2). While this provision generally permits an arbitrator to provide required information or notices to a party's attorney as that party's representative, a party's attorney should not be treated as a "party" for purposes of identifying matters that an arbitrator must disclose under standards 7 or 8, as those standards contain separate, specific requirements concerning the disclosure of relationships with a party's attorney.

Other terms that may be pertinent to these standards are defined in Code of Civil Procedure section 1280.

Standard 3. Application and effective date.

(a) Except as otherwise provided in this standard and standard 8, these standards apply to all persons who are appointed to serve as neutral arbitrators on or after July 1, 2002, in any arbitration under an arbitration agreement, if:

(1) The arbitration agreement is subject to the provisions of title 9 of part III of the Code of Civil Procedure (commencing with section 1280); or

(2) The arbitration hearing is to be conducted in California.

(b) These standards do not apply to:

(1) Party arbitrators, as defined in these standards; or

(2) Any arbitrator serving in:

(A) An international arbitration proceeding subject to the provisions of title 9.3 of part III of the Code of Civil Procedure;

(B) A judicial arbitration proceeding subject to the provisions of chapter 2.5 of title 3 of part III of the Code of Civil Procedure;

(C) An attorney-client fee arbitration proceeding subject to the provisions of article 13 of chapter 4 of division 3 of the Business and Professions Code;

(D) An automobile warranty dispute resolution process certified under California Code of Regulations title 16, division 33.1 or an informal dispute settlement procedure under Code of Federal Regulations title 16, chapter 1, part 703;

(E) An arbitration of a workers' compensation dispute under Labor Code sections 5270 through 5277;

(F) An arbitration conducted by the Workers' Compensation Appeals Board under Labor Code section 5308;

(G) An arbitration of a complaint filed against a contractor with the Contractors State License Board under Business and Professions Code sections 7085 through 7085.7;

(H) An arbitration conducted under or arising out of public or private sector labor-relations laws, regulations, charter provisions, ordinances, statutes, or agreements; or

(I) An arbitration proceeding governed by rules adopted by a securities self-regulatory organization and approved by the United States Securities and Exchange Commission under federal law.

(Subd (b) amended effective July 1, 2014.)

(c) The following persons are not subject to the standards or to specific amendments to the standards in certain arbitrations:

(1) Persons who are serving in arbitrations in which they were appointed to serve as arbitrators before July 1, 2002, are not subject to these standards in those arbitrations.

(2) Persons who are serving in arbitrations in which they were appointed to serve as arbitrators before January 1, 2003, are not subject to standard 8 in those arbitrations.

(3) Persons who are serving in arbitrations in which they were appointed to serve as arbitrators before July 1, 2014, are not subject to the amendments to standards 2, 7, 8, 12, 16, and 17 that took effect July 1, 2014 in those arbitrations.

(Subd (c) amended effective July 1, 2014.)

Standard 3 amended effective July 1, 2014.

Comment to Standard 3

With the exception of standard 8 and the amendments to standards 2, 7, 8, 12, 16, and 17 that took effect July 1, 2014, these standards apply to all neutral arbitrators appointed on or after July 1, 2002, who meet the criteria of subdivision (a). Arbitration provider organizations, although not themselves subject to these standards, should be aware of them when performing administrative functions that involve arbitrators who are subject to these standards. A provider organization's policies and actions should facilitate, not impede, compliance with the standards by arbitrators who are affiliated with the provider organization.

Subdivision (b)(2)(I) is intended to implement the decisions of the California Supreme Court in *Jevne v. Superior Court* ((2005) 35 Cal.4th 935) and of the United States Court of Appeals for the Ninth Circuit in *Credit Suisse First Boston Corp. v. Grunwald* ((9th Cir. 2005) 400 F.3d 1119).

Standard 4. Duration of duty.

(a) Except as otherwise provided in these standards, an arbitrator must comply with these ethics standards from acceptance of appointment until the conclusion of the arbitration.

(b) If, after the conclusion of the arbitration, a case is referred back to the arbitrator for reconsideration or rehearing, the arbitrator must comply with these ethics standards from the date the case is referred back to the arbitrator until the arbitration is again concluded.

Standard 5. General duty.

An arbitrator must act in a manner that upholds the integrity and fairness of the arbitration process. He or she must maintain impartiality toward all participants in the arbitration at all times.

Comment to Standard 5

This standard establishes the overarching ethical duty of arbitrators. The remaining standards should be construed as establishing specific requirements that implement this overarching duty in particular situations.

Maintaining impartiality toward all participants during all stages of the arbitration is central to upholding the integrity and fairness of the arbitration. An arbitrator must perform his or her duties impartially, without bias or prejudice, and must not, in performing these duties, by words or conduct manifest partiality, bias, or prejudice, including but not limited to partiality, bias, or prejudice based upon race, sex, religion, national origin, disability, age, sexual orientation, socioeconomic status, or the fact that a party might select the arbitrator to serve as an arbitrator in additional cases. After accepting appointment, an arbitrator should avoid entering into any relationship or acquiring any interest that might reasonably create the appearance of partiality, bias, or prejudice. An arbitrator does not become partial, biased, or prejudiced simply by having acquired knowledge of the parties, the issues or arguments, or the applicable law.

Standard 6. Duty to refuse appointment.

Notwithstanding any contrary request, consent, or waiver by the parties, a proposed arbitrator must decline appointment if he or she is not able to be impartial.

Standard 7. Disclosure.

(a) Intent

This standard is intended to identify the matters that must be disclosed by a person nominated or appointed as an arbitrator. To the extent that this standard addresses matters that are also addressed by statute, it is intended to include those statutory disclosure requirements, not to eliminate, reduce, or otherwise limit them.

(b) General provisions

For purposes of this standard:

(1) *Collective bargaining cases excluded*

The terms "cases" and "any arbitration" do not include collective bargaining cases or arbitrations conducted under or arising out of collective bargaining agreements between employers and employees or between their respective representatives.

(2) *Offers of employment or professional relationship*

(A) Except as provided in (B), if an arbitrator has disclosed to the parties in an arbitration that he or she will entertain offers of employment or of professional relationships from a party or lawyer for a party while the arbitration is pending as required by subdivision (b) of standard 12, the arbitrator is not also required under this standard to disclose to the parties in that arbitration any such offer from a party or lawyer for a party that he or she subsequently receives or accepts while that arbitration is pending.

(B) In a consumer arbitration, if an arbitrator has disclosed to the parties that he or she will entertain offers of employment or of professional relationships from a party or lawyer for a party while the arbitration is pending as required by subdivision (b) of standard 12 and has informed the parties in the pending arbitration about any such offer and the acceptance of any such offer as required by subdivision (d) of standard 12, the arbitrator is not also required under this standard to disclose that offer or the acceptance of that offer to the parties in that arbitration.

(3) *Names of parties in cases*

When making disclosures about other pending or prior cases, in order to preserve confidentiality, it is sufficient to give the name of any party who is not a party to the pending arbitration as "claimant" or "respondent" if the party is an individual and not a business or corporate entity.

(Subd (b) amended effective July 1, 2014.)

(c) Time and manner of disclosure

(1) *Initial disclosure*

Within 10 calendar days of service of notice of the proposed nomination or appointment, a proposed arbitrator must disclose to all parties in writing all matters listed in subdivisions (d) and (e) of this standard of which the arbitrator is then aware.

(2) *Supplemental disclosure*

If an arbitrator subsequently becomes aware of a matter that must be disclosed under either subdivision (d) or (e) of this standard, the arbitrator must disclose that matter to the parties in writing within 10 calendar days after the arbitrator becomes aware of the matter.

(Subd (c) amended effective July 1, 2014.)

(d) Required disclosures

A proposed arbitrator or arbitrator must disclose all matters that could cause a person aware of the facts to reasonably entertain a doubt that the arbitrator would be able to be impartial, including, but not limited to, all of the following:

(1) *Family relationships with party*

The arbitrator or a member of the arbitrator's immediate or extended family is:

(A) A party;

(B) The spouse or domestic partner of a party; or

(C) An officer, director, or trustee of a party.

(2) *Family relationships with lawyer in the arbitration*

(A) Current relationships

The arbitrator, or the spouse, former spouse, domestic partner, child, sibling, or parent of the arbitrator or the arbitrator's spouse or domestic partner is:

(i) A lawyer in the arbitration;

(ii) The spouse or domestic partner of a lawyer in the arbitration; or

(iii) Currently associated in the private practice of law with a lawyer in the arbitration.

(B) Past relationships

The arbitrator or the arbitrator's spouse or domestic partner was associated in the private practice of law with a lawyer in the arbitration within the preceding two years.

(3) *Significant personal relationship with party or lawyer for a party*

The arbitrator or a member of the arbitrator's immediate family has or has had a significant personal relationship with any party or lawyer for a party.

(4) *Service as arbitrator for a party or lawyer for party*

(A) The arbitrator is serving or, within the preceding five years, has served:

(i) As a neutral arbitrator in another prior or pending noncollective bargaining case involving a party to the current arbitration or a lawyer for a party.

(ii) As a party-appointed arbitrator in another prior or pending noncollective bargaining case for either a party to the current arbitration or a lawyer for a party.

(iii) As a neutral arbitrator in another prior or pending noncollective bargaining case in which he or she was selected by a person serving as a party-appointed arbitrator in the current arbitration.

(B) Case information

If the arbitrator is serving or has served in any of the capacities listed under (A), he or she must disclose:

(i) The names of the parties in each prior or pending case and, where applicable, the name of the attorney representing the party in the current arbitration who is involved in the pending case, who was involved in the prior case, or whose current associate is involved in the pending case or was involved in the prior case.

(ii) The results of each prior case arbitrated to conclusion, including the date of the arbitration award, identification of the prevailing party, the amount of monetary damages awarded, if any, and the names of the parties' attorneys.

(C) Summary of case information

If the total number of the cases disclosed under (A) is greater than five, the arbitrator must provide a summary of these cases that states:

(i) The number of pending cases in which the arbitrator is currently serving in each capacity;

(ii) The number of prior cases in which the arbitrator previously served in each capacity;

(iii) The number of prior cases arbitrated to conclusion; and

(iv) The number of such prior cases in which the party to the current arbitration, the party represented by the lawyer for a party in the current arbitration or the party represented by the party-arbitrator in the current arbitration was the prevailing party.

(5) *Compensated service as other dispute resolution neutral*

The arbitrator is serving or has served as a dispute resolution neutral other than an arbitrator in another pending or prior noncollective bargaining case involving a party or lawyer for a party and the arbitrator received or expects to receive any form of compensation for serving in this capacity.

(A) Time frame

For purposes of this paragraph (5), "prior case" means any case in which the arbitrator concluded his or her service as a dispute resolution neutral within two years before the date of the arbitrator's proposed nomination or appointment.

(B) Case information

If the arbitrator is serving or has served in any of the capacities listed under this paragraph (5), he or she must disclose:

(i) The names of the parties in each prior or pending case and, where applicable, the name of the attorney in the current arbitration who is involved in the pending case, who was involved in the prior case, or whose current associate is involved in the pending case or was involved in the prior case;

(ii) The dispute resolution neutral capacity (mediator, referee, etc.) in which the arbitrator is serving or served in the case; and

(iii) In each such case in which the arbitrator rendered a decision as a temporary judge or referee, the date of the decision, the prevailing party, the amount of monetary damages awarded, if any, and the names of the parties' attorneys.

(C) Summary of case information

If the total number of cases disclosed under this paragraph (5) is greater than five, the arbitrator must also provide a summary of the cases that states:

(i) The number of pending cases in which the arbitrator is currently serving in each capacity;

(ii) The number of prior cases in which the arbitrator previously served in each capacity;

(iii) The number of prior cases in which the arbitrator rendered a decision as a temporary judge or referee; and

(iv) The number of such prior cases in which the party to the current arbitration or the party represented by the lawyer for a party in the current arbitration was the prevailing party.

(6) *Current arrangements for prospective neutral service*

Whether the arbitrator has any current arrangement with a party concerning prospective employment or other compensated service as a dispute resolution neutral or is participating in or, within the last two years, has participated in discussions regarding such prospective employment or service with a party.

(7) *Attorney-client relationship*

Any attorney-client relationship the arbitrator has or has had with a party or lawyer for a party. Attorney-client relationships include the following:

(A) An officer, a director, or a trustee of a party is or, within the preceding two years, was a client of the arbitrator in the arbitrator's private practice of law or a client of a lawyer with whom the arbitrator is or was associated in the private practice of law;

(B) In any other proceeding involving the same issues, the arbitrator gave advice to a party or a lawyer in the arbitration concerning any matter involved in the arbitration; and

(C) The arbitrator served as a lawyer for or as an officer of a public agency which is a party and personally advised or in any way represented the public agency concerning the factual or legal issues in the arbitration.

(8) *Employee, expert witness, or consultant relationships*

The arbitrator or a member of the arbitrator's immediate family is or, within the preceding two years, was an employee of or an expert witness or a consultant for a party or for a lawyer in the arbitration.

(9) *Other professional relationships*

Any other professional relationship not already disclosed under paragraphs (2)–(8) that the arbitrator or a member of the arbitrator's immediate family has or has had with a party or lawyer for a party.

(10) *Financial interests in party*

The arbitrator or a member of the arbitrator's immediate family has a financial interest in a party.

(11) *Financial interests in subject of arbitration*

The arbitrator or a member of the arbitrator's immediate family has a financial interest in the subject matter of the arbitration.

(12) *Affected interest*

The arbitrator or a member of the arbitrator's immediate family has an interest that could be substantially affected by the outcome of the arbitration.

(13) *Knowledge of disputed facts*

The arbitrator or a member of the arbitrator's immediate or extended family has personal knowledge of disputed evidentiary facts relevant to the arbitration. A person who is likely to be a material witness in the proceeding is deemed to have personal knowledge of disputed evidentiary facts concerning the proceeding.

(14) *Membership in organizations practicing discrimination*

The arbitrator is a member of any organization that practices invidious discrimination on the basis of race, sex, religion, national origin, or sexual orientation. Membership in a religious organization, an official military organization of the United States, or a nonprofit youth organization need not be disclosed unless it would interfere with the arbitrator's proper conduct of the proceeding or would cause a person aware of the fact to reasonably entertain a doubt concerning the arbitrator's ability to act impartially.

(15) Any other matter that:

(A) Might cause a person aware of the facts to reasonably entertain a doubt that the arbitrator would be able to be impartial;

(B) Leads the proposed arbitrator to believe there is a substantial doubt as to his or her capacity to be impartial, including, but not limited to, bias or prejudice toward a party, lawyer, or law firm in the arbitration; or

(C) Otherwise leads the arbitrator to believe that his or her disqualification will further the interests of justice.

(Subd (d) amended effective July 1, 2014.)

(e) Other required disclosures

In addition to the matters that must be disclosed under subdivision (d), a proposed arbitrator or arbitrator must also disclose:

(1) *Professional discipline*

(A) If the arbitrator has been disbarred or had his or her license to practice a profession or occupation revoked by a professional or occupational disciplinary agency or licensing board, whether in California or elsewhere. The disclosure must specify the date of the revocation, what professional or occupational disciplinary agency or licensing board revoked the license, and the reasons given by that professional or occupational disciplinary agency or licensing board for the revocation.

(B) If the arbitrator has resigned his or her membership in the State Bar or another professional or occupational licensing agency or board, whether in California or elsewhere, while public or private disciplinary charges were pending. The disclosure must specify the date of the resignation, what professional or occupational disciplinary agency or licensing board had charges pending against the arbitrator at the time of the resignation, and what those charges were.

(C) If within the preceding 10 years public discipline other than that covered under (A) has been imposed on the arbitrator by a professional or occupational disciplinary agency or licensing board, whether in California or elsewhere. "Public discipline" under this provision means any disciplinary action imposed on the arbitrator that the professional or occupational disciplinary agency or licensing board identifies in its publicly available records or in response to a request for information about the arbitrator from a member of the public. The disclosure must specify the date the discipline was imposed, what professional or occupational disciplinary agency or licensing board imposed the discipline, and the reasons given by that professional or occupational disciplinary agency or licensing board for the discipline.

(2) *Inability to conduct or timely complete proceedings*

(A) If the arbitrator is not able to properly perceive the evidence or properly conduct the proceedings because of a permanent or temporary physical impairment; and

(B) Any constraints on his or her availability known to the arbitrator that will interfere with his or her ability to commence or complete the arbitration in a timely manner.

(Subd (e) amended effective July 1, 2014.)

(f) Continuing duty

An arbitrator's duty to disclose the matters described in subdivisions (d) and (e) of this standard is a continuing duty, applying from service of the notice of the arbitrator's proposed nomination or appointment until the conclusion of the arbitration proceeding.

Standard 7 amended effective July 1, 2014.

Comment to Standard 7

This standard requires proposed arbitrators to disclose to all parties, in writing within 10 days of service of notice of their proposed nomination or appointment, all matters they are aware of at that time that could cause a person aware of the facts to reasonably entertain a doubt that the proposed arbitrator would be able to be impartial as well as those matters listed under subdivision (e). This standard also requires that if arbitrators subsequently become aware of any additional such matters, they must make supplemental disclosures of these matters within 10 days of becoming aware of them. This latter requirement is intended to address both matters existing at the time of nomination or appointment of which the arbitrator subsequently becomes aware and new matters that arise based on developments during the arbitration, such as the hiring of new counsel by a party.

Timely disclosure to the parties is the primary means of ensuring the impartiality of an arbitrator. It provides the parties with the necessary information to make an informed selection of an arbitrator by disqualifying or ratifying the arbitrator following disclosure. See also standard 12, concerning disclosure and disqualification requirements relating to concurrent and subsequent employment or professional relationships between an arbitrator and a party or attorney in the arbitration. A party may disqualify an arbitrator for failure to comply with statutory disclosure obligations (see Code Civ. Proc., § 1281.91(a)). Failure to disclose, within the time required for disclosure, a ground for disqualification of which the arbitrator was then aware is a ground for *vacatur* of the arbitrator's award (see Code Civ. Proc., § 1286.2(a)(6)(A)).

The arbitrator's overarching duty under subdivision (d) of this standard, which mirrors the duty set forth in Code of Civil Procedure section 1281.9, is to inform parties about matters that could cause a person aware of the facts to reasonably entertain a doubt that the arbitrator would be able to be impartial. While the remaining subparagraphs of subdivision (d) require the disclosure of specific interests, relationships, or affiliations, these are only examples of common matters that could cause a person aware of the facts to reasonably entertain a doubt that the arbitrator would be able to be impartial. The fact that none of the interests, relationships, or affiliations specifically listed in the subparagraphs of (d) are present in a particular case does not necessarily mean that there is no matter that could reasonably raise a question about the arbitrator's ability to be impartial and that therefore must be disclosed. Similarly, the fact that a particular interest, relationship, or affiliation present in a case is not specifically enumerated in one of the examples given in these subparagraphs does not mean that it must not be disclosed. An arbitrator must make determinations concerning disclosure on a case-by-case basis, applying the general criteria for disclosure under subdivision (d): is the matter something that could cause a person aware of the facts to reasonably entertain a doubt that the arbitrator would be able to be impartial?

Code of Civil Procedure section 1281.85 specifically requires that the ethics standards adopted by the Judicial Council address the disclosure of interests, relationships, or affiliations that may constitute conflicts of interest, including prior service as an arbitrator or other dispute resolution neutral entity. Section 1281.85 further provides that the standards "shall be consistent with the standards established for arbitrators in the judicial arbitration program and may expand but may not limit the disclosure and disqualification requirements established by this chapter [chapter 2 of title 9 of part III, Code of Civil Procedure, sections 1281–1281.95]."

Code of Civil Procedure section 1281.9 already establishes detailed requirements concerning disclosures by arbitrators, including a specific requirement that arbitrators disclose the existence of any ground specified in Code of Civil Procedure section 170.1 for disqualification of a judge. This standard does not eliminate or otherwise limit those requirements; in large part, it simply consolidates and integrates those existing statutory disclosure requirements by topic area. This standard does, however, expand upon or clarify the existing statutory disclosure requirements in the following ways:

- Requiring arbitrators to make supplemental disclosures to the parties regarding any matter about which they become aware after the time for making an initial disclosure has expired, within 10 calendar days after the arbitrator becomes aware of the matter (subdivision (c)).
- Expanding required disclosures about the relationships or affiliations of an arbitrator's family members to include those of an arbitrator's domestic partner (subdivisions (d)(1) and (2); see also definitions of immediate and extended family in standard 2).
- Requiring arbitrators, in addition to making statutorily required disclosures regarding prior service as an arbitrator for a party or attorney for a party, to disclose both prior service as a neutral arbitrator selected by a party arbitrator in the current arbitration and prior compensated service as any other type of dispute resolution neutral for a party or attorney in the arbitration (e.g., temporary judge, mediator, or referee) (subdivisions (d)(4)(A)(iii) and (5)).
- If a disclosure includes information about five or more cases, requiring arbitrators to provide a summary of that information (subdivisions (d)(4)(C) and (5)(C).
- Requiring the arbitrator to disclose if he or she or a member of his or her immediate family is or, within the preceding two years, was an employee, expert witness, or consultant for a party or a lawyer in the arbitration (subdivision (d)(8)).
- Requiring the arbitrator to disclose if he or she or a member of his or her immediate family has an interest that could be substantially affected by the outcome of the arbitration (subdivision (d)(12)).
- Requiring arbitrators to disclose membership in organizations that practice invidious discrimination on the basis of race, sex, religion, national origin, or sexual orientation (subdivision (d)(14)).
- Requiring the arbitrator to disclose if he or she was disbarred or had his or her license to practice a profession or occupation revoked by a professional or occupational disciplinary agency or licensing board, resigned membership in the State Bar or another licensing agency or board while disciplinary charges were pending, or had any other public discipline imposed on him or her by a professional or occupational disciplinary agency or licensing board within the preceding 10 years (subdivision (e)(1)). The standard identifies the information that must be included in such a disclosure; however, arbitrators may want to provide additional information to assist parties in determining whether to disqualify an arbitrator based on such a disclosure.
- Requiring the arbitrator to disclose any constraints on his or her availability known to the arbitrator that will interfere with his or her ability to commence or complete the arbitration in a timely manner (subdivision (e)(2)).
- Clarifying that the duty to make disclosures is a continuing obligation, requiring disclosure of matters that were not known at the time of nomination or appointment but that become known afterward (subdivision (f)).

It is good practice for an arbitrator to ask each participant to make an effort to disclose any matters that may affect the arbitrator's ability to be impartial.

Standard 8. Additional disclosures in consumer arbitrations administered by a provider organization.

(a) General provisions

(1) *Reliance on information provided by provider organization*

Except as to the information in (c)(1), an arbitrator may rely on information supplied by the administering provider organization in making the disclosures required by this standard only if the provider organization represents that the information the arbitrator is relying on is current through the end of the immediately preceding calendar quarter or more recent. If the information that must be disclosed is available on the Internet, the arbitrator may comply with the obligation to disclose this information by providing in the disclosure statement required under standard 7(c)(1) the Internet address of the specific web page at which the information is located and notifying the party that the arbitrator will supply hard copies of this information upon request.

(2) *Reliance on representation that not a consumer arbitration*

An arbitrator is not required to make the disclosures required by this standard if he or she reasonably believes that the arbitration is not a consumer arbitration based on reasonable reliance on a consumer party's representation that the arbitration is not a consumer arbitration.

(Subd (a) amended effective July 1, 2014.)

(b) Additional disclosures required

In addition to the disclosures required under standard 7, in a consumer arbitration as defined in standard 2 in which a dispute resolution provider organization is coordinating, administering, or providing the arbitration services, a proposed arbitrator who is nominated or appointed as an arbitrator on or after January 1, 2003 must disclose the following within the time and in the same manner as the disclosures required under standard 7(c)(1):

(1) *Relationships between the provider organization and party or lawyer in arbitration*

Any significant past, present, or currently expected financial or professional relationship or affiliation between the administering dispute resolution provider organization and a party or lawyer in the arbitration. Information that must be disclosed under this standard includes:

(A) The provider organization has a financial interest in a party.

(B) A party, a lawyer in the arbitration, or a law firm with which a lawyer in the arbitration is currently associated is a member of or has a financial interest in the provider organization.

(C) Within the preceding two years the provider organization has received a gift, bequest, or favor from a party, a lawyer in the arbitration, or a law firm with which a lawyer in the arbitration is currently associated.

(D) The provider organization has entered into, or the arbitrator currently expects that the provider organization will enter into, an agreement or relationship with any party or lawyer in the arbitration or a law firm with which a lawyer in the arbitration is currently associated under which the provider organization will administer, coordinate, or provide dispute resolution services in other noncollective bargaining matters or will provide other consulting services for that party, lawyer, or law firm.

(E) The provider organization is coordinating, administering, or providing dispute resolution services or has coordinated, administered, or provided such services in another pending or prior noncollective bargaining case in which a party or lawyer in the arbitration was a party or a lawyer. For purposes of this paragraph, "prior case" means a case in which the dispute resolution neutral affiliated with the provider organization concluded his or her service within the two years before the date of the arbitrator's proposed nomination or appointment, but does not include any case in which the dispute resolution neutral concluded his or her service before July 1, 2002.

(2) *Case information*

If the provider organization is acting or has acted in any of the capacities described in paragraph (1)(E), the arbitrator must disclose:

(A) The names of the parties in each prior or pending case and, where applicable, the name of the attorney in the current arbitration who is involved in the pending case or who was involved in the prior case;

(B) The type of dispute resolution services (arbitration, mediation, reference, etc.) coordinated, administered, or provided by the provider organization in the case; and

(C) In each prior case in which a dispute resolution neutral affiliated with the provider organization rendered a decision as an arbitrator, a temporary judge appointed under article VI, §4 of the California Constitution, or a referee appointed under Code of Civil Procedure sections 638 or 639, the date of the decision, the prevailing party, the amount of monetary damages awarded, if any, and the names of the parties' attorneys.

(3) *Summary of case information*

If the total number of cases disclosed under paragraph (1)(E) is greater than five, the arbitrator must also provide a summary of these cases that states:

(A) The number of pending cases in which the provider organization is currently providing each type of dispute resolution services;

(B) The number of prior cases in which the provider organization previously provided each type of dispute resolution services;

(C) The number of such prior cases in which a neutral affiliated with the provider organization rendered a decision as an arbitrator, a temporary judge, or a referee; and

(D) The number of prior cases in which the party to the current arbitration or the party represented by the lawyer in the current arbitration was the prevailing party.

(Subd (b) amended effective July 1, 2014.)

(c) Relationship between provider organization and arbitrator

If a relationship or affiliation is disclosed under subdivision (b), the arbitrator must also provide information about the following:

(1) Any financial relationship or affiliation the arbitrator has with the provider organization other than receiving referrals of cases, including whether the arbitrator has a financial interest in the provider organization or is an employee of the provider organization;

(2) The provider organization's process and criteria for recruiting, screening, and training the panel of arbitrators from which the arbitrator in this case is to be selected;

(3) The provider organization's process for identifying, recommending, and selecting potential arbitrators for specific cases; and

(4) Any role the provider organization plays in ruling on requests for disqualification of the arbitrator.

(Subd (c) amended effective July 1, 2014.)

(d) Effective date

The provisions of this standard take effect on January 1, 2003. Persons who are serving in arbitrations in which they were appointed to serve as arbitrators before January 1, 2003, are not subject to this standard in those pending arbitrations.

Standard 8 amended effective July 1, 2014.

Comment to Standard 8

This standard only applies in consumer arbitrations in which a dispute resolution provider organization is administering the arbitration. Like standard 7, this standard expands upon the existing statutory disclosure requirements. Code of Civil Procedure section 1281.95 requires arbitrators in certain construction defect arbitrations to make disclosures concerning relationships between their employers or arbitration services and the parties in the arbitration. This standard requires arbitrators in all consumer arbitrations to disclose any financial or professional relationship between the administering provider organization and any party, attorney, or law firm in the arbitration and, if any such relationship exists, then the arbitrator must also disclose his or her relationship with the dispute resolution provider organization. This standard requires an arbitrator to disclose if the provider organization has a financial interest in a party or lawyer in the arbitration or if a party or lawyer in the arbitration has a financial interest in the provider organization even though provider organizations are prohibited under Code of Civil Procedure section 1281.92 from administering any consumer arbitration where any such relationship exists.

Subdivision (b). Currently expected relationships or affiliations that must be disclosed include all relationships or affiliations that the arbitrator, at the time the disclosure is made, expects will be formed. For example, if the arbitrator knows that the administering provider organization has agreed in concept to enter into a business relationship with a party, but they have not yet signed a written agreement formalizing that relationship, this would be a "currently expected" relationship that the arbitrator would be required to disclose.

Standard 9. Arbitrators' duty to inform themselves about matters to be disclosed.

(a) General duty to inform him or herself

A person who is nominated or appointed as an arbitrator must make a reasonable effort to inform himself or herself of matters that must be disclosed under standards 7 and 8.

(b) Obligation regarding extended family

An arbitrator can fulfill the obligation under this standard to inform himself or herself of relationships or other matters involving his or her extended family and former spouse that are required to be disclosed under standard 7 by:

(1) Seeking information about these relationships and matters from the members of his or her immediate family and any members of his or her extended family living in his or her household; and

(2) Declaring in writing that he or she has made the inquiry in (1).

(c) Obligation regarding relationships with associates of lawyer in the arbitration

An arbitrator can fulfill the obligation under this standard to inform himself or herself of relationships with any lawyer associated in the practice of law with the lawyer in the arbitration that are required to be disclosed under standard 7 by:

(1) Informing the lawyer in the arbitration, in writing, of all such relationships within the arbitrator's knowledge and asking the lawyer if the lawyer is aware of any other such relationships; and

(2) Declaring in writing that he or she has made the inquiry in (1) and attaching to this declaration copies of his or her inquiry and any response from the lawyer in the arbitration.

(d) Obligation regarding service as a neutral other than an arbitrator before July 1, 2002

An arbitrator can fulfill the obligation under this standard to inform himself or herself of his or her service as a dispute resolution neutral other than as an arbitrator in cases that commenced prior to July 1, 2002 by:

(1) Asking any dispute resolution provider organization that administered those prior services for this information; and

(2) Declaring in writing that he or she has made the inquiry in (1) and attaching to this declaration copies of his or her inquiry and any response from the provider organization.

(e) Obligation regarding relationships with provider organization

An arbitrator can fulfill his or her obligation under this standard to inform himself or herself of the information that is required to be disclosed under standard 8 by:

(1) Asking the dispute resolution provider organization for this information; and

(2) Declaring in writing that he or she has made the inquiry in (1) and attaching to this declaration copies of his or her inquiry and any response from the provider organization.

Comment to Standard 9

This standard expands arbitrators existing duty of reasonable inquiry that applies with respect to financial interests under Code of Civil Procedure section 170.1(a)(3), to require arbitrators to make a reasonable effort to inform themselves about all matters that must be disclosed. This standard also clarifies what constitutes a reasonable effort by an arbitrator to inform himself or herself about specified matters, including relationships or other matters concerning his or her extended family and relationships with attorneys associated in the practice of law with the attorney in the arbitration (such as associates encompassed within the term "lawyer for a party").

Standard 10. Disqualification.

(a) An arbitrator is disqualified if:

(1) The arbitrator fails to comply with his or her obligation to make disclosures and a party serves a notice of disqualification in the manner and within the time specified in Code of Civil Procedure section 1281.91;

(2) The arbitrator complies with his or her obligation to make disclosures within 10 calendar days of service of notice of the proposed nomination or appointment and, based on that disclosure, a party serves a notice of disqualification in the manner and within the time specified in Code of Civil Procedure section 1281.91;

(3) The arbitrator makes a required disclosure more than 10 calendar days after service of notice of the proposed nomination or appointment and, based on that disclosure, a party serves a notice of disqualification in the manner and within the time specified in Code of Civil Procedure section 1281.91; or

(4) A party becomes aware that an arbitrator has made a material omission or material misrepresentation in his or her disclosure and, within 15 days after becoming aware of the omission or misrepresentation and within the time specified in Code of Civil Procedure section 1281.91(c), the party serves a notice of disqualification that clearly describes the material omission or material misrepresentation and how and when the party became aware of this omission or misrepresentation; or

(5) If any ground specified in Code of Civil Procedure section 170.1 exists and the party makes a demand that the arbitrator disqualify himself or herself in the manner and within the time specified in Code of Civil Procedure section 1281.91(d).

(b) For purposes of this standard, "obligation to make disclosure" means an arbitrator's obligation to make disclosures under standards 7 or 8 or Code of Civil Procedure section 1281.9.

(c) Notwithstanding any contrary request, consent, or waiver by the parties, an arbitrator must disqualify himself or herself if he or she concludes at any time during the arbitration that he or she is not able to conduct the arbitration impartially.

Comment to Standard 10

Code of Civil Procedure section 1281.91 already establishes requirements concerning disqualification of arbitrators. This standard does not eliminate or otherwise limit those requirements or change existing authority or procedures for challenging an arbitrator's failure to disqualify himself or herself. The provisions of subdivisions (a)(1), (2), and (5) restate existing disqualification procedures under section 1281.91; (b) and (d) when an arbitrator makes, or fails to make, initial disclosures or where a section 170.1 ground exists. The provisions of subdivisions (a)(3) and (4) clarify the requirements relating to disqualification based on disclosure made by the arbitrator after appointment or based on the discovery by the party of a material omission or misrepresentation in the arbitrator's disclosure.

Standard 11. Duty to refuse gift, bequest, or favor.

(a) An arbitrator must not, under any circumstances, accept a gift, bequest, favor, or honoraria from a party or any other person or entity whose interests are reasonably likely to come before the arbitrator in the arbitration.

(b) From service of notice of appointment or appointment until two years after the conclusion of the arbitration, an arbitrator must not, under any circumstances, accept a gift, bequest, favor, or honoraria from a party or any other person or entity whose interests have come before the arbitrator in the arbitration.

(c) An arbitrator must discourage members of his or her family residing in his or her household from accepting a gift, bequest, favor, or honoraria that the arbitrator would be prohibited from accepting under subdivisions (a) or (b).

(d) This standard does not prohibit an arbitrator from demanding or receiving a fee for services or expenses.

Comment to Standard 11

Gifts and favors do not include any rebate or discount made available in the regular course of business to members of the public.

Standard 12. Duties and limitations regarding future professional relationships or employment.

(a) **Offers as lawyer, expert witness, or consultant**

From the time of appointment until the conclusion of the arbitration, an arbitrator must not entertain or accept any offers of employment or new professional relationships as a lawyer, an expert witness, or a consultant from a party or a lawyer for a party in the pending arbitration.

(b) **Offers for employment or professional relationships other than as a lawyer, expert witness, or consultant**

(1) In addition to the disclosures required by standards 7 and 8, within ten calendar days of service of notice of the proposed nomination or appointment, a proposed arbitrator must disclose to all parties in writing if, while that arbitration is pending, he or she will entertain offers of employment or new professional relationships in any capacity other than as a lawyer, expert witness, or consultant from a party or a lawyer for a party, including offers to serve as a dispute resolution neutral in another case.

(2) If the arbitrator discloses that he or she will entertain such offers of employment or new professional relationships while the arbitration is pending:

(A) In consumer arbitrations, the disclosure must also state that the arbitrator will inform the parties as required under (d) if he or she subsequently receives an offer while that arbitration is pending.

(B) In all other arbitrations, the disclosure must also state that the arbitrator will not inform the parties if he or she subsequently receives an offer while that arbitration is pending.

(3) A party may disqualify the arbitrator based on this disclosure by serving a notice of disqualification in the manner and within the time specified in Code of Civil Procedure section 1281.91(b).

(Subd (b) amended effective July 1, 2014.)

(c) **Acceptance of offers under (b) prohibited unless intent disclosed**

If an arbitrator fails to make the disclosure required by subdivision (b) of this standard, from the time of appointment until the conclusion of the arbitration the arbitrator must not entertain or accept any such offers of employment or new professional relationships, including offers to serve as a dispute resolution neutral.

(Subd (c) amended effective July 1, 2014.)

(d) **Required notice of offers under (b)**

If, in the disclosure made under subdivision (b), the arbitrator states that he or she will entertain offers of employment or new professional relationships covered by (b), the arbitrator may entertain such offers. However, in consumer arbitrations, from the time of appointment until the conclusion of the arbitration, the arbitrator must inform all parties to the current arbitration of any such offer and whether it was accepted as provided in this subdivision.

(1) The arbitrator in a consumer arbitration must notify the parties in writing of any such offer within five days of receiving the offer and, if the arbitrator accepts the offer, must notify the parties in writing within five days of that acceptance. The arbitrator's notice must identify the party or attorney who made the offer and provide a general description of the employment or new professional relationship that was offered including, if the offer is to serve as a dispute resolution neutral, whether the offer is to serve in a single case or multiple cases.

(2) If the arbitrator fails to inform the parties of an offer or an acceptance as required under (1), that constitutes a failure to comply with the arbitrator's obligation to make a disclosure required under these ethics standards.

(3) If an arbitrator has informed the parties in a pending arbitration about an offer as required under (1):

(A) Receiving or accepting that offer does not, by itself, constitute corruption in or misconduct by the arbitrator;

(B) The arbitrator is not also required to disclose that offer or its acceptance under standard 7; and

(C) The arbitrator is not subject to disqualification under standard 10(a)(2), (3), or (5) solely on the basis of that offer or the arbitrator's acceptance of that offer.

(4) An arbitrator is not required to inform the parties in a pending arbitration about an offer under this subdivision if:

(A) He or she reasonably believes that the pending arbitration is not a consumer arbitration based on reasonable reliance on a consumer party's representation that the arbitration is not a consumer arbitration;

(B) The offer is to serve as an arbitrator in an arbitration conducted under or arising out of public or private sector labor-relations laws, regulations, charter provisions, ordinances, statutes, or agreements; or

(C) The offer is for uncompensated service as a dispute resolution neutral.

(Subd (d) adopted effective July 1, 2014.)

(e) **Relationships and use of confidential information related to the arbitrated case**

An arbitrator must not at any time:

(1) Without the informed written consent of all parties, enter into any professional relationship or accept any professional employment as a lawyer, an expert witness, or a consultant relating to the case arbitrated; or

(2) Without the informed written consent of the party, enter into any professional relationship or accept employment in another matter in which information that he or she has received in confidence from a party by reason of serving as an arbitrator in a case is material.

(Subd (e) relettered effective July 1, 2014; adopted as subd (d).)
Standard 12 amended effective July 1, 2014.

Comment to Standard 12

Subdivision (d)(1). A party may disqualify an arbitrator for failure to make required disclosures, including disclosures required by these ethics standards (see Code Civ. Proc., § 1281.91(a) and standard 10(a)). Failure to disclose, within the time required for disclosure, a ground for disqualification of which the arbitrator was then aware is also a ground for *vacatur* of the arbitrator's award (see Code Civ. Proc., § 1286.2(a)(6)(A)).

Subdivision (d)(4)(B). The arbitrations identified under this provision are only those in which, under Code of Civil Procedure section 1281.85(b) and standard 3(b)(2)(H), the ethics standards do not apply to the arbitrator.

Standard 13. Conduct of proceeding.

(a) An arbitrator must conduct the arbitration fairly, promptly, and diligently and in accordance with the applicable law relating to the conduct of arbitration proceedings.

(b) In making the decision, an arbitrator must not be swayed by partisan interests, public clamor, or fear of criticism.

Comment to Standard 13

Subdivision (a). The arbitrator's duty to dispose of matters promptly and diligently must not take precedence over the arbitrator's duty to dispose of matters fairly.

Conducting the arbitration in a procedurally fair manner includes conducting a balanced process in which each party is given an opportunity to participate. When one but not all parties are unrepresented, an arbitrator must ensure that the party appearing without counsel has an adequate opportunity to be heard and involved. Conducting the arbitration promptly and diligently requires expeditious management of all stages of the proceeding and concluding the case as promptly as the circumstances reasonably permit. During an arbitration, an arbitrator may discuss the issues, arguments, and evidence with the parties or their counsel, make interim rulings, and otherwise to control or direct the arbitration. This standard is not intended to restrict these activities.

The arbitrator's duty to uphold the integrity and fairness of the arbitration process includes an obligation to make reasonable efforts to prevent delaying tactics, harassment of any participant, or other abuse of the arbitration process. It is recognized, however, that the arbitrator's reasonable efforts may not successfully control all conduct of the participants.

For the general law relating to the conduct of arbitration proceedings, see chapter 3 of title 9 of part III of the Code of Civil Procedure, sections 1282–1284.2, relating to the conduct of arbitration proceedings. See also Code of Civil Procedure section 1286.2 concerning an arbitrator's unreasonable refusal to grant a continuance as grounds for *vacatur* of the award.

Standard 14. Ex parte communications.

(a) An arbitrator must not initiate, permit, or consider any ex parte communications or consider other communications made to the arbitrator outside the presence of all of the parties concerning a pending or impending arbitration, except as permitted by this standard, by agreement of the parties, or by applicable law.

(b) An arbitrator may communicate with a party in the absence of other parties about administrative matters, such as setting the time and place of hearings or making other arrangements for the conduct of the proceedings, as long as the arbitrator reasonably believes that the communication will not result in a procedural or tactical advantage for any party. When such a discussion occurs, the arbitrator must promptly inform the other parties of the communication and must give the other parties an opportunity to respond before making any final determination concerning the matter discussed.

(c) An arbitrator may obtain the advice of a disinterested expert on the subject matter of the arbitration if the arbitrator notifies the parties of the person consulted and the substance of the advice and affords the parties a reasonable opportunity to respond.

Comment to Standard 14

See also Code of Civil Procedure sections 1282.2(e) regarding the arbitrator's authority to hear a matter when a party fails to appear and 1282.2(g) regarding the procedures that must be followed if an arbitrator intends to base an award on information not obtained at the hearing.

Standard 15. Confidentiality.

(a) An arbitrator must not use or disclose information that he or she received in confidence by reason of serving as an arbitrator in a case to gain personal advantage. This duty applies from acceptance of appointment and continues after the conclusion of the arbitration.

(b) An arbitrator must not inform anyone of the award in advance of the time that the award is given to all parties. This standard does not prohibit an arbitrator from providing all parties with a tentative or draft decision for review or from providing an award to an assistant or to the provider organization that is coordinating, administering, or providing the arbitration services in the case for purposes of copying and distributing the award to all parties.

Standard 16. Compensation.

(a) An arbitrator must not charge any fee for services or expenses that is in any way contingent on the result or outcome of the arbitration.

(b) Before accepting appointment, an arbitrator, a dispute resolution provider organization, or another person or entity acting on the arbitrator's behalf must inform all parties in writing of the terms and conditions of the arbitrator's compensation. This information must include any basis to be used in determining fees; any special fees for cancellation, research and preparation time, or other purposes; any requirements regarding advance deposit of fees; and any practice concerning situations in which a party fails to timely pay the arbitrator's fees, including whether the arbitrator will or may stop the arbitration proceedings.

(Subd (b) amended effective July 1, 2014.)
Standard 16 amended effective July 1, 2014.

Comment to Standard 16

This standard is not intended to affect any authority a court may have to make orders with respect to the enforcement of arbitration agreements or arbitrator fees. It is also not intended to require any arbitrator or arbitration provider organization to establish a particular requirement or practice concerning fees or deposits, but only to inform the parties if such a requirement or practice has been established.

Standard 17. Marketing.

(a) An arbitrator must be truthful and accurate in marketing his or her services. An arbitrator may advertise a general willingness to serve as an arbitrator and convey biographical information and commercial terms of employment but must not make any representation that directly or indirectly implies favoritism or a specific outcome. An arbitrator must ensure that his or her personal marketing activities and any activities carried out on his or her behalf, including any activities of a provider organization with which the arbitrator is affiliated, comply with this requirement.

(Subd (a) amended effective July 1, 2014.)

(b) An arbitrator must not solicit business from a participant in the arbitration while the arbitration is pending.

(c) An arbitrator must not solicit appointment as an arbitrator in a specific case or specific cases.

(Subd (c) adopted effective July 1, 2014.)

(d) As used in this standard, "solicit" means to communicate in person, by telephone, or through real-time electronic contact to any prospective participant in the arbitration concerning the availability for professional employment of the arbitrator in which a significant motive is pecuniary gain. The term solicit does not include: (1) responding to a request from all parties in a case to submit a proposal to provide arbitration services in that case; or (2) responding to inquiries concerning the arbitrator's availability, qualifications, experience, or fee arrangements.

(Subd (d) adopted effective July 1, 2014.)
Standard 17 amended effective July 1, 2014.

Comment to Standard 17

Subdivision (b) and (c). Arbitrators should keep in mind that, in addition to these restrictions on solicitation, several other standards contain related disclosure requirements. For example, under standard 7(d)(4)–(6), arbitrators must disclose information about their past, current, and prospective service as an arbitrator or other dispute resolution for a party or attorney in the arbitration. Under standard 8(b)(1)(C) and (D), in consumer arbitrations administered by a provider organization, arbitrators must disclose if the provider organization has coordinated, administered, or provided dispute resolution services, is coordinating, administering, or providing such services, or has an agreement to coordinate, administer, or provide such services for a party or attorney in the arbitration. And under standard 12 arbitrators must disclose if, while an arbitration is pending, they will entertain offers from a party or attorney in the arbitration to serve as a dispute resolution neutral in another case.

These provisions are not intended to prohibit an arbitrator from accepting another arbitration from a party or attorney in the arbitration while the first matter is pending, as long as the arbitrator complies with the provisions of standard 12 and there was no express solicitation of this business by the arbitrator.

Appendix A
Judicial Council Legal Forms List

Under Government Code section 68511, the Judicial Council may "prescribe" certain forms. Use of prescribed forms is mandatory. Under rule 1.31, each mandatory Judicial Council legal form is identified as mandatory by an asterisk (*) on the list of Judicial Council legal forms published in this appendix. Mandatory forms bear the word "adopted" in the lower left corner of the first page.

Optional forms bear the word "approved" in the lower left corner of the first page. Use of an approved (optional) form is not mandatory, but the form must be accepted by all courts in appropriate cases (rule 1.35(a)).

A local court may not reject any Judicial Council form, optional or mandatory, for any of the reasons listed in rule 1.42.

The forms are available on the California Courts Web site in both a fillable and a PDF format at *www.courts.ca.gov/forms*.

JUDICIAL COUNCIL FORMS

Form No.	Date	Title
		[Rev. Nov. 11, 2024]

ADOPTION

Form No.	Date	Title
ADOPT-050-INFO	1/1/2024	How to Adopt a Child in California
ADOPT-200*	1/1/2024	Adoption Request
ADOPT-205	1/1/2016	Declaration Confirming Parentage in Stepparent Adoption
ADOPT-206	1/1/2021	Declaration Confirming Parentage in Stepparent Adoption: Gestational Surrogacy
ADOPT-210*	1/1/2021	Adoption Agreement
ADOPT-215*	1/1/2024	Adoption Order
ADOPT-216*	7/1/2013	Verification of Compliance with Hague Adoption Convention Attachment
ADOPT-220*	7/1/2010	Adoption of Indian Child
ADOPT-225*	1/1/2005	Parent Of Indian Child Agrees To End Parental Rights
ADOPT-226*	1/1/2008	[Revoked] Notice of Adoption Proceedings for a Possible Indian Child
ADOPT-230*	1/1/2007	Adoption Expenses
ADOPT-310*	1/1/2024	Contact After Adoption Agreement
ADOPT-315*	1/1/2018	Request to: Enforce, Change, End Contact After Adoption Agreement
ADOPT-320*	1/1/2018	Answer to Request to: Enforce, Change, End Contact After Adoption Agreement
ADOPT-325*	1/1/2018	Judge's Order to: Enforce, Change, End Contact After Adoption Agreement
ADOPT-330*	1/1/2024	Request for Appointment of Confidential Intermediary
ADOPT-331*	1/1/2008	Order for Appointment of Confidential Intermediary

ALTERNATIVE DISPUTE RESOLUTION

Form No.	Date	Title
ADR-100*	7/1/2012	Statement of Agreement or Nonagreement
ADR-101*	3/1/1994	ADR Information Form
ADR-102	1/1/2012	Request for Trial De Novo After Judicial Arbitration
ADR-103	1/1/2024	Petition to Confirm, Correct, or Vacate Attorney-Client Fee Arbitration Award
ADR-104	1/1/2024	Rejection of Award and Request for Trial After Attorney-Client Fee Arbitration
ADR-105	1/1/2024	Information Regarding Rights After Attorney-Client Fee Arbitration
ADR-106	1/1/2024	Petition to Confirm, Correct, or Vacate Contractual Arbitration Award
ADR-107	7/1/2009	Attendance Sheet for Court-Program Mediation of Civil Case
ADR-109	1/1/2007	Stipulation or Motion For Order Appointing Referee
ADR-110	7/1/2011	Order Appointing Referee
ADR-111	1/1/2006	Report of Referee
ADR-200	1/1/2020	Mediation Disclosure Notification and Acknowledgement

APPELLATE

Form No.	Date	Title
APP-001	7/1/2015	[Revoked] Information on Appeal Procedures for Unlimited Civil Cases
APP-001-INFO	1/1/2025	Information on Appeal Procedures for Unlimited Civil Cases [renumbered from APP-001]
APP-002	1/1/2024	Notice of Appeal/Cross-Appeal (Unlimited Civil Case)
APP-003	1/1/2019	Appellant's Notice Designating Record on Appeal (Unlimited Civil Case)
APP-004*	1/1/2025	Civil Case Information Statement (Appellate)
APP-005	1/1/2017	Abandonment Of Appeal (Unlimited Civil Case)
APP-006	1/1/2025	Application for Extension of Time to File Brief—Unlimited Civil Case
APP-007	1/1/2017	Request for Dismissal of Appeal (Civil Case)
APP-008	1/1/2017	Certificate of Interested Entities or Persons
APP-009	1/1/2017	Proof of Service (Court of Appeal)
APP-009E	1/1/2017	Proof of Electronic Service
APP-009-INFO	1/1/2021	Information Sheet For Proof of Service (Court of Appeal)
APP-010	1/1/2024	Respondent's Notice Designating Record on Appeal—Unlimited Civil Case
APP-011	1/1/2024	[Revoked] Respondent's Notice Electing to Use an Appendix (Unlimited Civil Case)
APP-012	1/1/2017	Stipulation for Extension of Time to File Brief (Civil Case)
APP-013*	1/1/2020	Memorandum of Costs on Appeal
APP-014	1/1/2018	[Revoked] Proposed Statement on Appeal (Unlimited Civil Case)
APP-014	1/1/2021	Appellant's Proposed Settled Statement (Unlimited Civil Case)
APP-014A	1/1/2019	Other Party and Nonparty Witness Testimony and other Evidence Attachment (Unlimited Civil Case)
APP-014-INFO	1/1/2019	Information Sheet for Proposed Settled Statement
APP-015-INFO*	4/1/2024	Information Sheet on Waiver of Appellate Court Fees — Supreme Court, Court of Appeal, Appellate Division [same as FW-015-INFO*]
APP-016	7/1/2010	Order on Court Fee Waiver (Court of Appeal or Supreme Court) [same as FW-016]
APP-016-GC	1/1/2021	Order on Court Fee Waiver (Court of Appeal or Supreme Court) (Ward or Conservatee) [same as FW-016-GC]
APP-020	1/1/2019	Response to Appellant's Proposed Settled Statement (Unlimited Civil Case)
APP-022	1/1/2019	Order on Appellant's Proposed Settled Statement (Unlimited Civil Case)
APP-025	1/1/2019	Appellant Motion to Use a Settled Statement (Unlimited Civil Case)
APP-031A	1/1/2015	Attached Declaration (Court of Appeal)

---

* Adopted for mandatory use by all courts.

APP-060	1/1/2023	Notice of Appeal—Civil Commitment/Mental Health Proceedings
APP-101-INFO	1/1/2025	Information on Appeal Procedures for Limited Civil Cases
APP-102	1/1/2024	Notice of Appeal/Cross-Appeal—Limited Civil Case
APP-103	1/1/2021	Appellant's Notice Designating Record on Appeal (Limited Civil Case)
APP-104	1/1/2021	Proposed Statement on Appeal (Limited Civil Case)
APP-105	3/1/2014	Order Concerning Appellant's Proposed Statement on Appeal (Limited Civil Case)
APP-106	1/1/2025	Application for Extension of Time to File Brief—Limited Civil Case
APP-107	1/1/2017	Abandonment of Appeal (Limited Civil Case)
APP-108	1/1/2020	Notice of Waiver of Oral Argument (Limited Civil Case)
APP-109	1/1/2017	Proof of Service (Appellate Division)
APP-109E	1/1/2017	Proof of Electronic Service (Appellate Division)
APP-109-INFO	1/1/2021	What Is Proof of Service?
APP-110	1/1/2024	Respondent's Notice Designating Record on Appeal—Limited Civil Case
APP-111	1/1/2024	[Revoked] Respondent's Notice Electing to Use an Appendix (Limited Civil Case)
APP-150-INFO	1/1/2024	Information on Writ Proceedings in Misdemeanor, Infraction, and Limited Civil Cases
APP-151	1/1/2017	Petition for Writ (Misdemeanor, Infraction, or Limited Civil Case)
APP-200	1/1/2025	Appellant's Opening Brief—Limited Civil Case
APP-200-INFO	1/1/2025	How to Use Form APP-200 in Limited Civil Case
APP-201	1/1/2025	Respondent's Brief—Limited Civil Case
APP-201-INFO	1/1/2025	How to Use Form APP-201 in Limited Civil Case
APP-202	1/1/2025	Appellant's Reply Brief—Limited Civil Case
APP-202-INFO	1/1/2025	How to Use Form APP-202 in Limited Civil Case

ATTACHMENT

AT-105	7/1/2010	Application for Right to Attach Order, Temporary Protective Order, Etc.
AT-115	7/1/2010	Notice of Application and Hearing for Right to Attach Order and Writ of Attachment
AT-120	7/1/2010	Right to Attach Order After Hearing and Order for Issuance of Writ of Attachment
AT-125	7/1/2010	Ex Parte Right to Attach Order and Order for Issuance of Writ of Attachment (Resident)
AT-130	7/1/2010	Ex Parte Right to Attach Order and Order for Issuance of Writ of Attachment (Nonresident)
AT-135	1/1/2003	Writ of Attachment
AT-138*	10/1/2024	Application and Order for Appearance and Examination [same as EJ-125*]
AT-140	7/1/2011	Temporary Protective Order
AT-145	7/1/1983	Application and Notice of Hearing for Order to Terminate, Modify, or Vacate Temporary Protective Order
AT-150	7/1/1983	Order to Terminate, Modify, or Vacate Temporary Protective Order
AT-155	7/1/1983	Notice of Opposition to Right to Attach Order and Claim of Exemption
AT-160*	1/1/2006	Undertaking by Personal Sureties [same as CD-140*]
AT-165	1/1/2003	Notice of Attachment
AT-167	9/1/2022	Memorandum of Garnishee [same as EJ-152]
AT-170	7/1/1983	Application to Set Aside Right to Attach Order and Release Attached Property, Etc.
AT-175	7/1/1983	Order to Set Aside Attachment, to Substitute Undertaking, Etc.
AT-180	1/1/1985	Notice of Lien [same as EJ-185]

BIRTH, MARRIAGE, DEATH

BMD-001*	9/1/2018	Petition to Establish Fact, Time, and Place of Birth [renumbered from MC-361]
BMD-001A*	9/1/2018	Declaration in Support of Petition to Establish Fact, Time, and Place of Birth [renumbered from MC-361A]
BMD-002*	9/1/2018	Petition to Establish Fact, Date, and Place of Marriage [renumbered from MC-362]
BMD-002A*	9/1/2018	Declaration in Support of Petition to Establish Fact, Date, and Place of Marriage [renumbered from MC-362A]
BMD-003*	9/1/2018	Petition to Establish Fact, Time, and Place of Death [renumbered from MC-360]
BMD-003A*	9/1/2018	Declaration in Support of Petition to Establish Fact, Time, and Place of Death [renumbered from MC-360A]

CARE Act

CARE-050-INFO	9/1/2024	Information for Petitioners—About the CARE Act
CARE-060-INFO*	9/1/2024	Information for Respondents—About the CARE Act
CARE-100*	9/1/2024	Petition to Commence CARE Act Proceedings
CARE-101*	9/1/2024	Mental Health Declaration—CARE Act Proceedings
CARE-103	9/1/2024	Order to Provide Information to Respondent's Attorney in Related Proceedings
CARE-105*	9/1/2024	Order for CARE Act Report
CARE-106*	9/1/2024	Notice of Order for CARE Act Report
CARE-107	9/1/2023	Proof of Personal Service of Notice of Order for CARE Act Report
CARE-110*	9/1/2023	Notice of Initial Appearance—CARE Act Proceedings
CARE-111	9/1/2023	Proof of Personal Service of Notice of Initial Appearance—CARE Act Proceedings
CARE-113*	9/1/2024	Notice of Respondent's Rights—CARE Act Proceedings
CARE-115*	9/1/2023	Notice of Hearing—CARE Act Proceedings

---

* Adopted for mandatory use by all courts.

CARE-116	9/1/2023	Proof of Personal Service of Notice of Hearing—CARE Act Proceedings
CARE-120	9/1/2023	Request for New Order and Hearing—CARE Act Proceedings
CARE-130	9/1/2024	Order to Provide Information to Respondent's Attorney in Related Proceedings

CASE MANAGEMENT

CM-010*	1/1/2024	Civil Case Cover Sheet
CM-011*	9/1/2018	Confidential Cover Sheet False Claims Action *[renumbered from MC-060]*
CM-015	7/1/2007	Notice of Related Case
CM-020	1/1/2008	Ex Parte Application for Extension of Time to Serve Pleading and Orders
CM-110*	1/1/2024	Case Management Statement
CM-180*	1/1/2007	Notice of Stay of Proceedings
CM-181*	1/1/2007	Notice of Termination or Modification of Stay
CM-200*	1/1/2007	Notice of Settlement of Entire Case

CIVIL

CIV-010*	1/1/2024	Application and Order for Appointment of Guardian Ad Litem—Civil and Family Law *[same as FL-935*]*
CIV-011*	1/1/2024	Order Appointing Guardian Ad Litem—Civil and Family Law *[same as FL-936*]*
CIV-020	1/1/2022	*[Revoked]* Notice of Intent to Appear by Telephone
CIV-025	1/1/2007	Application and Order for Reissuance of Order to Show Cause and Temporary Restraining Order
CIV-050*	1/1/2007	Statement of Damages (Personal Injury or Wrongful Death)
CIV-090	1/1/2008	Offer to Compromise and Acceptance Under Code of Civil Procedure Section 998
CIV-100*	1/1/2023	Request for Entry of Default (Application to Enter Default)
CIV-105*	1/1/2023	Request for Entry of Default (Fair Debt Buying Practices Act)
CIV-110*	1/1/2025	Request for Dismissal
CIV-120*	1/1/2012	Notice of Entry of Dismissal and Proof of Service
CIV-130	1/1/2024	Notice of Entry of Judgment or Order
CIV-140	1/1/2019	Declaration of Demurring Party Regarding Meet and Confer
CIV-141	1/1/2019	Declaration of Demurring Party in Support of Automatic Extension
CIV-150*	9/1/2018	Notice of Limited Scope Representation *[renumbered from MC-950]*
CIV-151	9/1/2018	Application to Be Relieved as Attorney on Completion of Limited Scope Representation *[renumbered from MC-955]*
CIV-152	9/1/2018	Objection to Application to Be Relieved as Attorney on Completion of Limited Scope Representation *[renumbered from MC-956]*
CIV-153	9/1/2018	Order on Application to Be Relieved as Attorney on Completion of Limited Scope Representation *[renumbered from MC-958]*
CIV-160	9/1/2018	Petition for Order Striking and Releasing Lien, Etc. (Government Employee) *[renumbered from MC-100]*
CIV-161	9/1/2018	Order to Show Cause (Government Employee) *[renumbered from MC-101]*
CIV-165*	1/1/2025	Order on Unlawful Use of Personal Identifying Information
CIV-170*	1/1/2024	Petition and Declaration Regarding Unresolved Claims and Deposit of Undistributed Surplus Proceeds of Trustee's Sale *[renumbered from MC-095]*

CIVIL HARASSMENT PREVENTION

CH-100*	1/1/2025	Request for Civil Harassment Restraining Orders
CH-100-INFO	1/1/2025	Can a Civil Harassment Restraining Order Help Me?
CH-101*	7/1/2007	*[Revoked]* Request and Order for Free Service of Restraining Order (Sexual Assault or Stalking)
CH-102*	1/1/2012	*[Revoked]* Confidential CLETS Information (Domestic Violence, Civil Harassment, Elder Abuse, Juvenile Law)
CH-109*	1/1/2025	Notice of Court Hearing
CH-110*	1/1/2025	Temporary Restraining Order (CLETS—TCH)
CH-115*	1/1/2020	Request to Continue Court Hearing *[renumbered from CH-125*]*
CH-115-INFO	1/1/2020	How to Ask for a New Hearing Date
CH-116*	9/1/2022	Order on Request to Continue Hearing (Temporary Restraining Order) (CLETS—TCH)
CH-117*	9/1/2022	Order Granting Alternative Service
CH-120*	1/1/2025	Response to Request for Civil Harassment Restraining Orders
CH-120-INFO	1/1/2025	How Can I Respond to a Request for Civil Harassment Restraining Orders?
CH-125*	1/1/2005	*[Renumbered]* Reissue Temporary Restraining Order (Civil Harassment) *[renumbered to CH-115*]*
CH-130*	1/1/2025	Civil Harassment Restraining Order After Hearing (CLETS—CHO)
CH-131	1/1/2005	*[Renumbered]* Proof of Service by Mail (Civil Harassment) *[renumbered to CH-250]*
CH-135	1/1/2005	*[Renumbered]* What Is Proof of Service? (Civil Harassment) *[renumbered to CH-200-INFO]*
CH-140*	7/1/2007	*[Renumbered]* Restraining Order After Hearing to Stop Harassment (CLETS) (Civil Harassment) *[renumbered to CH-130*]*
CH-145	1/1/2005	*[Renumbered]* Proof of Firearms Turned in or Sold (Civil Harassment) *[renumbered to CH-800]*
CH-150	7/1/2007	*[Renumbered]* Can a Civil Harassment Restraining Order Help Me? (Civil Harassment) *[renumbered to CH-100-INFO]*

---

* Adopted for mandatory use by all courts.

CH-151	1/1/2005	*[Renumbered]* How Can I Answer a Request for Orders to Stop Harassment? (Civil Harassment) *[renumbered to CH-120-INFO]*
CH-160*	9/1/2020	Request to Keep Minor's Information Confidential
CH-160-INFO	9/1/2020	Privacy Protection for a Minor (Person Under 18 Years Old)
CH-165*	1/1/2021	Order on Request to Keep Minor's Information Confidential
CH-170*	9/1/2020	Notice of Order Protecting Information of Minor
CH-175*	9/1/2020	Cover Sheet for Confidential Information
CH-176*	9/1/2020	Request for Release of Minor's Confidential Information
CH-177*	1/1/2021	Notice of Request for Release of Minor's Confidential Information
CH-178*	9/1/2020	Response to Request for Release of Minor's Confidential Information
CH-179*	9/1/2020	Order on Request for Release of Minor's Confidential Information
CH-200	1/1/2023	Proof of Personal Service
CH-200-INFO	9/1/2022	What Is "Proof of Personal Service"?
CH-205-INFO	9/1/2022	What If the Person I Want Protection from Is Avoiding (Evading) Service or Cannot be Located?
CH-210*	9/1/2022	Summons (Civil Harassment Restraining Order)
CH-250	9/1/2022	Proof of Service of Response by Mail (CLETS)
CH-260	9/1/2022	*[Revoked]* Proof of Service of Order After Hearing by Mail
CH-600*	1/1/2018	Request to Modify/Terminate Civil Harassment Restraining Order
CH-610*	1/1/2018	Notice of Hearing on Request to Modify/Terminate Civil Harassment Restraining Order
CH-620*	1/1/2018	Response to Request to Modify/Terminate Civil Harassment Restraining Order
CH-630*	1/1/2018	Order on Request to Modify/Terminate Civil Harassment Restraining Order
CH-700*	1/1/2016	Request to Renew Restraining Order
CH-710*	1/1/2016	Notice of Hearing to Renew Restraining Order
CH-715*	1/1/2024	Request to Reschedule Hearing to Renew Restraining Order
CH-716*	1/1/2024	Order to Reschedule Hearing to Renew Restraining Order
CH-720*	1/1/2016	Response to Request to Renew Restraining Order
CH-730*	1/1/2012	Order Renewing Civil Harassment Restraining Order (CLETS)
CH-800	1/1/2023	Receipt for Firearms and Firearm Parts
CH-800-INFO	1/1/2023	How Do I Turn In, Sell, or Store My Firearms and Firearm Parts?

CLAIM AND DELIVERY

CD-100*	1/1/2006	Application for Writ of Possession
CD-110*	1/1/2006	Notice of Application for Writ of Possession and Hearing
CD-120*	1/1/2006	Order for Writ of Possession
CD-130*	1/1/2006	Writ of Possession
CD-140*	1/1/2006	Undertaking By Personal Sureties *[same as AT-160*]*
CD-160*	1/1/2006	Application and Notice of Application and Hearing for Order to Quash Ex Parte Writ of Possession
CD-170*	1/1/2006	Order for Release and Redelivery of Property
CD-180*	1/1/2006	Declaration for Ex Parte Writ of Possession
CD-190*	1/1/2006	Application for Temporary Restraining Order
CD-200*	1/1/2006	Temporary Restraining Order

CLETS

CLETS-001*	1/1/2025	Confidential Information for Law Enforcement

COURT RECORDS

REC-001(N)*[1]	1/1/2007	Notice of Intent to Destroy Superior Court Records; Offer to Transfer Possession *(formerly 982.8(1)(N))*
REC-001(R)*	1/1/2007	Request for Transfer or Extension of Time for Retention of Superior Court Records *(formerly 982.8(1)(R))*
REC-002(N)*[2]	1/1/2007	Notice of Hearing on Request for Transfer or Extension of Time for Retention of Superior Court Records; Court Record; Release and Receipt of Records *(formerly 982.8(2)(N))*
REC-002(R)*	1/1/2007	Release and Receipt of Superior Court Records *(formerly 982.8(2)(R))*
REC-003*	1/1/2007	Report to the Judicial Council: Superior Court Records Destroyed, Preserved, and Transferred *(formerly 982.8A)*
REC-033*	1/1/2018	*[Revoked]* Report to the Judicial Council: Superior Court Records Destroyed, Preserved, and Transferred

CRIMINAL

CR-100*	1/24/2012	Fingerprint Form
CR-101	1/1/2025	Plea Form, With Explanations and Waiver of Rights—Felony
CR-102	1/1/2025	Domestic Violence Plea Form With Waiver of Rights—Misdemeanor
CR-105	9/1/2023	Defendant's Financial Statement on Eligibility for Appointment of Counsel and Record on Appeal at Public Expense

---

* Adopted for mandatory use by all courts.

[1] Form REC-001(R) to be printed on reverse side of form REC-001(N).

[2] Form REC-002(R) to be printed on reverse side of form REC-002(N).

JUDICIAL COUNCIL LEGAL FORMS LIST

Form	Date	Title
CR-106	1/1/2020	Proof of Service—Criminal Record Clearing
CR-106-INFO	1/1/2020	Information on How to File a Proof of Service in Criminal Record Clearing Requests
CR-110	1/1/2023	Order for Victim Restitution [same as JV-790]
CR-111	7/1/2015	Abstract of Judgment—Restitution [same as JV-791]
CR-112	1/1/2023	Instructions: Order for Victim Restitution [same as JV-792]
CR-113	1/1/2014	Instructions: Abstract of Judgment—Restitution [same as JV-793]
CR-115*	1/1/2020	Defendant's Statement of Assets
CR-117	1/1/2004	Instructions: Defendant's Statement of Assets
CR-118	1/1/2005	Information Regarding Income Deduction Order (Pen. Code, §1202.42)
CR-119	1/1/2005	Order for Income Deduction (Pen. Code, §1202.42)
CR-120	1/1/2017	Notice of Appeal—Felony (Defendant)
CR-125*	7/1/2007	Order to Attend Court or Provide Documents: Subpoena/Subpoena Duces Tecum [same as JV-525*]
CR-126	1/1/2025	Application for Extension of Time to File Brief—Criminal Case
CR-130	1/1/2009	[Revoked] Notice of Appeal—Misdemeanor (Defendant)
CR-131-INFO	9/1/2020	Information on Appeal Procedures for Misdemeanors
CR-132	1/1/2020	Notice of Appeal (Misdemeanor)
CR-133	9/1/2023	Request for Court-Appointed Lawyer in Misdemeanor Appeal
CR-134	1/1/2020	Notice Regarding Record on Appeal (Misdemeanor)
CR-135	1/1/2021	Proposed Statement on Appeal (Misdemeanor)
CR-136	3/1/2014	Order Concerning Appellant's Proposed Statement on Appeal (Misdemeanor)
CR-137	1/1/2017	Abandonment of Appeal (Misdemeanor)
CR-138	1/1/2020	Notice of Waiver of Oral Argument (Misdemeanor)
CR-141-INFO	1/1/2020	Information on Appeal Procedures for Infractions
CR-142	1/1/2020	Notice of Appeal and Record on Appeal
CR-143	1/1/2021	Proposed Statement on Appeal (Infraction)
CR-144	3/1/2014	Order Concerning Appellant's Proposed Statement on Appeal (Infraction)
CR-145	1/1/2017	Abandonment of Appeal (Infraction)
CR-150*	1/1/2021	Certificate of Identity Theft: Judicial Finding of Factual Innocence
CR-151	1/1/2005	Petition for Certificate of Identity Theft (Pen. Code, §530.6)
CR-160*	1/1/2025	Criminal Protective Order—Domestic Violence (CLETS—CPO)
CR-161*	1/1/2025	Criminal Protective Order—Other Than Domestic Violence (CLETS—CPO)
CR-162*	1/1/2025	Order to Surrender Firearms in Domestic Violence Case (CLETS—CPO)
CR-165*	7/1/2016	Notice of Termination of Protective Order in Criminal Proceeding (CLETS—CANCEL)
CR-168	1/1/2007	Batterer Intervention Program Progress Report
CR-170	1/1/2020	Notification of Decision Whether to Challenge Recommendation (Pen. Code, § 2972.1)
CR-173	1/1/2022	Order for Commitment (Sexually Violent Predator) [renumbered from MC-280]
CR-174	1/1/2022	[Revoked] Order for Extended Commitment (Sexually Violent Predator)
CR-175	9/1/2018	[Renumbered] Notice and Request for Ruling (Criminal) [renumbered to HC-004]
CR-180	1/1/2024	Petition for Dismissal
CR-181	1/1/2024	Order for Dismissal
CR-183	1/1/2016	Petition for Dismissal (Military Personnel) [same as MIL-183]
CR-184	1/22/2019	Order for Dismissal (Military Personnel) [same as MIL-184]
CR-185	1/1/2009	Petition for Expungement of DNA Profiles and Samples (Pen. Code, §299) [same as JV-796]
CR-186	1/1/2009	Order for Expungement of DNA Profiles and Samples (Pen. Code, §299) [same as JV-798]
CR-187	9/21/2024	Motion to Vacate Conviction or Sentence
CR-188	9/21/2024	Order on Motion to Vacate Conviction or Sentence
CR-190*	1/1/2004	Order Appointing Counsel in Capital Case
CR-191*	1/22/2019	Declaration of Counsel for Appointment in Capital Case
CR-200	1/1/2021	Form Interrogatories—Crime Victim Restitution
CR-210	1/1/2025	Prohibited Persons Relinquishment Form Findings (Pen. Code, § 29810(c))
CR-220	1/22/2019	Proof of Enrollment or Completion Alcohol or Drug Program [renumbered from MC-400]
CR-221	1/1/2021	Order to Install Ignition Interlock Device [renumbered from ID-100]
CR-222	1/1/2021	Ignition Interlock Installation Verification [renumbered from ID-110]
CR-223	1/1/2021	Ignition Interlock Calibration Verification [renumbered from ID-120]
CR-224	1/1/2021	Ignition Interlock Noncompliance Report [renumbered from ID-130]
CR-225	1/1/2021	Ignition Interlock Removal and Modification to Probation Order [renumbered from ID-140]
CR-226	1/1/2021	Notice to Employers of Ignition Interlock Restriction [renumbered from ID-150]
CR-250*	11/1/2012	Notice and Motion for Transfer
CR-251*	3/14/2022	Order for Transfer
CR-252*	11/1/2012	Receiving Court Comment Form
CR-290*	5/1/2023	Felony Abstract of Judgment—Prison Commitment—Determinate
CR-290(A)*	7/1/2012	Felony Abstract of Judgment Attachment Page
CR-290.1*	7/1/2012	Felony Abstract of Judgment—Determinate Single, Concurrent, or Full-Term Consecutive Count Form
CR-292*	5/1/2023	Abstract of Judgment—Prison Commitment—Indeterminate
CR-300	1/1/2021	Petition for Revocation (Pen. Code, §§ 1170(h)(5)(B), 1203.2, 3000.08, and 3455)
CR-301	7/1/2013	Warrant Request and Order
CR-302	7/1/2013	Request and Order to Recall Warrant
CR-320	1/1/2025	Can't Afford to Pay Fine: Traffic and Other Infractions [same as TR-320]

---

* Adopted for mandatory use by all courts.

RULES OF COURT 606

CR-321	1/1/2025	Can't Afford to Pay Fine: Traffic and Other Infractions (Court Order) [same as TR-321]
CR-400	1/1/2024	Petition/Application Under Health and Safety Code Section 11361.8—Adult Crimes
CR-401	1/1/2024	Proof of Service for Petition/Application Under Health and Safety Code Section 11361.8—Adult Crimes
CR-402	1/1/2024	Prosecuting Agency Response to Petition/Application Under Health and Safety Code Section 11361.8—Adult Crimes
CR-403	1/1/2024	Order After Petition/Application Under Health and Safety Code Section 11361.8—Adult Crimes [renumbered from CR-188]
CR-404	1/1/2019	Petition/Application for Resentencing and Dismissal
CR-405	1/1/2019	Order After Petition/Application for Resentencing and Dismissal
CR-409	1/1/2024	Petition to Seal Arrest and Related Records
CR-409-INFO	1/1/2024	Information on How to File a Petition to Seal Arrest and Related Records
CR-410	1/1/2019	Order to Seal Arrest and Related Records (Pen. Code, sections 851.91, 851.92)
CR-412	1/1/2024	Petition for Resentencing Based on Health Conditions Due to Military Service Listed in Penal Code Section 1170.91(b) [same as MIL-412]
CR-415*	7/1/2021	Petition to Terminate Sex Offender Registration (Pen. Code, § 290.5)
CR-415-INFO	7/1/2021	Information on Filing a Petition to Terminate Sex Offender Registration
CR-416	7/1/2021	Proof of Service—Sex Offender Registration Termination (Pen. Code, § 290.5)
CR-417*	7/1/2021	Response by District Attorney to Petition to Terminate Sex Offender Registration
CR-418*	7/1/2021	Order on Petition to Terminate Sex Offender Registration (Pen. Code, § 290.5)
CR-425	1/1/2023	Request for Resentencing and Dismissal (Pen. Code, § 653.29)
CR-426	1/1/2023	Order After Request for Resentencing and Dismissal (Pen. Code, § 653.29)
CR-430	1/1/2024	Petition for Dismissal—Incarcerated Individual Hand Crew or Institutional Firehouse Participant
CR-430-INFO	1/1/2024	Information on Filing a Petition for Dismissal—Incarcerated Individual Hand Crew or Institutional Firehouse Participant
CR-431	1/1/2024	Court Cover Letter and Agency Certification—Incarcerated Individual Hand Crew or Institutional Firehouse Participant
CR-432	1/1/2024	Order on Petition—Incarcerated Individual Hand Crew or Institutional Firehouse Participant
CR-600*	4/25/2019	Capital Case Attorney Pretrial Checklist
CR-601*	4/25/2019	Capital Case Attorney List of Appearances
CR-602*	4/25/2019	Capital Case Attorney List of Exhibits
CR-603*	4/25/2019	Capital Case Attorney List of Motions
CR-604*	4/25/2019	Capital Case Attorney List of Jury Instructions
CR-605*	4/25/2019	Capital Case Attorney Trial Checklist

DISABILITY ACCESS LITIGATION

DAL-001*	7/1/2016	Important Advisory Information for Building Owners and Tenants
DAL-002	7/1/2016	Answer—Disability Access
DAL-005*	7/1/2016	Defendant's Application for Stay of Proceedings and Early Evaluation Conference, Joint Inspection
DAL-006*	7/1/2013	Confidential Cover Sheet and Declaration Re Documents for Stay and Early Evaluation Conference
DAL-010*	7/1/2016	Notice of Stay of Proceedings and Early Evaluation Conference, Joint Inspection
DAL-012	1/1/2016	Proof of Service—Disability Access Litigation
DAL-015*	1/1/2015	Application for Mandatory Evaluation Conference Under Civil Code Section 55.545
DAL-020*	7/1/2013	Notice of Mandatory Evaluation Conference

DISCOVERY

DISC-001	1/1/2024	Form Interrogatories—General
DISC-002	1/1/2009	Form Interrogatories—Employment Law
DISC-003	1/1/2014	Form Interrogatories—Unlawful Detainer [same as UD-106]
DISC-004	1/1/2007	Form Interrogatories—Limited Civil Cases (Economic Litigation)
DISC-005	7/1/2013	Form Interrogatories—Construction Litigation
DISC-010*	1/1/2024	Case Questionnaire—For Limited Civil Cases (Under $25,000)
DISC-015*	1/1/2024	Request For Statement Of Witnesses And Evidence—For Limited Civil Cases (Under $25,000)
DISC-020	1/1/2008	Request for Admission
DISC-030	1/1/2008	Commission to Take Deposition Outside California

DOMESTIC VIOLENCE PREVENTION

DV-100*	1/1/2025	Request for Domestic Violence Restraining Order
DV-101	1/1/2017	Description of Abuse
DV-105*	1/1/2024	Request for Child Custody and Visitation Orders
DV-105(A)*	1/1/2025	City and State Where Children Lived (Domestic Violence Prevention)
DV-108*	1/1/2023	Request for Order: No Travel with Children
DV-109*	1/1/2025	Notice of Court Hearing (Domestic Violence Prevention)
DV-110*	1/1/2025	Temporary Restraining Order (CLETS—TRO) (Domestic Violence Prevention)
DV-112	1/1/2012	Waiver of Hearing on Denied Request for Temporary Restraining Order
DV-115*	1/1/2020	Request to Continue Hearing (Temporary Restraining Order) [renumbered from DV-125*]
DV-115-INFO	1/1/2020	How to Ask for a New Hearing Date

---

* Adopted for mandatory use by all courts.

Form	Date	Title
DV-116*	1/1/2023	Order on Request to Continue Court Hearing (Temporary Restraining Order) (CLETS—TRO)
DV-117*	1/1/2020	Order Granting Alternative Service
DV-120*	1/1/2025	Response to Request for Domestic Violence Restraining Order
DV-120-INFO	1/1/2025	How Can I Respond to a Request for Domestic Violence Restraining Order?
DV-125*	1/1/2023	Response to Request for Child Custody and Visitation Orders (Domestic Violence Prevention)
DV-126-INFO	1/1/2012	*[Revoked]* How to Reissue a Temporary Restraining Order (Domestic Violence Prevention)
DV-130*	1/1/2025	Restraining Order After Hearing (Order of Protection)
DV-140*	1/1/2024	Child Custody and Visitation Order
DV-145*	1/1/2023	Order: No Travel With Children
DV-150*	1/1/2023	*[Revoked]* Supervised Visitation and Exchange Order
DV-160*	9/1/2020	Request to Keep Minor's Information Confidential
DV-160-INFO	1/1/2021	Privacy Protection for a Minor (Person Under 18 Years Old)
DV-165*	1/1/2021	Order on Request to Keep Minor's Information Confidential
DV-170*	9/1/2020	Notice of Order Protecting Information of Minor
DV-175*	9/1/2020	Cover Sheet for Confidential Information
DV-176*	9/1/2020	Request for Release of Minor's Confidential Information
DV-177*	1/1/2021	Notice of Request for Release of Minor's Confidential Information
DV-178*	9/1/2020	Response to Request for Release of Minor's Confidential Information
DV-179*	9/1/2020	Order on Request for Release of Minor's Confidential Information
DV-180*	7/1/2014	Agreement and Judgment of Parentage
DV-200	1/1/2023	Proof of Personal Service (CLETS)
DV-200-INFO	1/1/2020	What Is "Proof of Personal Service"? *[renumbered from DV-210-INFO]*
DV-205-INFO	1/1/2020	What if the Person I Want Protection From is Avoiding (Evading) Service?
DV-210*	1/1/2020	Summons (Domestic Violence Restraining Order)
DV-210-INFO	1/1/2010	*[Renumbered]* What is "Proof of Service"? (Domestic Violence Prevention) *[renumbered to DV-200-INFO]*
DV-250	1/1/2020	Proof of Service by Mail (CLETS)
DV-260*	1/1/2012	*[Revoked]* Confidential CLETS Information (Domestic Violence, Civil Harassment, Elder Abuse, Juvenile Law)
DV-290*	7/1/2007	*[Revoked]* Request and Order for Free Service of Restraining Order (Sexual Assault or Stalking)
DV-300*	1/1/2025	Request to Change or End Restraining Order
DV-300-INFO	1/1/2025	How Do I Ask to Change or End a Domestic Violence Restraining Order?
DV-305*	1/1/2025	Request to Change Child Custody and Visitation Orders
DV-310*	1/1/2025	Notice of Court Hearing and Temporary Order to Change or End Restraining Order
DV-315*	1/1/2025	Request to Reschedule Hearing to Change or End Restraining Order
DV-316*	1/1/2025	Order to Reschedule Hearing to Change or End Restraining Order
DV-320*	1/1/2025	Response to Request to Change or End Restraining Order
DV-325*	1/1/2025	Response to Request to Change Child Custody and Visitation Orders
DV-330*	1/1/2025	Order on Request to Change or End Restraining Order
DV-400*	1/1/2025	*[Revoked]* Findings and Order to Terminate Restraining Order After Hearing (CLETS—CANCEL)
DV-400-INFO	1/1/2025	*[Revoked]* How Do I Ask to Change or End a Domestic Violence Restraining Order After Hearing?
DV-500-INFO	1/1/2025	Can a Domestic Violence Restraining Order Help Me?
DV-505-INFO	1/1/2024	How to Ask for a Temporary Restraining Order
DV-510-INFO	1/1/2010	*[Renumbered]* I Filled Out the Forms—What Now? *[renumbered to DV-505-INFO]*
DV-520-INFO	1/1/2023	Get Ready for the Court Hearing
DV-530-INFO	1/1/2023	How to Enforce Your Restraining Order
DV-540-INFO	1/1/2010	*[Renumbered]* Information for the Restrained Person (Domestic Violence Prevention) *[renumbered to DV-120-INFO]*
DV-550-INFO	1/1/2012	*[Revoked]* Get Ready for Your Hearing (For Restrained Person) (Domestic Violence Prevention)
DV-560	1/1/2012	*[Revoked]* How Can I Make the Order Permanent? (Domestic Violence Prevention)
DV-570	1/1/2003	Which Financial Form—FL-155 or FL-150?
DV-600*	7/1/2015	Order to Register Out-of-State or Tribal Court Protective/Restraining Order (CLETS—OOS)
DV-610	7/1/2012	Fax Transmission Cover Sheet for Registration of Tribal Court Protective Order
DV-630*	1/22/2019	Order to Register Canadian Domestic Violence Protective/Restraining Order (Domestic Violence Prevention)
DV-700*	1/1/2024	Request to Renew Restraining Order
DV-700-INFO	1/1/2024	How Do I Ask the Court to Renew My Restraining Order? *[renumbered from DV-720-INFO]*
DV-710*	1/1/2024	Notice of Hearing to Renew Restraining Order
DV-715*	1/1/2024	Request to Reschedule Hearing to Renew Restraining Order
DV-716*	1/1/2024	Order to Reschedule Hearing to Renew Restraining Order
DV-720*	1/1/2024	Response to Request to Renew Restraining Order
DV-720-INFO	7/1/2006	*[Renumbered]* How Do I Ask the Court to Renew my Restraining Order? *[renumbered to DV-700-INFO]*
DV-730*	1/1/2024	Order to Renew Domestic Violence Restraining Order
DV-800	1/1/2023	Proof of Firearms Turned In, Sold, or Stored *[same as JV-270]*
DV-800-INFO	1/1/2024	How Do I Turn In, Sell, or Store My Firearms, Firearm Parts, and Ammunition? *[same as JV-270-INFO]*
DV-805*	7/1/2016	Proof of Enrollment for Batterer Intervention Program
DV-810	1/1/2003	*[Renumbered]* What Do I Do With My Gun or Firearm? *[renumbered to DV-800-INFO and JV-270-INFO]*

---

* Adopted for mandatory use by all courts.

DV-815	7/1/2016	Batterer Intervention Program Progress Report
DV-820*	1/1/2023	Prohibited Items Finding and Orders
DV-830*	1/1/2023	Noncompliance with Firearms and Ammunition Order, or Warrant
DV-840*	1/1/2024	Notice of Compliance Hearing for Firearms and Ammunition *[same as FL-840*]*
DV-900*	7/1/2016	Order Transferring Wireless Phone Account
DV-901*	7/1/2016	Attachment to Order Transferring Wireless Phone Account

ELDER OR DEPENDENT ADULT ABUSE PREVENTION

EA-100*	1/1/2025	Request for Elder or Dependent Adult Abuse Restraining Orders
EA-100-INFO	1/1/2025	Can a Restraining Order to Prevent Elder or Dependent Adult Abuse Help Me?
EA-102*	1/1/2012	*[Revoked]* Confidential CLETS Information
EA-109*	1/1/2025	Notice of Court Hearing (Elder or Dependent Adult Abuse Prevention)
EA-110*	1/1/2025	Temporary Restraining Order (CLETS—TEA or TEF)
EA-115*	1/1/2020	Request to Continue Court Hearing (Temporary Restraining Order) *[renumbered from EA-125*]*
EA-115-INFO	1/1/2020	How to Ask for a New Hearing Date
EA-116*	1/1/2020	Order on Request to Continue Hearing (Temporary Restraining Order) (CLETS—TEA or TEF)
EA-120*	1/1/2025	Response to Request for Elder or Dependent Adult Abuse Restraining Orders (Elder or Dependent Adult Abuse Prevention)
EA-120-INFO	1/1/2025	How Can I Respond to a Request for Elder or Dependent Adult Abuse Restraining Orders? (Elder or Dependent Adult Abuse Prevention)
EA-125*	1/1/2007	*[Renumbered]* Request and Order for Reissuance of Temporary Restraining Order (CLETS—TEA or TEF) *[renumbered to EA-115*]*
EA-130*	1/1/2025	Elder or Dependent Adult Abuse Restraining Order After Hearing
EA-140	1/1/2007	*[Renumbered]* Proof of Personal Service—CLETS *[renumbered to EA-200]*
EA-141	1/1/2007	*[Renumbered]* Proof of Service by Mail—CLETS *[renumbered to EA-250]*
EA-142-INFO	7/1/2008	*[Renumbered]* What Is "Proof of Service"? *[renumbered to EA-200-INFO]*
EA-145	1/1/2007	*[Renumbered]* Proof of Firearms Turned In or Sold *[renumbered to EA-800]*
EA-150	7/1/2008	*[Revoked]* Instructions on Petition for a Protective Order to Prevent Elder of Dependent Adult Abuse
EA-150-INFO	7/1/2008	*[Renumbered]* Can a Restraining Order To Prevent Elder or Dependent Adult Abuse Help Me? *[renumbered to EA-100-INFO; formerly EA-150]*
EA-151-INFO	1/1/2007	*[Renumbered]* How Can I Respond to a Request for Orders to Stop Elder or Dependent Adult Abuse? *[renumbered to EA-120-INFO]*
EA-200	1/1/2023	Proof of Personal Service
EA-200-INFO	1/1/2023	What Is "Proof of Personal Service"?
EA-250	1/1/2023	Proof of Service of Response by Mail
EA-260	1/1/2012	Proof of Service of Order After Hearing by Mail
EA-300*	1/1/2023	Request for Elder or Dependent Adult Restraining Order Allowing Contact
EA-300-INFO	1/1/2023	Can An Elder or Dependent Adult Restraining Order Allowing Contact Help Me?
EA-309*	1/1/2024	Notice of Court Hearing to Allow Contact
EA-315*	1/1/2023	Request to Continue Court Hearing on Request to Allow Contact
EA-315-INFO	1/1/2023	How to Ask for a New Date for a Hearing to Allow Contact
EA-316*	1/1/2023	Order on Request to Continue Hearing on Request to Allow Contact
EA-320*	1/1/2023	Response to Request for Elder or Dependent Adult Restraining Order Allowing Contact
EA-320-INFO	1/1/2023	How Can I Respond to a Request for an Elder or Dependent Adult Restraining Order Allowing Contact?
EA-330*	1/1/2024	Elder or Dependent Adult Restraining Order Allowing Contact After Hearing
EA-600*	1/1/2018	Request to Modify/Terminate Elder or Dependent Adult Abuse Restraining Order
EA-610*	1/1/2018	Notice of Hearing on Request to Modify/Terminate Elder or Dependent Adult Abuse Restraining Order
EA-620*	1/1/2018	Response to Request to Modify/Terminate Elder or Dependent Adult Abuse Restraining Order
EA-630*	1/1/2018	Order on Request to Modify/Terminate Elder or Dependent Adult Abuse Restraining Order
EA-700*	1/1/2012	Request to Renew Restraining Order
EA-710*	1/1/2012	Notice of Hearing to Renew Restraining Order
EA-715*	1/1/2024	Request to Reschedule Hearing to Renew Restraining Order
EA-716*	1/1/2024	Order to Reschedule Hearing to Renew Restraining Order
EA-720*	1/1/2012	Response to Request to Renew Restraining Order
EA-730*	1/1/2012	Order Renewing Elder or Dependent Adult Abuse Restraining Order (CLETS)
EA-800	1/1/2023	Receipt for Firearms and Firearm Parts
EA-800-INFO	1/1/2023	How Do I Turn In, Sell, or Store My Firearms and Firearm Parts?

ELECTRONIC FILING AND SERVICE

EFS-005	7/1/2016	*[Renumbered]* Consent to Electronic Service and Notice of Electronic Service Address *[renumbered to EFS-005-CV]*
EFS-005-CV	7/1/2016	Consent to Electronic Service and Notice of Electronic Service Address *[renumbered from EFS-005]*
EFS-005-JV*	1/1/2019	Electronic Service: Consent, Withdrawal of Consent, Address Change (Juvenile) *[same as JV-141*]*
EFS-006	1/1/2019	Withdrawal of Consent to Electronic Service

---

* Adopted for mandatory use by all courts.

EFS-007	7/1/2013	Request for Exemption from Mandatory Electronic Filing and Service
EFS-008	7/1/2013	Order of Exemption from Mandatory Electronic Filing and Service
EFS-010	1/1/2011	Notice of Change of Electronic Service Address
EFS-020*	2/1/2017	Proposed Order (Cover Sheet)
EFS-050	2/1/2017	Proof of Electronic Service [same as POS-050]
EFS-050(D)	1/1/2010	Attachment to Proof of Electronic Service (Documents Served) [same as POS-050(D)]
EFS-050(P)	2/1/2017	Attachment to Proof of Electronic Service (Persons Served) [same as POS-050(P)]

EMANCIPATION OF MINOR

EM-100*	9/1/2018	Petition for Declaration of Emancipation of Minor, Order Prescribing Notice, Declaration of Emancipation, and Order Denying Petition [renumbered from MC-300*]
EM-100-INFO	9/1/2018	Emancipation Pamphlet [renumbered from MC-301*]
EM-109*	9/1/2018	Notice of Hearing—Emancipation of Minor [renumbered from MC-305]
EM-115*	9/1/2018	Emancipation of Minor Income and Expense Declaration [renumbered from MC-306]
EM-130*	9/1/2018	Declaration of Emancipation of Minor After Hearing [renumbered from MC-310*]
EM-140	9/1/2018	Emancipated Minor's Application to California Department of Motor Vehicles [renumbered from MC-315]

EMERGENCY PROTECTIVE ORDER

EPO-001*	1/1/2025	Emergency Protective Order (CLETS—EPO)
EPO-002*	1/1/2025	Gun Violence Emergency Protective Order (CLETS—EGV)

ENFORCEMENT OF JUDGMENT

EJ-001*	7/1/2014	Abstract of Judgment—Civil and Small Claims
EJ-100	7/1/2014	Acknowledgment of Satisfaction of Judgment
EJ-105	7/1/1983	Application for Entry of Judgment on Sister-State Judgment
EJ-110	7/1/1983	Notice of Entry of Judgment on Sister-State Judgment
EJ-115*	7/1/2015	Notice of Application for Recognition and Entry of Tribal Court Money Judgment
EJ-125*	10/1/2024	Application and Order for Appearance and Examination [same as AT-138*]
EJ-130	9/1/2020	Writ of Execution
EJ-140-INFO*	1/1/2025	Information on Debtor's Examinations Regarding Consumer Debt [same as SC-136-INFO*]
EJ-141*	1/1/2025	Application and Order to Appear for Examination—Consumer Debt
EJ-143*	1/1/2025	Notice of Financial Statement—Consumer Debt
EJ-144*	1/1/2025	Financial Statement—Consumer Debt
EJ-146*	1/1/2025	Notice of Motion and Motion to Require Examination—Consumer Debt
EJ-147*	1/1/2025	Application and Order to Require Examination After Submission of Financial Statement—Consumer Debt
EJ-150	9/1/2020	Notice of Levy
EJ-152	9/1/2022	Memorandum of Garnishee [same as AT-167]
EJ-155*	9/1/2021	Exemptions From the Enforcement of Judgments
EJ-156	7/15/2024	Current Dollar Amounts of Exemptions From Enforcement of Judgments
EJ-157	1/1/2021	Ex Parte Application for Order on Deposit Account Exemption
EJ-157-INFO	9/1/2020	Instructions for Ex Parte Application for Order on Deposit Account Exemption
EJ-158	1/1/2021	Declaration Regarding Notice and Service for Ex Parte Application for Order on Deposit Account Exemption
EJ-159	1/1/2021	Order on Application for Designation of Deposit Account Exemption
EJ-160	1/1/2009	Claim of Exemption
EJ-165*	1/1/2007	Financial Statement [same as WG-007*]
EJ-170	7/1/1983	Notice of Opposition to Claim of Exemption
EJ-175	1/1/2007	Notice of Hearing on Claim of Exemption [same as WG-010]
EJ-180	1/1/1985	Notice of Hearing on Right to Homestead Exemption
EJ-182	1/1/1985	Notice of Rehearing on Right to Homestead Exemption
EJ-185	1/1/1985	Notice of Lien [same as AT-180]
EJ-186	4/1/2022	Current Dollar Amounts under Code of Civil Procedure Section 699.730(b)
EJ-190	1/1/2024	Application for and Renewal of Judgment
EJ-195*	1/1/2024	Notice of Renewal of Judgment

EXPEDITED JURY TRIAL

EJT-001-INFO*	7/1/2016	Expedited Jury Trial Information Sheet [renumbered from EJT-010-INFO*]
EJT-003*	7/1/2016	Request to Opt Out of Mandatory Expedited Jury Trial Procedures
EJT-004*	7/1/2016	Objection to Request to Opt Out of Mandatory Expedited Jury Trial Procedures
EJT-005	7/1/2016	Order on Request to Opt Out of Mandatory Expedited Jury Trial Procedures
EJT-010-INFO*	7/1/2016	[Renumbered] Expedited Jury Trial Information Sheet [renumbered to EJT-001-INFO*]
EJT-018	7/1/2016	Agreement of Parties (Mandatory Expedited Jury Trial Procedures)
EJT-020	7/1/2016	[Proposed] Consent Order for Voluntary Expedited Jury Trial

---

* Adopted for mandatory use by all courts.

EJT-020A	7/1/2016	*[Renumbered]* Attachment to [Proposed] Consent Order for Expedited Jury Trial *[renumbered to EJT-022A]*
EJT-022A	7/1/2016	Attachment to [Proposed] Consent Order or Agreement of Parties *[renumbered from EJT-020A]*

FAMILY LAW
Dissolution, Legal Separation and Annulment

FL-100*	1/1/2020	Petition—Marriage/Domestic Partnership
FL-103*	1/1/2015	*[Revoked]* Petition—Domestic Partnership/Marriage (Family Law)
FL-105*	1/1/2025	Declaration Under Uniform Child Custody Jurisdiction and Enforcement Act (UCCJEA) *[same as GC-120*]*
FL-105(A)*	1/1/2025	Attachment to Declaration Under Uniform Child Custody Jurisdiction and Enforcement Act (UCCJEA) *[same as GC-120(A)*]*
FL-107-INFO	1/1/2015	Legal Steps for a Divorce or Legal Separation
FL-110*	1/1/2015	Summons (Family Law)
FL-115	1/1/2021	Proof of Service of Summons
FL-117	1/1/2021	Notice and Acknowledgment of Receipt
FL-120*	1/1/2020	Response—Marriage/Domestic Partnership
FL-123*	1/1/2015	*[Revoked]* Response—Domestic Partnership/Marriage (Family Law)
FL-130	1/1/2023	Appearance, Stipulations, and Waivers
FL-130(A)	1/1/2023	Declaration and Conditional Waiver of Rights Under the Servicemembers Civil Relief Act of 2003
FL-140*	7/1/2013	Declaration of Disclosure
FL-141*	7/1/2013	Declaration Regarding Service of Declaration of Disclosure and Income and Expense Declaration
FL-142	1/1/2005	Schedule of Assets and Debts
FL-144	1/1/2007	Stipulation and Waiver of Final Declaration of Disclosure
FL-145	1/1/2006	Form Interrogatories—Family Law
FL-150*	9/1/2024	Income and Expense Declaration
FL-155	1/1/2004	Financial Statement (Simplified)
FL-157	1/1/2021	Spousal or Domestic Partner Support Declaration Attachment
FL-158	1/1/2012	Supporting Declaration for Attorney's Fees and Costs Attachment
FL-160*	7/1/2016	Property Declaration
FL-161*	1/1/2025	Continuation of Property Declaration
FL-165*	1/1/2023	Request to Enter Default
FL-170*	1/17/2020	Declaration for Default or Uncontested Dissolution or Legal Separation
FL-172	1/1/2012	Case Information—Family Law
FL-174	1/1/2012	Family Centered Case Resolution Order
FL-180*	7/1/2012	Judgment
FL-182	7/1/2012	Judgment Checklist—Dissolution/Legal Separation
FL-190*	1/1/2005	Notice of Entry of Judgment
FL-191*	7/1/2005	Child Support Case Registry Form
FL-192*	9/1/2024	Notice of Rights and Responsibilities Regarding Child Support
FL-195	1/22/2024	Income Withholding for Support
FL-196	1/22/2024	Income Withholding for Support—Instructions

FAMILY LAW
Parentage Actions

FL-200	9/1/2021	Petition to Determine Parental Relationship (Uniform Parentage)
FL-210*	1/1/2015	Summons
FL-211*	1/1/2023	Confidential Cover Sheet—Parentage Action Involving Assisted Reproduction
FL-220	9/1/2021	Response to Petition to Determine Parental Relationship (Uniform Parentage)
FL-230*	1/1/2020	Declaration for Default or Uncontested Judgment (Uniform Parentage, Custody and Support)
FL-235	1/1/2020	Advisement and Waiver of Rights Re: Determination of Parental Relationship
FL-240*	1/1/2021	Stipulation for Entry of Judgment Re: Determination of Parental Relationship
FL-250*	1/1/2020	Judgment (Uniform Parentage—Custody and Support)
FL-260*	9/1/2021	Petition for Custody and Support of Minor Children
FL-270*	1/1/2020	Response to Petition for Custody and Support of Minor Children
FL-272*	1/1/2020	Notice of Motion to Cancel (Set Aside) Judgment of Parentage
FL-273*	1/1/2020	Declaration in Support of Motion to Cancel (Set Aside) Judgment of Parentage
FL-274	1/1/2020	Information Sheet for Completing Notice of Motion to Cancel (Set Aside) Judgment of Parentage
FL-276*	1/1/2020	Response to Notice of Motion to Cancel (Set Aside) Judgment of Parentage
FL-278*	9/1/2021	Order After Hearing on Motion to Cancel (Set Aside) Judgment of Parentage (Family Law—Governmental)
FL-280*	1/1/2020	Request for Hearing and Application to Cancel (Set Aside) Voluntary Declaration of Parentage or Paternity
FL-281	1/1/2020	Information Sheet for Completing Request for Hearing and Application to Cancel (Set Aside) Voluntary Declaration of Parentage or Paternity
FL-285*	1/1/2020	Responsive Declaration to Application to Cancel (Set Aside) Voluntary Declaration of Parentage or Paternity

---

* Adopted for mandatory use by all courts.

FL-290*	1/1/2020	Order After Hearing on Motion to Cancel (Set Aside) Voluntary Declaration of Parentage or Paternity

FAMILY LAW
Motions and Attachments

FL-300*	1/1/2025	Request for Order
FL-300-INFO	1/1/2025	Information Sheet for Request for Order (Family Law)
FL-301*	7/1/2012	*[Revoked]* Notice of Motion
FL-302	9/1/2024	Earning Capacity Factors Attachment
FL-303	7/1/2020	Declaration Regarding Notice and Service of Request for Temporary Emergency (Ex Parte) Orders
FL-304-INFO	7/1/2020	How to Reschedule a Hearing in Family Court
FL-305*	7/1/2016	Temporary Emergency (Ex Parte) Orders
FL-306*	1/1/2014	*[Revoked]* Request and Order to Continue Hearing and Extend Temporary Emergency (Ex Parte) Orders
FL-306	7/1/2020	Request to Reschedule Hearing (Family Law—Governmental—Uniform Parentage—Custody and Support)
FL-307*	9/1/2017	*[Revoked]* Order on Request to Continue Hearing
FL-307	7/1/2020	Request to Reschedule Hearing Involving Temporary Emergency (Ex Parte) Orders (Family Law—Governmental—Uniform Parentage—Custody and Support)
FL-308	7/1/2020	Agreement and Order to Reschedule Hearing (Family Law—Governmental—Uniform Parentage—Custody and Support)
FL-309*	7/1/2020	Order on Request to Reschedule Hearing (Family Law—Governmental—Uniform Parentage—Custody and Support)
FL-310*	7/1/2012	*[Revoked]* Application for Order and Supporting Declaration
FL-310	7/1/2020	Responsive Declaration to Request to Reschedule Hearing (Family Law—Governmental—Uniform Parentage—Custody and Support)
FL-311	1/1/2023	Child Custody and Visitation (Parenting Time) Application Attachment
FL-312*	7/1/2016	Request for Child Abduction Prevention Orders
FL-313-INFO	1/1/2012	Child Custody Information Sheet—Recommending Counseling
FL-314-INFO	1/1/2012	Child Custody Information Sheet—Child Custody Mediation
FL-315*	1/1/2018	Request or Response to Request for Separate Trial
FL-316	7/1/2012	Request for Orders Regarding Noncompliance With Disclosure Requirements
FL-318-INFO	1/1/2009	Retirement Plan Joinder—Information Sheet (Family Law)
FL-319	1/1/2012	Request for Attorney's Fees and Costs Attachment (Family Law)
FL-320*	1/1/2025	Responsive Declaration to Request for Order
FL-320-INFO	1/1/2025	Information Sheet: Responsive Declaration to Request for Order
FL-321	7/1/2012	Witness List
FL-321-INFO	7/1/2017	*[Renumbered]* Attorney for Child in a Family Law Case—Information Sheet *[renumbered to FL-323-INFO]*
FL-322	1/1/2008	Declaration of Counsel for a Child Regarding Qualifications
FL-323*	1/1/2023	Order Appointing Counsel for a Child
FL-323-INFO	7/1/2017	Attorney for Child in a Family Law Case—Information Sheet *[renumbered from FL-321-INFO]*
FL-324	1/1/2014	*[Renumbered]* Declaration of Supervised Visitation Provider *[renumbered to FL-324(P)*]*
FL-324(NP)	1/1/2021	Declaration of Supervised Visitation Provider (Nonprofessional)
FL-324(P)*	9/1/2021	Declaration of Supervised Visitation Provider (Professional) *[renumbered from FL-324]*
FL-325*	1/1/2020	Declaration of Court-Connected Child Custody Evaluator Regarding Qualifications
FL-326*	1/1/2020	Declaration of Private Child Custody Evaluator Regarding Qualifications
FL-327*	9/1/2022	Order Appointing Child Custody Evaluator
FL-327(A)*	9/1/2022	Additional Orders Regarding Child Custody Evaluations Under Family Code Section 3118
FL-328*	9/1/2022	Notice Regarding Confidentiality of Child Custody Evaluation Report Under Family Code Section 3111
FL-329*	9/22/2022	Confidential Child Custody Evaluation Report Under Family Code Section 3118
FL-329-INFO	1/1/2010	Child Custody Evaluation Information Sheet
FL-330	1/1/2012	Proof of Personal Service
FL-330-INFO	1/1/2012	Information Sheet for Proof of Personal Service
FL-334	1/1/2025	Declaration Regarding Address Verification—Postjudgment Request to Modify a Child Custody, Visitation, or Child Support Order
FL-335	1/1/2012	Proof of Service by Mail
FL-335-INFO	1/1/2012	Information Sheet for Proof of Service by Mail
FL-336*	7/1/2016	Order to Pay Waived Court Fees and Costs (Superior Court)
FL-337*	7/1/2016	Application to Set Aside Order to Pay Waived Court Fees—Attachment
FL-338*	7/1/2009	Order After Hearing on Motion to Set Aside Order to Pay Waived Court Fees
FL-340*	1/1/2012	Findings and Order After Hearing
FL-341	1/1/2023	Child Custody and Visitation (Parenting Time) Order Attachment
FL-341(A)*	1/1/2015	Supervised Visitation Order
FL-341(B)*	7/1/2016	Child Abduction Prevention Order Attachment
FL-341(C)	7/1/2016	Children's Holiday Schedule Attachment
FL-341(D)	7/1/2016	Additional Provisions—Physical Custody Attachment
FL-341(E)	7/1/2016	Joint Legal Custody Attachment

---

* Adopted for mandatory use by all courts.

FL-342*	9/1/2024	Child Support Information and Order Attachment
FL-342(A)*	9/1/2024	Non-Guideline Child Support Findings Attachment
FL-343	1/1/2021	Spousal, Domestic Partner, or Family Support Order Attachment
FL-344*	1/1/2007	Property Order Attachment To Findings And Order After Hearing
FL-345	1/1/2021	Property Order Attachment To Judgment
FL-346	1/1/2012	Attorney's Fees and Costs Order Attachment
FL-347*	1/1/2018	Bifurcation of Status of Marriage or Domestic Partnership—Attachment
FL-348	1/1/2009	Pension Benefits—Attachment to Judgment *(Attach to form FL-180)*
FL-349	1/1/2021	Spousal or Domestic Partner Support Factors Under Family Code Section 4320—Attachment
FL-350*	1/1/2022	Stipulation to Establish or Modify Child Support and Order
FL-355	1/1/2004	Stipulation and Order for Custody and/or Visitation of Children
FL-356*	1/1/2021	Confidential Request for Special Immigrant Juvenile Findings—Family Law
FL-357*	7/1/2016	Special Immigrant Juvenile Findings *[same as JV-357*, GC-224*]*
FL-358*	7/1/2016	Confidential Response to Request for Special Immigrant Juvenile Findings
FL-360*	1/1/2007	Request For Hearing And Application To Set Aside Support Order Under Family Code Section 3691
FL-365*	1/1/2003	Responsive Declaration to Application to Set Aside Support Order
FL-367*	1/1/2003	Order After Hearing on Motion to Set Aside Support Order
FL-370*	1/1/2003	Pleading on Joinder—Employees Benefit Plan
FL-371*	1/1/2003	Notice of Motion and Declaration for Joinder
FL-372*	1/1/2003	Request for Joinder of Employee Benefit Plan Order
FL-373*	1/1/2003	Responsive Declaration to Motion for Joinder and Consent Order of Joinder
FL-374*	1/1/2003	Notice of Appearance and Response of Employee Benefit Plan
FL-375*	1/1/2003	Summons (Joinder)
FL-380	7/12/2024	*[Revoked]* Application for Expedited Child Support Order
FL-381	7/12/2024	*[Revoked]* Response to Application for Expedited Child Support Order and Notice of Hearing
FL-382	7/12/2024	*[Revoked]* Expedited Child Support Order
FL-390*	1/1/2003	Notice of Motion and Motion for Simplified Modification of Order for Child, Spousal, or Family Support
FL-391	7/1/2008	Information Sheet—Simplified Way to Change Child, Spousal, or Family Support
FL-392*	1/1/2003	Responsive Declaration to Motion for Simplified Modification of Order for Child, Spousal, or Family Support
FL-393	7/1/2008	Information Sheet—How to Oppose a Request to Change Child, Spousal, or Family Support
FL-395*	1/1/2003	Ex Parte Application for Restoration of Former Name After Entry of Judgment and Order (Family Law)
FL-396*	1/1/2003	Request for Production of an Income and Expense Declaration After Judgment
FL-397*	1/1/2003	Request for Income and Benefit Information From Employer
FL-398*	12/2/2005	Notice of Activation of Military Service and Deployment and Request to Modify a Support Order

FAMILY LAW
Enforcement

FL-400*	1/1/2025	Order for Child Support Security Deposit and Evidence of Deposit
FL-401*	1/1/2003	Application for Disbursement and Order for Disbursement From Child Support Security Deposit
FL-410*	1/1/2015	Order to Show Cause and Affidavit for Contempt
FL-411*	1/1/2003	Affidavit of Facts Constituting Contempt (Financial and Injunctive Orders)
FL-412*	1/1/2003	Affidavit of Facts Constituting Contempt
FL-415	7/1/2003	Findings and Order Regarding Contempt
FL-420*	1/1/2003	Declaration of Payment History
FL-421	7/1/2003	Payment History Attachment
FL-430*	1/1/2014	Ex Parte Application to Issue, Modify, or Terminate an Earnings Assignment Order
FL-435*	1/1/2005	Earnings Assignment Order for Spousal or Partner Support
FL-440	1/1/2003	Statement for Registration of California Support Order
FL-445*	1/1/2021	Request for Hearing Regarding Registration of California Support Order
FL-450*	7/1/2008	Request for Hearing Regarding Earnings Assignment
FL-455*	1/1/2003	Stay of Service of Earnings Assignment and Order
FL-460	1/1/2003	Qualified Domestic Relations Order for Support
FL-461	1/1/2003	Attachment to Qualified Domestic Relations Order for Support
FL-470*	1/1/2007	Application and Order For Health Insurance Coverage
FL-475*	1/1/2003	Employer's Health Insurance Return
FL-478*	1/1/2007	Request and Notice of Hearing Regarding Health Insurance Assignment
FL-478-INFO	1/1/2007	Information Sheet and Instructions for Request and Notice of Hearing Regarding Health Insurance Assignment
FL-480*	1/1/2015	Abstract of Support Judgment
FL-485*	7/1/2013	Notice of Delinquency
FL-490*	1/1/2024	Application to Determine Arrears

---

* Adopted for mandatory use by all courts.

FAMILY LAW
Interstate Actions

FL-500	1/1/2008	*[Revoked]* Uniform Support Petition
FL-505*	1/1/2008	*[Revoked]* Child Support Enforcement Transmittal #1—Initial Request
FL-510*	7/1/2017	Summons (UIFSA)
FL-511*	1/1/2017	*[Revoked]* Ex Parte Application for Order for Nondisclosure of Address and Order (UIFSA)
FL-515*	1/1/2017	*[Revoked]* Order to Show Cause (UIFSA)
FL-520*	1/1/2017	Response to Uniform Support Petition (UIFSA)
FL-525	1/1/2008	*[Revoked]* Affidavit in Support of Establishing Paternity
FL-526	1/1/2008	*[Revoked]* General Testimony
FL-530*	1/1/2020	Judgment Regarding Parental Obligations (UIFSA)
FL-530*	*1/1/2026*	Judgment Regarding Parental Obligations (UIFSA)
FL-540*	1/1/2023	Joint Application for Recognition of Tribal Court Order Dividing Retirement Plan or Other Deferred Compensation
FL-541*	1/1/2023	Application for Recognition of Tribal Court Order Dividing Retirement Plan or Other Deferred Compensation
FL-556	1/1/2008	*[Revoked]* Registration Statement
FL-557	1/1/2008	*[Revoked]* Child Support Enforcement Transmittal #2—Subsequent Actions
FL-558	1/1/2008	*[Revoked]* Locate Data Sheet
FL-559	1/1/2008	*[Revoked]* Child Support Enforcement Transmittal #3—Request for Assistance/Discovery
FL-560*	1/1/2017	Ex Parte Application for Transfer and Order (UIFSA)
FL-570	1/1/2020	Notice of Registration of Out-of-State Support Order
FL-571	1/1/2008	*[Revoked]* Notice of Determination of Controlling Order
FL-575*	1/1/2021	Request for Hearing Regarding Registration of Out-of-State Support Order
FL-580	1/1/2025	Registration of Out-of-State or Tribal Custody Order and Notice of Registration
FL-580-INFO	1/1/2025	How to Register and Request Enforcement of Your Out-of-State or Tribal Custody Order
FL-581	1/1/2025	Petition for Enforcement of Out-of-State or Tribal Custody Order and Application for Warrant to Take Physical Custody of Child
FL-585	1/1/2025	Request for Hearing Regarding Registration of Out-of-State or Tribal Custody Order
FL-590A*	7/1/2017	UIFSA Child Support Order Jurisdictional Attachment
FL-592*	7/1/2017	Notice of Registration of an International Hague Convention Support Order
FL-594*	1/1/2017	Request for Hearing Regarding Registration of an International Hague Convention Support Order

FAMILY LAW
Governmental Child Support

FL-600*	1/1/2020	Summons and Complaint or Supplemental Complaint Regarding Parental Obligations (Governmental)
FL-600*	*1/1/2026*	Summons and Complaint or Supplemental Complaint Regarding Parental Obligations (Governmental)
FL-605*	1/1/2007	Notice and Acknowledgment of Receipt
FL-610*	1/1/2020	Answer to Complaint or Supplemental Complaint Regarding Parental Obligations (Governmental)
FL-610*	*1/1/2026*	Answer to Complaint or Supplemental Complaint Regarding Parental Obligations (Governmental)
FL-611	1/1/2003	Information Sheet for Service of Process
FL-615*	1/1/2020	Stipulation for Judgment or Supplemental Judgment Regarding Parental Obligations and Judgment
FL-616*	1/1/2003	Declaration for Amended Proposed Judgment
FL-616*	*1/1/2026*	Declaration for Amended Proposed Judgment
FL-618*	1/1/2010	Request for Dismissal
FL-620*	1/1/2023	Request to Enter Default Judgment
FL-625*	1/1/2020	Stipulation and Order
FL-626	1/1/2009	Stipulation and Order Waiving Unassigned Arrears
FL-627*	1/1/2003	Order for Genetic (Parentage) Testing
FL-630*	1/1/2020	Judgment Regarding Parental Obligations
FL-630*	*1/1/2026*	Judgment Regarding Parental Obligations (Governmental)
FL-632*	9/1/2024	Notice Regarding Payment of Support
FL-632-INFO	9/1/2024	Information Sheet: Notice Regarding Payment of Support
FL-634*	1/1/2011	Notice of Change of Responsibility for Managing Child Support Case
FL-635*	7/1/2004	Notice of Entry of Judgment and Proof of Service by Mail
FL-635*	*1/1/2026*	Notice of Entry of Judgment and Proof of Service by Mail
FL-640*	1/1/2012	Notice and Motion to Cancel (Set Aside) Support Order Based on Presumed Income
FL-640*	*1/1/2026*	Notice and Motion to Cancel (Set Aside) Support Order Based on Presumed Income or Earning Capacity
FL-640-INFO	1/1/2012	Information Sheet for Notice and Motion to Cancel (Set Aside) Support Order Based on Presumed Income
FL-640-INFO	*1/1/2026*	Information Sheet for Notice and Motion to Cancel (Set Aside) Support Order Based on Presumed Income or Earning Capacity
FL-643	1/1/2007	Declaration Of Obligor's Income During Judgment Period—Presumed Income Set-Aside Request
FL-643	*1/1/2026*	Declaration About Parent's Income or Earning Capacity During Judgment Periods

---

* Adopted for mandatory use by all courts.

FL-645*	1/1/2003	Notice to Local Child Support Agency of Intent to Take Independent Action to Enforce Support Order
FL-646*	1/1/2003	Response of Local Child Support Agency to Notice of Intent to Take Independent Action to Enforce Support Order
FL-650*	1/1/2003	Statement for Registration of California Support Order
FL-651*	1/1/2004	Notice of Registration of California Support Order
FL-660*	1/1/2003	Ex Parte Motion by Local Child Support Agency and Declaration for Joinder of Other Parent
FL-661	1/1/2012	Notice of Motion and Declaration for Joinder of Other Parent in Governmental Action
FL-661-INFO	1/1/2012	Information Sheet for Notice of Motion and Declaration for Joinder of Other Parent in Governmental Action
FL-662*	1/1/2012	Responsive Declaration to Motion for Joinder of Other Parent—Consent Order of Joinder
FL-662-INFO	1/1/2012	Information Sheet for Responsive Declaration to Motion for Joinder of Other Parent—Consent Order of Joinder
FL-663*	1/1/2009	Stipulation and Order for Joinder of Other Parent
FL-665*	1/1/2020	Findings and Recommendation of Commissioner
FL-665*	*1/1/2026*	Findings and Recommendation of Commissioner (Governmental)
FL-666*	1/1/2003	Notice of Objection
FL-667*	1/1/2003	Review of Commissioner's Findings of Fact and Recommendation
FL-670*	1/1/2003	Notice of Motion for Judicial Review of License Denial
FL-675*	1/1/2003	Order After Judicial Review of License Denial
FL-676*	1/1/2024	Request for Determination of Support Arrears (Governmental)
FL-676-INFO	1/1/2024	Information Sheet: Request for Determination of Support Arrears (Governmental)
FL-677*	1/1/2012	Notice of Opposition and Notice of Motion on Claim of Exemption
FL-678*	1/1/2003	Order Determining Claim of Exemption or Third-Party Claim
FL-679*	1/1/2022	*[Revoked]* Request for Telephone Appearance
FL-679-INFO*	1/1/2022	*[Revoked]* Information Sheet—Request for Telephone Appearance
FL-680*	1/1/2012	Notice of Motion
FL-680*	*1/1/2026*	Notice of Motion
FL-681	7/1/2005	Clerk Calendar Cover Sheet (For Court Clerk Use Only)
FL-683*	7/1/2005	Order to Show Cause
FL-683*	*1/1/2026*	Order to Show Cause
FL-684*	1/1/2010	Request for Order and Supporting Declaration
FL-685*	1/1/2012	Response to Governmental Notice of Motion or Order to Show Cause
FL-686*	1/1/2020	Proof of Service by Mail
FL-687*	1/1/2020	Order After Hearing
FL-687*	*1/1/2026*	Order After Hearing (Governmental)
FL-688*	1/1/2022	Short Form Order After Hearing
FL-688*	*1/1/2026*	Short Form Order After Hearing (Governmental)
FL-692*	1/1/2020	Minutes and Order or Judgment
FL-692*	*1/1/2026*	Minutes and Order or Judgment (Governmental)
FL-693	1/1/2003	Guideline Findings Attachment
FL-693	*1/1/2026*	Guideline Findings Attachment
FL-694	1/1/2020	Advisement and Waiver of Rights for Stipulation
FL-697*	1/1/2003	Declaration for Default or Uncontested Judgment

FAMILY LAW
Summary Dissolutions

FL-800*	1/1/2024	Joint Petition for Summary Dissolution
FL-810*	1/1/2024	Summary Dissolution Information
FL-820*	1/1/2012	Request for Judgment, Judgment of Dissolution of Marriage, and Notice of Entry of Judgment
FL-825*	1/1/2012	Judgment of Dissolution and Notice of Entry of Judgment
FL-830*	7/1/2015	Notice of Revocation of Joint Petition for Summary Dissolution
FL-840*	1/1/2024	Notice of Compliance Hearing for Firearms and Ammunition *[same as DV-840*]*

FAMILY LAW
Miscellaneous

FL-910*	1/1/2020	Request of Minor to Marry or Establish a Domestic Partnership
FL-912	1/1/2020	Consent for Minor to Marry or Establish a Domestic Partnerhip
FL-915*	1/1/2020	Order and Notices to Minor on Request to Marry or Establish a Domestic Partnership
FL-920	1/1/2003	Notice of Consolidation
FL-935	1/1/2024	*[Revoked]* Application and Order for Appointment of Guardian Ad Litem of Minor—Family Law
FL-935*	1/1/2024	Application and Order for Appointment of Guardian Ad Litem—Civil and Family Law *[same as CIV-010*]*
FL-936*	1/1/2024	Order Appointing Guardian Ad Litem—Civil and Family Law *[same as CIV-011*]*
FL-940	1/1/2003	Office of the Family Law Facilitator Disclosure
FL-945	1/1/2003	Family Law Information Center Disclosure
FL-950*	9/1/2017	Notice of Limited Scope Representation
FL-955*	9/1/2017	Notice of Completion of Limited Scope Representation

---

* Adopted for mandatory use by all courts.

FL-955-INFO	9/1/2017	Information for Client About Notice of Completion of Limited Scope Representation
FL-956*	9/1/2017	Objection to Proposed Notice of Completion of Limited Scope Representation
FL-957*	9/1/2017	Response to Objection to Proposed Notice of Completion of Limited Scope Representation
FL-958*	1/1/2018	Order on Completion of Limited Scope Representation
FL-960*	1/1/2003	Notice of Withdrawal of Attorney of Record
FL-970*	1/1/2003	Request and Declaration for Final Judgment of Dissolution of Marriage
FL-980	1/1/2013	Application for Order for Publication or Posting
FL-982	1/1/2013	Order for Publication or Posting
FL-985	1/1/2013	Proof of Service by Posting

FEE WAIVER

FW-001*	4/1/2024	Request to Waive Court Fees
FW-001-GC*	4/1/2024	Request to Waive Court Fees (Ward or Conservatee)
FW-001-INFO	1/1/2024	Information Sheet on Waiver of Superior Court Fees and Costs
FW-002*	9/1/2023	Request to Waive Additional Court Fees (Superior Court)
FW-002-GC*	9/1/2015	Request to Waive Additional Court Fees (Superior Court) (Ward or Conservatee)
FW-003*	9/1/2019	Order on Court Fee Waiver (Superior Court)
FW-003-GC*	9/1/2019	Order on Court Fee Waiver (Superior Court) (Ward or Conservatee)
FW-004*	7/1/2009	[Revoked] Order on Application for Waiver of Additional Court Fees and Costs (formerly 982(a)(18.1))
FW-005*	9/1/2019	Notice: Waiver of Court Fees (Superior Court)
FW-005-GC*	9/1/2019	Notice: Waiver of Court Fees (Superior Court) (Ward or Conservatee)
FW-006*	7/1/2009	Request for Hearing About Court Fee Waiver Order (Superior Court)
FW-006-GC*	9/1/2015	Request for Hearing About Court Fee Waiver Order (Superior Court) (Ward or Conservatee)
FW-007*	1/1/2010	Notice on Hearing About Court Fees
FW-007-GC*	9/1/2015	Notice on Hearing About Court Fees (Ward or Conservatee)
FW-008*	9/1/2019	Order on Court Fee Waiver After Hearing (Superior Court)
FW-008-GC*	9/1/2019	Order on Court Fee Waiver After Hearing (Superior Court) (Ward or Conservatee)
FW-010*	7/1/2009	Notice to Court of Improved Financial Situation or Settlement
FW-010-GC*	9/1/2015	Notice to Court of Improved Financial Situation or Settlement (Ward or Conservatee)
FW-011*	7/1/2009	Notice to Appear for Reconsideration of Fee Waiver
FW-011-GC*	9/1/2015	Notice to Appear for Reconsideration of Fee Waiver (Ward or Conservatee)
FW-012*	9/1/2019	Order on Court Fee Waiver After Reconsideration Hearing (Superior Court)
FW-012-GC*	9/1/2019	Order on Court Fee Waiver After Reconsideration Hearing (Superior Court) (Ward or Conservatee)
FW-015-INFO*	4/1/2024	Information Sheet on Waiver of Appellate Court Fees — Supreme Court, Court of Appeal, Appellate Division [same as APP-015-INFO*]
FW-016	7/1/2010	Order on Court Fee Waiver (Court of Appeal or Supreme Court) [same as APP-016]
FW-016-GC	1/1/2021	Order on Court Fee Waiver (Court of Appeal or Supreme Court) (Ward or Conservatee) [same as APP-016-GC]
FW-020	1/1/2021	Request for Court Reporter by Party With Fee Waiver

GUARDIANSHIPS AND CONSERVATORSHIPS

GC-005	1/1/2019	Application for Appointment of Counsel
GC-006	1/1/2019	Order Appointing Legal Counsel
GC-010	1/1/2020	Certification of Attorney Qualifications
GC-011*	1/1/2020	[Revoked] Annual Certification of Court-Appointed Attorney
GC-015*	1/1/2020	Notice of Hearing on Petition to Determine Claim to Property [same as DE-115*]
GC-020*	7/1/2005	Notice of Hearing—Guardianship or Conservatorship
GC-020(C)*	7/1/2005	Clerk's Certificate of Posting Notice of Hearing—Guardianship or Conservatorship
GC-020(MA)	7/1/2005	Attachment to Notice of Hearing Proof of Service by Mail [same as DE-120(MA)]
GC-020(P)	7/1/2005	Proof of Personal Service of Notice of Hearing—Guardianship or Conservatorship
GC-020(PA)	7/1/2005	Attachment to Notice of Hearing Proof of Personal Service [same as DE-120(PA)]
GC-021*	1/1/1998	Order Dispensing with Notice
GC-022*	1/1/1998	Order Prescribing Notice [same as DE-200*]
GC-035*	1/1/1998	Request for Special Notice [same as DE-154*]
GC-040*	1/1/2007	Inventory and Appraisal [same as DE-160*]
GC-041*	1/1/1998	Inventory and Appraisal Attachment [same as DE-161*]
GC-042*	1/1/2008	Notice of Filing of Inventory and Appraisal and How to Object to the Inventory or the Appraised Value of Property
GC-042(MA)	1/1/2008	Attachment to Notice of Filing of Inventory and Appraisal and How to Object to the Inventory or the Appraised Value of Property
GC-045	1/1/2008	Objections to Inventory and Appraisal of Conservator or Guardian
GC-050*	1/1/2009	Notice of Taking Possession or Control of an Asset of Minor or Conservatee
GC-051*	7/1/2005	Notice of Opening or Changing a Guardianship or Conservatorship Account or Safe Deposit Box
GC-060*	1/1/2006	Report of Sale and Petition for Order Confirming Sale of Real Property [same as DE-260*]
GC-065*	1/1/2015	Order Confirming Sale of Real Property [same as DE-265*]
GC-070*	1/1/1998	Ex Parte Petition for Authority to Sell Securities and Order [same as DE-270*]
GC-075*	1/1/1998	Ex Parte Petition for Approval of Sale of Personal Property and Order [same as DE-275*]

---

* Adopted for mandatory use by all courts.

Form	Date	Title
GC-079*	1/1/2008	Pre-Move Notice of Proposed Change of Personal Residence of Conservatee or Ward
GC-079(MA)	1/1/2008	Attachment to Pre-Move Notice of Proposed Change of Personal Residence of Conservatee or Ward
GC-080*	1/1/2008	Change of Residence Notice
GC-080(MA)	1/1/2008	Attachment to Post-Move Notice of Change of Residence of Conservatee or Ward
GC-085*	1/1/2000	Petition to Fix Residence Outside the State of California
GC-090*	1/1/2000	Order Fixing Residence Outside the State of California
GC-100*	1/1/2024	Petition for Appointment of Guardian Ad Litem—Probate [same as DE-350*]
GC-101*	1/1/2024	Order Appointing Guardian Ad Litem—Probate [same as DE-351*]
GC-110*	7/1/2008	Petition for Appointment of Temporary Guardian
GC-110(P)*	1/1/2009	Petition for Appointment of Temporary Guardian of the Person
GC-111*	7/1/2008	Petition for Appointment of Temporary Conservator
GC-112	1/1/2009	Ex Parte Application for Good Cause Exception to Notice of Hearing on Petition for Appointment of Temporary Conservator
GC-112(A-1)	1/1/2009	Declaration in Support of Ex Parte Application for Good Cause Exception to Notice of Hearing on Petition for Appointment of Temporary Conservator
GC-112(A-2)	1/1/2009	Declaration Continuation Page
GC-115	1/1/2009	Order on Ex Parte Application for Good Cause Exception to Notice of Hearing on Petition for Appointment of Temporary Conservator
GC-120*	1/1/2025	Declaration Under Uniform Child Custody Jurisdiction and Enforcement Act (UCCJEA) [same as FL-105*]
GC-120(A)*	1/1/2025	Attachment to Declaration Under Uniform Child Custody Jurisdiction and Enforcement Act (UCCJEA) [same as FL-105(A)*]
GC-140*	1/1/2009	Order Appointing Temporary Guardian
GC-141*	1/1/2009	Order Appointing Temporary Conservator
GC-150*	1/1/2015	Letters of Temporary Guardianship or Conservatorship
GC-205*	1/1/2023	[Renumbered] Guardianship Pamphlet [renumbered to GC-205-INFO]
GC-205-INFO	1/1/2023	Information on Probate Guardianship of the Person
GC-206-INFO	1/1/2023	Information on Probate Guardianship of the Estate
GC-207-INFO*	1/1/2023	Comparison of Guardians With Other Nonparent Caregivers [same as JV-352-INFO*]
GC-210*	7/1/2016	Petition for Appointment of Guardian of Minor
GC-210(A-PF)*	7/1/2009	Professional Fiduciary Attachment to Petition for Appointment of Guardian or Conservator [same as GC-310(A-PF)*]
GC-210(CA)*	1/1/2022	Child Information Attachment to Probate Guardianship Petition (Probate—Guardianships and Conservatorships)
GC-210(P)*	7/1/2016	Petition for Appointment of Guardian of the Person
GC-210(PE)*	7/1/2016	Petition to Extend Guardianship of the Person
GC-211*	1/1/2004	Consent of Proposed Guardian, Nomination of Guardian, and Consent to Appointment of Guardian and Waiver of Notice
GC-212*	7/1/2009	Confidential Guardian Screening Form
GC-215	1/1/2023	Objection to Petition for Appointment of Guardian
GC-220*	1/1/2016	Petition for Special Immigrant Juvenile Findings
GC-224*	1/1/2016	[Revoked] Order Regarding Eligibility for Special Immigrant Juvenile Status—Probate Guardianship (Probate—Guardianships and Conservatorships)
GC-224*	7/1/2016	Special Immigrant Juvenile Findings [same as FL-357*, JV-357*]
GC-240*	7/1/2016	Order Appointing Guardian or Extending Guardianship of the Person
GC-248*	1/1/2001	Duties of Guardian (Probate)
GC-250*	7/1/2016	Letters of Guardianship
GC-251*	7/1/2003	Confidential Guardianship Status Report
GC-255*	1/1/2006	Petition for Termination of Guardianship
GC-260*	1/1/2006	Order Terminating Guardianship
GC-310*	1/1/2019	Petition for Appointment of Probate Conservator
GC-310(A-PF)*	7/1/2009	Professional Fiduciary Attachment to Petition for Appointment of Guardian or Conservator [same as GC-210(A-PF)*]
GC-312*	1/1/2024	Confidential Supplemental Information (Probate Conservatorship)
GC-313*	1/1/2019	Attachment Requesting Special Orders Regarding a Major Neurocognitive Disorder
GC-314*	7/1/2009	Confidential Conservator Screening Form
GC-320*	7/1/2016	Citation for Conservatorship
GC-322*	1/1/2006	Citation—Probate [same as DE-122*]
GC-325*	1/1/2025	Confidential Declaration on Medical Ability to Attend Hearing—Probate Conservatorship
GC-330	1/1/2023	Order Appointing Court Investigator
GC-331	1/1/2023	Order Appointing Court Investigator (Review and Successor Conservator Investigations)
GC-332	1/1/2023	[Revoked] Order Setting Biennial Review Investigation and Directing Status Report Before Review
GC-333*	1/1/2019	Ex Parte Application for Order Authorizing Completion of Capacity Declaration—HIPAA
GC-334*	1/1/2019	Ex Parte Order Re Completion of Capacity Declaration—HIPAA
GC-335*	1/1/2025	Confidential Capacity Assessment and Declaration—Probate Conservatorship
GC-335A*	1/1/2025	Everyday Activities Attachment to Confidential Capacity Assessment and Declaration—Probate Conservatorship
GC-336*	1/1/2009	Ex Parte Order Authorizing Disclosure of (Proposed) Conservatee's Health Information to Court Investigator—HIPAA

* Adopted for mandatory use by all courts.

JUDICIAL COUNCIL LEGAL FORMS LIST

Form	Date	Title
GC-340*	1/15/2016	Order Appointing Probate Conservator
GC-341*	1/1/2008	Notice of Conservatee's Rights
GC-341(MA)	1/1/2008	Attachment to Notice of Conservatee's Rights
GC-348*	1/1/2011	Duties of Conservator and Acknowledgment of Receipt of *Handbook for Conservators*
GC-350*	7/1/2015	Letters of Conservatorship
GC-355	1/1/2025	Confidential Conservatorship Care Plan—Part 1
GC-356*	1/1/2025	Confidential Conservatorship Care Plan—Part 2 (Medical Information)
GC-360*	1/1/2016	Conservatorship Registration Cover Sheet and Attestation of Conservatee's Non-Residence in California
GC-361*	1/1/2016	Notice of Intent to Register Conservatorship
GC-362*	1/1/2016	Conservatorship Registrant's Acknowledgment of Receipt of Handbook for Conservators
GC-363	1/1/2020	Petition for Transfer Orders (California Conservatorship Jurisdiction Act)
GC-364	1/1/2019	Provisional Order for Transfer (California Conservatorship Jurisdiction Act)
GC-365	1/1/2019	Final Order Confirming Transfer (California Conservatorship Jurisdiction Act)
GC-366	1/1/2020	Petition for Orders Accepting Transfer (California Conservatorship Jurisdiction Act)
GC-367	1/1/2019	Provisional Order Accepting Transfer (California Conservatorship Jurisdiction Act)
GC-368	1/1/2019	Final Order Accepting Transfer (California Conservatorship Jurisdiction Act)
GC-380*	1/1/2019	Petition for Exclusive Authority to Give Consent for Medical Treatment
GC-385*	1/1/2019	Order Authorizing Conservator to Give Consent for Medical Treatment
GC-395*	1/1/2006	Ex Parte Petition for Final Discharge and Order *[same as DE-295*]*
GC-399*	1/1/2017	Notice of the Conservatee's Death
GC-400(A)(1)	1/1/2008	Schedule A, Receipts, Dividends—Standard Account
GC-400(A)(2)	1/1/2008	Schedule A, Receipts, Interest—Standard Account
GC-400(A)(3)	1/1/2008	Schedule A, Receipts, Pensions, Annuities, and Other Regular Periodic Payments—Standard Account
GC-400(A)(4)	1/1/2008	Schedule A, Receipts, Rent—Standard Account
GC-400(A)(5)	1/1/2008	Schedule A, Receipts, Social Security, Veterans' Benefits, Other Public Benefits—Standard Account
GC-400(A)(6)	1/1/2008	Schedule A, Receipts, Other Receipts—Standard Account
GC-400(A)(C)	1/1/2008	Schedule A and C, Receipts and Disbursements Worksheet—Standard Account
GC-400(AP)	1/1/2008	Additional Property Received During Period of Account—Standard and Simplified Accounts *[same as GC-405(AP)]*
GC-400(B)	1/1/2015	Schedule B, Gains on Sales—Standard and Simplified Accounts *[same as GC-405(B)]*
GC-400(C)(1)	1/1/2008	Schedule C, Disbursements, Conservatee's Caregiver Expenses—Standard Account
GC-400(C)(2)	1/1/2008	Schedule C, Disbursements, Conservatee's Residential or Long-Term Care Facility Living Expenses—Standard Account
GC-400(C)(3)	1/1/2008	Schedule C, Disbursements, Ward's Education Expenses—Standard Account
GC-400(C)(4)	1/1/2008	Schedule C, Disbursements, Fiduciary and Attorney Fees—Standard Account
GC-400(C)(5)	1/1/2008	Schedule C, Disbursements, General Administration Expenses—Standard Account
GC-400(C)(6)	1/1/2008	Schedule C, Disbursements, Investment Expenses—Standard Account
GC-400(C)(7)	1/1/2008	Schedule C, Disbursements, Living Expenses—Standard Account
GC-400(C)(8)	1/1/2008	Schedule C, Disbursements, Medical Expenses—Standard Account
GC-400(C)(9)	1/1/2008	Schedule C, Disbursements, Property Sale Expenses—Standard Account
GC-400(C)(10)	1/1/2008	Schedule C, Disbursements, Rental Property Expenses—Standard Account
GC-400(C)(11)	1/1/2008	Schedule C, Disbursements, Other Expenses—Standard Account
GC-400(D)	1/1/2015	Schedule D, Losses on Sales—Standard and Simplified Accounts *[same as GC-405(D)]*
GC-400(DIST)	1/1/2008	Distributions to Conservatee or Ward—Standard and Simplified Accounts *[same as GC-405(DIST)]*
GC-400(E)(1)	1/1/2008	Cash Assets on Hand at End of Account Period—Standard and Simplified Accounts *[same as GC-405(E)(1)]*
GC-400(E)(2)	1/1/2008	Non-Cash Assets on Hand at End of Account Period—Standard and Simplified Accounts *[same as GC-405(E)(2)]*
GC-400(F)	1/1/2008	Schedule F, Changes in Form of Assets—Standard and Simplified Accounts *[same as GC-405(F)]*
GC-400(G)	1/1/2008	Schedule G, Liabilities at End of Account Period—Standard and Simplified Accounts *[same as GC-405(G)]*
GC-400(NI)	1/1/2008	Net Income From a Trade or Business—Standard Account
GC-400(NL)	1/1/2008	Net Loss From a Trade or Business—Standard Account
GC-400(OCH)	1/1/2008	Other Charges—Standard and Simplified Accounts *[same as GC-405(OCH)]*
GC-400(OCR)	1/1/2008	Other Credits—Standard and Simplified Accounts *[same as GC-405(OCR)]*
GC-400(PH)(1)	1/1/2008	Cash Assets on Hand at Beginning of Account Period—Standard and Simplified Accounts *[same as GC-405(PH)(1)]*
GC-400(PH)(2)	1/1/2008	Non-Cash Assets on Hand at Beginning of Account Period—Standard and Simplified Accounts *[same as GC-405(PH)(2)]*
GC-400(SUM)*	1/1/2008	Summary of Account—Standard and Simplified Accounts *[same as GC-405(SUM)*]*
GC-405(A)*	1/1/2008	Schedule A, Receipts—Simplified Account
GC-405(AP)	1/1/2008	Additional Property Received During Period of Account—Standard and Simplified Accounts *[same as GC-400(AP)]*
GC-405(B)	1/1/2015	Schedule B, Gains on Sales—Standard and Simplified Accounts *[same as GC-400(B)]*
GC-405(C)*	1/1/2008	Schedule C, Disbursements—Simplified Account
GC-405(D)	1/1/2015	Schedule D, Losses on Sales—Standard and Simplified Accounts *[same as GC-400(D)]*
GC-405(DIST)	1/1/2008	Distributions to Conservatee or Ward—Standard and Simplified Accounts *[same as GC-400(DIST)]*

---

* Adopted for mandatory use by all courts.

GC-405(E)(1)	1/1/2008	Cash Assets on Hand at End of Account Period—Standard and Simplified Accounts *[same as GC-400(E)(1)]*
GC-405(E)(2)	1/1/2008	Non-Cash Assets on Hand at End of Account Period—Standard and Simplified Accounts *[same as GC-400(E)(2)]*
GC-405(F)	1/1/2008	Schedule F, Changes in Form of Assets—Standard and Simplified Accounts *[same as GC-400(F)]*
GC-405(G)	1/1/2008	Schedule G, Liabilities at End of Account Period—Standard and Simplified Accounts *[same as GC-400(G)]*
GC-405(OCH)	1/1/2008	Other Charges—Standard and Simplified Accounts *[same as GC-400(OCH)]*
GC-405(OCR)	1/1/2008	Other Credits—Standard and Simplified Accounts *[same as GC-400(OCR)]*
GC-405(PH)(1)	1/1/2008	Cash Assets on Hand at Beginning of Account Period—Standard and Simplified Accounts *[same as GC-400(PH)(1)]*
GC-405(PH)(2)	1/1/2008	Non-Cash Assets on Hand at Beginning of Account Period—Standard and Simplified Accounts *[same as GC-400(PH)(2)]*
GC-405(SUM)*	1/1/2008	Summary of Account—Standard and Simplified Accounts *[same as GC-400(SUM)*]*
GC-410	1/1/2020	Request and Order for Waiver of Accounting
GC-505	7/1/2007	Forms You Need to Ask the Court to Appoint a Guardian of the Person
GC-510	7/1/2007	What is "Proof of Service" in a Guardianship?

GUN VIOLENCE PREVENTION

GV-009	1/1/2023	Notice of Court Hearing
GV-020*	1/1/2025	Response to Gun Violence Emergency Protective Order (Gun Violence Prevention)
GV-020-INFO	1/1/2025	How Can I Respond to a Gun Violence Emergency Protective Order?
GV-025	9/1/2019	Proof of Service by Mail
GV-030*	1/1/2025	Gun Violence Restraining Order After Hearing on EPO-002 (CLETS—HGV) (Gun Violence Prevention)
GV-100*	1/1/2025	Petition for Gun Violence Restraining Order
GV-100-INFO	1/1/2025	Can a Gun Violence Restraining Order Help Me?
GV-109*	1/1/2025	Notice of Court Hearing (Gun Violence Prevention)
GV-110*	1/1/2025	Temporary Gun Violence Restraining Order (CLETS—TGV) (Gun Violence Prevention)
GV-115*	1/1/2024	Request to Continue Court Hearing for Gun Violence Restraining Order (EPO-002 or Temporary Restraining Order) (Gun Violence Prevention)
GV-116*	1/1/2023	Order on Request to Continue Hearing (EPO-002 or Temporary Restraining Order) (CLETS—EGV or CLETS—TGV)
GV-120*	1/1/2025	Response to Petition for Gun Violence Restraining Order (Gun Violence Prevention)
GV-120-INFO	1/1/2025	How Can I Respond to a Petition for a Gun Violence Restraining Order? (Gun Violence Prevention)
GV-125*	1/1/2025	Consent to Gun Violence Restraining Order and Surrender of Firearms (Gun Violence Prevention)
GV-130*	1/1/2025	Gun Violence Restraining Order After Hearing or Consent to Gun Violence Restraining Order
GV-200	9/1/2019	Proof of Personal Service
GV-200-INFO	1/1/2019	What Is "Proof of Personal Service"?
GV-250	1/1/2019	Proof of Service by Mail
GV-600*	9/1/2020	Request to Terminate Gun Violence Restraining Order
GV-610*	9/1/2020	Notice of Hearing on Request to Terminate Gun Violence Restraining Order
GV-620*	1/1/2024	Response to Request to Terminate Gun Violence Restraining Order
GV-630*	9/1/2020	Order on Request to Terminate Gun Violence Restraining Order
GV-700*	1/1/2024	Request to Renew Gun Violence Restraining Order
GV-710*	1/1/2025	Notice of Hearing on Request to Renew Gun Violence Restraining Order (Gun Violence Prevention)
GV-715*	1/1/2024	Request to Reschedule Hearing to Renew Restraining Order
GV-716*	1/1/2024	Order to Reschedule Hearing to Renew Restraining Order
GV-720*	1/1/2019	Response to Request to Renew Gun Violence Restraining Order
GV-730*	1/1/2024	Order on Request to Renew Gun Violence Restraining Order
GV-800	1/1/2024	Receipt for Firearms, Firearm Parts, Ammunition, and Magazines
GV-800-INFO	1/1/2024	How Do I Turn In, Sell, or Store My Firearms, Firearm Parts, Ammunition, and Magazines?

HABEAS CORPUS

HC-001	9/1/2024	Petition for Writ of Habeas Corpus *[renumbered from MC-275]*
HC-002	9/1/2018	Petition for Writ of Habeas Corpus—LPS Act (Mental Health) *[renumbered from MC-265]*
HC-003	9/1/2018	Petition for Writ of Habeas Corpus—Penal Commitment (Mental Health) *[renumbered from MC-270]*
HC-004	9/1/2018	Notice and Request for Ruling *[renumbered from CR-175]*
HC-100*	4/25/2019	Declaration of Counsel Re Minimum Qualifications for Appointment in Death Penalty–Related Habeas Corpus Proceedings
HC-101*	4/25/2019	Order Appointing Counsel in Death Penalty–Related Habeas Corpus Proceeding
HC-200*	4/25/2019	Petitioner's Notice of Appeal—Death Penalty–Related Habeas Corpus Decision

---

* Adopted for mandatory use by all courts.

JUDICIAL COUNCIL LEGAL FORMS LIST

IGNITION INTERLOCK DEVICE

ID-100	7/1/2008	*[Renumbered]* Order to Install Ignition Interlock Device *[renumbered to CR-221]*
ID-110	7/1/2005	*[Renumbered]* Ignition Interlock Installation Verification *[renumbered to CR-222]*
ID-120	7/1/2005	*[Renumbered]* Ignition Interlock Calibration Verification and Tamper Report *[renumbered to CR-223]*
ID-130	1/1/2000	*[Renumbered]* Ignition Interlock Noncompliance Report *[renumbered to CR-224]*
ID-140	7/1/2008	*[Renumbered]* Ignition Interlock Removal and Modification to Probation Order *[renumbered to CR-225]*
ID-150	7/1/2005	*[Renumbered]* Notice to Employers of Ignition Interlock Restriction *[renumbered to CR-226]*

INDIAN CHILD WELFARE ACT

ICWA-005-INFO	1/1/2022	Information Sheet on Indian Child Inquiry Attachment and Notice of Child Custody Proceeding for Indian Child
ICWA-010(A)*	1/1/2020	Indian Child Inquiry Attachment
ICWA-020*	3/25/2020	Parental Notification of Indian Status
ICWA-030*	1/1/2021	Notice of Child Custody Proceeding for Indian Child
ICWA-030(A)	1/1/2008	Attachment to Notice of Child Custody Proceeding for Indian Child
ICWA-040	1/1/2020	Notice of Designation of Tribal Representative in a Court Proceeding Involving an Indian Child
ICWA-042	1/1/2024	Request for Tribal Participation
ICWA-050	1/1/2008	Notice of Petition and Petition to Transfer Case Involving an Indian Child to Tribal Jurisdiction
ICWA-060*	1/1/2020	Order on Petition to Transfer Case Involving an Indian Child to Tribal Jurisdiction
ICWA-070*	1/1/2020	Request for Ex Parte Hearing to Return Physical Custody of an Indian Child
ICWA-080*	1/1/2020	Order on Request for Ex Parte Hearing to Return Physical Custody of an Indian Child
ICWA-090*	1/1/2021	Order After Hearing on Ex Parte Request to Return Physical Custody of an Indian Child
ICWA-100	1/1/2021	Tribal Information Form
ICWA-100-INFO	1/1/2021	Instructions Sheet for Tribal Information Form
ICWA-101*	1/1/2021	Agreement of Parent or Indian Custodian to Temporary Custody of Indian Child

INTERPRETER

INT-001*	1/1/2009	Semiannual Report to the Judicial Council on the Use of Noncertified or Nonregistered Interpreters
INT-002(A)*	1/1/2009	Semiannual Report to the Judicial Council on the Use of Nonregistered Interpreters *(Attachment to INT-001)*
INT-100-INFO*	1/1/2018	*[Revoked]* Procedures and Guidelines to Appoint a Noncertified or Nonregistered Interpreter in Criminal and Juvenile Delinquency Proceedings
INT-100-INFO*	1/1/2025	Procedures to Appoint a Noncertified or Nonregistered Spoken Language Interpreter
INT-110*	1/1/2025	Provisional Qualifications of Noncertified or Nonregistered Spoken Language Interpreter
INT-120*	1/1/2025	Certification of Unavailability of Certified or Registered Interpreter and Availability of Provisionally Qualified Interpreter
INT-140	1/1/2025	Temporary Use of a Noncertified or Nonregistered Spoken Language Interpreter
INT-200	7/1/2008	Foreign Language Interpreter's Duties—Civil and Small Claims (For Noncertified and Nonregistered Interpreters)
INT-300	7/1/2016	Request for Interpreter (Civil)

JUDGMENT

JUD-100	1/1/2025	Judgment

JURY SELECTION

JURY-001	9/1/2018	Juror Questionnaire for Civil Cases/Code of Civil Procedure section 205(c)-(d) *[renumbered from MC-001]*
JURY-002	9/1/2018	Juror Questionnaire for Criminal Cases/Code of Civil Procedure section 205(c)-(d) *[renumbered from MC-002]*
JURY-003	9/1/2018	Juror Questionnaire for Expedited Jury Trials *[renumbered from MC-003]*
JURY-010	9/1/2018	Juror's Motion to Set Aside Sanctions and Order *[renumbered from MC-070]*

JUVENILE

JV-050	1/1/2015	*[Revoked]* Information for Parents (Juvenile Dependency)
JV-050-INFO	1/1/2015	What happens if your child is taken from your home?
JV-055	1/1/2015	*[Revoked]* Juvenile Court—The Dependency Court: How It Works
JV-060	9/1/2017	*[Renumbered]* Juvenile Court—Information for Parents *[renumbered to JV-060-INFO]*
JV-060-INFO	7/1/2023	Juvenile Justice Court: Information for Parents
JV-100*	2/1/2023	Juvenile Dependency Petition (Version One)
JV-101(A)*	2/1/2023	Additional Children Attachment—Juvenile Dependency Petition
JV-110*	2/1/2023	Juvenile Dependency Petition (Version Two)
JV-120	1/1/2007	Serious Physical Harm (§ 300(a))

---

* Adopted for mandatory use by all courts.

JV-121	2/1/2023	Failure to Protect (§ 300(b))
JV-122	1/1/2007	Serious Emotional Damage (§ 300(c))
JV-123*	1/1/2007	Sexual Abuse (§ 300(d))
JV-124	1/1/2007	Severe Physical Abuse (§ 300(e))
JV-125	1/1/2007	Caused Another Child's Death Through Abuse or Neglect (§ 300(f))
JV-126	1/1/2007	No Provision for Support (§ 300(g))
JV-127	1/1/2007	Freed for Adoption (§ 300(h))
JV-128	1/1/2007	Cruelty (§ 300(i))
JV-129	1/1/2007	Abuse of Sibling (§ 300(j))
JV-130*	1/1/2008	*[Revoked]* Parental Notification of Indian Status (Juvenile Court)
JV-130-INFO	1/1/2013	Paying for Lawyers in Dependency Court—Information for Parents and Guardians
JV-131	1/1/2013	Order to Appear for Financial Evaluation
JV-132	4/1/2024	Financial Declaration—Juvenile Dependency
JV-133	1/1/2013	Recommendation Regarding Ability to Repay Cost of Legal Services
JV-134	1/1/2013	Response to Recommendation Regarding Ability to Repay Cost of Legal Services
JV-135	1/1/2013	Order for Repayment of Cost of Legal Services
JV-136	1/1/2013	Juvenile Dependency—Cost of Appointed Counsel: Repayment Recommendation/Response/Order
JV-140*	1/1/2007	Notification of Mailing Address
JV-141*	1/1/2019	Electronic Service: Consent, Withdrawal of Consent, Address Change (Juvenile) *[same as EFS-005-JV*]*
JV-150*	1/1/2007	Supplemental Petition for More Restrictive Placement (Attachment) (Welfare and Institutions Code, § 387)
JV-172*	1/1/2024	Ex Parte Application for Voluntary Admission to Psychiatric Residential Treatment Facility
JV-173*	1/1/2024	Proof of Notice of Hearing on Application for Voluntary Admission to Psychiatric Residential Treatment Facility
JV-174*	1/1/2024	Order on Application for Voluntary Admission to Psychiatric Residential Treatment Facility
JV-175	1/1/2024	Review of Voluntary Admission of Child to Psychiatric Residential Treatment Facility
JV-176*	1/1/2024	Review of Voluntary Admission of Nonminor or Nonminor Dependent to Psychiatric Residential Treatment Facility
JV-177*	1/1/2024	Admission to Psychiatric Residential Treatment Facility by Consent of Conservator—Additional Findings and Orders
JV-180*	1/1/2020	Request to Change Court Order
JV-182*	1/1/2007	Confidential Information (Request to Change Court Order)
JV-183*	1/1/2016	Court Order on Form JV-180, *Request to Change Court Order*
JV-184*	1/1/2009	Order After Hearing on Form JV-180, *Request to Change Court Order*
JV-185	1/1/2016	Child's Information Sheet—Request to Change Court Order
JV-190*	1/1/2007	Waiver of Rights—Juvenile Dependency
JV-195*	7/1/1998	Waiver of Reunification Services
JV-200*	1/1/2016	Custody Order—Juvenile—Final Judgment
JV-205*	1/1/2016	Visitation (Parenting Time) Order—Juvenile
JV-206	1/1/2016	Reasons for No or Supervised Visitation—Juvenile
JV-210	1/1/2023	Application to Commence Juvenile Court Proceedings and Decision of Social Worker (Welf. & Inst. Code, § 329)
JV-212	9/1/2018	Application to Review Decision by Social Worker Not to Commence Proceedings (Welf. & Inst. Code, §331) *[renumbered from JV-215]*
JV-213*	1/1/2023	Probate Court Request for Juvenile Court Review of Decision Not to Commence Proceedings
JV-214*	9/1/2018	Request for Hearing on Waiver of Presumptive Transfer
JV-214(A)*	9/1/2018	Notice of and Order on Request for Hearing on Waiver of Presumptive Transfer
JV-214-INFO	9/1/2018	Instructions for Requesting a Hearing to Review Waiver of Presumptive Transfer of Specialty Mental Health Services
JV-215*	9/1/2018	Order After Hearing on Waiver of Presumptive Transfer
JV-216	9/1/2018	Order Delegating Judicial Authority Over Psychotropic Medication
JV-217-INFO	1/1/2019	Guide to Psychotropic Medication Forms
JV-218	7/1/2016	Child's Opinion About the Medicine
JV-219	1/1/2018	Statement About Medicine Prescribed
JV-219-INFO	7/1/2016	*[Renumbered]* Information About Psychotropic Medication Forms *[renumbered to JV-217-INFO]*
JV-220*	1/1/2018	Application For Psychotropic Medication
JV-220(A)*	1/1/2018	Physician's Statement—Attachment
JV-220(B)*	1/1/2018	Physician's Request to Continue Medication—Attachment
JV-221*	1/1/2021	Proof of Notice of Application
JV-222	1/1/2018	Input on Application for Psychotropic Medication
JV-223*	9/1/2020	Order on Application for Psychotropic Medication
JV-224*	1/1/2016	*[Revoked]* Order Regarding Eligibility for Special Immigrant Juvenile Status
JV-224*	9/1/2020	County Report on Psychotropic Medication
JV-225*	1/1/2014	Your Child's Health and Education
JV-226	7/1/2013	Authorization to Release Health and Mental Health Information (Dependency)
JV-227	1/1/2014	Consent to Release Education Information (Dependency)
JV-228	9/1/2020	Position on Release of Information to Medical Board of California
JV-228-INFO	1/1/2025	Background on Release of Information to Medical Board of California
JV-229*	9/1/2020	Withdrawal of Release of Information to Medical Board of California

---

* Adopted for mandatory use by all courts.

Form	Date	Title
JV-235*	1/1/2023	Placing Agency's Request for Review of Placement in Short-Term Residential Therapeutic Program or Community Treatment Facility
JV-236*	1/1/2023	Input on Placement in Short-Term Residential Therapeutic Program or Community Treatment Facility
JV-237*	1/1/2023	Proof of Service—Short-Term Residential Therapeutic Program or Community Treatment Facility Placement
JV-238	1/1/2023	Notice of Hearing on Placement in Short-Term Residential Therapeutic Program or Community Treatment Facility
JV-239*	1/1/2023	Order on Placement in Short-Term Residential Therapeutic Program or Community Treatment Facility
JV-240*	1/1/2024	Notice of Request for Approval of Short-Term Residential Therapeutic Program or Community Treatment Facility Without a Hearing
JV-245*	1/1/2025	Request for Juvenile Restraining Order
JV-247*	1/1/2025	Response to Request for Juvenile Restraining Order
JV-248*	1/1/2012	*[Revoked]* Confidential CLETS Information (Domestic Violence, Civil Harassment, Elder Abuse, Juvenile Law)
JV-249*	1/1/2025	Notice of Court Hearing
JV-250*	1/1/2025	Temporary Restraining Order—Juvenile (CLETS—TJV)
JV-251*	1/1/2023	Request to Reschedule Restraining Order Hearing
JV-252	1/1/2023	*[Renumbered]* Proof of Firearms Turned In, Sold, or Stored *[renumbered to JV-270]*
JV-252-INFO	1/1/2023	*[Renumbered]* How Do I Turn In, Sell, or Store My Firearms? *[renumbered to JV-270-INFO]*
JV-253*	1/1/2025	Order on Request to Reschedule Restraining Order Hearing
JV-255*	1/1/2025	Juvenile Restraining Order After Hearing (CLETS—OJV)
JV-257*	1/1/2025	Order to Change or End Restraining Order After Hearing—Juvenile (CLETS)
JV-258*	1/1/2025	Request for Juvenile Restraining Order Against a Child
JV-259*	1/1/2025	Response to Request for Juvenile Restraining Order Against a Child
JV-260*	1/1/2025	Temporary Restraining Order Against a Child (CLETS—TJC)
JV-265*	1/1/2025	Juvenile Restraining Order Against a Child—Order After Hearing (CLETS—OJC)
JV-268*	1/1/2025	Proof of Personal Service
JV-270	1/1/2023	Proof of Firearms Turned In, Sold, or Stored *[same as DV-800]*
JV-270-INFO	1/1/2024	How Do I Turn In, Sell, or Store My Firearms? *[same as DV-800-INFO]*
JV-272*	1/1/2025	Prohibited Items Finding and Orders
JV-274*	1/1/2023	Noncompliance With Firearms and Ammunition Order, or Warrant
JV-280*	1/1/2007	Notice of Review Hearing
JV-281	1/1/2014	Notice of Hearing—Nonminor
JV-282	1/1/2019	Proof of service—Nonminor
JV-285	9/1/2020	Relative Information
JV-287	9/1/2020	Confidential Information
JV-290	9/1/2020	Caregiver Information Form
JV-290-INFO	10/1/2007	Instruction Sheet for Caregiver Information Form
JV-291-INFO	9/1/2020	Information on Requesting Access to Records for Persons With a Limited Right to Appeal
JV-295*	9/1/2020	De Facto Parent Request
JV-296*	1/1/2007	De Facto Parent Statement
JV-297*	9/1/2019	De Facto Parent Order
JV-298*	1/1/2007	Order Ending De Facto Parent Status
JV-299	9/1/2019	De Facto Parent Pamphlet
JV-300*	7/1/2010	Notice of Hearing on Selection of a Permanent Plan
JV-305*	1/1/2007	Citation for Publication Under Welfare and Institutions Code Section 294
JV-310*	1/1/2019	Proof of Service Under Section 366.26 of the Welfare and Institutions Code
JV-320*	1/1/2023	Orders Under Welfare and Institutions Code Sections 366.24, 366.26, 727.3, 727.31
JV-321*	9/1/2020	Request for Prospective Adoptive Parent Designation
JV-322*	1/1/2007	Confidential Information—Prospective Adoptive Parent
JV-323*	1/1/2008	Notice of Intent to Remove Child
JV-324*	1/1/2008	Notice of Emergency Removal
JV-325*	1/1/2008	*[Revoked]* Proof of Notice of Hearing
JV-325*	9/1/2020	Objection to Removal
JV-325-INFO	1/1/2008	*[Revoked]* Instructions for Notice of Prospective Adoptive Parent Hearing
JV-326*	1/1/2019	Proof of Notice Under Section 366.26(n)
JV-326-INFO	1/1/2019	Instructions for Notice of Hearings Under Section 366.26(n)
JV-327*	7/1/2010	Prospective Adoptive Parent Designation Order
JV-328*	1/1/2008	Prospective Adoptive Parent Order After Hearing
JV-330*	9/1/2019	Letters of Guardianship (Juvenile)
JV-350*	9/1/2019	*[Renumbered]* Guardianship Pamphlet *[renumbered to JV-350-INFO*]*
JV-350-INFO*	1/1/2023	Information on Juvenile Court Guardianship
JV-352-INFO*	1/1/2023	Comparison of Guardians With Other Nonparent Caregivers *[same as GC-207-INFO*]*
JV-356*	1/1/2016	Request for Special Immigrant Juvenile Findings
JV-357*	7/1/2016	Special Immigrant Juvenile Findings *[same as FL-357*, GC-224*]*
JV-361*	1/1/2021	First Review Hearing After Youth Turns 16 Years of Age—Information, Documents, and Services
JV-362*	1/1/2023	Review Hearing for Youth Approaching 18 Years of Age—Information, Documents, and Services
JV-363*	1/1/2023	Review Hearing for Youth 18 Years of Age or Older—Information, Documents, and Services

* Adopted for mandatory use by all courts.

Form	Date	Title
JV-364*	1/1/2020	Termination of Dependency for Adoption
JV-365*	1/1/2023	Termination of Juvenile Court Jurisdiction—Nonminor
JV-367*	1/1/2021	Findings and Orders After Hearing to Consider Termination of Juvenile Court Jurisdiction Over a Nonminor
JV-400	1/1/2007	Visitation Attachment: Parent, Legal Guardian, Indian Custodian, Other Important Person
JV-401	1/1/2015	Visitation Attachment: Sibling
JV-402	1/1/2007	Visitation Attachment: Grandparent
JV-403	1/1/2016	Sibling Attachment: Contact and Placement
JV-405	1/1/2020	Continuance—Dependency Detention Hearing
JV-406	7/1/2011	Continuance—Dependency General
JV-410	1/1/2025	Findings and Orders After Detention Hearing (Welf. & Inst. Code, § 319)
JV-412	1/1/2020	Findings and Orders After Jurisdictional Hearing (Welf. & Inst. Code, § 356)
JV-415	1/1/2020	Findings and Orders After Dispositional Hearing (Welf. & Inst. Code, § 361 et seq.)
JV-416	7/1/2011	Dispositional Attachment: Dismissal of Petition With Or Without Informal Supervision (Welf. & Inst. Code, § 360(b))
JV-417	7/1/2011	Dispositional Attachment: In-Home Placement With Formal Supervision (Welf. & Inst. Code, § 361)
JV-418	1/1/2021	Dispositional Attachment: Appointment of Guardian (Welf. & Inst. Code, § 360(a))
JV-419	1/1/2007	Guardianship—Consent and Waiver of Rights
JV-419A	1/1/2007	Guardianship—Child's Consent and Waiver of Rights
JV-420	7/1/2011	Dispositional Attachment: Removal From Custodial Parent—Placement With Previously Noncustodial Parent (Welf. & Inst. Code, §§ 361, 361.2)
JV-421	1/1/2023	Dispositional Attachment: Removal From Custodial Parent—Placement With Nonparent (Welf. & Inst. Code, §§ 361, 361.2)
JV-425	7/1/2011	Findings and Orders After In-Home Status Review Hearing (Welf. & Inst. Code, § 364)
JV-426	7/1/2011	Findings and Orders After In-Home Status Review Hearing—Child Placed With Previously Noncustodial Parent (Welf. & Inst. Code, §§ 364, 366.21)
JV-430	1/1/2023	Findings and Orders After Six-Month Status Review Hearing (Welf. & Inst. Code, § 366.21(e))
JV-431	7/1/2011	Six-Month Prepermanency Attachment: Child Reunified (Welf. & Inst. Code, § 366.21(e))
JV-432	1/1/2023	Six-Month Permanency Attachment: Reunification Services Continued (Welf. & Inst. Code, § 366.21(e))
JV-433	1/1/2023	Six-Month Permanency Attachment: Reunification Services Terminated (Welf. & Inst. Code, § 366.21(e))
JV-435	1/1/2023	Findings and Orders After 12-Month Permanency Hearing (Welf. & Inst. Code, § 366.21(f))
JV-436	7/1/2011	Twelve-Month Permanency Attachment: Child Reunified (Welf. & Inst. Code, § 366.21(f))
JV-437	1/1/2023	Twelve-Month Permanency Attachment: Reunification Services Continued (Welf. & Inst. Code, § 366.21(f))
JV-438	1/1/2023	Twelve-Month Permanency Attachment: Reunification Services Terminated (Welf. & Inst. Code, § 366.21(f))
JV-440	1/1/2023	Findings and Orders After 18-Month Permanency Hearing (Welf. & Inst. Code, § 366.22)
JV-441	7/1/2011	Eighteen-Month Permanency Attachment: Child Reunified (Welf. & Inst. Code, § 366.22)
JV-442	1/1/2023	Eighteen-Month Permanency Attachment: Reunification Services Terminated (Welf. & Inst. Code, § 366.22)
JV-443	1/1/2023	Eighteen-Month Permanency Attachment: Reunification Services Continued (Welf. & Inst. Code, § 366.22)
JV-445	1/1/2023	Findings and Orders After Postpermanency Hearing—Parental Rights Terminated; Permanent Plan of Adoption (Welf. & Inst. Code, § 366.3)
JV-446	1/1/2023	Findings and Orders After Postpermanency Hearing—Permanent Plan Other Than Adoption (Welf. & Inst. Code, § 366.3)
JV-448	1/1/2006	Order Granting Authority to Consent to Medical, Surgical, and Dental Care (Welf. & Inst. Code, § 366.27)
JV-450*	1/1/2012	Order for Prisoner's Appearance at Hearing Affecting Parental Rights
JV-451*	1/1/2012	Prisoner's Statement Regarding Appearance at Hearing Affecting Parental Rights
JV-455	1/1/2023	Findings and Orders After 24-Month Permanency Hearing (Welf. & Inst. Code, § 366.25)
JV-456	7/1/2011	Twenty-Four-Month Permanency Attachment: Child Reunified (Welf. & Inst. Code, § 366.25)
JV-457	1/1/2023	Twenty-Four-Month Permanency Attachment: Reunification Services Terminated (Welf. & Inst. Code, § 366.25)
JV-459(A)	1/1/2023	Status Review Attachment: Sexual and Reproductive Health Services (Welf. & Inst. Code, §§ 366(a)(1)(F), 727.2(e)(7))
JV-460	1/1/2021	Attachment: Additional Findings and Orders For Child Approaching Majority—Dependency
JV-461*	1/1/2021	Findings and Orders After Nonminor Disposition Hearing
JV-461(A)*	1/1/2023	Dispositional Attachment: Nonminor Dependent
JV-462	1/1/2023	Findings and Orders After Nonminor Dependent Status Review Hearing
JV-463*	1/1/2021	Nonminor's Informed Consent to Hold Disposition Hearing
JV-464-INFO*	1/1/2019	How to Ask to Return to Juvenile Court Jurisdiction and Foster Care
JV-466*	1/1/2019	Request to Return to Juvenile Court Jurisdiction and Foster Care
JV-468*	7/1/2012	Confidential Information—Request to Return to Juvenile Court Jurisdiction and Foster Care
JV-469*	4/1/2023	Petition and Order to Exit and Reenter Jurisdiction—Nonminor Dependent
JV-470	1/1/2019	Findings and Orders Regarding Prima Facie Showing on Nonminor's Request to Reenter Foster Care

---

* Adopted for mandatory use by all courts.

Form	Date	Title
JV-471*	9/1/2022	Findings and Orders Regarding Exit and Reentry of Jurisdiction—Nonminor Dependent
JV-472	1/1/2019	Findings and Orders After Hearing to Consider Nonminor's Request to Reenter Foster Care
JV-474	1/1/2019	Nonminor Dependent—Consent to Copy and Inspect Nonminor Dependent Court File
JV-475	10/25/2013	Agreement of Adoption of Nonminor or Dependent
JV-477	10/25/2013	Consent of Spouse or Registered Domestic Partner to Adoption of Nonminor Dependent
JV-479	10/25/2013	Order of Adoption of Nonminor Dependent
JV-500*	1/1/2007	Parentage Inquiry
JV-501*	1/1/2007	Parentage—Findings and Judgment
JV-505*	1/1/2008	Statement Regarding Parentage
JV-510*	1/1/2019	Proof of Service—Juvenile
JV-510(A)	1/1/2019	Attachment to Proof of Service—Juvenile (Additional Persons Served)
JV-520*	1/1/2007	Fax Filing Cover Sheet
JV-525*	7/1/2007	Order to Attend Court or Provide Documents: Subpoena/Subpoena Duces Tecum [same as CR-125*]
JV-530*	7/1/2002	Certified Request for Pupil Records—Truancy
JV-531*	7/1/2002	Local Educational Agency Response to JV-530
JV-535*	1/1/2021	Order Designating Educational Rights Holder
JV-535(A)*	9/1/2021	Attachment to Order Designating Educational Rights Holder
JV-535-INFO	9/1/2020	Information on Educational Rights Holders
JV-536*	1/1/2014	Local Educational Agency Response to JV-535—Appointment of Surrogate Parent
JV-537	1/1/2014	Educational Rights Holder Statement
JV-538	1/1/2014	Findings and Orders Regarding Transfer from School of Origin
JV-539	1/1/2014	Request for Hearing Regarding Child's Access to Services
JV-540*	1/1/2014	Notice of Hearing on Joinder—Juvenile
JV-548*	1/1/2017	Motion for Transfer Out
JV-550*	1/1/2017	Juvenile Court Transfer-Out Orders
JV-552*	1/1/2017	Juvenile Court Transfer-Out Orders—Nonminor Dependent
JV-555	1/1/2020	Notice of Intent to Place Child Out of County
JV-556	1/1/2019	Objection to Out-of-County Placement and Notice of Hearing
JV-565	1/1/2013	Request for Assistance With Expedited Placement Under the Interstate Compact on the Placement of Children
JV-567*	1/1/2013	Expedited Placement Under the Interstate Compact on the Placement of Children: Findings and Orders
JV-569*	9/1/2020	Proof of Service—Petition for Access to Juvenile Case File
JV-570*	9/1/2020	Petition for Access to Juvenile Case File
JV-571*	9/1/2020	Notice of Petition for Access to Juvenile Case File
JV-572*	9/1/2020	Objection to Release of Juvenile Case File
JV-573*	1/1/2021	Order on Petition for Access to Juvenile Case File
JV-574*	1/1/2021	Order After Judicial Review on Petition for Access to Juvenile Case File
JV-575*	1/1/2007	Petition to Obtain Report of Law Enforcement Agency
JV-580*	1/1/2006	Notice to Child and Parent/Guardian RE: Release of Juvenile Police Records and Objection
JV-581	1/1/2022	Law Enforcement Notice on Sealing of Records (Welf. & Inst. Code, § 827.95)
JV-582	1/1/2022	Petition to Seal Juvenile Police Records
JV-589	1/1/2022	Acknowledgment of Juvenile Diversion Record Sealed (Welf. & Inst. Code, § 786.5)
JV-590	9/1/2018	Order to Seal Juvenile Records—Welfare and Institutions Code Section 781
JV-591	7/1/2016	Acknowledgment of Juvenile Record Sealed
JV-592	1/1/2021	Prosecutor Request for Access to Sealed Juvenile Case File
JV-593	1/1/2021	Notice of Prosecutor Request for Access to Sealed Juvenile Case File
JV-594	1/1/2021	Response to Prosecutor Request for Access to Sealed Juvenile Case File
JV-595	1/1/2021	Request to Seal Juvenile Records
JV-595-INFO*	1/1/2022	How to Ask the Court to Seal Your Records
JV-596	9/1/2018	Dismissal and Sealing of Records—Welfare and Institutions Code Section 786
JV-596-INFO*	1/1/2022	Sealing of Records for Satisfactory Completion of Probation
JV-597	1/1/2022	Probation Department Notice on Sealing of Records After Diversion Program (Welf. & Inst. Code § 786.5)
JV-598	9/1/2018	Petition to Review Denial of Sealing of Records After Diversion Program
JV-599	1/1/2021	Order on Prosecutor Request for Access to Sealed File
JV-600	1/1/2020	Juvenile Wardship Petition
JV-610	1/1/2007	Child Habitually Disobedient (§ 601(a))
JV-611	1/1/2007	Child Habitually Truant (§ 601(b))
JV-615	1/1/2012	Deferred Entry of Judgment Notice of Noncompliance
JV-618	7/1/2023	Waiver of Rights—Juvenile Justice
JV-620*	1/1/2007	Violation of Law By Child
JV-622	1/1/2006	Informal Probation Agreement
JV-624	1/1/2012	Terms and Conditions
JV-625	9/1/2018	Notice of Hearing—Juvenile Delinquency Proceeding
JV-635*	5/22/2017	Promise to Appear—Juvenile Delinquency (Juvenile 14 Years or Older)
JV-640	1/1/2012	Delinquency Court Proceeding Findings and Orders
JV-642	2/1/2023	Initial Appearance Hearing—Juvenile Delinquency
JV-644*	1/1/2012	Jurisdiction Hearing—Juvenile Delinquency

* Adopted for mandatory use by all courts.

JV-665	7/1/2023	Disposition—Juvenile Delinquency
JV-667	7/1/2023	Custodial and Out-of-Home Placement Disposition Attachment
JV-672	1/1/2024	Findings and Orders After Six-Month Prepermanency Hearing—Delinquency
JV-674	1/1/2023	Findings and Orders After Permanency Hearing—Delinquency (Welf. & Inst. Code, § 727.3)
JV-678	1/1/2023	Findings and Orders After Postpermanency Hearing—Delinquency (Welf. & Inst. Code, § 727.3)
JV-680	1/1/2021	Findings and Orders for Child Approaching Majority—Delinquency
JV-681	7/1/2012	Attachment: Hearing for Dismissal—Additional Findings and Orders—Foster Care Placement—Delinquency
JV-682	3/15/2019	*[Renumbered]* Findings and Orders After Hearing to Modify Delinquency Jurisdiction to Transition Jurisdiction for Child Younger Than 18 Years of Age *[renumbered to JV-688]*
JV-683	3/15/2019	Findings and Orders After Hearing to Modify Delinquency Jurisdiction to Transition Jurisdiction for Ward Older Than 18 Years of Age
JV-688	1/1/2014	Continuance—Juvenile Delinquency *[renumbered from JV-682]*
JV-690	7/1/2023	School Notification of Court Adjudication
JV-692	7/1/2023	Notification to Sheriff of Juvenile Delinquency Felony Adjudication
JV-700	7/1/2016	Declaration of Eligibility for Appointment to Represent Youth in Delinquency Court
JV-710	9/1/2023	Order to Transfer Juvenile to Criminal Court Jurisdiction (Welfare and Institutions Code, § 707)
JV-720	1/1/2008	*[Revoked]* Supplemental Petition for More Restrictive Placement (Attachment) (Welfare & Institutions Code, § 777(a))
JV-730	1/1/2008	*[Revoked]* Supplemental Petition for Commitment for 30 Days or Less (Attachment) (Welfare & Institutions Code, § 777(b))
JV-732*	7/1/2023	*[Revoked]* Commitment to the California Department of Corrections and Rehabilitation, Division of Juvenile Facilities
JV-733	7/1/2023	Commitment to Secure Youth Treatment Facility
JV-735	7/1/2023	Juvenile Notice of Violation of Probation
JV-740	1/1/2012	Petition to Modify, Change, or Set Aside Previous Orders—Change of Circumstances
JV-742	1/1/2019	Request to Vacate Disposition and Dismiss Penal Code Section 647f Adjudication
JV-743	1/1/2019	Order after Request to Vacate Disposition and Dismiss Penal Code Section 647f Adjudication
JV-744	7/1/2017	Request to Reduce Juvenile Marijuana Offense (Health and Safety Code, § 11361.8(m))
JV-744A	7/1/2017	Attachment to Request to Reduce Juvenile Marijuana Offense (Health and Safety Code, § 11361.8(m))
JV-745	7/1/2017	*[Revoked]* Juvenile Order After Request to Reduce Marijuana Offense
JV-745	7/1/2017	Prosecuting Agency Response to Request to Reduce Juvenile Marijuana Offense (Health and Safety Code, § 11361.8(m))
JV-746	7/1/2017	Order After Request to Reduce Juvenile Marijuana Offense (Health and Safety Code, § 11361.8(m))
JV-748	1/1/2019	Request to Expunge Arrest or Vacate Adjudication (Human Trafficking Victim) (Penal Code, § 236.14)
JV-749	1/1/2019	Order after Request to Expunge Arrest or Vacate Adjudication (Human Trafficking Victim) (Penal Code, § 236.14)
JV-750*	9/1/2018	Determination of Eligibility—Deferred Entry of Judgment—Juvenile
JV-751*	7/1/2023	Citation and Written Notification for Deferred Entry of Judgment—Juvenile
JV-755	1/1/2012	Deferred Entry of Judgment—Dismissal and Sealing of Juvenile Records
JV-760	1/1/2012	Deferred Entry of Judgment Order
JV-790	1/1/2023	Order for Victim Restitution *[same as CR-110]*
JV-791	7/1/2015	Abstract of Judgment—Restitution *[same as CR-111]*
JV-792	1/1/2023	Instructions: Order for Victim Restitution *[same as CR-112]*
JV-793	1/1/2014	Instructions: Abstract of Judgment—Restitution *[same as CR-113]*
JV-794	9/1/2017	Petition to Terminate Wardship and Order
JV-796	1/1/2009	Petition for Expungement of DNA Profiles and Samples (Pen. Code, §299) *[same as CR-185]*
JV-798	1/1/2009	Order for Expungement of DNA Profiles and Samples (Pen. Code, §299) *[same as CR-186]*
JV-800	1/1/2023	Notice of Appeal—Juvenile
JV-805-INFO	1/1/2020	Information Regarding Appeal Rights
JV-810	1/1/2021	Recommendation for Appointment of Appellate Attorney for Child
JV-816	1/1/2025	Application for Extension of Time to File Brief—Juvenile Justice Case
JV-817	1/1/2025	Application for Extension of Time to File Brief—Juvenile Dependency Case
JV-820	9/1/2020	Notice of Intent to File Writ Petition and Request for Record to Review Order Setting a Hearing Under Welfare and Institutions Code Section 366.26 (California Rules of Court, Rule 8.450)
JV-822	9/1/2020	Notice of Intent to File Writ Petition and Request for Record to Review Order Designating or Denying Specific Placement of a Dependent Child After Termination of Parental Rights (California Rules of Court, Rule 8.454)
JV-825	1/1/2017	Petition for Extraordinary Writ
JV-826	1/1/2007	Denial of Petition (California Rules of Court, Rules 8.452, 8.456)
JV-828	7/1/2010	Notice of Action (California Rules of Court, Rule 8.452)
JV-915*	9/1/2023	Petition to Terminate Juvenile Sex Offender Registration
JV-915-INFO	9/1/2023	Information on Filing a Petition to Terminate Juvenile Sex Offender Registration
JV-916	9/1/2023	Proof of Service—Juvenile Sex Offender Registration Termination
JV-917*	9/1/2023	Response by District Attorney to Petition to Terminate Juvenile Sex Offender Registration
JV-918*	9/1/2023	Order on Petition to Terminate Juvenile Sex Offender Registration

---

* Adopted for mandatory use by all courts.

LANGUAGE ACCESS

LA-350	9/1/2019	Notice of Available Language Assistance—Service Provider
LA-400	9/1/2019	Service Not Available in My Language: Request to Change Court Order
LA-450	9/1/2019	Service Not Available in My Language: Order

MENACING DOG

MD-100	9/1/2018	Petition to Determine If Dog Is Potentially Dangerous or Vicious [renumbered from MC-600]
MD-109	9/1/2018	Notice of Hearing [renumbered from MC-601]
MD-130	9/1/2018	Order After Hearing [renumbered from MC-602]
MD-140	9/1/2018	Notice of Appeal [renumbered from MC-603]

MILITARY SERVICE

MIL-010*	1/1/2012	Notice of Petition and Petition for Relief From Financial Obligation During Military Service
MIL-012*	7/24/2023	Order on Petition for Relief From Financial Obligations During Military Service
MIL-015*	1/1/2012	Declaration In Support of Petition for Relief From Financial Obligations During Military Service
MIL-020	1/1/2012	Order on Petition for Relief From Financial Obligations During Military Service
MIL-100	1/1/2025	Notification of Military Veteran/Reserve/Active Status
MIL-183	1/1/2016	Petition for Dismissal (Military Personnel) [same as CR-183]
MIL-184	1/22/2019	Order for Dismissal (Military Personnel) [same as CR-184]
MIL-412	1/1/2024	Petition for Resentencing Based on Health Conditions Due to Military Service Listed in Penal Code Section 1170.91(b) [same as CR-412]

MISCELLANEOUS

CP10	7/1/2017	Claim of Right to Possession and Notice of Hearing
CP10.5	6/15/2015	Prejudgment Claim of Right to Possession
GDC-001*	1/1/2019	Gender Discrimination Notice
MC-001	9/1/2018	[Renumbered] Juror Questionnaire for Civil Cases [renumbered to JURY-001]
MC-002	9/1/2018	[Renumbered] Juror Questionnaire for Criminal Cases/Capital Case Supplement [renumbered to JURY-002]
MC-003	9/1/2018	[Renumbered] Juror Questionnaire for Expedited Jury Trials [renumbered to JURY-003]
MC-005*	1/1/2007	Facsimile Transmission Cover Sheet (Fax Filing)
MC-010	1/1/2025	Memorandum of Costs (Summary)
MC-011	1/1/2025	Memorandum of Costs (Worksheet)
MC-012*	1/1/2024	Memorandum of Costs After Judgment, Acknowledgment of Credit, and Declaration of Accrued Interest
MC-013-INFO	1/1/2024	Information Sheet for Calculating Interest and Amount Owed on a Judgment
MC-020	1/1/1987	Additional Page [to be attached to any form]
MC-025	7/1/2009	Attachment to Judicial Council Form
MC-030	1/1/2006	Declaration
MC-031	7/1/2005	Attached Declaration
MC-040	1/1/2013	Notice of Change of Address or Other Contact Information
MC-050*	1/1/2009	Substitution of Attorney—Civil (Without Court Order)
MC-051*	1/1/2007	Notice of Motion and Motion to Be Relieved as Counsel—Civil
MC-052*	1/1/2007	Declaration in Support of Attorney's Motion to Be Relieved as Counsel—Civil
MC-053*	1/1/2007	Order Granting Attorney's Motion to Be Relieved as Counsel—Civil
MC-060*	9/1/2018	[Renumbered] Confidential Cover Sheet False Claims Action [renumbered to CM-011*]
MC-070	9/1/2018	[Renumbered] Juror's Motion to Set Aside Sanctions and Order [renumbered to JURY-010]
MC-095*	9/1/2018	[Renumbered] Petition and Declaration Regarding Unresolved Claims and Deposit of Undistributed Surplus Proceeds of Trustee's Sale [renumbered to CIV-170*]
MC-100	9/1/2018	[Renumbered] Petition for Order Striking and Releasing Lien, etc. (Government Employee) [renumbered to CIV-160]
MC-101	9/1/2018	[Renumbered] Order to Show Cause (Government Employee) [renumbered to CIV-161]
MC-120*	1/1/2017	Confidential Reference List of Identifiers
MC-125*	1/1/2019	Confidential Information From Under Civil Code Section 1708.85
MC-200	1/1/2018	Claim Opposing Forfeiture (Health & Saf. Code, § 11488.5)
MC-201	1/1/2009	Claim Opposing Forfeiture of Vehicle (Vehicle Code, § 14607.6)
MC-202	2/1/1995	Petition for Forfeiture of Vehicle and Notice of Hearing
MC-210	9/1/2018	[Renumbered] Defendant's Financial Statement on Eligibility for Appointment of Counsel and Reimbursement and Record on Appeal at Public Expense [renumbered to CR-105]
MC-245	1/1/2018	[Renumbered] Motion to Vacate Conviction or Sentence (Pen. Code, §§ 1016.5, 1473.7) [renumbered to CR-187]
MC-246	1/1/2018	[Renumbered] Order on Motion to Vacate Conviction or Sentence (Pen. Code, §§ 1016.5, 1473.7) [renumbered to CR-188]
MC-265	9/1/2018	[Renumbered] Petition for Writ of Habeas Corpus—LPS Act (Mental Health) [renumbered to HC-002]

---

* Adopted for mandatory use by all courts.

MC-270	9/1/2018	*[Renumbered]* Petition for Writ of Habeas Corpus—Penal Commitment (Mental Health) *[renumbered to HC-003]*
MC-275	9/1/2018	*[Renumbered]* Petition for Writ of Habeas Corpus *[renumbered to HC-001]*
MC-280	9/1/2018	*[Renumbered]* Order for Commitment (Sexually Violent Predator) *[renumbered to CR-173]*
MC-281	9/1/2018	*[Renumbered]* Order for Extended Commitment (Sexually Violent Predator) *[renumbered to CR-174]*
MC-300*	9/1/2018	*[Renumbered]* Petition for Declaration of Emancipation of Minor, Order Prescribing Notice, Declaration of Emancipation, and Order Denying Petition *[renumbered to EM-100*]*
MC-301*	9/1/2018	*[Renumbered]* Emancipation Pamphlet *[renumbered to EM-100-INFO]*
MC-305*	9/1/2018	*[Renumbered]* Notice of Hearing—Emancipation of Minor *[renumbered to EM-109*]*
MC-306*	9/1/2018	*[Renumbered]* Emancipation of Minor Income and Expense Declaration *[renumbered to EM-115*]*
MC-310*	9/1/2018	*[Renumbered]* Declaration of Emancipation of Minor After Hearing *[renumbered to EM-130*]*
MC-315	9/1/2018	*[Renumbered]* Emancipated Minor's Application to California Department of Motor Vehicles *[renumbered to EM-140]*
MC-350*	1/1/2021	Petition for Approval of Compromise of Claim or Action or Disposition of Proceeds of Judgment for Minor or Person With A Disability
MC-350(A-12b(5))	1/1/2021	Additional Medical Service Providers Attachment to Petition for Approval of Compromise of Claim or Action or Disposition of Proceeds of Judgment *[renumbered from MC-350(A-13b(5))]*
MC-350(A-13b(5))	1/1/2010	Medical Service Provider Attachment to Petition to Approve Compromise of Claim or Action or Disposition of Proceeds of Judgment *[renumbered to MC-350(A-12b(5))]*
MC-350EX*	1/1/2021	Petition for Expedited Approval of Compromise of Claim or Action or Disposition of Proceeds of Judgment for Minor or Person With a Disability
MC-351*	1/1/2021	Order Approving Compromise of Claim or Action or Disposition of Proceeds of Judgment for Minor or Person With a Disability
MC-355*	1/1/2021	Order to Deposit Funds in Blocked Account
MC-356*	1/1/2021	Acknowledgment of Receipt of Order and Funds for Deposit in Blocked Account
MC-357*	1/1/2021	Petition to Withdraw Funds From Blocked Account
MC-358*	1/1/2021	Order Authorizing Withdrawal of Funds From Blocked Account
MC-360*	9/1/2018	*[Renumbered]* Petition to Establish Fact, Time, and Place of Death (Miscellaneous) *[renumbered to BMD-003*]*
MC-360A*	9/1/2018	*[Renumbered]* Declaration in Support of Petition to Establish Fact, Time, and Place of Death (Miscellaneous) *[renumbered to BMD-003A*]*
MC-361*	9/1/2018	*[Renumbered]* Petition to Establish Fact, Time, and Place of Birth (Miscellaneous) *[renumbered to BMD-001*]*
MC-361A*	9/1/2018	*[Renumbered]* Declaration in Support of Petition to Establish Fact, Time, and Place of Birth (Miscellaneous) *[renumbered to BMD-001A*]*
MC-362*	9/1/2018	*[Renumbered]* Petition to Establish Fact, Date, and Place of Marriage (Miscellaneous) *[renumbered to BMD-002*]*
MC-362A*	9/1/2018	*[Renumbered]* Declaration in Support of Petition to Establish Fact, Date, and Place of Marriage (Miscellaneous) *[renumbered to BMD-002A*]*
MC-400	9/1/2018	*[Renumbered]* Proof of Enrollment or Completion (Alcohol or Drug Program) *[renumbered to CR-220]*
MC-410	1/1/2021	Disability Accommodation Request
MC-410-INFO	1/1/2021	How to Request a Disability Accommodation for Court
MC-500*	1/1/2007	Media Request to Photograph, Record, or Broadcast
MC-510*	1/1/2007	Order on Media Request to Permit Coverage
MC-600	9/1/2018	*[Renumbered]* Petition to Determine if Dog is Potentially Dangerous or Vicious (Menacing Dog) *[renumbered to MD-100]*
MC-600*	1/1/2024	Confidential Report of Findings and Orders Affecting Voting Rights
MC-600A	1/1/2024	Attachment to Confidential Report of Findings and Orders Affecting Voting Rights
MC-601	9/1/2018	*[Renumbered]* Notice of Hearing (Menacing Dog) *[renumbered to MD-109]*
MC-602	9/1/2018	*[Renumbered]* Order After Hearing (Menacing Dog) *[renumbered to MD-130]*
MC-603	9/1/2018	*[Renumbered]* Notice of Appeal (Menacing Dog) *[renumbered to MD-140]*
MC-700*	9/1/2018	*[Renumbered]* Prefiling Order—Vexatious Litigant *[renumbered to VL-100*]*
MC-701	9/1/2018	*[Renumbered]* Request to File New Litigation by Vexatious Litigant *[renumbered to VL-110]*
MC-702	9/1/2018	*[Renumbered]* Order to File New Litigation by Vexatious Litigant *[renumbered to VL-115]*
MC-703	9/1/2018	*[Renumbered]* Application for Order to Vacate Prefiling Order and Remove Plaintiff/Petitioner From Judicial Council Vexatious Litigant List *[renumbered to VL-120]*
MC-704	9/1/2018	*[Renumbered]* Order on Application to Vacate Prefiling Order and Remove Plaintiff/Petitioner From Judicial Council Vexatious Litigant List *[renumbered to VL-125]*
MC-800	1/1/2002	Court Clerks Office: Signage
MC-950*	9/1/2018	*[Renumbered]* Notice of Limited Scope Representation *[renumbered to CIV-150*]*
MC-955	9/1/2018	*[Renumbered]* Application to Be Relieved as Attorney on Completion of Limited Scope Representation *[renumbered to CIV-151]*
MC-956	9/1/2018	*[Renumbered]* Objection to Application to Be Relieved as Attorney on Completion of Limited Scope Representation *[renumbered to CIV-152]*
MC-958	9/1/2018	*[Renumbered]* Order on Application to Be Relieved as Attorney on Completion of Limited Scope Representation *[renumbered to CIV-153]*
MC-1000	1/1/2019	Request for Review of Denial of Request to Remove Name From Gang Database

---

* Adopted for mandatory use by all courts.

NAME CHANGES

NC-100*	1/1/2023	Petition for Change of Name
NC-100-INFO	1/1/2023	Instructions for Filing a Petition for Change of Name
NC-110*	1/1/2023	Name and Information About the Person Whose Name Is to Be Changed (Attachment to Petition for Change of Name)
NC-110G*	1/1/2001	Supplemental Attachment to Petition for Change of Name (Declaration of Guardian)
NC-120*	1/1/2023	Order to Show Cause—Change of Name
NC-121*	1/1/2019	Proof of Service of Order to Show Cause
NC-125*	1/1/2023	Order to Show Cause for Change of Name to Conform to Gender Identity *[same as NC-225*]*
NC-130*	9/1/2018	Decree Changing Name
NC-130G*	9/1/2018	Decree Changing Name of Minor (By Guardian)
NC-150	1/1/2023	Notice of Hearing on Petition
NC-200*	1/1/2023	*[Revoked]* Petition for Change of Name, Recognition of Change of Gender, and Issuance of New Birth Certificate
NC-210	9/1/2018	*[Revoked]* Declaration of Physician—Attachment to Petition (Change of Name and Gender/Change of Gender) *[same as NC-310]*
NC-220*	9/1/2018	*[Revoked]* Order to Show Cause for Change of Name
NC-225*	1/1/2023	Order to Show Cause for Change of Name to Conform to Gender Identity *[same as NC-125*]*
NC-230*	1/1/2023	*[Revoked]* Decree Changing Name and Order Recognizing Change of Gender and for Issuance of New Birth Certificate
NC-300	1/1/2023	Petition for Recognition of Change of Gender and Sex Identifier, Name Change, and Issuance of New Certificates
NC-300-INFO	1/1/2023	Instructions for Filing Petition for Recognition of Change of Gender and Sex Identifier, Name Change, and Issuance of New Certificates
NC-310	9/1/2018	*[Revoked]* Declaration of Physician—Attachment to Petition (Change of Name and Gender/Change of Gender) *[same as NC-210]*
NC-311*	1/1/2023	Birth Certificate for Child of Petitioner—Attachment
NC-312*	1/1/2023	Marriage License and Certificate—Attachment
NC-320	9/1/2018	*[Revoked]* Setting of Hearing on Petition for Change of Gender and Issuance of New Birth Certificate
NC-325*	1/1/2023	Order to Show Cause—Issuance of New Marriage License and Certificate
NC-330	1/1/2023	Order Recognizing Change of Gender and Sex Identifier, for Name Change, and for Issuance of New Certificates
NC-400*	1/1/2019	Confidential Cover Sheet—Name Change Proceeding Under Address Confidentiality Program (Safe at Home)
NC-400-INFO	1/1/2019	Information Sheet for Name Change Proceedings Under Address Confidentiality Program (Safe at Home)
NC-410*	1/1/2010	Application to File Documents Under Seal in Name Change Proceeding Under Address Confidentiality Program (Safe at Home)
NC-420*	1/1/2019	Declaration in Support of Application to File Documents Under Seal in Name Change Proceeding Under Address Confidentiality Program (Safe at Home)
NC-425	1/1/2010	Order on Application to File Documents Under Seal in Name Change Proceeding Under Address Confidentiality Program (Safe at Home)
NC-500*	1/1/2023	Petition for Recognition of Minor's Change of Gender and Sex Identifier and for Issuance of New Birth Certificate and Change of Name
NC-500-INFO	1/1/2023	Instructions for Filing Petition for Recognition of Minor's Change of Gender and Sex Identifier
NC-510G*	1/1/2023	Declaration of Guardian or Juvenile Attorney (Attachment to Form NC-500)
NC-520*	1/1/2023	Order to Show Cause for Recognition of Minor's Change of Gender and Issuance of New Birth Certificate
NC-530*	1/1/2023	Order Recognizing Minor's Change of Gender and Sex Identifier and for Issuance of New Birth Certificate
NC-530G*	1/1/2023	*[Revoked]* Order Recognizing Change of Gender and for Issuance of New Birth Certificate (By Guardian or Dependency Attorney)

PLEADING
General

PLD-050*	1/1/2024	General Denial *(formerly 982(a)(13))*

PLEADING
Contract

PLD-C-001	1/1/2024	Complaint—Contract *(formerly 982.1(20))*
PLD-C-001(1)	1/1/2007	Cause of Action—Breach of Contract *(formerly 982.1(21))*
PLD-C-001(2)	1/1/2009	Cause of Action—Common Counts *(formerly 982.1(22))*
PLD-C-001(3)	1/1/2007	Cause of Action—Fraud *(formerly 982.1(23))*
PLD-C-010	1/1/2007	Answer—Contract *(formerly 982.1(35))*
PLD-C-500*	1/1/2024	Complaint—Recovery of COVID-19 Rental Debt

---

* Adopted for mandatory use by all courts.

PLD-C-505*	1/1/2024	Answer—Recovery of COVID-19 Rental Debt
PLD-C-520*	11/1/2021	Verification by Plaintiff Regarding Rental Assistance—Recovery of COVID-19 Rental Debt

PLEADING
Personal Injury, Property Damage, Wrongful Death

PLD-PI-001	1/1/2024	Complaint—Personal Injury, Property Damage, Wrongful Death *(formerly 982.1(1))*
PLD-PI-001(1)	1/1/2007	Cause of Action—Motor Vehicle *(formerly 982.1(2))*
PLD-PI-001(2)	1/1/2007	Cause of Action—General Negligence *(formerly 982.1(3))*
PLD-PI-001(3)	1/1/2007	Cause of Action—Intentional Tort *(formerly 982.1(4))*
PLD-PI-001(4)	1/1/2007	Cause of Action—Premises Liability *(formerly 982.1(5))*
PLD-PI-001(5)	1/1/2007	Cause of Action—Products Liability *(formerly 982.1(6))*
PLD-PI-001(6)	1/1/2007	Exemplary Damages Attachment *(formerly 982.1(13))*
PLD-PI-002	1/1/2024	Cross-Complaint—Personal Injury, Property Damage, Wrongful Death *(formerly 982.1(14))*
PLD-PI-003	1/1/2007	Answer—Personal Injury, Property Damage, Wrongful Death *(formerly 982.1(15))*

PROBATE - DECEDENTS ESTATES

DE-111*	7/1/2017	Petition for Probate
DE-111(A-3d)*	7/1/2017	**[Renumbered]** Waiver of Bond by Heir or Beneficiary *[renumbered to DE-111(A-3e)]*
DE-111(A-3e)*	7/1/2017	Waiver of Bond by Heir or Beneficiary *[renumbered from DE-111(A-3d); same as DE-142*]*
DE-115*	1/1/2020	Notice of Hearing on Petition to Determine Claim to Property *[same as GC-015*]*
DE-120*	1/1/2020	Notice of Hearing—Decedent's Estate or Trust
DE-120(MA)	7/1/2005	Attachment to Notice of Hearing Proof of Service by Mail *[same as GC-020(MA)]*
DE-120(P)	7/1/2005	Proof of Personal Service of Notice of Hearing—Decedent's Estate or Trust
DE-120(PA)	7/1/2005	Attachment to Notice of Hearing Proof of Personal Service *[same as GC-020(PA)]*
DE-121*	1/1/2013	Notice of Petition to Administer Estate
DE-121(MA)	1/1/2006	Attachment to Notice of Petition to Administer Estate—Proof of Service by Mail
DE-122*	1/1/2006	Citation—Probate *[same as GC-322*]*
DE-125*	1/1/1998	Summons (Probate)
DE-131*	1/1/1998	Proof of Subscribing Witness
DE-135*	1/1/1998	Proof of Holographic Instrument
DE-140*	1/1/1998	Order for Probate
DE-142*	7/1/2017	Waiver of Bond by Heir or Beneficiary *[same as DE-111(A-3e)*]*
DE-147*	1/1/2002	Duties and Liabilities of Personal Representative
DE-150*	1/1/1998	Letters
DE-154*	1/1/1998	Request for Special Notice *[same as GC-035*]*
DE-157*	1/1/2013	Notice of Administration to Creditors
DE-160*	1/1/2007	Inventory and Appraisal *[same as GC-040*]*
DE-161*	1/1/1998	Inventory and Appraisal Attachment *[same as GC-041*]*
DE-165*	1/1/1998	Notice of Proposed Action (Objection—Consent)
DE-166*	1/1/1998	Waiver of Notice of Proposed Action
DE-172*	1/1/1998	Creditor's Claim
DE-174*	1/1/2009	Allowance or Rejection of Creditor's Claim
DE-200*	1/1/1998	Order Prescribing Notice *[same as GC-022*]*
DE-221*	1/1/2014	Spousal or Domestic Partner Property Petition
DE-226*	1/1/2015	Spousal or Domestic Partner Property Order
DE-260*	1/1/2006	Report of Sale and Petition for Order Confirming Sale of Real Property *[same as GC-060*]*
DE-265*	1/1/2015	Order Confirming Sale of Real Property *[same as GC-065*]*
DE-270*	1/1/1998	Ex Parte Petition for Authority to Sell Securities and Order *[same as GC-070*]*
DE-275*	1/1/1998	Ex Parte Petition for Approval of Sale of Personal Property and Order *[same as GC-075*]*
DE-295*	1/1/2006	Ex Parte Petition for Final Discharge and Order *[same as GC-395*]*
DE-300*	4/1/2022	Maximum Values For Small Estate Set-Aside & Disposition of Estate Without Administration
DE-305*	1/1/2023	Affidavit Re: Real Property of Small Value
DE-310*	1/1/2023	Petition to Determine Succession to Real Property
DE-315*	4/1/2022	Order Determining Succession to Real Property
DE-350*	1/1/2024	Petition for Appointment of Guardian Ad Litem—Probate *[same as GC-100*]*
DE-351*	1/1/2024	Order Appointing Guardian Ad Litem—Probate *[same as GC-101*]*

PROOF OF SERVICE

POS-010*	1/1/2007	Proof of Service of Summons
POS-015*	1/1/2005	Notice And Acknowledgment Of Receipt—Civil
POS-020	1/1/2005	Proof Of Personal Service—Civil (Proof of Service) / Information Sheet For Proof Of Personal Service—Civil
POS-020(D)	1/1/2005	Attachment to Proof of Personal Service—Civil (Documents Served) (Proof of Service)
POS-020(P)	1/1/2005	Attachment to Proof of Personal Service—Civil (Persons Served) (Proof of Service)
POS-030	1/1/2005	Proof of Service by First-Class Mail—Civil (Proof of Service) / Information Sheet for Proof of Service by First-Class Mail—Civil
POS-030(D)	1/1/2005	Attachment to Proof of Service by First-Class Mail—Civil (Documents Service) (Proof of Service)

---

* Adopted for mandatory use by all courts.

POS-030(P)	1/1/2005	Attachment to Proof of Service by First-Class Mail—Civil (Persons Served) (Proof of Service)
POS-040	1/1/2020	Proof of Service—Civil
POS-040(D)	1/1/2005	Attachment to Proof of Service—Civil (Documents Served)
POS-040(P)	2/1/2017	Attachment to Proof of Service—Civil (Persons Served)
POS-050	2/1/2017	Proof of Electronic Service *[same as EFS-050]*
POS-050(D)	1/1/2010	Attachment to Proof of Electronic Service (Documents Served) *[same as EFS-050(D)]*
POS-050(P)	2/1/2017	Attachment to Proof of Electronic Service (Persons Served) *[same as EFS-050(P)]*

RECEIVERSHIPs

RC-200	1/1/2007	Ex Parte Order Appointing Receiver and Order to Show Cause and Temporary Restraining Order—Rents, Issues, and Profits
RC-210	1/1/2007	Order Confirming Appointment of Receiver and Preliminary Injunction—Rents, Issues, and Profits
RC-300	1/1/2007	Order to Show Cause and Temporary Restraining Order—Rents, Issues, and Profits
RC-310	1/1/2007	Order Appointing Receiver After Hearing and Preliminary Injunction—Rents, Issues, and Profits

REMOTE APPEARANCE

RA-010*	1/1/2022	Notice of Remote Appearance
RA-015*	1/1/2022	Opposition to Remote Proceeding at Evidentiary Hearing or Trial
RA-020	1/1/2022	Order Regarding Remote Appearance
RA-025	1/1/2022	Request To Appear Remotely—Juvenile Dependency
RA-030	1/1/2022	Request To Compel Physical Presence—Juvenile Dependency

SAFE AT HOME

SH-001*	9/1/2020	Confidential Information Form Under Code of Civil Procedure Section 367.3
SH-020*	1/1/2021	Motion to Place Documents Under Seal Under Code of Civil Procedure Section 367.3
SH-020-INFO	1/1/2021	Instructions for Motion to Place Documents Under Seal Under Code of Civil Procedure Section 367.3
SH-022*	1/1/2021	Declaration in Support of Motion to Place Documents Under Seal Under Code of Civil Procedure Section 367.3
SH-025*	1/1/2021	Order on Motion to Place Documents Under Seal Under Code of Civil Procedure Section 367.3
SH-030*	1/1/2021	Ex Parte Application for Order Shortening Time for Hearing on Motion to Place Documents Under Seal Under Code of Civil Procedure Section 367.3
SH-032*	1/1/2021	Declaration Regarding Notice and Service of Ex Parte Application for Order Shortening Time for Hearing on Motion to Place Documents Under Seal Under Code of Civil Procedure Section 367.3
SH-035	1/1/2021	Order on Ex Parte Application for Order Shortening Time for Hearing on Motion to Place Documents Under Seal Under Code of Civil Procedure Section 367.3

SCHOOL VIOLENCE PREVENTION

SV-100*	1/1/2025	Petition for Private Postsecondary School Violence Restraining Orders (Private Postsecondary School Violence Prevention)
SV-100-INFO	1/1/2025	How Do I Get an Order to Prohibit Private Postsecondary School Violence? (Private Postsecondary School Violence Prevention)
SV-102*	1/1/2012	*[Revoked]* Confidential CLETS Information (Private Postsecondary School Violence Prevention)
SV-109*	1/1/2025	Notice of Court Hearing (Private Postsecondary School Violence Prevention)
SV-110*	1/1/2025	Temporary Restraining Order (CLETS—TSV)
SV-115*	1/1/2020	Request to Continue Court Hearing (Temporary Restraining Order) (Private Postsecondary School Violence Prevention)
SV-115-INFO	1/1/2020	How to Ask for a New Hearing Date (Private Postsecondary School Violence Prevention)
SV-116*	1/1/2020	Order on Request to Continue Hearing (Temporary Restraining Order) (CLETS—TSV) (Private Postsecondary School Violence Prevention)
SV-120*	1/1/2025	Response to Petition for Private Postsecondary School Violence Restraining Orders (Private Postsecondary School Violence Prevention)
SV-120-INFO	1/1/2025	How Can I Respond to a Petition for Private Postsecondary School Violence Restraining Orders? (Private Postsecondary School Violence Prevention)
SV-130*	1/1/2025	Private Postsecondary School Violence Restraining Order After Hearing (CLETS—SVO) (Private Postsecondary School Violence Prevention)
SV-200	1/1/2023	Proof of Personal Service
SV-200-INFO	1/1/2012	What Is "Proof of Personal Service"? (Private Postsecondary School Violence Prevention)
SV-250	1/1/2012	Proof of Service of Response by Mail (Private Postsecondary School Violence Prevention)
SV-260	1/1/2012	Proof of Service of Order After Hearing by Mail (Private Postsecondary School Violence Prevention)
SV-600*	1/1/2018	Request to Modify/Terminate Private Postsecondary School Violence Restraining Order
SV-610*	1/1/2018	Notice of Hearing on Request to Modify/Terminate Private Postsecondary School Violence Restraining Order
SV-620*	1/1/2018	Response to Request to Modify/Terminate Private Postsecondary School Violence Restraining Order

---

* Adopted for mandatory use by all courts.

SV-630*	1/1/2018	Order on Request to Modify/Terminate Private Postsecondary School Violence Restraining Order
SV-700*	1/1/2012	Request to Renew Restraining Order (Private Postsecondary School Violence Prevention)
SV-710*	1/1/2012	Notice of Hearing to Renew Restraining Order
SV-715*	1/1/2024	Request to Reschedule Hearing to Renew Restraining Order
SV-716*	1/1/2024	Order to Reschedule Hearing to Renew Restraining Order
SV-720*	1/1/2012	Response to Request to Renew Restraining Order
SV-730*	1/1/2012	Order Renewing Private Postsecondary School Violence Restraining Order (CLETS)
SV-800	9/1/2024	Receipt for Firearms and Firearm Parts
SV-800-INFO	1/1/2023	How Do I Turn In, Sell, or Store My Firearms and Firearm Parts?

SERVICE

SER-001*	1/1/2024	Request for Sheriff to Serve Court Papers
SER-001A*	1/1/2024	Special Instructions for Writs and Levies—Attachment

SMALL CLAIMS

SC-100*	1/1/2024	Plaintiff's Claim and ORDER to Go to Small Claims Court
SC-100-INFO*	1/1/2024	Information for the Small Claims Plaintiff (Small Claims)
SC-100A*	1/1/2017	Other Plaintiffs or Defendants (Attachment to Plaintiff's Claim and ORDER to Go to Small Claims Court)
SC-101*	1/1/2024	Attorney Fee Dispute (After Arbitration) (Attachment to Plaintiff's Claim and ORDER to Go to Small Claims Court)
SC-103	11/1/2021	Fictitious Business Name (Small Claims)
SC-104	1/1/2009	Proof of Service (Small Claims)
SC-104A	1/1/2006	Proof of Mailing (Substituted Service) (Small Claims)
SC-104B	11/1/2021	What Is "Proof of Service"? (Small Claims)
SC-104C	7/1/2017	How to Serve a Business or Public Entity
SC-105	1/1/2007	Request for Court Order and Answer
SC-105A	1/1/2007	Order on Request for Court Order
SC-106	1992	*[Revoked]* Request to Pay Judgment in Installments (Small Claims)
SC-107*	1/1/2000	Small Claims Subpoena for Personal Appearance and Production of Documents at Trial or Hearing and Declaration
SC-108	7/1/2011	Request to Correct or Cancel Judgment and Answer (Small Claims)
SC-108A	1/1/2007	Order on Request to Correct or Cancel Judgment
SC-109	1/1/2007	Authorization to Appear
SC-110	1/1/2004	*[Revoked]* Request to Postpone Small Claims Hearing
SC-111	1/1/2004	*[Revoked]* Order on Request to Postpone Small Claims Hearings
SC-112A	7/1/2010	Proof of Service by Mail (Small Claims)
SC-113A	7/1/2010	Clerk's Certificate of Mailing
SC-114	1/1/2004	Request to Amend Claim Before Hearing (Small Claims)
SC-120*	1/1/2011	Defendant's Claim and ORDER to Go to Small Claims Court (Small Claims)
SC-120A*	1/1/2007	Other Plaintiffs or Defendants (Attachment to Defendant's Claim and ORDER to Go to Small Claims Court)
SC-130*	1/1/2025	Notice of Entry of Judgment (Small Claims)
SC-132*	7/1/2010	Attorney-Client Fee Dispute (Attachment to Notice of Entry of Judgment)
SC-133*	1/1/2011	Judgment Debtor's Statement of Assets (Small Claims)
SC-134*	1/1/2025	Application and Order to Produce Statement of Assets and to Appear for Examination
SC-135	1/1/2007	Notice of Motion to Vacate Judgment and Declaration
SC-136*	1/1/2025	Application and Order to Produce Financial Statement or Appear for Examination—Consumer Debt
SC-136-INFO*	1/1/2025	Information on Debtor's Examinations Regarding Consumer Debt *[same as EJ-140-INFO*]*
SC-140	1/1/2007	Notice of Appeal
SC-145*	1/1/2007	Request to Pay Judgment to Court
SC-150*	7/1/2010	*[Revoked]* Information for the Small Claims Plaintiff
SC-150	7/1/2010	Request to Postpone Trial
SC-152	7/1/2010	Order on Request to Postpone Trial
SC-200*	1/1/2025	Notice of Entry of Judgment
SC-200-INFO	1/1/2025	What to Do After the Court Decides Your Small Claims Case
SC-202A*	7/1/2010	Decision on Attorney-Client Fee Dispute
SC-220	1/1/2024	Request to Make Payments
SC-220-INFO	1/1/2024	*[Revoked]* Payments in Small Claims Cases
SC-221	7/1/2013	Response to Request to Make Payments
SC-222	7/1/2013	Order on Request to Make Payments
SC-223	1/1/2024	Declaration of Default in Payment of Judgment
SC-224	1/1/2024	Response to Declaration of Default in Payment of Judgment
SC-225	7/1/2013	Order on Declaration of Default in Payments
SC-225A	7/1/2013	Attachment to Order on Declaration of Default in Payments
SC-290	7/1/2010	Acknowledgment of Satisfaction of Judgment
SC-300	3/15/2019	Petition for Writ (Small Claims)
SC-300-INFO	1/1/2016	Information on Writ Proceedings in Small Claims Cases

---

* Adopted for mandatory use by all courts.

SC-500*	1/1/2024	Plaintiff's Claim and ORDER to Go to Small Claims Court (COVID-19 Rental Debt)
SC-500-INFO	10/15/2021	COVID-19 Rental Debt in Small Claims Court
SC-500A*	11/1/2021	Other Plaintiffs or Defendants (COVID-19 Rental Debt)

SUBPOENA

SUBP-001*	1/1/2007	Civil Subpoena for Personal Appearance at Trial or Hearing
SUBP-002*	1/1/2012	Civil Subpoena (Duces Tecum) for Personal Appearance and Production of Documents, Electronically Stored Information, and Things at Trial or Hearing and Declaration
SUBP-010*	1/1/2012	Deposition Subpoena for Production of Business Records
SUBP-015*	1/1/2009	Deposition Subpoena for Personal Appearance
SUBP-020*	1/1/2009	Deposition Subpoena for Personal Appearance and Production of Documents and Things
SUBP-025*	1/1/2008	Notice to Consumer or Employee and Objection
SUBP-030*	1/1/2010	Application for Discovery Subpoena in Action Pending Outside California
SUBP-035*	1/1/2012	Subpoena for Production of Business Records in Action Pending Outside California
SUBP-040*	1/1/2010	Deposition Subpoena for Personal Appearance in Action Pending Outside California
SUBP-045*	1/1/2012	Deposition Subpoena for Personal Appearance and Production of Documents, Electronically Stored Information, and Things in Action Pending Outside California
SUBP-050*	1/1/2010	Subpoena for Inspection of Premises in Action Pending Outside California

SUMMONS

SUM-100*	7/1/2009	Summons
SUM-110*	7/1/2009	Summons—Cross-Complaint
SUM-120*	7/1/2009	Summons (Joint Debtor)
SUM-130*	1/1/2024	Summons—Eviction (Unlawful Detainer/Forcible Detainer/Forcible Entry)
SUM-140*	7/1/2016	*[Revoked]* Summons—Storage Lien Enforcement
SUM-145*	7/1/2009	Summons—Enforcement of State Housing Law
SUM-200(A)*	1/1/2007	Additional Parties Attachment (Attachment to Summons) *(formerly 982(a)(9)(A))*
SUM-300*	1/1/2007	Declaration of Lost Summons After Service *(formerly 982(a)(12))*

TRAFFIC

TR-100*	1/1/2004	Notice of Correction and Proof of Service
TR-106	1/1/2004	Continuation of Notice to Appear
TR-108	1/1/2004	Continuation of Citation
TR-115	6/26/2015	Automated Traffic Enforcement System Notice to Appear
TR-120	6/26/2015	Nontraffic Notice to Appear
TR-130	1/1/2024	Traffic/Nontraffic Notice to Appear
TR-135	1/1/2024	*[Revoked]* Electronic Traffic/Nontraffic Notice to Appear (4″ format)
TR-140	1/1/2024	Notice to Correct Violation
TR-145	1/1/2024	*[Revoked]* Electronic Traffic/Nontraffic Notice to Appear (3″ format)
TR-150	1/1/2009	*[Revoked]* Instructions on Appeal Procedures for Infractions
TR-155	1/1/2009	*[Revoked]* Notice of Appeal (Infraction)
TR-160	1/1/2009	*[Revoked]* Proposed Statement on Appeal (Infraction)
TR-165	1/1/2009	*[Revoked]* Abandonment of Appeal (Infraction)
TR-200*	1/1/1999	Instructions to Defendant
TR-205*	1/1/1999	Request for Trial by Written Declaration
TR-210*	1/1/1999	Notice and Instructions to Arresting Officer
TR-215*	1/1/1999	Decision and Notice of Decision
TR-220*	1/1/1999	Request for New Trial (Trial de Novo)
TR-225*	1/1/1999	Order and Notice to Defendant of New Trial (Trial de Novo)
TR-235*	1/1/2024	Officer's Declaration
TR-300*	1/1/2024	Agreement to Pay and Forfeit Bail in Installments
TR-300o*	1/1/2024	Online Agreement to Pay and Forfeit Bail in Installments
TR-310*	1/1/2024	Agreement to Pay Traffic Violator School Fees in Installments
TR-310o*	1/1/2024	Online Agreement to Pay Traffic Violator School Fees in Installments
TR-320	1/1/2025	Can't Afford to Pay Fine: Traffic and Other Infractions *[same as CR-320]*
TR-321	1/1/2025	Can't Afford to Pay Fine: Traffic and Other Infractions (Court Order) *[same as CR-321]*
TR-500-INFO	5/13/2022	*[Revoked]* Instructions to Defendant for Remote Video Proceeding
TR-505*	5/13/2022	*[Revoked]* Notice and Waiver of Rights and Request for Remote Video Arraignment and Trial
TR-510*	5/13/2022	*[Revoked]* Notice and Waiver of Rights and Request for Remote Video Proceeding
TR-INST	1/1/2025	Notice to Appear and Related Forms

TRANSITIONAL HOUSING MISCONDUCT

TH-100*	9/1/2018	Petition for Order Prohibiting Abuse or Program Misconduct
TH-110*	9/1/2018	Order to Show Cause and Temporary Restraining Order
TH-120*	9/1/2018	Participant's Response to Petition for Order Prohibiting Abuse or Program Misconduct
TH-130*	9/1/2018	Order After Hearing on Petition for Order Prohibiting Abuse or Program Misconduct

---

* Adopted for mandatory use by all courts.

TH-140*	9/1/2018	Proof of Personal Service
TH-190	9/1/2018	Restatement of Transitional Housing Misconduct Act (Civil Code section 1954.10 et seq.)
TH-200*	9/1/2018	Instructions for Program Operators (Civil Code section 1954.10 et seq.)
TH-210*	9/1/2018	Instructions for Participants (Civil Code section 1954.10 et seq.)

UNLAWFUL DETAINER (LANDLORD/TENANT)

UD-100	1/1/2024	Complaint—Unlawful Detainer
UD-101*	1/1/2024	Plaintiff's Mandatory Cover Sheet and Supplemental Allegations—Unlawful Detainer
UD-104	10/5/2020	Cover Sheet for Declaration of Covid-19—Related Financial Distress
UD-104(A)	10/5/2020	Attachment—Declaration of Covid-19—Related Financial Distress
UD-105	1/1/2024	Answer—Unlawful Detainer
UD-106	1/1/2014	Form Interrogatories—Unlawful Detainer [same as DISC-003]
UD-110	1/1/2024	Judgment—Unlawful Detainer
UD-110H	1/1/2024	Judgment—Unlawful Detainer Attachment [renumbered from UD-110S]
UD-110P	1/1/2024	Judgment—Unlawful Detainer Partial Eviction Attachment
UD-110S	1/1/2024	[Renumbered] Judgment—Unlawful Detainer Attachment [renumbered to UD-110H]
UD-115	1/1/2003	Stipulation for Entry of Judgment (Unlawful Detainer)
UD-116	7/1/2003	Declaration for Default Judgment by Court (Unlawful Detainer—Civ. Proc., §585(d))
UD-120*	7/16/2022	Verification by Landlord Regarding Rental Assistance—Unlawful Detainer
UD-125*	10/1/2021	Application to Prevent Forfeiture Due to COVID-19 Rental Debt
UD-150*	1/1/2005	Request/Counter-Request To Set Case For Trial—Unlawful Detainer
UD-155	1/1/2024	Eviction Case (Unlawful Detainer) Stipulation

VEXATIOUS LITIGANTS

VL-100*	9/1/2018	Prefiling Order—Vexatious Litigant [renumbered from MC-700*]
VL-110	9/1/2018	Request to File New Litigation by Vexatious Litigant [renumbered from MC-701]
VL-115	9/1/2018	Order to File New Litigation by Vexatious Litigant [renumbered from MC-702]
VL-120	9/1/2018	Application for Order to Vacate Prefiling Order and Remove Plaintiff/Petitioner From Judicial Council Vexatious Litigant List [renumbered from MC-703]
VL-125	9/1/2018	Order on Application to Vacate Prefiling Order and Remove Plaintiff/Petitioner From Judicial Council Vexatious Litigant List [renumbered from MC-704]

WAGE GARNISHMENT

WG-001*	1/1/2012	Application For Earnings Withholding Order (Wage Garnishment) (formerly 982.5(1))
WG-002*	9/1/2023	Earnings Withholding Order
WG-003*	9/1/2023	Employee Instructions
WG-004*	1/1/2012	Earnings Withholding Order For Support (Wage Garnishment) (formerly 982.5(3))
WG-005*	9/1/2017	Employer's Return (formerly 982.5(4))
WG-006	1/1/2009	Claim of Exemption (formerly 982.5(5))
WG-007*	1/1/2007	Financial Statement [same as EJ-165*]
WG-008*	1/1/2007	Notice of Filing of Claim of Exemption (formerly 982.5(6))
WG-009*	1/2/2012	Notice of Opposition to Claim of Exemption (Wage Garnishment)
WG-010	1/1/2007	Notice of Hearing on Claim of Exemption [same as EJ-175]
WG-011	1/1/2007	Order Determining Claim of Exemption (formerly 982.5(9))
WG-012	1/1/2012	Notice of Termination or Modification of Earnings Withholding Order (Wage Garnishment) (formerly 982.5(10))
WG-020*	1/1/2007	Application for Earnings Withholding Order for Taxes (State Tax Liability) (formerly 982.5(11))
WG-021*	1/1/2007	Confidential Supplement to Application for Earnings Withholding Order for Taxes (Wage Garnishment—State Tax Liability) (formerly 982.5(11S))
WG-022*	1/1/2007	Earnings Withholding Order for Taxes (Wage Garnishment—State Tax Liability) (formerly 982.5(12))
WG-023*	1/1/2007	Notice of Hearing—Earnings Withholding Order for Taxes (State Tax Liability) (formerly 982.5(13))
WG-024*	1/1/2007	Temporary Earnings Withholding Order for Taxes (State Tax Liability) (formerly 982.5(14))
WG-025*	1/1/2007	Confidential Supplement to Temporary Earnings Withholding Order for Taxes (State Tax Liability) (formerly 982.5(14S))
WG-026*	1/1/2007	Claim of Exemption and Financial Declaration (State Tax Liability) (formerly 982.5(15))
WG-030*	9/1/2023	Earnings Withholding Order for Elder or Dependent Adult Financial Abuse
WG-035*	1/1/2012	Confidential Statement of Judgment Debtor's Social Security Number

WORKPLACE VIOLENCE PREVENTION

WV-100*	1/1/2025	Petition for Workplace Violence Restraining Orders
WV-100-INFO	1/1/2025	How Do I Get an Order to Prohibit Workplace Violence?
WV-102*	1/1/2012	[Revoked] Confidential CLETS Information (Workplace Violence Prevention)
WV-109*	1/1/2025	Notice of Court Hearing (Workplace Violence Prevention)
WV-110*	1/1/2025	Temporary Restraining Order (CLETS—TWH)

---

* Adopted for mandatory use by all courts.

WV-115*	1/1/2025	Request to Continue Court Hearing (Temporary Restraining Order) (Workplace Violence Prevention)
WV-115-INFO	1/1/2020	How to Ask for a New Hearing Date
WV-116*	1/1/2025	Order on Request to Continue Hearing (Temporary Restraining Order)
WV-120*	1/1/2025	Response to Petition for Workplace Violence Restraining Orders
WV-120-INFO	1/1/2025	How Can I Respond to a Petition for Workplace Violence Restraining Orders?
WV-130*	1/1/2025	Workplace Violence Restraining Order After Hearing (CLETS—WHO)
WV-131	1/1/2011	*[Renumbered]* Proof of Service by Mail of Completed Response (Workplace Violence)
WV-132	1/1/2011	*[Revoked]* Proof of Service by Personal Delivery of Completed Response (Workplace Violence)
WV-140*	1/1/2011	*[Renumbered]* Order After Hearing on Petition of Employer for Injunction Prohibiting Violence or Threats of Violence Against Employee (CLETS) (Workplace Violence)
WV-145	1/1/2011	*[Renumbered]* Proof of Sale or Turning In of Firearms
WV-150-INFO*	1/1/2011	*[Renumbered]* Instructions for Petitions to Prohibit Workplace Violence
WV-200	1/1/2025	Proof of Personal Service (Workplace Violence Prevention)
WV-200-INFO	1/1/2012	What Is "Proof of Personal Service"? (Workplace Violence Prevention)
WV-250	1/1/2025	Proof of Service of Response by Mail *(formerly WV-131)*
WV-260	1/1/2025	Proof of Service of Order After Hearing by Mail
WV-600*	1/1/2018	Request to Modify/Terminate Workplace Violence Restraining Order
WV-610*	1/1/2018	Notice of Hearing on Request to Modify/Terminate Workplace Violence Restraining Order
WV-620*	1/1/2018	Response to Request to Modify/Terminate Workplace Violence Restraining Order
WV-630*	1/1/2018	Order on Request to Modify/Terminate Workplace Violence Restraining Order
WV-700*	1/1/2025	Request to Renew Restraining Order
WV-710*	1/1/2025	Notice of Hearing to Renew Restraining Order
WV-715*	1/1/2025	Request to Reschedule Hearing to Renew Restraining Order
WV-716*	1/1/2025	Order to Reschedule Hearing to Renew Restraining Order
WV-720*	1/1/2025	Response to Request to Renew Restraining Order
WV-730*	1/1/2025	Order Renewing Workplace Violence Restraining Order
WV-800	9/1/2024	Receipt for Firearms and Firearm Parts
WV-800-INFO	1/1/2023	How Do I Turn In, Sell, or Store My Firearms and Firearm Parts?

* Adopted for mandatory use by all courts.

Appendix B
Liability Limits of a Parent or Guardian Having Custody and Control of a Minor for the Torts of a Minor
(Civ. Code, § 1714.1)

Formula

Pursuant to Civil Code section 1714.1, the joint and several liability limit of a parent or guardian having custody and control of a minor under subdivisions (a) and (b) for each tort of the minor shall be computed and adjusted as follows:

$$\text{Adjusted limit} = \left[\frac{\text{Current CCPI} - \text{January 1, 1995, CCPI}}{\text{January 1, 1995, CCPI}} + 1 \right] \times \text{January 1, 1995, limit}$$

Definition

"CCPI" means the California Consumer Price Index, as established by the California Department of Industrial Relations.

July 1, 2021, calculation and adjustment

The joint and several liability of a parent or guardian having custody and control of a minor under Civil Code section 1714.1, subdivision (a) or (b), effective July 1, 2021, shall not exceed $47,100 for each tort.

The calculation is as follows:

$$\$47,081.68 = \left[\frac{285.315 - 151.5}{151.5} + 1 \right] \times \$25,000$$

Under section 1714.1, subdivision (c), the adjusted limit is rounded to the nearest hundred dollars, so the dollar amount of the adjusted limit is rounded to $47,100.

Appendix B amended effective July 1, 2021; adopted effective January 1, 1997; previously amended effective January 1, 1999, January 1, 2001, January 1, 2003, January 1, 2005, January 1, 2007, February 18, 2009, January 1, 2011, July 1, 2013, July 1, 2015, July 1, 2017, and July 1, 2019.

Appendix C
Guidelines for the Operation of Family Law Information Centers and Family Law Facilitator Offices

(1) *Independence and integrity*

An attorney and other staff working in a family law information center or family law facilitator office should, at all times, uphold the independence and integrity of the center or office in conjunction with its role within the court and the legal system.

(2) *Role as representative of the court*

An attorney and other staff working in a family law information center or family law facilitator office should recognize that they are representatives of the court and, as such, should avoid all acts of impropriety and the appearance of impropriety at all times.

(3) *Impartiality and diligence*

An attorney working in a family law information center or family law facilitator office should perform his or her duties impartially and diligently. Impartiality means delivering services to all eligible litigants in a neutral manner. Diligence requires that the attorney provide the litigants with pertinent information to allow them to bring their matter before the court. This may include appropriate referrals to other resources as well as direct information and assistance at the center or office. The attorney should require similar conduct of all personnel.

(4) *Respect and patience*

An attorney working in a family law information center or family law facilitator office should be aware of the social and economic differences that exist among litigants and maintain patience with and respect for the litigants who seek the services of the center or office. The attorney should require similar conduct of all personnel. However, if a litigant becomes unruly or disruptive, the attorney may ask the litigant to leave the center or office.

(5) *Bias and prejudice*

An attorney working in a family law information center or family law facilitator office should assist the litigants who seek assistance without exhibiting bias or prejudice based on race, sex, religion, national origin, disability, age, sexual orientation, socioeconomic status, or other similar factors, and should require similar conduct of all personnel.

(6) *Competent legal information*

An attorney working in a family law information center or family law facilitator office and his or her staff should provide the litigants who seek assistance with procedural and legal information and education so that the litigants will have increased access to the court. Family law information centers and family law facilitator offices are not intended to replace private counsel.

(7) *Full notification of limits of service*

An attorney working in a family law information center or family law facilitator office should ensure that conspicuous notice is given, as set forth in Family Code section 10013, that no attorney-client relationship exists between the center or office, or its staff, and the family law litigant. The notice should include the advice that the absence of an attorney-client relationship means that communications between the party and the family law information center or family law facilitator office are not privileged and that the services may be provided to the other party. Additionally, the family law information center must use *Family Law Information Center Disclosure* (form FL-945) or provide similar notice. The family law facilitator office must use *Office of the Family Law Facilitator Disclosure* (form FL-940) or provide similar notice of the warnings set forth in Family Code section 10015.

(8) *Public comment*

An attorney working in a family law information center or family law facilitator office and his or her staff must at all times comply with Family Code section 10014, and must not make any public comment about the litigants or about any pending or impending matter in the court.

(9) *Gifts or payments*

An attorney working in a family law information center or family law facilitator office and his or her staff should not accept any gifts, favors, bequests, or loans from the litigants whom they assist, since this may give the appearance of impropriety or partiality—except for nominal gifts such as baked goods, as allowed by local rules.

(10) *Communications with bench officer*

An attorney working in a family law information center or family law facilitator office and his or her staff should avoid all ex parte communications with a bench officer, except as provided in accordance with Family Code section 10005. In addition, an attorney should avoid all communications with a bench officer in which he or she offers an opinion on how the bench officer should rule on a pending case. Communications about purely procedural matters or the functioning of the court are allowed and encouraged.

(11) *Communications with represented litigants*

An attorney working in a family law information center or family law facilitator office and his or her staff should not assist a litigant who is represented by an attorney unless the litigant's attorney consents or the court has referred the litigant for assistance.

Advisory Committee Comment

These guidelines are promulgated as directed by former Family Code section 15010(f). They are intended to guide the attorneys providing assistance in family law information centers and family law facilitator offices created by Family Code sections 10000–10015.

These guidelines are not intended to be exclusive. Attorneys who work in the family law information centers and family law facilitator offices are also bound by the State Bar Act, the Rules of Professional Conduct, local and state court employee rules, and relevant opinions of the California courts to the extent that they apply.

The authorities that govern attorney conduct in California apply to all California attorneys regardless of the capacity in which they are acting in a particular matter. (*Librarian v. State Bar* 25 Cal.2d. 314 (1944).) "Permission" not to comply with these authorities may not be given by the State Bar. (*Sheffield v. State Bar* 22 Cal.2d. 627 (1943).)

Thus, California attorneys, regardless of the capacity in which they are performing in a particular matter, must conform their conduct to the governing California authorities. However, because the disciplinary authorities are activity-specific, not all authorities apply in all instances. For example, a transactional attorney who never appears in court is not likely to be at risk of violating the rules that govern court appearances. The transactional attorney is not immune from those rules; the nature of his or her practice simply minimizes the impact of those rules upon the services he or she performs. Thus, although center and facilitator attorneys will not be immune from the governing authorities, certain rules and requirements will apply more directly to the nature of the services being provided than will others.

Just as the Rules of Professional Conduct are activity-specific in general professional practice, so are center and facilitator office attorneys. Although the Rules of Professional Conduct and related authorities will apply generally, and will apply directly when the attorney is representing clients in an attorney-client relationship, they will not directly be invoked when a center or facilitator attorney provides assistance to a nonclient in a court-based program that does not, by definition, represent "clients."

To the extent that the above-mentioned Family Code sections establish by law that there is no attorney-client relationship or privilege for services provided by a family law information center or family law facilitator office, the Rules of Professional Conduct that specifically address the attorney-client relationship and the conduct of that relationship would not be invoked if the attorney were providing services within the scope of those sections. However, the Rules of Professional Conduct would govern attorneys employed by centers or facilitator offices who also continued to maintain a law practice and worked with actual clients in an attorney-client relationship.

Although center and facilitator office attorneys are not exempt from the Rules of Professional Conduct, the employing court may promulgate guidelines for the services provided by a center or facilitator office that are more applicable to the center or office than are some of the Rules of Professional Conduct, however, any such restrictions must still be fully consistent with the Rules of Professional Conduct. The principles set forth in the California Code of Judicial Ethics are often more applicable to the centers and facilitator offices and are consistent with the Rules of Professional Conduct. Those principles form the basis for the guidelines contained in these standards. The court may enforce these guidelines through its employee disciplinary process for court employees. Following are the areas of the Rules of Professional Conduct where these guidelines provide standards that are more applicable to the role of the family law information center or family law facilitator office as an entity of the court.

Rule 2-100 (Communication With a Represented Party)—see proposed guideline 11 (Communication with represented litigants).

Rule 2-400 (Prohibited Discriminatory Conduct in a Law Practice)—see proposed guideline 5 (Bias and prejudice);

Rule 3-110 (Failing to Act Competently)—see proposed guidelines 3 (Impartiality and diligence) and 6 (Competent legal information);

Rule 3-120 (Sexual Relations With Client)—see proposed guideline 2 (Role as representative of the court);

Rule 3-200 (Prohibited Objectives of Employment)—see proposed guideline 2 (Role as representative of the court);

Rule 3-210 (Advising the Violation of Law)—see proposed guideline 2 (Role as representative of the court);

Rule 3-320 (Relationship With Other Party's Lawyer)—see proposed guideline 2 (Role as representative of the court);

Rule 4-300 (Purchasing Property at a Foreclosure or a Sale Subject to Judicial Review)—see proposed guideline 2 (Role as representative of the court);

Rule 4-400 (Gifts From Client)—see proposed guideline 9 (Gifts or payments);

Rule 5-120 (Trial Publicity)—see proposed guideline 8 (Public comment);

Rule 5-220 (Suppression of Evidence)—see proposed guideline 2 (Role as representative of the court);

Rule 5-300 (Contact With Officials)—see proposed guideline 10 (Communications with bench officers);

Rule 5-310 (Prohibited Contact With Witnesses)—see proposed guideline 2 (Role as representative of the court); and

Rule 5-320 (Contact With Jurors)—see proposed guideline 2 (Role as representative of the court).

Appendix D
Judicial Council Governance Policies

MARCH 2021

Judicial Council Governance Policies

The Judicial Council is the policymaking body of the California courts, the largest court system in the nation. Under the leadership of the Chief Justice and in accordance with the California Constitution, the council is responsible for ensuring the consistent, independent, impartial, and accessible administration of justice. Members of the council are appointed by the Chief Justice. Appointees from the Board of Trustees of the State Bar of California and both houses of the Legislature also serve as members of the council. Together the members serve to carry out judicial branch goals. Judicial Council staff implements the council's policies, and the goals and priorities of the council are set forth in *The Strategic Plan for California's Judicial Branch*:

   I. Access, Fairness, and Diversity
   II. Independence and Accountability
   III. Modernization of Management and Administration
   IV. Quality of Justice and Service to the Public
   V. Education for Branchwide Professional Excellence
   VI. Branchwide Infrastructure for Service Excellence
   VII. Adequate, Stable, and Predictable Funding for a Fully Functioning Branch

GOVERNANCE PROCESS

1. Responsibilities of the Council

The council establishes goals and policies for California's judicial branch of government. The council is directly responsible for the following:

a. Establishing broad goals and policies that set the direction and priorities for the continuous improvement of California's system for the administration of justice. These goals and policies include fundamental goals such as promoting public access to the justice system, increasing responsiveness to the needs of court users of diverse backgrounds, and upholding the rule of law and the impartiality of judges as constitutional officers.

b. Establishing standards for the performance and accountability of the administrative operations and procedures of the branch. These standards address the diverse needs of court users, employ modern management practices that implement and sustain innovative ideas and effective practices, and report on judicial branch performance to the public, the Legislature, the Governor, and the courts.

c. Developing and maintaining administrative, technological, and physical infrastructures, including court facilities, that enhance accessibility to the courts and support the needs of the people of California and the judicial branch.

d. Taking all appropriate steps to develop and establish the judicial branch's fiscal priorities, secure appropriate funding for the judicial branch, establish fiscal and budget policies for the branch, allocate branch appropriations to the courts and the council, and ensure accountability through reporting on the use of its public resources to the legislative and executive branches of state government and to the public.

e. Sponsoring and taking positions on pending legislation consistent with the council's established goals and priorities to support consistent and effective statewide programs and policies that provide for the highest quality of administration of justice, and that promote an impartial judiciary.

f. Developing high-quality education and professional development opportunities for all judicial branch personnel to meet public needs and to enhance public trust and confidence in the courts.

g. Communicating with and reporting to the legislative and executive branches of state government to advance judicial branch goals, and account for the use of public funds and resources.

2. Council Policymaking

The Judicial Council establishes judicial branch policy for the improvement of an independent and impartial justice system that meets public needs and enhances public trust and confidence in the courts. The council develops policy in consultation with the people of California, court leadership, judicial officers, Judicial Council advisory bodies, employees in the judicial branch, the State Bar of California, advocacy groups, the Legislature, the Governor, and other government entities and justice system partners.

The principal focus of the Judicial Council is to establish policies that emphasize long-term strategic leadership and that align with judicial branch goals. Council policymaking is focused on the beneficiaries of the policy, the results to be achieved, the costs that may be incurred, and the corresponding judicial branch goals.

To enable the council to make well-informed strategic decisions, all policy proposals submitted for council consideration by internal committees, advisory bodies, the Administrative Director, and staff should address the following:

- Beneficiaries of the policy;
- Results to be achieved;
- Costs that may be incurred;
- Each corresponding judicial branch goal, objective, and anticipated outcome;
- Previous council action on the issue or policy;
- Comments from interested parties;
- Analysis of the benefits and risks of the proposals; and
- Analysis of the strengths and weaknesses of alternative options and an explanation of their implications.

3. Maintenance of Governance Policies and Principles

Every three years, the Judicial Council conducts a review of its governance policies and principles and determines whether any revisions are needed. The Executive and Planning Committee monitors the regular implementation of the governance policies and principles.

In order to ensure that new council members have the knowledge and understanding needed to perform their duties effectively, they are oriented to the council's governance policies and principles as well as the council's history of policymaking on key topics, such as court facilities, fiscal appropriations, and infrastructure initiatives. On an annual basis, the chair of the Executive and Planning Committee reviews the governance policies and principles at a council meeting with members.

4. Internal Committees

a. Executive and Planning Committee

The Executive and Planning Committee makes regular reports to the council on its actions. Its responsibilities are outlined in California Rules of Court, rule 10.11, and summarized below.

   i. Oversees the council's strategic planning process.
   ii. Oversees the council's policies and procedures regarding court facilities.
   iii. Establishes agendas for council meetings.
   iv. Develops a schedule of topics the council intends to consider for making policy.
   v. Makes recommendations to the council regarding governance.
   vi. Recommends candidates to the Chief Justice for appointment to the council and its advisory bodies.

b. Rules Committee

The Rules Committee makes regular reports to the council on its actions. Its responsibilities are outlined in California Rules of Court, rule 10.13, and summarized below.

   i. Identifies the need for new rules, standards, and forms.
   ii. Establishes and publishes procedures for the proposal, adoption, and approval of rules of court, forms, and standards of judicial administration that ensure that relevant input from the public is solicited and considered.
   iii. Reviews proposed rules, standards, and forms, and circulates those proposals for public comment in accordance with its procedures and guidelines.

iv. Provides guidelines for the style and format of rules, forms, and standards and ensures that proposals are consistent with the guidelines.
v. Ensures that proposals for new or amended rules, standards, and forms do not conflict with statutes or other rules.
vi. Determines whether proposals for new or amended rules, standards, or forms have complied with its procedures.

c. Legislation Committee

The Legislation Committee makes regular reports to the council on its actions. Its responsibilities are outlined in California Rules of Court, rule 10.12, and summarized below.
i. Represents the Judicial Council's position with other agencies and entities, such as the Legislature, the Governor's Office, the State Bar of California, local government, local bar associations, and other court-related professional associations.
ii. Reviews and makes recommendations on proposals for Judicial Council sponsored legislation; reviews pending bills; determines positions consistent with the council's previous policy decisions; and oversees advocacy for those positions.

d. Technology Committee

The Technology Committee makes regular reports to the council on its actions. Its responsibilities are outlined in California Rules of Court, rule 10.16, and summarized below.
i. Oversees the council's policies concerning technology and is responsible in partnership with the courts for coordinating with the Administrative Director and all internal committees, advisory committees, commissions, working groups, task forces, justice partners, and stakeholders on technological issues relating to the branch and the courts.
ii. Responsible for ensuring that council policies are complied with, and that specific projects proceed on schedule and within scope and budget.
iii. Seeks reports and recommendations from the Administrative Director, the courts, and stakeholders on technology issues. It ensures that technology reports to the council are clear, comprehensive, and provide relevant options so that the council can make effective final technology policy decisions.

e. Judicial Branch Budget Committee

The Judicial Branch Budget Committee makes regular reports to the council on its actions. Its responsibilities are outlined in California Rules of Court, rule 10.15, and summarized below.
i. Ensures that proposed judicial branch budgets, allocation schedules, and related budgetary issues are brought to the Judicial Council in a timely manner and in a format that permits the council to establish funding priorities in the context of the council's annual program objectives, statewide policies, and long-range strategic and operational plans.
ii. Reviews and makes recommendations annually to the council on submitted budget change proposals for the judicial branch, coordinates these budget change proposals, and ensures that they are submitted to the council in a timely manner.
iii. Reviews and makes recommendations on the use of statewide emergency funding for the judicial branch.
iv. Reviews and makes recommendations on the funding of grants on programs assigned to the committee.
v. Acts on other assignments referred to it by the council.

f. Litigation Management Committee

The Litigation Management Committee makes regular reports to the council on its actions. Its responsibilities are outlined in California Rules of Court, rule 10.14, and summarized below.
i. The committee oversees litigation and claims against trial and appellate courts, the Judicial Council, and employees of those bodies that seek recovery of $100,000 or more, or raise important policy issues.
ii. Important policy or court operations issues may include whether to initiate litigation on behalf of a court, when to defend a challenged court practice, or how to resolve disputes where the outcome might have statewide implications.

5. Role of Advisory Committees

Advisory committees under California Rules of Court, rule 10.34(a) are standing committees created by rule of court or the Chief Justice to make recommendations and offer policy alternatives to the Judicial Council for improving the administration of justice within their designated areas of focus by doing the following:
i. Identifying issues and concerns affecting court administration and recommending solutions to the council.
ii. Proposing necessary changes to rules, standards, forms, and jury instructions.
iii. Reviewing pending legislation and making recommendations to the Legislation Committee on whether to support or oppose it.
iv. Recommending new legislation to the council.
v. Recommending to the council pilot projects and other programs to evaluate new procedures or practices.
vi. Acting on assignments referred by the council or an internal committee.
vii. Making other appropriate recommendations to the council.

6. Council-Staff Relationship

Officially passed motions of the council, and decisions and instructions of the Chief Justice, are binding on the Administrative Director. Decisions or instructions of individual council members or internal and advisory bodies are binding on the Administrative Director if the council or its chair has specifically delegated such exercise of authority.

The Administrative Director has sole authority to assign, supervise, and direct staff. The Administrative Director is responsible for ensuring the completeness and quality of reports and other work product presented to the council. Council members may from time to time request information or assistance from staff, unless in the Director's opinion such requests require an unreasonable amount of staff time or become disruptive. Council members and advisory body members may individually provide information to the Administrative Director on the performance of staff or staff agency to the council.

The Administrative Director, as secretary to the council, may attend and participate in the meetings of each internal committee.

Appendix D amended effective March 12, 2021; previously amended effective January 1, 2016, January 1, 2018, and April 16, 2020.

2021 Note: The appendix, Operating Standards for Judicial Council Advisory Bodies, was removed as part of the amendment to Appendix D, effective March 12, 2021.

Appendix E
Guidelines for Determining Financial Eligibility for County Payment of the Cost of Counsel Appointed by the Court in Proceedings Under the Guardianship-Conservatorship Law

1. Purpose
2. Persons responsible for payment of the cost of appointed counsel
3. Cost of appointed counsel
4. Presumed eligibility for county payment
5. Determination of responsible person's obligation for the cost of appointed counsel
6. Apportionment
7. Private appointed counsel for conservatee under section 1470
8. Amount payable by the county

1. Purpose

These guidelines are adopted to implement Probate Code section 1470(c)(3), which provides that the Judicial Council shall adopt guidelines to assist in determining financial eligibility for county payment of all or part of the reasonable sum fixed by the court for compensation and expenses of counsel appointed by the court under chapter 4 of part 1 of division 4 of the Probate Code.

2. Persons responsible for payment of the cost of appointed counsel

Except to the extent that they are determined to be unable to pay for all or any portion of the cost of appointed counsel under paragraph 5 of these guidelines, the following persons or estates of persons (referred to collectively as the "responsible person") are responsible for the payment of that cost:

A. The estate of the ward or proposed ward in a guardianship proceeding under section 1470;

B. The parent or parents of the ward or proposed ward in a guardianship proceeding under section 1470;

C. The estate of a conservatee or proposed conservatee in a conservatorship proceeding under sections 1470–1472;

D. The conservatee or proposed conservatee, if he or she has no estate, in a conservatorship proceeding under sections 1471–1472;

E. The person alleged to lack legal capacity in a proceeding to authorize a particular transaction in community property under sections 1471–1472, to the extent the court does not order the cost paid from the proceeds of the transaction under section 1472(a)(3); and

F. The health care patient in a proceeding to determine his or her capacity to make a health care decision under sections 1471–1472.

3. Cost of appointed counsel

The cost of appointed counsel is the reasonable sum fixed by the court after the performance of legal services under Probate Code section 1470 or section 1472 for the compensation and expenses of appointed counsel.

4. Presumed eligibility for county payment

Except as provided in paragraph 7, the person responsible for payment of the cost of appointed counsel is presumed to be eligible for payment by the county of that cost if the person satisfies one or more of the following three conditions:

A. The responsible person is eligible for:

(1) Supplemental Security Income (SSI) and State Supplementary Payment (SSP);

(2) Medi-Cal;

(3) General Assistance or General Relief (GA/GR) Program (county general relief);

(4) Cash Assistance Program for [aged, blind, and disabled legal] Immigrants (CAPI);

(5) CalWORKs (California Work Opportunity and Responsibility to Kids) or Tribal (Native American) TANF (Temporary Assistance for Needy Families) grant program;

(6) CalFresh (Supplemental Nutrition Assistance Program (SNAP)) or California Food Assistance Program (CFAP), a California program for immigrants not eligible for federal SNAP; or

(7) In-Home Supportive Services (IHSS);

B. The responsible person's income is 125 percent or less of current federal poverty guidelines, updated periodically in the Federal Register by the United States Department of Health and Human Services; or

C. The responsible person, as individually determined by the court, cannot pay the cost of appointed counsel without using funds that would be normally used to pay for the common necessaries of life for the responsible person and his or her family.

5. Determination of responsible person's obligation for the cost of appointed counsel

If the court finds that the responsible person, including a responsible person described in paragraph 4, can pay all or a portion of the cost of appointed counsel, can pay those costs in installments, or can pay those costs under some other equitable arrangement without using money that normally would pay for the common necessaries of life for the responsible person and the responsible person's family, the court may order the responsible person to pay appointed counsel directly, reimburse the county for the costs of appointed counsel paid by the county, or both, in part or on such other terms as the court determines are fair and reasonable under the circumstances.

6. Apportionment

If the responsible person is the estate of a ward or proposed ward and one or both of his or her parents, the court may allocate the amount determined to be payable by the responsible person under paragraph 5 among them in any proportions the court deems just.

7. Private appointed counsel for conservatee under section 1470

A conservatee or proposed conservatee for whom private counsel is appointed under Probate Code section 1470 is ineligible for payment by the county of any portion of the cost of appointed counsel.

8. Amount payable by the county

Except as provided in paragraph 7, the amount payable by the county for the cost of appointed counsel is all or any part of the cost that the court determines that the responsible person cannot pay under paragraph 5.

Appendix E adopted effective January 1, 2013.

Advisory Committee Comment

The guidelines placed in Appendix E to the California Rules of Court are not rules of court. They are based in part on the conditions for granting an initial court fee waiver under Government Code section 68632(a)–(c). For the purposes of these guidelines as well as of that Government Code section, the term "common necessaries of life" has the same meaning it had in Code of Civil Procedure section 706.051(c)(1) before the amendment of that section effective on January 1, 2012. (Assem. Bill 1388; Stats. 2011, ch. 694, § 1.)

The 2012 amendment of section 706.051(c)(1) completely eliminated "common necessaries of life" from that code section. The deleted phrase referred to an exception to the exemption provided in the section from an earnings withholding order for amounts the debtor can prove are necessary to support himself or herself and his or her family, often referred to as the support exemption. In other words, under former section 706.051(c)(1), the support exemption of section 706.051(b) would not apply to shield the debtor from an earnings withholding order to collect a debt incurred to purchase the "common necessaries of life."

The following appellate cases discussed the meaning of "common necessaries of life" as that phrase was used in section 706.051(c)(1) and predecessor code sections that used the phrase for the same purpose:

- A debt for hospital services to defendant or his family was based on the common necessaries of life. (*J. J. MacIntyre Co. v. Duren* (1981) 118 Cal.App.3d Supp. 16.)
- The performance of legal services and the advancement of costs of litigation giving rise to award to an attorney in marriage dissolution action qualified as "common necessaries of life" for the benefit of the debtor's indigent wife, thereby permitting the attorney to enforce the award by writ of execution on

the husband's earnings against his claim of the support exemption. (*In re Marriage of Pallesi* (1977) 73 Cal.App.3d 424.)

- "Common necessaries of life," in former section 690.11 (repealed) exempting debts incurred for common necessaries of life from a statute protecting all of a judgment debtor's earnings from execution or attachment if earnings were necessary for the support of the debtor's family, did not refer to "necessaries" in the broad sense, but meant things that are ordinarily required for everyone's sustenance. (*Ratzlaff v. Portillo* (1971) 14 Cal.App.3d 1013.)
- Attorney's fees former wife incurred in obtaining divorce were not common "necessaries of life" within the meaning of former section 690.11 (repealed). (*Lentfoehr v. Lentfoehr* (1955) 134 Cal.App.2d Supp. 905.)
- "Common necessaries of life," as used in former section 690.11 (repealed), exempting all of the earnings of a debtor if necessary for the use or support of debtor's family residing within the state, except as against the collection of debts incurred by debtor, his wife, or family for common necessaries of life—meant those things that are commonly required by persons for their sustenance regardless of their employment or status. (*Los Angeles Finance Co. v. Flores* (1952) 110 Cal.App.2d Supp. 850.)
- In proceedings supplemental to execution, the debtor was required to pay one-half of a check for $47.50, which was in her possession, and which had been received as salary from the Works Progress Administration, in partial satisfaction of a judgment based on a necessary of life, although money may have been needed by debtor for the support of herself and her family. (*Medical Finance Association v. Short* (1939) 36 Cal.App.2d Supp. 745.)

Appendix F
Guidelines for the Juvenile Dependency Counsel Collections Program (JDCCP)

1. Legal Authority
2. Effective Date
3. Responsible Person—Definition
4. No Liability
5. Determination of Cost of Legal Services
6. Determination of Ability to Pay; Financial Evaluation Officer; Statewide Standard
7. Judicial Proceeding Following Determination of Ability to Reimburse Cost
8. Reevaluation of Ability to Pay
9. Frequency of Determination of Ability to Pay and Assessment
10. Collection Services
11. Recovery of Program Implementation Costs
12. Remittance and Reporting of Collected Revenue
13. Program Data Reporting
14. Allocation of Collected Funds to Trial Courts
15. Technical Assistance

1. Legal Authority

These guidelines are adopted under the authority of section 903.47 of the Welfare and Institutions Code,[1] which mandates that the Judicial Council "establish a program to collect reimbursements from the person liable for the costs of counsel appointed to represent parents or minors pursuant to Section 903.1 in dependency proceedings." (Welf. & Inst. Code, § 903.47(a).) As part of the program, the statute requires the council to "[a]dopt a statewide standard for determining [a responsible person's] ability to pay reimbursements for counsel." This standard must "at a minimum include the family's income, their necessary obligations, the number of people dependent on this income, and the cost-effectiveness of the program." (Ibid.) The statute also requires the council to "[a]dopt policies and procedures allowing a court to recover from the money collected the costs associated with implementing the reimbursements program."[2] These policies and procedures must, in turn, "limit the amount of money a court may recover to a reasonable proportion of the reimbursements collected and provide the terms and conditions under which a court may use a third party to collect reimbursements." (Ibid.)

Section 903.1 imposes liability on specified persons and estates for the cost of legal services provided to the child and directly to those persons in dependency proceedings. These responsible persons are jointly and severally liable for the cost of the child's representation. If the petition is dismissed at or before the jurisdictional hearing, though, no liability attaches.

Section 904 authorizes the trial court to determine the cost of dependency-related legal services using methods or procedures approved by the Judicial Council.

Under section 903.47(b), the court may designate a court financial evaluation officer (FEO) or, with the consent of the county, a county financial evaluation officer (FEO) to determine a responsible person's ability to pay the cost of court-appointed counsel. The court refers any responsible person to the designated FEO at the close of the dispositional hearing under section 903.45(b) unless that referral would not be cost-effective under section 903.47(a)(1)(A). The FEO then determines the responsible person's ability to pay all or part of the cost of dependency-related legal services under the procedures and within the limits set by section 903.45(b). The statutory scheme, particularly sections 901 and 903, prohibits the assessed amount from exceeding the actual cost of the legal services.

Sections 903.1(c) and 903.47(a)(2) direct each court to deposit collected reimbursements in the same manner as it deposits revenue collected under section 68085.1 of the Government Code. The Judicial Council must then transfer the remitted reimbursements to the Trial Court Trust Fund (TCTF).

Except as otherwise authorized by law, the Judicial Council must allocate the funds collected through the reimbursement program to reduce court-appointed attorney caseloads to the Judicial Council–approved standard. In determining allocations, the council must give priority to courts with the highest attorney caseloads that also demonstrate the ability to immediately improve outcomes for parents and children as the result of lower caseloads.

2. Effective Date

These guidelines are effective for all dependency proceedings filed on or after January 1, 2013. Amendments adopted after that date will take effect as specified by the Judicial Council, but no sooner than 30 days after the council meeting at which they are adopted.

3. Responsible Person—Definition

"Responsible person," as used in these guidelines, refers to the father, mother, spouse, or any other person liable for the support of a child; the estate of that person; or the estate of the child, as made liable under section 903.1(a) for the cost of dependency-related legal services rendered to the child or directly to that person.

4. No Liability

Under section 903.1(b), a responsible person is not liable for, and the court will not seek reimbursement of, the cost of legal services under section 903.1(a) if the dependency petition is dismissed at or before the jurisdictional hearing.

5. Determination of Cost of Legal Services

The court is charged with determining the cost of dependency-related legal services. In doing so, the court may adopt **one** of the three methods in (a)–(c). In no event will the court seek reimbursement of an amount that exceeds the actual cost of legal services already provided to the children and the responsible person in the proceeding. The court may update its determination of the cost of legal services on an annual basis, on the conclusion of the dependency proceedings in the juvenile court, or on the cessation of representation of the child or responsible person.

(a) Actual Cost

The court may determine the actual cost of the legal services provided to a child or responsible person in a dependency proceeding. The court should base this determination on the actual cost incurred per event in the proceeding, per hour billed, or per client represented.

(b) Cost Model

The court may determine the cost of legal services provided to a child or responsible person in a dependency proceeding by applying the Uniform Regional Cost Model available on *jrn.courts.ca.gov* or from *jdccp@jud.ca.gov*. Use of the cost model as described in this section will ensure that the court seeks reimbursement of an amount that most closely approximates, but does not exceed, the actual cost incurred by the court.

(1) *Time Allocated to Each Event per Attorney*

The court will calculate the time allocated to each event in a local dependency proceeding by

(A) Dividing the normative caseload of 141 clients per attorney by the actual caseload reported by the dependency attorneys in the county in which the court sits, and then

(B) Multiplying the result by the number of hours allocated to the type of event in question by the Dependency Counsel Caseload Study.[3]

(2) *Cost of Each Event per Attorney*

---

[1] Except as otherwise specified, all statutory references in these guidelines are to the Welfare and Institutions Code.

[2] This section defines *costs associated with implementing the reimbursements program* as the "court costs of assessing a parent's ability to pay for court-appointed counsel and the costs to collect delinquent reimbursements."

[3] See Center for Families, Children & Cts., Admin. Off. of Cts. Rep., *Court-Appointed Counsel: Caseload Standards, Service Delivery Models, and Contract Administration* (June 23, 2004), p. 3 & appen.

The court will then calculate the cost of each type of event by multiplying the time allocated to the event by

(A) The actual hourly rate billed to the court for the provision of dependency-related legal services, or

(B) The lowest actual hourly rate billed for dependency-related legal services in the region[4] in which the court is located as reported in the most recent survey of those rates, or

(C) The approved hourly rate for the region in which the court is located as provided in the Caseload Funding Model (CFM) approved by the Judicial Council in October 2007 and June 2008.[5]

(3) *Cost of Proceeding per Attorney*

The court will then calculate the cost of the services provided by an attorney in a dependency proceeding by adding together the costs of each event that has occurred in the proceeding at issue.

(c) Flat Rate Fee Structure

The court may adopt a flat rate fee structure for the cost of legal services in a dependency proceeding as long as the fees charged do not exceed the actual cost of the services provided in that proceeding up to and including the date of the determination and assessment.

6. Determination of Ability to Pay; Financial Evaluation Officer; Statewide Standard

(a) Referral for Financial Evaluation

At the close of the dispositional hearing, the court will order any responsible person present at the hearing to appear before a designated financial evaluation officer (FEO) for a determination of the responsible person's ability to pay reimbursement of all or part of the cost of legal services for which he or she is liable under section 903.1(a), unless the court finds that, given the resources of the court, evaluation by an FEO would not be a cost-effective method of determining the responsible person's ability to pay.

(1) *Responsible Person Not Present at Dispositional Hearing*

If a responsible person is not present at the dispositional hearing, the court will issue proper notice and an order for him or her to appear before an FEO for determination of his or her ability to pay reimbursement of all or part of the cost of legal services for which he or she is liable under section 903.1(a) unless the court finds that evaluation by an FEO would not be a cost-effective method of determining the responsible person's ability to pay given the resources of the court.

To issue proper notice to a responsible person not present at the hearing at which appearance for a financial evaluation is ordered, the court should send *Order to Appear for Financial Evaluation* (form JV-131) or the equivalent local form by first-class mail to that person's mailing address of record.

(2) *Alternative Methods*

If the court finds that evaluation by an FEO is not cost-effective, it may take whatever steps it deems cost-effective to determine the responsible person's ability to pay.

(3) *Failure to Appear for Financial Evaluation*

If a responsible person is ordered to appear for financial evaluation, has received proper notice, and fails to appear as ordered, the FEO will recommend that the court order the responsible person to pay the full cost of legal services as determined under section 5 of these guidelines unless the next paragraph applies.

If a responsible person is not present at the hearing at which the order to appear for a financial evaluation is made, has received proper notice and an order to appear, and responds to the order by submitting a declaration that he or she is involuntarily confined and therefore not able to attend or reschedule the evaluation, the FEO or the court may presume that he or she is unable to pay reimbursement and is eligible for a waiver of liability at that time.

(4) *Proper Notice*

Proper notice to a responsible person will contain notice of all of the following:

(A) His or her right to a statement of the costs as soon as it is available;

(B) His or her procedural rights under section 27755 of the Government Code;

(C) The time limit within which his or her appearance is required; and

(D) A warning that if he or she fails to appear before the FEO, the officer will recommend that the court order him or her to pay the full cost of legal services, and that the FEO's recommendation will be a sufficient basis for the court to order payment of an amount up to the full cost.

(b) Financial Evaluation Officer

The court may either designate a court FEO to determine responsible persons' ability to reimburse the cost of legal services or, with the consent of and under terms agreed to by the county, designate a county FEO to determine responsible persons' ability to reimburse the cost of legal services.

(c) Authority of Financial Evaluation Officer

The designated FEO will conduct the evaluation under the procedures outlined in section 903.45(b). The FEO may determine a referred responsible person's ability to pay all or part of the cost of legal services for which he or she is liable, negotiate a plan for reimbursement over a set period of time based on the responsible person's financial condition, enter into an agreement with the responsible person regarding the amount to be reimbursed and the terms of reimbursement, petition the court for an order of reimbursement according to the terms agreed to with the responsible person, and refer the responsible person back to court for a hearing in the event of a lack of agreement.

(d) Standard for Determining Ability to Pay

The FEO will determine the responsible person's ability to reimburse the cost of legal services using the following standard:

(1) *Presumptive Inability to Pay; Waiver*

If a responsible person receives qualifying public benefits or [1] **qualifies for a fee waiver under the criteria of Government Code section 68632(b)(1)** at the time of the inquiry, then [2] **the person** is presumed to be unable to pay reimbursement and is eligible for a waiver of liability.

(A) *Qualifying public benefits* include benefits under any of the programs listed in Government Code section 68632(a).

(2) *Further Inquiry*

If the court has concluded as a matter of policy that further inquiry into the financial condition of persons presumed unable to pay would not be warranted or cost-effective, the inquiry may end at this point with a determination that the person is unable to pay.

If the court has concluded as a matter of policy that further inquiry into the financial condition of persons presumed unable to pay is warranted notwithstanding the presumption, the FEO may proceed to a detailed evaluation under (d)(3).

(3) *Responsible Person's Financial Condition*

The FEO may, at any time following the close of the dispositional hearing, make a detailed evaluation of a referred responsible person's financial condition at that time under section 903.45(b). Based on any relevant information submitted by the responsible person, including but not limited to a completed *Financial Declaration—Juvenile Dependency* (form JV-132) or the equivalent local form, the FEO will assess the responsible person's household income, household needs and obligations (including other court-ordered obligations), and the number of persons dependent on the household income and will determine the person's ability to pay all or part of the cost of legal services without using funds that would normally be used to pay for the common necessaries of life.

When calculating a person's household income, the FEO must exclude from consideration any benefits received from a public assistance program that determines eligibility based on need.[6]

(e) Circumstances Requiring No Petition or Order for Reimbursement

Under section 903.45(b), the FEO may not petition the court to order reimbursement of the cost of legal services, and the court will not so order, if:

(1) The responsible person has been reunified with any of the children under a court order and the FEO determines that requiring repayment would harm his or her ability to support the children;

---

[4] California trial courts are grouped into four regions based on parity in cost of living, attorney salaries, and other factors among counties in a given region. See Center for Families, Children & Cts., Admin. Off. of Cts. Rep., *DRAFT Pilot Program and Court-Appointed Counsel* (Oct. 26, 2007), pp. 7–8.

[5] See *id.*, at pp. 7–10; Trial Court Budget Working Group Rep., *Court-Appointed Counsel Compensation Model and Workload-Based Funding Methodology* (June 10, 2008).

[6] *In re S.M.* (2012) 209 Cal.App.4th 21, 28–31.

(2) The responsible person is currently receiving reunification services and the court or the FEO determines that requiring repayment will pose a barrier to reunification; or

(3) The court determines that requiring repayment would be unjust under the circumstances of the case.

(f) Amount Assessed

The FEO may, consistent with the responsible person's ability to pay, assess any amount up to the full cost determined under section 5 of these guidelines, and may recommend reimbursement in a single lump sum or in multiple installments over a set period of time.

(g) Agreement; Petition

If the responsible person agrees in writing to the FEO's written determination of the amount that the responsible person is able to reimburse and the terms of reimbursement, the FEO will petition the court for an order requiring the responsible person to reimburse the court in a manner that is reasonable and compatible with the responsible person's financial condition.

(h) Dispute; Referral

If the responsible person disputes his or her liability for the cost of legal services, the amount of that cost, the FEO's determination of his or her ability to reimburse all or part of that cost, or the terms of reimbursement, the FEO will refer the matter, with his or her written determination, back to the juvenile court for a hearing.

7. Judicial Proceeding Following Determination of Ability to Reimburse Cost

On having made a determination of the responsible person's ability to reimburse all or part of the cost of legal services, the FEO will return the matter to the juvenile court as follows:

(a) Agreement; Order

If the responsible person agrees to reimburse the court as recommended by the FEO, the FEO will prepare an agreement to be signed by the responsible person. The agreement will reflect the amount to be reimbursed and the terms under which reimbursement will be paid. The juvenile court may order the responsible person to pay reimbursement under those terms without further notice to the responsible person.

(b) Dispute; Hearing

If the matter is deemed in dispute and the FEO has referred the matter back to the juvenile court under section 6(h), the court will set and conduct a hearing under section 903.45(b).

(c) Judicial Determination

If, at the conclusion of the hearing, the court determines that the responsible person is able to reimburse all or part of the cost of legal services—including the cost of any attorney appointed to represent the responsible person at that hearing—without using funds that would normally be used to pay for the common necessaries of life, the court will set the amount to be reimbursed and order the responsible person to pay that amount to the court in a manner that the court believes reasonable and compatible with the responsible person's financial condition.

8. Reevaluation of Ability to Pay

At any time before reimbursement is complete, a responsible person may petition the court to modify or vacate the reimbursement order based on a change in circumstances affecting his or her ability to pay. The court may deny the petition without a hearing if the petition fails to state a change of circumstances. The court may grant the petition without a hearing if the petition states a change of circumstances and all parties stipulate to the requested modification.

9. Frequency of Determination of Ability to Pay and Assessment

The initial evaluation and determination of a responsible person's ability to pay reimbursement may be conducted at any time following the conclusion of the dispositional hearing. The court may order a reevaluation of a responsible person's financial condition on an annual basis, on the conclusion of the dependency proceedings in the juvenile court, or on the cessation of court-appointed representation of the child or the responsible person.

If the FEO determines on reevaluation that the responsible person is able at that time to pay all or part of the cost of legal services, the FEO may, consistent with the responsible person's ability to pay without using funds that would normally be used to pay for the common necessaries of life, assess an amount up to the full cost, as determined under section 5, of any legal services provided to the child or the responsible person and may recommend reimbursement in a single lump sum or in multiple installments over a set period of time.

10. Collection Services

(a) Court-Based Collection Services

To the extent applicable and consistent with sections 903.1 and 903.47, a court should administer the collection, processing, and deposit of court-ordered reimbursement of the cost of dependency-related legal services under the procedures in policies FIN 10.01 and FIN 10.02 of the *Trial Court Financial Policies and Procedures Manual*.

(b) Outside Collection-Services Providers

When appropriate and consistent with policy FIN 10.01, a court may use an outside collection-services provider.

(1) *Collection Services Provided by County*

If collection services are provided by the county, the agreement should be formalized by a memorandum of understanding (MOU) between the court and county. Judicial Council staff will provide a sample MOU on request. An electronic copy of the MOU, including a scanned copy of the completed signature page, must be sent to *jdccp@jud.ca.gov*.

(2) *Collection Services Provided by Private Vendor*

A court that uses a private collection service should use a vendor that has entered into a master agreement with the Judicial Council to provide comprehensive collection services. A court that uses such a vendor should complete a participation agreement and send it to Judicial Council staff via e-mail to *jdccp@jud.ca.gov*. A court may contract directly with a private vendor only on terms and conditions substantially similar to those set forth in the master agreements for comprehensive collection services available at *jrn.courts.ca.gov/programs/collections/mva.htm*.

(3) *Court Option for Judicial Council Agreement with Collection-Services Provider*

At a court's request, the Judicial Council may directly enter into an MOU with the county or an agreement with a private collection-services vendor for services under this program.

(c) Agreements Between Courts

Nothing in this section is intended to preclude a court or courts from establishing an agreement with another court or courts for one or more courts to perform services under this program on behalf of other courts, or for one or more courts to combine collection efforts under this program.

11. Recovery of Program Implementation Costs

A court may recover, from the money it has collected, its eligible program implementation costs before remitting the balance of the collected funds to the state in the manner required by Government Code section 68085.1. Eligible costs are limited by statute to the cost of determining responsible persons' ability to repay the cost of court-appointed counsel and to the cost of collecting delinquent reimbursements. If a court's eligible costs in any given month exceed the amount of revenue it has collected in that month, the court may carry the excess costs forward within the same fiscal year until sufficient revenue is collected to recover the eligible costs in full. Any program costs recovered by the court must be documented by the court and reported monthly by e-mail to *jdccp@jud.ca.gov* in a format consistent with the Cost Recovery Template available on *jrn.courts.ca.gov* or from *jdccp@jud.ca.gov*.

(a) *Delinquent Reimbursement* Defined

For purposes of this section, *delinquent reimbursement* means any reimbursement payment not received within one business day of the date it is due.

12. Remittance and Reporting of Collected Revenue

A court will remit collected revenue, less recovered costs, to the state in the same manner as required under Government Code section 68085.1 and will report this revenue on row 130 of *Court Remittance Advice* (form TC-145). The Judicial Council will deposit the revenue received through this program into the Trial Court Trust Fund as required by statute.

(a) Judicial Council Collections Agreement Option

Where the Judicial Council has entered into an MOU or an agreement with a county or a private collection-services vendor under section 10(b)(3) of these guidelines, funds will be remitted directly to the Judicial Council under the terms of the MOU or the agreement.

13. Program Data Reporting

Each court should report JDCCP data to Judicial Council staff to ensure implementation of the Legislature's intent by determining the cost-effectiveness of the program and confirming that efforts to collect reimbursement do not negatively impact reunification; to provide a basis for projecting the amount of future reimbursements; and to evaluate the JDCCP's effectiveness both statewide and at the local level.

(a) Ongoing Reporting Requirement

To support the amount remitted to the Trial Court Trust Fund, each court will report collections data annually on or before September 30, beginning September 30, 2013. The first report should cover the period from January 1, 2013, to June 30, 2013. Each court should submit its completed report attached to an e-mail message to *jdccp@jud.ca.gov*.

(1) *Data Reporting*

Judicial Council staff will provide a reporting template that solicits the following information:

(A) Total number of responsible persons evaluated in the reporting period to determine their ability to pay

(B) Number of persons in (A) found unable to pay

(C) Number of persons in (A) found able to pay but not ordered to pay under section 6(e)

(D) Number of open accounts at the beginning of the reporting period

(E) Dollar amount in open accounts at the beginning of the reporting period

(F) Number of new accounts opened in the reporting period

(G) Dollar amount in accounts opened during the reporting period

(H) Total dollar amount collected from all accounts in the reporting period

(I) Number of accounts closed or discharged in the reporting period

(J) Number of open accounts at the end of the reporting period

(K) Dollar amount in open accounts at the end of the reporting period

(2) *JDCCP Implementation Review*

Within two years of the effective date of these guidelines and thereafter as needed, the Judicial Council will evaluate the progress of the JDCCP's statewide implementation and examine the impact of the program on court workload and finances. For this purpose, Judicial Council staff may survey the courts about their financial evaluation processes, including the time and resources needed to determine responsible persons' ability to pay, the number of such persons evaluated, the results of the evaluations as specified in 6(d)–(g), and the number of judicial hearings necessary under 7(b)–(c).

14. Allocation of Collected Funds to Trial Courts

(a) Eligibility for Allocation

A trial court is eligible to receive an allocation from the funds remitted through the JDCCP for the purpose of reducing its dependency-counsel caseload if it meets the following criteria.

(1) *Participation*

The court has demonstrated its participation in the JDCCP by

(A) adopting a local rule or policy requiring the juvenile court to inquire at or before the close of each dispositional hearing about each responsible person's ability to pay reimbursement and

(B) submitting annual reports under section 13.

(2) *Funding Need*

The court receives a base court-appointed counsel allocation that, viewed as a percentage of the available statewide funding, is less than its percentage share of the statewide court-appointed counsel funding need as estimated by the CFM.[7]

(b) Allocation Methodology

Remitted funds will be allocated annually, as part of the court-appointed counsel budget development process, to each eligible court in an amount equivalent to its need as a percentage of the estimated aggregate funding need of all eligible courts. Any allocation from the remitted funds is separate from, and in addition to, a court's allocation from the statewide court-appointed counsel funding base.

The Judicial Council provides a single funding allocation to the DRAFT program to support court-appointed counsel in participating courts. This funding is managed by the Judicial Council as part of the court-appointed counsel budget development and funding process. Collected reimbursements allocated to the DRAFT program will also be managed by the council through this process.

(c) Review of Determination of Funding Level

A court that believes that the amount of its allocation is due to an error in determining its funding need may request a review of that determination within 90 days. The request should clearly state the nature of the error.

The review will be conducted collaboratively by the court and the Judicial Council.

15. Technical Assistance

Judicial Council staff will provide technical assistance on request to courts that are in the process of implementing the JDCCP or that wish to coordinate collection efforts with other courts. Courts may send requests by e-mail to *jdccp@jud.ca.gov* to receive technical assistance, which can include (but is not limited to) services such as:

(a) Helping a court implement the reimbursement program within its current administrative structure;

(b) Advising a court on the application of the Uniform Cost Model under section 5(b) of these guidelines;

(c) Coordinating a regional reimbursement program among several courts; or

(d) Working with current collection-services providers who have entered into master agreements with the Judicial Council to ensure compliance with the JDCCP reporting requirements.

Appendix F amended effective April 1, 2024; adopted effective January 1, 2013; previously amended effective September 23, 2013, January 1, 2016, and July 1, 2016.

Appx. F 2024 Deletes. [1] has a household income 125 percent or less of the threshold established by the federal poverty guidelines in effect **[2]** he or she

---

[7] In October 2007, the TCBWG developed and the Judicial Council approved a need-based compensation or caseload funding model (CFM) for court-appointed dependency counsel practicing in courts under the DRAFT program. (See Trial Court Budget Working Group Rep., *supra* note 5.) In June 2008, the council's Executive and Planning Committee extended that methodology to appointed dependency counsel in all juvenile courts statewide. The CFM uses the number of data-supported clients in a county to determine the number of FTE attorneys needed to serve that population at the Judicial Council–approved caseload standard of 188 clients per FTE attorney. (See *id.*, at p. 4.) It then uses cost of living, county counsel salaries, and other economic factors to assign each court to one of four statewide groups. (See *id.*, at p. 5.) To promote equity in attorney compensation, each group of courts is assigned an attorney salary level based on the prevailing county counsel salary range in that group. Each court's appointed-counsel salary needs are determined by multiplying the mid-tier salary level by the number of FTE attorneys needed to serve the client population at the approved caseload. The cost of benefits and overhead, including support staff, are calculated at assigned percentages of the attorney salaries. Adding these elements together yields a precise estimate of the funding needed for a court to ensure competent representation of all parties in juvenile dependency proceedings under sections 317(c) and 317.5, as well as rule 5.660(d) of the California Rules of Court.

Appendix G
Parliamentary Procedures for the Judicial Council of California

Approved by the Judicial Council on December 14, 2012

I. Introduction
II. Establishing a Quorum
III. The Role of the Chair
IV. Voting Requirement for Judicial Council Action
V. Motions in General
   A. Substantive Motions
   B. Friendly Amendments
   C. Procedural Motions
   D. Motions to Reconsider
VI. Multiple Motions Before the Judicial Council
VII. Counting Votes
   A. Number of Votes Needed to Take Action
   B. Abstentions
   C. Examples
VIII. Alternative Methods of Voting
   A. Voting by Proxy
   B. Attending Meetings and Voting by Telephone or Teleconference
   C. Early Voting
IX. Courtesy and Decorum
X. Recess and Adjournment

I. Introduction

These parliamentary procedures are a set of rules for conducting business at Judicial Council meetings.

II. Establishing a Quorum

A quorum is defined as the minimum number of members of the body who must be present at a meeting for business to be legally transacted. The Judicial Council abides by a rule providing that a quorum is one more than half the *voting* members. Because there are 21 voting members on the council, there must be 11 voting members present to legally transact business. Even if the council has a quorum to begin the meeting, it can lose the quorum during the meeting when a member departs. When that occurs, the council loses its ability to transact business until and unless a quorum is reestablished.

III. The Role of the Chair

While all members of the council should know and understand the rules of parliamentary procedure, it is the Chair who is charged with applying the rules in the conduct of the meeting. The Chair, for all intents and purposes, makes the final ruling on the rules every time he or she states an action. In fact, all decisions by the Chair are final unless overruled by the council itself.

Because the Chair conducts the meeting, normally the Chair will play a less active role in the debate and discussion than other members of the council. This does not mean that the Chair should not participate in the debate or discussion. The Chair as a member of the council has the full right to participate in the debate, discussion, and decision making of the council. However, the Chair should generally look to other council members to make or second motions.

IV. Voting Requirement for Judicial Council Action

To take any substantive action, a majority of all voting members of the Judicial Council must vote in favor of the action. (See Gov. Code, § 68508.) Because there are 21 voting members on the council, there must be a quorum of at least 11 members voting to take any action, and a vote on a substantive motion (as defined below) requires 11 affirmative votes to pass.

Advisory members of the council may make or second motions and may fully participate in discussion and debate, but are not counted for purposes of quorum, and may not vote. (See Cal. Rules of Court, rule 10.3(b).)

V. Motions in General

Motions are made in a simple two-step process. First, the Chair should recognize the council member. Second, the member makes a motion by preceding his or her desired approach with the words, "I move ...." A typical motion might be: "I move that we adopt the committee's recommendation."

The Chair usually initiates the motion by doing one of the following:
1. Inviting the council members to make a motion. "A motion at this time would be in order."
2. Suggesting a motion to the members. "A motion would be in order that we adopt the committee's recommendation."
3. Making the motion. As noted, the Chair has every right as a council member to make a motion, but should normally do so only if he or she wishes to make a motion on an item but is convinced that no other member is willing to step forward to do so at a particular time.

After a vote is taken, the Chair should announce the result of the vote as well as the vote count. For example, the Chair might say: "The motion to create a five-member working group to develop parliamentary procedures for the council has passed. The vote was 11 in favor, 9 opposed, and 1 abstention." By announcing the result and the vote count, the Chair clarifies what the council has done for the benefit of the council and the public. Rather than making the announcement, the Chair may ask the Secretary to announce the result of the vote as well as the vote count.

A. Substantive Motions

There are three substantive motions that are the most common and recur often at meetings:

The basic motion. The basic motion is the one that puts forward a decision for the council's consideration. A basic motion might be: "I move that we create a five-member working group to develop parliamentary procedures for the council."

The motion to amend. If a member wants to change a basic motion that is before the body, he or she would move to amend it. A motion to amend might be: "I move that we amend the motion to have a ten-member working group." A motion to amend takes the basic motion that is before the council and seeks to change it in some way. The council would first vote on whether the motion should be amended. If that motion passes, the council would then vote on the motion itself as amended.

The substitute motion. If a member wants to completely do away with the basic motion that is before the council and put a new motion in its place, he or she would move to make a substitute motion. A substitute motion might be: "I move that we impose a moratorium against appointing new working groups."

Motions to amend and substitute motions are often confused. But they are quite different, and their effect (if passed) is also quite different. A motion to amend seeks to retain the basic motion on the floor, but modify it in some way. A substitute motion seeks to throw out the basic motion on the floor and substitute a new and different motion for it. The decision on whether a motion is really a motion to amend or a substitute motion is left to the Chair. So if a member makes what that member calls a motion to amend, but the Chair determines that it is really a substitute motion, the Chair's designation governs.

The basic rule of substantive motions is that they are subject to discussion and debate. Accordingly, basic motions, motions to amend, and substitute motions are all eligible for full discussion by the council. The debate can continue as long as council members wish to discuss an item, subject to the decision of the Chair that it is time to move on and take action.

For a substantive motion to pass, it requires the affirmative concurrence of a majority of voting members of the council. In other words, 11 voting members of the council must vote in favor of a substantive motion for it to pass. An abstention does not constitute a vote in favor of a motion. The order in which various motions are considered is addressed in section VI, Multiple Motions Before the Judicial Council, on pages 5–6.

B. Friendly Amendments

A "friendly amendment" is a practical parliamentary tool that is simple, informal, saves time, and avoids bogging down a meeting with numerous formal motions. It works as follows: During the discussion on a pending motion, it may appear that a change to the motion is desirable or may win support for the motion from some members. When that happens, a member who has the floor may simply say, "I would like to suggest a friendly amendment to the motion." The member suggests the friendly amendment, and if the maker and the person who seconded the motion pending on the floor accept the friendly amendment, that now becomes the pending motion on the floor. If either the maker or the person who seconded rejects the proposed friendly amendment, the proposer can formally move to amend.

C. Procedural Motions

In contrast to the substantive motions described above, which result in the council voting whether to take action, there are several types of procedural motions. These motions differ from substantive motions in both the applicability of the rule of free and open debate on motions and in the number of votes required to pass the motions. The procedural motions, all of which indicate a desire of the council to move on, are *not* debatable. Thus, when the motion is made and seconded, the Chair must immediately call for a vote without debate on the procedural motion.

As for votes on these motions, while substantive motions require the concurrence of 11 voting members, procedural motions require either a majority or a two-thirds vote (depending on the motion) of voting members who are present. For example, if 15 voting members are present, 8 votes are required to pass a motion that requires a majority vote, and 10 votes are required to pass a motion that requires a two-thirds vote. (The counting of votes is discussed in greater detail in section VII, Counting Votes, on pages 7–8.)

Procedural motions that require a **majority vote** include:

Motion to adjourn. This motion, if passed, requires the council to immediately adjourn to its next regularly scheduled meeting. It requires a simple majority vote of those present and voting to pass.

Motion to recess. This motion, if passed, requires the council to immediately take a recess. Normally, the Chair determines the length of the recess, which may be a few minutes or an hour. It requires a simple majority vote of those present and voting to pass.

Motion to fix the time to adjourn. This motion, if passed, requires the council to adjourn the meeting at the specific time set in the motion. For example, the motion might be: "I move we adjourn this meeting at 5 p.m." It requires a simple majority vote of those present and voting to pass.

Motion to table. This motion, if passed, requires discussion of the agenda item to be halted and the agenda item to be placed on "hold." The motion can contain a specific time in which the item can come back to the council: "I move we table this item until our regular meeting in October." Or the motion can contain no specific time for the return of the item, in which case a motion to take the item off the table and bring it back to the council will have to be taken at a future meeting. A motion to table an item (or to bring it back to the council) requires a simple majority vote of those present and voting to pass.

Procedural motions that require a **two-thirds vote** include:

Motion to object to consideration of an item. Normally, such a motion is unnecessary since the objectionable item can be tabled or simply defeated. However, when members of a body do not even want an item on the agenda to be considered, then such a motion is in order. It requires a two-thirds vote of those present and voting to pass.

Motion to limit debate. The most common form of this motion is to say: "I move the previous question" or "I move the question" or "I call the question" or simply "Question." As a practical matter, when a member calls out one of these phrases, the Chair can expedite things by treating it as a "request" rather than as a formal motion. The Chair can then simply inquire, "Is there any further discussion?" If no one wishes to discuss it further, the Chair can proceed to a vote on the underlying matter. On the other hand, if even one council member wishes further discussion and debate on the underlying matter, the Chair must treat the "call for the question" as a motion and proceed accordingly.

When a council member makes such a motion, he or she is really saying, "I've had enough debate. Let's get on with the vote." When such a motion is made, the Chair should ask for a second, stop debate, and vote on the motion to limit debate. Note that a motion to limit debate could include a time limit. For example: "I move we limit debate on this agenda item to 15 minutes." A motion to limit debate requires a two-thirds vote of those present and voting to pass.

D. Motions to Reconsider

There is a special and unique motion that requires a separate explanation: the motion to reconsider. A tenet of parliamentary procedure is finality. After vigorous discussion, debate, and a vote, there must be some closure to the issue. Thus, after a vote is taken, the matter is deemed closed, subject only to reopening if a proper motion to reconsider is made and passed.

A motion to reconsider is a procedural motion that requires only a majority vote of those voting members who are present to pass, but there are two special rules that apply only to the motion to reconsider.

First is the matter of timing. A motion to reconsider must be made at the meeting at which the item was first voted upon. A motion to reconsider made at a later time is untimely.

Second, a motion to reconsider may be made only by a member who voted *in the majority* on the original motion. If such a member has a change of heart, he or she may make the motion to reconsider. (Any other council member may second the motion.) If a member who voted *in the minority* seeks to make the motion to reconsider, it must be ruled out of order. The purpose of this rule is finality. If a member of the minority could make a motion to reconsider, the item could be brought back to the council again and again, which would defeat the purpose of finality.

If the motion to reconsider passes, then the original matter is back before the body, and a new original motion is in order. The matter may be discussed and debated as if it were on the floor for the first time.

VI. Multiple Motions Before the Judicial Council

There can be up to three motions on the floor at the same time. The Chair can reject a fourth motion until he or she has addressed the three that are on the floor and has resolved them. This rule has practical value. More than three motions on the floor at one time tends to be too confusing and unwieldy for most everyone, including the Chair.

When there are two or three motions on the floor (after motions and seconds) at the same time, the vote should proceed *first* on the *last* motion that was made. So, for example, assume the first motion is a basic motion to appoint a 5-member working group to develop parliamentary procedures for the council. During the discussion of this motion, a member might make a second motion to amend the basic motion so that a 10-member working group would be appointed instead of a 5-member working group. And perhaps, during that discussion, another member makes yet a third motion as a substitute motion to impose a moratorium against appointing new working groups. The proper procedure would be as follows:

First, the Chair would address the third (the last) motion on the floor, the substitute motion. After discussion and debate, a vote would be taken on the third motion. If the substitute motion *passed*, it would be a substitute for the basic motion and would eliminate it. The first motion would be moot, as would the second motion (which sought to amend the first motion), and the action on the agenda item would be completed on the passage by the council of the third motion (the substitute motion). No vote would be taken on the first or second motions.

Second, if the substitute motion failed, the Chair would address the second (now, the last) motion on the floor, the motion to amend. The discussion and debate would focus strictly on the amendment (whether the committee should be 5 members or 10 members). If the motion to amend *passed*, the Chair would now move to consider the main motion (the first motion) *as amended*. If the motion to amend *failed*, the Chair would now move to consider the main motion (the first motion) in its original format, not amended.

VII. Counting Votes

A. Number of Votes Needed to Take Action

As noted above, for substantive motions, a minimum of 11 voting members must be present to constitute a quorum, and a minimum of 11 votes are needed to pass such substantive motions. For procedural motions, a minimum of 11 voting members must be present to constitute a quorum, and there must be either a majority vote or a two-thirds vote of voting members, depending on the motion, to pass such procedural motions.

When a majority vote is needed to pass a motion, one vote more than 50 percent of those voting is required. If a two-thirds vote is needed to pass a motion, there is a formula to determine how many affirmative votes are required. The simple rule of thumb is to count the "no" votes and double that count to determine how many "yes" votes are needed to pass a particular motion. So, for example, if 6 members vote "no," then the "yes" vote of at least 12 members is required to achieve a two-thirds majority vote to pass the motion.

In the event of a tie vote, the motion always fails because an affirmative vote is required to pass any motion. For example, if the vote is 10 in favor and 10 opposed, with 1 member absent, the motion is defeated.

B. Abstentions

Members sometimes prefer to abstain from voting. Members who abstain are counted for purposes of determining whether there is a quorum, but the abstention votes on the motion are treated as if they do not exist. In other words, an abstention is not treated as either a "yes" vote or a "no" vote.

C. Examples

Here are a few examples to illustrate vote-counting under different circumstances:

Majority Vote Counting

Assume that 21 voting members of the council are present to vote on a substantive motion, which requires 11 votes to pass. If the vote on the motion is 11 to 10, the motion passes. If the motion is 10 to 10 with 1 abstention, the motion fails because the abstention is not counted as a "yes" vote.

Assume that 18 members are present and voting on a procedural motion that requires only a majority vote to pass (as opposed to 11 votes). If the vote is 10 to 8, the motion passes. If the vote is 9 to 9, the motion fails. If the vote is 9 to 8 with 1 abstention, the motion fails because 10 votes are required for the motion to pass (one vote more than 50 percent). Once again, the abstention vote is counted only for the purpose of determining quorum, but on the actual vote on the motion, it is as if the abstention vote did not occur.

Two-Thirds Vote Counting

Assume 21 members are present and voting on a motion that requires a two-thirds vote to pass. If the vote is 11 to 10, the motion fails for lack of a two-thirds majority. If the vote is 18 to 3, the motion passes with a clear two-thirds majority. If the vote is 13 to 8, the motion fails. Using the formula discussed above, the "no" votes are counted and doubled to determine whether there are enough "yes" votes to constitute a two-thirds majority. If the vote is 13 to 6 with 2 abstentions, the motion passes because the abstentions are treated as if they don't exist, and with 6 "no" votes, 12 votes are needed to pass the motion. Therefore, the motion passes with 13 votes.

Abstention

To cast an "abstention" vote, a member either votes "abstain" or says "I abstain." However, if a member votes "present," that is also treated as an abstention. The member is essentially saying, "Count me for purposes of a quorum, but my vote on the issue is abstain." In fact, any manifestation of intention to vote neither "yes" nor "no" on the pending motion may be treated by the Chair as an abstention.

Absence

Can a member vote "absent" or "count me as absent?" The ruling on this is up to the Chair. The better approach is for the Chair to count this as a vote to abstain if the person does not actually leave the boardroom. If, however, the member leaves the boardroom and is actually absent, the Chair should count the member as absent. That, of course, may affect the quorum.

VIII. Alternative Methods of Voting

A. Voting by Proxy

Voting by proxy is not permitted. A Judicial Council member, therefore, may not authorize another person to vote on his or her behalf.

B. Attending Meetings and Voting by Telephone or Teleconference

Council members are permitted to attend meetings and vote by telephone or teleconference.

C. Early Voting

On occasion, a voting member of the Judicial Council may be unable to attend a council meeting or must depart before the presentation of a discussion item or the ensuing exchange is completed. Subdivision (c) of rule 10.5 (Notice and agenda of council meeting) defines the term "business meetings" as meetings "at which a majority of voting members are present to discuss and decide matters within the council's jurisdiction." The rule contemplates that members will be present for a discussion of the agenda item. Accordingly, a council member is not permitted to vote before the discussion about the agenda item has ended.

IX. Courtesy and Decorum

The rules of order are meant to create an atmosphere where council members and the public can attend to business efficiently, fairly, and with full participation. At the same time, it is up to the Chair and the council members to maintain common courtesy and decorum. It is always best for only one person at a time to have the floor, and it is always best for every speaker to be first recognized by the Chair before speaking.

The Chair should ensure that discussion and debate of an agenda item focuses on the item and the policy in question. The Chair has the right to cut off discussion that diverges from the agenda item.

Debate and discussion should be focused, but free and open. In the interest of time, the Chair may, however, limit the time allotted to speakers, including council members.

Council members should not interrupt the speaker. There are, however, exceptions. A speaker may be interrupted for the following reasons:

Privilege. The proper interruption would be to say, "Point of privilege." The Chair would then ask the interrupter to "state your point." Appropriate points of privilege relate to anything that would interfere with the normal comfort of the meeting. For example, the room may be too hot or too cold, or a blowing fan might interfere with a person's ability to hear.

Order. The proper interruption would be to say, "Point of order." Again, the Chair would ask the interrupter to "state your point." Appropriate points of order relate to anything that would not be considered appropriate conduct of the meeting, such as the Chair moving on to a vote on a motion that permits debate without allowing that discussion or debate.

Appeal. If the Chair makes a ruling with which a member of the body disagrees, that member may appeal the ruling of the Chair. For example, if the Chair deems a motion to be a substitute motion and a member considers it to be a motion to amend, the member may appeal that ruling. If the motion is seconded and, after debate, it passes by a simple majority vote, the ruling of the Chair is deemed reversed. The motion to appeal the ruling of the Chair is considered a procedural motion.

Call for orders of the day. This is simply another way of saying, "Let's return to the agenda." If a member believes that the council has drifted from the agenda, such a call may be made. It does not require a vote. If the Chair discovers that the agenda has not been followed, the Chair simply reminds the council members to return to the agenda item properly before them. If the Chair fails to do so, the Chair's determination may be appealed.

Withdraw a motion. During debate and discussion of a motion, the maker of the motion on the floor, at any time, may interrupt a speaker to withdraw his or her motion from the floor. The motion is immediately deemed withdrawn, although the Chair may ask the person who seconded the motion if he or she wishes to make the motion, and any other member may make the motion if properly recognized.

X. Recess and Adjournment

Unless there is an objection, the Chair may recess the council meeting for a definite period of time and may adjourn the meeting.

Appendix G adopted effective December 14, 2012.

Appendix H
Amount of Civil Penalty to Cure Alleged Violation of Proposition 65 for Failure to Provide Certain Warnings (Health & Saf. Code, § [1] *25249.7(k)*)

Formula

Under Health and Safety Code section [2] 25249.7(k), the amount of civil penalty per facility or premises that an alleged violator may agree to pay within 14 days of service of a notice of violation under that section will be computed and adjusted as follows:

$$\text{Adjusted penalty amount} = \left[\frac{\text{annual CCPI (Dec. [3] 2023)} - \text{annual CCPI (Dec. [4] 2018)}}{\text{annual CCPI (Dec. [5] 2018)}} + 1 \right] \times \text{Previous dollar amount}$$

Definition

"CCPI" means the California Consumer Price Index for All Urban Comsumers, as established by the California Department of Industrial Relations.

Calculation and adjustment

Effective April 1, [6] 2024, the amount of civil penalty that an alleged violator may agree to pay within 14 days of service of a notice of violation under Health and Safety Code section [7] 25249.7(k)(2)(B)(ii) is [8] **$610** per facility or premises where the alleged violation occurred.

The calculation is as follows:

$$[9]\ \$608.79 = \left[\frac{[10]\ 331.804 - [11]\ 272.51}{[12]\ 272.51} + 1 \right] \times \$500$$

Under Health and Safety Code section [13] 25249.7(k)(2)(B)(ii), the adjusted penalty amount is rounded to the nearest $5, so the dollar amount of the adjusted limit is rounded to [14] **$610**.

[Appendix H amended effective April 1, 2024; adopted effective April 1, 2019]

Appx. H 2024 Deletes. [1] 26249.7(k) [2] 26249.7(k) [3] 2018 [4] 2013 [5] 2018 [6] 2019 [7] 26249.7(k)(2)(B)(ii) [8] $565 [9] $563.92 [10] 272.51 [11] 241.623 [12] 241.623 [13] 26249.7(k)(2)(B)(ii) [14] $565

Appendix I
Emergency Rules Related to COVID-19

[Appendix I amended effective March 11, 2022; adopted effective April 6, 2020; previously amended effective April 17, 2020, April 20, 2020, May 29, 2020, June 20, 2020, August 13, 2020, November 13, 2020, January 1, 2022, and January 21, 2022.]

Emergency rule 1. Unlawful detainers
Emergency rule 2. Judicial foreclosures—suspension of actions
Emergency rule 3. Use of technology for remote appearances
Emergency rule 5. Personal appearance waivers of defendants during health emergency
Emergency rule 6. Emergency orders: juvenile dependency proceedings
Emergency rule 7. Emergency orders: juvenile delinquency proceedings
Emergency rule 8. Emergency orders: temporary restraining or protective orders
Emergency rule 9. Tolling statutes of limitations for civil causes of action
Emergency rule 10. Extensions of time in which to bring a civil action to trial
Emergency rule 13. Effective date for requests to modify support

Emergency rule 1. Unlawful detainers

(a) Application

Notwithstanding any other law, including Code of Civil Procedure sections 1166, 1167, 1169, and 1170.5, this rule applies to all actions for unlawful detainer.

(b) Issuance of summons

A court may not issue a summons on a complaint for unlawful detainer unless the court finds, in its discretion and on the record, that the action is necessary to protect public health and safety.

(c) Entry of default

A court may not enter a default or a default judgment for restitution in an unlawful detainer action for failure of defendant to appear unless the court finds both of the following:

(1) The action is necessary to protect public health and safety; and

(2) The defendant has not appeared in the action within the time provided by law, including by any applicable executive order.

(d) Time for trial

If a defendant has appeared in the action, the court may not set a trial date earlier than 60 days after a request for trial is made unless the court finds that an earlier trial date is necessary to protect public health and safety. Any trial set in an unlawful detainer proceeding as of April 6, 2020 must be continued at least 60 days from the initial date of trial.

(e) Sunset of rule

This rule will remain in effect through September 1, 2020, or until amended or repealed by the Judicial Council. Notwithstanding Code of Civil Procedure section 1170.5 and this subdivision, any trial date set under (d) as of September 1, 2020, will remain as set unless a court otherwise orders.

(Subd (e) amended effective August 13, 2020; adopted effective April 6, 2020.)
Emergency Rule 1 amended effective August 13, 2000; adopted effective April 6, 2020.

Emergency rule 2. Judicial foreclosures—suspension of actions

Notwithstanding any other law, this rule applies to any action for foreclosure on a mortgage or deed of trust brought under chapter 1, title 10, of part 2 of the Code of Civil Procedure, beginning at section 725a, including any action for a deficiency judgment, and provides that, through September 1, 2020, or until this rule is amended or repealed by the Judicial Council:

(1) All such actions are stayed, and the court may take no action and issue no decisions or judgments unless the court finds that action is required to further the public health and safety.

(2) The period for electing or exercising any rights under that chapter, including exercising any right of redemption from a foreclosure sale or petitioning the court in relation to such a right, is extended.

Emergency Rule 2 amended effective August 13, 2020; adopted effective April 6, 2020.

Advisory Committee Comment

The provision for tolling any applicable statute of limitations, in prior subdivision (2), has been removed as unnecessary because the tolling provisions in emergency rule 9 apply to actions subject to this rule.

Emergency rule 3. Use of technology for remote appearances

(a) Remote appearances

Notwithstanding any other law, in order to protect the health and safety of the public, including court users, both in custody and out of custody defendants, witnesses, court personnel, judicial officers, and others, courts must conduct criminal proceedings and court operations as follows:

(1) Courts may require that criminal proceedings and court operations be conducted remotely.

(2) In criminal proceedings, courts must receive the consent of the defendant to conduct the proceeding remotely and otherwise comply with emergency rule 5. Notwithstanding Penal Code sections 865 and 977 or any other law, the court may conduct any criminal proceeding remotely. As used in this rule, "consent of the defendant" means that the consent of the defendant is required only for the waiver of the defendant's appearance as provided in emergency rule 5. For good cause shown, the court may require any witness to personally appear in a particular proceeding.

(3) Conducting criminal proceedings remotely includes, but is not limited to, the use of video, audio, and telephonic means for remote appearances; the electronic exchange and authentication of documentary evidence; e-filing and e-service; the use of remote interpreting; and the use of remote reporting and electronic recording to make the official record of an action or proceeding.

(Subd (a) amended effective January 1, 2022; adopted effective April 6, 2020.)

(b) Sunset of rule

This rule will sunset on June 30, 2022, unless otherwise amended or repealed by the Judicial Council.

(Subd (b) amended effective March 11, 2022; adopted effective April 6, 2020.)
Emergency Rule 3 amended effective March 11, 2022; adopted effective April 6, 2020; previously amended effective January 1, 2022.

Emergency rule 4. Emergency Bail Schedule [Repealed]

Emergency Rule 4 repealed effective June 20, 2020; adopted effective April 6, 2020.

Emergency rule 5. Personal appearance waivers of defendants during health emergency

(a) Application

Notwithstanding any other law, including Penal Code sections 865 and 977, this rule applies to all criminal proceedings except cases alleging murder with special circumstances and cases in which the defendant is currently incarcerated in state prison, as governed by Penal Code section 977.2.

(b) Types of personal appearance waivers

(1) With the consent of the defendant, the court must allow a defendant to waive his or her personal appearance and to appear remotely, either through video or telephonic appearance, when the technology is available.

(2) With the consent of the defendant, the court must allow a defendant to waive his or her appearance and permit counsel to appear on his or her behalf. The court must accept a defendant's waiver of appearance or personal appearance when:

(A) Counsel for the defendant makes an on the record oral representation that counsel has fully discussed the waiver and its implications with the defendant and the defendant has authorized counsel to proceed as counsel represents to the court;

(B) Electronic communication from the defendant as confirmed by defendant's counsel; or

(C) Any other means that ensures the validity of the defendant's waiver.

(c) Consent by the defendant

(1) For purposes of arraignment and entry of a not guilty plea, consent means a knowing, intelligent, and voluntary waiver of the right to appear personally in court. Counsel for the defendant must state on the record at each applicable hearing that counsel is proceeding with the defendant's consent.

(2) For purposes of waiving time for a preliminary hearing, consent also means a knowing, intelligent, and voluntary waiver of the right to hold a preliminary hearing within required time limits specified either in

Penal Code section 859b or under emergency orders issued by the Chief Justice and Chair of the Judicial Council.

(3) The court must accept defense counsel's representation that the defendant understands and agrees with waiving any right to appear unless the court has specific concerns in a particular matter about the validity of the waiver.

(d) Appearance through counsel

(1) When counsel appears on behalf of a defendant, courts must allow counsel to do any of the following:

(A) Waive reading and advisement of rights for arraignment.

(B) Enter a plea of not guilty.

(C) Waive time for the preliminary hearing.

(2) For appearances by counsel, including where the defendant is either appearing remotely or has waived his or her appearance and or counsel is appearing by remote access, counsel must confirm to the court at each hearing that the appearance by counsel is made with the consent of the defendant.

(e) Conduct of remote hearings

(1) With the defendant's consent, a defendant may appear remotely for any pretrial criminal proceeding.

(2) Where a defendant appears remotely, counsel may not be required to be personally present with the defendant for any portion of the criminal proceeding provided that the audio and/or video conferencing system or other technology allows for private communication between the defendant and his or her counsel. Any private communication is confidential and privileged under Evidence Code section 952.

(f) Sunset of rule

This rule will sunset on June 30, 2022, unless otherwise amended or repealed by the Judicial Council.

(Subd (f) amended effective March 11, 2022; adopted effective April 6, 2020.) Emergency Rule 5 amended effective March 11, 2022; adopted effective April 6, 2020.

Emergency rule 6. Emergency orders: juvenile dependency proceedings

(a) Application

This rule applies to all juvenile dependency proceedings filed or pending until the state of emergency related to the COVID-19 pandemic is lifted.

(b) Essential hearings and orders

The following matters should be prioritized in accordance with existing statutory time requirements.

(1) Protective custody warrants filed under Welfare and Institutions Code section 340.

(2) Detention hearings under Welfare and Institutions Code section 319. The court is required to determine if it is contrary to the child's welfare to remain with the parent, whether reasonable efforts were made to prevent removal, and whether to vest the placing agency with temporary placement and care.

(3) Psychotropic medication applications.

(4) Emergency medical requests.

(5) A petition for reentry of a nonminor dependent.

(6) Welfare and Institutions Code section 388 petitions that require an immediate response based on the health and safety of the child, which should be reviewed for a prima facie showing of change of circumstances sufficient to grant the petition or to set a hearing. The court may extend the final ruling on the petition beyond 30 days.

(c) Foster care hearings and continuances during the state of emergency

(1) A court may hold any proceeding under this rule via remote technology consistent with Code of Civil Procedure section 367.75 and rule 3.672.

(2) At the beginning of any hearing at which one or more participants appears remotely, the court must admonish all the participants that the proceeding is confidential and of the possible sanctions for violating confidentiality.

(3) The child welfare agency is responsible for notice of remote hearings unless other arrangements have been made with counsel for parents and children. Notice is required for all parties and may include notice by telephone or other electronic means. The notice must also include instructions on how to participate in the court hearing remotely.

(4) Court reports

(A) Attorneys for parents and children must accept service of the court report electronically.

(B) The child welfare agency must ensure that the parent and the child receive a copy of the court report on time.

(C) If a parent or child cannot receive the report electronically, the child welfare agency must deliver a hard copy of the report to the parent and the child on time.

(5) Nothing in this subdivision prohibits the court from making statutorily required findings and orders, by minute order only and without a court reporter, by accepting written stipulations from counsel when appearances are waived if the stipulations are confirmed on the applicable Judicial Council forms or equivalent local court forms.

(6) If a court hearing cannot occur either in the courthouse or remotely, the hearing may be continued up to 60 days, except as otherwise specified.

(A) A dispositional hearing under Welfare and Institutions Code section 360 should not be continued more than 6 months after the detention hearing without review of the child's circumstances. In determining exceptional circumstances that justify holding the dispositional hearing more than 6 months after the child was taken into protective custody, the impact of the state of emergency related to the COVID-19 pandemic must be considered.

i. If the dispositional hearing is continued more than 6 months after the start date of protective custody, a review of the child must be held at the 6-month date. At the review, the court must determine the continued necessity for and appropriateness of the placement; the extent of compliance with the case plan or available services that have been offered; the extent of progress which has been made toward alleviating or mitigating the causes necessitating placement; and the projected likely date by which the child may return home or placed permanently.

ii. The court may continue the matter for a full hearing on all dispositional findings and orders.

(B) A judicial determination of reasonable efforts must be made within 12 months of the date a child enters foster care to maintain a child's federal title IV-E availability. If a permanency hearing is continued beyond the 12-month date, the court must review the case to determine if the agency has made reasonable efforts to return the child home or arrange for the child to be placed permanently. This finding can be made without prejudice and may be reconsidered at a full hearing.

(7) During the state of emergency related to the COVID-19 pandemic, previously authorized visitation must continue, but the child welfare agency is to determine the manner of visitation to ensure that the needs of the family are met. If the child welfare agency changes the manner of visitation for a child and a parent or legal guardian in reunification, or for the child and a sibling(s), or a hearing is pending under Welfare and Institutions Code section 366.26, the child welfare agency must notify the attorneys for the children and parents within 5 court days of the change. All changes in manner of visitation during this time period must be made on a case by case basis, balance the public health directives and best interest of the child, and take into consideration whether in-person visitation may continue to be held safely. Family time is important for child and parent well-being, as well as for efforts toward reunification. Family time is especially important during times of crisis. Visitation may only be suspended if a detriment finding is made in a particular case based on the facts unique to that case. A detriment finding must not be based solely on the existence of the impact of the state of emergency related to the COVID-19 pandemic or related public health directives.

(A) The attorney for the child or parent may ask the juvenile court to review the change in manner of visitation. The child or parent has the burden of showing that the change is not in the best interest of the child or is not based on current public health directives.

(B) A request for the court to review the change in visitation during this time period must be made within 14 court days of the change. In reviewing the change in visitation, the court should take into consideration the factors in (c)(7).

(Subd (c) amended effective January 21, 2022; adopted effective April 6, 2020.)

(d) Sunset of rule

This rule will sunset on June 30, 2022, unless otherwise amended or repealed by the Judicial Council.

(Subd (d) amended effective March 11, 2022; adopted effective April 6, 2020.) Emergency Rule 6 amended effective March 11, 2022; adopted effective April 6, 2020; previously amended effective January 21, 2022.

Advisory Committee Comment

When courts are unable to hold regular proceedings because of an emergency that has resulted in an order as authorized under Government Code section 68115, federal timelines do not stop. Circumstances may arise where reunification services to the parent, including visitation, may not occur or be provided. The court must consider the circumstances of the emergency when deciding whether to extend or terminate reunification services and whether services were reasonable given the state of the emergency. (Citations: 42 U.S.C. § 672(a)(1)–(2), (5); 45 CFR § 1355.20; 45 CFR § 1356.21 (b) – (d); 45 C.F.R. § 1356.71(d)(1)(iii); Child Welfare Policy Manual, 8.3A.9 Title IV-E, Foster Care Maintenance Payments Program, Reasonable efforts, Question 2 (www.acf.hhs.gov/cwpm/public_html/programs/cb/laws_policies/laws/cwpm/policy_dsp.jsp?citID=92)]); Letter dated March 27, 2020, from Jerry Milner, Associate Commissioner, Children's Bureau, Administration for Children and Families, U.S. Department of Health and Human Services.)

Emergency rule 7. Emergency orders: juvenile delinquency proceedings

(a) **Application**

This rule applies to all proceedings in which a petition has been filed under Welfare and Institutions Code section 602 in which a hearing would be statutorily required during the state of emergency related to the COVID-19 pandemic.

(b) **Juvenile delinquency hearings and orders during the state of emergency**

(1) A hearing on a petition for a child who is in custody under Welfare and Institutions Code section 632 or 636 must be held within the statutory timeframes as modified by an order of the court authorized by Government Code section 68115. The court must determine if it is contrary to the welfare of the child to remain in the home, whether reasonable services to prevent removal occurred, and whether to place temporary placement with the probation agency if the court will be keeping the child detained and out of the home.

(2) If a child is detained in custody and an in-person appearance is not feasible due to the state of emergency, courts must make reasonable efforts to hold any statutorily required hearing for that case via remote appearance within the required statutory time frame and as modified by an order of the court authorized under Government Code section 68115 for that proceeding. If a remote proceeding is not a feasible option for such a case during the state of emergency, the court may continue the case as provided in (d) for the minimum period of time necessary to hold the proceedings.

(3) Without regard to the custodial status of the child, the following hearings should be prioritized during the state of emergency related to the COVID-19 pandemic:

(A) Psychotropic medication applications.

(B) All emergency medical requests.

(C) A petition for reentry of a nonminor dependent.

(D) A hearing on any request for a warrant for a child.

(E) A probable cause determination for a child who has been detained but has not had a detention hearing within the statutory time limits.

(4) Notwithstanding any other law, and except as described in (5), during the state of emergency related to the COVID-19 pandemic, the court may continue for good cause any hearing for a child not detained in custody who is subject to its juvenile delinquency jurisdiction until a date after the state of emergency has been lifted considering the priority for continued hearings in (d).

(5) For children placed in foster care under probation supervision, a judicial determination of reasonable efforts must be made within 12 months of the date the child enters foster care to maintain a child's federal title IV-E availability. If a permanency hearing is continued beyond the 12-month date, the court must nevertheless hold a review to determine if the agency has made reasonable efforts to return the child home or place the child permanently. This finding can be made without prejudice and may be reconsidered at a full hearing.

(c) **Proceedings with remote appearances during the state of emergency**

(1) A court may hold any proceeding under this rule via remote technology consistent with Code of Civil Procedure section 367.75 and rule 3.672.

(2) At the beginning of any hearing conducted with one or more participants appearing remotely, the court must admonish all the participants that the proceeding is confidential and of the possible sanctions for violating confidentiality.

(3) The court is responsible for giving notice of remote hearings, except for notice to a victim, which is the responsibility of the prosecuting attorney or the probation department. Notice is required for all parties and may include notice by telephone or other electronic means. The notice must also include instructions on how to participate in the hearing remotely.

(4) During the state of emergency, the court has broad discretion to take evidence in the manner most compatible with the remote hearing process, including but not limited to taking testimony by written declaration. If counsel for a child or the prosecuting attorney objects to the court's evidentiary procedures, that is a basis for issuing a continuance under (d).

(Subd (c) amended effective January 21, 2022; adopted effective April 6, 2020.)

(d) **Continuances of hearings during the state of emergency.**

Notwithstanding any other law, the court may for good cause continue any hearing other than a detention hearing for a child who is detained in custody. In making this determination, the court must consider the custody status of the child, whether there are evidentiary issues that are contested, and, if so, the ability for those issues to be fairly contested via a remote proceeding.

(e) **Extension of time limits under Welfare and Institutions Code section 709**

In any case in which a child has been found incompetent under Welfare and Institutions Code section 709 and that child is eligible for remediation services or has been found to require secure detention, any time limits imposed by section 709 for provision of services or for secure detention are tolled for the period of the state of emergency if the court finds that remediation services could not be provided because of the state of emergency.

(f) **Sunset of rule**

This rule will sunset on June 30, 2022, unless otherwise amended or repealed by the Judicial Council.

(Subd (f) amended effective March 11, 2022; adopted effective April 6, 2020.)
Emergency Rule 7 amended effective March 11, 2022; adopted effective April 6, 2020; previously amended effective January 21, 2022.

Advisory Committee Comment

This emergency rule is being adopted in part to ensure that detention hearings for juveniles in delinquency court must be held in a timely manner to ensure that no child is detained who does not need to be detained to protect the child or the community. The statutory scheme for juveniles who come under the jurisdiction of the delinquency court is focused on the rehabilitation of the child and thus makes detention of a child the exceptional practice, rather than the rule. Juvenile courts are able to use their broad discretion under current law to release detained juveniles to protect the health of those juveniles and the health and safety of the others in detention during the current state of emergency related to the COVID-19 pandemic.

Emergency rule 8. Emergency orders: temporary restraining or protective orders

(a) **Application**

Notwithstanding any other law, this rule applies to any emergency protective order, temporary restraining order, or criminal protective order that was requested, issued, or set to expire during the state of emergency related to the COVID-19 pandemic. This includes requests and orders issued under Family Code sections 6250 or 6300, Code of Civil Procedure sections 527.6, 527.8, or 527.85, Penal Code sections 136.2, 18125 or 18150, or Welfare and Institutions Code sections 213.5, 304, 362.4, or 15657.03, and including any of the foregoing orders issued in connection with an order for modification of a custody or visitation order issued pursuant to a dissolution, legal separation, nullity, or parentage proceeding under Family Code section 6221.

(b) **Duration of orders**

(1) Any emergency protective order made under Family Code section 6250 that is issued during the state of emergency must remain in effect for up to 30 days from the date of issuance.

(2) Any temporary restraining order or gun violence emergency protective order issued or set to expire during the state of emergency related to the COVID-19 pandemic must remain in effect for a period of time that the court determines is sufficient to allow for a hearing on the long-term order to occur, for up to 90 days.

(3) Any criminal protective order, subject to this rule, set to expire during the state of emergency, must be automatically extended for a period of 90 days, or until the matter can be heard, whichever occurs first.

(4) Upon the filing of a request to renew a restraining order after hearing that is set to expire during the state of emergency related to the COVID-19 pandemic, the current restraining order after hearing must

remain in effect until a hearing on the renewal can occur, for up to 90 days from the date of expiration.

(Subd (b) amended effective April 20, 2020.)

(c) Ex parte requests and requests to renew restraining orders

(1) Courts must provide a means for the filing of ex parte requests for temporary restraining orders and requests to renew restraining orders. Courts may do so by providing a physical location, drop box, or, if feasible, through electronic means.

(2) Any ex parte request and request to renew restraining orders may be filed using an electronic signature by a party or a party's attorney.

(Subd (c) amended effective April 20, 2020.)

(d) Service of Orders

If a respondent appears at a hearing by video, audio, or telephonically, and the court grants an order, in whole or in part, no further service is required upon the respondent for enforcement of the order, provided that the court follows the requirements of Family Code section 6384.

(e) Entry of orders into California Law Enforcement Telecommunications System

Any orders issued by a court modifying the duration or expiration date of orders subject to this rule, must be transmitted to the Department of Justice through the California Law Enforcement Telecommunications System (CLETS), as provided in Family Code section 6380, without regard to whether they are issued on Judicial Council forms, or in another format during the state of emergency.

(f) Sunset of rule

This rule will sunset on June 30, 2022, unless otherwise amended or repealed by the Judicial Council.

(Subd (f) adopted effective March 11, 2022.)

Emergency Rule 8 amended effective March 11, 2022; adopted effective April 6, 2020; previously amended effective April 20, 2020.

Emergency rule 9. Tolling statutes of limitations for civil causes of action

(a) Tolling statutes of limitations over 180 days

Notwithstanding any other law, the statutes of limitations and repose for civil causes of action that exceed 180 days are tolled from April 6, 2020, until October 1, 2020.

(Subd (a) lettered and amended effective May 29, 2020; adopted effective April 6, 2020.)

(b) Tolling statutes of limitations of 180 days or less

Notwithstanding any other law, the statutes of limitations and repose for civil causes of action that are 180 days or less are tolled from April 6, 2020, until August 3, 2020.

(Subd (b) adopted effective May 29, 2020.)

(c) Sunset of rule

This rule will sunset on June 30, 2022, unless otherwise amended or repealed by the Judicial Council. This sunset does not nullify the effect of the tolling of the statutes of limitation and repose under the rule.

(Subd (c) adopted effective March 11, 2022.)

Emergency Rule 9 amended effective March 11, 2022; adopted effective April 6, 2020; previously amended effective May 29, 2020.

Advisory Committee Comment

Emergency rule 9 is intended to apply broadly to toll any statute of limitations on the filing of a pleading in court asserting a civil cause of action. The term "civil causes of action" includes special proceedings. (See Code Civ. Proc., §§ 312, 363 ["action," as used in title 2 of the code (Of the Time of Commencing Civil Actions), is construed "as including a special proceeding of a civil nature"); special proceedings of a civil nature include all proceedings in title 3 of the code, including mandamus actions under §§ 1085, 1088.5, and 1094.5—all the types of petitions for writ made for California Environmental Quality Act (CEQA) and land use challenges]; see also Pub. Resources Code, § 21167(a)–(e) [setting limitations periods for civil "action[s]" under CEQA].)

The rule also applies to statutes of limitations on filing of causes of action in court found in codes other than the Code of Civil Procedure, including the limitations on causes of action found in, for example, the Family Code and Probate Code.

Subdivision (c). The sunset of the rule does not nullify the effect of the tolling of the statutes of limitation and repose established by the rule. Depending on the specific facts of the case and the applicable statute of limitation or repose, the effect of the tolling may survive beyond the sunset date of the rule. For example, if the right to file a cause of action subject to the four-year statute of limitation in Code of Civil Procedure section 337 first accrued on February 15, 2020, the statute of limitation, having been tolled from April 6, 2020, until October 1, 2020, under subdivision (a), would expire in August 2024 rather than February 2024.

Emergency rule 10. Extensions of time in which to bring a civil action to trial

(a) Extension of five years in which to bring a civil action to trial

Notwithstanding any other law, including Code of Civil Procedure section 583.310, for all civil actions filed on or before April 6, 2020, the time in which to bring the action to trial is extended by six months for a total time of five years and six months.

(b) Extension of three years in which to bring a new trial

Notwithstanding any other law, including Code of Civil Procedure section 583.320, for all civil actions filed on or before April 6, 2020, if a new trial is granted in the action, the three years provided in section 583.320 in which the action must again be brought to trial is extended by six months for a total time of three years and six months. Nothing in this subdivision requires that an action must again be brought to trial before expiration of the time prescribed in (a).

(c) Sunset of rule

This rule will sunset on June 30, 2022, unless otherwise amended or repealed by the Judicial Council. This sunset does not nullify the effect of the extension of time in which to bring a civil action to trial under the rule.

(Subd (c) adopted effective March 11, 2022.)

Emergency Rule 10 amended effective March 11, 2022; adopted effective April 6, 2020.

Advisory Committee Comment

The sunset of the rule does not nullify the effect of the six-month extension established by the rule for all civil actions filed on or before April 6, 2020. Depending on the specific facts of the case, the effect of the extension may survive beyond the sunset date of the rule. For example, if a civil action subject to Code of Civil Procedure section 583.310 was filed on February 15, 2020, the time in which to bring the action to trial would fall in August 2025, having been extended by six months for a total time of five years and six months, rather than February 2025.

Emergency rule 11. Depositions through remote electronic means [Repealed]

Emergency Rule 11 repealed effective November 13, 2020; adopted effective April 6, 2020.

Emergency rule 12. Electronic service [Repealed]

Emergency Rule 12 repealed effective November 13, 2020; adopted effective April 17, 2020.

Emergency rule 13. Effective date for requests to modify support

(a) Application

Notwithstanding any other law, including Family Code sections 3591, 3603, 3653, and 4333, this rule applies to all requests to modify or terminate child, spousal, partner, or family support. For the purpose of this rule, "request" refers to *Request for Order* (form FL-300), *Notice of Motion (Governmental)* (form FL-680), or other moving papers requesting a modification of support.

(b) Effective date of modification

Except as provided in Family Code section 3653(b), an order modifying or terminating a support order may be made effective as of the date the request and supporting papers are mailed or otherwise served on the other party, or other party's attorney when permitted. Nothing in this rule restricts the court's discretion to order a later effective date.

(c) Service of filed request

If the request and supporting papers that were served have not yet been filed with the court, the moving party must also serve a copy of the request and supporting papers after they have been filed with the court on the other party, or other party's attorney when permitted. If the moving party is the local child support agency and the unfiled request already has a valid court date and time listed, then subsequent service of the request is not required.

(d) Court discretion

Nothing in this rule is meant to limit court discretion or to alter rule 5.92 or 5.260 regarding which moving papers are required to request a modification of support.

(e) Sunset of rule

This rule will sunset on June 30, 2022, unless otherwise amended or repealed by the Judicial Council.

(Subd (e) amended effective March 11, 2022; adopted effective April 20, 2020.)

Emergency Rule 13 amended effective March 11, 2022; adopted effective April 20, 2020.

CALIFORNIA SUPREME COURT

California Code of Judicial Ethics.
Supreme Court Committee on Judicial Ethics Opinions Internal Operating Rules and Procedures.
Supreme Court Rules Regarding Electronic Filing. Rules 1-13.
Internal Operating Practices and Procedures of the California Supreme Court.
Supreme Court Policies Regarding Cases Arising From Judgments of Death. Policy Statements 1-4.
Appendix to Supreme Court Policies Regarding Cases Arising From Judgments of Death Concerning Appointed Counsel's Duties.
Payment Guidelines for Appointed Counsel Representing Indigent Criminal Appellants in the California Supreme Court.
Guidelines for Fixed Fee Appointments, On Optional Basis, to Automatic Appeals and Related Habeas Corpus Proceedings in the California Supreme Court.
Guidelines for the Commission on Judicial Appointments. Guidelines 1-8.

California Code of Judicial Ethics

[Adopted by the Supreme Court pursuant to article VI, section 18(m) of the California Constitution]

[Amended by the Supreme Court of California effective July 1, 2020; adopted effective January 15, 1996; previously amended March 4, 1999, December 13, 2000, December 30, 2002, June 18, 2003, December 22, 2003, January 1, 2005, June 1, 2005, July 1, 2006, January 1, 2007, January 1, 2008, April 29, 2009, January 1, 2013, January 21, 2015, August 19, 2015, December 1, 2016, and October 10, 2018]

Preface
Preamble
Terminology
Canon 1. A judge shall uphold the integrity and independence of the judiciary.
Canon 2. A judge shall avoid impropriety and the appearance of impropriety in all of the judge's activities.
Canon 3. A judge shall perform the duties of judicial office impartially, competently, and diligently.
Canon 4. A judge shall so conduct the judge's quasi-judicial and extrajudicial activities as to minimize the risk of conflict with judicial obligations.
Canon 5. A judge or candidate for judicial office shall not engage in political or campaign activity that is inconsistent with the independence, integrity, or impartiality of the judiciary.
Canon 6. Compliance with the Code of Judicial Ethics.

Preface

Formal standards of judicial conduct have existed for more than 65 years. The original Canons of Judicial Ethics promulgated by the American Bar Association were modified and adopted in 1949 for application in California by the Conference of California Judges (now the California Judges Association).

In 1969, the American Bar Association determined that then current needs and problems warranted revision of the canons. In the revision process, a special American Bar Association committee, headed by former California Chief Justice Roger Traynor, sought and considered the views of the bench and bar and other interested persons. The American Bar Association Code of Judicial Conduct was adopted by the House of Delegates of the American Bar Association August 16, 1972.

Effective January 5, 1975, the California Judges Association adopted a new California Code of Judicial Conduct adapted from the American Bar Association 1972 Model Code. The California code was recast in gender-neutral form in 1986.

In 1990, the American Bar Association Model Code was further revised after a lengthy study. The California Judges Association again reviewed the model code and adopted a revised California Code of Judicial Conduct on October 5, 1992.

Proposition 190 (amending Cal. Const., art. VI, §18, subd. (m), operative March 1, 1995) created a new constitutional provision that states, "The Supreme Court shall make rules for the conduct of judges, both on and off the bench, and for judicial candidates in the conduct of their campaigns. These rules shall be referred to as the Code of Judicial Ethics."

The Supreme Court formally adopted the 1992 Code of Judicial Conduct in March 1995, as a transitional measure pending further review.

The Supreme Court formally adopted the Code of Judicial Ethics effective January 15, 1996.

The Supreme Court has formally adopted amendments to the Code of Judicial Ethics on several occasions. The *Advisory Committee Commentary* is published by the Supreme Court Advisory Committee on the Code of Judicial Ethics.
(Preface amended effective August 19, 2015.)

Preamble

Our legal system is based on the principle that an independent, fair, and competent judiciary will interpret and apply the laws that govern us. The role of the judiciary is central to American concepts of justice and the rule of law. Intrinsic to this code are the precepts that judges, individually and collectively, must respect and honor the judicial office as a public trust and must strive to enhance and maintain confidence in our legal system. The judge is an arbiter of facts and law for the resolution of disputes and is a highly visible member of government under the rule of law.

The Code of Judicial Ethics ("code") establishes standards for ethical conduct of judges on and off the bench and for candidates for judicial office.* The code consists of broad declarations called canons, with subparts, and a terminology section. Following many canons is a commentary section prepared by the Supreme Court Advisory Committee on the Code of Judicial Ethics. The commentary, by explanation and example, provides guidance as to the purpose and meaning of the canons. The commentary does not constitute additional rules and should not be so construed. All members of the judiciary must comply with the code. Compliance is required to preserve the integrity* of the bench and to ensure the confidence of the public.

The canons should be read together as a whole, and each provision should be construed in context and consistent with every other provision. They are to be applied in conformance with constitutional requirements, statutes, other court rules, and decisional law. Nothing in the code shall either impair the essential independence* of judges in making judicial decisions or provide a separate basis for civil liability or criminal prosecution.

The code governs the conduct of judges and candidates for judicial office* and is binding upon them. Whether disciplinary action is appropriate, and the degree of discipline to be imposed, requires a reasoned application of the text and consideration of such factors as the seriousness of the transgression, if there is a pattern of improper activity, and the effect of the improper activity on others or on the judicial system.
(Preamble amended effective August 19, 2015.)

Terminology

Terms explained below are noted with an asterisk (*) in the canons where they appear. In addition, the canons in which these terms appear are cited after the explanation of each term below.

"Candidate for judicial office" is a person seeking election to or retention of a judicial office. A person becomes a candidate for judicial office as soon as he or she makes a public announcement of candidacy, declares or files as a candidate with the election authority, or authorizes solicitation or acceptance of contributions or support. See Preamble and Canons 3B(9) (*Commentary*), 3E(2)(b)(i), 3E(3)(a), 5, 5A, 5A (*Commentary*), 5B(1), 5B(2), 5B(3), 5B(4), 5B (*Commentary*), 5B(4) (*Commentary*) 5C, 5D, and 6E.

"Fiduciary" includes such relationships as executor, administrator, trustee, and guardian. See Canons 3E(5)(d), 4E(1), 4E(2), 4E(3), 4E (*Commentary*), 6B, and 6F (*Commentary*).

---

* Terms with an asterisk (*) are defined in the Terminology section.
* Terms with an asterisk (*) are defined in the Terminology section.

"Gender identity" means a person's internal sense of being male, female, a combination of male and female, or neither male nor female. See Canons 2C, 2C (*Commentary*), 3B(5), 3B(6), 3C(1), and 3C(3).

"Gender expression" is the way people communicate or externally express their gender identity to others, through such means as pronouns used, clothing, appearance, and demeanor. See Canons 2C, 2C (*Commentary*), 3B(5), 3B(6), 3C(1), and 3C(3).

"Gift" means anything of value to the extent that consideration of equal or greater value is not received, and includes a rebate or discount in the price of anything of value unless the rebate or discount is made in the regular course of business to members of the public without regard to official status. See Canons 4D(5), 4D(5) (*Commentary*), 4D(6), 4D(6)(a), 4D(6)(b), 4D(6)(b) (*Commentary*), 4D(6)(d), 4D(6)(f), 4D(6)(i), 4D(6)(i) (*Commentary*), 4D(6) and 4D(7) (*Commentary*), 4H (*Commentary*), 5A (*Commentary*), 5B(4) (*Commentary*), 6D(2)(c), and 6D(7).

"Impartial," "impartiality," and "impartially" mean the absence of bias or prejudice in favor of, or against, particular parties or classes of parties, as well as the maintenance of an open mind in considering issues that may come before a judge. See Canons 1, 1 (*Commentary*), 2A, 2 and 2A (*Commentary*), 2B (*Commentary*), 2C (*Commentary*), 3, 3B(9) (*Commentary*), 3B(10) (*Commentary*), 3B(12), 3B(12) (*Commentary*), 3C(1), 3C(5), 3E(4)(b), 3E(4)(c), 4A(1), 4A (*Commentary*), 4C(3)(b) (*Commentary*), 4C(3)(c) (*Commentary*), 4D(1) (*Commentary*), 4D(6)(a) (*Commentary*), 4D(6)(b) (*Commentary*), 4D(6)(g) (*Commentary*), 4D(6)(i) (*Commentary*), 4H (*Commentary*), 5, 5A, 5A (*Commentary*), 5B (*Commentary*), 5B(4) (*Commentary*), 6D(2)(a), and 6D(3)(a)(vii).

"Impending proceeding" is a proceeding or matter that is imminent or expected to occur in the near future. The words "proceeding" and "matter" are used interchangeably, and are intended to have the same meaning. See Canons 2 and 2A (*Commentary*), 3B(7), 3B(7)(a), 3B(9), 3B(9) (*Commentary*), 4H (*Commentary*), and 6D(6). "Pending proceeding" is defined below.

"Impropriety" includes conduct that violates the law, court rules, or provisions of this code, as well as conduct that undermines a judge's independence, integrity, or impartiality. See Canons 2, 2 and 2A (*Commentary*), 2B (*Commentary*), 2C (*Commentary*), 3B(9) (*Commentary*), 4D(1)(b) (*Commentary*), 4D(6)(g) (*Commentary*), 4D(6)(i) (*Commentary*), 4H, and 5.

"Independence" means a judge's freedom from influence or control other than as established by law. See Preamble, Canons 1, 1 (*Commentary*), 2C, 4C(2) (*Commentary*), 4D(6)(a) (*Commentary*), 4D(6)(g) (*Commentary*), 4D(6)(i) (*Commentary*), 4H(3) (*Commentary*), 5, 5A (*Commentary*), 5B (*Commentary*), and 6D(1).

"Integrity" means probity, fairness, honesty, uprightness, and soundness of character. See Preamble, Canons 1, 1 (*Commentary*), 2A, 2 and 2A (*Commentary*), 2B (*Commentary*), 2C (*Commentary*), 3B(9) (*Commentary*), 3C(1), 3C(5), 4D(6)(a) (*Commentary*), 4D(6)(b) (*Commentary*), 4D(6)(g) (*Commentary*), 4D(6)(i) (*Commentary*), 4H (*Commentary*), 5, 5A (*Commentary*), 5B (*Commentary*), and 6D(1).

"Knowingly," "knowledge," "known," and "knows" mean actual knowledge of the fact in question. A person's knowledge may be inferred from circumstances. See Canons 2B(2)(b), 2B(2)(e), 2C (*Commentary*), 3B(2) (*Commentary*), 3B(7)(a), 3B(7)(a) (*Commentary*), 3D(2), 3D(5), 3E(5)(f), 5B(1)(b), 6D(3)(a)(i), 6D(3)(a) (*Commentary*), 6D(4) (*Commentary*), and 6D(5)(a).

"Law" means constitutional provisions, statutes, court rules, and decisional law. See Canons 1 (*Commentary*), 2A, 2C (*Commentary*), 3A, 3B(2), 3B(7), 3B(7)(c), 3B(8), 3B(8) (*Commentary*), 3B(12) (*Commentary*), 3E(1), 4C(3)(c) (*Commentary*), 4F, and 4H.

"Law, the legal system, or the administration of justice." When a judge engages in an activity that relates to the law, the legal system, or the administration of justice, the judge should also consider factors such as whether the activity upholds the integrity, impartiality, and independence of the judiciary (Canons 1 and 2A), whether the activity impairs public confidence in the judiciary (Canon 2), whether the judge is allowing the activity to take precedence over judicial duties (Canon 3A), and whether engaging in the activity would cause the judge to be disqualified (Canon 4A(4)). See Canons 4B (*Commentary*), 4C(1), 4C(1) (*Commentary*), 4C(2), 4C(2) (*Commentary*), 4C(3)(a), 4C(3)(b) (*Commentary*), 4C(3)(d)(ii), 4C(3)(d) (*Commentary*), 4D(6)(d), 4D(6)(e), 5A (*Commentary*), 5D, and 5D (*Commentary*).

"Member of the judge's family" means a spouse, registered domestic partner, child, grandchild, parent, grandparent, or other relative or person with whom the judge maintains a close familial relationship. See Canons 2B(3)(c), 2B (*Commentary*), 4C(3)(d)(i), 4D(1) (*Commentary*), 4D(2), 4D(5) (*Commentary*), 4E(1), and 4G (*Commentary*).

"Member of the judge's family residing in the judge's household" means a spouse or registered domestic partner and those persons who reside in the judge's household and who are relatives of the judge, including relatives by marriage or persons with whom the judge maintains a close familial relationship. See Canons 4D(5), 4D(5) (*Commentary*), 4D(6), 4D(6)(b) (*Commentary*), 4D(6)(f) and 6D(2)(c).

"Nonpublic information" means information that, by law, is not available to the public. Nonpublic information may include, but is not limited to, information that is sealed by statute or court order, impounded, or communicated in camera, and information offered in grand jury proceedings, presentencing reports, dependency cases, or psychiatric reports. Nonpublic information also includes information from affidavits, jury results, or court rulings before it becomes public information. See Canons 3B(11) and 6D(8)(a).

"Pending proceeding" is a proceeding or matter that has commenced. A proceeding continues to be pending through any period during which an appeal may be filed and any appellate process until final disposition. The words "proceeding" and "matter" are used interchangeably, and are intended to have the same meaning. See Canons 2 and 2A (*Commentary*), 2B(3)(a), 3B(7), 3B(9), 3B(9) (*Commentary*), 3E(5)(a), 4H (*Commentary*), and 6D(6). "Impending proceeding" is defined above.

"Political organization" means a political party, political action committee, or other group, the principal purpose of which is to further the election or appointment of candidates to nonjudicial office. See Canon 5A.

"Registered domestic partner" means a person who has registered for domestic partnership pursuant to state law or who is recognized as a domestic partner pursuant to Family Code section 299.2. See Canons 3E(5)(d), 3E(5)(e), 3E(5)(i), 4D(6)(d), 4D(6)(f), 4D(6)(j), 4H(2), 5A (*Commentary*), 6D(3)(a)(v), and 6D(3)(a)(vi).

"Require." Any canon prescribing that a judge "require" certain conduct of others means that a judge is to exercise reasonable direction and control over the conduct of those persons subject to the judge's direction and control. See Canons 3B(3), 3B(4), 3B(6), 3B(8) (*Commentary*), 3B(9), 3C(3), 6D(1), 6D(2)(a), and 6D(6).

"Service organization" includes any organization commonly referred to as a "fraternal organization." See Canons 3E(5)(d), 4C(2) (*Commentary*), 4C(3)(b), 4C(3)(b) (*Commentary*), 4C(3)(d) (*Commentary*), 4D(6)(j), and 6D(2)(b).

"Subordinate judicial officer." A subordinate judicial officer is, for the purposes of this code, a person appointed pursuant to article VI, section 22 of the California Constitution, including, but not limited to, a commissioner, referee, and hearing officer. See Canons 3D(3), 4G (*Commentary*), and 6A.

"Temporary Judge" means an active or inactive member of the bar who, pursuant to article VI, section 21 of the California Constitution, serves or expects to serve as a judge once, sporadically, or regularly on a part-time basis under a separate court appointment for each period of service or for each case heard. See Canons 3E(5)(h), 4C(3)(d)(i), 4C(3)(d) (*Commentary*), 6A, and 6D.

"Third degree of relationship" includes the following persons: great-grandparent, grandparent, parent, uncle, aunt, brother, sister, child, grandchild, great-grandchild, nephew, and niece. See Canons 3E(5)(e), 3E(5)(i), and 6D(3)(a)(v).

(*Terminology amended effective July 1, 2020; previously amended effective August 19, 2015, January 21, 2016, and October 10, 2018.*)

Canon 1. A judge shall uphold the integrity* and independence* of the judiciary.

An independent, impartial,* and honorable judiciary is indispensable to justice in our society. A judge should participate in establishing, maintaining, and enforcing high standards of conduct, and shall personally observe those standards so that the integrity* and independence* of the judiciary is preserved. The provisions of this code are to be construed and applied to further that objective. A judicial decision or administrative act later determined to be incorrect legally is not itself a violation of this code.

ADVISORY COMMITTEE COMMENTARY: Canon 1

Deference to the judgments and rulings of courts depends upon public confidence in the integrity and independence* of judges. The integrity* and independence* of judges depend in turn upon their acting without fear or favor. Although* judges should be independent, they must comply with the law* and the provisions of this code. Public confidence in the impartiality* of the judiciary is maintained by the adherence of each judge to this responsibility. Conversely, violations of this code diminish public confidence in the judiciary and thereby do injury to the system of government under law.

The basic function of an independent, impartial,* and honorable judiciary is to maintain the utmost integrity* in decisionmaking, and this code should be read and interpreted with that function in mind.

(Canon 1 amended effective August 19, 2015; previously amended effective January 1, 2013.)

Canon 2. A judge shall avoid impropriety* and the appearance of impropriety* in all of the judge's activities.

A. Promoting Public Confidence

A judge shall respect and comply with the law* and shall act at all times in a manner that promotes public confidence in the integrity* and impartiality* of the judiciary. A judge shall not make statements, whether public or nonpublic, that commit the judge with respect to cases, controversies, or issues that are likely to come before the courts or that are inconsistent with the impartial* performance of the adjudicative duties of judicial office.

ADVISORY COMMITTEE COMMENTARY: Canons 2 and 2A

Public confidence in the judiciary is eroded by irresponsible or improper conduct by judges.

A judge must avoid all impropriety* and appearance of impropriety.* A judge must expect to be the subject of constant public scrutiny. A judge must therefore accept restrictions on the judge's conduct that might be viewed as burdensome by other members of the community and should do so freely and willingly.

A judge must exercise caution when engaging in any type of electronic communication, including communication by text or email, or when participating in online social networking sites or otherwise posting material on the Internet, given the accessibility, widespread transmission, and permanence of electronic communications and material posted on the Internet. The same canons that govern a judge's ability to socialize and communicate in person, on paper, or over the telephone apply to electronic communications, including use of the Internet and social networking sites. These canons include, but are not limited to, Canons 2B(2) (lending the prestige of judicial office), 3B(7) (ex parte communications), 3B(9) (public comment about pending* or impending proceedings*), 3E(2) (disclosure of information relevant to disqualification), and 4A (conducting extrajudicial activities to avoid casting doubt on the judge's capacity to act impartially,* demeaning the judicial office, or frequent disqualification).

The prohibition against behaving with impropriety* or the appearance of impropriety* applies to both the professional and personal conduct of a judge.

The test for the appearance of impropriety* is whether a person aware of the facts might reasonably entertain a doubt that the judge would be able to act with integrity,* impartiality,* and competence.

As to membership in organizations that practice invidious discrimination, see Commentary under Canon 2C.

As to judges making statements that commit the judge with respect to cases, controversies, or issues that are likely to come before the courts, see Canon 3B(9) and its commentary concerning comments about a pending proceeding,* Canon 3E(3)(a) concerning the disqualification of a judge who makes statements that commit the judge to a particular result, and Canon 5B(1)(a) concerning statements made during an election campaign that commit the candidate to a particular result. In addition, Code of Civil Procedure section 170.2, subdivision (b), provides that, with certain exceptions, a judge is not disqualified on the ground that the judge has, in any capacity, expressed a view on a legal or factual issue presented in the proceeding before the judge.

(Canon 2A amended effective October 10, 2018; previously amended effective January 1, 2013, and August 19, 2015.)

B. Use of the Prestige of Judicial Office

(1) A judge shall not allow family, social, political, or other relationships to influence the judge's judicial conduct or judgment, nor shall a judge convey or permit others to convey the impression that any individual is in a special position to influence the judge.

(2) A judge shall not lend the prestige of judicial office or use the judicial title in any manner, including any oral or written communication, to advance the pecuniary or personal interests of the judge or others. This canon does not prohibit the following:

(a) A judge may testify as a character witness, provided the judge does so only when subpoenaed.

(b) A judge may, without a subpoena, provide the Commission on Judicial Performance with a written communication containing (i) factual information regarding a matter pending before the commission or (ii) information related to the character of a judge who has a matter pending before the commission, provided that any such factual or character information is based on personal knowledge.* In commission proceedings, a judge shall provide information responsive to a subpoena or when officially requested to do so by the commission.

(c) A judge may provide factual information in State Bar disciplinary proceedings and shall provide information responsive to a subpoena or when officially requested to do so by the State Bar.

(d) A judge may respond to judicial selection inquiries, provide recommendations (including a general character reference relating to the evaluation of persons being considered for a judgeship), and otherwise participate in the process of judicial selection.

(e) A judge may serve as a reference or provide a letter of recommendation only if based on the judge's personal knowledge* of the individual. These written communications may include the judge's title and may be written on stationery that uses the judicial title.

(3) Except as permitted in subdivision (c) or otherwise authorized by law* or these canons:

(a) A judge shall not advance the pecuniary or personal interests of the judge or others by initiating communications with a sentencing judge or a representative of a probation department about a proceeding pending* before the sentencing judge, but may provide information in response to an official request. "Sentencing judge" includes a judge who makes a disposition pursuant to Welfare and Institutions Code section 725.

(b) A judge, other than the judge who presided over the trial of or sentenced the person seeking parole, pardon, or commutation of sentence, shall not initiate communications with the Board of Parole Hearings regarding parole or the Office of the Governor regarding parole, pardon, or commutation of sentence, but may provide these entities with information for the record in response to an official request.

(c) A judge may initiate communications concerning a member of the judge's family* with a representative of a probation department regarding sentencing, the Board of Parole Hearings regarding parole, or the Office of the Governor regarding parole, pardon, or commutation of sentence, provided the judge is not identified as a judge in the communication.

ADVISORY COMMITTEE COMMENTARY: Canon 2B

A strong judicial branch, based on the prestige that comes from effective and ethical performance, is essential to a system of government in which the judiciary functions independently of the executive and legislative branches. A judge should distinguish between proper and improper use of the prestige of office in all of his or her activities.

As to those communications that are permitted under this canon, a judge must keep in mind the general obligations to maintain high standards of conduct as set forth in Canon 1, and to avoid any impropriety* or the appearance of impropriety* as set forth in Canon 2. A judge must also be mindful of Canon 2A, which requires a judge to act at all times in a manner that promotes public confidence in the integrity* and impartiality* of the courts.

A judge must avoid lending the prestige of judicial office for the advancement of the private interests of the judge or others. For example, a judge must not use the judicial position to gain advantage in a civil suit involving a member of the judge's family,* or use his or her position to gain deferential treatment when stopped by a police officer for a traffic offense.

If a judge posts on social networking sites such as Facebook or crowdsourced sites such as Yelp or Trip Advisor, the judge may not lend the prestige of judicial office to advance the pecuniary or personal interests of the judge or others. For example, a judge may not comment on, recommend, or criticize businesses, products, or services on such sites if it is reasonably likely that the judge can be identified as a judge.

See canon 4C(3)(d)(iv) prohibiting the use of the prestige of judicial office for fundraising or membership solicitation, but allowing a judge to be a speaker, guest of honor, or recipient of an award for public or charitable service, provided the judge does not personally solicit funds and complies with Canons 4A(1), (2), (3), and (4).

As to the use of a judge's title to identify a judge's role in the presentation and creation of legal education programs and materials, see Commentary to Canon 4B. In contracts for publication of a judge's writings, a judge should retain control over the advertising, to the extent feasible, to avoid exploitation of the judge's office.

This canon does not afford a judge a privilege against testifying in response to any official summons.

See also Canons 3D(1) and 3D(2) concerning a judge's obligation to take appropriate corrective action regarding other judges who violate any provision of the Code of Judicial Ethics and attorneys who violate any provision of the Rules of Professional Conduct.

Except as set forth in Canon 2B(3)(a), this canon does not preclude consultations among judges. Additional limitations on such consultations among judges are set forth in Canon 3B(7)(a).

---

* Terms with an asterisk (*) are defined in the Terminology section.

(Canon 2B amended effective July 1, 2020; previously amended effective January 1, 2008, January 1, 2013, and August 19, 2015.)

C. Membership in Organizations

A judge shall not hold membership in any organization that practices invidious discrimination on the basis of race, sex, gender, gender identity,* gender expression,* religion, national origin, ethnicity, or sexual orientation.

This canon does not apply to membership in a religious organization.

ADVISORY COMMITTEE COMMENTARY: Canon 2C

Membership by a judge in an organization that practices invidious discrimination on the basis of race, sex, gender, religion, national origin, ethnicity, or sexual orientation gives rise to a perception that the judge's impartiality is impaired. The code prohibits such membership by judges to preserve the fairness, impartiality,* independence,* and honor of the judiciary, to treat all parties equally under the law,* and to avoid impropriety* and the appearance of impropriety.**

Previously, Canon 2C contained exceptions to this prohibition for membership in religious organizations, membership in an official military organization of the United States and, so long as membership did not violate Canon 4A, membership in a nonprofit youth organization. The exceptions for membership in an official military organization of the United States and nonprofit youth organizations have been eliminated as exceptions to the canon. The exception for membership in religious organizations has been preserved.

Canon 2C refers to the current practices of the organization. Whether an organization practices invidious discrimination is often a complex question to which judges should be sensitive. The answer cannot be determined from a mere examination of an organization's current membership rolls, but rather depends on how the organization selects members and other relevant factors, such as whether the organization is dedicated to the preservation of religious, ethnic, or cultural values of legitimate common interest to its members, or whether it is in fact and effect an intimate, purely private organization whose membership limitations could not be constitutionally prohibited. Absent such factors, an organization is generally said to discriminate invidiously if it arbitrarily excludes from membership on the basis of race, religion, sex, gender, gender identity, gender expression,* national origin, ethnicity, or sexual orientation persons who would otherwise be admitted to membership.*

Although Canon 2C relates only to membership in organizations that invidiously discriminate on the basis of race, sex, gender, gender identity, gender expression,* religion, national origin, ethnicity, or sexual orientation, a judge's membership in an organization that engages in any discriminatory membership practices prohibited by law* also violates Canon 2 and Canon 2A and gives the appearance of impropriety.* In addition, it would be a violation of Canon 2 and Canon 2A for a judge to arrange a meeting at a club that the judge knows* practices such invidious discrimination or for the judge to use such a club regularly. Moreover, public manifestation by a judge of the judge's knowing* approval of invidious discrimination on any basis gives the appearance of impropriety* under Canon 2 and diminishes public confidence in the integrity* and impartiality* of the judiciary in violation of Canon 2A.*

(Canon 2C amended effective October 10, 2018; previously amended effective June 18, 2003, January 1, 2013, and January 21, 2016.)

Canon 3. A judge shall perform the duties of judicial office impartially,* competently, and diligently.

A. Judicial Duties in General

All of the judicial duties prescribed by law* shall take precedence over all other activities of every judge. In the performance of these duties, the following standards apply.

B. Adjudicative Responsibilities

(1) A judge shall hear and decide all matters assigned to the judge except those in which he or she is disqualified.

ADVISORY COMMITTEE COMMENTARY: Canon 3B(1)

Canon 3B(1) is based upon the affirmative obligation contained in Code of Civil Procedure section 170.

(2) A judge shall be faithful to the law* regardless of partisan interests, public clamor, or fear of criticism, and shall maintain professional competence in the law.*

ADVISORY COMMITTEE COMMENTARY: Canon 3B(2)

Competence in the performance of judicial duties requires the legal knowledge, skill, thoroughness, and preparation reasonably necessary to perform a judge's responsibilities of judicial office. Canon 1 provides that an incorrect legal ruling is not itself a violation of this code.*

(3) A judge shall require* order and decorum in proceedings before the judge.

(4) A judge shall be patient, dignified, and courteous to litigants, jurors, witnesses, lawyers, and others with whom the judge deals in an official capacity, and shall require* similar conduct of lawyers and of all staff and court personnel under the judge's direction and control.

(5) A judge shall perform judicial duties without bias or prejudice. A judge shall not, in the performance of judicial duties, engage in speech, gestures, or other conduct that would reasonably be perceived as (a) bias, prejudice, or harassment, including but not limited to bias, prejudice, or harassment based upon race, sex, gender, gender identity,* gender expression,* religion, national origin, ethnicity, disability, age, sexual orientation, marital status, socioeconomic status, or political affiliation, or (b) sexual harassment.

(6) A judge shall require* lawyers in proceedings before the judge to refrain from (a) manifesting, by words or conduct, bias, prejudice, or harassment based upon race, sex, gender, gender identity,* gender expression,* religion, national origin, ethnicity, disability, age, sexual orientation, marital status, socioeconomic status, or political affiliation, or (b) sexual harassment against parties, witnesses, counsel, or others. This canon does not preclude legitimate advocacy when race, sex, gender, gender identity,* gender expression,* religion, national origin, ethnicity, disability, age, sexual orientation, marital status, socioeconomic status, political affiliation, or other similar factors are issues in the proceeding.

(7) A judge shall accord to every person who has a legal interest in a proceeding, or that person's lawyer, the full right to be heard according to law.* Unless otherwise authorized by law,* a judge shall not independently investigate facts in a proceeding and shall consider only the evidence presented or facts that may be properly judicially noticed. This prohibition extends to information available in all media, including electronic. A judge shall not initiate, permit, or consider ex parte communications, that is, any communications to or from the judge outside the presence of the parties concerning a pending* or impending* proceeding, and shall make reasonable efforts to avoid such communications, except as follows:

(a) Except as stated below, a judge may consult with other judges. A judge presiding over a case shall not engage in discussions about that case with a judge who has previously been disqualified from hearing that case; likewise, a judge who knows* he or she is or would be disqualified from hearing a case shall not discuss that matter with the judge assigned to the case. A judge also shall not engage in discussions with a judge who may participate in appellate review of the matter, nor shall a judge who may participate in appellate review of a matter engage in discussions with the judge presiding over the case.

A judge may consult with court personnel or others authorized by law,* as long as the communication relates to that person's duty to aid the judge in carrying out the judge's adjudicative responsibilities.

In any discussion with judges or court personnel, a judge shall make reasonable efforts to avoid receiving factual information that is not part of the record or an evaluation of that factual information. In such consultations, the judge shall not abrogate the responsibility personally to decide the matter.

For purposes of Canon 3B(7)(a), "court personnel" includes bailiffs, court reporters, court externs, research attorneys, courtroom clerks, and other employees of the court, but does not include the lawyers in a proceeding before a judge, persons who are appointed by the court to serve in some capacity in a proceeding, or employees of other governmental entities, such as lawyers, social workers, or representatives of the probation department.

ADVISORY COMMITTEE COMMENTARY: Canon 3B(7)(a)

Regarding communications between a judge presiding over a matter and a judge of a court with appellate jurisdiction over that matter, see Government Code section 68070.5.

Though a judge may have ex parte discussions with appropriate court personnel, a judge may do so only on matters that are within the proper performance of that person's duties. For example, a bailiff may inform the judge of a threat to the judge or to the safety and security of the courtroom, but may not tell the judge ex parte that a defendant was overheard making an incriminating statement during a court recess. A clerk may point out to the judge a technical defect in a proposed sentence, but may not suggest to the judge that a defendant deserves a certain sentence.

A sentencing judge may not consult ex parte with a representative of the probation department about a matter pending before the sentencing judge.

This canon prohibits a judge who is presiding over a case from discussing that case with another judge who has already been disqualified from hearing that case.

---

* Terms with an asterisk (*) are defined in the Terminology section.

A judge also must be careful not to talk to a judge whom the judge knows* would be disqualified from hearing the matter.

(b) A judge may initiate, permit, or consider ex parte communications, where circumstances require, for scheduling, administrative purposes, or emergencies that do not deal with substantive matters provided:

(i) the judge reasonably believes that no party will gain a procedural or tactical advantage as a result of the ex parte communication, and

(ii) the judge makes provision promptly to notify all other parties of the substance of the ex parte communication and allows an opportunity to respond.

(c) A judge may initiate, permit, or consider any ex parte communication when expressly authorized by law* to do so or when authorized to do so by stipulation of the parties.

(d) If a judge receives an unauthorized ex parte communication, the judge shall make provision promptly to notify the parties of the substance of the communication and provide the parties with an opportunity to respond.

ADVISORY COMMITTEE COMMENTARY: Canon 3B(7)

An exception allowing a judge, under certain circumstances, to obtain the advice of a disinterested expert on the law* has been eliminated from Canon 3B(7) because consulting with legal experts outside the presence of the parties is inconsistent with the core tenets of the adversarial system. Therefore, a judge shall not consult with legal experts outside the presence of the parties. Evidence Code section 730 provides for the appointment of an expert if a judge determines that expert testimony is necessary. A court may also invite the filing of amicus curiae briefs.

An exception allowing a judge to confer with the parties separately in an effort to settle the matter before the judge has been moved from this canon to Canon 3B(12).

This canon does not prohibit court personnel from communicating scheduling information or carrying out similar administrative functions.

A judge is statutorily authorized to investigate and consult witnesses informally in small claims cases. Code of Civil Procedure section 116.520, subdivision (c).

(8) A judge shall dispose of all judicial matters fairly, promptly, and efficiently. A judge shall manage the courtroom in a manner that provides all litigants the opportunity to have their matters fairly adjudicated in accordance with the law.*

ADVISORY COMMITTEE COMMENTARY: Canon 3B(8)

The obligation of a judge to dispose of matters promptly and efficiently must not take precedence over the judge's obligation to dispose of the matters fairly and with patience. For example, when a litigant is self-represented, a judge has the discretion to take reasonable steps, appropriate under the circumstances and consistent with the law* and the canons, to enable the litigant to be heard. A judge should monitor and supervise cases so as to reduce or eliminate dilatory practices, avoidable delays, and unnecessary costs.

Prompt disposition of the court's business requires a judge to devote adequate time to judicial duties, to be punctual in attending court and expeditious in determining matters under submission, and to require* that court officials, litigants, and their lawyers cooperate with the judge to those ends.

(9) A judge shall not make any public comment about a pending* or impending* proceeding in any court, and shall not make any nonpublic comment that might substantially interfere with a fair trial or hearing. The judge shall require* similar abstention on the part of staff and court personnel subject to the judge's direction and control. This canon does not prohibit judges from making statements in the course of their official duties or from explaining the procedures of the court, and does not apply to proceedings in which the judge is a litigant in a personal capacity. In connection with a judicial election or recall campaign, this canon does not prohibit any judge from making a public comment about a pending* proceeding, provided (a) the comment would not reasonably be expected to affect the outcome or impair the fairness of the proceeding, and (b) the comment is about the procedural, factual, or legal basis of a decision about which a judge has been criticized during the election or recall campaign. Other than cases in which the judge has personally participated, this canon does not prohibit judges from discussing, in legal education programs and materials, cases and issues pending in appellate courts. This educational exemption does not apply to cases over which the judge has presided or to comments or discussions that might interfere with a fair hearing of the case.

ADVISORY COMMITTEE COMMENTARY: Canon 3B(9)

The requirement that judges abstain from public comment regarding a pending* or impending* proceeding continues during any appellate process and until final disposition. A judge shall make reasonable efforts to ascertain whether a case is pending* or impending* before commenting on it. This canon does not prohibit a judge from commenting on proceedings in which the judge is a litigant in a personal capacity, but in cases such as a writ of mandamus where the judge is a litigant in an official capacity, the judge must not comment publicly.

"Making statements in the course of their official duties" and "explaining the procedures of the court" include providing an official transcript or partial official transcript of a court proceeding open to the public and explaining the rules of court and procedures related to a decision rendered by a judge.

The provision allowing a judge to make a public comment about a pending* decision that is the subject of criticism during an election campaign applies to all judicial elections, including recall elections. Depending on the circumstances, the judge should consider whether it may be preferable for a third party, rather than the judge, to respond or issue statements in connection with allegations concerning the decision. For purposes of this provision, a recall campaign begins when a judge is served with a notice of intention to circulate a recall petition (see Elec. Code, § 11006), and a judicial election campaign begins when a judge or candidate for judicial office* files a declaration of intention of candidacy for judicial office (see Elec. Code, § 8023).

Although this canon does not prohibit a judge from commenting on cases that are not pending* or impending* in any court, a judge must be cognizant of the general prohibition in Canon 2 against conduct involving impropriety* or the appearance of impropriety.* A judge should also be aware of the mandate in Canon 2A that a judge must act at all times in a manner that promotes public confidence in the integrity* and impartiality* of the judiciary. In addition, when commenting on a case pursuant to this canon, a judge must maintain the high standards of conduct, as set forth in Canon 1.

Although a judge is permitted to make nonpublic comments about pending* or impending* cases that will not substantially interfere with a fair trial or hearing, the judge should be cautious when making any such comments. There is always a risk that a comment can be misheard, misinterpreted, or repeated. A judge making such a comment must be mindful of the judge's obligation under Canon 2A to act at all times in a manner that promotes public confidence in the integrity* and impartiality* of the judiciary. When a judge makes a nonpublic comment about a case pending* before that judge, the judge must keep an open mind and not form an opinion prematurely or create the appearance of having formed an opinion prematurely.

(10) A judge shall not commend or criticize jurors for their verdict other than in a court order or opinion in a proceeding, but may express appreciation to jurors for their service to the judicial system and the community.

ADVISORY COMMITTEE COMMENTARY: Canon 3B(10)

Commending or criticizing jurors for their verdict may imply a judicial expectation in future cases and may impair a juror's ability to be fair and impartial* in a subsequent case.

(11) A judge shall not disclose or use, for any purpose unrelated to judicial duties, nonpublic information* acquired in a judicial capacity.

(12) A judge may participate in settlement conferences or in other efforts to resolve matters in dispute, including matters pending before the judge. A judge may, with the express consent of the parties or their lawyers, confer separately with the parties and/or their lawyers during such resolution efforts. At all times during such resolution efforts, a judge shall remain impartial* and shall not engage in conduct that may reasonably be perceived as coercive.

ADVISORY COMMITTEE COMMENTARY: Canon 3B(12)

While the judge plays an important role in overseeing efforts to resolve disputes, including conducting settlement discussions, a judge should be careful that efforts to resolve disputes do not undermine any party's right to be heard according to law.*

The judge should keep in mind the effect that the judge's participation in dispute resolution efforts may have on the judge's impartiality* or the appearance of impartiality* if the case remains with the judge for trial after resolution efforts are unsuccessful. Accordingly, a judge may wish to consider whether: (1) the parties or their counsel have requested or objected to the participation by the trial judge in such discussions; (2) the parties and their counsel are relatively sophisticated in legal matters or the particular legal issues involved in the case; (3) a party is unrepresented; (4) the case will be tried by the judge or a jury; (5) the parties will participate with their counsel in settlement discussions and, if so, the effect of personal contact between the judge and parties; and (6) it is appropriate during the settlement conference for the judge to express an opinion on the merits or worth of the case or express an opinion on the legal issues that the judge may later have to rule upon.

If a judge assigned to preside over a trial believes participation in resolution efforts could influence the judge's decisionmaking during trial, the judge may decline to engage in such efforts.

---

* Terms with an asterisk (*) are defined in the Terminology section.

Where dispute resolution efforts of any type are unsuccessful, the judge should consider whether, due to events that occurred during the resolution efforts, the judge may be disqualified under the law* from presiding over the trial. See, e.g., Code of Civil Procedure section 170.1, subdivision (a)(6)(A).

(Canon 3B amended effective July 1, 2020; previously amended effective December 22, 2003, January 1, 2008, January 1, 2013, August 19, 2015, and October 10, 2018.)

C. Administrative Responsibilities

(1) A judge shall diligently discharge the judge's administrative responsibilities impartially,* on the basis of merit, without bias or prejudice, free of conflict of interest, and in a manner that promotes public confidence in the integrity* of the judiciary. A judge shall not, in the performance of administrative duties, engage in speech, gestures, or other conduct that would reasonably be perceived as (a) bias, prejudice, or harassment, including but not limited to bias, prejudice, or harassment based upon race, sex, gender, gender identity,* gender expression,* religion, national origin, ethnicity, disability, age, sexual orientation, marital status, socioeconomic status, or political affiliation, or (b) sexual harassment.

ADVISORY COMMITTEE COMMENTARY: Canon 3C(1)

In considering what constitutes a conflict of interest under this canon, a judge should be informed by Code of Civil Procedure section 170.1, subdivision (a)(6).

(2) A judge shall maintain professional competence in judicial administration, and shall cooperate with other judges and court officials in the administration of court business.

(3) A judge shall require* staff and court personnel under the judge's direction and control to observe appropriate standards of conduct and to refrain from (a) manifesting bias, prejudice, or harassment based upon race, sex, gender, gender identity,* gender expression,* religion, national origin, ethnicity, disability, age, sexual orientation, marital status, socioeconomic status, or political affiliation, or (b) sexual harassment in the performance of their official duties.

(4) A judge with supervisory authority for the judicial performance of other judges shall take reasonable measures to ensure the prompt disposition of matters before them and the proper performance of their other judicial responsibilities.

(5) A judge shall not make unnecessary court appointments. A judge shall exercise the power of appointment impartially,* on the basis of merit, without bias or prejudice, free of conflict of interest, and in a manner that promotes public confidence in the integrity* of the judiciary. A judge shall avoid nepotism and favoritism. A judge shall not approve compensation of appointees above the reasonable value of services rendered.

ADVISORY COMMITTEE COMMENTARY: Canon 3C(5)

Appointees of a judge include assigned counsel and officials such as referees, commissioners, special masters, receivers, and guardians. Consent by the parties to an appointment or an award of compensation does not relieve the judge of the obligation prescribed by Canon 3C(5).

(Canon 3C amended effective October 10, 2018; previously amended effective December 22, 2003, April 29, 2009, January 1, 2013, and August 19, 2015.)

D. Disciplinary Responsibilities

(1) Whenever a judge has reliable information that another judge has violated any provision of the Code of Judicial Ethics, that judge shall take appropriate corrective action, which may include reporting the violation to the appropriate authority. (See Commentary to Canon 3D(2).)

(2) Whenever a judge has personal knowledge,* or concludes in a judicial decision, that a lawyer has committed misconduct or has violated any provision of the Rules of Professional Conduct, the judge shall take appropriate corrective action, which may include reporting the violation to the appropriate authority.

ADVISORY COMMITTEE COMMENTARY: Canons 3D(1) and 3D(2)

Appropriate corrective action could include direct communication with the judge or lawyer who has committed the violation, writing about the misconduct in a judicial decision, or other direct action, such as a confidential referral to a judicial or lawyer assistance program, or a report of the violation to the presiding judge, appropriate authority, or other agency or body. Judges should note that in addition to the action required by Canon 3D(2), California law imposes additional mandatory reporting requirements to the State Bar on judges regarding lawyer misconduct. See Business and Professions Code sections 6086.7 and 6086.8, subdivision (a), and California Rules of Court, rules 10.609 and 10.1017.

"Appropriate authority" means the authority with responsibility for initiation of the disciplinary process with respect to a violation to be reported.

(3) A judge shall promptly report in writing to the Commission on Judicial Performance when he or she is charged in court by misdemeanor citation, prosecutorial complaint, information, or indictment with any crime in the United States as specified below. Crimes that must be reported are: (1) all crimes, other than those that would be considered misdemeanors not involving moral turpitude or infractions under California law; and (2) all misdemeanors involving violence (including assaults), the use or possession of controlled substances, the misuse of prescriptions, or the personal use or furnishing of alcohol. A judge also shall promptly report in writing upon conviction of such crimes.

If the judge is a retired judge serving in the Temporary Assigned Judges Program, he or she shall promptly report such information in writing to the Chief Justice rather than to the Commission on Judicial Performance. If the judge is a subordinate judicial officer,* he or she shall promptly report such information in writing to both the presiding judge of the court in which the subordinate judicial officer* sits and the Commission on Judicial Performance.

(4) A judge shall cooperate with judicial and lawyer disciplinary agencies.

ADVISORY COMMITTEE COMMENTARY: Canons 3D(3) and 3D(4)

See Government Code section 68725, which requires judges to cooperate with and give reasonable assistance and information to the Commission on Judicial Performance, and rule 104 of the Rules of the Commission on Judicial Performance, which requires a respondent judge to cooperate with the commission in all proceedings in accordance with section 68725.

(5) A judge shall not retaliate, directly or indirectly, against a person known* or suspected to have assisted or cooperated with an investigation of a judge or a lawyer.

(Canon 3D amended effective July 1, 2020; adopted effective January 15, 1996; previously amended effective June 19, 1997, March 4, 1999, January 1, 2008, January 1, 2013, August 19, 2015, and October 10, 2018.)

E. Disqualification and Disclosure

(1) A judge shall disqualify himself or herself in any proceeding in which disqualification is required by law.*

ADVISORY COMMITTEE COMMENTARY: Canon 3E(1)

The term "proceeding" as used in this canon encompasses prefiling judicial determinations. Thus, if a judge has a disqualifying interest in a matter, the judge is disqualified from taking any action in the matter, even if it predates the actual filing of a case, such as making a probable cause determination, signing a search or arrest warrant, setting bail, or ordering an own recognizance release. Interpreting "proceeding" to include prefiling judicial determinations effectuates the intent of the canon because it assures the parties and the public of the integrity and fairness of the judicial process.*

(2) In all trial court proceedings, a judge shall disclose on the record as follows:

(a) Information relevant to disqualification

A judge shall disclose information that is reasonably relevant to the question of disqualification under Code of Civil Procedure section 170.1, even if the judge believes there is no actual basis for disqualification.

(b) Campaign contributions in trial court elections

(i) Information required to be disclosed

In any matter before a judge who is or was a candidate for judicial office* in a trial court election, the judge shall disclose any contribution or loan of $100 or more from a party, individual lawyer, or law office or firm in that matter as required by this canon, even if the amount of the contribution or loan would not require disqualification. Such disclosure shall consist of the name of the contributor or lender, the amount of each contribution or loan, the cumulative amount of the contributor's contributions or lender's loans, and the date of each contribution or loan. The judge shall make reasonable efforts to obtain current information regarding contributions or loans received by his or her campaign and shall disclose the required information on the record.

(ii) Manner of disclosure

The judge shall ensure that the required information is conveyed on the record to the parties and lawyers appearing in the matter before the judge. The judge has discretion to select the manner of disclosure, but the manner used shall avoid the appearance that the judge is soliciting campaign contributions.

(iii) Timing of disclosure

---

* Terms with an asterisk (*) are defined in the Terminology section.

Disclosure shall be made at the earliest reasonable opportunity after receiving each contribution or loan. The duty commences no later than one week after receipt of the first contribution or loan, and continues for a period of two years after the candidate takes the oath of office, or two years from the date of the contribution or loan, whichever event is later.

ADVISORY COMMITTEE COMMENTARY: Canon 3E(2)(b)

Code of Civil Procedure section 170.1, subdivision (a)(9)(C) requires a judge to "disclose any contribution from a party or lawyer in a matter that is before the court that is required to be reported under subdivision (f) of Section 84211 of the Government Code, even if the amount would not require disqualification under this paragraph." This statute further provides that the "manner of disclosure shall be the same as that provided in Canon 3E of the Code of Judicial Ethics." Canon 3E(2)(b) sets forth the information the judge must disclose, the manner for making such disclosure, and the timing thereof.

"Contribution" includes monetary and in-kind contributions. See Cal. Code Regs., tit. 2, § 18215, subd. (b)(3). See generally Government Code section 84211, subdivision (f).

Disclosure of campaign contributions is intended to provide parties and lawyers appearing before a judge during and after a judicial campaign with easy access to information about campaign contributions that may not require disqualification but could be relevant to the question of disqualification of the judge. The judge is responsible for ensuring that the disclosure is conveyed to the parties and lawyers appearing in the matter. The canon provides that the judge has discretion to select the manner of making the disclosure. The appropriate manner of disclosure will depend on whether all of the parties and lawyers are present in court, whether it is more efficient or practicable given the court's calendar to make a written disclosure, and other relevant circumstances that may affect the ability of the parties and lawyers to access the required information. The following alternatives for disclosure are non-exclusive. If all parties are present in court, the judge may conclude that the most effective and efficient manner of providing disclosure is to state orally the required information on the record in open court. In the alternative, again if all parties are present in court, a judge may determine that it is more appropriate to state orally on the record in open court that parties and lawyers may obtain the required information at an easily accessible location in the courthouse, and provide an opportunity for the parties and lawyers to review the available information. Another alternative, particularly if all or some parties are not present in court, is that the judge may disclose the campaign contribution in a written minute order or in the official court minutes and notify the parties and the lawyers of the written disclosure. See California Supreme Court Committee on Judicial Ethics Opinions, CJEO Formal Opinion No. 2013-002, pp. 7-8. If a party appearing in a matter before the judge is represented by a lawyer, it is sufficient to make the disclosure to the lawyer.

In addition to the disclosure obligations set forth in Canon 3E(2)(b), a judge must, pursuant to Canon 3E(2)(a), disclose on the record any other information that may be relevant to the question of disqualification. As examples, such an obligation may arise as a result of contributions or loans of which the judge is aware made by a party, lawyer, or law office or firm appearing before the judge to a third party in support of the judge or in opposition to the judge's opponent; a party, lawyer, or law office or firm's relationship to the judge or role in the campaign; or the aggregate contributions or loans from lawyers in one law office or firm.

Canon 3E(2)(b) does not eliminate the obligation of the judge to recuse himself or herself where the nature of the contribution or loan, the extent of the contributor's or lender's involvement in the judicial campaign, the relationship of the contributor or lender, or other circumstance requires recusal under Code of Civil Procedure section 170.1, and particularly section 170.1, subdivision (a)(6)(A).

(3) A judge shall disqualify himself or herself in accordance with the following:

(a) Statements that commit the judge to a particular result

A judge is disqualified if the judge, while a judge or candidate for judicial office,* made a statement, other than in a court proceeding, judicial decision, or opinion, that a person aware of the facts might reasonably believe commits the judge to reach a particular result or rule in a particular way in a proceeding.

(b) Bond ownership

Ownership of a corporate bond issued by a party to a proceeding and having a fair market value exceeding $1,500 is disqualifying. Ownership of a government bond issued by a party to a proceeding is disqualifying only if the outcome of the proceeding could substantially affect the value of the judge's bond. Ownership in a mutual or common investment fund that holds bonds is not a disqualifying financial interest.

ADVISORY COMMITTEE COMMENTARY: Canon 3E(3)(b)

The distinction between corporate and government bonds is consistent with the Political Reform Act (see Gov. Code, § 82034), which requires disclosure of corporate bonds, but not government bonds. Canon 3E(3) is intended to assist judges in complying with Code of Civil Procedure section 170.1, subdivision (a)(3) and Canon 3E(5)(d).

(4) An appellate justice shall disqualify himself or herself in any proceeding if for any reason:

(a) the justice believes his or her recusal would further the interests of justice; or

(b) the justice substantially doubts his or her capacity to be impartial;* or

(c) the circumstances are such that a reasonable person aware of the facts would doubt the justice's ability to be impartial.*

(5) Disqualification of an appellate justice is also required in the following instances:

(a) The appellate justice has served as a lawyer in the pending* proceeding, or has served as a lawyer in any other proceeding involving any of the same parties if that other proceeding related to the same contested issues of fact and law as the present proceeding, or has given advice to any party in the present proceeding upon any issue involved in the proceeding.

ADVISORY COMMITTEE COMMENTARY: Canon 3E(5)(a)

Canon 3E(5)(a) is consistent with Code of Civil Procedure section 170.1, subdivision (a)(2), which addresses disqualification of trial court judges based on prior representation of a party in the proceeding.

(b) Within the last two years, (i) a party to the proceeding, or an officer, director or trustee thereof, either was a client of the justice when the justice was engaged in the private practice of law or was a client of a lawyer with whom the justice was associated in the private practice of law; or (ii) a lawyer in the proceeding was associated with the justice in the private practice of law.

(c) The appellate justice represented a public officer or entity and personally advised or in any way represented that officer or entity concerning the factual or legal issues in the present proceeding in which the public officer or entity now appears.

(d) The appellate justice, his or her spouse or registered domestic partner,* or a minor child residing in the household, has a financial interest or is either a fiduciary* who has a financial interest in the proceeding, or is a director, advisor, or other active participant in the affairs of a party. A financial interest is defined as ownership of more than a 1 percent legal or equitable interest in a party, or a legal or equitable interest in a party of a fair market value exceeding $1,500. Ownership in a mutual or common investment fund that holds securities does not itself constitute a financial interest; holding office in an educational, religious, charitable, service,* or civic organization does not confer a financial interest in the organization's securities; and a proprietary interest of a policyholder in a mutual insurance company or mutual savings association or similar interest is not a financial interest unless the outcome of the proceeding could substantially affect the value of the interest. A justice shall make reasonable efforts to keep informed about his or her personal and fiduciary* interests and those of his or her spouse or registered domestic partner* and of minor children living in the household.

(e)(i) The justice or his or her spouse or registered domestic partner,* or a person within the third degree of relationship* to either of them, or the spouse or registered domestic partner* thereof, is a party or an officer, director, or trustee of a party to the proceeding, or

(ii) a lawyer or spouse or registered domestic partner* of a lawyer in the proceeding is the spouse, registered domestic partner,* former spouse, former registered domestic partner,* child, sibling, or parent of the justice or of the justice's spouse or registered domestic partner,* or such a person is associated in the private practice of law with a lawyer in the proceeding.

(f) The justice

(i) served as the judge before whom the proceeding was tried or heard in the lower court,

(ii) has personal knowledge* of disputed evidentiary facts concerning the proceeding, or

(iii) has a personal bias or prejudice concerning a party or a party's lawyer.

(g) A temporary or permanent physical impairment renders the justice unable properly to perceive the evidence or conduct the proceedings.

(h) The justice has a current arrangement concerning prospective employment or other compensated service as a dispute resolution neutral

---

* Terms with an asterisk (*) are defined in the Terminology section.

or is participating in, or, within the last two years has participated in, discussions regarding prospective employment or service as a dispute resolution neutral, or has been engaged in such employment or service, and any of the following applies:

(i) The arrangement is, or the prior employment or discussion was, with a party to the proceeding;

(ii) The matter before the justice includes issues relating to the enforcement of either an agreement to submit a dispute to an alternative dispute resolution process or an award or other final decision by a dispute resolution neutral;

(iii) The justice directs the parties to participate in an alternative dispute resolution process in which the dispute resolution neutral will be an individual or entity with whom the justice has the arrangement, has previously been employed or served, or is discussing or has discussed the employment or service; or

(iv) The justice will select a dispute resolution neutral or entity to conduct an alternative dispute resolution process in the matter before the justice, and among those available for selection is an individual or entity with whom the justice has the arrangement, with whom the justice has previously been employed or served, or with whom the justice is discussing or has discussed the employment or service.

For purposes of Canon 3E(5)(h), "participating in discussions" or "has participated in discussions" means that the justice (i) solicited or otherwise indicated an interest in accepting or negotiating possible employment or service as an alternative dispute resolution neutral, or (ii) responded to an unsolicited statement regarding, or an offer of, such employment or service by expressing an interest in that employment or service, making any inquiry regarding the employment or service, or encouraging the person making the statement or offer to provide additional information about that possible employment or service. If a justice's response to an unsolicited statement regarding a question about, or offer of, prospective employment or other compensated service as a dispute resolution neutral is limited to responding negatively, declining the offer, or declining to discuss such employment or service, that response does not constitute participating in discussions.

For purposes of Canon 3E(5)(h), "party" includes the parent, subsidiary, or other legal affiliate of any entity that is a party and is involved in the transaction, contract, or facts that gave rise to the issues subject to the proceeding.

For purposes of Canon 3E(5)(h), "dispute resolution neutral" means an arbitrator, a mediator, a temporary judge* appointed under article VI, section 21 of the California Constitution, a referee appointed under Code of Civil Procedure section 638 or 639, a special master, a neutral evaluator, a settlement officer, or a settlement facilitator.

(i) The justice's spouse or registered domestic partner* a person within the third degree of relationship* to the justice or his or her spouse or registered domestic partner,* or the person's spouse or registered domestic partner,* was a witness in the proceeding.

(j) The justice has received a campaign contribution of $5,000 or more from a party or lawyer in a matter that is before the court, and either of the following applies:

(i) The contribution was received in support of the justice's last election, if the last election was within the last six years; or

(ii) The contribution was received in anticipation of an upcoming election.

Notwithstanding Canon 3E(5)(j), a justice shall disqualify himself or herself based on a contribution of a lesser amount if required by Canon 3E(4).

The disqualification required under Canon 3E(5)(j) may be waived if all parties that did not make the contribution agree to waive the disqualification.

ADVISORY COMMITTEE COMMENTARY: Canon 3E

Canon 3E(1) sets forth the general duty to disqualify applicable to a judge of any court. Sources for determining when recusal or disqualification is appropriate may include the applicable provisions of the Code of Civil Procedure, other provisions of the Code of Judicial Ethics, the Code of Conduct for United States Judges, the American Bar Association's Model Code of Judicial Conduct, and related case law.

The decision whether to disclose information under Canon 3E(2) is a decision based on the facts of the case before the judge. A judge is required to disclose only information that is related to the grounds for disqualification set forth in Code of Civil Procedure section 170.1.

---

* Terms with an asterisk (*) are defined in the Terminology section.

Canon 3E(4) sets forth the general standards for recusal of an appellate justice. The term "appellate justice" includes justices of both the Courts of Appeal and the Supreme Court. Generally, the provisions concerning disqualification of an appellate justice are intended to assist justices in determining whether recusal is appropriate and to inform the public why recusal may occur.

The rule of necessity may override the rule of disqualification. For example, a judge might be required to participate in judicial review of a judicial salary statute, or might be the only judge available in a matter requiring judicial action, such as a hearing on probable cause or a temporary restraining order. In the latter case, the judge must promptly disclose on the record the basis for possible disqualification and use reasonable efforts to transfer the matter to another judge as soon as practicable.

In some instances, membership in certain organizations may have the potential to give an appearance of partiality, although membership in the organization generally may not be barred by Canon 2C, Canon 4, or any other specific canon. A judge holding membership in an organization should disqualify himself or herself whenever doing so would be appropriate in accordance with Canon 3E(1), 3E(4), or 3E(5) or statutory requirements. In addition, in some circumstances, the parties or their lawyers may consider a judge's membership in an organization relevant to the question of disqualification, even if the judge believes there is no actual basis for disqualification. In accordance with this canon, a judge should disclose to the parties his or her membership in an organization, in any proceeding in which that information is reasonably relevant to the question of disqualification under Code of Civil Procedure section 170.1, even if the judge concludes there is no actual basis for disqualification.

(6) It shall not be grounds for disqualification that the justice:

(a) Is or is not a member of a racial, ethnic, religious, sexual, or similar group and the proceeding involves the rights of such a group;

(b) Has in any capacity expressed a view on a legal or factual issue presented in the proceeding, except as provided in Canon 3E(5)(a), (b), or (c);

(c) Has as a lawyer or public official participated in the drafting of laws* or in the effort to pass or defeat laws,* the meaning, effect, or application of which is in issue in the proceeding unless the judge believes that his or her prior involvement was so well known* as to raise a reasonable doubt in the public mind as to his or her capacity to be impartial.*

ADVISORY COMMITTEE COMMENTARY: Canon 3E(6)

Canon 3E(6) is substantively the same as Code of Civil Procedure section 170.2, which pertains to trial court judges.

(Canon 3E amended effective December 1, 2016; adopted effective January 15, 1996; previously amended effective April 15, 1996, June 19, 1997, March 4, 1999, December 13, 2000, June 18, 2003, December 22, 2003, January 1, 2005, January 1, 2007, January 1, 2008, April 29, 2009, January 1, 2013, and August 19, 2015.)

Canon 4. A judge shall so conduct the judge's quasi-judicial and extrajudicial activities as to minimize the risk of conflict with judicial obligations.

A. Extrajudicial Activities in General

A judge shall conduct all of the judge's extrajudicial activities so that they do not

(1) cast reasonable doubt on the judge's capacity to act impartially,*
(2) demean the judicial office,
(3) interfere with the proper performance of judicial duties, or
(4) lead to frequent disqualification of the judge.

ADVISORY COMMITTEE COMMENTARY: Canon 4A

Complete separation of a judge from extrajudicial activities is neither possible nor wise; a judge should not become isolated from the community in which he or she lives. Expressions of bias or prejudice by a judge, even outside the judge's judicial activities, may cast reasonable doubt on the judge's capacity to act impartially* as a judge. Expressions that may do so include inappropriate use of humor or the use of demeaning remarks. See Canon 2C and accompanying Commentary.

Because a judge's judicial duties take precedence over all other activities (see Canon 3A), a judge must avoid extrajudicial activities that might reasonably result in the judge being disqualified.

(Canon 4A amended effective August 19, 2015; previously amended effective January 1, 2013.)

B. Quasi-Judicial and Avocational Activities

A judge may speak, write, lecture, teach, and participate in activities concerning legal and nonlegal subject matters, subject to the requirements of this code.

ADVISORY COMMITTEE COMMENTARY: Canon 4B

As a judicial officer and person specially learned in the law,* a judge is in a unique position to contribute to the improvement of the law, the legal system, and the administration of justice,* including revision of substantive and procedural law* and improvement of criminal and juvenile justice. To the extent that time permits, a judge may do so, either independently or through a bar or judicial association or other group dedicated to the improvement of the law.* It may be necessary to promote legal education programs and materials by identifying authors and speakers by judicial title. This is permissible, provided such use of the judicial title does not contravene Canons 2A and 2B.

Judges are not precluded by their office from engaging in other social, community, and intellectual endeavors so long as they do not interfere with the obligations under Canons 2C and 4A.

(Canon 4B amended effective August 19, 2015; previously amended effective January 1, 2013.)

C. Governmental, Civic, or Charitable Activities

(1) A judge shall not appear at a public hearing or officially consult with an executive or legislative body or public official except on matters concerning the law, the legal system, or the administration of justice,* or in matters involving the judge's private economic or personal interests.

ADVISORY COMMITTEE COMMENTARY: Canon 4C(1)

When deciding whether to appear at a public hearing or to consult with an executive or legislative body or public official on matters concerning the law, the legal system, or the administration of justice, a judge should consider if that conduct would violate any other provisions of this code. For a list of factors to consider, see the explanation of "law, the legal system, or the administration of justice" in the Terminology section. See also Canon 2B regarding the obligation to avoid improper influence.*

(2) A judge shall not accept appointment to a governmental committee or commission or other governmental position that is concerned with issues of fact or policy on matters other than the improvement of the law, the legal system, or the administration of justice.* A judge may, however, serve in the military reserve or represent a national, state, or local government on ceremonial occasions or in connection with historical, educational, or cultural activities.

ADVISORY COMMITTEE COMMENTARY: Canon 4C(2)

Canon 4C(2) prohibits a judge from accepting any governmental position except one relating to the law, legal system, or administration of justice as authorized by Canon 4C(3). The appropriateness of accepting extrajudicial assignments must be assessed in light of the demands on judicial resources and the need to protect the courts from involvement in extrajudicial matters that may prove to be controversial. Judges shall not accept governmental appointments that are likely to interfere with the effectiveness and independence* of the judiciary, or that constitute a public office within the meaning of article VI, section 17 of the California Constitution.*

Canon 4C(2) does not govern a judge's service in a nongovernmental position. See Canon 4C(3) permitting service by a judge with organizations devoted to the improvement of the law, the legal system, or the administration of justice and with educational, religious, charitable, service,* or civic organizations not conducted for profit. For example, service on the board of a public educational institution, other than a law school, would be prohibited under Canon 4C(2), but service on the board of a public law school or any private educational institution would generally be permitted under Canon 4C(3).*

(3) Subject to the following limitations and the other requirements of this code,

(a) a judge may serve as an officer, director, trustee, or nonlegal advisor of an organization or governmental agency devoted to the improvement of the law, the legal system, or the administration of justice* provided that such position does not constitute a public office within the meaning of article VI, section 17 of the California Constitution;

(b) a judge may serve as an officer, director, trustee, or nonlegal advisor of an educational, religious, charitable, service,* or civic organization not conducted for profit;

ADVISORY COMMITTEE COMMENTARY: Canon 4C(3)

Canon 4C(3) does not apply to a judge's service in a governmental position unconnected with the improvement of the law, the legal system, or the administration of justice. See Canon 4C(2).*

Canon 4C(3) uses the phrase, "Subject to the following limitations and the other requirements of this code." As an example of the meaning of the phrase, a judge permitted by Canon 4C(3) to serve on the board of a service organization may be prohibited from such service by Canon 2C or 4A if the institution practices invidious discrimination or if service on the board otherwise casts reasonable doubt on the judge's capacity to act impartially* as a judge.*

Service by a judge on behalf of a civic or charitable organization may be governed by other provisions of Canon 4 in addition to Canon 4C. For example, a judge is prohibited by Canon 4G from serving as a legal advisor to a civic or charitable organization.

Service on the board of a homeowners association or a neighborhood protective group is proper if it is related to the protection of the judge's own economic interests. See Canons 4D(2) and 4D(4). See Canon 2B regarding the obligation to avoid improper use of the prestige of a judge's office.

(c) a judge shall not serve as an officer, director, trustee, or nonlegal advisor if it is likely that the organization

(i) will be engaged in judicial proceedings that would ordinarily come before the judge, or

(ii) will be engaged frequently in adversary proceedings in the court of which the judge is a member or in any court subject to the appellate jurisdiction of the court of which the judge is a member.

ADVISORY COMMITTEE COMMENTARY: Canon 4C(3)(c)

The changing nature of some organizations and of their relationship to the law makes it necessary for the judge regularly to reexamine the activities of each organization with which the judge is affiliated to determine if it is proper for the judge to continue the affiliation. Some organizations regularly engage in litigation to achieve their goals or fulfill their purposes. Judges should avoid a leadership role in such organizations as it could compromise the appearance of impartiality.*

(d) a judge as an officer, director, trustee, nonlegal advisor, or as a member or otherwise

(i) may assist such an organization in planning fundraising and may participate in the management and investment of the organization's funds. However, a judge shall not personally participate in the solicitation of funds or other fundraising activities, except that a judge may privately solicit funds for such an organization from members of the judge's family* or from other judges (excluding court commissioners, referees, court-appointed arbitrators, hearing officers, temporary judges,* and retired judges who serve in the Temporary Assigned Judges Program, practice law, or provide alternative dispute resolution services);

(ii) may make recommendations to public and private fund-granting organizations on projects and programs concerning the law, the legal system, or the administration of justice;*

(iii) shall not personally participate in membership solicitation if the solicitation might reasonably be perceived as coercive or if the membership solicitation is essentially a fundraising mechanism, except as permitted in Canon 4C(3)(d)(i);

(iv) shall not permit the use of the prestige of his or her judicial office for fundraising or membership solicitation but may be a speaker, guest of honor, or recipient of an award for public or charitable service provided the judge does not personally solicit funds and complies with Canons 4A(1), (2), (3), and (4).

ADVISORY COMMITTEE COMMENTARY: Canon 4C(3)(d)

A judge may solicit membership or endorse or encourage membership efforts for an organization devoted to the improvement of the law, the legal system, or the administration of justice, or a nonprofit educational, religious, charitable, service,* or civic organization as long as the solicitation cannot reasonably be perceived as coercive and is not essentially a fundraising mechanism. Solicitation of funds or memberships for an organization similarly involves the danger that the person solicited will feel obligated to respond favorably if the solicitor is in a position of influence or control. A judge must not engage in direct, individual solicitation of funds or memberships in person, in writing, or by telephone except in the following cases: (1) a judge may solicit other judges (excluding court commissioners, referees, court-appointed arbitrators, hearing officers, temporary judges,* and retired judges who serve in the Temporary Assigned Judges Program, practice law, or provide alternative dispute resolution services) for funds or memberships; (2) a judge may solicit other persons for membership in the organizations described above if neither those persons nor persons with whom they are affiliated are likely ever to appear before the court on which the judge serves; and (3) a judge who is an officer of such an organization may send a general membership solicitation mailing over the judge's signature.*

When deciding whether to make recommendations to public and private fund-granting organizations on projects and programs concerning the law, the legal system, or the administration of justice, a judge should consider whether that conduct would violate any other provision of this code. For a list of factors to consider, see the explanation of "law, the legal system, or the administration of justice" in the Terminology section.*

Use of an organization's letterhead for fundraising or membership solicitation does not violate Canon 4C(3)(d), provided the letterhead lists only the judge's name and office or other position in the organization, and designates the judge's judicial title only if other persons whose names appear on the letterhead have comparable designations. In addition, a judge must also make reasonable efforts to ensure that the judge's staff, court officials, and others subject to the judge's direction and control do not solicit funds on the judge's behalf for any purpose, charitable or otherwise.

---

* Terms with an asterisk (*) are defined in the Terminology section.

(e) A judge may encourage lawyers to provide pro bono publico legal services.

ADVISORY COMMITTEE COMMENTARY: Canon 4C(3)(e)

In addition to appointing lawyers to serve as counsel for indigent parties in individual cases, a judge may promote broader access to justice by encouraging lawyers to participate in pro bono publico legal services, as long as the judge does not employ coercion or abuse the prestige of judicial office.

(Canon 4C amended effective July 1, 2020; previously amended effective January 1, 2013, and August 19, 2015.)

D. Financial Activities

(1) A judge shall not engage in financial and business dealings that

(a) may reasonably be perceived to exploit the judge's judicial position, or

(b) involve the judge in frequent transactions or continuing business relationships with lawyers or other persons likely to appear before the court on which the judge serves.

ADVISORY COMMITTEE COMMENTARY: Canon 4D(1)

The Time for Compliance provision of this code (Canon 6F) postpones the time for compliance with certain provisions of this canon in some cases.

A judge must avoid financial and business dealings that involve the judge in frequent transactions or continuing business relationships with persons likely to appear either before the judge personally or before other judges on the judge's court. A judge shall discourage members of the judge's family* from engaging in dealings that would reasonably appear to exploit the judge's judicial position or that would involve family members in frequent transactions or continuing business relationships with persons likely to appear before the judge. This rule is necessary to avoid creating an appearance of exploitation of office or favoritism and to minimize the potential for disqualification.

Participation by a judge in financial and business dealings is subject to the general prohibitions in Canon 4A against activities that tend to reflect adversely on impartiality,* demean the judicial office, or interfere with the proper performance of judicial duties. Such participation is also subject to the general prohibition in Canon 2 against activities involving impropriety* or the appearance of impropriety* and the prohibition in Canon 2B against the misuse of the prestige of judicial office.

In addition, a judge must maintain high standards of conduct in all of the judge's activities, as set forth in Canon 1.

(2) A judge may, subject to the requirements of this code, hold and manage investments of the judge and members of the judge's family,* including real estate, and engage in other remunerative activities. A judge shall not participate in, nor permit the judge's name to be used in connection with, any business venture or commercial advertising that indicates the judge's title or affiliation with the judiciary or otherwise lend the power or prestige of his or her office to promote a business or any commercial venture.

(3) A judge shall not serve as an officer, director, manager, or employee of a business affected with a public interest, including, without limitation, a financial institution, insurance company, or public utility.

ADVISORY COMMITTEE COMMENTARY: Canon 4D(3)

Although participation by a judge in business activities might otherwise be permitted by Canon 4D, a judge may be prohibited from participation by other provisions of this code when, for example, the business entity frequently appears before the judge's court or the participation requires significant time away from judicial duties. Similarly, a judge must avoid participating in any business activity if the judge's participation would involve misuse of the prestige of judicial office. See Canon 2B.

(4) A judge shall manage personal investments and financial activities so as to minimize the necessity for disqualification. As soon as reasonably possible, a judge shall divest himself or herself of investments and other financial interests that would require frequent disqualification.

(5) Under no circumstance shall a judge accept a gift,* bequest, or favor if the donor is a party whose interests have come or are reasonably likely to come before the judge. A judge shall discourage members of the judge's family residing in the judge's household* from accepting similar benefits from parties who have come or are reasonably likely to come before the judge.

ADVISORY COMMITTEE COMMENTARY: Canon 4D(5)

In addition to the prohibitions set forth in Canon 4D(5) regarding gifts,* other laws* may be applicable to judges, including, for example, Code of Civil Procedure section 170.9 and the Political Reform Act of 1974 (Gov. Code, § 81000 et seq.).

Canon 4D(5) does not apply to contributions to a judge's campaign for judicial office, a matter governed by Canon 5, although such contributions may give rise to an obligation by the judge to disqualify or disclose. See Canon 3E(2)(b) and accompanying Commentary and Code of Civil Procedure section 170.1, subdivision (a)(9).

Because a gift,* bequest, or favor to a member of the judge's family residing in the judge's household* might be viewed as intended to influence the judge, a judge must inform those family members of the relevant ethical constraints upon the judge in this regard and urge them to take these constraints into account when making decisions about accepting such gifts,* bequests, or favors. A judge cannot, however, reasonably be expected to know or control all of the financial or business activities of all family members residing in the judge's household.*

The application of Canon 4D(5) requires recognition that a judge cannot reasonably be expected to anticipate all persons or interests that may come before the court.

(6) A judge shall not accept and shall discourage members of the judge's family residing in the judge's household* from accepting a gift,* bequest, favor, or loan from anyone except as hereinafter set forth. Gifts* that are permitted by Canons 4D(6)(a) through (i) may only be accepted if the gift,* bequest, favor, or loan would neither influence nor reasonably be perceived as intended to influence the judge in the performance of judicial duties:

(a) a gift,* bequest, favor, or loan from a person whose preexisting relationship with the judge would prevent the judge under Canon 3E from hearing a case involving that person;

ADVISORY COMMITTEE COMMENTARY: Canon 4D(6)(a)

Upon appointment or election as a judge or within a reasonable period of time thereafter, a judge may attend an event honoring the judge's appointment or election as a judge provided that (1) the judge would otherwise be disqualified from hearing any matter involving the person or entity holding or funding the event, and (2) a reasonable person would not conclude that attendance at the event undermines the judge's integrity,* impartiality,* or independence.*

(b) a gift* for a special occasion from a relative or friend, if the gift* is fairly commensurate with the occasion and the relationship;

ADVISORY COMMITTEE COMMENTARY: Canon 4D(6)(b)

A gift* to a judge, or to a member of the judge's family residing in the judge's household,* that is excessive in value raises questions about the judge's impartiality* and the integrity* of the judicial office and might require disqualification of the judge where disqualification would not otherwise be required. See, however, Canon 4D(6)(a).

(c) commercial or financial opportunities and benefits, including special pricing and discounts, and loans from lending institutions in their regular course of business, if the same opportunities and benefits or loans are made available on the same terms to similarly situated persons who are not judges;

(d) any gift* incidental to a public testimonial, or educational or resource materials supplied by publishers on a complimentary basis for official use, or a discounted or complimentary membership in a bar-related association, or an invitation to the judge and the judge's spouse or registered domestic partner* or guest to attend a bar-related function or an activity devoted to the improvement of the law, the legal system, or the administration of justice;*

(e) advances or reimbursement for the reasonable cost of travel, transportation, lodging, and subsistence that is directly related to participation in any judicial, educational, civic, or governmental program or bar-related function or activity devoted to the improvement of the law, the legal system, or the administration of justice;*

ADVISORY COMMITTEE COMMENTARY: Canon 4D(6)(e)

Acceptance of an invitation to a law-related function is governed by Canon 4D(6)(d); acceptance of an invitation paid for by an individual lawyer or group of lawyers is governed by Canon 4D(6)(g). See also Canon 4H(2) and accompanying Commentary.

(f) a gift,* award, or benefit incident to the business, profession, or other separate activity of a spouse or registered domestic partner* or other member of the judge's family residing in the judge's household,* including gifts,* awards, and benefits for the use of both the spouse or registered domestic partner* or other family member and the judge;

(g) ordinary social hospitality;

ADVISORY COMMITTEE COMMENTARY: Canon 4D(6)(g)

Although Canon 4D(6)(g) does not preclude ordinary social hospitality, a judge should carefully weigh acceptance of such hospitality to avoid any appearance of impropriety* or bias or any appearance that the judge is misusing the prestige of judicial office. See Canons 2 and 2B. A judge should also consider whether

---

* Terms with an asterisk (*) are defined in the Terminology section.

acceptance would affect the integrity,* impartiality,* or independence* of the judiciary. See Canon 2A.

(h) an invitation to the judge and the judge's spouse, registered domestic partner,* or guest to attend an event sponsored by an educational, religious, charitable, service,* or civic organization with which the judge is associated or involved, if the same invitation is offered to persons who are not judges and who are similarly engaged with the organization.

(i) a nominal gift,* provided the gift* is not from a lawyer, law firm, or other person likely to appear before the court on which the judge serves, unless one or more of the exceptions in this canon applies.

ADVISORY COMMITTEE COMMENTARY: Canon 4D(6)(i)

For example, nominal gifts* include snacks or a token memento from jurors, keychains or pens provided by vendors at legal conferences, or handicrafts or art projects from students.

A judge should carefully weigh acceptance of any nominal gift to avoid any appearance of impropriety* or bias or any appearance that the judge is misusing the prestige of judicial office. See Canons 2 and 2B. A judge should also consider whether acceptance would affect the integrity,* impartiality,* or independence* of the judiciary. See Canon 2A.

(7) A judge may accept the following, provided that doing so would neither influence nor reasonably be perceived as intended to influence the judge in the performance of judicial duties:

(a) a scholarship or fellowship awarded on the same terms and based on the same criteria applied to other applicants;

(b) rewards and prizes given to competitors or participants in random drawings, contests, or other events that are open to persons who are not judges.

ADVISORY COMMITTEE COMMENTARY: Canons 4D(6) and 4D(7)

The references to such scholarships, fellowships, rewards, and prizes were moved from Canon 4D(6) to Canon 4D(7) because they are not considered to be gifts* under this code, and a judge may accept them.

(Canon 4D amended effective July 1, 2020; previously amended effective January 1, 2007, January 1, 2013, August 19, 2015, and October 10, 2018.)

E. Fiduciary* Activities

(1) A judge shall not serve as executor, administrator, or other personal representative, trustee, guardian, attorney in fact, or other fiduciary,* except for the estate, trust, or person of a member of the judge's family,* and then only if such service will not interfere with the proper performance of judicial duties. A judge may, however, act as a health care representative pursuant to an advance health care directive for a person whose preexisting relationship with the judge would prevent the judge from hearing a case involving that person under Canon 3E(1).

(2) A judge shall not serve as a fiduciary* if it is likely that the judge as a fiduciary* will be engaged in proceedings that would ordinarily come before the judge, or if the estate, trust, or minor or conservatee will be engaged in contested proceedings in the court on which the judge serves or one under its appellate jurisdiction.

(3) The same restrictions on financial activities that apply to a judge personally also apply to the judge while acting in a fiduciary* capacity.

ADVISORY COMMITTEE COMMENTARY: Canon 4E

The Time for Compliance provision of this code (Canon 6F) postpones the time for compliance with certain provisions of this canon in some cases.

The restrictions imposed by this canon may conflict with the judge's obligation as a fiduciary.* For example, a judge shall resign as trustee if detriment to the trust would result from divestiture of trust holdings the retention of which would place the judge in violation of Canon 4D(4).

(Canon 4E amended effective July 1, 2020; previously amended effective January 1, 2013, and August 19, 2015.)

F. Service as Arbitrator or Mediator

A judge shall not act as an arbitrator or mediator or otherwise perform judicial functions in a private capacity unless expressly authorized by law.*

ADVISORY COMMITTEE COMMENTARY: Canon 4F

Canon 4F does not prohibit a judge from participating in arbitration, mediation, or settlement conferences performed as part of his or her judicial duties.

(Canon 4F amended effective August 19, 2015.)

G. Practice of Law

A judge shall not practice law.

ADVISORY COMMITTEE COMMENTARY: Canon 4G

This prohibition refers to the practice of law in a representative capacity and not in a pro se capacity. A judge may act for himself or herself in all legal matters, including matters involving litigation and matters involving appearances before or other dealings with legislative and other governmental bodies. However, in so doing, a judge must not abuse the prestige of office to advance the interests of the judge or member of the judge's family.* See Canon 2B.

This prohibition applies to subordinate judicial officers,* magistrates, special masters, and judges of the State Bar Court.

(Canon 4G amended effective August 19, 2015; previously amended effective January 1, 2005.)

H. Compensation, Reimbursement, and Honoraria

A judge may receive compensation and reimbursement of expenses as provided by law* for the extrajudicial activities permitted by this code, if the source of such payments does not give the appearance of influencing the judge's performance of judicial duties or otherwise give the appearance of impropriety.*

(1) Compensation shall not exceed a reasonable amount nor shall it exceed what a person who is not a judge would receive for the same activity.

(2) Expense reimbursement shall be limited to the actual cost of travel, food, lodging, and other costs reasonably incurred by the judge and, where appropriate to the occasion, by the judge's spouse, registered domestic partner,* or guest. Any payment in excess of such an amount is compensation.

(3) No judge shall accept any honorarium. "Honorarium" means any payment made in consideration for a speech given, an article published, or attendance at any public or private conference, convention, meeting, social event, meal, or like gathering. "Honorarium" does not include earned income for personal services that are customarily provided in connection with the practice of a bona fide business, trade, or profession, such as teaching or writing for a publisher, and does not include fees or other things of value received pursuant to Penal Code section 94.5 for performance of a marriage. For purposes of this canon, "teaching" includes presentations to impart educational information to lawyers in events qualifying for credit under Minimum Continuing Legal Education, to students in bona fide educational institutions, and to associations or groups of judges.

ADVISORY COMMITTEE COMMENTARY: Canon 4H

Judges should not accept compensation or reimbursement of expenses if acceptance would appear to a reasonable person to undermine the judge's integrity,* impartiality,* or independence.*

A judge must assure himself or herself that acceptance of reimbursement or fee waivers would not appear to a reasonable person to undermine the judge's independence,* integrity,* or impartiality.* The factors a judge should consider when deciding whether to accept reimbursement or a fee waiver for attendance at a particular activity include whether:

(a) the sponsor is an accredited educational institution or bar association rather than a trade association or a for-profit entity;

(b) the funding comes largely from numerous contributors rather than from a single entity, and whether the funding is earmarked for programs with specific content;

(c) the content is related or unrelated to the subject matter of a pending* or impending* proceeding before the judge, or to matters that are likely to come before the judge;

(d) the activity is primarily educational rather than recreational, and whether the costs of the event are reasonable and comparable to those associated with similar events sponsored by the judiciary, bar associations, or similar groups;

(e) information concerning the activity and its funding sources is available upon inquiry;

(f) the sponsor or source of funding is generally associated with particular parties or interests currently appearing or likely to appear in the judge's court, thus possibly requiring disqualification of the judge;

(g) differing viewpoints are presented;

(h) a broad range of judicial and nonjudicial participants are invited; or

(i) the program is designed specifically for judges.

Judges should be aware of the statutory limitations on accepting gifts.*

(Canon 4H amended effective October 10, 2018; previously amended effective January 1, 2007, January 1, 2013, and August 19, 2015.)

Canon 5. A judge or candidate for judicial office* shall not engage in political or campaign activity that is inconsistent with the independence,* integrity,* or impartiality* of the judiciary.

Judges and candidates for judicial office* are entitled to entertain their personal views on political questions. They are not required to surrender their rights or opinions as citizens. They shall, however, not engage in

---

* Terms with an asterisk (*) are defined in the Terminology section.

political activity that may create the appearance of political bias or impropriety.* Judicial independence,* impartiality,* and integrity* shall dictate the conduct of judges and candidates for judicial office.*

Judges and candidates for judicial office* shall comply with all applicable election, election campaign, and election campaign fundraising laws* and regulations.

ADVISORY COMMITTEE COMMENTARY: Canon 5

The term "political activity" should not be construed so narrowly as to prevent private comment.

(Canon 5 Preface amended effective August 19, 2015; previously amended effective January 1, 2013.)

A. Political Organizations*

Judges and candidates for judicial office* shall not

(1) act as leaders or hold any office in a political organization;*

(2) make speeches for a political organization* or candidate for nonjudicial office, or publicly endorse or publicly oppose a candidate for nonjudicial office; or

(3) personally solicit funds for a political organization* or nonjudicial candidate; or make contributions to a political party or political organization* or to a nonjudicial candidate in excess of $500 in any calendar year per political party or political organization* or candidate, or in excess of an aggregate of $1,000 in any calendar year for all political parties or political organizations* or nonjudicial candidates.

ADVISORY COMMITTEE COMMENTARY: Canon 5A

This provision does not prohibit a judge or a candidate for judicial office* from signing a petition to qualify a measure for the ballot, provided the judge does not use his or her official title.

In judicial elections, judges are neither required to shield themselves from campaign contributions nor are they prohibited from soliciting contributions from anyone, including attorneys. Nevertheless, there are necessary limits on judges facing election if the appearance of impropriety* is to be avoided. In soliciting campaign contributions or endorsements, a judge shall not use the prestige of judicial office in a manner that would reasonably be perceived as coercive. See Canons 1, 2, 2A, and 2B. Although it is improper for a judge to receive a gift* from an attorney subject to exceptions noted in Canon 4D(6), a judge's campaign may receive attorney contributions.

Although attendance at political gatherings is not prohibited, any such attendance should be restricted so that it would not constitute an express public endorsement of a nonjudicial candidate or a measure not affecting the law, the legal system, or the administration of justice* otherwise prohibited by this canon.

Subject to the monetary limitation herein to political contributions, a judge or a candidate for judicial office* may purchase tickets for political dinners or other similar dinner functions. Any admission price to such a political dinner or function in excess of the actual cost of the meal will be considered a political contribution. The prohibition in Canon 5A(3) does not preclude judges from contributing to a campaign fund for distribution among judges who are candidates for reelection or retention, nor does it apply to contributions to any judge or candidate for judicial office.*

Under this canon, a judge may publicly endorse or oppose a candidate for judicial office.* Such positions are permitted because judicial officers have a special obligation to uphold the integrity,* impartiality,* and independence* of the judiciary and are in a unique position to know the qualifications necessary to serve as a competent judicial officer.

Although family members of the judge or candidate for judicial office* are not subject to the provisions of this code, a judge or candidate for judicial office* shall not avoid compliance with this code by making contributions through a spouse or registered domestic partner* or other family member.

(Canon 5A amended effective July 1, 2020; previously amended effective January 1, 2007, and August 19, 2015.)

B. Conduct During Judicial Campaigns and Appointment Process

(1) A candidate for judicial office* or an applicant seeking appointment to judicial office shall not:

(a) make statements to the electorate or the appointing authority that commit the candidate or the applicant with respect to cases, controversies, or issues that are likely to come before the courts, or

(b) knowingly,* or with reckless disregard for the truth, make false or misleading statements about the identity, qualifications, present position, or any other fact concerning himself or herself or his or her opponent or other applicants.

(2) A candidate for judicial office* shall review and approve the content of all campaign statements and materials produced by the candidate or his or her campaign committee before its dissemination. A candidate shall take appropriate corrective action if the candidate learns of any misrepresentations made in his or her campaign statements or materials. A candidate shall take reasonable measures to prevent any misrepresentations being made in his or her support by third parties. A candidate shall take reasonable measures to ensure that appropriate corrective action is taken if the candidate learns of any misrepresentations being made in his or her support by third parties.

(3) Every candidate for judicial office* shall complete a judicial campaign ethics course approved by the Supreme Court no earlier than one year before or no later than 60 days after the filing of a declaration of intention by the candidate, the formation of a campaign committee, or the receipt of any campaign contribution, whichever is earliest. If a judge appears on the ballot as a result of a petition indicating that a write-in campaign will be conducted for the office, the judge shall complete the course no later than 60 days after receiving notice of the filing of the petition, the formation of a campaign committee, or the receipt of any campaign contribution, whichever is earliest.

Unless a judge forms a campaign committee or solicits or receives campaign contributions, this requirement does not apply to judges who are unopposed for election and will not appear on the ballot. Unless an appellate justice forms a campaign committee or solicits or receives campaign contributions, this requirement does not apply to appellate justices.

ADVISORY COMMITTEE COMMENTARY: Canon 5B

The purpose of Canon 5B is to preserve the integrity* of the appointive and elective process for judicial office and to ensure that the public has accurate information about candidates for judicial office.* Compliance with these provisions will enhance the integrity,* impartiality,* and independence* of the judiciary and better inform the public about qualifications of candidates for judicial office.*

This code does not contain the "announce clause" that was the subject of the United States Supreme Court's decision in Republican Party of Minnesota v. White (2002) 536 U.S. 765. That opinion did not address the "commit clause," which is contained in Canon 5B(1)(a). The phrase "appear to commit" has been deleted because, although candidates for judicial office* cannot promise to take a particular position on cases, controversies, or issues prior to taking the bench and presiding over individual cases, the phrase may have been overinclusive.

Canon 5B(1)(b) prohibits knowingly making false or misleading statements during an election campaign because doing so would violate Canons 1 and 2A, and may violate other canons.

The time limit for completing a judicial campaign ethics course in Canon 5B(3) is triggered by the earliest of one of the following: the filing of a declaration of intention, the formation of a campaign committee, or the receipt of any campaign contribution. If a judge's name appears on the ballot as a result of a petition indicating that a write-in campaign will be conducted, the time limit for completing the course is triggered by the earliest of one of the following: the notice of the filing of the petition, the formation of a campaign committee, or the receipt of any campaign contribution. A financial contribution by a candidate for judicial office* to his or her own campaign constitutes receipt of a campaign contribution.

(4) In judicial elections, judges may solicit campaign contributions or endorsements for their own campaigns or for other judges and attorneys who are candidates for judicial office.* Judges are permitted to solicit such contributions and endorsements from anyone, including attorneys and other judges, except that a judge shall not solicit campaign contributions or endorsements from California state court commissioners, referees, court-appointed arbitrators, hearing officers, and retired judges serving in the Temporary Assigned Judges Program, or from California state court personnel. In soliciting campaign contributions or endorsements, a judge shall not use the prestige of judicial office in a manner that would reasonably be perceived as coercive. See Canons 1, 2, 2A, and 2B.

ADVISORY COMMITTEE COMMENTARY: Canon 5B(4)

Regarding campaign contributions for a judge's own campaign, see Canon 3E(2)(b) and accompanying Commentary addressing disclosure of campaign contributions. See also Code of Civil Procedure section 170.1, subdivision (a)(9), which provides that a judge is disqualified if the judge has received a campaign contribution exceeding $1,500 from a party or an attorney in the proceeding. Although it is improper for a judge to receive a gift* from an attorney subject to exceptions noted in Canon 4D(6), a judge's campaign may receive attorney contributions. See also Government Code section 8314, which prohibits any elected state or local officer from using public resources, including buildings, telephones, and state-compensated time, for a campaign activity. Under section 8314, subdivision (b)(2), "campaign activity" does not include "the incidental and minimal use of public resources, such as equipment or office space, for campaign

---

* Terms with an asterisk (*) are defined in the Terminology section.

purposes, including the referral of unsolicited political mail, telephone calls, and visitors to private political entities."

Even though it is permissible for a judge to solicit endorsements and campaign funds for attorneys who are candidates for judicial office,* the judge must be cautious. Such solicitation may raise issues of disqualification and disclosure under Code of Civil Procedure section 170.1, subdivision (a), and Canon 3E. Even if the judge is not disqualified, disclosure may be required under Canon 3E(2)(a). For example, a judge who has solicited campaign funds or endorsements for a candidate who is an attorney must consider disclosing that solicitation in all cases in which the attorney candidate appears before the judge. The judge should also consider Canon 4A(1) and Canon 4A(4), which require a judge to conduct extrajudicial activities so they do not cast reasonable doubt on the judge's capacity to act impartially* or lead to frequent disqualification.

"Judicial elections" includes recall elections.

(Canon 5B amended effective July 1, 2020; previously amended effective December 22, 2003, January 1, 2013, August 19, 2015, December 1, 2016, and October 10, 2018.)

C. Speaking at Political Gatherings

Candidates for judicial office* may speak to political gatherings only on their own behalf or on behalf of another candidate for judicial office.*

D. Measures to Improve the Law

A judge or candidate for judicial office* may engage in activity in relation to measures concerning improvement of the law, the legal system, or the administration of justice,* only if the conduct is consistent with this code.

ADVISORY COMMITTEE COMMENTARY: Canon 5D

When deciding whether to engage in activity relating to measures concerning the law, the legal system, or the administration of justice,* such as commenting publicly on ballot measures, a judge must consider whether the conduct would violate any other provisions of this code. See the explanation of "law, the legal system, or the administration of justice" in the Terminology section.

(Canon 5D amended effective August 19, 2015; previously amended effective January 1, 2013.)

Canon 6. Compliance with the Code of Judicial Ethics.

A. Judges

Anyone who is an officer of the state judicial system and who performs judicial functions including, but not limited to, a subordinate judicial officer,* a magistrate, a court-appointed arbitrator, a judge of the State Bar Court, a temporary judge,* or a special master, is a judge within the meaning of this code. All judges shall comply with this code except as provided below.

ADVISORY COMMITTEE COMMENTARY: Canon 6A

For the purposes of this canon, if a retired judge is serving in the Temporary Assigned Judges Program, the judge is considered to "perform judicial functions." Because retired judges who are privately retained may perform judicial functions, their conduct while performing those functions should be guided by this code.

(Canon 6A amended effective July 1, 2020; previously amended effective January 1, 2005, January 1, 2013, and August 19, 2015.)

B. Retired Judge Serving in the Temporary Assigned Judges Program

A retired judge who has filed an application to serve on assignment, meets the eligibility requirements set by the Chief Justice for service, and has received an acknowledgment of participation in the Temporary Assigned Judges Program shall comply with all provisions of this code, except for the following:

4C(2)—Appointment to governmental positions
4E—Fiduciary* activities

(Canon 6B amended effective July 1, 2020; previously amended effective January 1, 2005, and January 1, 2013.)

C. Retired Judge as Arbitrator or Mediator

A retired judge serving in the Temporary Assigned Judges Program is not required to comply with Canon 4F of this code relating to serving as an arbitrator or mediator, or performing judicial functions in a private capacity, except as otherwise provided in the *Standards and Guidelines for Judicial Assignments* promulgated by the Chief Justice.

ADVISORY COMMITTEE COMMENTARY: Canon 6C

Article VI, section 6 of the California Constitution provides that a "retired judge who consents may be assigned to any court" by the Chief Justice. Retired judges who are serving in the Temporary Assigned Judges Program pursuant to the above provision are bound by Canon 6B, including the requirement of Canon 4G barring the practice of law. Other provisions of California law,* and standards and guidelines for eligibility and service set by the Chief Justice, further define the limitations on who may serve on assignment.

(Canon 6C amended effective July 1, 2020; previously amended effective January 1, 2013, and August 19, 2015.)

D. Temporary Judge,* Referee, or Court-Appointed Arbitrator[1]

A temporary judge,* a person serving as a referee pursuant to Code of Civil Procedure section 638 or 639, or a court-appointed arbitrator shall comply only with the following code provisions:

(1) A temporary judge,* a referee, or a court-appointed arbitrator shall comply with Canons 1 [integrity* and independence* of the judiciary], 2A [promoting public confidence], 3B(3) [order and decorum], 3B(4) [patient, dignified, and courteous treatment], 3B(6) [require* lawyers to refrain from manifestations of any form of bias or prejudice], 3D(1) [action regarding misconduct by another judge], and 3D(2) [action regarding misconduct by a lawyer], when the temporary judge,* referee, or court-appointed arbitrator is actually presiding in a proceeding or communicating with the parties, counsel, or staff or court personnel while serving in the capacity of a temporary judge,* referee, or court-appointed arbitrator in the case.

(2) A temporary judge,* referee, or court-appointed arbitrator shall, from the time of notice and acceptance of appointment until termination of the appointment:

(a) Comply with Canons 2B(1) [not allow family or other relationships to influence judicial conduct], 3B(1) [hear and decide all matters unless disqualified], 3B(2) [be faithful to and maintain competence in the law*], 3B(5) [perform judicial duties without bias or prejudice], 3B(7) [accord full right to be heard to those entitled; avoid ex parte communications, except as specified], 3B(8) [dispose of matters fairly and promptly], 3B(12) [remain impartial* and not engage in coercive conduct during efforts to resolve disputes], 3C(1) [discharge administrative responsibilities without bias and with competence and cooperatively], 3C(3) [require* staff and court personnel to observe standards of conduct and refrain from bias and prejudice], and 3C(5) [make only fair, necessary, and appropriate appointments];

(b) Not personally solicit memberships or donations for religious, service,* educational, civic, or charitable organizations from the parties and lawyers appearing before the temporary judge,* referee, or court-appointed arbitrator;

(c) Under no circumstance accept a gift,* bequest, or favor if the donor is a party, person, or entity whose interests are reasonably likely to come before the temporary judge,* referee, or court-appointed arbitrator. A temporary judge,* referee, or court-appointed arbitrator shall discourage members of the judge's family residing in the judge's household* from accepting benefits from parties who are reasonably likely to come before the temporary judge,* referee, or court-appointed arbitrator.

(3) A temporary judge* shall, from the time of notice and acceptance of appointment until termination of the appointment, disqualify himself or herself in any proceeding as follows:

(a) A temporary judge*—other than a temporary judge solely conducting settlement conferences—is disqualified to serve in a proceeding if any one or more of the following are true:

(i) the temporary judge* has personal knowledge* (as defined in Code of Civil Procedure section 170.1, subdivision (a)(1)) of disputed evidentiary facts concerning the proceeding;

(ii) the temporary judge* has served as a lawyer (as defined in Code of Civil Procedure section 170.1, subdivision (a)(2)) in the proceeding;

(iii) the temporary judge,* within the past five years, has given legal advice to, or served as a lawyer (as defined in Code of Civil Procedure section 170.1, subdivision (a)(2)), except that this provision requires disqualification if the temporary judge* represented a party in the past five years rather than the two-year period specified in section 170.1, subdivision (a)(2)) for a party in the present proceeding;

ADVISORY COMMITTEE COMMENTARY: Canon 6D(3)(a)(iii)

The application of Canon 6D(3)(a)(iii), providing that a temporary judge* is disqualified if he or she has given legal advice or served as a lawyer for a party to the proceeding in the past five years, may depend on the type of assignment and the amount of time available to investigate whether the temporary judge* has previously represented a party. If time permits, the temporary judge* must conduct such an investigation. Thus, if a temporary judge* is privately compensated by the

---

* Terms with an asterisk (*) are defined in the Terminology section.

[1] Reference should be made to relevant commentary to analogous or individual canons cited or described in this canon and appearing elsewhere in this code.

parties or is presiding over a particular matter known* in advance of the hearing, the temporary judge* is presumed to have adequate time to investigate. If, however, a temporary judge* is assigned to a high volume calendar, such as traffic or small claims, and has not been provided with the names of the parties prior to the assignment, the temporary judge* may rely on his or her memory to determine whether he or she has previously represented a party.

(iv) the temporary judge* has a financial interest (as defined in Code of Civil Procedure sections 170.1, subdivision (a)(3), and 170.5) in the subject matter in the proceeding or in a party to the proceeding;

(v) the temporary judge,* or the spouse or registered domestic partner* of the temporary judge,* or a person within the third degree of relationship* to either of them, or the spouse or registered domestic partner* of such a person is a party to the proceeding or is an officer, director, or trustee of a party;

(vi) a lawyer or a spouse or registered domestic partner* of a lawyer in the proceeding is the spouse, former spouse, registered domestic partner,* former registered domestic partner,* child, sibling, or parent of the temporary judge* or the temporary judge's spouse or registered domestic partner,* or if such a person is associated in the private practice of law with a lawyer in the proceeding;

(vii) for any reason:

(A) the temporary judge* believes his or her recusal would further the interests of justice;

(B) the temporary judge* believes there is a substantial doubt as to his or her capacity to be impartial;* or

(C) a person aware of the facts might reasonably entertain a doubt that the temporary judge* would be able to be impartial.* Bias or prejudice toward an attorney in the proceeding may be grounds for disqualification; or

(viii) the temporary judge* has received a campaign contribution of $1,500 or more from a party or lawyer in a matter that is before the court and the contribution was received in anticipation of an upcoming election.

(b) A temporary judge* before whom a proceeding was tried or heard is disqualified from participating in any appellate review of that proceeding.

(c) If the temporary judge* has a current arrangement concerning prospective employment or other compensated service as a dispute resolution neutral or is participating in, or, within the last two years has participated in, discussions regarding prospective employment or service as a dispute resolution neutral, or has been engaged in such employment or service, and any of the following applies:

(i) The arrangement or current employment is, or the prior employment or discussion was, with a party to the proceeding;

(ii) The temporary judge* directs the parties to participate in an alternative dispute resolution process in which the dispute resolution neutral will be an individual or entity with whom the temporary judge* has the arrangement, is currently employed or serves, has previously been employed or served, or is discussing or has discussed the employment or service; or

(iii) The temporary judge* will select a dispute resolution neutral or entity to conduct an alternative dispute resolution process in the matter before the temporary judge,* and among those available for selection is an individual or entity with whom the temporary judge* has the arrangement, is currently employed or serves, has previously been employed or served, or is discussing or has discussed the employment or service.

For the purposes of Canon 6D(3)(c), the definitions of "participating in discussions," "has participated in discussions," "party," and "dispute resolution neutral" are set forth in Code of Civil Procedure section 170.1, subdivision (a)(8), except that the words "temporary judge" shall be substituted for the word "judge" in such definitions.

(d) A lawyer is disqualified from serving as a temporary judge* in a family law or unlawful detainer proceeding if in the same type of proceeding:

(i) the lawyer holds himself or herself out to the public as representing exclusively one side; or

(ii) the lawyer represents one side in 90 percent or more of the cases in which he or she appears.

ADVISORY COMMITTEE COMMENTARY: Canon 6D(3)(d)

Under Canon 6D(3)(d), "one side" means a category of persons such as landlords, tenants, or litigants exclusively of one gender.

(4) After a temporary judge* who has determined himself or herself to be disqualified from serving under Canon 6D(3)(a)–(d) has disclosed the basis for his or her disqualification on the record, the parties and their lawyers may agree to waive the disqualification and the temporary judge* may accept the waiver. The temporary judge* shall not seek to induce a waiver and shall avoid any effort to discover which lawyers or parties favored or opposed a waiver.

ADVISORY COMMITTEE COMMENTARY: Canon 6D(4)

Provisions addressing waiver of mandatory disqualifications or limitations, late discovery of grounds for disqualification or limitation, notification of the court when a disqualification or limitation applies, and requests for disqualification by the parties are located in rule 2.818 of the California Rules of Court. Rule 2.818 states that the waiver must be in writing, must recite the basis for the disqualification or limitation, and must state that it was knowingly* made. It also states that the waiver is effective only when signed by all parties and their attorneys and filed in the record.

(5) A temporary judge,* referee, or court-appointed arbitrator shall, from the time of notice and acceptance of appointment until termination of the appointment:

(a) In all proceedings, disclose in writing or on the record information as required by law,* or information that is reasonably relevant to the question of disqualification under Canon 6D(3), including personal or professional relationships known* to the temporary judge,* referee, or court-appointed arbitrator, that he or she or his or her law firm has had with a party, lawyer, or law firm in the current proceeding, even though the temporary judge,* referee, or court-appointed arbitrator concludes that there is no actual basis for disqualification; and

(b) In all proceedings, disclose in writing or on the record membership of the temporary judge,* referee, or court-appointed arbitrator in any organization that practices invidious discrimination on the basis of race, sex, gender, religion, national origin, ethnicity, or sexual orientation, except for membership in a religious organization.

(6) A temporary judge,* referee, or court-appointed arbitrator, from the time of notice and acceptance of appointment until the case is no longer pending in any court, shall not make any public comment about a pending* or impending* proceeding in which the temporary judge,* referee, or court-appointed arbitrator has been engaged, and shall not make any nonpublic comment that might substantially interfere with such proceeding. The temporary judge,* referee, or court-appointed arbitrator shall require* similar abstention on the part of staff and court personnel subject to his or her control. This canon does not prohibit the following:

(a) Statements made in the course of the official duties of the temporary judge,* referee, or court-appointed arbitrator; and

(b) Explanations about the procedures of the court.

(7) From the time of appointment and continuing for two years after the case is no longer pending* in any court, a temporary judge,* referee, or court-appointed arbitrator shall under no circumstances accept a gift,* bequest, or favor from a party, person, or entity whose interests have come before the temporary judge,* referee, or court-appointed arbitrator in the matter. The temporary judge,* referee, or court-appointed arbitrator shall discourage family members residing in the household of the temporary judge,* referee, or court-appointed arbitrator from accepting any benefits from such parties, persons or entities during the time period stated in this subdivision. The demand for or receipt by a temporary judge,* referee, or court-appointed arbitrator of a fee for his or her services rendered or to be rendered would not be a violation of this canon.

(8) A temporary judge,* referee, or court-appointed arbitrator shall, from the time of notice and acceptance of appointment and continuing indefinitely after the termination of the appointment:

(a) Comply with Canon 3B(11) [no disclosure of nonpublic information* acquired in a judicial capacity] (except as required by law*);

(b) Not commend or criticize jurors sitting in a proceeding before the temporary judge,* referee, or court-appointed arbitrator for their verdict other than in a court order or opinion in such proceeding, but may express appreciation to jurors for their service to the judicial system and the community; and

(c) Not lend the prestige of judicial office to advance his, her, or another person's pecuniary or personal interests and not use his or her judicial title in any written communication intended to advance his, her, or another person's pecuniary or personal interests, except to show his, her, or another person's qualifications.

---

* Terms with an asterisk (*) are defined in the Terminology section.

(9)(a) A temporary judge* appointed under rule 2.810 of the California Rules of Court, from the time of the appointment and continuing indefinitely after the termination of the appointment, shall not use his or her title or service as a temporary judge* (1) as a description of the lawyer's current or former principal profession, vocation, or occupation on a ballot designation for judicial or other elected office, (2) in an advertisement about the lawyer's law firm or business, or (3) on a letterhead, business card, or other document that is distributed to the public identifying the lawyer or the lawyer's law firm.

(b) This canon does not prohibit a temporary judge* appointed under rule 2.810 of the California Rules of Court from using his or her title or service as a temporary judge* on an application to serve as a temporary judge,* including an application in other courts, on an application for employment or for an appointment to a judicial position, on an individual resume or a descriptive statement submitted in connection with an application for employment or for appointment or election to a judicial position, or in response to a request for information about the public service in which the lawyer has engaged.

(10) A temporary judge,* referee, or court-appointed arbitrator shall comply with Canon 6D(2) until the appointment has been terminated formally or until there is no reasonable probability that the temporary judge,* referee, or court-appointed arbitrator will further participate in the matter. A rebuttable presumption that the appointment has been formally terminated will arise if, within one year from the appointment or from the date of the last hearing scheduled in the matter, whichever is later, neither the appointing court nor counsel for any party in the matter has informed the temporary judge,* referee, or court-appointed arbitrator that the appointment remains in effect.

(11) A lawyer who has been a temporary judge,* referee, or court-appointed arbitrator in a matter shall not accept any representation relating to the matter without the informed written consent of all parties.

(12) When by reason of serving as a temporary judge,* referee, or court-appointed arbitrator in a matter, he or she has received confidential information from a party, the person shall not, without the informed written consent of the party, accept employment in another matter in which the confidential information is material.

ADVISORY COMMITTEE COMMENTARY: Canon 6D

Any exceptions to the canons do not excuse a judicial officer's separate statutory duty to disclose information that may result in the judicial officer's recusal or disqualification.

(Canon 6D amended effective December 1, 2016; adopted effective January 15, 1996; previously amended effective April 15, 1996, March 4, 1999, July 1, 2006, January 1, 2007, January 1, 2008, January 1, 2013, August 19, 2015, and January 21, 2016.)

E. Judicial Candidate

A candidate for judicial office* shall comply with the provisions of Canon 5.

F. Time for Compliance

A person to whom this code becomes applicable shall comply immediately with all provisions of this code except Canons 4D(4) and 4E and shall comply with Canons 4D(4) and 4E as soon as reasonably possible and in any event within a period of one year.

ADVISORY COMMITTEE COMMENTARY: Canon 6F

If serving as a fiduciary when selected as a judge, a new judge may, notwithstanding the prohibitions in Canon 4E, continue to serve as a fiduciary* but only for that period of time necessary to avoid adverse consequences to the beneficiary of the fiduciary* relationship and in no event longer than one year.*

(Canon 6F amended effective August 19, 2015; previously amended effective January 1, 2013.)

G. Interim Rule Concerning Subordinate Judicial Officers

(Canon 6G repealed effective June 1, 2005; adopted December 30, 2002.)

H. Judges on Leave Running for Other Public Office

A judge who is on leave while running for other public office pursuant to article VI, section 17 of the California Constitution shall comply with all provisions of this code, except for the following, insofar as the conduct relates to the campaign for public office for which the judge is on leave:

2B(2)—Lending the prestige of judicial office to advance the judge's personal interest

4C(1)—Appearing at public hearings

5—Engaging in political activity (including soliciting and accepting campaign contributions for the other public office).

---

* Terms with an asterisk (*) are defined in the Terminology section.

ADVISORY COMMITTEE COMMENTARY: Canon 6H

These exceptions are applicable only during the time the judge is on leave while running for other public office. All of the provisions of this code will become applicable at the time a judge resumes his or her position as a judge.

Conduct during elections for judicial office is governed by Canon 5.

(Canon 6H amended effective August 19, 2015; adopted effective January 1, 2005; previously amended effective January 1, 2013.)

SUPREME COURT COMMITTEE ON JUDICIAL ETHICS OPINIONS INTERNAL OPERATING RULES AND PROCEDURES

Pursuant to California Rules of Court, rule 9.80(m), the following are the internal operating rules and procedures of the Supreme Court Committee on Judicial Ethics Opinions. (Adopted by the Committee on Judicial Ethics Opinions on January 6, 2012; approved by the Supreme Court on January 25, 2012.)

Rule 1. Purpose and Scope; Authority; Membership
Rule 2. Definitions
Rule 3. Meetings and Conferences
Rule 4. Referrals to California Judges Association Committee on Judicial Ethics
Rule 5. Confidentiality
Rule 6. Opinion Requests
Rule 7. Consideration of Requests; Response Procedures
Rule 8. Opinion Distribution
Rule 9. California Judges Association

Rule 1. Purpose and Scope; Authority; Membership

(a) Purpose and scope

The Committee on Judicial Ethics Opinions was established by the Supreme Court to provide judicial ethics advisory opinions on topics of interest to the judiciary, judicial officers, candidates for judicial office, and members of the public. In providing its opinions and advice, the committee acts independently of the Supreme Court, the Commission on Judicial Performance, the Judicial Council, the Administrative Office of the Courts, and all other entities.

The committee will not provide opinions or advice in matters known by a requester or the committee to be the subject of pending litigation or a pending Commission on Judicial Performance or State Bar disciplinary proceeding.

(b) Authority

The committee is authorized by California Rules of Court, rule 9.80, adopted by the Supreme Court, to provide ethics advice to judicial officers and candidates for judicial office, including formal written opinions, informal written opinions, and oral advice. The committee is also authorized to consider topics for opinions suggested by individuals and entities. California Rules of Court, rule 9.80, and these rules are not intended to prohibit or inhibit individuals from seeking advice from other sources.

The committee is specifically authorized to:

(1) Issue formal written opinions, informal written opinions, and oral advice on proper judicial conduct under the California Code of Judicial Ethics, the California Constitution, statutes, rules of court, and any other applicable authority;

(2) Make recommendations to the Supreme Court for amending the Code of Judicial Ethics, the California Rules of Professional Conduct, or California Rules of Court, rule 9.80;

(3) Make recommendations regarding appropriate subjects for judicial education programs offered by the Center for Judicial Education and Research, the California Judges Association, or other providers.

(4) Make other recommendations to the Supreme Court as deemed appropriate by the committee or as requested by the Court; and

(5) Adopt amendments to these internal operating rules and procedures, subject to approval by the Supreme Court.

(c) Membership

The committee consists of 12 members appointed by the Supreme Court, including at least one justice from a court of appeal and one member who is a subordinate judicial officer employed full-time by a superior court. The remaining members are justices of a court of appeal or

judges of a superior court, active or retired. No more than two retired justices or judges may be members of the committee at one time, except if an active justice or judge retires during his or her term, he or she may complete the term. A retired justice or judge committee member may not be an active member of the State Bar of California and may not be engaged in privately compensated dispute resolution activities.
(Adopted by the Committee on Judicial Ethics Opinions on January 6, 2012; approved by the Supreme Court on January 25, 2012.)

Rule 2.   Definitions

The following definitions apply, except where otherwise stated:

(a) "Committee" or "CJEO" means the Supreme Court Committee on Judicial Ethics Opinions.

(b) "Chair" means the member of the committee appointed as the chairperson by the Supreme Court pursuant to California Rules of Court, rule 9.80(g).

(c) "Vice-chair" means the member of the committee appointed as the vice-chairperson by the Supreme Court from the members of the committee pursuant to California Rules of Court, rule 9.80(g).

(d) "Judicial officer" means anyone who is an officer of the state judicial system, who performs judicial functions, and who is bound to comply with the California Code of Judicial Ethics adopted by the Supreme Court pursuant to the California Constitution, article VI, section 18(m).

(e) "Judicial candidate" means a person seeking election to or retention of judicial office by election. A person becomes a candidate for judicial office as soon as he or she makes a public announcement of candidacy, declares or files as a candidate with the election authority, or authorizes solicitation or acceptance of contributions or support. For purposes of these rules, the term "judicial candidate" includes any "candidate" bound to comply with the California Code of Judicial Ethics adopted by the Supreme Court pursuant to the California Constitution, article VI, section 18(m).

(f) "Requester" means an individual or entity who makes a request for an opinion or advice or who suggests a topic for the committee to consider as the subject of a formal opinion.

(g) "Committee counsel" means the legal advisor hired by the committee to serve as its staff and maintain the CJEO legal offices pursuant to these rules and as directed by the committee.

(h) "CJA" means the California Judges Association, a voluntary professional association of the state's judges, and "CJA Ethics Committee" means the California Judges Association Committee on Judicial Ethics.

(i) "CJEO Web site" means *www.JudicialEthicsOpinions.ca.org*, established and maintained by the committee pursuant to California Rules of Court, rule 9.80(n).

(j) "Toll-free CJEO line" means 1-855-854-5366, the toll-free telephone number operated by the committee pursuant to California Rules of Court, rule 9.80(n).

(k) "CJEO e-mail address" means Judicial.Ethics@jud.ca.gov, the e-mail address maintained by the committee pursuant to California Rules of Court, rule 9.80(n).

(*l*) "CJEO Opinion Request Form" means the form approved by the committee for use in making all requests for opinions, directly available on the CJEO Web site or by mail by calling the toll-free CJEO line.

(m) "CJEO Suggested Topic Form" means the form approved by the committee for use in submitting judicial ethics topics for consideration, directly available on the CJEO Web site or by mail by calling the toll-free CJEO line.

(n) "CJEO Confidentiality Waiver Form" means the form approved by the committee for use when a judicial officer or candidate for judicial office waives confidentiality pursuant to California Rules of Court, rule 9.80(h)(3), and rule 5(b) of these internal operating rules and procedures. This form is directly available on the CJEO Web site or by mail by calling the toll-free CJEO line.

(o) "Disciplinary proceedings" means any formal or informal matters that are being conducted by the Commission on Judicial Performance or the State Bar, including hearings, inquiries, and investigations.
(Adopted by the Committee on Judicial Ethics Opinions on January 6, 2012; approved by the Supreme Court on January 25, 2012.)

Rule 3.   Meetings and Conferences

(a) The chair will call committee meetings as needed, preside over those meetings, appoint subcommittees as needed, and otherwise coordinate the work of the committee. In the absence of the chair, the vice-chair will act as chair and will otherwise perform such duties as assigned by the chair.

(b) The committee should meet in person at least twice a year and, at the discretion of the chair, may confer either in writing, including electronic mail, by telephone, by videoconference, or by other available electronic means as often as needed to conduct committee business and resolve pending opinion requests.
(Adopted by the Committee on Judicial Ethics Opinions on January 6, 2012; approved by the Supreme Court on January 25, 2012.)

Rule 4.   Referrals to California Judges Association Committee on Judicial Ethics

(a) All requests for oral advice will be referred to the California Judges Association Committee on Judicial Ethics, with the following exceptions:

(1) A definitive answer to the request appears to be found in the resolution of an issue by the CJEO in a pending or prior formal or informal opinion;

(2) The requester declines to contact the CJA Judicial Ethics Committee; or

(3) When the request raises an issue that can be resolved by a statute, rule of court, canon, or other source, the committee will inform the requester of the particular source that may resolve the issue but will not provide oral advice. If the cited source does not resolve the issue for the requester, the committee will refer the requester to the CJA Ethics Committee.

(b) At its discretion, the committee will determine whether an exception applies and the oral advice to be given. Both determinations will be made by agreement of no fewer than three committee members who will serve on a rotating basis. Any serving member may request full committee discussion and vote on a determination, to be held at a time and by such means as determined by the chair. Upon such determinations, the chair will assign to one committee member the task of communicating the oral advice to the requester.
(Adopted by the Committee on Judicial Ethics Opinions on January 6, 2012; approved by the Supreme Court on January 25, 2012.)

Rule 5.   Confidentiality

(a) For purposes of this rule, "committee" includes committee members and their staff, committee counsel, and any additional staff hired by the committee.

(b) Pursuant to California Rules of Court, rule 9.80(h), all committee communications are confidential except as described in these rules. To ensure confidentiality, the following apply:

(1) All records of the committee, including all opinions, inquiries, replies, circulated drafts, documents, writings, files, communications with staff, and proceedings of the committee must be maintained as confidential and must not be disclosed outside of the committee unless confidentiality is waived or is otherwise provided for under these rules.

(2) All information electronically gathered by the committee, including on computers and electronic devices, on the CJEO Web site, in the CJEO e-mail accounts, and in the electronic files and e-mail accounts of the committee, must be maintained as confidential using available electronic security applications and other means, including password protections and access restrictions.

(3) The CJEO office, file cabinets, and computers must be maintained using security measures to restrict access and protect confidentiality as provided in these rules.

(4) All communications and documents regarding the opinions and advice of CJA forwarded by CJA to the committee pursuant to CJEO rule 9 are confidential as provided in these rules.

(c) The committee must not disclose outside the committee any confidential information obtained or developed by the committee, including identifying information concerning an individual whose inquiry or conduct has been the subject of any communication.

(d) The committee must not disclose within the committee any identifying information concerning an individual whose inquiry or conduct is the subject of any communication with the committee. In order to fulfill this mandate, the following procedures apply:

(1) Upon receipt of a request for an opinion or advice, committee counsel must assign a number to the request and remove the requester's name and identifying information. The committee members will deliber-

ate and respond to the request under the procedures provided in these rules without identification of the requester.

(2) Any person who learns the identity of the requester through direct contact with the requester or through number assignment and identification removal must maintain the confidentiality of the identifying information of the requester within the committee unless confidentiality is waived or is otherwise provided for under these rules.

(3) If the requester is an entity, such as CJA or the Commission on Judicial Performance, the requester's name need not be removed, but if the request includes identifying information concerning an individual, that information must be removed and maintained as confidential.

(e) A judicial officer or candidate for judicial office may waive confidentiality; any such waiver must be in writing using the CJEO Confidentiality Waiver Form, which is available on the CJEO Web site or by mail by calling the toll-free CJEO line. If the judicial officer or candidate making the request for an opinion or advice waives confidentiality or asserts reliance on an opinion or advice by the committee in judicial or attorney discipline proceedings, such request and opinion or advice no longer are confidential under these rules. Notwithstanding any waiver, committee deliberations and records are confidential.

(Adopted by the Committee on Judicial Ethics Opinions on January 6, 2012; approved by the Supreme Court on January 25, 2012.)

Rule 6. Opinion Requests

(a) The committee will issue formal written opinions on any subject it deems appropriate. Any person or entity may suggest, in writing, a topic for the committee to consider as the subject of a formal opinion. Topics must be submitted using the CJEO Topic Suggestion Form, which is available on the CJEO Web site or by mail by calling the toll-free CJEO line.

(b) Only judicial officers and candidates for judicial office may request informal written opinions and oral advice.

(c) Any judicial officer or candidate for judicial office may request a formal or informal written opinion from the committee. Requests must be submitted using the CJEO Opinion Request Form, which is available on the CJEO Web site or by mail by calling the toll-free CJEO line. The committee will consider only written requests for formal and informal opinions; the requests must describe the facts and discuss the issues presented in the request. The request should include citation to any constitutional provisions, statutes, rules of court, canons, advisory opinions, case law, or other authorities relevant to the request.

(d) A judicial officer or candidate for judicial office requesting oral advice may communicate in person, in writing (including by electronic mail), or by telephone with committee staff or any member of the committee, who must refer the request to the chair.

(e) A judicial officer or candidate for judicial office requesting an opinion or advice must disclose to the committee whether the issue that is the subject of the request is also the subject of:

(1) Pending litigation;

(2) A pending Commission on Judicial Performance disciplinary proceeding;

(3) A pending State Bar disciplinary proceeding; or

(4) An inquiry to, or an opinion provided by or pending from, the CJA Ethics Committee.

(f) The committee will inform an inquiring judicial officer or candidate for judicial office that he or she must disclose all relevant information as described in these rules and that any opinion or advice issued by the committee will be based on the premise that all relevant information has been disclosed, including whether another inquiry has been made and has been completed or is pending.

(Adopted by the Committee on Judicial Ethics Opinions on January 6, 2012; approved by the Supreme Court on January 25, 2012.)

Rule 7. Consideration of Requests; Response Procedures

(a) The committee must consider all requests for an opinion. An executive committee consisting of the chair, vice-chair, and two additional members appointed by the chair will review all requests and organize them into two lists comprised of high priority requests and other requests. The executive committee will present both lists to the committee for consideration. The executive committee may perform additional duties as directed by the chair.

(b) The committee will determine whether a request for an opinion should be accepted or declined, and if accepted, whether the committee will provide a formal written opinion, an informal written opinion, oral advice, or any combination of the discretionary options for response provided in these rules. If the committee decides to proceed by way of oral advice, the request shall be referred to the three-member oral advice subcommittee.

(c) Eight members of the committee must vote affirmatively to prepare a formal or informal written opinion. Upon a vote to proceed, the chair will appoint a subcommittee of four members, including at least one court of appeal justice, to analyze the issue and draft an opinion for consideration by the entire committee.

(d) Eight members of the committee must vote affirmatively to adopt a draft formal written opinion drafted by a subcommittee. The draft opinion will be posted and the public will be given notice and an opportunity to comment for at least 45 days on the CJEO Web site, unless the committee in its discretion decides an opinion should be issued in final form in less time or with no prior notice and opportunity to comment. After the public comment period has expired, the committee will decide whether the opinion should be published in its original form, modified, or withdrawn. Eight committee members must vote affirmatively on the final version of the opinion or to withdraw a formal written opinion.

(e) Eight members of the committee must vote affirmatively to adopt an informal written opinion. After the committee adopts an informal written opinion, it will be distributed to the requesting judicial officer or candidate for judicial office by committee counsel.

(Adopted by the Committee on Judicial Ethics Opinions on January 6, 2012; approved by the Supreme Court on January 25, 2012.)

Rule 8. Opinion Distribution

(a) The committee will, upon final adoption of a formal written opinion, distribute the opinion to all California judicial officers and other interested persons and entities by posting it on the CJEO Web site and by providing copies to the person or entity who requested the opinion. Committee counsel will maintain a list of interested persons and entities who request receipt of distributed CJEO opinions. The committee may withdraw, modify, or supersede an opinion at any time.

(b) The committee will periodically post summaries of its informal written opinions on the CJEO Web site and may, in its discretion, post summaries of its oral advice.

(c) Committee counsel must maintain records of committee determinations and opinions at the CJEO office.

(Adopted by the Committee on Judicial Ethics Opinions on January 6, 2012; approved by the Supreme Court on January 25, 2012.)

Rule 9. California Judges Association

The CJEO, working with the California Judges Association and its Ethics Committee, will develop procedures for the delivery to CJEO, on a continuing and timely basis, summaries of all "informal responses" issued by CJA. "Informal responses" are the written records maintained by the CJA Ethics Committee that contain a recitation of the oral inquiry and the response. The summaries provided by CJA to CJEO will not include the name of the inquiring judicial officer but will contain: (1) a full description of the inquiry; (2) all of the relevant circumstances; (3) a full description of the answer provided; (4) the reasoning in support of the answer; and (5) any relevant information that would be helpful to CJEO. CJA will begin providing CJEO with summaries on the date of the approval of these rules. After six months of such deliveries, CJEO will evaluate whether the information provided is sufficient to enable it to meet its responsibilities, including determining which topics merit formal written opinions. At that time, CJEO will report to the Supreme Court on its evaluation and may propose any amendments necessary to these rules to reflect the policies and procedures it determines are needed to provide the full scope of service intended by the court. All communications and documents regarding opinions and advice of CJA forwarded by CJA to the committee are confidential.

(Adopted by the Committee on Judicial Ethics Opinions on January 6, 2012; approved by the Supreme Court on January 25, 2012.)

Supreme Court Rules Regarding Electronic Filing

[Amended effective January 1, 2022; adopted effective September 1, 2017; previously amended February 1, 2018, May 1, 2018, and March 18, 2020.]

Application; electronic filing system. Rule 1.
Documents subject to electronic filing. Rule 2.
Mandatory electronic filing. Rule 3.
Voluntary electronic filing. Rule 4.
Submission of paper copies of electronically filed documents. Rule 5.
Excuse from electronic filing. Rule 6.
Registration of electronic filers. Rule 7.
Signatures. Rule 8.
Service. Rule 9.
Format and size of electronically filed documents. Rule 10.
Privacy Protection. Rule 11.
Fees. Rule 12.
Technical Failure of Electronic Filing System. Rule 13.

Rule 1. Application; electronic filing system.

These rules govern electronic filing in the Supreme Court under California Rules of Court, rules 8.70 – 8.79. The court's electronic filing system (EFS) is operated by ImageSoft TrueFiling (TrueFiling).
Rule 1 adopted effective September 1, 2017.

Rule 2. Documents subject to electronic filing.

Rules 3 and 4 identify the documents that must or may be filed electronically in the Supreme Court. Except as provided in this rule, no document other than those identified in rules 3 and 4 may be filed electronically in the Supreme Court. In certain circumstances, including but not limited to natural disasters, public health emergencies, and other situations substantially affecting the court's operations, the Supreme Court may direct the Clerk / Executive Officer of the Supreme Court to accept or require electronic filing of any document and / or to modify the requirements of rule 5 regarding the filing of paper copies. If the court so directs, the Clerk must promptly make reasonable efforts to provide adequate notice to affected parties and counsel, including identifying the type of documents that may or must be electronically filed and the duration of the expanded electronic procedures.
Rule 2 amended effective March 18, 2020; adopted effective September 1, 2017.

Rule 3. Mandatory electronic filing.

(a) Documents that attorneys must file electronically

Pursuant to California Rules of Court, rule 8.71, effective September 1, 2017, unless the court grants a motion for an excuse under rule 6, all attorneys representing a party in a matter before the court must file the documents listed in this subdivision electronically through the court's EFS.

(1) *Documents in proceedings under rules 8.495–8.498, 8.500–8.508, 9.13, and 9.60*

All documents filed before the court issues its decision to grant or deny review, including:

(A) Petitions for review; answers; replies;

(B) Applications to permit the filing of a petition, answer, reply, or attachment that exceeds the length limits set by California Rules of Court, rule 8.504(d);

(C) Applications to extend the time to file an answer or reply;

(D) Motions for relief from default for failure to timely file a petition, answer, or reply;

(E) All other applications and motions in these proceedings filed before the court issues its decision to grant or deny review; and

(F) Any correspondence filed in connection with the documents in (A) – (E).

(G) Amicus curiae letters under California Rules of Court, rule 8.500(g) and requests for depublication and related documents under California Rules of Court, rule 8.1125 may be filed electronically on a voluntary basis. (See Rule 4.)

(2) *Documents in proceedings under rules 8.380–8.385*

All documents filed before the court issues an order to show cause or its ruling on the petition, including:

(A) Petitions for writ of habeas corpus; informal responses, replies;

(B) Applications to permit the filing of a petition, informal response, reply, or attachment that exceeds the length limits set by California Rules of Court, rule 8.204(c);

(C) Applications to extend the time to file an informal response or reply;

(D) Motions for relief from default for failure to timely file an informal response, or reply;

(E) All other applications and motions in these proceedings filed before the court issues an order to show cause or its ruling on the petition; and

(F) Any correspondence filed in connection with the documents in (A) – (E).

(3) *Documents in proceedings under rules 8.485–8.486, and 9.13*

All documents filed before the court issues an alternative writ or its ruling on the petition, including:

(A) Petitions; preliminary responses, replies, and accusations against an attorney;

(B) Applications to permit the filing of a petition, preliminary response, reply, or attachment that exceeds the length limits set by California Rules of Court, rule 8.204(c);

(C) Applications to extend the time to file a preliminary response or reply;

(D) Motions for relief from default for failure to timely file a preliminary response, reply, or accusation against an attorney;

(E) All other applications and motions in these proceedings filed before the court issues an alternative writ or its ruling on the petition; and

(F) Any correspondence filed in connection with the documents in (A) – (E).

(4) *Documents in matters arising from a judgment of death*

All documents filed in these matters. For purposes of this subdivision:

(A) Matters arising from a judgment of death include:

(i) Automatic appeals under California Rules of Court, rules 8.600–8.642;

(ii) Habeas corpus proceedings in the court under California Rules of Court, rules 8.380–8.388 that involve a challenge to the validity of the petitioner's death judgment, including proceedings before any referee appointed by the court to conduct a hearing following the court's issuance of an order to show cause; and;

(ii) Other original writ proceedings in the court under California Rules of Court, rules 8.485–8.493 that relate to an automatic appeal or a habeas corpus proceeding challenging the validity of the death judgment, including proceedings on petitions for a writ of mandate under Penal Code section 1405, subdivision (k).

(B) Matters arising from a judgment of death do not include:

(i) Habeas corpus proceedings on petitions challenging only a capital inmate's conditions of confinement; and

(ii) Proceedings under California Rules of Court, rules 8.500–8.552 that relate to an automatic appeal or a habeas corpus proceeding challenging the validity of the death judgment, including petitions for review from lower court decisions regarding Penal Code section 1054.9 motions. These proceedings are governed by subdivision (a)(1) of this rule.

(C) A superior court judge who is appointed by the court as a referee in a proceeding under (A)(ii) is not considered a trial court for purposes of exemption from mandatory e-filing under California Rules of Court, rule 8.71(c).

(3) *Other documents on order of the court*

Any other document on order of the court.
(Subd (a) amended effective May 1, 2018; adopted effective September 1, 2017; previously amended effective February 1, 2018.)

(b) Application to new and pending cases

Electronic filing of the documents listed in (a) is mandatory as of September 1, 2017, including documents filed in cases commenced before that date.
(Subd (b) adopted effective September 1, 2017.)
Rule 3 amended effective May 1, 2018; adopted effective September 1, 2017; previously amended effective February 1, 2018.

Rule 4. Voluntary electronic filing.

(a) Individuals or entities exempt from mandatory electronic filing

Pursuant to California Rules of Court, rule 8.71(b) and (c), electronic filing is voluntary for:

(1) Self-represented litigants; and

(2) Trial courts.
(Subd (a) adopted effective September 1, 2017.)

(b) Amicus curiae letters and requests for depublication

Amicus curiae letters under California Rules of Court, rule 8.500(g) and requests for depublication and related documents under California Rules of Court, rule 8.1125 may be filed electronically on a voluntary basis.
(Subd (b) relettered from subd (c) effective February 1, 2018; adopted as subd (c) effective September 1, 2017.)
Rule 4 amended effective February 1, 2018; adopted effective September 1, 2017.

Rule 5. Submission of paper copies of electronically filed documents.

(a) Documents in proceedings under rules 8.380–8.385, 8.485–8.486, 8.495–8.498, 8.500–8.508, 9.13, and 9.60

Unless otherwise ordered by the court:

(1) For each electronically filed document in these proceedings, the filer must also submit to the court one unbound paper copy of the document.

(2) The paper copy must be mailed, delivered to a common carrier, or delivered to the court within two court days after the document is filed electronically with the court. If the filing requests an immediate stay, the paper copy must be delivered to court by the close of business the next court day after the document is filed electronically.

(Subd (a) amended effective May 1, 2018; adopted effective September 1, 2017; previously amended effective February 1, 2018.)

(b) Documents in matters arising from a judgment of death

Unless otherwise ordered by the court:

(1) For each electronically filed document in these matters, the filer must also submit to the court one unbound paper copy of the document.

(2) The paper copy must be mailed, delivered to a common carrier, or delivered to the court within two court days after the document is filed electronically with the court.

(Subd (b) adopted effective September 1, 2017.)

Rule 5 amended effective May 1, 2018; adopted effective September 1, 2017; previously amended effective February 1, 2018.

Rule 6. Excuse from electronic filing.

(a) Motion requesting excuse

A party wanting to be excused from the requirement to file a document electronically must file a motion in the court requesting to be excused. The motion must comply with California Rules of Court, rule 8.54 and must specify whether the party is requesting to be excused from electronically filing all documents or only a particular document or documents.

(Subd (a) adopted effective September 1, 2017.)

(b) Grounds for excuse

Pursuant to California Rules of Court, rule 8.71(d), the court will grant an excuse on a satisfactory showing that:

(1) The party will suffer undue hardship if required to file electronically;

(2) The party will suffer significant prejudice if required to file electronically; or

(3) It is not feasible for the party to convert a particular document to electronic form by scanning, imaging, or another means.

(Subd (b) adopted effective September 1, 2017.)

Rule 6 adopted effective September 1, 2017.

Rule 7. Registration of electronic filers.

(a) Obligation to register

Unless the court excuses the filer from this obligation under rule 6, every filer who is required or voluntarily chooses to file a document electronically under these rules must register as a TrueFiling user and obtain a username and password for access to TrueFiling. Registration with and access to the EFS is through the TrueFiling website at https://www.truefiling.com.

(Subd (a) adopted effective September 1, 2017.)

(b) Registered users' responsibilities

A registered TrueFiling user is responsible for all documents filed under the user's registered username and password. The registered user must also comply with the requirements of California Rules of Court, rule 8.32 regarding the duty to provide address and other contact information, and notice of any changes.

(Subd (b) adopted effective September 1, 2017.)

Rule 7 adopted effective September 1, 2017.

Rule 8. Signatures.

Rules 8.70 and 8.75 of the California Rules of Court govern the requirements for signatures on documents electronically filed with the court.

Rule 8 amended January 1, 2022; adopted effective September 1, 2017.

Rule 9. Service.

(a) Electronic service

In addition to the ways identified in California Rules of Court, rule 8.78 that a recipient may agree to accept electronic service, a recipient is deemed to have agreed to electronic service in a matter before this court if the recipient agreed to electronic service in the same matter in the Court of Appeal.

(Subd (a) adopted effective September 1, 2017.)

(b) Service by the court

Documents prepared by the court will be served on EFS users through the EFS or by electronic notification.

(Subd (b) adopted effective September 1, 2017.)

(c) Service of paper copies

When service of a document is required to be made on a person or entity that has not consented to electronic service, the server must comply with California Rules of Court, rule 8.25 regarding service of paper copies.

(Subd (c) adopted effective September 1, 2017.)

Rule 9 adopted effective September 1, 2017.

Rule 10. Format and size of electronically filed documents.

(a) Format

(1) *Text searchable format*

All documents filed electronically must be in text-searchable PDF (portable document format), or other searchable format approved by the court, while maintaining original document formatting. If an electronic filer must file a document the filer possesses only in paper format, the filer must convert the document to an electronic document that complies with this rule by scanning or other means. It is the filer's responsibility to ensure that any document filed is complete and readable. Except as otherwise specified in this rule, electronically filed documents must comply with the content and form requirements of the California Rules of Court applicable to the particular document, with the exception of those provisions dealing exclusively with requirements for paper documents.

(2) *Pagination*

The page numbering of documents filed electronically must comply with California Rules of Court, rule 8.74(b)(3).

(3) *Electronic Bookmarks*

Each document must include in the bookmarks panel of the electronic document a descriptive link (hereafter referred to as an electronic bookmark), to each heading, subheading and to the first page of any component of the document, including any table of contents, table of authorities, petition, verification, points and authorities, declaration, certificate of word count, certificate of interested entities or persons, proof of service, tab, exhibit, or attachment. Each electronic bookmark to a tab, exhibit, or attachment must include the letter or number of the tab, exhibit, or attachment and a description of the tab, exhibit, or attachment.

(4) *Capital Matter Notation*

All documents electronically filed in matters related to a case in which a judgment of death was entered against the defendant must include a clear and obvious notation on the cover page of the document that the filing is related to a capital case. This requirement does not apply to matters filed with the court during pretrial or trial proceedings when a death judgment is being sought by the prosecution but has not yet been entered by the superior court.

(Subd (a) amended effective January 1, 2022; adopted effective September 1, 2017.)

(b) Size

(1) An electronic filing may not be larger than 25 megabytes. This rule does not change the length limitations established by the California Rules of Court for petitions, answers, replies, briefs or any other document filed in the court.

(2) If a document exceeds the size limitation in (1), a party must submit the document in multiple files.

(A) These files must be paginated consecutively across all files in the document, including the cover pages required by (B).

(B) Each file must have a cover page that includes the following information:

(i) The total number of files constituting document;

(ii) The number of this file within the document;

(iii) The total number of pages in the document; and

(iv) The page numbers of the document contained in this file.

(C) The cover pages required by (B) must be included in the paper copies of the document submitted to the court under rule 5.

(Subd (b) adopted effective September 1, 2017.)

Rule 10 amended effective January 1, 2022; adopted effective September 1, 2017.

Rule 11. Privacy Protection.

(a) Personal Identifiers

Electronic filers must comply with California Rules of Court, rule 1.201 regarding exclusion or redaction of personal identifiers from all documents filed with the court. Neither TrueFiling nor the Clerk of the Court has any responsibility to review documents for compliance with these requirements.

(Subd (a) adopted effective September 1, 2017.)

(b) Sealed and Confidential Records

Electronic filers must comply with California Rules of Court, rules 8.45–8.47 regarding sealed and confidential records, with the exception of those requirments exclusively applicable to paper filings.

(Subd (b) adopted effective September 1, 2017.)
Rule 11 adopted effective September 1, 2017.

Rule 12. Fees.

(a) Collection of filing fees

For electronic filings, TrueFiling is designated as the court's agent for collection of filing fees required by law and any associated credit card or bank charges or convenience fees.

(Subd (a) adopted effective September 1, 2017.)

(b) Vendor fees

Pursuant to California Rules of Court, rule 8.73 and TrueFiling's contract with the court, in addition the filing fees required by law, TrueFiling will assess fees for each electronic filing in accordance with the schedule posted on the TrueFiling Web site, as approved by the court. These fees will be considered recoverable costs under rule 8.278(d)(1)(D).

(Subd (b) adopted effective September 1, 2017.)

(c) Exemption from vendor fees

The following are exempt from the fees charged for electronic filing under (b):

(1) *Parties with fee waivers*

A party who has been granted a fee waiver by the court who chooses to file documents electronically.

(2) *Government officers and entities*

The persons and entities identified in Government Code section 6103.

(Subd (c) adopted effective September 1, 2017.)
Rule 12 adopted effective September 1, 2017.

Rule 13. Technical Failure of Electronic Filing System.

The court is not responsible for malfunctions or errors occurring in the electronic transmission or receipt of electronically filed documents. The initial point of contact for anyone experiencing difficulty with TrueFiling is the toll-free telephone number posted on the TrueFiling Web site. California Rules of Court, rule 8.77, governs if a filer fails to meet a filing deadline imposed by court order, rule, or statute because of a failure at any point in the electronic transmission and receipt of a document. A motion under California Rules of Court, rule 8.77(d) to accept the document as timely filed must comply with rule 8.54.

Rule 13 adopted effective September 1, 2017.

INTERNAL OPERATING PRACTICES AND PROCEDURES OF THE CALIFORNIA SUPREME COURT

(Revised October 22, 2003, November 24, 2003, August 25, 2004, January 1, 2007, and April 22, 2015)[1]

I. Acting Chief Justice
II. Transfer of Cases
III. Conferences
IV. Conference Memoranda
V. Calendar Sessions for Oral Argument
VI. Calendars and Calendar Memoranda
VII. Submission
VIII. Assignments for Preparation of Opinions
IX. Circulation of Opinions
X. Filing of Opinions
XI. Review of Determinations by the Commission on Judicial Performance
XII. Temporary Absence of Justices
XIII. Disqualification of Justices and Assignment of Court of Appeal Justices
XIV. Applications for Recommendations for Executive Clemency, Habeas Corpus, and Stays
XV. Appointment of Attorneys in Criminal Cases
XVI. Communications From Counsel in Pending Cases
XVII. Suspension of Procedures

The following internal operating practices and procedures are observed by the California Supreme Court in the performance of its duties.[2]

I. ACTING CHIEF JUSTICE

An Acting Chief Justice performs the functions of the Chief Justice when the Chief Justice is absent or unable to participate in a matter. The Chief Justice, pursuant to constitutional authority (Cal. Const., art. VI, § 6), selects on a rotational basis an associate justice to serve as Acting Chief Justice.

II. TRANSFER OF CASES

A. All transfers to the Supreme Court of a cause in a Court of Appeal pursuant to article VI, section 12 of the California Constitution are accomplished by order of the Chief Justice made on a vote of four justices assenting thereto.

B. Unless otherwise ordered by the Chief Justice, all applications for writs of mandate and/or prohibition that have not previously been filed with the proper Court of Appeal are transferred to such court.

III. CONFERENCES

A. Unless otherwise directed by the Chief Justice, regular conferences are held each Wednesday, excluding the Wednesday of regular calendar sessions and the first Wednesday of July and August.

B. Special conferences may be called by the Chief Justice whenever deemed necessary or desirable.

C. Four justices constitute a quorum for any regular or special conference.

D. A judge assigned by the Chief Justice to assist the court, or to act in the place of a regular member of the court who is disqualified or otherwise unable to act, may be counted to obtain a quorum for a conference. A regular member of the court, present at a conference, who is not participating in a particular matter is not counted in determining a quorum for that matter.

E. A justice who has ascertained that he or she will not be present at a conference or will not be participating in a particular matter will notify the Chief Justice or the Calendar Coordinator, as specified by sections XII.C and XIII.A. The absent justice may communicate in writing to the Calendar Coordinator his or her votes on some or all of the matters on any given conference, and may be counted to constitute a quorum for each such conference matter on which a vote has been cast.

F. Matters in which time is of the essence may be considered by the court without a formal conference. In such matters, because time is of the essence, an order will be filed as soon as four justices vote for a particular disposition.

IV. CONFERENCE MEMORANDA

A. Unless otherwise directed by the Chief Justice, a conference memorandum is prepared for each petition requiring conference consideration or action.

B. Upon the filing of a petition, motion, or application, the Calendar Coordinator, under the direction of the Chief Justice, assigns it a conference date and refers it to one of the central staffs or a member of the court for preparation of a conference memorandum as follows:

---

[1] These practices and procedures may be amended from time to time, as needed, to facilitate the court's ability to discharge its duties. Amendments are reflected in updated versions of the practices and procedures on the California Courts Web site at <http://www.courtinfo.ca.gov/courts/supreme/iopp.htm>. Section VIII.D was amended October 22, 2003; sections III.E, IX, X, and XII were amended November 24, 2003; sections IV.J and XIII.B were amended August 25, 2004; and, rules references throughout were amended effective January 1, 2007, to reflect the reorganization and renumbering of the California Rules of Court effective on that date.

[2] Various provisions of the California Constitution, codes, and rules of court, as well as numerous provisions of the decisional law, bear on how the court functions. The court's internal operating practices and procedures should be considered in that context.

1. Petitions in civil cases, to the civil central staff.
2. Petitions in or derived from criminal cases, other than cases arising from judgments of death, to the criminal central staff.
3. Applications for writs of habeas corpus arising out of criminal proceedings, other than cases arising from judgments of death, to the criminal central staff.
4. Motions in criminal cases arising from judgments of death, to the six associate justices and the Chief Justice, or to the capital central staff.
5. Applications for writs of habeas corpus arising out of judgments of death, to the six associate justices and the Chief Justice, or to the capital central staff.
6. Applications to the Supreme Court pursuant to article V, section 8 of the California Constitution for a recommendation regarding the granting of a pardon or commutation to a person twice convicted of a felony, to the criminal central staff.
7. Petitions for review of State Bar proceedings pursuant to rule 9.13 et seq. of the California Rules of Court, to the civil central staff.
8. All other petitions and applications, to the six associate justices and the Chief Justice in rotation so that, at the end of a given period of time, each justice will have been assigned an equal number of petitions. Petitions for rehearing after decision in the Supreme Court are referred to a justice, other than the author, who concurred in the majority opinion.

C. The recommendation set forth in a conference memorandum will generally be one of the following: (1) "Grant," (2) "Grant and Hold," (3) "Grant and Transfer," (4) "Deny," (5) "Submitted," (6) "Denial Submitted," and (7) "Deny and Depublish." The designation "submitted" is used when the author believes the case warrants special discussion. The designation "denial submitted" is used when the author believes the petition should be denied, but nevertheless believes some ground exists that could arguably justify a grant, or an issue is raised that otherwise warrants discussion by the court. The designation "deny and depublish" is used when the author does not believe the decision warrants review, but nevertheless believes the opinion is potentially misleading and should not be relied on as precedent.

D. The author of the conference memorandum assigns it to either the "A" or the "B" list. Cases assigned to the "A" list include all those in which the recommendation is to grant or take affirmative action of some kind, e.g., "grant and transfer" or "deny and depublish," in which a dissenting opinion has been filed in the Court of Appeal, or in which the author believes denial is appropriate, but that the case poses questions that deserve special attention. Cases assigned to the "B" list concern routine matters, or application of settled law.

E. Conference memoranda are delivered by the author to the Calendar Coordinator for reproduction and distribution to the justices no later than the Tuesday of the week before the conference, thus providing ample time for the justices and their staffs to review the petition and the court's internal memoranda.

F. The court's Calendar Coordinator divides the weekly conference agenda into an "A" and "B" list, based on the designation appearing on each conference memorandum.

G. Matters appearing on the "A" list are called and considered at the conference for which they are scheduled. Before or after a vote is taken, any justice may request that a case be put over to a subsequent conference within the jurisdictional time limit for further study, preparation of a supplemental memorandum, or both. The time within which action thereon must be taken will be extended pursuant to rules 8.264 and 8.500 of the California Rules of Court, if necessary.

H. Matters appearing on the "B" list will be denied in accordance with the recommendation of the memorandum, at the conference at which they are scheduled, unless a justice requests that a case be put over to a subsequent conference within the jurisdictional time limit for further study, preparation of a supplemental memorandum, or both.

I. In any case in which the petition, application, or motion is denied, a justice may request that his or her vote be recorded in the court minutes.

J. When a justice is unavailable or disqualified to participate in a vote on a petition for review or other matter (see, e.g., section XIII.A., *post*), and four justices cannot agree on a disposition, the Chief Justice, pursuant to constitutional authority (Cal. Const., art. VI, § 6), assigns in alphabetical order (except as set forth below) a Court of Appeal justice as a pro tempore justice to participate in the vote on the petition or matter. The assigned justice is furnished all pertinent petitions, motions, applications, answers, briefs, memoranda, and other material. A newly-appointed Court of Appeal justice will be assigned as a pro tempore justice of the Supreme Court only after he or she has served on the Court of Appeal for one year. If a Court of Appeal justice is unable to serve on a particular case, the next justice on the alphabetical list will be assigned, and the Court of Appeal justice who was unable to serve will be assigned in the next case in which a pro tempore appointment is required.

K. Either at the time review is granted, or at any time thereafter, the court may specify which of the issues presented should be briefed and argued.

L. Within 15 days after review is granted in a civil case or a criminal case in which a corporate entity is a party, each party must file a "Certification of Interested Entities or Persons" that lists any persons, associations of persons, firms, partnerships, corporations (including parent and subsidiary corporations) or other entities other than the parties themselves known by the party to have either (i) a financial interest in the subject matter of the controversy or in a party to the proceeding; or (ii) any other kind of interest that could be substantially affected by the outcome of the proceeding. This requirement does not apply to any governmental entity or its agencies. The Clerk's Office shall notify all parties including real parties in interest in writing of this requirement at the time the parties are notified of the court's grant of review.

Revised effective January 1, 2007, and April 22, 2015.

V. CALENDAR SESSIONS FOR ORAL ARGUMENT

Regular sessions of the court are held each year, on a day or days as determined by the Chief Justice, in San Francisco, Los Angeles, and Sacramento. Special sessions may be held elsewhere by order of the Chief Justice or by order on a vote of four justices assenting thereto.

Unless otherwise ordered by the Chief Justice, the court convenes at 9:00 a.m.

Unless otherwise ordered, only one counsel may be heard for each side. Counsel wishing to divide the time for oral argument must request permission from the Court not later than ten days after the case has been set for oral argument. In no event shall oral argument be divided into segments of less than ten minutes, except that one counsel for the opening side (unless additional counsel are so authorized) may reserve a portion of his or her allotted time for rebuttal.

VI. CALENDARS AND CALENDAR MEMORANDA

A. The purpose of the calendar memorandum is to present the facts and legal issues, and to propose a resolution of the legal issues.

B. At the request of the justice preparing a calendar memorandum, or on direction of the Chief Justice, or on the affirmative vote of a majority of the court, the Clerk's Office will request counsel for the parties to be prepared to argue and to submit additional briefs on any points that are deemed omitted or inadequately covered by the briefs or in which the court is particularly interested.

C. In assigning cases for the preparation of calendar memoranda, the Chief Justice takes into account the following considerations, but may depart from these considerations for the purpose of equalizing the workload of the justices or expediting the work of the court:

1. The case is assigned to one of the justices who voted for review. If a case involves substantially the same issues as one already assigned for preparation of a calendar memorandum, it may be assigned to the justice who has the similar case. Preference in case assignments may be given to a justice who authored the conference memorandum or supplemental conference memorandum on which the petition was granted, unless other factors, such as equalization of workload, suggest a different assignment.

2. Granted petitions in other matters and State Bar proceedings originally referred to the central staffs are generally assigned to the justices in such a manner as to equalize each justice's allotment of cases.

3. Appeals in cases in which the death penalty has been imposed are assigned in rotation as they are filed.

4. When a rehearing has been granted and a supplemental calendar memorandum is needed, the matter will ordinarily be assigned to the justice who prepared the prior opinion if it appears that he or she can present the views of the majority. Otherwise, the case will be assigned to a justice who is able to do so.

D. The court's general procedures for circulation of calendar memoranda, etc., are as follows:

1. The justice to whom a case is assigned prepares and circulates a calendar memorandum within a prescribed time after the filing of the last brief. When the calendar memorandum circulates, the Calendar Coordi-

nator distributes copies of the briefs to each justice. The record remains with the Calendar Coordinator, to be borrowed as needed by a justice or his or her staff.

2. Within a prescribed time after the calendar memorandum circulates, each justice states his or her preliminary response to the calendar memorandum (i.e., that he or she concurs, concurs with reservations, is doubtful, or does not concur). Each justice also indicates whether he or she intends to write a separate concurring or dissenting calendar memorandum in the case. If it appears from the preliminary responses that a majority of the justices concur in the original calendar memorandum, the Chief Justice places the case on a pre-argument conference (§ VI.D.4, *post*). If it appears from the preliminary responses that a majority of the justices will probably not concur in the original calendar memorandum or a modified version of that memorandum, the Chief Justice places the matter on a conference for discussion or reassigns the case.

3. Each justice who wishes to write a concurring or dissenting calendar memorandum does so and circulates that memorandum within a prescribed time after the original calendar memorandum circulates. Soon after any concurring or dissenting calendar memorandum circulates, each justice either confirms his or her agreement with the original calendar memorandum or indicates his or her agreement with the concurring or dissenting calendar memorandum. If the original calendar memorandum thereby loses its tentative majority, the Chief Justice places the matter on a conference for discussion or reassigns the case.

4. The Chief Justice convenes a pre-argument conference at least once each month. The purpose of the conference is to identify those cases that appear ready for oral argument. The Chief Justice constructs the calendars from those cases.

The Chief Justice places on the agenda of the conference any case in which all concurring or dissenting calendar memoranda have circulated and the "majority" calendar memorandum has been approved by at least four justices or is likely to be approved by four justices at the conference. The Chief Justice also includes on the agenda any case in which discussion could facilitate resolution of the issues.

VII. Submission

A. A cause is submitted when the court has heard oral argument or has approved a waiver of argument and the time has passed for filing all briefs and papers, including any supplementary brief permitted by the court.

B. Submission may be vacated only by an order of the Chief Justice stating in detail the reasons therefor. The order shall provide for prompt resubmission of the cause.

VIII. Assignments for Preparation of Opinions

A. After argument the Chief Justice convenes a conference to determine whether the calendar memorandum continues to represent the views of a majority of the justices. In light of that discussion, the Chief Justice assigns the case for opinion.

B. The Chief Justice assigns the cases for preparation of opinions in the following manner:

1. If a majority of the justices agree with the disposition suggested in the calendar memorandum, ordinarily the case is assigned to the author of that memorandum.

2. If a majority of the justices disagree with the disposition reached in the memorandum, the case is reassigned to one of the majority.

3. When a case is argued on rehearing, it ordinarily remains with the justice who prepared the prior opinion or the supplemental calendar memorandum if it appears that he or she can express the majority view. If he or she does not agree with the majority view, the case is reassigned to a justice who is a member of the majority.

4. In making assignments pursuant to these guidelines, the Chief Justice takes several considerations into account, including the following: (a) the fair distribution of work among the members of the court; (b) the likelihood that a justice can express the view of the majority of the court in a particular case; (c) the amount of work he or she has done on that case or on the issues involved; and (d) the status of the unfiled cases theretofore assigned to him or her.

C. Every reasonable effort is made by the justices to agree on the substance of opinions, and whenever possible, dissents or special concurrence on minor matters are avoided. When a justice discovers that he or she objects to something in a proposed opinion, he or she will call it to the author's attention. In addition, the objecting justice may prepare and circulate a memorandum setting forth his or her concerns and suggestions for the purpose of giving the author an opportunity to conform to any proposed changes and to remove or meet the objections raised. These practices and filing policies (see § X, *post*) reflect the court's strong preference for assuring that each opinion author be allowed sufficient time to consider the views of every justice before the opinion is released for filing.

D. Unless otherwise ordered by the Chief Justice, all opinions in State Bar and Commission on Judicial Performance cases and all memorandum opinions are issued "By the Court." All other opinions identify the author and the concurring justices unless a majority of the court conclude that because substantial portions of the opinion have been drafted by a number of justices, or for other compelling reasons, the opinion should be issued "By the Court."

E. The rules of the *California Style Manual* are consulted in the preparation of opinions as well as conference and calendar memoranda.

IX. Circulation of Opinions

Within a prescribed time after submission, the justice to whom the case is assigned circulates the proposed majority opinion. Within a prescribed time after the proposed majority opinion circulates, all concurring or dissenting opinions circulate. If the author of the proposed majority opinion wishes to respond by change or by memorandum to any concurring or dissenting opinion, he or she does so promptly after that opinion circulates. The author of the concurring or dissenting opinion thereafter has a prescribed time in which to respond.

All opinions are cite-checked and proofread before circulating. Only copies of an opinion circulate; the original remains in the Calendar Coordination Office. A justice may indicate his or her concurrence in an opinion (including an opinion authored by the justice) by signing the original that is retained in the Calendar Coordination Office or by transmitting to the Calendar Coordinator, by facsimile, a signed copy of the signature page of the opinion, indicating the justice's concurrence. When possible, it is preferred that a justice indicate his or her concurrence by signing the original that is retained in the Calendar Coordination Office.

X. Filing of Opinions

When the circulation process has been completed, the Calendar Coordination Office shall notify the authoring justice of each proposed opinion that the matter appears ready for filing, and shall inquire whether each authoring justice is releasing his or her opinion for filing. When all opinions have been released for filing, the Calendar Coordination Office shall provide for the duplication of the opinion, and shall notify the Clerk of the Court and the Reporter of Decisions of the scheduled filing date. The Clerk of the Court shall file the opinion on the scheduled date at the San Francisco office of the Supreme Court.

Opinions are completed in time for reproduction and filing on a normal opinion-filing day. Unless good cause to vacate submission appears, the opinions are filed on or before the 90th day after submission. Internal circulation of an opinion after the 80th day following submission may result in the inability of the author of the proposed majority or of another timely circulated opinion to afford the views contained in the late circulated opinion full consideration and response. Such late circulated opinions will not be filed until at least 10 days but in no event more than 20 days after the filing of the majority opinion. At any time before the majority or lead opinion is final, the court may modify or grant rehearing pursuant to the applicable rules of court.

XI. Review of Determinations by the Commission on Judicial Performance

A petition for review of a determination by the Commission on Judicial Performance to retire, remove, censure, admonish, or disqualify a judge or former judge under subdivision (d) of section 18 of article VI of the California Constitution must address both the appropriateness of review and the merits of the commission's determination. The commission may file a response, and the petitioner a reply, within prescribed times. The petition is assigned by the Calendar Coordinator, under the direction of the Chief Justice, to the civil central staff. When briefing is complete, the staff prepares a conference memorandum in which the recommendation generally will be either to "Deny" or "Retain for Further Consideration."

If a majority of the justices vote to "deny," the petition is denied, and an order to that effect is filed forthwith. If a majority vote to "retain for further consideration," the Chief Justice assigns the case to a justice who voted to retain. This justice then prepares a memorandum on the merits, which will serve as a calendar memorandum if an order granting review subsequently is filed. The court's usual procedures for circulation of calendar memoranda then are followed. Once all concurring and dissenting memoranda have circulated, and it appears there is a majority for a particular disposition, the matter is considered at a conference. If a majority vote to deny review, an order to that effect is filed forthwith. If a majority vote to grant review, an order to that effect is filed, and the case is simultaneously set for oral argument at the soonest possible time under the court's usual scheduling rules. Because of the time limitations in subdivision (d) of section 18 of article VI of the California Constitution, continuance of oral argument rarely will be granted. Following oral argument and submission of the cause, the court's usual rules for preparation and circulation of opinions apply.

XII. Temporary Absence of Justices

A. As soon as a justice knows that he or she will not be attending a conference of the court, he or she will notify the Chief Justice. Any justice who will not be present at conference may communicate his or her votes on any given conference matter as set forth in section III.E. A justice may communicate such votes whether he or she is within or temporarily outside of California. A case may be assigned to a justice for the preparation of a calendar memorandum, under the procedures set forth in section VI, regardless of whether he or she is within or temporarily outside of California at the time the order granting review or issuing a writ or order to show cause is filed.

B. Any justice who is participating in the decision of a case, and who is temporarily outside of California, may communicate his or her concurrence in an opinion (including an opinion authored by that justice) by transmitting to the Calendar Coordinator, by facsimile, a signed copy of the signature page of the opinion, indicating the justice's concurrence, as set forth in section IX. If an opinion is concurred in by four justices, it may be filed as provided above in section X, even though one or more of the concurring justices are temporarily absent from the state and regardless of whether an absent justice is the author of the opinion.

XIII. Disqualification of Justices and Assignment of Court of Appeal Justices

A. Each justice has a duty to hear and decide all matters coming before the court in the absence of a ground of disqualification. (Cal. Code Jud. Ethics, canon 3B(1).) Although one ground of disqualification is presented when a justice has specified financial interests in a party to a proceeding (*id.*, canon 3E(5)(d)), recusal is not required based on a justice's financial interest in an entity that appears in a proceeding but is not a party (e.g., a nonparty entity or a nonparty member of a nonparty advocacy group that requests publication or depublication of a Court of Appeal opinion, or that writes in support of or in opposition to a petition for review, or that appears in a proceeding as amicus curiae), unless 'the justice believes his or her recusal would further the interests of justice' (*id.*, canon 3E(4)(a)), or 'the justice substantially doubts his or her capacity to be impartial' (*id.*, canon 3E(4)(b)), or 'the circumstances are such that a reasonable person aware of the facts would doubt the justice's ability to be impartial' (*id.*, canon 3E(4)(c)). As soon as a justice discovers that he or she is disqualified in any proceeding, he or she will notify the Calendar Coordinator.

B. When it is known after a case is granted but before argument that a justice for any reason is unable to participate in a matter, the Chief Justice pursuant to constitutional authority (Cal. Const., art. VI, § 6) assigns on an alphabetical rotational basis (under the procedure described *ante*, section IV.J) a Court of Appeal justice to assist the court in place of the nonparticipating justice. The assigned justice is furnished all pertinent petitions, motions, applications, answers, briefs, memoranda, and other material.

C. If an assigned justice has participated in the decision of a case before this court, that justice will also participate in any further proceedings — including requests for modification, petitions for rehearing, and rehearings — until such time as the decision has become final. This procedure is to be followed unless the original assignment was necessitated by the absence of a regular justice of this court, in which event a regular justice, if able to do so, will participate in lieu of the assigned justice in the consideration of any petition for rehearing and, if rehearing is granted, in any subsequent proceeding.

D. If a justice retires before a case in which he or she has heard oral argument is final, he or she may be assigned to continue to participate in the case. When a permanent replacement justice appointed to fill the vacancy created by the retirement of that justice has taken the oath of office, and the opinion has been filed, any petition for rehearing will be acted on by the permanent replacement justice.

Revised effective April 22, 2015.

XIV. Applications for Recommendations for Executive Clemency, Habeas Corpus, and Stays

A. An application for a recommendation for executive clemency comes before this court pursuant to article V, section 8, subdivision (a) of the California Constitution and Penal Code section 4851. When such applications are received by the Clerk's Office, they are given a file number, and the fact that they have been filed is a matter of public record. The papers and documents transmitted to the court by the Governor with the application often contain material that the Governor may have the right to withhold from the public. (See Gov. Code, § 6254, subds. (c), (f), & (*l*); Civ. Code, § 1798.40, subd. (c).) Accordingly, the court treats these files as confidential and does not make them available to the public.

Applications are denied unless four or more justices vote to recommend that clemency be granted. The Chief Justice informs the Governor by letter of the court's recommendation, and a copy of such letter is included in the court's file and considered a matter of public record. Pursuant to the provisions of Penal Code section 4852, the Clerk transmits the record to the office of the Governor if the court's recommendation is favorable to the applicant. Otherwise, the documents remain in the files of the court. (See Pen. Code, § 4852.)

B. When a defendant in a criminal case files a petition for review after denial without opinion by the Court of Appeal of a petition for prohibition or mandate attacking a Penal Code section 995 or section 1538.5 ruling, the matter will be placed on the agenda of a regular conference and will not be accelerated. Absent extraordinary circumstances, no order staying the trial will issue. If the case goes to trial and the matter becomes moot before the regular conference, the memorandum need only so state, and the petition may then be denied as moot without the necessity of considering its merits.

When the Court of Appeal has denied such a writ petition with opinion, a request to stay the trial pending action by the Supreme Court on the petition for review will be granted when necessary to prevent the matter from becoming moot.

C. When a misdemeanor conviction has become final on appeal or a final contempt order has been filed by a trial court and the defendant or contemner files a petition for review following denial of a timely habeas corpus or certiorari petition by a Court of Appeal or files a timely original petition, a stay of execution of the judgment or order will issue pending determination of the petition. The Chief Justice may condition the stay on the filing of a bond or on the continuation of an appeal bond, if any, if he or she deems it appropriate to do so. If the petition appears to lack merit, however, expedited consideration will be given to deny the petition in preference to releasing an incarcerated petitioner.

D. Pending disposition of a petition for writ of habeas corpus to review an order permitting extradition, the Chief Justice may stay extradition on behalf of the court. If the petition appears to lack merit, however, expedited consideration will be given to deny the petition in preference to staying the extradition proceedings.

E. In cases not covered by subdivisions B and C of this section, and when not precluded by subdivision G of this section, the Chief Justice may, in his or her discretion, grant applications for stays of judicial proceedings or orders pending regular conference consideration of the matters involved.

F. Except as provided in subdivisions B through E of this section and except in emergencies, petitions for habeas corpus, applications for stays of judicial proceedings or orders, and applications for stays of execution are to be resolved at the weekly case conference.

G. Stays governed by special provisions of statutes or rules of court will be issued only in compliance with such provisions. (See, e.g., Pub. Util. Code, §§ 1761–1766; Cal. Rules of Court, rule 8.112.)

H. Applications to stay actions by public agencies or private parties pending consideration of petitions for writs of mandate (i.e., *Emeryville*-type stays [see *People ex rel. S. F. Bay etc. Com. v. Town of Emeryville* (1968) 69 Cal.2d 533]) are to be resolved at the weekly case conference.

I. Upon receipt of a proper notice of bankruptcy relating to a pending petition for review in a creditor's action or an action that would diminish the relevant estate, the court will file an order noting the stay of proceedings and suspending the operation of the applicable rule 8.500 time period. (See 11 U.S.C. § 362(a)(1).) Thereafter, the parties will be directed to file quarterly status reports to apprise the court of the current status of the bankruptcy proceedings. Upon receipt of a proper notice terminating the bankruptcy stay, the court shall enter an order terminating the stay of proceedings and indicating that the applicable time period of rule 8.500(a) shall begin running anew from the date of the order.

Revised effective January 1, 2007.

XV. Appointment of Attorneys in Criminal Cases

A. In criminal matters, upon a verified or certified statement of indigency, the court, acting through the Clerk's Office, will appoint an attorney for a party in the following instances:

1. In a pending case in which the petition for review has been granted;
2. In a pending automatic appeal and/or related state habeas corpus/executive clemency proceedings;
3. In an original proceeding in which an alternative writ or an order to show cause has been issued;
4. In capital cases in the following proceedings:
   (a) Proceedings for appellate or other postconviction review of state court judgments in the United States Supreme Court, subject however to the power of that court to appoint counsel therein; and
   (b) Conduct of sanity hearings when indicated.

B. At or after the time the court appoints appellate counsel to represent an indigent appellant on direct appeal, the court also shall offer to appoint habeas corpus/executive clemency counsel for each indigent capital appellant. Following that offer, the court shall appoint habeas corpus/executive clemency counsel unless the court finds, after a hearing if necessary (held before a referee appointed by the court), that the appellant rejected the offer with full understanding of the legal consequences of the decision.

C. The court's Automatic Appeals Monitor is responsible for recruiting, evaluating, and recommending the appointment of counsel on behalf of indigent appellants in capital appeals and/or related state habeas corpus/executive clemency proceedings.

D. Counsel in automatic appeals and/or related state habeas corpus/executive clemency proceedings are compensated by one of two alternative methods: Under the "time and costs" method, counsel are compensated on an hourly basis and reimbursed for necessary expenses that were reasonably incurred. The court makes partial payments on counsel's fee claims while these claims are pending full review. Under the alternative optional "fixed fee and expenses" method, counsel are paid a fixed amount at regular stages of a case, according to a predetermined assessment of its difficulty.

E. Habeas corpus petitions in capital cases are governed by the timeliness and compensation standards set out in the "Supreme Court Policies Regarding Cases Arising From Judgments of Death." Habeas corpus counsel appointed in capital cases have the duty to investigate factual and legal grounds for the filing of a petition for a writ of habeas corpus, as delineated in those policies.

XVI. Communications From Counsel in Pending Cases

Whenever a matter is pending before the court, any communication to the court from counsel is to be addressed to the Clerk's Office, with copies to all counsel.

XVII. Suspension of Procedures

Whenever exceptional or emergency conditions require speedy action, or whenever there is other good cause for special action regarding any matter, the operation of these procedures may be temporarily suspended by affirmative vote of four justices.

The Chief Justice may extend any applicable time limit (except that stated in section X) on written request by a justice stating good cause and the date by which he or she expects to comply.

SUPREME COURT POLICIES REGARDING CASES ARISING FROM JUDGMENTS OF DEATH

(Adopted by the Supreme Court effective June 6, 1989.)

(Amended effective September 28, 1989, September 19, 1990, January 27, 1992, December 21, 1992, July 29, 1993, December 22, 1993, June 20, 1996, January 22, 1997, January 22, 1998, February 4, 1998, August 23, 2001, December 19, 2001, January 16, 2002, July 17, 2002, July 26, 2002, November 20, 2002, November 30, 2005, and January 1, 2008.)

Stays of execution. Policy Statement 1.
Withdrawal of counsel. Policy Statement 2.
Standards governing filing of habeas corpus petitions and compensation of counsel in relation to such petitions. Policy Statement 3.
Service of process by counsel for defendant. Policy Statement 4.

Policy Statement 1. Stays of execution.

The court will consider a motion for a stay of execution only if such a motion is made in connection with a petition for a writ of habeas corpus filed in this court, or to permit certiorari review by the United States Supreme Court.

Adopted June 6, 1989.

Policy Statement 2. Withdrawal of counsel.

In the absence of exceptional circumstances—for example, when an appointed counsel becomes mentally or physically incapacitated—the court will consider a motion to withdraw as attorney of record only if appropriate replacement counsel is ready and willing to accept appointment for the balance of the representation for which the withdrawing attorney has been appointed (i.e., appellate representation, habeas corpus/executive clemency representation, or both).

Adopted June 6, 1989; amended effective Jan. 22, 1998.

Policy Statement 3. Standards governing filing of habeas corpus petitions and compensation of counsel in relation to such petitions.

The Supreme Court promulgates these standards as a means of implementing the following goals with respect to petitions for writs of habeas corpus relating to capital cases: (i) ensuring that potentially meritorious habeas corpus petitions will be presented to and heard by this court in a timely fashion; (ii) providing appointed counsel some certainty of payment for authorized legal work and investigation expenses; and (iii) providing this court with a means to monitor and regulate expenditure of public funds paid to counsel who seek to investigate and file habeas corpus petitions.

For these reasons, effective June 6, 1989, all petitions for writs of habeas corpus arising from judgments of death, whether the appeals therefrom are pending or previously resolved, are governed by these standards:

1. Timeliness standards

1-1. Appellate counsel in a capital case shall take and maintain detailed, understandable and computerized transcript notes and shall compile and maintain a detailed list of potentially meritorious habeas corpus issues that have come to appellate counsel's attention. In addition, if appellate counsel's appointment does not include habeas corpus representation, until separate counsel is appointed for that purpose, appellate counsel shall preserve evidence that comes to the attention of appellate counsel if that evidence appears relevant to a potential habeas corpus investigation. If separate "post-conviction" habeas corpus/executive clemency counsel (hereafter "habeas corpus" counsel) is appointed, appellate counsel shall deliver to habeas corpus counsel copies of the list of potentially meritorious habeas corpus issues, copies of the transcript notes, and any preserved evidence relevant to a potential habeas corpus investigation, and thereafter shall update the issues list and transcript notes as warranted. Appellate counsel shall consult with and work cooperatively with habeas corpus counsel to facilitate timely investigation, and timely preparation and filing (if warranted) of a habeas corpus petition by habeas corpus counsel.

Habeas corpus counsel in a capital cases shall have a duty to investigate factual and legal grounds for the filing of a petition for a writ of habeas corpus. The duty to investigate is limited to investigating potentially meritorious grounds for relief that come to counsel's attention in the course of reviewing appellate counsel's list of potentially meritorious habeas corpus issues, the transcript notes prepared by appellate counsel, the appellate record, trial counsel's existing case files, and the appellate briefs, and in the course of making reasonable efforts to discuss the case with the defendant, trial counsel and appellate counsel. The duty to investigate does not impose on counsel an obligation to conduct, nor does it authorize the expenditure of public funds for, an unfocused investigation having as its object uncovering all possible factual bases for a collateral attack on the judgment. Instead, counsel has a duty to investigate potential habeas corpus claims only if counsel has become aware of information that might reasonably lead to actual facts supporting a potentially meritorious claim. All petitions for writs of habeas corpus should be filed without substantial delay.

[As amended effective July 29, 1993, and Jan. 22, 1998.]

1-1.1. A petition for a writ of habeas corpus will be presumed to be filed without substantial delay if it is filed within 180 days after the final due date for the filing of appellant's reply brief on the direct appeal or within 36 months after appointment of habeas corpus counsel, whichever is later.

[As amended effective Sept. 19, 1990, Jan. 22, 1998, July 17, 2002, and Nov. 30, 2005.]

1-1.2. A petition filed more than 180 days after the final due date for the filing of appellant's reply brief on the direct appeal, or more than 36 months after appointment of habeas corpus counsel, whichever is later, may establish absence of substantial delay if it alleges with specificity facts showing the petition was filed within a reasonable time after petitioner or counsel (a) knew, or should have known, of facts supporting a claim and (b) became aware, or should have become aware, of the legal basis for the claim.

[As amended effective Sept. 19, 1990, July 29, 1993, Jan. 22, 1998, July 17, 2002, and Nov. 30, 2005.]

Official Note No. 1: The amendments to standards 1-1.1 and 1-1.2, effective July 17, 2002, changing "90 days" to "180 days," shall apply to all petitions for a writ of habeas corpus arising from a judgment of death that were pending before the Supreme Court on July 17, 2002, and to all such petitions filed after that date. *[Note added by Supreme Court order, July 26, 2002.]*

Official Note No. 2: The amendments to standards 1-1.1 and 1-1.2, effective November 30, 2005, changing "24 months" to "36 months," shall apply to all petitions for a writ of habeas corpus arising from a judgment of death that were pending before the Supreme Court on November 30, 2005, and to all such petitions filed after that date. *[Note added by Supreme Court order, Nov. 30, 2005.]*

1-1.3. [Repealed effective Jan. 22, 1998]

1-2. If a petition is filed after substantial delay, the petitioner must demonstrate good cause for the delay. A petitioner may establish good cause by showing particular circumstances sufficient to justify substantial delay.

1-3. Any petition that fails to comply with these requirements may be denied as untimely.

1-4. The court may toll the 180-day period of presumptive timeliness for the filing of a capital-related habeas corpus petition (which begins to run from the final due date to file the appellant's reply brief in the appeal) when it authorizes the appellant to file supplemental briefing. The court will not toll before the 180-day presumptive timeliness period begins to run or after it has finished running.

Ordinarily, the court will toll the 180-day presumptive timeliness period only when the appellant is represented by the same counsel on appeal and also for related habeas corpus/executive clemency proceedings.

If the court determines that it will toll such 180-day presumptive timeliness period, it will so provide in its order authorizing the appellant to file supplemental briefing.

When the court provides for tolling of the 180-day presumptive timeliness period in its order authorizing the appellant to file supplemental briefing, it will determine a reasonable period of time for the appellant to devote to whatever supplemental briefing is authorized, add that period of time to the final due date to file the appellant's reply brief in the appeal, and indicate the new date by which the appellant may file a presumptively timely habeas corpus petition.

Other than under these circumstances, the court will not toll, or otherwise extend, the period in which to file a presumptively timely capital-related habeas corpus petition.

[Standard adopted effective Nov. 20, 2002.]

2. Compensation standards

2-1. This court's appointment of appellate counsel for a person under a sentence of death is for the following: (i) pleadings and proceedings related to preparation and certification of the appellate record; (ii) representation in the direct appeal before the California Supreme Court; (iii) preparation and filing of a petition for a writ of certiorari, or an answer thereto, in the United States Supreme Court and, if certiorari is granted, preparation and filing of a brief or briefs on the merits and preparation and presentation of oral argument; and (iv) representation in the trial court relating to proceedings pursuant to Penal Code section 1193.

This court's appointment of habeas corpus counsel for a person under a sentence of death shall be made simultaneously with appointment of appellate counsel or at the earliest practicable time thereafter. The appointment of habeas corpus counsel is for the following: (i) investigation, and preparation and filing (if warranted), of a habeas corpus petition in the California Supreme Court, including any informal briefing and evidentiary hearing ordered by the court and any petition to exhaust state remedies; (ii) representation in the trial court relating to proceedings pursuant to Penal Code section 1227; and (iii) representation in executive clemency proceedings before the Governor of California.

Absent prior authorization by this court, this court will not compensate counsel for the filing of any other motion, petition, or pleading in any other California or federal court or court of another state. Counsel who seek compensation for representation in another court should secure appointment by, and compensation from, that court.

[As amended effective Dec. 22, 1993, Jan. 22, 1998, and Feb. 4, 1998.]

2-2. Habeas corpus counsel should expeditiously investigate potentially meritorious bases for filing a petition for a writ of habeas corpus. If the timing of separate appointments permits, this investigation should be done concurrently with appellate counsel's review of the appellate record and briefing on appeal, and in any event, in cooperation with appellate counsel.

[As amended effective Dec. 21, 1992, and Jan. 22, 1998.]

2-2.1. In all cases in which counsel was appointed on or after the October 12, 1997, enactment of Senate Bill No. 513 (Stats. 1997, ch. 869), counsel, without prior authorization of the court, may incur expenses up to a total of $25,000 for habeas corpus investigation, and may submit claims to the court for reimbursement up to that amount. Investigative expenses include travel associated with habeas corpus investigation, and services of law clerks, paralegals, and others serving as habeas corpus investigators. The reasonable cost of photocopying defense counsel's trial files is not considered an investigative expense, and will be separately reimbursed. The court will reimburse counsel for expenses up to $25,000 that were reasonably incurred pursuant to the duty to investigate as described in standard 1-1, but it will not authorize counsel to expend, nor will it reimburse counsel for, habeas corpus investigation expenses exceeding $25,000 before the issuance of an order to show cause. This policy applies to both hourly ("time and costs") and fixed fee appointments.

The policy described in the foregoing paragraph shall also apply to those cases in which counsel was appointed prior to October 12, 1997 (the enactment of Sen. Bill No. 513), and in which, by January 22, 1998, the effective date of the above-described policy, the defendant has not filed a habeas corpus petition in this court and no more than 90 days [now 180 days] have passed since the final due date for the filing of the appellant's reply brief on direct appeal.

As to those cases in which, by January 1, 2008 (the effective date of Assem. Bill No. 1248), the defendant has not filed a capital-related habeas corpus petition in this court and the date by which to file a presumptively timely petition has not yet passed, counsel may be reimbursed up to $50,000 for those investigative services and expenses incurred on or after that date. Such investigative funding for expenses incurred after January 1, 2008, also is available in those cases in which a presumptively timely petition has been filed by January 1, 2008, but petitioner's reply to the informal response has not been filed and the time to do so (with any extensions of time) has not passed as of that date.

[As amended effective Jan. 16, 2002, and Jan. 1, 2008; standard adopted effective Jan. 22, 1998.]

2-2.2. In all cases in which counsel was appointed on an hourly basis prior to October 12, 1997, and in which, by January 22, 1998, either a petition for a writ of habeas corpus has been filed in this court, or more than 90 days have passed since the final due date for the filing of the appellant's reply brief on direct appeal, requests by appointed counsel for authorization to incur, and reimbursement of, investigation expenses shall be governed by the following standards (2-2.3 through 2-4.4):

2-2.3. Without prior authorization of the court, counsel may incur expenses up to a total of $3,000 for habeas corpus investigation relating to a death penalty judgment, and may submit claims to the court for reimbursement up to that amount. The court will reimburse counsel for expenses up to $3,000 that were reasonably incurred pursuant to the duty to investigate as described in standard 1-1.

2-2.4. If after incurring $3,000 in investigation expenses (or if $3,000 in reimbursement for investigation funds previously has been granted on behalf of the same defendant/petitioner with regard to the same underlying death penalty judgment), counsel determines it is necessary to incur additional expenses for which he or she plans to seek reimbursement from the court, counsel must seek and obtain prior authorization from the court. As a general rule, the court will *not* reimburse counsel for expenses exceeding $3,000, without prior authorization of the court. Requests by appointed counsel for prior authorization to incur investigation expenses shall be governed by the following standards.

2-3. Counsel shall file with this court a "Confidential request for authorization to incur expenses to investigate potential habeas corpus issues," showing good cause why the request was not filed on or before the date the appellant's opening brief on appeal was filed.

[As amended effective Dec. 21, 1992, and Jan. 22, 1998.]

2-4. The confidential request for authorization to incur expenses shall set out:

2-4.1. The issues to be explored;

2-4.2. Specific facts that suggest there may be an issue of possible merit;

2-4.3. An itemized list of the expenses requested for each issue of the proposed habeas corpus petition; and

2-4.4. (a) An itemized listing of all expenses previously sought from, and/or approved by any court of this state and/or any federal court in connection with any habeas corpus proceeding or investigation concerning the same judgment and petitioner; (b) A statement summarizing the status of any proceeding or investigation in any court of this state and/or any federal court concerning the same judgment and petitioner; and (c) A copy of any related petition previously filed in any trial and/or lower appellate court of this state and/or any federal court concerning the same judgment and petitioner.

[As amended effective Jan. 27, 1992, and Dec. 21, 1992.]

2-5. Counsel generally will not be awarded compensation for fees and expenses relating to matters that are clearly not cognizable in a petition for a writ of habeas corpus.

[As renumbered effective Dec. 21, 1992.]

2-6. When a petition is pending in this court to exhaust claims presented in a federal habeas corpus petition, a request by counsel for investigative funds to bolster or augment claims already presented in the petition normally will be denied absent a showing of strong justification for the request. A request for investigative funds may be granted if the petitioner demonstrates that he or she has timely discovered new and potentially meritorious areas of investigation not previously addressed in the petitioner's federal or state petitions. This has been the internal operating policy of the court since December 16, 1992.

[Standard adopted effective June 20, 1996.]

2-7. Each request for fees relating to a habeas corpus petition must be accompanied by: (a) An itemized listing of all fees previously sought from, and/or approved by any court of this state and/or any federal court in connection with any habeas corpus proceeding or investigation concerning the same judgment and petitioner; (b) A statement summarizing the status of any proceeding or investigation in any court of this state and/or any federal court concerning the same judgment and petitioner; and (c) A copy of any related petition previously filed in any trial and/or lower appellate court of this state and/or any federal court concerning the same judgment and petitioner.

[As renumbered and amended effective Dec. 21, 1992, and as renumbered effective June 20, 1996.]

2-8. In a case in which the court orders an evidentiary hearing, and counsel and the court do not enter into a "fixed fee and expenses agreement" covering the evidentiary hearing (see "Guideline 10" of the "Guidelines for Fixed Fee Appointments, on Optional Basis, to Automatic Appeals and Related Habeas Corpus Proceedings in the California Supreme Court"), requests for reimbursement of necessary and reasonable expenses incurred in preparation for and presentation of the evidentiary hearing shall be governed by the following standards:

2-8.1. Counsel may incur "incidental" expenses (i.e., travel to and from the evidentiary hearing and related hearings before the referee, meals and lodging during the hearing, telephone charges, photocopying, etc.) without prior approval, and the court will reimburse counsel for such itemized, reasonable and necessarily incurred expenses pursuant to the court's "Payment Guidelines for Appointed Counsel Representing Indigent Criminal Appellants in the California Supreme Court," part III ("Necessary Expenses").

2-8.2. Counsel should seek and obtain from this court prior approval for all investigation and witness expenses, including, but not limited to, investigator fees and costs, expert fees and costs, and expert witness fees and costs.

2-8.3. Counsel may submit requests for reimbursement of expenses every 60 days to this court, and will be reimbursed for necessary and reasonable expenses consistently with part III of the "Payment Guidelines," *supra*.

[Standard adopted effective Jan. 22, 1997.]

Policy Statement 4. Service of process by counsel for defendant.

Consistently with longstanding practice and court policy, except as specified below, counsel for the defendant must serve his or her client, any separate counsel of record in any matter related to the same judgment, counsel of record for every other party, the trial court, the assisting entity or attorney for counsel for the defendant and any separate counsel of record, and trial counsel, with a copy of each motion, request for extension of time, brief, petition or other public document filed in this court or in the trial court on the client's behalf, including any supporting declaration, with attached proof of service. A declaration submitted in support of any motion or request may refer to and incorporate by reference matters set forth in a current "confidential 60-day status report" simultaneously provided only to this court. Counsel also must serve any additional person or entity as requested by this court.

Counsel for the defendant need not serve (1) trial counsel with any matter upon or after the filing in this court of the certified record on appeal; (2) the trial court with any extension-of-time request related to appellate briefing; and (3) the trial court or trial counsel with any matter related to habeas corpus briefing.

If counsel for the defendant elects to serve the defendant personally with the document, counsel may indicate on the proof of service the date by which counsel will so serve the defendant (not to exceed 30 calendar days), and counsel shall thereafter notify the court in writing that the defendant has been served. In the alternative, counsel for the defendant need not serve the defendant with any specific document to be filed if counsel for the defendant attaches to the proof of service for that specific document (1) a declaration by the defendant stating that he or she does not wish to be served with that specific document, and (2) a declaration by counsel for the defendant stating that he or she has described to the defendant the substance and purpose of that specific document.

[Policy amended effective Dec. 19, 2001.]

SUPREME COURT OF CALIFORNIA

Appendix to Supreme Court Policies Regarding Cases Arising From Judgments of Death Concerning Appointed Counsel's Duties

Procedures and policies adopted by the California Supreme Court on August 22, 2001, as amended July 27, 2005, and May 18, 2011, and March 19, 2014

Counsel appointed in capital matters must be familiar with the duties set forth in the timeliness standards and compensation standards contained in the Supreme Court Policies Regarding Cases Arising From Judgments of Death, which are published periodically in Advance Pamphlets of the California Official Reports, in the "Rules" pages, and available on the website www.courts.ca.gov/5641.htm, and in desktop versions of the California Rules of Court. Important aspects of these policies are reiterated below in part I. Counsel is responsible for keeping up to date regarding any amendments to these policies. In addition, counsel must be familiar with the additional duties set forth in part II of this Appendix. For questions regarding the Policies or this Appendix, counsel should contact the court's Capital Appointment Coordinator/Advisor.

I. DUTIES STATED IN THE POLICIES

Appellate counsel in a capital case must take and maintain detailed, understandable, and computerized transcript notes, and must compile and maintain a detailed list of potentially meritorious habeas corpus issues that have come to appellate counsel's attention. Moreover, if appellate counsel's appointment does not include related habeas corpus/executive clemency representation, until separate postconviction habeas corpus/executive clemency counsel ("habeas corpus" counsel) is appointed, appellate counsel must preserve evidence that comes to his or her attention if that evidence appears relevant to a potential habeas corpus investigation. (Supreme Ct. Policies Regarding Cases Arising From Judgments of Death, policy 3, std. 1-1, 1st par.)

After separate habeas corpus counsel is appointed, appellate counsel must deliver to habeas corpus counsel copies of the list of potentially meritorious habeas corpus issues, copies of the transcript notes, and any preserved evidence relevant to a potential habeas corpus investigation, and thereafter must update the "issues list" and the computerized transcript notes as warranted. Moreover, appellate counsel must consult with and work cooperatively with habeas corpus counsel to facilitate a timely investigation, and the timely preparation and filing (if warranted) of a habeas corpus petition by appointed habeas corpus counsel. (Policy 3, std. 1-1, 1st par.)

Appointed appellate counsel's scope of representation includes the preparation and certification of the record on appeal; representation in the direct appeal before the California Supreme Court; preparation and filing of a petition for a writ of certiorari, or an answer thereto, in the United States Supreme Court, and, if certiorari is granted, preparation and filing of a brief or briefs on the merits, and preparation and presentation of oral argument; and representation in the trial court relating to proceedings to set an execution date pursuant to Penal Code section 1193. (Policy 3, std. 2-1, 1st par.)

Appointed habeas corpus counsel's scope of representation includes the investigation, and preparation and filing (if warranted), of a habeas corpus petition in the Supreme Court, including any informal briefing and evidentiary hearing ordered by the court and any petition to exhaust state remedies; representation in the trial court relating to proceedings to set an execution date pursuant to Penal Code section 1227; and representation in executive clemency proceedings before the Governor of California. (Policy 3, std. 2-1, 2d par.)

As noted, habeas corpus counsel in a capital case has a duty to investigate factual and legal grounds for the filing of a petition for a writ of habeas corpus. The duty to investigate is limited to investigating potentially meritorious grounds for relief that come to counsel's attention in the course of reviewing appellate counsel's list of potentially meritorious habeas corpus issues, the transcript notes prepared by appellate counsel, the appellate record, trial counsel's existing case files, and the appellate briefs, and in the course of making reasonable efforts to discuss the case with the defendant, trial counsel, and appellate counsel. (Policy 3, std. 1-1, 2d par.)

Habeas corpus counsel's duty to investigate does not impose on such counsel an obligation to conduct, nor does it authorize the expenditure of public funds for, an unfocused investigation having as its object uncovering all possible factual bases for a collateral attack on the judgment of death. Instead, habeas corpus counsel has a duty to investigate potential habeas corpus claims only if counsel has become aware of information that might reasonably lead to actual facts supporting a potentially meritorious claim. (Policy 3, std. 1-1, 2d par.) A petition for a writ of habeas corpus will be presumed to be filed without substantial delay if it is filed within 180 days after the final due date for the filing of the appellant's reply brief on the direct appeal, or within 36 months after appointment of habeas corpus counsel, *whichever is later*. (Policy 3, stds. 1-1.1 & 1-1.2, as amended eff. Nov. 30, 2005; see also, *In re Robbins* (1998) 18 Cal.4th 770.)

In the event that more than one counsel is appointed to represent the same defendant jointly, either in a capital appeal, in related habeas corpus/executive clemency proceedings in the Supreme Court or in both classes of proceedings upon an "appellate/habeas corpus" appointment, one such attorney must be designated as lead counsel for each *separate* appointment. Lead counsel is responsible for the overall conduct of the case (i.e., the capital appeal, the related habeas corpus/executive clemency proceedings or, in appellate/habeas corpus representation, both classes of proceedings) and for supervising the work of appointed associate counsel and any nonappointed, supervised counsel. (Cal. Rules of Court, rule 8.605(c)(2); see also, Advisory Com. com. to subd. (c).)

II. ADDITIONAL DUTIES OF APPOINTED COUNSEL

A. Cooperation with Assisting Entity or Counsel

Appellate counsel and habeas corpus counsel also have a duty to cooperate, as a condition of the appointment, with the assisting entity or counsel designated by the Supreme Court to provide outside consultation and resource assistance to appointed counsel. Appointed counsel's cooperation and close working relationship with his or her assisting entity or counsel are important to achieving the common goal of maintaining a high level of legal representation in all capital appeals and related habeas corpus/executive clemency proceedings.

The Supreme Court requires the assisting entity or counsel to report to it periodically and in detail on appointed counsel's case progress. The court places considerable weight on these reports in determining compensation of counsel and whether counsel should be given additional capital case appointments.

Assisting entities that may be designated in this capacity include, as appropriate, the California Appellate Project (CAP) in San Francisco, the Office of the State Public Defender (OSPD), and the Habeas Corpus Resource Center (HCRC). (See Cal. Rules of Court, rule 8.605(c)(5).) In the event the designated assisting entity or counsel has a conflict of interest, the Supreme Court will designate an alternative assisting entity, or an experienced private capital appellate and/or habeas corpus practitioner, as appropriate.

Appointed counsel's obligation to cooperate with other appointed counsel and the assisting entity or counsel includes the following duties:

1. Appellate counsel must promptly make available to the assisting entity or counsel, for review, the above-described computerized transcript notes and detailed list of potentially meritorious habeas corpus issues, as well as a list of potential issues on the direct appeal.
2. Upon a request from the assisting entity or counsel, and after consultation with the Capital Appointment Coordinator/Advisor, appellate counsel must either make a copy of relevant portions of the record available to that entity or counsel for its review, or permit the assisting entity or counsel to photocopy the record.
3. Both appellate and habeas corpus counsel must promptly initiate and maintain communication with the defendant/appellant, trial counsel, and any separately appointed counsel.
4. Both appellate and habeas corpus counsel must review carefully all manuals, newsletters, and other materials distributed by any assisting entity or counsel, and make appropriate use of the resources available in brief and information banks.
5. Unless the Supreme Court advises counsel otherwise, both appellate and habeas corpus counsel are expected to attend post-appointment training programs presented by the assisting entities or counsel.
6. Habeas corpus counsel must submit to the assisting entity or counsel a detailed outline of potential habeas corpus issues to be investigated and a proposed investigation plan, and must conduct a prompt investigation, as described above, of any potentially meritorious habeas corpus issues.
7. Appellate counsel must maintain ongoing consultation with the assisting entity or counsel regarding possible appellate issues; drafts of motions, pleadings, and briefs; and oral argument. The court anticipates that all appointed counsel will participate in a moot court in preparation for oral argument.
8. Both appellate and habeas corpus counsel must consult with the assisting entity or counsel regarding the amount of time appointed counsel plans to spend researching the direct appeal and/or conducting a habeas corpus investigation. In so doing, appointed counsel must consult, and be guided by, the Supreme Court's (a) Policy 3 timeliness standards and compensation standards, referenced above, as well as the court's (b) "time and costs" payment guidelines and (c) "fixed fee" guidelines. The time-and-costs payment guidelines

and the fixed fee guidelines are published periodically in Advance Pamphlets of the California Official Reports, in the "Rules" pages, together with the Policies. These and related materials are available on the website www.courts.ca.gov/5641.htm, and in desktop versions of the California Rules of Court. The court's Internal Operating Practices and Procedures are published periodically in Advance Pamphlets of the California Official Reports in the "Rules" pages, and are available on the website www.courts.ca.gov/2007_Supreme_Court_Booklet.pdf, and in desktop versions of the California Rules of Court.

9. Both appellate and habeas corpus counsel must submit drafts of all motions, pleadings, briefs, petitions and replies, investigation plans, etc., to the assisting entity or counsel for review, allowing sufficient time for that review and for incorporating appropriate suggested changes into the final document.

10. Both appellate and habeas corpus counsel must provide the assisting entity or counsel with copies of all court orders, motions, pleadings, briefs, petitions, replies and responses, etc., filed by appointed counsel and by counsel for the respondent.

The Supreme Court anticipates that all appointed counsel will comply with these duties and provide the foregoing level of cooperation with other appointed counsel and with the assisting entity or counsel. The court will consider appointed counsel's cooperation and compliance with these duties in determining counsel's compensation (either fixed fee or time-and-costs) and counsel's suitability for subsequent appointments. Also, unless counsel has substantially complied with these duties, the assisting entity or counsel may be unable to submit the substantial compliance letter required under fixed fee guideline 5 ("Progress Payments").

If appointed counsel, or the assisting entity or counsel, identifies problems in complying with these duties, appointed counsel, or the assisting entity or counsel, should promptly notify the Capital Appointment Coordinator/Advisor.

B. Other Duties of Appointed Counsel Procedures as adopted by the California Supreme Court on August 22, 2001, and amended July 27, 2005, May 18, 2011, and March 19, 2014

1. Contents of Declarations in Support of Extension of Time (EOT) Applications

Any declaration submitted in support of an EOT request must include the following:
a. The original due date for the uncompleted matter for which an EOT is sought; the total amount of time that has elapsed since that date; and the number of prior extensions requested and granted or denied.
b. The number of pages in the record on appeal, as follows: (a) the number of pages in the combined record on appeal, both reporter's and clerk's transcripts, *including* juror questionnaires, and (b) the number of pages in the combined record on appeal, *excluding* the juror questionnaires. (This information is not required if the EOT request concerns only habeas corpus briefing.)
c. A good faith estimate of the percentage of work accomplished to date, with regard to the uncompleted matter for which an EOT is sought. A good faith estimate of the amount of time required for the remaining work to be done, with regard to the uncompleted matter for which an EOT is sought, and a proposed target date for the filing of that matter.

Pursuant to the court's longstanding practice, extensions of time for briefing in automatic appeals and informal briefing and post-order to show cause briefing in habeas corpus proceedings will be granted in up to 60-day intervals.

2. Confidential Status Report (CSR) of Appointed Counsel and Assisting Entity or Counsel

In accordance with longstanding court practice, until appointed appellate counsel files the appellant's opening brief, and until appointed habeas corpus/executive clemency counsel files a capital-related state habeas corpus petition, a current CSR must be submitted every 60 days. Lead appointed counsel must serve a copy of the CSR on the assisting entity or attorney and on any appointed associate counsel, and must submit proof of service with the report. A CSR submitted by appointed counsel must include the following:
a. Current case status, including a good faith estimate of the percentage of work accomplished to date with regard to each pending uncompleted task.
b. Progress during the last 60 days.
c. Problems and reasons for any delay.
d. Future plans, including a good faith estimate of the amount of time it will take for the remaining work to be done as to each pending uncompleted task, and a proposed target date for completion of each such task.

Whenever appointed appellate counsel has filed a request for an EOT to file the appellant's opening brief or appellant's reply brief, or appointed habeas corpus/executive clemency counsel has filed a request for an EOT to file the reply to an informal response to a petition for a writ of habeas corpus, and the court has subsequently denied that request, appointed counsel must submit to the court and serve upon the assisting entity or attorney a CSR as described above 30 days after the court's order denying the request and every 30 days thereafter until the brief or reply has been filed.

In addition, the assisting entity or attorney must also submit to the court 30 days after the date of the court's order and every 30 days thereafter until the brief or reply is filed a CSR providing the following:
a. The assisting entity's or attorney's assessment of current case status, including a good faith estimate of the percentage of work accomplished to date with regard to each pending uncompleted task.
b. The assisting entity's or attorney's assessment of appointed counsel's progress during the last 30 days.
c. The assisting entity's or attorney's views regarding any problems and the reasons for delay.
d. Future plans and arrangements appointed counsel and the assisting entity or attorney have made, including the assisting entity's or attorney's good faith estimate of the date when the brief or reply will be filed.

The assisting entity or attorney must serve a copy of the CSR on the lead appointed counsel and any appointed associate counsel being assisted, and must submit proof of service with the report.

3. Supplemental Declarations and Confidential Status Reports

As appropriate, counsel of record may be requested to submit a supplemental declaration to establish good cause for any requested EOT. Similarly, appointed counsel, as appropriate, may be requested to submit a supplemental CSR.

4. Certification or Declaration of Contents of Confidential Status Reports are Made Under Penalty of Perjury

In all automatic appeals and capital-related habeas corpus proceedings in which appointed counsel of record is required to submit a periodic CSR, and in all such cases and proceedings in which appointed counsel is not required to submit a CSR but nevertheless chooses to do so, the CSR must contain a certification or declaration under penalty of perjury by lead counsel that the contents of the CSR are true and correct. (Code Civ. Proc., § 2015.5.)

5. Proof of Service

In all automatic appeals and capital-related habeas corpus proceedings in which counsel of record is required to provide the court with the original of a proof of service (Policy 4, Supreme Court Policies Regarding Cases Arising From Judgments of Death ["Service of process by counsel for defendant"]), such delivery must be evidenced by a certification or declaration under penalty of perjury. (Code Civ. Proc., § 2015.5.)

PAYMENT GUIDELINES FOR APPOINTED COUNSEL REPRESENTING INDIGENT CRIMINAL APPELLANTS IN THE CALIFORNIA SUPREME COURT

(Revised September 19, 1990, and December 22, 1993)

(Amended effective September 1, 1995, January 1, 1997, July 30, 1997, January 22, 1998, February 4, 1998, January 16, 2002, August 25, 2004, October 1, 2005, November 30, 2005, July 1, 2006, October 1, 2007, July 23, 2008, August 27, 2008, and March 5, 2012)

I. INTRODUCTION

The California Supreme Court determines the compensation of appointed counsel representing indigent criminal appellants. The guidelines set forth below are a general statement of the factors considered by the court in determining appropriate compensation for the time devoted to indigent criminal appeals (and related habeas corpus representation) and the reasonable and necessary expenses incurred by appointed counsel. In reviewing these guidelines, counsel should bear in mind the following:

A. Although most of the guidelines apply routinely, the application of others, such as the reimbursement of travel expenses or of the cost of expert witnesses and investigators, depends on the circumstances of each case.

B. The rates in the guidelines are subject to periodic change. These include the hourly compensation of appointed counsel, mileage and per diem rates for travel, and rates for the reimbursement of the cost of services by others.

C. For the most current information concerning these matters, and the payment guidelines generally, counsel are encouraged to contact the California Appellate Project (CAP). CAP is the appointed counsel administrator that assists private counsel with automatic appeals. CAP's address and telephone number are as follows:

California Appellate Project
101 Second Street, Suite 600
San Francisco, CA 94105
(415) 495-0500

II. REASONABLE COMPENSATION

A. Compensation rate The compensation rate for members of the State Bar of California who are appointed as counsel in indigent criminal appeals is the same allowable-hour rate appointed counsel received or was eligible to receive in the Court of Appeal, except for automatic appeals and/or related habeas corpus/executive clemency proceedings, for which the rate is $145 per allowable hour.

B. "Allowable hours" The compensation rate is multiplied by the number of "allowable hours" of appellate work to determine a reasonable sum for compensation. Benchmarks for "allowable hours" in capital cases (i.e., an estimate of the time an attorney experienced in the handling of criminal appeals might devote to the various stages of capital litigation) are set out below, in part II.*I.3*.

C. Recording of hours Appointed counsel should record the number of hours devoted to the following phases of appellate work:
1. Record review
2. Record correction
3. Motions and applications
4. Sixty-day status reports
5. Researching and writing opening brief
6. Researching and writing reply brief
7. Researching and writing supplemental brief(s)
8. Investigating and writing habeas corpus petition
9. Reply to response(s) to habeas corpus petition
10. Evidentiary hearing
11. Oral argument (includes preparation)
12. Post-oral argument representation
13. Rehearing petition or opposition
14. Certiorari petition or opposition (and briefing and argument in the United States Supreme Court after grant of certiorari; see post, subpart *I*.3.(i))
15. Client communication
16. Travel
17. Other services (specify)

D. Factors considered by the court The following factors are considered by the court in determining the number of allowable hours:
1. Whether the billed hours are within the benchmarks, or whether there exists good cause to depart from the benchmarks.
2. Length of the record.
3. Complexity and novelty of the legal issues.
4. Quality of work.

E. Exceptional procedural matters Counsel should provide the court with an explanation of the time spent on exceptional procedural matters, such as repeated applications for augmentation of the record on appeal.

F. Travel time Travel time will be compensated to the extent that the time could not reasonably be spent working on the case.

G. Circumstances warranting additional compensation If counsel believes there exist extraordinary circumstances that justify compensation beyond that set out in these guidelines, counsel should bring such factors to the attention of the court at the time a claim for payment of compensation and expenses is presented. Counsel's showing of justification should be commensurate with the extent to which he or she seeks to exceed the benchmarks.

H. Submission of payment requests Counsel may submit a request for payment of compensation and expenses every 90 days.

***I.* Special rules for capital cases** The following rules apply to capital cases only:

1. *Delay in certification of record or filing of brief* If delay in the certification of the record on appeal or in the filing of the appellant's opening brief (AOB) is due to a lack of diligence on the part of appointed counsel, payment of compensation will be deferred until the record is certified or the AOB is filed.

2. *Forms and reports* Counsel must submit a cumulative hours compensation form and the most recent status report with every request for payment. The cumulative hours compensation form will be provided by the court or may be obtained from CAP. Counsel should retain a copy of each cumulative hours compensation form submitted. These forms will facilitate completion of the data form for automatic appeals, which must accompany the request for final payment for services rendered in this court. Note that although a request for payment may be submitted every 90 days, a current status report must be submitted every 60 days.

3. *"Allowable hours" benchmarks* The court, after consultation with representatives of a cross-section of the criminal justice bar, has established the following benchmarks for the various stages of capital representation:

(i) APPEAL

Reading the record and producing detailed, understandable and computerized transcript notes:	40 pp./hr.
Record correction:	20–120 hrs.
Client communication:	15–30 hrs.
Appellant's opening brief (AOB):	260–600 hrs.
Appellant's reply brief (ARB):	55–160 hrs.
Oral argument:	40–80 hrs.
Supplemental briefs:	20–80 hrs.
Rehearing petition:	25–75 hrs.
Certiorari petition:	40–75 hrs.

Briefing and argument in the United States Supreme Court after grant of certiorari:

Counsel shall seek compensation for such services from the United States Supreme Court. Should that court deny compensation for such services, this court will authorize reasonable compensation for such services up to a maximum of $6,000.

(ii) HABEAS CORPUS

a. Investigation and Presentation of Petition

(For cases in which appellate counsel also handles habeas corpus responsibilities):

Client communication related to habeas corpus investigation:
Up to 60 hours, as follows: Up to 30 hrs. in the first year after appointment; and up to 15 hrs. per year thereafter.

Investigate and present habeas corpus petition: 140–400 hrs.

(For cases in which separate appointed counsel handles habeas corpus responsibilities):

Client communication related to habeas corpus investigation:
Up to 70 hours, as follows: Up to 40 hrs. in the first year after appointment; and up to 15 hrs. per year thereafter.

Record review: 50 pp./hr.

Investigate and present habeas corpus petition: 180–500 hrs.

For all cases:
  Informal reply: 50–120 hrs.
  Traverse: 50–120 hrs.

b. Habeas Corpus Evidentiary Hearing

Preparation: 150–600 hrs.
Evidentiary hearing: 72–144 hrs. (i.e., 3–6 days)

Post-hearing litigation before the referee: 75–125 hrs.

These benchmarks apply collectively to all counsel, appointed and supervised, who are engaged in work related to a habeas corpus evidentiary hearing, and are not multiplied, or otherwise increased, by virtue of the fact that more than one attorney is participating in this work.

c. Post-Hearing Briefs in the Supreme Court

Brief on the merits, response brief, and supplemental brief: 50–150 hrs.

d. Habeas Corpus Proceedings Returnable in Superior Court Following Order to Show Cause on Alleged Mental Retardation of Condemned Inmate

The "allowable hours" benchmark ranges for habeas corpus proceedings after issuance of an order to show cause, including any traverse to the return, and preparation for, or presentation at, an evidentiary hearing, as set forth in Payment Guideline II, subpart *I*.3.(ii), apply to all habeas corpus proceedings following an order to show cause issued by the Supreme Court, including any order to show cause returnable to the superior court regarding a condemned inmate's alleged mental retardation and resulting ineligibility for the death penalty within the meaning of *Atkins v. Virginia* (2002) 536 U.S. 304.

Before requesting compensation from the Supreme Court for attorney fees related to such *Atkins* litigation in superior court, appointed counsel first must obtain the superior court's recommendation for payment of the incurred hours. However, the superior court's recommendation is not binding on the Supreme Court, which will, in all cases, exercise independent review concerning attorney fees recommended for payment by the superior court.

These requirements apply to all such fee requests, for *Atkins* litigation in superior court, pending before the Supreme Court on or after March 5, 2012.

(iii) EXECUTIVE CLEMENCY

Representation in executive clemency proceedings before the Governor of California: 40–80 hrs.

These benchmarks are guidelines for the expected hours in "typical" cases, and are neither ceilings nor floors for fees in any given case. The court will continue to monitor its fee payment data to determine whether adjustment of the benchmarks is warranted in the future. Counsel is advised to review the benchmarks carefully, and to bear the following in mind throughout the course of representation (i.e., at each "stage" of the litigation):

a. *The "lower range" of the benchmarks* A case that has a relatively short record (i.e., 3,000–6,000 pages), and that raises standard (albeit fact-specific) issues already resolved in prior cases, should generally produce hours near or below the "lower range" of the benchmarks. Based on experience, the court expects a substantial percentage of cases to be completed under the lower range of the benchmarks. Counsel should determine at an early stage of representation whether the case meets the description of a "lower range" case. If counsel has such a case, and submits a fee request substantially exceeding the lower range of the benchmarks for any particular stage of the litigation, he or she must include in each request a detailed explanation of why fees exceeding the lower range of the benchmarks should be awarded. The court will award fees substantially exceeding the appropriate benchmark range only if it is convinced that on the facts of the case, such fees are warranted.

b. *The "upper range" of the benchmarks* Based on experience, the court anticipates a number of cases will produce fee hours at or near the upper range of the benchmarks, and occasionally, over that range. The following important caveats apply in such cases:

The upper range of the benchmarks is generally reserved for those cases with relatively long records (i.e., 10,000 or more pages), *and* that raise novel or difficult issues. The mere fact that the record may be long does *not* indicate that "upper range" or "over-benchmark" hours will be appropriate in any or each stage of the litigation.

If a case does not meet the above description of an "upper range" or "over-benchmark" case, counsel should not expect to receive "upper range" or "over-benchmark" fees. In order to secure such fees in a case not otherwise meeting the above description, counsel must include in the request a detailed explanation of why the fees requested should be awarded. The court will award fees near or exceeding the appropriate benchmark range only if it is convinced that on the facts of the case, such fees are warranted.

4. *Second counsel "override"* In cases in which appointed counsel deems it necessary to associate with second counsel, and the court approves the association, the court may in its discretion, and on a showing of good cause, approve compensation to appointed counsel for hours incurred exceeding the "appeal" through "habeas corpus briefing" benchmarks by 5-15 percent. As a general rule the court will allow the full 15 percent override in cases in which counsel divides the hours fairly evenly for the stage for which fees are sought. If counsel divides the work less evenly, the override will be diminished accordingly. The court will continue to monitor the cases to determine whether the 15 percent ceiling should be increased.

III. NECESSARY EXPENSES

A. Items not qualifying as expenses The hourly fee should cover all overhead related to a case, *including secretarial services, word processing, and the like.* Expenses listed below will be reimbursed to the extent they are itemized, reasonable, and necessarily incurred during the course of the appeal, and otherwise comply with the court's procedures (see below, part III.B). Note that these guidelines apply not only to appointed counsel, but to those persons, including experts and investigators, who assist appointed counsel with the appeal.

B. Prior approval Prior approval is required for extraordinary expenses, such as for out-of-state travel, expert witnesses and investigators. *In capital cases,* expense requests are governed by the court's "Standards Governing Filing of Habeas Corpus Petitions and Compensation of Counsel in Relation to Such Petitions," published in the Official Reports advance sheet pamphlets. (See *id.,* std. 2-1 et seq.)

C. Reimbursable expenses In general, when making a request for reimbursement, counsel must itemize *all* expenses, and must provide in the request the original receipts for the following: (i) travel expenses (airfare, car rental, hotel bills, etc.) over $47 per day; (ii) telephone and copying expenses over $50 and $100 per month, respectively (see below); and (iii) all other single transactions that exceed $100. Counsel should keep all receipts in the event documentation is later required.

1. *Photocopying* The cost of photocopying will be reimbursed, at not more than 10 cents per page, whether the copying is done inside or outside counsel's office. If counsel represents that photocopying was billed at 10 cents per page or less, receipts will not be required unless the expenses are in excess of $100 per month.

In addition to investigative expenses as set forth in the "Supreme Court Policies Regarding Cases Arising From Judgments of Death,"

Policy 3, standard 2-2.1, counsel appointed to handle habeas corpus/executive clemency representation will be reimbursed the reasonable cost of photocopying defense counsel's trial files, at the rate of not more than 10 cents per page, after filing of the certified record on appeal. Counsel must provide a receipt or invoice showing the number of pages copied, and the cost per page. Reimbursement will not be paid for photocopying of items already contained in the record on appeal, such as daily transcripts or exhibits.

2. *Postage and delivery costs* Expenses for express mail/messenger service will be reimbursed only on a showing that use of express mail/messenger service was necessary and reasonable.

3. *Telephone charges* Receipts will not be required unless the expenses are in excess of $50 per month.

4. *Travel expenses*

a. The court will determine the reasonableness and necessity of travel expenses on a case-by-case basis. Counsel are cautioned that travel expenses are not considered necessary when the purpose of a trip may reasonably be accomplished in another way, such as by telephone or correspondence. Further, counsel should use the least expensive alternative means of travel. For motor vehicles, the mileage rate is the prevailing amount established by the Administrative Office of the Courts.

b. When travel is required by appointed counsel or a person authorized to assist appointed counsel, reasonable and necessary meals and lodging may be claimed, to the extent allowed under State Board of Control rules. Counsel should contact CAP for further information.

c. Some of the lesser known provisions of the Board of Control rules are as follows:

(1) The per diem allowance does not apply for trips of 25 miles or less.
(2) Lunch is not covered unless the travel period is 24 hours or more.
(3) The cost of collision coverage in a contract for a rental car is not covered.

5. *Computerized legal research* The reasonable cost of computerized legal research (as opposed to the costs of installation and monthly access fees), when the use is specifically attributable to the case, will be reimbursed to the extent reasonably and necessarily incurred. Counsel must explain in writing the specific nature of the computer expenses (e.g., Shepard's, Autocite, issue searches, etc.), and must explain why computerized research was more efficient than the same research performed "manually."

6. *Services of law clerks, paralegals, and State Bar members*

a. Counsel shall be reimbursed for the compensation of the following individuals at a rate not to exceed the following:

(1) Law clerks who are not members of the State Bar of California at $40 per allowable hour.
(2) Paralegals at $40 per allowable hour.
(3) Members of the State Bar of California, who are not appointed to the case, at the rate of $98 per allowable hour.

b. Reimbursement of the compensation for all persons performing legal services, other than appointed counsel, shall be subject to the following conditions:

(1) In submitting a claim for reimbursement, counsel shall describe with specificity the legal services and number of hours of work performed by each other person so the court can evaluate the reasonableness of the services and expenses as part of appointed counsel's overall claim. *It is expected that the hours devoted to legal services by nonappointed counsel, and any "exceptionally high" hours attributed to law clerks and paralegals* (i.e., hours exceeding 30 percent of the benchmark hours for appointed counsel for any given stage), *will reduce the hours that appointed counsel will devote to those services.*

(2) Appointed counsel shall not delegate to others those functions that require the ability and experience for which counsel was appointed.

(3) Appointed counsel shall supervise and have full responsibility for the services performed by others.

7. *Services of investigators and experts*

a. An investigator or expert shall be compensated at a rate not to exceed the maximum rates listed below. Counsel must establish that use of an expert's services is reasonably necessary under the facts of the case. Counsel seeking to use the services of multiple experts relating to a single or common issue must demonstrate a compelling necessity for such use of multiple experts. In addition, counsel must include in the request for reimbursement a representation that the rate requested

(1) does not exceed the investigator's or expert's customary rates for the services performed, and
(2) does not exceed local prevailing rates for the services performed.

b. The maximum rates are as follows

(1) Investigators, $55-90 per hour.
(2) Penalty phase consultants, $60-125 per hour.
(3) Psychiatrists and other medically licensed mental health experts, $200-350 per hour.
(4) Other forensic experts, $125-225 per hour.
(5) Psychologists (Ph.D.'s), $150-275 per hour.
(6) Attorneys serving as experts, $125-145 per hour. (*Note:* Until an order to show cause is issued, *or* the People submit an expert declaration in their informal opposition to a habeas corpus petition, the court will not approve payment for attorney "expert opinion" in the form of declarations, etc.)
(7) Any expert listed above testifying at a court proceeding, eight times the hourly rate per day or four times the hourly rate per half day.

c. In exceptional circumstances, when the need for services at a greater rate of compensation is documented and prior authorization is obtained from the Supreme Court, compensation beyond the maximum may be paid.

8. *Proceedings returnable in superior court following order to show cause on alleged mental retardation of condemned inmate*

In proceedings pending in superior court pursuant to an order to show cause issued by the California Supreme Court, and returnable before the superior court, regarding a condemned inmate's alleged mental retardation and resulting ineligibility for the death penalty within the meaning of *Atkins v. Virginia* (2002) 536 U.S. 304 (see also *In re Hawthorne* (2005) 35 Cal.4th 40), the following practices apply to requests by counsel appointed in the California Supreme Court for the reimbursement of investigation services and expenses incurred in superior court for experts, investigators and law clerks/paralegals:

a. The superior court in which the *Atkins*-related proceedings are pending makes only a *recommendation* for pre-authorization to incur, and payment of, the expenses of investigators, experts, and other service providers for whom reimbursement is sought by appointed counsel. Thereafter, the Supreme Court independently determines, pursuant to its time-and-costs Payment Guidelines and the Policy 3 compensation standards (see Supreme Ct. Policies Regarding Cases Arising From Judgments of Death), whether the recommended funding is reasonable and, to the extent found reasonable, authorizes appointed counsel to incur such expenses and reimburses appointed counsel, as appropriate.

This provision will apply to all such funding requests pending before the Supreme Court on or after March 5, 2012.

b. Appointed counsel may engage experts, investigators and law clerks/paralegals either in the locality where counsel's offices are situated or in the locality where the superior court proceedings are being held, at counsel's option.

c. The California Supreme Court will pay for investigation services and expenses at the rate prevailing where the services are engaged, if otherwise permissible within the maximum hourly rates and other applicable provisions set forth within these payment guidelines.

IV. FEE AND EXPENSE DISALLOWANCES

The court will provide reasons in writing for fee disallowances of $1,000 or more, and expense disallowances of $500 or more.

V. COURT ACTION UPON NONPERFORMANCE OF WORK, AND REIMBURSEMENT OF FEES UPON AUTHORIZED WITHDRAWAL OF APPOINTED COUNSEL

A. Nonperformance of counsel In the rare circumstance in which appointed counsel ceases work on a case and refuses to complete the work with reasonable diligence, the court has had, and will continue to exercise as appropriate, the following nonexclusive options: The court may enforce its legal rights; the court may refer the matter to the State Bar; and finally, the court may institute contempt proceedings to enforce its orders.

B. Authorized withdrawal of counsel In the event that the court permits appointed counsel to withdraw before completion of counsel's duties in a case, the court will, as appropriate under the circumstances, authorize payment to counsel for legal work completed. Alternatively, the court may, as appropriate under the circumstances, order counsel to reimburse the court for fees paid, less a credit for work performed that is determined by the court to be of value to the court.

Adopted Jan. 1, 1991; amended Dec. 22, 1993; Sept. 1, 1995; Jan. 1, 1997; July 30, 1997; Jan. 22, 1998; Feb. 4, 1998; Jan. 16, 2002; Aug. 25, 2004; Oct. 1, 2005; Nov. 30, 2005; July 1, 2006; Oct. 1, 2007; July 23, 2008; Aug. 27, 2008; Mar. 5, 2012.

GUIDELINES FOR FIXED FEE APPOINTMENTS, ON OPTIONAL BASIS, TO AUTOMATIC APPEALS AND RELATED HABEAS CORPUS PROCEEDINGS IN THE CALIFORNIA SUPREME COURT

(Adopted by the Supreme Court December 14, 1993, effective January 1, 1994)

(Amended effective September 1, 1995, January 1, 1997, January 22, 1997, July 30, 1997, January 22, 1998, February 4, 1998, July 18, 2001, January 16, 2002, March 21, 2002, October 1, 2005, November 30, 2005, July 1, 2006, October 1, 2007, January 1, 2008, and March 5, 2012.)

Introduction

Presently, appointed counsel in automatic appeals are compensated on a "time and costs" basis, under the Payment Guidelines for Appointed Counsel Representing Indigent Criminal Appellants in the California Supreme Court (as revised) (hereafter Payment Guidelines). Under the Payment Guidelines, appointed counsel must submit a detailed and lengthy cumulative hours compensation form with every request for payment of fees and reimbursement of expenses. Moreover, "allowable hours" benchmarks limit the fees available for each stage of the capital representation; other provisions limit or exclude reimbursement for expenses. Requests for prior approval of extraordinary expenses are governed by the Supreme Court Policies Regarding Cases Arising From Judgments of Death (as revised).

In an effort to provide appointed counsel in capital cases greater predictability, consistency and control over compensation and expenses, and to reduce administrative burdens on both counsel and the Court, the Court has adopted an optional fixed fee and expenses payment system.

The categories of fixed fees set out below in Guidelines 1, 1.1, and 1.2 establish the compensation and responsibilities of appointed counsel for all services and "incidental expenses" (habeas corpus investigation expenses are separately provided for in Guideline 2):

(1) In cases in which counsel is appointed to represent the defendant both on appeal and in related habeas corpus/executive clemency proceedings, fixed fee compensation is for: (a) the direct appeal, through the filing of a certiorari petition to the United States Supreme Court, or an answer thereto (but not including any briefs or appearances in the United States Supreme Court after grant of certiorari or any briefs or appearances on remand to the California Supreme Court, which work would be compensated under the terms and limitations of the Payment Guidelines); (b) state habeas corpus investigation, and preparation and filing (if warranted) of a state habeas corpus petition and informal reply, and any subsequent habeas corpus petition, including any petition to exhaust state remedies, in the California Supreme Court (but not including any traverse, habeas corpus evidentiary hearing or post-hearing briefs in the California Supreme Court, which work would be compensated under the terms and limitations of the Payment Guidelines); (c) any trial court proceedings under Penal Code sections 1193 and 1227 to set an execution date; and (d) representation in executive clemency proceedings before the Governor of California. (See Cal. Supreme Ct., Policies Regarding Cases Arising From Judgments of Death, *supra*, Compensation Stds., std. 2-1.)

(2) In cases in which counsel is appointed to represent the defendant on appeal only, fixed fee compensation is for: (a) the direct appeal, through the filing of a certiorari petition to the United States Supreme Court, or an answer thereto (but not including any briefs or appearances in the United States Supreme Court after grant of certiorari or any briefs or appearances on remand to the California Supreme Court, which work would be compensated under the terms and limitations of the Payment Guidelines); and (b) any trial court proceedings under Penal Code section 1193 to set an execution date. (See Cal. Supreme Ct., Policies Regarding Cases Arising From Judgments of Death, *supra*, Compensation Stds., std. 2-1.)

(3) In cases in which counsel is appointed to represent the defendant in habeas corpus/executive clemency proceedings only, fixed fee compensation is for: (a) state habeas corpus investigation, and preparation and filing (if warranted) of a state habeas corpus petition and informal reply, and any subsequent habeas corpus petition, including any petition to exhaust state remedies, in the California Supreme Court (but not including any traverse, habeas corpus evidentiary hearing or post-hearing briefs in the California Supreme Court, which work would be compensated under the terms and limitations of the Payment Guidelines); (b) any trial court proceedings under Penal Code section 1227 to set an execution date; and (c) representation in executive clemency proceedings before the Governor of California. (See Cal. Supreme Ct., Policies Regarding Cases Arising From Judgments of Death, *supra*, Compensation Stds., std. 2-1.)

1. Fixed Fee Categories for Cases in Which Counsel Is Appointed to Handle the Appeal and Related Habeas Corpus/Executive Clemency Proceedings

Category I: $160,000

A. An appeal from a judgment based on a guilty plea and penalty phase; or

B. An appeal from a judgment on remand following a reversal limited to penalty.

C. Caveat: An appeal from a judgment on limited remand for a new hearing on the automatic motion to modify the death verdict (Pen. Code, § 190.4, subd. (e)) likely will be valued well below $160,000. (See also Guideline 4 [Case Evaluation], *post*.)

Category II: $231,000

A. An appeal from a judgment on remand following a reversal limited to the special circumstance finding(s) and penalty; or

B. An appeal otherwise in category I(A) or I(B) that presents a more complex case, in the Court's view, by reason of, but not limited to, one or more of the following factors: The combined record on appeal is 4,000 or more pages; there was more than one homicide victim, and the homicides occurred in more than one incident; there were numerous pretrial and/or penalty phase motions; there were multiple defendants and/or appellants; or

C. An initial appeal or an appeal from a judgment on remand following a reversal of guilt, in which the combined record on appeal is under 6,000 pages.

Category III: $283,000

A. An initial appeal or an appeal from a judgment on remand following a reversal of guilt, in which the combined record on appeal is between 6,000 and 12,000 pages; or

B. An appeal otherwise in category II(A) or II(C) that presents a more complex case, in the Court's view, by reason of, but not limited to, one or more of the following factors: The combined record on appeal is 5,000 or more pages; there was more than one homicide victim, and the homicides occurred in more than one incident; there were numerous pretrial and/or penalty phase motions; there were multiple defendants and/or appellants.

Category IV: $322,000

A. An initial appeal or an appeal from a judgment on remand following a reversal of guilt, in which the combined record on appeal is 12,000 or more pages; or

B. An appeal otherwise in category III(A) that presents a more complex case, in the Court's view, by reason of, but not limited to, one or more of the following factors: The combined record on appeal is 10,000 or more pages; there was more than one homicide victim, and the homicides occurred in more than one incident; there were numerous pretrial and/or penalty phase motions; there were multiple defendants and/or appellants.

Category V: $368,000 base fee

Exceptional cases that occur infrequently, involve many victims and incidents, and have a combined record on appeal of 25,000 or more pages. In this category, appointed counsel may present a justification at the outset for a fixed fee higher than the base fee.

1.1. Fixed Fee Categories for Cases in Which Counsel Is Appointed to Handle the Appeal Only

Category I: $65,000

A. An appeal from a judgment based on a guilty plea and penalty phase; or

B. An appeal from a judgment on remand following a reversal limited to penalty.

C. Caveat: An appeal from a judgment on limited remand for a new hearing on the automatic motion to modify the death verdict (Pen. Code, § 190.4, subd. (e)) likely will be valued well below $65,000. (See also Guideline 4 [Case Evaluation], *post*.)

Category II: $136,000

A. An appeal from a judgment on remand following a reversal limited to the special circumstance finding(s) and penalty; or

B. An appeal otherwise in category I(A) or I(B) that presents a more complex case, in the Court's view, by reason of, but not limited to, one or more of the following factors: The combined record on appeal is 4,000 or more pages; there was more than one homicide victim, and the homicides occurred in more than one incident; there were numerous pretrial and/or penalty phase motions; there were multiple defendants and/or appellants; or

C. An initial appeal or an appeal from a judgment on remand following a reversal of guilt, in which the combined record on appeal is under 6,000 pages.

Category III: $178,000

A. An initial appeal or an appeal from a judgment on remand following a reversal of guilt, in which the combined record on appeal is between 6,000 and 12,000 pages; or

B. An appeal otherwise in category II(A) or II(C) that presents a more complex case, in the Court's view, by reason of, but not limited to, one or more of the following factors: The combined record on appeal is 5,000 or more pages; there was more than one homicide victim, and the homicides occurred in more than one incident; there were numerous pretrial and/or penalty phase motions; there were multiple defendants and/or appellants.

Category IV: $219,000

A. An initial appeal or an appeal from a judgment on remand following a reversal of guilt, in which the combined record on appeal is 12,000 or more pages; or

B. An appeal otherwise in category III(A) that presents a more complex case, in the Court's view, by reason of, but not limited to, one or more of the following factors: The combined record on appeal is 10,000 or more pages; there was more than one homicide victim, and the homicides occurred in more than one incident; there were numerous pretrial and/or penalty phase motions; there were multiple defendants and/or appellants.

Category V: $263,000 base fee

Exceptional cases that occur infrequently, involve many victims and incidents, and have a combined record on appeal of 25,000 or more pages. In this category, appointed counsel may present a justification at the outset for a fixed fee higher than the base fee.

1.2. Fixed Fee Categories for Cases in Which Counsel Is Appointed to Handle Habeas Corpus/Executive Clemency Proceedings Only

Category I: $85,000, plus an additional fixed fee calculated at the rate of $145 for every 50 pages of transcript in the combined record on appeal.

A. Habeas corpus representation related to a case that would fall within Fixed Fee Guideline 1.1, Categories I or II.

B. Habeas corpus representation related to a case that would fall within Fixed Fee Guideline 1.1, Categories III, IV, or V, but that, for case-specific reasons, is of below-average complexity.

Category II: $110,000, plus an additional fixed fee calculated at the rate of $145 for every 50 pages of transcript in the combined record on appeal.

A. Habeas corpus representation related to a case that would fall within Fixed Fee Guideline 1.1, Categories III, IV, or V.

B. Habeas corpus representation related to a case that would fall within Fixed Fee Guideline 1.1, Categories I or II, but that, for case-specific reasons, nevertheless is of average complexity.

Category III: $127,000, plus an additional fixed fee calculated at the rate of $145 for every 50 pages of transcript in the combined record on appeal, for cases of above-average complexity.

For cases of exceptional complexity, appointed counsel may present a justification at the outset for a fixed fee higher than the $127,000 base fee.

1.3. Factors Affecting Fee Categories

The California Supreme Court considers four factors in determining the fee in fixed fee appointments in capital proceedings: *complexity, difficulty, extraordinary costs,* and *time-intensiveness.* The case-specific issues that influence the applicability of these factors often overlap, but examples of such issues include the following:

- Multiple defendants
- Motion for change of venue
- Joint or separate trials with co-defendants
- Multiple homicides or multiple incidents (including multiple victims in separate incidents)
- Mistrials and re-trial(s)
- Substitution of trial counsel; additional trial proceedings or phases (e.g., grand jury, competency phase, sanity phase)
- Multiple special circumstances
- Prior convictions or unadjudicated criminal conduct admitted at penalty phase
- Prosecution's use of informants
- Extensive litigation of the admissibility of evidence
- Forensic testing, analysis, and evidence (e.g., DNA, hair, fingerprint, blood, ballistics) introduced at trial or necessary for habeas investigation
- Mentally ill, mentally impaired, or mentally retarded capital defendants
- Non-English-speaking or foreign national capital defendant
- Non-English-speaking witnesses
- Minimal guilt and/or penalty phase investigation done for trial
- Investigation requirements in multiple locations and/or out of the state or country
- Extended elapsed time since offenses/trial
- Necessity of expert witnesses
- Necessity of using some fees to cover investigative and incidental expenses

- Length of record
- Number of trial witnesses

1.4. Suggested Format and Contents of Fixed Fee Requests

Counsel may submit requests for consideration of a case for a particular fixed fee category. Lengthy letters are not necessary or encouraged. Letters for the most complex cases should not exceed seven pages. A suggested format that will assist the Court in making a fixed fee determination includes the following elements:

Fixed fee request: An opening paragraph stating the fee category and base fee requested, plus additional amounts sought for transcript length and cases of exceptional complexity.

Short summary of the case: This paragraph should not extensively reiterate the facts of the case or the procedural history.

Discussion of the applicability of the four factors to this particular case: An explanation of why the appointed case is particularly complex, difficult, costly, and/or time-intensive.

2. Incidental and Investigative Expenses

All incidental expenses for the direct appeal and habeas corpus/executive clemency representation are included in the fixed fee. Incidental expenses include photocopying, postage, telephone charges, computerized legal research, travel (other than for habeas corpus investigation) and services of law clerks and paralegals (other than for habeas corpus investigation). In addition to the agreed-upon fixed fee, counsel may also incur up to $25,000 in habeas corpus investigative expenses, without prior Court authorization, subject to the Court's Payment Guidelines, *supra*, part III, subpart C, paragraphs 1-7, inclusive ("Reimbursable expenses"). Investigative expenses include travel associated with habeas corpus investigation, and services of law clerks, paralegals, and others serving as habeas corpus investigators. Counsel will be reimbursed for all such habeas corpus investigative expenses that were reasonably incurred, up to $25,000. The Court will not authorize or reimburse habeas corpus investigative expenses exceeding $25,000 prior to the issuance of an order to show cause.

As to those cases in which, by January 1, 2008 (the effective date of Assem. Bill No. 1248), the defendant has not filed a capital-related habeas corpus petition in this court and the date by which to file a presumptively timely petition has not yet passed, counsel may be reimbursed up to $50,000 for those investigative services and expenses incurred on or after that date. Such investigative funding for expenses incurred after January 1, 2008, also is available in those cases in which a presumptively timely petition has been filed by January 1, 2008, but petitioner's reply to the informal response has not been filed and the time to do so (with any extensions of time) has not passed as of that date. (See also Cal. Supreme Ct., Policies Regarding Cases Arising From Judgments of Death, *supra*, Timeliness Stds., std. 1-1, & Compensation Stds., std. 2-2.1.)

3. Requests for Additional Fees

In extraordinary and unique situations, the Court will entertain requests for additional fees based on exceptional circumstances (e.g., circumstances that were unforeseeable at the time of the appointment of counsel on a fixed fee basis). In such situations, counsel shall have the burden of proof to justify any additional fees.

4. Case Evaluation

There will be agreement on the fixed fee prior to the appointment of counsel. (See also, Guideline 6 [Conversion From Time and Costs Appointment to Fixed Fee], *post*.) Initially, applicant counsel selected to consider an appointment to a specific automatic appeal and/or habeas corpus/executive clemency proceedings will have the option of investigating that case for purposes of proposing a fixed fee pursuant to these alternative guidelines, rather than the traditional time and costs method. At any given time, there will be only one set of applicant counsel investigating a specific automatic appeal and/or habeas corpus/executive clemency proceedings for purposes of a possible appointment. Applicant counsel are encouraged to consult with trial counsel, examine any available transcript "dailies" prepared during the trial or other proceedings, and examine any available materials normally found in the clerk's transcript. Counsel are also encouraged to examine additional materials and information that may be available from the California Appellate Project in San Francisco.

Using these alternative guidelines, applicant counsel opting to be appointed on a fixed fee basis will propose a category and hence a fee for all services and expenses in the case. The Court's concurrence is required for any such appointment.

Discussions with applicant counsel regarding proposals for fixed fee appointments shall be conducted through the Automatic Appeals Monitor.

The fixed fee encompasses counsel's investigative costs in reviewing the case for purposes of considering an appointment. If counsel's proposal for a fixed fee is not accepted by the Court, counsel will not be reimbursed for those investigative costs; however, counsel may request an appointment to that case pursuant to the traditional time and costs method of the Payment Guidelines.

5. Progress Payments

Until appointed appellate counsel files the appellant's opening brief or appointed habeas corpus counsel files a petition, a current status report must be filed every 60 days. Other than reimbursement for habeas corpus investigative expenses, documentation and itemization of hours and expenses by appointed counsel are not required under these alternative fixed fee guidelines.

Counsel appointed for both the direct appeal *and* habeas corpus/executive clemency proceedings will receive progress payments after specified stages of representation as follows: (i) one-sixth of the fixed amount shortly after counsel is appointed; (ii) one-sixth after counsel (a) submits to the assisting entity or counsel (e.g., the Habeas Corpus Resource Center, the California Appellate Project, or other assisting counsel) detailed, understandable and computerized transcript notes, a list of potentially meritorious habeas corpus issues, and a draft first request for correction of the record (and, if appropriate, any motion for augmentation and/or settled statement), and (b) files this first request; (iii) one-sixth after certification of the record and filing of the record in this court (one-half of this progress payment will be advanced upon request after the trial court's order disposing of the consolidated motion to augment, correct, and settle the record on appeal); (iv) one-sixth after counsel (a) files a confidential declaration that he or she has made reasonable efforts to consult with defendant and trial counsel about potential habeas corpus issues, (b) submits to the assisting entity or counsel a detailed outline of potential habeas corpus issues to be investigated, and (c) files the appellant's opening brief (one-quarter of this progress payment will be advanced upon request after counsel's submission to the assisting entity or counsel of a complete draft of the statement of the case and statement of the facts portion of the appellant's opening brief; one-quarter after submission of a complete draft of the guilt phase and special circumstance issues portion of the appellant's opening brief; and one-quarter after submission of a complete draft of the penalty phase issues portion of the appellant's opening brief [counsel may request these advances before progress payment (iii) has been paid in full]); (v) one-sixth after counsel (a) submits to the assisting entity or counsel a draft reply brief, (b) files a reply brief, and (c) files a confidential declaration that counsel has substantially completed the habeas corpus investigation (to the extent possible given funding provided therefor), and has submitted for review to the assisting entity or counsel a draft habeas corpus petition with necessary exhibits and declarations (or, in the alternative, that counsel has submitted for review to the assisting entity or counsel a draft declaration indicating that all potential leads have been substantially pursued to the extent possible given funding provided therefor, and that it appears that no habeas corpus petition will be filed) (one-half of this progress payment will be advanced upon request after the following: (a) the Attorney General files the respondent's brief, and (b) counsel files a confidential declaration that counsel has completed approximately one-half of the anticipated habeas corpus investigation, and has submitted to the assisting entity or counsel a detailed outline of the remainder of the planned investigation); (vi) one-sixth, less $10,000, after counsel files a habeas corpus petition in this court on behalf of counsel's client, and after oral argument and submission of the matter on the direct appeal (except that if counsel files no petition, counsel must instead file a confidential declaration indicating that all potential leads have been pursued to the extent possible given funding provided therefor, and that no habeas corpus petition will be filed, after which counsel will receive no sixth progress payment, except upon a showing that in view of work performed, full or partial payment is warranted); and finally (vii) the sum of $10,000 after completion of representation in executive clemency proceedings before the Governor of California. With each request for payment except for those set forth above in (i), (vi), and (vii), counsel shall provide to the court a statement from the assisting entity or counsel that counsel's submission to the entity or counsel substantially complies with the conditions set forth for payment.

Counsel appointed for the direct appeal only will receive progress payments after specified stages of representation as follows: (i) one-sixth of the fixed amount shortly after counsel is appointed; (ii) one-sixth after counsel (a) submits to the assisting entity or counsel (e.g., the Habeas Corpus Resource Center, the California Appellate Project, or other assisting counsel) detailed, understandable and computerized transcript notes, and a draft first request for correction of the record (and, if appropriate, any motion for augmentation and/or settled statement), and (b) files this first request; (iii) one-sixth after certification of the record and filing of the record in this court (one-half of this progress payment will be advanced upon request after the trial court's order disposing of the consolidated motion to augment, correct, and settle the record on appeal); (iv) one-sixth after counsel files the appellant's opening brief (one-quarter of this progress payment will be advanced upon request after counsel's submission to the assisting entity or counsel of a complete draft of the statement of the case and statement of the facts portion of the appellant's opening brief; one-quarter after submission of a complete draft of the guilt phase and special circumstance issues portion of the appellant's opening brief; and one-quarter after submission of a complete draft of the penalty phase issues portion of the appellant's opening brief [counsel may request these advances before progress payment (iii) has been paid in full]); (v) one-sixth after counsel (a) submits to the assisting entity or counsel a draft of the appellant's reply brief, and (b) files the reply brief; and (vi) one-sixth after oral argument and submission of the matter on the direct appeal. With each request for payment except for those set forth above in (i) and (vi), counsel shall provide to the court a statement from the assisting entity or counsel that counsel's submission to the entity or counsel substantially complies with the conditions set forth for payment.

Counsel whose appointment is limited to habeas corpus/executive clemency proceedings will receive progress payments after specified stages of representation as follows: (i) one-fifth of the fixed amount shortly after counsel is appointed; (ii) one-fifth after counsel files a confidential declaration that counsel has reviewed the record on appeal and the detailed transcript notes and list of potentially meritorious habeas corpus issues provided by appointed counsel on the direct appeal, has made reasonable efforts to consult with defendant, appellate counsel and trial counsel, and has submitted to the assisting entity or counsel (e.g., the Habeas Corpus Resource Center, the California Appellate Project, or other assisting counsel) a detailed outline of potential habeas corpus issues to be investigated; (iii) one-fifth after counsel files a confidential declaration that counsel has completed approximately one-half of the anticipated habeas corpus investigation, and has submitted to the assisting entity or counsel a detailed outline of the remainder of the planned investigation; (iv) one-fifth after counsel files a confidential declaration that counsel has submitted for review to the assisting entity or counsel a draft habeas corpus petition with necessary exhibits and declarations (or, in the alternative, that counsel has submitted for review to the assisting entity or counsel a draft declaration indicating that all potential leads have been pursued to the extent possible given funding provided therefor, and that no habeas corpus petition will be filed) (one-half of this progress payment will be advanced upon request after counsel files a confidential declaration that counsel has completed the habeas corpus investigation to the extent possible given the funding provided therefor); (v) one-fifth, less $10,000, after counsel files a habeas corpus petition in this court on behalf of his or her client (except that if counsel files no petition, counsel must instead file a confidential declaration indicating that all potential leads have been pursued to the extent possible given funding provided therefor, and that no habeas corpus petition will be filed, after which counsel will receive no fifth progress payment, except upon a showing that in view of work performed, full or partial payment is warranted); and finally (vi) $10,000 after completion of representation in executive clemency proceedings before the Governor of California. With each request for payment except for those set forth above in (i), (v), and (vi), counsel shall provide to the court a statement from the assisting entity or counsel that counsel's submission to the entity or counsel substantially complies with the conditions set forth for payment.

Under limited circumstances (e.g., a delay in the certification of the record not due to a lack of diligence on the part of appointed counsel), the court will authorize partial payments before completion of the relevant stage(s) of representation.

In the event the proceedings terminate prior to the completion of all of the stages set forth in the progress payment schedule (as a result, for example, of the death of the defendant), appointed counsel shall memorialize all work completed and the court shall determine and pay an appropriate sum to compensate counsel for work performed prior to the termination of the proceedings.

6. Conversion From Time and Costs Appointment to Fixed Fee

Counsel appointed to an automatic appeal and/or habeas corpus/executive clemency proceedings under the traditional time and costs basis of the Payment Guidelines are encouraged to consider converting their method of compensation pursuant to this optional, fixed fee payment system. Any such conversion must take into account any payments previously made to counsel, and must be approved by the Court. Ordinarily, conversion will not be approved after the filing of the appellant's opening brief, or, in the case of habeas corpus/executive clemency counsel, after six months following counsel's appointment, whichever is later.

Counsel approved by the Court for an appointment to his/her first automatic appeal and/or habeas corpus/executive clemency proceedings should carefully consider an initial appointment under the time and costs basis of the Payment Guidelines. A conversion to a fixed fee appointment pursuant to these alternative guidelines may be more appropriate after such counsel has become familiar with the case.

7. Second Counsel

The Court encourages association with second counsel. Unlike the procedure under the traditional time and costs appointment scheme of the Payment Guidelines, the fixed fees provided by this optional payment system are intended to adequately compensate appointed counsel and any associate counsel. Hence, the Court will not recognize a "second counsel override" in fixed fee cases.

8. Valuation and Length of Record on Appeal

In determining the length of the combined record on appeal as part of the process whereby a case may be valued within a fixed fee category, the Court will take into consideration whether an unusual proportion of the record is comprised of jury voir dire and/or preliminary hearing transcript. When appropriate, the Court may treat the combined record as having a reduced length. Moreover, consistent with this court's historical practice, when determining the appropriate fixed fee category, the Court will not include, in determining the size of the combined record on appeal, the juror questionnaires completed by actual or prospective jurors.

9. Applicability of Supreme Court Policies Regarding Cases Arising From Judgments of Death

The Supreme Court Policies Regarding Cases Arising From Judgments of Death, as amended, apply to all automatic appeals and habeas corpus/executive clemency proceedings in which counsel has opted for a fixed fee pursuant to these alternative guidelines. However, standard 2-2.2 of the Compensation Standards, through standard 2-4.4 of the Compensation Standards (governing authorization to incur, and reimbursement of, habeas corpus investigation expenses), shall not apply to fixed fee cases.

10. Fixed Legal Fees and Expenses For Evidentiary Hearings

In a case in which the Court orders an evidentiary hearing, counsel may elect to enter a fixed legal fee and expenses agreement covering (i) preparation for the evidentiary hearing, (ii) presentation of the evidentiary hearing, (iii) post-hearing litigation before the referee, and (iv) post-hearing briefs and proceedings in this Court.

(1) **Fixed Legal Fee and Expense Categories.** The Court and counsel for petitioner will agree to fix legal fees and expenses within one of the following categories.

Each agreement shall specify one fixed dollar sum covering *all* legal fees and *all* expenses—"incidental" and investigative—(e.g., photocopying, postage, telephone charges, travel, computerized legal research, services of law clerks and paralegals, services of and witness fees for investigators and experts, and any other witness expenses).

The fixed sum agreement shall also specify separately a dollar amount for the "legal fee component" and the "expenses component" of the fixed sum.

Category A: $68,500 ($60,000 legal fees; $8,500 expenses).

A matter presenting a single issue or limited issues expected to require minimal additional investigation, minimal or no services of experts, and to consume 1-2 hearing days.

Category A(1): $74,000 ($60,000 legal fees; $14,000 expenses)

A matter otherwise within category A, but which is expected to require significant additional investigation and use of experts.

Category B: $108,000 ($94,000 legal fees; $14,000 expenses)

A matter expected to require significant additional investigation and/or significant use of experts, and to consume 3-4 hearing days.

Category B(1): $115,000 ($94,000 legal fees; $21,000 expenses)

A matter otherwise within category B, but which is expected to require substantial additional investigation and use of experts.

Category C: $156,000 ($135,000 legal fees; $21,000 expenses)

A matter expected to require substantial additional investigation and/or services of experts, and to consume 5-6 hearing days.

Category C(1): $165,000 ($135,000 legal fees; $30,000 expenses)

A matter otherwise within category C, but which is expected to require substantial additional investigation and use of experts.

Category D: $202,500 *base sum* ($167,500 base amount for legal fees; $35,000 base amount for expenses)

A matter that is expected to require substantial additional investigation and services of experts, and to consume 7 or more hearing days. In this category, counsel may present justification at the outset for a fixed sum higher than the base amount.

(2) **Requests for Additional Legal Fees.** In extraordinary and unique situations, the Court will entertain requests for additional fees based on exceptional circumstances, as set out *ante*, Fixed Fee Appointment Guideline 3.

(3) **Case Evaluation.** A fixed fee and expenses agreement shall be reached within 60 days after the Court issues its order appointing a referee. Discussions with applicant counsel regarding proposals for such an agreement shall be conducted through the Automatic Appeals Monitor.

(4) **Fixed Legal Fee and Expense Payments.**

Fixed legal fee payments. Counsel shall be entitled to be paid one-fourth of the *legal fee component* of the amount set out in the fixed legal fee and expenses agreement upon the filing of the Court's order making the fixed legal fee and expenses appointment. Thereafter, counsel will receive, on written request (but without the necessity of providing an itemization of hours), a one-fourth progress payment of the legal fee component after (i) the evidentiary hearing commences, (ii) the post-hearing litigation before the referee is completed, and (iii) the post-hearing briefing in this Court is completed. Under limited circumstances (e.g., substantial delay not due to lack of diligence on the part of counsel), the Court will authorize partial payments before completion of the aforementioned stages.

Expense payments. Every 30 days, counsel may request reimbursement from this Court for all necessary and reasonable expenses, up to the amount set out in the fixed legal fee and expenses agreement. Reimbursement shall be governed by and calculated in accordance with the Court's Payment Guidelines, *supra*, part III ("Necessary Expenses").

11. Court Action Upon Nonperformance of Work, and Reimbursement of Fees Upon Authorized Withdrawal of Appointed Counsel

The provisions of "Guideline V" of the "Payment Guidelines for Appointed Counsel Representing Indigent Criminal Appellants in the California Supreme Court" apply as well to counsel appointed on a "fixed fee" basis.

12. Reimbursement for Photocopying Defense Counsel's Trial Files

In addition to investigative expenses as set forth in the "Supreme Court Policies Regarding Cases Arising From Judgments of Death," Policy 3, standard 2-2.1, counsel appointed to handle habeas corpus/executive clemency representation will be reimbursed the reasonable cost of photocopying defense counsel's trial files, at the rate of not more than 10 cents per page, after filing of the certified record on appeal. Counsel must provide a receipt or invoice showing the number of pages copied, and the cost per page. Reimbursement will not be paid for photocopying of items already contained in the record on appeal, such as daily transcripts or exhibits.

Adopted Dec. 14, 1993, effective Jan. 1, 1994; amended Sept. 1, 1995; Jan. 1, 1997; Jan. 22, 1997; July 30, 1997; Jan. 22, 1998; Feb. 4, 1998; Jan. 16, 2002; March 21, 2002; Oct. 1, 2005; Nov. 30, 2005; July 1, 2006; Oct. 1, 2007; Jan. 1, 2008; and Mar. 5, 2012.

GUIDELINES FOR THE COMMISSION ON JUDICIAL APPOINTMENTS

(Adopted by the Commission on Judicial Appointments, effective May 18, 1999; amended effective July 1, 2005, March 1, 2006, February 23, 2007, and November 19, 2007.)

Definitions; commission headquarters. Guideline 1.
Commission membership (Cal. Const., art. VI, § 7). Guideline 2.
Commission chairperson. Guideline 3.
Pre-hearing procedures. Guideline 4.
Hearing procedures. Guideline 5.
Staff to the commission. Guideline 6.
Post-hearing procedures. Guideline 7.
Publication and distribution of these guidelines. Guideline 8.

Guideline 1. Definitions; commission headquarters.

(a) **[Definition]** "Nomination" and "nominee" also refer to appointments and appointees, as described in article VI, section 16(d), of the California Constitution.

Adopted effective May 18, 1999.

(b) **[Definition]** "Court days" refer to days on which the California courts are open for official business. Normally, Mondays through Fridays are counted as court days, except for judicial holidays.

Adopted effective May 18, 1999.

(c) **[Commission headquarters]** The headquarters and mailing address of the Commission on Judicial Appointments (commission) are:

Commission on Judicial Appointments
c/o Chief Justice of California
Supreme Court of California
350 McAllister Street
San Francisco, California 94102
Attention: The Secretary to the Commission

The commission's facsimile transmission (fax) number is (415) 865-7181, and its telephone number is (415) 865-7060.

Amended effective February 23, 2007; adopted effective May 18, 1999; previously amended effective March 1, 2006.

Guideline 2. Commission membership (Cal. Const., art. VI, § 7).

The commission consists of the Chief Justice of California, the Attorney General, and the presiding justice of the Court of Appeal of the affected district or, if there are two or more presiding justices, the one who has presided longest or, for a nomination to the Supreme Court, the presiding justice who has presided longest as a presiding justice on any Court of Appeal.

Amended effective July 1, 2005; adopted effective May 18, 1999.

Guideline 3. Commission chairperson.

(a) [Chairperson] The Chief Justice (or Acting Chief Justice) shall serve as chairperson of the commission.

Adopted effective May 18, 1999.

(b) [Powers] The chairperson shall preside at the confirmation hearing. The chairperson also is authorized to:

(1) act on behalf of the commission in all matters arising between hearings;

(2) adopt such internal guidelines and order measures as deemed appropriate to implement these guidelines, or for good cause extend or shorten the time periods set forth in these guidelines;

(3) set time limits for the testimony of witnesses;

(4) at the hearing, limit or terminate a witness's testimony for failure to comply with these guidelines;

(5) exclude any person from the hearing who disrupts the proceedings; and

(6) make security arrangements for the confirmation hearing.

Amended effective March 1, 2006; adopted effective May 18, 1999; previously amended effective July 1, 2005.

Guideline 4. Pre-hearing procedures.

(a) [Scheduling, notice, and location of public hearing] The chairperson shall schedule the confirmation hearing within a reasonable time after the nomination and shall issue a press release announcing the time, place, and subject of the hearing.

Adopted effective May 18, 1999.

(b) [Commission on Judicial Nominees Evaluation (Gov. Code, § 12011.5)] The chairperson shall request the Commission on Judicial Nominees Evaluation of the State Bar (JNE) to:

(1) submit to the commission as soon as practicable, but in no event later than the time specified in paragraph (d) of this guideline, its written recommendations to the commission concerning the nominee, and the reasons therefor, and, if specifically requested, all prior JNE recommendations, including the date of evaluation and the court for which the nominee was evaluated; and

(2) designate a representative to testify at the hearing as to the JNE evaluation of the nominee.

Adopted effective May 18, 1999.

(c) [Communications with the commission] All communications regarding a nominee must be made in writing to the commission and/or by testimony at the hearing. Communications regarding a nomination or nominee should be made to the commission as a whole rather than to any commission member individually, and shall be distributed promptly to the members of the commission. Communications may be sent to the commission by United States Mail, overnight delivery, messenger service, or fax, to arrive within the time specified in these guidelines. The commission generally will not formally acknowledge receipt of written presentations concerning a nominee's qualifications. Communications that are received by the commission after the time specified in these guidelines shall be returned to the sender by the secretary to the commission.

Amended effective March 1, 2006; adopted effective May 18, 1999.

(d) [Written presentations and requests to testify; time for submission]

(1) Individuals, including the nominee, who submit a written presentation or request to testify before the commission must identify themselves by name, address, and occupation, and, if applicable, shall identify the name, address, and purpose of any agency or organization for which they are acting in a representative capacity. Telephone numbers and any fax numbers of these individuals and organizations must be included.

(2) Except for the nominee's list of those witnesses whom he or she wishes to testify, as described under paragraph (g), all requests to testify before the commission must be in writing and must specifically state whether the witness will be testifying in support of or in opposition to the nominee, and describe the proposed testimony, its relevance to the nominee's qualifications, and the facts upon which the witness's testimony and opinion will be based. All written presentations or requests to testify must be received by the commission no later than 5:00 p.m. on the fifth court day before the hearing. (For example, if a hearing is to be held on a Monday, the fifth court day before the hearing would be the preceding Monday, unless a judicial holiday falls in between. Each intervening judicial holiday requires an additional court day's notice.)

Amended effective March 1, 2006; adopted effective May 18, 1999; previously amended effective July 1, 2005.

(e) [Permissible testimony] The commission shall review requests to testify and shall permit testimony that is relevant to the nominee's qualifications. Testimony relating to the judicial system generally or to the overall nomination or confirmation process will not be received. Testimony that is unduly cumulative to or repetitive of other testimony may be excluded. A person whose request to testify is denied shall be so informed by the commission as soon as possible before the hearing, by telephone or fax.

Amended effective March 1, 2006; adopted effective May 18, 1999.

(f) [Notice to nominee] The commission promptly shall provide the nominee with a copy of all the written presentations or requests to testify it receives and shall afford the nominee an opportunity to refute, clarify, or comment, either at the hearing or before the hearing in writing, or both. Similarly, if the commission receives any record, public or private, or any other communication relating to the nominee's qualifications, it promptly shall provide the nominee with a copy thereof, and afford the nominee an opportunity to refute, clarify, or comment on that record or communication (consistent with the provisions of Cal. Const. art. VI, § 18.5). All written responses by the nominee must be received by the commission no later than 5:00 p.m. on the third court day before the hearing.

Adopted effective May 18, 1999.

(g) [Nominee's witness list] The nominee shall present the commission with a list of any witnesses he or she wishes to testify at the hearing. This list must include the information required by paragraph (d)(1) and shall be received by the commission no later than 5:00 p.m. on the third court day before the hearing.

Adopted effective May 18, 1999.

(h) [Release of lists of speakers and communications] No later than 2:00 p.m. on the second court day before the scheduled hearing, the commission shall release to the public the following:

(1) the names of witnesses who will testify at the hearing;

(2) the names of any individuals or organizations that have submitted written communications to the commission;

(3) correspondence and public reports received by the commission concerning the nominee's qualifications, including any reports submitted by JNE pursuant to paragraph (b), and the nominee's Personal Data Questionnaire submitted by the Governor to the commission. The commission, however, shall delete any confidential personal information such as an individual's residential address, or Social Security or driver's license number. The written material released shall be made available for copying at the requesting party's expense.

Amended effective July 1, 2005; adopted effective May 18, 1999.

Guideline 5. Hearing procedures.

(a) [Conference] The commission members may confer before the confirmation hearing to consider procedural issues.

Adopted effective May 18, 1999.

(b) [Absence of commission member] Concurrence of at least two commission members present at the hearing is necessary to confirm a nominee. If the Chief Justice is recused or unavailable, the Acting Chief Justice shall serve as the chairperson. If the presiding justice described in Guideline 2 is recused or unavailable, the presiding justice of the affected district who has presided next longest as presiding justice, or, in districts with a single presiding justice, the acting presiding justice, or for a nomination to the Supreme Court, the presiding justice who has presided next longest as presiding justice on any Court of Appeal, shall serve. (See Cal. Const., art. VI, §§ 2, 3, and 7.) A request that a commission member not participate in proceedings of the commission shall be decided by that member alone. The hearing may proceed if two members of the commission are present.

Amended effective July 1, 2005; adopted effective May 18, 1999.

(c) [Witnesses] Witnesses shall be heard in the following order:

(1) witnesses in support of the nominee;

(2) witnesses in opposition to the nominee;

(3) the JNE representative;

(4) the nominee.

Adopted effective May 18, 1999.

(d) [Exhibits and demonstrative evidence] Witnesses must testify orally and have no right to present exhibits or demonstrative evidence at the hearing.

Adopted effective May 18, 1999.

(e) **[Record of hearing]** The hearing proceedings shall be recorded by audio or video recorder, court reporter, or any other means appropriate for preserving the testimony. A nominee who wishes to make his or her own arrangements to record the hearing by video recorder or other means shall notify the commission in writing. This notice must be received by the commission no later than 5:00 p.m. on the second court day before the hearing.

Adopted effective May 18, 1999.

(f) **[Public attendance and broadcasting]** The hearing shall be open to the public and to the media. Any request to broadcast, photograph, or record the hearing requires the approval of the chairperson, upon written application received no later than 5:00 p.m. on the second court day before the hearing. The request, as well as the broadcasting, photographing, and recording, shall comply with the provisions of California Rules of Court, rules 1.150 and 2.954, where applicable.

Amended effective November 19, 2007; adopted effective May 18, 1999; previously amended effective July 1, 2005.

(g) **[Announcement of decision]** The commission may deliberate privately, but shall announce its decision publicly at the hearing, as well as by subsequent news release. If necessary, the hearing may be continued to a future date for further proceedings.

Adopted effective May 18, 1999.

(h) **[Official record]** The commission's minutes shall be the official record of the hearing.

Adopted effective May 18, 1999.

Guideline 6. Staff to the commission.

The chairperson of the commission may designate a person to act as secretary to the commission and one or more persons to act as assistant secretaries. The secretary shall maintain custody of the commission's files. The Administrative Office of the Courts, at the chairperson's direction, shall provide additional staff and financial support as necessary to enable the commission to perform its duties.

Adopted effective May 18, 1999.

Guideline 7. Post-hearing procedures.

(a) **[Access to the commission's files]** Except as otherwise provided in paragraph (b) of this guideline, after the conclusion of any nomination proceedings of the commission subject to these guidelines, a person, agency, or organization, upon written request to the commission's secretary, may obtain access to the public portions of the commission's files, as defined in guideline 4(h), as well as any transcript of the hearing prepared by a court reporter as a record of those proceedings pursuant to guideline 5(e), for inspection and copying at the requesting party's expense.

(b) **[Audio or video recording]** Any audio or video recording prepared as a record of the hearing pursuant to guideline 5(e) shall be copyrighted and made available for viewing at a time and location specified by the commission's secretary, but shall not be available for copying by the requesting party unless such copying is authorized by the commission.

Amended effective July 1, 2005; adopted effective May 18, 1999.

Guideline 8. Publication and distribution of these guidelines.

(a) **[Official guidelines]** These guidelines for the Commission on Judicial Appointments shall be published by the Reporter of Decisions in the advance pamphlets of the California Official Reports and shall be made available on the judicial branch's Web site (at *www.courtinfo.ca.gov/reference/documents/guidelinescja.pdf*) or by calling the Public Information Office of the Administrative Office of the Courts at (415) 865-7740.

Amended effective November 19, 2007; adopted effective May 18, 1999; previously amended effective July 1, 2005.

(b) **[News release]** Information regarding access to these guidelines shall accompany each news release announcing a commission hearing.

Adopted effective May 18, 1999.

(c) **[Copies]** A copy of these guidelines shall be sent to the nominee with the notice of the hearing, and to each designated witness.

Adopted effective May 18, 1999.

CALIFORNIA COURTS OF APPEAL

LOCAL RULES AND INTERNAL OPERATING PRACTICES AND PROCEDURES OF THE COURTS OF APPEAL

First Appellate District. Rules 1-21; Internal Operating Practices and Procedures.
Second Appellate District. Rules 1-9; Internal Operating Practices and Procedures.
Third Appellate District. Rules 1-6; Internal Operating Practices and Procedures.
Fourth Appellate District. Rules 1-5; Internal Operating Practices and Procedures, Division One; Internal Operating Practices and Procedures, Division Two; Internal Operating Practices and Procedures, Division Three.
Fifth Appellate District. Rules 1-8; Local Court Form; Internal Operating Practices and Procedures.
Sixth Appellate District. Rules 1-4; Internal Operating Practices and Procedures.

FIRST APPELLATE DISTRICT LOCAL RULES

[Adopted effective August 23, 2019; amended February 28, 2020, June 24, 2022, and June 5, 2023]
[Previously adopted effective October 16, 2006; amended effective May 1, 2015, and October 12, 2018; repealed effective August 23, 2019]

Obligation of superior court clerk to prepare and file docketing statements in certain criminal, juvenile, dependency, and family matters. Rule 1.
Extensions of time for superior court clerk or court reporter to prepare transcripts. Rule 2.
Obligation of court reporters to include transcripts of specified proceedings in criminal and juvenile delinquency appeals. Rule 3.
Augmentations of the record. Rule 4.
Parties' stipulation to use original superior court file as the appellate record. Rule 5.
Requests for judicial notice. Rule 6.
Motions to consolidate. Rule 7.
Notification of settlement or basis for early resolution. Rule 8.
Settlement conferences in civil appeals. Rule 9.
Motions for stipulated reversal of judgment. Rule 10.
Extensions of time for filing briefs. Rule 11.
Electronic Filing. Rule 12.
Oral argument. Rule 13.
Focus Letters and Tentative Opinions. Rule 15.
New Authority Prior to Oral Argument. Rule 16.
Electronic Devices in the Courtroom. Rule 17.
Media Coverage of Oral Argument. Rule 18.
Abbreviated Opinions. Rule 19.
Circuit-riding Sessions. Rule 20.
Parties' Obligation to Notify Court of Bankruptcy Stays. Rule 21.
Internal Operating Practices and Procedures.

POLICY OF THE COURT OF APPEAL, FIRST APPELLATE DISTRICT, STATE OF CALIFORNIA ON PUBLIC USE OF ELECTRONIC DEVICES IN THE COURTROOM

The First District adopts the following policy, which allows for restricted public use of electronic devices in the courtroom during oral arguments before the court:

Only counsel and self-represented litigants may use laptop computers and electronic tablets in the courtroom. Such devices may be used only as an aid in presenting oral argument, and may not be used to display demonstrative evidence to the court or for any other purpose. Devices must be silenced and placed in "airplane mode" at all times. No cellular telephones or other electronic devices are permitted in the courtroom, except for assisted listening devices. No audio or video recording or photography is permitted in the courtroom, except in compliance with

California Rules of Court, rule 1.150. Failure to comply with these restrictions may result in the violator being removed from the courtroom.

(Adopted effective March 16, 2015)

Rule 1. Obligation of Superior Court Clerk to Prepare and File Docketing Statements in Certain Criminal, Juvenile, Dependency, and Family Matters

(a) **[Docketing Statements]** In all criminal appeals, juvenile appeals from proceedings arising under Welfare and Institutions Code sections 300, 601, or 602, in all writ proceedings challenging orders entered under Welfare and Institutions Code sections 366.26 and 366.28, and in proceedings under Family Code section 7800, the clerk of the superior court must, upon the filing of a notice of appeal or notice of intent to file a writ petition, prepare a docketing statement and promptly forward it to this court with (1) the notice of appeal or notice of intent to file a writ petition, and (2) a copy of the abstract of judgment, minutes, or order being appealed or challenged by writ.

(b) **[Forms]** The following forms of docketing statements shall be used:

(1) Docketing Statement for Criminal Notice of Appeal

(2) Docketing Statement for Juvenile Notice of Appeal and Juvenile Notice of Intent to File Writ Petition

These forms are available on the court's website at: http://www.courts.ca.gov/1954.htm.

(c) **[Sanctions]** The failure of a superior court clerk to file a docketing statement as required by this rule may result in the imposition of sanctions.

Rule 1 adopted, effective August 23, 2019.

Rule 2. Extensions of Time for Superior Court Clerk or Court Reporter to Prepare Transcripts

(a) **[Extension of Time for Clerk's Transcript]** A clerk's request for an extension of time to prepare a clerk's transcript on appeal will not be granted without a showing of good cause.

(b) **[Extension of Time for Reporter's Transcript]** A court reporter's request for an extension of time to file the reporter's transcript will not be granted without a showing of good cause and the approval of the Presiding Judge, or other duly authorized judge, of the superior court.

(1) Automatic Extension in Certain Criminal Appeals. Court reporters are granted one automatic extension of time of 30 days to prepare and file the reporter's transcript where the defendant appeals from a criminal judgment of conviction after trial. Thus, the reporter's transcript is due within 50 days of the filing of the notice of appeal. (See Cal. Rules of Court, rule 8.336.) This rule does not apply whenever the People appeal, or when a defendant appeals from the following:

- a postjudgment order;
- a judgment entered on a plea of not guilty or nolo contendere;
- a judgment pronounced on resentencing after remand from the appellate court;
- an order revoking probation or a judgment entered after the revocation of probation; and
- an order extending a defendant's term of commitment to a state hospital.

In these cases, the reporter's transcript is due no more than 20 days after the notice of appeal is filed. (See Cal. Rules of Court, rule 8.336(d)(3).)

(2) Automatic Extension in Certain Civil Appeals. Court reporters are granted one automatic extension of time of 30 days to prepare and certify the reporter's transcript where a party appeals from a civil judgment entered after trial by jury or by the court. Thus, the reporter's transcript must be prepared and certified within 60 days after the notice is sent in accordance with California Rules of Court, rule 8.130(d)(2). (See Cal. Rules of Court, rule 8.130(f)(1).) This rule does not apply when a party appeals from the following:

- a postjudgment order;
- a summary judgment;
- a judgment of dismissal after the sustaining of a demurrer without leave to amend;
- a default judgment;
- a judgment of dismissal for failure to proceed in a timely manner;
- any other appealable pretrial order; and
- an order declaring a minor free from the custody and control of his or her parents.

In these cases, the reporter's transcript is due no more than 30 days after the notice is sent in accordance with California Rules of Court, rule 8.130(d)(2). (See Cal. Rules of Court, rule 8.130(f)(1).)

(3) Juvenile Proceedings. Court reporters are not granted an automatic extension of time in appeals and writs from orders or judgments in juvenile proceedings. (Welf. & Inst. Code, §§ 300 et seq., 601, 602.)

In juvenile appeals, the reporter's transcript is due no more than 20 days after the notice of appeal is filed. (See Cal. Rules of Court, rules 8.409(c), 8.416(c)(1).) In juvenile writ proceedings under Welfare and Institutions Code sections 366.26 and 366.28, the reporter's transcript is due 12 calendar days after the notice of intent is filed. (See Cal. Rules of Court, rules 8.450(h)(1), 8.454(h)(1).)

(c) **[Reporter Defaults]** If a court reporter fails to timely file the reporter's transcript, this court may issue an order directing the court reporter to show cause why he or she should not be declared incompetent to act as an official reporter, under the provisions of section 69944 of the Government Code.

(d) **[Sanctions]** Sanctions may be imposed upon a clerk who fails to timely file a clerk's transcript, or upon a court reporter who fails to timely file a reporter's transcript. (See Cal. Rules of Court, rule 8.23.)

(e) **[Forms]** A clerk's request for an extension of time to file a clerk's transcript on appeal shall be substantially in the form of the Clerk's Affidavit and Order for Extension of Time to File Transcript on Appeal. A reporter's request for an extension of time to file the reporter's transcript shall be substantially in the form of the Reporter's Affidavit and Order for Extension of Time to File Transcript on Appeal. These forms are available on the court's website at: http://www.courts.ca.gov/1954.htm.

Rule 2 adopted, effective August 23, 2019.

Rule 3. Obligation of Court Reporters to Include Transcripts of Specified Proceedings in Criminal and Juvenile Delinquency Appeals

In addition to the transcripts designated in the California Rules of Court, transcripts of the following proceedings should be included as part of the record in appeals in criminal and juvenile delinquency cases:

(a) **[Proceedings on Defense Motions]** Reporter's transcripts of the proceedings held on all defense motions that were denied, in whole or in part, including but not limited to the following:

- motions to suppress identification of the defendant;
- motions to suppress evidence;
- motions to exclude evidence of defendant's prior offenses or other conduct;
- motions to suppress defendant's statements (e.g. *Miranda v. Arizona* (1966) 384 U.S. 436);
- motions to permit or preclude impeachment of defendant or witness with prior offenses;
- motions to determine defendant's competence;
- motions for severance or joinder;
- motions to change venue;
- motions for the discovery of police officer records (*Pitchess v. Superior Court* (1974) 11 Cal.3d 531);
- motions for self-representation (*Faretta v. California* (1975) 422 U.S. 806);
- motions in limine;
- motions to terminate or replace defense counsel under *People v. Marsden* (1970) 2 Cal.3d 118. When provided in paper format, an original and two copies of the sealed transcript shall accompany the record upon certification and delivery to this court. When provided in electronic format, a separately saved file containing only the confidential *Marsden* transcript shall be provided. The court will provide appellant's counsel with a copy of the transcript. If appellant raises a *Marsden* issue, a copy of the transcript will then be provided to the Attorney General in the manner prescribed in California Rules of Court, rule 8.47(b)(2).

(b) **[Proceedings on Prosecution Motions]** Reporter's transcripts of the proceedings held on the following prosecution motions should be included as part of the record when the motion was *granted* in whole or in part:

- motions for joinder;
- motions to impeach the defendant with prior offenses;
- motions for admission of defendant's prior offenses or conduct.

(c) **[Revocation of Probation—Plea Proceedings]** Transcripts of the hearings held on the following proceedings should be included as part of the record in appeals from decisions to revoke probation:

- the original sentencing proceeding at which probation was imposed;
- the proceedings at the time of entry of a guilty plea or nolo contendere plea if the original judgment of conviction is based on such plea; and
- the proceedings at which probation is revoked and the defendant is sentenced.

(d) **[In Camera Hearings]** Transcripts of hearings held in camera or under seal shall be transmitted to this court only, and no sealed copies shall be provided to counsel for either party except on application to and approval by this court. When provided in paper format, an original and two copies of the sealed transcript shall accompany the record upon certification and delivery to this court. When provided in electronic format, a separately saved file containing only the confidential transcript shall be provided.

Rule 3 adopted, effective August 23, 2019.

Rule 4. Augmentations of the Record

(a) **[General Principles]** Parties shall limit their augmentation requests to material that was filed or lodged in the trial court. Augmentation cannot be used to add material to the record on appeal that is outside of the superior court's record. (See, e.g., *Vons Companies, Inc. v. Seabest Foods, Inc.* (1996) 14 Cal.4th 434, 444, fn. 3.)

(b) **[Items Inadvertently Omitted]** If a party realizes that a required or designated item has been omitted from the record, the party shall, in accordance with California Rules of Court, rules 8.155(b), 8.340(c), or 8.410(b)(1), file a notice in the superior court requesting that the item be prepared, certified, and sent to this court. Such a notice should not be filed in this court in the first instance. In criminal and juvenile cases, if a superior court clerk or reporter realizes after a record has been certified that a required or designated item was omitted, the clerk or reporter shall, without the need for a court order, promptly prepare, certify, and send the item to this court in accordance with California Rules of Court, rules 8.340(b) and 8.410(a).

(c) **[Time for Seeking Augmentation in this Court]** Any motion filed in this court to augment a record shall be submitted on the earliest date practicable. Appellant should file any such request in one motion filed no later than 30 days after the record has been filed in this court, except in certain juvenile dependency appeals or writs that have a shorter deadline. (See Cal. Rules of Court, rules 8.416(d)(2), 8.452(e)(2), 8.456(e)(2).) Respondent should file any such request in one motion made within 30 days of the filing of appellant's opening brief. Thereafter, motions to augment will be considered only upon a showing of good cause.

(1) In cases in which the appellant or petitioner is represented by the First District Appellate Project, any request for an augmentation of the record shall be made within 30 days after the expiration of the 10-day administrative-review period.

(d) **[Clerk's Transcript]** A motion to augment the clerk's transcript must be accompanied by the proposed augmented document or identify the proposed document with specificity. The record can be augmented only with documents that were filed or lodged in the superior court. A motion to augment shall be accompanied by a declaration stating that the document was so filed or lodged.

(e) **[Reporter's Transcript]** A motion to augment the reporter's transcript shall identify with specificity the portion of the proceeding sought to be included in the appellate record, the name of the reporter and his or her CSR number if available, and the date or dates of the proceeding. Any such motion shall explain why the transcript may be useful for the appeal. Requests for transcripts of a jury voir dire must be specific and be limited to only the portion of the proceeding that may be useful for the appeal.

(f) **[Good Faith Required]** Repeated motions to augment are strongly disfavored. A motion to augment shall be made in good faith and shall not be made for the purpose of delay. A motion filed on or close to the date a brief is due may raise an inference that it was filed for the purpose of delay.

Rule 4 adopted, effective August 23, 2019.

Rule 5. Parties' Stipulation to Use Original Superior Court File as the Appellate Record

The procedures set forth in California Rules of Court, rule 8.128 allowing the parties to stipulate to using the original superior court file in lieu of the clerk's transcript are approved for use by the superior courts in this district in all civil cases in which the trial court retains no continuing jurisdiction. Any stipulation under this rule shall be substantially in the form of the Stipulation for Use of Original Superior Court File in Lieu of Clerk's Transcript, which is available on the court's website at: http://www.courts.ca.gov/1954.htm.

Rule 5 adopted, effective August 23, 2019.

Rule 6. Requests for Judicial Notice

(a) **[Form of Request]** Requests for judicial notice must comply with California Rules of Court, rule 8.252.

(b) **[Deferral of Ruling]** If a request for judicial notice is filed at the same time as the moving party's brief, or if the court has deferred ruling on a request for judicial notice, the parties may rely on the item sought to be judicially noticed in their briefs. If the court subsequently denies the request, however, it will not consider any such item in rendering its decision.

Rule 6 adopted, effective August 23, 2019.

Rule 7. Motions to Consolidate

Motions to consolidate appeals must include a statement indicating whether the other party or parties agree with the proposed consolidation.

Rule 7 adopted, effective August 23, 2019.

Rule 8. Notification of Settlement or Basis for Early Resolution

Parties shall notify the court as soon as possible when discussions between the parties suggest a reasonable likelihood the case may settle. (See Cal. Rules of Court, rule 8.244.) Likewise, parties shall notify the court as soon as possible if there is any basis for an early dismissal of the appeal. Unless and until the appeal is dismissed, the parties remain obligated to file briefs in a timely fashion and to complete all other tasks that are required by the rules of court. Parties may ask the court that any notice filed under this rule not appear on the public docket.

Rule 8 adopted, effective August 23, 2019.

Rule 9. Settlement Conferences in Civil Appeals

(a) **[Application of Rule]** This rule applies to all appeals in civil cases except appeals from proceedings under sections 601 and 602 of the Welfare and Institutions Code, appeals arising in proceedings involving jurisdiction over an abused or neglected child or to establish or terminate parental rights, and appeals from original proceedings ancillary to a criminal prosecution.

(b) **[Request or Order for Settlement Conference]**

(1) A settlement conference will be scheduled if requested in writing by counsel for all parties to the appeal. The request may be made at any time prior to the close of briefing and shall be addressed to the court's Clerk/Executive Officer. A request by counsel for any party that states all other parties join in the request is adequate for this purpose.

(2) At any time during the pendency of an appeal, the panel to which the appeal has been assigned may order a settlement conference even though none was requested.

(3) The pendency of settlement proceedings will not suspend preparation of the appellate record or briefing, unless the court has granted an extension of time or the parties have stipulated to an extension of time as provided in the California Rules of Court.

(c) **[The Settlement Conference]**

(1) A justice selected by the court from outside the division to which the appeal is assigned shall preside over the settlement conference. The Settlement Conference Justice will notify the parties of the date and time of the conference. All subsequent communications regarding the settlement conference shall be directed to the Settlement Conference Justice and shall not be entered in the court file. The Settlement Conference Justice may conduct the conference as he or she deems appropriate.

(2) All parties and their counsel of record must attend all settlement conference sessions in person with full settlement authority. If the party is not an individual, a party representative with full authority to settle all appeals and cross-appeals must attend all settlement conference sessions in person, in addition to counsel. If a party has potential insurance coverage applicable to any of the issues in dispute, a representative of each insurance carrier whose policy may apply must also attend all settlement conference sessions in person, with full settlement authority. Any party seeking an exception to these requirements must seek and obtain advance approval by the Settlement Conference Justice.

The Settlement Conference Justice may invite participation by any additional person or entity if he or she concludes that such participation would facilitate settlement.

(d) [Implementation of Settlement Agreements] The parties and their counsel shall promptly take the steps necessary to implement the agreements reached at the settlement conference. An appellant who has settled must immediately serve and file a notice of settlement in this court and thereafter seek abandonment or dismissal of the appeal as provided in California Rules of Court, rule 8.244.

(e) [Confidentiality] Except as otherwise required by law, information disclosed to the Settlement Conference Justice, the parties, counsel, or any other participant in the settlement conference shall be confidential and shall not be disclosed to anyone not participating in the settlement conference.

(f) [Appellate Process] Parties and counsel shall comply with all rules applicable to processing appeals while concurrently participating in settlement activities under this rule.

(g) [Sanctions] Monetary sanctions may be imposed by the Settlement Conference Justice or the Administrative Presiding Justice for failure to comply with these rules.

Rule 9 adopted, effective August 23, 2019.

Rule 10. Motions for Stipulated Reversal of Judgment

A stipulated motion to reverse or vacate a duly entered judgment will be considered only if it satisfies the requirements of Code of Civil Procedure section 128, subdivision (a)(8).

Such a motion must be accompanied by a copy of the judgment and a joint declaration by the parties or their counsel that:

(a) describes the parties and the factual and legal issues presented at trial;

(b) indicates whether the judgment involves important public rights or unfair, illegal or corrupt practices, or torts affecting a significant number of people, or otherwise affects a significant number of people who are not parties to the litigation;

(c) discloses whether the judgment exposes any person who is a state licensee to a possible disciplinary proceeding; and

(d) discloses whether the judgment may have collateral estoppel or other effects in potential future litigation and, if so, whether third parties who might be prejudiced by stipulated reversal of the judgment have received notice of the motion.

Rule 10 adopted, effective August 23, 2019.

Rule 11. Extensions of Time for Filing Briefs

(a) [Procedure] The deadlines for filing briefs in civil, criminal, and juvenile appeals are specified in the California Rules of Court. In civil cases, the parties may stipulate to extend the time for filing each brief not more than 60 days. In criminal proceedings, extensions of time by stipulation are not allowed. (See, e.g., Cal. Rules of Court, rule 8.360(c)(4).) Extensions of time will be granted by the court only on a showing of good cause. (See *id.*, rule 8.60(b).) In certain juvenile proceedings, extensions of time may be granted only on an exceptional showing of good cause. (See, e.g., *id.*, rules 8.416(f), 8.450(d), 8.454(d).) The factors the court considers when evaluating whether an applicant for an extension of time has shown good cause or has made an exceptional showing of good cause are identified in California Rules of Court, rule 8.63(b).

An application for an extension of time to file a brief is not necessary, either before or after a default notice is issued under the California Rules of Court, if the brief can be and is filed within the pertinent default period. The clerk shall accept such a brief as timely filed.

(b) [Forms] An application for an extension of time to file a brief shall be substantially in the form of one of the following:

(1) Application for Extension of Time to File Brief (Civil Case) (Judicial Council Forms, form APP-006.)

(2) Application for Extension of Time to File Brief (Criminal Case) (Judicial Council Forms, form CR-126.)

(3) Application for Extension of Time to File Brief (Juvenile Case) (Judicial Council Forms, form JV-816.)

These forms are available on the court's website at: http://www.courts.ca.gov/1954.htm.

(c) [Automatic Extension for Omitted Record] If a party asks the superior court to prepare an omitted part of the record under California Rules of Court, rules 8.155(b), 8.340(b), or 8.410(a), and provides this court with notice of the request, the deadline for filing the party's brief shall be automatically extended by 15 days from the date the omitted part of the record is filed. This extension shall not shorten any other extensions of time that are granted.

Rule 11 adopted, effective August 23, 2019.

Rule 12. Electronic Filing

In light of amended California Rule of Court, rule 8.74, some electronic formatting requirements of the First District's Local Rule 12(b) have been superseded. Parties are directed to rule 8.74 for any questions regarding electronic formatting requirements. Local Rule 12(b) is being amended to conform with California Rule of Court, rule 8.74.

Bookmarking and Pagination

Editor's Note: The document can be found here: https://www.courts.ca.gov/documents/1dca-Local-Rule-12-bookmarks-and-pagination.pdf.

Guide to Creating Electronic Appellate Documents

Editor's Note: The document can be found here: https://www.courts.ca.gov/documents/DCA-Guide-To-Electronic-Appellate-Documents.pdf.

All filings are to be made through the Court's electronic filing system (EFS) operated by ImageSoft TrueFiling (TrueFiling). Use of the EFS system is mandatory for all attorneys filing in this District, unless an exemption is granted, and is voluntary for all self-represented litigants. A filing in electronic format will be accepted in lieu of any paper copies otherwise required under California Rules of Court, rule 8.44, and constitutes the official record of the Court.

(a) [Registration]

(1) Obligation to Register. Each attorney of record in any proceeding in this District is obligated to become an EFS user and obtain a user ID and password for access to the TrueFiling system. Self-represented litigants must register if they wish to e-file. Attorneys and self-represented litigants may register at: https://tf3.truefiling.com/register.

(2) Obligation to Keep Account Information Current. An EFS user is responsible for all documents filed under the user's registered ID and password. Registered users are required to keep their e-mail address current and may update their e-mail address online via the TrueFiling Web site.

(b) [Format]

All documents filed electronically must comply with the format requirements of California Rules of Court, rule 8.74. Electronic briefs must comply with the content and form requirements of California Rules of Court, rules 8.74 and 8.204, with the exception of those provisions dealing exclusively with requirements for paper. Pleadings and exhibits not properly formatted may be rejected.

(Subd (b) amended, effective February 28, 2020.)

(c) [Signatures] A TrueFiling user ID and password is the equivalent of an electronic signature for a registered attorney or party. Any document displaying the symbol "/s/" with the attorney's or party's printed name shall be deemed signed by that attorney/party.

(d) [Trial Court Record]

(1) Appendices, Agreed Statements, and Settled Statements. Parties must submit any appendix filed pursuant to California Rules of Court, rule 8.124, any agreed statement filed pursuant to rule 8.134, or any settled statement filed pursuant to rule 8.137 in electronic form. Appendices should be submitted in a single volume if possible, with multiple volumes permitted only to the extent necessary to meet file size limitations in subdivision (b)(1) of this rule. If multiple volumes are required, they shall be consecutively paginated. Each volume shall clearly state the volume and page numbers included within that volume and include an index of contents, with a descriptive electronic bookmark, to the first page of each indexed document. Appendices exceeding 10 volumes should be delivered to the court on machine readable optical media in lieu of e-filing. A party submitting such an appendix shall file a notice of lodging via TrueFiling.

(2) Administrative Records. In addition to any administrative record provided by the trial court pursuant to California Rules of Court, rule 8.123, the party or parties seeking review must submit a copy of the administrative record in electronic form. An administrative record may be delivered to the court on machine readable optical media in lieu of e-filing.

(3) Reporter's Transcripts. Any party who orders a reporter's transcript of proceedings pursuant to California Rules of Court, rule 8.130, must also request a copy of the transcript in computer-readable format, as provided in Code of Civil Procedure section 271, subdivision (a), and submit an electronic copy to the Court. Should the reporter's transcript exceed the size limitations in subdivision (b)(1) of this rule, a party must either (i) submit the transcript in multiple parts, or (ii) provide the Court with the transcript in digital format on machine readable optical media.

(4) Submissions by the Trial Court.

(i) To the extent that a trial court is able to do so, the court shall submit the clerk's transcript and/or the reporter's transcript(s) in searchable PDF format, either through the TrueFiling system or a court provided portal, in lieu of paper copies otherwise required under the California Rules of Court, and make electronic versions available to parties willing to accept them in lieu of paper copies. One paper copy, in addition to any electronic copy, must be provided to an indigent criminal defendant or his/her counsel. Digital copies of clerk's transcripts and reporter's transcripts must comply with the California Rules of Court.

(ii) Notwithstanding subpart (4)(i) above if, prior to January 1, 2023, a trial court or the court's official reporter or reporter pro tempore lacks the technical ability to use or store a clerk or reporter's transcript in electronic form as prescribed in section 271 of the Code of Civil Procedure and the California Rules of Court, the trial court may provide advance notice of this fact to the Clerk of the Court and may file a paper original of the record or portion of the record that it cannot file electronically. If the proceedings in an action are transcribed by multiple court reporters, those who can deliver transcripts in electronic form must do so, while those who cannot, must notify this court before providing paper copies. All reporters who work on a single action must coordinate with each other to ensure that all transcripts, electronic and paper, are numbered sequentially.

(iii) In the event a paper original of the reporter's transcript is filed with the court and the transcript was produced with computer aided transcription equipment, upon notice by the court made within 120 days of the filing or delivery of the paper transcript, the official reporter or official reporter pro tempore shall provide an electronic copy of the transcript in full text-searchable PDF format.

(e) [Personal Identifiers and Privacy Issues] To protect personal privacy, parties and their attorneys must not include, or must redact where inclusion is necessary, personal identifiers such as social security numbers, driver's license numbers, and financial account numbers from all pleadings and other papers filed in the Court's public file, whether filed in paper or electronic form, unless otherwise provided by law or ordered by the Court. (Cal. Rules of Court, rule 1.201(a).) If an individual's social security number is required in a pleading or other paper filed in the public file, only the last four digits of that number shall be used. If financial account numbers are required in a pleading or other paper filed in the public file, only the last four digits of these numbers shall be used. Particularly sensitive confidential information such as medical records and proprietary or trade secret information should be filed only under seal as required by law or authorized pursuant to the California Rules of Court.

The responsibility for excluding or redacting identifiers from all documents filed with the Court rests solely with the parties and their attorneys. (Cal. Rules of Court, rule 1.201(b).) Neither TrueFiling nor the Clerk of the Court has any responsibility to review pleadings or other papers for compliance.

(f) [Filing Deadlines] Filing documents electronically does not alter any filing deadlines. In order to be timely filed on the day they are due, all electronic transmissions of documents must be completed (i.e., received completely by the Clerk of the Court) prior to midnight. Where a specific time of day is set for filing by Court order or stipulation, the electronic filing shall be completed by that time. Although EFS permits parties to submit documents electronically 24 hours a day, users should be aware that telephone or online assistance may not be available outside of normal Court business hours.

(g) [Completion of Filing] Electronic transmission of a document through TrueFiling in compliance with the California Rules of Court shall, upon confirmed receipt of the entire document by the Clerk of the Court, constitute filing of the document for all purposes.

(h) [Technical Failure/Motions for Late Filing] If a filer fails to meet a filing deadline imposed by Court order, rule, or statute because of a failure at any point in the electronic transmission and receipt of a document, the filer may file the document on paper or electronically as soon thereafter as practicable and accompany the filing with a motion to accept the document as timely filed. For good cause shown, the Court may enter an order permitting the document to be filed nunc pro tunc to the date the filer originally sought to transmit the document electronically.

The Clerk of the Court shall deem the EFS system to be subject to a technical failure whenever the system is unable to accept filings continuously or intermittently over the course of any period of time greater than one hour after 12:00 noon that day. Filings due on the day of a technical failure which were not filed solely due to such technical failure shall be due the next court day. Such delayed filings shall be accompanied by a declaration or affidavit attesting to at least two attempts by the filer to file electronically after 12:00 noon with each attempt at least one hour apart on each day of delay due to such technical failure. The initial point of contact for any practitioner experiencing difficulty filing a document into the EFS system shall be the toll-free number posted on the TrueFiling Web site.

The Court shall not be responsible for malfunction or errors occurring in electronic transmission or receipt of electronically filed documents.

(i) [Manual Filing] An EFS user may be excused from filing a particular document electronically if (1) it is not available in electronic format; (2) it must therefore be scanned to PDF; and (3) the file size of the scanned document exceeds the limit specified on the EFS Web site. Such a document instead shall be manually filed with the Clerk of Court and served upon the parties in accordance with the statutory requirements and the California Rules of Court applicable to service of paper documents. Parties manually filing a document shall file electronically a manual filing notification setting forth the reason why the document cannot be filed electronically.

(j) [Service] Attorneys or self-represented parties who have registered with TrueFiling to participate in EFS consent to service or delivery of all documents by any other party in a case through the system. (Cal. Rules of Court, rule 8.78.) Orders or other documents generated by the Court will be served only through the EFS or by e-mailed notification. Only self-represented litigants who are not registered EFS users will receive manual service or notification by other means.

(k) [Filing fees] TrueFiling is a private vendor under contract with the Court. TrueFiling will assess vendor fees for each filing in accordance with the schedule posted on its website, as approved by the Court. E-filing fees will be considered recoverable costs under California Rules of Court, rule 8.278(d)(1)(D). TrueFiling is designated as the Court's agent for collection of Court imposed fees where required for any filing, and any associated credit card or bank charges or convenience fees (Cal. Rules of Court, rule 8.78; Gov. Code, § 6159).

Self-represented parties are exempt from the requirement of electronic filing. However, should a self-represented party with a fee waiver opt to file documents electronically, that party is exempt from the fees and costs associated with electronic filing. The persons and entities identified in Government Code section 6103 also are exempt from the fees and costs associated with e-filing.

(l) [Exemptions] Self-represented parties may, but are not required to register for electronic filing, but must comply with this rule and the requirements of TrueFiling if they elect to register.

If this rule causes undue hardship or significant prejudice to any party, the party shall lodge the number of paper copies required by the California Rules of Court without regard to electronic filing, plus an additional unbound paper copy in lieu of the electronic copy, accompanied by a declaration setting forth facts that support the claim of hardship. Acceptance of the lodged papers for filing will be subject to further order of the Court. When it is not otherwise feasible for a party to convert a document to electronic form by scanning, imaging or other means, the document may be filed in paper form (Cal. Rules of Court, rule 8.71(g)), together with a declaration setting forth the reasons that electronic filing was not feasible.

(m) [Sanctions for Noncompliance] Failure of counsel to timely register or otherwise comply with EFS filing requirements, unless exempted, shall subject counsel to sanctions as may be imposed by the Court.

Rule 12 amended effective February 28, 2020; adopted effective August 23, 2019.

Rule 13. Oral Argument

(a) [Option to Waive Argument] After a case has been briefed and assigned to a judicial panel for resolution, the parties will be notified that they may elect to waive oral argument. The court attaches no significance to waiving argument, and it understands that oral argument may be unnecessary when the parties' positions have been fully briefed.

b) [Notice and Procedure] An election to present oral argument must be made in writing and must contain the following information: (1) the number and title of the case; (2) the name of the person who will present oral argument; (3) if that person is an attorney, the name of the party whom he or she is representing; and (4) whether the oral argument will be presented in person or remotely. If a party wishes to change from in person to remote argument, or vice versa, he or she must promptly inform the divisional deputy clerk and the opposing parties. If any party timely elects to proceed with oral argument, the court will notify the parties of the time and date of the argument. The oral argument will be conducted in accordance with the California Rules of Court.

(c) [Time] The amount of time allocated for each side to present oral argument may vary. Normally, the parties should plan on being allocated 15 minutes per side, although the court may expand or shorten this time before or at the oral argument.

(d) [Sharing Argument Time] In cases in which two or more parties have interests that are aligned, i.e., are on the same side, those parties shall confer before the oral argument on how they prefer to share their side's time during the oral argument. Multiple attorneys who share time should avoid repeating arguments made by other attorneys.

(e) [Oral Argument Dates] The court maintains a list of the currently scheduled oral argument dates for each division. The list is available on the court's web site at http://www.courts.ca.gov/11245.htm. The dates on the list are tentative and parties and their counsel should always verify them with the clerk of the division to which a case is assigned.

(f) [Recording and Streaming of Oral Argument] The court records and streams all oral arguments, including oral arguments presented remotely by video or by telephone conference call. A request for oral argument will be deemed consent to such recording and streaming.

(g) [Continuances] Any party who wishes to continue oral argument to a later date must submit a request, in writing, that includes: (1) an explanation as to why the request for continuance is being made; (2) confirmation that there was a meet and confer with all opposing parties (or an explanation why it was impracticable to meet and confer) in an attempt to select a mutually agreeable date and whether there is opposition to a continuance; and (3) a proposed new date no more than 45 days after the currently assigned date and that is on the list of already scheduled oral argument dates for the division in question. If the proposed new date is more than 45 days after the currently assigned date, the request for continuance must set forth, in detail, why argument on an earlier date is not possible. The court retains the discretion to deny any and all requests for a continuance.

Rule 13 adopted, effective August 23, 2019; amended, effective June 5, 2023.

Rule 14. Oral Argument by Teleconference [Repealed]
Rule 14 adopted, effective August 23, 2019; repealed, effective June 5, 2023.

Rule 15. Focus Letters and Tentative Opinions
(a) [Focus Letters] Panels may issue focus orders or letters in cases scheduled for oral argument. These orders or letters are issued before argument, and they notify the parties about particular issues the panel is interested in discussing.

(b) [Tentative Opinions] Panels may, in their sole discretion, issue tentative opinions in cases scheduled for oral argument. Any such tentative opinion will be issued before the argument, and the parties will be notified that the court is prepared to rule along the lines indicated in the tentative opinion. When a tentative opinion is issued, oral argument will be held only if a party that originally requested oral argument notifies the court, opposing counsel, and unrepresented parties, that they still wish to proceed with oral argument. If such a notification is given, oral argument will proceed as scheduled, and the views expressed in the tentative opinion will be subject to change. If no such notification is given, oral argument will not be held, and the court's final opinion will reflect the substance of the tentative opinion.

(Subd (b) amended effective June 24, 2022; adopted effective August 23, 2019.
Rule 15 amended effective June 24, 2022; adopted effective August 23, 2019.

Rule 16. New Authority Prior to Oral Argument
Parties submitting a letter of new authorities prior to oral argument under California Rules of Court, rule 8.254 must submit the letter when the authorities become available and as far in advance of any scheduled oral argument as possible. No argument or further discussion of those authorities is permitted in the letter.
Rule 16 adopted, effective August 23, 2019.

Rule 17. Electronic Devices in the Courtroom
Counsel and self-represented litigants may use laptop computers and electronic tablets to aid them in taking notes and presenting oral argument, but they may not use them for any other purpose, including displaying demonstrative evidence. Electronic devices must be silenced and placed in "airplane mode" at all times. No cellular telephones or other electronic devices are permitted in the courtroom, except for use as assisted-listening devices. No audio or video recording or photography is permitted in the courtroom, except in compliance with California Rule of Court, rule 1.150. Failure to comply with these restrictions may result in the violator being removed from the courtroom.
Rule 17 adopted, effective August 23, 2019; amended, effective June 5, 2023.

Rule 18. Media Coverage of Oral Argument
A request to photograph, record, or broadcast an oral argument must comply with California Rules of Court, rule 1.150 and be approved by written order of the presiding justice of the division to which a case is assigned.
Rule 18 adopted, effective August 23, 2019.

Rule 19. Abbreviated Opinions
In accordance with Standard 8.1 of the Standards of Judicial Administration, a memorandum or other abbreviated form of opinion may be issued in causes that (1) are determined by a controlling statute not challenged as unconstitutional and not presenting a substantial question of interpretation or application, (2) are determined by a controlling decision that does not require a reexamination or clarification of its principles or holdings, or (3) raise factual issues that are resolved by the substantial-evidence rule.
Rule 19 adopted, effective August 23, 2019.

Rule 20. Circuit-riding Sessions
The court will conduct its sessions in its courtroom in San Francisco, except that sessions may occasionally be held at educational institutions or elsewhere within the district.
Rule 20 adopted, effective August 23, 2019.

Rule 21. Parties' Obligation to Notify Court of Bankruptcy Stays
(a) [Conditions for Giving Notice] Any party to a matter pending before this court who is aware of a bankruptcy that could cause or impose a stay of proceedings in this court must promptly give notice of such bankruptcy, as set forth below.

(b) [Procedure for Notice] The notice required by subdivision (a) shall be filed with the court and served on all parties and shall include (1) a copy of the most recent order of the bankruptcy court and of any stay order issued by that court and (2) an explanation of whether a stay order or an automatic stay is in effect and why the stay applies to the pending appeal or writ proceeding. Any party disputing the notifying party's documentation or explanation shall promptly serve and file an opposing statement.

(c) [Status Reports] On the first court days of January, April, July, and October, the debtor or other party for whose benefit a stay of proceedings in this case has been taken must serve and file brief status reports informing the court of the status of the bankruptcy.

(d) [Notice to Proceed] Any party may, at any time, serve and file notice of any circumstances or orders permitting the stay of proceedings in this court to end, including evidence that the bankruptcy stay has been lifted, the bankruptcy proceeding has been dismissed, or the party has obtained relief from the stay.
Rule 21 adopted, effective August 23, 2019.

INTERNAL OPERATING PRACTICES AND PROCEDURES
FIRST APPELLATE DISTRICT

(Adopted effective April 2, 2007; amended March 18, 2024)

I. INTRODUCTION
   A. Purpose and Scope
   B. General Information

II. ORGANIZATION OF THE COURT
   A. Justices and Staff
   B. Clerk/Executive Officer, Clerk's Office Staff, and Administrative Support Staff
   C. Managing Attorney and Central Staff

III. PROCEDURES FOR PROCESSING CASES
   A. Assigning Cases to Divisions
   B. Processing Appeals
   C. Processing Writ Petitions

I. INTRODUCTION

A. Purpose and Scope

The purpose of [1] **these internal operating practices and procedures** is to [2] **provide information** about the organization of the court and its procedures for processing cases. [3] **These practices and procedures are not intended to [4] supplant** the California Rules of Court, the Local Rules of the First Appellate District, or the statutes and constitutional provisions governing [5] **court operations.**

B. General Information

The court's address is:

California Court of Appeal
First Appellate District
350 McAllister Street
San Francisco, CA 94102

The clerk's office is located on the first floor in Room [6] **1195. It** is open to the public from 9:00 a.m. to 5:00 p.m., Monday through Friday, exclusive of state holidays. Its [7] e-mail address is [8] first.district@jud.ca.gov.

The court's telephone numbers are:

(415) 865-7200 (Clerk's Office)
[9]
(415) 865-7300 [10] **(Main Number)**
[11]

The court's website is [12] **https://www.courts.ca.gov/1dca.htm.**

II. ORGANIZATION OF THE COURT

A. Justices and Staff

The First Appellate District [13] **consists** of five divisions, [14] **which functionally operate as discrete, differentiated units for the purpose of deciding cases. (Gov. Code, 69101.)** Each division consists of a presiding justice **(PJ)** and three associate justices. **If a justice position is vacant, the Chief Justice may appoint a judge pro tempore to sit by assignment for a designated period.** [15]

The PJ is responsible for managing the division's caseload, presiding over oral argument, and performing administrative tasks. In any case in which the PJ is not on the panel of justices assigned to a case, the senior associate justice of the division serves as the acting presiding justice.

One of the five presiding justices serves as the court's administrative presiding justice (APJ). Among other duties, the APJ is responsible for leading the court, establishing policies, promoting access to justice, providing a forum for the fair and expeditious resolution of disputes, and maximizing the use of judicial resources. (See Cal. Rules of Court, rule 10.1004.)

Each justice employs two research attorneys and one judicial assistant. Some justices also invite law student externs to assist them. Each division has an assigned writ attorney who is supervised by the PJ.

B. Clerk/[16] *Executive Officer***, Clerk's Office Staff, and Administrative Support Staff**

[17] **The court's clerk/executive officer (CEO) is selected by the justices and works under the general direction and supervision of the APJ.** The CEO manages the clerk's office and its personnel and supervises the court's administrative support staff. The CEO also oversees nonjudicial support activities, including personnel, budget, technology, and facilities. (See Cal. Rules of Court, rule 10.1020.)

C. Managing Attorney and Central Staff

The court's managing attorney is selected by the justices [18] **and** works under the general direction and supervision of the [19] **AJP.** The managing attorney serves as legal advisor to the court, its justices, and the clerk's office [20]. The managing attorney also supervises [21] a central staff of **research** attorneys and judicial assistants, **who are assigned on an as-needed basis to assist in processing appeals and writ petitions.**

[22]

III. PROCEDURES FOR PROCESSING CASES

A. [23] *Assigning* **Cases to Divisions**

[24] **Appeals are sequentially assigned to the divisions when the** clerk's office receives the notices of appeal from the superior court. Writ petitions are sequentially assigned to the divisions when the petitions are filed with the court. Appeals and petitions are assigned to divisions without regard to subject matter or complexity. However, when it is apparent to the clerk's office that an appeal or petition arises from the same trial court action that gave rise to an earlier proceeding in this court, the filing will be assigned to the same division that handled the earlier proceeding.

Appeals and writ petitions are sometimes assigned to a division before it becomes apparent that a different division previously handled a related proceeding. In these instances, the subsequent appeal or petition may be transferred to the division that handled the earlier proceeding. If the subsequent appeal or petition arose from the same trial court action that gave rise to the earlier proceeding, the APJ decides whether it should be transferred to the division that handled the earlier proceeding. If the appeal or petition arose from a different trial court action than gave rise to the earlier proceeding, the Supreme Court, upon request, decides whether it should be transferred to the division that handled the earlier proceeding. (Cal. Rules of Court, rule 10.1000.)

B. Processing [25] **Appeals**

[26] 1. *Motions.* Each PJ determines the process for resolving motions that are filed in an appeal before the case is fully briefed. Routine motions and requests for extensions of time are typically decided by the PJ; dispositive motions are decided by a majority of a panel of three justices.

2. *Vexatious Litigants.* Applications to appeal or file a writ petition submitted by self-represented litigants named on the vexatious litigant list maintained by the Judicial Council are assigned to "Division v"—a virtual division—and are decided by the APJ. If the APJ grants the application, the case is assigned to one of the court's five divisions as described above.

3. *Panel Assignments.* Fully briefed appeals are assigned to a panel of three justices for decision. To expedite their processing, appeals entitled to priority—such as juvenile dependency appeals—may be assigned before they are fully briefed. Appeals are assigned to a randomly selected panel, except that an appeal arising from a related proceeding already handled by a panel may be assigned to that same panel.

4. *Draft Opinions.* One justice on the panel is assigned to author the opinion. The author prepares a draft opinion, which typically includes a statement of the pertinent factual and procedural history, an analysis of the legal issues necessary to resolve the appeal, and a proposed disposition. In some appeals, the author may prepare a memorandum opinion with an abbreviated factual recitation and legal discussion. (See Cal. Stds. Jud. Admin., § 8.1.) Upon completion of the draft opinion, the author circulates it to the other panel members for their consideration. Conferencing practices vary among divisions.

5. *Focus Letters and Tentative Opinions.* In cases scheduled for oral argument, the panel may issue a focus letter or order to notify the parties about particular issues the panel is interested in discussing, in addition to any other issues the court and the parties may want to address. Panels may, in their sole discretion, issue tentative opinions in cases scheduled for oral argument. (See Ct. App., First Dist., Local Rules of Ct., rule 15(b).) Any party who originally requested oral argument, and who still wants to proceed with argument after receiving a tentative opinion, must reassert their desire for argument.

6. *Oral Argument and Submission.* When an appeal is assigned to a panel, the court notifies the parties that they may request oral argument within a designated time. If no party requests oral argument, argument will be deemed waived and the case will be submitted upon the court's approval of the waiver. If a party requests oral argument, or if the court determines that oral argument would be helpful regardless of whether a party has requested it, the clerk's office notifies the parties of the argument's date, time, and location. The court will continue oral argument only upon written application supported by a showing of good cause. At the conclusion of oral argument, the PJ or acting preseiding justice declares the matter submitted unless submission is deferred pending further briefing.

Opinions are filed within ninety days of the date the matter is submitted. (See Cal. Const., art. VI, § 19.)

7. *Preparing and Filing Opinions.* After the parties have waived oral argument or oral argument has concluded, the author prepares a final draft of the opinion. If the other justices on the panel concur in the opinion, they approve it and the opinion is filed. A justice who does not subscribe to the opinion's reasoning or disposition may file a separate opinion. If the author fails to obtain the concurrence of at least one other justice on the panel, authorship may be reassigned to another panel member. An opinion is published if a majority of the justices on the panel certifies it for publication.

8. *Rehearing.* A majority of the justices on a panel is required to decide a petition for rehearing. An order granting rehearing vacates the court's original opinion and sets the case for full reconsideration. Generally, the parties have no right to reargue the case. In some cases, however, the court may invite additional briefing or conduct another oral argument before resubmitting the matter and filing a new opinion.

C. Processing [27] *Writ Petitions*

[28] Upon filing, writ petitions are transmitted to the divisional writ attorney who typically researches the issues and provides legal analysis and recommendations to a panel of three justices. Before ruling on a petition, the court may request opposition. If the court decides that an opinion is required, the matter is assigned to a justice on the panel to author, and the matter is thereafter processed similarly to an appeal.

IOPPs 2024 Deletes. [1] this document [2] inform members of the bar and other interested persons [3] It is [4] duplicate [5] the processing of cases [6] 1185 and [7] internet [8] : [9] (415) 865-7209 (Clerk's Office Fax) [10] (Chambers' Receptionist) [11] (415) 865-7309 (Reception Fax) [12] : http://www.courtinfo.ca.gov/courts/courtsofappeal/1stDistrict/ [13] is comprised [14] each consisting [15] Each division operates as a separate unit for the purpose of hearing and deciding cases.

The presiding justice of each division convenes conferences and presides at hearings (oral arguments) in the division and has overall responsibility for calendaring cases, managing the caseload of the division, and all other divisional administrative matters. If the presiding justice is absent or disqualified or not a member of the three-justice panel assigned to decide a matter, the presiding justice usually designates the senior associate justice of the division to serve as acting presiding justice. The Chief Justice of California has designated one of the court's presiding justices to serve as its administrative presiding justice, as prescribed in the California Rules of Court.

Each of the court's justices employs a judicial assistant and two chambers attorneys. Some of the court's justices also utilize law student externs to assist in their individual chambers. In addition, each division employs a writ attorney and a divisional attorney, who are selected by the justices of the division and supervised by its presiding justice. [16] Administrator [17] The court's clerk/administrator is selected by the justices of the court and works under the general direction and supervision of the administrative presiding justice. The clerk/administrator is responsible for planning, organizing, coordinating, and directing the management of the clerk's office and its personnel. The clerk/administrator also supervises the court's administrative support staff. The clerk/administrator is responsible for all nonjudicial support activities, including personnel, budget, technology, and facilities. [18] of the court [19] administrative presiding justice [20] on a variety of issues, including personnel and matters of appellate procedure [21] the court's [22] D. Mediation Program Administrator and Support Staff

The court's mediation program administrator is selected by the administrative presiding justice and works under the general direction and supervision of the administrative presiding justice or a designated supervising justice. The mediation program administrator is responsible for the day-to-day administration of the court's mediation program and supervises its support staff. [23] Assignment of [24] 1. In General. Appeals are assigned to a division when the clerk's office receives the notices of appeal from the superior court where they were filed. Writ petitions are assigned to a division when they are filed with the clerk's office. Assignments are made in rotation, without regard to subject matter or complexity. Exceptions to the random assignment procedures are made if multiple appeals or writ petitions arise from the same trial court action or proceeding, in which case later appeals or writ petitions are assigned to the same division to which the first appeal or writ petition was assigned.

2. Transfer of Cases. If, subsequent to the initial assignment of an appeal or writ petition to a division, it is determined that it arises from the same trial court action or proceeding as a prior appeal or writ petition, the administrative presiding justice may transfer the later appeal or writ petition to the same division to which the first appeal or writ petition was assigned. If multiple appeals or writ petitions arise from different trial court actions or proceedings, but involve the same parties or co-parties and the same or related subject matter, transaction, or incident, the court may request that the Supreme Court transfer later appeals or writ petitions to the same division to which the first appeal or writ petition was assigned. [25] of [26]

1. Assignment of Appeals to Panels. When an appeal is fully briefed, it is ready for assignment to a panel of three justices for decision. The court maintains a computer-generated list of fully briefed civil appeals and a separate list of fully briefed criminal and juvenile appeals. The appeals are listed in the order in which they became fully briefed. Appeals entitled to priority on calendar are assigned first, followed by non-priority appeals in the order in which they became fully briefed. Appeals are assigned to panels in rotation, equalizing the number of cases in which each justice participates. One of the three justices on the panel is designated as the lead justice for each appeal. Appeals are assigned randomly, without regard to subject matter, except that an appeal may be assigned to the same panel to which a related appeal or writ petition was previously assigned.

2. Draft Opinions. After an appeal is assigned to a panel, the lead justice prepares a draft opinion. Although the format may vary somewhat from justice to justice or division to division, the draft opinion generally includes the following information: (1) a statement of the pertinent factual and procedural history of the case; (2) an analysis of each issue necessary to resolve the appeal; and (3) a proposed disposition. The primary purpose of the draft opinion is to provide the panel with all of the relevant information it needs to decide the appeal. Upon completion, the lead justice distributes the draft opinion to the other two justices on the panel for their review. The panel may also meet to discuss the case. Conferencing practices vary from division to division.

3. Oral Argument and Submission of the Cause. When an appeal is assigned to a panel of three justices for decision, the court initially notifies the parties that oral argument will be deemed waived unless one of the parties requests oral argument within the time designated in the notice. If the parties request oral argument, or if the court otherwise determines that oral argument would be helpful, the clerk's office then notifies the parties of the date, time, and place of the hearing. A continuance of oral argument will be granted only upon written application and a showing of good cause. Counsel may not stipulate to a continuance. At the conclusion of oral argument, the presiding justice or acting presiding justice will declare the matter submitted, unless submission is deferred pending further briefing.

4. Preparation and Filing of Opinions. After oral argument or the waiver of oral argument, the lead justice prepares a final draft of the opinion. If the other two justices on the panel concur in the opinion, they sign it and it is delivered to the clerk's office for filing. If an individual justice does not subscribe to all of the reasoning of an opinion, he or she may file a separate opinion. If the lead justice fails to obtain the concurrence of at least one of the other justices on the panel, the case may be reassigned to one of the other panel members for the preparation of an opinion. An opinion is published if a majority of the justices on the panel certifies it for publication.

5. Rehearings. When a petition for rehearing is filed, the clerk's office delivers the petition to the justice who authored the court's opinion. After reviewing the petition and conducting whatever research he or she deems necessary, the authoring justice circulates the petition to the other two justices on the panel with a recommended ruling. Two votes are necessary to grant or deny a petition for rehearing. A petition for rehearing normally will not be granted unless the court has requested an answer. An order granting rehearing vacates the court's original opinion and sets the case for full reconsideration. Generally, the parties have no right to reargue the case; however, the court, in its discretion, may invite either written briefing or oral argument, or both, before resubmitting the matter and filing its new opinion. [27] of Original Proceedings [28] After a writ petition has been filed, the clerk's office delivers the petition to the writ attorney for the division to which the writ is assigned. Depending upon the nature of the petition and its urgency, the writ attorney may present the petition to a panel of justices shortly after its filing, or may perform extensive research. In appropriate cases, the court may request opposition from the real party or parties in interest. If an opinion is required, the matter is assigned to one of the justices on the writ panel and is thereafter handled much like the court handles an appeal. The specific procedures governing various types of writ petitions are enumerated in the California Rules of Court.

SECOND APPELLATE DISTRICT LOCAL RULES

[Amended effective August 7, 2023; previously amended effective November 19, 2012, December 31, 2012, March 9, 2014, September 1, 2014, March 9, 2015, June 24, 2016, July 15, 2016, August 26, 2016, and October 30, 2017]

Contents of reporter's and clerk's transcripts. Rule 1.
Augmentation of record and correction of omissions from record. Rule 2.
Designation of the record in civil appeals under California Rules of Court, rules 8.120, 8.122, and 8.130. Rule 3.
Proposed orders. Rule 4.
Advance notice of request for immediate relief in juvenile dependency writ petitions. Rule 6.
Filing of an appeal in a dependency matter by a person who is not the child, parent, guardian or social services agency. Rule 8.
Record in later appeals in the same dependency cases. Rule 9.
Internal Operating Practices and Procedures.

Rule 1. Contents of reporter's and clerk's transcripts

(a) Criminal and Juvenile Delinquency Appeals

In addition to the normal record prescribed by rules 8.320, and 8.407 of the California Rules of Court, all records in defendants' criminal appeals and minors' juvenile delinquency appeals before the Court of Appeal, Second Appellate District, are hereby augmented under rule 8.340 and 8.410 of the California Rules of Court to include reporter's and clerk's transcripts of the following:

(1) [Jury examination and opening statement]

Except if a conviction was obtained by plea or admission, reporter's transcripts of (a) jury voir dire whenever a motion regarding the composition of the jury or jury panel (for example, a motion under *People v. Wheeler* (1978) 22 Cal.3d 258 [148 Cal.Rptr. 890, 583 P.2d 748]) or a motion for a mistrial was made during the jury voir dire and decided in whole or in part adversely to the defendant; and (b) opening statements.

(2) [Sealed and in camera hearings]

Except if a conviction was obtained by plea or admission, oral proceedings of all sealed and in camera hearings resulting in rulings adverse in whole or in part to the appellant. These transcripts shall be listed in the index to the reporter's transcript, and the original and two copies of the sealed transcripts shall be transmitted to this court in sealed envelopes marked "CONFIDENTIAL—MAY NOT BE EXAMINED WITHOUT COURT ORDER." This court shall provide a copy of the sealed transcripts, other than transcripts of a hearing from which the appellant and defense counsel were excluded, to the appellant's counsel on appeal, upon his or her application. If the appellant raises an issue on appeal relating to the sealed transcripts, copies of transcripts shall then be provided to the Attorney General upon their written request. Unless otherwise ordered by this court, the sealed transcripts of a hearing from which the appellant and defense counsel were excluded may be examined only by a justice of this court personally.

(3) [Waivers of constitutional rights]

Reporter's transcripts of oral proceedings at which the appellant's constitutional rights were waived.

(4) [Guilty or nolo contendere pleas and admissions]

Proceedings at which the appellant moved to withdraw a guilty or nolo contendere plea or a juvenile admission, and proceedings at which sentence or disposition was imposed.

(5) [Pretrial proceedings]

(A) The following pretrial proceedings: (i) proceedings to determine competence of the appellant (Pen. Code, § 1368); and (ii) motions for self-representation (*Faretta v. California* (1975) 422 U.S. 806 [95 S.Ct. 2525, 45 L.Ed.2d 562]).

(B) Except if a conviction or sustained petition was obtained by plea or admission, the following pretrial proceedings which were decided in whole or in part adversely to the appellant: (i) motions to suppress identification; (ii) motions to suppress statements of the appellant; (iii) motions to permit or preclude impeachment of the appellant or a witness with prior offenses (*People v. Castro* (1985) 38 Cal.3d 301 [211 Cal.Rptr. 719, 696 P.2d 111]); (iv) motions for severance or joinder; (v) motions for change of venue; (vi) motions for discovery of police officer records (*Pitchess v. Superior Court* (1974) 11 Cal.3d 531 [113 Cal.Rptr. 897, 522 P.2d 305]); and (vii) *in limine* motions.

(6) [Revocation of probation]

In appeals from revocation of probation: (a) the original sentencing or dispositional proceeding at which probation was imposed; (b) the proceedings at the time of entry of a guilty plea or nolo contendere plea or admission if the original judgment of conviction or sustained petition is based on such plea; and (c) the proceedings at which probation is revoked and the appellant is sentenced or disposition is imposed.

(7) [Documentary exhibits]

The Clerk's Transcript shall include all documentary exhibits admitted in evidence, refused, or lodged in the case in the superior court, including copies of any demonstrative exhibits that were shown to the trier of fact if those copies were lodged in the superior court. The demonstrative exhibits to be included in the clerk's transcript shall include copies of computer slide presentations (such as PowerPoint presentations) that were shown to the trier of fact, whether or not the presentations were marked as exhibits if copies were lodged in the superior court. Each admitted exhibit shall be clearly identified and sequentially numbered.

(Adopted Aug. 1, 1992; amended effective July 15, 2016; Aug. 7, 2023.)

(b) Juvenile dependency

In addition to the normal record prescribed by rules 8.407(a) and (b) of the California Rules of Court, the record in a juvenile *dependency* appeal before the Court of Appeal, Second Appellate District, is hereby augmented under rules 8.155(a), 8.410(b), and 8.416(d) of the California Rules of Court as follows:

(1) In all appeals under Welfare and Institutions Code section 395, subdivision (a) (1), a reporter's transcript of the detention hearing.

(2) For an appeal from an order terminating parental rights under Welfare and Institutions Code section 366.26, except in a case where a notice of intent was previously filed (Welf. & Inst. Code section 366.26 subd. (*l*) (1)), a reporter's transcript of the hearing at which the order setting a section 366.26 hearing was made.

(3) In all appeals under Welfare and Institutions Code section 395, subdivision (a) (1), a clerk's transcript containing the printed ICWA inquiry forms (ICWA 010; ICWA 020); all notices sent to an Indian tribe (ICWA 030); all signed return receipts for the mailing of the ICWA 030 notices; and, all responses from an Indian tribe.

(4) In all appeals under Welfare and Institutions Code section 395, subdivision (a) (1), a reporter's transcript of the oral proceedings for which the minutes indicate that the Indian Child Welfare Act (ICWA) was considered.

(Adopted effective July 15, 2016.)
Rule 1 adopted Aug. 1, 1992; amended Mar. 8, 1993; Jan. 1, 2005; Mar. 20, 2006; Jan. 1, 2007; Apr. 16, 2007; Apr. 27, 2009; July 15, 2016.

Rule 2. Augmentation of record and correction of omissions from record

(a) [Material inadvertently omitted]

Counsel should not file a motion to augment the record when items have been omitted from the designated (civil) or normal (criminal) record on appeal. In those cases counsel should immediately notify the clerk of the superior court, who shall forthwith comply with rule 8.340(b) of the California Rules of Court.

(Adopted Aug. 1, 1992; amended Jan. 1, 2007.)

(b) [When to file motion to augment]

Appellant should file requests for augmentation in one motion within 40 days of the filing of the record or the appointment of counsel. Respondent should file requests for augmentation in one motion made within 30 days of the filing of appellant's opening brief. Thereafter, motions to augment will not be granted except upon a showing of good cause for the delay.

(Adopted Aug. 1, 1992; amended Jan. 1, 2005; Jan. 1, 2007; Dec. 31, 2012.)

(c) [Clerk's transcript]

A motion to augment or correct the clerk's transcript shall be accompanied by the documents requested. If the documents are not provided, the motion must identify them with specificity and contain an explanation for their omission. The motion and the accompanying documents must be served simultaneously on opposing counsel. The requested augmented materials shall have been filed or lodged with the trial court and the declaration shall so state.

(Adopted Aug. 1, 1992.)

(d) [Reporter's transcript]

A motion to augment the reporter's transcript shall identify the portion of the record with specificity, including the reporter's name and the date of the hearing. The motion shall establish with some certainty how the requested materials may be useful on appeal.

(Adopted Aug. 1, 1992.)

(e) [Extensions of time]

The time to perform any act required or permitted by the California Rules of Court will not be automatically extended by the filing of or ruling on a motion to augment. If additional time is needed, counsel may request an extension of time in the motion to augment.

(Adopted Aug. 1, 1992.)

(f) [Good faith required]

A motion to augment shall be made in good faith and shall not be made for the purpose of delay.

(Adopted Aug. 1, 1992.)

(g) [Proposed order]

A motion to augment must be accompanied by a proposed order. The form *Order Re: Augmentation* may be used.

(Adopted Aug. 3, 1998.)

(h) [Attachments]

When more than one document or transcript are attached to or submitted with a motion to augment the record pursuant to California

Rules of Court, rule 8.155(a), the pages of the documents and transcripts must be consecutively numbered.
(Adopted Sept. 15, 2003; amended Jan. 1, 2007; Apr. 16, 2007.)
Rule 2 adopted Aug. 1, 1992; amended Aug. 3, 1998; Sept. 15, 2003; Jan. 1, 2005; Jan. 1, 2007; Apr. 16, 2007; Dec. 31, 2012.

Rule 3. Designation of the record in civil appeals under California Rules of Court, rules 8.120, 8.122, and 8.130

(a) [Contents of the notice and designation of record]

The notice to prepare a reporter's transcript and the designation of the contents of a clerk's transcript required to be filed with the clerk of the superior court by the California Rules of Court, rules 8.130, 8.120, and 8.122 shall include the following information:

(1) [Reporter's transcript]

The notice to prepare the reporter's transcript shall state for each oral proceeding to be included in the record (1) the date, (2) the department number, (3) the name of the reporter or electronic recording monitor, and (4) the nature of the proceeding.

(2) [Clerk's transcript]

The designation of the contents of the clerk's transcript shall state for each paper or record to be included (1) the title and (2) the date of filing. For each exhibit to be included in the clerk's transcript, the designation shall include (1) the exhibit number, (2) a brief description, and (3) the admission status.
(Adopted May 17, 1996; amended Jan. 1, 2007; Apr. 16, 2007; Apr. 27, 2009.)

(b) [Form to designate record]

The form *Designation of the Record on Appeal* may be used to designate the record in civil appeals.
(Adopted May 17, 1996.)

(c) [Sanctions]

Failure to comply with this local rule is a failure to properly designate the record under California Rules of Court, rules 8.130, 8.120, and 8.122 and may result in the dismissal of the appeal or the imposition of monetary sanctions.
(Adopted May 17, 1996; amended Jan. 1, 2007; Apr. 27, 2009.)
Rule 3 adopted May 17, 1996; amended Jan. 1, 2007; Apr. 16, 2007; Apr. 27, 2009.

Rule 4. Proposed orders

Any motion or application filed with this court must be accompanied by a proposed order. Failure to comply with this local rule may result in the denial of the motion or application.
Rule 4 adopted Aug. 3, 1998.

Rule 5. Requests for Judicial Notice [Repealed]
Rule 5 adopted Apr. 12, 1999; repealed Jan. 1, 2005.

Rule 5. Extensions of time for filing briefs [Repealed]
Rule 5 adopted effective May 5, 2008; repealed effective June 24, 2016.

Rule 6. Advance notice of request for immediate relief in juvenile dependency writ petitions

Before filing a petition for extraordinary writ with a request for immediate relief in a juvenile dependency proceeding, the petitioner must use best efforts to provide notice in person, by telephone, by facsimile or by e-mail to all parties at the earliest possible time and, when practical, at least 24 hours before filing. In addition, before filing such a petition, the petitioner must deliver to all parties in person, by facsimile, or by e-mail a copy of the petition. A declaration of notice and delivery, including the date, time, manner, name of the individual notified, any response of the individual notified, and whether any opposition will be filed, or a declaration stating the reasons why notice or delivery could not be accomplished, must accompany the petition. Noncompliance with this rule will not prevent the court from exercising its discretion in the best interest of the child.
Rule 6 adopted Sept. 15, 2003.

Rule 7. Copies of Briefs, Original Proceedings (Writs), Oppositions or Replies to a Writ Petition Including Any Exhibits or Appendices — Electronic or Paper [Repealed]
Rule 7 adopted Nov. 19, 2012; amended Sept. 1, 2014; Mar. 9, 2015; repealed Oct. 30, 2017.

Rule 8. Filing of an appeal in a dependency matter by a person who is not the child, parent, guardian or social services agency

In order to comply with Welfare and Institutions Code section 827, an appellant who is not the child, parent, guardian or social services agency must complete and file a JV-570 Judicial Council Form Request for Disclosure of Juvenile Court File (JV-570) as follows:

(1) The JV-570 must be filed in the juvenile court with a timely notice of appeal, or within 10 days after the notice of appeal is filed.

(2) The judge or referee in the dependency case shall rule on the JV-570 within the time limit set forth in Welfare and Institutions Code section 827, subdivision (a) (2) (F).

(3) If the JV-570 is denied, the clerk shall prepare a transcript containing the notice of appeal and the JV-570, the JV-571 [Notice of Request for Disclosure of Juvenile Case File], any JV-572 [Objection to Release of Juvenile Case File] and the JV-573 [Order on Request for Disclosure of Juvenile Case File] and/or JV-574 [Order After Judicial Review].

(4) If the Request is granted in whole or part, the clerk and the reporter shall prepare the record designated and approved by the judge or referee as set forth in the JV-574 Order After Judicial Review.

(5) If the JV-570 is not filed, the superior court clerk must promptly notify the petitioner in writing that if the form is not filed within 15 days after the notice is sent, the reviewing court will dismiss the appeal.
Rule 8 adopted effective July 15, 2016; revised effective August 26, 2016.

Rule 9. Record in later appeals in the same dependency cases

In a later appeal in a dependency case filed by a party in a prior appeal in the case, the record is augmented with the clerk's and reporter's transcripts in the previous appeal(s), and the record shall be prepared as follows:

(1) A clerk's transcript containing the items listed under California Rules of Court rule 8.407 (a) [normal clerk's transcript] which were filed *after* the judgment or order which was the subject of the prior appeal.

(2) A reporter's transcript of the oral proceedings at any hearing which resulted in the order that is the subject of the later appeal.
Rule 9 adopted effective July 15, 2016.

Policy Statement. Policy Statement for Voluntary Settlement Conference in Civil Appeals [Repealed]
Policy Statement adopted Feb. 16, 1984; repealed April 22, 2002.

INTERNAL OPERATING PRACTICES AND PROCEDURES
SECOND APPELLATE DISTRICT

(Revised effective September 30, 2016)

Purpose
Organization of the District
Processing of Cases
   Assignment of Cases
   Motions
   Appeals
      Preparation of Bench Memoranda
      Oral Argument
      Determination
      Rehearing
      Publication
   Writ Petitions
Assigned Justices
Externship Program
Settlement/Mediation Program
Local Rules

Purpose

The purpose of this document is to provide members of the bar and other interested persons with general information concerning the organization of the Second Appellate District and its procedures for processing cases.

Organization of the District

The Second Appellate District covers four counties and consists of eight divisions. Each division is a separate court for the purpose of hearing and deciding cases assigned to it. Divisions One through Five, Seven and Eight are located at 300 South Spring Street, Los Angeles, California, 90013 and handle all matters arising from Los Angeles County. Division Six is located at 200 East Santa Clara Street, Ventura, California, 93001 and handles all matters arising from Ventura, Santa Barbara, and San Luis Obispo Counties.

Each division consists of three Associate Justices and a Presiding Justice. The Chief Justice appoints one of the Presiding Justices to serve as Administrative Presiding Justice to perform the duties prescribed in the California Rules of Court.

Each justice maintains a chambers which consists of the justice, judicial attorneys, and a judicial assistant. In addition, each division is assigned other judicial attorneys, including writs attorneys, and other judicial assistants, judicial secretaries, and deputy clerks. A Managing Attorney provides direct assistance to the Administrative Presiding Justice and supervises attorneys and judicial assistants who are not assigned to a particular division. These include the staff responsible for Workers' Compensation matters.

A Clerk/Executive Officer is selected by the justices of the district and works under the general direction and supervision of the Administrative Presiding Justice. The Clerk/Executive Officer is responsible for planning, organizing, coordinating, and directing the management of the clerk's office and its personnel. The Clerk/Executive Officer also supervises the library, administrative, and computer services staffs. The Clerk/Executive Officer is responsible for all district support activities, including personnel, budget, technology, and facilities.

Processing of Cases

Assignment of Cases

Appeals and original proceedings (writ petitions) arising in Ventura, Santa Barbara, and San Luis Obispo Counties are assigned to Division Six. Appeals and writ petitions arising in Los Angeles County are assigned to the divisions in Los Angeles (One through Five, Seven and Eight) on a random, pro rata basis, unless an appeal or writ petition arises from a trial court action or proceeding from which an appeal or writ petition was previously filed in the district. In that case, the appeal or writ petition is generally assigned to the division to which the prior appeal or writ petition was assigned. On occasion and in order to equalize workload, Los Angeles cases may be assigned to Division Six and Division Six cases may be assigned to one of the Los Angeles divisions. Once a case has been assigned to a division it remains in that division for all further proceedings unless the clerk upon direction of the Presiding Justice, requests the Supreme Court or the Administrative Presiding Justice to transfer the case to another division or district, under rule 10.1000 of the California Rules of Court. If two or more justices in a division are recused from a case, the case is to be re-assigned to another division.

Motions

The Presiding Justice of each division determines the manner in which motions are handled within that division. Motions filed before a case is assigned to a division are designated "Division P" motions and are ruled upon by the Administrative Presiding Justice.

Appeals

Preparation of Bench Memoranda

After an appeal has been fully briefed, it is generally assigned on a random, pro rata basis to a three-justice panel. A change in the composition of the panel may be required when, for example, a conflict arises or to accommodate workload imbalances. The case is set for oral argument on an upcoming calendar. Oral argument may be waived by the parties. The court is not obligated to accept a waiver and may ask that the parties appear for oral argument.

The justices on the panel review the briefs and the record. Under the direction of the justices, judicial attorneys generally prepare bench memoranda in anticipation of oral argument. The memoranda discuss the procedural background, facts, and issues in the cases and may recommend various treatments and dispositions. The panel members review the memoranda in preparation for oral argument and the filing of written opinions.

If an issue arises that was not raised by the parties, a letter pursuant to Government Code section 68081 will be sent to the parties requesting briefing. The court may order additional briefing on any issue.

Oral Argument

Each division generally schedules hearings for two days each month and entertains argument on those matters for which oral argument has not been waived by the parties. The manner in which calendars are called and the order in which cases are scheduled for argument differ among the divisions. The composition of the panel assigned to each case is announced at the hearing.

Determination

If the parties have waived oral argument or oral argument does not change the justices' understanding of the case, and all justices on the panel agree with the bench memorandum, it may form the basis of the written opinion to be filed. If oral argument raises additional issues to be considered, or consensus among the panel justices does not exist, the bench memorandum may be altered or discarded and a new memorandum may be circulated. Concurring and dissenting opinions may also be prepared. Unless further briefing is allowed, generally cases are submitted at the close of oral argument. If further briefing is allowed, the date of submission will be ordered by the court.

Rehearing

Timely petitions for rehearing are presented to the court for review. If the court desires opposition, the clerk will be directed to call counsel and request that an answer be filed. In some instances, a modification may be issued and rehearing otherwise denied. Grant of a petition for rehearing may or may not result in a request for further briefing or additional oral argument.

Publication

An opinion or part of an opinion may be published if a majority of the panel rendering the decision determines that it meets the standards for publication contained within the California Rules of Court.

Writ Petitions

Writ petitions are reviewed by the justices of the division to which they are assigned, with the assistance of the division's writs attorneys. Writ petitions that do not seek immediate relief are discussed at periodic writ conferences, usually weekly. If the writ petition seeks immediate relief, a timely determination is made. In appropriate cases, the court may issue a stay or other order to preserve the status quo pending further action. The court may summarily deny a writ petition, either before or after receiving opposition. If a writ petition results in the issuance of an alternative writ or an order to show cause, a written opinion generally results unless the trial court complies with the alternative writ.

Assigned Justices

Upon request, the Chief Justice may assign a judge, retired judge, justice, or retired justice to sit as a justice pro tem in a particular division. Assigned justices assist with the court's workload in various situations, including judicial vacancies and disqualifications.

Externship Program

The Second District maintains a centralized unpaid externship program for law students who participate on a part-time or full-time basis and who may receive law school credit. Externs are recruited or may apply, and those selected are assigned to justices in the various divisions. Once assigned to a justice, externs work under the close supervision of the justice and the justice's staff. Individual justices may accept externship applications in addition to using the district's centralized recruitment and assignment program. Externs have come to the district from law schools throughout the United States.

Settlement/Mediation Program

The Second District participates in a district-wide voluntary settlement/mediation program. A volunteer attorney or mediator presides over the settlement/mediation process. If at any time the parties decide to explore the possibility of settlement/mediation, they should contact the clerk's office.

Local Rules

The Second District has adopted a number of local rules. (See Local Rules of the Second District Court of Appeal.)

Amended Jan. 1, 2007; Jan. 1, 2008; March 2009; Sept. 30, 2016.

THIRD APPELLATE DISTRICT LOCAL RULES

[As amended effective September 18, 2023; adopted effective January 1, 1977, and previously amended May 1, 1982, December 31, 1982, November 10, 1986, September 4, 1989, July 6, 1993; as amended, reorganized, and renumbered effective October 2, 2006; and previously amended March 2, 2007, May 29, 2009, December 2, 2013, September 14, 2015, September 26, 2016, May 26, 2017, December 11, 2017, October 1, 2018, May 31, 2019, April 10, 2020, and March 24, 2023]

Mediation in Civil Appeals. Rule 1.
Stipulation for use of original superior court file. Rule 2.
Time for oral argument. Rule 3.
Judicial notice of legislative history materials. Rule 4.
Electronic filing. Rule 5.
Appointed Attorney Deemed to Request a Paper Reporter's Transcript. Rule 6.
Internal Operating Practices and Procedures.

Rule 1. Mediation in Civil Appeals

(a) Mediation Program

To enable efficient case management and more expeditious resolution of appeals, the Court of Appeal, Third Appellate District (Court), has a Mediation Program (Program) for all civil appeals not exempt from the Program. Procedures for mediation and operation of the Program are promulgated by the Court of Appeal Mediation Program Committee (Committee).

(Subd (a) adopted eff. Oct. 2, 2006; amended eff. May 29, 2009, and Dec. 2, 2013.)

(b) Program administration

The Program is administered by the Mediation Program Administrator (Administrator) acting under the direction of the Committee and under the supervision of the Administrative Presiding Justice or a designated Supervising Associate Justice (Presiding Justice).

(Subd (b) adopted as part of subd (a) eff. October 2, 2006; relettered to subd (b) & amended eff. May 29, 2009; amended eff. December 2, 2013.)

(c) Civil Appeals exempt from the Program

Any appeal taken from a civil commitment order of the type referenced in rule 8.483(a)(1) of the California Rules of Court, a judgment or order entered in a conservatorship, guardianship, or sterilization proceeding, **or of the type referenced in rules 8.700 or 8.710 of the California Rules of Court,** is exempt from the Program.

(Subd (c) adopted as subd (b) eff. Oct. 2, 2006; relettered to subd (c) & amended eff. May 29, 2009; amended eff. Dec. 2, 2013, and Sept. 18, 2023.)

(d) Process prior to referral for assessment

(1) Upon filing a notice of appeal in a civil case not exempt from the Program, the provisions of rules 8.121, 8.124(a)(1), 8.128, and 8.216 of the California Rules of Court, requiring designation of the record, payment of estimated costs of preparation of the record, stipulating to proceeding with the original superior court file, and submission of a proposed briefing schedule, are suspended.

(2) These rules do not prohibit the superior court from collecting its deposit required by section 68926.1 of the Government Code and by rule 8.100(b)(2) of the California Rules of Court.

(3) Upon receiving notice of filing of a civil appeal in a case not exempt from the Program:

(A) The Appellant must file a Civil Case Information Statement form (Form APP-004), as required by rule 8.100(g) of the California Rules of Court, and an Appellant's Civil Appeal Mediation Statement form.

(B) The Respondent must file a Respondent's Civil Appeal Mediation Statement form.

(4) The Appellant's Civil Appeal Mediation Statement form must be served and filed within 15 days after the superior court clerk sends notification of the filing of the notice of appeal. Failure to timely file either the Appellant's Civil Case Information Statement or the Appellant's Civil Appeal Mediation Statement will result in dismissal of the appeal, without prejudice to reinstatement upon a showing of good cause.

(5) The Respondent's Civil Appeal Mediation Statement must be served and filed within 10 days after the Appellant's Civil Appeal Mediation Statement is filed. Failure to timely file a Respondent's Civil Appeal Mediation Statement will result in a Program selection decision without input from the respondent.

(6) Generally, multiple appeals from the same judgment or a related order are assigned the same appellate case number unless the record for the first notice of appeal has already been filed. (See Advisory Committee Comment to Cal. Rules of Court, rule 8.147.) Subsequent appellant's and respondent's Civil Appeal Mediation Statements will not be required when a second or subsequent notice of appeal has been filed within the same appellate case number.

(7) After Respondent's Civil Appeal Mediation Statement has been filed or was due to be filed, the Administrator shall promptly notify the parties whether the appeal has been selected for the Program.

(Subd (d) adopted as subd (c) eff. Oct. 2, 2006; repealed & adopted eff. May 29, 2009; amended eff. Dec. 2, 2013, and May 26, 2017.)

(e) Process for referral, assessment, and selection for the Program

(1) If a civil appeal is not exempt from the Program, the Presiding Justice may refer the appeal to the Administrator for assessment.

(2) Upon referral for assessment, the Administrator will communicate with counsel and/or non-represented parties to assess whether the peal is amenable to mediation. Based on the assessment, the Administrator will recommend to the Presiding Justice whether the appeal should be selected for the Program.

(3) The Presiding Justice will then decide whether to select the appeal for the Program.

(Subd (e) adopted eff. May 29, 2009; amended eff. Dec. 2, 2013.)

(f) Stipulation and order for placement in the Program

(1) A civil appeal exempt from, or not selected for, the Program may nonetheless be placed in the Program by stipulation and order.

(2) If an appeal is exempt from the Program, the stipulation must be served on the superior court and filed with the Court within 30 days after filing of the notice of appeal. If an appeal was not selected for the Program, the stipulation must be served on the superior court and filed with the Court within 10 days after notification that the appeal was not selected.

(3) The original signature of at least one party must appear on the stipulation filed in the Court. The signatures of the other parties may be in the form of copies of the signed signature page of the stipulation.

(4) Upon receipt of the stipulation by the superior court, the provisions of rules 8.121, 8.124(a)(1), 8.128, and 8.216 of the California Rules of Court, requiring designation of the record, payment of estimated costs of preparation of the record, stipulating to proceeding with the original superior court file, and submission of a proposed briefing schedule, are suspended.

(5) The Court will decide whether to sign the stipulation and order and place the appeal in the Program.

(6) If the appeal is placed in the Program by stipulation and order, suspension of rules 8.121, 8.124(a)(1), 8.128, and 8.216 of the California Rules of Court will remain in effect until the earlier of completion of mediation, other order of the Court lifting the suspension, or the lapse of a period of nine months from the filing of the stipulation with the Court.

(7) If the proposed stipulation is not approved by the Court and the appeal is not placed in the Program, the Administrator must notify the parties, the superior court, and the Court, in writing, that suspension of rules 8.121, 8.124(a)(1), 8.128, and 8.216 of the California Rules of Court is terminated.

(Subd (f) adopted as subd (d) eff. Oct. 2, 2006; amended eff. March 2, 2007; relettered to subd (f) & amended eff. May 29, 2009; amended eff. Dec. 2, 2013, and Sept. 18, 2023.)

(g) Process following selection decision and prior to mediation

(1) *Upon selection of an appeal for the Program*

(A) The Court will issue an order directing that the appeal has been selected for the Program.

(B) The Administrator will:

(i) Notify the parties that the appeal will be mediated.

(ii) Assign a mediator to the appeal. The Administrator may replace a selected mediator upon request by a party or the mediator based on good cause.

(iii) Furnish the parties with the name, address, and telephone number of the mediator, and three dates when the mediator is available for the mediation sessions.

(C) Within 10 days after receipt of notice of the dates the mediator is available, the parties must mutually confer and advise the Administrator and the mediator of their scheduling preferences.

(2) *Suspension of rules following selection decision*

(A) If an appeal is selected for the Program, suspension of rules 8.121, 8.124(a)(1), 8.128, and 8.216 of the California Rules of Court will remain in effect until the earlier of completion of the mediation, other order of the Court lifting the suspension, or the lapse of a period of nine months from the referral of the appeal to the Administrator for assessment as described in subdivision (e) supra.

(B) If an appeal is not selected for the Program, the Court will enter an order to this effect. The Administrator must notify the parties and the superior court by providing a copy of the Court's order not selecting the case for mediation and that suspension of rules 8.121, 8.124(a)(1), 8.128, and 8.216 of the California Rules of Court is terminated. Upon notification by the Court or the Administrator that an appeal was not selected for the Program, the parties' obligation to comply with the requirements of rules 8.121, 8.124(a)(1), 8.128 and 8.216 of the California Rules of Court commences as if notice of appeal was filed on the date specified in the notification.

(Subd (g) adopted as subd (e) eff. Oct. 2, 2006; relettered to subd (g) & amended eff. May 29, 2009; amended eff. Dec. 2, 2013, and Sept. 18, 2023.)

(h) **Mediation and mediation preparation**

(1) *Costs and fees for mediation preparation and services*

(A) Mediators will not charge the parties any fee for the premediation conference call, the mediator's premediation preparation time, and for the first four hours of the initial mediation session.

(B) Notwithstanding subparagraph (h)(1)(A) above, in exceptional cases, the parties and the mediator may agree before the start of the mediation session, in a writing pursuant to Business and Professions Code section 6148, to a fee to be paid by the parties to the mediator for the mediator's additional preparation time.

(C) Prior to the start of the mediation session, the parties and the mediator may agree, in a writing pursuant to Business and Professions Code section 6148, to a fee to be paid by the parties to the mediator to continue the mediation beyond the initial four hours.

(2) *Continuation of mediation sessions*

For good cause and with approval of the Administrator, the mediator and the parties may continue a mediation session to a date certain.

(3) *Mediator communications with parties and counsel*

(A) The mediator may at any time communicate with any counsel or unrepresented parties with or without notice to the other parties or their counsel.

(B) The mediator may require counsel or unrepresented parties to furnish information, documents, records, or other items specified by the mediator.

(4) *Full authority to settle*

(A) Counsel, parties, and persons with full authority to settle the appeal must personally attend the mediation, unless excused in writing by the mediator for good cause. If any consent to settle is required for any reason, the party or person with that consensual authority must be personally present at the mediation.

(B) If a party has potential insurance coverage applicable to any of the issues in dispute, a representative of each insurance carrier whose policy may apply must attend all mediation sessions in person, with full settlement authority. The party with such potential insurance coverage and that party's counsel shall serve timely notice to each insurance carrier with potential insurance coverage informing the carrier: (i) that appellate mediation has been ordered; (ii) that the carrier must have a representative with full settlement authority attend all mediation sessions in person; and (iii) of the date, time, and place of all mediation sessions. (See *Campagnone v. Enjoyable Pools & Spas Service & Repairs, Inc.* (2008) 163 Cal.App.4th 566.)

(C) The mediator may invite participation by any additional person or entity if the mediator concludes that such participation would facilitate mediation.

(5) *Submission of mediation attendance form*

Prior to the start of mediation, the parties and the mediator shall submit to the Administrator a Mediation Attendance Form, listing all participants in the mediation.

(6) *Completion of mediation*

Within 10 days after completion of mediation, the mediator shall submit to the Administrator a Mediator's Statement notifying the Administrator whether an agreement was reached, and the parties and their counsel must separately complete and submit to the Administrator confidential evaluations of the mediation and the mediator on a form provided by the Administrator.

(7) *Appeal not resolved by mediation*

(A) If completion of mediation does not result in disposition of the appeal or if the parties are unable to resolve the appeal within nine months of referral for assessment or from the filing of a stipulation for mediation as described in this rule, the Administrator must, within 10 days after notice of completion of the mediation or lapse of the nine-month period, notify the parties, the superior court, and the Court, in writing, that suspension of rules 8.121, 8.124(a)(1), 8.128, and 8.216 of the California Rules of Court is terminated.

(B) The parties' obligation to comply with the requirements of rules 8.121, 8.124(a)(1), 8.128 and 8.216 of the California Rules of Court commences as if notice of appeal was filed on the date specified in the notification.

(8) *Appeal resolved by mediation*

(A) Pursuant to California Rules of Court, rule 8.244(a) and (b), if the mediation results in a disposition of the appeal and the record has not been filed in the Court, the appellant must promptly file a notice of settlement with the Court and, within 45 days thereafter, file an abandonment of the appeal in the superior court.

(B) Pursuant to California Rules of Court, rule 8.244(a) and (c), if the mediation results in a disposition of the appeal and the record has been filed in the Court, the appellant must promptly file a notice of settlement in the Court and must, within 45 days thereafter, serve and file in the Court a request for dismissal of the appeal.

(9) *Confidentiality*

Except as otherwise provided by law, information disclosed to the mediator, the parties, counsel, or any other participant in the mediation including the Administrator, is confidential.

(10) *Ethical Standards*

Mediators must adhere to the rules of conduct for mediators in court-sponsored mediation programs for civil cases, as set forth in the California Code of Civil Procedure and the California Rules of Court.

(11) *Sanctions*

Monetary sanctions may be imposed following a noticed motion by a party seeking sanctions for failure to comply with the rules or upon the Court's own motion.

(Subd (h) adopted as subd (f) eff. Oct. 2, 2006; relettered to subd (h) & amended eff. May 29, 2009; amended eff. December 2, 2013, May 31, 2019, and Sept. 18, 2023.)

Rule 1 adopted eff. October 2, 2006; amended eff. March 2, 2007; May 29, 2009; Dec. 2, 2013; May 26, 2017; May 31, 2019; Sept. 18, 2023.

Rule 2. Stipulation for use of original superior court file

Rule 8.128 of the California Rules of Court provides for the use of the original superior court file in lieu of the clerk's transcript on appeal in those civil cases where the parties so stipulate. In accordance with rule 8.128 of the California Rules of Court, the procedure therein is approved for use by the superior courts within this district.

Rule 2 adopted as Rule 22, eff. Sept. 4, 1989; renumbered from rule 22 eff. October 2, 2006; amended eff. March 2, 2007.

Rule 3. Time for oral argument

Each side is allowed 15 minutes for oral argument. Where there are more than two parties, a "side" consists of all parties whose interests are not adverse. If there are more than two parties represented by separate counsel who request oral argument, or if counsel for amicus curiae requests oral argument, the court may apportion or expand the time according to the respective interests of the parties and of amicus curiae. Any request for additional time for oral argument must be made by written application submitted to the court within 10 calendar days of the date of the order setting oral argument. The application must be served contemporaneously on all other parties and must specify the amount of time requested and the issues to which additional oral argument will be addressed. When an application is granted, the time allotted to the other side or sides will be similarly enlarged. All parties will be advised of the disposition of any such application prior to hearing.

Rule 3 adopted, eff. April 10, 1998; renumbered from rule 23 eff. October 2, 2006.

Rule 4. Judicial notice of legislative history materials

A party making a motion to have the Court take judicial notice of legislative history documents must identify each such document as a separate exhibit and must provide legal authority supporting the consideration of each document as cognizable legislative history. (See *Kaufman & Broad Communities, Inc. v. Performance Plastering, Inc.* (2005) 133 Cal.App.4th 26.)

Rule 4 adopted eff. October 2, 2006.

Rule 5. Electronic Filing.

(a) Definitions

As used in this local rule, unless the context otherwise requires:

(1) "Court" means the Court of Appeal for the Third Appellate District.

(2) "Electronic filing" and "document" are as defined in rule 8.70(c), California Rules of Court.

(3) A "file" is a unit of electronic information with a filename.

(4) "TrueFiling" is the court's electronic filing portal for registered users.

(5) "Registered user" and "registered users" refer to a person or persons registered to use TrueFiling.

(6) "EFS" means the court's electronic filing system, which includes, but is not limited to, TrueFiling and the court's file transfer protocol (FTP) server.

(7) "EFS user" and "EFS users" refer to a user or users of the court's electronic filing system.

(Subd (a) amended eff. April 10, 2020; previously amended eff. September 26, 2016.)

(b) Mandatory electronic filing

Electronic filing is mandatory for all attorneys filing with the court unless an exemption is granted; electronic filing is voluntary for all non-attorney self-represented litigants. Electronic filers must use the court's EFS.

(Subd (b) amended eff. April 10, 2020; previously amended eff. September 26, 2016, and December 11, 2017.)

(c) Registration

(1) *Obligation to Register.* Each attorney in any proceeding in this court is obligated to become a registered user and obtain a username and password for access to TrueFiling unless an exemption is granted. Non-attorney self-represented litigants must become registered users if they wish to file electronically. Attorneys and non-attorney self-represented litigants may become registered users by registering at <http://www.truefiling.com>.

(2) *Responsibility; Obligation to Keep Account Information Current.* A registered user is responsible for all documents filed under the user's registered username and password. The registered user must comply with the requirements of the California Rules of Court.

(Subd (c) amended eff. December 11, 2017; adopted as subd (a) eff. September 14, 2015; previously amended and relettered eff. September 26, 2016.)

(d) Signatures

For registered users, a registered username and password is the equivalent of an electronic signature.

(Subd (d) amended and relettered eff. April 10, 2020; adopted as subd (d) eff. September 14, 2015; previously amended and relettered as subd (f) eff. September 26, 2016.)

(e) Superior Court Record

(1) *Record of Administrative Proceedings.* In addition to any administrative record provided by the trial court pursuant to the California Rules of Court, registered users seeking review of an administrative determination must submit an electronic copy of the administrative record to the court in compliance with rule 8.74 of the California Rules of Court.

(2) *Reporter's Transcript.* A registered user who orders a reporter's transcript of proceedings must also request a copy of the transcript in electronic format and must submit an electronic copy to the court in compliance with rule 8.74 of the California Rules of Court.

(3) *Transmissions by the Superior Court.* The court authorizes and encourages the superior courts within the Third Appellate District to engage in the electronic service and electronic filing of documents, including, but not limited to, the clerk's transcript and reporter's transcripts. If a superior court transmits an electronic document to the court, it shall also make the electronic document available to the parties. If a superior court transmits electronic documents to the court in lieu of paper, the court will accept electronic documents complying with the California Rules of Court and this local rule.

(Subd (e) amended and relettered eff. April 10, 2020; adopted as subd (e) eff. September 14, 2015; previously amended and relettered as subd (g) eff. September 26, 2016; previously amended eff. December 11, 2017.)

(f) Personal Identifiers and Privacy Issues

To protect personal privacy and other legitimate interests, parties and their attorneys must not include, or must redact where inclusion is necessary, personal identifiers such as Social Security numbers, driver's license numbers, and financial account numbers from all documents filed as part of the court's public record, whether filed in paper or electronic format, unless otherwise provided by law or ordered by the court. If an individual's Social Security number or financial account number is required in a document filed as part of the court's public record, only the last four digits of the number shall be used.

The responsibility for excluding or redacting identifiers from all documents filed with the court rests solely with the parties and their attorneys. Neither TrueFiling nor the Clerk of the Court has any responsibility to review documents for compliance.

(Subd (f) relettered eff. April 10, 2020; adopted as subd (f) eff. September 14, 2015; previously amended and relettered as subd (h) eff. September 26, 2016; previously amended eff. December 11, 2017.)

(g) Filing Deadlines

Electronic filing does not alter any filing deadlines. An electronic filing not completely received by the court by 11:59 p.m. will be deemed to have been received on the next court day. If a specific time of day is set for filing by court order or stipulation, the electronic filing shall be completed by that time. Although the EFS permits users to transmit electronic documents 24 hours a day, EFS users should be aware that telephone or online assistance may not be available outside of normal court business hours, and requests for immediate relief made after the close of the court's normal business hours may not be addressed until the next court day.

(Subd (g) amended and relettered eff. April 10, 2020; adopted as subd (h) eff. September 14, 2015; previously amended and relettered as subd (j) eff. September 26, 2016.)

(h) Motion to Accept Filing as Timely Following TrueFiling Technical Failure

If a registered user fails to meet a filing deadline imposed by court order, rule or law because of a TrueFiling failure, the registered user may file the document in electronic or paper format as soon thereafter as practicable and accompany the filing with a motion to accept the document as timely filed. A late submission that missed a jurisdictional deadline will be accepted for filing pursuant to this subparagraph only if the deadline was missed due to a TrueFiling failure. The initial point of contact for anyone experiencing difficulty with TrueFiling shall be the toll-free telephone number posted on the TrueFiling Web site.

The court is not responsible for malfunctions or errors occurring in the electronic transmission or receipt of electronically filed documents.

(Subd (h) relettered eff. April 10, 2020; adopted as subd (i) eff. September 14, 2015; previously amended and relettered as subd (k) eff. September 26, 2016.)

(i) Service

Registration with TrueFiling manifests affirmative consent to receive service through the EFS. Documents prepared by the court will be served on EFS users through the EFS or by electronic notification.

(Subd (i) amended and relettered eff. April 10, 2020; adopted as subd (k) eff. September 14, 2015; previously amended and relettered (l) eff. September 26, 2016; previously amended eff. December 11, 2017.)

(j) Filing Fees

TrueFiling is operated by a vendor pursuant to a contract with the court. The vendor will assess fees for each electronic filing via TrueFiling in accordance with the schedule posted on the TrueFiling Web site, as approved by the court. TrueFiling fees will be considered recoverable costs under the California Rules of Court. The vendor is designated as the court's agent for collection of court-imposed fees where required for any electronic filing made by registered users, and any associated credit card or bank charges or convenience fees.

If a non-attorney self-represented litigant with a fee waiver chooses to file documents electronically, that litigant is exempt from the fees and costs associated with electronic filing. The persons and entities identified in Government Code section 6103 are also exempt from the fees and costs associated with the EFS.

(Subd (j) relettered eff. April 10, 2020; adopted as subd (l) eff. September 14, 2015; previously amended and relettered as subd (m) eff. September 26, 2016.)

(k) Exemptions

(1) Non-attorney self-represented litigants may, but are not required to, register for electronic filing. Non-attorney self-represented litigants who opt to register for electronic filing must comply with the California Rules of Court, this local rule, and the requirements of the EFS.

(2) When it is not feasible for a registered user to convert a document to electronic format in compliance with rule 8.74 of the California Rules of Court, the document may be filed in paper format with a declaration setting forth the reason that electronic filing was not feasible.

(3) If the requirements of this local rule cause undue hardship or significant prejudice to any registered user, the registered user may file a motion for an exemption from the requirements of this local rule.

(Subd (k) amended and relettered eff. April 10, 2020; adopted as subd (m) eff. September 14, 2015; previously amended and relettered as subd (n) eff. September 26, 2016; previously amended eff. December 11, 2017.)

(*l*) Rejection of an Electronic Filing for Noncompliance

The court will reject an electronic filing if it does not comply with the requirements of the California Rules of Court and this local rule.

(Subd (l) amended and relettered eff. April 10, 2020; adopted as subd (n) eff. September 14, 2015; previously amended and relettered as subd (o) eff. September 26, 2016.)

(m) Sanctions for Noncompliance

Failure of counsel to timely register, and failure of any registered user to comply with electronic filing requirements, unless exempted, may be subject to sanctions imposed by the court.

(Subd (m) relettered eff. April 10, 2020; adopted as subd (o) eff. September 14, 2015; previously amended and relettered as subd (p) eff. September 26, 2016.)

(n) Original Documents

The court may scan any paper document into an electronic format, in which case the electronic document will be deemed the original for purposes of the court record.

(Subd (n) relettered eff. April 10, 2020; adopted as subd (q) eff. September 26, 2016.)

(o) Posting and Publication

The Clerk of the Court is directed to post a copy of this local rule on the court's Web site and submit a copy to the Reporter of Decisions for publication.

(Subd (o) relettered eff. April 10, 2020; adopted as subd (p) eff. September 14, 2015; previously amended and relettered as subd (r) eff. September 26, 2016.)
Rule 5 amended eff. April 10, 2020; adopted eff. September 14, 2015; previously amended eff. September 26, 2016, and December 11, 2017.

Rule 6. Appointed Attorney Deemed to Request a Paper Reporter's Transcript

Prior to January 1, 2026, an appointed attorney is deemed to request, pursuant to Code of Civil Procedure section 271, subdivision (a)(1), that the reporter's transcript be delivered in paper form.

Rule 6 adopted effective October 1, 2018; amended effective March 24, 2023.

Rule 7. The Settlement Conference [Repealed]

Rule 7 adopted Jan. 1, 1977; amended May 1, 1982; Dec. 31, 1982; repealed eff. Oct. 2, 2006.

Rule 8. Conference Without Appellate Record [Repealed]

Rule 8 adopted Jan. 1, 1977; amended May 1, 1982; Dec. 31, 1982; Nov. 10, 1986; Sept. 4, 1989; repealed eff. Oct. 2, 2006.

Rule 9. Exclusion From Conference Requirement [Repealed]

Rule 9 amended Nov. 10, 1986; repealed eff. Oct. 2, 2006.

Rule 10. Disqualification of Conference Justice [Repealed]

Rule 10 repealed eff. Oct. 2, 2006.

Rule 21. Tabbing of Exhibits [Repealed]

Rule 21 adopted Jan. 1, 1977; repealed eff. July 6, 1993.

Rule 22. Stipulation for Use of Original Superior Court File [Renumbered]

Rule 22 adopted Sept. 4, 1989; renumbered to rule 2 eff. Oct. 2, 2006.

Rule 23. Time for Oral Argument [Renumbered]

Rule 23 adopted Apr. 10, 1998; renumbered to rule 3 eff. Oct. 2, 2006.

Rule 31. Location of Hearings [Repealed]

Rule 31 repealed eff. Oct. 2, 2006.

INTERNAL OPERATING PRACTICES AND PROCEDURES
THIRD APPELLATE DISTRICT

[Revised effective March 24, 2023; previously amended effective June 24, 2016, and July 12, 2019]

I. INTRODUCTION
II. STRUCTURE OF THE COURT
III. FILINGS
IV. ORGANIZATION AND DUTIES OF STAFF ATTORNEYS
V. WRIT PETITIONS, MOTIONS AND OTHER APPLICATIONS
VI. JUDICIAL ASSIGNMENTS IN APPEALS
VII. PREPARATION OF A DRAFT OPINION
VIII. ORAL ARGUMENT
IX. CALENDAR
X. FILING OF THE COURT'S DECISION; REHEARING
XI. MEDIATION OF CIVIL APPEALS

I. INTRODUCTION

The purpose of this publication is to advise the bar and interested members of the public regarding the internal rules and general operating practices of this court. No attempt is made to restate or amplify the California Rules of Court or constitutional provisions and statutes governing the practices and procedures of a Court of Appeal. This publication supersedes previous statements of the court's Internal Operating Practices and Procedures.

II. STRUCTURE OF THE COURT

The Third Appellate District is authorized eleven justices: an administrative presiding justice and ten associate justices.

There are no divisions of this court. The court operates in three-justice panels selected at random on a rotational basis.

The courtroom, judicial offices, and Clerk's Office are located in the Stanley Mosk Library and Courts Building, 914 Capitol Mall, Sacramento, California 95814. The Clerk's Office is located on the fourth floor and is open to the public Monday through Friday, from 8:30 a.m. to 4:30 p.m., except for judicial holidays.

III. FILINGS

All matters are filed with the Clerk's Office. The Clerk's Office processes and files the documents, distributing matters to the court when judicial action is required.

Routine motions or applications, such as requests for extensions of time, are referred to the Administrative Presiding Justice. More substantive motions and extraordinary writ petitions are referred to a three-justice panel.

Generally, upon the completion of briefing, appeals are evaluated and designated for handling by the court based on the number and apparent complexity of the issues raised, the subject matter, and the length of the record. In order to expedite certain proceedings, evaluation of an appeal may be done upon the filing of the last respondent's brief.

IV. ORGANIZATION AND DUTIES OF STAFF ATTORNEYS

Each justice is authorized two staff attorneys who work exclusively for the justice. Some of the justices also utilize law student externs who work under their direct supervision.

In addition, the court maintains a central staff of attorneys: a managing attorney who counsels the court and directs the work of the staff, attorneys who specialize in writs, attorneys who specialize in dependency cases, and other central staff attorneys. All central staff attorneys, including the managing attorney, work under the general supervision of the administrative presiding justice and are responsible to the entire court.

The primary responsibility of staff attorneys assigned to an individual justice is the preparation of memoranda for the appeals that are assigned to the justice's chambers. The attorney studies the record and the briefs, analyzes and researches the legal issues, discusses the issues with the justice, and then prepares a legal memorandum with guidance from the justice. The memorandum is prepared for the exclusive use of the court.

The central staff has two main functions. Some central staff attorneys study and familiarize themselves with nonroutine motions, writ petitions, and other extraordinary applications filed with the court. After analyzing and researching the matter, these attorneys present the motion, petition, or application to a three-justice panel of the court for its determination. The other central staff attorneys are assigned appeals that may be authored by any one of the eleven justices. These appeals are concurrently assigned to a central staff attorney and a panel with a designated author-justice. The central staff attorney studies the record and the briefs, analyzes and researches the legal issues, confers with the author-justice, and then prepares a legal memorandum with guidance from the author-justice. The memorandum is prepared for the exclusive use of the court.

V. WRIT PETITIONS, MOTIONS AND OTHER APPLICATIONS

At the weekly writ conference, usually held on Thursdays, a three-justice panel rules on pending writ petitions, nonroutine motions, and other applications. The writ panel varies from week to week, with each justice participating approximately the same number of times during the year as the other justices.

Central staff attorneys make an oral presentation on each matter, and the writ panel considers the parties' written submissions as needed. The panel discusses each matter and decides what action to take. Unless it summarily denies a writ petition, the panel will issue an alternative writ, an order to show cause, or a writ of review, or the panel will notify the parties that it is considering issuing a peremptory writ in the first instance. If an alternative writ, an order to show cause, or a writ of review is issued, the matter is assigned to one of the justices on the writ panel and is thereafter handled much like the court does with an appeal (see discussion, *post*).

At times, the court is presented with a writ petition, motion, or application that purportedly requires urgent or immediate action. Such matters are promptly assigned to a central staff writ attorney for review. If immediate action is required, a panel of three justices is assembled to hear the matter.

VI. JUDICIAL ASSIGNMENTS IN APPEALS

Assignments of appeals to individual justices are not governed by fixed rules or set formula. Each appeal is evaluated and assigned a weight to reflect its relative complexity. Effort is made to fairly apportion the caseload so that no justice is assigned a disproportionate number of the more difficult or less difficult appeals. Subject matter is not a basis for assignment of an appeal to a particular justice, except that, where a justice has been assigned to the same case in an earlier appeal, a new appeal in that case often will be assigned to the same justice.

The three-justice panels are selected at random in order to vary their composition so that over a period of time each justice will participate with all other members of the court in the multiple combinations possible.

The initial designation of the author of the opinion in an appeal is done on a random basis at the time the case is assigned to chambers or to central staff. Each justice is initially designated to author approximately the same number of opinions that will be authored by each of the other justices during the course of the year. Of course, whether the justice initially designated to author an opinion ultimately does so depends upon whether the justice obtains the concurrence of at least one other member of the panel. If the justice fails to do so, one of the other panel members will take over the responsibility of authoring the opinion of the court.

VII. PREPARATION OF A DRAFT OPINION

A legal memorandum prepared by a staff attorney is submitted to the justice initially designated to author the opinion in the appeal. After examining and evaluating the record, the parties' briefs, and the staff attorney memorandum, and after engaging in any necessary independent research and analysis, the justice prepares a draft opinion for the exclusive use of the court. A copy of the draft opinion, the briefs, and the record are then circulated, in order of seniority, to the other two participating justices. Each of the other participating justices indicates his or her tentative concurrence or dissent, or otherwise recommends changes to the draft opinion. All three justices also indicate their tentative positions on whether the ultimate opinion of the court should be certified for publication. The decision to publish the opinion requires approval by a majority of the three-justice panel.

VIII. ORAL ARGUMENT

When the draft opinion is circulated, each justice assigned to the case indicates whether he or she wants the case calendared for oral argument or whether a waiver of oral argument should be solicited by the court. At the request of one justice, the case will be calendared for oral argument.

If the justices agree to solicit a waiver of oral argument, the Clerk's Office sends the parties a letter indicating that the court is prepared to decide the case without oral argument and that oral argument will be waived unless it is requested by either counsel within ten days. If neither counsel requests oral argument within ten days, the court at that time approves the waiver of oral argument and the matter is deemed submitted for decision.

If either counsel requests oral argument, the case is placed on calendar. With the court's approval, a party may waive its appearance at oral argument requested by another party. Continuances are disfavored and will not be granted in the absence of a showing of unusually compelling circumstances. Oral argument will not be continued by stipulation of parties. The matter is deemed submitted for decision at the conclusion of oral argument or, if supplemental briefing is requested by the court, at the time the last brief is filed.

The panel holds a post argument conference, in most cases on the same day that the case is heard. Often the case is finally decided at this conference, and suggestions may be made to the assigned author concerning the content of the opinion. If there is not agreement at this stage, areas of disagreement may be identified and refined.

An opinion will be filed within ninety days of the date of submission.

IX. CALENDAR

The court sits twelve times a year, once each month. The calendar is usually set to begin on the third Monday or Tuesday of each month and generally lasts for five or six days. Special calendars, although rare, may be held by the court.

Each calendar consists of both civil and criminal appeals and other proceedings ready for decision. The administrative presiding justice is responsible for the final composition of the calendar.

X. FILING OF THE COURT'S DECISION; REHEARING

After oral argument or waiver of oral argument, a final draft opinion is circulated among the participating justices. A justice may indicate conditional approval if certain changes are made or otherwise forward comments on the draft to the author and the other participating justice. If there are to be separate concurring or dissenting opinions, they are circulated in final draft form among the participating justices. At the same time, the panel makes a final decision on publication.

Before the opinion is put in final form for filing, transcript references and citations are verified again.

When the opinion is signed, it is transmitted to the Clerk's Office, where it is filed as a decision and opinion of the court. Counsel of record are sent copies of the opinion on that same day. Copies also are available in the Clerk's Office for the news media and interested members of the public.

For sixty days, the Reporter of Decisions posts published opinions of the Court of Appeal, Third Appellate District, at:
http://www.courts.ca.gov/opinions-slip.htm?Courts=C

Unpublished opinions of the court are posted for sixty days at http://www.courts.ca.gov/opinions-nonpub.htm?Courts=C

Timely petitions for rehearing are immediately presented to the author of the opinion and the other panel members for review. If the petition lacks merit, it is denied. In some cases, the opinion may be modified and rehearing otherwise denied. The granting of a petition for rehearing may or may not result in a request by the court for additional briefing or oral argument.

XI. MEDIATION OF CIVIL APPEALS

In October 2006, the court initiated a mediation program for civil appeals governed by its Local Rule 1.

Revised effective March 24, 2023; previously amended effective June 24, 2016, and July 12, 2019.

FOURTH APPELLATE DISTRICT LOCAL RULES

[Amended effective November 1, 2024; previously amended January 1, 2007, November 9, 2007, August 13, 2010, July 1, 2015, April 1, 2016, January 3, 2017, February 23, 2019, January 1, 2023, and August 19, 2024.]

Writ proceedings. Rule 1.
Automatic Extensions for Briefs in Omitted Records. Rule 2.
Stipulation for Use of Original Superior Court File. Rule 3.
Civil Settlement Conference Procedures (Division Two Only). Rule 4.
Reporter's Transcripts in Felony Appeals. Rule 5.
Internal Operating Practices and Procedures for the Fourth Appellate District, Division One.
Internal Operating Practices and Procedures Fourth Appellate District, Division Two.
Internal Operating Practices and Procedures Fourth Appellate District, Division Three.

Rule 1. Writ Proceedings

(a) [Request for immediate stay] A request that an immediate stay be issued or other immediate relief be granted is to be served on the respondent and each real party in interest by (1) personal delivery or (2) an expeditious method consented to in advance by the party served. If the respondent or any real party in interest is not served personally or by an expeditious method consented to in advance by the party served, the court will not act on the request for five days, except to deny it summarily, absent a showing of good cause. The document cover must state conspicuously "STAY REQUESTED" or "IMMEDIATE RELIEF REQUESTED" or words of similar effect.

The court may issue a stay or other order necessary to preserve the status quo or the court's jurisdiction without opposition. However, a request for immediate relief, other than a stay or other order necessary to preserve the status quo or the court's jurisdiction, will not be granted unless the court has received an unsolicited opposition or, alternatively, has requested opposition.

(b) [Preliminary opposition] In an extraordinary proceeding involving a petition for writ of mandate, certiorari or prohibition pursuant to California Rules of Court, rules 8.485–8.493, the real party in interest need not file a preliminary opposition as provided in rule 8.487(a) unless requested to do so by the court. Except as provided in subdivision (a) of this rule, the court will not take any action on a writ petition, other than to summarily deny it, without first giving the real party in interest an opportunity to respond.

(Amended, eff. Aug. 13, 2010; adopted, eff. Oct. 29, 2004.)

Rule 2. Automatic Extensions for Briefs in Omitted Records

If a party requests the superior court to prepare an omitted part of the record under California Rules of Court, rule [1] *8.340(b)* and the party provides this court with notice of the request, the deadline for filing the party's brief shall be automatically extended by 15 days from the date the omitted part of the record is filed with this court. This extension shall not shorten any other extensions of time that are granted.

(Previously repealed, eff. Jan. 1, 2023. Adopted, eff. Aug. 19, 2024. As amended, eff. Nov. 1, 2024.)

Rule 2. 2024 Deletes. [1] 8.155(b)

Rule 3. Stipulation for Use of Original Superior Court File

Rule 8.128 of the California Rules of Court provides for the use of the original superior court file in lieu of the clerk's transcript on appeal in those civil cases where the parties so stipulate. In accordance with rule 8.128 of the California Rules of Court, the procedure therein is approved for use by the superior courts within this district unless the Court of Appeal orders otherwise in a particular case.

(Formerly Rule 10, adopted, eff. April 26, 1992. Renumbered Rule 3, eff. Oct. 29, 2004. As amended, eff. Jan. 1, 2007.)

Rule 4. Civil Settlement Conference Procedures (Division Two Only)

(a) [Application of rule] This rule is adopted pursuant to rule 8.248, California Rules of Court, and shall apply to all civil cases except appeals from proceedings under sections 300, 601, and 602 of the Welfare and Institutions Code, appeals from proceedings under sections 221 and 232 of the Civil Code, and appeals from original proceedings ancillary to a criminal prosecution.

(b) [Notice of availability of conference] Upon receipt of notice of the filing of a notice of appeal, the clerk of this court shall mail a copy of this rule to counsel for all parties.

(c) [General settlement conference procedure]

(1) The presiding justice may schedule a settlement conference and order the parties' attendance at any time during the pendency of an appeal.

(2) Written notice of the date and time of the settlement conference will be given by the court.

(3) Immediately upon accepting a case for the settlement conference procedure, all further proceedings, including the filing of briefs, shall be suspended until further order of the court. However, this rule shall not suspend preparation of the appellate record unless a specific order is issued directing suspension of record preparation.

(d) [Prebriefing settlement conference procedure and sanctions]

(1) A request for a settlement conference to be held prior to completion of briefing shall be served and filed within 30 days from the date of mailing of the notice specified in subdivision (b). Opposition to a request for a settlement conference must be served and filed within 15 days after the request's filing date.

(2) If the court orders a settlement conference prior to the completion of briefing, the parties shall each serve and file an original and one copy of a settlement conference statement at least 15 days before the settlement conference. The parties may file by the same date a joint settlement conference statement in lieu of separate statements. Failure to timely serve and file a settlement conference statement complying with this rule may result in the imposition of sanctions including dismissal of the appeal. Every settlement conference statement shall contain the following:

(A) The trial court name and case title and number;

(B) The name of the judge who rendered the judgment or order appealed and the date of its entry;

(C) The date the notice of appeal was filed;

(D) The names, address, and telephone numbers of counsel for all parties to the appeal;

(E) A brief description of the judgment or order appealed;

(F) A concise statement of the case, including a brief procedural history and all facts material to consideration of the issues presented; and,

(G) The issues expected to be raised in the briefs.

(e) [Postbriefing settlement conference procedure and sanctions] After briefing is completed, the court may request the parties to provide information helpful to the court in deciding whether to order the parties to participate in a settlement conference. The parties shall complete all post-briefing settlement conference questionnaires and respond to all confidential settlement conference inquiries within 15 days of mailing by the clerk of the court. Failure to timely respond to a settlement conference inquiry or questionnaire may result in the imposition of sanctions including dismissal of the appeal.

(f) [Settlement conference and sanctions]

(1) The court shall maintain a list of attorneys who have developed expertise in specified areas of law, are generally respected in the legal community, and are willing to mediate settlement conferences at this court. These attorneys shall be designated as settlement conference mediators and preside over every settlement conference unless otherwise ordered. A justice or assigned justice may be designated as a settlement conference mediator and preside over a settlement conference if so ordered.

(2) The mediator presiding over a settlement conference may in his or her discretion continue it from time to time to allow for further negotiation.

(3) Counsel for every party to the appeal and their clients shall attend any settlement conference. Failure to attend a settlement conference may result in the imposition of sanctions against any party or counsel, including dismissal.

(4) The settlement conference mediator may invite parties to the action who are not parties to the appeal, or any person who has an interest in the action, to attend the settlement conference if it appears to the mediator that their presence may facilitate settlement of the case. Any party to the appeal may serve and file a written request for the attendance of such a party or person at least 15 days before the settlement conference.

(5) Counsel shall confer with their clients in advance and be thoroughly familiar with the case and prepared to present their contentions in detail.

(6) The presiding justice, a justice designated by the presiding justice, or the settlement conference mediator may excuse a client's personal attendance upon request and a showing that hardship or unusual circumstances make the client's attendance impossible or impractical. If personal attendance is excused, counsel either shall have obtained full authority to agree to a settlement that binds the client or the client shall be available for consultation by telephone.

(7) Where settlement cannot be reached, partial settlement will be sought. Any settlement shall be reduced to writing and signed by counsel. After a complete settlement has been agreed to in writing, the parties shall promptly file a stipulation to dismiss the appeal on the ground that the case has been settled. The stipulation shall specify the allocation of costs on appeal and state whether the remittitur is to issue immediately.

(g) [Disqualification of settlement conference justice]

(1) A justice or assigned justice who participates in a settlement conference that does not result in complete settlement shall not thereafter participate in any way in the consideration or disposition of the case on its merits.

(2) A justice or assigned justice of the court will not be disqualified to participate in the consideration or disposition of a case on its merits because he or she has ruled on a request for a settlement conference,

ordered that a settlement conference be held, signed orders granting relief from default for an act required by a party under this rule, extended or shortened any time period specified in this rule, or otherwise signed an order concerning a procedural aspect of the settlement conference process. Only mediating a settlement conference shall disqualify a justice from consideration or disposition of the case on its merits.
(Adopted, eff. Oct. 13, 1992. As amended, eff. Oct. 29, 2004; Jan. 1, 2007.)

Rule 5. Reporter's Transcripts in Felony Appeals

(a) Defendant's counsel is deemed to have requested under Code of Civil Procedure section 271(a)(1) that his or her copy of the reporter's transcript be delivered in paper form.
(Adopted, eff. Feb. 23, 2018. Previously repealed eff. Jan. 1, 2017.)

Rule 6. Writ Petitions: Supporting Records and Stay Requests [Repealed]
Rule 6 adopted, eff. May 18, 1987; repealed, eff. Sept. 9, 1996.

Rule 7. Civil Settlement Conference Procedures (Division Three Only) [Repealed]
Rule 7 adopted, eff. Sept. 14, 1989; repealed, eff. Dec. 1, 2003.

Rule 8. Attachments to Briefs (Division One Only) [Repealed]
Rule 8 adopted, eff. April 2, 1990; repealed, eff. Oct. 29, 2004.

Rule 9. Civil Docketing Statement; Form [Repealed]
Rule 9 adopted, eff. Jan. 3, 1997; repealed, eff. March 10, 2003.

Rule 10. Stipulation for Use of Original Superior Court File [Renumbered]
Rule 10 adopted, eff. April 26, 1992; renumbered to rule 3, eff. Oct. 29, 2004.

INTERNAL OPERATING PRACTICES AND PROCEDURES FOR THE FOURTH APPELLATE DISTRICT, DIVISION ONE

(Revised effective January 27, 2012; September 19, 2014; June 1, 2017; March 1, 2019; June 4, 2024)

I. INTRODUCTION
  A. Purpose
  B. Organization of the District
  C. Justices and Judicial Staff
  D. Clerk/Executive Officer, Clerk's Office Staff and Administrative Support Staff
  E. Managing Attorney and Central Staff
  F. The Clerk's Office

II. THE WORK OF THE COURT
  A. Original Proceedings (Writs)
  B. Appeals
    1. Case Screening
    2. Case Assignment/Processing
    3. Oral Argument
    4. Submission of Cases
  C. Filing of the Court's Decision; Rehearing
    1. Signed Opinions
    2. Concurring or Dissenting Opinions
    3. Publication of Opinions
    4. Rehearing
  D. Posting of Opinions
  E. Motions

III. CIVIL MEDIATION PROGRAM
IV. EXTERN PROGRAM
V. LOCAL RULES

I. INTRODUCTION

A. Purpose

The purpose of this document is to provide members of the bar and other interested persons with general information concerning the organization of the Fourth Appellate District, Division One and its procedures for processing cases. It is not intended to duplicate the California Rules of Court, the Local Rules of the Fourth Appellate District, or the statutes and constitutional provisions governing the processing of cases. This document describes the internal operating practices and procedures of Division One for review of appeals and original proceedings. This publication supersedes previous statements of the court's Internal Operating Practices and Procedures.

B. Organization of the District

The Court of Appeal for the Fourth Appellate District consists of three divisions. Division One, which generally hears appeals in cases from San Diego and Imperial Counties, is located in San Diego. Division Two, which generally hears appeals in cases from Riverside, San Bernardino and Inyo Counties, is located in Riverside. Division Three, which generally hears appeals in cases from Orange County, is located in Santa Ana. Cases filed in one division may be transferred to another division to equalize the workload of the three courts.

The courtroom and Office of the Clerk are located at 750 B Street, Suite 300, San Diego, California 92101.

C. Justices and Judicial Staff

Each division consists of associate justices and a presiding justice. The Chief Justice appoints one of the presiding justices to serve as administrative presiding justice to perform the duties prescribed in the California Rules of Court, rule 10.1004. Division One has 10 justices. Each justice maintains a chamber which consists of the justice, judicial attorneys, and a judicial assistant. The court also has a central staff consisting of judicial attorneys, including writs attorneys, and other judicial assistants who work for each of the justices on a rotating basis.

D. Clerk/Executive Officer, Clerk's Office Staff and Administrative Support Staff

A clerk/executive officer is selected by the presiding justices of the district and works under the general direction and supervision of the administrative presiding justice. The clerk/executive officer is responsible for planning, organizing, coordinating, and directing the management of the clerk's office and all nonjudicial support activities as prescribed in the California Rules of Court, rule 10.1020. The clerk/executive officer is responsible for all district support activities, including personnel, budget, technology, and facilities.

E. Managing Attorney and Central Staff

The court's managing attorney is selected by the justices of the court and works under the general direction and supervision of the administrative presiding justice. The managing attorney serves as legal advisor to the court, its justices, and the clerk's office on a variety of issues, including matters of appellate procedure. The managing attorney also supervises the court's central staff attorneys and judicial assistants who are not assigned to a particular chambers.

F. The Clerk's Office

Each appeal or writ petition filed in Division One is assigned a six-digit identification number that is preceded by a "D" (e.g., D000000). A digit deputy is assigned two of the numbers from zero to nine and is responsible for processing all filings in cases that end in either of those numbers. (For example, the digit deputy that is assigned the numbers "1" and "2" is responsible for processing all filings in cases that have a number ending in a "1" or a "2".) Thus, parties or practitioners seeking information or assistance in their cases should ask to speak with the appropriate digit deputy, unless the case has been placed on a court calendar, in which case they should speak to the calendaring [1] staff.

II. THE WORK OF THE COURT

A. Original Proceedings (Writs)

Writs are reviewed and decided by a panel of three justices, the composition of which rotates on a monthly basis. The clerk's office forwards all writ petitions to the writ department, which is staffed by central staff attorneys. The supervising writ attorney reviews each petition to determine its urgency. If an immediate stay or other form of urgent action appears to be necessary, a writ attorney may orally present the petition to the writ panel; otherwise, petitions are generally processed in order of their filing, subject to adjustments for impending hearing or trial dates. Normally, a writ attorney reviews the petition without waiting for a response, although one may be solicited; the attorney thereafter prepares a written memorandum evaluating the petition and circulates it to the writ panel.

After a writ petition is presented (whether orally or in writing), the justices on the writ panel may:

(1) request a response;
(2) deny the petition (regardless of whether a response has been requested or filed);
(3) issue a peremptory writ in the first instance without oral argument, but only after a response has been requested or filed and the parties have been notified in writing [2] of its possible issuance; or
(4) issue an alternative writ or order to show cause.

It is the court's practice to request an initial response to a petition before issuing an alternative writ or an order to show cause. If the panel issues an alternative writ or an order to show cause, the real party in interest is given an opportunity to file a formal response, and the [3] **case** will be placed on calendar. Generally, the writ attorney who presented the petition to the writ panel assists the lead justice in drafting the opinion when the court issues a peremptory writ in the first instance. When the panel has issued an alternative writ or an order to show cause, the matter is assigned to the lead justice's chambers for the drafting of the opinion.

B. Appeals

1. *Case Screening*

In civil cases, the California Rules of Court require an appellant to file a Civil Case Information Statement (Cal. Rules of Court, rule 8.100(g)), which is reviewed by a central staff attorney to determine if there is any issue regarding the timeliness of the appeal or the appealability of the challenged judgment or order, whether the case is entitled to calendar priority, whether there has been a previous writ or appeal in the same case or in a closely related case, and whether the appeal is affected by a pending bankruptcy. It is the court's practice to grant priority on its own motion to matters involving child custody or visitation.

In all appeals, after the respondent's brief is filed or the time for filing such a brief has run in a case, the managing attorney or a designated staff attorney screens the case and estimates the amount of time that the preparation of a draft opinion is likely to take.

Criminal appeals involving issues that can be resolved with little difficulty based upon well-established law and that do not present a likelihood of dispute as to how the law applies to the facts are designated as "by the court" ("BC") cases. In criminal appeals in which the appellant's counsel is unable to discern any reasonably arguable issues to raise, the court must independently review the record in accordance with *People v. Wende* (1979) 25 Cal.3d 436; **those** [4] are accordingly designated as "*Wende*" appeals.

All other appeals are assigned a numerical value based on the likely amount of time to research the case. These assigned "weights" are used in assigning cases to chambers and to central staff **attorneys**, to balance [5] **workload** throughout the court.

2. *Case Assignment/Processing*

BCs, *Wendes*, juvenile dependency cases, and cases weighted 10 or higher are generally assigned by the managing attorney to central staff attorneys for processing. Priority is given to cases as required by law and, within the priority classification on a first-in, first-out basis. These cases are assigned randomly, in rotation, to a lead justice, who supervises the preparation of a draft opinion.

All other types of appeals are usually assigned by the managing attorney to a lead justice's chambers. Absent unusual circumstances, these assignments are made on a random basis to the justices. The internal procedures for assigning cases to chambers attorneys and for preparing draft opinions varies from one chambers to another.

3. *Oral Argument*

Once a draft opinion has been prepared in a case, its path is determined by whether a party or parties have requested oral argument. In cases where oral argument is waived, the draft opinion is circulated in order of seniority to the other justices assigned to the panel for that case, for their review.

In cases for which oral argument is requested, the draft opinion is placed in a calendar book. The calendar book contains the draft opinions for those cases on which the justice is participating. The justices hear oral argument and then confer immediately after argument takes place.

Oral argument is generally held during the second full week of the month, although occasionally cases are calendared for argument at other times, if necessitated by urgency or other good cause. Argument is limited to 15 minutes per side, unless the court grants a party's advance written request for more time pursuant to Miscellaneous Order 061218 **at** https://www.courts.ca.gov/documents/4dca-div1-061218-Oral-Argument-Time-Limit-Order.pdf.

4. *Submission of Cases*

Cases that are orally argued are normally submitted at the conclusion of argument. Where oral argument is waived, the case is submitted at the conclusion of the argument calendar for the month to which it is assigned. Submission of the case triggers the 90-day rule for the filing of the opinion. (Cal. Const., art. VI, § 19.)

C. Filing of the Court's Decision; Rehearing

1. *Signed Opinions*

Unless the two other participating justices disagree with the disposition proposed by the assigned author, the justice assigned will prepare the majority opinion. When a proposed majority opinion has been drafted, it is circulated to the other participating justices. They indicate approval, disapproval, or proposed changes. Differences of opinion as to the language of the opinion or the ultimate disposition of the case may be taken up in conference. The opinion may then be modified in a manner acceptable to the justices. If two justices agree, a written opinion is filed.

2. *Concurring or Dissenting Opinions*

Where a difference of opinion exists among the justices participating in a case, a justice who agrees with the result reached but not with the reasoning of the majority may write a separate concurring opinion or may merely indicate concurrence only in the judgment reached by the majority. Likewise, a justice who disagrees with the result reached by the majority may write a dissenting opinion. Each panel member has a full opportunity to consider the views of associates prior to the completion and filing of the opinion.

3. *Publication of Opinions*

A decision of the court is not published in the official reports unless it is certified for publication by a majority of the participating justices. The criteria for publication and publication requests are set forth in rules 8.1105 and 8.1120, respectively, of the California Rules of Court.

4. *Rehearing*

The procedure for filing a petition for rehearing is governed by rule 8.268 of the California Rules of Court. When a petition for rehearing is filed, the petition is routed to the justice who authored the opinion with copies to the participating justices. The authoring justice reviews the petition, and then indicates whether he or she votes to grant or deny the petition. The petition, along with any staff memorandum, is then circulated to the other two justices on the panel for their decisions. Two votes are necessary to grant or deny a petition for rehearing.

D. Posting of Opinions

For 60 days, the Reporter of Decisions posts published opinions of the Court of Appeal at: [6] **http://www.courts.ca.gov/opinions-slip.htm?Courts=C.** Unpublished opinions of the court are posted for 60 days at [7] **http://www.courts.ca.gov/opinions-nonpub.htm?Courts=C.**

E. Motions

Routine applications and motions are reviewed and ruled on by the Presiding or Acting Presiding Justice. Dispositive motions, such as motions to dismiss an appeal, are ruled on by a panel of three justices. Requests for extensions of time to file briefs or other papers are ruled on by the Presiding Justice. Motions in writ proceedings are not held for opposition absent a request by the parties.

III. [8] CIVIL MEDIATION PROGRAM

The general information packet sent to parties at the commencement of [9] **a civil** appeal includes guidelines for the [10] **court's Civil Mediation Program. Participation is voluntary, and the agreement of all parties is required. Mediation requests may be initiated by the parties prior to the filing of any briefs or at any time up to 30 days following the filing of the final brief by submitting the Confidential Mediation Request Form which is available at https://www.courts.ca.gov/2519.htm#panel7901. The court may reach out informally to parties to make them aware of the court's mediation option when the parties have indicated an interest in potential mediation but have not requested mediation through the court's program. The commencement of mediation procedures will ordinarily not permit the interruption or extension of the brief filing schedule.**

Upon receipt of a stipulated mediation request, and with approval from the Administrative Presiding Justice, the court will request an appointment of a mediator from the Temporary Assigned Judges Program (TAJP). The parties stipulating to mediation procedures may request the appointment of a specific retired justice in the TAJP. However, selection of the mediation justice shall be at the discretion of the court and the TAJP. The court also reserves the right to decline to initiate mediation procedures in any specific case. If mediation proves unsuccessful, the parties are obligated to adhere to the California Rules of Court until final resolution of the matter.

IV. EXTERN PROGRAM

The court has an unpaid extern program for select law school students three times a year (fall, spring, and summer sessions). Each justice who participates in the program selects the extern who will work for [11] them, usually for 20 to 40 hours per week during the session. A central staff attorney supervises the program, which includes a general orientation about the court and its work, a series of substantive and procedural law lectures, and monthly group meetings. Once assigned to a justice, externs work under the close supervision of the justice and the justice's staff. Students who participate in the extern program as part of their school's extern/clinic program may earn course credit for their work at the court.

V. LOCAL RULES

The Fourth District has adopted a number of local rules. (See Local Rules of the Fourth District Court of Appeal.)

(Adopted Sept. 1, 2004; amended Jan. 1, 2005; Jan. 1, 2007; Jan. 1, 2008; Feb. 15, 2010; Jan. 27, 2012; Sept. 19, 2014; June 1, 2017; Mar. 1, 2019; June 4, 2024.)

IOPPs. 2024 Deletes. [1] clerk [2] , [3] cause [4] and [5] workloads [6] http://www.courts.ca.gov/opinions-slip.htm?Courts=D [7] http://www.courts.ca.gov/opinions-nonpub.htm?Courts=D [8] SETTLEMENT CONFERENCES [9] the [10] settlement program and an appellate settlement request form. The program is voluntary and available at the request of both parties or, should there be more than two parties, at the request of any two opposing parties. The request for a settlement conference may be made as soon as the notice of appeal is filed, and settlement proceedings may commence before briefing but, in any event, the request must be received no later than 30 days after the filing of the last brief. The request normally does not affect or extend the normal briefing schedule. In selecting the justice to participate in the settlement conference, the presiding justice considers any request by the parties for a particular justice. If settlement efforts prove unsuccessful, the settlement justice recuses from hearing the appeal in the case and all settlement papers are maintained as strictly confidential, kept separate from the appellate record and not considered by the attorneys or justices assigned to work on the appeal. [11] him or her

INTERNAL OPERATING PRACTICES AND PROCEDURES
FOURTH APPELLATE DISTRICT, DIVISION TWO

(June 2023 Revision)

SECTION I. INTRODUCTION
SECTION II. THE COURT
SECTION III. ORIGINAL PROCEEDINGS
SECTION IV. CIVIL CASE INFORMATION STATEMENT
SECTION V. CIVIL APPELLATE SETTLEMENT PROGRAM
SECTION VI. EXTENSIONS TO FILE BRIEFS
SECTION VII. CASE ASSIGNMENT
SECTION VIII. TENTATIVE OPINIONS AND ORAL ARGUMENT
SECTION IX. FILING OPINIONS
SECTION X. PRESIDING JUSTICE
SECTION XI. STAFF

SECTION I. INTRODUCTION

To implement the rules governing appellate court procedure, each district and division of the Court of Appeal has developed local customs and practices that may be similar to or different from other districts and divisions. This statement of the internal operating procedures and practices describes the more important customs of this court. The purpose of the statement is to inform the public and the bar of the general manner in which this court conducts its business.

SECTION II. THE COURT

Division Two of the Fourth District is located in Riverside and operates with almost complete autonomy from Division One located in San Diego and Division Three located in Santa Ana. Division Two handles all appellate matters arising in Inyo, Riverside, and San Bernardino Counties. Additionally, cases originating in one division of the Fourth District may be transferred to another division by the Administrative Presiding Justice if required because of recusals or decision of an earlier case by a different division. (See Cal. Rules of Court, rule 10.1000(b).)

SECTION III. ORIGINAL PROCEEDINGS

Original proceedings are assigned to panels of three justices selected each month by rotation. The court's writ attorneys assist the justices by preparing written summaries. The justices review the summaries and meet informally or formally as necessary to decide the case.

More urgent writ matters, including those requesting immediate stays, are the subject of immediate action by the justices facilitated by oral summaries by writ attorneys. If an alternative writ or order to show cause is issued, the issuing justice normally prepares the tentative opinion (see Section VIII., below).

SECTION IV. CIVIL CASE INFORMATION STATEMENT

California Rules of Court, rule 8.100(f), requires the filing of a civil case information statement in the Court of Appeal with a copy of the judgment or order appealed in all civil appeals within 10 days after the clerk mails the notice to do so and the required form. Under the supervision of the Presiding Justice, a central staff attorney reviews the civil case information statement to determine appealability, timeliness, appellate case title and the parties to the appeal.

This court uses the civil case information statement to implement this court's policy to honor its jurisdictional limitations. Thus, this court will not construe a nonappealable ruling to include language of judgment or dismissal. (See *Shpiller v. Harry C's Redlands* (1993) 13 Cal.App.4th 1177, 1179-1181; *Passavanti v. Williams* (1990) 225 Cal.App.3d 1602, 1608-1610.) This court also uses the civil case information statement to initially screen cases for the court's settlement program. (See Section V., below.)

SECTION V. CIVIL APPELLATE SETTLEMENT PROGRAM

Division Two of the Fourth District began its civil appellate settlement program using volunteer attorney mediators in June 1991, the first program of its kind in California. The program helped dramatically in reducing backlog by freeing justices to work on cases that could not be settled. The program received the 1997 Kleps Award for court administration.

Volunteer attorney mediators chosen and scheduled by the Presiding Justice in cooperation with the court's settlement coordinator conduct most of the settlement conferences for civil appeals. On occasion, justices also act as mediators in selected cases. The volunteer mediators are experienced and respected attorneys from Riverside and San Bernardino Counties who are assigned cases for settlement according to their areas of expertise. The Settlement Coordinator selects cases for settlement based on settlement conference information forms filed by counsel and the availability of an appropriate mediator. Once a case has been selected by the court for settlement proceedings, participation is mandatory.

Settlement conferences may be held either before or after briefing is completed. Postbriefing settlement conferences were the rule when the court was using the program to reduce its backlog in the early and mid-1990's, but since the court has eliminated its backlog, prebriefing conferences are the rule and postbriefing conferences are rare and generally discouraged. When cases are selected for a prebriefing settlement conference, generally the court permits a record produced by the superior court to be filed but stays filing of the briefs. Parties file a settlement conference statement within 10 days after notice that the case has been selected. Settlement conferences are held over a period of time before settlement is achieved or determined not to be possible. All documents relating to settlement proceedings are retained in a separate, confidential file for the case, and the proceedings and results are confidential and not revealed to the panel that decides the case if settlement is not achieved. Court of Appeal, Fourth District, Division Two, Local Rules of Court, rule 4 authorizes the program.

SECTION VI. EXTENSIONS TO FILE BRIEFS

Extensions to file briefs are granted or denied based on the factors listed in California Rules of Court, rule 8.63(b). When further extensions on the usual grounds (the existence of other time-limited commitments, the size of the record and number and complexity of the issues, and planned vacations) are no longer appropriate, counsel is so notified in an order granting the last extension on the usual grounds. Thereafter, no extensions will be granted except upon other factors listed in rule 8.63(b). If a further extension is obtained on one or more of those grounds, counsel is again notified that no further extensions will be granted on the usual grounds or the grounds stated in the application. A request for an extension on an excluded ground will be denied, and the clerk directed to issue a notice of default in failing to timely file the brief. (Cal. Rules of Court, rule 8.220(a)(1), (2).)

SECTION VII. CASE ASSIGNMENT

When a case is ready for assignment, the record is checked to see if any justice was involved in trial court proceedings or for other reasons should not be involved in deciding the case. The court maintains a confidential recusal list, which is reviewed prior to final case assignment. Cases are divided into six categories: unusually difficult chambers cases, chambers cases, "fast track" dependency cases (Cal. Rules of Court, rule 8.416(a)(1)(A)), dependency writs reviewing orders setting a hearing under Welfare and Institutions Code section 336.26 (Cal. Rules of Court, rules 8.450–8.452), death penalty habeas appeals and central staff cases. The cases are randomly assigned to a justice as author, and those in the categories of the unusually difficult, "fast track" dependency, death penalty habeas and rules 8.450–8.452 writs are assigned by a rotation. Assignments to authors are usually made monthly, except "fast track" cases and rules 8.450–8.452 writs are assigned immediately, and central staff cases are assigned weekly. When the author has prepared the tentative opinion (see Section VIII., below), the case is randomly assigned to a panel.

SECTION VIII. TENTATIVE OPINIONS AND ORAL ARGUMENT

A tentative opinion is the preliminary draft of the court's decision prepared by the author and reviewed by the panel members. The author circulates the tentative opinion with a cover sheet to the other two justices and notes a recommendation for or against oral argument. The two panel justices consider the briefs and record and note on the cover sheet their preliminary responses and evaluation of the need for oral argument.

Depending on the author's and panel justices' evaluation of the need for oral argument, one of two notices regarding oral argument is transmitted to counsel or self represented parties with the tentative opinion. The first notice invites participation in oral argument and informs counsel that a notice of the date and time of argument will be mailed at least 30 days in advance of the date and time of oral argument. The second notice informs counsel that, while "[t]he court is not unalterably bound by the tentative opinion and is willing to amend or discard the tentative opinion if counsel's arguments persuade the court that the tentative opinion is incorrect in any way," "*at present, in this case the court believes that the record and briefs thoroughly present the facts and legal arguments such that the court is prepared to rule as set forth in the tentative opinion without oral argument.*" The notice advises the parties that oral argument will be deemed waived unless the clerk of the court receives a request for oral argument on the form attached to the notice on or before 12 days after the date of the notice.

Oral argument is held on the first Tuesday and Wednesday of each month, with slight adjustments occasionally made for holidays. If a party requests oral argument or the justices have decided that oral argument would be helpful, the clerk prepares the calendar and mails it to counsel at least 30 days in advance of the hearing. Two or three weeks before oral argument, the justices discuss the cases set for oral argument at a calendar conference.

SECTION IX. FILING OPINIONS

After oral argument, or waiver of oral argument, authors and panel justices develop the tentative opinions and preliminary responses into the opinions, concurrences, and dissents filed as the final decisions. If oral argument is deemed waived in a case, the opinion is circulated for approval and signature to the other panel members as soon as it is signed by the author. The opinion is filed as soon as it is signed by all members of the panel.

Argued cases are deemed submitted on the date of oral argument, and the opinions are generally filed within the same month.

SECTION X. PRESIDING JUSTICE

In addition to the regular duties of an associate justice, the Presiding Justice handles the administrative operation of the court including the functions designated in California Rules of Court, rule 10.1012. In so doing, the Presiding Justice performs a number of tasks essential to the functioning of the court. These include without limitation policymaking, personnel, budgeting, oversight of facilities, grounds, furnishings, and equipment, case assignment, calendar preparation, case management, decision of all motions and applications until the case is assigned to an author, appointments of counsel, supervision and selection of cases for the settlement program, and supervision of the central staff and clerk's office. Staff assist in these tasks when necessary in the Presiding Justice's discretion.

SECTION XI. STAFF

Each justice has 2 research attorneys and a judicial assistant who work exclusively for the justice. In addition, the court has a central staff consisting of a managing attorney, supervising attorney, writ attorneys, research attorneys and judicial assistants. All central staff personnel are under the supervision of the Presiding Justice, who assigns a research attorney to a particular justice to research and draft opinions.

The clerk's office includes an assistant clerk executive officer, supervising deputy clerks and a number of deputy clerks. A settlement coordinator manages the volunteer attorney mediator settlement conference program. Two systems administrators maintain the court's computer systems. A librarian organizes and updates a central library, distributes materials to the justices' and attorneys' libraries, assists justices and attorneys with legal research, and prepares a library budget for approval by the Presiding Justice. The judicial assistants facilitate case flow and perform secretarial services for the justices and attorneys.

(Amended June 1, 2023.)

INTERNAL OPERATING PRACTICES AND PROCEDURES
FOURTH APPELLATE DISTRICT, DIVISION THREE

(Revised effective January 1, 2008; June 4, 2024)

SECTION I. INTRODUCTION
SECTION II. STRUCTURE OF COURT AND ORGANIZATION OF STAFF
SECTION III. ETHICAL SCREENS
SECTION IV. PROCEDURES FOR PROCESSING CASES
   A. Filing
   B. Screening of New Cases
   C. Motions and Applications
   D. Original Proceedings, etc.
   E. Appeals – Oral Argument and Decision
SECTION V. SETTLEMENT
   A. Settlement Notices
   B. Stipulated Requests for Dismissal
   C. Stipulated Requests for Reversal (Code Civ. Proc., §128, subd. (a)(8).)
   D. Settlement Conferences

SECTION I. INTRODUCTION

This document describes [1] internal operating practices and procedures of this court. These practices and procedures supplement the statutes, **California Rules of Court, and Fourth Appellate District Local Rules** [2] that otherwise govern the court's business.

This court is located at 601 W. Santa Ana Blvd., Santa Ana, California 92701. The Clerk's Office is open to the public from 9:00 a.m. to 4:30 p.m. The phone number for the Clerk's Office is (714) 571-2600. The website for the Fourth Appellate District is located at https://www.courts.ca.gov/4dca.htm

SECTION II. STRUCTURE OF COURT AND ORGANIZATION OF STAFF

Division Three of the Fourth Appellate District is currently authorized eight justices — a presiding justice and seven associate justices. The Chairperson of the Judicial Council **may** periodically [3] **assign** pro tem justices to assist the court.

Each [4] **chambers** staff consists of two or three judicial attorneys and a judicial assistant. **Many of the justices also utilize law student externs who may receive academic credit, without pay, while working at the court.**

The managing appellate court attorney supervises a separate central staff. The managing appellate court attorney and central staff work under the direction and supervision of the presiding justice. They review original proceedings, motions, and **applications (such as** extension [5]**). They also** act as counsel for the clerk's office [6] and assist in the evaluation of cases. [7]

The assistant clerk/[8] **court executive officer** supervises the court's administrative staff under the direction of the presiding justice. The court's administrative staff consists of deputy clerks, **a librarian,** court systems administrators, and office assistants.

SECTION [9] *III.* ETHICAL SCREENS

The court maintains an ethical screening process for its judicial attorneys, judicial assistants, clerks, externs, and other staff members in order to maintain and preserve public confidence in the judicial system. The purpose of this process is to inform the justices at the earliest possible opportunity of any circumstances of an actual or potential conflict of interest involving a court staff member that could give rise to the need for an ethical screen. If applicable, the ethical screen is promptly implemented.

SECTION [10] *IV.* PROCEDURES FOR PROCESSING CASES

[11] A. Filing

All documents are filed with the clerk's office, which processes the documents, identifies formatting defects in the documents, communicates with counsel, and distributes the filed documents to the appropriate court employees.

The court has implemented mandatory electronic filing. The California Rules of Court, rules 8.70–8.79, require all filings to be made through the court's electronic filing system, unless an exemption applies.

Prior to the completion of briefing and assignment of a case to a designated Justice's chambers, filings that request a ruling are distributed to the managing attorney and central staff. Once a matter is assigned to a designated justice and panel for decision, additional filings are routed to chambers.

B. Screening of New Cases

All notices of appeal and civil case information statements are reviewed promptly by central staff. This initial review is designed to identify facially apparent concerns regarding appealability or the timeliness of the notice of appeal. In appropriate cases, the court will consider on its own motion whether to dismiss appeals in full or in part. In such instances, the parties will be provided an opportunity to file letter briefs or other responses to concerns identified by the court. A failure to oppose a motion may be deemed a consent to the granting of the motion. (Cal. Rules of Court, rule 8.54(c).) The parties should not consider this preliminary review to be conclusive when it does not result in dismissal, but should address any appealability and timeliness concerns by way of motions or in their briefs.

C. Motions and Applications

1. With the exception of motions filed prior to appellant's opening brief in criminal appeals and juvenile appeals, the court's general practice is to hold motions on appeals (Cal. Rules of Court, rule 8.54) in the clerk's office until (1) an opposition has been served and filed, or (2) the time has passed to serve and file an opposition, whichever is earlier. To expedite the processing of an unopposed motion, the moving party should file a stipulation of non-opposition from the other party or parties.

2. Motions in writ proceedings are immediately transmitted to central staff and are not necessarily held for opposition, depending on the circumstances.

3. Following the dismissal of an appeal for a procedural default, parties are encouraged to file motions to vacate the dismissal and to reinstate the appeal as early as possible. This court loses jurisdiction to vacate dismissal and reinstate the appeal 30 days after the appeal is dismissed. (Cal. Rules of Court, rule 8.264(b)(1).) However, if a motion to vacate dismissal and reinstate the appeal is filed near the jurisdictional deadline, the motion will not be held for opposition as there would be insufficient time to rule prior to losing jurisdiction. Parties opposing reinstatement of the appeal should immediately contact the clerk's office, communicate their intent to file opposition, and file opposition promptly thereafter if they intend to oppose such a motion.

4. Applications (Cal. Rules of Court, rule 8.50), including applications for extensions of time (Cal. Rules of Court, rule 8.60), generally are not held by the clerk's office for opposition to be filed. Parties intending to file opposition to an application should immediately notify the clerk's office, communicate their intent to oppose the application, and promptly file opposition thereafter.

5. Consistent with the presiding justice's duty to maximize the use of judicial resources and increase the efficiency of court operations (Cal. Rules of Court, rule 10.603(a)), rulings on motions are often deferred to be decided in conjunction with the decision on appeal. Examples include but are not limited to: (a) motions to dismiss the appeal that appear to require the expenditure of court resources similar to the determination of the merits of the appeal itself; (b) requests for judicial notice that appear to require a full understanding of the record or issues in dispute in order to rule on the request; and (c) motions filed after briefing is substantially underway.

D. Original Proceedings, etc.

1. The presiding justice assigns on a quarterly basis three justices to serve as the court's primary "writ panel" for a three-month period. Alternates are also assigned to cover absences and conflicts. Furthermore, consistent with the presiding justice's responsibility to ensure fair and expeditious resolution of disputes (Cal. Rules of Court, rule 10.603(a)), "prior panels" are often utilized when a pending petition or motion is related to a prior appeal or petition handled by that panel.

2. In addition to original proceedings, the writ panel also rules on supersedeas petitions, transfer petitions, petitions for interlocutory appeals, and motions requiring rulings by a three-justice panel prior to the final decision in an appeal.

3. The clerk's office notifies central staff when a matter requiring their attention is filed. Central staff determines the urgency of the relief sought. The matter is calendared for a weekly writ panel conference if court action is not required immediately. Impromptu writ conferences are held when court action is required earlier. Either way, central staff attorneys prepare written summaries, which are provided to the writ panel members. Under the supervision and by order of the presiding justice, informal briefing may be solicited from the parties prior to the submission of the matter to the writ panel for a decision.

4. If the writ panel decides to issue an order to show cause, alternative writ, or writ of review, the matter typically is assigned to a single justice on the writ panel as tentative author. The matter is thereafter treated similarly to an appeal as described below. Other matters, such as peremptory writs in the first instance and dismissals of appeals, may be resolved by per curiam opinions or orders, with the assistance of central staff.

E. Appeals – Oral Argument and Decision

1. When the respondent's brief is filed (or the time expires for the filing of a respondent's brief), the clerk's office sends out a notice to the parties who have appeared to give them an opportunity to request oral argument. (Cal. Rules of Court, rules 8.220(a), 8.256(c).) Each side is allowed up to 15 minutes for oral argument. Where there are more than two parties, a side consists of all parties whose interests are not adverse. If there are more than two parties represented by separate counsel who request oral argument, or if counsel for amicus curiae requests oral argument, the court may apportion or expand the time according to the respective interests of the parties and of amicus curiae. Any request for additional time for oral argument must be made by written application submitted to the court within 10 calendar days of the date of the order setting oral argument. The application must be served contemporaneously on all other parties

and must specify the amount of time requested and the issues to which additional oral argument will be addressed. When an application is granted, the time allotted to the other side or sides will be similarly enlarged.

2. Cases are generally scheduled for oral argument once briefing is completed and in order of the requests for argument. Statutory priorities are enforced, and parties claiming calendar preference must promptly serve and file a motion for preference. (Cal. Rules of Court, rule 8.240.) Non-oral argument cases are similarly assigned once briefing is completed and in order based on the date oral argument is waived. Panels, including a justice tentatively designated to author the opinion, are generally assigned on a random rotating basis, subject to the presiding justice's responsibility to ensure fair and expeditious resolution of disputes, and to promote access to justice for all members of the public. (Cal. Rules of Court, rule 10.603(a).).

3. A confidential written summary is prepared by the authoring justice and provided to each panel member prior to oral argument. The panel usually conferences on a case before argument occurs and sometimes after argument is completed. Thereafter, a proposed final opinion circulates among the panel members for comments and/or approval. Proposed opinions for cases in which oral argument has been waived generally circulate among panel members without a formal conference. All cases may routinely be discussed among the justices and staff members informally on an as-needed basis.

4. A monthly oral argument calendar is planned and announced a month ahead of time. Oral argument dates are typically scheduled for the third full week of each month.

5. All requests for continuances of oral argument must be in writing and contain a particularized showing of compelling circumstances. The written request must inform the court of opposing counsel's position regarding any continuance. No request will be forwarded to the presiding justice until the court is made aware of opposing counsel's position. Counsel's stipulation to continue oral argument is not sufficient in the absence of a showing of compelling cause. Oral argument continuance requests are particularly disfavored if they are filed fewer than 15 days prior to the scheduled date of argument.

6. The court conducts in-person oral argument in all cases in which argument has been requested and the presiding justice will grant permission to appear remotely only in extraordinary cases. A party requesting a remote appearance must file the request and a supporting declaration promptly. Remote appearance requests are particularly disfavored if they are filed fewer than 15 days prior to the scheduled date of argument.

7. Any post-briefing citation of additional authorities must be made by letter to the court, without further legal argument, and served upon opposing counsel. (Cal Rules of Court, rule 8.254.) The court retains discretion to strike or disregard untimely citations of authority as they deprive the court and opposing counsel of sufficient opportunity to prepare for oral argument.

[12]

SECTION V. *SETTLEMENT* [13]

A. Notice of Settlements.

The settling appellants shall immediately serve and file notices of settlement of any pending civil appeal, and telephone the court if the case has been calendared for oral argument. (See Cal. Rules of Court, rule 8.244(a) for other requirements concerning notice of settlements.) [14]

B. Stipulated Requests for Dismissal.

Counsel should promptly serve and file stipulated requests for dismissal [15]. The stipulation should specify the allocation of costs on appeal and whether the remittitur is to issue immediately. (Cal. Rules of Court, rules 8.244(c), **8.272(c)(1), 8.278**.)

C. Stipulated Requests for Reversal. (Code Civ. Proc., §128, subd. (a)(8).)

Stipulated requests for a reversal of the judgment ordinarily are heard by the writ panel [16] unless the appeal already has been assigned to a panel for decision.

1. GOOD CAUSE. The parties must provide a sufficient showing to satisfy the statutory criteria in Code of Civil Procedure section 128, subdivision (a)(8). A copy of the judgment shall accompany the motion.

2. JOINT DECLARATION. The motion shall include a joint declaration of counsel that (1) describes the parties and the factual and legal issues presented at trial; (2) indicates whether the judgment involves important public rights or unfair, illegal or corrupt practices, or torts affecting a significant number of persons, or otherwise affects the public or a significant number of persons not parties to the litigation (if the judgment is against a state licensee, the declaration must also disclose whether it exposes such person to any possible disciplinary proceeding); (3) discloses whether the judgment sought to be reversed may have collateral estoppel or other effects in potential future litigation and, if so, whether any third parties who might be prejudiced by stipulated reversal of the judgment have received notice of the motion; and (4) discloses whether the judgment involves discretionary determinations by the trial court that cannot be reversed by stipulation of the parties alone without independent appellate review. [17]

3. NOTICE TO PARTY. The joint declaration shall include a certification that a copy of the stipulation and joint declaration has been delivered to the [18] **parties**. The certification need not include the address of the [19] **parties** notified. In a class action, the copy required need be delivered to only one represented party.

D. Settlement Conferences

Although the court discontinued its formal Judicial Settlement Program (pursuant to Misc. Order 2011-04, entered July 11, 2011), the presiding justice retains discretion to facilitate ad hoc settlement conferences in appropriate cases.

(Amended Apr. 14, 2004; Mar. 1, 2005; Jan. 1, 2007; Jan. 1, 2008; June 4, 2024.)

IOPPs. 2024 Deletes. [1] the general [2] and rules of court [3] assigns [4] justice's [5] requests, [6] , [7] Many of the justices also utilize law student externs who may receive academic credit, without pay, while working at the court. [8] administrator [9] VI. [10] III. [11] A. Appeals.

1. When an appeal is fully briefed, the clerk's office sends out a notice to the parties who have appeared to give them an opportunity to request oral argument. (Cal. Rules of Court, rule 8.220(a).) Cases are generally scheduled for oral argument in order of the requests. Statutory priorities are enforced, and parties claiming calendar preference must promptly serve and file a motion for preference. (Cal. Rules of Court, rule 8.240.) Non-oral argument cases are similarly assigned in order based on the date oral argument is waived. Panels, including a justice tentatively designated to author the opinion, are generally assigned on a random rotating basis, subject to the presiding justice's responsibility to ensure that the court's resources are allocated in an effective and efficient manner to fairly and expeditiously resolve disputes, and to promote access to justice for all members of the public. (Cal. Rules of Court, rule 10.603(a).).

2. A confidential written summary is prepared by the authoring justice and provided to each panel member prior to oral argument. The panel may conference on a case before argument and always conferences after oral argument is completed. Thereafter, a proposed final opinion circulates among the panel members for comments and/or approval. Proposed opinions for cases in which oral argument has been waived generally circulate among panel members without a formal conference. All cases may routinely be discussed among the justices and staff members informally on an as-needed basis.

3. All requests for continuances of oral argument must be in writing and contain a particularized showing of compelling circumstances. The written request must inform the court of opposing counsel's position regarding any continuance. No request will be forwarded to the presiding justice until the court is made aware of opposing counsel's position. Counsel's stipulation to continue oral argument is not sufficient in the absence of a showing of compelling cause.

4. Any post-briefing citation of additional authorities must be made by letter to the court, without further legal argument, and served upon opposing counsel. The court retains discretion to strike or disregard late-filed or untimely citations of authority as they deprive the court and opposing counsel of sufficient opportunity to prepare for oral argument.

5. The court offers remote video appearances for oral argument on criminal matters, allowing counsel to appear via video from Division One in San Diego.

B. Original Proceedings.

1. The presiding justice assigns on a quarterly basis three justices to serve as the court's writ panel for a three-month period. The writ panel members also rule on motions requiring a three-judge panel.

2. The clerk's office notifies the managing appellate court attorney when an original proceeding is filed. The managing appellate court attorney determines the urgency of the relief sought. The matter is calendared for the weekly writ panel conference if court action is not required before then. Impromptu writ conferences are held when court action is required earlier. The managing appellate court

attorney and central staff attorneys prepare written summaries of original proceedings which are provided to the writ panel members before their weekly conference.

C. Motions.

1. The court's practice is to hold motions on appeals (Cal. Rules of Court, rule 8.54) in the clerk's office until (1) an opposition has been served and filed, or (2) the time has passed to serve and file an opposition, whichever is earlier. To expedite the processing of an unopposed motion, the moving party should file a stipulation of nonopposition from other counsel.

2. Motions in writ proceedings are not generally held for opposition absent a request by the parties.

D. Filings by Facsimile, E-mail or Other Electronic Means

The court does not accept filings by facsimile, e-mail or other electronic means unless specifically authorized by court order or court rule. Local Rule 5 provides for a voluntary fax filing pilot project throughout the Fourth Appellate District for specified documents, but not briefs. [12] SECTION IV. JUDICIAL SETTLEMENT PROGRAM

A. Purpose and Structure.

1. The court has established a judicial settlement program to mediate appellate disputes, and, where appropriate, to establish briefing schedules, to simplify appellate issues, and to address procedural concerns. The court encourages appellate mediations and settlement conferences, and will make its resources available to parties who attempt in good faith to resolve a dispute on appeal.

2. The judicial settlement program is directed by the presiding justice, who appoints a supervising judicial attorney to administer the program and to conduct settlement conferences. In addition, a senior clerk schedules the settlement conferences and provides an interface between the public and the court.

B. Filings.

All papers pertaining to the judicial settlement program should be filed with the clerk's office at the courthouse, located at 925 No. Spurgeon Street, or mailed to the court at the following address:

California Court of Appeal
Fourth Appellate District, Division Three
P.O. Box 22055
Santa Ana, CA 92702
Attn: Judicial Settlement Program

These papers ordinarily are retained separately from the other documents filed on appeal, and, where appropriate, are confidential and for the purposes of the Judicial Settlement Program only.

C. Location and Telephone.

1. The judicial settlement program is physically housed in the Civic Center Professional Plaza, about one-half mile from the Spurgeon Street courthouse. The street address is:

Civic Center Professional Plaza
500 West Santa Ana Blvd., Room 400
Santa Ana, CA 92701

2. The telephone number is (714) 564-3600. The fax number is (714) 567-6060. Callers also may use the court's general telephone number: (714) 558-6777.

D. Settlement Conference Information Forms (SCIF's).

1. The presiding justice may order any pending civil appeal to be scheduled for a settlement conference pursuant to the California Rules of Court, rule 8.248. This decision is based upon the court's review of Settlement Conference Information Forms (SCIF), which are prepared by the parties and filed with the court. Preference is given to any stipulated requests for a settlement conference.

2. Request or stipulation for SCIF orders should be made in writing, directed to the Judicial Settlement Program. Requests may be made in confidence.

E. Settlement Conferences.

1. TIMING. Settlement conferences may be ordered before, during or after briefing. The court generally does not schedule a conference after an appeal has been set for oral argument except for good cause. The court tries to accommodate stipulations for specific day or dates. Parties may ascertain available settlement conference dates by telephoning the settlement conference clerk.

2. SETTLEMENT CONFERENCE OFFICER. The presiding justice appoints the person who conducts the settlement conference. In addition to the supervising attorney who manages the judicial settlement program, the settlement conference officer may be an individual justice, assigned pro tem justice, or other judicial attorney.

3. PERSONAL ATTENDANCE. Unless otherwise specified, all parties and their counsel must attend any settlement conference in person, and must have full settlement authority. Attendance by counsel claiming settlement authority is not sufficient. Any exceptions must be approved in advance by the court.

a. INSTITUTIONAL LITIGANTS. If the party is not an individual, then a party representative with full authority to settle must personally attend all settlement conferences in person, in addition to counsel.

b. INSURANCE. If a party has potential insurance coverage applicable to any of the issues in dispute, a representative of each insurance carrier whose policy may apply also must personally attend all settlement conferences, with full settlement authority.

c. TELEPHONIC APPEARANCES. The court prefers in-person settlement conferences and does not ordinarily grant requests for telephonic appearances. Parties who desire to participate by telephone must promptly serve and file a written request at least five court days before any settlement conference explaining why the attendee's personal presence is impossible or impracticable.

4. ADDITIONAL PARTICIPANTS. The court may order other necessary persons (whether or not a party to the appeal) to personally attend settlement conferences. In addition, the conference officer may invite parties to the action who are not parties to the appeal, or any person or entity having interest in the action, to attend. Any party may serve and file a written request for the attendance of such a party or person at least five court days before any settlement conference. No other person may attend a settlement conference without the permission of the conference officer.

5. SETTLEMENT BRIEFS. If a settlement conference is held before appellate briefing or record preparation, the conference officer may direct that the parties provide settlement conference briefs, or other appropriate documents, to facilitate a meaningful and productive settlement conference.

6. PRE-CONFERENCE PREPARATION. Counsel should confer with their clients in advance of any settlement conference and be thoroughly familiar with the case and prepared to present their contentions in detail. Counsel should review their SCIFs for completeness and accuracy and promptly notify the conference officer of any material changes or omissions at least three court days before the settlement conference.

7. LOCATION. Settlement conferences generally are held at the court's settlement conference facilities. (See IVC, above for address.) Settlement conferences also may be held at the Spurgeon Street courthouse. Participants should carefully check the notice of a settlement conference for the correct location.

8. DURATION. Participants should be prepared to remain for the duration of the day, or until dismissed by the conference officer. No person who has been ordered to appear may leave without permission of the conference officer. At the conclusion of a prehearing conference, the conference officer may continue the conference to another date to allow for further discussions.

9. CONTINUANCES. Parties who seek to continue a settlement conference should attempt to do so by stipulation, with a mutually agreeable alternative date. Any request for continuances should be made in writing, with reasons stated, and served and filed at least five court days before the conference. Continuances are not granted, except for good cause.

10. EX PARTE COMMUNICATIONS. The conference officer may communicate with any of the parties or their counsel with or without notice to the other parties or their counsel.

11. CONFIDENTIALITY. All discussions and information imparted during the settlement conference are confidential, and the conference officer cannot testify about them.

F. "Workout" Conferences.

The presiding justice may order that a prehearing "workout" conference be held for any of the following purposes: (1) to simplify issues on appeal, (2) to establish a briefing schedule, (3) to address procedural questions, issues or outstanding motions or applications, (4) to lay the groundwork for a future settlement conference, (5) to facilitate ongoing settlement discussions, (6) to monitor the progress of a pending settlement or private mediation, or (7) for any other reason or reasons. Unlike settlement conferences, workout conferences are conducted either in person or by telephone. Generally, only counsel, not clients, participate in "workout" conferences.

G. Private Mediations.

The presiding justice entertains stipulated requests to stay of appellate proceedings to allow private mediations. Stay requests shall not exceed 60 days except for good cause. Any such stipulated request shall specify the identity of the mediator, the scheduled day or dates for mediation, and any other pertinent factors.

H. Stays; Tolling.

Appeals are not automatically stayed merely because parties are ordered to prepare a SCIF, or to choose dates for a settlement conference. The tolling provisions for briefs (Cal. Rules of Court, rule 8.248(d)) commence to run only when the court mails notice of a settlement conference for a specific date and time. Record preparation is not automatically stayed without a court order. The court's policy is to conduct settlement conferences as expeditiously as possible, and to issue a rule 8.248(d) notice lifting any stay or tolling order within 90 days from the date of the notice of the settlement conference.

I. Disqualification.

Disqualification of justices is governed by the Canon 3E of the California Code of Judicial Ethics. Justices are not disqualified to hear appeals merely because they rule on settlement conference requests or sign orders pertaining to procedural aspects of the settlement conference process. If appeals do not settle, neither the conference officer nor any other court personnel present at a conference will participate further in the determination of the appeal on the merits. (Cal. Rules of Court, rule 8.248(c)(2).)

J. Sanctions.

The judicial settlement program shall not be employed by any party in bad faith or for purposes of delay. The court may impose sanctions for (1) failure to appear at a prehearing (settlement) conference, (2) failure to participate in good faith in the judicial settlement program, or to cooperate in good faith with the conference officer, or (3) failure to comply with a court order or court rule. Sanctions may include monetary awards, or, in the case of an appellant's failure to comply, dismissal of the appeal. [13] NOTICES & STIPULATIONS [14] Settling appellants also should e-mail or telephone the settlement conference clerk if the appeal has been placed in the judicial settlement program. **[15]** because of settlements **[16]**, **[17]** (see, e.g., *Garabedian v. Los Angeles Cellular Telephone Co.* (2004) 118 Cal.App.4th 123; *Stewart v. Stewart* (1955) 130 Cal.App.2d 186, 193.) **[18]** client **[19]** party

FIFTH APPELLATE DISTRICT LOCAL RULES

[As amended effective September 27, 2021; adopted, effective July 1, 1981; and previously amended February 25, 1983, February 8, 1985, October 2, 1992, November 15, 1993, June 25, 1999, August 25, 2003, January 1, 2007, August 17, 2007, September 1, 2011, February 10, 2012, November 1, 2012, December 1, 2014, May 11, 2015, February 19, 2016, August 1, 2016, and June 5, 2017.]

Augmentation of record and correction of omissions from record. Rule 1.
Mediation program for civil appeals. Rule 2.
Writ petitions: supporting records and stay requests. Rule 3.
Telephonic oral argument. Rule 4.
Record preparation in juvenile appeals and writs. Rule 7.
Electronic filing. Rule 8.
Appellate Court Writ Petition Information Sheet. Local court form.
Internal Operating Practices and Procedures.

Order Regarding Penal Code section 4019 Amendment Supplemental Briefing

February 11, 2010

In pending appeals in which an appellant arguably is entitled to additional presentence custody credits under the January 25, 2010 amendments to Penal Code section 4019, the court will deem the following issues raised without additional briefing:

(1) Under amended Penal Code section 4019, appellant is entitled to recalculation of presentence work and custody credits;

(2) To hold otherwise would violate equal protection principles.

This order applies to all appeals. If the court deems supplemental briefing necessary from either the appellant or the respondent, it will request a letter brief from counsel.

JAMES A. ARDAIZ, P.J.

Order Regarding Supplemental Briefing
February 21, 2007

In cases remanded from the United States Supreme Court for further consideration in light of *Cunningham v. California* (2007) 549 U.S. — [127 S.Ct. 856, 2007 U.S. Lexis 1324]:

(1) Within 30 days after of the order remanding the case to the Court of Appeal for further proceedings, appellant may serve and file a supplemental opening brief in the Court of Appeal. Within 30 days after such a brief is filed, the respondent may serve and file a supplemental responding brief.

(2) Supplemental briefs must be limited to matters arising after the previous Court of Appeal decision in the cause.

JAMES A. ARDAIZ, P.J.

Amended Order Regarding Cunningham Briefing
February 16, 2007

If the appellant has raised an issue challenging the imposition of the upper term, in reliance on *Blakely v. Washington* (2004) 542 U.S. 296 or *Apprendi v. New Jersey* (2000) 530 U.S. 466, it shall be deemed that the appellant is also relying on *Cunningham v. California* (2007) 549 U.S. — [127 S.Ct. 856, 2007 U.S. LEXIS 1324].

If the court deems supplemental briefing necessary from either the appellant or the respondent to address related issues such as forfeiture, waiver, prejudice, etc., it will request a letter brief from counsel. Any request to file supplemental briefing will be considered on a case-by-case basis.

JAMES A. ARDAIZ, P.J.

Rule 1. Augmentation of Record and Correction of Omissions from Record

(a) [Material inadvertently omitted] Counsel should not file a motion to augment the record when items have been omitted from the normal (criminal) record on appeal. In those cases counsel should immediately notify the clerk of the superior court, who shall comply with rule 8.155(b) of the California Rules of Court.

(b) [When to file motion to augment] Appellant should file requests for augmentation in one motion within 40 days of the filing of the record. Respondent should file requests for augmentation in one motion made within 30 days of the filing of appellant's opening brief. Thereafter, motions to augment will not be granted except upon a showing of good cause for the delay.

(c) [Clerk's transcript] A motion to augment or correct the clerk's transcript shall be accompanied either by certified copies of the documents requested, or, if the documents are not provided, the motion must identify them with specificity and contain an explanation for their omission. When submitting an electronic motion to augment or correct the clerk's transcript, a party must electronically submit the documents requested as a separate .pdf file at the same time as the motion and ensure the documents are formatted in compliance with this court's Local Rule 8. When electronically submitting a motion to augment or correct the clerk's transcript, a party may exceed the 300-page limit, contained in California Rules of Court, rules 8.124(d)(1) and 8.144(c)(1), as long as the file size is 25 megabytes or smaller.

(d) [Reporter's transcript] A motion to augment the reporter's transcript shall identify the portion of the record with specificity, including the reporter's name and the date of the hearing. The motion shall establish with some certainty how the requested materials may be useful on appeal.

(e) [Extension of time] The time to perform any act required or permitted by the California Rules of Court will not be automatically extended in civil cases by the filing of or ruling on a motion to augment. If additional time is needed, counsel may request an extension of time in the motion to augment.

(f) [Good faith required] A motion to augment shall be made in good faith and shall not be made for the purpose of delay.

Rule 1 adopted Nov. 15, 1993; renumbered from Rule 2 Aug. 25, 2003; amended Jan. 1, 2007; Aug. 17, 2007; Feb. 19, 2016.

Rule 2. Mediation Program for Civil Appeals

The Court has established a Judicial Mediation Program to assist parties to resolve appellate disputes in civil cases the Court finds suitable.

(a) Rule application: This rule applies to all civil appeals except those under Welfare and Institutions Code sections 300, 601, and 602 and Family Code section 7802, appeals in conservatorship and guardianship matters, and appeals from original proceedings ancillary to a criminal prosecution.

(Subd (a) adopted effective Sept. 1, 2011.)

(b) Questionnaire: When a notice of appeal is filed in any civil case to which this rule applies, the Clerk will promptly mail or e-mail to appellant and respondent instructions for the filing of the non-confidential Civil Appeal Case Screening Questionnaire. [Downloadable form available on the Court's website http://www.courts.ca.gov/5dca.htm.] Within 10 calendar days after the Clerk mails or e-mails instructions regarding the Civil Appeal Case Screening Questionnaire, each party must complete, sign, and serve the Questionnaire, and file it electronically.

The Questionnaire will assist the Court in selecting a case for mediation with a sitting Justice of this Court. The Court will select a case promptly after the Questionnaire is submitted and before the parties have incurred the expense of record preparation and appellate briefing. The Court recognizes the parties are asked to prepare the Questionnaire very early in the appellate process and may not be able to identify all appellate contentions. The Court will not deem an omission to be a waiver or forfeiture of any claim on appeal.

Failure to return the Questionnaire timely on appellant's part may result in dismissal of the appeal, without prejudice to reinstatement on a showing of good cause, or in imposition of monetary sanctions pursuant to subdivision (e).

Failure to return the Questionnaire timely on respondent's part may result in the appeal being considered for mediation suitability without input from respondent, or in imposition of monetary sanctions pursuant to subdivision (e).

(Subd (b) amended effective Feb. 19, 2016; adopted effective Sept. 1, 2011; previously amended Feb. 10, 2012.)

(c) Mediation/Settlement Process:

(1) Effective upon the filing of any civil notice of appeal to which the rule applies, the provisions of rules 8.121, 8.124 and 8.216 of the California Rules of Court requiring designation of the record, payment of estimated costs for preparation of the record, and submission of a proposed briefing schedule are suspended, pending the Court's decision to select or not select the civil appeal for mediation.

These rules do not prohibit the superior court from collecting the deposit required by Government Code section 68926.1 and by California Rules of Court, rule 8.100(b)(2).

(2) Within 14 calendar days after the Court receives the Civil Appeal Case Screening Questionnaires, it will notify the parties in writing, by telephone, or by e-mail whether the Court has or has not selected the civil appeal for mediation. If a civil appeal is selected for mediation, the Court's Mediation Coordinator will provide the parties with three dates on which the Justice is available for the mediation session. At the same time, the Court will furnish the Justice mediator with copies of the Civil Appeal Case Screening Questionnaires. Within 14 calendar days after receipt of the dates the Justice mediator is available, the parties must advise the Court's Mediation Coordinator of their scheduling preferences. The Justice mediator will promptly select the date for the mediation session and the Mediation Coordinator will notify the parties by e-mail.

If a civil appeal is selected for mediation, suspension of rules 8.121, 8.124, and 8.216 of the California Rules of Court will remain in effect until the mediation process is complete.

If a civil appeal is not selected for mediation, the Court will notify the parties and the superior court, in writing, that the suspension of rules 8.121, 8.124, and 8.216 of the California Rules of Court is terminated. The parties must comply with the requirements of rules 8.121, 8.124, and 8.216 as if the notice of appeal had been filed on the date specified in the Court's notice.

If a civil appeal is not selected for mediation, the parties may thereafter electronically file a stipulation for entry into the mediation program. The Court will promptly decide whether or not to accept the case into the mediation program and the Mediation Coordinator will notify the parties of the Court's decision.

(3) The Justice mediator may, for good cause, continue a mediation session to a date certain. The Justice may also continue the mediation from time-to-time to allow further opportunity for negotiation and agreement.

(4) The parties shall submit in writing, directly to the Justice mediator, a CONFIDENTIAL Mediation Statement at least seven (7) calendar days before the scheduled mediation. The statement shall provide:

(A) The names of parties and their attorneys.

(B) A statement regarding the existence of any applicable insurance, and, if so, the identity of the carrier, the amount of the applicable insurance policy limits, and the nature of any insurance coverage disputes/issues.

(C) A statement indicating whether or not a board, council or other committee must approve any settlement, and, if so, the identity of that body.

(D) The identification of any person not named as a party whose consent is necessary to achieve settlement.

(E) The dates and results of prior arbitration, mediation, and most recent settlement discussions.

(F) The dates and amounts of any Code of Civil Procedure section 998 offers.

(G) A statement identifying and discussing in detail all facts and law pertinent to the issues of liability and damages involved in the case as to that party.

(H) An itemization of all economic and noneconomic damages claimed by the plaintiff.

(I) A description of any liens and their amounts.

(J) A statement whether there is any claim for recovery of attorney's fees, and, if so, the amount incurred to date.

(K) A statement of any additional information that might assist the Justice mediator.

(5) All parties and their counsel of record must attend all mediation sessions in person and with full settlement authority. If a party is not an individual, then a party representative with full authority to settle all appeals and cross-appeals must attend all mediation sessions in person, in addition to counsel. If a party has potential insurance coverage applicable to any of the issues in dispute, a representative of each insurance carrier whose policy may apply also must attend all mediation sessions in person, with full settlement authority. Any exception to this requirement must be approved in writing by the Justice mediator. The Justice mediator may invite participation by any additional person or entity if the mediator concludes that such participation would facilitate mediation.

(6) If completion of mediation does not result in disposition of the appeal, the Court will immediately notify the parties and the superior court in writing or e-mail that suspension of rules 8.121, 8.124, and 8.216 of the California Rules of Court is terminated. The parties must comply with the requirements of rules 8.121, 8.124, and 8.216 as if the notice of appeal had been filed on the date specified in the Court's notice.

(Subd (c) amended effective Feb. 19, 2016; adopted effective Sept. 1, 2011; previously amended effective Feb. 10, 2012.)

(d) Confidentiality: Except as otherwise required by law, information disclosed to the Justice mediator, the parties, counsel, or any other participant in the mediation, or in the Mediation Statement, is confidential and must not be disclosed to anyone not participating in the program. The parties are required to sign a confidentiality agreement in a form designated by the Court.

(Subd (d) adopted effective Sept. 1, 2011.)

(e) Sanctions: Monetary sanctions may be imposed following an electronically filed noticed motion by a party seeking sanctions for failure to comply with the rules or on the Court's own motion. Any date selected for a motion for sanctions must be cleared in advance with the Court's Mediation Coordinator at 5DC_Mediation@jud.ca.gov.

(Subd (e) amended effective Feb. 19, 2016; adopted effective Sept. 1, 2011.)

(f) Disqualification of Justice Mediator: Any Justice who participates in a mediation shall not thereafter participate in the consideration or disposition of the appeal on its merits.

(Subd (f) amended effective Feb. 19, 2016; adopted effective Sept. 1, 2011.)
Rule 2 amended effective Feb. 19, 2016; adopted effective Sept. 1, 2011; former rule 2, Settlement Conferences in Civil Appeals, repealed effective Sept. 1, 2011; previously amended effective Feb. 10, 2012.

Rule 3. Writ Petitions: Supporting Records and Stay Requests

(a) [Information Sheet] All petitions for extraordinary writs, other than habeas corpus, shall be accompanied by a properly completed face sheet, the *Appellate Court Writ Petition Information Sheet*. This form is available through TrueFiling on the Court's website and from the clerk of the court.

(Subd (a) amended effective Aug. 1, 2016; previously amended Nov. 1, 2012 and May 11, 2015.)

(b) [Required Exhibits] A petition for an extraordinary writ that seeks review of a trial court ruling shall be accompanied by the following:

(1) a copy of the order or judgment from which relief is sought;

(2) copies of all documents submitted to the trial court supporting and opposing petitioner's position; and

(3) a transcript of the proceedings leading to the order or judgment below, or if a transcript is unnecessary or unavailable, a declaration by counsel (i) explaining why a transcript is unnecessary or unavailable and (ii) fairly summarizing the proceedings, including arguments by counsel and the basis of the trial court's decision, if stated.

(Subd (b) amended effective Nov. 1, 2012.)

(c) [Copies of Filed Documents] A party who electronically files any petition, answer, opposition, reply, or other response to a petition, including any supporting documents, according to the requirements of Local Rule 8, is exempt from submitting copies of such documents. A self-represented party may electronically file such documents according to the requirements of Local Rule 8, but is not required to do so.

Otherwise and in lieu of the requirements contained in California Rules of Court, rule 8.44(b)(3) and (5), a party who files a petition, answer, opposition, reply, or other response to a petition, including any supporting documents, in paper form shall file an original and one paper copy that is unbound, printed on white paper and does not contain tabs or a red cover.

A self-represented person who files a petition for writ of habeas corpus is only required to file the original petition.

(Subd (c) amended effective Aug. 1, 2016; adopted effective Nov. 1, 2012; previously amended May 11, 2015.)

(d) [Stay Request] A petitioner who requests an immediate stay shall explain in the petition the reasons for the urgency and set forth all relevant time constraints. If a petitioner does not submit the required record and explanations or does not present facts sufficient to excuse the failure to submit them, the Court may summarily deny the stay request.

(Subd (d) amended effective Aug. 1, 2016; previously amended Nov. 1, 2012.)
Rule 3 adopted Nov. 15, 1993; amended and renumbered from Rule 5 Aug. 25, 2003; amended effective Nov. 1, 2012; May 11, 2015; Aug. 1, 2016.

Rule 4. Telephonic Oral Argument

Telephonic oral argument is available to all parties.

Telephonic Oral Argument Procedures

1. A party who requests oral argument must return to the court a questionnaire designating the time requested. The questionnaire must

designate the attorney arguing the case, if the party is represented by counsel, or the name(s) of the litigant(s) who will appear if the party is self-represented.

2. The process for appearing telephonically for oral argument is described on the court's website.

3. A party, if self-represented, or a party's designated counsel is expected to be available during the time oral argument has been scheduled and until such time as it has been completed.

Failure to be available to participate in telephonic oral argument, once requested, will be treated in the same manner as a failure to personally appear for scheduled oral argument.

4. Parties are encouraged to use a landline telephone for telephonic oral argument because landlines typically facilitate better two-way communication. If a party must use a cellular phone, pausing occasionally during the argument is critical to allow the Justices to ask questions.

5. Any deviation by appointed or retained counsel from these procedures shall not be permitted except by express prior approval of the court.
Rule 4 adopted Nov. 15, 1993; renumbered from Rule 6 Aug. 25, 2003; amended Aug. 17, 2007; June 5, 2017.

Rule 5. Writ Petitions: Supporting Records and Stay Requests [Renumbered]
Rule 5 adopted Nov. 15, 1993; renumbered to Rule 3 Aug. 25, 2003.

Rule 5. Stipulation for Use of Original Superior Court File [Repealed]
Rule 5 adopted Oct. 16, 2006; repealed Aug. 1, 2016.

Rule 6. The Teleconference Oral Argument Option [Renumbered]
Rule 6 adopted Nov. 15, 1993; renumbered to Rule 4 Aug. 25, 2003.

Rule 7. Record Preparation in Juvenile Appeals and Writs

(a) [Application]

This rule applies to record preparation in:

(1) Appeals from judgments or appealable orders in:

(A) Cases under Welfare and Institutions Code sections 300, 601, and 602; and

(B) Actions to free a child from parental custody and control under Family Code section 7800 et seq.; and

(2) Writ petitions under Welfare and Institutions Code sections 366.26 and 366.28.

(Subd (a) adopted effective Dec. 1, 2014.)

(b) [Sending the Record]

Within 20 days after a notice of appeal or notice of intent is filed, the clerk of the superior court shall send, by the most expeditious method, the original record to this court, noting the sending date on each original.

In appeals, copies of the record shall be sent at the same time to counsel pursuant to California Rules of Court, rules 8.409(e)(1)(B), (e)(2) and 8.416(c)(2)(B), (c)(3), as applicable.

In writ proceedings under Welfare and Institutions Code sections 366.26 and 366.28, copies of the record shall be sent at the same time to counsel or any unrepresented party pursuant to California Rules of Court, rules 8.450(i)(2) and 8.454(i)(2), as applicable.

(Subd (b) adopted effective Dec. 1, 2014.)

(c) [Enforcement]

In the event this court does not receive the original record within 23 calendar days after a notice of appeal or notice of intent is filed, this court shall issue an order directed to the superior court executive officer to deliver the original transcripts to this court within 2 court days. If the superior court executive officer does not comply with this court's order, an order to show cause may issue.

(Subd (c) adopted effective Dec. 1, 2014.)
Rule 7 adopted Dec. 1, 2014.

Rule 8. Electronic Filing

Pursuant to California Rules of Court, rule 8.71, the Court will require all filings in this District be made through the Court's electronic filing system (EFS) operated by ImageSoft TrueFiling (TrueFiling). Use of the EFS system is mandatory for all attorneys filing in this District, unless an exemption is granted, and is voluntary for all self-represented litigants. A filing in electronic format will be accepted in lieu of any paper copies otherwise required under California Rules of Court, rule 8.44 and constitutes the official record of the Court.

(a) [Registration]

(1) Obligation to Register. Each attorney of record in any proceeding in this District is obligated to become an EFS user and obtain a user ID and password for access to the TrueFiling system. Self-represented litigants must register if they wish to e-file. Attorneys and self-represented litigants may register at: https://tf3.truefiling.com/register

(2) Obligation to Keep Account Information Current. An EFS user is responsible for all documents filed under the user's registered ID and password. Registered users are required to keep their e-mail address current and may update their e-mail address online via the TrueFiling Web site. The user also must comply with the requirements of California Rules of Court, rule 8.32.

(Subd (a) amended effective September 27, 2021; adopted effective Dec. 1, 2014; previously amended effective May 11, 2015.)

(b) [Format]

Documents filed electronically must be in PDF format, or readily capable of conversion to PDF format while maintaining original document formatting by TrueFiling to permit text searches and to facilitate transmission and retrieval. If the filer possesses only a paper copy of a document, it may be scanned to convert it to a searchable PDF format. It is the filer's responsibility to ensure that any document filed is complete and readable. No single document shall exceed a total file size of 25 MB. Document pages must be consecutively numbered beginning from the cover page of the document and using only the Arabic numbering system, as in 1, 2, 3.

Briefs must comply with the content and format requirements of California Rules of Court, rule 8.204, with the exception of those provisions dealing exclusively with requirements for paper. The table of contents for each brief shall include electronic bookmarks to each heading in the text. All original proceedings must include electronic bookmarks from the table of contents for each hearing in the text, and to the first page of any exhibit(s), with a description of the exhibit included in the bookmark.

(Subd (b) amended effective September 27, 2021; adopted effective Dec. 1, 2014; previously amended effective May 11, 2015.)

(c) [Signatures]

A TrueFiling user ID and password is the equivalent of an electronic signature for a registered attorney or party. Any document displaying the symbol "/s/" with the attorney's or party's printed name shall be deemed signed by that attorney/party.

(Subd (c) adopted effective Dec. 1, 2014.)

(d) [Trial Court Record]

(1) Appendices, Agreed Statements, and Settled Statements. Parties must submit any appendix filed pursuant to California Rules of Court, rule 8.124, any agreed statement filed pursuant to California Rules of Court, rule 8.134, or any settled statement filed pursuant to California Rules of Court, rule 8.137 in electronic form. Each part of the record submitted in any appendix shall clearly state the volume and page numbers included within that part and include an index of contents, with a descriptive electronic bookmark to the first page of each indexed document.

(2) Administrative Records. In addition to any administrative record provided by the trial court pursuant to California Rules of Court, rule 8.123, the party or parties seeking review of a board case under California Rules of Court, rule 8.728(b) must submit a copy of the administrative record in electronic form.

(3) Reporter's Transcripts. Any party who orders a reporter's transcript of proceedings pursuant to California Rules of Court, rule 8.130 must also request a copy of the transcript in computer-readable format, as provided in California Rules of Court, rule 8.144(d)(1), and submit an electronic copy to the Court.

(Subd (d) amended effective September 27, 2021; adopted effective Dec. 1, 2014; previously amended effective May 11, 2015.)

(e) [Personal Identifiers and Privacy Issues]

To protect personal privacy, parties and their attorneys must not include, or must redact where inclusion is necessary, personal identifiers such as social security numbers and financial account numbers from all pleadings and other papers filed in the Court's public file, whether filed in paper or electronic form, unless otherwise provided by law or ordered by the Court. (Cal. Rules of Court, rule 1.201(a).) If an individual's social security number is required in a pleading or other paper filed in the public file, only the last four digits of that number shall be used. If financial account numbers are required in a pleading or other paper filed in the public file, only the last four digits of these numbers shall be used.

The responsibility for excluding or redacting identifiers from all documents filed with the Court rests solely with the parties and their attorneys. (Cal. Rules of Court, rule 1.201(b).) Neither TrueFiling nor the Clerk of the Court has any responsibility to review pleadings or other papers for compliance.

(Subd (e) amended effective September 27, 2021; adopted effective Dec. 1, 2014; previously amended effective May 11, 2015.)

(f) [Sealed or Confidential Material]

All filers must comply with California Rules of Court, rules 8.46 and 8.47 pertaining to sealed and confidential material.

(Subd (f) adopted effective May 11, 2015.)

(g) [Filing Deadlines]

Filing documents electronically does not alter any filing deadlines. In order to be timely filed on the day they are due, all electronic transmissions of documents must be completed (i.e., received completely by the Clerk of the Court) prior to midnight. Where a specific time of day is set for filing by Court order or stipulation, the electronic filing shall be completed by that time. Although EFS permits parties to submit documents electronically 24 hours a day, users should be aware that telephone or online EFS assistance may not be available outside of normal Court business hours.

(Subd (g) repealed, amended and relettered from subd (f) effective May 11, 2015; adopted effective Dec. 1, 2014.)

(h) [Technical Failure/Motions for Late Filing]

If a filer fails to meet a filing deadline imposed by Court order, rule, or statute because of a failure at any point in the electronic transmission and receipt of a document, the filer may file the document as soon thereafter as practicable and accompany the filing with a motion to accept the document as timely filed. (See Cal. Rules of Court, rule 8.77(d).)

The Clerk of the Court shall deem the EFS system to be subject to a technical failure whenever the system is unable to accept filings continuously or intermittently over the course of any period of time greater than one hour after 12:00 noon that day. Filings due on the day of a technical failure which were not filed solely due to such technical failure shall be due the next court day. The initial point of contact for any practitioner experiencing difficulty filing a document into the EFS system shall be the toll-free number posted on the TrueFiling Web site.

The Court shall not be responsible for malfunction or errors occurring in electronic transmission or receipt of electronically filed documents.

(Subd (h) amended effective September 27, 2021; adopted effective Dec. 1, 2014; previously amended effective May 11, 2015.)

(i) [Service]

An attorney's registration with TrueFiling to participate in EFS constitutes consent to service or delivery of all documents by any other party in a case through the system. (Cal. Rules of Court, rule 8.78(a)(2)(B).)

(Subd (i) amended effective September 27, 2021; adopted effective Dec. 1, 2014; previously repealed, amended and relettered from subd (j) effective May 11, 2015.)

(j) [Filing Fees]

TrueFiling is a private vendor under contract with the Court. TrueFiling will assess vendor fees for each filing in accordance with the schedule posted on its Web site, as approved by the Court. e-Filing fees will be considered recoverable costs under California Rules of Court, rule 8.278(d)(1)(D). TrueFiling is designated as the Court's agent for collection of Court imposed fees where required for any filing, and any associated credit card or bank charges or convenience fees (Cal. Rules of Court, rules 8.73(b), 8.76; Gov. Code, § 6159).

Should a self-represented party with a fee waiver opt to file documents electronically, that party is exempt from the fees and costs associated with electronic filing. The persons and entities identified in Government Code section 6103 also are exempt from the fees and costs associated with e-Filing.

(Subd (j) amended effective September 27, 2021; adopted effective Dec. 1, 2014; previously amended and relettered from subd (k) effective May 11, 2015.)

(k) [Exemptions]

Self-represented parties may, but are not required to, register for electronic filing. If they elect to register, they must comply with this rule and the requirements of TrueFiling.

If electronic filing and/or service causes undue hardship or significant prejudice to any party, the party may file a motion for an exemption from the requirements of this rule. (See Cal. Rules of Court, rule 8.71(d).) When it is not otherwise feasible for a party to convert a document to electronic form by scanning, imaging or other means, the document may be filed in paper form (Cal. Rules of Court, rule 8.71(g)), together with a declaration setting forth the reasons that electronic filing was not feasible.

(Subd (k) amended effective September 27, 2021; adopted effective Dec. 1, 2014; previously amended and relettered from subd (l) effective May 11, 2015.)

(l) [Sanctions for Noncompliance]

Failure of counsel to timely register or otherwise comply with EFS filing requirements, unless exempted, shall subject counsel to sanctions as may be imposed by the Court.

(Subd (l) relettered from subd (m) effective May 11, 2015; adopted effective Dec. 1, 2014.)

Rule 8 amended effective September 27, 2021; adopted Dec. 1, 2014; previously amended effective May 11, 2015.

Local Court Form. Appellate Court Writ Petition Information Sheet

By order dated November 23, 1982, all petitions for extraordinary writs, other than habeas corpus, shall be accompanied by a properly completed face sheet, the *Appellate Court Writ Petition Information Sheet*. This form is available from the clerk of the court, and also is available on the court Web site.

Local Court Form amended Aug. 25, 2003; amended Aug. 17, 2007.

INTERNAL OPERATING PRACTICES AND PROCEDURES
FIFTH APPELLATE DISTRICT

(Adopted August 1993, revised February 2005, January 1, 2007)

I. INTRODUCTION
II. STRUCTURE OF COURT AND ORGANIZATION OF STAFF
III. PRACTICES AFFECTING THE DECISIONAL PROCESS
    A. Regular Appeals
    B. Routine Dispositions
    C. Writs
    D. Motions
    E. Petitions for Rehearing and Applications for Publication
    F. Settlement Conferences in Civil Cases.
IV. TELEPHONIC ORAL ARGUMENT OPTION
V. PRELIMINARY REVIEW OF APPELLANT'S OPENING BRIEF IN CIVIL CASES

I. INTRODUCTION

The purpose of this memorandum is to acquaint the bar and litigants with the general internal operating procedures of this court. It does not duplicate the California Rules of Court nor the statutes that govern the processes of the Courts of Appeal.

II. STRUCTURE OF COURT AND ORGANIZATION OF STAFF

The court is currently authorized ten judges — a presiding justice and nine associate justices.

The court is not divided into divisions and normally operates with three panels. The justices are rotated among the panels each month so that over time each justice will sit an equal number of times with every other justice on the court.

Each justice is authorized two staff attorneys. In addition, the court has a central staff consisting of experienced attorneys who write draft opinions in cases that are screened for routine disposition. The court also employs experienced writ and motion attorneys. The central staff and writ and motion attorneys work under the direction and supervision of the presiding justice.

III. PRACTICES AFFECTING THE DECISIONAL PROCESS

The workload of the court is divided into six principal categories: regular appeals (those not screened for routine disposition treatment); routine disposition appeals; writs; motions; petitions for rehearing and applications for publication; and settlement conferences in civil cases.

A. Regular Appeals.

When the appellant's reply brief has been filed or the time for filing that brief has passed, the case is ready for disposition by written opinion. The cases are placed on the ready list in the order in which they become ready and are set in that order absent a granted motion to advance or a statutory priority. Although the clerk attempts to note those cases that are entitled to statutory priority, counsel is advised to remind the court of any particular case that is entitled to priority.

When placed on the ready list, the managing attorney screens all cases under the supervision of the presiding justice. Those cases subject to routine disposition in accordance with the procedure described below are so designated on the list of ready cases. The balance of the cases are designated as regular appeals.

During the last two weeks of each month the managing attorney under the supervision of the presiding justice prepares a list of the cases to be set on the regular calendar in the third following month. For example, cases to be set in April are selected in the last two weeks of January. In order to equalize the workload among the justices, the managing attorney assigns a weight to all cases according to degree of difficulty. Consistent with the goal of achieving an equal caseload for each justice, and absent a compelling reason to the contrary, the cases are then assigned at random to the individual justices for authorship. The total weight of the cases assigned to each justice is approximately equal. Two other justices from the same panel are assigned to participate in deciding each case. The cases are then calendared for oral argument, and notices of the settings are sent to the attorneys of record. The court does not look with favor upon requests for continuance of the hearing date and will normally refuse to grant a continuance unless a request is received within five days of the time the notice is sent and good cause is shown for the continuance.

If oral argument is requested, counsel may utilize the telephonic oral argument option which is available in this court (Oral argument by telephone option — see Section IV, post.)

When a case is calendared for oral argument, one of the staff attorneys for the justice to whom the case is assigned prepares a memorandum of facts and law in that case. Memoranda in all cases are normally completed during the month following the setting. For example, memoranda for cases calendared for April are completed in February. When completed, the memorandum is distributed to the three justices assigned to decide the case. The authoring justice will normally prepare a proposed opinion in each case to be distributed to the other two justices assigned to that case prior to the pre-argument conference which is held shortly before the date set for oral argument. Each of the justices will have read the briefs, as much of the record as they deem necessary, the case memorandum and the proposed opinion, if any, prior to the pre-argument conference.

Well in advance of oral argument, each case is reviewed by the court to determine if the issues can be narrowed or if the court will accept waiver of oral argument. In the former case, the court may advise counsel by letter of the particular issues upon which the court would like to hear oral argument. In the latter case, the court will advise counsel by letter that it is willing to accept a waiver of oral argument.

As a result of the court's preparation for oral argument, the justices are thoroughly familiar with the facts and issues before oral argument commences. The court normally asks questions of counsel during oral argument in an effort to pinpoint those issues that are particularly troublesome, to clear up any areas of confusion or uncertainty, and to further narrow the issues. Occasionally, supplementary briefing is permitted or requested. Otherwise, cases are submitted for decision at the conclusion of oral argument. (See Cal. Rules of Court, rule 8.256(d).)

After argument, the participating justices hold a post-argument conference. Thereafter, the authoring justice circulates a draft opinion to the other justices on the panel for their concurrence or dissent. In the event a majority of the justices do not eventually concur in the opinion of the justice to whom the case was assigned for authorship, a non-concurring justice prepares the majority opinion.

Discussion as to whether an opinion qualifies for full or partial publication under California Rules of Court, rules 8.1105 or 8.1110, normally occurs at the pre and post-oral argument conferences, though the question remains open until the opinion becomes final.

If oral argument is waived, the case is ordered removed from the calendar and submitted for decision. The opinion may be filed any time thereafter. The decisional process is substantially the same as that outlined above except for the pre-oral argument conference.

B. Routine Dispositions.

A routine disposition is a case on appeal which raises no new or novel questions of law, is not of wide public interest, and can be disposed of by the application of settled principles of law to the facts. The draft opinion is written by an experienced attorney assigned to the central staff or by a justice.

The court is sensitive to the concern that the judicial input into this type of case may be diluted and therefore carefully supervises these cases. First, the presiding justice supervises the initial selection of the case for treatment as a routine disposition. Second, a panel of three justices is selected at random to participate on the case. Third, in each case a lead justice will read the briefs, the record where indicated, and approve or disapprove the draft opinion in writing. If the lead justice approves the draft opinion either as written or with changes, the two other justices must read and approve the opinion in writing. Fourth, if any justice so requests, a conference will be held among the justices and the author of the draft opinion. If, after a conference, any justice is of the opinion the case is inappropriate for routine disposition treatment, its designation as a regular appeal is restored and the case is processed in accordance with the procedure for regular appeals.

Last, when a draft opinion is approved by the justices, counsel are sent a letter indicating the court is willing to accept waiver of oral argument. Counsel are free to request oral argument and, if requested, the case is then placed on the oral argument calendar. Oral argument is requested in only a small percentage of these cases.

Appointed counsel are advised that the court will consider the extent to which requested oral argument was a reasonable consideration by counsel and the extent to which such argument, if presented, adds to or enhances the arguments presented in the briefs in evaluating compensation claimed for preparation time and travel time. If oral argument is requested, counsel should consider utilizing the telephonic oral argument option, which is available in this court. (See Section IV, post.)

If oral argument is waived or if oral argument is requested, after argument and post-argument conference, the opinion as written or as modified may be filed either as a signed opinion or as an unsigned per curiam opinion. In the latter case, the participating justices' names appear at the bottom of the first page.

C. Writs.

The term "writs" as used here includes the traditional writs (mandamus, prohibition, certiorari, supersedeas, habeas corpus, error coram vobis), also writs of review, petitions in Workers' Compensation Appeals Board cases, Agricultural Labor Relations Board matters, Public Employment Relations Board, Alcoholic Beverage Control Board, and Public Utilities Commission cases.

The court has two writ panels of three justices each, the membership of which is rotated among all the justices from month to month. Writs are assigned to the panels so as to approximately equalize the workload. Writ conferences are held by each panel at least once per week, usually on Thursday mornings.

When a writ petition is filed, copies are distributed to the writ attorneys who, under the supervision of the presiding justice, assign them to the panels. A memorandum is prepared in each case by the writ attorney and delivered to each justice on the assigned panel prior to the writ conference. Emergency writs, usually involving a request for a stay of a proceeding in the trial court, are by necessity considered and disposed of as required by the particular circumstances, the constraints of time involved, and other court business. Other than issuance of a temporary stay order, writs will not be issued prior to the receipt of a response from parties who would be adversely affected or unless such parties inform the court that no response will be filed. A petition for a writ may be denied without a response being filed.

If it appears the matter is one in which relief may be appropriate but a peremptory grant would be inappropriate, an order to show cause or alternative writ is issued and the case may be calendared for oral argument. The case is then handled in accordance with the procedure for regular appeals.

Occasionally, if the issuance of a peremptory writ in the first instance has been prayed, and the facts are clear, and the case has been fully briefed and nothing would be added by oral argument, relief by way of peremptory writ may be granted without the issuance of an order to show cause or alternative writ. In these cases, a short opinion or a written order with reasons stated will be filed. Summary denials are more frequent, in which event, the law of the case doctrine does not apply. (See *Kowis v. Howard* (1992) 3 Cal.4th 888.)

California Rules of Court, rule 8.452 writ petitions taken from orders setting a hearing under Welfare and Institutions Code section 366.26 are handled on the writ calendar. Such cases, generated by the filing of a notice of intent to file a writ petition are distributed to a central staff attorney specializing in juvenile dependency law and rule 8.452 writ practice. The central staff attorney works under the supervision of the presiding justice and assigns such cases to panels on a rotating basis. Once the time passes under rule 8.452 for the filing of a response to such a writ petition, the central staff attorney prepares an Order to Show Cause setting the case for oral argument with the proviso that, in the event the parties do not advise this court of their desire to orally argue the case within seven days' time, the matter will be submitted. Thereafter, the central staff attorney prepares a memorandum, which in most cases addresses the merits of the writ petition, and delivers the memorandum to each justice on the assigned panel prior to the writ conference. The case is then handled in accordance with the procedure for routine dispositions.

Petitions for review of Agricultural Labor Relations Board decisions, of orders and awards of the Workers' Compensation Appeals Board, the Public Employment Relations Board, the Public Utilities Commission, and the Alcoholic Beverage Control Board, and review of decisions of appellate divisions of superior courts pursuant to California Rules of Court, rule 8.1002, are handled on the writ calendar. If a petition for review is granted, or the certification under rule 8.1005 is accepted, the case is set for oral argument after briefing is completed. The case is then disposed of in accordance with the procedure for handling regular appeals.

D. Motions.

Non-routine motions and applications, including applications for bail, are processed in accordance with the procedure for handling writs.

Applications in routine matters (see Cal. Rules of Court, rules 8.50, 8.57), including motions to augment or correct the record, requests for extensions of time, and disciplinary proceedings against attorneys and court reporters for failure to timely file briefs and records, are normally disposed of by the presiding justice with the assistance of a writ attorney.

E. Petitions for Rehearing and Applications for Publication.

Petitions for rehearing and applications for publication are assigned for disposition to the same panel members who participated in the initial opinion.

F. Settlement Conferences in Civil Cases.

Upon stipulation of all parties to a civil case pending in the court or on the presiding justice's own motion, a settlement conference will be calendared and held pursuant to California Rules of Court, rule 8.284. Notice of availability of a settlement conference is sent to counsel at the time the record on appeal is filed. For further details, see local rule 2 on settlement conferences in civil appeals, a copy of which will be furnished upon request.

IV. TELEPHONIC ORAL ARGUMENT OPTION

The court has in place a teleconferencing system that allows up to five attorneys in different offices to present their argument over the telephone in a single case. Attorneys selecting this option remains in their office until the clerk notifies them that their case has been called. The attorneys will then come on the line and are part of a telephone conference call. The system broadcasts the attorney's voice over the courtroom public address system as well as to other counsel appearing by telephone. The justices are convened in open court and speak into microphones which broadcast into court and through the telephone system. Counsel can hear each other and the court. The system allows one or more attorneys to appear in court and argue while other counsel listen and present their argument over the telephone. The argument is tape-recorded just as if all attorneys were present in court.

The teleconferencing option was implemented to accommodate counsel's time and to provide a significant cost savings to clients and the state by eliminating travel time and costs, as well as time spent waiting for a case to be called. Retained counsel selecting the telephonic oral argument receive a nominal billing from the court following the argument to cover the cost of the conference call and administrative time involved.

Details of the practices and procedures related to the telephonic oral argument option are available from the clerk upon request and may be found in the California Rules of Court, Local Rules of the Courts of Appeal.

V. PRELIMINARY REVIEW OF APPELLANT'S OPENING BRIEF IN CIVIL CASES

The court presumes that briefs filed by counsel will comply with applicable standards. (See Cal. Rules of Court, rule 8.204 [Contents and form of briefs]). Unfortunately, many briefs do not. This adds to the court's workload and delays resolution of appeals.

Therefore, in civil appeals in this court:

(1.) After appellant's opening brief is filed, the managing attorney reviews the brief for basic compliance with pertinent rules, statutes, and case law. The review is non-substantive; the court does not engage in advocacy for the parties.

(2.) Should the brief fail to comply with minimum standards, the court may strike or return the brief and give counsel the opportunity to file an adequate brief within a specified time.

(3.) Should a subsequent brief continue to fail minimum standards, the court may dismiss the appeal without further notice. (*In re S.C.* (2006) 138 Cal.App. 4th 396, 406-407.)

The same standards apply to briefs filed by pro se appellants. A party proceeding inpropria persona is treated like any other party and is entitled to the same, but no greater consideration than other litigants and attorneys. A propria persona litigant is held to the same rules of procedure as an attorney. (*First American Title Co. v. Mirzaian* (2003) 108 Cal.App.4th 956, 958, fn. 1.)

(Amended Jan. 1, 2007.)

SIXTH APPELLATE DISTRICT LOCAL RULES

(Amended effective September 20, 2021; revised effective January 16, 2016; amended effective June 5, 2017; February 13, 2018; April 16, 2018; December 28, 2020)

Mediation. Rule 1.
Electronic filing. Rule 2.
Reporter's transcripts in felony appeals — Exception to California Code of Civil Procedure section 271(a). Rule 3.
Establishing appellate jurisdiction, civil case information statement, required attachments. Rule 4.

POLICY REGARDING *IN RE PHOENIX H.* BRIEFS IN LIGHT OF NEW EFILING REQUIREMENT

Effective immediately, the Sixth District Court of Appeal will no longer require compliance with California Rules of Court, rule 8.360 (a) for briefs filed Pursuant to *In re Phoenix H.* (2009) 47 Cal.4th 835. Court-appointed counsel should now submit a *Phoenix H.* brief in letter format when court-appointed counsel find no arguable issue to be pursued on appeal. All letter briefs filed pursuant to *In re Phoenix H.* shall be electronically filed. All other procedures and requirements associated with *Phoenix H.* briefs shall remain unchanged.

Dated: May 10, 2012

Conrad L. Rushing P.J.

Rule 1. Mediation

(a) [Application of rule] This rule is adopted pursuant to rule 8.248, California Rules of Court, and shall apply to all civil appeals filed in the Sixth District Court of Appeal.

(Subd (a) adopted effective February 5, 2010.)

(b) [Purpose of Mediation Program] To aid the expeditious and just resolution of civil appeals, the Court of Appeal for the Sixth District has established a mediation Program ("Program"). The Program shall be administered by the Administrative Presiding Justice or a designated Supervising Justice, and their designated staff.

(Subd (b) amended effective April 16, 2018; adopted effective February 5, 2010.)

(c) [Scope of Mediation Program] At the court's discretion, any civil appeal may be placed in the Program upon the agreement of all parties to the appeal. The Court may, at its discretion, remove an appeal from the Program.

(Subd (c) amended effective April 16, 2018; adopted effective February 5, 2010.)

(d) [Mediators]

1. The court shall maintain a list of attorneys who have developed expertise in specified areas of law, are generally respected in the legal community, and are willing to mediate cases at this court. These attorneys shall be designated as mediators and preside over mediations conducted within the scope of the Program.

2. A justice or assigned justice of this court may, at the court's discretion, be designated as a mediator and preside over a mediation. A justice or assigned justice who participates in a mediation that does not

result in complete settlement shall not thereafter participate in any way in the consideration or disposition of the case on its merits.

3. A justice or assigned justice of the court will not be disqualified to participate in the consideration or disposition of a case on its merits because he or she has ruled on a request for a mediation, ordered that a mediation be held, signed orders granting relief from default for an act required under this rule, extended or shortened any time period specified in this rule, or otherwise signed an order concerning a procedural aspect of the mediation process.

(Subd (d) amended effective June 11, 2010; adopted effective February 5, 2010.)

(e) [General Mediation Program Procedure]

1. All parties in a civil appeal shall file a Mediation Statement Form within 15 days of the date the Clerk of this court sends notice that the court has received the notice of appeal. Each party shall also serve a copy of their completed Mediation Statement Form on all other parties.

2. The Mediation Statement Form shall be transmitted by the Clerk to the Program and shall not be entered into the court file.

3. Within 15 days of receipt of the Mediation Statement Forms, the court shall notify the parties when a case is selected for mediation and furnish the name, address and telephone number of the mediator selected for the mediation. The court shall provide three possible dates for mediation.

4. The parties shall meet and confer to agree on the date of mediation, and inform the court within 5 days of the date selected for mediation. The court will issue written notice of the date and time of the mediation. The mediator, with the approval of the Court, may, for good cause, postpone or continue a mediation session to a date certain.

5. The Court may replace a selected mediator upon written request by a party supported by a showing of good cause or upon request of the mediator.

6. Immediately upon acceptance of a case into the Program, all further proceedings, including the filing of briefs, shall be suspended for 90 days. However, this rule shall not suspend preparation of the appellate record unless a specific order is issued directing suspension of record preparation. Upon the expiration of the stay, the appeal shall be reinstated to active status on the court's docket. Any request for further stay shall be granted only upon written application to the court and only upon a showing of good cause.

7. Mediation services shall be furnished by the Court without fee to the parties for up to a total of 4 hours. Any further mediation services shall be at the discretion of the mediator, on such terms as the mediator and the parties may agree upon, and consistent with the provisions of this rule.

(Subd (e) amended effective April 16, 2018; adopted effective February 5, 2010; previously amended effective June 11, 2010.)

(f) [Mediation Hearing and Sanctions]

1. All parties and their counsel of record must attend all mediation sessions in person with full settlement authority. If the party is not an individual, then a party representative with full authority to settle all appeals and cross-appeals must attend all mediation sessions in person, in addition to counsel. If a party has potential insurance coverage applicable to any of the issues in dispute, a representative of each insurance carrier whose policy may apply must also attend all mediation sessions in person, with full settlement authority. Any exception to this requirement must be approved in writing by the Court. Failure to attend may result in the imposition of sanctions against any party or counsel, up to and including immediate termination from the Program or dismissal of the appeal.

2. The mediator may invite parties to the action who are not parties to the appeal, or any person who has an interest in the action, to attend the mediation if it appears to the mediator that their presence may facilitate settlement of the case. Any party to the appeal may serve and file a written request for the attendance of such a party or person at least 15 days before the mediation.

3. Counsel shall confer with their clients in advance and be thoroughly familiar with the case and prepared to present their contentions in detail.

4. The presiding justice, a justice designated by the presiding justice, or the mediator may excuse a client's personal attendance upon request and a showing that hardship or unusual circumstances make the client's attendance impossible or impractical. If personal attendance is excused, counsel either shall have obtained full authority to agree to a settlement that binds the client or the client shall be available for consultation by telephone.

5. The mediator may require parties or their counsel to furnish information, documents, records or other items specified by the mediator.

(Subd (f) amended effective April 16, 2018; adopted effective February 5, 2010; previously amended effective June 11, 2010.)

(g) [Post Mediation Procedure]

1. No later than 10 days after completion of mediation, the mediator shall submit to the Court a Mediation Attendance Form, listing all participants in the mediation, and a brief summary of the procedural outcome of the mediation.

2. Each party and their counsel shall separately complete and submit to the Court evaluations of the mediation and the mediator on a form provided by the Court.

3. The parties and their counsel shall promptly take the steps necessary to implement the agreements reached in mediation. An appellant who has settled must immediately serve and file a notice of settlement in the Court of Appeal and, thereafter, must seek abandonment or dismissal of the appeal as provided in the California Rules of Court. The notice of settlement shall specify the allocation of costs on appeal and state whether the remittitur is to issue immediately.

4. Upon receiving notification that no agreement was reached at mediation, this court will immediately vacate the stay and reinstate the appeal to active status on the court's docket.

(Subd (g) adopted effective February 5, 2010.)

(h) [Confidentiality] Except as otherwise required by law, information disclosed to the mediator, the parties, counsel, or any other participant in the mediation, shall be confidential and shall not be disclosed to anyone not participating in the mediation Program.

(Subd (h) adopted effective February 5, 2010.)

(i) [Ethical Standards] Mediators shall adhere to the Rules of Conduct for Mediators in Court-Connected Mediation Programs for Civil Cases set forth in the California Rules of Court.

(Subd (i) adopted effective February 5, 2010.)

(j) [Appellate Process] Parties and counsel shall comply with all rules applicable to processing appeals while concurrently participating in the mediation Program.

(Subd (j) adopted effective February 5, 2010.)

(k) [Sanctions] Monetary sanctions may be imposed by the Administrative Presiding Justice or Supervising Justice for failure to comply with these rules.

(Subd (k) adopted effective February 5, 2010.)

Rule 1 reinstated effective November 13, 2013; suspended effective April 2, 2013; amended effective June 11, 2010; April 16, 2018; adopted effective February 5, 2010; former Rule 1 repealed effective March 2, 2007.

2013 Note: The Publisher received the following court order dated April 2, 2013 through November 12, 2013, "IT IS HEREBY ORDERED that the Mediation Program pursuant to Local Rule 1 is suspended."

Rule 2. Electronic Filing

Pursuant to California Rules of Court, rule 8.72, the Court of Appeal for the Sixth Appellate District (court) adopts the following requirements for electronic filing in this district.

1. **Registration.**

1. *Obligation to Register.* The court's electronic filing system (EFS) is operated by ImageSoft, Inc. (ImageSoft), and may be accessed via the TrueFiling portal (TrueFiling). In order to access TrueFiling, each attorney of record in any proceeding pending in this court is obligated to become an EFS user and obtain a username and password. Self-represented litigants must register if they wish to file electronically. Attorneys and self-represented litigants may register at https://tf3.truefiling.com/register.

2. *Obligation to Keep Account Information Current.* Registered users are required to keep their e-mail addresses current and must update their e-mail addresses online via the TrueFiling web site. Updating TrueFiling does not relieve the user of the notice of change requirements in California Rules of Court, rule 8.32, subdivision (b).

2. **Format.**

The formatting requirements enumerated in California Rules of Court, rule 8.74(a)-(d) are incorporated herein by reference and shall apply to all documents electronically filed in the Sixth District. For more information and examples, you can refer to [Pending Link to the COA FAQs document].

3. **Record on Appeal and Writ Proceedings.**

1. *Appendix.* Parties must submit any appendix filed pursuant to California Rules of Court, rule 8.124 in electronic format. Each part of the appendix shall comply with the format, pagination and bookmark requirements enumerated in subparagraph (b) of this rule. If submitted in

multiple parts, the cover of each part of the record submitted in any appendix or exhibit volume shall clearly state the volume and page numbers included within that part, and include an index of contents.

2. *Administrative Record.* In addition to any administrative record provided by the trial court pursuant to California Rules of Court, rule 8.123, the party or parties seeking review of an administrative determination must submit a copy of the administrative record as an electronic text-searchable PDF. An administrative record may be delivered to the court on CD, DVD, or flash drive.

3. *Reporter's Transcript.* Any party who orders a reporter's transcript of proceedings pursuant to California Rules of Court, rule 8.130, which is provided in paper format, must also request a copy of the transcript in electronic format, as provided in Code of Civil Procedure section 271, and must submit an electronic copy to the court.

4. *Writ Proceedings.* All documents and exhibits submitted in writ proceedings must be submitted in electronic format and must comply with the requirements enumerated in subparagraph (b) of this rule.

5. *Transmissions by the Superior Court.* The court authorizes and encourages the superior courts within the Sixth Appellate District to engage in the electronic service and electronic filing of documents, including, but not limited to, the clerk's transcript and reporter's transcripts. If a superior court transmits an electronic document to the court, it shall also make the electronic document available to the parties. If a superior court transmits electronic documents to the court in lieu of paper, the court will accept electronic documents complying with the California Rules of Court and this local rule.

4. **Electronic Version Deemed Original Record.** The court may scan any paper document into an electronic format, in which case the electronic document will be deemed the original for purposes of the court record. The original electronic record will be maintained by the court in compliance with all statutory requirements, and the court may elect to destroy the paper documents.

5. **Filing Deadlines.** Consistent with California Rules of Court, rules 8.71(f)(2) and 8.77, filing documents electronically does not alter any filing deadlines. A document that is received electronically by the court after 11:59 p.m. is deemed to have been received on the next court day. In order to be timely filed on the day they are due, all electronic transmissions of documents must be completed prior to midnight. Although EFS permits parties to submit documents electronically 24 hours a day, users should be aware that telephone or online assistance may not be available outside of normal court business hours.

6. **Motion to Accept Filing as Timely Following TrueFiling Technical Failure.** If a filer fails to meet a filing deadline imposed by court order, rule or law because of a failure of the EFS, the filer may file a paper or electronic document as soon thereafter as practicable and accompany the filing with a motion to accept the document as timely filed pursuant to California Rules of Court, rule 8.77(d).

7. **Service.** An attorney's registration with TrueFiling to participate in the EFS constitutes consent to service or delivery of all documents by any other party in a case through the system. (Cal. Rules of Court, rule 8.78.) Orders or other documents generated by the court will be served only through the EFS or by e-mailed notification. Only those exempted from the EFS pursuant to subparagraph (l) will receive manual service or notification by other means.

8. **Signatures.** The signature requirements enumerated in California Rules of Court, rule 8.75 are incorporated herein by reference and shall apply to all documents electronically filed in the Sixth District.

9. **Filing Fees.** ImageSoft is a private vendor under contract with the court. ImageSoft will assess EFS fees for each filing in accordance with the schedule posted on the TrueFiling web site, as approved by the court. EFS fees will be considered recoverable costs under California Rules of Court, rule 8.278(d)(1)(D). ImageSoft is designated as the court's agent for collection of court-imposed fees where required for any filing, and any associated credit card or bank charges or convenience fees. (Cal. Rules of Court, rule 8.76; Gov. Code, § 6159.) If a party with a fee waiver chooses to file documents electronically, that party is exempt from the fees and costs associated with electronic filing. The persons and entities identified in Government Code section 6103 are also exempt from the fees and costs associated with the EFS.

10. **Exemptions.**

1. Self-represented parties are exempt from mandatory electronic filing. Self-represented parties who opt to register for electronic filing must comply with this rule and the requirements of TrueFiling.

2. When it is not feasible for a party to convert a document to electronic form by scanning, imaging, or other means, the document may be filed in paper form, with a declaration setting forth the reasons why electronic filing was not feasible. The paper documents shall be filed and served upon the parties in accordance with all statutory requirements and the California Rules of Court applicable to paper documents.

3. If electronic filing and/or service causes undue hardship or significant prejudice to any party, the party may file a motion for an exemption from the requirements of this rule. (See Cal. Rules of Court, rule 8.54(a)(1) & (2).) Pursuant to California Rules of Court, rule 8.71(d), the court will grant relief from some or all of these requirements on a satisfactory showing of undue hardship or significant prejudice.

11. **Rejection of Electronic Filing for Noncompliance.** The court will reject an electronic filing if it does not comply with the requirements of this rule pursuant California Rules of Court, rule 8.77(b).

12. **Sanctions for Noncompliance.** Failure of counsel to timely register, and failure of any registered user to comply with EFS filing requirements, unless exempted, may be subject to sanctions imposed by the court.

13. **Posting and Publication.** The Clerk of the Court is directed to post a copy of this rule on the court's web site pursuant to California Rules of Court, rule 8.72(a), and to submit a copy to the Reporter of Decisions for publication pursuant to California Rules of Court, rule 10.1030(a).

Rule 2 amended effective September 20, 2021; adopted effective January 16, 2016; previously amended effective June 5, 2017, and April 16, 2018.

Rule 3. Reporter's Transcripts in Felony Appeals — Exception to California Code of Civil Procedure section 271(a)

a. Effective February 13, 2018, except as provided in subsection (b) below, counsel for a defendant in a felony appeal shall be deemed to have requested that his or her copy of the reporter's transcript be delivered in paper form pursuant to Code of Civil Procedure section 271(a)(1).

(Adopted, effective February 13, 2018.)

b. Notwithstanding the exception set forth in subsection (a) above, defendant's counsel, or, if the defendant is not yet represented by appellate counsel, the district appellate project, may request that his or her copy of the reporter's transcript be delivered in electronic form as provided in California Code of Civil Procedure section 271(a) by serving the lead court reporter and the superior court with a written request within 15 days after the notice of appeal is filed.

(Adopted, effective February 13, 2018.)
Rule 3 adopted effective February 13, 2018.

Rule 4. Establishing Appellate Jurisdiction, Civil Case Information Statement, Required Attachments

(a) An appellant filing a completed *Civil Case Information Statement* (Form APP-004) in this District pursuant to California Rules of Court, rule 8.100, subdivision (g), must attach the following documents:

(1) A copy of the judgment or order being appealed, including:

(A) A judgment of dismissal, if the appeal challenges a judgment entered after:

i. an order granting summary judgment, or

ii. an order sustaining a demurrer without leave to amend, or

iii. an order granting judgment on the pleadings;

(B) If appealing an order made after judgment (Code of Civ. Proc. §904.1, subd. (a)(2)), a copy of the final judgment or order of dismissal that predated the order being appealed (see Code Civ. Proc., §§ 577, 581d);

(2) A copy of the proof of service from the clerk of the superior court or any party's notice of entry of the order or judgment being appealed; or if neither the clerk of the superior court nor any party served a proof of service or notice of entry, a statement that no such document exists;

(3) If claiming an extension of time to file the appeal pursuant to California Rules of Court, rule 8.108, subdivision (b), (c), (d) or (e), a copy of the trial court's order granting or denying the applicable motion;

(4) The proof of service or notice of entry of any order listed in (3); or, if neither the clerk of the superior court nor any party served a proof of service or notice of entry, a statement that no such document exists;

(5) Any additional documents that may be necessary to establish appellate jurisdiction pursuant to Code of Civil Procedure section 904.1 and California Rules of Court, rules 8.104 and 8.108.

(Subd (a) adopted effective December 28, 2020.)

(b) If appellant fails to comply with this rule, or if the court requires additional documents to verify appellate jurisdiction, the court will notify the appellant in writing of any omission or additional request. If any requested document is unavailable or does not exist, appellant shall so notify the court in writing with a statement why the document(s) cannot be provided. If appellant fails to comply with the court's request within the specified time, the court may, on its own motion or upon motion of any party, issue an order to show cause why the appeal should not be dismissed.

(Subd (b) adopted effective December 28, 2020.)
Rule 4 adopted effective December 28, 2020.

INTERNAL OPERATING PRACTICES AND PROCEDURES
SIXTH APPELLATE DISTRICT

(Revised effective January 1, 2009)

Introduction
I. STRUCTURE OF THE COURT AND ORGANIZATION OF STAFF
  A. Justices
  B. Presiding Justice
  C. Clerk/Administrator
  D. Research Attorneys
    1. Attorneys Assigned to Justices
    2. Writ Attorneys
    3. Central Staff
    4. Externs
  E. Law Librarian
  F. Judicial Assistants to Appellate Court Justices
II. PROCESSING APPEALS
  A. In General
    1. Assignment of Cases
    2. Preliminary Case Conferences
    3. Oral Argument
    4. Post-Oral Argument Conference
  B. Preparation and Filing of Opinions
    1. Signed Opinions
    2. Concurring or Dissenting Opinions
    3. Publication of Opinions
  C. Rehearings
  D. Original and Discretionary Proceedings
  E. Communications with Counsel or Parties
  F. Settlement

Introduction

The purpose of this document is to acquaint the bar and interested members of the public with the general operating practices of the Court of Appeal, Sixth Appellate District.

The internal procedures of the Court of Appeal are largely governed by the California Constitution, statutes, and the appellate rules adopted by the Judicial Council. The Court of Appeal may adopt and publish its own rules that do not conflict with a statute or rule adopted by the Judicial Council.

I. STRUCTURE OF THE COURT AND ORGANIZATION OF STAFF

A. JUSTICES

The court has seven authorized judicial positions, consisting of a presiding justice and six associate justices.

The Chief Justice, as Chairperson of the Judicial Council, may assign a retired justice or judge, or an active trial court judge to serve temporarily on a Court of Appeal. Justices pro tem may be assigned (1) when there is a judicial vacancy, or (2) when a Court of Appeal justice is absent or unable to serve, or is disqualified in a given case, or (3) when the court needs assistance in reducing a backlog of cases.

Justices sit in panels of three that change periodically.

The courtroom and office of the clerk of the court are located in the Comerica Bank building at 333 West Santa Clara Street, Suite 1060, San Jose, California 95113.

B. PRESIDING JUSTICE

The presiding justice convenes conferences and presides at hearings (oral argument) when he or she is a member of the three-justice panel assigned to hear a case. The presiding justice has specific authority under rule 10.1012 of the California Rules of Court to grant or deny applications and to extend time for filing of records and briefs on appeal. The rule also gives the presiding justice limited authority to dismiss an appeal for noncompliance with the Rules of Court and to grant relief from default. The presiding justice also has overall responsibility for the calendaring of cases, the management of the caseload within the district, and the scheduling of oral arguments.

If the presiding justice is absent or disqualified, or not a member of the three-justice panel that is to decide a matter, the presiding justice designates the senior associate justice to serve as acting presiding justice.

C. CLERK/ADMINISTRATOR

The Clerk/Administrator is responsible for maintaining the court's public records and files and for advising litigants, counsel, and the public of the status of matters before the court.

Appointed by the court, the clerk assists in the preparation of the court's calendar, dockets its cases, and supervises other administrative functions required for the court's operation. The clerk is aided by an assistant clerk/administrator, six deputy clerks and a support staff.

D. RESEARCH ATTORNEYS

1. Attorneys Assigned to Justices

Each justice is currently authorized to employ two permanent research attorneys.

Research attorneys employed by or assigned to a justice work primarily on appeals assigned to the justice. The attorney's work involves legal research, examination of the trial court record, conferring with the justices assigned to the case, and preparing written memoranda and draft opinions.

2. Writ Attorneys

The court is currently authorized to employ two writ attorneys who assist the court in reviewing petitions for various writs, such as mandate, prohibition, certiorari or review, habeas corpus, and error coram vobis.

3. Central Staff

In addition to the writ attorneys and research attorneys assigned to justices, the court employs a staff of several senior research attorneys. This staff is known as the "central staff" because it provides research and analysis assistance for the justices of the court. Central staff attorneys are assigned to individual justices by the court and provide the same research and assistance required of the justices' permanent research staff.

4. Externs

The Sixth Appellate District cooperates with law schools in enabling law students to earn academic credits by working one semester, without pay, performing research for individual justices. These law students are selected and supervised by individual justices.

E. LAW LIBRARIAN

The court's law library collection of approximately 30,000 volumes is maintained by a professional Law Librarian. The collection includes the latest technological developments in legal research such as: a wide variety of CD-ROM's on the Local Area Network (LAN); access to various online research services including the Internet; and a selection of microforms, audio tapes and video tapes, in addition to the books. The Law Librarian is also responsible for keeping current on technology and legal trends, which affords the court staff the opportunity to do efficient and effective research on all issues before the court.

F. JUDICIAL ASSISTANTS TO APPELLATE COURT JUSTICES

Each justice is authorized to employ one judicial assistant who is responsible for the timely processing of the justice's opinions, including circulating draft opinions for review by other members of the panel, typing judicial correspondence, cite-checking and shepardizing draft opinions, and delivering opinions to the clerk for filing. The court employs other secretarial support staff as needed.

II. PROCESSING APPEALS

A. In General

When a criminal or civil appeal is fully briefed, it is identified on a computer-generated list indicating the case is ready for analysis and decision. The appeals are considered by the court after they are fully briefed. Decisions may be made and the opinions filed in a different order depending on factors such as the complexity of the litigation and whether oral argument is requested. The California Constitution requires the filing of a written opinion in every appeal.

1. Assignment of Cases

Assignment of cases to individual justices is generally made by rotation from the list of ready cases. The justice assigned to a particular case then has lead or primary responsibility for that case in the course of conference discussions, research and preparation of the opinion.

2. Preliminary Case Conferences

In the course of preparing an opinion, conferences are held at the request of the author or other panel members. In difficult or complex cases, more than one conference may be held. Conferences are generally not held in cases involving routine issues.

3. Oral Argument

When a case is ready for possible argument, the clerk will write and ask the parties whether they desire to exercise their right to appear personally for oral argument or to argue by teleconference. [The Sixth District Court of Appeal Teleconferencing Oral Argument Procedures Manual is available from the clerk's office upon request.] If oral argument is requested, the case is placed on an oral argument calendar.

After the case is scheduled for oral argument, any party or counsel for a party may contact the clerk's office and be informed of the names of the justices assigned to the case.

The order in which cases are to be argued is determined by the presiding justice. Because of the considerable investment of court time and resources necessary to prepare a case for oral argument, continuances are disfavored and will be granted only on a showing of good cause. Oral argument will not be continued by stipulation of counsel absent a showing of good cause. If no appearance is made, the case may be ordered submitted.

The order and the time allotted for counsel to make their presentations are specified in rule 8.256 of the California Rules of Court.

In most instances, the presiding justice will inform counsel at the beginning of each session that the court has reviewed the briefs and is familiar with the facts and issues. The court requests that counsel not merely reiterate the argument contained in his or her brief. Oral argument is generally most helpful and effective when reasonably brief and when counsel focuses on the decisive issues, succinctly clarifies the facts as they relate to a given issue, or clarifies the holding or reasoning of potentially applicable or controlling authority.

The court disfavors the submission of untimely citations of authority as it deprives the court and opposing counsel of sufficient opportunity to prepare for oral argument. The court retains discretion to strike or disregard such citations.

When oral argument has concluded in a given case, the justice presiding will declare the cause submitted, unless submission has been deferred for additional briefing.

4. Post-Oral Argument Conference

A post-oral argument conference is held in which the justices again discuss the case and finally determine the decision to be reached.

B. Preparation and Filing of Opinions

1. Signed Opinions

Unless the two other participating justices disagree with the disposition proposed by the assigned author, the justice assigned will prepare the majority opinion. When a proposed majority opinion has been drafted, it is circulated to the other participating justices. They indicate approval, disapproval, or proposed changes. Differences of opinion as to the language of the opinion or the ultimate disposition of the case may be taken up in conference. The opinion may then be modified in a manner acceptable to the justices. If two justices agree, a written opinion is filed.

2. Concurring or Dissenting Opinions

Where a difference of opinion exists among the justices participating in a case, a justice who agrees with the result reached but not with the reasoning of the majority may write a separate concurring opinion, or may merely indicate concurrence only in the judgment reached by the majority. Likewise, a justice who disagrees with the result reached by the majority may write a dissenting opinion. Each panel member has a full opportunity to consider the views of associates prior to the completion and filing of the opinion.

3. Publication of Opinions

A decision of the court is not published in the official reports unless it is certified for publication by a majority of the participating justices. The criteria for publication and publication requests are set forth in rules 8.1105 and 8.1120, respectively, of the California Rules of Court.

C. Rehearings

The procedure for filing a petition for rehearing is governed by rule 8.268 of the California Rules of Court. When a petition for rehearing is filed, the petition is routed to the justice who authored the opinion with copies to the participating justices. The authoring justice reviews the petition, and then indicates whether he or she votes to grant or deny the petition. The petition, along with any staff memorandum, is then circulated to the other two justices on the panel for their decisions. Two votes are necessary to grant or deny a petition for rehearing.

D. Original and Discretionary Proceedings

Petitions for writ of mandate, prohibition, certiorari, and habeas corpus, statutory review petitions, other miscellaneous applications to the original jurisdiction of the court, and applications for supersedeas or other relief pending appeal under Code of Civil Procedure section 923 or other statutory provisions are normally handled independently of the court's appellate caseload.

In original proceedings the court expects counsel to comply with the provisions of rules 8.486–8.488 of the California Rules of Court and all applicable time limitations, to explain any substantial delay in seeking relief in matters to which specific time limits do not apply, and to lodge with the court (and serve on adverse parties) a properly organized and indexed record sufficient to permit informed review. Any request for a stay of proceedings must be clearly labeled as such (Cal. Rules of Court, rule 8.116), and circumstances that require expedited consideration should be clearly identified in the petition or application and noted on its cover. Counsel should advise the clerk of the next trial court date at the time the petition or application is filed.

Parties to statutory writ review proceedings should comply with applicable briefing schedules (for example, Cal. Rules of Court, rules 8.495(b), 8.498(c)). The court will strictly apply those schedules, absent a timely application for exception supported by a showing of good cause.

In habeas corpus matters, the court in appropriate cases will request an informal response and provide for a reply to the response under rule 8.385(b) of the California Rules of Court.

In other original proceedings it is the court's policy not to grant affirmative relief (beyond a temporary stay) without first giving adverse parties an opportunity to submit a memorandum of points and authorities in opposition. Opposition need not be submitted in these matters unless expressly requested by the court. If requested, opposition must be submitted on or before the date stated in the request, unless an extension is obtained before that date.

Original proceedings are referred to the writ attorney for initial review. The writ attorney thereafter communicates with the court concerning the matter. The court will conduct a writ conference and meet specially when necessary. All written submissions by any party, and any written staff memoranda, are distributed to and reviewed by all participating justices.

If affirmative relief is to be granted, the Sixth District will issue an alternative writ of mandate or prohibition, which directs the relief prayed for in the petition or, in the alternative, that the respondent appear and show cause why the relief should not be granted. An order to show cause may be issued without the alternative writ. In limited circumstances, the court may issue a peremptory writ in the first instance without allowing oral argument.

Counsel seeking writ relief should carefully review the "Sixth District Court of Appeal Outline on Original Proceedings and Relief Ancillary to Appeal," which is available on request from the clerk's office or available for download in .pdf or .doc format from the court's website.

E. Communications with Counsel or Parties

Except in oral argument, the justices do not communicate directly with counsel or parties concerning pending cases. Any necessary communications are handled by the clerk.

Attorneys employed by the court do not communicate with counsel or parties concerning pending cases.

F. Settlement

The parties must immediately notify the court of the settlement of any pending case (Cal. Rules of Court, rule 8.244).

Upon the request of all parties to a pending case, the court will schedule and conduct a settlement conference. The conference will be conducted before a justice of the court or an assigned judge. The settlement conference must be attended by the parties unless counsel or another authorized representative in attendance have full authority to settle.

No justice conducting a settlement conference will participate in deciding the case or discuss the case with any justice deciding the case if the case is not settled.

(Amended Jan. 1, 2007; Jan. 1, 2008; Jan. 1, 2009.)

CALIFORNIA RULES OF PROFESSIONAL CONDUCT

2025 EDITION

Rules of Professional Conduct adopted by the Board of Trustees of the State Bar and approved by the Supreme Court with revisions operative June 1, 2020. Prior version adopted by the Board of Governors of the State Bar and approved by the Supreme Court operative May 27, 1989.

Rules of Professional Conduct promulgated by the Board of Trustees of the State Bar and approved by the Supreme Court with amendments current through November 11, 2024.

Rules of Professional Conduct are reprinted with permission from the State Bar of California. No part of this work may be reproduced, stored in a retrieval system, or transmitted in any medium without prior written permission of the State Bar of California.

CONTENTS

RULES OF PROFESSIONAL CONDUCT

	Rules
Purpose and Function of the Rules of Professional Conduct	1.0
Terminology	1.0.1
Chapter 1. Lawyer-Client Relationship	1.1 – 1.18
Chapter 2. Counselor	2.1 – 2.4.1
Chapter 3. Advocate	3.1 – 3.10
Chapter 4. Transactions with Persons Other Than Clients	4.1 – 4.4
Chapter 5. Law Firms and Associations	5.1 – 5.6
Chapter 6. Public Service	6.3 – 6.5
Chapter 7. Information About Legal Services	7.1 – 7.5
Chapter 8. Maintaining the Integrity of the Profession	8.1 – 8.5

CALIFORNIA RULES OF PROFESSIONAL CONDUCT

Purpose and Function of the Rules of Professional Conduct. Rule 1.0. Terminology. Rule 1.0.1.

Rule 1.0 Purpose and Function of the Rules of Professional Conduct

(a) Purpose.

The following rules are intended to regulate professional conduct of lawyers through discipline. They have been adopted by the Board of Trustees of the State Bar of California and approved by the Supreme Court of California pursuant to Business and Professions Code sections 6076 and 6077 to protect the public, the courts, and the legal profession; protect the integrity of the legal system; and promote the administration of justice and confidence in the legal profession. These rules together with any standards adopted by the Board of Trustees pursuant to these rules shall be binding upon all lawyers.

(b) Function.

(1) A willful violation of any of these rules is a basis for discipline.

(2) The prohibition of certain conduct in these rules is not exclusive. Lawyers are also bound by applicable law including the State Bar Act (Bus. & Prof. Code, § 6000 et seq.) and opinions of California courts.

(3) A violation of a rule does not itself give rise to a cause of action for damages caused by failure to comply with the rule. Nothing in these rules or the Comments to the rules is intended to enlarge or to restrict the law regarding the liability of lawyers to others.

(c) Purpose of Comments.

The comments are not a basis for imposing discipline but are intended only to provide guidance for interpreting and practicing in compliance with the rules.

(d) These rules may be cited and referred to as the "California Rules of Professional Conduct."

Comment

[1] The Rules of Professional Conduct are intended to establish the standards for lawyers for purposes of discipline. (See *Ames v. State Bar* (1973) 8 Cal.3d 910, 917 [106 Cal.Rptr. 489].) Therefore, failure to comply with an obligation or prohibition imposed by a rule is a basis for invoking the disciplinary process. Because the rules are not designed to be a basis for civil liability, a violation of a rule does not itself give rise to a cause of action for enforcement of a rule or for damages caused by failure to comply with the rule. (*Stanley v. Richmond* (1995) 35 Cal.App.4th 1070, 1097 [41 Cal.Rptr.2d 768].) Nevertheless, a lawyer's violation of a rule may be evidence of breach of a lawyer's fiduciary or other substantive legal duty in a non-disciplinary context. (*Ibid.*; see also *Mirabito v. Liccardo* (1992) 4 Cal.App.4th 41, 44 [5 Cal.Rptr.2d 571].) A violation of a rule may have other non-disciplinary consequences. (See, e.g., *Fletcher v. Davis* (2004) 33 Cal.4th 61, 71-72 [14 Cal.Rptr.3d 58] [enforcement of attorney's lien]; *Chambers v. Kay* (2002) 29 Cal.4th 142, 161 [126 Cal.Rptr.2d 536] [enforcement of fee sharing agreement].)

[2] While the rules are intended to regulate professional conduct of lawyers, a violation of a rule can occur when a lawyer is not practicing law or acting in a professional capacity.

[3] A willful violation of a rule does not require that the lawyer intend to violate the rule. (*Phillips v. State Bar* (1989) 49 Cal.3d 944, 952 [264 Cal.Rptr. 346]; and see Bus. & Prof. Code, § 6077.)

[4] In addition to the authorities identified in paragraph (b)(2), opinions of ethics committees in California, although not binding, should be consulted for guidance on proper professional conduct. Ethics opinions and rules and standards promulgated by other jurisdictions and bar associations may also be considered.

[5] The disciplinary standards created by these rules are not intended to address all aspects of a lawyer's professional obligations. A lawyer, as a member of the legal profession, is a representative and advisor of clients, an officer of the legal system and a public citizen having special responsibilities for the quality of justice. A lawyer should be aware of deficiencies in the administration of justice and of the fact that the poor, and sometimes persons* who are not poor cannot afford adequate legal assistance. Therefore, all lawyers are encouraged to devote professional time and resources and use civic influence to ensure equal access to the system of justice for those who because of economic or social barriers cannot afford or secure adequate legal counsel. In meeting this responsibility of the profession, every lawyer should aspire to render at least fifty hours of pro bono publico legal services per year. The lawyer should aim to provide a substantial* majority of such hours to indigent individuals or to nonprofit organizations with a primary purpose of providing services to the poor or on behalf of the poor or disadvantaged. Lawyers may also provide financial support to organizations providing free legal services. (See Bus. & Prof. Code, § 6073.)

(Adopted Sept. 26, 2018, eff. Nov. 1, 2018.)

Rule 1.0.1 Terminology

(a) "Belief" or "believes" means that the person* involved actually supposes the fact in question to be true. A person's* belief may be inferred from circumstances.

(b) [Reserved]

(c) "Firm" or "law firm" means a law partnership; a professional law corporation; a lawyer acting as a sole proprietorship; an association authorized to practice law; or lawyers employed in a legal services organization or in the legal department, division or office of a corporation, of a government organization, or of another organization.

(d) "Fraud" or "fraudulent" means conduct that is fraudulent under the law of the applicable jurisdiction and has a purpose to deceive.

(e) "Informed consent" means a person's* agreement to a proposed course of conduct after the lawyer has communicated and explained (i) the relevant circumstances and (ii) the material risks, including any actual and reasonably* foreseeable adverse consequences of the proposed course of conduct.

(e-1) "Informed written consent" means that the disclosures and the consent required by paragraph (e) must be in writing.*

(f) "Knowingly," "known," or "knows" means actual knowledge of the fact in question. A person's* knowledge may be inferred from circumstances.

(g) "Partner" means a member of a partnership, a shareholder in a law firm* organized as a professional corporation, or a member of an association authorized to practice law.

(g-1) "Person" has the meaning stated in Evidence Code section 175.

(h) "Reasonable" or "reasonably" when used in relation to conduct by a lawyer means the conduct of a reasonably prudent and competent lawyer.

(i) "Reasonable belief" or "reasonably believes" when used in reference to a lawyer means that the lawyer believes the matter in question and that the circumstances are such that the belief is reasonable.

(j) "Reasonably should know" when used in reference to a lawyer means that a lawyer of reasonable prudence and competence would ascertain the matter in question.

(k) "Screened" means the isolation of a lawyer from any participation in a matter, including the timely imposition of procedures within a law firm* that are adequate under the circumstances (i) to protect information that the isolated lawyer is obligated to protect under these rules or other law; and (ii) to protect against other law firm* lawyers and nonlawyer personnel communicating with the lawyer with respect to the matter.

(*l*) "Substantial" when used in reference to degree or extent means a material matter of clear and weighty importance.

(m) "Tribunal" means: (i) a court, an arbitrator, an administrative law judge, or an administrative body acting in an adjudicative capacity and authorized to make a decision that can be binding on the parties involved; or (ii) a special master or other person* to whom a court refers one or more issues and whose decision or recommendation can be binding on the parties if approved by the court.

(n) "Writing" or "written" has the meaning stated in Evidence Code section 250. A "signed" writing includes an electronic sound, symbol, or process attached to or logically associated with a writing and executed, inserted, or adopted by or at the direction of a person* with the intent to sign the writing.

Comment

Firm or Law Firm*

---

* An asterisk (*) identifies a word or phrase defined in the terminology rule, rule 1.0.1.

[1] Practitioners who share office space and occasionally consult or assist each other ordinarily would not be regarded as constituting a law firm.* However, if they present themselves to the public in a way that suggests that they are a law firm* or conduct themselves as a law firm,* they may be regarded as a law firm* for purposes of these rules. The terms of any formal agreement between associated lawyers are relevant in determining whether they are a firm,* as is the fact that they have mutual access to information concerning the clients they serve.

[2] The term "of counsel" implies that the lawyer so designated has a relationship with the law firm,* other than as a partner* or associate, or officer or shareholder, that is close, personal, continuous, and regular. Whether a lawyer who is denominated as "of counsel" or by a similar term should be deemed a member of a law firm* for purposes of these rules will also depend on the specific facts. (Compare *People ex rel. Department of Corporations v. Speedee Oil Change Systems, Inc.* (1999) 20 Cal.4th 1135 [86 Cal.Rptr.2d 816] with *Chambers v. Kay* (2002) 29 Cal.4th 142 [126 Cal.Rptr.2d 536].)

Fraud

[3] When the terms "fraud"* or "fraudulent"* are used in these rules, it is not necessary that anyone has suffered damages or relied on the misrepresentation or failure to inform because requiring the proof of those elements of fraud* would impede the purpose of certain rules to prevent fraud* or avoid a lawyer assisting in the perpetration of a fraud,* or otherwise frustrate the imposition of discipline on lawyers who engage in fraudulent conduct. The term "fraud"* or "fraudulent"* when used in these rules does not include merely negligent misrepresentation or negligent failure to apprise another of relevant information.

Informed Consent and Informed Written Consent**

[4] The communication necessary to obtain informed consent* or informed written consent* will vary according to the rule involved and the circumstances giving rise to the need to obtain consent.

*Screened**

[5] The purpose of screening* is to assure the affected client, former client, or prospective client that confidential information known* by the personally prohibited lawyer is neither disclosed to other law firm* lawyers or nonlawyer personnel nor used to the detriment of the person* to whom the duty of confidentiality is owed. The personally prohibited lawyer shall acknowledge the obligation not to communicate with any of the other lawyers and nonlawyer personnel in the law firm* with respect to the matter. Similarly, other lawyers and nonlawyer personnel in the law firm* who are working on the matter promptly shall be informed that the screening* is in place and that they may not communicate with the personally prohibited lawyer with respect to the matter. Additional screening* measures that are appropriate for the particular matter will depend on the circumstances. To implement, reinforce and remind all affected law firm* personnel of the presence of the screening,* it may be appropriate for the law firm* to undertake such procedures as a written* undertaking by the personally prohibited lawyer to avoid any communication with other law firm* personnel and any contact with any law firm* files or other materials relating to the matter, written* notice and instructions to all other law firm* personnel forbidding any communication with the personally prohibited lawyer relating to the matter, denial of access by that lawyer to law firm* files or other materials relating to the matter, and periodic reminders of the screen* to the personally prohibited lawyer and all other law firm* personnel.

[6] In order to be effective, screening* measures must be implemented as soon as practical after a lawyer or law firm* knows* or reasonably should know* that there is a need for screening.*

(Adopted Sept. 26, 2018, eff. Nov. 1, 2018.)

CHAPTER 1
LAWYER-CLIENT RELATIONSHIP

Competence. Rule 1.1.
Scope of Representation and Allocation of Authority. Rule 1.2.
Advising or Assisting the Violation of Law. Rule 1.2.1.
Diligence. Rule 1.3.
Communication with Clients. Rule 1.4.
Communication of Settlement Offers. Rule 1.4.1.
Disclosure of Professional Liability Insurance. Rule 1.4.2.
Fees for Legal Services. Rule 1.5.
Fee Divisions Among Lawyers. Rule 1.5.1.
Confidential Information of a Client. Rule 1.6.
Conflict of Interest: Current Clients. Rule 1.7.
Business Transactions with a Client and Pecuniary Interests Adverse to a Client. Rule 1.8.1.
Use of Current Client's Information. Rule 1.8.2.
Gifts from Client. Rule 1.8.3.
Payment of Personal or Business Expenses Incurred by or for a Client. Rule 1.8.5.
Compensation from One Other than Client. Rule 1.8.6.
Aggregate Settlements. Rule 1.8.7.
Limiting Liability to Client. Rule 1.8.8.
Purchasing Property at a Foreclosure or a Sale Subject to Judicial Review. Rule 1.8.9.
Sexual Relations with Current Client. Rule 1.8.10.
Imputation of Prohibitions Under Rules 1.8.1 to 1.8.9. Rule 1.8.11.
Duties to Former Clients. Rule 1.9.
Imputation of Conflicts of Interest: General Rule. Rule 1.10.
Special Conflicts of Interest for Former and Current Government Officials and Employees. Rule 1.11.
Former Judge, Arbitrator, Mediator, or Other Third-Party Neutral. Rule 1.12.
Organization as Client. Rule 1.13.
Safekeeping Funds and Property of Clients and Other Persons. Rule 1.15.
Declining or Terminating Representation. Rule 1.16.
Sale of a Law Practice. Rule 1.17.
Duties to Prospective Client. Rule 1.18.

Rule 1.1 Competence

(a) A lawyer shall not intentionally, recklessly, with gross negligence, or repeatedly fail to perform legal services with competence.

(b) For purposes of this rule, "competence" in any legal service shall mean to apply the (i) learning and skill, and (ii) mental, emotional, and physical ability reasonably* necessary for the performance of such service.

(c) If a lawyer does not have sufficient learning and skill when the legal services are undertaken, the lawyer nonetheless may provide competent representation by (i) associating with or, where appropriate, professionally consulting another lawyer whom the lawyer reasonably believes* to be competent, (ii) acquiring sufficient learning and skill before performance is required, or (iii) referring the matter to another lawyer whom the lawyer reasonably believes* to be competent.

(d) In an emergency a lawyer may give advice or assistance in a matter in which the lawyer does not have the skill ordinarily required if referral to, or association or consultation with, another lawyer would be impractical. Assistance in an emergency must be limited to that reasonably* necessary in the circumstances.

Comment

[1] The duties set forth in this rule include the duty to keep abreast of the changes in the law and its practice, including the benefits and risks associated with relevant technology.

[2] This rule addresses only a lawyer's responsibility for his or her own professional competence. See rules 5.1 and 5.3 with respect to a lawyer's disciplinary responsibility for supervising subordinate lawyers and nonlawyers.

[3] See rule 1.3 with respect to a lawyer's duty to act with reasonable* diligence.

(Amended Feb. 18, 2021, eff. Mar. 22, 2021; Adopted Sept. 26, 2018, eff. Nov. 1, 2018.)

Rule 1.2 Scope of Representation and Allocation of Authority

(a) Subject to rule 1.2.1, a lawyer shall abide by a client's decisions concerning the objectives of representation and, as required by rule 1.4, shall reasonably* consult with the client as to the means by which they are to be pursued. Subject to Business and Professions Code section 6068, subdivision (e)(1) and rule 1.6, a lawyer may take such action on behalf of the client as is impliedly authorized to carry out the representation. A lawyer shall abide by a client's decision whether to settle a matter. Except as otherwise provided by law in a criminal case, the lawyer shall abide by the client's decision, after consultation with the lawyer, as to a plea to be entered, whether to waive jury trial and whether the client will testify.

(b) A lawyer may limit the scope of the representation if the limitation is reasonable* under the circumstances, is not otherwise prohibited by law, and the client gives informed consent.*

Comment

Allocation of Authority between Client and Lawyer

[1] Paragraph (a) confers upon the client the ultimate authority to determine the purposes to be served by legal representation, within the limits imposed by law and the lawyer's professional obligations. (See, e.g., Cal. Const., art. I, § 16; Pen. Code, § 1018.) A lawyer retained to represent a client is authorized to act on behalf of the client, such as in procedural matters and in making certain tactical decisions. A lawyer is not authorized merely by virtue of the lawyer's retention to impair the client's substantive rights or the client's claim itself. (*Blanton v. Womancare, Inc.* (1985) 38 Cal.3d 396, 404 [212 Cal.Rptr. 151, 156].)

[2] At the outset of, or during a representation, the client may authorize the lawyer to take specific action on the client's behalf without further consultation. Absent a material change in circumstances and subject to rule 1.4, a lawyer may rely on such an advance authorization. The client may revoke such authority at any time.

---

* An asterisk (*) identifies a word or phrase defined in the terminology rule, rule 1.0.1.

Independence from Client's Views or Activities

[3] A lawyer's representation of a client, including representation by appointment, does not constitute an endorsement of the client's political, economic, social or moral views or activities.

Agreements Limiting Scope of Representation

[4] All agreements concerning a lawyer's representation of a client must accord with the Rules of Professional Conduct and other law. (See, e.g., rules 1.1, 1.8.1, 5.6; see also Cal. Rules of Court, rules 3.35-3.37 [limited scope rules applicable in civil matters generally], 5.425 [limited scope rule applicable in family law matters].)

(Adopted Sept. 26, 2018, eff. Nov. 1, 2018.)

Rule 1.2.1 Advising or Assisting the Violation of Law

(a) A lawyer shall not counsel a client to engage, or assist a client in conduct that the lawyer knows* is criminal, fraudulent,* or a violation of any law, rule, or ruling of a tribunal.*

(b) Notwithstanding paragraph (a), a lawyer may:

(1) discuss the legal consequences of any proposed course of conduct with a client; and

(2) counsel or assist a client to make a good faith effort to determine the validity, scope, meaning, or application of a law, rule, or ruling of a tribunal.*

Comment

[1] There is a critical distinction under this rule between presenting an analysis of legal aspects of questionable conduct and recommending the means by which a crime or fraud* might be committed with impunity. The fact that a client uses a lawyer's advice in a course of action that is criminal or fraudulent* does not of itself make a lawyer a party to the course of action.

[2] Paragraphs (a) and (b) apply whether or not the client's conduct has already begun and is continuing. In complying with this rule, a lawyer shall not violate the lawyer's duty under Business and Professions Code section 6068, subdivision (a) to uphold the Constitution and laws of the United States and California or the duty of confidentiality as provided in Business and Professions Code section 6068, subdivision (e)(1) and rule 1.6. In some cases, the lawyer's response is limited to the lawyer's right and, where appropriate, duty to resign or withdraw in accordance with rules 1.13 and 1.16.

[3] Paragraph (b) authorizes a lawyer to advise a client in good faith regarding the validity, scope, meaning or application of a law, rule, or ruling of a tribunal* or of the meaning placed upon it by governmental authorities, and of potential consequences to disobedience of the law, rule, or ruling of a tribunal* that the lawyer concludes in good faith to be invalid, as well as legal procedures that may be invoked to obtain a determination of invalidity.

[4] Paragraph (b) also authorizes a lawyer to advise a client on the consequences of violating a law, rule, or ruling of a tribunal* that the client does not contend is unenforceable or unjust in itself, as a means of protesting a law or policy the client finds objectionable. For example, a lawyer may properly advise a client about the consequences of blocking the entrance to a public building as a means of protesting a law or policy the client believes* to be unjust or invalid.

[5] If a lawyer comes to know* or reasonably should know* that a client expects assistance not permitted by these rules or other law or if the lawyer intends to act contrary to the client's instructions, the lawyer must advise the client regarding the limitations on the lawyer's conduct. (See rule 1.4(a)(4).)

[6] Paragraph (b) permits a lawyer to advise a client regarding the validity, scope, and meaning of California laws that might conflict with federal or tribal law. In the event of such a conflict, the lawyer may assist a client in drafting or administering, or interpreting or complying with, California laws, including statutes, regulations, orders, and other state or local provisions, even if the client's actions might violate the conflicting federal or tribal law. If California law conflicts with federal or tribal law, the lawyer must inform the client about related federal or tribal law and policy and under certain circumstances may also be required to provide legal advice to the client regarding the conflict (see rules 1.1 and 1.4).

(Adopted Sept. 26, 2018, eff. Nov. 1, 2018.)

Rule 1.3 Diligence

(a) A lawyer shall not intentionally, repeatedly, recklessly or with gross negligence fail to act with reasonable diligence in representing a client.

(b) For purposes of this rule, "reasonable diligence" shall mean that a lawyer acts with commitment and dedication to the interests of the client and does not neglect or disregard, or unduly delay a legal matter entrusted to the lawyer.

Comment

[1] This rule addresses only a lawyer's responsibility for his or her own professional diligence. See rules 5.1 and 5.3 with respect to a lawyer's disciplinary responsibility for supervising subordinate lawyers and nonlawyers.

[2] See rule 1.1 with respect to a lawyer's duty to perform legal services with competence.

(Adopted Sept. 26, 2018, eff. Nov. 1, 2018.)

Rule 1.4 Communication with Clients

(a) A lawyer shall:

(1) promptly inform the client of any decision or circumstance with respect to which disclosure or the client's informed consent* is required by these rules or the State Bar Act;

(2) reasonably* consult with the client about the means by which to accomplish the client's objectives in the representation;

(3) keep the client reasonably* informed about significant developments relating to the representation, including promptly complying with reasonable* requests for information and copies of significant documents when necessary to keep the client so informed; and

(4) advise the client about any relevant limitation on the lawyer's conduct when the lawyer knows* that the client expects assistance not permitted by the Rules of Professional Conduct or other law.

(b) A lawyer shall explain a matter to the extent reasonably* necessary to permit the client to make informed decisions regarding the representation.

(c) A lawyer may delay transmission of information to a client if the lawyer reasonably believes* that the client would be likely to react in a way that may cause imminent harm to the client or others.

(d) A lawyer's obligation under this rule to provide information and documents is subject to any applicable protective order, non-disclosure agreement, or limitation under statutory or decisional law.

Comment

[1] A lawyer will not be subject to discipline under paragraph (a)(3) of this rule for failing to communicate insignificant or irrelevant information. (See Bus. & Prof. Code, § 6068, subd. (m).) Whether a particular development is significant will generally depend on the surrounding facts and circumstances. **For example, a lawyer's receipt of funds on behalf of a client requires communication with the client pursuant to rule 1.15, paragraphs (d)(1) and (d)(4) and ordinarily is also a significant development requiring communication with the client pursuant to this rule.**

[2] A lawyer may comply with paragraph (a)(3) by providing to the client copies of significant documents by electronic or other means. This rule does not prohibit a lawyer from seeking recovery of the lawyer's expense in any subsequent legal proceeding.

[3] Paragraph (c) applies during a representation and does not alter the obligations applicable at termination of a representation. (See rule 1.16(e)(1).)

[4] This rule is not intended to create, augment, diminish, or eliminate any application of the work product rule. The obligation of the lawyer to provide work product to the client shall be governed by relevant statutory and decisional law.

(Adopted Sept. 26, 2018, eff. Nov. 1, 2018; amended Oct. 24, 2022, eff. Jan. 1, 2023.)

Rule 1.4.1 Communication of Settlement Offers

(a) A lawyer shall promptly communicate to the lawyer's client:

(1) all terms and conditions of a proposed plea bargain or other dispositive offer made to the client in a criminal matter; and

(2) all amounts, terms, and conditions of any written* offer of settlement made to the client in all other matters.

(b) As used in this rule, "client" includes a person* who possesses the authority to accept an offer of settlement or plea, or, in a class action, all the named representatives of the class.

Comment An oral offer of settlement made to the client in a civil matter must also be communicated if it is a "significant development" under rule 1.4.

(Adopted Sept. 26, 2018, eff. Nov. 1, 2018.)

Rule 1.4.2 Disclosure of Professional Liability Insurance

(a) A lawyer who knows* or reasonably should know* that the lawyer does not have professional liability insurance shall inform a client in writing,* at the time of the client's engagement of the lawyer, that the lawyer does not have professional liability insurance.

(b) If notice under paragraph (a) has not been provided at the time of a client's engagement of the lawyer, the lawyer shall inform the client in writing* within thirty days of the date the lawyer knows* or reasonably should know* that the lawyer no longer has professional liability insurance during the representation of the client.

(c) This rule does not apply to:

(1) a lawyer who knows* or reasonably should know* at the time of the client's engagement of the lawyer that the lawyer's legal representa-

---

* An asterisk (*) identifies a word or phrase defined in the terminology rule, rule 1.0.1.

tion of the client in the matter will not exceed four hours; provided that if the representation subsequently exceeds four hours, the lawyer must comply with paragraphs (a) and (b);

(2) a lawyer who is employed as a government lawyer or in-house counsel when that lawyer is representing or providing legal advice to a client in that capacity;

(3) a lawyer who is rendering legal services in an emergency to avoid foreseeable prejudice to the rights or interests of the client;

(4) a lawyer who has previously advised the client in writing* under paragraph (a) or (b) that the lawyer does not have professional liability insurance.

Comment

[1] The disclosure obligation imposed by paragraph (a) applies with respect to new clients and new engagements with returning clients.

[2] A lawyer may use the following language in making the disclosure required by paragraph (a), and may include that language in a written* fee agreement with the client or in a separate writing:

"Pursuant to rule 1.4.2 of the California Rules of Professional Conduct, I am informing you in writing that I do not have professional liability insurance."

[3] A lawyer may use the following language in making the disclosure required by paragraph (b):

"Pursuant to rule 1.4.2 of the California Rules of Professional Conduct, I am informing you in writing that I no longer have professional liability insurance."

[4] The exception in paragraph (c)(2) for government lawyers and in-house counsels is limited to situations involving direct employment and representation, and does not, for example, apply to outside counsel for a private or governmental entity, or to counsel retained by an insurer to represent an insured. If a lawyer is employed by and provides legal services directly for a private entity or a federal, state or local governmental entity, that entity is presumed to know* whether the lawyer is or is not covered by professional liability insurance.

(Adopted Sept. 26, 2018, eff. Nov. 1, 2018.)

Rule 1.5 Fees for Legal Services

(a) A lawyer shall not make an agreement for, charge, or collect an unconscionable or illegal fee.

(b) Unconscionability of a fee shall be determined on the basis of all the facts and circumstances existing at the time the agreement is entered into except where the parties contemplate that the fee will be affected by later events. The factors to be considered in determining the unconscionability of a fee include without limitation the following:

(1) whether the lawyer engaged in fraud* or overreaching in negotiating or setting the fee;

(2) whether the lawyer has failed to disclose material facts;

(3) the amount of the fee in proportion to the value of the services performed;

(4) the relative sophistication of the lawyer and the client;

(5) the novelty and difficulty of the questions involved, and the skill requisite to perform the legal service properly;

(6) the likelihood, if apparent to the client, that the acceptance of the particular employment will preclude other employment by the lawyer;

(7) the amount involved and the results obtained;

(8) the time limitations imposed by the client or by the circumstances;

(9) the nature and length of the professional relationship with the client;

(10) the experience, reputation, and ability of the lawyer or lawyers performing the services;

(11) whether the fee is fixed or contingent;

(12) the time and labor required; and

(13) whether the client gave informed consent* to the fee.

(c) A lawyer shall not make an agreement for, charge, or collect:

(1) any fee in a family law matter, the payment or amount of which is contingent upon the securing of a dissolution or declaration of nullity of a marriage or upon the amount of spousal or child support, or property settlement in lieu thereof; or

(2) a contingent fee for representing a defendant in a criminal case.

(d) A lawyer may make an agreement for, charge, or collect a fee that is denominated as "earned on receipt" or "non-refundable," or in similar terms, only if the fee is a true retainer and the client agrees in writing* after disclosure that the client will not be entitled to a refund of all or part of the fee charged. A true retainer is a fee that a client pays to a lawyer to ensure the lawyer's availability to the client during a specified period or on a specified matter, but not to any extent as compensation for legal services performed or to be performed.

(e) A lawyer may make an agreement for, charge, or collect a flat fee for specified legal services. A flat fee is a fixed amount that constitutes complete payment for the performance of described services regardless of the amount of work ultimately involved, and which may be paid in whole or in part in advance of the lawyer providing those services.

Comment

Prohibited Contingent Fees

[1] Paragraph (c)(1) does not preclude a contract for a contingent fee for legal representation in connection with the recovery of post-judgment balances due under child or spousal support or other financial orders.

Payment of Fees in Advance of Services

[2] Rule 1.15(a) and (b) govern whether a lawyer must deposit in a trust account a fee paid in advance.

[3] When a lawyer-client relationship terminates, the lawyer must refund the unearned portion of a fee. (See rule 1.16(e)(2).)

Division of Fee

[4] A division of fees among lawyers is governed by rule 1.5.1.

Written Fee Agreements*

[5] Some fee agreements must be in writing* to be enforceable. (See, e.g., Bus. & Prof. Code, §§ 6147 and 6148.)

(Adopted Sept. 26, 2018, eff. Nov. 1, 2018.)

Rule 1.5.1 Fee Divisions Among Lawyers

(a) Lawyers who are not in the same law firm* shall not divide a fee for legal services unless:

(1) the lawyers enter into a written* agreement to divide the fee;

(2) the client has consented in writing,* either at the time the lawyers enter into the agreement to divide the fee or as soon thereafter as reasonably* practicable, after a full written* disclosure to the client of: (i) the fact that a division of fees will be made; (ii) the identity of the lawyers or law firms* that are parties to the division; and (iii) the terms of the division; and

(3) the total fee charged by all lawyers is not increased solely by reason of the agreement to divide fees.

(b) This rule does not apply to a division of fees pursuant to court order.

Comment

The writing* requirements of paragraphs (a)(1) and (a)(2) may be satisfied by one or more writings.*

(Adopted Sept. 26, 2018, eff. Nov. 1, 2018.)

Rule 1.6 Confidential Information of a Client

(a) A lawyer shall not reveal information protected from disclosure by Business and Professions Code section 6068, subdivision (e)(1) unless the client gives informed consent,* or the disclosure is permitted by paragraph (b) of this rule.

(b) A lawyer may, but is not required to, reveal information protected by Business and Professions Code section 6068, subdivision (e)(1) to the extent that the lawyer reasonably believes* the disclosure is necessary to prevent a criminal act that the lawyer reasonably believes* is likely to result in death of, or substantial* bodily harm to, an individual, as provided in paragraph (c).

(c) Before revealing information protected by Business and Professions Code section 6068, subdivision (e)(1) to prevent a criminal act as provided in paragraph (b), a lawyer shall, if reasonable* under the circumstances:

(1) make a good faith effort to persuade the client: (i) not to commit or to continue the criminal act; or (ii) to pursue a course of conduct that will prevent the threatened death or substantial* bodily harm; or do both (i) and (ii); and

(2) inform the client, at an appropriate time, of the lawyer's ability or decision to reveal information protected by Business and Professions Code section 6068, subdivision (e)(1) as provided in paragraph (b).

(d) In revealing information protected by Business and Professions Code section 6068, subdivision (e)(1) as provided in paragraph (b), the lawyer's disclosure must be no more than is necessary to prevent the criminal act, given the information known* to the lawyer at the time of the disclosure.

(e) A lawyer who does not reveal information permitted by paragraph (b) does not violate this rule.

---

* An asterisk (*) identifies a word or phrase defined in the terminology rule, rule 1.0.1.

Comment

Duty of confidentiality

[1] Paragraph (a) relates to a lawyer's obligations under Business and Professions Code section 6068, subdivision (e)(1), which provides it is a duty of a lawyer: "To maintain inviolate the confidence, and at every peril to himself or herself to preserve the secrets, of his or her client." A lawyer's duty to preserve the confidentiality of client information involves public policies of paramount importance. (*In Re Jordan* (1974) 12 Cal.3d 575, 580 [116 Cal.Rptr. 371].) Preserving the confidentiality of client information contributes to the trust that is the hallmark of the lawyer-client relationship. The client is thereby encouraged to seek legal assistance and to communicate fully and frankly with the lawyer even as to embarrassing or detrimental subjects. The lawyer needs this information to represent the client effectively and, if necessary, to advise the client to refrain from wrongful conduct. Almost without exception, clients come to lawyers in order to determine their rights and what is, in the complex of laws and regulations, deemed to be legal and correct. Based upon experience, lawyers know* that almost all clients follow the advice given, and the law is upheld. Paragraph (a) thus recognizes a fundamental principle in the lawyer-client relationship, that, in the absence of the client's informed consent,* a lawyer must not reveal information protected by Business and Professions Code section 6068, subdivision (e)(1). (See, e.g., *Commercial Standard Title Co. v. Superior Court* (1979) 92 Cal.App.3d 934, 945 [155 Cal.Rptr.393].)

Lawyer-client confidentiality encompasses the lawyer-client privilege, the work-product doctrine and ethical standards of confidentiality

[2] The principle of lawyer-client confidentiality applies to information a lawyer acquires by virtue of the representation, whatever its source, and encompasses matters communicated in confidence by the client, and therefore protected by the lawyer-client privilege, matters protected by the work product doctrine, and matters protected under ethical standards of confidentiality, all as established in law, rule and policy. (See *In the Matter of Johnson* (Rev. Dept. 2000) 4 Cal. State Bar Ct. Rptr. 179; *Goldstein v. Lees* (1975) 46 Cal.App.3d 614, 621 [120 Cal.Rptr. 253].) The lawyer-client privilege and work-product doctrine apply in judicial and other proceedings in which a lawyer may be called as a witness or be otherwise compelled to produce evidence concerning a client. A lawyer's ethical duty of confidentiality is not so limited in its scope of protection for the lawyer-client relationship of trust and prevents a lawyer from revealing the client's information even when not subjected to such compulsion. Thus, a lawyer may not reveal such information except with the informed consent* of the client or as authorized or required by the State Bar Act, these rules, or other law.

Narrow exception to duty of confidentiality under this rule

[3] Notwithstanding the important public policies promoted by lawyers adhering to the core duty of confidentiality, the overriding value of life permits disclosures otherwise prohibited by Business and Professions Code section 6068, subdivision (e)(1). Paragraph (b) is based on Business and Professions Code section 6068, subdivision (e)(2), which narrowly permits a lawyer to disclose information protected by Business and Professions Code section 6068, subdivision (e)(1) even without client consent. Evidence Code section 956.5, which relates to the evidentiary lawyer-client privilege, sets forth a similar express exception. Although a lawyer is not permitted to reveal information protected by section 6068, subdivision (e)(1) concerning a client's past, completed criminal acts, the policy favoring the preservation of human life that underlies this exception to the duty of confidentiality and the evidentiary privilege permits disclosure to prevent a future or ongoing criminal act.

Lawyer not subject to discipline for revealing information protected by Business and Professions Code section 6068, subdivision (e)(1) as permitted under this rule

[4] Paragraph (b) reflects a balancing between the interests of preserving client confidentiality and of preventing a criminal act that a lawyer reasonably believes* is likely to result in death or substantial* bodily harm to an individual. A lawyer who reveals information protected by Business and Professions Code section 6068, subdivision (e)(1) as permitted under this rule is not subject to discipline.

No duty to reveal information protected by Business and Professions Code section 6068, subdivision (e)(1)

[5] Neither Business and Professions Code section 6068, subdivision (e)(2) nor paragraph (b) imposes an affirmative obligation on a lawyer to reveal information protected by Business and Professions Code section 6068, subdivision (e)(1) in order to prevent harm. A lawyer may decide not to reveal such information. Whether a lawyer chooses to reveal information protected by section 6068, subdivision (e)(1) as permitted under this rule is a matter for the individual lawyer to decide, based on all the facts and circumstances, such as those discussed in Comment [6] of this rule.

Whether to reveal information protected by Business and Professions Code section 6068, subdivision (e) as permitted under paragraph (b)

[6] Disclosure permitted under paragraph (b) is ordinarily a last resort, when no other available action is reasonably* likely to prevent the criminal act. Prior to revealing information protected by Business and Professions Code section 6068, subdivision (e)(1) as permitted by paragraph (b), the lawyer must, if reasonable* under the circumstances, make a good faith effort to persuade the client to take steps to avoid the criminal act or threatened harm. Among the factors to be considered in determining whether to disclose information protected by section 6068, subdivision (e)(1) are the following:

(1) the amount of time that the lawyer has to make a decision about disclosure;

(2) whether the client or a third-party has made similar threats before and whether they have ever acted or attempted to act upon them;

(3) whether the lawyer believes* the lawyer's efforts to persuade the client or a third person* not to engage in the criminal conduct have or have not been successful;

(4) the extent of adverse effect to the client's rights under the Fifth, Sixth and Fourteenth Amendments of the United States Constitution and analogous rights and privacy rights under Article I of the Constitution of the State of California that may result from disclosure contemplated by the lawyer;

(5) the extent of other adverse effects to the client that may result from disclosure contemplated by the lawyer; and

(6) the nature and extent of information that must be disclosed to prevent the criminal act or threatened harm.

A lawyer may also consider whether the prospective harm to the victim or victims is imminent in deciding whether to disclose the information protected by section 6068, subdivision (e)(1). However, the imminence of the harm is not a prerequisite to disclosure and a lawyer may disclose the information protected by section 6068, subdivision (e)(1) without waiting until immediately before the harm is likely to occur.

Whether to counsel client or third person not to commit a criminal act reasonably* likely to result in death or substantial* bodily harm*

[7] Paragraph (c)(1) provides that before a lawyer may reveal information protected by Business and Professions Code section 6068, subdivision (e)(1), the lawyer must, if reasonable* under the circumstances, make a good faith effort to persuade the client not to commit or to continue the criminal act, or to persuade the client to otherwise pursue a course of conduct that will prevent the threatened death or substantial* bodily harm, including persuading the client to take action to prevent a third person* from committing or continuing a criminal act. If necessary, the client may be persuaded to do both. The interests protected by such counseling are the client's interests in limiting disclosure of information protected by section 6068, subdivision (e) and in taking responsible action to deal with situations attributable to the client. If a client, whether in response to the lawyer's counseling or otherwise, takes corrective action — such as by ceasing the client's own criminal act or by dissuading a third person* from committing or continuing a criminal act before harm is caused — the option for permissive disclosure by the lawyer would cease because the threat posed by the criminal act would no longer be present. When the actor is a nonclient or when the act is deliberate or malicious, the lawyer who contemplates making adverse disclosure of protected information may reasonably* conclude that the compelling interests of the lawyer or others in their own personal safety preclude personal contact with the actor. Before counseling an actor who is a nonclient, the lawyer should, if reasonable* under the circumstances, first advise the client of the lawyer's intended course of action. If a client or another person* has already acted but the intended harm has not yet occurred, the lawyer should consider, if reasonable* under the circumstances, efforts to persuade the client or third person* to warn the victim or consider other appropriate action to prevent the harm. Even when the lawyer has concluded that paragraph (b) does not permit the lawyer to reveal information protected by section 6068, subdivision (e)(1), the lawyer nevertheless is permitted to counsel the client as to why it may be in the client's best interest to consent to the attorney's disclosure of that information.

Disclosure of information protected by Business and Professions Code section 6068, subdivision (e)(1) must be no more than is reasonably necessary to prevent the criminal act*

[8] Paragraph (d) requires that disclosure of information protected by Business and Professions Code section 6068, subdivision (e) as permitted by paragraph (b), when made, must be no more extensive than is necessary to prevent the criminal act. Disclosure should allow access to the information to only those persons* who the lawyer reasonably believes* can act to prevent the harm. Under some circumstances, a lawyer may determine that the best course to pursue is to make an anonymous disclosure to the potential victim or relevant law-enforcement authorities. What particular measures are reasonable* depends on the circumstances known* to the lawyer. Relevant circumstances include the time available, whether the victim might be unaware of the threat, the lawyer's prior course of dealings with the client, and the extent of the adverse effect on the client that may result from the disclosure contemplated by the lawyer.

Informing client pursuant to paragraph (c)(2) of lawyer's ability or decision to reveal information protected by Business and Professions Code section 6068, subdivision (e)(1)

[9] A lawyer is required to keep a client reasonably* informed about significant developments regarding the representation. (See rule 1.4; Bus. & Prof. Code, § 6068, subd. (m).) Paragraph (c)(2), however, recognizes that under certain circumstances, informing a client of the lawyer's ability or decision to reveal information protected by section 6068, subdivision (e)(1) as permitted in paragraph (b) would likely increase the risk of death or substantial* bodily harm, not only to the originally-intended victims of the criminal act, but also to the client or members

---

* An asterisk (*) identifies a word or phrase defined in the terminology rule, rule 1.0.1.

of the client's family, or to the lawyer or the lawyer's family or associates. Therefore, paragraph (c)(2) requires a lawyer to inform the client of the lawyer's ability or decision to reveal information protected by section 6068, subdivision (e)(1) as permitted in paragraph (b) only if it is reasonable* to do so under the circumstances. Paragraph (c)(2) further recognizes that the appropriate time for the lawyer to inform the client may vary depending upon the circumstances. (See Comment [10] of this rule.) Among the factors to be considered in determining an appropriate time, if any, to inform a client are:

(1) whether the client is an experienced user of legal services;
(2) the frequency of the lawyer's contact with the client;
(3) the nature and length of the professional relationship with the client;
(4) whether the lawyer and client have discussed the lawyer's duty of confidentiality or any exceptions to that duty;
(5) the likelihood that the client's matter will involve information within paragraph (b);
(6) the lawyer's belief,* if applicable, that so informing the client is likely to increase the likelihood that a criminal act likely to result in the death of, or substantial* bodily harm to, an individual; and
(7) the lawyer's belief,* if applicable, that good faith efforts to persuade a client not to act on a threat have failed.

Avoiding a chilling effect on the lawyer-client relationship

[10] The foregoing flexible approach to the lawyer's informing a client of his or her ability or decision to reveal information protected by Business and Professions Code section 6068, subdivision (e)(1) recognizes the concern that informing a client about limits on confidentiality may have a chilling effect on client communication. (See Comment [1].) To avoid that chilling effect, one lawyer may choose to inform the client of the lawyer's ability to reveal information protected by section 6068, subdivision (e)(1) as early as the outset of the representation, while another lawyer may choose to inform a client only at a point when that client has imparted information that comes within paragraph (b), or even choose not to inform a client until such time as the lawyer attempts to counsel the client as contemplated in Comment [7]. In each situation, the lawyer will have satisfied the lawyer's obligation under paragraph (c)(2), and will not be subject to discipline.

Informing client that disclosure has been made; termination of the lawyer-client relationship

[11] When a lawyer has revealed information protected by Business and Professions Code section 6068, subdivision (e) as permitted in paragraph (b), in all but extraordinary cases the relationship between lawyer and client that is based on trust and confidence will have deteriorated so as to make the lawyer's representation of the client impossible. Therefore, when the relationship has deteriorated because of the lawyer's disclosure, the lawyer is required to seek to withdraw from the representation, unless the client has given informed consent* to the lawyer's continued representation. The lawyer normally must inform the client of the fact of the lawyer's disclosure. If the lawyer has a compelling interest in not informing the client, such as to protect the lawyer, the lawyer's family or a third person* from the risk of death or substantial* bodily harm, the lawyer must withdraw from the representation. (See rule 1.16.)

Other consequences of the lawyer's disclosure

[12] Depending upon the circumstances of a lawyer's disclosure of information protected by Business and Professions Code section 6068, subdivision (e)(1) as permitted by this rule, there may be other important issues that a lawyer must address. For example, a lawyer who is likely to testify as a witness in a matter involving a client must comply with rule 3.7. Similarly, the lawyer must also consider his or her duties of loyalty and competence. (See rules 1.7 and 1.1.)

Other exceptions to confidentiality under California law

[13] This rule is not intended to augment, diminish, or preclude any other exceptions to the duty to preserve information protected by Business and Professions Code section 6068, subdivision (e)(1) recognized under California law.

(Adopted Sept. 26, 2018, eff. Nov. 1, 2018.)

Rule 1.7 Conflict of Interest: Current Clients

(a) A lawyer shall not, without informed written consent* from each client and compliance with paragraph (d), represent a client if the representation is directly adverse to another client in the same or a separate matter.

(b) A lawyer shall not, without informed written consent* from each affected client and compliance with paragraph (d), represent a client if there is a significant risk the lawyer's representation of the client will be materially limited by the lawyer's responsibilities to or relationships with another client, a former client or a third person,* or by the lawyer's own interests.

(c) Even when a significant risk requiring a lawyer to comply with paragraph (b) is not present, a lawyer shall not represent a client without written* disclosure of the relationship to the client and compliance with paragraph (d) where:

(1) the lawyer has, or knows* that another lawyer in the lawyer's firm* has, a legal, business, financial, professional, or personal relationship with or responsibility to a party or witness in the same matter; or

(2) the lawyer knows* or reasonably should know* that another party's lawyer is a spouse, parent, child, or sibling of the lawyer, lives with the lawyer, is a client of the lawyer or another lawyer in the lawyer's firm,* or has an intimate personal relationship with the lawyer.

(d) Representation is permitted under this rule only if the lawyer complies with paragraphs (a), (b), and (c), and:

(1) the lawyer reasonably believes* that the lawyer will be able to provide competent and diligent representation to each affected client;

(2) the representation is not prohibited by law; and

(3) the representation does not involve the assertion of a claim by one client against another client represented by the lawyer in the same litigation or other proceeding before a tribunal.

(e) For purposes of this rule, "matter" includes any judicial or other proceeding, application, request for a ruling or other determination, contract, transaction, claim, controversy, investigation, charge, accusation, arrest, or other deliberation, decision, or action that is focused on the interests of specific persons,* or a discrete and identifiable class of persons.*

Comment

[1] Loyalty and independent judgment are essential elements in the lawyer's relationship to a client. The duty of undivided loyalty to a current client prohibits undertaking representation directly adverse to that client without that client's informed written consent.* Thus, absent consent, a lawyer may not act as an advocate in one matter against a person* the lawyer represents in some other matter, even when the matters are wholly unrelated. (See *Flatt v. Superior Court* (1994) 9 Cal.4th 275 [36 Cal.Rptr.2d 537].) A directly adverse conflict under paragraph (a) can arise in a number of ways, for example, when: (i) a lawyer accepts representation of more than one client in a matter in which the interests of the clients actually conflict; (ii) a lawyer, while representing a client, accepts in another matter the representation of a person* who, in the first matter, is directly adverse to the lawyer's client; or (iii) a lawyer accepts representation of a person* in a matter in which an opposing party is a client of the lawyer or the lawyer's law firm.* Similarly, direct adversity can arise when a lawyer cross-examines a non-party witness who is the lawyer's client in another matter, if the examination is likely to harm or embarrass the witness. On the other hand, simultaneous representation in unrelated matters of clients whose interests are only economically adverse, such as representation of competing economic enterprises in unrelated litigation, does not ordinarily constitute a conflict of interest and thus may not require informed written consent* of the respective clients.

[2] Paragraphs (a) and (b) apply to all types of legal representations, including the concurrent representation of multiple parties in litigation or in a single transaction or in some other common enterprise or legal relationship. Examples of the latter include the formation of a partnership for several partners* or a corporation for several shareholders, the preparation of a pre-nuptial agreement, or joint or reciprocal wills for a husband and wife, or the resolution of an "uncontested" marital dissolution. If a lawyer initially represents multiple clients with the informed written consent* as required under paragraph (b), and circumstances later develop indicating that direct adversity exists between the clients, the lawyer must obtain further informed written consent* of the clients under paragraph (a).

[3] In *State Farm Mutual Automobile Insurance Company v. Federal Insurance Company* (1999) 72 Cal.App.4th 1422 [86 Cal.Rptr.2d 20], the court held that paragraph (C)(3) of predecessor rule 3-310 was violated when a lawyer, retained by an insurer to defend one suit, and while that suit was still pending, filed a direct action against the same insurer in an unrelated action without securing the insurer's consent. Notwithstanding *State Farm*, paragraph (a) does not apply with respect to the relationship between an insurer and a lawyer when, in each matter, the insurer's interest is only as an indemnity provider and not as a direct party to the action.

[4] Even where there is no direct adversity, a conflict of interest requiring informed written consent* under paragraph (b) exists if there is a significant risk that a lawyer's ability to consider, recommend or carry out an appropriate course of action for the client will be materially limited as a result of the lawyer's other responsibilities, interests, or relationships, whether legal, business, financial, professional, or personal. For example, a lawyer's obligations to two or more clients in the same matter, such as several individuals seeking to form a joint venture, may materially limit the lawyer's ability to recommend or advocate all possible positions that each might take because of the lawyer's duty of loyalty to the other clients. The risk is that the lawyer may not be able to offer alternatives that would otherwise be available to each of the clients. The mere possibility of subsequent harm does not itself require disclosure and informed written consent.* The critical questions are the likelihood that a difference in interests exists or will eventuate and, if it does, whether it will materially interfere with the lawyer's independent professional judgment in considering alternatives or foreclose courses of action that reasonably* should be pursued on behalf of each client. The risk that the lawyer's representation may be materially limited may also arise from present or past relationships between the lawyer, or another member of the lawyer's firm*,

---

* An asterisk (*) identifies a word or phrase defined in the terminology rule, rule 1.0.1.

with a party, a witness, or another person* who may be affected substantially by the resolution of the matter.

[5] Paragraph (c) requires written* disclosure of any of the specified relationships even if there is not a significant risk the relationship will materially limit the lawyer's representation of the client. However, if the particular circumstances present a significant risk the relationship will materially limit the lawyer's representation of the client, informed written consent* is required under paragraph (b).

[6] Ordinarily paragraphs (a) and (b) will not require informed written consent* simply because a lawyer takes inconsistent legal positions in different tribunals* at different times on behalf of different clients. Advocating a legal position on behalf of a client that might create precedent adverse to the interests of another client represented by a lawyer in an unrelated matter is not sufficient, standing alone, to create a conflict of interest requiring informed written consent.* Informed written consent* may be required, however, if there is a significant risk that: (i) the lawyer may temper the lawyer's advocacy on behalf of one client out of concern about creating precedent adverse to the interest of another client; or (ii) the lawyer's action on behalf of one client will materially limit the lawyer's effectiveness in representing another client in a different case, for example, when a decision favoring one client will create a precedent likely to seriously weaken the position taken on behalf of the other client. Factors relevant in determining whether the clients' informed written consent* is required include: the courts and jurisdictions where the different cases are pending, whether a ruling in one case would have a precedential effect on the other case, whether the legal question is substantive or procedural, the temporal relationship between the matters, the significance of the legal question to the immediate and long-term interests of the clients involved, and the clients' reasonable* expectations in retaining the lawyer.

[7] Other rules and laws may preclude the disclosures necessary to obtain the informed written consent* or provide the information required to permit representation under this rule. (See, e.g., Bus. & Prof. Code, § 6068, subd. (e)(1) and rule 1.6.) If such disclosure is precluded, representation subject to paragraph (a), (b), or (c) of this rule is likewise precluded.

[8] Paragraph (d) imposes conditions that must be satisfied even if informed written consent* is obtained as required by paragraphs (a) or (b) or the lawyer has informed the client in writing* as required by paragraph (c). There are some matters in which the conflicts are such that even informed written consent* may not suffice to permit representation. (See *Woods v. Superior Court* (1983) 149 Cal.App.3d 931 [197 Cal.Rptr. 185]; *Klemm v. Superior Court* (1977) 75 Cal.App.3d 893 [142 Cal.Rptr. 509]; *Ishmael v. Millington* (1966) 241 Cal.App.2d 520 [50 Cal.Rptr. 592].)

[9] This rule does not preclude an informed written consent* to a future conflict in compliance with applicable case law. The effectiveness of an advance consent is generally determined by the extent to which the client reasonably* understands the material risks that the consent entails. The more comprehensive the explanation of the types of future representations that might arise and the actual and reasonably* foreseeable adverse consequences to the client of those representations, the greater the likelihood that the client will have the requisite understanding. The experience and sophistication of the client giving consent, as well as whether the client is independently represented in connection with giving consent, are also relevant in determining whether the client reasonably* understands the risks involved in giving consent. An advance consent cannot be effective if the circumstances that materialize in the future make the conflict nonconsentable under paragraph (d). A lawyer who obtains from a client an advance consent that complies with this rule will have all the duties of a lawyer to that client except as expressly limited by the consent. A lawyer cannot obtain an advance consent to incompetent representation. (See rule 1.8.8.)

[10] A material change in circumstances relevant to application of this rule may trigger a requirement to make new disclosures and, where applicable, obtain new informed written consents.* In the absence of such consents, depending on the circumstances, the lawyer may have the option to withdraw from one or more of the representations in order to avoid the conflict. The lawyer must seek court approval where necessary and take steps to minimize harm to the clients. See rule 1.16. The lawyer must continue to protect the confidences of the clients from whose representation the lawyer has withdrawn. (See rule 1.9(c).)

[11] For special rules governing membership in a legal service organization, see rule 6.3; and for work in conjunction with certain limited legal services programs, see rule 6.5.

(Adopted Sept. 26, 2018, eff. Nov. 1, 2018.)

Rule 1.8.1 Business Transactions with a Client and Pecuniary Interests Adverse to a Client

A lawyer shall not enter into a business transaction with a client, or knowingly* acquire an ownership, possessory, security or other pecuniary interest adverse to a client, unless each of the following requirements has been satisfied:

(a) the transaction or acquisition and its terms are fair and reasonable* to the client and the terms and the lawyer's role in the transaction or acquisition are fully disclosed and transmitted in writing* to the client in a manner that should reasonably* have been understood by the client;

(b) the client either is represented in the transaction or acquisition by an independent lawyer of the client's choice or the client is advised in writing* to seek the advice of an independent lawyer of the client's choice and is given a reasonable* opportunity to seek that advice; and

(c) the client thereafter provides informed written consent* to the terms of the transaction or acquisition, and to the lawyer's role in it.

Comment

[1] A lawyer has an "other pecuniary interest adverse to a client" within the meaning of this rule when the lawyer possesses a legal right to significantly impair or prejudice the client's rights or interests without court action. (See *Fletcher v. Davis* (2004) 33 Cal.4th 61, 68 [14 Cal.Rptr.3d 58]; see also Bus. & Prof. Code, § 6175.3 [Sale of financial products to elder or dependent adult clients; Disclosure]; Fam. Code, §§ 2033-2034 [Attorney lien on community real property].) However, this rule does not apply to a charging lien given to secure payment of a contingency fee. (See *Plummer v. Day/Eisenberg, LLP* (2010) 184 Cal.App.4th 38 [108 Cal.Rptr.3d 455].)

[2] For purposes of this rule, factors that can be considered in determining whether a lawyer is independent include whether the lawyer: (i) has a financial interest in the transaction or acquisition; and (ii) has a close legal, business, financial, professional or personal relationship with the lawyer seeking the client's consent.

[3] Fairness and reasonableness under paragraph (a) are measured at the time of the transaction or acquisition based on the facts that then exist.

[4] In some circumstances, this rule may apply to a transaction entered into with a former client. (Compare *Hunniecutt v. State Bar* (1988) 44 Cal.3d 362, 370-71 ["[W]hen an attorney enters into a transaction with a former client regarding a fund which resulted from the attorney's representation, it is reasonable to examine the relationship between the parties for indications of special trust resulting therefrom. We conclude that if there is evidence that the client placed his trust in the attorney because of the representation, an attorney-client relationship exists for the purposes of [the predecessor rule] even if the representation has otherwise ended [and] It appears that [the client] became a target of [the lawyer's] solicitation because he knew, through his representation of her, that she had recently received the settlement fund [and the court also found the client to be unsophisticated]."] with *Wallis v. State Bar* (1942) 21 Cal.2d 322 [finding lawyer not subject to discipline for entering into business transaction with a former client where the former client was a sophisticated businesswoman who had actively negotiated for terms she thought desirable, and the transaction was not connected with the matter on which the lawyer previously represented her].)

[5] This rule does not apply to the agreement by which the lawyer is retained by the client, unless the agreement confers on the lawyer an ownership, possessory, security, or other pecuniary interest adverse to the client. Such an agreement is governed, in part, by rule 1.5. This rule also does not apply to an agreement to advance to or deposit with a lawyer a sum to be applied to fees, or costs or other expenses, to be incurred in the future. Such agreements are governed, in part, by rules 1.5 and 1.15.

[6] This rule does not apply: (i) where a lawyer and client each make an investment on terms offered by a third person* to the general public or a significant portion thereof; or (ii) to standard commercial transactions for products or services that a lawyer acquires from a client on the same terms that the client generally markets them to others, where the lawyer has no advantage in dealing with the client.

(Adopted Sept. 26, 2018, eff. Nov. 1, 2018.)

Rule 1.8.2 Use of Current Client's Information

A lawyer shall not use a client's information protected by Business and Professions Code section 6068, subdivision (e)(1) to the disadvantage of the client unless the client gives informed consent,* except as permitted by these rules or the State Bar Act.

Comment

A lawyer violates the duty of loyalty by using information protected by Business and Professions Code section 6068, subdivision (e)(1) to the disadvantage of a current client.

(Adopted Sept. 26, 2018, eff. Nov. 1, 2018.)

Rule 1.8.3 Gifts from Client

(a) A lawyer shall not:

(1) solicit a client to make a substantial* gift, including a testamentary gift, to the lawyer or a person* related to the lawyer, unless the lawyer or other recipient of the gift is related to the client, or

(2) prepare on behalf of a client an instrument giving the lawyer or a person* related to the lawyer any substantial* gift, unless (i) the lawyer or other recipient of the gift is related to the client, or (ii) the client has been advised by an independent lawyer who has provided a certificate of

---

* An asterisk (*) identifies a word or phrase defined in the terminology rule, rule 1.0.1.

independent review that complies with the requirements of Probate Code section 21384.

(b) For purposes of this rule, related persons* include a person* who is "related by blood or affinity" as that term is defined in California Probate Code section 21374, subdivision (a).

Comment

[1] A lawyer or a person* related to a lawyer may accept a gift from the lawyer's client, subject to general standards of fairness and absence of undue influence. A lawyer also does not violate this rule merely by engaging in conduct that might result in a client making a gift, such as by sending the client a wedding announcement. Discipline is appropriate where impermissible influence occurs. (See *Magee v. State Bar* (1962) 58 Cal.2d 423 [24 Cal.Rptr. 839].)

[2] This rule does not prohibit a lawyer from seeking to have the lawyer or a partner* or associate of the lawyer named as executor of the client's estate or to another potentially lucrative fiduciary position. Such appointments, however, will be subject to rule 1.7(b) and (c).

(Adopted Sept. 26, 2018, eff. Nov. 1, 2018.)

Rule 1.8.4 [Reserved]

Rule 1.8.5 Payment of Personal or Business Expenses Incurred by or for a Client

(a) A lawyer shall not directly or indirectly pay or agree to pay, guarantee, or represent that the lawyer or lawyer's law firm* will pay the personal or business expenses of a prospective or existing client.

(b) Notwithstanding paragraph (a), a lawyer may:

(1) pay or agree to pay such expenses to third persons,* from funds collected or to be collected for the client as a result of the representation, with the consent of the client;

(2) after the lawyer is retained by the client, agree to lend money to the client based on the client's written* promise to repay the loan, provided the lawyer complies with rules 1.7(b), 1.7(c), and 1.8.1 before making the loan or agreeing to do so;

(3) advance the costs of prosecuting or defending a claim or action, or of otherwise protecting or promoting the client's interests, the repayment of which may be contingent on the outcome of the matter; and

(4) pay the costs of prosecuting or defending a claim or action, or of otherwise protecting or promoting the interests of an indigent person* in a matter in which the lawyer represents the client.

(c) "Costs" within the meaning of paragraphs (b)(3) and (b)(4) are not limited to those costs that are taxable or recoverable under any applicable statute or rule of court but may include any reasonable* expenses of litigation, including court costs, and reasonable* expenses in preparing for litigation or in providing other legal services to the client.

(d) Nothing in this rule shall be deemed to limit the application of rule 1.8.9.

(Adopted Sept. 26, 2018, eff. Nov. 1, 2018.)

Rule 1.8.6 Compensation from One Other than Client

A lawyer shall not enter into an agreement for, charge, or accept compensation for representing a client from one other than the client unless:

(a) there is no interference with the lawyer's independent professional judgment or with the lawyer-client relationship;

(b) information is protected as required by Business and Professions Code section 6068, subdivision (e)(1) and rule 1.6; and

(c) the lawyer obtains the client's informed written consent* at or before the time the lawyer has entered into the agreement for, charged, or accepted the compensation, or as soon thereafter as reasonably* practicable, provided that no disclosure or consent is required if:

(1) nondisclosure or the compensation is otherwise authorized by law or a court order; or

(2) the lawyer is rendering legal services on behalf of any public agency or nonprofit organization that provides legal services to other public agencies or the public.

Comment

[1] A lawyer's responsibilities in a matter are owed only to the client except where the lawyer also represents the payor in the same matter. With respect to the lawyer's additional duties when representing both the client and the payor in the same matter, see rule 1.7.

[2] A lawyer who is exempt from disclosure and consent requirements under paragraph (c) nevertheless must comply with paragraphs (a) and (b).

[3] This rule is not intended to abrogate existing relationships between insurers and insureds whereby the insurer has the contractual right to unilaterally select counsel for the insured, where there is no conflict of interest. (See *San Diego Navy Federal Credit Union v. Cumis Insurance Society* (1984) 162 Cal.App.3d 358 [208 Cal.Rptr. 494].).

[4] In some limited circumstances, a lawyer might not be able to obtain client consent before the lawyer has entered into an agreement for, charged, or accepted compensation, as required by this rule. This might happen, for example, when a lawyer is retained or paid by a family member on behalf of an incarcerated client or in certain commercial settings, such as when a lawyer is retained by a creditors' committee involved in a corporate debt restructuring and agrees to be compensated for any services to be provided to other similarly situated creditors who have not yet been identified. In such limited situations, paragraph (c) permits the lawyer to comply with this rule as soon thereafter as is reasonably* practicable.

[5] This rule is not intended to alter or diminish a lawyer's obligations under rule 5.4(c).

(Adopted Sept. 26, 2018, eff. Nov. 1, 2018.)

Rule 1.8.7 Aggregate Settlements

(a) A lawyer who represents two or more clients shall not enter into an aggregate settlement of the claims of or against the clients, or in a criminal case an aggregate agreement as to guilty or nolo contendere pleas, unless each client gives informed written consent.* The lawyer's disclosure shall include the existence and nature of all the claims or pleas involved and of the participation of each person* in the settlement.

(b) This rule does not apply to class action settlements subject to court approval.

(Adopted Sept. 26, 2018, eff. Nov. 1, 2018.)

Rule 1.8.8 Limiting Liability to Client

A lawyer shall not:

(a) Contract with a client prospectively limiting the lawyer's liability to the client for the lawyer's professional malpractice; or

(b) Settle a claim or potential claim for the lawyer's liability to a client or former client for the lawyer's professional malpractice, unless the client or former client is either:

(1) represented by an independent lawyer concerning the settlement; or

(2) advised in writing* by the lawyer to seek the advice of an independent lawyer of the client's choice regarding the settlement and given a reasonable* opportunity to seek that advice.

Comment

[1] Paragraph (b) does not absolve the lawyer of the obligation to comply with other law. (See, e.g., Bus. & Prof. Code, § 6090.5.)

[2] This rule does not apply to customary qualifications and limitations in legal opinions and memoranda, nor does it prevent a lawyer from reasonably* limiting the scope of the lawyer's representation. (See rule 1.2(b).)

(Adopted Sept. 26, 2018, eff. Nov. 1, 2018.)

Rule 1.8.9 Purchasing Property at a Foreclosure or a Sale Subject to Judicial Review

(a) A lawyer shall not directly or indirectly purchase property at a probate, foreclosure, receiver's, trustee's, or judicial sale in an action or proceeding in which such lawyer or any lawyer affiliated by reason of personal, business, or professional relationship with that lawyer or with that lawyer's law firm* is acting as a lawyer for a party or as executor, receiver, trustee, administrator, guardian, or conservator.

(b) A lawyer shall not represent the seller at a probate, foreclosure, receiver, trustee, or judicial sale in an action or proceeding in which the purchaser is a spouse or relative of the lawyer or of another lawyer in the lawyer's law firm* or is an employee of the lawyer or the lawyer's law firm.*

(c) This rule does not prohibit a lawyer's participation in transactions that are specifically authorized by and comply with Probate Code sections 9880 through 9885, but such transactions remain subject to the provisions of rules 1.8.1 and 1.7.

Comment

A lawyer may lawfully participate in a transaction involving a probate proceeding which concerns a client by following the process described in Probate Code sections 9880-9885. These provisions, which permit what would otherwise be impermissible self-dealing by specific submissions to and approval by the courts, must be strictly followed in order to avoid violation of this rule.

(Adopted Sept. 26, 2018, eff. Nov. 1, 2018.)

---

* An asterisk (*) identifies a word or phrase defined in the terminology rule, rule 1.0.1.

Rule 1.8.10 Sexual Relations with Current Client

(a) A lawyer shall not engage in sexual relations with a current client who is not the lawyer's spouse or registered domestic partner, unless a consensual sexual relationship existed between them when the lawyer-client relationship commenced.

(b) For purposes of this rule, "sexual relations" means sexual intercourse or the touching of an intimate part of another person* for the purpose of sexual arousal, gratification, or abuse.

(c) If a person* other than the client alleges a violation of this rule, no Notice of Disciplinary Charges may be filed by the State Bar against a lawyer under this rule until the State Bar has attempted to obtain the client's statement regarding, and has considered, whether the client would be unduly burdened by further investigation or a charge.

Comment

[1] Although this rule does not apply to a consensual sexual relationship that exists when a lawyer-client relationship commences, the lawyer nevertheless must comply with all other applicable rules. (See, e.g., rules 1.1, 1.7, and 2.1.)

[2] When the client is an organization, this rule applies to a lawyer for the organization (whether inside counsel or outside counsel) who has sexual relations with a constituent of the organization who supervises, directs or regularly consults with that lawyer concerning the organization's legal matters. (See rule 1.13.)

[3] Business and Professions Code section 6106.9, including the requirement that the complaint be verified, applies to charges under subdivision (a) of that section. This rule and the statute impose different obligations.

(Adopted Sept. 26, 2018, eff. Nov. 1, 2018.)

Rule 1.8.11 Imputation of Prohibitions Under Rules 1.8.1 to 1.8.9

While lawyers are associated in a law firm,* a prohibition in rules 1.8.1 through 1.8.9 that applies to any one of them shall apply to all of them.

Comment

A prohibition on conduct by an individual lawyer in rules 1.8.1 through 1.8.9 also applies to all lawyers associated in a law firm* with the personally prohibited lawyer. For example, one lawyer in a law firm* may not enter into a business transaction with a client of another lawyer associated in the law firm* without complying with rule 1.8.1, even if the first lawyer is not personally involved in the representation of the client. This rule does not apply to rule 1.8.10 since the prohibition in that rule is personal and is not applied to associated lawyers.

(Adopted Sept. 26, 2018, eff. Nov. 1, 2018.)

Rule 1.9 Duties to Former Clients

(a) A lawyer who has formerly represented a client in a matter shall not thereafter represent another person* in the same or a substantially related matter in which that person's* interests are materially adverse to the interests of the former client unless the former client gives informed written consent.*

(b) A lawyer shall not knowingly* represent a person* in the same or a substantially related matter in which a firm* with which the lawyer formerly was associated had previously represented a client

(1) whose interests are materially adverse to that person;* and

(2) about whom the lawyer had acquired information protected by Business and Professions Code section 6068, subdivision (e) and rules 1.6 and 1.9(c) that is material to the matter;

unless the former client gives informed written consent.*

(c) A lawyer who has formerly represented a client in a matter or whose present or former firm* has formerly represented a client in a matter shall not thereafter:

(1) use information protected by Business and Professions Code section 6068, subdivision (e) and rule 1.6 acquired by virtue of the representation of the former client to the disadvantage of the former client except as these rules or the State Bar Act would permit with respect to a current client, or when the information has become generally known;* or

(2) reveal information protected by Business and Professions Code section 6068, subdivision (e) and rule 1.6 acquired by virtue of the representation of the former client except as these rules or the State Bar Act permit with respect to a current client.

Comment

[1] After termination of a lawyer-client relationship, the lawyer owes two duties to a former client. The lawyer may not (i) do anything that will injuriously affect the former client in any matter in which the lawyer represented the former client, or (ii) at any time use against the former client knowledge or information acquired by virtue of the previous relationship. (See *Oasis West Realty, LLC v. Goldman* (2011) 51 Cal.4th 811 [124 Cal.Rptr.3d 256]; *Wutchumna Water Co. v. Bailey* (1932) 216 Cal. 564 [15 P.2d 505].) For example, (i) a lawyer could not properly seek to rescind on behalf of a new client a contract drafted on behalf of the former client and (ii) a lawyer who has prosecuted an accused person* could not represent the accused in a subsequent civil action against the government concerning the same matter. (See also Bus. & Prof. Code, § 6131; 18 U.S.C. § 207(a).) These duties exist to preserve a client's trust in the lawyer and to encourage the client's candor in communications with the lawyer.

[2] For what constitutes a "matter" for purposes of this rule, see rule 1.7(e).

[3] Two matters are "the same or substantially related" for purposes of this rule if they involve a substantial* risk of a violation of one of the two duties to a former client described above in Comment [1]. For example, this will occur: (i) if the matters involve the same transaction or legal dispute or other work performed by the lawyer for the former client; or (ii) if the lawyer normally would have obtained information in the prior representation that is protected by Business and Professions Code section 6068, subdivision (e) and rule 1.6, and the lawyer would be expected to use or disclose that information in the subsequent representation because it is material to the subsequent representation.

[4] Paragraph (b) addresses a lawyer's duties to a client who has become a former client because the lawyer no longer is associated with the law firm* that represents or represented the client. In that situation, the lawyer has a conflict of interest only when the lawyer involved has actual knowledge of information protected by Business and Professions Code section 6068, subdivision (e) and rules 1.6 and 1.9(c). Thus, if a lawyer while with one firm* acquired no knowledge or information relating to a particular client of the firm,* and that lawyer later joined another firm,* neither the lawyer individually nor lawyers in the second firm* would violate this rule by representing another client in the same or a related matter even though the interests of the two clients conflict. See rule 1.10(b) for the restrictions on lawyers in a firm* once a lawyer has terminated association with the firm.*

[5] The fact that information can be discovered in a public record does not, by itself, render that information generally known* under paragraph (c). (See, e.g., *In the Matter of Johnson* (Review Dept. 2000) 4 Cal. State Bar Ct. Rptr. 179.)

[6] With regard to the effectiveness of an advance consent, see rule 1.7, Comment [9]. With regard to imputation of conflicts to lawyers in a firm* with which a lawyer is or was formerly associated, see rule 1.10. Current and former government lawyers must comply with this rule to the extent required by rule 1.11.

(Adopted Sept. 26, 2018, eff. Nov. 1, 2018.)

Rule 1.10 Imputation of Conflicts of Interest: General Rule

(a) While lawyers are associated in a firm,* none of them shall knowingly* represent a client when any one of them practicing alone would be prohibited from doing so by rules 1.7 or 1.9, unless

(1) the prohibition is based on a personal interest of the prohibited lawyer and does not present a significant risk of materially limiting the representation of the client by the remaining lawyers in the firm;* or

(2) the prohibition is based upon rule 1.9(a) or (b) and arises out of the prohibited lawyer's association with a prior firm,* and

(i) the prohibited lawyer did not substantially participate in the same or a substantially related matter;

(ii) the prohibited lawyer is timely screened* from any participation in the matter and is apportioned no part of the fee therefrom; and

(iii) written* notice is promptly given to any affected former client to enable the former client to ascertain compliance with the provisions of this rule, which shall include a description of the screening* procedures employed; and an agreement by the firm* to respond promptly to any written* inquiries or objections by the former client about the screening* procedures.

(b) When a lawyer has terminated an association with a firm,* the firm* is not prohibited from thereafter representing a person* with interests materially adverse to those of a client represented by the formerly associated lawyer and not currently represented by the firm,* unless:

(1) the matter is the same or substantially related to that in which the formerly associated lawyer represented the client; and

(2) any lawyer remaining in the firm* has information protected by Business and Professions Code section 6068, subdivision (e) and rules 1.6 and 1.9(c) that is material to the matter.

(c) A prohibition under this rule may be waived by each affected client under the conditions stated in rule 1.7.

(d) The imputation of a conflict of interest to lawyers associated in a firm* with former or current government lawyers is governed by rule 1.11.

Comment

[1] In determining whether a prohibited lawyer's previously participation was substantial,* a number of factors should be considered, such as the lawyer's level

---

* An asterisk (*) identifies a word or phrase defined in the terminology rule, rule 1.0.1.

of responsibility in the prior matter, the duration of the lawyer's participation, the extent to which the lawyer advised or had personal contact with the former client, and the extent to which the lawyer was exposed to confidential information of the former client likely to be material in the current matter.

[2] Paragraph (a) does not prohibit representation by others in the law firm* where the person* prohibited from involvement in a matter is a nonlawyer, such as a paralegal or legal secretary. Nor does paragraph (a) prohibit representation if the lawyer is prohibited from acting because of events before the person* became a lawyer, for example, work that the person* did as a law student. Such persons,* however, ordinarily must be screened* from any personal participation in the matter. (See rules 1.0.1(k) and 5.3.)

[3] Paragraph (a)(2)(ii) does not prohibit the screened* lawyer from receiving a salary or partnership share established by prior independent agreement, but that lawyer may not receive compensation directly related to the matter in which the lawyer is prohibited.

[4] Where a lawyer is prohibited from engaging in certain transactions under rules 1.8.1 through 1.8.9, rule 1.8.11, and not this rule, determines whether that prohibition also applies to other lawyers associated in a firm* with the personally prohibited lawyer.

[5] The responsibilities of managerial and supervisory lawyers prescribed by rules 5.1 and 5.3 apply to screening* arrangements implemented under this rule.

[6] Standards for disqualification, and whether in a particular matter (1) a lawyer's conflict will be imputed to other lawyers in the same firm,* or (2) the use of a timely screen* is effective to avoid that imputation, are also the subject of statutes and case law. (See, e.g., Code Civ. Proc., § 128, subd. (a)(5); Pen. Code, § 1424; *In re Charlisse C.* (2008) 45 Cal.4th 145 [84 Cal.Rptr.3d 597]; *Rhaburn v. Superior Court* (2006) 140 Cal.App.4th 1566 [45 Cal.Rptr.3d 464]; *Kirk v. First American Title Ins. Co.* (2010) 183 Cal.App.4th 776 [108 Cal.Rptr.3d 620].)

(Adopted Sept. 26, 2018, eff. Nov. 1, 2018.)

Rule 1.11 Special Conflicts of Interest for Former and Current Government Officials and Employees

(a) Except as law may otherwise expressly permit, a lawyer who has formerly served as a public official or employee of the government:

(1) is subject to rule 1.9(c); and

(2) shall not otherwise represent a client in connection with a matter in which the lawyer participated personally and substantially as a public official or employee, unless the appropriate government agency gives its informed written consent* to the representation. This paragraph shall not apply to matters governed by rule 1.12(a).

(b) When a lawyer is prohibited from representation under paragraph (a), no lawyer in a firm* with which that lawyer is associated may knowingly* undertake or continue representation in such a matter unless:

(1) the personally prohibited lawyer is timely screened* from any participation in the matter and is apportioned no part of the fee therefrom; and

(2) written* notice is promptly given to the appropriate government agency to enable it to ascertain compliance with the provisions of this rule

(c) Except as law may otherwise expressly permit, a lawyer who was a public official or employee and, during that employment, acquired information that the lawyer knows* is confidential government information about a person,* may not represent a private client whose interests are adverse to that person* in a matter in which the information could be used to the material disadvantage of that person.* As used in this rule, the term "confidential government information" means information that has been obtained under governmental authority, that, at the time this rule is applied, the government is prohibited by law from disclosing to the public, or has a legal privilege not to disclose, and that is not otherwise available to the public. A firm* with which that lawyer is associated may undertake or continue representation in the matter only if the personally prohibited lawyer is timely screened* from any participation in the matter and is apportioned no part of the fee therefrom.

(d) Except as law may otherwise expressly permit, a lawyer currently serving as a public official or employee:

(1) is subject to rules 1.7 and 1.9; and

(2) shall not:

(i) participate in a matter in which the lawyer participated personally and substantially while in private practice or nongovernmental employment, unless the appropriate government agency gives its informed written consent;* or

(ii) negotiate for private employment with any person* who is involved as a party, or as a lawyer for a party, or with a law firm* for a party, in a matter in which the lawyer is participating personally and substantially, except that a lawyer serving as a law clerk to a judge, other adjudicative officer or arbitrator may negotiate for private employment as permitted by rule 1.12(b) and subject to the conditions stated in rule 1.12(b).

Comment

[1] Rule 1.10 is not applicable to the conflicts of interest addressed by this rule.

[2] For what constitutes a "matter" for purposes of this rule, see rule 1.7(e).

[3] Paragraphs (a)(2) and (d)(2) apply regardless of whether a lawyer is adverse to a former client. Both provisions apply when the former public official or employee of the government has personally and substantially participated in the matter. Personal participation includes both direct participation and the supervision of a subordinate's participation. Substantial* participation requires that the lawyer's involvement be of significance to the matter. Participation may be substantial* even though it is not determinative of the outcome of a particular matter. However, it requires more than official responsibility, knowledge, perfunctory involvement, or involvement on an administrative or peripheral issue. A finding of substantiality should be based not only on the effort devoted to the matter, but also on the importance of the effort. Personal and substantial* participation may occur when, for example, a lawyer participates through decision, approval, disapproval, recommendation, investigation or the rendering of advice in a particular matter.

[4] By requiring a former government lawyer to comply with rule 1.9(c), paragraph (a)(1) protects information obtained while working for the government to the same extent as information learned while representing a private client. This provision applies regardless of whether the lawyer was working in a "legal" capacity. Thus, information learned by the lawyer while in public service in an administrative, policy, or advisory position also is covered by paragraph (a)(1).

[5] Paragraph (c) operates only when the lawyer in question has actual knowledge of the information; it does not operate with respect to information that merely could be imputed to the lawyer.

[6] When a lawyer has been employed by one government agency and then moves to a second government agency, it may be appropriate to treat that second agency as another client for purposes of this rule, as when a lawyer is employed by a city and subsequently is employed by a federal agency. Because conflicts of interest are governed by paragraphs (a) and (b), the latter agency is required to screen* the lawyer. Whether two government agencies should be regarded as the same or different clients for conflict of interest purposes is beyond the scope of these rules. (See rule 1.13, Comment [6]; see also *Civil Service Commission v. Superior Court* (1984) 163 Cal.App.3d 70, 76-78 [209 Cal.Rptr. 159].)

[7] Paragraphs (b) and (c) do not prohibit a lawyer from receiving a salary or partnership share established by prior independent agreement, but that lawyer may not receive compensation directly relating the lawyer's compensation to the fee in the matter in which the lawyer is personally prohibited from participating.

[8] Paragraphs (a) and (d) do not prohibit a lawyer from jointly representing a private party and a government agency when doing so is permitted by rule 1.7 and is not otherwise prohibited by law.

[9] A lawyer serving as a public official or employee of the government may participate in a matter in which the lawyer participated substantially while in private practice or non-governmental employment only if: (i) the government agency gives its informed written consent* as required by paragraph (d)(2)(i); and (ii) the former client gives its informed written consent* as required by rule 1.9, to which the lawyer is subject by paragraph (d)(1).

[10] This rule is not intended to address whether in a particular matter: (i) a lawyer's conflict under paragraph (d) will be imputed to other lawyers serving in the same governmental agency; or (ii) the use of a timely screen* will avoid that imputation. The imputation and screening* rules for lawyers moving from private practice into government service under paragraph (d) are left to be addressed by case law and its development. (See *City & County of San Francisco v. Cobra Solutions, Inc.* (2006) 38 Cal.4th 839, 847, 851-54 [43 Cal.Rptr.3d 776]; *City of Santa Barbara v. Superior Court* (2004) 122 Cal.App.4th 17, 26-27 [18 Cal.Rptr.3d 403].) Regarding the standards for recusals of prosecutors in criminal matters, see Penal Code section 1424; *Haraguchi v. Superior Court* (2008) 43 Cal.4th 706, 711-20 [76 Cal.Rptr.3d 250]; and *Hollywood v. Superior Court* (2008) 43 Cal.4th 721, 727-35 [76 Cal.Rptr.3d 264]. Concerning prohibitions against former prosecutors participating in matters in which they served or participated in as prosecutor, see, e.g., Business and Professions Code section 6131 and 18 United States Code section 207(a).

(Adopted Sept. 26, 2018, eff. Nov. 1, 2018.)

Rule 1.12 Former Judge, Arbitrator, Mediator, or Other Third-Party Neutral

(a) Except as stated in paragraph (d), a lawyer shall not represent anyone in connection with a matter in which the lawyer participated personally and substantially as a judge or other adjudicative officer, judicial staff attorney or law clerk to such a person* or as an arbitrator, mediator, or other third-party neutral, unless all parties to the proceeding give informed written consent.*

---

* An asterisk (*) identifies a word or phrase defined in the terminology rule, rule 1.0.1.

(b) A lawyer shall not seek employment from any person* who is involved as a party or as lawyer for a party, or with a law firm* for a party, in a matter in which the lawyer is participating personally and substantially as a judge or other adjudicative officer or as an arbitrator, mediator, or other third party neutral. A lawyer serving as a judicial staff attorney or law clerk to a judge or other adjudicative officer may seek employment from a party, or with a lawyer or a law firm* for a party, in a matter in which the staff attorney or clerk is participating personally and substantially, but only with the approval of the court.

(c) If a lawyer is prohibited from representation by paragraph (a), other lawyers in a firm* with which that lawyer is associated may knowingly* undertake or continue representation in the matter only if:

(1) the prohibition does not arise from the lawyer's service as a mediator or settlement judge;

(2) the prohibited lawyer is timely screened* from any participation in the matter and is apportioned no part of the fee therefrom; and

(3) written* notice is promptly given to the parties and any appropriate tribunal* to enable them to ascertain compliance with the provisions of this rule.

(d) An arbitrator selected as a partisan of a party in a multimember arbitration panel is not prohibited from subsequently representing that party.

Comment

[1] Paragraphs (a) and (b) apply when a former judge or other adjudicative officer, or a judicial staff attorney or law clerk to such a person,* or an arbitrator, mediator, or other third-party neutral, has personally and substantially participated in the matter. Personal participation includes both direct participation and the supervision of a subordinate's participation, as may occur in a chambers with several staff attorneys or law clerks. Substantial* participation requires that the lawyer's involvement was of significance to the matter. Participation may be substantial* even though it was not determinative of the outcome of a particular case or matter. A finding of substantiality should be based not only on the effort devoted to the matter, but also on the importance of the effort. Personal and substantial* participation may occur when, for example, the lawyer participated through decision, recommendation, or the rendering of advice on a particular case or matter. However, a judge who was a member of a multi-member court, and thereafter left judicial office to practice law, is not prohibited from representing a client in a matter pending in the court, but in which the former judge did not participate, or acquire material confidential information. The fact that a former judge exercised administrative responsibility in a court also does not prevent the former judge from acting as a lawyer in a matter where the judge had previously exercised remote or incidental administrative responsibility that did not affect the merits, such as uncontested procedural duties typically performed by a presiding or supervising judge or justice. The term "adjudicative officer" includes such officials as judges pro tempore, referees, and special masters.

[2] Other law or codes of ethics governing third-party neutrals may impose more stringent standards of personal or imputed disqualification. (See rule 2.4.)

[3] Paragraph (c)(2) does not prohibit the screened* lawyer from receiving a salary or partnership share established by prior independent agreement, but that lawyer may not receive compensation directly related to the matter in which the lawyer is personally prohibited from participating.

(Adopted Sept. 26, 2018, eff. Nov. 1, 2018.)

Rule 1.13 Organization as Client

(a) A lawyer employed or retained by an organization shall conform his or her representation to the concept that the client is the organization itself, acting through its duly authorized directors, officers, employees, members, shareholders, or other constituents overseeing the particular engagement.

(b) If a lawyer representing an organization knows* that a constituent is acting, intends to act or refuses to act in a matter related to the representation in a manner that the lawyer knows* or reasonably should know* is (i) a violation of a legal obligation to the organization or a violation of law reasonably* imputable to the organization, and (ii) likely to result in substantial* injury to the organization, the lawyer shall proceed as is reasonably* necessary in the best lawful interest of the organization. Unless the lawyer reasonably believes* that it is not necessary in the best lawful interest of the organization to do so, the lawyer shall refer the matter to higher authority in the organization, including, if warranted by the circumstances, to the highest authority that can act on behalf of the organization as determined by applicable law.

(c) In taking any action pursuant to paragraph (b), the lawyer shall not reveal information protected by Business and Professions Code section 6068, subdivision (e).

(d) If, despite the lawyer's actions in accordance with paragraph (b), the highest authority that can act on behalf of the organization insists upon action, or fails to act, in a manner that is a violation of a legal obligation to the organization or a violation of law reasonably* imputable to the organization, and is likely to result in substantial* injury to the organization, the lawyer shall continue to proceed as is reasonably* necessary in the best lawful interests of the organization. The lawyer's response may include the lawyer's right and, where appropriate, duty to resign or withdraw in accordance with rule 1.16.

(e) A lawyer who reasonably believes* that he or she has been discharged because of the lawyer's actions taken pursuant to paragraph (b), or who resigns or withdraws under circumstances described in paragraph (d), shall proceed as the lawyer reasonably believes* necessary to assure that the organization's highest authority is informed of the lawyer's discharge, resignation, or withdrawal.

(f) In dealing with an organization's constituents, a lawyer representing the organization shall explain the identity of the lawyer's client whenever the lawyer knows* or reasonably should know* that the organization's interests are adverse to those of the constituent(s) with whom the lawyer is dealing.

(g) A lawyer representing an organization may also represent any of its constituents, subject to the provisions of rules 1.7, 1.8.2, 1.8.6, and 1.8.7. If the organization's consent to the dual representation is required by any of these rules, the consent shall be given by an appropriate official, constituent, or body of the organization other than the individual who is to be represented, or by the shareholders.

Comment

The Entity as the Client

[1] This rule applies to all forms of private, public and governmental organizations. (See Comment [6].) An organizational client can only act through individuals who are authorized to conduct its affairs. The identity of an organization's constituents will depend on its form, structure, and chosen terminology. For example, in the case of a corporation, constituents include officers, directors, employees and shareholders. In the case of other organizational forms, constituents include the equivalents of officers, directors, employees, and shareholders. For purposes of this rule, any agent or fiduciary authorized to act on behalf of an organization is a constituent of the organization.

[2] A lawyer ordinarily must accept decisions an organization's constituents make on behalf of the organization, even if the lawyer questions their utility or prudence. It is not within the lawyer's province to make decisions on behalf of the organization concerning policy and operations, including ones entailing serious risk. A lawyer, however, has a duty to inform the client of significant developments related to the representation under Business and Professions Code section 6068, subdivision (m) and rule 1.4. Even when a lawyer is not obligated to proceed in accordance with paragraph (b), the lawyer may refer to higher authority, including the organization's highest authority, matters that the lawyer reasonably believes* are sufficiently important to refer in the best interest of the organization subject to Business and Professions Code section 6068, subdivision (e) and rule 1.6.

[3] Paragraph (b) distinguishes between knowledge of the conduct and knowledge of the consequences of that conduct. When a lawyer knows* of the conduct, the lawyer's obligations under paragraph (b) are triggered when the lawyer knows* or reasonably should know* that the conduct is (i) a violation of a legal obligation to the organization, or a violation of law reasonably* imputable to the organization, and (ii) likely to result in substantial* injury to the organization.

[4] In determining how to proceed under paragraph (b), the lawyer should consider the seriousness of the violation and its potential consequences, the responsibility in the organization and the apparent motivation of the person* involved, the policies of the organization concerning such matters, and any other relevant considerations. Ordinarily, referral to a higher authority would be necessary. In some circumstances, however, the lawyer may ask the constituent to reconsider the matter. For example, if the circumstances involve a constituent's innocent misunderstanding of law and subsequent acceptance of the lawyer's advice, the lawyer may reasonably* conclude that the best interest of the organization does not require that the matter be referred to higher authority. If a constituent persists in conduct contrary to the lawyer's advice, it will be necessary for the lawyer to take steps to have the matter reviewed by a higher authority in the organization. If the matter is of sufficient seriousness and importance or urgency to the organization, referral to higher authority in the organization may be necessary even if the lawyer has not communicated with the constituent. For the responsibility of a subordinate lawyer in representing an organization, see rule 5.2.

[5] In determining how to proceed in the best lawful interests of the organization, a lawyer should consider the extent to which the organization should be informed of the circumstances, the actions taken by the organization with respect to the matter and the direction the lawyer has received from the organizational client.

---

* An asterisk (*) identifies a word or phrase defined in the terminology rule, rule 1.0.1.

Governmental Organizations

[6] It is beyond the scope of this rule to define precisely the identity of the client and the lawyer's obligations when representing a governmental agency. Although in some circumstances the client may be a specific agency, it may also be a branch of government or the government as a whole. In a matter involving the conduct of government officials, a government lawyer may have authority under applicable law to question such conduct more extensively than that of a lawyer for a private organization in similar circumstances. Duties of lawyers employed by the government or lawyers in military service may be defined by statutes and regulations. In addition, a governmental organization may establish internal organizational rules and procedures that identify an official, agency, organization, or other person* to serve as the designated recipient of whistle-blower reports from the organization's lawyers, consistent with Business and Professions Code section 6068, subdivision (e) and rule 1.6. This rule is not intended to limit that authority.

(Adopted Sept. 26, 2018, eff. Nov. 1, 2018.)

Rule 1.14 [Reserved]

Rule 1.15 Safekeeping Funds and Property of Clients and Other Persons*

(a) All funds received or held by a lawyer or law firm* for the benefit of a client, or other person* to whom the lawyer owes a contractual, statutory, or other legal duty, including advances for fees, costs and expenses, shall be deposited in one or more identifiable bank accounts labeled "Trust Account" or words of similar import, maintained in the State of California, or, with written* consent of the client, in any other jurisdiction where there is a substantial* relationship between the client or the client's business and the other jurisdiction.

(b) Notwithstanding paragraph (a), a flat fee paid in advance for legal services may be deposited in a lawyer's or law firm's operating account, provided:

(1) the lawyer or law firm* discloses to the client in writing* (i) that the client has a right under paragraph (a) to require that the flat fee be deposited in an identified trust account until the fee is earned, and (ii) that the client is entitled to a refund of any amount of the fee that has not been earned in the event the representation is terminated or the services for which the fee has been paid are not completed; and

(2) if the flat fee exceeds $1,000.00, the client's agreement to deposit the flat fee in the lawyer's operating account and the disclosures required by paragraph (b)(1) are set forth in a writing* signed by the client.

(c) Funds belonging to the lawyer or the law firm* shall not be deposited or otherwise commingled with funds held in a trust account except:

(1) funds reasonably* sufficient to pay bank charges; and

(2) funds belonging in part to a client or other person* and in part presently or potentially to the lawyer or the law firm,* in which case the portion belonging to the lawyer or law firm* must be withdrawn at the earliest reasonable* time after the lawyer or law firm's interest in that portion becomes fixed. However, if a client or other person* disputes the lawyer or law firm's right to receive a portion of trust funds, the disputed portion shall not be withdrawn until the dispute is finally resolved.

(d) A lawyer shall:

(1) absent good cause, notify a client or other person* no later than 14 days of the receipt of funds, securities, or other property in which the lawyer knows* or reasonably should know* the client or other person* has an interest;

(2) identify and label securities and properties of a client or other person* promptly upon receipt and place them in a safe deposit box or other place of safekeeping as soon as practicable;

(3) maintain complete records of all funds, securities, and other property of a client or other person* coming into the possession of the lawyer or law firm;*

(4) promptly account in writing* to the client or other person* for whom the lawyer holds funds or property;

(5) preserve records of all funds and property held by a lawyer or law firm* under this rule for a period of no less than five years after final appropriate distribution of such funds or property;

(6) comply with any order for an audit of such records issued pursuant to the Rules of Procedure of the State Bar; and

(7) promptly distribute [2] any undisputed funds or property in the possession of the lawyer or law firm* that the client or other person* is entitled to receive.

(e) The Board of Trustees of the State Bar shall have the authority to formulate and adopt standards as to what "records" shall be maintained by lawyers and law firms* in accordance with subparagraph (d)(3). The standards formulated and adopted by the Board, as from time to time amended, shall be effective and binding on all lawyers.

(f) For purposes of determining a lawyer's compliance with paragraph (d)(7), unless the lawyer, and the client or other person* agree in writing that the funds or property will continue to be held by the lawyer, there shall be a rebuttable presumption affecting the burden of proof as defined in Evidence Code sections 605 and 606 that a violation of paragraph (d)(7) has occurred if the lawyer, absent good cause, fails to distribute undisputed funds or property within 45 days of the date when the funds become undisputed as defined by paragraph (g). This presumption may be rebutted by proof by a preponderance of evidence that there was good cause for not distributing funds within 45 days of the date when the funds or property became undisputed as defined in paragraph (g).

(g) As used in this rule, "undisputed funds or property" refers to funds or property, or a portion of any such funds or property, in the possession of a lawyer or law firm* where the lawyer knows* or reasonably should know* that the ownership interest of the client or other person* in the funds or property, or any portion thereof, has become fixed and there are no unresolved disputes as to the client's or other person's* entitlement to receive the funds or property.

Standards:

Pursuant to this rule, the Board of Trustees of the State Bar adopted the following standards, effective November 1, 2018, as to what "records" shall be maintained by lawyers and law firms* in accordance with paragraph (d)(3).

(1) A lawyer shall, from the date of receipt of funds of the client or other person* through the period ending five years from the date of appropriate disbursement of such funds, maintain:

(a) a written* ledger for each client or other person* on whose behalf funds are held that sets forth:

(i) the name of such client or other person;*

(ii) the date, amount and source of all funds received on behalf of such client or other person;*

(iii) the date, amount, payee and purpose of each disbursement made on behalf of such client or other person;* and

(iv) the current balance for such client or other person;*

(b) a written* journal for each bank account that sets forth:

(i) the name of such account;

(ii) the date, amount and client [4] affected by each debit and credit; and

(iii) the current balance in such account;

(c) all bank statements and cancelled checks for each bank account; and

(d) each monthly reconciliation (balancing) of (a), (b), and (c).

(2) A lawyer shall, from the date of receipt of all securities and other properties held for the benefit of client or other person* through the period ending five years from the date of appropriate disbursement of such securities and other properties, maintain a written* journal that specifies:

(a) each item of security and property held;

(b) the person* on whose behalf the security or property is held;

(c) the date of receipt of the security or property;

(d) the date of distribution of the security or property; and

(e) person* to whom the security or property was distributed.

Comment

[1] Whether a lawyer owes a contractual, statutory or other legal duty under paragraph (a) to hold funds on behalf of a person* other than a client in situations where client funds are subject to a third-party lien will depend on the relationship between the lawyer and the third-party, whether the lawyer has assumed a contractual obligation to the third person* and whether the lawyer has an independent obligation to honor the lien under a statute or other law. In certain circumstances, a lawyer may be civilly liable when the lawyer has notice of a lien and disburses funds in contravention of the lien. (See *Kaiser Foundation Health Plan, Inc. v. Aguiluz* (1996) 47 Cal.App.4th 302 [54 Cal.Rptr.2d 665].) However, civil liability by itself does not establish a violation of this rule. (Compare *Johnstone v. State Bar of California* (1966) 64 Cal.2d 153, 155-156 [49 Cal.Rptr. 97] [" 'When an attorney assumes a fiduciary relationship and violates his duty in a manner that would justify disciplinary action if the relationship had been that of attorney and client, he may properly be disciplined for his misconduct.' "] with *Crooks v. State Bar* (1970) 3 Cal.3d 346, 358 [90 Cal.Rptr. 600] [lawyer who agrees

---

* An asterisk (*) identifies a word or phrase defined in the terminology rule, rule 1.0.1.

to act as escrow or stakeholder for a client and a third-party owes a duty to the nonclient with regard to held funds].)

[2] As used in this rule, "advances for fees" means a payment intended by the client as an advance payment for some or all of the services that the lawyer is expected to perform on the client's behalf. With respect to the difference between a true retainer and a flat fee, which is one type of advance fee, see rule 1.5(d) and (e). Subject to rule 1.5, a lawyer or law firm* may enter into an agreement that defines when or how an advance fee is earned and may be withdrawn from the client trust account.

[3] Absent written* disclosure and the client's agreement in a writing* signed by the client as provided in paragraph (b), a lawyer must deposit a flat fee paid in advance of legal services in the lawyer's trust account. Paragraph (b) does not apply to advance payment for costs and expenses. Paragraph (b) does not alter the lawyer's obligations under paragraph (d) or the lawyer's burden to establish that the fee has been earned.

[4] Subparagraph (d)(7) is not intended to apply to a fee or expense the client has agreed to pay in advance, or the client file, or any other property that the client or other person* has agreed in writing that the lawyer will keep or maintain. Regarding a lawyer's refund of a fee or expense paid in advance, see rule 1.16(e)(2). Regarding the release of a client's file to the client, see rule 1.16(e)(1).

[5] Upon rebuttal by proof by a preponderance of the evidence of the presumption set forth in paragraph (f), a violation of paragraph (d)(7) must be established by clear and convincing evidence without the benefit of the rebuttable presumption.

[6] Whether or not the rebuttable presumption in paragraph (f) applies, a lawyer must still comply will all other applicable provisions of this rule. This includes a lawyer's duty to take diligent steps to initiate and complete the resolution of disputes concerning a client's or other person's* entitlement to funds or property received by a lawyer.

[7] Under paragraph (g), possible disputes requiring resolution may include, but are not limited to, disputes concerning entitlement to funds arising from: medical liens; statutory liens; prior attorney liens; costs or expenses; attorney fees; a bank's policies and fees for clearing a check or draft; any applicable conditions on entitlement such as a plaintiff's execution of a release and dismissal; or any legal proceeding, such as an interpleader action, concerning the entitlement of any person to receive all or a portion of the funds or property.

(Adopted Sept. 26, 2018, eff. Nov. 1, 2018; amended Oct. 24, 2022, eff. Jan. 1, 2023.)

Rule 1.16 Declining or Terminating Representation

(a) Except as stated in paragraph (c), a lawyer shall not represent a client or, where representation has commenced, shall withdraw from the representation of a client if:

(1) the lawyer knows* or reasonably should know* that the client is bringing an action, conducting a defense, asserting a position in litigation, or taking an appeal, without probable cause and for the purpose of harassing or maliciously injuring any person;*

(2) the lawyer knows* or reasonably should know* that the representation will result in violation of these rules or of the State Bar Act;

(3) the lawyer's mental or physical condition renders it unreasonably difficult to carry out the representation effectively; or

(4) the client discharges the lawyer.

(b) Except as stated in paragraph (c), a lawyer may withdraw from representing a client if:

(1) the client insists upon presenting a claim or defense in litigation, or asserting a position or making a demand in a non-litigation matter, that is not warranted under existing law and cannot be supported by good faith argument for an extension, modification, or reversal of existing law;

(2) the client either seeks to pursue a criminal or fraudulent* course of conduct or has used the lawyer's services to advance a course of conduct that the lawyer reasonably believes* was a crime or fraud;*

(3) the client insists that the lawyer pursue a course of conduct that is criminal or fraudulent;*

(4) the client by other conduct renders it unreasonably difficult for the lawyer to carry out the representation effectively;

(5) the client breaches a material term of an agreement with, or obligation, to the lawyer relating to the representation, and the lawyer has given the client a reasonable* warning after the breach that the lawyer will withdraw unless the client fulfills the agreement or performs the obligation;

(6) the client knowingly* and freely assents to termination of the representation;

(7) the inability to work with co-counsel indicates that the best interests of the client likely will be served by withdrawal;

(8) the lawyer's mental or physical condition renders it difficult for the lawyer to carry out the representation effectively;

(9) a continuation of the representation is likely to result in a violation of these rules or the State Bar Act; or

(10) the lawyer believes* in good faith, in a proceeding pending before a tribunal,* that the tribunal* will find the existence of other good cause for withdrawal.

(c) If permission for termination of a representation is required by the rules of a tribunal,* a lawyer shall not terminate a representation before that tribunal* without its permission.

(d) A lawyer shall not terminate a representation until the lawyer has taken reasonable* steps to avoid reasonably* foreseeable prejudice to the rights of the client, such as giving the client sufficient notice to permit the client to retain other counsel, and complying with paragraph (e).

(e) Upon the termination of a representation for any reason:

(1) subject to any applicable protective order, non-disclosure agreement, statute or regulation, the lawyer promptly shall release to the client, at the request of the client, all client materials and property. "Client materials and property" includes correspondence, pleadings, deposition transcripts, experts' reports and other writings,* exhibits, and physical evidence, whether in tangible, electronic or other form, and other items reasonably* necessary to the client's representation, whether the client has paid for them or not; and

(2) the lawyer promptly shall refund any part of a fee or expense paid in advance that the lawyer has not earned or incurred. This provision is not applicable to a true retainer fee paid solely for the purpose of ensuring the availability of the lawyer for the matter.

Comment

[1] This rule applies, without limitation, to a sale of a law practice under rule 1.17. A lawyer can be subject to discipline for improperly threatening to terminate a representation. (See *In the Matter of Shalant* (Review Dept. 2005) 4 Cal. State Bar Ct. Rptr. 829, 837.)

[2] When a lawyer withdraws from the representation of a client in a particular matter under paragraph (a) or (b), the lawyer might not be obligated to withdraw from the representation of the same client in other matters. For example, a lawyer might be obligated under paragraph (a)(1) to withdraw from representing a client because the lawyer has a conflict of interest under rule 1.7, but that conflict might not arise in other representations of the client.

[3] Withdrawal under paragraph (a)(1) is not mandated where a lawyer for the defendant in a criminal proceeding, or the respondent in a proceeding that could result in incarceration, or involuntary commitment or confinement, defends the proceeding by requiring that every element of the case be established. (See rule 3.1(b).)

[4] Lawyers must comply with their obligations to their clients under Business and Professions Code section 6068, subdivision (e) and rule 1.6, and to the courts under rule 3.3 when seeking permission to withdraw under paragraph (c). If a tribunal* denies a lawyer permission to withdraw, the lawyer is obligated to comply with the tribunal's* order. (See Bus. & Prof. Code, §§ 6068, subd. (b) and 6103.) This duty applies even if the lawyer sought permission to withdraw because of a conflict of interest. Regarding withdrawal from limited scope representations that involve court appearances, compliance with applicable California Rules of Court concerning limited scope representation satisfies paragraph (c).

[5] Statutes may prohibit a lawyer from releasing information in the client materials and property under certain circumstances. (See, e.g., Pen. Code, §§ 1054.2 and 1054.10.) A lawyer in certain criminal matters may be required to retain a copy of a former client's file for the term of his or her imprisonment. (See, Pen. Code, § 1054.9.)

[6] Paragraph (e)(1) does not prohibit a lawyer from making, at the lawyer's own expense, and retaining copies of papers released to the client, or to prohibit a claim for the recovery of the lawyer's expense in any subsequent legal proceeding.

(Amended Apr. 23, 2020, eff. June 1, 2020; Adopted Sept. 26, 2018, eff. Nov. 1, 2018.)

Rule 1.17 Sale of a Law Practice

All or substantially* all of the law practice of a lawyer, living or deceased, including goodwill, may be sold to another lawyer or law firm* subject to all the following conditions:

(a) Fees charged to clients shall not be increased solely by reason of the sale.

(b) If the sale contemplates the transfer of responsibility for work not yet completed or responsibility for client files or information protected by Business and Professions Code section 6068, subdivision (e)(1), then;

(1) if the seller is deceased, or has a conservator or other person* acting in a representative capacity, and no lawyer has been appointed to

---

* An asterisk (*) identifies a word or phrase defined in the terminology rule, rule 1.0.1.

act for the seller pursuant to Business and Professions Code section 6180.5, then prior to the transfer;

(i) the purchaser shall cause a written* notice to be given to each client whose matter is included in the sale, stating that the interest in the law practice is being transferred to the purchaser; that the client has the right to retain other counsel; that the client may take possession of any client materials and property, as required by rule 1.16(e)(1); and that if no response is received to the notice within 90 days after it is sent, or if the client's rights would be prejudiced by a failure of the purchaser to act during that time, the purchaser may act on behalf of the client until otherwise notified by the client, and

(ii) the purchaser shall obtain the written* consent of the client. If reasonable* efforts have been made to locate the client and no response to the paragraph (b)(1)(i) notice is received within 90 days, consent shall be presumed until otherwise notified by the client.

(2) in all other circumstances, not less than 90 days prior to the transfer;

(i) the seller, or the lawyer appointed to act for the seller pursuant to Business and Professions Code section 6180.5, shall cause a written* notice to be given to each client whose matter is included in the sale, stating that the interest in the law practice is being transferred to the purchaser; that the client has the right to retain other counsel; that the client may take possession of any client materials and property, as required by rule 1.16(e)(1); and that if no response is received to the notice within 90 days after it is sent, or if the client's rights would be prejudiced by a failure of the purchaser to act during that time, the purchaser may act on behalf of the client until otherwise notified by the client, and

(ii) the seller, or the lawyer appointed to act for the seller pursuant to Business and Professions Code section 6180.5, shall obtain the written* consent of the client prior to the transfer. If reasonable* efforts have been made to locate the client and no response to the paragraph (b)(2)(i) notice is received within 90 days, consent shall be presumed until otherwise notified by the client.

(c) If substitution is required by the rules of a tribunal* in which a matter is pending, all steps necessary to substitute a lawyer shall be taken.

(d) The purchaser shall comply with the applicable requirements of rules 1.7 and 1.9.

(e) Confidential information shall not be disclosed to a nonlawyer in connection with a sale under this rule.

(f) This rule does not apply to the admission to or retirement from a law firm,* retirement plans and similar arrangements, or sale of tangible assets of a law practice.

Comment

[1] The requirement that the sale be of "all or substantially* all of the law practice of a lawyer" prohibits the sale of only a field or area of practice or the seller's practice in a geographical area or in a particular jurisdiction. The prohibition against the sale of less than all or substantially* all of a practice protects those clients whose matters are less lucrative and who might find it difficult to secure other counsel if a sale could be limited to substantial* fee-generating matters. The purchasers are required to undertake all client matters sold in the transaction, subject to client consent. This requirement is satisfied, however, even if a purchaser is unable to undertake a particular client matter because of a conflict of interest.

[2] Under paragraph (a), the purchaser must honor existing arrangements between the seller and the client as to fees and scope of work and the sale may not be financed by increasing fees charged for client matters transferred through the sale. However, fee increases or other changes to the fee arrangements might be justified by other factors, such as modifications of the purchaser's responsibilities, the passage of time, or reasonable* costs that were not addressed in the original agreement. Any such modifications must comply with rules 1.4 and 1.5 and other relevant provisions of these rules and the State Bar Act.

[3] Transfer of individual client matters, where permitted, is governed by rule 1.5.1. Payment of a fee to a nonlawyer broker for arranging the sale or purchase of a law practice is governed by rule 5.4(a).

(Adopted Sept. 26, 2018, eff. Nov. 1, 2018.)

Rule 1.18 Duties to Prospective Client

(a) A person* who, directly or through an authorized representative, consults a lawyer for the purpose of retaining the lawyer or securing legal service or advice from the lawyer in the lawyer's professional capacity, is a prospective client.

(b) Even when no lawyer-client relationship ensues, a lawyer who has communicated with a prospective client shall not use or reveal information protected by Business and Professions Code section 6068, subdivision (e) and rule 1.6 that the lawyer learned as a result of the consultation, except as rule 1.9 would permit with respect to information of a former client.

(c) A lawyer subject to paragraph (b) shall not represent a client with interests materially adverse to those of a prospective client in the same or a substantially related matter if the lawyer received from the prospective client information protected by Business and Professions Code section 6068, subdivision (e) and rule 1.6 that is material to the matter, except as provided in paragraph (d). If a lawyer is prohibited from representation under this paragraph, no lawyer in a firm* with which that lawyer is associated may knowingly* undertake or continue representation in such a matter, except as provided in paragraph (d).

(d) When the lawyer has received information that prohibits representation as provided in paragraph (c), representation of the affected client is permissible if:

(1) both the affected client and the prospective client have given informed written consent,* or

(2) the lawyer who received the information took reasonable* measures to avoid exposure to more information than was reasonably* necessary to determine whether to represent the prospective client; and

(i) the prohibited lawyer is timely screened* from any participation in the matter and is apportioned no part of the fee therefrom; and

(ii) written* notice is promptly given to the prospective client to enable the prospective client to ascertain compliance with the provisions of this rule.

Comment

[1] As used in this rule, a prospective client includes a person's* authorized representative. A lawyer's discussions with a prospective client can be limited in time and depth and leave both the prospective client and the lawyer free, and sometimes required, to proceed no further. Although a prospective client's information is protected by Business and Professions Code section 6068, subdivision (e) and rule 1.6 the same as that of a client, in limited circumstances provided under paragraph (d), a law firm* is permitted to accept or continue representation of a client with interests adverse to the prospective client. This rule is not intended to limit the application of Evidence Code section 951 (defining "client" within the meaning of the Evidence Code).

[2] Not all persons* who communicate information to a lawyer are entitled to protection under this rule. A person* who by any means communicates information unilaterally to a lawyer, without reasonable* expectation that the lawyer is willing to discuss the possibility of forming a lawyer-client relationship or provide legal advice is not a "prospective client" within the meaning of paragraph (a). In addition, a person* who discloses information to a lawyer after the lawyer has stated his or her unwillingness or inability to consult with the person* (*People v. Gionis* (1995) 9 Cal.4th 1196 [40 Cal.Rptr.2d 456]), or who communicates information to a lawyer without a good faith intention to seek legal advice or representation, is not a prospective client within the meaning of paragraph (a).

[3] In order to avoid acquiring information from a prospective client that would prohibit representation as provided in paragraph (c), a lawyer considering whether or not to undertake a new matter must limit the initial interview to only such information as reasonably* appears necessary for that purpose.

[4] Under paragraph (c), the prohibition in this rule is imputed to other lawyers in a law firm* as provided in rule 1.10. However, under paragraph (d)(1), the consequences of imputation may be avoided if the informed written consent* of both the prospective and affected clients is obtained. (See rule 1.0.1(e-1) [informed written consent].) In the alternative, imputation may be avoided if the conditions of paragraph (d)(2) are met and all prohibited lawyers are timely screened* and written* notice is promptly given to the prospective client. Paragraph (d)(2)(i) does not prohibit the screened* lawyer from receiving a salary or partnership share established by prior independent agreement, but that lawyer may not receive compensation directly related to the matter in which the lawyer is prohibited.

[5] Notice under paragraph (d)(2)(ii) must include a general description of the subject matter about which the lawyer was consulted, and the screening* procedures employed.

(Adopted Sept. 26, 2018, eff. Nov. 1, 2018.)

CHAPTER 2
COUNSELOR

Advisor. Rule 2.1.
Lawyer as Third-Party Neutral. Rule 2.4.
Lawyer as Temporary Judge, Referee, or Court-Appointed Arbitrator. Rule 2.4.1.

---

* An asterisk (*) identifies a word or phrase defined in the terminology rule, rule 1.0.1.

Rule 2.1 Advisor

In representing a client, a lawyer shall exercise independent professional judgment and render candid advice.

Comment

[1] A lawyer ordinarily has no duty to initiate investigation of a client's affairs or to give advice that the client has indicated is unwanted, but a lawyer may initiate advice to a client when doing so appears to be in the client's interest.

[2] This rule does not preclude a lawyer who renders advice from referring to considerations other than the law, such as moral, economic, social and political factors that may be relevant to the client's situation.

(Adopted Sept. 26, 2018, eff. Nov. 1, 2018.)

Rule 2.2 [Reserved]

Rule 2.3 [Reserved]

Rule 2.4 Lawyer as Third-Party Neutral

(a) A lawyer serves as a third-party neutral when the lawyer assists two or more persons* who are not clients of the lawyer to reach a resolution of a dispute, or other matter, that has arisen between them. Service as a third-party neutral may include service as an arbitrator, a mediator or in such other capacity as will enable the lawyer to assist the parties to resolve the matter.

(b) A lawyer serving as a third-party neutral shall inform unrepresented parties that the lawyer is not representing them. When the lawyer knows* or reasonably should know* that a party does not understand the lawyer's role in the matter, the lawyer shall explain the difference between the lawyer's role as a third-party neutral and a lawyer's role as one who represents a client.

Comment

[1] In serving as a third-party neutral, the lawyer may be subject to court rules or other law that apply either to third-party neutrals generally or to lawyers serving as third-party neutrals. Lawyer neutrals may also be subject to various codes of ethics, such as the Judicial Council Standards for Mediators in Court Connected Mediation Programs or the Judicial Council Ethics Standards for Neutral Arbitrators in Contractual Arbitration.

[2] A lawyer who serves as a third-party neutral subsequently may be asked to serve as a lawyer representing a client in the same matter. The conflicts of interest that arise for both the individual lawyer and the lawyer's law firm* are addressed in rule 1.12.

[3] This rule is not intended to apply to temporary judges, referees or court-appointed arbitrators. (See rule 2.4.1.)

(Adopted Sept. 26, 2018, eff. Nov. 1, 2018.)

Rule 2.4.1 Lawyer as Temporary Judge, Referee, or Court-Appointed Arbitrator

A lawyer who is serving as a temporary judge, referee, or court-appointed arbitrator, and is subject to canon 6D of the California Code of Judicial Ethics, shall comply with the terms of that canon.

Comment

[1] This rule is intended to permit the State Bar to discipline lawyers who violate applicable portions of the California Code of Judicial Ethics while acting in a judicial capacity pursuant to an order or appointment by a court.

[2] This rule is not intended to apply to a lawyer serving as a third-party neutral in a mediation or a settlement conference, or as a neutral arbitrator pursuant to an arbitration agreement. (See rule 2.4.)

(Adopted Sept. 26, 2018, eff. Nov. 1, 2018.)

CHAPTER 3
ADVOCATE

Meritorious Claims and Contentions. Rule 3.1.
Delay of Litigation. Rule 3.2.
Candor Toward the Tribunal. Rule 3.3.
Fairness to Opposing Party and Counsel. Rule 3.4.
Contact with Judges, Officials, Employees, and Jurors. Rule 3.5.
Trial Publicity. Rule 3.6.
Lawyer as Witness. Rule 3.7.
Special Responsibilities of a Prosecutor. Rule 3.8.
Advocate in Nonadjudicative Proceedings. Rule 3.9.
Threatening Criminal, Administrative, or Disciplinary Charges. Rule 3.10.

Rule 3.1 Meritorious Claims and Contentions

(a) A lawyer shall not:

(1) bring or continue an action, conduct a defense, assert a position in litigation, or take an appeal, without probable cause and for the purpose of harassing or maliciously injuring any person;* or

(2) present a claim or defense in litigation that is not warranted under existing law, unless it can be supported by a good faith argument for an extension, modification, or reversal of the existing law.

(b) A lawyer for the defendant in a criminal proceeding, or the respondent in a proceeding that could result in incarceration, or involuntary commitment or confinement, may nevertheless defend the proceeding by requiring that every element of the case be established.

(Adopted Sept. 26, 2018, eff. Nov. 1, 2018.)

Rule 3.2 Delay of Litigation

In representing a client, a lawyer shall not use means that have no substantial* purpose other than to delay or prolong the proceeding or to cause needless expense.

Comment

See rule 1.3 with respect to a lawyer's duty to act with reasonable* diligence and rule 3.1(b) with respect to a lawyer's representation of a defendant in a criminal proceeding. See also Business and Professions Code section 6128, subdivision (b).

(Adopted Sept. 26, 2018, eff. Nov. 1, 2018.)

Rule 3.3 Candor Toward the Tribunal*

(a) A lawyer shall not:

(1) knowingly* make a false statement of fact or law to a tribunal* or fail to correct a false statement of material fact or law previously made to the tribunal* by the lawyer;

(2) fail to disclose to the tribunal* legal authority in the controlling jurisdiction known* to the lawyer to be directly adverse to the position of the client and not disclosed by opposing counsel, or knowingly* misquote to a tribunal* the language of a book, statute, decision or other authority; or

(3) offer evidence that the lawyer knows* to be false. If a lawyer, the lawyer's client, or a witness called by the lawyer, has offered material evidence, and the lawyer comes to know* of its falsity, the lawyer shall take reasonable* remedial measures, including, if necessary, disclosure to the tribunal,* unless disclosure is prohibited by Business and Professions Code section 6068, subdivision (e) and rule 1.6. A lawyer may refuse to offer evidence, other than the testimony of a defendant in a criminal matter, that the lawyer reasonably believes* is false.

(b) A lawyer who represents a client in a proceeding before a tribunal* and who knows* that a person* intends to engage, is engaging or has engaged in criminal or fraudulent* conduct related to the proceeding shall take reasonable* remedial measures to the extent permitted by Business and Professions Code section 6068, subdivision (e) and rule 1.6.

(c) The duties stated in paragraphs (a) and (b) continue to the conclusion of the proceeding.

(d) In an ex parte proceeding where notice to the opposing party in the proceeding is not required or given and the opposing party is not present, a lawyer shall inform the tribunal* of all material facts known* to the lawyer that will enable the tribunal* to make an informed decision, whether or not the facts are adverse to the position of the client.

Comment

[1] This rule governs the conduct of a lawyer in proceedings of a tribunal,* including ancillary proceedings such as a deposition conducted pursuant to a tribunal's* authority. See rule 1.0.1(m) for the definition of "tribunal."

[2] The prohibition in paragraph (a)(1) against making false statements of law or failing to correct a material misstatement of law includes citing as authority a decision that has been overruled or a statute that has been repealed or declared unconstitutional, or failing to correct such a citation previously made to the tribunal* by the lawyer.

Legal Argument

[3] Legal authority in the controlling jurisdiction may include legal authority outside the jurisdiction in which the tribunal* sits, such as a federal statute or case that is determinative of an issue in a state court proceeding or a Supreme Court decision that is binding on a lower court.

[4] The duties stated in paragraphs (a) and (b) apply to all lawyers, including defense counsel in criminal cases. If a lawyer knows* that a client intends to testify falsely or wants the lawyer to introduce false evidence, the lawyer should seek to persuade the client that the evidence should not be offered and, if unsuccessful, must refuse to offer the false evidence. If a criminal defendant insists on testifying, and the lawyer knows* that the testimony will be false, the lawyer may offer the

---

* An asterisk (*) identifies a word or phrase defined in the terminology rule, rule 1.0.1.

testimony in a narrative form if the lawyer made reasonable* efforts to dissuade the client from the unlawful course of conduct and the lawyer has sought permission from the court to withdraw as required by rule 1.16. (See, e.g., *People v. Johnson* (1998) 62 Cal.App.4th 608 [72 Cal.Rptr.2d 805]; *People v. Jennings* (1999) 70 Cal.App.4th 899 [83 Cal.Rptr.2d 33].) The obligations of a lawyer under these rules and the State Bar Act are subordinate to applicable constitutional provisions.

Remedial Measures

[5] Reasonable* remedial measures under paragraphs (a)(3) and (b) refer to measures that are available under these rules and the State Bar Act, and which a reasonable* lawyer would consider appropriate under the circumstances to comply with the lawyer's duty of candor to the tribunal.* (See, e.g., rules 1.2.1, 1.4(a)(4), 1.16(a), 8.4; Bus. & Prof. Code, §§ 6068, subd. (d), 6128.) Remedial measures also include explaining to the client the lawyer's obligations under this rule and, where applicable, the reasons for the lawyer's decision to seek permission from the tribunal* to withdraw, and remonstrating further with the client to take corrective action that would eliminate the need for the lawyer to withdraw. If the client is an organization, the lawyer should also consider the provisions of rule 1.13. Remedial measures do not include disclosure of client confidential information, which the lawyer is required to protect under Business and Professions Code section 6068, subdivision (e) and rule 1.6.

Duration of Obligation

[6] A proceeding has concluded within the meaning of this rule when a final judgment in the proceeding has been affirmed on appeal or the time for review has passed. A prosecutor may have obligations that go beyond the scope of this rule. (See, e.g., rule 3.8(f) and (g).)

Ex Parte Communications

[7] Paragraph (d) does not apply to ex parte communications that are not otherwise prohibited by law or the tribunal.*

Withdrawal

[8] A lawyer's compliance with the duty of candor imposed by this rule does not require that the lawyer withdraw from the representation. The lawyer may, however, be required by rule 1.16 to seek permission of the tribunal* to withdraw if the lawyer's compliance with this rule results in a deterioration of the lawyer-client relationship such that the lawyer can no longer competently and diligently represent the client, or where continued employment will result in a violation of these rules. A lawyer must comply with Business and Professions Code section 6068, subdivision (e) and rule 1.6 with respect to a request to withdraw that is premised on a client's misconduct.

[9] In addition to this rule, lawyers remain bound by Business and Professions Code sections 6068, subdivision (d) and 6106.

(Adopted Sept. 26, 2018, eff. Nov. 1, 2018.)

Rule 3.4 Fairness to Opposing Party and Counsel

A lawyer shall not:

(a) unlawfully obstruct another party's access to evidence, including a witness, or unlawfully alter, destroy or conceal a document or other material having potential evidentiary value. A lawyer shall not counsel or assist another person* to do any such act;

(b) suppress any evidence that the lawyer or the lawyer's client has a legal obligation to reveal or to produce;

(c) falsify evidence, counsel or assist a witness to testify falsely, or offer an inducement to a witness that is prohibited by law;

(d) directly or indirectly pay, offer to pay, or acquiesce in the payment of compensation to a witness contingent upon the content of the witness's testimony or the outcome of the case. Except where prohibited by law, a lawyer may advance, guarantee, or acquiesce in the payment of:

(1) expenses reasonably* incurred by a witness in attending or testifying;

(2) reasonable* compensation to a witness for loss of time in attending or testifying; or

(3) a reasonable* fee for the professional services of an expert witness;

(e) advise or directly or indirectly cause a person* to secrete himself or herself or to leave the jurisdiction of a tribunal* for the purpose of making that person* unavailable as a witness therein;

(f) knowingly* disobey an obligation under the rules of a tribunal* except for an open refusal based on an assertion that no valid obligation exists; or

(g) in trial, assert personal knowledge of facts in issue except when testifying as a witness, or state a personal opinion as to the guilt or innocence of an accused.

Comment

[1] Paragraph (a) applies to evidentiary material generally, including computerized information. It is a criminal offense to destroy material for purpose of impairing its availability in a pending proceeding or one whose commencement can be foreseen. (See, e.g., Pen. Code, § 135; 18 U.S.C. §§ 1501-1520.) Falsifying evidence is also generally a criminal offense. (See, e.g., Pen. Code, § 132; 18 U.S.C. § 1519.) Applicable law may permit a lawyer to take temporary possession of physical evidence of client crimes for the purpose of conducting a limited examination that will not alter or destroy material characteristics of the evidence. Applicable law may require a lawyer to turn evidence over to the police or other prosecuting authorities, depending on the circumstances. (See *People v. Lee* (1970) 3 Cal.App.3d 514, 526 [83 Cal.Rptr. 715]; *People v. Meredith* (1981) 29 Cal.3d 682 [175 Cal.Rptr. 612].)

[2] A violation of a civil or criminal discovery rule or statute does not by itself establish a violation of this rule. See rule 3.8 for special disclosure responsibilities of a prosecutor.

(Adopted Sept. 26, 2018, eff. Nov. 1, 2018.)

Rule 3.5 Contact with Judges, Officials, Employees, and Jurors

(a) Except as permitted by statute, an applicable code of judicial ethics or code of judicial conduct, or standards governing employees of a tribunal,* a lawyer shall not directly or indirectly give or lend anything of value to a judge, official, or employee of a tribunal.* This rule does not prohibit a lawyer from contributing to the campaign fund of a judge or judicial officer running for election or confirmation pursuant to applicable law pertaining to such contributions.

(b) Unless permitted to do so by law, an applicable code of judicial ethics or code of judicial conduct, a rule or ruling of a tribunal,* or a court order, a lawyer shall not directly or indirectly communicate with or argue to a judge or judicial officer upon the merits of a contested matter pending before the judge or judicial officer, except:

(1) in open court;

(2) with the consent of all other counsel and any unrepresented parties in the matter;

(3) in the presence of all other counsel and any unrepresented parties in the matter;

(4) in writing* with a copy thereof furnished to all other counsel and any unrepresented parties in the matter; or

(5) in ex parte matters.

(c) As used in this rule, "judge" and "judicial officer" shall also include: (i) administrative law judges; (ii) neutral arbitrators; (iii) State Bar Court judges; (iv) members of an administrative body acting in an adjudicative capacity; and (v) law clerks, research attorneys, or other court personnel who participate in the decision-making process, including referees, special masters, or other persons* to whom a court refers one or more issues and whose decision or recommendation can be binding on the parties if approved by the court.

(d) A lawyer connected with a case shall not communicate directly or indirectly with anyone the lawyer knows* to be a member of the venire from which the jury will be selected for trial of that case.

(e) During trial, a lawyer connected with the case shall not communicate directly or indirectly with any juror.

(f) During trial, a lawyer who is not connected with the case shall not communicate directly or indirectly concerning the case with anyone the lawyer knows* is a juror in the case.

(g) After discharge of the jury from further consideration of a case a lawyer shall not communicate directly or indirectly with a juror if:

(1) the communication is prohibited by law or court order;

(2) the juror has made known* to the lawyer a desire not to communicate; or

(3) the communication involves misrepresentation, coercion, or duress, or is intended to harass or embarrass the juror or to influence the juror's actions in future jury service.

(h) A lawyer shall not directly or indirectly conduct an out of court investigation of a person* who is either a member of a venire or a juror in a manner likely to influence the state of mind of such person* in connection with present or future jury service.

(i) All restrictions imposed by this rule also apply to communications with, or investigations of, members of the family of a person* who is either a member of a venire or a juror.

(j) A lawyer shall reveal promptly to the court improper conduct by a person* who is either a member of a venire or a juror, or by another toward a person* who is either a member of a venire or a juror or a member of his or her family, of which the lawyer has knowledge.

---

* An asterisk (*) identifies a word or phrase defined in the terminology rule, rule 1.0.1.

(k) This rule does not prohibit a lawyer from communicating with persons* who are members of a venire or jurors as a part of the official proceedings.

(*l*) For purposes of this rule, "juror" means any empaneled, discharged, or excused juror.

Comment

[1] An applicable code of judicial ethics or code of judicial conduct under this rule includes the California Code of Judicial Ethics and the Code of Conduct for United States Judges. Regarding employees of a tribunal* not subject to judicial ethics or conduct codes, applicable standards include the Code of Ethics for the Court Employees of California and 5 United States Code section 7353 (Gifts to Federal employees). The statutes applicable to adjudicatory proceedings of state agencies generally are contained in the Administrative Procedure Act (Gov. Code, § 11340 et seq.; see Gov. Code, § 11370 [listing statutes with the act].) State and local agencies also may adopt their own regulations and rules governing communications with members or employees of a tribunal.*

[2] For guidance on permissible communications with a juror in a criminal action after discharge of the jury, see Code of Civil Procedure section 206.

[3] It is improper for a lawyer to communicate with a juror who has been removed, discharged, or excused from an empaneled jury, regardless of whether notice is given to other counsel, until such time as the entire jury has been discharged from further service or unless the communication is part of the official proceedings of the case.

(Adopted Sept. 26, 2018, eff. Nov. 1, 2018.)

Rule 3.6 Trial Publicity

(a) A lawyer who is participating or has participated in the investigation or litigation of a matter shall not make an extrajudicial statement that the lawyer knows* or reasonably should know* will (i) be disseminated by means of public communication and (ii) have a substantial* likelihood of materially prejudicing an adjudicative proceeding in the matter.

(b) Notwithstanding paragraph (a), but only to the extent permitted by Business and Professions Code section 6068, subdivision (e) and rule 1.6, lawyer may state:

(1) the claim, offense or defense involved and, except when prohibited by law, the identity of the persons* involved;

(2) information contained in a public record;

(3) that an investigation of a matter is in progress;

(4) the scheduling or result of any step in litigation;

(5) a request for assistance in obtaining evidence and information necessary thereto;

(6) a warning of danger concerning the behavior of a person* involved, when there is reason to believe* that there exists the likelihood of substantial* harm to an individual or to the public but only to the extent that dissemination by public communication is reasonably* necessary to protect the individual or the public; and

(7) in a criminal case, in addition to paragraphs (1) through (6):

(i) the identity, general area of residence, and occupation of the accused;

(ii) if the accused has not been apprehended, the information necessary to aid in apprehension of that person;*

(iii) the fact, time, and place of arrest; and

(iv) the identity of investigating and arresting officers or agencies and the length of the investigation.

(c) Notwithstanding paragraph (a), a lawyer may make a statement that a reasonable* lawyer would believe* is required to protect a client from the substantial* undue prejudicial effect of recent publicity not initiated by the lawyer or the lawyer's client. A statement made pursuant to this paragraph shall be limited to such information as is necessary to mitigate the recent adverse publicity.

(d) No lawyer associated in a law firm* or government agency with a lawyer subject to paragraph (a) shall make a statement prohibited by paragraph (a).

Comment

[1] Whether an extrajudicial statement violates this rule depends on many factors, including: (i) whether the extrajudicial statement presents information clearly inadmissible as evidence in the matter for the purpose of proving or disproving a material fact in issue; (ii) whether the extrajudicial statement presents information the lawyer knows* is false, deceptive, or the use of which would violate Business and Professions Code section 6068, subdivision (d) or rule 3.3; (iii) whether the extrajudicial statement violates a lawful "gag" order, or protective order, statute, rule of court, or special rule of confidentiality, for example, in juvenile, domestic, mental disability, and certain criminal proceedings, (see Bus. & Prof. Code, § 6068, subd. (a) and rule 3.4(f), which require compliance with such obligations); and (iv) the timing of the statement.

[2] This rule applies to prosecutors and criminal defense counsel. See rule 3.8(e) for additional duties of prosecutors in connection with extrajudicial statements about criminal proceedings.

(Adopted Sept. 26, 2018, eff. Nov. 1, 2018.)

Rule 3.7 Lawyer as Witness

(a) A lawyer shall not act as an advocate in a trial in which the lawyer is likely to be a witness unless:

(1) the lawyer's testimony relates to an uncontested issue or matter;

(2) the lawyer's testimony relates to the nature and value of legal services rendered in the case; or

(3) the lawyer has obtained informed written consent* from the client. If the lawyer represents the People or a governmental entity, the consent shall be obtained from the head of the office or a designee of the head of the office by which the lawyer is employed.

(b) A lawyer may act as advocate in a trial in which another lawyer in the lawyer's firm* is likely to be called as a witness unless precluded from doing so by rule 1.7 or rule 1.9.

Comment

[1] This rule applies to a trial before a jury, judge, administrative law judge or arbitrator. This rule does not apply to other adversarial proceedings. This rule also does not apply in non-adversarial proceedings, as where a lawyer testifies on behalf of a client in a hearing before a legislative body.

[2] A lawyer's obligation to obtain informed written consent* may be satisfied when the lawyer makes the required disclosure, and the client gives informed consent* on the record in court before a licensed court reporter or court recorder who prepares a transcript or recording of the disclosure and consent. See definition of "written" in rule 1.0.1(n).

[3] Notwithstanding a client's informed written consent,* courts retain discretion to take action, up to and including disqualification of a lawyer who seeks to both testify and serve as an advocate, to protect the trier of fact from being misled or the opposing party from being prejudiced. (See, e.g., *Lyle v. Superior Court* (1981) 122 Cal.App.3d 470 [175 Cal.Rptr. 918].)

(Adopted Sept. 26, 2018, eff. Nov. 1, 2018.)

Rule 3.8 Special Responsibilities of a Prosecutor

The prosecutor in a criminal case shall:

(a) not institute or continue to prosecute a charge that the prosecutor knows* is not supported by probable cause;

(b) make reasonable* efforts to assure that the accused has been advised of the right to, and the procedure for obtaining, counsel and has been given reasonable* opportunity to obtain counsel;

(c) not seek to obtain from an unrepresented accused a waiver of important pretrial rights unless the tribunal* has approved the appearance of the accused in propria persona;

(d) make timely disclosure to the defense of all evidence or information known* to the prosecutor that the prosecutor knows* or reasonably should know* tends to negate the guilt of the accused, mitigate the offense, or mitigate the sentence, except when the prosecutor is relieved of this responsibility by a protective order of the tribunal;* and

(e) exercise reasonable* care to prevent persons* under the supervision or direction of the prosecutor, including investigators, law enforcement personnel, employees or other persons* assisting or associated with the prosecutor in a criminal case from making an extrajudicial statement that the prosecutor would be prohibited from making under rule 3.6.

(f) When a prosecutor knows* of new, credible and material evidence creating a reasonable* likelihood that a convicted defendant did not commit an offense of which the defendant was convicted, the prosecutor shall:

(1) promptly disclose that evidence to an appropriate court or authority, and

(2) if the conviction was obtained in the prosecutor's jurisdiction,

(i) promptly disclose that evidence to the defendant unless a court authorizes delay, and

(ii) undertake further investigation, or make reasonable* efforts to cause an investigation, to determine whether the defendant was convicted of an offense that the defendant did not commit.

(g) When a prosecutor knows* of clear and convincing evidence establishing that a defendant in the prosecutor's jurisdiction was con-

---

* An asterisk (*) identifies a word or phrase defined in the terminology rule, rule 1.0.1.

victed of an offense that the defendant did not commit, the prosecutor shall seek to remedy the conviction.

Comment

[1] A prosecutor has the responsibility of a minister of justice and not simply that of an advocate. This responsibility carries with it specific obligations to see that the defendant is accorded procedural justice, that guilt is decided upon the basis of sufficient evidence, and that special precautions are taken to prevent and to rectify the conviction of innocent persons.* This rule is intended to achieve those results. All lawyers in government service remain bound by rules 3.1 and 3.4.

[2] Paragraph (c) does not forbid the lawful questioning of an uncharged suspect who has knowingly* waived the right to counsel and the right to remain silent. Paragraph (c) also does not forbid prosecutors from seeking from an unrepresented accused a reasonable* waiver of time for initial appearance or preliminary hearing as a means of facilitating the accused's voluntary cooperation in an ongoing law enforcement investigation.

[3] The disclosure obligations in paragraph (d) are not limited to evidence or information that is material as defined by *Brady v. Maryland* (1963) 373 U.S. 83 [83 S.Ct. 1194] and its progeny. For example, these obligations include, at a minimum, the duty to disclose impeachment evidence or information that a prosecutor knows* or reasonably should know* casts significant doubt on the accuracy or admissibility of witness testimony on which the prosecution intends to rely. Paragraph (d) does not require disclosure of information protected from disclosure by federal or California laws and rules, as interpreted by case law or court orders. Nothing in this rule is intended to be applied in a manner inconsistent with statutory and constitutional provisions governing discovery in California courts. A disclosure's timeliness will vary with the circumstances, and paragraph (d) is not intended to impose timing requirements different from those established by statutes, procedural rules, court orders, and case law interpreting those authorities and the California and federal constitutions.

[4] The exception in paragraph (d) recognizes that a prosecutor may seek an appropriate protective order from the tribunal* if disclosure of information to the defense could result in substantial* harm to an individual or to the public interest.

[5] Paragraph (e) supplements rule 3.6, which prohibits extrajudicial statements that have a substantial* likelihood of prejudicing an adjudicatory proceeding. Paragraph (e) is not intended to restrict the statements which a prosecutor may make which comply with rule 3.6(b) or 3.6(c).

[6] Prosecutors have a duty to supervise the work of subordinate lawyers and nonlawyer employees or agents. (See rules 5.1 and 5.3.) Ordinarily, the reasonable* care standard of paragraph (e) will be satisfied if the prosecutor issues the appropriate cautions to law enforcement personnel and other relevant individuals.

[7] When a prosecutor knows* of new, credible and material evidence creating a reasonable* likelihood that a person* outside the prosecutor's jurisdiction was convicted of a crime that the person* did not commit, paragraph (f) requires prompt disclosure to the court or other appropriate authority, such as the chief prosecutor of the jurisdiction where the conviction occurred. If the conviction was obtained in the prosecutor's jurisdiction, paragraph (f) requires the prosecutor to examine the evidence and undertake further investigation to determine whether the defendant is in fact innocent or make reasonable* efforts to cause another appropriate authority to undertake the necessary investigation, and to promptly disclose the evidence to the court and, absent court authorized delay, to the defendant. Disclosure to a represented defendant must be made through the defendant's counsel, and, in the case of an unrepresented defendant, would ordinarily be accompanied by a request to a court for the appointment of counsel to assist the defendant in taking such legal measures as may be appropriate. (See rule 4.2.) Statutes may require a prosecutor to preserve certain types of evidence in criminal matters. (See Pen. Code, §§ 1417.1-1417.9.) In addition, prosecutors must obey file preservation orders concerning rights of discovery guaranteed by the Constitution and statutory provisions. (See *People v. Superior Court (Morales)* (2017) 2 Cal.5th 523 [213 Cal.Rptr.3d 581]; *Shorts v. Superior Court* (2018) 24 Cal.App.5th 709 [234 Cal.Rptr.3d 392].)

[8] Under paragraph (g), once the prosecutor knows* of clear and convincing evidence that the defendant was convicted of an offense that the defendant did not commit, the prosecutor must seek to remedy the conviction. Depending upon the circumstances, steps to remedy the conviction could include disclosure of the evidence to the defendant, requesting that the court appoint counsel for an unrepresented indigent defendant and, where appropriate, notifying the court that the prosecutor has knowledge that the defendant did not commit the offense of which the defendant was convicted.

[9] A prosecutor's independent judgment, made in good faith, that the new evidence is not of such nature as to trigger the obligations of paragraphs (f) and (g), though subsequently determined to have been erroneous, does not constitute a violation of this rule.

(Amended Apr. 23, 2020, eff. June 1, 2020; Adopted Sept. 26, 2018, eff. Nov. 1, 2018.)

Rule 3.9 Advocate in Nonadjudicative Proceedings

A lawyer representing a client before a legislative body or administrative agency in connection with a pending nonadjudicative matter or proceeding shall disclose that the appearance is in a representative capacity, except when the lawyer seeks information from an agency that is available to the public.

Comment

This rule only applies when a lawyer represents a client in connection with an official hearing or meeting of a governmental agency or a legislative body to which the lawyer or the lawyer's client is presenting evidence or argument. It does not apply to representation of a client in a negotiation or other bilateral transaction with a governmental agency or in connection with an application for a license or other privilege or the client's compliance with generally applicable reporting requirements, such as the filing of income-tax returns. This rule also does not apply to the representation of a client in connection with an investigation or examination of the client's affairs conducted by government investigators or examiners. Representation in such matters is governed by rules 4.1 through 4.4. This rule does not require a lawyer to disclose a client's identity.

(Adopted Sept. 26, 2018, eff. Nov. 1, 2018.)

Rule 3.10 Threatening Criminal, Administrative, or Disciplinary Charges

(a) A lawyer shall not threaten to present criminal, administrative, or disciplinary charges to obtain an advantage in a civil dispute.

(b) As used in paragraph (a) of this rule, the term "administrative charges" means the filing or lodging of a complaint with any governmental organization that may order or recommend the loss or suspension of a license, or may impose or recommend the imposition of a fine, pecuniary sanction, or other sanction of a quasi-criminal nature but does not include filing charges with an administrative entity required by law as a condition precedent to maintaining a civil action.

(c) As used in this rule, the term "civil dispute" means a controversy or potential controversy over the rights and duties of two or more persons* under civil law, whether or not an action has been commenced, and includes an administrative proceeding of a quasi-civil nature pending before a federal, state, or local governmental entity.

Comment

[1] Paragraph (a) does not prohibit a statement by a lawyer that the lawyer will present criminal, administrative, or disciplinary charges, unless the statement is made to obtain an advantage in a civil dispute. For example, if a lawyer believes* in good faith that the conduct of the opposing lawyer or party violates criminal or other laws, the lawyer may state that if the conduct continues the lawyer will report it to criminal or administrative authorities. On the other hand, a lawyer could not state or imply that a criminal or administrative action will be pursued unless the opposing party agrees to settle the civil dispute.

[2] This rule does not apply to a threat to bring a civil action. It also does not prohibit actually presenting criminal, administrative or disciplinary charges, even if doing so creates an advantage in a civil dispute. Whether a lawyer's statement violates this rule depends on the specific facts. (See, e.g., *Crane v. State Bar* (1981) 30 Cal.3d 117 [177 Cal.Rptr. 670].) A statement that the lawyer will pursue "all available legal remedies," or words of similar import, does not by itself violate this rule.

[3] This rule does not apply to: (i) a threat to initiate contempt proceedings for a failure to comply with a court order; or (ii) the offer of a civil compromise in accordance with a statute such as Penal Code sections 1377 and 1378.

[4] This rule does not prohibit a government lawyer from offering a global settlement or release-dismissal agreement in connection with related criminal, civil or administrative matters. The government lawyer must have probable cause for initiating or continuing criminal charges. (See rule 3.8(a).)

[5] As used in paragraph (b), "governmental organizations" includes any federal, state, local, and foreign governmental organizations. Paragraph (b) exempts the threat of filing an administrative charge that is a prerequisite to filing a civil complaint on the same transaction or occurrence.

(Adopted Sept. 26, 2018, eff. Nov. 1, 2018.)

CHAPTER 4
TRANSACTIONS WITH PERSONS* OTHER THAN CLIENTS

Truthfulness in Statements to Others. Rule 4.1.
Communication with a Represented Person. Rule 4.2.
Communicating with an Unrepresented Person. Rule 4.3.
Duties Concerning Inadvertently Transmitted Writings. Rule 4.4.

Rule 4.1 Truthfulness in Statements to Others

In the course of representing a client a lawyer shall not knowingly:*

(a) make a false statement of material fact or law to a third person;* or

---

* An asterisk (*) identifies a word or phrase defined in the terminology rule, rule 1.0.1.

(b) fail to disclose a material fact to a third person* when disclosure is necessary to avoid assisting a criminal or fraudulent* act by a client, unless disclosure is prohibited by Business and Professions Code section 6068, subdivision (e)(1) or rule 1.6.

Comment

[1] A lawyer is required to be truthful when dealing with others on a client's behalf, but generally has no affirmative duty to inform an opposing party of relevant facts. A misrepresentation can occur if the lawyer incorporates or affirms the truth of a statement of another person* that the lawyer knows* is false. However, in drafting an agreement or other document on behalf of a client, a lawyer does not necessarily affirm or vouch for the truthfulness of representations made by the client in the agreement or document. A nondisclosure can be the equivalent of a false statement of material fact or law under paragraph (a) where a lawyer makes a partially true but misleading material statement or material omission. In addition to this rule, lawyers remain bound by Business and Professions Code section 6106 and rule 8.4.

[2] This rule refers to statements of fact. Whether a particular statement should be regarded as one of fact can depend on the circumstances. For example, in negotiation, certain types of statements ordinarily are not taken as statements of material fact. Estimates of price or value placed on the subject of a transaction and a party's intentions as to an acceptable settlement of a claim are ordinarily in this category, and so is the existence of an undisclosed principal except where nondisclosure of the principal would constitute fraud.*

[3] Under rule 1.2.1, a lawyer is prohibited from counseling or assisting a client in conduct that the lawyer knows* is criminal or fraudulent.* See rule 1.4(a)(4) regarding a lawyer's obligation to consult with the client about limitations on the lawyer's conduct. In some circumstances, a lawyer can avoid assisting a client's crime or fraud* by withdrawing from the representation in compliance with rule 1.16.

[4] Regarding a lawyer's involvement in lawful covert activity in the investigation of violations of law, see rule 8.4, Comment [5].

(Adopted Sept. 26, 2018, eff. Nov. 1, 2018.)

Rule 4.2 Communication with a Represented Person*

(a) In representing a client, a lawyer shall not communicate directly or indirectly about the subject of the representation with a person* the lawyer knows* to be represented by another lawyer in the matter, unless the lawyer has the consent of the other lawyer.

(b) In the case of a represented corporation, partnership, association, or other private or governmental organization, this rule prohibits communications with:

(1) A current officer, director, partner,*or managing agent of the organization; or

(2) A current employee, member, agent, or other constituent of the organization, if the subject of the communication is any act or omission of such person* in connection with the matter which may be binding upon or imputed to the organization for purposes of civil or criminal liability.

(c) This rule shall not prohibit:

(1) communications with a public official, board, committee, or body; or

(2) communications otherwise authorized by law or a court order.

(d) For purposes of this rule:

(1) "Managing agent" means an employee, member, agent, or other constituent of an organization with substantial* discretionary authority over decisions that determine organizational policy.

(2) "Public official" means a public officer of the United States government, or of a state, county, city, town, political subdivision, or other governmental organization, with the comparable decision-making authority and responsibilities as the organizational constituents described in paragraph (b)(1).

Comment

[1] This rule applies even though the represented person* initiates or consents to the communication. A lawyer must immediately terminate communication with a person* if, after commencing communication, the lawyer learns that the person* is one with whom communication is not permitted by this rule.

[2] "Subject of the representation," "matter," and "person" are not limited to a litigation context. This rule applies to communications with any person,* whether or not a party to a formal adjudicative proceeding, contract, or negotiation, who is represented by counsel concerning the matter to which the communication relates.

[3] The prohibition against communicating "indirectly" with a person* represented by counsel in paragraph (a) is intended to address situations where a lawyer seeks to communicate with a represented person* through an intermediary such as an agent, investigator or the lawyer's client. This rule, however, does not prevent represented persons* from communicating directly with one another with respect to the subject of the representation, nor does it prohibit a lawyer from advising a client concerning such a communication. A lawyer may also advise a client not to accept or engage in such communications. The rule also does not prohibit a lawyer who is a party to a legal matter from communicating on his or her own behalf with a represented person* in that matter.

[4] This rule does not prohibit communications with a represented person* concerning matters outside the representation. Similarly, a lawyer who knows* that a person* is being provided with limited scope representation is not prohibited from communicating with that person* with respect to matters that are outside the scope of the limited representation. (See, e.g., Cal. Rules of Court, rules 3.35 – 3.37, 5.425 [Limited Scope Representation].)

[5] This rule does not prohibit communications initiated by a represented person* seeking advice or representation from an independent lawyer of the person's* choice.

[6] If a current constituent of the organization is represented in the matter by his or her own counsel, the consent by that counsel to a communication is sufficient for purposes of this rule.

[7] This rule applies to all forms of governmental and private organizations, such as cities, counties, corporations, partnerships, limited liability companies, and unincorporated associations. When a lawyer communicates on behalf of a client with a governmental organization, or certain employees, members, agents, or other constituents of a governmental organization, however, special considerations exist as a result of the right to petition conferred by the First Amendment of the United States Constitution and article I, section 3 of the California Constitution. Paragraph (c)(1) recognizes these special considerations by generally exempting from application of this rule communications with public boards, committees, and bodies, and with public officials as defined in paragraph (d)(2) of this rule. Communications with a governmental organization constituent who is not a public official, however, will remain subject to this rule when the lawyer knows* the governmental organization is represented in the matter and the communication with that constituent falls within paragraph (b)(2).

[8] Paragraph (c)(2) recognizes that statutory schemes, case law, and court orders may authorize communications between a lawyer and a person* that would otherwise be subject to this rule. Examples of such statutory schemes include those protecting the right of employees to organize and engage in collective bargaining, employee health and safety, and equal employment opportunity. The law also recognizes that prosecutors and other government lawyers are authorized to contact represented persons,* either directly or through investigative agents and informants, in the context of investigative activities, as limited by relevant federal and state constitutions, statutes, rules, and case law. (See, e.g., *United States v. Carona* (9th Cir. 2011) 630 F.3d 917; *United States v. Talao* (9th Cir. 2000) 222 F.3d 1133.) The rule is not intended to preclude communications with represented persons* in the course of such legitimate investigative activities as authorized by law. This rule also is not intended to preclude communications with represented persons* in the course of legitimate investigative activities engaged in, directly or indirectly, by lawyers representing persons* whom the government has accused of or is investigating for crimes, to the extent those investigative activities are authorized by law.

[9] A lawyer who communicates with a represented person* pursuant to paragraph (c) is subject to other restrictions in communicating with the person.* (See, e.g. Bus. & Prof. Code, § 6106; *Snider v. Superior Court* (2003) 113 Cal.App.4th 1187, 1213 [7 Cal.Rptr.3d 119]; *In the Matter of Dale* (2005) 4 Cal. State Bar Ct. Rptr. 798.)

(Adopted Sept. 26, 2018, eff. Nov. 1, 2018.)

Rule 4.3 Communicating with an Unrepresented Person*

(a) In communicating on behalf of a client with a person* who is not represented by counsel, a lawyer shall not state or imply that the lawyer is disinterested. When the lawyer knows* or reasonably should know* that the unrepresented person* incorrectly believes* the lawyer is disinterested in the matter, the lawyer shall make reasonable* efforts to correct the misunderstanding. If the lawyer knows* or reasonably should know* that the interests of the unrepresented person* are in conflict with the interests of the client, the lawyer shall not give legal advice to that person,* except that the lawyer may, but is not required to, advise the person* to secure counsel.

(b) In communicating on behalf of a client with a person* who is not represented by counsel, a lawyer shall not seek to obtain privileged or other confidential information the lawyer knows* or reasonably should know* the person* may not reveal without violating a duty to another or which the lawyer is not otherwise entitled to receive.

Comment

[1] This rule is intended to protect unrepresented persons,* whatever their interests, from being misled when communicating with a lawyer who is acting for a client.

---

* An asterisk (*) identifies a word or phrase defined in the terminology rule, rule 1.0.1.

[2] Paragraph (a) distinguishes between situations in which a lawyer knows* or reasonably should know* that the interests of an unrepresented person* are in conflict with the interests of the lawyer's client and situations in which the lawyer does not. In the former situation, the possibility that the lawyer will compromise the unrepresented person's* interests is so great that the rule prohibits the giving of any legal advice, apart from the advice to obtain counsel. A lawyer does not give legal advice merely by stating a legal position on behalf of the lawyer's client. This rule does not prohibit a lawyer from negotiating the terms of a transaction or settling a dispute with an unrepresented person.* So long as the lawyer discloses that the lawyer represents an adverse party and not the person,* the lawyer may inform the person* of the terms on which the lawyer's client will enter into the agreement or settle the matter, prepare documents that require the person's* signature, and explain the lawyer's own view of the meaning of the document and the underlying legal obligations.

[3] Regarding a lawyer's involvement in lawful covert activity in the investigation of violations of law, see rule 8.4, Comment [5].

(Adopted Sept. 26, 2018, eff. Nov. 1, 2018.)

Rule 4.4 Duties Concerning Inadvertently Transmitted Writings*

Where it is reasonably* apparent to a lawyer who receives a writing* relating to a lawyer's representation of a client that the writing* was inadvertently sent or produced, and the lawyer knows* or reasonably should know* that the writing* is privileged or subject to the work product doctrine, the lawyer shall:

(a) refrain from examining the writing* any more than is necessary to determine that it is privileged or subject to the work product doctrine, and

(b) promptly notify the sender.

Comment

[1] If a lawyer determines this rule applies to a transmitted writing,* the lawyer should return the writing* to the sender, seek to reach agreement with the sender regarding the disposition of the writing,* or seek guidance from a tribunal.* (See *Rico v. Mitsubishi* (2007) 42 Cal.4th 807, 817 [68 Cal.Rptr.3d 758].) In providing notice required by this rule, the lawyer shall comply with rule 4.2.

[2] This rule does not address the legal duties of a lawyer who receives a writing* that the lawyer knows* or reasonably should know* may have been inappropriately disclosed by the sending person.* (See *Clark v. Superior Court* (2011) 196 Cal.App.4th 37 [125 Cal.Rptr.3d 361].)

(Adopted Sept. 26, 2018, eff. Nov. 1, 2018.)

CHAPTER 5
LAW FIRMS* AND ASSOCIATIONS

Responsibilities of Managerial and Supervisory Lawyers. Rule 5.1.
Responsibilities of a Subordinate Lawyer. Rule 5.2.
Responsibilities Regarding Nonlawyer Assistants. Rule 5.3.
Employment of Disbarred, Suspended, Resigned, or Involuntarily Inactive Lawyer. Rule 5.3.1.
Financial and Similar Arrangements with Nonlawyers. Rule 5.4.
Unauthorized Practice of Law; Multijurisdictional Practice of Law. Rule 5.5.
Restrictions on a Lawyer's Right to Practice. Rule 5.6.

Rule 5.1 Responsibilities of Managerial and Supervisory Lawyers

(a) A lawyer who individually or together with other lawyers possesses managerial authority in a law firm,* shall make reasonable* efforts to ensure that the firm* has in effect measures giving reasonable* assurance that all lawyers in the firm* comply with these rules and the State Bar Act.

(b) A lawyer having direct supervisory authority over another lawyer, whether or not a member or employee of the same law firm,* shall make reasonable* efforts to ensure that the other lawyer complies with these rules and the State Bar Act.

(c) A lawyer shall be responsible for another lawyer's violation of these rules and the State Bar Act if:

(1) the lawyer orders or, with knowledge of the relevant facts and of the specific conduct, ratifies the conduct involved; or

(2) the lawyer, individually or together with other lawyers, possesses managerial authority in the law firm* in which the other lawyer practices, or has direct supervisory authority over the other lawyer, whether or not a member or employee of the same law firm,* and knows* of the conduct at a time when its consequences can be avoided or mitigated but fails to take reasonable* remedial action.

Comment
Paragraph (a) – Duties Of Managerial Lawyers To Reasonably Assure Compliance with the Rules*

[1] Paragraph (a) requires lawyers with managerial authority within a law firm* to make reasonable* efforts to establish internal policies and procedures designed, for example, to detect and resolve conflicts of interest, identify dates by which actions must be taken in pending matters, account for client funds and property, and ensure that inexperienced lawyers are properly supervised.

[2] Whether particular measures or efforts satisfy the requirements of paragraph (a) might depend upon the law firm's structure and the nature of its practice, including the size of the law firm,* whether it has more than one office location or practices in more than one jurisdiction, or whether the firm* or its partners* engage in any ancillary business.

[3] A partner,* shareholder or other lawyer in a law firm* who has intermediate managerial responsibilities satisfies paragraph (a) if the law firm* has a designated managing lawyer charged with that responsibility, or a management committee or other body that has appropriate managerial authority and is charged with that responsibility. For example, the managing lawyer of an office of a multi-office law firm* would not necessarily be required to promulgate firm-wide policies intended to reasonably* assure that the law firm's lawyers comply with the rules or State Bar Act. However, a lawyer remains responsible to take corrective steps if the lawyer knows* or reasonably should know* that the delegated body or person* is not providing or implementing measures as required by this rule.

[4] Paragraph (a) also requires managerial lawyers to make reasonable* efforts to assure that other lawyers in an agency or department comply with these rules and the State Bar Act. This rule contemplates, for example, the creation and implementation of reasonable* guidelines relating to the assignment of cases and the distribution of workload among lawyers in a public sector legal agency or other legal department. (See, e.g., State Bar of California, Guidelines on Indigent Defense Services Delivery Systems (2006).)

Paragraph (b) – Duties of Supervisory Lawyers

[5] Whether a lawyer has direct supervisory authority over another lawyer in particular circumstances is a question of fact.

Paragraph (c) – Responsibility for Another's Lawyer's Violation

[6] The appropriateness of remedial action under paragraph (c)(2) would depend on the nature and seriousness of the misconduct and the nature and immediacy of its harm. A managerial or supervisory lawyer must intervene to prevent avoidable consequences of misconduct if the lawyer knows* that the misconduct occurred.

[7] A supervisory lawyer violates paragraph (b) by failing to make the efforts required under that paragraph, even if the lawyer does not violate paragraph (c) by knowingly* directing or ratifying the conduct, or where feasible, failing to take reasonable* remedial action.

[8] Paragraphs (a), (b), and (c) create independent bases for discipline. This rule does not impose vicarious responsibility on a lawyer for the acts of another lawyer who is in or outside the law firm.* Apart from paragraph (c) of this rule and rule 8.4(a), a lawyer does not have disciplinary liability for the conduct of a partner,* associate, or subordinate lawyer. The question of whether a lawyer can be liable civilly or criminally for another lawyer's conduct is beyond the scope of these rules.

(Adopted Sept. 26, 2018, eff. Nov. 1, 2018.)

Rule 5.2 Responsibilities of a Subordinate Lawyer

(a) A lawyer shall comply with these rules and the State Bar Act notwithstanding that the lawyer acts at the direction of another lawyer or other person.*

(b) A subordinate lawyer does not violate these rules or the State Bar Act if that lawyer acts in accordance with a supervisory lawyer's reasonable* resolution of an arguable question of professional duty.

Comment

When lawyers in a supervisor-subordinate relationship encounter a matter involving professional judgment as to the lawyers' responsibilities under these rules or the State Bar Act and the question can reasonably* be answered only one way, the duty of both lawyers is clear and they are equally responsible for fulfilling it. Accordingly, the subordinate lawyer must comply with his or her obligations under paragraph (a). If the question reasonably* can be answered more than one way, the supervisory lawyer may assume responsibility for determining which of the reasonable* alternatives to select, and the subordinate may be guided accordingly. If the subordinate lawyer believes* that the supervisor's proposed resolution of the question of professional duty would result in a violation of these rules or the State Bar Act, the subordinate is obligated to communicate his or her professional judgment regarding the matter to the supervisory lawyer.

(Adopted Sept. 26, 2018, eff. Nov. 1, 2018.)

Rule 5.3 Responsibilities Regarding Nonlawyer Assistants

With respect to a nonlawyer employed or retained by or associated with a lawyer:

(a) a lawyer who individually or together with other lawyers possesses managerial authority in a law firm,* shall make reasonable* efforts

---

* An asterisk (*) identifies a word or phrase defined in the terminology rule, rule 1.0.1.

to ensure that the firm* has in effect measures giving reasonable* assurance that the nonlawyer's conduct is compatible with the professional obligations of the lawyer;

(b) a lawyer having direct supervisory authority over the nonlawyer, whether or not an employee of the same law firm,* shall make reasonable* efforts to ensure that the person's* conduct is compatible with the professional obligations of the lawyer; and

(c) a lawyer shall be responsible for conduct of such a person* that would be a violation of these rules or the State Bar Act if engaged in by a lawyer if:

(1) the lawyer orders or, with knowledge of the relevant facts and of the specific conduct, ratifies the conduct involved; or

(2) the lawyer, individually or together with other lawyers, possesses managerial authority in the law firm* in which the person* is employed, or has direct supervisory authority over the person,* whether or not an employee of the same law firm,* and knows* of the conduct at a time when its consequences can be avoided or mitigated but fails to take reasonable* remedial action.

Comment

Lawyers often utilize nonlawyer personnel, including secretaries, investigators, law student interns, and paraprofessionals. Such assistants, whether employees or independent contractors, act for the lawyer in rendition of the lawyer's professional services. A lawyer must give such assistants appropriate instruction and supervision concerning all ethical aspects of their employment. The measures employed in instructing and supervising nonlawyers should take account of the fact that they might not have legal training.

(Adopted Sept. 26, 2018, eff. Nov. 1, 2018.)

Rule 5.3.1 Employment of Disbarred, Suspended, Resigned, or Involuntarily Inactive Lawyer

(a) For purposes of this rule:

(1) "Employ" means to engage the services of another, including employees, agents, independent contractors and consultants, regardless of whether any compensation is paid;

(2) "Member" means a member of the State Bar of California;

(3) "Involuntarily inactive member" means a member who is ineligible to practice law as a result of action taken pursuant to Business and Professions Code sections 6007, 6203, subdivision (d)(1), or California Rules of Court, rule 9.31(d);

(4) "Resigned member" means a member who has resigned from the State Bar while disciplinary charges are pending; and

(5) "Ineligible person" means a member whose current status with the State Bar of California is disbarred, suspended, resigned, or involuntarily inactive.

(b) A lawyer shall not employ, associate in practice with, or assist a person* the lawyer knows* or reasonably should know* is an ineligible person to perform the following on behalf of the lawyer's client:

(1) Render legal consultation or advice to the client;

(2) Appear on behalf of a client in any hearing or proceeding or before any judicial officer, arbitrator, mediator, court, public agency, referee, magistrate, commissioner, or hearing officer;

(3) Appear as a representative of the client at a deposition or other discovery matter;

(4) Negotiate or transact any matter for or on behalf of the client with third parties;

(5) Receive, disburse or otherwise handle the client's funds; or

(6) Engage in activities that constitute the practice of law.

(c) A lawyer may employ, associate in practice with, or assist an ineligible person to perform research, drafting or clerical activities, including but not limited to:

(1) Legal work of a preparatory nature, such as legal research, the assemblage of data and other necessary information, drafting of pleadings, briefs, and other similar documents;

(2) Direct communication with the client or third parties regarding matters such as scheduling, billing, updates, confirmation of receipt or sending of correspondence and messages; or

(3) Accompanying an active lawyer in attending a deposition or other discovery matter for the limited purpose of providing clerical assistance to the active lawyer who will appear as the representative of the client.

(d) Prior to or at the time of employing, associating in practice with, or assisting a person* the lawyer knows* or reasonably should know* is an ineligible person, the lawyer shall serve upon the State Bar written* notice of the employment, including a full description of such person's current bar status. The written* notice shall also list the activities prohibited in paragraph (b) and state that the ineligible person will not perform such activities. The lawyer shall serve similar written* notice upon each client on whose specific matter such person* will work, prior to or at the time of employing, associating with, or assisting such person* to work on the client's specific matter. The lawyer shall obtain proof of service of the client's written* notice and shall retain such proof and a true and correct copy of the client's written* notice for two years following termination of the lawyer's employment by the client.

(e) A lawyer may, without client or State Bar notification, employ, associate in practice with, or assist an ineligible person whose sole function is to perform office physical plant or equipment maintenance, courier or delivery services, catering, reception, typing or transcription, or other similar support activities.

(f) When the lawyer no longer employs, associates in practice with, or assists the ineligible person, the lawyer shall promptly serve upon the State Bar written* notice of the termination.

Comment

If the client is an organization, the lawyer shall serve the notice required by paragraph (d) on its highest authorized officer, employee, or constituent overseeing the particular engagement. (See rule 1.13.)

(Adopted Sept. 26, 2018, eff. Nov. 1, 2018.)

Rule 5.4 Financial and Similar Arrangements with Nonlawyers

(a) A lawyer or law firm* shall not share legal fees directly or indirectly with a nonlawyer or with an organization that is not authorized to practice law, except that:

(1) an agreement by a lawyer with the lawyer's firm,* partner,* or associate may provide for the payment of money or other consideration over a reasonable* period of time after the lawyer's death, to the lawyer's estate or to one or more specified persons;*

(2) a lawyer purchasing the practice of a deceased, disabled or disappeared lawyer may pay the agreed-upon purchase price, pursuant to rule 1.17, to the lawyer's estate or other representative;

(3) a lawyer or law firm* may include nonlawyer employees in a compensation or retirement plan, even though the plan is based in whole or in part on a profit-sharing arrangement, provided the plan does not otherwise violate these rules or the State Bar Act;

(4) a lawyer or law firm* may pay a prescribed registration, referral, or other fee to a lawyer referral service established, sponsored and operated in accordance with the State Bar of California's Minimum Standards for Lawyer Referral Services;

(5) a lawyer or law firm* may share with or pay a court-awarded legal fee to a nonprofit organization that employed, retained, recommended, or facilitated employment of the lawyer or law firm* in the matter; or

(6) a lawyer or law firm* may share with or pay a legal fee that is not court-awarded but arises from a settlement or other resolution of the matter with a nonprofit organization that employed, retained, recommended, or facilitated employment of the lawyer or law firm* in the matter provided:

(i) the nonprofit organization qualifies under section 501(c)(3) of the Internal Revenue Code;

(ii) the lawyer or law firm* enters into a written* agreement to divide the fee with the nonprofit organization;

(iii) the lawyer or law firm* obtains the client's consent in writing,* either at the time the lawyer or law firm* enters into the agreement with the nonprofit organization to divide the fee or as soon thereafter as reasonably* practicable, after a full written* disclosure to the client of the fact that a division of fees will be made, the identity of the lawyer or law firm* and the nonprofit organization that are parties to the division, and the terms of the division, including the restriction imposed under paragraph (a)(6)(iv); and

(iv) the total fee charged by the lawyer or law firm* is not increased solely by reason of the agreement to divide fees.

(b) A lawyer shall not form a partnership or other organization with a nonlawyer if any of the activities of the partnership or other organization consist of the practice of law.

---

* An asterisk (*) identifies a word or phrase defined in the terminology rule, rule 1.0.1.

(c) A lawyer shall not permit a person* who recommends, employs, or pays the lawyer to render legal services for another to direct or regulate the lawyer's independent professional judgment or interfere with the lawyer-client relationship in rendering legal services.

(d) A lawyer shall not practice with or in the form of a professional corporation or other organization authorized to practice law for a profit if:

(1) a nonlawyer owns any interest in it, except that a fiduciary representative of a lawyer's estate may hold the lawyer's stock or other interest for a reasonable* time during administration;

(2) a nonlawyer is a director or officer of the corporation or occupies a position of similar responsibility in any other form of organization; or

(3) a nonlawyer has the right or authority to direct or control the lawyer's independent professional judgment.

(e) The Board of Trustees of the State Bar shall formulate and adopt Minimum Standards for Lawyer Referral Services, which, as from time to time amended, shall be binding on lawyers. A lawyer shall not accept a referral from, or otherwise participate in, a lawyer referral service unless it complies with such Minimum Standards for Lawyer Referral Services.

(f) A lawyer shall not practice with or in the form of a nonprofit legal aid, mutual benefit or advocacy group if the nonprofit organization allows any third person* to interfere with the lawyer's independent professional judgment, or with the lawyer-client relationship, or allows or aids any person* to practice law in violation of these rules or the State Bar Act.

Comment

[1] Paragraph (a) does not prohibit a lawyer or law firm* from paying a bonus to or otherwise compensating a nonlawyer employee from general revenues received for legal services, provided the arrangement does not interfere with the independent professional judgment of the lawyer or lawyers in the firm* and does not violate these rules or the State Bar Act. However, a nonlawyer employee's bonus or other form of compensation may not be based on a percentage or share of fees in specific cases or legal matters.

[2] Paragraph (a) also does not prohibit payment to a nonlawyer third-party for goods and services provided to a lawyer or law firm;* however, the compensation to a nonlawyer third-party may not be determined as a percentage or share of the lawyer's or law firm's overall revenues or tied to fees in particular cases or legal matters. A lawyer may pay to a nonlawyer third-party, such as a collection agency, a percentage of past due or delinquent fees in concluded matters that the third-party collects on the lawyer's behalf.

[3] Paragraph (a)(5) permits a lawyer to share with or pay court-awarded legal fees to nonprofit legal aid, mutual benefit, and advocacy groups that are not engaged in the unauthorized practice of law. (See *Frye v. Tenderloin Housing Clinic, Inc.* (2006) 38 Cal.4th 23 [40 Cal.Rptr.3d 221]; see also rule 6.3.) Under the specified circumstances, paragraph (a)(6) permits a lawyer to share with or pay legal fees arising from a settlement or other resolution of the matter to 501(c)(3) organizations, such as nonprofit legal aid and charitable groups that are not engaged in the unauthorized practice of law. Paragraphs (a)(5) and (a)(6) include the concept of a nonprofit organization facilitating the employment of a lawyer to provide legal services. One example of such facilitation is a nonprofit organization's operation of a law practice incubator program.

[4] A lawyer or law firm* who has agreed to share with or pay legal fees to a qualifying organization under paragraphs (a)(5) or (a)(6) remains obligated to exercise independent professional judgment in the client's best interest. See rules 1.7 and 2.1. Regarding a lawyer's contribution of legal fees to a legal services organization, see rule 1.0, Comment [5] on financial support for programs providing pro bono legal services.

[5] Nothing in paragraphs (a)(5) or (a)(6) is intended to alter the regulation of lawyer referral activity set forth in Business and Professions Code section 6155. In addition, a lawyer must comply with rules 5.4(a)(4) and 7.2(b).

[6] This rule is not intended to affect case law regarding the relationship between insurers and lawyers providing legal services to insureds. (See, e.g., *Gafcon, Inc. v. Ponsor Associates* (2002) 98 Cal.App.4th 1388 [120 Cal.Rptr.2d 392].)

[7] Paragraph (c) is not intended to alter or diminish a lawyer's obligations under rule 1.8.6 (Compensation from One Other Than Client).

(Amended Feb. 18, 2021, eff. Mar. 22, 2021; Adopted Sept. 26, 2018, eff. Nov. 1, 2018.)

Rule 5.5   Unauthorized Practice of Law; Multijurisdictional Practice of Law

(a) A lawyer admitted to practice law in California shall not:

(1) practice law in a jurisdiction where to do so would be in violation of regulations of the profession in that jurisdiction; or

(2) knowingly* assist a person* in the unauthorized practice of law in that jurisdiction.

(b) A lawyer who is not admitted to practice law in California shall not:

(1) except as authorized by these rules or other law, establish or maintain a resident office or other systematic or continuous presence in California for the practice of law; or

(2) hold out to the public or otherwise represent that the lawyer is admitted to practice law in California.

Comment

Paragraph (b)(1) prohibits lawyers from practicing law in California unless otherwise entitled to practice law in this state by court rule or other law. (See, e.g., Bus. & Prof. Code, § 6125 et seq.; see also Cal. Rules of Court, rules 9.40 [counsel pro hac vice], 9.41 [appearances by military counsel], 9.42 [certified law students], 9.43 [out-of-state attorney arbitration counsel program], 9.44 [registered foreign legal consultant], 9.45 [registered legal services attorneys], 9.46 [registered in-house counsel], 9.47 [attorneys practicing temporarily in California as part of litigation], 9.48 [non-litigating attorneys temporarily in California to provide legal services].)

(Adopted Sept. 26, 2018, eff. Nov. 1, 2018.)

Rule 5.6   Restrictions on a Lawyer's Right to Practice

(a) Unless authorized by law, a lawyer shall not participate in offering or making:

(1) a partnership, shareholders, operating, employment, or other similar type of agreement that restricts the right of a lawyer to practice after termination of the relationship, except an agreement that concerns benefits upon retirement; or

(2) an agreement that imposes a restriction on a lawyer's right to practice in connection with a settlement of a client controversy, or otherwise.

(b) A lawyer shall not participate in offering or making an agreement which precludes the reporting of a violation of these rules.

(c) This rule does not prohibit an agreement that is authorized by Business and Professions Code sections 6092.5, subdivision (i) or 6093.

Comment

[1] Concerning the application of paragraph (a)(1), see Business and Professions Code section 16602; *Howard v. Babcock* (1993) 6 Cal.4th 409, 425 [25 Cal.Rptr.2d 80].

[2] Paragraph (a)(2) prohibits a lawyer from offering or agreeing not to represent other persons* in connection with settling a claim on behalf of a client.

[3] This rule does not prohibit restrictions that may be included in the terms of the sale of a law practice pursuant to rule 1.17.

(Adopted Sept. 26, 2018, eff. Nov. 1, 2018.)

Rule 5.7   [Reserved]

CHAPTER 6
PUBLIC SERVICE

Membership in Legal Services Organization. Rule 6.3.
Limited Legal Services Programs. Rule 6.5.

Rule 6.1   [Reserved]

Rule 6.2   [Reserved]

Rule 6.3   Membership in Legal Services Organization

A lawyer may serve as a director, officer or member of a legal services organization, apart from the law firm* in which the lawyer practices, notwithstanding that the organization serves persons* having interests adverse to a client of the lawyer. The lawyer shall not knowingly* participate in a decision or action of the organization:

(a) if participating in the decision or action would be incompatible with the lawyer's obligations to a client under Business and Professions Code section 6068, subdivision (e)(1) or rules 1.6(a), 1.7, 1.9, or 1.18; or

(b) where the decision or action could have a material adverse effect on the representation of a client of the organization whose interests are adverse to a client of the lawyer.

Comment

Lawyers should support and participate in legal service organizations. A lawyer who is an officer or a member of such an organization does not thereby have a lawyer-client relationship with persons* served by the organization. However, there is potential conflict between the interests of such persons* and the interests of the lawyer's clients. If the possibility of such conflict disqualified a lawyer from

---

* An asterisk (*) identifies a word or phrase defined in the terminology rule, rule 1.0.1.

serving on the board of a legal services organization, the profession's involvement in such organizations would be severely curtailed.

(Adopted Sept. 26, 2018, eff. Nov. 1, 2018.)

Rule 6.4 [Reserved]

Rule 6.5 Limited Legal Services Programs

(a) A lawyer who, under the auspices of a program sponsored by a court, government agency, bar association, law school, or nonprofit organization, provides short-term limited legal services to a client without expectation by either the lawyer or the client that the lawyer will provide continuing representation in the matter:

(1) is subject to rules 1.7 and 1.9(a) only if the lawyer knows* that the representation of the client involves a conflict of interest; and

(2) is subject to rule 1.10 only if the lawyer knows* that another lawyer associated with the lawyer in a law firm* is prohibited from representation by rule 1.7 or 1.9(a) with respect to the matter.

(b) Except as provided in paragraph (a)(2), rule 1.10 is inapplicable to a representation governed by this rule.

(c) The personal disqualification of a lawyer participating in the program will not be imputed to other lawyers participating in the program.

Comment

[1] Courts, government agencies, bar associations, law schools and various nonprofit organizations have established programs through which lawyers provide short-term limited legal services — such as advice or the completion of legal forms that will assist persons* in addressing their legal problems without further representation by a lawyer. In these programs, such as legal-advice hotlines, advice-only clinics or pro se counseling programs, whenever a lawyer-client relationship is established, there is no expectation that the lawyer's representation of the client will continue beyond that limited consultation. Such programs are normally operated under circumstances in which it is not feasible for a lawyer to systematically screen* for conflicts of interest as is generally required before undertaking a representation.

[2] A lawyer who provides short-term limited legal services pursuant to this rule must secure the client's informed consent* to the limited scope of the representation. (See rule 1.2(b).) If a short-term limited representation would not be reasonable* under the circumstances, the lawyer may offer advice to the client but must also advise the client of the need for further assistance of counsel. Except as provided in this rule, these rules and the State Bar Act, including the lawyer's duty of confidentiality under Business and Professions Code section 6068, subdivision (e)(1) and rules 1.6 and 1.9, are applicable to the limited representation.

[3] A lawyer who is representing a client in the circumstances addressed by this rule ordinarily is not able to check systematically for conflicts of interest. Therefore, paragraph (a)(1) requires compliance with rules 1.7 and 1.9(a) only if the lawyer knows* that the representation presents a conflict of interest for the lawyer. In addition, paragraph (a)(2) imputes conflicts of interest to the lawyer only if the lawyer knows* that another lawyer in the lawyer's law firm* would be disqualified under rules 1.7 or 1.9(a).

[4] Because the limited nature of the services significantly reduces the risk of conflicts of interest with other matters being handled by the lawyer's law firm,* paragraph (b) provides that imputed conflicts of interest are inapplicable to a representation governed by this rule except as provided by paragraph (a)(2). Paragraph (a)(2) imputes conflicts of interest to the participating lawyer when the lawyer knows* that any lawyer in the lawyer's firm* would be disqualified under rules 1.7 or 1.9(a). By virtue of paragraph (b), moreover, a lawyer's participation in a short-term limited legal services program will not be imputed to the lawyer's law firm* or preclude the lawyer's law firm* from undertaking or continuing the representation of a client with interests adverse to a client being represented under the program's auspices. Nor will the personal disqualification of a lawyer participating in the program be imputed to other lawyers participating in the program.

[5] If, after commencing a short-term limited representation in accordance with this rule, a lawyer undertakes to represent the client in the matter on an ongoing basis, rules 1.7, 1.9(a), and 1.10 become applicable.

(Adopted Sept. 26, 2018, eff. Nov. 1, 2018.)

CHAPTER 7
INFORMATION ABOUT LEGAL SERVICES

Communications Concerning a Lawyer's Services. Rule 7.1.
Advertising. Rule 7.2.
Solicitation of Clients. Rule 7.3.
Communication of Fields of Practice and Specialization. Rule 7.4.
Firm Names and Trade Names. Rule 7.5.

Rule 7.1 Communications Concerning a Lawyer's Services

(a) A lawyer shall not make a false or misleading communication about the lawyer or the lawyer's services. A communication is false or misleading if it contains a material misrepresentation of fact or law, or omits a fact necessary to make the communication considered as a whole not materially misleading.

(b) The Board of Trustees of the State Bar may formulate and adopt standards as to communications that will be presumed to violate rule 7.1, 7.2, 7.3, 7.4 or 7.5. The standards shall only be used as presumptions affecting the burden of proof in disciplinary proceedings involving alleged violations of these rules. "Presumption affecting the burden of proof" means that presumption defined in Evidence Code sections 605 and 606. Such standards formulated and adopted by the Board, as from time to time amended, shall be effective and binding on all lawyers.

Comment

[1] This rule governs all communications of any type whatsoever about the lawyer or the lawyer's services, including advertising permitted by rule 7.2. A communication includes any message or offer made by or on behalf of a lawyer concerning the availability for professional employment of a lawyer or a lawyer's law firm* directed to any person.*

[2] A communication that contains an express guarantee or warranty of the result of a particular representation is a false or misleading communication under this rule. (See also Bus. & Prof. Code, § 6157.2, subd. (a).)

[3] This rule prohibits truthful statements that are misleading. A truthful statement is misleading if it omits a fact necessary to make the lawyer's communication considered as a whole not materially misleading. A truthful statement is also misleading if it is presented in a manner that creates a substantial* likelihood that it will lead a reasonable* person* to formulate a specific conclusion about the lawyer or the lawyer's services for which there is no reasonable* factual foundation. Any communication that states or implies "no fee without recovery" is also misleading unless the communication also expressly discloses whether or not the client will be liable for costs.

[4] A communication that truthfully reports a lawyer's achievements on behalf of clients or former clients, or a testimonial about or endorsement of the lawyer, may be misleading if presented so as to lead a reasonable* person* to form an unjustified expectation that the same results could be obtained for other clients in similar matters without reference to the specific factual and legal circumstances of each client's case. Similarly, an unsubstantiated comparison of the lawyer's services or fees with the services or fees of other lawyers may be misleading if presented with such specificity as would lead a reasonable* person* to conclude that the comparison can be substantiated. An appropriate disclaimer or qualifying language often avoids creating unjustified expectations.

[5] This rule prohibits a lawyer from making a communication that states or implies that the lawyer is able to provide legal services in a language other than English unless the lawyer can actually provide legal services in that language or the communication also states in the language of the communication the employment title of the person* who speaks such language.

[6] Rules 7.1 through 7.5 are not the sole basis for regulating communications concerning a lawyer's services. (See, e.g., Bus. & Prof. Code, §§ 6150–6159.2, 17000 et seq.) Other state or federal laws may also apply.

(Adopted Sept. 26, 2018, eff. Nov. 1, 2018.)

Rule 7.2 Advertising

(a) Subject to the requirements of rules 7.1 and 7.3, a lawyer may advertise services through any written,* recorded or electronic means of communication, including public media.

(b) A lawyer shall not compensate, promise or give anything of value to a person* for the purpose of recommending or securing the services of the lawyer or the lawyer's law firm,* except that a lawyer may:

(1) pay the reasonable* costs of advertisements or communications permitted by this rule;

(2) pay the usual charges of a legal services plan or a qualified lawyer referral service. A qualified lawyer referral service is a lawyer referral service established, sponsored and operated in accordance with the State Bar of California's Minimum Standards for a Lawyer Referral Service in California;

(3) pay for a law practice in accordance with rule 1.17;

(4) refer clients to another lawyer or a nonlawyer professional pursuant to an arrangement not otherwise prohibited under these Rules or the State Bar Act that provides for the other person* to refer clients or customers to the lawyer, if:

(i) the reciprocal referral arrangement is not exclusive; and

(ii) the client is informed of the existence and nature of the arrangement;

(5) offer or give a gift or gratuity to a person* having made a recommendation resulting in the employment of the lawyer or the lawyer's law firm,* provided that the gift or gratuity was not offered or

---

* An asterisk (*) identifies a word or phrase defined in the terminology rule, rule 1.0.1.

given in consideration of any promise, agreement, or understanding that such a gift or gratuity would be forthcoming or that referrals would be made or encouraged in the future.

(c) Any communication made pursuant to this rule shall include the name and address of at least one lawyer or law firm* responsible for its content.

Comment

[1] This rule permits public dissemination of accurate information concerning a lawyer and the lawyer's services, including for example, the lawyer's name or firm* name, the lawyer's contact information; the kinds of services the lawyer will undertake; the basis on which the lawyer's fees are determined, including prices for specific services and payment and credit arrangements; a lawyer's foreign language ability; names of references and, with their consent, names of clients regularly represented; and other information that might invite the attention of those seeking legal assistance. This rule, however, prohibits the dissemination of false or misleading information, for example, an advertisement that sets forth a specific fee or range of fees for a particular service where, in fact, the lawyer charges or intends to charge a greater fee than that stated in the advertisement.

[2] Neither this rule nor rule 7.3 prohibits communications authorized by law, such as court-approved class action notices.

Paying Others to Recommend a Lawyer

[3] Paragraph (b)(1) permits a lawyer to compensate employees, agents, and vendors who are engaged to provide marketing or client-development services, such as publicists, public-relations personnel, business-development staff, and website designers. See rule 5.3 for the duties of lawyers and law firms* with respect to supervising the conduct of nonlawyers who prepare marketing materials and provide client development services.

[4] Paragraph (b)(4) permits a lawyer to make referrals to another lawyer or nonlawyer professional, in return for the undertaking of that person* to refer clients or customers to the lawyer. Such reciprocal referral arrangements must not interfere with the lawyer's professional judgment as to making referrals or as to providing substantive legal services. (See rules 2.1 and 5.4(c).) Conflicts of interest created by arrangements made pursuant to paragraph (b)(4) are governed by rule 1.7. A division of fees between or among lawyers not in the same law firm* is governed by rule 1.5.1.

(Adopted Sept. 26, 2018, eff. Nov. 1, 2018.)

Rule 7.3   Solicitation of Clients

(a) A lawyer shall not by in-person, live telephone or real-time electronic contact solicit professional employment when a significant motive for doing so is the lawyer's pecuniary gain, unless the person* contacted:

(1) is a lawyer; or

(2) has a family, close personal, or prior professional relationship with the lawyer.

(b) A lawyer shall not solicit professional employment by written,* recorded or electronic communication or by in-person, telephone or real-time electronic contact even when not otherwise prohibited by paragraph (a), if:

(1) the person* being solicited has made known* to the lawyer a desire not to be solicited by the lawyer; or

(2) the solicitation is transmitted in any manner which involves intrusion, coercion, duress or harassment.

(c) Every written,* recorded or electronic communication from a lawyer soliciting professional employment from any person* known* to be in need of legal services in a particular matter shall include the word "Advertisement" or words of similar import on the outside envelope, if any, and at the beginning and ending of any recorded or electronic communication, unless the recipient of the communication is a person* specified in paragraphs (a)(1) or (a)(2), or unless it is apparent from the context that the communication is an advertisement.

(d) Notwithstanding the prohibitions in paragraph (a), a lawyer may participate with a prepaid or group legal service plan operated by an organization not owned or directed by the lawyer that uses in-person, live telephone or real-time electronic contact to solicit memberships or subscriptions for the plan from persons* who are not known* to need legal services in a particular matter covered by the plan.

(e) As used in this rule, the terms "solicitation" and "solicit" refer to an oral or written* targeted communication initiated by or on behalf of the lawyer that is directed to a specific person* and that offers to provide, or can reasonably* be understood as offering to provide, legal services.

Comment

[1] A lawyer's communication does not constitute a solicitation if it is directed to the general public, such as through a billboard, an Internet banner advertisement, a website or a television commercial, or if it is in response to a request for information or is automatically generated in response to Internet searches.

[2] Paragraph (a) does not apply to situations in which the lawyer is motivated by considerations other than the lawyer's pecuniary gain. Therefore, paragraph (a) does not prohibit a lawyer from participating in constitutionally protected activities of bona fide public or charitable legal-service organizations, or bona fide political, social, civic, fraternal, employee or trade organizations whose purposes include providing or recommending legal services to its members or beneficiaries. (See, e.g., *In re Primus* (1978) 436 U.S. 412 [98 S.Ct. 1893].)

[3] This rule does not prohibit a lawyer from contacting representatives of organizations or groups that may be interested in establishing a bona fide group or prepaid legal plan for their members, insureds, beneficiaries or other third parties for the purpose of informing such entities of the availability of and details concerning the plan or arrangement which the lawyer or lawyer's firm* is willing to offer.

[4] Lawyers who participate in a legal service plan as permitted under paragraph (d) must comply with rules 7.1, 7.2, and 7.3(b). (See also rules 5.4 and 8.4(a).)

(Adopted Sept. 26, 2018, eff. Nov. 1, 2018.)

Rule 7.4   Communication of Fields of Practice and Specialization

(a) A lawyer shall not state that the lawyer is a certified specialist in a particular field of law, unless:

(1) the lawyer is currently certified as a specialist by the Board of Legal Specialization, or any other entity accredited by the State Bar to designate specialists pursuant to standards adopted by the Board of Trustees; and

(2) the name of the certifying organization is clearly identified in the communication.

(b) Notwithstanding paragraph (a), a lawyer may communicate the fact that the lawyer does or does not practice in particular fields of law. A lawyer may also communicate that his or her practice specializes in, is limited to, or is concentrated in a particular field of law, subject to the requirements of rule 7.1.

(Adopted Sept. 26, 2018, eff. Nov. 1, 2018.)

Rule 7.5   Firm* Names and Trade Names

(a) A lawyer shall not use a firm* name, trade name or other professional designation that violates rule 7.1.

(b) A lawyer in private practice shall not use a firm* name, trade name or other professional designation that states or implies a relationship with a government agency or with a public or charitable legal services organization, or otherwise violates rule 7.1.

(c) A lawyer shall not state or imply that the lawyer practices in or has a professional relationship with a law firm* or other organization unless that is the fact.

Comment

The term "other professional designation" includes, but is not limited to, logos, letterheads, URLs, and signature blocks.

(Adopted Sept. 26, 2018, eff. Nov. 1, 2018.)

Rule 7.6   [Reserved]

CHAPTER 8
MAINTAINING THE INTEGRITY OF THE PROFESSION

False Statement Regarding Application for Admission to Practice Law. Rule 8.1.
Compliance with Conditions of Discipline and Agreements in Lieu of Discipline. Rule 8.1.1.
Judicial Officials. Rule 8.2.
Reporting Professional Misconduct. Rule 8.3.
Misconduct. Rule 8.4.
Prohibited Discrimination, Harassment and Retaliation. Rule 8.4.1.
Disciplinary Authority; Choice of Law. Rule 8.5.

Rule 8.1   False Statement Regarding Application for Admission to Practice Law

(a) An applicant for admission to practice law shall not, in connection with that person's* own application for admission, make a statement of material fact that the lawyer knows* to be false, or make such a statement with reckless disregard as to its truth or falsity.

---

* An asterisk (*) identifies a word or phrase defined in the terminology rule, rule 1.0.1.

(b) A lawyer shall not, in connection with another person's* application for admission to practice law, make a statement of material fact that the lawyer knows* to be false.

(c) An applicant for admission to practice law, or a lawyer in connection with an application for admission, shall not fail to disclose a fact necessary to correct a statement known* by the applicant or the lawyer to have created a material misapprehension in the matter, except that this rule does not authorize disclosure of information protected by Business and Professions Code section 6068, subdivision (e) and rule 1.6.

(d) As used in this rule, "admission to practice law" includes admission or readmission to membership in the State Bar; reinstatement to active membership in the State Bar; and any similar process relating to admission or certification to practice law in California or elsewhere.

Comment

[1] A person* who makes a false statement in connection with that person's* own application for admission to practice law may be subject to discipline under this rule after that person* has been admitted. (See, e.g., *In re Gossage* (2000) 23 Cal.4th 1080 [99 Cal.Rptr.2d 130].)

[2] A lawyer's duties with respect to a *pro hac vice* application or other application to a court for admission to practice law are governed by rule 3.3.

[3] A lawyer representing an applicant for admission to practice law is governed by the rules applicable to the lawyer-client relationship, including Business and Professions Code section 6068, subdivision (e)(1) and rule 1.6. A lawyer representing a lawyer who is the subject of a disciplinary proceeding is not governed by this rule but is subject to the requirements of rule 3.3.

(Adopted Sept. 26, 2018, eff. Nov. 1, 2018.)

Rule 8.1.1 Compliance with Conditions of Discipline and Agreements in Lieu of Discipline

A lawyer shall comply with the terms and conditions attached to any agreement in lieu of discipline, any public or private reproval, or to other discipline administered by the State Bar pursuant to Business and Professions Code sections 6077 and 6078 and California Rules of Court, rule 9.19.

Comment

Other provisions also require a lawyer to comply with agreements in lieu of discipline and conditions of discipline. (See, e.g., Bus. & Prof. Code, § 6068, subds. (k), (*l*).)

(Adopted Sept. 26, 2018, eff. Nov. 1, 2018.)

Rule 8.2 Judicial Officials

(a) A lawyer shall not make a statement of fact that the lawyer knows* to be false or with reckless disregard as to its truth or falsity concerning the qualifications or integrity of a judge or judicial officer, or of a candidate for election or appointment to judicial office.

(b) A lawyer who is a candidate for judicial office in California shall comply with canon 5 of the California Code of Judicial Ethics. For purposes of this rule, "candidate for judicial office" means a lawyer seeking judicial office by election. The determination of when a lawyer is a candidate for judicial office by election is defined in the terminology section of the California Code of Judicial Ethics. A lawyer's duty to comply with this rule shall end when the lawyer announces withdrawal of the lawyer's candidacy or when the results of the election are final, whichever occurs first.

(c) A lawyer who seeks appointment to judicial office shall comply with canon 5B(1) of the California Code of Judicial Ethics. A lawyer becomes an applicant seeking judicial office by appointment at the time of first submission of an application or personal data questionnaire to the appointing authority. A lawyer's duty to comply with this rule shall end when the lawyer advises the appointing authority of the withdrawal of the lawyer's application.

Comment

To maintain the fair and independent administration of justice, lawyers should defend judges and courts unjustly criticized. Lawyers also are obligated to maintain the respect due to the courts of justice and judicial officers. (See Bus. & Prof. Code, § 6068, subd. (b).)

(Adopted Sept. 26, 2018, eff. Nov. 1, 2018.)

Rule 8.3 Reporting Professional Misconduct

(a) A lawyer shall, without undue delay, inform the State Bar, or a tribunal* with jurisdiction to investigate or act upon such misconduct, when the lawyer knows* of credible evidence that another lawyer has committed a criminal act or has engaged in conduct involving dishonesty, fraud,* deceit, or reckless or intentional misrepresentation or misappropriation of funds or property that raises a substantial* question as to that lawyer's honesty, trustworthiness, or fitness as a lawyer in other respects.

(b) Except as required by paragraph (a), a lawyer may, but is not required to, report to the State Bar a violation of these Rules or the State Bar Act.

(c) For purposes of this rule, "criminal act" as used in paragraph (a) excludes conduct that would be a criminal act in another state, United States territory, or foreign jurisdiction, but would not be a criminal act in California.

(d) This rule does not require or authorize disclosure of information gained by a lawyer while participating in a substance use or mental health program, or require disclosure of information protected by Business and Professions Code section 6068, subdivision (e) and rules 1.6 and 1.8.2; mediation confidentiality; the lawyer-client privilege; other applicable privileges; or by other rules or laws, including information that is confidential under Business and Professions Code section 6234.

Comment

[1] This rule does not abrogate a lawyer's obligations to report the lawyer's own conduct as required by these rules or the State Bar Act. (See, e.g., rule 8.4.1(d) and (e); Bus. & Prof. Code, § 6068, subd. (o).)

[2] The duty to report under paragraph (a) is not intended to discourage lawyers from seeking counsel. This rule does not apply to a lawyer who is consulted about or retained to represent a lawyer whose conduct is in question, or to a lawyer consulted in a professional capacity by another lawyer on whether the inquiring lawyer has a duty to report a third-party lawyer under this rule. The duty to report under paragraph (a) does not apply if the report would involve disclosure of information that is gained by a lawyer while participating as a member of a state or local bar association ethics hotline or similar service.

[3] The duty to report without undue delay under paragraph (a) requires the lawyer to report as soon as the lawyer reasonably believes* the reporting will not cause material prejudice or damage to the interests of a client of the lawyer or a client of the lawyer's firm.* The lawyer should also consider the applicability of other rules such as rules 1.4 (the duty to communicate), 1.7(b) (material limitation conflict), 5.1 (responsibilities of managerial and supervisorial lawyers), and 5.2 (responsibilities of a subordinate lawyer).

[4] This rule limits the reporting obligation to those offenses that a self-regulating profession must vigorously endeavor to prevent. A measure of judgment is, therefore, required in complying with the provisions of this rule. The term "substantial* question" refers to the seriousness of the possible offense and not the quantum of evidence of which the lawyer is aware.

[5] Information about a lawyer's misconduct or fitness may be received by a lawyer while participating in a substance use or mental health program, including but not limited to the Attorney Diversion and Assistance Program. (See Bus. & Prof. Code, § 6234.) In these circumstances, providing for an exception to the reporting requirement of paragraph (a) of this rule encourages lawyers to seek treatment through such programs. Conversely, without such an exception, lawyers may hesitate to seek assistance from these programs, which may then result in additional harm to their professional careers and additional injury to the welfare of clients and the public.

[6] The rule permits reporting to either the State Bar or to "a tribunal* with jurisdiction to investigate or act upon such misconduct." A determination whether to report to a tribunal,* instead of the State Bar, will depend on whether the misconduct arises during pending litigation and whether the particular tribunal* has the power to "investigate or act upon" the alleged misconduct. Where the litigation is pending before a non-judicial tribunal,* such as a private arbitrator, reporting to the tribunal* may not be sufficient. If the tribunal* is a proper reporting venue, evidence of lawyer misconduct adduced during those proceedings may be admissible evidence in subsequent disciplinary proceedings. (*Caldwell v. State Bar* (1975) 13 Cal.3d 488, 497.) Furthermore, a report to the proper tribunal* may also trigger obligations for the tribunal* to report the misconduct to the State Bar or to take other "appropriate corrective action." (See Bus. & Prof. Code, §§ 6049.1, 6086.7, 6068.8; and Cal. Code of Jud. Ethics, canon 3D(2).)

[7] A report under this rule to a tribunal* concerning another lawyer's criminal act or fraud* may constitute a "reasonable* remedial measure" within the meaning of rule 3.3(b).

[8] In addition to reporting as required by paragraph (a), a report may also be made to another appropriate agency. A lawyer must not threaten to present criminal, administrative or disciplinary charges to obtain an advantage in a civil dispute in violation of rule 3.10.

[9] A lawyer may also be disciplined for participating in an agreement that precludes the reporting of a violation of the rules. (See rule 5.6(b); and Bus. & Prof. Code, § 6090.5.)

[10] Communications to the State Bar relating to lawyer misconduct are "privileged, and no lawsuit predicated thereon may be instituted against any person." (Bus. & Prof. Code, § 6094.) However, lawyers may be subject to criminal

---

* An asterisk (*) identifies a word or phrase defined in the terminology rule, rule 1.0.1.

penalties for false and malicious reports or complaints filed with the State Bar or be subject to discipline or other penalties by offering false statements or false evidence to a tribunal.* (See rule 3.3(a); Bus. & Prof. Code, §§ 6043.5, subd. (a), 6068, subd. (d).)

(Adopted June 21, 2023, eff. Aug. 1, 2023.)

Rule 8.4 Misconduct

It is professional misconduct for a lawyer to:

(a) violate these rules or the State Bar Act, knowingly* assist, solicit, or induce another to do so, or do so through the acts of another;

(b) commit a criminal act that reflects adversely on the lawyer's honesty, trustworthiness, or fitness as a lawyer in other respects;

(c) engage in conduct involving dishonesty, fraud,* deceit, or reckless or intentional misrepresentation;

(d) engage in conduct that is prejudicial to the administration of justice;

(e) state or imply an ability to influence improperly a government agency or official, or to achieve results by means that violate these rules, the State Bar Act, or other law; or

(f) knowingly* assist, solicit, or induce a judge or judicial officer in conduct that is a violation of an applicable code of judicial ethics or code of judicial conduct, or other law. For purposes of this rule, "judge" and "judicial officer" have the same meaning as in rule 3.5(c).

Comment

[1] A violation of this rule can occur when a lawyer is acting in propria persona or when a lawyer is not practicing law or acting in a professional capacity.

[2] Paragraph (a) does not prohibit a lawyer from advising a client concerning action the client is legally entitled to take.

[3] A lawyer may be disciplined for criminal acts as set forth in Business and Professions Code sections 6101 et seq., or if the criminal act constitutes "other misconduct warranting discipline" as defined by California Supreme Court case law. (See *In re Kelley* (1990) 52 Cal.3d 487 [276 Cal.Rptr. 375].)

[4] A lawyer may be disciplined under Business and Professions Code section 6106 for acts involving moral turpitude, dishonesty, or corruption, whether intentional, reckless, or grossly negligent.

[5] Paragraph (c) does not apply where a lawyer advises clients or others about, or supervises, lawful covert activity in the investigation of violations of civil or criminal law or constitutional rights, provided the lawyer's conduct is otherwise in compliance with these rules and the State Bar Act.

[6] This rule does not prohibit those activities of a particular lawyer that are protected by the First Amendment to the United States Constitution or by Article I, section 2 of the California Constitution.

(Adopted Sept. 26, 2018, eff. Nov. 1, 2018.)

Rule 8.4.1 Prohibited Discrimination, Harassment and Retaliation

(a) In representing a client, or in terminating or refusing to accept the representation of any client, a lawyer shall not:

(1) unlawfully harass or unlawfully discriminate against persons* on the basis of any protected characteristic; or

(2) unlawfully retaliate against persons.*

(b) In relation to a law firm's operations, a lawyer shall not:

(1) on the basis of any protected characteristic,

(i) unlawfully discriminate or knowingly* permit unlawful discrimination;

(ii) unlawfully harass or knowingly* permit the unlawful harassment of an employee, an applicant, an unpaid intern or volunteer, or a person* providing services pursuant to a contract; or

(iii) unlawfully refuse to hire or employ a person*, or refuse to select a person* for a training program leading to employment, or bar or discharge a person* from employment or from a training program leading to employment, or discriminate against a person* in compensation or in terms, conditions, or privileges of employment; or

(2) unlawfully retaliate against persons.*

(c) For purposes of this rule:

(1) "protected characteristic" means race, religious creed, color, national origin, ancestry, physical disability, mental disability, medical condition, genetic information, marital status, sex, gender, gender identity, gender expression, sexual orientation, age, military and veteran status, or other category of discrimination prohibited by applicable law, whether the category is actual or perceived;

(2) "knowingly permit" means to fail to advocate corrective action where the lawyer knows* of a discriminatory policy or practice that results in the unlawful discrimination or harassment prohibited by paragraph (b);

(3) "unlawfully" and "unlawful" shall be determined by reference to applicable state and federal statutes and decisions making unlawful discrimination or harassment in employment and in offering goods and services to the public; and

(4) "retaliate" means to take adverse action against a person* because that person* has (i) opposed, or (ii) pursued, participated in, or assisted any action alleging, any conduct prohibited by paragraphs (a)(1) or (b)(1) of this rule.

(d) A lawyer who is the subject of a State Bar investigation or State Bar Court proceeding alleging a violation of this rule shall promptly notify the State Bar of any criminal, civil, or administrative action premised, whether in whole or part, on the same conduct that is the subject of the State Bar investigation or State Bar Court proceeding.

(e) Upon being issued a notice of a disciplinary charge under this rule, a lawyer shall:

(1) if the notice is of a disciplinary charge under paragraph (a) of this rule, provide a copy of the notice to the California Department of Fair Employment and Housing and the United States Department of Justice, Coordination and Review Section; or

(2) if the notice is of a disciplinary charge under paragraph (b) of this rule, provide a copy of the notice to the California Department of Fair Employment and Housing and the United States Equal Employment Opportunity Commission.

(f) This rule shall not preclude a lawyer from:

(1) representing a client alleged to have engaged in unlawful discrimination, harassment, or retaliation;

(2) declining or withdrawing from a representation as required or permitted by rule 1.16; or

(3) providing advice and engaging in advocacy as otherwise required or permitted by these rules and the State Bar Act.

Comment

[1] Conduct that violates this rule undermines confidence in the legal profession and our legal system and is contrary to the fundamental principle that all people are created equal. A lawyer may not engage in such conduct through the acts of another. (See rule 8.4(a).) In relation to a law firm's operations, this rule imposes on all law firm* lawyers the responsibility to advocate corrective action to address known* harassing or discriminatory conduct by the firm* or any of its other lawyers or nonlawyer personnel. Law firm* management and supervisorial lawyers retain their separate responsibility under rules 5.1 and 5.3. Neither this rule nor rule 5.1 or 5.3 imposes on the alleged victim of any conduct prohibited by this rule any responsibility to advocate corrective action.

[2] The conduct prohibited by paragraph (a) includes the conduct of a lawyer in a proceeding before a judicial officer. (See Cal. Code Jud. Ethics, canon 3B(6) ["A judge shall require lawyers in proceedings before the judge to refrain from manifesting, by words or conduct, bias or prejudice based upon race, sex, gender, religion, national origin, ethnicity, disability, age, sexual orientation, marital status, socioeconomic status, or political affiliation against parties, witnesses, counsel, or others."].) A lawyer does not violate paragraph (a) by referring to any particular status or group when the reference is relevant to factual or legal issues or arguments in the representation. While both the parties and the court retain discretion to refer such conduct to the State Bar, a court's finding that peremptory challenges were exercised on a discriminatory basis does not alone establish a violation of paragraph (a).

[3] A lawyer does not violate this rule by limiting the scope or subject matter of the lawyer's practice or by limiting the lawyer's practice to members of underserved populations. A lawyer also does not violate this rule by otherwise restricting who will be accepted as clients for advocacy-based reasons, as required or permitted by these rules or other law.

[4] This rule does not apply to conduct protected by the First Amendment to the United States Constitution or by Article I, section 2 of the California Constitution.

[5] What constitutes a failure to advocate corrective action under paragraph (c)(2) will depend on the nature and seriousness of the discriminatory policy or practice, the extent to which the lawyer knows* of unlawful discrimination or harassment resulting from that policy or practice, and the nature of the lawyer's relationship to the lawyer or law firm* implementing that policy or practice. For example, a law firm* non-management and non-supervisorial lawyer who becomes aware that the law firm* is engaging in a discriminatory hiring practice may advocate corrective action by bringing that discriminatory practice to the attention of a law firm* management lawyer who would have responsibility under rule 5.1 or 5.3 to take reasonable* remedial action upon becoming aware of a violation of this rule.

---

* An asterisk (*) identifies a word or phrase defined in the terminology rule, rule 1.0.1.

[6] Paragraph (d) ensures that the State Bar and the State Bar Court will be provided with information regarding related proceedings that may be relevant in determining whether a State Bar investigation or a State Bar Court proceeding relating to a violation of this rule should be abated.

[7] Paragraph (e) recognizes the public policy served by enforcement of laws and regulations prohibiting unlawful discrimination, by ensuring that the state and federal agencies with primary responsibility for coordinating the enforcement of those laws and regulations is provided with notice of any allegation of unlawful discrimination, harassment, or retaliation by a lawyer that the State Bar finds has sufficient merit to warrant issuance of a notice of a disciplinary charge.

[8] This rule permits the imposition of discipline for conduct that would not necessarily result in the award of a remedy in a civil or administrative proceeding if such proceeding were filed.

[9] A disciplinary investigation or proceeding for conduct coming within this rule may also be initiated and maintained if such conduct warrants discipline under California Business and Professions Code sections 6106 and 6068, the California Supreme Court's inherent authority to impose discipline, or other disciplinary standard.

(Adopted Sept. 26, 2018, eff. Nov. 1, 2018.)

Rule 8.5 Disciplinary Authority; Choice of Law

(a) Disciplinary Authority.

A lawyer admitted to practice in California is subject to the disciplinary authority of California, regardless of where the lawyer's conduct occurs. A lawyer not admitted in California is also subject to the disciplinary authority of California if the lawyer provides or offers to provide any legal services in California. A lawyer may be subject to the disciplinary authority of both California and another jurisdiction for the same conduct.

(b) Choice of Law.

In any exercise of the disciplinary authority of California, the rules of professional conduct to be applied shall be as follows:

(1) for conduct in connection with a matter pending before a tribunal,* the rules of the jurisdiction in which the tribunal* sits, unless the rules of the tribunal* provide otherwise; and

(2) for any other conduct, the rules of the jurisdiction in which the lawyer's conduct occurred, or, if the predominant effect of the conduct is in a different jurisdiction, the rules of that jurisdiction shall be applied to the conduct. A lawyer shall not be subject to discipline if the lawyer's conduct conforms to the rules of a jurisdiction in which the lawyer reasonably believes* the predominant effect of the lawyer's conduct will occur.

Comment

Disciplinary Authority

The conduct of a lawyer admitted to practice in California is subject to the disciplinary authority of California. (See Bus. & Prof. Code, §§ 6077, 6100.) Extension of the disciplinary authority of California to other lawyers who provide or offer to provide legal services in California is for the protection of the residents of California. A lawyer disciplined by a disciplinary authority in another jurisdiction may be subject to discipline in California for the same conduct. (See, e.g., § 6049.1.)

(Adopted Sept. 26, 2018, eff. Nov. 1, 2018.)

---

* An asterisk (*) identifies a word or phrase defined in the terminology rule, rule 1.0.1.

RULES AND POLICY DECLARATIONS OF THE COMMISSION ON JUDICIAL PERFORMANCE

2025 EDITION

The Rules of the Commission on Judicial Performance were adopted at the commission's October 22-23, 1996 meeting. The rules are effective December 1, 1996, and supersede Rules 901–922 of the Rules of Court.

The Policy Declarations of the Commission on Judicial Performance were approved by the commission on May 28, 1997.

The Rules and Policy Declarations of the Commission on Judicial Performance promulgated and adopted by the commission with amendments from November 20, 2023 through November 11, 2024.

The Rules of the Commission on Judicial Performance were last amended February 1, 2024. The Policy Declarations of the Commission on Judicial Performance were last amended December 7, 2022.

PREFACE

From 1961 to 1994, the Judicial Council was responsible for promulgating rules of procedure for the Commission on Judicial Performance. The Judicial Council adopted rules 901–922 of the Rules of Court as rules for the censure, removal, retirement or private admonishment of judges.

Since its early history, the commission has deliberated on and recorded in its minutes its resolutions regarding significant policy issues. These resolutions address areas not detailed in its governing provisions (California Constitution, Rules of Court, and Government Code) including internal organization and management, staff functions, and implementation of the rules and statutes regarding formal proceedings and disability matters. In 1984, the commission collected the statements of existing policy in a single, amendable document entitled Policy Declarations of the Commission on Judicial Performance.

Proposition 190, approved by California voters in the November 1994 general election, took effect March 1, 1995. One of the most significant changes implemented by Proposition 190 was a change in authority for promulgating rules regarding commission procedures and confidentiality. The commission now has the authority to promulgate its own rules.

In April 1995, the commission adopted rules 901–922 of the Rules of Court as interim rules pending a comprehensive review of the rules. The commission also adopted Policy Declarations 1.1 through 4.4, amended rule 917 to require a vote of six members of the commission, and adopted transitional Rules 1, 2 and 3. The commission adopted two new rules, Rules 120 and 127, as interim rules in May 1996.

At its October 22-23, 1996 meeting, the commission adopted the Rules of the Commission on Judicial Performance. The commission Rules took effect December 1, 1996 and replaced rules 901–918 and 922 of the Rules of Court and transitional Rules 1, 2 and 3. Rules 919, 920 and 921 concern Supreme Court review of commission determinations and were not reviewed by the commission.

The Policy Declarations of the Commission on Judicial Performance were approved by the commission on May 28, 1997.

**Table Showing Changes Promulgated by the Commission on Judicial Performance
From November 20, 2023 Through November 11, 2024**

Rules of the Commission on Judicial Performance

Rule	Effect	Date
121(f)	Amended	Feb. 1, 2024

RULES OF THE COMMISSION ON JUDICIAL PERFORMANCE

Interested party. Rule 101.
Confidentiality and disclosure. Rule 102.
Protection from liability for statements. Rule 103.
Duty to cooperate; response by respondent judge. Rule 104.
Medical examination. Rule 105.
Judge's representation by counsel. Rule 106.
Notice requirements. Rule 107.
Extensions of time. Rule 108.
Commencement of commission action. Rule 109.
Preliminary investigation. Rule 111.
Legal error. Rule 111.4.
Monitoring. Rule 112.
Notice of tentative advisory letter, private admonishment, or public admonishment. Rule 113.
Advisory letter, private admonishment, and public admonishment procedure. Rule 114.
Negotiated settlement during preliminary investigation. Rule 116.5.
Records disposition program. Rule 117.
Notice of formal proceedings. Rule 118.
Answer. Rule 119.
Filing with the commission during formal proceedings. Rule 119.5.
Disqualification. Rule 120.
Suspension; termination of suspension; removal of suspended judge. Rule 120.5.
Setting for hearing before commission or masters. Rule 121.
Discovery procedures. Rule 122.
Hearing. Rule 123.
Media at hearing. Rule 124.
Evidence. Rule 125.
Exhibits at hearing. Rule 125.5.
Procedural rights of judge in formal proceedings. Rule 126.
Discipline by consent. Rule 127.
Amendments to notice or answer; dismissals. Rule 128.
Report of masters. Rule 129.
Briefs to the commission. Rule 130.
Participation by non-parties. Rule 131.
Appearance before commission. Rule 132.
Hearing additional evidence. Rule 133.
Commission vote. Rule 134.
Rule of necessity. Rule 134.5.
Record of commission proceedings. Rule 135.
Finality. Rule 136.
Retroactivity. Rule 137.
Definitions. Rule 138.

Rule 101. Interested Party.

Judges who are members of the commission or of the Supreme Court may not participate as such in any commission proceedings involving themselves.

Adopted Oct. 24, 1996, effective Dec. 1, 1996.

Rule 102. Confidentiality and Disclosure.

(a) (Scope of rule) Except as provided in this rule, all papers filed with and proceedings before the commission shall be confidential. Nothing in this rule prohibits the respondent judge or anyone other than a commission member or member of commission staff from making statements regarding the judge's conduct underlying a complaint or proceeding.

(b) (Disclosure after institution of formal proceedings) When the commission institutes formal proceedings, the following shall not be confidential:

(1) The notice of formal proceedings and all subsequent papers filed with the commission and the special masters, all stipulations entered, all findings of fact and conclusions of law made by the special masters and by the commission, and all determinations of removal, censure and public admonishment made by the commission;

(2) The formal hearing before the special masters and the appearance before the commission.

(c) (Explanatory statements) The commission may issue explanatory statements under article VI, section 18(k) of the California Constitution.

(d) (Submission of proposed statement of clarification and correction regarding commission proceedings by judge) Notwithstanding rule 102(a), if public reports concerning a commission proceeding result in substantial unfairness to the judge involved in the proceeding, including unfairness resulting from reports which are false or materially misleading or inaccurate, the involved judge may submit a proposed statement of clarification and correction to the commission and request its issuance. The commission shall either issue the requested statement, advise the judge in writing that it declines to issue the requested statement, or issue a modified statement.

(e) (Disclosure to complainant) Upon completion of an investigation or proceeding, the commission shall disclose to the person complaining against the judge that the commission (1) has found no basis for action against the judge or determined not to proceed further in this matter, (2) has taken an appropriate corrective action, the nature of which shall not be disclosed, or (3) has publicly admonished, censured, removed, or retired the judge, or has found the person unfit to serve as a subordinate judicial officer. Where a matter is referred to the commission by a presiding judge or other public official in his or her official capacity, disclosure under this subdivision concerning that matter shall be made to the individual serving in that office at the time the matter is concluded. The name of the judge shall not be used in any written communication to the complainant, unless formal proceedings have been instituted or unless the complainant is a presiding judge or other public official in his or her official capacity. Written communications in which the judge's name is not used shall include the date of the complaint as a cross-reference.

(f) (Public safety) When the commission receives information concerning a threat to the safety of any person or persons, information concerning such a threat may be provided to the person threatened, to persons or organizations responsible for the safety of the person threatened, and to law enforcement and/or any appropriate prosecutorial agency.

(g) (Disclosure of information to prosecuting authorities) The commission may release to prosecuting authorities at any time information which reveals possible criminal conduct by the judge or former judge or by any other individual or entity.

(h) (Disclosure of records to public entity upon request or consent of judge) If a judge or former judge requests or consents to release of commission records to a public entity, the commission may release that judge's records.

(i) (Disclosure of records of disciplinary action to appointing authorities) The commission shall, upon request, provide to the Governor of any State of the Union, the President of the United States, or the Commission on Judicial Appointments the text of any private admonishment or advisory letter issued after March 1, 1995 or any other disciplinary action together with any information that the commission deems necessary to a full understanding of the commission's action, with respect to any applicant under consideration for any judicial appointment, provided that:

(1) The request is in writing; and

(2) Any information released to the appointing authority is simultaneously provided to the applicant.

All information disclosed to appointing authorities under this subdivision remains privileged and confidential. Private admonishments and advisory letters issued before March 1, 1995 shall only be disclosed under this section with the judge's written consent.

(j) (Disclosure of information regarding pending proceedings to appointing authorities) The commission may, upon request, in the interest of justice or to maintain public confidence in the administration of justice, provide to the Governor of any State of the Union, the President of the United States, the Commission on Judicial Appointments, or any other state or federal authorities responsible for judicial appointments information concerning any pending investigation or proceeding with respect to any applicant under consideration for any judicial appointment, provided that:

(1) The request is in writing; and
(2) Any information released to the appointing authority is simultaneously provided to the applicant.

If a disclosure about a pending matter is made and that matter subsequently is closed by the commission without discipline being imposed, disclosure of the latter fact shall be made promptly to the appointing authority and the judge.

All information disclosed to appointing authorities under this subdivision remains privileged and confidential.

(k) **(Disclosure of information to the State Bar upon retirement or resignation)** If a judge retires or resigns from office or if a subordinate judicial officer retires, resigns or is terminated from employment after a complaint is filed with the commission, or if a complaint is filed with the commission after the retirement, resignation or termination, the commission may, in the interest of justice or to maintain public confidence in the administration of justice, release information concerning the complaint, investigation and proceedings to the State Bar, provided that the commission has commenced a preliminary investigation or other proceeding and the judge or subordinate judicial officer has had an opportunity to respond to the commission's inquiry or preliminary investigation letter.

(l) **(Disclosure of information about subordinate judicial officers to presiding judges)** The commission may release to a presiding judge or his or her designee information concerning a complaint, investigation or disposition involving a subordinate judicial officer, including the name of the subordinate judicial officer, consistent with the commission's jurisdiction under article VI, section 18.1 of the California Constitution.

(m) **(Disclosure of information regarding disciplinary action and pending proceedings to the Chief Justice)** With respect to any judge who is under consideration for judicial assignment following retirement or resignation, or is sitting on assignment, the commission may, upon the request of the Chief Justice of California and with the consent of that judge, in the interest of justice or to maintain public confidence in the administration of justice, provide the Chief Justice information concerning any record of disciplinary action or any pending investigation or proceeding with respect to that judge, provided that:

(1) The request and consent are in writing;
(2) If the disclosure involves a pending investigation or proceeding, the judge has had an opportunity to respond to the pending investigation or proceeding; and
(3) Any information released to the Chief Justice is simultaneously provided to the judge seeking assignment.

If the disclosure involves disciplinary action, the commission may include any information the commission deems necessary to a full understanding of its action.

If a disclosure about a pending matter is made and that matter subsequently is closed by the commission without discipline being imposed, disclosure of the latter fact shall be made promptly to the Chief Justice and the judge.

All information disclosed to the Chief Justice under this subdivision remains privileged and confidential.

(n) **(Disclosure of information to presiding judges about possible lack of capacity or other inability to perform)** The commission may release to a presiding judge or his or her designee information concerning an investigation involving possible lack of capacity or other inability to perform judicial duties on the part of a judge of that court, except that no confidential medical information concerning the judge may be released.

(o) **(Disclosure of closing to judge who provides information to the commission)** Upon completion of the commission's review of a complaint or an investigation, the commission may notify a judge who is the subject of a complaint and has voluntarily provided information to the commission concerning the complaint, that the commission has found no basis for action against the judge or determined not to proceed further in the matter. The notification shall be in writing.

(p) **(Disclosure of information to regulatory agencies)** The commission may in the interest of justice, to protect the public, or to maintain public confidence in the administration of justice, release to a federal, state or local regulatory agency information which reveals a possible violation of a law or regulation within the agency's jurisdiction by a judge, former judge, subordinate judicial officer or former subordinate judicial officer, provided the commission has commenced a preliminary investigation.

In the event information is revealed under this subsection, the agency must be admonished that the fact that the commission has undertaken an investigation of the judge must remain confidential unless formal proceedings have been instituted.

(q) **(Disclosure of information to mentor judge)** When a judge has agreed to participate in a mentoring program, the commission may provide the mentor judge with the specifications of the allegations before the commission, any materials concerning the allegations the commission deems relevant and necessary for the mentor to perform his or her services, and any prior discipline, including private discipline, imposed on the judge for similar misconduct. The mentor judge will not be given the complaint or witness statements, but may be given a summary of information provided in the complaint and witness statements.

If a judge who participated in mentoring is found to have engaged in subsequent misconduct, any resulting discipline, including public discipline, on the subsequent matter may include a discussion of the prior matter that was the subject of the mentoring and that the judge participated in mentoring.

(r) **(Disclosure to California State Auditor)** The commission shall provide to the California State Auditor, or an authorized employee of the Auditor, access to confidential commission records pursuant to the provisions of Government Code sections 8545.1 and 8545.2 in connection with an audit mandated by statute or requested by the California State Legislature. This subdivision applies to confidential records in the commission's possession prior to the enactment of subdivision (r) of section 102.

(s) **(Disclosure to respondent in formal proceedings)** In compliance with discovery obligations in formal proceedings, the commission may provide to a judge who is the respondent in formal proceedings pursuant to rule 118 et seq., or to the judge's counsel, any relevant items that might otherwise be confidential under rule 102, including (i) some or all of the written or oral statements of another judge made or obtained during or after a staff inquiry under former rule 110 or preliminary investigation of that judge, (ii) any writings or physical items of evidence submitted by or on behalf of the other judge during or after such staff inquiry under former rule 110 or preliminary investigation, and (iii) relevant portions of the staff inquiry under former rule 110 and preliminary investigation letter(s) sent to that judge. Prior to providing discovery of confidential statements to a respondent judge in formal proceedings, the commission shall give notice and an opportunity to be heard to the judge whose confidential statements are being provided. To the extent possible, steps will be taken to protect the confidentiality of the judge who provided the relevant information (e.g., by redacting or sealing documents).

Adopted Oct. 24, 1996, effective Dec. 1, 1996; amended Oct. 8, 1998, Feb. 11, 1999; interim amendment May 9, 2001; amended Jan. 29, 2003; amended and interim amendment Aug. 26, 2004; amended Oct. 25, 2005, May 23, 2007, Jan. 28, 2009, Mar. 23, 2011, May 13, 2015; interim amendment June 29, 2016, Mar. 28, 2018; amended Sept. 20, 2018; interim amendment Jan. 29, 2020, Mar. 24, 2021, Mar. 23, 2022; amended Dec. 7, 2022.

Rule 103. Protection From Liability for Statements.

The making of statements to the commission, the filing of papers with or the giving of testimony before the commission, or before the masters appointed by the Supreme Court pursuant to rule 121, shall not give rise to civil liability for the person engaged in such acts. This privilege extends to any motions or petitions filed in the Supreme Court, as well as papers filed in connection therewith. No other publication of such statements, papers or proceedings shall be so privileged.

Adopted Oct. 24, 1996, effective Dec. 1, 1996.

Rule 104. Duty to Cooperate; Response by Respondent Judge.

(a) A respondent judge shall cooperate with the commission in all proceedings in accordance with Government Code section 68725. The judge's cooperation or lack of cooperation may be considered by the commission in determining the appropriate disciplinary sanction or disposition as well as further proceedings to be taken by the commission but may not be considered in making evidentiary determinations.

(b) A respondent judge shall, within the time limits set forth in rule 111(a), respond to the merits of a preliminary investigation letter.

(c) A respondent judge shall, within the time limits set forth in rule 119(b), file an answer to a notice of formal proceedings which comports with the requirements set forth in rule 119(c).

(d) A respondent judge shall file all other responses and documents required in commission proceedings within such reasonable time as the commission may prescribe, and shall comply with all other requirements of commission proceedings, including the discovery requirements set forth in rule 122.

(e) In accordance with California Evidence Code section 913, no inference shall be drawn as to any matter in issue or to the credibility of the judge based on a refusal to respond as required by this rule or to respond to a question at a hearing under rule 123 when such refusal is based on the exercise of the privilege against self-incrimination or of any other Evidence Code privilege or of any other privilege recognized by law.

Adopted Oct. 24, 1996, effective Dec. 1, 1996; amended Oct. 25, 2005, Dec. 7, 2022.

Rule 105. Medical Examination.

A judge shall, upon a finding of good cause by seven members of the commission and within such reasonable time as the commission may prescribe, submit to a medical examination ordered by the commission. The examination must be limited to the conditions stated in the finding of good cause. No examination by a specialist in psychiatry may be required without the consent of the judge.

Adopted Oct. 24, 1996, effective Dec. 1, 1996.

Rule 106. Judge's Representation by Counsel.

A judge may be represented by counsel in all commission proceedings. The written communications of counsel shall be deemed to be the written communications of the judge. Counsel has the authority to bind the judge as to all matters except a stipulation as to discipline.

Any paper filed with the commission and any written statement made to the commission or to its staff must be signed by the judge or the judge's counsel. A stipulation as to discipline must be signed by the judge. The signing of any document or statement warrants that the signer has personal knowledge of the matter contained in the document or statement or has investigated the matter and has a good faith belief in the accuracy of the representations contained in the document or statement.

This rule applies to the filing of responses to preliminary investigation letters under rule 111, to the filing of answers in formal proceedings under rule 119, and to all other filings with the commission and the masters and all other correspondence with the commission.

Adopted Oct. 24, 1996, effective Dec. 1, 1996; amended Dec. 7, 2022.

Rule 107. Notice Requirements.

(a) (**Notices of preliminary investigation, tentative advisory letter, tentative private admonishment, and tentative public admonishment**) All notices of a preliminary investigation, or tentative advisory letter, private admonishment or public admonishment shall be sent to a judge at chambers or at his or her residence unless otherwise requested, and a copy thereof shall be mailed to counsel of record. If a judge does not occupy chambers and his or her place of residence is unknown, the notice shall be sent to the judge's last known address. The notice shall be given by prepaid (1) certified mail return receipt requested, or (2) overnight mail delivery with a proof of delivery service, or (3) personal service with proof of service. If the judge's last known address is outside of the United States, service shall be made by recorded delivery. Envelopes containing such notices shall be marked "personal and confidential"; the inscription "Commission on Judicial Performance" shall not be used on the envelopes. In the event of service by certified or recorded mail, service is complete at the time of mailing.

(b) (**Service of notice of formal proceedings, other notices and correspondence in connection with formal proceedings**) After institution of formal proceedings, the service of the notice of formal proceedings shall be made as set forth in rule 118, and the giving of notice or sending of other correspondence in connection with the formal proceedings shall be accomplished as set forth in rule 126.

Adopted Oct. 24, 1996, effective Dec. 1, 1996; amended Oct. 25, 2005, June 26, 2019, Dec. 7, 2022.

Rule 108. Extensions of Time.

(a) (**Extensions for response to preliminary investigation letter and for answer to notice of formal proceedings**) Upon a showing of good cause submitted by the judge, the chairperson may extend the time for filing a response to a preliminary investigation letter under rule 111 or for filing an answer to a notice of formal proceedings.

(b) (**Extension of time for commencing hearing before the special masters**) In order to maintain public confidence in the integrity of the judiciary and protect the welfare of the public, all hearings before the special masters shall be heard at the earliest possible time after the issuance under rule 118 of the notice of formal proceedings. In accordance with this policy, extensions of time for commencing a hearing before the special masters are disfavored. The chairperson of the commission or the presiding master may extend the time for commencing a hearing before the special masters upon a showing of good cause, supported by declaration detailing specific facts showing that a continuance is necessary. Good cause does not include the ordinary press of business.

(c) (**Extension of time for filing report of the masters**) The chairperson may, upon request of the masters, extend the time for the filing of the report of the masters under rule 129.

(d) (**Other extensions of time**) Any other or further extension of time, other than to demand an appearance before the commission to object to a tentative advisory letter, or to a tentative private or public admonishment pursuant to rule 114(b), or to demand formal proceedings pursuant to rule 114(c), may be granted by the chairperson only upon a showing of good cause.

(e) (**Alternative authority**) The chairperson may delegate his or her authority under this rule to another member, and the commission may designate any member to act instead of the chairperson.

Adopted Oct. 24, 1996, effective Dec. 1, 1996; amended Oct. 8, 1998, Jan. 26, 2000, Oct. 25, 2005; interim amendment Jan. 31, 2007; amended May 23, 2007, Jan. 28, 2009, Oct. 19, 2011, Dec. 7, 2022.

Rule 109. Commencement of Commission Action.

(a) (**Receipt of written statement**) Upon receiving a written statement alleging facts indicating that a judge is guilty of willful misconduct in office, persistent failure or inability to perform the duties of office, habitual intemperance in the use of intoxicants or drugs, or conduct prejudicial to the administration of justice that brings the judicial office into disrepute, or that the judge has a disability that seriously interferes with the performance of the duties of office and is or is likely to become permanent, or that the judge has engaged in an improper action or a dereliction of duty, the commission may:

(1) In an appropriate case, determine that the statement is obviously unfounded or frivolous and dismiss the proceeding;

(2) If the statement is not obviously unfounded or frivolous, make a preliminary investigation to determine whether formal proceedings should be instituted and a hearing held.

(b) (**Preliminary investigation on commission's own motion**) The commission may make a preliminary investigation on the basis of information received by the commission not contained in a written report indicating that a judge is guilty of willful misconduct in office, persistent failure or inability to perform the duties of office, habitual intemperance in the use of intoxicants or drugs, or conduct prejudicial to the administration of justice that brings the judicial office into disrepute, or that the judge has a disability that seriously interferes with the performance of the duties of office and is or is likely to become permanent, or that the judge has engaged in an improper action or a dereliction of duty.

(c) (**Preliminary investigation of subordinate judicial officers**) The commission may make a preliminary investigation of a subordinate judicial officer whenever:

(1) The commission receives from a complainant a written request within 30 days after the date of mailing of notice to the complainant by the local court of the disposition of a complaint against a subordinate judicial officer, and the commission concludes that the local court may have abused its discretion in its disposition of such complaint;

(2) The commission receives from a local court a request that the commission investigate or adjudicate a complaint against a subordinate judicial officer;

(3) The commission receives from a local court information that a complaint resulted in the written reprimand, suspension, or removal of the subordinate judicial officer;

(4) The commission receives from a local court information that a subordinate judicial officer resigned while an investigation was pending and before a final decision was made by the local court; or

(5) The commission receives a complaint concerning a subordinate judicial officer who resigned or retired before the local court received the complaint.

Subsection (c) applies only to complaints about a subordinate judicial officer received in the local court on or after June 3, 1998; subdivision (1) of subsection (c) applies only in cases in which the complainant was apprised by the local court of the 30-day time limit for seeking review by the commission.

(d) (Notification of disposition at the judge's request) Upon request from a judge who is the subject of a complaint before the commission, the commission shall notify the judge in writing of the disposition of the complaint if:

(1) The judge's request to the commission specifically describes the underlying incident giving rise to the complaint;

(2) The pendency of the complaint has become generally known to the public; or

(3) The judge has received written notice of the complaint from someone who is not associated with the commission.

Adopted Oct. 24, 1996, effective Dec. 1, 1996; amended Oct. 8, 1998; interim amendment Feb. 11, 1999; amended Jan. 29, 2003, Oct. 25, 2005, Mar. 23, 2011, Dec. 7, 2022.

Rule 110. Staff Inquiry; Advisory Letter after Staff Inquiry. [Repealed]

Repealed Dec. 7, 2022; adopted Oct. 24, 1996, effective Dec. 1, 1996; amended May 8, 2013.

Rule 111. Preliminary Investigation.

(a) (Notice) If the commission commences a preliminary investigation, the judge shall be notified of the investigation and the nature of the charge, and shall be afforded a reasonable opportunity in the course of the preliminary investigation to present such matters as the judge may choose. A reasonable time for a judge to respond to a preliminary investigation letter shall be 20 days from the date the letter was mailed to the judge unless the time is extended pursuant to rule 108.

(b) (Preliminary investigation letter) A preliminary investigation letter shall include specification of the allegations, including, to the extent possible: the date of the conduct; the location where the conduct occurred; and, if applicable, the name(s) of the case(s) or identification of the court proceeding(s) in relation to which the conduct occurred. If the investigation concerns statements made by or to the judge, the letter shall include the text or summaries of the comments.

(c) (Termination of investigation) If the preliminary investigation does not disclose sufficient cause to warrant further proceedings, the commission shall terminate the investigation and notify the judge in writing.

Adopted Oct. 24, 1996, effective Dec. 1, 1996; amended May 8, 2013, Dec. 7, 2022.

Rule 111.4. Legal Error.

Discipline shall not be imposed for mere legal error without more. However, a judge who commits legal error which, in addition, clearly and convincingly reflects bad faith, bias, abuse of authority, disregard for fundamental rights, intentional disregard of the law, or any purpose other than the faithful discharge of judicial duty is subject to investigation and discipline.

Adopted May 8, 2013; amended Dec. 7, 2022.

Rule 111.5. Correction of Advisory Letter. [Repealed]

Repealed Dec. 7, 2022; adopted Oct. 25, 2005; interim amendment Mar. 23, 2011; amended Oct. 19, 2011, May 8, 2013.

Rule 112. Monitoring.

The commission may defer termination of a preliminary investigation for a period not to exceed two years for observation and review of a judge's conduct. The judge shall be advised in writing of the type of behavior for which the judge is being monitored. (Such disclosure shall not limit the commission's consideration of misconduct involving other types of behavior which may be observed or reported during the period of monitoring.)

Adopted Oct. 24, 1996, effective Dec. 1, 1996.

Rule 113. Notice of Tentative Advisory Letter, Private Admonishment, or Public Admonishment.

If after a preliminary investigation the commission determines that there is good cause for an advisory letter, private admonishment, or public admonishment, the commission may issue a notice of tentative discipline to the judge by certified mail. The notice shall include a statement of facts and the reasons for the tentative discipline. The notice shall also contain an advisement as to the judge's options under rule 114. The notice may cite any discipline that was imposed on the judge prior to issuance of the notice.

Adopted Oct. 24, 1996, effective Dec. 1, 1996; amended Feb. 11, 1999, May 23, 2007, June 26, 2019, Dec. 7, 2022.

Rule 114. Advisory Letter, Private Admonishment, and Public Admonishment Procedure.

A judge who receives a notice of tentative advisory letter, private admonishment, or public admonishment pursuant to rule 113 has the following options:

(a) (Acceptance of tentative discipline) The judge may choose not to object to the tentative discipline. If the judge does not demand formal proceedings (if applicable) or an appearance before the commission to object to the tentative discipline within 30 days after the mailing of a notice of tentative advisory letter, private admonishment, or public admonishment, the discipline becomes effective.

(b) (Appearance before the commission) The judge may, within 30 days of the mailing of a notice of tentative advisory letter, private admonishment, or public admonishment, file with the commission a written demand for an appearance before the commission to object to the tentative discipline, waiving any right to formal proceedings under rule 118 (if applicable) and review by the Supreme Court. A judge who demands an appearance before the commission shall, within 30 days of the mailing of the notice of tentative advisory letter, private admonishment, or public admonishment, submit a written statement of the basis of the judge's objections to the tentative discipline.

After the time set for the appearance before the commission, the commission may:

(1) Close the matter without disciplinary action;

(2) Issue the tentative discipline; or

(3) Issue a lesser discipline.

If the commission determines to issue discipline after an appearance under this rule, it may in its final decision modify the notice in response to the judge's written objections and any oral presentation.

An appearance before the commission under this rule is not an evidentiary hearing. Factual representations or information, including documents, letters, or witness statements, not previously presented to the commission during the preliminary investigation will not be considered unless it is shown that the new factual information is either: (1) (a) material to the question of whether the judge engaged in misconduct or the appropriate level of discipline, and (b) could not have been discovered and presented to the commission with reasonable diligence during the preliminary investigation, (2) offered to correct an error of fact in the notice of tentative discipline, or (3) necessary to prevent a miscarriage of justice.

To be considered under this rule, new factual information must be presented at the time the judge submits written objections to the tentative discipline. When newly presented factual information meets the criteria for consideration under this rule, the commission may investigate the new information before proceeding with its disposition pursuant to the appearance process. If this investigation discloses information of possible other misconduct, that information will not be considered in the disposition of the pending notice but may be the subject of a new preliminary investigation.

(c) (Formal proceedings) The judge may, within 30 days of the mailing of a notice of tentative private or public admonishment, file with the commission a demand for formal proceedings pursuant to rule 118.

(d) (Extensions of time) The 30 days provided to demand formal proceedings or an appearance before the commission to object to a tentative advisory letter, private admonishment, or public admonishment pursuant to subdivisions (b) and (c) may not be extended. The time for filing a written statement of the judge's objections to the tentative discipline pursuant to subdivision (b) may be extended by the chairperson or the chairperson's designee upon a showing of good cause, if the judge has, within 30 days of the mailing of the notice, filed a demand for an appearance with any applicable personal waiver of the right to formal proceedings and to review by the Supreme Court.

Adopted Oct. 24, 1996, effective Dec. 1, 1996; amended Jan. 29, 2003, Oct. 25, 2005, Jan. 31, 2007, Jan. 28, 2009; interim amendment Mar. 23, 2011; amended Oct. 19, 2011, May 8, 2013, June 26, 2019, Dec. 7, 2022.

Rule 115. Notice of Tentative Public Admonishment. [Repealed]

Repealed Dec. 7, 2022; adopted Oct. 24, 1996, effective Dec. 1, 1996; amended Feb. 11, 1999, May 23, 2007, June 26, 2019.

Rule 116. Public Admonishment Procedure. [Repealed]

Repealed Dec. 7, 2022; adopted Oct. 24, 1996, effective Dec. 1, 1996; amended Jan. 29, 2003, Oct. 25, 2005, Jan. 28, 2009; interim amendment Mar. 23, 2011; amended Oct. 19, 2011, May 8, 2013, June 26, 2019.

Rule 116.5. Negotiated Settlement During Preliminary Investigation.

At any time during a preliminary investigation or discipline proceeding under rules 113 and 114, the commission may authorize legal staff or other designated attorney to negotiate with the judge a resolution of any matter at issue. The judge may also initiate settlement discussions with legal staff or other designated attorney. A proposed resolution agreed to by the judge and legal staff or other designated attorney shall be jointly submitted to the commission, which may accept it, reject it or return it to the judge and legal staff or other designated attorney to consider modifications to it. No agreement between the judge and legal staff or other designated attorney is binding unless approved by the commission. A settlement proposal rejected by the commission cannot be used against the judge in any proceedings. After formal proceedings are instituted, settlement negotiations are governed by rule 127.

Adopted May 23, 2007; amended June 28, 2017, Dec. 7, 2022.

Rule 117. Records Disposition Program.

The commission shall adopt a records disposition program designed to dispose of records of complaints against a judge. The commission's records disposition program shall be consistent with constitutional language and case law and shall be published in the Policy Declarations of the Commission on Judicial Performance.

Adopted Oct. 24, 1996, effective Dec. 1, 1996; amended Jan. 31, 2018.

Rule 118. Notice of Formal Proceedings.

(a) (Issuance of notice) After the preliminary investigation has been completed, if the commission concludes that formal proceedings should be instituted, the commission shall without delay issue a written notice to the judge advising the judge of the institution of formal proceedings to inquire into the charges against the judge. Such proceedings shall be entitled:

"BEFORE THE COMMISSION ON JUDICIAL PERFORMANCE Inquiry Concerning Judge _____, No. _____."

(b) (Content of notice) The notice shall specify in ordinary and concise language the charges against the judge and the alleged facts upon which such charges are based, and shall advise the judge of the duty to file a written answer to the charges within 20 days after service of the notice upon the judge.

(c) (Service of notice) After a notice of formal proceedings is signed by the chairperson of the commission, the chairperson's designee or other member designated by the commission, the notice shall be served by personal service of a copy thereof on the judge, unless the judge personally or through counsel waives personal service and consents to service by mail. If there is no consent to service by mail and it appears to the chairperson of the commission upon affidavit that, after reasonable effort for a period of 10 days, personal service could not be had, service may be made upon the judge by mailing, by prepaid certified mail, copies of the notice addressed to the judge at the judge's chambers and last known residence. In the event of service by certified mail, service is complete at the time of mailing.

(d) (Public announcement) Not less than five days after service of the notice of formal proceedings as set forth above, the commission shall issue a public announcement advising that formal proceedings have been instituted, and shall make public the notice of formal proceedings. The public announcement shall set forth the date the judge's answer to the notice of formal proceedings is due, and shall indicate that the answer to the notice of formal proceedings will be made public.

Adopted Oct. 24, 1996, effective Dec. 1, 1996; amended Feb. 11, 1999, Oct. 25, 2005, Oct. 17, 2007.

Rule 119. Answer.

(a) (Pleadings and motions) The notice of formal proceedings and answer shall constitute the pleadings. No further pleadings shall be filed and no motion or demurrer shall be filed against any of the pleadings.

(b) (Filing of answer) Within 20 days after service of the notice of formal proceedings the judge shall serve, in accordance with rule 119.5, and file with the commission an answer, which shall be verified and shall conform in style to subdivision (b) of rule 8.204 of the California Rules of Court. The chairperson, the chairperson's designee or other member designated by the commission may grant an extension of time only upon timely written request establishing good cause for an extension of time.

(c) (Content of answer) The answer shall be as complete and straightforward as the information reasonably available to the respondent judge permits. The answer shall (1) admit each allegation which is true, (2) deny each allegation which is untrue, and (3) specify each allegation as to the truth of which the judge lacks sufficient information or knowledge. If a respondent judge gives lack of information or knowledge as a reason for a failure to admit or deny any allegation, the respondent judge shall state in the answer that a reasonable inquiry concerning the matter in the particular allegation has been made, and that the information known or readily obtainable is insufficient to enable the respondent judge to admit or deny the matter.

Adopted Oct. 24, 1996, effective Dec. 1, 1996; amended Jan. 26, 2000, Jan. 29, 2003, Jan. 31, 2007.

Rule 119.5. Filing with the Commission During Formal Proceedings.

(a) (Procedures for filing) After the institution of formal proceedings, all briefs and other documents to be filed shall be filed with the commission by electronic transmission as provided in this rule, and shall be accompanied by a proof of service of the document upon the other party or parties, and upon the special masters if they have been appointed in the matter. This includes documents submitted in conjunction with a hearing before the special masters, other than exhibits to be admitted at the hearing. Exhibits admitted at a hearing before the masters shall be transmitted to the commission office pursuant to rule 125.5. A document is deemed filed with the commission as set forth in subparagraph (c)(1) below. The commission's agent for purposes of filing documents after institution of formal proceedings is the Legal Advisor to Commissioners or the Legal Advisor's designee. A filing may be evidenced by a conformed copy of the cover page of each document submitted for filing.

(b) (Electronic filing) Electronic filing means the transmission of a document by electronic service to the electronic address of the commission, directed to the Legal Advisor to Commissioners or the Legal Advisor's designee. The electronic address for filing pursuant to these rules is filings@cjp.ca.gov.

(c) (Conditions for electronic filing) After the institution of formal proceedings, parties or non-parties pursuant to rule 131 shall file documents with the commission electronically, subject to the following conditions:

(1) A document transmitted electronically shall be deemed filed on the date received, or the next court day if received on a non-court day or after 5:00 p.m.

(2) The document shall be considered filed, for purposes of filing deadlines and the time to respond under these rules, as set forth in subsection (1) of this subdivision.

(3) Upon receipt of an electronically filed document, the commission shall promptly send the filer confirmation that the document was received.

(4) Electronically filed documents must be text searchable when technologically feasible without impairment of the document's image.

(5) By electronically filing a document, the party filing represents that the original signed document is in the party's possession or control. Notwithstanding any provision of law to the contrary, including Evidence Code sections 255 and 260, a signature produced in an electronic filing is deemed to be an original.

(d) (Signatures) When the document to be filed requires the signature of any person, the document shall be deemed to have been signed by that person if filed electronically.

(e) (Signatures under penalty of perjury) When a document to be filed electronically provides for a signature under penalty of perjury of any person, the document is deemed to have been signed by that person if filed electronically, provided that the declarant, before filing, has physically signed a printed form of the document. By electronically filing the document, electronic filers certify that they will produce the original, signed document upon request by the Legal Advisor.

(f) (Electronic service) After the institution of formal proceedings, documents shall be served by electronic means on another party, a party's attorney, or the special masters.

(g) (**Document in paper form**) When it is not feasible for a party or other person to convert a document to electronic form by scanning, imaging, or another means, the commission may, upon request, allow the party to file the document in paper form via either hand delivery or by mail.

Adopted Feb. 11, 1999; amended Oct. 25, 2005; interim amendment Jan. 31, 2007; amended May 23, 2007; interim amendment Oct. 17, 2012; amended May 8, 2013; interim amendment Feb. 2, 2022; amended Dec. 7, 2022.

Rule 120. Disqualification.

(a) (**Disqualification upon determination to remove, retire or bar from assignments**) If the commission determines that a judge should be removed or retired from office, the commission will, in its order of removal or retirement, also order pursuant to article VI, section 18(b) of the California Constitution that the judge be disqualified from acting as a judge, without loss of salary, until the commission's determination becomes final or until any decision by the Supreme Court on any petition for review becomes final. If the commission determines to censure and bar a former judge from receiving assignments, the commission will, in its order of censure, also order that the judge be barred from receiving assignments until the commission's determination becomes final or until any decision by the Supreme Court on any petition for review becomes final.

(b) (**Disqualification upon notice of formal proceedings**) Before the commission has reached a determination regarding removal or retirement of a judge, the commission may temporarily disqualify a judge without loss of salary upon notice of formal proceedings pursuant to article VI, section 18(b) of the California Constitution if the commission determines that there is substantial evidence that the continued service of the judge poses a threat of serious harm to the public or to the administration of justice.

If good cause for disqualification is apparent, the commission may issue a notice of intention to temporarily disqualify the judge along with a notice of formal proceedings. Subsequent to the filing of a notice of formal proceedings, the examiner may file with the commission a motion to temporarily disqualify the judge. The commission's notice of intention to disqualify or the examiner's motion to disqualify shall be by personal service or service upon the judge's counsel. If such service cannot be effectuated, service shall be by prepaid certified mail upon the judge at his or her chambers and last known residence. If service is by mail, the notice shall be accompanied by an affidavit or certificate of mailing and an affidavit shall be filed regarding the inability to effectuate personal service or service upon counsel.

The judge shall have an opportunity to respond in writing within 10 days of receipt of the commission's notice of intention to disqualify or the examiner's motion to disqualify, or within 15 days after the mailing of the notice, whichever occurs first. The time for filing a response shall not be subject to extension under rule 108. The judge's response may include points and authorities in support of any legal arguments, and may include verified statements, other testimony, medical or other expert reports and any other evidence in opposition to the facts on which the commission's notice of intention to disqualify or the examiner's motion to disqualify is based. Upon the filing of a response or expiration of time for filing a response, the commission may issue an order of temporary disqualification.

(c) (**Accelerated disposition of charges**) In cases in which a judge is temporarily disqualified under rule 120(b) the disposition of the charges in the notice of formal proceedings shall be accelerated and the formal proceedings shall proceed without appreciable delay. In such cases, the commission may reduce the number of days provided in rules 122, 129, and 130 for the filing of papers in connection with the formal proceedings.

(d) (**Duration of temporary disqualification**) An order for temporary disqualification of a judge under subdivision (b) of this rule shall remain in effect until further order of the commission or until the pending formal proceedings have been concluded by the commission.

Adopted Oct. 24, 1996, effective Dec. 1, 1996; amended Oct. 8, 1998, Feb. 11, 1999, June 28, 2017.

Rule 120.5. Suspension; Termination of Suspension; Removal of Suspended Judge.

(a) (**Felony**) When the commission receives proof that a judge has pled guilty or no contest to, or has been found guilty of, a felony under California or federal law, the commission shall promptly issue an order suspending the judge from office without salary.

(b) (**Crime punishable as a felony or that involves moral turpitude**) When the commission receives proof that a judge has pled guilty or no contest to, or has been found guilty of, a crime that is not a felony under California or federal law but is punishable as a felony under that law or involves moral turpitude under that law, the commission shall promptly issue a notice of intention to suspend the judge without salary in accordance with subdivision (e) of this rule.

(c) (**Reversal of conviction**) If a judge is suspended by reason of article VI, section 18, subdivision (c) of the California Constitution, and the commission receives proof that the conviction has been reversed, the commission shall promptly issue a notice of intention to terminate the suspension in accordance with subdivision (e) of this rule.

(d) (**Finality of conviction**) If a judge is suspended by reason of article VI, section 18, subdivision (c) of the California Constitution, and the commission receives proof that the conviction is final, the commission shall promptly issue a notice of intention to remove the judge from office in accordance with subdivision (e) of this rule.

(e) (**Notice**) Any notice issued pursuant to this rule shall be in accordance with the following:

(1) The notice shall be given to the judge or judge's counsel and to the examiner or other attorney designated by the commission to receive notice in the matter.

(2) The notice shall be by personal service or service upon the judge's counsel. If such service cannot be effectuated, service shall be by prepaid certified mail upon the judge at his or her chambers and last known residence. If service is by mail, the notice shall be accompanied by an affidavit or certificate of mailing and an affidavit shall be filed regarding the inability to effectuate personal service or service upon counsel. If the service is by certified mail, service is complete at the time of mailing.

(3) The judge shall have an opportunity to respond in writing within 10 days of receipt by the judge of a notice of intended suspension under subdivision (b) or a notice of intended removal under subdivision (d), or within 15 days after the mailing of the notice, whichever occurs first. Within five days after receipt of the judge's response, or within 20 days of the mailing of the notice if no response is filed, whichever occurs first, the examiner or other attorney designated by the commission may present points and authorities respecting the notice and in reply to any response. The commission may request additional briefing. Extensions of time under this subdivision are disfavored and will be granted only upon a specific and affirmative showing of good cause. Good cause does not include ordinary press of business.

(4) The examiner or other attorney designated by the commission shall have an opportunity to respond in writing within 10 days of receipt of a notice of intended termination of suspension under subdivision (c). Within five days after receipt of the response of the examiner or other attorney designated by the commission, or within 15 days of the mailing of the notice if no response is filed, whichever occurs first, the judge may present points and authorities respecting the notice and in reply to any response. The commission may request additional briefing. Extensions of time under this subdivision are disfavored and will be granted only upon a specific and affirmative showing of good cause. Good cause does not include ordinary press of business.

(5) Upon receipt of the points and authorities or reply or the expiration of the time for the filing thereof, whichever occurs first, or upon receipt of any additional briefs as may be requested by the commission, the commission shall promptly issue its order if it concludes that the relevant standards specified in article VI, section 18, subdivision (c) of the California Constitution have been met.

Adopted Oct. 25, 2005; amended Jan. 31, 2007.

Rule 121. Setting for Hearing Before Commission or Masters.

(a) (**Time for setting for hearing**) On filing or on expiration of the time for filing an answer, the commission shall set the matter for hearing.

(b) (**Appointment of special masters or master**) Unless the commission determines to hold the hearing before itself, the commission may request the Supreme Court to appoint three special masters to hear and take evidence in the matter, and to report to the commission. On a vote of seven members of the commission and with the consent of the judge involved, the commission may request the Supreme Court to appoint one special master in place of three special masters. Consent of the judge shall be defined as (1) written agreement by the judge or counsel of record, or (2) failure to object in writing within 30 days of notice of the commission's intention to request the appointment of one special master.

(c) **(Requirements for special masters)** Special masters shall be judges. When there are three special masters, not more than two of them may be retired judges from courts of record.

(d) **(Notice to respondent judge of appointment of special masters and examiner)** Upon appointment of special masters or a single special master by the Supreme Court and appointment of an examiner by the commission, the respondent judge shall be given notice of the orders appointing the masters and the examiner, and the examiner shall be given notice of the order appointing the special masters.

(e) **(Notice of hearing)** The commission shall set a time and place for hearing before itself or before the masters and shall give notice by mail confirming the date and place of the hearing to the judge and the examiner at least 20 days before the hearing.

(f) **(Remote testimony during hearing)** Prior to the commencement of the hearing, the respondent judge or the examiner may request that a witness whom the party intends to call be allowed to testify at the hearing via remote video technology. The commission, if the hearing is before itself, or the special masters, after considering any objection by the other party, may, upon good cause shown, permit the testimony of the witness to be taken via remote video technology, provided that the place of the hearing can reasonably accommodate the request; that all parties can simultaneously see and hear the witness; that the witness is in a private, enclosed space with no one else present during their testimony; and that the witness has immediate access to exhibits or other records that might be used during the examination of the witness. If these conditions are not met during the remote testimony, the commission or the special masters may require the witness to appear in person at a hearing and may strike the witness's remote testimony if the witness does not appear in person.

In a hearing regarding a disability application, remote testimony may be taken only by stipulation of the parties.

Adopted Oct. 24, 1996, effective Dec. 1, 1996; interim amendment Feb. 1, 2024.

Rule 122. Discovery Procedures.

(a) **(Exclusive procedures)** The procedures in this rule shall constitute the exclusive procedures for discovery. Discovery may be obtained only after a written notice of formal proceedings is issued.

(b) **(Applicability to both parties)** The examiner and the judge are each entitled to discovery from the other in accordance with these procedures.

(c) **(Initial discovery provided by trial counsel)** At the time of service of the notice of formal proceedings, the judge shall be provided copies of all documents and other information specified in rule 122(e) which is not privileged and is in the possession of the commission. Such information shall be made available at the commission offices. Alternatively, if a judge requests that the materials be sent to a specific address, the commission shall provide the judge with copies of said documents and information at that address.

(d) **(Discovery requests)** Discovery requests may be made in writing at any time after the filing of the notice of formal proceedings. All requests for discovery must be made in writing to the opposing side within 30 days after service of the answer to the written notice of formal proceedings or within 30 days after service of the written notice of formal proceedings if no answer has yet been filed, or within 15 days after service of any amendment to the notice.

(e) **(Inspection and copying)** The following items may be inspected or copied by the side requesting discovery:

(1) The names, and if known, the business addresses and business telephone numbers of persons the opposing side then intends to call as witnesses at the hearing;

(2) The names, and if known, the business addresses and business telephone numbers of those persons who may be able to provide substantial material information favorable to the judge. Substantial material information favorable to the judge is evidence bearing directly on the truth of the charges or relevant to the credibility of a witness intended to be called;

(3) All statements about the subject matter of the proceedings, including any impeaching evidence, made by any witness then intended to be called by either side;

(4) All statements about the subject matter of the proceedings made by a person named or described in the notice, or amendment to the notice, other than the judge when it is claimed that an act or omission of the judge as to the person described is a basis for the formal proceeding;

(5) All investigative reports made by or on behalf of the commission, the examiner, or the judge, about the subject matter of the proceeding;

(6) All writings, including reports of mental, physical, and blood examinations, then intended to be offered in evidence by the opposing side;

(7) All physical items of evidence then intended to be offered in evidence;

(8) All writings or physical items of evidence which would be admissible in evidence at the hearing.

(f) **(Compliance with request)** If either side receives a written request for discovery in accordance with these procedures, the side receiving the request shall have a continuing duty to provide discovery of items listed in the request until proceedings before the masters are concluded. When a written request for discovery is made in accordance with these rules, discovery shall be provided within a reasonable time after any discoverable items become known to the side obligated to provide discovery.

(g) **(Depositions)** After the filing of the notice of formal proceedings, depositions shall be allowed as provided in this subdivision. The party requesting the deposition shall bear all costs for service of process, reporter, transcripts and facility usage, and in the case of a videotaped deposition to perpetuate testimony under subpart (1), all direct costs incurred in videotaping the deposition.

(1) **(Depositions to perpetuate testimony)** The commission or the special masters shall order the taking of the deposition of any person upon a showing by the side requesting the deposition that the proposed deponent is a material witness who is unable or cannot be compelled to attend the hearing. If a deposition is ordered, the procedures stated in Government Code section 68753 shall be followed. Depositions to perpetuate testimony may be videotaped.

(2) **(Discovery depositions)** In addition to depositions to perpetuate testimony provided for under subpart (1) of this subdivision, discovery depositions are permitted as provided in this subpart (2). Discovery depositions may not be videotaped.

a. The judge shall have the right to take depositions of up to four material witnesses, and the examiner shall have the right to take depositions of the judge and up to three other material witnesses. Depositions of commission members or staff are not permitted. Bench officers, other than the respondent judge, and court staff shall be afforded counsel for the deposition, upon request, by the Judicial Council.

b. If the examiner and judge stipulate in writing that a deposition may be taken as a matter of right under subpart (a), the commission shall issue a subpoena for such deposition. If the examiner and judge are unable to agree that a witness is material, or unable to agree concerning the manner, time and place of a deposition, the party seeking the deposition may file a request for deposition subpoena with the commission. Objections shall be filed within five days of filing the request. The commission may place restrictions or conditions on the manner, time and place of any deposition.

c. Each deposition upon oral examination is limited to one day of seven hours. Any objection during a deposition upon oral examination must be stated concisely and in a non-argumentative and non-suggestive manner. A person may instruct a deponent not to answer only when necessary to preserve a privilege, to enforce a limitation directed by the commission, or to present a motion to the commission that the deposition is being conducted in bad faith or in such manner unreasonably to annoy, embarrass or oppress the deponent or party.

d. Depositions shall be completed 30 days prior to the hearing, unless a cut-off time otherwise is set by the commission or by stipulation of the examiner and the judge.

e. Any motion under this subpart (2) shall be presented to the commission. The commission may designate the chairperson or the chairperson's designee to perform all or any part of its duties under this subdivision. If special masters have been appointed pursuant to rule 121, subdivision (b), the chairperson may designate one or more of them to perform all or any part of the commission's duties under this subpart.

(h) **(Subpoenas for the production of documents)** After the filing of the notice of formal proceedings, subpoenas for the production of documents by nonparties shall be allowed as provided in this subdivision. The party requesting the subpoena shall bear all costs for service of process of the subpoena on a nonparty.

(1) The parties shall have the right to the issuance of up to four subpoenas for the production of documents to nonparties, subject to the requirements of this rule. The parties may seek more than four subpoenas only upon a showing of good cause for the issuance of the additional subpoena(s). Subpoenas issued to commission members or staff under this rule are not permitted. Commission files and records are not subject to a subpoena for production of documents.

(2) If the examiner and judge stipulate in writing that a subpoena for the production of documents may issue, the commission shall issue the subpoena. If the examiner and judge are unable to agree to the issuance of a particular subpoena, the party seeking the subpoena may file an application for the issuance of that subpoena with the commission. The application shall be made on a form provided by the commission and shall include a declaration from the party or the party's attorney establishing good cause and including (a) an itemization, with reasonable particularity, of each document requested, (b) facts establishing why each document is relevant to the issues raised in the formal proceeding, and (c) facts establishing that the witness has the documents requested in the witness's custody or control. A copy of the proposed subpoena shall be attached to the application. The application must be served on the other party. Upon a finding of good cause based on the foregoing factors, the chairperson of the commission, the chairperson's designee, or the special masters may issue the subpoena.

Objections to an application for a subpoena for the production of documents shall be filed within seven days of the filing of the application. The commission or the special masters may place restrictions or conditions on the manner, time, and place of the document production.

(3) Applications for subpoenas for the production of documents shall be made in sufficient time for service of the subpoena and the production of documents to be completed 30 days prior to the hearing, unless a later cut-off time otherwise is set by the commission or by stipulation of the examiner and the judge.

(4) If an application for a subpoena seeks documents that are personal records as defined by Code of Civil Procedure section 1985.3, or employment records as defined by Code of Civil Procedure section 1985.6, the application shall include a "notice of privacy rights" advising the individual whose records are sought of the subpoena and of the individual's right to object within seven days of receipt of the notice. The notice of privacy rights shall state that the documents sought may be protected by a right to privacy; that any objection to the subpoena may be filed with the commission, with copies sent to the examiner and the respondent, within seven days of receipt of the notice; and that if the party seeking the documents will not agree to cancel or limit the subpoena, an attorney should be consulted about the recipient's privacy rights. If the subpoena is issued, the subpoena, accompanied by the notice of privacy rights, shall first be served on the individual whose records are sought by the subpoena. The notice of privacy rights must be personally served or acknowledged in writing by the individual upon whom the notice was served. A proof of service, or a written acknowledgment of receipt, shall be filed with the commission. The recipient of a notice of privacy rights has seven days to file an objection. If no objection is filed by the individual within seven days, the subpoena may be served on the nonparty custodian of the individual's records.

(5) Documents shall be produced within 15 days of service of the subpoena, unless an objection has been filed with the commission. If an objection is filed, no documents that are the subject of the objection shall be produced in response to a subpoena until the objection has been considered by the chairperson of the commission or an appropriate designee has considered the objection and ordered the documents to be produced. Unless otherwise directed by the commission, copies of any documents produced in response to a subpoena issued pursuant to this rule shall be provided to the opposing party within seven days of the party's receipt of the documents.

(6) Any motions under this subdivision shall be presented to the chairperson. The commission may designate the commission or the special masters to perform all or any part of the chairperson's duties under this subdivision.

(i) (**Failure to comply with discovery request**) If any party fails to comply with a discovery request as authorized by these procedures, the items withheld shall be suppressed or, if the items have been admitted into evidence, shall be stricken from the record. If testimony is elicited during direct examination and the side eliciting the testimony withheld any statement of the testifying witness in violation of these discovery procedures, the testimony shall be ordered stricken from the record. Upon a showing of good cause for failure to comply with a discovery request, the commission, master, or masters may admit the items withheld or direct examination testimony of a witness whose statement was withheld upon condition that the side against whom the evidence is sought to be admitted is granted a reasonable continuance to prepare against the evidence, or may order the items or testimony suppressed or stricken from the record. The commission may, upon review of any hearing, order any evidence stricken from the record for violation of a valid discovery request if the evidence could have been ordered stricken by the masters for violation of a valid discovery request.

(j) (**Applicable privileges**) Nothing in these procedures shall authorize the discovery of any writing or thing which is privileged from disclosure by law or is otherwise protected or made confidential as the work product of the attorney, including memoranda by commission staff and examiners. Statements of any witness interviewed by the examiner, by any investigators for either side, by the judge, or by the judge's attorney shall not be protected as work product.

(k) (**Definition of statement**) For purposes of these procedures, "statement" shall mean either (1) a written statement prepared by or at the direction of the declarant or signed by the declarant, or (2) an oral statement of the declarant which has been recorded stenographically, mechanically, or electronically, or which has been videotaped, transcribed, or summarized in writing.

(*l*) (**Return of discovery, continued confidentiality of discovery**) Upon the completion or termination of commission proceedings, the respondent judge shall return to the commission all materials provided to the judge under this rule that have not become part of the public record. All items provided in discovery pursuant to this rule remain confidential under rule 102 until and unless those items become part of the public record.

(m) (**Protective orders**) The commission or the masters may, upon application supported by a showing of good cause, issue protective orders to the extent necessary to maintain in effect such privileges and other protections as are otherwise provided by law.

Adopted Oct. 24, 1996, effective Dec. 1, 1996; amended Jan. 29, 2003, Oct. 17, 2007, Mar. 23, 2011, Dec. 5, 2012, June 28, 2017, June 26, 2019, July 1, 2020.

Rule 123. Hearing.

(a) (**Hearing without answer or appearance by judge**) At the time and place set for hearing, the commission, or the masters when the hearing is before masters, shall proceed with the hearing whether or not the judge has filed an answer or appears at the hearing. The examiner shall present the case in support of the charges in the notice of formal proceedings.

(b) (**Consideration of failure to answer, appear, or respond to questions**) The failure of the judge to answer the charges or to appear at the hearing shall not, standing alone, be taken as evidence of the truth of the facts alleged to constitute grounds for censure, removal, retirement, public or private admonishment, or an advisory letter. In accordance with California Evidence Code section 413, in reviewing the evidence and facts in the case against the judge, the commission and the masters may consider the judge's failure to explain or deny evidence or facts in the case or any willful suppression of evidence if that is the case, unless the failure or suppression is due to the judge's exercise of any legally recognized privilege. A lack of cooperation by the judge may be considered by the commission under rule 104.

(c) (**Reporting of hearing**) A verbatim record shall be made of the proceedings at the hearing.

(d) (**Number of commission members at hearing**) When the hearing is before the commission, not fewer than six members shall be present when the evidence is produced.

Adopted Oct. 24, 1996, effective Dec. 1, 1996; amended Oct. 25, 2005, Dec. 7, 2022.

Rule 124. Media at Hearing.

All applications for film or electronic coverage of hearings in formal proceedings are to be submitted to the commission a reasonable time prior to the commencement of the hearing. The commission shall promptly inform the respondent judge of any requests for film or electronic coverage of the hearing. Applications for film or electronic coverage of the hearing are to be decided by the chairperson of the commission or the chairperson's designee after conferring with the masters or presiding master, if masters have been appointed.

Rule 125. Evidence.

(a) **(Applicable law and agreed statement)** The California Evidence Code shall be applicable to all hearings before the commission or masters. Oral evidence shall be taken only on oath or affirmation. The examiner or the judge may propose to the other party an agreed statement in place of all or a part of the testimony. An agreed statement shall not foreclose argument to the commission or masters.

(b) **(Prior disciplinary action)** Any prior disciplinary action may be received in evidence to prove that conduct is persistent or habitual or to determine what action should be taken regarding discipline. Prior disciplinary action includes any disciplinary action which is in effect before the conclusion of a commission proceeding, including review by the Supreme Court.

(c) **(Settlement discussions)** Evidence of any settlement offer made by the judge, the examiner, or the commission to resolve any or all of the charges against the judge, or of any written or oral statements made during settlement discussions between the judge and the examiner or commission staff, shall be inadmissible in all public proceedings before the commission or masters. Nothing in this rule shall limit the admissibility, during formal proceedings, of the written responses of the judge or the judge's counsel to preliminary investigation or staff inquiry (under former rule 110) letters.

Adopted Oct. 24, 1996, effective Dec. 1, 1996; amended Oct. 9, 2020, Dec. 7, 2022.

Rule 125.5. Exhibits at Hearing.

Original exhibits admitted at a hearing before the special masters shall be transmitted by the masters to the commission office at the completion of the evidentiary portion of the hearing, unless the masters determine that there is reason to retain the original exhibit or exhibits to assist in the preparation of their report to the commission. Any original exhibits retained by the masters shall be transmitted to the commission at or before the time the report of the masters is submitted to the commission.

Adopted as interim rule Jan. 31, 2007; adopted May 23, 2007.

Rule 126. Procedural Rights of Judge in Formal Proceedings.

(a) **(Enumeration of rights, subpoenas)** When formal proceedings have been instituted, a judge shall have the right and reasonable opportunity to defend against the charges by the introduction of evidence, to be represented by counsel, and to examine and cross-examine witnesses. The judge shall have the right to the issuance of subpoenas for attendance of witnesses to testify or produce books, papers, and other evidentiary matter. The judge shall also have the right to the issuance of subpoenas for the production of documents, as set forth in rule 122. Subpoenas are to be issued by the chairperson of the commission, the chairperson's designee, or the special masters. Subpoenas addressed to the commission or its staff may only be obtained from the special masters upon a showing of good cause with notice to the commission.

(b) **(Transcripts)** When a transcript of the testimony has been prepared at the expense of the commission, a copy thereof shall be provided to the judge in connection with the proceedings. The judge shall have the right, without any order or approval, to have all or any portion of the testimony in the proceedings transcribed at the judge's expense.

(c) **(Manner of service)** Subject to rule 118(c), concerning service of a notice of formal proceedings, all notices and correspondence in connection with formal proceedings shall be sent to the judge's chambers, unless otherwise requested, and a copy thereof shall be mailed to counsel of record.

(d) **(Appointment of conservator)** If the judge is adjudged to be of unsound mind or incompetent, or if it appears to the commission at any time during the proceedings that the judge is not competent to act for himself or herself, the commission may petition a court of competent jurisdiction for the appointment of a conservator unless the judge has a conservator who will represent the judge. If a conservator is or has been appointed for a judge, the conservator may claim and exercise any right and privilege and make any defense for the judge with the same force and effect as if claimed, exercised, or made by the judge, if competent, and whenever these rules provide for serving, giving notice or sending any matter to the judge, such notice or matter shall be served, given, or sent to the conservator.

Adopted Oct. 24, 1996, effective Dec. 1, 1996; amended Jan. 31, 2007, May 23, 2007, June 28, 2017, June 26, 2019, Dec. 7, 2022.

Rule 127. Discipline by Consent.

(a) **(Negotiations)** Either respondent or the examiner may initiate negotiations on discipline by consent. Both the examiner and respondent must agree to any proposed disposition before submission to the commission. No agreement between the examiner and respondent is binding until approved by the commission.

(b) **(Submission to commission)** At any time after the initiation of formal charges and before final disposition, the respondent may agree with the examiner that the respondent shall admit to any or all of the charges in exchange for a stated sanction. The agreement shall be submitted to the commission, which shall accept or reject the agreement.

(c) **(Rejection of agreement)** If the stated sanction is rejected by the commission, the admission shall be withdrawn and cannot be used against the respondent in any proceedings.

(d) **(Affidavit of consent)** A respondent who consents to a stated sanction shall personally execute an affidavit stating that:

(1) The respondent consents to the sanction;
(2) The consent is freely and voluntarily rendered;
(3) The respondent admits the truth of the charges as alleged; and
(4) The respondent waives review by the Supreme Court.

Adopted Oct. 24, 1996, effective Dec. 1, 1996.

Rule 128. Amendments to Notice or Answer; Dismissals.

(a) **(Amendments)** The commission, at any time prior to its determination, may allow or require amendments to the notice of formal proceedings and may allow amendments to the answer. During the evidentiary hearing, the special masters may allow amendments to the notice to conform to proof. If a motion to amend the notice to set forth additional facts not presented at the hearing is made during the evidentiary hearing, the chairperson of the commission, or the chairperson's designee, shall determine whether the motion shall be determined by the full commission or the special masters. In case such an amendment is made, the judge shall be given reasonable time both to answer the amendment and to prepare and present his or her defense against the matters charged thereby.

(b) **(Dismissals by examiner)** At any time after the filing of formal charges and before final disposition, where exigent circumstances prevent consideration by the full commission, the examiner, with the concurrence of the director–chief counsel and the chairperson, may dismiss any charge from the notice of formal proceedings, if it appears that the available evidence is insufficient to sustain the charge or that dismissal is otherwise in the interest of justice, and such dismissal is not tantamount to dismissal of the proceedings as a whole.

(c) **(Dismissals by special masters)** The special masters may not dismiss any charge contained in the notice of formal proceedings.

Adopted Oct. 24, 1996, effective Dec. 1, 1996; amended June 26, 2019, Oct. 9, 2020.

Rule 129. Report of Masters.

(a) **(Transcript)** Upon the completion of the presentation of evidence at a hearing before the masters, a transcript of the hearing shall be promptly prepared and submitted to the Legal Advisor, who shall promptly mail a copy to each of the special masters, the examiner and the respondent judge.

(b) **(Submission of proposed findings of fact and conclusions of law)** Unless the masters specify an earlier date, the examiner and the respondent judge shall submit to the masters proposed findings of fact and conclusions of law, with citations to the transcript and exhibits, no later than 30 days after mailing of the transcript described in rule 129(a). Submission to the masters shall occur by a delivery method that results in actual receipt by them of the documents on or before the specified due date for submission. The masters may waive the submission of such proposed findings and conclusions.

(c) **(Preparation of report of masters)** Within 45 days after mailing of the transcript described in rule 129(a) or within 15 days after submission of the parties' proposed findings of fact and conclusions of law, whichever occurs later, the masters shall submit a report to the commission. Prior to the submission of their report, the masters may require such additional briefing and argument by the examiner and the respondent judge as the masters may desire. Upon request of the presiding master, the chair of the commission or the chair's designee may grant additional time for the submission of the report of the masters to the commission.

(d) **(Content of report of masters)** The report of the masters shall contain findings of fact and conclusions of law, along with an analysis of the evidence and reasons for the findings and conclusions, but shall not contain a recommendation as to discipline.

(e) **(Copy of report to judge and examiner)** Upon receiving the report of the masters, the commission shall promptly mail a copy to the judge and the examiner.

Adopted Oct. 24, 1996, effective Dec. 1, 1996; amended Jan. 29, 2003, Oct. 25, 2005, Mar. 23, 2011, Oct. 9, 2020.

Rule 130. Briefs to the Commission.

(a) **(Filing of opening briefs)** Within 15 days after the date of mailing of the copy of the masters' report to the judge as reflected on the proof of service by mail, the examiner or the judge may file with the commission opening briefs which may consist of objections to the report of the special masters and points and authorities concerning the issues in the matter, including the issue of sanctions. Objections to the masters' report and all factual statements shall be specific and shall be supported by reference to the book and page number of the record. Briefs shall conform in style to subdivision (b) of rule 8.204 of the California Rules of Court, shall follow the length limitations set forth in subdivision (c) of rule 8.204 of the California Rules of Court, and, when filed by the examiner, a copy shall be sent by first-class mail to the judge.

(b) **(Response to briefs)** Within 10 days after the filing of opening briefs, the examiner or the judge may file with the commission a response.

Adopted Oct. 24, 1996, effective Dec. 1, 1996; amended Jan. 29, 2003, Jan. 31, 2007, Mar. 23, 2011.

Rule 131. Participation by Non-Parties.

Briefs of amicus curiae will be considered by the commission if they present legal issues or represent perspectives not otherwise presented or represented by the parties. An amicus curiae brief may not be used to present inadmissible or non-admitted evidentiary materials to the commission.

A brief of an amicus curiae may be filed only if accompanied by the written consent of all parties, or upon a motion demonstrating to the chairperson of the commission or the chairperson's designee that the filing of the brief would be helpful to the commission in the resolution of the pending matter. When consent to the filing of a brief of an amicus curiae is refused by a party to the case, a motion for leave to file the brief, accompanied by the proposed brief, may be presented to the chairperson or the chairperson's designee. The motion shall concisely state the nature of the applicant's interest and set forth facts or questions of law that have not been, or reasons for believing that they will not be, presented by the parties and their relevancy to the disposition of the case. The motion may be in letter form but may not exceed four pages. The commission shall forward copies of any such motion and proposed brief to both the examiner and the judge.

The cover of the amicus brief must identify the party supported, and the brief shall not exceed 50 pages in length. Evidentiary references shall include citation to the record before the commission.

An amicus brief shall be submitted or filed within the time limits prescribed for the party that the brief supports. No reply briefs or briefs of an amicus curiae in support of reconsideration shall be received.

Any brief of an amicus curiae that fails to comply with this rule will not be considered by the commission.

Adopted Oct. 24, 1996, effective Dec. 1, 1996.

Rule 132. Appearance Before Commission.

Upon receipt of the masters' report and any objections, the commission shall give the judge and the examiner an opportunity to be heard orally before the commission, and written notice of the time and place of such hearing shall be mailed to the judge, at least 10 days prior thereto.

Adopted Oct. 24, 1996, effective Dec. 1, 1996.

Rule 133. Hearing Additional Evidence.

(a) The commission may order a hearing for the taking of additional evidence at any time while the matter is pending before it. The order shall set the time and place of hearing and shall indicate the matters on which the evidence is to be taken. A copy of such order shall be sent by mail to the judge at least 10 days prior to the date of hearing.

(b) In any case in which masters have been appointed, the hearing of additional evidence may be before such masters or before the commission, and the proceedings therein shall be in conformance with the provisions of rules 121 to 130, inclusive.

Adopted Oct. 24, 1996, effective Dec. 1, 1996; amended Jan. 29, 2003.

Rule 134. Commission Vote.

The commission may issue an advisory letter to, privately or publicly admonish, censure, remove or retire a judge, or find a person unfit to serve as a subordinate judicial officer. The affirmative vote of six members of the commission who have considered the record and report of the masters and who were present at any oral hearing as provided in rule 132 or, when the hearing was before the commission without masters, of six members of the commission who have considered the record, and at least four of whom were present when the evidence was produced, is required for an advisory letter, private or public admonishment, censure, removal or retirement of a judge, or a finding that a person is unfit to serve as a subordinate judicial officer, or for dismissal of the proceedings.

Adopted Oct. 24, 1996, effective Dec. 1, 1996; amended Oct. 8, 1998, Feb. 11, 1999, Jan. 29, 2003, Dec. 7, 2022.

Rule 134.5. Rule of Necessity.

A commission member shall not be subject to disqualification based on an actual or potential conflict of interest if his or her disqualification would prevent the existence of a quorum. This rule does not apply if a quorum can be convened with members who are not actually present. The basis of the commission member's actual or potential conflict and the reason the member's participation was necessary shall be recorded in the minutes and included in any resulting discipline.

Adopted May 23, 2007.

Rule 135. Record of Commission Proceedings.

The commission shall maintain records of all actions taken by the commission concerning a judge. Notice of any disciplinary determination and notice of any disqualification under article VI, section 18(b) of the California Constitution shall be mailed to the judge. In all formal proceedings, the commission shall prepare a transcript of the testimony and of all proceedings and shall make written findings of fact and conclusions of law.

Adopted Oct. 24, 1996, effective Dec. 1, 1996.

Rule 136. Finality.

A commission determination to impose discipline upon a judge following formal proceedings under rule 118 shall become final 30 days after the date of the order regarding the disciplinary determination.

Adopted Oct. 24, 1996, effective Dec. 1, 1996.

Rule 137. Retroactivity.

Those cases in which formal proceedings have been instituted on or before February 28, 1995 will be governed by the provisions of article VI, section 18 of the California Constitution which are operative and in effect as of February 28, 1995. Those cases in which formal proceedings are instituted on or after March 1, 1995 will be governed by the provisions of article VI, section 18 of the California Constitution operative as of March 1, 1995.

Adopted Oct. 24, 1996, effective Dec. 1, 1996.

Rule 138. Definitions.

In these rules, unless the context or subject matter otherwise requires:

(a) "Commission" means the Commission on Judicial Performance.

(b) "Judge" means a judge of any court of this state or a retired judge who has elected to serve on senior judge status or former judge as provided in California Constitution, article VI, section 18(d). For purposes of these rules, "judge" also means a court commissioner or referee, included as subordinate judicial officers in the commission's jurisdiction under California Constitution, article VI, section 18.1.

(c) "Chairperson" includes the acting chairperson.

(d) "Masters" means the special master or special masters appointed by the Supreme Court upon request of the commission.

(e) "Presiding master" means the master so designated by the Supreme Court or, if no designation is made, the judge selected by the panel.

(f) "Examiner" means the counsel designated by the commission to gather and present evidence before the masters or commission with respect to the charges against a judge.

(g) "Shall" is mandatory and "may" is permissive.

(h) "Mail" and "mailed" include ordinary mail, email, and personal delivery.

(i) "Filing" means delivering to commission staff at the commission office during regular business hours. A filing may be evidenced by a conformed copy of the cover page of each document submitted for filing. To be filed, a document must be accompanied by a proof of service of the document upon the other party or parties.

Adopted Oct. 24, 1996, effective Dec. 1, 1996; amended Oct. 8, 1998, Feb. 11, 1999, Oct. 9, 2020.

POLICY DECLARATIONS OF THE COMMISSION ON JUDICIAL PERFORMANCE

Div. I. Complaints and Investigations. Policy Declarations 1.1–1.14.
Div. II. Discipline, Appearances and Formal Proceedings. Policy Declarations 2.1–2.7.
Div. III. Commission Administration. Policy Declarations 3.1–3.14.
Div. IV. Disclosure of Information. Policy Declarations 4.1–4.6.
Div. V. Disability Retirement Applications. Policy Declarations 5.1–5.6.
Div. VI. Code of Ethics for Commission Members. Policy Declarations 6.1–6.5.
Div. VII. Discipline. Policy Declaration 7.1.

PREAMBLE

In consideration of the need for both uniformity and continuity of procedure and equitable, expeditious resolution of recurrent and detailed issues of procedure, the commission has authorized the formulation of the following policy declarations detailing commission policies, procedures and practices. These policy declarations are to reflect internal procedural detail neither duplicative of nor inconsistent with constitutional mandate or statutes or commission rules. These policy declarations are based upon concepts of utility, experience, and fair hearing of matters before the commission.

Rules referred to in the policy declarations are Rules of the Commission on Judicial Performance.

TITLE

These policy declarations shall be known and may be cited as the Policy Declarations of the Commission on Judicial Performance.

DIVISION I
COMPLAINTS AND INVESTIGATIONS

Anonymous complaints. Policy Declaration 1.1.
Reconsideration of complaints closed upon initial review. Policy Declaration 1.1.5.
Preliminary investigations. Policy Declaration 1.4.
Preliminary investigation letters. Policy Declaration 1.5.
Authorization for preliminary investigations between meetings. Policy Declaration 1.6.
Authorization for supplemental preliminary investigation letters between meetings. Policy Declaration 1.6.5.
Preliminary investigation letters not authorized or determined not to be warranted. Policy Declaration 1.7.
Cases removed from active calendar. Policy Declaration 1.8.
Admonishments to persons giving interviews and statements. Policy Declaration 1.9.
Consent, preservation of witness interviews and statements. Policy Declaration 1.10.
Independent record of witness statements. Policy Declaration 1.11.
Investigation subpoenas. Policy Declaration 1.12.
Witness statements under oath. Policy Declaration 1.13.
Submission of character letters. Policy Declaration 1.14.

Policy Declaration 1.1. Anonymous Complaints.

Staff will evaluate anonymous complaints for merit; if a complaint is deemed sufficiently meritorious, it will be placed on the oversight agenda for consideration by the commission as to whether or not it should be docketed.

Approved May 28, 1997.

Policy Declaration 1.1.5. Reconsideration of Complaints Closed Upon Initial Review.

If a matter is closed by the commission at initial review because a complaint does not state sufficient facts or information to establish a prima facie case of misconduct, the complainant shall be informed that if further new information is provided, it will be reviewed and, if sufficient, the complaint will be reconsidered.

Approved June 28, 2017.

Policy Declaration 1.2. Staff Inquiries. [Repealed]

Repealed Dec. 7, 2022; Approved May 28, 1997.

Policy Declaration 1.3. Staff Inquiry Letters. [Repealed]

Repealed Dec. 7, 2022; Approved May 28, 1997.

Policy Declaration 1.4. Preliminary Investigations.

The purpose of a preliminary investigation is to determine whether formal proceedings should be instituted and a hearing held.

At the conclusion of a preliminary investigation, or at the conclusion of a period of monitoring under rule 112, the commission may take any of the following actions:

(1) Close the matter;
(2) Issue a notice of tentative advisory letter, private admonishment or public admonishment; or
(3) Institute formal proceedings.

A judge must receive a preliminary investigation letter and be afforded an opportunity to respond before a notice of tentative advisory letter, private admonishment or public admonishment may issue or formal proceedings may be instituted.

Approved May 28, 1997; amended June 26, 2019, Dec. 7, 2022.

Policy Declaration 1.5. Preliminary Investigation Letters.

A preliminary investigation letter provides the judge notice of the investigation and the nature of the charge under review and may include: the date of the conduct; the location(s) where the conduct occurred; if applicable, the name of the case(s) or identification of the court proceeding(s) in relation to which the conduct occurred. If the investigation concerns statements made by or to the judge, the letter may also include the text or summaries of the comments.

The purpose of the preliminary investigation letter is to afford the judge an opportunity to provide such matters as the judge may choose including information about the factual aspects of the allegations and other relevant comment.

Approved May 28, 1997.

Policy Declaration 1.6. Authorization for Preliminary Investigations Between Meetings.

In instances where a matter comes to the attention of the commission between meetings, which on its face appears to warrant a preliminary investigation and there has already been direct communication with the subject judge or other exigent circumstances exist, an effort should be made, whenever possible, to poll all of the commission members for authorization of a preliminary investigation. If, in the discretion of the chairperson or acting chairperson, polling all of the members is not feasible, the chairperson or acting chairperson may authorize the preliminary investigation. When a preliminary investigation is authorized without a poll of the members, the members shall be promptly notified of the action taken.

Approved May 28, 1997; amended Dec. 7, 2022.

Policy Declaration 1.6.5. Authorization for Supplemental Preliminary Investigation Letters Between Meetings.

When a judge's response to a preliminary investigation letter fails to respond to an allegation in the letter or reveals additional instances or a variation of the same conduct that is the subject of the commission's investigation, the chairperson or acting chairperson may authorize staff to send a supplemental letter to obtain the judge's explanation concerning the omitted, additional or variation of the allegations.

Approved Feb. 1, 2017; amended Dec. 7, 2022.

Policy Declaration 1.7.   Preliminary Investigation Letters Not Authorized or Determined Not to Be Warranted.

At the time a preliminary investigation is authorized by the commission, the authorization may or may not include writing the judge a letter, in addition to other investigation. If information acquired during the preliminary investigation establishes that there is no basis for further proceedings, the preliminary investigation may be closed without the judge being contacted. A preliminary investigation letter authorized by the commission need not be sent if information obtained by staff before the letter is sent shows that the letter may not be warranted.

Approved May 28, 1997; amended Dec. 7, 2022.

Policy Declaration 1.8.   Cases Removed From Active Calendar.

The commission may defer its consideration of a pending preliminary investigation and direct that the matter be removed from the commission's active calendar. Circumstances which may warrant deferral in the commission's consideration of a matter include: when the case from which the complaint arose is still pending before the judge; when an appeal or ancillary proceeding is pending in which factual issues or claims relevant to the complaint are to be resolved; when criminal or other proceedings involving the judge are pending. In appropriate cases, the complainant may be notified that the commission has deferred action on the complaint.

When a matter is removed from the commission's active calendar, it shall be placed on the commission agenda at every meeting, and subject to active consideration at the discretion of the commission.

Approved May 28, 1997; amended Mar. 22, 2017, Dec. 7, 2022.

Policy Declaration 1.9.   Admonishments to Persons Giving Interviews and Statements.

In the course of a preliminary investigation, persons questioned or interviewed to ascertain the validity of allegations shall be admonished that the investigation is confidential under the California Constitution and commission rules. When it appears that there may be use of the elicited information in connection with possible testimony or discovery, the person providing the information shall be so advised.

Approved May 28, 1997; amended Dec. 7, 2022.

Policy Declaration 1.10.   Consent, Preservation of Witness Interviews and Statements.

Consent to mechanical recording may be obtained from interviewees. Statements and interviews may be transcribed and preserved, and may be submitted to interviewees for signature and verification.

Approved May 28, 1997.

Policy Declaration 1.11.   Independent Record of Witness Statements.

Where a witness statement or interview is not transcribed or recorded, it is not to be conveyed, commented upon or otherwise communicated to the commission by commission staff unless an independent memorialization of the statement has been prepared by staff (a writing other than a case memorandum or report from staff to the commission).

Approved May 28, 1997.

Policy Declaration 1.12.   Investigation Subpoenas.

Commission investigation subpoenas may issue upon application to the commission chairperson, vice-chairperson or the designee of either, stating the name, address and title, if any, of the person from whom information is sought, and whether or not a statement under oath is to be taken.

Approved May 28, 1997.

Policy Declaration 1.13.   Witness Statements Under Oath.

When the statement of a witness is taken under oath pursuant to Government Code section 68750, the witness may be given an opportunity to review and make corrections to the transcript of the witness's testimony at the office of the court reporter before whom the statement was taken. A copy of the statement shall not otherwise be furnished to the witness unless formal proceedings are instituted in the matter in which the testimony was given and the witness's statement is discoverable under rule 122.

Approved June 25, 1998.

Policy Declaration 1.14.   Submission of Character Letters.

(1)   Written communications submitted during preliminary investigation

During a preliminary investigation, written communications containing information related to the character of a judge who has a matter pending before the commission may be submitted to the commission. Such written communications must be delivered to the commission office, and shall not be delivered to individual commission members.

In determining the weight to be given to written character references, the commission may consider, but is not limited to, the following list of factors:

(a)   The length of time the author of the written communication has known the judge, and the nature and extent of the author's contact with the judge;

(b)   Whether the character reference is submitted in the form of a declaration signed under penalty of perjury; and

(c)   Whether the information provided by a person other than a judge or subordinate judicial officer is based on personal knowledge.

Pursuant to canon 2B, character references submitted by judges or subordinate judicial officers must be based on personal knowledge.

(2)   Written communications submitted after the initiation of formal proceedings

After the initiation of formal proceedings, written communications related to the character of the respondent judge may only be submitted by stipulation of the parties at the hearing held pursuant to rule 123 or rule 133. After the completion of the evidentiary hearing pursuant to rule 123 or 133, such communications shall not be accepted by the commission.

Approved May 22, 2008; amended Dec. 7, 2022.

DIVISION II
DISCIPLINE, APPEARANCES AND FORMAL PROCEEDINGS

Opposition to tentative advisory letter, tentative private admonishment and tentative public admonishment; statement of objections and appearance. Policy Declaration 2.1.
Date of hearing. Policy Declaration 2.2.
Prehearing proceedings. Policy Declaration 2.3.
Deposition transcripts taken pursuant to Rule 122(g). Policy Declaration 2.3.5.
Agreed statement and discipline by consent. Policy Declaration 2.4.
Order barring assignments to former judges. Policy Declaration 2.5.
Modification of decision following formal proceedings. Policy Declaration 2.6.
Citation of commission decisions. Policy Declaration 2.7.

Policy Declaration 2.1.   Opposition to Tentative Advisory Letter, Tentative Private Admonishment and Tentative Public Admonishment; Statement of Objections and Appearance.

An appearance before the commission to object to the imposition of a tentative advisory letter, a tentative private admonishment or a tentative public admonishment under rule 114, means an opportunity for a judge to informally object to the imposition of discipline in argument before the commission based on the proceedings which resulted in the issuance of a notice of tentative discipline and the judge's statement of objections.

A judge's demand for an appearance after notice of a tentative advisory letter, tentative private admonishment, or tentative public admonishment under rule 114, shall include a written statement of the basis of the judge's objections to the tentative discipline. The appearance before the commission will be scheduled after receipt of the judge's demand for appearance and statement of objections. The commission may request further briefing.

At the appearance before the commission, the judge may appear with or without counsel. The appearance is not an evidentiary hearing and there is no testimony by witnesses. Argument shall be limited to oral presentation not to exceed thirty (30) minutes by the judge and thirty (30) minutes by trial counsel or other attorney designated by the commission to present argument in support of the discipline.

Approved May 28, 1997; amended Oct. 6, 2009, Oct. 19, 2011, June 26, 2019, Dec. 7, 2022.

Policy Declaration 2.1.5.   Limitation on Requests for Correction of Advisory Letters. [Repealed]

Repealed Dec. 7, 2022; Approved June 30, 2010.

Policy Declaration 2.2.   Date of Hearing.

Absent unusual circumstances, the evidentiary hearing on the charges set forth in a notice of formal proceedings shall be set to commence two to four months following the issuance under rule 118 of the notice of formal proceedings.

Approved May 28, 1997; amended Aug. 26, 2004.

Policy Declaration 2.3. Prehearing Proceedings.

The commission or the special masters may require prehearing status statements, briefs or conferences (either by telephone or in person), or require any other appropriate prehearing proceeding. The purpose of such prehearing proceedings is to provide the commission or the special masters with pertinent information for prehearing and to ensure that the hearing proceeds efficiently. The masters may issue appropriate prehearing orders and may determine whether any such order needs be in writing.

Approved May 28, 1997; amended Aug. 26, 2004.

Policy Declaration 2.3.5. Deposition Transcripts Taken Pursuant to Rule 122(g).

The following procedures apply to the transcription of depositions taken pursuant to rule 122(g):

(1) The party noticing the deposition shall arrange for a court reporter.

(2) The party noticing the deposition shall bear the cost of the transcription.

(3) The court reporter shall send written notice to the deponent, the judge, and the examiner when the original transcript of the deposition is available.

(4) The court reporter shall certify on the transcript of the deposition that the deponent was duly sworn and that the transcript is a true record of the testimony given.

(5) The original transcript shall be transmitted to the party noticing the deposition, at that party's expense. The other party and the deponent may obtain a copy of the transcript from the court reporter upon request and at the expense of that party or deponent.

(6) A copy of the transcript shall not be filed with the commission unless admitted at a hearing held pursuant to rule 123 or rule 133, or as an exhibit to a motion filed with the commission or the special masters.

Approved Jan. 30, 2013.

Policy Declaration 2.4. Agreed Statement and Discipline by Consent.

An agreed statement under rule 125(a) may be offered by the respondent judge and the examiner in place of all or part of the evidence after institution of formal proceedings. An agreement between the respondent judge and the examiner for discipline by consent under rule 127 may be submitted to the commission after institution of formal proceedings. The examiner is responsible for handling negotiations with the respondent judge or respondent judge's counsel concerning agreed statements and agreements for discipline by consent.

Approved May 28, 1997.

Policy Declaration 2.5. Order Barring Assignments to Former Judges.

If the commission determines to bar a former judge from receiving an assignment, appointment to or reference of work from any California state court, pursuant to article VI, section 18(d) of the California Constitution, the order barring the judge from receiving assignments will be included in the commission's order of censure.

Notice of an order barring a former judge from receiving assignments shall be given to the Chief Justice and to the Judicial Council for distribution to the presiding judges of the state courts.

Approved June 25, 1998; amended Dec. 7, 2022.

Policy Declaration 2.6. Modification of Decision Following Formal Proceedings.

At any time before a commission determination to impose discipline upon a judge following formal proceedings becomes final under rule 136, the commission may modify the order regarding the disciplinary determination to eliminate any erroneous statement of fact or law in the order.

Adopted June 29, 2005.

Policy Declaration 2.7. Citation of Commission Decisions.

Citations to commission decisions following formal proceedings should be to the CJP Supplement to the Official California Reports in the following form: Inquiry Concerning _____ (year) (volume) Cal.4th CJP Supp. (page). Citations to public decisions not reported in the Official California Reports should be in the following form: [Censure/Censure and Bar/Public Admonishment] of Judge _____ (year) (page).

Approved June 30, 2010.

DIVISION III
COMMISSION ADMINISTRATION

Setting regular and special meetings. Policy Declaration 3.1.
Organizational meeting; election of chairperson and vice-chairperson. Policy Declaration 3.2.
Preparation of annual report. Policy Declaration 3.3.
Availability of commission rules and policy declarations. Policy Declaration 3.4.
Review of commission rules, proposed changes. Policy Declaration 3.5.
Policy declarations. Policy Declaration 3.6.
Staff authorization for announcements between meetings. Policy Declaration 3.7.
Announcement at conclusion of previously-announced investigation. Policy Declaration 3.7.5.
Duties of trial counsel. Policy Declaration 3.8.
Legal advisor to commissioners. Policy Declaration 3.9.
Records disposition policy. Policy Declaration 3.10.
Biennial adjustment of gift limitation amount. Policy Declaration 3.11.
Extensions of time. Policy Declaration 3.12.
Procedures and standards for staff recusal. Policy Declaration 3.13.
Certification applications; Confidentiality. Policy Declaration 3.14.

Policy Declaration 3.1. Setting Regular and Special Meetings.

(1) Before the end of each calendar year, staff will propose a choice of dates for each meeting for the next calendar year. At its March organizational meeting, the commission will approve the meeting dates for the remainder of the year.

(2) A special meeting shall be called (a) upon not less than five (5) days notice by the chairperson or acting chairperson, or (b) upon notice of request of not less than four (4) members.

Approved May 28, 1997.

Policy Declaration 3.2. Organizational Meeting; Election of Chairperson and Vice-Chairperson.

At its March meeting each year, the commission shall organize itself for the conduct of business for the ensuing year and shall select a chairperson and vice-chairperson.

Approved May 28, 1997.

Policy Declaration 3.3. Preparation of Annual Report.

At the end of each calendar year, staff will prepare a draft annual report for circulation to the commission or such members as the commission delegates for review of the draft report. After the draft report is reviewed and suggestions made, staff will revise the draft report in accordance therewith and will submit the report in final form to the chairperson for approval for publication within the first quarter of the calendar year.

Approved May 28, 1997; amended Feb. 11, 1999.

Policy Declaration 3.4. Availability of Commission Rules and Policy Declarations.

The rules and policy declarations of the commission will be published by the commission and distributed to the public upon request. The commission's rules and policy declarations are also to be published, to the extent possible, in legal publications including the California Official Reports Advance Sheets and other legal publications and on-line services.

Approved May 28, 1997; amended Feb. 11, 1999.

Policy Declaration 3.5. Review of Commission Rules, Proposed Changes.

(1) Biennial Rules Review

Every two years, in even-numbered years, the commission shall review its rules, and any rule enactments, amendments or repeals proposed by commission members or staff, or third parties. Proposed changes to the rules by commission members or staff, or third parties which are received by the commission other than during its biennial rules review may be considered by the commission and either deferred to the next review of the rules or, in the commission's discretion, acted upon prior to the next biennial rules review pursuant to the procedures specified in this policy declaration.

(2) Submission of Rule Proposals

Proposed rules, amendments and repeals must be submitted in writing to the commission's office and include a statement of the specific purpose of the proposed rule, amendment or repeal and explain how the proposal would achieve the intended purpose. The commission or a designated member of staff may, in writing, solicit further information or clarification from the proponent of the rule, amendment or repeal.

(3) Public Comment

All rule proposals submitted to the commission pursuant to subdivision (2) or by a member of the commission or commission staff shall be reviewed by the commission or the commission's rules committee. If, after review, the commission is considering the adoption of a proposed rule or amendment or the repeal of an existing rule, the proposal must be circulated for public comment. The invitation to comment shall include the express language of the proposal or proposed change and an explanation of the reason for the proposed change. There shall be a 60-day comment period, the expiration of which shall be noticed in the invitation to comment. The time to comment may be shortened to 30 days or extended to 90 days for good cause. Within 30 days after the expiration of the initial comment period, responses to comments submitted during the initial comment period may be submitted. The period to respond to comments may be shortened for good cause. All comments and responses shall be submitted in writing. The commission shall not consider any further comments or input after the expiration of the comment and response periods.

The commission may determine that exigent circumstances require it to adopt, amend, or suspend a rule on an interim basis without first circulating it for public comment. Before the rule is enacted, amended or repealed on a permanent basis, it shall be circulated for public comment according to the provisions of this policy declaration.

The commission may correct inadvertent, non-substantive errors in commission rules without circulating the revision for public comment and issuing a public report.

(4) Commission Action on Proposal

As soon as feasible after the expiration of the comment and response periods, the commission shall review and consider all written comments and responses received and vote to adopt, modify, or reject the proposal. The commission may modify the proposed rule or amendment in view of the comments received and other considerations without seeking further public comment, unless the modification results in a significant change to the substance of the proposal. The adoption, amendment, or repeal of a rule becomes effective as of the date of the commission's action, unless otherwise specified.

(5) Public Report

A final public report shall be issued as promptly as possible after the commission votes to adopt, reject or modify the proposed rule. The report shall include the express language of the rule or amendment adopted by the commission and the language of any rule that was repealed by the commission. The report shall include a summary of any written comment submitted during the comment and response periods together with an explanation of why a change was made to accommodate the comment or the reasons for making no change. The commission may respond to repetitive comments as a group or summarily dismiss irrelevant comments.

(6) Public File

The commission shall maintain a public rules file. The file shall include copies of any rule proposals submitted to the commission pursuant to this policy declaration, written correspondence with proponents of a rule amendment, the invitation to comment circulated by the commission, any comments received during the public comment and response periods, the final public report, and any external reports, studies or documentary evidence relied on by the commission in reaching its determination on a proposed rule, amendment or repeal. Confidential information included in a public comment shall be redacted from the copy placed in the public file. Copies of any materials contained in the public file shall be provided to any member of the public upon request, subject to a reasonable administrative fee.

Approved May 28, 1997; amended Feb. 4, 2004, Dec. 5, 2013, July 11, 2018, July 1, 2020.

Policy Declaration 3.6. Policy Declarations.

When there is commission approval for staff to draft a policy declaration, any proposed enactment, amendment or repeal shall be submitted to each commission member for consideration at a duly convened meeting of the commission at which a vote thereon is taken. The commission may have the proposed enactment, amendment or repeal reviewed by the rules committee prior to a vote by the commission.

Approved May 28, 1997; amended Jan. 30, 2013.

Policy Declaration 3.7. Staff Authorization for Announcements Between Meetings.

When the director believes an announcement pursuant to California Constitution, article VI, section 18(k) or pursuant to rule 102(c) is appropriate between meetings in a particular proceeding, the director shall so advise the chairperson or acting chairperson. An effort should be made, whenever possible, to poll all of the members for authorization of the announcement. If, in the discretion of the chairperson or acting chairperson, polling all of the members is not feasible, the chairperson or acting chairperson may authorize the announcement. When an announcement is authorized without a poll of the members, the members shall be promptly notified of the action taken.

Approved May 28, 1997.

Policy Declaration 3.7.5. Announcement at Conclusion of Previously-Announced Investigation.

When the commission has issued a public statement announcing or confirming that a matter is under investigation pursuant to article VI, section 18(k) or pursuant to rule 102(c), at the conclusion of the investigation, the commission shall issue a public statement indicating that the previously-announced investigation has been completed. If the matter has been concluded by the commission, the announcement shall so state. If the commission has instituted formal proceedings, the announcement shall so state, and the announcement may include an explanation of formal proceedings.

Approved Feb. 11, 1999.

Policy Declaration 3.8. Duties of Trial Counsel.

Trial counsel shall serve as examiner in formal proceedings instituted by the commission and shall represent the commission in litigation before the California Supreme Court and other courts when directed to do so by the commission. Trial counsel shall serve under the direction of the commission's director-chief counsel.

Approved May 28, 1997.

Policy Declaration 3.9. Legal Advisor to Commissioners.

The commission has established the position of legal advisor to commissioners and shall designate an attorney to serve in that capacity. The legal advisor reports directly to the commission and shall assist the commission in its adjudicatory function, including in its consideration and adjudication of matters in which formal proceedings have been instituted and matters in which judges demand an appearance before the commission to object to a tentative advisory letter, private admonishment or public admonishment.

The legal advisor shall not participate in the investigation of complaints or prosecution of charges against judges. If the legal advisor previously participated in an investigation or adversarial proceeding in another capacity as an attorney for the commission, he or she shall not assist the commission in its deliberations or adjudication of that matter absent a written waiver by the judge.

The legal advisor shall present to the commission proposals for disposition of matters in which formal proceedings have been instituted which have been jointly offered by trial counsel and the judge or judge's counsel. After institution of formal proceedings, the legal advisor shall be responsible for requesting the appointment of special masters by the Supreme Court and shall serve as the commission's liaison to special masters appointed in formal proceedings.

The legal advisor shall perform such additional duties as may be assigned by the commission that do not require or cause the legal advisor to participate in the commission's investigatory or prosecutorial functions.

Approved May 28, 1997; amended Aug. 26, 2004, Oct. 19, 2011, June 26, 2019, Dec. 7, 2022.

Policy Declaration 3.10. Records Disposition Policy.

At the beginning of each calendar year, the commission shall destroy all files which did not result in an advisory letter, public or private admonishment, public reproval, censure, removal or involuntary retirement, resignation or retirement with proceedings pending, or finding that a person was unfit to serve as a subordinate judicial officer as follows:

(1) Files involving complaints against municipal or superior court judges dated or docketed by the commission in the thirteenth year prior to the new calendar year; and

(2) Files involving complaints against appellate or Supreme Court justices dated or docketed by the commission in the nineteenth year prior to the new calendar year; and

(3) Files involving complaints against subordinate judicial officers dated or docketed by the commission in the thirteenth year prior to the new calendar year.

Approved May 28, 1997; amended Feb. 11, 1999.

Policy Declaration 3.11. Biennial Adjustment of Gift Limitation Amount.

(1) Code of Civil Procedure section 170.9(a) limits to $250 the total value of gifts that an individual judge may accept from any single source in any calendar year. Section 170.9(d) requires that the commission adjust that amount biennially to reflect changes in the Consumer Price Index, rounded to the nearest $10. Since section 170.9(d) took effect January 1, 1995, an adjustment must be made in subsequent odd-numbered years (commencing in 1997).

(2) The adjusted gift limitation amount shall apply as of January 1 of the year in which the adjustment is announced and shall remain in effect until January 1 of the next odd-numbered year.

(3) The adjusted gift limitation amount shall be calculated by the commission as follows:

(a) The base dollar amount ($250) shall be increased or decreased by the percentage change in the annual average California Consumer Price Index (CCPI) for all urban consumers from the base year (1994) to the end of the calendar year immediately preceding the year of adjustment.

(b) Formula: The base dollar amount ($250) is multiplied by a fraction whose numerator is the annual average CCPI for the even-numbered year preceding the year of adjustment and whose denominator is the 1994 annual average CCPI (151.5). The resulting dollar amount is rounded to the nearest $10, unless that amounts ends in the numeral five with no cents, in which case it is not rounded in either direction.

Approved May 28, 1997.

Policy Declaration 3.12. Extensions of Time.

Unnecessary delay in commission proceedings is incompatible with the commission's mandate to protect the public and the judiciary in general. Accordingly, extensions of time are disfavored.

Approved Aug. 26, 2004.

Policy Declaration 3.13. Procedures and Standards for Staff Recusal.

(1) The chairperson of the commission or the chairperson's designee shall be informed if any member of legal staff, the director, or the legal advisor has any possible conflicts of interest involving either a case assigned to him or her or any other case pending before the commission and of information that might be considered relevant to the question of disqualification, even if the attorney believes there is no actual basis for disqualification.

(2) The chairperson or the chairperson's designee shall make a determination as to whether the attorney shall be recused or other action taken. The commission shall be appraised at each meeting of any conflicts or potential conflicts brought to the attention of the chairperson. The commission may overrule or modify any resolution of a conflict by the chairperson.

(3) An attorney shall be recused under the following circumstances:

(a) The attorney in the course of a previous representation of a client has received confidential information that has any relevance to a commission investigation;

(b) The attorney has personal knowledge of disputed evidentiary facts concerning the proceedings;

(c) The attorney has a current personal, financial, or professional relationship with the judge, the judge's counsel, or the complainant;

(d) The attorney has a previous personal, financial, or professional relationship with the judge, the judge's counsel, or the complainant which casts a substantial doubt on the attorney's ability to be impartial;

(e) The attorney's spouse or partner has a personal, financial, or professional relationship with the judge, the judge's counsel, or the complainant which casts a substantial doubt on the attorney's ability to be impartial;

(f) Where a reasonable person aware of the facts would entertain a substantial doubt that the attorney would be impartial.

(4) In the event an attorney other than the director is recused, the recused attorney shall not review any materials concerning the matter or discuss the matter with commission staff. The recusal shall be noted prominently in the file and commission staff shall be directed not to circulate any materials concerning the matter to the recused attorney, not to consult with the recused attorney concerning the matter and not to discuss the matter in the presence of the recused attorney. The entire legal staff need not be recused from the matter unless the commission determines that the recused attorney's conflict casts a substantial doubt on the ability of the entire staff to be impartial. The recusal of the attorney shall be noted in the commission's minutes.

(5) In the event the director is recused, the entire legal staff, excluding the legal advisor, shall be recused. The commission may obtain outside counsel to handle intake, investigation, and any further proceedings involving the case, including acting as media contact, without consultation with the director or legal staff. The recusal of the director shall be noted in the commission's minutes.

(6) In the case of a recusal of the legal advisor or trial counsel, the commission may designate a member of legal staff or obtain outside counsel to advise the commission or act as examiner.

Approved June 30, 2010.

Policy Declaration 3.14. Certification Applications: Confidentiality.

The commission shall treat as confidential any information which is presented to the commission by a former judge or justice for certification to administer oaths or affirmations pursuant to Code of Civil Procedure Section 2093 and Government Code Section 1225 for retirement purposes, except the fact that a certification is in effect may be revealed.

Approved Dec. 1, 2015.

DIVISION IV
DISCLOSURE OF INFORMATION

Public safety. Policy Declaration 4.1.
Disclosure of information to prosecuting authorities. Policy Declaration 4.2.
Disclosure of disciplinary records to public entity upon request/with consent of judge. Policy Declaration 4.3.
Disclosure of records of disciplinary action to appointing authorities. Policy Declaration 4.4.
Disclosure of information regarding pending proceedings to appointing authorities. Policy Declaration 4.5.
Limitation on disclosure to appointing authorities—Complaints not yet reviewed by the commission. Policy Declaration 4.5.5.
Disclosure of information to public entities. Policy Declaration 4.6.

Policy Declaration 4.1. Public Safety.

The disclosure of information concerning a threat to public safety under rule 102(f) may be made by the chairperson, the director or the designee of either.

Approved May 28, 1997.

Policy Declaration 4.2. Disclosure of Information to Prosecuting Authorities.

When, in the course of evaluating complaints or conducting investigations, commission staff acquires information revealing possible criminal conduct by a judge, former judge or by any other individual or entity, such information shall be brought to the attention of the commission at the earliest possible opportunity for consideration of a referral of the information to prosecuting authorities. Such a referral requires a vote of a majority of the commission members.

Approved May 28, 1997.

Policy Declaration 4.3. Disclosure of Disciplinary Records to Public Entity Upon Request/With Consent of Judge.

When a judge requests or consents to the release of commission records of disciplinary action under rule 102(h), the judge's request must be made in writing to the commission office. If the judge is consenting to a request by a public entity for records of disciplinary action, the judge's written consent and a copy of the entity's request must be received by the commission office. Copies of any information released to the public entity shall be provided simultaneously to the judge requesting or consenting to the release of records.

Approved May 28, 1997.

Policy Declaration 4.4. Disclosure of Records of Disciplinary Action to Appointing Authorities.

Requests by an appointing authority for records of disciplinary action pursuant to California Constitution, article VI, section 18.5 or rule 102(i) must be made in writing to the commission office. Copies of any information provided to the appointing authority shall be provided simultaneously to the applicant judge.

Approved May 28, 1997.

Policy Declaration 4.5. Disclosure of Information Regarding Pending Proceedings to Appointing Authorities.

Requests by an appointing authority for information regarding pending investigations or proceedings pursuant to rule 102(j) must be made in writing to the commission office. Copies of any information provided to the appointing authority shall be provided simultaneously to the applicant judge.

Approved May 28, 1997.

Policy Declaration 4.5.5. Limitation on Disclosure to Appointing Authorities—Complaints Not Yet Reviewed by the Commission.

When responding to a request for information regarding pending investigations from appointing authorities (rule 102(j)), the director-chief counsel shall state that the commission's discretionary authority to release information concerning pending investigations does not encompass comment on any complaint that may have been received by the commission and has not yet been reviewed by the commission to determine whether or not to authorize an investigation or whether any such complaint exists.

Approved Mar. 13, 2002.

Policy Declaration 4.6. Disclosure of Information to Public Entities.

The release of information to a public entity, pursuant to rule 102, subsections (k) or (p), requires a vote of a majority of the commission members. The commission may, in its discretion, notify the judge, former judge, subordinate judicial officer or former subordinate judicial officer, that such disclosure is being made. Copies of any information being disclosed to the public entity may, in the commission's discretion, be made available to the judge, former judge, subordinate judicial officer or former subordinate judicial officer, who is the subject of the disclosure.

Approved May 28, 1997; amended Jan. 29, 2003, Dec. 6, 2017.

DIVISION V
DISABILITY RETIREMENT APPLICATIONS

Disability applications: confidentiality. Policy Declaration 5.1.
Disability applications: medical consultants. Policy Declaration 5.2.
Reexamination of judges retired for disability. Policy Declaration 5.3.
Procedure in disability retirement matters. Policy Declaration 5.4.
Disability applications: burden of proof. Policy Declaration 5.5.
Procedure in restoration to capacity matters. Policy Declaration 5.6.

Policy Declaration 5.1. Disability Applications: Confidentiality.

The commission shall treat as confidential any information which is presented to the commission by a judge for retirement purposes, except as follows:

(1) The fact and date that an application has been filed and has been approved or rejected or remains pending may be revealed.

(2) If the Judges' Retirement System (JRS) submits a written request for information concerning a particular disability retirement application pursuant to Government Code section 75080(d) or 75580(a), the commission shall provide to JRS any information that the commission deems necessary to a full understanding of the commission's action, in furtherance of the statutory scheme embodied in articles 3 and 4 of the Judges' Retirement Law and articles 4 and 6 of the Judges' Retirement System II (JRS II). The commission shall furnish the judge in question with a copy of any documents provided to JRS. All information released under this section shall remain confidential and privileged.

Approved May 28, 1997; amended June 21, 2000, Aug. 26, 2004, Jan. 30, 2013.

Policy Declaration 5.2. Disability Applications: Medical Consultants.

The commission may arrange with the University of California Medical Centers and/or other qualified medical practitioners for medical consultants to provide independent medical examinations for disability retirement applicants, to assist the commission as necessary in evaluating disability retirement applications under Government Code sections 75060 and 75560.1, making findings under policy declaration 5.4(4) in order to facilitate implementation of Government Code sections 75080(d) and 75580(a), and/or reevaluating the medical status of a judge retired on disability under Government Code sections 75060.6 and 75560.6.

Approved May 28, 1997; amended June 21, 2000, Jan. 30, 2013.

Policy Declaration 5.3. Reexamination of Judges Retired for Disability.

When approving a request for disability retirement, the commission shall decide on a case-by-case basis whether and when the judge shall be required to be reexamined pursuant to Government Code section 75060.6 or 75560.6. Notwithstanding such decision, a judge retired for disability may be required to undergo reexamination pursuant to Government Code section 75060.6 or 75560.6.

Approved May 28, 1997; amended Jan. 30, 2013.

Policy Declaration 5.4. Procedure in Disability Retirement Matters.

(1) An application for disability retirement must include: a consent to disability retirement, executed by the judge or, in an application by a JRS II judge, a family member or legal representative acting on behalf of the judge pursuant to Government Code section 75560.1(a), and a medical certificate of disability, executed under penalty of perjury by a licensed physician. To complete the application, the commission ordinarily will require a medical report prepared by that physician in support of certification, which shall include a statement specifying the nature of the judicial duties that cannot be efficiently discharged due to the judge's disability, and all pertinent medical documentation.

A judge seeking the disability retirement allowance provided under Government Code section 75560.4(b) must inform the commission in the judge's consent to disability retirement that the judge is seeking a determination by the commission whether the disability is predominantly a result of injury arising out of and in the course of judicial service. The commission will not make a determination whether the injury is predominantly a result of injury arising out of and in the course of judicial service if the judge is entitled to 65 percent of the judge's final compensation on the effective date of the disability retirement under Government Code section 75560.4(a).

(2) When a judge submits an application for disability retirement, the commission will advise the judge if the certifying physician's report or other medical documentation supporting the application is inadequate, and will give the judge thirty (30) days to supply more complete data. The judge shall cooperate in obtaining any medical/psychiatric records the commission or the special master needs in evaluating the judge's disability application.

(3) Following receipt of a complete application, the commission may request review of medical reports and documents by independent consultants and/or medical examiners. One or more independent medical examinations and/or additional medical information may be requested within one hundred twenty (120) days of the first commission meeting after receipt of complete medical records. This time may be extended for good cause. If an independent medical examination is conducted, the commission will provide a copy of the examiner's report to the judge. If the examiner concludes that the judge suffers from a disability that precludes the efficient discharge of judicial duties and is permanent or likely to become so, the examiner's report shall include a statement specifying the nature of the judicial duties that cannot be efficiently discharged due to the disability.

If the judge has informed the commission that the judge is seeking a disability retirement allowance pursuant to Government Code section 75560.4(b), the examiner's report shall also set forth the examiner's opinion whether the disability is predominantly a result of injury arising out of and in the course of judicial service and the basis for that opinion.

(4) Within sixty (60) days of the first commission meeting after receipt of all reports by consultants and medical examiners, the commission will: approve the application, or tentatively deny it, or extend its time to act on the application for good cause, "good cause" to include circumstances in which the judge's condition cannot yet be deemed permanent or likely to become so, within the meaning of Government

Code section 75060 or 75560.1. If the commission extends its time to act, notice of such extension shall be provided to the judge.

(5) If the commission approves the application, the commission will refer the application to the Chief Justice. If the Chief Justice approves the application, the Judges' Retirement System will be informed that the disability application has been approved. The commission may also prepare a statement of findings specifying the nature of the judicial duties that cannot be efficiently discharged due to the disability.

(6) If the commission tentatively denies the application, or approves the application but tentatively determines that the disability is not predominantly a result of injury arising out of and in the course of judicial service, the commission will within thirty (30) days issue a tentative decision setting forth the reasons for the denial. The tentative decision will be provided to the judge upon issuance.

(7) If the commission approves the disability application, but tentatively determines that the disability is not predominantly a result of injury arising out of and in the course of judicial service, the commission will refer the application to the Chief Justice. If the Chief Justice approves the application, Judges' Retirement System will be informed that the disability application has been approved, subject to a pending determination whether or not the disability is predominantly a result of injury arising out of and in the course of judicial service.

(8) A tentative denial of the disability application or a tentative determination that the disability is not predominantly a result of injury arising out of and in the course of judicial service becomes final thirty (30) days after issuance unless, within thirty (30) days of the tentative denial, or tentative determination, the judge (1) files a request to submit additional information to the commission, or (2) files a request for an evidentiary hearing to contest the tentative denial or tentative determination. A request to submit additional information shall explain the relevance of the additional information to the commission's determination(s). A request to submit additional information does not preclude the judge from requesting an evidentiary hearing if, after considering the additional information, the commission does not change its tentative denial of the disability application, or tentative determination that the disability is not predominantly a result of injury arising out of and in the course of judicial service. A request for an evidentiary hearing shall specify the factual and legal issues to be contested at the evidentiary hearing.

(9) If a judge's request to submit additional information is granted, the commission shall reconsider the tentative denial of the application or tentative work-related determination based on the new information submitted. Within sixty (60) days of the first commission meeting after receipt of the new information, the commission shall make a decision approving the application and referring it to the Chief Justice, or issue a tentative denial of the application. If requested, within sixty (60) days of the first commission meeting after receipt of the new information, the commission shall make a determination either that the disability is work-related and advise the Judges' Retirement System, or issue a tentative determination that the disability is not work-related.

(10) Within thirty (30) days of the first commission meeting after a judge requests an evidentiary hearing, the commission will appoint a special master authorized to take evidence on the matter, and to report to the commission. The proceedings before the special master are not a de novo review of the basis for the commission's tentative denial of the disability application or tentative determination regarding work-relatedness. The special master's report to the commission shall contain proposed findings of fact and conclusions of law on the issues specified in the judge's request for an evidentiary hearing and on any other issues raised by the parties during the proceedings, as deemed relevant by the special master.

(11) Upon appointment, the special master shall be given a copy of the judge's application for disability retirement, the commission's tentative denial of the application or tentative determination that the disability is not predominantly a result of injury arising out of and in the course of judicial service, and any medical and/or psychiatric reports considered by the commission. These documents may be considered by the special master in reaching proposed findings and conclusions.

(12) The special master may require briefing from the parties before and after the evidentiary hearing. The judge and the examiner shall submit a list of witnesses and exhibits to be presented at the evidentiary hearing within ten days prior to the hearing, unless otherwise specified by the special master.

(13) The California Evidence Code shall be applicable to an evidentiary hearing before a special master held pursuant to policy declaration 5.4(10).

(14) Within one hundred twenty (120) days after the appointment of a special master, the master will refer the matter back to the commission with a report containing proposed findings, unless the special master requests and is granted an extension of time from the chairperson or another member designated by the chairperson or the commission.

(15) Within sixty (60) days of the first commission meeting following such referral, the commission will make a decision approving the application and referring it to the Chief Justice or denying the application and advising the Chief Justice, or, pursuant to Government Code section 75560.4(b), determining either that the disability is predominantly a result of injury arising out of and in the course of judicial service or that it is not such an injury and advising Judges' Retirement System.

Approved May 28, 1997; amended June 21, 2000, Jan. 30, 2013, Mar. 22, 2017, Dec. 7, 2022.

Policy Declaration 5.5. Disability Applications: Burden of Proof.

Unless Government Code section 75062, 75063, or 75064, 75562, 75563 or 75564 applies, a judge seeking disability retirement must establish by a preponderance of the evidence that the judge is eligible for disability retirement under section 75560 or 75560.1 and that the judge is unable to discharge efficiently the duties of judicial office by reason of mental or physical disability that is or is likely to become permanent. A judge seeking benefits under section 75560.4(b) must establish by a preponderance of the evidence that the disability is predominantly a result of injury arising out of and in the course of judicial service.

Approved May 28, 1997; amended Jan. 30, 2013, Feb. 1, 2017.

Policy Declaration 5.6. Procedure in Restoration to Capacity Matters.

(1) An application for restoration to capacity must be in writing, executed by the judge, and be accompanied by one or more medical reports sufficient to establish that the judge is no longer mentally or physically incapacitated and is capable of discharging efficiently the duties of judicial office.

(2) When a judge submits an application for restoration to capacity, the commission will advise the judge if the certifying physician's report or other medical documentation supporting the application is inadequate, and will give the judge thirty (30) days to supply more complete data.

(3) Following receipt of a complete application, the commission may request review of medical reports and documents by independent consultants and/or medical examiners. One or more independent medical examinations may be requested within one hundred twenty (120) days of the first commission meeting after receipt of complete medical records. This time may be extended for good cause. If an independent medical examination is conducted, the commission will provide a copy of the examiner's report to the judge.

(4) Within sixty (60) days of the first commission meeting after receipt of all reports by consultants and medical examiners, the commission will either approve the application or tentatively deny it.

(5) If the commission tentatively denies the application, the commission will within thirty (30) days issue a tentative decision setting forth the reasons for the denial. The tentative decision will be provided to the judge upon issuance.

(6) A tentative denial becomes final thirty (30) days after issuance unless, within thirty (30) days of the tentative denial, the judge files a request to present additional evidence. Within thirty (30) days of the first commission meeting after such filing, the commission will appoint a special master authorized to take evidence, obtain additional medical information, and take any other steps the special master deems necessary to resolve the matter.

(7) Within one hundred eighty (180) days after the appointment of a special master, the master will refer the matter back to the commission with a report containing proposed findings.

(8) Within ninety (90) days of the first commission meeting following such referral, the commission will make a decision either approving the application for restoration to capacity or denying it.

Approved May 28, 1997.

DIVISION VI
CODE OF ETHICS FOR COMMISSION MEMBERS

Recusal. Policy Declaration 6.1.

Confidentiality. Policy Declaration 6.2.
Ex parte contacts. Policy Declaration 6.3.
Judicial election activities. Policy Declaration 6.4.
Impropriety and appearance of impropriety. Policy Declaration 6.5.

Preface

As the agency charged with enforcing standards of judicial conduct in order to maintain the integrity and independence of the judiciary, the California Commission on Judicial Performance (commission) recognizes the importance of observing high standards of ethical conduct in the performance of its responsibilities. The Code of Ethics (Code) set forth in these policy declarations describes ethical standards expected of a commission member. The Code does not confer any substantive or procedural due process rights other than those provided by law, or create a separate basis for civil liability or criminal prosecution.

For purposes of this Code, the judge who is the subject of a complaint, an investigation, or formal proceedings before the commission shall be referred to as the "subject judge."

Adopted Jan. 31, 2007; amended Dec. 13, 2007.

Policy Declaration 6.1. Recusal.

(1) A commission member shall recuse himself or herself if:
(a) The member does not think he or she is able to act fairly and impartially in a matter;
(b) The member or an immediate family member is the subject of the investigation;
(c) The member served as a lawyer or a judge in any proceedings that are the subject of the investigation;
(d) The member has a case pending before the subject judge either as a litigant or in the member's capacity as a lawyer;
(e) A lawyer with whom the member practices is involved in the complaint;
(f) The member has a bias or prejudice for or against the subject judge; or
(g) A reasonable person aware of the facts would entertain a substantial doubt that the member would be able to be impartial.

(2) If a member determines to recuse himself or herself:
(a) The member shall recuse himself or herself promptly;
(b) The recused member may, but is not required to, state the reason(s) for his or her recusal;
(c) The recused member shall leave the room, not comment further or otherwise participate in the commission's consideration of the matter from which the member is recused; and
(d) The recused member shall not receive further written materials on the matter from which the member is recused while the matter is pending before the commission.

Adopted Jan. 31, 2007; amended Jan. 30, 2013, Dec. 7, 2022.

Policy Declaration 6.2. Confidentiality.

(1) Confidentiality shall be maintained with regard to all new, pending, and closed matters pursuant to rule 102 and other applicable legal requirements.

(2) Members shall ensure that all confidential documents are secured. When the members are notified in writing (e.g., through the meeting minutes) that documents in selected matters may be discarded, members who choose to discard such documents shall ensure that they are destroyed. Members who choose to retain such documents shall ensure that they are secured.

(3) A member shall not use or disclose, for any purpose unrelated to commission duties, non-public or confidential information acquired in his or her capacity as a commission member.

Adopted Jan. 31, 2007.

Policy Declaration 6.3. Ex Parte Contacts.

(1) A member shall not initiate, permit, or consider ex parte communications regarding a matter pending or impending before the commission, other than authorized communications with other commission members and staff.

(2) If a member is contacted about a new or pending matter by a subject judge, a judge's attorney or other agent, or a subject judge's family or friends, the member shall not discuss the matter, but may refer the person to the director-chief counsel.

(3) If a member is contacted by a complainant, witness, or potential witness about a new, pending, or closed matter, the member shall not discuss the matter, but may refer the person to the director-chief counsel. Correspondence from complainants about commission business shall be referred to the director-chief counsel for acknowledgement and disposition.

(4) After the initiation of formal proceedings, commission members shall not initiate communications with or receive communications from the director-chief counsel, investigative staff, or trial counsel concerning the matter except as provided by commission rules or stipulation of all parties in the proceeding.

Adopted Jan. 31, 2007; amended Dec. 13, 2007.

Policy Declaration 6.4. Judicial Election Activities.

(1) A member of the commission shall not publicly support or oppose a candidate for election to judicial office in California while a member of the commission. For purposes of this guideline, both incumbent judges and attorneys seeking election to a judicial position are considered candidates for judicial office.

(2) A member of the commission shall not personally contribute funds directly to any candidate for election to judicial office in California while a member of the commission. If a commission member is a member of a partnership or professional corporation that contributes funds to candidates for judicial office in California, the commission member should not participate in such contribution decisions. If a commission member is assessed a portion of any contribution made to a candidate for judicial office by the member's firm, the commission member's recusal from matters involving the judge may be appropriate under some circumstances. In assessing whether to recuse, relevant factors include: whether the amount of money assessed from the commission member is de minimis (less than $10), whether the commission member's name is included in the firm name, the number of other partners in the member's firm, and the total number of judges in the county in which the judicial candidate was elected.

(3) A member of the commission who is also a member of the board of an organization which is involved in judicial election activities in California should exercise caution over his or her participation in such activities. A member of the commission should not participate in the organization's endorsements of or opposition to specific judicial candidates in California. Ideally, any publication of the organization's endorsement of or opposition to specific judicial candidates would state that the commission member on the board of the organization had not participated in the endorsement or opposition. In some instances, depending on the size of the organization, its purpose and its activities, the commission member should consider resigning from the organization's board if an appearance of conflict of interest or other impropriety cannot otherwise be avoided.

Adopted Jan. 31, 2007; amended Mar. 28, 2018.

Policy Declaration 6.5. Impropriety and Appearance of Impropriety.

(1) A member shall not lend the prestige of his or her commission office to advance his or her private interests or the interests of others; nor shall the member convey or permit others to convey the impression that they are in a special position to influence the commission.

(2) A member shall not be swayed by partisan interests, public clamor, or fear of criticism with respect to the conduct of commission business.

(3) In conducting commission business, a member shall refrain from manifesting by word or action bias or prejudice on the basis of a protected characteristic or on membership in a group or class as identified in canon 3B(5) against parties, witnesses, counsel, or others.

Adopted Jan. 31, 2007; amended Dec. 7, 2022.

DIVISION VII
DISCIPLINE

Policy Declaration 7.1. Non-Exclusive Factors Relevant to Sanctions.

The following non-exclusive factors may be relevant in considering the appropriate discipline to be ordered. Because each case is considered on its own facts, the applicability and weight given to any factor is within the discretion of the commission.

(1) Characteristics of Misconduct:
(a) The number of acts of misconduct;
(b) The nature and seriousness of the misconduct;

(c) Whether the misconduct occurred in the judge's official capacity or in the judge's private life;

(d) Whether the misconduct involved dishonesty or lack of integrity;

(e) Whether the misconduct was intentional, premeditated, negligent, or spontaneous;

(f) The nature and extent to which the misconduct has been injurious to other persons;

(g) Whether the judge was motivated by a desire to satisfy a personal or venal interest, vindictiveness, or an interest in justice, or compassion;

(h) Whether the misconduct undermines the integrity of the judiciary, respect for the judiciary or the administration of justice;

(i) Whether the misconduct involves unequal application of justice on the basis of a protected characteristic or on membership in a group or class as identified in canon 3B(5).

(2) Service and Demeanor of the Judge:

(a) Whether the judge has acknowledged the acts occurred and has shown an appreciation of the impropriety of his or her acts;

(b) Whether the judge cooperated fully and honestly in the commission proceedings;

(c) Whether the judge has evidenced an effort to change or modify the conduct;

(d) The judge's length of service in a judicial capacity;

(e) Whether there has been prior disciplinary action concerning the judge;

(f) Whether there are exceptional personal circumstances that warrant consideration;

(g) The judge's reputation for administering his or her judicial duties in a fair, impartial, and dignified manner and for making positive contributions to the court or community.

Approved Oct. 22, 2008; amended Dec. 7, 2022.

INDEX

CIVIL CODE

CODE OF CIVIL PROCEDURE

EVIDENCE CODE

FAMILY CODE

PROBATE CODE

RULES OF COURT

RULES OF PROFESSIONAL CONDUCT

RULES OF COMMISSION ON JUDICIAL PERFORMANCE

GOVERNMENT CODE [ADMINISTRATIVE PROCEDURE ACT,
GOVERNMENT CLAIMS ACT & MISCELLANEOUS FEE PROVISIONS]

ABBREVIATIONS

CC	Civil Code
CCP	Code of Civil Procedure
Ev	Evidence Code
Fam	Family Code
Gov	Government Code
Pro	Probate Code
JudPerR	Rules of Commission on Judicial Performance
JudPerPolicy	Policy Declarations of the Commission on Judicial Performance
ProfC	Rules of Professional Conduct
CRC	Rules of Court
CRCAppx	Rules of Court Appendix
CRCSupp	Rules of Court Supplement
CRC ArbEthicsStand	Rules of Court Ethics Standards for Neutral Arbitrators in Contractual Arbitration
CRC JudAdminStand	Rules of Court Standards of Judicial Administration
CRCSupp JudEthicsCanon	Code of Judicial Ethics

INDEX TO THE CIVIL, CIVIL PROCEDURE, EVIDENCE, FAMILY, PROBATE CODES, RULES OF COURT, RULES OF PROFESSIONAL CONDUCT, RULES OF COMMISSION ON JUDICIAL PERFORMANCE, GOVERNMENT CODE [ADMINISTRATIVE PROCEDURE ACT, GOVERNMENT CLAIMS ACT & MISCELLANEOUS FEE PROVISIONS]

Abbreviations used in references are listed in Table of Abbreviations on facing page.

A

ABANDONED CHILDREN
Adoption
    Proceedings for abandoned child   Fam §8607

ABANDONED SPOUSES
Marital privilege
    Waiver   Ev §§972, 985

ABANDONMENT
Adoption proceedings for abandoned child   Fam §§7822, 8606, 8607
Animals   CC §1834.5
Appellate rules
    Superior court appeals (See **APPELLATE RULES, SUPERIOR COURT APPEALS**)
Children (See **PARENT AND CHILD**)
Customer records
    Disposition of abandoned records
        Immunity   CC §1798.84
Decedent's estate, abandonment of personal property of (See **ADMINISTRATION OF ESTATES**)
Easements (See **EASEMENTS**)
Eminent domain proceedings   CCP §1268.510
Escheat after (See **ESCHEAT**)
Floating homes (See **FLOATING HOMES**)
Homestead property, abandonment of   CCP §§704.980, 704.990
Infants (See **PARENT AND CHILD**)
Landlord and tenant
    Abandoned personal property, disposition of
        Commercial real property   CC §§1993 to 1993.09
Landlord disposing tenant's property   CCP §1174
Leased premises abandoned by lessee   CC §§1951 to 1951.7, CCP §415.47
Marital privilege
    Waiver   Ev §§972, 985
Mineral rights (See **MINERALS AND MINERAL RIGHTS**)
Minor children (See **PARENT AND CHILD**)
Mobilehome, sale of   CC §798.61
Money orders   CCP §§1511, 1513, 1542, 1581
Parents (See **PARENT AND CHILD**)
Retirement funds (See **RETIREMENT**)
Statute of limitation, effect of   CCP §1476
Tenant's abandoned property after termination of tenancy, disposition of   CC §§1980 to 1991
Traveler's checks   CCP §§1511, 1513, 1542, 1581
Unclaimed property (See **UNCLAIMED PROPERTY**)

ABATEMENT
Bequests, abatement of (See **ADMINISTRATION OF ESTATES**)
Cause of action, abatement of
    Disability of party during pending action or proceeding, effect of   CCP §375
    Transfer of interests, effect of   CCP §368.5
Nuisances, abatement of (See **NUISANCES**)

ABBREVIATIONS
Use in legal papers   CCP §186

ABDUCTION (See **KIDNAPPING AND CHILD ABDUCTION**)

ABETTING (See **AIDING AND ABETTING**)

ABILITY TO PAY PROGRAM   Gov §§68645 to 68645.7
Infractions
    Appearances
        Alternatives to personal appearance   Gov §68645.1
    Clerk making ability to pay determinations   Gov §68645.3
    Funding estimate   Gov §68645.7
    Online tool for adjudication of infraction violations   Gov §68645
        Deadline for offering tool   Gov §68645.2
        Electronic verification of public benefits   Gov §68645.3
        Establishing inability to pay   Gov §68645.2
        Languages available when using tool   Gov §68645.2
        Payment recommendations   Gov §68645.2
    Online trial   Gov §68645.4
    Report by judicial council to legislature   Gov §68645.5
Traffic violator school eligibility   Gov §68645.15

ABORTIONS
Commercial blockage tort affecting medical care facilities   CC §§3427 to 3427.4
Confidentiality of medical information
    Restrictions on release of medical information related to abortion   CC §§56.108, 56.110
Consumer privacy rights
    Personal information restrictions of persons at or near family planning center   CC §1798.99.90
Genetic defects, failure of parent to abort on discovery of   CC §43.6
Legally protected health care services   CC §§1798.300 to 1798.308
    Action for relief from abusive litigation infringing on protected activity   CC §1798.303
        Jurisdiction of court   CC §§1798.306, 1798.308
        Measure of damages   CC §1798.305
    Constitutional and statutory protections   CC §1798.301
    Definitions   CC §1798.300
    Foreign jurisdictions, interference with rights   CC §1798.302
    Laws governing   CC §1798.307
    Subpoena issued in connection with abusive litigation, motion to modify or quash   CC §1798.304
Medical records
    Restrictions on release of medical information related to abortion   CC §§56.108, 56.110
Minor, consent required for abortion by   Fam §6925
Parental consent   Fam §6925
Physicians and surgeons
    Release of medical information related to abortion
        Restrictions   CC §§56.108, 56.110

ABROGATION
Enactment of code, effect on existing statutes of   CCP §18

ABSENCE
Adjournment for absence of judge   CCP §139
Annulment of marriage after first spouse found to be alive   Fam §2210
Claims against decedents' estates, deposit of funds for absent claimants with   Pro §11428
Conservatees (See **CONSERVATORS**)
Cotrustee, absence as grounds for incapacity of   Pro §15622
Defendant absent from state, tolling statutes of limitation against   CCP §351
Judge's absence, adjournment on   CCP §139
Judicial arbitration proceedings, absence of party to   CRC 3.821
Military (See **MILITARY**)
Missing persons (See **MISSING PERSONS**)
Personal representatives of decedents' estates (See **EXECUTORS AND ADMINISTRATORS**)
Unknown persons (See **UNKNOWN PERSONS**)

ABSENCE—Cont.
Witness   Ev §240

ABSOLUTE FEE (See **FEE SIMPLE**)

ABSOLUTE OWNERSHIP
Definition   CC §§678, 679

ABSTRACT OF JUDGMENT
Generally   CCP §674
Additional recordation fees collected from lienors   Gov §27387
Amendment to abstract of judgment, requirements for   CCP §674
Child support, recordation of abstract of judgment for   Fam §4506.1
Claims against decedents' estate, filing abstract of judgment for purposes of   Pro §9301
Deposit of real property to secure future child support payments   Fam §4617
Enforcement of judgments (See **ENFORCEMENT OF JUDGMENTS**)
Family support   Fam §4506
Fees
    Superior court fees, specified services   Gov §70626
Public entities or state agencies, abstract of judgment filed with
    Generally   CCP §§708.730 to 708.750
    Filing fees for   CCP §708.785
Small claims courts, issuance by clerk   CCP §116.820
Support orders   Fam §4506

ABSTRACT OF TITLE (See **TITLE AND OWNERSHIP**)

ABUSE
Children (See **CHILD ABUSE**)
Domestic violence (See **DOMESTIC VIOLENCE**)
Elder abuse (See **SENIOR CITIZENS**)
Judicial discretion (See **DISCRETION OF COURT**)
Sexual abuse (See **SEX OFFENSES**)
Substance abuse (See **SUBSTANCE ABUSE**)

ACADEMIC RECORDS
Truancy mediation program, disclosure of records for
    Juvenile court proceedings   CRC 5.652

ACCELERATION OF LOANS
Generally   CC §711.5
Automobile sales   CC §2983.3
Homestead property, prohibition against acceleration of debt liability for lien on   CCP §704.810
Trust deed or mortgage, loan secured by   CC §§711.5, 2924.5, 2924.6, 2954.10

ACCEPTANCE
Contracts (See **CONTRACTS AND AGREEMENTS**)
Trusts (See **TRUSTS**)
Wills accepted for deposit by attorney   Pro §713

ACCESS
Construction-related accessibility claims   CC §§55.3 to 55.57 (See **CONSTRUCTION-RELATED ACCESSIBILITY CLAIMS**)
Disabled persons' right to full and equal access to public facilities   CC §54.1
    Construction or application of provisions in issue, solicitor general notified   CC §55.2
Eminent domain, access to premises for preliminary studies for   CCP §§1245.010 to 1245.060
Landlord preventing access to tenant   CC §789.3

ACCESSION
Ownership of   CC §732
Personal property   CC §§1025 to 1033
Real property acquired through   CC §§1000, 1013 to 1019

ACCESSORY DWELLING UNITS
Common interest developments
    Construction or use on single-family residential lot
        Restrictions prohibited   CC §4751
Covenants, conditions, and restrictions
    Unenforceability of accessory dwelling unit prohibitions   CC §714.3

ACCESS TO CLINICS AND CHURCHES
Force, threat or other obstruction of access to health facilities or school grounds   CC §1708.9

ACCIDENTS AND ACCIDENT REPORTS
Arbitration proceedings, reports admissible in   CRC 3.823

ACCORD AND SATISFACTION
Acceptance constituting   CC §1523

ACCORD AND SATISFACTION—Cont.
Definition   CC §1521
Disputed amounts, effect of payments by check of   CC §1526
Mechanics' liens
    Effect of waiver and release provisions   CC §8130
Performance   CC §§1522, 1524
Uncontested amounts, payments of   CC §1525

ACCOUNTS AND ACCOUNTING
Accountants
    Sexual harassment, civil action for
        Construction or application of provisions in issue, solicitor general notified   CC §51.1
Administrators (See **EXECUTORS AND ADMINISTRATORS**)
Admissibility of accounts   Ev §§1270 to 1272
Automobile repossession, requirements after   CC §2983.2
Blocked accounts, withdrawal of funds
    Petition
        Memorandum in support of petition not required   CRC 3.1114
Book accounts (See **BOOK ACCOUNTS**)
Business records (See **BUSINESS RECORDS**)
Common interest developments (See **COMMON INTEREST DEVELOPMENTS**)
Community property, court order requiring accounting of   Fam §1101
Confidentiality of accounts, accountants maintaining   CC §§1799 to 1799.2
Conservators (See **CONSERVATORS**)
Damages for unlawful disclosure of information   CC §1799.2
Definitions   Pro §§21 to 23, 46
Earnings assignment for support   Fam §5236
Enforcement of judgments (See **ENFORCEMENT OF JUDGMENTS**)
Escheated property accounts separated by controller   CCP §§1314, 1319
Executors (See **EXECUTORS AND ADMINISTRATORS**)
Fiduciary income and principal act
    Receipts, allocation   Pro §16342
Fire, destruction by   CCP §§1953.10 to 1953.13
Guardianship (See **GUARDIAN AND WARD**)
Insurance underwriting committee, liability of accountant member of   CC §43.7
Mortgage financial statement   CC §§2943, 2954, 2954.2
Multiple-party accounts (See **MULTIPLE-PARTY ACCOUNTS**)
Natural disaster, destruction by   CCP §§1953.10 to 1953.13
Peer review committees, liability of   CC §43.7
Pleadings, allegations in   CCP §454
Power of attorney, duty to maintain accounts under   Pro §4236
Professional committee's proceeding against accountant, action for damages from   CC §43.7
Referee to examine or take account, appointment of   CCP §639
Review committees, liability of   CC §43.7
Seller assisted marketing plan, keeping records for   CC §1812.213
Special administrators rendering accounting   Pro §8546
Statutes of limitation
    Generally   CCP §337
    Accrual of cause on open account   CCP §344
    Book account defined   CCP §337a
    State or county hospitals, actions on accounts for support of patients at   CCP §345
    Unlawful disclosure by accounting companies   CC §1799.2
Stay of order to inspect corporate books   CCP §917.8
Transient occupancy in common interest developments, apartment buildings or single-family homes, recordkeeping required for accepting reservations or money for   CC §1864
Trust deed financial statements   CC §§2943, 2954, 2954.2
Trusts (See **TRUSTS**)
Uniform Transfers to Minors Act, petition for accounting by custodian under   Pro §3919
Veterans Administration, notice requirement for   Pro §1461.5

ACCRETION
Islands formed by, ownership of   CC §§1016, 1017
Land formed by, ownership of   CC §1014

ACCRUAL
Embezzlement   CCP §338
Fraud   CCP §338
Lapse of time for bringing action under laws of state where action has arisen, effect of   CCP §361
Open account, accrual of cause on   CCP §344

ACCURATE RECORDS UNDER INFORMATION PRACTICES ACT (See **INFORMATION PRACTICES ACT**)

ACKNOWLEDGMENTS
Assignment of judgment   CCP §673
Automobiles (See **AUTOMOBILES**)

ACKNOWLEDGMENTS—Cont.
Certificates
- Generally   CC §1188
- Fees
  - Superior court fees, specified services   Gov §70626
- Foreign countries   CC §1183
- Mistakes, correction of   CC §1202
- Other states' requirements for acknowledgments, California notaries' authorization to comply with   CC §1189
- Out-of-state acknowledgments   CC §§1182, 1189
- Proof of execution   CC §1200
- Signatures   CC §1193
- Writing as presumed authentication   Ev §1451

Chief Clerk of the Assembly, acknowledgments taken by   CC §§1180, 1181
Child born out of wedlock, prior acknowledgment of paternity by father maintaining action for injury to   CCP §376
City attorney, acknowledgments taken by   CC §1181
Clerks of court
- Generally   CC §§1180 to 1182
- Fees   Gov §26855

Commissioner, acknowledgments taken by   CC §§1182, 1183
Conservator, acknowledging receipt of information regarding duties and liabilities of   Pro §1834
Defects affecting notice of title   CC §1207
Deputies, acknowledgments taken by   CC §1184
District attorney, acknowledgments taken by   CC §1181
Enforcement of judgments (See **ENFORCEMENT OF JUDGMENTS**)
Failure of notary to obtain satisfactory evidence   CC §1185
Foreign countries, acknowledgment of instruments in   CC §§1183, 1183.5, 1189
Forms
- General form   CC §1189
- Notarial acts by officers in armed services   CC §1183.5

Hague Convention, acknowledgment in foreign countries affected by   CC §1183
Identification of person making acknowledgment   CC §§1185, 1196, 1197
Judges, acknowledgments taken by   CC §§1180 to 1183
Local officers, acknowledgments taken by   CC §1181
Military officers, acknowledgments taken by   CC §1183.5
Notaries public, acknowledgments taken by   CC §§1181 to 1183.5
- Scope of certification   CC §1189

Other states' requirements for acknowledgments, California notaries' authorization to comply with   CC §1189
Out-of-state acknowledgments   CC §§1182, 1189
Personal representatives filing acknowledgment of statement of duties and liabilities of office   CRC 7.150, Pro §8404
Proof of execution
- Generally   CC §1195
- Action for   CC §1203
- Authority of officer   CC §1201
- Certificate of proof   CC §§1195, 1200, 1202
- Facts to be proved   CC §1199
- Form for certificate of proof   CC §1195
- Handwriting as   CC §1198
- Recordation of instrument   CC §1204
- Retroactive laws   CC §§1205, 1206
- Subscribing witness   CC §§1196 to 1198

Recordation (See **RECORDS AND RECORDING**)
Renewing liability, acknowledgment or promise   CCP §360
Satisfaction of judgments (See **SATISFACTION OF JUDGMENTS**)
Seals
- Generally   CC §1193
- Military officers   CC §1183.5

Secretary of State, acknowledgments taken by   CC §§1180, 1181
Signatures of certificates by officers   CC §1193
Supervisors, county board of   CC §1181
Unacknowledged instruments (See within this heading, **"Proof of execution"**)
Wills (See **WILLS**)
Witnesses to   CC §1185

ACQUIRED IMMUNE DEFICIENCY SYNDROME (AIDS)
Employee's HIV status, limited confidentiality of   CC §56.31
Marriage license applicants informed about   Fam §358
Sale of real property, disclosure regarding occupant afflicted with AIDS on   CC §1710.2

ACTIONS
Abatement of (See **ABATEMENT**)
Age-appropriate design code
- No private actions to enforce provisions   CC §1798.99.35

As class of judicial remedy   CCP §21
Automated license plate recognition systems (ALPR), data security
- Breach of security   CC §1798.90.54

ACTIONS—Cont.
Automated license plate recognition systems (ALPR), data security—Cont.
- Unauthorized access or use of information   CC §1798.90.54

Basis of civil actions   CCP §25
Booking photographs
- Commercial use of booking photographs   CC §1798.91.1

Children and minors
- Immigration status irrelevant   CC §3339.5
- Minor maintaining action   Fam §6601

Child support enforcement   Fam §§4000, 4002
Civil actions (See **CIVIL ACTIONS**)
Coerced debt
- Causing another to incur coerced debt   CC §1798.97.2
  - Establishing debt as coerced   CC §1798.97.3
  - Notice of intent to file action   CC §1798.97.2

Commencement of actions (See **COMMENCEMENT OF ACTIONS**)
Commercial and industrial common interest developments
- Common areas, damage to common area   CC §6858
  - Comparative fault to reduce measure of damages   CC §6860
- Construction defects litigation
  - Member meeting prior to filing action   CC §6876
  - Settlement agreements   CC §6874
- Declarations, actions to enforce covenants and restrictions   CC §6856
  - Standing of association   CC §6858
- Separate interests, damage to separate interest   CC §6858
  - Comparative fault to reduce measure of damages   CC §6860

Common interest developments   CC §§5975 to 5986
- Alternative dispute resolution   CC §§5925 to 5965
- Board meetings
  - Actions for declaratory or equitable relief to enforce provisions   CC §4955
- Comparative fault reducing damage recovery   CC §5985
- Declarants, developers or builders, legal proceedings against   CC §5986
- Dispute resolution for disputes between association and member
  - Good faith engagement by association in dispute resolution required for association to file action   CC §5910.1
- Member elections
  - Action for declaratory or equitable relief to enforce   CC §5145
- Record inspection
  - Actions to enforce member rights   CC §5235
- Standing of association   CC §5980

Construction defects   CC §§895 to 945.5 (See **CONSTRUCTION DEFECTS, ACTIONS FOR**)
Consumer privacy rights
- Actions for damages, injunctions, declaratory relief, etc
  - Security practices and procedures not in place   CC §1798.150
- California privacy protection agency
  - Unpaid fines, actions to collect   CC §1798.199.75

Continuances
- Criminal cases   CRC 4.113, 4.115

Coordination of actions (See **COORDINATION OF ACTIONS**)
Credit reports
- Discouraging or prohibiting consumer access to credit report
  - State action for civil penalty   CC §1785.10.1

Criminal actions (See **CRIMINAL ACTIONS AND PROCEEDINGS**)
Customer records
- Disclosure of personal information of customer   CC §§1798.83, 1798.84

Dams
- Actions to restrain violations
  - Cost and fee awards to attorney general prevailing in actions   CCP §1021.8

Defined   CCP §22
Easements
- Failure of owner to pay cost of maintenance or repair of right of way   CC §845
- Owner or occupant, actions by   CC §§809, 810

Economic litigation procedures (See **ECONOMIC LITIGATION PROCEDURES**)
Electronic recording delivery systems
- Voidable transactions
  - Action for relief   Gov §27396

Embryos
- Unauthorized use or misuse of sperm, ova or embryo   CC §1708.5.6

Escrow agent rating service
- Agent's action to enforce obligations of service   CC §§1785.28, 1785.28.6

Evidence
- Preservation of evidence or perpetuation of testimony prior to filing action   CCP §§2035.010 to 2035.060

Fair debt buying practices
- Complaints
  - Contents   CC §1788.58

ACTIONS—Cont.
Fair debt buying practices—Cont.
Statute of limitations on debt
Actions brought after expiration of statute, prohibition CC §1788.56
Violation of provisions CC §1788.62
Fair debt settlement practices
Consumers
Actions to enforce CC §1788.305
Firearms and other weapons
Firearm industry standards of conduct
Actions against industry members for violation of standards CC §3273.52
Firearm manufacturer liability
Digital firearm manufacturing codes
Distribution to unauthorized persons CC §3273.61
Regulation or restriction of firearms
Recovery of attorney fees CCP §1021.11
Form of civil actions CCP §307
Genetic privacy
Enforcement of provisions CC §56.182
Groundwater rights actions CCP §§830 to 852 (See **GROUNDWATER RIGHTS ACTIONS**)
Health facilities
Force, threat or other obstruction of access to facility
Damages or injunctions, actions to enforce provisions CC §1708.9
Hospitals
Force, threat or other obstruction of access to facility
Damages or injunctions, actions to enforce provisions CC §1708.9
Hotels and motels
Cancellation of reservations, refunds
Action for violation of provisions CC §1748.83
Sex trafficking activity, hotel permitting or benefiting from
Actions against hotel for sex trafficking activity CC §52.65
Human trafficking CC §52.5
Entertainment facility tickets CC §52.66
Sex trafficking activity, hotel permitting or benefiting from
Actions against hotel for sex trafficking activity CC §52.65
Immigration status
Disclosure in open court
Civil actions Ev §351.3
Injury
As basis for action CCP §25
Types CCP §§27 to 29
Joinder of actions (See **JOINDER OF ACTIONS**)
Judicial arbitration CCP §§1141.11, 1141.12
When required CRC 3.811
Landlord and tenant
COVID-19 rental debt, actions to recover CCP §§871.10 to 871.12
Unduly influencing tenant to vacate CC §1940.2
Law and motion proceedings CRC 3.1100 to 3.1372 (See **LAW AND MOTION PROCEEDINGS**)
Legally protected health care services
Action for relief from abusive litigation infringing on protected activity CC §1798.303
Jurisdiction of court CC §§1798.306, 1798.308
Measure of damages CC §1798.305
Lien on cause of action CRC 3.1360
Limitation of actions (See **STATUTES OF LIMITATION**)
Limited civil cases (See **LIMITED CIVIL CASES**)
Marriage, action to establish validity Fam §309
Mechanics' liens, enforcement
Action to enforce lien CC §§8460 to 8470
Stop payment notices, enforcement of claim stated in notice CC §§8550 to 8560, 9500 to 9510
Merger of civil and criminal actions prohibited CCP §32
Minor maintaining Fam §6601
Nonimprisonment for debt or tort CCP §501
Object of action CCP §30
Obligation arising from contract or operation of law as basis CCP §26
Obscene and harmful matter
Electronic messages depicting obscene material
Knowingly sending unsolicited messages CC §1708.88
Unauthorized obscene material
Distribution CC §52.8
One form only CCP §307
Online violence prevention
Violent posts, removal
Order to remove, action seeking CC §1798.99.22
Ova
Unauthorized use or misuse of sperm, ova or embryo CC §1708.5.6

ACTIONS—Cont.
Parentage
Actions to determine parent and child relationship
Who may bring action Fam §7630
Parental authority, action for abuse Fam §7507
Parent's right to support, county to enforce Fam §4403
Parties
Designation of parties CCP §308
Generally (See **PARTIES**)
Pending actions (See **PENDENCY OF ACTIONS**)
Photographs of dead bodies, use in civil proceedings CCP §129
Pleadings (See **PLEADINGS**)
Political campaigns
Sale and manufacture of political items
Misrepresentation as to originality CC §1739.4
Preservation of evidence or perpetuation of testimony prior to filing action CCP §§2035.010 to 2035.060
Privacy
Customer use data for electrical or natural gas usage CC §1798.99
Photographs, films, etc., exposing intimate body parts or sexual acts of another without permission, distribution
Actions for injunctions, damages, etc CC §1708.85
Confidential information form CRCAppx A
Private student loan collections reform
Actions against creditor, lender or collector for violations of provisions CC §1788.208
Actions to collect
Complaints CC §1788.205
Real estate transfer disclosure statements
Actions, claims for damages, etc CC §1102.6
Rental passenger vehicle transactions
Actions for violation of provisions CC §1939.25
School grounds
Force, threat or other obstruction of access to facility
Damages or injunctions, actions to enforce provisions CC §1708.9
Sex trafficking activity, hotel permitting or benefiting from
Actions against hotel for sex trafficking activity CC §52.65
Sexual exploitation
Commercial sexual exploitation, minor or nonminor dependent victims CC §3345.1
Sexually explicit depiction of individual, creation or disclosure
Cause of action CC §1708.86
Sexual orientation violence CC §52.45
Short-term vacation rentals
Cancellation of reservations, refunds
Action for violation of provisions CC §1748.83
Small claims court (See **SMALL CLAIMS COURTS**)
Sperm
Unauthorized use or misuse of sperm, ova or embryo CC §1708.5.6
Spousal support, action to enforce right to Fam §4303
Stay of proceedings
Notice of stay, filing of CRC 3.650
Student borrower bill of rights
Enforcement of compliance with rights CC §1788.103
Subcutaneous implanting of identification device, requiring of another CC §52.7
Summary adjudication as to CCP §437c
Survival of actions (See **SURVIVAL OF ACTIONS**)
Time for commencing actions (See **STATUTES OF LIMITATION**)
Transfer of actions (See **TRANSFER OF ACTIONS**)
Types of actions CCP §24
Unclaimed deposits and payments, controller bringing up actions on CCP §1572
Unlimited civil cases
Appellate forms CRCAppx A
Usury
Payment of illegal interest
Rights of person paying CC §1916.12-3
Vexatious litigants (See **VEXATIOUS LITIGANTS**)
Video recordings of dead bodies, use in civil proceedings CCP §129
Witnesses
Preservation of evidence or perpetuation of testimony prior to filing action CCP §§2035.010 to 2035.060

ACTORS AND ACTRESSES
Child performers
Extras, background performers, etc
Trusts for percentage of earnings, exceptions to requirements Fam §6752
Vlogging, minors engaged in the work of Fam §§6650 to 6656
Employer and employee
Commercial online entertainment employment service providers
Age information of subscribers, restriction on disclosure CC §1798.83.5

ACTORS AND ACTRESSES—Cont.
Injunctive relief, applicability of   CCP §526
Minor's contracts for artistic services   Fam §§6750 to 6753

ACTORS FUND OF AMERICA
Minors, employment
   Arts, entertainment, and professional sports, contracts for employment in
      Trust for portion of gross earnings, fund's duties as to   Fam §6752

ACTS (See **CITATION OF ACTS**)

ACTS OF GOD (See **NATURAL CATASTROPHES**)

ACUPUNCTURISTS
Discovery of records of health care professional review committees   Ev §1157
Monetary liability of   CC §43.7

ADDING MACHINES
Serial number destroyed or altered prior to sale   CC §1710.1

ADDITIONAL WRITS OF ATTACHMENT (See **ATTACHMENT**)

ADDRESS
Adoption proceedings, address information of birth parent in (See **ADOPTION**)
Adoption proceedings, address of birth parents   Fam §§8702, 8703, 8818, 8819
Apartment building owner, notice of address of   CC §§1962, 1962.5
Appellate rules, superior court appeals
   Address of record
      Notice of change   CRC 8.816
Change of address
   Appeals
      Electronic filing, when required   CRCSupp 1st AppDist
      Service and filing notice of change   CRC 8.32
   Conservators
      Residence of conservatee   CRC 7.1063
   Credit card issuers
      Notice to cardholder   CC §1799.1b
      Verification of change of address for offeree or cardholder   CC §1747.06
   Earnings assignment for support   Fam §5237
   Electronic filing and service rules
      Change of electronic service address   CRC 2.251
   Guardian and ward
      Ward's residence, change   CRC 7.1013
   Service and filing of notice of   CRC 2.200
   Telephone accounts
      Notice to account holder   CC §1799.1b
Common interest developments
   Record inspection
      Safe at home program participants, duties of association   CC §5216
Confidentiality
   Reproductive health care service providers
      Address confidentiality for reproductive health care service providers, employees, volunteers and patients   Gov §§6215 to 6218.5
   Victims of certain crimes   Gov §§6205 to 6211
      Actions, confidentiality requirements for protected persons in civil proceeding   CCP §367.3
      Judicial council forms   CRCAppx A, Fam §6226.5
      Name change proceedings under address confidentiality program   CRC 2.575 to 2.577
Credit card issuers
   Change of address requests
      Notice to cardholder   CC §1799.1b
      Verification of change of address for offeree or cardholder   CC §1747.06
Domestic violence
   Emergency protective orders
      Prohibition on obtaining address or location of protected person   Fam §6252.5
   Ex parte protective orders
      Prohibition on obtaining address or location of protected person   Fam §6322.7
   Protection order, address of applicant for   Fam §6225
Electronic filing and service rules
   Change of electronic service address   CRC 2.251
Executor residing out of state as required to furnish address   Pro §8573
Family rules
   Default
      Service address requirement   CRC 5.402
Identity theft
   Credit reports
      Verification of addresses by users of credit reports   CC §1785.20.3
Information Practices Act (See **INFORMATION PRACTICES ACT**)

ADDRESS—Cont.
Intangible personalty escheated, determining address of owner of   CCP §1510
Juror personal information (See **JURY**)
Letters correctly addressed and posted presumed to be received   Ev §641
Marriage licenses
   Options for address   Fam §§351.5, 351.6
Money orders, determining address of purchaser of   CCP §§1511, 1513, 1542, 1581
Sex offenses, exclusion as evidence of address and telephone number of victims of   Ev §352.1
Telephone accounts
   Change of address requests
      Notice to account holder   CC §1799.1b
Traveler's checks, determining address of purchaser of   CCP §§1511, 1513, 1542, 1581
Trial court rules
   Attorneys, address
      Papers, first page format and content   CRC 2.111
   Service and filing notice of change of party or attorney address   CRC 2.200
Unknown address
   Family rules
      Service of process by publication or posting   CRC 5.72
   Missing persons (See **MISSING PERSONS**)
   Service of papers (See **SERVICE OF PAPERS**)

ADEQUATE REMEDY AT LAW
Injunction in absence of   CC §3422, CCP §526
Specific performance of   CC §3387

ADHESION, CONTRACTS OF
Time for performance
   Reasonable time required in contracts of adhesion   CC §1657.1

ADJACENT COUNTIES
Small claims court advisory services   CCP §116.940

ADJACENT LANDOWNERS
Appurtenance   CC §662
Boundaries   CC §§829 to 835 (See **BOUNDARIES**)
Covenants, duties under   CC §§1469, 1470
Easement rights to natural support   CC §801
Electrified security fences   CC §835
Excavations endangering   CC §832
Fences (See **FENCES**)
Fixtures mistakenly placed on adjoining land   CC §1013.5
Good faith improver (See **GOOD FAITH IMPROVER**)
Lateral support from adjoining property, right to   CC §832
Overhanging trees, ownership of   CC §§833, 834
Streets and highways (See **STREETS AND HIGHWAYS**)
Support from   CC §832
Trees with roots extending on adjacent land, ownership of   CC §§833, 834

ADJOURNMENTS
Arbitration (See **ARBITRATION**)
Courts of appeal   CCP §42
Judge's absence   CCP §139
Judicial holidays, effect of   CCP §136
Jury absence permitting   CCP §617
Superior court adjournments construed as recesses   CCP §74
Supreme Court   CCP §42
U.S.Congress (See **CONGRESS**)

ADJUSTABLE RATE MORTGAGE LOANS (See **TRUST DEEDS AND MORTGAGES**)

ADMINISTRATION OF ESTATES (See also **EXECUTORS AND ADMINISTRATORS; WILL PROBATE**)
Abandonment of property
   Generally   Pro §9780
   Consent to   Pro §9785
   Court authorization   Pro §9781
   Independent administration   Pro §10513
   Notice requirements   Pro §§9782, 9785, 9786
   Objecting party
      Generally   Pro §9783
      Tender of property to   Pro §9788
   Order restraining   Pro §9784
   Tender of property to objecting party   Pro §9788
   Waiver
      Court review waived   Pro §9787
      Notice, waiver of   Pro §9785

ADMINISTRATION OF ESTATES—Cont.
Abatement of bequests
    Class of legatees, order of priority for abatement of bequests within   Pro §21403
    Contributions by devisees and legatees after sale of estate property, requirement of   Pro §21405
    Debts and expenses of estate administration, priority of   Pro §21400
    Rules applicable to   Pro §21401
    Transitional provision   Pro §21406
Accounting
    Executors and administrators (See **EXECUTORS AND ADMINISTRATORS**)
Additional or further notice, requirements of   Pro §1202
Administrators with will annexed (See **ADMINISTRATORS WITH WILL ANNEXED**)
Advice of proposed action (See **INDEPENDENT ADMINISTRATION OF ESTATES ACT**)
Affidavits
    Admissible evidence   Pro §1022
    Publication of notice of hearing, affidavit of   Pro §8124
Alien or foreign citizen, notice of death of   Pro §8113
Ancillary administration (See **ANCILLARY ADMINISTRATION**)
Annuities, will instruction authorizing purchase of   Pro §9733
Appeals
    Generally   Pro §§1300, 1303
    Costs on appeal   Pro §1002
    Executors and administrators (See **EXECUTORS AND ADMINISTRATORS**)
    Judgment roll for   Pro §1050
    Stay on appeal   Pro §1310
Appraisals
    Generally   Pro §8900
    Attorney, compensation for appraisal as extraordinary services by   Pro §8907
    Binding effect of agreement to partition by   CCP §873.970
    Bond, statement concerning sufficiency of   CRC 7.501
    Change of ownership statement, filing of   Pro §8800
    Compensation for appraisal as extraordinary services by personal representative or attorney   Pro §8907
    Filing requirements   Pro §§8800 to 8804
        Compliance with filing provisions   Pro §1456.5
    Grazing land, sale of   Pro §10207
    Independent expert, appraisal by   Pro §§8900, 8904
    Objection to   Pro §8906
    Personal representative, appraisal by
        Generally   Pro §8900
        Compensation of appraisal as extraordinary services   Pro §8907
        Items subject to appraisal   Pro §8901
    Probate referee, appraisal by
        Generally   Pro §§8900, 8902
        Reports by   Pro §8908
        Retention of records   Pro §8909
        Waiver of   Pro §8903
    Small estates, appraisal of (See **SMALL ESTATES WITHOUT ADMINISTRATION**)
    Status report   Pro §§8940, 8941
    Transitional provision   Pro §8980
    Verification of   Pro §8905
Assignment of real property sales contract after confirmation   Pro §10314
Attorney General, notice to   Pro §§1209, 8111
Attorneys' fees
    Generally   Pro §10810
    Accounting actions, defense of   Pro §11003
    Appraisal of property as extraordinary services, compensation for   Pro §8907
    Extraordinary services
        Generally   Pro §10811
        Appraisal of property, compensation for   Pro §8907
        Special administrator, attorney for   Pro §8547
    In excess of statutory amount, validity of compensation where   Pro §10813
    Order for reduction of   Pro §12205
    Ordinary services, compensation for   Pro §10810
    Personal representative as attorney, compensation of   Pro §10804
    Special administrator, extraordinary services for   Pro §8547
    Two or more attorneys, apportionment of compensation for   Pro §10814
    Will provision for compensation, effect of   Pro §10812
Auctions
    Public sales generally (See within this heading, "**Public sales**")
Beneficiaries
    Death
        Notice   CRC 7.51

ADMINISTRATION OF ESTATES—Cont.
Bonds, corporate
    Depositories for   Pro §9702
    Investment in   Pro §9730
    Sales   Pro §10200
    Subscription rights   Pro §§9735, 10200
Bonds, surety (See **EXECUTORS AND ADMINISTRATORS**)
Borrowing money
    Loans generally (See within this heading, "**Loans**")
Brokers
    Compensation of   Pro §§10161 to 10166
    Employment   CRC 7.453, Pro §10150
Businesses
    Continuation (See within this heading, "**Continuation of business**")
Change of ownership statement for property owned at time of death, filing of   Pro §8800
Citations, issuance of   Pro §§1240 to 1242
Claims against decedents' estates (See **CLAIMS AGAINST ESTATES**)
Class of legatees, priority of abatement of bequests within   Pro §21403
Closing estate administration, procedure for   Pro §§12200 to 12206
Commodities sold short   Pro §9735
Common trust funds, investment in   Pro §9730
Community property not requiring administration (See **SMALL ESTATES WITHOUT ADMINISTRATION**)
Compensation
    Attorneys' fees (See within this heading, "**Attorneys' fees**")
    Personal representatives (See **EXECUTORS AND ADMINISTRATORS**)
Compromise and settlement of claims (See **EXECUTORS AND ADMINISTRATORS**)
Conditional sales of personalty   Pro §§10257, 10258
Confirmation
    Generally   Pro §9611
    Conveyance of property after confirmation   Pro §10314
    Default of purchaser, vacating confirmation of sale on   Pro §§10350, 10351
    Notice of hearing
        Personal property sales   Pro §10260
        Real property sales   Pro §10308
    Objections
        Personal property sales, objections to   Pro §10261
        Real property sales, objections to   Pro §10310
    Partnership interest of decedent, sale of   Pro §10261
    Perishables, sale of   Pro §10259
    Personal property sales
        Generally   Pro §10260
        Bids at confirmation hearing, offer of   Pro §10262
        Exceptions to confirmation requirement   Pro §10259
        Objection to confirmation   Pro §10261
        Partnership interest, sale of   Pro §10261
        Perishables, sale of   Pro §10259
        Petition   Pro §10260
        Procedural errors, effect of   Pro §10264
        Proof of notice of sale   Pro §10263
        Refusal by fiduciary to show property to prospective buyers, effect of   CRC 7.451
        Vacating sale after confirmation, court order for   Pro §§10350, 10351
    Petition for hearing
        Attorney or petitioner presence required at confirmation hearing   CRC 7.452
        Personal property sales   Pro §10260
        Real property sales   Pro §10308
    Real property sales   Pro §§10308 to 10310
        Appearance at confirmation hearing   CRC 7.452
        Assignment of property after   Pro §10314
        Bids at confirmation hearing, offer of   Pro §10311
        Conveyance of property after   Pro §10314
        Issuance of order for   Pro §10313
        Objections to   Pro §10310
        Petition   Pro §10308
        Procedural errors, effect of   Pro §10316
        Proof of notice of sale   Pro §10312
        Refusal by fiduciary to show property to prospective buyers   CRC 7.451
        Vacating order of confirmation   Pro §§10350, 10351
    Small estates without administration (See **SMALL ESTATES WITHOUT ADMINISTRATION**)
    Vacating order of confirmation   Pro §§10350, 10351
Consent
    Abandonment of property, consent to   Pro §9785
    Sale of estate property to personal representative, consent of heirs to   Pro §9881
Conservatorships (See **CONSERVATORS**)

ADMINISTRATION OF ESTATES—Cont.
  Continuance or postponement
    Hearings
      Generally   Pro §1045
      Notice of continued or postponed hearings   Pro §1205
    Sales, postponement of
      Personal property sales   Pro §10254
      Real property sales   CRC 7.451, Pro §10305
  Continuation of business
    Additional powers of independent administrator   Pro §10534
    Advice of proposed action   Pro §10512
    Court authorizing   Pro §9760
    Partnerships   Pro §§9762, 9763
  Contracts
    Personal representative, validity of contracts with decedent for purchase of estate property by   Pro §9884
    Real property sales generally (See within this heading, **"Real property sales"**)
  Contributions by devisees and legatees after sale of estate property for purposes of abatement, requirement of   Pro §21405
  Control of decedent's property during   Pro §§7000, 7001
  Conveyance or transfer of property claimed by decedent or other person   Pro §§805 to 859
  Corporate bonds (See within this heading, **"Bonds, corporate"**)
  Corporate stock
    Generally   Pro §10200
    Commodities sold short   Pro §9735
    Completion of securities transaction initiated by decedent   Pro §9735
    Conversion of securities   Pro §10200
    Depository for   Pro §9702
    Holder of securities, personal representative as
      Generally   Pro §9736
      Independent administrator   Pro §10560
    Independent administrator, authority of   Pro §10560
    Investment of estate funds in   Pro §9730
    Redemption of   Pro §10200
    Sales
      Generally   Pro §10200
      Completion of sales transactions initiated by decedent   Pro §9735
      Mutual capital certificates   Pro §10201
      Short sales   Pro §9735
    Short sales   Pro §9735
    Subscription rights   Pro §§9735, 10200
    Undelivered securities   Pro §9735
    Voting
      Generally   Pro §9655
      Independent administrators   Pro §10560
  Costs
    Generally   Pro §1002
    Claims against decedent's estate (See **CLAIMS AGAINST ESTATES**)
    Family allowance proceedings   Pro §6544
    Personal representative, liability of   CCP §1026
    Preliminary distribution proceedings   Pro §11624
  Cotenancy interest, estate sale of   Pro §10006
  County treasurer
    Copy of decree of distribution to   Pro §11853
    Deposit of funds with   Pro §§11850 to 11854
  Court supervision of (See **EXECUTORS AND ADMINISTRATORS**)
  Creditors' claims (See **CLAIMS AGAINST ESTATES**)
  Credit sales of estate property
    Personal property sales   Pro §§10257, 10258
    Real property sales   Pro §10315
  Cum testamento annexo (See **ADMINISTRATORS WITH WILL ANNEXED**)
  Damages
    Sales   Pro §10380
      Liquidated damages   Pro §10381
  De bonis non administration   Pro §12252
  Debts
    Generally   Pro §9650
    Abatement of estate property in satisfaction of   Pro §21401
    Accounting, generally (See **EXECUTORS AND ADMINISTRATORS**)
    Claims presented on (See **CLAIMS AGAINST ESTATES**)
    Continuation of administration in satisfaction of   Pro §11640
    Contribution for abatement by beneficiaries   Pro §21405
    Funeral expenses (See **FUNERALS**)
    Last illness (See **LAST ILLNESS**)
    Loans to estate
      Loans generally (See within this heading, **"Loans"**)
    Sale of property for satisfaction of   Pro §10000
    Unpaid debts after first order for payment, satisfaction of   Pro §11640
  Deceased distributees   Pro §§11801, 11802

ADMINISTRATION OF ESTATES—Cont.
  Decrees
    Judgments and decrees
      Claims against estates (See **CLAIMS AGAINST ESTATES**)
      Generally (See within this heading, **"Judgments and decrees"**)
  Deeds, execution of
    Completion of decedent's contract to convey by personal representative   Pro §§850 to 859
    Confirmation of sale, pursuant to order of   Pro §10314
  Delivery costs as expenses of   Pro §11754
  Deposit of funds
    County treasurer, deposit with   Pro §§11850 to 11854
    Direct distribution by depository   Pro §9704
    Independent administration   Pro §10533
    Insured accounts   Pro §§8401, 9700
    Interest on deposits in trust companies   Pro §9705
    Personal property, deposit of   Pro §9701
    Petitioner for letters, effect of deposits by   Pro §8401
    Securities, deposit of   Pro §9702
    State of California, deposit with   Pro §§11900 to 11904
    Unclaimed property (See **UNCLAIMED PROPERTY**)
    Withdrawal of accounts be subject to court order, personal representative requesting   Pro §9703
  Disclaimer of testamentary interest   Pro §§260 to 295
  Discovery
    Conveyance or transfer of property claimed by decedent or other person   Pro §851.1
    Law and motion rules
      Applicable to discovery proceedings in probate   CRC 3.1100
  Distributions
    Ancillary administration (See **ANCILLARY ADMINISTRATION**)
    Assignment of beneficiary's interest   Pro §11604.5
    Character of property, allegations in petition   CRC 7.652
    Deceased distributees   Pro §§11801, 11802
    Deposit of funds generally (See within this heading, **"Deposit of funds"**)
    Discharge of executors and administrators   Pro §§12250 to 12252
    Final distribution (See within this subheading, "Final distribution")
    General provisions   Pro §§11750 to 11753
    Heirship, determination of   Pro §§11700 to 11705
    Income during administration, accrual of   Pro §§12000 to 12007
    Notice of hearing   Pro §11601
    Orders   Pro §§11603 to 11605
    Petition
      Generally   Pro §11600
      Parties with standing to oppose   Pro §11602
      Property description in petition for distribution   CRC 7.651
    Preliminary distribution   Pro §§11620 to 11624
      Ancillary administration   Pro §12540
    Testamentary trust, decree of distribution establishing   CRC 7.650
  Encumbrances
    Liens
      Claims based on liens (See **CLAIMS AGAINST ESTATES**)
      Generally (See within this heading, **"Liens"**)
  Enforcement of judgments
    Claims against estates (See **CLAIMS AGAINST ESTATES**)
    Generally (See within this heading, **"Judgments and decrees"**)
  Entry and filing of orders   Pro §1048
  Escheat proceedings (See **ESCHEAT**)
  Estate tax (See **ESTATE TAX**)
  Exchange of property
    Generally   Pro §9920
    Notice of hearing on   Pro §§1200, 9922
    Petition for   Pro §9921
    Procedural errors, effect of   Pro §9923
  Exempt property, petition to set aside   Pro §§6510, 6511
  Ex parte communications
    Restrictions   Pro §1051
  Expenses of administration
    Abatement of estate property in satisfaction of   Pro §21401
    Attorneys' fees (See within this heading, **"Attorneys' fees"**)
    Auctioneer's fees   Pro §§10160 to 10168
    Broker's fees   Pro §§10160 to 10166
    Costs
      Claims against estates (See **CLAIMS AGAINST ESTATES**)
      Generally (See within this heading, **"Costs"**)
    Executors and administrators, compensation of (See **EXECUTORS AND ADMINISTRATORS**)
  Extension and shortening of time
    Continuances or postponements (See within this heading, **"Continuance or postponement"**)
    Notices, shortening time of (See within this heading, **"Notices"**)

ADMINISTRATION OF ESTATES—Cont.
Fact of death proceedings combined with administration of estate proceedings Pro §202
Family allowance (See **FAMILY ALLOWANCE**)
Family home, right to temporary possession of Pro §§6500, 6501
Final distribution
    Generally Pro §§11640 to 11642
    Ancillary administration Pro §12540
    Claims against estate, listing CRC 7.403
    Newly acquired property
        De bonis non administration of Pro §12252
        Final distribution order, effect on Pro §11642
    Report CRC 7.403, Pro §§12200 to 12202
    Testamentary trust, decree of distribution establishing CRC 7.650
    Time limit
        Statutory limits on administration Pro §12200
        Testator's time limits on administration, effect of Pro §12206
    Unpaid creditors after final distribution, rights of Pro §11429
    Whereabouts unknown of distributee Pro §11603
Floating homes, sale of CC §800.88
Foreign citizen, notice of death of Pro §8113
Foreign wills, administration pursuant to Pro §§12520, 12521, 12523, 12524
Fraud
    Discovery of decedent's assets wrongfully held by another, personal representative's petition for Pro §§8870 to 8873
    Sale of estate assets by personal representative, limitation of actions to recover property in cases of fraudulent Pro §10382
    Voidable transactions by decedent, recovering property transferred under Pro §9653
Good faith, attempt to comply with publication requirements in Pro §8122
Guardianships (See **GUARDIAN AND WARD**)
Hearings
    Clerk, matter set for hearing by Pro §1041
    Continuance or postponement (See within this heading, **"Continuance or postponement"**)
    Conveyance or transfer of property claimed by decedent or other person Pro §851
        Discovery Pro §851.1
    Heirship determination Pro §11704
    Lease transactions, authorization for Pro §9945
    Loans, authorization for Pro §9804
    Missing person presumed dead, estate of (See **MISSING PERSONS**)
    Necessity for sale of estate property, hearing for determining Pro §10001
    Notices of (See within this heading, **"Notices"**)
    Partition before distribution Pro §11952
    Postponement Pro §1205
    Rules of procedure governing Pro §1040
    Trials generally (See within this heading, **"Trials"**)
Heirship proceedings (See **HEIRS**)
Homesteads (See **HOMESTEADS**)
Income
    Accrual of income during administration Pro §§12000 to 12007
    Collection of Pro §§9650, 9651
Incompetent's share, deposit of Pro §§11850 to 11854
Independent Administration of Estates Act (See **INDEPENDENT ADMINISTRATION OF ESTATES ACT**)
Inheritance tax (See **INHERITANCE TAX**)
Insurance
    Liability insurance
        Claims against estates (See **CLAIMS AGAINST ESTATES**)
        Obtaining Pro §9656
Interested parties
    Conservatee as interested person Pro §1210
    Request for special notices by Pro §§1250 to 1252
    United States as Pro §7280
    Ward as interested person Pro §1210
Interest income
    Legacies and devises, interest on Pro §§12000 to 12007
    Trust companies, interest on deposits in Pro §9705
Inventory
    Bond, statement concerning sufficiency of CRC 7.501
    Change of ownership statement, filing of Pro §8800
    Concealed property Pro §§8870 to 8873
    Contents of Pro §8850
    Discharge of debt by will devise, effect of Pro §8851
    Filing requirements Pro §§8800 to 8804
        Compliance with filing requirements Pro §1456.5
    Oath of personal representative Pro §8852
    Small estates, summary administration of (See **SMALL ESTATES WITHOUT ADMINISTRATION**)
    Transitional provision Pro §8980

ADMINISTRATION OF ESTATES—Cont.
Investments
    Bonds Pro §9730
    Cash in possession, duty to invest Pro §9652
    Common trust fund Pro §9730
    Mutual funds Pro §9730
    Surplus moneys Pro §9732
    United States obligations, investments in Pro §§9730, 9731
Judge, disqualification of
    Generally Pro §7060
    Transfer of proceedings resulting from Pro §§7070 to 7072
Judgment roll of proceedings Pro §1050
Judgments and decrees Pro §§1046 to 1051
    Claims against estates (See **CLAIMS AGAINST ESTATES**)
    Escheat CCP §1423
    Final distribution, order for Pro §11640
    Final judgment, effect of Pro §7250
    Judgment roll Pro §1050
Jurisdiction
    Generally Pro §§7050, 7051
    Ancillary administration Pro §§12590, 12591
    Loan authorization and enforcement Pro §9806
    Missing person presumed dead, estate of Pro §12403
    Transfer of proceedings Pro §§7070 to 7072
Jury trial, right to Pro §825
Known heirs or devisees, notice to Pro §§1206, 8110
Law and motion rules
    Applicable to discovery proceedings in probate CRC 3.1100
Leases
    Defined Pro §9940
    Execution of lease by personal representative Pro §9948
    Maximum period of Pro §9947
    Oil and gas leases (See within this heading, **"Oil and gas leases"**)
    Procedure for obtaining lease Pro §§9941 to 9948
    Sale of leasehold interest Pro §10203
    Short term lease Pro §9941
    Terms of lease agreements Pro §9946
Letters of administration (See **EXECUTORS AND ADMINISTRATORS**)
Liability insurance
    Claims against estate, effect on (See **CLAIMS AGAINST ESTATES**)
    General provision for obtaining liability insurance Pro §9656
Liens
    Claims based on (See **CLAIMS AGAINST ESTATES**)
    Independent administrator Pro §10514
    Sale of property subject to Pro §§10360 to 10363
    Special administrators paying Pro §8544
Lis pendens, filing notice of Pro §§1004, 9354
Loans
    Deficiency judgment Pro §9807
    Hearing on petition to encumber estate property Pro §9804
    Independent administrator, authorization for Pro §10514
    Notes, authority for executing Pro §§9805, 9806
    Notice of hearing for Pro §9803
    Order authorizing borrowing money Pro §9804
    Petition for authorization Pro §9802
    Sale of estate assets on credit
        Personal property Pro §§10257, 10258
        Real property Pro §10315
    Security interest, authorizing estate property as Pro §§9800, 9801
    Shift-in-land-use loans Pro §10207
    Special administrator, authority of Pro §8544
Mailing of notice
    General requirements for mailing notices Pro §§1215, 1217
    Hearing, mailing notice of Pro §1220
    Proof of mailing of notice Pro §1261
Minor's share, deposit of Pro §§11850 to 11854
Missing persons (See **MISSING PERSONS**)
Mobilehomes, sale of CC §798.78
Mortgages
    Trust deeds
        Claims against estates (See **CLAIMS AGAINST ESTATES**)
        Generally (See within this heading, **"Trust deeds"**)
Mutual funds, investment in Pro §9730
Newly acquired property after final distribution
    De bonis non administration Pro §12252
    Effect on final distribution order Pro §11642
Newspapers of general circulation, publishing notice of administration of estate in Pro §8121
New trial, motion for Pro §7220

ADMINISTRATION OF ESTATES—Cont.
Nonresidents
    Ancillary administration of nonresident decedent's estate (See **ANCILLARY ADMINISTRATION**)
    Executor or administrator, nonresident as   Pro §§8572 to 8577
    Jurisdiction for nonresident decedent's estate   Pro §7052
    Notice of death of foreign citizen   Pro §8113
    Surviving spouse's right of election in California real property of nondomiciliary decedent   Pro §120
No property subject to administration, petition to terminate further estate proceedings where   Pro §12251
Notes, authority for executing   Pro §§9805, 9806
Notices
    Generally   Pro §1042
    Abandonment proceedings   Pro §§9782, 9785, 9786
    Additional or further notice, requirements of   Pro §1202
    Address unknown, procedure for notice where   Pro §1212
    Advice of proposed action   Pro §10510
    Attorney as proper recipient of notices to parties   Pro §1214
    Attorney General, notice to   Pro §§1209, 8111
    Citations, issuance of   Pro §§1240 to 1242
    Confirmation proceedings, notice of hearing   Pro §§10260, 10308
    Contents of notice
        Hearing, notice of   Pro §1230
        Personal property sales   Pro §10253
        Real property sales   Pro §10304
    Continued or postponed hearings, notice of   Pro §1205
    Creditors filing claims against estate, notice to (See **CLAIMS AGAINST ESTATES**)
    Credit sales of personal property   Pro §10258
    Delivery of notice
        Methods   Pro §1215
    Distribution of assets, notice of hearing   Pro §11601
    Encumbered property, notice of hearing to determine administration expenses payable from proceeds of sale of   Pro §10361.6
    Evidence at hearing of proof of notice   Pro §1266
    Exceptions
        Parent-child relationships   Pro §1207
        Petitioners in action   Pro §1201
    Foreign citizen, notice of death of   Pro §8113
    Further notice, requirements of   Pro §1202
    General notice provisions   Pro §§1200 to 1214
    Good faith, attempt to comply with notice requirements in   Pro §8122
    Governing law   Pro §1200
    Heirship determination proceedings   Pro §11701
    Known heirs or devisees, notice to   Pro §§1206, 8110
    Lease transactions, notice of hearing on petition to authorize   Pro §9944
    Lis pendens, filing notice of   Pro §§1004, 9354
    Loans, application for   Pro §9803
    Mailing of (See within this heading, **"Mailing of notice"**)
    Missing persons (See **MISSING PERSONS**)
    Necessity of estate property sales, hearing to determine   Pro §10001
    Nonresident decedents' estate   Pro §§12510, 12521
    Parent-child relationship, giving notice where   Pro §1207
    Partition before distribution, proceedings for   Pro §11952
    Personal delivery
        Proof of   Pro §1264
    Petitioner, requirement of notice to   Pro §1201
    Petition, notice of
        Publication of notice of petition to administer estate   CRC 7.54
    Posting or publication of notice (See within this heading, **"Posting or publication"**)
    Postponed hearing, notice of   Pro §1205
    Procedure for giving   Pro §§1200 to 1266
    Proof of notice
        Evidence at hearing of   Pro §1266
        Hearing, proof of notice of   Pro §1260
        Personal delivery   Pro §1264
    Publication of notices (See within this heading, **"Posting or publication"**)
    Public entity claimants, notification of   Pro §8112
    Realty sales   Pro §§10300 to 10304
    Request for special notice   Pro §§1250 to 1252
    Service of   Pro §§8110 to 8113
    Shortening time of notice
        Hearing, notice of   Pro §1203
        Personal property sales, notice of   Pro §10251
        Real property sales, notice of   Pro §10302
    Special notice, request for   Pro §§1250 to 1252
    Statutory form of notice of hearing   Pro §1211
    Surety, notice to   Pro §1213

ADMINISTRATION OF ESTATES—Cont.
Notices—Cont.
    Title and ownership, third party claims to   Pro §851
        Discovery   Pro §851.1
    Trust beneficiaries, notice to   Pro §1208
    Type size requirements   Pro §8123
    Unspecified mode of giving notice of hearing, procedure for   Pro §1221
    Waiver of   Pro §1204
Oil and gas leases
    Generally   Pro §§9946, 9947
    Principal and income allocations   CC §731.11
    Sale of leasehold interest   Pro §10203
Opening estate administration   Pro §§8000 to 8577
Options
    Conveyance of property pursuant to option in will, procedure for   Pro §§9980 to 9983
    Final distribution subject to   Pro §11603
    Independent administrator, options exercised by (See **INDEPENDENT ADMINISTRATION OF ESTATES ACT**)
    Nontransferable options rights held by decedent's estate, personal representative exercising   Pro §9734
    Personal representative
        Nontransferable options rights to be exercised by   Pro §9734
        Purchase of options by personal representative, will provision authorizing   Pro §9885
    Real property options
        Generally   Pro §9960
        Minimum purchase price   Pro §9962
        Notice of hearing   Pro §9963
        Order granting   Pro §9964
        Petition   Pro §9961
        Procedural errors, effect of   Pro §9966
        Recorded option, effect of expiration of   Pro §9965
    Testamentary disposition of options
        Generally   Pro §9980
        Creditors' rights, protection of   Pro §9982
        Notice of hearing on   Pro §9981
        Personal representative, will authorizing purchase by   Pro §9885
        Petition   Pro §9981
        Procedural errors, effect of   Pro §9983
Orders
    Generally   Pro §1046
    Borrowing money, order authorizing   Pro §9804
    Closing of estate   Pro §§12200 to 12206
    Contents of   Pro §1047
    County treasurer, copy of decree of distribution to   Pro §11853
    Distribution of estate   Pro §§11603 to 11605
    Encumbering estate property, order authorizing   Pro §9804
    Enforcement of   Pro §1049
    Entry and filing of   Pro §1048
    Final distribution order   Pro §§11640 to 11642
    Final orders, effect of   Pro §7250
    Judgments and decrees generally (See within this heading, **"Judgments and decrees"**)
    Lease transactions, order authorizing   Pro §9945
    Preliminary distribution order   Pro §11603
    Prior law, effect of   Pro §3
    Recital of jurisdictional facts in   Pro §1047
    Recordation of orders affecting real property   Pro §7263
    Rules of procedure governing   Pro §1040
    Vacating sale
        Defaulting purchaser, order vacating sale   Pro §§10350, 10351
        Real property sales, order vacating   Pro §10313
Ownership
    Title generally (See within this heading, **"Title"**)
Parties
    Interested parties (See within this heading, **"Interested parties"**)
Partition proceedings
    Appraisal, binding effect of partition by   CCP §873.970
    Heirs, proceedings for distribution of estate to   Pro §§11950 to 11956
    Joinder of personal representative   CCP §872.530
    Personal representative as party against cotenants in partition of decedent's undivided interest   Pro §9823
Partnership interests
    Generally   Pro §§9761, 9763
    Sale of interest
        Generally   Pro §10204
        Confirmation of   Pro §10261
Perishable property, sale of   Pro §§10252, 10259
Personal delivery of notice
    Proof of notice   Pro §1264

ADMINISTRATION OF ESTATES—Cont.
  Personal property
    Sale of
      Ex parte application for order   CRC 7.454
    Specific performance of contract to transfer personal property, action for   Pro §§850 to 859
  Personal representatives in general (See **EXECUTORS AND ADMINISTRATORS**)
  Petitions
    Confirmation of sale   Pro §§10260, 10308
    Deposited shares of estate, petition to recover   Pro §11854
    Disclaimer of interest   Pro §§260 to 295
    Distribution of assets (See within this heading, **"Distributions"**)
    Encumbered property, petition to determine administration expenses payable from proceeds of sale of   Pro §§10361.5, 10361.6
    Exchange of property, authorization for   Pro §9921
    Executor or administrator's fees, partial allowance of   Pro §10830
    Exempt property, set aside of   Pro §§6510, 6511
    Hearing to order sale of assets, petition for   Pro §10001
    Heirship determination   Pro §11700
    Lease by estate   Pro §9943
    Loans obtained by estate   Pro §9802
    Missing person presumed dead (See **MISSING PERSONS**)
    Nonresident decedents' estate   Pro §§12510, 12521
    Notice of petition to administer estate
      Publication   CRC 7.54
    Options
      Real property options (See within this heading, **"Options"**)
    Specific performance to convey or transfer property claimed by decedent or other person   Pro §850
    Temporary possession of family home and property, right to   Pro §6501
    Termination of further estate proceedings, petition for   Pro §12251
    Title and ownership, third party claims to   Pro §850
    Verification generally (See within this heading, **"Verification"**)
    Writing requirements   Pro §1020
  Posthumous children (See **POSTHUMOUS CHILDREN**)
  Posting or publication
    Generally   Pro §§1230, 8120
    Affidavit of publication, filing of   Pro §8124
    Courthouse, posting at   Pro §1230
    Creditors, notices to   Pro §§8112, 9001
    General requirements for posting notice of hearing   Pro §1230
    Good faith attempt to comply with notice requirements, sufficiency of   Pro §8122
    Missing person's estates, hearing on   Pro §12405
    Newspapers in general circulation, notice of hearing in   Pro §8121
    Proof of posting   Pro §1263
    Proof of publication   Pro §1262
    Specific performance, notice of hearing for   Pro §851
    Subsequent publication of notice, requirements for   Pro §8125
  Postponements (See within this heading, **"Continuance or postponement"**)
  Preliminary distribution
    Generally   Pro §§11620 to 11624
    Ancillary administration   Pro §12540
  Principal and income allocations   CC §§731 to 731.05
    Animals   CC §731.10
    Bonds or obligations to pay money   CC §731.08
    Continuation of business, use of principal for   CC §731.09
    Corporate assets   CC §§731.05, 731.07
    Definitions   CC §731.03
    Delayed income   CC §731.13
    Depletion, property subject to   CC §731.12
    Expenses of administration   CC §731.15
    Governing law   CC §731.02
    Mortgages and acquisition of property   CC §731.14
    Natural resources   CC §731.11
    Termination of income interest   CC §731.06
  Priorities and preferences
    Claims against estates, payment of   Pro §§11420, 11421
    Executors and administrators (See **EXECUTORS AND ADMINISTRATORS**)
  Prior law, effect of   Pro §3
  Private sales
    Personal property
      Generally   Pro §10255
      Bids in compliance with notice of sale   Pro §10256
    Real property
      Generally   Pro §10306
      Minimum bids   Pro §10309
      Notice of sale terms, bids in compliance with   Pro §10307
      Overbids   Pro §10311

ADMINISTRATION OF ESTATES—Cont.
  Probate referees
    Appraisals by (See within this heading, **"Appraisals"**)
    Commission and expenses of   Pro §§8960 to 8964
    Designation of   Pro §§8920 to 8922
    Prior law, effect of   Pro §3
    Removal of   Pro §8924
  Probate rules   CRC 7.1 to 7.1105
  Proof of notice (See within this heading, **"Notices"**)
  Public administrators (See **PUBLIC ADMINISTRATORS**)
  Publication (See within this heading, **"Posting or publication"**)
  Public entity claimants, notification of   Pro §8112
  Public guardians (See **PUBLIC GUARDIANS**)
  Public sales
    Generally   Pro §§10003, 10254
    Auctioneers
      Compensation of   Pro §§10160 to 10168
      Employment of   Pro §10151
    Bids   Pro §10256
    Real property sales generally (See within this heading, **"Real property sales"**)
  Real property sales
    Generally   Pro §10305
    Ancillary administration   Pro §12541
    Assignment of property   Pro §10314
    Change of ownership statement, filing of   Pro §8800
    Confirmation of sale (See within this heading, **"Confirmation"**)
    Consolidated Farm and Rural Development Act, realty sales pursuant to   Pro §10207
    Defaulting purchaser, court order for sale   Pro §§10350, 10351
    Equitable interest in real property sales contract made during decedent's lifetime, sale of   Pro §10206
    Grazing associations, realty sales to   Pro §10207
    New sale, court order for   Pro §10313
    Notices
      Contents of notice of sale   Pro §10304
      $5000, notice of sale for property less than   Pro §10301
      Publication of notice of sale   Pro §10300
      Shortening time of notice   Pro §10302
      Will instructions, effect of sales pursuant to   Pro §10303
    Options (See within this heading, **"Options"**)
    Pasture associations, realty sales to   Pro §10207
    Private sales (See within this heading, **"Private sales"**)
    Public auctions generally (See within this heading, **"Public sales"**)
    Report of sale   Pro §10308
    Resale after vacating sale to defaulting purchaser, court order for   Pro §§10350, 10351
    Specific performance of contract to convey real property, action for   Pro §§850 to 859
    Vacating order
      Confirmation of sale on default of purchaser, order vacating   Pro §§10350, 10351
      Property sale, court order vacating   Pro §10313
  Recordation
    Orders affecting real property, generally   Pro §7263
    State, orders distributing property to   Pro §11902
  Referees
    Appraisals (See within this heading, **"Appraisals"**)
    Generally (See within this heading, **"Probate referees"**)
  Rent, collection of   Pro §§9650, 9651
  Repairs
    Generally   Pro §9650
    Independent administrator   Pro §10562
  Reports
    Final distribution, status report of   Pro §§12200 to 12202
    Sale, report of   Pro §§10260, 10308, 10351
  Requests for special notice   Pro §§1250 to 1252
  Resale of property   Pro §10350
  Revocation of letters (See **EXECUTORS AND ADMINISTRATORS**)
  Royalties under oil and gas leases   Pro §§9946, 9947
  Sales
    Appraisals generally (See within this heading, **"Appraisals"**)
    Auctioneer, acquiring services of   Pro §10151
    Bids   Pro §§10262, 10306, 10311
    Bonds   Pro §10200
    Brokers
      Employment   CRC 7.453, Pro §10150
    Certificates of deposit   Pro §10200
    Chose in action   Pro §10205
    Confirmation of (See within this heading, **"Confirmation"**)

ADMINISTRATION OF ESTATES—Cont.
  Sales—Cont.
    Continuance or postponement
      Personal property sales   Pro §10254
      Real property sales   CRC 7.451, Pro §10305
    Corporate stock (See within this heading, **"Corporate stock"**)
    Cotenancy interest, sale of   Pro §10006
    Credit sales
      Personal property sales   Pro §§10257, 10258
      Real property sales   Pro §10315
    Damages
      Generally   Pro §10380
      Liquidated damages   Pro §10381
    Debts, payment of   Pro §10000
    Default by purchaser   Pro §10350
    Discretion of personal representative regarding property to be sold   Pro §10003
    Down payment, requirements for   Pro §§10257, 10258
    Exclusive listing, contents of petition for approval   CRC 7.453
    Floating homes, sale of   CC §800.88
    Grazing associations, sales to   Pro §10207
    Hearings   Pro §10001
    Independent administrators (See **INDEPENDENT ADMINISTRATION OF ESTATES ACT**)
    Investment trust certificates   Pro §10200
    Leasehold interest   Pro §10203
    Liens, payment of   Pro §§10360 to 10363
    Limitation of actions to set aside   Pro §10382
    Liquidated damages, liability of personal representative for   Pro §10381
    Losses, liability of personal representative for   Pro §§9657, 10005
    Mobilehomes, sale of   CC §798.78
    Mode of selling   Pro §10003
    Mortgages   Pro §§10360 to 10363
    Oil and gas lease, interest under   Pro §10203
    Options generally (See within this heading, **"Options"**)
    Partition before distribution   Pro §11953
    Partnership interests, sale   Pro §10204
      Confirmation of sale   Pro §10261
    Pasture associations, sales to   Pro §10207
    Perishables   Pro §§10252, 10259
    Personal property
      Ex parte application for order authorizing   CRC 7.454
    Personal representative, purchase by
      Generally   Pro §9880
      Consent of heirs to   Pro §9881
      Contract of decedent, purchase by personal representative pursuant to   Pro §9884
      Grounds for court order authorizing   Pro §9882
      Option to purchase estate property by personal representative, will authorizing   Pro §9885
      Petition   Pro §9883
    Postponement of
      Personal property sales   Pro §10254
      Real property sales   CRC 7.451, Pro §10305
    Profits, liability of personal representative for   Pro §§9657, 10005
    Public sales
      Generally (See within this heading, **"Public sales"**)
      Real property sales (See within this heading, **"Real property sales"**)
    Quick sale   Pro §§10252, 10259
    Realty (See within this heading, **"Real property sales"**)
    Refusal to show property to prospective buyers   CRC 7.451
    Report required   Pro §§10260, 10308, 10351
    Resales   Pro §10350
    Savings and loan securities   Pro §10200
    Stock (See within this heading, **"Corporate stock"**)
    Title generally (See within this heading, **"Title"**)
    Trust deeds   Pro §§10360 to 10363
    Unit sales authorized   Pro §10004
    Vacating sale
      Defaulting purchaser, order vacating sales   Pro §§10350, 10351
      Real property sales, order vacating   Pro §10313
    Wills, sale under authority of   Pro §§10000, 10002, 10252
  Savings account, withdrawal of   Pro §10201
  Settlement of claims (See **EXECUTORS AND ADMINISTRATORS**)
  Severance of matters associated with proceedings and actions under Probate Code   Pro §801
  Shipping costs as expenses of   Pro §11754
  Signature
    Verification generally (See within this heading, **"Verification"**)
  Small estates
    Ancillary administration of (See **ANCILLARY ADMINISTRATION**)

ADMINISTRATION OF ESTATES—Cont.
  Small estates—Cont.
    Escheat of   CCP §1415
    Summary administration of (See **SMALL ESTATES WITHOUT ADMINISTRATION**)
  Special administrators   Pro §§8540 to 8547
  Special notice, request for   Pro §§1250 to 1252
  Specific performance to convey or transfer property claimed by decedent or other person   Pro §§850 to 859
  State of California
    Claims against decedent's estate filed by   Pro §§9200 to 9205
    Deposit of funds with   Pro §§11900 to 11904
    Escheat of estate property to (See **ESCHEAT**)
  State securities, investment in   Pro §§9730, 9731
  Stay on appeal   Pro §1310
  Stock (See within this heading, **"Corporate stock"**)
  Storage costs as expenses of   Pro §11754
  Summary administration of small estates
    Generally (See **SMALL ESTATES WITHOUT ADMINISTRATION**)
    Ancillary administration (See **ANCILLARY ADMINISTRATION**)
  Surviving spouse (See **SURVIVING SPOUSE**)
  Temporary possession of family home and property, right to   Pro §§6500, 6501
  Termination of further estate proceedings   Pro §12251
  Time
    Final distribution, time limit
      Statutory limits on administration   Pro §12200
      Testator's time limits on administration, effect   Pro §12206
  Title
    Generally   Pro §§7000, 7001, 7260 to 7263
    Action on third party claims to   Pro §§850 to 859
    Confirmation of sale, requirement of
      Generally   Pro §§10260, 10308
      Exceptions to   Pro §12059
    Instrument executed pursuant to court order   Pro §§7261, 10314
    Perishables   Pro §§10252, 10259
    Securities   Pro §10200
    Transaction defined   Pro §7261
  Treasurer (See within this heading, **"County treasurer"**)
  Trials   Pro §§1000 to 1051
    Costs   Pro §1002
    Jury trial, right to   Pro §825
    New trial motions   Pro §7220
    Procedural rules of practice governing   Pro §§1000, 1001
  Trust deeds
    Authority for executing   Pro §9805
    Chattel mortgage securing sale of personalty   Pro §§10257, 10258
    Claims based on (See **CLAIMS AGAINST ESTATES**)
    Credit sales, security for   Pro §10315
    Foreign executors satisfying mortgages   CC §2939.5
    Loans, security for   Pro §§9800, 9801
    Mutual capital certificates, sale of   Pro §10201
    Notes   Pro §9806
    Sales of property subject to   Pro §§10360 to 10363
    Security interest, authorizing estate property as   Pro §§9800, 9801
    Special administrators, authority of   Pro §8544
  Trust funds, investments in   Pro §9730
  Unclaimed property (See **UNCLAIMED PROPERTY**)
  United States
    Investments in United States obligations   Pro §§9730, 9731
    Status of government agencies as interested person to proceedings   Pro §7280
  Vacating sale
    Defaulting purchaser, order vacating sales involving   Pro §§10350, 10351
    Real property sales, order vacating   Pro §10313
  Valuation
    Appraisals generally (See within this heading, **"Appraisals"**)
    Testamentary gifts   Pro §21118
  Venue
    Generally   Pro §7051
    Nondomiciliary decedent, venue for   Pro §7052
  Verification
    Generally   Pro §1021
    Attorney, signing and verification by   Pro §1023
    Evidentiary use of verified petition   Pro §1022
  Vouchers
    Accounting of payments by personal representative, vouchers for   Pro §10901
    Claims against estate, vouchers to support   Pro §9151
  Waiver
    Abandonment of property
      Court review, waiver   Pro §9787

ADMINISTRATION OF ESTATES—Cont.
Waiver—Cont.
    Abandonment of property —Cont.
        Notice, waiver Pro §9785
    Notices, waiver of Pro §1204

ADMINISTRATIVE ADJUDICATION
Generally Gov §§1400.10, 11400
Accusations
    Generally Gov §11503
    Amended accusation
        Generally Gov §11507
        After submission of case for decision Gov §11516
    Form of notice of defense, accusation including Gov §11505
    Response (See within this heading, **"Response to accusation"**)
    Service of Gov §11505
    Statement of issues, applicability of procedural requirements to Gov §§11504, 11504.5
    Supplemental accusations, filing of Gov §11507
Administrative law judges
    Appointment of Gov §§11370.3, 11502
    Assignment to cases by director Gov §11370.3
    Continuance of adjudicatory proceedings by Gov §11524
    Decision of case Gov §11517
    Default by respondent, authority to award reasonable expenses after Gov §11455.30
    Defined Gov §11500
    Delegation of agency's powers to conduct hearings Gov §11512
    Disqualification Gov §11512
    Ethics, Administrative Adjudication Code of Gov §§11475 to 11475.70
    Evidence, ALJ's authority to rule on admissibility of Gov §11512
    Health and Safety Code proceedings, special qualifications for Gov §11502.1
    Medical licensees, authority to hear disciplinary proceedings involving Gov §11372
    Medical Quality Hearing Panel, qualifications for Gov §11371
    Oaths, authority to administer Gov §11528
    Official acts, certification of Gov §11528
    Powers of Gov §11512
    Prehearing conferences Gov §11511.5
    Proposed decisions by Gov §11517
    Pro tempore administrative law judges, appointment of Gov §11370.3
    Qualifications
        Generally Gov §11502
        Health and Safety Code proceedings, special qualifications for Gov §11502.1
        Medical Quality Hearing Panel, qualifications for Gov §11371
Admissibility of evidence
    Evidence generally (See within this heading, **"Evidence"**)
Adoption of regulations
    Generally Gov §§11400.20, 11400.21
    Alternative dispute resolution, model regulations governing Gov §11420.20
    Conversion of proceedings, regulations providing for Gov §11470.50
    Declaratory decision procedures, model regulations for Gov §11465.70
    Emergency decisions, regulations providing for Gov §11460.20
    Office of Administrative Hearings' authority to adopt rules and regulations Gov §11370.5
Affidavits as admissible evidence in Gov §11514
Alternative dispute resolution
    Generally Gov §11420.10
    De novo proceeding after nonbinding arbitration Gov §11420.10
    Evidence admissible outside of ADR, effect on Gov §11420.30
    Model regulations, adoption of Gov §11420.20
    Open to public, applicability of requirement that hearing be Gov §11420.20
    Prehearing conference, conversion of Gov §11511.5
    Protected communications Gov §11420.30
Alternative procedure for decision not requiring adjudicative proceeding Gov §11415.50
Appeals
    Judicial review generally (See within this heading, **"Judicial review"**)
Applicability of administrative adjudication provisions Gov §§11410.10 to 11410.50
Arbitration
    Alternative dispute resolution generally (See within this heading, **"Alternative dispute resolution"**)
Attorney general, notice of petition for license reinstatement or reduction of penalty to Gov §11522
Attorney professional conduct
    Threatening criminal, administrative or disciplinary charges ProfC 3.10

ADMINISTRATIVE ADJUDICATION—Cont.
Attorneys' fees
    Bad faith or frivolous tactics, award based on Gov §11455.30
    Default by respondent, award based on Gov §11520
Bill of rights Gov §§11425.10 to 11425.60
Certified interpreters Gov §§11435.30 to 11435.50
Code of Ethics, Administrative Adjudication Gov §§11475 to 11475.70
Communications
    Alternative dispute resolution, protected communications in Gov §11420.30
    Privileged communications, generally (See **PRIVILEGED COMMUNICATIONS**)
    Prohibited communications Gov §§11430.40 to 11430.50
Contempt sanction
    Bad faith or frivolous action causing delay, enforcement of order awarding expenses for Gov §11455.30
    Grounds for Gov §11455.10
    Procedure Gov §11455.20
    Subpoena, failure to comply with Gov §11450.20
Continuance of Gov §11524
Conversion of proceedings
    Adoption of governing regulations Gov §11470.50
    Authority for Gov §11470.10
    Cross-examination required, conversion of informal hearing when Gov §11445.50
    Duties of presiding officer after conversion Gov §11470.40
    Notice requirements Gov §11470.40
    Prehearing conference Gov §11511.5
    Record of original proceeding, use of Gov §11470.30
    Successor officer to preside over new proceeding, appointment of Gov §11470.20
Correction of mistake or clerical error in decision Gov §11518.5
Cross-examination
    Affiant, waiver of right to cross-examine Gov §11514
    Informal hearings, use in Gov §11445.50
Deaf or hard-of-hearing party, language assistance for Gov §11435.10
Decisions
    Alternative procedures for decision not requiring adjudicative proceeding Gov §11415.50
    Alternative treatments of decision Gov §11440.10
    Compliance Gov §11519
    Contested case Gov §11517
    Correction of mistake or clerical error Gov §11518.5
    Declaratory decisions (See within this heading, **"Declaratory decisions"**)
    Defined Gov §11405.50
    Delivery to parties Gov §11518
    Effective date of Gov §11519
    Emergency decisions (See within this heading, **"Emergency decisions"**)
    Findings of fact Gov §11425.50
    Judicial review generally (See within this heading, **"Judicial review"**)
    Motion to vacate Gov §11520
    Precedent decisions Gov §11425.60
    Probation Gov §11519
    Proposed decision of ALJ Gov §11517
    Reconsideration of decision Gov §11521
        Judicial review, effect of failure to request agency reconsideration Gov §11523
    Restitution Gov §11519
    Stay of execution Gov §11519
    Time limits for adoption Gov §11517
    Writing requirement Gov §11425.50
Declaratory decisions
    Generally Gov §11465.20
    Alternative responses to application Gov §11465.50
    Applicability of hearing procedures Gov §11465.40
    Authority to conduct Gov §11465.10
    Contents of decision Gov §11465.60
    Issuance of Gov §11465.20
    Model regulations, adoption of Gov §11465.70
    Notice of application Gov §11465.30
    Status of decision Gov §11465.60
Default by respondent Gov §11520
Defense to accusations
    Response generally (See within this heading, **"Response to accusation"**)
Definitions Gov §§11405.10 to 11405.80, 11500
Delaying tactics, order of reasonable expenses for Gov §11455.30
Delegation of agency's powers relating to conduct of proceedings Gov §11512
De novo proceeding after nonbinding arbitration Gov §11420.10
Depositions Gov §11511
Disclosure of prohibited communications Gov §§11430.40 to 11430.50

ADMINISTRATIVE ADJUDICATION—Cont.
Discovery
    Generally   Gov §11507.6
    Depositions   Gov §11511
    Exclusivity of discovery procedure under APA   Gov §11507.5
    Motion or petition to compel   Gov §11507.7
    Sexual harassment, assault, or battery, limits in cases involving   Gov §11440.40
Disqualification
    Administrative law judges   Gov §11512
    Presiding officer   Gov §11425.40
        Prohibited communications, receipt   Gov §11430.60
District statement of reduction in force
    Amended statement   Gov §11507
        After submission of case for decision   Gov §11516
    Filing   Gov §11503
    Form of notice of defense, accusation including   Gov §11505
    Service of   Gov §11505
    Supplemental statements   Gov §11507
Electronic means (See within this heading, **"Telephone, television or electronic means"**)
Emergency decisions
    Adoption of regulations providing for   Gov §11460.20
    Authority for   Gov §§11460.10, 11460.20
    Grounds for   Gov §11460.30
    Health care professional disciplinary proceedings, limits on use in   Gov §11529
    Hearing   Gov §11460.40
    Issuance of   Gov §11460.50
    Judicial review   Gov §11460.80
    Limits on   Gov §§11460.30, 11529
    Notice requirements   Gov §§11460.40, 11460.50
    Official record   Gov §11460.70
    Subsequent proceeding   Gov §11460.60
English, proceedings in   Gov §11435.20
Ethics, Administrative Adjudication Code of   Gov §§11475 to 11475.70
Evidence
    Generally   Gov §11513
    Administrative law judge's authority to rule on admissibility of   Gov §11512
    Affidavits, admissibility of   Gov §11514
    Alternative dispute resolution   Gov §11420.30
    Disclosure of source of written communication submitted to state agency in quasi-judicial proceeding, requirement for   Gov §11440.60
    Discovery procedure (See within this heading, **"Discovery"**)
    Exclusion of   Gov §§11512, 11513
    Hearsay   Gov §11513
    Official notice of matters, agency taking   Gov §11515
    Prehearing conference   Gov §11511.5
    Privileged communications, generally (See **PRIVILEGED COMMUNICATIONS**)
    Settlement negotiation, admissibility of   Gov §11415.60
    Sexual harassment, assault or battery, proceedings alleging   Gov §11440.40
Exclusion of evidence   Gov §§11512, 11513
Exempt agency adopting administrative adjudication provisions   Gov §11410.40
Ex parte communications   Gov §§11430.10 to 11430.80
Expenses and expenditures
    Agency funds, expenditures authorized as legal charges against   Gov §11527
    Bad faith or frivolous tactics, authority to award reasonable expenses for   Gov §11455.30
    Default by respondent, authority to award reasonable expenses after   Gov §11520
    Judicial review, costs for preparation of record for   CCP §§1094.5, 1094.6, Gov §11523
    Language assistance, costs and fees   Gov §§11435.25, 11435.45
    Witness fees   Gov §11450.40
Factual basis for decision, statement of   Gov §11425.50
Filing requirements
    Accusations, filing of   Gov §11503
    Continuance, application for   Gov §11524
    Defense, notice of   Gov §11506
    Discovery, motion or petition to compel   Gov §11507.7
    District statement of reduction in force   Gov §11503
    Hearing involving licenses and privileges   Gov §§11503, 11504
    Petitions generally (See within this heading, **"Petitions"**)
    Statement of issues, filing of   Gov §11504
First Amendment rights, expedited procedures for review of permit or entitlement decision implicating   CCP §1094.8
Foreign states, deposition of witnesses in   Gov §11511
Form or report required by state agency, challenge to   Gov §11380

ADMINISTRATIVE ADJUDICATION—Cont.
Frivolous actions or tactics, award of reasonable expenses for   Gov §11455.30
Governing definitions   Gov §§11405.10 to 11405.80, 11500
Governing procedure   Gov §§11415.10, 11415.20, 11425.10
Governor
    Applicability of adjudicative provisions   Gov §11410.20
    Authority to suspend or adopt procedures to avoid loss of federal funds   Gov §11415.30
Health care professionals disciplinary proceedings
    Generally   Gov §§11372, 11373
    Applicability of APA   Gov §11373
    Emergency decision procedure, limit on use of   Gov §11529
    Facilities and support personnel, Office of Administrative Hearings to provide   Gov §11373.3
    Interim orders   Gov §11529
    Medical Quality Hearing Panel   Gov §11371
    Right to counsel   Gov §11529
Hearings
    Administrative law judges generally (See within this heading, **"Administrative law judges"**)
    Change in place of hearing, motion for   Gov §11508
    Consolidation of proceedings   Gov §11507.3
    Continuance of   Gov §11524
    Cross-examination
        Affiant, waiver of right to cross-examine   Gov §11514
        Informal hearings   Gov §11445.50
    Electronic means, hearing conducted by   Gov §§11425.20, 11440.30, 11508
    Emergency decisions   Gov §11460.40
    Evidence generally (See within this heading, **"Evidence"**)
    Health care professionals disciplinary proceedings (See within this heading, **"Health care professionals disciplinary proceedings"**)
    Informal hearing procedure (See within this heading, **"Informal hearings"**)
    Joint hearing   Gov §11507.3
    Language assistance generally (See within this heading, **"Language assistance"**)
    Notice of
        Informal hearings   Gov §115445.30
        Respondent, notice to   Gov §11509
    Oaths
        Authority to administer oath   Gov §11528
        Refusal to take oath, contempt   Gov §11455.10
    Office of Administrative Hearings (See **ADMINISTRATIVE PROCEDURE ACT**)
    Open to public   Gov §11425.20
    Place of   Gov §11508
    Postponement of   Gov §11505
    Prehearing conference   Gov §11511.5
        Public meetings, exception to requirement   Gov §11425.30
    Record of   Gov §11512
    Respondent's request for   Gov §11505
    Telephone, television or electronic means, hearing conducted by   Gov §§11425.20, 11440.30
    Time of   Gov §11508
    Witnesses (See within this heading, **"Witnesses"**)
Informal hearings
    Authority for   Gov §11445.10
    Cross-examination, use of   Gov §11445.50
    Duty of presiding officer   Gov §11445.40
    Eligible proceedings   Gov §11445.20
    Legislative declaration concerning   Gov §11445.10
    Material facts in dispute   Gov §11445.60
    Notice of   Gov §11445.30
    Objection to   Gov §11445.30
    Prehearing conference, conversion of   Gov §11511.5
    Procedures   Gov §11445.40
Interim decision (See within this heading, **"Emergency decisions"**)
Interim regulations governing   Gov §§11400.20, 11400.21
Interpreters (See within this heading, **"Language assistance"**)
Intervention   Gov §11440.50
Joint hearing   Gov §11507.3
Judicial review
    Appeals from denial of writ   CCP §1094.5
    Applicability of provisions for judicial review   CCP §1094.5
    Bad faith or frivolous tactics, presiding officer's order awarding expenses for   Gov §11455.30
    Continuance denied by agency   Gov §11524
    Costs for preparation of record   CCP §§1094.5, 1094.6, Gov §11523
    Cross-examination in informal hearings, presiding officer's actions concerning use of   Gov §11470.10
    Emergency decisions   Gov §11460.80

ADMINISTRATIVE ADJUDICATION—Cont.
  Judicial review—Cont.
    First Amendment rights, expedited procedures for review of permit or entitlement decision implicating   CCP §1094.8
    Local agency decision, procedural requirements for review of   CCP §1094.6
    Procedure for obtaining   CCP §§1094.5, 1094.6, Gov §11523
    Reconsideration of agency decision, effect of failure to seek   Gov §11523
  Language assistance
    Generally   Gov §11435.20
    Alternate interpreter   Gov §11435.55
    Certified interpreters   Gov §§11435.30 to 11435.50
    Confidentiality   Gov §11435.65
    Costs and fees
      Interpreter examination and certification renewal   Gov §11435.45
      Payment of interpreters   Gov §11435.25
    Deaf or hard-of-hearing party   Gov §11435.10
    Defined   Gov §11435.05
    Notice of right to   Gov §11435.60
    Removal of name from certified interpreter list   Gov §11435.50
    State agencies providing   Gov §11435.15
  Legislature
    Applicability of adjudicative provisions   Gov §11410.20
    Suspension or adoption of procedures to avoid loss of federal funds, Governor's report of   Gov §11415.30
  Licenses and privileges
    Accusations against holder of (See within this heading, **"Accusations"**)
    Decisions (See within this heading, **"Decisions"**)
    Hearings involving (See within this heading, **"Hearings"**)
    Informal hearings, availability of   Gov §11445.20
    Medical disciplinary proceedings (See within this heading, **"Health care professionals disciplinary proceedings"**)
    Regulatory agencies subject to formal hearing provisions   Gov §11501
    Reinstatement of license or reduction of penalty, petition for   Gov §11522
    Response to accusations (See within this heading, **"Response to accusation"**)
    Settlement, timing of   Gov §11415.60
    Statement of issues
      Generally   Gov §11504
      Procedural requirements for accusations, applicability of   Gov §§11504, 11504.5
  Local agency
    Applicability of provisions to   Gov §11410.30
    Judicial review, procedure for obtaining   CCP §1094.6
  Mail and mailing
    Notice of defense, mailing of   Gov §11505
    Notice of participation, mailing   Gov §11505
    Service by   Gov §11440.20
      Subpoenas   Gov §11450.20
    Voting by agency members   Gov §11526
  Mediation
    Alternative dispute resolution generally (See within this heading, **"Alternative dispute resolution"**)
  Medical disciplinary proceedings (See within this heading, **"Health care professionals disciplinary proceedings"**)
  Medical examination, language assistance provided for (See within this heading, **"Language assistance"**)
  Mistake or clerical error in decision, correction of   Gov §11518.5
  New proceeding after nonbinding arbitration   Gov §11420.10
  Nonbinding arbitration
    Alternative dispute resolution generally (See within this heading, **"Alternative dispute resolution"**)
  Notice
    Accusation amended after submission for decision   Gov §11516
    Affidavits as evidence, notice to introduce   Gov §11514
    Conversion of proceeding   Gov §11470.40
    Declaratory decision, application for   Gov §11465.30
    Defense, notice of
      Responses generally (See within this heading, **"Response to accusation"**)
    District statement of reduction in force amended after submission for decision   Gov §11516
    Emergency decision   Gov §§11460.40, 11460.50
    Hearings generally (See within this heading, **"Hearings"**)
    Language assistance, right to   Gov §11435.60
    Official notice of matters as evidence   Gov §11515
    Reduction of penalty, notice to Attorney General of petition for   Gov §11522
    Subpoenas, written notice in lieu of   Gov §11450.50
  Notice of defense
    Responses generally (See within this heading, **"Response to accusation"**)

ADMINISTRATIVE ADJUDICATION—Cont.
  Oaths
    Authority to administer oath   Gov §11528
    Refusal to take oath as grounds for contempt   Gov §11455.10
  Office of Administrative Hearings (See **ADMINISTRATIVE PROCEDURE ACT**)
  Official notice of matters as evidence, agency taking   Gov §11515
  Orders
    Contempt generally (See within this heading, **"Contempt sanction"**)
    Deposition, order to appear for   Gov §11511
    Judicial review of orders generally (See within this heading, **"Judicial review"**)
    Prehearing orders   Gov §11511.5
  Penalties
    Agency's authority to reduce penalty proposed by ALJ   Gov §11517
    Limitation on   Gov §11425.50
    Reduction, petition for   Gov §11522
  Pending proceedings, communications regarding   Gov §§11430.10 to 11430.80
  Petitions
    License reinstatement, petition for   Gov §11522
    Penalty reduction, petition for   Gov §11522
    Reconsideration of agency decision, petition for   Gov §11521
  Physician disciplinary proceedings (See within this heading, **"Health care professionals disciplinary proceedings"**)
  Place of hearing   Gov §11508
  Podiatric Medicine Board disciplinary proceedings, generally (See within this heading, **"Health care professionals disciplinary proceedings"**)
  Postponement   Gov §11505
  Precedent decisions   Gov §11425.60
  Prehearing conferences
    Generally   Gov §11511.5
    Public meeting requirement, exception to   Gov §11425.20
  Presiding officers
    Bad faith or frivolous tactics, authority to award expenses for   Gov §11455.30
    Cross-examination in informal hearings, actions concerning use of   Gov §11445.50
    Disqualification
      Generally   Gov §11425.40
      Prohibited communications, receipt of   Gov §11430.60
    Eligibility   Gov §11425.30
    Ethics, Administrative Adjudication Code of   Gov §§11475 to 11475.70
    Exclusion of evidence, authority for   Gov §11513
    Informal hearings, regulation of   Gov §11445.40
    Prohibited communications   Gov §§11430.10 to 11430.80
    Subpoena powers   Gov §§11450.20, 11450.30
  Prevailing law   Gov §11415.20
  Privileged communications, generally (See **PRIVILEGED COMMUNICATIONS**)
  Probation   Gov §11519
  Prohibited communications   Gov §§11430.10 to 11430.80
  Quash subpoena, motion to   Gov §11450.30
  Quasi-public entity, applicability of administrative adjudication provisions to   Gov §11410.60
  Reconsideration of decision
    Generally   Gov §11521
    Judicial review, effect of failure to request agency reconsideration on   Gov §11523
  Record of proceedings
    Converted proceeding, use of original record in   Gov §11470.30
    Decision based on   Gov §11517
    Emergency decision   Gov §11460.70
    Formal hearing   Gov §11512
    Judicial review, preparation of record for   CCP §§1094.5, 1094.6, Gov §11523
    Public record   Gov §11517
  Regulatory agencies subject to formal hearing provisions   Gov §11501
  Reinstatement of license, petition for   Gov §11522
  Request for hearing by respondent   Gov §11505
  Response to accusation
    Generally   Gov §11506
    Amended or supplemental accusation, response to   Gov §11507
    Failure to file notice of defense, effect of   Gov §11520
    Objection to   Gov §11506
    Request for hearing   Gov §§11505, 11506
  Response to district statement of reduction in force
    Generally   Gov §11506
    Amended or supplemental statement, response   Gov §11507
    Objection to   Gov §11506
    Request for hearing   Gov §11506
  Restitution   Gov §11519

ADMINISTRATIVE ADJUDICATION—Cont.
Sanctions
- Bad faith or frivolous action causing delay, award of expenses for   Gov §11455.30
- Contempt sanction (See within this heading, **"Contempt sanction"**)
- Settlement including   Gov §11415.60

Service of electronic document   Gov §11440.20

Service of papers
- Accusations, service of   Gov §11505
- Corrected decision   Gov §11518.5
- Decision   Gov §11518
- Discovery, motion or petition to compel   Gov §11507.7
- Mail, service by
  - Generally   Gov §11440.20
  - Subpoenas   Gov §11450.20
- Manner of   Gov §11440.20
- Statement of issues, service of   Gov §11504
- Subpoenas   Gov §11450.20
- Written notice in lieu of subpoena   Gov §11450.50

Settlement
- Conference   Gov §11511.7
- Decision by   Gov §11415.60
- License, timing of settlement of proceeding involving   Gov §11415.60
- Public hearing requirement, applicability of   Gov §11425.20
- Sanctions included in   Gov §11415.60

Sexual harassment, assault or battery, evidence in proceedings alleging   Gov §11440.40

Statements
- Factual basis for decision   Gov §11425.50
- License or privilege action, statement of issues in   Gov §11504
  - Procedural requirements for accusations, applicability   Gov §§11504, 11504.5
- Respondent, statement to   Gov §11505

Stay of execution
- Generally   Gov §11519
- Pending judicial review   CCP §1094.5

Subpoenas
- Applicability of procedures   Gov §11450.05
- Issuance of   Gov §§11450.10, 11450.20
- Mileage and fees of witness   Gov §11450.40
- Objection to   Gov §11450.30
- Presiding officers, subpoena powers of   Gov §§11450.20, 11450.30
- Quash, motion to   Gov §11450.30
- Satisfaction of subpoena duces tecum   Gov §11450.10
- Service of   Gov §11450.20
- Written notice in lieu of   Gov §11450.50

Supplemental accusations, filing of   Gov §11507
Supplemental district statement of reduction in force   Gov §11507

Sympathy expressed to accident victim or family
- Evidentiary effect   Gov §11440.45

Telephone, television or electronic means
- Hearings, generally   Gov §§11425.20, 11440.30
- Prehearing conference conducted by   Gov §11511.5
- Settlement conference conducted by   Gov §11511.7

Television (See within this heading, **"Telephone, television or electronic means"**)

Temporary decision
- Emergency decisions generally (See within this heading, **"Emergency decisions"**)

Time
- Hearing   Gov §11508

Translators (See within this heading, **"Language assistance"**)
Vacate decision, motion to   Gov §11520

Verification
- Accusations, verification of   Gov §11503
- Statement of issues, verification of   Gov §11504

Voting by agency members
- Adjudicatory proceedings, voting on decisions in   Gov §11517
- Mail, voting by   Gov §11526

Waiver of rights, generally   Gov §11415.40

Witnesses
- Deposition of   Gov §11511
- Examination
  - Generally   Gov §11513
  - Affiants, cross-examination of   Gov §11514
- Exchange of witness lists at prehearing conference   Gov §11511.5
- Mileage and fees   Gov §11450.40
- Oaths generally (See within this heading, **"Oaths"**)

Written decision   Gov §11425.50

ADMINISTRATIVE CODE (See **ADMINISTRATIVE PROCEDURE ACT**)

ADMINISTRATIVE LAW
Generally (See **ADMINISTRATIVE PROCEDURE ACT**)
Adjudicative proceedings (See **ADMINISTRATIVE ADJUDICATION**)
Environmental quality act
- Petitions under environmental quality act, civil rules governing   CRC 3.1365, 3.2200 to 3.2240

ADMINISTRATIVE OFFICE OF THE COURTS (See **JUDICIAL COUNCIL**)

ADMINISTRATIVE PRESIDING JUSTICE
Appellate rules, supreme court and courts of appeal (See **APPELLATE RULES, SUPREME COURT AND COURTS OF APPEAL**)
Superior courts
- Presiding judge (See **SUPERIOR COURTS**)

ADMINISTRATIVE PROCEDURE ACT
Adjudicative proceedings (See **ADMINISTRATIVE ADJUDICATION**)
Administrative Code (See within this heading, **"Code of Regulations"**)
Administrative Code Supplement (See within this heading, **"Regulatory Code Supplement"**)
Administrative law judges
- Adjudicative proceedings (See **ADMINISTRATIVE ADJUDICATION**)
- Appointment of   Gov §§11370.3, 11502

Administrative Notice Register (See within this heading, **"Regulatory Notice Register"**)
Administrative review of regulations
- Office of Administrative Law generally (See within this heading, **"Office of Administrative Law"**)

Adoption of regulations
- Adjudicative proceedings, regulations governing (See **ADMINISTRATIVE ADJUDICATION**)
- Building standard regulations, applicability of procedural rulemaking requirements to   Gov §11356
- Consistent with statutory authorization, agency regulations adopted as   Gov §11342.2
- Definitions   Gov §§11342.510 to 11342.610
- Effective dates
  - Generally   Gov §11343.4
  - Emergency regulations   Gov §11346.1
- Effect on statutory authority to regulate by state agency   Gov §11342.1
- Electronic communication   Gov §11340.85
- Emergency regulations, procedural requirements for   Gov §11346.1
- Exempt regulations   Gov §11346.1
- File of rulemaking proceedings (See within this heading, **"Rulemaking file for proposed regulation"**)
- Filing requirements
  - Generally   Gov §11343
  - Emergency regulations   Gov §11346.1
  - OAL approval or disapproval of proposed regulation, notice of   Gov §11349.3
  - Resubmission of proposed regulations   Gov §11349.4
  - Style for filing, conformity of   Gov §11343.1
- Fire safety regulations requiring approval of state fire marshal   Gov §11359
- 45-day public comment period   Gov §11346.4
- Governor's review of Office of Administrative Law decision   Gov §11349.5
- Judicial notice of   Ev §451, Gov §§11343.6, 11344.6
- Notice of proposed action (See within this heading, **"Notice of proposed action"**)
- Petitions
  - Regulatory action, petition for   Gov §11340.7
  - Rulemaking file, copy of petition included   Gov §11347.3
- Presumption of validity of text of regulation published in   Gov §11344.6
- Public Utilities Commission, applicability of agency rulemaking requirements to   Gov §11351
- "Reasonably necessary" to effectuate purpose of agency as grounds for   Gov §11342.2
- Rulemaking file (See within this heading, **"Rulemaking file for proposed regulation"**)
- Scope of coverage of agency rulemaking requirements   Gov §11346
- Statement of reasons
  - Contents   Gov §11346.2
  - Final statement   Gov §11346.9
- Withdrawal of proposed regulation
  - Before decision of office of administrative law   Gov §11349.3
  - Resubmission after   Gov §11349.4
- Workers' Compensation Appeals Board and Division of Workers' Compensation, applicability of rulemaking requirements to   Gov §11351

Alternative dispute resolution of adjudicative proceedings (See **ADMINISTRATIVE ADJUDICATION**)

ADMINISTRATIVE PROCEDURE ACT—Cont.
Amendment of regulations
    Emergency regulations, amendment of regulations by adoption of   Gov §11346.1
Appeals
    Adjudicative proceeding (See **ADMINISTRATIVE ADJUDICATION**)
    Form or report required by state agency, appeal of certification of   Gov §11380
Appointments
    Administrative law judge, appointment of   Gov §§11370.3, 11502
    Directors, appointment of
        Office of Administrative Hearings, director of   Gov §11370.2
        Office of Administrative Law, director of   Gov §11340.2
    Office of Administrative Hearings (See within this heading, **"Office of Administrative Hearings"**)
Archiving of rulemaking file   Gov §11347.3
Attorney professional conduct
    Nonadjudicative proceedings
        Advocacy in nonadjudicative proceedings   ProfC 3.9
Automobiles
    Weight
        Vehicle weight impacts and ability of manufacturers and operators to comply with weight laws   Gov §11343.3
Bill of rights for administrative adjudication   Gov §§11425.10 to 11425.60
Blind persons
    Narrative description of proposed regulation upon request   Gov §11346.6
Building standard regulations
    Fire safety regulations, state fire marshal's approval of   Gov §11359
    General rulemaking requirements, applicability of   Gov §11356
    Transmittal of proposed regulations for approval by Building Standards Commission   Gov §11343
Certificates and certification
    Interpreters   Gov §§11435.30 to 11435.50
    Official acts, authority to certify   Gov §11528
    Proposed regulations, certification by head of state agency of   Gov §11343
    Reporting requirement of state agency, appeal from certification of   Gov §11380
Citation of Act   Gov §11370
Claims, adjudication of (See **ADMINISTRATIVE ADJUDICATION**)
Clerk
    County clerk
        Code of Regulations, repository for   Gov §§11343.5, 11344.2
        Regulatory Code Supplement, repository for   Gov §11344.2
Code of Regulations
    County clerk as repository for   Gov §§11343.5, 11344.2
    Official name for   Gov §11344.9
    Presumption of validity of regulation published in   Gov §11344.6
    Publication
        Official publication and printing   Gov §11344
        Other authorized printers   Gov §11344.7
        Presumption of validity of published regulation   Gov §11344.6
    Public inspection, distribution to libraries for   Gov §11344.2
    Sales price
        Public sales   Gov §11344.4
        State agencies, sales to   Gov §11344.7
Contempt sanction in adjudicative proceedings (See **ADMINISTRATIVE ADJUDICATION**)
Continuance of proceedings
    Adjudicative proceedings   Gov §11524
    Proposed agency action proceedings   Gov §11346.8
County clerk
    Code of Regulations, repository for   Gov §§11343.5, 11344.2
    Regulatory Code Supplement, repository for   Gov §11344.2
Decisions
    Administrative adjudication (See **ADMINISTRATIVE ADJUDICATION**)
    OAL, decision of (See within this heading, **"Office of Administrative Law"**)
Declaratory decision procedure (See **ADMINISTRATIVE ADJUDICATION**)
Declaratory relief
    Generally   Gov §§11350, 11350.3
    Grounds for invalidity of regulation   Gov §11350
    Public Utilities Commission regulations, relief inapplicable to   Gov §11351
    Workers' Compensation Appeals Board and Division of Workers' Compensation regulations, relief inapplicable to   Gov §11351
Default by respondent in adjudicative proceedings   Gov §11520
Definitions
    Adjudicative proceedings   Gov §§11405.10 to 11405.80, 11500
    Administrative regulations and rulemaking   Gov §§11342.510 to 11342.610, 11344.9, 11349

ADMINISTRATIVE PROCEDURE ACT—Cont.
Directors
    Office of Administrative Hearings (See within this heading, **"Office of Administrative Hearings"**)
    Office of Administrative Law
        Appointment and qualifications of director   Gov §11340.2
        Staff and employees of director   Gov §11340.3
Disabilities, persons with
    Visual or communication disability
        Narrative description of proposed regulation upon request   Gov §11346.6
Disclosure
    Prohibited communications in adjudicative proceedings   Gov §§11430.40 to 11430.50
Discovery in administrative adjudication proceedings (See **ADMINISTRATIVE ADJUDICATION**)
Economic impact statements
    Adverse impact on business, proposed regulations having potential for   Gov §11346.5
    Jobs, assessment of new regulations on creation of   Gov §11346.3
    State agency requirements   Gov §11346.3
Effective dates
    Decision in contested case, date of   Gov §11519
Emergency regulatory procedures
    Generally   Gov §11346.1
    Declaratory judgment on validity of regulation, action for   Gov §11350
    Review of emergency regulation   Gov §11349.6
English
    Adjudication proceedings   Gov §11435.20
    Plain English
        Defined   Gov §§11342, 11342.580
        Policy statement on drafting regulations   Gov §11343.2
Evidence
    Adjudicative proceedings (See **ADMINISTRATIVE ADJUDICATION**)
    Judicial notice of agency regulations filed with secretary of state   Gov §§11343.6, 11344.6
Expenses and expenditures
    Adjudicative proceedings (See **ADMINISTRATIVE ADJUDICATION**)
File of rulemaking proceedings (See within this heading, **"Rulemaking file for proposed regulation"**)
Filing requirements
    Adjudicative proceedings (See **ADMINISTRATIVE ADJUDICATION**)
Finance, Department of
    Exemption for actions relating to statement budget by Department of Finance   Gov §11342.5
    Guidelines for assessing cost of regulations   Gov §11357
Fire safety regulations, state fire marshal's approval of   Gov §11359
Foreign states, deposition of witnesses in   Gov §11511
Form or report required by state agency, challenge to   Gov §11380
45-day public comment period for adoption, amendment or repeal of agency regulation   Gov §11346.4
Governor
    Adjudicative proceedings (See **ADMINISTRATIVE ADJUDICATION**)
    Office of Administrative Hearings
        Directors, appointment   Gov §11370.2
        Reporting recommendations to governor   Gov §11370.5
    Office of Administrative Law
        Action by governor (See within this heading, **"Office of Administrative Law"**)
Health care professionals disciplinary proceedings (See **ADMINISTRATIVE ADJUDICATION**)
Hearings
    Adjudicative proceedings (See **ADMINISTRATIVE ADJUDICATION**)
    Office of Administrative Hearings (See within this heading, **"Office of Administrative Hearings"**)
    Proposed agency action, public hearing on   Gov §11346.8
Identification number system to track regulatory actions   Gov §§11341, 11345
Inspection of rulemaking file for proposed regulation   Gov §11347.3
Internet
    California Code of Regulations, legislature's intent to establish access to   Gov §§11340.1, 11344
    Proposed agency action, public comments by fax or email on   Gov §11340.8
    Public agencies, websites for
        Electronic publication or distribution of written materials   Gov §11340.85
        Exempt agencies or regulations not required to be posted   Gov §11340.9
        Proposed agency actions, publication and posting of   Gov §11340.8
        Regulatory Notice Register, weekly website posting of   Gov §§11344.1, 11345

ADMINISTRATIVE PROCEDURE ACT—Cont.
Internet—Cont.
- Small Business Advocate, maintaining website link to   Gov §11346.7

Interpreters in adjudicative proceedings (See **ADMINISTRATIVE ADJUDICATION**)

Jobs, assessment of new regulations on creation of   Gov §11346.3

Judges (See within this heading, "**Administrative law judges**")

Judicial notice of agency regulations filed with secretary of state   Ev §451, Gov §§11343.6, 11344.6

Judicial remedies
- Adjudicative proceedings (See **ADMINISTRATIVE ADJUDICATION**)
- Declaratory relief (See within this heading, "**Declaratory relief**")

Language assistance in adjudicative proceedings (See **ADMINISTRATIVE ADJUDICATION**)

Legislature
- Adjudicative proceedings (See **ADMINISTRATIVE ADJUDICATION**)
- Office of Administrative Hearings, recommendations of   Gov §11370.5
- Office of Administrative Law, legislative purpose for establishing   Gov §§11340, 11340.1

Licenses and privileges, administrative adjudication involving (See **ADMINISTRATIVE ADJUDICATION**)

Local agencies
- Administrative adjudication (See **ADMINISTRATIVE ADJUDICATION**)
- Failure to include economic impact statement in rulemaking file, effect of   Gov §11349.1
- Notice of cost or savings estimate imposed by proposed regulation on   Gov §11346.5

Major regulations
- Defined   Gov §11342.548
- Regulatory impact assessment   Gov §11346.3
- Statement of reasons   Gov §11346.2

Medical Board disciplinary proceedings (See **ADMINISTRATIVE ADJUDICATION**)

Notice of proposed action
- Generally   Gov §11346.4
- Business enterprises, information concerning adverse economic impact of proposed regulations on   Gov §11346.5
- Contents of   Gov §11346.5
- Jobs, information on adverse economic impact of proposed regulations on   Gov §11346.3
- Plain English regulations, policy statement on   Gov §11343.2
- Public discussion by interested parties prior to notice of proposed action   Gov §11346.45
- Substantial changes to notice provisions, effect of   Gov §11346.8
- Termination of proposed action   Gov §11347

Notices
- Adjudicative proceedings (See **ADMINISTRATIVE ADJUDICATION**)
- Approval or disapproval of proposed regulation, notice of   Gov §11349.3
- Proposed agency action, notice of (See within this heading, "**Notice of proposed action**")
- Repeal, notice of   Gov §§11349.8, 11349.9

Oaths
- Adjudicative proceedings (See **ADMINISTRATIVE ADJUDICATION**)
- Proposed agency action proceedings, authority to administer oath in   Gov §11346.8

Office of Administrative Hearings
- Appeal of certification of form or report required by state agency   Gov §11380
- Appointment
  - Administrative law judge   Gov §§11370.3, 11502
  - Director   Gov §11370.2
  - Staff employees   Gov §11370.3
- Authority to adopt rules and regulations   Gov §11370.5
- Director
  - Administrative law judges, appointment and assignment of   Gov §§11370.3, 11502
  - Defined   Gov §11370.1
  - Governor, appointment by   Gov §11370.2
  - Qualifications of   Gov §11370.2
  - Staff employees, appointment of   Gov §11370.3
- Governor
  - Director, appointment of   Gov §11370.2
  - Report of recommendations to   Gov §11370.5
- Medical Quality Hearing Panel   Gov §11371
- Operating costs of   Gov §11370.4
- Reporting requirements   Gov §11370.5
- Study and research of administrative adjudication   Gov §11370.5

Office of Administrative Law
- Access to agency records   Gov §11340.4
- Approval or disapproval of regulations
  - Generally   Gov §11349.3

ADMINISTRATIVE PROCEDURE ACT—Cont.
Office of Administrative Law—Cont.
- Approval or disapproval of regulations—Cont.
  - Emergency regulations, procedure for   Gov §11349.6
  - Resubmission after disapproval   Gov §11349.4
- Code of Regulations generally (See within this heading, "**Code of Regulations**")
- Decision
  - Judicial review of   Gov §11350
  - Notice of   Gov §11349.3
  - Withdrawal of proposed regulation before   Gov §11349.3
- Definitions   Gov §§11342.510 to 11342.610, 11349
- Director
  - Appointment and qualifications of   Gov §11340.2
  - Staff and other employees of   Gov §11340.3
- Discretion to file rules and regulations not subject to Act   Gov §11343.8
- Emergency regulations, procedure for (See within this heading, "**Emergency regulatory procedures**")
- Enabling provision for authority of   Gov §11359
- Filing requirements for regulations   Gov §11340.5
- Governor, action by
  - Director, appointment of   Gov §11340.2
  - Regulatory Code Supplement, reporting decision in   Gov §11344
  - Request for governor's review   Gov §11349.5
- Identification number system to track regulatory actions   Gov §§11341, 11345
- Legislative purpose for establishing   Gov §§11340, 11340.1
- Performance standard regulations   Gov §§11340, 11340.1
- Petitions, capacity to file   Gov §11340.6
- Prescriptive standard regulations   Gov §§11340, 11340.1
- Presumption of approval of proposed regulation after 30 days without action by   Gov §11349.3
- Priority review of agency regulations   Gov §11349.7
- Purpose   Gov §11340.4
- Regulatory Code Supplement (See within this heading, "**Regulatory Code Supplement**")
- Repeal of regulations (See within this heading, "**Repeal of regulations**")
- Resubmission after denial or withdrawal of proposed regulation   Gov §11349.4
- Review procedure   Gov §11349.7
- Rulemaking file (See within this heading, "**Rulemaking file for proposed regulation**")
- Secretary of state generally (See within this heading, "**Secretary of State**")
- Staff and other employees of   Gov §11340.3
- Standards for review of agency regulations   Gov §11349.1
- Status of regulations, determination of   Gov §11340.5
- Withdrawal of proposed regulation
  - Before decision by Office   Gov §11349.4
  - Resubmission after withdrawal   Gov §11349.3

Office of Administrative Procedure
- Office of Administrative hearings generally (See within this heading, "**Office of Administrative Hearings**")

Official notice of matters in adjudicatory hearings, evidence of   Gov §11515

Out-of-state witnesses, deposition of   Gov §11511

Penalties in adjudicative proceedings (See **ADMINISTRATIVE ADJUDICATION**)

Performance standard regulations, legislative intent regarding   Gov §§11340, 11340.1

Petitions
- Adjudicative proceedings (See **ADMINISTRATIVE ADJUDICATION**)
- Regulatory action, petition for   Gov §11340.7
- Rulemaking file, copy of petition in   Gov §11347.3

Physician disciplinary proceedings (See **ADMINISTRATIVE ADJUDICATION**)

Plain English
- Defined   Gov §§11342, 11342.580
- Policy statement on drafting regulations   Gov §11343.2

Postponement
- Adjudicatory proceedings   Gov §11505
- Proposed agency action proceedings   Gov §11346.8

Prehearing conferences (See **ADMINISTRATIVE ADJUDICATION**)

Prescriptive standard regulations, legislative intent regarding   Gov §§11340, 11340.1

Presiding officer at administrative proceeding (See **ADMINISTRATIVE ADJUDICATION**)

Presumptions
- Approval of regulation after 30 days without action by Office of Administrative Law, presumption of   Gov §11349.3
- Validity of agency regulations filed with secretary of state, rebuttable presumption of   Gov §§11343.6, 11344.6

Privileged communications in adjudicatory proceedings (See **PRIVILEGED COMMUNICATIONS**)

ADMINISTRATIVE PROCEDURE ACT—Cont.
Proposed agency action
    Contents of statement of   Gov §11346.2
    Economy, assessment of impact on   Gov §11346.3
    Hearings   Gov §11346.8
    Identification number system for tracking regulatory actions   Gov §§11341, 11345
    Notice of (See within this heading, **"Notice of proposed action"**)
    Public discussion by interested parties prior to notice of proposed action   Gov §11346.45
    Regulatory Notice Register, publication in   Gov §11344.1
    Statement of proposed action
        Final statement, contents   Gov §11364.9
        Substantial changes to statement   Gov §11346.8
    Statement of reasons
        Contents   Gov §11346.2
        Final statement   Gov §11346.9
    Visual or communications disability
        Narrative description of proposed regulation upon request   Gov §11346.6
Publication
    Code of Regulations (See within this heading, **"Code of Regulations"**)
    Proposed action, notice of   Gov §11346.4
    Regulatory Code Supplement
        Authorized printers   Gov §11344.7
        Official publication   Gov §11344
    Regulatory Notice Register (See within this heading, **"Regulatory Notice Register"**)
Public comment on regulations
    Fax or email from general public   Gov §11340.8
    Time period for   Gov §11346.4
Public hearings
    Hearings generally (See within this heading, **"Hearings"**)
Public inspection of rulemaking file for proposed regulation   Gov §11347.3
Public Utilities Commission, applicability of agency rulemaking procedures to   Gov §11351
Record of rulemaking proceedings (See within this heading, **"Rulemaking file for proposed regulation"**)
Regulatory action, petition for   Gov §§11340.6, 11340.7
Regulatory Code Supplement
    Contents of   Gov §11344
    County clerk as repository for   Gov §§11343.5, 11344.2
    Notice of proposed action, publication of   Gov §11346.4
    Official name for   Gov §11344.9
    Presumption of validity of regulation published in   Gov §11344.6
    Publication
        Official publication   Gov §11344
        Other authorized printers   Gov §11344.7
    Sales price
        Public sales   Gov §11344.4
        State agencies, sales to   Gov §11344.7
Regulatory impact assessment   Gov §11346.3
    Analyses
        Regulations for conducting   Gov §11346.36
        Review and report   Gov §11349.1.5
    Failure to complete   Gov §§11349.1, 11349.1.5
Regulatory Notice Register
    Contents of   Gov §11344.1
    Official name for   Gov §11344.9
    Publication
        Official publication   Gov §11344.1
        Other authorized printers   Gov §11344.7
        Time of publication for documents   Gov §11344.3
        Website posting   Gov §§11344.1, 11345
    Sales price
        Public sales   Gov §11344.4
        State agencies, sales to   Gov §11344.7
    Time of publication for documents in   Gov §11344.3
Repeal of regulations
    Emergency regulations, effect of repeal by   Gov §11346.1
    Order of repeal defined   Gov §§11342, 11342.560
    Statutory authority repealed, procedure to review repeal of regulation where   Gov §§11349.8, 11349.9
Reporting requirement of state agency, challenge to   Gov §11380
Respondent in adjudicative proceedings (See **ADMINISTRATIVE ADJUDICATION**)
Resubmission of proposed regulation after denial or withdrawal   Gov §11349.4
Review
    Administrative review of regulations, generally (See within this heading, **"Office of Administrative Law"**)

ADMINISTRATIVE PROCEDURE ACT—Cont.
Rulemaking file for proposed regulation
    Additional material
        After publication of notice of proposed action, inclusion of   Gov §11347.1
        After public hearing, inclusion of   Gov §11346.8
        After submission to OAL, inclusion of   Gov §11349.2
    Archiving of file   Gov §11347.3
    Central location for current and pending rulemaking actions, maintaining of   Gov §11348
    Contents of   Gov §11347.3
    Copies of petitions by interested parties, inclusion of   Gov §11347.3
    Notice of deficiency for documents omitted in   Gov §11349.1
Sales of printed codes or supplement and notice register   Gov §11344.4
San Francisco Bay Conservation and Development Commission   Gov §11354.1
School districts
    Failure to include economic impact statement in rulemaking file, effect of   Gov §11349.1
    Notice of cost or savings estimate imposed by proposed regulation on   Gov §11346.5
Secretary of State
    Emergency regulations, filing of   Gov §11346.1
    Endorsement and filing with   Gov §11343.2
    General discussion of procedure for filing regulations with   Gov §11343
    Style and procedures for agency regulations filed with   Gov §11343.1
    30th day after filing, regulation or repeal effective on   Gov §11343.4
Service of papers
    Adjudicative proceedings (See **ADMINISTRATIVE ADJUDICATION**)
    Notices generally (See within this heading, **"Notices"**)
Settlement of adjudicative proceedings (See **ADMINISTRATIVE ADJUDICATION**)
Small businesses
    Adverse impact on small business, proposed regulations having potential for   Gov §11346.5
    Defined   Gov §§11342, 11342.610
    Website link to Small Business Advocate   Gov §11346.7
Standards for review of agency regulations   Gov §11349.1
State budget, exemption for Finance Department actions relating to   Gov §11342.5
Statement of proposed action
    Final statement of proposed action, contents of   Gov §11364.9
    Substantial changes to statement, effect of   Gov §11346.8
Statement of reasons
    Contents of   Gov §11346.2
    Final statement   Gov §11346.9
Statements
    Adjudicative proceeding (See **ADMINISTRATIVE ADJUDICATION**)
    Proposed action, statement of
        Final statement   Gov §11364.9
        Substantial changes   Gov §11346.8
    Reasons, statement of
        Contents   Gov §11346.2
        Final statement   Gov §11346.9
Stay of execution in adjudicative proceeding   Gov §11519
Subpoenas in adjudicative proceedings (See **ADMINISTRATIVE ADJUDICATION**)
30th day after filing, regulation or repeal effective on   Gov §11343.4
Translators in adjudicative proceedings (See **ADMINISTRATIVE ADJUDICATION**)
Unconstitutionality of regulation, judgment declaring
    Attorney general notified   CRC 2.1100
Validity of regulations
    Declaratory relief, action for (See within this heading, **"Declaratory relief"**)
    Presumption of (See within this heading, **"Presumptions"**)
Villaraigosa-Keely Act, rulemaking exclusion under   Gov §11361
Visual or communication disability
    Narrative description of proposed regulation upon request   Gov §11346.6
Water quality control plans
    Drinking water
        Contamination of public water system notification, inapplicability to proceedings concerning   Gov §11352
        Periodic water analysis, inapplicability to proceedings concerning   Gov §11352
        Report to department, inapplicability to proceedings concerning   Gov §11352
    Municipal stormwater management, inapplicability of provisions   Gov §11352
    Pending court actions before June 1, 1992, applicability to   Gov §11354
    State policy, guidelines or water quality control plans, applicability to   Gov §11353

ADMINISTRATIVE PROCEDURE ACT—Cont.
Water quality control plans—Cont.
    Waste discharge requirements and permits, inapplicability to proceedings concerning   Gov §11352
    Water quality certification, inapplicability to proceedings concerning   Gov §11352
Withdrawal of proposed regulation
    Before decision by Office of Administrative Law   Gov §11349.3
    Resubmission after   Gov §11349.4
Witnesses in adjudicative proceedings (See **ADMINISTRATIVE ADJUDICATION**)
Workers' Compensation Appeals Board and Division of Workers' Compensation, applicability of agency rulemaking procedure to   Gov §11351
Writ of mandate in adjudicative proceedings (See **ADMINISTRATIVE ADJUDICATION**)

ADMINISTRATIVE REGULATIONS (See **ADMINISTRATIVE PROCEDURE ACT**)

ADMINISTRATORS (See **EXECUTORS AND ADMINISTRATORS**)

ADMINISTRATORS WITH WILL ANNEXED
Generally   Pro §8440
Appointment
    Generally   Pro §8440
    Priority for   Pro §8441
Bond requirements   Pro §§8480 to 8488
De bonis non administration, subsequent letters issued for purposes of   Pro §12252
Form of letters   Pro §8405
Named executor, failure to qualify by   Pro §§8440, 8522
Newly discovered property after final settlement, subsequent letters issued for administration of   Pro §12252
Nonresident personal representatives   Pro §§8570 to 8577
Powers and duties   Pro §8442
Priority for appointment   Pro §8441
Secretary of state, service of   Pro §8574

ADMIRALTY
Bottomry (See **BOTTOMRY**)
Foreign decrees, binding effect of   CCP §1914
Judicial notice of admiralty rules   Ev §451
Respondentia (See **LOANS UPON RESPONDENTIA**)
Sealed documents of admiralty courts presumed to be genuine   Ev §1452

ADMISSIBILITY OF EVIDENCE (See also **EVIDENCE**)
Administrative adjudication (See **ADMINISTRATIVE ADJUDICATION**)
Arbitration proceedings (See **ARBITRATION**)
Best and secondary evidence (See **BEST AND SECONDARY EVIDENCE**)
Blood tests   Ev §712
Character evidence (See **CHARACTER AND REPUTATION**)
Child welfare services case plan, parent signing or accepting services under   Ev §1228.1
Chiropractic review board records, exemption of   Ev §1157
Civil resolution of criminal matter, evidence relating to offer for   Ev §1153.5
Claim, conduct or statements made in negotiation of   Ev §1154
Compromise offers, evidence of (See **SETTLEMENT AND COMPROMISE**)
Computer information (See **COMPUTERS**)
Conduct, evidence admissible to prove   Ev §§1100 to 1106
Confusing evidence, exclusion of   Ev §352
Court determining   Ev §§402, 403, 405
Definition   Ev §§400, 401
Dental review board records   Ev §1157
Domestic violence (See **DOMESTIC VIOLENCE**)
Economic litigation provisions for exclusion of evidence   CCP §97
Electronic transactions, admissibility of evidence of records and signatures related to   CC §1633.13
Error on appeal regarding   Ev §§353, 354
Guilty pleas   Ev §1153
Hearsay rule, exceptions to (See **HEARSAY**)
Hypnosis of witness   Ev §795
Insurance, admissibility of evidence of (See **INSURANCE**)
Liability insurance, evidence of   Ev §1155
Limited purposes, admission of evidence for   Ev §355
Mediation, communications associated with (See **MEDIATION**)
Medical records   Ev §§1156 to 1158
Misleading evidence, exclusion of   Ev §352
Podiatric review board records   Ev §1157
Polygraph evidence, exclusion of   Ev §351.1
Prejudicial evidence, exclusion of   Ev §352

ADMISSIBILITY OF EVIDENCE—Cont.
Preliminary fact, determination of   Ev §§402 to 406
Privileged communications (See **PRIVILEGED COMMUNICATIONS**)
Proffered evidence
    Definitions   Ev §§400, 401
    Preliminary fact, determination of   Ev §§402 to 405
Relevant evidence   Ev §§350, 351
Reputation evidence (See **CHARACTER AND REPUTATION**)
Settlement negotiations, evidence of (See **SETTLEMENT AND COMPROMISE**)
Sex offenses (See **SEX OFFENSES**)
Subsequent safety measures, evidence of   Ev §1151
Sympathy or benevolent expressions as admission for civil liability, inadmissibility of   Ev §1160
Time-consuming evidence, exclusion of   Ev §352
Verdict, evidence impeaching or supporting   Ev §1150

ADMISSIONS
Admissibility, determination of   Ev §402
Child welfare services case plan, effect of parent signing or accepting services under   Ev §1228.1
Confessions (See **CONFESSIONS**)
Hearsay evidence   Ev §§1220, 1230
Material allegations, failure to respond   CCP §§431.20, 431.30
Requests for (See **REQUEST FOR ADMISSION**)
Service of process, written proof of   CCP §§417.10, 417.20
Summary judgments, admissions in support or opposition of motion for   CCP §437c
Third party, statement by   Ev §1224

ADMISSIONS DAY
Judicial holidays, excluded from days designated as   CCP §135

ADMITTED SURETY INSURERS (See **SURETYSHIP, BONDS AND UNDERTAKINGS**)

ADMONISHMENT (See **JUDGES**)

ADOPTION
Abandonment of child   Fam §§7822, 8606, 8607
Accounting report   Fam §8610
Address of birth parents   Fam §§8702, 8703, 8818, 8819
Adoption facilitators
    Education of public on unlicensed adoption agencies
        Website, creation   Fam §8625
Adoption service provider
    Defined   Fam §8502
    Duties   Fam §§8801.3 to 8801.7
Adoptive parents
    Age difference between child and   Fam §8601
    Appearance by counsel
        Absence for military, charitable, or religious service   Fam §8613
        Waiver of personal appearance when impossible or impracticable   Fam §8613.5
    Consent of spouse   Fam §8603
    Defined   Fam §8503
    Disqualifying factors   Fam §8712
    Investigation of   Fam §8712
Adult adoptions
    Generally   Fam §9300
    Agreement for adoption   Fam §§9320, 9321
    Appearance at hearing   Fam §§9323, 9324
    Consent required   Fam §§9301, 9302
    Developmentally disabled persons   Fam §§9326, 9327
    Examination of parties   Fam §9328
    Hearings   Fam §§9307, 9322, 9323
    Investigations and reports   Fam §§9325, 9327
    Name of adopted person   Fam §9304
    Notice of hearing   Fam §§9323, 9326
    Petition
        Approval of adoption   Fam §9321
        Termination of parent-child relationship   Fam §9340
    Termination of birth parents rights and obligations   Fam §9306
    Unrelated adults, limit on number that may be adopted in one year   Fam §9303
    Venue for petitions   Fam §9321.5
Advertising
    Unlicensed persons or agencies   Fam §8609
Affidavits
    Brothers and sisters, request for contact between   Fam §9205
    Identity of birth parents, request for   Fam §9203

ADOPTION—Cont.
Age
    Disclosure of identity of birth parents to child attaining age of 21   Fam §§8702, 8818, 9203
    Minimum age difference between adoptive parents and child   Fam §8601
Agency adoptions
    Accreditation of full service adoption agencies   Fam §8521
        Noncustodial adoption agencies   Fam §8533
    Appeal of unfavorable recommendation   Fam §8720
    Appearance at hearing   Fam §8718
    Attorney for petitioner, reports and findings submitted to   Fam §8717
    Concealment of child   Fam §8713
    Consent generally (See within this heading, **"Consent"**)
    County agencies
        Custody and control of child   Fam §8704
        Deceased parents, adoption of child of   Fam §8705
        Definition of county adoption agency   Fam §8513
        Delegated county adoption agency defined   Fam §8515
        Fees   Fam §8716
        Foster parent or relative caregiver as prospective parent   Fam §§8730, 8732, 8733, 8735
        Investigation of prospective adoptive parents   Fam §8712
        Photo-listing service   Fam §8707
        Relinquishment of child to agency   Fam §§8700, 8700.5, 8702
        Reporting requirements for agency adoptions   Fam §§8715, 8717
        Sibling contact   Fam §9205
        Unfavorable report   Fam §8720
    Custody and control of child   Fam §§8704, 8705
    Deceased parents, consent where   Fam §8705
    Defined   Fam §8506
    Delegated county adoption agency
        Defined   Fam §8515
    Denial of petition   Fam §8720
    Disclosure of information   Fam §9201
    Dismissal of petition   Fam §8719
    DNA testing on blood samples provided by biological parents   Fam §§8706, 9202.5
    Fees   Fam §8716
    Foster care license or certification
        When not required   Fam §8704.5
    Foster parent adoptions generally (See within this heading, **"Foster parents, adoption by"**)
    Full-service adoption agency   Fam §8521
    Information concerning adoption issues and specific needs of child, requirement that adoptive parent be provided with   Fam §8733
    Intercounty adoptions
        Discrimination in placement, prohibition   Fam §8708
        Statewide exchange system   Fam §§8710.1 to 8710.4
    Interstate adoptions generally (See within this heading, **"Interstate adoptions"**)
    Investigation of prospective adoptive parent
        Copy of report and findings given to petitioner's attorney   Fam §8717
        Criminal investigations   Fam §§8712, 8730
        Foster parents seeking to adopt   Fam §§8730 to 8732
        Relative caregiver seeking to adopt   Fam §§8730, 8732
        Submission of report to court   Fam §8715
    Medical information generally (See within this heading, **"Medical information"**)
    Noncustodial adoption agency   Fam §8533
    Order of adoption   Fam §8714
    Petition for adoption
        Generally   Fam §§8704, 8714
        Denial of   Fam §8720
        Withdrawal of   Fam §8719
    Photo-listing service   Fam §8707
    Placement preference rules generally (See within this heading, **"Placement preference rules"**)
    Presumption concerning adoptive placement   Fam §8704
    Relative adoptions generally (See within this heading, **"Relatives"**)
    Relinquishment of child (See within this heading, **"Relinquishment of child"**)
    Relinquishment of child to agency   Fam §8700
        Revocation of right to relinquish, waiver   Fam §8700.5
        Statement to birth parents at time of relinquishment   Fam §8702
    Removal of child from adoptive home   Fam §8704
    Removal of child from county during   Fam §8713
    Reports submitted to court   Fam §§8715, 8717
    Training programs for prospective adoptive parents, policy statement concerning   Fam §8734
    Unfavorable recommendation by agency or department   Fam §8720
    Withdrawal of petition   Fam §8719

ADOPTION—Cont.
Agreements
    Adoption placement agreement   Fam §8801.3
    Adoptive parents to treat child as lawful child   Fam §8612
    Adult adoptee and adoptive parents, agreement between   Fam §§9320, 9321
    Intercountry adoptions   Fam §8905
    Judicial council forms   CRCAppx A
    Kinship and postadoption contact agreements with birth parent   CRC 5.451, Fam §§8616.5, 8714, 8714.5
    Kinship and postadoption contact agreements with siblings   CRC 5.451
American Indian ancestry, certificate pertaining to   Fam §8619
Appeals
    Agency adoptions, review of unfavorable report   Fam §8720
    Alleged father's consent, appeal from order requiring or dispensing with   Fam §7669
    Independent adoptions (See within this heading, **"Independent adoptions"**)
    Intercountry adoptions, review of unfavorable agency report   Fam §8917
    Order requiring or dispensing with alleged father's consent   Fam §7669
    Withdrawal of consent to adoption   Fam §9005
Appearance
    Agency adoptions   Fam §8718
    Attorney appearing for adoptive parent
        Absence of parent for military, charitable, or religious service   Fam §8613
        Waiver of personal appearance when impossible or impracticable   Fam §8613.5
    Independent adoption proceedings   Fam §8823
    Intercountry adoptions   Fam §8913
    Remote electronic means, appearance by   Fam §8613.5
    Stepparent adoptions   Fam §9007
Applicants
    Defined   Fam §8509
Attorneys
    Adoptive parent's appearance by counsel
        Absence for military, charitable, or religious service   Fam §8613
        Waiver of personal appearance when impossible or impracticable   Fam §8613.5
    Counsel for child, CASA programs   CRC 5.655
    Independent adoption proceedings, attorney-client relationship in   Fam §8800
    Petitioner's attorney, agency reports submitted to   Fam §§8717, 8821, 8915
Best interest of child
    Petitions to set aside adoption
        Consideration of best interest in ruling on petition   Fam §9102
Birth certificates
    Deceased spouse as parent on new birth certificate, inclusion of   Fam §8615
    Readopted child originally adopted in foreign country   Fam §8919
Birth parents
    Address of   Fam §§8702, 8703, 8818, 8819
    Adult adoptee and adult adoptee's birth parents, consent for contact between   Fam §9204
    Consent
        Generally   Fam §§8604, 8606
        Stepparent adoptions (See within this heading, **"Stepparent adoptions"**)
    Deceased birth parents, adoption of child of   Fam §8705
    Defined   Fam §8512
    Disclosure of identity to child attaining age of 21   Fam §§8702, 8818, 9203
    Effect of adoption on   Fam §8617
    Inheritance rights   Pro §6451
    Medical history   Fam §§8702, 8706, 8817, 8818, 8909
    Name of birth parents stricken from documents   Fam §9200
    Notice to birth parent of termination of parental rights   Fam §8819
    Rights, requirement that birth parents be advised of   Fam §§8801.3, 8801.5
    Statement to birth parents at time consent to adoption is signed   Fam §8818
    Statement to parents at time of relinquishment   Fam §8702
    Status of adoption, information on   Fam §§8701, 8813
    Termination of parental rights, notice of   Fam §§8703, 8819
Brothers and sisters
    Adult adoptions, limit on number of   Fam §9303
    Disclosure of information on sibling of adoptee   Fam §9205
        Request for sibling contact information   CRC 5.460
    Exception to age difference required between child and adoptive parents   Fam §8601
    Postadoption contact agreements   Fam §8616.5
    Readoption in state of child originally adopted in foreign country
        Sibling separation, visitation with separated siblings   Fam §8920
    Request for sibling contact information   CRC 5.460

ADOPTION—Cont.
  Certificate of adoption
    Generally   Fam §8614
    Contents of   Fam §9200
  Certification of out-of-state group homes pursuant to Interstate Compact on the Placement of Children   Fam §7911.1
  Certification of prospective adoptive parents by private agency, preplacement evaluation as basis of   Fam §8811.5
  Civil unions
    Stepparent adoptions
      Birth of child during marriage, domestic partnership or civil union   Fam §9000.5
  Closed hearings   Fam §8611
  Concealment of child   Fam §§8713, 8803
    Intercountry adoptions   Fam §8910
  Confidential intermediaries   Fam §9205
    Sibling contacts
      Request for sibling contact information   CRC 5.460
  Confidentiality of records   Fam §9200
    Disclosures generally (See within this heading, **"Disclosures"**)
  Conflict of interest of attorney representing both parties in independent adoptions   Fam §8800
  Conflict of laws
    Adult adoptions   Fam §9321.5
    Jurisdiction   Fam §9210
      Interstate adoptions   Fam §9212
  Consent
    Adult adoptee and adult adoptee's birth parents, consent for contact between   Fam §9204
    Adult adoptions   Fam §§9301, 9302
    Appealability of order on withdrawal of consent   Fam §9005
    Birth parents   Fam §§8604, 8606
      Stepparent adoptions (See within this heading, **"Stepparent adoptions"**)
    Deceased parents, consent where   Fam §8705
    Independent adoptions (See within this heading, **"Independent adoptions"**)
    Indian child's parents   Fam §8606.5
    Minor birth parent's consent   Fam §§8814, 9003
    Mother's consent   Fam §8605
    Other parent, relinquishment or consent by other parent   Fam §7661
    Presumed father   Fam §8604
    Revocation of   Fam §8814.5
    Spouse of married adoptive parent   Fam §8603
    Stepparent adoptions (See within this heading, **"Stepparent adoptions"**)
    12-year-old child or older, consent of   Fam §8602
  County adoption agencies
    Custody and control of child   Fam §8704
    Deceased birth parents, adoption of child of   Fam §8705
    Defined   Fam §8513
    Delegated county adoption agency defined   Fam §8515
    Diversity of potential adoptive parents   Fam §8707.1
    Fees   Fam §8716
    Foster parent or relative caregiver as prospective parent
      Assessment or home study requirements   Fam §§8730, 8732
      Denial, notice to agency responsible for foster care placement   Fam §8735
      Information to prospective parents   Fam §8733
      Medical reports included in assessment   Fam §8732
    Investigation of prospective adoptive parents   Fam §8712
    Photo-listing service
      Establishing service for use by agencies   Fam §8707
    Relinquishment of child to agency   Fam §8700
      Revocation of right to relinquish, waiver   Fam §8700.5
      Statement to birth parents at time of relinquishment   Fam §8702
    Reporting requirements for agency adoptions   Fam §§8715, 8717
    Sibling contact
      Criteria for information release   Fam §9205
    Unfavorable report
      Review in court   Fam §8720
  Criminal records (See within this heading, **"Fingerprints and criminal records"**)
  Cruelly treated child   Fam §7823
  Custody and control of child
    Agency adoptions   Fam §§8704, 8705
    Deceased parents, consent where   Fam §8705
    Intercountry adoptions   Fam §8903
  Days defined for   Fam §8514
  Deceased birth parents, adoption of child of   Fam §8705
  Deceased spouse named as parent in new birth certificate   Fam §8615
  Definitions   Fam §§8500 to 8548
  Delegated county adoption agency defined   Fam §8515
  Delinquent children, placement in institution in another state   Fam §7908

ADOPTION—Cont.
  Department of Social Services   Fam §8518
  Dependent children
    Authorization for adoption, permanency planning hearing   CRC 5.706 to 5.740
    Form   CRC 5.730
    Orders
      Judicial council form   CRCAppx A
    Permanent plan, selection   CRC 5.725
    Petition
      Where filed   Fam §8714
    Prospective adoptive parent designation   CRC 5.726
  Deposition to examine adoptive parent   Fam §§8613, 8613.5
  Descent and distribution (See within this heading, **"Inheritance rights, effect on"**)
  Desertion of child   Fam §8606
  Developmentally disabled persons
    Adult adoption proceedings   Fam §§9326, 9327
    Setting aside adoption, petition for   Fam §9100
  Disabled persons
    Adult adoptions, limit on number of   Fam §9303
    Developmentally disabled
      Adult adoption proceedings   Fam §§9326, 9327
      Setting aside adoption, petition   Fam §9100
  Disclosures
    Confidential intermediaries   Fam §9205
    Confidentiality of records, generally   Fam §9200
    Home study and updates to home study
      Resource family status of prospective adoptive parents, release to gain approval of status   Fam §9203.1
    Identity of birth parents   Fam §§8702, 8818, 9203
    Information Practices Act, disclosures under   CC §1798.24
    Medical reports   Fam §9202
    Public agencies or licensed adoption agencies, disclosure of information by   Fam §9201
    Siblings
      Names and addresses   CRC 5.460, Fam §9205
    Statewide exchange system   Fam §8710.4
    Waiver of confidentiality   Fam §§9204, 9205
      Request for sibling contact information   CRC 5.460
  Discrimination in placement, prohibition of   Fam §8708
  Diversity of potential adoptive parents
    Agency adoptions   Fam §8707.1
  DNA testing
    Access to stored blood samples provided by biological parents   Fam §9202.5
    Agency adoptions, storing of blood samples from biological parents in   Fam §8706
    Independent adoptions, storing of blood samples from biological parents in   Fam §8817
    Intercountry adoptions, storing of blood samples from biological parents in   Fam §8909
  Domestic partner adoption
    Stepparent adoptions
      Birth of child during marriage, domestic partnership or civil union   Fam §9000.5
  Ethnic background of child
    Placement preference rules generally (See within this heading, **"Placement preference rules"**)
  Examination of parties
    Generally   Fam §8612
    Adult adoption proceedings   Fam §9328
    Depositions   Fam §§8613, 8613.5
  Exchange system for interjurisdictional adoptions   Fam §§8710.1 to 8710.4
  Expenses, accounting report of   Fam §8610
  Facilitators (See within this heading, **"Adoption facilitators"**)
  Family rules
    Hague adoption convention, adoptions under   CRC 5.490 to 5.492
    Intercountry adoptions   CRC 5.490 to 5.493
  Father
    Birth parents (See within this heading, **"Birth parents"**)
    Identification of natural father   Fam §7663
    Termination of parental rights (See within this heading, **"Termination of parental rights"**)
  Fees
    Accounting reports   Fam §8610
    Agency adoptions   Fam §8716
    Brothers and sisters, request for contact between   Fam §9205
    Identity of birth parents, request for   Fam §9203
    Independent adoption proceedings   Fam §§8810, 8812
    Intercountry adoptions   Fam §8907

ADOPTION—Cont.
Fees—Cont.
Payment by adoptive parents, birth parent's request for Fam §8812
Stepparent adoptions Fam §9002
Termination of parental rights of father, filing fees for petition for Fam §7670
Filing of postadoption contact agreements with court Fam §8616.5
Agency adoptions Fam §8714
Independent adoption Fam §8802
Intercountry adoption Fam §8912
Stepparent adoptions Fam §9000
Fingerprints and criminal records
Agency adoptions Fam §§8712, 8730
Foster parents and relative caregivers seeking to adopt Fam §8730
Independent adoption proceedings Fam §8811
Intercountry adoptions Fam §8908
Foreign country adoptions Fam §§8900 to 8920
Hague adoption convention, adoptions under CRC 5.490 to 5.492
Intercountry adoptions generally CRC 5.490 to 5.493 (See within this heading, **"Intercountry adoptions"**)
Forms
Agency adoptions, form authorizing disclosure of birth parent's name and address Fam §8702
Dependent children CRC 5.730
Independent adoptions, form authorizing disclosure of birth parent's name and address Fam §8818
Judicial council legal forms CRCAppx A
Release of child from health facility Fam §8607
Foster parents, adoption by
Generally Fam §8710
Agency adoptions
    Foster care license or certification, when not required Fam §8704.5
Assessment or home study of foster parent or relative caregiver seeking to adopt Fam §§8730 to 8732
Denial of approval for adoption by foster parent or relative caregiver, foster care placement agency notified of Fam §8735
Medical assessment of foster parent or relative caregiver seeking to adopt Fam §8732
Pre-1999 placement with foster parent or relative caregiver, effect of current law on Fam §8736
Full-service adoption agency Fam §8521
Guardian adopting
Child free from parental custody and control
    Proceeding to declare Pro §1516.5
Petition for adoption Fam §8802
Hague adoption convention, adoptions under CRC 5.490 to 5.492
Child residents of foreign country, Hague convention party
    US resident adopting CRC 5.492
Child residents of US
    Foreign country not party to convention CRC 5.491
    Foreign country party to convention CRC 5.490
Hague adoption certificate
    Defined Fam §8900.5
    Recognition as final adoption Fam §8925
Hague custody declaration
    Defined Fam §8900.5
    Recognition as final adoption Fam §8925
Intercountry adoptions generally CRC 5.490 to 5.493, Fam §§8900 to 8920 (See within this heading, **"Intercountry adoptions"**)
Health (See within this heading, **"Medical information"**)
Health facility, forms for release of child from Fam §8607
Health insurance
Notice of reduced-cost options through California health benefit exchange or no-cost Medi-Cal
    Court notice to petitioners for adoption Fam §8613.7
Hearings
Adult adoptions Fam §§9307, 9322, 9323
Appearance generally (See within this heading, **"Appearance"**)
Closed hearings Fam §8611
Termination of parental rights Fam §§7667, 7668
Home studies
Disclosure by department or adoption agency
    Resource family status of prospective adoptive parents, release to gain approval of status Fam §9203.1
Intercountry adoptions
    Readoption in state of child originally adopted in foreign country Fam §8919
Interstate situations Fam §§7901.1, 7906.5
Identification of birth parents Fam §§8702, 8818, 9203
Alleged fathers and presumed parents Fam §7663

ADOPTION—Cont.
Independent adoptions
Address of birth parents Fam §§8818, 8819
Appeals
    Adverse agency action, appeal of Fam §8820
    Unfavorable agency report, review of Fam §8822
    Withdrawal of consent Fam §8815
Appearance at hearing Fam §8823
Attorney-client relationship Fam §8800
Attorney for petitioner, reports and findings given to Fam §8821
Concealment of child Fam §8803
Consent requirements
    Agency or department Fam §8816
    Birth parents Fam §8814
    Duty to accept Fam §8806
    Failure or refusal of county agency to consent Fam §8820
    Request to sign consent in presence of court Fam §8809
    Withdrawal of consent Fam §8815
Defined Fam §8524
Denial of petition Fam §8822
Disclosure of birth parent's name and address Fam §8818
Dismissal of petition Fam §8804
Disqualifying factors for prospective adoptive parents Fam §8811
DNA testing of blood samples provided by biological parents Fam §§8817, 9202.5
Duty of department or agency Fam §8806
Fees Fam §§8810, 8812
Fingerprints of adoptive parents Fam §8811
Health problems of birth parents Fam §§8817, 8819
Investigation of prospective adoptive parent
    Generally Fam §8807
    Criminal records Fam §8811
    Interview by department or agency Fam §§8808, 8809
    Preplacement certification by private agency, investigation in connection with Fam §8811.5
Medical reports on child and biological parents Fam §§8817 to 8819, 9202.5
Notice to birth parent of termination of parental rights Fam §8819
Order of adoption Fam §8802
Personal knowledge of prospective adoptive parents Fam §8801
Petition for adoption
    Generally Fam §8802
    Denial of Fam §8822
    Withdrawal of Fam §8804
Removal of child from adoptive home Fam §8805
Removal of child from county Fam §8803
Reports and findings submitted to court Fam §8821
Return of child to birth parents Fam §8815
Selection of prospective adoptive parents Fam §8801
Statement to birth parents at time consent to adoption is signed Fam §8818
Status of adoption, request for information on Fam §8813
Unfavorable recommendation by department or agency Fam §8822
Withdrawal of petition Fam §8804
Indian child
Involuntary placements, rules governing CRC 5.480 to 5.488 (See **INDIAN CHILD WELFARE ACT INVOLUNTARY PLACEMENTS**)
Judicial council forms CRCAppx A
Native Americans generally (See within this heading, **"Native Americans"**)
Information concerning adoption issues and specific needs of child, requirement that adoptive parent be provided with Fam §8733
Information Practices Act, disclosures under CC §1798.24
Inheritance rights, effect on
Adoptive parents and child, relationship between Pro §6450
Judicial doctrine of equitable adoption, precedence of Pro §6455
Natural parents and child, severance of relationship between Pro §6451
Stepparent adoptions Fam §9004, Pro §6451
Intercountry adoptions
Accredited agencies
    Defined Fam §8900.5
Adoption of regulations Fam §8901
Adoption service
    Defined Fam §8900.5
    Emigration of child from California to convention country, duties of provider of adoption service Fam §8924
Agreements with other adoption agencies Fam §8905
Appeal of unfavorable agency report Fam §8917
Appearance at hearing Fam §8913
Attorney of petitioner, reports given to Fam §8915
Central authority
    Defined Fam §8900.5
Concealment of child Fam §8910

ADOPTION—Cont.
  Intercountry adoptions—Cont.
    Convention
      Defined   Fam §8900.5
    Convention adoption
      Complaints, applicable provisions   Fam §8923
      Defined   Fam §8900.5
      Facilitation, bond   Fam §8921
    Convention country
      Defined   Fam §8900.5
      Emigration of child from California to convention country, adoption service provider duties   Fam §8924
    Custody and control of child   Fam §8903
    Definitions   Fam §§527, 8900.5
    Dismissal of petition   Fam §8916
    Disqualifying factors to prospective adoptive parents   Fam §8908
    DNA testing on blood samples provided by biological parents   Fam §§8909, 9202.5
    Exempted providers
      Defined   Fam §8900.5
    Fees   Fam §8907
    Financial responsibility of child, agreement to share   Fam §8906
    Foreign country, adoptions finalized in   Fam §8904
      Child born in foreign country
        Request to adopt under California law   CRC 5.493
    Hague adoption convention, adoptions under   CRC 5.490 to 5.492
      Child residents of Hague convention foreign country, US resident adopting   CRC 5.492
      Child residents of US adopted by resident of foreign country not party to convention   CRC 5.491
      Child residents of US adopted by resident of foreign country party to convention   CRC 5.490
      Definition of Hague adoption certificates and Hague custody declarations   Fam §8900.5
      Judicial council forms   CRCAppx A
      Recognition of Hague adoption certificates and Hague custody declarations as final adoption   Fam §8925
    Investigation of prospective adoptive parents
      Generally   Fam §8902
      Criminal investigations   Fam §8908
    Legal service
      Defined   Fam §8900.5
    Licensing of private adoption agencies engaged in   Fam §§8900, 8902
    Medi-Cal eligibility   Fam §8903
    Medical report on child and biological parents   Fam §§8909, 9202.5
    Order of adoption   Fam §8912
    Primary providers
      Defined   Fam §8900.5
    Public domestic authority
      Defined   Fam §8900.5
    Readoption in state of child originally adopted in foreign country   Fam §8919
      Arrival of adoptee, report to department   Fam §8919.5
      Sibling separation, visitation with separated siblings   Fam §8920
    Regulation of   Fam §8901
    Removal of child from adoptive home   Fam §8918
    Removal of child from county   Fam §8910
    Reports and findings submitted to court   Fam §§8914, 8915
    Request for adoption   Fam §8912
      Time to file   Fam §8911
      Withdrawal   Fam §8916
    Request to adopt under California law
      Child born in foreign country when adoption finalized in foreign country   CRC 5.493
    Secretary
      Defined   Fam §8900.5
    Services provided by agency   Fam §8902
    Supervised providers
      Defined   Fam §8900.5
    Unfavorable recommendation by adoption agency   Fam §8917
    Withdrawal of petition   Fam §8916
  Intercounty adoptions
    Discrimination in placement, prohibition of   Fam §8708
    Statewide exchange system   Fam §§8710.1 to 8710.4
  Interstate adoptions
    Determination of placement by agency   Fam §7913
    Discrimination in placement, prohibition of   Fam §8708
    Home environment study request from another state   Fam §7901.1
    Custody of child in requesting state   Fam §7906.5

ADOPTION—Cont.
  Interstate adoptions—Cont.
    Interstate Compact on Placement of Children   CRC 5.616, Fam §§7900 to 7913
      Children covered by compact   Fam §7907.5
    Relinquishment by parent residing in other state   Fam §8700
  Interviews
    Examination of parties generally (See within this heading, "**Examination of parties**")
    Independent adoption proceedings   Fam §§8808, 8809
  Investigations
    Adult adoption proceedings   Fam §§9325, 9327
    Agency adoptions (See within this heading, "**Agency adoptions**")
    Criminal investigations (See within this heading, "**Fingerprints and criminal records**")
    Independent adoptions (See within this heading, "**Independent adoptions**")
    Intercountry adoptions   Fam §8902
      Criminal investigations   Fam §8908
    Interstate Compact on the Placement of Children, oversight of placement arrangements pursuant to   Fam §§7911 to 7912
    Stepparent adoptions   Fam §9001
      Cost of investigation   Fam §9002
  Jurisdiction   Fam §§8714, 9210
    Interstate adoptions   Fam §9212
  Juvenile court proceedings (See **JUVENILE COURTS**)
  Juvenile rules
    Hague adoption convention, adoptions under   CRC 5.490 to 5.492
  Juvenile wardship proceedings, freeing wards for adoption   CRC 5.825
  Kinship adoption agreements with birth parent   CRC 5.451, Fam §§8616.5, 8714, 8714.5
  Kinship adoption agreements with siblings   CRC 5.451
  Letters in possession of adoption agency, release of   Fam §9206
  Licensed adoption agency
    Agency adoptions generally (See within this heading, "**Agency adoptions**")
    Defined   Fam §8530
    Education of public on unlicensed adoption agencies
      Website, creation   Fam §8625
    Intercountry adoptions   Fam §§8900, 8902
    Regulation of   Fam §8621
  Marriage
    Stepparent adoption
      Birth of child during marriage, domestic partnership, etc   Fam §9000.5
  Medical care
    Eligibility of dependent child for Medi-Cal   Fam §8903
    Intercountry adoption proceedings, care of child involved in   Fam §8903
    Release of child from health facility, forms for   Fam §8607
  Medi-Cal eligibility of child   Fam §8903
  Medical information
    Generally   Fam §§8702, 8703, 8818, 8819
    Birth parents notifying department of health problems   Fam §§8702, 8818
    Disclosure of report upon request to certain persons   Fam §9202
    DNA testing of blood samples provided by biological parents (See within this heading, "**DNA testing**")
    Foster parent seeking to adopt, medical assessment of   Fam §8732
    Independent adoption proceedings   Fam §§8817 to 8819, 9202.5
    Information Practices Act, disclosures under   CC §1798.24
    Intercountry adoptions   Fam §§8909, 9202.5
    Regulations   Fam §8608
    Relative seeking to adopt, medical assessment of   Fam §8732
    Submitted to adoptive parents   Fam §§8706, 8817
  Mentally ill persons
    Developmentally disabled persons generally (See within this heading, "**Developmentally disabled persons**")
    Setting aside adoption, petition for   Fam §9100
  Military service, adoptive parent absent because of   Fam §8613
  Names
    Adopted child's name   Fam §8618
    Adult adoptee   Fam §9304
    Order of adoption containing child's adopted name   Fam §§8714, 8802, 8912, 9000
  Native Americans
    Certificate of ancestry   Fam §8619
    Consent to adoption
      Parental consent   Fam §8606.5
    Final orders
      Copy to secretary of interior   Fam §9208
    Involuntary placements, rules governing   CRC 5.480 to 5.488 (See **INDIAN CHILD WELFARE ACT INVOLUNTARY PLACEMENTS**)
    Placement preferences and standards   Fam §8710
    Postadoption contract agreements   Fam §8616.5

ADOPTION—Cont.
  Native Americans—Cont.
    Prospective adoptive parents
      Designation   CRC 5.726
    Termination of parental rights of father
      Waiver of rights to notice of adoption procedures   Fam §7660.5
    Tribal customary adoptions
      Defined   CRC 5.502
      Disposition hearings, consideration of tribal custom adoptions   CRC 5.690
      Emergency removal   CRC 5.728
      Permanency hearings   CRC 5.715, 5.720, 5.722
      Permanent plan selection   CRC 5.725
      Post-permanency review hearings   CRC 5.740
      Proposed removal   CRC 5.727
      Review hearings   CRC 5.708
    Tribe or organization membership of child
      Information as to tribal affiliation   Fam §9209
      Status information obtained by specified entities   Fam §8620
    Unmarried minors, adoption of
      Provisions applicable when Indian children involved   CRC 5.730, Fam §8600.5
    Vacating or setting aside decree of adoption
      Return of custody, petition for   Fam §8619.5
  Natural parents
    Birth parents generally (See within this heading, **"Birth parents"**)
  Neglected child   Fam §7823
  Noncustodial adoption agency   Fam §8533
  Nondependent minors
    Venue
      Request for filing request for adoption or readoption of nondependent minor, locations for filing   Fam §8609.5
  Nonminor dependents
    Forms   CRCAppx A
  Notices
    Adult adoption proceedings   Fam §§9323, 9326
    Dispensing with notice to biological father   Fam §7666
    Father notified of adoption proceedings   Fam §§7664, 7666
    Foster parent or relative caregiver, foster care placement agency notified of denial of approval for adoption by   Fam §8735
    Presumed parent notified of adoption proceedings   Fam §7660
      Manner of giving notice   Fam §7666
      Voluntary waiver of notice   Fam §7660.5
    Stepparent adoptions, notice to birth parent of   Fam §9004
    Termination of parental rights   Fam §§8703, 8819
  Order of adoption   Fam §8612
    Agency adoptions   Fam §8714
    Independent adoption proceedings   Fam §8802
    Intercountry adoptions   Fam §8912
    Judicial council forms   CRCAppx A
    Nunc pro tunc orders   Fam §8601.5
    Stepparent adoptions   Fam §9000
    Vacation of adoption order   Fam §§9101, 9102
  Other states (See within this heading, **"Interstate adoptions"**)
  Parent and child relationship, establishment of   Fam §7610
  Personal property in possession of adoption agency, release of   Fam §9206
  Petition for adoption
    Adult adoption, petition for approval of   Fam §9321
    Agency adoptions (See within this heading, **"Agency adoptions"**)
    Independent adoption proceedings (See within this heading, **"Independent adoptions"**)
    Intercountry adoptions (See within this heading, **"Intercountry adoptions"**)
    Postadoption contact agreement with birth parent, filing with   Fam §§8714, 8714.5
    Stepparent adoptions   Fam §9000
  Petition for termination of parental rights of alleged father
    Multiple alleged fathers of same child
      Single petition   Fam §7671
    Multiple biological siblings
      Single petition   Fam §7671
  Petitions
    Setting aside adoption, petition for   Fam §9100
    Termination of parental rights of father   Fam §7662
  Photographs in possession of adoption agency, release of   Fam §9206
  Photo-listing service   Fam §8707
  Place for adoption defined   Fam §8539
  Placement for adoption requirements   Fam §8801.3
  Placement preference rules
    Applicability of criteria   Fam §8711
    Foster parents, consideration of   Fam §8710
    Prohibited discrimination   Fam §8708

ADOPTION—Cont.
  Placement preference rules—Cont.
    Regulations, adoption of   Fam §8711.5
    Relative, preference for placement with   Fam §8710
    Religious background, consideration of   Fam §8709
  Postadoption contact agreements   CRC 5.451
    Birth parent   CRC 5.451, Fam §§8616.5, 8714, 8714.5
      Independent adoption petitions
        Attachment of agreement to petition   Fam §8802
      Intercounty adoption petitions
        Attachment of agreement to petition   Fam §8912
      Stepparent or domestic partner adoption petitions
        Attachment of agreement to petition   Fam §9000
    Siblings   CRC 5.451
  Presumed father
    Consent   Fam §8604
  Prospective adoptive parents
    Defined   Fam §8542
    Designation   CRC 5.726
  Qualified court investigator defined   Fam §8543
  Racial background of child
    Placement preference rules generally (See within this heading, **"Placement preference rules"**)
  Readoption in state of child originally adopted in foreign country   Fam §8919
    Arrival of adoptee, report to department   Fam §8919.5
    Sibling separation, visitation with separated siblings   Fam §8920
  Relationship between adopted child and adoptive parents   Fam §§8616, 9305
  Relatives
    Adoption by   Fam §§8714.5, 8802
    Age difference between child and adoptive parents, exception to requirements concerning   Fam §8601
    Assessment or home study of foster parent or relative caregiver seeking to adopt   Fam §§8730, 8732
    Consent to adoption of child when both birth parents deceased   Fam §8705
    Denial of approval for adoption by foster parent or relative caregiver, foster care placement agency notified of   Fam §8735
    Kinship adoption agreement   CRC 5.451
    Medical assessment of foster parent or relative caregiver seeking to adopt   Fam §8732
    Postadoption contact agreement with birth parent   CRC 5.451, Fam §8616.5
    Postadoption contact agreement with siblings   CRC 5.451
    Pre-1999 placement with foster parent or relative caregiver, effect of current law on   Fam §8736
    Preference for placement with   Fam §8710
    Siblings (See within this heading, **"Brothers and sisters"**)
  Religious background, consideration of   Fam §8709
  Relinquishment of child
    Agency, relinquishment to   Fam §8700
      Effect of relinquishment   Fam §7662
      Exception to requirement of parental consent   Fam §8606
      Filing of   Fam §8700
      Minor birth parent   Fam §8700
      Other states, birth parent residing in   Fam §8700
      Rescission of   Fam §8700
      Revocation of right to relinquish, waiver   Fam §8700.5
      Statement to birth parents at time of relinquishment   Fam §8702
    Other parent, relinquishment or consent by other parent   Fam §7661
  Removal of child from adoptive home
    Agency adoptions   Fam §8704
    Independent adoption proceedings   Fam §8805
    Intercountry adoptions   Fam §8918
  Removal of child from county
    Agency adoptions   Fam §8713
    Independent adoptions   Fam §8803
    Intercountry adoptions   Fam §8910
  Reports
    Agency adoptions, reporting requirements   Fam §§8715, 8717
    Developmentally disabled persons, adoption of   Fam §9327
    Independent adoptions, reports and findings submitted to court given to petitioner's attorney   Fam §8821
    Intercountry adoptions   Fam §§8914, 8915
    Investigation of prospective adoptive parent in independent adoption proceedings   Fam §8807
    Medical reports
      Medical information generally (See within this heading, **"Medical information"**)
  Request for adoption
    Agency adoptions
      Venue for filing request   Fam §8714
    Forms   CRCAppx A

ADOPTION—Cont.
Request for adoption—Cont.
Independent adoptions
Venue for filing request   Fam §8802
Rescission of relinquishment of child to adoption agency   Fam §8700
Revocation of right to relinquish, waiver   Fam §8700.5
Revocation
Birth parents' consent to adoption   Fam §8814.5
Setting aside adoption (See within this heading, **"Vacation of adoption"**)
Siblings (See within this heading, **"Brothers and sisters"**)
Special-needs child defined   Fam §8545
Statewide exchange system   Fam §§8710.1 to 8710.4
Statute of limitation to vacation of adoption proceedings   Fam §9102
Stepparent adoptions   Fam §8548
Appeal of withdrawal of consent to adoption   Fam §9005
Appearance at hearings   Fam §9007
Birth of child during marriage, domestic partnership or civil union   Fam §9000.5
Confirmation of parentage
Declaration, forms   CRCAppx A
Consent requirement
Birth parent's consent   Fam §9003
Inheritance rights of child   Fam §9004
Notice to birth parent   Fam §9004
Refusal of birth parent to give   Fam §9006
Withdrawal of consent   Fam §9005
Defined   Fam §8548
Dismissal of petition   Fam §9006
Fees   Fam §9002
Home study   Fam §9001
Inheritance rights, effect on   Fam §9004, Pro §6451
Investigations
Generally   Fam §9001
Cost of   Fam §9002
Judicial council forms   CRCAppx A
Notice to birth parent   Fam §9004
Order of adoption   Fam §9000
Petition for adoption
Generally   Fam §9000
Withdrawal of   Fam §9006
Withdrawal of petition   Fam §9006
Temporary custody orders   Fam §8604
Termination of parental rights   Fam §§7660 to 7671
Alleged fathers
Appeal from order requiring or dispensing with alleged father's consent   Fam §7669
Determination and order concerning parental rights   Fam §7664
Ex parte order terminating   Fam §7667
Multiple alleged fathers of same child, single petition   Fam §7671
Multiple biological siblings, single petition   Fam §7671
Notice requirements for mother relinquishing child for adoption   Fam §§7660, 7660.5, 7664, 7666
Petitions   Fam §§7662, 9340
Preference for trial   Fam §7667
Relinquishment, effect   Fam §7662
Setting for hearing   Fam §7667
Unknown biological father   Fam §7665
Voluntary waiver of notice for mother relinquishing child for adoption   Fam §7660.5
Filing fee   Fam §7670
Referral for adoption following termination   Fam §7893
Termination of parent-child relationship
Generally   Fam §§8703, 8819
Adult adoption proceedings   Fam §§9306, 9340
Costs, petitioner's liability for   Fam §7851.5
Father's rights (See within this heading, **"Termination of parental rights"**)
Training programs for prospective adoptive parents, policy statement concerning   Fam §8734
Uniform parentage act
Vacation or setting aside of judgment
Effect of provisions on adoption   Fam §7648.8
Unlicensed persons or agencies, advertising by   Fam §8609
Education of public on unlicensed adoption agencies
Website, creation   Fam §8625
Unmarried minors, adoption of   CRC 5.730, Fam §8600
Vacation of adoption
Birth parents not advised of rights, effect of   Fam §8801.5
Indian children
Return of custody, petition for   Fam §8619.5
Order   Fam §9101
Petition to set aside adoption   Fam §9100

ADOPTION—Cont.
Vacation of adoption—Cont.
Statutes of limitation   Fam §9102
Venue
Agency adoptions   Fam §8714
Independent adoptions   Fam §8802
International adoption or readoption requests   Fam §8912
Nondependent minors
Request for filing request for adoption or readoption of nondependent minor, locations for filing   Fam §8609.5
Visitation rights
Deceased parent, effect of adoption on visitation rights of relatives of   Fam §3102
Kinship adoption agreements   CRC 5.451
Postadoption contact agreement with birth parent   Fam §8616.5
Readoption in state of child originally adopted in foreign country
Separated siblings, visitation   Fam §8920
Waiver of right to revoke consent   Fam §8814.5
Will, adopted persons included in class for disposition under   Pro §21115

ADR PROGRAMS (See **ALTERNATIVE DISPUTE RESOLUTION**)

ADULT
Adoption of (See **ADOPTION**)
Child support for adult children (See **CHILD SUPPORT**)

ADULT-ORIENTED BUSINESSES
Human trafficking or slavery
Signs, businesses required to post notice concerning relief from slavery or human trafficking   CC §52.6

ADULT SCHOOLS (See **SCHOOLS; UNIVERSITIES AND COLLEGES**)

AD VALOREM TAX (See **TAXATION**)

ADVANCEMENTS
Ademption distinguished   Pro §6409
Death of recipient prior to distribution   Pro §6409
Hearings for   Pro §11640

ADVANCES
Loans (See **PREPAYMENTS**)

ADVERSE PARTY
Authentication of document   Ev §1414
Hearsay declarant, examination of   Ev §1203
Opinion evidence, examination of   Ev §804
Witnesses (See **WITNESSES**)

ADVERSE POSSESSION (See also **QUIETING TITLE**)
Absence of written instrument or judgment, extent of possession in   CCP §324
Actual continued occupation under claim of title not founded on written instrument or judgment   CCP §324
Alienation pending suit for possession   CCP §747
Claim of title
Founded on written instrument or judgment   CCP §§322, 323
Not founded on written instrument or judgment   CCP §§324, 325
Complaint in quieting title action specifying   CCP §761.020
Continued occupation and possession under claim of title based on written instrument or judgment   CCP §§322, 323
Cultivation of land
Not founded on written instrument or judgment, adverse possession by person claiming title   CCP §325
Sufficiency of possession, use and inclosure for claim based on written instrument, judgment   CCP §323
Damages for withholding property   CCP §§740, 741
Death of adverse possessor   CCP §327
Description of property in complaint   CCP §455
Disabilities tolling statute   CCP §328
Entry upon real estate deemed sufficient or valid as claim   CCP §320
Fences   CCP §§323, 325
Five years
Cessation of disability, commencement of action or making defense on   CCP §328
Continued occupation and possession under claim of title based on written instrument or judgment   CCP §322
Entry upon real estate deemed sufficient or valid as claim   CCP §320
Mortgaged premises, adverse possession of   CCP §346
Not founded on written instrument or judgment, adverse possession by person claiming title   CCP §325
Seisin or possession within five years of commencement of action   CCP §§318, 319

ADVERSE POSSESSION—Cont.
Five years—Cont.
    Subordinate occupation presumption   CCP §321
    Tenant, adverse possession by   CCP §326
Imprisonment tolling statute   CCP §328
Improvement of land
    Not founded on written instrument or judgment, adverse possession by person claiming title   CCP §325
    Sufficiency of possession, use and inclosure for claim based on written instrument, judgment   CCP §323
Inclosure of land
    Not founded on written instrument or judgment, adverse possession by person claiming title   CCP §325
    Sufficiency of possession, use and inclosure for claim based on written instrument, judgment   CCP §323
Legal capacity lacking
    Tolling of statute   CCP §328
Minority tolling statute   CCP §328
Mortgaged premises, adverse possession of   CCP §346
Mortgage, effect on   CC §2921
Occupancy
    Actual continued occupation under claim of title not founded on written instrument or judgment   CCP §324
    Continued occupation and possession under claim of title based on written instrument or judgment   CCP §§322, 323
    Subordination to legal title, presumption of   CCP §321
Presumptions
    Continued occupation and possession under claim of title based on written instrument or judgment   CCP §322
    Subordinate occupation presumption   CCP §321
    Tenant, adverse possession by   CCP §326
Public improvement liens, effect of   CCP §§801.1 to 801.15
Seisin or possession within five years of commencement of action   CCP §§318, 319
Statutes of limitation
    Disabilities tolling statute   CCP §328
    Five years (See within this heading, "**Five years**")
    Legal capacity lacking
        Tolling of statute   CCP §328
Subordinate occupation presumption   CCP §321
Sufficiency of possession, use and inclosure for claim based on written instrument, judgment   CCP §323
Taxes levied and assessed upon land, payment of   CCP §325
Tenant, adverse possession by   CCP §326
Title to real property
    Claim of title   CCP §§322 to 325
    Seisin or possession within five years of commencement of action arising out of   CCP §319
    Subordination to legal title, presumption of   CCP §321
Transfer of property   CC §1047
Venue in action for recovery of real property   CCP §392

ADVERTISING
Adoptions (See **ADOPTION**)
Asian language contracts, regulating advertising as to   CC §1632
Attorney professional conduct   ProfC 7.2
    Communications about lawyer's services generally   ProfC 7.1 to 7.5
    Solicitation of clients   ProfC 7.3
Auctions   CC §1812.607
Automobile leases   CC §§2985.71, 2989.4
Campaign advertising (See **CANDIDATES FOR OFFICE**)
Consumer protection in   CC §1770
Dating services   CC §1694.4
Debt collectors advertising name of debtor   CC §1788.12
Deceased personality's name, voice, signature, photograph, or likeness, unauthorized use of   CC §3344.1
Deceptive advertising prohibited   CC §1770
Discount buying services   CC §1812.120
Employment agencies, advertising practices of   CC §1812.508
Employment counseling services, advertising requirements for   CC §1812.513
Enforcement of judgments (See **ENFORCEMENT OF JUDGMENTS**)
Floating homes and floating home marinas (See **FLOATING HOMES**)
Grey market goods, advertising requirements for   CC §1797.82
Invoice or statement of account due, restrictions on solicitations resembling   CC §1716
Job listing services, advertising requirements of   CC §1812.520
Judges
    Name
        Use in advertising   CRCSupp JudEthicsCanon 4
Levied property, advertising sale of   CCP §701.545
Membership camping contract, advertisements for   CC §1812.301

ADVERTISING—Cont.
Mobilehomes, sale or rent of   CC §§798.70, 799.1.5
Name used without authorization   CC §§3344, 3344.1
Nurses' registries, advertising by   CC §1812.533
Photograph used without authorization   CC §§3344, 3344.1
Political advertising, sale of items involving   CC §1739.1
Realty sale signs   CC §§712, 713
Rental passenger vehicle transactions
    Quotes and additional mandatory charges
        Disclaimers   CC §1939.19
        Unfair practices, exception   CC §1939.20
Rental-purchase contracts, advertising of   CC §1812.630
Retail installment contract interest rate, required statement of   CC §1803.11
Sales tax notice included in   CC §1656.1
Signature used without authorization   CC §§3344, 3344.1
Signs and billboards (See **SIGNS AND BILLBOARDS**)
Social security numbers
    Sale of numbers
        Prohibition of sale, advertising for sale or offering for sale of number of another   CC §1798.85
Spanish language contracts, regulating advertising as to   CC §1632
Statute of limitation   CCP §338
Unassembled furniture   CC §1770
Unclaimed property fund appropriations for   CCP §1325
Veterans benefits or entitlements
    Workshops, presentations, events, etc regarding veterans benefits or entitlements
        Advertising or promoting without certain disclosures as unfair or deceptive practice   CC §1770
Voice used without authorization   CC §§3344, 3344.1
Weight loss programs   CC §1694.9

ADVICE OF PROPOSED ACTION (See **INDEPENDENT ADMINISTRATION OF ESTATES ACT**)

ADVISORY COMMITTEES
Judicial Council, advisory committees of (See **JUDICIAL COUNCIL**)

ADVISORY SERVICE
Small claims court (See **SMALL CLAIMS COURTS**)

AERONAUTICS BOARD
Eminent domain taking by   CCP §1245.210

AEROSOL PAINT CONTAINERS
Minors, sale to
    Verification of age for sale of age-restricted products   CC §1798.99.1

AESTHETIC CONSIDERATIONS
Eminent domain taking to preserve   CCP §§1240.120, 1240.680

AFDC (See **CHILD SUPPORT**)

AFFIDAVITS
Generally   CCP §2002
Administrative hearings, admissibility of affidavits at   Gov §11514
Adoption (See **ADOPTION**)
Attachment (See **ATTACHMENT**)
Attorney discipline
    Compliance, affidavit   CRC 9.20
Automobile conditional sales contract, venue affidavit in suit on   CC §2984.4
Blood test, affidavit stating technique in taking   Ev §712
Business records as evidence, affidavit accompanying   Ev §§1561, 1562
Caption   CRC 3.1115
Caregiver's authorization and affidavit for medical treatment of minors   Fam §§6550, 6552
Case, title of   CCP §1046
Claim and delivery (See **CLAIM AND DELIVERY**)
Claims against decedent's estate, affidavits in support of   Pro §9151
Confession of judgments   CCP §1138
Contempt proceedings   CCP §§1211, 1211.5
Continuance of trial requiring showing of need by   CCP §595.4
Coordination of actions   CCP §404
County clerk (See **CLERKS OF COURT**)
Decedents' estates
    Administration of (See **ADMINISTRATION OF ESTATES**)
    Claims against estate, affidavit in support of   Pro §9151
    Will probate   Pro §§1022, 8220, 8221
Declaration or certification of written instrument executed under penalty of perjury   CCP §2015.5
Default judgments (See **DEFAULT JUDGMENTS**)

AFFIDAVITS—Cont.
Defined   CCP §2003
Destroyed land records, action to reestablish   CCP §751.09
Dissolution of marriage (See **DISSOLUTION OF MARRIAGE**)
Domestic violence restraining orders   Fam §6300
Economic litigation provision for use of affidavit in lieu of direct testimony   CCP §98
Enforcement of judgments (See **ENFORCEMENT OF JUDGMENTS**)
Fact of death (See **FACT OF DEATH**)
Family law rules (See **FAMILY RULES**)
Fees for taking of affidavits (See **CLERKS OF COURT**)
Filing   CCP §2011
Foreign countries, taking in   CCP §§2014, 2015
Identity of judgment debtor, judgment creditor executing affidavit of   CCP §§680.135, 699.545
Indirect contempt proceeding   CCP §§1211, 1211.5
Injunctions, affidavits supporting   CCP §527
Innkeeper's lien, writ of possession on   CC §§1861.8, 1861.9, 1861.27
Inspection warrants   CCP §1822.51
Joint-debtor proceedings   CCP §991
Judge, form of affidavit for peremptory challenge of   CCP §170.6
Judicial officer's power to take and certify   CCP §179
Law and motion hearing, evidence received at   CRC 3.1306
Legal separation, proof of grounds for   Fam §2336
Libel, supporting motion to shorten time to answer charge of   CCP §460.5
Marriage license   Fam §§355, 505
    Identification of applicants
        Use of affidavit in lieu of photo identification   Fam §354
Mechanics' liens
    Public works, summary proceeding for release of funds
        Counter-affidavit of claimant   CC §9406
        Pleadings, affidavits to constitute   CC §9410
        Service of affidavit on claimant   CC §9404
        Service of affidavit on public entity   CC §9402
New trial (See **NEW TRIAL**)
Notices served, proof of   CCP §1013a
Orders refused, application for reconsideration of   CCP §1008
Other states, taking in   CCP §§2013, 2015
Parties   CCP §§2012 to 2015.5
Partition action   CCP §872.530
Penalty of perjury, declaration or certification of written instrument executed under   CCP §2015.5
Personal sureties, affidavit of qualifications by   CCP §995.520
Pleading verification by   CCP §446
Police officer's personnel record, good cause for discovery of   Ev §1043
Preference, motion for   CCP §36.5
Process (See **PROCESS AND SERVICE OF PROCESS**)
Publication, proof of   CCP §2010
Quieting title action, deceased defendant in   CCP §762.030
Retail installment sales contract, affidavit required with complaint in action on   CC §1812.10
Small estates without administration (See **SMALL ESTATES WITHOUT ADMINISTRATION**)
State agency hearings, admissibility of affidavits at   Gov §11514
Subpoena duces tecum (See **SUBPOENA DUCES TECUM**)
Summary judgments, affidavits in support or opposition of motion for   CCP §437c
Survival of actions, affidavit of successor in interest as party to   CCP §377.32
Traffic court, trial by written declaration in   CRC 4.210
Trusts (See **TRUSTS**)
Unknown persons as defendants   CCP §474
Venue, affidavit or complaint stating facts indicating   CCP §396a
Verification by use of   CCP §2009
Will probate   Pro §§1022, 8220, 8221

AFFINITY
Challenge of juror for implied bias   CCP §229
Defined   CCP §17
Referees, disqualification of   CCP §641

AFFIRMANCE OF JUDGMENT
Authority of Supreme Court and Courts of Appeal to affirm, reverse or modify judgment or order appealed from   CCP §43
Condition, affirmance on   CRC 8.264
Costs on appeal   CRC 8.278
Entering judgment of reviewing court in records of trial court   CCP §912
General powers of reviewing court   CCP §906
Review by supreme court, decision of cause on   CRC 8.516

AFFIRMATION
Oath defined to include   CCP §17

AFTER-ACQUIRED PROPERTY
Conveyances   CC §1106
Liens covering   CC §2883
Mortgages, coverage under   CC §2930

AFTER-BORN CHILDREN (See **POSTHUMOUS CHILDREN**)

AGE
Adoption proceedings (See **ADOPTION**)
Adult, age of   Fam §§6501, 6502
Burden of proof to establish age of accused   CRC 4.116
Discrimination
    Judicial ethics code
        Administrative responsibilities of judge, impartial discharge   CRCSupp JudEthicsCanon 3
        Attorneys, judges to require to refrain from manifesting   CRCSupp JudEthicsCanon 3
        Bias, prejudice or harassment in performance of judicial duties   CRCSupp JudEthicsCanon 3
        Court personnel and staff under direction of judge, standards of conduct enforced by judge   CRCSupp JudEthicsCanon 3
Domestic partners
    Age requirement   Fam §297
        Younger than minimum age, order of court granting permission   Fam §297.1
Entertainment industry
    Commercial online entertainment employment service providers
        Age information of subscribers, restriction on disclosure   CC §1798.83.5
Housing discrimination
    Age discrimination in housing, generally   CC §51.2
    Mobilehome parks (See **MOBILEHOMES**)
    Senior citizen housing, requirements for (See **SENIOR CITIZENS**)
Marriage, capacity to consent to   Fam §301
Minor, age of   Fam §§6500, 6502
Preference, motion for   CCP §36
Sale of age-restricted products
    Verification of age for sale of age-restricted products   CC §1798.99.1
Senior citizens (See **SENIOR CITIZENS**)
Spousal support   Fam §4320

AGE-APPROPRIATE DESIGN CODE   CC §§1798.99.28 to 1798.99.40
Applicability of provisions   CC §1798.99.40
Children's data protection working group
    Composition   CC §1798.99.32
    Duties   CC §1798.99.32
    Internal operation   CC §1798.99.32
    Meetings   CC §1798.99.32
    Purpose   CC §1798.99.32
Confidentiality of medical information act
    Applicability of code provisions   CC §1798.99.40
Dark patterns
    Prohibited acts   CC §1798.99.31
Data protection impact assessment
    Completion by providers of online services, products or features likely to be accessed by children   CC §1798.99.31
        Deadline   CC §1798.99.33
    Defined   CC §1798.99.30
    Online services, products or features likely to be accessed by children
        Actions required of businesses providing   CC §1798.99.31
    Purpose   CC §1798.99.31
Definitions   CC §1798.99.29
Enforcement of provisions   CC §1798.99.35
Geolocation information
    Prohibited acts   CC §1798.99.31
Legislative findings and intent   CC §1798.99.29
Online services, products or features likely to be accessed by children
    Actions required of businesses providing   CC §1798.99.31
    Definitions   CC §1798.99.30
Personal information
    Prohibited acts   CC §1798.99.31
Profiling
    Prohibited acts   CC §1798.99.31
Short title   CC §1798.99.28

AGED PERSONS (See **SENIOR CITIZENS**)

AGENCIES FOR ADOPTIONS (See **ADOPTION**)

AGENCY
Actual agency   CC §§2298, 2299
Administration of estates (See **ADMINISTRATION OF ESTATES**)

AGENCY

AGENCY—Cont.
Arbitration award against principal affecting surety CC §2855
Art dealer as agent of artist CC §1738.6
Attorney in fact (See **POWER OF ATTORNEY**)
Auctioneer, agency relationship of CC §§2362, 2363
Authority of agent CC §§2019, 2304, 2305; 2315 to 2326, 2330 to 2339
Automobile sales, agency loan financing CC §2983.4
Bills and notes (See **BILLS AND NOTES**)
Brokers (See **BROKERS**)
Business management by CC §2319
Challenge of juror for implied bias, relationships giving rise to CCP §229
Consideration requirements CC §2308
Corporations (See **CORPORATE OFFICERS AND EMPLOYEES**)
Damages for breach of warranty of authority of CC §3318
Death terminating CC §§2355, 2356
Defined CC §2295
Delegation of authority CC §§2304, 2349 to 2351
Digital assets of principal, agent's access to
    Agent defined Pro §871
    Authority over content of electronic communications Pro §879.1
    Catalogue of electronic communications, disclosure to agent Pro §879.2
Discretionary powers CC §2320
Eligibility of agency CC §2296
Extinguishment of CC §§2355, 2356
Factors, agency relationship of CC §§2367 to 2369
General terms, authority in CC §§2321, 2322
Incapacity of parties CC §§2355, 2356
Indemnity contracts covering agency CC §2775
Information to agent CC §2020
Mechanics' liens
    Scope of agency and authority of agents CC §8066
Negligence CC §§2338, 2339
Notes (See **BILLS AND NOTES**)
Oral authorization for CC §2309
Ostensible agents CC §§2298, 2300, 2317
Parol, authority granted by CC §2309
Payment, authority to receive CC §§2325, 2326
Personal liability of agency CC §2343
Power of attorney (See **POWER OF ATTORNEY**)
Ratification of acts CC §§2307, 2310 to 2314
Real estate brokers (See **BROKERS**)
Real property
    Agency listings for transfer of property CC §§1086 to 1089.5
Referees, disqualification of CCP §641
Representations by CC §2319
Revocation of authority CC §2356
Sale of realty (See **VENDOR AND PURCHASER**)
Scope of authority, acts within CC §§2330, 2343
Special agents CC §2297
Special terms, authority in CC §2321
Statute of frauds CC §1624, CCP §1971
Subagents CC §2022
Termination of CC §§2355, 2356
Third parties, transactions with CC §§2342 to 2345
Undisclosed principal CC §2336

AGING DEPARTMENT
Supportive care pilot projects
    Medical information disclosures CC §56.10

AGISTER'S LIENS (See **PASTURES**)

AGISTMENT (See **PASTURES**)

AGREED CASE
Appeals CCP §1140
Applicable cases CCP §1138
Enforcement of judgment CCP §1140
Entry in judgment roll CCP §1139
Family rules
    Rescheduling hearings
        Written agreements to reschedule CRC 5.95
Hearing and determination CCP §1138
Submission of CCP §1138
Summary judgment CCP §437c

AGREED STATEMENT
Appellate rules, superior court appeals
    Limited civil cases in appellate division
        Record on appeal CRC 8.836
Appellate rules, supreme court and courts of appeal (See **APPELLATE RULES, SUPREME COURT AND COURTS OF APPEAL**)

AGRICULTURAL LABOR RELATIONS BOARD
Judicial review of ALRB orders CRC 8.728

AGRICULTURE (See **FARMS AND FARMERS**)

AID FOR DEPENDENT CHILDREN (See **CHILD SUPPORT**)

AIDING AND ABETTING
Attorney-client privilege, applicability of Ev §956
Identification of person aiding in crime, admissibility of hearsay evidence concerning Ev §1238
Physician's services aiding in commission of crime, absence of privilege where Ev §997
Privilege claim in obtaining services of lawyer to aid in commission of crime Ev §§956, 981
Psychotherapist's services aiding in commission of crime, absence of privilege where Ev §1018

AIDS (See **ACQUIRED IMMUNE DEFICIENCY SYNDROME (AIDS)**)

AIR
Appurtenance CC §662
Easement rights to CC §801
Realty including airspace CC §659

AIR CONDITIONING
Construction defects, actions for
    Actionable defects CC §896
Home improvement goods and services CC §1689.8
Landlord terminating CC §789.3

AIRCRAFT AND AVIATION (See also **AIRPORTS**)
Blind persons having equal access rights to CC §§54.1, 54.3, 54.4, 55
    Construction or application of provisions in issue, solicitor general notified CC §55.2
Disabled persons having equal access rights to CC §§54.1, 54.3, 54.4, 55
    Construction or application of provisions in issue, solicitor general notified CC §55.2
Drones Gov §§853 to 853.5
    Emergency response
        Drones or unmanned aircraft systems damaged by emergency responder, immunity from liability for damage to drone interfering with emergency response CC §43.101
Guide dogs permitted aboard CC §§54.2, 54.3
    Construction or application of provisions in issue, solicitor general notified CC §55.2
Liens
    Assignment of CCP §1208.63
    Federal statutes, applicability of CCP §1208.70
    Fraud, loss by CCP §§1208.64, 1208.69
    Notice of CCP §1208.62
    Repairs CCP §1208.61
    Sale to satisfy CCP §§1208.65 to 1208.68
    Storage CCP §1208.61
Retail installment sales of aircraft CC §1801.4
Terrorism
    September 11, 2001 terrorist attacks
        Statute of limitations on actions CCP §340.10
Unmanned aircraft
    Emergency response
        Drones or unmanned aircraft systems damaged by emergency responder, immunity from liability for damage to drone interfering with emergency response CC §43.101
Unruh Act, exclusion of aircraft sales from CC §1801.4

AIR FORCE (See **MILITARY**)

AIRPLANES (See **AIRCRAFT AND AVIATION**)

AIR POLLUTION (See **ENVIRONMENTAL HAZARDS**)

AIRPORTS (See also **AIRCRAFT AND AVIATION**)
Eminent domain CCP §§1240.110, 1240.125
Human trafficking
    Signs, businesses required to post notice concerning relief from slavery or human trafficking CC §52.6
Indemnity contract for construction of CC §2783
Nuisance, actions to abate CCP §§731a, 731b
Real Estate Transfer Disclosure Statements, form of
    Proximity of airport, localities adopting different or additional disclosure CC §1102.6a

AIRPORTS—Cont.
Rental passenger vehicle transactions
> Personal vehicle sharing programs
>> Airports, regulation of access and fees at airport facilities   CC §1939.38

Slavery
> Signs, businesses required to post notice concerning relief from slavery or human trafficking   CC §52.6

AIR QUALITY (See ENVIRONMENTAL HAZARDS)

AIR RESOURCES BOARD
Gasoline stations, emission standards for   CC §1952.8

ALAMEDA COUNTY
Unlawful detainer actions
> Controlled substances as nuisance
>> Pilot program   CC §3486.5

ALARMS
Burglar alarms
> Electronic transactions
>> Applicability of electronic transactions provisions   CC §1633.3
> Home improvement goods   CC §1689.8
> Public liability for failure of police to respond to   Gov §845

Electrified security fences
> Interface between fence and monitored alarm device   CC §835

ALCOHOLIC BEVERAGES
Abuse (See SUBSTANCE ABUSE)
Commercial motor vehicle employer for vehicle accident caused by intoxicated employee, damages recoverable from   CC §3333.7
Custody of children
> Drug or alcohol abuse as custody determination factor
>> Testing for alcohol or controlled substance use ordered by court   Fam §3041.5

Decedent's estate, filing tax claims against   Pro §§9200 to 9205
Guardian and ward, custody of child
> Drug or alcohol abuse as custody determination factor
>> Testing for alcohol or controlled substance use ordered by court   Fam §3041.5

Human trafficking
> Signs, businesses required to post notice concerning relief from slavery or human trafficking   CC §52.6

Ignition interlock orders   CRC 4.325
Marriage license denied to persons under influence of   Fam §352
On-sale licenses
> Human trafficking
>> Signs, businesses required to post notice concerning relief from slavery or human trafficking   CC §52.6

Public nuisances, attorney's fees recoverable for enjoining unlawful sales or distribution of alcoholic liquor as   CC §3496
Rape, use to accomplish
> Statute of limitations on sexual assault damages   CCP §340.16

Satisfaction of judgment, interest in alcoholic beverage license applied to   CCP §708.630
Slavery
> Signs, businesses required to post notice concerning relief from slavery or human trafficking   CC §52.6

Social host's liability to third parties after serving   CC §1714
Third party liability of social host after serving   CC §1714
Voidable transactions provisions, applicability to sale of wine   CC §3440

ALCOHOLISM (See SUBSTANCE ABUSE)

ALE (See ALCOHOLIC BEVERAGES)

ALIAS WRITS
Attachments writs   CCP §482.090

ALIENATION OF AFFECTION
Generally   CC §43.5
Foster parent, action against   CC §43.56

ALIENATION, RESTRAINTS ON (See PERPETUITIES AND RESTRAINTS ON ALIENATION)

ALIENS
Attorneys
> Registered foreign legal consultants admitted to practice as attorney   CRC 9.44
> Fingerprinting of special admission attorneys   CRC 9.9.5

Child custody
> Immigration status, effect   Fam §3040

Children and minors
> Actions for damages
>> Discovery into immigration status prohibited   CC §3339.5
>> Immigration status irrelevant   CC §3339.5

Citizenship (See CITIENSHIP)
Contracts
> Local government or law enforcement agency contracts to detain noncitizens for civil immigration custody
>> Prohibition   CC §1670.9

Damages
> Children and minors
>> Immigration status irrelevant   CC §3339.5
> Civil rights enforcement, irrelevance of immigration status   CC §3339

Death of foreign citizen, notice of   Pro §8113
Discrimination prohibited   CC §51
Forcible entry and detainer
> Immigration or citizenship status irrelevant to issue of liability or remedy   CC §3339.10

Foreign legal consultants   CRC 9.44
> Fingerprinting of special admission attorneys   CRC 9.9.5

Jury service, exceptions to eligibility for   CCP §203
Landlord and tenant
> Immigration or citizenship status of persons
>> Actions to recover possession, restrictions on landlord actions based in immigration or citizenship status   CCP §1161.4
>> Definition of immigration or citizenship status   CC §1940.05
>> Involuntary quit by tenant, restrictions on landlord actions based in immigration or citizenship status   CCP §1161.4
>> Prohibited acts based on   CC §§1940.3, 1940.35
>> Retaliation against tenant by reporting or threatening to report to immigration authorities   CC §1942.5
>> Unduly influencing tenant to vacate by threatening disclosures relating to immigration or citizenship status   CC §1940.2

Probate proceedings
> Inheritance by non-citizens or non-nationals   Pro §6411

ALIMONY (See SPOUSAL SUPPORT)

ALLEGATIONS (See PLEADINGS)

ALTERATION OF CLOTHING (See TAILORS)

ALTERATION OF INSTRUMENTS (See MODIFICATION)

ALTERNATE JURORS (See JURY)

ALTERNATIVE DISPUTE RESOLUTION
Administration of ADR program by trial court   CRC 10.780 to 10.783
ADR committee
> Administration of program   CRC 10.783

ADR program information, court to furnish   CRC 10.781
Attorney professional conduct
> Former judges, arbitrators, mediators, etc, restrictions on representation of clients   ProfC 1.12
> Service by attorney as third-party neutral   ProfC 2.4

Civil action mediation program   CRC 3.890 to 3.898
Civil rules
> Information package
>> Papers to be filed   CRC 3.221

Committee
> ADR committee
>> Administration of program   CRC 10.783

Common interest developments
> Associations and members, disputes between   CC §§5900 to 5920 (See COMMON INTEREST DEVELOPMENTS)
> Generally   CC §§5925 to 5965 (See COMMON INTEREST DEVELOPMENTS)

Construction defects, actions for
> Prelitigation procedures generally   CC §§910 to 938 (See CONSTRUCTION DEFECTS, ACTIONS FOR)

Coordination by trial courts   CRC JudAdminStand 10.70
Court officers and employees
> Labor relations
>> Submission for dispute resolution   CRC 10.659

Criteria for referring cases to dispute resolution providers   CRC JudAdminStand 10.72
Definitions   CRC 3.800

ALTERNATIVE DISPUTE RESOLUTION—Cont.
Family law
    Mediators and evaluators
        Ex parte communications   Fam §216
Forms
    Judicial council legal forms   CRCAppx A
Informational statements to parties
    Papers to be filed   CRC 3.221
Judges
    Employment or prospective employment as a dispute resolution neutral as basis for disqualification of judges   CCP §§170.1, 1281.9
Judicial administration standards
    Committees to oversee ADR programs   CRC JudAdminStand 10.71
    Coordination of ADR programs, judicial council guidelines   CRC JudAdminStand 10.70
    Criteria for referring cases to ADR providers, judicial council guidelines   CRC JudAdminStand 10.72
Judicial arbitration   CRC 3.810 to 3.830
Mediation Act   CRC 3.890 to 3.898
Mediators standards of conduct
    Ethical standards for conduct of mediators   CRC 3.850 to 3.860
        Complaints about court-program mediators   CRC 3.865 to 3.872
Neutrals, list of   CRC 10.781
Plaintiff, ADR information provided   CRC 3.221
Privilege to serve as neutral   CRC 10.781
Programs   CCP §1775
    Administrative adjudication (See **ADMINISTRATIVE ADJUDICATION**)
    Arbitration (See **ARBITRATION**)
    Common interest developments (See **COMMON INTEREST DEVELOPMENTS**)
    Eminent domain proceedings postponed for ADR purposes   CCP §1250.430
    Hazardous releases, procedures for resolving liability for (See **ENVIRONMENTAL HAZARDS**)
    Information   CRC 3.221
    Judicial administration standards (See **JUDICIAL ADMINISTRATION STANDARDS**)
    Judicial arbitration (See **JUDICIAL ARBITRATION**)
    Mediation (See **MEDIATION**)
    Trial court administration   CRC 10.780 to 10.783
        ADR committee   CRC 10.783
        ADR program administrator   CRC 10.783
        Applicability of rules   CRC 10.780
        Information reporting   CRC 10.782
        Neutrals, listing   CRC 10.781
        Privilege to serve as neutral   CRC 10.781
Settlement and compromise
    Notice to neutral of settlement of case   CRC 3.1385
    Time-limited demands   CCP §§999 to 999.5
Stipulation to ADR
    Form   CRC 3.221

ALTERNATIVE WRITS
Court commissioner's powers to hear and determine   CCP §259

ALZHEIMER'S DISEASE
Neurocognitive disorders
    Major neurocognitive disorder conservatorships   Pro §2356.5

AMBASSADORS
Affidavits taken before   CCP §2014
Signature of secretary on documents presumed to be genuine   Ev §§1454, 1530

AMBER ALERT
Rental passenger vehicle transactions
    Electronic surveillance technology
        Exceptions to restrictions on use   CC §1939.23

AMBIGUITIES (See **CERTAINTY**)

AMBULANCES
Public health and safety labor or service providers
    Logo or identifying mark of public agency, display   CC §3273

AMENDMENTS
Administrative regulations (See **ADMINISTRATIVE PROCEDURE ACT**)
Bill of Rights
    Fourth Amendment (See **SEARCH AND SEIZURE**)
Common interest developments, amended declaration for (See **COMMON INTEREST DEVELOPMENTS**)
Complaints (See **COMPLAINTS**)

AMENDMENTS—Cont.
Contempt proceedings, rules to amend affidavit or statement of facts in   CCP §1211.5
Decedent's estate, amendment of creditors' claims filed against   Pro §9104
Eminent domain action, pleading amendments in   CCP §1250.340
Judge's removal or censure, amendment to pleadings in proceedings for   JudPerR 128
Mobilehome park rules   CC §798.25
Personal data records   CC §§1798.22, 1798.26
Pleadings (See **PLEADINGS**)
Premarital agreements   Fam §1614
Pretrial conference orders   CCP §576
Small claims actions (See **SMALL CLAIMS COURTS**)
State agency regulations, amendment procedure for (See **ADMINISTRATIVE PROCEDURE ACT**)

AMERICAN INDIANS (See **NATIVE AMERICANS**)

AMERICAN RED CROSS
Adoption proceedings, absence of adoptive parent serving in Red Cross   Fam §8613

AMERICANS WITH DISABILITIES ACT COMPLIANCE
Civil rights violation, ADA violation as
    Construction or application of provisions in issue
        Solicitor general notified   CC §51.1
Courts   CRC 1.100
Interrogation of hard of hearing, use of interpreter   Ev §754
Transportation, equal access to
    Construction or application of provisions in issue, solicitor general notified   CC §55.2

AMICUS CURIAE
Appellate rules, supreme court and courts of appeal
    Certiorari, mandate and prohibition
        Attorney general and other amicus briefs   CRC 8.487
    Death penalty
        Habeas corpus, appeals from superior court decisions in habeas cases involving death penalty   CRC 8.396
Briefs   CRC 8.200
    Appellate rules, supreme court and courts of appeal
        Habeas corpus, appeals from superior court decisions in habeas cases involving death penalty   CRC 8.396
    Attorney general's amicus brief   CRC 8.200
    Capital cases   CRC 8.630
    Criminal appeals   CRC 8.360
    Juvenile case appeals   CRC 8.412
Filing of documents
    Number   CRC 8.44
Judges, proceedings against   JudPerR 131
Supreme court
    Filing briefs in   CRC 8.520
    Oral argument   CRC 8.524
        Habeas corpus   CRC 8.386
    Review of amicus curiae letters   CRC 8.500

AMMUNITION
Firearm industry responsibility, industry standards of conduct
    Definition of ammunition   CC §3373.50
Firearms and other weapons generally (See **FIREARMS AND OTHER WEAPONS**)

AMOUNT IN CONTROVERSY
Attachment (See **ATTACHMENT**)
General denial   CCP §431.40
Judicial arbitration (See **JUDICIAL ARBITRATION**)
Limited civil cases   CCP §85
Mediation of civil actions   CCP §1775.5, CRC 3.891
Small claims court (See **SMALL CLAIMS COURTS**)

AMUSEMENT MACHINES (See **VENDING MACHINES**)

AMUSEMENT PARKS (See **FAIRS AND EXPOSITIONS**)

ANABOLIC STEROIDS
Mandatory warning statement in rental agreement with athletic facilities regarding   CC §1812.97 (Title 2.55 version of section)

ANAPHYLAXIS
Epinephrine auto-injector administration for first aid
    Immunity from civil liability of lay rescuers or prehospital emergency medical care providers   CC §1714.23

ANATOMICAL GIFTS
Drivers' licenses
    Encoded information
        Use of encoded information by organ procurement organizations   CC §1798.90.1
Health care decisions
    Advance health care directives
        Form of statutory advance health care directive   Pro §4701

ANCESTRY
Bible entries as evidence   Ev §1312
Church records as evidence of   Ev §1315
Discrimination   CC §§51 to 53
Family friends, statements concerning ancestry by   Ev §1311
Hearsay evidence, acceptance of   Ev §1310
Relative's statements concerning   Ev §1311
Reputation among family members concerning   Ev §1313

ANCIENT DOCUMENTS
Admissibility of   Ev §1331
Authentication   Ev §1419
Presumed authentic   Ev §643

ANCILLARY ADMINISTRATION
Generally   Pro §12540
Affidavit procedure for collection of property (See within this heading, **"Small estates without ancillary administration"**)
Commencement of proceedings   Pro §12510
Construction and interpretation   Pro §12500
Definitions   Pro §§12501 to 12507
Distributions
    Insolvent decedent's estate in sister state, effect of distribution to   Pro §12542
    Preliminary and final distribution, order for   Pro §12540
    Real property proceeds, distribution of   Pro §12541
Foreign nation
    Defined   Pro §12502
    Personal representative
        Defined   Pro §12503
        Jurisdiction over   Pro §§12590, 12591
    Will probate in   Pro §12523
Governing law   Pro §12530
Immunity of sister state personal representative taking of small estate property by affidavit   Pro §12573
Insolvent decedent's estate in sister state, effect of distributions to   Pro §12542
Jurisdiction over foreign personal representatives   Pro §§12590, 12591
Local personal representative
    Appointment
        Petition for   Pro §12510
        Priorities for   Pro §12513
    Defined   Pro §12504
Notices, generally   Pro §12512
Personal representatives
    Foreign nation personal representative (See within this heading, **"Foreign nation"**)
    Local personal representative (See within this heading, **"Local personal representative"**)
    Sister state personal representative (See within this heading, **"Sister state personal representative"**)
Petitions
    Appointment of local personal representative, petition for   Pro §12510
    Will probate, petition for   Pro §12510
        Contents   Pro §12521
Priorities for appointment of local personal representative   Pro §12513
Sister state
    Personal representative (See within this heading, **"Sister state personal representative"**)
    Will probate in   Pro §12522
Sister state personal representative
    Defined   Pro §12507
    Distributions of property to (See within this heading, **"Distributions"**)
    Jurisdiction over   Pro §§12590, 12591
    Small estate property, collection of (See within this heading, **"Small estates without ancillary administration"**)
Small estates without ancillary administration
    Collection of property by affidavit   Pro §12570
    Immunity of sister state personal representative taking property by affidavit   Pro §12573
    Transfers to personal representative   Pro §12572
Venue of proceedings   Pro §12511

ANCILLARY ADMINISTRATION—Cont.
Will probate
    California, effect of will admitted in   Pro §12524
    Foreign nation, probate of will in   Pro §12523
    Petition
        Generally   Pro §12510
        Contents of   Pro §12521
    Procedure for   Pro §12520
    Sister state, probate of will in   Pro §12522

ANESTHESIA
Battery on anesthetized person
    Statute of limitations on sexual assault damages   CCP §340.16
Rape, use to accomplish
    Statute of limitations on sexual assault damages   CCP §340.16
Sexual battery against anesthetized person
    Statute of limitations on sexual assault damages   CCP §340.16

ANIMALS
Abandoned animals, care of   CC §1834.5
Animal shelters (See within this heading, **"Depositaries of animals"**)
Animal testing, restrictions against   CC §1834.9
    Cosmetics developed or manufactured using animal testing   CC §1834.9.5
    Pesticides or chemical substances
        Canine and feline toxicological experiments   CC §1834.9.3
Assignment for benefit of creditors, property exempt from   CCP §1801
Borrowed animals, treatment of   CC §1887
Cattle (See **LIVESTOCK**)
Common interest developments, pets in
    Restrictions on limitations, prohibitions   CC §4715
Cosmetics developed or manufactured using animal testing   CC §1834.9.5
Cruelty
    Borrowed animals   CC §1887
    Damages for   CC §3340
    Motion pictures depicting   CC §§3504 to 3508.2
    Prevention of   CC §1834
Damages for injury to   CC §3340
Dealers
    Definition of animal dealer   CC §1834.7
    Living animals, transfer for research, experimentation, etc
        Shelter prohibited from transfer   CC §1834.7
    Transfer of carcass to research facility or animal dealer
        Euthanizing for transport, prohibition   CC §1834.7
Declawing or devocalizing animals
    Landlord and tenant
        Discouraging or denying application for occupancy for refusal of animal owner to declaw or devocalize animal   CC §1942.7
Depositaries of animals
    Abandonment following deposit   CC §1834.5
    Duties of animal depositary   CC §§1834, 1846
    Euthanasia, prohibition against subjecting adoptable and treatable animals to   CC §1834.4
    Finder as depositary for owner   CC §2080
    Involuntary deposit of live animal   CC §§1815, 1845
        Notification of animal control officials   CC §1816
    Rewards, acceptance of   CC §1845
Dogs (See **DOGS**)
Domestic violence
    Protective orders on behalf of animals   Fam §6320
        California law enforcement telecommunications (CLETS) information form, confidentiality and use of information   CRC 1.51, CRCAppx A
        Denial of petition for ex parte order, reasons to be provided   Fam §6320.5
Euthanasia
    Prohibition against subjecting adoptable and treatable animals to   CC §1834.4
    Transfer of carcass to research facility or animal dealer
        Prohibition on euthanizing for transport   CC §1834.7
    Use of euthanized animals used for research or to supply blood or other biological products
        Sign and statement   CC §1834.7
Fights between animals
    Property used for dog or cock fighting as nuisance   CC §3482.8
        Unlawful detainer actions   CCP §1161
Finder of animal as depositary for owner   CC §2080
Fish (See **FISH AND FISHING**)
Gratuitous depositaries, duties of   CC §1846
Guide dogs (See **DOGS**)

ANIMALS—Cont.
Harassment, order prohibiting
    Permissible orders regarding animal of petitioner   CCP §527.6
        COVID-19, emergency rule   CRCAppx I Emer Rule 8
Horses (See **HORSES**)
Hunters (See **HUNTERS AND HUNTING**)
Impoundment (See within this heading, "Depositaries of animals")
Inspection warrants (See **INSPECTION WARRANTS**)
Involuntary deposit of live animal   CC §§1815, 1845
    Notification of animal control officials   CC §1816
Liens   CCP §1208.5
Livestock (See **LIVESTOCK**)
Loaned animals, treatment of   CC §1887
Medical research
    Traditional and nontraditional test methods, when used   CC §1834.9
Mobilehome parks, pets in   CC §798.33
Motion pictures depicting cruelty to   CC §§3504 to 3508.2
Motor vehicles
    Leaving or confining animals in unattended vehicles
        Rescue of animal trapped in closed vehicle, immunity from civil or criminal liability for damage to vehicle   CC §43.100
Payment for care of   CC §1853
Pedigree   CC §3064.1
Pets
    Divorce
        Division of property   Fam §2605
    Legal separation
        Division of property   Fam §2605
Poultry (See **POULTRY**)
Principal and income allocations   CC §731.10
Products liability cases involving motor vehicles, inadmissibility of evidence pertaining to live animal experimentations in   Ev §1159
Rescue of animal trapped in closed vehicle
    Immunity from civil or criminal liability for damage to vehicle   CC §43.100
Research facilities
    Definition of research facility   CC §1834.7
    Living animals, transfer for research, experimentation, etc
        Shelter prohibited from transfer   CC §1834.7
    Transfer of carcass to research facility or animal dealer
        Euthanizing for transport, prohibition   CC §1834.7
Rewards offered by owners, involuntary depositary's acceptance of   CC §1845
Seeing eye dogs (See **DOGS**)
Service dogs, disabled persons using   CC §§54.1, 54.2
    Construction or application of provisions in issue, solicitor general notified   CC §55.2
Shelters
    Definition of animal shelter entity   CC §1834.7
    Euthanized animals used for research or to supply blood or other biological products
        Sign and statement   CC §1834.7
    Living animals, transfer for research, experimentation, etc
        Prohibition   CC §1834.7
Statute of limitation against veterinarians or persons boarding   CCP §340
Title and ownership
    Generally   CC §655
    Fur bearing animals   CC §996
    Wild animals   CC §§656, 996
Trust for care of domestic or pet animals   Pro §15212
    Trust decanting, uniform act   Pro §19523
Zoos (See **ZOOS**)

ANNEXATION
Procedure for validation   CCP §349.4

ANNUAL INTEREST RATES (See **INTEREST ON MONEY**)

ANNUAL PERCENTAGE RATE
Automobile conditional sales contract, requirements in   CC §2982

ANNUITIES
Beneficiary, trustee named in will designated as   Pro §§6320 to 6330
Decedent's estate representative to purchase annuities, will instruction authorizing   Pro §9733
Disclaimer of interest   Pro §§260 to 295
Employee benefit plan including   Fam §80
Interest, accrual of   Pro §12004
Spousal support, annuity to provide continued   Fam §4360
Statutory form power of attorney, powers under   Pro §4457
Testamentary gift of   Pro §21117

ANNUITIES—Cont.
Transmutation of marital property, waiver of right to annuity as evidence of   Fam §853
Unclaimed deposits and payments   CCP §1515

ANNULMENT
Generally   Fam §2000
Absence of first spouse, subsequent marriage in   Fam §2210
Action for breach of fiduciary duty between spouses   Fam §1101
Attorney professional conduct
    Contingent fees
        Circumstances where contingent fee agreement impermissible   ProfC 1.5
Attorney's fees and costs   Fam §§270 to 274, 2010, 2030 to 2034, 2040, 2255
    Allocation of fees and costs   Fam §§2032, 2034
    Financial need basis   CRC 5.427
Child support, consolidation of actions   CRC 5.365
Concealment of property, prohibition against   Fam §§2040 to 2045
Conciliation petition affecting stay on filing petition for nullity   Fam §1840
Consent, absence of   Fam §2210
Conservators   Fam §2211
Court commissioner's powers   CCP §259
Custody of children   Fam §2253
Death of first spouse, subsequent marriage in belief in   Fam §2210
Default judgment, procedure for   Fam §2338.5
Domestic partnerships
    Procedure for obtaining annulment   CRC 5.76
Encumbrance of property, restrictions on   Fam §§754, 2040 to 2045
Family centered case resolution   CRC 5.83, Fam §§2450 to 2452
Family rules
    Domestic partnerships
        Dissolution, legal separation, or annulment   CRC 5.76
    Parties
        Husband and wife or domestic partners as parties   CRC 5.16
    Statutes of limitation
        Quash, request for order   CRC 5.63
    Title IV-D support enforcement
        Consolidation of support orders   CRC 5.365
Fees
    Superior court fees
        First paper, filing   Gov §§70602.5, 70602.6, 70670
Financial assets and liabilities
    Sealing pleadings concerning financial assets and liabilities   Fam §2024.6
Force used in obtaining consent   Fam §2210
Forms
    Judicial council legal forms   CRCAppx A
Grounds for nullity   Fam §2210
Health coverage
    Notice of reduced-cost options through California health benefit exchange or no-cost Medi-Cal
        Court notice to parties upon filing for annulment, divorce, etc   Fam §2024.7
Impotency   Fam §2210
Incest   Fam §2200
Income and expenses declaration   Fam §§2100 to 2113
Joinder of parties   Fam §2021
Judgment of nullity
    Division of property   Fam §§2251, 2252
    Effect of   Fam §§310, 2212
    Notice to parties advising review of wills, insurance policies, etc   Fam §2024
    Protective orders, judgment including   Fam §§2049, 6360, 6361
    Relief from   Fam §§2120 to 2129
Jurisdiction   Fam §§2010 to 2013
Maiden name, restoration of   Fam §§2080 to 2082
Mental illness   Fam §2210
Military personnel, waiver of respondent's filing fees for   Gov §70673
Minors incapable of consent   Fam §2210
Notice of entry of judgment   CRC 5.413, 5.415
Pendency of proceeding, recording notice of   Fam §754
Petition for   Fam §2250
    Financial assets and liabilities
        Sealing pleadings concerning financial assets and liabilities   Fam §2024.6
    Social security numbers
        Redaction to ensure privacy   Fam §2024.5
Power of attorney, termination of   Pro §§3722, 4154
Protective and restraining orders
    Ex parte orders   Fam §§240 to 246, 2045
    Judgment, orders in   Fam §§2049, 6360, 6361
    Notice and hearing, orders after   Fam §2047

ANNULMENT—Cont.
Protective and restraining orders—Cont.
    Summons, inclusion of restraining order in   Fam §§231 to 235, 2040, 2041
Putative spouse   Fam §§2251, 2252, 2254
Responsive pleading, time for filing   Fam §2020
Restoration of former name   Fam §§2080 to 2082
Same sex marriage
    Residence requirements   Fam §2320
Social security numbers
    Confidentiality of persons involved in annulment, dissolution or legal separation
        Redaction of numbers from documents   Fam §2024.5
Spousal support   Fam §2254
Statistical information collected by Judicial Council and reported to legislature   Fam §2348
Statutes of limitation   Fam §2211
    Family rules
        Quash, request for order   CRC 5.63
Summary dissolution of marriage (See **SUMMARY DISSOLUTION OF MARRIAGE**)
Summons, inclusion of restraining order in   Fam §§231 to 235, 2040 to 2041
Transfer of causes
    Retention of jurisdiction to issue protective orders   CCP §399
    Subsequent to final judgment   CCP §397.5
    Time frames for transferring jurisdiction
        Family law actions or proceedings   CRC 5.97
Transfer of property, restrictions on   Fam §2045
Venue, improper joinder to fix   CCP §395
Wills (See **WILLS**)

ANONYMOUS WITNESS PROGRAM
Immunity for   CC §48.9

ANSWERS
Generally   CCP §431.30
Admission of material allegations by failure to deny   CCP §§431.20, 431.30
Affirmative relief   CCP §431.30
Amended answer   CCP §471.5
Appearance by filing   CCP §1014
Appellate rules, supreme court and courts of appeal (See **APPELLATE RULES, SUPREME COURT AND COURTS OF APPEAL**)
Arbitration petition in lieu of answer to complaint, defendant filing   CCP §1281.7
Capacity of complainant party to sue, lack of   CCP §430.10
Certiorari   CCP §1069.1
Child support enforcement services, answers to complaints in actions brought by   Fam §§17400, 17404
Contents of   CCP §431.30
Decedent's estate proceedings   Pro §§1043, 8004, 8251
Default judgments   CCP §§585, 586
Defenses separately stated   CCP §431.30
Demurrers (See **DEMURRERS**)
Denial of allegations
    Generally   CCP §431.30
    Property not exceeding $1000, general denial in action involving   CCP §431.40
Depositions (See **DEPOSITIONS**)
Dissolution of marriage proceedings (See **DISSOLUTION OF MARRIAGE**)
Earthquakes, answer to complaint to reestablish boundary after   CCP §751.56
Economic litigation provisions for limited civil cases   CCP §92
Eminent domain action   CCP §1250.320
Enlarging time for   CCP §473
Fact issues joined on   CCP §590
Filing fees
    Generally   Gov §§70612, 70614
    Children's waiting room in courthouse, surcharge to fund   Gov §70640
    Riverside County
        Courthouse seismic repair costs, additional filing fees authorized to defray   Gov §70622
    Supplemental fees for first paper filing   Gov §§70602.5, 70602.6
Forcible entry and detainer   CCP §§1167, 1167.3, 1170
General grounds for objection to complaint   CCP §§430.10, 430.30
Injunctions   CCP §528
Judges, censure, removal or admonishment of (See **JUDGES**)
Judgment on the pleadings, motion for   CCP §438
Judicial Council to develop and approve official forms   CCP §425.12
Jury commissioner inquiry or summons   CCP §196
Mandamus   CCP §§1089, 1089.5
Material allegations
    Generally   CCP §431.10
    Admission of material allegation by failure to deny   CCP §431.20

ANSWERS—Cont.
Material allegations—Cont.
    Denial in answer   CCP §431.30
New matter in defense   CCP §§431.20, 431.30
Objection to answer, grounds for   CCP §430.20
Offsetting cross-demand, answer asserting defense of   CCP §431.70
Partition action   CCP §§872.410 to 872.430
Pending actions on same causes, alleging   CCP §430.10
Quieting title action   CCP §761.030
Relief from judgment application accompanied by pleading proposed to be filed therein   CCP §473
Remand from federal court, time for response after   CCP §430.90
Service of
    Time for service   CRC 3.110
Shortened time to respond (See **SHORTENING TIME**)
Strike, motion to (See **MOTION TO STRIKE**)
Summons, time to respond to   CCP §412.20
Supplemental answers   CCP §464
Third-party defendant filing special answer   CCP §428.70
Unlawful detainer   CCP §§1167, 1167.3, 1170
Waiver of objections to pleadings   CCP §430.80
Water diversion cases   CCP §534

ANTENNAS
Commercial and industrial common interest developments
    Protected uses   CC §6708

ANTENUPTIAL AGREEMENTS (See **PROPERTY SETTLEMENT AGREEMENTS**)

ANTI-HEART BALM STATUTE   CC §43.5

APARTMENTS
Common interest developments generally   CC §§4000 to 6150 (See **COMMON INTEREST DEVELOPMENTS**)
Covered multifamily dwellings
    Service of papers or subpoena, access to covered multifamily dwelling   CCP §415.21
Demolition of residential dwellings
    Notice of application to demolish   CC §1940.6
Lien of keeper of (See **ENFORCEMENT OF JUDGMENTS**)
Manager of building, procedure for identifying   CC §§1961 to 1962.7
Owner of building, procedure for identifying   CC §§1961 to 1962.7
Statute of limitation for recovery or conversion of personal property left at   CCP §341a
Transient occupancy in dwelling unit of apartment buildings, recordkeeping required for accepting reservations or money for   CC §1864

APOTHECARIES (See **PHARMACISTS AND PHARMACIES**)

APPEAL BONDS   CCP §§917.9 to 922

APPEALS
Generally   CCP §§904 to 914
Administrative appeals
    Adjudicative proceedings (See **ADMINISTRATIVE ADJUDICATION**)
    Rules and regulations (See **ADMINISTRATIVE PROCEDURE ACT**)
Adoption proceedings (See **ADOPTION**)
Affirmance of judgment (See **AFFIRMANCE OF JUDGMENT**)
Agreed case   CCP §1140
Appellate court rules
    Superior court, appellate division proceedings   CRC 8.800 to 8.936 (See **APPELLATE RULES, SUPERIOR COURT APPEALS**)
    Supreme court and courts of appeal, rules on appeal to   CRC 8.1 to 8.642 (See **APPELLATE RULES, SUPREME COURT AND COURTS OF APPEAL**)
Arbitration proceedings   CCP §§1291, 1294, 1294.2
Capital cases (See **CAPITAL PUNISHMENT**)
Certificates
    Superior court fees   Gov §70620
Child support orders (See **CHILD SUPPORT**)
Conservators, orders concerning (See **CONSERVATORS**)
Costs
    Frivolous appeals   CCP §907
    Recovery of costs on appeal   CCP §1034
    Supreme Court and Courts of Appeal, rules on appeal to (See **APPELLATE RULES, SUPREME COURT AND COURTS OF APPEAL**)
Courts of Appeal
    Generally (See **COURTS OF APPEAL**)
    Appellate rules, supreme court and courts of appeal   CRC 8.1 to 8.642 (See **APPELLATE RULES, SUPREME COURT AND COURTS OF APPEAL**)
Death penalty cases (See **CAPITAL PUNISHMENT**)

APPEAL INDEX

APPEALS—Cont.
Demurrer sustained without leave to amend   CCP §472c
Dismissal
    Generally   CCP §913
    Superior court, rules on appeal to
        Abandonment and dismissal (See **APPELLATE RULES, SUPERIOR COURT APPEALS**)
    Supreme Court and Courts of Appeal, rules on appeal to (See **APPELLATE RULES, SUPREME COURT AND COURTS OF APPEAL**)
Disregard of nonprejudicial error   CCP §475
Entering judgment of reviewing court in records of trial court   CCP §912
Exceptions, orders and rulings reserved without   CCP §647
Executors and administrators, orders concerning (See **EXECUTORS AND ADMINISTRATORS**)
Family Code, general provision concerning appealable orders under   CCP §904.1
Findings contrary to or in addition to those of trial court   CCP §909
Forcible entry and detainer   CCP §§1176, 1178
Frivolous appeals   CCP §907
Guardian and ward, orders concerning (See **GUARDIAN AND WARD**)
Injunctions   CCP §§904.1, 904.2
Interlocutory judgments
    Generally   CCP §§904.1, 904.2
    Special defense, separate trial of   CCP §597
Irrigation, mandamus affecting   CCP §1110a
Justice courts (See **JUSTICE COURTS**)
Juvenile appeals (See **JUVENILE COURTS**)
Juvenile rules
    Representation of child on appeal   CRC 5.661
Modification of judgment (See **MODIFICATION OF JUDGMENT**)
Monetary sanctions against party or attorney, appeal of   CCP §904.1
New trial motion   CCP §657
Nonjury trials   CCP §909
Notice of appeal
    Indigent appeal   CCP §936.1
    Small claims court (See **SMALL CLAIMS COURTS**)
    Superior courts, appellate rules (See **APPELLATE RULES, SUPERIOR COURT APPEALS**)
    Supreme court and courts of appeal, appellate rules (See **APPELLATE RULES, SUPREME COURT AND COURTS OF APPEAL**)
    Withdrawal of legal service agency attorney for indigent client, effect on time limitations of   CCP §285.3
Notwithstanding verdict, motion for judgment   CCP §629
Parties to action   CCP §902
Perpetuation of testimony pending appeal   CCP §§2036.010 to 2036.050
Power of attorney, orders concerning   Pro §§1302, 1302.5, 1310
Powers of reviewing court   CCP §906
Prejudicial error required for reversal   CCP §475
Public improvement assessments, appeal of judgment in action contesting validity of   CCP §329.5
Quash, motion to   CCP §§904.1 to 904.2
Record on appeal
    Death of reporter as preventing preparation of   CCP §914
    Felony case, preparation of record for   CCP §269
    Loss or destruction of   CCP §1953.06
    Superior courts, appellate rules (See **APPELLATE RULES, SUPERIOR COURT APPEALS**)
    Supreme court and courts of appeal, appellate rules (See **APPELLATE RULES, SUPREME COURT AND COURTS OF APPEAL**)
Rehearings
    Superior courts, appellate rules (See **APPELLATE RULES, SUPERIOR COURT APPEALS**)
    Supreme court and courts of appeal, appellate rules (See **APPELLATE RULES, SUPREME COURT AND COURTS OF APPEAL**)
Reversal of judgment (See **REVERSAL OF JUDGMENT**)
Rules of court
    Superior court, appellate division proceedings   CRC 8.800 to 8.936 (See **APPELLATE RULES, SUPERIOR COURT APPEALS**)
    Supreme court and courts of appeal, appellate rules   CRC 8.1 to 8.642 (See **APPELLATE RULES, SUPREME COURT AND COURTS OF APPEAL**)
Small claims court (See **SMALL CLAIMS COURTS**)
Statute of limitation extended where judgment for plaintiff reversed on appeal   CCP §355
Striking of pleading as issue on appeal   CCP §472c
Summary judgment proceeding, review of determination in   CCP §437c
Superior courts
    Appellate division
        Generally (See **APPELLATE DIVISION OF SUPERIOR COURT**)
        Proceedings in appellate division   CRC 8.800 to 8.936 (See **APPELLATE RULES, SUPERIOR COURT APPEALS**)

APPEALS—Cont.
Support proceedings, appeal of judgment in   Fam §3554
Supreme court (California)
    Generally (See **SUPREME COURT, CALIFORNIA**)
    Appellate rules, supreme court and courts of appeal   CRC 8.1 to 8.642 (See **APPELLATE RULES, SUPREME COURT AND COURTS OF APPEAL**)
Termination of parental rights   Fam §§7893 to 7895
Trusts, orders concerning (See **TRUSTS**)
Unlawful detainer actions   CCP §§1176, 1178
Validation proceedings   CCP §870
Water supply, mandamus affecting   CCP §1110a
Will probate, orders concerning (See **WILL PROBATE**)
Witnesses
    Perpetuation of testimony pending appeal   CCP §§2036.010 to 2036.050

APPEARANCE
Generally   CCP §1014
Ability to pay program
    Infractions
        Alternatives to personal appearance   Gov §68645.1
Adoption proceedings (See **ADOPTION**)
Answer, appearance by filing   CCP §1014
Arbitration proceedings (See **ARBITRATION**)
Attorney, appearance through
    Waiver of personal appearance
        COVID-19, emergency rule   CRCAppx I Emer Rule 5
Child support
    Show cause orders   Fam §17404.1
    Title IV-D support actions
        Telephone appearances   CRC 3.670, 3.672, 5.324
Citation to appear (See **CITATION TO APPEAR**)
Conservatee   CCP §372
Conservators
    Termination
        Appearance of conservatee at hearing   Pro §1863
Criminal cases
    Traffic offenses
        Bail, when deposit required   CRC 4.105
        Notice to appear forms   CRC 4.103
Death penalty
    Lists of appearances, exhibits and motions   CRCAppx A
    Pretrial proceedings   CRC 4.119
    Trial, additional requirements   CRC 4.230
Discovery
    Interstate and international depositions and discovery act
        Choice of law to resolve disputes, appearance fees   CCP §2029.610
Dissolution of marriage (See **DISSOLUTION OF MARRIAGE**)
Enforcement of judgments (See **ENFORCEMENT OF JUDGMENTS**)
Ex parte applications, consideration without appearance by applicant or counsel
    Remote appearances generally   CRC 3.672
Ex parte proceedings
    Generally (See **EX PARTE PROCEDURE**)
Family centered case resolution orders
    Without appearance   CRC 5.83
Family rules   CRC 5.62
    Emergency or ex parte orders, requests
        Appearance at hearing   CRC 5.169
    General appearance, effect   CRC 5.68
    Telephone appearance   CRC 3.672, 5.9
Guardians ad litem
    Pseudonym, appointment under
        Leave to appear under pseudonym, ex parte request   CCP §372.5
Inconvenient forum, effect of general appearance on motion to stay or dismiss on grounds of   CCP §410.30
Indian child welfare act involuntary placements
    Tribal appearance by telephone or other remote means   CRC 3.672, 5.482
Judges, proceedings against   JudPerR 114, 123
Jurisdiction, motion to quash service of summons for lack of   Fam §2012
Juvenile rules
    Telephone appearances   CRC 3.672, 5.531
        Nonminor dependents, retention of jurisdiction   CRC 3.672, 5.900
Juvenile wardship proceedings
    Remote appearances   CRC 3.672
        COVID-19, emergency rule   CRCAppx I Emer Rule 7
Legal capacity lacking   CCP §372
Mediation sessions   CRC 3.894
Military counsel, appearance by   CRC 9.41
Military spouses
    Registered military spouse attorney   CRC 9.41.1

APPEARANCE—Cont.
Minors CCP §372
    Mature minors, appearances to obtain protective orders
        Domestic violence Fam §6229
Notice to appear forms CRC 4.103
    Judicial council legal forms CRCAppx A
Personal appearance
    Waiver
        COVID-19, emergency rule CRCAppx I Emer Rule 5
    When required CRC 3.670
Personal service of summons, general appearance equivalent to CCP §410.50
Quieting title proceedings CCP §762.050
Remote appearances, technology use
    Civil cases generally CRC 3.672
    COVID-19, emergency rule CRCAppx I Emer Rule 3
    Domestic violence restraining order
        Remote appearance of party, support person or witness Fam §6308
        Service requirements CRC 5.496
    Equal and fair access to justice
        Working group for statewide framework for remote proceedings CCP §367.9
    Notice CCP §367.75
    Open court proceedings
        Limiting public access when remote access available, restrictions CCP §124
    Permitted CCP §367.75
    Report on use of remote technology CCP §367.8
    Service requirements
        Restraining orders CRC 3.1162, 5.496
Service of process
    Motions to quash service CCP §418.10
    Remote appearances
        Restraining orders CRC 3.1162, 5.496
Small claims court (See **SMALL CLAIMS COURTS**)
Sterilization proceedings, attendance required by party to be sterilized at Pro §1956
Subpoenas (See **SUBPOENA**)
Telephone appearances CRC 3.670
    Child support
        Title IV-D support actions CRC 3.670, 5.324
    Dependent children
        Nonminor disposition hearings CRC 5.697
    Family rules CRC 5.9
    Hardware CRC JudAdminStand 3.1
    Indian child, dependency matters
        Tribal appearance by telephone or other remote means CRC 3.672, 5.531
    Indian child welfare act involuntary placements
        Tribal appearance by telephone or other remote means CRC 3.672, 5.482
    Judicial council standards CRC JudAdminStand 3.1
    Juvenile rules CRC 3.672, 5.531
        Nonminor dependents, retention of jurisdiction CRC 3.672, 5.900
    Remote appearances
        Civil cases CRC 3.672
        COVID-19, emergency rule CRCAppx I Emer Rule 3
        Restraining orders
            Service requirements CRC 3.1162
Traffic offenses
    Notice to appear forms CRC 4.103
Uniform Child Custody Jurisdiction and Enforcement Act (See **UNIFORM CHILD CUSTODY JURISDICTION AND ENFORCEMENT ACT**)

APPEARANCE BONDS (See **BAIL**)

APPELLATE DIVISION OF SUPERIOR COURT CCP §77
Appealable rulings CCP §904.2
Appellate court rules CRC 8.800 to 8.936 (See **APPELLATE RULES, SUPERIOR COURT APPEALS**)
Gangs and gang membership
    Designation of person as member, associate, etc
        Appeal of designation CRC 3.2300
Judgments
    Statement of reasons for judgment CCP §77
Judicial administration rules
    Administration of appellate division CRC 10.1100 to 10.1108
Mandamus
    Appeal of judgment involving mandamus or prohibition directed to superior court CCP §904.3
Original jurisdiction of appellate division
    Petition for writ
        Fee Gov §§70602.5, 70602.6, 70621

APPELLATE DIVISION OF SUPERIOR COURT—Cont.
Peremptory challenge of judge, inapplicability of provision for CCP §170.7
Prohibition, writ of
    Appeal of judgment involving mandamus or prohibition directed to superior court CCP §904.3
Small claims appeals CRC 8.950 to 8.966 (See **APPELLATE RULES, SUPERIOR COURT APPEALS**)
Transfers from appellate division to court of appeal CRC 8.1000 to 8.1018

APPELLATE REVIEW IN CIVIL CASES
Administration of appellate courts, supreme court and courts of appeal CRC 10.1000 to 10.1030
Arbitration proceedings
    Elder and dependent adult civil protection act
        Expedited appeals process CCP §1294.4, CRC 8.710 to 8.717
Attorneys' fees, notice of motion to claim CRC 3.1702
Capitol building annex project
    Environmental impact report on building annex project, judicial review
        Petitions under environmental quality act, civil rules governing CRC 3.2220 to 3.2237
Conservators Pro §§1300, 1301
    Appeal bonds CCP §919
    Effect of appeal Pro §§1310 to 1312
    Limited civil cases in appellate division
        Compromise of claims, approval CRC 8.825
    Order establishing conservatorships CRC 8.480
    Reversal of appointment order, effect of Pro §1311
    Stay on appeal Pro §1310
    Sterilization of conservatee, judgment authorizing conservator to consent CRC 8.482
    Sterilization orders Pro §§1962, 1965
Conservatorship jurisdiction act, appeals under Pro §1301.5
Consumer privacy rights
    California privacy protection agency
        Complaints, fines, etc, judicial review CC §1798.199.85
Courts of appeal
    Rules governing appellate review in supreme court and courts of appeal CRC 8.4 to 8.276
Dependent child proceedings
    Hearing orders, long-term placement
        Judicial council form for orders CRCAppx A
Environmental quality act cases under public resources code CRC 8.700 to 8.705
Fees
    Waiver
        Judicial council legal forms CRCAppx A
Foreign country judgments
    Stay of enforcement pending appeal CCP §1720
Forms
    Judicial council legal forms CRCAppx A
Memorandum opinions CRC JudAdminStand 8.1
Record on appeal
    Designating record on appeal
        Judicial council forms CRCAppx A
    Electronic recordings CRC 2.952
Rules
    Supreme court and courts of appeal, rules governing review in CRC 8.4 to 8.276
Supreme court
    Rules governing appellate review in supreme court and courts of appeal CRC 8.4 to 8.276
Transfers of cases from superior court appellate division to court of appeal CRC 8.1000 to 8.1018

APPELLATE REVIEW IN CRIMINAL CASES
Administration of appellate courts, supreme court and courts of appeal CRC 10.1000 to 10.1030
Certificate of probable cause for appeal, when required CRC 8.304
Courts of appeal
    Rules governing review in CRC 8.300 to 8.398
Defendants, appeal by CRC 8.304
    Judgments appealable CRC 8.304
Forms
    Judicial council legal forms CRCAppx A
Juvenile court appeals CRC 5.585
    Supreme court and courts of appeals CRC 8.400 to 8.470
Juvenile wardship proceedings CRC 5.585
Misdemeanor cases
    Oral argument, waiver
        Forms, judicial council CRCAppx A
Nolo contendere plea, appeal from conviction following CRC 8.304

APPELLATE REVIEW IN CRIMINAL CASES—Cont.
Notification to defendant of rights   CRC 4.305, 4.306
Probation
    Revocation on admission of violation, appeal by defendant   CRC 8.304
Record on appeal
    Communications from or with jury   CRC 2.1030
    Electronic recordings   CRC 2.952
Rules
    Supreme court and courts of appeals reviews   CRC 8.300 to 8.398
Supreme court
    Rules governing review in   CRC 8.300 to 8.398

APPELLATE REVIEW IN JUVENILE CASES
Forms, judicial council   CRCAppx A
Rules governing appellate review   CRC 5.585 to 5.595
Supreme court and courts of appeal   CRC 8.400 to 8.474
    Generally (See **APPELLATE RULES, SUPREME COURT AND COURTS OF APPEAL**)

APPELLATE RULES
Forms
    Appellate forms
        Judicial council legal forms   CRCAppx A
Miscellaneous appeals and writs   CRC 8.720 to 8.730 (See **APPELLATE RULES, MISCELLANEOUS APPEALS AND WRITS**)
Publication of appellate opinions   CRC 8.1100 to 8.1125
Small claims appeals   CRC 8.950 to 8.966
Superior court appeals
    Generally   CRC 8.800 to 8.966 (See **APPELLATE RULES, SUPERIOR COURT APPEALS**)
Supreme court and courts of appeal
    Generally   CRC 8.1 to 8.642
Title of rules   CRC 8.1
Transfers from superior court appellate division to court of appeal   CRC 8.1000 to 8.1018

APPELLATE RULES, MISCELLANEOUS APPEALS AND WRITS   CRC 8.720 to 8.730
Agricultural Labor Relations Board cases, review   CRC 8.728
Answer
    Public Utilities Commission reviews   CRC 8.724
    Workers' Compensation Appeals Board cases, review   CRC 8.720
Briefs
    Agricultural Labor Relations Board cases, review of   CRC 8.728
    Certificates of interested entities or persons
        Agricultural labor relations board cases, review of   CRC 8.728
        Public utilities commission reviews   CRC 8.724
        Workers' compensation appeals board cases, review of   CRC 8.720
    Public Employment Relations Board cases, review of   CRC 8.728
    Public Utilities Commission orders, review of   CRC 8.724
    Workers' Compensation Appeals Board cases, review of   CRC 8.720
Copies
    Public Utilities Commission review petition   CRC 8.724
    Workers' Compensation Appeals Board cases, petition to review   CRC 8.720
Filing
    Agricultural Labor Relations Board cases, review of   CRC 8.728
    Public Employment Relations Board cases, review of   CRC 8.728
    Public Utilities Commission review petition   CRC 8.724
    Workers' Compensation Appeals Board cases, petition to review   CRC 8.720
Petition
    Agricultural Labor Relations Board cases, review of   CRC 8.728
    Public Employment Relations Board cases, review of   CRC 8.728
    Public Utilities Commission decisions, review of   CRC 8.724
    Workers' Compensation Appeals Board cases, review of   CRC 8.720
Public Employment Relations Board cases, review of   CRC 8.728
Public Utilities Commission decisions, review of   CRC 8.724
Record on appeal
    Agricultural Labor Relations Board cases, review of   CRC 8.728
    Public Employment Relations Board cases, review of   CRC 8.728
Remittitur
    Review, writs of   CRC 8.730
Reply
    Public Utilities Commission reviews   CRC 8.724
    Workers' Compensation Appeals Board cases, review of   CRC 8.720
Service
    Public Utilities Commission review petition   CRC 8.724
    Workers' Compensation Appeals Board cases, petition to review   CRC 8.720

APPELLATE RULES, MISCELLANEOUS APPEALS AND WRITS—Cont.
Time
    Public Utilities Commission review petition, filing of   CRC 8.724
    Workers' Compensation Appeals Board cases, filing for review of   CRC 8.720
Workers' Compensation Appeals Board cases   CRC 8.720

APPELLATE RULES, SUPERIOR COURT APPEALS   CRC 8.800 to 8.966
Abandonment and dismissal   CCP §913
    Infraction case appeals   CRC 8.904
        Record on appeal, failure to procure   CRC 8.924
    Limited civil cases in appellate division   CRC 8.825
        Record on appeal, failure to procure   CRC 8.842
    Misdemeanor appeals   CRC 8.855
        Record on appeal, failure to procure   CRC 8.874
    Small claims appeals   CRC 8.963
Address of record   CRC 8.816
Administration of appellate division   CRC 10.1100 to 10.1108
    Assignments to division   CRC 10.1100
    Judicial assignments to division   CRC 10.1100
    Presiding judge   CRC 10.1104
    Sessions   CRC 10.1108
Agreed statement
    Limited civil cases in appellate division
        Record on appeal   CRC 8.836
Amendments to rules   CRC 8.805
Amicus curiae briefs   CRC 8.882
Applicability of provisions   CRC 8.800
Applications
    Content   CRC 8.806
    Disposition of application   CRC 8.806
    Envelopes to accompany   CRC 8.806
    Extension of time   CRC 8.810
    Filing   CRC 8.806
    Service   CRC 8.806
Arbitration proceedings   CCP §§1291, 1294, 1294.2
Argument
    Gang database removal, appeal proceedings   CRC 3.2300
    Oral argument   CRC 8.885
        Applicability of provisions   CRC 8.880
        Infraction case appeals   CRC 8.929
Attorneys
    Address of record   CRC 8.816
    Email, notice of change   CRC 8.816
    Fax number, notice of change   CRC 8.816
    Misdemeanor appeals
        Appointment of appellate counsel   CRC 8.851
    Substitution   CRC 8.814
    Telephone number of record   CRC 8.816
    Withdrawal   CRC 8.814
    Writ proceedings within original jurisdiction of appellate division
        Petition filed by attorney for party   CRC 8.932
Augmentation of record on appeal
    Infraction case appeals   CRC 8.923
    Limited civil cases in appellate division   CRC 8.841
    Misdemeanor appeals   CRC 8.873
Bonds, surety
    Costs
        Recoverable costs   CRC 8.891
Briefs
    Amicus curiae briefs   CRC 8.882
    Applicability of provisions   CRC 8.880
    Contents   CRC 8.883
        Infraction case appeals   CRC 8.928
    Costs
        Recoverable costs   CRC 8.891
    Extensions of time   CRC 8.882
    Failure to file   CRC 8.882
        Infraction case appeals   CRC 8.927
    Form   CRC 8.883
        Infraction case appeals   CRC 8.928
    Infraction case appeals
        Applicability of provisions   CRC 8.925
        Content   CRC 8.928
        Failure to file brief   CRC 8.927
        Filing   CRC 8.927
        Form of brief   CRC 8.928
        Length of brief   CRC 8.928
        Noncomplying briefs   CRC 8.928
        Schedule   CRC 8.926

APPELLATE RULES, SUPERIOR COURT APPEALS—Cont.
  Briefs—Cont.
    Infraction case appeals—Cont.
      Service   CRC 8.927
      Time to file   CRC 8.927
    Length   CRC 8.883
      Infraction case appeals   CRC 8.928
    Nonconforming briefs   CRC 8.883
      Infraction case appeals   CRC 8.928
    Parties
      Appellant and respondent, party as both   CRC 8.884
      Briefs by party   CRC 8.882
    Schedule
      Infraction case appeals   CRC 8.926
      Notice of briefing schedule   CRC 8.881
      Party as both appellant and respondent   CRC 8.884
    Service and filing   CRC 8.882
      Infraction case appeals   CRC 8.927
  Calendar
    Oral argument   CRC 8.885
  Certification of opinions for publication   CRC 8.887
  Certiorari (See **CERTIORARI**)
  Clerk
    Infraction case appeals
      Record on appeal, clerk's transcript   CRC 8.912, 8.913
    Misdemeanor appeals
      Abandonment of appeal, duties of clerk   CRC 8.855
    Remittitur
      Duties of clerk   CRC 8.890
    Small claims appeals
      Abandonment and dismissal, duties of clerk   CRC 8.963
    Transcript
      Limited civil cases in appellate division, record on appeal   CRC 8.832
  Construction   CRC 8.802
    Statutes referenced considered to be as amended   CRC 8.805
  Correction
    Infraction case appeals
      Record on appeal   CRC 8.923
    Limited civil cases in appellate division
      Record on appeal   CRC 8.841
    Misdemeanor appeals
      Record on appeal   CRC 8.873
  Costs
    Applicability of provisions   CRC 8.880
    Claiming
      Procedure for claiming or opposing   CRC 8.891
    Judgment for costs   CRC 8.891
    Limited civil cases in appellate division
      Clerk's transcript as part of record on appeal   CRC 8.832
      Reporter's transcript as part of record on appeal   CRC 8.834
      Trial court file in lieu of clerk's transcript for record on appeal   CRC 8.833
    Opposing costs
      Procedure for claiming or opposing   CRC 8.891
    Recoverable costs   CRC 8.891
    Right to costs   CRC 8.891
    Waiver of fees and costs   CRC 8.818
    Writ proceedings within original jurisdiction of appellate division   CRC 8.936
  Criminal appeals
    Infraction case appeals generally   CRC 8.900 to 8.929 (See within this heading, **"Infraction case appeals"**)
    Misdemeanor appeals generally   CRC 8.850 to 8.874 (See within this heading, **"Misdemeanor appeals"**)
  Cross appeal
    Infraction case appeals
      Notice of appeal   CRC 8.902
    Limited civil cases in appellate division
      Extending time to appeal   CRC 8.823
      Notice of cross appeal   CRC 8.806
    Misdemeanor appeals
      Notice of appeal   CRC 8.853
  Decisions on appeal
    Applicability of provisions   CRC 8.880
    Certification of opinions for publication   CRC 8.887
    Filing   CRC 8.887
    Finality   CRC 8.888
    Gang database removal, appeal proceedings   CRC 3.2300
    Increase or decrease in amount of judgment
      Consent   CRC 8.888

APPELLATE RULES, SUPERIOR COURT APPEALS—Cont.
  Decisions on appeal—Cont.
    Infraction case appeals
      Applicability of provisions   CRC 8.925
    Modification   CRC 8.888
    Writ proceedings within original jurisdiction of appellate division
      Filing of decision   CRC 8.935
      Finality of decision   CRC 8.935
      Modification of decisions   CRC 8.935
    Written opinions   CRC 8.887
  Default, relief from   CRC 8.812
    Infraction case appeals
      Record on appeal, failure to procure   CRC 8.924
    Limited civil cases in appellate division
      Record on appeal, failure to procure   CRC 8.842
    Misdemeanor appeals
      Record on appeal, failure to procure   CRC 8.874
  Definitions   CRC 8.803
  Dismissal (See within this heading, **"Abandonment and dismissal"**)
  Electronically filed documents
    Signatures on electronically filed documents   CRC 8.804
  Evidence questions   Ev §§353, 354
  Exhibits
    Infraction case appeals   CRC 8.921
    Misdemeanor appeals
      Record on appeal   CRC 8.870
  Extensions of time   CRC 8.810
    Briefs   CRC 8.882
    Factors considered in determining   CRC 8.811
    Limited civil cases in appellate division   CRC 8.823
      Agreed statement for record on appeal   CRC 8.836
    Misdemeanor appeals
      Statement on appeal as record   CRC 8.869
    Policies   CRC 8.811
    Rehearing
      No extensions for granting or denying petition   CRC 8.889
  Family allowance orders   Pro §6545
  Fees
    Costs
      Recoverable costs   CRC 8.891
    Limited civil cases in appellate division
      Notice of appeal   CRC 8.821
    Waiver of fees and costs   CRC 8.818
  Filing   CRC 8.817
    Abandonment and dismissal
      Small claims cases   CRC 8.963
    Applications   CRC 8.806
    Briefs   CRC 8.882
      Infraction case appeals   CRC 8.927
    Costs
      Recoverable costs   CRC 8.891
    Form of filed documents   CRC 8.815
    Infraction case appeals
      Record on appeal   CRC 8.922
    Misdemeanor appeals
      Record on appeal   CRC 8.872
    Motions   CRC 8.808
    Signatures on electronically filed documents   CRC 8.804
    Small claims appeals   CCP §116.750, CRC 8.954
  Forms
    Appellate forms
      Judicial council legal forms   CRCAppx A
  Frivolous appeals
    Sanctions   CRC 8.891
  Gang database removal, appeal proceedings   CRC 3.2300
    Applicability   CRC 3.2300
    Decision   CRC 3.2300
    Definitions   CRC 3.2300
    Judges
      Designated judge for petitions under rule   CRC 3.2300
    Oral argument   CRC 3.2300
    Order to remove name
      Service on attorney general   CRC 3.2300
    Petition
      Fees   CRC 3.2300
      Filing   CRC 3.2300
      Form   CRC 3.2300
      Service   CRC 3.2300
    Record   CRC 3.2300
    Written argument   CRC 3.2300

APPELL INDEX 38

APPELLATE RULES, SUPERIOR COURT APPEALS—Cont.
Gender
    Construction of terms   CRC 8.802
Headings of provisions
    Substantive nature of headings   CRC 8.802
Indexes
    Limited civil cases in appellate division
        Record on appeal   CRC 8.838
Infraction case appeals   CRC 8.900 to 8.929
    Abandonment of appeal   CRC 8.904
    Applicability of provisions   CRC 8.900
    Briefs
        Applicability of provisions   CRC 8.925
        Content   CRC 8.928
        Failure to file brief   CRC 8.927
        Filing   CRC 8.927
        Form of brief   CRC 8.928
        Length of brief   CRC 8.928
        Noncomplying briefs   CRC 8.928
        Schedule   CRC 8.926
        Service   CRC 8.927
        Time to file   CRC 8.927
    Decisions
        Applicability of provisions   CRC 8.925
    Electronic recording of trial court proceedings   CRC 8.917
    Exhibits   CRC 8.921
    Limited record   CRC 8.910, 8.920
    Notice of appeal   CRC 8.901
        Cross appeal   CRC 8.902
        Late notice of appeal   CRC 8.902
        Normal time   CRC 8.902
        Premature notice of appeal   CRC 8.902
        Time to file   CRC 8.902
    Notice when proceedings below not electronically recorded or otherwise cannot be transcribed   CRC 8.917, 8.919
    Oral argument   CRC 8.929
    Oral proceedings, record of   CRC 8.915
    Proposed statement on appeal
        Judicial council form   CRCAppx A
    Record on appeal   CRC 8.910 to 8.924
        Augmentation of record   CRC 8.923
        Clerk's transcript   CRC 8.912, 8.913
        Correction of record   CRC 8.923
        Electronic recording of trial court proceedings   CRC 8.917
        Exhibits   CRC 8.921
        Failure to procure record   CRC 8.924
        Filing record   CRC 8.922
        Limited record   CRC 8.910, 8.920
        Normal record   CRC 8.910
        Notice when proceedings below not electronically recorded or otherwise cannot be transcribed   CRC 8.917, 8.919
        Oral proceedings, record of   CRC 8.915
        Prosecuting attorney's notice as to nonreceipt of record   CRC 8.911
        Reporter's transcript   CRC 8.918, 8.919
        Sending record   CRC 8.922
        Statement on appeal   CRC 8.916
        Trial court file in lieu of clerk's transcript   CRC 8.914
    Statement on appeal   CRC 8.916
    Stay of execution   CRC 8.903
    Trial court file in lieu of clerk's transcript for record on appeal   CRC 8.914
Judge
    Appellate division assignments   CCP §77, CRC 10.1100
Judgment notwithstanding verdict
    Limited civil cases in appellate division
        Motion for judgment notwithstanding verdict extending time to appeal   CRC 8.823
Judgments
    Costs on appeal   CRC 8.891
    Decrease in amount
        Consent   CRC 8.888
    Increase in amount
        Consent   CRC 8.888
    Modification as part of appellate decision   CRC 8.888
    Vacation of judgment, motion
        Limited civil cases in appellate division   CRC 8.823
Judicial administration rules
    Administration of appellate division   CRC 10.1100 to 10.1108
Judicial notice   CRC 8.809
Limited civil cases in appellate division   CRC 8.820 to 8.845
    Abandonment of appeal   CRC 8.825
    Applicability of provisions   CRC 8.820

APPELLATE RULES, SUPERIOR COURT APPEALS—Cont.
Limited civil cases in appellate division —Cont.
    Briefs, hearings and decisions   CRC 8.880 to 8.891
    Dismissal
        Voluntary dismissal   CRC 8.825
    Extending time to appeal   CRC 8.823
    Notice of appeal   CRC 8.821
        Late notice   CRC 8.822
        Premature notice   CRC 8.822
    Record on appeal   CRC 8.830 to 8.845
        Agreed statement   CRC 8.836
        Appendix, use   CRC 8.845
        Augmentation   CRC 8.841
        Clerk's transcript   CRC 8.832
        Completeness of record, determining   CRC 8.840
        Correction of record   CRC 8.841
        Electronic recording of proceedings   CRC 8.835
        Failure to procure record   CRC 8.842
        Filing record   CRC 8.840
        Form of record   CRC 8.838
        Multiple appeals   CRC 8.839
        Normal record   CRC 8.830
        Notice designating record   CRC 8.831
        Notice when electronic recording of proceedings not available or transcript not possible   CRC 8.835
        Reporter's transcript   CRC 8.834
        Statement on appeal   CRC 8.837
        Trial court file in lieu of clerk's transcript   CRC 8.833
    Supersedeas   CRC 8.824
    Time to appeal   CRC 8.822
May
    Construction of term   CRC 8.802
May not
    Construction of terms   CRC 8.802
Misdemeanor appeals   CRC 8,850 to 8.874
    Abandonment of appeal   CRC 8.855
    Applicability of provisions   CRC 8.850
    Attorneys
        Appointment of appellate counsel   CRC 8.851
    Briefs, hearings and decisions   CRC 8.880 to 8.891
    Notice of appeal   CRC 8.852
        Late notice of appeal   CRC 8.853
        Normal time to appeal   CRC 8.853
        Premature notice of appeal   CRC 8.853
        Time to appeal   CRC 8.853
    Oral argument, waiver
        Forms, judicial council   CRCAppx A
    Proposed statement on appeal
        Judicial council form   CRCAppx A
    Record on appeal   CRC 8.860 to 8.874
        Additions to limited normal record   CRC 8.867
        Augmentation of record   CRC 8.873
        Clerk's transcript   CRC 8.861, 8.862
        Contents of clerk's transcript   CRC 8.861
        Contents of reporter's transcript   CRC 8.865
        Correction of record   CRC 8.873
        Demurrers or other appealable orders, limited normal record   CRC 8.867
        Electronic record   CRC 8.864, 8.868
        Exhibits   CRC 8.870
        Failure to procure record   CRC 8.874
        Filing record   CRC 8.872
        Juror-identifying information   CRC 8.871
        Limited record   CRC 8.860, 8.867
        Normal record on appeal   CRC 8.860
        Notice when proceedings not reported or cannot be transcribed   CRC 8.866, 8.868
        Oral proceedings, record of   CRC 8.864
        Preparation of clerk's transcript   CRC 8.862
        Preparation of reporter's transcript   CRC 8.866
        Probation condition appeals   CRC 8.867
        Reporter's transcript   CRC 8.864 to 8.866
        Sending record   CRC 8.872
        Statement on appeal   CRC 8.869
        Suppression of evidence or return of seized property, limited normal record   CRC 8.867
        Trial court file in lieu of clerk's transcript   CRC 8.863
    Release on appeal   CRC 8.854
    Stay of execution   CRC 8.854

APPELLATE RULES, SUPERIOR COURT APPEALS—Cont.
Motions
    Attorneys
        Withdrawal   CRC 8.814
    Disposition   CRC 8.808
    Filing   CRC 8.808
    Judicial notice   CRC 8.809
    Parties
        Substitution   CRC 8.814
    Service   CRC 8.808
Multiple appeals
    Limited civil cases in appellate division
        Record on appeal   CRC 8.839
Must
    Construction of term   CRC 8.802
New trial
    Limited civil cases in appellate division
        Motion for new trial   CRC 8.823
Notice
    Abandonment and dismissal
        Small claims cases   CRC 8.963
    Appeal, notice of (See within this heading, **"Notice of appeal"**)
    Briefs
        Schedule for briefing   CRC 8.881
    Extension of time
        Application, notice of   CRC 8.810
    Infraction case appeals
        Clerk's notification of filing of notice of appeal   CRC 8.901
    Limited civil cases, appeal to appellate division
        Notification of appeal   CRC 8.821
    Limited civil cases in appellate division
        Record on appeal, designation   CRC 8.831
    Misdemeanor appeals
        Notice of appeal filed   CRC 8.852
    Oral argument   CRC 8.885
        Infraction case appeals   CRC 8.929
    Remittitur   CRC 8.890
    Writ proceedings within original jurisdiction of appellate division
        Notice if writ issues   CRC 8.934
Notice of appeal
    Default, relief from
        Not given   CRC 8.812
    Infraction case appeals   CRC 8.901
        Cross appeal   CRC 8.902
        Late notice of appeal   CRC 8.902
        Normal time   CRC 8.902
        Premature notice of appeal   CRC 8.902
        Time to file   CRC 8.902
    Limited civil cases in appellate division   CRC 8.821
        Late notice   CRC 8.822
        Premature notice   CRC 8.822
    Misdemeanor appeals   CRC 8.852
        Late notice of appeal   CRC 8.853
        Normal time to appeal   CRC 8.853
        Premature notice of appeal   CRC 8.853
        Time to appeal   CRC 8.853
    Small claims appeals   CCP §116.750, CRC 8.954
    Validation proceedings   CCP §870
Numbers
    Construction of terms   CRC 8.802
Opinions
    Written opinions   CRC 8.887
Oral argument   CRC 8.885
    Applicability of provisions   CRC 8.880
    Gang database removal, appeal proceedings   CRC 3.2300
    Infraction case appeals   CRC 8.929
    Misdemeanor appeals
        Waiver of oral argument, judicial council form   CRCAppx A
Party
    Address and telephone number of record   CRC 8.816
    Briefs   CRC 8.882
        Appellant and respondent, party as both   CRC 8.884
    Substitution   CRC 8.814
Petitions
    Limited civil cases in appellate division
        Supersedeas   CRC 8.824
    Writ proceedings within original jurisdiction of appellate division
        Attorney filing petition for party   CRC 8.932
        Opposition to petition   CRC 8.933
        Pro se petitions   CRC 8.931

APPELLATE RULES, SUPERIOR COURT APPEALS—Cont.
Premature notice of appeal
    Infraction case appeals   CRC 8.902
    Limited civil cases in appellate division   CRC 8.822
    Misdemeanor appeals   CRC 8.853
    Small claims cases   CRC 8.954
Presiding judge
    Administration of appellate division   CRC 10.1104
Publication of appellate opinions   CRC 8.1100 to 8.1125
    Authority for rules governing   CRC 8.1100
    Certification of opinions for publication   CRC 8.887
    Citation of opinions   CRC 8.1115
    Depublication of published opinions   CRC 8.1125
    Editing of opinions   CRC 8.1105
    Partial publication of appellate opinions   CRC 8.1110
    Procedure for publication of appellate opinions   CRC 8.1105
    Review of published opinion granted   CRC 8.1115
    Standards for publication of opinions   CRC 8.1105
    Unpublished opinions
        Citation   CRC 8.1115
        Effect   CRC 8.1115
        Request for publication   CRC 8.1120
Reconsideration of appealable orders
    Limited civil cases in appellate division
        Motion for reconsideration extending time to appeal   CRC 8.823
Record on appeal
    Costs
        Recoverable costs   CRC 8.891
    Extension of time for preparation   CRC 8.810
    Gang database removal, appeal proceedings   CRC 3.2300
    Infraction case appeals   CRC 8.910 to 8.924
        Augmentation of record   CRC 8.923
        Clerk's transcript   CRC 8.912, 8.913
        Correction of record   CRC 8.923
        Electronic recording of trial court proceedings   CRC 8.917
        Exhibits   CRC 8.921
        Failure to procure record   CRC 8.924
        Filing record   CRC 8.922
        Limited record   CRC 8.910, 8.920
        Normal record   CRC 8.910
        Notice when proceedings below not electronically recorded or otherwise cannot be transcribed   CRC 8.917, 8.919
        Oral proceedings, record of   CRC 8.915
        Prosecuting attorney's notice as to nonreceipt of record   CRC 8.911
        Reporter's transcript   CRC 8.918, 8.919
        Sending record   CRC 8.922
        Statement on appeal   CRC 8.916
        Trial court file in lieu of clerk's transcript   CRC 8.914
    Limited civil cases in appellate division   CRC 8.830 to 8.845
        Agreed statement   CRC 8.836
        Appendix, use   CRC 8.845
        Augmentation   CRC 8.841
        Clerk's transcript   CRC 8.832
        Completeness of record, determining   CRC 8.840
        Correction of record   CRC 8.841
        Electronic recording of proceedings   CRC 8.835
        Failure to procure record   CRC 8.842
        Filing record   CRC 8.840
        Form of record   CRC 8.838
        Multiple appeals   CRC 8.839
        Normal record   CRC 8.830
        Notice designating record   CRC 8.831
        Notice when electronic recording of proceedings not available or transcript not possible   CRC 8.835
        Reporter's transcript   CRC 8.834
        Statement on appeal   CRC 8.837
        Trial court file in lieu of clerk's transcript   CRC 8.833
    Misdemeanor appeals   CRC 8.860 to 8.874
        Additions to limited normal record   CRC 8.867
        Augmentation of record   CRC 8.873
        Clerk's transcript   CRC 8.861, 8.862
        Contents of clerk's transcript   CRC 8.861
        Contents of reporter's transcript   CRC 8.865
        Correction of record   CRC 8.873
        Demurrers or other appealable orders, limited normal record   CRC 8.867
        Electronic record   CRC 8.864, 8.868
        Exhibits   CRC 8.870
        Failure to procure record   CRC 8.874
        Filing record   CRC 8.872
        Juror-identifying information   CRC 8.871

APPELLATE RULES, SUPERIOR COURT APPEALS—Cont.
  Record on appeal—Cont.
    Misdemeanor appeals —Cont.
      Limited record   CRC 8.860, 8.867
      Normal record on appeal   CRC 8.860
      Notice when proceedings not reported or cannot be transcribed   CRC 8.866, 8.868
      Oral proceedings, record of   CRC 8.864
      Preparation of clerk's transcript   CRC 8.862
      Preparation of reporter's transcript   CRC 8.866
      Probation condition appeals   CRC 8.867
      Reporter's transcript   CRC 8.864 to 8.866
      Sending record   CRC 8.872
      Statement on appeal   CRC 8.869
      Suppression of evidence or return of seized property, limited normal record   CRC 8.867
      Trial court file in lieu of clerk's transcript   CRC 8.863
    Small claims   CRC 8.957
  Records
    Sealing of records   CRC 8.819
  Rehearing
    Answer   CRC 8.889
    Applicability of provisions   CRC 8.880
    Effect of granting rehearing   CRC 8.889
    Extensions of time
      No extensions for granting or denying petition   CRC 8.889
    Ordering rehearing   CRC 8.889
    Petition for rehearing   CRC 8.889
    Writ proceedings within original jurisdiction of appellate division   CRC 8.935
  Remittitur   CRC 8.890
    Applicability of provisions   CRC 8.880
    Writ proceedings within original jurisdiction of appellate division   CRC 8.935
  Sanctions   CRC 8.891
    Infraction case appeals
      Record on appeal, failure to procure   CRC 8.924
    Limited civil cases in appellate division
      Record on appeal, failure to procure   CRC 8.842
    Misdemeanor appeals
      Record on appeal, failure to procure   CRC 8.874
  Sealed records
    Applicable rules   CRC 8.819
  Service   CRC 8.817
    Applications   CRC 8.806
    Briefs   CRC 8.882
      Infraction case appeals   CRC 8.927
  Sessions of appellate division
    Administration of appellate division   CRC 10.1108
  Shortening time   CRC 8.813
  Should
    Construction of terms   CRC 8.802
  Small claims cases   CRC 8.950 to 8.966
    Abandonment of appeal   CRC 8.963
    Applicability of provisions   CRC 8.950
    Compromise of case involving wards or conservatees, approval   CRC 8.963
    Continuance   CRC 8.960
    Cross examination   CRC 8.966
    Definitions   CRC 8.952
    Dismissal
      Delay in bringing case to trial   CCP §116.795, CRC 8.963
      Notice   CRC 8.963
      Request for   CRC 8.963
      Stipulation for   CRC 8.963
    Examination and cross examination   CRC 8.966
    Filing of appeal   CCP §116.750, CRC 8.954
    Incompetent persons, approval for compromise of case involving   CRC 8.963
    Minors, approval for compromise of case involving   CRC 8.963
    Notice of appeal   CCP §116.750
      Notification of filing of notice of appeal   CRC 8.954
      Premature notice   CRC 8.954
    Record on appeal   CCP §116.770, CRC 8.957
    Setting for hearing   CCP §116.770
    Small claims courts generally (See **SMALL CLAIMS COURTS**)
    Transmitting record   CRC 8.957
    Writ petitions   CRC 8.970 to 8.977
      Applicability of provisions   CRC 8.970
      Attorney filing for party   CRC 8.973
      Costs   CRC 8.977

APPELLATE RULES, SUPERIOR COURT APPEALS—Cont.
  Small claims cases —Cont.
    Writ petitions —Cont.
      Decisions   CRC 8.976
      Definitions   CRC 8.971
      Notice to small claims court   CRC 8.975
      Opposition   CRC 8.974
      Pro se petitions   CRC 8.972
      Remittitur   CRC 8.976
      Return or opposition   CRC 8.974
      Telephone notice to small claims court   CRC 8.975
  Statement on appeal
    Infraction case appeals   CRC 8.916
    Limited civil cases in appellate division
      Record on appeal   CRC 8.837
    Misdemeanor appeals
      Record on appeal   CRC 8.869
  Stay of execution
    Infraction case appeals   CRC 8.903
    Misdemeanor appeals   CRC 8.854
  Stay of proceedings
    Limited civil cases in appellate division
      Supersedeas   CRC 8.824
  Stipulations
    Attorneys
      Substitution   CRC 8.814
    Infraction case appeals
      Limited record on appeal   CRC 8.910
    Misdemeanor appeals
      Limited record on appeal   CRC 8.860
  Submission of cause   CRC 8.886
    Applicability of provisions   CRC 8.880
  Supersedeas
    Limited civil cases in appellate division   CRC 8.824
  Telephone number of record   CRC 8.816
  Tenses
    Construction of terms   CRC 8.802
  Transcript
    Clerk's transcript
      Infraction case appeals, record on appeal   CRC 8.912, 8.913
      Limited civil cases in appellate division, record on appeal   CRC 8.832
      Misdemeanor appeals, record on appeal   CRC 8.861, 8.862
    Electronic recording of proceedings, transcript from
      Infraction case appeals   CRC 8.917
      Limited civil cases in appellate division, record on appeal   CRC 8.835
    Reporter's transcript
      Infraction case appeals, record on appeal   CRC 8.918, 8.919
      Limited civil cases in appellate division, record on appeal   CRC 8.834
      Misdemeanor appeals, record on appeal   CRC 8.864 to 8.866
  Transfers from superior court appellate division to court of appeal   CRC 8.1000 to 8.1018
    Appellate division proceedings after certification or transfer   CRC 8.1014
    Applicability of rules   CRC 8.1000
    Arguments
      Issues to be argued   CRC 8.1012
    Authority of court of appeal   CRC 8.1002
    Briefs   CRC 8.1012
    Certification   CRC 8.1005
      Appellate division proceedings after certification or transfer   CRC 8.1014
    Decision by court of appeal in transferred case
      Filing, finality and modification   CRC 8.1018
    Denial of transfer
      Finality   CRC 8.1018
    Disposition of transferred case   CRC 8.1016
    Grounds for transfer   CRC 8.1002
    Order for transfer   CRC 8.1008
      Vacating transfer order   CRC 8.1018
    Petitions   CRC 8.1006
    Record on transfer   CRC 8.1007
    Remittitur   CRC 8.1018
    Retransfer without decision
      Disposition of transferred case   CRC 8.1016
    Scope of rules   CRC 8.1000
    Time   CRC 8.1008
      Certification   CRC 8.1005

APPELLATE RULES, SUPERIOR COURT APPEALS—Cont.
Unlimited civil cases
    Forms
        Judicial council legal forms   CRCAppx A
Vacation of judgment, motion
    Limited civil cases in appellate division
        Extending time to appeal   CRC 8.823
Vacation of submission of cause   CRC 8.886
Videoconferencing
    Oral argument by videoconference   CRC 8.885
    Infraction case appeals   CRC 8.929
Waiver of fees and costs   CRC 8.818
Will
    Construction of terms   CRC 8.802
Writ proceedings within original jurisdiction of appellate division   CRC 8.930 to 8.936
    Applicability of provisions   CRC 8.930
    Costs   CRC 8.936
    Filing of decision   CRC 8.935
    Finality of decision   CRC 8.935
    Modification of decisions   CRC 8.935
    Notice if writ issues   CRC 8.934
    Opposition to petition   CRC 8.933
    Petitions
        Attorney filing petition for party   CRC 8.932
        Pro se petitions   CRC 8.931
    Pro se petitions   CRC 8.931
    Rehearings   CRC 8.935
    Remittitur   CRC 8.935
    Small claims cases, writ petitions   CRC 8.970 to 8.977
    Telephone notice if writ issues   CRC 8.934

APPELLATE RULES, SUPREME COURT AND COURTS OF APPEAL   CRC 8.1 to 8.642
Abandonment of appeal (See within this heading, **"Dismissal"**)
Additional evidence on appeal, application for   CRC 8.252
    Costs, items recoverable as   CRC 8.278
Additional record
    Criminal appeals   CRC 8.324
Addresses
    Change notice, service and filing   CRC 8.32
        Electronic filing, when required   CRCSupp 1st AppDist
    Record, address of   CRC 8.32
Administration of appellate courts   CRC 10.1000 to 10.1030
    Administrative presiding judge, court of appeals   CRC 10.1004
    Attorney misconduct triggering notification to state bar
        Justice's duties   CRC 10.1017
    Clerk/executive officers
        Education, minimum   CRC 10.471
        Education of judicial branch, duties as to   CRC 10.452
        Role and duties   CRC 10.1020
    Divisions of court of appeals
        Assignment of cases to balance workload   CRC 10.1008
    Judicial duties, failure to perform   CRC 10.1016
    Local rules of courts of appeal   CRC 10.1030
    Minutes
        Court of appeal minutes   CRC 10.1024
    Progress of appeals, supervision   CRC 10.1012
    Records
        Preservation and destruction of court of appeals records   CRC 10.1028
    Transfer of causes   CRC 10.1000
Administrative presiding justice   CRC 10.1004
    Clerk/executive officer, role and duties   CRC 10.1020
        Education of clerk/executive officer, minimum   CRC 10.471
        Education of judicial branch, duties as to   CRC 10.452
    Duties   CRC 10.1004
    Failure of court judge to perform judicial duties, notification   CRC 10.1016
    Oversight of   CRC 10.1014
    Progress of appeals, supervision   CRC 10.1012
    Transfer of cases   CRC 10.1000
Administrative proceedings
    Record of proceedings
        Availability to other party   CRC 8.123
        Content of record on appeal   CRC 8.120
        Designation for inclusion   CRC 8.123
        Return by reviewing court   CRC 8.123
        Transmittal to reviewing court   CRC 8.123
Agreed statement
    Civil appeals   CRC 8.134
        Transcript not available   CRC 8.130

APPELLATE RULES, SUPREME COURT AND COURTS OF APPEAL—Cont.
Agreed statement—Cont.
    Content of record on appeal   CRC 8.120
    Criminal appeals   CRC 8.344
    E-filing in supreme court and courts of appeal
        Format of electronic documents   CRC 8.74
    Juvenile case appeals   CRC 8.407
Amendment of rules by Judicial Council   CRC 8.13
Amicus curiae (See **AMICUS CURIAE**)
Answer
    Failure to conform to requirements re form   CRC 8.18
    Removal to supreme court before decision in court of appeal   CRC 8.552
    Supreme court review of court of appeal decision   CRC 8.500
Appellant
    Defined   CRC 8.10
Appendix designated as record on appeal   CRC 8.124
    Content of record on appeal   CRC 8.120
    E-filing in supreme court and courts of appeal
        Format of electronic documents   CRC 8.74
Applicability of provisions   CRC 8.4
    Documents filed and served electronically and via paper   CRC 8.11
Applications   CRC 8.50
    Extension of time   CRC 8.60
        Electronic filing, when required   CRCSupp 1st AppDist
    Fees for filing   CRC 8.25
Argument
    Juvenile case appeals
        Dependency appeals, certain counties   CRC 8.416
        Order designating specific placement of dependent child, writ petition to review   CRC 8.456
        Orders setting hearing in termination cases, writ petition to review   CRC 8.452
        Termination of parental rights, appeal from   CRC 8.416
        Transfer of minor to court of criminal jurisdiction   CRC 8.417
    Media coverage of oral argument
        1st Appellate District local rules   CRCSupp 1st AppDist
    Oral arguments   CRC 8.256
        Amicus, argument by   CRC 8.524
        Applicability   CRC 8.524
        Attorneys, number   CRC 8.524
        Calendar sessions   CRCSupp SupCtIOPP V
        Capital cases   CRC 8.638
        Death penalty, supreme court review   CRC 8.638
        Elder and dependent adult civil protection act, expedited appeals process   CRC 8.716
        Environmental quality act cases under public resources code   CRC 8.702
        Habeas corpus   CRC 8.386
        Juvenile case appeals   CRC 8.417
        Media coverage of oral argument   CRCSupp 1st AppDist
        Notice of argument   CRC 8.524
        Place of argument   CRC 8.524
        Request, electronic filing   CRCSupp 1st AppDist
        Sequence of argument   CRC 8.524
        Submission of cause   CRC 8.524
        Time for argument   CRC 8.524, CRCSupp 4th AppDist Misc Order 15-6, 4th AppDist Misc Order 16-6, 4th AppDist Misc Order 17-6, 4th AppDist Misc Order 18-6
    Teleconference system, oral arguments via   CRCSupp 5th AppDist
        5th Appellate District local rules   CRCSupp 5th AppDist
    Time for oral argument   CRC 8.500, CRCSupp 3rd AppDist
    Time of submission of cause   CRC 8.256, 8.386
    Transfers from superior court appellate division to court of appeal
        Issues to be considered   CRC 8.1012
Attach
    Defined   CRC 8.10
Attachments
    Defined   CRC 8.10
Attorney general
    Briefs, service of   CRC 8.29, 8.212
    Certification of state-law questions to California Supreme Court by federal appellate courts, notice to Attorney General   CRC 8.548
Attorneys
    Appointed attorneys
        Reporter's transcript, request for paper presumed   CRCSupp 3rd AppDist
    Attorney General
        Briefs, service   CRC 8.29, 8.212
        Certification of state-law questions to California Supreme court by federal appellate courts, notice to Attorney General   CRC 8.548

APPELLATE RULES, SUPREME COURT AND COURTS OF APPEAL—Cont.
  Attorneys—Cont.
    Capital cases
      Qualifications of counsel   CRC 8.605
    Conservatorships
      Sterilization of conservatee, judgment authorizing conservator to consent   CRC 8.482
    Criminal appeals cases, appointment in   CRC 8.300
      4th Appellate District local rules   CRCSupp 4th AppDist Misc Order 15-5, 4th AppDist Misc Order 16-5, 4th AppDist Misc Order 17-5, 4th AppDist Misc Order 18-5
      Supreme court appointment   CRCSupp SupCtIOPP XV
    Disciplinary action against attorney, review of (See **ATTORNEYS**)
    Electronic court records, public access
      Attorney access   CRC 8.81
    Habeas corpus, capital cases
      Appeals from superior court decisions in habeas cases involving death penalty, ineffective assistance of trial counsel   CRC 8.397
      Appointment   CRC 8.605
      Qualifications of counsel   CRC 8.652
    Juvenile case appeals
      4th Appellate District local rules   CRCSupp 4th AppDist Misc Order 15-5, 4th AppDist Misc Order 16-5, 4th AppDist Misc Order 17-5, 4th AppDist Misc Order 18-5
      Appointment   CRC 8.403
    Non-appealing minor's counsel, automatic appointment
      4th Appellate District local rules   CRCSupp 4th AppDist Misc Order 15-13, 4th AppDist Misc Order 16-13, 4th AppDist Misc Order 17-13, 4th AppDist Misc Order 18-13
    Retained counsel, determination of representation by Appellate Defenders, Inc
      4th Appellate District local rules   CRCSupp 4th AppDist Misc Order 15-10, 4th AppDist Misc Order 16-10, 4th AppDist Misc Order 17-10, 4th AppDist Misc Order 18-10
    Staff attorneys
      3rd Appellate District local rules
        Internal operating practices and procedures (IOPP)   CRCSupp 3rd AppDist
    Substitution   CRC 8.36
      4th Appellate District local rules   CRCSupp 4th AppDist Misc Order 15-7, 4th AppDist Misc Order 16-7, 4th AppDist Misc Order 17-7, 4th AppDist Misc Order 18-7
      Electronic filing, when required   CRCSupp 1st AppDist
    Withdrawal of   CRC 8.36
  Augmentation of record   CRC 8.155
    1st Appellate District local rules   CRCSupp 1st AppDist
    2nd Appellate District local rules   CRCSupp 2nd AppDist
    5th Appellate District local rules   CRCSupp 5th AppDist
    6th Appellate District local rules   CRCSupp 6th AppDist Misc Order 17-1
    Criminal appeals   CRC 8.340
    Death penalty appeals   CRC 8.634
      Habeas corpus, appeals from superior court decisions in habeas cases involving death penalty   CRC 8.395
    Juvenile case appeals   CRC 8.410, 8.416
      Orders setting hearing in termination cases, writ petition to review   CRC 8.452
      Transfer of minor to court of criminal jurisdiction   CRC 8.417
    Motion to augment
      4th Appellate District local rules   CRCSupp 4th AppDist Misc Order 15-16, 4th AppDist Misc Order 16-16, 4th AppDist Misc Order 17-16, 4th AppDist Misc Order 18-16
  Authority of Judicial Council to prescribe procedure, generally   CCP §901
  Bail on appeal   CRC 8.312
  Bankruptcy proceedings pending, duty of party to inform court of   CRCSupp 1st AppDist
  Briefs
    Additional or supplemental briefs upon permission   CRC 8.200
    Amicus curiae briefs   CRC 8.200
      Capital cases   CRC 8.630
      Certiorari, mandate and prohibition   CRC 8.487
      Criminal appeals   CRC 8.360
      Habeas corpus, appeals from superior court decisions in habeas cases involving death penalty   CRC 8.396
      Juvenile case appeals   CRC 8.412
    Appellant's opening brief   CRC 8.200
    Attachments
      Supreme court briefs   CRC 8.520
    Bar numbers, requirement for   CRC 8.204
    Briefs on the merits in supreme court   CRC 8.520

APPELLATE RULES, SUPREME COURT AND COURTS OF APPEAL—Cont.
  Briefs—Cont.
    Certificates of interested entities or persons   CRC 8.208
      Criminal appeals   CRC 8.361
      Electronic filing, when required   CRCSupp 1st AppDist
    Certification of state-law questions to California Supreme Court by federal appellate courts and other states' courts of last resort
      Letters in support or opposition   CRC 8.548
    Certiorari   CRC 8.487
    Conservatorships, appeal from order establishing   CRC 8.480
    Copies
      2nd Appellate district local rules   CRCSupp 2nd AppDist
    Costs, items recoverable as   CRC 8.278
    Court's request
      Capital cases   CRC 8.630
    Cover, requirements for   CRC 8.204
    Criminal appeals   CRC 8.360
    Cross appeal   CRC 8.216
    Cunningham briefing   CRCSupp 5th AppDist
    Death penalty appeals   CRC 8.630, 8.631
      Habeas corpus, appeals from superior court decisions in habeas cases involving death penalty   CRC 8.396
    Defined   CRC 8.10
    E-filing in supreme court and courts of appeal
      Format of electronic documents   CRC 8.74
    Elder and dependent adult civil protection act, expedited appeals process   CRC 8.715
    Electronic copies   CRC 8.212
      Paper documents, electronic copies   CRC 8.44
    Environmental quality act cases under public resources code
      Appellate review of CEQA cases   CRC 8.702
    Failure to file brief   CRC 8.220
      Juvenile case appeals   CRC 8.412, 8.416
    Filing   CRC 8.212
      Electronic filing and service   CRCSupp 1st AppDist, 6th AppDist
      Fees   CRC 8.25
    Form
      Capital cases   CRC 8.630
      Criminal appeals   CRC 8.360
      Supreme court cases   CRC 8.520
    Format   CRC 8.204
    Judge's copies   CRC 8.212
    Judicial notice
      Capital cases   CRC 8.630
    Juvenile case appeals   CRC 8.412
      Contents   CRC 8.412
      Dependency appeals, certain counties   CRC 8.416
      Failure to file   CRC 8.412, 8.416
      Form   CRC 8.412
      Length   CRC 8.412
      Service   CRC 8.412
      Terminations of parental rights, appeal from   CRC 8.416
      Time to file   CRC 8.412, 8.416
      Transfer of minor to court of criminal jurisdiction   CRC 8.417
    Late briefs, permission to file   CRC 8.220
    Length limitation   CRC 8.204
      Capital cases   CRC 8.630, 8.631
      Criminal appeals   CRC 8.360
    Local court of appeal rule imposing other requirements, effect   CRC 8.20
    New authority discovered after filing of brief   CRC 8.254
    Noncomplying briefs   CRC 8.204
    Number of copies   CRC 8.44
    Overlength briefs, application to file
      Capital cases   CRC 8.631
    Paper briefs
      Format   CRC 8.204
    Presentence custody credit
      Recalculation   CRCSupp 3rd AppDist, 5th AppDist
    Reply brief   CRC 8.216
    Respondent   CRC 8.200
    Service   CRC 8.212
      Capital cases   CRC 8.630
      Elder and dependent adult civil protection act, expedited appeals process   CRC 8.715
      Electronic filing and service   CRCSupp 6th AppDist
    State bar numbers, requirement for   CRC 8.204
    Supplemental briefs
      Capital cases   CRC 8.630
      Remand or transfer from supreme court, supplemental briefs after   CRC 8.200

APPELLATE RULES, SUPREME COURT AND COURTS OF APPEAL—Cont.
  Briefs—Cont.
    Supreme court briefs   CRC 8.520
    Time to file   CRC 8.212
      1st Appellate District local rules   CRCSupp 1st AppDist
      Capital cases   CRC 8.630
      Criminal appeals   CRC 8.360
      Elder and dependent adult civil protection act, expedited appeals process   CRC 8.715
      Transfer from supreme court to court of appeals for further proceedings   CRC 8.528
      Transfers from superior court appellate division to court of appeal   CRC 8.1012
      Trial judge to receive   CRC 8.212
    Wende briefs
      Electronic filings   CRCSupp 1st AppDist
  Calendar
    Memoranda, supreme court   CRCSupp SupCtIOPP VI
    Oral arguments, supreme court   CRCSupp SupCtIOPP V
    Preference on calendar   CRC 8.240
  Capital case appeals
    Death penalty appeals generally   CRC 8.601 to 8.652
  Certification
    Federal appellate courts, certification of state-law questions to California Supreme Court by   CRC 8.548
    Other states' courts of last resort, certification of state-law questions to California Supreme Court by   CRC 8.548
    Transfers from superior court appellate division to court of appeal   CRC 8.1005
      Appellate division proceedings after certification or transfer   CRC 8.1014
  Certiorari   CRC 8.485 to 8.493
    Amicus briefs   CRC 8.487
    Applicability of provisions   CRC 8.485
    Briefs   CRC 8.487
    Certificate of interested entities or persons   CRC 8.488
      Electronic filing, when required   CRCSupp 1st AppDist
    Costs
      Award and recovery   CRC 8.493
    Decisions   CRC 8.490
    Environmental quality act cases under public resources code
      Writ proceedings   CRC 8.703
    Filing of decision   CRC 8.490
    Finality of decision   CRC 8.490
    Modification of decision   CRC 8.490
    Notice if writ issues   CRC 8.489
    Notice of sanctions   CRC 8.492
    Opposition   CRC 8.487, CRCSupp 4th AppDist
      Sanctions   CRC 8.492
    Oral argument
      Sanctions   CRC 8.492
    Petition
      Contents   CRC 8.486
      Supporting documents   CRC 8.486
    Rehearings   CRC 8.490
    Remittitur   CRC 8.490
    Sanctions   CRC 8.492
    Sealed or confidential records   CRC 8.486
    Service of petition and supporting documents   CRC 8.486
    Writs of mandate, certiorari and prohibition in supreme court or court of appeal   CRC 8.485 to 8.493
  Chief Justice
    Administrative presiding justice, appointment   CRC 10.1004
    Education of judicial branch
      Additional education recommendations for certain judicial assignments   CRC 10.469
      Duties of chief judge   CRC 10.452
  Circuit-riding sessions   CRCSupp 1st AppDist
  Civil appeals   CRC 8.100 to 8.276
    Briefs
      Court of appeals, briefs in   CRC 8.200 to 8.224
      Civil case information statements, attachments
        6th Appellate District local rules   CRCSupp 6th AppDist
      Hearing and decision in court of appeals   CRC 8.240 to 8.276
      Record on appeal   CRC 8.120 to 8.163
      Taking appeal   CRC 8.100 to 8.116
  Civil case information statement   CRC 8.100
    Electronic filing, when required   CRCSupp 1st AppDist
    Judicial council forms   CRCAppx A

APPELLATE RULES, SUPREME COURT AND COURTS OF APPEAL—Cont.
  Civil commitment
    Appeal from order of civil commitment   CRC 8.483
  Clerk/executive officer
    Advance collection of fees   Gov §68847
    Certificate under seal, fees for   Gov §68930
    Comparing documents for certification, fees for   Gov §68929
    Copies, fees for   Gov §68928
    Copies of notice of appeal sent to   CRC 8.100
    Criminal appeals
      Abandonment of appeal   CRC 8.316
    Juvenile case appeals
      Abandonment of appeal, duties of clerk   CRC 8.411
    Other non-specified services, fees for   Gov §68932
    Payment of fees, method of   CRC 8.100
    Receipts issued by   CRC 8.100
    Remittitur, issuance   CRC 8.272
      Supreme court   CRC 8.540
    Role and duties   CRC 10.1020
      Education of clerk/administrator, minimum   CRC 10.471
      Education of judicial branch, duties as to   CRC 10.452
    Transfers from superior court appellate division to court of appeal
      Duties of clerk/executive officer   CRC 8.1008
  Clerk, lower court
    Breach of duties   CRC 8.23
    Criminal appeals
      Abandonment of appeal   CRC 8.316
      Notice   CRC 8.308
      Record on appeal   CRC 8.320
    Elder and dependent adult civil protection act, expedited appeals process
      Notice of appeal, superior court clerk duties   CRC 8.714
    Environmental quality act cases under public resources code
      Appellate review of CEQA cases, superior court duties   CRC 8.702
    Habeas corpus petition records filing   CRC 8.384
    Interference with proceedings   CRC 8.23
    Juvenile case appeals
      Abandonment of appeal, duties of clerk   CRC 8.411
      Notice of appeal, duties of clerk upon filing   CRC 8.405
      Termination cases   CRC 8.450
    Notification of filing of notices of appeal   CRC 8.100
    Record on appeal
      Sanctioning reporter or clerk for delay   CRC 8.23
    Reporter's transcript
      Duties of clerk   CRC 8.130
    Transmission of record on appeal to reviewing court   CRC 8.147
  Clerk's transcript   CRC 8.122
    Appendix in lieu of   CRC 8.124
    Augmentation or correction   CRCSupp 5th AppDist
    Benoit orders
      4th Appellate District local rules   CRCSupp 4th AppDist Misc Order 15-2, 4th AppDist Misc Order 16-2, 4th AppDist Misc Order 17-2, 4th AppDist Misc Order 18-2
    Binding and cover   CRC 8.144
      4th Appellate District local rules   CRCSupp 4th AppDist
    Commitment
      Appeal from order of civil commitment   CRC 8.483
    Content of record on appeal   CRC 8.120
    Copies   CRC 8.122
    Correction   CRC 8.155
    Costs   CRC 8.122
    Criminal appeals
      2nd Appellate District local rules   CRCSupp 2nd AppDist
      Capital cases   CRC 8.610, 8.616
      Normal record on appeal   CRC 8.320
      Preparing, certifying and sending record   CRC 8.336
      Sealed or confidential records, form of record on appeal   CRC 8.336
    Death penalty appeals
      Habeas corpus, appeals from superior court decisions in habeas cases involving death penalty   CRC 8.395
    Deposit by appellant   Gov §68926.1
    Designation of papers and records for inclusion in clerk's transcript   CRC 8.122
    E-filing in supreme court and courts of appeal
      Format of electronic documents   CRC 8.74
    Failure of party to procure   CRC 8.140
    Filing of record   CRC 8.122
    Indexes   CRC 8.144
    Joint appendix in lieu of   CRC 8.124
    Juror-identifying information, redaction   CRC 8.332
      Capital cases   CRC 8.610, 8.611

APPELLATE RULES, SUPREME COURT AND COURTS OF APPEAL—Cont.
Clerk's transcript —Cont.
Juvenile case appeals
2nd Appellate District local rules CRCSupp 2nd AppDist
4th Appellate District local rules CRCSupp 4th AppDist Misc Order 15-8, 4th AppDist Misc Order 16-8, 4th AppDist Misc Order 17-8, 4th AppDist Misc Order 18-8
Normal record CRC 8.407
Preparing and certifying CRC 8.409
Multiple defendant appeals, non-capital cases
4th Appellate District local rules CRCSupp 4th AppDist Misc Order 15-12, 4th AppDist Misc Order 16-12, 4th AppDist Misc Order 17-12, 4th AppDist Misc Order 18-12
Pagination CRC 8.144
Paper and format CRC 8.144
4th Appellate District local rules CRCSupp 4th AppDist
Police reports
4th Appellate District local rules CRCSupp 4th AppDist Misc Order 15-11, 4th AppDist Misc Order 16-11, 4th AppDist Misc Order 17-11, 4th AppDist Misc Order 18-11
Preparation of CRC 8.122
Sealed or confidential records
Form of record, compliance with sealed or confidential records provisions CRC 8.144
Settled statement in lieu of CRC 8.137
Superior court file in lieu of clerk's transcript, filing CRC 8.128
Timely preparation
1st Appellate District local rules CRCSupp 1st AppDist
Commitment
Appeal from order of civil commitment CRC 8.483
Compromise of case involving minor or incompetent, requirements for approval CRC 8.244
Conference prior to hearing CRC 8.248
Civil settlement conference procedures
4th Appellate District local rules CRCSupp 4th AppDist
Confidential records CRC 8.47
Access to records CRC 8.45
4th Appellate District local rules CRCSupp 4th AppDist Misc Order 15-4, 4th AppDist Misc Order 16-4, 4th AppDist Misc Order 17-4, 4th AppDist Misc Order 18-4
Administrative presiding justices and presiding justices
Oversight of CRC 10.1014
Applicability of provisions CRC 8.45, 8.47
Certiorari, mandate and prohibition CRC 8.486
Criminal appeals
Capital cases CRC 8.610
Record on appeal, form of record CRC 8.336
Definitions CRC 8.45
E-filing in supreme court and courts of appeal
Format of electronic documents CRC 8.74
Electronic filing CRCSupp 5th AppDist
Format of records CRC 8.45
Habeas corpus CRC 8.380 to 8.385
Supporting documents accompanying petition CRC 8.380, 8.384
In-camera proceedings CRC 8.47
Juvenile case appeals
Access to filed documents and records CRC 8.401
Documents filed with court CRC 8.401
Record on appeal, transcripts CRC 8.409
Maintaining confidentiality CRC 8.47
Marsden hearing records CRC 8.47
Record on appeal
Form of record, compliance with sealed or confidential records provisions CRC 8.144
Transmission of records CRC 8.45
Waiver of fees and costs CRC 8.26
Conflicts of interest
Briefs
Certificates of interested entities or persons CRC 8.208, 8.361, 8.488
Consent to modification of judgment CRC 8.264, 8.532
Conservatorships
Order establishing, appeal from CRC 8.480
Sterilization of conservatee, judgment authorizing conservator to consent CRC 8.482
Construction CRC 8.7
Amendments by Judicial Council CRC 8.13
Statute references include subsequent amendments CRC 8.16
Copies
Briefs CRC 8.212
2nd Appellate district local rules CRCSupp 2nd AppDist

APPELLATE RULES, SUPREME COURT AND COURTS OF APPEAL—Cont.
Copies—Cont.
Costs recoverable CRC 8.278
Defined CRC 8.10
Electronic court records, public access
Fees for copies of electronic records CRC 8.85
Notice of appeal to be sent to review court clerk, copies CRC 8.100
Transcripts CRC 8.122, 8.130, 8.150
Coronavirus
Emergency rules related to COVID-19 CRCAppx I Emer Rules 1 to 13
Tolling or extension of time for public health emergencies CRC 8.66
Corrections
Appendix CRC 8.155
Record on appeal CRC 8.155
2nd Appellate District local rules CRCSupp 2nd AppDist
Criminal appeals CRC 8.340
Habeas corpus, appeals from superior court decisions in habeas cases involving death penalty CRC 8.395
Juvenile case appeals CRC 8.410, 8.416, 8.417, 8.452
Transcripts CRC 8.155
Costs
Appendix in lieu of transcript, preparation CRC 8.124
Award of costs CRC 8.278
Certiorari, mandate and prohibition
Award and recovery of costs CRC 8.493
Cross appeal, deposit of estimated costs for record on CRC 8.147
Entry of judgment CRC 8.278
Environmental impact reports, jobs and economic improvement through environmental leadership act of 2021
Appellate review of CEQA cases CRC 8.703
Frivolous appeals CRC 8.276
Criminal appeals CRC 8.366
Items recoverable as CRC 8.278
Joint appendix in lieu of transcript, preparation CRC 8.124
Memorandum of costs CRC 8.278
Multiple appeal, deposit of estimated costs for record on CRC 8.147
Procedure for claiming CRC 8.278
Remittitur to contain provision for CRC 8.276
Criminal appeals CRC 8.366
Reporter's transcript
Dispute over costs of transcript CRC 8.130
Supreme court review CRC 8.544
Transcripts, preparation CRC 8.122, 8.130
Waiver of costs and fees CRC 8.26
Family law proceedings in supreme court or court of appeals, applicable rules CRC 5.46
Will probate cases CRC 8.278, Pro §1002
Courtroom protocols
2nd Appellate District local rules CRCSupp 2nd AppDist
Cover of briefs and other papers, requirements CRC 8.204
Color CRC 8.40
Definition of cover CRC 8.10
Information on cover CRC 8.40
COVID-19
Emergency rules related to COVID-19 CRCAppx I Emer Rules 1 to 13
Tolling or extension of time for public health emergencies CRC 8.66
Criminal appeals CRC 8.300 to 8.398
Abandonment of appeal CRC 8.316
Additional record CRC 8.324
Agreed statement CRC 8.344
Attorneys, appointment CRC 8.300
4th Appellate District local rules CRCSupp 4th AppDist Misc Order 15-5, 4th AppDist Misc Order 16-5, 4th AppDist Misc Order 17-5, 4th AppDist Misc Order 18-5
Bail CRC 8.312
Briefs CRC 8.360
Capital cases CRC 8.630, 8.631
Cross appeals
Time to appeal CRC 8.308
Death penalty appeals CRC 8.601 to 8.652
Decision in court of appeal
Applicable rules CRC 8.366
Decision in supreme court
Applicable rules CRC 8.368
Diagnostic reports ordered by court
Preparing, certifying and sending record CRC 8.336
Docketing statements
1st Appellate District local rules CRCSupp 1st AppDist

APPELLATE RULES, SUPREME COURT AND COURTS OF APPEAL—Cont.
Criminal appeals —Cont.
Entity as defendant
Certificate of interested entities or persons   CRC 8.361, CRCSupp 1st AppDist
Exhaustion of state remedies, petition in supreme court to accomplish   CRC 8.508
Applicable provisions   CRC 8.504
Exhibits
Record on appeal   CRC 8.316
Extension of time
Electronic filing, when required   CRCSupp 1st AppDist
Filing appeal   CRC 8.304
E-filing, 5th Appellate District   CRCSupp 5th AppDist
Finality of court of appeals decisions   CRC 8.366
Guilty pleas
Appeal after conviction following   CRC 8.304
Preparing, certifying and sending record   CRC 8.336
Hearing in court of appeal
Applicable rules   CRC 8.366
Juror-identifying information in record on criminal appeal, sealing   CRC 8.332
Capital cases   CRC 8.610, 8.611
Late notice of appeal   CRC 8.308
Limited record on appeal   CRC 8.320
Nolo contendere plea
Appeal after conviction following   CRC 8.304
Preparing, certifying and sending record   CRC 8.336
Normal time to appeal   CRC 8.308
Notice of appeal   CRC 8.304
Late notice of appeal   CRC 8.308
Premature notice   CRC 8.308
Oral argument
Capital cases   CRC 8.638
Probation violation
Appeal after admission   CRC 8.304
Preparing, certifying and sending record   CRC 8.336
Record on appeal   CRC 8.320 to 8.346
Addition to normal record   CRC 8.324
Agreed statement as record   CRC 8.344
Augmenting or correcting record in court of appeal   CRC 8.340
Capital cases   CRC 8.608 to 8.622, 8.634
Juror-identifying information   CRC 8.332, 8.610, 8.611
Normal record   CRC 8.320, 8.324
Preparing, certifying and sending record   CRC 8.336
Settled statement as record   CRC 8.346
Rehearing
Capital cases   CRC 8.642
Release on appeal   CRC 8.312
Remittitur
Capital cases   CRC 8.642
Sealed records
Capital cases   CRC 8.610
Juror-identifying information   CRC 8.332, 8.610, 8.611
Settled statement   CRC 8.346
Stay of execution   CRC 8.312
Stipulations
Partial transcript for record on appeal   CRC 8.320
Submission of cause
Capital cases   CRC 8.638
Taking appeal   CRC 8.300 to 8.316
Time to appeal   CRC 8.308
Transcripts
Juror-identifying information   CRC 8.332, 8.610, 8.611
Normal record   CRC 8.320
Preparing, certifying and sending record   CRC 8.336
Voluntary dismissal of appeal   CRC 8.316
Cross appeal
Briefs   CRC 8.216
Criminal appeals
Time to appeal   CRC 8.308
Environmental quality act cases under public resources code
Appellate review of CEQA cases   CRC 8.702
Juvenile case appeals   CRC 8.406
Notice   CRC 8.100, 8.104
Record on   CRC 8.147
Time limit for filing record   CRC 8.147
Death penalty appeals   CRC 8.601 to 8.652
Attorneys for capital cases
Qualifications   CRC 8.605

APPELLATE RULES, SUPREME COURT AND COURTS OF APPEAL—Cont.
Death penalty appeals —Cont.
Automatic appeals
Supreme court, automatic appeal to   CRC 8.603
Briefs   CRC 8.630, 8.631
Habeas corpus, appeals from superior court decisions in habeas cases involving death penalty   CRC 8.396
Capital punishment generally (See **CAPITAL PUNISHMENT**)
Decisions   CRC 8.642
Exhibits
Transmission in death penalty appeals   CRC 8.634
Extension of time limit on
Electronic filing, when required   CRCSupp 1st AppDist
Filing of decision   CRC 8.642
Finality of decision   CRC 8.642
Habeas corpus, appeals from superior court decisions in habeas cases involving death penalty   CRC 8.390 to 8.398
Amici curiae briefs   CRC 8.396
Appealability, certificate   CRC 8.392, 8.398
Applicability of provisions   CRC 8.390
Attorneys, appointment and qualifications   CRC 8.391, 8.605, 8.652
Attorneys, ineffective assistance of trial counsel not previously raised   CRC 8.397
Augmenting or correcting record   CRC 8.395
Briefs   CRC 8.396
Clerk's transcript   CRC 8.395
Denial of certificate of appealability, finality   CRC 8.398
Extension of time to prepare record   CRC 8.395
Filing appeal   CRC 8.392
Finality of decision   CRC 8.398
Ineffective assistance of trial counsel not previously raised   CRC 8.397
Judicial notice   CRC 8.395
Notice of appeal   CRC 8.392
Notification of filing of notice of appeal, distribution   CRC 8.392
Record on appeal   CRC 8.395
Reporter's transcript   CRC 8.395
Service of briefs   CRC 8.396
Stay of execution on appeal   CRC 8.394
Successive petition cases, appeal of denial of relief   CRC 8.392
Time for appeal   CRC 8.393
Transcripts, partial   CRC 8.395
Judgment
Copies, distribution   CRC 8.603
Modification of decision   CRC 8.642
Oral argument
Supreme court review   CRC 8.638
Record on appeal   CRC 8.608 to 8.622
Accuracy of trial record   CRC 8.622
Augmenting record in supreme court   CRC 8.634
Completeness of trial record   CRC 8.619
Content   CRC 8.610
Extensions of time   CRC 8.608
Form   CRC 8.610
Habeas corpus, appeals from superior court decisions in habeas cases involving death penalty   CRC 8.395
Juror-identifying information, protection   CRC 8.610, 8.611
Preliminary proceedings, record   CRC 8.613
Preparing trial record   CRC 8.616
Supervision of preparation of record   CRC 8.608
Transcripts, delivery date   CRC 8.608
Trial record   CRC 8.616 to 8.622
Rehearing   CRC 8.642
Remittitur   CRC 8.642
Supreme court   CRC 8.540
Submission of cause   CRC 8.638
Death penalty cases
Generally (See **CAPITAL PUNISHMENT**)
Decision of reviewing court
Certiorari, mandate and prohibition   CRC 8.490
Criminal appeals
Capital cases   CRC 8.642
Decision in court of appeal, applicable rules   CRC 8.366
Decision in supreme court, applicable rules   CRC 8.368
Finality   CRC 8.264, 8.532
Criminal appeals   CRC 8.366
Habeas corpus   CRC 8.387
Habeas corpus
Filing decision   CRC 8.387
Finality of decision   CRC 8.387

APPELLATE RULES, SUPREME COURT AND COURTS OF APPEAL—Cont.

Decision of reviewing court—Cont.
- Juvenile case appeals
  - Court of appeals, applicable rules   CRC 8.470
  - Order designating specific placement of dependent child, writ petition to review   CRC 8.454, 8.456
  - Orders setting hearing in termination cases, writ petition to review   CRC 8.452
  - Supreme court, applicable rules   CRC 8.472
- Modification   CRC 8.264, 8.532
- Supreme court decision   CRC 8.528

Default, notice
- Record on appeal
  - Failure to procure record   CRC 8.140

Default relief   CRC 8.60

Definitions   CRC 8.10
- Sealed and confidential records   CRC 8.45

Dependent adults
- Elder and dependent adult civil protection act, expedited appeals process   CRC 8.710 to 8.717

Dismissal
- After filing record   CRC 8.244
- Before filing record   CRC 8.244
- Brief, failure to file opening   CRC 8.220
- Criminal appeals
  - Abandonment of appeal   CRC 8.316
- Failure to procure filing of record   CRC 8.140
- Filing fee, failure to pay   CRC 8.100
- Finality of involuntary dismissal order   CRC 8.264, 8.532
  - Habeas corpus   CRC 8.387
- Juvenile case appeals
  - Abandonment of appeal   CRC 8.411
- Late notice of appeal   CRC 8.104
- Noncompliance with rules, dismissal because of   CRC 10.1012
- Notice   CRC 8.244
- Record on appeal
  - Motion to dismiss prior to filing record   CRC 8.57
- Supreme court review   CRC 8.528
- Voluntary abandonment and dismissal   CRC 8.244
  - Criminal appeals   CRC 8.316

Divisions of appellate court
- Assignment of cases to divisions   CRC 10.1008
- Geographically separate divisions
  - Presiding justice, powers and duties   CRC 10.1004

E-filing in supreme court and courts of appeal   CRC 8.70 to 8.79, CRCSupp 6th AppDist
- 1st Appellate District local rules   CRCSupp 1st AppDist
- Agreed statement
  - Format of electronic documents   CRC 8.74
- Appendix to brief
  - Format of electronic documents   CRC 8.74
- Applicability of provisions   CRC 8.70
- Briefs
  - Format of electronic documents   CRC 8.74
- Capital matter notation   CRCSupp SuprCtE-file 10
- Clerk's transcript
  - Format of electronic documents   CRC 8.74
- Close of business
  - Documents received after close of business   CRC 8.77
- Confirmation of receipt and filing
  - Court's actions   CRC 8.77
  - Duties of electronic filing service providers   CRC 8.73
- Construction of provisions   CRC 8.70
- Court
  - Defined   CRC 8.70
- Court responsibilities   CRC 8.72
- Definitions   CRC 8.70
- Delayed delivery   CRC 8.77
- Digital signature of documents   CRC 8.75
- Documents
  - Defined   CRC 8.70
  - Format   CRC 8.74
  - Reliability and integrity of documents served by electronic notification   CRC 8.78
  - Signatures   CRC 8.75
  - Supreme court-specific rules, documents subject to e-filing   CRCSupp SuprCtE-file 2 to CRCSupp SuprCtE-file 4
- Elder and dependent adult civil protection act, expedited appeals process   CRC 8.711

APPELLATE RULES, SUPREME COURT AND COURTS OF APPEAL—Cont.

E-filing in supreme court and courts of appeal—Cont.
- Electronic filers
  - Defined   CRC 8.70
- Electronic filings
  - Defined   CRC 8.70
- Electronic filing service providers
  - Contracts with providers   CRC 8.73
  - Defined   CRC 8.70
  - Duties   CRC 8.73
- Electronic notification
  - Defined   CRC 8.70
- Electronic service
  - Defined   CRC 8.70
- Electronic service address
  - Defined   CRC 8.70
- Electronic signatures
  - Defined   CRC 8.70
- Electronic transmission
  - Defined   CRC 8.70
- Endorsement
  - Court's actions upon filing   CRC 8.77
- Exhibits
  - Format of electronic documents   CRC 8.74
- Fees for filing   CRC 8.76
- Fee waivers   CRC 8.76
  - Application may be filed electronically   CRC 8.71
- Filer responsibilities   CRC 8.72
- Format of documents   CRC 8.74
  - Supreme court-specific rules   CRCSupp SuprCtE-file 10
- Hardship
  - Excuse from mandatory electronic filing for undue hardship or significant prejudice   CRC 8.71
- Judicial notice, request
  - Format of electronic documents   CRC 8.74
- Judicial signature of documents   CRC 8.75
- Mandatory electronic filing   CRC 8.71
- Notice of problems with electronic filing   CRC 8.72
- Order of court requiring electronic service   CRC 8.79
- Paper documents
  - Serving in paper form   CRC 8.79
  - Supreme court-specific rules   CRCSupp SuprCtE-file 5
  - When filing paper documents permitted   CRC 8.71
- Perjury
  - Signatures of documents under penalty of perjury   CRC 8.75
- Prejudice
  - Excuse from mandatory electronic filing for undue hardship or significant prejudice   CRC 8.71
- Privacy
  - Supreme court-specific rules   CRCSupp SuprCtE-file 11
- Pro se parties
  - Exemption from mandatory electronic filing   CRC 8.71
- Publication of electronic filing requirements   CRC 8.72
- Purpose of rules   CRC 8.70
- Receipt of document complying with filing requirements
  - Date and time of filing   CRC 8.77
- Rejection of document for filing
  - Court's actions upon receipt   CRC 8.77
- Reporter's transcript
  - Format of electronic documents   CRC 8.74
- Sealed and confidential records
  - Format of electronic documents   CRC 8.74
- Secure electronic signatures
  - Defined   CRC 8.70
- Service, electronic
  - Address changes   CRC 8.78
  - Authorization for electronic service   CRC 8.78
  - Court, service on   CRC 8.78
  - Court's use of electronic service   CRC 8.78
  - Definition of electronic service   CRC 8.70
  - Lists, maintenance   CRC 8.78
  - Order of court requiring electronic service   CRC 8.79
  - Parties' responsibilities   CRC 8.78
  - Proof of service   CRC 8.78
  - Supreme court-specific rules   CRCSupp SuprCtE-file 9
- Settled statement
  - Format of electronic documents   CRC 8.74
- Signatures of documents   CRC 8.75
  - Electronic signatures defined   CRC 8.70
  - Secure electronic signatures defined   CRC 8.70

APPELLATE RULES, SUPREME COURT AND COURTS OF APPEAL—Cont.
E-filing in supreme court and courts of appeal —Cont.
    Signatures of documents —Cont.
        Supreme court-specific rules   CRCSupp SuprCtE-file 8
    Supreme court-specific rules   CRCSupp SuprCtE-file 1 to CRCSupp SuprCtE-file 13
        Applicability of rules   CRCSupp SuprCtE-file 1
        Confidential records, privacy protection   CRCSupp SuprCtE-file 11
        Documents subject to e-filing   CRCSupp SuprCtE-file 2 to CRCSupp SuprCtE-file 4
        Excuse from electronic filing   CRCSupp SuprCtE-file 6
        Fees   CRCSupp SuprCtE-file 12
        Format of electronically filed documents   CRCSupp SuprCtE-file 10
        Mandatory electronic filing   CRCSupp SuprCtE-file 3
        Paper copies filed with electronically filed documents   CRCSupp SuprCtE-file 5
        Personal identifiers, privacy protection   CRCSupp SuprCtE-file 11
        Privacy protection   CRCSupp SuprCtE-file 11
        Registration of electronic filers   CRCSupp SuprCtE-file 7
        Sealed records, privacy protection   CRCSupp SuprCtE-file 11
        Service   CRCSupp SuprCtE-file 9
        Signatures   CRCSupp SuprCtE-file 8
        Size of electronically filed documents   CRCSupp SuprCtE-file 10
        Technical failure of system   CRCSupp SuprCtE-file 13
        Voluntary electronic filing   CRCSupp SuprCtE-file 4
    Transmission of filing
        Duties of electronic filing service providers   CRC 8.73
    Trial courts
        Exemption from mandatory electronic filing   CRC 8.71
Elder and dependent adult civil protection act, expedited appeals process   CRC 8.710 to 8.717
    Appellate rules governing civil rules, applicability   CRC 8.710
    Applicability of provisions   CRC 8.710
    Briefs   CRC 8.715
    Electronic filing   CRC 8.711
    Extensions of time
        Good cause and promotion of interest of justice as grounds   CRC 8.717
    Notice of appeal   CRC 8.712
        Superior court clerk duties   CRC 8.714
    Oral argument   CRC 8.716
    Record
        Oral proceedings   CRC 8.713
        Written documents   CRC 8.713
    Service   CRC 8.711
Electronic court records, public access   CRC 8.80 to 8.85
    Applicability of provisions   CRC 8.81
    Attorney access   CRC 8.81
    Benefits of electronic access   CRC 8.80
    Bulk distributions
        Defined   CRC 8.82
        When permitted   CRC 8.83
    Case-by-case access   CRC 8.83
    Conditions   CRC 8.84
    Courthouse electronic access for certain records   CRC 8.83
    Definitions   CRC 8.82
    Electronic access to extent feasible   CRC 8.83
        Defined   CRC 8.82
    Fees for copies of electronic records   CRC 8.85
    Limitations   CRC 8.84
    Means or methods of access   CRC 8.84
    Notice to persons accessing records   CRC 8.84
    Official or unofficial nature of records accessed   CRC 8.84
    Party access   CRC 8.81
    Privacy policy
        Posting   CRC 8.84
    Purpose of provisions   CRC 8.80
    Records made inaccessible by court order or operation of law
        Limitation of court's duties   CRC 8.83
    Remote electronic access
        When permitted   CRC 8.83
    Right of access   CRC 8.83
    Use of records, conditions   CRC 8.84
Entry
    Costs, judgment for   CRC 8.278
    Notice of appeal filed prior to entry of judgment   CRC 8.104
    Time for appeal affected by entry of judgment or appealable order   CRC 8.104

APPELLATE RULES, SUPREME COURT AND COURTS OF APPEAL—Cont.
Environmental quality act cases under public resources code
    Appellate review of CEQA cases   CRC 8.700 to 8.705
        Applicable provisions   CRC 8.700, 8.702
Evidence
    Additional evidence on appeal, application for   CRC 8.252
    Costs, items recoverable as   CRC 8.278
Exhaustion of state remedies
    Criminal appeals
        Petition for review solely to exhaust   CRC 8.504, 8.508
Exhibits
    Commitment
        Appeal from order of civil commitment   CRC 8.483
    Criminal appeals
        Record on appeal   CRC 8.320
    Death penalty appeals
        Transmission in death penalty appeals   CRC 8.634
    Designation for inclusion in clerk's transcript   CRC 8.122
    E-filing in supreme court and courts of appeal
        Format of electronic documents   CRC 8.74
    Electronic submission
        2nd Appellate District local rules   CRCSupp 2nd AppDist
    1st Appellate District local rule   CRCSupp 1st AppDist
    Juvenile case appeals
        Transmitting exhibits   CRC 8.407
    Transmission to reviewing court   CRC 8.224
Expenses
    Costs on appeal (See within this heading, **"Costs"**)
Extension of time   CRC 8.60
    Agreed statement, effect of filing stipulation for   CRC 8.134
    Applications   CRC 8.50, 8.60
        Electronic filing, when required   CRCSupp 1st AppDist
    Briefs, filing   CRC 8.212
    Criminal appeals
        Record on appeal, preparing, certifying and sending record   CRC 8.336, 8.613
        Trial record, capital cases   CRC 8.616 to 8.622
    Elder and dependent adult civil protection act, expedited appeals process
        Good cause and promotion of interest of justice as grounds for extension   CRC 8.717
    Emergencies   CRC 8.66
    Environmental quality act cases under public resources code
        Appellate review of CEQA cases   CRC 8.702
    Good cause
        Factors considered   CRC 8.63
    Juvenile case appeals
        Briefs   CRC 8.412, 8.416
        Orders setting hearing in termination case, writ petition to review   CRC 8.450
        Record on appeal   CRC 8.409
        Time to appeal   CRC 8.406
        Transfer of minor to court of criminal jurisdiction   CRC 8.417
    Policy statement on   CRC 8.63
    Supreme court review, filing of petition for   CRC 8.500
Fax filings
    1st Appellate District local rules   CRCSupp 1st AppDist
Fees
    Electronic court records, public access
        Fees for copies of electronic records   CRC 8.85
    Inclusion of fee with filing   CRC 8.25
    Notice of appeal, filing fees for (See within this heading, **"Notice of appeal"**)
    Original jurisdiction of Supreme Court and courts of appeal, filing fees for writ petitions within   Gov §68926
    Recoverable costs   CRC 8.278
    State law library special account, civil filing fees, deposit into   Gov §68926.3
    Supreme Court petition, filing fees for   Gov §§68926, 68927
    Transcripts, preparation   CRC 8.122, 8.130
    Waiver of costs and fees   CRC 8.26
        Family law proceedings in supreme court or court of appeals, applicable rules   CRC 5.46
5th Appellate District local rules   CRCSupp 5th AppDist
    Internal operating practices and procedures   CRCSupp 5th AppDist
Filing   CRC 8.25
    Agreed statement   CRC 8.134
    Answer to petition for supreme court review   CRC 8.500
    Appendix in lieu of clerk's transcript   CRC 8.124
    Calendar preference, motion for   CRC 8.240
    Courts of appeal petition, filing fees for   Gov §68926

APPELL INDEX 48

APPELLATE RULES, SUPREME COURT AND COURTS OF
APPEAL—Cont.
Filing—Cont.
Criminal appeals CRC 8.304
Dismissal of appeal (See within this heading, "Dismissal")
Documents filed in reviewing court
Electronic copies of paper documents CRC 8.44
Number CRC 8.44
E-filing in supreme court and courts of appeal CRC 8.70 to 8.79,
CRCSupp 1st AppDist, 5th AppDist, 6th AppDist
Applicability of rules CRC 8.11
Elder and dependent adult civil protection act, expedited appeals
process CRC 8.711
Supreme court-specific rules CRCSupp SuprCtE-file 1 to CRCSupp
SuprCtE-file 13
Elder and dependent adult civil protection act, expedited appeals process
CRC 8.711
Electronic copies of paper documents CRC 8.44
Emergencies, effect CRC 8.66
Failure to conform to requirements CRC 8.18
Habeas corpus decision CRC 8.387
Habeas corpus petition records CRC 8.384
Juvenile case appeals CRC 8.405
Notice of appeal CRC 8.100
Time CRC 8.104
Record on appeal filed in reviewing court CRC 8.150
Rehearing, proceedings for CRC 8.268
Habeas corpus CRC 8.387
Supreme court CRC 8.536
Review court judgment modification CRC 8.264, 8.532
Settled statement CRC 8.137
State law library special account, civil filing fees, deposit into Gov
§68926.3
Superior court file in lieu of clerk's transcript CRC 8.128
Supersedeas writ CRC 8.112
Supreme court petition for review of court of appeals decision CRC 8.500
Transcripts CRC 8.122, 8.130
Writ, filing fee for Gov §68926
Finality of judgment CRC 8.264, 8.532
Certiorari, mandate and prohibition CRC 8.490
Habeas corpus CRC 8.387
Findings, request for CRC 8.252
Fires
Extension of time CRC 8.66
1st Appellate District local rules CRCSupp 1st AppDist
Internal operating practices and procedures CRCSupp 1st AppDist
Focus letters and tentative opinions
1st Appellate District local rules CRCSupp 1st AppDist
Forms
Appellate forms
Judicial council legal forms CRCAppx A
4th Appellate District local rules CRCSupp 4th AppDist
Internal operating practices and procedures, divisions 1 to 3 CRCSupp 4th
AppDist
Frivolous appeals CRC 8.276
Guardian of mentally ill persons or infants, compromise for CRC 8.244
Habeas corpus CRC 8.380 to 8.398
Appeal from order granting relief CRC 8.388
Death penalty cases
Appeals from superior court decisions in habeas cases involving death
penalty CRC 8.390 to 8.398
Attorney appointment CRC 8.605
Attorney qualifications CRC 8.652
Filing decision CRC 8.387
Finality of decision CRC 8.387
Noncapital cases, appointed attorney qualifications CRC 4.553
Petitions
Attorney filing for party CRC 8.384
Proceedings after petition CRC 8.385
Pro se petitions CRC 8.380
Rehearing CRC 8.387
Remittitur in habeas proceedings CRC 8.387
Hearing
Criminal appeals
Hearing in court of appeal, applicable rules CRC 8.366
Hearing in supreme court, applicable rules CRC 8.368
Juvenile case appeals
Court of appeals, applicable rules CRC 8.470
Order designating specific placement of dependent child, writ petition
to review CRC 8.454, 8.456

APPELLATE RULES, SUPREME COURT AND COURTS OF
APPEAL—Cont.
Hearing—Cont.
Juvenile case appeals—Cont.
Orders setting hearing in termination cases, writ petition to review
CRC 8.450, 8.452
Supreme court, applicable rules CRC 8.472
Prehearing conference CRC 8.248
Rehearings CRC 8.268
Habeas corpus CRC 8.387
Supreme court CRC 8.536
Supreme court review CRC 8.516, 8.552
In camera proceedings
Confidential records CRC 8.47
Indigent persons (See INDIGENT PERSONS)
Internal operating practices procedures (IOPP)
1st Appellate District local rules CRCSupp 1st AppDist
2nd Appellate District local rules CRCSupp 2nd AppDist
3rd Appellate District local rules CRCSupp 3rd AppDist
4th Appellate District local rules CRCSupp 4th AppDist
5th Appellate District local rules CRCSupp 5th AppDist
6th Appellate District local rules CRCSupp 6th AppDist
Issues on review, supreme court specification of CRC 8.516
Joint appendix in lieu of transcript CRC 8.124
Content of record on appeal CRC 8.120
Judges (See within this heading, "Justices")
Judgment notwithstanding verdict, effect on time for filing notice of appeal of
motion for CRC 8.108
Judgments
Affirmance on condition CRC 8.264
Consent to modification CRC 8.264
Defined CRC 8.10
Entry of judgment (See within this heading, "Entry")
Finality of decisions CRC 8.264, 8.532
Habeas corpus CRC 8.387
Vacate, effect of motion to CRC 8.108
Judicial notice CRC 8.252
1st Appellate District local rules CRCSupp 1st AppDist
Death penalty appeals
Habeas corpus, appeals from superior court decisions in habeas cases
involving death penalty CRC 8.395
E-filing in supreme court and courts of appeal
Format of electronic documents CRC 8.74
Habeas corpus CRC 8.386
Legislative history materials
3rd Appellate District local rules CRCSupp 3rd AppDist
Requests
4th Appellate District local rules CRCSupp 4th AppDist Misc Order
15-16, 4th AppDist Misc Order 16-16, 4th AppDist Misc Order
17-16, 4th AppDist Misc Order 18-16
Justices
Administrative Presiding Justice (See within this heading, "Administrative
presiding justice")
Chief Justice (See within this heading, "Chief Justice")
Conflicts of interest
Briefs, certificates of interested entities or persons CRC 8.208, 8.361,
8.488, CRCSupp 1st AppDist
Education of judicial branch
Additional education recommendations for certain judicial assignments
CRC 10.469
Duties of justices, clerk/executive officers, managing attorneys and
supervisors CRC 10.452
Failure to perform judicial duties, notice of CRC 10.1016
Juvenile case appeals CRC 8.400 to 8.474
2nd Appellate District local rules CRCSupp 2nd AppDist
Abandoning appeal CRC 8.411
Agreed statement CRC 8.407
Alternate procedure, local adoption CRC 8.416
Applicability of rules CRC 8.400
Attorneys, appointment CRC 8.403
4th Appellate District local rules CRCSupp 4th AppDist Misc Order
15-5, 4th AppDist Misc Order 16-5, 4th AppDist Misc Order 17-5,
4th AppDist Misc Order 18-5
Augmentation of record CRC 8.410, 8.416
Orders setting hearing in termination cases, writ petition to review
CRC 8.452
Transfer of minor to court of criminal jurisdiction CRC 8.417
Briefs
Contents CRC 8.412
Dependency appeals, certain counties CRC 8.416
Failure to file CRC 8.412, 8.416

APPELLATE RULES, SUPREME COURT AND COURTS OF APPEAL—Cont.
Juvenile case appeals —Cont.
- Briefs—Cont.
  - Form   CRC 8.412
  - Length   CRC 8.412
  - Service   CRC 8.412
  - Terminations of parental rights, appeal from   CRC 8.416
  - Time to file   CRC 8.412, 8.416
  - Transfer of minor to court of criminal jurisdiction   CRC 8.417
- Certification of record   CRC 8.416
- Clerk's duties   CRC 8.405
  - Abandonment of appeal   CRC 8.411
  - Termination cases   CRC 8.450
- Clerk's transcript   CRC 8.407
  - Preparing and certifying   CRC 8.409
- Confidentiality
  - Access to filed documents and records   CRC 8.401
  - Documents filed with court   CRC 8.401
  - Oral arguments   CRC 8.401
  - Record on appeal   CRC 8.401
- Correcting the record   CRC 8.410, 8.416
  - Orders setting hearing in termination cases, writ petition to review   CRC 8.452
  - Transfer of minor to court of criminal jurisdiction   CRC 8.417
- Cross-appeal
  - Time to appeal   CRC 8.406
- Data to evaluate effectiveness of rules   CRC 8.474
- Decision
  - Court of appeals, applicable rules   CRC 8.470
  - Order designating specific placement of dependent child, writ petition to review   CRC 8.456
  - Orders setting hearing in termination cases, writ petition to review   CRC 8.452
  - Supreme court, applicable rules   CRC 8.472
- Dependency cases
  - Alternate procedure, local adoption   CRC 8.416
  - Certain counties   CRC 8.416
- Docketing statements
  - 1st Appellate District local rules   CRCSupp 1st AppDist
- Exhibits
  - Transmitting exhibits   CRC 8.407
- Extension of time
  - Transfer of minor to court of criminal jurisdiction   CRC 8.417
- Failure to file brief   CRC 8.412, 8.416
- Filing appeal   CRC 8.405
  - E-filing, 5th Appellate District   CRCSupp 5th AppDist
- Forms, judicial council   CRCAppx A
- Hearings
  - Court of appeals, applicable rules   CRC 8.470
  - Order designating specific placement of dependent child, writ petition to review   CRC 8.456
  - Orders setting hearing in termination cases, writ petition to review   CRC 8.450, 8.452
  - Supreme court, applicable rules   CRC 8.472
- Late notice of appeal   CRC 8.406
- Limited rights to appeal
  - Access to juvenile records, judicial council forms   CRCAppx A
- Normal time   CRC 8.406
- Notice of appeal   CRC 8.405
- Omissions in record   CRC 8.410
- Oral arguments   CRC 8.416
  - Confidentiality   CRC 8.401
  - Dependency appeals, certain counties   CRC 8.416
  - Order designating specific placement of dependent child, writ petition to review   CRC 8.456
  - Orders setting hearing in termination cases, writ petition to review   CRC 8.452
  - Terminations of parental rights, appeal from   CRC 8.416
  - Transfer of minor to court of criminal jurisdiction   CRC 8.417
- Order designating specific placement of dependent child, writ petition to review   CRC 8.456
  - Notice of intent to file   CRC 8.450, 8.454
- Orders setting hearing in termination cases, writ petition to review   CRC 8.452
  - Intent to file writ petition to review, notice   CRC 8.450
  - Notice of intent to file   CRC 8.450
- Premature notice of appeal   CRC 8.406
- Preparation of record   CRC 8.409, 8.416, 8.450
- Proceedings to which applicable   CRC 8.400

APPELLATE RULES, SUPREME COURT AND COURTS OF APPEAL—Cont.
Juvenile case appeals —Cont.
- Record on appeal
  - Access to filed documents and records   CRC 8.401
  - Additions to normal record   CRC 8.407
  - Augmentation of record   CRC 8.410, 8.416, 8.452
  - Certification of record   CRC 8.416, 8.450
  - Confidentiality   CRC 8.401
  - Correcting the record   CRC 8.410, 8.416, 8.452
  - Cover of record   CRC 8.416
  - Dependency appeals, certain counties   CRC 8.416
  - Extension of time to prepare record   CRC 8.409
  - Multiple appeals in same case   CRC 8.408
  - Normal record   CRC 8.407
  - Omissions in record   CRC 8.410
  - Order designating specific placement of dependent child, writ petition to review   CRC 8.454, 8.456
  - Orders setting hearing in termination cases, writ petition to review   CRC 8.450, 8.452
  - Preparation of record   CRC 8.409, 8.416, 8.450, CRCSupp 5th AppDist
  - Procedures to identify records and expedite processing of matters   CRC 8.474
  - Sending record   CRC 8.409, 8.416, 8.450
  - Terminations of parental rights, appeal from   CRC 8.416
  - Transfer of minor to court of criminal jurisdiction   CRC 8.417
- Reporter's transcript   CRC 8.407
  - Preparing and certifying   CRC 8.409
- Sending record   CRC 8.409, 8.416, 8.450
- Service of briefs   CRC 8.412
- Settled statement   CRC 8.407
- Stays   CRC 8.404
  - Order designating specific placement of dependent child, writ petition to review   CRC 8.456
  - Orders setting hearing in termination cases, writ petition to review   CRC 8.452
- Submission of cause
  - Dependency appeals, certain counties   CRC 8.416
  - Terminations of parental rights, appeal from   CRC 8.416
- Termination of parental rights   CRC 8.416
  - Order designating specific placement of dependent child, writ petition to review   CRC 8.454, 8.456
  - Orders setting hearing in termination cases, writ petition to review   CRC 8.450, 8.452
  - Prerequisites for appeal   CRC 8.403
- Time to appeal   CRC 8.406
- Transcripts
  - Preparing and certifying   CRC 8.409
- Transfer of minor to court of criminal jurisdiction   CRC 8.417
  - Time to appeal order transferring minor   CRC 8.406
- Lending record on appeal   CRC 8.153
- Limited issues, decision on   CRC 8.516
- Local rules
  - 1st Appellate District local rules   CRCSupp 1st AppDist
  - 2nd Appellate District local rules   CRCSupp 2nd AppDist
  - 3rd Appellate District local rules   CRCSupp 3rd AppDist
  - 4th Appellate District local rules   CRCSupp 4th AppDist
  - 5th Appellate District local rules   CRCSupp 5th AppDist
  - 6th Appellate District local rules   CRCSupp 6th AppDist
  - Administration of appellate courts
    - Local rules of courts of appeal   CRC 10.1030
  - Effect of local rules   CRC 8.20
- Mandate, writ of   CRC 8.485 to 8.493
  - Amicus briefs   CRC 8.487
  - Applicability of provisions   CRC 8.485
  - Attorney general amicus brief   CRC 8.487
  - Briefs   CRC 8.487
  - Certificate of interested entities or persons   CRC 8.488
    - Electronic filing, when required   CRCSupp 1st AppDist
  - Costs
    - Award and recovery   CRC 8.493
  - Decisions   CRC 8.490
  - Denial of petition for writ
    - Time to file responsive pleading in trial court   CRC 8.491
  - Environmental quality act cases under public resources code
    - Writ proceedings   CRC 8.703
  - Filing of decision   CRC 8.490
  - Finality of decision   CRC 8.490
  - Modification of decision   CRC 8.490
  - Notice if writ issues   CRC 8.489

APPELLATE RULES, SUPREME COURT AND COURTS OF APPEAL—Cont.
- Mandate, writ of —Cont.
    - Notice of sanctions CRC 8.492
    - Opposition CRC 8.487, CRCSupp 4th AppDist
        - Sanctions CRC 8.492
    - Oral argument
        - Sanctions CRC 8.492
    - Petition
        - Contents CRC 8.486
        - Supporting documents CRC 8.486
    - Rehearings CRC 8.490
    - Remittitur CRC 8.490
    - Sanctions CRC 8.492
    - Sealed or confidential records CRC 8.486
    - Service of petition and supporting documents CRC 8.486
    - Writs of mandate, certiorari and prohibition in supreme court or court of appeal CRC 8.485 to 8.493
- Marsden hearings
    - Confidential records CRC 8.47
- Mediation of civil appeals
    - 3rd appellate district local rules CRCSupp 3rd AppDist
    - 5th appellate district local rules CRCSupp 5th AppDist
    - 6th appellate district local rules CRCSupp 6th AppDist
- Mental illness, compromise of case CRC 8.244
- Minors
    - Compromise of case CRC 8.244
    - Supersedeas writ CRC 8.112
- Minutes
    - Court of appeal minutes CRC 10.1024
- Modification of judgment CCP §908, CRC 8.264, 8.532
    - Certiorari, mandate and prohibition CRC 8.490
    - Habeas corpus CRC 8.387
- Monitoring progress of appeal CRC 10.1012
- Motions CRC 8.54
    - Calendar preference, motion for CRC 8.240
    - Dismissal of appeal prior to filing of record CRC 8.57
    - Electronic copies of paper documents CRC 8.44
    - Electronic filing
        - List of motions requiring electronic filing CRCSupp 1st AppDist
    - Extension of time CRC 8.60
        - Electronic filing, when required CRCSupp 1st AppDist
    - Local court of appeal rule imposing other requirements, effect CRC 8.20
    - Number of copies CRC 8.44
    - Shortening time CRC 8.68
- Multiple appeals in same case
    - Juvenile case appeals
        - Record on appeal, single record suffices CRC 8.408
- Natural catastrophes
    - Extension of time CRC 8.66
- New authorities, discovery after brief
    - Letter to court CRC 8.254
- New trial
    - Notice of appeal, extension of time to file CRC 8.108
        - Electronic filing, when required CRCSupp 1st AppDist
        - Environmental quality act cases under public resources code CRC 8.702
- Notice of appeal CRC 8.100
    - Clerk, filing with CRC 8.100
    - Construction, towards sufficiency CRC 8.100
    - Copies of notice of appeal to be sent to review court clerk CRC 8.100
    - Criminal appeals CRC 8.304
        - Time to appeal CRC 8.308
    - Cross appeals CRC 8.100, 8.108
    - Death penalty
        - Habeas corpus, appeals from superior court decisions in habeas cases involving death penalty CRC 8.392
    - Elder and dependent adult civil protection act, expedited appeals process CRC 8.712
        - Superior court clerk duties CRC 8.714
    - Environmental quality act cases under public resources code
        - Appellate review of CEQA cases CRC 8.702
    - Extension of time to file CRC 8.108
        - Electronic filing, when required CRCSupp 1st AppDist
    - Fees for filing CRC 8.25, 8.100, Gov §68926
        - Deposit by appellant Gov §68926.1
        - State law library special account, deposit of civil filing fees into Gov §68926.3
    - Filing requirements CRC 8.100, 8.104
        - 4th Appellate District local rules CRCSupp 4th AppDist Misc Order 15-1, 4th AppDist Misc Order 16-1, 4th AppDist Misc Order 17-1, 4th AppDist Misc Order 18-1

APPELLATE RULES, SUPREME COURT AND COURTS OF APPEAL—Cont.
- Notice of appeal —Cont.
    - Judgment notwithstanding verdict, effect on time for filing notice of appeal of motion for CRC 8.108
    - Juvenile case appeals CRC 8.405
        - Late notice of appeal CRC 8.406
        - Premature notice of appeal CRC 8.406
    - Notification of filing CRC 8.100
    - Premature notice CRC 8.104
    - Signature CRC 8.100
    - Time of filing CRC 8.104
        - Elder and dependent adult civil protection act, expedited appeals process CRC 8.712
    - Vacate, effect of motion to CRC 8.108
    - Vexatious litigants
        - 4th Appellate District local rules CRCSupp 4th AppDist Misc Order 15-15, 4th AppDist Misc Order 16-15, 4th AppDist Misc Order 17-15, 4th AppDist Misc Order 18-15
- Notices
    - Appeal, notice of (See within this heading, **"Notice of appeal"**)
    - Appendix in lieu of transcript, notice of election for CRC 8.124
    - Death penalty cases (See **CAPITAL PUNISHMENT**)
    - Deposit by appellant Gov §68926.1
    - Designation of papers and records CRC 8.122
    - Dismissal of appeal CRC 8.244
    - Exhibits to be transmitted to reviewing court, notice specifying CRC 8.224
    - Judge's failure to perform duties, notice of CRC 10.1016
    - Missing or omitted material, notice to clerk or reporter to prepare and transmit CRC 8.155
    - Record on appeal
        - Designation of record CRC 8.121
    - Remittitur, notice of issuance of CRC 8.272
    - Reporter's transcript, notice to prepare CRC 8.130
    - Settlement following filing of notice of appeal, notice to court of CRC 8.244
    - Transmission of record CRC 8.150
    - Voluntary abandonment and dismissal CRC 8.244
- Opinions
    - Abbreviated opinions
        - 1st Appellate District local rules CRCSupp 1st AppDist
    - Habeas corpus CRC 8.387
    - Modification of CRC 8.264, 8.532
    - Privacy in opinions
        - Names, use in court opinions CRC 8.90
    - Publication of appellate opinions CRC 8.1100 to 8.1125 (See within this heading, **"Publication of appellate opinions"**)
    - Tentative opinions
        - 1st Appellate District local rules CRCSupp 1st AppDist
- Oral arguments CRC 8.256, 8.524
    - 3rd Appellate District local rules
        - Internal operating procedures CRCSupp 3rd AppDist
    - Calendar sessions, supreme court CRCSupp SupCtIOPP V
    - Death penalty, supreme court review CRC 8.638
    - Elder and dependent adult civil protection act, expedited appeals process CRC 8.716
    - Environmental quality act cases under public resources code
        - Appellate review of CEQA cases CRC 8.702
    - Habeas corpus CRC 8.386
    - Juvenile case appeals CRC 8.416
        - Confidentiality CRC 8.401
        - Orders setting hearing in termination cases, writ petition to review CRC 8.452
        - Transfer of minor to court of criminal jurisdiction CRC 8.417
    - Media coverage of oral argument
        - 1st Appellate District local rules CRCSupp 1st AppDist
    - Request, electronic filing CRCSupp 1st AppDist
    - Sanctions
        - Certiorari, mandate and prohibition CRC 8.492
        - Combining arguments as to sanctions with argument on merits CRC 8.276, 8.366
    - Teleconference system, oral arguments via
        - 5th Appellate District local rules CRCSupp 5th AppDist
    - Time for oral argument
        - 3rd Appellate District local rules CRCSupp 3rd AppDist
        - 4th Appellate District local rules CRCSupp 4th AppDist Misc Order 15-6, 4th AppDist Misc Order 16-6, 4th AppDist Misc Order 17-6, 4th AppDist Misc Order 18-6
- Oral proceedings in trial court
    - Content of record on appeal CRC 8.120

APPELLATE RULES, SUPREME COURT AND COURTS OF APPEAL—Cont.

Original proceedings in reviewing courts
    Habeas corpus   CRC 8.380 to 8.398
Oversight of administrative presiding justices and presiding justices   CRC 10.1014
Pandemics
    Emergency rules related to COVID-19   CRCAppx I Emer Rules 1 to 13
    Tolling or extension of time for public health emergencies   CRC 8.66
Party
    Defined   CRC 8.10
    Electronic court records, public access
        Party access   CRC 8.81
    Extension of time
        Notice to party of extension of time   CRC 8.60
    Substitution   CRC 8.36
Petition
    Criminal appeals
        Exhaustion of state remedies   CRC 8.504, 8.508
    Electronic copies of paper documents   CRC 8.44
    Failure to conform to requirements   CRC 8.18
    5th Appellate District rules re writ petitions   CRCSupp 5th AppDist
    Filing fees   CRC 8.25, Gov §68926
        State law library special account, deposit of fees into   Gov §68926.3
        Supreme court   Gov §68927
    Habeas corpus (See **HABEAS CORPUS**)
    Local court of appeal rule imposing other requirements, effect   CRC 8.20
    Number of copies filed   CRC 8.44
    Rehearing (See within this heading, **"Rehearing"**)
    Removal to supreme court before decision in court of appeal   CRC 8.552
    Supersedeas, writ of   CRC 8.112, 8.116
    Supreme court review of court of appeal decisions   CRC 8.500, 8.516
    Transfers from superior court appellate division to court of appeal   CRC 8.1006
    Writ petitions
        Copies   CRCSupp 1st AppDist, 6th AppDist
Preference on calendar, motion for   CRC 8.240
Prehearing conference   CRC 8.248
Privacy
    Opinions
        Names, use in court opinions   CRC 8.90
    Protection of privacy in documents and records   CRC 1.201, 8.41
Progress of appeal, procedure for monitoring   CRC 10.1012
Prohibition, writ of   CRC 8.485 to 8.493
    Amicus briefs   CRC 8.487
    Applicability of provisions   CRC 8.485
    Attorney general amicus brief   CRC 8.487
    Briefs   CRC 8.487
    Certificate of interested entities or persons   CRC 8.488
        Electronic filing, when required   CRCSupp 1st AppDist
    Costs
        Award and recovery   CRC 8.493
    Decisions   CRC 8.490
    Environmental quality act cases under public resources code
        Writ proceedings   CRC 8.703
    Filing of decision   CRC 8.490
    Finality of decision   CRC 8.490
    Modification of decision   CRC 8.490
    Notice if writ issues   CRC 8.489
    Notice of sanctions   CRC 8.492
    Opposition   CRC 8.487, CRCSupp 4th AppDist
        Sanctions   CRC 8.492
    Oral argument
        Sanctions   CRC 8.492
    Petition
        Contents   CRC 8.486
        Supporting documents   CRC 8.486
    Rehearings   CRC 8.490
    Remittitur   CRC 8.490
    Sanctions   CRC 8.492
    Sealed or confidential records   CRC 8.486
    Service of petition and supporting documents   CRC 8.486
    Writs of mandate, certiorari and prohibition in supreme court or court of appeal   CRC 8.485 to 8.493
Public access to electronic court records   CRC 8.80 to 8.85
Publication of appellate opinions   CRC 8.1100 to 8.1125
    Authority for rules governing   CRC 8.1100
    Citation of opinions   CRC 8.1115
    Depublication of published opinions   CRC 8.1125
    Editing of opinions   CRC 8.1105
    Partial publication of appellate opinions   CRC 8.1110

APPELLATE RULES, SUPREME COURT AND COURTS OF APPEAL—Cont.

Publication of appellate opinions —Cont.
    Procedure for publication of appellate opinions   CRC 8.1105
    Review of published opinion granted   CRC 8.1115
    Standards for publication of opinions   CRC 8.1105
    Unpublished opinions
        Citation   CRC 8.1115
        Effect   CRC 8.1115
        Request for publication of   CRC 8.1120
Public health emergencies
    Emergency rules related to COVID-19   CRCAppx I Emer Rules 1 to 13
    Tolling or extension of time   CRC 8.66
Receipts for payment of fees   CRC 8.100
Reconsideration of appealable orders
    Environmental quality act cases under public resources code
        Appellate review of CEQA cases   CRC 8.702
Record on appeal
    Additional record
        Criminal appeals   CRC 8.324
    Administrative proceedings, record of
        Availability to other party   CRC 8.123
        Content of record on appeal   CRC 8.120
        Designation   CRC 8.123
    Agreed statement as record   CRC 8.134
        Content of record on appeal   CRC 8.120
        Criminal appeals   CRC 8.344
        Transcript not available   CRC 8.130
    Appendix designated as record on appeal
        Content of record on appeal   CRC 8.120
    Appendix in lieu of clerk's transcript   CRC 8.124
    Augmentation   CRC 8.155
        1st Appellate District local rules   CRCSupp 1st AppDist
        2nd Appellate District local rules   CRCSupp 2nd AppDist
        5th Appellate District local rules   CRCSupp 5th AppDist
        6th Appellate District local rules   CRCSupp 6st AppDist Misc Order 17-1
        Criminal appeals   CRC 8.340
        Death penalty appeals   CRC 8.634
    Civil appeals   CRC 8.120 to 8.163
    Clerk's transcript   CRC 8.122
        Content of record on appeal   CRC 8.120
    Completion of record
        Determining when record complete   CRC 8.149
    Confidential records
        Form of record, compliance with sealed or confidential records provisions   CRC 8.144
    Conservatorships, appeal from order establishing   CRC 8.480
    Content of record on appeal   CRC 8.120
    Copies   CRC 8.150
    Corrections   CRC 8.155
        2nd Appellate District local rules   CRCSupp 2nd AppDist
        Criminal appeals   CRC 8.340
    Costs, items recoverable as   CRC 8.278
    Criminal appeals   CRC 8.320 to 8.346
        Addition to normal record   CRC 8.324
        Agreed statement as record   CRC 8.344
        Augmentation of record   CRC 8.340
        Capital cases   CRC 8.608 to 8.622, 8.634
        Correction of record   CRC 8.340
        Juror-identifying information in record on criminal appeal, sealing   CRC 8.332, 8.610, 8.611
        Normal record   CRC 8.320, 8.324
        Preparing, certifying and sending record   CRC 8.336
        Settled statement as record   CRC 8.346
    Cross appeal   CRC 8.147
    Death penalty appeals   CRC 8.608 to 8.622
        Accuracy of trial record   CRC 8.622
        Augmenting record in supreme court   CRC 8.634
        Completeness of trial record   CRC 8.619
        Content   CRC 8.610
        Extensions of time   CRC 8.608
        Form   CRC 8.610
        Habeas corpus, appeals from superior court decisions in habeas cases involving death penalty   CRC 8.395
        Juror-identifying information, protection   CRC 8.610, 8.611
        Preliminary proceedings, record   CRC 8.613
        Preparing trial record   CRC 8.616
        Supervision of preparation of record   CRC 8.608
        Transcripts, delivery date   CRC 8.608
        Trial record   CRC 8.616 to 8.622

APPELLATE RULES, SUPREME COURT AND COURTS OF APPEAL—Cont.
- Record on appeal—Cont.
  - Default for failure to procure record   CRC 8.140
  - Delay
    - Sanctioning reporter or clerk for delay   CRC 8.23
  - Designation of record
    - 2nd Appellate District local rules   CRCSupp 2nd AppDist
    - Administrative proceedings, record of   CRC 8.123
    - Notice designating record on appeal   CRC 8.121
  - Dismissal of appeal
    - Failure to procure record on appeal   CRC 8.140
    - Motion to dismiss prior to filing record   CRC 8.57
  - Elder and dependent adult civil protection act, expedited appeals process
    - Oral proceedings   CRC 8.713
    - Written documents   CRC 8.713
  - Electronic filing, when required   CRCSupp 1st AppDist
  - Environmental quality act cases under public resources code
    - Appellate review of CEQA cases   CRC 8.702
  - Exhibits (See within this heading, **"Exhibits"**)
  - Extension of time   CRC 8.60
    - Death penalty appeals   CRC 8.608
    - Electronic filing, when required   CRCSupp 1st AppDist
  - Form of record   CRC 8.144
    - 4th Appellate District local rules   CRCSupp 4th AppDist
  - Habeas corpus
    - Writ granted, appeal from   CRC 8.388
  - Incomplete records presumed complete for judgment   CRC 8.163
  - Juror-identifying information in record on criminal appeal, sealing of   CRC 8.332
    - Death penalty appeals   CRC 8.610, 8.611
  - Juvenile case appeals
    - Access to filed documents and records   CRC 8.401
    - Augmenting record   CRC 8.410, 8.416, 8.452
    - Certification of record   CRC 8.409, 8.416
    - Clerk's transcript   CRC 8.407
    - Confidentiality   CRC 8.401
    - Correcting the record   CRC 8.410, 8.416, 8.452
    - Cover of record   CRC 8.416
    - Dependency appeals, certain counties   CRC 8.416
    - Extension of time to prepare record   CRC 8.409
    - Multiple appeals in same case   CRC 8.408
    - Normal record   CRC 8.407
    - Omissions in record   CRC 8.410
    - Order designating specific placement of dependent child, writ petition to review   CRC 8.454, 8.456
    - Orders setting hearing in termination cases, writ petition to review   CRC 8.450, 8.452
    - Preparation of record   CRC 8.409, 8.416, 8.450, CRCSupp 5th AppDist
    - Procedures to identify records and expedite processing of matters   CRC 8.474
    - Sending record   CRC 8.409, 8.416, 8.450
    - Terminations of parental rights, appeal from   CRC 8.416
    - Transfer of minor to court of criminal jurisdiction   CRC 8.417
  - Lending record   CRC 8.153
  - Motions prior to filing record   CRC 8.57
  - Multiple appeals from same judgment   CRC 8.147
  - Oral proceedings in trial court included
    - Completion of record, determining   CRC 8.149
  - Presumption from record   CRC 8.163
  - Proposed settled statement   CRC 8.137
    - Judicial council legal forms   CRCAppx A
  - Reporter's transcript   CRC 8.130
    - Content of record on appeal   CRC 8.120
    - Electronic filing, when required   CRCSupp 1st AppDist
  - Sealed records   CRC 8.46
    - Form of record, compliance with sealed or confidential records provisions   CRC 8.144
  - Settled statement as record   CRC 8.137
    - Content of record on appeal   CRC 8.120
    - Criminal appeals   CRC 8.346
    - Reporter's transcript unavailable   CRC 8.130
  - Subsequent appeals in same case   CRC 8.147
  - Superior court file in lieu of clerk's transcript   CRC 8.128
    - Content of record on appeal   CRC 8.120
  - Transcripts (See within this heading, **"Transcripts"**)
  - Transfers from superior court appellate division to court of appeal
    - Record on transfer   CRC 8.1007
  - Transmission to reviewing court   CRC 8.150

APPELLATE RULES, SUPREME COURT AND COURTS OF APPEAL—Cont.
- Record on appeal—Cont.
  - Written documents
    - Completion of record, determining   CRC 8.149
    - Content of record on appeal   CRC 8.120
- Records of court of appeals
  - Destruction   CRC 10.1028
  - Electronic court records, public access   CRC 8.80 to 8.85
  - Preservation   CRC 10.1028
- Referees, production of additional evidence before   CRC 8.252
- Rehearing
  - Capital cases   CRC 8.642
  - Certiorari, mandate and prohibition   CRC 8.490
  - Effect of granting
    - Supreme court   CRC 8.536
  - Electronic filings   CRCSupp 1st AppDist
  - Extensions of time
    - Electronic filing, when required   CRCSupp 1st AppDist
    - Supreme court   CRC 8.536
  - Habeas corpus   CRC 8.387
  - Petition and answer
    - Form   CRC 8.268, CRCSupp 6th AppDist
    - Supreme court   CRC 8.536
    - Time for filing   CRC 8.268
  - Power to grant   CRC 8.268
    - Supreme court   CRC 8.536
- Remittitur   CRC 8.272
  - Capital cases   CRC 8.642
  - Certiorari, mandate and prohibition   CRC 8.490
  - Exhibits returned to superior court   CRC 8.224
  - Habeas corpus proceedings   CRC 8.387
  - Immediate issuance   CRC 8.272
  - Issuance   CRC 8.272, 8.552
  - Judgment for costs inserted in   CRC 8.278
    - Criminal appeals   CRC 8.366
  - Juvenile case appeals
    - Orders setting hearing in termination cases, writ petition to review   CRC 8.452
  - Recall   CRC 8.272
  - Stay of issuance   CRC 8.272
  - Supreme court   CRC 8.540
  - Transfers from superior court appellate division to court of appeal   CRC 8.1018
- Removal of cases (See within this heading, **"Transfer of cases"**)
- Reporter
  - Interference with proceedings   CRC 8.23
  - No notes, notice
    - 4th Appellate District local rules   CRCSupp 4th AppDist Misc Order 15-14, 4th AppDist Misc Order 16-14, 4th AppDist Misc Order 17-14, 4th AppDist Misc Order 18-14
  - Notice
    - 4th Appellate District local rules   CRCSupp 4th AppDist Misc Order 15-14, 4th AppDist Misc Order 16-14, 4th AppDist Misc Order 17-14, 4th AppDist Misc Order 18-14
  - Not normal record, notice
    - 4th Appellate District local rules   CRCSupp 4th AppDist Misc Order 15-14, 4th AppDist Misc Order 16-14, 4th AppDist Misc Order 17-14, 4th AppDist Misc Order 18-14
  - Opinions furnished to Reporter of Decisions   CRC 8.1105
  - Record on appeal
    - Sanctioning reporter or clerk for delay   CRC 8.23
- Reporter's transcript
  - Appointed counsel
    - Paper receipt of transcript   CRCSupp 3rd AppDist, 5th AppDist Misc Order 17-1
  - Binding and cover   CRC 8.144
    - 4th Appellate District local rules   CRCSupp 4th AppDist
  - Clerk of superior court, duties   CRC 8.130
  - Commitment
    - Appeal from order of civil commitment   CRC 8.483
  - Confidential transcripts
    - 4th Appellate District local rules   CRCSupp 4th AppDist Misc Order 15-9, 4th AppDist Misc Order 16-9, 4th AppDist Misc Order 17-9, 4th AppDist Misc Order 18-9
  - Content of record on appeal   CRC 8.120
  - Costs
    - Dispute over costs of transcript   CRC 8.130
  - Covers
    - 4th Appellate District local rules   CRCSupp 4th AppDist Misc Order 15-9, 4th AppDist Misc Order 16-9, 4th AppDist Misc Order 17-9, 4th AppDist Misc Order 18-9

APPELLATE RULES, SUPREME COURT AND COURTS OF APPEAL—Cont.
Reporter's transcript—Cont.
 Criminal appeals
  1st Appellate District local rules CRCSupp 1st AppDist
  2nd Appellate District local rules CRCSupp 2nd AppDist
  Capital cases CRC 8.613, 8.616
  Felony appeals CRCSupp 4th AppDist, 6th AppDist
  Juror-identifying information CRC 8.332, 8.610, 8.611
  Normal record on appeal CRC 8.320
  Preparing, certifying and sending record CRC 8.336
  Sealed or confidential records, form of record on appeal CRC 8.336
 Death penalty appeals
  Habeas corpus, appeals from superior court decisions in habeas cases involving death penalty CRC 8.395
 E-filing in supreme court and courts of appeal
  Format of electronic documents CRC 8.74
 Electronic filing, when required CRCSupp 1st AppDist
 Extension of time to file
  4th Appellate District local rules CRCSupp 4th AppDist Misc Order 15-3, 4th AppDist Misc Order 16-3, 4th AppDist Misc Order 17-3, 4th AppDist Misc Order 18-3
 Indexes CRC 8.144
  4th Appellate District local rules CRCSupp 4th AppDist Misc Order 15-9, 4th AppDist Misc Order 16-9, 4th AppDist Misc Order 17-9, 4th AppDist Misc Order 18-9
 Juvenile case appeals
  1st Appellate District local rules CRCSupp 1st AppDist
  2nd Appellate District local rules CRCSupp 2nd AppDist
  4th Appellate District local rules CRCSupp 4th AppDist Misc Order 15-8, 4th AppDist Misc Order 16-8, 4th AppDist Misc Order 17-8, 4th AppDist Misc Order 18-8
  Normal record CRC 8.407
  Preparing and certifying CRC 8.409
 Multiple defendant appeals, non-capital cases
  4th Appellate District local rules CRCSupp 4th AppDist Misc Order 15-12, 4th AppDist Misc Order 16-12, 4th AppDist Misc Order 17-12, 4th AppDist Misc Order 18-12
 Notice to prepare and preparation CRC 8.130
 Page limits
  4th Appellate District local rules CRCSupp 4th AppDist Misc Order 15-9, 4th AppDist Misc Order 16-9, 4th AppDist Misc Order 17-9, 4th AppDist Misc Order 18-9
 Pagination CRC 8.144
 Paper and format CRC 8.144
  4th Appellate District local rules CRCSupp 4th AppDist
 Reimbursement of reporter's fees from transcript reimbursement fund CRC 8.130
 Respondent may not require reporter's transcript CRC 8.130
 Sealed or confidential records
  Form of record, compliance with sealed or confidential records provisions CRC 8.144
 Timely preparation
  1st Appellate District local rules CRCSupp 1st AppDist
Respondent
 Defined CRC 8.10
Reviewing court
 Clerk/executive officer
  Authority and duties CRC 10.1020
  Education, minimum CRC 10.471
  Education of judicial branch, duties as to CRC 10.452
 Defined CRC 8.10
Review of court of appeal decision
 Remittitur
  Supreme court CRC 8.540
Sanctions, procedure for requesting CRC 8.276
 Certiorari, mandate and prohibition CRC 8.492
 Criminal appeals CRC 8.366
 Supreme court review CRC 8.544
Sealed records CRC 8.46
 Access to records CRC 8.45
 Applicability of provisions CRC 8.45
 Confidential records generally CRC 8.47
 Criminal appeals
  Capital cases CRC 8.610
  Juror-identifying information CRC 8.332, 8.610, 8.611
  Record on appeal, form of record CRC 8.336
 Definitions CRC 8.45
 Denial of motion or application to seal record CRC 8.46

APPELLATE RULES, SUPREME COURT AND COURTS OF APPEAL—Cont.
Sealed records—Cont.
 Disclosure of nonpublic material in public filings
  Public redacted version CRC 8.46
  Unredacted version CRC 8.46
 E-filing in supreme court and courts of appeal
  Format of electronic documents CRC 8.74
 Electronic filing CRCSupp 5th AppDist
 Format of records CRC 8.45
 Habeas corpus CRC 8.380 to 8.385
  Supporting documents accompanying petition CRC 8.380, 8.384
 Juvenile case appeals
  Access to filed documents and records CRC 8.401
  Documents filed with court CRC 8.401
  Record on appeal, transcripts CRC 8.409
 Record on appeal
  Form of record, compliance with sealed or confidential records provisions CRC 8.144
 Transmission of records CRC 8.45
2nd Appellate District local rules CRCSupp 2nd AppDist
 Internal operating practices and procedures CRCSupp 2st AppDist
Service CRC 8.25
 Address change notice, service and filing CRC 8.32
  Electronic filing, when required CRCSupp 1st AppDist
 Amicus curiae briefs CRC 8.200
 Appendix in lieu of transcript, notice of election for CRC 8.124
 Attorneys
  Substitution CRC 8.36
  Withdrawal CRC 8.36
 Briefs CRC 8.200, 8.212
  Attorney general, when required to serve CRC 8.29
  Capital cases CRC 8.630
  Criminal appeals CRC 8.360
  Elder and dependent adult civil protection act, expedited appeals process CRC 8.715
 Certiorari
  Service of petition and supporting documents CRC 8.486
 Clerk's transcript, notice designating papers and records for inclusion in CRC 8.122
 Criminal appeals
  Briefs CRC 8.360
  Exhaustion of state remedies, petition for review CRC 8.508
 Cross appeal notices CRC 8.108
 Elder and dependent adult civil protection act, expedited appeals process CRC 8.711
 Environmental quality act cases under public resources code CRC 8.701
 Juvenile case appeals
  Briefs CRC 8.412
  Orders setting hearing in termination cases, writ petition to review CRC 8.452
 New authorities, discovery after brief
  Letter to court CRC 8.254
 Notice of appeal CRC 8.100
 Opening briefs CRC 8.212
 Parties, substitution CRC 8.36
 Reporter's transcript, notice to prepare CRC 8.130
 Settled statement notice CRC 8.137
  Criminal appeals CRC 8.346
 Supersedeas writ CRC 8.112
 Telephone number change CRC 8.32
 Transfers from superior court appellate division to court of appeal
  Briefs CRC 8.1012
Sessions CRC 8.256
Settled statement CRC 8.137
 Content of record on appeal CRC 8.120
 Criminal appeals CRC 8.346
 E-filing in supreme court and courts of appeal
  Format of electronic documents CRC 8.74
 Juvenile case appeals CRC 8.407
 Proposed settled statement CRC 8.137
  Judicial council legal forms CRCAppx A
 Reporter's transcript unavailable CRC 8.130
  Criminal appeals CRC 8.346
Settlement of cases pending on appeal (See **SETTLEMENT AND COMPROMISE**)
Settlements
 1st Appellate District local rules CRCSupp 1st AppDist
 Civil settlement conference procedures
  4th Appellate District local rules CRCSupp 4th AppDist

APPELLATE RULES, SUPREME COURT AND COURTS OF APPEAL—Cont.
Settlements—Cont.
    Notice to court of settlement following filing of notice of appeal   CRC 8.244
Shortening time   CRC 8.68
    Applications   CRC 8.50
Signature
    E-filing in supreme court and courts of appeal   CRC 8.75
    Entry of appealable order determined by   CRC 8.104
    Multiple parties' signatures required   CRC 8.42
        E-filed documents   CRC 8.75
    Notice of appeal   CRC 8.100
6th Appellate District local rules   CRCSupp 6th AppDist
    Internal operating practices and procedures   CRCSupp 6th AppDist
Statements
    Agreed statement (See within this heading, **"Agreed statement"**)
    Appellant's opening brief, contents of   CRC 8.204
    Settled statement (See within this heading, **"Settled statement"**)
Stay of proceedings   CRC 8.112, 8.116
    Criminal appeals, stay of execution pending   CRC 8.312
    Death penalty appeals
        Habeas corpus, appeals from superior court decisions in habeas cases involving death penalty   CRC 8.394
    Immediate stay   CRCSupp 4th AppDist
    Juvenile case appeals
        Order designating specific placement of dependent child, writ petition to review   CRC 8.456
        Orders setting hearing in termination cases, writ petition to review   CRC 8.452
        Stay pending appeal   CRC 8.404
    Other cause before court, supreme court order deferring action pending disposition of   CRC 8.512
    Remittitur
        Supreme court   CRC 8.540
Stipulation
    Commitment, appeal from order
        Partial transcript   CRC 8.483
    Criminal appeals
        Partial transcript for record on appeal   CRC 8.320
    Judgment, stipulated reversal
        1st Appellate District local rules   CRCSupp 1st AppDist
    Original superior court file, use in lieu of clerk's transcript
        1st Appellate District local rules   CRCSupp 1st AppDist
        3rd Appellate District local rules   CRCSupp 3rd AppDist
        4th Appellate District local rules   CRCSupp 4th AppDist
    Partial transcripts   CRC 8.130
    Signatures
        Multiple signatures   CRC 8.42, 8.75, 8.77
    Superior court file in lieu of clerk's transcript, use of   CRC 8.128
    Voluntary abandonment of appeal   CRC 8.244
Submission of cause
    Courts of appeal, submission in   CRC 8.256, 8.386
    Juvenile case appeals
        Dependency appeals, certain counties   CRC 8.416
        Terminations of parental rights, appeal from   CRC 8.416
    Supreme court, submission in   CRCSupp SupCtIOPP VII
Subsequent appeals in same case
    Record on appeal   CRC 8.147
Substitution
    Attorney   CRC 8.36
        4th Appellate District local rules   CRCSupp 4th AppDist Misc Order 15-7, 4th AppDist Misc Order 16-7, 4th AppDist Misc Order 17-7, 4th AppDist Misc Order 18-7
        Electronic filing, when required   CRCSupp 1st AppDist
    Parties   CRC 8.36
Superior court
    Defined   CRC 8.10
    Extension of time
        Record on appeal, no extensions on preparation time   CRC 8.60
Supersedeas, writ of   CRC 8.112, 8.116
Supreme court, proceedings in   CRC 8.500 to 8.552
Surety bond premiums as recoverable cost   CRC 8.278
Teleconference system, oral arguments via   CRCSupp 5th AppDist
Telephone number
    Change
        Service and filing notice of change   CRC 8.32
    Record, telephone number of   CRC 8.32
Temporary stay   CRC 8.112, 8.116
3rd Appellate District local rules   CRCSupp 3rd AppDist
    Internal operating practices and procedures   CRCSupp 3rd AppDist

APPELLATE RULES, SUPREME COURT AND COURTS OF APPEAL—Cont.
Time
    Agreed statement, filing   CRC 8.134
    Application to extend time
        Electronic filing, when required   CRCSupp 1st AppDist
    Briefs   CRC 8.212, 8.360
        Capital cases   CRC 8.630
    Calendar preference, motion for   CRC 8.240
    Computation   CRC 8.60
    Costs, procedure for claiming   CRC 8.278
    Criminal appeals
        Notice of appeal   CRC 8.308
    Cross appeal, filing   CRC 8.108
    Default relief by review court   CRC 8.60
    Dismissal for failure to pay filing fee or procure record within time allowed   CRC 8.140
    Elder and dependent adult civil protection act, expedited appeals process
        Time to appeal   CRC 8.712
    Environmental quality act cases under public resources code   CRC 8.701, 8.702
    Extension of time (See within this heading, **"Extension of time"**)
    Finality of decisions   CRC 8.264, 8.532
    Judge's failure to perform duties, excessive absence as basis for   CRC 10.1016
    Judgment notwithstanding verdict, effect on time for filing notice of appeal of motion for   CRC 8.108
    Juvenile case appeals
        Record on appeal   CRC 8.409
        Time to appeal   CRC 8.406
    Monitoring appeal to determine need for extensions   CRC 10.1012
    Multiple appeals, record on   CRC 8.147
    Notice of appeal, filing   CRC 8.104
    Oral arguments   CRCSupp 3rd AppDist
    Rehearings   CRC 8.268
        Supreme court   CRC 8.536
    Reporter's transcript, notice to prepare   CRC 8.130
    Sessions of court   CRC 8.256
    Settled statements   CRC 8.137
        Criminal appeals   CRC 8.346
    Shortening time   CRC 8.68
    Submission of cause   CRC 8.256, 8.386
    Supreme court review of court of appeals case prior to decision   CRC 8.552
    Supreme court review of court of appeals decision   CRC 8.512
    Transcripts, preparation   CRC 8.122
    Transfers from superior court appellate division to court of appeal   CRC 8.1008
        Briefs   CRC 8.1012
        Certification   CRC 8.1005
    Vacate, effect of motion to   CRC 8.108
Transcripts
    Benoit orders
        4th Appellate District local rules   CRCSupp 4th AppDist Misc Order 15-2, 4th AppDist Misc Order 16-2, 4th AppDist Misc Order 17-2, 4th AppDist Misc Order 18-2
    Clerk's transcript (See within this heading, **"Clerk's transcript"**)
    Commitment, appeal from order
        Partial transcript, stipulation as to   CRC 8.483
    Conservatorships
        Appeal from order establishing   CRC 8.480
        Sterilization of conservatee, judgment authorizing conservator to consent   CRC 8.482
    Content of record on appeal   CRC 8.120
    Criminal appeals
        Capital cases   CRC 8.613
        Juror-identifying information   CRC 8.332, 8.610, 8.611
        Normal record on appeal   CRC 8.320
        Preparing, certifying and sending record   CRC 8.336
        Reporter's transcript, felony appeals   CRCSupp 4th AppDist, 6th AppDist
        Sealed or confidential records, form of record on appeal   CRC 8.336
    Death penalty appeals
        Delivery date of transcript   CRC 8.608
        Habeas corpus, appeals from superior court decisions in habeas cases involving death penalty   CRC 8.395
    Death penalty cases
        Record on appeal generally (See **CAPITAL PUNISHMENT**)
    E-filing in supreme court and courts of appeal
        Format of electronic documents   CRC 8.74

APPELLATE RULES, SUPREME COURT AND COURTS OF APPEAL—Cont.
Transcripts—Cont.
  Extension of time to file
    4th Appellate District local rules   CRCSupp 4th AppDist Misc Order 15-3, 4th AppDist Misc Order 16-3, 4th AppDist Misc Order 17-3, 4th AppDist Misc Order 18-3
  Form of record   CRC 8.144
  Juvenile case appeals
    4th Appellate District local rules   CRCSupp 4th AppDist Misc Order 15-8, 4th AppDist Misc Order 16-8, 4th AppDist Misc Order 17-8, 4th AppDist Misc Order 18-8
  Preparing and certifying   CRC 8.409
  Multiple defendant appeals, non-capital cases
    4th Appellate District local rules   CRCSupp 4th AppDist Misc Order 15-12, 4th AppDist Misc Order 16-12, 4th AppDist Misc Order 17-12, 4th AppDist Misc Order 18-12
  Police reports
    4th Appellate District local rules   CRCSupp 4th AppDist Misc Order 15-11, 4th AppDist Misc Order 16-11, 4th AppDist Misc Order 17-11, 4th AppDist Misc Order 18-11
  Reporter's transcript (See within this heading, **"Reporter's transcript"**)
  Sealed or confidential records
    Form of record, compliance with sealed or confidential records provisions   CRC 8.144
Transfer of cases
  Administrative presiding justice, transfer of case by   CRC 10.1000
  Dismissal of review   CRC 8.528
  Divisions of appellate court
    Assignment of cases to divisions   CRC 10.1008
  Instructions, transfer with   CRC 8.528
  Remaining issues, transfer for decision   CRC 8.528
  Retransfer of cause not decided   CRC 8.528
  Superior court appellate division to court of appeal   CRC 8.1000 to 8.1018
  Supreme court, transfers by   CRC 10.1000
  Supreme court, transfer to before decision in court of appeal   CRC 8.552
Transfers from superior court appellate division to court of appeal   CRC 8.1000 to 8.1018
  Appellate division proceedings after certification or transfer   CRC 8.1014
  Applicability of rules   CRC 8.1000
  Argument
    Issues to be considered   CRC 8.1012
  Authority of court of appeal   CRC 8.1002
  Briefs   CRC 8.1012
  Certification   CRC 8.1005
    Appellate division proceedings after certification or transfer   CRC 8.1014
  Decision by court of appeal in transferred case
    Filing, finality and modification   CRC 8.1018
  Disposition of transferred case   CRC 8.1016
  Grounds for transfer   CRC 8.1002
  Limited issues
    Disposition of transferred case   CRC 8.1016
  Order for transfer   CRC 8.1008
    Vacating transfer order   CRC 8.1018
  Petitions   CRC 8.1006
  Record on transfer   CRC 8.1007
  Remittitur   CRC 8.1018
  Retransfer without decision
    Disposition of transferred case   CRC 8.1016
  Scope of rules   CRC 8.1000
  Time   CRC 8.1008
    Certification   CRC 8.1005
Typewritten documents
  Briefs   CRC 8.204
  Transcripts (See within this heading, **"Transcripts"**)
Unsealing records in reviewing court   CRC 8.46
Vacate judgment, time for filing notice of appeal extended by motion to   CRC 8.108
  Environmental quality act cases under public resources code
    Appellate review of CEQA cases   CRC 8.702
Vacation of submission   CRC 8.256
Vexatious litigants
  Notice of appeal
    4th Appellate District local rules   CRCSupp 4th AppDist Misc Order 15-15, 4th AppDist Misc Order 16-15, 4th AppDist Misc Order 17-15, 4th AppDist Misc Order 18-15
Violation of court rules, dismissal   CRC 10.1012
Voluntary abandonment of appeal (See within this heading, **"Dismissal"**)

APPELLATE RULES, SUPREME COURT AND COURTS OF APPEAL—Cont.
Waiver of costs and fees   CRC 8.26
  Family law proceedings in supreme court or court of appeals, applicable rules   CRC 5.46
Waiver of oral argument, submission after   CRC 8.256
Will
  Construction   CRC 8.10
Will probate cases, costs on appeal of   CRC 8.278, Pro §1002
Withdrawal
  Abandonment of suit (See within this heading, **"Dismissal"**)
  Attorney, withdrawal   CRC 8.36
Writing
  Defined   CRC 8.10
Writ panels
  3rd Appellate District local rules
    Internal operating practices and procedures (IOPP)   CRCSupp 3rd AppDist
Written
  Defined   CRC 8.10

APPLIANCES
Serial number altered or destroyed prior to sale   CC §1710.1
Warranties on   CC §§1790 to 1795.8

APPLICATIONS
Appellate rules, superior court appeals   CRC 8.806
  Extension of time   CRC 8.810
    Electronic filing, when required   CRCSupp 1st AppDist
Attachment (See **ATTACHMENT**)
Automobile lien sale, application for conducting   CC §3071
Change of names   CCP §1276
Claim and delivery, possession writ   CCP §512.010
Default judgments   CCP §§585.5, 587
Family law rules (See **FAMILY RULES**)
Filing fees   Gov §§70611, 70613
  Amendment of complaint or other subsequent pleadings
    Effect on filing fee   Gov §70613.5
  Permissible additional fees   Gov §70603
  Superior court fees
    Hearings, filing motion, application or paper filed which would require   Gov §70617
  Supplemental fees for first paper filing   Gov §§70602.5, 70602.6
Garnishment (See **GARNISHMENT**)
Homestead property, application for order for sale of   CCP §§704.750, 704.760
Intervention, complaint in   CCP §387
Motion, application for order as   CCP §1003
Sister State Money-Judgment Act   CCP §§1710.15, 1710.20
Superior courts (See **SUPERIOR COURTS**)

APPOINTMENT
Administrative Procedure Act (See **ADMINISTRATIVE PROCEDURE ACT**)
Administrators of decedents' estates (See **EXECUTORS AND ADMINISTRATORS**)
Arbitrators   CCP §1281.6
Conservators (See **CONSERVATORS**)
Executors of decedents' estates (See **EXECUTORS AND ADMINISTRATORS**)
Guardian ad litem (See **GUARDIAN AD LITEM**)
Guardians (See **GUARDIAN AND WARD**)
International commercial arbitrators and conciliators (See **INTERNATIONAL COMMERCIAL ARBITRATION AND CONCILIATION**)
Jury commissioner, appointment of   CCP §195
Partition referees   CCP §§872.630, 873.010 to 873.050
Power of appointment (See **POWER OF APPOINTMENT**)
Probate referees (See **PROBATE REFEREES**)
Public guardians (See **PUBLIC GUARDIANS**)
Receivers (See **RECEIVERS AND RECEIVERSHIP**)
Referees (See **REFEREES**)
Small claims advisory committee, appointments to   CCP §116.950
Special administrators   Pro §§8540, 8541
Sterilization proceedings (See **STERILIZATION**)
Superior courts (See **SUPERIOR COURTS**)
Trustees (See **TRUSTS**)

APPORTIONMENT
Covenant, benefits under   CC §§1467, 1469
Freightage   CC §§2140, 2141
Partition proceedings, costs of   CCP §§874.040, 874.050, 874.110

APPRAISALS
Administration of decedents' estates (See **ADMINISTRATION OF ESTATES**)
Conservatorship estates (See **CONSERVATORS**)
Decedents' estates (See **ADMINISTRATION OF ESTATES**)

APPRAISALS—Cont.
Deficiency judgment proceeding on foreclosure of mortgages   CCP §§580a, 726
Eminent domain (See **EMINENT DOMAIN**)
Foreclosure, deficiency judgment proceeding on   CCP §§580a, 726
Guardianship estates (See **GUARDIAN AND WARD**)
Improper influence of appraisal or valuation   CC §1090.5
Inverse condemnation action, appraisal fees in   CCP §1036
Liens   CCP §726
Mortgages
   Refinancing
      Disclosure as to unbiased appraisal and complaint process   CC §1102.6g
Multiple listing service   CC §§1086 to 1089.5
Partition by   CCP §§873.910 to 873.980
Partition of real property act
   Valuation of property   CCP §874.316
Sale or other transfer of real estate
   Disclosures
      Unbiased appraisal and complaint process   CC §1102.6g
Sexual harassment, civil action for
   Construction or application of provisions in issue, solicitor general notified   CC §51.1

APPROPRIATION OF WATERS (See **WATERS**)

APPROPRIATIONS
State aid (See **PUBLIC FINANCE**)

APPROVAL
Surety bonds and sureties (See **SURETYSHIP, BONDS AND UNDERTAKINGS**)

APPURTENANCES (See **REAL PROPERTY**)

AQUACULTURE (See **FISH AND FISHING**)

ARBITRATION (See also **INTERNATIONAL COMMERCIAL ARBITRATION AND CONCILIATION; JUDICIAL ARBITRATION**)
Generally   CCP §§1280, 1280.2
Adjournment
   Generally   CCP §1282.2
   Judicial arbitration   CRC 3.824
Administrative adjudication (See **ADMINISTRATIVE ADJUDICATION**)
Admissibility of evidence
   Former testimony at proceedings as hearsay exception at subsequent trial   Ev §§1290 to 1292
   Hearings, admissibility of evidence at   CCP §1282.2
Affiliations of arbitrator, disclosure of   CCP §1281.95
Agreements
   Enforcement   CCP §§1281 to 1281.99
   Setting forth provisions in petition to compel   CRC 3.1330
Answer to complaint, defendant filing petition to compel arbitration in lieu of   CCP §1281.7
Appeals   CCP §§1291, 1294, 1294.2
   Elder and dependent adult civil protection act
      Expedited appeals process   CCP §1294.4, CRC 8.710 to 8.717
Appearance
   Waiver of notice by   CCP §1282.2
Arbitrators (See **ARBITRATORS**)
Attachment orders, party's rights under arbitration agreement on filing for   CCP §1281.8
Attorney professional conduct
   Former judges, arbitrators, mediators, etc
      Restrictions on representation of clients   ProfC 1.12
   Service as temporary judge, referee or court-appointed arbitrator, applicability of judicial ethics canon 6D   ProfC 2.4.1
   Service by attorney as third-party neutral   ProfC 2.4
Attorneys
   Attorney's fees disputes, arbitration of (See **ATTORNEY'S FEES**)
   Representation by counsel in arbitration proceedings
      Generally   CCP §1282.4
      Judicial arbitration   CRC 3.821
      Out-of-state attorneys   CCP §1282.4, CRC 9.43
Awards
   Confirmation (See within this heading, "**Confirmation of awards**")
   Contents   CCP §1283.4
   Contracts, effect as   CCP §1287.6
   Correction (See within this heading, "**Correction of awards**")
   Form   CCP §1283.4
   Fraud   CCP §1286.2

ARBITRATION—Cont.
Awards—Cont.
   Judgment in conformity with award, entry of   CCP §1287.4
   Judicial arbitration (See **JUDICIAL ARBITRATION**)
   Law and motion rules applicable to proceedings to enforce   CRC 3.1103
   Objections to   CCP §§1283.8, 1284
   Postponement by arbitrator   CCP §1286.2
   Principal, surety affected by award against   CC §2855
   Rehearings   CCP §1287
   Service of   CCP §1283.6
   Surety affected by award against principal   CC §2855
   Time for   CCP §1283.8
   Unconfirmed and unvacated awards, effect of   CCP §1287.6
   Vacation (See within this heading, "**Vacation of awards**")
Civil rules
   Case management
      Determination as to arbitration or other ADR   CRC 3.722
      Stipulation as to arbitration or other ADR   CRC 3.726
Claims against decedent's estate, summary determination of   Pro §9621
Collective bargaining agreement, representation by non-attorney in arbitration arising under   CCP §1282.4
Commercial arbitration (See **INTERNATIONAL COMMERCIAL ARBITRATION AND CONCILIATION**)
Common interest developments
   Alternative dispute resolution (See **COMMON INTEREST DEVELOPMENTS**)
Compelling arbitration
   Generally   CCP §1281.2
   Answer to complaint, petition to compel in lieu of   CCP §1281.7
   Arbitration agreement provisions, incorporation into petition of   CRC 3.1330
   Law and motion rules, applicability   CRC 3.1103
Confirmation of awards
   Generally   CCP §§1285, 1286
   Contents of petition   CCP §1285.4
   Dismissal of proceedings   CCP §§1286, 1287.2
   Judgment in conformity with award, entry of   CCP §1287.4
   Response to petition   CCP §§1285.2, 1285.6
   Small claims action for attorney fees   CCP §116.220
   Time limits for serving and filing of papers   CCP §§1288 to 1288.8
   Unconfirmed and unvacated awards, effect of   CCP §1287.6
Conflicts of interest
   Disclosures by and disqualification of arbitrators   CCP §§1281.9 to 1281.95
   Judges' employment or prospective employment as a dispute resolution neutral as basis for disqualification of judges   CCP §§170.1, 1281.9
Consolidation of actions   CCP §1281.3
Construction contracts (See **BUILDING CONSTRUCTION; BUILDING CONTRACTORS**)
Consumer arbitration
   Definition of consumer arbitration
      Arbitrators, ethics standards for neutral arbitrators   CRC ArbEthicsStand 2
   Disclosures by arbitrator
      Openness to offers of employment or professional relationship   CRC ArbEthicsStand 7
      Provider organizations administering arbitration   CRC ArbEthicsStand 8
   Disqualification of arbitrator
      Financial interests of private arbitration companies in consumer arbitrations   CCP §1281.92
   Drafting party breach of arbitration agreement
      Consequences   CCP §1281.98
      Monetary sanctions against breaching party   CCP §1281.99
      Nonpayment of fees   CCP §1281.97
   Fees and costs in consumer proceedings   CCP §1284.3
      Drafting party obligation   CCP §1281.97
   Private arbitration companies
      Disclosures   CCP §1281.96
Consumer contract awareness act   CC §§1799.208, 1799.209
Continuances
   COVID-19, cases extended pursuant to   CCP §599
   Refusal as grounds for vacating award   CCP §1286.2
Contracts
   Ethics standards for neutral arbitrators   CRC ArbEthicsStand 1 to CRC ArbEthicsStand 17
   Time period specified for commencement of arbitration
      Tolling by filing of civil action   CCP §1281.12
Correction of awards
   Generally   CCP §§1285, 1286
   Contents of petition   CCP §§1285.4, 1285.8

ARBITRATION—Cont.
  Correction of awards—Cont.
    Dismissal of proceedings   CCP §§1286, 1287.2
    Grounds   CCP §1286.6
    Notice requirement   CCP §1286.8
    Requisites   CCP §1286.8
    Response to petition   CCP §§1285.2, 1285.6, 1285.8
    Small claims action for attorney fees   CCP §116.220
    Time limits for serving and filing of papers   CCP §§1288 to 1288.8
  Costs
    Generally   CCP §§1284.2, 1293.2
    Consumer arbitration
      Fees and costs in consumer proceedings   CCP §1284.3
    Judicial arbitration
      Fees of arbitrator   CRC 3.819
      Trial, costs after   CRC 3.826
    Offer to compromise, effect of refusal of   CCP §998
  Court-ordered arbitration (See **JUDICIAL ARBITRATION**)
  Decedents' estates, summary determination of claims against   Pro §9621
  Depositions   CCP §§1283, 1283.05
  Disclosures required   CCP §§1281.9, 1281.91, 1281.95
    Data collection and reports available to public   CCP §1281.96
  Discovery
    Generally   CCP §1283.05
    Judicial arbitration (See **JUDICIAL ARBITRATION**)
    List of witnesses and documents   CCP §1282.2
  Division of property on dissolution of marriage   Fam §2554
  Documents intended to be introduced at hearing   CCP §1282.2
  Easement, apportionment of maintenance costs for   CC §845
  Eminent domain proceedings (See **EMINENT DOMAIN**)
  Employment arbitration
    Drafting party breach of arbitration agreement
      Consequences   CCP §1281.98
      Monetary sanctions against breaching party   CCP §1281.99
      Nonpayment of fees   CCP §1281.97
    Fees and costs in employment proceedings
      Drafting party obligation   CCP §1281.97
  Enforcement of agreements   CCP §§1281 to 1281.99
  Ethics standards for arbitrators   CCP §1281.85
  Evidence, admissibility
    Former testimony at proceedings   Ev §§1290 to 1292
    Hearings, admissibility of evidence   Ev §1282.2
  Expert witnesses, list of   CCP §1282.2
  Family law proceedings
    Appointment of arbitrators
      Applicable guidelines for appointment   CRC JudAdminStand 5.30
  Fees
    Generally   CCP §1284.2
    Consumer arbitration
      Fees and costs in consumer proceedings   CCP §1284.3
    Employment arbitration or consumer arbitration
      Drafting party obligation   CCP §1281.97
    Judicial arbitrators   CCP §1141.28, CRC 3.819
  Firefighters and law enforcement officers
    Costs and expenses, party liable for   CCP §1299.9
    Decisions by arbitration panel   CCP §1299.7
    Definitions   CCP §1299.3
    Hearings, generally   CCP §1299.5
    Legislative findings and intent   CCP §1299
    Procedural requirements   CCP §1299.6
    Rejection of decision   CCP §1299.7
    Request to submit to arbitration   CCP §1299.4
    Selection of arbitration panel   CCP §1299.4
    Statutory provisions
      General arbitration provisions, applicability of   CCP §1299.8
      Specific arbitration provisions, applicability of   CCP §1299.2
    Strikes, prohibition against   CCP §1299.4
    Subpoena power of arbitration panel   CCP §1299.5
  Health care providers (See **PHYSICIANS AND SURGEONS**)
  Hearings
    Generally   CCP §1282.2
    Administrative hearings (See **ADMINISTRATIVE ADJUDICATION**)
    International commercial arbitration (See **INTERNATIONAL COMMERCIAL ARBITRATION AND CONCILIATION**)
    Judicial arbitration (See **JUDICIAL ARBITRATION**)
    Rehearings   CCP §1287
    Summary hearings on petitions, general provisions for   CCP §1290.2
    Vacation of award   CCP §1286.4
  Injunctive relief, party's rights under arbitration agreement on filing for   CCP §1281.8
  International commercial arbitration (See **INTERNATIONAL COMMERCIAL ARBITRATION AND CONCILIATION**)

ARBITRATION—Cont.
  Joinder of parties   CCP §1281.2
  Judges, service as arbitrators   CRCSupp JudEthicsCanons 3 to 6
  Judicial Arbitration   CRC 3.810 to 3.830 (See **JUDICIAL ARBITRATION**)
  Jurisdiction   CCP §§86, 116.220, 1292.4 to 1293
  Labor and labor unions
    Collective bargaining agreement, representation by non-attorney in arbitration arising under   CCP §1282.4
    Firefighters and law enforcement officers (See within this heading, "**Firefighters and law enforcement officers**")
  Law and motion proceedings
    Motions concerning arbitration   CRC 3.1330
  Leases, violation of   CC §§1942.1, 1942.5
  Medical malpractice (See **MALPRACTICE**)
  Motor vehicle warranties, actions involving   CC §1793.22
  Nonresident attorneys, representation in arbitration proceedings by   CCP §1282.4, CRC 9.43
  Notice
    Correction of award, prospective   CCP §1286.8
    Hearing   CCP §1282.2
    Motor vehicle warranties, actions involving   CC §1793.22
    Petition   CCP §1290.4
    Vacation of award, prospective   CCP §1286.4
  Oaths   CCP §1282.8
  Objections and exceptions
    Award in arbitration, objection to   CCP §§1283.8, 1284
    Judicial arbitration   CCP §1141.15
  Offer to compromise, costs chargeable against party refusing   CCP §998
  Other states, representation in arbitration proceedings by attorneys from   CCP §1282.4, CRC 9.43
  Out-of-state attorney arbitration counsel   CRC 9.43
  Petitions
    Compelling arbitration (See within this heading, "**Compelling arbitration**")
    Consolidation of proceedings   CCP §1281.3
    Correction of awards (See within this heading, "**Correction of awards**")
    General provisions   CCP §§1290 to 1293.2
    Jurisdiction   CCP §§86, 1292.4 to 1293
    Notice of hearing   CCP §1290.4
    Service   CCP §§1290.4, 1290.6, 1290.8
    Stay of proceedings (See within this heading, "**Stay of proceedings**")
    Summary hearings   CCP §1290.2
    To compel arbitration   CRC 3.1330
    Vacation of awards (See within this heading, "**Vacation of awards**")
    Venue   CCP §§1292, 1292.2
  Physicians and surgeons (See **PHYSICIANS AND SURGEONS**)
  Pretrial arbitration (See **JUDICIAL ARBITRATION**)
  Principal, surety affected by award against   CC §2855
  Priority of proceedings   CCP §1291.2
  Private arbitration companies
    Disclosures   CCP §1281.96
  Provisional remedies, party's rights under arbitration agreement on filing for   CCP §1281.8
  Public agency, construction contract with   CC §1670, CCP §1296
  Real estate contracts, arbitration of (See **REAL ESTATE CONTRACT ARBITRATION**)
  Receiver, party's rights under arbitration agreement on appointment of   CCP §1281.8
  Reports
    Data collection and reports available to public   CCP §1281.96
  Request to arbitrate pursuant to written agreement   CCP §1281.1
  Rules of court arbitration (See **JUDICIAL ARBITRATION**)
  Separate proceedings   CCP §1281.3
  Service
    Awards   CCP §1283.6
    Petitions   CCP §1290.4
    Responses   CCP §§1290.6, 1290.8
    Witnesses, list of   CCP §1282.2
  Settlements
    Notice to neutral of settlement of case   CRC 3.1385
    Time-limited demands   CCP §§999 to 999.5
  Small claims jurisdiction to confirm, correct or vacate award   CCP §116.220
  Solicitation
    Disclosure   CCP §1281.9
    Not to be made party to   CCP §1281.93
  Stay of proceedings
    Generally   CCP §1281.4
    Arbitration agreement provisions set forth in petition for   CRC 3.1330
    Construction lien claim, effect of filing application for   CCP §1281.5
    Jurisdiction   CCP §1292.8
    Pending actions, effect of   CCP §1281.2
    Provisional remedies, effect of filing for   CCP §1281.8

ARBITRATION—Cont.
Submission of controversy to arbitration, party's request for   CCP §1281.1
Subpoenas   CCP §1282.6
Subpoenas duces tecum   CCP §1282.6
Surety, effect of award against principal on   CC §2855
Time for proceedings   CCP §1283.8
   Tolling by filing of civil action   CCP §1281.12
Transcripts
   Certified shorthand reporters
      Party's right   CCP §1282.5
Uninsured motorist cases
   Differential case management rules, applicability   CRC 3.712
   Rules for arbitration of   Gov §68609.5
Vacation of awards
   Generally   CCP §§1285, 1286
   Contents of petition   CCP §§1285.4, 1285.8
   Dismissal of proceedings   CCP §§1286, 1287.2
   Grounds   CCP §1286.2
   Judicial arbitration   CCP §1141.22, CRC 3.828
   Notice requirement   CCP §1286.4
   Rehearing before new arbitrators   CCP §1287
   Requisites   CCP §1286.4
   Response to petition   CCP §§1285.2, 1285.6, 1285.8
   Small claims action for attorney fee award   CCP §116.220
   Time limits for serving and filing of papers   CCP §§1288 to 1288.8
   Unconfirmed and unvacated awards, effect of   CCP §1287.6
Venue of proceedings   CCP §§1292, 1292.2
Waiver of arbitration
   Construction lien claim, effect of filing application for   CCP §1281.5
   Provisional remedies, effect of filing for   CCP §1281.8
Warranties on motor vehicles, actions involving   CC §1793.22
Witnesses
   Generally   CCP §1282.2
   Fees of   CCP §1283.2
   List of   CCP §1282.2
   Subpoenas for attendance of   CCP §1282.6
Writ of possession, party's rights under arbitration agreement on filing for   CCP §1281.8

ARBITRATORS
Affiliations, disclosure of   CCP §1281.95
Appointment   CCP §1281.6
Attorney professional conduct
   Former judges, arbitrators, mediators, etc
      Restrictions on representation of clients   ProfC 1.12
   Service as temporary judge, referee or court-appointed arbitrator, applicability of judicial ethics canon 6D   ProfC 2.4.1
   Service by attorney as third-party neutral   ProfC 2.4
Co-arbitrators, authority of   CCP §1282
Conflicts of interest
   Disclosures by and disqualification of arbitrators   CCP §§1281.9 to 1281.95
   Judges' employment or prospective employment as a dispute resolution neutral as basis for disqualification of judges   CCP §§170.1, 1281.9
Consumer arbitration
   Definition of consumer arbitration
      Arbitrators, ethics standards for neutral arbitrators   CRC ArbEthicsStand 2
   Disclosures by arbitrator
      Openness to offers of employment or professional relationship   CRC ArbEthicsStand 7
      Provider organizations administering arbitration   CRC ArbEthicsStand 8
   Disqualification
      Financial interests of private arbitration companies in consumer arbitrations   CCP §1281.92
Contracts
   Ethics standards for neutral arbitrators   CRC ArbEthicsStand 1 to CRC ArbEthicsStand 17
Corruption of   CCP §1286.2
Court-appointed arbitrators, compliance with Code of Judicial Ethics   CRCSupp JudEthicsCanon 6
Disciplinary action
   Ethics standards
      Disclosures   CRC ArbEthicsStand 7
Discovery, power to compel   CCP §1283.05
Discrimination, prohibition against in court appointments   CRC 10.611, CRC JudAdminStand 10.21
Disqualification   CCP §§1281.9, 1281.91, 1281.95
   Financial interests of private arbitration companies in consumer arbitrations   CCP §1281.92

ARBITRATORS—Cont.
Disqualification —Cont.
   Judges' employment or prospective employment as a dispute resolution neutral as basis for disqualification of judges   CCP §§170.1, 1281.9
Ethics standards   CCP §1281.85, CRC ArbEthicsStand 1 to CRC ArbEthicsStand 17
   Applicability of provisions   CRC ArbEthicsStand 3
   Bequests
      Refusal   CRC ArbEthicsStand 11
   Compensation   CRC ArbEthicsStand 16
   Conducting proceedings   CRC ArbEthicsStand 13
   Confidentiality   CRC ArbEthicsStand 15
   Construction of provisions   CRC ArbEthicsStand 1
   Consumer arbitrations done by provider organizations, disclosures   CRC ArbEthicsStand 8
   Contents of rules of court   CRC 1.4
   Continuing duty to disclose   CRC ArbEthicsStand 7
   Definitions   CRC ArbEthicsStand 2
   Disclosures   CRC ArbEthicsStand 7
      Consumer arbitrations done by provider organizations   CRC ArbEthicsStand 8
      Duty of arbitrator as to matters disclosed   CRC ArbEthicsStand 8
   Disqualification   CRC ArbEthicsStand 10
   Duration of ethical duty   CRC ArbEthicsStand 4
   Effective date   CRC ArbEthicsStand 3
   Ex parte communications   CRC ArbEthicsStand 14
   Fairness of process   CRC ArbEthicsStand 5
   Favors
      Refusal   CRC ArbEthicsStand 11
   Future professional relationships
      Duties and limitations   CRC ArbEthicsStand 12
   Gifts
      Refusal   CRC ArbEthicsStand 11
   Integrity of process   CRC ArbEthicsStand 5
   Intent of provisions   CRC ArbEthicsStand 1
   Judges as private arbitrators   CRCSupp JudEthicsCanon 4
   Marketing   CRC ArbEthicsStand 17
   Purpose of provisions   CRC ArbEthicsStand 1
   Refusal of appointment
      When required   CRC ArbEthicsStand 6
   Soliciting business   CRC ArbEthicsStand 17
   Time for disclosure   CRC ArbEthicsStand 7
Ex parte communications with
   Judicial arbitration   CRC 3.820
Immunity from civil liability   CCP §1297.119
Intervenors   CCP §1281.2
Judge serving as
   Employment or prospective employment as a dispute resolution neutral as basis for disqualification of judges   CCP §§170.1, 1281.9
Judicial arbitration (See **JUDICIAL ARBITRATION**)
Misconduct of   CCP §1286.2
Neutral arbitrators, authority of   CCP §§1282 to 1282.8
Postponement of hearings   CCP §1286.2
Pretrial arbitration (See **JUDICIAL ARBITRATION**)
Qualifications   CCP §1281.6
Reports
   Data collection and reports available to public   CCP §1281.96
Standards for neutral arbitrators
   Ethics standards for neutral arbitrators   CRC ArbEthicsStand 1 to CRC ArbEthicsStand 17
Unanimous agreement   CCP §1282

ARCHITECTS
Bond required to secure costs in action against   CCP §1029.5
Certificate of merit in negligence action against   CCP §§411.35, 430.10
Construction defects, actions for   CC §§895 to 945.5 (See **CONSTRUCTION DEFECTS, ACTIONS FOR**)
Design professionals' liens   CC §§8300 to 8319 (See **LIENS**)
Indemnity against loss from design defects   CC §§2783, 2784
   Public agencies, contracts with   CC §2782.8
Latent deficiencies in planning or construction of improvement to real property, statute of limitation for damages for   CCP §337.15
Late payment penalty in lieu of interest, contract provision for   CC §3319
Liens   CC §§8300 to 8319 (See **LIENS**)
Mechanics' liens   CC §§8000 to 9566 (See **MECHANICS' LIENS**)
Patent deficiencies in planning or construction of improvement to real property, statute of limitation for injury or death from   CCP §337.1
Public agencies, payment schedule for   CC §3320
Stipulated judgments in construction defect actions   CCP §664.7
Subcontractor design professionals, payments to   CC §3321
Withholding disputed amount   CC §§3320, 3321

AREIAS CREDIT CARD FULL DISCLOSURE ACT CC §§1748.10, 1748.11

AREIAS RETAIL INSTALLMENT ACCOUNT FULL DISCLOSURE ACT CC §§1810.20, 1810.21

AREIAS-ROBBINS CHARGE CARD FULL DISCLOSURE ACT CC §§1748.20 to 1748.23

ARGUMENT AND COMMENT OF COUNSEL
Appellate division of superior court
    Transfer from division to court of appeals
        Issues to be considered   CRC 8.1012
Appellate rules, superior court appeals
    Oral argument   CRC 8.885
        Applicability of provisions   CRC 8.880
        Infraction case appeals   CRC 8.929
Closing argument (See **CLOSING ARGUMENT**)
Court reporters to take down all arguments of prosecuting attorney   CCP §269
Judgment by stipulation   CCP §665
Order of proceedings   CCP §607
Rules on appeal
    Supreme court and courts of appeal (See **APPELLATE RULES, SUPREME COURT AND COURTS OF APPEAL**)

ARMED FORCES (See **MILITARY**)

ARMENIA
Limitations period for action by Armenian genocide victims
    Banks and other financial institutions   CCP §354.45
    Insurers, actions against   CCP §354.4

ARRAIGNMENT   CRC 4.100
Court reporters to take down all arraignments, pleas and sentences in felony cases   CCP §269
Criminal case management, trial courts   CRC 10.951
Hearsay evidence, sufficient cause based upon   Ev §1203.1
Judicial holiday, proceedings on   CCP §134
Time for arraignment   CRC 4.110

ARREST
Bench warrants to secure attendance of witnesses   CCP §§1993, 1994
    Fee for processing civil warrant   Gov §26744.5
    Release of arrested witness   CCP §1993.1
        Failure of released witness to appear   CCP §1993.2
Booking
    Commercial use of booking photographs   CC §1798.91.1
Children and minors
    Dependency proceedings   CRC 5.526
    Sealing arrest records of juvenile delinquents
        Order on prosecutor request for access   CRCAppx A
        Prosecuting attorney request to access sealed juvenile case files   CRC 5.860
Claims against law enforcement officers (See **CLAIMS AGAINST PUBLIC ENTITIES AND EMPLOYEES**)
Contempt proceedings   CCP §§1212, 1214, 1220
Courthouses
    Civil arrest at courthouse
        Judicial officer's power to protect privilege from civil arrest at court house   CCP §177
        Restrictions on arrest at courthouse of person attending court proceeding or attending to legal business in courthouse   CC §43.54
Credit reporting (See **CREDIT REPORTING**)
Debt collectors threatening   CC §1788.10
Dogs used in police or military work, injuries inflicted by   CC §§3342, 3342.5
Employment investigations, notification of subsequent arrests
    Attorneys, fingerprinting   CRC 9.9.5
Examination proceedings for purposes of enforcement of judgments, failure to appear at   CCP §708.170
Informer, disclosure of   Ev §1042
Marital privilege
    Knowledge of prior arrest   Ev §972
Presumption of official duty regularly performed   Ev §664
Sealing and destruction of arrest records
    Judicial council legal forms   CRCAppx A
    Juvenile records
        Order on prosecutor request for access   CRCAppx A
        Prosecuting attorney request to access sealed juvenile case files   CRC 5.860
Sheriff's fees for serving bench warrants   Gov §26744

ARREST—Cont.
Small claims court judgment, sanctions for failure to disclose assets for purposes of enforcement of   CCP §116.830
Warrants
    Bench warrants to secure attendance of witnesses   CCP §§1993, 1994
        Failure of released witness to appear   CCP §1993.2
        Fee for processing civil warrant   Gov §26744.5
        Release of arrested witness   CCP §1993.1
    Dependent child proceedings   CRC 5.526
    Juvenile wardship proceedings
        COVID-19, emergency rule   CRCAppx I Emer Rule 7
    Liability for arrest based on warrant regular on its face   CC §43.55
    Minors, dependency or wardship proceedings   CRC 5.526
    Parents or guardians, dependency or wardship proceedings   CRC 5.526
    Presumption of official duty regularly performed, effect of lack of warrant on   Ev §664
    Seal of court, documents requiring   CCP §153
    Witnesses, bench warrants to secure attendance of   CCP §§1993, 1994
        Failure of released witness to appear   CCP §1993.2
        Fee for processing civil warrant   Gov §26744.5
        Release of arrested witness   CCP §1993.1
Witnesses, bench warrants to secure attendance of   CCP §§1993, 1994
    Fee for processing civil warrant   Gov §26744.5
    Release of arrested witness   CCP §1993.1
        Failure of released witness to appear   CCP §1993.2

ART AND ARTISTS
California Art Preservation Act   CC §987
Charitable organizations exempt from disclosure requirements for sale   CC §1742.6
Commissions, right to   CC §986
Consignment of works to dealers   CC §§1738.5, 1738.6
Copyrights for reproductions of fine art   CC §982
Dealers (See **ART DEALERS**)
Defined   CC §§986, 1738
Destruction or defacement of art works, liability for   CC §987
Enforcement of judgment, exemption from   CC §986, CCP §704.040
Expropriated art
    Holocaust
        Limitation of actions   CCP §338
    Political persecution
        Limitation of actions   CCP §338.2
Holocaust-era artwork
    Action to recover Holocaust-era artwork   CCP §354.3
Infringement, action for   CCP §429.30
Injunctive relief to preserve or restore integrity of fine art work   CC §989
Literary property (See **LITERARY PROPERTY**)
Minor's contracts for artistic services   Fam §§6750 to 6753
Nazi Germany
    Action to recover Holocaust-era artwork   CCP §354.3
Ownership
    Generally   CC §980
    Proportion of   CC §981
    Publication, dedication by   CC §983
    Reservation of ownership rights in reproduced, displayed, or performed work of art   CC §988
    Transfer of right of reproduction   CC §982
Porcelain painting as fine art   CC §997
Residual rights   CC §986
Retroactive laws affecting   CC §1738.9
Sales, general provisions for   CC §§1740 to 1745.5
Sound recordings (See **RECORDING OF SOUND**)
Statutes of limitation
    Sale of fine prints, limitation statute for action involving   CC §1745
    Theft of articles of historic or artistic importance   CCP §338
Waiver of rights of artists to dealers   CC §1738.8

ART DEALERS
Bona fide purchasers, sales to   CC §1738.7
Commissions for sales, artists' rights to   CC §986
Consignment of works to   CC §§1738.5, 1738.6
Definition   CC §1738
Requirements for sales by   CC §§1738.5, 1738.6
Retroactive laws affecting   CC §1738.9
Waiver of rights by artist to   CC §1738.8

ARTICLES
Conflicting articles in codes   CC §§23.5, 23.6

ARTIFICIAL INSEMINATION (See **ASSISTED REPRODUCTION**)

ARTISAN'S LIENS
Generally   CC §§3051, 3051a
Alternative lien-sale procedure for charges not exceeding $150   CC §3052b

ARTS COUNCIL
Missing artists, money owed to   CC §986

ASBESTOS
Depositions
    Time limits for witness examination
        Mesothelioma or silicosis, actions involving   CCP §2025.295
School district's liability for exposure to   Gov §905.5
Statute of limitation based on exposure to   CCP §340.2

ASIAN LANGUAGES
Contracts in Chinese, Tagalog, Vietnamese or Korean languages   CC §1632
Mortgages of residential property, foreign language summaries of terms   CC §1632.5

AS IS SALES
Generally   CC §§1790 to 1793, 1795.7
Defined   CC §1791.3

ASSAULT AND BATTERY
Anesthetized persons, sexual battery against
    Statute of limitations on sexual assault damages   CCP §340.16
Breach of peace   CCP §1209
Domestic violence (See **DOMESTIC VIOLENCE**)
Hearsay exception for statement concerning infliction or threat of physical injury upon declarant   Ev §1370
Injunctions
    Dependency proceeding
        Forms for firearm relinquishment   CRCAppx A
Institutionalized persons, sexual battery against
    Statute of limitations on sexual assault damages   CCP §340.16
Invasion of privacy
    Assault with intent to capture visual image or sound recording   CC §1708.8
Medically incapacitated persons, sexual battery against
    Statute of limitations on sexual assault damages   CCP §340.16
Postsecondary educational institutions
    Orders against violence threatened on campus or facility
        COVID-19, emergency rule   CRCAppx I Emer Rule 8
        Requests for protective orders   CRC 3.1160
    Protection orders against violence threatened on campus or facility   CCP §527.85
        California law enforcement telecommunications (CLETS) information form, confidentiality and use of information   CRC 1.51, CRCAppx A
        Judicial council legal forms   CRCAppx A
        Memorandum in support of petition not required   CRC 3.1114
Prostitution, evidence
    Extortion, serious felony, assault, domestic violence, human trafficking, sexual battery or stalking, victims or witnesses
        Inadmissibility of evidence of prostitution in prosecution for prostitution   Ev §1162
Sedated persons, sexual battery against
    Statute of limitations on sexual assault damages   CCP §340.16
Sex offenses (See **SEX OFFENSES**)
Sexual battery
    Statute of limitations on sexual assault damages   CCP §340.16
Statutes of limitation   CCP §335.1
    Torture, genocide, crimes against humanity, etc   CCP §354.8

ASSAULT WEAPONS
Nuisance abatement
    Unlawful weapons or ammunition purpose   CC §3485
Unlawful detainer actions
    Illegal weapons or ammunition on real property   CC §3485

ASSEMBLY
Labor disputes, limitation on enjoining acts relating to   CCP §527.3

ASSESSMENTS
Commercial and industrial common interest developments   CC §§6800 to 6828
    (See **COMMERCIAL AND INDUSTRIAL COMMON INTEREST DEVELOPMENTS**)
Common interest developments (See **COMMON INTEREST DEVELOPMENTS**)
Taxation (See **TAXATION**)

ASSIGNMENT FOR BENEFIT OF CREDITORS
Attachment (See **ATTACHMENT**)
Claim filing period for creditors   CCP §1802
Defined   CCP §§493.010, 1800
Exempt property   CCP §1801
Insolvency defined   CCP §1800
Liens
    Generally   CCP §§493.010 to 493.060
    Judicial liens   CCP §1800
Notice to assignor's creditors and other parties interest, requirement of   CCP §1802
Occupation of premises under   CC §1954.05
Partnership property   CCP §1800
Preferences, recovery of   CCP §1800
Priorities
    Generally   CCP §493.010
    Wage claims   CCP §§1204, 1204.5
Recovery of preferences   CCP §1800
Subrogation of assignee's rights under liens terminated by   CCP §493.060
Transfers by assignor, assignee recovering   CCP §1800
Wage claims, priority of   CCP §§1204, 1204.5

ASSIGNMENT OF CASES
Judges (See **JUDGES**)

ASSIGNMENT OF WAGES
Conservatee, payment of support to   Pro §3088
Deeds of trust and mortgages
    Modification or workout plan to avoid foreclosure
        Disabled person victim of prohibited acts, punishment   CC §2944.8
        Prohibited acts   CC §2944.7
        Senior citizen victim of prohibited acts, punishment   CC §2944.8
        Statute of limitations to enforce protections   CC §2944.10
Ex parte proceedings
    Termination of order   Fam §4324.5
Family support forms   CRCAppxs A (CRCFL-430), (CRCFL-435), (CRCFL-455)
    Hearings
        Request for hearing   CRCAppx A (CRCFL-450)
Forms, Judicial Council   CRCAppxs A (CRCFL-430), (CRCFL-435)
Mortgage foreclosure consultants taking   CC §2945.4
Support orders, enforcement of (See **EARNINGS ASSIGNMENT FOR SUPPORT**)

ASSIGNMENTS
Generally   CC §955.1
Aircraft liens   CCP §1208.63
Automobiles (See **AUTOMOBILES**)
Benefit of creditors (See **ASSIGNMENT FOR BENEFIT OF CREDITORS**)
Child support (See **CHILD SUPPORT**)
Commercial and industrial common interest developments
    Assessments
        Assignment of right to collect payments   CC §6826
Common interest developments
    Collection of assessments
        Assignment or pledge of right to collect   CC §5735
Dance studio contracts, defenses against assignee of   CC §1812.56
Earnings assignment for support (See **EARNINGS ASSIGNMENT FOR SUPPORT**)
Enforcement of judgments (See **ENFORCEMENT OF JUDGMENTS**)
Estates, distribution
    Beneficiary's interest, assignment   Pro §11604.5
Health studio contracts, defenses against assignee of   CC §1812.88
Judgment, recording assignment of   CCP §673
Leases
    Generally (See **LEASES**)
    Creditors, assignment for benefit of (See **ASSIGNMENT FOR BENEFIT OF CREDITORS**)
    Landlord-tenant relationship (See **LANDLORD AND TENANT**)
Livestock service liens   CC §3080.22
Mortgages (See **TRUST DEEDS AND MORTGAGES**)
Nonnegotiable instruments, transfer of   CC §955
Oil and gas liens   CCP §1203.64
Real property sales contract of decedent, assignment of   Pro §10314
Retail installment sales contracts (See **RETAIL INSTALLMENT SALES**)
Right to payment due judgment debtor, assignment of   CCP §§708.510 to 708.560
Seller assisted marketing plan   CC §1812.211
Small claims court, restriction on assignee filing claim in   CCP §116.420
Support (See **CHILD SUPPORT**)
Surety bonds, assignment of cause of action for enforcement of liability on   CCP §996.430

ASSIGNMENTS—Cont.
Wages
    Assignment of wages generally (See **ASSIGNMENT OF WAGES**)
    Support, assignment for (See **EARNINGS ASSIGNMENT FOR SUPPORT**)

ASSISTED REPRODUCTION
Embryo donation
    Effect on parent-child relationship   Fam §7613
    Renunciation of legal interest in embryos
        Agreement between non-married persons sharing legal control over disposition   Fam §7613
Father of resulting child   Fam §7613
Forms for assisted reproduction   Fam §7613.5
Gestational carriers, agreements
    Contents   Fam §7962
    Jurisdiction   Fam §7620
    Venue   Fam §7620
Parent-child relationship, effect on   Fam §7613
Renunciation of legal interest in embryos
    Agreement between non-married persons sharing legal control over disposition   Fam §7613
Semen not provided through physician or licensed sperm bank
    Parental relationship of donor and child   Fam §7613
Surrogacy or donor facilitators   Fam §§7960, 7961
Unauthorized use or misuse of sperm, ova or embryo
    Civil action for damages   CC §1708.5.6
Uniform parentage act   Fam §7613
    Assisted reproduction
        Defined   Fam §7606
        Forms for assisted reproduction   Fam §7613.5
    Vacation or setting aside of judgment
        Effect of provisions on paternity determinations   Fam §7648.9

ASSISTIVE DEVICES
Warranties on   CC §§1791, 1791.1, 1792.2, 1793.02

ASSOCIATIONS
Appellate rules, supreme court and courts of appeal
    Briefs
        Certificates of interested entities or persons   CRC 8.208, 8.361, 8.488, CRCSupp 1st AppDist
Attorney professional conduct
    Law firms and associations generally   ProfC 5.1 to 5.6
    Organization or entity as client   ProfC 1.13
Attorneys
    Registered in-house counsel   CRC 9.46
        Fingerprinting of special admission attorneys   CRC 9.9.5
Camping clubs, regulation of membership   CC §§1812.300 to 1812.309
Capacity to sue or be sued   CCP §369.5
Certiorari
    Briefs
        Certificates of interested entities or persons   CRC 8.488, CRCSupp 1st AppDist
Common interest developments (See **COMMON INTEREST DEVELOPMENTS**)
Dating services (See **DATING SERVICES**)
Enforcement of judgments (See **ENFORCEMENT OF JUDGMENTS**)
Good faith improver provisions, applicability of   CCP §871.2
Grazing associations, sale of decedent's land to   Pro §10207
In-house counsel
    Registered in-house counsel   CRC 9.46
        Fingerprinting of special admission attorneys   CRC 9.9.5
Judges' membership in organizations, Code of Judicial Ethics provisions concerning   CRCSupp JudEthicsCanon 2
Judgment based on personal liability of member   CCP §369.5
Lessees' associations   CC §1942.5
Mandate
    Briefs
        Certificates of interested entities or persons   CRC 8.488, CRCSupp 1st AppDist
Marital status, denial of credit because of   CC §1812.32
Pasture associations, sale of decedent's land to   Pro §10207
Professional societies (See **PROFESSIONAL SOCIETIES**)
Prohibition, writ of
    Briefs
        Certificates of interested entities or persons   CRC 8.488, CRCSupp 1st AppDist
Public trail, enjoining closure of   CCP §731.5
Registered in-house counsel   CRC 9.46
    Fingerprinting of special admission attorneys   CRC 9.9.5

ASSOCIATIONS—Cont.
Service of process
    Generally   CCP §416.40
    Individual member, service on   CCP §§369.5, 412.30
    Manner of service of business organizations
        Leaving summons and complaint at office, mailing copy   CCP §415.95
    Summons   CCP §412.30
Tenants' associations   CC §1942.5
Unclaimed deposits and payments escheated   CCP §1517
Venue in actions against   CCP §§395.2, 395.5
Weight loss centers (See **WEIGHT LOSS PROGRAMS**)
Wills, taking under   Pro §6102

ASYLUMS (See **MENTAL HOSPITALS**)

ATHLETICS
Anabolic steroids, posting warning statements regarding   CC §1812.97 (Title 2.55 version of section)
Autographed memorabilia
    Certificates of authenticity   CC §1739.7
    Sale   CC §1739.7
Easement for use of land   CC §801
Health studios services contracts (See **HEALTH STUDIO SERVICES CONTRACTS**)
Minor's contract for services as participant or player   Fam §§6750 to 6753
Owner's liability for recreational land   CC §846

AT-ISSUE MEMORANDUM
Case management
    Civil rules   CRC 3.700 to 3.771 (See **CIVIL RULES**)
    Class actions   CRC 3.760 to 3.771 (See **CLASS ACTIONS**)
    Complex litigation   CRC 3.750, 3.751
    Coordination of actions
        Differential case management rules, applicability   CRC 3.712
        Initial case management conference   CRC 3.541
        Telephone appearance at case management conferences   CRC 3.670
    Criminal actions and proceedings   CRC 10.950 to 10.953
        Judicial council legal forms   CRCAppx A
    False claims act cases   CRC 2.573
    Judges
        Case management and delay reduction of trial, consideration of   CRC JudAdminStand 2.1
    Judicial administration standards
        Case management and delay reduction procedures   CRC JudAdminStand 2.1, CRC JudAdminStand 2.2, CRCAppx A
    Judicial arbitration, case management conference   CRC 3.812
        Telephone appearance at case management conferences   CRC 3.670
    Mistrial
        Short cause cases, case management   CRC 3.735
    Pretrial conferences, case management   CRC 3.722, 3.723
        Complex cases   CRC 3.750
        Setting trial date   CRC 3.729
        Subjects considered   CRC 3.727
        Telephone appearances   CCP §367.6, CRC 3.670
    Short causes
        Case management   CRC 3.735
    Trial court delay reduction
        Case disposition time goals   CRC JudAdminStand 2.2
        Civil case management   CRC 3.700 to 3.771
        Plans   Gov §68603

ATTACHMENT
Account debtor defined   CCP §481.020
Accounts receivable
    Generally   CCP §488.470
    Defined   CCP §481.030
Additional writs
    Application for   CCP §§484.310, 484.520
    Exemption claims   CCP §§484.340, 484.350
    Ex parte procedure   CCP §§485.510 to 485.540
    Findings   CCP §484.370
    Foreign corporations applying for   CCP §§492.060, 492.070
    Notices of action on   CCP §484.340
    Oaths, applications under   CCP §484.320
    Opposition to exemption claims   CCP §484.360
    Other states applying for   CCP §§492.060, 492.070
    Process   CCP §484.330
    Service of papers   CCP §484.330
Adverse interest claim by third party   CCP §491.170

ATTACHMENT—Cont.
Affidavits
    Additional writs, support in ex parte procedure   CCP §485.530
    Applications support by   CCP §§484.030, 484.510, 485.210
    Exemption claims, support of   CCP §§484.050, 484.070, 484.350
    Facts, use of   CCP §482.040
    Foreign corporations   CCP §492.020
    Injury as grounds for issuing writ   CCP §485.010
    Opposition to exemption claims   CCP §§484.070, 484.360
    Original writ, supporting application for   CCP §484.030
    Other states   CCP §492.020
    Protective orders, supporting applications for   CCP §486.010
Alias writs   CCP §482.090
Amount in controversy
    Generally   CCP §483.010
    Appeal for increase in bonds   CCP §489.410
    Bonds   CCP §489.220
Amount secured by   CCP §§483.015, 483.020
Appeals
    Generally   CCP §§904.1, 904.2
    Bonds   CCP §§489.410, 489.420, 921
    Undertaking, execution of   CCP §921
Appearance requirement   CCP §§491.140, 491.160
Applications
    Generally   CCP §484.020
    Additional writs   CCP §§484.310, 485.520
    Affidavits supporting   CCP §§484.030, 484.510, 485.210
    Attorneys' fees, estimate of   CCP §482.110
    Ex parte procedure   CCP §§484.510, 485.210
    Foreign corporations   CCP §492.020
    Nonresident attachment   CCP §§492.020, 492.070
    Notices on   CCP §§484.050, 484.340
    Oaths, executing under   CCP §§484.020, 484.320
    Original writs   CCP §484.010
    Protective orders   CCP §§486.010, 486.030, 489.320
    Statement and description in   CCP §§484.020, 484.320
    Undertaking substituted for attachment   CCP §489.310
Arbitration agreements, effect of filing for attachment orders by party subject to   CCP §1281.8
Assignment for benefit of creditors
    Generally   CCP §493.010
    Release of attachment on   CCP §493.040
Attorneys' fees
    Costs generally (See within this heading, **"Costs and fees"**)
Automobiles
    Going business, attachment of equipment   CCP §488.385
    Levy of vehicle, method   CCP §488.425
Availability   CCP §483.010
Bailee, attaching goods in possession   CCP §488.365
Bankruptcy
    Generally   CCP §493.010
    Applications for   CCP §§484.020, 484.320
    Reinstatement of terminated attachment   CCP §493.050
    Release of   CCP §493.040
    Termination of   CCP §493.030
Banks
    Definition of financial institution   CCP §481.113
    Deposits generally (See within this heading, **"Deposits"**)
Bonds
    Amount in controversy   CCP §489.220
    Appeals on   CCP §§489.410, 489.420, 921
    Approval of   CCP §489.060
    Delivery of   CCP §488.740
    Governing law   CCP §489.010
    Notice   CCP §489.230
    Protective orders, filing before issuance of   CCP §489.210
    Release of   CCP §§489.310, 489.320
    Right to attach order requiring undertaking   CCP §917.65
    Substituting undertaking for attachment   CCP §489.310
    Wrongful attachments, liability on   CCP §490.020
Burden of proof   CCP §482.100
Ceasing of force of   CCP §488.510
Chattel paper
    Generally   CCP §§487.010, 488.435
    Defined   CCP §481.040
Checks issued under temporary protective order, effect of   CCP §486.060
Citation   CCP §482.010
Cities   CCP §481.200
Claims against estate involving   Pro §9304
Commercial coach, attachment of   CCP §488.425
Compromise of attachment, consent of plaintiff to   CCP §491.440

ATTACHMENT—Cont.
Conforming with instructions, liability of levying officer for   CCP §488.140
Consent of plaintiff to settlement of pending action   CCP §491.440
Contempt for failing to transfer possession   CCP §482.080
Contents of writ   CCP §488.010
Copy of original attachment notice sufficing as notice   CCP §488.065
Corporation property subject to   CCP §487.010
Costs and fees
    Availability of   CCP §482.110
    Award of costs to prevailing party   CCP §1033.5
    Creditor's suit   CCP §491.370
    Defined   CCP §481.055
    Garnishee's memorandum   CCP §488.610
    Property keeper fees   Gov §26726
        Recovery of costs by prevailing party   CCP §1033.5
    Sheriff's fees (See within this heading, **"Sheriff's fees"**)
    Superior court fees, specified services   Gov §70626
Cotton   CCP §481.110
Creditor's suit for   CCP §§491.310 to 491.370
Credit unions
    Financial institutions generally (See within this heading, **"Financial institutions"**)
Crops (See within this heading, **"Farm products, timber or minerals"**)
Damages
    Generally   CCP §§490.060, 493.040
    Subordinate judicial duty, action as   CCP §482.060
Death
    Deposit account, pay-on-death provision in   CCP §488.455
    Party to action, effect of death of   CCP §488.510
    Personalty of decedent's estate, attachment of interest in   CCP §488.485
Debts   CCP §481.020
Defense, waiver of   CCP §484.110
Definitions   CCP §§481.010 to 481.225, 488.300, 488.600
Denial of claim of exemption   CCP §484.530
Deposits
    Generally   CCP §§487.010, 488.455
    Defined   CCP §481.080
    Expenses of attachment, deposit for   CCP §488.050
    Safe deposit box, property in   CCP §§488.460, 488.465
Determination of court, effect of   CCP §484.100
Direction of writ to county levying officer   CCP §488.030
Discovery rights of plaintiff allowed under attachment order   CCP §485.230
Districts   CCP §481.200
Duty of levying officer   CCP §488.020
Dwelling attachment of personalty used as   CCP §488.415
Earnings
    Garnishment (See **GARNISHMENT**)
    Salaries and wages generally (See within this heading, **"Salaries and wages"**)
Endorsement of instrument for payment   CCP §488.710
Entry of judgment in pending action, consent of plaintiff for   CCP §491.440
Equipment
    Generally   CCP §487.010
    Defined   CCP §481.100
    Going business   CCP §488.375
Excessive amount of property interest, effect of   CCP §§482.120, 488.720
Excessive levy   CCP §482.120
Exemption
    Generally   CCP §§485.010, 487.020
    Affidavits supporting claims of   CCP §§484.050, 484.070, 484.350
    Art dealers holding money for payment of artists   CC §986
    Bonuses   CCP §487.020
    Compensation   CCP §487.020
    Denial of claim   CCP §484.530
    Homesteads   CCP §487.025
    Notice of opposition to claims of   CCP §§484.070, 484.360
    Original writs, claims in   CCP §§484.050, 484.070
    Pending action, defendant's application for exemption from lien in   CCP §491.470
    Points and authorities supporting claims of   CCP §§484.070, 484.350, 484.360
    Procedure for   CCP §§482.100, 487.030
    Salaries   CCP §§486.060, 487.020
    Subordinate judicial duty, contested claim as   CCP §482.060
    Time for claiming   CCP §485.610
    Veterans' federal disability benefits
        Exemptions from attachment and other legal process   CCP §483.013
    Wrongful attachments   CCP §490.010
Ex parte procedure
    Additional writs in   CCP §§485.510 to 485.540
    Affidavits supporting applications for   CCP §§484.510, 485.210

ATTACHMENT—Cont.
  Ex parte procedure—Cont.
    Application for   CCP §§484.510, 484.520, 485.210
    Exemptions   CCP §§482.100, 484.530
    Findings   CCP §§484.520, 485.220, 485.540
    Injury as grounds for issuing writ   CCP §485.010
    Protective orders, effect of ex parte application on   CCP §486.100
    Quash, motion to   CCP §485.240
    Release, motion for   CCP §485.240
    Setting aside, motion for   CCP §485.240
  Extension of lien   CCP §488.510
  Farm products, timber or minerals
    Generally   CCP §§481.110, 487.010
    Going business, attachment of farm products of   CCP §§488.395, 488.405
    Levy procedure   CCP §488.325
    Transfer of property   CCP §486.050
  Fees (See within this heading, **"Costs and fees"**)
  Filing, plaintiff requesting secrecy of   CCP §482.050
  Final money judgments   CCP §488.480
  Financial institutions
    Defined   CCP §481.113
    Deposits with (See within this heading, **"Deposits"**)
  Findings
    Generally   CCP §§484.090, 484.100
    Additional writs   CCP §§484.370, 485.540
    Amount attaching   CCP §492.090
    Ex parte procedure   CCP §§484.520, 485.220
    Foreign corporations, grounds for issuance of writ   CCP §492.030
    Other states, grounds for issuance of writ   CCP §492.030
    Protective orders   CCP §486.020
  Foreign attachment (See within this heading, **"Other states"**)
  Forms
    Judicial council legal forms   CRCAppx A
  Furniture, use determining wrongful attachment   CCP §490.010
  Garnishment (See **GARNISHMENT**)
  General intangibles
    Generally   CCP §488.470
    Defined   CCP §481.115
  Going business
    Equipment, attachment of   CCP §488.375
    Farm products, attachment of   CCP §488.395
    Inventory, attachment of   CCP §§488.395, 488.405
    Vehicle, attachment of   CCP §488.385
  Hearings
    Continuance of   CCP §484.080
    Findings   CCP §§484.090, 484.100, 484.370, 484.520
    Notices on   CCP §§484.040, 484.050, 484.340, 1005
    Original writs   CCP §484.040
    Service of notice of application and hearing for writ, time for   CCP §1005
    Time   CCP §482.100
  Homesteads, right to attach   CCP §487.025
  Household purposes, claim based on sale, services or loan for   CCP §483.010
  Injunctive relief, effect on   CCP §482.020
  Insolvency (See within this heading, **"Bankruptcy"**)
  Instructions
    Conforming with instructions, liability of levying officer for   CCP §488.140
    Name and address of plaintiff in   CCP §488.040
    Writing, requirement for   CCP §488.030
  Instruments
    Generally   CCP §488.440
    Defined   CCP §481.117
    Endorsement and presentation of instrument for payment   CCP §488.710
    Negotiable instruments   CCP §§487.010, 488.445
  Intervention by plaintiff in pending action   CCP §491.430
  Inventory
    Generally   CCP §§481.120, 487.010
    Going business, attaching inventory of   CCP §§488.395, 488.405
    Return of writ including   CCP §488.130
    Transfer of property   CCP §486.050
  Issuance of writ
    Notice of opposition against right to attach orders, filing of   CCP §§484.060, 484.070
  Joinder of defendant   CCP §491.320
  Judicial and subordinate judicial duties   CCP §482.060
  Judicial Council forms and rules, generally   CCP §482.030
  Jurisdiction for third party examination   CCP §491.150
  Jurors, attachment of   CCP §209
  Jury trial on creditor's suit   CCP §491.350
  Law and motion rules, applicability   CRC 3.1103

ATTACHMENT—Cont.
  Levy
    By registered process server   CCP §488.080
    Exemption generally (See within this heading, **"Exemption"**)
    General provisions   CCP §§488.010 to 488.140
    Liens generally (See within this heading, **"Liens"**)
    Methods of levy   CCP §§488.300 to 488.485
    Temporary protective order
      Protective orders generally (See within this heading, **"Protective orders"**)
    Third persons, duties and liabilities after levy   CCP §§488.600 to 488.620
  Liens
    Generally   CCP §483.010
    Continuation of lien on transfer or encumbrance of property   CCP §491.200
    Extension of   CCP §488.510
    Failure to serve notice, effect of   CCP §488.120
    Homesteads   CCP §487.025
    Levying officer, possessing lien of   CCP §488.100
    Mortgages
      Availability of attachment on claim secured by mortgage   CCP §483.010
      Foreclosure action, viability of attachment   CCP §483.012
    Pending actions generally (See within this heading, **"Pending actions"**)
    Priority of   CCP §488.500
    Protective order's effect on   CCP §§486.110, 493.030 to 493.050
    Termination of   CCP §§493.030 to 493.050
    Third parties holding   CCP §491.110
    Trust deeds
      Foreclosure action, viability of attachment in conjunction with   CCP §483.012
      General provision concerning availability of attachment on claim secured by mortgage   CCP §483.010
  Livestock (See within this heading, **"Farm products, timber or minerals"**)
  Logs (See within this heading, **"Farm products, timber or minerals"**)
  Mechanics' lien claimant, right to writ   CC §8468
  Memorandum of garnishee, request for   CCP §488.610
  Milk   CCP §481.110
  Minerals (See within this heading, **"Farm products, timber or minerals"**)
  Mobilehomes
    Going business, attaching mobilehome of   CCP §488.385
    Method of levy, generally   CCP §488.425
  Money judgment, finality of attachment of   CCP §488.480
  Mortgages
    Foreclosure action, viability of attachment in conjunction with   CCP §483.012
    General provision concerning availability of attachment on claim secured by mortgage   CCP §483.010
  Motions
    Ex parte proceedings   CCP §485.240
    Quash, motion to   CCP §492.050
      Ex parte procedure   CCP §485.240
    Time for service of notice of application and hearing for writ   CCP §1005
    Vacation   CCP §492.050
      Ex parte procedure   CCP §485.240
  Motor vehicles
    Going business concern, attachment of equipment of   CCP §488.385
    Method of levy of vehicle   CCP §488.425
  Negotiable instruments   CCP §§487.010, 488.445
  Nonresident attachment (See within this heading, **"Other states"**)
  Notices
    Generally   CCP §488.060
    Applications   CCP §§484.050, 484.340
    Bonds   CCP §489.230
    Copies of original sufficing as   CCP §488.065
    Exemption claim, notice of opposition to   CCP §§484.070, 484.360
    Hearings   CCP §§484.050, 484.340
    Issuance of right to attach order, notice opposing   CCP §§484.050, 484.060
    Oaths   CCP §§481.010, 484.020, 484.320
    Opposition against right to attach orders, filing notice of   CCP §§484.060, 484.070
    Real property, attaching of   CCP §488.315
    Release, request for   CCP §493.040
    Service of   CCP §488.305
    Time for service of notice of application and hearing for writ   CCP §1005
  Opposition against right to attach orders, notice of   CCP §§484.060, 484.070
  Original writs
    Affidavits supporting applications for   CCP §484.030
    Application for   CCP §484.010
    Continuance of hearings   CCP §484.080
    Exemption claims   CCP §§484.050, 484.070

ATTACHMENT—Cont.
Original writs—Cont.
- Findings CCP §§484.090, 484.100
- Hearings for CCP §§484.040, 484.080
- Notices of action on CCP §484.050
- Oath, application under CCP §§484.020, 484.320
- Opposition to issuance of CCP §§484.050, 484.060
- Process CCP §484.040
- Service of papers CCP §484.040

Other states
- Generally CCP §492.010
- Additional writs CCP §§492.060, 492.070
- Affidavits supporting applications CCP §492.020
- Application requirements CCP §§492.020, 492.070
- Denial of order CCP §492.030
- Findings CCP §§492.030, 492.090
- Foreign-money claims CCP §676.11
- Levy procedure CCP §492.040
- Quash, motion to CCP §492.050
- Release, motion for CCP §492.050
- Setting aside order motion for CCP §492.050

Partnerships' property subject to CCP §487.010
Payment, presentation of instruments for CCP §488.710
Pending actions
- Generally CCP §488.475
- Consent of plaintiff, requirement for CCP §491.440
- Contents of notice of lien CCP §491.420
- Exemption from lien, application by defendant for CCP §491.470
- Intervention by plaintiff CCP §491.430
- Judgments in CCP §§491.415, 491.460
- Procedure for obtaining lien by notice of lien CCP §491.410

Perishables
- Protective orders generally (See within this heading, **"Protective orders"**)

Points and authorities supporting claims for exemptions CCP §§484.070, 484.350, 484.360
Prejudgment attachment
- Sealing records
  - Delayed public disclosure CRC 2.580

Presentation of instrument for payment CCP §488.710
Priorities and preferences
- Attachment lien, priority of CCP §488.500
- Earnings assignment order for support Fam §5243
- Wage claims CCP §§1206 to 1208

Private place of defendant, requirements when personal property is located in CCP §488.070
Process server (See within this heading, **"Registered process server"**)
Process, service of (See within this heading, **"Service"**)
Property keeper fees
- Generally Gov §26726
- Costs, recovery by prevailing party as CCP §1033.5

Protective orders
- Affidavits supporting application CCP §486.010
- Application CCP §§486.010, 486.030, 489.320
- Bonds filed before issuance of CCP §489.210
- Checks, effect on amount of CCP §486.060
- Contents of CCP §486.040
- Defendant, effect on CCP §486.070
- Denied application, substitution for CCP §486.030
- Expiration of CCP §486.090
- Findings CCP §486.020
- Liens CCP §§486.110, 493.030 to 493.050
- Modification of CCP §486.100
- Property, transfer of CCP §486.050
- Provisions of CCP §486.040
- Service of papers CCP §486.080
- Termination of order, application for CCP §489.320
- Third party examination procedures CCP §491.180
- Time of expiration CCP §486.090
- Vacated CCP §486.100
- Wrongful attachments CCP §490.010

Quash, motion to
- Generally CCP §492.050
- Ex parte procedure CCP §485.240

Real property
- Generally CCP §488.315
- Defined CCP §481.203
- Sheriff's fees for writ on (See within this heading, **"Sheriff's fees"**)

Receivers, appointment of CCP §488.700
Records
- Public inspection, unavailability for CCP §482.050
- Wrongful attachments, records determining CCP §490.010

ATTACHMENT—Cont.
Recovery of judgment, delivery of undertaking on CCP §488.740
Referee examining third parties CCP §491.130
Registered process server
- Defined CCP §481.205
- Levy by CCP §488.080
- Liability of CCP §488.140

Release
- Generally CCP §§488.720, 699.060
- Appeal CCP §489.420
- Assignment on benefit of creditors, release on CCP §493.040
- Bankruptcy CCP §493.040
- Bonds for CCP §§489.310, 489.320
- Damages payment for improper release CCP §493.040
- Directions for CCP §488.730
- Excessive amount of defendant's interest, release for CCP §488.720
- Foreign corporations motioning for CCP §492.050
- Liability of levying officer for CCP §488.730
- Notice of request for CCP §493.040
- Other states motioning for CCP §492.050

Return of writ CCP §488.130
Safe deposit box, property in CCP §§488.460, 488.465
Salaries and wages
- Generally (See **GARNISHMENT**)
- Earnings assignment order for support Fam §5243
- Exemptions CCP §§486.060, 487.020
- Preference to wage claims upon levy of attachment CCP §§1206 to 1208

Sales
- Costs, recovery of CCP §491.370
- Homesteads CCP §487.025
- Joinder of defendants on CCP §491.320
- Jury trial on creditor's suit for CCP §491.350
- Limitations on creditor's suit for CCP §491.330
- Restrictions on CCP §491.330
- Sheriff's fees
  - Conducting or postponing property sales Gov §26746
  - Notice of forced sale of personal property Gov §26725.1
- Third party in possession of property, effect of CCP §491.310
- Transfers, orders restraining CCP §491.340

Satisfaction of judgment in pending action, consent of plaintiff to CCP §491.440
Savings and loan associations
- Financial institutions generally (See within this heading, **"Financial institutions"**)

Second writ
- Additional writs generally (See within this heading, **"Additional writs"**)

Securities, attachment of CCP §§487.010, 488.450
Security interests
- Generally CCP §483.010
- Bonds (See within this heading, **"Bonds"**)
- Defined CCP §481.223
- Stock CCP §§487.010, 488.450

Service
- Generally CCP §488.305
- Additional writs CCP §484.330
- Definition of registered process server CCP §481.205
- Deposit accounts
  - Writ, service CCP §488.455
- Exemption claims CCP §482.100
- Failure to serve notice, effect of attachment lien where CCP §488.120
- Garnishee's memorandum CCP §488.610
- Hearing requirements CCP §484.040
- Levy of attachment by process server CCP §488.080
- Manner of service CCP §482.070
- Protective orders CCP §486.080
- Sheriff's fees (See within this heading, **"Sheriff's fees"**)
- Third parties, improper service on CCP §491.160

Sheriff's fees
- Generally Gov §§26725, 26746
- Additional notices Gov §§26725.1, 26728.1
- Cancellation of execution Gov §26736
- Conducting or postponing property sales Gov §26730
- Copy fees Gov §26727
- Forced sale of personal property, notice of Gov §§26728, 26728.1
- Levy on personal property Gov §26734
- Property keeper fees Gov §26726
  - Costs, recovery by prevailing party CCP §1033.5
- Sales
  - Conducting or postponing property sales Gov §26730
  - Notice of forced sale of personal property Gov §§26728, 26728.1
- Service of writ
  - Generally Gov §§26725, 26746

ATTACHMENT—Cont.
Sheriff's fees—Cont.
    Service of writ—Cont.
        Additional notices, fees for   Gov §26725.1
        Cancellation of execution   Gov §26736
Statutory construction   CCP §481.010
Stay pending appeal   CCP §921
Stock, attachment of   CCP §§487.010, 488.450
Stores and storekeepers   CCP §481.120
Subject property   CCP §487.010
Subordinate judicial duty, attachment as   CCP §482.060
Summons, service of   CCP §§482.070, 484.040
Surety bonds (See within this heading, "**Bonds**")
Taking property into custody, manner of   CCP §488.090
Tangible personal property
    Availability on claim secured by interest in personal property   CCP §483.010
    Bailee's possession, attaching of goods in   CCP §488.365
    Defendant, attachment of tangible personal property in possession of   CCP §488.335
    Defined   CCP §481.225
    Levying officer, attaching personal property in custody of   CCP §488.355
    Third person, attachment of personal property in possession of   CCP §488.345
Temporary protective orders
    Protective orders generally (See within this heading, "**Protective orders**")
Third persons
    Adverse interest claim by   CCP §491.170
    Appearance requirement   CCP §491.140
    Deposit accounts, attachment of   CCP §488.455
    Duties and liabilities after levy   CCP §§488.600 to 488.620
    Failure to appear   CCP §491.160
    Garnishment memorandum, liability of third party giving   CCP §488.620
    General provisions for examination   CCP §491.110
    Judgment establishing liability of   CCP §491.360
    Jurisdiction for examining of   CCP §491.150
    Procedure for making claim   CCP §488.110
    Safe deposit box property in names of third party, attachment of   CCP §488.465
    Sales where third party in possession   CCP §491.310
    Tangible personal property in possession of third person, attaching of   CCP §488.345
    Temporary protective orders on examination of   CCP §491.180
    Witnesses, testimony by   CCP §491.120
Timber (See within this heading, "**Farm products, timber or minerals**")
Time
    Exemptions, claiming of   CCP §485.610
    Hearings   CCP §482.100
    Service of notice of application and hearing for writ   CCP §1005
Transfers
    Generally   CCP §486.050
    Adverse interest claims by third parties, restraint on transfers involving   CCP §491.170
    Liens continued on   CCP §491.200
    Possession of property sought for attachment, order directing transfer of   CCP §482.080
    Sales, provisional order restraining transfer on   CCP §491.340
Trust beneficiary, attachment of deposit account of   CCP §488.455
Trust deeds
    Foreclosure action, viability of attachment in conjunction with   CCP §483.012
    General provision concerning availability of attachment on claim secured by trust deed   CCP §483.010
Undertakings (See within this heading, "**Bonds**")
University of California   CCP §481.200
Unlawful detainer   CCP §483.020
Vacation of order
    Generally   CCP §492.050
    Ex parte procedure   CCP §485.240
Vessels
    Going business, attaching vessel of   CCP §488.385
    Method of levy, generally   CCP §488.425
Veterans' federal disability benefits
    Exemptions from attachment and other legal process   CCP §483.013
Wages
    Garnishment generally (See **GARNISHMENT**)
    Generally (See within this heading, "**Salaries and wages**")
Waiver of defense   CCP §484.110
Witnesses testifying for third party   CCP §491.120

ATTACHMENT—Cont.
Wrongful attachments
    Generally   CCP §§489.130, 490.010 to 490.060
    Damages (See within this heading, "**Damages**")

ATTEMPTS TO COMMIT CRIME
Murder
    Attempting or soliciting murder of spouse
        Damages for injuries to married person   Fam §782.5
        Support award to convicted spouse prohibited   Fam §4324

ATTENDANCE
Jurors (See **JURY**)
Subpoenas (See **SUBPOENA**)
Witnesses (See **WITNESSES**)

ATTESTING WITNESSES (See **WILLS**)

ATTORNEY DISCIPLINE   CRC 9.10 to 9.23
Affidavit of compliance   CRC 9.20
Agreement in lieu of discipline
    Compliance with discipline or agreements in lieu of discipline   ProfC 8.1.1
    Restrictions on lawyer's right to practice
        Permitted agreements   ProfC 5.6
Assessment for attorney discipline
    Interim special regulatory assessment of attorneys   CRC 9.2, 9.9
Attorney professional conduct
    Compliance with discipline or agreements in lieu of discipline   ProfC 8.1.1
    Disciplinary authority
        Jurisdictional considerations   ProfC 8.5
    Law firm employment of disbarred, suspended, resigned or involuntarily inactive lawyers   ProfC 5.3.1
    Threatening criminal, administrative or disciplinary charges   ProfC 3.10
    Violation as grounds for discipline   ProfC 1.0
Attorney work product, discovery   CCP §2018.070
Chief trial counsel
    Petition for review   CRC 9.14
Child support payments, suspension for delinquency in   CRC 9.22
Client protection   CRC 9.20
    Reimbursement to client security fund
        Enforcement of orders for payment of reimbursements money judgment   CRC 9.23
Construction-related accessibility claims
    Demand letters
        Violation of provisions as grounds for discipline   CC §55.32
Contempt
    Attorney misconduct triggering notification to state bar
        Appellate justice's duties   CRC 10.1017
        Trial judge duties   CRC 10.609
Continuing legal education
    Minimum continuing legal education requirements, failure to comply with   CRC 9.31
Conviction proceedings
    State bar court
        Authority   CRC 9.10
Costs
    Enforcement of orders for payment of costs as money judgment   CRC 9.23
Court's assumption of jurisdiction over practice   CCP §§353.1, 473.1
Criminal convictions
    Attorney subject to   CRC 9.10
    Disciplinary proceedings   CRC 9.10
Definitions   CRC 9.1
Disbarment
    Attorney professional conduct
        Law firm employment of disbarred, suspended, resigned or involuntarily inactive lawyers   ProfC 5.3.1
Discovery
    Attorney work product   CCP §2018.070
Discovery abuses, sanctions for
    Reporting sanction to state bar   CCP §2023.050
Duties of attorney subject to   CRC 9.20
Effective date of disciplinary orders   CRC 9.18
Foreign legal consultants, suspension of   CRC 9.44
Grounds for discipline
    Construction-related accessibility claims
        Demand letters, violations   CC §55.32
    Notification to state bar of attorney misconduct
        Appellate justice's duties   CRC 10.1017
        Judge's duties   CRC 10.609
Health care provider's negligence, noncompliance with notice requirement for commencement of action for   CCP §365

ATTORNEY DISCIPLINE—Cont.
Hearings
  Testimony by judges   CRCSupp JudEthicsCanon 2
Inactive enrollment, involuntary transfer to
  Attorney professional conduct
    Law firm employment of disbarred, suspended, resigned or involuntarily inactive lawyers   ProfC 5.3.1
Incompetent representation
  Attorney misconduct triggering notification to state bar
    Appellate justice's duties   CRC 10.1017
    Trial judge duties   CRC 10.609
Judges
  Competency to testify in State Bar investigations   Ev §703.5
    Factual information in state bar disciplinary proceedings   CRCSupp JudEthicsCanon 2
  Disciplinary responsibilities of judge   CRCSupp JudEthicsCanon 3
Minimum continuing legal education requirements, failure to comply with   CRC 9.31
Misrepresentation
  Attorney misconduct triggering notification to state bar
    Appellate justice's duties   CRC 10.1017
    Trial judge duties   CRC 10.609
Petitions
  Reinstatement   CRC 9.10
Probate rules
  Guardianships or conservatorships
    Appointed counsel qualifications, notification of disciplinary action   CRC 7.1105
Probation order   CRC 9.10
Professional conduct rules   ProfC 1.0 to 8.5 (See **ATTORNEY PROFESSIONAL CONDUCT**)
Professional responsibility exam
  State bar court
    Authority   CRC 9.10
Proof of compliance   CRC 9.20
Public or private reprovals
  Conditions   CRC 9.19
Readmission and reinstatement   CRC 9.10
  Petitions and hearings   CRC 9.10
  Support payments, suspension for delinquency in   CRC 9.22
Reimbursement to client security fund
  Enforcement of orders for payment of reimbursements money judgment   CRC 9.23
Rejection of resignation by supreme court   CRC 9.21
Remand of action to state bar court or state bar   CRC 9.17
Reprovals
  Conditions   CRC 9.19
Resignation
  Attorney professional conduct
    Law firm employment of disbarred, suspended, resigned or involuntarily inactive lawyers   ProfC 5.3.1
  Charges pending   CRC 9.21
Review department
  Independent review of record   CRC 9.12
Rules of professional conduct   ProfC 1.0 to 8.5 (See **ATTORNEY PROFESSIONAL CONDUCT**)
Settlements
  Sex offense cases, civil case settlements
    Confidentiality agreements, discipline of attorneys insisting on agreement contrary to legal restrictions   CCP §1002
    Restrictions on nondisclosure agreements (NDAs) in certain cases   CCP §1001
Specialist certification, suspension or revocation or denial   CRC 9.35
Special masters
  Special master's attorney discipline fund   CRC 9.2, 9.9
State Bar Court judges, appointment and qualifications   CRC 9.11
Support payments, suspension for delinquency   CRC 9.22
Supreme court
  Inherent power of supreme court   CRC 9.10
  Rejection of resignation   CRC 9.21
Supreme court review
  Chief trial counsel's petition for review   CRC 9.14
  Committee of bar examiners' petition for review   CRC 9.15
  Grounds for   CRC 9.16
  Orders, effective date   CRC 9.18
  Petition for review   CRC 9.13
    Chief trial counsel's petition   CRC 9.14
    State bar petition   CRC 9.15
  Remand of action to state bar court or to state bar   CRC 9.17

ATTORNEY DISCIPLINE—Cont.
Suspension or disbarment
  Attorney professional conduct
    Law firm employment of disbarred, suspended, resigned or involuntarily inactive lawyers   ProfC 5.3.1
  License fees, suspension for nonpayment
    Expungement of suspension, state bar recommendation   CRC 9.8

ATTORNEY GENERAL
Administration of decedents' estates, notice of   Pro §§1209, 8111
Amicus curiae briefs
  Filing   CRC 8.200
    Supreme court, filing in   CRC 8.520
Appellate rules, supreme court and courts of appeal
  Briefs
    Service of   CRC 8.29
  Briefs, service of   CRC 8.212
  Certification of state-law questions to California supreme court by federal appellate courts, notice to attorney general   CRC 8.548
  Certiorari, mandate and prohibition
    Amicus brief of attorney general and others   CRC 8.487
California coastal act
  Civil actions to enforce provisions
    Fees and costs for attorney general   CCP §1021.8
Change of venue of actions by or against state   CCP §401
Charitable trusts, supervision of trustees
  Civil actions to enforce provisions
    Fees and costs for attorney general   CCP §1021.8
Civil rights violation, bringing action for   CC §§52, 52.1
  Construction or application of civil rights provisions in issue, solicitor general notified   CC §51.1
  Fees and costs for attorney general   CCP §1021.8
Constitutional challenge to state law, Attorney General's intervention in appeal of   CCP §§664.5, 902.1
Consumer privacy rights
  Actions for damages, injunctions, declaratory relief, etc
    Notice to attorney general of action   CC §1798.150
  Businesses, service providers, contractors, etc, violation
    Actions for injunctions, civil penalties, etc, by attorney general   CC §1798.199.90
  Rulemaking to implement provisions   CC §1798.185
    California privacy protection agency takeover of rulemaking responsibility   CC §1798.199.40
Containers, fair packaging and labeling
  Civil actions to enforce provisions
    Fees and costs for attorney general   CCP §1021.8
Disabled persons access, actions to enforce
  Fees and costs for attorney general   CCP §1021.8
Electronic court records, remote access
  Government entities, access by
    List of government entities which may be authorized to receive access   CRC 2.540
Electronic recording delivery systems
  Evaluation of system   Gov §27398
  Monitoring system   Gov §27396
  Regulation and oversight costs
    County responsibility for attorney general regulation and oversight   Gov §27397
  Rulemaking to implement provisions   Gov §27393
  System certification
    Required   Gov §27392
  Voidable transactions
    Action for relief   Gov §27396
Eminent domain summons served on   CCP §1250.140
Environmental protection
  Civil actions to enforce provisions
    Fees and costs for attorney general   CCP §1021.8
  Pollution action, Attorney General to be provided copy of pleading by party filing   CCP §388
Escheat (See **ESCHEAT**)
False claims actions
  Filing records under seal   CRC 2.570 to 2.573
Felon's story, action regarding proceeds from sale of   CC §2225
Firearms and other weapons
  Firearm industry standards of conduct
    Actions against industry members for violation of standards   CC §3273.52
Firefighting liability
  Civil actions to enforce provisions
    Fees and costs for attorney general   CCP §1021.8

ATTORNEY GENERAL—Cont.
  Fish and wildlife laws
    Civil actions to enforce provisions
      Fees and costs for attorney general   CCP §1021.8
  Gang database removal, appeal proceedings
    Order to remove name
      Service on attorney general   CRC 3.2300
  Genetic privacy
    Enforcement of provisions   CC §56.182
  Hazardous substances, underground storage
    Civil actions to enforce provisions
      Fees and costs for attorney general   CCP §1021.8
  Housing discrimination
    Civil actions to enforce provisions
      Fees and costs for attorney general   CCP §1021.8
  Immigration consultants
    Civil actions to enforce provisions
      Fees and costs for attorney general   CCP §1021.8
  Information Practices Act, obtaining injunctive relief under   CC §1798.47
  Interstate family support
    Duties of state officials, compelling performance   Fam §5700.308
  Labor disputes, action for violence during   CC §52
  Marital status, action for denial of credit because of   CC §§1812.32, 1812.33
  Online marketplaces
    Actions to enforce provisions   CC §1749.8.4
    Attorney general actions to enforce provisions   CC §1749.8.4
  Police officers (See **LAW ENFORCEMENT OFFICERS**)
  Price discrimination based on gender
    Price differences for substantially similar goods based on gender of marketing audience
      Enforcement of provisions   CC §51.14
  Quo warranto proceedings brought by   CCP §803
  San Francisco Bay conservation and development commission
    Civil actions to enforce provisions
      Fees and costs for attorney general   CCP §1021.8
  Small claims advisory committee, composition of   CCP §116.950
  Smokeless tobacco nonsale distribution
    Civil actions to enforce provisions
      Fees and costs for attorney general   CCP §1021.8
  Smoking, tobacco sales and distribution
    Civil actions to enforce provisions
      Fees and costs for attorney general   CCP §1021.8
  Solicitor general
    Civil rights actions
      Construction or application of civil rights provisions in issue, solicitor general notified   CC §51.1
    Disabled, blind, deaf, etc., equal access provisions
      Construction of application of provisions in issue, solicitor general notified   CC §55.2
  Terrorism
    September 11, 2001 terrorist attacks
      Identification of participants and conspirators   CCP §340.10
  Trusts (See **TRUSTS**)
  Unclaimed deposits and payments   CCP §§1574, 1575
  Unruh Civil Rights Act, bringing action under   CC §52
  Water, federal water pollution control act enforcement
    Civil actions to enforce provisions
      Fees and costs for attorney general   CCP §1021.8
  Water, unauthorized diversion or use
    Civil actions to enforce provisions
      Fees and costs for attorney general   CCP §1021.8
  Water, waste or unreasonable use
    Civil actions to enforce provisions
      Fees and costs for attorney general   CCP §1021.8
  Water, water quality enforcement
    Civil actions to enforce provisions
      Fees and costs for attorney general   CCP §1021.8
  Water, water rights enforcement
    Civil actions to enforce provisions
      Fees and costs for attorney general   CCP §1021.8
  Will probate proceedings, notice of   Pro §§1209, 8111

ATTORNEY IN FACT (See **POWER OF ATTORNEY**)

ATTORNEY PROFESSIONAL CONDUCT   ProfC 1.0 to 8.5
  Admission to practice
    False statements regarding application for admission   ProfC 8.1
  Advertising   ProfC 7.2
    Solicitation of clients   ProfC 7.3
  Advising client to or assisting client to violate law   ProfC 1.2.1
  Advocacy role   ProfC 3.1 to 3.10

ATTORNEY PROFESSIONAL CONDUCT—Cont.
  Aggregate settlements involving multiple clients   ProfC 1.8.7
    Law firms
      Imputation to all members of firm of violations of certain provisions   ProfC 1.8.11
  Allocation between attorney and client of authority   ProfC 1.2
  Associations
    Law firms and associations generally   ProfC 5.1 to 5.6
    Organization or entity as client   ProfC 1.13
  Business expenses incurred by or for client
    Law firms
      Imputation to all members of firm of violations of certain provisions   ProfC 1.8.11
    Restrictions on attorney payment of client's business or personal expenses   ProfC 1.8.5
  Business transactions with clients   ProfC 1.8.1
    Law firms
      Imputation to all members of firm of violations of certain provisions   ProfC 1.8.11
  Candid advice   ProfC 2.1
  Candor towards the tribunal   ProfC 3.3
  Client-lawyer relationship   ProfC 1.0 to 1.18
  Comments to rules
    Purpose of official comments   ProfC 1.0
  Communications concerning lawyer's services   ProfC 7.1
  Communications with clients
    Duties and standards   ProfC 1.4
    Malpractice insurance lacking
      Duty to inform client   ProfC 1.4.2
    Settlement offers
      Prompt communication   ProfC 1.4.1
  Competence
    Defined   ProfC 1.1
    Methods of providing competent representation   ProfC 1.1
    Required   ProfC 1.1
  Confidential information
    Client's information   ProfC 1.6
      Conflicts of interest, use of client information in fashion adverse to interest of client   ProfC 1.8.2
      Law firms, imputation to all members of firm of violations of certain provisions   ProfC 1.8.11
    Prospective clients
      Duties to prospective clients   ProfC 1.18
  Conflicts of interest
    Aggregate settlements involving multiple clients   ProfC 1.8.7
    Business transactions with clients   ProfC 1.8.1
    Current clients   ProfC 1.7
      Information of client, use to disadvantage of client   ProfC 1.8.2
    Foreclosure sale, judicial sale, etc
      Purchase by attorney of property at foreclosure or judicial sale   ProfC 1.8.9
    Former clients
      Duties to former clients   ProfC 1.9
    Former judges, arbitrators, mediators, etc   ProfC 1.12
    Gifts from client to attorney
      Influencing client to give   ProfC 1.8.3
    Government officials or employees, former and current   ProfC 1.11
    Law firms
      Imputation of conflict of one member to other members of firm   ProfC 1.10
      Imputation to all members of firm of violations of certain provisions   ProfC 1.8.11
    Limitation of attorney liability to client
      Prohibitions   ProfC 1.8.8
    Nonclient, compensation from   ProfC 1.8.6
    Pecuniary interests adverse to client   ProfC 1.8.1
    Prospective clients
      Duties to prospective clients   ProfC 1.18
  Contacts with judges, jurors, tribunal officials or employees, etc   ProfC 3.5
  Contingent fees
    Circumstances where contingent fee agreement impermissible   ProfC 1.5
  Counselor role of attorney
    Advisor   ProfC 2.1
    Candid advice   ProfC 2.1
    Independent professional judgment   ProfC 2.1
    Temporary judge, referee or court-appointed arbitrator, service as   ProfC 2.4.1
    Third-party neutral, service as   ProfC 2.4
  Court officials or employees
    Contacts with judges, jurors, tribunal officials or employees, etc   ProfC 3.5

ATTORNEY PROFESSIONAL CONDUCT—Cont.
Criminal law and procedure
    Confidential information, revealing
        Prevention of criminal act   ProfC 1.6
    Contingent fees
        Circumstances where contingent fee agreement impermissible   ProfC 1.5
    Professional misconduct, conduct constituting
        Criminal acts affecting honesty, trustworthiness or fitness as attorney   ProfC 8.4
    Proof of every element of case
        Defense may require   ProfC 3.1
    Prosecutor's responsibilities   ProfC 3.8
    Threatening criminal, administrative or disciplinary charges   ProfC 3.10
Declining to represent   ProfC 1.16
Definitions   ProfC 1.0.1
    Candidates for judicial office
        Integrity of profession   ProfC 8.2
    Competence   ProfC 1.1
    Employ
        Law firm employment of disbarred, suspended, resigned or involuntarily inactive lawyers   ProfC 5.3.1
    Ineligible persons
        Law firm employment of disbarred, suspended, resigned or involuntarily inactive lawyers   ProfC 5.3.1
    Involuntarily inactive members
        Law firm employment of disbarred, suspended, resigned or involuntarily inactive lawyers   ProfC 5.3.1
    Member
        Law firm employment of disbarred, suspended, resigned or involuntarily inactive lawyers   ProfC 5.3.1
    Reasonable diligence   ProfC 1.3
    Resigned members
        Law firm employment of disbarred, suspended, resigned or involuntarily inactive lawyers   ProfC 5.3.1
    Sexual relations
        Current clients, relations with   ProfC 1.8.10
Delay of litigation   ProfC 3.2
Diligence
    Reasonable diligence
        Defined   ProfC 1.3
    Representation of client in diligent manner   ProfC 1.3
Discipline
    Agreement in lieu of discipline
        Compliance with agreement   ProfC 8.1.1
        Restrictions on lawyer's right to practice, permitted agreements   ProfC 5.6
    Compliance with discipline   ProfC 8.1.1
    Disciplinary authority
        Jurisdictional considerations   ProfC 8.5
    Law firm employment of disbarred, suspended, resigned or involuntarily inactive lawyers   ProfC 5.3.1
Discrimination
    Prohibited discrimination, harassment and retaliation   ProfC 8.4.1
Evidence
    False evidence
        Candor towards the tribunal   ProfC 3.3
    Obstructing access to evidence, witness, etc
        Fairness to opposing party and counsel   ProfC 3.4
Expenses incurred by or for client
    Law firms
        Imputation to all members of firm of violations of certain provisions   ProfC 1.8.11
    Restrictions on attorney payment of client's business or personal expenses   ProfC 1.8.5
Extrajudicial statements
    Trial publicity   ProfC 3.6
Fairness to opposing party and counsel   ProfC 3.4
False statements of law or fact to tribunal
    Candor towards the tribunal   ProfC 3.3
Fees for legal services
    Contingency fee agreements
        Circumstances where contingent fee agreement impermissible   ProfC 1.5
    Law firms
        Financial and other arrangements with nonattorneys   ProfC 5.4
    Nonclient, compensation from   ProfC 1.8.6
        Law firms, imputation to all members of firm of violations of certain provisions   ProfC 1.8.11
    Splitting fees   ProfC 1.5.1
    Unconscionable fees   ProfC 1.5

ATTORNEY PROFESSIONAL CONDUCT—Cont.
Fields of practice, communications as to   ProfC 7.4
Foreclosure sales
    Purchase by attorney of property at foreclosure or judicial sale
        Law firms, imputation to all members of firm of violations of certain provisions   ProfC 1.8.11
        Restrictions   ProfC 1.8.9
Former clients
    Duties to former clients   ProfC 1.9
Fraud
    Professional misconduct, conduct constituting   ProfC 8.4
Function of rules   ProfC 1.0
Gifts from client
    Law firms
        Imputation to all members of firm of violations of certain provisions   ProfC 1.8.11
    Restrictions   ProfC 1.8.3
Harassment
    Prohibited discrimination, harassment and retaliation   ProfC 8.4.1
Imputation to all members of firm of conflict of one member   ProfC 1.10
Imputation to all members of firm of violations of certain provisions   ProfC 1.8.11
Inactive enrollment, involuntary transfer to
    Law firm employment of disbarred, suspended, resigned or involuntarily inactive lawyers   ProfC 5.3.1
Independent professional judgment   ProfC 2.1
Information about legal services   ProfC 7.1 to 7.5
    Advertising   ProfC 7.2
    Communications concerning lawyer's services   ProfC 7.1
    Fields of practice, communications as to   ProfC 7.4
    Firm names   ProfC 7.5
    Solicitation of clients   ProfC 7.3
    Specialization, communications as to   ProfC 7.4
    Trade names   ProfC 7.5
Integrity of profession, maintaining   ProfC 8.1 to 8.5
    Admission to practice
        False statements regarding application for admission   ProfC 8.1
    Compliance with discipline and agreements in lieu of discipline   ProfC 8.1.1
    Disciplinary authority
        Jurisdictional considerations   ProfC 8.5
    Discrimination, harassment and retaliation   ProfC 8.4.1
    Judicial officers   ProfC 8.2
    Professional misconduct, conduct constituting   ProfC 8.4
Judges
    Appointment to judicial office, lawyer seeking   ProfC 8.2
    Candidates for judicial office
        Applicable provisions   ProfC 8.2
    Contacts with judges, jurors, tribunal officials or employees, etc   ProfC 3.5
    False statements as to qualifications or integrity   ProfC 8.2
    Former judges, arbitrators, mediators, etc
        Restrictions on representation of clients   ProfC 1.12
    Professional misconduct, conduct constituting
        Assisting, inducing, etc, judge to violate judicial ethics, code of judicial conduct, etc   ProfC 8.4
    Service as temporary judge, referee or court-appointed arbitrator
        Judicial ethics canon 6D, when applicable   ProfC 2.4.1
Judicial sales
    Purchase by attorney of property at foreclosure or judicial sale
        Law firms, imputation to all members of firm of violations of certain provisions   ProfC 1.8.11
        Restrictions   ProfC 1.8.9
Jurors
    Contacts with judges, jurors, tribunal officials or employees, etc   ProfC 3.5
Law firms   ProfC 5.1 to 5.6
    Defined   ProfC 1.0.1
    Disbarred or suspended lawyers
        Employment of disbarred, suspended, resigned or involuntarily inactive lawyers   ProfC 5.3.1
    Financial and other arrangements with nonattorneys   ProfC 5.4
    Imputation to all members of firm of violations of certain provisions   ProfC 1.8.11
    Inactive status, involuntary
        Employment of disbarred, suspended, resigned or involuntarily inactive lawyers   ProfC 5.3.1
    Managerial lawyers
        Nonlawyer assistants, responsibilities of firm   ProfC 5.3
        Responsibilities   ProfC 5.1
    Multijurisdictional practice of law   ProfC 5.5
    Names of law firms   ProfC 7.5

ATTORNEY PROFESSIONAL CONDUCT—Cont.
  Law firms —Cont.
    Nonlawyer assistants
      Responsibilities of firm ProfC 5.3
    Resigned lawyers
      Employment of disbarred, suspended, resigned or involuntarily inactive lawyers ProfC 5.3.1
    Restricting lawyer's right to practice
      Agreements restricting ProfC 5.6
    Sale of law practice ProfC 1.17
    Subordinate lawyers
      Responsibilities ProfC 5.2
    Supervisory lawyers
      Nonlawyer assistants, responsibilities of firm ProfC 5.3
      Responsibilities ProfC 5.1
    Unlawful practice of law ProfC 5.5
  Legal services organizations
    Membership in organization ProfC 6.3
  Legal services programs
    Limited legal services programs, service in ProfC 6.5
  Limitation of attorney liability to client
    Law firms
      Imputation to all members of firm of violations of certain provisions ProfC 1.8.11
    Prohibitions ProfC 1.8.8
  Limited scope of representation
    Attorney authorized to limit ProfC 1.2
  Managerial lawyers
    Nonlawyer assistants, responsibilities of firm ProfC 5.3
    Responsibilities ProfC 5.1
  Meritorious claims and contentions ProfC 3.1
  Misconduct
    Professional misconduct, conduct constituting ProfC 8.4
  Multijurisdictional practice of law ProfC 5.5
  Names of law firms ProfC 7.5
  Nonadjudicative proceedings
    Advocacy in nonadjudicative proceedings ProfC 3.9
  Nonclients, transactions with ProfC 4.1 to 4.4
    Represented persons
      Communications with represented persons ProfC 4.2
    Truthfulness in statements to others while representing client ProfC 4.1
    Unrepresented persons
      Communications with unrepresented persons ProfC 4.3
    Writings inadvertently transmitted
      Duties of attorney receiving ProfC 4.4
  Nonlawyer assistants
    Responsibilities of firm ProfC 5.3
  Obstructing access to evidence, witness, etc
    Fairness to opposing party and counsel ProfC 3.4
  Organization or entity as client ProfC 1.13
  Pecuniary interests adverse to client ProfC 1.8.1
    Law firms
      Imputation to all members of firm of violations of certain provisions ProfC 1.8.11
  Probable cause to bring or defend claim
    Meritorious claims and contentions ProfC 3.1
  Prolonging the proceedings ProfC 3.2
  Prosecutors
    Special responsibilities of prosecutor ProfC 3.8
  Prospective clients
    Duties to prospective clients ProfC 1.18
  Purpose of rules ProfC 1.0
  Records
    Trust accounts
      Safekeeping of funds and property of clients ProfC 1.15
  Represented persons
    Communications with represented persons ProfC 4.2
  Resigned attorney
    Law firm employment of disbarred, suspended, resigned or involuntarily inactive lawyers ProfC 5.3.1
  Restricting lawyer's right to practice
    Agreements restricting ProfC 5.6
  Retainer fees ProfC 1.5
  Retaliation
    Prohibited discrimination, harassment and retaliation ProfC 8.4.1
  Safekeeping of funds and property of clients ProfC 1.15
  Sale of law practice ProfC 1.17
  Scope of representation ProfC 1.2
  Settlements
    Aggregate settlements involving multiple clients ProfC 1.8.7
      Law firms, imputation to all members of firm of violations of certain provisions ProfC 1.8.11

ATTORNEY PROFESSIONAL CONDUCT—Cont.
  Settlements—Cont.
    Client's decision to settle
      Attorney to abide ProfC 1.2
    Communications with clients
      Prompt communication of settlement offers ProfC 1.4.1
    Limitation of attorney liability to client
      Law firms, imputation to all members of firm of violations of certain provisions ProfC 1.8.11
      Prohibitions ProfC 1.8.8
  Sexual relations
    Current clients, relations with
      Law firms, imputation to all members of firm of violations of certain provisions ProfC 1.8.11
      Restrictions ProfC 1.8.10
  Solicitation of clients ProfC 7.3
  Specialization, communications as to ProfC 7.4
  Splitting fees ProfC 1.5.1
  Subordinate lawyers at law firms
    Responsibilities ProfC 5.2
  Supervisory lawyers
    Nonlawyer assistants, responsibilities of firm ProfC 5.3
    Responsibilities ProfC 5.1
  Terminating representation ProfC 1.16
  Third-party neutral
    Attorney as third-party neutral ProfC 2.4
  Threatening criminal, administrative or disciplinary charges ProfC 3.10
  Trade names ProfC 7.5
  Trial publicity ProfC 3.6
  Trust accounts
    Safekeeping of funds and property of clients ProfC 1.15
  Unconscionable fees ProfC 1.5
  Unlawful practice of law ProfC 5.5
  Unrepresented persons
    Communications with unrepresented persons ProfC 4.3
  Violations of rules or state bar act
    Advising client to or assisting client to violate law ProfC 1.2.1
    Professional misconduct, conduct constituting ProfC 8.4
  Withdrawal from representation ProfC 1.16
  Witnesses
    Attorney as witness ProfC 3.7
    Obstructing access to evidence, witness, etc
      Fairness to opposing party and counsel ProfC 3.4
  Writings inadvertently transmitted
    Duties of attorney receiving ProfC 4.4

ATTORNEYS
Active and inactive status
  Continuing legal education, noncompliance leading to inactive status
    Expungement of record of inactive enrollment CRC 9.31
  Fingerprinting
    Active licensed attorneys CRC 9.9.5
    Inactive status attorneys prior to becoming active status CRC 9.9.5
Address records
  Change of address, notice to parties CRC 2.200
    Electronic filing, when required CRCSupp 1st AppDist
Admission to practice CRC 9.3 to 9.9.5
  Attorney professional conduct
    False statements regarding application for admission ProfC 8.1
  Bar examination (See **BAR EXAMINATION**)
  Counsel pro hac vice CRC 9.40
  Law students
    Provisional licensure of 2020 law school graduates CRC 9.49
      Pathway to full licensure, provisional licensure with CRC 9.49.1
  Military counsel, appearance by CRC 9.41
  Military spouses
    Registered military spouse attorney CRC 9.41.1
  Oath of allegiance
    Required oath upon admission to practice CRC 9.7
  Provisional licensure of 2020 law school graduates CRC 9.49
    Pathway to full licensure, provisional licensure with CRC 9.49.1
  Roll of attorneys admitted to practice CRC 9.8
    Online reporting of information by attorneys CRC 9.9
  Supreme Court inherent power CRC 9.3
Adoption (See **ADOPTION**)
Affidavit of compliance, disciplinary action CRC 9.20
Appearance at court proceedings (See **APPEARANCE**)
Appellate briefs, inclusion of State Bar membership number CRC 8.204
Appellate counsel, qualifications
  Death penalty appeals CRC 8.605

ATTORNEYS—Cont.
Appellate counsel, qualifications—Cont.
    Death penalty habeas proceedings   CRC 8.652
Appellate rules, superior court appeals
    Address and telephone number of record   CRC 8.816
    Misdemeanor appeals
        Appointment of appellate counsel   CRC 8.851
    Substitution for attorney   CRC 8.814
        Electronic filing, when required   CRCSupp 1st AppDist
    Withdrawal of attorney   CRC 8.814
    Writ proceedings within original jurisdiction of appellate division
        Petition filed by attorney for party   CRC 8.932
Appellate rules, supreme court and courts of appeal (See **APPELLATE RULES, SUPREME COURT AND COURTS OF APPEAL**)
Appointment by court
    Appellate rules, supreme court and courts of appeal
        Juvenile case appeals   CRC 8.403
    Capital punishment
        Habeas proceedings, qualifications of appointed counsel   CRC 8.652
        Trial counsel, qualifications   CRC 4.117
    Criminal appeals   CRC 8.300
    Death penalty
        Appellate counsel appointments   CRC 8.605
        Appellate counsel qualifications   CRC 8.605
        Declaration of counsel for appointment, form   CRCAppx A
        Habeas counsel appointments   CRC 8.605
        Habeas counsel qualifications   CRC 8.652
        Trial counsel qualifications   CRC 4.117
    Family law
        Compensation, judicial administration standards   CRC JudAdminStand 5.30
        Custody and visitation cases   CRC 5.240 to 5.242, Fam §§3150 to 3153
        Ex parte communications   Fam §216
    Fixed fee appointments   CRCSupp FixedFeeAppoint
    Forms
        Judicial council legal forms   CRCAppx A
    Habeas proceedings
        Capital cases, appointments   CRC 8.605
        Qualifications of appointed counsel
            Capital cases   CRC 8.652
            Noncapital cases   CRC 4.553
    Indigent criminal appellants in supreme court, payment guidelines
        Disallowed fees and expenses   CRCSupp PayGuideAppoint
        Expenses   CRCSupp PayGuideAppoint
        Habeas corpus proceedings   CRCSupp PayGuideAppoint
        Nonperformance of work   CRCSupp PayGuideAppoint
        Reasonable compensation, factors   CRCSupp PayGuideAppoint
        Withdrawal, reimbursement   CRCSupp PayGuideAppoint
    Judicial administration standards (See **JUDICIAL ADMINISTRATION STANDARDS**)
    Juvenile dependency proceedings
        Counsel collections program guidelines   CRCAppx F
    Misdemeanor appeals   CRC 8.851
    Nondiscrimination in court appointments   CRC 10.611, CRC JudAdminStand 10.21
    Termination of parental rights
        Indigent appellant, appointment of counsel for   Fam §7895
Arbitration (See **ARBITRATION**)
Assumption of jurisdiction over practice
    Extension of limitations period   CCP §353.1
    Relief from judgment or other proceedings   CCP §473.1
Attorney-client privilege (See **PRIVILEGED COMMUNICATIONS**)
Attorney general (See **ATTORNEY GENERAL**)
Attorney's fees (See **ATTORNEY'S FEES**)
Authority to bind client   CCP §283
Bad faith actions, assessment against attorney of expenses and attorney fees incurred as result of (See **SANCTIONS**)
Bar examination (See **BAR EXAMINATION**)
Capital cases (See **CAPITAL PUNISHMENT**)
CASA programs in juvenile courts   CRC 5.655
Cellular telephone conversations, attorney-client privilege for   Ev §952
Certificates
    Foreign legal consultants, certificate of registration of   CRC 9.44
    Meritorious cause of action, certificate for (See **CERTIFICATE OF MERIT**)
    Specialist, certification as   CRC 9.35
Certified law student program   CRC 9.42
Cessation of practice
    State bar, resignation from with pending disciplinary action   CRC 9.21

ATTORNEYS—Cont.
Challenges to jury panel, services of legal counsel in connection with   CCP §225
Change of attorneys (See within this heading, "**Substitution of attorney**")
Child support
    Representation in child support proceedings (See **CHILD SUPPORT**)
Child support obligation, failure to pay   CRC 9.22
City attorney (See **CITY ATTORNEYS**)
Civil rules
    Limited scope representation   CRC 3.35 to 3.37
Client funds account management
    State bar client trust account protection program   CRC 9.8.5
Communications
    Attorney-client privilege (See **PRIVILEGED COMMUNICATIONS**)
    Jurors, communications with (See **JURY**)
Competency standards
    Juvenile proceedings   CRC 5.660
Conduct, judicial notice of   Ev §451
Confession of judgment, attorneys signing certificates for   CCP §1132
Conflicts of interest
    Dependent child of court
        Siblings, conflict of interest guidelines when representing   CRC 5.660
Conservators (See **CONSERVATORS**)
Conspiring with client, action against attorney for   CC §1714.10
Construction-related accessibility claims
    Advisory filed along with complaint or demand for money by attorney   CC §55.3
    Complaints
        Duties of attorney upon sending or serving complaint   CC §55.32
    Demand letters
        Allegation of construction-related accessibility claim   CC §55.32
        Answer forms to be included   CC §55.3
        Contents of demand letters   CC §55.3
    Prelitigation letters to education entities   CC §54.27
    Stay and early evaluation conference
        Notice to defendant of rights to, attorney duties as to   CC §55.54
Contempt orders, stay of execution of   CCP §§128, 1209
Continuance of trial, agreement on   CCP §595.2
Continuing legal education
    Delinquency cases
        Training of attorneys representing children in delinquency cases   CRC 5.664
    Discipline   CRC 9.31
    Noncompliance
        Inactive status
            Expungement of record of inactive enrollment   CRC 9.31
Coordination proceedings   CRC 3.550
Counsel pro hac vice   CRC 9.40
County counsel (See **COUNTY COUNSEL**)
Court's assumption of jurisdiction over practice
    Extension of limitations period   CCP §353.1
    Relief from judgment or other proceedings   CCP §473.1
Criminal history information records
    Fingerprinting of attorneys
        Active licensed attorneys   CRC 9.9.5
        Foreign countries, active attorneys residing in   CRC 9.9.5
        Inactive status prior to becoming active status   CRC 9.9.5
        Special admissions attorneys   CRC 9.9.5
    Subsequent arrest notifications
        Fingerprinting of attorneys   CRC 9.9.5
Cross complaint served on   CCP §428.60
Custody of children (See **CUSTODY OF CHILDREN**)
Damages, liability of legal professional societies for   CC §§43.7, 43.95
Death of attorney
    New attorney appointed by client on death of attorney   CCP §286
    Practice administrator appointed by personal representative on death of attorney   Pro §§9764, 17200
Death of client, availability of attorney-client privilege following   Ev §957
Death penalty
    Appointed counsel
        Appellate counsel appointments   CRC 8.605
        Appellate counsel qualifications   CRC 8.605
        Habeas counsel appointments   CRC 8.605
        Habeas counsel qualifications   CRC 8.652
    Habeas corpus
        Attorney appointments for death penalty cases   CRC 4.561
Debt collection, false representations in   CC §§1788.13, 1788.16
Decedents' estates
    Probate attorneys
        Education requirements   CRC 10.478

ATTORNEYS—Cont.
　Decedents' estates—Cont.
　　Probate attorneys —Cont.
　　　Qualifications　CRC 10.776, 10.777
　Delaying tactics, assessment against attorney of expenses and attorney fees incurred as result of (See **SANCTIONS**)
　Deliberation and verdict, post-trial discussions with jurors regarding　CCP §206
　Dependent children
　　Collection for reimbursement of appointed attorneys
　　　Guidelines for juvenile dependency counsel collections program　CRCAppx F
　　Guardian ad litem
　　　Child abuse and treatment act (CAPTA) guardians ad litem　CRC 5.662
　　Legal costs, liability for
　　　Juvenile dependency counsel collections program, guidelines　CRCAppx F
　Depositions
　　Subpoenas
　　　Issuance by attorney of record　CCP §2020.210
　Deposit of estate-planning documents with attorney (See **TRUSTS; WILLS**)
　Disability of attorney, appointment of practice administrator in event of　Pro §§2468, 17200
　Disability of plaintiff tolling statute of limitation for legal malpractice actions　CCP §340.6
　Discipline
　　Attorney discipline generally (See **ATTORNEY DISCIPLINE**)
　　Rules of professional conduct generally (See **ATTORNEY PROFESSIONAL CONDUCT**)
　Discovery (See **DISCOVERY**)
　Discrimination
　　Court appointment　CRC 10.611, CRC JudAdminStand 10.21
　Dismissal, consent of or notice to attorney of　CCP §581
　Disqualification of judges (See **JUDGES, DISQUALIFICATION OF**)
　Domestic violence
　　Appointment of attorney in domestic violence proceedings　Fam §6340
　　Victim representatives　Fam §6228
　Donative transfers
　　Presumption of fraud or undue influence
　　　Duties of counsel　Pro §21384
　Electronic court records
　　Remote access
　　　Parties, designees, attorneys, court-appointed persons or persons working in legal organization or qualified legal services project, access by　CRC 2.515 to 2.528
　Electronic filing and service rules
　　Fees
　　　Sanctions for attorney's failure to pay provider fees　CCP §411.20.5
　Emancipation of children (See **EMANCIPATION OF MINORS**)
　Enforcement of judgments (See **ENFORCEMENT OF JUDGMENTS**)
　Executors and administrators (See **EXECUTORS AND ADMINISTRATORS**)
　Ex parte proceedings
　　Identification of attorney or party　CRC 3.1202
　Extension of time
　　Court's assumption of jurisdiction over practice　CCP §353.1
　　Legislature, time extension for attorneys attending　CCP §1054.1
　Fair debt settlement practices
　　Exemptions from provisions　CC §1788.304
　Family law facilitators, minimum standards　CRC 5.430
　Family law proceedings
　　Appointment by court
　　　Applicable guidelines for appointment　CRC JudAdminStand 5.30
　　　Compensation of court-appointed attorneys　CRC JudAdminStand 5.30
　　Limited basis representation
　　　Notice　CRCAppx A (CRCFL-950)
　　　Objection to application for relief from　CRCAppx A (CRCFL-956)
　　　Order deciding issue of relief　CRCAppx A (CRCFL-958)
　　　Relief as counsel, application　CRCAppx A (CRCFL-955)
　　Limited scope representation　CRC 5.425
　　Service of papers on attorney of record　Fam §215
　　Title IV-D support enforcement
　　　Attorney of record in support actions　CRC 5.320
　　Withdrawal of attorney of record
　　　Notice of withdrawal　CRCAppx A (CRCFL-960)
　Fax transmissions, attorney-client privilege for　Ev §952
　Fees (See **ATTORNEY'S FEES**)
　Fingerprinting
　　Active licensed attorneys　CRC 9.9.5
　　Foreign countries, active attorney residing in　CRC 9.9.5
　　Inactive status attorneys prior to becoming active status　CRC 9.9.5

ATTORNEYS—Cont.
　Fingerprinting—Cont.
　　Special admissions attorneys　CRC 9.9.5
　Foreign countries, licensed attorneys residing in
　　Fingerprinting　CRC 9.9.5
　Foreign legal consultants　CRC 9.44
　　Fingerprinting of special admission attorneys　CRC 9.9.5
　Frivolous actions, assessment against attorney of expenses and attorney fees incurred as result of (See **SANCTIONS**)
　Guardianship (See **GUARDIAN AND WARD**)
　Habeas corpus
　　Attorney appointments
　　　Death penalty cases　CRC 4.561, 8.391
　　Attorney qualifications
　　　Death penalty cases　CRC 4.562, 8.391, 8.652
　　Ineffective assistance
　　　Death penalty cases, appeals from superior court habeas proceedings　CRC 8.397
　　Petitions filed by attorneys　CRC 8.384
　Health care provider's negligence, noncompliance with notice requirement for commencement of action for　CCP §365
　Incompetent representation
　　Attorney misconduct triggering notification to state bar
　　　Appellate justice's duties　CRC 10.1017
　　　Trial judge duties　CRC 10.609
　Indigent persons (See **INDIGENT PERSONS**)
　Ineffective assistance
　　Habeas corpus, capital cases
　　　Appeals from superior court decisions in habeas cases involving death penalty　CRC 8.397
　In-house counsel
　　Registered in-house counsel　CRC 9.46
　　Fingerprinting of special admission attorneys　CRC 9.9.5
　Inspection of records by (See **INSPECTION**)
　Insurance (See **INSURANCE**)
　Interest on lawyers trust accounts (IOLTA)
　　Unclaimed property
　　　Administration of funds escheated from IOLTA accounts　CCP §1564.5
　International wills, authorized persons re　Pro §§6388, 6389
　Internet website accessibility violations
　　Complaints or demand letter
　　　Duties of attorney upon sending or serving　CC §55.32
　Interstate family support
　　Private counsel authorized　Fam §5700.309
　Judge advocate, appearance in state court　CRC 9.41
　Judges
　　Practice of law　CRCSupp JudEthicsCanons 3, 4
　　Temporary judges
　　　Appointment of attorney as temporary judge　CRC 2.810, 2.812
　Judges' right to representation in proceedings for censure, removal or admonishment　JudPerR 106, 126
　Judicial arbitration proceedings　CRC 3.821
　Jurisdiction over practice
　　Extension of limitations period on　CCP §353.1
　　Relief from judgment or other proceedings　CCP §473.1
　Juvenile rules
　　Appeals
　　　Representation of child on appeal　CRC 5.661
　　Delinquency proceedings
　　　Responsibilities of children's counsel in delinquency proceedings　CRC 5.663
　　　Training requirements for children's counsel　CRC 5.664
　　Electronic service
　　　Consent by child, consultation with and notification by attorney　CRC 5.523
　Law and motion rules
　　Relieving counsel, motion for order　CRC 3.1362
　Law practice
　　In-house counsel
　　　Registered in-house counsel　CRC 9.46
　　Rules governing law practice, attorneys and judges　CRC 9.0 to 9.90
　　　Attorney discipline　CRC 9.10 to 9.22
　　　Authority for rules　CRC 9.0
　　　Contents of rules　CRC 1.4
　　　Continuing legal education　CRC 9.31
　　　Definitions　CRC 9.1
　　　Legal specialists, certification　CRC 9.35
　　　Non-bar members, appearances and practice by　CRC 9.40 to 9.49.1
　　　Oath taken upon admission to practice　CRC 9.7
　　　Title of rules　CRC 9.0

ATTORNEYS—Cont.
  Law practice—Cont.
    Rules governing law practice, attorneys and judges —Cont.
      Unaccredited law schools, study in   CRC 9.30
  Law schools not accredited, study in   CRC 9.30
  Law students (See **LAW STUDENTS**)
  Lawyer referral service, immunity from liability for referrals by   CC §43.95
  Legal service programs
    Registered legal aid attorneys   CRC 9.45
      Fingerprinting of special admission attorneys   CRC 9.9.5
  Legislature
    Extension of time for attorneys attending   CCP §1054.1
    Legislative continuance   CCP §595
  License fees
    Suspension for nonpayment
      Expungement of suspension, state bar recommendation   CRC 9.8
  Limitation of actions (See within this heading, **"Statutes of limitation"**)
  Limited scope representation   CRC 3.35 to 3.37
    Applicability of provisions   CRC 3.35
    Definition of limited scope representation   CRC 3.35
    Family rules   CRC 5.425
    Forms
      Judicial council forms   CRCAppx A
    Noticed representation
      Providing notice   CRC 3.36
      Relief as attorney, request   CRC 3.36
      Types of limited scope representation   CRC 3.35
    Undisclosed representation
      Attorneys' fees sought   CRC 3.37
      Drafting or other preparation of court documents   CRC 3.37
      Types of limited scope representation   CRC 3.35
  Malpractice (See **MALPRACTICE**)
  Mandatory continuing legal education requirements   CRC 9.31
  Mediation
    Confidentiality of communications, admissions, etc, in mediation proceedings
      Disclosure by attorney to client of confidentiality requirements   Ev §1129
  Medical records, inspection of   CCP §1985.7, Ev §1158
  Military counsel, appearance by   CRC 9.41
  Military spouses
    Registered military spouse attorney   CRC 9.41.1
  Minimum continuing legal education requirements   CRC 9.31
  Misrepresentation by attorney
    Attorney misconduct triggering notification to state bar
      Appellate justice's duties   CRC 10.1017
      Trial judge duties   CRC 10.609
  Mistake, inadvertence, surprise or excusable neglect, relief from judgment based on attorney's   CCP §473
  Monetary sanctions against attorney, appeal of   CCP §904.1
  Multijurisdictional practice   ProfC 5.5
    In-house counsel
      Fingerprinting of special admission attorneys   CRC 9.9.5
      Registered in-house counsel   CRC 9.46
    Legal aid attorneys
      Fingerprinting of special admission attorneys   CRC 9.9.5
      Registered legal aid attorneys   CRC 9.45
    Temporarily in California as part of litigation   CRC 9.47
    Temporarily in California providing nonlitigation services   CRC 9.48
  New attorney training, state bar   CRC 9.32
  Newspapers and magazines (See **NEWSPAPERS AND MAGAZINES**)
  Nonresidents (See within this heading, **"Other states"**)
  Notice
    Appointment of new attorney on attorney's death, removal or suspension   CCP §286
    Limited scope representation
      Noticed representation, notice of   CRC 3.36
    Pendency of action, notice of   CCP §405.21
    Service of notice on attorney   CCP §1011
    Substitution of attorney   CCP §285
  Other states
    Appearance as counsel pro hac vice   CRC 9.40
    Arbitration counsel   CRC 9.43
    Arbitration proceedings, representation by nonresident attorney in   CCP §1282.4, CRC 9.43
    Foreign legal consultants   CRC 9.44
      Fingerprinting of special admission attorneys   CRC 9.9.5
    Military counsel, representation by   CRC 9.41
    Military spouses
      Registered military spouse attorney   CRC 9.41.1
    Pro hac vice counsel, representation by   CRC 9.40

ATTORNEYS—Cont.
  Other states—Cont.
    Serving attorneys of nonresidents   CCP §1015
  Partition (See **PARTITION**)
  Peer review committees, liability of   CC §43.7
  Pendency of actions (See **PENDENCY OF ACTIONS**)
  Personal representatives (See **EXECUTORS AND ADMINISTRATORS**)
  Pleadings verification by   CCP §446
  Power of attorney (See **POWER OF ATTORNEY**)
  Practice administrator
    Death of attorney, practice administrator appointed in event of   Pro §§9764, 17200
    Disability of attorney, practice administrator appointed in event of   Pro §§2468, 17200
  Practice of law
    In-house counsel
      Fingerprinting of special admission attorneys   CRC 9.9.5
      Registered in-house counsel   CRC 9.46
    Multijurisdictional practice of law   ProfC 5.5
    Provisional licensure of 2020 law school graduates   CRC 9.49
      Pathway to full licensure, provisional licensure with   CRC 9.49.1
    Registered legal aid attorney   CRC 9.45
      Fingerprinting of special admission attorneys   CRC 9.9.5
    Restricting lawyer's right to practice
      Agreements restricting   ProfC 5.6
    Rules governing law practice, attorneys and judges   CRC 9.0 to 9.90
      Attorney discipline   CRC 9.10 to 9.22
      Authority for rules   CRC 9.0
      Continuing legal education   CRC 9.31
      Definitions   CRC 9.1
      Legal specialists, certification   CRC 9.35
      Military spouses   CRC 9.41.1
      Non-bar members, appearances and practice by   CRC 9.40 to 9.49.1
      Oath taken upon admission to practice   CRC 9.7
      Title of rules   CRC 9.0
      Unaccredited law schools, study in   CRC 9.30
    Supreme court
      Inherent jurisdiction   CRC 9.3
    Temporarily in California
      Litigation, in connection with   CRC 9.47
      Nonlitigation services, providing   CRC 9.48
    Unauthorized practice of law   ProfC 5.5
  Private child support collectors   Fam §§5610 to 5616
  Privileged communications (See **PRIVILEGED COMMUNICATIONS**)
  Probate proceedings
    Compensation for guardians and conservators
      Advance payments   CRC 7.755
      Contingency fee agreements   CRC 7.753
      Petitions for orders to allow compensation   CRC 7.751
    Compensation of personal representatives and attorneys   CRC 7.700 to 7.707
    Ex parte communications
      Prohibition on communications   CRC 7.10
      Notice to attorney   CRC 7.51
  Professional committees, liability of   CC §§43.7, 43.95
  Professional conduct   ProfC 1.0 to 8.5 (See **ATTORNEY PROFESSIONAL CONDUCT**)
  Professional conduct, rules of (See **ATTORNEY PROFESSIONAL CONDUCT**)
  Professional negligence (See **MALPRACTICE**)
  Pro hac vice counsel   CRC 9.40
    Filing fee, application to appear   Gov §70617
  Prosecuting attorney (See **DISTRICT ATTORNEY**)
  Provisional licensure of 2020 law school graduates   CRC 9.49
    Pathway to full licensure, provisional licensure with   CRC 9.49.1
  Public defender (See **PUBLIC DEFENDER**)
  Public guardians, employment by (See **PUBLIC GUARDIANS**)
  Public officers and employees
    Quieting title to improperly encumbered property of public officer or employee, proceedings for
      Counsel for officer or employee supplied by employer   CCP §765.060
  Radio and television (See **RADIO AND TELEVISION**)
  Receive money claimed by client, authority to   CCP §283
  Receivers, employment by   CRC 3.1180
    Compensation
      Claim for compensation of attorney in final account   CRC 3.1184
  Referral services
    Privileged communications
      Crime, using service to enable   Ev §968
      Definitions   Ev §965
      Description of privilege   Ev §966

ATTORNEYS—Cont.
  Referral services—Cont.
    Privileged communications —Cont.
      Fraud, using service to enable   Ev §968
      Lawyer referral service-client privilege   Ev §§965 to 968
      Mandatory claim of privilege by service   Ev §967
      Prevention of criminal act likely to result in death or bodily harm, disclosure   Ev §968
      Waiver of attorney referral service-client privilege   Ev §912
      Who may claim privilege   Ev §966
  Registered foreign legal consultants   CRC 9.44
    Fingerprinting of special admission attorneys   CRC 9.9.5
  Registered in-house counsel   CRC 9.46
    Fingerprinting of special admission attorneys   CRC 9.9.5
  Registered legal aid attorney   CRC 9.45
    Fingerprinting of special admission attorneys   CRC 9.9.5
  Registered military spouse attorney   CRC 9.41.1
  Resignation
    State bar, resignation from with pending disciplinary action   CRC 9.21
  Review committees, liability of   CC §43.7
  Roll of attorneys admitted to practice   CRC 9.8
    Online reporting of information by attorneys   CRC 9.9
  Rules of professional conduct   ProfC 1.0 to 8.5 (See **ATTORNEY PROFESSIONAL CONDUCT**)
  Service of process and papers
    Affidavit of compliance, discipline   CRC 9.20
    Foreign legal consultants, service on   CRC 9.44
    Nonresidents, serving attorneys of   CCP §1015
    Remote appearances
      Restraining orders   CRC 3.1162, 5.496
    Service on attorney   CRC 1.21
  Sexual assault of minor, certificate of merit requirement in action for   CCP §§340.1, 340.11
  Sexual harassment, civil action for
    Construction or application of provisions in issue, solicitor general notified   CC §51.1
  Sexual relations with clients
    Attorney professional conduct   ProfC 1.8.10
      Law firms, imputation to all members of firm of violations of certain provisions   ProfC 1.8.11
  Small claims courts (See **SMALL CLAIMS COURTS**)
  Specialist, certification as   CRC 9.35
    Attorney professional conduct
      Communications as to specialization or fields of practice   ProfC 7.4
  Statutes of limitation
    Court assuming jurisdiction over practice, extension on   CCP §353.1
    Professional services, action for wrongful act or omission arising in performance of   CCP §340.6
    Withdrawal of legal service agency attorney for indigent client, effect of   CCP §285.3
  Sterilization proceedings (See **STERILIZATION**)
  Subpoena duces tecum, attorney issuing   CCP §1985
  Substitution of attorney
    Appellate proceedings   CRC 8.36
      Electronic filing, when required   CRCSupp 1st AppDist
    Consent to   CCP §284
    Motion to be relieved as counsel   CCP §284, CRC 3.1362
    Notice to adversary of   CCP §285
    Order for substitution on application of client or attorney   CCP §284
  Summons containing statement re obtaining advice of attorney   CCP §412.20
  Superior courts (See **SUPERIOR COURTS**)
  Support of children
    Disciplinary action against attorney for delinquency in support payments   CRC 9.22
    Representation in child support proceedings (See **CHILD SUPPORT**)
  Telephone, appearance by (See **APPEARANCE**)
  Temporarily in California
    Litigation, in connection with   CRC 9.47
    Nonlitigation services, providing   CRC 9.48
  Temporary judges
    Appointment of attorney as temporary judge   CRC 2.810
    Qualifications of attorney   CRC 2.812
  Termination of parental rights
    Appointment of counsel   Fam §§7860 to 7864
  Training for new attorneys, state bar   CRC 9.32
  Trial court rules
    Change of address
      Service and filing of notice of   CRC 2.200
    Name, address, telephone number, bar membership number, etc
      Papers, first page format and content   CRC 2.111

ATTORNEYS—Cont.
  Trust accounts, IOLTA
    Provisional licensure of 2020 law school graduates
      Access to client trust accounts restricted   CRC 9.49
  Trust accounts, state bar client trust account protection program   CRC 9.8.5
  Trust deeds and mortgages (See **TRUST DEEDS AND MORTGAGES**)
  Trusts
    Probate attorneys
      Education requirements   CRC 10.478
      Qualifications   CRC 10.776, 10.777
  Unauthorized practice of law   ProfC 5.5
    Certified law students   CRC 9.42
  Verification of pleadings   CCP §446
  Vexatious litigant provisions, plaintiff defined for purposes of   CCP §391
  Voir dire examination of prospective jurors (See **JURY**)
  Withdrawal of attorney
    Appellate proceedings   CRC 8.36
    Domestic relations matters   CCP §285.1
    Indigent client, withdrawal of legal service agency attorney for   CCP §§285.2 to 285.4
    Law and motion rule for   CRC 3.1362
    Limited scope representation
      Relief as attorney, request   CRC 3.36
    Motion to be relieved as counsel   CCP §284, CRC 3.1362
      Limited scope representation   CRC 3.36
      Memorandum in support of motion not required   CRC 3.1114

ATTORNEY'S FEES
Generally   CCP §§1021, 1033.5
Administration of estates (See **ADMINISTRATION OF ESTATES**)
Administrative adjudication (See **ADMINISTRATIVE ADJUDICATION**)
Annulment of marriage   Fam §§270 to 274, 2010, 2030 to 2034, 2040, 2255
  Financial need basis   CRC 5.427
Appeals
  Before rendition of judgment, fees for   CRC 3.1702
  Notice of motion to claim fees for   CRC 3.1702
Appointment of counsel
  Fixed fee appointments   CRCSupp FixedFeeAppoint
  Indigent criminal appellants in supreme court, payment guidelines
    Disallowed fees and expenses   CRCSupp PayGuideAppoint
    Expenses   CRCSupp PayGuideAppoint
    Habeas corpus proceedings   CRCSupp PayGuideAppoint
    Nonperformance of work   CRCSupp PayGuideAppoint
    Purpose of provisions   CRCSupp PayGuideAppoint
    Reasonable compensation, factors   CRCSupp PayGuideAppoint
    Withdrawal, reimbursement   CRCSupp PayGuideAppoint
  Probate proceedings, guardianship-conservatorship law
    Financial eligibility for court appointed counsel, guidelines   CRCAppx E
Arbitration of fees
  Jurisdiction in matters concerning   CCP §§86, 116.220
  Small claims action concerning award   CCP §116.220
Asian language contracts, translations   CC §1632
Attachment (See **ATTACHMENT**)
Attorney in fact
  Undue influence or financial abuse of elder or dependent adult to take, conceal, etc, property of principal
    Liability for attorney fees   Pro §4231.5
Attorney professional conduct
  Contingency fee agreements
    Circumstances where contingent fee agreement impermissible   ProfC 1.5
  Law firms
    Financial and other arrangements with nonattorneys   ProfC 5.4
  Nonclient, compensation from   ProfC 1.8.6
    Law firms, imputation to all members of firm of violations of certain provisions   ProfC 1.8.11
  Retainer fees   ProfC 1.5
  Splitting fees   ProfC 1.5.1
  Unconscionable fees   ProfC 1.5
Automated license plate recognition systems (ALPR)
  Data security
    Breach of security   CC §1798.90.54
    Unauthorized access or use of information   CC §1798.90.54
Automobile lease contracts, award on action on   CC §2988.9
Bad-faith actions or tactics, award of expenses and attorney's fees incurred as result of (See **SANCTIONS**)
Bad faith claims under government claims act or for contribution or indemnity   CCP §1038
Blind persons, violating rights of   CC §55
Book accounts, action on   CC §1717.5

ATTORNEY'S FEES—Cont.
Booking photographs
    Commercial use of booking photographs
        Actions to enforce prohibition   CC §1798.91.1
Capital cases, compensation for investigation and filing of habeas corpus petitions in   CRCSupp SupCtPolicy
Carpenter-Katz Small Business Equal Access to Justice Act   CCP §1028.5
Change of venue   CCP §396b
Children and minors
    Services to minors and incompetent persons   CRC 7.955
Child support proceedings (See **CHILD SUPPORT**)
Civil rights actions   CC §§52, 52.1, 54.3
    Construction or application of provisions in issue, solicitor general notified   CC §§51.1, 55.2
Claims against public entities (See **CLAIMS AGAINST PUBLIC ENTITIES AND EMPLOYEES**)
Common interest developments
    Record inspection
        Actions to enforce member rights   CC §5235
Conservation easements, action involving   CC §815.7
Conservatorships (See **CONSERVATORS**)
Construction-related accessibility claims
    Factors considered in awarding attorneys' fees   CC §55.55
Consumer credit
    Holder rule
        Attorneys' fees for exercise of rights under holder rule   CC §1459.5
Contemnor ordered to pay   CCP §1218
Contract actions
    Motion for attorney's fees as costs in   CC §1717, CRC 3.1702
Costs in actions on contract, motion for attorney's fees as   CC §1717, CRC 3.1702
Credit, actions based on denial of (See **CREDIT**)
Credit card holders action based on billing errors   CC §1747.50
Credit reports, action for   CC §1785.31
Crimes against humanity
    Assault and battery, wrongful death, etc constituting torture, genocide, crimes against humanity, etc   CCP §354.8
Custody of children   Fam §3153
    Access to legal representation by requiring party to provide for other party's attorney fees   Fam §7605
        Financial need basis for fees   CRC 5.427
    Court-appointed counsel for minor
        Compensation   CRC 5.241
    Exclusive custody, action for
        Financial need basis for fees   CRC 5.427
        Ordering party to provide for legal representation of other party   Fam §3121
Dealership law, discrimination under   CC §86
Debt collectors falsely claiming   CC §1788.13
Deeds of trust and mortgages
    Foreclosure prevention
        Enforcement   CC §2924.12
Default judgments   CCP §585
    Fee schedules   CRC 3.1800
Delay, award of fees incurred as result of bad-faith actions or tactics solely intended to cause (See **SANCTIONS**)
Dependent children
    Juvenile dependency counsel collections program, guidelines   CRCAppx F
Deposit of estate-planning documents with attorney (See **TRUSTS; WILLS**)
Disabled persons, violating rights of   CC §55
Discount buying services, breach of contract   CC §1812.123
Disputes between attorney and client
    Limitation of actions   CCP §340.6
Dissolution of marriage   Fam §§270 to 274, 2010, 2030 to 2034, 2040
    Domestic violence misdemeanors by spouse against spouse
        Consequences in divorce proceedings   Fam §4325
    Financial need basis   CRC 5.427
    Violent sexual felony or domestic violence felony by spouse against spouse
        Consequences in divorce proceedings   Fam §4324.5
Domestic violence cases   Fam §§6344, 6386
    Tort liability for domestic violence   CC §1708.6
Donative transfers
    Presumption of fraud or undue influence
        Costs and attorney's fees   Pro §21380
Doxing victims' recourse   CC §1708.89
Eminent domain action   CCP §1235.140
Enforcement of judgments (See **ENFORCEMENT OF JUDGMENTS**)
Expedited jury trials
    Applicable provisions   CCP §630.10

ATTORNEY'S FEES—Cont.
Expedited jury trials—Cont.
    Mandatory expedited jury trials, limited civil cases
        Applicability of rules governing costs and attorney fees   CCP §630.27
        Opting out of expedited process   CCP §630.20
    Post-trial motions   CCP §630.09
Fair debt buying practices
    Violation of provisions   CC §1788.62
Family law proceedings   Fam §§270 to 274, 2030 to 2034
    Amount, determination of just and reasonable amount   Fam §2034
    Financial need basis   CRC 5.427
    Limited scope representation, attorneys
        Nondisclosure of attorney assistance in document preparation   CRC 5.425
Fee agreements
    Contingency fee agreements
        Circumstances where contingent fee agreement impermissible   ProfC 1.5
    Time for filing motion for fees under contractual provision   CRC 3.1702
Felons, recovery of attorney's fees in action for damages against   CCP §1021.4
Firearms and other weapons
    Actions to prevent enforcement of laws
        Award to prevailing party   CCP §1021.11
    Firearm industry standards of conduct
        Actions against industry members for violation of standards   CC §3273.52
Fixtures, ownership of   CC §1013.5
Floating homes and floating home marinas   CC §800.200
Foreclosure proceedings   CCP §§580c, 730
Frivolous actions or tactics, award of fees incurred as result of (See **SANCTIONS**)
Garnishment exemptions
    Unavailability of exemption for certain attorneys' fees   CCP §706.051
Genocide
    Assault and battery, wrongful death, etc constituting torture, genocide, crimes against humanity, etc   CCP §354.8
Greenway easements
    Enforcement of easement   CC §816.62
Guardian ad litem, payment of expenses of   CCP §373.5
Guardianships (See **GUARDIAN AND WARD**)
Habeas corpus petitions in capital cases, compensation for investigation and filing of   CRCSupp SupCtPolicy
Home equity sales contracts   CC §1695.7
Housing cooperatives and housing cooperative trusts
    Actions against boards and members
        Attorneys' fees and costs for successful plaintiffs   CC §817.4
Human trafficking
    Actions for human trafficking   CC §52.5
Incompetent persons
    Services to minors and incompetent persons   CRC 7.955
Indemnity action   CCP §1021.6
Indigent persons (See **INDIGENT PERSONS**)
Information Practices Act proceedings (See **INFORMATION PRACTICES ACT**)
Interpleader   CCP §386.6
Interstate family support   Fam §5700.313
Invasion of privacy action   CC §§1798.53, 3344, 3344.1
Inverse condemnation action   CCP §1036
Jenkins act claims   CCP §1021.10
Judgment lien on property of misidentified owner, release of   CCP §§697.410, 697.660
Juvenile proceedings
    Dependency
        Juvenile dependency counsel collections program, guidelines   CRCAppx F
Landlord and tenant
    COVID-19
        Rental debt, action to recover   CCP §871.11
    Immigration or citizenship status of tenant, occupant, etc
        Disclosures to immigration authorities with intent to intimidate or harass   CC §1940.35
    Rent control litigation   CC §1947.15
    Retaliatory eviction, liability   CC §1942.5
    Tenant's action against landlord   CC §789.3
Legal separation proceedings   Fam §§270 to 274, 2010, 2030 to 2034, 2040
    Financial need basis   CRC 5.427
Libel and slander action   CCP §1021.7
Licensees and state regulatory agencies, actions between   CCP §1028.5
Lien foreclosure cases, fees in   CCP §730

INDEX

ATTORNEY'S FEES—Cont.
  Limited scope representation
    Undisclosed representation
      Attorneys' fees sought   CRC 3.37
  Mechanics' liens
    Release of property from claim of lien   CC §8488
    Stop payment notices
      Enforcement of claim stated   CC §8558
  Mediator awarded fees and costs against party attempting to compel testimony or production of documents concerning mediation   Ev §1127
  Membership camping contracts, actions on   CC §1812.306
  Mineral rights, actions involving preservation of   CC §883.250
  Minor's contract for   Fam §6602
  Mistake, inadvertence, surprise or excusable neglect, award of costs and fees on grant of relief from judgment based on   CCP §473
  Mobilehome parks, actions involving   CC §798.85
  Mortgages (See **TRUST DEEDS AND MORTGAGES**)
  Nuisance abatement
    Controlled substances activities
      Unlawful detainer actions   CC §3486
  Nuisance abatement actions   CC §3496
    Controlled substances activities
      Unlawful detainer actions   CC §3486.5
    Illegal weapons on real property
      Unlawful detainer actions   CC §3485
  Obscene and harmful matter
    Unauthorized obscene material
      Actions for distribution   CC §52.8
  Online marketplaces
    Attorney general actions to enforce provisions   CC §1749.8.4
  Online violence prevention
    Violent posts, removal
      Order to remove, action seeking   CC §1798.99.22
  Paint, recovery from parent for minor defacing property by use of   CC §1714.1
  Partition (See **PARTITION**)
  Police officers, actions against   CCP §1021.7
  Power of attorney (See **POWER OF ATTORNEY**)
  Private child support collectors
    Civil actions   Fam §5615
  Probate proceedings
    Appointed counsel under guardianship-conservatorship law
      Financial eligibility guidelines   CRCAppx E
  Public administrator, compensation of attorney for   Pro §7622
  Public defender in conservatorship proceedings   Pro §§1471, 1472
  Public interest, award to prevailing party for action in   CCP §1021.5
  Public nuisances, actions enjoining (See **NUISANCES**)
  Public trails, action to enjoin closure of   CCP §731.5
  Recreational user's action against public entity or private owner contractually related to public or nonprofit agency, administrative claim for attorney's fees in   CC §846.1
  Recreational vehicle parks, actions involving   CC §799.78
  Rental-purchase contracts, breach of   CC §1812.636
  Request for admission
    Failure to admit
      Expense incurred to prove matters not admitted   CCP §2033.420
  Retail installment sales (See **RETAIL INSTALLMENT SALES**)
  Retaliatory eviction action   CC §1942.5
  Salaries and wages, action for   CCP §1031
  Satisfaction of judgments (See **SATISFACTION OF JUDGMENTS**)
  Sexual assault of minor, failure to comply with certificate of merit requirement in action for   CCP §§340.1, 340.11
  Sexually explicit depiction of individual, creation or disclosure
    Element of damages   CC §1708.86
  Sexual orientation violence
    Civil actions   CC §52.45
  SLAPP suits
    Motions to strike
      Defendants prevailing on special motions to strike   CCP §425.16
  Small business and regulatory agency, action between   CCP §1028.5
  Small claims courts (See **SMALL CLAIMS COURTS**)
  Spanish language translation of contracts for   CC §1632
  Special administrators, attorney for   Pro §8547
  Splitting fees   ProfC 1.5.1
  Spousal support proceedings (See **SPOUSAL SUPPORT**)
  Statutory fees, claims for   CRC 3.1702
  Sterilization proceedings   Pro §1963
  Subcutaneous implanting of identification device, requiring of another   CC §52.7
  Subpoenas, motion to quash   CCP §1987.2
  Support of children proceedings (See **CHILD SUPPORT**)
  Telephone appearance, effect on award based on   CRC JudAdminStand 3.1
  Termination of parental rights, appointment of counsel   Fam §7863

ATTORNEY'S FEES—Cont.
  Torture
    Assault and battery, wrongful death, etc constituting torture, genocide, crimes against humanity, etc   CCP §354.8
  Trade secrets, claims of misappropriation of   CC §3426.4
  Trespass to land under agricultural use   CCP §1021.9
  Trial court rules
    Sanctions for failure to comply with rules
      Civil cases   CRC 2.30
  Trust deeds (See **TRUST DEEDS AND MORTGAGES**)
  Trust deposited with attorney (See **TRUSTS**)
  Trustees and associates of trustees, restrictions on legal fees for   Pro §15687
  Unconscionable fee
    Attorney professional conduct   ProfC 1.5
  Uniform Parentage Act, actions under   Fam §7640
  Unlawful detainer action   CCP §1174.2
    Nuisances
      Controlled substances activities   CC §§3486, 3486.5
      Weapons or ammunition on real property   CC §3485
    Rent default, untenantable dwellings
      Landlord liability for costs and attorney fees   CCP §1174.21
  Unperformed contracts for sale of realty   CC §886.020
  Unruh Civil Rights Act, violation of   CC §§52, 52.1
  Unsolicited goods, mailing and attempted collection for   CC §§1584.5, 1584.6
  Vexatious litigant, undertaking to assure payment of expenses incurred in connection with litigation instituted by   CCP §391
  Void or voidable marriage, proceedings to have marriage judged   Fam §2255
  Wage claims   CCP §1031
  War crimes
    Assault and battery, wrongful death, etc constituting torture, genocide, crimes against humanity, etc   CCP §354.8
  Warranties on goods sold, violation of   CC §1794.1
  Wholesale sales representatives, actions involving   CC §1738.16
  Will deposited with attorney (See **WILLS**)

ATTORNMENT
  Tenant attorning to stranger   CC §1948
  Transfer not requiring   CC §1111

AUCTIONS   CC §§1812.600 to 1812.610 (See also **BIDS AND BIDDING**)
  Abandoned property of tenant, sale of   CC §1988
  Administration of decedents' estates (See **ADMINISTRATION OF ESTATES**)
  Advertising requirements   CC §1812.607
  Agency relationship of auctioneer   CC §§2362, 2363
  Authority of auctioneer for sale of property   CC §2362
  Autographed collectibles
    Applicability of provisions   CC §1739.7
  Bids intended only to increase sale price   CC §1812.610
  Bond requirement for auctioneers   CC §1812.600
  Conservatorship, sale of assets of   Pro §2543
  Contract between auctioneer and owner of goods   CC §1812.608
  Decedents' estates, sale of assets of (See **ADMINISTRATION OF ESTATES**)
  Deceptive statements as to highest bid by auctioneer   CC §1812.610
  Definitions   CC §1812.601
  Deposit by auctioneer in lieu of bond   CC §1812.600
  Deposits and payments unclaimed, public auction of   CCP §1563
  Deposits of clients' funds, maintenance of   CC §1812.607
  Disclosure requirements   CC §1812.607
  Duties of auctioneer and auction company   CC §1812.605
  Fine art, sale of   CC §986
  Funds received from auction, requirements for   CC §1812.607
  Guardianship, sale of assets of   Pro §2543
  Horses, notice required at auction of   CC §1834.8
  Injunctions to restrain violative conduct   CC §1812.602
  Innkeeper's lien   CC §§1861.19, 1861.24
  Liability of auctioneer and auction company   CC §§1812.606
  Liens or encumbrances on items, disclosure of   CC §1812.607
  Livestock service liens, sale under   CC §§3080.02 to 3080.22
  Mortgage foreclosure (See **TRUST DEEDS AND MORTGAGES**)
  Notification of changes in auction company   CC §1812.607
  Partition (See **PARTITION**)
  Penalties for violations   CC §§1812.604, 1812.607, 1812.608
  Real property auctions
    Bids intended only to increase sale price   CC §1812.610
  Recordkeeping required   CC §1812.607
  Refunds and deposits   CC §1812.607
  Reserve bids
    Seller bidding to increase sale price   CC §1812.610
  Restitution, order for   CC §1812.603
  Seller's bids
    Disclosures   CC §1812.610

AUCTIONS—Cont.
Terms of auction, announcement of   CC §1812.607
Trust deeds, sale under (See **TRUST DEEDS AND MORTGAGES**)
Unclaimed property (See **UNCLAIMED PROPERTY**)
Waiver of protections   CC §1812.609

AUDIOTAPING
Court proceedings, recording   CRC 2.950 to 2.954
    Media coverage   CRC 1.150
    Notice
        Limitation on papers filed   CRC 3.250
Recording of sound generally (See **RECORDING OF SOUND**)
Transcripts of recordings offered as evidence   CRC 2.1040

AUDIT
Royalties
    Sound recording royalty audits   CC §§2500, 2501

AUDITOR, STATE
Judicial performance, commission on
    Censure, removal, admonishment or retirement of judges
        Confidentiality of proceedings, exceptions for audits   JudPerR 102

AUTHENTICATION OF WRITINGS
Generally   Ev §§1400 to 1454
Clerks of court, fee for authentication of documents by   Gov §70629

AUTHORITY
Joint authority, effect of grant of   CCP §15
Jury commissioner   CCP §195

AUTHORIZED SURETY COMPANY (See **SURETYSHIP, BONDS AND UNDERTAKINGS**)

AUTHORS
Assignment of rights   CC §982
Compositions subject to ownership   CC §655
Infringement, action for   CCP §429.30
Title to created works   CC §§980, 981

AUTOGRAPHS
Memorabilia   CC §1739.7
Signatures generally (See **SIGNATURES**)

AUTOMATED EXTERNAL DEFIBRILLATORS
Immunity from liability for emergency care   CC §1714.21

AUTOMATED LICENSE PLATE RECOGNITION SYSTEMS (ALPR)
Data security   CC §§1798.90.5 to 1798.90.55
    Breach of security
        Remedies   CC §1798.90.54
    Definitions   CC §1798.90.5
    End users
        Definition of ALPR end users   CC §1798.90.5
        Duties   CC §1798.90.53
    Operators
        Definition of ALPR operator   CC §1798.90.5
        Duties   CC §1798.90.51
    Public agencies
        Defined   CC §1798.90.5
        Duties   CC §1798.90.55
        Public comment prior to agency implementation of system   CC §1798.90.55
    Records of access to information   CC §1798.90.52
    Unauthorized access or use of information
        Remedies   CC §1798.90.54
    Usage and privacy policy   CC §1798.90.51
        End users   CC §1798.90.53
        Operators   CC §1798.90.51

AUTOMATED TELLER MACHINES (ATMS) (See **DEBIT CARDS**)

AUTOMATED TRAFFIC ENFORCEMENT SYSTEMS
Intersections and places driver required to stop
    Evidentiary effect of printed representations of computer information
        Applicability to systems   Ev §1552
    Evidentiary effect of printed representations of images stored on video or digital medium
        Applicability to systems   Ev §1553

AUTOMATED TRANSACTIONS (See **ELECTRONIC TRANSACTIONS**)

AUTOMATIC CHECKOUT SYSTEMS
Grocery store point-of-sale systems   CC §§7100 to 7106

AUTOMATIC RENEWAL CLAUSE
Lease, requirements for printing in   CC §1945.5

AUTOMOBILE ACCIDENTS
Property damage
    Time-limited demands   CCP §§999 to 999.5
Vehicle history reports
    Contents   CC §1784.1

AUTOMOBILE DEALERS AND MANUFACTURERS
Buy-here-pay-here auto dealers
    Automobile sales finance
        Obligations of dealers   CC §2983.37
    Consumer warranty protection
        Used vehicles, obligations of dealers   CC §1795.51
Consumer privacy rights
    Inapplicability to vehicle or ownership information shared between dealer and manufacturer   CC §1798.145
Consumer warranty protection
    Used vehicles
        Buy-here-pay-here dealers' obligations   CC §1795.51

AUTOMOBILE INSURANCE
Amortization of amounts advanced to obtain insurance   CC §2982.8
Arbitration of liability coverage disputes
    Agreements to arbitrate   CCP §1784
    Amount in controversy   CCP §1777
    Court-ordered mediation or arbitration, relief from obligation to participate in   CCP §1780
    Definitions   CCP §1776
    Presumption of insurer's good faith   CCP §§1778, 1779
    Removal from arbitration   CCP §1779
    Requests for arbitration   CCP §1777
    Tolling of limitations periods and suspension of case-management requirements   CCP §1780
Claims
    Time-limited demands   CCP §§999 to 999.5
Conditional sale contract provisions as to   CC §§2982, 2982.8, 2984.1, 2984.2
Finance charges on amounts advanced to obtain insurance   CC §2982.8
Juvenile offenders, use of sealed records
    Prosecuting attorney request to access sealed juvenile case files   CRC 5.860
        Order on prosecutor request for access   CRCAppx A
Liability insurance
    Arbitration (See within this heading, "**Arbitration of liability coverage disputes**")
    Conditional sales contracts, coverage under   CC §§2982, 2982.8
    Public liability insurance requirements, warning notice of   CC §2984.1
    Third-party cause of action for unfair claims settlement practices   CC §§2870, 2871
Negligence, inadmissible evidence to prove   Ev §1155
Sales contract, notice of coverage under   CC §§2982, 2982.8, 2984.1, 2984.2
Uninsured motorist cases, rules for arbitration of   Gov §68609.5

AUTOMOBILE LEASES
Generally   CC §§2985.7 to 2993 (See **AUTOMOBILES**)
Rental passenger vehicle transactions generally   CC §§1939.01 to 1939.39 (See **RENTAL PASSENGER VEHICLE TRANSACTIONS**)

AUTOMOBILES
Acceleration of loans   CC §2983.3
Accounting after repossession   CC §2983.2
Acknowledgment of delivery of documents
    Conditional sales contract   CC §2984.3
    Leases   CC §2986.4
Adjustment programs   CC §§1795.90 to 1795.93
Advertising of automobile leases   CC §§2985.71, 2989.4
Animal experimentations, inadmissibility of evidence in products liability actions based on   Ev §1159
Animals
    Leaving or confining animals in unattended vehicles
        Rescue of animal trapped in closed vehicle, immunity from civil or criminal liability for damage to vehicle   CC §43.100
Arbitration of warranty disputes   CC §1793.22
Assignments
    Benefit of creditors, property exempt from assignment for   CCP §1801
    Leases   CC §2986.10

AUTOMOBILES—Cont.
Assignments—Cont.
    Sales contracts   CC §§2983.1, 2983.5
        Consideration for assignment   CC §2982.10
Attachment (See **ATTACHMENT**)
Attorneys' fees recoverable on action on lease   CC §2988.9
Bailment
    Sales contract distinguished   CC §2981.5
Blind persons having equal rights to use of   CC §§54.1, 54.3, 54.4, 55
Conditional sales
    Sales generally (See within this heading, **"Sales"**)
Confidentiality agreements concerning terms of reacquisition by manufacturer or distributor, restrictions on   CC §1793.26
Cosigner's liability
    Generally   CC §§1799.90 to 1799.103
    Repossession, delinquency notice to cosigner prior to   CC §2983.35
Costs
    Conditional sales contract, recovery under   CC §2983.4
    Lease violation, recovery for   CC §2988.5
Crimes
    Lease violations   CC §2989.8
    Sale of automobiles, crimes in   CC §2983.6
Deferment of sales agreement   CC §2982.3
Department of Motor Vehicles (See **MOTOR VEHICLES DEPARTMENT**)
Disabled persons having equal right to use of   CC §§54.1, 54.3, 54.4, 55
Emergency vehicles (See **EMERGENCIES**)
Enforcement of judgments (See **ENFORCEMENT OF JUDGMENTS**)
    Health aids as exempt property
        Conversion of steering, wheelchair lift, or motorized steps   CCP §704.050
Express warranties, nonconformity to   CC §1793.22
Extension of time
    Arbitration of warranty disputes   CC §1793.22
    Sales agreement   CC §2982.3
Fee for repossession notice   Gov §26751
Finance charges
    Conditional sales contract provisions regarding   CC §2982
    Defined   CC §2981
    Insurance obtained by holder   CC §2982.8
Fraud, revival of possessory lien on vehicle lost by   CC §3070
Guide dogs permitted in   CC §§54.2, 54.3
History
    Vehicle history reports
        Contents   CC §1784.1
        Provider duties   CC §1784.1
Industrial loan companies, loans through   CC §2982.8
Information Practices Act, disclosure under   CC §1798.26
Inspection of lease records   CC §2989.5
Installment sales
    Sales generally (See within this heading, **"Sales"**)
Insurance (See **AUTOMOBILE INSURANCE**)
Investment property pledged as collateral on consumer credit contract, restrictions concerning   CC §1799.103
Jurors, Department of Motor Vehicles list of licensed drivers as source for selection of   CCP §197
Kickbacks in automobile leases, prohibition against   CC §2986.12
Labor and materials, lien on vehicle for   CC §3069
Leases   CC §§2985.7 to 2993
    Acknowledgment of delivery of documents, requirements for   CC §2986.4
    Advance payment refund requirements   CC §2986.13
    Advertising   CC §§2985.71, 2989.4
    Asian language contracts, translations   CC §1632
    Assignee, rights of   CC §2986.10
    Attorneys' fees   CC §2988.9
    Chinese language
        Foreign language translations of notice requirement   CC §1799.91
    Confession of judgment prohibited   CC §2986.3
    Constant yield method of computing rent charges   CC §2985.7
    Construction of provisions as to   CC §2985.7
    Consumer credit contract, lease as   CC §1799.90
    Contents of contract   CC §§2985.8, 2986.3
    Contracts   CC §§2985.7 to 2993
        Contents of contract   CC §§2985.8, 2986.3
        Distinguishing between lease contract and sale contract   CC §§2981, 2981.5
    Cooling off period as unavailable   CC §2985.8
    Cosigner's liability, required notice of   CC §§1799.91 to 1799.96
    Crimes   CC §2989.8
    Damages
        Generally   CC §2988.5
        Unlawful subleases, recovery for   CC §3343.5

AUTOMOBILES—Cont.
Leases—Cont.
    Defined   CC §§1799.90, 2985.7
    Early termination of lease, computation of penalty and notice requirements for   CC §2987
    Estimated residual value   CC §2988
    Federal civil action previously filed, effect of   CC §2989
    Gap liability notice   CC §2985.8
    Inspection of records   CC §2989.5
    Kickbacks, prohibition against   CC §2986.12
    Korean language
        Foreign language translations of notice requirement   CC §1799.91
    Lemon law   CC §§1793.2 to 1793.26
    Notices
        Contract, notice in   CC §2985.8
        Early termination, notices required in event of   CC §2987
        Foreign language translations of notice requirement   CC §1799.91
        Sale of vehicle on lease expiration, notice to lessees and guarantors of   CC §2989.2
    Other documents and agreements not required in lease contract   CC §2985.9
    Preprinted forms
        Generally   CC §2992
        Spanish translation required   CC §2991
    Prohibited provisions in   CC §2986.3
    Public policy, declaration of   CC §2988
    Rebates   CC §2986.12
    Refund of down-payment when contract not executed   CC §2986.13
    Registration requirements   CC §2989.4
    Regulation M defined   CC §2985.7
    Regulations by DMV, authorization for   CC §2989.6
    Rental passenger vehicle transactions generally   CC §§1939.01 to 1939.39
        (See **RENTAL PASSENGER VEHICLE TRANSACTIONS**)
    Rescission   CC §2988.7
    Risk of loss   CC §2988
    Sales of vehicle on expiration of lease   CC §2989.2
    Setoffs   CC §2988.5
    Single recovery authorized   CC §2988.5
    Spanish language translation
        Foreign language translations of notice requirement   CC §1799.91
    Spanish language translation requirements   CC §§1632, 2991
    Spanish translation required   CC §2991
    Tagalog language
        Foreign language translations of notice requirement   CC §1799.91
    Title transfer fee, limitation on   CC §2986.5
    Unlawful subleases, action for damages for   CC §3343.5
    Vehicle Code requirements, vehicle complying with   CC §2986.5
    Vietnamese language
        Foreign language translations of notice requirement   CC §1799.91
Lemon law
    Dispute resolution process   CC §1793.22
    Notice to subsequent purchaser   CC §§1793.23, 1793.24
    Presumption regarding reasonable attempts to repair   CC §1793.22
    Reacquisition terms, restrictions on confidentiality agreements concerning   CC §1793.26
    Restitution or replacement of new motor vehicle under warranty   CC §1793.2
    Sales or use tax refunded, reimbursement of manufacturer for   CC §1793.25
Liens
    Apartment housekeeper's lien, exemption from   CC §1861a
    Application to conduct lien sale   CC §§3071, 3072
    Assignment of lien for labor and materials   CC §3069
    Consent of legal owner, services performed without   CC §3068
    Documentation entitling person to possession of vehicle   CC §3068.1
    Extension of lien period, conditions for   CC §3068.1
    Extinguishing of lien, conditions for   CC §3068.1
    Fee for lien-sale preparation   CC §3074
    Fraud, possessory lien on vehicle lost by   CC §3070
    Procedure for conducting lien sales   CC §§3068.1, 3071, 3072
    Proceeds from sale, disposition of   CC §3073
    Repairs, liens for   CC §§3067 to 3074
    Revival of lien by repossession of vehicle   CC §3070
    Security interest for loans   CC §2982.5
    Storage of vehicles, lien for   CC §§3068, 3068.1, 3069
    Towed vehicles
        Expenses for towed vehicle, lien sale to recover   CC §3068.1
        Improper towing or removal to acquire lienhold interest, liability for   CC §3070
        Storage costs, tow truck operator's lien to recover   CC §3068.2

AUTOMOBILES—Cont.
  Liens—Cont.
    Value of vehicle used as basis for conduct of lien sales   CC §§3068.1, 3071, 3072
  Manufacturers, transporters, dealers and sales professionals
    Restitution ordered against licensee, effect   Gov §11519.1
  Notices
    Adjustment programs, manufacturer's notice on   CC §1795.91
    Arbitration of warranty disputes   CC §1793.22
    Deceptive practices, notice concerning   CC §2982
    Leases (See within this heading, "**Leases**")
    Lemon Law Buyback   CC §§1793.23, 1793.24
    Lien sale, notice of   CC §§3071, 3072
    Repossession
      Co-signer, delinquency notice   CC §2983.35
      Intention to sell repossessed vehicle   CC §2983.2
    Sales (See within this heading, "**Sales**")
    Service bulletins, dealer's notice on obtaining   CC §1795.91
  Ownership certificate inscribed with Lemon Law Buyback notation   CC §§1793.23, 1793.24
  Parking (See **PARKING FACILITIES**)
  Pollution control, sales contract notification concerning   CC §2982
  Presumption concerning express warranties   CC §1793.22
  Reacquisition by manufacturer or distributor, restrictions on confidentiality agreements concerning terms of   CC §1793.26
  Reasonable attempts to repair   CC §§1793.2, 1793.22
  Rees-Levering Act
    Sales generally (See within this heading, "**Sales**")
  Refunds
    Leases   CC §2986.13
    Sales   CC §2982.7
  Registration
    Leases
      Optional DMV electronic filing fee, disclosures as to   CC §2985.8
    Sales contracts
      Optional DMV electronic filing fee, disclosures as to   CC §2982
  Reimbursement of manufacturer for sales or use tax refunded to buyer of new motor vehicle under warranty   CC §1793.25
  Rental passenger vehicle transactions generally   CC §§1939.01 to 1939.39
  Repairs
    Adjustment programs   CC §§1795.90 to 1795.93
    Liens for repairs   CC §§3067 to 3074
    Reasonable number of attempts to repair new motor vehicle   CC §§1793.2, 1793.22
    Restitution or replacement of new motor vehicle under warranty   CC §1793.2
    Sales or use tax refunded to buyer of vehicle under warranty, reimbursement of manufacturer for   CC §1793.25
    Service contracts, warranties under   CC §1794.41
  Repossession
    Accounting after repossession   CC §2983.2
    Fee for receipt and filing of repossession report   Gov §26751
    Finance charge, nonpayment of   CC §2982
    Improper towing or removal, liability for   CC §3070
    Notices
      Co-signer, delinquency notice to   CC §2983.35
      Intention to sell repossessed vehicle, notice of   CC §2983.2
    Reinstatement of contract   CC §2983.3
    Revival of possessory lien lost by fraud   CC §3070
  Rescue of child from vehicle
    Immunity from liability for damage or trespass to vehicle   CC §43.102
  Restitution or replacement of new motor vehicle under warranty   CC §1793.2
  Sales
    Acceleration of maturity   CC §2983.3
    Accounting by holder after resale under repossession   CC §2983.2
    Acknowledgment of delivery of documents, requirements for   CC §2984.3
    Amortization   CC §2982.8
    Annual percentage rate, necessity for stating   CC §2982
    Application fees, prohibition against   CC §2982
    Asian language contracts, translations   CC §1632
    Assignee of contract, rights of   CC §§2983.1, 2983.5
    Assignment of contract
      Consideration for assignment   CC §2982.10
      Document retention   CC §2984.5
    Attorneys' fees under conditional sales contract   CC §2983.4
    Bailment contract distinguished   CC §2981.5
    Cancellation option agreement sold with automobile
      Itemized price in contract   CC §2982.2
    Certificate of compliance   CC §2982
    Complaints regarding deceptive trade practices   CC §§2982, 2982.05

AUTOMOBILES—Cont.
  Sales—Cont.
    Confession of judgment, prohibition against contract provision for   CC §2983.7
    Construction of provisions regulating   CC §2981
    Contents of contract for   CC §§2982, 2982.05
    Contract of sale
      Document retention   CC §2984.5
      Itemized prices for separate items sold   CC §2982.2
    Copies of documents   CC §§2982, 2984.3
    Correction of errors   CC §§2983, 2983.1
    Cosigner's liability   CC §§1799.90 to 1799.103
      Repossession, delinquency notice to cosigner   CC §2983.35
    Costs under conditional sales contract   CC §2982.5
    Credit checks
      Document retention   CC §2984.5
    Crimes   CC §2983.6
    Customer receiving copy of contract   CC §2984.3
    Debt cancellation agreements sold with automobile
      Itemized price in contract   CC §2982.2
    Deceptive practices, notice concerning   CC §§2982, 2982.05
    Defenses of buyer, prohibition against contract provision precluding   CC §2983.7
    Deferred agreements   CC §2982.3
    Deficiency recovery after sale of repossessed vehicle   CC §2983.2
    Definitions   CC §2981
    Delinquency charges   CC §2982
    Delivery presumed   CC §2984.3
    Dishonored check, fee for return of   CC §2982
    Document preparation fees, imposition of   CC §2982
    Document retention   CC §2984.5
    Down payment, recovery of   CC §§2982, 2983
    Enforceability of contract   CC §§2983, 2983.1
    Express warranties   CC §1793.22
    Extended agreements   CC §2982.3
    Finance (See **AUTOMOBILE SALES FINANCE**)
    First-class mail, extension request transmitted by   CC §2983.2
    Full disclosure requirements   CC §§2982, 2983
    Insurance, contract provisions as to   CC §§2982, 2982.8, 2984.1, 2984.2
      Itemized price in contract   CC §2982.2
    Investment property pledged as collateral on consumer credit contract, restrictions concerning   CC §1799.103
    Itemization of amount financed
      Disclosures   CC §2982
    Itemized prices for separate items sold   CC §2982.2
    Lease distinguished   CC §§2981, 2981.5
    Lemon law (See within this heading, "**Lemon law**")
    Liability to purchaser of assignee   CC §2983.5
    Licenses for automobile manufacturers, transporters, dealers and sales professionals
      Restitution, licensee ordered to pay   Gov §11519.1
    Liens generally (See within this heading, "**Liens**")
    Limitation on liability of assignee   CC §2983.5
    Mailing of notice after repossession   CC §§2982, 2982.8, 2983.2, 2983.3
    Mistakes, correction of   CC §2984
    No cooling off period, notice of   CC §2982
    Notices
      Contractual notifications, generally   CC §2982
      Insurance, notifications concerning   CC §§2982, 2982.8
      Pollution control compliance, notifications concerning   CC §2982
    Other property, conditional sales contract affecting   CC §2984.2
    Permissible property for   CC §2984.2
    Pollution control, contractual notifications regarding   CC §2982
    Precomputed basis finance charge   CC §§2981, 2981.8, 2982
    Prepayment of indebtedness   CC §2982
    Recovery by buyer   CC §§2983, 2983.1
    Rees-Levering motor vehicles sales and finance act   CC §§2981 to 2984.5
    Refund to buyer   CC §2982.7
    Registration of vehicle
      Optional DMV electronic filing fee, disclosures as to   CC §2982
    Regulation, applicability of   CC §2981
    Repossession generally (See within this heading, "**Repossession**")
    Rescission   CC §§2982.5, 2983.1
    Sales or use tax refunded to buyer or lessee of new motor vehicle under warranty, manufacturer's reimbursement   CC §1793.25
    Service contracts
      Itemized price in contract   CC §2982.2
    Signature   CC §2982
    Simple-interest basis finance charge   CC §§2981, 2981.7, 2982
    Small claims court, assignee's standing to file claim in   CCP §116.420
    Spanish language, contract in   CC §1632

AUTOMOBILES—Cont.
  Sales—Cont.
    Supervised financial organization, loans by CC §2982.5
    Supervised financial organizations CC §2982.5
    Surface protection products sold with automobile
      Itemized price in contract CC §2982.2
    Theft deterrent devices sold with automobile
      Itemized price in contract CC §2982.2
    Third parties financing purchase of CC §2982.5
    Trade-in calculation and disclosure CC §2982
    Truth-in-Lending Act, applicability of CC §2982
    Type-size requirements for contract CC §2981.9
    Unfair trade practices CC §§2982, 2982.05
    Used vehicles
      Cooling off period CC §2982
    Validity of contract CC §§2983, 2983.1
    Venue of action CC §2984.4, CCP §396a
    Wage assignment clause, prohibition against CC §2983.7
    Waiver of rights by buyer, prohibition against contract provision for CC §2983.7
    Writing required for contract of CC §§2981.9, 2982
  Sales or use tax refunded, reimbursement of manufacturer for CC §1793.25
  Security interests, types of CC §2982.5
  Service bulletins in adjustment programs CC §§1795.90, 1795.91
  Service contracts CC §§1793.2, 1794.41
  Small claims court (See **SMALL CLAIMS COURTS**)
  Small estates without administration Pro §13050
  Special county sheriff's fund for fees collected from inspection of motor vehicles requiring certificate of correction Gov §26746.1
  Starter interrupt technology
    Buy-here-pay-here auto dealers
      Automobile sales finance, restrictions on use of technology CC §2983.37
  Storage liens CC §§3067 to 3074
  Supervised financial organizations, loans by CC §2982.5
  Vehicle history reports
    Contents CC §1784.1
    Provider duties CC §1784.1
  Vehicle identification numbers
    Vehicle history reports
      Contents CC §1784.1
  Warranty
    Lemon law
      Sales or use tax refunded, reimbursement of manufacturer CC §1793.25
    Military
      Motor vehicle purchased in US, applicability of California warranty provisions CC §1791.8
    Restitution or replacement actions CCP §§871.20 to 871.28
      Applicability of provisions CCP §871.20
      Civil penalties CCP §871.27
      Damages CCP §871.27
      Definitions CCP §871.22
      Depositions CCP §871.26
      Discovery CCP §871.26
      Duties and obligations cumulative CCP §871.28
      Limitation of actions CCP §871.21
      Notice CCP §871.24
      Offsets CCP §871.27
      References to manufacturers CCP §871.23
      Standardized SBA release CCP §871.25
    Sale of personal information, opting out
      Information shared between new vehicle dealer and manufacturer for warranty or recall purposes CC §1798.145
    Used vehicles
      Buy-here-pay-here dealers' obligations CC §1795.51
  Weight
    Administrative regulations
      Vehicle weight impacts and ability of manufacturers and operators to comply with weight laws Gov §11343.3
  Written declaration, trial by for infractions offenses CRC 4.210

AUTOMOBILE SALES FINANCE CC §2982.5
  Buy-here-pay-here dealers
    Obligations of dealers CC §2983.37
  Contracts
    Electric vehicle charging stations included in contract
      Disclosures CC §2982.11
  Dealers
    Buy-here-pay-here dealers
      Obligations of dealers CC §2983.37

AUTOMOBILE SALES FINANCE—Cont.
  Disclosures
    Electric vehicle charging stations included in contract CC §2982.11
  Electric vehicles
    Charging stations included in contract
      Disclosures CC §2982.11
  Finance charge CC §§2981, 2981.7, 2981.8, 2982, 2982.8
  Guaranteed asset protection waiver
    Conditional sales contracts
      Offer, sale, etc, of guaranteed asset protection waiver in connection with contract CC §2982.12
    Defined CC §2981
    Disclosures CC §§2982, 2982.2
  Notices
    Guaranteed asset protection waiver
      Offer, sale, etc, of guaranteed asset protection waiver in connection with conditional sales contract CC §§2982.12, 2983.1

AUTOMOBILE THEFT
Keys left in parked vehicle, liability affected by CC §1630.5
Limitation on liability, effect of signs stating CC §1630
Parking facility, liability of CC §1630.5

AUTOPSIES
Child victims
  Sealing autopsy report and evidence CCP §130
  Restriction on reproducing photograph or video taken in course of CCP §129

AVIATION (See **AIRCRAFT AND AVIATION**)

AVOIDANCE
Voidable transactions CC §3439.07

AWARDS
Attorneys' fees (See **ATTORNEY'S FEES**)
International commercial arbitration awards (See **INTERNATIONAL COMMERCIAL ARBITRATION AND CONCILIATION**)
Judicial arbitration awards (See **JUDICIAL ARBITRATION**)
Non-judicial arbitration awards (See **ARBITRATION**)

B

BABYSITTING AND BABYSITTERS (See **CHILD CARE**)

BACKGROUND
Expert witnesses Ev §802

BAD CHECKS (See **CHECKS**)

BAD FAITH
Award of expenses and attorney's fees incurred as result of bad-faith actions or tactics (See **SANCTIONS**)
Landlord, bad faith retention of deposits by CC §1950.7
Powers of attorney
  Bad faith of attorney in fact Pro §§4231, 4231.5
Small claims court judgment, award of attorney's fees on appeal from CCP §116.790
Summary judgment motion support or opposition presented in bad faith CCP §437c

BAGGAGE
Bus, liability for loss by operator of CC §2205
Common carriers liens for fares CC §2191
Delivery requirements CC §2183
Foreclosure of deposit liens CC §1857
Free carriage of CC §§2180, 2181
Higher value declaration CC §§2177, 2205
Hotel, apartment, lodging or hospital, limitation of action for recovery or conversion of personal property left at CCP §341a
Hotel keeper's lien on CC §1861
Lien for rent CC §§1861, 1861a
Limitation on liability
  Carrier's liability CC §§2178, 2182
  Innkeeper's liability CC §1859
Notice of valuable goods CC §2177
Place for carrying CC §2183
Tagging requirements CC §2205

BAIL
Amount of bail
  Jury trial, request for as affecting amount CRC 4.101

BAIL—Cont.
Amount of bail—Cont.
  Schedules CRC 4.102
Appeal, bail pending CRC 8.312
  Finality of court of appeals ruling on bail CRC 8.366
Boating violations
  Bail schedule CRC 4.102
Business licensing violations, bail schedule CRC 4.102
Check, payment by means of CRC 10.821
Contempt proceedings CCP §§1213, 1215, 1216
Fish and game violations, bail schedule CRC 4.102
Forestry violations, bail schedule CRC 4.102
Jury trial request, effect of CRC 4.101
Parks and recreation violations, bail schedule CRC 4.102
Payment CRC 10.821
Public utilities violations, bail schedule CRC 4.102
Reduction of bail
  Pending appeal CRC 8.312
Schedules CRC 4.102
Uniform Bail and Penalty Schedules CRC 4.102

BAILIFFS
Appointment CRCSupp JudEthicsCanon 3
Juvenile court proceedings CRC 5.530

BAILMENT
Automobiles (See **AUTOMOBILES**)
Death of party to CC §1934
Default on obligations by lessor CC §1957
Delivery of property under CC §1955
Demand for return of property loaned CC §1894
Deposits (See **DEPOSITS**)
Enforcement of judgments (See **ENFORCEMENT OF JUDGMENTS**)
Expenses and upkeep CC §§1956, 2078
Fitness requirement of property held under CC §1955
Gratuitous bailee CC §§1505, 2078
Hiring contracts CC §§1925 to 1935
Indemnity requirements CC §§1893, 1894
Loss from early termination of CC §§1894, 1935
Negligence CC §§1888, 1928, 2078
Notice of expenditures CC §1957
Offer of contract CC §1503
Place for redelivery of property held under CC §§1896, 1958
Possession, transfer of CC §1925
Quiet enjoyment, right of CC §1955
Repairs CC §§1889, 1929
Return of bailed property CC §1958
Termination of agreement CC §§1894 to 1896, 1931 to 1934
Use, bailment for CC §§1884 to 1896
Vessels held under charter-party agreement CC §1959

BALLOON PAYMENTS (See **TRUST DEEDS AND MORTGAGES**)

BALLOT MEASURES
Precedence to cases involving certification of CCP §35

BANK ACCOUNTS
Community property accounts of spouses
  Statutory language for creating particular types of accounts Pro §5203
Electronic transactions
  Exceptions to applicability of electronic transactions provisions CC §1633.3
Joint accounts
  Excess withdrawal by party
    Claim for recovery Pro §5301
    Proportional ownership interest in other parties Pro §5301
Pay-on-death accounts
  Excess withdrawal by party
    Claim for recovery Pro §5301
    Proportional ownership interest in other parties Pro §5301
Tenancy in common account
  Statutory language for creating particular types of accounts Pro §5203
Totten trust accounts
  Excess withdrawal by party
    Claim for recovery Pro §5301
    Proportional ownership interest in other parties Pro §5301

BANK ACCOUNTS—Cont.
Trust accounts
  Excess withdrawal by party
    Proportional ownership interest in other parties Pro §5301

BANK DRAFTS (See **CHECKS**)

BANKING (See **BANKS AND BANKING**)

BANKRUPTCY (See also **INSOLVENCY**)
Assignment for benefit of creditors (See **ASSIGNMENT FOR BENEFIT OF CREDITORS**)
Attachment (See **ATTACHMENT**)
Automobile sales finance
  Acceleration of loans
    Proceedings in bankruptcy not to be used to accelerate loan CC §2983.3
  Repossession
    Proceedings in bankruptcy not to be used to justify repossession CC §2983.3
Child support obligations discharged in Fam §4013
Credit reporting (See **CREDIT REPORTING**)
Debt collectors, effect on CC §1788.14
Enforcement of judgments (See **ENFORCEMENT OF JUDGMENTS**)
1st Appellate District local rule, duty of party to inform court of pending bankruptcy proceedings pursuant to CRCSupp 1st AppDist
Fraudulent transfers (See **VOIDABLE TRANSACTIONS**)
Gift certificates
  Issuer's duty to honor CC §1749.6
Homestead exemption, applicability of CCP §703.140
  Amount of exemption, determination CCP §703.150
Investigative agencies, restrictions on information of CC §1785.18
Judicial notice of general orders and forms in Ev §451
Landlord, priority of deposits by tenant to CC §1950.7
Liens, effect on CCP §§493.030 to 493.050
Property settlement agreements, discharge of obligations in Fam §3592
Small claims court, trustee in bankruptcy filing in CCP §116.420
Voidable transactions (See **VOIDABLE TRANSACTIONS**)

BANKS AND BANKING
Administrators of decedents' estates (See **EXECUTORS AND ADMINISTRATORS**)
Armenian genocide victims, claims against banks
  Limitation of actions CCP §354.45
Attachment (See **ATTACHMENT**)
Attorney professional conduct
  Trust accounts
    Safekeeping of funds and property of clients ProfC 1.15
Banker's liens CC §3054
Blocked accounts (See **BLOCKED ACCOUNTS**)
Business days CC §9
Check accounts (See **CHECKS**)
Child support payments (See **CHILD SUPPORT**)
Collection agencies, regulations on CC §§1788 to 1788.32
Conservators
  Banks acting as conservators (See **CONSERVATORS**)
  Opening or changing name on conservatee's account, responsibilities of conservator CRC 7.1061
Creditors, deposit of money due CC §1500
Debit cards, cardholder's liability for unauthorized use
  Waiver of protections
    Void CC §1748.32
Deposits
  Attachment (See **ATTACHMENT**)
  Beneficiaries, direct payment to Pro §9704
  Blocked accounts (See **BLOCKED ACCOUNTS**)
  Child support security deposits CC §710
  Creditors, money due CC §1500
  Decedent's estate, deposits for Pro §§8401, 9700 to 9705
  Definitions Pro §§21, 46
  Enforcement of judgments (See **ENFORCEMENT OF JUDGMENTS**)
  Escheat CCP §1513
  Heirs, direct payment of estate funds to Pro §9704
  Liens on CC §3054
  Married person's earnings held in deposit account Fam §911, Pro §§5305 to 5307
  Multiple-party accounts (See **MULTIPLE-PARTY ACCOUNTS**)

BANKS AND BANKING—Cont.
  Deposits—Cont.
    Performance of contract by making   CC §1500
    Seller assisted marketing plans, claims against deposit accounts of   CC §1812.221
    Surety making   CC §2811
    Unclaimed deposits   CCP §§1513, 1513.5, 1516
  Discount buying organization establishing trust account in   CC §1812.116
  Enforcement of judgments (See **ENFORCEMENT OF JUDGMENTS**)
  Escheat of deposits   CCP §§1513, 1513.5
  Executors of decedents' estates (See **EXECUTORS AND ADMINISTRATORS**)
  Extension of credit for overdrawn accounts   CC §§1747.02, 1747.03
  Federal banks, rules applicable to   CC §1916.12
  Financial contracts, statute of frauds provisions concerning   CC §1624
  Financial protection and innovation commissioner
    Interest rate regulatory authority   CC §1916.5
    Superior court hearings on sale of properties of savings and loan association who's properties and assets are in possession of   CCP §§73c, 73d
    Unclaimed Property Law, investigatory powers under   CCP §1571
  Forged or raised check, limitation of action for payment of   CCP §340
  Guardians
    Banks as guardians (See **GUARDIAN AND WARD**)
    Opening or changing name on accounts, responsibilities of guardian   CRC 7.1011
  Heirs, direct payment to   Pro §9704
  Holidays for banks   CC §§7.1, 9
  Identity theft
    Business entity filings   CC §§1798.200 to 1798.203
  Impound accounts, interest on   CC §2954.8
  Interest on impound accounts   CC §2954.8
  Joint tenancy in bank deposits   CC §683
  Judgments, enforcement
    Service of process
      Central locations of financial institutions, designation for service of process   CCP §684.115
      Manner of service   CCP §684.110
      Third-party agents, designation for service of process   CCP §684.115
  Liens   CC §3054
  Liquidation, limitations period for recovery of money or property deposited applicable to banks in process of   CCP §348
  Minors
    Multiple-party accounts, payments from   Pro §5407
    Uniform Transfers to Minors Act (See **UNIFORM TRANSFERS TO MINORS ACT**)
  Multiple-party accounts (See **MULTIPLE-PARTY ACCOUNTS**)
  Negotiable instruments (See **NEGOTIABLE INSTRUMENTS**)
  NOW accounts, escheat of   CCP §1513
  Optional bank holidays   CC §7.1
  P.O.D Accounts (See **MULTIPLE-PARTY ACCOUNTS**)
  Power of attorney (See **POWER OF ATTORNEY**)
  Process, officers receiving service of   CCP §416.10
  Public administrators (See **PUBLIC ADMINISTRATORS**)
  Public officers and employees
    Quieting title to improperly encumbered property of public officer or employee, proceedings for
      Financial institution claims, applicability of provisions   CCP §765.050
  Recovery of money or property deposited, limitation of actions for   CCP §348
  Safe deposit boxes (See **SAFETY DEPOSIT BOXES**)
  Saturday holidays affecting   CC §9
  Seller assisted marketing plans   CC §§1812.204, 1812.206, 1812.214
  Sexual harassment, civil action for
    Construction or application of provisions in issue, solicitor general notified   CC §51.1
  Shared appreciation loans (See **SHARED APPRECIATION LOANS**)
  Small businesses
    Commercial financing transactions   CC §§1799.300 to 1799.304
  Social security numbers
    Confidentiality
      Continued use by financial institutions   CC §1786.60
  Statutes of limitation
    Forged or raised check, action against bank for payment of   CCP §340
    Recovery of money or property deposited, actions for   CCP §348
  Totten trust accounts   Pro §§5404, 5406
  Trustee, financial institutions as   Pro §16015
  Variable interest rates (See **INTEREST ON MONEY**)

BANK SUPERINTENDENT
Interest variables, prescribing regulations for   CC §1916.5

BAPTISMAL CERTIFICATES
Birth, evidence of   Ev §1315

BAR ASSOCIATION (See **ATTORNEYS**)

BARBERING AND COSMETOLOGY
Gender
  Prohibition against charging different price for services of similar or like kind based solely on   CC §51.6
  Small business gender discrimination in pricing services compliance act   CC §§55.61 to 55.63
Human trafficking
  Signs, businesses required to post notice concerning relief from slavery or human trafficking   CC §52.6

BAR EXAMINATION
Analysis of validity of examination   CRC 9.6
Committee of Bar Examiners
  Appointments   CRC 9.4
  Duties as to bar examination   CRC 9.6
  Nominations   CRC 9.4
  Rules adopted by committee and approved by trustees
    Supreme court review and approval   CRC 9.5
Supreme court
  Approval by supreme court   CRC 9.6

BARLEY
Crusher, lien for use of   CC §3061
Storage regulations after sale of   CC §§1880 to 1881.2

BARS (See **COCKTAIL LOUNGES**)

BASTARDS (See **PARENT AND CHILD**)

BATTERED WOMAN OR INTIMATE PARTNER BATTERING EFFECTS
Admissibility of expert testimony of   Ev §1107
Child victims, 12 or older
  Medical care and treatment
    Consent   Fam §6930
Domestic violence generally (See **DOMESTIC VIOLENCE**)
Mitigation of circumstances   CRC 4.423

BATTERY (See **ASSAULT AND BATTERY**)

BB DEVICES
Sale to minor
  Verification of age for sale of age-restricted products   CC §1798.99.1

BEACHES
Public entity's liability for   Gov §831.21
Public use of private land   CC §1009

BEAUTY SALONS (See **BARBERING AND COSMETOLOGY**)

BED AND BREAKFAST LODGING
Human trafficking or slavery
  Signs, businesses required to post notice concerning relief from slavery or human trafficking   CC §52.6

BED BUG INFESTATIONS
Landlord and tenant   CC §§1954.600 to §CC 1954.605
  Current infestation
    Showing, renting or leasing of premises prohibited   CC §1954.602
  Information on bed bugs provided to prospective tenants   CC §1954.603
  Inspections
    Entry by landlord to inspect   CC §1954.604
    Findings, notice to tenant   CC §1954.605
  Legislative findings and intent   CC §1954.600
  Notice by tenant of suspected infestation
    Retaliatory eviction or other retaliatory actions, prohibitions   CC §1942.5
  Pest control operators
    Defined   CC §1954.601

BEEF (See **LIVESTOCK**)

BEER (See **ALCOHOLIC BEVERAGES**)

BENEFICIARIES
Life insurance (See **LIFE INSURANCE**)
Power of attorney (See **POWER OF ATTORNEY**)
Trusts (See **TRUSTS**)
Wills (See **WILLS**)

BEST AND SECONDARY EVIDENCE
Generally   Ev §§1520 to 1522
Business records, admissibility of (See **BUSINESS RECORDS**)
Certified copies   Ev §1531
Computer information, printed representations of (See **COMPUTERS**)
Deeds   Ev §§1600 to 1605
Duplicate defined   Ev §260
Lost or destroyed original, secondary evidence of contents of   Ev §§1523, 1551
Microphotographed files, records, photographs, etc., in custody of criminal justice agency
     Reproductions, admissibility   Ev §1550.1
Numerous accounts or writings, admissibility of oral evidence representing   Ev §1523
Official records   Ev §§1530 to 1532
Oral evidence, admissibility of   Ev §1523
Original defined   Ev §255

BEST INTEREST OF CHILD (See **CUSTODY OF CHILDREN**)

BEVERAGES (See **ALCOHOLIC BEVERAGES**)

BEYOND REASONABLE DOUBT
Criminal proceedings   Ev §§501, 502
Presumptions, effect on   Ev §607
Requirement for burden of proof   Ev §115
Sterilization proceedings, findings in   Pro §1958

BIAS AND PREJUDICE
Court commissioners, disqualification of   CCP §170.6
Disqualification of judges (See **JUDGES, DISQUALIFICATION OF**)
Disregard of nonprejudicial error   CCP §475
Evidence excluded for creating   Ev §352
     Creative expressions, admissibility   Ev §352.2
Judges   CRCSupp JudEthicsCanons 3, 4 (See **JUDGES**)
Judicial administration standards
     Appointments by court, nondiscrimination in   CRC JudAdminStand 10.21
     Duty of court to prevent bias   CRC JudAdminStand 10.20
Jury
     Civil cases, judicial administration standards   CRC JudAdminStand 3.25
     Peremptory challenge to juror based on bias   CCP §§231.5, 231.7
     Voir dire examination calculated to discover   CCP §222.5
Petit jurors
     Civil cases, judicial administration standards   CRC JudAdminStand 3.25
Pleadings and proof, material variance in   CCP §469
Presumption against prejudice   CCP §475
Referees, disqualification of   CCP §§170.6, 639, 641

BIBLE
Ancestry, family entries as evidence   Ev §1312

BICYCLES
Common carriers transporting   CC §2181
Electric bicycles
     Landlord and tenant
         Personal micromobility devices, rights of tenants   CC §1940.41
     Shared mobility devices   CC §§2505 to 2506
Serial numbers destroyed or altered prior to sale   CC §1710.1
Shared mobility devices   CC §§2505 to 2506

BIDS AND BIDDING (See also **AUCTIONS**)
Administration of estates (See **ADMINISTRATION OF ESTATES**)
Enforcement of judgments (See **ENFORCEMENT OF JUDGMENTS**)
Homestead exemption, effect of bids failing to exceed amount of   CCP §704.800
Leases on city property   CC §719
Mortgages, sales under   CC §§2924g, 2924h
     Prospective owner-occupant as bidder   CC §2924m
Partition sales   CCP §873.680

BIFURCATION
Family law rules (See **FAMILY RULES**)
Motion of court for   CCP §§597, 597.5
New trial motion following bifurcated trial   CRC 3.1591
Statement of decision   CRC 3.1591

BIGAMY
Spousal testimony in bigamy proceedings, admissibility of   Ev §§972, 985

BILLBOARDS (See **SIGNS AND BILLBOARDS**)

BILLING COMPANIES
Medical claims, release of information for   CC §56.16

BILLING CYCLE (See **RETAIL INSTALLMENT SALES**)

BILL OF EXCEPTIONS
Extensions of time   CCP §§1054, 1054.1
New trial, loss as grounds for   CCP §663.1

BILL OF LADING
Apportionment of freightage under   CC §2140
Limitation on liability   CC §2176

BILL OF PARTICULARS
Demand and response
     Limitation on papers filed   CRC 3.250

BILL OF RIGHTS
Fourth Amendment (See **SEARCH AND SEIZURE**)

BILL OF SALE
Generally   CC §1053
Cancellation   CC §1058
Consignment (See **COMMON CARRIERS**)
Constructive delivery   CC §1059
Delivery   CC §§1054 to 1056, 1059
Escrow, transfer through   CC §§1057, 1057.5
Grain sold by bill of sale without delivery   CC §§1880.3 to 1880.6, 1880.8, 1880.9
Hearsay rule affecting admissibility of statements in   Ev §1330
Mining machinery   CC §1631
Redelivery   CC §1058
Unclaimed property, controller executing bills of sale for   CCP §1376
Vessels   CC §1135

BILLS AND NOTES
Accrual of interest on promissory note secured by trust deed   CC §2948.5
Administrator executing notes   Pro §§9805, 9806
Attachment (See **ATTACHMENT**)
Common carrier's liability for transporting   CC §2200
Dance studio, defenses on notes given for lessons by   CC §1812.55
Discount buying services   CC §1812.113
Executors executing notes   Pro §§9805, 9806
Guardianship (See **GUARDIAN AND WARD**)
Health studio fees, defenses against holders of notes given for   CC §1812.87
Joinder of parties, costs in absence of   CCP §1022
Nonprobate transfers (See **NONPROBATE TRANSFERS**)
Possession of note as presumption of payment   Ev §634
Retail installment sales notes, defenses against holders of   CC §1810.7
Seller assisted marketing plan   CC §1812.210
Trust deeds and mortgages, notes secured by (See **TRUST DEEDS AND MORTGAGES**)
Unsolicited goods, billing statements sent for   CC §§1584.5, 1584.6
Variable interest note, requirements of notice for   CC §1916.5

BILLS OF EXCHANGE
Generally (See **NEGOTIABLE INSTRUMENTS**)
Checks (See **CHECKS**)
Joinder of parties, costs in absence of   CCP §1022

BINDING
Attorney's authority to bind client   CCP §283

BINS
Grain storage after sale, regulation of   CC §§1880 to 1881.2

BIRTH
Adoption proceedings (See **ADOPTION**)
Bible entries as evidence   Ev §1312
Certificates of birth (See **BIRTH CERTIFICATES**)
Church records as evidence   Ev §1315
Community reputation concerning   Ev §1314
Declarant unavailable, admissibility of statement of   Ev §1310
Family friends, statements concerning birth by   Ev §1311
Genetic defects, failure of parent to abort on discovery of   CC §43.6
Neighbor's testimony concerning   Ev §1314
Paternity suits (See **PATERNITY**)
Records as proof of   Ev §1281
Relative's statements concerning   Ev §1311
Reputation among family members concerning   Ev §1313
Statutes of limitation for personal injuries to minor sustained during birth   CCP §340.4

BIRTH CERTIFICATES
Adoption proceedings (See **ADOPTION**)
Change of name
     Application to change name or child's name on California birth certificate   CCP §1276

BIRTH CERTIFICATES—Cont.
Evidence concerning family history Ev §§1315, 1316
Forms
 Judicial council legal forms CRCAppx A
Parentage, voluntary declarations Fam §§7570 to 7581
 Challenge to declaration
  New certificates, issuance in light of ruling Fam §7578
Recordation of (See **RECORDS AND RECORDING**)

BIRTH CONTROL
Abortion (See **ABORTIONS**)
Sterilization (See **STERILIZATION**)

BIRTH NAME
Dissolution and annulment proceedings, restoration of former name in Fam §§2080 to 2082, 2401
Refusal to do business with person due to use of birth name CCP §1279.6

BIRTH PARENTS (See **ADOPTION**)

BLACKLISTING
Civil rights protection
 Construction or application of provisions in issue, solicitor general notified CC §51.1

BLIND PERSONS
Administrative procedure act
 Visual or communication disability
  Narrative description of proposed regulation upon request Gov §11346.6
Commercial and industrial common interest developments
 Disabled access
  Modification of separate interests CC §6714
Definition of visually impaired CC §54.6
Discrimination (See **DISCRIMINATION**)
Equal access to public facilities CC §§54, 54.1, 54.3, 54.4, 55
 Construction or application of provisions in issue, solicitor general notified CC §55.2
Guide dogs for (See **DOGS**)
Housing, denial of CC §54.1
 Construction or application of provisions in issue, solicitor general notified CC §55.2
Injunctions for violation of equal rights CC §55
Internet website-related accessibility claims CC §55.33
Jury (See **JURY**)
Negligence, failure to use white cane or guide dog as not constituting CC §54.4
Privacy
 Touch screen devices for self-service check-in at hotels or transportation facilities CC §54.9
Public restrooms, right to use of CC §55
Telephone facilities, use of CC §54.1
 Construction or application of provisions in issue, solicitor general notified CC §55.2
Touch screen devices
 Self-service check-in at hotels or passenger transportation facilities CC §54.9
Visually impaired defined CC §54.6
White cane
 Day set aside for CC §54.5
 Negligence in failure to use CC §54.4

BLOCKED ACCOUNTS
Conservators and guardians, reduction of surety bond amount required for Pro §2328
Executors and administrators, reduction of surety bond amount required for Pro §8483

BLOOD TESTS
Admissibility of evidence from Ev §712
Adoption
 DNA testing (See **ADOPTION**)
Parentage
 Genetic testing to determine parentage Fam §§7550 to 7562 (See **PATERNITY**)

BLUE LAWS (See **SUNDAYS**)

BLUNT WRAPS
Minors
 Verification of age for sale of age-restricted products CC §1798.99.1

BOARDING FACILITIES AND STABLES
Statutes of limitation for injury to animal CCP §340

BOARDINGHOUSES
Blind persons CC §§54.1, 54.3, 54.4, 55
 Construction or application of provisions in issue, solicitor general notified CC §55.2
Demolition
 Notice of application to demolish CC §1940.6
Disabled persons CC §§54.1, 54.3, 54.4, 55
 Construction or application of provisions in issue, solicitor general notified CC §55.2
Forcible entry statute, protection under CCP §1159
Guide dogs permitted in CC §§54.2, 54.3
 Construction or application of provisions in issue, solicitor general notified CC §55.2
Liens CC §§1861 to 1861.28
Loss of property, liability of housekeeper for CC §§1859, 1860
Monthly tenancy presumed CC §1944
Occupancy, right to CC §1940.1
Rent control ordinances, effect of substantial compliance with CC §1947.7
Statute of limitation for recovery or conversion of personal property left at CCP §341a
Tenants, classification as CC §1940
Termination, notice of CC §1946.5

BOARD OF SUPERVISORS (See **SUPERVISORS**)

BOARDS
Agricultural Labor Relations Board, judicial review of decisions CRC 8.728
Public Employment Relations Board, judicial review of decisions CRC 8.728
Service of process on CCP §416.50
Validation proceedings CCP §§860 to 870
Workers' Compensation Appeals Board, judicial review of decisions CRC 8.720

BOATING TRAILS
Closure of CCP §731.5

BOATS (See **VESSELS**)

BODYWORKERS
Human trafficking or slavery
 Signs, businesses required to post notice concerning relief from slavery or human trafficking CC §52.6

BOGUS CHECKS (See **CHECKS**)

BOLTS
Fixtures attached to real property by CC §660

BOMB SHELTERS
Personal injury liability of governmental agency to parties using CC §1714.5

BONA FIDE PURCHASERS
Art works sold by dealer to CC §1738.7
Home equity sales contracts CC §1695.12
Nonprobate transfers to former spouse Pro §5044
Partition sales CCP §873.690
Voidable transactions CC §3439.08

BONDING COMPANY (See **SURETYSHIP, BONDS AND UNDERTAKINGS**)

BONDS
Appeal bonds CCP §§917.9 to 922
Appellate rules, superior court appeals
 Costs
  Recoverable costs CRC 8.891
Attachment (See **ATTACHMENT**)
Child custody
 Orders
  Risk of abduction findings and preventative measures Fam §3048
Claims against public entities and employees, requirement for bonds to pay Gov §§975.2 to 978.8
Common interest developments
 Directors, officers and employees
  Association to maintain bond or insurance coverage for directors, officers and employees CC §5806
Conservators CRC 7.207
Corporate sureties, prerequisites to acceptance of CRC 3.1130
Decedents' estates (See **ADMINISTRATION OF ESTATES**)
Defined CCP §349.2
Enforcement of bond
 Deposit in lieu of bond
  Collection, sale, etc, to enforce liability CCP §995.760
Enforcement of judgments (See **ENFORCEMENT OF JUDGMENTS**)

BONDS—Cont.
Fax filing and service
    Excluded documents and papers from   CRC 2.300
Fidelity bonds (See **SURETYSHIP, BONDS AND UNDERTAKINGS**)
Guardians   CRC 7.207
Injunctions (See **INJUNCTIONS**)
Law and motion rules
    Acceptance of corporate sureties, prerequisites to   CRC 3.1130
Mechanics' liens   CC §§8150 to 8154, 8424 (See **MECHANICS' LIENS**)
Official bonds (See **BONDS OF PUBLIC OFFICIALS**)
Partition sale proceeds invested in government obligations   CCP §873.810
Payment bonds (See **PAYMENT BONDS**)
Power of attorney, statutory form   Pro §4453
Preliminary injunction, bond requirements   CRC 3.1150
Principal and income allocations   CC §§731 to 731.15
Public officials (See **BONDS OF PUBLIC OFFICIALS**)
Receivers (See **RECEIVERS AND RECEIVERSHIP**)
Statutes of limitation
    California-issued bonds
        No limitation   CCP §348.5
    Contesting validity of bonds   CCP §349.2
    Corporate bonds, notes or debentures, action upon   CCP §336a
    Exception to limitation   CCP §337.6
    General obligation bonds, action upon   CCP §§337.5, 337.6
    State bonds, action on   CCP §337.5
Surety bonds (See **SURETYSHIP, BONDS AND UNDERTAKINGS**)
Validation
    Authorization and existence of bonds, dates of   CCP §864
    Procedure for validation   CCP §349.4
    Statute of limitation contesting validity of bonds   CCP §349.2
    Taxes pledged for bond payments by agency other than agency imposing tax, notice requirements concerning   CCP §870.5
Vexatious litigants   CCP §§391 to 391.8
Voidable transactions, undertaking and action to set aside   CC §§3445 to 3449
Withdrawal of bond   CRC 3.1130
Wrongfully enjoining public improvement or utility, damages for   CCP §526b

BONDS OF PUBLIC OFFICIALS
Generally   CCP §§995.810 to 995.850
Commissioner handling property or money   CCP §571
Court reporter taking down and transcribing at cost of county   CCP §274a
Indemnity rights, bond as basis for   CCP §1055
Referee handling property or money   CCP §571
Statute of limitation upon bond of public official   CCP §338

BONUSES
Attachments, exemption from   CCP §487.020

BOOK ACCOUNTS
Attorney's fees in action on book accounts, recovery of   CC §1717.5
Defined   CCP §337a

BOOKING PHOTOGRAPHS
Commercial use of booking photographs   CC §1798.91.1

BOOKKEEPING (See **ACCOUNTS AND ACCOUNTING**)

BOOKS (See also **LITERARY PROPERTY**)
Admissibility of statements in   Ev §§1340, 1341
Assignment for benefit of creditors, property exempt from   CCP §1801
Bible, evidence of ancestry   Ev §1312
County recorder's books   CC §1171
Infringement, action for   CCP §429.30
Judges' writings, Code of Judicial Ethics provisions concerning   CRCSupp JudEthicsCanons 2, 4
Law books, presumptions of accuracy of   Ev §645
Presumptions of printing or publishing of   Ev §644
Privacy
    Reader privacy act   CC §§1798.90, 1798.90.05
Trial publicity
    Court proceedings, restrictions on media coverage of   CRC 1.150

BOTTOMRY
Discharge provisions applicable to mortgages, exception to   CC §2942
Lien statutes applicable to   CC §2877
Priority rule, exception from   CC §2897

BOULEVARDS (See **STREETS AND HIGHWAYS**)

BOUNDARIES
Adjoining landowners   CC §§829 to 835

BOUNDARIES—Cont.
Burden of proof in dispute involving state   Ev §523
Cities (See **CITIES AND MUNICIPALITIES**)
Common interest developments   CC §4220
Condominiums   CC §§783, 4220
Construction of instrument to determine   CCP §2077
Counties (See **COUNTIES**)
Disclosure of written evidence in dispute involving state   CCP §2031.510
Districts (See **DISTRICTS**)
Earthquake, reestablishing after   CCP §§751.50 to 751.65
Groundwater rights actions
    Basin boundaries   CCP §841
Improvement districts (See **PUBLIC ENTITIES**)
Maintenance of   CC §841
Monuments
    Repairs   CC §841
    Surveyors erecting   CC §846.5
Public entities (See **PUBLIC ENTITIES**)
Quieting title (See **QUIETING TITLE**)
Reputation as evidence of   Ev §§1322, 1323
Slides and other earth movement, boundary reestablishment after   CCP §§751.50 to 751.65
Special districts (See **PUBLIC ENTITIES**)
State, dispute over boundary involving   CCP §2031.510, Ev §523
Statute of limitation to contest change of boundaries of city, county or other public entity   CCP §349.1
Surveyor's rights   CC §846.5
Validation procedure for change of boundaries of city, county or other public entity   CCP §349.4

BOYCOTTS
Discrimination
    Business transactions, prohibition against discrimination in   CC §51.5

BRACEROS
Actions to recover savings fund amounts   CCP §354.7

BREACH OF CONTRACT (See **CONTRACTS AND AGREEMENTS**)

BREACH OF PROMISE OF MARRIAGE
Action for   CC §43.5

BREASTFEEDING
Jury service deferral   CCP §210.5, CRC 2.1006
Right to breast-feed in public and private places where mother and child are otherwise authorized to be present   CC §43.3

BREEDER'S LIEN
Generally   CC §§3062 to 3064.1

BRIDGES
Indemnity coverage for construction of   CC §2783

BRIEFS   CRC 8.200 to 8.224
Amicus briefs   CRC 8.200
    Attorney general's brief   CRC 8.200
    Juvenile case appeals   CRC 8.412
Appellant's opening brief   CRC 8.200, 8.220
Appellate division of superior court
    Rules applicable to appellate division proceedings (See **APPELLATE RULES, SUPERIOR COURT APPEALS**)
    Transfer from division to court of appeals   CRC 8.1012
Attachments   CRC 8.204
Attorney general, service on   CRC 8.212
Certificates of interested entities or persons   CRC 8.208
    Criminal appeals   CRC 8.361
    Electronic filing, when required   CRCSupp 1st AppDist
Certiorari   CRC 8.487
Copies and duplicates
    Service   CRC 8.212
Covers
    Required information   CRC 8.204
Criminal cases   CRC 8.360
Cross-appeals   CRC 8.216
    Contents of briefs   CRC 8.216
    Extensions of time   CRC 8.216
    Sequence of briefs   CRC 8.216
    Time for filing briefs   CRC 8.216
Cunningham briefing   CRCSupp 5th AppDist
Death penalty appeals   CRC 8.630, 8.631
    Habeas corpus, appeals from superior court decisions in habeas cases involving death penalty   CRC 8.396

BRIEFS—Cont.
Defective briefs   CRC 8.204
E-filing in supreme court and courts of appeal
    Format of electronic documents   CRC 8.74
Elder and dependent adult civil protection act, expedited appeals process   CRC 8.715
Electronic copies   CRC 8.212
Environmental quality act
    Appellate review of CEQA cases
        Jobs and economic improvement through environmental leadership act of 2021   CRC 8.702
        Sacramento downtown arena project, CEQA challenges   CRC 8.702
    Petitions under environmental quality act, civil rules governing
        Jobs and economic improvement through environmental leadership act of 2011   CRC 3.2227
        Sacramento downtown arena project, CEQA challenges   CRC 3.2227
Family rules
    Setting trials and long-cause hearings
        Trial or hearing briefs   CRC 5.394
Filing
    Cross-appeal   CRC 8.216
    Electronic filing and service   CRCSupp 1st AppDist, 6th AppDist
    Failure to file   CRC 8.220
        Juvenile case appeals   CRC 8.412, 8.416
Format specifications   CRC 8.204
Headings   CRC 8.204
Judges, proceedings against (See **JUDGES**)
Juvenile case appeals   CRC 8.412
Length   CRC 8.204
    Capital cases   CRC 8.630, 8.631
    Criminal appeals   CRC 8.360
Local rules, effect   CRC 8.20
New authority discovered after filing of brief   CRC 8.254
Noncomplying   CRC 8.204
Opening brief   CRC 8.200
Overlength briefs
    Application to file
        Capital cases   CRC 8.631
Paper briefs
    Format   CRC 8.204
Presentence custody credit
    Recalculation   CRCSupp 3rd AppDist, 5th AppDist
Printed briefs   CRC 8.204
Respondent's brief   CRC 8.200, 8.220
Service of process and papers
    Criminal cases   CRC 8.360
    Electronic filing and service   CRCSupp 1st AppDist, 6th AppDist
    Time of service   CRC 8.212, 8.220
State bar disciplinary actions against attorneys   CRC 9.13
Style specifications   CRC 8.204
Summary judgment motions
    Supplemental briefs   CCP §437c
Supreme court   CRC 8.520
    Service on   CRC 8.212
Time of service and filing   CRC 8.212, 8.220, 8.360
    Extension of time to file
        Electronic filing, when required   CRCSupp 1st AppDist
Transfer of appeals
    Supreme court appeal to court of appeal   CRC 8.528
Typewritten briefs   CRC 8.204, 8.360
Wende **briefs**
    Electronic filings   CRCSupp 1st AppDist

BROADBAND ACCESS
Digital equity bill of rights   CC §§3120 to CC 3123 (See **DIGITAL EQUITY BILL OF RIGHTS**)
Net neutrality generally   CC §§3100 to 3104 (See **NET NEUTRALITY**)

BROADCASTING (See **RADIO AND TELEVISION**)

BROKERS
Generally   CC §§2323, 2324
Administrators employing brokers for sale of estate assets (See **ADMINISTRATION OF ESTATES**)
Agency
    Acknowledgment of receipt of disclosure form   CC §2079.14
    Listings   CC §§1086 to 1089.5
    Refusal to acknowledge receipt of disclosure regarding agency relationship   CC §2079.15
Agreements for services   CC §§1086 to 1089.5
    Representation agreements   CC §1670.50

BROKERS—Cont.
Associate real estate licensees
    Disclosure requirements generally (See within this heading, "**Disclosure requirements**")
Bureau of real estate
    Information Practice Act, applicability to   CC §1798.3
Buyer's agents
    Disclosure
        Acknowledgment of receipt of disclosure form   CC §2079.14
        Duties   CC §2079.14
    Representation agreements   CC §1670.50
Commercial real property
    Duties owed to prospective purchaser
        Definition of commercial real property   CC §2079.13
Compensation of agent not determinative of relationship   CC §2079.19
Confidential information
    Dual agency or representation
        Restrictions on disclosure of confidential information   CC §2079.21
Construction trucking services brokers
    Transportation charges, payment   CC §3322
Contract modification to agency relationship permitted   CC §2079.23
Definitions   CC §§1086, 2079.13
Disclosure requirements   CC §§1102 to 1103.15
    Agency   CC §§2079.12 to 2079.25
        Acknowledgment of receipt of disclosure form   CC §2079.14
    AIDS, disclosures regarding prior occupant afflicted with   CC §1710.2
    Amendment of disclosure   CC §§1102.9, 1103.9
    Applicability of requirements   CC §§1089, 1102, 1102.18, 1103, 1103.15, 2079.25
    Death of prior occupant occurring within three years, disclosures regarding   CC §1710.2
    Delivery of disclosure statements   CC §§1102.3, 1102.12, 1103.3, 1103.10, 1103.12
    Earthquake hazard   CC §§1103 to 1103.15
        Consumer information handbooks   CC §§2079.8, 2079.9, 2079.11
    Electrical inspections   CC §1102.6i
    Environmental hazards, complying with requirements to inform transferee of   CC §§2079.7, 2079.11
    Errors or omissions, liability for   CC §§1102.4, 1102.5, 1103.4
    Explosive munitions in neighborhood area, written notice of   CC §1102.15
    Fire hazard disclosure   CC §§1103 to 1103.15
    Flood hazard disclosure   CC §§1103 to 1103.15
    Forms
        General form of transfer disclosure statement   CC §1102.6
        Local requirements, disclosure statement reflecting   CC §1102.6a
        Natural hazards, disclosure concerning   CC §1103.2
    Gas powered appliances   CC §1102.6j
    Home energy ratings, information regarding   CC §2079.10
    Industrial use zoning   CC §1102.17
    Inspection of property, duty to disclose findings concerning   CC §2079
    Legislative intent   CC §1102.1
    Mello-Roos Community Facilities Act, disclosure regarding special tax liens on transfer of property pursuant to   CC §1102.6b
    Mobilehome sales   CC §§1102 to 1102.18
    Natural hazard disclosure statements   CC §§1103 to 1103.15
    Other laws, effect   CC §1103.8
    Registered sex offenders, notification concerning statewide database of locations of   CC §2079.10a
    Taxation
        Supplemental property tax bills   CC §1102.6c
    Transfer fees, property subject to   CC §1102.6e
    Water conservation   CC §2079.10
        Plumbing retrofits, disclosures as to noncompliant plumbing fixtures   CC §1102.155
    Water storage tanks   CC §1102.156
    Window security bars and safety release mechanism   CC §1102.16
Dual agency   CC §§2079.21, 2079.22
Duties owed to prospective purchasers
    Associate real estate licensee's duty equivalent to that owed by broker   CC §2079.13
    Disclosure requirements (See within this heading, "**Disclosure requirements**")
    Real estate agency relationship, disclosure regarding   CC §§2079.12 to 2079.25
Earthquake hazards (See within this heading, "**Disclosure requirements**")
Environmental hazards, complying with requirements to inform transferee of   CC §§2079.7, 2079.11
Exclusive listing agreements
    Restrictions   CC §1670.12
Executors employing brokers for sale of estate assets (See **ADMINISTRATION OF ESTATES**)

BROKERS—Cont.

Explosive munitions in neighborhood area, disclosure of   CC §1102.15
Fire hazard, disclosure of   CC §§1103 to 1103.15
Flood hazard, disclosure of   CC §§1103 to 1103.15
Home energy ratings, disclosure of information regarding   CC §2079.10
Home improvement financing, unfair trade practice constituted by mortgage broker negotiating through contractor to arrange terms of   CC §1770
Industrial use zoning, disclosure of   CC §1102.17
Inspection of residential property
    Generally   CC §2079
    Buyer's duty of reasonable care, effect of   CC §2079.5
    Disclosure of inspection, form of   CC §§1102.6, 1102.6a
    Inaccessible areas or unaffected units, liability for   CC §2079.3
    Lease transactions, applicability of article to   CC §2079.1
    New subdivisions, duty to inspect inapplicable to   CC §2079.6
    Standard of care for   CC §2079.2
    Statute of limitations for breach of duty   CC §2079.4
Late payment charges   CC §2954.4
Listing agents
    Agency relationship, required disclosure regarding   CC §§2079.12 to 2079.25
    Compensation   CC §2079.19
    Exclusive listing agreements, restrictions   CC §1670.12
    Multiple listing service   CC §§1086 to 1089.5
Loans arranged or made by brokers, exemption from usury laws for   CC §1916.1
Mello-Roos Community Facilities Act, disclosure regarding special tax liens on transfer of property pursuant to   CC §1102.6b
Membership camping contract brokers   CC §1812.314
Multiple listing services   CC §§1086 to 1089.5
New subdivisions, broker's duty to inspect residential property inapplicable to   CC §2079.6
Partition
    Heirs property, uniform act
        Broker offering property for open market sale, report requirement   CCP §874.321
        Referees contracting with   CCP §873.110
Peer review societies, immunity of   CC §43.91
Prepaid rental listing services
    Exclusive listing agreements, restrictions   CC §1670.12
Privileged communications, professional societies protected under   CC §43.91
Professional societies, liability of   CC §43.91
Real Estate Transfer Disclosures
    Statements, form   CC §§1102.6, 1102.6a
    Taxation
        Supplemental property tax bills   CC §1102.6c
Record retention for listings   CC §1088
Registered sex offenders, notification concerning statewide database of locations of   CC §2079.10a
Representation agreements   CC §1670.50
Securities broker-dealer, contract formation by electronic submission of application to   CC §1633
Seller's agents
    Acknowledgment of receipt of disclosure form   CC §2079.14
    Buyer's agents, seller's agent acting as   CC §2079.22
    Contents of required disclosure regarding agency relationship   CC §2079.16
    Definitions   CC §2079.13
    Delivery of required disclosure regarding agency relationship   CC §2079.14
    Disclosure as to status as seller's agent or as dual agent   CC §2079.17
Sexual harassment, civil action for
    Construction or application of provisions in issue, solicitor general notified   CC §51.1
Statute of limitation for breach of duty to inspect property   CC §2079.1
Transient occupancy in common interest developments, apartment buildings or single-family homes, recordkeeping required for accepting reservations or money for   CC §1864
Usury laws, exemption from   CC §1916.1
Water conservation disclosure requirements   CC §2079.10
    Plumbing retrofits, disclosures as to noncompliant plumbing fixtures   CC §1102.155
Water storage tank disclosures   CC §1102.156
Window security bars and safety release mechanism, disclosure of   CC §1102.16
Written contracts for employment of   CC §1624

BROTHERS AND SISTERS

Administrators, priority for serving as   Pro §8461
Adoption proceedings (See **ADOPTION**)
Inheritance by   Pro §§6402, 6402.5
Visitation rights of   Fam §3102

BUCKER

Lien   CC §§3065 to 3065c

BUDGETS, COURT

Judicial Administration Rules (See **JUDICIAL ADMINISTRATION RULES**)

BUDGETS, STATE

Consumer privacy rights
    California privacy protection agency
        Appropriations to fund agency   CC §1798.199.95

BUILDING AND LOAN ASSOCIATIONS (See SAVINGS AND LOANS)

BUILDING CODES

Inspection warrants to determine violations   CCP §1822.50

BUILDING CONSTRUCTION

Arbitration
    Lien claim as affecting arbitration rights   CCP §1281.5
    Out-of-state arbitration, invalidity of contract provision requiring   CCP §410.42
    Public contracts   CC §1670, CCP §§1281.5, 1296
Bond required to secure costs in action against designers   CCP §1029.5
Burden of proving necessity for zoning ordinances limiting   Ev §669.5
Common interest developments (See **COMMON INTEREST DEVELOPMENTS**)
Construction defects, action for (See **CONSTRUCTION DEFECTS, ACTIONS FOR**)
Construction trucking services brokers
    Transportation charges, payment   CC §3322
Contractors (See **BUILDING CONTRACTORS**)
Covenants prohibiting prefabricated modular homes, validity of   CC §714.5
Damages for intentional destruction of property under construction   CC §1721
Defects in construction
    Actions for construction defects   CC §§895 to 945.5 (See **CONSTRUCTION DEFECTS, ACTIONS FOR**)
Good faith improver of property of another (See **GOOD FAITH IMPROVER**)
Indemnity agreements   CC §§2782 to 2784
    January 1, 2013, contracts on or after   CC §2782.05
    Subcontractor's defense or indemnity obligation   CC §2782.05
    Void or unenforceable provisions, insertion   CC §2782.05
Injunction, security for costs incurred as result of delay   CCP §§529.1, 529.2
Insurance
    Wrap-up insurance covering, indemnity agreements   CC §2782.9
        Private residential improvements   CC §2782.95
        Public works   CC §2782.96
Latent deficiencies in planning or construction, limitation of actions for damages for   CCP §337.15
Mechanics' liens (See **MECHANICS' LIENS**)
Notice of pendency of action to declare building uninhabitable   CCP §405.7
Out-of-state arbitration or litigation of disputes, invalidity of contract provision requiring   CCP §410.42
Patent deficiencies in planning or construction, limitation of actions for injury or death from   CCP §337.1
Prefabricated modular homes, validity of covenants prohibiting   CC §714.5
Public contracts and works (See **PUBLIC CONTRACTS AND WORKS**)
Residential building permits
    Quality reviewers
        Immunity from liability   CC §43.99
Residential construction, indemnity agreements   CC §2782
    Wrap-up insurance policies applicable   CC §2782.9
        Private residential improvement covered   CC §2782.95
Small business action, costs in   CCP §1028.5
Statutes of limitation
    Latent deficiencies in planning or construction, damages for   CCP §337.15
    Patent deficiencies in planning or construction, injury or death from   CCP §337.1
Stipulated judgments in construction defect actions   CCP §664.7
Subdivisions (See **SUBDIVISIONS**)
Substantial completion for purposes of running of limitations period   CCP §§337.1, 337.15

BUILDING CONTRACTORS

Arbitration
    Lien claim as affecting arbitration rights   CCP §1281.5
    Out-of-state arbitration, invalidity of contract provisions requiring   CCP §410.42
    Public contracts   CC §1670, CCP §§1281.5, 1296

BUILDING CONTRACTORS—Cont.
Bonds
    Injunction, motion for security re   CCP §529.1
Common interest developments (See **COMMON INTEREST DEVELOPMENTS**)
Construction defects, actions for   CC §§895 to 945.5 (See **CONSTRUCTION DEFECTS, ACTIONS FOR**)
Excavation (See **EXCAVATIONS**)
Indemnity agreements   CC §§2782 to 2784
Mechanics' liens (See **MECHANICS' LIENS**)
Out-of-state arbitration or litigation of disputes, invalidity of contract provisions requiring   CCP §410.42
Public contracts and works (See **PUBLIC CONTRACTS AND WORKS**)
Release from liability, agreements for   CC §2782.5
Residential construction
    Indemnity agreements   CC §2782
Service and repair contracts
    Commencement of work
        Effect on contract   CC §1689.15
    Rescission   CC §1689.15
Support from adjacent land   CC §832

BUILDING INSPECTORS
Witnesses, subpoenaed as   Gov §§68097.1, 68907.2

BUILDING PERMITS
Burden of proving necessity for zoning ordinances limiting   Ev §669.5
Mechanics' liens
    Requirements   CC §8172

BUILDINGS
Generally   CC §660
Bins (See **BINS**)
Condominiums (See **COMMON INTEREST DEVELOPMENTS**)
Elevators (See **ELEVATORS**)
Life tenant's duty to repair   CC §840
Prefabricated modular homes, validity of covenants prohibiting   CC §714.5
Public buildings (See **PUBLIC BUILDINGS**)
Solar energy systems (See **SOLAR ENERGY**)
Walls (See **WALLS**)
Windows (See **WINDOWS**)

BUILDING STANDARDS
Accessibility standards
    Construction-related accessibility claims   CC §§55.3 to 55.57 (See **CONSTRUCTION-RELATED ACCESSIBILITY CLAIMS**)
Inspections
    Exterior elevated elements
        Landlord entry of building to comply with provisions   CC §1954
Regulations (See **ADMINISTRATIVE PROCEDURE ACT**)

BULK SALES
Storage of grain after sale in bulk   CC §§1880 to 1881.2
Voidable transactions (See **VOIDABLE TRANSACTIONS**)
Wage claims, preference for   CCP §1205

BUNGALOW COURT
Limitation of actions for recovery or conversion of personal property left at   CCP §341a

BUPRENORPHINE
Minors
    Consent to treatment for opioid use disorder   Fam §6929.1

BURDEN OF GOING FORWARD
Generally   Ev §§550, 630
Definition   Ev §110
Mechanics' liens
    Release of property from claim of lien
        Hearing   CC §8488
Official records, presumptions of existence of   Ev §1530
Presumptions affecting   Ev §§603, 604, 630

BURDEN OF PRODUCING EVIDENCE (See **BURDEN OF GOING FORWARD**)

BURDEN OF PROOF
Generally   Ev §§500, 520 to 522
Age of accused person   CRC 4.116
Attachments   CCP §482.100
Beyond reasonable doubt (See **BEYOND REASONABLE DOUBT**)

BURDEN OF PROOF—Cont.
Boundary dispute involving state   Ev §523
Clear and convincing evidence (See **CLEAR AND CONVINCING EVIDENCE**)
Confidential communication, claim for   Ev §917
Contract consideration   CC §1615
Criminal proceedings   Ev §501
Definition   Ev §115
Degree of proof required in proceedings   Ev §115
Enforcement of judgment, third party claim of ownership or security interest in property subject to   CCP §720.360
Equalization, state board
    Evasion or fraud cases, penalty sought   Ev §524
Foreign country judgments   CCP §1715
Good faith improver   CCP §871.3
Grants of land involving state, dispute over   Ev §523
Housing limits, proving necessity for zoning ordinances setting   Ev §669.5
Interstate family support
    Contest of validity or enforcement of registered order
        Defenses and burdens of proof applicable   Fam §5700.607
Jury instructions   Ev §502
Mechanic's liens
    Public works
        Summary proceeding for release of funds   CC §9410
    Release of property from claim of lien
        Hearing   CC §8488
Missing person, presumption of death of   Ev §667
Motion pictures depicting cruelty, actions against   CC §3507.1
Necessary degree of proof required in proceedings except where higher degree of proof otherwise required by law, preponderance of evidence as   Ev §115
Parentage
    Voluntary declaration of parentage
        Challenge by nonsignatories of declaration   Fam §7578
Preliminary fact, proof of   Ev §405
Preponderance of evidence
    Jury instructions on   Ev §502
    Requisite degree of proof required except where higher degree of proof otherwise required by law, preponderance of evidence as   Ev §115
Presumptions affecting   Ev §§601, 605, 606, 660 to 669.5
Reasonable doubt (See **BEYOND REASONABLE DOUBT**)
Small claims actions, effect of defendant's failure to appear in   CCP §116.520
Summary judgment, grant or denial of motion for   CCP §437c
Tribal court civil money judgment act
    Objections
        Applicant's and objector's burdens   CCP §1737
oning ordinances limiting housing, proving necessity for   Ev §669.5

BUREAU OF INDIAN AFFAIRS
Adoption proceedings, documents pertaining to Indian blood and tribal enrollment   Fam §8619

BURGLAR ALARMS
Electronic transactions
    Applicability of electronic transactions provisions   CC §1633.3
Home improvement goods   CC §1689.8
Public liability for failure of police to respond to   Gov §845

BURIAL (See **CEMETERIES**)

BUSES
Baggage, liability for loss of   CC §2205
Blind persons having equal right to use of   CC §§54.1, 54.3, 54.4, 55
    Construction or application of provisions in issue, solicitor general notified   CC §55.2
Charter bus transportation companies
    Customer records, privacy
        Duties of companies   CC §53.5
Disabled persons having equal right to use of   CC §§54.1, 54.3, 54.4, 55
    Construction or application of provisions in issue, solicitor general notified   CC §55.2
Guide dogs permitted on   CC §§54.2, 54.3
    Construction or application of provisions in issue, solicitor general notified   CC §55.2
Human trafficking
    Signs, businesses required to post notice concerning relief from slavery or human trafficking   CC §52.6
        Training for employees who might interact with victims   CC §52.6
Overcrowding, applicability of code provisions as to   CC §§2184, 2185
Private or charter bus transportation companies
    Customer records, privacy
        Duties of companies   CC §53.5

BUSES—Cont.
Slavery
> Signs, businesses required to post notice concerning relief from slavery or human trafficking CC §52.6
>> Training for employees who might interact with victims CC §52.6

Stations
> Human trafficking or slavery
>> Signs, businesses required to post notice concerning relief from slavery or human trafficking CC §52.6

BUSINESS
Accounting business, confidentiality requirements CC §§1799 to 1799.2
Administration of estates (See **ADMINISTRATION OF ESTATES**)
Agents managing CC §2319
Attachment of going business (See **ATTACHMENT**)
Birth name of customer, use of CCP §1279.6
Carpenter-Katz Small Business Equal Access to Justice Act CCP §1028.5
Community property business, management of Fam §1100
Continuation of decedent's business (See **ADMINISTRATION OF ESTATES**)
Discrimination CC §§51 to 53
Easement rights for transaction of CC §801
Enforcement of judgments (See **ENFORCEMENT OF JUDGMENTS**)
Escheat of unclaimed funds and property held by business associations CCP §§1511, 1513, 1516, 1520, 1520.5, 1542, 1581
Exemption for purposes of enforcement of judgments of property used in CCP §704.060
Goodwill of business, eminent domain compensation for loss of CCP §§1263.510 to 1263.530
> Leaseback agreements CCP §1263.510

Investment advisers CC §3372
Marital status, denial of credit because of CC §1812.32
Seller assisted marketing plans CC §§1812.200 to 1812.221
Slander by injury to CC §46
Small business, costs in action involving CCP §1028.5
Statutory form power of attorney, powers under Pro §4456
Trusts (See **TRUSTS**)

BUSINESS AND OCCUPATIONAL LICENSES
Fines and penalties, bail schedule CRC 4.102

BUSINESS DAYS
Civil Code statute CC §§9, 11
Judicial business transacted, days when CCP §133

BUSINESS OF THE COURTS
Superior courts (See **SUPERIOR COURTS**)

BUSINESS OVERSIGHT COMMISSIONER
Superior court hearings on sale of properties of savings and loan association whose business, properties and assets are in possession of CCP §§73c, 73d

BUSINESS RECORDS
Admissible evidence
> Affidavits accompanying records, admissibility of Ev §1562
> Copies, admissibility of Ev §§1550, 1562
> Hearsay rule, exception to Ev §§1270 to 1272

Affidavits
> Admissibility of Ev §1562
> Custodian's affidavit Ev §§1561, 1562

Book accounts (See **BOOK ACCOUNTS**)
Confidentiality
> Bookkeeping services, duty of nondisclosure of personal information maintained by CC §§1799 to 1799.2
> Social security numbers, prohibiting posting or display to general public of CC §1798.85
>> Financial institutions, continued use CC §1786.60
>> Waiver of protections CC §1798.86
> Video recording sales or rental services, duty of nondisclosure of personal information maintained by CC §1799.3

Copies
> Admissible evidence Ev §§1550, 1562
> Production of records in response to subpoena Ev §§1560, 1564

Custodian of records, subpoena of (See **SUBPOENA DUCES TECUM**)
Customer records (See **CUSTOMER RECORDS**)
Electronic transactions (See **ELECTRONIC TRANSACTIONS**)
Employment agencies, recordkeeping requirements of CC §1812.522
Fire, destruction by CCP §§1953.10 to 1953.13
Inspection of records
> Employment and job listing services, business records of CC §1812.522
> Subpoena duces tecum for (See **SUBPOENA DUCES TECUM**)

Job listing services, recordkeeping requirements of CC §1812.522

BUSINESS RECORDS—Cont.
Natural disaster, destruction by CCP §§1953.10 to 1953.13
Nurses' registries, duty to maintain log sheets and records by CC §1812.529
Photographic copies Ev §1550
Privacy of (See within this heading, "**Confidentiality**")
Production of (See **SUBPOENA DUCES TECUM**)
Small claims action, evidence in CCP §116.540
Social security numbers, prohibiting posting or display to general public of CC §1798.85
> Financial institutions, continued use CC §1786.60
> Waiver of protections CC §1798.86

Subpoena of (See **SUBPOENA DUCES TECUM**)

BUSINESS, TRANSPORTATION AND HOUSING AGENCY
Mortgage loans, regulation of CC §1918.5

BUTTONS
Sale of campaign buttons CC §1739.1

BUYER'S CHOICE ACT CC §§1103.20 to 1103.22

BUY-HERE-PAY-HERE AUTO DEALERS
Automobile sales finance
> Obligations of dealers CC §2983.37

Consumer warranty protection
> Used vehicles
>> Buy-here-pay-here dealers' obligations CC §1795.51

C

CABLE TELEVISION COMPANIES
Cancellation of utility, cable, etc, services on behalf of deceased person
> In-person cancellation not to be required Pro §217

Service or repairs during specified time period where subscriber's presence required, liability for failure to provide CC §1722

CABS (See **TAXIS**)

CADAVERS (See **DEAD BODIES**)

CALAMITIES (See **EMERGENCIES**)

CALENDAR
Appeals
> Superior court appeals
>> Oral argument CRC 8.885
> Supreme court and courts of appeal cases (See **APPELLATE RULES, SUPREME COURT AND COURTS OF APPEAL**)

Coordination of actions, standards for CCP §404.1
Court calendars (See **COURT CALENDARS**)
Judicial holidays, effect of CCP §136
Preference in setting for trial or hearing (See **PRIORITIES AND PREFERENCES**)
Pretrial arbitration, trial de novo after CCP §1141.20
Superior courts (See **SUPERIOR COURTS**)

CALIFORNIA AGE-APPROPRIATE DESIGN CODE CC §§1798.99.28 to 1798.99.40 (See **AGE-APPROPRIATE DESIGN CODE**)

CALIFORNIA COASTAL ACT
Attorney general, civil actions to enforce provisions
> Fees and costs for attorney general CCP §1021.8

CALIFORNIA CONSERVATORSHIP JURISDICTION ACT
Interstate jurisdiction, transfer and recognition Pro §§1980 to 2033 (See **CONSERVATORS**)

CALIFORNIA CONSUMER PRIVACY ACT OF 2018 CC §§1798.100 to 1798.199.100

CALIFORNIA FAMILY SUPPORT COUNCIL
Child support, reporting of delinquencies for Fam §§4700, 4701

CALIFORNIA FORECLOSURE PREVENTION ACT CC §2924

CALIFORNIA HEALTH BENEFIT EXCHANGE
Adoption
> Health insurance
>> Notice of reduced-cost options through California health benefit exchange or no-cost Medi-Cal Fam §8613.7

Annulment of marriage
> Health insurance
>> Notice of reduced-cost options through California health benefit exchange or no-cost Medi-Cal Fam §2024.7

CALIFORNIA HEALTH BENEFIT EXCHANGE—Cont.
Divorce
    Health insurance
        Notice of reduced-cost options through California health benefit exchange or no-cost Medi-Cal   Fam §2024.7
Legal separation
    Health insurance
        Notice of reduced-cost options through California health benefit exchange or no-cost Medi-Cal   Fam §2024.7

CALIFORNIA-MADE
Made in California program
    Unfair competition or deceptive trade practices   CC §1770

CALIFORNIA NATIONAL GUARD
Immunity of public entity for injury arising from action of   Gov §816

CALIFORNIA PARENT LOCATOR SERVICE
Earnings assignment for support, whereabouts of obligor unknown   Fam §5280

CALIFORNIA PRIVACY PROTECTION AGENCY   CC §§1798.199.10 to 1798.199.100 (See CONSUMER PRIVACY RIGHTS)

CALIFORNIA RESEARCH BUREAU
Frivolous actions
    Motions for sanctions, etc
        Copy of motion to bureau   CCP §128.5
Unlawful detainer actions
    Reports to bureau
        Controlled substances as nuisance   CC §§3486, 3486.5
        Firearms or weapons as nuisance   CC §3485

CALIFORNIA RULES OF COURT
Rules applicable to all courts   CRC 1.1 to 1.201 (See RULES OF COURT)

CALIFORNIA STATE UNIVERSITY
Claims against public entities and employees
    Payments by trustees   Gov §935.9
    Presentation of claims
        Applicable provisions   Gov §905.9
    Trustees' actions on claims   Gov §912.5
Construction-related accessibility claims
    Attorney prelitigation letter to education entities   CC §54.27
Social security numbers
    Public posting or display
        Implementation of provisions   CC §1798.85
Unclaimed property
    Disposition   CC §2080.8
        Claim not required for controller to transfer property to state or local agencies   CCP §1540

CALIFORNIA STATUTORY WILL (See WILLS)

CALLING CARDS
Gift certificate provisions inapplicable   CC §1749.45

CALWORKS
Child support
    Local child support agencies
        Assigned support payments made for CalWORKs recipients, notice   Fam §17504.4
        Duties for CalWORKs cases   Fam §3680.5

CAMPAIGN BUTTONS
Sale of   CC §1739.1

CAMPERS
Mobilehomes (See MOBILEHOMES)
Recreational vehicles (See RECREATIONAL VEHICLES)

CAMPING
Liability of owner for recreational land   CC §846
Membership camping contracts   CC §§1812.300 to 1812.309
    Waiver of protections   CC §1812.316
Special occupancy parks
    Danger imminent, requiring guests to move   CC §1867
    Eviction of overstaying guests   CC §1866
    Minors
        Conditions for minors staying   CC §1866

CANADA
Domestic violence protective orders, recognition and enforcement   Fam §§6450 to 6460

CANALS
Public liability for injury caused by condition of   Gov §831.8

CANCELLATION OF ASSESSMENT
Public improvement assessment, action to determine adverse interests in real property arising out of   CCP §801.15

CANCELLATION OF INSTRUMENTS
Action for   CC §§3412 to 3415
Credit cards   CC §1747.85
Dance studio contracts   CC §1812.54
Discount buying services contracts   CC §1812.118
Electronic transaction, notice of right to cancel   CC §1633.16
Health studio contracts   CC §§1812.85, 1812.89
Home equity sales contracts (See HOME EQUITY SALES CONTRACTS)
Home solicitation sales contracts (See HOME SOLICITATION SALES CONTRACTS)
Intent to cancel contract   CC §1699
Membership camping contracts   CC §§1812.303, 1812.304, 1812.314
Mortgage foreclosure consultants contract   CC §§2945.2, 2945.3
Parties bound by   CC §1700
Private child support collectors   Fam §5613
    Notice of cancellation form   Fam §5611
Seller assisted marketing plans   CC §§1812.208, 1812.209, 1812.215
Seminar sales solicitation contracts (See SEMINAR SALES SOLICITATION CONTRACTS)

CANDIDATES FOR OFFICE
Advertising, superimposition of photographs
    Precedence of proceedings involving elections   CCP §35
Damages for misleading advertising
    Candidate's cause of action based on false depiction of representations of official public documents   CC §3344.6
    Unauthorized signatures in campaign advertisements, action for damages for   CC §3344.5
Precedence to cases involving elections proceedings (See ELECTIONS AND ELECTIONS PROCEEDINGS)
Radio or television broadcast libelous to character of candidate   CC §48.5
Shortening of time to respond to complaint in action for libel alleged to have occurred during election campaign   CCP §460.7
Unauthorized signatures in campaign advertisements, action for damages for   CC §3344.5

CANONS OF JUDICIAL ETHICS (See JUDGES)

CAPACITY
Contracts (See CONTRACTS AND AGREEMENTS)
Due Process in Competence Determinations Act   Pro §§810, 813, 1801, 1881, 3201, 3204, 3208, 3208.5
Emancipated minors   Fam §7050
Judicial determinations, generally   Pro §§810 to 813
Marriage (See MARRIAGE)
Medical decisions (See MEDICAL TREATMENT)
Standing to sue (See CAPACITY TO SUE)
Wills, capacity to make   Pro §§810 to 812, 6100, 6100.5

CAPACITY TO SUE
Contract made for benefit of another   CCP §369
Decedent's estate, personal representative to (See EXECUTORS AND ADMINISTRATORS)
De facto parents   CRC 5.534
Emancipated minors   Fam §7050
Executors and administrators (See EXECUTORS AND ADMINISTRATORS)
Limited conservatees   Pro §1872
Married persons   CCP §370
Objection to complaint or cross-complaint, lack of capacity as grounds for   CCP §430.10
Parents maintaining action for injury of child   CCP §376
Partners and partnerships   CCP §369.5
Third party beneficiary contracts   CCP §369
Unincorporated associations   CCP §369.5

CAPITAL PUNISHMENT
Appeals   CRC 8.601 to 8.652
    Automatic appeals
        Supreme court, automatic appeal to   CRC 8.603
    Briefs   CRC 8.630, 8.631
    Decision, filing, finality and modification
        Applicability   CRC 8.642
    Exhibits
        Transmission of exhibits in death penalty appeals   CRC 8.634

CAPITAL PUNISHMENT—Cont.
  Appeals —Cont.
    Extension of time limit
      Electronic filing, when required   CRCSupp 1st AppDist
    Judgment
      Copies, distribution   CRC 8.603
    Oral argument   CRC 8.638
    Record on appeal   CRC 8.608 to 8.622
      Accuracy of trial record on appeal, certification   CRC 8.622
      Augmenting record in supreme court   CRC 8.634
      Completeness of record on appeal, certification   CRC 8.619
      Confidential records   CRC 8.610
      Contents   CRC 8.610
      Extensions of time   CRC 8.608
      Juror-identifying information   CRC 8.610, 8.611
      Preliminary proceedings, preparing and certifying record   CRC 8.613
      Sealed record   CRC 8.610
      Supervision of preparation of record   CRC 8.608
      Transcripts, delivery date   CRC 8.608
      Trial record   CRC 8.616 to 8.622
    Rehearings
      Applicable provisions   CRC 8.642
    Remittitur   CRC 8.642
    Submission of cause   CRC 8.638
    Supreme court, practices and policies   CRCSupp SuprCtPract
    Transcripts
      Notice to prepare   CRC 8.613
  Appearance
    Lists of appearances, exhibits and motions   CRCAppx A
      Pretrial proceedings   CRC 4.119
      Trial, additional requirements   CRC 4.230
  Attorneys for capital cases   CRC 4.561, 4.562
    Appeals, appointments   CRC 8.605
    Appeals, qualifications   CRC 8.605
    Appointed counsel
      Appellate counsel appointments   CRC 8.605
      Appellate counsel qualifications   CRC 8.605
      Declaration of counsel for appointment, form   CRCAppx A
      Habeas counsel appointments   CRC 8.605
      Habeas counsel qualifications   CRC 8.652
      Trial counsel qualifications   CRC 4.117
    Compensation   CRCSupp SupCtPolicy
    Habeas corpus proceedings (See **HABEAS CORPUS**)
    Habeas counsel, appointments   CRC 8.605
    Habeas counsel, qualifications   CRC 8.652
    Record on appeal
      Preliminary proceedings   CRC 8.613
    Supreme court
      Habeas corpus petitions, compensation of attorneys   CRCSupp FixedFeeAppoint
      Withdrawal of counsel   CRCSupp FixedFeeAppoint
    Withdrawal from representation   CRCSupp SupCtPolicy
  Checklist   CRCAppx A
    Pretrial proceedings   CRC 4.119
    Trial, additional requirements   CRC 4.230
  Electronic recordings presented or offered into evidence
    Pretrial proceedings   CRC 4.119
    Trial, additional requirements   CRC 4.230
  Evidence
    Electronic recordings presented or offered into evidence
      Pretrial proceedings   CRC 4.119
      Trial, additional requirements   CRC 4.230
  Execution
    Date for   CRC 4.315
  Exhibits
    Lists of appearances, exhibits and motions   CRCAppx A
      Pretrial proceedings   CRC 4.119
      Trial, additional requirements   CRC 4.230
  Fixed fee guidelines for appointed counsel in automatic appeals   CRCSupp FixedFeeAppoint
  Habeas corpus
    Appointment of counsel   CRC 8.605
    Compensation of attorney   CRCSupp SupCtPolicy
    Death penalty-related proceedings in superior court   CRC 4.560 to 4.577
      Appeals from superior court decisions in habeas cases involving death penalty   CRC 8.390 to 8.398
    Duty to investigate, attorney's   CRCSupp SupCtPolicy
    Fixed fee guidelines for appointed counsel in automatic appeals and related habeas corpus proceedings   CRCSupp FixedFeeAppoint
    Forms, judicial council   CRCAppx A
    Qualifications of counsel   CRC 8.652

CAPITAL PUNISHMENT—Cont.
  Habeas corpus—Cont.
    Supreme court policies   CRCSupp SupCtPolicy
    Time for filing   CRCSupp SupCtPolicy
  Indigents, Supreme Court guidelines for compensating counsel appointed for   CRCSupp PayGuideAppoint
  Judges
    Education of judicial branch
      Additional education recommendations for certain judicial assignments   CRC 10.469
  Jury instructions
    Lists of appearances, exhibits, motions and jury instructions   CRCAppx A
      Trial, additional requirements   CRC 4.230
  Jury selection in death penalty cases (See **JURY**)
  Justices
    Education of judicial branch
      Additional education recommendations for certain judicial assignments   CRC 10.469
  Motions
    Lists of appearances, exhibits and motions   CRCAppx A
      Pretrial proceedings   CRC 4.119
      Trial, additional requirements   CRC 4.230
  Policies of Supreme Court   CRCSupp SupCtPolicy
  Pretrial proceedings   CRC 4.119
  Procedure in capital cases
    Pretrial proceedings   CRC 4.119
    Trial
      Additional requirements in capital cases   CRC 4.230
  Record on appeal   CRC 8.608 to 8.622
    Augmenting record in supreme court   CRC 8.634
    Certification
      Accuracy of trial record on appeal   CRC 8.622
      Completeness of trial record on appeal   CRC 8.619
      Preliminary proceedings   CRC 8.613
    Confidential records   CRC 8.610
    Contents   CRC 8.610
    Extensions of time   CRC 8.608
    Juror-identifying information   CRC 8.610, 8.611
    Preliminary proceedings
      Preparation and certification of record   CRC 8.613
    Sealed record   CRC 8.610
    Supervision of preparation of record   CRC 8.608
    Transcripts
      Delivery date   CRC 8.608
      Preparation, notice   CRC 8.613
      Review daily by counsel during trial   CRC 4.230
    Trial record
      Accuracy of trial record on appeal, certification   CRC 8.622
      Completeness of trial record on appeal, certification   CRC 8.619
      Preparation   CRC 8.616
  Remittitur   CRC 8.642
  Setting date for execution in death penalty cases   CRC 4.315
  Stay of execution, appeal as
    Supreme court policies   CRCSupp SupCtPolicy
  Supreme court
    Habeas corpus petitions   CRCSupp SupCtPolicy
    Stays of execution   CRCSupp SupCtPolicy
    Withdrawal of counsel   CRCSupp SupCtPolicy
  Transcripts (See within this heading, **"Record on appeal"**)
  Withdrawal of counsel   CRCSupp SupCtPolicy

CAPITOL BUILDINGS
Annex
  Environmental impact report on building annex project, judicial review
    Petitions under environmental quality act, civil rules governing   CRC 3.2220 to 3.2240

CAPPERS AND RUNNERS
Unlawful detainer filings, public access to   CCP §1161.2

CAPTIONS
Conciliation court petition   Fam §1832
Pleadings   CCP §422.30

CAPTIVES
Records of captive persons in other countries as admissible   Ev §1283

CARCASS (See **ANIMALS**)

CARDIOPULMONARY RESUSCITATION
General provisions concerning immunity from liability for emergency care   CC §§1714.2, 1714.21

CARDIOPULMONARY RESUSCITATION—Cont.
Request to regarding resuscitative measures   Pro §§4780 to 4786

CARNIVALS (See **FAIRS AND EXPOSITIONS**)

CARPENTER-KATZ SMALL BUSINESS EQUAL ACCESS TO JUSTICE ACT   CCP §1028.5

CARPETS
Home improvement goods and services   CC §1689.8

CARRIAGE OF GOODS OR PERSONS (See **COMMON CARRIERS**)

CARRIERS (See **COMMON CARRIERS**)

CASA PROGRAM (See **COURT-APPOINTED SPECIAL ADVOCATES (CASA)**)

CASEFLOW MANAGEMENT   CRC 3.700 to 3.771
False claims act
    Filing records under seal   CRC 2.573

CASE QUESTIONNAIRES
Economic litigation provisions for limited civil cases   CCP §93

CASE TRANSFER (See **TRANSFER OF ACTIONS**)

CATALOG SALES (See **MAIL ORDER SALES**)

CATS
Sales contracts
    Payments subsequent to transfer of possession to transfer ownership, void contracts   CC §1670.10

CATTLE (See **LIVESTOCK**)

CATTLE GUARDS
Eminent domain compensation for   CCP §1263.450

CAUSE, CHALLENGE FOR (See **JURY**)

CAUSE OF ACTION (See **ACTIONS**)

CAVES
Spelunking, injuries from   CC §846

CEDAR FIRE, SAN DIEGO COUNTY
Reconstruction contracts
    Construction defects, actions for
        Incorporation of construction defects actions provisions in contracts for reconstruction   CC §945.6

CELLULAR TELEPHONES
Attorney-client privilege for conversations on   Ev §952
Child sexual abuse hosted on social media platform   CC §§3273.65 to 3273.69
Commercial sexual exploitation of minor by social media platform   CC §3345.1
Domestic violence victims
    Cell phone billing responsibility, transfer upon request   Fam §6347
Security for connected devices   CC §§1798.91.04 to 1798.91.06

CEMENT
Fixtures attached to real property by   CC §660

CEMETERIES
Easement right to burial   CC §§801, 802
Exempt property for purposes of enforcement of judgments   CCP §704.200

CENSURE (See **JUDGES**)

CEREMONIAL MARRIAGES (See **MARRIAGE**)

CERTAINTY
Contracts, construction of   CC §1654
Damages, determination of   CC §3301
Partition action   CCP §872.520
Pleadings, uncertainty of   CCP §§430.10, 430.20
Wills (See **WILLS**)

CERTIFICATE OF MERIT
Architect, engineer or land surveyor, certificate of merit in negligence action against   CCP §§411.35, 430.10
Objections to complaint or cross-complaint on grounds of lack of certificate of merit   CCP §430.10

CERTIFICATE OF MERIT—Cont.
Sexual assault of minor, certificate of merit requirement in action for   CCP §§340.1, 340.11

CERTIFICATE OF TITLE
Lemon Law Buyback   CC §§1793.23, 1793.24
Statute of limitation founded upon contract or obligation evidenced by   CCP §339

CERTIFICATES AND CERTIFICATION
Abstract of judgment, certification of   CCP §674
Acknowledgment certificates (See **ACKNOWLEDGMENTS**)
Administrative Procedure Act (See **ADMINISTRATIVE PROCEDURE ACT**)
Admitted surety insurer, certificate of authorization for   CCP §995.640
Adoption (See **ADOPTION**)
Appellate rules
    Superior court appeals
        Opinions, certification for publication   CRC 8.887
    Supreme court and courts of appeal (See **APPELLATE RULES, SUPREME COURT AND COURTS OF APPEAL**)
Attorneys (See **ATTORNEYS**)
Autographed sports memorabilia, certificate of authenticity to be furnished in sale of   CC §1739.7
Baptismal certificates   Ev §1315
Birth certificates (See **BIRTH CERTIFICATES**)
Clerks of court (See **CLERKS OF COURT**)
Confession of judgment, attorneys signing certificates for   CCP §1132
Death (See **DEATH**)
Divorce certificate as evidence concerning family history   Ev §§1315, 1316
Enforcement of judgments (See **ENFORCEMENT OF JUDGMENTS**)
ERISA pension funds, loans of   CC §1917.210
Family history, certificates as evidence of   Ev §§1315, 1316
International will, execution of   Pro §§6384, 6385
Interpreters (See **TRANSLATORS AND INTERPRETERS**)
Marriage certificates (See **MARRIAGE**)
Meritorious cause of action (See **CERTIFICATE OF MERIT**)
Missing status of federal personnel, certificate reporting   Pro §3700
Penalty of perjury, certification of written instruments executed under   CCP §2015.5
Power of attorney, certified copy of   Pro §4307
Public administrators, certificate of possession and control of decedent's property by   Pro §7603
Public guardians, written certification for taking possession and control of property by   Pro §2901
Public officials, fee for certificate as to official capacity of   Gov §26852
Realty sales contracts, certificate of compliance for   CC §2985.51
Rehabilitation (See **PARDONS**)
Rent control ordinances, certification of rent levels permitted under   CC §1947.8
Sexual assault counselor, certificate for   Ev §1035.2
Sheriff's certificate (See **SHERIFF**)
Temporary restraining order, certification of attempt to notify party of   CCP §527
Transcripts
    Court reporters generally (See **COURT REPORTERS**)
Translators and interpreters (See **TRANSLATORS AND INTERPRETERS**)
Trust deeds and mortgages, discharge of   CC §§2939, 2940 to 2941.7
Trustees (See **TRUSTS**)
Written instrument executed under penalty of perjury, certification of   CCP §2015.5

CERTIFIED MAIL (See **MAIL AND MAILING**)

CERTIFIED QUESTIONS
Requests to and answers by supreme court   CRC 8.548

CERTIORARI   CRC 8.485 to 8.493
Amicus briefs   CRC 8.487
Answer   CCP §1069.1
Appellate rules, superior court appellate division
    Small claims courts, writ petitions   CRC 8.970 to 8.977
    Writ proceedings within original jurisdiction of appellate division   CRC 8.930 to 8.936
Appellate rules, supreme court and court of appeal
    Opposition   CRCSupp 4th AppDist
    Writ proceedings in supreme court or court of appeal   CRC 8.485 to 8.493
        Environmental quality act cases under public resources code   CRC 8.703
Applicability of provisions   CRC 8.485
Briefs   CRC 8.487
Certificate of interested entities or persons   CRC 8.488
    Electronic filing, when required   CRCSupp 1st AppDist

CERTIORARI—Cont.
Costs CCP §1027
    Award and recovery CRC 8.493
Decisions CRC 8.490
Defective returns CCP §1075
Defined CCP §1067
Demurrer CCP §1069.1
Environmental quality act cases under public resources code
    Writ proceedings CRC 8.703
Filing of decision CRC 8.490
Finality of decision CRC 8.490
Judgment signed by clerk CCP §1077
Jurisdiction for CCP §1068
Modification of decision CRC 8.490
Notice if writ issues CRC 8.489
Notice of sanctions CRC 8.492
Notice to adverse party CCP §1069
Opposition CRC 8.487
    Sanctions CRC 8.492
Oral argument
    Sanctions CRC 8.492
Petition CCP §1069
    Contents CRC 8.486
    Supporting documents CRC 8.486
Record, procedure for transferring CCP §§1070, 1071
Rehearings CRC 8.490
Remittitur CCP §1076, CRC 8.490
Return by demurrer or answer CCP §§1069.1, 1108
Review authorized CCP §1074
Sanctions CRC 8.492
Sealed or confidential records CRC 8.486
Service of petition and supporting documents CRC 8.486
Service of writ CCP §§1073, 1107
Small claims courts
    Writ petitions CRC 8.970 to 8.977
Stay of proceedings CCP §1072
Superior court appellate division
    Writ proceedings within original jurisdiction of appellate division CRC 8.930 to 8.936
Writs of mandate, certiorari and prohibition in supreme court or court of appeal CRC 8.485 to 8.493
    Environmental quality act cases under public resources code
        Writ proceedings CRC 8.703

CESAR CHAVEZ DAY
Designation as judicial holiday CCP §135

CHALLENGES
International commercial arbitrators, challenges of (See **INTERNATIONAL COMMERCIAL ARBITRATION AND CONCILIATION**)
Jury challenges (See **JURY**)

CHAMBERS
Courts of Appeal, powers and duties at chambers of justices of CCP §165
Judges, powers and duties of CCP §166
Supreme Court justices, powers and duties at chambers of CCP §165

CHANGE OF NAMES
Adoption proceedings (See **ADOPTION**)
Application for CCP §1276
Birth certificates
    Application to change name or child's name on California birth certificate CCP §1276
Common law right for any person to change one's name, no abrogation of CCP §1279.5, Fam §2082
Confidential marriage licenses, certificates, etc
    Application to change name on California confidential marriage license, etc CCP §1276
Conservator taking possession of assets of conservatee held by financial institutions Pro §§2891, 2893
Domestic partnership
    Declaration of domestic partnership form to provide for Fam §298
    Election to change name Fam §298.6
    Permissible names Fam §298.6
    Registration of declaration to indicate new name and previous name Fam §298.5
Domestic violence address confidentiality program, spouse-participant in CCP §1277
    Trial court rules CRC 2.575 to 2.577
Former name of spouse restored following dissolution of marriage Fam §§2080 to 2082, 2401

CHANGE OF NAMES—Cont.
Forms
    Judicial council legal forms CRCAppx A
Gender identity, change to conform name to identity CCP §1277
    Objection CCP §1277.5
    Procedure CCP §1277.5
    Publication of proceeding not required CCP §1277.5
Guardian taking possession of assets of ward held by financial institutions Pro §§2891, 2893
Hearings CCP §1278
Infants CCP §1276
Joint consent of minor's parents, best-interest determination in absence of CCP §1278.5
Jurisdiction CCP §1275
Maiden name of wife restored following dissolution of marriage Fam §§2080 to 2082, 2401
Marriage
    Amendment to correct clerical errors Fam §306.5
    Election to change name Fam §306.5
    Licenses, certificates, etc
        Application to change name on California marriage license, etc CCP §1276
    Marriage license to allow for Fam §355
    Permissible names Fam §306.5
Notice CCP §1277
Petitions CCP §1276
    Memorandum in support of petition not required CRC 3.1114
Prisoners and parolees, name-change restrictions on CCP §1279.5
Procedure for CCP §§1275 to 1279.6
Publication CCP §1277
    Gender identity, change to conform name to identity, publication not required CCP §1277.5
Refusal to do business with person using birth or former name CCP §1279.6
Sex offenders, restrictions on CCP §1279.5
Show cause order, notice of CCP §1277
Uniform Parentage Act, actions under Fam §7638
Witness Protection Program, change of name under CCP §1277

CHANGE OF VENUE (See **VENUE**)

CHAPTERS
Conflicting chapters in codes CC §§23.4, 23.6

CHARACTER AND REPUTATION
Generally Ev §1100
Community reputation concerning family history Ev §1314
Conduct, character evidence as proof of Ev §1101
Credibility, attack on
    Generally Ev §§780, 785, 786, 790
    Felony convictions Ev §788
    Previous consistent statements Ev §791
    Religious beliefs Ev §789
    Sexual assault victim, procedures regarding Ev §§782, 783
    Specific instances of conduct Ev §787
Criminal cases
    Generally Ev §1102
    Conduct of victim Ev §§782, 1103
    Conviction of crime Ev §788
    Sexual assault (See within this heading, **"Sexually oriented offenses"**)
Family history, reputation among other family members concerning Ev §1313
History of community as evidence Ev §1320
Information Practices Act, protection under CC §1798.38
Judges
    Testimony by CRCSupp JudEthicsCanon 2
Professional persons, investigation of CC §§43.7, 43.8
Sexually oriented offenses
    Administrative adjudication proceedings alleging sexual harassment, assault or battery Gov §11440.40
    Commission of other sexual offense, admissibility of evidence of Ev §1108
    Conduct of victim, admissibility of evidence regarding Ev §§1103, 1106
    Credibility of victim, procedures for attacking Ev §§782, 783
Time of particular character trait, proof of Ev §1324

CHARGE CARDS (See **CREDIT CARDS**)

CHARGE TO JURY (See **JURY**)

CHARITABLE ORGANIZATIONS
Exemption for purposes of enforcement of judgments of aid from CCP §704.170

CHARITABLE ORGANIZATIONS—Cont.
Eyeglasses
    Immunity from liability
        Nonprofit charitable organization and volunteer eye care professionals donating screening, eyeglasses, etc   CC §1714.26
Fine prints sale, charities exempt from disclosure requirements for   CC §1742.6
Judges
    Office of judge in organization not a financial interest for purposes of disqualification   CCP §170.5
        Participation in charitable activities   CRCSupp JudEthicsCanon 4
Nonprofit corporations (See **NONPROFIT CORPORATIONS AND ASSOCIATIONS**)
Trusts for charitable purposes (See **TRUSTS**)
Uniform prudent management of institutional funds act   Pro §§18501 to 18510 (See **INSTITUTIONAL FUNDS MANAGEMENT**)
Vision screenings, eyeglasses, etc
    Immunity from liability
        Nonprofit charitable organization and volunteer eye care professionals donating screening, eyeglasses, etc   CC §1714.26

CHARITABLE TRUSTS
Annuity trusts   Pro §21540
Applicability of Trust Law provisions   Pro §15004
Attorney general
    Beneficiaries' rights, enforcement   Pro §17210
    Civil actions to enforce provisions
        Fees and costs for attorney general   CCP §1021.8
    Disposal of all or substantially all of charitable assets
        Trustee notice to attorney general prior to disposal   Pro §16110
Charitable lead trust provisions, construction   Pro §21541
Charitable remainder trust provisions, construction   Pro §21540
Cy pres doctrine   Pro §21220
Decanting of trusts, uniform act   Pro §§19501 to 19530 (See **TRUST DECANTING, UNIFORM ACT**)
Defined   Pro §16100
Disposal of all or substantially all of charitable assets
    Trustee notice to attorney general prior to disposal   Pro §16110
Distributions under   Pro §16101
Duties of trustees   Pro §§16100 to 16110
Honorary trusts   Pro §15211
Lead trusts   Pro §21541
Petition for administration of estate, service on Attorney General   Pro §8111
Proceedings under Tax Reform Act, procedure for   Pro §16105
Remainder unitrusts   Pro §21540
Restrictions   Pro §16102
Statutory provisions   Pro §16104
Trust Law, applicability   Pro §15004
Uniform prudent management of institutional funds act   Pro §§18501 to 18510 (See **INSTITUTIONAL FUNDS MANAGEMENT**)

CHARTERED CITIES
Assessment against real property for public improvements, time limit for contesting validity of   CCP §329.5

CHARTERED COUNTIES (See **COUNTIES**)

CHARTERS
Vessels held under   CC §1959

CHASTITY
Slander by imputing absence of   CC §46

CHATTEL MORTGAGES (See also **CONDITIONAL SALES; SECURED TRANSACTIONS**)
Administrators executing   Pro §9805
Apartment housekeeper's lien subordinate to rights under   CC §1861a
Attachment (See **ATTACHMENT**)
Automobiles (See **AUTOMOBILES**)
Decedents' estates, securing credit sale of personalty of   Pro §§10257, 10258
Enforcement of judgments (See **ENFORCEMENT OF JUDGMENTS**)
Executors executing   Pro §9805
Foreclosure, stay of proceedings   CCP §917.2

CHECK CASHERS
Amount cashed for person during year requiring report to IRS   CC §1789.30
Deferred deposit of personal check, agreement for   CC §1789.35
Defined   CC §1789.31
Fines for operating without permit   CC §1789.37
Government checks, limitations on fees charged for cashing   CC §1789.35
Identification   CC §1789.35
Payroll checks, limitations on fees charged for cashing   CC §1789.35

CHECK CASHERS—Cont.
Penalties for operating without permit   CC §1789.37
Permit, application procedures for   CC §1789.37
Personal checks, terms for cashing   CC §1789.35
Posting of fee schedules   CC §§1789.30, 1789.32
Registration of check cashers with Department of Justice   CC §1789.37
Remedies and damages against check cashers   CC §1789.35
Unfair business practices related to posting of information   CC §1789.32
Waiver of protections   CC §1789.38

CHECKS
Accord and satisfaction, effect of check payments of disputed amounts for purposes of   CC §1526
Attachment of   CCP §486.060
Bad checks
    Filing fees, consequences of paying with bad check   CCP §411.20
    Liability for making   CC §1719
Check cashers (See **CHECK CASHERS**)
Court clerks, checks for making payments to   CCP §411.20, CRC 8.100, 10.821
    Underpayment   CCP §411.21
Credit card issuer extending credit to cardholder by means of preprinted check or draft, required disclosures by   CC §1748.9
Credit card number as identification for negotiable instruments, use of   CC §1725
Debit cards, cardholder's liability for unauthorized use
    Waiver of protections
        Void   CC §1748.32
Demand for payment following dishonor   CC §1719
Dissemination of information regarding consumer checking accounts, liability for   CC §1785.5
Forged or raised check, limitation of action for payment of   CCP §340
Good faith dispute requirement for stop payments   CC §1719
"Insufficient funds" defined   CC §1719
Presumption of evidence for check payments in dispute   Ev §670
Protective order's effect on amount of   CCP §486.060
Stop payments, notice requirements and damages for   CC §1719
Traveler's checks (See **TRAVELER'S CHECKS**)
Treble damages for making bad checks   CC §1719

CHEMICALS
Animal testing, restrictions against
    Pesticides or chemical substances
        Canine and feline toxicological experiments   CC §1834.9.3

CHICKENS (See **POULTRY**)

CHIEF JUSTICE
Appellate duties and powers of (See **APPELLATE RULES, SUPREME COURT AND COURTS OF APPEAL**)
Education of judicial branch
    Additional education recommendations for certain judicial assignments   CRC 10.469
    Duties of chief judge   CRC 10.452

CHIEF OF POLICE (See **LAW ENFORCEMENT OFFICERS**)

CHILD ABDUCTION (See **CUSTODY OF CHILDREN**)

CHILD ABUSE
Character of defendant, admission of other-acts evidence to establish
    Previous child abuse   Ev §1109
Custody and visitation, effect of child abuse conviction on   Fam §3030
Domestic Violence Protection Act, protection against child abuse and abduction under (See **DOMESTIC VIOLENCE**)
Government tort liability
    Childhood sexual abuse damage claims   Gov §831.8
Hearsay rule, exceptions to   Ev §§1228, 1253, 1293, 1360
Libel and slander action by person accused of   CC §48.7
Mediators, continuing education of   Fam §1816
Medical diagnosis or treatment, admissibility of statements made for purposes of   Ev §1253
Parental control, grounds in actions to declare child free from   Fam §§7820 to 7827
Privileged communications between sexual assault victim and counselor
    Name change proceedings under address confidentiality program   CRC 2.575 to 2.577
Reliability of minor's statement, determination of   Ev §1360
Reports
    Human trafficking victim-caseworker privilege
        Duty to report not diminished by provisions   Ev §1038.3
Resource guidelines for court practice   CRC JudAdminStand 5.45

CHILD ABUSE—Cont.
Sanctions for false accusation of   Fam §3027.1
Sentences
    Abuse and neglect as mitigating circumstance   CRC 4.423
Sexual abuse (See **SEX OFFENSES**)
Termination of parental rights
    Generally   Fam §§7800 to 7895 (See **TERMINATION OF PARENTAL RIGHTS**)
    Circumstances where proceedings may be brought   Fam §7823
Visitation
    Supervised   CRC JudAdminStand 5.20
Visitation and custody, effect of child abuse conviction on   Fam §3030

CHILD CARE
Adoption agencies (See **ADOPTION**)
Child support award including costs of child care   Fam §§4061 to 4063
Criminal history checks on child care providers by child care provider trustline registry   CC §1812.5093
Employment agencies
    Trustline registry for child care providers, requirements concerning   CC §1812.5093
    Verification of work experience or training of person seeking babysitting job   CC §1812.509
Trustline registry for child care providers   CC §1812.5093

CHILD CUSTODY (See **CUSTODY OF CHILDREN**)

CHILD EMANCIPATION (See **EMANCIPATION OF MINORS**)

CHILDHOOD SEXUAL ABUSE (See **SEX OFFENSES**)

CHILD LABOR
Trusts for percentage of earnings, mandatory
    Extras, background performers, etc
        Trusts for percentage of earnings, exceptions to requirements   Fam §6752
Vlogging, minors engaged in the work of   Fam §§6650 to 6656

CHILD PLACEMENT AGENCIES (See **ADOPTION**)

CHILDREN
Minors generally (See **MINORS**)
Parent and child generally (See **PARENT AND CHILD**)

CHILDREN BORN OUT OF WEDLOCK (See **PARENT AND CHILD; PATERNITY**)

CHILD SUPPORT   Fam §§4000 to 4077
Generally   Fam §§3900 to 3902
Abstract of judgment
    Liens
        Digital form of lien record   Fam §17523.5
    Right to record   Fam §§4506, 4506.1
Abuse of parental authority, duty to support after finding of   Fam §7507
Additional support, provision for   Fam §§3901, 4061 to 4063
Adult child
    Agreement to support   Fam §3587
    Compensation, entitlement to   Fam §3910
    Incapacity of   Fam §3910
AFDC
    Welfare generally (See within this heading, "**Welfare**")
Agreement between parents, support order based on   Fam §§3585 to 3587
Allowance to parent out of child's property   Fam §3902
Amount of support
    Generally   Fam §§3830, 4055 to 4057
    Simplified income and expense form for determining child support, development of   Fam §4068
Annual gross income, computation of   Fam §4058
Annual net disposable income, computation of   Fam §4059
Appeals
    Generally   CCP §904.1, Fam §3554
    Attorney General's appeal in case brought by child support agency   Fam §17407
Arrears in payment
    Deposit of assets (See within this heading, "**Deposit of assets to secure future payment**")
    Deposit of money to secure future support payments, use of   Fam §§4570 to 4573
    Government support enforcement services
        Compromise of arrears program   Fam §17560
        Statement of arrearages required by   Fam §§17524, 17526
    Interest on   CCP §695.211

CHILD SUPPORT—Cont.
Arrears in payment—Cont.
    Judgments for fees on amounts in arrears   Fam §5616
    Limitations period for recovery of   Fam §4503
    Notice of delinquency   Fam §§4722 to 4724, 4731
    Penalty provisions   Fam §§4720 to 4733
    Perjury, allegations of arrearages under penalty of   Fam §5230.5
    Vacating when paternity determination vacated   Fam §7648.4
Assets, deposit of (See within this heading, "**Deposit of assets to secure future payment**")
Assignment
    Benefit of creditors, effect of assignment for   CCP §§1800, 1801
    Earnings assignment for support (See **EARNINGS ASSIGNMENT FOR SUPPORT**)
    Government support enforcement services
        Assigned support payments made for CalWORKs recipients, notice   Fam §17504.4
        Impact of passthrough payments, report   Fam §17504.6
        Passthrough payments of assigned obligation to former recipient of aid   Fam §17504.2
    Health and medical insurance   Fam §§3760 to 3773
Attorney professional conduct
    Contingent fees
        Circumstances where contingent fee agreement impermissible   ProfC 1.5
Attorneys
    Attorney as support obligor, failure to pay   CRC 9.22
Attorney's fees and costs
    Modification of support orders   Fam §3652
    Person awarded fees, court determination of   Fam §3557
        Financial need basis for fees   CRC 5.427
    Temporary orders for award of   Fam §2031
Avoiding payment
    Knowingly assisting obligor   CC §1714.4
        Conduct constituting   CC §1714.41
Bank accounts
    Electronic funds transfer, account for   Fam §4508
    Writ of execution, financial institution designation of central location for service of   CCP §689.040
Bankruptcy, effect of discharge in   Fam §4013
Bond securing performance of   Fam §§4012, 4615
CalWORKs program
    Local child support agencies
        Duties for CalWORKs cases   Fam §3680.5
Case registry forms   CRC 5.330
Change of award (See within this heading, "**Modification**")
Child care costs   Fam §§4061 to 4063
Child for whom support may be ordered   Fam §58
Child Support Case Registry Form, requirement for filing   CRC 5.330
Child Support Collections Recovery Fund   Fam §17402.5
Child support commissioners, judicial education   CRC 5.340
Child Support Delinquency Reporting Law   Fam §§4700, 4701
Child support obligee defined   Fam §4550
Child support payment trust fund   Fam §17311
Child Support Services Advance fund   Fam §17703
Circumstances of parent, obligation based on   Fam §4075
Collection and payment
    Local agency responsibility   Fam §§17500 to 17560
    Passthrough payments of assigned obligation to former recipient of aid   Fam §17504.2
    Impact of passthrough payments, report   Fam §17504.6
Collections
    Delinquency   Fam §17450
        Financial institution data match   Fam §17453
        Reciprocal agreements with other states   Fam §17460
        Tax return data, use to collect   Fam §17452
        Transmittal of delinquency amounts without court order   Fam §17456
        Withholding   Fam §§17454, 17456
    Private child support collectors   Fam §§5610 to 5616
    Trust agreement to receive or disburse   Fam §17311.5
Combined summons and complaint, filing by clerks   CRC 5.325
Commissioners, judicial education for   CRC 5.340
Community property liable for   Fam §§915, 4008
Compensation of other parent or relatives for voluntary support to child   Fam §3951
Computers
    Software used to determine support amount   CRC 5.275, Fam §3830
    System authorized to provide standardized information   CCP §1062.20
Conciliation Courts, orders of   Fam §1839
Confidentiality of child support enforcement agency records   Fam §§17212, 17514

CHILD SUPPORT—Cont.
Consolidation of actions   CRC 5.365
Contempt
    Generally   CCP §1209.5
    Deposit of money to secure future support payments, failure to comply with order for   Fam §4571
    Limitations period in action for   CCP §1218.5
    Willful failure to obey support order   Fam §7641
Contingent period of time, support ordered for   Fam §4007
Costs (See within this heading, **"Attorney's fees and costs"**)
County agencies enforcing support (See within this heading, **"Government support enforcement services"**)
County officer forwarding support payment to designated payee   Fam §3555
County officer or local child support agency as designated payee   Fam §§4200 to 4205
    State disbursement unit as payee   Fam §§4200, 4201, 4204
Court clerks
    Minimum training standards   CRC 5.355
    Staff, minimum training required   Fam §3555
Court commissioners
    Generally   Fam §4250
    Appointment of child support commissioners   Fam §4252
    Default orders entered by commissioners   Fam §4253
    Education requirements   CRC 5.340
    Funding of commissioners   Fam §17712
    Judicial Council role   Fam §4252
    Powers of commissioners, generally   CCP §259
    Procedure for reference to and hearing by commissioners   Fam §4251
    Title IV-D cases, commissioners to hear   Fam §§4250, 4251
Court reporter taking down and transcribing at cost of county   CCP §274a
Crediting money judgments for support   CCP §695.221
Creditors, direct payment to   Fam §2023
Credit reporting agencies
    Information not to be contained in credit report   CC §1785.13
    Reporting delinquencies to   Fam §§4700, 4701
Criminal information concerning parent, purging local child support agency case files of   Fam §17531
Custodial parent's failure to implement rights of noncustodial parent, effect of   Fam §3556
Death of child, effect of   Fam §5240
Decedent's estate, liability for support payments out of   Fam §3952
Default judgments
    Generally (See **FAMILY RULES**)
    Government support enforcement services, action brought by   Fam §§17430, 17433
    Referee or commissioner, default orders by   Fam §4253
Deferred sale of family home, request of custodial parent for   Fam §§3800 to 3810
Definitions   Fam §§150, 3500, 3515
Delay in bringing dissolution action to trial, effect of dismissal for   CCP §583.161
Delinquency
    Collection of delinquency   Fam §17450
        Financial institution data match   Fam §17453
        Reciprocal agreements with other states   Fam §17460
        Tax return data, use to collect   Fam §17452
        Transmittal of delinquency amounts without court order   Fam §17456
        Withholding   Fam §§17454, 17456
    Definition of delinquency   Fam §17450
    Earnings
        Defined   Fam §17450
        Notice   Fam §§4722 to 4724, 4731, 17525
Department of child support services   Fam §§17000 to 17325
    Administrative service fees   Fam §17208
    Child support payment trust fund   Fam §17311
    Collections
        Trust agreement to receive or disburse   Fam §17311.5
    Definitions   Fam §17000
    Deposit of payments
        Qualifying account requirement   Fam §17325
    Director   Fam §§17300 to 17325
    Establishment and purpose   Fam §§17000 to 17325
    Local child support agencies, establishment and transition to   Fam §§17304, 17305
    Organization of   Fam §§17200 to 17212
    Payments
        Recipients   Fam §17311.7
    State disbursement unit   Fam §17309
        Recipients of payments   Fam §17311.7
        Timing of support payments, remedy for effects of timing change   Fam §17307

CHILD SUPPORT—Cont.
Deposit of assets to secure future payment
    Generally   Fam §§4600 to 4604
    Bond in lieu of deposit   Fam §4615
    Deposit holder defined   Fam §4601
    Ex parte restraining orders   Fam §§4610, 4620
    Fees and costs incurred by deposit holder   Fam §4604
    Grounds for defense to allegation that obligor-parent in arrears   Fam §§4612, 4632
    Order for deposit   Fam §§4610 to 4617
    Presumptions   Fam §4611
    Release of real property   Fam §4641
    Return of assets to obligor   Fam §§4640, 4641
    Sale of assets   Fam §§4616, 4630 to 4632
    Stop motions   Fam §4631
    Use or sale of assets   Fam §§4630 to 4632
Deposit of money to secure future support payments
    Generally   Fam §§4550 to 4554
    Application to reduce or eliminate deposit   Fam §§4565 to 4567
    Child support security deposit   Fam §4560
    Court controlled account   Fam §4561
    Delinquent payments, use of deposit to make   Fam §§4570 to 4573
    Dissolution of account and disposition of remaining funds   Fam §4563
    Evidence of deposit   Fam §4562
    Hardship, deposit to impose   Fam §4567
    Order for deposit of money   Fam §§4560 to 4563
Deposit of payments
    Qualifying account requirement   Fam §17325
Discovery
    Law and motion rules applicable to discovery proceedings in family law   CRC 3.1100
    Modification of support order   Fam §§3660 to 3668
    Tax returns   Fam §3552
    Termination of support order   Fam §§3660 to 3668
Dismissal of dissolution of marriage petition for delay in prosecution, effect of child support orders on   CCP §583.161
Dissolution of marriage
    Consolidation of actions   CRC 5.365
Domestic violence protective order requiring presumed natural father to pay support   Fam §6341
    Parentage, agreement and judgment
        Agreement and judgment of parentage in domestic violence prevention act cases   CRC 5.380
Drivers' licenses
    Suspension or denial of license for noncompliance with support obligation   Fam §17520
        Lower-income obligors   Fam §17520.5
Duration of duty   Fam §3901
Duty of support of minor child   Fam §§3900, 3901
Earning capacity of parent
    Determination   Fam §4058
Earnings assignment for support (See **EARNINGS ASSIGNMENT FOR SUPPORT**)
Earnings, child support payments as   CC §1812.30
Earnings withholding order for support (See **GARNISHMENT**)
Education of child, costs of   Fam §§4061 to 4063
Electronic funds transfer for payments
    Accounts for   Fam §4508
    State disbursement unit
        Employer payment of withholding   Fam §17309.5
Emancipated minor   Fam §§5240, 7050
Employment Development Department information concerning obligors, access to   Fam §§17508, 17509, 17518
Enforcement
    Generally   Fam §§290, 291, 4000, 4500 to 4508
    Abstract of judgment, recordation of   Fam §§4506, 4506.1
    Arrears
        Judgments for fees on arrears   Fam §5616
    Attorneys at law   CRC 9.22
    Contempt action, Judicial Council forms for   Fam §292
    Creditor of public entity, judgment debtor as   CCP §§708.730, 708.740, 708.780
    Credit reporting agencies, reporting delinquencies to   Fam §§4700, 4701
    Defenses by obligor alleged to be in arrears
        Laches as to portion owed to state   Fam §291
    Deposit of assets (See within this heading, **"Deposit of assets to secure future payment"**)
    Deposit of money (See within this heading, **"Deposit of money to secure future support payments"**)
    Earnings assignment for support (See **EARNINGS ASSIGNMENT FOR SUPPORT**)
    Earnings withholding order for support (See **GARNISHMENT**)

CHILD SUPPORT—Cont.
  Enforcement—Cont.
    Employee benefit plan, enforcement for support against   Fam §5103
    Execution, writ of   Fam §§5100 to 5104
    Exemptions applied to judgment, generally   CCP §703.070
    Family support order, generally   Fam §4501
    Forms, adoption by judicial council   Fam §17432.5
    Garnishment (See **GARNISHMENT**)
    Government support enforcement services (See within this heading, **"Government support enforcement services"**)
    Liens (See within this heading, **"Liens"**)
    Limited civil cases, unavailability of enforcement through   CCP §580
    Local agency responsibility   Fam §§17500 to 17560
    Local child support agencies (See within this heading, **"Government support enforcement services"**)
    Lottery winnings owed judgment debtor, claim for support arrearages filed against state for   CCP §§708.730, 708.740
    Modified support order, effect on judgment lien of   CCP §697.360
    Notice generally (See within this heading, **"Notice"**)
    Parent Locator Service and Central Registry   Fam §17506
    Penalties (See within this heading, **"Penalties"**)
    Period of enforceability for possession or sale of property   Fam §§291, 4502
    Private child support collectors   Fam §§5610 to 5616
    Relief from support judgments or orders   Fam §§2120 to 2129, 3690 to 3693, 17432
    Renewal requirements, judgments exempt from   CCP §683.310, Fam §§291, 4502
    Retirement benefits of judgment debtor   CCP §§704.110, 704.114, 704.115, Fam §17528
    Satisfaction of money judgment for child support, priorities for crediting money received in   CCP §695.221
    Self-help materials   Fam §291
    Social security payments   Fam §§4504, 17516
    Tax refund owed judgment debtor, claim against   CCP §§708.730, 708.740, 708.780
    Unemployment compensation benefits, enforcement against   CCP §704.120, Fam §17518
    Workers' compensation benefits, enforcement against   CCP §704.160, Fam §17510
  Enforcement of judgments
    Levy and execution
      Application for writ of execution, priority   CCP §699.510
  Equal responsibility of parents for   Fam §4001
  Escrow relating to support judgment lien, demand statement needed to close   CCP §697.360
  Evasion of obligation
    Knowingly assisting obligor   CC §1714.4
      Conduct constituting   CC §1714.41
  Evidence
    Admissibility of income and benefit information provided by employer in proceeding to modify or terminate support   Ev §1567
    Deposit of money to secure future payments   Fam §4562
    Title IV-D support enforcement cases
      Tribal court, transfers   CRC 5.372
  Execution writ to enforce support order   Fam §§5100 to 5104
  Ex parte restraining orders   Fam §§4610, 4620
  Expenses
    Added to amount of support   Fam §§4061 to 4063
    County, expenses and fees charged to   Fam §4203
    Declaration (See within this heading, **"Income and expense declaration"**)
    Travel expenses for visitation   Fam §§4061, 4062
  Family home, rental value of   Fam §4057
  Family law facilitators for unrepresented parties   Fam §§10000 to 10015
  Family law information centers for unrepresented low-income litigants   Fam §§15000 to 15012
  Family law rules (See **FAMILY RULES**)
  Family support defined   Fam §92
  Federal law, compliance with   Fam §4553
  Fees
    Department of child support services
      Administrative service fees   Fam §17208
    Title IV-D child support agency involved   Gov §70672
    Waiver of fees and costs
      Repayment of waived fees in support actions   CRC 5.45
  Financial hardship (See within this heading, **"Hardship"**)
  Financial institution match system
    Delinquency
      Collection of delinquency   Fam §17453
  Findings
    Nonguideline findings attachment   CRCAppx A (CRCFL-342(A))

CHILD SUPPORT—Cont.
  Findings—Cont.
    Request of party   Fam §4005
  Foreign country judgments   CCP §1715
  Forms, simplified complaints and answers
    Judicial council forms   CRCAppx A
  Formulas for award calculation (See within this heading, **"Statewide uniform guidelines"**)
  Garnishment (See **GARNISHMENT**)
  Government support enforcement services   CRC 5.300 to 5.375, Fam §§4002, 4200 to 4205, 4351
    Abduction records, disclosure of   Fam §17514
    Abstract of judgment, recordation of   Fam §4506.1
    Actions under Social Security Act Title IV-D   CRC 5.320
    Address of obligor, requirements on receipt of   Fam §17401
    Agreement, judgment based on   Fam §17416
    Answers to complaints in actions brought by local support agencies   Fam §§17400, 17404
    Appeals by Attorney General   Fam §17407
    Appearance in actions   CRC 5.360
    Appropriations augmenting local funding for child support agencies   Fam §17555
    Assigned support payments made for CalWORKs recipients
      Impact of passthrough payments, report   Fam §17504.6
      Notice by local child support agency   Fam §17504.4
      Passthrough payments of assigned obligation to former recipient of aid   Fam §17504.2
    Attorney-client relationship, disclaimer of   Fam §17406
    Attorney of record for actions under Social Security Act Title IV-D   CRC 5.320
    Attorneys' fees award against governmental agency   Fam §273
    Child Support Collections Recovery Fund   Fam §17402.5
    Child Support Services Advance fund   Fam §17703
    Civil procedure for enforcement actions, generally   Fam §§17400, 17404
    Commissioners (See within this heading, **"Court commissioners"**)
    Complaints
      Local support agencies, complaints against by custodial and noncustodial parents   Fam §§17800 to 17804
      Local support agencies, complaints and answers in actions brought by   CRC 5.325, Fam §§17400, 17404, 17428
    Compromise of arrears program   Fam §17560
    Confidentiality of records   Fam §§17212, 17514
    Consolidation of support orders   Fam §17408
    County assessments
      Compliance by county with standards, assessment   Fam §17702
    Data collection and reporting by local support agencies   Fam §17600
    Debt compromise of obligor parent's liabilities for public assistance   Fam §§17550, 17552
    Declaration of state reciprocity by attorney general   Fam §17407.5
    Deduction of support payment from aid received by obligee, first $50 as exempt from requirement for   Fam §17504
    Default judgment in enforcement action   Fam §§17430, 17433
    Definitions   Fam §17000
    Delinquency notice   Fam §17525
    Departmental regulations to be promulgated for case referrals to local child support agencies   Fam §17552
    Department of Child Support Services (See within this heading, **"Department of child support services"**)
    Designation of local child support agency as assigned payee   Fam §§3030, 3752, 4200 to 4205, 17000
      State disbursement unit as payee   Fam §§4200, 4201, 4204
    Disabled obligor, modification of child support enforcement order for   Fam §17400.5
    Earnings assignment for support, enforcement of   CCP §704.114, Fam §§5212, 5244 to 5247, 17420
    Earnings withholding order for support, enforcement by local child support agency of   CCP §706.030, Fam §17509
    Effective date of support order in proposed judgment   Fam §17400.5
    Electronic copy of original signed pleadings   CRC 2.257
    Electronic court records, remote access
      Access by government entities   CRC 2.540
      Government entities, access by   CRC 2.540
    Electronic filing of pleadings signed by agent of local child support agency   Fam §17400
    Electronic fund transfers for employer payment of withholding   Fam §17309.5
    Electronic signatures
      Substitution for original signatures   Fam §17400
    Employment and training services for noncustodial parents, administration of   Fam §17211
    Erroneous enforcement action, remediation of   Fam §§17433, 17530

CHILD SUPPORT—Cont.
  Government support enforcement services —Cont.
    Expedited modification of support order   Fam §17441
    Failure of defendant to answer or appear, default judgment   Fam §17430
    Family law facilitator's role where local child support agency enforcing support   Fam §10008
    Filing requirements for actions   CRC 5.320
    Forms, adoption by judicial council   Fam §17432.5
    Forms of pleadings   Fam §17400
      Judicial council legal forms   CRCAppx A
    Funding of county programs   Fam §§17701 to 17714
      Appropriations augmenting funding   Fam §17555
    Health and disability benefits, limitation on withholding of   CCP §704.130
    Health insurance
      Medical insurance form, requirements concerning   Fam §§17422, 17424
      Notification requirements   Fam §§3752, 3771, 3773
    Incentive programs established for local and state agencies   Fam §§17600, 17704, 17706, 17708
    Independent enforcement actions by parents, availability of   Fam §17404
    Information provided to public   Fam §§17400, 17434
    Intercounty support obligations
      Custodial and supporting parents residing in different counties   Fam §§4202, 4203
      Registration of support orders   Fam §§5600 to 5604
    Intervention in family law cases, local child support agencies' authority and procedure for   Fam §17400
    Interview of custodial parent   Fam §17405
    Levies   CCP §§689.020 to 689.050, Fam §17522
      Liquidation of financial assets pursuant to   Fam §17522.5
    Licenses and permits of noncompliant obligors, denial or suspension of   Fam §§17520, 17521
    Lien for child support   Fam §17523
    Local child support agencies
      Funding   Fam §17306.1
    Mistaken identity, remedies for enforcement action based on   Fam §§17433, 17530
    Modification of child support enforcement order
      Disabled obligor   Fam §17400.5
      Expedited modification of support order   Fam §17441
      Military deployment   Fam §17440
    Notices
      Change of payee on support order   Fam §17404.4
      Intention to appear   CRC 5.360
      Recipients of support services   Fam §§17401.5, 17406
    Number of children requiring support, inquiry concerning   Fam §17418
    Other agencies, cooperation of   Fam §§17505, 17508, 17510, 17518, 17528
    Outreach by local child support agencies   Fam §§17400, 17434
    Parentage determinations in enforcement actions   Fam §§7558, 17404, 17406, 17410 to 17416
      Genetic testing to determine parentage   Fam §7558
    Penalties, prohibition on use of   Fam §4729
    Performance standards for local child support agencies   Fam §17602
    Pleadings in actions brought by local support agencies   CRC 5.325, Fam §§17400, 17404, 17428
    Presumed income for purposes of support order, notice to defendant concerning   Fam §17400
    Public social service benefits or payments under Social Security Act as exempt from support enforcement   Fam §17516
    Quality assurance and performance improvement program   Fam §17701
    Referrals by Welfare Department   Fam §17415
    Regulations, adoption of   Fam §§17306, 17310, 17312
    Reimbursement of aid to family during period of separation or desertion, enforcement of noncustodial parent's obligation for   Fam §17402
    Relief from judgments and orders   Fam §17432
    Remittance of federal and state public assistance child support payments by local child support agencies   Fam §17402.1
    Remote participation in hearings by electronic means   Fam §17404.3
    Reports to legislature   Fam §17556
    Retirement benefits, enforcement against   Fam §17528
    Sanction against local agency for noncompliance with state plan   Fam §17604
    Show cause orders   Fam §17404.1
    Spousal support enforcement in conjunction with enforcement of child support   Fam §§4351, 17000, 17604
    Statement of arrearages   Fam §§17524, 17526
    Substitution of payee, recordation of   Fam §§4506.2 to 4506.3
    Summons and complaint   CRC 5.325
    Temporary support, order for   Fam §17400
    Time limit for filing claims   Fam §17540

CHILD SUPPORT—Cont.
  Government support enforcement services —Cont.
    Title IV-D obligations of child support agency, generally   Fam §17500
    Transfer of case if tribunal inappropriate   Fam §17404.2
    Transition from enforcement by district attorneys to enforcement by local child support agencies   Fam §17305
    Uncollectible amounts   Fam §17400
    Undeliverable payments, return to obligor of   Fam §17502
    Unemployment compensation benefits, enforcement against   Fam §17518
    Venue for actions brought by local child support agencies   Fam §17400
    Voluntary acknowledgment of paternity   Fam §§17410 to 17414
    Warrant or notice of levy, local child support agency levying against property pursuant to   CCP §§689.020, 689.030
    Welfare recipients receiving support
      State disbursement unit, directing support payments to   Fam §4200
    Workers' compensation benefits, enforcement against   CCP §704.160, Fam §17510
  Grandchild, duty to support   Fam §3930
  Guidelines   Fam §§4050 to 4077 (See within this heading, **"Statewide uniform guidelines"**)
  Hardship
    Generally   Fam §§4070 to 4073
    Deposit of money to secure future support payments as imposing hardship   Fam §4567
    Maximum hardship deduction, formula for calculating   Fam §4059
  Health and disability benefits, limitation on withholding of   CCP §704.130
  Health and medical insurance
    Generally   Fam §§3751, 3753, 4006
    Additional insurance obtained by parent, reimbursement for   Fam §4063
    Assignment of health care coverage   Fam §§3760 to 3773
    Continuation of coverage
      When required   Fam §3752.5
    Defined   Fam §3750
    Family law facilitators for unrepresented parties   Fam §§10000 to 10015
    Government support enforcement services
      Medical insurance form, requirements   Fam §§17422, 17424
      Notification requirements   Fam §§3752, 3771, 3773
    Improper grounds for insurer's or employer's denial of child's enrollment   Fam §3751.5
    Judicial Council forms   Fam §3772
    Notification from obligor to obligee of insurance status   Fam §3752.5
    Uninsured health costs added to amount of support   Fam §4062
  Hearings
    Commissioners, hearings before   Fam §4251
    Deposit of money to secure future support payments as imposing hardship   Fam §4567
    Government enforcement of support obligation, civil procedure for   Fam §§17404, 17406
    Remote participation in hearings by electronic means   Fam §17404.3
  Hiding assets to avoid payment of obligation
    Knowingly assisting obligor   CC §1714.4
      Conduct constituting   CC §1714.41
  High school student, duty to support   Fam §3901
  Illness of obligor   Fam §4726
  Income and benefit information provided by employer admissible in proceeding to modify or terminate support   Ev §1567
  Income and expense declaration
    Defined   Fam §95
    Employer, request for information from   Fam §3664
    Request for   Fam §3664
    Sanctions for incomplete or inaccurate   Fam §3667
  Income withholding orders, hearings on   CRC 5.335
    Forms for income withholding   CRCAppx A
  Information and order attachment   CRCAppx A (CRCFL-342)
  Intercounty enforcement (See within this heading, **"Other counties"**)
  Interest on money judgment or support order   CCP §695.211
    Accrual of interest   Fam §17433.5
  Interstate family support   Fam §§5700.101 to 5700.903
  Interstate income withholding orders, hearings on   CRC 5.335
  Joint responsibility of parents for   Fam §4001
  Judgments and orders for support
    Enforcement generally (See within this heading, **"Enforcement"**)
    Suspension
      Incarceration or institutionalization of obligee   Fam §4007.5
  Judicial Council
    Delinquencies   Fam §4732
    Deposit of money to secure future support payments   Fam §4552
    Forms   CRCAppxs A, A (CRCFL-140 to CRCFL-196), (CRCFL-380 to CRCFL-393), Fam §3668
    Penalty provisions   Fam §4732

CHILD SUPPORT—Cont.
  Judicial Council—Cont.
    Simplified income and expense form for determining child support, development of Fam §4068
    Study and reports on guidelines Fam §4054
  Jurisdiction Fam §§2010 to 2013
    Deferred sale of family home order Fam §3809
    Interstate family support Fam §§5700.201 to 5700.211
  Law and motion rules
    Discovery
      Applicable to discovery proceedings in family law CRC 3.1100
  Levies CCP §§689.020 to 689.050, Fam §17522
    Liquidation of financial assets pursuant to Fam §17522.5
  Licenses and permits of noncompliant obligees, denial or suspension of Fam §§17520, 17521
  Liens
    Judgments, abstract of
      Digital form of lien record Fam §17523.5
    Personal property liens imposed in actions brought by government support enforcement services Fam §17523
    Real property liens CCP §§697.320, 697.350, 697.360, 697.380 to 697.400
  Limitations statutes
    Arrearages, recovery Fam §4503
    Contempt actions for failure to pay support CCP §1218.5
  Liquidation of financial assets pursuant to levy Fam §17522.5
  Local child support agencies
    Electronic court records, remote access
      Government entities, access by CRC 2.540
    Funding Fam §17306.1
    Government support enforcement services generally (See within this heading, "**Government support enforcement services**")
  Marital privilege Fam §3551
  Medical insurance coverage (See within this heading, "**Health and medical insurance**")
  Military
    Government support enforcement services
      Compromise of arrears program Fam §17560
      Modification of support upon activation into service Fam §17440
  Minimum training standards for court clerks CRC 5.355
  Mistaken identity
    Remediation of child support agency's enforcement action based on Fam §§17433, 17530
    Support obligor CRC 5.375
  Modification
    Generally Fam §§3650 to 3654
    Admissibility of income and benefit information provided by employer Ev §1567
    Child Support Case Registry Form, requirement for filing CRC 5.330
    Deferred sale of family home order Fam §3807
    Discovery procedures Fam §§3660 to 3668
    Domestic violence prevention act proceedings CRC 5.381
    Effective dates for modification and requests for modification CRCAppx I Emer Rule 13
    Expedited modification of support order Fam §17441
    Income of subsequent spouse or nonmarital partner affecting Fam §4057.5
    Information on procedures for Fam §4010
    Judgment lien, effect of modified support order on CCP §697.360
    Military service activation and deployment, notice of CRCAppx A (CRCFL-398)
    Notice requirements, generally Fam §215
    Penalties, consideration of Fam §4730
    Phase-in provision for conforming to uniform guidelines Fam §4076
    Retroactivity of Fam §3653
    Simplified procedures for unrepresented parents, legislative intent concerning development of Fam §§3680, 3680.5
    Temporary support orders Fam §3603
  Monthly net disposable income Fam §§4056, 4060
  More than 2 parents
    Guidelines for child support Fam §4052.5
    Presumptions
      Amount established by formula as correct amount Fam §4057
  Necessaries, third person providing Fam §3950
  Notice
    Delinquency, notice of Fam §§4722 to 4724, 4731, 17525
    Deposit of money to secure future support payments as imposing hardship Fam §§4566, 4567
    Earnings assignment for support (See **EARNINGS ASSIGNMENT FOR SUPPORT**)
    Government support enforcement services, general provision for notices to recipients of Fam §17406

CHILD SUPPORT—Cont.
  Notice—Cont.
    Licenses and permits of noncompliant obligees, denial or suspension of Fam §§17520, 17521
    Local child support agency, notice for payment to Fam §4506.3
    Modification requirements, generally Fam §215
    Public entity creditor, notice of support arrearage issued to support obligor who is CCP §§708.730, 708.780
    Tax refund owed to support obligor, notice of support arrearage issued when CCP §§708.730, 708.780
  Obligee, generally Fam §3550
  Obligor, generally Fam §3550
  Orders
    Generally Fam §4001
    Child Support Case Registry Form, requirement for filing CRC 5.330
    Creditors, payment to Fam §2023
    Deferred sale of family home Fam §§3800 to 3810
    Defined Fam §155
    Dismissal of dissolution of marriage petition for delay in prosecution, effect of child support orders on CCP §583.161
    Enforcement generally (See within this heading, "**Enforcement**")
    Modification (See within this heading, "**Modification**")
    Registration
      Hearings, request form CRCAppx A
      Statement of registration CRCAppx A (CRCFL-440)
    Retroactivity, generally Fam §4009
    Setting aside
      Order deciding issues CRCAppx A (CRCFL-367)
      Request for hearing CRCAppx A (CRCFL-360)
      Responsive declaration CRCAppx A (CRCFL-365)
    Show cause orders Fam §17404.1
    Statewide registry of support orders Fam §§17390 to 17393
    Subsequent orders, rights with respect to Fam §3604
    Suspension
      Incarceration or institutionalization of obligee Fam §4007.5
    Vacating when paternity determination vacated Fam §7648.4
  Other counties
    Custodial and supporting parents residing in different counties Fam §§4202, 4203
    Registration of support orders Fam §§5600 to 5604
  Parent Locator Service and Central Registry Fam §17506
  Paternity determinations (See **PATERNITY**)
  Payment trust fund Fam §17311
  Penalties
    Delinquent payments Fam §§4720 to 4733
    Earnings assignment order for support, noncompliance with Fam §5241
    Government support enforcement services, prohibition on imposition of penalties by Fam §4729
  Pendente lite support (See within this heading, "**Temporary support**")
  Personal information required to be filed by obligor and obligee Fam §4014
  Pilot projects (See **FAMILY LAW PILOT PROJECTS**)
  Preference for separate trial on issue of support Fam §4003
  Presumed natural father ordered to pay child support Fam §6341
    Parentage, judgment and agreement
      Agreement and judgment of parentage in domestic violence prevention act cases CRC 5.380
  Presumptions
    Amount established by formula as correct amount Fam §4057
    Deposit of assets to secure future payment Fam §4611
  Priority of support payments Fam §4011
  Private child support collectors Fam §§5610 to 5616
    Attorneys Fam §§5610, 5615
    Cancellation of contract Fam §5613
      Notice of cancellation form Fam §5611
    Civil actions Fam §5615
    Contract terms Fam §5611
    Definition Fam §5610
    Disclosures required Fam §5612
    Duties Fam §5614
    Judgments for fees on arrears Fam §5616
    Money judgment in court order Fam §5616
    Penalties for violations Fam §5615
    Prohibited acts Fam §5614
  Privilege, spousal
    Inapplicability of spousal testimony privilege Fam §3551
  Probate proceedings
    Power of appointment, claims against powerholder's property subject to Pro §684
  Property of child, allowance for support out of Fam §3902

CHILD SUPPORT—Cont.
Property settlement agreement, distributions as to   Fam §3585
Public assistance (See within this heading, **"Welfare"**)
Public enforcement of support obligations (See within this heading, **"Government support enforcement services"**)
Public entity's obligation to judgment debtor, application to satisfaction on money judgment of   CCP §§708.710 to 708.795
Public social service benefits or payments under Social Security Act as exempt from support enforcement   Fam §17516
Quasi-community property liable for   Fam §4008
Railroad Retirement Act, payments by government pursuant to   Fam §4504
Reconciliation of parties, effect of   Fam §3602
Referees
    Court commissioners generally (See within this heading, **"Court commissioners"**)
Refund of tax owed judgment debtor, filing against public entity for   CCP §§708.730, 708.740, 708.795
Registration of support orders
    Hearings, request
        Forms, judicial council   CRCAppx A
    Other counties   Fam §§5600 to 5604
    Statewide registry of support orders   Fam §§17390 to 17393
Registry form, requirement for filing   CRC 5.330
Regulations governing public enforcement of support, adoption of   Fam §§17306, 17310, 17312
Reimbursement
    Additional support costs, reimbursement of other parent for   Fam §4063
    County furnishing support to child   Fam §4002
    Voluntary support provided by other parent or relatives   Fam §3951
Relief from support judgments or orders   Fam §§2120 to 2129, 3690 to 3693, 17432
Remarriage, effect of   Fam §3808
Residence of obligor   Fam §3550
Retirement benefits of judgment debtor   CCP §§704.110, 704.114, 704.115, Fam §17528
Retroactive application
    Modification of support order   Fam §3653
    Order for support   Fam §4009
Salaries and wages
    Generally   Fam §§4050 to 4068
    Assignment of wages (See **EARNINGS ASSIGNMENT FOR SUPPORT**)
    Deduction from salaries and wages   Fam §4507
    Garnishment (See **GARNISHMENT**)
    Government support enforcement services, obligation of employers to cooperate with   Fam §17512
    Name and address of employer, notification to other parent of   Fam §4014
Sale of family home to be deferred, request of custodial parent for   Fam §§3800 to 3810
Satisfaction of money judgment for support, crediting of   CCP §695.221
Seasonal or fluctuating income, consideration of   Fam §4064
Security for
    Generally   Fam §4012
    Assets deposited (See within this heading, **"Deposit of assets to secure future payment"**)
    Money deposited (See within this heading, **"Deposit of money to secure future support payments"**)
    Performance bond   Fam §4615
Separate property liable for   Fam §4008
Separate trial on issue of support   Fam §4003
Separation agreement, provisions for support in   Fam §3580
Service of papers
    Deposit of money to secure future support payments, application and order for   Fam §§4571, 4572
    Notice of delinquency   Fam §§4724, 4731
Settlement and compromise
    Government support enforcement services
        Compromise of arrears program   Fam §17560
Sex offense or child abuse, child support payments from noncustodial parent convicted of   Fam §3030
Show cause orders   Fam §17404.1
Simplified income and expense form for determining child support, development of   Fam §4068
Social security payments   Fam §§4504, 17516
    Title IV-D support actions, rules for   CRC 5.300 to 5.375
Software used to determine support amount   Fam §3830
Spousal privilege   Fam §3551
Spousal support
    Termination of child support
        Changed circumstances as result of termination justifying modification   Fam §4326

CHILD SUPPORT—Cont.
State disbursement unit   Fam §17309
    Designation as payee   Fam §§4200, 4201, 4204
    Electronic fund transfers for employer payment of withholding   Fam §17309.5
    Government support enforcement services
        Earnings withholding order for support, payments to levying officer or state disbursement unit   CCP §706.030
    Timing of support payments, remedy for effects to change   Fam §17307
Statewide registry of support orders   Fam §§17390 to 17393
    Data acquisition and maintenance   Fam §17391
    Forms
        Judicial council duties   Fam §§17392, 17393
    Implementation plan   Fam §17391
    Information transmitted by clerks of court
        Requirements   Fam §17392
    Legislative declaration and intent   Fam §17390
Statewide uniform guidelines   Fam §§4050 to 4077
    Applicability   Fam §4074
    Certification of statewide uniform calculators   CRC 5.275
    Difference between awarded amount and guideline formula amount   Fam §4056
    Federal child support regulations, compliance
        Report on state legislative response   Fam §4077
    Formula for determining support   Fam §4055
    Judicial Council study and reports on   Fam §4054
    Legislature to review   Fam §4067
    Low-income adjustment, requirements for   Fam §4055
    Modification of orders entered before guideline's effective date   Fam §4069
    More than 2 parents   Fam §4052.5
    Phase-in provision for modification of prior orders   Fam §4076
    Principles   Fam §4053
    Spousal support and separate maintenance payments unaffected by   Fam §4075
Statutes of limitation
    Arrearages, limitations period for recovery of   Fam §4503
    Contempt actions for failure to pay support   CCP §1218.5
Stipulated agreement for award   Fam §§4057, 4065
Stranger providing   Fam §3951
Substitution of payee, right of enforcing agency to record   Fam §§4506.2, 4506.3
Supplemental complaint for   Fam §2330.1
Surety bond   Fam §§4012, 4615
Taxation
    Refund owed judgment debtor, filing against public entity for   CCP §§708.730, 708.740, 708.795
    Returns (See within this heading, **"Tax returns"**)
Tax returns
    Generally   Fam §3552
    Modification of award   Fam §§3665, 3667
Telephone appearances
    Title IV-D support actions   CRC 3.670, 3.672, 5.324
Temporary support
    Generally   Fam §3600
    Termination of   Fam §§3601, 3603
    Transfer of venue, determining support issues prior to determination of motion for   CCP §§396b, 397
Termination
    Generally   Fam §§3650 to 3654
    Admissibility of income and benefit information provided by employer   Ev §1567
    Contingency, termination on happening of   Fam §4007
    Discovery procedures   Fam §§3660 to 3668
    Effective dates for termination and requests for termination   CRCAppx I Emer Rule 13
    Relief from support judgment or order   Fam §§2120 to 2129, 3690 to 3693, 17432
    Retroactivity of   Fam §3653
    Spousal support modification on grounds of changed circumstances   Fam §4326
    Temporary support   Fam §§3601, 3603
Third parties providing necessaries   Fam §3950
Title IV-D support actions   CRC 5.300
    Attorney of record, district attorney as   CRC 5.320
    Child Support Case Registry Form, filing procedure for   CRC 5.330
    Child support commissioners, requirement of judicial education   CRC 5.340
    Complaint and summons   CRC 5.325
    Consolidation of child support orders   CRC 5.365
    Court clerk staff assigned to Title IV-D cases, minimum training standards   CRC 5.355

CHILD SUPPORT—Cont.
  Title IV-D support actions —Cont.
    Fees
      Title IV-D child support agency involved Gov §70672
    Forms, use of CRC 5.7, 5.310
      New and revised governmental forms, implementation by local child support agencies CRC 5.311
    Indian child
      Transfer of title IV-D cases from tribal court CRC 5.372
      Transfer of title IV-D cases to tribal court CRC 5.372
    Interstate income withholding orders, procedure for hearings CRC 5.335
    Judges, duties CRC 5.305
    Judgment regarding parental obligations
      Form, implementation of new form CRC 5.311
    Local child support agency, appearance by CRC 5.360
    Memorandum of points and authorities not required CRC 5.315
    Mistaken identity of support obligor, procedure for filing motion regarding CRC 5.375
    Parentage or paternity, hearing to cancel or set aside voluntary declaration CRC 5.350
    Party designation in caption for transfer of interstate and intrastate cases CRC 5.370
    Telephone appearances CRC 3.670, 3.672, 5.324
      Audibility of proceedings CRC 3.670, 5.324
      Communication of information about telephone appearances CRC 5.324
      Conference call providers CRC 3.670, 5.324
      Defined CRC 5.324
      Equipment required to implement rule CRC 5.324
      Need for personal appearance determined CRC 5.324
      Notice by court of decision on telephone appearance CRC 5.324
      Opposition to telephone appearance CRC 5.324
      Purpose of provision CRC 5.324
      Reporting of proceedings CRC 5.324
      Request for telephone appearance CRC 5.324
      Shortening time CRC 5.324
      Vendors providing services CRC 3.670, 5.324
      When disallowed CRC 5.324
      When permitted CRC 5.324
  Transfer of causes
    Subsequent to final judgment CCP §397.5
  Transfer of venue, determining support issues prior to determination of motion for CCP §§396b, 397
  Travel expenses for visitation Fam §4062
  Unemployed obligor
    Jobs programs, court-ordered participation in Fam §3558
    Listing of employment applications, requirement for Fam §4505
    Retroactivity of modification order to date of unemployment Fam §3653
    Showing required to avoid penalties Fam §4726
    Unemployment compensation benefits, enforcement against CCP §704.120, Fam §17518
  Uniform guidelines Fam §§4050 to 4077
  Uniform interstate family support act Fam §§5700.101 to 5700.903
  Uniform Parentage Act Fam §7637
    Local child support agency
      Action to determine paternity Fam §7634
    Vacation or setting aside of judgment
      Genetic testing Fam §7648.2
      Orders vacated when paternity determination vacated Fam §7648.4
  Venue in actions to enforce CCP §395
  Voluntary declaration of parentage, action based on Fam §7644
  Wages
    Assignment (See **EARNINGS ASSIGNMENT FOR SUPPORT**)
    Garnishment generally (See **GARNISHMENT**)
    Generally (See within this heading, "**Salaries and wages**")
  Welfare
    Commissioners to hear Title IV-D cases Fam §§4250, 4251
    County officer as designated payee Fam §§4200 to 4205
      State disbursement unit as payee Fam §§4200, 4201, 4204
    Court clerk staff assigned to Title IV-D cases, minimum training standards for CRC 5.355
    Crediting of money judgment for support, priorities for CCP §695.221
    Earnings assignment for support in Title IV-D cases (See **EARNINGS ASSIGNMENT FOR SUPPORT**)
    Government enforcement of support obligations to welfare recipients (See within this heading, "**Government support enforcement services**")
    Information provided to court Fam §4004
    Judges hearing Title IV-D cases under exceptional circumstances CRC 5.305
    Parent's obligation, effect of welfare on Fam §3951
    Satisfaction of money judgment for support, crediting of CCP §695.221

CHILD SUPPORT—Cont.
  Welfare—Cont.
    Spousal support enforcement in conjunction with enforcement of child support Fam §§4351, 17000, 17604
    State disbursement unit
      Directing support payments to unit Fam §4200
  Withdrawal of attorney in domestic relations matter CCP §285.1
  Withholding
    Collection of delinquency
      Court order not required Fam §17456
      Notice of withholding Fam §17454
    Forms CRCAppx A
  Witnesses
    Live testimony
      When received CRC 5.113, Fam §217
  Workers' compensation benefits, enforcement against CCP §704.160, Fam §17510
  Worksheets for calculating amount Fam §4068

CHINAWARE
Common carrier's liability for CC §2200

CHINESE
Contracts in Chinese, Tagalog, Vietnamese or Korean languages CC §1632
  Consumer credit contracts
    Federal notice requirement CC §1799.96
    Foreign language translations of notice requirement CC §1799.91
Gender tax repeal act preventing charging different prices for services of similar or like kind based on gender
  Consumer affairs department pamphlet for affected businesses and other notice of requirements of provisions CC §51.63
  Licensing authority notice of provisions to licensee upon issuance or renewal CC §51.6
Mortgages of residential property, foreign language summaries of terms CC §1632.5

CHIROPODY (See **PODIATRY AND PODIATRISTS**)

CHIROPRACTORS
Bond required to secure costs in action against CCP §1029.6
Damages (See **DAMAGES**)
Discovery proceedings, exemption of records from Ev §1157
Malpractice (See **MALPRACTICE**)
Mandamus
  Administrative order of agency issuing licenses, review of CCP §1094.5
  Licensing board decisions, review of CC §1094.5
Medical records, attorney's authorized inspection of CCP §1985.7, Ev §1158
Review committees, liability of CC §§43.7, 43.8

CHOICE OF LAW
Attorney professional conduct
  Disciplinary authority ProfC 8.5
Construction contract provisions requiring arbitration or litigation of disputes outside of California, invalidity of CCP §410.42
Discovery
  Interstate and international depositions and discovery act
    Choice of law to resolve disputes CCP §§2029.600 to 2029.650
Foreign corporations, actions against CCP §410.40
Interstate family support
  Registration for enforcement Fam §5700.604
Nonresident persons, actions against CCP §410.40

CHOSE IN ACTION
Decedents' estates, sale of interest of Pro §10205
Defined CC §953
Genetic defects of child, cause of action for CC §43.6
Transfer of CC §954

CHURCHES
Easement rights for pew CC §§801, 802
Family history, church records concerning Ev §1315

CIGARETTES (See **SMOKING**)

CINEMA (See **MOTION PICTURES**)

CITATION OF ACTS
Administrative Procedure Act Gov §11370
Areias Credit Card Full Disclosure Act CC §1748.10
Areias Retail Installment Account Full Disclosure Act CC §1810.20
Areias-Robbins Charge Card Full Disclosure Act CC §1748.20
Attachment Law CCP §482.010

CITATION OF ACTS—Cont.
Automotive Consumer Notification Act   CC §§1793.23, 1793.24
Bond and Undertaking Law   CCP §995.010
Carpenter-Katz Small Business Equal Access to Justice Act   CCP §1028.5
Child Support Delinquency Reporting Law   Fam §4700
Civil Code   CC §21
Confidentiality of Medical Information Act   CC §56
Consumer Contract Awareness Act   CC §1799.200
Consumer Credit Reporting Act   CC §1785.1
Consumers Legal Remedies Act   CC §1750
Credit reports, statutes affecting   CC §1785.2
Credit Services Act   CC §1789.10
Cullen Earthquake Act   CCP §751.65
Destroyed Land Records Relief Law   CCP §751.01
Domestic Violence Prevention Law   Fam §6200
Due Process in Competence Determinations Act   Pro §§810, 813, 1801, 1881, 3201, 3204, 3208
Electronic Commerce Act   CC §1789.1
Emancipation of Minors Law   Fam §7000
Eminent domain statutes   CCP §1230.010
Employment Agency, Employment Counseling, and Job Listing Services Act   CC §1812.500
Enforcement of Judgments Law   CCP §680.010
Family Conciliation Court Law   Fam §1800
Fiduciaries' Wartime Substitution Law   Pro §350
Floating Home Residency Law   CC §800
Guardianship-Conservatorship Law   Pro §1400
Health Care Decisions Law   Pro §4600
Independent Administration of Estates Act   Pro §10400
Independent Wholesale Sales Representatives Contractual Relations Act   CC §1738.11
Information Practices Act   CC §1798
Investigative Consumer Reporting Agencies Act   CC §1786.1
Legal Estates Principal and Income Law   CC §731
Multiple-party Accounts Law   Pro §5100
Oil and Gas Lien Act   CCP §1203.50
Private Bulk Grain Storage Law   CC §1880
Probate Code   Pro §1
Recreational Vehicle Park Occupancy Law   CC §799.20
Rosenthal Fair Debt Collection Practices Act   CC §1788
Small Claims Act   CCP §116.110
Song-Beverly Consumer Warranty Act   CC §1790
Song-Beverly Credit Card Act   CC §1747
Tanner Consumer Protection Act   CC §1793.22
Trial Jury Selection and Management Act   CCP §190
Trust Law   Pro §15000
Unclaimed Property Law   CCP §1500
Uniform Child Custody Jurisdiction and Enforcement Act   Fam §3400
Uniform Divorce Recognition Act   Fam §§2090 to 2093
Uniform Federal Lien Registration Act   CCP §2107
Uniform Foreign-Money Claims Act   CCP §676
Uniform Parentage Act   Fam §7600
Uniform Premarital Agreement Act   Fam §1600
Uniform Prudent Management of Institutional Funds Act   Pro §18501
Uniform Trade Secrets Act   CC §3426
Uniform Transfers to Minors Act   Pro §3900
Unruh Act   CC §1801
Unruh Civil Rights Act   CC §51
Wage Garnishment Law   CCP §706.010

CITATION OF CASES
Depublication of published opinions, request procedure for   CRC 8.1125
Law and motion proceedings
    Memorandum in support of motion   CRC 3.1113
Partial publication of appellate opinions   CRC 8.1110
Review of published opinion granted   CRC 8.1115
Unpublished opinions   CRC 8.1115
    Publication of unpublished opinions, request procedure for   CRC 8.1120

CITATION OF CODES
Code of Civil Procedure   CCP §19
Family Code   Fam §1

CITATION TO APPEAR
Conservatorship proceedings   Pro §§1823, 1824
Juvenile court proceedings   CRC 5.526
Notice to appear
    Electronic citation forms   CRC 4.103
Termination of parental rights   Fam §§7880 to 7883
Will probate proceedings   Pro §§1240 to 1242

CITIES AND MUNICIPALITIES
Attachment proceedings   CCP §481.200
Attorney professional conduct
    Organization or entity as client   ProfC 1.13
Bonds issued by (See **BONDS**)
Boundaries
    Limitation of actions to contest change of   CCP §349.1
    Validation procedure for change in   CCP §349.4
Building restrictions, burden of proving necessity for   Ev §669.5
Charter cities
    Marriage solemnization by city clerk
        Local government officials, authority to solemnize   Fam §400
Charters (See **CHARTERED CITIES**)
Claim and delivery   CCP §511.100
Conservation easements held by   CC §815.3
Consolidation
    Contesting consolidation, statute of limitation for   CCP §349.1
    Validation procedure   CCP §349.4
Contracts
    Immigration and naturalization
        Prohibition of contracts by local government or law enforcement agency to detain noncitizens for civil immigration custody   CC §1670.9
Costs, liability for   CCP §1029
Counties defined to include   CCP §17
Decedent's estate, filing claims against   Pro §§9200 to 9205
Design professionals
    Indemnification, public agencies   CC §2782.8
Dissolution
    Contesting dissolution, limitation of actions for   CCP §349.1
    Validation procedure   CCP §349.4
Districts (See **DISTRICTS**)
Escheat of unclaimed deposits and payments   CCP §1519
Formation
    Contesting formation, statute of limitation for   CCP §349.1
    Validation procedure   CCP §349.4
Greenway easements
    Entities permitted to acquire and hold easement   CC §816.56
Groundwater rights actions
    Intervention in comprehensive adjudication   CCP §837
Holiday for purposes of computing time if public office closed   CCP §12b
Human trafficking or slavery
    Ordinances preventing, effect   CC §52.6
Immigration and naturalization
    Contracts by local government or law enforcement agency to detain noncitizens for civil immigration custody
        Prohibition   CC §1670.9
Injunctions against   CC §3423, CCP §526
Judicial district defined to include   CCP §17
Leases
    Abandonment provisions, applicability of   CC §1952.6
    Limitations on   CC §§718, 719
Ordinances and regulations (See **ORDINANCES**)
Personal information, disclosure of   CC §§1798 to 1798.42
Pleadings verification by   CCP §446
Presentation of claims as prerequisite to commencement of actions against governmental agencies   CCP §313
Public health and safety labor or service providers
    Logo or identifying mark of public agency, display restrictions   CC §3273
Reorganization
    Contesting reorganization, limitation of actions for   CCP §349.1
    Validation procedure   CCP §349.4
Service of process on   CCP §416.50
Shared mobility devices
    Agreements with or permits from local government   CC §2505
    Authorization   CC §2505
Statutes of limitation
    Boundaries, actions to contest change of   CCP §349.1
    Contesting formation, dissolution, consolidation or change of organization   CCP §349.1
Superior court appellate division in every county and city and county   CCP §77
Superior court fees
    Services to local, state and federal governments   Gov §70633
Unclaimed property, disposition of   CC §2080.6
Validation proceedings   CCP §§860 to 870
Venue in actions by or against   CCP §394
Wills, taking under   Pro §6102

CITIZENSHIP
Contracts
    Local government or law enforcement agency contracts to detain noncitizens for civil immigration custody
        Prohibition   CC §1670.9

CITIZENSHIP—Cont.
Discrimination prohibited   CC §51
Forcible entry and detainer
    Immigration or citizenship status irrelevant to issue of liability or remedy   CC §3339.10
Jury service obligation   CCP §191
Landlord and tenant
    Immigration or citizenship status of persons
        Actions to recover possession, restrictions on landlord actions based in immigration or citizenship status   CCP §1161.4
        Definition of immigration or citizenship status   CC §1940.05
        Involuntary quit by tenant, restrictions on landlord actions based in immigration or citizenship status   CCP §1161.4
        Prohibited acts based on   CC §§1940.3, 1940.35
        Retaliation against tenant by reporting or threatening to report to immigration authorities   CC §1942.5
        Unduly influencing tenant to vacate by threatening disclosures relating to immigration or citizenship status   CC §1940.2
Ownership of property regardless of citizenship status   CC §671
Property rights regardless of citizenship status   CC §671

CITY ATTORNEYS
Acknowledgment of instruments by   CC §1181
Civil rights actions, bringing of   CC §§52, 52.1
    Construction or application of civil rights provisions in issue, solicitor general notified   CC §51.1
Dog bites, actions pertaining to   CC §3342.5
Electronic court records, remote access
    Government entities, access by
        List of government entities which may be authorized to receive access   CRC 2.540
Firearm industry standards of conduct
    Actions against industry members for violation of standards   CC §3273.52
Unruh Civil Rights Act, bringing action under   CC §52

CITY CLERK
Acknowledgment of instruments   CC §1181

CIVIC ORGANIZATIONS
Judge's office in organization not a financial interest for purposes of disqualification   CCP §170.5

CIVIL ACTION MEDIATION (See MEDIATION)

CIVIL ACTIONS
Actions generally (See **ACTIONS**)
Commencement of actions (See **COMMENCEMENT OF ACTIONS**)
Coordination of actions (See **COORDINATION OF ACTIONS**)
Economic litigation procedures (See **ECONOMIC LITIGATION PROCEDURES**)
Generally (See **ACTIONS**)
Law and motion proceedings   CRC 3.1100 to 3.1372 (See **LAW AND MOTION PROCEEDINGS**)
Limitation of actions (See **STATUTES OF LIMITATION**)
Limited civil cases (See **LIMITED CIVIL CASES**)
Parties (See **PARTIES**)
Pleadings (See **PLEADINGS**)
Time for commencing actions (See **STATUTES OF LIMITATION**)
Vexatious litigants (See **VEXATIOUS LITIGANTS**)

CIVIL ACTIVE LIST
Superior courts (See **SUPERIOR COURTS**)

CIVIL COMMITMENT
Appeals
    Notice of appeal
        Form, judicial council   CRCAppx A
    Order of civil commitment, appeal from   CRC 8.483

CIVIL DISCOVERY ACT   CCP §§2016.010 to 2036.050

CIVIL HARASSMENT (See HARASSMENT)

CIVIL PROCEDURE
Citation of code   CCP §19
Construing Code of Civil Procedure (See **CONSTRUING AND INTERPRETATION**)
Effective date of Code of Civil Procedure   CCP §2
Judicial officers   CCP §§165 to 187
Jurors and court commissioners   CCP §§190 to 259
Ministerial officers and powers   CCP §§262 to 286
Organization and jurisdiction of courts   CCP §§33 to 153

CIVIL PROCEDURE—Cont.
Preliminary provisions   CCP §§2 to 32
Title and division of Code of Civil Procedure   CCP §1

CIVIL RIGHTS (See DISCRIMINATION)

CIVIL RULES   CRC 3.1 to 3.2240
Alternative dispute resolution   CRC 3.800 to 3.878, 3.890 to 3.898
    Definitions   CRC 3.800
    Information package
        Papers to be filed   CRC 3.221
    Judicial arbitration   CRC 3.810 to 3.830
    Mediation
        Applicability of provisions   CRC 3.835
        Civil action mediation   CRC 3.890 to 3.898
        Complaints about court-program mediators   CRC 3.865 to 3.872
        Reports or statements of mediator   CRC 3.845
        Standards of conduct for mediators   CRC 3.850 to 3.860
Appearances
    Remote appearances   CRC 3.672
    Telephone appearances   CRC 3.670
Applicability of rules   CRC 3.10
Arbitration
    Case management conference
        Determination as to arbitration   CRC 3.722
        Telephone appearance at case management conferences   CRC 3.670
    Judicial arbitration   CRC 3.810 to 3.830
Assignment of judges
    Case management   CRC 3.734
Attorneys' fees   CRC 3.1702
Attorneys, limited scope representation   CRC 3.35 to 3.37
    Applicability of provisions   CRC 3.35
    Definition of limited scope representation   CRC 3.35
    Noticed representation
        Providing notice   CRC 3.36
        Relief as attorney, request   CRC 3.36
        Types of limited scope representation   CRC 3.35
    Undisclosed representation
        Attorneys' fees sought   CRC 3.37
        Drafting or other preparation of court documents   CRC 3.37
        Types of limited scope representation   CRC 3.35
Bifurcated trials
    Statement of decision, judgment and motion for new trial following   CRC 3.1591
Case management   CRC 3.700 to 3.771
    Additional case management conferences   CRC 3.723
    Alternative dispute resolution
        Initial conference, determination as to ADR   CRC 3.722
        Stipulation   CRC 3.726
        Telephone appearance at case management conferences   CRC 3.670
    Applicability of case management rules   CRC 3.720
    Assignment of judges   CRC 3.734
    Class actions   CRC 3.760 to 3.771
    Collections cases   CRC 3.740, 3.741
        Civil case cover sheet to be checked   CRC 3.740
        Default judgment, time for   CRC 3.740
        Definitions   CRC 3.740
        Failure to serve in timely manner   CRC 3.740
        Settlement   CRC 3.741
        Time for service of complaint   CRC 3.740
    Complex cases   CRC 3.750, 3.751
        Judicial administration standards   CRC JudAdminStand 3.10
    Conferences   CRC 3.722
        Additional case management conferences   CRC 3.723
        Applicability of case management rules when conference set   CRC 3.720
        Class actions   CRC 3.762
        Complex cases   CRC 3.750
        Judicial arbitration   CRC 3.812
        Subjects considered at conferences   CRC 3.727
        Telephone appearance at case management conferences   CRC 3.670
    Differential case management   CRC 3.710 to 3.715
    Environmental quality act
        Petitions under environmental quality act, civil rules governing   CRC 3.2220
    Forms
        Judicial council legal forms   CRCAppx A
    Initial conference   CRC 3.722
        Complex cases   CRC 3.750
        Telephone appearance at case management conferences   CRC 3.670
    Joint case management statement   CRC 3.725

CIVIL RULES—Cont.
  Case management —Cont.
    Judge assignment   CRC 3.734
    Meet and confer
      Complex cases   CRC 3.750
      Duty to meet and confer   CRC 3.724
      Judicial council legal forms   CRCAppx A
    Orders
      Appearance at conference not required for order   CRC 3.722
      Contents of case management order   CRC 3.728
      Controlling effect of order   CRC 3.730
    Review of case
      Time for review   CRC 3.721
    Scope and purpose of case management rules   CRC 3.700
    Short cause cases   CRC 3.735
    Statement   CRC 3.725
      Form   CRCAppx A
    Suspension of case management rules for certain cases   CRC 3.720
    Trial date
      Setting   CRC 3.729
  Class actions
    Case management   CRC 3.760 to 3.771
      Certifying or decertifying class, motions   CRC 3.764
      Class notices   CRC 3.766
      Complaint form   CRC 3.761
      Conducting class action, orders   CRC 3.767
      Conferences   CRC 3.762
      Discovery   CRC 3.768
      Dismissal of action   CRC 3.770
      Governing rules   CRC 3.760
      Judgments   CRC 3.771
      Order certifying, amending, etc, class   CRC 3.765
      Order upon conclusion of conference   CRC 3.763
      Settlement of class actions   CRC 3.769
      Telephone appearance at case management conferences   CRC 3.670
  Collections cases, management   CRC 3.740, 3.741
    Civil case cover sheet to be checked   CRC 3.740
    Default judgment, time for   CRC 3.740
    Definitions   CRC 3.740
    Failure to serve in timely manner   CRC 3.740
    Settlement   CRC 3.741
    Time for service of complaint   CRC 3.740
  Complex cases
    Coordination of actions   CRC 3.501 to 3.550
    Counterdesignations   CRC 3.402
    Defined   CRC 3.400
    Designations
      Court's action designating   CRC 3.403
      Joint complex designations   CRC 3.402
      Plaintiff's designation of action as complex   CRC 3.401
    Electronic filing and service   CRC 3.751
    Environmental quality act
      Petitions under environmental quality act, civil rules governing   CRC 3.2220
    Factors making case complex   CRC 3.400
    Initial case management conference   CRC 3.750
      Telephone appearance at case management conferences   CRC 3.670
    Joint complex designations   CRC 3.402
    Judicial administration standards   CRC JudAdminStand 3.10
    Management   CRC 3.750, 3.751
    Noncomplex counterdesignation   CRC 3.402
    Related cases   CRC 3.300
  Conferences
    Case management   CRC 3.722, 3.723
      Class actions   CRC 3.762
      Complex cases   CRC 3.750
      Subjects considered at conferences   CRC 3.727
      Telephone appearance at case management conferences   CRC 3.670
    Related cases
      Notice of related case   CRC 3.300
  Consolidation of cases   CRC 3.350
    Related cases   CRC 3.300
  Contents of rules of court   CRC 1.4
  Coordination of actions   CRC 3.500 to 3.550
    Complex actions   CRC 3.501 to 3.550
    Consolidation of cases   CRC 3.350
      Noncomplex actions   CRC 3.500
    Differential case management rules, applicability   CRC 3.712
    Noncomplex actions   CRC 3.500
    Related cases
      Notice of related case   CRC 3.300

CIVIL RULES—Cont.
  Coordination of actions —Cont.
    Transfer of noncomplex cases   CRC 3.500
  Coordination of complex actions   CRC 3.501 to 3.550
    Add-on cases
      Determining whether to coordinate add-ons   CRC 3.544
      Identification of potential add-ons   CRC 3.531
      Petition for coordination when cases already coordinated   CRC 3.532
    Ancillary proceedings, court for   CRC 3.545
    Appeals   CRC 3.505
    Applicable provisions in coordination proceedings   CRC 3.504
      Procedural rules   CRC 3.510 to 3.515
    Attorneys
      Coordination attorneys   CRC 3.550
    Case number   CRC 3.550
    Contents of petition   CRC 3.521
    Coordination attorneys   CRC 3.550
    Coordination motion judges
      Order assigning   CRC 3.524, 3.532
    Coordination trial judges
      Assignment   CRC 3.540
      Duties   CRC 3.541
    Definitions   CRC 3.501
    Denial of coordination   CRC 3.529
    Determination as to whether case is complex   CRC 3.502
    Differential case management rules, applicability   CRC 3.712
    Dismissal of action   CRC 3.545
    Electronic submission of documents to judicial council   CRC 3.512
    Evidence presented at hearings   CRC 3.514
    Finality of judgment   CRC 3.545
    Grant of coordination   CRC 3.529
      Petition for coordination when cases already coordinated   CRC 3.532
    Hearing on petition
      Notice of hearing   CRC 3.527
      Separate hearing on certain issues   CRC 3.528
      Timing   CRC 3.527
    Hearing on request to coordinate add-on   CRC 3.544
    Hearing on transfer motions   CRC 3.543
    Initial case management conference   CRC 3.541
      Telephone appearance at case management conferences   CRC 3.670
    Judges
      Coordination motion judges   CRC 3.524, 3.532
      Coordination trial judges   CRC 3.540, 3.541
      Disqualification   CRC 3.516
    Judgments   CRC 3.545
    Judicial administration standards   CRC JudAdminStand 3.10
    Judicial council staff
      General administration of coordinated actions   CRC 3.550
    Liaison counsel
      Appointment   CRC 3.506
      Defined   CRC 3.501
      Service on liaison counsel   CRC 3.510
    Management of proceedings   CRC 3.541
    Motions   CRC 3.520
    Notice of submission of petition   CRC 3.522, 3.523
    Opposition to petition   CRC 3.525
    Orders
      Add-on cases, order on request to coordinate   CRC 3.544
      Denial of coordination   CRC 3.529
      Grant of coordination   CRC 3.529
      Transfer of action or claim   CRC 3.543
    Papers
      Electronic submission of documents to judicial council   CRC 3.512
      Judicial council, submission to   CRC 3.511
    Permission to submit petition   CRC 3.520
    Petitions   CRC 3.520 to 3.532
    Proof of filing and service of petition   CRC 3.521
    Remand of action or claim   CRC 3.542
    Service of process   CRC 3.510
      Coordination motion judges, order assigning   CRC 3.524
      Memoranda and declarations   CRC 3.513
      Notice of submission   CRC 3.523
    Settlement of action   CRC 3.545
    Site of coordination proceedings   CRC 3.530
    Stays   CRC 3.515, 3.529
    Summary judgments   CRC 3.545
    Support of petition   CRC 3.526
    Termination of action   CRC 3.545
    Time
      Extending or shortening   CRC 3.503
    Title of proceeding   CRC 3.550

CIVIL INDEX

CIVIL RULES—Cont.
Coordination of complex actions —Cont.
    Transfer of action or claim   CRC 3.543
Costs
    Attorneys' fees   CRC 3.1702
    Forma pauperis, application for fee and cost waivers   CRC 3.50 to 3.58
        Waiver of fees generally   Gov §§68630 to 68641
    Prejudgment costs   CRC 3.1700
    Unlawful detainer proceedings
        Supplemental costs   CRC 3.2000
    Waiver of fees and costs   Gov §§68630 to 68641
        Application for fee and cost waivers   CRC 3.50 to 3.58
        Bench warrants to secure attendance of witnesses, applicability of waiver provisions   Gov §26744.5
        Remote appearance fees   CRC 3.672
Cover sheets
    Collections cases   CRC 3.740
    False claims actions
        Judicial council legal forms   CRCAppx A
    Forms   CRCAppx A
    Papers to be filed   CRC 3.220
Default judgments   CRC 3.110, 3.1800
Differential case management   CRC 3.710 to 3.715
    Applicability   CRC 3.712
    Authority for rules   CRC 3.710
    Delay reduction goals   CRC 3.713
        Differentiation of cases to reach   CRC 3.714
    Disposition time
        Goals   CRC 3.714
    Emergency suspension of rules
        Applicability of differential case management provisions absent suspension   CRC 3.712
    Evaluation factors   CRC 3.715
    General civil cases
        Applicability   CRC 3.712
    Goals   CRC 3.713
        Differentiation of cases to reach   CRC 3.714
    Judges
        Delay reduction goals   CRC 3.713
    Local court rules
        Required   CRC 3.711
Discovery
    Conduct of discovery   CRC 3.1010
    Format of discovery   CRC 3.1000
    Motions   CRC 3.1345 to 3.1348
    Telephone appearance at hearings on discovery motions   CRC 3.670
Dismissal of actions
    Hearings to review dismissal
        Telephone appearance at hearings to review dismissal   CRC 3.670
    Notice of entry
        Service and filing   CRC 3.1390
Duration of case, remote appearance
    Notice of intent to appear remotely for duration of case   CRC 3.672
Environmental quality act
    Petitions under environmental quality act   CRC 3.2200 to 3.2240
Family proceedings
    Applicability of rules   CRC 3.10
Fees
    Waiver of fees and costs   Gov §§68630 to 68641
        Application for fee and cost waivers   CRC 3.50 to 3.58
        Bench warrants to secure attendance of witnesses, applicability of waiver provisions   Gov §26744.5
        Remote appearance fees   CRC 3.672
Filing
    Fees
        Credit card or debit card payments   CRC 3.100
Injunctions and other provisional relief   CRC 3.1140 to 3.1184
Judges
    Assignment of judges
        Case management   CRC 3.734
    Coordination of complex actions
        Coordination motion judges   CRC 3.524, 3.532
        Coordination trial judges   CRC 3.540, 3.541
    Differential case management
        Delay reduction goals   CRC 3.713
Judgments   CRC 3.1800 to 3.1806
    Default judgments   CRC 3.110, 3.1800
    Interest
        Inclusion   CRC 3.1802
    Periodic payment of judgments
        Public entities, judgments against   CRC 3.1804

CIVIL RULES—Cont.
Judgments —Cont.
    Renewal
        Notice of renewal of judgment   CRC 3.1900
    Signature and notation on written instrument of fact of judgment   CRC 3.1806
    Vacation of judgment
        Motion to vacate, hearing   CRC 3.1602
Judicial arbitration   CRC 3.810 to 3.830
Jury trial   CRC 3.1540
    Instructions to jurors
        Applicable provisions   CRC 3.1560
    Special verdicts   CRC 3.1580
Juvenile proceedings
    Applicability of rules   CRC 3.10
    Dependency proceedings
        Remote appearances   CRC 3.672
Law and motion proceedings   CRC 3.1100 to 3.1372
Limitation on filing of papers   CRC 3.250
Local rules of court
    Remote appearances   CRC 3.672
Management of cases   CRC 3.700 to 3.771
    Class actions   CRC 3.760 to 3.771
    Collections cases   CRC 3.740, 3.741
    Complex cases   CRC 3.750, 3.751
    Differential case management   CRC 3.710 to 3.715
    Judicial council legal forms   CRCAppx A
Mediation
    Civil action mediation   CRC 3.890 to 3.898
        Applicability of rules   CRC 3.835
    Reports or statements of mediator   CRC 3.845
    Standards of conduct for mediators   CRC 3.850 to 3.860
        Complaints about court-program mediators   CRC 3.865 to 3.872
Meet and confer requirement   CRC 3.724
    Complex cases   CRC 3.750
    Judicial council legal forms   CRCAppx A
New trial
    Notice of intention to move for
        Memorandum in support of   CRC 3.1600
Papers   CRC 3.220 to 3.222
    Clerk
        Service of papers on clerk when party's address unknown   CRC 3.252
    Coordination of complex actions
        Electronic submission of documents to judicial council   CRC 3.512
        Judicial council, submission of papers to   CRC 3.511
    Limitation on filing of papers   CRC 3.250
Parties
    List of parties   CRC 3.254
Pleadings
    Motions concerning pleading and venue   CRC 3.1320 to 3.1326
Probate proceedings
    Applicability of rules   CRC 3.10
Process and service of process
    Coordination of complex actions   CRC 3.510
        Memoranda and declarations   CRC 3.513
    Papers   CRC 3.220 to 3.222
        Party's address unknown, service of papers on clerk   CRC 3.252
    Related case
        Notice of related case   CRC 3.300
    Remote appearances
        Restraining orders   CRC 3.1162, 5.496
    Stay of proceedings   CRC 3.650
    Time for service of complaints, cross-complaints and responses   CRC 3.110
Referees
    Agreement, reference by   CRC 3.900 to 3.907
        Documents and exhibits, applicable provisions   CRC 3.930
        Intervention, motion for leave to file complaint   CRC 3.932
        Notice by and contact information for referee   CRC 3.931
        Open proceedings   CRC 3.931
        Sealing of records, motion or application   CRC 3.932
        Site for proceedings   CRC 3.931
    Court-ordered reference   CRC 3.920 to 3.926
        Documents and exhibits, applicable provisions   CRC 3.930
        Intervention, motion for leave to file complaint   CRC 3.932
        Notice by and contact information for referee   CRC 3.931
        Open proceedings   CRC 3.931
        Sealing of records, motion or application   CRC 3.932
        Site for proceedings   CRC 3.931

CIVIL RULES—Cont.
  Related cases
    Notice of related case   CRC 3.300
  Remote appearances   CRC 3.672
    Restraining orders
      Service requirements   CRC 3.1162, 5.496
  Setting trial date   CRC 3.729
  Settlements
    Collections cases
      Case management, effect of settlement   CRC 3.741
    Conditional settlement   CRC 3.1385
    Disabilities, persons with
      Claim of persons with disabilities   CRC 3.1382
    Good faith settlement and dismissal   CRC 3.1382
    Minor's claims   CRC 3.1382
    Notice of settlement of entire case   CRC 3.1385
  Short cause cases
    Case management   CRC 3.735
  Show cause orders
    Responsive papers
      Time to serve   CRC 3.110
  Small claims   CRC 3.2100 to 3.2120 (See **SMALL CLAIMS COURTS**)
  Statement of decision
    New trial following bifurcated trial   CRC 3.1591
    Tentative decision   CRC 3.1590
  Stay of proceedings   CRC 3.650
  Telephone appearances   CRC 3.670
  Title of rules   CRC 3.1
  Trial
    Jury trial   CRC 3.1540
      Instructions to jurors   CRC 3.1560
      Special verdicts   CRC 3.1580
    Remote appearances for evidentiary hearing or trial   CRC 3.672
  Trial date
    Setting   CRC 3.729
  Unlawful detainer proceedings
    Costs
      Supplemental costs   CRC 3.2000
  Vacation of judgments
    Motion to vacate, hearing   CRC 3.1602
  Venue
    Motions concerning pleading and venue   CRC 3.1320 to 3.1326
  Verdict
    Special verdicts   CRC 3.1580
  Waiver of fees and costs, application   CRC 3.50 to 3.58
    Applicability of provisions   CRC 3.50
    Bench warrants to secure attendance of witnesses
      Fee for processing civil warrant, applicability of waiver provisions   Gov §26744.5
    Confidentiality
      Access to application   CRC 3.54
    Decision-making procedure   CRC 3.52
    Forms for application   CRC 3.51
      Judicial council legal forms   CRCAppx A
    Grant of application unless otherwise determined by court   CRC 3.53
    Independent consideration of application   CRC 3.54
    Lien for waived costs and fees   CRC 3.57
    List of fees and costs waived
      Additional fees and costs waived   CRC 3.56
      Initial application   CRC 3.55
    Notice of right to apply for waiver   CRC 3.58
    Presumed grant of application unless court acts   CRC 3.53
    Remote appearance fees   CRC 3.672
    Waiver of fees generally   Gov §§68630 to 68641

CIVIL SERVICE
Judicial notice of regulations by state personnel board   Ev §451

CIVIL UNIONS
Adoption
  Stepparent adoptions
    Birth of child during marriage, domestic partnership or civil union   Fam §9000.5

CLAIM AND DELIVERY (See also **CONVERSION**)
Generally   CCP §§511.010 to 511.100, 516.040
Affidavits
  Hearings, support in   CCP §512.050
  Requirements for   CCP §516.030
Alternative judgment in replevin   CCP §667

CLAIM AND DELIVERY—Cont.
Arbitration agreements, effect of filing for writ of possession by party subject to CCP §1281.8
Bonds
  Acceptance of sureties for   CCP §515.030
  Execution of   CCP §515.010
  Payment in lieu of   CCP §515.020
California, state of   CCP §511.100
Cities   CCP §511.100
Cotton   CCP §511.040
Counties   CCP §511.100
Crops   CCP §511.040
Damages   CCP §627
Districts   CCP §511.100
Eggs   CCP §511.040
Ex parte procedure
  Hearings for issuance of writ   CCP §512.020
  Seizure of property, endorsement on writ   CCP §512.090
Forms
  Judicial council legal forms   CRCAppx A
Hearings
  Affidavits   CCP §512.050
  Ex parte procedure for issuance of writ   CCP §512.020
  Notice of application and hearing   CCP §§512.030, 512.040, 1005
  Points and authorities in   CCP §512.050
  Time for service of notice of application and hearing   CCP §1005
Injunctive relief, effect on   CCP §516.050
Inventory   CCP §511.050
Judicial Council rules on   CCP §§516.010, 516.020
Jury verdict   CCP §627
Levying officers
  Generally   CCP §511.060
  Custody of property held by   CCP §514.010
  Delivery of writ   CCP §514.020
  Disposition of property by   CCP §514.030
  Perishables, sale of   CCP §514.030
  Possession writs directed by   CCP §512.080
  Return of writs to court   CCP §514.040
  Seizure of property, endorsement on writ   CCP §512.090
Livestock   CCP §511.040
Milk   CCP §511.040
Possession
  Alternative judgment   CCP §667
  Application for writ, form of   CCP §512.010
  Arbitration agreements, effect of filing for writ of possession by party subject to   CCP §1281.8
  Delivery of writ   CCP §514.020
  Ex parte procedure for issuance of writ   CCP §512.020
  Findings   CCP §512.110
  Grounds for issuance of writ   CCP §512.060
  Hearings for issuance of writ   CCP §512.020
  Levying officers directing   CCP §512.080
  Notice of application and hearing   CCP §§512.030, 512.040
  Oaths for applications   CCP §512.010
  Process   CCP §512.030
  Requirements for writ   CCP §512.080
  Return of writ to court   CCP §514.040
  Seizure of property, endorsement on writ   CCP §512.090
  Temporary restraining order   CCP §512.120
  Transfer of   CCP §512.070
  Waiver of writ   CCP §512.100
Probable validity   CCP §511.090
Service of notice of application and hearing, time for   CCP §1005
Storage of property taken by   CCP §514.030
Sureties (See within this heading, "**Bonds**")
Temporary restraining orders   CCP §§512.120, 513.010, 513.020
Third party claiming property after levy   CCP §514.050
Time for service of notice of application and hearing for   CCP §1005
Undertakings (See within this heading, "**Bonds**")
University of California regents   CCP §511.100
Wool   CCP §511.040

CLAIMS
Decedents' estates (See **CLAIMS AGAINST ESTATES**)
Escheat (See **ESCHEAT**)
Government, claims against (See **CLAIMS AGAINST PUBLIC ENTITIES AND EMPLOYEES**)
Interpleader (See **INTERPLEADER**)
Money payment as inadmissible evidence to prove invalidity of claim   Ev §1154
Small claims courts (See **SMALL CLAIMS COURTS**)
Special administrator collecting   Pro §8544

CLAIMS INDEX 106

CLAIMS—Cont.
Third party claims   CCP §1050
Tort Claims Act (See **CLAIMS AGAINST PUBLIC ENTITIES AND EMPLOYEES**)
Unclaimed deposits and payments escheated   CCP §1541

CLAIMS AGAINST ESTATES
Absent claimants, deposit of funds for   Pro §11428
Abstract of judgment, filing of   Pro §9301
Accounting by representative (See **EXECUTORS AND ADMINISTRATORS**)
Action on claim
    Continuation of action pending at time of death, requirements for   Pro §9370
    Liability insurance coverage (See within this heading, "Liability insurance")
    Lienholders, action on claim by   Pro §9391
    Mortgage or judgment lien cases, claim filing exception for   Pro §9391
    Pending action against decedent   Pro §9370
        Notice of lis pendens filed in real property action   Pro §§1004, 9354
        Small estates without administration (See **SMALL ESTATES WITHOUT ADMINISTRATION**)
    Prerequisite to bringing action   Pro §9351
    Statute of limitations
        Generally   Pro §9353
        Tolling of   Pro §9352
    Transitional provisions   Pro §9399
    Venue of proceedings   Pro §9354
Affidavits supporting   Pro §9151
Alcoholic beverage tax, claims for   Pro §§9200 to 9205
Allowed claims   CRC 7.401, 7.402, Pro §§9250 to 9252
    Contested allowance of claim   Pro §9254
    Endorsement by personal representative   Pro §9250
    Judge, determination by (See within this heading, "Judges")
    Partial allowance of   Pro §9255
    Personal representative as creditor, procedure for claims filed by   Pro §9252
    Statute of limitations, effect of (See within this heading, "Statutes of limitation")
Amended claims, filing of   Pro §9104
Arbitration, summary determination of disputes by   Pro §9621
Attachment lien converted to judgment lien   Pro §9304
Automobile taxes, claims for   Pro §§9200 to 9205
Cigarette tax, claims for   Pro §§9200 to 9205
Compromise of claims (See **EXECUTORS AND ADMINISTRATORS**)
Consolidation of actions involving liability insurer and decedent's estate   Pro §552
Contested allowance of claims   Pro §9254
Contingent, disputed or not due debts
    Generally   Pro §11460
    Agreement of parties regarding   Pro §11462
    Continuation of administration until debt resolution   Pro §11467
    Deposit of amount in financial institution   Pro §11463
    Distributee
        Bond requirements   Pro §11466
        Personal liability, assumption of   Pro §11464
    Notice of hearing on   Pro §11461
    Orders dealing with   Pro §11461
    Trustee appointed to receive payments of   Pro §11465
Continuing action pending at time of death, requirements for   Pro §9370
Contract claims   Pro §9000
Conversion of attachment liens to judgment liens   Pro §9304
Copies filed with claims, requirement for   Pro §9152
Costs
    Appeal costs   Pro §1002
    Partial allowance of claim, recovery of costs in action on   Pro §9255
    Personal liability of representative for   CCP §1026
Counties, claims filed by   Pro §§9200 to 9205
Damages recoverable from liability insurer of decedent   Pro §554
Definitions   Pro §§9000, 11400 to 11402
Denial of claim (See within this heading, "Rejection of claim")
Deposit in court of funds for absent claimant   Pro §11428
Disputed debts (See within this heading, "Contingent, disputed or not due debts")
Distributee
    Contingent and disputed debts, liability for
        Bond requirements   Pro §11466
        Personal liability, assumption   Pro §11464
    Creditors, personal liability to   Pro §§9203, 9392
Due course of administration, judgments payable in   Pro §9300
Endorsement by personal representative of allowance or rejection of claim filed, requirement of   Pro §9250
Enforcement of judgments (See within this heading, "Judgments")

CLAIMS AGAINST ESTATES—Cont.
Escheat of unclaimed deposits for payment of   Pro §11428
Exception to claim filing requirements
    Distributee's personal liability to creditors   Pro §9392
    Insurance claims, action on   Pro §9390
    Mortgage or judgment liens, action on   Pro §9391
Exoneration of encumbered property   Pro §21404
Failure to file, claims barred for   Pro §9002
Failure to give notice to creditors, liability for   Pro §9053
Final report or petition for final distribution, listing of claims in   CRC 7.403
Foreclosure, accepting deed in lieu of   Pro §9850
Forms
    Judicial Council claim form, use of   Pro §9153
    Notice to creditors to file claims   Pro §9052
Funeral expenses (See **FUNERALS**)
Gasoline tax, claims for   Pro §§9200 to 9205
General requirements for filing   Pro §9150
Good faith payment of claims not properly filed by personal representative   Pro §11005
Governing law   Pro §§9004, 11405
Health care services department
    Medi-Cal beneficiary's death, notification of   Pro §9202
Health Services Department
    Filing claims against estate by   Pro §§9200, 9205
Heirship, determination of (See **HEIRS**)
Homestead, liability of   Pro §6526
Income tax, claims for   Pro §§9200 to 9205
Individual liability of personal representative   Pro §§11424, 11429
Insurance coverage
    Liability insurance (See within this heading, "Liability insurance")
Interest on debts   Pro §11423
Judges
    Allowance or rejection of claim
        No independent administrator of estate, judge determining merits of claims where   Pro §9251
        Personal representative as creditor, judge determining merits of claims filed by   Pro §9252
        Refusal or failure to act on claim as rejection   Pro §9256
    Temporary judge, summary determination of disputes by   Pro §9620
Judgment liens
    Attachment lien into judgment lien, conversion of   Pro §9304
    Enforcement of   Pro §9391
Judgments
    Generally   CCP §§686.010, 686.020, Pro §§9300 to 9304
    Attachment of personalty   CCP §488.485
    Escheat of estate   CCP §1423
    Levy on judgment debtor's interest in personal property of decedent's estate   CCP §700.200
    Liability of personal representative   Pro §11424
    Liens
        Attachment lien into judgment lien, conversion   Pro §9304
        Enforcement of judgment lien   Pro §9391
    Money claims, judgment on   Pro §§9300, 9301
    Nonmoney judgments, enforcement of   Pro §9302
    Unvested interest of judgment debtor applied to satisfaction of money judgment   CCP §709.020
Judicial Council claim form, use of   Pro §9153
Last illness (See **LAST ILLNESS**)
Late claims, filing of   Pro §9103
Liability insurance
    Claim filing requirements for claims covered by insurance   Pro §9390
    Consolidation of actions involving   Pro §552
    Damages recoverable in action against liability insurer of decedent   Pro §554
    Defenses of insurer   Pro §553
    Establishing decedent's liability as exception to claim filing requirement in action for   Pro §9390
    Name of defendants in action   Pro §552
    Parties to action to establish decedent's covered liability   CCP §377.50, Pro §550
    Statute of limitations   Pro §551
Liens
    Action on claim by lienholders   Pro §9391
    Claims based on   CCP §686.010, Pro §9152
    Description of   Pro §9152
    Exoneration of encumbered property, effect on   Pro §21404
    Judgment liens
        Attachment lien, conversion into judgment lien   Pro §9304
        Enforcement   Pro §9391
    Part payment   Pro §9851

CLAIMS AGAINST ESTATES—Cont.
  Liens—Cont.
      Specific devise used for satisfaction of   Pro §21404
  Limitation of actions (See within this heading, **"Statutes of limitation"**)
  Lis pendens   Pro §9370
      Notice of lis pendens filed in real property action   Pro §§1004, 9354
      Small estates without administration (See **SMALL ESTATES WITHOUT ADMINISTRATION**)
  Litigation, claims in (See within this heading, **"Action on claim"**)
  Medi-Cal beneficiary's death, notice to health care services department   Pro §9202
  Money judgments   Pro §§9300, 9301
  Mortgages
    Action on claim by mortgage holders   Pro §9391
    Deed in lieu of foreclosure of   Pro §9850
    Description of   Pro §9152
    Exoneration of encumbered property   Pro §21404
    Part payment   Pro §9851
    Specific devise for satisfaction of   Pro §21404
    Sufficiency of reference to   Pro §9152
  Municipalities, claims filed by   Pro §§9200 to 9205
  Nonmoney judgments, enforcement of   Pro §9302
  Not due debts (See within this heading, **"Contingent, disputed or not due debts"**)
  Notices
    Creditors, notice to (See within this heading, **"Notice to creditors"**)
    Health care services department, notice of Medi-Cal beneficiary's death   Pro §9202
    Lis pendens, filing notice of   Pro §§1004, 9354
  Notice to creditors
    Generally   Pro §9050
    Exceptions   Pro §9054
    Failure to give notice, liability for   Pro §9053
    Form of   Pro §9052
    Immunity of personal representative for giving or failing to give notice   Pro §9053
    Posting or publication of   Pro §9001
    Time requirement for giving   Pro §9051
  Partial allowance of claim   Pro §9255
  Payment of claims
    Generally   Pro §9003
    Absent claimants, deposit of funds for   Pro §11428
    Interest   Pro §11423
    Judgments for (See within this heading, **"Judgments"**)
    Missing creditor, deposit with county treasurer for   Pro §11428
    Orders for payment   Pro §§11422, 11424
    Priority for payment   Pro §§11420, 11421
    Promise to pay debts by personal representative, enforceability of   Pro §9604
    Surviving spouse, allocation of debts with   Pro §§11440 to 11446
    Unpaid creditor after final distribution, rights of   Pro §11429
  Pending litigations
    Generally   Pro §9370
    Notice of lis pendens filed in real property action   Pro §§1004, 9354
    Small estates without administration (See **SMALL ESTATES WITHOUT ADMINISTRATION**)
  Personal injury claims   Pro §9000
    Compromise and settlement of claims
      Time-limited demands   CCP §§999 to 999.5
  Personal representative
    Costs in action prosecuted or defended by personal representative, liability for   CCP §1026
    Late claims against estate, petition for filing of   Pro §9103
    Notice to creditors, immunity of personal representative for giving or failing to give   Pro §9053
    Service of claim on personal representative   Pro §9150
    Waiver of defects in filing by creditors   Pro §9154
  Petition to determine claim to property, notice of hearing
    Form, judicial council   CRCAppx A
  Presentation of claim
    Generally   Pro §§9150 to 9154
    Public entities, claims filed by   Pro §§9200 to 9205
    Time for filing (See within this heading, **"Time for filing claims"**)
  Priority for payment of claims   Pro §§11420, 11421
  Public administrator paying   Pro §7662
  Publication of notice to creditors to file claims   Pro §9001
  Public entities, claims filed by   Pro §§9200 to 9205
  Quieting title action   CCP §762.030, Pro §9654
  Refusal or failure to act on claim filed by personal representative or judge as rejection of claim   Pro §9256

CLAIMS AGAINST ESTATES—Cont.
  Rejection of claim
    Judge, determination by (See within this heading, **"Judges"**)
    Limitations period to bring action after   Pro §9353
    Partial allowance of claim   Pro §9255
    Personal representative as creditor, procedure for claims filed by   Pro §9252
    Procedure for   CRC 7.401, 7.402, Pro §9250
    Refusal or failure to act on claim filed as   Pro §9256
  Representatives, personal liability of   Pro §§11424, 11429
  Revised claims, filing of   Pro §9104
  Sales and use tax, claims for   Pro §§9200 to 9205
  Service of claim on personal representatives   Pro §9150
  Settlement of claims (See **EXECUTORS AND ADMINISTRATORS**)
  Small estates without administration (See **SMALL ESTATES WITHOUT ADMINISTRATION**)
  Special administrator's duties regarding   Pro §8546
  State of California, claims filed by   Pro §§9200 to 9205
  Statute of frauds applicable   Pro §9604
  Statutes of limitation
    Bar of claims not filed
      Generally   Pro §§9002, 9253
      Public entities, claims by   Pro §§9200, 9201
    Enforcement of claims to distribution of estate, action for   CCP §366.3
    Liability insurer, action against   Pro §551
    Litigation, claims in, generally (See within this heading, **"Action on claim"**)
    Rejected claims, bringing action on   Pro §9353
  Summary dispute determination
    Arbitration, submission of disputes to   Pro §9621
    Temporary judge, submission of disputes to   Pro §9620
  Survival of actions (See **SURVIVAL OF ACTIONS**)
  Surviving spouse, allocation of debts with
    Generally   Pro §11440
    Agreement with personal representative   Pro §11444
    Characterization of debt as separate or community   Pro §11444
    Funeral expenses   Pro §11446
    Inventory of surviving spouse's property   Pro §11442
    Last illness expenses   Pro §11446
    Notice of hearing   Pro §11443
    Order by court   Pro §11445
    Petition   Pro §11441
  Taxes unpaid, claims for   Pro §§9200 to 9205
  Temporary judges, summary determination of disputes by   Pro §9620
  Time
    Filing of claims (See within this heading, **"Time for filing claims"**)
    Notice to creditors, time requirement for giving   Pro §9051
    Refusal or failure to act on claim filed, effect of   Pro §9256
    Rejected claims, time for bringing action on   Pro §9353
    Service on personal representative, time for   Pro §9150
    Statute of limitations (See within this heading, **"Statutes of limitation"**)
  Time for filing claims
    Generally   Pro §9002
    Amended or revised claims   Pro §9104
    Late claims   Pro §9103
    Limitation periods
      Generally   Pro §9100
      Vacancy in office of personal representative, effect of creditors filing claims during   Pro §9101
    Status of claims filed before expiration of   Pro §9102
    Vacancy in office of personal representative, effect of claims filed during   Pro §9101
  Title and ownership, third party action on claims involving   Pro §§850 to 859
  Tort claims   Pro §9000
  Trust deeds (See within this heading, **"Mortgages"**)
  Trust estates, claims against (See **TRUSTS**)
  Unemployment insurance tax, claims for   Pro §§9200 to 9205
  Unpaid creditor after final distribution, rights of   Pro §11429
  Victims and victims rights
    Director of victim compensation and government claims board
      Notice of death of decedent with imprisoned heir   Pro §9202
  Vouchers in support of claim, filing of   Pro §9151
  Waiver of defects in filing procedure   Pro §9154
  Welfare claims   Pro §§9200 to 9205
  Written instruments, filing requirements for claims based on   Pro §9152

CLAIMS AGAINST PUBLIC ENTITIES AND EMPLOYEES
Acceptance of amount allowed by claimant, effect of   Gov §946
Accrual of cause of action, date of   Gov §901
Actions
  Compromise or settlement of pending action   Gov §§948, 949
  Construction of   Gov §§942 to 944

CLAIMS INDEX

CLAIMS AGAINST PUBLIC ENTITIES AND EMPLOYEES—Cont.
Actions—Cont.
  Definitions   Gov §§940 to 940.6
  Local public entities, special provisions relating to actions against   Gov §§960 to 960.8
  Petition for relief from bar to suit for failure to present timely claim   Gov §946.6
  Public employees, actions against   Gov §§950 to 951
  Public entities, actions against   Gov §§945 to 949
  State, special provisions relating to actions against   Gov §§955 to 956
Administrative adjudication (See **ADMINISTRATIVE ADJUDICATION**)
Adoption or enforcement of laws, immunity from liability for   Gov §§818.2, 821
Agreements
  Claims procedures established by   Gov §§930 to 930.6
  Tort liability under agreements between public entities   Gov §§895 to 895.8
Amendment of claims   Gov §910.6
Amount allowed in claims   Gov §906
Appeals of disapproved claims   Gov §§926.4, 926.6
  Time for appeal   CRC 8.108, 8.823
Appropriations   Gov §965
Arrest, liability for failure to make   Gov §846
Asbestos exposure, liability of school district for   Gov §905.5
Attorney General notification to Controller of payment   Gov §965.3
Attorney's fees
  Law enforcement officers, actions against   CCP §1021.7
  Recreational user's action against public entity, administrative claim to recover attorney's fees expended in   CC §846.1
Audits as prerequisite to Controller's drawing warrant for claim   Gov §925.6
Authority for settlement of claim   Gov §935.4
Authorized entry on property, liability for   Gov §821.8
Bad faith
  Cost award based on determination of bad faith   CCP §1038
  Unconstitutional enactments
    Immunity of public employee acting in good faith under apparent authority of enactment   Gov §820.6
Beaches deemed in natural unimproved condition   Gov §831.21
Board, defined   Gov §§900.2, 940.2
Bomb shelters, injuries sustained in   CC §1714.5
Bonds, funding judgments against local entities with   Gov §§975.2 to 978.8
Burglar alarm, failure of police to respond to   Gov §845
California National Guard activity, immunity for injury arising from   Gov §816
California state university
  Payments by trustees   Gov §935.9
  Presentation of claims
    Applicable provisions   Gov §905.9
    Trustees' actions on claims   Gov §912.5
Canal, liability for injury caused by condition of   Gov §831.8
Capacity to present claim   Gov §910
Cargo tank vehicles traveling through tunnels, immunity from liability for failure to prohibit or restrict   Gov §821.5
Childhood sexual abuse damage claims   Gov §831.8
Child protection workers, extent of civil immunity of   Gov §820.21
Civil rights, actions to enforce against peace officer or custodial officer
  Immunity
    Inapplicability of state immunity provisions   CC §52.1
Claims presentation
  False claims, civil liability for making
    Filing false claims act records under seal   CRC 2.570 to 2.573
  Required presentation of claims   Gov §905
  State mandates commission, eligibility of claim for consideration
    No submission of claim to general services department   Gov §905.3
Claims procedures
  Agreement, claims procedures established by   Gov §§930 to 930.6
  Forms   Gov §910.4
  Public entities, claims procedures established by   Gov §§935 to 935.9
Collateral source payments in personal injury or wrongful death actions   Gov §985
Commencement of action against public entity   Gov §§945.6, 945.8
Compromise or settlement
  State, claims against
    General services department authority to allow certain claims   Gov §965.1
Conduit, liability for injury caused by condition of   Gov §§831.8, 831.9
Constitutionality of claim, procedures for determining   Gov §§920 to 920.8
Contents of claim   Gov §910
Contractual liability, applicability of public entity liability provisions to   Gov §814
Contribution or indemnification in agreements between public entities   Gov §§895.4, 895.6

CLAIMS AGAINST PUBLIC ENTITIES AND EMPLOYEES—Cont.
Controlled substances violation, liability of schools for publication or reports or photographs of persons convicted of   Gov §818.7
Controller
  Attorney General notification to Controller of payment   Gov §965.3
  Department of Transportation Claims   Gov §956.2
  Late payment by state agencies
    Failure of agency to file correct claim with controller   Gov §927.13
  Presentation of claims to   Gov §§925 to 926.10
    Audit prior to presentation   Gov §925.6
  Time for payments   Gov §927.13
Correctional facility, liability for failure to provide   Gov §845.2
Costs award, bad faith as basis of   CCP §1038
Criminal cases
  Defense of employee, public entity providing   Gov §995.8
  Pending criminal charges, prohibition against bringing civil action against peace officer when   Gov §945.3
Custodial officers
  Personnel records, disclosure   Ev §1043
    Inclusions and exclusions from disclosure   Ev §1045
    Officer not present for alleged conduct   Ev §1047
Custody, liability for injury from failure to retain person in   Gov §846
Dangerous condition of public property
  Public property generally (See within this heading, **"Public property"**)
Defense of public employees   Gov §§995 to 996.6
Definitions governing   Gov §§810 to 811.9
Department of Motor Vehicles' liability for injury to lienholder   Gov §818.5
Department of Transportation
  Controller's duty to draw warrant for claims against   Gov §965.2
  Payment of claims by   Gov §935.7
Director of Finance, report of actions to   Gov §965.65
Discretion of public employee, liability for act or omission resulting from exercise of   Gov §820.2
Dog parks owned or operated by public entity
  Death or injury caused by actions of dog
    Immunity of public entity   Gov §831.7.5
Drain, liability for injury caused by condition of   Gov §§831.8, 831.9
Earnings assignment for support, immunity from prosecution for enforcing   Fam §5247
Earthquake or volcanic prediction, immunity from liability for   Gov §955.1
Emergency facilities, injuries sustained in   CC §1714.5
Emergency vehicle, liability for operation of traffic signals controlled by   Gov §830.9
Emotional distress resulting from land failure of unimproved public property   Gov §831.25
Employment, assessment of new regulations on creation of   Gov §11346.3
Escaped person, liability from injuries caused by   Gov §§845.8, 856.2
Exemplary damages
  Generally   Gov §818
  Indemnification of public employees   Gov §825
Failure or refusal to defend public employee   Gov §996.4
Failure to discharge statutory duty, liability of public entity for   Gov §815.6
False arrest or imprisonment, liability of officer for   Gov §820.4
Federal agency's claim against credits owing to State by debtor   Gov §926.8
Fifty thousand dollars, executive officer allowing claim filings not exceeding   Gov §965.1
Filing claims (See within this heading, **"Presentation of claim"**)
Fire protection, liability from injuries resulting from   Gov §§850 to 850.8
First aid stations, injuries sustained in   CC §1714.5
Flood control and water conservation facilities, liability for injuries caused by   Gov §§831.8, 831.9
Form and contents of notice of action taken   Gov §913
Fraud, corruption or malice of employee, indemnification of public entity for act or omission due to   Gov §825.6
Good faith
  Cost award based on determination of bad faith   CCP §1038
  Unconstitutional enactments, immunity of public employee acting in good faith under apparent authority of   Gov §820.6
Grading or maintenance of road, liability for injury caused by   Gov §831.3
Gradual earth movement, liability for activities to abate   Gov §§865 to 867
Harassment, liability for   Gov §815.3
Hazardous recreational activity, liability for injury to participant or spectator in   Gov §831.7
Health or safety hazard, liability for failure to make inspection of property to determine   Gov §§816.6, 821.4
Hearing on determination for payment of judgment   Gov §976
Hospitals (See within this heading, **"Medical or mental facilities"**)
Impending peril, liability for activities to abate an   Gov §§865 to 867
Indemnification
  Generally   Gov §825
  Agreements between public entities, indemnity provisions in   Gov §895.4

CLAIMS AGAINST PUBLIC ENTITIES AND EMPLOYEES—Cont.
Indemnification—Cont.
 Amount of payment of claim or judgment by public employee, right to recover Gov §825.2
 Fraud, corruption or malice of employee, indemnification of public entity for act or omission due to Gov §825.6
 Health care providers Gov §827
 Liability of public employee to indemnify public entity Gov §825.4
Independent contractor, liability for tortious act or omission of Gov §815.4
Insurance for local public entities Gov §§989 to 991.2
Intentional infliction of emotional distress, liability for Gov §815.3
Intentional torts by public official Gov §815.3
Interest on amount of judgments Gov §965.5
Interest on liquidated claim against public entity by individual or other public entity Gov §§926.10, 927.12
Inverse condemnation actions Gov §905.1
Jail, failure to provide Gov §845.2
Joint and several liability of public entities in mutual agreement Gov §895.2
Judges and subordinate judicial officers, claims affecting Gov §811.9
Judgments
 Payment of claims and judgments
  Local entities, general provisions concerning payment of judgments against Gov §§970 to 971.2
  Time limit for enforcement Gov §§965.5, 970.1
Judicial branch entities Gov §905.7
 Actions against public employees and entities
  Definition of judicial branch entity Gov §940.3
  Judicial relief from nonpresentation of claims Gov §946.6
  Settlement of claims Gov §948.1
  Summons, service Gov §955.9
 Claims and claims presentation
  Adjustment and payment of claims Gov §935.8
  Defined Gov §900.3
  Forms Gov §910.4
  Rule of court to determine action on claim against Gov §912.7
 Compromise or settlement
  Judicial council settlement Gov §948.1
 Payment of claims and judgments Gov §§965, 965.2
  Conditions for payment Gov §965.6
  Reports on remedial measures Gov §965.65
Judicial or administrative proceedings, immunity from liability for instituting or prosecuting Gov §821.6
Juvenile court system
 Report of abuse or neglect, time for filing late claim as extended by agency's failure to make timely Gov §911.4
 Social workers and child protection workers, extent of civil immunity of Gov §820.21
Late claims, presentation of Gov §§911.4 to 912.4
Late payment by state agencies
 Appropriation requests for payment of penalties Gov §927.8
 Definitions under prompt payment provisions Gov §927.2
 Disputing invoices, procedure for Gov §927.3
 Expedited payment of prime contractors Gov §927.10
 Grants Gov §927.1
  Defined Gov §927.2
 Interest on liquidated claims, inapplicability of provisions for Gov §927.12
 Justifiable delays in payment Gov §927.11
 Legislative intent underlying prompt payment provisions Gov §927
 Medi-Cal claims, exemption for Gov §927.5
 Penalties
  Generally Gov §927.1
  Appropriation requests for payment of penalties Gov §927.8
  Penalty rates Gov §§927.6, 927.7
  Reporting of late payment penalties Gov §927.9
  Suspension of penalty provisions Gov §927.11
  Time limit for payment to avoid penalties Gov §927.4
 Refunds or other payments due
  Definition of notice of refund or other payment due Gov §927.2
  Failure of agency to file correct claim with controller Gov §927.13
  Submission of notice to controller Gov §927.3
 Reporting of late payment penalties Gov §927.9
Law enforcement officers
 Attorneys' fees in actions against peace officers CCP §1021.7
 Burglar alarm, failure of police to respond to Gov §845
 Civil rights, actions to enforce against peace officer or custodial officer
  Immunity, inapplicability CC §52.1
 Criminal charges pending, prohibition against action while Gov §945.3
 Discovery of personnel records of peace officers CCP §1005, Ev §§1043 to 1047
 Dogs used in police work, injuries inflicted by CC §§3342, 3342.5
 False arrest or imprisonment, liability of officer for Gov §820.4

CLAIMS AGAINST PUBLIC ENTITIES AND EMPLOYEES—Cont.
Law enforcement officers—Cont.
 Killed in line of duty, survivors as immune from liability for officer's actions in line of duty when officer was Gov §823
 Medical history of officer, access to Ev §1044
 Nonnegligent act or omission, liability for Gov §820.4
 Prisoners, actions involving Gov §§844 to 846
 Psychological history, access to Ev §1044
 Scene of accident, discretion of officer to leave Gov §820.25
 Sexual assault by officer
  Presentation of claim, requirements Gov §945.9
 Statutes of limitation on actions against officer to recover damages for seizure of property for statutory forfeiture CCP §340
 Survivors of officer killed in line of duty as immune from liability for officer's actions in line of duty Gov §823
 Warrant regular on its face, protection against liability for arrest based on CC §43.55
Leave of absence from mental facility, liability for injury resulting from Gov §856
Legislature
 Appeals to Gov §926.6
 Declarations and public access programs, liability for Gov §831.5
 Exemption of claims for expenses Gov §925.2
 Report of claim to Gov §912.8
Liability, generally
 Public employees Gov §820
 Public entities Gov §§815 to 818.9
Licenses and permits, immunity from liability for decisions as to Gov §§818.4, 821.2
Limits on award against governmental agency Fam §273
Local public entity defined Gov §§900.2, 940.4
Mailing claim, manner of Gov §915.2
Mandamus
 Compelling performance of act by writ of mandate Gov §§965.7, 965.8
 Preservation of right to resort to writ of mandate Gov §942
Mass care centers, injuries sustained in CC §1714.5
Medical care to prisoner, liability for failure to provide Gov §845.6
Medi-Cal claims, late payment of Gov §927.5
Medical or mental facilities
 Generally Gov §854.8
 Adequate equipment or personnel, failure to maintain Gov §855
 Agnews developmental center
  Continuity of care for clients Gov §854.1
 Confining person for mental illness or addiction, injury resulting from decision for Gov §856
 Definitions pertaining to Gov §§854 to 854.5
 Diagnosis, injury from failure to Gov §855.8
 Escaped person, injury resulting from Gov §856.2
 Failure to admit person to facility, injury resulting from Gov §856.4
 Indemnification of health care providers Gov §827
 Insurance for volunteer health professionals Gov §990.9
 Judicial determination or review of legality of confinement, interference with right of inmate to obtain Gov §855.2
 Lanterman developmental center
  Continuity of care for clients Gov §854.1
 National Influenza Program, immunity of public entity or employee participating in Gov §856.6
 Physical or mental examination, injury on failure to make Gov §855.6
 Prisoners, public entity's liability for failure to provide medical care to Gov §845.6
 Public health or disease prevention acts, injury resulting from decision about Gov §855.4
Minors
 Juvenile court system
  Report of abuse or neglect, time for filing late claim as extended by agency failure to make timely Gov §911.4
  Social workers and child protection workers, extent of civil immunity Gov §820.21
 Late claims, computation of time period for permissible Gov §911.4
Misrepresentations by employee, immunity of public entity for Gov §§818.8, 822.2
National Influenza Program, immunity of public entity or employee participating in Gov §856.6
Navigable waters, liability for injuries on portions of Gov §831.6
Notices
 Attorney General notification to Controller of payment Gov §965.3
 Dangerous condition of public property Gov §§835.2, 840.4
 Form and contents of notice of action taken Gov §913
 Insufficiency of claims Gov §910.8
 Methods of notification by board Gov §915.4
 Payment of judgment, notice of hearing on Gov §§975.4, 975.6

CLAIMS INDEX

CLAIMS AGAINST PUBLIC ENTITIES AND EMPLOYEES—Cont.
Notices—Cont.
    Secretary of State, notice to public agency by   Gov §960.4
    Untimely filed claim, notice of   Gov §911.3
    Waiver of defense as to sufficiency of claim by failure to give   Gov §911
Offsets of   Gov §§907, 965.6
Omnibus claim appropriation   Gov §§920 to 920.8
Parole of release determinations, liability for injury resulting from   Gov §§845.8, 856
Partition proceedings in which State has interest   Gov §956
Payment of claims and judgments
    Bonds, funding judgments against local entities with   Gov §§975 to 978.8
    Collateral source payments   Gov §985
    Elected official's intentional torts, payment of deficiency in action based on   Gov §815.3
    Late payment by state agencies (See within this heading, **"Late payment by state agencies"**)
    Local entities, general provisions concerning payment of judgments against   Gov §§970 to 971.2
    Periodic payment of judgments   CRC 3.1804
    Periodic payments   Gov §984
    State agency payments   Gov §935.6
    State entities, general provisions concerning payment of claims and judgments against   Gov §§965 to 965.8
Peace officers (See within this heading, **"Law enforcement officers"**)
Penalties for late payment of claims by state agencies (See within this heading, **"Late payment by state agencies"**)
Periodic payments, payment by   Gov §984
Personal injury or wrongful death actions, collateral source payments in   Gov §985
Pesticides, liability for use of   Gov §862
Petition for relief from bar to suit for failure to present timely claim   Gov §946.6
Physical or mental examination, injury on failure to make   Gov §855.6
Presentation of claim
    Appropriations made or state funds available, presentation of claim against State where   Gov §925.4
    Capacity to present claim   Gov §910
    Fees for filing
        State, claims against   Gov §905.2
    Filing of claim   Gov §915.2
    Late claims, presentation of   Gov §§911.4 to 912.4
        Grant or denial of application to present   Gov §911.6
    Law enforcement officers
        Sexual assault by officer, requirements for presentation   Gov §945.9
    Mailing of claim   Gov §915.2
    Manner of   Gov §915
    Prohibition of suit against public entity until   Gov §945.4
    State, claims against   Gov §§905.2, 910.8, 911
    Time limits on   Gov §911.2
Prisoners
    Generally   Gov §§844 to 846
    Commencement of action by   Gov §945.6
    Public employee, actions against   Gov §950.6
Private property, venue in action against State for taking or damages of   Gov §955
Procedure for claims   Gov §§912.6, 912.8
Prompt payment provisions
    Late payments generally (See within this heading, **"Late payment by state agencies"**)
Proximate cause of injury, liability of public entity where employee is   Gov §815.2
Public entities, presentation of claims for inverse condemnation against   Gov §905.1
Public health or disease prevention acts, injury resulting from decision about   Gov §855.4
Public property
    Generally   Gov §835
    Attorney's fees in recreational user's action against public entity, administrative claim for recovery of   CC §846.1
    Authorized entry on property, liability for   Gov §821.8
    Beaches deemed in natural unimproved condition   Gov §831.21
    Court's determination that condition not dangerous   Gov §830.2
    Definition of dangerous condition   Gov §835.2
    Definitions involving dangerous condition of   Gov §830
    Emotional distress resulting from land failure of unimproved public property   Gov §831.25
    Hazardous recreational activity, liability for injury to participant or spectator in   Gov §831.7
    Impending peril, liability for activities to abate an   Gov §§865 to 867
    Legislative declarations and public access programs, liability for   Gov §831.5

CLAIMS AGAINST PUBLIC ENTITIES AND EMPLOYEES—Cont.
Public property—Cont.
    Natural condition of unimproved public property, liability for   Gov §§831.2, 831.21
    Notice of dangerous condition, definition of   Gov §§835.2, 840.4
    Plan, design, construction or improvement of public property, injury caused by   Gov §830.7
    Public employees, liability of   Gov §§840 to 840.2
    Reasonableness of act or omission causing dangerous condition, effect of   Gov §§835.4, 840.6
    Res ipsa loquitur doctrine, applicability of   Gov §830.5
    Safety improvements by special assessment districts not constituting   Gov §830.1
    Schools (See within this heading, **"Schools"**)
    Signs or roadway markings, failure to provide   Gov §830.4
    Streets and highways (See within this heading, **"Streets and highways"**)
    Traffic signals (See within this heading, **"Traffic signals"**)
Punitive damages   Gov §818
    Indemnification of public employees   Gov §825
Real property
    Public property generally (See within this heading, **"Public property"**)
Recreational property, liability for injuries on unpaved roads or trails providing access to   Gov §831.4
Refusal of public entity to defend action against employee   Gov §995.2
Reimbursement of state employee for costs of defense   Gov §955.3
Rejected claim, reexamination of   Gov §913.2
Reservoir, liability for injury caused by condition of   Gov §831.8
Res ipsa loquitur doctrine   Gov §830.5
Roads (See within this heading, **"Streets and highways"**)
Safety improvements by special assessment districts not constituting public property   Gov §830.1
Scene of accident, discretion of law enforcement officer to leave   Gov §820.25
Schools
    Asbestos exposure, liability of school district for   Gov §905.5
    Controlled substances violation, liability of schools for publication or reports or photographs of persons convicted of   Gov §818.7
    Prohibition on submission of claims by school district   Gov §905.3
    Publications of school, liability for   Gov §818.7
    Unsold school lands, liability for injuries on   Gov §831.6
Secretary of State, actions involving   Gov §§960.3, 960.4
Service of summons
    Order allowing service on Secretary of State   Gov §960.3
    Registry of Public Agencies, service in conformity with statement in   Gov §960.8
    Required filings concerning public agency, service in absence of   Gov §960.2
    State, service in action against   Gov §955.4
Sexual battery, liability for   Gov §815.3
Signature on claim   Gov §910.2
Signs (See within this heading, **"Traffic signals"**)
Signs or roadway markings, failure to provide   Gov §830.4
Small claims court advisors, immunity for   CCP §116.940, Gov §818.9
Social workers and child protection workers, extent of civil immunity of   Gov §820.21
State, claims against
    Presentation of claims   Gov §§905.2, 910.8, 911
State Controller (See within this heading, **"Controller"**)
State defined   Gov §§900.6, 940.6
Statutes of limitation for actions against peace officer, criminal charges tolling   Gov §945.3
Statutory liability of public entities   Gov §815
Streets and highways
    Grading or maintenance of road, liability for injury caused by   Gov §831.3
    Traffic signals (See within this heading, **"Traffic signals"**)
    Unpaved roads or trails providing access to unimproved property, liability for   Gov §831.4
    Weather conditions, liability for effect of   Gov §831
Submerged lands, liability for injuries on portions of   Gov §831.6
Suits (See within this heading, **"Actions"**)
Summons, service
    Judicial branch entities, service on   Gov §955.9
Survivors of law enforcement officer slain in line of duty as immune from liability for officer's actions in line of duty   Gov §823
Tax law administration, liability for   Gov §§860 to 860.4
Theft of money from employee's official custody, liability for   Gov §822
Third persons, liability of employee for acts or omissions of   Gov §820.8
Tidelands, liability for injuries on portions of   Gov §831.6
Time limits on presentation of claim   Gov §911.2
Tort liability under agreements between public entities   Gov §§895 to 895.8
Traffic signals
    Generally   Gov §830.4

CLAIMS AGAINST PUBLIC ENTITIES AND EMPLOYEES—Cont.
Traffic signals—Cont.
  Dangerous conditions, failure to provide traffic or warning signals of Gov §830.8
  Emergency vehicle, liability for operation of traffic signals controlled by Gov §830.9
Transportation Department
  Controller's duty to draw warrant for claims against Gov §965.2
  Payment of claims by department Gov §935.7
Trial court employees, claims affecting Gov §811.9
United States Treasurer, issuance of warrant payable to Gov §926.8
Unpaved roads or trails providing access to unimproved property, liability for Gov §831.4
Untimely filed claim, notice of Gov §911.3
Venue
  City, county or agency's action against State, venue in Gov §955.3
  Death or injury to person or property within State, venue in action for Gov §955.2
  Relief from bar to suit for failure to present timely claim, venue in action for Gov §946.6
  State, venue in action for claims against Gov §§955, 955.2, 955.3
Vicarious liability of local public officials Gov §820.9
Victim compensation and government claims board
  Claims for consideration by board Gov §905.3
Volcanic prediction, immunity from liability for Gov §955.1
Waiver of defense as to sufficiency of claim Gov §911
Water Resources, actions arising out of work of Department of Gov §956
Weather conditions, liability for effect on streets and highways of Gov §831
Witness, conditions under which public entity may indemnify or defend Gov §995.9
Workers' compensation provisions, no implied repeal of Gov §814.2

CLASS ACTIONS
Authorizing provision CCP §382
Case management CRC 3.760 to 3.771
  Certification or decertification of class
    Motion CRC 3.764
    Order CRC 3.765
  Complaint form CRC 3.761
  Conducting class action, orders CRC 3.767
  Conferences CRC 3.762
    Order upon conclusion of conference CRC 3.763
    Telephone appearance at case management conferences CRC 3.670
  Discovery from unnamed class members CRC 3.768
  Dismissal of action CRC 3.770
  Governing rules CRC 3.760
  Judgments CRC 3.771
  Judicial council legal forms CRCAppx A
  Notices
    Class members, notice to CRC 3.766
    Settlement of class actions CRC 3.769
Certification or decertification of class
  Motion CRC 3.764
  Order CRC 3.765
Complex litigation defined CRC 3.400
Conducting class action
  Orders CRC 3.767
Construction defects, actions for
  Prelitigation procedures
    Combined claims covering items not covered under chapter CC §931
Consumer privacy rights
  Actions for damages, injunctions, declaratory relief, etc
    Security practices and procedures not in place CC §1798.150
Consumer protection CC §§1752, 1781
Credit reporting CC §1785.31
Decertification of class
  Motion CRC 3.764
  Order CRC 3.765
Discovery from unnamed class members CRC 3.768
Dismissal of action, party or cause of action CCP §581, CRC 3.770
Initial case management conference in coordinated actions CRC 3.541
  Telephone appearance at case management conferences CRC 3.670
Judgments CRC 3.771
  Jurisdiction retained to enforce CRC 3.769
  Settlement of class actions CRC 3.769
Judicial arbitration
  Exemption from arbitration CRC 3.811
Management of class actions CRC 3.760 to 3.771
Notices
  Case management
    Conference, notice of CRC 3.762

CLASS ACTIONS—Cont.
Notices—Cont.
  Class members, notice to CRC 3.766
  Dismissal of class actions CRC 3.770
  Settlement of class actions CRC 3.769
Orders
  Case conference orders CRC 3.763
  Certification or decertification of class CRC 3.765
  Conduct of class action, orders in directing CRC 3.767
  Settlement of class actions CRC 3.769
Preliminary injunctions or temporary restraining orders in CCP §527
Private student loan collections reform
  Actions against creditor, lender or collector for violations of provisions CC §1788.208
Settlement of class actions CRC 3.769
Surety bonds, class of persons seeking enforcement of liability on CCP §996.410
Unpaid residue, distribution of CCP §384

CLEAR AND CONVINCING EVIDENCE
Jury instructions on Ev §502
Legal title owner presumed to be full beneficial title owner, evidence rebutting Ev §662
Requirement for burden of proof Ev §115
Termination of parental rights, burden of proof required Fam §7821

CLEMENCY
Generally (See **PARDONS**)
Supreme court
  Application for recommendation for executive clemency CRCSupp SupCtIOPP XIV

CLERGYPERSONS
Conciliation court proceedings Fam §1838
Family history, clergyman's certificates as evidence of Ev §1316
Marriage, solemnization of Fam §400
Privileges for penitent in court proceedings (See **PRIVILEGED COMMUNICATIONS**)

CLERICAL ERRORS
Administrative adjudication, decision in Gov §11518.5
Judgments, correction of clerical errors in CCP §473
Small claims court, grounds for vacating judgment of CCP §116.725

CLERKS OF COURT
Acknowledgment of instruments (See **ACKNOWLEDGMENTS**)
Adjournment on judge's absence CCP §139
Administrative Procedure Act (See **ADMINISTRATIVE PROCEDURE ACT**)
Affidavits, fees for taking of (See within this heading, **"Fees"**)
Appellate duties, failure to perform CRC 8.23
Appellate rules, superior court appeals (See **APPELLATE RULES, SUPERIOR COURT APPEALS**)
Appellate rules, supreme court and courts of appeal (See **APPELLATE RULES, SUPREME COURT AND COURTS OF APPEAL**)
Arbitration award filed with CCP §1141.20, CRC 3.825
Assignment of judgment, recording CCP §673
Certificates
  Effect of certificate of court clerk CCP §2015.3
  Fees (See within this heading, **"Fees"**)
Change of venue, transmittal of papers and pleadings pursuant to order for CCP §399
  Time frames for transferring jurisdiction
    Family law actions or proceedings CRC 5.97
Check or other negotiable instrument, payment of fees by CCP §411.20, CRC 8.100, 10.821
  Underpayment CCP §411.21
Child support cases under Title IV-D, minimum training standards for court clerks assigned to CRC 5.355
Citation to appear, issuance of (See **CITATION TO APPEAR**)
Combined summons and complaint, filing CRC 5.325
Contempt CCP §1209
Copies
  Fees (See within this heading, **"Fees"**)
Court operations costs, salaries and benefits included as CRC 10.810
Criminal cases
  Service of briefs CRC 8.360
Diversion of criminal defendants
  Traffic violators CRC 4.104
Drop boxes for filing documents CRC 2.210
Ethics programs CRC JudAdminStand 10.16
Exhibits (See **EXHIBITS**)
Family law rules (See **FAMILY RULES**)

CLERKS OF COURT—Cont.
Family rules
   Request for orders
      Time frames for transferring jurisdiction   CRC 5.97
Fees
   Generally   Gov §26820
   Acknowledgment of instruments, fees for   Gov §26855
   Administrative charges
      Returned checks, handling   CCP §411.20
      Underpayment   CCP §411.21
   Admitted surety insurer, fees for (See **SURETYSHIP, BONDS AND UNDERTAKINGS**)
   Affidavits
      Generally   Gov §26853
      Pension claimants, waiver of fees for   Gov §26858
      Superior court fees, specified services   Gov §70626
   Amendment of complaint or other subsequent pleadings, effect on filing fee   Gov §70613.5
   Appeal certificates required by Courts of Appeal or Supreme Court   Gov §70620
   Authentication fee   Gov §70629
   Certification fees
      Generally   Gov §26833
      Admitted surety insurer, certificate of authority of   Gov §26855.3
      Appeals to courts of appeal or Supreme Court   Gov §70620
      Comparing copy presented with original on file, fee for   Gov §26837
      Public official, certificate as to official capacity of   Gov §26852
      Revivor   Gov §26847
      Unspecified certificates   Gov §26836
   Change of venue   Gov §70618
   Checks or other negotiable instruments, payment by   CCP §411.20, CRC 8.100, 10.821
      Underpayment   CCP §411.21
   Child custody cases   Gov §70678
   Comparing copy presented with original on file, fees for   Gov §26837
   Conservators (See **CONSERVATORS**)
   Copies
      Certifying, superior court fees, specified services   Gov §70626
      Domestic partnership dissolution record, fee for certified copy of   Gov §70674
      General fees   Gov §26831
      Indigent plaintiff, copy fee waived for   Gov §70676
      Marriage dissolution record, fee for certified copy of   Gov §70674
   Credit cards in payment of court fees, use of   CRC 10.820
   Exemplification of documents   Gov §26839
   Exemptions from fee payment   Gov §26857
   Family conciliation services fees   Gov §26840.3
   Filing fees
      Answers   Gov §70612
      Change of venue   Gov §70618
      Check returned unpaid   CCP §411.20
      Children's waiting room in courthouse, surcharge to fund   Gov §70640
      Conservators (See **CONSERVATORS**)
      Courthouse seismic repair costs in Riverside County, surcharge to defray   Gov §70622
      Initial filing fees   Gov §§70611, 70614
      Insufficient amount tendered   CCP §411.21
      Permissible additional fees   Gov §70603
      Probate petition   Gov §§70602.5, 70602.6, 70650
      Supplemental fees for first paper filing   Gov §§70602.5, 70602.6
      Underpayment   CCP §411.21
      Unspecified papers, fee for indexing and filing   Gov §26850
   Indexing and filing unspecified papers, fee for   Gov §26850
   Initial petition, filing fees for   Gov §§70611, 70613, 70614
      Permissible additional fees   Gov §70603
      Supplemental fees for first paper filing   Gov §§70602.5, 70602.6
   Insufficient amount tendered   CCP §411.21
   Marriage (See **MARRIAGE**)
   Notary public, filing bond by   Gov §26849.1
   Pension claimants, waiver of affidavit fees for   Gov §26858
   Probate petition   Gov §70650
      Supplemental fees for first paper filing   Gov §§70602.5, 70602.6
   Recording fees for licenses and certificates   Gov §26851
   Registration fees for licenses and certificates   Gov §26851
   Revivor, fees for certificate of   Gov §26847
   Search of records, fees for   Gov §26854
   Underpayment   CCP §411.21
   Unspecified certificates   Gov §26836
Filing fees (See within this heading, **"Fees"**)
Indexes, court, maintenance   CRC 10.851

CLERKS OF COURT—Cont.
Judges performing duties of   CCP §167
Justice courts (See **JUSTICE COURTS**)
Letters of administration signed by   Pro §8405
Marriage (See **MARRIAGE**)
Notice of pendency of action (See **PENDENCY OF ACTIONS**)
Notices served, clerk's proof of   CCP §1013a
Oaths, administering   CCP §2093
Partition referees, clerks as   CCP §873.050
Register of actions
   Judgment, entry of   CCP §668.5
Retention or destruction of exhibits or depositions   CCP §§1952, 1952.3
Salaries and benefits included as court operations costs   CRC 10.810
Service of process
   Party's address unknown
      Papers served on clerk   CRC 3.252
Signature on judgment   CRC 3.1806
Signature on summons   CCP §412.20
Small claims courts
   Court clerk's role in assisting litigants   CRC 3.2110
Superior courts (See **SUPERIOR COURTS**)
Tentative decision, service of   CRC 3.1590
Trial court rules
   Drop boxes for filing documents   CRC 2.210
   Records of court
      Original documents filed with clerk   CRC 2.400
Unpaid, check for filing fees returned   CCP §411.20
Vexatious litigant subject to prefiling order, clerk shall not file litigation presented by   CCP §391.7
Will delivered to clerk for probate   Pro §8200

CLIENT PRIVILEGES (See PRIVILEGED COMMUNICATIONS)

CLINICAL LABORATORY TECHNOLOGISTS
Blood tests, affidavit stating technique of taking   Ev §712
Bond required to secure costs in action against   CCP §1029.6
Malpractice (See **MALPRACTICE**)
Medical records, attorney's authorized inspection of   CCP §1985.7, Ev §1158

CLINICAL SOCIAL WORKER (See PRIVILEGED COMMUNICATIONS)

CLINICS
Medical claims data error correction   CC §57

CLOCKS
Common carrier's liability for transporting   CC §2200

CLOSED HEARINGS
Adoption proceedings   Fam §8611
Termination of parental rights   Fam §7884

CLOSING ARGUMENT   CCP §607

CLOTHESLINES
Common interest developments
   Governing documents not to prohibit clotheslines or drying racks in owner's backyard   CC §4753
Landlord and tenant
   Tenant use clothesline or drying rack in private areas   CC §1940.20

CLOTHING
Defined   CC §1791
Hotel, apartment, lodging or hospital, limitation of action for recovery or conversion of personal property left at   CCP §341a
Lien for work on   CC §3066
Prisoners (See **PRISONERS**)
Return of clothing to retail seller   CC §1793.35
Survivors of family having possession of   Pro §6500
Warranties on sale of   CC §§1790 to 1793, 1795.5

CLOUD ON TITLE
Quieting title (See **QUIETING TITLE**)

CLUB CARDS
Supermarket club cards
   Waiver of protections   CC §1749.66

CLUBS (See ASSOCIATIONS)

COCKFIGHTING
Property used for dog or cock fighting as nuisance   CC §3482.8
   Unlawful detainer actions   CCP §1161

COCKTAIL LOUNGES
Unruh Civil Rights Act   CC §§51, 52

CODICIL
Generally (See **WILLS**)
Will defined to include   CCP §17

COERCED DEBT   CC §§1798.97.1 to 1798.97.6
Applicability of provisions   CC §1798.97.4
    Incurring debt on or after July 1, 2023   CC §1798.97.5
Causing another to incur coerced debt   CC §1798.97.2
    Establishing debt as coerced   CC §1798.97.3
    Notice of intent to file action   CC §1798.97.2
Collection activities
    Notice to claimant of coerced debt
        Effect on activities   CC §1798.97.2
Definitions   CC §1798.97.1
Establishing debt as coerced, action or cross-complaint   CC §1798.97.3
Incurring debt on or after July 1, 2023
    Applicability of provisions   CC §1798.97.5
Notice to claimant of coerced debt   CC §1798.97.2
Secured debt
    Inapplicability of provisions   CC §1798.97.4
Severability of provisions   CC §1798.97.6

COERCION
Mitigating circumstances   CRC 4.423
Privileged matter disclosed   Ev §919
Real estate appraisal
    Improper influence of appraisal   CC §1090.5
Transfer on death deeds
    Fraud, undue influence, etc, creation of deed
        Applicability of other provisions penalizing conduct   Pro §5698

COHABITATION
Battered cohabitant, sentencing   CRC 4.423
Domestic partners
    Confidential domestic partnership
        Establishment of process to enter   Fam §298.7
Domestic violence protective orders   Fam §§2045 to 2049, 7710 to 7730
    Denial of petition for ex parte order, reasons to be provided   Fam §6320.5
Fraudulent promise, action for damages for   CC §43.4
Presumption concerning child of marriage   Fam §§7540, 7541, 7611
Spousal support affected by supported spouse cohabiting with opposite sex   Fam §4323

COLLABORATIVE JUSTICE COURTS
Judicial council advisory committee   CRC 10.56

COLLABORATIVE LAW PROCESS
Family law matters   Fam §2013

COLLATERAL ATTACK
Letters of administration, limitation on attack on orders granting   Pro §8007

COLLATERAL ESTOPPEL
Citation of unpublished opinions   CRC 8.1115
Economic litigation provision   CCP §99

COLLATERAL KINDRED
Claims of   Pro §§6402, 6402.5

COLLATERAL SOURCE RULE   CC §3333.1

COLLECTIBLES
Autographed memorabilia   CC §1739.7

COLLECTION
Attachment (See **ATTACHMENT**)
Enforcement of judgment (See **ENFORCEMENT OF JUDGMENTS**)

COLLECTION AGENCIES
Generally   CC §§1788 to 1788.32, 2021
Identity theft
    Debt collector's duties upon notice from victim of identity theft   CC §1788.18
Mortgage or deed of trust, notice by agent for collection under promissory note secured by   CC §2924.3
Notice
    Consumer collection notice   CC §§1812.700 to 1812.702
Scope of duties of collection agent   CC §2021

COLLECTION AGENCIES—Cont.
Sexual harassment, civil action for
    Construction or application of provisions in issue, solicitor general notified   CC §51.1

COLLECTION CASE MANAGEMENT   CRC 3.740, 3.741

COLLECTIVE BARGAINING BY PUBLIC EMPLOYEES
PERB decisions, appellate review   CRC 8.728

COLLEGES (See **UNIVERSITIES AND COLLEGES**)

COMMENCEMENT OF ACTIONS
Filing complaint   CCP §411.10
Filing fees   CCP §411.20
    Underpayment   CCP §411.21
Governmental agencies, presentation of claims as prerequisite to commencement of actions against   CCP §313
Health care provider's professional negligence, notice of intention to commence action based on   CCP §364
Objection to jurisdiction   CCP §§418.10, 418.11
Pleadings, generally (See **PLEADINGS**)
Quieting title   CCP §761.010
Service of process (See **PROCESS AND SERVICE OF PROCESS**)
Summons (See **PROCESS AND SERVICE OF PROCESS**)
Survival of actions (See **SURVIVAL OF ACTIONS**)
Time for commencing actions (See **STATUTES OF LIMITATION**)

COMMENT OF COUNSEL (See **ARGUMENT AND COMMENT OF COUNSEL**)

COMMERCIAL AND INDUSTRIAL COMMON INTEREST DEVELOPMENTS   CC §§6500 to 6876
Access to member's separate interest
    Denial prohibited   CC §6654
Antennas
    Protected uses   CC §6708
Applicability of provisions   CC §6582
    Effective date   CC §6505
Articles of incorporation
    Conflicts between different governing documents
        Articles of incorporation and declaration   CC §6600
        Bylaws and articles of incorporation or declaration   CC §6600
        Operating rules and bylaws of articles of incorporation or declaration   CC §6600
    Contents   CC §6622
Assessments   CC §§6800 to 6828
    Assignment of right to collect payments   CC §6826
    Collection   CC §§6820 to 6828
    Debt of owner of separate interest   CC §6808
    Effective date for assessment provisions   CC §6828
    Establishment and imposition   CC §§6800, 6804
    Exemption from execution   CC §6804
    Liens
        Common areas, damage   CC §6824
        Contents   CC §6814
        Enforcement of lien   CC §6820
        Governing documents, no lien for noncompliance   CC §6824
        Noncompliance with procedures for liens   CC §6819
        Pre-lien notice to owner   CC §6812
        Priority   CC §6816
        Release of lien   CC §6818
        Sale to enforce lien   CC §§6820, 6822
    Overnight payments   CC §6810
    Payment and delinquency   CC §§6808 to 6819
    Pre-lien notice to owner   CC §6812
    Receipts for payments   CC §6810
    Regular assessments   CC §6800
    Special assessments   CC §6800
Associations
    Conflicts of interest   CC §6758
    Defined   CC §6528
    Governance   CC §§6750 to 6760
    Incorporation   CC §6750
    Information filed with secretary of state   CC §6760
    Nonprofit mutual benefit corporations
        Exercise by association of powers granted to nonprofit mutual benefit corporations   CC §6752
    Records
        Change in member information   CC §6756
    Unincorporated associations   CC §6750

COMMERCIAL AND INDUSTRIAL COMMON INTEREST DEVELOPMENTS—Cont.
- Board of directors
  - Definition of board   CC §6530
- Bylaws
  - Conflicts between different governing documents
    - Bylaws and articles of incorporation or declaration   CC §6600
    - Operating rules and bylaws of articles of incorporation or declaration   CC §6600
- Charging stations for electric vehicles
  - Protected uses   CC §6713
- Collection of assessments   CC §§6820 to 6828
- Common areas
  - Access to member's separate interest
    - Denial prohibited   CC §6654
  - Damage to common area
    - Actions   CC §6858
    - Comparative fault to reduce measure of damages   CC §6860
    - Lien   CC §6824
  - Defined   CC §6532
  - Egress, right of   CC §6652
  - Exclusive use common areas
    - Defined   CC §6550
  - Forced vacation of separate or common interest
    - Termites or other wood-destroying pests   CC §6720
  - Ingress, right of   CC §6652
  - Insurance covering common areas   CC §6840
  - Lien for work performed on common area   CC §6658
  - Maintenance
    - Responsibility for maintenance   CC §6716
  - Ownership   CC §6650
  - Partition
    - Prohibited   CC §6656
  - Support, right of   CC §6652
- Common interest development
  - Defined   CC §6534
- Condominium plans   CC §§6624 to 6628
  - Amendment   CC §6628
  - Consent to recordation of plan
    - Signatures, required persons   CC §6626
  - Contents   CC §6624
  - Creation of common interest development   CC §6580
  - Defined   CC §6540
  - Liberal construction   CC §6602
  - Physical boundaries prevail over description in deed, plan, etc   CC §6604
  - Revocation   CC §6628
- Condominium projects
  - Defined   CC §6542
- Conflicts of interest   CC §6758
- Construction defects litigation
  - Actions
    - Member meeting prior to filing action   CC §6876
  - Settlement agreements   CC §6874
- Contracts
  - Conflicts of interest   CC §6758
- Covenants
  - Restrictive covenants   CC §6606
- Creation of common interest development   CC §6580
- Declarants
  - Defined   CC §6544
- Declarations   CC §§6614 to 6620
  - Actions to enforce covenants and restrictions   CC §6856
    - Standing of association   CC §6858
  - Amendment
    - Capability of declaration to be amended   CC §6616
    - Process for amendment   CC §6620
  - Conflicts between different governing documents
    - Articles of incorporation and declaration   CC §6600
    - Bylaws and articles of incorporation or declaration   CC §6600
    - Operating rules and bylaws of articles of incorporation or declaration   CC §6600
  - Contents of declaration   CC §6614
  - Creation of common interest development   CC §6580
  - Defined   CC §6546
  - Extension of termination date   CC §6618
  - Liberal construction   CC §6602
  - Restrictive covenants   CC §6606
  - Termination date
    - Extension of termination date   CC §6618
  - Updating statutory references in light of enactment of provisions   CC §6610

COMMERCIAL AND INDUSTRIAL COMMON INTEREST DEVELOPMENTS—Cont.
- Deeds
  - Liberal construction   CC §6602
  - Physical boundaries prevail over description in deed, plan, etc   CC §6604
- Definitions   CC §§6526 to 6566
  - Display of flag of the United States   CC §6702
  - Operating rule   CC §6630
  - Statutory construction governed by definitions   CC §6526
- Delivery of documents to association   CC §6512
  - Electronic delivery in writing   CC §6520
  - Electronic means   CC §6518
  - Individual delivery   CC §6514
  - Individual notice   CC §6514
  - Mail delivery   CC §6518
- Developers
  - Deletion from governing documents of provisions relevant to developer   CC §6608
- Directors
  - Board of directors
    - Definition of board   CC §6530
  - Defined   CC §6548
- Disabled access
  - Modification of separate interests   CC §6714
- Documents
  - Applicability of provisions
    - Effective date   CC §6505
  - Delivery to association   CC §6512
    - Electronic delivery in writing   CC §6520
    - Electronic means   CC §6518
    - Individual delivery   CC §6514
    - Individual notice   CC §6514
    - Mail delivery   CC §6518
- Egress
  - Right of ingress, egress and support   CC §6652
- Electric vehicle charging stations
  - Protected uses   CC §6713
- Exclusive use common areas
  - Defined   CC §6550
  - Sale or other transfer   CC §6668
- Flags
  - United States flag displays
    - Protected uses   CC §6702
- Forced vacation of separate or common interest
  - Termites or other wood-destroying pests   CC §6720
- Governance of associations   CC §§6750 to 6760
- Governing documents   CC §§6600 to CC§6632
  - Articles of incorporation
    - Contents   CC §6622
  - Condominium plans generally   CC §§6624 to 6628
  - Conflicts between different governing documents   CC §6600
  - Conflicts between laws and documents   CC §6600
  - Declarations generally   CC §§6614 to 6620
  - Defined   CC §6552
  - Developers
    - Deletion of provisions relevant to developer   CC §6608
  - Liberal construction   CC §6602
  - Noncompliance
    - Lien for noncompliance, restrictions   CC §6824
    - Monetary penalty   CC §§6850, 6854
  - Operating rules   CC §§6630, 6632
  - Physical boundaries prevail over description in deed, plan, etc   CC §6604
  - Restrictive covenants   CC §6606
  - Updating statutory references in light of enactment of provisions   CC §6610
- Individual notice
  - Defined   CC §6553
- Ingress
  - Right of ingress, egress and support   CC §6652
- Insurance
  - Common areas, coverage   CC §6840
- Liens
  - Assessments
    - Common areas, damage   CC §6824
    - Contents   CC §6814
    - Enforcement of lien   CC §6820
    - Governing documents, no lien for noncompliance   CC §6824
    - Noncompliance with procedures for liens   CC §6819
    - Pre-lien notice to owner   CC §6812
    - Priority   CC §6816
    - Release of lien   CC §6818

COMMERCIAL AND INDUSTRIAL COMMON INTEREST DEVELOPMENTS—Cont.
Liens—Cont.
   Assessments —Cont.
      Sale to enforce lien   CC §§6820, 6822
   Claim of lien served on association   CC §8119
      Notice by association to owners   CC §6660
   Scope   CC §6658
Maintenance   CC §§6716 to 6722
   Responsibility for maintenance   CC §6716
   Telephone wiring   CC §6722
   Termites or other wood-destroying pests
      Forced vacation of separate or common interest   CC §6720
      Responsibility for maintenance   CC §6718
Majority of quorum
   Approval by majority of quorum   CC §6524
Majority vote   CC §6522
Maps
   Creation of common interest development   CC §6580
Marketing of individual interest
   Protected uses   CC §6710
Mechanics' liens
   Claim of lien served on association   CC §8119
      Notice by association to owners   CC §6660
Members
   Defined   CC §6554
   Majority vote   CC §6522
   Records
      Change in member information   CC §6756
Modification of separate interests   CC §6714
Operating rules
   Conditions for validity and enforceability   CC §6632
   Conflicts between different governing documents
      Operating rules and bylaws of articles of incorporation or declaration   CC §6600
   Defined   CC §6630
Ownership rights and interests   CC §§6650 to 6654
Partition
   Common areas
      Prohibition on partition   CC §6656
   Entire project   CC §6656
Persons
   Defined   CC §6560
Pets
   Protected uses   CC §6706
Planned developments
   Defined   CC §6562
   Sale or other transfer   CC §6664
Protected uses   CC §§6700 to 6713
   Antennas   CC §6708
   Electric vehicle charging stations   CC §6713
   Marketing of individual interest   CC §6710
   Pets   CC §6706
   Separate interests
      Restrictions on regulation of separate interest   CC §6700
   Signs
      Noncommercial signage display   CC §6704
   United States flag displays   CC §6702
   Water-efficient landscaping   CC §6712
Quorum
   Majority of quorum, approval by   CC §6524
Records
   Change in member information   CC §6756
Restrictive covenants   CC §6606
Sale or other transfer
   Marketing of individual interest
      Protected uses   CC §6710
   Separate interests   CC §6662
      Exclusive use common areas   CC §6668
      Planned development sale   CC §6664
      Stock cooperatives   CC §6666
   Severability of component interests
      Restrictions   CC §6670
Satellite dishes
   Protected uses   CC §6708
Separate interests
   Damage to separate interest
      Actions   CC §6858
      Comparative fault to reduce measure of damages   CC §6860
   Defined   CC §6564

COMMERCIAL AND INDUSTRIAL COMMON INTEREST DEVELOPMENTS—Cont.
Separate interests—Cont.
   Forced vacation of separate or common interest
      Termites or other wood-destroying pests   CC §6720
   Maintenance
      Responsibility for maintenance   CC §6716
   Modification   CC §6714
   Restrictions on regulation of separate interest   CC §6700
   Sale or other transfer   CC §6662
      Exclusive use common areas   CC §6668
      Planned development sale   CC §6664
      Stock cooperatives   CC §6666
Short title of provisions   CC §6500
Signs
   Noncommercial signage display   CC §6704
Small claims courts
   Appearance by association managing development   CCP §116.540
Special assessments   CC §6800
Statutory construction
   Hierarchy headings in code not considered law   CC §6502
Stock cooperatives
   Defined   CC §6566
   Sale or other transfer   CC §6666
Support
   Right of ingress, egress and support   CC §6652
Telephone wiring
   Maintenance   CC §6722
Termites or other wood-destroying pests
   Forced vacation of separate or common interest   CC §6720
   Responsibility for maintenance   CC §6718
United States flag displays
   Protected uses   CC §6702
Water-efficient landscaping
   Protected uses   CC §6712
Zoning
   Like structures, lots, etc, to be treated alike
      Local zoning requirements   CC §6510

COMMERCIAL CREDIT REPORTING (See **CREDIT REPORTING**)

COMMERCIAL FISHING
Fines and penalties
   Bail schedule   CRC 4.102

COMMERCIAL REAL PROPERTY LEASES (See **LEASES**)

COMMINGLING
Sales contracts   CC §1497

COMMISSION (See **COMPENSATION; FEES; SALARIES AND WAGES**)

COMMISSIONERS
Acknowledgment of instruments   CC §§1182, 1183
Bond executed by   CCP §571
Court commissioners (See **COURT COMMISSIONERS**)
Innkeeper's liens, writ of possession on   CC §1861.28
Jury commissioner (See **JURY COMMISSIONER**)
Public utilities (See **PUBLIC UTILITIES COMMISSION**)
Service of process on   CCP §416.50

COMMISSION MERCHANTS (See **FACTORS AND COMMISSION MERCHANTS**)

COMMISSION ON JUDICIAL PERFORMANCE (See **JUDGES**)

COMMITTEES
Judicial council
   Advisory bodies, working groups and task forces   CRC 10.30 to 10.70 (See **JUDICIAL COUNCIL**)
Medical review committees not subject to discovery proceedings   Ev §§1157, 1157.5
Peer review committees (See **PEER REVIEW COMMITTEES**)
Professional committee's proceeding against staff member, action for damages from   CC §§43.7, 43.8
State Bar Court judges, Applicant Evaluation and Nomination Committee   CRC 9.11

COMMON ACCIDENT CAUSING DEATH (See **SIMULTANEOUS DEATH**)

COMMON AREAS
Common interest developments
  Commercial and industrial common interest developments generally   CC §§6500 to 6876 (See **COMMERCIAL AND INDUSTRIAL COMMON INTEREST DEVELOPMENTS**)
  Generally   CC §§4000 to 6150 (See **COMMON INTEREST DEVELOPMENTS**)
Condominiums
  Partition, transfer restrictions   CC §4610
Mobilehome parks   CC §798.24

COMMON CARRIERS
Aircraft (See **AIRCRAFT AND AVIATION**)
Apportionment of freightage   CC §§2140, 2141
Baggage, liens for fares   CC §2191
Bill of lading (See **BILL OF LADING**)
Blind and handicapped persons
  Equal access rights
    Construction or application of provisions in issue, solicitor general notified   CC §55.2
  Guide dog admittance of
    Construction or application of provisions in issue, solicitor general notified   CC §55.2
Blind persons having equal rights for use of   CC §§54.1, 54.3, 54.4, 55
Buses (See **BUSES**)
Carrier of passengers act   CC §§2213 to 2218
  Applicability   CC §§2215, 2217
  Civil actions and penalties   CC §2216
  Definitions   CC §2214
  Severability   CC §2218
Charges for shipping   CC §§2110, 2136 to 2144
Consignment
  Definitions   CC §2110
  Factors, consigning property to   CC §2027
Contract of carriage defined   CC §2085
Damages for breach of contract by   CC §§3315 to 3317
Defined   CC §2168
Delay in transportation
  Standard of care for   CC §2196
  Storage or rental equipment charges from delay caused by consignor or consignee, liability for   CC §§2197, 2197.5
Delivery of goods   CC §§2118 to 2121
Disabled persons having equal rights for use of   CC §§54.1, 54.3, 54.4, 55
  Construction or application of provisions in issue, solicitor general notified   CC §55.2
Discrimination
  Law enforcement officer, firefighter or search and rescue dog handlers serving outside jurisdiction
    Lodging, eating or transportation, prohibition on discrimination   CC §54.25
Easement rights for stopping   CC §801
Elevators (See **ELEVATORS**)
Fitness of vehicle, requirements for   CC §2101
Freightage
  Generally   CC §§2110, 2136 to 2144
  Lien on   CC §§2144, 3051.5, 3051.6
Gratuitous carriers, duties of   CC §§2090, 2096
Guide dogs permitted on   CC §§54.2, 54.3
  Construction or application of provisions in issue, solicitor general notified   CC §55.2
Higher value declaration   CC §§2177, 2200, 2205
Hospital liens, exclusion from   CC §3045.6
Inland carriers   CC §§2086, 2087
Liens
  Baggage of passenger, lien on   CC §2191
  Freight, lien on   CC §§2144, 3051.5, 3051.6
Marine carriers   CC §§2086 to 2088
Motor carriers (See **MOTOR CARRIERS**)
Negligence
  Freight transported   CC §§2194, 2195
  Gratuitous carriers   CC §§2090, 2096
  Limiting liability   CC §§2174 to 2178
  Payment for carriage, effect of   CC §§2100 to 2102
  Property transported   CC §2114
Notices
  Arrival of goods   CC §2120
  Storage of goods after delivery refused   CC §2121
  Valuables, requirements for notice of   CC §§2177, 2200
Overcrowding prohibited   CC §§2102, 2184, 2185
Passengers
  Bicycles transported by   CC §2181

COMMON CARRIERS—Cont.
Passengers—Cont.
  Blind and visually impaired persons
    Touch screen devices for self-service check-in at hotels or passenger transportation facilities   CC §54.9
  Courtesy, requirements for   CC §2103
  Delay in transporting   CC §2104
  Fare, payment of   CC §§2173, 2187 to 2191
  Free carriage of baggage for   CC §§2180, 2181
  Overcrowding prohibited   CC §§2102, 2184, 2185
  Payment of fare by   CC §§2173, 2187 to 2191
  Rules of conduct, obedience to   CC §2186
  Seats required   CC §2185
Perishables, sale of   CC §2204
Preferential treatment   CC §§2170, 2171
Priority in transportation by   CC §§2170, 2171
Railroads (See **RAILROADS**)
Service rendered in carriage of freight   CC §2203
Shipping instructions, compliance with   CC §2115
Space flight liability and immunity   CC §§2210 to 2212
  Definitions   CC §2210
  Entity liability   CC §2212
  Warning and acknowledgment statements   CC §2211
Speed of vehicle, requirements for   CC §2104
Standard of care required
  Negligence generally (See within this heading, **"Negligence"**)
Storage or rental equipment charges from delay caused by consignor or consignee, liability for   CC §§2197, 2197.5
Street railways (See **STREET RAILWAYS**)
Telephones and telegraphs (See **TELEPHONES AND TELEGRAPHS**)
Time schedule requirements   CC §§2170, 2172
Treatment of passengers   CC §2103
Unclaimed property, sale of   CC §§2081 to 2081.4
Valuable goods, liability for loss of   CC §§2177, 2200
Vessels (See **VESSELS**)
Weight certification, carrier's lien for fines resulting from owner's false   CC §§2144, 3051.6

COMMON INTEREST DEVELOPMENTS   CC §§4000 to 6150
Accessory dwelling units
  Construction or use on single-family residential lot
    Restrictions prohibited   CC §4751
Access to separate interest
  Barring access to separate interest   CC §4510
Accounts and accounting
  Budgets (See within this heading, **"Budget of association"**)
  Finances
    Large transfers, board approval   CC §5502
    Monthly review by board   CC §5500
    Review by board   CC §§5500 to 5502
    Satisfaction of review requirements   CC §5501
  Financial documents
    Availability of financial statement, notice   CC §5320
    Budgets (See within this heading, **"Budget of association"**)
    Review of financial statement   CC §5305
  Managing agent, disposition of association funds by   CC §5380
Actions   CC §§5975 to 5986
  Alternative dispute resolution   CC §§5925 to 5965
  Comparative fault reducing damage recovery   CC §5985
  Covenants and restrictions, enforcement   CC §5975
  Declarants, developers or builders, legal proceedings against
    Governing documents not to restrict   CC §5986
    Limitations of actions not extended   CC §5986
  Notice to owners   CC §6150
  Standing of association   CC §5980
Agent for receipt of payments
  Record notice of agent   CC §4210
Agents, managing   CC §§5375 to 5385
Agriculture
  Personal agriculture by homeowner
    Unreasonable restrictions in governing documents, void   CC §4750
Airport influence areas
  Disclosure requirements
    Special disclosures in declaration   CC §4255
Alternative dispute resolution   CC §§5925 to 5965
  Assessment liens
    Pre-lien dispute resolution   CC §5670
  Definitions   CC §5925
  Developer, action against   CC §6000
  Dispute resolution for disputes between association and member generally   CC §§5900 to 5920

COMMON INTEREST DEVELOPMENTS—Cont.
Alternative dispute resolution —Cont.
    Enforcement action
        Certificates required at commencement   CC §5950
        Costs and fees, effect of refusal to engage in dispute resolution   CC §5960
        Defined   CC §5925
        Filing preceded by attempt at dispute resolution   CC §5930
        Reference to dispute resolution after filing   CC §5955
    Evidence code applicability   CC §5940
    Filing enforcement action preceded by attempt at dispute resolution   CC §5930
    Foreclosure   CC §5705
    Reference to dispute resolution after filing of enforcement action   CC §5955
    Request for resolution
        Contents   CC §5935
        Service   CC §5935
    Summary to members of provisions   CC §5965
        Dispute resolution for disputes between association and member, content of summary   CC §5920
    Time to complete dispute resolution   CC §5940
    Tolling statute of limitations   CC §5945
Amendment of declaration
    Authorized   CC §4260
    Extension of term of declaration   CC §4265
    Judicial authorization of amendment   CC §4275
    Procedure for amendment   CC §4270
American flag display
    Restrictions on limitations, prohibitions   CC §4705
Annual policy statement   CC §5310
    Alternative dispute resolution
        Summary to members of provisions   CC §§5920, 5965
    Availability, notice   CC §5320
    Collection of assessment
        Statement of collection procedure included in policy statement   CC §5730
    Defined   CC §4078
Annual reports   CC §§5300 to 5320
    Annual policy statement   CC §5310
        Availability, notice   CC §5320
    Budget
        Annual budget report   CC §5300
        Availability, notice   CC §5320
    Financial statement
        Review   CC §5305
Applicability of provisions
    Prospective application   CC §4010
Arbitration (See within this heading, **"Alternative dispute resolution"**)
Architectural review and decisionmaking
    Improvements to separate interests
        Standards when review required   CC §4765
Articles of incorporation, requirements for   CC §4280
    Bylaws
        Consistency with articles and declaration   CC §4205
        Consistency with declaration   CC §4205
        Governing documents defined to include declarations, bylaws, etc   CC §4150
    Operating rules
        Consistency with declaration, articles and bylaws   CC §4205
Artificial turf
    Architectural guidelines not to prohibit   CC §4735
Assembly by and communication among owners, guests, residents, etc
    Permitted activities   CC §4515
Assessments   CC §§5600 to 5740
    Alternative dispute resolution for assessment disputes
        Operating rules changes, types of rules to which provisions applicable   CC §4355
    Approvals   CC §5605
        Emergency exception to requirements   CC §5610
    Assignment or pledge of right to collect   CC §5735
    Collection process   CC §§5700 to 5740
        Applicability of provisions   CC §5740
        Assignment or pledge of right to collect   CC §5735
        Common area damage, limitation on foreclosure for penalties or damages   CC §5725
        Foreclosure, decisionmaking   CC §5705
        Limitation on foreclosure   CC §5720
        Manner of enforcing lien   CC §5700
        Redemption after trustee sale   CC §5715
        Sale under foreclosure   CC §5710

COMMON INTEREST DEVELOPMENTS—Cont.
Assessments —Cont.
    Collection process —Cont.
        Statement of collection procedure   CC §5730
    Debt of owner   CC §5650
    Deed-restricted affordable housing units   CC §5605
    Delinquent assessments
        Costs recovery   CC §5650
        Notice of delinquent assessment   CC §§5675, 5690
        Operating rules changes, types of rules to which provisions applicable   CC §4355
        Redemption, right of   CCP §729.035
        Time after assessment due before delinquency occurs   CC §5650
    Emergency exception to approval requirements   CC §5610
    Establishment and imposition   CC §§5600 to 5625
    Exemption from execution   CC §5620
    Foreclosure
        Common area damage, limitation on foreclosure for penalties or damages   CC §5725
        Dispute resolution   CC §5705
        Limitation on foreclosure   CC §5720
        Notice of foreclosure   CC §5705
        Redemption after trustee sale   CC §5715
        Sale under foreclosure   CC §5710
    Increases
        Approvals   CC §5605
        Notice   CC §5615
    Levy
        Association's duty and power   CC §5600
    Liens
        Manner of enforcing lien   CC §5700
        Pre-lien dispute resolution   CC §5670
        Pre-lien notice   CC §5660
        Priority of lien   CC §5680
        Recordation, decisionmaking   CC §5673
        Redemption, right of   CCP §729.035
    Limits on assessment   CC §5605
    Notice of assessments and foreclosure
        Delinquent assessments   CC §§5675, 5690
        Foreclosure notice   CC §5705
    Payment and delinquency   CC §§5650 to 5690
        Application of payments   CC §5655
        Decision to record lien considered board decision   CC §5673
        Method of payment   CC §5655
        Notice of delinquent assessment   CC §§5675, 5690
        Plan for payment   CC §5665
        Pre-lien dispute resolution   CC §5670
        Pre-lien notice   CC §5660
        Priority of lien   CC §5680
        Procedural noncompliance, effect   CC §5690
        Protest, payment under   CC §5658
        Release of lien   CC §5685
    Plan for payment   CC §5665
    Property tax value as basis   CC §5625
    Prospective purchaser, disclosure to   CC §4525
        Form for billing disclosures   CC §4528
    Protest, payment under   CC §5658
    Release of lien   CC §5685
    Separate interests within development
        Levy of assessments, when permitted   CC §5625
    Statement of collection procedure
        Annual policy statement, collection procedure included   CC §5730
Assignments
    Collection of assessments
        Assignment or pledge of right to collect   CC §5735
Association   CC §§4800 to 4820
    Accounts and accounting (See within this heading, **"Accounts and accounting"**)
    Action for damages (See within this heading, **"Damages, action for"**)
    Assessments generally (See within this heading, **"Assessments"**)
    Canvassing and petitioning members, board and residents
        Permitted activities   CC §4515
    Community associations
        References to association as owner's association or community association   CC §4800
    Defined   CC §4080
    Delivery of documents to association
        General rule   CC §4035
    Identification of common interest developments
        Information submitted to secretary of state   CC §5405

COMMON INTEREST DEVELOPMENTS—Cont.
  Association —Cont.
    Joint neighborhood associations
      Members of participating associations, powers CC §4820
    Notice to association
      Annual notice to association of contact information and information about status of unit CC §4041
      Preferred method for receiving notice from association CC §4041
    Owner's association
      References to association as owner's association or community association CC §4800
    Powers CC §4805
    Protected uses of separate interests
      Restrictions on association regulation of separate interest use CC §§4700 to 4753
    Transfer disclosure
      Information provided by association CC §4530
  Banners
    Noncommercial signs, posters, flags or banners
      Restrictions on limitations, prohibitions CC §4710
  Blanket encumbrance, notice to purchaser or lessee of CC §1133
  Board meetings CC §§4900 to 4955
    Actions for declaratory or equitable relief to enforce provisions CC §4955
    Agenda
      Content of meeting CC §4930
    Attendance and participation CC §4925
    Canvassing and petitioning members, board and residents
      Permitted activities CC §4515
    Conduct of meetings CC §4930
    Defined CC §4090
    Electronic transmissions
      Restrictions CC §4910
    Emergencies or disasters
      Teleconference for meetings where in person is unsafe or impossible due disaster or emergency CC §5450
    Emergency meetings
      Calling, procedure CC §4923
      Electronic transmissions to conduct emergency meeting CC §4910
      Grounds CC §4923
      Notice CC §4920
    Executive session
      Grounds CC §4935
      Notice CC §4920
    Extra-meeting actions
      Prohibited CC §4910
    Minutes
      Distribution and approval CC §4950
      Executive session, notation in minutes CC §4935
    Notice CC §4920
    Open meetings
      Attendance and participation CC §4925
      Short title CC §4900
    Remote meeting by teleconference CC §4926
  Board of directors
    Bonds, surety
      Association to maintain bond or insurance coverage for directors, officers and employees CC §5806
    Conflicts of interest
      Interested directors CC §5350
    Contracts or transactions authorized, ratified, etc, by board
      Conflicts of interest CC §5350
    Definition of board CC §4085
    Definition of directors CC §4140
    Finances
      Large transfers, board approval CC §5502
      Monthly review by board CC §5500
      Review by board CC §§5500 to 5502
      Satisfaction of review requirements CC §5501
    Foreclosure
      Decision to initiate foreclosure as board decision CC §5705
    Liens
      Decision to record lien as board decision CC §§5673, 5690
    Operating rules
      Change of rules, approval by board CC §4360
    Training course for directors CC §5400
    Volunteer directors and officers, tort liability CC §5800
  Boundaries of units CC §4220
  Budget of association
    Annual budget report CC §5300
      Availability, notice CC §5320
      Defined CC §4076

COMMON INTEREST DEVELOPMENTS—Cont.
  Builders
    Actions or legal proceedings against declarants, developers or builders CC §5986
  Building construction
    Prefiling requirements in actions against builders and developers CC §§6000, 6150
    Settlement agreement with builder, disclosure to association members concerning CC §6100
    Volunteer officer's or director's protection from personal liability, decisions concerning actions against contractors as within scope of CC §5800
  Bylaws
    Assembly by and communication among owners, guests, residents, etc, permitted activities
      Restriction of rights not permitted in governing documents CC §4515
    Consistency with articles and declaration CC §4205
    Governing documents defined to include declarations, bylaws, etc CC §4150
    Operating rules
      Consistency with declaration, articles and bylaws CC §4205
  Citation of Act CC §4000
  Clotheslines
    Governing documents not to prohibit clotheslines or drying racks in owner's backyard CC §4753
  Collection of assessments CC §§5700 to 5740
  Commercial and industrial developments
    Generally CC §§6500 to 6876 (See **COMMERCIAL AND INDUSTRIAL COMMON INTEREST DEVELOPMENTS**)
    Inapplicability of residential provisions CC §4202
  Common areas
    Access to separate interest by means of
      Barring access to separate interest CC §4510
    Assembly by and communication among owners, guests, residents, etc
      Permitted activities CC §4515
    Condominium projects
      Partition, transfer restrictions CC §4610
    Damage to common area
      Limitation on foreclosure for penalties or damages CC §5725
    Defects in, settlement between association and builder CC §6100
    Defined CC §4095
    Easements appurtenant to CC §4505
    Exclusive use, granting
      Action for violation of provisions CC §4605
      Definition of exclusive use common areas CC §4145
      Procedure CC §4600
      Transfer of separate interests CC §4645
    Maintenance and repair of CC §4775
      Communications wiring CC §4790
      Termite work CC §§4780, 4785
    Member elections
      Meeting space access CC §5105
    Operating rules changes
      Types of rules to which provisions applicable CC §4355
    Ownership of
      Tenants in common CC §4500
    Partition
      Condominiums, transfer restrictions CC §4610
    Pest control
      Notice of pesticide application when not applied by licensed pest control operator CC §4777
    Requirements CC §4201
    Solar energy systems, restrictions on CC §714.1
      Provisions outside of common interest development law limiting association's regulation of member's separate interest CC §4700
    Tenancy in common CC §4500
  Community apartment projects
    Common interest development defined to include CC §4100
    Defined CC §4105
    Transfer of separate interest CC §4625
  Community associations
    Associations generally CC §§4800 to 4820
    References to association as owner's association or community association CC §4800
  Community service organizations
    Definition of community service organization or similar entities CC §4110
    Fees collected with transfer of title CC §4525
    Reserve funds
      Planning, community service organization report CC §5580
  Conciliation (See within this heading, "**Alternative dispute resolution**")

COMMON INTEREST DEVELOPMENTS—Cont.
Condominiums
    Blanket encumbrance, notice to purchaser or lessee of   CC §1133
    Boundaries   CC §§783, 4220
    Common areas, partition action involving   CC §4610
    Common interest development defined to include condominium project   CC §4100
    Defects, disclosure of   CC §1134
    Definitions   CC §783
    Disclosure of defects by developer   CC §1134
    Earthquake insurance, loans requiring   CC §2955.1
    Estate interest in   CC §783
    Floating homes and floating home marinas (See **FLOATING HOMES**)
    Mobilehome condominiums (See **MOBILEHOMES**)
    Partition actions, restrictions on
        Transfer restrictions   CC §4610
    Plans   CC §§4285 to 4295
        Amendment   CC §4295
        Contents   CC §4285
        Definition of condominium plan   CC §4120
        Liberal construction   CC §4215
        Recording   CC §4290
        Revocation   CC §4295
    Projects
        Definition of condominium project   CC §4125
        Transfer of separate interest   CC §4630
    Recording condominium plan
        Applicability of provisions   CC §4200
    Stock cooperative defined   CC §783.1
    Transfer of separate interest   CC §4630
Conflicts of interest   CC §5350
    Disclosure requirements
        Managing agent's disclosures to board before entering into management agreement   CC §5375.5
Construction and interpretation
    Governing documents, deeds, condominium plans, etc
        Liberal construction   CC §4215
    Headings of sections and hierarchical elements
        Effect   CC §4005
    Local zoning ordinances   CC §4020
    Prospective application of provisions   CC §4010
Construction defects, actions for
    Prelitigation procedures
        Nonduplication of prelitigation procedures   CC §935
Construction of development (See within this heading, **"Building construction"**)
Contractors
    Building construction generally (See within this heading, **"Building construction"**)
Contracts
    Board of directors
        Contracts or transactions authorized, ratified, etc, by board   CC §5350
Conveyances
    Transfer of interests generally (See within this heading, **"Transfer of interests"**)
Covenants and restrictions   CC §5975
    Housing development projects using authorized floor area ratio standards
        Unenforceable   CC §4747
    Restrictive covenants   CC §§782, 782.5
        Deletion of unlawful restrictive covenants   CC §4225
        Provisions outside of common interest development law limiting association's regulation of member's separate interest   CC §4700
Creation of common interest development
    Applicability of provisions   CC §4200
Damages, action for
    Alternative dispute resolution   CC §§5925 to 5965
    Comparative fault reducing damage recovery   CC §5985
    Liquidated damages provisions, residential property   CC §1675
    Owner, limitation of liability   CC §5805
    Standing of association   CC §5980
    Volunteer officers and directors, limitation on liability of   CC §5800
Declarants
    Actions or legal proceedings against declarants, developers or builders   CC §5986
    Defined   CC §4130
    Governing documents
        Deletion of declarant provisions from documents   CC §4230
Declarations   CC §§4250 to 4275
    Amendment   CC §4260
        Extension of term of declaration   CC §4265
        Judicial authorization of amendment   CC §4275
        Procedure for amendment   CC §4270

COMMON INTEREST DEVELOPMENTS—Cont.
Declarations —Cont.
    Articles of incorporation
        Consistency with declaration   CC §4205
    Bylaws
        Consistency with articles and declaration   CC §4205
    Contents of
        Required contents   CC §4250
    Covenants and restrictions in   CC §5975
        Unlawful restrictive covenants, deletion   CC §4225
    Defined   CC §4135
    Disclosures   CC §4255
    Extension of term
        Amendment of declaration   CC §4265
    Governing documents defined to include declarations, bylaws, etc   CC §4150
    Liberal construction   CC §4215
    Operating rules
        Consistency with declaration, articles and bylaws   CC §4205
    Recording
        Applicability of provisions   CC §4200
Deeds
    Liberal construction   CC §4215
Deeds of trust and mortgages
    Power of sale
        Transfer of property in CID, recording   CC §2924.1
Defects in design or construction
    Damages generally (See within this heading, **"Damages, action for"**)
Defects in design or construction, action against builder   CC §§6000 to 6150
Definitions   CC §§4075 to 4190
    Applicability of definitions   CC §4075
    Association records
        Record inspection   CC §5200
    Change of rules   CC §4340
    Common interest development defined   CC §4100
    Enhanced association records
        Record inspection   CC §5200
    Identity theft
        Record inspection, withholding or redacting information from records   CC §5215
    Member elections, proxies   CC §5130
    Operating rules   CC §4340
Delinquent assessments
    Operating rules, changes
        Types of rules to which provisions applicable   CC §4355
    Payment of assessments, delinquency
        Generally   CC §§5650 to 5690
    Redemption, right of   CCP §729.035
Delivery of documents or notice
    Associations   CC §4035
    Electronic delivery
        Written information requirement satisfied by electronic delivery   CC §4055
    General delivery or notice
        Methods of delivery   CC §4045
    Individuals   CC §4040
    Proof of delivery   CC §4050
    Time of delivery   CC §4050
Developers
    Actions or legal proceedings against declarants, developers or builders   CC §5986
    Governing documents
        Updating by deleting provisions benefiting developer after development complete   CC §4230
Directors
    Board meetings   CC §§4900 to 4955 (See within this heading, **"Board meetings"**)
    Board of directors (See within this heading, **"Board of directors"**)
    Defined   CC §4140
    Liabilities
        Limitation of volunteer liability   CC §5800
    Training course for directors   CC §5400
Disabilities, persons with
    Discrimination by refusing to permit modification of premises
        Provisions outside of common interest development law limiting association's regulation of member's separate interest   CC §4700
Disciplinary actions against member   CC §5850
    Effect of provisions on board authority to impose penalties   CC §5865
    Hearings   CC §5855
    Operating rules, changes
        Types of rules to which provisions applicable   CC §4355

COMMON INTEREST DEVELOPMENTS—Cont.
- Disclosure requirements CC §§4525 to 4545
  - Blanket encumbrance, notice to purchaser or lessee of CC §1133
  - Form for billing disclosures CC §4528
  - List of documents to be provided to prospective purchaser CC §4525
  - Managing agent's disclosures to board before entering into management agreement CC §5375
    - Conflicts of interest CC §5375.5
    - Delivery of disclosures, facilitation CC §5376
  - Newly converted condominium, defects statement prior to sale of first unit in CC §1134
  - Reserve funds
    - Assessment and reserve funding disclosure CC §5570
  - Settlement agreement with builder, disclosure to association members concerning CC §6100
  - Special disclosures in declaration CC §4255
  - Transfer disclosures
    - Billing disclosures CC §§4528, 4530
    - Enforcement of disclosure requirements CC §4540
    - Information provided by association CC §4530
    - List of documents to be provided to prospective purchaser CC §4525
    - Separate interests CC §4535
    - Title not affected by transfers in violation of provisions CC §4545
- Discriminatory restrictive covenants
  - Unlawful restrictive covenants, deletion CC §4225
- Dispute resolution
  - Alternative dispute resolution generally CC §§5925 to 5965
  - Associations and members, disputes between CC §§5900 to 5920
- Dispute resolution for disputes between association and member CC §§5900 to 5920
  - Action by association when member requests dispute resolution
    - Good faith engagement by association in dispute resolution required to file action CC §5910.1
  - Applicability of provisions CC §5900
  - Meet and confer procedure CC §5915
  - Notice of alternative dispute resolution process CC §5965
  - Procedure
    - Fair, reasonable and expeditious CC §§5905, 5910
    - Standard procedure for association not providing one CC §5915
- Documents and papers
  - Declarations CC §§4250 to 4275 (See within this heading, **"Declarations"**)
  - Delivery methods
    - Associations CC §4035
    - General notice CC §4045
    - Individual notice CC §4040
    - Time and proof of delivery CC §4050
  - Electronic delivery
    - Written information requirement satisfied by electronic delivery CC §4055
  - Financial documents
    - Review of financial documents CC §§5305, 5320
  - Governing documents other than declaration
    - Enforcement CC §5975
  - Operating rules CC §§4340 to 4370
  - Prospective purchaser, documents to be provided to CC §4525
    - Form for billing disclosures CC §4528
  - Record inspection generally CC §§5200 to 5240
- Drought emergency
  - Pressure washing of exterior of separate interest
    - Requirement to pressure wash during drought emergency void CC §4736
- Drying racks
  - Governing documents not to prohibit clotheslines or drying racks in owner's backyard CC §4753
- Earthquake insurance
  - Disclosure requirements for condominium loans requiring CC §2955.1
- Easement for access, right of CC §4505
- Elder housing
  - Deed restrictions, prohibitions CC §§782, 782.5
- Elections procedures
  - Assembly by and communication among owners, guests, residents, etc
    - Permitted activities CC §4515
  - Common areas, granting exclusive use
    - When election required CC §4060
  - Majority approval, all members
    - Requirements CC §4065
  - Majority approval, quorum of members
    - Requirements CC §4070
  - Member elections CC §§5100 to 5145

COMMON INTEREST DEVELOPMENTS—Cont.
- Elections procedures—Cont.
  - Operating rules changes, types of rules to which provisions applicable CC §4355
- Electric vehicle charging stations
  - Architectural guidelines not to prohibit
    - Restrictions on limitations, prohibitions CC §4745
  - Common areas, granting exclusive use
    - Action for declaratory or equitable relief to enforce procedure CC §4605
    - Election, when required CC §4600
  - Time of use (TOU) meters, covenants, restrictions, etc on installation or use, void CC §4745.1
- Equitable servitudes CC §5975
- Exclusive use common areas
  - Defined CC §4145
  - Transfer restrictions CC §4600
    - Action for declaratory or equitable relief to enforce procedure CC §4605
    - Separate interests, transfer CC §4645
- Factory-built structures
  - Provisions outside of common interest development law limiting association's regulation of member's separate interest CC §4700
- Family day care homes, operation
  - Provisions outside of common interest development law limiting association's regulation of member's separate interest CC §4700
- Fees
  - Transfer disclosure
    - Information provided by association CC §4530
  - Transfer of owner's interest
    - Exemption from fee limitations CC §4580
    - Limitations of transfer fees charged by association, etc CC §4575
    - Restrictions on owner's marketing of interest CC §4730
- Finances CC §§5500 to 5580
  - Reserve funds CC §§5510 to 5520
    - Assessment and reserve funding disclosure CC §5570
    - Community service organization report CC §5580
    - Contents of reserve funding plan CC §5560
    - Litigation as use for funds CC §5520
    - Planning CC §§5550 to 5580
    - Summary of association reserves CC §5565
    - Temporary transfer of reserve funds CC §5515
    - Use of reserve funds CC §5510
- Financial documents
  - Budgets (See within this heading, **"Budget of association"**)
  - Review of financial statement
    - Annual reports CC §5305
    - Availability, notice CC §5320
- Flag display
  - Restrictions on limitations, prohibitions
    - Noncommercial signs, posters, flags or banners CC §4710
    - US flag CC §4705
- Floating homes and floating home marinas (See **FLOATING HOMES**)
- Foreclosure
  - Common area damage
    - Limitation on foreclosure for penalties or damages CC §5725
  - Dispute resolution CC §5705
  - Limitation on foreclosure CC §5720
  - Notice of foreclosure CC §5705
  - Sale under foreclosure CC §5710
    - Redemption after trustee sale CC §5715
- Gardens
  - Personal agriculture by homeowner
    - Unreasonable restrictions in governing documents, void CC §4750
- General delivery or notice
  - Definition of general notice CC §4148
  - Methods of delivery CC §4045
- Governance CC §§4800 to 5405
  - Annual reports CC §§5300 to 5320
  - Association CC §§4800 to 4820
  - Board meeting CC §§4900 to 4955
  - Conflicts of interest CC §5350
  - Government assistance CC §§5400 to 5405
  - Managing agents CC §§5375 to 5385
  - Member elections CC §§5100 to 5145
  - Member meetings CC §5000
  - Record inspection CC §§5200 to 5240
  - Recordkeeping CC §5260
- Governing documents
  - Actions
    - Declarants, developers or builders, legal proceedings against not to be restricted by governing documents CC §5986

COMMON INTEREST DEVELOPMENTS—Cont.
Governing documents—Cont.
  Actions by association to enforce
    Emergency declaration, effect   CC §5875
  Agent for receipt of payments
    Record notice of agent   CC §4210
  Articles of incorporation
    Consistency with declaration   CC §4205
    Contents   CC §4280
  Assembly by and communication among owners, guests, residents, etc., permitted activities
    Restriction of rights not permitted in governing documents   CC §4515
  Bylaws
    Consistency with articles and declaration   CC §4205
  Clotheslines
    Governing documents not to prohibit clotheslines or drying racks in owner's backyard   CC §4753
  Compliance with law   CC §4205
  Condominium plans   CC §§4285 to 4295
  Covenants
    Unlawful restrictive covenants, deletion   CC §4225
  Declarant provisions
    Deletion   CC §4230
  Declarations generally   CC §§4250 to 4275
  Defined   CC §4150
  Drying racks
    Governing documents not to prohibit clotheslines or drying racks in owner's backyard   CC §4753
  Leases and rental agreements
    Governing documents not to prohibit   CC §4741
  Liberal construction   CC §4215
  Operating rules   CC §§4340 to 4370
    Consistency wit declaration, articles and bylaws   CC §4205
  Protected uses of separate interests
    Restrictions on association regulation of separate interest use   CC §§4700 to 4753
  Statutory references in documents
    Correction in light of enactment of new provisions   CC §4235
  Violation of governing documents or association rules, monetary penalties for
    Effect of provisions on board authority to impose penalties   CC §5865
    Hearings   CC §5855
    Schedule   CC §5850
Government assistance   CC §§5400 to 5405
  Registry of common interest developments   CC §5405
  Training course for directors   CC §5400
Homeowners' association
  Associations generally   CC §§4800 to 4820 (See within this heading, "**Association**")
Identification
  Information submitted to secretary of state   CC §5405
Improvements and modifications   CC §4760
  Architectural review and decisionmaking, standards when required   CC §4765
Individual delivery of documents   CC §4040
  Definition of individual notice   CC §4153
Industrial and commercial developments
  Commercial and industrial developments generally   CC §§6500 to 6876
  (See **COMMERCIAL AND INDUSTRIAL COMMON INTEREST DEVELOPMENTS**)
  Inapplicability of residential provisions   CC §4202
Ingress, egress, and support   CC §4505
  Access to separate interest denied   CC §4510
Inspection of premises
  Reserve funds, planning
    Exterior elevated elements, visual inspection   CC §5551
    Inspection of premises and components   CC §5550
Inspection of records   CC §§5200 to 5240
Insurance requirements
  Earthquake insurance
    Disclosure requirements for condominium loans requiring   CC §2955.1
  Officers' liabilities
    Association to maintain bond or insurance coverage for directors, officers and employees   CC §5806
  Owner, requirements for limitation on tort action against   CC §5805
  Policy summaries distributed to members   CC §5810
  Volunteer officer or director, liability insurance coverage for   CC §5800

COMMON INTEREST DEVELOPMENTS—Cont.
Internal dispute resolution
  Dispute resolution for disputes between association and member generally   CC §§5900 to 5920
Items of business
  Defined   CC §4155
Joint neighborhood associations
  Members of participating associations, powers   CC §4820
Junior accessory dwelling units
  Construction or use on single-family residential lot
    Restrictions prohibited   CC §4751
Leases and rental agreements
  Governing documents not to prohibit   CC §§4740, 4741
Liability of officers and directors
  Volunteers
    Limitation of volunteer liability   CC §5800
Liability of owners of separate interests
  Limitation of member liability   CC §5805
Liens
  Assessment liens
    Manner of enforcing lien   CC §5700
    Pre-lien dispute resolution   CC §5670
    Pre-lien notice   CC §5660
    Priority of lien   CC §5680
    Recording lien, decisionmaking   CC §§5673, 5690
    Redemption, right of   CCP §729.035
    Release of lien   CC §5685
  Association served with claim of lien   CC §8119
    Notice to members   CC §4620
  Blanket encumbrance, notice to purchaser or lessee of   CC §1133
  Labor performed or materials furnished   CC §4615
Litigation, notice to owners of proposed civil actions by association   CC §6150
Low water-using plants
  Architectural guidelines not to prohibit   CC §4735
Maintenance
  Common areas and separate interests   CC §4775
    Communications wiring access   CC §4790
  Communications wiring access   CC §4790
  Pesticide application, notice when not applied by licensed pest control operator   CC §4777
  Termite work   CC §4780
    Temporary removal of occupants   CC §4785
Management
  Governance generally   CC §§4800 to 5405
  Managing agent   CC §§5375 to 5385
    Association funds, disposition   CC §5380
    Association funds, disposition of   CC §5380
    Defined   CC §4158
    Disclosure requirements for prospective managing agent   CC §§5375 to 5376
  Small claims courts
    Appearance by association managing development   CCP §116.540
Managing agents   CC §§5375 to 5385
  Defined   CC §4158
  Full-time employees of association not included within meaning of managing agent   CC §5385
  Prospective managing agents
    Disclosures   CC §5375
  Trust fund account for association funds   CC §5380
Marketing owner's interest
  Restrictions on
    Restrictions on limitations, prohibitions   CC §4730
Mechanics' liens
  Association served with claim of lien   CC §8119
    Notice to members   CC §4620
  Labor or material furnished to owner   CC §4615
Mediation (See within this heading, "**Alternative dispute resolution**")
Meetings
  Board meetings generally   CC §§4900 to 4955
  Builder, meetings prior to filing action against   CC §§6000, 6150
  Definition of board meetings   CC §4090
  Member meetings   CC §5000
  Operating rules, changes
    Reversal of rule change at special member meeting   CC §4365
Member elections   CC §§5100 to 5145
  Acclamation, election by   CC §5103
  Action for declaratory or equitable relief to enforce   CC §5145
  Applicability of provisions   CC §5100
  Ballots
    Counting   CC §5120
    Retention   CC §5125

COMMON INTEREST DEVELOPMENTS—Cont.
  Member elections —Cont.
    Ballots—Cont.
      Voting procedures   CC §5115
    Campaign-related information
      Association funds, restrictions on use   CC §5135
    Candidates numbering not more than number of vacancies
      Acclamation, election by   CC §5103
    Common areas
      Meeting space access   CC §5105
    Counting ballots   CC §5120
    Directors
      Acclamation, election by   CC §5100
      Requirement of election for seats on board of directors   CC §5100
    Disqualifications from nominations   CC §§5100, 5105
    Inspectors of elections
      Ballots, retention   CC §5125
      Duties   CC §5110
      Independent third parties serving as inspectors   CC §5110
      Selection method   CC §5105
    Media access for candidates or members   CC §5105
    Nominating procedures
      Communication   CC §5105
      Deadline for submission   CC §5115
    Notice of election   CC §5115
    Proxies   CC §5130
    Qualifications of candidates
      Communication   CC §5105
    Quorum required by governing documents   CC §5115
    Results
      Reporting   CC §5120
    Retention of ballots   CC §5125
    Retention of registration list and voter list   CC §§5105, 5125
    Voter envelopes
      Retention   CC §5125
    Voting
      Procedures   CC §5115
      Qualifications, communication   CC §5105
  Member meetings
    Parliamentary procedure   CC §5000
  Members
    Defined   CC §4160
    Dispute resolution for disputes between association and member   CC §§5900 to 5920
    Elections
      Member elections   CC §§5100 to 5145
    Personal information of members
      Sale by association or managing agent without consent   CC §5230
      Transmitting by association or managing agent to third party without consent   CC §5230
    Record inspection, membership lists
      Opting out of sharing information for list   CC §5220
      Request for list   CC §5225
  Mobilehome condominiums (See **MOBILEHOMES**)
  Modification of separate interests   CC §§4760, 4765
  Money management
    Trust fund account for association funds
      Managing agent's duties as to   CC §5380
  Motor vehicles
    Electric vehicle charging stations
      Action for declaratory or equitable relief to enforce procedure for granting exclusive use of common area   CC §4605
      Architectural guidelines not to prohibit   CC §4745
      Common areas, granting exclusive use   CC §4600
      Time of use (TOU) meters, covenants, restrictions, etc on installation or use, void   CC §4745.1
  Negligence actions (See within this heading, **"Damages, action for"**)
  Notice
    Assessments
      Delinquent assessments   CC §§5675, 5690
      Increases   CC §5615
      Pre-lien notice   CC §5660
    Association
      Annual notice to association of contact information and information about status of unit   CC §4041
    Board meetings   CC §4920
      Emergencies or disasters, meetings entirely by teleconference   CC §5450
    Foreclosure
      Notice of foreclosure   CC §5705

COMMON INTEREST DEVELOPMENTS—Cont.
  Notice—Cont.
    General delivery or notice
      Definition of general notice   CC §4148
      Methods of delivery   CC §4045
    Individual notice
      Defined   CC §4153
      Methods of delivery   CC §4040
    Maintenance
      Pesticide application, notice when not applied by licensed pest control operator   CC §4777
    Operating rules
      Change of rules   CC §4360
  Officers' liabilities
    Bonds, surety or insurance
      Association to maintain bond or insurance coverage for directors, officers and employees   CC §5806
    Volunteers
      Limitation of volunteer liability   CC §5800
  Open Meetings Act
    Board meetings generally   CC §§4900 to 4955
    Short title   CC §4900
  Operating rules   CC §§4340 to 4370
    Assembly by and communication among owners, guests, residents, etc, permitted activities
      Restriction of rights not permitted in governing documents   CC §4515
    Authorized
      Conditions for validity and enforceability   CC §4350
    Change of rules
      Approval by board   CC §4360
      Definition of rule change   CC §4340
      Effective date of provisions   CC §4370
      Notice   CC §4360
      Reversal, member meeting   CC §4365
      Types of rules to which provisions applicable   CC §4355
    Conditions for validity and enforceability   CC §4350
    Consistency with declaration, articles and bylaws   CC §4205
    Definitions   CC §4340
    Enacted, amended or repealed in good faith and in compliance with provisions
      Conditions for validity and enforceability   CC §4350
    Legal
      Conditions for validity and enforceability   CC §4350
    Prospective purchaser, documents to be provided to   CC §4525
    Reasonableness
      Conditions for validity and enforceability   CC §4350
    Violation of governing documents or association rules, monetary penalties for
      Effect of provisions on board authority to impose penalties   CC §5865
      Hearings   CC §5855
      Schedule   CC §5850
    Written
      Conditions for validity and enforceability   CC §4350
  Owners' association
    Accounts and accounting (See within this heading, **"Accounts and accounting"**)
    Action for damages (See within this heading, **"Damages, action for"**)
    Assessments generally (See within this heading, **"Assessments"**)
    Associations generally   CC §§4800 to 4820 (See within this heading, **"Association"**)
    References to association as owner's association or community association   CC §4800
  Ownership rights and interests   CC §§4500 to 4515
    Appurtenant rights   CC §4505
    Assembly by and communication with one another and others
      Permitted activities   CC §4515
    Common areas
      Tenants in common   CC §4500
    Easements   CC §4505
    Separate interest property
      Access   CC §4510
    Transfers
      Disclosures   CC §§4525 to 4545
      Fees   CC §§4575, 4580
      Restrictions on transfer   CC §§4600 to 4605
      Separate interests   CC §§4625 to 4650
  Partition actions
    Condominiums
      Transfer restrictions   CC §4610

COMMON INTEREST DEVELOPMENTS—Cont.
Payment of assessments   CC §§5650 to 5690
Penalties
    Operating rules, changes
       Types of rules to which provisions applicable   CC §4355
    Violation of governing documents or association rules, monetary penalties for
       Effect of provisions on board authority to impose penalties   CC §5865
       Hearings   CC §5855
       Schedule   CC §5850
Personal agriculture by homeowner
    Unreasonable restrictions in governing documents, void   CC §4750
Persons
    Defined   CC §4170
Pest control
    Notice of pesticide application when not applied by licensed pest control operator   CC §4777
    Termite work   CC §4780
       Temporary relocation for pest control work   CC §4785
Petitions
    Canvassing and petitioning members, board and residents
       Permitted activities   CC §4515
Pets
    Restrictions on limitations, prohibitions   CC §4715
Physical changes to common areas or separate interests
    Alternative dispute resolution for assessment disputes
       Operating rules changes, types of rules to which provisions applicable   CC §4355
    Reviewing proposed changes
       Architectural review and decisionmaking, standards when required   CC §4765
Planned developments
    Common interest development defined to include planned development   CC §4100
    Defined   CC §4175
    Transfer of separate interest   CC §4635
Plants
    Low water-using plants
       Architectural guidelines not to prohibit   CC §4735
Pledge
    Collection of assessments
       Assignment or pledge of right to collect   CC §5735
Political activities
    Assembly by and communication among owners, guests, residents, etc
       Permitted activities   CC §4515
Posters
    Noncommercial signs, posters, flags or banners
       Restrictions on limitations, prohibitions   CC §4710
Pressure washing of exterior of separate interest
    Drought emergency declared
       Requirement to pressure wash during drought emergency void   CC §4736
Prospective purchaser, provision of documents to   CC §4525
Protected uses of separate interests   CC §§4700 to 4753
    Accessory or junior accessory dwelling units
       Restrictions on construction or use prohibited   CC §4751
    Applicability of provisions   CC §4700
    Electric vehicle charging stations   CC §4745
       Time of use (TOU) meters, covenants, restrictions, etc on installation or use, void   CC §4745.1
    Flag display   CC §4705
    Housing development projects using authorized floor area ratio standards
       Covenants or restrictions unenforceable   CC §4747
    Leasing or rental restrictions   CC §§4740, 4741
    Marketing of property   CC §4730
    Owner of separate interest in common interest development   CC §4739
    Pets   CC §4715
    Provisions outside of common interest development law limiting association's regulation of member's separate interest   CC §4700
    Roofing materials
       Requiring fire-retardant coverings   CC §4720
    Satellite dishes   CC §4725
    Signs
       Noncommercial signs   CC §4710
    Solar energy systems on multifamily common area roofs   CC §4746
    Television antennas   CC §4725
    Water conservation
       Low water-using plants   CC §4735

COMMON INTEREST DEVELOPMENTS—Cont.
Real estate brokers
    Exclusive relationship with broker effecting restriction on owner's marketing of interest
       Restrictions on limitations, prohibitions   CC §4730
Record inspection   CC §§5200 to 5240
    Actions to enforce member rights   CC §5235
    Applicability of provisions   CC §5240
    Association records
       Defined   CC §5200
    Availability
       Parameters   CC §5205
       Time for availability   CC §5210
    Commercial use of records
       Restrictions   CC §5230
    Cost of copying documents   CC §5205
    Definitions   CC §5200
    Electronic availability of documents   CC §5205
    Enhanced association records
       Defined   CC §5200
    Membership lists
       Opting out of sharing information for list   CC §5220
       Request for list   CC §5225
    Redacting information from records
       Grounds   CC §5215
    Safe at home program participants
       Duties of association   CC §5216
    Sale of records
       Use of records, restrictions   CC §5230
    Use of records, restrictions   CC §5230
    Withholding information from records
       Grounds   CC §5215
Recordkeeping   CC §5260
    Requests related to records
       Mailing-related requests   CC §5260
Registry of common interest developments   CC §5405
Regular assessments
    Assessments generally (See within this heading, **"Assessments"**)
Religious items displayed on dwelling entry
    Governing documents not to restrict   CC §4706
    Restrictions unenforceable   CC §1940.45
Repair of premises
    Common areas or separate interests   CC §4775
    Communications wiring access   CC §4790
    Religious items displayed on dwelling entry
       Temporary removal to accommodate repair   CC §4706
    Termite work   CC §4780
       Temporary relocation for pest control work   CC §4785
Reports
    Annual reports   CC §§5300 to 5320
Reserve accounts, statement of
    Definition of reserve accounts   CC §4177
    Requirements
       Definition of reserve account requirements   CC §4178
Reserve funds   CC §§5510 to 5520
    Assessment and reserve funding disclosure   CC §5570
    Litigation
       Use for litigation   CC §5520
    Planning   CC §§5550 to 5580
       Assessment and reserve funding disclosure   CC §5570
       Community service organization report   CC §5580
       Contents of reserve funding plan   CC §5560
       Exterior elevated elements, visual inspection   CC §5551
       Inspection of premises and components   CC §5550
       Study of reserve needs   CC §5550
       Summary of association reserves   CC §5565
    Temporary transfer of reserve funds   CC §5515
    Use of reserve funds   CC §5510
Roofs
    Fire retardant roof coverings
       Restrictions on limitations, prohibitions   CC §4720
Rules
    Operating rules   CC §§4340 to 4370
Sale of interest
    Restrictions on owner's marketing of interest   CC §4730
San Francisco Bay conservation and development commission jurisdiction
    Disclosure requirements
       Special disclosures in declaration   CC §4255
Satellite dish restrictions
    Restrictions on limitations, prohibitions   CC §4725
Senior citizen housing developments, generally   CC §§51.2 to 51.4

COMMON INTEREST DEVELOPMENTS—Cont.
Separate interests
    Access to separate interest   CC §4510
    Assessments
        Levy on separate interests within development, when permitted   CC §5625
    Defined   CC §4185
    Improvements to separate interests   CC §4760
        Architectural review and decisionmaking, standards when required   CC §4765
    Maintenance   CC §4775
    Modification   CC §§4760, 4765
    Operating rules, changes
        Types of rules to which provisions applicable   CC §4355
    Owner of separate interest in common interest development
        Protected uses of separate interests   CC §4739
    Pest control
        Notice of pesticide application when not applied by licensed pest control operator   CC §4777
    Protected uses of separate interests   CC §§4700 to 4753
    Religious items displayed on dwelling entry
        Governing documents not to restrict   CC §4706
    Transfer disclosures   CC §4535
        Enforcement of disclosure requirements   CC §4540
    Transfers   CC §§4625 to 4650
Settlement agreement with builder, disclosure to association members concerning   CC §6100
Signs
    For sale signs on property
        Provisions outside of common interest development law limiting association's regulation of member's separate interest   CC §4700
    Noncommercial signs, posters, flags or banners
        Restrictions on limitations, prohibitions   CC §4710
Small claims courts
    Appearance
        Associations managing development   CCP §116.540
Solar energy systems installed in common areas, restrictions on   CC §714.1
    Approvals
        Determinations of applications   CC §714
Solar energy systems, restrictions on installation
    Common areas, exclusive use grants   CC §4600
    Protected uses of separate interests
        Solar energy systems on multifamily common area roofs   CC §4746
    Provisions outside of common interest development law limiting association's regulation of member's separate interest   CC §4700
Statutes of limitation
    Alternative dispute resolution
        Tolling statute of limitations   CC §5945
    Declarants, developers or builders, legal proceedings against
        Limitations of actions not extended   CC §5986
    Notice requirements for actions against developer, effect of   CC §§6000, 6150
Stock cooperatives
    Common interest development defined to include stock cooperatives   CC §4100
    Defined   CC §4190
    Transfer of separate interest   CC §4640
Telephone wiring, access to
    Communications wiring access   CC §4790
Television antennas, restrictions on installation or use of
    Restrictions on limitations, prohibitions   CC §4725
Temporary relocation for pest control work
    Termite work   CC §4785
Termite damage, liability for   CC §4780
    Temporary removal of occupant   CC §4785
Tort action (See within this heading, **"Damages, action for"**)
Tort liability based on interest in common area   CC §5805
Transfer of interests
    Billing disclosures
        Form   CC §4528
        Information provided by association   CC §4530
    Disclosures   CC §§4525 to 4545 (See within this heading, **"Disclosure requirements"**)
    Exclusive use of common area, granting
        Action for declaratory or equitable relief to enforce procedure   CC §4605
        Restrictions on granting   CC §4600
    Fees
        Exemption from transfer fee limitations   CC §4580
        Permitted fees   CC §4575

COMMON INTEREST DEVELOPMENTS—Cont.
Transfer of interests—Cont.
    Lien for work performed in project
        Restrictions on transfer   CC §4615
    Partition of condominium   CC §4610
    Restricting marketing of owner's interest   CC §4730
    Restrictions on transfer   CC §§4600 to 4605
    Separate interests   CC §§4625 to 4650
        Community apartment projects   CC §4625
        Condominium projects   CC §4630
        Disclosures   CC §4535
        Enforcement of disclosure requirements   CC §4540
        Exclusive use common areas   CC §4645
        Planned developments   CC §4635
        Severability of interests   CC §4650
        Stock cooperatives   CC §4640
    Title to property transferred in violation of provisions   CC §4545
Transient occupancy in dwelling unit of common interest development, recordkeeping requirements for person accepting reservations or money for   CC §1864
Trust deeds and mortgages
    Redemption
        Foreclosure by association for nonpayment of assessments   CCP §729.035
Trust fund account for association funds
    Managing agent's duties as to   CC §5380
United States flag
    Display
        Restrictions on limitations, prohibitions   CC §4705
Video or television antennas, restrictions on installation or use of
    Restrictions on limitations, prohibitions   CC §4725
Volunteer officer or director, limited liability of   CC §5800
Water use
    Artificial turf
        Restrictions on water efficiency measures prohibited   CC §4735
    Low water-using plants
        Restrictions on water efficiency measures prohibited   CC §4735
Zones and zoning ordinances
    Local zoning ordinances, interpretation of   CC §4020

COMMON LAW
Applicability of common-law rule construing code   CCP §4
Change of name   CCP §1279.5
Civil Code, effect on   CC §§4, 5
Rule against perpetuities, validity of   Pro §21201
Rule of decision in courts   CC §22.2
Trusts, applicability of common law to   Pro §15002
Will probate
    No contest clauses
        Common law governing no contest clauses   Pro §21313

COMMON LAW DOMESTIC PARTNERSHIP
Confidential domestic partnership
    Establishment of process to enter   Fam §298.7

COMMUNICABLE DISEASES (See **CONTAGIOUS DISEASES**)

COMMUNICATIONS
Attorney-client privilege (See **PRIVILEGED COMMUNICATIONS**)
Attorneys, generally (See **ATTORNEYS**)
Jurors, communications with (See **JURY**)
Privileged communications (See **PRIVILEGED COMMUNICATIONS**)

COMMUNITY APARTMENT PROJECTS (See **COMMON INTEREST DEVELOPMENTS**)

COMMUNITY-BASED TRANSITIONAL HOUSING
Misconduct by participants   CC §§1954.10 to 1954.18

COMMUNITY CARE FACILITIES
Out-of-state residential facilities, placements in   Fam §§7910, 7911
    Investigations of threats to child health or safety   Fam §7911.1
    Licensing of facilities   Fam §7911.1
Wards of juvenile court, facilities for
    Community treatment facilities, placement review hearing   CRC 5.618
    Short-term residential therapeutic program, placement review hearing   CRC 5.618

COMMUNITY COLLEGES
Construction-related accessibility claims
    Attorney prelitigation letter to education entities   CC §54.27

COMMUNITY COLLEGES—Cont.
Social security numbers
    Public posting or display
        Implementation of provisions   CC §1798.85

COMMUNITY PROPERTY
Generally   Fam §§751, 760
Acceleration of loan, absence of   CC §2924.6
Accounting, court order of   Fam §1101
Administration of estates
    Distributions
        Character of property, allegations in petition   CRC 7.652
Annuity as evidence of transmutation of marital property, waiver of right to   Fam §853
Appeals, authority for   CCP §904.1
Application of definitions   Fam §900
Arbitration proceedings for division of   Fam §2554
Attorney's fees   Fam §1102
Bank accounts   Fam §911
Breach of fiduciary duty between spouses, action for   Fam §1101
Business or interest in business, management of   Fam §1100
Characterization of marital property   Fam §§760 to 853
Child support   Fam §§915, 4008
Commingling of separate and community property   Fam §852
Consent
    Court to dispense with requirement of   Fam §1101
    Gift of community personal property requiring   Fam §1100
    Transmutation of property   Fam §850
Conservatorship, management and disposition of community property in   Fam §1103, Pro §§3000 to 3154
    Authorization of transaction, findings and order   Pro §3144
Consideration, surviving spouse recovering property transferred in absence of   Pro §102
Conveyances
    Dissolution or annulment of marriage or legal separation, temporary restraining orders in connection with   Fam §§2040, 2041, 2045
    Execution of instruments   Fam §1102
    Separate property   Fam §770
Damages (See within this heading, **"Personal injury damages"**)
Death caused by other spouse, liability of married person for wrongful death damages when   Fam §1000
Death of spouse (See **SURVIVING SPOUSE**)
Debts
    Generally   Fam §§910, 930
    Defined   Fam §902
    Division of community estate on dissolution   Fam §916
    Income tax liability, joint   Fam §2628
    Incurred after entry of judgment of dissolution   Fam §2624
    Incurred after marriage but before separation   Fam §2622
    Incurred after separation but before judgment   Fam §2623
    Incurred before marriage   Fam §2621
    Necessaries   Fam §914
    Personal injury damages   Fam §1000
    Premarital debts   Fam §§910, 911
    Quasi-community property liable for   Fam §912
    Quasi-marital property   Fam §§2251, 2252
    Reimbursement
        Generally   Fam §§920, 931
        Debts paid after separation but before trial   Fam §2626
    Separate debts   Fam §2625
    Separate property liable for   Fam §§913, 916
    Support obligations not arising out of marriage   Fam §915
    Time debt incurred   Fam §903
Defined   CC §§687, 5110, Fam §§65, 760, Pro §§28, 3002
Deposit accounts   Fam §911, Pro §§5305 to 5307
Dissolution of marriage (See **DISSOLUTION OF MARRIAGE**)
Division of property   Fam §§2600 to 2605
    Generally (See **DISSOLUTION OF MARRIAGE**)
    Debts, liability after property division   Fam §916
    Pet animals   Fam §2605
    Quasi-marital property   Fam §§2251, 2252
Domestic partners
    Death of person in registered domestic partnership
        Community and decedent property   Pro §100
Domestic violence
    Personal injury damages
        Enforcement against abusive spouse's share of community property   Fam §2603.5
Dwellings
    Disposition of separate property residence, limitation on   Fam §754
    Excluding one spouse from other's dwelling   Fam §§753, 2035, 2036.5

COMMUNITY PROPERTY—Cont.
Earnings of married person, liability of   Fam §911
Education
    Contribution to spouse's education, reimbursement for   Fam §2641
    Loans, liability for   Fam §2627
Employee benefit plans
    Adverse claims, discharge of plan from   Fam §755
    Definition of employee pension benefit plan   Fam §80
    Dissolution of marriage (See **DISSOLUTION OF MARRIAGE**)
    Murder
        Attempting or soliciting murder of spouse   Fam §782.5
Encumbrances
    Attorney's fees (See **ATTORNEY'S FEES**)
    Community personal property encumbered by spouse   Fam §§1100, 2033, 2034
    Dissolution or annulment of marriage or legal separation, temporary restraining orders in connection with   Fam §§2040, 2041, 2045
    Execution of instruments   Fam §1102
    Security for debt incurred by spouse   Fam §913
Enforcement of money judgments subject to   CCP §§695.020, 703.020
Equal interests in   Fam §751
Escheat, taking by representation for prevention of   Pro §§103, 6402
Ex parte orders restraining disposing of   Fam §§2045 to 2049
Expectancy, restoration of   Pro §102
Fiduciary relationship
    Breach of duty between spouses   Fam §1101
    Management and control of community property   Fam §1100
Gifts
    Consent of spouse to gift of community personal property   Fam §1100
    Transmutation provisions not applicable to   Fam §852
Homesteads (See **HOMESTEADS**)
Incapacitated spouse
    Wrongful death damages, liability of married person for death caused by other spouse   Fam §1000
Income tax liability, joint   Fam §2628
Incompetent spouse, management and control of property of   Fam §1103
Indemnity contracts   Fam §782
Inventory for decedent's estate, inclusion in   Pro §8850
Jointly-owned deposit accounts, presumptions regarding   Pro §§5305 to 5307
Jurisdiction
    Continuing jurisdiction over unadjudicated property   Fam §2556
    Quasi-community property   Fam §2011
    Service of summons   Fam §2011
Leases, execution of   Fam §1102
Liquidation under court order   Fam §2108
Management and control   Fam §§1100 to 1103
Misappropriation of assets   Fam §2602
Mortgages (See **TRUST DEEDS AND MORTGAGES**)
Multiple-party accounts, ownership of   Pro §§5305, 5307
Necessaries, debt incurred for   Fam §914
Negligent or wrongful act of spouse causing injury to other spouse   Fam §782
Nonprobate transfers
    Former spouse, transfer   Pro §§5040 to 5048
Other states
    Division of marital property where real property located in   Fam §2660
    Domicile of spouse in other state, effect of   Pro §120
    Property located in other state, descent of   Pro §66
Partition (See **PARTITION**)
Pension benefits
    Employee benefit plans
        Dissolution of marriage (See **DISSOLUTION OF MARRIAGE**)
        Generally (See within this heading, **"Employee benefit plans"**)
Personal injury damages
    Assignment to injured spouse on dissolution of marriage   Fam §2603
    Characterization as community property   Fam §780
    Concurrent negligence of spouse   Fam §783
    Domestic violence
        Enforcement against abusive spouse's share of community property   Fam §2603.5
    Liability of married person for injuries caused by other spouse   Fam §1000
    Liability of tortfeasor spouse to injured spouse   Fam §782
    Negligent or wrongful act of spouse causing injury to other spouse   Fam §782
    Separate property, damages characterized as   Fam §781
Personal property, management and control of   Fam §1100
Pet animals
    Division of property   Fam §2605
Presumptions
    Dissolution of marriage more than four years before death   Fam §802
    Joint title, property held in   Fam §2581
    Multiple-party accounts, ownership of   Pro §§5305, 5307

COMMUNITY PROPERTY—Cont.
Presumptions—Cont.
    Property acquired by married woman before 1975   Fam §803
Property settlement agreements (See **PROPERTY SETTLEMENT AGREEMENTS**)
Putative spouse, quasi-marital property   Fam §§2251, 2252
Quasi-community property
    Child support   Fam §4008
    Death of spouse (See **SURVIVING SPOUSE**)
    Debts, liability for   Fam §912
    Defined   Fam §125, Pro §66
    Jurisdiction over   Fam §2011
    Partition (See **PARTITION**)
    Revocable trusts, transfers to   Pro §104.5
    Spousal support, liability for   Fam §4338
Quasi-marital property   Fam §§2251, 2252
Real property
    Division of property where real property located in other state   Fam §2660
    Management and control of   Fam §1102
Recordation
    Generally   Fam §1102
    Transmutation of real property   Fam §852
Reimbursement
    Acquisition of property, separate property contributions for   Fam §2640
    Debts   Fam §§920, 931
        Debts paid after separation but before trial   Fam §2626
    Education and training, community contributions for   Fam §2641
Relief from judgment   Fam §§2120 to 2129
Restoration of expectancy by surviving spouse   Pro §102
Retirement
    Employee benefit plans
        Dissolution of marriage (See **DISSOLUTION OF MARRIAGE**)
        Generally (See within this heading, "**Employee benefit plans**")
    Tribal court orders, payments pursuant to   Fam §2611
Revocable transfer on death deeds   Pro §§5600 to 5698
Revocable trusts, property in   Fam §761, Pro §§104, 104.5, 13504
Rule against perpetuities, spouse's right to exercise joint power of appointment with respect to   Pro §21211
Salary of married person, liability of   Fam §911
Sale of property
    Consent of spouse to sale of community personal property   Fam §1100
    Execution of instruments   Fam §1102
Separate property
    Administration of estates, distributions
        Character of property, allegations in petition   CRC 7.652
    Child support   Fam §4008
    Conveyance of   Fam §770
    Debts incurred during marriage but not for benefit of community   Fam §2625
    Debts, liability for   Fam §913
    Defined   Fam §§130, 770, 2502, 3515
    Disposition of separate property residence, limitation on   Fam §754
    Earnings and accumulations while living separate and apart   Fam §§771, 772
    Excluding one spouse from other's dwelling   Fam §§753, 2035, 2036.5
    Homesteads (See **HOMESTEADS**)
    Interest of spouses in   Fam §752
    Intestate distribution of   Pro §§6400 to 6402.5
    Personal injury damages   Fam §781
    Presumption concerning property acquired by married woman before 1975   Fam §803
    Spousal support, liability for   Fam §§915, 4301, 4320 to 4322, 4338
Spousal support, liability for   Fam §§915, 4301, 4320 to 4322, 4338
Summary dissolution of marriage   Fam §2400
    Security interests to avoid frustration of postmortem enforcement of community property rights   Fam §2337
Surviving spouse (See **SURVIVING SPOUSE**)
Survivor benefits as evidence of transmutation of marital property, waiver of rights to   Fam §853
Time of valuation of   Fam §2552
Title and ownership of property
    Generally   CC §§682, 682.1, 5104
    Court to determine   Fam §1101
    Joint title, holding property in   Fam §§2580, 2581
Tort liability   Fam §2627
Transfer on death deeds   Pro §§5600 to 5698
Transmutation of marital property
    Generally   Fam §850
    Form of transmutation   Fam §852
    Specific acts   Fam §853
    Voidable transactions laws applicable   Fam §851

COMMUNITY PROPERTY—Cont.
Trust property   Fam §761, Pro §§104, 104.5, 13504
Valuation of assets   Fam §2552
Wages of married persons   Fam §911
Whereabouts of spouse unknown   Fam §2604
Wrongful death damages, liability of married person for death caused by other spouse   Fam §1000

COMMUNITY SERVICE
Contempt, punishment   CCP §1218

COMPACTS
Interstate Compact on Placement of Children   CRC 5.616, Fam §§7900 to 7913
    Children covered by compact   Fam §7907.5
    Indian children, applicability of compact   Fam §7907.3

COMPENSATION (See also **COSTS; FEES**)
Generally   CC §3274
Attachments, exemption from   CCP §487.020
Attorneys' fees (See **ATTORNEY'S FEES**)
Child support provided voluntarily by other parent or relatives   Fam §3951
Conservators (See **CONSERVATORS**)
Court commissioners   CCP §259
Custody of children (See **CUSTODY OF CHILDREN**)
Damages (See **DAMAGES**)
Eminent domain (See **EMINENT DOMAIN**)
Execution of process by coroner or elisor   CCP §262.10
Executors and administrators (See **EXECUTORS AND ADMINISTRATORS**)
Expert witnesses (See **EXPERT AND OPINION EVIDENCE**)
Guardian ad litem, payment of expenses of   CCP §373.5
Guardians, generally (See **GUARDIAN AND WARD**)
Judicial arbitrators   CCP §§1141.18, 1141.28
Jurors (See **JURY**)
Jury commissioner   CCP §195
Mediators under provisions for civil action mediation   CCP §1775.8
Mortgage foreclosure consultants   CC §2945.4
Public administrators (See **PUBLIC ADMINISTRATORS**)
Salaries (See **SALARIES AND WAGES**)
Trustees (See **TRUSTS**)
Trusts (See **TRUSTS**)
Uniform Transfers to Minors Act, compensation of custodian under   Pro §3915
Wills (See **WILLS**)

COMPETENCE TO STAND TRIAL
Commitment to state hospital or other facility
    Appeal from order of civil commitment   CRC 8.483
Dismissal of underlying prosecution
    Posttrial procedure   CRC 4.130
Diversion of individuals with mental disorders
    Generally   CRC 4.130
    Reinstatement of proceedings   CRC 4.130
Examination of defendant   CRC 4.130
Hearing on
    Posttriial hearings on competence   CRC 4.130
Posttriial hearings on competence   CRC 4.130
Probable cause as to commission of crime, determination
    Proceedings to determine   CRC 4.131
Proceedings to determine   CRC 4.130
    Applicable provisions   CRC 4.130
    Effect of initiation   CRC 4.130
    Examination of defendant   CRC 4.130
    Initiation by court   CRC 4.130
    Trial on issue of mental competency   CRC 4.130
Reinstatement of felony proceedings   CRC 4.130
Remote proceedings
    Conditions for proceeding through use of remote technology   CCP §367.76
Request for a determination of probable cause
    Procedure for proceedings to determine   CRC 4.131
Trial on issue of competence   CRC 4.130

COMPETITION, UNFAIR (See **UNFAIR COMPETITION**)

COMPLAINTS
Amendment
    Amendment as of course   CCP §472
    Answers   CCP §471.5
    Cross-complaints (See **CROSS-COMPLAINTS**)
    Filing fee   Gov §70614
        Amendment of complaint or other subsequent pleadings, effect on filing fee   Gov §70613.5
        Supplemental fees for first paper filing   Gov §§70602.5, 70602.6

COMPLAINTS—Cont.
Amendment—Cont.
Health care providers, amended pleadings for punitive damages against CCP §425.13
Service on defendant   CCP §471.5
True name of defendant designated as unknown   CCP §474
Art, infringement   CCP §429.30
Attorney conspiring with client, complaint or pleading alleging   CC §1714.10
Authors, infringement   CCP §429.30
Books, infringement   CCP §429.30
Case cover sheets   CRC 3.220
Forms   CRCAppx A
Certificate of merit (See **CERTIFICATE OF MERIT**)
Child support enforcement services, complaints in actions brought by government   Fam §§17400, 17404, 17428
Compulsory joinder, complaint stating names of persons subject to   CCP §389
Construction defects, actions for   CCP §425.50
High-frequency litigants
Contents of complaint filed by high-frequency litigant   CCP §425.50
Construction-related accessibility claims
Advisory to defendant building owner, tenant, etc to be included by attorney with complaint or demand for money   CC §55.3
High-frequency litigants
Defined   CCP §425.55
Fees   Gov §70616.5
Contents of   CCP §425.10
Courts
Bias or prejudice, prevention by courts, judges, etc
Complaint procedure   CRC JudAdminStand 10.20
Criminal complaints (See **INDICTMENT, INFORMATION AND COMPLAINT**)
Cross-complaints (See **CROSS-COMPLAINTS**)
Default judgments (See **DEFAULT JUDGMENTS**)
Defined   CCP §426.10
Demurrers to (See **DEMURRERS**)
Description of property   CCP §455
Destroyed land records relief law proceedings   CCP §751.04
Earthquakes, boundary reestablishment after   CCP §751.53
Economic litigation provisions for limited civil cases   CCP §92
Eminent domain proceedings   CCP §1250.110
Fair debt buying practices
Actions on consumer debt
Contents of complaint   CC §1788.58
Filing
Amended complaint
Effect of amended complaint or other subsequent pleading on filing fee   Gov §70613.5
Fee for filing   Gov §26826.01
Check for filing fees
Returned unpaid   CCP §411.20
Underpayment   CCP §411.21
Children's waiting room in courthouse, surcharge to fund   Gov §70640
Cover sheet requirement   CRC 3.220
Cross-complaint, fee for filing   Gov §26826.01
Initial filing fees   Gov §§70611, 70613
Permissible additional fees   Gov §70603
Supplemental fees for first paper filing   Gov §§70602.5, 70602.6
Riverside County
Courthouse seismic repair costs, additional filing fees authorized to defray   Gov §70622
TRO or OSC sought   CRC 3.1150
Forcible entry and detainer proceedings   CCP §§1166, 1166a, 1167.3, 1173
Grounds for objection to   CCP §430.10
Groundwater rights actions
Contact information of persons reporting extractions
Plaintiff request of information following approval of notice   CCP §836.5
Definition of complaint   CCP §832
Notice of complaint   CCP §835
Lodging other notice materials with court   CCP §836
Health care providers, amended pleading for punitive damages against   CCP §425.13
Indictment (See **INDICTMENT, INFORMATION AND COMPLAINT**)
Initial filing fees   Gov §§70611, 70613
Permissible additional fees   Gov §70603
Supplemental fees for first paper filing   Gov §§70602.5, 70602.6
Injunction granted at any time prior to judgment on   CCP §527
Interplead and litigate claims, complaint to compel conflicting claimants to   CCP §386
Intervention, complaint in   CCP §387

COMPLAINTS—Cont.
Judgment on the pleadings, motion for   CCP §438
Meet and confer prior to moving for judgment on the pleadings   CCP §439
Judicial Council to develop and approve official forms   CCP §425.12
Libel and slander (See **LIBEL AND SLANDER**)
Literary property, infringement   CCP §429.30
Medical personnel, complaints from public concerning   CC §43.96
Motion for supplemental complaints   CCP §464
Music, infringement   CCP §429.30
Names of parties in title of   CCP §422.40
Objections to allegations in   CCP §§430.10, 430.30
Paintings, infringement   CCP §429.30
Parties, names of   CCP §422.40
Partition (See **PARTITION**)
Permissible pleadings   CCP §422.10
Permissive joinder of causes of action   CCP §427.10
Personal injuries   CCP §§425.10 to 425.12
Process and service of process
Time for service   CRC 3.110
Public improvement assessment, action to determine adverse interests in real property arising out of   CCP §§801.2, 801.3
Quieting title action   CCP §§761.010, 761.020
Quo warranto proceedings   CCP §804
Real property, description of   CCP §455
Sculpture rights, infringement   CCP §429.30
Service of complaints (See **PROCESS AND SERVICE OF PROCESS**)
Strike, motion to (See **MOTION TO STRIKE**)
Subordinate judicial officers, complaints against   CRC 10.703
Supplemental complaints   CCP §464
True name of defendant designated as unknown, amendments to add   CCP §474
Unknown persons as defendants   CCP §474
Unlawful detainer (See **UNLAWFUL DETAINER**)
Venue, affidavit or complaint stating facts indicating   CCP §396a
Voided filing
Check for filing fees returned unpaid   CCP §411.20
Underpayment of filing fee   CCP §411.21
Wrongful death actions   CCP §§425.10 to 425.12

COMPLEX LITIGATION
Case management   CRC 3.750, 3.751
Coordination of complex actions   CRC 3.501 to 3.550
Add-on cases
Determining whether to coordinate add-ons   CRC 3.544
Identification of potential add-ons   CRC 3.531
Petition for coordination when cases already coordinated   CRC 3.532
Ancillary proceedings, court for   CRC 3.545
Appeals   CRC 3.505
Applicable provisions in coordination proceedings   CRC 3.504
Procedural rules   CRC 3.510 to 3.515
Attorneys
Coordination attorneys   CRC 3.550
Case number   CRC 3.550
Contents of petition   CRC 3.521
Coordination attorneys   CRC 3.550
Coordination motion judges
Order assigning   CRC 3.524, 3.532
Coordination trial judges
Assignment   CRC 3.540
Duties   CRC 3.541
Definitions   CRC 3.501
Denial of coordination   CRC 3.529
Determination as to whether case is complex   CRC 3.502
Differential case management rules, applicability   CRC 3.712
Dismissal of action   CRC 3.545
Electronic submission of documents to judicial council   CRC 3.512
Evidence presented at hearings   CRC 3.514
Finality of judgment   CRC 3.545
Grant of coordination   CRC 3.529
Petition for coordination when cases already coordinated   CRC 3.532
Hearing on petition
Notice of hearing   CRC 3.527
Separate hearing on certain issues   CRC 3.528
Timing   CRC 3.527
Hearing on request to coordinate add-on   CRC 3.544
Hearing on transfer motions   CRC 3.543
Initial case management conference   CRC 3.541
Telephone appearance at case management conferences   CRC 3.670
Judges
Coordination motion judges, order assigning   CRC 3.524, 3.532
Coordination trial judges   CRC 3.540, 3.541
Disqualification   CRC 3.516

COMPLEX LITIGATION—Cont.
Coordination of complex actions —Cont.
    Judgments   CRC 3.545
    Judicial administration standards   CRC JudAdminStand 3.10
    Judicial council staff
        General administration of coordinated actions   CRC 3.550
    Liaison counsel
        Appointment   CRC 3.506
        Defined   CRC 3.501
        Service on liaison counsel   CRC 3.510
    Management of proceedings   CRC 3.541
    Motions   CRC 3.520
    Notice of submission of petition   CRC 3.522, 3.523
    Opposition to petition   CRC 3.525
    Orders
        Add-on cases, order on request to coordinate   CRC 3.544
        Denial of coordination   CRC 3.529
        Grant of coordination   CRC 3.529
        Transfer of action or claim   CRC 3.543
    Papers, submission to judicial council   CRC 3.511
        Electronic submission of documents to judicial council   CRC 3.512
    Permission to submit petition   CRC 3.520
    Petitions   CRC 3.520 to 3.532
    Proof of filing and service of petition   CRC 3.521
    Remand of action or claim   CRC 3.542
    Service of process   CRC 3.510
        Coordination motion judges, order assigning   CRC 3.524
        Memoranda and declarations   CRC 3.513
        Notice of submission   CRC 3.523
    Settlement of action   CRC 3.545
    Site of coordination proceedings   CRC 3.530
    Stays   CRC 3.515, 3.529
    Summary judgments   CRC 3.545
    Support of petition   CRC 3.526
    Termination of action   CRC 3.545
    Time
        Extending or shortening   CRC 3.503
    Title of proceeding   CRC 3.550
    Transfer of action or claim   CRC 3.543
Counterdesignations   CRC 3.402
Court action   CRC 3.403
Definition   CRC 3.400
Depositions
    Time limits for witness examination
        Exception for complex cases   CCP §2025.290
Designation as complex litigation
    Court's action to designate   CRC 3.403
    Joint complex designations   CRC 3.402
    Plaintiff designating action   CRC 3.401
Electronic filing and service   CRC 3.751
Environmental quality act
    Petitions under environmental quality act, civil rules governing
        Exemption from complex case rules   CRC 3.2220
Fees
    Designation fee
        Permissible additional fees   Gov §70603
Groundwater rights actions
    Comprehensive adjudications
        Presumption that comprehensive adjudication is complex action   CCP §838
Joint complex designations   CRC 3.402
Judges
    Selection   CRC JudAdminStand 3.10
Judicial administration standards   CRC JudAdminStand 3.10
Juror notebooks
    Preparation for benefit of jurors   CRC 2.1032
Management of complex cases   CRC 3.750, 3.751
Noncomplex counterdesignation   CRC 3.402
Provisional designation   CRC 3.400
Related cases   CRC 3.300
Report to legislature and governor concerning Centers for Complex Litigation   Gov §68617

COMPOSITIONS
Ownership, subject to   CC §655
Publication   CC §§983, 984

COMPROMISE AND SETTLEMENTS (See **SETTLEMENT AND COMPROMISE**)

COMPTOMETERS
Serial number destroyed or altered prior to sale   CC §1710.1

COMPUTATION OF TIME
Holidays (See **HOLIDAYS**)
Limitation of actions (See **STATUTES OF LIMITATION**)

COMPUTERS
Automated teller machines (ATMs) (See **DEBIT CARDS**)
Blind and visually impaired persons
    Internet website-related accessibility claims   CC §55.33
Child sexual abuse hosted on social media platform   CC §§3273.65 to 3273.69
Child support
    Software used to determine amount   CRC 5.275
Commercial sexual exploitation of minor by social media platform   CC §3345.1
Conviction records generated by computer, judicial notice of   Ev §452.5
Court records
    Entry of judgment in judgment book, alternatives to   CCP §668.5
    Judicial Council standards for automated recordkeeping   CRC 10.870
    Judicial notice of computer-generated records relating to criminal conviction   Ev §452.5
    Maintenance and update of court indexes   CRC 10.851
Courts
    Surplus technology equipment, disposal   CRC 10.830
Crimes related to computers
    Data or access to data illegally obtained or accessed
        Purchase by unauthorized person   CC §1724
        Sale   CC §1724
Electronic commercial services (See **ELECTRONIC COMMERCIAL SERVICES**)
Electronic filing and service (See **ELECTRONIC FILING AND SERVICE**)
Electronic funds transfers (See **ELECTRONIC FUNDS TRANSFERS**)
Electronic transactions (See **ELECTRONIC TRANSACTIONS**)
Entry of judgment in judgment book, alternatives to   CCP §668.5
Evidence
    Electronic transactions, admissibility of evidence of records and signatures related to   CC §1633.13
    Judicial notice of computer-generated records relating to criminal conviction   Ev §452.5
    Printed representations, presumption of accuracy of
        Computer information or program   Ev §1552
        Digital medium, images stored   Ev §1553
Information technology provided directly to courts, costs reported as   CRC 10.810
Judicial council
    Information technology advisory committee   CRC 10.53
Judicial notice of computer-generated records relating to criminal conviction   Ev §452.5
Medical records confidentiality
    Businesses organized to maintain medical information
        Digital services offered to consumers   CC §56.06
            Limitation of access to information about gender affirming care, abortion, or contraception information   CC §56.101
Point-of-sale systems   CC §§7100 to 7106
Presumption of accuracy of printed representations
    Computer information or computer program, generally   Ev §1552
    Images stored on digital medium   Ev §1553
Pro per court documents, interactive computer system authorized to prepare standardized   CCP §1062.20
Schools, terms for leasing or selling equipment to   CC §998
Secondary evidence
    Computer information or program   Ev §1552
    Digital medium, images stored   Ev §1553
Security for connected devices   CC §§1798.91.04 to 1798.91.06
Standardized information, system authorized to provide   CCP §1062.20
Support payments, use of software to determine   CRC 5.275, Fam §3830
Trial court automation   CRC 10.870
Year 2000 Problem (See **YEAR 2000 PROBLEM**)

CONCEALMENT
Adoption proceedings, concealment of child   Fam §§8713, 8803
    Intercountry adoptions   Fam §8910
Attorney's performance of professional services, concealment tolling statute of limitation for actions arising out of   CCP §340.6
Dissolution of marriage proceedings, concealment of property in   Fam §§2040 to 2045
Executors and administrators (See **EXECUTORS AND ADMINISTRATORS**)
Family law proceedings, temporary restraining orders in   Fam §§2040 to 2045
Health care providers, intentional concealment tolling statute of limitation for actions against   CCP §340.5

CONCESSIONAIRES
Disclosure of personal information by law enforcement agencies to city or county agencies screening prospective concessionaires   CC §1798.24a

CONCILIATION COURTS Fam §§1800 to 1802
Child custody Fam §§1841, 3089
Citation to act Fam §1800
Confidentiality of hearings, conferences, and papers Fam §1818
Coordination of mediation and conciliation services Fam §§1850 to 1852
Costs
    Court operations, salaries and benefits of court personnel included as costs of CRC 10.810
    Petition, filing fees for Fam §1835
Counselors of conciliation
    Appointment of Fam §§1814 to 1816
    Continuing education programs Fam §1816
    Powers and duties of Fam §1814
    Qualification of Fam §1815
    Salaries and benefits as costs of court operations CRC 10.810
Court agreements with other courts to provide joint services Fam §1820
Custody of child proceedings Fam §§1841, 3089
Destruction of records Fam §1819
Domestic violence, jurisdiction in cases of Fam §1834
Experts, assistance of Fam §1838
Fees for filing petition Fam §1835
Functional budget categories CRC 10.810
Hearings
    Confidentiality of Fam §1818
    Informality of Fam §1838
    Notice of Fam §1836
    Time and place of Fam §1837
Informal hearings Fam §1838
Joint conciliation court services Fam §1820
Joint custody of children Fam §3089
Judges Fam §§1811 to 1813
Judicial council, duties of Fam §§1850 to 1852
Jurisdiction
    Generally Fam §§1810, 1830
    Domestic violence cases Fam §1834
Mediators Fam §§1816, 3160, 3164
Medical specialists, assistance of Fam §1838
Minor child, transfer of proceedings involving Fam §1841
Notice of hearings Fam §1836
Orders Fam §1839
Pastors, assistance of Fam §1838
Pendency of other proceeding affecting Fam §1840
Petitions
    Generally Fam §1831
    Caption Fam §1832
    Contents of Fam §1833
    Filing fee Fam §1835
    Preparation of Fam §1834
Place of hearings Fam §1837
Probation officers Fam §1817
Purpose of act Fam §1801
Reconciliation agreements Fam §1839
Secretary, appointment of Fam §1814
Sessions, number of Fam §1811
Stay on filing petition for dissolution of marriage Fam §1840
Substitute judges Fam §1813
Summary dissolution of marriage, brochure on Fam §2406
Support orders Fam §1839
Time of hearings Fam §1837
Transfer of proceedings Fam §§1812, 1841, 1842

CONCILIATION OF INTERNATIONAL COMMERCIAL DISPUTES (See INTERNATIONAL COMMERCIAL ARBITRATION AND CONCILIATION)

CONCLUSIONS OF LAW
Statement of decision in lieu of CCP §632

CONCURRENT JURISDICTION (See JURISDICTION)

CONDEMNATION (See EMINENT DOMAIN)

CONDITIONAL ESTATES
Conditions precedent (See CONDITIONS PRECEDENT)
Conditions subsequent (See CONDITIONS SUBSEQUENT)
Fee, limitations on CC §764
Marriage restraints CC §710
Possibility of reverter CC §1045

CONDITIONAL ESTATES—Cont.
Time of enjoyment CC §707

CONDITIONAL SALES (See also CHATTEL MORTGAGES; SECURED TRANSACTIONS)
Administration of decedents' estates, sale of personal property of Pro §§10257, 10258
Automobiles (See AUTOMOBILES)
Household goods and personal property as collateral, use of CC §1799.100
Religious materials as security interest CC §1799.97
Residential property, disclosures required for sale of CC §§2956 to 2968
Unlawful detainer, holding over after sale pursuant to default provisions as act constituting CCP §1161a

CONDITION OF SENTENCE
Attorney reprovals CRC 9.19
Juveniles CRC 5.790

CONDITIONS PRECEDENT
Generally CC §708
Contracts, pleadings alleging facts as to CCP §457
Offer CC §1498
Pleadings alleging performance of CCP §§457, 459
Specific performance in absence of performing CC §3392
Vesting of title CC §1110
Wrongful act CC §709

CONDITIONS SUBSEQUENT
Generally CC §708
Reconveyance requirement CC §1109
Transfer of property for breach of CC §1046

CONDOMINIUMS
Common interest developments
    Commercial and industrial common interest developments generally CC §§6500 to 6876 (See COMMERCIAL AND INDUSTRIAL COMMON INTEREST DEVELOPMENTS)
    Generally CC §§4000 to 6150 (See COMMON INTEREST DEVELOPMENTS)

CONDOMS
Possession of condoms to prove certain crimes
    Evidence of possession of condoms
        Inadmissibility Ev §782.1
Sexual battery
    Damages liability for sexual battery generally CC §1708.5
    Stealthing or nonconsensual condom removal CC §1708.5

CONDUCT
Admissibility of evidence to prove Ev §§1100 to 1106
Family law proceedings, award of attorney's fees and costs as sanctions based on conduct of party or attorney Fam §271
Misleading conduct or statement of party, evidentiary effect of Ev §623

CONDUITS
Public liability for injury caused by condition of Gov §§831.8, 831.9

CONFERENCES
Family centered case resolution conferences CRC 5.83
Pretrial conferences (See PRETRIAL CONFERENCES)

CONFESSION OF JUDGMENTS CCP §1132
Automobile sales contract, prohibited provision in CC §2983.7

CONFESSIONS
Generally Ev §§1220 to 1228
Admissibility of Ev §402

CONFIDENTIAL DOMESTIC PARTNERSHIP Fam §298.7

CONFIDENTIAL MARRIAGES Fam §§500 to 511
Change of name on confidential marriage licenses, certificates, etc
    Application to change name on California confidential marriage license, etc CCP §1276
Informational brochures Fam §§358, 505
Notaries public
    Issuance of confidential marriage licenses Fam §§530 to 536
Remote licensing and solemnization
    Issuance of license using remote technology Fam §550

CONFIDENTIAL MATTERS
Adoption records (See ADOPTION)

CONFIDENTIAL MATTERS—Cont.
Appellate rules, superior court appeals
    Waiver of fees and costs   CRC 8.818
Appellate rules, supreme court and courts of appeal
    Sealed and confidential records   CRC 8.45 to 8.47
    Waiver of fees and costs   CRC 8.26
Automobile reacquisition by manufacturer or distributor, restrictions on confidentiality agreements concerning terms of   CC §1793.26
Change of name
    Financial institutions, change of name information for conservatorship and guardianship assets as filed by   Pro §§2891, 2893
    Witness Protection Program or domestic violence address confidentiality program   CCP §1277
Child support enforcement agency records   Fam §§17212, 17514
Civil rules
    Waiver of fees
        Application   CRC 3.54
Conciliation Court hearings, conferences, and papers   Fam §1818
Custody of children, mediation proceedings   Fam §3177
Driver's licenses
    Encoded information use   CC §1798.90.1
Fax filing of court documents and papers (See **FAX FILING AND SERVICE**)
Indian child welfare act involuntary placements
    Adoption
        Affidavit of confidentiality to bureau of Indian affairs   CRC 5.487
International commercial conciliation proceedings, confidentiality of statements made in   CCP §1297.371
International wills   Pro §6389
Judges
    Committee on judicial ethics opinions   CRCSupp JudEthicsOpinionsIOP 5
        Communications to and from committee   CRC 9.80
    Proceedings against   JudPerR 102
Judicial performance, commission on
    Ethics code for commission members
        Confidentiality of proceedings   JudPerPolicy 6.2
Juvenile court records (See **JUVENILE COURTS**)
Marriages, confidential   Fam §§500 to 511
    Informational brochures   Fam §§358, 505
    Notaries public
        Issuance of confidential marriage licenses   Fam §§530 to 536
Mediation (See **MEDIATION**)
Medical information   CC §§56.101, 56.104, 56 to 56.37
    Employer release   CC §56.21
    Marketing
        Defined   CC §56.05
        Disclosure of information for use in marketing   CC §56.10
        Pharmaceutical company requiring disclosure as condition of receiving pharmaceuticals   CC §56.102
Privacy protection (See **INFORMATION PRACTICES ACT**)
Privileged communications (See **PRIVILEGED COMMUNICATIONS**)
Protective orders
    California law enforcement telecommunications (CLETS) information form, confidentiality and use of information   CRC 1.51, CRCAppx A
Rent control provisions, confidentiality of tenant information disclosed for purposes of establishing compliance with   CC §1947.7
Social security numbers
    Annulment, dissolution of marriage or legal separation
        Confidentiality of persons involved   Fam §2024.5
    Prohibiting posting or display to general public of   CC §1798.85
Uniform Parentage Act (See **UNIFORM PARENTAGE ACT**)

CONFIRMATION
Arbitration awards (See **ARBITRATION**)
Decedent's property, sale of (See **ADMINISTRATION OF ESTATES**)
Receivers, sale by   CCP §568.5
Small estates without administration (See **SMALL ESTATES WITHOUT ADMINISTRATION**)

CONFLICTING TESTIMONY (See **WITNESSES**)

CONFLICT OF INTERESTS
Administrators   Pro §9880
Adoption proceedings, attorney representing both parties in independent adoption   Fam §8800
Appellate rules, supreme court and courts of appeal
    Briefs
        Certificates of interested entities or persons   CRC 8.208, 8.361, 8.488, CRCSupp 1st AppDist
Arbitration and arbitrators
    Ethical standards for neutral arbitrators   CRC ArbEthicsStand 1 to CRC ArbEthicsStand 17

CONFLICT OF INTERESTS—Cont.
Arbitration and arbitrators—Cont.
    Judicial arbitration   CRC 3.816
Attorney professional conduct
    Aggregate settlements involving multiple clients   ProfC 1.8.7
    Business transactions with clients   ProfC 1.8.1
    Current clients   ProfC 1.7
        Information of client, use to disadvantage of client   ProfC 1.8.2
    Foreclosure sale, judicial sale, etc
        Purchase by attorney of property at foreclosure or judicial sale   ProfC 1.8.9
    Former clients
        Duties to former clients   ProfC 1.9
    Former judges, arbitrators, mediators, etc   ProfC 1.12
    Gifts from client to attorney
        Influencing client to give   ProfC 1.8.3
    Government officials or employees, former and current   ProfC 1.11
    Law firms
        Imputation of conflict of one member to other members of firm   ProfC 1.10
        Imputation to all members of firm of violations of certain provisions   ProfC 1.8.11
    Limitation of attorney liability to client
        Prohibitions   ProfC 1.8.8
    Nonclient, compensation from   ProfC 1.8.6
    Pecuniary interests adverse to client   ProfC 1.8.1
    Prospective clients
        Duties to prospective clients   ProfC 1.18
Certiorari
    Briefs
        Certificates of interested entities or persons   CRC 8.488, CRCSupp 1st AppDist
Commercial and industrial common interest developments   CC §6758
Common interest developments   CC §5350
    Disclosure requirements
        Managing agent's disclosures to board before entering into management agreement   CC §5375.5
Conservators
    Estate, conservatorship of
        Standards of conduct   CRC 7.1059
Consumer privacy rights
    California privacy protection agency
        Board   CC §1798.199.15
Depositions
    Officer conducting proceedings   CCP §2025.320
Executors   Pro §9880
Guardianships
    Estate, guardianship of
        Standards of conduct   CRC 7.1009
Insurance defense cases, insured's right to independent counsel resulting from conflict of interests in   CC §2860
Interpreters   CRC 2.890
Judicial arbitrators   CRC 3.816
Judicial ethics
    Code of judicial ethics generally (See **JUDGES**)
    Disqualification   CRCSupp JudEthicsCanon 3
Judicial performance, commission on   JudPerR 101
    Censure, removal, admonishment or retirement of judges
        Disqualification of commission member unless quorum prevented by disqualification   JudPerR 134.5
    Ethics code for commission members
        Recusal, conditions requiring   JudPerPolicy 6.1
    Recusal of commission staff   JudPerPolicy 3.13
Jury challenges (See **JURY**)
Juvenile court proceedings
    Dependent child of court
        Attorneys, conflict of interest guidelines when representing siblings   CRC 5.660
Mandate
    Briefs
        Certificates of interested entities or persons   CRC 8.488, CRCSupp 1st AppDist
Mediation
    Ethical standards for conduct of mediators   CRC 3.850 to 3.860
        Complaints about court-program mediators   CRC 3.865 to 3.872
Prohibition, writ of
    Briefs
        Certificates of interested entities or persons   CRC 8.488, CRCSupp 1st AppDist

CONFLICT OF INTERESTS—Cont.
Referees, disqualification of   CCP §641
    Disclosures by referee
        Agreement, reference by   CRC 3.904
        Court-ordered reference   CRC 3.924
Small claims court advisory services   CCP §116.940, CRC 3.2120
Trustee   Pro §§16004, 16005

CONFLICT OF LAWS
Adoption
    Adult adoptions   Fam §9321.5
    Jurisdiction   Fam §9210
        Interstate adoptions   Fam §9212
Consumer contract awareness act   CC §1799.208
Consumer privacy rights
    Conflict with other provisions   CC §1798.175
Contracts, construction of   CC §1646
Escheat, effect on   Pro §§6803, 6805
Genetic privacy
    Effect of provisions on other laws   CC §56.184
Greenway easements
    Effect of other provisions   CC §816.64
International commercial arbitration and conciliation   CCP §1297.282
Interstate family support
    Registration for enforcement   Fam §5700.604
Partition
    Partition of real property act
        Governance of act   CCP §874.313
Settlement and compromise
    Time-limited demands   CCP §999.4
Will construction   Pro §§6113, 6141

CONFRONTATION
Witnesses   Ev §711

CONGRESS
Judicial notice of acts by   Ev §§451, 452
Marriage, members of Congress as authorized to solemnize   Ev §400

CONNECTED DEVICES, SECURITY   CC §§1798.91.04 to 1798.91.06
Definitions   CC §1798.91.05
Manufacturer's duties   CC §1798.91.04
    Third party software or applications   CC §1798.91.06
Reasonable security features
    Manufacturer's duties   CC §1798.91.04
Third party software or applications
    Manufacturer's duties   CC §1798.91.06

CONSANGUINITY
Challenge of juror for implied bias   CCP §229
Degree of kinship or consanguinity   Pro §13
Disqualification of judges, grounds for   CCP §170.1
Referees, disqualification   CCP §641

CONSENT
Administration of decedents' estates (See **ADMINISTRATION OF ESTATES**)
Adoption   Fam §§8602 to 8606 (See **ADOPTION**)
Annulment in absence of consent   Fam §2210
Community property, consent to transfer of (See **COMMUNITY PROPERTY**)
Conservatorship (See **CONSERVATORS**)
Contracts   CC §§1565 to 1590 (See **CONTRACTS AND AGREEMENTS**)
Co-representatives of decedents' estates, majority consent of   Pro §9630
Court where action commenced, consent to keeping action in   CCP §§396a, 396b
Direct marketing, medical information used for   CC §1798.91
Dismissal   CCP §581
Electronic filing and service rules
    Express consent   CRC 2.251
    Withdrawal of consent
        Judicial council legal forms   CRCAppx A
Genetic privacy
    Direct-to-consumer genetic testing companies
        Express consent from consumer   CC §56.181
Guardianships
    Wards 19 or 20 years of age, extension of guardianship   CRC 7.1002.5
Joint tenancy severance without   CC §683.2
Judges, proceedings against (See **JUDGES**)
Juvenile rules
    Electronic service
        Child's consent   CRC 5.523

CONSENT—Cont.
Legal separation, consent required for   Fam §2345
Marriage (See **MARRIAGE**)
Medical treatment (See **MEDICAL TREATMENT**)
Minor's medical treatment (See **MINORS**)
Nonprobate transfers of property (See **NONPROBATE TRANSFERS**)
Personal information collected by government agencies, disclosure of   CC §1798.24
Public guardians appointed as guardian or conservator, consent required for   Pro §2922
Rape and other sex offenses
    Consent not deemed defense in cases of adults in position of authority over minors   CC §1708.5.5
Referees (See **REFEREES**)
Rescission, requirements for   CC §1689
Spouse called as adverse witness   Ev §971
Sterilization proceedings (See **STERILIZATION**)
Suretyship liability in absence of   CC §2788
Trusts (See **TRUSTS**)

CONSERVATION
Easements
    Conservation easements generally (See **CONSERVATION EASEMENTS**)
    Greenway easements generally   CC §§816.50 to 816.66 (See **GREENWAY EASEMENTS**)
Eminent domain statutes affecting property reserved for   CCP §§1240.670, 1240.680
Water conservation
    Brokers
        Disclosure requirements   CC §2079.10
    Government tort liability
        Injuries caused by condition of facilities   Gov §831.8
    Water conserving plumbing retrofits   CC §§1101.1 to 1101.9

CONSERVATION EASEMENTS
Acquisition   CC §815.3
Definition   CC §815.1
Effect   CC §815.2
Eminent domain
    Property subject to conservation easement, acquisition by eminent domain   CCP §1240.055
Greenway easements generally   CC §§816.50 to 816.66 (See **GREENWAY EASEMENTS**)
Indian tribes holding   CC §815.3
Legislative intent   CC §815
Limitation on interest conveyed   CC §815.4
Remedies   CC §815.7

CONSERVATORS   Pro §§1400 to 1491
Absentees
    Admissible evidence of status as   Pro §1844
    Estates of   Pro §1803
    Missing conservatee (See within this heading, **"Missing conservatee"**)
    Rules for appointment for   Pro §§1840 to 1844
    Spouse of absentee, appointment of   Pro §1813
    Terminating conservatorship for   Pro §1864
Absent from hearing, conservatee as   Pro §1826
Abuse
    Civil penalty for abuse of conservatee   Pro §2112
    Investigation of allegations of abuse
        Petitions to investigate, persons authorized to petition   Pro §1851.6
Accounts and accounting   CRC 7.575
    Generally   Pro §§1060 to 1064, 2620
    Account statement
        Format   Pro §2620
    Allowances to conservatees   Pro §2421
    Approval, petition for   Pro §1064
    Attorney presenting account of estate on death of conservator   Pro §2632
    Blocked account   Pro §2328
    Compensation, allowance for   Pro §2623
    Conservatee's accounts
        Opening or changing name on account, responsibilities of conservator   CRC 7.1061
    Conservator defined   Pro §2600
    Contents of   Pro §§1061 to 1063
    Death of conservatee   Pro §§2620, 2630 to 2631
    Death or disability of conservator   Pro §§2630, 2632
    Exhausted estate   Pro §2626
    Expenses, allowance for   Pro §2623
    Failure to file   Pro §2620.2
    Final account of conservator of estate   CRC 7.576

CONSERVATORS—Cont.
  Accounts and accounting —Cont.
    Form, development of
      Judicial council forms   CRC 7.575, CRCAppx A
    Forms   Pro §2620
    Fraud detection investigations   Pro §2620.1
    Funeral expenses   Pro §2631
    Incapacity of guardian   Pro §2632
    Investigation and review of findings   Pro §1851.2
    Jurisdiction retained on settlement of   Pro §2630
    Last illness, expenses of   Pro §2631
    Notice re hearing on   Pro §2621
    Objections
      Generally   Pro §§2622, 2622.5
      Surety, notice to   Pro §1213
    Personal representative's incorporation by reference of conservator's accounting   Pro §10902
    Practice administrator appointed in event of attorney disability, accounting by   Pro §2468
    Purchases, court reviewing   Pro §2625
    Reimbursement of conservators   Pro §2623
    Remaining assets after death, transfer of   Pro §2631
    Salary of ward   Pro §2601
    Sales, court review re   Pro §2625
    Sanctions for bad-faith objections   Pro §2622.5
    Settlement, petition for   Pro §2630
    Small estates receiving public assistance   Pro §2628
    Supporting documentation   Pro §2620
    Temporary conservators   Pro §2255
    Termination of relationship   Pro §§2630 to 2633
    Waiver of accounting, request and order
      Forms, judicial council   CRCAppx A
    Welfare payments, estate consisting of   Pro §2628
  Acknowledgment of receipt of information regarding duties and liabilities   Pro §1834
  Actions by or against conservatee, generally
    Fee waivers, civil actions on behalf of conservatee or ward   CRC 7.5
  Administration of decedent's estate
    Appointment of conservator as administrator   Pro §§8464, 8469
    Interested party to action, status of conservator as   Pro §1210
    Service of notice on conservator, effect of   Pro §1210
    Summary administration of small estates by conservator   Pro §13051
  Advance health care directive under Health Care Decisions Law, guardian or conservator nomination in   Pro §4672
  Allowances to conservatees   Pro §2421
  Annual assessment of conservatees for investigation and review expenses   Pro §1851.5
  Annuities   Pro §2459
  Annulment of marriage   Fam §2211
  Appeals
    Generally   Pro §§1300, 1301
    Jurisdiction
      Appeals under conservatorship jurisdiction act   Pro §1301.5
    Limited civil cases in appellate division
      Compromise of claims, approval   CRC 8.825
    Order establishing conservatorships   CRC 8.480
    Reversal of appointment order, effect of   Pro §1311
    Stay on appeal   Pro §1310
    Sterilization of conservatee, judgment authorizing conservator to consent   CRC 8.482
  Appearance of conservatee by conservator or guardian ad litem   CCP §372
  Appointment
    Generally   Pro §1801
    Absentees generally (See within this heading, **"Absentees"**)
    Conservatee nominating person for   Pro §1810
    Creditors petitioning for   Pro §1820
    Decedent's estate, appointment of conservator as administrator to   Pro §§8464, 8469
    Disabled persons' claims, payments pursuant to
      Attorneys' fees for services to minors and persons with disabilities   CRC 7.955
      Trusts, payment into   CRC JudAdminStand 7.10
    Discretion of court   Pro §1812
    Domestic partner, appointment of   Pro §1813.1
    Fee waivers   CRC 3.50 to 3.53, 7.5
    Form of petition for   Pro §1821
    Guidelines re priority for   Pro §1812
    Joint conservators   Pro §2105
    Medical treatment, appointment of conservator for person lacking capacity to give informed consent to   Pro §§1880 to 1898

CONSERVATORS—Cont.
  Appointment—Cont.
    Minor's or person with disabilities, payment of claims pursuant to   Pro §§3600 to 3613
      Definition of person with disability   Pro §3603
      Express consent of protected person to court orders, when required   Pro §3613
    Missing conservatee generally (See within this heading, **"Missing conservatee"**)
    Nonprofit charitable corporation, appointment of   Pro §2104
    Order, contents of   Pro §1830
    Priority for   Pro §§1810 to 1813
    Public conservators (See **PUBLIC GUARDIANS**)
    Relative nominating person for   Pro §1811
    Several conservatees, one conservator for   Pro §2106
    Spouse, appointment of   Pro §1813
    Successor conservators generally (See within this heading, **"Successor conservators"**)
    Temporary conservators   Pro §§2250 to 2258
    Trust companies as conservators   Pro §300
    Voluntary request for   Pro §1802
  Appraisals
    Assessor, copy to   Pro §2612
    Conservator defined   Pro §2600
    Developmental services department, copy to   Pro §2611
    Failure to file   Pro §2614.5
    Fee schedule or other compensation
      Professional fiduciary to file proposed hourly fee schedule or statement of proposed compensation   Pro §2614.7
    Hearing on objections to   Pro §2614
    Independent   Pro §2614
    Later discovered property   Pro §2613
    Method for preparing   Pro §2610
    Notice, mailing to family   Pro §2610
    Objections to   Pro §2614
    Petition to object to   Pro §2616
    Public guardians, appraisal by   Pro §2943
    State department of state hospitals, copy to   Pro §2611
    Supplemental   Pro §2613
    Temporary conservators   Pro §2255
    Termination, effect on   Pro §2633
    Time for   Pro §§2610, 2613
  Arbitration of claims   Pro §§2405, 2406
  Assets
    Personal property generally (See within this heading, **"Personal property"**)
    Taking possession of conservatee's assets, responsibilities of conservator   CRC 7.1061
  Attendance at hearing   Pro §1825
  Attorneys
    Accounting of estate by   Pro §2632
    Appointed counsel   CRC 7.1101 to 7.1105, Pro §§1470 to 1472
      Alternatives to experience requirements   CRC 7.1102, 7.1103
      Annual certification of attorney qualifications   CRC 7.1105
      Certification of attorney qualifications   CRC 7.1105
      Compensation of appointed counsel   Pro §1472
      Confidentiality of certifications, supporting documentations, etc   CRC 7.1105
      Conservatorship termination   Pro §1861.5
      Continuing education   CRC 7.1102, 7.1103
      Disciplinary action against attorney, notification   CRC 7.1105
      Discretionary appointment of legal counsel   Pro §1470
      Experience requirements   CRC 7.1102, 7.1103
      Financial eligibility determinations, guidelines   CRCAppx E
      Inability to afford counsel   Pro §1474
      Initial certification of attorney qualifications   CRC 7.1105
      Judicial council legal forms   CRCAppx A
      Legal capacity of conservatee, proposed conservatee or person lacking, requirements for appointed attorney   CRC 7.1103
      Local court administration   CRC 7.1104
      Mandatory appointment of legal counsel   Pro §1471
      Qualifications   CRC 7.1101 to 7.1103
    Attorneys' fees (See within this heading, **"Attorneys' fees"**)
    Disability of attorney, conservator's appointment of practice administrator in event of   Pro §§2468, 17200
    Discharge   Pro §2356.5
    Education of court-employed staff attorneys
      Rule of court implementing, judicial council duties   Pro §1456
    Indians, proceedings for
      Inability to afford counsel   Pro §1474
    Probate attorneys
      Education requirements   CRC 10.478

CONSERVATORS—Cont.
  Attorneys—Cont.
    Probate attorneys—Cont.
      Qualifications   CRC 10.776, 10.777
      Sterilization of conservatee, judgment authorizing conservator to consent
        Appeal from judgment   CRC 8.482
      Withdrawal from representation of conservator, notice to surety required on
        Pro §1213
  Attorneys' fees
    Conservator acting as attorney, court approval of legal fees for   Pro §2645
    Contingency fee contract   Pro §2644
    Court-appointed counsel   Pro §§1470, 1472
      Financial eligibility determinations, guidelines   CRCAppx E
    Disclosure of relationships   Pro §2645
    Expense payable from principal and income of estate, general discussion of
      legal fees as   Pro §2430
    Extraordinary fees for accounting of estate   Pro §2632
    Payment from estate   Pro §2647
    Periodic payment   Pro §2643
    Petitions
      By attorney   Pro §2642
      By conservator of estate   Pro §2640
      By conservator of person   Pro §2641
    Practice administrator appointed in event of attorney disability, compensa-
      tion for   Pro §2468
  Bankruptcy, commencing actions in   Pro §2462
  Banks as trust companies
    Trust companies generally (See within this heading, "**Trust companies**")
  Blocked accounts, placing money or property in   Pro §2328
  Bona fide purchasers of real property in conservatorship estate, validity of
    transactions by   Pro §§1875, 3074
  Bonds   CRC 7.207, Pro §§2300, 2320 to 2330, 2333 to 2335
    Additional bond, requirements for   Pro §§2320.2, 2330, 2334
    Conservator of the person   Pro §2322
    Discharge of surety   Pro §2335
    Ex parte application to increase amount of bond   Pro §2320.1
    Insufficient bond   CRC 7.204, Pro §2334
    Inventory, failure to file   Pro §2615
    Joint conservators   CRC 7.203, Pro §2326
    Multiple conservatees, bonding requirement for   Pro §2327
    Nonprofit charitable corporation   Pro §2325
    Notice to surety   Pro §1213
    Practice administrator appointed in event of attorney disability, bond posted
      by   Pro §2468
    Public benefit payments, estates receiving   Pro §2323
    Public conservators (See **PUBLIC GUARDIANS**)
    Reduction of   Pro §§2328 to 2329
    Small estates   Pro §2323
    Stay on appeal, bond requirement for   Pro §1310
    Substitution or discharge of surety   Pro §2335
    Temporary conservators   Pro §2251
    Trust companies as conservators, bond requirements for   Pro §301
    Waiver by conservatees   Pro §2321
  Borrowing money   Pro §§2550 to 2552
  Breach of fiduciary duty
    Estate value, conservator's liability for   Pro §§2401.3, 2401.6
    Interest on loss, conservator's liability for   Pro §§2401.5, 2401.6
    Other remedies for   Pro §2401.7
  California conservatorship jurisdiction act   Pro §§1980 to 2033
    Judicial council legal forms   CRCAppx A
  Capacity
    Generally   Pro §§1870 to 1901
    Approval or avoidance of conservatee's transactions   Pro §1873
    Authorized transactions   Pro §1873
    Binding transactions   Pro §§1870 to 1876
    Bona fide purchasers of realty   Pro §1875
    Health care decisions   Pro §§1880 to 1898, 2354, 2355
    Law governing   Pro §1876
    Marry, conservatee's right to
      General conservatee's right to marry   Pro §§1900, 1901
      Limited conservatee's right to marry   Pro §2351.5
    Medical treatment, consent to   Pro §§1880 to 1898, 2354, 2355
    Rights affected by lack of   Pro §1871
    Transaction defined   Pro §1870
    Vote, right to   Pro §§1865, 1910
  Change of address
    Residence of conservatee, change   CRC 7.1063
  Charitable corporations as   Pro §2104
  Children's property, disposition where no conservatorship
    Attorneys' fees for services to minors and disabled persons   CRC 7.955
    Trusts, payment into   CRC JudAdminStand 7.10

CONSERVATORS—Cont.
  Citations, use of   Pro §§1823, 1824
  Claims
    Disputed claims   Pro §§2405, 2406
    Payment of   Pro §§2430, 2431
    Petition to determine claim to property, notice of hearing
      Form, judicial council   CRCAppx A
  Community property as conservatorship estate, management and disposition of
    Fam §1103, Pro §§3000 to 3154
    Authorization of transaction, findings and order   Pro §3144
  Compensation   Pro §§2430, 2640 to 2647
    Accounts including   Pro §2623
    Attorneys (See within this heading, "**Attorneys' fees**")
    Fees payable from estate of conservatee, determination limited to   Pro
      §2646
    Just and reasonable compensation, standards for determining   CRC 7.756
    Person who petitioned for appointment but was not appointed   Pro §2640.1
    Practice administrator appointed in event of attorney disability, compensa-
      tion for   Pro §2468
    Probate rules
      Compensation for guardians, conservators and trustees   CRC 7.750 to
        7.776
  Compromise (See within this heading, "**Settlement and compromise**")
  Conduct
    Standards of conduct   Pro §2410
  Confidential Conservator Screening Form, use   CRC 7.1050
  Confirmation of acts of   Pro §§2359, 2403
  Consent to medical treatment
    Medical treatment generally (See within this heading, "**Medical treatment**")
    Sterilization (See **STERILIZATION**)
  Conservatorship alternatives program   Pro §1836
  Consulting proposed conservatee   Pro §1828
  Contempt for disobeying court order, removal for   Pro §2655
  Continuances
    Successor conservator, hearing for   Pro §2686
    Support of conservatee's spouse, action for   Pro §3086
  Contracts to convey property, procedure re   Pro §§2521 to 2528
  Control and regulation of   Pro §2102
  Convulsive therapy   Pro §2356
  Costs in action prosecuted or defended by   CCP §1026
  Court employees obtaining estate property, prohibition against   Pro §2111.5
  Court investigator
    Appointment
      Forms   CRC 7.1060
    Defined   Pro §1419
    Education requirements   CRC 10.478
    Electronic court records, remote access
      Government entities, access by   CRC 2.540
    Qualification and appointment of   CRC 10.776, 10.777, Pro §1454
    Report of investigation   CRC 7.1060, Pro §1826
  Courts
    Court investigators, probate attorneys and probate examiners
      Education of judicial branch personnel   CRC 10.478
      Qualifications   CRC 10.776, 10.777
  Creditors' petitions for appointment of   Pro §1820
  Custodial parent defined   Pro §1419.5
  Death
    Accounting on death of conservatee   Pro §§2620, 2630 to 2631
    Accounting on death of conservator   Pro §§2630, 2632
    Duty on death of conservatee   Pro §2467
      Notice   Pro §2361
    Limited conservatee   Pro §1860.5
    Notice   Pro §2361
    Termination on death of conservatee   Pro §1860
  Debts
    Collecting   Pro §2451
    Payment of   Pro §§2430, 2431
  Decedent's estate, administration of (See within this heading, "**Administration of
    decedent's estate**")
  Dedication of property   Pro §2556
  Deed, acceptance of   Pro §2464
  Deficiency judgment against estate property   Pro §2551
  Definitions   Pro §§29, 30, 1400.1 to 1446, 1490, 3004 to 3008
  Dependents, support of   Pro §§2420 to 2423
  Deposit of funds
    Generally   Pro §2453
    Checks and drafts   Pro §2452
    Order authorizing deposit or withdrawal of money or property   Pro §2456
    Personal property   Pro §2454
    Public guardians   Pro §2940
    Securities   Pro §2455

CONSERVATORS—Cont.
Destroyed land records, action to reestablish   CCP §§751.09, 751.21, 751.28
Developmentally disabled persons
    Generally   Pro §1801
    Assessment report on proposed conservatee   Pro §1827.5
    Decision at hearing   Pro §1828.5
    Defined   Pro §1420
    Hearing
        Generally   Pro §1828.5
        Notice of hearing   Pro §§1461, 1461.4, 1822
    Limited conservatorship
        Court review   Pro §1850.5
    Notice of hearing   Pro §§1461, 1461.4, 1822
    Objections to petition   Pro §1823
    Order, contents of   Pro §1830
    Petition
        Contents of   Pro §1821
        Objections to   Pro §1823
    Report on proposed conservatee   Pro §1827.5
    Sterilization of (See **STERILIZATION**)
Developmental Services Department, notice to   Pro §§1461, 1461.4, 1822
Digital assets of conservatee, access to   Pro §879.3
    Conservator defined   Pro §871
Disability of conservator, accounting on   Pro §2632
Discharge
    Assets transferred out of state   Pro §2808
    Exhausted estate   Pro §2626
    Temporary conservators   Pro §2258
Disclaimer of interest   Pro §§260 to 295
Disclosure by spouse of conservatee of legal separation, dissolution, or annulment   Pro §1813
Dissolution of marriage proceedings, representation of incapacitated spouse   Fam §2332
Distribution
    Incompetent person without conservator, distribution involving   Pro §§11850 to 11854
    Surplus income   Pro §2423
Domestic partnerships
    Appointment of domestic partner as conservator   Pro §1813.1
    General conservatee's right to enter into domestic partnership   Pro §§1900, 1901
    Limited conservatee's right to enter into domestic partnership   Pro §2351.5
Domestic violence
    Victim representatives   Fam §6228
Drugs   Pro §2356
Due Process in Competence Determinations Act   Pro §§1801, 1881
Duties and liabilities statement, acknowledgment of receipt   CRC 7.1051
Duties of Conservator handbook, conservator to acknowledge receipt   CRC 7.1051
Easements   Pro §2556
Education
    Appointment of person to make educational decisions for minor   Pro §2662
Effectiveness of court in conservatorship cases
    Study, reporting by judicial council   Pro §1458
Elections
    Voting by conservatee   Pro §§1823, 1828, 1851, 1865, 1910
Emergency removal of conservatees from place of residence   Pro §2254
Employment of conservatee   Pro §2601
Encumbering personal property   Pro §§2550 to 2552
Enforcement of judgment against estate   CCP §709.030
Establishment of conservatorship   Pro §§1820 to 1830
Estate, conservatorship of
    Conflicts of interest
        Standards of conduct   CRC 7.1059
    Incapacitated professional fiduciary   Pro §2469
    Management of conservatorship estate   CRC 7.1059
    Powers of conservators, generally   Pro §§2450 to 2469
    Standards of conduct   CRC 7.1059
Estate management powers   Pro §§2450 to 2469
Estate plan of conservatee   Pro §§2583, 2586
Examination of estate assets
    Citation to appear, issuance of   Pro §§2616, 2619
    Interrogatories for   Pro §2617
    Petition for   Pro §2616
    Witnesses for   Pro §2618
Exchanges of property   Pro §§2545, 2550, 2557
Expenses, payment of   Pro §§2430, 2431, 2623
Family, surplus income distributed to   Pro §2423
Fees
    Filing fees in probate proceedings generally   Gov §§70650 to 70663

CONSERVATORS—Cont.
Fees—Cont.
    Waivers of fees in probate cases   CRC 7.5
        Appeals in supreme court and court of appeals   CRC 8.26
        Applicable provisions   CRC 3.50
        Application for waiver   CRC 3.51
        Determination of application   CRC 3.52
        Expiration   CRC 7.5
        Financial condition of conservatee, determination   CRC 7.5
        Grant of application unless acted on by court   CRC 3.53
        Judicial council forms   CRCAppx A
        Termination or modification of previously granted waivers   CRC 7.5
Fiduciary relationship   Pro §§2101, 2113
    Professional fiduciaries generally   Pro §§60.1, 2340, 2341
Filing fees
    Public conservator, etc., or State Mental Health Department employee, filing by   Gov §70659
    Riverside County
        Courthouse seismic repair costs, additional filing fees authorized to defray   Gov §70622
Financial institutions
    Banks
        Trust companies generally (See within this heading, **"Trust companies"**)
    Savings and loan associations
        Definitions   Pro §1490
        Surety bond of conservator, funds blocked account excluded   Pro §2328
    Trust companies (See within this heading, **"Trust companies"**)
Foreclosure on estate property   Pro §2551
Foreign conservators
    Defined   Pro §2800
    Removal of nonresident conservatee's property from state   Pro §§3800 to 3803
Foreign countries
    Interstate jurisdiction, transfer and recognition   Pro §§1980 to 2033
        Judicial council legal forms   CRCAppx A
Foreign judgments, effect of   CCP §1913
Forms
    Confidential Conservator Screening Form, use of   CRC 7.1050
    Judicial council legal forms   CRCAppx A
    Letters of conservatorship   Pro §2311
Fraud detection investigations   Pro §2620.1
Funeral expenses   Pro §2631
General plan, filing with court
    Judicial council rules   Pro §1456.5
Gifts to minors (See **UNIFORM TRANSFERS TO MINORS ACT**)
Governing law
    Generally   Pro §2100
    Prior law, effect of   Pro §3
Guardian ad litem (See **GUARDIAN AD LITEM**)
Health care (See within this heading, **"Medical treatment"**)
Health facilities, moving conservatees to   Pro §§2253, 2254
Hearings
    Appraisement of estate, objection to   Pro §2614
    Conservatee's attendance   Pro §1825
    Disclaimer of interest   Pro §277
    Disputed claims   Pro §§2405, 2406
    Interviewing absent conservatees   Pro §1826
    Limited conservatorships
        Conduct of hearing   Pro §1828
        Notice of hearing   Pro §1822
    Loans, authorization of   Pro §§2550 to 2551
    Missing conservatee, petition hearings on   Pro §§1461.7, 1847
    Notices generally (See within this heading, **"Notices"**)
    Persons allowed to attend   Pro §1829
    Procedure   Pro §1827
    Property disputes   Pro §§2521 to 2528
    Removal of conservators   Pro §§2650 to 2654
    Residence of conservatee, change of   Pro §§2253, 2254
    Substituted judgment provisions, proposed action under   Pro §2581
    Temporary conservators   Pro §2250
        Proposed temporary conservator, attendance   Pro §2250.4
    Termination of conservatorship   Pro §1863
    Transferring assets out of state   Pro §§2800 to 2808
    Venue change   Pro §§2210 to 2217
Home of conservatee   Pro §§2457, 2571
Homestead property as conservatorship estate, management and disposition of   Pro §§3000 to 3154
    Authorization of transaction, findings and order   Pro §3144

CONSERVATORS—Cont.
Incapacitated persons
    Security freezes, credit reports
        Protected consumer security freezes   CC §§1785.11.9 to 1785.11.11
Incapacitated professional fiduciary   Pro §2469
Independent exercise of powers   Pro §§2408, 2590 to 2595
Indians, proceedings for
    Applicability of Indian Child Welfare Act   CRC 7.1015, Pro §1459.5
        Notice requirements   CRC 7.51
    Attorneys, inability to afford   Pro §1474
    Interstate jurisdiction, transfer and recognition
        Generally   Pro §§1980 to 2033
        Judicial council legal forms   CRCAppx A
        Provisions specific to federally recognized Indian tribes   Pro §§2031 to 2033
    Involuntary placements
        Indian Child Welfare Act, rules governing   CRC 5.480 to 5.488
        (See **INDIAN CHILD WELFARE ACT INVOLUNTARY PLACEMENTS**)
    Legislative findings and intent   Pro §1459
    Notices
        Indian children as proposed conservatee   Pro §1460.2
    Registration and recognition of orders from other states
        Tribal courts (California tribes), applicability of provisions   Pro §2019
    Transfers of conservatorships
        Tribal courts (California tribes), transfers to or from   Pro §2003
    Tribal membership of conservatee
        Petition, contents   Pro §§1821, 1826
Indigent persons
    Waiver of fees   CRC 7.5, Gov §68631
        Appeals in supreme court and court of appeals   CRC 8.26
        Applicable provisions   CRC 3.50
        Application for waiver   CRC 3.51
        Definitions   Gov §68631.5
        Determination of application   CRC 3.52
        Expiration   CRC 7.5
        Financial condition of conservatee, determination   CRC 7.5
        Grant of application unless acted on by court   CRC 3.53
        Judicial council forms   CRCAppx A
        Termination or modification of previously granted waivers   CRC 7.5
Informational material on rights, duties, limitations, and responsibilities of conservator, county to furnish   Pro §§1834 to 1835.5
Information Practices Act, obtaining information under   CC §1798.24
Informed consent to medical treatment
    Major neurocognitive disorders, conservator's authority to act   Pro §2356.5
    Medical treatment generally (See within this heading, **"Medical treatment"**)
Instructions, petition for   Pro §§1455, 2359, 2403
Insurance, powers re   Pro §§2459, 2460
Interested person defined   Pro §1424
Interstate jurisdiction, transfer and recognition   Pro §§1980 to 2033
    Applicability of provisions   Pro §1981
        Effective or operative date of provisions   Pro §2024
    Appropriateness of forum, considerations   Pro §1996
    California conservatorship jurisdiction act
        Short title of provisions   Pro §1980
    Conduct as reason to decline jurisdiction   Pro §1997
    Continuing jurisdiction   Pro §1995
    Costs
        Requests for assistance between courts, travel expenses   Pro §1985
    Court rules and forms
        Judicial council to develop   Pro §2023
    Declining jurisdiction
        Appropriateness of forum, considerations   Pro §1996
        Conduct as reason to decline   Pro §1997
    Definitions   Pro §§1982, 1991
        Indian tribes, federally recognized   Pro §2031
    Emergency
        Defined   Pro §1991
        Special jurisdiction   Pro §1994
    Exclusive jurisdiction   Pro §1995
    Exclusivity of provisions in determining jurisdiction   Pro §1992
    Foreign country considered as state for purposes of applicability of provisions   Pro §1983
    Forms
        Judicial council legal forms   CRCAppx A
    Home state
        Defined   Pro §1991
        Determinations, factors   Pro §1993
    Indian tribes, federally recognized   Pro §§2031 to 2033
        Definitions   Pro §2031

CONSERVATORS—Cont.
Interstate jurisdiction, transfer and recognition —Cont.
    Indian tribes, federally recognized —Cont.
        Dismissal of petitions due to conservatee membership in tribe with jurisdiction   Pro §2033
        Inapplicability of general jurisdiction provisions when tribe has jurisdiction   Pro §2032
    Legislative intent   Pro §1980
    Multiple states with ongoing proceedings
        Commencing or staying, considerations   Pro §1999
    Notice of proceedings
        Both states, requirements of notice   Pro §1998
    Other states' courts
        Communications with courts of other states   Pro §1984
        Requests for assistance between courts   Pro §1985
    Registration and recognition of orders from other states   Pro §§2011 to 2019
        Authority of conservator upon registration   Pro §2016
        Estate, conservatorship   Pro §2012
        Informing conservator of rights, duties, etc, court's duties   Pro §2015
        Intent to register   Pro §2014
        Notice of intent to register   Pro §2014
        Person and estate, conservatorship   Pro §2013
        Person, conservatorship   Pro §2011
        Recordation of registration   Pro §2018
        Settlement and compromise, jurisdiction   Pro §2505
        Third party reliance on registered orders, immunity   Pro §2017
        Tribal courts (California tribes), applicability of provisions   Pro §2019
    Removal of conservator, grounds   Pro §2650
    Short title of provisions   Pro §1980
    Significant-connection state
        Defined   Pro §1991
        Determinations, factors   Pro §§1991, 1993
    Special jurisdiction   Pro §1994
    Statutory construction
        Electronic Signatures in Global and National Commerce Act, relation between acts   Pro §2022
        Uniform application and construction   Pro §2021
    Transfers of conservatorships   Pro §§2001 to 2003
        Change of residence of conservatee, petition for transfer   Pro §2352
        Other state, transfer from   Pro §2002
        Other state, transfer to   Pro §2001
        Tribal courts (California tribes), transfers to or from   Pro §2003
    Witnesses
        Other state, testimony in   Pro §1986
Interviewing absent conservatees   Pro §1826
Inventory
    Appraisals generally (See within this heading, **"Appraisals"**)
    Assessor, copy to   Pro §2612
    Conservator defined   Pro §2600
    Contents of   Pro §2610
    Developmental Services Department, copy to   Pro §2611
    Failure to file   Pro §§2614.5, 2615
    Fee schedule or other compensation
        Professional fiduciary to file proposed hourly fee schedule or statement of proposed compensation   Pro §2614.7
    Later discovered property   Pro §2613
    Liability for failure to file   Pro §2615
    Notice, mailing to family   Pro §2610
    Oath with   Pro §2610
    State department of state hospitals, copy to   Pro §2611
    Supplemental   Pro §2613
    Temporary conservators   Pro §2255
    Termination, effect on   Pro §§2602, 2633
    Time for   Pro §2610
Investigations
    Absent from hearing, investigation where conservatee is   Pro §1826
    Abuse allegations
        Petitions to investigate, persons authorized to petition   Pro §1851.6
    Accountings, filing   Pro §1851.2
    Annual assessment of conservatees for costs of   Pro §1851.5
    Court investigator (See within this heading, **"Court investigator"**)
    Education of investigators
        Rule of court implementing, judicial council duties   Pro §1456
    Electronic court records, remote access
        Government entities, access by   CRC 2.540
    Fraud detection investigations   Pro §2620.1
    Major neurocognitive disorders, conservator's powers where conservatee suffers from   Pro §2356.5
    Periodic investigations   Pro §§1850 to 1853

CONSERVATORS—Cont.
  Investigations—Cont.
    Prefiling investigations Pro §§2910, 2911
    Pre-hearing duties of court investigator Pro §2250.6
    Reimbursement for costs Pro §1851.5
    Report of Pro §1826
    Successor conservator proceedings Pro §§2684, 2686
    Transfers of conservatorships
      Investigation and review upon acceptance of transfer from another jurisdiction Pro §1851.1
  Investments
    Generally Pro §§2547, 2570, 2573, 2574
    Public guardians Pro §2940
  Joint conservators
    Generally Pro §2105
    Bond requirements Pro §2326
    Liability of Pro §2105.5
    Terminal illness of custodial parent as grounds for appointing parent and parent's nominee as joint conservators Pro §2105
  Joint purchase of real property Pro §2572
  Judges
    Appointment of conservators in proceedings against JudPerR 126
    Education as to conservatorship and guardianship matters CRC 10.468
      Rule of court implementing, judicial council duties Pro §1456
    Education of judges and subordinate judicial officers regularly assigned to probate cases
      Domestic violence issues CRC 10.464
  Judgments
    Enforcement of judgments against conservatorship estate CCP §709.030
    Finality of Pro §2103
    Foreign judgments, effect of CCP §1913
    Payments pursuant to judgment in favor of minor or disabled person, disposition of
      Attorneys' fees for services to minors and disabled person CRC 7.955
      Trusts, payment into CRC JudAdminStand 77.10
    Payments pursuant to judgment in favor of minor or person with disability, disposition of Pro §§3600 to 3613
      Definition of person with disability Pro §3603
      Express consent of protected person to court orders, when required Pro §3613
    Removing conservators Pro §2653
    Terminating conservatorship Pro §1863
  Jurisdiction
    Generally Pro §2200
    California conservatorship jurisdiction act Pro §§1980 to 2033
      Judicial council legal forms CRCAppx A
    Interstate jurisdiction, transfer and recognition Pro §§1980 to 2033
      Judicial council legal forms CRCAppx A
    More than one county, proceedings commencing in Pro §2203
    Real property disputes Pro §§2524 to 2526
    Settlement and compromise Pro §2505
    Termination, retention after Pro §2630
  Jury
    Challenge of juror for implied bias, relationships giving rise to CCP §229
    Conservatees ineligible for jury service CCP §203
    Trial by jury, conservatees' right to Pro §§825, 1452, 1453, 1823, 1826 to 1828, 1863
  Last illness, expenses of Pro §2631
  Leases Pro §2550
  Legislative intent Pro §1800
  Letters
    Generally Pro §2310
    Administration letters, grant of Pro §§8464, 8469
    Form Pro §2311
    Powers stated in Pro §2594
    Public guardians Pro §2922
    Recordation of Pro §2313
    Revoking Pro §§2650 to 2654
    Temporary conservatorship Pro §2251
  Liens on personalty, borrowing secured by Pro §§2550 to 2552
  Limitation on actions
    Sold property, action to recover Pro §2548
    Sureties, actions against Pro §2333
  Limited conservatorships Pro §1800.3
    Generally Pro §1801
    Attorneys, appointment of Pro §1471
      Financial eligibility guidelines for court appointment CRCAppx E
    Continuation or termination, recommendations on Pro §1851
    Contracts, limited conservatee's right to make Pro §1872
    Court review Pro §1850.5

CONSERVATORS—Cont.
  Limited conservatorships—Cont.
    Death of limited conservatee Pro §1860.5
    Developmentally disabled persons
      Court review Pro §1850.5
      Generally (See within this heading, "**Developmentally disabled persons**")
    Disputed claims Pro §2405
    Hearing
      Conduct of Pro §1828
      Notice of Pro §1822
    Legal capacity of conservatee Pro §1872
    Modification of Pro §2351.5
    Notice of hearing Pro §1822
    Objections to petition Pro §1823
    Order, contents of Pro §1830
    Ordinary duty of care requirements Pro §2401
    Petition
      Contents of Pro §1821
      Objections to Pro §1823
    Powers of conservator Pro §2351.5
    Proceedings to establish Pro §1431
    Public defender, appointment of Pro §§1471, 1472
    Sterilization proceedings (See **STERILIZATION**)
    Termination
      Generally Pro §1860.5
      Recommendations on Pro §1851
  Lis pendens, filing notice of Pro §1004
  Loans Pro §§2550 to 2552
  Location of property, duty to disclose Pro §2529
  Mail, rules on use of Pro §1467
  Marriage
    General conservatee's right to marry Pro §§1900, 1901
    Limited conservatee's right to marry Pro §2351.5
  Medical information, authorization for release of CC §56.10
  Medical treatment
    Generally Pro §§2354, 2355
    Appointment of conservator for person lacking capacity to give informed consent Pro §§1880 to 1898
    Existing or continuing condition, petition for order authorizing treatment for Pro §§2356.5, 2357
    Informed consent for
      Major neurocognitive disorders, conservator's authority to act where conservatee suffers from Pro §2356.5
      Judicial determination that conservatee unable to give informed consent Pro §1881
    Moving conservatees for Pro §§2253, 2254
    Pre-employment physical, disclosure of information from CC §56.10
    Sterilization (See **STERILIZATION**)
  Mental health facilities, placing conservatee in Pro §2356
  Mining leases Pro §§2553 to 2555
  Minor who is or has been married, establishment of conservatorship for Pro §1800.3
  Missing conservatee
    Generally Pro §§1804, 1845, 1853
    Grounds for appointment Pro §§1845, 1847, 1849
    Hearing, notice of Pro §§1461.7, 1847
    Initial petition requirements Pro §1846
    Post-appointment notice Pro §1461.7
    Procedure for appointment of conservator Pro §§1846 to 1849.5
  Modification of powers Pro §2350
    Limited conservatorships Pro §2351.5
  Mortgages Pro §§2550 to 2552
  Mutual funds
    Generally Pro §2459
    Sale of mutual funds without beneficiary designation Pro §2544.5
  Nature and location of property, duty to disclose Pro §2529
  Neurocognitive disorders
    Major neurocognitive disorder conservatorships Pro §2356.5
  New trial motion Pro §1453
  Nomination of Pro §§1488, 1489, 1810, 1811
  Non-professional conservators or guardians
    Educational program Pro §1457
  Nonprofit charitable corporations as Pro §2104
  Nonresident conservatees
    Generally Pro §2107
    Foreign conservators
      Defined Pro §2800
      Removal of nonresident conservatee's property from state Pro §§3800 to 3803
      Removal of property from state Pro §§3800 to 3803

CONSERVATORS—Cont.
Nonresident conservatees—Cont.
    Restrictions on establishment of conservatorship over nonresident   Pro §1800.3
Notices   CRC 7.51, Pro §§1460 to 1469
    Absentee conservatee   Pro §§1842, 1853
    Accounts, hearings on allowance and settlement of   Pro §2621
    Additional notice, court requiring   Pro §1462
    Bond, reduction of   Pro §2329
    Change of residence   Pro §2352
    Citations to appear   Pro §§1823, 1824
    Decedent's estate proceedings, effect of notice served on conservator regarding   Pro §1210
    Developmentally disabled persons, hearings involving   Pro §§1461, 1461.4, 1822
    Developmental Services Department   Pro §§1461, 1822
    Disclaimer of interest, hearing on   Pro §277
    Financial institutions, conservator's taking possession of assets held by   Pro §§2890 to 2893
    Hearing re proposed conservatorship   Pro §1822
    Indian children as proposed conservatee   Pro §1460.2
    Interstate jurisdiction, transfer and recognition
        Both states, requirements of notice   Pro §1998
        Intent to register orders from other states   Pro §2014
    Inventory and appraisal
        Mailing to family   Pro §2610
    Limited conservatorship, hearing on   Pro §1822
    Mailing, rules re   Pro §1467
    Medical treatment, hearing on consent of conservator to   Pro §1892
    Property disputes, hearings on   Pro §2521
    Proposed action, hearing on   Pro §2581
    Removal of conservators   Pro §2652
    Residence, request to change conservatee's place of   Pro §§2253, 2254
    Sales   Pro §2543
    Service of   Pro §1824
    Special notice   Pro §§2700 to 2702
    State hospital patient   Pro §§1461, 1461.4, 1822
        Ward or conservatee as patient, notice to state department of state hospitals   Pro §1461
    Substituted judgment provisions, hearing on proposed action under   Pro §2581
    Successor conservator, hearing on   Pro §2683
    Support of conservatee's spouse, hearing on   Pro §3081
    Surety, notice to   Pro §1213
    Temporary conservators, petitions for   Pro §2250
    Termination hearing   Pro §1862
    Transferring assets out of state, hearing on   Pro §2804
    12 years old, notice to child under   Pro §1460.1
    Venue change hearing   Pro §2214
    Veterans Administration   Pro §§1461.5, 1822
Oaths
    Generally   Pro §2300
    Inventory   Pro §2610
    Temporary conservators   Pro §2251
Objections
    Accounts   Pro §§2622, 2622.5
        Surety, notice to   Pro §1213
    Appraisals, objection to   Pro §2614
    Transfer of assets out of state   Pro §2805
Orders
    Additional security   Pro §2334
    Appeal from orders (See within this heading, **"Appeals"**)
    Appointing conservator   Pro §1830
    Authorizing transactions by conservatee   Pro §1873
    Blocked accounts, placing money or property in   Pro §2328
    Compensation of services rendered, order for   Pro §2643
    Deposit or withdraw money or property in trust companies   Pro §2456
    Disclaimer of interest, order to file   Pro §277
    Failure to perform duties   Pro §2404
    Finality of   Pro §2103
    Independent exercise of powers   Pro §§2590 to 2595
    Loans and security   Pro §2551
    Nonobligatory acts, order for conservator to perform   Pro §§2358, 2402
    Nonobligatory acts, order for guardian to perform   Pro §§2358, 2402
    Property transfers   Pro §§2527, 2528
    Removing conservators   Pro §2653
    Residence, change of   Pro §§2253, 2254
    Substituted judgment provisions, authorization for proposed actions under   Pro §2584
    Successor conservator, appointment of   Pro §2688
    Surplus income distribution   Pro §2423

CONSERVATORS—Cont.
Orders—Cont.
    Termination of conservatorship   Pro §1860
    Transactions, authorizing or directing   Pro §2111
    Trust companies, deposit or withdraw money or property in   Pro §2456
    Wage claims, failure to pay   Pro §2431
Other states
    Interstate jurisdiction, transfer and recognition   Pro §§1980 to 2033
        Judicial council legal forms   CRCAppx A
Partition proceedings (See **PARTITION**)
Personal liability on contracts by conservator as fiduciary   Pro §2110
Personal property
    Contracts to transfer personal property, court approval of   Pro §§2521 to 2528
    Court employees obtaining estate property, prohibition against   Pro §2111.5
    Depositing and withdrawing   Pro §§2454, 2456
    Examination of estate assets (See within this heading, **"Examination of estate assets"**)
    Out-of-state transfer of assets   Pro §§2800 to 2808
    Sales generally (See within this heading, **"Sales"**)
Personal residence of conservatee (See within this heading, **"Residence of conservatee"**)
Person, conservatorship   Pro §§2350 to 2361
Petitions
    Accounts, approval of   Pro §1064
    Additional security by conservator, request for   Pro §2334
    Appointment of conservator   Pro §1820
    Appraisement of estate, objection to   Pro §2616
    Attorneys' fees   Pro §§2640 to 2642 (See within this heading, **"Attorneys' fees"**)
    Borrowing money, authorization for   Pro §2551
    Compensation for services rendered, petition for   Pro §§2430, 2640 to 2647
    Contents of   Pro §1821
    Creditors   Pro §1820
    Defined   Pro §1430
    Disclaimer of interest, order for   Pro §277
    Examination of estate assets   Pro §2616
    Harassment
        Unmeritorious petitions intended to annoy or harass   Pro §1970
    Independent powers, grant of   Pro §2592
    Limited conservatorship, petition for   Pro §§1821, 1827.5
    Major neurocognitive disorders, petition for authority to act where conservatee suffers from   Pro §2356.5
    Medical treatment for existing or continuing condition, authorization for   Pro §§2356.5, 2357
    Perform duties, order to   Pro §2404
    Practice administrator for disabled attorney, petition for appointment of   Pro §§2468, 17200
    Private professional conservators
        Petition to include registration information   Pro §2250
    Property transfers, authority re   Pro §2526
    Relatives, petition requiring identification of   Pro §1821
    Removal of conservators   Pro §2651
    Residence change for conservatees   Pro §§2253, 2254
    Service on proposed conservatee   Pro §1824
    Settlement or compromise, court approval of   Pro §2506
    Temporary conservators   Pro §§2250, 2250.2
    Termination of conservatorship   Pro §§1861, 1864
    Transactions by conservatee, order authorizing   Pro §§1873, 1874
    Transfer of assets out-of-state   Pro §§2802, 2803
    Venue change   Pro §§2211 to 2213
Photographs
    Conservatee, annual photograph   Pro §2360
Plan filing with court
    Care, custody, and control of conservatee   Pro §2351.2
Possession of property disputed   Pro §§2521 to 2528
Power of attorney (See **POWER OF ATTORNEY**)
Powers
    Generally   Pro §§2350, 2351, 2450
    Annuities   Pro §2459
    Authorization, exercise without   Pro §2450
    Bankruptcy   Pro §2462
    Borrowing money   Pro §§2550 to 2552
    Care plan, filing with court   Pro §2351.2
    Checks, cashing and depositing   Pro §2452
    Civil actions   Pro §2462
    Community property   Pro §3056
    Contracts   Pro §2451.5
    Death of conservatee   Pro §2467
    Debt and benefit collection   Pro §2451

CONSERVATORS—Cont.
Powers—Cont.
    Dedication of property   Pro §2556
    Deed to mortgaged property, acceptance of   Pro §2464
    Easements, dedicating or granting   Pro §2556
    Employment of professionals   Pro §2451.5
    Encumbering personal property   Pro §§2550 to 2552
    Exercise of powers, confirming acts in   Pro §2403
    Health care decisions   Pro §§2354, 2355, 2356.5
    Homestead property   Pro §3056
    Independent exercise of   Pro §§2408, 2590 to 2595
    Insurance   Pro §§2459, 2460
    Investments   Pro §§2570 to 2574
    Leases   Pro §§2550, 2552.5 to 2555
    Limited conservators   Pro §2351.5
    Limits on   Pro §§2351, 2450
    Loans   Pro §§2550 to 2552
    Medical treatment, consent to   Pro §§2354, 2355, 2356.5
    Modification
        Generally   Pro §2350
        Limited conservatorships   Pro §2351.5
    Mutual funds   Pro §2459
    Nonresident conservatees   Pro §2107
    Ownership rights   Pro §2458
    Partition actions   Pro §2463
    Property, valueless   Pro §2465
    Purchase of property   Pro §2451.5
    Real property transactions   Pro §2111
    Residence change for conservatees   Pro §§2253, 2254, 2352
    Retirement plans, continuing   Pro §2459
    Sales generally (See within this heading, **"Sales"**)
    Surrender during removal proceedings   Pro §2654
    Taxes   Pro §2461
    Temporary conservators   Pro §2252
    Transactions under court order   Pro §2111
    Welfare payments, acting as payee for   Pro §2452
    Withdrawal of independent powers   Pro §2593
Powers of appointment   Pro §§600 to 695
Practice administrator appointed in event of attorney disability   Pro §§2468, 17100
Pre-employment physical of minor ward, disclosure of information from   CC §56.10
Priority in appointment of   Pro §§1810 to 1813
Prior law   Pro §§1488 to 1490
Private sale of assets   Pro §2543
Probate attorneys
    Education requirements   CRC 10.478
    Qualifications   CRC 10.776, 10.777
Probate conservator appointment
    Order appointing   CRCAppx A
Probate examiners
    Education requirements   CRC 10.478
    Qualifications   CRC 10.776, 10.777
Probate rules
    Generally   CRC 7.1 to 7.1105
Procedure for conservatorship hearings   Pro §1827
Proceeding defined   Pro §3008
Process (See within this heading, **"Service of process"**)
Professional fiduciaries
    Deceased professional fiduciary   Pro §9765
    Fee schedule or compensation, proposed
        Inventory and appraisal of estate   Pro §2614.7
        Submission of new schedule or statement   Pro §2614.8
    Periodic payments for services rendered
        Petition   Pro §2643.1
    Petition for conservatorship
        Contents   Pro §1510
    Temporary conservators
        Petition for temporary guardian or conservator, contents   Pro §2250
Property disputes, procedure re   Pro §§2521 to 2528
Public assistance (See within this heading, **"Welfare payments"**)
Public auctions   Pro §2543
Public conservators
    Electronic court records, remote access
        Government entities, access by   CRC 2.540
Public defender, appointment and compensation of   Pro §§1471, 1472
Purchases, accounting for   Pro §2625
Real property
    Generally   Pro §§1875, 2111
    Bona fide purchasers of   Pro §§1875, 3074
    Contracts to convey real property, court approval of   Pro §§2521 to 2528

CONSERVATORS—Cont.
Real property—Cont.
    Court employees obtaining estate property, prohibition against   Pro §2111.5
    Foreign jurisdictions, property in
        Determining conservatee's interests, standard of care   Pro §2401.1
    Interested persons, response to petition by   Pro §2522
    Lis pendens, filing notice of   Pro §1004
    Sales generally (See within this heading, **"Sales"**)
Recordation
    Interstate jurisdiction, transfer and recognition
        Registration and recognition of orders from other states   Pro §2018
    Letters of conservatorship   Pro §2313
    Real property transactions   Pro §2111
Records destroyed in fire or calamity   CCP §1953.05
Referees
    Disqualification as referee, conservatorship relationship as grounds for   CCP §641
Registration of conservators
    Petition to include registration information   Pro §2250
Reimbursement of   Pro §§2466, 2623
    Investigations   Pro §1851.5
Relatives
    Nominations by   Pro §1811
    Petition, requirement of identification of relatives in   Pro §1821
    Surplus income distributed to   Pro §2423
Removal   Pro §§2650 to 2654
    Cause, removal for   Pro §2653
    Contempt for disobeying court order, removal for   Pro §2655
    Inventory, failure to provide   Pro §2614.5
    Investigation upon conservatee wish to remove conservator and appoint successor conservator   Pro §1851
    Professional fiduciaries, removal for cause
        Report to professional fiduciaries bureau   Pro §2653
    Surety, notice to   Pro §1213
    Surrendering estate during proceedings for   Pro §2654
    Temporary conservators   Pro §2258
Rent on leases arranged by   Pro §§2553 to 2555
Residence of conservatee
    Generally   Pro §2352
    Change of   CRC 7.1063, Pro §§2253, 2254
    Least restrictive appropriate residence   Pro §2352.5
    Sale of   Pro §2540
Resignation
    Generally   Pro §2660
    Appointment of person to make educational decisions for minor   Pro §2662
    Temporary conservators   Pro §2258
Review of conservatorship   Pro §§1850 to 1853
Revocation of letters   Pro §§2650 to 2654
Rights of conservatee   Pro §§1823, 1828
Rights of conservators
    County to furnish information regarding   Pro §§1834 to 1835.5
Safe deposit boxes
    Opening or changing name on account, responsibilities of conservator   CRC 7.1061
Salaries and wages
    Claims for wages, conservator paying   Pro §2431
    Compensation generally (See within this heading, **"Compensation"**)
    Conservatees   Pro §2601
Sales
    Accounting and court review of   Pro §2625
    Appraisals   Pro §2543
    Auction sales   Pro §2543
    Authorization to sell personal residence   Pro §2541.5
    Bona fide purchasers of realty   Pro §§1875, 3074
    Bond requirements for realty sales   Pro §2330
    Conduct of   Pro §2543
    Confirmation requirements   Pro §§2540, 2544 to 2545
    Exchanges   Pro §§2545, 2550, 2557
    Exclusive listing, contents of petition for approval of   CRC 7.453
    Furniture   Pro §2545
    Mortgages or trust deeds and   Pro §2542
    Mutual funds without beneficiary designation   Pro §2544.5
    Notices re   Pro §§2540, 2543
    Permitted sales   Pro §2541
    Personal effects   Pro §2545
    Personal residence, sale of   Pro §2540
    Private sales   Pro §2543
    Proceeds, investment of   Pro §§2547, 2570 to 2574
    Public auctions   Pro §2543
    Recovery action by conservatee   Pro §2548

CONSERVATORS—Cont.
  Sales—Cont.
    Refusal to show property to prospective buyers   CRC 7.451
    Residence of conservatee
      Authorization to sell personal residence   Pro §2541.5
    Securities   Pro §2544
    Tangible personalty under $5,000   Pro §2545
    Terms of   Pro §2542
      Best interest of conservatee   Pro §2591.5
  Savings and loan associations
    Definitions   Pro §1490
    Funds deposited in
      Deposit of funds generally (See within this heading, **"Deposit of funds"**)
      Surety bond of conservator, funds in blocked account excluded in determining   Pro §2328
  Screening forms   CRC 7.1050
  Securities
    Deposits   Pro §§2455, 2456
    Sales   Pro §2544
    Shareholder rights, exercise of   Pro §2458
  Separate property (See **COMMUNITY PROPERTY**)
  Service of citation and petition on proposed conservatee   Pro §1824
  Service of process
    Generally   CCP §§416.60, 416.70
    Decedent's estate proceedings, notice served on conservator regarding   Pro §1210
  Settlement and compromise   Pro §§2500, 2507
    Attorneys' fees for services to minors and incompetent persons   CRC 7.955
    Conservatee and conservator, dispute between   Pro §2503
    Court approval for   Pro §§2500 to 2507
    Disposition of property or money paid pursuant to
      Trusts, payment into   CRC JudAdminStand 7.10
    Forms
      Judicial council forms   CRC 7.101
    Jurisdiction re   Pro §2505
    Law governing   Pro §2507
    Notice of settlement of entire case
      Minor's or disabled person's claims involved   CRC 3.1385
    Payments pursuant to   Pro §§3600 to 3613
      Express consent of protected person to court orders, when required   Pro §3613
      Trusts, payment into   CRC JudAdminStand 7.10
    Personal injury claims   Pro §2504
    Real property matters   Pro §2501
    Support and maintenance claims   Pro §2504
    Wrongful death claims   Pro §2504
  Shares (See within this heading, **"Securities"**)
  Small estates, authority of conservator regarding summary administration of   Pro §13051
  Spouses
    Appointment of spouse for proposed conservatee   Pro §1813
    Community property, management and control of   Pro §§3000 to 3154
      Authorization of transaction, findings and order   Pro §3144
    Disclosure by spouse of conservatee of legal separation, dissolution, or annulment   Pro §1813
    Surplus income distribution to   Pro §2423
  Standards of conduct   Pro §2410
  State hospitals
    Ward or conservatee as patient
      Notice to state department of state hospitals   Pro §§1461, 1511
  Statutes of limitation
    Sold property, action to recover   Pro §2548
    Sureties, actions against   Pro §2333
  Stay of order, bond requirements for   CCP §919
  Sterilization
    Appeals
      Sterilization of conservatee, judgment authorizing conservator to consent   CRC 8.482
  Sterilization proceedings (See **STERILIZATION**)
  Substituted judgment
    Considerations for court determination on proposed action   Pro §§2583, 2586
    Estate plan of conservatee as consideration for authorizing proposed action   Pro §§2583, 2586
    Findings of court required for authorization of proposed action   Pro §2582
    Liability of conservator for failure to propose actions under substituted judgment provisions   Pro §2585
    Notice of hearing on proposed action   Pro §2581
    Order authorizing proposed action   Pro §2584
    Petition for authorization for proposed action   Pro §2580

CONSERVATORS—Cont.
  Successor conservators
    Absentee conservatee   Pro §2689
    Appearance, persons making   Pro §2687
    Capacity to petition for   Pro §2681
    Contents of petition for   Pro §2682
    Continuance for failure of conservatee to appear   Pro §2686
    Failure of conservatee to appear at hearing   Pro §2686
    Investigation requirements   Pro §§2684, 2686
    Nature of hearing, court informing conservatee of   Pro §2685
    Notice of hearing   Pro §2683
    Order appointing   Pro §2688
    Procedure for appointment   Pro §2680
    Substitution during wartime (See **FIDUCIARIES' WARTIME SUBSTITUTION LAW**)
  Support of conservatee
    Generally   Pro §§2420 to 2423
    Spouse of conservatee (See within this heading, **"Support of spouse of conservatee"**)
  Support of spouse of conservatee
    Capacity to file support petition   Pro §3080
    Citation of managerial spouse   Pro §3082
    Continuances   Pro §3086
    Declarations required   Pro §3084
    Division of community property for   Pro §3089
    Enforcement of orders   Pro §3090
    Ex parte orders   Pro §3085
    Judicial Council authority   Pro §3091
    Managerial spouse, examination of   Pro §3082
    Method for payment   Pro §3088
    Modification of orders   Pro §§3083, 3088
    Notice of hearing   Pro §3081
    Order for payment   Pro §3088
    Pending determination, payments while   Pro §3083
    Revocation of orders   Pro §§3083, 3088
    Status of property, determination of   Pro §3087
  Sureties
    Bonds generally (See within this heading, **"Bonds"**)
  Surplus income, distribution of   Pro §2423
  Surrendering estate during removal proceedings   Pro §2654
  Suspension
    Mismanagement, allegations of   Pro §2334
    Removal of conservators, suspension during proceedings for   Pro §2654
    Surety, notice to   Pro §1213
    Temporary conservators   Pro §2258
  Taxation   Pro §2461
  Temporary conservators   Pro §§2250 to 2258
    Good cause exception to notice of hearing on petition for appointment   CRC 7.1062
    Indian child, temporary guardianships or conservatorships   CRC 7.1015
    Interstate jurisdiction, transfer and recognition
      Special jurisdiction   Pro §1994
  Terminal illness of custodial parent as grounds for appointing parent and parent's nominee as joint conservators   Pro §2105
  Termination
    Generally   Pro §§1860 to 1865
    Absentees, conservatorship for   Pro §1864
    Appearance of conservatee at hearing   Pro §1863
    Appointment of counsel   Pro §1861.5
    Appraisals   Pro §2633
    Assets transferred out of state   Pro §2808
    Court order for   Pro §1860
    Death of conservatee   Pro §1860
    Discharge (See within this heading, **"Discharge"**)
    Exhausted estate   Pro §2626
    Funeral expenses   Pro §2631
    Inventory, filing of   Pro §2633
    Investigation upon conservatee wish to terminate conservatorship   Pro §1851
    Jurisdiction retained following   Pro §2630
    Last illness, expenses of   Pro §2631
    Limited conservatorships   Pro §1860.5
      Recommendations on termination   Pro §1851
    Married minors   Pro §1860
    New proceedings, effect of   Pro §1863
    Notice of hearing   Pro §1862
    Petition for   Pro §1861
    Remaining assets after death of conservatee, transfer of   Pro §2631
    Removal   Pro §§2650 to 2654 (See within this heading, **"Removal"**)
    Temporary conservators   Pro §2257
    Unknown location of conservatee   Pro §1853

CONSERVATORS—Cont.
Termination—Cont.
    Voting rights, restoration of   Pro §1865
Testamentary dispositions (See **WILL CONSTRUCTION**)
Transaction defined   Pro §§1870, 2111
Transfer of assets out-of-state   Pro §§2800 to 2808
Transfers of conservatorships
    Change of residence of conservatee
        Petition for transfer   Pro §2352
    Interstate jurisdiction, transfer and recognition   Pro §§2001 to 2003
    Investigation and review upon acceptance of transfer from another jurisdiction   Pro §1851.1
    Other state, transfer from   Pro §2002
    Other state, transfer to   Pro §2001
    Tribal courts (California tribes), transfers to or from   Pro §2003
Transitional provisions   Pro §§1488 to 1490
Trial by jury, conservatees' right to   Pro §§1452, 1453, 1823, 1826 to 1828, 1863
Trust companies
    Generally   Pro §§2453, 2453.5, 2454, 2456
    Appointment as conservator   Pro §300
    Blocked accounts   Pro §2328
    Bond requirement as conservators   Pro §301
    Defined   Pro §83
    Fiduciary duties, restriction on investments   Pro §2401
    Notice to court upon conservator's taking possession of assets held by financial institutions   Pro §§2890 to 2893
    Order authorizing deposit or withdrawal of money or property in   Pro §2456
Trust deeds, executing notes and   Pro §§2550 to 2552
Undue influence, persons unable to resist
    Wrongful taking, concealment, etc of property of conservatee, minor, elder, dependent adult, etc   Pro §859
Uniform Transfers to Minors Act (See **UNIFORM TRANSFERS TO MINORS ACT**)
Venue
    Action against conservator   CCP §395.1
    Change of venue   Pro §§2210 to 2217
    Nonresident conservatee, proceedings for   Pro §2202
    Resident conservatee, proceedings for   Pro §2201
Veterans Administration, notice to   Pro §§1461.5, 1822
Vexatious litigants
    Petitions
        Unmeritorious petitions intended to annoy or harass   Pro §1970
Vote, conservatee's right to   Pro §1910
    Periodic review of conservatorship
        Determining ability to complete voter registration affidavit   Pro §1851
Wage claims, rules re   Pro §2431
Wartime substitution of (See **FIDUCIARIES' WARTIME SUBSTITUTION LAW**)
Waste, actions for recovery of treble damages for   CCP §732
Welfare payments
    Accounting when estate consists of   Pro §2628
    Bond requirement on estates involving   Pro §2323
    Payee, conservator as   Pro §2452
Will for conservatee, conservator making   Pro §§6100, 6100.5, 6110
Will probate proceedings, effect of notice served on conservator regarding   Pro §1210
Withdrawal
    Independent authority of conservator   Pro §2593
Wrongful taking, concealment, etc of property of conservatee, minor, elder, dependent adult, etc   Pro §859

CONSIDERATION
Generally (See **CONTRACTS AND AGREEMENTS**)
Voidable transactions   CC §§3439.03, 3439.04

CONSIGNMENTS
Art works delivered to dealers for   CC §§1738.5, 1738.6
Common carriers (See **COMMON CARRIERS**)
Definitions   CC §1738

CONSOLIDATED FARM AND RURAL DEVELOPMENT ACT
Shift-in-land-use loans, sale of decedent's land for   Pro §10207

CONSOLIDATION
Deeds, consolidation of   CC §1093
Support orders   Fam §17408

CONSOLIDATION OF ACTIONS   CRC 3.350
Arbitration actions   CCP §1281.3

CONSOLIDATION OF ACTIONS—Cont.
Authority for   CCP §1048
Common questions of law and fact   CCP §1048
Coordination petition
    Motions (See **COORDINATION OF ACTIONS**)
Decedent's estate, consolidation of actions involving liability insurer for   Pro §552
Family law proceedings
    Notice of consolidation   CRCAppx A (CRCFL-920)
Filing requirements   CRC 3.350
Motion requirements   CRC 3.350
Noncomplex actions, transfer and consolidation   CRC 3.500
Related cases   CRC 3.300
Validation proceedings, consolidation of actions in   CCP §865
Wrongful death (See **WRONGFUL DEATH**)

CONSOLIDATION OF ENTITIES
Cities (See **CITIES AND MUNICIPALITIES**)
Counties (See **COUNTIES**)
Districts (See **DISTRICTS**)
Public entities (See **PUBLIC ENTITIES**)

CONSPIRACY
Attorney conspiring with client, action against   CC §1714.10
Hearsay statements concerning conspiracy to commit crime, admissibility of   Ev §1223
Indictment (See **INDICTMENT, INFORMATION AND COMPLAINT**)

CONSTITUTIONAL LAW
Self-incrimination, privilege against
    Dependent child proceedings   CRC 5.534
Unconstitutionality of statute or regulation, notice to Attorney General   CRC 2.1100

CONSTRUCTION (See **BUILDING CONSTRUCTION**)

CONSTRUCTION AND INTERPRETATION
Generally   CCP §1858
Adoption proceedings, provisions for freeing minor from parental custody and control   Fam §7801
Ancillary administration   Pro §12500
Appellate rules
    Superior court appeals   CRC 8.802
        Statutes referenced considered to be as amended   CRC 8.805
    Supreme court and courts of appeal (See **APPELLATE RULES, SUPREME COURT AND COURTS OF APPEAL**)
Attachment proceedings   CCP §481.010
Automobile Sales Finance Act   CC §2981
Civil Code   CC §§5, 13, 21
Common interest developments
    Governing documents, deeds, condominium plans, etc
        Liberal construction   CC §4215
    Headings of sections and hierarchical elements
        Effect   CC §4005
    Local zoning ordinances   CC §4020
    Prospective application of provisions   CC §4010
Common-law rule construing code abrogated   CCP §4
Consumers Legal Remedy Act   CC §1760
Contempt proceedings, rules to construe affidavit or statement of facts in   CCP §1211.5
Continuation of existing statutes   CCP §5
Contracts (See **CONTRACTS AND AGREEMENTS**)
Conveyances   CCP §2077
Deeds   CC §§1066 to 1070, CCP §2077
Definitions applicable   Ev §§100 to 250
1872 Codes   CC §§23 to 23.6
Electronic filing and service rules
    Construction of rules   CRC 2.250
Emancipation of minors, legislative intent for declaration of   Fam §7110
Eminent domain law   CCP §§1235.010 to 1235.070
Evidence Code   Ev §§1 to 12
Execution of document, applicability of laws of place of   CCP §1857
Existing laws, code provisions construed as continuations of   CCP §5
Family code   Fam §§3, 6, 9 to 12
Favored party   CCP §1864
Fiduciaries' Wartime Substitution Law (See **FIDUCIARIES' WARTIME SUBSTITUTION LAW**)
Foreign country judgments
    Uniformity of law among states enacting provisions   CCP §1722
Gender   CCP §17

CONSTRUCTION AND INTERPRETATION—Cont.
Groundwater rights actions
    Factors used to construe provisions   CCP §830
Home equity sales contracts   CC §1695
Indemnity contracts   CC §2778
Information Practices Act   CC §§1798.63, 1798.70 to 1798.78
Institutional funds management
    Electronic signatures in global and national commerce act
        Effect of provisions on federal act   Pro §18509
    Uniform construction of provisions   Pro §18510
Intent of legislature controlling   CCP §1859
International commercial arbitration and conciliation
    General principles of law   CCP §1297.20
International Wills Act   Pro §6387
Joint and several liability   CC §§1430 to 1432
Judges, rules governing removal or censure of   JudPerR 138
Judicial arbitration statute   CCP §1141.30
Judicial districts, statutory references to   CCP §§17, 38
Landlord and tenant
    Commercial real property tenancies, disposition of property remaining upon termination
        Notice of abandonment provision, relation to disposition provisions   CC §1993.09
    Deposits by tenant to   CC §1950.5
Liberally construed, code provisions to be   CCP §4
Mobilehome evictions   CC §798.55
Natural rights favored   CCP §1866
Notices   CCP §1865
Oil and gas liens, statute governing   CCP §1203.66
Particular provisions controlling general   CCP §1859
Picketing, limiting injunctions for   CCP §527.3
Pleadings   CCP §452
Plural   CCP §17
Power of attorney (See **POWER OF ATTORNEY**)
Privileged communication provisions   Ev §§900 to 905
Probate Code   Pro §§1 to 13, 20
Retail installment sales statute   CC §1802
Rules of court   CRC 1.5
Sentencing in superior court, rules governing   CRC 4.405
Singular   CCP §17
Sterilization   Pro §1950
Suretyship agreement   CC §§2799 to 2802, 2837
Technical language
    Appropriate meaning or definition, technical words and phrases construed according to   CCP §16
    Contracts, use in   CC §1645
    Parol evidence proving meaning of   CCP §1861
Tense   CCP §17
Time of code effect   CC §23
Trusts (See **TRUSTS**)
Uniform International Wills Act   Pro §6387
Vehicle Leasing Act   CC §2985.7
Voidable transactions   CC §3440.9
Wills (See **WILL CONSTRUCTION**)
Words and phrases construed according to context and approved usage   CCP §16
Written words controlling printed words   CCP §1862

CONSTRUCTION CONTRACTS
Indemnity agreements   CC §§2782 to 2784
Mechanics' liens   CC §§8000 to 9566 (See **MECHANICS' LIENS**)

CONSTRUCTION DEFECTS, ACTIONS FOR   CC §§895 to 945.5
Actionable defects   CC §§896, 897
    Contracting to limit liability or diminish standards   CC §901
    Evidence required to prove   CC §942
Actual moisture barriers
    Defined   CC §895
Affirmative defenses   CC §945.5
Air conditioning
    Actionable defects   CC §896
Architects
    Additional liability not created by   CC §937
    Affirmative defenses   CC §945.5
    Applicability to subcontractors, suppliers, designers, etc   CC §936
    Certificate of merit
        Requirement not abrogated by provisions   CC §937
Attached structures
    Actionable defects   CC §896
Builders
    Comparative fault   CC §945.5
    Defenses   CC §945.5

CONSTRUCTION DEFECTS, ACTIONS FOR—Cont.
Builders—Cont.
    Defined   CC §911
    Prelitigation procedures
        Duties of builder   CC §912
        Nonparticipation in prelitigation process   CC §915
Cedar fire, San Diego county
    Reconstruction contracts
        Incorporation of construction defects actions provisions in contracts for reconstruction   CC §945.6
Claimants
    Defined   CC §895
Close of escrow
    Defined   CC §895
Commercial and industrial common interest developments   CC §§6874, 6876
Common interest developments
    Construction defect litigation generally   CC §§6000 to 6150
Comparative fault   CC §945.5
Complex litigation, factors determining   CRC 3.400
Damages   CC §943
    Measure   CC §944
Definitions   CC §895
    Actions   CC §941
Designed moisture barriers
    Defined   CC §895
Designers
    Additional liability not created by   CC §937
    Affirmative defenses   CC §945.5
    Applicability to subcontractors, suppliers, designers, etc   CC §936
    Certificate of merit
        Requirement not abrogated by provisions   CC §937
Discovery of claims
    Prelitigation procedures
        Subsequently discovered claims   CC §932
Drainage systems
    Actionable defects   CC §896
Driveways
    Actionable defects   CC §896
Dryer ducts
    Actionable defects   CC §896
Effective date   CC §938
Electrical issues
    Actionable defects   CC §896
Enhanced protection agreements   CC §902
    Consequences of election to offer or use   CC §906
    Disputes
        Bifurcation   CC §905
    Greater or equal protection than in provisions   CC §904
    Writing   CC §903
Evidence
    Residential construction standards, failure to meet   CC §942
Fences
    Actionable defects   CC §896
Fire protection issues
    Actionable defects   CC §896
General contractors
    Affirmative defenses   CC §945.5
    Applicability to subcontractors, suppliers, contractors, etc   CC §936
Heating
    Actionable defects   CC §896
Homeowners
    Defined   CC §895
    Maintenance obligations   CC §907
Inspections
    Prelitigation procedures   CC §916
Irrigation systems
    Actionable defects   CC §896
Limitation of actions   CC §941
    Prelitigation procedures
        Tolling statute of limitations   CC §927
Maintenance
    Homeowners' maintenance obligations   CC §907
Manufactured products or components
    Actionable defects   CC §896
    Affirmative defenses   CC §945.5
Materials suppliers
    Affirmative defenses   CC §945.5
    Applicability to subcontractors, suppliers, designers, etc   CC §936
Mediation
    Prelitigation procedures
        Offer to mediate   CC §919

CONSTRUCTION DEFECTS, ACTIONS FOR—Cont.
Mediation—Cont.
    Prelitigation procedures —Cont.
        Undergoing mediation   CC §928
Mitigation of damages, failure of homeowner
    Defenses of builder   CC §945.5
Ordinary wear and tear
    Defenses of builder   CC §945.5
Original purchasers
    Binding of original purchasers and successors   CC §945
Paint
    Actionable defects   CC §896
Patios
    Actionable defects   CC §896
Prelitigation procedures   CC §§910 to 938
    Alternative nonadversarial procedures   CC §914
    Applicability to subcontractors, suppliers, designers, etc   CC §936
    Builders
        Duties   CC §912
        Nonparticipation in prelitigation process   CC §915
    Cash settlements   CC §929
    Combined claims covering items not covered under chapter   CC §931
    Common interest developments
        Nonduplication of prelitigation procedures   CC §935
    Conduct of parties during prelitigation process
        Evidence at subsequent actions   CC §934
    Inspections   CC §916
    Mediation
        Offer to mediate   CC §919
        Undergoing mediation   CC §928
    Mixed claims covering items not covered under chapter   CC §931
    Nonadversarial nature   CC §914
    Notice   CC §910
        Acknowledgment of receipt   CC §§913, 915
    Repairs
        Accepting offer   CC §918
        Access to information about repair   CC §923
        Failure to offer   CC §920
        Observation   CC §922
        Offer to repair   CC §917
        Scheduling and effecting repair   CC §921
        Undertaking some but not all repairs   CC §924
        Unsuccessful repairs   CC §933
        Untimely repairs   CC §925
        Waiver or release from provisions   CC §926
    Strict construction of time periods and other provisions   CC §930
    Subsequently discovered claims
        Applicability of provisions   CC §932
    Time limits
        Strict construction of time periods and other provisions   CC §930
    Tolling statute of limitations   CC §927
Releases
    Defenses of builder   CC §945.5
Repairs
    Defenses of builder   CC §945.5
    Prelitigation procedures
        Accepting offer   CC §918
        Access to information about repair   CC §923
        Failure to offer   CC §920
        Observation   CC §922
        Offer to repair   CC §917
        Scheduling and effecting repair   CC §921
        Undertaking some but not all repairs   CC §924
        Unsuccessful repairs   CC §933
        Untimely repairs   CC §925
        Waiver or release from provisions   CC §926
Scope of actions permitted   CC §943
Settlements
    Prelitigation procedures
        Cash settlements   CC §929
        Time-limited demands   CCP §§999 to 999.5
Sidewalks
    Actionable defects   CC §896
Soil issues
    Actionable defects   CC §896
Stains
    Actionable defects   CC §896
Structural issues
    Actionable defects   CC §896
Structures
    Defined   CC §895

CONSTRUCTION DEFECTS, ACTIONS FOR—Cont.
Subcontractors
    Affirmative defenses   CC §945.5
    Applicability to subcontractors, suppliers, designers, etc   CC §936
Unforeseen act of nature
    Defenses of builder   CC §945.5
Unintended water
    Defined   CC §895
Warranties   CC §900
    Fit and finish   CC §900
Water issues
    Actionable defects   CC §896

CONSTRUCTION LIENS   CC §§8000 to 9566 (See **MECHANICS' LIENS**)

CONSTRUCTION PROJECTS
Mechanics' liens   CC §§8000 to 9566 (See **MECHANICS' LIENS**)

CONSTRUCTION-RELATED ACCESSIBILITY CLAIMS   CC §§55.3 to 55.57
Answers
    Demand letters to include answer forms   CC §55.3
Attorneys at law
    Prelitigation letters to education entities   CC §54.27
Attorneys' fees
    Factors considered in awarding   CC §55.55
Certified access specialists (CASp)
    Defined   CC §55.52
    Duties   CC §55.53
Complaints   CCP §425.50
    Advisory to defendant building owner, tenant, etc to be included by attorney with complaint or demand for money   CC §55.3
    Attorneys at law
        Duties of attorney upon sending or serving complaint   CC §55.32
    High-frequency litigants
        Contents of complaint filed by high-frequency litigant   CCP §425.50
        Defined   CCP §425.55
        Fees   Gov §70616.5
Compliance with standards   CC §§55.51 to 55.54
    Applicability of provisions   CC §55.51
    Citation of provisions   CC §55.51
    Definitions   CC §55.52
Conflicting state and federal standards
    More protective provision to be applied   CC §55.53
Correction of violations
    Reduction of damage liability   CC §55.56
Costs of suit
    Factors considered in determining recoverable costs   CC §55.55
Definitions
    Advisory to defendant included with complaint or demand for money   CC §55.3
    Compliance with standards   CC §55.52
Demand letters
    Allegation of construction-related accessibility claim   CC §55.31
    Answer forms included with demand letters   CC §55.3
    Attorneys
        Answer forms included with demand letters   CC §55.3
        Contents of demand letters   CC §55.3
        Requirements of attorneys sending demand letters   CC §55.32
    Contents   CC §55.3
    Definition of demand letter   CC §55.3
Demands for money
    Advisory to defendant building owner, tenant, etc to be included by attorney with complaint or demand for money   CC §55.3
Effective date of provisions   CC §55.57
Evaluation conferences
    Mandatory evaluation conference   CC §55.545
        Notice   CRC 3.682
    Stay and early evaluation conference   CC §55.54
Forms
    Judicial council legal forms   CRCAppx A
High-frequency litigants
    Complaints
        Contents of complaint filed by high-frequency litigant   CCP §425.50
        Notice to defendant of rights to stay and early evaluation conference   CC §55.54
    Defined   CCP §425.55
    Fees   Gov §70616.5
Inspections
    Certified access specialists (CASp)
        Duties   CC §55.53

CONSTRUCTION-RELATED ACCESSIBILITY CLAIMS—Cont.
Landlord and tenant
    Commercial real property tenancies
        Certified access specialist (CASp) inspections, statements, inspection certificates and inspection reports   CC §1938
Mandatory evaluation conference   CC §55.545
    Process and service of process   CRC 3.682
Mitigation of statutory damages   CC §55.56
Schools and education
    Attorneys at law
        Prelitigation letters to education entities   CC §54.27
Settlements
    Demand letters
        Allegation of construction-related accessibility claim   CC §55.31
Statutory damages
    Liability   CC §55.56
Stay and early evaluation conference
    Notice to defendant of rights to   CC §55.54
    Service of notice   CRC 3.680
Technical violations
    Presumptions   CC §55.56

CONSTRUCTIVE NOTICE (See RECORDS AND RECORDING)

CONSTRUCTIVE TRUSTS
Generally   CC §§2223, 2224
Applicability of Trust Law to   Pro §15003
Attorney general actions
    Statute of limitations   CC §2224.5

CONSULS AND CONSULATES
Acknowledgment of instruments   CC §1183
Affidavits taken before   CCP §2014
Death of foreign citizen, notice of   Pro §8113
International wills   Pro §6380
Signature of consul general   Ev §§1454, 1530

CONSULTANTS
Health care service plans, immunity from prosecution for consultants to Managed Health Care Department overseeing statutory compliance of   CC §43.98
Mortgage foreclosure consultants   CC §§2945 to 2945.11

CONSUMER AFFAIRS DEPARTMENT
Asian language contracts, translations   CC §1632
Spanish language, contracts written in   CC §1632

CONSUMER ARBITRATION
Definition of consumer arbitration
    Arbitrators, ethics standards for neutral arbitrators   CRC ArbEthicsStand 2
Disclosures by arbitrator
    Openness to offers of employment or professional relationship   CRC ArbEthicsStand 7
    Provider organizations administering arbitration   CRC ArbEthicsStand 8
Disqualification of arbitrator
    Financial interests of private arbitration companies in consumer arbitrations   CCP §1281.92
Fees and costs in consumer proceedings   CCP §1284.3

CONSUMER CONTRACT AWARENESS ACT
Arbitration   CC §§1799.208, 1799.209
Citation of Act   CC §1799.200
Conflict of laws   CC §1799.208
Definitions   CC §1799.201
Delivery of copies of
    To consumer   CC §1799.202
    To guarantor   CC §1799.206
    To multiple parties of contract   CC §1799.204
Guarantor, seller's obligation to furnish contract copy to   CC §1799.206
Liability of seller failing to comply with requirement to furnish copies of   CC §1799.205
Multiple parties, seller's obligation to furnish copies to   CC §1799.204
Transactions requiring seller to furnish copies of   CC §1799.203
Waiver of protections   CC §1799.207

CONSUMER CREDIT CONTRACTS
Adverse credit information on cosigner   CC §1799.101
Attorneys' fees
    Holder rule
        Attorneys' fees for exercise of rights under holder rule   CC §1459.5
Chinese language
    Foreign language translations of notice requirement   CC §1799.91
        Federal notice requirement   CC §1799.96

CONSUMER CREDIT CONTRACTS—Cont.
Cosigner
    Consumer credit contract, notice of   CC §1799.91
    Damages recoverable by cosigner for creditor's violation of collection procedure   CC §1799.101
    Obligations of payment   CC §1799.101
Credit denial disclosure act
    Waiver of protections   CC §1787.4
Definitions   CC §§1799.90, 1799.101
Holder rule
    Attorneys' fees for exercise of rights under holder rule   CC §1459.5
Household goods, security interests in   CC §1799.100
Investment property pledged as collateral on consumer credit contract, restrictions concerning   CC §1799.103
Korean language
    Foreign language translations of notice requirement   CC §1799.91
        Federal notice requirement   CC §1799.96
Marital relationships, effect on   CC §1799.98
Medical debts   CC §§1785.20.6, 1785.27
Notice
    Form of notice   CC §1799.92
Notice requirement
    Action or enforcement prohibited against person entitled to notice but not given notice   CC §1799.95
    Contents of   CC §1799.91
    Federal notice requirement
        Actions against person subject to   CC §1799.99
        Applicability of   CC §1799.96
    Federal notice requirement, applicability of   CC §1799.96
    Placement or inclusion of notice within sales agreement   CC §1799.92
    Rights and obligations of parties, effect on   CC §1799.94
Personal property, security interests in   CC §1799.100
Religious books and materials, validity of security interests in   CC §1799.97
Signatures required   CC §1799.93
Spanish language
    Foreign language translations of notice requirement   CC §1799.91
        Federal notice requirement   CC §1799.96
Suretyship transactions, effect on   CC §1799.98
Tagalog language
    Foreign language translations of notice requirement   CC §1799.91
        Federal notice requirement   CC §1799.96
Vietnamese language
    Foreign language translations of notice requirement   CC §1799.91
        Federal notice requirement   CC §1799.96
Waiver of protections   CC §1799.104

CONSUMER DEBT COLLECTION   CC §§1788 to 1788.33
Common counts, use prohibited   CCP §425.30
Communications practices   CC §§1788.10 to 1788.185
Dismissal of civil actions
    Consumer debt
        Plaintiff debt buyer failing to appear or prepare to proceed   CCP §581.5
Exemption of principal residence from execution of judgment lien   CCP §699.730
Fair debt buying generally   CC §§1788.50 to 1788.66 (See FAIR DEBT BUYING PRACTICES)
Hospital debt
    Collection practices and required communications   CC §1788.14
    Complaints brought be debt collector
        Allegations required   CC §1788.185
        Confidential information, redaction   CC §1788.185
        Contents included with complaint   CC §1788.185
    Default judgments   CC §1788.185
Notice for consumer collections   CC §§1812.700 to 1812.702
    Change of notice   CC §1812.701
    Third party debt collector notice to debtor   CC §1812.700
    Violations of provisions   CC §1812.702
Statement by debt collector
    Contents   CC §1788.14.5
    Required statement upon debtor request   CC §1788.14.5
Time-barred debt, attempts to collect
    Communications with debtor   CC §1788.14
Waiver of protections   CC §1788.33

CONSUMER FINANCIAL PROTECTION
Solicitation of consumer for consumer financial product or service
    Disclosures   CC §1770
    Unfair competition and trade practices   CC §1770

CONSUMER GOODS AND SERVICES
Venue in actions founded on obligations for   CCP §§395, 396a

CONSUMER LEGAL REMEDIES ACT
Disclosures to consumers in solicitation to consumer for consumer financial products or services   CC §1770

CONSUMER PRIVACY RIGHTS   CC §§1798.100 to 1798.199.100
Actions for damages, injunctions, declaratory relief, etc
    Security practices and procedures not in place   CC §1798.150
Applicability of provisions   CC §1798.146
California privacy protection agency   CC §§1798.199.10 to 1798.199.100
    Appropriations to fund agency   CC §1798.199.95
    Board
        Compensation   CC §1798.199.25
        Composition   CC §1798.199.15
        Delegation of authority to chair or executive director   CC §1798.199.35
        Duties   CC §1798.199.15
        Governance of agency   CC §1798.199.10
        Qualifications of members   CC §1798.199.15
        Terms of members   CC §1798.199.20
    Cease and desist
        Orders upon violation of provisions   CC §1798.199.55
    Cure of violation
        Agency authority to work with business towards one-time cure   CC §1798.199.45
    Data broker registration
        Access of accessible deletion mechanism   CC §1798.99.86
        Annual registration   CC §1798.99.82
        Generally   CC §§1798.99.80 to 1798.99.89
        Information provided for registration
            Access by public to information filed   CC §1798.99.84
        Rulemaking by agency   CC §1798.99.87
    Duties of agency   CC §1798.199.35
    Established   CC §1798.199.10
    Executive director
        Appointment   CC §1798.199.30
        Duties   CC §1798.199.30
    Fines for violations   CC §1798.199.55
        Actions to collect unpaid fines   CC §1798.199.75
        Good faith of business, service provider, contractor, etc, consideration by agency   CC §1798.199.100
        Judgment to collect, application by agency for   CC §1798.199.80
        Judicial review of complaint or fine   CC §1798.199.85
    Good faith of business, service provider, contractor, etc
        Consideration by agency   CC §1798.199.100
    Investigation of violations   CC §1798.199.45
    Judicial review of complaint or fine   CC §1798.199.85
    Limitation of actions for administrative actions   CC §1798.199.70
    Notice of violation   CC §1798.199.50
    Orders upon violation of provisions   CC §1798.199.55
    Probable cause to believe violation of provisions
        Due process requirements for finding   CC §1798.199.50
        Hearing upon finding of probable cause   CC §1798.199.55
        Judicial review of complaint or fine   CC §1798.199.85
    Purpose   CC §1798.199.10
    Rejection of administrative law judge decision
        Statement of reasons   CC §1798.199.60
    Staffing of agency   CC §1798.199.95
    Subpoenas
        Authority of agency   CC §1798.199.65
    Witnesses
        Subpoenas, agency authority   CC §1798.199.65
Cease and desist
    Orders upon violation of provisions   CC §1798.199.55
Compliance with provisions
    Penalties for noncompliance   CC §1798.155
Conflict with other provisions   CC §1798.175
Consumer privacy fund
    Established   CC §1798.160
    Investment of money in fund   CC §1798.160
    Offsetting costs of enforcement, use of fund   CC §1798.160
    Use of money in fund   CC §1798.160
Cure of violation
    California privacy protection agency
        Agency authority to work with business towards one-time cure   CC §1798.199.45
Data broker registration
    Generally   CC §§1798.99.80 to 1798.99.89
    Statutory construction of data broker registration provisions with consumer privacy act   CC §1798.99.88
Definitions   CC §1798.140
Discrimination against consumer for exercise of rights   CC §1798.125

CONSUMER PRIVACY RIGHTS—Cont.
Effect of obligations on businesses   CC §1798.145
Exemptions   CC §1798.145
Family planning centers
    Personal information restrictions of persons at or near   CC §1798.99.90
Financial incentives for collection, sale or deletion of personal information   CC §1798.125
Fines for violations   CC §1798.199.55
    Actions to collect unpaid fines   CC §1798.199.75
    Businesses, service providers, contractors, etc   CC §1798.199.90
    Good faith of business, service provider, contractor, etc, consideration by agency   CC §1798.199.100
    Judgment to collect, application by agency for   CC §1798.199.80
    Judicial review of complaint or fine   CC §1798.199.85
Injunctions against violations
    Businesses, service providers, contractors, etc   CC §1798.199.90
Investigation of violations
    California privacy protection agency   CC §1798.199.45
Liberal construction of provisions   CC §1798.194
Limitation of actions
    California privacy protection agency
        Administrative actions   CC §1798.199.70
Limits of business obligations   CC §1798.145
Multiple-step transactions designed to avoid or evade provisions   CC §1798.190
Notice of violation   CC §1798.199.50
Operative date of provisions   CC §1798.198
    Preemption of local provisions   CC §1798.199
Opt in consent by consumer for financial incentive programs   CC §1798.125
Opt out rights of consumer   CC §1798.120
    Business implementation of opt out mechanism   CC §1798.135
Orders upon violation of provisions   CC §1798.199.55
Personal information collected by business
    Correction of inaccurate personal information
        Compliance with request   CC §1798.130
        Right of consumer to correct   CC §1798.106
    Deletion of information collected
        Financial incentives for collection, sale or deletion of personal information   CC §1798.125
        Request   CC §1798.105
    Disclosures by businesses collecting
        Categories of information to which consumer entitled   CC §1798.110
        Compliance with request   CC §1798.130
        Correction of inaccurate personal information, right of consumer to correct to be disclosed   CC §1798.106
        Deletion of information collected
            Right to deletion to be disclosed   CC §1798.105
        Duties of businesses   CC §1798.100
        Time for disclosure   CC §1798.100
    Duties of businesses collecting   CC §1798.100
    Financial incentives for collection, sale or deletion of personal information   CC §1798.125
    Loyalty or other awards, premiums, discounts, etc
        Permitted   CC §1798.125
    Notice of categories collected   CC §1798.100
    Opt in consent by consumer for financial incentive programs   CC §1798.125
    Records
        Deletion of information collected, record of requests   CC §1798.105
    Request by consumer for information   CC §1798.100
        Compliance with request   CC §1798.130
        Contents of request   CC §1798.110
    Sale or sharing of information by business
        Children's information, restrictions on sale or disclosure   CC §1798.120
        Deletion of information collected, notice to buyers or sharers   CC §1798.105
        Disclosures upon consumer request   CC §1798.115
        Elimination of monetary or other consideration to avoid provisions   CC §1798.190
        Opt out rights of consumer   CC §1798.120
    Sensitive personal information
        Defined   CC §1798.140
        Limiting use and disclosure, consumer's right   CC §1798.121
        Methods of limiting use and disclosure   CC §1798.135
Preemption of local provisions   CC §1798.180
    Operative date   CC §1798.199
Privacy protection agency   CC §§1798.199.10 to 1798.199.100
Probable cause to believe violation of provisions
    Due process requirements for finding   CC §1798.199.50
    Hearing upon finding of probable cause   CC §1798.199.55
    Judicial review of complaint or fine   CC §1798.199.85

CONSUMER PRIVACY RIGHTS—Cont.
Reidentification of deidentified information, prohibitions   CC §1798.148
Requests regarding personal information
    Methods for requests provided by businesses   CC §1798.130
    Notice of rights to make requests   CC §1798.130
    Time for response   CC §1798.130
Rulemaking to implement provisions   CC §1798.185
    California privacy protection agency
        Duties of agency   CC §1798.199.35
Sale or sharing of personal information
    Children's information
        Restrictions on sale or disclosure   CC §1798.120
    Disclosures upon consumer request   CC §1798.115
        Compliance with request   CC §1798.130
    Elimination of monetary or other consideration to avoid provisions   CC §1798.190
    Financial incentives for collection, sale or deletion of personal information   CC §1798.125
    Loyalty or other awards, premiums, discounts, etc
        Permitted   CC §1798.125
    Opt in consent by consumer for financial incentive programs   CC §1798.125
    Opt out rights of consumer   CC §1798.120
        Business implementation of opt out mechanism   CC §1798.135
Scope of obligations imposed on businesses   CC §1798.145
Sensitive personal information
    Defined   CC §1798.140
    Limiting use and disclosure, consumer's right   CC §1798.121
        Methods   CC §1798.135
Service providers to business
    Deletion of information collected   CC §1798.105
    Violations by providers, attribution to business   CC §1798.145
Statutory construction
    Harmony with state and federal law   CC §1798.196
    Liberal construction of provisions   CC §1798.194
Student grades, educational scores or test results
    Limits on obligations on businesses   CC §1798.145
Subpoenas, compliance
    Exemptions on businesses to comply with subpoenas   CC §1798.145
Time for business to respond to and honor consumer rights
    Extensions   CC §1798.145
Waiver or limitation of consumer rights
    Contracts or agreements void   CC §1798.192

CONSUMER PROTECTION
Generally   CC §§1750 to 1756
Actions authorized   CC §§1780 to 1784
Aged persons, remedies for   CC §§1780, 3345
Arbitration and arbitrators
    Disqualification of arbitrator
        Financial interests of private arbitration companies in consumer arbitrations   CCP §1281.92
    Drafting party breach of arbitration agreement
        Consequences   CCP §1281.98
        Monetary sanctions against breaching party   CCP §1281.99
        Nonpayment of fees   CCP §1281.97
    Fees and costs in consumer proceedings   CCP §1284.3
        Drafting party obligation   CCP §1281.97
    Private arbitration companies
        Disclosures   CCP §1281.96
Autographed memorabilia, dealer's sale   CC §1739.7
Class actions   CC §§1752, 1781
Commencement of action   CC §1780
Conditional sales (See **CONDITIONAL SALES**)
Consumer contract awareness act (See **CONSUMER CONTRACT AWARENESS ACT**)
Credit cards (See **CREDIT CARDS**)
Credit contracts (See **CONDITIONAL SALES**)
Credit reports (See **CREDIT REPORTING**)
Credit services organizations (See **CREDIT SERVICES ORGANIATIONS**)
Damages
    Generally   CC §1780
    Warranties, recovery on   CC §§1794, 1794.1
Deceptive practices   CC §1770
Definitions   CC §1761
Delivery of goods purchased under retail sales contract within 4-hour period   CC §1722
Demand for correction or repair as prerequisite to action for damages by consumer   CC §1782
Disabled persons, remedies for   CC §§1780, 3345

CONSUMER PROTECTION—Cont.
Discount buying services contracts   CC §§1812.100 to 1812.129
Electronic commercial services (See **ELECTRONIC COMMERCIAL SERVICES**)
Garnishment regulated by Consumer Credit Protection Act   CCP §706.151
Gift certificates, prohibition against expiration dates on   CC §1749.5
    Bankruptcy of issuer, duty to honor   CC §1749.6
    Waiver of protections
        Void   CC §1749.51
Grey market goods sales (See **GREY MARKET GOODS**)
Home Equity Loan Disclosure Act   CC §§2970 to 2971
Home solicitation sales contracts (See **HOME SOLICITATION SALES CONTRACTS**)
Injunctive relief   CC §1782
Installment sales regulated (See **RETAIL INSTALLMENT SALES**)
Layaway plans   CC §§1749 to 1749.4
Leased consumer goods, warranties for   CC §§1791, 1795.4
Married women, discrimination against   CC §§1812.30, 1812.31
Products liability (See **PRODUCTS LIABILITY**)
Rent-to-own transactions   CC §§1812.620 to 1812.650
Repair and replacement
    Demand for correction or repair as prerequisite to action for damages by consumer   CC §1782
    Presence of consumer required during repair or service, 4-hour time period for commencement of contracted repairs when   CC §1722
    Warranty, goods under   CC §§1793.2, 1793.3, 1793.6
Retail installment sales (See **RETAIL INSTALLMENT SALES**)
Return of goods under warranty   CC §1793.2
Seller assisted marketing plans   CC §§1812.200 to 1812.221
Senior citizens, remedies for   CC §§1780, 3345
Small claims court judges, bench book availability   CCP §116.930
Small claims courts
    Selection of forum outside of state
        Contracts for personal, family or household purposes   CCP §116.225
Subpoena of consumer's records   CCP §§1985.3, 1985.4
Unsolicited goods   CC §§1584.5, 1584.6
Venue of consumer actions   CC §1780
Veterans
    Remedies   CC §3345
Warranties (See **WARRANTIES**)

CONSUMER REFUNDS
Prepaid debit card, refund offered by
    Alternative method required to be offered   CC §1748.41
    Definitions   CC §1748.40

CONSUMER REPORTS
Consumer privacy rights
    Exemptions from privacy requirements   CC §1798.145
Credit reports generally (See **CREDIT REPORTING**)
Escrow agent rating service
    Applicability of consumer credit reporting agency provisions to rating service   CC §§1785.28, 1785.28.6
Landlord and tenant
    Consumer reports regarding rent payments   CC §1954.07
Personal information protection
    Consumer credit reporting agencies
        Software updates and other measures to address security vulnerability   CC §1798.81.6
Private student loan collections reform
    Actions against creditor, lender or collector for violations of provisions
        Correction of consumer report, removal of derogatory information, etc   CC §1788.208

CONSUMER REPRESENTATIVES
Small claims advisory committee, composition of   CCP §116.950

CONSUMER WARRANTY PROTECTION
Cancellation of month-to-month or periodic service contracts by contractor   CC §1794.4
Delivery of consumer goods
    Manufacturer's express warranties prior to delivery
        Prohibition   CC §1793.01
Electronic online warranty
    Disclosures   CC §1793.1
Hearing aids and accessories
    Extension of warranty period during service or repairs   CC §1795.6
    Return to seller for adjustment, replacement or refund   CC §1793.02
Manufacturer's express warranties
    Prior to delivery of consumer good
        Prohibition of express warranty   CC §1793.01

CONSUMER WARRANTY PROTECTION—Cont.
Month-to-month or periodic service contracts in lieu of warranty   CC §1794.4
Product registration card
    Disclosures   CC §1793.1
Service contract to buyer, sale of
    Retailers' duties under service contracts   CC §1794.45
Used vehicles
    Buy-here-pay-here dealers' obligations   CC §1795.51

CONTAGIOUS DISEASES
Libel and slander   CC §46
Medical information disclosures by providers
    Prevention or controlling of diseases, injuries, etc   CC §56.10
Minor's treatment of   Fam §6926

CONTAINERS
Fair packaging and labeling
    Attorney general, civil actions to enforce provisions
        Fees and costs for attorney general   CCP §1021.8

CONTEMPT
Acts and omissions constituting   CCP §1209
Administrative adjudication (See **ADMINISTRATIVE ADJUDICATION**)
Affidavit in indirect contempt proceeding   CCP §§1211, 1211.5
Arrest   CCP §§1212, 1214, 1220
Attachments, failing to transfer possession   CCP §482.080
Attorney fees and costs, contemnor ordered to pay   CCP §1218
Attorney misconduct triggering notification to state bar
    Appellate justice's duties   CRC 10.1017
    Trial judge duties   CRC 10.609
Attorneys, stay of contempt orders against   CCP §§128, 1209
Bail   CCP §§1213, 1215, 1216
Breach of peace during trial   CCP §1209
Children
    Imprisonment or physical confinement
        Circumstances where imprisonment barred   CCP §1219
    Refusal to testify   CCP §1219.5
Child support proceedings (See **CHILD SUPPORT**)
Clerks of court   CCP §1209
Community service imposed on contemner   CCP §1218
Concealment of assets by estate representative   Pro §§8870, 8873
Construe, amend and review affidavit or statement of facts, rules to   CCP §1211.5
County government officials, contempt orders against   CCP §128
Decedent's representative (See **EXECUTORS AND ADMINISTRATORS**)
Deposition proceedings (See **DEPOSITIONS**)
Deposits in court, refusal to make   CCP §574
Direct contempt   CCP §1211
Disorderly conduct during trial   CCP §1209
Dissolution of marriage proceedings   Fam §2026
Domestic violence victim, contempt orders against   CCP §§128, 1219
Earnings assignment for support, employer's noncompliance under   Fam §5241
Enforcement of judgments   CCP §717.010
Examination proceedings for purposes of enforcement of judgments, failure to appear at   CCP §708.170
Family law proceedings   Fam §§290, 292, 2026
    Affidavits
        Facts constituting contempt   CRCAppxs A (CRCFL-411), (CRCFL-412)
    Findings and order   CRCAppx A (CRCFL-415)
    Orders to show cause   CRCAppx A (CRCFL-410)
Fines for   CCP §1218
Illness affecting person under arrest for   CCP §1221
Imprisonment for failure to comply with court order   CCP §1219
Indirect contempt   CCP §§1211, 1211.5
Journalists failing to testify, procedural requirements as to   CCP §1986.1
Judges
    Competency to testify as to statement or conduct that gave rise to contempt   Ev §703.5
    Power to punish for contempt   CCP §178
    Responsibility to maintain order and decorum   CRCSupp JudEthicsCanon 3
Judgments and decrees
    Disobedience to   CCP §1209
    Finality of orders on contempt   CCP §1222
Judicial council form of order to show cause and affidavit for contempt (family law)   CCP §1211, Fam §292
Judicial officer's power to punish for   CCP §178
Jury summons, failure to respond to   CCP §209
    Motion to set aside sanctions imposed by default   CRC 2.1010
Mediator's competency to testify as to act that gave rise to contempt   Ev §703.5

CONTEMPT—Cont.
Minors
    Imprisonment or physical confinement
        Circumstances where imprisonment barred   CCP §1219
    Refusal to testify   CCP §1219.5
Newspapers and magazines (See **NEWSPAPERS AND MAGAZINES**)
Order made on subsequent application, violation of requirements for   CCP §1008
Penalties for   CCP §1218
Possession, re-entry after removal from   CCP §1210
Privileged communication, contempt for person claiming   Ev §914
Proof of execution of instruments, contempt in proceedings for   CC §1201
Public safety employees, stay of contempt orders against   CCP §128
Punishment for   CCP §1218
Remote proceedings
    Conditions for proceeding through use of remote technology   CCP §367.76
Sentences for   CCP §1218
Service requirements, exception to   CCP §1016
Sexual assault victims, contempt orders against   CCP §§128, 1219
Show cause orders
    Family law cases   CRCAppx A (CRCFL-410)
Small claims court judgment, sanctions for failure to disclose assets for purposes of enforcement of   CCP §116.830
State agency hearings (See **ADMINISTRATIVE ADJUDICATION**)
Statement of facts by judicial officer   CCP §§1211, 1211.5
Stay of execution of contempt order pending filing of petition for extraordinary relief   CCP §128
Subpoena disobeyed   CCP §§1985.1, 1991 to 1992
Summary punishment of contempt committed in court's presence   CCP §1211
Support proceedings (See **CHILD SUPPORT**)
Termination of parental rights, failure to comply with citation to appear at hearing   Fam §7883
Trial for   CCP §1217
Uniform Parentage Act, failure to obey judgment in action brought under   Fam §7641
Vexatious litigant's disobedience of order prohibiting filing of new litigation   CCP §391.7

CONTEST OF WILL   Pro §§21300 to 21308, 21310 to 21315, 21320 to 21322

CONTEXT
Civil Code, construction of   CC §13

CONTIGUOUS PROPERTY (See **ADJACENT LANDOWNERS**)

CONTINGENT FEES
Attorneys fees generally (See **ATTORNEY'S FEES**)
Mediation
    Standards of conduct for mediators   CRC 3.859

CONTINGENT LIABILITY
Confession of judgment for purpose of securing person against   CCP §1132

CONTINGENT REMAINDER (See **REMAINDERS**)

CONTINUANCES   CCP §§594a to 599
Administration of estates (See **ADMINISTRATION OF ESTATES**)
Administrative Procedure Act, continuances under (See **ADMINISTRATIVE PROCEDURE ACT**)
Adoption proceedings, hearing on termination of parental rights of alleged father   Fam §7668
Affidavits showing need for   CCP §595.4
Amendment of pleadings, postponement due to   CCP §473
Appellate rules, supreme court and courts of appeal
    Oral arguments   CRCSupp 1st AppDist
Arbitration   CCP §1286.2
    Judicial arbitration   CRC 3.818
Attachments, hearings on   CCP §484.080
Attorneys' agreement for   CCP §595.2
Conservators (See **CONSERVATORS**)
Costs   CCP §1024
COVID-19, cases extended pursuant to   CCP §599
Criminal cases   CRC 4.113
    Trial, cases set for   CRC 4.113, 4.115
Decedent's estates, administration of (See **ADMINISTRATION OF ESTATES**)
Depositions   CCP §§595.1, 596
Discovery proceedings, proceedings in court defined to include   CCP §595.1
Dissolution of marriage proceedings   Fam §2334
Evidence, absence of   CCP §595.4
Ex parte temporary restraining orders, hearing   Fam §245
Family rules
    Live testimony
        Determination of whether continuance necessary or desirable   CRC 5.113

CONTINUANCES—Cont.
Family rules—Cont.
  Request for orders
    Temporary emergency orders   CRC 5.94
  Rescheduling hearings
    Definition of rescheduling the hearing   CRC 5.2
    Failure to request order   CRC 5.94
    Requesting to reschedule hearing   CRC 5.95
Grounds   CRC 3.1332
Harassment
  Protection order proceedings   CCP §527.6
    COVID-19, emergency rule   CRCAppx I Emer Rule 8
Indian child welfare act involuntary placements   CRC 5.482
  Commencement of proceedings
    Time for commencement   CRC 5.482
  Dispositional hearings when court knows or has reason to know Indian child involved
    Limits on continuances   CRC 5.550
Interrogatories, proceedings in court defined to include   CCP §595.1
Judicial arbitration   CRC 3.818
Jury fees refunded   CCP §631.3
Law and motion rules of court regarding motions for   CRC 3.1332
Legislative continuance   CCP §595
Mining claims   CCP §595.3
Motions for   CRC 3.1332
Preference, effect of grant of motion for   CCP §36
Pretrial conferences, proceedings in court defined to include   CCP §595.1
Protective orders
  Requests for protective orders   CRC 3.1160
Small claims court actions
  Appeal   CRC 8.960
State agency proceedings (See **ADMINISTRATIVE PROCEDURE ACT**)
Summary judgment motions   CCP §437c
Superior courts (See **SUPERIOR COURTS**)
Termination of parental rights   Fam §7871
  Appointment of counsel   Fam §7864
Trial court delay reduction programs (See **TRIAL COURT DELAY REDUCTION**)
Will probate proceedings (See **WILL PROBATE**)
Workplace violence or threat of violence
  Protection order proceedings
    COVID-19, emergency rule   CRCAppx I Emer Rule 8

CONTINUATION OF PENDING ACTION OR PROCEEDING (See **PENDENCY OF ACTIONS**)

CONTINUING EDUCATION
Administrative office of the courts
  Executives, managers, supervisors, etc, education requirements   CRC 10.491
Attorneys at law
  Custody and visitation cases
    Court-appointed counsel for minor, qualifications for appointment   CRC 5.242
  Delinquency cases
    Training of attorneys representing children in delinquency cases   CRC 5.664
  Discipline
    Minimum continuing legal education requirements, failure to comply with   CRC 9.31
  Guardianship and conservatorship proceedings
    Court appointed attorneys in probate proceedings   CRC 7.1102, 7.1103
  Interpreters   CRC 2.890
  Mandatory status   CRC 9.31
Child custody evaluators and investigators   CRC 5.225
  Supervisors of investigators and evaluators   CRC 5.220
Clerk/executive officers for supreme court and courts of appeals
  Minimum education requirements   CRC 10.471
  Providers and course criteria approval   CRC 10.481
Court investigators
  Probate court investigators   CRC 10.478
Dependency mediators
  Count-connected dependency mediation   CRC 5.518
Family rules
  Title IV-D support enforcement
    Child support commissioners   CRC 5.340
Judges
  Additional education recommendations for certain judicial assignments   CRC 10.469
  Family law judges and subordinate judicial officers   CRC 10.463

CONTINUING EDUCATION—Cont.
Judges—Cont.
  Probate cases, judges and subordinate judicial officers regularly assigned to   CRC 10.468
    Domestic violence issues   CRC 10.464
  Providers and course criteria approval   CRC 10.481
  Temporary judges   CRC 2.815
  Trial courts   CRC 10.462
    Executive officers   CRC 10.473
    Managers, supervisors and personnel   CRC 10.474
    Subordinate judicial officers   CRC 10.462
Judicial administration rules
  Education of judicial officers
    Delivery methods to satisfy continuing education requirements   CRC 10.493
Judicial council   CRC 10.491
  Temporary extension and reduction of education requirements, content-based and hours-based requirements   CRC 10.492
Justices
  Additional education recommendations for certain judicial assignments   CRC 10.469
  Minimum education requirements   CRC 10.461
  Providers and course criteria approval   CRC 10.481
Managing attorneys
  Minimum education requirements for managing attorneys, supervisors, etc of supreme court and courts of appeals   CRC 10.472
  Providers and course criteria approval   CRC 10.481
Probate attorneys   CRC 10.478
Probate court investigators   CRC 10.478
Probate examiners   CRC 10.478
Public administrators   Pro §7605
Public conservators   Pro §1456.2
Public guardians   Pro §2923
Small claims court
  Temporary judges   CCP §116.240
Supervisors
  Minimum education requirements for managing attorneys, supervisors, etc of supreme court and courts of appeals   CRC 10.472
  Providers and course criteria approval   CRC 10.481

CONTRACTOR RELATIONS   CC §§8000 to 9566 (See **MECHANICS' LIENS**)

CONTRACTORS
Building construction generally (See **BUILDING CONSTRUCTION**)
Building contractors
  Mechanics' liens   CC §§8000 to 9566
  Payment bonds
    Private works   CC §§8600 to 8614
    Public works   CC §§9550 to 9566
Mechanics' liens   CC §§8000 to 9566

CONTRACTS AND AGREEMENTS
Acceptance
  Generally   CC §1584
  Accord and satisfaction   CC §1523
  Benefits, acceptance of   CC §1589
  Conditional acceptance   CC §1582
  Indemnity contracts   CC §2795
  Qualified acceptance   CC §1585
  Retail installment account agreement   CC §1810
  Seller assisted marketing plan   CC §1812.202
  Voidable contract   CC §1588
Accord and satisfaction (See **ACCORD AND SATISFACTION**)
Adhesion, contracts of
  Time for performance
    Reasonable time required in contracts of adhesion   CC §1657.1
Administration of estates (See **ADMINISTRATION OF ESTATES**)
Adoption of child, agreements for (See **ADOPTION**)
Alteration
  Forgery (See **FORGERY**)
  Modification   CC §1698
    Copies of contract, effect of altering   CC §1701
Alternative performance   CC §§1448 to 1451
Appellate rules, supreme court and courts of appeal
  E-filing in supreme court and courts of appeal
    Electronic filing service providers, contracts with   CRC 8.73
Arbitration
  Generally (See **ARBITRATION**)
Asian language contracts   CC §1632
  Mortgages of residential property, foreign language summaries of terms   CC §1632.5

CONTRACTS AND AGREEMENTS—Cont.
Assisted reproduction
    Embryo donation
        Renunciation of legal interest in embryos
            Agreement between non-married persons sharing legal control over disposition   Fam §7613
Attorney's fees
    Generally (See **ATTORNEY'S FEES**)
Auction contract   CC §1812.608
Automobile sales contract, contents   CC §§2982, 2982.05
    Electric vehicle charging stations included in contract
        Disclosures   CC §2982.11
    Itemized prices for separate items sold   CC §2982.2
Breach
    Anticipatory breach   CC §1440
    Injunction against   CC §3423, CCP §526
    Interest awarded for breach of   CC §3288
    Judicial Council to develop and approve official forms   CCP §425.12
    Secured lender's action against borrower for violation of environmental provisions relating to real property security   CCP §736
Building construction
    Indemnity agreements   CC §§2782 to 2784
    January 1, 2013, contracts on or after   CC §2782.05
    Subcontractor's defense or indemnity obligation   CC §2782.05
    Void or unenforceable provisions, insertion   CC §2782.05
Camping contracts   CC §§1812.300 to 1812.309
    Waiver of protections   CC §1812.316
Cancellation
    Generally (See **CANCELLATION OF INSTRUMENTS**)
    Extinguishment
        Accord and satisfaction (See **ACCORD AND SATISFACTION**)
        Generally   CC §§1682 to 1689 (See within this heading, **"Extinguishment"**)
    Rescission (See within this heading, **"Rescission"**)
Capacity to make contract   CC §§1556, 1557, Fam §§6700, 6701, Pro §§810 to 812
Capacity to sue with regard to contract made for benefit of another   CCP §369
Carriage, contract of   CC §2085
Cats
    Sales of dogs and cats
        Payments subsequent to transfer of possession to transfer ownership, void contracts   CC §1670.10
Certainty, construction of contract   CC §1654
Child support
    Private child support collectors
        Terms of contracts   Fam §5611
Choice of law provisions in contractual disputes (See **CHOICE OF LAW**)
Civil actions, obligations arising from contract as basis for   CCP §26
Civil rights, persons prohibited from making contracts if deprived of   CC §1556
Commercial and industrial common interest developments
    Conflicts of interest   CC §6758
Common interest developments
    Conflicts of interest
        Board of directors authorizing, ratifying, etc, contracts   CC §5350
Conditional sales (See **CONDITIONAL SALES**)
Conditions
    Acceptance   CC §1582
    Performance   CC §1494
Conflict of laws   CC §1646
Consent
    Absence of   CC §§1567 to 1579
    Communicated consent   CC §1581
    Fraud, generally (See within this heading, **"Fraud"**)
    Free   CC §§1565 to 1567
    Parental or guardian consent
        Minor's representation that parent or guardian has consented not considered consent   CC §1568.5
    Time element   CC §1583
Conservatees making   Pro §1872
Consideration
    Agency relationship in absence of   CC §2308
    Alteration requiring   CC §1698
    Amount   CC §§1611 to 1613
    Burden of showing want of   CC §1615
    Defined   CC §1605
    Determination of   CC §§1611 to 1613
    Discount buying services   CC §1812.101
    Executory   CC §§1609, 1610
    Failure of consideration   CC §1689
    Health studio services   CC §1812.86
    Illegal   CC §§1607, 1608

CONTRACTS AND AGREEMENTS—Cont.
Consideration—Cont.
    Impossibility of performance   CC §§1612, 1613
    Premarital agreements   Fam §1611
    Ratable proportion, debtor receiving   CC §1514
    Realty sales (See **VENDOR AND PURCHASER**)
    Release   CC §1541
    Return of consideration by party rescinding   CC §§1691 to 1693
    Specific performance denied because of inadequacy of   CC §3391
    Suretyship contracts   CC §2792
    Trusts, requirement for   Pro §15208
    Unclaimed property, agreement to locate   CCP §1582
    Void consideration, rescission because of   CC §1689
    Written instrument, consideration presumed under   CC §1614
Construction of terms (See within this heading, **"Interpretation"**)
Consumer contracts
    Statements by consumer about seller, lessor, goods or services
        Waiver of consumer rights, prohibited contract provisions   CC §§1670.8, 1670.8.5
Consumer credit contracts (See **CONSUMER CREDIT CONTRACTS**)
Convicted or incarcerated persons as lacking capacity to make   CC §1556
Copies of consumer contracts, seller to furnish (See **CONSUMER CONTRACT AWARENESS ACT**)
Costs
    Action on contract, enforcement of contract provision awarding costs to prevailing party in   CC §1717
    Attorney's fees as costs, recovery of   CC §1717, CRC 3.1702
Credit reporters, creditors contracting with   CC §1785.1
Credit services organizations   CC §1789.16 (See **CREDIT SERVICES ORGANIATIONS**)
Custody of children (See **CUSTODY OF CHILDREN**)
Customer records
    Security procedures to protect personal information
        Third party users of records to be contractually obligated to provide security procedures   CC §1798.81.5
Damages (See **DAMAGES**)
Dance studios, regulating contracts with   CC §§1812.50 to 1812.69
Dating services (See **DATING SERVICES**)
Death of proposer, revocation of offer on   CC §1587
Declaratory judgments determining rights under   CCP §1060
Default judgments   CCP §§585, 585.5
Defined   CC §1549
Delivery
    Applicability of code sections governing   CC §1627
    Time of effect of contract as governed by   CC §1626
Description, errors in   CC §1690
Dogs
    Sales of dogs and cats
        Payments subsequent to transfer of possession to transfer ownership, void contracts   CC §1670.10
Duress, acts constituting   CC §1569
Electronic court records
    Vendors, contracts with to provide public access   CRC 2.505
Electronic filing and service rules
    Electronic filing manager contracts   CRC 2.255
    Service provider contracts   CRC 2.255
Electronic recording delivery systems
    Authorized submitters
        Contracting to be authorized submitter   Gov §27397.5
    Computer security auditors
        Use to audit system   Gov §27394
    County recorder authority as to contracts   Gov §27391
Electronic transactions (See **ELECTRONIC TRANSACTIONS**)
Employment agencies (See **EMPLOYMENT AGENCIES**)
Employment counseling services (See **EMPLOYMENT COUNSELING SERVICES**)
"Endless chain" schemes, right to rescind by participants to   CC §1689.2
Enforcement of judgments (See **ENFORCEMENT OF JUDGMENTS**)
Express contracts
    Generally   CC §1619
    Definition   CC §1620
Extinguishment
    Generally   CC §§1682 to 1689
    Accord and satisfaction (See **ACCORD AND SATISFACTION**)
    Dance studio contracts, authority to terminate   CC §1812.54
    Destruction of instrument for purpose of   CC §1699
    Rescission (See within this heading, **"Rescission"**)
Fair debt settlement practices
    Contracts between providers and consumers   CC §1788.302
Foreclosure consulting contracts
    Spanish or Asian languages   CC §1632

CONTRACTS AND AGREEMENTS—Cont.
- Fraud
    - Actual fraud   CC §§1571, 1572, 1574
    - Constructive fraud   CC §§1571, 1573
    - Exemption from liability, validity of contracts for   CC §1668
    - Obtaining consent by   CC §§1567, 1568
    - Statute of frauds (See **STATUTE OF FRAUDS**)
    - Written contracts prevented   CC §1623
- Gifts of unsolicited goods   CC §§1584.5, 1584.6
- Good faith   CC §1493
- Governing law   CC §1646
- Guardian and ward (See **GUARDIAN AND WARD**)
- Health studio services contracts (See **HEALTH STUDIO SERVICES CONTRACTS**)
- Home equity sales contracts (See **HOME EQUITY SALES CONTRACTS**)
- Home solicitation sales contracts (See **HOME SOLICITATION SALES CONTRACTS**)
- Husband and wife contracting to alter legal relationship to each other   Fam §1620
- Identification of parties   CC §1558
- Illegal contracts   CC §§1596 to 1599, 1607, 1608, 1667 to 1670.12
    - Telemarketing in violation of provisions   CC §1670.6
- Immigration and naturalization
    - Local government or law enforcement agency contracts to detain noncitizens for civil immigration custody
        - Prohibition   CC §1670.9
- Implied contracts
    - Generally   CC §1619
    - Definition   CC §1621
- Impossibility of performance
    - Generally   CC §§1596 to 1598, 1612, 1613
    - Alternative act required   CC §1451
- Incapacity of persons with unsound mind   CC §§38 to 40, 1556, 1557
- Indemnity contracts (See **INDEMNITY**)
- Independent collateral contracts   CC §1698
- Injunction against breach of   CC §3423, CCP §526
- Interest on money
    - Award for breach of   CC §3288
    - Rate of interest   CC §1916.12-1
- Interpleader in actions upon   CCP §386
- Interpretation
    - Ambiguities, construction against party causing   CC §1654
    - Conflict of laws as to   CC §1646
    - Entire instrument considered   CC §§1641, 1642
    - Extrinsic aids for   CC §1647
    - Inconsistent language   CC §§1650, 1652, 1653
    - Indemnity contracts   CC §§2778, 2782
    - Intent governing   CC §§1636, 1637, 1648 to 1650
    - Joint and several liability, determination of   CC §§1659, 1660
    - Language employed   CC §§1638, 1644, 1645, 1812.303
    - Law applicable   CC §1646
    - Lawfulness of agreement, construction favoring   CC §1643
    - Mistakes, correction of   CC §1640
    - Ordinary meaning given to words used   CC §1644
    - Particular clauses, general clauses controlling   CC §1650
    - Printed statements, written statements controlling   CC §1651
    - Public contracts subject to rules governing   CC §1635
    - Repugnancy, duty to reconcile   CC §1652
    - State law, agreement of parties to be governed by   CC §1646.5
    - Suretyship contracts   CC §§2799 to 2802, 2837
    - Technical language   CC §1645
    - Time of performance, implied requirements for   CC §1657
    - Two or more instruments constituting single contract   CC §1642
    - Usage, conformity with   CC §§1655, 1656
    - Waiver, effect on right of   CC §3268
    - Written contracts   CC §1639
- Job listing services (See **JOB LISTING SERVICES**)
- Judicial administration rules
    - Former employees
        - Limitations on contracting with   CRC 10.104
    - Indemnification   CRC 10.203
    - Intrabranch contracting
        - Limitations   CRC 10.103
- Judicial determination that person lacks legal capacity to contract   Pro §§810 to 812
- Jurisdiction over persons liable on   CCP §410.70
- Kinship adoption agreements   CRC 5.451, Fam §§8616.5, 8714, 8714.5
- Landlord and tenant
    - COVID-19 rental debt, action to recover
        - Breach of contract actions filed before October 2020   CCP §871.10

CONTRACTS AND AGREEMENTS—Cont.
- Legal incapacity to make decision
    - Revocation of proposal   CC §1587
- Liens created by   CC §2881
- Limitation of actions
    - Generally (See within this heading, **"Statutes of limitation"**)
    - Rescission
        - Parol contract   CCP §339
        - Written instrument, contract founded on   CCP §337
- Marijuana
    - Medical cannabis/marijuana
        - Commercial activity in relation to marijuana as lawful object of contract   CC §1550.5
    - Retail marijuana
        - Commercial activity in relation to marijuana as lawful object of contract   CC §1550.5
- Marriage (See **MARRIAGE**)
- Medical cannabis/marijuana
    - Commercial activity in relation to marijuana as lawful object of contract   CC §1550.5
- Membership camping contracts   CC §§1812.300 to 1812.309
    - Waiver of protections   CC §1812.316
- Menace, acts constituting   CC §1570
- Mentally impaired persons   CC §§38 to 40, 1556, 1557, Pro §§810 to 812
- Minors
    - Artistic services   Fam §§6750 to 6753
    - Attorney's fees   Fam §6602
    - Capacity to make contract   CC §§1556, 1557, Fam §§6700, 6701
    - Disaffirmance of contracts   Fam §§6710 to 6713, 6751
    - Emancipated minors   Fam §7050
    - Entertainment   Fam §§6750 to 6753
    - Good faith purchaser, protection of   Fam §6713
    - Necessaries   Fam §6712
    - Professional sports   Fam §§6750 to 6753
    - Sex acts, contract for payment to minor victim of   CC §§1169.5, 1169.7
    - Vlogging, minors engaged in the work of   Fam §§6650 to 6656 (See **VLOGGING**)
- Mistakes
    - Generally   CC §§1567, 1577 to 1579
    - Correction of contract   CC §1640
    - Description of goods subject to contract, rescission due to mistake in   CC §1690
    - Rescission because of   CC §1689
- Mobilehome rental agreement (See **MOBILEHOMES**)
- Modification
    - Generally   CC §1698
    - Copies of contract, effect of altering   CC §1701
    - Forgery (See **FORGERY**)
- Mortgage foreclosure consultants   CC §§2945 to 2945.11
- Mortgages of residential property, foreign language summaries of terms   CC §1632.5
- Mutuality   CC §1580
- Novation (See **NOVATION**)
- Nurses' registries (See **NURSES**)
- Object of contracts   CC §§1595 to 1599
    - Marijuana
        - Commercial activity in relation to marijuana as lawful object of contract   CC §1550.5
- Offers
    - Acceptance (See within this heading, **"Acceptance"**)
    - Bailment relationship   CC §1503
    - Business place, offer made at   CC §1489
    - Conditions precedent   CC §1498
    - Extinguishing obligation   CC §1485
    - Interest payments   CC §1504
    - Legal incapacity to make decision
        - Revocation of proposal   CC §1587
    - Partial performance   CC §1486
    - Party to   CC §§1487, 1488
    - Place for   CC §1489
    - Residence, offer made at   CC §1489
    - Revocation of   CC §§1586, 1587
    - Seller assisted marketing plan   CC §1812.202
    - Time for   CC §§1490, 1491
    - Unsolicited goods   CC §§1584.5, 1584.6
    - Waiver of objection by creditor   CC §1501
- Oral contracts, limitation of actions on   CCP §339
- Parking facilities for motor vehicles   CC §§1630, 1630.5
- Parol contracts, limitation of actions on   CCP §339
- Parol evidence (See **PAROL EVIDENCE**)

CONTRACTS AND AGREEMENTS—Cont.
Parties
    Convicted or incarcerated persons as lacking capacity to make   CC §1556
    Existence of contract, contracting parties as element for   CC §1550
    Identity of   CC §1558
    Mentally impaired persons as   CC §§38 to 40, 1556, 1557
    Third parties (See within this heading, **"Third party beneficiaries"**)
    Waiver in contract or settlement of right to testify concerning criminal conduct or sexual harassment   CC §1670.11
Partition referees making   CCP §§873.110 to 873.160
Performance
    Ability to perform   CC §1495
    Accord and satisfaction   CC §§1522, 1524
    Alternative performance   CC §§1448 to 1451
    Anticipatory breach   CC §1440
    Conditions   CC §1494
    Defenses   CC §1511
    Delay in   CC §1492
    Deposit constituting   CC §1500
    Executed contract   CC §1661
    Full performance   CC §1473
    Good faith   CC §1493
    Impossibility of   CC §§1596 to 1598, 1612, 1613
        Alternative act required   CC §1451
    Joint creditors   CC §1476
    Jointly liable parties   CC §1474
    Natural disasters, preventing of   CC §1511
    Parties performance   CC §1477
    Payment   CC §§1478, 1479
    Postponement from holiday to next business day   CCP §13
    Prevention of   CC §§1511 to 1515
    Sureties, exoneration of   CC §§2839, 2846
    Time for   CC §1657
    Two or more obligees   CC §1475
    Unperformed contracts for sale of realty (See **TITLE AND OWNERSHIP**)
    Willingness to perform   CC §1495
Pleadings (See **PLEADINGS**)
Postadoption contact agreement with birth parent   CRC 5.451, Fam §§8616.5, 8714, 8714.5
Postadoption contact agreement with siblings   CRC 5.451
Prisoners as lacking capacity to make contracts   CC §1556
Private child support collectors
    Terms of contracts   Fam §5611
Proposals
    Acceptance generally (See within this heading, **"Acceptance"**)
    Offers generally (See within this heading, **"Offers"**)
Public contracts (See **PUBLIC CONTRACTS AND WORKS**)
Public policy, agreements contrary to   CC §§1667 to 1670.12
Real property
    Exclusive listing agreements   CC §1670.12
Realty sales
    Generally (See **VENDOR AND PURCHASER**)
    Installment contracts (See **REAL PROPERTY SALES CONTRACTS**)
    Text message or instant message format communications, insufficiency to constitute contract to convey realty   CC §1624
Record maintenance under Information Practices Act, contract for   CC §1798.19
Release (See **RELEASE**)
Renewing liability, acknowledgment or promise   CCP §360
Rental passenger vehicle transactions generally   CC §§1939.01 to 1939.39
Rental-purchase contracts, Karnette Rental-Purchase Act for   CC §§1812.620 to 1812.650
Rescission
    Alteration of contract affecting   CC §1698
    Asian language contracts, translations   CC §1632
    Assistive devices, sale of   CC §1793.02
    Automobile conditional sale contracts   CC §§2982.5, 2983.1
    Automobile lease   CC §2988.7
    Cancellation of instruments (See **CANCELLATION OF INSTRUMENTS**)
    Damages, recovery of   CC §1692
    Dental plan or services   CC §1689.3
    Description, errors in   CC §1690
    Discount buying services contracts   CC §1812.121
    Effect of   CC §1688
    "Endless chain" schemes, right to rescind by participants to   CC §1689.2
    Grounds for   CC §1689
    Home solicitation sales contracts (See **HOME SOLICITATION SALES CONTRACTS**)
    Insurance (See **INSURANCE**)
    Marriage dowry recoverable   CC §1590
    Membership camping contracts   CC §1812.306

CONTRACTS AND AGREEMENTS—Cont.
Rescission—Cont.
    Minors generally (See within this heading, **"Minors"**)
    Notice requirements   CC §1691
    Novation   CC §1533
    Retail installment sales conditioned on buyer obtaining financing   CC §1803.9
    Return of consideration   CC §§1691 to 1693
    Seminar sales solicitation contracts (See **SEMINAR SALES SOLICITATION CONTRACTS**)
    Spanish language, violation of requirements for   CC §1632
    Statutes of limitation
        Parol contract   CCP §339
        Written instrument, contract founded on   CCP §337
    Unsound mind, contract of person with   CC §39
Retail installment sales contract (See **RETAIL INSTALLMENT SALES**)
Retail marijuana
    Commercial activity in relation to marijuana as lawful object of contract   CC §1550.5
Roof repairs (See **ROOFING WARRANTIES**)
Safe deposit boxes rented in joint tenancy   CC §683.1
Sale of goods
    Consumer contracts
        Waiver by consumer of rights to make statements about seller, lessor, goods or services, prohibited contract provisions   CC §§1670.8, 1670.8.5
    Sales generally (See **SALES**)
Sale of realty (See **SALE OF REALTY**)
Sales (See **SALES**)
Seals, requirements for   CC §§1628, 1629
Seller assisted marketing plans   CC §§1812.200 to 1812.221
Seminar sales solicitation contracts (See **SEMINAR SALES SOLICITATION CONTRACTS**)
Service contracts (See **REPAIRS**)
Signature, destruction of   CC §1699
Spanish language contracts (See **SPANISH**)
Spanish language translation requirements   CC §§1632, 2991
Specific performance (See **SPECIFIC PERFORMANCE**)
Spousal support, court order based on agreement of parties   Fam §§3590 to 3593
Spouses' legal relationship, contracts altering   Fam §1620
Standing to sue with regard to contract made for benefit of another   CCP §369
State law, agreement of parties to be governed by   CC §1646.5
Statute of frauds (See **STATUTE OF FRAUDS**)
Statutes of limitation
    Certificate, abstract or guaranty of title, actions founded upon contract or obligation evidenced by   CCP §339
    Parol contracts   CCP §339
    Rescission
        Parol contract   CCP §339
        Written instrument, contract founded on   CCP §337
    Written instrument, action upon contract founded on   CCP §337
Succession to inheritance, contract regarding   CC §1624, Pro §21700
Successive actions on new causes on   CCP §1047
Sundays and holidays, performance on   CC §11
Suretyship contracts   CC §§2792 to 2795
Telemarketing
    Unlawfulness of contracts generated by unlawful telemarketing   CC §1670.6
Termination
    Extinguishment
        Accord and satisfaction generally (See **ACCORD AND SATISFACTION**)
        Generally   CC §§1682 to 1689 (See within this heading, **"Extinguishment"**)
        Rescission generally (See within this heading, **"Rescission"**)
Third party beneficiaries
    Generally   CC §1559
    Original undertakings   CC §2794
    Standing to sue   CCP §369
Timber, recording of contracts for   CC §1220
Time
    Adhesion, contracts of
        Reasonable time required in contracts of adhesion   CC §1657.1
Transportation costs
    Wage deductions for costs of transporting immigrant to U.S
        Void contracts   CC §1670.7
Unclaimed property (See **UNCLAIMED PROPERTY**)
Unconscionable contracts
    Generally   CC §§1670.5, 1770
    Premarital agreements   Fam §1615
Undue influence, acts constituting   CC §1575

CONTRACTS AND AGREEMENTS—Cont.

Unlawful contracts   CC §§1667 to 1670.12
Unperformed contracts for sale of realty (See **TITLE AND OWNERSHIP**)
Unsound mind, incapacity of persons with   CC §§38 to 40, 1556, 1557, Pro §§810 to 812
Venue in actions founded on contract obligation   CCP §395
Violence
    Freedom from violence or intimidation based on sex, race, religion, etc
        Coerced or involuntary waiver of rights   CC §51.7
Voiding contract for illegality of object   CC §§1598, 1599
Waiver of rights under   CC §3268
Warranties (See **WARRANTIES**)
Weight loss programs (See **WEIGHT LOSS PROGRAMS**)
Wholesale sales representatives, contractual agreements with (See **WHOLESALE SALES REPRESENTATIVES**)
Wills, contracts for making   CC §1624, Pro §21700
Witnesses
    Waiver in contract or settlement of right to testify concerning criminal conduct or sexual harassment   CC §1670.11
Writing
    Asian language contracts, translations   CC §1632
    Effect of written contracts   CC §1625
    Fraud preventing contract in   CC §1623
    Health studio services   CC §1812.82
    Presumption of consideration   CC §1614
    Seller assisted marketing plan   CC §1812.207
    Spanish language   CC §1632
    Statute of frauds (See **STATUTE OF FRAUDS**)
    Superiority of written contract   CC §1625

CONTRIBUTION

Generally   CC §1432, CCP §§881 to 883
Heirs, abatement of bequests by contributions from   Pro §21405
Partition (See **PARTITION**)
Public entities, contribution provisions in agreements between   Gov §§895.4, 895.6
Release   CC §1543, CCP §§875 to 880
Sureties (See **SURETYSHIP, BONDS AND UNDERTAKINGS**)
Tort action, judgments in   CCP §§875 to 880

CONTROLLED SUBSTANCES (See **NARCOTICS AND DANGEROUS DRUGS**)

Minors
    Consent to treatment for opioid use disorder   Fam §§6929, 6929.1

CONTROLLER

Claims against public entities and employees (See **CLAIMS AGAINST PUBLIC ENTITIES AND EMPLOYEES**)
Escheat (See **ESCHEAT**)
Notice of default on property subject to lien for postponed property taxes   CC §2924b
Unclaimed property (See **UNCLAIMED PROPERTY**)

CONVALESCENT HOSPITALS (See **NURSING HOMES**)

CONVENIENCE

Change of venue, grounds for   CCP §397
Coordination of actions   CCP §404.1
Separate trial of issues   CCP §598

CONVERSION (See also **CLAIM AND DELIVERY**)

Damages for   CC §§3336 to 3338
Demand for return   CC §1713
Involuntary trusts
    Attorney general actions
        Statute of limitations   CC §2224.5
Statutes of limitation
    Generally   CCP §338
    Hotel, apartment, lodging or hospital, action for recovery or conversion of personal property left at   CCP §341a

CONVEYANCES

Generally   CC §§1044, 1052, 1053
Acknowledgments (See **ACKNOWLEDGMENTS**)
Adverse possession, transfer of property held by   CC §1047
After-acquired title   CC §1106
Appraisals
    Improper influence on appraisal   CC §1090.5
Bill of sale (See **BILL OF SALE**)
Cancellation   CC §1058

CONVEYANCES—Cont.

Capacity to make conveyance   Pro §§810 to 812
Chattel mortgages (See **CHATTEL MORTGAGES**)
Common interest developments (See **COMMON INTEREST DEVELOPMENTS**)
Community property (See **COMMUNITY PROPERTY**)
Conclusive against grantor   CC §1107
Condition subsequent, transfer for breach of   CC §1046
Condominiums (See **COMMON INTEREST DEVELOPMENTS**)
Construction of   CCP §2077
Constructive delivery   CC §1059
Contract for sale of realty   CC §§2985 to 2985.6
    Statute of frauds
        Text message or instant message format communications, insufficiency to constitute contract to convey realty   CC §1624
Damages (See **DAMAGES**)
Dedication (See **DEDICATION**)
Deeds (See **DEEDS**)
Delivery
    Generally   CC §§1054 to 1056, 1058, 1059
    Disclosure statement   CC §§1102.3, 1102.10
    Governing law   CC §1627
Disclosure requirements (See **BROKERS; VENDOR AND PURCHASER**)
Discriminatory restrictions   CC §§53, 782, 782.5
Donative transfers
    Presumption of fraud or undue influence   Pro §§21360 to 21392 (See **DONATIVE TRANSFERS**)
Dwelling houses
    Disclosure requirements generally   CC §§1102 to 1103.15 (See **BROKERS**)
    Fee limitations for transfer of title   CC §1097
Easements   CC §1104
Escrow
    Agents' liability for disclosure statements   CC §1102.11
    Transfers through   CC §§1057, 1057.5
Explosive munitions in neighborhood area, disclosure of   CC §1102.15
Fee limitations for transfer of residential title   CC §1097
Fee-simple title, presumption of   CC §1105
Fraudulent transfers (See **VOIDABLE TRANSACTIONS**)
Home equity sales contracts, presumptions regarding conveyances with option to repurchase by equity purchaser in   CC §1695.12
Implied covenants   CC §1113
Judicial determination that person lacks legal capacity to make conveyance   Pro §§810 to 812
Judicial officer's power to take and certify proof and acknowledgment of conveyance   CCP §179
Leases (See **LEASES**)
Life estate owner transferring estate greater than held   CC §1108
Minors, gifts to (See **UNIFORM TRANSFERS TO MINORS ACT**)
Mortgages (See **TRUST DEEDS AND MORTGAGES**)
Partition (See **PARTITION**)
Perpetuities and restraints on alienation (See **PERPETUITIES AND RESTRAINTS ON ALIENATION**)
Pest control inspection report, requirement of   CC §1099
Possibility of reverter   CC §1045
Quit claim deeds (See **QUITCLAIM DEEDS**)
Real property acquired through   CC §1000
Recording of instruments (See **RECORDS AND RECORDING**)
Recovery of real property, conveyance during pendency of action for   CCP §747
Residential property
    Disclosure requirements generally   CC §§1102 to 1103.15 (See **BROKERS**)
    Fee limitations for transfer of title   CC §1097
Restraints (See **PERPETUITIES AND RESTRAINTS ON ALIENATION**)
Secured transactions (See **SECURED TRANSACTIONS**)
Sheriff, conveyances on sale of real estate by   CCP §262.4
Specific performance to convey or transfer property subject to administration by personal representative, conservator, or guardian   Pro §§850 to 859
Statute of frauds   CC §1624, CCP §1971
    Insufficiency of text message or instant message format communications to constitute contract to convey realty   CC §1624
Stay of judgment for   CCP §917.4
Transfer fees   CC §§1098, 1098.5
    Disclosure of property subject to   CC §1102.6e
    New transfer fees banned   CC §1098.6
Trust deeds (See **TRUST DEEDS AND MORTGAGES**)
Trustee, presumption of conveyance by   Ev §642
Uniform Transfers to Minors Act (See **UNIFORM TRANSFERS TO MINORS ACT**)

CONVEYANCES—Cont.
Valuation
    Improper influence on valuation   CC §1090.5
Voidable transactions (See **VOIDABLE TRANSACTIONS**)
Water conserving plumbing retrofits
    Disclosures as to noncompliant plumbing fixtures   CC §§1101.4, 1102.155
Water storage tank disclosures   CC §1102.156
Window security bars and safety release mechanism, disclosure of   CC §1102.16
Writing
    Generally   CC §1091, CCP §1971
    Statute of frauds   CC §1624, CCP §1971

CONVICTION OF CRIME
Administrator of decedent's estate, disqualification as   Pro §8402
Adoption proceeding investigations (See **ADOPTION**)
Adverse possession, disabilities tolling statute of limitations in actions for   CCP §328
Aggravation, prior convictions as circumstance in   CRC 4.421
Attorney's fees in action for damages against felons, award of   CCP §1021.4
Computer-generated conviction record, judicial notice of   Ev §452.5
Contracts after   CC §1556
Credibility of witness attacked by introducing record of prior felony conviction   Ev §788
Credit reporting (See **CREDIT REPORTING**)
Discount buying organization officer, disclosure of conviction of   CC §1812.106
Electronically digitized copy of official conviction record
    Evidence, admissibility   Ev §452.5
Executor, disqualification as   Pro §8402
Felons and felonies
    Juvenile wardship proceedings
        Declaration of offense as misdemeanor after hearing   CRC 5.795
        Misdemeanor or felony, finding of offense as   CRC 5.790
    Sentencing to jail, mandatory supervision
        Criteria affecting mandatory supervision   CRC 4.415
    Story of felon, creation of involuntary trust for proceeds resulting from sale   CC §2225
Firearms and other weapons
    Felony convicts
        Forms for relinquishment of firearms   CRCAppx A
    Relinquishment of firearms
        Forms for firearm relinquishment   CRCAppx A
Hearsay rule as applied to official record of conviction   Ev §452.5
Immediate preparation of record on appeal following felony conviction   CCP §269
Judges
    Censure, removal or admonishment
        Suspension   JudPerR 120.5
Judicial notice of computer-generated conviction record   Ev §452.5
Jury service, exceptions to eligibility for   CCP §203
Libel and slander (See **LIBEL AND SLANDER**)
Other states (See **OTHER STATES**)
Profits from felon's story, creation of involuntary trust for proceeds resulting from   CC §2225
Punitive damages award against felon bringing suit against victim of crime on which felony conviction was based   CCP §§128.5, 128.7
Record of conviction, admissibility of   Ev §452.5
Report to Justice Department by courts, requirements for   CRC 4.320
Restitution judgments awarded in felony convictions, trust assets used in satisfaction of   Pro §15305.5
Slander by charging conviction   CC §46
Statute of limitation for damages against person based on commission of felony offense   CCP §340.3
Termination of parental rights
    Circumstances where proceedings may be brought   Fam §7825
Trusts
    Felon's story, creation of involuntary trust for proceeds resulting from sale of   CC §2225
    Restitution judgments, trust assets used in satisfaction of   Pro §15305.5

COOPERATIVES
Housing cooperatives
    Housing cooperatives and housing cooperative trusts generally   CC §§817 to 817.4
Mobilehome cooperatives   CC §§799 to 799.11 (See **MOBILEHOMES**)
Residential stock cooperatives (See **COMMON INTEREST DEVELOPMENTS**)

COORDINATION OF ACTIONS   CRC 3.500 to 3.550
Add-on cases   CRC 3.544
    Definition   CRC 3.501

COORDINATION OF ACTIONS—Cont.
Add-on cases —Cont.
    Petitions   CRC 3.521
        Request to coordinate add-on case when cases already ordered coordinated   CRC 3.532
    Potential add-on cases   CRC 3.531
Affidavit stating facts showing that actions meet required standards   CCP §404
Ancillary proceedings, court for   CRC 3.545
Appeals   CCP §404.2, CRC 3.505
Assignment of judges
    Coordination motion judge   CCP §404, CRC 3.524
    Coordination trial judge   CCP §404.3, CRC 3.540
Central depository for evidentiary material and documents   CRC 3.541
Class actions, schedule for   CRC 3.541
Common question of fact or law   CCP §§404, 404.1
Coordination attorney   CRC 3.550
    Defined   CRC 3.501
Coordination motion judge
    Assignment of   CRC 3.524
    Definition   CRC 3.501
    Orders pending assignment of trial judge   CRC 3.529
    Recommendation of site for coordination proceedings   CRC 3.530
    Termination of authority   CRC 3.529
Coordination trial judge   CRC 3.540 to 3.545
    Definition   CRC 3.501
    Management of proceedings   CRC 3.541
    Order assigning   CRC 3.540
    Remand of action or claim   CRC 3.542
    Termination of action   CRC 3.545
    Transfer of action or claim   CRC 3.543
Declarations   CRC 3.500
    Opposing petition   CRC 3.525
    Service, time for   CRC 3.513
    Supporting petition   CRC 3.521
Definitions   CRC 3.501
Delegation of authority by presiding judge   CCP §404.9
Denial of coordination   CRC 3.529, 3.544
Determination of complexity of case   CRC 3.502
Differential case management rules, applicability   CRC 3.712
Discovery
    Schedule for   CRC 3.541
Dismissal of action   CRC 3.545
Evidence at hearings   CRC 3.514
Expenses   CCP §404.8
Extension of time, request or stipulation for   CRC 3.503
    Electronic filing, when required   CRCSupp 1st AppDist
Finality of judgment   CRC 3.545
General civil law, applicability   CRC 3.504
Grant of coordination, order for   CRC 3.529, 3.544
Hearings   CRC 3.527
    Add-on cases   CRC 3.544
    Evidence   CRC 3.514
    Separate hearing on specified issues   CRC 3.528
Initial case management conference   CRC 3.541
    Telephone appearance at case management conferences   CRC 3.670
Judges
    Assignment (See within this heading, **"Assignment of judges"**)
    Delegation of authority by presiding judge   CCP §404.9
    Disqualification   CRC 3.516
    List of active and retired judges available   CRC 3.550
Judgment   CRC 3.545
Judicial Council   CCP §§404.7, 404.9
    Complex actions, coordination
        Electronic submission of documents to council   CRC 3.512
        Papers submitted to chair   CRC 3.511
        Petition for coordination, permission   CRC 3.520
        Report to council when petition not timely decided   CRC 3.527
    General administration by staff   CRC 3.550
    Petition for coordination   CRC 3.521
Jurisdiction
    Final disposition, until   CRC 3.545
    Severable claims, continuing over   CRC 3.529
    Transferred case   CRC 3.543
Liaison counsel
    Appointment   CRC 3.506, 3.541
    Defined   CRC 3.501
    Service of papers on   CRC 3.510
Local rules, compliance with   CRC 3.504
Memorandums
    Objections   CRC 3.525
    Petition for coordination   CRC 3.521

COORDINATION OF ACTIONS—Cont.
  Memorandums—Cont.
      Time for submission and service   CRC 3.513
  Motions   CRC 3.520
      Coordination petition, motion to submit   CRC 3.520
      Stay of proceedings   CRC 3.515
      Submit petition, motion to   CCP §404
      Transfer and consolidation
          Coordination of cases sharing common issue of law or fact   CCP §§404, 404.3
          Non-complex actions, transfer of   CCP §403, CRC 3.500
  Notice
      Hearing on petition, notice   CRC 3.527
      Potential add-on cases   CRC 3.531
      Related case, notice   CRC 3.300
      Submission of petition, notice   CRC 3.522, 3.523
  Numbers for cases   CRC 3.550
  Opposition to petition   CRC 3.525
  Orders   CRC 3.529
      Coordination, order of   CCP §404.4
      Stay of proceedings   CRC 3.515
  Petitions   CCP §404, CRC 3.520 to 3.532
      Add-on cases, coordination when cases already ordered coordinated   CRC 3.532
      Judicial Council petitions   CRC 3.521
      Notice of submission of petition   CRC 3.522, 3.523
      Opposition to   CRC 3.525
      Statement in support of   CRC 3.526
      Trial court motions   CRC 3.520
  Procedural rules   CRC 3.510 to 3.515
  Process and service of process   CRC 3.510 to 3.515
      Liaison counsel, service on   CRC 3.506, 3.510
      Memorandums and declarations, time for service   CRC 3.513
      Notice of submission of petition   CRC 3.523
      Opposition to petition for coordination   CRC 3.525, 3.544
      Order granting or denying coordination   CRC 3.529, 3.544
      Proof of filing and service of petition for coordination   CRC 3.510, 3.521
      Support of petition for coordination   CRC 3.526
  Register of proceeding   CRC 3.550
  Related cases   CRC 3.300
  Remand of action or claim   CRC 3.542
      Definition of remand   CRC 3.501
  Reviewing court selection   CCP §404.2, CRC 3.505
  Separate trial of issue or defense   CRC 3.541
  Settlement of action   CRC 3.545
  Shortening of time, request   CRC 3.503
  Site of coordination proceedings   CRC 3.530
  Standards for   CCP §404.1
  Stay of proceedings   CCP §404.5, CRC 3.515
      Add-on case   CRC 3.544
      Grant or denial of coordination, effect of   CRC 3.529
      Pending request for coordination   CRC 3.520
      Report on status   CRC 3.527
  Summary judgments   CRC 3.545
  Termination of action   CRC 3.545
  Titles of cases   CRC 3.550
  Transfer and consolidation motion (See within this heading, "**Motions**")
  Transfer of action or claim   CRC 3.543
      Definition of transfer   CRC 3.501
  Writ of mandate   CCP §404.6

COPIES (See also **PHOTOGRAPHS AND PHOTOCOPIES**)
  Appellate rules
      Supreme court and courts of appeal (See **APPELLATE RULES, SUPREME COURT AND COURTS OF APPEAL**)
  Attachment, copy of original sufficing as notice of   CCP §488.065
  Automobile conditional sales contracts   CC §2984.3
  Best and secondary evidence (See **BEST AND SECONDARY EVIDENCE**)
  Claims against decedents' estates, filing copy of written instrument in support of (See **CLAIMS AGAINST ESTATES**)
  Consumer contracts, seller's obligation to furnish copies of (See **CONSUMER CONTRACT AWARENESS ACT**)
  Co-signer's liability, copy of notice of   CC §1799.93
  County clerk's fees (See **CLERKS OF COURT**)
  Court indexes accessible by   CRC 10.851
  Dance studio contract, customer receiving copy of   CC §1812.52
  Discovery
      Demand for inspection, copying, testing or sampling
          Inspection demands generally   CCP §§2031.010 to 2031.510 (See **INSPECTION DEMANDS**)
  Enforcement of judgments (See **ENFORCEMENT OF JUDGMENTS**)

COPIES—Cont.
  Escheat orders received by controller   CCP §1312
  Fax transmissions (See **FACSIMILE TRANSMISSIONS**)
  Health studio contract, customer receiving copy of   CC §1812.82
  Information Practices Act, furnishing under   CC §1798.34
  Judges (See **JUDGES**)
  Medical records, fees charged for copying of   Ev §1158
  Photocopies (See **PHOTOGRAPHS AND PHOTOCOPIES**)
  Pleadings, loss of   CCP §1045
  Postmortem examination or autopsy, restriction on reproducing photograph or video taken at scene of death or in course of   CCP §129
  Records and recordings (See **RECORDS AND RECORDING**)
  Retail installment sales contract, buyer receiving copy of   CC §1803.7
  Subpoena duces tecum (See **SUBPOENA DUCES TECUM**)
  Superior courts (See **SUPERIOR COURTS**)
  Trust deed sale and default notices, procedure for obtaining copies of   CC §2924b
  Venue (See **VENUE**)
  Wills (See **WILL PROBATE**)

COPYRIGHT
  Generally   CC §§980 to 986, 988
  Art and artists (See **ART AND ARTISTS**)
  Judgment debtor, assignment of right to payment due   CCP §§708.510 to 708.560
  Literary property (See **LITERARY PROPERTY**)
  Patent of invention (See **PATENT OF INVENTION**)
  Recording of sound (See **RECORDING OF SOUND**)

CO-REPRESENTATIVES OF ESTATES (See **EXECUTORS AND ADMINISTRATORS**)

CORN
Storage regulations after sale of   CC §§1880 to 1881.2

CORONAVIRUS (See **COVID-19**)

CORONER
Execution of process
      Compensation for   CCP §262.10
      Sheriff is party to action, execution by coroner where   CCP §262.6
Juries of inquest (See **JURIES OF INQUEST**)
Medical records, disclosure to coroners, medical examiners or forensic pathologists   CC §56.10
Photographs or video recordings, prohibition against copying   CCP §129
Process
      Execution of process
          Compensation   CCP §262.10
          Sheriff as party to action   CCP §262.6
Small estates liable for fees for return of property found on decedent by   Pro §13114
Statute of limitation against   CCP §339
Witness fees   Gov §68095

CORPORATE DISSOLUTION
Jurisdiction over trustees and stockholders   CCP §410.60
Receivers appointed for   CCP §§564, 565
Service of process on dissolved corporation   CCP §416.20
Statute of limitation to set aside any action taken by trustees of dissolved corporation   CCP §341

CORPORATE MERGER
Executor of decedent's estate, appointment of successor trust company after merger as   Pro §8423

CORPORATE OFFICERS AND EMPLOYEES
Challenge of juror for implied bias, relationships giving rise to   CCP §229
Eminent domain, officers giving evidence for valuation under   Ev §813
Party to action   Ev §777
Process against corporation   CCP §416.10
Service of summons on corporation by serving   CCP §416.10
Small claims court (See **SMALL CLAIMS COURTS**)
Statute of limitation against corporate directors to recover penalty or forfeiture or enforce liability   CCP §359
Volunteer officers and directors of nonprofit corporations, action against   CCP §425.15

CORPORATE SHARES AND SHAREHOLDERS
Administration of estates (See **ADMINISTRATION OF ESTATES**)
Attachment of securities   CCP §§487.010, 488.450
Briefs, certificates in interested entities or persons   CRC 8.208, 8.361, 8.488
      Electronic filing, when required   CRCSupp 1st AppDist

CORPORATE SHARES AND SHAREHOLDERS—Cont.
Broker-dealer, contract formation by electronic submission of application to CC §1633
Conservators (See **CONSERVATORS**)
Decedent's estate
    Administration of estates (See **ADMINISTRATION OF ESTATES**)
    Registration in beneficiary form   Pro §§5500 to 5512
    Stock bonus or employee savings plan, nonprobate transfer of   Pro §§6321 to 6330
    Trusts (See **TRUSTS**)
Dividends
    Escheat to state   CCP §1516
    Principal and income allocations   CC §731.07
Electronic submission of application to securities broker-dealer, contract formation by   CC §1633
Emancipated minor holding stock   Fam §7052
Employee benefit plan including stock options   Fam §80
Employee savings plan or stock bonus, nonprobate transfer of   Pro §§6321 to 6330
Enforcement of judgments (See **ENFORCEMENT OF JUDGMENTS**)
Gifts to minors (See **UNIFORM TRANSFERS TO MINORS ACT**)
Jurisdiction over trustees and stockholders of corporation forfeiting charter   CCP §410.60
Marital status, denial of credit because of   CC §1812.32
Minors, transfers to (See **UNIFORM TRANSFERS TO MINORS ACT**)
Partition sales of securities   CCP §873.660
Power of attorney, statutory form   Pro §4453
Principal and income allocations   CC §731.07
Proxies, estate representative exercising (See **EXECUTORS AND ADMINISTRATORS**)
Receivers depositing   CCP §568.1
Statute of limitation against shareholders to recover penalty or forfeiture or enforce liability   CCP §359
Stay of order to inspect books   CCP §917.8
Trusts (See **TRUSTS**)
Uniform TOD Security Registration Act   Pro §§5500 to 5512
Uniform Transfers to Minors Act (See **UNIFORM TRANSFERS TO MINORS ACT**)

CORPORATIONS
Acknowledgment of instruments   CC §§1185, 1190, 1190.1
Administrators (See **EXECUTORS AND ADMINISTRATORS**)
Admitted surety insurer (See **SURETYSHIP, BONDS AND UNDERTAKINGS**)
Agents (See **CORPORATE OFFICERS AND EMPLOYEES**)
Appellate rules, supreme court and courts of appeal
    Briefs
        Certificates in interested entities or persons   CRC 8.361, 8.488, CRCSupp 1st AppDist
Attachments, corporate assets subject to   CCP §487.010
Attorney professional conduct
    Organization or entity as client   ProfC 1.13
Attorneys
    Registered in-house counsel   CRC 9.46
        Fingerprinting of special admission attorneys   CRC 9.9.5
Bonds (See **BONDS**)
Common interest developments (See **COMMON INTEREST DEVELOPMENTS**)
Crimes and penalties
    Electronic summons, issuance   CRC 2.259
Depositions, procedure for
    Economic litigation procedures   CCP §94
    Notice of deposition
        Description of matters on which examination requested   CCP §2025.230
Directors and officers
    Briefs, certificates of interested entities or persons   CRC 8.208, 8.361, 8.488
        Electronic filing, when required   CRCSupp 1st AppDist
    Judges, service as directors or officers   CRCSupp JudEthicsCanon 4
Dissolution (See **CORPORATE DISSOLUTION**)
Eminent domain, officers giving evidence on valuation for   Ev §813
Enforcement of judgments (See **ENFORCEMENT OF JUDGMENTS**)
Executors (See **EXECUTORS AND ADMINISTRATORS**)
Filing of instruments
    Identity theft in business entity filings   CC §§1798.200 to 1798.203
Foreign corporations (See **FOREIGN CORPORATIONS**)
Forfeiture of charter or right to do business
    Jurisdiction over trustees and stockholders   CCP §410.60
    Service of process on corporation   CCP §416.20
Health care providers, access to medical information maintained by corporation deemed as   CC §§56.06, 56.07

CORPORATIONS—Cont.
Identity theft in business entity filings   CC §§1798.200 to 1798.203
Inclusions in definition   CCP §17
In-house counsel
    Registered in-house counsel   CRC 9.46
        Fingerprinting of special admission attorneys   CRC 9.9.5
Injunctions suspending business of   CCP §531
Jurisdiction when charter is forfeited   CCP §410.60
Marital status, denial of credit because of   CC §1812.32
Medical information corporations, access to medical records maintained by   CC §§56.06, 56.07
Municipal corporations (See **CITIES AND MUNICIPALITIES**)
Nonprofit corporations (See **NONPROFIT CORPORATIONS AND ASSOCIATIONS**)
Person defined to include   CCP §17
Pleadings verification by   CCP §446
Process
    Default against corporation   CCP §412.30
    Designated agent receiving service of   CCP §416.10
    Forfeit of charter or right to do business   CCP §416.20
    Manner of service of business organizations
        Leaving summons and complaint at office, mailing copy   CCP §415.95
    Notice   CCP §412.30
    Officer receiving service of   CCP §416.10
    Trustee of corporation, service on   CCP §416.20
Public trail, enjoining closure of   CCP §731.5
Registered in-house counsel   CRC 9.46
    Fingerprinting of special admission attorneys   CRC 9.9.5
Seal, affixed   CC §1628
Service of process
    Process generally (See within this heading, "**Process**")
Statutes of limitation
    Corporate bonds, notes or debentures, actions upon   CCP §336a
    Directors or shareholders, actions against   CCP §359
    Dissolved corporation, action to set aside any action taken by trustees of   CCP §341
Stock (See **CORPORATE SHARES AND SHAREHOLDERS**)
Surety capacity (See **SURETYSHIP, BONDS AND UNDERTAKINGS**)
Tax liens and other federal liens, filing of notice of   CC §2101
Venue in actions against   CCP §395.5
Verifications of pleadings   CCP §446

CORPORATIONS SOLE
Attorney professional conduct
    Organization or entity as client   ProfC 1.13

CORPSES (See **DEAD BODIES**)

CORRECTIONS OF ERRORS
Appellate rules
    Superior court appeals (See **APPELLATE RULES, SUPERIOR COURT APPEALS**)
    Supreme court and courts of appeal (See **APPELLATE RULES, SUPREME COURT AND COURTS OF APPEAL**)
Information Practices Act (See **INFORMATION PRACTICES ACT**)
Libel by newspaper or radio, correction demand to avoid   CC §48a

CORRESPONDENCE (See **LETTERS**)

COSMETICS
Animal testing to develop or manufacture   CC §1834.9.5

COSMETOLOGY (See **BARBERING AND COSMETOLOGY**)

COSTA-HAWKINS RENTAL HOUSING ACT   CC §§1954.50 to 1954.53

COSTS (See also **COMPENSATION; FEES**)
Generally   CCP §§1032, 1033, 1033.5
Administration of decedents' estates
    Generally (See **ADMINISTRATION OF ESTATES**)
    Claims against decedents' estates (See **CLAIMS AGAINST ESTATES**)
Administrative law and procedure
    Adjudicative proceedings (See **ADMINISTRATIVE ADJUDICATION**)
    Economic impact of regulation, assessment of (See **ADMINISTRATIVE PROCEDURE ACT**)
Annulment of marriage   Fam §§270 to 274, 2010, 2030 to 2034, 2255
    Financial need basis   CRC 5.427
Appeals
    Certiorari, mandate and prohibition
        Award and recovery of costs   CRC 8.493
    Superior court appeals (See **APPELLATE RULES, SUPERIOR COURT APPEALS**)
    Supreme court and courts of appeal (See **APPELLATE RULES, SUPERIOR COURT APPEALS**)
Arbitration (See **ARBITRATION**)

COSTS (—Cont.)

Architects, undertaking required to secure costs in action against   CCP §1029.5
Attachment (See **ATTACHMENT**)
Attorney discipline
    Enforcement of orders for payment of costs as money judgment   CRC 9.23
Attorney general
    Civil actions enforcing public rights   CCP §1021.8
Attorneys' fees (See **ATTORNEY'S FEES**)
Automobiles (See **AUTOMOBILES**)
Bad faith actions or appeals
    Commencement of action by party in   CCP §1038
    Government claim act cases   CCP §1038
Bond filed by estate representative, amount allowed as cost of   Pro §8486
Carpenter-Katz Small Business Equal Access to Justice Act   CCP §1028.5
Certiorari   CCP §1027
    Award and recovery of costs   CRC 8.493
Change of venue   CCP §399
    Time frames for transferring jurisdiction
        Family law actions or proceedings   CRC 5.97
Child support proceedings (See **CHILD SUPPORT**)
Civil rules
    Waiver of fees and costs   Gov §§68630 to 68641
        Application   CRC 3.50 to 3.58
Claims against decedents' estates (See **CLAIMS AGAINST ESTATES**)
Common interest developments
    Alternative dispute resolution
        Enforcement action, effect of refusing to engage in dispute resolution   CC §5960
Compromise, costs of litigation charged to party refusing offer of   CCP §998
Conciliation courts (See **CONCILIATION COURTS**)
Confession of judgments   CCP §1139
Conservators
    Interstate jurisdiction, transfer and recognition
        Requests for assistance between courts, travel expenses   Pro §1985
Construction-related accessibility claims
    Factors considered in determining recoverable costs   CC §55.55
Consumer arbitration
    Fees and costs of private arbitration company   CCP §1284.3
Contemnor ordered to pay   CCP §1218
Continuance of trial   CCP §1024
Contract actions, recovery in   CC §1717
Counties, liability of
    Generally   CCP §1029
    Judicial arbitration, administrative costs of   CCP §1141.28
Court reporters (See **COURT REPORTERS**)
Credit card holder's action based on billing errors   CC §1747.50
Credit denied because of marital status, costs in action for   CC §1812.34
Credit reports as basis for action   CC §1785.31
Crimes against humanity
    Assault and battery, wrongful death, etc constituting torture, genocide, crimes against humanity, etc   CCP §354.8
Custody of children (See **CUSTODY OF CHILDREN**)
Dealership law, discrimination violating   CC §86
Decedents' estates
    Administration of decedents' estates
        Generally (See **ADMINISTRATION OF ESTATES**)
    Claims against decedents' estates (See **CLAIMS AGAINST ESTATES**)
Default, costs on   CRC 3.1700
Definitions   CCP §1032
Depositions (See **DEPOSITIONS**)
Deposits by defendant   CC §1717, CCP §1025
Designers, undertaking required to secure costs in action against   CCP §1029.5
Directed verdict, granting defense costs on   CCP §1038
Discount buying services, breach of contract   CC §1812.123
Dismissal of action   CC §1717
    Consumer debt cases
        Plaintiff debt buyer failing to appear or prepare to proceed   CCP §581.5
Dissolution of marriage   Fam §§270 to 274, 2010, 2030 to 2034
    Financial need basis   CRC 5.427
Districts, liability of   CCP §1029
Domestic violence cases   Fam §§6344, 6386
Donative transfers
    Presumption of fraud or undue influence   Pro §21380
Doxing victims' recourse   CC §1708.89
Eminent domain (See **EMINENT DOMAIN**)
Enforcement of judgments (See **ENFORCEMENT OF JUDGMENTS**)
Engineers, undertaking required to secure costs in action against   CCP §1029.5
Entry of   CRC 3.1700

COSTS (—Cont.)

Environmental quality act
    Jobs and economic improvement through environmental leadership act of 2021
        Appellate review of CEQA cases   CRC 8.705
    Petitions under environmental quality act, civil rules governing
        Environmental leadership development projects   CRC 3.2240
        Environmental leadership development transit projects   CRC 3.2240
        Inglewood arena project   CRC 3.2240
        Oakland sports and mixed use project   CRC 3.2240
Escheated property, recording notice of action for   CCP §1410
Executors and administrators   CCP §1026
Exhibits   CCP §1033.5
Expedited jury trials
    Applicable provisions   CCP §630.10
    Mandatory expedited jury trials, limited civil cases
        Applicability of rules governing costs and attorney fees   CCP §630.27
    Post-trial motions   CCP §630.09
Extension of time for filing costs memorandum or motion to strike or tax costs   CRC 3.1700
    Electronic filing, when required   CRCSupp 1st AppDist
Fair debt buying practices
    Violation of provisions   CC §1788.62
Family law proceedings   Fam §§270 to 274, 2030 to 2034
    Allocation of fees and costs   Fam §§2032, 2034
    Financial need basis   CRC 5.427
    Sanctions may include expenses for parties aggrieved by rules violation   CRC 5.14
Filing fees
    Check for filing fees returned unpaid   CCP §411.20
    Fee waiver
        Economically unable to pay   Gov §§68630 to 68641
    Prevailing party, recovery by   CCP §1033.5
    Underpayment   CCP §411.21
Foreign corporation as plaintiff, security for costs for   CCP §1030
Garnishment, costs included in final withholding order for   CCP §706.028
Genocide
    Assault and battery, wrongful death, etc constituting torture, genocide, crimes against humanity, etc   CCP §354.8
Government claims act, bad faith actions under   CCP §1038
Greenway easements
    Enforcement of easement   CC §816.62
Homestead exemption, recovery of judgment creditor's cost in action involving   CCP §704.840
Human trafficking
    Actions for human trafficking   CC §52.5
Indemnity, action for   CC §2778
Indigent persons, waiver   Gov §§68630 to 68641
    Abstract of judgment or writ of execution
        Payment of waived fees   Gov §68638
    Application for initial fee waiver   Gov §68633
    Change in financial circumstances
        Person granted waiver, notice   Gov §68636
    Conservatorships and guardianships   Gov §68631
    Court clerk copying fees   Gov §70676
    Expiration of initial fee waiver   Gov §68639
    Family law case
        Payment of waived fees   Gov §68637
    Granting initial fee waiver   Gov §68631
    Hearing on eligibility for waiver   Gov §68636
    Initial fee waiver   Gov §68631
    Installment payments
        Rules allowing payment   Gov §68640
    Judicial Council application form
        Application for initial fee waiver   Gov §68633
    Legislative findings and declarations   Gov §68630
    Payment of waived fees by party against whom judgment entered
        Trial court fees   Gov §68637
    Person granted waiver not entitled   Gov §68636
    Persons granted permission to proceed without paying   Gov §68632
    Persons sentenced to state prison or county jail
        Trial court fees   Gov §68635
    Processing and determination of application for waiver
        Appellate courts   Gov §68634.5
        Trial courts   Gov §68634
    Recovery of waived fees or costs   Gov §68636
    Rules, adoption   Gov §§68640, 68641
    Settlement, compromise, award or other recovery
        Payment of fees from   Gov §68637
    Sheriff's fees   Gov §26720.5

COSTS (—Cont.
Indigent persons, waiver —Cont.
 Trial courts fees Gov §§68635, 68637
  Determination of waiver Gov §68634
 In forma pauperis applications
  Waiver of fees and costs Gov §§68630 to 68641
   Application CRC 3.50 to 3.58
    Bench warrants to secure attendance of witnesses, applicability of waiver provisions Gov §26744.5
Information Practices Act, recovery in proceeding under CC §§1798.46, 1798.47
Initial fee waiver
 Economically unable to pay Gov §§68630 to 68641
International commercial arbitration and conciliation (See **INTERNATIONAL COMMERCIAL ARBITRATION AND CONCILIATION**)
Interpleader CCP §386.6
Interpreters
 Court interpreter fees CCP §1033.5
Interstate family support Fam §5700.313
Inverse condemnation action CCP §1036
Jenkins act claims CCP §1021.10
Joinder of parties, costs in absence of CCP §1022
Judicial arbitration (See **JUDICIAL ARBITRATION**)
Jury (See **JURY**)
Legal separation proceedings Fam §§270 to 274, 2010, 2030 to 2034
 Financial need basis CRC 5.427
Mandate CCP §§1094.5, 1095
 Award and recovery of costs CRC 8.493
Mechanic's liens
 Actions to enforce CC §8464
 Stop payment notices, enforcement of claim stated CC §8558
Mediation of civil actions, administration of CCP §1775.8
Medical records, inspection of Ev §1158
Medical services, undertaking required to secure costs in action alleging negligence in performance of CCP §1029.5
Memorandum of costs CRC 3.1700
 Appellate court rules for CRC 8.278
Mileage (See **MILEAGE**)
Mistake, inadvertence, surprise or excusable neglect, award of costs and fees on grant of relief from judgment based on CCP §473
Mobilehomes, actions involving CC §798.85
Mortgages (See **TRUST DEEDS AND MORTGAGES**)
Municipal corporations, liability of CCP §1029
Nonresident as plaintiff, security for costs for CCP §1030
Nonsuit, granting defense costs on CCP §1038
Nuisance abatement actions
 Illegal weapons on real property CC §3485
Obscene and harmful matter
 Unauthorized obscene material
  Actions for distribution CC §52.8
Online violence prevention
 Violent posts, removal
  Order to remove, action seeking CC §1798.99.22
Paint, recovery from parent for child defacing property by use of CC §1714.1
Partition (See **PARTITION**)
Poor persons, waiver for (See **INDIGENT PERSONS**)
Postponement of trial CCP §1024
Prejudgment costs CCP §1034, CRC 3.1700
Pretrial arbitration (See **JUDICIAL ARBITRATION**)
Prevailing party defined CCP §1032
Process, service of (See **PROCESS AND SERVICE OF PROCESS**)
Professional persons, bond securing costs in actions against CCP §§1029.5, 1029.6
Prohibition, writ of
 Award and recovery of costs CRC 8.493
Public entities and employees, claims against (See **CLAIMS AGAINST PUBLIC ENTITIES AND EMPLOYEES**)
Public guardians (See **PUBLIC GUARDIANS**)
Quo warranto proceedings CCP §810
Recovery of CCP §§1032, 1033
Reduction of court operations under trial court coordination plans (See **JUDICIAL ADMINISTRATION STANDARDS**)
Referees' fees CCP §1023
Rental-purchase contracts, breach of CC §1812.636
Retail installment sales price, recovery of CC §§1810.4, 1811.1
Settlement, costs of litigation charged to party refusing offer of CCP §998
Small business and regulatory agency, action between CCP §1028.5
Small claims cases
 Writ petitions CRC 8.977
Small claims courts (See **SMALL CLAIMS COURTS**)
Spousal support proceedings (See **SPOUSAL SUPPORT**)
State agency proceedings (See **ADMINISTRATIVE PROCEDURE ACT**)

COSTS (—Cont.
State of California, liability of CCP §1028
Sterilization proceedings Pro §1963
Subpoenas duces tecum Ev §1563
Summary judgment
 Defense costs, granting CCP §1038
Superior courts
 Appellate division proceedings (See **APPELLATE RULES, SUPERIOR COURT APPEALS**)
Supreme court and courts of appeal (See **APPELLATE RULES, SUPREME COURT AND COURTS OF APPEAL**)
Surety bonds (See **SURETYSHIP, BONDS AND UNDERTAKINGS**)
Surveyors, undertaking required to secure costs in action against CCP §1029.5
Taxing costs
 Items allowable as costs CCP §1033.5
 Motion and notice of motion CRC 3.1700
Tender and deposit, effect of CC §1717, CCP §1025
Termination of parent-child relationship, liability for costs in action for Fam §7851.5
Torture
 Assault and battery, wrongful death, etc constituting torture, genocide, crimes against humanity, etc CCP §354.8
Trade secrets, misappropriation
 Expert witness and other recoverable costs CC §3426.4
Transcripts CCP §1033.5
Transfer of causes
 Time frames for transferring jurisdiction
  Family law actions or proceedings CRC 5.97
Translators
 When required Ev §753
Trial court coordination plan, cost reductions under (See **JUDICIAL ADMINISTRATION STANDARDS**)
Trial court rules
 Sanctions for noncompliance
  Civil cases CRC 2.30
Trial de novo, costs on CCP §1141.21
 Judicial arbitration CRC 3.826
Trust deeds (See **TRUST DEEDS AND MORTGAGES**)
Trust proceedings (See **TRUSTS**)
Uniform Parentage Act, actions under Fam §7640
Unlawful detainer (See **UNLAWFUL DETAINER**)
Unperformed contracts for sale of realty, title requirements for CC §886.020
Validation proceedings CCP §868
Venue, change of
 Criminal cases, reimbursement guidelines CRC 4.155
Vexatious litigants, security for costs CCP §§391 to 391.8
Voidable transactions by decedent, proceedings to recover property transferred under Pro §9653
Void or voidable marriage, proceedings to have marriage judged Fam §2255
Waiver of court costs and fees
 Appellate rules, supreme court and courts of appeal
  E-filing in supreme court and courts of appeal, eligibility for filing CRC 8.76
 Civil rules governing waiver of fees and costs CRC 3.50 to 3.58 (See **CIVIL RULES**)
 Court reporters
  Request for reporter if granted fee waiver CRC 2.956
 Economically unable to pay Gov §§68630 to 68641
 Forms
  Judicial council legal forms CRCAppx A
 Remote appearance fees CRC 3.672
War crimes
 Assault and battery, wrongful death, etc constituting torture, genocide, crimes against humanity, etc CCP §354.8
Wholesale sales representatives, costs awarded in actions involving CC §1738.16
Will probate proceedings (See **WILL PROBATE**)
Witnesses' fees (See **WITNESSES**)

COTENANCY
Joint tenancy (See **JOINT TENANCY**)
Ouster, establishment of CC §843
Partition (See **PARTITION**)
Tenancy in common (See **TENANCY IN COMMON**)

COTTON
Attachment proceedings CCP §481.110
Claim and delivery CCP §511.040

COUNSELING
Conciliation counselors (See **CONCILIATION COURTS**)

COUNSELING—Cont.
Domestic violence cases, order for counseling in   Fam §6343
Marriage counselors, privileged communication with (See **PRIVILEGED COMMUNICATIONS**)
Sexual assault victim-counselor privilege (See **PRIVILEGED COMMUNICATIONS**)
Vocational training   Fam §4331

COUNSELORS AT LAW (See **ATTORNEYS**)

COUNSEL, RIGHT TO
Appeals
    Appointment of counsel for   CRC 8.300
    Misdemeanor appeals
        Appointment of appellate counsel   CRC 8.851
Appointment of counsel
    Death penalty
        Appellate counsel appointments   CRC 8.605
        Appellate counsel qualifications   CRC 8.605
        Declaration of counsel for appointment, form   CRCAppx A
        Habeas counsel appointments   CRC 8.605
        Habeas counsel qualifications   CRC 8.652
        Trial counsel qualifications   CRC 4.117
    Fixed fee appointments   CRCSupp FixedFeeAppoint
    Indigent criminal appellants in supreme court, payment guidelines
        Disallowed fees and expenses   CRCSupp PayGuideAppoint
        Expenses   CRCSupp PayGuideAppoint
        Nonperformance of work   CRCSupp PayGuideAppoint
        Purpose of provisions   CRCSupp PayGuideAppoint
        Reasonable compensation, factors   CRCSupp PayGuideAppoint
        Withdrawal, reimbursement   CRCSupp PayGuideAppoint
    Trial counsel, qualifications   CRC 4.117
Competency standards, juvenile proceedings   CRC 5.660
Dependency proceedings   CRC 5.660
Juvenile cases
    CASA programs   CRC 5.655
Mediation sessions   CRC 3.894

COUNTERCLAIMS
Abolition of   CCP §428.80

COUNTIES
Adjacent counties (See **ADJACENT COUNTIES**)
Appellate briefs
    Attorney general representing state or county, service of brief on   CRC 8.29
Attachment proceedings   CCP §481.200
Attorney professional conduct
    Organization or entity as client   ProfC 1.13
Bonds issued by (See **BONDS**)
Boundaries
    Limitation of actions to contest change of   CCP §349.1
    Validation procedure for change in   CCP §349.4
Building restrictions, burden of proving necessity for   Ev §669.5
Cardiopulmonary resuscitation, courses in   CC §1714.2
Child support arrearages, restrictions on information concerning   Fam §4002
Child welfare agencies
    Electronic court records, remote access
        Government entities, access by   CRC 2.540
Claim and delivery   CCP §511.100
Clerks (See **CLERKS OF COURT**)
Compensation for expert witnesses   Ev §731
Conservation easements held by   CC §815.3
Consolidation
    Contesting consolidation, limitation of actions for   CCP §349.1
    Validation procedure   CCP §349.4
Contempt orders against county government officials   CCP §128
Contracts
    Immigration and naturalization
        Prohibition of contracts by local government or law enforcement agency to detain noncitizens for civil immigration custody   CC §1670.9
Costs, liability for (See **COSTS**)
Court operations
    Costs   CRC 10.810
    Notice of change in court-county relationship   CRC 10.805
Court reporter taking down and transcribing at cost of county   CCP §274a
Decedent's estate, claims against   Pro §§9200 to 9205
Defined   Fam §67
Design professionals
    Indemnification, public agencies   CC §2782.8

COUNTIES—Cont.
Dissolution
    Contesting dissolution, limitation of actions for   CCP §349.1
    Validation procedure   CCP §349.4
District attorney (See **DISTRICT ATTORNEY**)
Execution of process, effect of creation of new county on   CCP §262.11
Formation
    Contesting formation, limitation of actions for   CCP §349.1
    Validation procedure   CCP §349.4
Greenway easements
    Entities permitted to acquire and hold easement   CC §816.56
Groundwater rights actions
    Intervention in comprehensive adjudication   CCP §837
Holiday for purposes of computing time if public office closed   CCP §12b
Human trafficking or slavery
    Ordinances preventing, effect   CC §52.6
Immigration and naturalization
    Contracts by local government or law enforcement agency to detain noncitizens for civil immigration custody
        Prohibition   CC §1670.9
Inclusions in definition   CCP §17
Jails (See **PRISONERS**)
Judicial arbitration, county payments for   CCP §1141.28
Judicial district defined to include   CCP §§17, 38
Jury commissioner, appointment of   CCP §195
Leased abandonment provisions, applicability of   CC §1952.6
Marriage solemnization by county supervisor
    Local government officials, authority to solemnize   Fam §400
Ordinances and regulations (See **ORDINANCES**)
Pleadings verification   CCP §446
Presentation of claims as prerequisite to commencement of actions against governmental agencies   CCP §313
Process
    Creation of new county, effect of   CCP §262.11
    Service of process   CCP §416.50
Public health services
    Providers of public health and safety labor or service
        Logo or identifying mark of public agency, display restrictions   CC §3273
Reorganization
    Contesting reorganization, limitation of actions for   CCP §349.1
    Validation procedure   CCP §349.4
Shared mobility devices
    Agreements with or permits from local government   CC §2505
Statutes of limitation
    Applicability to actions brought in name of or for benefit of   CCP §345
    Boundaries, actions to contest change of   CCP §349.1
    Contesting formation, dissolution, consolidation or change of organization   CCP §349.1
Superintendent of Schools (See **SCHOOLS**)
Superior court appellate division in every county and city and county   CCP §77
Superior court fees
    Services to local, state and federal governments   Gov §70633
Supervisors (See **SUPERVISORS**)
Trial court coordination within counties (See **JUDICIAL ADMINISTRATION STANDARDS**)
Unclaimed property, disposition of   CC §2080.6
Validation proceedings   CCP §§860 to 870
Venue in actions by or against   CCP §394
Wills, taking under   Pro §6102

COUNTY CLERK (See **CLERKS OF COURT**)

COUNTY COUNSEL
Acknowledgment of instruments   CC §1181
Electronic court records, remote access
    Government entities, access by   CRC 2.540
Firearm industry standards of conduct
    Actions against industry members for violation of standards   CC §3273.52
Unruh Civil Rights Act, bringing action under   CC §52

COUNTY HOSPITALS
Statute of limitation on accounts for support of patients at   CCP §345

COUNTY MENTAL HEALTH DIRECTOR (See **MENTAL HOSPITALS**)

COUNTY RECORDER
Electronic recording delivery systems   Gov §§27390 to 27399 (See **ELECTRONIC RECORDING DELIVERY SYSTEMS**)
Fees for official services   Gov §§27360 to 27388.2
Generally (See **RECORDS AND RECORDING**)

COUNTY RECORDER—Cont.
Truncation of social security numbers, program for
    Generally   Gov §§27300 to 27307 (See **SOCIAL SECURITY**)

COUNTY SHERIFF (See **SHERIFF**)

COUNTY TREASURER (See **TREASURER**)

COUNTY TREASURY (See **TREASURY**)

COURSE OF EMPLOYMENT (See **AGENCY**)

COURT-APPOINTED SPECIAL ADVOCATES (CASA)   CRC 5.655
Confidentiality of case information, records, etc
    Plan   CRC 5.655
Dependency proceeding, appointment of advocate as guardian ad litem   CRC 5.660
    Child abuse and treatment act (CAPTA) guardians ad litem   CRC 5.662
Designation by presiding judge
    Memorandum of understanding between designating court and program   CRC 5.655
    Necessity of designation to serve in county   CRC 5.655
Finance, facility and risk management plans   CRC 5.655
Judicial rules   CRC 5.655
Volunteers
    Appointment of volunteers   CRC 5.655
    Oath   CRC 5.655
    Prohibited activities   CRC 5.655
    Removal, resignation or termination   CRC 5.655
    Screening, standards   CRC 5.655
    Supervision, support, etc   CRC 5.655
    Training   CRC 5.655

COURT ARBITRATION (See **JUDICIAL ARBITRATION**)

COURT CALENDARS
Causes under submission, monitoring of   CRC 10.603
Criminal cases
    Assignments   CRC 4.115
    Continuances   CRC 4.115
    Master calendar   CRC 4.115
Differential case management rules   CRC 3.710 to 3.715

COURT CLERK (See **CLERKS OF COURT**)

COURT COMMISSIONERS
Arbitrators, qualification as   CCP §1141.18
Child support matters (See **CHILD SUPPORT**)
Code of Judicial Conduct, compliance with   CRCSupp JudEthicsCanon 6
Complaints against, procedures for handling   CRC 10.603
Court operations, salaries and benefits as costs of   CRC 10.810
Disciplinary actions
    Censure and removal procedures, applicability of   JudPerR 138
    Complaints against subordinate judicial officers, procedures   CRC 10.703
Disqualification for prejudice   CCP §170.6
Ethics programs   CRC JudAdminStand 10.166
Judicial arbitration panels, appointment of retired commissioners   CRC 3.814
Powers of   CCP §259
Social Security Act Title IV-D support actions, rules for   CRC 5.300 to 5.375

COURTESY
Passengers on common carriers, requirements for treatment of   CC §2103

COURT OF CLAIMS
Judicial notice of rules of   Ev §451

COURT OFFICERS AND EMPLOYEES
Accommodation of disabilities
    Reasonable accommodation   CRC JudAdminStand 10.25
County clerk (See **CLERKS OF COURT**)
Court reporters (See **COURT REPORTERS**)
Courts of appeal
    Ethics code for court employees   CRC JudAdminStand 10.16
Disabilities, employees with
    Reasonable accommodation   CRC JudAdminStand 10.25
Discrimination
    Nondiscrimination in application and selection procedures   CRC JudAdminStand 10.21
Education of judicial branch   CRC 10.451 to 10.493
    Recommendations for appellate and trial court personnel   CRC 10.479
Ethics code for court employees, adoption of   CRC JudAdminStand 10.16

COURT OFFICERS AND EMPLOYEES—Cont.
Ethics orientation for judicial branch employees   CRC 10.455
Interpreters (See **TRANSLATORS AND INTERPRETERS**)
Judicial administration standards
    Accommodation of employees' disabilities
        Reasonable accommodation   CRC JudAdminStand 10.25
    Court interpreters   CRC JudAdminStand 2.10, CRC JudAdminStand 2.11
    Ethics code for court employees, adoption   CRC JudAdminStand 10.16
Labor relations of court employees   CRC 10.650 to 10.660
    Applicable law   CRC 10.655, 10.657, 10.659
    Collective bargaining
        Construction of provisions not to make applicable to court employees   CRC 10.657
    Definitions   CRC 10.652
    Dues deduction   CRC 10.659
    Interpretation   CRC 10.651, 10.657, 10.658
    Mediation and dispute resolution   CRC 10.659
    Meet-and-confer, right and obligation to   CRC 10.653
    Purpose of provisions   CRC 10.651
    Scope of representation   CRC 10.654
    Title of rules   CRC 10.650
    Transition provisions   CRC 10.656
    Writ for mandate or prohibition, hearing on petition for   CRC 10.660
Ministerial officers
    Power of court to control conduct of   CCP §128
    Sheriff (See **SHERIFF**)
Personnel plans   CRC 10.670
Probation officers and deputies (See **PROBATION OFFICERS AND DEPUTIES**)
Recruitment procedures, nondiscrimination   CRC JudAdminStand 10.21
Sheriff (See **SHERIFF**)
Subordinate judicial officers   CRC 10.700 to 10.703
    Complaints against subordinate judicial officers   CRC 10.703
    Education of judicial branch employees   CRC 10.451 to 10.493
        Additional education recommendations for certain judicial assignments   CRC 10.469
        Trial court subordinate judicial officers   CRC 10.462
    Law practice of subordinate judicial officers   CRC 10.702
    Qualifications and education   CRC 10.701
    Role   CRC 10.700
Translators (See **TRANSLATORS AND INTERPRETERS**)
Workers' compensation
    Judicial branch workers' compensation program advisory committee   CRC 10.67

COURT REPORTERS (See also **SUPERIOR COURTS**)
Appellate rules
    Supreme court and courts of appeal (See **APPELLATE RULES, SUPREME COURT AND COURTS OF APPEAL**)
Appointments   CRCSupp JudEthicsCanon 3
    Judges, appointments by   CRCSupp JudEthicsCanon 3
Arbitration proceedings, report
    Certified shorthand reporters
        Party's right   CCP §1282.5
    Judicial arbitration   CRC 3.824
Audio taping
    Electronic recordings generally (See within this heading, "**Electronic recordings**")
Automated recordkeeping (See **COMPUTERS**)
Availability of reporting services   CRC 2.956
Certificates
    Electronic recording of court proceedings, certificate for reels required for   CRC 2.952
Certification
    Prima facie evidence of testimony and proceedings, certified transcript as   CCP §273
Certified shorthand reporter, use   CRC 2.956
Computerized recordkeeping (See **COMPUTERS**)
Cost of county, matters that may be reported at   CCP §274a
Court operations costs, salaries and benefits as   CRC 10.810
Death or disability of court reporter, effect of   CCP §§657.1, 914
Delay in preparation of record on appeal   CRC 8.23
Depositions, transcripts and other recordings of
    Transcript of deposition   CCP §2025.510
        Notice of availability for reading, correcting and signing   CCP §2025.520
Electronic recordings
    Evidence, admission into   CRC 2.1040
    Fees for verbatim reporting services   CRC 2.958
    Official court records, use in   CRC 2.952, 2.954

COURT REPORTERS—Cont.
Electronic recordings—Cont.
    Transcripts
        Delivery in electronic form   CCP §271
Electronic records (See **COMPUTERS**)
Ethics programs   CRC JudAdminStand 10.16
Evidence, reports as   CCP §273
Fees   CRC 2.956
    Reporting testimony and proceedings   Gov §69947
        Contested proceedings   Gov §69948
        Criminal proceedings   Gov §69952
        Default or uncontested proceedings   Gov §69949
        Equal payment by parties, other proceedings requiring   Gov §69953
        Juvenile proceedings   Gov §69952
        Lanterman-Petris-Short Act proceedings   Gov §69952
        Recovery of costs by prevailing party   CCP §1033.5
        Termination of parental rights   Gov §69952
    Transcription
        Generally   Gov §69950
        Additional phonographic reporters   Gov §69953.5
        Computer-assisted transcripts   Gov §69954
        Costs, prevailing party recovering transcript fees as   CCP §1033.5
        Reimbursement from transcript reimbursement fund   CRC 8.130
        Special daily service   Gov §69951
        Uniformity in transcription rate expenditures, report on recommendations   Gov §69950.5
Felony case, preparation of record on appeal for   CCP §269
Functional budget categories   CRC 10.810
Historic court records preservation program   CRC 10.855
Judges, censure, removal or admonishment of (See **JUDGES**)
Juvenile proceedings   CCP §274a
    Transcription of hearings   CRC 5.532
Law and motion proceedings   CRC 3.1310
List of reporters working on case   CRC 2.950
Low-income litigants, provision of services to   CRC 8.130
Mandamus (See **MANDAMUS**)
New trial (See **NEW TRIAL**)
Official court reporter, availability   CRC 2.956
Presumed correct   CCP §273
Record on appeal
    Delay in preparation   CRC 8.23
    Form of transcript   CRC 8.144
Reporter's transcript
    Fees   Gov §69950
    Uniformity in transcription rate expenditures, report on recommendations   Gov §69950.5
Rough draft of transcript, prohibition on use of   CCP §273
Salaries and benefits as court operations costs   CRC 10.810
Sentencing proceedings, recording   CRC 4.431
Sound recordings
    Electronic recordings generally (See within this heading, "**Electronic recordings**")
Superior courts (See **SUPERIOR COURTS**)
Trade secrets, protection of   Ev §1063
Transcript reimbursement fund   CRC 8.130
Trial court reporting services   CRC 2.956
Videotaping
    Electronic recordings generally (See within this heading, "**Electronic recordings**")
Views, presence at   CCP §651
Waiver of court fees and costs
    Request for reporter if granted fee waiver   CRC 2.956
        Judicial council forms   CRCAppx A

COURTROOMS
Assistive listening systems for hard-of-hearing persons, courtroom use of   CC §54.8
Children waiting rooms   CRC JudAdminStand 10.24
Facilities
    Court facilities standards   CRC 10.180
    Modification
        Trial court facility modification advisory committee   CRC 10.65
Facility modification
    Trial court facility modification advisory committee   CRC 10.65
Photographing in   CRC 1.150
Radio and television   CRC 1.150
Riverside County, additional filing fees authorized to defray courthouse seismic repair costs   Gov §70622
Security
    Court security advisory committee   CRC 10.61
Smoking policy   CRC 10.504

COURTROOMS—Cont.
Sound recording   CRC 1.150
Television   CRC 1.150
Witness, exclusion of   Ev §777

COURT RULES (See **RULES OF COURT**)

COURTS
Abbreviations, use in legal papers of   CCP §186
Access to courthouses and court proceedings
    Prohibition of activities threatening access to courthouses and court proceedings
        Judge's authority   CCP §177
Administer oaths, power to   CCP §128
Administration
    Judicial Administration Rules (See **JUDICIAL ADMINISTRATION RULES**)
    Judicial Administration Standards (See **JUDICIAL ADMINISTRATION STANDARDS**)
Administrative office of the courts
    References to administrative office of courts   CRC 10.81
Appeal, Courts of (See **COURTS OF APPEAL**)
Arrest
    Civil arrest at courthouse
        Judicial officer's power to protect privilege from civil arrest at courthouse   CCP §177
        Restrictions on arrest at courthouse of person attending court proceeding or attending to legal business in courthouse   CC §43.54
Attorney professional conduct
    Court officials or employees
        Contacts with judges, jurors, tribunal officials or employees, etc   ProfC 3.5
Bias, prevention   CRC JudAdminStand 10.20
Broadcasting, photographing, or recording proceedings   CRC 1.150
Budget and management information
    Maintenance by superior court   CRC 10.501
Budget appropriations   CRC 10.810
Business days   CCP §133
Caseflow management   CRC 3.700 to 3.771
Change of venue (See **VENUE**)
Chapter heading not limiting   CCP §182
Compel obedience to its judgments, orders and process, power to   CCP §128
Conciliation courts (See **CONCILIATION COURTS**)
Contempt of court (See **CONTEMPT**)
Courtesy   CRC JudAdminStand 10.17
Courtrooms (See **COURTROOMS**)
Criminal departments and divisions   CRC 10.950, 10.951
Disabled personnel, reasonable accommodation   CRC JudAdminStand 10.25
Discrimination, prohibition against in court appointments   CRC 10.611, CRC JudAdminStand 10.21
Electronic court records   CRC 2.500 to 2.545
Employee labor relations   CRC 10.650 to 10.660
Employees of (See **COURT OFFICERS AND EMPLOYEES**)
English language in judicial proceedings   CCP §185, Ev §§750 to 757
Executive committees   CRC 10.605
Executive officers, duties   CRC 10.610
Expert witnesses, appointment of   Ev §§722, 730 to 733
Facilities
    Acquisition, space planning, construction and design   CRC 10.184
    Court facilities advisory committee   CRC 10.62
    Judicial council recommendations for policies, procedures and standards   CRC 10.181
    Judicial council staff
        Operation and maintenance of facilities   CRC 10.182
    Operation and maintenance of facilities   CRC 10.182
    Security
        Court security advisory committee   CRC 10.61
        Court security committees   CRC 10.173
        Memoranda of understanding, petitions regarding disputes   CRC 10.174
        Plans for court security   CRC 10.172
    Smoking in court facilities   CRC 10.504
    Standards for court facilities   CRC 10.180
    Transfer of responsibilities to judicial council   CRC 10.183
    Trial court facility modification advisory committee   CRC 10.65
Family Conciliation Court Law (See **CONCILIATION COURTS**)
Federal courts (See **FEDERAL COURTS**)
Fees
    Setting fees by court for products and services   CRC 10.815
Gender-neutral language in rules, forms, etc   CRC 10.612

COURTS — INDEX

COURTS—Cont.
  Government tort liability
    Actions against judicial branch entities
      Definition of judicial branch entity   Gov §940.3
      Judicial relief from nonpresentation of claims   Gov §946.6
      Settlement of claims   Gov §948.1
      Summons, service   Gov §955.9
    Claims and claims presentation against judicial branch entity
      Adjustment and payment of claims   Gov §935.8
      Definition of judicial branch entity   Gov §900.3
      Rule of court to determine action on claim against   Gov §912.7
    Payment of claims and judgments against judicial branch entities   Gov §§965, 965.2
      Appropriations   Gov §965
      Conditions for payment   Gov §965.6
      Reports on remedial measures   Gov §965.65
  Implied powers to effectuate conferred powers   CCP §187
  Independent Administration of Estates Act, court supervision under (See **INDEPENDENT ADMINISTRATION OF ESTATES ACT**)
  Injunction staying proceedings   CCP §526
  Judges (See **JUDGES**)
  Judicial branch statistical information system (JBSIS)   CRC 10.400
  Judicial branch workers' compensation program advisory committee   CRC 10.67
  Judicial business transacted, days when   CCP §133
  Judicial council
    Public access to judicial administrative records   CRC 10.500
  Judicial holidays (See **HOLIDAYS**)
  Judicial notice (See **JUDICIAL NOTICE**)
  Jury
    Complaints of jurors
      Receipt and response mechanism   CRC JudAdminStand 10.51
    Generally (See **JURY**)
  Justice courts (See **JUSTICE COURTS**)
  Juvenile courts (See **JUVENILE COURTS**)
  Language access services
    Collaboration and technology to provide services   CRC 1.300
    Court-ordered and court-provided programs, services and professionals   CRC 1.300
  Limited English proficient court litigants
    Language access services
      Collaboration and technology to provide services   CRC 1.300
      Court-ordered and court-provided programs, services and professionals   CRC 1.300
  Mediation of employment disputes   CRC 10.659
  Numerals, use in legal papers of   CCP §186
  Officers of (See **COURT OFFICERS AND EMPLOYEES**)
  Operations   CRC 10.810
  Performance standards   CRC JudAdminStand 10.17
  Powers in conduct of proceedings   CCP §128
  Preference, motion for (See **PRIORITIES AND PREFERENCES**)
  Probation officers and deputies (See **PROBATION OFFICERS AND DEPUTIES**)
  Process, power to amend and control   CCP §128
  Public, sittings to be   CCP §124
  Quality service to court users
    Education of judicial branch
      Recommendations for appellate and trial court personnel   CRC 10.479
  Records   CRC 2.400
    Court records
      Public access to judicial administrative records   CRC 10.500
    Electronic court records   CRC 2.500 to 2.545
    Forms
      Judicial council legal forms   CRCAppx A
    Judicial administration standards
      Court records management standards   CRC JudAdminStand 10.80
    Public access to judicial administrative records   CRC 10.500
  Remote appearances   CCP §367.75
    COVID-19, emergency rule   CRCAppx I Emer Rule 3
    Equal and fair access to justice
      Working group for statewide framework for remote proceedings   CCP §367.9
    Open court proceedings
      Limiting public access when remote access available, restrictions   CCP §124
    Report on use of remote technology   CCP §367.8
  Reporters (See **COURT REPORTERS**)
  Seal of court (See **SEAL**)
  Security of court facilities
    Court security advisory committee   CRC 10.61
    Court security committees   CRC 10.173

COURTS—Cont.
  Security of court facilities—Cont.
    Memoranda of understanding
      Disputes related to MOU, petitions regarding   CRC 10.174
    Plans for court security   CRC 10.172
  Self-help centers   CRC 10.960
  Service of process, court directing manner of   CCP §413.30
  Small claims court (See **SMALL CLAIMS COURTS**)
  Smoking in court facilities   CRC 10.504
  Statutory powers   CCP §128
  Superior courts (See **SUPERIOR COURTS**)
  Support staff ethics program   CRC JudAdminStand 10.16
  Supreme Court (See **SUPREME COURT, CALIFORNIA**)
  Testify, power to compel attendance of persons to   CCP §128
  Trial courts, judicial administration
    Automation of trial courts   CRC 10.870
    Employment protection and governance
      Writ petitions in labor relations disputes   CRC 10.660
    Funding of trial courts
      Notice of change in court-county relationship   CRC 10.805
    Litigation management   CRC 10.202
    Management of trial courts   CRC 10.601 to 10.953
  Trial generally (See **TRIAL**)
  Tribal courts
    Judicial council
      Tribal court-state court forum   CRC 10.60
    Money judgments
      Tribal court civil money judgment act   CCP §§1730 to 1741
    Title IV-D support actions
      Transfer of title IV-D cases from tribal court   CRC 5.372
      Transfer of title IV-D cases to tribal court   CRC 5.372
  Vacancy in office of all or any judges or justices, effect on proceedings of   CCP §184
  Workers' compensation program
    Judicial council workers' compensation program for trial courts   CRC 10.350

COURT SELF-HELP CENTERS   CRC 10.960

COURTS OF APPEAL
  Adjournments construed as recesses   CCP §42
  Administrative presiding justices
    Education of judicial officers
      Duties of administrative presiding justices   CRC 10.452
  Agricultural Labor Relations Board, judicial review of decisions   CRC 8.728
  Appellate rules   CRC 8.1 to 8.642 (See **APPELLATE RULES, SUPREME COURT AND COURTS OF APPEAL**)
  Assignment of cases to divisions   CRC 10.1008
  Authority to affirm, reverse or modify judgment or order appealed from   CCP §43
  Contested election cases, preference to   CCP §44
  Conveyance of real property, justice's power to take and certify proof and acknowledgment of   CCP §179
  Decisions
    Finality   CRC 8.264
      Habeas corpus   CRC 8.387
    Memorandum opinions   CRC JudAdminStand 8.1
    Modifications   CRC 8.264
  Declaration, justice's power to take and certify   CCP §179
  Districts and divisions
    Assignment of cases to divisions   CRC 10.1008
  Education of judicial branch
    Administrative presiding justices
      Duties   CRC 10.452
    Justices
      Additional education recommendations for certain judicial assignments   CRC 10.469
      Minimum requirements   CRC 10.461
    Recommendations for appellate and trial court personnel   CRC 10.479
  E-filing in supreme court and courts of appeal
    Generally   CRC 8.70 to 8.79
    Supreme court-specific rules   CRCSupp SuprCtE-file 1 to CRCSupp SuprCtE-file 13
  Environmental quality act cases under public resources code   CRC 8.700 to 8.705
  Ethics
    Code for court employees   CRC JudAdminStand 10.16
    Training for judicial branch employees   CRC 10.455
  Family rules
    Waiver of fees and costs in supreme court and court of appeal   CRC 5.46

COURTS OF APPEAL—Cont.
Fees
    Waiver
        Judicial council legal forms   CRCAppx A
Judicial notice, motion requesting   CRC 8.252
    Habeas corpus   CRC 8.386
Jurisdiction
    Original jurisdiction
        Habeas corpus   CRC 8.380 to 8.398
        Mandate, certiorari and prohibition   CRC 8.485 to 8.493
Justices
    Affidavit, power to take and certify   CCP §179
    Appellate rules (See **APPELLATE RULES, SUPREME COURT AND COURTS OF APPEAL**)
    Chambers, powers and duties at   CCP §165
    Conveyance of real property, power to take and certify proof and acknowledgment of   CCP §179
    Education of judicial branch
        Additional education recommendations for certain judicial assignments   CRC 10.469
        Duties of justices, clerk/administrators, managing attorneys and supervisors   CRC 10.452
        Minimum requirements   CRC 10.461
    Failure to perform duties   CRC 10.1016
    Satisfaction of judgment, power to take and certify acknowledgment of   CCP §179
    Vacancy in office of all or any justices, effect on proceedings of   CCP §184
Libel or slander actions by person holding elective office or by candidate, preference to   CCP §44
Local rules of court (See **APPELLATE RULES, SUPREME COURT AND COURTS OF APPEAL**)
Managing attorneys
    Education of judicial branch
        Minimum education requirements for managing attorneys, supervisors, etc   CRC 10.472
New trial, authority to direct   CCP §43
Original writs, procedural rules
    Habeas corpus   CRC 8.380 to 8.398
    Mandate, certiorari and prohibition in supreme court or court of appeal   CRC 8.485 to 8.493
        Environmental quality act cases under public resources code   CRC 8.703
Presiding justices and acting presiding justices
    Administrative presiding justices
        Education of judicial officers, duties of administrative presiding justices   CRC 10.452
Probate proceedings, preference to   CCP §44
Public Employment Relations Board, judicial review of decisions   CRC 8.728
Records
    Public access to judicial administrative records   CRC 10.500
Rehearings   CRC 8.268
    Habeas corpus   CRC 8.387
Satisfaction of judgment, justice's power to take and certify acknowledgment of   CCP §179
Statutory powers, listing of   CCP §128
Supervisors
    Education of judicial branch
        Minimum education requirements for managing attorneys, supervisors, etc   CRC 10.472
Support staff ethics program   CRC JudAdminStand 10.16
Time
    Appellate rules (See **APPELLATE RULES, SUPREME COURT AND COURTS OF APPEAL**)
    Transact business at any time, courts may   CCP §41
Transfer of cause   CRC 10.1000
    Wrong court, appeal or petition filed in   CCP §396
Travel expense reimbursement for judicial officers and employees   CRC 10.106
Vacancy in office of all or any justices, effect on proceedings of   CCP §184

COURT TECHNOLOGY
Indexes, automated maintenance   CRC 10.851
Judicial Branch Statistical Information System (JBSIS)   CRC 10.400
Trial court automation   CRC 10.870

COVENANTS AND CONDITIONS
Accessory dwelling units
    Unenforceability of accessory dwelling unit prohibitions   CC §714.3
Adjacent property   CC §§1469, 1470
Affordable housing developments
    Recorded restrictive covenants, unenforceability in face of approved and recorded restrictive covenant affordable housing modification document   CC §714.6

COVENANTS AND CONDITIONS—Cont.
Apportionment   CC §§1467, 1469
Appurtenances   CC §1460
Breach, liability for   CC §1466
Commercial and industrial common interest developments
    Restrictive covenants   CC §6606
Common interest developments   CC §5975
    Housing development projects using authorized floor area ratio standards
        Unenforceability of restrictions   CC §4747
    Unlawful restrictive covenants, deletion   CC §4225
Consent for transfer   CC §1457
Contracts (See **CONTRACTS AND AGREEMENTS**)
Creation, time of   CC §749
Defined   CC §1462
Discriminatory restrictions   CC §§53, 782, 782.5
    Common interest developments
        Unlawful restrictive covenants, deletion   CC §4225
Environmental covenants   CC §1471
Foreclosure sale
    Final sale
        Recorded covenants for purchased property   CC §2924o
Hazardous materials, lands containing   CC §1471
Implied from deed   CC §1113
Junior accessory dwelling units
    Unenforceability of accessory dwelling unit prohibitions   CC §714.3
Leases   CC §§1469, 1470
Parties bound by   CC §1465
Prefabricated modular homes, validity of covenants restricting use of   CC §714.5
Quiet enjoyment   CC §1463
Racial covenants   CC §§53, 782, 782.5
    Common interest developments
        Unlawful restrictive covenants, deletion   CC §4225
Recordation   CC §1468
    Affordable housing developments
        Recorded restrictive covenants, unenforceability in face of approved and recorded restrictive covenant affordable housing modification document   CC §714.6
Repairs   CC §1468
Restrictions defined   CC §784
Restrictive covenants
    Affordable housing developments
        Recorded restrictive covenants, unenforceability in face of approved and recorded restrictive covenant affordable housing modification document   CC §714.6
    Commercial and industrial common interest developments   CC §6606
Running with land   CC §§1460 to 1463
Satellite dishes in common interest developments
    Restrictions on limitations, prohibitions   CC §4725
Solar energy systems, invalidity of covenants prohibiting use of   CC §714
Successive owners bound by   CC §1468
Taxes, payment of   CC §1468

COVENANTS, CONDITIONS, AND RESTRICTIONS
Affordable housing developments
    Sale of unit to nonprofit housing corporation after unit not purchased by income-qualifying person or family within time period   CC §714.7

COVENANTS NOT TO SUE
Contribution among joint tortfeasors, effect on   CCP §877

COVID-19
Appellate rules, supreme court and courts of appeal
    E-filing in supreme court and courts of appeal
        Documents subject to e-filing in Supreme Court, modifications in light of emergencies   CRCSupp SuprCtE-file 2
    Tolling or extension of time for public health emergencies   CRC 8.66
Continuances in civil cases
    Cases extended pursuant to state of emergency   CCP §599
Deeds of trust and mortgages
    Small landlord and homeowner relief act   CC §§3273.01 to 3273.16
Emergency rules related to COVID-19   CRCAppx I Emer Rules 1 to 13
Fair debt buying practices
    COVID-19 rental debt
        Sale or assignment, prohibition for debt of rental assistance recipients   CC §1788.66
Landlord and tenant
    COVID-19 rental housing recovery act   CCP §§1179.08 to 1179.15 (See **UNLAWFUL DETAINER**)
    COVID-19 tenant relief act   CCP §§1179.01 to 1179.07 (See **UNLAWFUL DETAINER**)

COVID-19—Cont.
  Landlord and tenant—Cont.
    Rental debt, action to recover   CCP §§871.10 to 871.12
      Attorneys' fees   CCP §871.11
      Breach of contract actions filed before October 2020   CCP §871.10
      Good faith effort by plaintiff to seek rental assistance   CCP §871.10
      Reduction in damages for refusal to obtain rental assistance   CCP §871.10
      Small claims court jurisdiction   CCP §116.223
      Sunset of provisions   CCP §871.12
      Time to commence action   CCP §871.10
      Unlawful detainer actions, applicability of provisions   CCP §871.10
    Rental debt, fees or service reductions   CC §1942.9
    Rental debt, negative use in evaluating housing applications by housing providers, tenant screening companies, etc   CC §1785.20.4
  Mortgages
    Small landlord and homeowner relief act   CC §§3273.01 to 3273.16
  Small claims courts
    Jurisdiction for action to recover COVID-19 rental debt   CCP §116.223

CPR (See **CARDIOPULMONARY RESUSCITATION**)

CREDIBILITY (See **WITNESSES**)

CREDIT
Attorneys' fees in action for denial of credit
  Marital status, action for denial because of   CC §1812.34
  Reasons for denial, action for failure to state   CC §1787.3
Childbearing age affecting extension of   CC §1812.30
Conditional sales (See **CONDITIONAL SALES**)
Consumer protection (See **CONSUMER PROTECTION**)
Cosigner's liability   CC §§1799.90 to 1799.103
Costs in action for denial of credit because of marital status   CC §1812.34
Debt collectors affecting   CC §§1788.20 to 1788.22
Definition   CC §1812.30
Denial   CC §§1787.1 to 1787.3
  Waiver of protections   CC §1787.4
Electronic fund transfers   CC §§1747.02, 1747.03
Fines and penalties for denial of credit because of marital status   CC §1812.33
Grey market goods, buyer's right to credit on return of   CC §1797.85
Injunctions against denial of credit because of marital status   CC §§1812.32, 1812.33
Marital status of applicant, discrimination because of   CC §§1812.30 to 1812.35
Notice of denial   CC §§1787.1 to 1787.3
  Waiver of protections   CC §1787.4
Partition sales on credit   CCP §873.630
Reasons for denial, disclosure of   CC §§1787.1 to 1787.3
  Waiver of protections   CC §1787.4
Retail installment sales (See **RETAIL INSTALLMENT SALES**)
Separate accounts, applications by married persons for   CC §1812.30
Services organizations (See **CREDIT SERVICES ORGANIZATIONS**)
Statute of limitation for denial of credit because of marital status   CC §1812.35
Women, transactions involving   CC §§1812.30 to 1812.35

CREDIT CARDS
Generally   CC §§1747 to 1748.95
Account numbers printed on receipts, restrictions concerning   CC §1747.09
Activation process   CC §1747.05
Address change for offeree or cardholder
  Notice to cardholder of request   CC §1799.1b
  Verification by issuer   CC §1747.06
Annual statement of finance charges at cardholder request   CC §1748.5
Appellate rules, supreme court and courts of appeal
  E-filing in supreme court and courts of appeal
    Fees for filing, methods of payment   CRC 8.76
Billing errors
  Correction of   CC §§1747.50 to 1747.65
  Defined   CC §1747.02
Cancellation notice   CC §1747.85
Charge card
  Definitions   CC §1748.21
  Disclosure requirements   CC §1748.22
Check or draft as means of extending credit to cardholder, disclosures required for   CC §1748.9
Courts
  Acceptance of credit card payments   CRC 10.820
Defenses of cardholder to disputes   CC §1747.90
Definitions   CC §§1747.02, 1748.12
Depositing or processing charges without furnishing or agreeing to furnish goods or services subject of charge, liability for   CC §1748.7

CREDIT CARDS—Cont.
Disability insurance, creditor remedies regarding   CC §1812.405
Disclosure requirements
  Generally   CC §1748.11
  Charge card application   CC §1748.22
  Marketing information, cardholder's right to prohibit release of   CC §1748.12
  Minimum payment warning on billing statements   CC §1748.13
  Retail installment account credit   CC §1810.21
  Secured credit cards   CC §1747.94
  Waiver of protections
    Void   CC §§1748.14, 1748.23
Discounts to cash customers   CC §§1748, 1748.1
Discrimination in issuance
  Generally   CC §1747.80
  Marital status of applicant   CC §1812.30
Electronic filing and service rules
  Fees, payment of   CRC 2.258
Employees of organization, liability for unauthorized use where issuance to   CC §1747.20
False information concerning holders of   CC §1747.70
Fax filing of court papers and documents, payment by credit card authorized for   CCP §1010.5, CRC 2.304
Filing fees
  Credit card payments   CRC 3.100
Finance charges annual statement at cardholder request   CC §1748.5
Fines and penalties for denial of credit because of marital status   CC §1812.33
Full disclosure
  Disclosure requirements generally (See within this heading, **"Disclosure requirements"**)
Identification for negotiable instruments, use of credit card number as   CC §1725
Inactive status, cardholder's account placed on   CC §1747.85
Information personal to cardholder, prohibition against vendor eliciting   CC §1747.08
Inquiry by card holder concerning account   CC §§1747.02, 1747.40
Interest paid, cardholder's right to request annual statement concerning   CC §1748.5
Investigative agencies, credit cards as identification   CC §1786.22
Loss of   CC §1747.20
Marital status of applicant, discrimination because of   CC §1812.30
Membership fee when used in connection with retail installment account   CC §1810.4
Minimum payment warning to consumer on billing statements   CC §1748.13
Notation of credit card as condition of acceptance of negotiable instrument   CC §1725
Notices
  Adequate notice defined   CC §1747.02
  Cancellation of card   CC §1747.85
  Loss of   CC §1747.20
  Marketing information, notice to cardholder of right to prohibit release of   CC §1748.12
  Third person, termination of authorization for use by   CC §1747.02
Racial discrimination in issuance   CC §1747.80
Receipts, printing of account numbers on   CC §1747.09
Recovery in disputes involving credit card transactions   CC §1747.90
Retail installment account credit, disclosure requirements for   CC §1810.21
Secured credit cards   CC §1747.94
Separate accounts, applications by married persons for   CC §1812.30
Song-Beverly credit card act   CC §§1747 to 1748.95
Surcharge on credit card transaction, prohibition against   CC §1748.1
Termination of authorization for use by third person   CC §1747.02(f)
Theft of   CC §1747.20
Third person, authorization by cardholder for use by   CC §1747.02
Trial courts, acceptance of credit cards   CRC 10.820
Truth in Lending Act, relation to   CC §1747.01
Unauthorized person, credit card application using person's name by   CC §1748.95
Unauthorized use
  Defined   CC §1747.02
  Liability of cardholder   CC §§1747.10, 1747.20
Waiver of protections
  Void   CC §1747.04

CREDIT DISABILITY INSURANCE
Generally   CC §1812.400
Applicability of law   CC §1812.404
Constitutionality of law   CC §1812.410
Definitions   CC §§1812.401, 1812.405, 1812.406
Disclosure requirements   CC §1812.402
Interest in debtor's property, effect of law on   CC §1812.409
Key person, special coverage for   CC §1812.406

CREDIT DISABILITY INSURANCE—Cont.
Nonpayment of required sum, effect of   CC §1812.407
Open-end credit plan as creditor's remedy   CC §1812.405
Recertification of temporary disability, remedy available where debtor's failure to submit forms for   CC §1812.403
Rights and obligations of debtor, creditor, and insurer   CC §1812.402
Waiver, effect of   CC §1812.408

CREDITORS
Administrators, priority for appointment as   Pro §8461
Assignment for benefit of creditors (See **ASSIGNMENT FOR BENEFIT OF CREDITORS**)
Banks, deposit of money due in   CC §1500
Challenge of juror for implied bias, relationships giving rise to   CCP §229
Collection agencies, regulations on   CC §§1788 to 1788.32
Cosigned credit contracts, liability for adverse credit reporting on   CC §§1799.101, 1799.102
Creditor's suit (See **ENFORCEMENT OF JUDGMENTS**)
Credit services organizations
    Communication with credit services organizations about accounts   CC §1789.134
Debt settlements
    Fair debt settlement practices   CC §§1788.300 to 1788.307
Decedents' estates, presenting claims against (See **CLAIMS AGAINST ESTATES**)
Defined   CC §§1799.90, 3430
Disability of debtor (See **CREDIT DISABILITY INSURANCE**)
Fair debt buying generally   CC §§1788.50 to 1788.66 (See **FAIR DEBT BUYING PRACTICES**)
Family law proceeding, payment of obligation directly to creditor   Fam §2023
Fraudulent transfers (See **VOIDABLE TRANSACTIONS**)
Gifts made in view of death, recovery for benefit of creditors of   Pro §5705
Homesteads (See **HOMESTEADS**)
Inquiry to creditor concerning debt, time for answering   CC §1720
Judgment creditors (See **ENFORCEMENT OF JUDGMENTS**)
Power of appointment, claims involving (See **POWER OF APPOINTMENT**)
Presumption of money owed from creditor possessing obligation   Ev §635
Savings and loan association, deposit of money due in   CC §1500
Small estates without administration (See **SMALL ESTATES WITHOUT ADMINISTRATION**)
Survival of actions (See **SURVIVAL OF ACTIONS**)
Title, debtor transferring   CC §1502
Trusts (See **TRUSTS**)
Voidable transactions (See **VOIDABLE TRANSACTIONS**)

CREDIT REPORTING
Adverse action defined   CC §1785.3
Arrest information, restrictions on
    Consumer credit reports   CC §1785.13
    Investigative consumer reports   CC §1786.18
Attorneys' fees in action against   CC §1785.31
Bankruptcies
    Consumer credit reports, restrictions on   CC §1785.13
    Investigative consumer reports, restrictions on   CC §1786.18
Blocking of reported transactions allegedly resulting from unauthorized use of consumer's identifying information to obtain goods or services   CC §1785.16
    Resellers of credit information, applicability to   CC §1785.16.3
Certification of purposes by prospective users of credit information, requirement for   CC §1785.14
Child support arrearages (See **CHILD SUPPORT**)
Citation of statutes affecting   CC §1785.2
Class actions   CC §1785.31
Closure requirement   CC §1785.25
Codes explained, requirements for   CC §1785.15
Commercial credit reports
    Availability of report to subject   CC §1785.43
    Consumer Credit Reporting Agencies Act, exclusion from   CC §1785.41
    Definitions   CC §1785.42
    Errors or inaccuracies, correction of   CC §1785.43
    Protecting sources of information   CC §1785.43
    Waiver of protections   CC §1785.44
Consumer privacy rights
    Exemptions from privacy requirements   CC §1798.145
Contracts between creditors and credit reporters   CC §1785.1
Conviction of crime
    Consumer credit report, restrictions on disclosing convictions in   CC §1785.13
    Investigative consumer report, restrictions on disclosing convictions in   CC §1786.18
Correction of records   CC §§1785.16, 1785.30
Cosigned credit contracts, liability for adverse credit reports on   CC §1799.101

CREDIT REPORTING—Cont.
Costs in action against   CC §1785.31
"Credit score" information
    Home loans, required notice to consumer applying for   CC §1785.20.2
    Requests by consumer   CC §§1785.15.1, 1785.15.2
Damages recoverable
    Consumer credit reporting agencies, actions against   CC §1785.31
    Investigative consumer reporting agencies, actions against   CC §1786.50
Debt collector representing himself as agency for   CC §1788.13
Definitions   CC §1785.3
Deletion of information   CC §§1785.16, 1785.30
Delinquent accounts, collection of   CC §1785.25
Denial of credit based on   CC §1785.1
Disclosures required only for consumers with mailing address in state   CC §1785.6
Discouraging or prohibiting consumer access to credit report   CC §1785.10.1
Disputed information
    Consumer credit reports
        Consumer, request for investigation by   CC §§1785.16, 1785.25
        User of credit reporting agency, request for investigation by   CC §1785.21
    Investigative consumer reports   CC §1786.24
Employment information
    Bad credit, claim of   CC §1785.20.5
    Furnishing information   CC §1785.11
    Inspection of files   CC §§1785.10, 1785.15
    Investigative agencies (See **INVESTIGATIVE CONSUMER REPORTING AGENCIES**)
    Notice of agency giving adverse information   CC §1785.20
    Notice of report to person involved   CC §1785.20.5
    Procedures   CC §1785.18
    Prohibited reporting of information on age or race or religion   CC §1785.18
Escrow agent rating service
    Applicability of consumer credit reporting agency provisions to rating service   CC §§1785.28, 1785.28.6
Exemptions from statutes affecting   CC §1785.4
Federal statutes, action under   CC §1785.34
Fees charged consumers
    Consumer credit reporting agencies   CC §1785.17
    Investigative consumer reporting agencies   CC §1786.26
Freezes
    Check services company, exemption of   CC §1785.11.6
    Deposit account information service company, exemption of   CC §1785.11.6
    Effect of freeze on obligations of reporting agency   CC §1785.15
    Fees assessed for placing, removing, etc   CC §1785.11.2
        Identity theft victims, prohibition on fees   CC §1785.15
    Fraud prevention services, exemption   CC §1785.11.6
    Free copy of consumer's credit report   CC §1785.11.3
    Placing alerts and freezes in report   CC §§1785.11.1 to 1785.11.11
    Protected consumer security freezes   CC §§1785.11.9 to 1785.11.11
        Applicability of provisions   CC §1785.11.10
        Definitions   CC §1785.11.9
        Exceptions to provisions   CC §1785.11.10
        Placement, requirements   CC §1785.11.11
        Removal, procedure   CC §1785.11.11
    Reseller of credit information, exemption of   CC §1785.11.4
Governing law   CC §1785.41
Governmental agencies, credit reports furnished to   CC §1785.12
Grounds for furnishing   CC §1785.11
Housing providers
    COVID-19 rental debt
        Negative use in evaluating housing applications prohibited   CC §1785.20.4
Husband and wife, regulating joint accounts for   CC §1812.30
Identification of party requesting information
    Consumer credit reports   CC §§1785.14, 1785.15, 1785.21
    Investigative consumer reports   CC §§1786.20, 1786.22
Identity theft
    Blocking access to fraudulent data   CC §1785.15
    Deletion of inquiries for credit report resulting from identity theft   CC §1785.16.1
    Fees for security freezes for victims prohibited   CC §1785.15
    Prohibition against selling consumer debt of victim of identity theft   CC §1785.16.2
    Security alerts or freezes   CC §§1785.11.1 to 1785.11.11
    Verification of consumer address for identity theft by users of consumer credit report   CC §1785.20.3
    Victims to be provided information as to statutory rights   CC §1785.15.3
Incomplete or inaccurate information   CC §1785.25

CREDIT INDEX

CREDIT REPORTING—Cont.
Indictments
    Consumer credit reports, restrictions on disclosing indictments in   CC §1785.13
    Investigative consumer reports, restrictions on disclosing indictments in CC §1785.13
Injunctions   CC §1785.31
Inspection of files
    Consumer credit reporting agencies   CC §§1785.10, 1785.15
    Discouraging consumer access   CC §1785.10.1
    Investigative consumer reporting agencies   CC §§1786.10, 1786.22
    Prohibiting consumer access   CC §1785.10.1
Insurance
    Furnishing information   CC §1785.11
    Investigative consumer reporting agencies (See **INVESTIGATIVE CONSUMER REPORTING AGENCIES**)
    Notice of adverse information   CC §1785.20
Invasion of privacy
    Consumer credit reporting agency, action against   CC §1785.32
    Investigative consumer reporting agency, action against   CC §1786.52
Investigative consumer reporting agencies (See **INVESTIGATIVE CONSUMER REPORTING AGENCIES**)
Joint credit accounts, requirements for   CC §1812.30
Libel and slander action
    Consumer credit reports   CC §1785.32
    Investigative consumer reports   CC §1786.52
Mailing address in state, notices and disclosures required only for consumers with   CC §1785.6
Mailing requests for copy   CC §1785.15
Married persons maintaining joint accounts, regulation of   CC §1812.30
Medical debts   CC §§1785.20.6, 1785.27
Medical information restrictions   CC §1785.13
Misuse of credit information, penalty for   CC §1785.19
Mobilehome park sales, fees charged for credit report in   CC §798.74
Name and address from listing, procedure for removal of   CC §1785.11
Negative credit information submitted to agency, consumer notified regarding   CC §1785.26
Negligence, action for   CC §§1785.31, 1785.32
New investigations   CC §1785.16
Notice
    Address in state, notices required only for consumers with mailing   CC §1785.6
    Adverse information   CC §1785.20
    Disputed information   CC §1785.16
    Employment information report, notice to person involved in   CC §1785.20.5
    Inspection request   CC §1785.15
    Investigative consumer reporting agencies (See **INVESTIGATIVE CONSUMER REPORTING AGENCIES**)
    Negative credit information submitted to agency, consumer notified regarding   CC §1785.26
    Removal of consumer's name from credit card solicitation list   CC §1785.11.8
Parties entitled to   CC §§1785.11, 1785.12
Personal information protection
    Consumer credit reporting agencies
        Software updates and other measures to address security vulnerability   CC §1798.81.6
Preventing improper use of credit information, procedure for   CC §1785.19.5
Procedural requirements for credit reporting agencies   CC §§1785.14, 1785.18
Prohibition against creditor selling consumer debt involving blocked information or victim of identity theft   CC §1785.16.2
Public officer or employee, prohibition against reporting stricken or released encumbrance against   CC §1785.135
Public policy affecting   CC §1785.1
Punitive damages   CC §1785.31
Purchase money liens on residential property, disclosures on   CC §§2956 to 2968
Recorded documents, disclosure of   CC §1785.35
Reinvestigation   CC §1785.16
Removal of consumer's name from credit card solicitation list   CC §1785.11.8
Removal of information   CC §§1785.16, 1785.30
Rental-purchase contracts, restrictions on reporting of   CC §§1812.640 to 1812.642
Rent applications, use of credit reports in screening of   CC §1950.6
Resale of report   CC §1785.22
Res judicata operation of federal judgment   CC §1785.34
Restrictions on information in report   CC §1785.13
Security alerts
    Generally   CC §1785.11.1
    Check services company, exemption of   CC §1785.11.6

CREDIT REPORTING—Cont.
Security alerts—Cont.
    Deposit account information service company, exemption of   CC §1785.11.6
    Fraud prevention services, exemption   CC §1785.11.6
    Free copy of consumer's credit report   CC §1785.11.3
    Placing alerts and freezes in report   CC §§1785.11.1 to 1785.11.11
    Protected consumer security freezes   CC §§1785.11.9 to 1785.11.11
    Reseller of credit information, exemption of   CC §1785.11.4
Security freezes
    Generally   CC §1785.11.2
    Check services company, exemption of   CC §1785.11.6
    Deposit account information service company, exemption of   CC §1785.11.6
    Effect of freeze on obligations of reporting agency   CC §1785.15
    Fees assessed for placing, removing, etc
        Identity theft victims, prohibition on fees   CC §1785.15
    Fraud prevention services, exemption   CC §1785.11.6
    Free copy of consumer's credit report   CC §1785.11.3
    Placing alerts and freezes in report   CC §§1785.11.1 to 1785.11.11
    Protected consumer security freezes   CC §§1785.11.9 to 1785.11.11
        Applicability of provisions   CC §1785.11.10
        Definitions   CC §1785.11.9
        Exceptions to provisions   CC §1785.11.10
        Placement, requirements   CC §1785.11.11
        Removal, procedure   CC §1785.11.11
    Reseller of credit information, exemption of   CC §1785.11.4
Single persons, prohibiting discrimination against   CC §1812.30
Solicitation and offer of credit in transaction not initiated by consumer, statement regarding prequalifying information required for   CC §1785.20.1
Solicitation list, removal of consumer's name from   CC §1785.11.8
Source of information   CC §§1785.18, 1785.30
Spousal support arrearages, restrictions on information concerning   CC §1785.13
Statutes of limitation
    Consumer credit reporting agencies, actions against   CC §1785.33
    Investigative consumer reporting agencies, actions against   CC §1786.52
Subpoena duces tecum of consumer's records   CCP §§1985.3, 1985.4
Tax liens
    Consumer credit reports, restrictions on disclosing tax liens in   CC §§1785.13, 1785.18
    Investigative consumer reports, restrictions on disclosing tax liens in   CC §1786.18
Telephone requests for copies   CC §1785.15
Transaction not initiated by consumer, use of report in connection with   CC §1785.20.1
Unauthorized use of consumer's identifying information to obtain goods or services, blocking of reported transactions allegedly resulting from   CC §1785.16
United States statutes, action under   CC §1785.34
Unlawful detainer actions
    Consumer credit report, restrictions on inclusion of unlawful detainer actions in   CC §1785.13
    Investigative consumer report, restrictions on inclusion of unlawful detainer actions in   CC §1786.18
Unmarried persons, discrimination against   CC §1812.30
User, identification of   CC §1785.21
Verification of consumer address for identity theft by users of consumer credit report   CC §1785.20.3
Waiver of protections   CC §1785.36
Wrongful acquisition of credit information, penalty for   CC §1785.19

CREDIT SALES
Automobile conditional sale contracts   CC §§2981 to 2984.4
Consumer credit contracts   CC §§1799.90 to 1799.103
Credit cards (See **CREDIT CARDS**)
Retail installment sales (See **RETAIL INSTALLMENT SALES**)

CREDIT SERVICES ORGANIZATIONS
Breach of contract   CC §1789.17
Citation of Act   CC §1789.10
Communication with credit services organizations about accounts   CC §1789.134
Compliance with contract   CC §1789.22
Consumer credit reporting agencies
    Communication with credit services organizations about accounts   CC §1789.134
    Defined   CC §1789.12
Creditors
    Communication with credit services organizations about accounts   CC §1789.134
Damages, action for recovery of   CC §1789.21

CREDIT SERVICES ORGANIZATIONS—Cont.
Debt buyers
    Communication with credit services organizations about accounts   CC §1789.134
Debt collectors
    Communication with credit services organizations about accounts   CC §1789.134
Definitions   CC §1789.12
Deposit in lieu of bond   CC §§1789.24, 1789.26
Fees
    Bond or deposit in lieu of bond, fee for filing   CC §1789.26
    Registration fee   CC §1789.25
General provisions regarding contract requirements   CC §1789.16
Injunctive relief, action for   CC §1789.21
Invalid provisions of Act, effect of   CC §1789.23
Misdemeanor, violation of governing Act as   CC §1789.20
Personal information
    Protection of personal information   CC §1789.135
Prohibited practices of   CC §1789.13
Purpose of law governing   CC §1789.11
Registration of   CC §1789.25
Surety bonds
    Generally   CC §1789.18
    Deposit in lieu of bond   CC §§1789.24, 1789.26
Waiver of rights by consumer   CC §1789.19
Written statement for consumer, requirement   CC §§1789.14, 1789.15

CREDIT UNIONS
Attachment (See **ATTACHMENT**)
Definitions   Pro §§22, 46
Guardians
    Opening or changing name on accounts, responsibilities of guardian   CRC 7.1011
Interest on impound accounts   CC §2954.8
Late payment charges   CC §2954.4
Multiple-party accounts (See **MULTIPLE-PARTY ACCOUNTS**)
Recovery of money or property deposited, limitation of actions for   CCP §348

CREEKS (See **RIVERS AND STREAMS**)

CRIMES AGAINST HUMANITY
Attorney's fees
    Assault and battery, wrongful death, etc constituting torture, genocide, crimes against humanity, etc   CCP §354.8
Statutes of limitations
    Assault and battery, wrongful death, etc constituting torture, genocide, crimes against humanity, etc   CCP §354.8

CRIME VICTIM'S REPARATION (See **RESTITUTION**)

CRIMINAL ACTIONS AND PROCEEDINGS   CCP §31
Age of accused person, hearing to determine   CRC 4.116
Aircraft lien, fraudulent possession to cause loss of   CCP §1208.69
Appeals
    Infraction case appeals in appellate division   CRC 8.900 to 8.929 (See **APPELLATE RULES, SUPERIOR COURT APPEALS**)
    Misdemeanor appeals in appellate division   CRC 8.850 to 8.874 (See **APPELLATE RULES, SUPERIOR COURT APPEALS**)
    Rules for supreme court and courts of appeal proceedings   CRC 8.300 to 8.398 (See **APPELLATE RULES, SUPREME COURT AND COURTS OF APPEAL**)
    Supreme court and courts of appeal
        Criminal appeals   CRC 8.300 to 8.388 (See **APPELLATE RULES, SUPREME COURT AND COURTS OF APPEAL**)
Appearances
    Personal appearance waivers
        COVID-19, emergency rule   CRCAppx I Emer Rule 5
    Remote appearances, technology use
        COVID-19, emergency rule   CRCAppx I Emer Rule 3
Attorney professional conduct
    Confidential information, revealing
        Prevention of criminal act   ProfC 1.6
    Contingent fees
        Circumstances where contingent fee agreement impermissible   ProfC 1.5
    Professional misconduct, conduct constituting
        Criminal acts affecting honesty, trustworthiness or fitness as attorney   ProfC 8.4
    Proof of every element of case
        Defense may require   ProfC 3.1
    Prosecutor's responsibilities   ProfC 3.8

CRIMINAL ACTIONS AND PROCEEDINGS—Cont.
Attorney professional conduct—Cont.
    Threatening criminal, administrative or disciplinary charges   ProfC 3.10
Attorney referral service-client privilege
    Use of service to perpetrate fraud or crime   Ev §968
Attorneys
    Capital cases
        Appointments, qualification of trial counsel   CRC 4.117
Attorneys participating in crime or fraud
    Discovery of attorney work product
        Not protected   CCP §2018.050
Case management, trial courts   CRC 10.950 to 10.953
    Judicial council legal forms   CRCAppx A
Character and reputation evidence (See **CHARACTER AND REPUTATION**)
Child care providers trustline registry providing criminal history checks on child care providers   CC §1812.5093
Child removed from state without consent or court order   Fam §§233, 2030
Civil resolution in lieu of filing criminal complaint, prosecuting attorney assisting in   CCP §33
Confidential marriages, violation by notaries to authorize   Fam §530
Contracts
    Waiver of right to testify concerning criminal conduct or sexual harassment   CC §1670.11
Conviction (See **CONVICTION OF CRIME**)
Criminal case assignments   CRC 4.115
Criminal master calendar   CRC 4.115
Criminal rules   CRC 4.1 to 4.601
    Pretrial proceedings   CRC 4.100 to 4.117
Damages (See **DAMAGES**)
Dance studio contracts, violation of provisions regulating   CC §1812.63
Discount buying services contracts   CC §1812.125
Domestic violence orders, violation   Fam §6388
    Firearm ownership or possession by person subject to protective order, prohibition on
        Determining violation   Fam §6322.5
    Gun ownership or possession by person subject to protective order, prohibition on   Fam §6389
Electronic court records
    Remote electronic access in individual criminal cases   CRC 2.503
Employment agencies, violations by   CC §1812.523
Employment counseling services, violations by   CC §1812.523
Examination for purposes of enforcement of judgments, willfully making improper service of order for   CCP §708.170
Expert testimony, payment of costs for   Ev §§731, 733
Family law proceedings
    Paternity proceedings
        Genetic tests to determine paternity, application to criminal actions   Fam §7556
Forms
    Judicial council legal forms   CRCAppx A
Gang-related crimes, decedent's sworn statement concerning (See **GANG VIOLENCE**)
Genetic characteristics, disclosure of test results for   CC §56.17
Grain storage after bulk sale, violation of requirements for notice of   CC §1881.1
Guilty plea (See **GUILTY PLEA**)
Harassment, injunction or order prohibiting
    Address or location of complaining party or family, prohibition on enjoined party from obtaining   CCP §527.10
    California law enforcement telecommunications (CLETS) information form, confidentiality and use of information   CRC 1.51, CRCAppx A
    Firearm purchases or possession while order in effect   CCP §§527.6, 527.9
Hearsay rules (See **HEARSAY**)
Home equity sales contracts   CC §1695.8
Husband and wife, privileged communications of (See **MARITAL PRIVILEGE**)
Identification documents
    Radio frequency identification (RFID) to remotely read identification document without knowledge or consent   CC §1798.79
Immigration status
    Disclosure of immigration status in open court, criminal cases   Ev §351.4
Inspection warrant, refusal to comply with   CCP §1822.57
Interpreters for criminal proceedings, appointment of noncertified   CRC 2.894
Job listing services, violations by   CC §1812.523
Judges
    Education of judges
        Domestic violence issues   CRC 10.464
Judicial administration standards for criminal cases   CRC JudAdminStand 4.10 to CRC JudAdminStand 4.42
Judicial holiday, proceedings on   CCP §134
Judicial notice of federal rules   Ev §451
Jury (See **JURY**)
Manslaughter (See **MANSLAUGHTER**)
Marriage, criminal penalties involving (See **MARRIAGE**)

CRIMINAL ACTIONS AND PROCEEDINGS—Cont.
Marriages (confidential), violation by notaries to authorize   Fam §530
Medical records, criminal liability for wrongful disclosure of   CC §§56.36, 1798.57
Merger of civil and criminal actions prohibited   CCP §32
Mortgages (See **TRUST DEEDS AND MORTGAGES**)
Nolo contendere plea (See **NOLO CONTENDERE PLEAS**)
Photographs of dead bodies, use in criminal proceedings of   CCP §129
Polygraph evidence, exclusion of   Ev §351.1
Preference in civil action where damages caused during commission of felony offense   CCP §37
Probation officers and deputies (See **PROBATION OFFICERS AND DEPUTIES**)
Public entity or employee, claim against (See **CLAIMS AGAINST PUBLIC ENTITIES AND EMPLOYEES**)
Readiness conferences   CRC 4.112
Real property sales contract provisions, violation of   CC §§2985.2, 2985.3
Remote appearances, technology use
    COVID-19, emergency rule   CRCAppx I Emer Rule 3
Remote hearings
    Waiver of personal appearance
        COVID-19, emergency rule   CRCAppx I Emer Rule 5
Reports on crime, immunity for persons or organizations making   CC §48.9
Retail installment sales provisions, violation of   CC §1812.6
Retired judge not qualified to try criminal case, stipulation that   CCP §170.65
Right to counsel (See **ATTORNEYS**)
Rules
    Factual innocence form   CRC 4.601
    Generally   CRC 4.1 to 4.601 (See **CRIMINAL RULES**)
    Postconviction   CRC 4.510 to 4.552
    Pretrial proceedings   CRC 4.100 to 4.155
    Sentencing   CRC 4.305 to 4.480
    Trials   CRC 4.200 to 4.230
Self-incrimination (See **SELF-INCRIMINATION**)
Settlements
    Waiver of right to testify concerning criminal conduct or sexual harassment   CC §1670.11
Statute of limitation for damages against person based on commission of felony offense   CCP §340.3
Subordinate judicial officers
    Education of judges and subordinate judicial officers
        Domestic violence issues   CRC 10.464
Superior courts (See **SUPERIOR COURTS**)
Traffic regulations and violations (See **TRAFFIC REGULATIONS AND VIOLATIONS**)
Transitional housing program misconduct
    Injunctions or temporary restraining orders
        Willful disobedience as misdemeanor   CC §1954.14
Trial court case management   CRC 10.950 to 10.953
    Judicial council legal forms   CRCAppx A
Trust deeds (See **TRUST DEEDS AND MORTGAGES**)
Usury
    Criminal penalties   CC §1916.12-3
    Loan sharking liability   CC §1916.12-3
Video recordings of dead bodies, use in criminal proceedings of   CCP §129
Withheld earnings, failure of employer to pay over   CCP §706.152
Workplace violence or threats of violence, injunctions or orders against
    Address or location of complaining party or family, prohibition on enjoined party from obtaining   CCP §527.10
    Firearm possession or purchase by person subject to   CCP §§527.8, 527.9

CRIMINAL APPEALS
Infraction case appeals in appellate division   CRC 8.900 to 8.929 (See **APPELLATE RULES, SUPERIOR COURT APPEALS**)
Misdemeanor appeals in appellate division   CRC 8.850 to 8.874 (See **APPELLATE RULES, SUPERIOR COURT APPEALS**)
Supreme court and courts of appeal, appellate rules governing   CRC 8.300 to 8.398 (See **APPELLATE RULES, SUPREME COURT AND COURTS OF APPEAL**)

CRIMINAL CONVERSATION
Action for   CC §43.5
Employees   CC §49

CRIMINAL HISTORY INFORMATION RECORDS
Adoption
    Fingerprints and criminal records generally (See **ADOPTION**)
Attorneys at law
    Fingerprinting
        Active licensed attorneys   CRC 9.9.5
        Foreign countries, active attorneys residing in   CRC 9.9.5

CRIMINAL HISTORY INFORMATION RECORDS—Cont.
Attorneys at law—Cont.
    Fingerprinting—Cont.
        Inactive status prior to becoming active status   CRC 9.9.5
        Special admissions attorneys   CRC 9.9.5
Child custody
    Supervised visitation and exchange programs
        Providers, standards   Fam §3200.5
Clearing records
    Proof of service
        Forms, judicial council   CRCAppx A
Electronic recording delivery systems
    Computer security auditors
        Eligibility to serve as   Gov §27395
Juvenile records   CRC 5.552
Microphotographed files, records, photographs, etc., in custody of criminal justice agency
    Reproductions, admissibility   Ev §1550.1
Public guardians   Pro §2920.5

CRIMINAL RULES   CRC 4.1 to 4.601
Age of defendant
    Certification to juvenile court   CRC 4.116
Appeals
    Right to appeal, notification   CRC 4.305, 4.306
Appearances
    Notice to appear forms   CRC 4.103
    Traffic infraction cases
        Appearance without deposit of bail   CRC 4.105
        Bail, when deposit required   CRC 4.105
Applicability of provisions   CRC 4.2
Arraignment   CRC 4.100
    Case management   CRC 10.951
    Time for arraignment   CRC 4.110
Assignments of criminal cases   CRC 4.115
Bail
    Amount
        Jury trial or lack of jury trial not to affect   CRC 4.101
    Traffic infraction cases
        Appearance without deposit of bail   CRC 4.105
        Deposit of bail, when required   CRC 4.105
    Uniform bail and penalty schedules   CRC 4.102
Change of venue   CRC 4.150 to 4.155
    Appeals following change   CRC 4.150
    Applicable rules   CRC 4.150
    Costs
        Reimbursement guidelines   CRC 4.155
    Motion for change   CRC 4.151
    Order upon change   CRC 4.153
    Receiving court, proceedings in   CRC 4.154
    Reimbursement of costs in change of venue, guidelines   CRC 4.155
    Rules for transfers   CRC 4.150 to 4.155
    Selection of court and trial judge   CRC 4.152
    Transferring courts, proceedings in   CRC 4.150
Competence to stand trial
    Probable cause that defendant committed crime, determination
        Procedure   CRC 4.131
Conferences
    Pre-voir dire conference   CRC 4.200
    Readiness conference   CRC 4.112
Continuances   CRC 4.113, 4.115
Death penalty
    Attorneys
        Appointed trial counsel, qualifications   CRC 4.117
    Date of execution
        Setting   CRC 4.315
    Habeas corpus
        Death penalty-related proceedings in superior court   CRC 4.560 to 4.577
    Pretrial proceedings   CRC 4.119
    Trials, additional requirements   CRC 4.230
Demurrers
    Time for plea or notice of intent to demur   CRC 4.110
Determinate sentencing   CRC 4.401 to 4.480
    Aggravation
        Circumstances in aggravation   CRC 4.421
        Hate crimes   CRC 4.427
        Statements in aggravation and mitigation   CRC 4.437
    Applicability of rules   CRC 4.403
    Base term of imprisonment   CRC 4.420

CRIMINAL RULES—Cont.
  Determinate sentencing —Cont.
    Concurrent or consecutive sentences
      Factors affecting determination   CRC 4.425
      Foreign jurisdiction, sentence consecutive to or concurrent with term in   CRC 4.451
      Indeterminate term, sentence consecutive to or concurrent with   CRC 4.451
      Multiple punishment, applicability of prohibition against multiple punishments   CRC 4.424
      Prior determinate sentence, determinate sentence consecutive to   CRC 4.452
    Definitions   CRC 4.405
    Double jeopardy
      Agreement to punishment as abandonment of claim   CRC 4.412
      Concurrent or consecutive sentences, applicability of prohibition against multiple punishments   CRC 4.424
    Enhancements
      Factors affecting imposition   CRC 4.428
      Hate crimes   CRC 4.427
      Stay of execution on excessive or prohibited portion of sentence resulting from enhancement   CRC 4.447
    Factors listed in rules
      Not exhaustive   CRC 4.408
      Relevant factors, mandatory consideration   CRC 4.409
    Hate crimes   CRC 4.427
    Hearing
      Matters considered at time set for sentencing   CRC 4.433
    Lesser included offenses
      Agreement to punishment as abandonment of claim   CRC 4.412
    Mandatory supervision
      Criteria affecting imposition   CRC 4.415
      Revocation, sentencing upon   CRC 4.435
    Mitigation
      Circumstances in mitigation   CRC 4.423
      Statements in aggravation and mitigation   CRC 4.437
    Objectives in sentencing   CRC 4.410
    Post-release community supervision
      Revocation, sentencing upon   CRC 4.435
    Presentence custody time credit   CRC 4.472
    Presentence investigations and reports   CRC 4.411
      Probation officer's report   CRC 4.411.5
    Probation
      Criteria affecting   CRC 4.414
      Presumptively ineligible defendant, granting probation   CRC 4.413, CRC JudAdminStand 4.35
      Revocation, sentencing upon   CRC 4.435
    Reasons for sentence choice   CRC 4.406
    Repeat offenders
      Violent sex crimes   CRC 4.426
    Reporting of sentencing proceedings   CRC 4.431
    Risk/needs assessment
      Court use in sentencing   CRC JudAdminStand 4.35
    Sex crimes
      Violent sex crimes   CRC 4.426
    Statement of views of judge and district attorney   CRC 4.480
    Statutory authority for rules   CRC 4.401
    Supervision
      Mandatory supervision, criteria affecting imposition   CRC 4.415
  Factual innocence
    Judicial finding of factual innocence form
      Confidentiality   CRC 4.601
  Firearms and other weapons
    Protective orders
      Firearm relinquishment procedures   CRC 4.700
      Forms for firearms relinquishment   CRCAppx A
  Habeas corpus   CRC 4.545 to 4.577
    Applicability of provisions   CRC 4.550
    Appointed counsel, qualifications in noncapital cases   CRC 4.553
    Court in which petition heard   CRC 4.552
    Death penalty-related proceedings in superior court   CRC 4.560 to 4.577
      Appealability, certificate   CRC 4.576
      Applicability of provisions   CRC 4.560
      Attorneys, appointment   CRC 4.561, 4.562
      Briefing following order to show cause   CRC 4.574
      Deadline extensions following order to show cause   CRC 4.574
      Denial following order to show cause   CRC 4.574
      Evidentiary hearing following order to show cause   CRC 4.574
      Filing petition   CRC 4.571
      Informal response and reply to petition   CRC 4.573
      Proceedings after filing of petition   CRC 4.573

CRIMINAL RULES—Cont.
  Habeas corpus —Cont.
    Death penalty-related proceedings in superior court —Cont.
      Proceedings after order to show cause   CRC 4.574
      Return after order to show cause   CRC 4.574
      Ruling on petition   CRC 4.571, 4.574
      Service of petition   CRC 4.571
      Show cause, order   CRC 4.573, 4.574
      Statement of decision on petition   CRC 4.575
      Submission of cause for purposes of compensation of judges, determination   CRC 4.574
      Successive petitions   CRC 4.576
      Transfer of attorney files to appellate counsel for appeals taken   CRC 4.577
      Transfer of petition   CRC 4.572
    Definitions   CRC 4.545
    Denial   CRC 4.551
    Evidentiary hearing   CRC 4.551
    Jurisdiction   CRC 4.552
    Petitions   CRC 4.551
    Responses   CRC 4.551
    Return   CRC 4.551
    Show cause, order to   CRC 4.551
    Single judge deciding petition   CRC 4.552
    Time, extending or shortening   CRC 4.551
    Transfer of petition   CRC 4.552
  Hate crimes
    Aggravating circumstances   CRC 4.427
      Sentencing considerations   CRC 4.421
    Determinate sentencing generally   CRC 4.427
    Misdemeanor hate crimes
      Sentencing considerations   CRC 4.330
  Ignition interlock installation orders
    Interest of justice exception, statement of reason for finding   CRC 4.325
  Indictments or informations
    Time for information   CRC 4.110
  Infractions
    Ability-to-pay determinations   CRC 4.335
      Confidential can't afford to pay fine forms   CRC 4.336, CRCAppx A
    Installment payment agreements   CRC 4.108
    Notice to appear
      Ability-to-pay determinations   CRC 4.335
      Confidential can't afford to pay fine form used with ability-to-pay determination   CRC 4.336, CRCAppx A
      Failure to appear or failure to pay for notice to appear   CRC 4.106
      Mandatory reminder notices   CRC 4.107
  Jury
    Voir dire   CRC 4.201
      Opening statement by counsel to panel   CRC 4.202
      Pre-voir dire conference   CRC 4.200
  Juvenile matters
    Certification to juvenile court   CRC 4.116
    Reverse remand of juvenile convicted as adult   CRC 4.510
  Memoranda in support of motions
    Pretrial motions   CRC 4.111
  Mental competency proceedings   CRC 4.130
  Mental health case protocols   CRC 10.951
  Motions
    Pretrial motions   CRC 4.111
      Case management   CRC 10.951
  Pleas
    Guilty pleas
      Certification for sentence and reference to probation officer   CRC 4.114
    No contest pleas
      Certification for sentence and reference to probation officer   CRC 4.114
    Time for plea or notice of intent to demur   CRC 4.110
  Postrelease community supervision
    Revocation procedure
      Sentencing upon revocation   CRC 4.435
      Supervising agency reports as to compliance with provisions   CRC 4.541
  Presentence custody time credit   CRC 4.310
    Determinate sentencing   CRC 4.472
  Pretrial diversion
    Traffic violator school   CRC 4.104
  Pretrial proceedings   CRC 4.100 to 4.117
    Case management   CRC 10.951

CRIMINAL RULES—Cont.
Probable cause
    Competence to stand trial
        Determination of probable cause of commission of crime, procedure CRC 4.131

Probation
    Criteria affecting   CRC 4.414
    Out-of-county transfers   CRC 4.530
    Presumptively ineligible defendant, granting probation   CRC 4.413
        Risk/needs assessment, court use in sentencing   CRC JudAdminStand 4.35
    Revocation, sentencing upon   CRC 4.435
    Suitability for probation
        Aggravating and mitigating factors, consideration   CRC 4.414

Protective orders
    Firearm relinquishment procedures   CRC 4.700
        Judicial council legal forms   CRCAppx A

Readiness conference   CRC 4.112
    Case management   CRC 10.951
        Telephone appearance at case management conferences   CRC 3.670

Sentencing   CRC 4.300 to 4.336
    Determinate sentencing   CRC 4.401 to 4.480

Statutory references in rules   CRC 4.3
Title of rules   CRC 4.1

Traffic court
    Written declaration, trial by   CRC 4.210

Traffic infraction proceedings
    Bail
        Appearance in traffic infraction cases, deposit of bail   CRC 4.105

Traffic violator school
    Pretrial diversion   CRC 4.104

Trial   CRC 4.200 to 4.230 (See **CRIMINAL TRIALS**)
Voir dire   CRC 4.201
    Opening statement by counsel to panel   CRC 4.202
    Pre-voir dire conference   CRC 4.200

CRIMINAL TRIALS   CRC 4.200 to 4.230
Case management   CRC 10.950 to 10.953
    Arraignments   CRC 10.951
    Judicial administration standards for criminal cases   CRC JudAdminStand 4.10 to CRC JudAdminStand 4.42
    Judicial council legal forms   CRCAppx A
    Meetings concerning criminal court system, designating judges to attend   CRC 10.952
    Mental health case protocols   CRC 10.951
    Preliminary hearings
        Disposition of cases prior to preliminary hearing, procedures   CRC 10.953
    Pretrial motions   CRC 10.951
    Readiness conferences   CRC 10.951
        Telephone appearance at case management conferences   CRC 3.670
    Supervising judge
        Duties   CRC 10.951
    Telephone appearance at case management conferences   CRC 3.670
    Three or more judges in court, organization   CRC 10.950

Criminal rules governing trials   CRC 4.200 to 4.230
Death penalty
    Additional requirements for trial in capital cases   CRC 4.230

Electronic filing and service of documents   CRC 2.251, 2.252
    Electronic summons, issuance   CRC 2.259
    Fees not chargeable in some criminal actions   CRC 2.255
    Permissive electronic filing by local rule   CRC 2.253

Evidence
    Creative expressions
        Admissibility   Ev §352.2
    Probative value *vs.* prejudicial effect
        Creative expressions, admissibility   Ev §352.2

Judicial administration standards for criminal cases   CRC JudAdminStand 4.10 to CRC JudAdminStand 4.42
Management rules for trial courts   CRC 10.950 to 10.953
Pretrial motions, time for making and disposition   CRC 4.111
Rules of court
    Criminal rules governing trials   CRC 4.200 to 4.230
Setting case for trial, time for   CRC 4.110

CROPS (See **FARMS AND FARMERS**)

CROSS APPEAL
Appellate rules, superior court appeals
    Environmental quality act
        Appellate review of CEQA cases   CRC 8.702

CROSS APPEAL—Cont.
Appellate rules, superior court appeals—Cont.
    Infraction case appeals
        Notice of appeal   CRC 8.902
    Limited civil cases in appellate division
        Extending time to appeal   CRC 8.823
        Notice of cross appeal   CRC 8.806
    Misdemeanor appeals
        Notice of appeal   CRC 8.853

Appellate rules, supreme court and courts of appeal (See **APPELLATE RULES, SUPREME COURT AND COURTS OF APPEAL**)

CROSS-CLAIMS (See **SMALL CLAIMS COURTS**)

CROSS-COMPLAINTS
Amendment
    Service   CCP §471.5, CRC 3.222
Attorney, service on   CCP §428.60
Coerced debt
    Establishing debt as coerced, action or cross-complaint   CC §1798.97.3
Compulsory cross-complaint
    Generally   CCP §426.30
    Declaratory relief, applicability in proceedings for   CCP §426.60
    Eminent domain proceedings, applicability in   CCP §426.70
    Exceptions to compulsory joinder requirement   CCP §426.40
    Jurisdictional requirements   CCP §§426.30, 426.40
    Leave of court required to file cross-complaint to assert unpleaded cause   CCP §426.50
    Small claims action, applicability in   CCP §426.60
    Special proceedings, applicability in   CCP §426.60
    Time for filing
        Generally   CCP §426.30
        Unpleaded cause, cross-complaint to assert   CCP §426.50
Compulsory joinder, cross-complaint stating names of persons subject to   CCP §389
Contents of   CCP §425.10
Counterclaims, substitution of cross-complaint pleadings for   CCP §428.80
Default judgments from failure to respond to   CCP §585
Defined   CCP §426.10
Demur, time to   CCP §432.10
Dismissal prohibited   CCP §581
Economic litigation provisions for limited civil cases   CCP §92
Eminent domain proceedings   CCP §426.70
Exceeding demand of opposing party, judgment for party asserting claim   CCP §666
Failure to allege related cause of action, effect of   CCP §426.30
Filing fee   Gov §26826.01
Grounds for objection to   CCP §430.10
Improvements made in good faith by third party   CCP §871.3
Interpleader   CCP §386
Joinder of actions
    Compulsory joinder, exceptions to   CCP §426.40
    Permissive joinder   CCP §427.10
Joinder of parties
    Compulsory joinder   CCP §389
    Permissive joinder   CCP §428.20
Judgment on the pleadings, motion for   CCP §438
    Meet and confer prior to moving for judgment on the pleadings   CCP §439
Judicial arbitration   CRC 3.812
Judicial Council to develop and approve official forms   CCP §425.12
Objections to allegations in   CCP §§430.10, 430.30
Papers to be served on cross-defendants   CRC 3.222
Permissible pleadings   CCP §422.10
Permissive cross-complaint
    Generally   CCP §428.10
    Joinder of action   CCP §§427.10, 428.30
    Joinder of parties
        Compulsory joinder   CCP §389
        Permissive joinder   CCP §428.20
    Separate document, requirement of cross-complaint as   CCP §428.40
    Service generally (See within this heading, **"Service"**)
    Third party pleadings   CCP §428.70
    Time for filing   CCP §428.50
Process, service of (See within this heading, **"Service"**)
Quieting title action   CCP §761.040
Related cause of action alleged by   CCP §426.30
Response, time for filing   CCP §432.10
Service
    Generally   CCP §428.60
    Amended complaints   CCP §471.5
    Papers to be served on cross-defendants   CRC 3.222

CROSS-COMPLAINTS—Cont.
Service—Cont.
Time for service   CRC 3.110
Small claims courts
Filing cross-complaints   CRC 3.2104
Strike, motion to (See **MOTION TO STRIKE**)
Third party pleadings   CCP §428.70
Time
Compulsory cross-complaints   CCP §426.30
Unpleaded cause, assertion in cross-complaint   CCP §426.50
Permissive cross-complaint, time for filing   CCP §428.50
Response, time for   CCP §432.10
Unpleaded cause, permission to assert   CCP §426.50

CROSS-EXAMINATION
Generally   Ev §773
Administrative adjudication proceedings (See **ADMINISTRATIVE ADJUDICATION**)
Adverse party called as witness   Ev §776
Court control over interrogation of witness   Ev §765
Custody of children, restrictions on waiver of right to cross examine court-appointed investigator in proceedings to establish   Fam §§3115, 3117
Definition   Ev §761
Depositions
Cross-examination of deponent   CCP §2025.330
Expert witnesses   Ev §§721, 732
Hearsay declarant, examination of   Ev §1203
Inconsistent statements by witnesses (See **WITNESSES**)
Leading questions   Ev §767
Recross examination
Defined   Ev §763
Leading questions   Ev §767
Refreshing memory, witness' use of writings for   Ev §771
Responsive answers by witnesses   Ev §766

CROSS-SECTIONAL REPRESENTATION
Jury selection   CCP §§197, 205

CRUELTY
Animals (See **ANIMALS**)
Children (See **CHILD ABUSE**)

CULLEN EARTHQUAKE ACT   CCP §§751.50 to 751.65

CULTIVATION OF LAND
Adverse possession (See **ADVERSE POSSESSION**)

CUM TESTAMENTO ANNEXO (See **ADMINISTRATORS WITH WILL ANNEXED**)

CUMULATIVE REMEDIES
Consumer protection   CC §1752
Information Practices Act   CC §§1798.49, 1798.53
Layaway plans   CC §1749.2

CURRENCY (See **MONEY**)

CURTESY
Abolished   Pro §6412

CUSTODIAL OFFICERS
Civil rights, actions to enforce against peace officer or custodial officer
Immunity
Inapplicability of state immunity provisions   CC §52.1
Personnel records, disclosure   Ev §1043
Inclusions and exclusions from disclosure   Ev §1045
Officer not present for alleged conduct   Ev §1047

CUSTODY AND CONTROL
Borrowed property   CC §1891
Child custody (See **CUSTODY OF CHILDREN**)
Enforcement of judgments (See **ENFORCEMENT OF JUDGMENTS**)
Guardian (See **GUARDIAN AND WARD**)
Habeas corpus (See **HABEAS CORPUS**)
Uniform Transfers to Minors Act (See **UNIFORM TRANSFERS TO MINORS ACT**)

CUSTODY OF CHILDREN
Generally   Fam §3010
Abduction of child
Concealment generally (See within this heading, "**Concealment of child**")
Missing party or child generally (See within this heading, "**Missing party or child**")

CUSTODY OF CHILDREN—Cont.
Absence or relocation of parent from family residence as consideration for court in awarding custody or visitation   Fam §3046
Military deployment   Fam §3047
Adoption (See **ADOPTION**)
Agreement of parties
Generally   Fam §3061
Joint custody presumed   Fam §3080
Alcohol abuse
Substance abuse generally (See within this heading, "**Substance abuse**")
Annulment decrees   Fam §2253
Appearance by minor without guardian ad litem   CCP §372
Application attachment   CRCAppx A (CRCFL-311)
Application of child custody provisions   Fam §§3021, 3403 to 3405
Attorneys
Court-appointed counsel for minor   CRC 5.240 to 5.242, Fam §§3114, 3150 to 3153, 3184
Ability of party to pay   CRC 5.241
Compensation   CRC 5.241
Complaints   CRC 5.240
Continuing education   CRC 5.242
Education and training   CRC 5.242
Experience requirements   CRC 5.242
Factors considered by court   CRC 5.240
Inability of party to pay   CRC 5.241
Orders appointing   CRC 5.240
Panel of eligible counsel   CRC 5.240
Qualifications of appointed counsel   CRC 5.242
Request for appointment   CRC 5.240
Responsibilities of counsel   CRC 5.242
Rights of counsel on behalf of child   CRC 5.242
Termination of appointment   CRC 5.240
Mediation proceedings, exclusion of counsel from   Fam §3182
Withdrawal of attorney in domestic relations matters   CCP §285.1
Attorney's fees   Fam §3153
Access to legal representation by requiring party to provide for other party's attorney fees   Fam §7605
Financial need basis for fees   CRC 5.427
Exclusive custody, action for
Financial need basis for fees   CRC 5.427
Ordering party to provide for legal representation of other party   Fam §3121
Best interest of child
Generally   Fam §§3011, 3020
Appointed counsel to represent   CRC 5.242, Fam §3151
Children's participation and testimony in family court proceedings
Determining child's best interest   CRC 5.250
Counseling requirement   Fam §3190
Joint custody, presumption for   Fam §3080
Mediation, standards for   Fam §§3162, 3180
Supervised visitation services, consideration in provision of   CRC JudAdminStand 5.20, Fam §3200
Bifurcated proceedings
Appeals   CCP §904.1
Child abuse or neglect
Allegations of child abuse made during custody proceedings, effect of   Fam §3027
Court-appointed evaluator to investigate allegations of child sexual abuse made during custody proceedings   Fam §3118
Orders regarding evaluations   CRCAppx A
Reports   CRCAppx A
False accusations, effect of   Fam §§3022.5, 3027.1, 3027.5
Sexual abuse report, effect of false   Fam §3027.5
Sexual offenses, denial of custody or visitation on ground of   Fam §3030
Supervised visitation and exchange programs   CRC JudAdminStand 5.20, Fam §3200
Child protective services agencies, release of reports of   Fam §3152
Child's wishes   Fam §3042
Children's participation and testimony in family court proceedings   CRC 5.250
Compensation
Failure to assume caretaker responsibility   Fam §3028
Thwarting other parent's visitation or custody rights   Fam §3028
Concealment of child
Generally   Fam §3062
Action to locate   Fam §§3130 to 3135, 3455, 3456
Hague Convention on Civil Aspects of International Child Abduction, order for return of child under   Fam §§3441, 3442, 3455
Missing parties (See within this heading, "**Missing party or child**")
Parent Locator Service and Central Registry   Fam §17506
Conciliation courts   Fam §§1841, 3089

CUSTODY OF CHILDREN—Cont.

Confidentiality
    Custodial parent's place of residence and employment   Fam §3030
    Psychological evaluation of child involved in custody or visitation proceedings   Fam §3025.5

Continuing education requirements for supervisors of investigators and evaluators   Fam §3165

Conviction of child abuse or molestation   Fam §3044

Costs and expenses
    Expenses generally (See within this heading, "Expenses")

Counseling
    Children's participation and testimony in family court proceedings
        Responsibilities of court-connected or appointed professionals   CRC 5.250
    Group counseling programs   Fam §§3200 to 3204
    Requirement   Fam §§3190 to 3193

Court-appointed counsel for minor   CRC 5.240 to 5.242, Fam §§3114, 3150 to 3153, 3184

Court-appointed investigators
    Investigations generally (See within this heading, "Investigations")

Court-appointed mediators or evaluators
    Ex parte communications   CRC 5.235
    Interns used in evaluation   CRC 5.225

Court commissioner's powers to hear and report findings and conclusions in preliminary matters including petitions for   CCP §259

Court-connected mediators or evaluators
    Declaration of evaluator concerning qualifications   CRCAppx A (CRCFL-325)
    Ex parte communications   CRC 5.235
    Interns used in evaluation   CRC 5.225
    Order appointing evaluator   CRCAppx A (CRCFL-327)
    Qualifications for evaluators   CRC 5.225

Court-ordered counseling   Fam §§3190 to 3193

Court-ordered evaluations
    Confidential written report   CRC 5.220
    Findings
        Presentation   CRC 5.220
    Qualifications of evaluators   CRC 5.220
    Service of evaluation report   CRC 5.220
    Standards of practice   CRC 5.220

Court reporter taking down and transcribing at cost of county   CCP §274a

Cross-examination of court-appointed investigator   Fam §§3115, 3117

Deferred sale of family home, request of custodial parent for   Fam §§3800 to 3810

Definitions   Fam §§3000 to 3007

Delay in prosecution   CCP §583.161

Dental records, access to   Fam §3025

Dependent children
    Out-of-county placements   CRC 5.614
        Judicial council legal forms   CRCAppx A
    Placement of
        Community treatment facility placements, hearings, review, etc   CRC 5.618
        Out-of-county placements   CRC 5.614, CRCAppx A
        Short-term residential therapeutic program placements, hearings, review, etc   CRC 5.618
    Protective custody   CRC 5.526
    Termination of jurisdiction
        Orders as to custody and visitation   CRC 5.700

Deportation
    Electronic testimony or participation allowed in deportation cases   Fam §3012

Detention
    Electronic testimony or participation allowed in detention cases   Fam §3012

Disabled parents
    Codification of decision in In re Marriage of Carney   Fam §3049

Dismissal of petition for delay in prosecution, effect   CCP §583.161

District attorney to locate missing party or child   Fam §§3130 to 3135, 3455, 3457

Domestic violence
    Generally (See **DOMESTIC VIOLENCE**)
    Custody investigations (See within this heading, "Investigations")
    Family court services, protocol   CRC 5.215
    Mediation proceedings   Fam §§3170, 3181, 3182
    Modification of orders
        Domestic violence prevention act proceedings   CRC 5.381
    Presumption that custody award to perpetrator of domestic violence is not in child's best interest   Fam §3044

Drug abuse
    Substance abuse generally (See within this heading, "Substance abuse")

CUSTODY OF CHILDREN—Cont.

Earnings of child   Fam §§3010, 7500, 7503, 7504

Education programs for parents and children   Fam §§3200 to 3204

Evaluations
    Investigations generally (See within this heading, "Investigations")

Evaluators and investigators
    Children's participation and testimony in family court proceedings
        Responsibilities of court-connected or appointed professionals   CRC 5.250
    Declaration of private evaluator regarding qualifications   CRCAppx A (CRCFL-326)
    Domestic violence training protocol   CRC 5.215
    Interns used in evaluation   CRC 5.225
    Judicial council forms   CRCAppx A
    Licensing, education, experience and training standards   CRC 5.225
    Order appointing evaluator   CRCAppx A (CRCFL-327)
    Training
        Domestic violence training standards   CRC 5.230
    Uniform standards of practice for evaluations   CRC 5.220

Evidence
    Report of court-appointed investigator   Fam §3111
    Uniform Child Custody Jurisdiction and Enforcement Act, procedures for gathering evidence under   Fam §§3411, 3412

Exclusive custody, action for   Fam §3120
    Attorney's fees
        Financial need basis for fees   CRC 5.427
        Ordering party to provide for legal representation of other party   Fam §3121

Ex parte communications   CRC 5.235

Ex parte orders   Fam §§3062 to 3064

Expenses
    Appointed counsel, compensation of   Fam §3153
    Compensation for failure to assume caretaker responsibility   Fam §3028
    Custody investigations   Fam §3112
    District attorney's expenses in locating missing party or child   Fam §§3130, 3134, 3457

Failure of custodial parent to implement rights of noncustodial parent   Fam §3556

Failure to exercise caretaker responsibility   Fam §3028

False accusation of child abuse or neglect   Fam §§3022.5, 3027.1, 3027.5

Family court services, protocol for   CRC 5.215

Family law facilitators for unrepresented parties   Fam §§10000 to 10015

Family law information centers for unrepresented low-income litigants   Fam §§15000 to 15012

Family reunification services   Fam §3026

Family rules
    Declarations under uniform child custody jurisdiction and enforcement act (UCCJEA)   CRC 5.52
    Domestic violence
        Communication protocol for domestic violence and child custody orders   CRC 5.445
        Family court services protocol   CRC 5.215
    Evaluations   CRC 5.220
    Investigators and evaluators
        Domestic violence training standards   CRC 5.230
        Licensing, education, experience, and training standards   CRC 5.225
    Judgments
        Entry of judgment   CRC 5.413
        Notice of entry of judgment   CRC 5.415
    Mediation   CRC 5.210

Fees charged in custody proceedings   Gov §70678

Friend of court, office of   Fam §§10101 to 10102

Grandparent's visitation rights   Fam §§3102 to 3104, 3171, 3176, 3185

Guardian adoptions
    Child declared free from parental custody and control
        Proceeding to declare   Pro §1516.5

Guardians
    Jurisdiction   Pro §2205
    Nomination by parent   Fam §3043
    Venue
        Communications between/among courts involved with custody, visitation and guardianship involving ward   CRC 7.1014
        Multiple counties, proceedings in   Pro §2204
    Visitation
        Former legal guardians   CRC 7.1008, Fam §3105, Pro §1602
        Orders following termination of juvenile court or probate court proceedings   CRC 5.475

Hearings
    Cross-examination of court-appointed investigator   Fam §§3115, 3117

CUSTODY OF CHILDREN—Cont.
  Hearings—Cont.
    Uniform Child Custody Jurisdiction and Enforcement Act, hearings under
      (See **UNIFORM CHILD CUSTODY JURISDICTION AND ENFORCEMENT ACT**)
      Visitation rights   Fam §§3176, 3185
  Immediate harm to child, risk of   Fam §3064
  Indian child
    Generally (See within this heading, **"Native Americans"**)
    Indian Child Welfare Act, compliance   Fam §§170 to 185, 3401
      Forms, judicial council   CRCAppx A
      Involuntary placements   CRC 5.480 to 5.488 (See **INDIAN CHILD WELFARE ACT INVOLUNTARY PLACEMENTS**)
  Indian children
    Tribal participation   Fam §185
  Injunctions against determinations in marital dissolution proceedings
    Custody or visitation orders following termination of juvenile court or probate court proceedings   CRC 5.475
  Interactive computer system authorized to prepare standardized pro per court documents   CCP §1062.20
  Interpreters for child custody proceedings, public provision of   Fam §3032
  Interstate compact on placement of children   Fam §§7900 to 7913
    Children covered by compact   Fam §7907.5
    Home environment study request from another state   Fam §7901.1
      Custody of child in requesting state   Fam §7906.5
  Investigations   Fam §§3111, 3116
    Children's participation and testimony in family court proceedings
      Responsibilities of court-connected or appointed professionals   CRC 5.250
    Continuing education
      Supervisors of investigators and evaluators   CRC 5.220, Fam §3165
    Cross-examination of court-appointed investigator   CRC 5.220, Fam §§3115, 3117
    Definitions   CRC 5.220, Fam §3110
    Domestic violence
      Family court services, domestic violence protocol   CRC 5.215
      Separate meetings with investigators where history of domestic violence   Fam §3113
      Training standards for court-appointed investigators and evaluators   CRC 5.230
    Education, experience, and training standards for investigators and evaluators   CRC 5.225
    Ex parte communications   CRC 5.235
    Expenses   Fam §3112
    Joint custody absent parental agreement   Fam §3081
    Other jurisdictions, cooperation with   CRC 5.220
    Qualifications of custody evaluators   Fam §3110.5
    Recommendation for appointment of counsel for child   Fam §3114
    Reports   CRC 5.220, Fam §3111
    Standards for investigations   CRC 5.220, Fam §3117
    Training
      Domestic violence protocol for family court services   CRC 5.215
      Domestic violence training standards generally   CRC 5.230
    Uniform Child Custody Jurisdiction and Enforcement Act, custody evaluations under   Fam §3412
  Joint custody
    Absent agreement of parents   Fam §3081
    Attachment for joint legal custody   CRCAppx A (CRCFL-341(E))
    Defined   Fam §3002
    Grant or denial of joint custody, reasons of court for   Fam §3082
    Modification of orders   Fam §§3087, 3088
    Presumption of   Fam §3080
    Primary parent, order specifying   Fam §3086
  Joint legal custody
    Content and effect of order for   Fam §3083
    Defined   Fam §3003
    Without granting joint physical custody   Fam §3085
  Joint physical custody
    Content of order   Fam §3084
    Defined   Fam §3004
    Joint legal custody granted without   Fam §3085
  Jurisdiction   Fam §§2010 to 2013
    Uniform Child Custody Jurisdiction and Enforcement Act (See **UNIFORM CHILD CUSTODY JURISDICTION AND ENFORCEMENT ACT**)
  Juvenile courts
    Exclusive jurisdiction   CRC 5.510
    Generally (See **JUVENILE COURTS**)
  Legislative findings and declarations   Fam §3020
  Mediation proceedings
    Generally   Fam §§3160 to 3188
    Adoption of mediation program by courts   Fam §3188

CUSTODY OF CHILDREN—Cont.
  Mediation proceedings—Cont.
    Children's participation and testimony in family court proceedings
      Responsibilities of court-connected or appointed professionals   CRC 5.250
    Contested cases   Fam §§3170 to 3173
    Continuing education requirements for mediators   CRC 5.210, Fam §3165
    Destruction of records   Fam §1819
    Domestic violence cases   Fam §§3170, 3181, 3182
    Ex parte communications involving court-appointed or court-connected evaluators or mediators   CRC 5.235
    Family court services, domestic violence protocol   CRC 5.215
    Functional budget categories   CRC 10.810
    Grandparent's visitation   Fam §§3171, 3176, 3185
    Judicial Council standards   CRC 5.210
    Recommendation by mediator to court   Fam §3183
    Scheduling   Fam §3175
    Stepparent visitation   Fam §§3171, 3176, 3185
    Uniform standards for mediation services   CRC 5.210
  Medical records, access to   Fam §3025
  Military duty, deployment, etc
    Effect on custody   Fam §3047
  Minor's appearance without guardian ad litem   CCP §372
  Missing party or child
    Action to locate   Fam §§3130 to 3135, 3455, 3456
    Birth certificate of child   Fam §3140
    Child support enforcement agency, use of abduction records by   Fam §17514
    Parent Locator Service and Central Registry   Fam §17506
    Uniform Parentage Act   Fam §7603
  Modification of orders
    Domestic violence prevention act proceedings   CRC 5.381
    False accusations of abuse   Fam §3022.5
    Joint custody, modification of custody order to   Fam §3088
    Joint custody order, modification of   Fam §3087
    Notice requirements, generally   Fam §215
    Sex offenses
      Effect of committing offense requiring registration by custodian or person residing with   Fam §3030.5
    Uniform Child Custody Jurisdiction and Enforcement Act (See **UNIFORM CHILD CUSTODY JURISDICTION AND ENFORCEMENT ACT**)
  More than 2 parents
    Allocation of custody and visitation based on best interests of child   Fam §3040
  Murder of one parent by other, custody and visitation determinations following   Fam §3030
  Native Americans
    Abandoned children
      Transfer by parent of care, custody and control to Indian custodian as not constituting abandonment   Fam §7822
    Alcohol or drug abuse as custody determination factor   Fam §3041
    Applicability of California provisions   Fam §177
    Applicability of Indian Child Welfare act   Pro §1459.5
    Indian Child Welfare Act, compliance with   Fam §§170 to 185, 3041
      Forms, judicial council   CRCAppx A
      Involuntary placements   CRC 5.480 to 5.488 (See **INDIAN CHILD WELFARE ACT INVOLUNTARY PLACEMENTS**)
    Interstate compact on placement of children
      Applicability to Indian children   Fam §7907.3
    Legislative findings and intent   Fam §175, Pro §1459
    Nonminor dependents, retention of jurisdiction
      Request for court to resume jurisdiction   CRC 5.906
      Status review hearings   CRC 5.903
    Notice   Fam §180
    Returning physical custody of Indian child, ex parte hearings
      Forms, judicial council   CRCAppx A
    Temporary custody of Indian child, agreement   CRCAppx A
    Termination of parental rights   Fam §7892.5
    Tribe of child
      Consideration of connection to tribal community   Fam §170
      Determination   Pro §1449
      Participation by tribe in proceedings   Fam §185
    Uniform Child Custody Jurisdiction and Enforcement Act, applicability of   Fam §3404
  Nonparent, custody awarded to   Fam §§3040, 3041
  Notice
    Change of residence of child   Fam §3024
    Indian child custody proceedings   Fam §180
    Risk of abduction findings and preventative measures   Fam §3048
    Uniform Child Custody Jurisdiction and Enforcement Act, notice requirements under   Fam §§3408, 3425

CUSTODY OF CHILDREN—Cont.
Orders
    Generally Fam §3022
    Ex parte orders Fam §§3062 to 3064
    Mediation of existing order Fam §3173
    Modification (See within this heading, **"Modification of orders"**)
    Registration of orders
        Out-of-state orders CRCAppxs A (CRCFL-580), (CRCFL-585)
    Response to request for custody and visitation orders
        Judicial council forms CRCAppx A
    Risk of abduction findings and preventative measures Fam §3048
    Show cause orders
        Compensation for failure to exercise visitation or custody rights Fam §3028
        Temporary custody Fam §3062
    Statement explaining basis of court decision Fam §3022.3
    Temporary restraining orders Fam §§2040, 2041
        Removal of child from state Fam §3063
Other states (See **UNIFORM CHILD CUSTODY JURISDICTION AND ENFORCEMENT ACT**)
Paternity at issue Fam §3172
Petition for grandparental visitation Fam §§3103, 3104
Physical custody attachment CRCAppx A (CRCFL-341(D))
Preference in award of custody Fam §3040
Presumption of joint custody Fam §3080
Priority on calendar
    Trial on issue of custody Fam §3023
    Uniform Child Custody Jurisdiction and Enforcement Act, challenge to jurisdiction under Fam §3407
Probation officers making investigations Fam §§3110 to 3116
Pro per court documents, interactive computer system authorized to prepare standardized CCP §1062.20
Property of child, parent's control over Fam §7502
Protective custody warrant for unlawfully detained or concealed child Fam §3134.5
Psychological evaluation of child involved in custody or visitation proceedings
    Confidentiality Fam §3025.5
Public assistance eligibility, specifying primary parent for Fam §3086
Public policy Fam §3020
Reconsideration of custody order based on false accusations of abuse Fam §3022.5
Records
    Parental access to records Fam §3025
    Supervised visitation records CRC JudAdminStand 5.20
    Uniform Child Custody Jurisdiction and Enforcement Act, requirements under (See **UNIFORM CHILD CUSTODY JURISDICTION AND ENFORCEMENT ACT**)
Registered sex offenders, denial of custody and visitation to Fam §3030
Removal of child from state Fam §§233, 2030, 3063, 3064
Reports
    Child protective services agencies, release of reports of Fam §3152
    Custody evaluations CRC 5.220, Fam §3111
Residence of child
    Absence or relocation of parent from family residence as consideration for court in awarding custody or visitation Fam §3046
        Military deployment Fam §3047
    Notice to other parent of change of child's residence Fam §3024
    Right of custodial parent to change child's residence Fam §7501
Sale of family home to be deferred, request of custodial parent for Fam §§3800 to 3810
Sanctions for false accusation of child abuse or neglect Fam §3027.1
School records, access to Fam §3025
Separate trial on issue of custody Fam §3023
Sex offenders
    Household membership of or permitting contact by registered sex offender Fam §3030
    Modification or termination of custody upon commission of offense requiring registration by custodian or person residing with Fam §3030.5
Sexual abuse
    Child abuse or neglect generally (See within this heading, **"Child abuse or neglect"**)
Show cause orders
    Compensation for failure to exercise visitation or custody rights Fam §3028
    Temporary custody Fam §3062
Siblings, visitation rights of Fam §3102
Sole legal custody defined Fam §3006
Sole physical custody
    Defined Fam §3007
    Missing party or child, action to locate Fam §3133
Spousal support, denial of Fam §4321

CUSTODY OF CHILDREN—Cont.
Statement explaining basis of court decision Fam §3022.3
Stay of execution of judgment affecting custody CCP §917.7
Stepparent's visitation rights Fam §§3101, 3171, 3176, 3185
Stipulation and order CRCAppx A (CRCFL-355)
Substance abuse
    Best interest of child, factor in determining Fam §3011
    Determining factor in custody
        Testing for alcohol or controlled substance use ordered by court Fam §3041.5
    Termination of parental rights
        Circumstances where proceedings may be brought Fam §7824
Supervised visitation and exchange programs CRC JudAdminStand 5.20, Fam §§3200 to 3204
    Administration of programs
        Definitions Fam §3201.5
    Compliance with provisions Fam §3202
    Grant funds
        Administration Fam §3204
    Providers, standards Fam §3200.5
        Declaration of provider, form CRCAppx A
    Superior courts as supervised visitation and exchange locations Fam §3200
Temporary custody
    Agreement, custody awarded in accordance with Fam §3061
    Ex parte orders Fam §§3062 to 3064
    Military deployment, duty, etc
        Effect on custody orders of temporary deployment, duty, etc Fam §3047
    Petition for Fam §3060
    Uniform Parentage Act Fam §7604
Temporary guardian appointment as affecting visitation rights Pro §2250
Temporary restraining orders
    Generally Fam §§2040, 2041
    Removal of child from state Fam §3063
Termination of parental rights (See **TERMINATION OF PARENTAL RIGHTS**)
Thwarting other parent's visitation or custody rights Fam §3028
Transfer of causes
    Retention of jurisdiction to issue protective orders CCP §399
    Subsequent to final judgment CCP §397.5
    Time frames for transferring jurisdiction
        Family law actions or proceedings CRC 5.97
Translators for child custody proceedings, public provision of Fam §3032
Uniform Child Custody Jurisdiction and Enforcement Act (See **UNIFORM CHILD CUSTODY JURISDICTION AND ENFORCEMENT ACT**)
Uniform Parentage Act Fam §§7604, 7637
Visitation
    Generally Fam §3100
    Absence or relocation of parent from family residence as consideration for court in awarding custody or visitation Fam §3046
        Military deployment Fam §3047
    Adoption of child, effect of (See **ADOPTION**)
    Application attachment CRCAppx A (CRCFL-311)
    Attorney's fees
        Access to legal representation by requiring party to provide for other party's attorney fees Fam §7605
        Financial need basis for fees CRC 5.427
    Bifurcated proceedings
        Appeals CCP §904.1
    Child abuse generally (See within this heading, **"Child abuse or neglect"**)
    Children's participation and testimony in family court proceedings CRC 5.250
    Confidentiality
        Psychological evaluation of child involved in custody or visitation proceedings Fam §3025.5
    Domestic violence prevention orders, effect of (See **DOMESTIC VIOLENCE**)
    Expenses added to child support award Fam §4062
    Failure to exercise rights Fam §3028
    Forms
        Judicial council legal forms CRCAppx A
    Friend of court, office of Fam §§10101 to 10102
    Grandparents Fam §§3102 to 3104, 3171, 3176, 3185
    Guardians
        Former legal guardians CRC 7.1008, Fam §3105, Pro §1602
        Jurisdiction Pro §2205
        Orders following termination of juvenile court or probate court proceedings CRC 5.475
        Venue, multiple counties with pending proceedings CRC 7.1014, Pro §2204

CUSTODY OF CHILDREN—Cont.
Visitation—Cont.
    Guardians—Cont.
        Ward's participation and testimony in probate guardianship proceedings   CRC 7.1016
    Hearings on   Fam §§3176, 3185
    Holiday schedule attachment   CRCAppx A (CRCFL-341(C))
    Interactive computer system authorized to prepare standardized pro per court documents   CCP §1062.20
    Mediation proceedings generally (See within this heading, **"Mediation proceedings"**)
    Modification of orders
        Domestic violence prevention act proceedings   CRC 5.381
    Murder of one parent by other, custody and visitation determinations following   Fam §3030
    Other state's visitation provisions, temporary order enforcing   Fam §3444
    Physical custody attachment   CRCAppx A (CRCFL-341(D))
    Psychological evaluation of child involved in custody or visitation proceedings
        Confidentiality   Fam §3025.5
    Reasons for no or for supervised visitation
        Form   CRCAppx A
    Registered sex offenders
        Denial of custody and visitation to   Fam §3030
        Modification or termination of order upon commission of offense requiring registration by custodian or person residing with   Fam §3030.5
    Risk of abduction findings and preventative measures   Fam §3048
    Siblings, visitation rights of   Fam §3102
    Stepparents   Fam §§3101, 3171, 3176, 3185
    Stipulation and order   CRCAppx A (CRCFL-355)
    Substance abuse as custody determining factor
        Testing for alcohol or controlled substance use ordered by court   Fam §3041.5
    Supervised visitation   CRC JudAdminStand 5.20, Fam §§3200 to 3204
        Declaration of provider, form   CRCAppx A
        Order   CRCAppx A (CRCFL-341(A))
        Providers, standards   Fam §3200.5
        Reasons for no or for supervised visitation, form   CRCAppx A
        Superior courts as supervised visitation and exchange locations   Fam §3200
    Temporary guardian, effect of appointment of   Pro §2250
    Thwarting other parent's visitation rights   Fam §3028
    Virtual visitation, presence of third person   Fam §3100
Warrant for unlawfully detained or concealed child   Fam §§3134.5, 3451
Welfare eligibility, specifying primary parent for   Fam §3086
Wishes of child   Fam §3042
    Children's participation and testimony in family court proceedings   CRC 5.250
Withdrawal of attorney in domestic relations matters   CCP §285.1
Witnesses
    Child as witness   Fam §3042
        Children's participation and testimony in family court proceedings   CRC 5.250
    Live testimony
        When received   CRC 5.113, Fam §217

CUSTOM AND USAGE
Admissible evidence to prove conduct   Ev §1105
Contracts conforming to   CC §§1655, 1656
International commercial arbitration, applicability of custom and usage of trade rules in   CCP §1297.285
Rent, effect on time for payment of   CC §1947

CUSTOMER RECORDS
Abandoned customer records
    Disposition of abandoned records
        Immunity   CC §1798.84
Computerized personal information owned or licensed by businesses
    Release to unauthorized persons by breach in security system
        Disclosures to persons affected   CC §§1798.82, 1798.84
            Identity theft protection and mitigation services, offering by source of breach   CC §1798.82
Contracts
    Security procedures to protect personal information
        Third party users of records to be contractually obligated to provide security procedures   CC §1798.81.5
Definitions   CC §1798.80
Disclosure of personal information of customer   CC §1798.83
    Commercial online entertainment employment service providers
        Age information of subscribers, restriction on disclosure   CC §1798.83.5

CUSTOMER RECORDS—Cont.
Disclosure of personal information of customer —Cont.
    Remedies of customer   CC §1798.84
Disposition of customer's records containing personal information, requirement for   CC §1798.81
Remedies available to customer injured by failure to destroy customer records containing personal information   CC §§1798.82, 1798.84
Security procedures to protect personal information   CC §1798.81.5
Social security numbers, prohibiting posting or display to general public of   CC §1798.85
    Financial institutions, continued use   CC §1786.60
    Waiver of protections   CC §1798.86
Waiver of protections   CC §1798.84

CUSTOMS COURT
Judicial notice of rules of   Ev §451

CY PRES
Charitable trusts   Pro §21220
Institutional funds management
    Restrictions in gift instruments
        Release   Pro §18506
Rule against perpetuities, effect on   Pro §21220
Transfer on death deeds
    Reformation of deed
        Cy pres doctrine to reform deed   Pro §5658

D

DAIRIES AND DAIRY PRODUCTS
Attachments proceedings   CCP §481.110
Claim and delivery   CCP §511.040
Nuisance, dairy operations as   CC §§3482.5, 3482.6

DALKON SHIELD
Limitations statute extension for claims resulting from use of   CCP §340.7

DAMAGES   CC §§3281 to 3361
Accounting companies, disclosure of information by   CC §1799.2
Additur of damages
    Consent to on appeal   CRC 8.264
Administrators of decedents' estates
    Generally (See **ADMINISTRATION OF ESTATES**)
    Executors and administrators, liability of (See **EXECUTORS AND ADMINISTRATORS**)
Adverse possession   CCP §§740, 741
Advertising, unauthorized use of name or likeness in   CC §§3344, 3344.1
Advisers on investments, liability of   CC §3372
Agent's authority, breach of warranty of   CC §3318
Alcoholic beverages
    Commercial motor vehicle employer for vehicle accident caused by intoxicated employee   CC §3333.7
    Social host's liability after serving   CC §1714
Aliens
    Children and minors
        Immigration status irrelevant   CC §3339.5
    Civil rights enforcement, irrelevance of immigration status   CC §3339
Alternative judgment in replevin   CCP §667
Animals
    Cruelty to   CC §3340
    Dogs (See **DOGS**)
Artists, seller of art withholding payment to   CC §986
Art works, destruction or defacement of   CC §987
Attachment (See **ATTACHMENT**)
Attorneys' professional societies, liability of   CC §§43.7, 43.95
Automated license plate recognition systems (ALPR)
    Data security
        Breach of security   CC §1798.90.54
        Unauthorized access or use of information   CC §1798.90.54
Automobile lease violations (See **AUTOMOBILES**)
Automobile warranties
    Restitution or replacement actions   CCP §871.27
Bad checks, liability for making   CC §1719
Booking photographs
    Commercial use of booking photographs   CC §1798.91.1
Breach of contract   CC §§1671, 1675 to 1681, 3300 to 3322
Buyer's loss, determination of   CC §3354
Cable television companies (See **CABLE TELEVISION COMPANIES**)
Campaign advertising (See **CANDIDATES FOR OFFICE**)
Certainty of   CC §3301

DAMAGES—Cont.
- Child sexual abuse hosted on social media platform
    - Liability for failure to comply with provisions   CC §3273.67
- Child support, assisting obligor in avoiding payment   CC §§1714.4, 1714.41
- Chiropractor (See **MALPRACTICE**)
- Civil rights actions   CC §§52, 52.1, 54.3
    - Construction or application of provisions in issue, solicitor general notified   CC §§51.1, 55.2
    - Gender violence   CC §52.4
- Claim and delivery   CCP §627
- Claims against public entities and employees (See **CLAIMS AGAINST PUBLIC ENTITIES AND EMPLOYEES**)
- Commencement of action, injury sustained after   CC §3283
- Commercial and industrial common interest developments
    - Actions for damage to separate or common areas
        - Comparative fault   CC §6860
- Commercial blockage tort affecting health care facility, damages for   CC §3427.2
- Commercial financing transactions with small businesses
    - Prohibited fees
        - Remedies for violations   CC §1799.303
- Common carriers, breach of contract by   CC §§3315 to 3317
- Common interest developments (See **COMMON INTEREST DEVELOPMENTS**)
- Community property (See **COMMUNITY PROPERTY**)
- Conservation easement, impairment of   CC §815.7
- Construction defects, actions for   CC §943
    - Measure of damages   CC §944
- Construction, intentional destruction of property under   CC §1721
- Construction-related accessibility claims
    - Statutory damages
        - Liability   CC §55.56
- Consumer privacy rights
    - Actions for damages, injunctions, declaratory relief, etc
        - Security practices and procedures not in place   CC §1798.150
- Consumer protection actions (See **CONSUMER PROTECTION**)
- Contracts
    - Breach of contract   CC §§1671, 1675 to 1681, 3300 to 3322
    - Conveyance   CC §3306
    - Interest rate for breach of contract   CC §3288
    - Rescission of   CC §1692
    - Sales contracts   CC §§3353, 3354
        - Realty (See within this heading, "**Sale of realty**")
- Contribution among joint defendants (See **CONTRIBUTION**)
- Conversion   CC §§3336 to 3338
- Conveyances
    - Contract to convey land, breach of   CC §3306
    - Right to convey land, breach of covenant of   CC §3304
- Conviction
    - Criminal acts generally (See within this heading, "**Criminal acts**")
- Costs of suit, recovery of (See **COSTS**)
- COVID-19 small landlord and homeowner relief act
    - Action by borrower harmed by violation of provisions   CC §3273.15
- Credit card holder, damages against vendor for eliciting personal information concerning   CC §1747.08
- Credit card violations, recovery for   CC §§1747.50 to 1747.80
- Credit denial, failure to state reasons for   CC §1787.2
- Credit reporting (See **CREDIT REPORTING**)
- Credit services organizations, action against   CC §1789.21
- Criminal acts
    - Attorney's fees in action against felons for damages, award of   CCP §1021.4
    - Homicide, liability for exemplary damages for   CC §3294
    - Sexual battery, exemplary damages for   CC §1708.5
    - Victim sued by felon for injuries arising from crime on which felony conviction based, exemplary damages for   CCP §§128.5, 128.7
- Cruelty to animals   CC §3340
- Dance studio contracts, violation of provisions regulating   CC §1812.62
- Dating service contracts, injury sustained under   CC §1694.4
- Death
    - Advertising, unauthorized use of deceased personality's name or likeness in   CC §3344.1
    - Estate of decedent, claims against (See **CLAIMS AGAINST ESTATES**)
    - Survival of actions (See **SURVIVAL OF ACTIONS**)
    - Wrongful death (See **WRONGFUL DEATH**)
- Debt collectors, illegal practices by   CC §§1788.30 to 1788.32
- Deeds of trust and mortgages
    - Enforcement of foreclosure prevention   CC §2924.12
- Default judgments (See **DEFAULT JUDGMENTS**)

DAMAGES—Cont.
- Delivery of goods during specified time period where consumer's presence required, retailer's liability for failure in   CC §1722
- Dentists (See **MALPRACTICE**)
- Depositions
    - Subpoenas
        - Disobedience of subpoena   CCP §2020.240
- Deposits (See **DEPOSITS**)
- Detriment defined   CC §3282
- Disabled persons denied access or admittance to public facilities, damages recoverable by   CC §54.3
    - Construction or application of provisions in issue, solicitor general notified   CC §55.2
- Discount buying services, breach of contract for   CC §1812.123
- Disfigurement, recovery for   CC §3333.2
- Dogs (See **DOGS**)
- Domestic partners, right to damages for negligent infliction of emotional distress recoverable by   CC §1714.01
- Domestic violence
    - Community property
        - Enforcement against abusive spouse's share of community property   Fam §2603.5
    - Tort liability for domestic violence   CC §1708.6
- Doxing victims' recourse   CC §1708.89
- Electric companies (See **ELECTRICITY AND ELECTRIC COMPANIES**)
- Embryos
    - Unauthorized use or misuse of sperm, ova or embryo
        - Civil action for damages   CC §1708.5.6
- Eminent domain (See **EMINENT DOMAIN**)
- Employment agencies, action against   CC §1812.523
- Employment counseling services, action against   CC §1812.523
- Encumbrances, breach of covenant against   CC §3305
- Enforcement of judgments (See **ENFORCEMENT OF JUDGMENTS**)
- Escrow companies specified by developer, use of   CC §2995
- Excavation damage to adjacent land   CC §832
- Execution-sale purchaser recovering   CCP §746
- Executors of decedents' estates, liability of (See **EXECUTORS AND ADMINISTRATORS**)
- Exemplary damages
    - Generally   CC §3294
    - Advertising, unauthorized use of name or likeness in   CC §§3344, 3344.1
    - Art works, destruction or defacement of   CC §987
    - Automated license plate recognition systems (ALPR)
        - Data security, breach   CC §1798.90.54
    - Blind or disabled persons, interference with rights
        - Construction or application of provisions in issue, solicitor general notified   CC §55.2
    - Campaign advertisements, use of unauthorized signatures in   CC §3344.5
    - Claims against public entities and employees (See **CLAIMS AGAINST PUBLIC ENTITIES AND EMPLOYEES**)
    - Credit reporting   CC §1785.31
    - Criminal acts generally (See within this heading, "**Criminal acts**")
    - Death (See **WRONGFUL DEATH**)
    - Default judgments, reservation of right to seek punitive damages on   CCP §§425.12, 425.115
    - Domestic violence
        - Tort liability for domestic violence   CC §1708.6
    - Employer's liability for   CC §3294
    - Employment agencies, action against   CC §1812.523
    - Employment counseling services, action against   CC §1812.523
    - Expedited jury trials
        - Mandatory expedited jury trials, limited civil cases, opting out of expedited process   CCP §630.20
    - Felonies (See within this heading, "**Criminal acts**")
    - Financial condition of defendant, admissibility of evidence of   CC §3295
    - Fire hydrants
        - Junk dealers or recyclers, wrongful possession of hydrants or fire department connections   CC §3336.5
    - Gender violence   CC §52.4
    - Health care providers, punitive damage claims against   CCP §425.13
    - Home equity sales contracts, violation of   CC §1695.7
    - Human trafficking   CC §52.5
    - Information Practices Act, violation of   CC §1798.53
    - Insurer, special notice of punitive damages award against   CC §3296
    - Job listing services, action against   CC §1812.523
    - Libel by newspaper or radio station   CC §48a
    - Measure of compensatory damages, exclusion of exemplary damages in determining   CC §3357
    - Mobilehomes   CC §798.86
    - Mortgage foreclosure consultants contracts   CC §2945.6
    - Nurses' registries, action against   CC §1812.523

DAMAGES—Cont.
  Exemplary damages—Cont.
    Pleading   CCP §425.10
    Prima facie case of liability   CC §3295
    Protective order re plaintiff's proof   CC §3295
    Public benefit trust fund
        Allocation of punitive damage awards to fund   CC §3294.5
    Religious corporations, claim for punitive damage against   CCP §425.14
    Rental-purchase contracts, breach of   CC §1812.636
    Reservation of right to seek punitive damages on default   CCP §§425.12, 425.115
    Sexual battery   CC §1708.5
    Sexual exploitation
        Commercial sexual exploitation, minor or nonminor dependent victims   CC §3345.1
    Sexually explicit depiction of individual, creation or disclosure   CC §1708.86
    Special verdict rendered in action   CCP §625
    Subcutaneous implanting of identification device, requiring of another   CC §52.7
    Trustee, action against   Pro §16442
    Unlicensed person, action for injury caused by   CCP §1029.8
    Valuations, exemplary damages added to   CC §3357
    Wholesale sales representatives, actions involving   CC §1738.15
    Wrongful death (See **WRONGFUL DEATH**)
  Fair debt buying practices
    Violation of provisions   CC §1788.62
  Fair debt settlement practices
    Consumers
        Actions to enforce   CC §1788.305
  Felonies (See within this heading, **"Criminal acts"**)
  Financial condition of defendant for purposes of exemplary damages, admissibility of evidence of   CC §3295
  Fines and penalties (See **FINES AND PENALTIES**)
  Firearms
    Discharged by child, limitation on parent's liability for firearm   CC §1714.3
    Firearm industry standards of conduct
        Actions against industry members for violation of standards   CC §3273.52
  Fire hydrants
    Junk dealers or recyclers
        Wrongful possession of hydrants or fire department connections   CC §3336.5
  Fixtures, removal of   CC §1013.5
  Forcible entry   CCP §§735, 1174
  Fraud (See **FRAUD**)
  Freight, breach of contract to transport   CC §§3315 to 3317
  Gas companies (See **GAS COMPANIES**)
  Gender violence   CC §52.4
  Greenway easements
    Enforcement of easement   CC §816.62
  Guardians (See **GUARDIAN AND WARD**)
  Guide dogs, owner's liability for damages caused by   CC §54.2
    Construction or application of provisions in issue, solicitor general notified   CC §55.2
  Health care providers (See **MALPRACTICE**)
  Health facilities
    Force, threat or other obstruction of access to facility   CC §1708.9
  Health studio contracts, violation of provisions regulating   CC §1812.94
  Home equity sales contracts, breach of   CC §1695.7
  Homicide, punitive damages for   CC §3294
  Hospitals
    Force, threat or other obstruction of access to facility   CC §1708.9
    Lien on damages award to injured party for payment of emergency treatment   CC §§3045.1 to 3045.6
    Malpractice (See **MALPRACTICE**)
  Human trafficking
    Actions   CC §52.5
  Husband and wife (See **COMMUNITY PROPERTY**)
  Identity theft, damages recoverable in actions involving   CC §1798.93
  Immigration and naturalization
    Children and minors
        Immigration status irrelevant   CC §3339.5
    Civil rights enforcement, irrelevance of immigration status   CC §3339
  Immunity (See **IMMUNITY**)
  Inconvenience   CC §3333.2
  Indemnification against loss   CC §2779
  Information Practices Act, recovery under   CC §§1798.48, 1798.53, 1798.77
  Injunctions (See **INJUNCTIONS**)
  Injury sustained, damages for   CC §3281

DAMAGES—Cont.
  Insurer, special notice of punitive damages award against   CC §3296
  Interest
    Generally   CC §3287
    Jury award of   CC §3288
    Prejudgment interest, award of   CC §3291
    Rate of interest
        Generally   CC §3289
        Retail installment contracts   CC §3289.5
    Trustee, action against   Pro §§16440, 16441
    Waiver of   CC §3290
  Invasion of privacy   CC §1708.8
    Generally (See **INVASION OF PRIVACY**)
  Investigative consumer reporting agencies   CC §1786.50
  Investment advisers, liability of   CC §3372
  Job listing services, action against   CC §1812.523
  Joint and several liability (See **JOINT AND SEVERAL LIABILITY**)
  Judgment lien on property of misidentified owner, release of   CCP §§697.410, 697.660
  Labor disputes, inciting violence during   CC §52
  Landlord and tenant (See **LANDLORD AND TENANT**)
  Leases (See **LEASES**)
  Legally protected health care services
    Action for relief from abusive litigation infringing on protected activity
        Measure of damages   CC §1798.305
  Liability insurer of decedent, damages recoverable from   Pro §554
  Libel suit against newspaper or radio station   CC §48a
  Lien conversions   CC §3338
  Limitations on amount of   CC §§3333.2, 3358
  Liquidated damages   CC §§1670, 1671
    Sexually explicit depiction of individual, creation or disclosure   CC §1708.86
  Malice (See **MALICE**)
  Mandamus   CCP §1095
  Market value as basis for   CC §3353
  Material used without permission in making personal property, liability for   CC §1033
  Measure of damages   CC §§3300 to 3361
    Agent's authority, breach of warranty of   CC §3318
    Animals, cruelty to   CC §3340
    Buyer's loss   CC §3354
    Certainty of damages, requirement of   CC §3301
    Common carriers, breach of contract by   CC §§3315 to 3317
    Conversion   CC §§3336, 3337, 3338
    Conveyances
        Contract to convey, breach   CC §3306
        Right to convey land, breach of covenant   CC §3304
    Dogs (See **DOGS**)
    Earnings, lost or impaired capacity
        Race, ethnicity or gender not to serve as basis for reduction in damages   CC §3361
    Encumbrances, breach of covenant against   CC §3305
    Exemplary damages excluded in determining   CC §3357
    Fraud   CC §3343
    Health care provider, action against   CC §3333.2
    Immigration status not to affect   CC §3339
    Impaired earning capacity
        Race, ethnicity or gender not to serve as basis for reduction in damages   CC §3361
    Interest included as   CC §3302
    Lease, breach of   CC §3308
    Liens on personal property   CC §3338
    Life estate in real property, termination of   CC §3335
    Lost earnings
        Race, ethnicity or gender not to serve as basis for reduction in damages   CC §3361
    Peculiar value to owner   CC §3355
    Proximate cause, requirement of   CC §§3300, 3333
    Quiet enjoyment, breach of covenant of   CC §3304
    Seisin, breach of covenant of   CC §3304
    Seller's loss   CC §3353
    Sexually explicit depiction of individual
        Creation or disclosure   CC §1708.86
    Title in real property, breach of covenant of   CC §3304
    Trusts (See **TRUSTS**)
    Warranty in real property breach of covenant of   CC §3304
    Written instrument, value of   CC §3356
    Wrongful use or occupation of land   CC §3334
  Minors (See **MINORS**)
  Mitigation of damages (See **MITIGATION OF DAMAGES**)

DAMAGES—Cont.

Mobilehomes
   Damages in actions concerning   CC §798.86
   Park, awards against
      Rent increases for prohibited   CC §798.39.5
Mortgage foreclosure consultant contracts   CC §2945.6
Nameplate removed from article sold   CC §1710.1
New trial (See **NEW TRIAL**)
Nominal damages   CC §3360
Nurses' registries, action against   CC §1812.523
Obscene and harmful matter
   Electronic messages depicting obscene material
      Knowingly sending unsolicited messages   CC §1708.88
Occupation of land in wrongful manner   CC §§3334, 3335
Opticians and optometrists (See **MALPRACTICE**)
Osteopaths (See **MALPRACTICE**)
Ova
   Unauthorized use or misuse of sperm, ova or embryo
      Civil action for damages   CC §1708.5.6
Pain and suffering   CC §3333.2
Paint, parent's liability for minor defacing property by use of   CC §1714.1
Parent's imputed liability for willful misconduct of children   CC §1714.1, CRCAppx B
Passenger carriage, breach of contract for   CC §3315
Peculiar value   CC §3355
Peer review committee, damages for communications of proceedings   CC §§43.7, 43.8
Penal damages (See **FINES AND PENALTIES**)
Personal injury actions (See **PERSONAL INJURIES**)
Pharmacies, violation of provisions for fee study by   CC §2528
Physician-patient privilege, applicability to action for damages for conduct of patient of   Ev §999
Physicians and surgeons (See **MALPRACTICE**)
Pipeline corporation's absolute liability for damages caused by discharge or leaking of oil   CC §3333.5
Pleadings, generally   CCP §425.10
Podiatrists (See **MALPRACTICE**)
Police officers, attorney's fee award in action against   CCP §1021.7
Political items, illegal sale of   CC §1739.4
Possession wrongfully held   CC §§3334 to 3336
Prejudgment interest, award of   CC §3291
Prescribed burns
   Immunity from damages   CC §3333.8
Prima facie case of liability for exemplary damages, burden on plaintiff to produce   CC §3295
Privacy
   Invasion of privacy   CC §1708.8
   Photographs, films, etc, exposing intimate body parts or sexual acts of another without permission, distribution
      Actions for injunctions, damages, etc   CC §1708.85
      Confidential information form   CRCAppx A
Private child support collectors
   Civil actions   Fam §5615
Private student loan collections reform
   Actions against creditor, lender or collector for violations of provisions   CC §1788.208
Professional societies (See **PROFESSIONAL SOCIETIES**)
Proximate cause   CC §§3300, 3333
Psychotherapists (See **MALPRACTICE**)
Public utilities (See **PUBLIC UTILITIES**)
Punitive damages
   Claims against public entities and employees (See **CLAIMS AGAINST PUBLIC ENTITIES AND EMPLOYEES**)
   Criminal acts generally (See within this heading, "Criminal acts")
   Exemplary damages generally (See within this heading, "Exemplary damages")
Purchaser's loss, determination of   CC §3354
Quiet enjoyment, breach of warranty of   CC §3304
Quiet title action   CCP §§740, 741
Quitclaim deed, breach of agreement to execute   CC §3306a
Realty contracts (See within this heading, "Sale of realty")
Reasonableness requirements   CC §3359
Rental passenger vehicle transactions
   Actions for violation of provisions   CC §1939.25
Rental-purchase contracts, breach of   CC §1812.636
Rent collection for untenantable dwelling, landlord's liability for   CC §1942.4
   Attorneys' fees and cost of suit, landlord liability   CCP §1174.21
Rent control ordinances, violation of (See **RENT CONTROL**)
Request for statement of damages being sought   CCP §§425.11, 425.12
Rescission of contract, recovery of damages under claim for   CC §1692
Retail installment sales (See **RETAIL INSTALLMENT SALES**)

DAMAGES—Cont.

Retaliatory eviction   CC §1942.5
Sale of realty
   Convey land, contract to   CC §3306
   Purchase land, contract to   CC §3307
   Quitclaim deed, nondelivery of   CC §3306a
Sales contracts
   Generally   CC §§3353, 3354
   Realty (See within this heading, "Sale of realty")
School grounds
   Force, threat or other obstruction of access to facility   CC §1708.9
Seisin, breach of covenant of   CC §3304
Seller assisted marketing plans, breach of contract   CC §1812.218
Seller's loss, determination of   CC §3353
Serial number removed from article sold   CC §1710.1
Sexual battery   CC §1708.5
Sexually explicit depiction of individual
   Creation or disclosure   CC §1708.86
Sexual orientation violence
   Civil actions   CC §52.45
Signal dogs, owner's liability for damages caused by   CC §54.2
   Construction or application of provisions in issue, solicitor general notified   CC §55.2
Small estates without administration (See **SMALL ESTATES WITHOUT ADMINISTRATION**)
Social host's liability after serving alcoholic beverages   CC §1714
Specific performance (See **SPECIFIC PERFORMANCE**)
Sperm
   Unauthorized use or misuse of sperm, ova or embryo
      Civil action for damages   CC §1708.5.6
Stalking   CC §1708.7
Statement of damages being sought, request for   CCP §§425.11, 425.12
   Limitation on papers filed   CRC 3.250
Stop payment orders on checks, damages for   CC §1719
Student borrower bill of rights
   Enforcement of compliance with rights   CC §1788.103
Subcutaneous implanting of identification device, requiring of another   CC §52.7
Subdivision Map Act, noncompliance with   CC §2985.51
Summary judgment
   Summary adjudication of issues, claims, causes, etc within action   CCP §437c
Survival of actions (See **SURVIVAL OF ACTIONS**)
Timber, injury to   CC §3346, CCP §§733, 734
Trade secret, damages for loss caused by misappropriation of   CC §3426.3
Treble damages (See **TREBLE DAMAGES**)
Trees, injury to   CC §3346, CCP §733
Trusts (See **TRUSTS**)
Unauthorized signatures in campaign advertisement, action for damages for   CC §3344.5
Unclaimed property, delivery of   CCP §1321
Uniform Foreign-Money Claims Act   CCP §§676 to 676.16
Unlawful detainer (See **UNLAWFUL DETAINER**)
Unlicensed person, action for injury caused by   CCP §1029.8
Unperformed contracts for sale of realty, effect of   CC §886.020
Unruh Act, rate of interest under   CC §3289.5
Unruh Civil Rights Act violations   CC §§52, 52.1
   Construction or application of civil rights provisions in issue, solicitor general notified   CC §51.1
Untenantable dwelling, landlord's liability for rent collection for   CC §1942.4
   Attorneys' fees and cost of suit, landlord liability   CCP §1174.21
Valuation of property
   Measure of damages generally (See within this heading, "Measure of damages")
Verdict determining amount of recovery   CCP §626
Waiver of interest on damages recoverable   CC §3290
Warranties on goods sold, violation of   CC §§1794, 1794.1
Waste, actions for recovery of treble damages for   CCP §732
Water diversion cases   CCP §534
Weight loss programs, injury sustained under   CC §1694.9
Wholesale sales representatives, actions involving   CC §1738.15
Written instruments, loss of   CC §3356
Wrongful death actions (See **WRONGFUL DEATH**)

DAMS

Actions to restrain violations
   Cost and fee awards to attorney general prevailing in actions   CCP §1021.8
Easement rights to flow of water over land without obstruction from   CC §801
Public liability for injury caused by condition of reservoir   Gov §831.8

DANCERS

Minor's contracts for artistic services   Fam §§6750 to 6753

DANCE STUDIOS
Contracts regulated   CC §§1812.50 to 1812.69

DANGEROUS PREMISES   CC §846

DATA ANALYTICS
Judicial council advisory committee   CRC 10.68

DATA BROKER REGISTRATION   CC §§1798.99.80 to 1798.99.89
Administrative actions, time for bringing   CC §1798.99.89
Annual registration   CC §1798.99.82
Audits for compliance with deletion requests   CC §1798.99.86
Compilation and disclosure of metrics   CC §1798.99.85
Consumer privacy act
     Statutory construction of data broker registration provisions with consumer privacy act   CC §1798.99.88
Definitions   CC §1798.99.80
Deletion of data
     Accessible mechanism   CC §1798.99.86
     Duties of data broker on request of consumer   CC §1798.99.86
Enforcement of registration requirement   CC §1798.99.82
Fee for registration   CC §1798.99.82
Fines, enforcement of registration requirement   CC §1798.99.82
Fund   CC §1798.99.81
Information provided for registration   CC §1798.99.82
     Access by public to information filed   CC §1798.99.84
Injunction to enforce registration   CC §1798.99.82
Requirement of registration   CC §1798.99.82
Rulemaking by agency   CC §1798.99.87

DATA, ILLEGALLY OBTAINED OR ACCESSED
Purchase by unauthorized person   CC §1724
Sale   CC §1724

DATA PROCESSING (See COMPUTERS)

DATA SECURITY BREACH NOTICE
Customer records   CC §1798.82
Information practices   CC §1788.61

DATING SERVICES
Cancellation of agreement
     Buyer's right to cancel   CC §1694.1
     Noncompliance with statute, cancellation for   CC §1694.2
Damages recoverable   CC §1694.4
Death or disability of buyer, effect of   CC §1694.3
Defined   CC §1694
False and misleading advertisement, liability for   CC §1694.4
Installment payments
     Generally   CC §1694.2
     Refund or credit, buyer's right to   CC §1694.4
Online dating services
     Cancellation of agreement
         Method of cancellation   CC §1694.1
         Notice of right to cancel   CC §1694.2
     Dating safety awareness information
         Access   CC §1694.3
     Defined   CC §1694
     Reporting behavior of other users
         Providing mechanism for reporting by service   CC §1694.3
     Written contract requirement   CC §1694.2
Refund or credit of payments, buyer's right to   CC §1694.4
Relocation of buyer's residence, effect of   CC §1694.3
Terms of agreement   CC §1694.2
Void and unenforceable contracts, grounds for   CC §1694.4

DATING VIOLENCE
Victim service providers, personal information protection   CC §§1798.79.8 to 1798.79.95
     Definitions   CC §1798.79.8
     Disclosing personal information
         Grants, requiring disclosure as condition   CC §1798.79.9
         Injunctions to prevent   CC §1798.79.95
         Prohibited   CC §1798.79.9

DAVIS-STIRLING COMMON INTEREST DEVELOPMENT ACT
Common interest developments generally   CC §§4000 to 6150 (See **COMMON INTEREST DEVELOPMENTS**)

DAYCARE (See CHILD CARE)

DEAD BODIES
Juries of inquest (See **JURIES OF INQUEST**)

DEAD BODIES—Cont.
Restriction on reproducing photograph or video taken at scene of death or in course of postmortem examination or autopsy   CCP §129

DEADLOCK OF JURY
Discharge   CCP §616

DEAD MAN'S STATUTE   Ev §1261

DEAF AND HARD OF HEARING PERSONS
Access to public facilities   CC §54.1
     Construction or application of provisions in issue, solicitor general notified   CC §55.2
Administrative adjudicative proceeding, interpreters in   Gov §11435.10
Assistive listening systems in judicial proceedings   CC §54.8
Commercial and industrial common interest developments
     Disabled access
         Modification of separate interests   CC §6714
Court personnel, disabled, reasonable accommodation for   CRC JudAdminStand 10.25
Courts, access rights   CC §54.8
Criminal cases
     Admissibility of oral or written statements by deaf or hard-of-hearing persons in   Ev §754
Defined   CC §54.8, Ev §754
Interpreters
     Appointment by court or parties   Ev §754
     Assistive listening systems in judicial proceedings   CC §54.8
     Certification programs for interpreters, guidelines for   CRC 2.892
     Court-appointed interpreters for   Ev §754
     Generally (See **TRANSLATORS AND INTERPRETERS**)
     Guidelines   Ev §754
     Jurors, interpreters for   CCP §224
     Privileged communication, effect of interpreter's presence during   Ev §754.5
Jury (See **JURY**)
Jury service
     Eligibility for   CCP §§203, 228
     Sign language interpreters and other assistance   CC §54.8, CCP §224
Mobilehome parks, restrictions as to signal dogs in   CC §798.33
Privileged communications   Ev §754.5
     Effect of interpreter's presence during   Ev §754.5
Signal dogs, right to   CC §54.2
Speech-to-text equipment
     Court, access rights   CC §54.8
Telephone facilities, use of   CC §54.1
     Construction or application of provisions in issue, solicitor general notified   CC §55.2

DEALERS
Art dealers (See **ART DEALERS**)
Autographed sports memorabilia, sale of   CC §1739.7
Automobile manufacturers, transporters, dealers and sales professionals
     Restitution, licensee ordered to pay
         Effect of order for restitution   Gov §11519.1
Fair dealership law   CC §§80 to 86

DEATH
Administration of estates (See **ADMINISTRATION OF ESTATES**)
Administrator (See **EXECUTORS AND ADMINISTRATORS**)
Advance health care directives   Pro §§4670 to 4679 (See **HEALTH CARE DECISIONS LAW**)
Advancement, death of heir after receipt of   Pro §6409
Adverse possessor, death of   CCP §327
Advertising, unauthorized use of name or likeness of deceased personality in   CC §3344.1
Agency, termination of   CC §§2355, 2356
Annulment when spouse that was believed dead is living   Fam §2210
Appeal, right of   CCP §903
Attachment (See **ATTACHMENT**)
Attorneys (See **ATTORNEYS**)
Bailment, death of party to   CC §1934
Bank accounts, effect of death on multiple-party   Pro §§5302, 5405
Bible entries as evidence   Ev §1312
Cancellation of utility, cable, etc, services on behalf of deceased person
     In-person cancellation not to be required   Pro §217
Capital punishment (See **CAPITAL PUNISHMENT**)
Certificates
     Evidence of family history   Ev §§1315, 1316
     Forms
         Judicial council legal forms   CRCAppx A

DEATH—Cont.
  Certificates—Cont.
    International wills Pro §6389
    Records and recordings (See **RECORDS AND RECORDING**)
  Child support terminated on death of child Fam §2023
  Child victims
    Sealing autopsy report and evidence CCP §130
  Church records as evidence of Ev §1315
  Common accident causing (See **SIMULTANEOUS DEATH**)
  Community reputation concerning Ev §1314
  Conservators
    Generally (See **CONSERVATORS**)
    Notice of death of conservatee Pro §2361
  Contracts (See **CONTRACTS AND AGREEMENTS**)
  Convalescent home contract, death of patient terminating CC §1934.5
  Court reporter's death, effect of CCP §§657.1, 914
  Damages (See **DAMAGES**)
  Dance studio contract, refund under CC §1812.57
  Dating service contracts, payment liability under CC §1694.3
  Dissolution of marriage (See **DISSOLUTION OF MARRIAGE**)
  Enforcement of judgments (See **ENFORCEMENT OF JUDGMENTS**)
  Estates (See **DECEDENTS' ESTATES**)
  Executor (See **EXECUTORS AND ADMINISTRATORS**)
  Fact of death (See **FACT OF DEATH**)
  Family friends, statements concerning death by Ev §1311
  Fiduciary income and principal act
    Death of individual resulting in creation of estate or trust
      Beneficiary portion of net income Pro §16371
      Distributions Pro §16370
  Gang-related crime, decedent's sworn statement concerning (See **GANG VIOLENCE**)
  Gifts in view of death
    Creditors, recovery of property for benefit of Pro §5705
    Defined Pro §§5700, 5702
    Governing law Pro §5701
    Presumption of Pro §5703
    Revocability of CC §1148, Pro §5704
  Guardianship (See **GUARDIAN AND WARD**)
  Health care decisions (See **HEALTH CARE DECISIONS LAW**)
  Health care powers of attorney
    Notice of death of principal Pro §4691
  Health studios refunding fees because of CC §1812.89
  Homestead property owner, protection from lien on death of CCP §704.995
  Immunity of landowner for death of person committing felony on property CC §847
  Intestate succession (See **INTESTATE SUCCESSION**)
  Judgments and decrees
    Establishing fact of death Pro §204
    Rendering after death CCP §669
  Juries of inquest (See **JURIES OF INQUEST**)
  Landowner's immunity for death of person committing felony on property CC §847
  Malpractice judgment against health care provider, effect of death of judgment creditor on periodic payments under CCP §667.7
  Missing persons presumed dead (See **MISSING PERSONS**)
  Mobilehome tenant, rights of heirs of CC §798.78
  Multiple-party accounts, effect of death on Pro §§5302, 5405
  Neighbor's testimony concerning Ev §1314
  New trial, court reporter's death as grounds for CCP §657.1
  Nonprobate transfers (See **NONPROBATE TRANSFERS**)
  Nursing home contract, death of patient terminating CC §1934.5
  Power of appointment (See **POWER OF APPOINTMENT**)
  Power of attorney (See **POWER OF ATTORNEY**)
  Presumption of death of person missing person Ev §§667, 1282, Pro §12401
  Principal, death of CC §§2355, 2356
  Prisoners (See **PRISONERS**)
  Professional fiduciaries
    Deceased professional fiduciary Pro §9765
  Records as proof of Ev §§1281 to 1283, Pro §§210 to 212
  Relative's statements concerning Ev §1311
  Rent recovery after CC §825
  Reputation among family members concerning Ev §1313
  Sale of real property, failure to disclose death of prior occupant to buyer in connection with CC §1710.2
  Simultaneous death (See **SIMULTANEOUS DEATH**)
  Spousal support affected by death of party (See **SPOUSAL SUPPORT**)
  Statutes of limitation (See **STATUTES OF LIMITATION**)
  Superior courts (See **SUPERIOR COURTS**)
  Survival of actions (See **SURVIVAL OF ACTIONS**)
  Surviving spouse (See **SURVIVING SPOUSE**)

DEATH—Cont.
  Telegrams, priority for transmitting CC §2207
  Title and ownership (See **TITLE AND OWNERSHIP**)
  Transfer or sale of real property, failure to disclose death of prior occupant to buyer in connection with CC §1710.2
  Weight loss programs, payment liability under CC §1694.8
  Will probate (See **WILL PROBATE**)
  Wills (See **WILLS**)
  Witnesses unavailable due to Ev §240
  Wrongful death (See **WRONGFUL DEATH**)

DEATH PENALTY (See **CAPITAL PUNISHMENT**)

DEBENTURES (See **BONDS**)

DEBIT CARDS
Account numbers printed on receipts, restrictions concerning CC §1747.09
Appellate rules, supreme court and courts of appeal
  E-filing in supreme court and courts of appeal
    Fees for filing, methods of payment CRC 8.76
Cardholder's liability for unauthorized use
  Waiver of protections
    Void CC §1748.32
Consumer refunds offered by prepaid debit card
  Alternative method of receiving refund to be provided CC §1748.41
  Definitions CC §1748.40
Definitions CC §1748.30
Fax filing and service
  Fees paid by debit or credit card CRC 2.304
Filing fees
  Debit card payments CRC 3.100
Public utilities
  Surcharge on credit or debit card transaction, prohibition against
    Exception for electrical, gas or water corporation CC §1748.1
Receipts, printing of account numbers on CC §1747.09
Unauthorized use of card, cardholder's liability for CC §1748.31
  Waiver of protections
    Void CC §1748.32

DEBT BUYING
Credit services organizations
  Debt buyers
    Communication with credit services organizations about accounts CC §1789.134
Dismissal of civil actions
  Consumer debt
    Plaintiff debt buyer failing to appear or prepare to proceed CCP §581.5
Fair debt buying practices CC §§1788.50 to 1788.66 (See **FAIR DEBT BUYING PRACTICES**)

DEBT COLLECTION
Consumer debt collection CC §§1788 to 1788.33 (See **CONSUMER DEBT COLLECTION**)
Credit services organizations
  Debt collectors
    Communication with credit services organizations about accounts CC §1789.134
Educational debt collection practices CC §§1788.90 to 1788.94
  Definitions CC §1788.92
  Legislative findings and intent CC §1788.91
  Prohibited debt collection practices by schools CC §1788.93
  Short title of act CC §1788.90
  Transcript used as leverage to collect debt
    Prohibited debt collection practices by schools CC §1788.93
  Waivers CC §1788.94
Fair debt buying generally CC §§1788.50 to 1788.66 (See **FAIR DEBT BUYING PRACTICES**)
Private student loan collections reform CC §§1788.200 to 1788.211
Student loans
  Private student loan collections reform CC §§1788.200 to 1788.211

DEBTORS
Attachment (See **ATTACHMENT**)
Challenge of juror for implied bias, relationships giving rise to CCP §229
Child support
  Private child support collectors Fam §§5610 to 5616
Collection agencies (See **COLLECTION AGENCIES**)
Confession of judgments (See **CONFESSION OF JUDGMENTS**)
Creditors (See **CREDITORS**)

DEBTORS—Cont.
Defined   CC §3429
Joint debtors (See **JOINT DEBTORS**)

DEBTS
Administration of decedents' estates
   Generally (See **ADMINISTRATION OF ESTATES**)
   Claims against decedents' estates, debts arising from (See **CLAIMS AGAINST ESTATES**)
Attachment (See **ATTACHMENT**)
Bonds (See **BONDS**)
Claims against decedents' estates (See **CLAIMS AGAINST ESTATES**)
Coerced debt   CC §§1798.97.1 to 1798.97.6 (See **COERCED DEBT**)
Collection agencies (See **COLLECTION AGENCIES**)
Community property, debt liability of (See **COMMUNITY PROPERTY**)
Confession of judgments (See **CONFESSION OF JUDGMENTS**)
Consumer debt collection
   Fair debt buying generally   CC §§1788.50 to 1788.64 (See **FAIR DEBT BUYING PRACTICES**)
   Generally   CC §§1788 to 1788.33 (See **CONSUMER DEBT COLLECTION**)
Contractual basis for   CC §1428
Defined   CC §1788.2
Dismissal of civil actions
   Consumer debt
      Plaintiff debt buyer failing to appear or prepare to proceed   CCP §581.5
Dissolution of marriage (See **DISSOLUTION OF MARRIAGE**)
Enforcement of judgments (See **ENFORCEMENT OF JUDGMENTS**)
Fair debt buying practices   CC §§1788.50 to 1788.66 (See **FAIR DEBT BUYING PRACTICES**)
Fair debt settlement practices   CC §§1788.300 to 1788.307 (See **FAIR DEBT SETTLEMENT PRACTICES**)
Fraudulent transfers (See **VOIDABLE TRANSACTIONS**)
Fraud, validity in absence of   CC §3431
Homestead property, prohibition against acceleration of debt liability for lien on   CCP §704.810
Human trafficking
   Debts of victim attributable to human trafficking, findings as to   CC §52.5
Identity theft
   Collector's duties upon notice from victim of identity theft   CC §1788.18
Imprisonment because of   CCP §501
Inquiry by debtor, requirements for answering   CC §1720
Intestate share, effect on   Pro §6410
Joint debtors under judgment (See **JUDGMENTS**)
Legal process, false simulation of   CC §1788.16
Marital property, debt liability of (See **COMMUNITY PROPERTY**)
Medical debts   CC §1788.12
   Consumer credit reports   CC §§1785.20.6, 1785.27
Nonimprisonment in civil action for debt or tort   CCP §501
Obligations delivered to debtor as presumed paid   Ev §633
Preexisting debt   Ev §1152
Preferences   CC §3432
Reporting as to consumer credit, regulation of   CC §§1785.1 to 1785.4
Rosenthal Fair Debt Collection Practices Act   CC §§1788 to 1788.32
Separate property of spouse, debt liability of (See **COMMUNITY PROPERTY**)
Settlements
   Fair debt settlement practices   CC §§1788.300 to 1788.307
Small estates without administration (See **SMALL ESTATES WITHOUT ADMINISTRATION**)
Voidable transactions (See **VOIDABLE TRANSACTIONS**)

DECANTING OF TRUSTS
Uniform act   Pro §§19501 to 19530 (See **TRUST DECANTING, UNIFORM ACT**)

DECEDENTS' ESTATES
Accounts and accounting
   Waiver of accounting
      Effect   CRC 7.550
Administration (See **ADMINISTRATION OF ESTATES**)
Appointment of personal representatives
   Fee waivers   CRC 3.50 to 3.53, 7.5
Attorneys
   Probate attorneys
      Education requirements   CRC 10.478
      Qualifications   CRC 10.776, 10.777
Beneficiaries
   Death
      Notice   CRC 7.51

DECEDENTS' ESTATES—Cont.
Child support payments out of estate   Fam §3952
Claims against (See **CLAIMS AGAINST ESTATES**)
Consanguinity
   Degree of kinship or consanguinity   Pro §13
Continuances (See **CONTINUANCES**)
Corporate shares (See **CORPORATE SHARES AND SHAREHOLDERS**)
Courts
   Court investigators, probate attorneys and probate examiners
      Education of judicial branch personnel   CRC 10.478
      Qualifications   CRC 10.776, 10.777
   Supervision of   Pro §§9610 to 9614
Custody of children (See **CUSTODY OF CHILDREN**)
Dead man's statute   Ev §1261
Distribution
   Heirship determinations
      Executors and administrators, participation   Pro §11704
Donative transfers
   Presumption of fraud or undue influence   Pro §§21360 to 21392 (See **DONATIVE TRANSFERS**)
Escheat (See **ESCHEAT**)
Executors (See **EXECUTORS AND ADMINISTRATORS**)
Ex parte communications
   Restrictions   Pro §1051
Fees
   Filing fees in probate proceedings generally   Gov §§70650 to 70663
   Waivers of fees in probate cases   CRC 7.5
      Applicable provisions   CRC 3.50
      Judicial council forms   CRCAppx A
Fiduciary income and principal act
   Applicability of provisions   Pro §16322
      Place of administration as basis of applicability   Pro §16323
   Generally   Pro §§16320 to 16383
Forms
   Judicial council legal forms   CRCAppx A
   Notice to creditors to file claims against   Pro §9052
Guardian ad litem
   Accounting
      Waiver of accounting   CRC 7.550
   Disclosures   Pro §1003
Heirs
   Generally   Pro §§248 to 249.8
   Partition of real property act   CCP §§874.311 to 874.323
Homesteads (See **HOMESTEADS**)
Incapacitated professional fiduciary   Pro §2469
Interest on money
   Small estates without administration
      Real property succession, excuse from liability for interest   Pro §13211
      Surviving spouse, excuse from liability for interest   Pro §13565
Intestate succession (See **INTESTATE SUCCESSION**)
Judges
   Education of judges and subordinate judicial officers regularly assigned to probate cases   CRC 10.468
      Domestic violence issues   CRC 10.464
Kinship
   Degree of kinship or consanguinity   Pro §13
Liens and encumbrances against estate property
   Small estates, affidavit procedure   Pro §§13100 to 13117
Marital privilege   Ev §984
Nonprobate transfers
   Former spouses   Pro §§5040 to 5048
Notice   Pro §§1200 to 1266
   Delivery of notice
      Methods of delivery   Pro §1215
   Proof of   Pro §§1260 to 1266
Partition
   Partition of real property act   CCP §§874.311 to 874.323
Partnerships (See **PARTNERSHIPS**)
Personal property of estates
   Small estate dispositions without administration   Pro §§13100 to 13117
Physician-patient privilege   Ev §1000
Powers of appointment   Pro §§600 to 695
Predeceased spouse
   Defined   Pro §59
Probate attorneys
   Education requirements   CRC 10.478
   Qualifications   CRC 10.776, 10.777
Probate examiners
   Education requirements   CRC 10.478
   Qualifications   CRC 10.776, 10.777

DECEDENTS' ESTATES—Cont.
Probate rules generally   CRC 7.1 to 7.1105
Property of estates
    Liability for decedent's property   Pro §§13560 to 13565
    Restitution of decedent's property by surviving spouse   Pro §§13560 to 13565
Real property of estates
    Small estate dispositions without administration   Pro §§13200 to 13211
Restitution of decedent's property by surviving spouse   Pro §§13560 to 13565
Revocable transfer on death deeds   Pro §§5600 to 5698 (See **TRANSFER ON DEATH DEEDS**)
Securities (See **CORPORATE SHARES AND SHAREHOLDERS**)
Severance of matters associated with proceedings and actions under Probate Code   Pro §801
Small estates (See **SMALL ESTATES**)
Small estate set-aside
    Forms
        Judicial council forms   CRCAppx A
    Periodic adjustment of dollar amounts   Pro §890
Small estates without administration (See **SMALL ESTATES WITHOUT ADMINISTRATION**)
Special notice   Pro §§1260 to 1266
Spousal privilege   Ev §984
Surviving domestic partners
    Health insurance
        Survivors of firefighters and peace officers, continuance   Pro §13600
Surviving spouses
    Health insurance
        Survivors of firefighters and peace officers, continuance   Pro §13600
    Liability for decedent's property   Pro §§13560 to 13565
Taxation, generally (See **ESTATE TAX**)
Tax liens and other federal liens, filing of notice of   CCP §2101
Testate succession (See **WILLS**)
Transfer on death deeds   Pro §§5600 to 5698
Trusts (See **TRUSTS**)
Undue influence
    Definition of undue influence   Pro §86
    Wrongful taking, concealment, etc of property of conservatee, minor, elder, dependent adult, etc   Pro §859
Uniform Parentage Act
    Vacation or setting aside of judgment
        Payments made in good faith by estate, trustees, insurers, etc., based on paternity judgment   Fam §7649.5
Voidable transactions
    Executor's duty to recover fraudulently conveyed estate property   Pro §9653
    Recovering property for creditors of   Pro §9653
    Small estate dispositions without administration   Pro §§13100 to 13117
Waivers
    Accounting
        Effect   CRC 7.550
Wrongful taking, concealment, etc of property of conservatee, minor, elder, dependent adult, etc   Pro §859

DECEIT (See **FRAUD**)

DECENCY (See **INDECENCY AND OBSCENITY**)

DECEPTIVE PRACTICES   CC §1770

DECISIONS
Generally (See **JUDGMENTS**)
Administrative agencies
    Adjudicative proceeding (See **ADMINISTRATIVE ADJUDICATION**)
    Office of Administrative Law (See **ADMINISTRATIVE PROCEDURE ACT**)
Findings of fact (See **FINDINGS**)
Statement of decision (See **STATEMENT OF DECISION**)

DECLARATION AGAINST INTEREST (See **ADMISSIONS**)

DECLARATIONS
Child support, income and expense declaration (See **CHILD SUPPORT**)
Common interest developments (See **COMMON INTEREST DEVELOPMENTS**)
Defined   CCP §116.130
Dissolution of marriage (See **DISSOLUTION OF MARRIAGE**)
Economic litigation provision for use of declaration in lieu of direct testimony   CCP §98
Emancipation of minors (See **EMANCIPATION OF MINORS**)
Homesteads (See **HOMESTEADS**)

DECLARATIONS—Cont.
Identity of judgment debtor, declaration under penalty of perjury executed by judgment creditor as to   CCP §680.135
Judicial officer's power to take and certify   CCP §179
Legal separation, assets and liabilities disclosure required for   Fam §§2100 to 2113
Mortgages, satisfaction of   CC §2941.7
Oath defined to include declaration   CCP §17
Part offered in evidence   Ev §356
Penalty of perjury, declaration of written instrument executed under   CCP §2015.5
Property   Fam §2330.5
Property declarations defined   Fam §115
Small claims court (See **SMALL CLAIMS COURTS**)
Survival of actions, execution of supporting declaration in (See **SURVIVAL OF ACTIONS**)
Trust deeds, satisfaction of   CC §2941.7
Written instrument executed under penalty of perjury, declaration of   CCP §2015.5

DECLARATORY JUDGMENTS
Administrative law
    Action for declaratory relief (See **ADMINISTRATIVE PROCEDURE ACT**)
    Adjudication proceeding, declaratory decision in (See **ADMINISTRATIVE ADJUDICATION**)
Coerced debt
    Establishing debt as coerced, action or cross-complaint   CC §1798.97.3
Common interest developments
    Board meetings
        Actions for declaratory or equitable relief to enforce provisions   CC §4955
    Member elections
        Action for declaratory or equitable relief to enforce   CC §5145
Consumer privacy rights
    Actions for damages, injunctions, declaratory relief, etc
        Security practices and procedures not in place   CC §1798.150
Contracts, determining rights under   CCP §1060
Cross-complaint provisions, applicability of   CCP §426.60
Cumulative remedies   CCP §1062
Deeds, determining rights under   CCP §1060
Health care providers, insurer of   CCP §1062.5
Identity theft, declaratory relief in actions involving   CC §1798.93
Income tax liability of nonresident   CCP §1060.5
Limited civil cases, unavailability of declaratory relief in   CCP §580
Necessary relief   CCP §1061
Parks, purpose in taking for   CCP §1240.700
Precedence over other matters   CCP §1062.3
Professional liability insurer's liability   CCP §1062.5
Rivers, determining natural flow of   CCP §1060
Will probate
    Construction of writing   CCP §1060
    No contest clauses, declaratory relief   Pro §§21320 to 21322

DECREES (See **JUDGMENTS**)

DEDICATION
Decedent's estate, property of   Pro §§9900, 9901
Prescriptive use   CC §§813, 1007
Public land, private property used as   CC §1009
Quieting title action, effect on   CCP §§771.010, 771.020
Title held under   CC §670
Trust property   Pro §16230

DEEDS (See also **COVENANTS AND CONDITIONS**)
Acknowledgments
    Superior court fees, specified services   Gov §70626
Administrators of decedents' estates (See **EXECUTORS AND ADMINISTRATORS**)
Adverse possession by person claiming title founded on written instrument   CCP §§322, 323
Advertising for sale, restrictions on   CC §712
Boundary determination   CCP §2077
Commercial and industrial common interest developments
    Liberal construction   CC §6602
    Physical boundaries prevail over description in deed, plan, etc   CC §6604
Conclusive against grantor   CC §1107
Conflicting clauses   CC §1070
Consolidation of   CC §1093
Construction of   CC §§1066 to 1070, CCP §2077
Copies, admissibility of   Ev §§1600 to 1605

DEEDS (—Cont.)
Declaratory judgments determining rights under   CCP §1060
Delivery   CC §§1054 to 1056, 1059, 1627
Description   CCP §2077
Executors of decedents' estates (See **EXECUTORS AND ADMINISTRATORS**)
Fee-simple title presumed   CC §1105
Form for transfer   CC §1092
Hearsay rule affecting admissibility of statements in   Ev §1330
Highways, deed for land bordering   CC §1112
Implied covenants   CC §1113
Inheritance, use of words of   CC §1072
Mortgage, deed shown as   CC §§2925, 2950
Names
    Changed by grantee   CC §1096
    Unnamed party as grantee   CC §1085
Partition action   CCP §873.230
Presumptions of authenticity   Ev §643
Privileged communications in determining validity of   Ev §§959 to 961, 1002, 1003, 1021, 1022
Quiet enjoyment under   CC §1463
Quitclaim deeds (See **QUITCLAIM DEEDS**)
Recording (See **RECORDS AND RECORDING**)
Redelivery   CC §1058
Revocable transfer on death deeds   Pro §§5600 to 5696 (See **TRANSFER ON DEATH DEEDS**)
Sheriff's deed (See **ENFORCEMENT OF JUDGMENTS**)
Statute of limitation   CC §1067
Title to   CC §994
Transfer on death deeds   Pro §§5600 to 5696 (See **TRANSFER ON DEATH DEEDS**)
Trust deeds and mortgages (See **TRUST DEEDS AND MORTGAGES**)
Unclaimed property, controller executing deeds for   CCP §1376

DEEDS OF TRUST (See **TRUST DEEDS AND MORTGAGES**)

DEEPFAKES
Sexually explicit depiction of individual, creation or disclosure
    Actions for damages   CC §1708.86

DEFACEMENT OF PROPERTY
Art works, defacement of   CC §987
Parent's liability for acts of minor children   CC §1714.1

DEFAMATION (See **LIBEL AND SLANDER**)

DEFAULT JUDGMENTS   CCP §585, CRC 3.110
Administrative adjudication, default by respondent in   Gov §11520
Affidavits
    Civil Code provisions, stating action not subject to   CCP §585.5
    Copy of application mailed to defendant, stating that   CCP §587
    Evidence presented by   CCP §585
Answers to complaint   CCP §§585, 586
Application for entry of default   CCP §§585 to 587
Associations   CCP §412.30
Attorney's fees   CCP §585
    Fee schedules   CRC 3.1800
Case management
    Collections cases
        Time for default judgment   CRC 3.740
Child support proceedings (See **CHILD SUPPORT**)
Complaint
    Conformity to pleadings   CCP §580
    Defined   CCP §587.5
    Failure to respond   CCP §§585, 586, CRC 3.110
Conformity to pleadings   CCP §580
Consumer debt collection
    Hospital debt   CC §1788.185
Contracts   CCP §§585, 585.5
Corporations   CCP §412.30
Costs   CRC 3.1700
Court reporter's fees   Gov §69949
Damages
    Determination of damages   CCP §585
    Reservation of right to seek punitive damages on default   CCP §§425.12, 425.115
Definitions   CCP §587.5
Demurrer to complaint   CCP §§585, 586
Destroyed land records relief law proceedings   CCP §751.14
Disallowed before expiration of time to respond   CCP §418.10
Dismissal, motions for   CCP §§585, 586
Dissolution of marriage (See **DISSOLUTION OF MARRIAGE**)

DEFAULT JUDGMENTS—Cont.
Documents to be submitted   CRC 3.1800
Eminent domain proceedings   CCP §1250.125
Employee benefit plan joined as party in family law proceeding   Fam §2065
Enforcement of judgments (See **ENFORCEMENT OF JUDGMENTS**)
Excusable neglect, relief from   CCP §473
Exemplary damages, reservation of right to seek   CCP §§425.12, 425.115
Fair debt buying practices
    Default judgments against debtor   CC §1788.60
        Setting aside default and leave to defend, motion and grounds   CC §1788.61
Family law rules (See **FAMILY RULES**)
Fee schedules   CRC 3.1800
Fictitious name, requirement for entry of default against person sued under   CCP §474
Forcible entry and detainer proceedings   CCP §1169
Grounds   CCP §§585, 586
Homestead, default at hearing on application for sale of   CCP §704.790
Judge's power to act, effect of proceedings for disqualification on   CCP §170.4
Judicial council form
    Mandatory use   CRC 3.1800
Law and motion rules applicable to proceedings to obtain or set aside   CRC 3.1103
Local rules of superior court, failure to comply with   CCP §575.2
Mistake, inadvertence, surprise or excusable neglect, relief from   CCP §473
Nonjury cases   CCP §636
Opening default
    Setting aside generally (See within this heading, **"Setting aside"**)
Partnerships   CCP §412.30
Paternity proceedings under uniform parentage act
    Default judgment of parentage
        Reconsideration   Fam §7646
Possession of real property   CCP §585
Prescriptive rights   CCP §585
Private student loan collections reform
    Actions against creditor, lender or collector for violations of provisions   CC §1788.208
    Actual notice not provided
        Motion to set aside default   CC §1788.207
    Requirements for default judgments against debtor   CC §1788.206
Procedure   CCP §585
Publication, service by   CCP §585
Punitive damages, reservation of right to seek   CCP §§425.12, 425.115
Quash, motion to   CCP §§585, 586
Quieting title action   CCP §764.010
Real property, recovery of   CCP §585
Relief granted, conformity to pleadings of   CCP §580
Relief of default (See within this heading, **"Setting aside"**)
Request for entry of default
    Judicial council legal forms   CRCAppx A
Setting aside
    Action commenced in improper court   CCP §585.5
    Mistake, inadvertence, surprise or excusable neglect, relief from   CCP §473
    Reviewing court relieving from default occasioned by failure to comply with rules   CRC 8.60
    Service of summons too late to defend action   CCP §473.5
Small claims court motions to vacate default judgments   CCP §§116.710 to 116.798
State agency proceedings, default by respondent in   Gov §11520
Stay of proceedings, motion for   CCP §§585, 586
Striking of pleadings, motions for   CCP §§585, 586
Summons not timely served as grounds to set aside   CCP §473.5
Supporting affidavits (See within this heading, **"Affidavits"**)
Time limits
    Entry of default on expiration of time to answer   CCP §585
Title, recovery of   CCP §585
Transfer, motion for   CCP §§585, 586
Unknown persons   CCP §474
Unlawful detainer   CCP §1169
    COVID-19, emergency rule   CRCAppx I Emer Rule 1
Vacation of (See within this heading, **"Setting aside"**)

DEFECTS
Disregard of nonprejudicial error   CCP §475

DEFENDANT
Complaints amended, service of   CCP §471.5
Designation of parties   CCP §308
Interpleader (See **INTERPLEADER**)
One defendant, judgment for or against   CCP §§578, 579

DEFENDANT—Cont.
Permissive joinder   CCP §379
Process (See **PROCESS AND SERVICE OF PROCESS**)
Protective order's effect on   CCP §486.070
Unknown defendants (See **UNKNOWN PERSONS**)
Unwilling plaintiff made defendant   CCP §382
Venue in county of residence of defendant   CCP §395
Witness in criminal case, calling defendant as   Ev §§930, 940

DEFENSE OF MARRIAGE
Gay marriage ban
    Recognition of certain same sex marriages contracted in other jurisdictions
        Dissolution, annulment or legal separation, jurisdiction   Fam §§2010, 2320
    Repeal   Fam §300

DEFENSES
Answer, defenses separately stated in   CCP §431.30
Assignees, action by   CCP §368
Construction defects, actions for
    Builders   CC §945.5
Fair debt buying practices
    Violation of provisions   CC §1788.62
Fair debt settlement practices
    Actions to enforce
        Unintentional violation   CC §1788.305
Firearms and other weapons
    Actions to prevent enforcement of laws
        What defenses not permitted   CCP §1021.11
Interstate family support
    Contest of validity or enforcement of registered order
        Defenses and burdens of proof applicable   Fam §5700.607
    Nonparentage as defense, prohibition   Fam §5700.315
Private student loan collections reform
    Actions against creditor, lender or collector for violations of provisions
        Unintentional violation defense   CC §1788.208
Public employees, defenses of   Gov §§995 to 996.6
Rape and other sex offenses
    Consent not deemed defense in cases of adults in position of authority over minors   CC §1708.5.5
Spouses sued together   CCP §370
Summary judgment motion where action is without merit or defense   CCP §437c
Unlawful detainer   CCP §1164
    Immigration or citizenship status as motivator of landlord action   CCP §1161.4
    Lease provisions penalizing good faith summoning of law enforcement or emergency assistance   CC §1946.8
Violent video games
    Minors
        Sale or rental to minor   CC §1746.1

DEFENSES IN CIVIL ACTIONS
Directed trusts
    Breach of trust   Pro §16624

DEFERRED COMPENSATION PLANS
Employee pension benefit plan defined   Fam §80

DEFIBRILLATORS
Entertainment facility
    Notice regarding human trafficking   CC §52.66
Immunity from liability for emergency care   CC §1714.21

DEFICIENCY JUDGMENTS
Automobile conditional sales contracts, recovery under   CC §2983.2
COVID-19, emergency rule   CRCAppx I Emer Rule 2
First mortgage or deed of trust on dwelling of less than 4 units
    When deficiency judgment prohibited   CCP §580e
Foreclosure proceedings
    COVID-19, emergency rule   CRCAppx I Emer Rule 2
Liens, foreclosure on   CCP §726
Mechanic's lien
    Action to enforce   CC §8466
Mobilehome, repossession of   CC §2983.8
Mortgages, foreclosure on   CCP §§580a to 580e, 726
Refinancing purchase money loans
    No deficiency judgment   CCP §580b
Retail installment sales, repossession after   CC §1812.5
Trust deeds, foreclosure on   CCP §§580a to 580e, 726
When not appropriate   CCP §580b
    Sale under deed of trust, mortgage, etc   CCP §580d

DEFINITIONS
Absentee   Pro §§1403, 3700
Absolute ownership   CC §§678, 679
Abuse   Ev §1037.7
    Restraining orders, juvenile rules   CRC 5.630
    Transitional housing program misconduct   CC §1954.12
Abuse against a child
    Child custody   Fam §3011
Abused
    Conservatorships   Pro §2112
Abuse or violence
    Change of lock upon request by eligible tenant   CC §1941.5
    Landlord and tenant   CCP §1161.3
    Screening of tenants   CC §1946.9
Abusive litigation
    Legally protected health care services   CC §1798.300
Accepted debit card
    Consumer refunds offered by prepaid debit card   CC §1748.40
Accommodation
    Persons with disabilities, accommodations requested of courts   CRC 1.100
Accord   CC §1521
Account debtor   CCP §§481.020, 680.120
Accounting period
    Fiduciary income and principal act   Pro §16321
Accounts   Pro §§21 to 23, 5122
    Child support delinquency, financial institution match system   Fam §17453
    Fiduciary access to digital assets   Pro §871
Accounts receivable   CCP §§481.030, 680.130
Account statements
    Conservators and guardians   Pro §2620
Accredited agencies
    Intercountry adoptions   Fam §8900.5
Accredited educational institution
    Probate cases, qualifications of personnel responsible for   CRC 10.776
Act
    Guardianship and conservatorship, Indian child welfare act applicability   CRC 7.1015
Action   CC §2132b, CCP §§22, 337.15, 363
    Appellate rules, superior court appeals   CRC 8.803
    Civil discovery act   CCP §2016.020
    Civil rules, coordination of complex actions   CRC 3.501
    Construction defects, limitation of actions   CC §941
    Family rules   CRC 5.2
    Rules of court   CRC 1.6
Active attorney in good standing of bar of a United States state, jurisdiction, possession, territory or dependency
    Attorney temporarily in California as part of litigation   CRC 9.47
    Attorney temporarily in California providing nonlitigation services   CRC 9.48
Active licensee in good standing of bar of a United States state, jurisdiction, possession, territory or dependency
    Attorney practice, registered military spouse attorneys   CRC 9.41.1
    Registered in-house counsel   CRC 9.46
    Registered legal aid attorneys   CRC 9.45
Actual agency   CC §§2298, 2299
Actual authority of agent   CC §2316
Actual cost
    Domestic violence, protection orders   CCP §527.9
Actual fraud   CC §1572
Actual malice   CC §48a
Actual moisture barrier
    Construction defects, actions for   CC §895
Actual notice   CC §18
Additional charges
    Rental passenger vehicle transactions, business program sponsors   CC §1939.21
Additional financial information
    Mobilehome parks, management approval of mobilehome purchaser   CC §798.74
Additional mandatory charges
    Rental passenger vehicle transactions   CC §1939.01
Add-on-case
    Civil rules, coordination of complex actions   CRC 3.501
Adequate documentation
    Coerced debt   CC §1798.97.1
Adequate notice   CC §1747.02
Adjacent
    Greenway easements   CC §816.52
Adjacent dwelling unit
    Pesticides   CC §1940.8.5

DEFINITIONS—Cont.
Adjoining
    Fences, boundaries and monuments, adjoining landowners CC §841
Adjudicative records
    Court records, public access CRC 10.500
Adjustment programs CC §1795.90
Administrative law judge
    Administrative adjudications, formal hearings Gov §11500
Admissibility or inadmissibility of evidence Ev §400
Admitted surety insurer CCP §995.120
    Mechanics' liens CC §8002
Adoptee
    Adoption, sibling contact information requests CRC 5.460
Adoption service
    Intercountry adoptions Fam §8900.5
Adoption service provider Fam §8502
Adoptive parent Fam §8503
ADR process
    Civil rules CRC 3.800
Adult Fam §6501
    Conservators, interstate jurisdiction, transfer and recognition Pro §1982
Adverse actions
    Investigative consumer reporting agencies, disclosures when not using agency CC §1786.53
    Screening of tenants CC §1946.9
Adverse information CC §1799.101
Adverse possession CCP §325
Advertisements
    Rental-purchase contracts CC §1812.622
Advertising and marketing
    Consumer privacy rights CC §1798.140
Advisory bodies
    Judicial council advisory bodies, meetings CRC 10.75
Affidavit CCP §2003
Affidavit of identity CCP §680.135
Affiliate CCP §1800
    Vehicle history reports CC §1784.1
Affinity CCP §17
    Juvenile rules CRC 5.502
Affinity, in marriage relation Fam §6205
Affirmative authorization
    Genetic privacy CC §56.18
Affordable housing developments
    Recorded restrictive covenants, unenforceability in face of approved and recorded restrictive covenant affordable housing modification document CC §714.6
Affordable rent
    Recorded restrictive covenants, unenforceability in face of approved and recorded restrictive covenant affordable housing modification document CC §714.6
Agency CC §§1798.3, 2295
    Administrative adjudications, formal hearings Gov §11500
Agency adoption Fam §8506
Agency members
    Administrative adjudications, formal hearings Gov §11500
Agent CC §§1086, 2295, Pro §5124
    Fiduciary access to digital assets Pro §871
    Motor vehicle liens CC §3068.1
Age of majority
    Vlogging, minors Fam §6650
Aggravation
    Sentencing rules, determinate sentencing CRC 4.405
Aggregate consumer information
    Consumer privacy rights CC §1798.140
Aggrieved person
    Settlement of employment disputes CCP §1002.5
Aggrieved person, provider, or other entity
    Legally protected health care services CC §1798.300
Agreements
    Arbitration CCP §1280
    Parol evidence rule CCP §1856
Airport concession fees
    Rental passenger vehicle transactions CC §1939.01
ALPR end users
    Automated license plate recognition systems (ALPR), data security CC §1798.90.5
ALPR information
    Automated license plate recognition systems (ALPR), data security CC §1798.90.5

DEFINITIONS—Cont.
ALPR operators
    Automated license plate recognition systems (ALPR), data security CC §1798.90.5
ALPR systems
    Automated license plate recognition systems (ALPR), data security CC §1798.90.5
Altered depictions
    Sexually explicit depiction of individual, actions for damages CC §1708.86
Alternate confidential intermediary
    Adoption, sibling contact information requests CRC 5.460
Alternative dispute resolution
    Common interest developments CC §5925
Alternative dispute resolution process CRC 3.800
Alternative test method
    Animal testing, restrictions against CC §1834.9.3
Amenability
    Judicial administration, risk/needs assessment use in sentencing CRC JudAdminStand 4.35
Amended pleading
    Family rules CRC 5.74
    Probate rules CRC 7.3
Amendment to a pleading
    Family rules CRC 5.74
    Probate rules CRC 7.3
Ammunition
    Firearm industry standards of conduct CC §3273.50
Amount financed
    Automobile sales finance CC §2981
Anabolic steroids CC §1812.97 (Title 2.55 version of section)
Anaphylaxis
    Epinephrine auto-injector administration, immunity from liability CC §1714.23
Ancillary administration Pro §12501
Animal CC §3504
    Animal research and testing limitations CC §1834.9
    Landlord and tenant, requiring declawing or devocalizing animals as condition of occupancy CC §1942.7
Animal test
    Cosmetics, animal testing to develop or manufacture CC §1834.9.5
Animal trusts
    Decanting of trusts, trusts for care of animals Pro §19523
An individual who would have a conflict of interest
    Guardians and conservators Pro §2662
Anonymous witness program CC §48.9
Antiques CC §1799.100
Appear remotely
    Remote appearances, civil cases generally CRC 3.672
Appellant CCP §902
    Appeals CRC 8.10
    Appellate rules, superior court appeals CRC 8.803
    Small claims appeals CRC 8.952
Appliances
    Rental-purchase contracts CC §1812.622
Applicable express warranty
    Automobile warranties CCP §871.21
Applicable law
    Arbitrators, ethics standards for neutral arbitrators CRC ArbEthicsStand 2
Applicable value
    Fiduciary income and principal act, unitrust Pro §16330
Applicant
    Adoption Fam §8509
    Fee waivers, conservatorships or guardianships Gov §68631.5
    Juries and jurors, permanent medical excuse CRC 2.1009
    Landlord and tenant, reusable tenant screening report CC §1950.1
    Persons with disabilities, accommodations requested of courts CRC 1.100
    Tribal court civil money judgment act CCP §1732
Application
    Interstate family support
        Convention support proceedings Fam §5700.701
Application-agnostic
    Net neutrality CC §3100
Application for occupancy
    Landlord and tenant, requiring declawing or devocalizing animals as condition of occupancy CC §1942.7
Application for stay and early evaluation conference
    Construction-related accessibility claims, compliance with standards CC §55.52
Application screening fee
    Landlord and tenant, reusable tenant screening report CC §1950.1

DEFINITIONS—Cont.

Appointed attorney
    Death penalty appeals and habeas corpus proceedings   CRC 8.601
    Guardianship or conservatorship proceedings, attorney qualifications   CRC 7.1101

Appointed counsel
    Death penalty appeals and habeas corpus proceedings   CRC 8.601
    Guardianship or conservatorship proceedings, attorney qualifications   CRC 7.1101

Appointee
    Power of appointment   Pro §610

Appointing authorities
    Interpreters and translators   Ev §754

Appointive property
    Power of appointment   Pro §610
    Trust decanting, uniform act   Pro §19502

Apportionment rate   CCP §1268.350

Appropriate trade premises
    Home solicitation sales contracts   CC §1689.5

Approved applications
    COVID-19 rental housing recovery act   CCP §1179.09

Appurtenances   CC §662

Arbitrators
    Ethics standards for neutral arbitrators   CRC ArbEthicsStand 22

Armenian genocide victim
    Limitation of actions   CCP §§354.4, 354.45

Arrearages   Fam §5201
Art dealer   CC §1740

Artistic or creative services
    Minors' employment contracts, artistic, entertainment or professional sports   Fam §6750

Artists   CC §986

Artwork or other personal property
    Limitation of actions   CCP §338.2

Ascertainable standard
    Trust decanting, uniform act   Pro §19502

As is sales   CC §1791.3

Assessments
    Court-ordered child custody evaluation   CRC 5.220

Asset-backed securities
    Fiduciary income and principal act   Pro §16321

Assets of a debtor
    Voidable transactions   CC §3439.01

Assigned judge
    Civil rules, coordination of complex actions   CRC 3.501

Assigned obligee   Fam §5214
Assignment for benefit of creditors   CCP §§493.010, 1800
Assignment order   Fam §5202

Assisted housing development
    Rent setting and limitations   CC §1947.13

Assisted reproduction
    Uniform parentage act   Fam §7606

Assisted reproduction agreement
    Surrogacy or donor facilitators   Fam §7960
    Uniform parentage act   Fam §7606

Assisting counsel or entity
    Death penalty appeals and habeas corpus proceedings   CRC 8.601

Assistive devices   CC §1791

Assistive technology device
    Shared mobility devices   CC §2505

Associate counsel
    Death penalty appeals and habeas corpus proceedings   CRC 8.601

Associated waterproofing systems
    Common interest developments, financial reserve planning   CC §5551

Association
    Commercial and industrial common interest developments   CC §6528
    Common interest developments, construction defect dispute resolution   CC §6000

Association election materials
    Common interest developments, fiscal matters   CC §5200

Association records
    Common interest developments, fiscal matters   CC §5200

Asynchronous education
    Judicial administration rules, continuing education of judicial branch   CRC 10.493

At-death transfer
    Will construction   Pro §21104

At risk of entering foster care
    Juvenile rules   CRC 5.502

Attach
    Appellate rules, superior court appeals   CRC 8.803

DEFINITIONS—Cont.

Attach—Cont.
    Appellate rules, supreme court and courts of appeals   CRC 8.10

Attachment   CCP §§481.010 to 481.225
    Appellate rules, superior court appeals   CRC 8.803
    Appellate rules, supreme court and courts of appeals   CRC 8.10

Attorney
    Appellate rules, superior court appeals   CRC 8.803
    Family rules   CRC 5.2
    Rules of court   CRC 1.6

Attorney general
    False claims act, filing records under seal   CRC 2.570

Auction company
    Autographed memorabilia   CC §1739.7

Auctioneer
    Autographed memorabilia   CC §1739.7

Auctions   CC §1812.601

Authentication
    Connected devices, security   CC §1798.91.05

Authorized agent
    Data broker registration   CC §1798.99.80
    Pesticides   CC §1940.8.5

Authorized driver
    Rental passenger vehicle transactions   CC §1939.01

Authorized fiduciary
    Trust decanting, uniform act   Pro §19502

Authorized person
    Electronic court records   CRC 2.502

Authorized representative
    Juries and jurors, permanent medical excuse   CRC 2.1009
    Sexually explicit depiction of individual, actions for damages   CC §1708.86

Authorized submitter
    Electronic recording delivery systems   Gov §27390

Authorized surety company   CCP §995.120

Authorized to appear
    Attorney temporarily in California as part of litigation   CRC 9.47

Autographed collectibles
    Autographed memorabilia   CC §1739.7

Automated clearinghouse   CCP §1532
    Commercial financing transactions with small businesses   CC §1799.300

Automated clearinghouse credit   CCP §1532
Automated clearinghouse debit   CCP §1532

Automated license plate recognition end-users
    Automated license plate recognition systems (ALPR), data security   CC §1798.90.5

Automated license plate recognition information
    Automated license plate recognition systems (ALPR), data security   CC §1798.90.5

Automated license plate recognition operators
    Automated license plate recognition systems (ALPR), data security   CC §1798.90.5

Automated license plate recognition systems
    Automated license plate recognition systems (ALPR), data security   CC §1798.90.5

Awards
    Arbitration   CCP §1280

Away court
    Court interpreters, cross-assignments   CRC 10.762

Baggage   CC §2181
Bail   CC §2780, CCP §995.185
Balloon payment loans   CC §§2924i, 2957
Bank-offered spot rate   CCP §676.1

Banks
    Limitation of actions, Armenian genocide victims   CCP §354.45

Base term
    Sentencing rules, determinate sentencing   CRC 4.405

Basin
    Groundwater rights actions   CCP §832

Belief
    Attorney professional conduct   ProfC 1.0.1

Believes
    Attorney professional conduct   ProfC 1.0.1

Beneficial owner
    Landlord and tenant
        Year's continuous, lawful occupation acting as limitation on termination of tenancy   CC §1946.2

Beneficiary   Pro §§24, 262, 5126
    Equity lines of credit, suspending and closing line on borrower's instruction   CC §2943.1
    Fiduciary income and principal act   Pro §16321

DEFINITIONS—Cont.
- Beneficiary —Cont.
  - Mortgages and deeds of trust   CC §2943
  - Transfer on death deeds   Pro §5608
  - Trust decanting, uniform act   Pro §19502
- Beneficiary form
  - TOD security registration act   Pro §5501
- Beneficiary statement   CC §2943
- Beneficiary with disability
  - Trust decanting, uniform act   Pro §19513
- Best interest of child
  - Court-ordered child custody evaluation   CRC 5.220
  - Custody of children, mediation   CRC 5.210
  - Family rules   CRC 5.2
- Bill   CC §2132b
- Billing agents
  - Landlord and tenant, water service in multifamily residential rental buildings   CC §1954.202
  - Mobilehomes and mobilehome parks, water service billing   CC §798.40
- Billing error   CC §1747.02
- Bill of sale   CC §1053
- Biological samples
  - Genetic privacy   CC §56.18
- Biometric information
  - Consumer privacy rights   CC §1798.140
- Birth parent   Fam §8512
- Blanket encumbrance   CC §1812.300
- Board
  - Commercial and industrial common interest developments   CC §6530
- Board meetings
  - Common interest developments   CC §4090
- Bonding company   CCP §995.120
- Bonds   CCP §349.2
- Bondsman   CCP §995.185
- Book account   CCP §337a
- Booking photographs
  - Commercial use of booking photographs   CC §1798.91.1
- Bookkeeping services   CC §1799
- Books
  - Reader privacy act   CC §1798.90
- Book service
  - Reader privacy act   CC §1798.90
- Borrower   CC §3030
  - COVID-19 small landlord and homeowner relief act   CC §3273.1
  - Deeds of trust and mortgages, secured party access to inspect for environmental damage   CC §2929.5
  - Mortgages   CC §2920.5
  - Private student loan collections reform   CC §1788.201
  - Receivers   CCP §564
  - Student borrower bill of rights   CC §1788.100
- Borrower's instruction to suspend and close equity line of credit
  - Equity lines of credit, suspending and closing line on borrower's instruction   CC §2943.1
- Borrower with disabilities
  - Student borrower bill of rights   CC §1788.100
- Borrower working in public service
  - Student borrower bill of rights   CC §1788.100
- Bracero
  - Actions to recover savings fund amounts   CCP §354.7
- Breach of security system
  - Customer records, computerized personal information   CC §§1798.82, 1798.84
  - Information practices, breach of security system   CC §1798.29
- Breach of trust
  - Directed trusts   Pro §16602
- Brief legal services
  - Electronic court records   CRC 2.502
- Broadband
  - Digital equity bill of rights   CC §3122
- Broadband internet access service
  - Net neutrality   CC §3100
- Broadcast application
  - Pesticides   CC §1940.8.5
- Broadcasting
  - Court proceedings, photographing, recording and broadcasting   CRC 1.150
- Broker
  - Commercial financing transactions with small businesses   CC §1799.300
- Broker of construction trucking services
  - Construction trucking services brokers, payment of transportation charges   CC §3322

DEFINITIONS—Cont.
- Budget meetings
  - Judicial council meetings   CRC 10.5
- Builder
  - Common interest developments, construction defect dispute resolution   CC §6000
  - Construction defects, actions for   CC §911
- Building operating costs
  - Commercial real property tenancies   CC §1950.9
- Bulk distribution
  - Appellate rules, supreme court and courts of appeal, public access to electronic court records   CRC 8.82
  - Electronic court records, public access   CRC 2.503
- Bundled sales
  - Foreclosure sales, purchases from institutions foreclosing on specified number of residential properties   CC §2924p
- Burden of proof   Ev §115
- Business
  - Consumer privacy rights   CC §1798.140
  - Consumer refunds offered by prepaid debit card   CC §1748.40
  - Customer record, disposition   CC §1798.80
  - Driver's licenses, encoded information use   CC §1798.90.1
  - Personal information restrictions of persons at or near family planning center   CC §1798.99.90
  - Privacy of customer electrical or natural gas usage data   CC §1798.98
    - Actions and other remedies of customer   CC §1798.99
- Business associate
  - Consumer privacy rights   CC §1798.146
- Business associations   CCP §1501
- Business controller information
  - Consumer privacy rights, commercial credit reporting agencies   CC §1798.145
- Business day   CC §9
  - Home solicitation sales contracts   CC §1689.5
- Business entity filings
  - Identity theft, business entity filings   CC §1798.200
- Business program
  - Rental passenger vehicle transactions, business program sponsors   CC §1939.21
- Business program sponsor
  - Rental passenger vehicle transactions, business program sponsors   CC §1939.21
- Business purpose
  - Consumer privacy rights   CC §1798.140
- Business renters
  - Rental passenger vehicle transactions, business program sponsors   CC §1939.21
- Buy-back   CC §1812.201
- Buyer
  - Automobile sales finance   CC §2981
  - Consumer warranty protection   CC §1791
- Buyer-broker representation agreement
  - Real estate brokers and sales persons   CC §2079.13
- Calendar preferences
  - Appeals in supreme court or courts of appeals   CRC 8.240
- California courts web site
  - Rules of court   CRC 1.6
- California tribe
  - Conservators, interstate jurisdiction, transfer and recognition   Pro §2031
- Call provision   CC §2924i
- Campground   CC §1812.300
- Camping cabin
  - Special occupancy parks   CC §1866
- Camping site   CC §1812.300
- Campsite
  - Special occupancy parks   CC §1866
- Canadian domestic violence protection orders   Fam §6451
- Candidate for judicial office
  - Attorney professional conduct   ProfC 8.2
  - Judicial ethics code   CRCSupp JudEthicsTerminology
- Canine or feline toxicological experiments
  - Animal testing, restrictions against   CC §1834.9.3
- Capable of performing jury service
  - Juries and jurors, permanent medical excuse   CRC 2.1009
- Capital building annex project
  - Petitions under environmental quality act, civil rules governing   CRC 3.2220
- Capital distribution
  - Fiduciary income and principal act, allocation of receipts   Pro §16340
- Cardholder   CC §1748.12
  - Consumer refunds offered by prepaid debit card   CC §1748.40

DEFINITIONS—Cont.

Care custodian
    Donative transfers   Pro §21362

Caregiver
    Intergenerational housing developments   CC §51.3.5

Carriage, contract of   CC §2085

Carrier of passengers   CC §2214

Carries
    Fiduciary access to digital assets   Pro §871

CASA
    Juvenile rules   CRC 5.502

Case
    Appellate rules, superior court appeals   CRC 8.803
    Rules of court   CRC 1.6

Cases involving child custody and visitation
    Family rules, communication protocol for domestic violence and child custody orders   CRC 5.445

Cash
    Gift certificates   CC §1749.5

Cash equivalent
    TOD security registration act   Pro §5501

Cash price   CC §2981
    Rental-purchase contracts   CC §1812.622

CASp
    Construction-related accessibility claims, compliance with standards   CC §55.52

Cat
    Animal testing, restrictions against   CC §1834.9.3

Catalog sale   CC §1791

Catalogue of electronic communications
    Fiduciary access to digital assets   Pro §871

CCPI
    Children and minors, calculations for imputed liability for willful misconduct of minor   CRCAppx B

Central authority
    Intercountry adoptions   Fam §8900.5
    Interstate family support
        Convention support proceedings   Fam §5700.701

Certificate
    Appellate briefs, certificate of interested entities or persons   CRC 8.208

Certificate of authenticity   CC §1740

Certificate of missing status   Pro §3700

Certified access specialist
    Construction-related accessibility claims, compliance with standards   CC §55.52

Certified interpreter
    Interpreters, appointment in court proceedings   CRC 2.893

Certiorari writ   CCP §1067

Chair
    Judges, committee on judicial ethics opinions   CRCSupp JudEthicsOpinionsIOP 2
    Judicial council advisory bodies, meetings   CRC 10.75

Chairperson
    Judicial performance commission rules   JudPerR 138

Challenge   CCP §225

Charge card   CC §1748.21

Charged
    Sentencing rules, determinate sentencing   CRC 4.405

Charged-off consumer debt
    Fair debt buying practices   CC §1788.50

Charges
    Mobilehome parks, management approval of mobilehome purchaser   CC §798.74

Charging stations
    Commercial lease restrictions   CC §1952.7
    Lessee installation, landlord approval   CC §1947.5

Charitable interest
    Trust decanting, uniform act   Pro §19502

Charitable organization
    Trust decanting, uniform act   Pro §19502

Charitable purpose
    Uniform prudent management of institutional funds act   Pro §18502

Charitable remainder trust   Pro §16061.7

Charitable trust   Pro §16100

Charter party   CC §1959

Charter-party carrier of passengers   CC §2214

Chattel interests   CC §765

Chattel paper   CCP §§481.040, 680.140

Chattels real   CC §765

Check cashers   CC §1789.31

DEFINITIONS—Cont.

Chemical substance
    Animal testing, restrictions against   CC §1834.9.3

Chief administrative officer
    Postsecondary educational institutions, protection orders against violence threatened on campus or facility   CCP §527.85

Chief justice
    Rules of court   CRC 1.6

Chief trial counsel
    Attorneys, judges and law practice, rules governing   CRC 9.1

Child   Pro §26
    Age-appropriate design code   CC §1798.99.30
    Interstate compact on placement of children   CRC 5.616
    Interstate family support   Fam §5700.102
    Juvenile rules   CRC 5.502
    Uniform Parentage Act, vacation or setting aside of judgment   Fam §7645

Child abuse
    Criminal action, evidence   Ev §1109

Child abuse prevention and treatment act (CAPTA) guardian ad litem for child subject to juvenile dependency petition
    Juvenile rules   CRC 5.502

Childcare items
    Gender neutral section or area for display of toys and childcare items, retailer duties   CC §55.8

Child custody evaluation
    Child custody evaluators, qualifications for appointment   CRC 5.225
    Court-ordered child custody evaluation   CRC 5.220

Child custody evaluators   CRC 5.225
    Court-ordered child custody evaluation   CRC 5.220

Child for whom support may be ordered   Fam §58

Childhood sexual assault   CCP §§340.1, 340.11

Child pornography
    Child sexual abuse hosted on social media platform   CC §3273.65

Children
    Age-appropriate design code   CC §1798.99.30
    Gender neutral section or area for display of toys and childcare items, retailer duties   CC §55.8

Child sexual abuse material
    Child sexual abuse hosted on social media platform   CC §3273.65

Child support   CCP §680.145

Child support delinquency   Fam §17450

Child support obligee   Fam §4550

Child support order
    Interstate family support   Fam §5700.102

Chose in action   CC §953

Circumstances in aggravation
    Sentencing rules, determinate sentencing   CRC 4.405

Circumstances in mitigation
    Sentencing rules, determinate sentencing   CRC 4.405

Civil action   CCP §30, Ev §120

Civil action for injury or illness based upon exposure to a hazardous material or toxic substance
    Statutes of limitation   CCP §340.8

Civil action or proceeding
    Tribal court civil money judgment act   CCP §1732

Civil case
    Appellate rules, superior court appeals   CRC 8.803
    Remote appearances, civil cases generally   CRC 3.672
    Rules of court   CRC 1.6

Civil petitions
    Rules of court   CRC 1.6

CJA
    Judges, committee on judicial ethics opinions   CRCSupp JudEthicsOpinionsIOP 2

CJEO
    Judges, committee on judicial ethics opinions   CRCSupp JudEthicsOpinionsIOP 2

CJEO confidentiality waiver form
    Judges, committee on judicial ethics opinions   CRCSupp JudEthicsOpinionsIOP 2

CJEO email address
    Judges, committee on judicial ethics opinions   CRCSupp JudEthicsOpinionsIOP 2

CJEO opinion request form
    Judges, committee on judicial ethics opinions   CRCSupp JudEthicsOpinionsIOP 2

CJEO suggested topic form
    Judges, committee on judicial ethics opinions   CRCSupp JudEthicsOpinionsIOP 2

DEFINITIONS—Cont.
  CJEO web site
    Judges, committee on judicial ethics opinions   CRCSupp JudEthicsOpinionsIOP 2
  Claimant
    Coerced debt   CC §1798.97.1
    Construction defects, actions for   CC §895
    Family rules, joinder of parties   CRC 5.24
    Mechanics' liens   CC §8004
  Claims
    Claims against estates   Pro §19000
    Coerced debt   CC §1798.97.1
    Undisputed claims, penalty against state for failure to pay   Gov §927.2
    Voidable transactions   CC §3439.01
  Class of internet content, application, service or device
    Net neutrality   CC §3100
  Claws
    Landlord and tenant, requiring declawing or devocalizing animals as condition of occupancy   CC §1942.7
  Clear and conspicuous
    Consumer warranty protection   CC §1791
    Direct marketing, medical information used for   CC §1798.91
  Clearly and conspicuously
    Consumer warranty protection   CC §1791
  Clergy   Ev §1030
  Clerk
    Civil rules, coordination of complex actions   CRC 3.501
    Juvenile rules   CRC 5.502
  Client   Ev §951
    Attorney referral service-client privilege   Ev §965
    Discovery, attorney work product   CCP §2018.010
  Close of business
    Electronic filing and service rules   CRC 2.250
  Close of escrow
    Construction defects, actions for   CC §895
  Clotheslines
    Common interest developments, governing document restrictions   CC §4753
    Tenant use of clothesline or drying rack in private areas   CC §1940.20
  Clothing   CC §1791
  Coerced debt   CC §1798.97.1
  Cohabitant   CC §51.3, Fam §6209
    Donative transfers   Pro §21364
  Collateral   CC §1799.100
  Collected
    Consumer privacy rights   CC §1798.140
  Collectible
    Autographed memorabilia   CC §1739.7
  Collection
    Consumer privacy rights   CC §1798.140
  Collection action   CC §1799.101
  Collections cases
    Civil rules, case management   CRC 3.740
  Collectors
    Drug take-back bins, limitation of liability   CC §1714.24
  Collects
    Consumer privacy rights   CC §1798.140
      Personal information restrictions of persons at or near family planning center   CC §1798.99.90
  Combined relationship index
    Genetic testing to determine parentage   Fam §7550.5
  Commercial and industrial common interest developments   CC §6531
  Commercial blockage   CC §3427.1
  Commercial credit report   CC §1785.42
  Commercial credit reporting agency   CC §1785.42
    Consumer privacy rights, commercial credit reporting agencies   CC §1798.145
  Commercial financing
    Commercial financing transactions with small businesses   CC §1799.300
  Commercial online entertainment employment service providers
    Age information of subscribers, restriction on disclosure   CC §1798.83.5
  Commercial property
    Commercial real property tenancies   CC §1938
  Commercial purposes   CC §1798.3
    Consumer privacy rights   CC §1798.140
  Commercial real property   CC §1954.26
    Commercial real property tenancies   CC §1950.9
    Commercial real property tenancies, disposition of property remaining upon termination   CC §1993
    Leases and contracts   CC §§827, 1632

DEFINITIONS—Cont.
  Commercial real property —Cont.
    Real estate brokers and sales persons, duties owed to prospective purchaser   CC §2079.13
    Water conserving plumbing retrofits   CC §1101.3
  Commercial sexual exploitation
    Minor or nonminor dependent victims   CC §3345.1
  Commercial use
    Court records, public access   CRC 10.500
  Commission
    Judicial performance commission rules   JudPerR 138
  Committee
    Death penalty appeals and habeas corpus proceedings   CRC 8.601
  Committee counsel
    Judges, committee on judicial ethics opinions   CRCSupp JudEthicsOpinionsIOP 2
  Common area
    Commercial and industrial common interest developments   CC §6532
  Common carriers   CC §2168
  Common count
    Consumer debt collection   CCP §425.30
  Common interest developments
    Commercial and industrial common interest developments   CC §6534
    Construction defect dispute resolution   CC §6000
  Communications
    Child custody, ex parte communications   CRC 5.235
  Community-based corrections programs
    Sentencing rules, determinate sentencing   CRC 4.405
  Community property   CC §§687, 5110, 5111, 5120.020, Fam §§65, 760, Pro §§28, 3002
  Community property address
    Common interest developments, record inspection involving safe at home program participants   CC §5216
  Compensation   CC §3274
    Drug take-back bins, limitation of liability   CC §1714.24
  Competence
    Attorney professional conduct   ProfC 1.1
  Competent counsel
    Juvenile rules, representation of parties   CRC 5.660
    Juvenile rules, training of counsel for child in delinquency proceedings   CRC 5.664
  Complainant
    Mediation, complaints about court-program mediators   CRC 3.866
  Complaining witness   Ev §1103
  Complaint   CCP §§426.10, 481.060
    Appellate rules, superior court appeals   CRC 8.803
    Blind and visually impaired persons
      Internet website-related accessibility claims   CC §55.33
    Construction-related accessibility claims
      Advisory   CC §55.3
      Education entities, prelitigation letters   CC §54.27
    Groundwater rights actions   CCP §832
    Mediation, complaints about court-program mediators   CRC 3.866
  Complaint committee
    Mediation, complaints about court-program mediators   CRC 3.866
  Complaint coordinator
    Mediation, complaints about court-program mediators   CRC 3.866
  Complaint procedure
    Mediation, complaints about court-program mediators   CRC 3.866
  Complaint proceeding
    Mediation, complaints about court-program mediators   CRC 3.866
  Comprehensive adjudications
    Groundwater rights actions   CCP §832
  Computer security auditor
    Electronic recording delivery systems   Gov §27390
  Computer systems
    Rental-purchase contracts   CC §1812.622
  Conclusion of the arbitration
    Arbitrators, ethics standards for neutral arbitrators   CRC ArbEthicsStand 2
  Conditionally sealed
    Sealed and confidential records, appellate rules for supreme court and courts of appeal   CRC 8.45
  Conditional sales contract   CC §2981
  Condition concurrent   CC §1437
  Condition of long-term overdraft
    Groundwater rights actions   CCP §832
  Condition precedent   CC §1436
  Condominium plan
    Commercial and industrial common interest developments   CC §6540
  Condominium project
    Commercial and industrial common interest developments   CC §6542

DEFINITIONS—Cont.
Condominiums   CC §783
Confidential
    Sealed and confidential records, appellate rules for supreme court and courts of appeal   CRC 8.45
Confidential commercial and financial information
    Court records, public access   CRC 10.500
Confidential communication   Ev §1037.2
    Human trafficking victim-caseworker privilege   Ev §1038.2
Confidential communication between client and lawyer referral service
    Attorney referral service-client privilege   Ev §965
Confidential communications request
    Confidentiality of medical information   CC §56.05
Confidential data
    Commercial financing transactions with small businesses   CC §1799.300
Confidential information   CCP §1798.3
    Real estate brokers and salespersons, dual agency   CC §2079.21
Confidential intermediaries
    Adoption, sibling contact information requests   CRC 5.460
Confidential name change petitioners
    Name change proceedings under address confidentiality program   CRC 2.575
Confined
    Prisoner as heir, notice of death   Pro §216
Connected devices
    Security for connected devices   CC §1798.91.05
Consent
    Adoption, sibling contact information requests   CRC 5.460
    Consumer privacy rights   CC §1798.140
    Sexually explicit depiction of individual, actions for damages   CC §1708.86
Consent order
    Expedited jury trials   CRC 3.1545
Conservatee   Pro §§29, 2357
    Conservators, interstate jurisdiction, transfer and recognition   Pro §1982
    Ex parte communication, probate proceedings   CRC 7.10
    Fiduciary access to digital assets   Pro §871
Conservatee's personal residence
    Change of conservatee residence   CRC 7.1063
Conservatee's residence
    Change of conservatee residence   CRC 7.1063
Conservation easements   CC §815
    Eminent domain to acquire property subject to conservation easement   CCP §1240.055
Conservator   Pro §§30, 1490, 2350, 2357, 2400, 3004
    Fiduciary access to digital assets   Pro §871
    Interstate jurisdiction, transfer and recognition   Pro §1982
    Inventory and accounts   Pro §2600
Conservator of the estate
    Interstate jurisdiction, transfer and recognition   Pro §1982
Conservator of the person
    Interstate jurisdiction, transfer and recognition   Pro §1982
Conservator of the person and estate
    Interstate jurisdiction, transfer and recognition   Pro §1982
Conservatorship orders
    Interstate jurisdiction, transfer and recognition   Pro §1982
Conservatorship proceeding
    Interstate jurisdiction, transfer and recognition   Pro §1982
Consignee   CC §§2110, 2123b
Consignment   CC §1738
Consignor   CC §§2110, 2123b
Conspicuously displays
    Health and safety labor or service providers to public agencies, logo display restrictions   CC §3273
Construction contract   CC §2783
Construction lender
    Mechanics' liens   CC §8006
Construction-related accessibility claims
    Advisory filed along with complaint or demand for money   CC §55.3
    Compliance with standards   CC §55.52
    Education entities, prelitigation letters   CC §54.27
Construction-related accessibility standards
    Construction-related accessibility claims, compliance with standards   CC §55.52
Constructive delivery   CC §1059
Constructive fraud   CC §1573
Construed according to context and approved usage   CCP §16
Consumables   CC §1791
Consumer   CC §§1785.3, 1786.2
    Arbitration   CCP §1280
    Autographed memorabilia   CC §1739.7

DEFINITIONS—Cont.
Consumer —Cont.
    Consumer privacy rights   CC §1798.140
    Credit services organizations   CC §1789.12
    Escrow agent rating services   CC §1785.28
    Fair debt settlement practices   CC §1788.301
    Genetic privacy   CC §56.18
    Rental-purchase contracts   CC §1812.622
Consumer arbitration
    Arbitrators, ethics standards for neutral arbitrators   CRC ArbEthicsStand 2
Consumer commodity
    Point-of-sale systems   CC §7100
Consumer contract   CC §1799.201
Consumer credit contract   CC §1799.90
Consumer credit report   CC §1785.3
Consumer credit reporting agency   CC §§1748.12, 1785.3
    Credit services organizations   CC §1789.12
    Mobilehome parks, management approval of mobilehome purchaser   CC §798.74
Consumer debt
    Book accounts, statute of limitations for recovery on   CCP §337a
    Consumer debt collection   CCP §425.30
    Enforcement of judgments and orders   CCP §708.111
Consumer financial product or service
    Unfair competition and trade practices   CC §1770
Consumer goods   CC §1749.1
Consumer party
    Arbitrators, ethics standards for neutral arbitrators   CRC ArbEthicsStand 2
Consumer price index for all urban consumers for all items
    Floating homes, cap on rent increases   CC §800.40.5
    Landlord and tenant
        Rent increase limitations   CC §1947.12
    Mobilehomes and mobilehome parks, rent restrictions   CC §798.30.5
Consumer product
    Online marketplaces   CC §1749.8
Consumer report
    Landlord and tenant, reusable tenant screening report   CC §1950.1
    Private student loan collections reform   CC §1788.201
Consumer reporting agency
    Landlord and tenant, reusable tenant screening report   CC §1950.1
    Private student loan collections reform   CC §1788.201
Contact
    Online violence prevention   CC §1798.99.20
Contactless identification document system
    Radio frequency identification (RFID) to remotely read identification document without knowledge or consent   CC §1798.795
Contains
    Child support, computer software used to determine support amount   CRC 5.275
Content, applications or services
    Net neutrality   CC §3100
Content-based education requirements
    Judicial administration rules, temporary extension and reduction of judicial education requirements   CRC 10.492
Content creator
    Minors' employment contracts, artistic, entertainment or professional sports   Fam §6750
Content of an electronic communication
    Fiduciary access to digital assets   Pro §871
Contest
    No contest clauses for wills, trusts, etc   Pro §§21300, 23310
Contested matters
    Guardianship or conservatorship proceedings, attorney qualifications   CRC 7.1101
Continuation statement
    Judgment liens, personal property   CCP §697.510
Continuing guaranty   CC §2814
Continuing jurisdiction of the court
    Trusts funded by court order   CRC 7.903
Contract of carriage   CC §2085
Contractor
    Consumer privacy rights   CC §1798.140
    Mechanics' liens   CC §8012
    Reconstruction contract provisions, Cedar fire   CC §945.6
Contract price
    Mechanics' liens   CC §8010
Contracts   CC §1549
    Mechanics' liens   CC §8008
    Mortgage foreclosure consultants   CC §2945.1
Contract testing facility
    Animal research and testing limitations   CC §1834.9

DEFINITIONS—Cont.
Controversy
    Arbitration   CCP §1280
Convention
    Intercountry adoptions   Fam §8900.5
    Interstate family support   Fam §5700.102
Convention adoption
    Intercountry adoptions   Fam §8900.5
Convention country
    Intercountry adoptions   Fam §8900.5
Convention support order
    Interstate family support
        Convention support proceedings   Fam §5700.701
Conveyances   CC §§1053, 1215
    Voidable transactions   CC §3439.01
Coordinated action
    Civil rules, coordination of complex actions   CRC 3.501
Coordination attorney
    Civil rules, coordination of complex actions   CRC 3.501
Coordination motion judge
    Civil rules, coordination of complex actions   CRC 3.501
Coordination proceedings
    Civil rules, coordination of complex actions   CRC 3.501
Coordination trial judge
    Civil rules, coordination of complex actions   CRC 3.501
Copies
    Appellate rules, superior court appeals   CRC 8.803
    Appellate rules, supreme court and courts of appeal   CRC 8.10
Corporate securities   CCP §995.120
Cosigner   CC §1799.101
    Private student loan collections reform   CC §1788.201
Cosmetics
    Animal testing to develop or manufacture   CC §1834.9.5
Cost impact   Gov §11342.535
Cost of rental
    Rental-purchase contracts   CC §1812.622
Costs   CCP §§481.055, 680.150, 1033.5, 1235.140
Counsel
    Appellate rules, superior court appeals   CRC 8.803
    Rules of court   CRC 1.6
County   CCP §17, Fam §67
County adoption agencies
    Adoption   Fam §8513
County jails
    Sentencing rules, determinate sentencing   CRC 4.405
County of principal residence
    Jury selection   CCP §197
Course of conduct
    Harassment, protection orders   CCP §527.6
    Postsecondary educational institutions, protection orders against violence threatened on campus or facility   CCP §527.85
    Workplace violence, protection orders   CCP §527.8
Court
    Appellate rules, e-filing in supreme court and courts of appeal   CRC 8.70
    Civil discovery act   CCP §2016.020
    Court proceedings, photographing, recording and broadcasting   CRC 1.150
    Family rules, communication protocol for domestic violence and child custody orders   CRC 5.445
    Fiduciary access to digital assets   Pro §871
    Fiduciary income and principal act   Pro §16321
    Juvenile rules   CRC 5.502
    Labor relations of court employees   CRC 10.652
    Revocation of supervision, probation, etc   CRC 4.541
    Trial court rules   CRC 2.3
    Trust decanting, uniform act   Pro §19502
Court-appointed investigator   Fam §3110
    Court-appointed child custody investigators and evaluators, domestic violence training standards   CRC 5.230
Court-appointed mediator or evaluator
    Child custody, ex parte communications   CRC 5.235
Court-appointed temporary judge   CRC 2.810
Court-connected evaluators
    Child custody evaluators, qualifications for appointment   CRC 5.225
Court-connected mediator or evaluator
    Child custody, ex parte communications   CRC 5.235
Court employees
    Labor relations of court employees   CRC 10.652
Court facilities
    Trial court rules, court records   CRC 2.400
Court investigators
    Education of personnel responsible for probate cases   CRC 10.478

DEFINITIONS—Cont.
Court investigators—Cont.
    Qualifications of personnel responsible for probate cases   CRC 10.776
Court-issued subpoenas, warrants or orders
    Privacy of customer records, duties of carriers and innkeepers   CC §53.5
Court litigants
    Language access services   CRC 1.300
Court operations
    Judicial administration rules, trial court budget and fiscal management   CRC 10.810
Court order
    Change of lock upon request by protected tenant   CC §1941.6
Court-ordered services
    Juvenile rules   CRC 5.502
Court-ordered treatment program
    Juvenile rules   CRC 5.502
Court personnel
    Judicial ethics code, consultations between judge and others   CRCSupp JudEthicsCanon 3
Court-program mediators
    Mediation, complaints about court-program mediators   CRC 3.866
Court-provided programs, services and professionals
    Language access services   CRC 1.300
Court record
    Appellate rules, supreme court and courts of appeal, public access to electronic court records   CRC 8.82
    Electronic court records   CRC 2.502
    Judicial administration rules, trial court records management   CRC 10.850
        Sampling of records   CRC 10.855
Court supervision   Pro §10400
Court supervision under probate code
    Trusts funded by court order   CRC 7.903
Covenant running with land   CC §§1460 to 1463
Covered commercial credit
    Consumer debt collection   CC §1788.2
Covered commercial credit transaction
    Consumer debt collection   CC §1788.2
Covered commercial debt
    Consumer debt collection   CC §1788.2
Covered credit
    Consumer debt collection   CC §1788.2
Covered debt
    Consumer debt collection   CC §1788.2
Covered entity
    Commercial financing transactions with small businesses   CC §1799.300
    Consumer privacy rights   CC §1798.146
Covered multifamily dwellings
    Service of papers or subpoena, access to covered multifamily dwelling   CCP §415.21
Covered person
    Unfair competition and trade practices   CC §1770
Covered time period
    COVID-19 tenant relief act   CCP §1179.02
Covers
    Appellate rules, superior court appeals   CRC 8.803
    Appellate rules, supreme court and courts of appeals   CRC 8.10
Cover up
    Childhood sexual assault, civil actions for damages   CCP §§340.1, 340.11
    Sexual assault, actions for damages   CCP §340.16
COVID-19 recovery period rental debt
    COVID-19 rental housing recovery act   CCP §1179.09
COVID-19-related financial distress
    COVID-19 tenant relief act   CCP §1179.02
COVID-19 rental debt
    COVID-19 rental housing recovery act   CCP §1179.09
    COVID-19 tenant relief act   CCP §1179.02
Creating instruments
    Power of appointment   Pro §610
Creative expressions
    Evidence, admissibility   Ev §352.2
Credible threat
    Stalking
        Tort   CC §1708.7
Credible threat of violence
    Harassment, protection orders   CCP §527.6
    Postsecondary educational institutions, protection orders against violence threatened on campus or facility   CCP §527.85
    Workplace violence, protection orders   CCP §527.8
Credit   CC §1812.30
Credit cards   CC §§1747.02, 1748.12
Credit disability insurance   CC §1812.401

DEFINITIONS—Cont.
- Credit life insurance   CC §1812.401
- Creditor   CC §§1799.90, 1812.401, 3430
  - Claims against estates   Pro §19000
  - Fair debt settlement practices   CC §1788.301
  - Private student loan collections reform   CC §1788.201
  - Probate   Pro §9000
  - Voidable transactions   CC §§3439.01, 3445
- Credit score
  - Mobilehome parks, management approval of mobilehome purchaser   CC §798.74
- Credit services organizations   CC §1789.12
- Crimes against humanity
  - Limitation of actions for assault and battery constituting genocide, crimes against humanity, etc   CCP §354.8
- Crime stopper organizations
  - Identity of informer, privilege to refuse to disclose   Ev §1041
- Criminal cases
  - Appellate rules, superior court appeals   CRC 8.803
  - Rules of court   CRC 1.6
- Criminal court protective order
  - Family rules, communication protocol for domestic violence and child custody orders   CRC 5.445
- Criminal sexual assault
  - Enrollment agreements, disaffirmance by minor of provisions purporting to waive rights or remedies arising out of sexual assault or battery of minor   CCP §1002.7
- Criminal sexual battery
  - Enrollment agreements, disaffirmance by minor of provisions purporting to waive rights or remedies arising out of sexual assault or battery of minor   CCP §1002.7
- Cross-assign or cross assignment
  - Court interpreters, cross-assignments   CRC 10.762
- Cross-complaint   CCP §426.10
- Cross-context behavioral advertising
  - Consumer privacy rights   CC §1798.140
- Cross-examination   Ev §761
- Cultural burn
  - Prescribed burns, immunity from damages   CC §3333.8
- Cultural fire practitioners
  - Prescribed burns, immunity from damages   CC §3333.8
- Current beneficiary
  - Trust decanting, uniform act   Pro §19502
- Current income beneficiary
  - Fiduciary income and principal act   Pro §16321
- Custodial property   Pro §3901
- Custodian   Pro §§3901, 6206
  - Fiduciary access to digital assets   Pro §871
- Customer   CC §1140
  - Customer record, disposition   CC §1798.80
  - Customer records, disclosure of personal information   CC §1798.83
  - Privacy of customer electrical or natural gas usage data   CC §1798.98
- Customer facility charge
  - Rental passenger vehicle transactions   CC §1939.01
- Daily or weekly news publications
  - Defamation   CC §48a
- Damages   CC §3281, CCP §917.9
- Damage waiver
  - Rental passenger vehicle transactions   CC §1939.01
- Dark pattern
  - Consumer privacy rights   CC §1798.140
  - Genetic privacy   CC §56.18
- Data
  - Privacy of customer electrical or natural gas usage data   CC §1798.98
  - Radio frequency identification (RFID) to remotely read identification document without knowledge or consent   CC §1798.795
- Data brokers
  - Data broker registration   CC §1798.99.80
- Data furnisher
  - Credit services organizations   CC §1789.12
- Data message
  - International commercial arbitration and conciliation   CCP §1297.73
- Data protection impact assessment
  - Age-appropriate design code   CC §1798.99.30
- Date of separation
  - Family law   Fam §70
  - Necessaries, spousal liability   Fam §914
- Date the child entered foster care
  - Juvenile rules   CRC 5.502
- Dating relationship   Fam §6210
- Dating service contracts   CC §1694

DEFINITIONS—Cont.
- Day
  - Mechanics' liens   CC §8058
- Dealers
  - Autographed memorabilia   CC §1739.7
  - Vehicle history reports   CC §1784.1
- Dealerships   CC §81
- Debit card
  - Consumer refunds offered by prepaid debit card   CC §1748.40
- Debt
  - Fair debt settlement practices   CC §1788.301
- Debt buyers
  - Consumer debt collection, statements by debt collector to debtor   CC §1788.14.5
  - Fair debt buying practices   CC §1788.50
- Debt collection   CC §1788.2
- Debtors   CC §§1812.401, 3429
  - Coerced debt   CC §1798.97.1
  - Private student loan collections reform   CC §1788.201
  - Rate of interest on judgments   CCP §685.010
  - Renewal of judgments   CCP §683.110
  - Voidable transactions   CC §3439.01
- Debts   CC §5120.030, Fam §902, Pro §11401
  - Claims against estates   Pro §19000
  - Educational debt collection practices   CC §1788.92
  - Voidable transactions   CC §3439.01
- Debt settlement providers
  - Fair debt settlement practices   CC §1788.301
- Debt settlement services
  - Fair debt settlement practices   CC §1788.301
- Decanting power
  - Trust decanting, uniform act   Pro §19502
- Deceased personality   CC §3344.1
- Deceased settlors
  - Claims against estates   Pro §19000
- Deceit   CC §1710
- Declarant   Ev §135
  - Commercial and industrial common interest developments   CC §6544
- Declaration   CCP §116.130
  - Appellate rules, superior court appeals   CRC 8.803
  - Commercial and industrial common interest developments   CC §6546
  - Rules of court   CRC 1.6
- Declaration of COVID-19 related financial distress
  - COVID-19 tenant relief act   CCP §1179.02
- Declawing
  - Landlord and tenant, requiring declawing or devocalizing animals as condition of occupancy   CC §1942.7
- De facto parent
  - Juvenile rules   CRC 5.502
- Defamation   CC §44
- Default
  - Age-appropriate design code   CC §1798.99.30
- Defaulting occupants
  - Recreational vehicle parks   CC §799.22
- Defaulting residents
  - Recreational vehicle parks   CC §799.23
- Defaulting tenants
  - Recreational vehicle parks   CC §799.24
- Default settings
  - Child support, computer software used to determine support amount   CRC 5.275
- Defendant   CCP §§116.130, 308, 1063
  - Intervention   CCP §387
  - Small claims appeals   CRC 8.952
- Deferred jurors   CCP §194
- Deferred payment price   CC §1802.9
- Deidentified
  - Consumer privacy rights   CC §1798.140
- Delegated county adoption agency   Fam §8515
- Delinquent debt
  - Consumer debt collection, statements by debt collector to debtor   CC §1788.14.5
- Delinquent reimbursement
  - Juvenile dependency proceedings, counsel collections program guidelines   CRCAppx F
- Deliver   CC §1954.26
- Delivery
  - Mortgages and deeds of trust   CC §2943
- Demand for money
  - Construction-related accessibility claims, advisory   CC §55.3

DEFINITIONS—Cont.
Demand letter
    Blind and visually impaired persons
        Internet website-related accessibility claims   CC §55.33
    Construction-related accessibility claims, advisory   CC §55.3
    Small business gender discrimination in pricing services compliance act   CC §55.62
Denial
    Habeas corpus   CRC 4.545
Dental care   Fam §6901
Department of FISCal
    Undisputed claims, penalty against state for failure to pay   Gov §927.2
Dependency mediation
    Juvenile rules   CRC 5.518
Dependent adult
    Donative transfers   Pro §21366
Dependent person   Ev §177
Depicted individual
    Sexually explicit depiction of individual, actions for damages   CC §1708.86
Deployment
    Child custody, temporary military duty, deployment, etc   Fam §3047
Depose   CCP §17
Deposit account   CCP §§481.080, 680.170
Deposited assets
    Limitation of actions, Armenian genocide victims   CCP §354.45
Deposit for exchange   CC §1818
Deposit holder   Fam §4601
Deposition   CCP §2004
Deposition officer
    Subpoena duces tecum for employment records   CCP §1985.6
Depository   CC §1858
Depository institution
    Commercial financing transactions with small businesses   CC §1799.300
Depreciation
    Fiduciary income and principal act, allocation of disbursements   Pro §16362
Derivative
    Fiduciary income and principal act, allocation of receipts   Pro §16353
Descendants   Pro §6205
Description
    Autographed memorabilia   CC §1739.7
Designated language
    Interpreters, appointment in court proceedings   CRC 2.893
Designated methods of submitting requests
    Consumer privacy rights   CC §1798.140
Designated person
    At-death transfers, class gifts   Pro §21114
Designated recipient
    Fiduciary access to digital assets   Pro §871
Designed moisture barrier
    Construction defects, actions for   CC §895
Design professional
    Indemnity, contracts with public agencies   CC §2782.8
    Mechanics' liens   CC §§8014, 8300
Despicable conduct
    Sexually explicit depiction of individual, actions for damages   CC §1708.86
Detained
    Juvenile rules   CRC 5.502
Determinable charitable interest
    Trust decanting, charitable interest protection   Pro §19514
Determination of value
    Partition, heirs property   CCP §874.312
    Partition of real property   CCP §874.312
Detriment   CC §3282
Developer   CC §1954.26
Developmental disability   Pro §1420
Device
    Consumer privacy rights   CC §1798.140
Devise   Pro §32
Devisee   Pro §34
Devocalizing
    Landlord and tenant, requiring declawing or devocalizing animals as condition of occupancy   CC §1942.7
Differential domestic violence assessment
    Child custody, domestic violence protocol for family court services   CRC 5.215
    Juvenile rules   CRC 5.518
Digital assets
    Fiduciary access to digital assets   Pro §871

DEFINITIONS—Cont.
Digital electronic record
    Electronic recording delivery systems   Gov §27390
Digital firearm manufacturing code
    Firearm manufacturer liability   CC §3273.60
Digitization
    Sexually explicit depiction of individual, actions for damages   CC §1708.86
Digitized electronic record
    Electronic recording delivery systems   Gov §27390
Direct care service   CC §1812.540
Direct contest
    No contest clauses for wills, trusts, etc   Pro §§21300, 23310
Direct contract
    Mechanics' liens   CC §8016
Direct contractor
    Mechanics' liens   CC §8018
Directed trust   Pro §16602
Directed trustee   Pro §16602
Direct evidence   Ev §410
Direct examination   Ev §760
Direct marketing purposes
    Customer records, disclosure of personal information   CC §1798.83
    Direct marketing, medical information used for   CC §1798.91
Director
    Commercial and industrial common interest developments   CC §6548
    Consumer privacy rights
        Commercial credit reporting agencies   CC §1798.145
        Personnel or work records or communications   CC §1798.145
Direct request
    Interstate family support
        Convention support proceedings   Fam §5700.701
Direct-to-consumer genetic testing company
    Genetic privacy   CC §56.18
Disability claim period   CC §1812.401
Disabled person   CC §1761
    Deeds of trust and mortgages, modification or workout plan to avoid foreclosure   CC §2944.8
Disciplinary proceedings
    Judges, committee on judicial ethics opinions   CRCSupp JudEthicsOpinionsIOP 2
Disclaimant beneficiary   Pro §264
Disclose   CC §1798.3
    Customer records, disclosure of personal information   CC §1798.83
    Sexually explicit depiction of individual, actions for damages   CC §1708.86
Discount buying organization   CC §1812.101
Discount prices   CC §1812.101
Discretionary services organization
    Domestic violence ex parte protective orders   Fam §6323.5
Disembarkation
    Carriers of passengers   CC §2214
Display of flag of the United States
    Commercial and industrial common interest developments   CC §6702
    Common interest developments   CC §4705
Disposable earnings
    Garnishment   CCP §706.011
Disposal
    Abandoned mobilehomes   CC §798.61
Dispose
    Abandoned mobilehomes   CC §798.61
Disposition
    Family centered case resolution   CRC 5.83
Dispute resolution neutral
    Arbitrators, ethics standards for neutral arbitrators   CRC ArbEthicsStand 2
    Disqualification of judges   CCP §170.1
Dispute resolution provider organization
    Arbitrators, ethics standards for neutral arbitrators   CRC ArbEthicsStand 2
Dissolution
    Family rules   CRC 5.2
Dissolution of marriage   Pro §36
Distribution
    Fiduciary income and principal act   Pro §16321
Distribution proceedings   CCP §676.1
Distributor   CC §1738.12
    Automobile warranties   CCP §871.21
Disturbing the peace of the other party
    Domestic violence, ex parte protective orders   Fam §6320
Document   CCP §481.090
    Appellate rules, e-filing in supreme court and courts of appeal   CRC 8.70
    Civil discovery act   CCP §2016.020

DEFINITIONS—Cont.
  Document —Cont.
    Electronic filing and service rules   CRC 2.250
  Documentation entitling person to possession of vehicle
    Motor vehicle liens   CC §3068.1
  Documentation or evidence of abuse or violence
    Landlord and tenant   CCP §1161.3
  Document of title   CCP §§481.090, 680.180
  Dog
    Animal testing, restrictions against   CC §1834.9.3
  Doing business in this state
    Slavery and human trafficking in supply chain, disclosures by businesses of efforts to eradicate   CC §1714.43
  Domestic partners   Fam §297, Pro §37
    Donative transfers   Pro §21368
    Juvenile rules   CRC 5.502
    Wrongful death   CCP §377.60
  Domestic protection order
    Canadian domestic violence protection orders, recognition and enforcement   Fam §6451
  Domestic violence   Fam §6211
    Child custody, domestic violence protocol for family court services   CRC 5.215
    Contempt, enforcement against victims for refusal to testify   CCP §1219
    Family rules, settlement service providers   CRC 5.420
  Domestic violence counselor   Ev §1037.1
    Contempt, enforcement against victims for refusal to testify   CCP §1219
  Domestic violence felony
    Divorce, violent sexual felony or domestic violence felony by spouse against spouse   Fam §4324.5
  Domestic violence misdemeanors
    Divorce, domestic violence misdemeanors by spouse against spouse   Fam §4325
  Domestic violence victim service organizations   Ev §1037.1
  Dominant tenement   CC §803
  Donors
    Power of appointment   Pro §610
    Surrogacy or donor facilitators   Fam §7960
  Down payment   CC §2981
  Doxes
    Doxing victims' recourse   CC §1708.89
  Drafting party
    Arbitration   CCP §1280
  Drying racks
    Common interest developments, governing document restrictions   CC §4753
    Tenant use of clothesline or drying rack in private areas   CC §1940.20
  Due or owning
    Rate of interest on judgments   CCP §685.010
    Renewal of judgments   CCP §683.110
  Due process
    Tribal court civil money judgment act   CCP §1732
  Duplicate   Ev §260
  Duress   CC §1569
  During marriage
    Community property, premarital debts   Fam §910
  Duty of support
    Interstate family support   Fam §5700.102
  Dwelling   CCP §704.710
  Dwelling unit   CC §1940
  Dynamic risk factors
    Judicial administration, risk/needs assessment use in sentencing   CRC JudAdminStand 4.35
  Earnings   CCP §706.011, Fam §5206
    Child support delinquency   Fam §17450
  Earnings assignment order for support   CCP §706.011, Fam §5208
    Enforcement of money judgments, exempt property   CCP §704.070
  Earnings withholding order for elder or dependent adult financial abuse
    Garnishment   CCP §706.011
  Earnings withholding orders
    Enforcement of money judgments, exempt property   CCP §704.070
  Easements   CC §§801, 887.010
  Edge providers
    Net neutrality   CC §3100
  Education about protecting children during family disruption
    Supervised visitation and exchange programs, administration of programs   Fam §3201.5
  Educational institutions
    Enrollment agreements, disaffirmance by minor of provisions purporting to waive rights or remedies arising out of sexual assault or battery of minor   CCP §1002.7

DEFINITIONS—Cont.
  Educational rights holder
    Juvenile rules   CRC 5.502
  Educational standardized assessment or educational assessment
    Consumer privacy rights, deletion of personal information related to student grades, scores, etc   CC §1798.145
  Education entities
    Construction-related accessibility claims, attorney prelitigation letters to education entity   CC §54.27
  Effective time period
    COVID-19 small landlord and homeowner relief act   CC §3273.1
  E-learning
    Judicial administration rules, continuing education of judicial branch   CRC 10.493
  Electrical corporation
    Privacy of customer electrical or natural gas usage data   CC §1798.98
  Electric utility
    Solar easements   CC §801.5
  Electric vehicle charging stations
    Commercial and industrial common interest developments, protected use for charging stations   CC §6713
    Commercial lease restrictions   CC §1952.7
    Lessee installation, landlord approval   CC §1947.6
  Electrified security fences
    Adjoining or adjacent landowners   CC §835
  Electronic
    Civil discovery act   CCP §2016.020
    Fiduciary access to digital assets   Pro §871
    Voidable transactions   CC §3439.01
  Electronic access   CRC 2.502
    Appellate rules, supreme court and courts of appeal, public access to electronic court records   CRC 8.82
  Electronically digitized copy
    Convictions, official records   Ev §452.5
  Electronically stored information
    Civil discovery act   CCP §2016.020
  Electronic commerce   CC §1789.2
  Electronic communication
    Doxing victims' recourse   CC §1708.89
    Fiduciary access to digital assets   Pro §871
    International commercial arbitration and conciliation   CCP §1297.73
  Electronic communication device
    Doxing victims' recourse   CC §1708.89
    Stalking
      Tort   CC §1708.7
  Electronic communication services
    Fiduciary access to digital assets   Pro §871
  Electronic delivery
    Pesticides   CC §1940.8.5
  Electronic device
    Rental-purchase contracts   CC §1812.622
  Electronic filer
    Appellate rules, e-filing in supreme court and courts of appeal   CRC 8.70
    Electronic filing and service rules   CRC 2.250
  Electronic filing
    Appellate rules, e-filing in supreme court and courts of appeal   CRC 8.70
    Electronic filing and service rules   CCP §1010.6, CRC 2.250
  Electronic filing manager
    Electronic filing and service rules   CRC 2.250
  Electronic filing service provider
    Appellate rules, e-filing in supreme court and courts of appeal   CRC 8.70
    Electronic filing and service   CRC 2.250
  Electronic funds transfer
    Escheat of unclaimed property   CCP §1532
    Landlord and tenant, payments for rent and security deposits   CC §1947.3
  Electronic health record
    Confidentiality   CC §56.101
  Electronic mail
    Levying officer electronic transactions act   CCP §263.1
  Electronic medical record
    Confidentiality   CC §56.101
  Electronic notification
    Appellate rules, e-filing in supreme court and courts of appeal   CRC 8.70
    Electronic filing and service rules   CCP §1010.6, CRC 2.250
  Electronic notification address
    Electronic filing and service rules   CRC 2.250
  Electronic recording delivery systems   Gov §27390
  Electronic records   CRC 2.502
    Appellate rules, supreme court and courts of appeal, public access to electronic court records   CRC 8.82
    Levying officer electronic transactions act   CCP §263.1

DEFINITIONS—Cont.
Electronic service
    Appellate rules, e-filing in supreme court and courts of appeal   CRC 8.70
    Electronic filing and service rules   CCP §1010.6, CRC 2.250
Electronic service address
    Appellate rules, e-filing in supreme court and courts of appeal   CRC 8.70
    Electronic filing and service rules   CRC 2.250
Electronic set
    Rental-purchase contracts   CC §1812.622
Electronic signatures   CCP §17
    Appellate rules, e-filing in supreme court and courts of appeal   CRC 8.70
    Levying officer electronic transactions act   CCP §263.1
Electronic surveillance technology
    Rental passenger vehicle transactions   CC §1939.01
Electronic transmission
    Appellate rules, e-filing in supreme court and courts of appeal   CRC 8.70
    Electronic filing and service rules   CCP §1010.6, CRC 2.250
Eligible bidders
    Foreclosure sales   CC §2924m
        Purchases from institutions foreclosing on specified number of residential properties   CC §2924p
Eligible housing development
    Housing development projects using authorized floor area ratio standards, unenforceability of restrictions   CC §4747
Eligible legal aid organization
    Registered legal aid attorneys   CRC 9.45
Eligible providers
    Child custody evaluators, education and training   CRC 5.225
    Supervised visitation and exchange programs, compliance with provisions   Fam §3202
Eligible tenant
    Change of lock upon request by eligible tenant   CC §1941.5
Eligible tenant buyer
    Foreclosure sales   CC §2924m
Eligible to serve
    Demographic data on regular grand jurors   CRC 10.625
Email
    Levying officer electronic transactions act   CCP §263.1
Emergency
    Administrative rulemaking   Gov §11342.545
    Conservators, interstate jurisdiction, transfer and recognition   Pro §1991
    Mineral rights interest owner's entry on land, notice   CC §848
Emergency protective order   Fam §6217
Emergency responders
    Immunity from liability for damage done to drone interfering with emergency response   CC §43.101
Employ
    Attorney professional conduct
        Law firm employment of disbarred, suspended, resigned or involuntarily inactive lawyers   ProfC 5.3.1
Employee   CCP §706.011
    Arbitration   CCP §1280
    Postsecondary educational institutions, protection orders against violence threatened on campus or facility   CCP §527.85
    Subpoena duces tecum for employment records   CCP §1985.6
    Workplace violence, protection orders   CCP §527.8
Employee benefit plan   Pro §266
Employee pension benefit plan   Fam §80
Employees who regularly have contact with customers
    Customer records, disclosure of personal information   CC §1798.83
Employer   Fam §5210
    Postsecondary educational institutions, protection orders against violence threatened on campus or facility   CCP §527.85
    Workplace violence, protection orders   CCP §527.8
Employment agencies   CC §1812.501
Employment counseling services   CC §1812.501
Employment records
    Subpoena duces tecum for employment records   CCP §1985.6
Encrypted
    Customer records, computerized personal information   CC §1798.82
    Information practices, breach of security system   CC §1798.29
Encryption key
    Customer records, computerized personal information   CC §1798.82
    Information practices, breach of security system   CC §1798.29
Encumbered property   Pro §10320
Encumbrance   CC §1114
Endowment funds
    Uniform prudent management of institutional funds act   Pro §18502
End users
    Net neutrality   CC §3100

DEFINITIONS—Cont.
Enforcement action
    Common interest developments, alternative dispute resolution   CC §5925
Enforcement of judgments   CCP §§680.110 to 680.380
Engage in the business
    Student borrower bill of rights   CC §1788.100
Enhanced association records
    Common interest developments, fiscal matters   CC §5200
Enhancement
    Sentencing rules, determinate sentencing   CRC 4.405
Enrollee
    Confidentiality of medical information   CC §56.05
Enrollment agreements
    Disaffirmance by minor of provisions purporting to waive rights or remedies arising out of sexual assault or battery of minor   CCP §1002.7
Enterprise service offering
    Net neutrality   CC §3100
Entitled person   CC §2943
    Equity lines of credit, suspending and closing line on borrower's instruction   CC §2943.1
Entity
    Appellate briefs, certificate of interested entities or persons   CRC 8.208
    Fiduciary income and principal act, allocation of receipts   Pro §16340
    Quieting title   CCP §765.010
    Sexual assault, actions for damages   CCP §340.16
Entity distributions
    Fiduciary income and principal act, allocation of receipts   Pro §16340
Environmental leadership development project
    Appellate review of CEQA cases   CRC 8.700
    Petitions under environmental quality act, civil rules governing   CRC 3.2220
Environmental leadership transit project
    Appellate review of CEQA cases   CRC 8.700
    Petitions under environmental quality act, civil rules governing   CRC 3.2220
Epinephrine auto-injectors
    Immunity from liability for administration   CC §1714.23
Equal access
    Digital equity bill of rights   CC §3122
Equity   CCP §680.190
Equity lines of credit
    Suspending and closing line on borrower's instruction   CC §2943.1
Equity purchaser   CC §1695.1
Equity seller   CC §1695.1
Escheat   CCP §1300
Escrow   CC §1057
    Escrow agent rating services   CC §1785.28
Escrow agent
    Escrow agent rating services   CC §1785.28
Escrow agent rating services   CC §1785.28
Escrow service
    Buyer's choice act   CC §1103.22
Essential care providers
    Domestic violence ex parte protective orders   Fam §6323.5
Established business relationship
    Customer records, disclosure of personal information   CC §1798.83
Estate   Pro §353
    Fiduciary income and principal act   Pro §16321
    Guardians and conservators of the estate   Pro §2400
    Inventory and accounts of guardians and conservators   Pro §2600
Estate plan of conservatee   Pro §2586
Estimated time for repair
    Rental passenger vehicle transactions   CC §1939.01
Estimated time for replacement
    Rental passenger vehicle transactions   CC §1939.01
Ethnic or racial group
    Genetic testing to determine parentage   Fam §7550.5
Evaluation
    Child custody, domestic violence protocol for family court services   CRC 5.215
    Court-ordered child custody evaluation   CRC 5.220
Evidence-based practices
    Sentencing rules, determinate sentencing   CRC 4.405
Evidence demonstrating existence of tenancy
    Foreclosure sales   CC §2924m
Evidence of sexual conduct
    Sexual conduct evidence, use to attack credibility of witness   Ev §782
Evidentiary hearing
    Habeas corpus   CRC 4.545
Evidentiary hearing or trial
    Remote appearances, civil cases generally   CRC 3.672

DEFINITIONS—Cont.

Examiner
    Judicial performance commission rules   JudPerR 138
Exception   CCP §646
Excited delirium
    Term not to be admitted in civil action   Ev §1156.5
Exclusive listing agreement
    Residential exclusive listing agreements act   CC §1670.12
Exclusive use common area
    Commercial and industrial common interest developments   CC §6550
Excused jurors   CCP §194
Executed contract   CC §1661
Execution of instruments   CCP §1933
Executor   Pro §6203
Executory contract   CC §1661
Exemplary damages   CC §48a
Exempted providers
    Intercountry adoptions   Fam §8900.5
Exempt entity
    Private student loan collections reform   CC §1788.201
Expanded capitol building annex project
    Appellate review of CEQA cases   CRC 8.700
    Petitions under environmental quality act, civil rules governing   CRC 3.2220
Expanded distributive discretion
    Trust decanting, uniform act   Pro §19502
Ex parte communication
    Child custody, ex parte communications   CRC 5.235
    Probate proceedings, rule governing ex parte communications   CRC 7.10
Expedited jury trial   CCP §630.01, CRC 3.1545
Expenses
    Civil rules, coordination of complex actions   CRC 3.501
Expert witnesses
    Groundwater rights actions   CCP §832
Expiration date or event
    Confidentiality of medical information   CC §56.05
Expiration of rental restriction
    Rent setting and limitations   CC §1947.13
Express consent
    Genetic privacy   CC §56.18
    Rental-purchase contracts   CC §1812.622
Express contracts   CC §1620
Express unitrust
    Fiduciary income and principal act, unitrust   Pro §16330
Express warranty   CC §1791.2
Extended family member
    Indian children   Fam §170
Extension of credit
    Credit services organizations   CC §1789.12
Exterior elevated elements
    Common interest developments, financial reserve planning   CC §5551
Extracontractual damages
    Time-limited demands   CCP §999
Facilitating the sharing or renting of vehicles
    Rental passenger vehicle transactions   CC §1939.38
Facilities that provide pediatric care
    Human trafficking or slavery, businesses required to post signs concerning   CC §52.6
Facility
    Force, threat or other obstruction of access to facility   CC §1708.9
Factors   CC §§2026, 2367
Failure to appear
    Infractions, failure to appear or failure to pay for notice to appear   CRC 4.106
Failure to maintain
    Foreclosure, maintaining vacant residential property   CC §2929.3
Failure to pay
    Infractions, failure to appear or failure to pay for notice to appear   CRC 4.106
Family
    Vlogging, minors   Fam §6650
Family allowance   Pro §38
Family centered case resolution conference   CRC 5.83
Family centered case resolution process   CRC 5.83
Family code
    Family rules   CRC 5.2
Family court services
    Child custody, domestic violence protocol for family court services   CRC 5.215

DEFINITIONS—Cont.

Family finding
    Family finding and notice performed by social worker or probation officer   CRC 5.637
Family member
    Dead bodies   CCP §129
Family of absentee   Pro §3700
Family planning center
    Personal information restrictions of persons at or near family planning center   CC §1798.99.90
Family support   Fam §92
Family trust
    Landlord and tenant
        Security deposit, retention by landlord   CC §1950.5
        Year's continuous, lawful occupation acting as limitation on termination of tenancy   CC §1946.2
Farm machinery   CC §1718
Farm products   CCP §481.110
Fax
    Fax filing and service   CRC 2.301
    Levying officer electronic transactions act   CCP §263.1
Fax filing   CRC 2.301
Fax filing agency
    Fax filing and service   CRC 2.301
Fax machine
    Fax filing and service   CRC 2.301
    Levying officer electronic transactions act   CCP §263.1
Fax transmission
    Fax filing and service   CRC 2.301
    Levying officer electronic transactions act   CCP §263.1
Feasible
    Electronic court records, public access   CRC 2.503
Federally licensed firearms manufacturer
    Firearm manufacturer liability   CC §3273.60
Fedwire
    Escheat of unclaimed property   CCP §1532
Fee estate   CC §762
Fees
    Rental-purchase contracts   CC §1812.622
Fee simple   CC §762
Felony   CC §2225
FFA
    Foster family agency accountability   CCP §1062.32
Fiduciary   Pro §39
    Ex parte communications, probate proceedings   CRC 7.10
    Fiduciary access to digital assets   Pro §871
    Fiduciary income and principal act   Pro §16321
    Judicial ethics code   CRCSupp JudEthicsTerminology
Fiduciary decision
    Fiduciary income and principal act, remedies for abuse of discretion   Pro §16326
15-passenger van
    Rental passenger vehicle transactions, advisories for renders   CC §1939.35
Filed documents
    Juvenile case appeals, confidentiality   CRC 8.401
Filing   CCP §697.590
    Judicial performance commission rules   JudPerR 138
Final decision
    COVID-19 rental housing recovery act   CCP §1179.09
Final judgments in eminent domain   CCP §1235.120
Finance charge   CC §1802.10
    Automobile sales finance   CC §2981
Financial institutions   CCP §§481.113, 680.200, Pro §§40, 3901
    Child support delinquency   Fam §17450
    Conservators, taking possession of conservatee's assets   CRC 7.1061
    Consumer debt, exemption of principal residence from execution of judgment lien   CCP §699.730
    Guardianships, taking possession of ward's assets   CRC 7.1011
Financial interest   CCP §170.5
    Arbitrators, ethics standards for neutral arbitrators   CRC ArbEthicsStand 2
    Conservators   Pro §2351
Financial organizations   CCP §1501
Fine art   CC §986
Fine art multiple   CC §1740
Fine print   CC §1740
Firearm
    Domestic violence prevention   Fam §6216
    Firearm industry standards of conduct   CC §3273.50
    Firearm manufacturer liability   CC §3273.60
Firearm accessory
    Firearm industry standards of conduct   CC §3273.50

DEFINITIONS—Cont.
- Firearm industry member
  - Firearm industry standards of conduct CC §3273.50
- Firearm precursor part
  - Domestic violence prevention Fam §6216
  - Firearm industry standards of conduct CC §3273.50
- Firearm-related product
  - Firearm industry standards of conduct CC §3273.50
- Firefighters CCP §1299.3
- Firm
  - Attorney professional conduct ProfC 1.0.1
  - Attorneys at law, provisional licensure of 2020 law school graduates CRC 9.49
    - Pathway to full licensure, provisional licensure with CRC 9.49.1
- First liens
  - Mortgages CC §2920.5
- First trust
  - Trust decanting, uniform act Pro §19502
- First trust instrument
  - Trust decanting, uniform act Pro §19502
- Fixed broadband internet access service
  - Net neutrality CC §3100
- Fixed internet service provider
  - Net neutrality CC §3100
- Fixed lien special assessment CCP §1265.250
- Fixtures CC §660
- Floating home CC §800.3
- Floating home marina CC §800.4
- Follows
  - Stalking, tort CC §1708.7
- Food additive
  - Animal testing, restrictions against CC §1834.9.3
- Food bank
  - Donations of food, immunity CC §1714.25
- Food facility
  - Donations of food, immunity CC §1714.25
- For a commercial purpose
  - Invasion of privacy CC §1708.8
- Forcible detainer CCP §1160
- Forcible entry CCP §1159
- Foreclosure consultant CC §2945.1
- Foreclosure prevention alternatives
  - Mortgages CC §2920.5
- Foreign central authority
  - Interstate family support
    - Convention support proceedings Fam §5700.701
- Foreign country
  - Foreign country money judgments recognition CCP §1714
  - Interstate family support Fam §5700.102
- Foreign-country judgment
  - Foreign country money judgments recognition CCP §1714
- Foreign jurisdiction
  - Discovery, interstate and international CCP §2029.200
- Foreign money CCP §676.1
- Foreign nation Pro §12502
- Foreign nation personal representative Pro §12503
- Foreign penal civil action
  - Discovery, interstate and international CCP §2029.200
- Foreign protective order Fam §6401
- Foreign subpoenas
  - Discovery, interstate and international CCP §2029.200
- Foreign support agreement
  - Interstate family support
    - Convention support proceedings Fam §5700.701
- Foreign support order
  - Interstate family support Fam §5700.102
- Foreign tribunal
  - Interstate family support Fam §5700.102
- Formal legal proceeding
  - Attorney temporarily in California as part of litigation CRC 9.47
- Formal probation
  - Revocation of supervision, probation, etc CRC 4.541
- Former cohabitant Fam §6209
- Foster care
  - Juvenile rules CRC 5.502
- Foster parent
  - Juvenile rules CRC 5.502
- Found
  - Sentencing rules, determinate sentencing CRC 4.405
- Fraud CC §3294
  - Attorney professional conduct ProfC 1.0.1

DEFINITIONS—Cont.
- Fraud —Cont.
  - Coerced debt CC §1798.97.1
- Fraudulent
  - Attorney professional conduct ProfC 1.0.1
- Fraudulent concealment
  - Consumer privacy rights, limitation of actions for administrative actions CC §1798.199.70
- Fraudulent transfer
  - Voidable transactions CC §3439.05
- Freehold CC §765
- Freight CC §2110
- Full and equal access
  - Public facilities, access for persons with disabilities CC §54.1
- Full evaluation, investigation or assessment
  - Child custody evaluators, qualifications for appointment CRC 5.225
  - Court-ordered child custody evaluation CRC 5.220
- Full service adoption agencies
  - Agency adoptions Fam §8521
- Fund
  - Mechanics' liens CC §8020
- Fund management agreement
  - Surrogacy or donor facilitators Fam §7960
- Future damages CCP §667.7
- Future interest CC §690
- Gas corporation
  - Privacy of customer electrical or natural gas usage data CC §1798.98
- Gender
  - Unruh civil rights act CC §§51, 52.4
- Gender-affirming health care
  - Legally protected health care services CC §1798.300
  - Medical information confidentiality CC §56.109
- Gender-affirming mental health care
  - Legally protected health care services CC §1798.300
  - Medical information confidentiality CC §56.109
- Gender discrimination pricing services claims
  - Small business gender discrimination in pricing services compliance act CC §55.62
- Gender expression
  - Judicial ethics code CRCSupp JudEthicsTerminology
- Gender identity
  - Judicial ethics code CRCSupp JudEthicsTerminology
- Gender violence
  - Civil rights actions CC §52.4
- General agent CC §2297
- General civil case
  - Rules of court CRC 1.6
- General counsel
  - Attorneys, judges and law practice, rules governing CRC 9.1
- General damages CC §48a
- General intangibles CCP §§481.115, 680.210
- General jurisdiction
  - Juvenile rules CRC 5.502
- General liens CC §§2873, 2874
- General personal representative Pro §42
  - Will probate Pro §58
- General power of appointment
  - Trust decanting, uniform act Pro §19502
- Generation-skipping transfer tax Pro §20200
- Genetic data
  - Customer records, computerized personal information CC §1798.82
  - Customer records, security procedures to protect personal information CC §1798.81.5
  - Genetic privacy CC §56.18
  - Information practices, breach of security system CC §1798.29
- Genetic information
  - Unruh civil rights act CC §51
- Genetic testing
  - Genetic privacy CC §56.18
  - Genetic testing to determine parentage Fam §7550.5
- Geophysical location tracking technology
  - Rental-purchase contracts CC §1812.622
- Gestational carriers
  - Surrogacy or donor facilitators Fam §7960
- Gift CC §1146
  - Arbitrators, ethics standards for neutral arbitrators CRC ArbEthicsStand 2
  - Judicial ethics code CRCSupp JudEthicsTerminology
- Gift certificates CC §1749.45
- Gift instrument
  - Uniform prudent management of institutional funds act Pro §18502
- Gifts in view of death Pro §§5700, 5702

DEFINITIONS—Cont.
Gleaner
    Donations of food, immunity   CC §1714.25
Golden State Energy
    Action by Golden State Energy for acquisition of PG&E property   CCP §1240.655
Good cause   CCP §116.130
    Tribal court civil money judgment act   CCP §1732
    Unlawful detainer, access to court records   CCP §1161.2
Good faith   CC §2132b
Good faith improver   CCP §871.1
Goods   CC §1802.1
    Home solicitation sales contracts   CC §1689.5
Goods or services   CC §1798.2
Goodwill of business   CCP §1263.510
Governing documents
    Commercial and industrial common interest developments   CC §6552
    Common interest development, pet provisions   CC §4715
Governmental benefits
    Trust decanting, beneficiaries with a disability   Pro §19513
Governmental emergency organization
    Disaster service workers, immunity from liability   CC §1714.5
Government entity
    Electronic court records   CRC 2.502
    Reader privacy act   CC §1798.90
Government-issued identification
    Verification of age for sale of age-restricted products   CC §1798.99.1
Government rental assistance program
    COVID-19 rental housing recovery act   CCP §1179.09
Governor
    Interstate family support   Fam §5700.801
Grand jury   CCP §192
Grant   CC §1053
    Claims against public entities and employees, late payment   Gov §927.2
Grantor trust
    Trust decanting, tax situations   Pro §19519
Gratuitous deposit   CC §1844
Greenway
    Greenway easements   CC §816.52
Greenway easements   CC §816.52
Grey market goods   CC §1797.8
Grocery department
    Point-of-sale systems   CC §7100
Grocery store
    Point-of-sale systems   CC §7100
Gross earnings
    Minors' employment contracts, artistic, entertainment or professional sports   Fam §6750
Gross receipts
    Slavery and human trafficking in supply chain, disclosures by businesses of efforts to eradicate   CC §1714.43
Groundwater
    Groundwater rights actions   CCP §832
Groundwater extraction facilities
    Groundwater rights actions   CCP §832
Groundwater recharge
    Groundwater rights actions   CCP §832
Guaranteed asset protection waiver
    Motor vehicle sales finance   CC §2981
Guarantor   CCP §995.185
Guaranty   CC §2787
Guardian   Pro §§1490, 2350, 2400
    Inventory and accounts   Pro §2600
    Juvenile rules   CRC 5.502
Guardian or conservator
    Termination of temporary guardianship or conservatorship   Pro §2357
Guest
    Recreational vehicle parks   CC §799.25
    Special occupancy parks   CC §1866
Guest records
    Privacy, duties of hotels, motels, inns, etc   CC §53.5
Guide dog   CC §54.1
Hague adoption certificate
    Intercountry adoptions   Fam §8900.5
Hague custody declaration
    Intercountry adoptions   Fam §8900.5
Handler of a search and rescue dog
    Discrimination in lodging, eating or transportation   CC §54.25
Harass
    Quieting title   CCP §765.010
    Stalking, tort   CC §1708.7

DEFINITIONS—Cont.
Harassment
    Doxing victims' recourse   CC §1708.89
    Protection orders   CCP §527.6
    Workplace violence, protection orders   CCP §527.8
Hard-of-hearing person   CC §54.8, Ev §754
Harm-reduction
    Interim homelessness programs, occupancy   CC §1954.08
Has participated in discussions
    Judges, disqualification due to prospective service as dispute resolution neutral   CCP §170.1
Have a common residence
    Domestic partnership   Fam §297
Hazardous material   CC §2782.6
Hazardous substance
    Deeds of trust and mortgages, secured party access to inspect for environmental damage   CC §2929.5
    Receivers   CCP §564
Head of family   CCP §704.710
Health and social services
    Donative transfers   Pro §21362
Health care decision
    Health care powers of attorney   Pro §4617
Health care institutions
    Medical negligence, limitation on damages   CC §3333.2
Health care provider   CC §§43.9, 56.05, 1714.8, 3333.1, CCP §§56.05, 340.5, 364, 667.7, 1295
    Arbitration of professional negligence, contracts for medical services requiring   CCP §1295
    Juries and jurors, permanent medical excuse   CRC 2.1009
    Medical malpractice, limitation on damages   CC §3333.2
Health care service plan   CC §56.05
Health insurance coverage   Fam §3750
Health insurance information
    Customer records, computerized personal information   CC §1798.82
    Customer records, security procedures to protect personal information   CC §1798.81.5
    Information practices, breach of security system   CC §1798.29
Health practitioner
    Change of lock upon request by eligible tenant   CC §1941.5
    Landlord and tenant, restrictions on termination of tenancy of victims of certain crimes   CC §1946.7
Health studio services   CC §1812.81
Hearing briefs
    Family rules, setting trials and long-cause hearings   CRC 5.393
Hearings   Ev §145
    Juvenile rules   CRC 5.502
Hearsay   Ev §§150, 1200
Heirs   Pro §44
High-income tenant
    COVID-19 tenant relief act   CCP §1179.02.5
High/low agreement
    Expedited jury trial   CRC 3.1545
    Mandatory expedited jury trial   CCP §630.21
    Voluntary expedited jury trial   CCP §630.01
High-volume third-party sellers
    Online marketplaces   CC §1749.8
Hiring   CC §1925
Holder   CC §2132b, CCP §1501
    Motor vehicle sales finance   CC §2981
Holder of a conservation easement
    Eminent domain to acquire property subject to conservation easement   CCP §1240.055
Holder of decedent's property   Pro §13002
Holder of privilege
    Attorney referral service-client privilege   Ev §965
    Domestic violence counselor-victim privilege   Ev §1037.4
    Human trafficking victim-caseworker privilege   Ev §1038.2
Holidays   CCP §12a
Holographic will   Pro §6111
Home appliances   CC §1791
Home court
    Court interpreters, cross-assignments   CRC 10.762
Home equity loan   CC §2970
Home-generated pharmaceutical waste
    Drug take-back bins, limitation of liability   CC §1714.24
Homeless person
    Transitional housing program misconduct   CC §1954.12
Homeowner
    Construction defects, actions for   CC §895

DEFINITIONS—Cont.

Homepage
    Consumer privacy rights   CC §1798.140
Home solicitation contract or offer   CC §1689.5
Home state
    Conservators, interstate jurisdiction, transfer and recognition   Pro §1991
    Interstate family support   Fam §5700.102
Homestead   CCP §704.710
Homestead designation   CCP §704.910
Honorarium
    Arbitrators, ethics standards for neutral arbitrators   CRC ArbEthicsStand 2
    Judges, ethics   CRCSupp JudEthicsCanon 4
Hosting platforms
    Private residence rental listings
        Cancellation of reservations, refunds   CC §1748.80
Hotel
    Blind and visually impaired persons, touch screen devices for self-service check-in at hotels or passenger transportation facilities   CC §54.9
    Cancellation of reservations, refunds   CC §1748.80
    Sex trafficking activity, action against hotel   CC §52.65
Hours-based education requirement
    Judicial administration rules, temporary extension and reduction of judicial education requirements   CRC 10.492
Household
    Consumer privacy rights   CC §1798.140
Household goods   CC §1799.100
Household member
    Change of lock upon request by eligible tenant   CC §1941.5
    Screening of tenants   CC §1946.9
Household members
    Landlord and tenant, restrictions on termination of tenancy of victims of certain crimes   CC §1946.7
Human trafficking caseworker
    Human trafficking victim-caseworker privilege   Ev §1038.2
Human trafficking victims
    Expert testimony on effect of human trafficking on victim   Ev §1107.5
Human trafficking victim service organizations
    Human trafficking victim-caseworker privilege   Ev §1038.2
Hypothesized genetic relationship
    Genetic testing to determine parentage   Fam §7550.5
ICCVAM
    Animal research and testing limitations   CC §1834.9
Identifiable minor
    Child sexual abuse hosted on social media platform   CC §3273.65
Identifiable private information
    Consumer privacy rights   CC §1798.146
Identification devices
    Subcutaneous implanting of identification device, requiring of another   CC §52.7
Identification documents
    Radio frequency identification (RFID) to remotely read identification document without knowledge or consent   CC §1798.795
Identifying characteristics
    Doxing victims' recourse   CC §1708.89
    Photographs, films, etc, exposing intimate body parts or sexual acts of another without permission, distribution, actions   CC §1708.85
Identity theft   CC §1798.92
    Common interest developments, withholding or redacting information from records   CC §5215
Image
    Obscene material, unsolicited electronic messages depicting   CC §1708.88
Immaterial allegation   CCP §431.10
Immediate family member
    Change of lock upon request by eligible tenant   CC §1941.5
    Coerced debt   CC §1798.97.1
    Landlord and tenant, restrictions on termination of tenancy of victims of certain crimes   CC §1946.7
    Screening of tenants   CC §1946.9
Immigration or citizenship status
    Landlord and tenant   CC §1940.05, CCP §1164.1
Imminent danger
    Special occupancy parks, danger requiring move   CC §1866
Immovable property   CC §658
Impairing or degrading lawful internet traffic on basis of internet content, application or services, or use of nonharmful device
    Net neutrality   CC §3100
Impartial
    Judicial ethics code   CRCSupp JudEthicsTerminology
Impartiality
    Judicial ethics code   CRCSupp JudEthicsTerminology

DEFINITIONS—Cont.

Impartially
    Judicial ethics code   CRCSupp JudEthicsTerminology
Impending proceedings
    Judicial ethics code   CRCSupp JudEthicsTerminology
Implied contracts   CC §1621
Implied warranty   CC §1791.1
Impression   CC §1740
Imprisonment
    Sentencing rules, determinate sentencing   CRC 4.405
Improper question   CCP §222.5
Impropriety
    Judicial ethics code   CRCSupp JudEthicsTerminology
Incapacitated principal
    Wills, transfer or encumbrance of specific gift, rights of transferee   Pro §21134
Incarcerated or involuntarily institutionalized
    Child support, suspension of orders or judgments   Fam §4007.5
Included action
    Civil rules, coordination of complex actions   CRC 3.501
Income
    Fiduciary income and principal act   Pro §16321
    Interstate family support   Fam §5700.102
Income and expense declaration   Fam §95
Income interest
    Fiduciary income and principal act   Pro §16321
Income of property   CC §748
Income trust
    Fiduciary income and principal act, unitrust   Pro §16330
Income-withholding order
    Family rules, interstate income withholding orders   CRC 5.335
    Interstate family support   Fam §5700.102
Indemnity   CC §2772
Independence
    Judicial ethics code   CRCSupp JudEthicsTerminology
Independent adoptions   Fam §8524
Independent attorney
    Donative transfers   Pro §21370
Independent contractor
    Consumer privacy rights, personnel or work records or communications   CC §1798.145
Independent person
    Fiduciary income and principal act   Pro §16321
Independent repair or service facility   CC §1791
Indian
    Indian children   Fam §170
Indian child
    Indian children   Fam §170
    Juvenile rules   CRC 5.502
Indian child custody proceeding   Pro §1449
    Indian children   Fam §170
Indian child's tribe
    Indian children   Fam §170
    Juvenile rules   CRC 5.502
Indian custodian
    Indian children   Fam §170
Indian organization
    Indian children   Fam §170
Indian tribe
    Indian children   Fam §170
Indian tribe with jurisdiction
    Conservators, interstate jurisdiction, transfer and recognition   Pro §2031
Indigent defendants
    Electronic filing and service, criminal cases   CRC 2.255
Indirect contest
    Wills, no contest clauses   Pro §21300
Individual   CCP §116.130
    Customer record, disposition   CC §1798.80
    Sexually explicit depiction of individual, actions for damages   CC §1708.86
Individual in an emergency
    Lease provisions penalizing summoning emergency assistance   CC §1946.8
Individually identifiable health information
    Consumer privacy rights   CC §1798.146
Individual notice
    Commercial and industrial common interest developments   CC §6553
Individual who is deaf or hard of hearing
    Interpreters and translators   Ev §754

DEFINITIONS—Cont.
Ineligible persons
  Attorney professional conduct
    Law firm employment of disbarred, suspended, resigned or involuntarily inactive lawyers   ProfC 5.3.1
Infer
  Consumer privacy rights   CC §1798.140
Inference   Ev §600
  Consumer privacy rights   CC §1798.140
Information
  Fiduciary access to digital assets   Pro §871
Information processing systems
  Levying officer electronic transactions act   CCP §263.1
Informed consent
  Attorney professional conduct   ProfC 1.0.1
Informed written consent
  Attorney professional conduct   ProfC 1.0.1
Infrastructure project
  Appellate review of CEQA cases   CRC 8.700
  Petitions under environmental quality act, civil rules governing   CRC 3.2220
Inglewood arena project
  Appellate review of CEQA cases   CRC 8.700
  Petitions under environmental quality act, civil rules governing   CRC 3.2220
Ingredient
  Cosmetics, animal testing to develop or manufacture   CC §1834.9.5
Initial fee waiver
  Civil rules governing waiver of fees and costs   CRC 3.50
Initial removal
  Juvenile rules   CRC 5.502
Initiating tribunal
  Interstate family support   Fam §5700.102
Injunctions   CCP §525
Injured spouse
  Divorce, domestic violence misdemeanors by spouse against spouse   Fam §4325
  Divorce, violent sexual felony or domestic violence felony by spouse against spouse   Fam §4324.5
Injury to person   CCP §§28, 29
Injury to property   CCP §28
Inland carriers   CC §2087
In place transfer
  Floating homes, cap on rent increases   CC §800.40.5
Inquiry
  Mediation, complaints about court-program mediators   CRC 3.866
Insider   CCP §1800
Insolvent   CC §3439.02, CCP §1800
  Voidable transactions   CC §3439.02
Inspected by a CASp
  Construction-related accessibility claims, compliance with standards   CC §55.52
Inspection warrants   CCP §1822.50
Institution
  Foreclosure sales, purchases from institutions foreclosing on specified number of residential properties   CC §2924p
Institutional funds
  Uniform prudent management of institutional funds act   Pro §18502
Institutions
  Conservators, taking possession of conservatee's assets   CRC 7.1061
  Guardianships, taking possession of ward's assets   CRC 7.1011
  Uniform prudent management of institutional funds act   Pro §18502
Instruction
  Levying officer electronic transactions act   CCP §263.1
Instructor-led training
  Judicial administration rules, continuing education of judicial branch   CRC 10.493
Instrument   CCP §680.220, Pro §45
Insured depository financial institution
  Child support, deposit of payments into qualifying account   Fam §17325
Integrity
  Judicial ethics code   CRCSupp JudEthicsTerminology
Intended occupant
  Landlord and tenant
    Year's continuous, lawful occupation acting as limitation on termination of tenancy   CC §1946.2
Intended parents
  Surrogacy or donor facilitators   Fam §7960
Intensive treatment
  CARE act rules   CRC 7.2205

DEFINITIONS—Cont.
Intentionally interacts
  Consumer privacy rights   CC §1798.140
Intercountry adoption   Fam §8527
Interest   CC §1915, Pro §267
Interested person   Pro §§48, 354, 1424
  Termination of parental rights, petitions by   Fam §7841
Interfere
  Force, threat or other obstruction of access to facility   CC §1708.9
Intermediary interpreters
  Evidence, interpreters and translators   Ev §754
Internal income of separate fund
  Fiduciary income and principal act
    Marital trusts, allocation of receipts   Pro §16348
International funds transfer
  Escheat of unclaimed property   CCP §1532
International will   Pro §6380
Internet service providers
  Net neutrality   CC §3100
Internet website-related accessibility claim
  Blind and visually impaired persons   CC §55.33
Internet website-related accessibility standard
  Blind and visually impaired persons   CC §55.33
Interpreters
  Evidence, interpreters and translators   Ev §754
In this state
  Student borrower bill of rights   CC §1788.100
Intimate body part
  Photographs, films, etc, exposing intimate body parts or sexual acts of another without permission, distribution, actions   CC §1708.85
Intimate partner violence
  Consent to medical treatment, minors   Fam §6930
Intimidate
  Force, threat or other obstruction of access to facility   CC §1708.9
Intimidation by threat of violence
  Civil rights   CC §51.7
Inventory   CCP §§481.120, 1800
Investigation
  Court-ordered child custody evaluation   CRC 5.220
Investigative consumer report   CC §1785.2
Investment adviser   CC §3372
Invoice
  Claims against public entities and employees, late payment   Gov §927.2
Involuntarily inactive members
  Attorney professional conduct
    Law firm employment of disbarred, suspended, resigned or involuntarily inactive lawyers   ProfC 5.3.1
In writing
  Direct marketing, medical information used for   CC §1798.91
ISP traffic exchange
  Net neutrality   CC §3100
ISP traffic exchange agreement
  Net neutrality   CC §3100
Issue   Pro §50
Issuing court
  Canadian domestic violence protection orders, recognition and enforcement   Fam §6451
Issuing foreign country
  Interstate family support   Fam §5700.102
Issuing state
  Interstate family support   Fam §5700.102
Issuing tribunal
  Interstate family support   Fam §5700.102
IV-D Case   Fam §5212
Jeopardize the validity and reliability of that educational standardized assessment or educational assessment
  Consumer privacy rights, deletion of personal information related to student grades, scores, etc   CC §1798.145
Jobbers   CC §1738.12
Job listing services   CC §1812.501
Joint account   Pro §5130
Joint authority   CC §12, CCP §15
Joint custody   Fam §3002
Joint interests   CC §683
Joint legal custody   Fam §3003
Joint physical custody   Fam §3004
Joint tenancy   CC §683
Judge
  Appellate rules, superior court appeals   CRC 8.803
  Court proceedings, photographing, recording and broadcasting   CRC 1.150
  Judicial performance commission rules   JudPerR 138

DEFINITIONS—Cont.
Judge—Cont.
    Rules of court   CRC 1.6
Judgment
    Appellate rules, superior court appeals   CRC 8.803
    Appellate rules, supreme court and court of appeals   CRC 8.10
    Uniform Parentage Act, vacation or setting aside of judgment   Fam §7645
Judgment creditor   CCP §§116.130, 680.240, 689.050, 706.011
Judgment debtor   CCP §§116.130, 680.240, 689.050, 706.011
Judgments   CCP §§577, 680.230, 1064, Fam §100
Judicial administrative records
    Court records, public access   CRC 10.500
Judicial branch employees
    Ethics training for judicial branch employees   CRC 10.455
Judicial branch entity
    Court records, public access   CRC 10.500
    Government tort liability, actions against public employees and entities   Gov §940.3
    Government tort liability, claims and claims presentation   Gov §900.3
Judicial branch personnel
    Court records, public access   CRC 10.500
Judicial candidates
    Judges, committee on judicial ethics opinions   CRCSupp JudEthicsOpinionsIOP 2
Judicial districts   CCP §§17, 38
Judicial liens   CCP §1800
Judicial officer   Fam §6240
    Judges, committee on judicial ethics opinions   CRCSupp JudEthicsOpinionsIOP 2
Judicial records   CCP §1904
Judicial remedies   CCP §20
Jurisdiction   CCP §410.10
    Child placement, interstate compact on   Fam §7908.5
Juror pool   CCP §194
Jury of inquest   CCP §194
Just cause
    Landlord and tenant, year's continuous, lawful occupation acting as limitation on termination of tenancy   CC §1946.2
Juvenile case files
    Confidentiality of juvenile records   CRC 5.552
Key person   CC §1812.407
Keys
    Radio frequency identification (RFID) to remotely read identification document without knowledge or consent   CC §1798.795
Kin
    Family finding and notice performed by social worker or probation officer   CRC 5.637
Knowingly
    Attorney professional conduct   ProfC 1.0.1
    Judicial ethics code   CRCSupp JudEthicsTerminology
Knowledge
    Judicial ethics code   CRCSupp JudEthicsTerminology
Known
    Attorney professional conduct   ProfC 1.0.1
    Judicial ethics code   CRCSupp JudEthicsTerminology
Knows
    Attorney professional conduct   ProfC 1.0.1
    Judicial ethics code   CRCSupp JudEthicsTerminology
Labor dispute   CCP §527.3
Laborer
    Mechanics' liens   CC §8024
Labor organization
    Subpoena duces tecum for employment records   CCP §1985.6
Labor, service, equipment or material
    Mechanics' liens   CC §8022
Land   CC §659
Landlord
    Commercial real property tenancies, disposition of property remaining upon termination   CC §1993
    COVID-19 tenant relief act   CCP §1179.02
    Landlord and tenant, reusable tenant screening report   CC §1950.1
    Landlord and tenant, water service in multifamily residential rental buildings   CC §1954.202
    Pesticides   CC §1940.8.5
Landowners
    Fences, boundaries and monuments, adjoining landowners   CC §841
Language services
    Language access services   CRC 1.300
Latent deficiencies in planning or construction of real property   CCP §337.15
Latent deficiency   CCP §337.15

DEFINITIONS—Cont.
Law   CC §22
    Interstate family support   Fam §5700.102
    Judicial ethics code   CRCSupp JudEthicsTerminology
Law and motion
    Civil rules governing law and motion proceedings   CRC 3.1103
Law enforcement agency
    Gang database removal, appeal proceedings   CRC 3.2300
Law enforcement entity
    Reader privacy act   CC §1798.90
Law enforcement officer   CCP §1299.3, Fam §6240
    Canadian domestic violence protection orders, recognition and enforcement   Fam §6451
Law firm
    Attorney professional conduct   ProfC 1.0.1
    Attorneys at law, provisional licensure of 2020 law school graduates   CRC 9.49
        Pathway to full licensure, provisional licensure with   CRC 9.49.1
Law, legal system or administration of justice
    Judicial ethics code   CRCSupp JudEthicsTerminology
Lawyer for a party
    Arbitrators, ethics standards for neutral arbitrators   CRC ArbEthicsStand 2
Lawyer in the arbitration
    Arbitrators, ethics standards for neutral arbitrators   CRC ArbEthicsStand 2
Layaway   CC §1749.1
Lead counsel
    Death penalty appeals and habeas corpus proceedings   CRC 8.601
Leadership project
    Appellate review of CEQA cases   CRC 8.700
    Petitions under environmental quality act, civil rules governing   CRC 3.2220
Leading question   Ev §764
Lead paint abatement program   CC §3494.5
Lease contracts   CC §§1799.90, 2985.7
Legal entity
    Levying officer electronic transactions act   CCP §263.1
Legal guardian
    Civil harassment protective proceedings, confidentiality of minor's information   CRC 3.1161
Legally protected health care activity   CC §1798.300
Legally responsible
    Sexual assault, actions for damages   CCP §340.16
Legal organization
    Electronic court records   CRC 2.502
Legal practice
    Attorneys at law, provisional licensure of 2020 law school graduates
        Pathway to full licensure, provisional licensure with   CRC 9.49.1
Legal process
    Attachment, manner of service   CCP §482.070
    Enforcement of judgments and orders, manner of service   CCP §684.110
Legal service
    Intercountry adoptions   Fam §8900.5
Lessee   CC §2985.7
Lessor   CC §2985.7
    Rental-purchase contracts   CC §1812.622
Lessor's cost
    Rental-purchase contracts   CC §1812.622
Letters of administration   Pro §52
Letters testamentary   Pro §52
Levying officer   CCP §§481.140, 680.260
    Levying officer electronic transactions act   CCP §263.1
Levying officer instructions
    Levying officer electronic transactions act   CCP §263.1
Liaison counsel
    Civil rules, coordination of complex actions   CRC 3.501
Libel   CC §45
License
    Customer records, security procedures to protect personal information   CC §1798.81.5
Licensed adoption agency   Fam §8530
    Adoption, sibling contact information requests   CRC 5.460
Licensed person
    Mortgage brokers, fiduciary duties   CC §2923.1
Licensed pest control applicator
    Pesticides   CC §1940.8.5
Licensee
    Attorneys, judges and law practice, rules governing   CRC 9.1
    Student borrower bill of rights   CC §1788.100
Lienholder
    COVID-19 small landlord and homeowner relief act   CC §3273.1

DEFINITIONS—Cont.
Liens   CC §2872, CCP §§1180, 1265.210
   Mechanics' liens   CC §8026
   Voidable transactions   CC §3439.01
Likely to be accessed by children
   Age-appropriate design code   CC §1798.99.30
Limited civil cases
   Rules of court   CRC 1.6
Limited distributive discretion
   Trust decanting, uniform act   Pro §19512
Limited edition
   Autographed memorabilia   CC §1739.7
Limited English proficient
   Language access services   CRC 1.300
Limited-equity housing cooperative
   Housing cooperatives and housing cooperative trusts   CC §817
Limited interest   CC §692
Limited scope representation
   Attorneys, civil rules   CRC 3.35
   Family rules   CRC 5.425
Liquidating assets
   Fiduciary income and principal act, allocation or receipts   Pro §16349
List of resident state tax filers
   Jury selection   CCP §197
Litigation   CCP §391
   Vexatious litigants   CCP §391.7
Litigation expenses
   Eminent domain, final offer and demand   CCP §1250.410
Livestock   CC §3080
Load-bearing components
   Common interest developments, financial reserve planning   CC §5551
Loan for exchange   CC §1902
Loan for money   CC §1912
Loan for use   CC §1844
Local agency   CCP §394
   Greenway easements   CC §816.52
   Illegal expenditure, waste, etc, of public funds   CCP §526a
Local child support agency   Fam §17000
Local court interpreter coordinator
   Court interpreters, cross-assignments   CRC 10.762
Local emergency
   Emergency declaration, transfer of property within geographic limits of declared area   CC §2968
Local publicly owned electric utility
   Privacy of customer electrical or natural gas usage data   CC §1798.98
Local rule   CRC 10.613
   Appellate rules, superior court appeals   CRC 8.803
   Family rules   CRC 5.2
   Rules of court   CRC 1.6
Local supervision
   Sentencing rules, determinate sentencing   CRC 4.405
Lock
   Change of lock upon request by eligible tenant   CC §1941.5
   Change of lock upon request by protected tenant   CC §1941.6
Lodged
   Name change proceedings under address confidentiality program   CRC 2.575
   Sealed and confidential records, appellate rules for supreme court and courts of appeal   CRC 8.45
   Trial court rules, sealed records   CRC 2.550
Lodger   CC §1946.5
Logo
   Health and safety labor or service providers to public agencies, logo display restrictions   CC §3273
Long-cause hearings
   Family rules, setting trials and long-cause hearings   CRC 5.393
Looted assets
   Limitation of actions, Armenian genocide victims   CCP §354.45
Lot
   Special occupancy parks   CC §1866
Lower income households
   Foreclosure sales, recorded covenants for purchased property   CC §2924o
   Recorded restrictive covenants, unenforceability in face of approved and recorded restrictive covenant affordable housing modification document   CC §714.6
LPS Act
   Ex parte communication, probate proceedings   CRC 7.10
   Guardianship or conservatorship proceedings, attorney qualifications   CRC 7.1101
LPS conservatorship
   Ex parte communication, probate proceedings   CRC 7.10

DEFINITIONS—Cont.
Luggage   CC §2181
Mail   CCP §116.130
   Judicial performance commission rules   JudPerR 138
Mailed
   Judicial performance commission rules   JudPerR 138
Maintains
   Drug take-back bins, limitation of liability   CC §1714.24
Major life activities   CC §1761
Major regulation
   Administrative regulations and rulemaking   Gov §11342.548
Malice   CC §3294
   Sexually explicit depiction of individual, actions for damages   CC §1708.86
Management
   Mobilehomes and mobilehome parks, rent restrictions   CC §798.30.5
   Recreational vehicle parks   CC §799.26
Management employee
   Consumer privacy rights, commercial credit reporting agencies   CC §1798.145
Mandamus   CCP §1084
Mandatory expedited jury trial   CCP §630.21, CRC 3.1545
Mandatory income interest
   Fiduciary income and principal act   Pro §16321
Mandatory supervision
   Sentencing rules, determinate sentencing   CRC 4.405
Manufacturer
   Automobile warranties   CCP §871.21
Manufacturers   CC §1791
   Animal research and testing limitations   CC §1834.9
   Connected devices, security   CC §1798.91.05
   Consumer warranty protection   CC §1791
   Cosmetics, animal testing to develop or manufacture   CC §1834.9.5
   Slavery and human trafficking in supply chain, disclosures by businesses of efforts to eradicate   CC §1714.43
Marine carriers   CC §2087
Marital deduction gifts   Pro §21520
Marital trust
   Fiduciary income and principal act
      Marital trusts, allocation of receipts   Pro §16348
Market
   Commercial and industrial common interest developments, marketing of individual interest   CC §6710
Marketing
   Commercial and industrial common interest developments, marketing of individual interest   CC §6710
   Medical information, confidentiality   CC §56.05
Marketing information   CC §1748.12
Marketplace
   Marketplace sales and sellers, commercial relationships, terms and conditions   CC §1749.7
Marketplace seller
   Marketplace sales and sellers, commercial relationships, terms and conditions   CC §1749.7
Marriage   Fam §300
Mass market
   Net neutrality   CC §3100
Master
   Judicial performance commission rules   JudPerR 138
Master list   CCP §194
Material allegation   CCP §431.10
Material facts
   Summary judgment motions   CRC 3.1350
Material supplier
   Mechanics' liens   CC §8028
Matter then pending in court
   Ex parte communication, probate proceedings   CRC 7.10
Media
   Court proceedings, photographing, recording and broadcasting   CRC 1.150
Media agency
   Court proceedings, photographing, recording and broadcasting   CRC 1.150
Media coverage
   Court proceedings, photographing, recording and broadcasting   CRC 1.150
Mediation   CCP §§1731, 1775.1
   Child custody, domestic violence protocol for family court services   CRC 5.215
   Civil rules   CRC 3.800
   Mediators, standards of conduct   CRC 3.852
Mediation communication
   Mediation, complaints about court-program mediators   CRC 3.866

DEFINITIONS—Cont.
Mediator
    Mediators, standards of conduct   CRC 3.852
Medical care   Fam §6902
Medical debt
    Consumer credit reporting agencies   CC §1785.3
Medical examiner, forensic pathologist or coroner
    Medical records, disclosures   CC §56.10
Medical information   CC §1786.2
    Consumer privacy rights   CC §1798.146
    Customer records, computerized personal information   CC §1798.82
    Customer records, security procedures to protect personal information   CC §1798.81.5
    Direct marketing, medical information used for   CC §1798.91
    Information practices, breach of security system   CC §1798.29
Medi-Cal program
    Claims against public entities and employees, late payment   Gov §927.2
Medical providers
    Medical records, inspection   Ev §1158
Medical research
    Animal research and testing limitations   CC §1834.9
    Animal testing, restrictions against   CC §1834.9.3
Medical service, product or device
    Consumer credit reporting agencies   CC §1785.3
Medical staff members
    Consumer privacy rights, personnel or work records or communications   CC §1798.145
Meet and confer in good faith
    Labor relations of court employees   CRC 10.652
Meets applicable standards
    Construction-related accessibility claims, compliance with standards   CC §55.52
Member
    Attorney professional conduct
        Law firm employment of disbarred, suspended, resigned or involuntarily inactive lawyers   ProfC 5.3.1
    Commercial and industrial common interest developments   CC §6554
Member of the arbitrator's extended family
    Arbitrators, ethics standards for neutral arbitrators   CRC ArbEthicsStand 2
Member of the arbitrator's immediate family
    Arbitrators, ethics standards for neutral arbitrators   CRC ArbEthicsStand 2
Member of the armed forces
    Consumer warranty protection   CC §1791
Member of the household
    Juvenile rules   CRC 5.502
Member of the judge's family
    Judicial ethics code   CRCSupp JudEthicsTerminology
Member of the judge's family residing in the judge's household
    Judicial ethics code   CRCSupp JudEthicsTerminology
Membership camping contracts   CC §1812.300
Membership program
    Rental passenger vehicle transactions   CC §1939.01
Memorandum
    Rules of court   CRC 1.6
Menace   CC §1570
Mental health application information
    Confidentiality of medical information   CC §56.05
Mental health digital service
    Confidentiality of medical information   CC §56.05
Mental health records
    Confidentiality of medical records, dependent children removed from parental custody   CC §56.016
Mental health treatment or counseling services
    Consent by minor to mental health treatment, counseling or residential shelter services   Fam §6924
Merchantability, warranty of   CC §1791.1
Microenterprise
    Commercial real property tenancies   CC §1950.9
    Leases and contracts   CC §§827, 1632
Military borrower
    Student borrower bill of rights   CC §1788.100
Military spouse attorney
    Attorney practice, non-California bar members   CRC 9.41.1
Mineral rights   CC §883.110
Mines
    Mining liens   CC §3060
Minor   Fam §6500
    Child sexual abuse hosted on social media platform   CC §3273.65
    Violent video games   CC §1746
    Vlogging, minors   Fam §6650
Minor child   Pro §6601

DEFINITIONS—Cont.
Mint condition
    Autographed memorabilia   CC §1739.7
Misappropriation of trade secrets   CC §3426.1
Missing persons   Pro §12400
Mistake of fact   CC §1577
Mistake of law   CC §1578
Mitigation
    Sentencing rules, determinate sentencing   CRC 4.405
Mobile broadband internet access service
    Net neutrality   CC §3100
Mobilehomes   CC §§798.1 to 798.12, 799
    Abandoned mobilehomes   CC §798.61
    Consumer warranty protection   CC §1791
Mobile internet service providers
    Net neutrality   CC §3100
Mobile station
    Net neutrality   CC §3100
Mobilization
    Child custody, temporary military duty, deployment, etc   Fam §3047
Modification document
    Recorded restrictive covenants, unenforceability in face of approved and recorded restrictive covenant affordable housing modification document   CC §714.6
Modification of parental rights
    Juvenile rules   CRC 5.502
Money   CCP §676.1
Money judgment   CCP §680.270
Monitor
    Records of court proceedings, electronic   CRC 2.952
Monitoring technology
    Rental-purchase contracts   CC §1812.622
Month   CCP §17
Mortgage brokerage services
    Fiduciary duties of mortgage brokers   CC §2923.1
Mortgage brokers
    Fiduciary duties of mortgage brokers   CC §2923.1
Mortgages   CC §§2920, 2924
Mortgage servicer
    COVID-19 small landlord and homeowner relief act   CC §3273.1
    Emergency declaration, transfer of property within geographic limits of declared area   CC §2968
    Mortgages   CC §2920.5
Motel or hotel
    Interim homelessness programs, occupancy   CC §1954.08
Motions   CCP §§116.130, 1003
    Summary judgment motions   CRC 3.1350
Motor carrier of property in dump truck equipment
    Construction trucking services brokers, payment of transportation charges   CC §3322
Motor vehicle
    Automobile sales finance   CC §2981
    Automobile warranties   CCP §871.21
    Carriers of passengers   CC §2214
    Special occupancy parks   CC §1866
Multifamily residential real property
    Water conserving plumbing retrofits   CC §1101.3
Multiphasic screening unit   CC §43.9
Multiple listing service   CC §1087
Multiple-party accounts   Pro §5132
Mutual foreign protective order   Fam §6401
Mutuality of consent   CC §1580
National medical support notice   Fam §3760
Natural parents
    Uniform parentage act   Fam §7601
Natural person
    Landlord and tenant
        Security deposit, retention by landlord   CC §1950.5
        Year's continuous, lawful occupation acting as limitation on termination of tenancy   CC §1946.2
Necessary technology
    Blind and visually impaired persons, touch screen devices for self-service check-in at hotels or passenger transportation facilities   CC §54.9
Net fair market value of a trust
    Fiduciary income and principal act, unitrust   Pro §16330
Net income
    Fiduciary income and principal act   Pro §16321
Neural data
    Consumer privacy rights   CC §1798.140
Neutral arbitrators
    Arbitration   CCP §1280

DEFINITIONS—Cont.

Neutral arbitrators—Cont.
    Arbitrators, ethics standards for neutral arbitrators   CRC ArbEthicsStand 2

New construction
    Mobilehome residency   CC §798.7

New mobilehome park construction
    Mobilehome residency   CC §798.7

New qualified buyers
    Default in real property purchase contract, liquidated damages   CC §1675

Newspaper of general circulation
    Foreclosure sales, publication of notice   CC §2924f

New trial   CCP §656

New value   CCP §1800

90-day transition plan
    Juvenile rules   CRC 5.502

911 service
    Immunity from liability, telecommunications services   CC §1714.55

NIST conforming labeling scheme
    Connected devices, security   CC §1798.91.05

No contest clause
    Wills, trusts, etc   Pro §§21300, 23310

No-fault just cause
    Landlord and tenant
        Year's continuous, lawful occupation acting as limitation on termination of tenancy   CC §1946.2

Nonattorney surrogacy or donor facilitators   Fam §7960

Noncertified interpreters
    Interpreters, appointment in court proceedings   CRC 2.893

Noncompliant plumbing fixtures
    Water conserving plumbing retrofits   CC §1101.3

Noncontingent rights
    Trust decanting, expanded distributive discretion   Pro §19511

Noncustodial adoption agency   Fam §8533

Nondomiciliary decedent   Pro §12505

Nongrantor trusts
    Trust decanting, tax situations   Pro §19519

Nonminor dependents
    Commercial sexual exploitation, minor or nonminor dependent victims   CC §3345.1
    Juvenile rules   CRC 5.502

Nonminors
    Juvenile rules   CRC 5.502

Non-personalized advertising
    Consumer privacy rights   CC §1798.140

Nonprobate transfer
    Dissolution of marriage   Fam §2040

Nonprofessional providers
    Child custody, supervised visitation   Fam §3200.5
    Supervised visitation services providers, standards   CRC JudAdminStand 5.20

Nonprofit charitable organization
    Donations of food, immunity   CC §1714.25
    Vision screening and eyeglass donations   CC §1714.26

Nonprofit organization
    Claims against public entities and employees, late payment   Gov §927.2
    Commercial real property tenancies   CC §1950.9
    Leases and contracts   CC §§827, 1632

Nonprofit public benefit corporation
    Claims against public entities and employees, late payment   Gov §927.2

Nonprofit service organization
    Claims against public entities and employees, late payment   Gov §927.2

Nonprofit, special use property in eminent domain proceedings   CCP §1235.155

Nonpublic information
    Judicial ethics code   CRCSupp JudEthicsTerminology

Nonregistered interpreters
    Interpreters, appointment in court proceedings   CRC 2.893

Nonrelative extended family member
    Family finding and notice performed by social worker or probation officer   CRC 5.637

Nonresident personal representative   Pro §8570

Nonviolent
    Force, threat or other obstruction of access to facility   CC §1708.9

Notice   CC §18
    Customer records, computerized personal information   CC §§1798.82, 1798.84
    Information practices, breach of security system   CC §1798.29
    Juvenile rules   CRC 5.502

Notice of pendency   CCP §405.2

Notice of refund or other payment due
    Claims against public entities and employees, late payment   Gov §927.2

DEFINITIONS—Cont.

Notify
    Juvenile rules   CRC 5.502

Novation   CC §1530

Nude
    Sexually explicit depiction of individual, actions for damages   CC §1708.86

Nuisances   CC §3479

Nurses' registries   CC §1812.524

Nursing services   CC §§1812.524, 1812.540

Oakland ballpark project
    Appellate review of CEQA cases   CRC 8.700
    Petitions under environmental quality act, civil rules governing   CRC 3.2220

Oakland sports and mixed-use project
    Appellate review of CEQA cases   CRC 8.700
    Petitions under environmental quality act, civil rules governing   CRC 3.2220

Oaths   CCP §17

Obligation   CC §1427

Obligee   Fam §5214
    Interstate family support   Fam §5700.102

Obligor   Fam §5216
    Consumer warranty protection   CC §1791
    Interstate family support   Fam §5700.102

Obscene material
    Distribution of unauthorized obscene material, actions   CC §52.8
    Unsolicited electronic messages depicting obscene material   CC §1708.88

Obscene matter
    Child sexual abuse hosted on social media platform   CC §3273.65

Occupancy
    Recreational vehicle parks   CC §799.27

Occupant
    Lease provisions penalizing summoning emergency assistance   CC §1946.8
    Recreational vehicle parks   CC §799.28
    Special occupancy parks   CC §1866

Occupy
    Recreational vehicle parks   CC §799.27

Of a harassing nature
    Doxing victims' recourse   CC §1708.89

Offense
    Sentencing rules, determinate sentencing   CRC 4.405

Offensive contact   CC §1708.5

Officer
    Consumer privacy rights
        Commercial credit reporting agencies   CC §1798.145
        Personnel or work records or communications   CC §1798.145

Official records
    Social security number truncation program   Gov §27300

Older borrower
    Student borrower bill of rights   CC §1788.100

Old Town Center project
    Appellate review of CEQA cases   CRC 8.700
    Petitions under environmental quality act, civil rules governing   CRC 3.2220

Old Town Center transit and transportation facilities project
    Appellate review of CEQA cases   CRC 8.700
    Petitions under environmental quality act, civil rules governing   CRC 3.2220

On call
    Jury service, duration   CRC 2.1002

One day
    Jury service, duration   CRC 2.1002

One trial
    Jury service, duration   CRC 2.1002

Online dating services
    Dating services   CC §1694

Online identifiers
    Doxing victims' recourse   CC §1708.89

Online marketplaces   CC §1749.8

Online platform
    Minors' employment contracts, artistic, entertainment or professional sports   Fam §6750
    Vlogging, minors   Fam §6650

Online service, product or feature
    Age-appropriate design code   CC §1798.99.30

Online tools
    Fiduciary access to digital assets   Pro §871

Open-end credit card account   CC §1748.13

Open-end credit plan   CC §1812.405

DEFINITIONS—Cont.
Open proceedings
    Ex parte communication, probate proceedings   CRC 7.10
Operating rule
    Commercial and industrial common interest developments   CC §6630
    Common interest developments, operating rules   CC §4340
Opioid antagonist
    Opioid antagonist administered for drug overdose, immunity from liability   CC §1714.22
Opioid overdose prevention and treatment training program
    Opioid antagonist administered for drug overdose, immunity from liability   CC §1714.22
Oral testimony
    Remote appearances, civil cases generally   CRC 3.672
Order after hearing
    Harassment, protection orders   CCP §527.6
    Workplace violence, protection orders   CCP §527.8
Order of repeal   Gov §§11342, 11342.560
Order on writ of habeas corpus
    Habeas corpus   CRC 4.545
Orders   CCP §§1003, 1064, Fam §100
    Adoption, sibling contact information requests   CRC 5.460
Order to show cause
    Habeas corpus   CRC 4.545
Organization
    Voidable transactions   CC §3439.01
Organ procurement organization
    Drivers' licenses, use of encoded information   CC §1798.90.1
Original   Ev §255
Original creditor
    Private student loan collections reform   CC §1788.201
Ostensible agent   CC §2300
Ostensible authority of agent   CC §2317
Out-of-state residential facilities
    Interstate compact on placement of children, refusals to approve certain placements   Fam §7910
Outside this state
    Interstate family support   Fam §5700.102
Overpayment
    Student borrower bill of rights   CC §1788.100
Owner
    Commercial real property tenancies, disposition of property remaining upon termination   CC §1993
    Consumer privacy rights, personnel or work records or communications   CC §1798.145
    Landlord and tenant
        Rent increase limitations   CC §1947.12
        Requiring declawing or devocalizing animals as condition of occupancy   CC §1942.7
        Year's continuous, lawful occupation acting as limitation on termination of tenancy   CC §1946.2
    Mechanics' liens   CC §§8182, 8188, 8190
    Mortgage foreclosure consultants   CC §2945.1
    Unclaimed property claims   CCP §1540
Owner of qualifying residential property
    Parking, unbundling from price of rent   CC §1947.1
Owner or owners
    Consumer privacy rights, commercial credit reporting agencies   CC §1798.145
Ownership   CC §654
Ownership information
    Consumer privacy rights
        Scope of rights involving information shared between vehicle dealer and manufacturer   CC §1798.145
Owns
    Customer records, security procedures to protect personal information   CC §1798.81.5
Pacific Gas and Electric Company
    Action by Golden State Energy for acquisition of PG&E property   CCP §1240.655
Paid earnings   CCP §704.070
Paid prioritization
    Net neutrality   CC §3100
Panel
    Death penalty appeals and habeas corpus proceedings   CRC 8.601
Papers
    Trial court rules   CRC 2.3
Parent   Pro §54
    Indian children   Fam §170
    Interstate compact on placement of children   CRC 5.616
Parent and child relationship   Fam §7601

DEFINITIONS—Cont.
Parenting plan
    Custody of children, mediation   CRC 5.210
Parenting time
    Family rules   CRC 5.2
Parent or guardian   Fam §6903
Park trailer
    Special occupancy parks   CC §1866
Partial evaluation, investigation or assessment
    Child custody evaluators, qualifications for appointment   CRC 5.225
    Court-ordered child custody evaluation   CRC 5.220
Partial payment
    Student borrower bill of rights   CC §1788.100
Participant
    Mediators, standards of conduct   CRC 3.852
    Space flight liability and immunity   CC §2211
    Transitional housing program misconduct   CC §1954.12
Participant injury
    Space flight liability and immunity   CC §2211
Participating in discussions
    Judges, disqualification due to prospective service as dispute resolution neutral   CCP §170.1
Partition by sale
    Partition, heirs property   CCP §874.312
    Partition of real property   CCP §874.312
Partition in kind
    Partition, heirs property   CCP §874.312
    Partition of real property   CCP §874.312
Partner
    Attorney professional conduct   ProfC 1.0.1
Partnership interest   CC §684
Party   CCP §116.130
    Administrative adjudications, formal hearings   Gov §11500
    Appeals   CRC 8.10
    Appellate rules, superior court appeals   CRC 8.803
    Arbitrators, ethics standards for neutral arbitrators   CRC ArbEthicsStand 2
    Civil rules, coordination of complex actions   CRC 3.501
    Conservators, interstate jurisdiction, transfer and recognition   Pro §1982
    Disqualification of judges   CCP §170.1
    Electronic court records   CRC 2.502
    Ex parte communications, probate proceedings   CRC 7.10
    Family rules   CRC 5.2
    Mediators, standards of conduct   CRC 3.852
    Participation and testimony in probate guardianship proceedings   CRC 7.1016
    Remote appearances, civil cases generally   CRC 3.672
    Rules of court   CRC 1.6
Party-arbitrator
    Arbitrators, ethics standards for neutral arbitrators   CRC ArbEthicsStand 2
Party to the arbitration
    Arbitration   CCP §1280
Passenger manifest record
    Privacy, duties of carriers   CC §53.5
Passenger vehicle
    Rental passenger vehicle transactions   CC §1939.01
Patent deficiencies in planning or construction of real property   CCP §337.1
Patient information
    Consumer privacy rights   CC §1798.146
Pattern of conduct
    Stalking, tort   CC §1708.7
Payment
    Commercial online entertainment employment service providers, age information of subscribers   CC §1798.83.5
    Fiduciary income and principal act
        Marital trusts, allocation of receipts   Pro §16348
    Undisputed claims, penalty against state for failure to pay   Gov §927.2
Payment bond
    Mechanics' liens   CC §8030
Payment processing services
    Fair debt settlement practices   CC §1788.301
Payment processor
    Fair debt settlement practices   CC §1788.301
Payoff demand statement
    Equity lines of credit, suspending and closing line on borrower's instruction   CC §2943.1
Pay-on-death account   Pro §§55, 5140
Peace officer's or firefighter's dog
    Discrimination against officer or firefighter in lodging, eating, or transportation   CC §54.25

DEFINITIONS—Cont.
Penalties
    Lease provisions penalizing summoning emergency assistance   CC §1946.8
Pending proceeding
    Judicial ethics code   CRCSupp JudEthicsTerminology
Penitent   Ev §1031
Per capita   Pro §§245, 247
Percentage change in cost of living
    Floating homes, cap on rent increases   CC §800.40.5
    Landlord and tenant, rent increase limitations   CC §1947.12
    Mobilehomes and mobilehome parks, rent restrictions   CC §798.30.5
Perfection   CCP §697.590
Performance standard   Gov §11342.570
Permanent escheat   CCP §1300
Permanent medical excuse
    Juries and jurors, permanent medical excuse   CRC 2.1009
Permissible appointee
    Power of appointment   Pro §610
Permitted health care resident   CC §51.3
Perpetual interest   CC §691
Person   CCP §§17, 116.130, Fam §105
    Animal research and testing limitations   CC §1834.9
    Appellate rules, superior court appeals   CRC 8.803
    Attorney professional conduct   ProfC 1.0.1
    Autographed memorabilia   CC §1739.7
    Automated license plate recognition systems (ALPR), data security   CC §1798.90.5
    Automobile sales finance   CC §2981
    Canadian domestic violence protection orders, recognition and enforcement   Fam §6451
    Coerced debt   CC §1798.97.1
    Commercial and industrial common interest developments   CC §6560
    Commercial use of booking photographs   CC §1798.91.1
    Conservators, interstate jurisdiction, transfer and recognition   Pro §1982
    Consumer privacy rights   CC §1798.140
    Court records, public access   CRC 10.500
    Credit services organizations   CC §1789.12
    Discovery, interstate and international   CCP §2029.200
    Donations of food, immunity   CC §1714.25
    Electronic court records   CRC 2.502
    Ex parte communications, probate proceedings   CRC 7.10
    Fair debt settlement practices   CC §1788.301
    Family rules   CRC 5.14
    Fiduciary access to digital assets   Pro §871
    Fiduciary income and principal act   Pro §16321
    Gender-affirming health care or mental health care, restrictions on release of medical information   CC §56.109
    Genetic privacy   CC §56.18
    Groundwater rights actions   CCP §832
    Identity theft, business entity filings   CC §1798.200
    Interstate family support   Fam §5700.102
    Investigative consumer reporting agencies, disclosures when not using agency   CC §1786.53
    Mechanics' liens   CC §8032
    Mortgage foreclosure consultants   CC §2945.1
    Rules of court   CRC 1.6
    Sexually explicit depiction of individual, actions for damages   CC §1708.86
    Student borrower bill of rights   CC §1788.100
    Subcutaneous implanting of identification device, requiring of another   CC §52.7
    Uniform prudent management of institutional funds act   Pro §18502
    Violent video games   CC §1746
    Voidable transactions   CC §3439.01
Personal agriculture
    Common interest developments, homeowner engaging in   CC §4750
    Landlord and tenant, personal agriculture by tenant   CC §1940.10
Personal debt
    Rate of interest on judgments   CCP §685.010
    Renewal of judgments   CCP §683.110
Personal identifying information
    Guardians ad litem, appointment under pseudonym   CCP §372.5
    Identity theft
        Business entity filings   CC §1798.200
Personal information
    Consumer privacy rights   CC §1798.140
    Customer record, disposition   CC §1798.80
    Customer records, computerized personal information   CC §§1798.82, 1798.84
    Customer records, disclosure of personal information   CC §1798.83

DEFINITIONS—Cont.
Personal information—Cont.
    Customer records, security procedures to protect personal information   CC §1798.81.5
    Information practices, breach of security system   CC §1798.29
    Personal information restrictions of persons at or near family planning center   CC §1798.99.90
    Reader privacy act   CC §1798.90
    Subcutaneous implanting of identification device, requiring of another   CC §52.7
Personally identifying information
    Victim service providers, personal information protection   CC §1798.79.8
Personal micromobility device
    Landlord and tenant   CC §1940.41
Personal property   CC §663, CCP §17, Ev §180
Personal representatives   Pro §58
    Fiduciary access to digital assets   Pro §871
    Fiduciary income and principal act   Pro §16321
Personal vehicle sharing program
    Rental passenger vehicle transactions   CC §1939.01
Person or entity
    Victim service providers, personal information protection   CC §1798.79.8
Person who is at risk of homelessness
    Landlord and tenant, temporary residence by persons at risk of homelessness in dwelling unit of tenant   CC §1942.8
Person with a disability
    Accommodations requested of courts   CRC 1.100
    Guardians or conservators, payments pursuant to compromise or judgment   Pro §3603
    Juries and jurors, permanent medical excuse   CRC 2.1009
Per stirpes   Pro §§245, 246
Pertinent government rental assistance program
    COVID-19 rental housing recovery act   CCP §1179.09
Pest
    Pesticides   CC §1940.8.5
Pest control operators
    Landlord and tenant, bed bug infestations   CC §1954.601
Pesticide   CC §1940.8.5
    Animal testing, restrictions against   CC §1834.9.3
Pet
    Common interest development   CC §4715
Petition
    Adoption, sibling contact information requests   CRC 5.460
    Gang database removal, appeal proceedings   CRC 3.2300
    Small claims courts, writ petitions   CRC 8.971
Petitioner   Fam §126
    Fee waivers, conservatorships or guardianships   Gov §68631.5
    Guardianship and conservatorship, Indian child welfare act applicability   CRC 7.1015
    Harassment, protection orders   CCP §527.6
    Juvenile rules   CRC 5.502
    Postsecondary educational institutions, protection orders against violence threatened on campus or facility   CCP §527.85
    Small claims courts, writ petitions   CRC 8.971
    Workplace violence, protection orders   CCP §527.8
Petition for coordination
    Civil rules, coordination of complex actions   CRC 3.501
Pharmaceutical
    Drug take-back bins, limitation of liability   CC §1714.24
Pharmaceutical company
    Confidentiality of medical information   CC §56.05
Photographing
    Court proceedings, photographing, recording and broadcasting   CRC 1.150
Physical confinement
    Contempt   CCP §1219
Physical obstruction
    Force, threat or other obstruction of access to facility   CC §1708.9
Physician orders for life sustaining treatment form
    Resuscitative measures, requests regarding   Pro §4780
Physicians' negligence   CC §3333.1, CCP §§340.5, 364, 667.7, 1295
Place for adoption   Fam §8539
Placement
    Interstate compact on placement of children   CRC 5.616
Place of business   CC §1791
Place of public accommodation
    Construction-related accessibility claims, compliance with standards   CC §55.52
Place under surveillance
    Stalking, tort   CC §1708.7
Plain English   Gov §§11342, 11342.580

DEFINITIONS—Cont.
Plaintiff   CCP §§116.130, 308, 1063, Fam §126
    Groundwater rights actions   CCP §832
    Intervention   CCP §387
    Sexually explicit depiction of individual, actions for damages   CC §1708.86
    Small claims appeals   CRC 8.952
Planned development
    Commercial and industrial common interest developments   CC §6562
Plant crop
    Landlord and tenant, personal agriculture by tenant   CC §1940.10
Pleadings   CCP §420
    Ex parte communications, probate proceedings   CRC 7.10
    Family rules   CRC 5.74
    No contest clauses for wills, trusts, etc   Pro §23310
    Probate rules   CRC 7.3
Pledge of property   CC §2924
P.O.D accounts   Pro §§5101, 5140
Point-of-sale systems   CC §7100
Political items   CC §1739.2
Political organizations
    Judicial ethics code   CRCSupp JudEthicsTerminology
Political persecution
    Limitation of actions   CCP §338.2
Position of authority
    Rape and other sex offenses   CC §1708.5.5
Postrelease community supervision
    Sentencing rules, determinate sentencing   CRC 4.405
Postsecondary educational institutions
    Postsecondary educational institutions, protection orders against violence threatened on campus or facility   CCP §527.85
Post-trial motions
    Expedited jury trial   CCP §630.01, CRC 3.1545
Potential juror   CCP §194
Powerholders
    Power of appointment   Pro §610
    Trust decanting, uniform act   Pro §19502
Power of appointment   Pro §§610 to 613
Power of attorney
    Fiduciary access to digital assets   Pro §871
Power of direction
    Directed trusts   Pro §16602
Power of termination   CC §885.010
Preadoptive parent
    Juvenile rules   CRC 5.502
Precise geolocation
    Consumer privacy rights   CC §1798.140
        Personal information restrictions of persons at or near family planning center   CC §1798.99.90
Predeceased spouse   Pro §59
Preliminary fact   Ev §400
Preliminary notice
    Mechanics' liens   CC §8034
Prelitigation letter
    Construction-related accessibility claims, attorney prelitigation letters to education entity   CC §54.27
Premarital agreement   Fam §1610
Premises
    Commercial real property tenancies, disposition of property remaining upon termination   CC §1993
Prepaid account
    Child support, deposit of payments into qualifying account   Fam §17325
Prepaid debit card
    Consumer refunds offered by prepaid debit card   CC §1748.40
Prescriptive standard   Gov §11342.590
Present interest   CC §689
Presently exercisable power of appointment
    Trust decanting, uniform act   Pro §19502
Presiding judge
    Appellate rules, superior court appeals   CRC 8.803
    Judicial administration rules, complaints against subordinate judicial officers   CRC 10.703
    Rules of court   CRC 1.6
Presiding justice
    Rules of court   CRC 1.6
Presiding master
    Judicial performance commission rules   JudPerR 138
Presumption   Ev §600
Presumptive remainder beneficiary
    Trust decanting, expanded distributive discretion   Pro §19511
Prevailing party   CCP §1032

DEFINITIONS—Cont.
Previous homeowner
    Mobilehomes and mobilehome parks destroyed by natural disaster, offers of renewed tenancy   CC §798.62
Previously established father
    Uniform Parentage Act, vacation or setting aside of judgment   Fam §7645
Previously established mother
    Uniform Parentage Act, vacation or setting aside of judgment   Fam §7645
Primary providers
    Intercountry adoptions   Fam §8900.5
Principal
    Fiduciary access to digital assets   Pro §871
    Fiduciary income and principal act   Pro §16321
Principal amount of judgment   CCP §680.300
Principal residence
    Jury selection   CCP §197
Principal term
    Sentencing rules, determinate sentencing   CRC 4.405
Priority housing development
    Actions challenging priority housing development projects   CCP §425.19
Private area
    Landlord and tenant, personal agriculture by tenant   CC §1940.10
    Tenant use of clothesline or drying rack in private areas   CC §1940.20
Private child support collector   Fam §5610
Private duty nurses   CC §1812.524
Private education lenders
    Private student loan collections reform   CC §1788.201
Private education loan collection action
    Private student loan collections reform   CC §1788.201
Private education loan collectors
    Private student loan collections reform   CC §1788.201
Private education loans
    Private student loan collections reform   CC §1788.201
Privately compensated
    Temporary judges, party request   CRC 2.830
Private, personal, and familial activities
    Invasion of privacy   CC §1708.8
Private practice of law   CCP §170.5
Private programs, services and professionals
    Language access services   CRC 1.300
Privileged information
    Court records, public access   CRC 10.500
Probabilistic identifier
    Consumer privacy rights   CC §1798.140
Probability of parentage
    Genetic testing to determine parentage   Fam §7550.5
Probate attorneys
    Education of personnel responsible for probate cases   CRC 10.478
    Qualifications of personnel responsible for probate cases   CRC 10.776
Probate conservatorship
    Guardianship or conservatorship proceedings, attorney qualifications   CRC 7.1101
Probate estate
    Claims against estates   Pro §19000
Probate examiners
    Education of personnel responsible for probate cases   CRC 10.478
    Qualifications of personnel responsible for probate cases   CRC 10.776
Probate guardianship
    Guardianship or conservatorship proceedings, attorney qualifications   CRC 7.1101
Probate proceedings
    Education of personnel responsible for probate cases   CRC 10.478
    Judges and subordinate judicial officers, education   CRC 10.468
    Qualifications of personnel responsible for probate cases   CRC 10.776
Probation officer
    Juvenile rules   CRC 5.502
Proceeding   Fam §110
    Family rules   CRC 5.2
    Participation and testimony in probate guardianship proceedings   CRC 7.1016
    Remote appearances, civil cases generally   CRC 3.672
Process   CCP §17
Processing
    Consumer privacy rights   CC §1798.140
Professional fiduciaries
    Conservatorships, abuse   Pro §2112
    Probate code   Pro §60.1
Professional negligence   CCP §§340.5, 364
    Arbitration of professional negligence, contracts for medical services requiring   CCP §1295
    Medical negligence, limitation on damages   CC §3333.2

DEFINITIONS—Cont.
Professional person
  Consent by minor to mental health treatment, counseling or residential shelter services   Fam §6924
Professional provider
  Child custody, supervised visitation   Fam §3200.5
  Supervised visitation services providers, standards   CRC JudAdminStand 5.20
Proffered evidence   Ev §401
Profiling
  Age-appropriate design code   CC §1798.99.30
  Consumer privacy rights   CC §1798.140
Profiteer of the felony   CC §2225
Program misconduct
  Transitional housing program misconduct   CC §1954.12
Program operators
  Transitional housing program misconduct   CC §1954.12
Program-related asset
  Uniform prudent management of institutional funds act   Pro §18502
Program sites
  Transitional housing program misconduct   CC §1954.12
Prohibition writ   CCP §1102
Promoter
  Autographed memorabilia   CC §1739.7
Proof   Ev §190
Proof of income
  COVID-19 tenant relief act   CCP §1179.02.5
Proof of service
  Rules applicable to all courts   CRC 1.21
Property   CCP §§17, 680.310, Ev §185, Fam §113, Pro §62
  Civil code   CC §14
  Emergency declaration, transfer of property within geographic limits of declared area   CC §2968
  Family rules   CRC 5.2
  Landlord and tenant, water service in multifamily residential rental buildings   CC §1954.202
  Voidable transactions   CC §3439.01
Property appropriated to public use
  Eminent domain to acquire property subject to conservation easement   CCP §1240.055
Property declaration   Fam §115
Property owner
  Lead paint abatement program   CC §3494.5
  Religious items displayed on dwelling entry, property owner restrictions   CC §1940.45
Proposed action   Gov §11342.595
  Trustees, notice of proposed actions   Pro §16500
Proposed conservatee
  Conservators, interstate jurisdiction, transfer and recognition   Pro §1982
Proposed nomination
  Arbitrators, ethics standards for neutral arbitrators   CRC ArbEthicsStand 2
Prosecuting attorney
  Appellate rules, superior court appeals   CRC 8.803
Prosecuting authority
  False claims act, filing records under seal   CRC 2.570
Prospective adoptive parent   Fam §8542
Prospective juror   CCP §194
Prospective owner-occupant
  Foreclosure sales   CC §2924m
    Purchases from institutions foreclosing on specified number of residential properties   CC §2924p
Prospective regular grand juror
  Demographic data on regular grand jurors   CRC 10.625
Protected consumers
  Protected consumer security freezes   CC §1785.11.9
Protected health information
  Consumer privacy rights   CC §1798.146
Protected individual   Fam §6401
  Canadian domestic violence protection orders, recognition and enforcement   Fam §6451
  Confidentiality of medical information   CC §56.05
Protected instruments
  No contest clauses for wills, trusts, etc   Pro §23310
Protected tenant
  Change of lock upon request by protected tenant   CC §1941.6
Protected time period
  COVID-19 tenant relief act   CCP §1179.02
Protective order   Fam §§6218, 6401
  Child custody, domestic violence protocol for family court services   CRC 5.215
  Family rules, settlement service providers   CRC 5.420

DEFINITIONS—Cont.
Protectors
  Decanting of trusts, trusts for care of animals   Pro §19523
Protocols
  Juvenile rules   CRC 5.518
Provide employment services
  Commercial online entertainment employment service providers, age information of subscribers   CC §1798.83.5
Provider
  Commercial financing transactions with small businesses   CC §1799.300
  Shared mobility devices   CC §2505
Provider of health care
  Consumer privacy rights   CC §1798.146
Providers
  Medical claims data error correction   CC §57
  Reader privacy act   CC §1798.90
  Supervised visitation services providers, standards   CRC JudAdminStand 5.20
Provisionally licensed lawyer
  Attorneys at law, provisional licensure of 2020 law school graduates   CRC 9.49
    Pathway to full licensure, provisional licensure with   CRC 9.49.1
Provisionally qualified
  Interpreters, appointment in court proceedings   CRC 2.893
Proxies
  Common interest developments, member elections   CC §5130
Pseudonymization
  Consumer privacy rights   CC §1798.140
Pseudonymize
  Consumer privacy rights   CC §1798.140
Psychiatric advance directive   Pro §4679
Psychotherapist   CC §43.93, Ev §1010
  Confidentiality of medical information   CC §56.104
  Confidentiality of medical records, dependent children removed from parental custody   CC §56.016
Psychotropic medication
  Juvenile rules   CRC 5.640
Public agencies   CCP §1240.140
  Automated license plate recognition systems (ALPR), data security   CC §1798.90.5
  Health and safety labor or service providers to public agencies, logo display restrictions   CC §3273
Public domestic authority
  Intercountry adoptions   Fam §8900.5
Public employee   Ev §195
Public entities   CCP §§481.200, 1235.190, Ev §200
  Commercial use of booking photographs   CC §1798.91.1
  Lead paint abatement program   CC §3494.5
  Mechanics' liens   CC §8036
Public entity
  Foster family agency accountability   CCP §1062.32
Public health and safety labor or services
  Health and safety labor or service providers to public agencies, logo display restrictions   CC §3273
Publicly available
  Consumer privacy rights   CC §1798.140
Publicly display
  Social security numbers   CC §1798.85
Public nuisance   CC §3480
Public or semipublic internet-based service or application
  Online violence prevention   CC §1798.99.20
Public records
  Investigative consumer reporting agencies, disclosures when not using agency   CC §1786.53
  Social security number truncation program   Gov §27300
Public safety agency
  911 service, telecommunications services, immunity from liability   CC §1714.55
Public social services
  Unfair or deceptive competition   CC §1770
  Unreasonable fees to assist applicants for public social services as deceptive practice   CC §1770
Public trail   CCP §731.5
Public water systems
  Groundwater rights actions   CCP §832
Public works contract
  Mechanics' liens   CC §8038
Punishment
  Juvenile rules   CRC 5.502
Purchase order
  Automobile sales finance   CC §2981

DEFINITIONS—Cont.
Purpose of housing onsite employees
    Mobilehomes and mobilehome parks, management employees   CC §798.23
Putative spouse   CCP §377.60
Qualified beneficiary
    Trust decanting, uniform act   Pro §19502
Qualified benefits property
    Trust decanting, tax situations   Pro §19519
Qualified business rental
    Rental passenger vehicle transactions, business program sponsors   CC §1939.21
Qualified commercial tenant
    Commercial real property tenancies   CC §1950.9
    Leases and contracts   CC §§827, 1632
Qualified court investigator   Fam §8543
Qualified defendants
    Construction-related accessibility claims, compliance with standards   CC §55.52
Qualified interpreter
    Evidence, interpreters and translators   Ev §754
Qualified juror   CCP §194
Qualified juror list   CCP §194
Qualified legal services project
    Electronic court records   CRC 2.502
Qualified mobilehome park
    Mobilehomes and mobilehome parks, rent restrictions   CC §798.30.5
Qualified ownership   CC §§654, 678, 680
Qualified permanent resident   CC §51.3
Qualified request
    Student borrower bill of rights   CC §1788.100
Qualified third parties
    Landlord and tenant, restrictions on termination of tenancy of victims of certain crimes   CC §1946.7
Qualified third party
    Change of lock upon request by eligible tenant   CC §1941.5
Qualified third-party professional;
    Coerced debt   CC §1798.97.1
Qualified written request
    Student borrower bill of rights   CC §1788.100
Qualifying accounts
    Child support, deposit of payments into qualifying account   Fam §17325
Qualifying institution
    Registered in-house counsel   CRC 9.46
Qualifying residential property
    Parking, unbundling from price of rent   CC §1947.1
Quasi-community property   Fam §125, Pro §66
Quasi-marital property   Fam §2251
Quasi-public entity
    Eminent domain   CCP §1245.320
Qui tam plaintiff
    False claims act, filing records under seal   CRC 2.570
Quote
    Rental passenger vehicle transactions   CC §1939.01
        Business program sponsor rentals   CC §1939.21
Race
    Unruh civil rights act   CC §51
Race or ethnicity
    Demographic data on regular grand jurors   CRC 10.625
Radio frequency identification
    Radio frequency identification (RFID) to remotely read identification document without knowledge or consent   CC §1798.795
Random   CCP §194
Ranking
    Marketplace sales and sellers, commercial relationships, terms and conditions   CC §1749.7
Ratio utility billing system
    Landlord and tenant, water service in multifamily residential rental buildings   CC §1954.202
Readers
    Radio frequency identification (RFID) to remotely read identification document without knowledge or consent   CC §1798.795
Readoption
    Adoption, visitation with adopted siblings   Fam §8920
Real party in interest
    Small claims courts, writ petitions   CRC 8.971
Real property   CC §§658, 659, CCP §§17, 680.320, Ev §205
    Transfer on death deeds   Pro §5610
Real property sales contracts   CC §2995

DEFINITIONS—Cont.
Real property security
    Deeds of trust and mortgages, secured party access to inspect for environmental damage   CC §2929.5
    Receivers   CCP §564
Reasonable
    Attorney professional conduct   ProfC 1.0.1
Reasonable belief
    Attorney professional conduct   ProfC 1.0.1
    Commercial real property tenancies, disposition of property remaining upon termination   CC §1993
Reasonable cause
    Claims against public entities and employees, late payment   Gov §927.2
Reasonable controls
    Firearm industry standards of conduct   CC §3273.50
Reasonable costs
    Business records, costs of production   Ev §1563
    Electric vehicle charging stations, commercial lease restrictions   CC §1952.7
    Medical records, inspection   Ev §1158
Reasonable diligence
    Attorney professional conduct   ProfC 1.3
Reasonable efforts
    Juvenile rules   CRC 5.502
Reasonable network management
    Net neutrality   CC §3100
Reasonable restrictions
    Commercial and industrial common interest developments, protected use for charging stations   CC §6713
    Common interest developments, restrictions on accessory or junior accessory dwelling units   CC §4751
    Covenants, unenforceability of accessory dwelling unit prohibitions   CC §714.3
    Electric vehicle charging stations, commercial lease restrictions   CC §1952.7
    Housing development projects using authorized floor area ratio standards, unenforceability of restrictions   CC §4747
    Personal agriculture by common interest development homeowner   CC §4750
Reasonable standards
    Electric vehicle charging stations, commercial lease restrictions   CC §1952.7
Reasonably
    Attorney professional conduct   ProfC 1.0.1
Reasonably available
    Adoption service provider   Fam §8502
Reasonably definite standard
    Trust decanting, uniform act   Pro §19502
Reasonably should know
    Attorney professional conduct   ProfC 1.0.1
Receivables   CCP §1800
Received by a state agency
    Claims against public entities and employees, late payment   Gov §927.2
Receiving court
    Probation, out-of-county transfers   CRC 4.530
Recipient
    Commercial financing transactions with small businesses   CC §1799.300
Reciprocal assignment orders
    Trial court management   CRC 10.630
Recognized employee organization
    Labor relations of court employees   CRC 10.652
Record
    Canadian domestic violence protection orders, recognition and enforcement   Fam §6451
    Commercial real property tenancies, disposition of property remaining upon termination   CC §1993
    Conservators, interstate jurisdiction, transfer and recognition   Pro §1982
    Customer record, disposition   CC §1798.80
    Fiduciary access to digital assets   Pro §871
    Interstate family support   Fam §5700.102
    Landlord and tenant, abandoned personal property disposition   CC §1980
    Levying officer electronic transactions act   CCP §263.1
    Name change proceedings under address confidentiality program   CRC 2.575
    Partition, heirs property   CCP §874.312
    Protected consumer security freezes   CC §1785.11.9
    Sealed and confidential records, appellate rules for supreme court and courts of appeal   CRC 8.45
    Trial court rules, sealed records   CRC 2.550
    Uniform prudent management of institutional funds act   Pro §18502
    Voidable transactions   CC §3439.01

DEFINITIONS—Cont.
Recorded
    Transfer on death deeds   Pro §5612
Recordings
    Court proceedings, photographing, recording and broadcasting   CRC 1.150
Record on appeal
    Juvenile case appeals, confidentiality   CRC 8.401
Record on writ petition
    Juvenile case appeals, confidentiality   CRC 8.401
Record owners   CCP §1255.450
Records
    Fiduciary income and principal act   Pro §16321
    Partition of real property   CCP §874.312
Records in the juvenile case file
    Juvenile case appeals, confidentiality   CRC 8.401
Recreational vehicle parks   CC §§799.29, 799.30
Recreational vehicles
    Special occupancy parks   CC §1866
Recross-examination   Ev §763
Redacted version
    Sealed and confidential records, appellate rules for supreme court and courts of appeal   CRC 8.45
Redirect examination   Ev §762
Reel
    Records of court proceedings, electronic   CRC 2.952
Referral
    Commercial financing transactions with small businesses   CC §1799.300
Refund
    Consumer refunds offered by prepaid debit card   CC §1748.40
Regional court interpreter coordinator
    Court interpreters, cross-assignments   CRC 10.762
Register
    Interstate family support   Fam §5700.102
    TOD security registration act   Pro §5501
Registered domestic partner
    Judicial ethics code   CRCSupp JudEthicsTerminology
Registered interpreter
    Interpreters, appointment in court proceedings   CRC 2.893
Registered process server   CCP §§481.205, 680.330
Registering entity
    TOD security registration act   Pro §5501
Registering tribunal
    Interstate family support   Fam §5700.102
Regular filing hours
    Electronic filing and service rules   CRC 2.250
Regular grand jury
    Demographic data on regular grand jurors   CRC 10.625
Regularly assigned to hear probate proceedings
    Probate cases, education of judges and subordinate judicial officers regularly assigned to   CRC 10.468
Regulation   Gov §§11342, 11342.600
Regulation Z
    Automobile sales finance   CC §2981
Regulatory agency
    Information practices   CC §1798.3
Related by blood or affinity
    Donative transfers   Pro §21374
Related cases
    Civil rules   CRC 3.300
    Family rules, coordination of court resources   CRC 5.440
Related cause of action   CCP §426.10
Relationship index
    Genetic testing to determine parentage   Fam §7550.5
Relative
    Juvenile rules   CRC 5.502
Relative caregiver   Fam §17550
Release
    Deeds of trust and mortgages, secured party access to inspect for environmental damage   CC §2929.5
    Receivers   CCP §564
Relevant evidence   Ev §210
Religion
    Discrimination   CC §51
Religious items
    Religious items displayed on dwelling entry, property owner restrictions   CC §1940.45
Remainder   CC §769
Remainderman   CC §731.03
Remand
    Civil rules, coordination of complex actions   CRC 3.501

DEFINITIONS—Cont.
Remote access
    Electronic court records   CRC 2.502
Remote appearance
    Remote appearances, civil cases generally   CRC 3.672
Remote-computing services
    Fiduciary access to digital assets   Pro §871
Remotely
    Radio frequency identification (RFID) to remotely read identification document without knowledge or consent   CC §1798.795
Remote proceeding
    Remote appearances, civil cases generally   CRC 3.672
Remote technical assistance
    Rental-purchase contracts   CC §1812.622
Remote technology
    Marriage, remote licensing and solemnization   Fam §560
    Remote appearances, civil cases generally   CRC 3.672
Removal
    Juvenile rules   CRC 5.502
Rental agreement
    Landlord and tenant, water service in multifamily residential rental buildings   CC §1954.202
Rental company
    Rental passenger vehicle transactions   CC §1939.01
Rental debt
    COVID-19 rental housing recovery act   CCP §1179.09
Rental debt that accumulated due to COVID-19 hardship
    COVID-19 rental housing recovery act   CCP §1179.09
Rental payment
    COVID-19 tenant relief act   CCP §1179.02
Rental-purchase agreement   CC §1812.622
Renter
    Rental passenger vehicle transactions   CC §1939.01
Renting
    Landlord and tenant, water service in multifamily residential rental buildings   CC §1954.202
Rent skimming   CC §890
Repair service facility   CC §1791
Reporting user
    Child sexual abuse hosted on social media platform   CC §3273.65
Representation
    Autographed memorabilia   CC §1739.7
Representative
    Protected consumer security freezes   CC §1785.11.9
Representative of the news media
    Court records, public access   CRC 10.500
Representative of victim
    Domestic violence, access to reports   Fam §6228
Reproductive health care services
    Legally protected health care services   CC §1798.300
Reproductive or sexual health application information
    Confidentiality of medical information   CC §56.05
Reproductive or sexual health digital service
    Confidentiality of medical information   CC §56.05
Requester
    Judges, committee on judicial ethics opinions   CRCSupp JudEthicsOpinionsIOP 2
Request for hearing
    Family rules, interstate income withholding orders   CRC 5.335
Request for review
    Gang database removal, appeal proceedings   CRC 3.2300
Request regarding resuscitative measures   Pro §4780
Require
    Judicial ethics code   CRCSupp JudEthicsTerminology
Require, coerce or compel
    Subcutaneous implanting of identification device, requiring of another   CC §52.7
Required payment approval date
    Claims against public entities and employees, late payment   Gov §927.2
Reschedule the hearing
    Family rules   CRC 5.2
Research
    Consumer privacy rights   CC §1798.140
Reservation
    Indian children   Fam §170
Residence
    Guardians and conservators of the person   Pro §2350
Residence in foreclosure
    Mortgage foreclosure consultants   CC §2945.1
Resident
    Illegal expenditure, waste, etc, of public funds   CCP §526a

DEFINITIONS—Cont.
  Resident—Cont.
    Intergenerational housing developments CC §51.3.5
    Lease provisions penalizing summoning emergency assistance CC §1946.8
    Recreational vehicle parks CC §799.31
  Residential mortgage loan
    Fiduciary duties of mortgage brokers CC §2923.1
  Residential real property CC §2924.6
    Landlord and tenant
      Rent increase limitations CC §1947.12
      Year's continuous, lawful occupation acting as limitation on termination of tenancy CC §1946.2
  Residential shelter services
    Consent by minor to mental health treatment, counseling or residential shelter services Fam §6924
  Resigned members
    Attorney professional conduct
      Law firm employment of disbarred, suspended, resigned or involuntarily inactive lawyers ProfC 5.3.1
  Resource conservation districts
    Undisputed claims, penalty against state for failure to pay Gov §927.2
  Respondent Fam §127
    Administrative adjudications, formal hearings Gov §11500
    Appeals CRC 8.10
    Appellate rules, superior court appeals CRC 8.803
    Canadian domestic violence protection orders, recognition and enforcement Fam §6451
    Harassment, protection orders CCP §527.6
    Postsecondary educational institutions, protection orders against violence threatened on campus or facility CCP §527.85
    Small claims courts, writ petitions CRC 8.971
    Tribal court civil money judgment act CCP §1732
    Workplace violence, protection orders CCP §527.8
  Responding state
    Interstate family support Fam §5700.102
  Responding tribunal
    Interstate family support Fam §5700.102
  Responsible party
    Lead paint abatement program CC §3494.5
  Responsible person
    Juvenile dependency proceedings, counsel collections program guidelines CRCAppx F
  Restrictive covenants
    Recorded restrictive covenants, unenforceability in face of approved and recorded restrictive covenant affordable housing modification document CC §714.6
  Results of a risk/needs assessment
    Judicial administration, risk/needs assessment use in sentencing CRC JudAdminStand 4.35
  Retail credit card CC §1748.13
  Retail installment sales CC §1802.5
  Retail motor fuel dispenser
    Credit cards CC §1747.02
  Retail motor fuel payment island automated cashier
    Credit cards CC §1747.02
  Retail seller CC §1749.1
    Slavery and human trafficking in supply chain, disclosures by businesses of efforts to eradicate CC §1714.43
  Retirement plan
    Execution, property exempt from CCP §704.115
  Return
    Habeas corpus CRC 4.545
  Returned
    Marriage licenses Fam §359
  Return to retail seller
    Consumer warranty protection CC §1791
  Reusable tenant screening report CC §1950.1
  Reversion CC §768
  Review department
    Attorneys, judges and law practice, rules governing CRC 9.1
  Reviewing court
    Appeals CRC 8.10
    Appellate rules, superior court appeals CRC 8.803
  Revocable TOD deeds
    Transfer on death deeds Pro §69
  Revocable transfer on death deeds
    Transfer on death deeds Pro §§69, 5614
  Revolving fund
    Claims against public entities and employees, late payment Gov §927.2

DEFINITIONS—Cont.
  RFID
    Radio frequency identification (RFID) to remotely read identification document without knowledge or consent CC §1798.795
  Right of representation, distribution by Pro §§245, 246
  Risk
    Judicial administration, risk/needs assessment use in sentencing CRC JudAdminStand 4.35
  Risk factors
    Judicial administration, risk/needs assessment use in sentencing CRC JudAdminStand 4.35
  Risk/needs assessment
    Sentencing rules, determinate sentencing CRC 4.405
  Risk score
    Judicial administration, risk/needs assessment use in sentencing CRC JudAdminStand 4.35
  Royalty recipient
    Audits of sound recording royalty reporting parties CC §2500
  Royalty reporting party
    Audits of sound recording royalty reporting parties CC §2500
  Rule
    Appellate rules, superior court appeals CRC 8.803
    Rules of court CRC 1.6
  Rule change
    Common interest developments, operating rules CC §4340
  Rules of conduct
    Mediation, complaints about court-program mediators CRC 3.866
  Sacramento arena project
    Appellate review of CEQA cases CRC 8.700
    Petitions under environmental quality act, civil rules governing CRC 3.2220
  Sacramento entertainment and sports center project
    Appellate review of CEQA cases CRC 8.700
    Petitions under environmental quality act, civil rules governing CRC 3.2220
  Safe at home participant
    Common interest developments, record inspection involving safe at home program participants CC §5216
  Safe at home program
    Common interest developments, record inspection involving safe at home program participants CC §5216
  Safety and best interest of the child
    Juvenile rules CRC 5.518
  Safety of family members
    Juvenile rules CRC 5.518
  Sale
    Consumer privacy rights CC §1798.140
  Sale or transfer
    Water conserving plumbing retrofits CC §1101.3
  Sanctions
    Family rules CRC 5.14
  Satisfactory evidence
    Acknowledgments CC §1185
  Savings fund
    Actions to recover savings fund amounts CCP §354.7
  School
    Educational debt collection practices CC §1788.92
  School-linked services coordinator
    Medical records, disclosures CC §56.10
  Screened
    Attorney professional conduct ProfC 1.0.1
  Seal CCP §14
  Sealed
    Sealed and confidential records, appellate rules for supreme court and courts of appeal CRC 8.45
    Trial court rules, sealing records CRC 2.550
  Search and rescue dogs
    Discrimination in lodging, eating or transportation CC §54.25
  Search and review time
    Court records, public access CRC 10.500
  Second trust
    Trust decanting, uniform act Pro §19502
  Second trust instrument
    Trust decanting, uniform act Pro §19502
  Secretary
    Intercountry adoptions Fam §8900.5
  Section CCP §17
    Juvenile rules CRC 5.502
    Sentencing rules, determinate sentencing CRC 4.405

DEFINITIONS—Cont.
Secured lender
    Deeds of trust and mortgages, secured party access to inspect for environmental damage   CC §2929.5
    Receivers   CCP §564
Secured party   CCP §680.340
Secure drug take-back bins
    Drug take-back bins, limitation of liability   CC §1714.24
Secure electronic signature
    Appellate rules, e-filing in supreme court and courts of appeal   CRC 8.70
Secure, long-term storage
    Personal micromobility devices, landlord and tenant   CC §1940.41
Security   CC §§680.345, 1950.5
    TOD security registration act   Pro §5501
Security account
    TOD security registration act   Pro §5501
Security agreement   CCP §1800
Security alerts   CC §1785.11.1
Security and integrity
    Consumer privacy rights   CC §1798.140
Security credentials
    Customer records, computerized personal information   CC §1798.82
    Information practices, breach of security system   CC §1798.29
Security features
    Connected devices, security   CC §1798.91.05
Security freezes   CC §1785.11.2
    Protected consumer security freezes   CC §1785.11.9
Security interests   CCP §§680.360, 1800
Security testing
    Electronic recording delivery systems   Gov §27390
Self-directed study
    Judicial administration rules, continuing education of judicial branch   CRC 10.493
Self-exit
    Interim homelessness programs, occupancy   CC §1954.08
Self-represented
    Electronic filing and service rules   CRC 2.250
Sell
    Consumer privacy rights   CC §1798.140
        Personal information restrictions of persons at or near family planning center   CC §1798.99.90
    Real estate brokers and sales persons   CC §2079.13
Seller
    Automobile sales finance   CC §2981
    Buyer's choice act   CC §1103.22
Seller assisted marketing plan   CC §1812.201
Seller's agent
    Real estate brokers and sales persons   CC §2079.13
Selling
    Consumer privacy rights   CC §1798.140
Seminar solicitation sales contracts   CC §1689.24
Senior citizen
    Deeds of trust and mortgages, modification or workout plan to avoid foreclosure   CC §2944.8
    Home solicitation sales contracts   CC §1689.5
    Intergenerational housing developments   CC §51.3.5
    Seminar solicitation sales contracts   CC §1689.24
Senior citizen housing developments   CC §51.3
Sensitive personal information
    Consumer privacy rights   CC §1798.140
Sensitive services
    Confidentiality of medical information   CC §56.05
Sentence choice
    Sentencing rules, determinate sentencing   CRC 4.405
Separate fund
    Fiduciary income and principal act
        Marital trusts, allocation of receipts   Pro §16348
Separate interest
    Commercial and industrial common interest developments   CC §6564
Separate property   Fam §§130, 770, 2502, 3515
Separate residential units
    Mechanics' liens   CC §8448
Serve and file
    Civil rules, coordination of complex actions   CRC 3.501
    Rules applicable to all courts   CRC 1.21
Service
    Appellate rules, superior court appeals   CRC 8.803
    Cancellation of utility, cable, etc, services on behalf of deceased person   Pro §217
    Consumer privacy rights   CC §1798.140
    Home solicitation sales contracts   CC §1689.5

DEFINITIONS—Cont.
Service—Cont.
    Mortgage foreclosure consultants   CC §2945.1
    Rules of court   CRC 1.6
Service bulletins   CC §1795.90
Service by fax
    Fax filing and service   CRC 2.301
Service contract   CC §1791
    Automobile sales finance   CC §2981
Service contract administrator
    Consumer warranty protection   CC §1791
Service contract seller
    Consumer warranty protection   CC §1791
Service member
    Attorney practice, registered military spouse attorneys   CRC 9.41.1
Service organizations
    Judicial ethics code   CRCSupp JudEthicsTerminology
Service provider
    Consumer privacy rights   CC §1798.140
    Genetic privacy   CC §56.18
Service provider for disabled juror   CCP §224
Servicing
    Student borrower bill of rights   CC §1788.100
Servient tenement   CC §803
Settlement account
    Fair debt settlement practices   CC §1788.301
Settlement services
    Family rules, settlement service providers   CRC 5.420
Settlor
    Directed trusts   Pro §16602
    Fiduciary income and principal act   Pro §16321
    Trust decanting, uniform act   Pro §19502
Several ownership   CC §681
Sex
    Discrimination   CC §51
Sex, race, color, religion, ancestry, national origin, disability, medical condition, genetic information, marital status or sexual orientation
    Discrimination   CC §51
Sex trafficking
    Hotels, actions against for sex trafficking activity   CC §52.65
Sexual assault
    Actions for damages   CCP §340.16
    Contempt, enforcement against victims for refusal to testify   CCP §1219
    Settlement of employment disputes   CCP §1002.5
Sexual battery   CC §1708.5
Sexual conduct
    Sexually explicit depiction of individual, actions for damages   CC §1708.86
Sexual contact   CC §43.93
Sexual harassment
    Settlement of employment disputes   CCP §1002.5
Sexually explicit material
    Sexually explicit depiction of individual, actions for damages   CC §1708.86
Sexual orientation
    Discrimination   CC §51
Sexual orientation violence
    Unruh civil rights act   CC §52.45
Sexual relations
    Attorney professional conduct   ProfC 1.8.10
Shall
    Judicial performance commission rules   JudPerR 138
Share
    Consumer privacy rights   CC §1798.140
        Personal information restrictions of persons at or near family planning center   CC §1798.99.90
Shared
    Consumer privacy rights   CC §1798.140
Shared appreciation loans   CC §1917
Shared mobility device   CC §2505
Shared mobility service providers
    Shared mobility devices   CC §2505
Sharing
    Consumer privacy rights   CC §1798.140
Shelter program
    Interim homelessness programs, occupancy   CC §1954.08
Shelter program administrator
    Interim homelessness programs, occupancy   CC §1954.08
Shelter program operator
    Interim homelessness programs, occupancy   CC §1954.08

DEFINITIONS—Cont.
  Shelter program participants
      Interim homelessness programs, occupancy CC §1954.08
  Sheriff CCP §17
      Rules of court CRC 1.6
  Short cause cases
      Civil rules, case management CRC 3.735
  Short-pay agreements
      Mortgages and deeds of trust CC §2943
  Short-pay demand statements
      Mortgages and deeds of trust CC §2943
  Short-pay requests
      Mortgages and deeds of trust CC §2943
  Short-term rental
      Cancellation of reservations, refunds CC §1748.80
  Sibling
      Adoption, sibling contact information requests CRC 5.460
      Adoption, visitation with adopted siblings Fam §8920
  Sibling group
      Juvenile rules CRC 5.502
  Side
      Civil rules, coordination of complex actions CRC 3.501
  Sign
      Voidable transactions CC §3439.01
  Signatures CCP §17
  Signed
      Attorney professional conduct ProfC 1.0.1
      Common interest developments, member elections CC §5130
  Significant-connection state
      Conservators, interstate jurisdiction, transfer and recognition Pro §1991
  Significant personal relationship
      Arbitrators, ethics standards for neutral arbitrators CRC ArbEthicsStand 2
  Simple-interest basis
      Automobile sales finance CC §2981
  Single-family, owner-occupied dwelling CC §2954.4
  Single-family residential property
      Real estate brokers and salespersons CC §2079.13
      Residential exclusive listing agreements act CC §1670.12
  Single-family residential real property
      Real estate brokers and salespersons CC §2079.13
      Water conserving plumbing retrofits CC §1101.3
  Sister state judgment CCP §1710.10
  Site
      Construction-related accessibility claims, compliance with standards CC §55.52
      Mechanics' liens CC §8040
      Special occupancy parks CC §1866
  Site improvement
      Mechanics' liens CC §8042
  Slander CC §46
  Sliding scale recovery agreements CCP §877.5
  Small business CCP §1028.5, Gov §§11342, 11342.610
      Claims against public entities and employees, late payment Gov §927.2
      Commercial financing transactions with small businesses CC §1799.300
  Small claims court
      Small claims appeals CRC 8.952
      Writ petitions in small claims courts CRC 8.971
  Smoking
      Landlord and tenant, prohibition of smoking CC §1947.5
  Social media company
      Child sexual abuse hosted on social media platform CC §3273.65
  Social media platform
      Child sexual abuse hosted on social media platform CC §3273.65
      Commercial sexual exploitation of minor by social media platform CC §3345.1
      Online violence prevention CC §1798.99.20
  Social study
      Juvenile rules CRC 5.502
  Social workers
      Juvenile rules CRC 5.502
  Software
      Child support, computer software used to determine support amount CRC 5.275
  Solar energy system CC §801.5
  Sold
      Consumer privacy rights CC §1798.140
  Sole legal custody Fam §3006
  Sole ownership CC §681
  Sole physical custody Fam §3007
  Solicit
      Arbitrators, ethics standards on marketing CRC ArbEthicsStand 17

DEFINITIONS—Cont.
  Solicitation
      Arbitration CCP §1281.9
      Unfair competition and trade practices CC §1770
  Source code
      Electronic recording delivery systems Gov §27390
  Source list CCP §194
  Space
      Special occupancy parks, danger requiring move CC §1866
  Space flight activities
      Space flight liability and immunity CC §2211
  Space flight entities
      Space flight liability and immunity CC §2211
  Special agent CC §2297
  Special damages CC §48a
  Special liens CC §§2873, 2875
  Special-needs child Fam §8545
  Special needs fiduciary
      Trust decanting, beneficiaries with a disability Pro §19513
  Special needs trusts
      Duty to maintain incapacitated child Fam §3910
      Trust decanting, beneficiaries with a disability Pro §19513
  Special occupancy parks CC §1866
      Danger requiring move CC §1866
  Special proceedings CCP §23
  Special tax benefit
      Fiduciary income and principal act Pro §16321
  Spousal support CCP §680.365, Fam §142
  Spousal support order
      Interstate family support Fam §5700.102
  Spouse
      Registered domestic partner
          Inclusion in definition of spouse CC §14, CCP §17, Ev §215, Fam §143, Pro §72
  State CCP §17, Fam §145
      Canadian domestic violence protection orders, recognition and enforcement Fam §6451
      Conservators, interstate jurisdiction, transfer and recognition Pro §1982
      Discovery, interstate and international CCP §2029.200
      Earnings withholding order for taxes CCP §706.070
      Interstate family support Fam §5700.102
      Trust decanting, uniform act Pro §19502
  State agency Gov §§11342.520, 11500
  State bar court
      Attorneys, judges and law practice, rules governing CRC 9.1
  State of emergency
      Emergency declaration, transfer of property within geographic limits of declared area CC §2968
  State small water systems
      Groundwater rights actions CCP §832
  State tax liability
      Earnings withholding order for taxes CCP §706.070
  Static risk factors
      Judicial administration, risk/needs assessment use in sentencing CRC JudAdminStand 4.35
  Statistically significant samples
      Common interest developments, financial reserve planning CC §5551
  Status conference
      Family centered case resolution CRC 5.83
  Statutory liens CCP §1800
  Stepparent adoption Fam §8548
  Stock cooperatives CC §783.1
      Commercial and industrial common interest developments CC §6566
      Transfer on death deeds Pro §5614.5
  Stop payment notice
      Mechanics' liens CC §8044
  Stop work notice
      Mechanics' liens CC §8830
  Streamlined CEQA projects
      Petitions under environmental quality act, civil rules governing CRC 3.2220
  Structure
      Construction defects, actions for CC §895
      Default in real property purchase contract, liquidated damages CC §1675
  Structure or area inspected
      Construction-related accessibility claims, correction of violations CC §55.56
  Student loan
      Student borrower bill of rights CC §1788.100
  Student loan account
      Student borrower bill of rights CC §1788.100

DEFINITIONS—Cont.
Student loan borrower
  Private student loan collections reform   CC §1788.201
Student loan debt
  Consumer debt, exemption of principal residence from execution of judgment lien   CCP §699.730
Student loan servicer
  Student borrower bill of rights   CC §1788.100
Students
  Postsecondary educational institutions, protection orders against violence threatened on campus or facility   CCP §527.85
Subcontractor
  Mechanics' liens   CC §8046
Subcutaneous
  Subcutaneous implanting of identification device, requiring of another   CC §52.7
Subdivision
  Juvenile rules   CRC 5.502
Subject individuals
  Commercial use of booking photographs   CC §1798.91.1
Submeter
  Landlord and tenant, water service in multifamily residential rental buildings   CC §1954.202
  Mobilehomes and mobilehome parks, water service billing   CC §798.40
Subordinate judicial officers
  Complaints against subordinate judicial officers   CRC 10.703
  Educational requirements for trial court judges and subordinate judicial officers   CRC 10.462
  Judicial administration rules, trial court management   CRC 10.701
  Judicial ethics code   CRCSupp JudEthicsTerminology
Subordinate term
  Sentencing rules, determinate sentencing   CRC 4.405
Subpoena
  Discovery, interstate and international   CCP §2029.200
Subpoenaing party
  Subpoena duces tecum for employment records   CCP §1985.6
Subpoenas duces tecum   CCP §1985
Subscriber
  Commercial online entertainment employment service providers, age information of subscribers   CC §1798.83.5
  Confidentiality of medical information   CC §56.05
Subscribing witness   CCP §1935
  Transfer on death deeds   Pro §5615
Subscription   CCP §17
Substantial
  Attorney professional conduct   ProfC 1.0.1
Substantial emotional distress
  Stalking, tort   CC §1708.7
Substantial likelihood
  Jurors, peremptory challenges   CCP §231.7
Substantially remodel
  Landlord and tenant
    Year's continuous, lawful occupation acting as limitation on termination of tenancy   CC §1946.2
Successive interest
  Fiduciary income and principal act   Pro §16321
Successor beneficiaries
  Fiduciary income and principal act   Pro §16321
  Trust decanting, expanded distributive discretion   Pro §19511
Successor of decedent   Pro §13006
Sufficient proof of authority
  Protected consumer security freezes   CC §1785.11.9
Suitability
  Judicial administration, risk/needs assessment use in sentencing   CRC JudAdminStand 4.35
Summons list   CCP §194
Superior court
  Appeals   CRC 8.10
  Family rules, title IV-D cases transferred to tribal court   CRC 5.372
Supervised counsel
  Death penalty appeals and habeas corpus proceedings   CRC 8.601
Supervised financial organization   CC §1801.6
Supervised persons
  Revocation of supervision, probation, etc   CRC 4.541
Supervised providers
  Intercountry adoptions   Fam §8900.5
Supervised visitation
  Services providers, standards   CRC JudAdminStand 5.20
Supervising agency
  Revocation of supervision, probation, etc   CRC 4.541

DEFINITIONS—Cont.
Supervising lawyer
  Attorneys at law, provisional licensure of 2020 law school graduates   CRC 9.49
    Pathway to full licensure, provisional licensure with   CRC 9.49.1
Supervision
  Judicial administration, risk/needs assessment use in sentencing   CRC JudAdminStand 4.35
Supervisory employee
  Hotels, actions against for sex trafficking activity   CC §52.65
Supplement to a pleading
  Family rules   CRC 5.74
  Probate rules   CRC 7.3
Supplier
  Cosmetics, animal testing to develop or manufacture   CC §1834.9.5
  Medical claims data error correction   CC §57
Support   Fam §150
Support enforcement agency
  Interstate family support   Fam §5700.102
Support order   Fam §155
  Interstate family support   Fam §5700.102
Sureties   CC §2787
Surface protection product
  Automobile sales finance   CC §2981
Surrogacy or donor facilitators   Fam §7960
Surrogates
  Surrogacy or donor facilitators   Fam §7960
Surviving spouse   Pro §78
Suspend
  Child support, suspension of orders or judgments   Fam §4007.5
  Equity lines of credit, suspending and closing line on borrower's instruction   CC §2943.1
Sustainable groundwater management act
  Groundwater rights actions   CCP §832
Sworn written certification
  Coerced debt   CC §1798.97.1
System certification
  Electronic recording delivery systems   Gov §27390
Taking control
  Conservators, taking possession of conservatee's assets   CRC 7.1061
  Guardianships, taking possession of ward's assets   CRC 7.1011
Taking possession
  Conservators, taking possession of conservatee's assets   CRC 7.1061
  Guardianships, taking possession of ward's assets   CRC 7.1011
Tangible personal property   CCP §680.370
Technical words and phrases, construction of   CCP §16
Telephone appearance
  Title IV-D support hearings   CRC 5.324
Telephone standby
  Jury service, duration   CRC 2.1002
Temporary duty
  Child custody, temporary military duty, deployment, etc   Fam §3047
Temporary interpreters
  Interpreters, appointment in court proceedings   CRC 2.893
Temporary judges   CRC 2.810
  Judicial ethics code   CRCSupp JudEthicsTerminology
  Rules of court   CRC 1.6
Temporary restraining order
  Harassment, protection orders   CCP §527.6
  Postsecondary educational institutions, orders against violence threatened on campus or facility   CCP §527.85
  Postsecondary educational institutions, protection orders against violence threatened on campus or facility   CCP §527.85
  Workplace violence, protection orders   CCP §527.8
Tenancy   CC §798.12
  Landlord and tenant
    Rent increase limitations   CC §1947.12
    Year's continuous, lawful occupation acting as limitation on termination of tenancy   CC §1946.2
Tenant   CC §1954.26
  Change of lock upon request by eligible tenant   CC §1941.5
  Change of lock upon request by protected tenant   CC §1941.6
  Commercial real property tenancies, disposition of property remaining upon termination   CC §1993
  COVID-19 tenant relief act   CCP §1179.02
  Recreational vehicle parks   CC §799.32
  Screening of tenants   CC §1946.9
Tenant screening   CC §1946.9
Tent
  Special occupancy parks   CC §1866

DEFINITIONS—Cont.
Terms of a trust
    Directed trusts   Pro §16602
    Fiduciary income and principal act   Pro §16321
Terms-of-service agreement
    Fiduciary access to digital assets   Pro §871
Terms of the trust
    Trust decanting, uniform act   Pro §19502
Terrorist victim
    September 11, 2001 terrorist attacks   CCP §340.10
Testator   Pro §6201
Testify   CCP §17
Testing facilities
    Animal testing, restrictions against   CC §1834.9.3
The court
    Appellate rules, E-filing in supreme court and courts of appeal   CRC 8.70
The decanting power
    Trust decanting, uniform act   Pro §19502
The public
    Appellate rules, supreme court and courts of appeal, public access to electronic court records   CRC 8.82
    Electronic court records   CRC 2.502
These rules
    Sentencing rules, determinate sentencing   CRC 4.405
Third degree of relationship
    Judicial ethics code   CRCSupp JudEthicsTerminology
Third party
    Consumer privacy rights   CC §1798.140
Third-party agent
    Enforcement of judgments and orders   CCP §684.115
Third-party booking service
    Cancellation of reservations, refunds   CC §1748.80
Third-party defendant   CCP §428.70
Third-party plaintiff   CCP §428.70
Third-party seller
    Online marketplaces   CC §1749.8
Third-party service providers
    Privacy of customer records, duties of carriers and innkeepers   CC §53.5
Three-dimensional printer
    Firearm manufacturer liability   CC §3273.60
Threshold amount
    Commercial real property tenancies, disposition of property remaining upon termination   CC §1993.07
Time-limited demand
    Settlement and compromise   CCP §999
Timely payment   Fam §5220
Title insurance
    Buyer's choice act   CC §1103.22
Title IV-D child support cases
    Family rules, title IV-D cases transferred to tribal court   CRC 5.372
Title IV-D support actions
    Family rules   CRC 5.300
Tobacco products
    Landlord and tenant, prohibition of smoking   CC §1947.5
Toll-free CJEO line
    Judges, committee on judicial ethics opinions   CRCSupp JudEthicsOpinionsIOP 2
Total of payments
    Automobile sales finance   CC §2981
    Rental-purchase contracts   CC §1812.622
To the extent it is feasible to do so
    Appellate rules, supreme court and courts of appeal, public access to electronic court records   CRC 8.82
Totten trust account   Pro §80
Tourism commission assessment
    Rental passenger vehicle transactions   CC §1939.01
Toy
    Gender neutral section or area for display of toys and childcare items, retailer duties   CC §55.8
Trade secret
    Court records, public access   CRC 10.500
Traditional animal test method   CC §1834.9
Traditional surrogates
    Surrogacy or donor facilitators   Fam §7960
Transaction or other nonlitigation matter
    Attorney temporarily in California providing nonlitigation services   CRC 9.48
Transfer   CC §1039
    Civil rules, coordination of complex actions   CRC 3.501
    Voidable transactions   CC §§3439.01, 3445

DEFINITIONS—Cont.
Transferee
    Small estates without administration   Pro §13202.5
    Affidavit procedure   Pro §13100.5
    Voidable transactions   CC §3445
    Wills, issue of deceased transferee taking under instrument   Pro §21110
Transfer fee
    Conveyance of property   CC §1098.6
    Conveyance of real property   CC §1098
Transferor   Pro §81
    Transfer on death deeds   Pro §5616
Transferred property
    Small estates without administration   Pro §13202.5
    Affidavit procedure   Pro §13100.5
Transferring court
    Probation, out-of-county transfers   CRC 4.530
Transition age youth
    Intergenerational housing developments   CC §51.3.5
Transitional housing programs
    Transitional housing program misconduct   CC §1954.12
Transitional independent living case plan
    Juvenile rules   CRC 5.502
Transitional independent living plan
    Juvenile rules   CRC 5.502
Transition dependents
    Juvenile rules   CRC 5.502
Transition jurisdiction
    Juvenile rules   CRC 5.502
Transition time period
    COVID-19 tenant relief act   CCP §1179.02
Transmission record
    Fax filing and service   CRC 2.301
    Levying officer electronic transactions act   CCP §263.1
Trauma-informed
    Interim homelessness programs, occupancy   CC §1954.08
Trauma kit
    Emergency medical care using trauma kit, limitation of liability   CC §1714.29
Travel trailer
    Automobile warranties   CCP §871.21
    Consumer warranty protection   CC §1791
Traverse
    Habeas corpus   CRC 4.545
Trial
    Guardianship or conservatorship proceedings, attorney qualifications   CRC 7.1101
Trial briefs
    Family rules, setting trials and long-cause hearings   CRC 5.393
Trial counsel
    Death penalty appeals and habeas corpus proceedings   CRC 8.601
Trial court
    Appellate rules, superior court appeals   CRC 8.803
Trial court system
    Jury service, duration   CRC 2.1002
Trial day
    Family rules, setting trials and long-cause hearings   CRC 5.393
Trial jurors   CCP §194
Trial jury   CCP §194
Trial jury panel   CCP §194
Tribal court
    Family rules, title IV-D cases transferred to tribal court   CRC 5.372
    Indian children   Fam §170
    Tribal court civil money judgment act   CCP §1732
Tribal customary adoption
    Juvenile rules   CRC 5.502
Tribal land
    Conservators, interstate jurisdiction, transfer and recognition   Pro §2031
Tribunal
    Attorney professional conduct   ProfC 1.0.1
    Canadian domestic violence protection orders, recognition and enforcement   Fam §6451
    Interstate family support   Fam §5700.102
Trier of fact   Ev §235
Truck stops
    Human trafficking or slavery, businesses required to post signs concerning   CC §52.6
Truncate
    Social security number truncation program   Gov §27300
Truncated social security number
    Social security number truncation program   Gov §27300

DEFINITIONS—Cont.

Trust Pro §82
    Claims against estates Pro §19000
    Fiduciary income and principal act Pro §16321

Trust director
    Directed trusts Pro §16602

Trustee Pro §§84, 6204
    Fiduciary access to digital assets Pro §871
    Fiduciary income and principal act Pro §16321

Trustee's fees Pro §15686

Trust estates
    Claims against estates Pro §19000

Trust funded by court order CRC 7.903

Trust instrument
    Trust decanting, uniform act Pro §19502

Trustline provider
    Supervised visitation services providers, standards CRC JudAdminStand 5.20

2020 law school graduate
    Attorneys at law, provisional licensure of 2020 law school graduates CRC 9.49

Typewriting
    Trial court rules CRC 2.3

Typewritten
    Trial court rules CRC 2.3

Unaffiliated
    Medical negligence, limitation on damages CC §3333.2

Unauthorized
    Distribution of unauthorized obscene material, actions CC §52.8

Unauthorized access, destruction, use, modification or disclosure
    Connected devices, security CC §1798.91.05

Unavailable as witness Ev §240

Unbundled parking
    Landlord and tenant CC §1947.1

Unclaimed property CCP §1300

Unconditional
    Trust decanting, charitable interest protection Pro §19514

Unconscious bias
    Jurors, peremptory challenges CCP §231.7

Under threat of eminent domain
    Eminent domain CCP §1263.025

Undisputed funds or property
    Attorney professional conduct, safekeeping of funds and property of clients ProfC 1.15

Undistributed income
    Fiduciary income and principal act, apportionment at beginning and end of income interest Pro §16377

Undue influence CC §1575
    Probate code Pro §86

Unintended water
    Construction defects, actions for CC §895

Unique identifier
    Consumer privacy rights CC §1798.140

Unique personal identifier
    Consumer privacy rights CC §1798.140

United States central authority
    Interstate family support
        Convention support proceedings Fam §5700.701

Unitrust
    Fiduciary income and principal act Pro §16330

Unitrust amount
    Fiduciary income and principal act, unitrust Pro §16330

Unitrust plan
    Fiduciary income and principal act, unitrust Pro §16330

Unitrust rate
    Fiduciary income and principal act, unitrust Pro §16330

Unlawful violence
    Harassment, protection orders CCP §527.6
    Postsecondary educational institutions, orders against violence threatened on campus or facility CCP §527.85
    Workplace violence, protection orders CCP §527.8

Unlawful weapons or ammunition purpose
    Nuisance abatement CC §3485

Unlimited civil cases
    Appellate rules, superior court appeals CRC 8.803
    Rules of court CRC 1.6

Unpaid balance
    Automobile sales finance CC §2981

Unperformed contract for sale of realty CC §886.010

DEFINITIONS—Cont.

Unreasonable fee
    Unreasonable fees to assist applicants for public social services as deceptive practice CC §1770

Unredacted version
    Sealed and confidential records, appellate rules for supreme court and courts of appeal CRC 8.45

Unsecured debt
    Small estates without administration Pro §13202.5
        Affidavit procedure Pro §13100.5
    Transfer on death deeds Pro §5618

Unsolicited
    Obscene material, unsolicited electronic messages depicting CC §1708.88

Urbanized area
    Greenway easements CC §816.52

Urban waterways
    Greenway easements CC §816.52

Users
    Electronic court records CRC 2.502
    Fiduciary access to digital assets Pro §871
    Online violence prevention CC §1798.99.20
    Reader privacy act CC §1798.90

Vacancy decontrol
    Rent control, professional fees recoverable by owners CC §1947.15

Validated risk/needs assessment instrument
    Judicial administration, risk/needs assessment use in sentencing CRC JudAdminStand 4.35

Valid liens
    Voidable transactions CC §3439.01

Valuation
    Real estate appraisal, improper influence of appraisal or valuation CC §1090.5

Vehicle
    Rental passenger vehicle transactions CC §1939.01
    Vehicle history reports CC §1784.1

Vehicle history database
    Vehicle history reports CC §1784.1

Vehicle history information
    Vehicle history reports CC §1784.1

Vehicle history report provider
    Vehicle history reports CC §1784.1

Vehicle history reports CC §1784.1

Vehicle information
    Consumer privacy rights
        Scope of rights CC §1798.145

Vehicle license fee
    Rental passenger vehicle transactions CC §1939.01

Vehicle license recovery fees
    Rental passenger vehicle transactions CC §1939.01

Vehicle registration fees
    Rental passenger vehicle transactions CC §1939.01

Verifiable consumer request
    Consumer privacy rights CC §1798.140

Verify
    Online marketplaces CC §1749.8

Vessel information
    Consumer privacy rights, commercial credit reporting agencies CC §1798.145

Vested interests
    Trust decanting, expanded distributive discretion Pro §19511

Vexatious litigant CCP §391

Vice-chair
    Judges, committee on judicial ethics opinions CRCSupp JudEthicsOpinionsIOP 2

Victim
    Domestic violence incident reports, access Fam §6228
    Human trafficking victim-caseworker privilege Ev §1038.2

Victim of abuse
    Lease provisions penalizing summoning emergency assistance CC §1946.8

Victim of crime
    Lease provisions penalizing summoning emergency assistance CC §1946.8

Victim of identity theft CC §1798.92

Victim of violent crime advocate
    Change of lock upon request by eligible tenant CC §1941.5
    Landlord and tenant, restrictions on termination of tenancy of victims of certain crimes CC §1946.7

Victim service providers
    Personal information protection CC §1798.79.8

DEFINITIONS—Cont.
Video game
  Violent video games   CC §1746
Violent post
  Online violence prevention   CC §1798.99.20
Violent sexual felony
  Divorce, violent sexual felony or domestic violence felony by spouse against spouse   Fam §4324.5
Violent video games   CC §1746
Virtual visitation
  Child custody   Fam §3100
Vision care   Fam §6904
Vision screening
  Donation of vision screening and eyeglasses   CC §1714.26
Visual inspection
  Common interest developments, financial reserve planning   CC §5551
Visually impaired   CC §54.6
Vlog
  Minors   Fam §6650
Vlogger
  Minors   Fam §6650
Vlogging
  Minors   Fam §6650
Voluntary expedited jury trial   CRC 3.1545
Voluntary transfer   CC §1040
Wage claims   Pro §11402
Waiver
  Adoption, sibling contact information requests   CRC 5.460
Ward or conservatee
  Termination of temporary guardianship or conservatorship   Pro §2357
Wards
  Ex parte communications, probate proceedings   CRC 7.10
  Participation and testimony in probate guardianship proceedings   CRC 7.1016
Ward's personal residence
  Guardian and ward, change of ward's residence   CRC 7.1013
Ward's residence
  Guardian and ward, change of ward's residence   CRC 7.1013
Warrant of arrest regular upon its face
  Arrest, liability based on warrant regular on its face   CC §43.55
Warrantor
  Automobile warranties   CCP §871.21
Water-conserving plumbing fixtures
  Water conserving plumbing retrofits   CC §1101.3
Water purveyors
  Landlord and tenant, water service in multifamily residential rental buildings   CC §1954.202
  Mobilehomes and mobilehome parks, water service billing   CC §798.40
Water service
  Landlord and tenant, water service in multifamily residential rental buildings   CC §1954.202
  Mobilehomes and mobilehome parks, water service billing   CC §798.40
Weight loss contracts   CC §1694.5
Wholesale sales representatives   CC §1738.12
Will   CCP §17
  Fiduciary access to digital assets   Pro §871
  Fiduciary income and principal act   Pro §16321
Withholding order for support   CCP §706.030
Witnesses   CCP §1878
Work
  Mechanics' liens   CC §8048
Workforce housing cooperative trust
  Housing cooperatives and housing cooperative trusts   CC §817
Working in a qualified legal services project
  Electronic court records, remote access   CRC 2.522
Work of art   CC §988
Work of improvement
  Mechanics' liens   CC §8050
Writ   CCP §17
  Small claims courts, writ petitions   CRC 8.971
Writing   CCP §17, Ev §250
  Appellate rules, superior court appeals   CRC 8.803
  Appellate rules, supreme court and courts of appeal   CRC 8.10
  Attorney professional conduct   ProfC 1.0.1
  Civil discovery act   CCP §2016.020
  Court records, public access   CRC 10.500
  Trial court rules   CRC 2.3
Written
  Appellate rules, superior court appeals   CRC 8.803
  Appellate rules, supreme court and courts of appeal   CRC 8.10
  Attorney professional conduct   ProfC 1.0.1

DEFINITIONS—Cont.
Written—Cont.
  Trial court rules   CRC 2.3
Written agreement
  Arbitration   CCP §1280
Written consent
  Direct marketing, medical information used for   CC §1798.91
Written reprimand
  Judicial administration rules, complaints against subordinate judicial officers   CRC 10.703
Youth
  Juvenile rules   CRC 5.502
Zero-rating
  Net neutrality   CC §3100

DEGREES OF PROOF
Beyond reasonable doubt (See **BEYOND REASONABLE DOUBT**)
Clear and convincing evidence (See **CLEAR AND CONVINCING EVIDENCE**)
Preponderance of evidence (See **PREPONDERANCE OF EVIDENCE**)

DELAY
Appeal taken solely for   CCP §907
Award of expenses and attorney's fees as result of frivolous or bad-faith actions or tactics solely intended to cause (See **SANCTIONS**)
Common carriers, delay in transit by   CC §§2104, 2196
Continuances (See **CONTINUANCES**)
Court orders to prevent   CCP §379.5
Dismissal for delay in prosecution (See **DISMISSAL**)
Enjoining construction project, security for costs incurred as result of   CCP §529.1
Prosecutions
  COVID-19, emergency rule   CRCAppx I Emer Rule 10
Small claims court (See **SMALL CLAIMS COURTS**)
Summary judgment motion support or opposition presented solely for purposes of delay   CCP §437c
Surety's liability affected by creditor's delay in pursuing remedies   CC §§2823, 2845
Trial procedures, delay reduction of (See **TRIAL COURT DELAY REDUCTION**)
Uniform Transfers to Minors Act, delay in transfer of custodial property under   Pro §3920.5
Vexatious litigant engaging in tactics solely intended to cause   CCP §391

DELEGATION OF POWER
Agency   CC §§2304, 2349 to 2351
Executor, delegating authority for naming   Pro §8422
Factors   CC §2367

DELIBERATION
Jury (See **JURY**)

DELINQUENCY CHARGES
Attorneys at law
  Juvenile court rules
    Training requirements for children's counsel   CRC 5.664
Judges
  Education of judges and subordinate judicial officers
    Domestic violence issues   CRC 10.464
Retail installment sales   CC §§1803.6, 1806.3, 1810.12

DELINQUENT CHILDREN (See **JUVENILE DELINQUENCY**)

DELIVERY
Action to compel delivery to owner of personalty   CC §3380
Automobile conditional sales contracts   CC §2984.3
Bailment, delivery under contract of   CC §1955
Bill of sale   CC §§1054 to 1056, 1059
Claim and delivery (See **CLAIM AND DELIVERY**)
Common carrier, duty to deliver goods by   CC §§2118 to 2121
Contracts (See **CONTRACTS AND AGREEMENTS**)
Conveyances (See **CONVEYANCES**)
Decedent's property in possession of third party to surviving spouse, delivery of   Pro §330
Deeds   CC §§1054 to 1056, 1059, 1627
Discount buying services contracts   CC §1812.116
Failure to deliver merchandise within specified 4-hour period requiring consumer's presence, retailer's liability for   CC §1722
Gifts   CC §1147
Grain sold in bulk in absence of   CC §§1880.3 to 1880.6, 1880.8, 1880.9

DELIVERY—Cont.

Retail goods and services, retailer's liability for failure to deliver within specified 4-hour period   CC §1722
Sale of goods   CC §1496
Stay of proceedings (See **STAY OF PROCEEDINGS**)
Things capable of delivery as subject to ownership   CC §655
Trust property to successor trustee, delivery of   Pro §15644
Unclaimed deposits and payments escheated delivered to controller   CCP §1532
Voidable transaction presumed in absence of   CC §3440
Will delivered for probate   Pro §§8200 to 8203

DEMAND FOR JURY   CCP §631

DEMAND FOR RETURN
Conversion of property   CC §1713
Deposited property, demand for return of   CC §§1822, 1823

DEMANDS TO PRODUCE DOCUMENTS (See **INSPECTION DEMANDS**)

DEMONSTRATION PROJECTS (See **PILOT AND DEMONSTRATION PROJECTS**)

DEMONSTRATIONS, PARADES AND MEETINGS
Enjoining acts relating to labor disputes, limitation on   CCP §527.3
Petition for injunction to limit picketing, description of premises in   CRC 3.1151
Violence
    Construction or application of provisions in issue, solicitor general notified   CC §51.1
    Waiver of right to freedom from violence, coerced or involuntary   CC §51.7

DEMURRERS   CRC 3.1320
All or part of pleading, demurrer may be taken to   CCP §430.50
Amendments after
    Dismissal following failure to amend   CRC 3.1320
Answer
    Generally   CCP §472a
    Alleging lack of sufficient facts for   CCP §430.20
    Amended answer, demurrer to   CCP §471.5
    Demurrer to answer overruled, effect of   CCP §472a
    Filed after ruling on demurrer   CCP §§472a, 472b
    Filed at same time as demurrer   CCP §472a
Appeal of order sustaining demurrer without leave to amend   CCP §472c
Appearance by filing   CCP §1014
Appellate rules, superior court appeals
    Misdemeanor appeals
        Limited normal record in appeal from demurrer or other appealable orders   CRC 8.867
Captions   CRC 3.1320
Certiorari   CCP §1069.1
Child abuse, libel and slander action by person accused of   CC §48.7
Default judgments   CCP §§585, 586
Discretion to grant leave to amend pleadings where demurrer sustained   CCP §472a
Dismissal of actions
    Based on demurrer   CCP §581, CRC 3.1320
    Failure to amend   CRC 3.1320
Economic litigation provisions for limited civil cases   CCP §92
Eminent domain action   CCP §§1250.350 to 1250.370
Enlarging time for   CCP §473
Exceptions, orders and rulings reserved without   CCP §647
Face of pleading, appearance of grounds on   CCP §430.30
Failure to appear at hearing   CRC 3.1320
Failure to file memorandum in support of special demurrer, effect   CRC 3.1113
Family rules
    No use of demurrers or summary judgment motions in family law actions   CRC 5.74
Forcible detainer   CCP §1170
    Meet and confer prerequisite to filing
        Inapplicability of meet and confer requirement in forcible entry, forcible detainer or unlawful detainer cases   CCP §430.41
Forcible entry   CCP §1170
    Meet and confer prerequisite to filing
        Inapplicability of meet and confer requirement in forcible entry, forcible detainer or unlawful detainer cases   CCP §430.41
Grounds for demurrer   CCP §§430.10, 430.60, CRC 3.1320
    Sustaining demurrer, grounds shown in order   CCP §472d
Issue at law   CCP §589
Judicial notice   CCP §§430.30, 430.70
Jurisdiction, alleging lack of   CCP §430.10

DEMURRERS—Cont.
Law and motion rules   CRC 3.1320
    Applicability   CRC 3.1103
    Failure to file memorandum in support of special demurrer, effect   CRC 3.1113
Leave to amend pleadings where demurrer sustained   CCP §472a, CRC 3.1320
Local rules of court
    Preemption of local rules   CRC 3.20
Mandamus   CCP §1089
Meet and confer prerequisite to filing
    Judicial council legal forms   CRCAppx A
Notice of hearing   CRC 3.1320
Overruling, effect of   CCP §472a
Permissible pleadings   CCP §422.10
Pleadings
    Time for pleading after demurrer   CRC 3.1320
Preemption of local rules   CRC 3.20
Remand from federal court, time to demur after   CCP §430.90
Setting for hearing   CRC 3.1320
Sexual assault of minor, failure to comply with certificate of merit requirement in action for   CCP §§340.1, 340.11
Specify grounds upon which objections are taken, requirement to   CCP §430.60
Strike, motion to (See **MOTION TO STRIKE**)
Striking of complaint
    Time for motion to strike after demurrer   CRC 3.1320
Sustaining, effect of   CCP §472a
Time   CRC 3.1320
Time limits and requirements   CCP §§430.40, 432.10, 471.5, 472a, 472b
Unlawful detainer   CCP §1170
    Meet and confer prerequisite to filing
        Inapplicability of meet and confer requirement in forcible entry, forcible detainer or unlawful detainer cases   CCP §430.41
Waiver
    Answer filed at same time as demurrer, effect of   CCP §472a
    Failure to appear in support of special demurrer   CRC 3.1320
    Failure to object, effect of   CCP §430.80
    Issue of law, effect of failure to prosecute demurrer   CCP §591
    Memorandum in support of special demurrer, effect of failure to file   CRC 3.1113
Whole instrument attacked   CCP §430.50
Will contests, use in   Pro §8251
Without leave to amend, sustaining demurrer   CCP §472c

DE NOVO PROCEEDING
Administrative adjudication, de novo proceeding after nonbinding arbitration in   Gov §11420.10
Trial (See **NEW TRIAL**)

DENTAL CARE
Caregiver authorization and affidavit for dental treatment of minors   Fam §§6550, 6552
Emancipated minor's consent   Fam §7050
Minors, care of (See **MINORS**)
Noncustodial parent's access to child's dental records   Fam §3025

DENTAL HYGIENISTS
Discovery, review committee records exempt from   Ev §1157
Liability of review committees   CC §§43.7, 43.8

DENTISTS
Bond required to secure costs in action against   CCP §1029.6
Confidentiality of records   CC §§56.101, 56 to 56.37
Discovery, dental committee records subject to   Ev §§1156, 1157
Electronic medical records
    System requirements   CC §56.101
Inspection of records by attorneys   CCP §1985.7, Ev §1158
Insurance underwriting committee, liability of dentist member of   CC §§43.7, 43.8
Malpractice (See **MALPRACTICE**)
Minors, diagnosis and treatment   Fam §§6920 to 6930
Noncustodial parent's right to dental records   Fam §3025
Peer review committees, liability of   CC §§43.7, 43.8
Professional committees, liability of   CC §§43.7, 43.8
Rescission of dental plan or services   CC §1689.3
Review committees, liability of   CC §§43.7, 43.8
Sexual harassment, civil action for
    Construction or application of provisions in issue, solicitor general notified   CC §51.1

DEPARTMENT OF CHILD SUPPORT SERVICES (See **CHILD SUPPORT**)

DEPARTMENT OF CONSUMER AFFAIRS
Small claims court administration   CCP §§116.920, 116.930, 116.950

DEPARTMENT OF CORRECTIONS
Exemption for funds of incarcerated judgment debtors   CCP §704.090
Small claims court (See **SMALL CLAIMS COURTS**)

DEPARTMENT OF MOTOR VEHICLES (See **MOTOR VEHICLES DEPARTMENT**)

DEPARTMENT OF TRANSPORTATION
Claims against public entities and employees (See **CLAIMS AGAINST PUBLIC ENTITIES AND EMPLOYEES**)

DEPARTMENT OF WATER RESOURCES
Actions arising out of work of   Gov §956

DEPARTMENT STORES
Gender neutral retail departments
    Childcare items
        Gender neutral section or area for display, retailer duties   CC §55.8
    Legislative findings and declarations   CC §55.7
    Toys
        Gender neutral section or area for display, retailer duties   CC §55.8

DEPENDENT ADULTS
Abuse of elder or dependent adult
    Arbitration, appeals
        Expedited process   CCP §1294.4, CRC 8.710 to 8.717
    Coerced debt   CC §§1798.97.1 to 1798.97.6 (See **COERCED DEBT**)
    Domestic violence reports
        Access to domestic violence incident reports   Fam §6228
    Forms
        Judicial council forms   CRCAppx A
    Protective orders to prevent
        Appellate court opinions, privacy protection as to use of names in opinions   CRC 8.90
        Requests for protective orders   CRC 3.1160
    Unlawful detainer
        Restrictions on termination of tenancy   CC §1946.7, CCP §1161.3
Discovery
    Elder abuse and dependent adult civil protection act   CCP §§2017.310, 2017.320
Financial abuse
    Attorney in fact
        Taking, concealing, etc property of principal   Pro §4231.5
    Garnishment
        Earnings withholding orders   CCP §§706.011, 706.023
Forms
    Judicial council legal forms   CRCAppx A
Landlord and tenant
    Abuse of elder or dependent adult
        Restrictions on termination of tenancy   CC §1946.7, CCP §1161.3
Undue influence
    Wrongful taking, concealment, etc of property of conservatee, minor, elder, dependent adult, etc   Pro §859
Wrongful taking, concealment, etc of property of conservatee, minor, elder, dependent adult, etc   Pro §859

DEPENDENT CHILDREN
Adoption proceedings   CRC 5.730
    Permanent plan, selection   CRC 5.725
    Prospective adoptive parent designation   CRC 5.726
Advice of hearing rights   CRC 5.534, 5.682
Appeals   CRC 5.585 to 5.595
    Advisement of rights   CRC 5.590
    Juvenile case appeals
        Certain counties, applicable rules   CRC 8.416
        Forms, judicial council   CRCAppx A
    Precedence for appeal of order freeing dependent child of court from parental custody and control   CCP §45
    Representation of child on appeal   CRC 5.661
    Stay pending appeal
        Conditions   CRC 5.595
    Transfer of case between counties   CRC 5.610
Approaching majority review hearings   CRC 5.707
Arrest warrant against custodial parent or guardian   CRC 5.526
Assessments
    Joint assessment procedure   CRC 5.512
Attorneys
    Collection for reimbursement of appointed attorneys
        Guidelines for juvenile dependency counsel collections program   CRCAppx F

DEPENDENT CHILDREN—Cont.
Caregivers
    Notice of proceedings to current caregivers   CRC 5.534
Change of name   CCP §§1276, 1277
Child advocate
    Court-appointed Special Advocate (CASA) program   CRC 5.655
    Notice of proceedings   CRC 5.524, 5.710
Child welfare services
    Case plan for child welfare services   CRC 5.690
Child welfare services case plan, parents' failure to cooperate in   Ev §1228.1
Citation to appear in addition to notice   CRC 5.526
Commencement of hearing   CRC 5.668
Community care facility, placement
    Community treatment facilities
        Hearings, review, etc   CRC 5.618
    Short term, specialized and intensive treatment
        Hearings, review, etc   CRC 5.618
    Temporary custody and detention
        Community treatment facilities   CRC 5.618
        Short term, specialized and intensive treatment   CRC 5.618
Competence of child subject to juvenile proceeding, doubt as to
    Evaluation of competence   CRC 5.645
Competence of child to cooperate with counsel   CRC 5.643
Continuances
    Dependent child of court proceedings
        Restraining orders   CRC 5.630
    Detention hearings   CRC 5.672
    Disposition hearings   CRC 5.684
        Indian child known to be involved or court having reason to know, limits on continuance   CRC 5.550
        Restrictions on delays   CRC 5.690
    Educational and developmental services decisionmaking rights of children   CRC 5.651
    Initial hearings   CRC 5.672
    Jurisdictional hearings   CRC 5.550
Control by parents or guardians, limitation by court   CRC 5.695
Counseling
    Family reunification services, order for   CRC 5.695
    Notice of requirement   CRC 5.526
Court Appointed Special Advocate (CASA)
    Appointment of as guardian ad litem   CRC 5.660
Court orders
    Disposition hearings   CRC 5.695
Cross-examination
    Right of   CRC 5.674
Custody of
    Order determining custody   CRC 5.475
    Stay of judgment affecting custody   CCP §917.7
Deceased child
    Juvenile case file of deceased child, release   CRC 5.553
De facto parents
    Defined   CRC 5.502
    Standing to participate in proceedings   CRC 5.534
Definitions   CRC 5.502
Delinquent children
    Placement under interstate compact   CRC 5.616
Delinquent-dependent dual status
    Modification of jurisdiction   CRC 5.812
Dependent child of court proceedings
    Admission of petition allegations at initial hearing   CRC 5.674
    Appeals   CRC 5.585 to 5.595
        Certain counties   CRC 8.416
        Stay pending appeal   CRC 5.595
        Supreme court and courts of appeal   CRC 8.400 to 8.474
    Appearance by minor without guardian ad litem   CCP §372
    Appearance by remote means   CRC 3.672
    Application to probation officer or social worker to commence   CRC 5.520
    Approaching majority review hearings   CRC 5.707
    Attendance at proceedings   CRC 5.530
    Attorneys
        Appointment   CRC 5.534, 5.660
        CASA programs   CRC 5.655
        Client complaints concerning representation   CRC 5.660
        Compensation   CRC JudAdminStand 5.40
        Competency standards   CRC 5.660
        Conflict of interest guidelines when representing siblings   CRC 5.660
        County counsel or DA, appearance   CRC 5.530
        Discrimination, prohibition against in appointments   CRC JudAdminStand 5.40
        District attorney representing petitioner   CRC 5.530
        Doubt as to capacity to cooperate with   CRC 5.643

DEPENDENT CHILDREN—Cont.
Dependent child of court proceedings—Cont.
- Attorneys—Cont.
  - Guidelines for juvenile dependency counsel collections program CRCAppx F
  - Local rules CRC 5.660
  - Qualifications of attorneys CRC 5.660
  - Representation, right to CRC 5.534, 5.660
- CASA volunteers, requirements CRC 5.655
- Commencement of CRC 5.510 to 5.526
- Competence of minor subject to juvenile proceedings, doubt as to
  - Evaluation of competence CRC 5.645
- Court performance measurement CRC 5.505
- Custody of child
  - Order determining custody CRC 5.620
  - Termination of jurisdiction, orders as to custody and visitation CRC 5.700
- Declaration of dependency
  - Disposition hearing, order of CRC 5.695
  - 18-month review hearing CRC 5.720
  - 6-month review hearing CRC 5.710
  - 12-month review hearing CRC 5.715
  - 24-month review hearing CRC 5.722
- Disposition orders
  - Legal guardian, appointment of CRC 5.695
  - Limitation on parental control CRC 5.695
  - Removal of child, grounds for CRC 5.695
  - Reunification services, order for CRC 5.695
  - Termination of jurisdiction, orders as to custody or visitation CRC 5.700
- Due process and court procedures, court performance measurement CRC 5.505
- Educational and developmental services decisionmaking rights of children CRC 5.651
- Educational rights holder, appointment for children with special needs CRC 5.534, 5.650
  - Definition of educational rights holder CRC 5.502
  - Identification of holder CRC 5.649
  - Orders concerning rights holder and educational decisionmaking CRC 5.649
  - Qualifications CRC 5.650
  - Training of rights holder CRC 5.650
  - Transfer of parent or guardian's educational rights to rights holder CRC 5.650
- 18-month review hearing CRC 5.720
- Emancipation of dependents and wards of court, rules of court for CRC 3.1370, 5.605
- Evidence requirements
  - Detention hearing CRC 5.676
  - Disposition hearing CRC 5.690
  - Jurisdiction hearing CRC 5.684
- Ex parte restraining orders
  - Forms for firearm relinquishment CRCAppx A
- Family-finding determination CRC 5.695
- Family maintenance review hearings CRC 5.706
- Findings
  - Detention hearing CRC 5.678
  - Disposition hearing CRC 5.695
  - Jurisdiction hearing CRC 5.682
- Forms
  - Judicial council legal forms CRCAppx A
- Guardianship
  - Disposition hearing, appointment of legal guardian at CRC 5.620, 5.695
  - Permanent plan, appointment of legal guardian pursuant to CRC 5.620, 5.735
  - Review hearings after permanent plan CRC 5.740
  - Termination or modification CRC 5.620, 5.740
- Incarcerated parents, participation CRC 5.530
- Indian Child Welfare Act
  - Intervene as party, tribe's right to CRC 5.534
  - Required notice under CRC 5.565, 5.725
  - Rules governing involuntary placements CRC 5.480 to 5.488 (See **INDIAN CHILD WELFARE ACT INVOLUNTARY PLACEMENTS**)
  - Tribal information form CRCAppx A
- Initial hearing
  - Admission of petition allegations CRC 5.674
  - Commencement of hearing CRC 5.668
  - Continuances CRC 5.550, 5.672
  - Evidence requirements in detention cases CRC 5.676

DEPENDENT CHILDREN—Cont.
Dependent child of court proceedings—Cont.
- Initial hearing—Cont.
  - Examination by court in detention cases CRC 5.674
  - Findings requirements in detention cases CRC 5.676, 5.678
  - Grounds for detention CRC 5.678
  - In-court notice to appear in subsequent proceedings CRC 5.667
  - Jurisdiction hearing, setting of CRC 5.674
  - No contest plea CRC 5.674
  - Notice of hearing, in-court CRC 5.667
  - Rights of child and parent or guardian in detention cases CRC 5.674
  - Setting of initial hearing CRC 5.670
  - Setting of jurisdiction hearing at initial hearing CRC 5.670, 5.674
  - Submission of jurisdictional determination and waiver of further hearing CRC 5.674
  - Visitation determination CRC 5.670
- Judicial education for dependency court officers
  - Additional education recommendations for certain judicial assignments CRC 10.469
  - Domestic violence issues CRC 10.464
- Juvenile court performance measures CRC 5.505
- Limitations on parental control CRC 5.695
- Marital communication privilege, inapplicability CRC 5.684
- Mediation proceedings CRC 5.518
- Mental health of child before court, inquiry into CRC 5.643
- Minor's appearance without guardian ad litem CCP §372
- No contest plea at initial hearing CRC 5.674
- Noncustodial parent, placement with
  - Review hearings CRC 5.708
- Notice of hearing CRC 5.524
  - In-court notice to appear in subsequent proceedings CRC 5.667
  - Permanent plan, hearing on CRC 5.725
  - 6-month review hearing CRC 5.710
  - Sufficiency of CRC 5.534
- Orders
  - Custody orders CRC 5.620
  - Declaration of dependency, order for CRC 5.695
  - Forms for firearm relinquishment CRCAppx A
  - Restraining orders CRC 5.620, 5.630
  - Termination of jurisdiction CRC 5.700
- Parentage determination CRC 5.635, 5.668
- Participation by child in hearing CRC 5.534
- Performance measures for juvenile dependency court CRC 5.505
- Permanent plan
  - 18-month review hearing CRC 5.720
  - Measurement of court performance CRC 5.505
  - 6-month review hearings CRC 5.710
  - 12-month review hearing CRC 5.715
  - 24-month review hearing CRC 5.722
- Relatives
  - Detention with relative, consideration of CRC 5.678
  - Presence at proceedings CRC 5.534
- Remote appearances in juvenile dependency proceedings CRC 3.672
- Resource guidelines of National Council of Juvenile and Family Court Judges CRC JudAdminStand 5.45
- Restraining orders CRC 5.620, 5.630
  - Forms for firearm relinquishment CRCAppx A
- Reunification services, order for CRC 5.695
- Review of status of dependent child of court
  - Hearings CRC 5.708
- Siblings
  - Review hearings CRC 5.708
- 6-month review hearing CRC 5.710
- Social study CRC 5.690
- Special education needs
  - Limitations on parental control CRC 5.695
- Stay of order or judgment
  - Educational and developmental services decisionmaking rights of children CRC 5.651
- Subpoenas, issuance CRC 5.526
- Surrogate parents, appointment for children with special needs CRC 5.650
- Telephone appearances CRC 5.531
  - Remote appearances generally CRC 3.672
- Timeliness of hearings
  - Performance measures CRC 5.505
- 12-month review hearing CRC 5.715
- 24-month review hearing CRC 5.722
- Venue CRC 5.510

DEPENDENT CHILDREN—Cont.
  Dependent child of court proceedings—Cont.
    Visitation rights   CRC 5.620
      Initial hearing on dependency petition, visitation determination in CRC 5.670
      Sibling visitation   CRC 5.670
  Detention hearing
    Admission of petition allegations   CRC 5.674
    Commencement of hearing   CRC 5.668
    Continuances   CRC 5.550, 5.672
    Detention alternatives   CRC 5.678
    Evidence requirements   CRC 5.676
    Findings   CRC 5.676, 5.678
      Making findings and orders on record   CRC 5.674
    Grounds for detention   CRC 5.678
    Indian children
      Active efforts   CRC 5.678
      Evidence   CRC 5.676
      Findings necessary to detain   CRC 5.674, 5.678
      Placement preferences   CRC 5.678
    No contest plea   CRC 5.674
    Orders
      Making findings and orders on record   CRC 5.674
    Parent or guardian not present or not notified   CRC 5.674
    Prima facie case, establishment of   CRC 5.676
      Request for prima facie hearing   CRC 5.674
    Relative, consideration of detention with   CRC 5.678
    Rights of child and parent or guardian   CRC 5.674
    Setting of detention hearing   CRC 5.670
    Setting of jurisdiction hearing at detention hearing   CRC 5.674
    Sibling visitation   CRC 5.670
    Submission of jurisdictional determination and waiver of further hearing CRC 5.674
    Supplemental petition for removal, detention pending adjudication
      Notice   CRC 5.565
    Visitation determination   CRC 5.670
  Discovery rights   CRC 5.546
  Disposition hearings   CRC 5.690 to 5.705
    Approaching majority review hearings   CRC 5.707
    Case plan for child welfare services   CRC 5.690
      Nonminor disposition hearings   CRC 5.697
    Continuance of disposition hearing   CRC 5.684
      Indian child known to be involved or court having reason to know, limits on continuance   CRC 5.550
      Restrictions on delays   CRC 5.690
    De facto parents, participation as parties   CRC 5.534
    Evidentiary requirements   CRC 5.690
      Nonminor disposition hearings   CRC 5.697
    Family-finding determination   CRC 5.695
    Family maintenance review hearings   CRC 5.706
    Findings and orders of court, alternative dispositions
      Judicial council form for orders   CRCAppx A
    Independent living case plan
      Nonminor disposition hearings   CRC 5.697
    Nonminor disposition hearings   CRC 5.697
      Judicial council forms   CRCAppx A
    Notices
      Nonminor disposition hearings   CRC 5.697
    Social study   CRC 5.690
      Nonminor disposition hearings   CRC 5.697
    Timing   CRC 5.690
  Domestic violence proceedings involving minor party, jurisdiction over   CCP §374.5
  Educational decisions
    Disposition hearings   CRC 5.695
    Educational and developmental services decisionmaking rights of children CRC 5.651
    Educational rights holder for child   CRC 5.534, 5.650
      Appointment   CRC 5.650
      Defined   CRC 5.502
      Identification of holder   CRC 5.649
      Judicial council forms   CRCAppx A
      Orders concerning rights holder and educational decisionmaking CRC 5.649
      Qualifications   CRC 5.650
      Training   CRC 5.650
      Transfer of parent or guardian's educational rights to rights holder CRC 5.650
    Review hearings   CRC 5.708

DEPENDENT CHILDREN—Cont.
  Educational decisions—Cont.
    Special education needs
      Educational and developmental services decisionmaking rights of children   CRC 5.651
      Educational rights holder appointment   CRC 5.502, 5.534, 5.650
      Identification of educational rights holder   CRC 5.649
      Orders concerning rights holder and educational decisionmaking CRC 5.649
      Surrogate parent appointment   CRC 5.650
  Emancipation petition   CRC 3.1370, 5.605
  Emergency orders
    COVID-19, emergency rule   CRC 3.672, CRCAppx I Emer Rule 6
  Evidence
    Detention hearings   CRC 5.676
    Disposition hearings
      Nonminor disposition hearings   CRC 5.697
  Ex parte injunctions or orders
    Firearm relinquishment procedures
      Forms for firearm relinquishment   CRCAppx A
  Expedited placement under Interstate Compact   CRC 5.616
  Family maintenance review hearings   CRC 5.706
  Financial evaluations
    Form for financial declaration   CRCAppx A
  Findings
    Disposition hearing
      Nonminor disposition hearings   CRC 5.697
  Forms
    Judicial council legal forms   CRCAppx A
  Grandparents' visitation rights   CRC 5.695
  Grounds for detention   CRC 5.678
  Guardian ad litem
    Child abuse and treatment act (CAPTA) guardians ad litem   CRC 5.662
  Guardians
    Appointment   CRC 5.735
    Disposition hearings generally   CRC 5.690 to 5.705
    Investigation and recommendation concerning proposed guardianship Pro §1513
    Notice of address   CRC 5.534
    Procedure for requesting   CRC 5.735
    Termination of guardianship   CRC 5.620
  Harassment proceedings brought against or initiated by minor, jurisdiction over CCP §374.5
  Health care of minor in temporary custody
    Psychotropic medication or drugs administered to child, court authorization for
      Forms, judicial council   CRCAppx A
  Hearings
    Community treatment facility placements
      Hearings, review, etc   CRC 5.618
    Educational and developmental services decisionmaking rights of children CRC 5.651
    Essential hearings and orders
      COVID-19, emergency rule   CRCAppx I Emer Rule 6
    Paternity inquiry   CRC 5.668
    Persons entitled to be present   CRC 5.530
    Preliminary hearing, admissibility of testimony of minor child at   Ev §1293
    Short term, specialized and intensive treatment
      Hearings, review, etc   CRC 5.618
    Transfer of case, hearing by receiving court   CRC 5.612
      Date of transfer-in hearing   CRC 5.610
      Nonminor dependents   CRC 5.613
  Immunity, grants of   CRC 5.548
  Independent Living Program
    Disposition hearings
      Nonminor disposition hearings, independent living case plan   CRC 5.697
  Indian children
    Detention hearing
      Active efforts   CRC 5.678
      Evidence required for detention of Indian child   CRC 5.676
      Findings necessary to detain   CRC 5.674, 5.678
      Placement preferences   CRC 5.678
    Emergency removal
      Hearing for return of custody when emergency ends   CRC 5.678
    Inquiry as to Indian status at first appearance   CRC 5.668
    Intake process
      Purposes of intake process   CRC 5.510
    Rules governing involuntary placements   CRC 5.480 to 5.488 (See **INDIAN CHILD WELFARE ACT INVOLUNTARY PLACEMENTS**)
    Telephone or computerized remote appearances by tribe   CRC 3.672, 5.531

DEPENDENT CHILDREN—Cont.
  Indian children—Cont.
    Termination of juvenile court jurisdiction
      Nonminor dependents or wards in foster care   CRC 5.555
    Tribal customary adoptions
      Defined   CRC 5.502
      Disposition hearings, consideration of tribal custom adoptions   CRC 5.690
      Orders, judicial council form   CRCAppx A
      Permanency hearings   CRC 5.715, 5.720, 5.722
      Permanent plan selection   CRC 5.725
      Post-permanency review hearings   CRC 5.740
      Review hearings   CRC 5.708
  Indian Child Welfare Act
    Required notice under   CRC 5.565, 5.570, 5.725
  Initial hearings   CRC 5.667 to 5.678
    Advice as to rights   CRC 5.668
    Explanation of proceedings   CRC 5.668
    Notice
      In-court notice to appear in subsequent proceedings   CRC 5.667
  Initial removal defined   CRC 5.502
  Intake program   CRC 5.514
    Settlement at intake   CRC 5.516
  Intercounty transfer of cases   CRC 5.610 to 5.616
  Interstate Compact on Placement of Children   CRC 5.616, Fam §§7900 to 7913
    Definitions   CRC 5.616
    Expedited placement   CRC 5.616
    Home environment study request from another state   Fam §7901.1
      Custody of child in requesting state   Fam §7906.5
  Joint assessment procedure   CRC 5.512
  Judge assignments
    Education of judicial branch
      Additional education recommendations for certain judicial assignments   CRC 10.469
  Judges, training standards for
    Education of judges and subordinate judicial officers
      Domestic violence issues   CRC 10.464
  Judgments   CRC 5.695
  Jurisdictional hearings
    Admissions   CRC 5.682
    Contested hearings   CRC 5.684
    Continuances   CRC 5.550
    Counsel   CRC 3.177, 3.1175, 5.530, 5.534, 5.660
    Evidence and findings   CRC 5.534, 5.682, 5.684
    No contest, entry of   CRC 5.682
    Persons present at   CRC 5.530
    Prosecuting witness and family members, attendance by   CRC 5.530
    Public, exclusion from   CRC 5.530
    Separate session of juvenile court for   CRC 5.530
    Setting   CRC 5.674
    Submission of jurisdictional determination and waiver of further hearing   CRC 5.682
    Termination of juvenile court jurisdiction
      Nonminor dependents or wards in foster care   CRC 5.555
    Transcript of proceedings   CRC 5.532
    Victim and support persons, attendance by   CRC 5.530
  Legal costs, liability for
    Juvenile dependency counsel collections program
      Guidelines   CRCAppx F
  Long-term placement hearing
    Orders
      Judicial council form   CRCAppx A
  Maintenance of family
    Family maintenance review hearings   CRC 5.706
  Marital communication privilege, inapplicability in dependency proceedings   CRC 5.684
  Mediation programs
    Court-connected dependency mediation   CRC 5.518
  Mental health or condition of child
    Competence of minor subject to juvenile proceedings, doubt as to
      Evaluation of competence   CRC 5.645
    Court procedures   CRC 5.643
  Modification of judgments and orders   CRC 5.560 to 5.580
  Name changes   CCP §§1276, 1277
  Nonminor dependents
    Dismissal of dependency or transition jurisdiction and immediate resumption
      Petitions   CRC 5.570
    Disposition hearings
      Judicial council forms   CRCAppx A
    Inspection and copying file
      Consent form   CRCAppx A

DEPENDENT CHILDREN—Cont.
  Nonminor dependents—Cont.
    Interstate compact on placement of children   CRC 5.616
    Request for retention of jurisdiction   CRC 5.906
    Retention of jurisdiction generally   CRC 5.900 to 5.906
    Termination of juvenile court jurisdiction
      Nonminor dependents or wards in foster care   CRC 5.555
    Transfers of jurisdiction   CRC 5.613
  Nonminors
    Disposition hearings
      Judicial council forms   CRCAppx A
      Nonminor disposition hearings   CRC 5.697
  Notices   CRC 5.534
    Dependency proceedings   CRC 5.524
    Indian Child Welfare Act requirements   CRC 5.565, 5.570
    Initial hearings
      In-court notice to appear in subsequent proceedings   CRC 5.667
    Out-of-county placements   CRC 5.614
      Judicial council legal forms   CRCAppx A
    Permanency hearings   CRC 5.706 to 5.740
    Petition to commence proceedings
      Subsequent petitions   CRC 5.565
    Status review hearings   CRC 5.710
  Orders   CRC 5.620 to 5.630
    Appeals from   CRC 5.585 to 5.595
    Custody orders   CRC 5.475
    Disposition hearings   CRC 5.695
      Nonminor disposition hearings   CRC 5.697
    Emergency orders
      COVID-19, emergency rule   CRCAppx I Emer Rule 6
    Modification   CRC 5.560 to 5.580
    Psychotropic medication or drugs administered to child, court authorization for
      Forms, judicial council   CRCAppx A
    Restraining orders
      Forms for firearm relinquishment   CRCAppx A
  Parentage
    Declarations   CRC 5.635
    Determinations   CRC 5.534
    Inquiry
      Commencement of hearings   CRC 5.668
      Duty to inquire   CRC 5.635
    Voluntary declaration   CRC 5.635
  Parents or guardians
    Address of parent appearing in proceedings, notice of   CRC 5.534
    Appearance by parent in proceedings, notice of address   CRC 5.534
    Arrest warrant against   CRC 5.526
    Citation to appear in addition to notice   CRC 5.526
    Counseling or education program, duty to participate in   CRC 5.526
    De facto parents   CRC 5.534
      Defined   CRC 5.502
    Rights, advisements as to   CRC 5.534
    Subpoenas, issuance on request of   CRC 5.526
    Surrogate parents, appointment for children with special needs
      Juvenile court proceedings   CRC 5.650
    Visitation with child   CRC 5.695
  Permanency planning hearing   CRC 5.706 to 5.740
    Adoption, consideration of   CRC 5.740
      Prospective adoptive parent designation   CRC 5.726
    Guardianship, consideration of   CRC 5.740
    Judicial council forms   CRCAppx A
    Notices   CRC 5.725
    Removal from prospective or designated adoptive parent
      Emergency removal   CRC 5.728
      Proposed removal   CRC 5.727
    Review hearing   CRC 5.740
    Supplemental petition, following sustaining of   CRC 5.565
    Termination of rights of one parent   CRC 5.725
  Permanency review hearing   CRC 5.720
    Subsequent permanency review hearing   CRC 5.722
  Permanency success
    Measurement of court performance   CRC 5.505
  Permanent plan
    Measurement of court performance   CRC 5.505
    Permanency review hearings
      Subsequent permanency review hearing   CRC 5.722
    Selection   CRC 5.725
    Subsequent hearings   CRC 5.565, 5.740
  Petition to commence proceedings   CRC 5.524
    Discretion of probation officer or social worker   CRC 5.514

DEPENDENT CHILDREN—Cont.
  Petition to commence proceedings —Cont.
    Notices
      Subsequent petitions   CRC 5.565
      Subsequent petition, new facts or circumstances   CRC 5.560, 5.565
  Placement   CRC 5.695
    Community treatment facilities
      Hearings, review, etc   CRC 5.618
    Indian children
      Detention, placement preferences   CRC 5.678
    Measurement of court performance   CRC 5.505
    Noncustodial parent, placement with
      Review hearings   CRC 5.708
    Out-of-county placements   CRC 5.614
      Judicial council legal forms   CRCAppx A
    Out of home placement
      Notice of proceedings to current caregivers   CRC 5.534
    Relatives, placement with   CRC 5.678
    Short term, specialized and intensive treatment
      Hearings, review, etc   CRC 5.618
  Postadoption contact agreements   CRC 5.451
  Preference to appeal from judgment freeing minor from parental custody and control   CCP §45
  Prima facie hearings
    When ordered   CRC 5.674
  Probation officers
    Application to commence dependency proceedings   CRC 5.520
    Informal supervision   CRC 5.514
    Social studies, preparation of   CRC 5.684
  Probation supervision
    Informal   CRC 5.514
  Process and service of process
    Petition and notice of hearing   CRC 5.524
    Subpoenas   CRC 5.526
  Protective custody   CRC 5.526
  Psychotropic medication   CRC 5.640
    Forms, judicial council   CRCAppx A
    Prescriptions
      Release of psychotropic medication prescription information to medical board, authorization   CRC 5.642
  Relatives
    Presence at hearings   CRC 5.534
  Release from temporary custody or detention
    Initial petition hearing, after   CRC 5.670
  Relocation of family unit
    Interstate compact on placement of children   CRC 5.616
  Remote appearances
    Juvenile dependency cases   CRC 3.672
  Removal from parent or guardian
    Emergency removal
      Indian children, hearing for return of custody after emergency ends   CRC 5.678
    Family finding and notice performed by social worker or probation officer   CRC 5.637
      Family-finding determination   CRC 5.695
    Grounds for   CRC 5.695
    Mental health records
      Protection from disclosure   CC §56.016
    Notice to parent regarding termination of rights   CRC 5.695
    Required findings   CRC 5.695
    Status review hearing   CRC 5.695, 5.706 to 5.740
  Reports by probation officers and social workers
    Admissibility in jurisdictional hearings   CRC 5.684
    Disposition hearings   CRC 5.690
  Residence of minor   CRC 5.510, 5.610
  Restraining orders   CRC 5.630
    Firearm relinquishment procedures
      Forms for firearm relinquishment   CRCAppx A
  Reunification services, requirement of   CRC 5.695
    Termination
      Findings   CRC 5.570
      Indian child, findings   CRC 5.570
  Review hearing
    Judicial council forms   CRCAppx A
  Review of status of dependent child of court
    Hearings   CRC 5.708
    Nonminor dependents, retention of jurisdiction   CRC 5.903
      Disposition hearings   CRCAppx A
    Review hearings   CRC 5.706 to 5.740
  Right to counsel, competency standards   CRC 5.660

DEPENDENT CHILDREN—Cont.
  Safety and well-being of child
    Measurement of court performance   CRC 5.505
  Sealing of juvenile court records
    Forms, judicial council   CRCAppx A
  Self-incrimination rights   CRC 5.534, 5.548, 5.674, 5.682
  Sexual abuse
    Family reunification services precluded   CRC 5.695
  Siblings
    Groups
      Definition   CRC 5.502
      Reunification services for   CRC 5.695
    Review hearings   CRC 5.708
    Visitation   CRC 5.670
  Social study
    Admissibility in jurisdictional hearing   CRC 5.684
    Cross-examination of preparer   CRC 5.684
    Definition   CRC 5.502
    Disposition hearings   CRC 5.690
      Nonminor disposition hearings   CRC 5.697
    Hearsay in report   CRC 5.684
    Weight   CRC 5.684
  Social workers
    Reports, persons entitled to receive   CRC 5.534
  Special education needs
    Educational and developmental services decisionmaking rights of children   CRC 5.651
    Educational rights holder appointment   CRC 5.534, 5.650
      Definition of educational rights holder   CRC 5.502
      Identification of holder   CRC 5.649
      Orders concerning rights holder and educational decisionmaking   CRC 5.649
      Qualifications   CRC 5.650
      Training   CRC 5.650
      Transfer of parent or guardian's educational rights to rights holder   CRC 5.650
    Surrogate parent appointment   CRC 5.650
  Status review hearings   CRC 5.695, 5.710
    Nonminor dependents, retention of jurisdiction   CRC 5.903
      Disposition hearings   CRCAppx A
  Stay of order or judgment   CCP §917.7
    Educational and developmental services decisionmaking rights of children   CRC 5.651
  Subpoenas   CRC 5.526
  Subsequent permanency review hearing   CRC 5.722
  Surrogate parents, appointment for children with special needs
    Juvenile court proceedings   CRC 5.650
  Telephone appearances   CRC 3.672, 5.531
    Disposition hearings
      Nonminor disposition hearings   CRC 5.697
    Nonminor dependents, retention of jurisdiction   CRC 3.672, 5.900
  Temporary custody and detention
    Review   CRC 5.695
  Temporary restraining orders
    Firearm relinquishment procedures
      Forms for firearm relinquishment   CRCAppx A
    Remote appearances
      Service requirements   CRC 5.496
    Violent behavior against parent or caretaker
      Forms for firearm relinquishment   CRCAppx A
  Termination of dependency   CRC 5.710
  Termination of juvenile court jurisdiction
    Nonminor dependents or wards in foster care   CRC 5.555
  Termination of parental rights, applicability of provisions for   Fam §7808
  Termination of rights of one parent
    Disposition hearings   CRC 5.695
      Setting hearing to consider termination   CRC 5.705
  Transcripts of proceedings   CRC 5.532
  Transfers
    Intercounty   CRC 5.610
      Nonminor dependents   CRC 5.613
  Transition age youth
    Intergenerational housing developments   CC §51.3.5
  Transitional arrangements
    Approaching majority review hearings
      Transitional independent living case plan   CRC 5.502, 5.707
  Transition jurisdiction
    Defined   CRC 5.502
    Hearings   CRC 5.812
    Modification to transition jurisdiction   CRC 5.813
      Age of ward between 17 years 5 months and 18   CRC 5.814

DEPENDENT CHILDREN—Cont.
Transition jurisdiction—Cont.
    Modification to transition jurisdiction —Cont.
        Forms, judicial council   CRCAppx A
    Transition dependent defined   CRC 5.502
Treatment programs, court-ordered
    Defined   CRC 5.502
Visitation
    Detained child, visitation with   CRC 5.670
        Grandparent visitation   CRC 5.695
    Sibling visitation   CRC 5.670
Warrants   CRC 5.526
Witnesses
    Immunity, granting of   CRC 5.548
Youth 18 years of age
    Permanency planning hearing
        Review hearing, 16 years or older   CRC 5.740

DEPORTATION
Child custody
    Electronic testimony or participation allowed in cases of   Fam §3012

DEPOSE
Inclusions in definition   CCP §17

DEPOSITIONS (See also INTERROGATORIES; REQUEST FOR ADMISSION)
Administrative adjudicative proceeding   Gov §11511
Admissibility as evidence   Ev §§1290 to 1292
Adoptive parents, deposition to examine   Fam §§8613, 8613.5
Answer
    Audiotaping depositions, procedure for
        Changing answers, time for   CCP §2025.530
    Motions to compel   CCP §2025.480, CRC 3.1345
        Notice of deposition, motion to compel compliance   CCP §2025.450
        Production of documents   CCP §2025.480
        Service on nonparty deponent   CRC 3.1346
    Transcript of deposition
        Changing answers, time for   CCP §2025.520
Arbitration proceedings   CCP §§1283, 1283.05
    Judicial arbitration
        Admissibility of depositions   CRC 3.823
Attendance
    Failure of party giving notice to attend
        Sanctions   CCP §2025.430
    Subpoena not served, causing failure to attend
        Sanctions   CCP §2025.440
Attorneys of record
    Subpoenas
        Issuance   CCP §2020.210
Attorney work product
    Written questions, depositions by
        Objections based on privilege   CCP §2028.050
Audiotaping depositions, procedure for   CCP §2025.340
    Copies, furnishing   CCP §2025.570
    Notice of availability of recording for review   CCP §2025.530
    Party access to recording   CCP §2025.560
    Retention by operator   CCP §2025.560
Automobile warranties
    Restitution or replacement actions   CCP §871.26
Business records, production of
    Methods of discovery
        Nonparty discovery   CCP §2020.010
    Notice of deposition   CCP §2025.220
    Subpoenas
        Attendance and testimony also commanded, requirements of subpoena   CCP §2020.510
        Business records produced for copying   CCP §§2020.410 to 2020.440
Clerk of court
    Subpoenas
        Issuance   CCP §2020.210
Complex cases
    Time limits for witness examination
        Exception for complex cases   CCP §2025.290
    Conduct of deposition   CCP §§2025.310 to 2025.340
        Cross-examination of deponent   CCP §2025.330
        Examination of deponent   CCP §2025.330
        Oath of deponent   CCP §2025.330
        Officer conducting proceedings   CCP §2025.320
        Recording, audio or video   CCP §2025.340
        Stenographic taking of testimony and objections   CCP §2025.330

DEPOSITIONS—Cont.
Conduct of deposition —Cont.
    Telephonic or other remote electronic means   CCP §2025.310
    Written questions propounded to deponent   CCP §2025.330
Contempt
    Subpoena, disobedience of   CCP §1991.1
Continuance of trial   CCP §§595.1, 596
Costs   CCP §1032.7
    Transcribing or video recording depositions, recovery of costs for   CCP §1033.5
Cross-examination of deponent   CCP §2025.330
    Written questions, depositions by
        Cross questions   CCP §2028.030
Destroyed land records relief law proceedings   CCP §751.18
Destruction of   CCP §§1952 to 1952.3
Disposition of   CCP §§1952 to 1952.3
Distance
    Fees for mileage   CCP §§1986.5, 2020
Economic litigation provisions for limited civil cases, permissible forms of discovery under   CCP §94
Electronic oral depositions
    Remote electronic means of taking depositions   CCP §2025.310, CRC 3.1010
        Notice of intention to take   CRC 3.250
Employer and employee
    Time limits for witness examination
        Exceptions for cases arising out of employment relationship   CCP §2025.290
Evidence
    Use of depositions as evidence   CCP §2025.620
        Preservation of evidence or perpetuation of testimony prior to filing action   CCP §2035.060
Examination of deponent   CCP §2025.330
    Time limits
        Witness examination   CCP §2025.290
Exhibit, deposition used as   CRC 3.1116
Expert witnesses   CCP §§2034.410 to 2034.470
    Fees of expert for time at deposition   CCP §§2034.430 to 2034.470
    Notice for deposition accompanied by tender of fee, effect   CCP §2034.460
    Order setting fee, motion for   CCP §2034.470
    Place to take deposition   CCP §2034.420
    Production of materials called for by deposition notice   CCP §2034.415
    Right to depose listed witnesses   CCP §2034.410
    Tendering fees   CCP §2034.450
    Time limits for witness examination   CCP §2025.290
    Workers' compensation cases, fees   CCP §2034.430
Family rules
    Discovery   CRC 5.12
Fees
    Generally   CCP §§1986.5, 2020
    Mileage fees   Ev §§1563, 1986.5, 2020
    Peace officers, deposition fees for   Gov §68097.6
    Production of business records   CCP §1563
    Witness fees and mileage   CCP §2020.230
Foreign countries
    Taking depositions in California for use in foreign country   CRC 3.1015
Foreign states or nations
    Interstate and international depositions and discovery act   CCP §§2029.100 to 2029.900 (See **DISCOVERY**)
    Taking depositions in   CCP §2027.010
Interstate and international depositions and discovery act   CCP §§2029.100 to 2029.900 (See **DISCOVERY**)
Judges
    Disciplinary proceedings against   JudPerR 122
Judicial arbitration
    Admissibility of depositions   CRC 3.823
Methods of discovery   CCP §2019.010
    Nonparty discovery   CCP §2020.010
Mileage
    Fees for mileage   CCP §§1986.5, 2020
Missing person, deposition regarding whereabouts of   Pro §12406
Motion to compel
    Answer to question or production of document   CCP §2025.480
    Notice of deposition, motion to compel compliance   CCP §2025.450
    Production of documents   CCP §2025.480
    Separate document setting forth item to which further response, answer or production is requested   CRC 3.1345
    Service of papers on nonparty deponent   CRC 3.1346
Nonparty deponents
    Personal service of motion to compel   CRC 3.1346

DEPOSITIONS—Cont.

Nonparty discovery
    Methods of discovery   CCP §2020.010
    Subpoenas   CCP §2020.020
Notice of deposition   CCP §§2025.210 to 2025.295
    Consumer records
        Service of notice on consumer   CCP §2025.240
    Contents   CCP §2025.220
    Corporations and other non-natural person deponents
        Description of matters on which examination requested   CCP §2025.230
    Limitation on papers filed   CRC 3.250
    Method for notice   CCP §2025.210
    Noncompliance with notice
        Sanctions   CCP §2025.450
    Parties appearing
        Providing notice to all parties appearing   CCP §2025.240
    Place for taking deposition   CCP §2025.250
        More distant location, motion and ruling   CCP §2025.260
    Scheduling deposition, interval between notice or subpoena   CCP §2025.270
    Service, effect   CCP §2025.280
    Subpoena served with notice   CCP §2025.240
        When deposition subpoena required   CCP §2025.280
    Unlawful detainer actions
        Time for taking deposition   CCP §2025.270
    Written questions, deposition by
        Delivery to officer conducting   CCP §2028.080
        Notice of written deposition   CCP §2028.020
        Questions accompany notice   CCP §2028.030
Oath of deponent   CCP §2025.330
Objections
    Errors and irregularities at deposition   CCP §2025.460
    Privileged and protected information
        Waiver absent objection   CCP §2025.460
        Written questions, depositions by   CCP §2028.050
    Service of written objection   CCP §2025.410
    Written questions, deposition by
        Attorney work product, objection based on   CCP §2028.050
        Form of question, objection to   CCP §2028.040
        Privilege, objection based on   CCP §2028.050
Officer conducting proceedings   CCP §2025.320
    Recording, audio or video
        Copies, furnishing   CCP §2025.570
    Subpoenas
        Business records produced for copying   CCP §§2020.420, 2020.430
    Transcript of deposition
        Certification by deposition officer   CCP §2025.540
        Copies, furnishing   CCP §2025.570
    Written questions, depositions by
        Notice and questions delivered to officer   CCP §2028.080
Oral depositions
    Inside California   CCP §§2025.010 to 2025.620
        Conduct of deposition   CCP §§2025.310 to 2025.340
        Notice   CCP §§2025.210 to 2025.295
        Objections, sanctions, protective orders, etc   CCP §§2025.410 to 2025.480
        Post-deposition procedures   CCP §§2025.610, 2025.620
        Transcript or recording   CCP §§2025.510 to 2025.570
    Methods of discovery   CCP §2019.010
        Nonparty discovery   CCP §2020.010
    Outside California   CCP §§2026.010, 2026.020
    Telephone, videoconference or other remote electronic means   CRC 3.1010
        Superior court fees   Gov §70630
Other states
    Administrative adjudicative proceeding, out-of-state witness in   Gov §11511
    Commission to take deposition in another state
        Superior court fees, specified services   Gov §70626
    Interstate and international depositions and discovery act   CCP §§2029.100 to 2029.900 (See **DISCOVERY**)
    Taking depositions in California for out-of-state use   CRC 3.1015
    Taking out-of-state depositions   CCP §2026.010
Peace officers, deposition fees for   Gov §68097.6
Perpetuation of testimony
    Actions, prior to filing
        Preservation of evidence or perpetuation of testimony prior to filing action   CCP §2035.060
    Appeal pending
        Use of deposition in later proceeding   CCP §2036.050
Persons deposable   CCP §2025.010

DEPOSITIONS—Cont.

Place for taking deposition   CCP §2025.250
    More distant location, motion and ruling   CCP §2025.260
Post-deposition procedures   CCP §§2025.610, 2025.620
    Evidence, use of deposition as   CCP §2025.620
    Subsequent depositions   CCP §2025.610
Prisoners   CCP §§1995 to 1997
Privileged and protected information
    Waiver   CCP §2025.460
    Written questions, depositions by
        Objections based on privilege   CCP §2028.050
Production, motion to compel
    Subpoenas
        Attendance and testimony also commanded, requirements of subpoena   CCP §2020.510
Production of business records
    Methods of discovery
        Nonparty discovery   CCP §2020.010
    Notice of deposition   CCP §2025.220
    Subpoenas
        Business records produced for copying   CCP §§2020.410 to 2020.440
Production of documents and things
    Motion to compel or quash   CRC 3.1345
        Service on nonparty deponent   CRC 3.1346
Protective orders
    Motion for protective order   CCP §2025.420
Recording, audio or video   CCP §2025.340
    Copies, furnishing   CCP §2025.570
    Notice of availability of recording for review   CCP §2025.530
    Party access to recording   CCP §2025.560
    Retention by operator   CCP §2025.560
Redirect
    Written questions, depositions by
        Redirect questions   CCP §2028.030
Rough draft transcript
    Use prohibited   CCP §2025.540
Sanctions
    Attendance
        Failure of party giving notice to attend   CCP §2025.430
        Subpoena not served, causing failure to attend   CCP §2025.440
    Generally (See **DISCOVERY**)
    Motion to compel answer or production
        Unsuccessfully making or opposing   CCP §2025.480
    Notice of deposition
        Failure to comply   CCP §2025.450
    Objections
        Unsuccessfully making or opposing objection   CCP §2025.410
    Protective orders
        Unsuccessfully making or opposing motion   CCP §2025.420
    Written questions, depositions by
        Objections   CCP §§2028.040, 2028.050
Scheduling deposition
    Interval between notice or subpoena   CCP §2025.270
Service
    Nonparties, subpoena of   CRC 3.1346
    Subpoenas   CCP §2020.220
Stenographic record of deposition
    Testimony and objections   CCP §2025.330
    Timely payment for services   CCP §2025.510
    Transcript of deposition
        Official record, stenographic testimony as   CCP §2025.510
        Retaining stenographic notes   CCP §2025.510
Stipulations
    Suspension of taking deposition   CCP §2025.470
Subpoena duces tecum
    Business records produced for copying   CCP §§2020.410 to 2020.440
Subpoenas
    Deposition subpoenas generally   CCP §§2020.210 to 2020.240 (See **DEPOSITION SUBPOENAS**)
Subsequent depositions, taking of   CCP §2025.610
Summary judgments, depositions in support or opposition of motion for   CCP §437c
Suspension of taking deposition   CCP §2025.470
Taking oral deposition   CCP §2025.010
Telephone oral depositions   CRC 3.1010
    Conduct of depositions   CCP §2025.310
Territories
    Oral depositions inside California for use outside California   CRC 3.1015
    Oral depositions outside California   CCP §2026.010
Time limitations for taking
    Discovery time limitation generally   CCP §§2024.010 to 2024.060

DEPOSITIONS—Cont.

Time limitations for taking—Cont.
    Scheduling deposition
        Interval between notice or subpoena   CCP §2025.270
Time limits for administering
    Witness examination   CCP §2025.290
        Mesothelioma or silicosis, actions involving   CCP §2025.295
Transcript of deposition   CCP §2025.510
    Certification by deposition officer   CCP §2025.540
    Changing answers, time for   CCP §2025.520
    Copies, furnishing   CCP §2025.570
    Notice of availability for reading, correcting and signing   CCP §2025.520
    Recording
        Notice of availability of recording for review   CCP §2025.530
    Retention by attorney   CCP §2025.550
    Rough draft transcript
        Use prohibited   CCP §2025.540
    Transmittal to attorney   CCP §2025.550
Videoconferencing
    Oral depositions   CRC 3.1010
    Superior court fees   Gov §70630
Video or audio depositions
    Copies, furnishing   CCP §2025.570
    Costs, recovery of   CCP §1033.5
    Notice of availability of recording for review   CCP §2025.530
    Party access to recording   CCP §2025.560
    Procedure   CCP §2025.340
    Retention by operator   CCP §2025.560
Will probate based on deposition of subscribing witness   Pro §8220
Witness fees   CCP §2020.230
Written questions, depositions by   CCP §§2028.010 to 2028.050
    Applicable procedures   CCP §2028.010
    Cross questions   CCP §2028.030
    Forwarding questions to deponent prior to deposition   CCP §2028.060
    Methods of discovery   CCP §2019.010
        Nonparty discovery   CCP §2020.010
    Notice of written deposition   CCP §2028.020
        Delivery to officer conducting   CCP §2028.080
    Objections
        Form of question   CCP §2028.040
        Privilege   CCP §2028.050
        Work product   CCP §2028.050
    Officer conducting proceedings
        Notice and questions delivered to officer   CCP §2028.080
    Orders issued by court   CCP §2028.070
    Propounding written question to deponent at oral deposition   CCP §2025.330
    Questions accompany notice   CCP §2028.030
    Redirect questions   CCP §2028.030

DEPOSITION SUBPOENAS   CCP §§2020.210 to 2020.240

Attendance and testimony commanded   CCP §2020.310
    Business records production also requested, requirements of subpoena   CCP §2020.510
Attorney of record
    Issuance   CCP §2020.210
Business records produced for copying   CCP §§2020.410 to 2020.440
    Affidavit   CCP §2020.430
    Attendance and testimony also commanded, requirements of subpoena   CCP §2020.510
    Consumer records   CCP §2020.410
    Contents   CCP §2020.410
    Custody of records   CCP §2020.430
    Delivery to officer   CCP §2020.430
    Description of records   CCP §2020.410
    Notice of deposition   CCP §2025.220
    Officer for deposition   CCP §2020.420
    Providing copies to specified parties   CCP §2020.440
Clerk of court
    Issuance   CCP §2020.210
Contempt for disobedience of   CCP §§1991.1, 2020.240
Damages for disobedience   CCP §2020.240
Electronically stored information (ESI)   CCP §2020.020
    Attendance and testimony commanded
        Business records production also requested, requirements of subpoena   CCP §2020.510
    Business records, production for copying
        Specifying form for ESI   CCP §2020.410
    Notice
        Contents of deposition notice   CCP §2025.220
        Service, effect   CCP §2025.280

DEPOSITION SUBPOENAS—Cont.

Electronically stored information (ESI) —Cont.
    Objection as to form of ESI to be provided   CCP §2020.220
    Service of deposition subpoena   CCP §2020.220
Failure to serve causing deponent to fail to attend
    Sanctions   CCP §2025.440
Forfeiture for disobedience   CCP §2020.240
Issuance   CCP §2020.210
Nonparty discovery   CCP §§2020.020, 2020.030
Notice of deposition served with subpoena   CCP §2025.240
    When deposition subpoena required   CCP §2025.280
Scheduling deposition, interval between notice or subpoena   CCP §2025.270
Service of deposition subpoena   CCP §2020.220
Witness fees and mileage   CCP §2020.230

DEPOSIT OF ESTATE-PLANNING DOCUMENTS (See TRUSTS; WILLS)

DEPOSITS

Generally   CC §§1813 to 1818
Administration of decedents' estates, deposit of funds for purposes of (See **ADMINISTRATION OF ESTATES**)
Animals, depositaries of (See **ANIMALS**)
Bank deposits (See **BANKS AND BANKING**)
Claim and delivery, property taken by   CCP §514.030
Conservatorship property, deposits of (See **CONSERVATORS**)
Court (See **DEPOSITS IN COURT**)
Damages recoverable
    Generally   CC §1836
    Indemnity for   CC §1833
    Limitation on amount recoverable   CC §1840
Decedent's estate, assets of (See **ADMINISTRATION OF ESTATES**)
Demand for redelivery   CC §§1822, 1823
Duties of depositary   CC §1839
Enforcement of judgments (See **ENFORCEMENT OF JUDGMENTS**)
Escheat generally (See **ESCHEAT**)
Exchange, deposit for   CC §§1818, 1878
Gratuitous deposits   CC §§1844 to 1847
Guardianship property, deposits of (See **GUARDIAN AND WARD**)
Hire, deposits for   CC §§1851 to 1857
Hotels and motels (See **HOTELS AND MOTELS**)
Impound accounts, requirement for   CC §2954.1
Indemnification requirements   CC §1833
Involuntary deposit
    Defined   CC §1815
    Gratuitous, as   CC §1845
Joint depositors, delivery to   CC §1827
Liens
    Generally   CC §1856
    Sale for satisfaction of   CC §1857
    Special lien on storage charges   CC §§3051, 3051a, 3052
Loss of property deposited   CC §1838
Negligence
    Limitation of liability for   CC §1840
    Loss of property   CC §1838
    Ordinary care, use of   CC §1852
Notices
    Third party claims   CC §1825
    True owner, notice of deposit   CC §1826
Perishable goods, sale of   CC §1837
Public administrators, deposit of assets from decedent's estate by (See **PUBLIC ADMINISTRATORS**)
Receivers (See **RECEIVERS AND RECEIVERSHIP**)
Rent deposits (See **RENT**)
Repair, deposit for purpose of   CC §§1858 to 1858.3
Return of property   CC §§1822 to 1828
Sales
    Lien, satisfaction of   CC §1857
    Perishables   CC §1837
Savings and loan associations (See **SAVINGS AND LOANS**)
Special lien on storage charges   CC §§3051, 3051a, 3052
Surety bond, deposit in lieu of (See **SURETYSHIP, BONDS AND UNDERTAKINGS**)
Survivorship rights   CC §1828
Termination of   CC §§1854, 1855
Third party claims, notice of   CC §1825
Trust funds   Pro §16225
Unclaimed property (See **UNCLAIMED PROPERTY**)
Use of property deposited   CC §1835
Voluntary deposit defined   CC §1814

DEPOSITS IN COURT

Admissions requiring   CCP §572
Child support payments, deposits to secure (See **CHILD SUPPORT**)

DEPOSITS IN COURT—Cont.
Contempt for refusing to deposit   CCP §574
Costs, deposits by defendant for   CC §1717, CCP §1025
Eminent domain proceedings (See **EMINENT DOMAIN**)
Interpleader (See **INTERPLEADER**)
Order for   CCP §572
Refusal, action for   CCP §574
Subject of litigation, delivery of   CCP §572
Surety bond, deposit in lieu of (See **SURETYSHIP, BONDS AND UNDERTAKINGS**)
Treasury of court
    Deposit with treasury   CCP §573

DEPOTS (See **RAILROADS**)

DEPRECIABLE PROPERTY (See **PERISHABLE AND DEPRECIABLE PROPERTY**)

DEPUTIES (See **PROBATION OFFICERS AND DEPUTIES**)

DERAIGNMENT OF TITLE (See **HEIRS**)

DERELICTION OF DUTY
Judges, unfitness of   JudPerR 109

DERIVATIVE SUITS (See **CLASS ACTIONS**)

DERIVATIVE TRANSACTIONS
Fiduciary income and principal act
    Receipts, allocation   Pro §16353

DESCENT AND DISTRIBUTION (See **INTESTATE SUCCESSION**)

DESCRIPTIONS
Complaints, real property described in   CCP §455
Deed   CCP §2077
Easements, description of premises in petition for injunction to protect   CRC 3.1151
Foreclosure sales, requirements in notice of   CC §§2924.8, 2924f
Grey market goods, reasonableness of language used for disclosures regarding   CC §1797.83
Inspection warrants (See **INSPECTION WARRANTS**)
Partition (See **PARTITION**)
Picketing, description of premises in petition for injunction to limit   CRC 3.1151
Quieting title complaint containing   CCP §761.020
Rescission of contract because of mistake in   CC §1690
Sale of property under mortgage or trust deed   CC §§2924.8, 2924f
Solar easements   CC §801.5

DESERTION OF CHILD
Adoption proceedings   Fam §8606

DESIGN
Jury deliberation rooms   CCP §216

DESIGN PROFESSIONALS
Architects (See **ARCHITECTS**)
Bonds required to secure costs in action against   CCP §1029.5
Building construction, generally (See **BUILDING CONSTRUCTION**)
Engineers (See **ENGINEERING**)
Land surveyors (See **SURVEYS AND SURVEYORS**)
Liens   CC §§8300 to 8319 (See **LIENS**)

DESTROYED LAND RECORDS RELIEF LAW   CCP §§751.01 to 751.28

DESTRUCTION OF INSTRUMENTS AND RECORDS
Conciliation court proceedings   Fam §1819
Contract extinguished by destroying instrument   CC §1699
Copies of contract, effect of destroying   CC §1701
Customer records containing personal information, disposition   CC §1798.81
Depositions   CCP §§1952 to 1952.3
Deposit of estate-planning documents with attorney (See **TRUSTS; WILLS**)
Destroyed land records relief law   CCP §§751.01 to 751.28
Exhibits   CCP §§1952 to 1952.3
Maps replaced   CCP §1855
Marriage licenses   Fam §360
    Confidential marriage licenses   Fam §510
Nunc pro tunc filing where public records lost or destroyed   CCP §1046a
Oral evidence of contents of destroyed writing, admissibility of   Ev §1523
Parties bound by   CC §1700
Photographic copies as evidence   Ev §1551
Restoration, action for   CC §3415

DESTRUCTION OF INSTRUMENTS AND RECORDS—Cont.
Secondary evidence of contents of destroyed writing   Ev §§1523, 1551
Superior court records destroyed   CRC 10.855, 10.856
Trust documents deposited with attorney (See **TRUSTS**)
Wills (See **WILLS**)

DESTRUCTION OF PROPERTY
Art works, defacement of   CC §987
Construction, damages for intentional destruction of property under   CC §1721
Escheated property   CCP §1379
Ex parte order enjoining   Fam §6320
    California law enforcement telecommunications (CLETS) information form, confidentiality and use of information   CRC 1.51, CRCAppx A
Sale of realty, risk of loss under contract for   CC §1662

DETAINER
Forcible entry and detainer (See **FORCIBLE ENTRY AND DETAINER**)
Unlawful detainer (See **UNLAWFUL DETAINER**)

DETENTION
Child custody
    Electronic testimony or participation allowed in cases of   Fam §3012

DETERMINABLE ESTATES   CC §§739 to 742

DETINUE
Statute of limitation   CCP §338

DETRIMENT
Damage award, effect on   CC §§3282, 3304 to 3318

DEVALUATION OF CURRENCY
Loan repayment, effect on   CC §1913

DEVELOPERS (See **BUILDING CONSTRUCTION**)

DEVELOPMENTALLY DISABLED PERSONS
Adoption of (See **ADOPTION**)
Conservatorship for (See **CONSERVATORS**)
Criminal offenders
    Judicial commitment
        Appeal from order of civil commitment   CRC 8.483
Defined   Pro §1420
Guardianship for (See **GUARDIAN AND WARD**)
Housing discrimination against disabled persons
    Construction or application of provisions in issue, solicitor general notified   CC §55.2
Information Practices Act, disclosure to patients' rights protection agency under   CC §1798.24b
Judicial commitment
    Appeal from order of civil commitment   CRC 8.483
    Remote proceedings
        Conditions for proceeding through use of remote technology   CCP §367.76
Juvenile court, inquiry into mental health of child before   CRC 5.643
    Competence of minor subject to juvenile proceedings, doubt as to
        Evaluation of competence   CRC 5.645
Payments pursuant to compromise or judgment for minor or person with disability
    Trusts, payment into   CRC JudAdminStand 7.10
Rape victim incapable of giving consent due to illness, proof that
    Statute of limitations on sexual assault damages   CCP §340.16
Special needs trusts (See **SPECIAL NEEDS TRUSTS**)
Sterilization proceedings (See **STERILIZATION**)
Termination of parental rights, parent declared developmentally disabled or mentally ill
    Circumstances where proceedings may be brought   Fam §7826

DEVELOPMENTAL SERVICES DEPARTMENT
Conservatorship proceedings involving state hospital patient, notice of   Pro §§1461, 1461.4, 1822
Guardianship proceedings involving state hospital patient, notice of   Pro §§1461, 1461.4, 1511
Special needs trust for minor or person with disability, notice of   Pro §§3602, 3605, 3611
    Definition of person with disability   Pro §3603
    Express consent of protected person to court orders, when required   Pro §3613

DEVISEES (See **WILLS**)

DIES, MOLDS AND FORMS
Ownership of   CC §1140

DIETITIANS
Review committees, liability of   CC §§43.7, 43.8

DIFFERENTIAL CASE MANAGEMENT (See CIVIL RULES)

DIFFERENTIAL CASE MANAGEMENT RULES (See TRIAL COURT DELAY REDUCTION)

DIGITAL ASSETS, FIDUCIARY ACCESS   Pro §§870 to 884 (See FIDUCIARY ACCESS TO DIGITAL ASSETS)

DIGITAL EQUITY BILL OF RIGHTS   CC §§3120 to CC 3123
Citation of provisions   CC §3120
Definitions   CC §3122
Effect of provisions   CC §3123
Enumeration of rights   CC §3122
Legislative findings   CC §3121
Obligations and rights not created by laws   CC §3123
Policy of state   CC §3122

DINING FACILITIES (See RESTAURANTS)

DIPLOMATS
Ambassadors (See AMBASSADORS)
Consuls (See CONSULS AND CONSULATES)

DIRECTED TRUSTS   Pro §§16600 to 16632
Applicability of provisions   Pro §16604
    Exceptions   Pro §16606
    Uniform application and construction   Pro §16630
Construction of provisions
    Electronic signatures in global and national commerce act, relation to   Pro §16632
    Uniform application and construction   Pro §16630
Cotrustees
    Relief from liability   Pro §16620
Definitions   Pro §16602
Directed trustee
    Actions outside scope of duties   Pro §16618
    Breach of trust
        Defenses asserted   Pro §16624
        Limitation of actions   Pro §16622
        When released from liability   Pro §16614
    Compliance with power of direction   Pro §16614
    Consent required for appointment   Pro §16605
    Information between director and trustee   Pro §16616
Legislative findings   Pro §16600
Principal place of administration   Pro §16604
Title of provisions   Pro §16600
Trust director
    Actions outside scope of duties   Pro §16618
    Breach of trust
        Defenses asserted   Pro §16624
        Limitation of actions   Pro §16622
        When released from liability   Pro §16614
    Charitable interest in trust
        Rules applicable   Pro §16610
    Consent required for appointment   Pro §16605
    Fiduciary duties and liability   Pro §16612
    Imposition of liability by terms of trust   Pro §16612
    Information between director and trustee   Pro §16616
    Payback provision to comply with Medicaid and Social Security Act
        Rules applicable   Pro §16610
    Personal jurisdiction over   Pro §16626
    Powers   Pro §16608
    Rules applicable to director in certain instances   Pro §§16610, 16628

DIRECTED VERDICT (See VERDICT)

DIRECT EXAMINATION
Adverse party called as witness   Ev §776
Court control over interrogation of witnesses   Ev §765
Definition   CCP §2005, Ev §760
Documents   Ev §768
Expert witnesses   Ev §732
Inconsistent statements by witnesses (See WITNESSES)
Leading questions   Ev §§764, 767
Redirect examination (See REDIRECT EXAMINATION)
Refreshing memory, witness' use of writings for   Ev §771
Responsive answers from witnesses   Ev §766

DIRECTORIES
Admissibility of   Ev §1340

DIRECTORS
Corporate directors (See CORPORATE OFFICERS AND EMPLOYEES)

DISABILITIES, GENERALLY (See DISABLED PERSONS)

DISABILITY BENEFITS
Assignment for benefit of creditors, property exempt from   CCP §1801
Exempt property for purposes of enforcement of judgments   CCP §704.130

DISABLED OR HANDICAPPED PERSONS
Landlord and tenant
    Rent control
        Moving tenant with permanent physical disability to accessible floor of property   CC §1954.53
Rent control
    Moving tenant with permanent physical disability to accessible floor of property   CC §1954.53

DISABLED PERSONS
Accessibility of buildings and facilities
    Attorney general, civil actions to enforce
        Fees and costs for attorney general   CCP §1021.8
        Construction or application of provisions in issue, solicitor general notified   CC §55.2
    Construction-related accessibility claims   CC §§55.3 to 55.57, CRCAppx A (See CONSTRUCTION-RELATED ACCESSIBILITY CLAIMS)
Accommodations requested of courts, requirements for   CRC 1.100
    Forms
        Judicial council forms   CRCAppx A
Administrative procedure act
    Visual or communication disability
        Narrative description of proposed regulation upon request   Gov §11346.6
Adoption (See ADOPTION)
Attorney's disability, appointment of practice administrator in event of   Pro §§2468, 17200
Attorney's performance of professional services, plaintiff's disability tolling statute of limitation for actions arising out of   CCP §340.6
Blindness (See BLIND PERSONS)
Building access
    Construction or application of provisions in issue, solicitor general notified   CC §55.2
Commercial and industrial common interest developments
    Disabled access
        Modification of separate interests   CC §6714
Compromise and settlement
    Court approval of compromise
        Appellate court opinions, privacy protection as to use of names in opinions   CRC 8.90
        Forms, use of judicial council forms   CRC 7.101
        Notice of settlement   CRC 3.1385
    Electronic court records
        Courthouse electronic access   CRC 2.503
Construction-related accessibility claims   CC §§55.3 to 55.57 (See CONSTRUCTION-RELATED ACCESSIBILITY CLAIMS)
Consumer protection provisions, remedies for disabled persons under   CC §§1780, 3345
Court personnel, reasonable accommodation for disabled   CRC JudAdminStand 10.25
Court reporter's disability as grounds for new trial   CCP §657.1
Courts
    Accommodations by   CRC 1.100
Credit disability insurance (See CREDIT DISABILITY INSURANCE)
Custody of children
    Disabled parents
        Codification of decision in In re Marriage of Carney   Fam §3049
Dance studio contract, refund under   CC §1812.57
Dating service contract, payment liability under   CC §1694.8
Deaf persons (See DEAF AND HARD OF HEARING PERSONS)
Deeds of trust and mortgages
    Modification or workout plan to avoid foreclosure
        Disabled person victim of prohibited acts, punishment   CC §2944.8
        Statute of limitations to enforce protections   CC §2944.10
Developmentally disabled persons (See DEVELOPMENTALLY DISABLED PERSONS)
Discrimination (See DISCRIMINATION)
Earnings, disability payments as   CC §1812.30
Enhancement of fines for injury resulting from deceptive consumer sales practices   CC §3345
Equal access rights to public facilities   CC §54
    Construction or application of provisions in issue, solicitor general notified   CC §55.2

DISABLED PERSONS—Cont.

Family allowance, disabled adult children receiving   Pro §§6540 to 6543
Health studios refunding fees to   CC §1812.89
Housing accommodations
    Modification of condominium unit   CC §4760
        Architectural review and decisionmaking, standards when required   CC §4765
Housing discrimination
    Construction or application of provisions in issue, solicitor general notified   CC §55.2
Injunctions for violation of equal rights   CC §§55, 55.1
Judgments in favor of minor or disabled person   Pro §§3600 to 3613
    Attorneys' fees for services to minors and person with disability   CRC 7.955
    Disposition of proceeds, court approval
        Expedited approval, petition   CRC 7.950.5
        Petition   CRC 7.950, 7.950.5
    Express consent of protected person to court orders, when required   Pro §3613
    Person with disability defined   Pro §3603
    Trusts, payment into   CRC JudAdminStand 7.10
Jurors (See **JURY**)
Jury service
    Disability as ground for excuse   CRC 2.1008
        Permanent medical excuse from jury service   CRC 2.1009
Mobilehomes and mobilehome parks
    Installation of ramps, handrails and other accommodations, permission of homeowner   CC §798.29.6
        Subdivisions, cooperatives and condominiums   CC §799.11
Modification of condominium unit   CC §4760
    Architectural review and decisionmaking, standards when required   CC §4765
Party to action disabled during pending action or proceeding, effect of   CCP §375
Payments pursuant to compromise or judgment for minor or person with disability
    Trusts, payment into   CRC JudAdminStand 7.10
Property tax exemptions (See **TAXATION**)
Public facilities, right to equal access to   CC §54
    Construction or application of provisions in issue, solicitor general notified   CC §55.2
Rules of court
    Accommodation by courts of persons with disability   CRC 1.100
Service dogs, use of   CC §§54.1, 54.2
    Construction or application of provisions in issue, solicitor general notified   CC §55.2
Sex offense against
    Proof that sex crime victim incapable of giving consent due to disability
        Statute of limitations on sexual assault damages   CCP §340.16
    Sexual battery against disabled person
        Statute of limitations on sexual assault damages   CCP §340.16
    Statute of limitations on sexual assault damages   CCP §340.16
Support of adult child   Fam §3910
Telephone facilities, use of   CC §54.1
    Construction or application of provisions in issue, solicitor general notified   CC §55.2
Trust decanting, uniform act
    Beneficiary with disability
        Trust for beneficiary with disability   Pro §19513
Weight loss programs, payment liability under   CC §1694.3

DISASTER RELIEF (See **NATURAL CATASTROPHES**)

DISASTER RELIEF ORGANIZATIONS

Medical information disclosed to   CC §57.10

DISASTERS (See **NATURAL CATASTROPHES**)

DISCHARGE

Jurors (See **JURY**)
Release and discharge (See **RELEASE**)

DISCIPLINARY ACTION

Attorneys (See **ATTORNEY DISCIPLINE**)
Judges (See **JUDGES**)

DISCLAIMER OF ESTATE INTEREST

Generally   Pro §§260 to 295
Attorney in fact, authority of   Pro §4264
Independent administrators of decedents' estates, authority of   Pro §10519
Trust beneficiaries, disclaimer of interest by   Pro §§260 to 295, 15309

DISCLOSURE

Administrative law and procedure (See **ADMINISTRATIVE PROCEDURE ACT**)
Adoption (See **ADOPTION**)
Agency
    Acknowledgment of receipt of disclosure form   CC §2079.14
AIDS, disclosures to buyer of real property regarding affliction of prior occupant with   CC §1710.2
Auctioneers, requirements for   CC §1812.607
Automobile leases
    Registration of vehicle
        Optional DMV electronic filing fee, disclosures as to   CC §2985.8
Automobile sales contracts   CC §§2982, 2983
    Registration of vehicle
        Optional DMV electronic filing fee, disclosures as to   CC §2982
Bookkeeping services   CC §§1799 to 1799.1a
Boundary dispute involving state, disclosure of written evidence in   CCP §2031.510
Brokers, disclosures by (See **BROKERS**)
Common interest developments (See **COMMON INTEREST DEVELOPMENTS**)
Conditional sales of residential property, disclosures required for   CC §§2956 to 2968
Consumer debt collection
    Statement by debt collector
        Contents   CC §1788.14.5
Conveyances (See **CONVEYANCES**)
Credit card accounts (See **CREDIT CARDS**)
Credit, reasons for denial of   CC §§1787.1 to 1787.3
    Waiver of protections   CC §1787.4
Customer records
    Personal information of customer   CC §1798.83
        Remedies of customer for violation   CC §1798.84
Death within three years of prior occupant, disclosure to buyer of real property concerning   CC §1710.2
Disability insurance claims   CC §1812.402
Discount buying services   CC §1812.106
Discovery (See **DISCOVERY**)
Earthquake hazards
    Real estate sales   CC §§1103 to 1103.15
Electronic Commerce Act, disclosure required under   CC §1789.3
Fair debt settlement practices
    Debt settlement providers   CC §1788.302
Fine prints, sale of   CC §§1742 to 1744
Flood and fire hazards   CC §§1103 to 1103.15
Forest fire hazard areas, real estate sales   CC §§1103 to 1103.15
Garnishment (See **GARNISHMENT**)
Genetic characteristics, test results for   CC §56.17
Grand jury (See **GRAND JURIES**)
Grant of land, disclosure of written evidence in dispute with state involving   CCP §2031.510
Grey market goods, sale of (See **GREY MARKET GOODS**)
Home Equity Loan Disclosure Act   CC §§2970 to 2971
Home equity sales contracts, disclosure requirement in   CC §1695.5
Home solicitation sales contracts, disclosure requirement in   CC §1689.7
Information Practices Act (See **INFORMATION PRACTICES ACT**)
Inspection of residential property, disclosure to prospective buyer required following   CC §2079
International commercial arbitration and conciliation (See **INTERNATIONAL COMMERCIAL ARBITRATION AND CONCILIATION**)
Investigative consumer reporting agencies (See **INVESTIGATIVE CONSUMER REPORTING AGENCIES**)
Mediation
    Standards of conduct for mediators
        Complaints about mediator conduct, disclosures concerning proceedings   CRC 3.860
Medical records (See **MEDICAL RECORDS**)
Membership camping contracts   CC §1812.302
Mobilehomes (See **MOBILEHOMES**)
Natural hazards, real estate sales   CC §§1103 to 1103.15
Personal records (See **INFORMATION PRACTICES ACT**)
Private student loan collections reform
    Statement to debtor by lender or loan collector
        Information required prior to statement   CC §1788.202
Privileged communications (See **PRIVILEGED COMMUNICATIONS**)
Public guardians, duty to disclose property information to   Pro §2901
Public policy affecting   Ev §§1040 to 1042
Real estate transfer disclosure statements (See **VENDOR AND PURCHASER**)
Renegotiable interest rates   CC §1916.8

DISCLOSURE—Cont.
Rental-purchase contracts, Karnette Rental-Purchase Act for   CC §§1812.620 to 1812.650
Sale or other transfer of real estate (See **REAL ESTATE SALES**)
Seller assisted marketing plans   CC §§1812.203, 1812.205, 1812.206
Seminar sales contracts, disclosure requirement in   CC §1689.21
Sex offenses
    Disclosure requirements for transactions involving sex offenders   CC §2079.10a
Shared appreciation loans (See **SHARED APPRECIATION LOANS**)
Sliding scale recovery agreement between joint tortfeasors   CCP §877.5
Social security numbers, prohibiting posting or display to general public of   CC §1798.85
    Financial institutions, continued use   CC §1786.60
    Waiver of protections   CC §1798.86
Transfer or sale of residential property, disclosure statements involving (See **VENDOR AND PURCHASER**)
Trust deeds and mortgages (See **TRUST DEEDS AND MORTGAGES**)
Unemployment insurance administration, information obtained through   Ev §1040
Vendor and purchaser (See **VENDOR AND PURCHASER**)
Waiver of privilege   Ev §919
Wheelchairs offered for sale or lease, defects in returned   CC §1793.025

DISCOUNTS
Credit card, discount for purchase by means other than   CC §§1748, 1748.1
Discount buying services contracts   CC §§1812.100 to 1812.129
Supermarket club cards (See **GROCERY STORES**)

DISCOVERY   CRC 3.1000, 3.1010
Abuse of discovery process, sanctions for (See **DISCOVERY ABUSES, SANCTIONS FOR**)
Accounting companies disclosing information during   CC §1799.1
Actions
    Defined   CCP §2016.020
Administration of estates
    Conveyance or transfer of property claimed by decedent or other person   Pro §851.1
    Law and motion rules
        Applicable to discovery proceedings in probate   CRC 3.1100
Administrative adjudication (See **ADMINISTRATIVE ADJUDICATION**)
Aliens
    Children and minors
        Discovery into immigration status prohibited   CC §3339.5
Appeals
    Discovery pending appeal
        Perpetuation of testimony or preservation of information pending appeal   CCP §§2036.010 to 2036.050
    Interstate and international depositions and discovery act
        Choice of law to resolve disputes, appeal for extraordinary writ   CCP §2029.650
Arbitration   CCP §§1283 to 1283.8
    Judicial arbitration (See **JUDICIAL ARBITRATION**)
Attachment order, discovery by plaintiff allowed pursuant to   CCP §485.230
Attorney work product   CCP §§2018.010 to 2018.080
    Breach of attorney-client relationship   CCP §2018.080
    Clients
        Defined   CCP §2018.010
    Construction of provisions to restate existing law   CCP §2018.040
    Crime or fraud, participation by attorney
        No protection of work product   CCP §2018.050
    Deposition on written question
        Objection to question based on work product   CCP §2028.050
    Disciplinary proceedings of state bar   CCP §2018.070
    Electronically stored information (ESI)
        Applicable rules   CCP §2020.220
        Subpoenas, applicability of privilege   CCP §1985.8
    In camera hearings   CCP §2018.060
    Inspection demands for electronically stored information
        Privilege claimed or attorney work product protection requested   CCP §2031.285
    Mental examinations, discovery procedure for
        Reports of examination, waiver of work product privilege   CCP §§2032.610, 2032.630
    Physical examinations, discovery procedure for
        Reports of examination, waiver of work product privilege   CCP §§2032.610, 2032.630
    Policy of state   CCP §2018.020
    When discoverable   CCP §2018.030
  Automobile warranties
    Restitution or replacement actions   CCP §871.26

DISCOVERY—Cont.
Boundary dispute involving state, disclosure of written evidence in   CCP §2031.510
Censure, removal or admonishment of judges (See **JUDGES**)
Child support (See **CHILD SUPPORT**)
Chiropractic review boards, exemption of records of   Ev §1157
Civil discovery act   CCP §§2016.010 to 2036.050
    Short title of provisions   CCP §2016.010
Class actions   CRC 3.768
Conduct of discovery
    Civil rules   CRC 3.1010
Contempt   CCP §1991.1
Continuance of trial proceedings includes   CCP §595.1
Coordinated actions   CRC 3.541
Copies
    Demand for inspection, copying, testing or sampling
        Inspection demands generally   CCP §§2031.010 to 2031.510 (See **INSPECTION DEMANDS**)
Courts
    Defined   CCP §2016.020
Custodial officer's personnel records   Ev §§1043 to 1047
Dead bodies
    Video recordings or photographs of dead bodies taken by coroners   CCP §129
Declaration for additional discovery
    Limitation on papers filed   CRC 3.250
Definitions   CCP §2016.020
Demand for inspection of documents, tangible things, land or other property (See **INSPECTION DEMANDS**)
Dental committee records subject to discovery   Ev §§1156, 1157
Dental hygienist review committee records exempt from   Ev §1157
Dependent adults
    Elder abuse and dependent adult civil protection act   CCP §§2017.310, 2017.320
Depositions
    Generally (See **DEPOSITIONS**)
    Methods of discovery   CCP §2019.010
Documents and records
    Definition of document   CCP §2016.020
    Inspection
        Demand for inspection of documents, tangible things, etc (See **INSPECTION DEMANDS**)
        Methods of discovery   CCP §2019.010
Domestic violence
    Restraining order discovery   Fam §6309
Economic litigation procedures (See **ECONOMIC LITIGATION PROCEDURES**)
Elder abuse and dependent adult civil protection act   CCP §§2017.310, 2017.320
Electronic
    Defined   CCP §2016.020
Electronically stored information (ESI)
    Applicability of civil discovery act provisions to ESI   CCP §2019.040
    Compelling discovery, motion   CCP §2025.480
    Defined   CCP §2016.020
    Deposition subpoenas   CCP §2020.020
        Contents of deposition notice   CCP §2025.220
        Effect of service of notice   CCP §2025.280
        Failure to comply with deposition notice   CCP §2025.450
        Objection as to form of ESI to be provided   CCP §2020.220
        Service of deposition subpoena   CCP §2020.220
    Inspection demands   CCP §§2031.010, 2031.030
        Compelling discovery despite burden of providing   CCP §2031.310
        Inaccessibility claimed   CCP §§2031.060, 2031.210
        Objections   CCP §2031.240
        Privilege claimed or attorney work product protection requested   CCP §2031.285
        Response, form of information furnished   CCP §2031.280
        Sanctions for failure to provide, circumstances avoiding   CCP §§2031.300, 2031.320
    Outside California, discovery in foreign jurisdictions   CCP §2026.010
        Foreign nations   CCP §2027.010
    Protective orders   CCP §2025.420
    Sanctions for failure to provide
        Good faith operation of electronic information system preventing provision of ESI, defense to sanctions   CCP §§2017.020, 2020.220
    Scope of discovery   CCP §2017.010
    Subpoenas   CCP §1985.8
    Undue burden or expense to produce   CCP §2020.220
        Objections to production   CCP §2025.460
    Work product
        Applicable rules   CCP §2020.220

DISCOVERY—Cont.
Electronic depositions
    Remote electronic means of taking oral depositions   CRC 3.1010
Electronic discovery act   CCP §1985.8
Electronic documents
    Inspection demands   CCP §§2031.010, 2031.030
        Compelling discovery despite burden of providing   CCP §2031.310
        Inaccessibility claimed   CCP §§2031.060, 2031.210
        Objections   CCP §2031.240
        Privilege claimed or attorney work product protection requested   CCP §2031.285
        Response, form of information furnished   CCP §2031.280
        Sanctions for failure to provide, circumstances avoiding   CCP §§2031.300, 2031.320
Eminent domain proceedings (See **EMINENT DOMAIN**)
Evidence, preservation prior to filing action   CCP §§2035.010 to 2035.060
    Attorney, appointment to represent expected adverse party   CCP §2035.040
    Depositions taken, use   CCP §2035.060
    Methods of perpetuation or preservation   CCP §2035.020
    Order authorizing discovery   CCP §2035.050
    Right to obtain discovery   CCP §2035.010
    Service of notice of petition   CCP §2035.040
    Verified petition   CCP §§2035.030, 2035.040
Expedited jury trials
    Pretrial proceedings   CRC 3.1548
Expert witnesses, discovery of
    Discovery by simultaneous information exchange (See **EXPERT AND OPINION EVIDENCE**)
Extent of discovery
    Limitation   CCP §2019.030
Failure to confer
    Sanctions   CCP §§2023.010, 2023.020
Family law proceedings
    Code provisions applicable to discovery   CRC 5.12
    Court rules provisions applicable to discovery   CRC 5.12
    Law and motion rules
        Applicability to discovery proceedings in family law proceedings   CRC 3.1100
    Postjudgment discovery   Fam §218
    Request for orders   CRC 5.12
Forcible entry and detainer
    Motion for discovery   CCP §1170.8, CRC 3.1347
        Judicial council, rules as to   CCP §1170.9
Foreign states or nations
    Interstate and international depositions and discovery act   CCP §§2029.100 to 2029.900
Format of discovery
    Civil rules   CRC 3.1000
Forms
    Judicial council legal forms   CRCAppx A
Frequency of discovery
    Limitation   CCP §2019.030
Frivolous actions
    Inapplicability   CCP §128.5
Grant of land, disclosure of written evidence in dispute with state involving   CCP §2031.510
Immigration and naturalization
    Children and minors
        Discovery into immigration status prohibited   CC §3339.5
Informal discovery conference   CCP §2016.080
Information Practices Act, effect of   CC §1798.71
Initial disclosures without awaiting discovery request   CCP §2016.090
Inspection
    Demand for inspection of documents, tangible things, land or other property (See **INSPECTION DEMANDS**)
    Methods of discovery   CCP §2019.010
Inspection demands
    Generally   CCP §§2031.010 to 2031.510 (See **INSPECTION DEMANDS**)
    Interstate and international depositions and discovery act (See within this heading, "**Interstate and international depositions and discovery act**")
Insurance coverage, discovery of   CCP §2017.210
Interrogatories
    Generally (See **INTERROGATORIES**)
    Methods of discovery   CCP §2019.010
Interstate and international depositions and discovery act   CCP §§2029.100 to 2029.900
    Applicability of discovery provisions   CCP §2029.500
    California version of uniform act   CCP §2029.700
    Choice of law to resolve disputes   CCP §2029.600
        Appeal for extraordinary writ   CCP §2029.650

DISCOVERY—Cont.
Interstate and international depositions and discovery act —Cont.
    Choice of law to resolve disputes —Cont.
        Appearance fees   CCP §2029.610
        Circumstances not requiring dispute resolution mechanism   CCP §2029.640
        Petitions, filing, notice and service   CCP §2029.630
        Procedure to resolve disputes   CCP §2029.610
        Subsequent petitions   CCP §2029.620
    Citation of provisions   CCP §2029.100
    Definitions   CCP §2029.200
    Foreign jurisdictions
        Defined   CCP §2029.200
        Proceedings pending, discovery requirements for party   CCP §2029.640
    Foreign penal civil action
        Defined   CCP §2029.200
    Foreign subpoenas
        Defined   CCP §2029.200
    Operative date of provisions   CCP §§2029.800, 2029.900
    Person
        Defined   CCP §2029.200
    Protective orders
        Choice of law to resolve disputes   CCP §2029.600
    State
        Defined   CCP §2029.200
    Subpoenas
        Application form   CCP §2029.390
        Choice of law to resolve disputes   CCP §2029.600
        Circumstances not requiring subpoena   CCP §2029.640
        Defined   CCP §2029.200
        Foreign subpoena   CCP §§2029.300, 2029.350
        Forms   CCP §2029.390
        Issuance   CCP §2029.350
        Request   CCP §§2029.300, 2029.390
        Service   CCP §2029.400
Interstate family support
    Assistance from tribunal of other state   Fam §5700.318
Judges, proceedings against (See **JUDGES**)
Judicial arbitration (See **JUDICIAL ARBITRATION**)
Juvenile court proceedings   CRC 5.546
Law and motion rules
    Family law, applicability to discovery proceedings in   CRC 3.1100
    Probate, applicability to discovery proceedings in   CRC 3.1100
Licensed professional clinical counselors
    Peer review or discipline records and proceedings, discovery
        Restrictions   Ev §1157
Local rules of court
    Preemption of local rules   CRC 3.20
Mediation (See **MEDIATION**)
Mediation proceedings
    Confidentiality
        Attorney disclosure to client of confidentiality standards in mediation proceedings   Ev §1129
Medical records
    Health care professional review committees, findings of   Ev §§1157 to 1157.7
    Hospital mortality studies, documents related to   Ev §§1156 to 1156.1
    Inspection by attorney, written authorization for   CCP §1985.7, Ev §1158
Meet and confer
    Declaration
        Contents   CCP §2016.040
    Failure to reach informal resolution
        Informal discovery conference at request of party or on court's own motion   CCP §2016.080
    Forms
        Judicial council legal forms   CRCAppx A
Mental examinations, discovery procedure for   CCP §§2032.010 to 2032.650
    Applicability of provisions   CCP §2032.010
    Attorney presence   CCP §2032.530
    Conduct of examination   CCP §§2032.510 to 2032.530
    Failure to produce another for examination
        Sanctions   CCP §2032.420
    Failure to submit
        Sanctions   CCP §2032.410
    Methods of discovery   CCP §2019.010
    Motions for examinations   CCP §§2032.310, 2032.320
        Grounds for granting   CCP §2032.320
        Leave of court   CCP §2032.310
    Physicians performing   CCP §2032.020
    Psychologists performing   CCP §2032.020

DISCOVERY—Cont.
- Mental examinations, discovery procedure for —Cont.
  - Recording examination   CCP §2032.530
  - Reports of examination   CCP §§2032.610 to 2032.650
    - Attorney work product waived for demand for report   CCP §§2032.610, 2032.630
    - Demanding report   CCP §2032.610
    - Existing and later reports of same condition, demand recipient's right to   CCP §§2032.640, 2032.650
    - Failure to timely deliver   CCP §2032.620
    - Motion to compel   CCP §§2032.620, 2032.650
  - Right to discovery   CCP §2032.020
  - Sexual abuse of minor
    - Duration of examination of minor aged 14 years or less   CCP §2032.340
    - Qualifications of examiner for examinee aged 14 or less   CCP §2032.020
- Methods of   CCP §2019.010
  - Nonparty discovery   CCP §2020.010
  - Trade secrets   CCP §2019.210
- Minors
  - Discovery into immigration status prohibited   CC §3339.5
  - Mental examinations
    - Sexual abuse of minor, duration of examination of minor aged 14 years or less   CCP §2032.340
- Misuse of discovery, acts constituting
  - Sanctions   CCP §§2023.010, 2023.030
- Motions
  - Civil rules   CRC 3.1345 to 3.1348
  - Format   CRC 3.1345
  - Service, methods   CCP §2016.050
  - Telephone appearance at hearings on discovery motions   CRC 3.670
- Motion to compel
  - Depositions (See **DEPOSITIONS**)
  - Inspection of documents (See **INSPECTION DEMANDS**)
  - Interrogatories (See **INTERROGATORIES**)
  - Mental examinations, discovery procedure for
    - Reports of examination   CCP §§2032.620, 2032.650
  - Physical examinations, discovery procedure for
    - Reports of examination   CCP §§2032.620, 2032.650
  - Requests for admissions (See **REQUEST FOR ADMISSION**)
  - Telephone appearance at hearings on discovery motions   CRC 3.670
- Nonparty discovery   CCP §§2020.010 to 2020.510
- Perpetuation of testimony
  - Actions, prior to filing   CCP §§2035.010 to 2035.060
    - Attorney, appointment to represent expected adverse party   CCP §2035.040
    - Depositions taken, use   CCP §2035.060
    - Methods of perpetuation or preservation   CCP §2035.020
    - Order authorizing discovery   CCP §2035.050
    - Right to obtain discovery   CCP §2035.010
    - Service of notice of petition   CCP §2035.040
    - Verified petition   CCP §§2035.030, 2035.040
  - Appeal pending   CCP §§2036.010 to 2036.050
    - Depositions, use in later proceeding   CCP §2036.050
    - Grounds for authorizing discovery   CCP §2036.040
    - Methods of discovery available   CCP §2036.020
    - Motion for leave to conduct discovery   CCP §2036.030
    - Right to discovery   CCP §2036.010
- Pharmacist review boards
  - Exemption of records   Ev §1157
- Physical examinations, discovery procedure for   CCP §§2032.010 to 2032.650
  - Applicability of provisions   CCP §2032.010
  - Attorney attendance   CCP §2032.510
  - Conduct of examination   CCP §§2032.510 to 2032.530
  - Failure to produce another for examination
    - Sanctions   CCP §2032.420
  - Failure to submit
    - Sanctions   CCP §2032.410
  - Methods of discovery   CCP §2019.010
  - Monitoring   CCP §2032.510
  - Motions for examination   CCP §§2032.310, 2032.320
    - Grounds for granting   CCP §2032.320
    - Leave of court   CCP §2032.310
  - Physicians performing   CCP §2032.020
  - Plaintiffs, personal injury cases   CCP §§2032.210 to 2032.260
    - Conditions for examination   CCP §2032.220
    - Definitions   CCP §2032.210
    - Failure to timely respond   CCP §2032.240
    - Grounds for seeking examination   CCP §2032.220
    - Motion for compliance with demand   CCP §2032.250

DISCOVERY—Cont.
- Physical examinations, discovery procedure for —Cont.
  - Plaintiffs, personal injury cases —Cont.
    - Response to demand   CCP §2032.230
    - Retention of demand, proof of service and response   CCP §2032.260
    - Sanctions   CCP §§2032.240, 2032.250
  - Protective orders
    - Suspension of examination pending motion   CCP §2032.510
  - Recording   CCP §2032.510
  - Reports of examination   CCP §§2032.610 to 2032.650
    - Attorney work product waived for demand for report   CCP §§2032.610, 2032.630
    - Demanding report   CCP §2032.610
    - Existing and later reports of same condition, demand recipient's right to   CCP §§2032.640, 2032.650
    - Failure to timely deliver   CCP §2032.620
    - Motion to compel   CCP §§2032.620, 2032.650
  - Right to discovery   CCP §2032.020
  - X-rays
    - Consent to additional x-rays   CCP §2032.520
- Podiatric records and proceedings   Ev §1157
- Police officer's personnel record   CCP §1005, Ev §§1043 to 1047
- Pre-arbitration proceedings   CRC 3.822
- Preemption of local rules   CRC 3.20
- Prehospital emergency medical care personnel review committee records exempt   Ev §1157
- Preservation of evidence prior to filing of action   CCP §§2035.010 to 2035.060
- Pretrial arbitration proceedings   CRC 3.822
- Probate proceedings
  - Law and motion rules
    - Applicability to discovery proceedings in probate   CRC 3.1100
- Production of documents and things (See **INSPECTION DEMANDS**)
- Protective orders
  - Attorney work product
    - Disciplinary action by state bar   CCP §2018.070
  - Class actions   CRC 3.768
  - Elder abuse and dependent adult civil protection act   CCP §2017.320
  - Electronically stored information (ESI)   CCP §2025.420
  - Interstate and international depositions and discovery act
    - Choice of law to resolve disputes   CCP §2029.600
  - Mental examinations, discovery procedure for
    - Suspension of examination pending motion   CCP §2032.510
  - Physical examinations, discovery procedure for
    - Suspension of examination pending motion   CCP §2032.510
  - Unsuccessfully making or opposing motion for protective order   CCP §2017.020
- Reference and referees
  - Discovery referees
    - Court-ordered reference   CRC 3.920
- Requests for admissions
  - Generally (See **REQUEST FOR ADMISSION**)
  - Methods of discovery   CCP §2019.010
- Sampling
  - Demand for inspection, copying, testing or sampling
    - Inspection demands generally   CCP §§2031.010 to 2031.510 (See **INSPECTION DEMANDS**)
- Sanctions (See **DISCOVERY ABUSES, SANCTIONS FOR**)
- Scope of discovery   CCP §§2017.010 to 2017.320
  - Elder abuse and dependent adult civil protection act
    - Confidential settlements   CCP §2017.310
    - Protective order to protect certain information   CCP §2017.320
  - Insurance information   CCP §2017.210
  - Limiting scope   CCP §2017.020
  - Protective orders
    - Elder abuse and dependent adult civil protection act   CCP §2017.320
    - Limiting scope of discovery   CCP §2017.020
  - Sexual conduct of plaintiff in certain actions   CCP §2017.220
  - Standard scope   CCP §2017.010
- Sequence of discovery   CCP §2019.020
  - Trade secrets   CCP §2019.210
- Service
  - Interstate and international depositions and discovery act
    - Choice of law to resolve disputes, petitions   CCP §2029.630
    - Subpoenas   CCP §2029.400
  - Mail or fax, service by   CCP §2016.050
- Sexual conduct
  - Administrative adjudication, sexual conduct of complainant in   Gov §11440.40
  - Plaintiff's sexual conduct   CCP §2017.220

DISCOVERY—Cont.

Small claims courts, pre-trial discovery procedures not permitted in   CCP §116.310
Spousal support proceedings (See **SPOUSAL SUPPORT**)
State agency proceedings (See **ADMINISTRATIVE ADJUDICATION**)
Stipulations
    Limitation on papers filed   CRC 3.250
    Modification of discovery procedures   CCP §2016.030
Summary judgment motions   CCP §437c
Supplemental and further discovery, format rules   CRC 3.1000
Telephone appearance at hearings on discovery motions   CRC 3.670
    Fees   CCP §367.6
Testing
    Demand for inspection, copying, testing or sampling
        Inspection demands generally   CCP §§2031.010 to 2031.510 (See **INSPECTION DEMANDS**)
Time limitations on   CCP §§2024.010 to 2024.060
    Completion of discovery   CCP §2024.020
        When complete   CCP §2024.010
    Early completion, motion for   CCP §2024.050
    Eminent domain, time for completion   CCP §2024.040
    Expert witnesses, time for completion   CCP §2024.030
    Extension of time for completion
        Agreement of parties   CCP §2024.060
    Forcible entry and detainer, time for completion   CCP §2024.040
    Judicial arbitration, time for completion   CCP §2024.040
    Reopening discovery after trial date set   CCP §2024.050
        Agreement of parties   CCP §2024.060
    Saturday, Sunday or holiday, deadline falling on   CCP §2016.060
Timing of discovery   CCP §2019.020
Trade secrets, discovery for misappropriation of
    Method and sequence   CCP §2019.210
Trusts
    Judicial proceedings against trusts   Pro §17201.1
Uniform interstate depositions and discovery act   CCP §§2029.100 to 2029.900
Unlawful detainer
    Motion for discovery   CCP §1170.9, CRC 3.1347
        Judicial council, rules as to   CCP §1170.9
Vexatious litigant conducting unnecessary discovery   CCP §391
Videoconferencing
    Superior court fees   Gov §70630
Withdrawal of legal service agency attorney for indigent client, effect on time limitations of   CCP §285.3
Work product doctrine
    Attorney work product generally   CCP §§2018.010 to 2018.080
    Electronically stored information (ESI)
        Applicable rules   CCP §2020.220
Writings
    Defined   CCP §2016.020

DISCOVERY ABUSES, SANCTIONS FOR

Abuse of discovery procedure   CCP §2023.010
Amount of sanction   CCP §2023.050
Electronically stored information (ESI)
    Sanctions for failure to provide
        Good faith operation of electronic information system preventing provision of ESI, defense to sanctions   CCP §§2017.020, 2023.030, 2025.410, 2025.450
Failure to confer   CCP §§2023.010, 2023.020
Failure to provide discovery   CRC 3.1348
Inspection demands, abuses as to
    Electronically stored information
        Circumstances where sanctions for failure to provide are avoided   CCP §§2031.300, 2031.320
    Failure to permit inspection in accord with demand   CCP §2031.320
    Protective orders and sanctions   CCP §2031.060
    Response to demand
        Failure to file timely response   CCP §2031.300
        Further response, motion to compel   CCP §2031.310
Juvenile court proceedings   CRC 5.546
Mental examinations, discovery procedure for
    Failure to produce another for examination   CCP §2032.420
    Failure to submit   CCP §2032.410
    Protective orders, unsuccessfully making or opposing motion for   CCP §2032.510
    Reports of examination   CCP §2032.650
Misuse of discovery process   CCP §§2023.010, 2023.030
Objections
    Unsuccessfully making or opposing objection
        Electronically stored information (ESI), good faith operation of electronic information system as defense to sanctions   CCP §2025.410

DISCOVERY ABUSES, SANCTIONS FOR—Cont.

Physical examinations, discovery procedure for
    Failure to produce another for examination   CCP §2032.420
    Failure to submit   CCP §2032.410
    Plaintiffs, personal injury cases   CCP §§2032.240, 2032.250
    Protective orders, unsuccessfully making or opposing motion for   CCP §2032.510
    Reports of examination   CCP §§2032.620, 2032.650
Procedure for imposition of sanction   CCP §2023.050
Pro se litigants
    Presumption of good faith of natural, unrepresented person   CCP §2023.050
Protective orders
    Unsuccessfully making or opposing motion for protective order   CCP §2017.020
Request for sanctions   CCP §2023.040
Sexual conduct of plaintiff
    Unsuccessfully making or opposing motions   CCP §2017.220

DISCRETION OF COURT

Amendment of pleadings, generally   CCP §473
Demurrer sustained, discretion to grant leave to amend pleadings where   CCP §472a
Evidence, probative value *vs.* **prejudicial effect**
    Creative expressions, admissibility   Ev §352.2
Mandamus proceedings determining abuse of discretion   CCP §1094.5
Motion to strike granted, discretion to grant leave to amend pleadings where   CCP §472a
New trial, abusing discretion as grounds for   CCP §657
Prejudicial evidence, exclusion   Ev §352
    Creative expressions, admissibility   Ev §352.2
Separate trial of issues   CCP §598
Voir dire examination of prospective jurors   CCP §§222.5, 223

DISCRIMINATION

Adoption, prohibited discrimination in placement for   Fam §8708
Aliens
    Discrimination prohibited   CC §51
    Enforcement of employment law not dependent on immigration status   CC §3339
Attorney general
    Civil rights violation, bringing action for
        Fees and costs for attorney general   CCP §1021.8
Attorney professional conduct
    Prohibited discrimination, harassment and retaliation   ProfC 8.4.1
Attorney's fees   CC §§52, 52.1, 54.3
    Construction or application of provisions in issue, solicitor general notified   CC §§51.1, 55.2
Businesses providing safe and welcoming environments for customers
    Pilot program to recognize   CC §51.17
Business transactions, prohibition against discrimination in   CC §51.5
    Construction or application of provisions in issue, solicitor general notified   CC §51.1
Citizenship   CC §51
    Discrimination prohibited   CC §51
Civil penalties   CC §§52, 52.1
    Construction or application of civil rights provisions in issue, solicitor general notified   CC §51.1
Consumer privacy rights
    Consumer exercise of rights   CC §1798.125
Court appointments, prohibition against discriminatory   CRC 10.611, CRC JudAdminStand 10.21
Court performance standards   CRC JudAdminStand 10.17
Courts
    Workplace conduct policies
        Courts' duties   CRC 10.351
Covenants based on race   CC §§53, 782, 782.5
Credit cards (See **CREDIT CARDS**)
Credit transactions by women   CC §§1812.30 to 1812.35
Damages for discriminatory acts   CC §§52, 52.1, 54.3
    Construction or application of civil rights provisions in issue, solicitor general notified   CC §51.1
    Gender violence   CC §52.4
    Measure of damages
        Immigration status not to affect   CC §3339
        Lost earnings or impaired earning capacity, race, ethnicity or gender not to serve as basis for reduction in damages   CC §3361
Dealerships, granting of   CC §§80 to 86
Defamation, privileges
    Sexual assault, harassment, or discrimination
        Communications made without malice regarding incidents   CC §47.1

DISCRIMINATION—Cont.
Disabled persons
  Construction or application of provisions in issue, solicitor general notified   CC §55.2
  Judicial ethics code
    Administrative responsibilities of judge, impartial discharge   CRCSupp JudEthicsCanon 3
    Attorneys, judges to require to refrain from manifesting   CRCSupp JudEthicsCanon 3
    Bias, prejudice or harassment in performance of judicial duties   CRCSupp JudEthicsCanon 3
    Court personnel and staff under direction of judge, standards of conduct enforced by judge   CRCSupp JudEthicsCanon 3
Dogs
  Law enforcement officers, firefighters or search and rescue dog handlers serving outside jurisdiction
    Prohibition on discrimination in lodging, eating, or transportation due to dog   CC §54.25
Equality of accommodations in business establishments
  Construction or application of provisions in issue
    Solicitor general notified   CC §51.1
Equal protection
  Political structure equal protection   CC §53.7
Foster care placement   Fam §7950
Franchises, granting of   CC §51.8
Gender discrimination
  Judicial ethics code
    Administrative responsibilities of judge, impartial discharge   CRCSupp JudEthicsCanon 3
    Attorneys, judges to require to refrain from manifesting   CRCSupp JudEthicsCanon 3
    Bias, prejudice or harassment in performance of judicial duties   CRCSupp JudEthicsCanon 3
    Court personnel and staff under direction of judge, standards of conduct enforced by judge   CRCSupp JudEthicsCanon 3
    Membership in discriminatory organizations   CRCSupp JudEthicsCanon 2
  Notice
    Judicial council legal forms   CRCAppx A
  Price differences for substantially similar goods based on gender of marketing audience   CC §51.14
  Small business gender discrimination in pricing services   CC §§55.61 to 55.63
Gender expression discrimination
  Judicial ethics code
    Administrative responsibilities of judge, impartial discharge   CRCSupp JudEthicsCanon 3
    Attorneys, judges to require to refrain from manifesting   CRCSupp JudEthicsCanon 3
    Bias, prejudice or harassment in performance of judicial duties   CRCSupp JudEthicsCanon 3
    Court personnel and staff under direction of judge, standards of conduct enforced by judge   CRCSupp JudEthicsCanon 3
    Membership in discriminatory organizations   CRCSupp JudEthicsCanon 2
Gender identity discrimination
  Judicial ethics code
    Administrative responsibilities of judge, impartial discharge   CRCSupp JudEthicsCanon 3
    Attorneys, judges to require to refrain from manifesting   CRCSupp JudEthicsCanon 3
    Bias, prejudice or harassment in performance of judicial duties   CRCSupp JudEthicsCanon 3
    Court personnel and staff under direction of judge, standards of conduct enforced by judge   CRCSupp JudEthicsCanon 3
    Membership in discriminatory organizations   CRCSupp JudEthicsCanon 2
Gender violence
  Actions for damages   CC §52.4
Genetic information   CC §51
Housing
  Age discrimination in housing   CC §51.2
    Deed restrictions, applicability of prohibitions on restrictions to housing for elderly   CC §§782, 782.5
  Covenants based on race   CC §§53, 782, 782.5
  Disabled persons' equal access to housing accommodations   CC §§54, 54.1, 54.3, 54.4, 55
    Construction or application of provisions in issue, solicitor general notified   CC §55.2
  Senior citizen housing, requirements for (See **SENIOR CITIZENS**)

DISCRIMINATION—Cont.
Housing—Cont.
  Unruh Civil Rights Act   CC §51
    Construction or application of provisions in issue, solicitor general notified   CC §51.1
Immigration status   CC §51
  Discrimination prohibited   CC §51
  Enforcement of employment law not dependent on immigration status   CC §3339
Independent civil actions
  Construction or application of civil rights provisions in issue, solicitor general notified   CC §51.1
Injunctive relief, availability of   CC §52.1
  Construction or application of civil rights provisions in issue, solicitor general notified   CC §51.1
Interference with exercise of rights
  Construction or application of civil rights provisions in issue, solicitor general notified   CC §51.1
Intimidation
  Threat of violence
    Construction or application of provisions in issue, solicitor general notified   CC §51.1
    Waiver of right to freedom from violence, coerced or involuntary   CC §51.7
Judges
  Administrative responsibilities of judge, impartial discharge   CRCSupp JudEthicsCanon 3
  Attorneys, judges to require to refrain from manifesting   CRCSupp JudEthicsCanon 3
  Bias, prejudice or harassment   CRCSupp JudEthicsCanon 3
  Court personnel and staff under direction of judge, standards of conduct enforced by judge   CRCSupp JudEthicsCanon 3
Judicial administration rules
  Workplace conduct policies
    Courts' duties   CRC 10.351
Judicial administration standards
  Appointments by court, nondiscrimination in   CRC JudAdminStand 10.21
  Duty of court to prevent bias   CRC JudAdminStand 10.20
Jurisdiction for civil rights actions   CC §52.2
Jury
  Peremptory challenge to juror based on bias   CCP §§231.5, 231.7
Marital status   CC §51
  Judicial ethics code
    Administrative responsibilities of judge, impartial discharge   CRCSupp JudEthicsCanon 3
    Attorneys, judges to require to refrain from manifesting   CRCSupp JudEthicsCanon 3
    Court personnel and staff under direction of judge, standards of conduct enforced by judge   CRCSupp JudEthicsCanon 3
Mobilehome park, club membership in   CC §798.20
National origin discrimination   CC §§51 to 53
  Judicial ethics code
    Administrative responsibilities of judge, impartial discharge   CRCSupp JudEthicsCanon 3
    Attorneys, judges to require to refrain from manifesting   CRCSupp JudEthicsCanon 3
    Court personnel and staff under direction of judge, standards of conduct enforced by judge   CRCSupp JudEthicsCanon 3
    Membership in discriminatory organizations   CRCSupp JudEthicsCanon 2
Penal damages for   CC §52
Political affiliation discrimination   CC §§51.7, 52
  Construction or application of provisions in issue, solicitor general notified   CC §51.1
  Judicial ethics code
    Administrative responsibilities of judge, impartial discharge   CRCSupp JudEthicsCanon 3
    Attorneys, judges to require to refrain from manifesting   CRCSupp JudEthicsCanon 3
    Court personnel and staff under direction of judge, standards of conduct enforced by judge   CRCSupp JudEthicsCanon 3
Political structure equal protection   CC §53.7
Price difference for services of similar or like kind based solely on gender   CC §51.6
Primary language   CC §51
Probate referees, appointment of   Pro §401
Public facilities, disabled persons' equal access to   CC §§54, 54.1, 54.3, 54.4, 55
  Disabled persons' equal access to housing accommodations
    Construction or application of provisions in issue, solicitor general notified   CC §55.2

DISCRIMINATION—Cont.
Religion   CC §§51 to 53
   Judicial ethics code
      Administrative responsibilities of judge, impartial discharge   CRCSupp JudEthicsCanon 3
      Attorneys, judges to require to refrain from manifesting   CRCSupp JudEthicsCanon 3
      Court personnel and staff under direction of judge, standards of conduct enforced by judge   CRCSupp JudEthicsCanon 3
      Membership in discriminatory organizations   CRCSupp JudEthicsCanon 2
Sex discrimination
   Courts, avoidance of bias based on gender or sexual orientation   CRC JudAdminStand 10.20
   Judicial ethics code
      Administrative responsibilities of judge, impartial discharge   CRCSupp JudEthicsCanon 3
      Attorneys, judges to require to refrain from manifesting   CRCSupp JudEthicsCanon 3
      Court personnel and staff under direction of judge, standards of conduct enforced by judge   CRCSupp JudEthicsCanon 3
      Membership in discriminatory organizations   CRCSupp JudEthicsCanon 2
   Jury instructions, gender-neutral language in   CRC 2.1055
   Settlement
      Restrictions on nondisclosure agreements (NDAs) in certain cases   CCP §1001
   Small business gender discrimination in pricing services   CC §§55.61 to 55.63
Sexual harassment, elements of cause of action for   CC §51.9
   Construction or application of provisions in issue, solicitor general notified   CC §51.1
Sexual orientation   CC §51
   Judicial ethics code
      Membership in discriminatory organizations   CRCSupp JudEthicsCanon 2
   Violence
      Civil actions   CC §52.45
Small business gender discrimination in pricing services   CC §§55.61 to 55.63
Small claims court, civil rights actions in   CC §52.2
Statutes of limitation
   Violence based on prejudice, right of all persons to be free of   CC §52, CCP §338
Unruh Civil Rights Act   CC §51
   Construction or application of provisions in issue, solicitor general notified   CC §51.1
Violence based on prejudice, right of all persons to be free of   CC §51.7
   Construction or application of provisions in issue, solicitor general notified   CC §51.1
   Waiver of right to freedom from violence, coerced or involuntary   CC §51.7
Violence based on victim characteristic
   Construction or application of provisions in issue, solicitor general notified   CC §51.1
   Waiver of right to freedom from violence, coerced or involuntary   CC §51.7
Workplace harassment or discrimination
   Restrictions on nondisclosure agreements (NDAs) in certain cases   CCP §1001

DISEASES
Contagious diseases (See **CONTAGIOUS DISEASES**)
Genetic information generally (See **GENETIC INFORMATION**)
Inspection warrants for purposes of eradication of (See **INSPECTION WARRANTS**)

DISFIGUREMENT (See MAYHEM)

DISMISSAL
Generally   CCP §581
Abandonment of prosecution   CCP §581
Appellate rules, superior court appeals
   Infraction case appeals
      Record on appeal, failure to procure   CRC 8.924
   Limited civil cases in appellate division
      Record on appeal, failure to procure   CRC 8.842
      Voluntary dismissal   CRC 8.825
   Misdemeanor appeals
      Record on appeal, failure to procure   CRC 8.874
   Small claims appeals   CRC 8.963
Appellate rules, supreme court and courts of appeal (See **APPELLATE RULES, SUPREME COURT AND COURTS OF APPEAL**)

DISMISSAL—Cont.
Attorney, consent of or notice to   CCP §581
Authority for   CCP §583.150
Bill of costs upon granting of   CCP §1033
Bonds, disposition of   CCP §581
Child support orders, dismissal of dissolution of marriage action for delay in prosecution affected by   CCP §583.161
Civil case management, trial courts
   Trial or dismissal of assigned cases   CRC 10.910
Class actions   CCP §581, CRC 3.770
Clerk's register, entry in   CCP §581d
Compulsory joinder, nonjoinder of person subject to   CCP §389
Consent to   CCP §581
Consumer debt
   Plaintiff debt buyer failing to appear or prepare to proceed   CCP §581.5
Contribution among joint tortfeasors, effect on   CCP §877
Coordination of complex actions   CRC 3.545
Criminal appeals
   Finality of ruling in court of appeals   CRC 8.366
Cross-complaint prohibiting   CCP §581
Default judgments   CCP §§585, 586
Delay in prosecution
   Generally   CCP §418.10
   Applicability of law   CCP §§583.120, 583.140, 583.160, 583.161
   Authority of court to dismiss action   CCP §583.150
   Bringing trial to action, mandatory time for   CCP §§583.310 to 583.360
      COVID-19, emergency rule   CRCAppx I Emer Rule 10
   Child support orders affecting dismissal of dissolution of marriage action for   CCP §583.161
   Compliance of parties with court's terms   CCP §583.430
   Conditionally settled, requirement that action not brought to trial   CRC 3.1340
   Conditions for dismissal   CCP §583.420
   Definitions   CCP §583.110
   Diligence requirement   CCP §583.130
   Discretionary dismissal   CCP §§583.410 to 583.430, CRC 3.1340, 3.1342
   Dissolution of marriage actions, exception to dismissal of   CCP §583.161
   Mediation of civil actions, tolling provisions for   CCP §1775.7
   New trial, mandatory time for bringing action to   CCP §583.320
   Relevant matters, consideration   CRC 3.1342
   Service of summons, mandatory time for (See **PROCESS AND SERVICE OF PROCESS**)
   Time to serve and file notice of motion, opposition, response and reply   CRC 3.1342
Demurrers
   Failure to answer after sustaining of   CRC 3.1320
   Sustained   CCP §581
Destruction or retention of exhibits and depositions held by clerk after case dismissal   CCP §1952
Dissolution of marriage proceedings   CCP §583.161, Fam §2338
Eminent domain (See **EMINENT DOMAIN**)
Enforcement of judgment, dismissal of third party claim of ownership or security interest in property subject to   CCP §720.370
Entry of dismissal   CCP §581d
   Service of notice   CRC 3.1390
Excusable neglect, relief from judgment for   CCP §473
Family rules
   Waiver of fees and costs
      Denial of waiver   CRC 5.43
Forms
   Judicial council legal forms   CRCAppx A
Garnishment proceedings, restrictions on dismissal of employee during   Pro §3088
Grounds for   CCP §581
Hearings to review dismissal
   Telephone appearance at hearings to review dismissal   CRC 3.670
Inconvenient forum doctrine (See **INCONVENIENT FORUM**)
Indian child welfare act involuntary placements
   Tribal court having exclusive jurisdiction   CRC 5.483
Indictments (See **INDICTMENT, INFORMATION AND COMPLAINT**)
Interpleader, dismissal of stakeholder   CCP §386.5
Judgments, dismissal orders constituting   CCP §581d
Law and motion rules
   Failure to prosecute, motion to dismiss for   CRC 3.1340, 3.1342
   Notices
      Entry of dismissal, service and filing of notice   CRC 3.1390
      Motion for dismissal, notice   CRC 3.1342
Mandamus petition in action for eminent domain   CCP §1245.255
Mechanics' liens
   Action to enforce lien, dismissal for want of prosecution   CC §8462

DISMISSAL—Cont.
Mechanics' liens—Cont.
> Stop payment notices, enforcement of claim stated   CC §8554
>> Effect of dismissal   CC §8556
>> Public works   CC §9508

Mediation affecting running of time period under provisions for delay in prosecution   CCP §1775.7
Memorandum of costs upon granting of   CCP §1033
Military personnel
> Order for dismissal
>> Form   CRCAppx A
> Petition for dismissal
>> Form   CRCAppx A

Mistake, inadvertence or surprise, application for relief from judgment for   CCP §473
Motion to dismiss
> Inconvenient forum, motion to dismiss for   CCP §418.10

New trial, time limit for   CCP §583.320
Notices
> Entry of dismissal, service and filing of notice of   CRC 3.1390
> Motion for dismissal, notice of   CRC 3.1342

Power of attorney, dismissal of petitions regarding   Pro §4543
Prejudice, dismissal with   CCP §581
Procedure for   CCP §581
Settlement of case, dismissal after   CRC 3.1385
Small claims actions (See **SMALL CLAIMS COURTS**)
Superior courts (See **SUPERIOR COURTS**)
Telephone appearance at hearing on issue
> Fees   CCP §367.6

Time
> Commencement of trial, dismissal before or after   CCP §581
> Delay in prosecution (See within this heading, **"Delay in prosecution"**)

Transfer of case, pendency of motion for   CCP §581
Trial
> Effect of commencement   CCP §581
> Time for bringing case to trial
>> COVID-19, emergency rule   CRCAppx I Emer Rule 10

Unlawful detainer actions
> Service of summons
>> Proof not timely filed   CCP §1167.1
> Venue
>> Stay or dismissal of action for inconvenient forum   CRC 3.1327

Venue
> Filing in wrong state court not grounds for dismissal   CCP §396

Vexatious litigants (See **VEXATIOUS LITIGANTS**)

DISMISSAL OF CIVIL ACTIONS
Coerced debt
> Establishing debt as coerced, action or cross-complaint   CC §1798.97.3

DISORDERLY CONDUCT
Contempt   CCP §1209
Domestic violence (See **DOMESTIC VIOLENCE**)

DISORDERLY HOUSES (See **PROSTITUTION**)

DISQUALIFICATION
Arbitrators   CCP §§1281.9, 1281.91, 1281.95
Court commissioner disqualified for prejudice   CCP §170.6
Judges (See **JUDGES, DISQUALIFICATION OF**)
Judicial arbitrators   CCP §1141.18
Jurors (See **JURY**)
Referees (See **REFEREES**)
Witnesses   Ev §701

DISSOLUTION OF CORPORATIONS (See **CORPORATE DISSOLUTION**)

DISSOLUTION OF MARRIAGE   Fam §2000
Absence of one spouse   Fam §2604
Acceleration of loan prohibited on   CC §2924.6
Action for breach of fiduciary duty between spouses   Fam §1101
Affidavits
> Default judgment, proof of grounds required for   Fam §2336
> Privileged publication, status as   CC §47

American Indians   Fam §295
Animals
> Pet animals
>> Division of property   Fam §2605

Annulment (See **ANNULMENT**)
Answers
> Alternative affirmative relief, request   Fam §213

DISSOLUTION OF MARRIAGE—Cont.
Answers—Cont.
> Time to file responsive pleading   Fam §2020

Appeals
> Bifurcated issues   CRC 5.392, Fam §2025
> Disposition of community estate   Fam §2555
> Effect of   Fam §2341
> Summary dissolution of marriage, effect of judgment of   Fam §2404

Appearance
> Affidavit of proof in lieu of appearance   Fam §2336
> Conversion of separation proceeding to dissolution proceeding   Fam §2321
> Employee benefit plan joined as party   Fam §§2063, 2072
> Special appearance during pendency of motion   Fam §2012

Armed forces personnel, waiver of filing fees for   Gov §70673
Assets and liabilities, disclosure of   Fam §§2100 to 2113
Assignment of cases within court   Fam §2330.3
Assignment of earnings for support (See **EARNINGS ASSIGNMENT FOR SUPPORT**)
Attorney professional conduct
> Contingent fees
>> Circumstances where contingent fee agreement impermissible   ProfC 1.5

Attorney's fees   Fam §§270 to 274, 2010, 2030 to 2034, 2040
> Allocation of fees and costs   Fam §§2032, 2034
> Financial need basis   CRC 5.427

Bifurcation of issues
> Appeal of bifurcated issue, procedure for   Fam §2025
> Certification of appeals   CRC 5.392
> Conditions imposed by court until judgment entered on all remaining issues   Fam §2337
> Early and separate trial on dissolution issue   Fam §2337

Birth name restored   Fam §§2080 to 2082, 2401
Case resolution   Fam §§2450 to 2452
> Family centered case resolution   CRC 5.83

Certified copy of marriage dissolution record, fee for   Gov §70674
Child support   Fam §§4000 to 4077
> Consolidation of actions   CRC 5.365
> Generally (See **CHILD SUPPORT**)

Community property
> Domestic violence misdemeanors by spouse against spouse
>> Consequences in divorce proceedings   Fam §4325
> Violent sexual felony by spouse against spouse
>> Consequences in divorce proceedings   Fam §4324.5

Concealment of property   Fam §§2040 to 2045
Conciliation courts (See **CONCILIATION COURTS**)
Conservator to represent incapacitated spouse   Fam §2332
Contempt   CCP §1218, Fam §2026
> Show cause orders   CRCAppx A (CRCFL-410)

Continuances   Fam §2334
Conveyances during pendency of proceeding   Fam §§754, 2040 to 2045
Costs   Fam §2010
Court commissioner's powers   CCP §259
Custody of children (See **CUSTODY OF CHILDREN**)
Date of separation
> Defined   Fam §70

Date of termination   Fam §§2340, 2343
Death of party
> Generally   Fam §310
> Entry of judgment, death after   Fam §2344
> More than four years before death, effect on community property presumption of dissolution   Fam §802
> Warning in summons concerning effect of death of party before property division   Fam §2040

Debts and liabilities
> Characterization of liabilities as separate or community   Fam §2551
> Confirming or assigning debts to parties   Fam §§2551, 2620 to 2627
> Division of   Fam §§2620 to 2627
> Payment of obligation directly to creditors   Fam §2023
> Reimbursement for debts paid after separation but before trial   Fam §2626
> Valuation date for liabilities   Fam §2552

Decision of court on   Fam §2338
Declarations
> Assets and liabilities   Fam §§2100 to 2113
> Property   Fam §2330.5

Default judgment
> Declaration for default or uncontested dissolution or legal separation
>> Judicial council forms   CRCAppx A
> No requirement for financial declaration where petition makes no demand   Fam §2330.5
> Procedure for   CRC 5.401, 5.402, Fam §§2335.5, 2338.5

DISSOLUTION OF MARRIAGE—Cont.
  Default judgment—Cont.
    Proof required for   CRC 5.401, Fam §2336
      Hearing on default judgments submitted on basis of declaration or affidavit   CRC 5.409
      Review of default submitted on basis of declaration or affidavit   CRC 5.407
    Waiver of final declaration of financial disclosure   Fam §2110
  Defaults   CRC 5.122, 5.401, 5.402
  Deferred sale of family home, request of custodial parent for   Fam §§3800 to 3810
  Disclosure of assets and liabilities   Fam §§2100 to 2113
  Discovery
    Law and motion rules applicable to discovery proceedings in family law   CRC 3.1100
  Dismissal of proceeding   CCP §583.161, Fam §2338
  Division of property   Fam §§2600 to 2605
    Acquisition of property, reimbursement of separate property contributions to   Fam §2640
    Appeal of   Fam §2555
    Arbitration   Fam §2554
    Award of asset to one party to effect substantially equal division   Fam §2601
    Award of estate to one party where less than $5,000 and other spouse cannot be located   Fam §2604
    Continuing jurisdiction   Fam §2556
    Debts and liabilities generally (See within this heading, **"Debts and liabilities"**)
    Definitions   Fam §§2500 to 2502
    Education, reimbursement of contributions for   Fam §2641
    Equal division   Fam §2550
    Income tax liability, joint   Fam §2628
    Interactive computer system authorized to prepare standardized pro per court documents   CCP §1062.20
    Joint form, presumption concerning property held in   Fam §2581
    Jointly held property   Fam §2650
    Liabilities, characterization of   Fam §2551
    Orders   Fam §2553
    Personal injury damages   Fam §2603
    Pet animals   Fam §2605
    Real property located in other state   Fam §2660
    Retirement benefits   Fam §2610
      Tribal court orders, payments pursuant to   Fam §2611
    Special rules governing   Fam §§2600 to 2605
    Valuation date for assets and liabilities   Fam §2552
    Violent sexual felony by spouse against spouse
      Consequences in divorce proceedings   Fam §4324.5
  Domestic partnership, termination or dissolution
    Armed forces personnel, waiver of filing fees for   Gov §70673
    Certified copy of dissolution record
      Fee   Gov §70674
    Default judgment
      Hearing on default judgments submitted on basis of declaration or affidavit   CRC 5.409
      Review of default submitted on basis of declaration or affidavit   CRC 5.407
    Equal rights, benefits and protections   Fam §297.5
    Family rules   CRC 5.76
    Marriage and partnership terminating
      Single proceeding   Fam §299
    Notice of termination of domestic partnership
      Filing to terminate partnership   Fam §299
      Forms   Fam §298
    Procedure   Fam §299
    Superior court fees
      First paper, filing   Gov §§70602.5, 70602.6, 70670
    Surviving domestic partner after death of partner, rights of   Pro §37
    Wills, effect of termination on testamentary provisions of   Pro §6122.1
  Domestic relations case investigators, duties
    Orders regarding custody evaluations   CRCAppx A
    Reports   CRCAppx A
  Domestic violence felony by spouse against spouse
    Attorney fees of convicted spouse not responsibility of separate estate of victim   Fam §4324.5
    Definition of violent sexual felony   Fam §4324.5
    Injured spouse defined   Fam §4324.5
    Legal separation date, determination   Fam §4324.5
    Pension and retirement benefits, community property disposition   Fam §4324.5
    Support award to perpetrator prohibited   Fam §4324.5

DISSOLUTION OF MARRIAGE—Cont.
  Domestic violence misdemeanors by spouse against spouse
    Attorneys' fees, payment from community assets   Fam §4325
    Definition of domestic violence misdemeanors   Fam §4325
    Division of property
      Effect of conviction   Fam §4325
    Legal separation date, determination   Fam §4325
    Pension and retirement benefits
      Effect of conviction   Fam §4325
    Support, effect of conviction   Fam §4325
  Domestic violence prevention (See **DOMESTIC VIOLENCE**)
  Dwelling house, exclusion from   Fam §§753, 2035, 2036.5
  Early and separate trial on dissolution issue   Fam §2337
  Earnings assignment for support (See **EARNINGS ASSIGNMENT FOR SUPPORT**)
  Eavesdropping, admissibility of evidence from   Fam §2022
  Educational loans   Fam §2627
  Employee benefit plan
    Appearance at hearing   Fam §§2063, 2072
    Default of   Fam §2065
    Division of retirement benefits   Fam §2610
    Domestic violence misdemeanors by spouse against spouse
      Consequences in divorce proceedings   Fam §4325
    Filing fees   Fam §2064
    Joinder of plan   CRC 5.29, Fam §§2021, 2060 to 2065
      Pleading on joinder   CRCAppx A (CRCFL-370)
      Separate trial of termination of marriage or domestic partnership, joinder as prerequisite   CRC 5.390
      Summary dissolution of marriage proceedings, court order to designate beneficiary   Fam §2337
    Modification of orders affecting plan   Fam §2074
    Notice of effect of judgment on   Fam §2024
    Orders affecting plan   Fam §§2073, 2074
    Property settlement, notice of proposed   Fam §2071
    Provisions governing proceeding in which plan has been joined   Fam §2070
    Setting aside orders   Fam §2074
    Severance of dissolution issue, conditions imposed on   Fam §2337
    Support orders, enforcement of   Fam §5103
    Tribal court orders, payments pursuant to   Fam §2611
    Violent sexual felony or domestic violence felony by spouse against spouse
      Consequences in divorce proceedings   Fam §4324.5
  Encumbering property, restrictions on   Fam §§754, 2040 to 2045
  Evidence of acts of misconduct   Fam §2335
  Excluding party from dwelling of other party   Fam §§753, 2035, 2036.5
  Ex parte protective orders   Fam §§240 to 246, 2045
  Expenses and income, disclosure of   Fam §§2100 to 2113
  Extension of time   Fam §2339
  Extraordinary expenditures, notice of   Fam §§2040, 2045
  Family allowance, loss of rights to   Fam §2337
  Family centered case resolution   CRC 5.83, Fam §§2450 to 2452
  Family law information centers for unrepresented low-income litigants   Fam §§15000 to 15012
  Family law rules (See **FAMILY RULES**)
  Fees
    Armed forces personnel, waiver of filing fees for   Gov §70673
    Attorney's fees   Fam §§270 to 274, 2010, 2030 to 2034
      Financial need basis   CRC 5.427
    Certified copy of marriage dissolution record, fee for   Gov §70674
    Employee benefit plan as not required to pay filing fees   Fam §2064
    Filing fees in family law cases   Gov §§70670 to 70676
    Superior court fees
      First paper, filing   Gov §§70602.5, 70602.6, 70670
  Financial declarations   Fam §2330.5
    Sealing pleadings concerning financial assets and liabilities   Fam §2024.6
  Foreign judgments
    Applicability of foreign country provisions   CCP §1715
  Former name restored   Fam §§2080 to 2082, 2401
  Forms
    Family rules generally (See **FAMILY RULES**)
    Judicial council legal forms   CRCAppx A
  Grounds for dissolution   Fam §§2310 to 2313
  Guardian or guardian ad litem to represent incapacitated spouse   Fam §2332
  Health insurance
    Notice of reduced-cost options through California health benefit exchange or no-cost Medi-Cal
      Court notice to parties upon filing for annulment, divorce, etc   Fam §2024.7
  Hearsay evidence, acceptance of   Ev §§1310 to 1314
  Homestead exemption
    Effect of pending divorce on exemption   CCP §704.720

DISSOLUTION OF MARRIAGE—Cont.
Incapacity
    Legal incapacity to make decisions
        Effect on support obligation   Fam §2313
        Grounds for dissolution   Fam §2310
        Proof   Fam §2312
        Service of petition   Fam §2332
Income and expenses, disclosure of   Fam §§2100 to 2113
Income tax liability, joint   Fam §2628
Individual retirement accounts
    Deferred distribution, preservation by means of assignment   Fam §2337
Injunctions   CRC 5.18
Insane spouse
    Representation of incapacitated spouse by guardian or conservator   Fam §2332
Insurance policies
    Conditions imposed on granting severance on issue of dissolution   Fam §2337
    Judgment, notice of entry and requirements of   Fam §§2051 to 2053
    Notice of effect of judgment on   Fam §2024
    Notice to insurance carriers of pending litigation   Fam §§2050, 2052, 2053
Interactive computer system authorized to prepare standardized pro per court documents   CCP §1062.20
Interlocutory judgments   Fam §§2338 to 2344
Irreconcilable differences   Fam §§2310, 2311, 2333
Joinder of parties   CRC 5.24, 5.29, Fam §2021
    Employee benefit plan   Fam §§2021, 2060 to 2065
        Pleading on joinder   CRCAppx A (CRCFL-370)
    Separate trial of termination of marriage or domestic partnership, joinder as prerequisite   CRC 5.390
    Family rules   CRC 5.24, 5.29
Joint petition for dissolution of marriage or for legal separation   Fam §2330
    Procedure   Fam §2342.5
        Rulemaking   Fam §2342.5.1
    Service deemed upon filing   Fam §2331
Judges, duration of assignment of   Fam §2330.3
Judgments
    Generally   Fam §2338
    Date of termination   Fam §§2340, 2343
    Effect of   Fam §§310, 2300
    Final   Fam §§2339, 2342
    Insurance carriers, notice of entry of judgment and requirements thereof   Fam §§2051 to 2053
    Interlocutory   Fam §§2338 to 2344
    Nunc pro tunc   Fam §2346
    Protective orders included in   Fam §§2049, 6360, 6361
    Relief from   Fam §§2120 to 2129
    Renewal   Fam §291
Jurisdiction   Fam §§2010 to 2013
    Division of property, continuing jurisdiction for   Fam §2556
    Retention of jurisdiction over date of termination   Fam §2343
    Same sex marriages
        Residence requirements   Fam §2320
Law and motion rules
    Applicable to discovery proceedings in family law   CRC 3.1100
Legal separation proceeding converted to dissolution proceeding   Fam §2321
Libel and slander action, accusations privileged from   CC §47
Maiden name restored after   Fam §§2080 to 2082
Mental illness
    Representation of incapacitated spouse by guardian or conservator   Fam §2332
Military personnel, waiver of respondent's filing fees for   Gov §70673
Misappropriation of money or property   Fam §2602
Misconduct, limitation on proving specific acts of   Fam §2335
Modification of orders after entry of judgment   Fam §215
Name
    Restoration   CRCAppx A (CRCFL-395)
Native Americans   Fam §295
New trial
    Effect of motion   Fam §2341
    Summary dissolution of marriage, effect of judgment of   Fam §2404
Nonprobate transfers
    Beneficiary designation
        Summary dissolution of marriage proceedings, court order to designate   Fam §2337
Notice
    Effect of judgment on will, insurance, etc   Fam §2024
    Entry of judgment   CRC 5.413, 5.415
    Insurance carriers, notice of pending litigation involving policies   Fam §§2050, 2052, 2053
    Jurisdiction, retention of   Fam §2343

DISSOLUTION OF MARRIAGE—Cont.
Notice—Cont.
    Modification of orders after entry of judgment   Fam §215
Nunc pro tunc judgment   Fam §2346
Orders
    Division of property, orders for   Fam §2553
    Modification of orders after entry of judgment   Fam §215
    Protective and restraining orders (See within this heading, **"Protective and restraining orders"**)
Out-of-state divorces   Fam §§2090 to 2093
Pendency of proceeding, recording notice of   Fam §754
Pension plans
    Employee benefit plan generally (See within this heading, **"Employee benefit plan"**)
Pension plans, joinder as party
    Judicial Council forms   CRCAppx A (CRCFL-372 to CRCFL-375)
Personal injury damages, assignment of   Fam §2603
Pet animals
    Division of property   Fam §2605
Petition
    Generally   Fam §2330
    Contents of   Fam §2330
    Dismissal of petition for delay in prosecution, effect of child support orders on   CCP §583.161
    Family law rules (See **FAMILY RULES**)
    Financial declarations
        Sealing pleadings concerning financial assets and liabilities   Fam §2024.6
    Notice of effect of judgment on will, insurance, etc   Fam §2024
    Service on other spouse   Fam §2331
    Social security numbers
        Redaction to ensure privacy   Fam §2024.5
Petitions
    Joint petition for dissolution of marriage or for legal separation   Fam §2330
        Procedure   Fam §2342.5
            Rulemaking   Fam §2342.5.1
        Service deemed upon filing   Fam §2331
Pleading
    Answer
        Alternative affirmative relief, request   Fam §213
        Time to file responsive pleading   Fam §2020
    Employee benefit plan joined as party   Fam §2061
    Petition generally (See within this heading, **"Petition"**)
    Social security numbers
        Redaction to ensure privacy   Fam §2024.5
Power of attorney, termination of (See **POWER OF ATTORNEY**)
Probate homestead, termination of other party's right to   Fam §2337
Proper court documents, interactive computer system authorized to prepare standardized   CCP §1062.20
Property declarations   Fam §2330.5
Property orders
    Attachments   CRCAppx A (CRCFL-344)
Property settlement agreements (See **PROPERTY SETTLEMENT AGREEMENTS**)
Protective and restraining orders
    Ex parte orders   Fam §§240 to 246, 2045
    Judgment, orders in   Fam §§2049, 6360, 6361
    Notice and hearing, orders after   Fam §2047
    Summons, inclusion of restraining order in   Fam §§231 to 235, 2040, 2041
Quasi-community property (See **COMMUNITY PROPERTY**)
Real estate contract arbitration clause, effect of   CCP §1298.5
Reconciliation of parties
    Conciliation court proceedings (See **CONCILIATION COURTS**)
    Contempt of existing court order, effect of reconciliation on   Fam §2026
    Continuance for   Fam §2334
    Temporary support order, effect on   Fam §3602
Remarriage
    Deferred sale of family home order, effect of remarriage on   Fam §3808
    Earnings assignment for support   Fam §5240
    Spousal support affected by   Fam §4337
Reservation of jurisdiction   CRC 5.18
Residence requirements   Fam §§2320 to 2322
    Family rules
        Quash, request for order, failure to meet residence requirements   CRC 5.63
    Same sex marriages   Fam §2320
Respondent
    Alternative affirmative relief, request for   Fam §213
    Time for filing responsive pleading   Fam §2020

DISSOLUTION OF MARRIAGE—Cont.
Restoration of former name Fam §§2080 to 2082, 2401
Restraining orders (See within this heading, **"Protective and restraining orders"**)
Retirement plans
    Employee benefit plan generally (See within this heading, **"Employee benefit plan"**)
Rules of procedure
    Family rules generally (See **FAMILY RULES**)
Same sex marriages
    Residence requirements Fam §2320
Separate trial on issue of dissolution Fam §2337
Separation
    Agreements Fam §3580
    Date of separation
        Defined Fam §70
    Judgment, dissolution subsequent to Fam §2347
    Proceedings, conversion to dissolution proceeding Fam §2321
Service of papers
    Assets and liabilities disclosure Fam §2103
    Employee benefit plan joined as party Fam §2062
    Incapacitated spouse, service on Fam §2332
    Petition served on other spouse Fam §2331
Severance of disputed issues
    Appeal of bifurcated issue, procedure for Fam §2025
    Certification of appeals CRC 5.392
    Conditions imposed by court until judgment entered on all remaining issues Fam §2337
    Early and separate trial on dissolution issue Fam §2337
Sexual offense by spouse against spouse
    Violent sexual felony
        Attorney fees of convicted spouse not responsibility of separate estate of victim Fam §4324.5
        Definition of violent sexual felony Fam §4324.5
        Injured spouse defined Fam §4324.5
        Legal separation date, determination Fam §4324.5
        Pension and retirement benefits, community property disposition Fam §4324.5
        Support award to perpetrator prohibited Fam §4324.5
Social security benefits, loss of Fam §2337
Social security numbers
    Confidentiality of persons involved in annulment, dissolution or legal separation
        Redaction of numbers from documents Fam §2024.5
Special appearance during pendency of motion Fam §2012
Statistical information collected by Judicial Council and reported to legislature Fam §2348
Stipulation for retention of jurisdiction Fam §2343
Summary dissolution Fam §§2400 to 2406 (See **SUMMARY DISSOLUTION OF MARRIAGE**)
Summons, inclusion of restraining order in Fam §§231 to 235, 2040, 2041
Support (See **CHILD SUPPORT; SPOUSAL SUPPORT**)
Taxes, conditions imposed on granting severance on issue of dissolution Fam §2337
Temporary restraining orders (See within this heading, **"Protective and restraining orders"**)
Temporary support (See **CHILD SUPPORT; SPOUSAL SUPPORT**)
Termination date stated in judgment Fam §§2340, 2343
Tort liability Fam §2627
Uncontested cases
    Declaration for default or uncontested dissolution or legal separation
        Judicial council forms CRCAppx A
Uniform Divorce Recognition Act Fam §§2090 to 2093
Venue
    Generally CCP §395
    Both parties moved from county rendering decree CCP §397.5
    Change of venue
        Retention of jurisdiction to issue protective orders CCP §399
        Time frames for transferring jurisdiction CRC 5.97
    Grounds for change of CCP §397
    Temporary support issues determined prior to determination of motion for transfer of CCP §§396b, 397
Wills (See **WILLS**)
Withdrawal of attorney in domestic relations matter CCP §285.1
Witnesses
    Live testimony
        When received CRC 5.113, Fam §217

DISSOLUTION OF PUBLIC ENTITIES (See **PUBLIC ENTITIES**)

DISTRIBUTION OF PROCEEDS
Administration of estates (See **ADMINISTRATION OF ESTATES**)
Enforcement of judgments (See **ENFORCEMENT OF JUDGMENTS**)

DISTRIBUTION OF PROCEEDS—Cont.
Homestead, sale of CCP §704.850

DISTRICT ATTORNEY
Acknowledgment of instruments CC §1181
Appellate rules, superior court appeals
    Infraction case appeals
        Record on appeal, prosecutor's notice as to nonreceipt of record CRC 8.911
Assisting in civil resolution in lieu of filing criminal complaint CCP §33
Attorney professional conduct
    Special responsibilities of prosecutor ProfC 3.8
Briefs in criminal appeals, delivery to CRC 8.360
Civil rights actions, bringing of CC §§52, 52.1
    Construction or application of civil rights provisions in issue, solicitor general notified CC §51.1
Custody proceedings, location of missing party or child for purposes of Fam §§3130 to 3135, 3455, 3457
Deaf or hard of hearing victim
    Interpreter services Ev §754
Dog bites, actions pertaining to CC §3342.5
Earnings assignment for support (See **EARNINGS ASSIGNMENT FOR SUPPORT**)
Electronic court records, remote access
    Government entities, access by
        List of government entities which may be authorized to receive access CRC 2.540
Electronic filing and service of documents
    Criminal actions
        Fees not chargeable in some criminal actions CRC 2.255
    Electronic summons, issuance CRC 2.259
Family law pilot projects (See **FAMILY LAW PILOT PROJECTS**)
Filings for Social Security Act Title IV-D support actions CRC 5.320
Indigent parents, adult child's petition to be relieved of obligation to support Fam §4413
Information Practices Act (See **INFORMATION PRACTICES ACT**)
Juvenile court proceedings
    Sealing of records, notification of petition
        Forms, judicial council CRCAppx A
        Order on prosecutor request for access CRCAppx A
        Prosecuting attorney request to access sealed juvenile case files CRC 5.860
Juvenile court records, access to
    Prosecuting attorney request to access sealed juvenile case files CRC 5.860
    Order on prosecutor request for access CRCAppx A
Juvenile wardship proceedings
    Appearance CRC 5.530
    Discretion whether to file petition CRC 5.520
    Mandatory referrals CRC 5.514
Marital status, action for denial of credit because of CC §§1812.32, 1812.33
Public administrator's bond, enforcing liability on Pro §7624
Real Estate Fraud Prosecution Trust Fund, procedures for distributions from Gov §27388
Summons
    Electronic filing and service of documents
        Electronic summons, issuance CRC 2.259
Unruh Civil Rights Act, bringing action under CC §52
Witness, district attorney inspector subpoenaed as Gov §§68097.1, 68907.2

DISTRICT OF COLUMBIA
State defined to include CCP §17

DISTRICTS
Attachment proceedings CCP §481.200
Bonds issued by (See **BONDS**)
Boundaries
    Limitation of actions to contest change of CCP §349.1
    Validation procedure for change in CCP §349.4
Cardiopulmonary resuscitation, courses in CC §1714.2
Claim and delivery CCP §511.100
Conservation easements held by CC §815.3
Consolidation
    Contesting consolidation, limitation of actions for CCP §349.1
    Validation procedure CCP §349.4
Costs, liability for CCP §1029
Dissolution
    Contesting dissolution, limitation of actions for CCP §349.1
    Validation procedure CCP §349.4
Formation
    Contesting formation, limitation of actions for CCP §349.1

DISTRICTS—Cont.
Formation—Cont.
    Validation procedure CCP §349.4
Greenway easements
    Entities permitted to acquire and hold easement CC §816.56
Lease abandonment provisions, applicability of CC §1952.6
Pleadings verification by CCP §446
Presentation of claims as prerequisite to commencement of actions against governmental agencies CCP §313
Reorganization
    Contesting reorganization, limitation of actions for CCP §349.1
    Validation procedure CCP §349.4
School districts (See **SCHOOL DISTRICTS**)
Service of process on CCP §416.50
Statutes of limitation
    Boundaries, actions to contest change of CCP §349.1
    Contesting formation, dissolution, consolidation or change of organization CCP §349.1
Unclaimed deposits and payments escheated CCP §1519
Unclaimed property, disposition of CC §2080.6
Validation proceedings CCP §§860 to 870
Venue in actions by or against CCP §394

DIVERSION OF CRIMINAL DEFENDANTS
Juvenile wardship proceedings
    Diversion services
        Satisfactory completion, determination CRC 5.850
        Sealing of records upon satisfactory completion of informal supervision, diversion, etc CRC 5.850
        Unsatisfactory completion, juvenile court review CRC 5.850
Mental disorders, individuals with
    Pretrial diversion CRC 4.130
    Reinstatement of felony proceedings CRC 4.130
Traffic violators CRC 4.104

DIVIDENDS
Corporate shareholders (See **CORPORATE SHARES AND SHAREHOLDERS**)
Income of property CC §748

DIVISION OF CODES (See **TITLES AND DIVISION OF CODES**)

DIVISION OF MARITAL PROPERTY (See **COMMUNITY PROPERTY; DISSOLUTION OF MARRIAGE**)

DIVORCE (See **DISSOLUTION OF MARRIAGE**)

DMV (See **MOTOR VEHICLES DEPARTMENT**)

DNA TESTING
Genetic information generally (See **GENETIC INFORMATION**)
Genetic privacy CC §§56.18 to 56.186 (See **GENETIC PRIVACY**)
Parentage
    Genetic testing to determine parentage Fam §§7550 to 7562 (See **PATERNITY**)

DOCKS (See **WHARVES**)

DOCTORS
Generally (See **PHYSICIANS AND SURGEONS**)
Chiropractors (See **CHIROPRACTORS**)
Dentists (See **DENTISTS**)
Opticians and optometrists (See **OPTICIANS AND OPTOMETRISTS**)
Osteopaths (See **OSTEOPATHS**)
Podiatry and podiatrists (See **PODIATRY AND PODIATRISTS**)
Psychotherapists (See **PSYCHOTHERAPISTS**)
Veterinarians (See **VETERINARIANS AND VETERINARY TECHNICIANS**)

DOCUMENTARY EVIDENCE
Ancient documents, admissibility of Ev §1331
Arbitration proceedings
    Judicial arbitration CRC 3.823
Attorney-client privilege applicable in determining validity of Ev §§959 to 961
Authentication Ev §§403, 1400 to 1454
Best and secondary evidence (See **BEST AND SECONDARY EVIDENCE**)
Business records (See **BUSINESS RECORDS**)
Cancellation of instruments (See **CANCELLATION OF INSTRUMENTS**)
Certificates (See **CERTIFICATES AND CERTIFICATION**)
Contracts (See **CONTRACTS AND AGREEMENTS**)
Copies (See **BEST AND SECONDARY EVIDENCE**)
Duplicate defined Ev §260

DOCUMENTARY EVIDENCE—Cont.
Examination as to contents of documents Ev §768
Exhibits (See **EXHIBITS**)
Hearsay rule, writing previously made by witness as admissible under Ev §1237
Inspection demands during discovery (See **INSPECTION DEMANDS**)
Literary property (See **LITERARY PROPERTY**)
Lost instruments (See **LOST INSTRUMENTS**)
Medical records (See **MEDICAL RECORDS**)
Newspapers and periodicals, presumption regarding publications purporting to be Ev §645.1
Original defined Ev §255
Part of writing offered, entire instrument examined Ev §356
Petitions (See **PETITIONS**)
Presumptions
    Authenticity Ev §643
    Date Ev §640
    Newspapers and periodicals, publications purporting to be Ev §645.1
    Truth of recitals in Ev §622
Privilege claims concerning attested documents Ev §§959, 1002, 1003, 1021, 1022
Refreshing memory, witness' use of writings for Ev §771
Statute of frauds (See **STATUTE OF FRAUDS**)

DOCUMENTARY FILMS
Animals depicted in CC §3508

DOCUMENTARY TRANSFER TAX
Records and recording
    Fees
        Effect of tax on additional fees Gov §27388

DOCUMENTS AND PAPERS
Abbreviations in legal papers CCP §186
Best evidence (See **BEST AND SECONDARY EVIDENCE**)
Change of venue, transfer of pleadings and papers on CCP §399
Claims against decedent's estate based on written instruments, filing requirements for Pro §9152
Common carrier's liability for CC §2200
Common interest developments (See **COMMON INTEREST DEVELOPMENTS**)
Deposit of estate-planning documents with attorney (See **TRUSTS; WILLS**)
Destruction (See **DESTRUCTION OF INSTRUMENTS AND RECORDS**)
English language, papers and proceedings to be in CCP §185
Evidence (See **DOCUMENTARY EVIDENCE**)
Fact of death (See **FACT OF DEATH**)
FAX filing of legal documents (See **FAX FILING AND SERVICE**)
Inspection of documents and things (See **INSPECTION DEMANDS**)
Jury taking into jury room CCP §612
Medical records (See **MEDICAL RECORDS**)
Numerals in legal papers CCP §186
Privacy protection CRC 1.20
Records and recordings (See **RECORDS AND RECORDING**)
Recycled paper (See **RECYCLED PRODUCTS**)
Request for production of (See **INSPECTION DEMANDS**)
Seal of court, documents requiring CCP §153
Service of (See **SERVICE OF PAPERS**)
Superior court fees
    Hearings, filing motion, application or paper filed which would require Gov §70617
Superior court rules (See **SUPERIOR COURTS**)

DOGS
Biting dogs
    Duty of owner to protect others from CC §3342.5
    Liability of owner CC §3342
Claims against public entities and employees
    Dog parks owned or operated by public entity
        Death or injury caused by actions of dog, immunity of public entity Gov §831.7.5
Damages
    Animals, injury to CC §3341
    Biting by dogs CC §3342
Dangerous and vicious
    Forms
        Judicial council legal forms CRCAppx A
    Liability of owner CC §§3341 to 3342.5
    Licensing and regulation
        Judicial council legal forms CRCAppx A
Deaf persons, signal dogs for CC §§54.1, 54.2
    Construction or application of provisions in issue, solicitor general notified CC §55.2

INDEX

DOGS—Cont.
Discrimination
    Law enforcement officers, firefighters, or search and rescue dog handlers serving outside jurisdiction
        Lodging, eating, or transportation, prohibition on discrimination   CC §54.25
Fighting
    Property used for dog or cock fighting as nuisance   CC §3482.8
        Unlawful detainer actions   CCP §1161
Firefighters
    Assignment of firefighter to canine unit serving outside jurisdiction
        Prohibition on discrimination in lodging, eating, or transportation due to dog   CC §54.25
Guide dogs (See within this heading, **"Seeing eye dogs"**)
Police or military dogs   CC §§3342, 3342.5
    Assignment of police officer to canine unit serving outside jurisdiction
        Prohibition on discrimination in lodging, eating, or transportation due to dog   CC §54.25
Sales
    Contracts
        Payments subsequent to transfer of possession to transfer ownership, void contracts   CC §1670.10
Search and rescue dogs
    Handlers serving outside jurisdiction
        Lodging, eating, or transportation, prohibition on discrimination   CC §54.25
Seeing eye dogs
    Generally   CC §§54.1 to 54.4, 55
    Construction or application of provisions in issue, solicitor general notified   CC §55.2
    Disabled persons using
        Construction or application of provisions in issue, solicitor general notified   CC §55.2
    oos and wild animal parks, admitted into   CC §54.7
Signal dogs   CC §§54.1, 54.2
    Construction or application of provisions in issue, solicitor general notified   CC §55.2
Vicious and dangerous
    Appeal of determination
        Superior court fees, specified services   Gov §70626
    Forms
        Judicial council legal forms   CRCAppx A
    Liability of owner   CC §§3341 to 3342.5

DOMESTIC FIXTURES
Fixtures removable   CC §1019

DOMESTIC PARTNERSHIP
Adoption
    Stepparent adoptions
        Birth of child during marriage, domestic partnership or civil union   Fam §9000.5
Age requirement   Fam §297
    Younger than minimum age
        Counseling prior to issuance of order granting permission   Fam §297.1
        Declaration of domestic partnership   Fam §297.1
        Emancipation of minor on entering into valid domestic partnership   Fam §7002
        Information provided upon issuance of order   Fam §297.1
        Order of court granting permission   Fam §297.1
Change of name
    Declaration of domestic partnership form to provide for   Fam §298
    Election to change name   Fam §298.6
    Permissible names   Fam §298.6
    Registration of declaration to indicate new name and previous name   Fam §298.5
Children and minors
    Age requirement   Fam §297
        Younger than minimum age, order of court granting permission   Fam §297.1
    Equal rights and obligations as to   Fam §297.5
    Family rule governing minor's request to establish domestic partnership   CRC 5.448
Children of domestic partner
    Equal rights and obligations as to   Fam §297.5
Community property
    Enforcement of judgments
        Exemption claims by domestic partner of judgment debtor   CCP §703.020

DOMESTIC PARTNERSHIP—Cont.
Confidential domestic partnership
    Establishment of process to enter   Fam §298.7
Conservators
    Appointment of domestic partner as   Pro §1813.1
    General conservatee's right to enter into domestic partnership   Pro §§1900, 1901
    Inventory and appraisal
        Notice, mailing to domestic partner   Pro §2610
    Limited conservatee's right to enter into domestic partnership   Pro §2351.5
Damages for negligent infliction of emotional distress, right to recover   CC §1714.01
Date of marriage
    Statutory references deemed to mean registration date   Fam §297.5
Death of person in registered domestic partnership
    Community and decedent property   Pro §100
    Quasi-community property   Pro §§101, 103
Declaration of domestic partnership
    Filing
        Required for domestic partnership   Fam §297
    Filling out   Fam §298
    Forms   Fam §298
    Registration of declaration   Fam §298.5
Definition and requirements   Fam §297
Dissolution
    Armed forces personnel, waiver of filing fees for   Gov §70673
    Certified copy of dissolution record
        Fee   Gov §70674
    Default judgment
        Hearing on default judgments submitted on basis of declaration or affidavit   CRC 5.409
        Review of default submitted on basis of declaration or affidavit   CRC 5.407
    Equal rights, benefits and protections   Fam §297.5
    Notice of termination of domestic partnership
        Filing to terminate partnership   Fam §299
        Forms   Fam §298
    Procedure   Fam §299
    Separate trial
        Joinder of pension plans as prerequisite to separate trial on termination of marriage or partnership   CRC 5.390
    Superior court fees
        First paper, filing   Gov §§70602.5, 70602.6, 70670
    Surviving domestic partner after death of partner, rights of   Pro §37
    Wills, effect of termination on testamentary provisions of   Pro §6122.1
Domestic abuse
    Equality in prevention and services for domestic abuse fund   Fam §298
Domestic violence
    Distribution of brochure to persons qualifying as domestic partner   Fam §358
Emancipation of minor on entering into valid domestic partnership   Fam §7002
Equality in prevention and services for domestic abuse fund   Fam §298
Equal rights, protections and benefits
    Marriage, equality to   Fam §297.5
Family rules
    Dissolution, legal separation, or annulment   CRC 5.76
        Default, hearing when submitted on basis of declaration or affidavit   CRC 5.409
        Default, review when submitted on basis of declaration or affidavit   CRC 5.407
    Support
        Change of prior support orders   CRC 5.260
        Financial declarations   CRC 5.260
        Judgment for support   CRC 5.260
Forms
    Judicial council legal forms   CRCAppx A
Guardian and ward
    Inventory and appraisal
        Notice, mailing to domestic partner   Pro §2610
Health care decisions for incapacitated partner   Pro §4716
Legal unions formed in other jurisdiction
    Recognition of legal unions as domestic partnership   Fam §299.2
Marriage, equal rights, protections and benefits for domestic partnership   Fam §297.5
Medical information disclosures by providers   CC §56.1007
Nonprobate transfers   Pro §§5000 to 5152
Other states
    Legal unions formed in other jurisdiction
        Recognition of legal unions as domestic partnership   Fam §299.2
Preemption of local ordinances and laws   Fam §299.6
Privileged communications   Ev §980

DOMESTIC PARTNERSHIP—Cont.
Probate rules
    Spousal property petitions   CRC 7.301
Registration   Fam §§298, 298.5
    Date
        Statutory references to date of marriage deemed to mean registration date   Fam §297.5
    Declaration of domestic partnership
        Registration of declaration   Fam §298.5
Spousal property petitions   CRC 7.301
Spouse defined to include registered domestic partner   CC §14, CCP §17, Ev §215, Fam §143, Pro §72
Statistics on domestic partnerships
    Document regarding
        Secretary of state to prepare   Fam §298.8
Summary dissolution of partnership   CRC 5.76
Support
    Modification or termination
        Effective dates for modification/termination and requests for modification/termination   CRCAppx I Emer Rule 13
    Orders, attachment   CRCAppx A (CRCFL-343)
Survivors
    Decedents' estates, survivorship   Pro §§13500 to 13542
    Definition of surviving spouse   Pro §78
    Equal rights, benefits and protections   Fam §297.5
Termination or dissolution of domestic partnership
    Equal rights, benefits and protections   Fam §297.5
    Family rules   CRC 5.76
    Marriage and partnership terminating
        Single proceeding   Fam §299
    Notice of termination of domestic partnership
        Filing to terminate partnership   Fam §299
        Forms   Fam §298
    Procedure   Fam §299
    Surviving domestic partner after death of partner, rights of   Pro §37
    Wills, effect of termination on testamentary provisions of   Pro §6122.1
Wrongful death
    Eligibility of domestic partner to bring action for wrongful death   CCP §377.60

DOMESTIC RELATIONS INVESTIGATORS
Custody proceedings, investigations for   Fam §§3110 to 3116

DOMESTIC RELATIONS RULES (See FAMILY RULES)

DOMESTIC SERVICES
Employment agencies (See EMPLOYMENT AGENCIES)

DOMESTIC VIOLENCE
Abduction defined   Fam §6240
Abuse defined   Fam §6203
Access to incident reports   Fam §6228
Address of applicant   Fam §6225
Affinity defined   Fam §6205
Animals
    Protective orders on behalf of animals   Fam §6320
        California law enforcement telecommunications (CLETS) information form, confidentiality and use of information   CRC 1.51, CRCAppx A
        Denial of petition for ex parte order, reasons to be provided   Fam §6320.5
Appellate court opinions
    Privacy, use of names in opinions   CRC 8.90
Application of domestic violence provisions   Fam §6221
Assault and battery
    Ex parte order enjoining   Fam §6320
        California law enforcement telecommunications (CLETS) information form, confidentiality and use of information   CRC 1.51, CRCAppx A
        Denial of petition for ex parte order, reasons to be provided   Fam §6320.5
Attempted murder
    Attorney fees and costs awarded to victim   Fam §274
    Retirement benefits, effect on award of community interest in   Fam §782.5
    Support award to convicted spouse prohibited   Fam §4324
Attorneys
    Petitioner, representing in enforcement proceedings   Fam §6386
    Victim representatives   Fam §6228
Attorney's fees   Fam §§274, 6344, 6386
Tort liability for domestic violence   CC §1708.6

DOMESTIC VIOLENCE—Cont.
Battered woman or intimate partner battering effects, admissibility of expert testimony of   Ev §1107
Batterer's programs
    Mandatory orders to participate   Fam §6343
    Orders   Fam §6343
Campus safety, emergency protective order where threat to   Fam §6250.5
Cell phone billing responsibility, transfer to victim   Fam §6347
Change of name for spouse-participant in address confidentiality program   CCP §1277
    Trial court rules   CRC 2.575 to 2.577
Child support
    Modification of orders
        Domestic violence prevention act proceedings   CRC 5.381
    Order for presumed natural father to pay   Fam §6341
        Parentage determinations, agreement and judgment in domestic violence prevention act cases   CRC 5.380
Citation of act   Fam §6200
Coerced debt   CC §§1798.97.1 to 1798.97.6
Cohabitant defined   Fam §6209
Commencement of civil action based on   CCP §340.15
Community interest in pension benefits, effect of attempted murder on award of   Fam §782.5
Community property
    Damages for domestic violence
        Enforcement against abusive spouse's share of community property   Fam §2603.5
Conciliation court proceedings   Fam §1834
Confidentiality
    Address confidentiality for victims
        Actions, confidentiality requirements for protected persons in civil proceeding   CCP §367.3
        Judicial council forms   CRCAppx A
        Name change proceedings under address confidentiality program   CRC 2.575 to 2.577
Conservators
    Victim representatives   Fam §6228
Contempt orders issued against victim of domestic violence   CCP §§128, 1219
Conviction of domestic violence
    Rebuttable presumption against award of spousal support to spouse for   Fam §4325
Costs   Fam §§6344, 6386
Counseling
    Limitation on court ordered treatments, programs, or services   Fam §3193
Counseling, order for   Fam §6343
Criminal violation of protective orders   Fam §6388
Custody and visitation orders
    Application of child custody provisions   Fam §3021
    Conditions of custody or visitation on establishment of domestic violence   Fam §3031
    Counseling, recommendation for separate   Fam §3192
    Court-appointed investigators, separate meetings with   Fam §3113
    Emergency protective orders   Fam §§3031, 3100, 6252 to 6253
    Ex parte orders   Fam §§3064, 6252 to 6253, 6323
    Family law facilitators for unrepresented parties   Fam §§10000 to 10015
    Governing law   Fam §6223
    Limitation on court ordered treatments, programs, or services   Fam §3193
    Mediation   Fam §§3170, 3181, 3182
    Modification of orders
        Domestic violence prevention act proceedings   CRC 5.381
    Other states (See UNIFORM CHILD CUSTODY JURISDICTION AND ENFORCEMENT ACT)
    Parentage determinations
        Agreement and judgment of parentage in domestic violence prevention act cases   CRC 5.380
    Stay of execution of judgment affecting custody   CCP §917.7
    Supervised visitation and exchange programs   CRC JudAdminStand 5.20, Fam §§3200 to 3204
        Providers, standards   Fam §3200.5
        Superior courts as supervised visitation and exchange locations   Fam §3200
    Temporary custody or visitation rights   Fam §§3064, 6252 to 6253, 6323
    Uniform Parentage Act, establishing parent-child relationship under   Fam §§6323, 6346
    Visitation rights, generally   Fam §3100
Damages
    Tort liability for domestic violence   CC §1708.6
Dating relationship defined   Fam §6210
Definitions   Fam §§6201 to 6218
Demonstration project to identify best practices   Fam §6219
Department of Justice, notice to   Fam §§6380, 6385

DOMESTIC VIOLENCE—Cont.
Divorce
    Domestic violence felony by spouse against spouse
        Consequences in divorce proceedings   Fam §4324.5
    Domestic violence misdemeanors by spouse against spouse
        Consequences in divorce proceedings   Fam §4325
Domestic partnership
    Distribution of brochure to persons qualifying as domestic partner   Fam §358
    Equality in prevention and services for domestic abuse fund   Fam §298
Duration of protective orders granted after notice and hearing   Fam §6345
Dwelling exclusion orders
    Firearm relinquishment procedures
        Forms for firearm relinquishment   CRCAppx A
Elder abuse (See **SENIOR CITIZENS**)
Emergency protective orders   Fam §§6240 to 6275
    Address or location of protected person
        Prohibition on obtaining   Fam §6252.5
    Child in danger   Fam §6257
    Contents of   Fam §6253
    COVID-19, emergency rule   CRCAppx I Emer Rule 8
    Custody or visitation of children   Fam §§3031, 3100, 6252 to 6253
    Defined   Fam §6217
    Enforcement of   Fam §6272
    Entry into database   Fam §6271
    Ex parte protective orders   Fam §§6250 to 6257
    Expiration of   Fam §6256
    Fees for service of   Gov §26721
    Finding required to issue order   Fam §6251
    Firearms emergency protective order   CRCAppx A
    Forms
        Judicial council legal forms   CRCAppx A
    Issuance of   Fam §§6241, 6250
    Law enforcement officers
        Request and enforcement of order   Fam §6250.3
        Responding officer, duties   Fam §6275
    Multiple protective orders issued
        Priority when one is emergency protective order   Fam §6383
    Service of   Fam §§6271, 6384
    Stalking   Fam §6274
    Types of orders   Fam §6252
    Validity   Fam §6250.3
Enforcement of domestic violence order
    Generally   Fam §§6380 to 6388
    Court appointed counsel to represent petitioner in   Fam §6386
    Emergency protective orders   Fam §6272
    Firearm relinquishment procedures
        Forms for firearm relinquishment   CRCAppx A
    Statewide enforcement   Fam §6381
    Uniform Interstate Enforcement of Domestic Violence Protection Orders Act (See within this heading, "**Uniform Interstate Enforcement of Domestic Violence Protection Orders Act**")
Equality in prevention and services for domestic abuse fund   Fam §298
Evidence
    Battered woman or intimate partner battering effects, admissibility of expert testimony of   Ev §1107
    Other domestic violence committed by defendant, admissibility of evidence of   Ev §1109
Excluding party from dwelling   Fam §§6321, 6340
Ex parte protective orders
    Generally   Fam §§2045, 6320 to 6327
    Address and location of protected person
        Prohibition on obtaining   Fam §6322.7
    Assault and harassment   Fam §6320
    California law enforcement telecommunications (CLETS) information form, confidentiality and use of information   CRC 1.51, CRCAppx A
    Denial of petition for ex parte order, reasons to be provided   Fam §6320.5
    COVID-19, emergency rule   CRCAppx I Emer Rule 8
    Denial of petition for ex parte order, reasons to be provided   Fam §6320.5
    Electronic submission of petitions   Fam §§6306.5, 6307
    Emergency orders   Fam §§6250 to 6257
    Exclusion of party from residence or dwelling   Fam §§6321, 6340
    Firearms or ammunition possessed by restrained person
        Determination if violation of restraining order   Fam §6322.5
    Insurance
        Restraining changes to, cashing in, etc, of insurance   Fam §6325.5
    Liens, order determining payment of   Fam §6324

DOMESTIC VIOLENCE—Cont.
Ex parte protective orders—Cont.
    Minor child/children of parties
        Restraining access to records and information concerning minor child   Fam §6323.5
    Notice not required   Fam §§6300, 6326
    Notice to restrained party   Fam §6302
    Property, orders affecting   Fam §§6324, 6325
    Remote appearance of party, support person or witness   Fam §6308
    Reproductive coercion, orders preventing disturbing peace of other party   Fam §6320
    Self-help services
        Posting information on services on superior court website   Fam §6306.6
    Service
        Alternative service where respondent evades service   Fam §6340
    Specific behavior, order enjoining   Fam §6322
    Stalking, ex parte order enjoining   Fam §§6274, 6320
        California law enforcement telecommunications (CLETS) information form, confidentiality and use of information   CRC 1.51, CRCAppx A
        Denial of petition for ex parte order, reasons to be provided   Fam §6320.5
    Temporary custody   Fam §§3064, 6252 to 6253, 6323
    Uniform Parentage Act, proceedings under   Fam §7710
False arrest immunity for officers enforcing facially regular protective or restraining orders   Fam §6383
Family law information centers for unrepresented low-income litigants   Fam §§15000 to 15012
Family reunification
    Limitation on court ordered treatments, programs, or services   Fam §3193
Family rules
    Child custody
        Communication protocol for domestic violence and child custody orders   CRC 5.445
        Family court services protocol   CRC 5.215
    Parties in domestic violence prevention proceedings   CRC 5.16
    Registration of foreign protection orders
        Tribal court orders   CRC 5.386
    Settlement service providers, court-connected   CRC 5.420
Fees   Fam §6222
    Marriage license and certificate fees used for domestic violence centers
        Alameda county   Gov §26840.10
        Shelter-based programs   Gov §§26840.7, 26840.8
        Solano county   Gov §26840.11
    Waiver of   Fam §6222
Final judgment of dissolution including protective order   Fam §§2049, 6360, 6361
Firearms and other weapons
    Confiscation
        Determining whether order violated   Fam §6322.5
        Forms for firearm relinquishment   CRCAppx A
    Definition of firearm   Fam §6216
    Emergency protective orders
        Form for firearms emergency protective order   CRCAppx A
    Ex parte protective orders
        Possessed by restrained person of firearm or ammunition, determination whether in violation of order   Fam §6322.5
    Firearm relinquishment procedures
        Forms for firearm relinquishment   CRCAppx A
    Orders, hearings
        Determination whether subject of order has registered firearm prior to hearing   Fam §6306
    Ownership or possession by person subject to protective order   Fam §6389
        Determining violation   Fam §6322.5
        Forms for firearm relinquishment   CRCAppx A
        Relinquishment of firearm, procedures   CRC 4.700
    Precursor part
        Definition of firearm precursor part   Fam §6216
    Prohibition on possession
        Determining violation   Fam §6322.5
        Forms for firearm relinquishment   CRCAppx A
    Relinquishment, records   Fam §6306
    Surrender of firearms
        Judicial council forms   CRCAppx A
    Taking temporary custody of firearms at scene of domestic violence incident
        Authority of peace officer at scene   Fam §6383
        Peace officers, authority at scene   Fam §6383
Former cohabitant defined   Fam §6209
Forms approved by Judicial Council   Fam §6226
    List of judicial council legal forms   CRCAppx A

DOMESTIC VIOLENCE—Cont.
  Guardian ad litem for minor party to proceedings to restrain or enjoin violence   CCP §§372, 374
    Appearance of minor under 12 to request or oppose temporary order   Fam §6229
  Gun ownership or possession by person subject to protective order, prohibition on   Fam §6389
    Determining violation   Fam §6322.5
    Firearm relinquishment procedures
      Forms for firearm relinquishment   CRCAppx A
  Hearing
    Firearms
      Determination whether subject of order has registered firearm prior to hearing   Fam §6306
    Orders issuable after   Fam §§2047, 6340 to 6345, 7720
    Petition for protective order   Fam §§6340 to 6345, 7720
    Search for prior criminal convictions or restraining orders prior to hearing   Fam §6306
    Service
      Alternative service where respondent evades service   Fam §6340
  Homicide attempt (See within this heading, **"Attempted murder"**)
  Incident reports, access to   Fam §6228
  Injunctions (See within this heading, **"Temporary restraining order"**)
  Insurance
    Ex parte protective orders
      Restraining changes to, cashing in, etc, of insurance   Fam §6325.5
  Intimate partner battering effects, admissibility of expert testimony of   Ev §1107
  Judges
    Education of judges and subordinate judicial officers
      Domestic violence issues   CRC 10.464
  Judgments, protective orders included in   Fam §§2049, 6360, 6361
  Judicial officer defined   Fam §6240
  Landlord and tenant
    Documentation or evidence of abuse or violence   CCP §1161.3
    Termination of tenancy
      Victims of domestic violence, sexual assault or stalking   CC §1946.7, CCP §1161.3
    Unlawful detainer proceedings, nuisance committed by tenant as grounds
      Presumption of nuisance   CCP §1161
  Law enforcement agency
    Notice to Department of Justice   Fam §6385
    Transmittal of orders to   Fam §6380
  Law enforcement officers
    Defined   Fam §6240
    Emergency protective orders   Fam §§6270 to 6275
    Firearms and other weapons
      Taking temporary custody of firearms at scene of domestic violence incident   Fam §6383
    Foreign protection orders, enforcement of (See within this heading, **"Uniform Interstate Enforcement of Domestic Violence Protection Orders Act"**)
    Immunity from prosecution for false arrest or false imprisonment   Fam §6383
    Information concerning order made available to   Fam §6382
    Service of restraining order by   Fam §6383
  Leaving household, effect of endangered person   Fam §§6254, 6301
  Loss of earnings, restitution for   Fam §§6342, 7720
  Marriage license applicants, information disseminated to   Fam §358
  Mediation
    Continuing education of mediators   Fam §1816
    Custody and visitation proceedings   Fam §§3170, 3181, 3182
    Family law facilitators, mediation by   Fam §§10005, 10015
    Support person for victims   Fam §§3182, 6303
  Minor's appearance in proceedings to restrain or enjoin violence   CCP §§372, 374, 374.5
    Appearance of minor under 12 to request or oppose temporary order   Fam §6229
  Minor's information in protective order proceedings
    Confidentiality of minor's information in protective order proceedings   Fam §6301.5
      Releasing confidential information   CRC 5.382
      Request to make confidential   CRC 5.382
    Privacy protection
      Form, judicial council   CRCAppx A
  Mitigating circumstance
    Superior court sentencing rules, subjection to abuse as   CRC 4.423
  Murder attempt (See within this heading, **"Attempted murder"**)
  Mutual restraining order   Fam §§2047, 6305, 6306, 7720
  Notice
    Orders issued after notice and hearing   Fam §§2047, 6340 to 6345
    Restrained party, notice to   Fam §6302

DOMESTIC VIOLENCE—Cont.
  Notice—Cont.
    Service
      Alternative service where respondent evades service   Fam §6340
  Orders
    Address confidentiality program
      Amendment of judicial council form to include information on program   Fam §6326.5
    Canadian orders, recognition and enforcement   Fam §§6450 to 6460
      Applicability of provisions   Fam §6459
      Definitions   Fam §6451
      Electronic signatures n global and national commerce act, effect of provisions   Fam §6458
      Emergency protective orders   Fam §6457
      Enforcement   Fam §§6452, 6455, 6457
      Immunity of officer enforcing order   Fam §6455
      Law enforcement officer enforcement   Fam §§6452, 6455, 6457
      Multiple orders, enforcement   Fam §6457
      Nonexclusive nature of remedy under provisions   Fam §6456
      Order to register order, form   CRCAppx A
      Priority in enforcing multiple orders   Fam §6457
      Registration of order in California   Fam §6454
      Severability of provisions   Fam §6460
      Short title of provisions   Fam §6450
      Tribunal's orders enforcing or refusing to enforce, applications for orders   Fam §6453
    Confidentiality of minor's information in protective order proceedings   Fam §6301.5
      Release of confidential information   CRC 5.382
      Request to make confidential   CRC 5.382
    Contempt
      Noncompliance with orders, action for contempt   CCP §1218
      Orders for contempt against victim of domestic violence, stay of   CCP §128
    Copies of   Fam §6387
    Custody (See within this heading, **"Custody and visitation orders"**)
    Denial
      Statement of reasons   Fam §6340
    Department of Justice, notification of   Fam §§6380, 6385
    Duration of order granted after notice and hearing   Fam §6345
    Emergency orders (See within this heading, **"Emergency protective orders"**)
    Enforcement (See within this heading, **"Enforcement of domestic violence order"**)
    Ex parte orders (See within this heading, **"Ex parte protective orders"**)
    Ex parte protective orders   Fam §§6320 to 6327
      COVID-19, emergency rule   CRCAppx I Emer Rule 8
      Electronic submission of petitions   Fam §§6306.5, 6307
      Minor child/children of parties, restrictions on access to information and records   Fam §6323.5
      Notice not required   Fam §§6300, 6326
      Remote appearance of party, support person or witness   Fam §6308
    Firearm ownership or possession by person subject to protective order, prohibition on   Fam §6389
      Determining violation   Fam §6322.5
      Forms for firearm relinquishment   CRCAppx A
    Forms
      Judicial council legal forms   CRCAppx A, Fam §§6326, 6326.5
    Guardian ad litem for minor party to proceedings to restrain or enjoin violence   CCP §§372, 374
      Appearance of minor under 12 to request or oppose temporary order   Fam §6229
    Inclusion in judgments   Fam §§2049, 6360, 6361
    Information provided to parties in court concerning terms and effect of order   Fam §6304
    Law enforcement agency, transmittal of orders to   Fam §6380
    Minor's appearance in proceedings to restrain or enjoin violence   CCP §§372, 374, 374.5
      Appearance of minor under 12 to request or oppose temporary order   Fam §6229
    Minor's information, confidentiality   Fam §6301.5
      Judicial council legal forms   CRCAppx A
      Release of confidential information   CRC 5.382
      Request to make information confidential   CRC 5.382
    Mutual restraining order   Fam §§2047, 6305, 6306, 7720
    Notice and hearing   Fam §§2047, 6340 to 6345
    Personal conduct restraining order
      Dismissal of petition, when not appropriate   CCP §583.161
    Protective order defined   Fam §6218
    Registry of orders, maintenance   Fam §6380
      Out of state or tribal court orders, order to register   CRCAppx A

DOMESTIC VIOLENCE—Cont.
Orders—Cont.
    Remote appearance of party, support person or witness   Fam §6308
    Search for prior criminal convictions or restraining orders prior to hearing   Fam §6306
    Self-help services
        Posting information on services on superior court website   Fam §6306.6
    Service of orders (See within this heading, **"Service of papers"**)
    Statement required in order   Fam §6224
    Temporary restraining orders (See within this heading, **"Temporary restraining order"**)
    Termination or modification of order, action for
        Forms for requesting modification   Fam §6345
        Notice requirements   Fam §6345
    Totality of circumstances considered   Fam §6301
    Uniform Parentage Act, proceedings under   Fam §§7710 to 7730
Other domestic violence committed by defendant, admissibility of evidence of   Ev §1109
Other remedies   Fam §6227
Out-of-pocket expenses, restitution for   Fam §§6342, 7720
Parents
    Victim representatives   Fam §6228
Paternity
    Agreement and judgment of parentage in domestic violence prevention act cases   CRC 5.380
    Orders during pendency of paternity suits   Fam §§7710 to 7730
Personal property
    Use, possession and control
        Orders determining   Fam §6342.5
Petitioner, attorney to represent   Fam §6386
Pets
    Protective orders on behalf of animals   Fam §6320
        California law enforcement telecommunications (CLETS) information form, confidentiality and use of information   CRC 1.51, CRCAppx A
        Denial of petition for ex parte order, reasons to be provided   Fam §6320.5
Phone harassment protective orders
    Denial of petition for ex parte order, reasons to be provided   Fam §6320.5
Photographs
    Incident reports, inclusion of photographs   Fam §6228
Pleas
    Judicial council forms   CRCAppx A
Privileged communications of victim in court proceedings (See **PRIVILEGED COMMUNICATIONS**)
Prostitution, evidence
    Extortion, serious felony, assault, domestic violence, human trafficking, sexual battery or stalking, victims or witnesses
        Inadmissibility of evidence of prostitution in prosecution for prostitution   Ev §1162
Protective orders (See within this heading, **"Orders"**)
    Discovery requests   Fam §6309
Public records
    Address confidentiality for victims
        Actions, confidentiality requirements for protected persons in civil proceeding   CCP §367.3
        Judicial council forms   CRCAppx A
        Name change proceedings under address confidentiality program   CRC 2.575 to 2.577
Punitive damages
    Tort liability for domestic violence   CC §1708.6
Purpose of statute   Fam §6220
Rape of spouse
    Statute of limitations on sexual assault damages   CCP §340.16
Real property
    Use, possession and control
        Orders determining   Fam §6342.5
Rebuttable presumption against award of spousal support to spouse convicted of domestic violence   Fam §4325
Registry of protective orders, maintenance of   Fam §6380
Reproductive coercion
    Ex parte protective orders
        Orders preventing disturbing peace of other party   Fam §6320
Restitution for loss of earnings and out-of-pocket expenses   Fam §§6342, 7720
Restraining orders
    COVID-19, emergency rule   CRCAppx I Emer Rule 8
    Denial of petition for ex parte order, reasons to be provided   Fam §6320.5
    Dependent child proceedings   CRC 5.620, 5.630
        Firearm relinquishment procedures   CRC 5.630
        Forms for firearm relinquishment   CRCAppx A

DOMESTIC VIOLENCE—Cont.
Restraining orders—Cont.
    Discovery process   Fam §6309
    Ex parte protective orders   Fam §§6320 to 6327
    Firearm relinquishment
        Forms for firearm relinquishment   CRCAppx A
        Procedures   CRC 4.700
    Forms
        Judicial council forms   CRCAppx A
    Remote appearance of proposed restrained person
        Service requirements   CRC 5.496
    Restraining and protective order system   Fam §§6380 to 6389
    Self-help services
        Posting information on services on superior court website   Fam §6306.6
    Service
        Alternative service where respondent evades service   Fam §6340
        Remote appearance of proposed restrained person   CRC 5.496
    Stalking
        Name change proceedings under address confidentiality program   CRC 2.575 to 2.577
    Summons
        Forms, judicial council   CRCAppx A
Retirement benefits, effect of attempted murder on award of community interest in   Fam §782.5
Service of papers
    Alternative service where respondent evades service   Fam §6340
    Order granting, form   CRCAppx A
    Emergency protective order   Fam §§6271, 6383, 6384
    Restraining orders   Fam §§6383, 6384
Shelters
    Rape of spouse, payments to shelter as condition of probation for
        Statute of limitations on sexual assault damages   CCP §340.16
Siblings
    Victim representatives   Fam §6228
Solicitation of murder
    Retirement benefits, effect on award of community interest in   Fam §782.5
    Support award to convicted spouse prohibited   Fam §4324
Spousal support
    Emotional distress from history of domestic violence as factor in support decisions   Fam §4320
    Murder
        Attempting or soliciting murder of spouse, denial of support   Fam §4324
    Rebuttable presumption against award of spousal support to abusive spouse   Fam §4325
Stalking
    Ex parte order enjoining   Fam §§6274, 6320
        California law enforcement telecommunications (CLETS) information form, confidentiality and use of information   CRC 1.51, CRCAppx A
        Denial of petition for ex parte order, reasons to be provided   Fam §6320.5
    Name change proceedings under address confidentiality program   CRC 2.575 to 2.577
    Protective orders
        Denial of petition for ex parte order, reasons to be provided   Fam §6320.5
Statute of limitation for civil action based on   CCP §340.15
    Felony offenses, damage actions based on commission of   CCP §340.3
Support person for victim of domestic violence   CCP §527.6, Fam §§3182, 6303
    COVID-19, emergency rule   CRCAppx I Emer Rule 8
    Possession of firearms   CCP §527.11
    Service of order   CCP §527.12
Temporary custody or visitation rights   Fam §§3064, 6252 to 6253, 6323
Temporary restraining order
    Affidavit showing reasonable proof of past acts of abuse   Fam §6300
    COVID-19, emergency rule   CRCAppx I Emer Rule 8
    Duration of order granted after notice and hearing   Fam §6345
    Ex parte (See within this heading, **"Ex parte protective orders"**)
    Ex parte orders
        Notice not required   Fam §6300
    Guardian ad litem for minor party to proceedings to restrain violence   CCP §§372, 374
        Appearance of minor under 12 to request or oppose temporary order   Fam §6229
    Harassment generally
        Address or location of complaining party or family, prohibition on enjoined party from obtaining   CCP §527.10

DOMESTIC VIOLENCE—Cont.
Temporary restraining order—Cont.
    Harassment generally—Cont.
        California law enforcement telecommunications (CLETS) information form, confidentiality and use of information   CRC 1.51, CRCAppx A
        Firearm relinquishment and disposition   CCP §527.9, CRCAppx A
        Minor's information confidentiality, request in civil harassment proceedings   CRC 3.1161
        Requests for protective orders   CRC 3.1160
    Harassment generally, temporary restraining order and injunction prohibiting   CCP §527.6
        COVID-19, emergency rule   CRCAppx I Emer Rule 8
        Forms for firearm relinquishment   CRCAppx A
        Hearing to renew restraining order
            Reschedule request and order   CRCAppx A
        Minor's information confidentiality, request in civil harassment proceedings   CRCAppx A
        Possession of firearms   CCP §527.11
        Service of order   CCP §527.12
    Hearing to renew restraining order
        Reschedule request and order   CRCAppx A
    Law enforcement officers
        Foreign orders, enforcement (See within this heading, **"Uniform Interstate Enforcement of Domestic Violence Protection Orders Act"**)
        Generally (See within this heading, **"Law enforcement officers"**)
    Minor's appearance in proceedings to restrain violence   CCP §§372, 374.5, 377
        Appearance of minor under 12 to request or oppose temporary order   Fam §6229
    Persons who may be granted   Fam §6301
    Possession of firearms   CCP §527.11
    Purpose of   Fam §6300
    Service of   Fam §§6383, 6384
    Termination
        Findings and order   CRCAppx A
    Willful violation of   Fam §6388
    Workplace violence or threat of violence, injunctive relief against
        COVID-19, emergency rule   CRCAppx I Emer Rule 8
        Forms for firearm relinquishment   CRCAppx A
        Hearing to renew restraining order
            Reschedule request and order   CRCAppx A
        Possession of firearms   CCP §527.11
    Workplace violence or threat of violence, protection orders   CCP §527.8, CRC 3.1160
        Address or location of complaining party or family, prohibition on enjoined party from obtaining   CCP §527.10
        California law enforcement telecommunications (CLETS) information form, confidentiality and use of information   CRC 1.51, CRCAppx A
        Firearm relinquishment and disposition   CCP §527.9
        Forms for firearm relinquishment   CRCAppx A
        Judicial council legal forms   CRCAppx A
        Memorandum in support of petition for order not required   CRC 3.1114
        Requests for protective orders   CRC 3.1160
Tort of domestic violence   CC §1708.6
Translation
    Court orders, translation of   CCP §185
Uniform Interstate Enforcement of Domestic Violence Protection Orders Act
    Citation of act   Fam §6400
    Definitions   Fam §6401
    Effective date   Fam §6409
    Emergency protective orders
        Multiple protective orders, priority of enforcement   Fam §6405
    Law enforcement officers
        Duty to enforce foreign protection order by   Fam §6403
        Liability of   Fam §6405
        Multiple orders, priority of enforcement   Fam §6405
    Legal and equitable remedies of protected person   Fam §6406
    Registration of foreign protection order   Fam §6404
        Tribal court protective orders   CRC 5.386
    Severability of provisions   Fam §6408
    State tribunals, enforcement of foreign protection order in   Fam §6402
    Uniformity of law in application and construction   Fam §6407
Uniform Parentage Act (See **UNIFORM PARENTAGE ACT**)
Unlawful detainer proceedings
    Domestic violence victims
        Abuse or violence against tenant, remedies   CCP §1174.27

DOMESTIC VIOLENCE—Cont.
Unlawful detainer proceedings—Cont.
    Limitations on termination of or refusal to renew tenancy of victims   CC §1946.7, CCP §1161.3
    Nuisance committed by tenant as grounds
        Presumption of nuisance   CCP §1161
Victim representatives   Fam §6228
Victims
    Coerced debt   CC §§1798.97.1 to 1798.97.6
Victim service providers, personal information protection   CC §§1798.79.8 to 1798.79.95
    Definitions   CC §1798.79.8
    Disclosing personal information
        Grants, requiring disclosure as condition   CC §1798.79.9
        Injunctions to prevent   CC §1798.79.95
        Prohibited   CC §1798.79.9
Visitation orders (See within this heading, **"Custody and visitation orders"**)
Willful violation of restraining order   Fam §6388
Wireless telephone billing responsibility, transfer to victim   Fam §6347
Workplace violence or threat of violence, protection orders   CCP §527.8, CRC 3.1160
    Address or location of complaining party or family, prohibition on enjoined party from obtaining   CCP §527.10
    California law enforcement telecommunications (CLETS) information form, confidentiality and use of information   CRC 1.51, CRCAppx A
    COVID-19, emergency rule   CRCAppx I Emer Rule 8
    Firearm relinquishment and disposition   CCP §527.9
        Forms for firearm relinquishment   CRCAppx A
    Judicial council legal forms   CRCAppx A
    Memorandum in support of petition for order not required   CRC 3.1114
    Possession of firearms   CCP §527.8
    Requests for protective orders   CRC 3.1160

DOMESTIC VIOLENCE PREVENTION LAW (See **DOMESTIC VIOLENCE**)

DOMICILE
Divorce obtained in other state by parties domiciled in California   Fam §§2090 to 2093
Personalty governed by law of owner's domicile   CC §946

DOMINANT TENEMENT
Easement   CC §803

DONATIONS (See **GIFTS**)

DONATIVE TRANSFERS
Presumption of fraud or undue influence   Pro §§21360 to 21392
    Attorneys
        Duty of counsel   Pro §21384
    Certificate of independent review
        Form   Pro §21384
    Costs and attorney's fees   Pro §21380
    Definitions   Pro §§21360 to 21374
    Gifts not subject to provisions   Pro §21384
    Gifts subject to provisions   Pro §21386
    Inapplicability to specified interests and transfers   Pro §21382
    Irrevocable instruments
        Applicability of provisions   Pro §21392
    Liability for transfer   Pro §21388
    Notice of contested instrument   Pro §21388
    Public policy   Pro §21392
    Transfer of property subject to presumption   Pro §21388
    Transfer to specific persons deemed under prohibition   Pro §21380
    Waiver of applicability
        Prohibition   Pro §21390

DOORS
Forcible entry by breaking   CCP §1159

DOOR-TO-DOOR SALES (See **HOME SOLICITATION SALES CONTRACTS**)

DOUBLE OR FORMER JEOPARDY
Concurrent or consecutive sentencing
    Applicability of prohibition against multiple punishments   CRC 4.424
Juvenile courts
    Certification cases   CRC 4.116
Multiple prosecutions for same act   CRC 4.412

DOWER
Abolished   Pro §6412

DOWN PAYMENT
Automobile sales, recovery under   CC §§2982, 2983
Retail installment sales contract provision   CC §1803.3
Seller assisted marketing plan   CC §§1812.201, 1812.210

DOWRY
Contract rescission, dowry recoverable after   CC §1590

DOXING
Victims' recourse   CC §1708.89

DRAFTS
Bill of exchange (See **BILLS OF EXCHANGE**)
Bills and notes (See **BILLS AND NOTES**)

DRAINS
Public liability for injury caused by condition of   Gov §§831.8, 831.9

DRAMA
Child star contracts   Fam §§6750 to 6753

DRAPERIES
Warranty for   CC §1793.35

DRAWING OF JURY (See **JURY**)

DRAWINGS
Commissions for sale of   CC §986

DRINKING WATER (See **WATER SUPPLY**)

DRIVER'S LICENSES
Abstract of judgment requiring identification number   CCP §674
Age-restricted products, sales
   Verification of age for sale of age-restricted products
      Government-issued identification   CC §1798.99.1
Anatomical gifts
   Encoded information
      Use of encoded information by organ procurement organizations   CC §1798.90.1
Child support obligation, suspension or denial of license for noncompliance with   Fam §§17520, 17521
   Lower-income obligors   Fam §17520.5
Commercial licenses
   Traffic violator schools, eligibility to attend   CRC 4.104
Encoded information, use   CC §1798.90.1
Information Practices Act, disclosures under   CC §1798.26
Investigative agencies requiring identification number   CC §1786.22
Privacy
   Encoded information, use   CC §1798.90.05
Radio frequency identification (RFID)
   Use to remotely read identification document without knowledge or consent   CC §§1798.79, 1798.795
Suspension or revocation
   Child support obligation, suspension or denial of license for noncompliance with   Fam §§17520, 17521
   Infractions
      Nonpayment of fine for infraction   CRC 4.106
   Request for stay   CRC 3.1142
   Small claims judgment, suspension for failure to satisfy   CCP §§116.870, 116.880
   Stay of suspension, request for   CRC 3.1142
Theft (See **AUTOMOBILE THEFT**)
Title inscribed with Lemon Law Buyback notation   CC §§1793.23, 1793.24
Towing of vehicles
   Liens (See **AUTOMOBILES**)
Trade-in calculation and disclosure   CC §2982
Traffic regulations and violations (See **TRAFFIC REGULATIONS AND VIOLATIONS**)
Venue, conditional sales action   CC §2984.4, CCP §396a
Warranty   CC §§1792 to 1795.8
   Adjustment programs   CC §§1795.90 to 1795.93
   Lemon law (See **AUTOMOBILES**)
   Repairs under warranty (See **AUTOMOBILES**)

DRIVER'S PRIVACY PROTECTION ACT
Consumer privacy rights
   Relation between act and consumer privacy provisions   CC §1798.145

DRONES   Gov §§853 to 853.5
Emergency response
   Drones or unmanned aircraft systems damaged by emergency responder
      Provision of emergency services by responder and interference with services by drone, immunity from liability for damage to drone or system   CC §43.101

DROP BOXES
Court document filing   CRC 2.210

DROUGHTS AND WATER SHORTAGES
Common interest developments
   Pressure washing of exterior of separate interest
      Requirement to pressure wash during drought emergency void   CC §4736

DRUG DIVERSION PROGRAMS
Guidelines for diversion drug court programs   CRC JudAdminStand 4.10
Preguilty plea drug court program
   Guidelines   CRC JudAdminStand 4.10

DRUGS (See **NARCOTICS AND DANGEROUS DRUGS**)

DRUGS AND NARCOTICS
Minors
   Consent to treatment for opioid use disorder   Fam §§6929, 6929.1

DRUGSTORES (See **PHARMACISTS AND PHARMACIES**)

DRUG TAKE-BACK BINS, SECURE
Liability of collector, limitation   CC §1714.24

DRUNKARDS (See **SUBSTANCE ABUSE**)

DRYCLEANERS
Gender, prohibition against charging different price for services of similar or like kind based solely on   CC §51.6
Lien for services of   CC §§3051, 3066
Small business gender discrimination in pricing services compliance act   CC §§55.61 to 55.63

DRYING RACKS
Common interest developments
   Governing documents not to prohibit clotheslines or drying racks in owner's backyard   CC §4753
Landlord and tenant
   Tenant use clothesline or drying rack in private areas   CC §1940.20

DUE CARE, LACK OF (See **NEGLIGENCE**)

DUE-ON-SALE CLAUSES
Public entity housing loans exempt from prohibition against   CC §711.5
Trust deed or mortgage, loan secured by   CC §2954.10

DUE PROCESS
Tribal court civil money judgment act
   Objections
      Grounds for objection   CCP §1737

DUMP TRUCKS
Construction trucking services brokers
   Transportation charges, payment   CC §3322

DUPLICATE WRITINGS (See **COPIES**)

DURABLE POWER OF ATTORNEY (See **POWER OF ATTORNEY**)

DURESS
Consent for contract obtained under   CC §§1567, 1569
Debt collection by use of   CC §1788.10
Debts
   Coerced debt   CC §§1798.97.1 to 1798.97.6
Domestic violence (See **DOMESTIC VIOLENCE**)
Forcible detainer   CCP §1160
Gender violence
   Civil rights actions   CC §52.4
Health care facilities
   Force, threat or other obstruction of access to health facilities or school grounds   CC §1708.9
Landlord and tenant
   Unduly influencing tenant to vacate   CC §1940.2
Mitigating circumstances   CRC 4.423
Parentage
   Voluntary declaration of parentage
      Challenge of declaration based on fraud, duress or material mistake of fact   Fam §7576
Rescission of contract because of   CC §1689
Schools
   Force, threat or other obstruction of access to health facilities or school grounds   CC §1708.9

DURESS—Cont.
Sodomy, commission by
    Statute of limitations
        Civil damages   CCP §340.16
Transfer on death deeds
    Fraud, undue influence, etc, creation of deed
        Applicability of other provisions penalizing conduct   Pro §5698
Wills, general discussion of effect on   Pro §6104

DUTIES
Jury commissioner   CCP §196

DWELLING HOUSES
Aged persons, housing for (See **SENIOR CITIZENS**)
Apartments (See **APARTMENTS**)
Blind persons, housing for (See **BLIND PERSONS**)
Common interest developments (See **COMMON INTEREST DEVELOPMENTS**)
Community property (See **COMMUNITY PROPERTY**)
Construction and building
    Residential building permit quality reviewers
        Immunity from liability   CC §43.99
Construction defects, actions for   CC §§895 to 945.5 (See **CONSTRUCTION DEFECTS, ACTIONS FOR**)
Conveyance of (See **CONVEYANCES**)
Covenants prohibiting prefabricated modular homes, validity of   CC §714.5
Demolition
    Notice of application to demolish   CC §1940.6
Discriminatory restrictions   CC §§53, 782, 782.5
Enforcement of judgments (See **ENFORCEMENT OF JUDGMENTS**)
Excluding spouse or other party from   Fam §§6321, 6340
Family home (See **FAMILY HOME**)
Forcible entry   CCP §1159
Home Equity Loan Disclosure Act   CC §§2970 to 2971
Homesteads (See **HOMESTEADS**)
Housing projects, injunctions against   CCP §529.2
Inspection warrants   CCP §1822.50
Mortgages (See **TRUST DEEDS AND MORTGAGES**)
Multifamily dwellings
    Service of papers or subpoena, access to covered multifamily dwelling   CCP §415.21
Residential building permits
    Quality reviewers
        Immunity from liability   CC §43.99
Room in dwelling, tenant's possession of   CC §1950
Senior citizens, housing for (See **SENIOR CITIZENS**)
Service of process at   CCP §415.20
Shared appreciation loans (See **SHARED APPRECIATION LOANS**)
State agencies, adoption of building standard regulations by (See **ADMINISTRATIVE PROCEDURE ACT**)
Transfer of (See **CONVEYANCES**)
Transient occupancy in single-family homes, recordkeeping required for accepting reservations or money for   CC §1864
Trust deeds (See **TRUST DEEDS AND MORTGAGES**)
Untenantable premises   CC §§1941 to 1942
Walls (See **WALLS**)
Windows (See **WINDOWS**)
oning ordinances limiting housing, burden of proving necessity for   Ev §669.5

DWELLINGS
Conditional sales of residential property, disclosure requirements for   CC §§2956 to 2968

DYING DECLARATIONS
Admissibility of   Ev §1242

E

EARNINGS
Generally (See **SALARIES AND WAGES**)
Defined   Fam §5206
Emancipated minor   Fam §7050
Married person's earnings   Fam §911
Parent and child (See **PARENT AND CHILD**)
Separate property   Fam §§771, 772

EARNINGS ASSIGNMENT FOR SUPPORT
Accounting by employer   Fam §5236
Arrearages
    Computation and liquidation of   Fam §§5230, 5238, 5239
    Defined   Fam §5201

EARNINGS ASSIGNMENT FOR SUPPORT—Cont.
Assigned obligee defined   Fam §5214
Assignment order defined   Fam §5202
Change of address of obligee   Fam §5237
Consolidated check, payment of amounts owed in   Fam §5236
Contempt   Fam §5241
Death of obligee   Fam §5240
Definitions   Fam §§5200 to 5220
Due date of support payments   Fam §5204
Earnings defined   Fam §5206
Earnings withholding order, priority over   CCP §706.031
Effective date of order   Fam §5231
Emancipated minor   Fam §5240
Employer
    Accounting by   Fam §5236
    Adverse employment actions   Fam §5290
    Change of employer, notification of   Fam §5281
    Consolidated check, payment of amounts owed by   Fam §5236
    Discharge of obligor, grounds for   Fam §5290
    Disciplinary action against employee obligor   Fam §5290
    Duties of   Fam §5235
    Future employers, order binding on   Fam §5231
    Identity unknown   Fam §5280
    Notice generally (See within this heading, "**Notice**")
    Penalty for noncompliance by   Fam §5241
    Promotions denied due to assignment   Fam §5290
    Refusal to hire obligor   Fam §5290
    Service of assignment order on   Fam §5232
    Withholding by   Fam §5233
Employer defined   Fam §5210
Government support enforcement services under Title IV-D   Fam §§5212, 5244 to 5247, 17420
Health and disability benefits, limitation on withholding of   CCP §704.130
Immunity of local child support agency and employers acting under earnings assignment provisions   Fam §5247
Intercounty support obligations   Fam §§5600 to 5604
Interstate support obligations
    California law, applicability   Fam §5230.1
Judicial Council forms   Fam §5295
Lien created by service of order   Fam §5242
Local child support agency's role, generally   Fam §5244
Modification of order to reflect correct or allowable amount   Fam §5272
Notice
    Change of address of obligee   Fam §5237
    Change of employer, notification of   Fam §5281
    In lieu of assignment order in Title-IV cases, service on employer of notice of assignment   Fam §5246
    Termination of employment, employer notifying obligee of obligor's   Fam §5282
Obligee defined   Fam §5214
Obligor defined   Fam §5216
Order for assignment
    Generally   Fam §5230
    Application for order   Fam §§5250 to 5252
    Before July 1, 1990, procedure for   Fam §5250
    Defined   Fam §5208
    Delivery of copy of order and statement of rights to obligor   Fam §5234
    Existing or future employer of obligor, as binding on   Fam §5231
    Issuance of   Fam §5253
    Modification of order to reflect correct or allowable amount   Fam §5272
    Notice of assignment served on employer in lieu of assignment order in Title-IV cases   Fam §5246
    Procedures for   Fam §§5250 to 5253
    Service of   Fam §§5232, 5242
    Termination of   Fam §5240
Other counties' earnings assignment orders, registration of   Fam §§5600 to 5604
Other remedies, use of   Fam §5245
Other states' orders
    Applicability of California law, generally   Fam §5230.1
Parent locator service   Fam §5280
Priorities
    Attachment, execution, or other assignment, priority of earnings assignment order over   CCP §706.031, Fam §5243
    Current and past-due support and/or multiple assignment orders, priorities among   Fam §5238
Quash, motion to
    Grounds for   Fam §5270
    Procedure   Fam §§5246, 5271
Registration of earnings assignment orders
    Other counties   Fam §§5600 to 5604
Remarriage of spouse   Fam §5240

EARNINGS ASSIGNMENT FOR SUPPORT—Cont.
Retirement benefits
    Private retirement benefits   CCP §704.115
    Public retirement benefits   CCP §§704.110, 704.114
Stay of order
    Generally   Fam §5260
    Termination of stay   Fam §§5240, 5261
Termination of order   Fam §5240
Timely payments   Fam §5220
Whereabouts of obligor unknown   Fam §5280
Withholding by employer   Fam §§5233, 5235
Workers' compensation temporary disability benefits   CCP §704.160

EARNINGS PROTECTION LAW (See GARNISHMENT)

EARNINGS WITHHOLDING ORDERS (See GARNISHMENT)

EARTHQUAKES
Appellate court procedures, earthquake emergency rules applicable to   CRC 8.66
Boundaries, reestablishment of   CCP §§751.50 to 751.65
Broker's duty to disclose hazards (See **BROKERS**)
Common interest developments insurance (See **COMMON INTEREST DEVELOPMENTS**)
Construction defects, actions for
    Unforeseen act of nature
        Defenses of builder   CC §945.5
Consumer information booklets   CC §§2079.8, 2079.9, 2079.11
Cullen Act   CCP §§751.50 to 751.65
Destroyed land records relief law   CCP §§751.01 to 751.28
Northridge earthquake of 1994, extended limitations period for insurance claims arising out of   CCP §340.9
Nunc pro tunc filing where public records lost or destroyed   CCP §1046a
Private records destroyed by   CCP §§1953.10 to 1953.13
Public records destroyed by   CCP §§1953 to 1953.06
Purchasers, disclosures   CC §§1103 to 1103.15
Real estate transfers
    Disclosures to purchasers   CC §§1103 to 1103.15
Sale of realty, disclosure requirements for (See **VENDOR AND PURCHASER**)
State's immunity from liability for prediction of   Gov §955.1

EASEMENTS
Abandoned easements
    Applicability of chapter   CC §§887.020, 887.090
    Clear record title, action to   CC §887.040
    Common law, effect of   CC §887.030
    Conditions constituting   CC §887.050
    Effect of   CC §887.080
    Fact of abandoned easement, action establishing   CC §887.040
    Preservation of easements
        General notice of intent   CC §887.060
        Late notice of intent   CC §887.070
Actions
    Failure of owner to pay cost of maintenance or repair of right of way   CC §845
    Owner or occupant, action by   CC §§809, 810
Air   CC §801
Burial   CC §§801, 802
Business transactions   CC §801
Common interest developments   CC §4505
Conservation easements   CC §§815 to 816
    Greenway easements generally   CC §§816.50 to 816.66 (See **GREENWAY EASEMENTS**)
Conveyance of   CC §1104
Decedent's estate, property of   Pro §§9900, 9901
Definitions   CC §§784, 801, 887.010
Dominant tenement defined   CC §803
Eminent domain
    Compensation for taking   CCP §1263.450
    Private owner acquiring appurtenant easement for utility service   CC §1001, CCP §1245.325
Enjoyment   CC §806
Fences   CC §801
Fishing rights   CC §§801, 802
Flooding land   CC §801
Future estates   CC §808
Greenway easements   CC §§816.50 to 816.66 (See **GREENWAY EASEMENTS**)
Heat   CC §801
Highways   CC §802
Hunting   CC §§801, 802
Injunctions to protect, petitions for   CRC 3.1151

EASEMENTS—Cont.
Light   CC §801
Minerals, taking of   CC §§801, 802
Multiple owners
    Costs of maintenance and repair
        Apportionment   CC §845
Natural support from adjacent land   CC §801
Partition sales   CC §807, CCP §873.710
Pasturage rights   CC §§801, 802
Pew rights   CC §§801, 802
Possession, enforcing right of   CC §810
Prescriptive use   CC §§813, 1008
Preservation of easements
    Abandoned easements, preservation
        General notice of intent   CC §887.060
        Late notice of intent   CC §887.070
Public use of private land   CC §813
Railroads (See **RAILROADS**)
Recreational use, limitation of liability for   CC §846
Rents, right of collecting   CC §§802, 808
Repair, duty of   CC §845
Restrictions defined   CC §784
Right of way
    Generally   CC §§801, 802
    Repairs   CC §845
Riparian rights   CC §801
Servient tenement defined   CC §803
Snow removal   CC §845
Solar easements   CC §§801, 801.5
Sports, using land for   CC §801
Statute of frauds   CC §1624, CCP §1971
Streets   CC §802
Termination   CC §811
Timber, taking of   CC §§801, 802
Tolls, right to collect   CC §802
Vested estate, easement in   CC §§804, 805
Walls, use of   CC §801
Waste, easement affecting right to prevent   CC §808
Water   CC §§801, 802

EAVESDROPPING AND WIRETAPPING
Dissolution of marriage proceedings, inadmissibility of evidence in   Fam §2022

E-BOOKS
Privacy
    Reader privacy act   CC §§1798.90, 1798.90.05

ECOLOGY (See ENVIRONMENTAL HAZARDS)

ECONOMIC LITIGATION PROCEDURES
Affidavit or declaration, prepared testimony by   CCP §98
Appeal, right to   CCP §100
Applicability of economic litigation provisions   CCP §91
Applicability of law for civil actions generally   CCP §90
Case questionnaires   CCP §93
Conclusive effect of judgment or final order   CCP §99
Discovery
    Additional discovery, motion or stipulation for   CCP §95
    Case questionnaire   CCP §93
    Permissible forms of discovery   CCP §94
    Request for statement identifying witnesses and evidence   CCP §96
    Sanctions for failure to respond to case questionnaire   CCP §93
Exclusion of evidence or witnesses not included in statement   CCP §97
Forms
    Case questionnaires   CCP §93
    Request for statement identifying witnesses and evidence   CCP §96
Permissible pleadings and motions   CCP §92
Prepared testimony by affidavit or declaration   CCP §98
Request for statement identifying witnesses and evidence   CCP §96
Sanctions for failure to respond to case questionnaire   CCP §93
Withdrawal of action from economic litigation requirements   CCP §91

ECONOMIC STATUS
Jury service exemption not allowed based on   CCP §204

ECONOMY AND EFFICIENCY
Separate trial of issues   CCP §598

EDITORS
Contempt charge for refusal to reveal source of information   Ev §1070

EDUCATION
Child custody mediators and investigators, continuing education requirements for Fam §3165
Community property rights regarding (See **COMMUNITY PROPERTY**)
Conciliation Court counselors, continuing education programs Fam §1816
Conservators
 Appointment of person to make educational decisions for minor Pro §2662
 Court staff Pro §1456
 Non-professional conservators or guardians, educational program Pro §1457
Expert witnesses, qualification of Ev §§720, 801
Guardianships
 Appointment of person to make educational decisions for minor Pro §2662
 Court staff Pro §1456
 Non-professional conservators or guardians, educational program Pro §1457
Judges
 Domestic violence issues CRC 10.464
 Family law matters CRC 10.463, CRC JudAdminStand 5.30
 Judicial branch education generally CRC 10.451 to 10.493
 Probate cases, judges and subordinate judicial officers regularly assigned to CRC 10.468
  Domestic violence issues CRC 10.464
 Temporary judges
  Training programs CRC 2.813
 Trial Court Delay Reduction Act, training program under Gov §68610
Judicial officers' education (See **JUDGES**)
Law students (See **LAW STUDENTS**)
Spousal support, consideration of education and training of supported spouse Fam §4320

EDUCATIONAL DEBT COLLECTION PRACTICES CC §§1788.90 to 1788.94
Definitions CC §1788.92
Legislative findings and intent CC §1788.91
Prohibited debt collection practices by schools CC §1788.93
Short title of act CC §1788.90
Transcript used as leverage to collect debt, prohibition CC §1788.93
Waivers CC §1788.94

EDUCATIONAL ORGANIZATIONS
Judge's office in organization not a financial interest for purposes of disqualification CCP §170.5

EFFECTIVE DATES
Code of Civil Procedure CCP §2

E-FILING
Appellate rules, supreme court and courts of appeal
 E-filing in supreme court and courts of appeal CRC 8.70 to 8.79
  Supreme court-specific rules CRCSupp SuprCtE-file 1 to CRCSupp SuprCtE-file 13
Electronic filing and service generally CCP §1010.6, CRC 2.250 to 2.261 (See **ELECTRONIC FILING AND SERVICE**)

EGG DONATION FOR FERTILITY TREATMENTS
Parent-child relationship, effect on Fam §7613

EGRESS (See **ACCESS**)

ELDER ABUSE (See **SENIOR CITIZENS**)

ELDERLY PERSONS (See **SENIOR CITIZENS**)

ELECTION CONTESTS
Voting rights
 Report of findings and orders affecting CRC 10.970, CRCAppx A

ELECTION OF RIGHTS OR REMEDIES
Judicial arbitration, election for (See **JUDICIAL ARBITRATION**)
Small claims court advisory services, election with respect to CCP §116.940

ELECTION OF SURVIVING SPOUSE
Small estates without administration (See **SMALL ESTATES WITHOUT ADMINISTRATION**)
Will, election to take against (See **WILLS**)

ELECTION PRECINCTS AND DISTRICTS
Redistricting and reapportionment
 Precedence of cases involving CCP §35

ELECTIONS AND ELECTIONS PROCEEDINGS
Campaign funds
 Judges, contributions by CRCSupp JudEthicsCanon 5

ELECTIONS AND ELECTIONS PROCEEDINGS—Cont.
Campaigns
 Judges, political activities by CRCSupp JudEthicsCanon 5
Candidates for office (See **CANDIDATES FOR OFFICE**)
Conservatee's right to vote Pro §§1865, 1910
Judicial elections
 Campaign contributions
  Disclosures CRCSupp JudEthicsCanon 3
  Disqualification from case, contribution as grounds CCP §170.1
 Code of judicial ethics
  Disclosures of campaign contributions CRCSupp JudEthicsCanon 3
  Leave, applicability of code to judge on leave to pursue election to other office CRCSupp JudEthicsCanon 6
 Ethical obligations of candidates CRCSupp JudEthicsCanon 6
 Judicial performance, commission on
  Ethics code for commission members JudPerPolicy 6.4
 Political activities by judges CRCSupp JudEthicsCanon 5
Mobilehomes
 Signs, placement of
  Political campaign signs CC §§798.51, 799.10
Political vote, evidentiary privilege to refuse disclosure of Ev §1050
Precedence
 Certification of ballot measures, cases involving CCP §35
 Certification of candidates, cases involving CCP §35
 Contested elections cases CCP §§35, 44
 Courts of appeal and Supreme Court, hearings in CCP §44
 Libel or slander action by candidate CCP §§44, 460.7
 Voter registration, cases involving CCP §35
Registration of voters
 Action to compel registration
  Fees, clerk not to charge Gov §70633
Sale of political items CC §§1739 to 1739.4
Service of process CCP §416.80
Shortening of time to respond to complaint in action for libel alleged to have occurred during election campaign CCP §460.7
Signs
 Landlord and tenant
  Political signs, restrictions on prohibition CC §1940.4
Unauthorized signatures in campaign advertisements, action for damages for CC §3344.5
U.S Congress, members of (See **CONGRESS**)

ELECTIVE OFFICE
Preference in courts of appeal and Supreme Court in hearing actions for libel or slander by person holding elective office or by candidate CCP §44
Shortening of time to respond to complaint in action for libel alleged to have occurred during election campaign CCP §460.7

ELECTRIC APPLIANCES (See **APPLIANCES**)

ELECTRIC BICYCLES
Landlord and tenant
 Personal micromobility devices, rights of tenants CC §1940.41

ELECTRICITY AND ELECTRIC COMPANIES
Cancellation of utility, cable, etc, services on behalf of deceased person
 In-person cancellation not to be required Pro §217
Credit cards
 Surcharge on credit card transaction, prohibition against
  Exception for electrical, gas or water corporation CC §1748.1
Debit cards
 Surcharge on debit card transaction, prohibition against
  Exception for electrical, gas or water corporation CC §1748.1
Diversion or tampering with electrical utility services, action for CC §§1882 to 1882.6
Electrical consumption data
 Privacy of customer electrical or natural gas usage data CC §1798.98
 Actions and other remedies of customer CC §1798.99
Home energy ratings, duty of seller or broker to disclose information regarding CC §2079.10
Indemnity coverage for construction, repair, renovation, maintenance or demolition of lines CC §2783
Inspection warrants to determine violations CCP §1822.50
Landlord and tenant (See **LANDLORD AND TENANT**)
Local publicly owned electric utilities
 Privacy of customer electrical or natural gas usage data CC §1798.98
  Actions and other remedies of customer CC §1798.99
Real estate sales
 Disclosures regarding electrical inspections CC §1102.6i
Repairs or service during specified time period where subscriber's presence required, liability for failure to provide CC §1722

ELECTRICITY AND ELECTRIC COMPANIES—Cont.
Small business action, costs in CCP §1028.5

ELECTRIC VEHICLES
Automobile sales finance
    Charging stations
        Disclosures when charging stations included in contract CC §2982.11
Charging stations
    Automobile sales finance
        Disclosures when charging stations included in contract CC §2982.11
    Commercial and industrial common interest developments
        Protected uses CC §6713
    Common interest developments
        Action for declaratory or equitable relief to enforce procedure for granting exclusive use of common area CC §4605
        Architectural guidelines not to prohibit CC §4745
        Common areas, granting exclusive use CC §4600
        Time of use (TOU) meters, covenants, restrictions, etc on installation or use, void CC §4745.1
    Landlord and tenant
        Commercial leases, lease terms prohibiting or restricting void CC §1952.7
        Installation by lessee, approval by landlord CC §1947.6
Common interest developments
    Electric vehicle charging stations
        Action for declaratory or equitable relief to enforce procedure for granting exclusive use of common area CC §4605
        Architectural guidelines not to prohibit CC §4745
        Common areas, granting exclusive use CC §4600
        Time of use (TOU) meters, covenants, restrictions, etc on installation or use, void CC §4745.1

ELECTROLOGISTS
Human trafficking
    Signs, businesses required to post notice concerning relief from slavery or human trafficking CC §52.6

ELECTRONICALLY STORED INFORMATION (ESI)
Deposition subpoenas CCP §2020.020
    Attendance and testimony commanded
        Business records production also requested, requirements of subpoena CCP §2020.510
    Business records, production for copying
        Specifying form for ESI CCP §2020.410
    Notice
        Contents of deposition notice CCP §2025.220
        Service, effect CCP §2025.280
    Objection as to form of ESI to be provided CCP §2020.220
    Service of deposition subpoena CCP §2020.220
Discovery
    Applicability of civil discovery act provisions to ESI CCP §2019.040
    Compelling discovery, motion CCP §2025.480
    Deposition subpoenas
        Failure to comply with deposition notice CCP §2025.450
    Inspection demands
        Objections CCP §2031.240
    Objection as to form of ESI to be provided CCP §2020.220
    Outside California, discovery in foreign jurisdictions CCP §2026.010
        Foreign nations CCP §2027.010
    Protective orders CCP §2025.420
    Sanctions for failure to provide
        Good faith operation of electronic information system preventing provision of ESI, defense to sanctions CCP §§2017.020, 2020.220, 2023.030
    Scope of discovery CCP §2017.010
    Undue burden or expense to produce CCP §2020.220
        Objections to production CCP §2025.460
    Work product
        Applicable rules CCP §2020.220
Subpoena duces tecum requiring production CCP §1985
    Employment records defined to include ESI CCP §1985.6
    Lost, damaged, etc, information caused by good faith operation of electronic information system
        No sanctions for failure to provide information CCP §1987.2
    Objection to form of production CCP §1985.8
    Personal records defined to include ESI CCP §1985.3
    Witness subpoena may include request to bring ESI and other things CCP §1987

ELECTRONIC CIGARETTES
Minors
    Verification of age for sale of age-restricted products CC §1798.99.1

ELECTRONIC COMMERCIAL SERVICES
Generally CC §1789
Applicability of Electronic Commerce Act CC §§1789.7, 1789.8
Citation CC §1789.1
Definitions CC §1789.2
Disclosure requirements CC §1789.3
Liability of provider CC §1789.6
Penalties for violation of Electronic Commerce Act CC §1789.5
Waiver of protections CC §1789.9

ELECTRONIC COURT RECORDS
Access CRC 2.501
    Calendars CRC 2.507
    Fees for electronic access CRC 2.506
    Indexes CRC 2.507
    Notice to persons accessing records CRC 2.504
    Public access CRC 2.503
        Criminal cases, remote electronic access in individual criminal cases CRC 2.503
    Registers of actions CRC 2.507
Applicability of provisions CRC 2.501
Bulk distribution CRC 2.503
Calendars
    Electronic access CRC 2.507
Conditions on use CRC 2.504
Contracts with vendors to provide public access CRC 2.505
Court calendars
    Electronic access CRC 2.507
Criminal cases
    Remote electronic access in individual criminal cases CRC 2.503
Definitions CRC 2.502
    Bulk distribution CRC 2.503
    Feasible CRC 2.503
Fees for electronic access CRC 2.506
Indexes
    Electronic access CRC 2.507
Limitations and conditions of use CRC 2.504
Notice to persons accessing records CRC 2.504
Off-site access CRC 2.503
Privacy policy
    Posting CRC 2.504
Public access CRC 2.503
    Criminal cases
        Remote electronic access in individual criminal cases CRC 2.503
    Fees for electronic access CRC 2.506
    Notice to persons accessing records CRC 2.504
Registers of actions
    Electronic access CRC 2.507
Remote access
    Audit trails
        Government entities, access by CRC 2.543
        Parties, designees, attorneys, court-appointed persons or persons working in legal organization or qualified legal services project, access by CRC 2.526
    Court termination of remote access
        Government entities, access by CRC 2.545
        Parties, designees, attorneys, court-appointed persons or persons working in legal organization or qualified legal services project, access by CRC 2.528
    Criminal cases
        Extraordinary criminal cases CRC 2.503
    Government entities, access by CRC 2.540 to 2.545
        Applicability of provisions CRC 2.540
        Audit trails CRC 2.543
        Court termination of remote access CRC 2.545
        Encryption to secure confidential or sealed information CRC 2.542
        Identity verification and management CRC 2.541
        List of government entities which may be authorized to receive access CRC 2.540
        Security of confidential information CRC 2.542
        Termination of remote access CRC 2.545
        Terms and conditions of access CRC 2.540, 2.544
    Identity verification and management
        Government entities, access by CRC 2.541
        Parties, designees, attorneys, court-appointed persons or persons working in legal organization or qualified legal services project, access by CRC 2.523

ELECTRONIC COURT RECORDS—Cont.
Remote access—Cont.
    Parties, designees, attorneys, court-appointed persons or persons working in legal organization or qualified legal services project, access by CRC 2.515 to 2.528
        Applicability of provisions   CRC 2.515
        Attorney of party, remote access   CRC 2.519
        Audit trails   CRC 2.526
        Conditions of access, court imposition   CRC 2.527
        Court-appointed persons, remote access   CRC 2.521
        Court termination of remote access   CRC 2.528
        Court to provide remote access to extent possible   CRC 2.516
        Designee of party, remote access   CRC 2.518
        Encryption to secure confidential or sealed information   CRC 2.524
        Identity verification and management   CRC 2.523
        Legal organization of attorney of party, remote access by workers in organization   CRC 2.520, 2.523
        Legal services projects providing brief legal services, remote access for persons working in project   CRC 2.522, 2.523
        Levels of access, enforcement   CRC 2.525
        Party remote access   CRC 2.517
        Scope of provisions   CRC 2.515
        Security of confidential information   CRC 2.524
        Termination of remote access   CRC 2.528
        Unauthorized access, duties of user   CRC 2.525
    Security of confidential information
        Government entities, access by   CRC 2.542
        Parties, designees, attorneys, court-appointed persons or persons working in legal organization or qualified legal services project, access by CRC 2.524
    Termination of remote access
        Government entities, access by   CRC 2.545
        Parties, designees, attorneys, court-appointed persons or persons working in legal organization or qualified legal services project, access by CRC 2.528
Statement of purpose   CRC 2.500

ELECTRONIC DATA BASES
Access to databases for service of process purposes   CCP §415.50
Court indexes   CRC 10.851
Decisional law   CRC 8.1115
Opinions of appellate courts   CRC 8.1115
Restraining and protective order system   Fam §§6380 to 6389

ELECTRONIC DATA PROCESSING
Records of trial proceedings   CRC 2.952

ELECTRONIC DATA TRANSMISSION
Trial court filings
    Proof of service   CCP §1013b

ELECTRONIC DEPOSITIONS
Remote electronic means of taking depositions   CCP §2025.310, CRC 3.1010

ELECTRONIC DISCOVERY ACT   CCP §1985.8

ELECTRONIC DOCUMENTS
Discovery
    Inspection demands   CCP §§2031.010, 2031.030
        Compelling discovery despite burden of providing   CCP §2031.310
        Inaccessibility claimed   CCP §§2031.060, 2031.210
        Objections   CCP §2031.240
        Privilege claimed or attorney work product protection requested CCP §2031.285
        Response, form of information furnished   CCP §2031.280
        Sanctions for failure to provide, circumstances avoiding   CCP §§2031.300, 2031.320
    Subpoenas   CCP §1985.8

ELECTRONIC FILING AND SERVICE   CCP §1010.6, CRC 2.250 to 2.261
Appellate rules, supreme court and courts of appeal
    E-filing in supreme court and courts of appeal   CRC 8.70 to 8.79
        Supreme court-specific rules   CRCSupp SuprCtE-file 1 to CRCSupp SuprCtE-file 13
Attorneys
    Relief as counsel, motion for
        Declaration as to electronic service address   CRC 3.1362
Authorization for electronic service   CRC 2.251
Certified mail
    Electronic service not available when registered or certified mail required CCP §1020

ELECTRONIC FILING AND SERVICE—Cont.
Change of electronic service address
    Service of process   CRC 2.251
    When electronic filing required   CRCSupp 1st AppDist
Close of business, filing by
    Local rule providing for receipt by midnight as being filed on that day CRC 2.259
Completion of service
    Determining when service complete   CRC 2.251
    Proof of electronic service   CCP §1013b
        Probate cases   Pro §1265
Complex litigation   CRC 3.751
Conditions of filing
    Filer responsibilities   CRC 2.256
Confirmation
    Court action upon receipt   CRC 2.259
Consent
    Express consent to electronic service   CRC 2.251
    Withdrawal of consent
        Judicial council legal forms   CRCAppx A
Construction of rules   CRC 2.250
Contracts
    Electronic filing manager contracts   CRC 2.255
    Service provider contracts   CRC 2.255
Court order requiring   CRC 2.253
    Requiring electronic service by local rule or court order   CRC 2.251
Court responsibilities   CRC 2.254
Criminal trials   CRC 2.251, 2.252
    Electronic summons, issuance   CRC 2.259
    Fees not chargeable in some criminal actions   CRC 2.255
    Permissive electronic filing by local rule   CRC 2.253
Definitions   CRC 2.250
Digital signature not required   CRC 2.257
Direct electronic filing   CRC 2.252
Documents appropriate for electronic filing   CRC 2.252
Effect of electronic filing   CRC 2.252
Electronic filing managers
    Contracts with electronic filing managers   CRC 2.255
    Definition of electronic filing manager   CRC 2.250
Electronic service lists
    Court to maintain   CRC 2.251
Electronic signatures   CRC 2.257
Endorsement
    Court action upon receipt   CRC 2.259
Environmental quality act
    Appellate review of CEQA cases
        Jobs and economic improvement through environmental leadership act of 2021   CRC 8.701
        Sacramento downtown arena project, CEQA challenges   CRC 8.701
    Petitions under environmental quality act, civil rules governing
        Jobs and economic improvement through environmental leadership act of 2021   CRC 3.2222
        Sacramento downtown arena project, CEQA challenges   CRC 3.2222
Exhibits
    Electronic exhibits
        Law and motion proceedings   CRC 3.1110
    Filing with electronically filed papers   CRC 2.114, 2.256
Fees
    Attorney's failure to pay provider fees
        Sanctions   CCP §411.20.5
    Costs and fees   CCP §1033.5
    Payment of filing fees   CRC 2.258
Filer responsibilities   CRC 2.256
Format of documents
    Filer responsibilities   CRC 2.256
Forms
    Judicial council forms   CRCAppx A
        Applicable requirements   CRC 2.140, 2.256
    Modification of judicial council forms   CRC 2.261
Hosting of electronic documents
    Costs and fees   CCP §1033.5
Indirect electronic filing   CRC 2.252
Judicial performance, commission on
    Censure, removal, admonishment or retirement of judges
        Filing with Commission   JudPerR 119.5
Juvenile rules
    Electronic filing   CRC 5.522
    Electronic service   CRC 5.523
        Address for electronic service to be provided to court on first appearance   CRC 5.534

ELECTRONIC FILING AND SERVICE—Cont.
Local rules
    Adoption   CCP §1010.6
    Close of business, filing by
        Local rule providing for receipt by midnight as being filed on that day   CRC 2.259
Mandatory electronic filing   CRC 2.253
    Exemption request
        Judicial council forms   CRCAppx A
    Order for exemption
        Judicial council forms   CRCAppx A
Modification of judicial council forms   CRC 2.261
Paper filing
    Circumstances allowing   CRC 2.252
    Electronic format of papers   CRC 2.100
Parties
    Service by parties   CRC 2.251
Perjury, documents filed under penalty of   CRC 2.257
Permissive electronic filing   CRC 2.253
Probate
    Contested probate proceedings   CRC 7.802
Problems with filing
    Court responsibilities   CRC 2.254
Proof of service   CCP §1013b, CRC 2.251
    Probate cases   Pro §1265
Public assess to filed documents
    Court responsibilities   CRC 2.254
Publication of requirements
    Court responsibilities   CRC 2.254
Receipt of filing
    Court action upon   CRC 2.259
Registered mail
    Electronic service not available when registered or certified mail required   CCP §1020
Rejection of document
    Court action upon receipt   CRC 2.259
Remote appearances, technology use
    COVID-19, emergency rule   CRCAppx I Emer Rule 3
Service of process   CRC 2.251
    Court use of electronic service   CRC 2.251
    Proof of electronic service   CCP §1013b
        Probate cases   Pro §1265
Service providers
    Contracts with electronic filing service providers   CRC 2.255
    Definition of electronic service filing provider   CRC 2.250
    Filer accounts
        Establishing with service provider   CRC 2.255
Signatures   CRC 2.257
Small claims courts
    Claims, electronic filing   CCP §116.320
Summons
    Issuance of electronic summons   CRC 2.259
Supreme court
    E-filing in supreme court and courts of appeal   CRC 8.70 to 8.79
        Supreme court-specific rules   CRCSupp SuprCtE-file 1 to CRCSupp SuprCtE-file 13
Uniform rules, adoption of   CCP §1010.6
Waiver of fees   CRC 2.258
Withdrawal of consent
    Forms
        Judicial council legal forms   CRCAppx A

ELECTRONIC FILING SYSTEMS
Complex litigation   CRC 3.751
Mandatory electronic service   CCP §1010.6
Proof of service   CCP §1013b
    Probate cases   Pro §1265
Rules for electronic service and filing   CRC 2.250 to 2.261

ELECTRONIC FUNDS TRANSFERS
Appellate rules, supreme court and courts of appeal
    E-filing in supreme court and courts of appeal
        Fees for filing, methods of payment   CRC 8.76
Child support payments
    Accounts for   Fam §4508
    State disbursement unit
        Electronic fund transfers for employer payment of withholding   Fam §17309.5
Debit cards (See **DEBIT CARDS**)
Electronic transactions
    Exceptions to applicability of electronic transactions provisions   CC §1633.3

ELECTRONIC FUNDS TRANSFERS—Cont.
Landlord and tenant
    Alternative forms of payment   CC §1947.3

ELECTRONIC MAIL (See **EMAIL**)

ELECTRONIC RECORDING DELIVERY SYSTEMS   Gov §§27390 to 27399
Authorized submitters
    Contracting to be authorized submitter   Gov §27397.5
    Defined   Gov §27390
Citation of provisions   Gov §27390
Computer security auditors
    Defined   Gov §27390
    Eligibility to serve as   Gov §27395
    Use to audit system   Gov §27394
Contracts
    Authorized submitters
        Contracting to be authorized submitter   Gov §27397.5
    Computer security auditors
        Use to audit system   Gov §27394
    County recorder authority as to   Gov §27391
County recorders
    Authority to establish system   Gov §27391
Definitions   Gov §27390
Digital electronic records
    Defined   Gov §27390
Digitized electronic records
    Defined   Gov §27390
Evaluation of system   Gov §27398
Monitoring system   Gov §27396
Regulation and oversight costs
    County responsibility for attorney general regulation and oversight   Gov §27397
Rulemaking to implement provisions   Gov §27393
Security testing
    Defined   Gov §27390
Source code
    Defined   Gov §27390
Statutory construction   Gov §27399
System certification
    Defined   Gov §27390
    Required   Gov §27392
Voidable transactions
    Action for relief   Gov §27396

ELECTRONIC RECORDINGS
Administrative adjudication proceedings conducted by electronic means (See **ADMINISTRATIVE ADJUDICATION**)
Court reporters (See **COURT REPORTERS**)
Discovery
    Inspection demands for electronically stored information   CCP §§2031.010, 2031.030
        Compelling discovery despite burden of providing   CCP §2031.310
        Inaccessibility claimed   CCP §§2031.060, 2031.210
        Objections   CCP §2031.240
        Privilege claimed or attorney work product protection requested   CCP §2031.285
        Response, form of information furnished   CCP §2031.280
        Sanctions for failure to provide, circumstances avoiding   CCP §§2031.300, 2031.320
    Subpoenas of electronically stored information   CCP §1985.8
Radio and television coverage of trials (See **RADIO AND TELEVISION**)
Sound, recording of (See **RECORDING OF SOUND**)
Transcripts   CRC 2.952
    Court reporters generally (See **COURT REPORTERS**)
    Delivery of transcript in electronic form   CCP §271
Trial court rules
    Official status of electronic recordings   CRC 2.952
Video recordings (See **VIDEO RECORDINGS**)

ELECTRONIC SERVICE OF PROCESS
Appellate rules, supreme court and courts of appeal
    E-filing in supreme court and courts of appeal   CRC 8.78
        Order for electronic service   CRC 8.79
Generally   CCP §1010.6, CRC 2.250 to 2.261 (See **ELECTRONIC FILING AND SERVICE**)
Groundwater rights actions
    Parties
        Disclosures of parties appearing   CCP §842
    Pleadings and papers   CCP §839

ELECTRONIC SIGNATURES
Child support
    Government support enforcement services
        Electronic filing of pleadings signed by agent of local child support agency   Fam §17400
Defined   CCP §17
Effectiveness   CCP §34
Electronic filing and service rules   CRC 2.257
Fiduciary access to digital assets
    Electronic signatures in global and national commerce act
        Relationship between provisions and act   Pro §882
Fiduciary income and principal act
    Electronic signatures in global and national commerce act
        Effect of provisions on act   Pro §16381
Partition
    Real property partition
        Electronic signature in global and national commerce act, effect of provisions   CCP §874.323

ELECTRONIC TRANSACTIONS
Acknowledgment of receipt by information processing system, effect of   CC §1633.15
Admissibility of evidence of electronic records and signatures   CC §1633.13
Application of Act   CC §§1633.3 to 1633.5
Attribution of electronic signature or record to particular person   CC §1633.9
Cancellation rights, satisfaction of requirements under other law for notification of   CC §1633.16
Change or error in electronic record, effect of   CC §1633.10
Citation of Act   CC §1633.1
Conservators
    Interstate jurisdiction, transfer and recognition
        Electronic Signatures in Global and National Commerce Act, relation between acts   Pro §2022
Definitions   CC §1633.2
Discovery
    Inspection demands for electronically stored information   CCP §§2031.010, 2031.030
        Compelling discovery despite burden of providing   CCP §2031.310
        Inaccessibility claimed   CCP §§2031.060, 2031.210
        Objections   CCP §2031.240
        Privilege claimed or attorney work product protection requested   CCP §2031.285
        Response, form of information furnished   CCP §2031.280
        Sanctions for failure to provide, circumstances avoiding   CCP §§2031.300, 2031.320
    Subpoena of electronically stored information   CCP §1985.8
Enforceability of electronic record or signature   CC §1633.7
Error or change in electronic record, effect of   CC §1633.10
Formation of contracts by electronic means   CC §§1633, 1633.14
Formatting and transmission requirements under other law, satisfaction of   CC §1633.8
Government agency not party to transaction, prohibition against regulation of electronic signature by   CC §1633.17
Health care directives or powers of attorney   Pro §4673
Institutional funds management
    Electronic signatures in global and national commerce act
        Effect of provisions on federal act   Pro §18509
Notarization of electronic signature   CC §1633.11
Notice of right to cancel, satisfaction of requirements under other law for   CC §1633.16
Place of sending and receiving electronic records   CC §1633.15
Retention of records, satisfaction of requirements under other law for   CC §1633.12
Securities broker-dealer, contract formation by electronic submission of application to   CC §1633
Service of process
    Levying officer electronic transactions act   CCP §§263 to 263.7
Subpoena of electronically stored information   CCP §1985.8
Time of sending and receiving electronic records   CC §1633.15
Writing requirements under other law, satisfaction of   CC §§1633.7, 1633.8

ELEEMOSYNARY ORGANIZATIONS (See CHARITABLE ORGANIZATIONS)

ELEMENTARY SCHOOLS (See SCHOOLS)

ELEVATORS
Apartment building owner, posting notice of   CC §1962.5
Landlord terminating service   CC §789.3

ELIGIBILITY (See QUALIFICATIONS)

ELISOR
Compensation for execution of process   CCP §262.10
Execution of process by   CCP §§262.8 to 262.10

EMAIL
Administrative procedure act
    Proposed agency action, public comments by fax or email on   Gov §11340.8
Appeals courts
    Certiorari, mandate and prohibition
        Notice by email   CRC 8.489
Attorneys
    Online reporting of information for inclusion in roll of attorneys   CRC 9.9
Change of address
    Appeals
        Service and filing notice of change   CRC 8.32
    Appellate rules, superior court appeals
        Notice of change   CRC 8.816
    Service and filing of notice of   CRC 2.200
Common interest developments
    Board meetings
        Restriction on use of electronic transmissions to conduct meetings   CC §4910
    Preferred method for receiving notice from association
        Notice to association   CC §4041
Discovery
    Inspection demands for electronically stored information   CCP §§2031.010, 2031.030
        Compelling discovery despite burden of providing   CCP §2031.310
        Inaccessibility claimed   CCP §§2031.060, 2031.210
        Objections   CCP §2031.240
        Privilege claimed or attorney work product protection requested   CCP §2031.285
        Response, form of information furnished   CCP §2031.280
        Sanctions for failure to provide, circumstances avoiding   CCP §§2031.300, 2031.320
Groundwater rights actions
    Notice of complaint   CCP §835
Health studio contracts
    Cancellation by email   CC §§1812.84, 1812.85
    Copy of contract, health studio customer receiving   CC §1812.82
Judicial council advisory body meetings
    Action by email between meetings   CRC 10.75
Judicial ethics code
    Public confidence in judiciary
        Electronic communications, care in using   CRCSupp JudEthicsCanon 2
Judicial ethics opinions
    Committee contact information   CRC 9.80
Obscene and harmful matter
    Electronic messages depicting obscene material
        Knowingly sending unsolicited messages   CC §1708.88
Rental passenger vehicle transactions
    Electronic communications between company and renter
        Agreement by renter in rental or lease agreement   CC §1939.22
Stalking conduct
    COVID-19, emergency rule   CRCAppx I Emer Rule 8
Trial court rules, email address
    Papers, first page format and content   CRC 2.118
        Acceptance of noncomplying papers for filing   CRC 2.118

EMANCIPATION OF MINORS
Generally   Fam §§7000 to 7002
Adult, emancipated minor considered as   Fam §7050
Capacity of emancipated minor   Fam §7050
Citation of law   Fam §7000
Declaration of emancipation
    Identification cards   Fam §§7140 to 7143
    Issuance of   Fam §7122
    Legislative intent   Fam §7110
    Mandamus   Fam §7123
    Notice   CRC 3.1370, 5.605, Fam §7121
    Petition for   CRC 3.1370, 5.605, Fam §7120
        Memorandum in support of petition not required   CRC 3.1114
    Rescission of declaration, petition for   Fam §§7130, 7132 to 7135
    Voiding declaration, petition for   Fam §§7130, 7131, 7133 to 7135
    Welfare benefits, effect on   Fam §7111
Earnings assignment for support   Fam §5240
Earnings of emancipated minor   Fam §7050
Effect of emancipation   Fam §7050

EMANCIPATION OF MINORS—Cont.
Forms
    Judicial council legal forms   CRCAppx A
Fraud, declaration obtained by   Fam §7130
Identification cards   Fam §§7140 to 7143
Indigent minors   Fam §7130
Insurance contracts   Fam §7051
Intent of law   Fam §7001
Mandamus   Fam §7123
Nonprofit corporation membership   Fam §7052
Notice
    Declaration of emancipation, hearing on   CRC 3.1370, 5.605, Fam §7121
    Department of Motor Vehicles, notice of rescinded or voided declaration   Fam §7143
    Voiding or rescinding declaration   Fam §7133
Petition   CRC 3.1370, 5.605
    Declaration of emancipation, petition for   CRC 3.1370, 5.605, Fam §7120
        Memorandum in support of petition not required   CRC 3.1114
    For declaration   CRC 3.1370, 5.605
    To rescind declaration
        Court order rescinding declaration   Fam §7134
    To void declaration
        Court order voiding declaration   Fam §7134
    Voiding or rescinding declaration   Fam §§7130 to 7135
Purpose of law   Fam §7001
Rescission of declaration   Fam §§7130, 7132 to 7135
Stock held by emancipated minor   Fam §7052
Support of emancipated minor   Fam §7050
Torts of emancipated minor, liability for   Fam §7050
Welfare benefits, effect of declaration on   Fam §7111
Wills, capacity to make   Fam §7050

EMBARRASSMENT
Court orders to prevent   CCP §379.5

EMBEZZLEMENT (See also **THEFT**)
Accrual of cause of action   CCP §338
Decedents' estates, embezzled property from   Pro §§8870 to 8873
Discount buying organization officer   CC §1812.106
Public employees (See **PUBLIC OFFICERS AND EMPLOYEES**)

EMBLEMENTS
Severable   CC §660

EMBRYO DONATION
Assisted reproduction
    Effect of donation on parent-child relationship   Fam §7613
    Renunciation of legal interest in embryos
        Agreement between non-married persons sharing legal control over disposition   Fam §7613

EMERGENCIES (See also **NATURAL CATASTROPHES**)
Administrative adjudicative proceedings under emergency decision procedure   Gov §§11460.10 to 11460.80
Anaphylaxis
    Epinephrine auto-injector administration for first aid
        Immunity from civil liability of lay rescuers, prehospital emergency medical care providers or authorized entities   CC §1714.23
Appellate courts
    E-filing in supreme court and courts of appeal
        Documents subject to e-filing in Supreme Court, modifications in light of emergencies   CRCSupp SuprCtE-file 2
    Special time rule   CRC 8.66
Appellate courts, special time rule   CRC 8.66
Automated external defibrillators
    Immunity from liability for emergency care   CC §1714.21
Cardiopulmonary resuscitation, immunity from liability for emergency care through   CC §§1714.2, 1714.21
Common interest developments
    Board meetings
        Emergencies or disasters, meetings entirely by teleconference   CC §5450
    Governing documents
        Actions by association to enforce, effect of emergency declaration   CC §5875
COVID-19
    Emergency rules related to COVID-19   CRCAppx I Emer Rules 1 to 13
Defibrillator, immunity from liability for emergency care using   CC §1714.21
Deposit of goods during time of   CC §1815
Disclosure of medical information during   CC §56.10
Domestic violence, emergency protective orders (See **DOMESTIC VIOLENCE**)

EMERGENCIES—Cont.
Drones   Gov §§853 to 853.5
Eminent domain for emergency projects   CCP §1245.230
Epinephrine auto-injectors
    Administration for first aid
        Immunity from civil liability of lay rescuers, prehospital emergency medical care providers or authorized entities   CC §1714.23
Family rules
    Request for emergency or ex parte orders   CRC 5.92, 5.151 to 5.170
Hazardous material emergency response
    Public health and safety labor or service providers
        Logo or identifying mark of public agency, display   CC §3273
Home solicitation contract provisions, emergency services excepted from   CC §1689.13
Hospital lien for emergency treatment   CC §§3045.1 to 3045.6
Human trafficking or slavery
    Signs, businesses required to post notice concerning relief from slavery or human trafficking   CC §52.6
Immunity from liability
    Drones or unmanned aircraft systems damaged by emergency responder
        Provision of emergency services by responder and interference with services by drone   CC §43.101
Injured emergency personnel, liability to   CC §1714.9
Juvenile court proceedings
    Adoption of child
        Prospective adoptive parents, emergency removal from   CRC 5.728
Landlord and tenant
    Entry by landlord because of emergency   CC §1954
    Lease provision penalizing good faith summoning of law enforcement or emergency assistance   CC §1946.8
Landlord entering because of   CC §1954
Psychotropic medications, administering to minors   CRC 5.640
    Forms, judicial council   CRCAppx A
    Prescriptions
        Release of psychotropic medication prescription information to medical board, authorization   CRC 5.642
Public health and safety labor or service providers
    Logo or identifying mark of public agency, display   CC §3273
Public health emergencies
    Emergency rules related to COVID-19   CRCAppx I Emer Rules 1 to 13
Resuscitative measures, requests regarding   Pro §§4780 to 4786
    Health care providers   Pro §4781
Slavery
    Signs, businesses required to post notice concerning relief from slavery or human trafficking   CC §52.6
Statutory violations in complying with governor's orders under   CC §1714.6
Supreme court e-filing rules
    Emergency situations, modifications to rules governing documents subject to electronic filing   CRCSupp SuprCtE-file 2
Traffic control signal controlled by emergency vehicle, public entity liability for operation of   Gov §830.9
Trauma kit, rendering emergency aid using
    Good Samaritan law, applicability   CC §1714.29

EMERGENCY MEDICAL CARE
Immunity from liability
    Trauma kit, rendering emergency aid using
        Good Samaritan law, applicability   CC §1714.29
Prehospital emergency medical care personnel
    Discovery, review committee records exempt from   Ev §1157
Trauma kit, rendering emergency aid using
    Good Samaritan law, applicability   CC §1714.29

EMERGENCY PROTECTIVE ORDERS (See **PROTECTIVE ORDERS**)

EMERGENCY ROOMS
Human trafficking or slavery
    Signs, businesses required to post notice concerning relief from slavery or human trafficking   CC §52.6

EMINENT DOMAIN
Generally   CCP §§1230.020 to 1230.060, Ev §§810 to 822
Abandonment of proceedings   CCP §1268.510
Acquisition (See within this heading, **"Taking"**)
Agreement specifying manner of payment of compensation   CCP §1263.015
Alternative dispute resolution, postponement of eminent domain proceedings for   CCP §1250.430
Apportionment of taxes (See within this heading, **"Taxes"**)
Appraisals
    Fee payment for   CCP §1235.140

EMINENT DOMAIN—Cont.
  Appraisals—Cont.
    Offer to purchase under threat of eminent domain
      Independent appraisal following offer   CCP §1263.025
    Valuation data, appraisal report used for   CCP §1258.260
  Arbitration
    Compensation for taking, arbitration of controversies as to   CCP §§1273.010 to 1273.050
    Referral of eminent domain proceedings to arbitrator   CCP §1250.420
  Award (See within this heading, **"Compensation"**)
  Benefits derived   Ev §812
  Citation of statutes   CCP §1230.010
  Comparable property as basis for opinion evidence   Ev §816
  Compensation
    Generally   CCP §§1263.010, 1263.020
    Agreement specifying manner of payment of   CCP §1263.015
    Appraisal following offer to purchase under threat of eminent domain   CCP §1263.025
    Arbitration of controversies as to compensation for taking   CCP §§1273.010 to 1273.050
    Crops   CCP §1263.250
    Date of valuation   CCP §§1263.110 to 1263.150
    Deposit in court
      After entry of judgment   CCP §§1268.110 to 1268.170
      Before entry of judgment   CCP §§1255.010 to 1255.080
    Evidence affecting   CCP §1260.210
    Fair market value   CCP §§1263.310 to 1263.330
    Final judgments, payment of   CCP §§1268.010 to 1268.030
    Final offer and demand for   CCP §1250.410
    Future interests   CCP §§1265.410, 1265.420
    Goodwill for business, compensation of   CCP §§1263.510 to 1263.530
      Leaseback agreements   CCP §§1263.510, 1263.615
    Interest on money judgment   CCP §§1263.015, 1268.310 to 1268.360
    Leaseback agreements, when required   CCP §1263.615
    Liens, impairment of security for   CCP §§1265.210 to 1265.240
    Measure of   CCP §§1263.310 to 1263.330
    Other interests, compensation for   CCP §1265.010
    Possession after judgment   CCP §§1268.210 to 1268.240
    Probable amount of compensation, deposit of   CCP §§1255.010 to 1255.080
    Remainder property
      Incomplete improvement or partial installation of machinery, compensation   CCP §1263.620
      Injury to remainder, compensation   CCP §§1263.410 to 1263.450
    Separation of assessments   CCP §§1260.220, 1260.230
    Severance, damages for   CCP §1240.150
    Valuation data, exchange of   CCP §§1258.210 to 1258.300
    Withdrawal of deposit for   CCP §§1255.210 to 1255.280, 1268.110 to 1268.170
  Complaints in proceedings for   CCP §1250.110
  Conservation easements
    Property subject to conservation easement, acquisition by eminent domain   CCP §1240.055
  Corporate officers giving evidence on value   Ev §813
  Costs
    Definition of   CCP §1235.140
    Inverse condemnation proceedings   CCP §1036
    Litigation expenses, payment of   CCP §§1250.410, 1268.610, 1268.620
    Payment of   CCP §§1268.710, 1268.720
  Crops, compensation for   CCP §1263.250
  Cross complaints in proceedings for   CCP §426.70
  Damages (See within this heading, **"Compensation"**)
  Date of valuation   CCP §§1263.110 to 1263.150
  Default judgments in proceedings for   CCP §1250.125
  Defendants in action for   CCP §§1250.220 to 1250.240
  Definitions   CCP §§1235.110 to 1235.210
  Demurrers   CCP §§1250.350 to 1250.370
  Deposit in court
    After entry of judgment   CCP §§1268.110 to 1268.170
    Before entry of judgment   CCP §§1255.010 to 1255.080
  Discovery
    Generally   CCP §§1258.010 to 1258.030
    Expert testimony (See within this heading, **"Expert testimony"**)
    Time for completion of discovery   CCP §2024.040
  Dismissal
    Mandamus petition   CCP §1245.255
    Taxes unpaid, effect on   CCP §1268.420
  Easements (See **EASEMENTS**)
  Electric utility property
    Public utilities generally (See within this heading, **"Public utilities"**)
  Emergency projects   CCP §1245.230

EMINENT DOMAIN—Cont.
  Evidence   CCP §1260.210, Ev §§810 to 822
  Excess condemnation   CCP §§1240.410 to 1240.430
  Exchange of property   CCP §§1240.310 to 1240.350
  Existing use, new taking affecting   CCP §§1240.510 to 1240.530
  Expert testimony
    Deposit in court, expert appraisal of compensation for   CCP §1255.010
    Knowledge of witness as basis for opinion testimony on value of property   Ev §813
    List of expert witnesses (See within this heading, **"List of expert witnesses"**)
    Price of property taken, opinion evidence based on   Ev §§814 to 816, 822
    Rental value of property as basis for opinion evidence on value   Ev §§817 to 819, 822
    Simultaneous information exchange about expert witnesses, discovery by means of   CCP §2034.010
    Statement of valuation data (See within this heading, **"Statement of valuation data"**)
  Fair market value   CCP §§1263.310 to 1263.330
  Final judgments   CCP §§1235.120, 1268.010 to 1268.030
  Form for exchange of valuation data   CCP §1258.210
  Franchise
    Taking for toll bridge   CCP §1240.110
    Toll Bridge Authority, takings by   CCP §1245.210
  Gas utility property
    Public utilities generally (See within this heading, **"Public utilities"**)
  Goodwill, value of   CCP §§1263.510 to 1263.530
    Leaseback agreements
      Effect on goodwill   CCP §1263.510
      When required   CCP §1263.615
  Hazardous substances on property acquired by school districts (See **SCHOOL DISTRICTS**)
  Hearings
    Generally   CCP §1245.235
    Conservation easements
      Property subject to conservation easement, acquisition by eminent domain   CCP §1240.055
    Quasi-public entity, actions by   CCP §1245.350
    Superior court proceedings   CCP §1250.010
  Heirs as parties to action   CCP §1260.240
  Highways (See **STREETS AND HIGHWAYS**)
  Improvements
    Compensation for   CCP §§1263.205 to 1263.270
    Crops, compensation for   CCP §1263.250
    Disputes on improvements as realty   CCP §1260.030
    Hardships, compensation for   CCP §1263.240
    Machinery, compensation for   CCP §§1263.205, 1263.620
    Private owners exercising power for   CC §1002, CCP §1245.326
    Public utilities compensated for   CCP §1263.240
    Value of   Ev §§816, 820, 821
  Injury to remainder, compensation for   CCP §§1263.410 to 1263.450
  Interest on money judgment   CCP §§1263.015, 1268.310 to 1268.360
  Intervention in action for   CCP §1250.230
  Inverse condemnation proceedings
    Costs, award of   CCP §1036
    Interest on award, computation of   CCP §1268.311
    Public entities, presentation of claims against   Gov §905.1
  Joinder of parties in action for   CCP §1250.240
  Judge's power to act, effect of proceedings for disqualification on   CCP §170.4
  Jurisdiction   CCP §1250.010
  Jury
    Fees   CCP §631.5
    Voir dire   CRC JudAdminStand 3.25
  Just compensation, determination of   Ev §§811, 812
  Later use
    Second use (See within this heading, **"Second use"**)
  Leaseback agreements, when required   CCP §1263.615
  Leases
    Alternatives to eminent domain   CCP §1240.120
    Compensation for loss of   CCP §§1265.110 to 1265.160
    Deposit of probable amount of compensation for   CCP §1255.050
    Rental value of lease, consideration of   Ev §§817 to 819, 822
    Termination of lease   CCP §1265.110
  Liens
    Allocation among junior and senior lienholders   CCP §1265.230
    Deduction of indebtedness from judgment   CCP §1265.220
    Defined   CCP §1265.210
    Prepayment payment, effect of   CCP §1265.240
    Tax lien, effect of   CCP §§1250.250, 1265.250
  Limitations on exercise of power   CCP §§1240.010 to 1240.055

EMINENT DOMAIN—Cont.
Lis pendens
    Place for recording notice of pendency of eminent domain proceeding   CCP §§405.6, 1250.150
    Valuation of leased property
        Effect of filing of lis pendens   Ev §817
List of expert witnesses
    Contents of   CCP §1258.240
    Date of exchange   CCP §1258.220
    Demand to exchange list   CCP §§1258.210, 1258.230
    Incomplete list, effect of   CCP §§1258.280, 1258.290
    Notice of changes   CCP §1258.270
    Simultaneous information exchange about expert witnesses, discovery by means of
        Applicability of provisions   CCP §2034.010
Mandamus action for review of resolution   CCP §1245.255
Mediator, referral of eminent domain disputes to   CCP §1250.420
Mobilehome park, termination of tenancy in   CC §798.56
New use (See within this heading, **"Second use"**)
Nonprofit, special use property
    Defined   CCP §1235.155
    Determining valuation without comparable market   CCP §1263.321
    Presumption of best and most necessary public use   CCP §1240.670
Notices
    Conservation easements
        Property subject to conservation easement, acquisition by eminent domain   CCP §1240.055
    Deposit in court, notice of   CCP §§1255.020, 1268.120
    Hearings generally (See within this heading, **"Hearings"**)
    Pendency of eminent domain proceeding
        Place for recording notice of pendency of eminent domain proceeding   CCP §§405.6, 1250.150
        Valuation of leased property, effect of filing of lis pendens   Ev §817
    Process   CCP §§1250.120 to 1250.150
        Complaint on failure to serve process within 6 months   CCP §1245.260
Opinion testimony of value
    Statement of valuation data (See within this heading, **"Statement of valuation data"**)
Owner of property testifying as to value   Ev §813
Pacific Gas and Electric Company
    Action by Golden State Energy for acquisition of PG&E property   CCP §1240.655
Parks
    Declaratory relief action   CCP §1240.700
    Highest and best use of land presumed   CCP §1240.680
Partial taking
    Generally   CCP §1240.410
    Compensation for   CCP §§1263.410 to 1263.450
    Leases   CCP §§1265.110 to 1265.160
    Valuation data in   CCP §1258.250
Parties to   CCP §§1250.210 to 1250.240
Partners giving evidence for valuation   Ev §813
Payments
    Compensation generally (See within this heading, **"Compensation"**)
Pendency of proceeding
    Place for recording notice of pendency of eminent proceeding   CCP §§405.6, 1250.150
    Valuation of leased property, effect of filing lis pendens on   Ev §817
Personal property, valuation of   Ev §811
Plaintiff in action for   CCP §§1250.210 to 1250.240
Pleadings
    Generally   CCP §§1250.310 to 1250.345
    Amendments in   CCP §1250.340
    Answer   CCP §1250.320
    Complaints   CCP §1250.110
Possession, orders for   CCP §§1255.410 to 1255.480
Preliminary studies for   CCP §§1245.010 to 1245.060
Presumptions
    Best and more necessary public use   CCP §§1240.640 to 1240.680
    Local public entity use presumed as more necessary than other or similar public use   CCP §1240.660
    Nonprofit organizations, best and most necessary public use by   CCP §1240.670
    Public entity use presumed as more necessary than other or similar public use   CCP §1240.650
    Resolution of necessity, effect of local governing board adopting   CCP §1245.250
    State use presumed as more necessary than other or similar public use   CCP §1240.640
    Types of best and most necessary public use   CCP §1240.680

EMINENT DOMAIN—Cont.
Priority of proceedings for   CCP §1260.010
Private owners exercising power of   CC §1002, CCP §1245.326
Process
    Generally   CCP §§1250.120 to 1250.150
    Complaint on failure to serve process within six months   CCP §1245.260
Proposed construction as basis for opinion testimony in value of property   Ev §813
Public agencies, definition of   CCP §1240.140
Publication, process served by   CCP §1250.125
Public entities
    Defined   CCP §1235.195
    Inverse condemnation proceedings   CCP §1245.260
    Quasi-public entities (See within this heading, **"Quasi-public entities"**)
    Resolution of necessity
        Additional property, taking of   CCP §1250.340
        Bribes involving adoption, effect of   CCP §1245.270
        Contents of   CCP §1245.230
        Emergency projects   CCP §1245.230
        Failure to use acquired property in conformity with resolution   CCP §1245.245
        "Governing body" defined for purposes of   CCP §1245.210
        Judicial review of   CCP §1245.255
        New use for property subject to resolution, when new resolution required   CCP §1245.245
        Notice and hearing   CCP §1245.235
        Prerequisite to exercising power of eminent domain   CCP §§1240.040, 1245.220
        Presumptions created after adoption of   CCP §1245.250
        Rescission of   CCP §1245.260
        Two-thirds vote requirement   CCP §1245.240
Public utilities
    Electric, gas, or water public utility property
        Defined   CCP §1235.193
        Rebuttable presumption of more necessary public use   CCP §§1240.650, 1245.250
    Improvements made by public utilities, compensation for   CCP §1263.240
    Private owner acquiring appurtenant easement for   CC §1001, CCP §1245.325
    Taking for   CCP §§1240.110, 1240.125
Quasi-public entities
    Compliance with other requirements imposed by law   CCP §1245.380
    Definitions   CCP §§1245.310, 1245.320
    Easement for utility services, private landowner's power of eminent domain to acquire   CCP §1245.325
    Resolution for consent to acquisition
        Contents of   CCP §1245.340
        Costs incurred, quasi-public entity's liability for   CCP §1245.370
        Damages, effect on liability of city or county for   CCP §1245.390
        Notice and hearing on   CCP §1245.350
        Prerequisite to exercising power of eminent domain   CCP §1245.330
        Two-thirds vote requirement   CCP §1245.360
    Temporary right of entry to repair, private landowner's power of eminent domain to acquire   CCP §1245.326
Real estate contract arbitration clause, effect of   CCP §1298.5
Recordation
    Definition of record owner   CCP §1255.450
    Place of recording for commencement of proceedings   CCP §1250.150
    Valuation data, recordation of   CCP §1258.260
Record owner defined   CCP §1255.450
Recreation areas
    Parks
        Declaratory relief action   CCP §1240.410
        Highest and best use of land presumed   CCP §1240.680
Relocation of business   CCP §1263.610
Remainder property
    Incomplete improvement or partial installation of machinery, compensation for   CCP §1263.620
    Injury to remainder, compensation for   CCP §§1263.410 to 1263.450
Rental value, consideration of   Ev §§817 to 819, 822
Repair or reconstruction
    Improvements generally (See within this heading, **"Improvements"**)
Resolutions
    Generally   CCP §§1245.220 to 1245.270
    Defined   CCP §1235.195
    Public entities, resolution of necessity by (See within this heading, **"Public entities"**)
    Quasi-public entities, resolution for consent to acquisition by (See within this heading, **"Quasi-public entities"**)
Retroactive laws   CCP §§1230.065, 1230.070

EMINENT DOMAIN—Cont.
Right of entry
    Conditions   CCP §1245.326
    Consent to and order for entry   CCP §1245.020
    Damage to or interference with possession and use of property   CCP §1245.060
Right to take, limitations on   CCP §§1240.010 to 1240.055
School districts, hazardous substances on property acquired by (See **SCHOOL DISTRICTS**)
Second use
    Greater use   CCP §§1240.610 to 1240.700
    More necessary use   CCP §§1240.610 to 1240.700
    Similar use, taking for   CCP §§1240.510 to 1240.530, 1260.020
Separate valuation, application for   CCP §1268.450
Service of process   CCP §§1250.120 to 1250.150
    Complaint on failure to serve within 6 months   CCP §1245.260
Settlement offers   CCP §1250.410
Size of property as basis for opinion testimony as to value   Ev §816
Statement of valuation data
    Generally   CCP §1258.250
    Changes, notice of   CCP §1258.270
    Contents of   CCP §1258.260
    Inadmissibility as evidence   CCP §§1258.280, 1258.290, Ev §822
    Procedures adopted by superior courts   CCP §1258.300
Statutory construction   CCP §§1235.010 to 1235.070
Streets (See **STREETS AND HIGHWAYS**)
Substitute condemnation   CCP §§1240.310 to 1240.350
Suitability of property as basis for opinion testimony as to value   Ev §816
Summons, service of   CCP §§1250.120 to 1250.150
    Complaint on failure to serve process within 6 months   CCP §1245.260
Taking
    Generally   CCP §§1240.110 to 1240.160
    Airports, taking for   CCP §§1240.110, 1240.125
    Demurrer stating objections to   CCP §1250.350
    Entry on premises for preliminary work   CCP §§1245.010 to 1245.060
    Existing use, taking for   CCP §§1240.510 to 1240.530, 1260.020
    Future use, taking for   CCP §§1240.210 to 1240.250
    Improvements (See within this heading, "**Improvements**")
    Notice of   CCP §1245.235
    Objections to right to take   CCP §§1250.350 to 1250.370, 1260.110, 1260.120
    Partial taking (See within this heading, "**Partial taking**")
    Public use   CCP §§1240.010 to 1240.055
    Resolutions   CCP §§1245.220 to 1245.270
        Defined   CCP §1235.195
        Public entities (See within this heading, "**Public entities**")
        Quasi-public entities (See within this heading, "**Quasi-public entities**")
    Second use (See within this heading, "**Second use**")
    Sewers, taking for   CCP §1240.125
    Transportation purposes   CCP §1245.210
    Valuation data   CCP §1258.250
    Water supply, taking for facilities for   CCP §§1240.110, 1240.125
Taxes
    Basis for value, assessments establishing   Ev §822
    Certification requirements   CCP §1260.250
    Defendant, joinder of lienholder as   CCP §1250.250
    Erroneous collection of taxes   CCP §1268.440
    Exempt property   CCP §§1268.420, 1268.440
    Proration of   CCP §§1268.410 to 1268.430
    Separate valuation, application for   CCP §1268.450
    Special assessment liens, payment of holders of   CCP §1265.250
Time, complaint for failure to serve process within stated   CCP §1245.260
Unknown persons as parties to action   CCP §1260.240
Utility service, real property owner acquiring easement for   CC §1001
Value of property
    Expert testimony generally (See within this heading, "**Expert testimony**")
    Fair market value   CCP §§1263.310 to 1263.330
    Nonprofit, special use property without comparable market, valuation of   CCP §1263.321
    No relevant, comparable market value for nonprofit or special use property, method for determining value of property where   Ev §824
    Statement of valuation data (See within this heading, "**Statement of valuation data**")
Venue of action for   CCP §§1250.020 to 1250.040
Verification in action for   CCP §1250.330
View of property as basis for opinion testimony on value   Ev §813
Water public utility property (See within this heading, "**Public utilities**")
oning, valuation data affected by   CCP §1258.260

EMOTIONAL DISTRESS
Child's emotional distress as grounds for court intervention   CRC 5.678
Genetic characteristics, disclosure of test results for   CC §56.17
Intentional infliction of emotional distress, public entity's liability for   Gov §815.3
Obscene and harmful matter
    Electronic messages depicting obscene material
        Knowingly sending unsolicited messages, damages for emotional distress   CC §1708.88
Public property, liability for emotional distress resulting from land failure of   Gov §831.25

EMOTIONAL STATE
Hearsay testimony showing   Ev §§1250 to 1252

EMPLOYEE BENEFIT PLANS
Community property interest (See **COMMUNITY PROPERTY**)
Dissolution, division of benefits or rights
    Tribal court orders, payments pursuant to   Fam §2611
Dissolution of marriage (See **DISSOLUTION OF MARRIAGE**)

EMPLOYEE HOUSING
Immigration status
    Enforcement of law not dependent on immigration status   CC §3339

EMPLOYEE RETIREMENT INCOME SECURITY ACT (See **ERISA**)

EMPLOYER AND EMPLOYEE
Agricultural Labor Relations Board cases, appellate review   CRC 8.728
Alien status
    Enforcement of employment law not dependent on immigration status   CC §3339
Applicant for employment, privileged communications concerning job performance of   CC §47
Arbitration
    Drafting party breach of arbitration agreement
        Consequences   CCP §1281.98
        Monetary sanctions against breaching party   CCP §1281.99
        Nonpayment of fees   CCP §1281.97
    Fees and costs in employment proceedings
        Drafting party obligation   CCP §1281.97
Arrests
    Subsequent arrests, notification
        Attorneys, fingerprinting   CRC 9.9.5
Challenge of juror for implied bias, relationships giving rise to   CCP §229
Children (See **MINORS**)
Commercial online entertainment employment service providers
    Age information of subscribers, restriction on disclosure   CC §1798.83.5
Consumer privacy rights
    Communications or transactions, applicability of rights   CC §1798.145
    Personnel records, applicability of rights   CC §1798.145
Court employee labor relations   CRC 10.650 to 10.660
Court employees (See **COURT OFFICERS AND EMPLOYEES**)
Credit cards issued to employees, liability for unauthorized use where   CC §1747.20
Credit reports (See **CREDIT REPORTING**)
Debt collectors communicating with employer   CC §1788.12
Depositions
    Time limits for witness examination
        Exceptions for cases arising out of employment relationship   CCP §2025.290
Earnings assignment for support (See **EARNINGS ASSIGNMENT FOR SUPPORT**)
Employment agencies (See **EMPLOYMENT AGENCIES**)
Employment counseling services (See **EMPLOYMENT COUNSELING SERVICES**)
Entertainment industry
    Commercial online entertainment employment service providers
        Age information of subscribers, restriction on disclosure   CC §1798.83.5
Exemplary damages, employer's liability for   CC §3294
Garnishment (See **GARNISHMENT**)
Health insurance coverage assignment for supported child of employee   Fam §§3760 to 3773
Immigration status
    Enforcement of employment law not dependent on immigration status   CC §3339
Injunctive relief action by employer for threats of violence towards employees
    COVID-19, emergency rule   CRCAppx I Emer Rule 8
    Firearm relinquishment and disposition
        Forms for firearm relinquishment   CRCAppx A

EMPLOYER AND EMPLOYEE—Cont.
Injunctive relief action by employer for threats of violence towards employees—Cont.
    Requests for protective orders   CRC 3.1160
Injury to servant affecting ability to serve   CC §49
Inspection of personnel files
    Investigative consumer reporting agencies
        Law on employee access to files not changed by provisions   CC §1786.55
Inspection warrants for working place   CCP §§1822.50, 1822.56
Interpreters
    Cross-assignments for court interpreter employees   CRC 10.762
    Regional court interpreter employment relations   CRC 10.761
Investigative consumer reporting agencies (See **INVESTIGATIVE CONSUMER REPORTING AGENCIES**)
Job listing services (See **JOB LISTING SERVICES**)
Job performance of applicant for employment, privileged communications concerning   CC §47
Labor relations (See **LABOR AND LABOR UNIONS**)
Libel and slander action   CC §§47, 48
Medical information, disclosure of   CC §§56.20 to 56.24
Minors (See **MINORS**)
Personnel files
    Inspection by employees
        Investigative consumer reporting agencies law not to change law on employee access to files   CC §1786.55
Power of attorney affecting third person conducting activities through employees   Pro §4308
Privileged communications concerning job performance of applicant for employment   CC §47
Protection of employee   CC §50
Protection orders, action by employer for threats of violence towards employees   CCP §527.8
    Address or location of complaining party or family, prohibition on enjoined party from obtaining   CCP §527.10
    California law enforcement telecommunications (CLETS) information form, confidentiality and use of information   CRC 1.51, CRCAppx A
    Firearm relinquishment and disposition   CCP §527.9
    Judicial council legal forms   CRCAppx A
    Memorandum in support of petition for order not required   CRC 3.1114
Public Employment Relations Board cases, appellate review   CRC 8.728
Public officers and employees (See **PUBLIC OFFICERS AND EMPLOYEES**)
Punitive damages, employer's liability for   CC §3294
Referees, disqualification of   CCP §641
Retirement (See **RETIREMENT**)
Settlement of employment disputes
    Prohibited terms in agreements settling employment disputes   CCP §1002.5
Sex offenses
    Sexual battery by employer
        Statute of limitations on sexual assault damages   CCP §340.16
Sexual orientation violence
    Limitation of liability   CC §52.45
Small claims action, appearance of employee for plaintiff in   CCP §116.540
Subpoena duces tecum for employment records   CCP §1985.6
Temporary restraining order to prevent violence toward employee, employer's action for
    COVID-19, emergency rule   CRCAppx I Emer Rule 8
    Requests for protective orders   CRC 3.1160
Threat of violence toward employee, employer's action for protection orders   CCP §527.8
    Address or location of complaining party or family, prohibition on enjoined party from obtaining   CCP §527.10
    California law enforcement telecommunications (CLETS) information form, confidentiality and use of information   CRC 1.51, CRCAppx A
    COVID-19, emergency rule   CRCAppx I Emer Rule 8
    Firearm relinquishment and disposition   CCP §527.9
        Forms for firearm relinquishment   CRCAppx A
    Judicial council legal forms   CRCAppx A
    Memorandum in support of petition for order not required   CRC 3.1114
    Requests for protective orders   CRC 3.1160
Trade secrets (See **TRADE SECRETS**)
Unemployment compensation (See **UNEMPLOYMENT COMPENSATION**)
Violence toward employee, employer's action for protection orders   CCP §527.8, CRC 3.1160
    Address or location of complaining party or family, prohibition on enjoined party from obtaining   CCP §527.10
    California law enforcement telecommunications (CLETS) information form, confidentiality and use of information   CRC 1.51, CRCAppx A
    COVID-19, emergency rule   CRCAppx I Emer Rule 8

EMPLOYER AND EMPLOYEE—Cont.
Violence toward employee, employer's action for protection orders —Cont.
    Firearm relinquishment and disposition   CCP §527.9
        Forms for firearm relinquishment   CRCAppx A
    Judicial council legal forms   CRCAppx A
    Memorandum in support of petition for order not required   CRC 3.1114
    Requests for protective orders   CRC 3.1160
Workers' compensation (See **WORKERS' COMPENSATION**)
Workplace violence, employer's action to prevent   CCP §527.8, CRC 3.1160
    Address or location of complaining party or family, prohibition on enjoined party from obtaining   CCP §527.10
    California law enforcement telecommunications (CLETS) information form, confidentiality and use of information   CRC 1.51, CRCAppx A
    COVID-19, emergency rule   CRCAppx I Emer Rule 8
    Firearm relinquishment and disposition   CCP §527.9
        Forms for firearm relinquishment   CRCAppx A
    Judicial council legal forms   CRCAppx A
    Memorandum in support of petition for order not required   CRC 3.1114
    Requests for protective orders   CRC 3.1160

EMPLOYMENT AGENCIES (See also **EMPLOYMENT COUNSELING SERVICES; JOB LISTING SERVICES**)
Advertising by   CC §1812.508
Bonding requirements   CC §1812.503
Child care (See **CHILD CARE**)
Defined   CC §1812.501
Domestic work
    Agency not considered employer of domestic worker, conditions under which   CC §1812.5095
    Work experience of jobseeker for to be verified by agency   CC §1812.509
Exempt activities   CC §1812.502
Fees
    Refund of fees to jobseeker   CC §§1812.504, 1812.506, 1812.523
    Schedule of employment agency fees   CC §1812.505
Fraud and misrepresentation, liability for   CC §§1812.508, 1812.523
Job orders   CC §1812.507
Minors, job placement for   CC §1812.509
Nursing services
    Long-term health care facilities
        Employment agencies, referrals from (See **NURSING HOMES**)
    Registries (See **NURSES**)
Recordkeeping requirements   CC §1812.522
Refund of employment agency fees to jobseeker   CC §§1812.504, 1812.506, 1812.523
Remedies available   CC §1812.523
Service agreements with jobseeker, requirements of   CC §1812.504
Union contract or labor troubles at jobsite, notification of jobseeker of   CC §1812.509

EMPLOYMENT COUNSELING SERVICES (See also **EMPLOYMENT AGENCIES; JOB LISTING SERVICES**)
Advertising by   CC §1812.513
Bonding requirements of   CC §1812.510
Defined   CC §1812.501
Exempt activities   CC §1812.502
Fees
    Refund of fees to jobseeker   CC §1812.523
    Schedule of counseling service fees   CC §1812.512
Fraud and misrepresentation, liability for   CC §§1812.513, 1812.523
Recordkeeping requirements   CC §1812.522
Remedies available   CC §1812.523
Service agreements with customers, requirements of   CC §1812.511

EMPLOYMENT DEVELOPMENT DEPARTMENT
Access to information collected by   Fam §§17508, 17509

ENCLOSURES
Fences (See **FENCES**)

ENCUMBRANCES
Administration of decedents' estates (See **ADMINISTRATION OF ESTATES**)
Annulment of marriage, restrictions on encumbrance of property   Fam §2045
Attorney's fees in family law proceedings (See **ATTORNEY'S FEES**)
Auctioned items, disclosure of encumbrances on   CC §1812.607
Blanket encumbrance, required notice to purchaser or lessee of   CC §1133
Community property (See **COMMUNITY PROPERTY**)
Damages for breach of covenant against   CC §3305
Definition   CC §1114

ENCUMBRANCES—Cont.
Discriminatory clauses in written instruments encumbering real property, prohibition against   CC §§53, 782
Enforcement of judgments (See **ENFORCEMENT OF JUDGMENTS**)
Liens (See **LIENS**)
Mechanics' liens   CC §§8000 to 9566 (See **MECHANICS' LIENS**)
Mortgages (See **TRUST DEEDS AND MORTGAGES**)
Trust deeds (See **TRUST DEEDS AND MORTGAGES**)

âc;ENDLESS CHAIN" SCHEMES
Right to rescind by participant to   CC §1689.2

ENDORSEMENTS
Non-negotiable instruments transferred   CC §1459

ENDOWMENT FUNDS
Uniform prudent management of institutional funds act   Pro §§18501 to 18510 (See **INSTITUTIONAL FUNDS MANAGEMENT**)

ENDS OF JUSTICE
Amending pleadings   CCP §473
Change of venue, grounds for   CCP §397
Coordination of actions   CCP §§404.1, 404.2
Separate trial of issues   CCP §598

ENERGY
Electricity (See **ELECTRICITY AND ELECTRIC COMPANIES**)
Landlord and tenant
  Clotheslines
    Tenant use clothesline or drying rack in private areas   CC §1940.20
  Drying racks
    Tenant use clothesline or drying rack in private areas   CC §1940.20
Solar energy (See **SOLAR ENERGY**)
Waters (See **WATERS**)

ENFORCEMENT OF JUDGMENTS
Generally   CCP §681.010
Accounts receivable
  Attachment (See **ATTACHMENT**)
  Collected rather than sold, levied property to be   CCP §701.520
  Defined   CCP §680.130
  Duties of account debtor after levy   CCP §701.050
  General method of levy on   CCP §700.170
  Judgment lien on personal property   CCP §697.530
  Registered process server, levy by   CCP §699.080
Administration of estates (See **ADMINISTRATION OF ESTATES**)
Advertisement
  Posting or publication of sale of levied property   CCP §701.555
Affidavits
  Execution writ to enforce support orders   Fam §5104
  Identity, judgment creditor executing affidavit   CCP §§680.135, 699.545
  Proof of service   CCP §684.220
  Public entities, collection from   CCP §§708.730, 708.740, 708.770, 708.780
  Statutes of limitation, affidavit to enforce after expiration of time allowed by   CCP §683.040
Agreed case   CCP §1140
Agricultural liens
  Priorities   CCP §697.590
Alcoholic beverage license applied to satisfaction of judgment, receivers appointed where   CCP §708.630
Alimony as exempt property   CCP §704.111
Apartment housekeeper's lien, third party claims on property levied for   CC §1861.25
Appeals
  Attachment proceedings (See **ATTACHMENT**)
  Exemption claims, appeal from orders in actions involving   CCP §703.600
  Stay of enforcement generally (See within this heading, "**Stay of enforcement**")
  Third party claims   CCP §720.420
Appearance
  Attachment, appearance requirement for   CCP §491.140
  Examination proceedings (See within this heading, "**Examination proceedings**")
Assignments
  Acknowledgment of assignment of judgment   CC §954.5
  Benefit of creditor, assignment for (See **ASSIGNMENT FOR BENEFIT OF CREDITORS**)
  Enforcement by judgment assignee   CCP §681.020
  Pending action or proceedings, lien in
    Attachment (See **ATTACHMENT**)
    Generally (See within this heading, "**Pending action or proceedings**")

ENFORCEMENT OF JUDGMENTS—Cont.
Assignments—Cont.
  Priority of   CCP §708.530
  Right to payment
    Application for assignment to judgment creditor of   CCP §708.510
    Exemption claim   CCP §708.550
    Governing law   CCP §708.530
    Modifying or setting aside assignment of   CCP §708.560
    Obligor's right, effect on   CCP §708.540
    Priority of assignment   CCP §708.530
    Restraint on assignment of right, application for order for   CCP §708.520
  Unassignable property not subject to enforcement   CCP §695.030
Associations
  Examination proceedings, appearance at   CCP §708.150
  Order charging interest in partnership required for satisfaction against partner   CCP §§708.310, 708.320
Attachment (See **ATTACHMENT**)
Attorneys
  Child support judgments against   CRC 9.22
  Disciplinary orders for payment of costs and for reimbursements to client security fund
    Money judgment, enforcement as   CRC 9.23
  Fees (See within this heading, "**Attorney's fees**")
  Service on   CCP §§684.010 to 684.050
Attorney's fees
  Collection of attorney's fees as costs in enforcing judgment   CCP §§685.040, 685.070
  Garnishee's memorandum, failure to respond to request for   CCP §488.610
  Nonappearance at enforcement proceedings, award for   CCP §708.170
  Stay of enforcement
    Perfection of appeal in family code cases not to stay award   CCP §917.75
Automobiles
  Attachment (See **ATTACHMENT**)
  Exemption claim for   CCP §704.010
  General method of levy on   CCP §700.090
Bailee
  Attachment on goods in possession of   CCP §488.365
  Levy on goods in possession of   CCP §700.060
Bank accounts
  Deposit accounts
    Attachment (See **ATTACHMENT**)
    Generally (See within this heading, "**Deposit accounts**")
Bankruptcy
  Insolvency proceedings
    Attachments (See **ATTACHMENT**)
    Generally (See within this heading, "**Insolvency proceedings**")
Beneficiary of trust, enforcement of judgment against   CCP §709.010, Pro §§15300 to 15309
Bidders at sale (See within this heading, "**Sales**")
Binding effect of execution sale   CCP §701.680
Bonds (See within this heading, "**Undertakings**")
Burden of proof in hearings on third party claims   CCP §720.360
Businesses
  Going businesses
    Attachment (See **ATTACHMENT**)
    Generally (See within this heading, "**Going businesses**")
Cause of action
  Generally   CCP §695.030
  Exemption claims generally (See within this heading, "**Exemption claims**")
  Pending action or proceedings, lien in
    Attachment (See **ATTACHMENT**)
    Generally (See within this heading, "**Pending action or proceedings**")
Certificates
  Foreclosure sale, certificate of   CCP §729.040
  Personal property, certificate for sale of   CCP §§701.650, 701.670
  Satisfaction of judgment, issuance and contents of certificate of   CCP §724.100
Chattel paper
  Attachment (See **ATTACHMENT**)
  Collected rather than sold, levied property to be   CCP §701.520
  Defined   CCP §680.140
  Duties of account debtor after levy   CCP §701.050
  Judgment lien on personal property   CCP §697.530
  Method of levy on   CCP §700.100
Child support (See **CHILD SUPPORT**)
Citation   CCP §680.010
Claims against estates (See **CLAIMS AGAINST ESTATES**)

ENFORCEMENT OF JUDGMENTS—Cont.
Collection
- Public entity, collection involving (See within this heading, **"Public entities"**)
- Sale, collection of property in lieu of CCP §701.520

Commercial and industrial common interest developments
- Assessments
  - Exemption from execution CC §6804

Commercial coach, attachment of CCP §488.425
Community property CCP §§695.020, 703.020
Consent to receive service, attorney for judgment debtor giving CCP §684.020
Conservatorship estate property CCP §709.030
Consumer Credit Protection Act of 1968 affecting wage garnishment law CCP §706.151
Consumer debt, exemption of principal residence from execution of judgment lien CCP §699.730
Contempt, enforcement of otherwise unenforceable judgment by CCP §717.010
Continuation of enforcement proceedings upon renewal of judgment CCP §683.200
Continuation of judgment liens
- Notwithstanding disposition of property CCP §697.610
- Statements CCP §697.510

Contracts
- Deemed made in recognition of state's power to repeal, alter or add exemptions CCP §703.060
- Waiver of exemptions CCP §703.040

Corporations and associations
- Examination proceedings, appearance at CCP §708.150
- Order charging interest in partnership required for satisfaction against partner CCP §§708.310, 708.320

Costs
- Generally CCP §685.050
- Attachment (See **ATTACHMENT**)
- Attorney's fees generally (See within this heading, **"Attorney's fees"**)
- Claimable costs of judgment creditor CCP §685.070
- Defined CCP §680.150
- Deposit by judgment creditor CCP §685.100
- Earnings withholding order (See **GARNISHMENT**)
- Exempted property, recovery of costs where levy made on CCP §703.090
- Homestead exemption, recovery of judgment creditor's cost in action involving CCP §704.840
- Incorporation of costs into judgment CCP §685.090
- Interest on judgments (See within this heading, **"Interest on judgment"**)
- Items allowed as CCP §685.070
- Judgment creditor's right to CCP §685.040
- Levy and execution fees Gov §70626
- Levying officer, special lien of CCP §687.050
- Memorandum of costs CCP §§685.070, 685.090
- Partition, enforcement for unpaid costs of CCP §874.140
- Procedure for claiming CCP §685.080
- Renewal of judgments
  - Filing fee CCP §683.150
  - Service CCP §§685.095, 699.080
    - Memorandum CCP §§685.070, 685.090
- Sheriff's fees (See within this heading, **"Sheriff's fees"**)
- Small claims court CCP §116.820
- Stay of enforcement CCP §917.1
  - Perfection of appeal in family code cases not to stay award CCP §917.75
- Suit by creditor, prohibition on recovery of costs in CCP §708.290
- Superior court fees, specified services Gov §70626
- Tax costs, judgment debtor's motion to CCP §685.070

Creditor's suit (See within this heading, **"Suit by creditor"**)
Crops, timber or minerals
- Attachment (See **ATTACHMENT**)
- Execution liens, transferal or encumbering of property subject to CCP §697.750
- General method of levy on CCP §700.020
- Pending action or proceeding, levy on property subject of CCP §700.180
- Registered process server, levy by CCP §699.080

Custody of property
- Attachment (See **ATTACHMENT**)
- Deposit by judgment creditor as prerequisite to taking CCP §685.100
- General methods for taking CCP §687.030
- Personal property in custody of levying officer, method of levy on CCP §700.050
- Release
  - Attachment (See **ATTACHMENT**)
  - Generally (See within this heading, **"Release and discharge"**)
- Sale of property CCP §1161a
- Writ of possession generally (See within this heading, **"Writ of possession"**)

ENFORCEMENT OF JUDGMENTS—Cont.
Damages
- Acknowledgment proceedings, entitlement to damages in CCP §724.090
- Sale, execution purchasers right to damages for injury after CCP §746

Death
- Claims against decedent's estate (See **CLAIMS AGAINST ESTATES**)
- Declared homestead owner, protection from lien where death of CCP §704.995
- Judgment creditor, enforcement after death of CCP §686.010
- Judgment debtor, enforcement after death of CCP §686.020
- Transfer of property subject to lien, death of judgment debtor after CCP §695.070

Declared homesteads (See **HOMESTEADS**)
Deed of sale of real property (See within this heading, **"Sales"**)
Default
- Highest bidder at sale, default by CCP §701.600
- Homestead, hearing on application for sale of CCP §704.790

Definitions CCP §§680.110 to 680.380
Demand by creditor for filing of third party claims (See within this heading, **"Third party claims"**)
Deposit
- Attachment writ, deposit of money for CCP §488.050
- Controller making deposit for satisfaction of judgment against public entity CCP §§708.740 to 708.770
- Election of highest bidder to treat sale as credit transaction CCP §§701.590, 701.600
- Judgment creditor's deposit, generally CCP §685.100
- Proceeds of sale deposited with court where conflicting claims CCP §701.830
- Redemption of property, deposit for CCP §729.060
- Security interest or lien on personal property, deposit of creditor where third party claiming CCP §720.290

Deposit accounts
- Attachment (See **ATTACHMENT**)
- Defined CCP §§680.170, 704.080
- Exemption claim for CCP §704.080
- General method of levy on CCP §700.140
- Registered process server, levy by CCP §699.080
- Third person and debtor, levy where property in name of CCP §700.160

Depreciable property CCP §699.070
Discharge (See within this heading, **"Release and discharge"**)
Disciplinary proceedings for failure to appear at examination proceedings CCP §708.170
Dismissal of hearings for third party claims CCP §720.370
Distribution of proceeds
- General provisions for execution sale proceeds CCP §§701.810 to 710.830
- Homestead, sale of CCP §704.850

Dwellings, personalty used as
- Attachment of CCP §488.415
- General method of levy on CCP §700.080

Earnings
- Attachment (See **ATTACHMENT**)
- Garnishment (See **GARNISHMENT**)
- Generally (See within this heading, **"Salaries and wages"**)

Earnings assignment for support (See **EARNINGS ASSIGNMENT FOR SUPPORT**)
Earnings withholding order (See **GARNISHMENT**)
Encumbered property
- Transfer or encumbrance of property
  - Attachment (See **ATTACHMENT**)
  - Generally (See within this heading, **"Transfer or encumbrance of property"**)

Entry of judgment, interest commencing on date of CCP §685.020
Escheat of decedent's estate CCP §1423
Evidentiary effect of declaration of homestead CCP §704.940
Examination proceedings
- Adverse claim to property by third party, effect of CCP §708.180
- Appearance
  - Generally CCP §708.110
  - Corporation, partnership, association, or other organizations served, appearance when CCP §708.150
  - Failure to appear, effect of CCP §708.170
  - Third party, application for order requiring appearance by CCP §708.120
  - Witnesses, appearance of CCP §708.130
- Consumer debt awarded on or after January 1, 2025 CCP §708.111
- Exemption claim made pursuant to CCP §§708.120, 708.140
- Intervention, right of CCP §708.190
- Judgment lien on property created by order requiring appearance at CCP §708.120
- Protective orders, availability of CCP §708.200

ENFORCEMENT OF JUDGMENTS—Cont.
Examination proceedings—Cont.
   Referee conducting   CCP §708.140
   Third party
      Adverse claim to property by   CCP §708.180
      Application for order requiring appearance by   CCP §708.120
      Satisfaction by order applying debtor's interest in property possessed or controlled by   CCP §708.205
   Venue for   CCP §708.160
   Willful improper service as misdemeanor   CCP §708.170
Execution liens
   Creation   CCP §697.710
   Duration   CCP §697.710
   Extinguishment upon release of levied property   CCP §699.060
   Priority as between execution lien and security interest   CCP §701.040
   Transferal or encumbering of property subject to   CCP §§697.720 to 697.750
Execution sales
   Sales generally (See within this heading, **"Sales"**)
Executors (See **ADMINISTRATION OF ESTATES**)
Exemption claims
   After levy, procedure for claiming exemptions
      Generally   CCP §§703.510, 703.520
      Appeal, right of   CCP §703.600
      Copy and notice of claim, service of   CCP §703.540
      Disposition of property subject to claim   CCP §703.610
      Extension of time, right to and notice of   CCP §703.590
      Financial statement requirement   CCP §703.530
      Opposition notice and application for order determining claim, procedure for   CCP §§703.550 to 703.580
   Alimony   CCP §704.111
   Alterations or additions to exemptions   CCP §703.060
   Application of exemptions   CCP §§703.010, 703.020
   Art works   CC §986, CCP §704.040
   Assignment for benefit of creditors, property exempt from   CCP §1801
   Attachment (See **ATTACHMENT**)
   Automobiles   CCP §704.010
   Bankruptcy law, applicability of exemptions in   CCP §§703.130, 703.140
      Amount of exemption, determination   CCP §703.150
   Cause of actions
      Personal injury   CCP §704.140
      Wrongful death   CCP §704.150
   Cemetery plots   CCP §704.200
   Charitable organization, aid from   CCP §704.170
   Community property   CCP §703.020
   Consumer debt, exemption of principal residence from execution of judgment lien   CCP §699.730
   Contractual waiver of exemptions   CCP §§703.040, 703.060
   Deposit accounts   CCP §704.080
      Judicial council forms   CRCAppx A
   Determination whether property is exempt, time for   CCP §703.100
   Examination proceedings, claim made pursuant to   CCP §§708.120, 708.140
   Execution, property not subject to   CCP §699.720
   Family and cemetery plots   CCP §704.200
   Federal emergency management agency (FEMA), money provided by   CCP §704.230
   Financial aid of institution of higher education   CCP §704.190
   Financial circumstances of judgment debtor, effect of change in   CCP §703.100
   Forms
      Judicial council legal forms   CRCAppx A
   Fraternal benefit society, aid from   CCP §704.170
   Garnishment (See **GARNISHMENT**)
   General time considerations for determinations on   CCP §703.100
   Golden State scholarshare trust act, money held pursuant to   CCP §704.105
   Governing law for determination of exemptions   CCP §703.050
   Health aids   CCP §704.050
   Health and disability benefits   CCP §704.130
   Hearings on application for order determining claim   CCP §§703.570, 703.580
   Heirlooms   CCP §704.040
   Homestead exemptions (See **HOMESTEADS**)
   HOPE trust accounts   CCP §704.235
   Household furnishings, appliances, provisions, and personal effects   CCP §704.020
   Incarcerated judgment debtor, funds of   CCP §704.090
   In effect at time of enforcement, application of exemptions and procedures   CCP §703.060
   Jewelry   CCP §704.040
   Judicial council forms   CRCAppx A

ENFORCEMENT OF JUDGMENTS—Cont.
Exemption claims—Cont.
   Life insurance policy   CCP §704.100
   Marital status of judgment debtor affecting applicability of   CCP §703.110
   Money in judgment debtor's deposit account   CCP §704.220
      Judicial council forms   CRCAppx A
      Support of debtor, spouse and dependents   CCP §704.225
   Motor vehicles   CCP §704.010
   Paid earnings   CCP §704.070
   Pending action or proceeding, lien in   CCP §708.450
   Personal debt   CCP §§703.580, 703.610
   Personal injury cause of action, settlement, or award   CCP §704.140
   Property not subject to enforcement of money judgments   CCP §§695.040, 704.210
   Public entities
      Judgment debtor as creditor of public entity   CCP §708.770
      Retirement benefits   CCP §§704.110, 704.114
   Recovery of costs where levy made on exempted property   CCP §703.090
   Release of property due to failure to claim exemption within time provided by law   CCP §703.580
   Relocation benefits   CCP §704.180
   Repair or improvement of residence, material applied to   CCP §704.030
   Retirement benefits generally (See within this heading, **"Retirement benefits"**)
   Right to payment, assignment of debtor's   CCP §708.550
   Separate maintenance   CCP §704.111
   Spousal support   CCP §704.111
   State tax liability, action to enforce   CCP §688.030
   Suit by creditor   CCP §708.260
      Determinations made by court   CCP §708.280
   Support of child or spouse, application of exemptions to judgments for   CCP §703.070
   Time and manner for   CCP §703.030
   Tools   CCP §704.060
   Tracing of exempt funds   CCP §703.080
   Trade, business, or profession, specified personal property used in   CCP §704.060
   Unemployment compensation disability and unemployment benefits   CCP §704.120
   Use of property, change in   CCP §703.100
   Vacation credits   CCP §704.113
   Value of property, change in   CCP §703.100
   Waiver of exemption, considerations for   CCP §§703.040, 703.060
   Who may claim   CCP §703.020
   Workers' compensation claim, award, or payment   CCP §704.160
   Wrongful death cause of action, settlement, or award   CCP §704.150
Extending and shortening time
   Attachment lien   CCP §488.510
   Exemption claims after levy   CCP §703.590
   Mail, service by   CCP §684.120
Fees
   Costs generally (See within this heading, **"Costs"**)
Fictitious business name, levy on deposit account under   CCP §700.160
Filing of papers   CCP §681.040
Final money judgment
   Attachment of   CCP §488.480
   Collected rather than sold, levied property to be   CCP §701.520
   General method of levy on   CCP §700.190
   Payment to levying officer   CCP §701.070
Financial statement
   Exemption claim after levy, requirement where   CCP §703.530
   Wage garnishment law, contents of financial statement under   CCP §706.124
Findings
   Attachment (See **ATTACHMENT**)
   Third party claims, hearings on   CCP §720.400
   Wage garnishment law   CCP §706.106
Fixtures, attachment liens on   CCP §§488.375, 488.385
Foreclosure of mortgages (See **TRUST DEEDS AND MORTGAGES**)
Foreign judgments
   Foreign country money judgments generally   CCP §§1713 to 1725 (See **FOREIGN JUDGMENTS**)
   Sister state money judgments generally   CCP §§1710 to 1710.65 (See **FOREIGN JUDGMENTS**)
Forms
   Generally   CCP §681.030
   Garnishment (See **GARNISHMENT**)
   Judgment liens on personal property   CCP §697.670
   Judicial council legal forms   CRCAppx A

ENFORCEMENT OF JUDGMENTS—Cont.

Franchise, enforcement against
    Application for order applying franchise to satisfaction of judgment   CCP §708.920
    Definitions   CCP §708.910
    Governing law   CCP §708.930
Garnishment (See **GARNISHMENT**)
General intangibles
    Attachment (See **ATTACHMENT**)
    Collected rather than sold, levied property to be   CCP §701.520
    Defined   CCP §680.210
    Duties of account debtor after levy   CCP §701.050
    General method of levy on   CCP §700.170
Going businesses
    Attachment (See **ATTACHMENT**)
    Execution lien, property subject to   CCP §697.730
    Fictitious business name, levy on deposit account under   CCP §700.160
    General method of levy on   CCP §700.070
Guardianship estate property   CCP §709.030
Health and disability benefits, exemption for   CCP §704.130
Health care provider, real property lien based on action involving   CCP §§697.320, 697.350, 697.380 to 697.400
Hearings
    Attachment, information in notice of   CCP §§484.050, 484.340
    Declared homestead, hearing on application for sale of   CCP §§704.770 to 704.790
    Garnishment (See **GARNISHMENT**)
    Proof of service of notice of   CCP §684.210
    Third party claims (See within this heading, **"Third party claims"**)
    Undertakings, hearings on objections to   CCP §§720.770, 922
Homestead exemption (See **HOMESTEADS**)
Identity of judgment debtor, judgment creditor executing affidavit of   CCP §§680.135, 699.545
Incarcerated judgment debtor, exemption claim for funds of   CCP §704.090
Incorporation of costs into judgment   CCP §685.090
Injunctive relief (See within this heading, **"Temporary injunctive relief"**)
Insolvency proceedings
    Attachments (See **ATTACHMENT**)
    Exemptions, applicability of   CCP §§703.130, 703.140
        Amount of exemption, determination   CCP §703.150
    Judgment lien on personal property continues in proceeds of property   CCP §697.620
Inspection demands of judgment creditor   CCP §708.030
Inspection of filed notices of judgment liens on personal property   CCP §697.580
Installment judgments
    Acknowledgment of satisfaction of matured installments under   CCP §§724.210 to 724.260
    Amount of real property judgment lien   CCP §697.350
    Crediting of money received, priorities for   CCP §§695.220, 695.221
    Health care providers, creation of judgment lien on real property based on judgments against   CCP §§697.320, 697.350
    Interest on judgments   CCP §685.020
    Period of enforcement   CCP §683.030
    Priorities of judgment liens   CCP §697.380
    Support, creation of judgment lien on real property based on judgments for   CCP §§697.320, 697.350
Instructions
    Attachments (See **ATTACHMENT**)
    Garnishment (See **GARNISHMENT**)
    Levying officer's instructions, form, content and effect of   CCP §687.010
Instruments
    Attachment (See **ATTACHMENT**)
    Collected rather than sold, levied property to be   CCP §701.520
    Defined   CCP §680.220
    Duties of obligor after levy   CCP §701.060
    General method for levy on   CCP §700.110
    Negotiable document of title, method of levy on   CCP §700.120
    Procedure for levy of   CCP §687.020
Interest on judgment   CC §§3287, 3291, CCP §§685.010 to 685.030, 685.050, CRC 3.1802
    Cessation of accrual of   CCP §685.030
    Entry of judgment, interest commencing on date of   CCP §685.020
    Installment judgments   CCP §685.020
    Local entities, payment of judgments against   Gov §970.1
    Prejudgment interest   CCP §685.110
    Rate interest accrues   CCP §685.010
    Satisfied in levy under writ, amount of interest to be   CCP §685.050
    Support obligations
        Accrual of interest   Fam §17433.5
Interrogatories served on judgment debtor   CCP §§708.010 to 708.030

ENFORCEMENT OF JUDGMENTS—Cont.

Intervention
    Examination proceedings   CCP §708.190
    Pending action or proceeding
        Attachment action   CCP §491.430
        Judgment creditor having obtained lien   CCP §491.430
Invalidity of certain provisions, effect of   CCP §681.050
Judgment lien on personal property
    Acknowledgment of satisfaction of   CCP §697.640
    Alternative or additional remedy, lien as   CCP §697.520
    Amount of   CCP §697.540
    Continuation of liens
        Disposition of property, effect   CCP §697.610
        Statements   CCP §697.510
    Creation and duration of judgment lien based on money judgment   CCP §697.510
    Definitions   CCP §697.590
    Examination proceedings, lien created by order for appearance at   CCP §708.120
    Execution liens generally (See within this heading, **"Execution liens"**)
    Federal court judgments   CCP §697.060
    Forms prescribed for   CCP §697.670
    Inspection of filed notices of lien, right of   CCP §697.580
    Misidentified owner's right to release of   CCP §697.660
    Notice of lien
        Filing of   CCP §697.570
        Inspection of filed notices of lien, right of   CCP §697.580
        Requirements and content of   CCP §697.550
        Service of copy of lien   CCP §697.560
    Priorities (See within this heading, **"Preferences and priorities"**)
    Property attached   CCP §697.530
    Release of   CCP §§697.650, 697.660
    Subordination of   CCP §697.650
Judgment lien on real property
    Amount of   CCP §697.350
    Attachment of property by   CCP §697.340
    Creation and duration of judgment lien based on money judgment   CCP §697.310
    Examination proceedings, lien created by order for appearance at   CCP §708.120
    Execution liens generally (See within this heading, **"Execution liens"**)
    Extinguishment upon recording of satisfaction of judgment or release   CCP §697.400
    Federal court judgments   CCP §697.060
    Health care provider, lien based on action involving   CCP §§697.320, 697.350, 697.380 to 697.400
    Homestead declaration affecting   CCP §704.950
    Misidentified owner's right to release of   CCP §697.410
    Modified judgment affecting   CCP §697.360
    Priorities (See within this heading, **"Preferences and priorities"**)
    Release of property subject to   CCP §§697.370, 697.400, 697.410
    Spousal or child support payments, lien based on judgment for   CCP §§697.320, 697.350, 697.380 to 697.400
    Transfer or encumbrance of property subject to lien, effect of   CCP §697.390
    Workers' compensation award, lien based on   CCP §697.330
Judicial Council rules and forms   CCP §681.030
Jurisdiction
    Attachment, third party examination for   CCP §491.150
    State tax liability, action to enforce   CCP §688.010
Jury trial
    Suit by creditor   CCP §§491.350, 708.270
    Third party claims   CCP §720.410
Labor claims, priority of   CCP §§1206 to 1208
Labor commissioner enforcement of judgments   CCP §§690.020 to 690.050
Law and motion rules, applicability of   CRC 3.1103
Lessee's interest in real property subject to   CCP §695.035
Levy and execution
    Generally   CCP §699.010
    Application for writ of execution   CCP §699.510, Fam §5104
    Attachment (See **ATTACHMENT**)
    Claiming exemptions after levy (See within this heading, **"Exemption claims"**)
    Commencement of levy, service of papers upon   CCP §700.010
    Contents of writ of execution   CCP §699.520
    Costs of service of writ included in judgment   CCP §§685.095, 699.080
    Delivery of writ and instructions, execution upon   CCP §699.530
    Deposit accounts
        Attachment (See **ATTACHMENT**)
        Generally (See within this heading, **"Deposit accounts"**)
    Execution liens generally (See within this heading, **"Execution liens"**)
    Exemption claims generally (See within this heading, **"Exemption claims"**)

ENFORCEMENT OF JUDGMENTS—Cont.
Levy and execution—Cont.
    Failure to post, serve, or mail copy of writ, effect of   CCP §699.550
    Fees for issuance of writ
        Superior court fees, specified services   Gov §70626
    Garnishment (See **GARNISHMENT**)
    Homestead exemption law, preservation of right of levy and sale pursuant to   CCP §704.970
    Incorrect levy in good faith, liability where   CCP §699.090
    Instruments (See within this heading, "**Instruments**")
    Labor commissioner enforcement of judgments
        Exemptions   CCP §690.040
        Performance by commissioner of levying officer duties   CCP §690.050
        Third party claims   CCP §690.040
    Levying officer (See within this heading, "**Levying officer**")
    Methods of levy (See within this heading, "**Methods of levy**")
    Private place, levy on personalty in   CCP §699.030
    Process server (See within this heading, "**Process servers**")
    Return of writ of execution, time for   CCP §699.560
    Sale of levied property (See within this heading, "**Sales**")
    Sheriff's fees generally (See within this heading, "**Sheriff's fees**")
    Support order for child, family, or spouse   Fam §§5100 to 5104
    Third parties generally (See within this heading, "**Third parties**")
    Transfer of property or title subject to writ following issuance, motion for   CCP §699.040
Levying officer
    Attachment (See **ATTACHMENT**)
    Commencement of levy, service of papers upon   CCP §700.010
    Costs collected by   CCP §685.050
    Deed of sale (See within this heading, "**Sales**")
    Defined   CCP §680.260
    Delivery of writ and instructions, execution upon   CCP §699.530
    Deposit by judgment creditor with   CCP §685.100
    Distribution of proceeds of sale or collection   CCP §§701.810 to 701.830
    Execution liens, transferal or encumbering of property subject to   CCP §§697.730, 697.740
    Ex parte application for transfer of property or title to   CCP §699.040
    Filing papers with   CCP §681.040
    General methods for taking custody of property   CCP §687.030
    Immediate possession of property, fees for taking   Gov §26722
    Incorporation of costs into judgment   CCP §685.090
    Instructions for levying officer, form, content and effect of   CCP §687.010
    Labor commissioner enforcement of judgments
        Performance by commissioner of levying officer duties   CCP §690.050
    Liability of   CCP §687.040
    Methods of levy generally (See within this heading, "**Methods of levy**")
    Payments made to   CCP §701.070
    Personal property in custody of levying officer, method of levy on   CCP §700.050
    Possession, execution of writ of   CCP §715.040
    Preservation of property value   CCP §699.070
    Registered process server (See within this heading, "**Process servers**")
    Release of property levied upon, procedure for   CCP §699.060
    Restriction on purchase by officer at execution sale   CCP §701.610
    Special lien of   CCP §687.050
    State agency or department performing duties in action to enforce state tax liability   CCP §688.030
Licenses and permits
    Generally   CCP §695.060
    Collected rather than sold, levied property to be   CCP §701.520
    Receiver appointed where alcoholic beverage license applied to satisfaction of judgment   CCP §708.630
Liens
    Agricultural liens
        Priorities   CCP §697.590
    Amount of lien, generally   CCP §697.010
    Apartment housekeeper's lien   CC §1861.25
    Attachment (See **ATTACHMENT**)
    Charging order, liens created by   CCP §§697.910, 697.920
    Continuation statements   CCP §697.510
    Creation upon recording of abstract of judgment   CCP §697.310
    Creditor's demand for claims by lienholder (See within this heading, "**Third party claims**")
    Creditor's suit, liens created by   CCP §§697.910, 697.920
    Declared homesteads (See **HOMESTEADS**)
    Deemed created in recognition of state's power to repeal, alter or add to governing law   CCP §703.060
    Examination proceedings, liens created by   CCP §§697.910, 697.920
    Execution liens (See within this heading, "**Execution liens**")

ENFORCEMENT OF JUDGMENTS—Cont.
Liens—Cont.
    Exempt, time for determination whether property is   CCP §703.100
    Extinguishment of lien, release of property following   CCP §697.050
    Garnishment (See **GARNISHMENT**)
    Homesteads (See **HOMESTEADS**)
    Levying officer, special lien of   CCP §687.050
    Limited liability companies
        Lien created by order charging interest in   CCP §708.320
    Lottery prize, procedure for enforcement of lien against   CCP §708.755
    Motion for lien on judgment   CRC 3.1360
    Partnership, lien created by order charging interest in   CCP §708.320
    Pending action or proceedings (See within this heading, "**Pending action or proceedings**")
    Period of effectiveness   CCP §697.030
    Personal property (See within this heading, "**Judgment lien on personal property**")
    Priority of lien   CCP §697.020
    Real property (See within this heading, "**Judgment lien on real property**")
    Renewal of judgments, extension of lien following   CCP §§683.180, 683.190
    Sale of property extinguishing   CCP §701.630
    Statutes of limitation   CCP §683.020
    Stay of judgment, effect on lien of   CCP §697.040
    Suit by creditor, lien created by service of summons in   CCP §708.250
    Tax lien pursuant to enforcement of state tax liability   CCP §688.050
    Third party claims (See within this heading, "**Third party claims**")
    Transferred or encumbered property generally (See within this heading, "**Transfer or encumbrance of property**")
    Transitional provisions for   CCP §694.080
Limitation of actions (See within this heading, "**Statutes of limitation**")
Lottery winnings owed judgment debtor
    Claim for support arrearages filed against state for   CCP §§708.30, 708.740
    Procedure for enforcement of lien against   CCP §708.755
Mail, service by
    Attachment lien affected by failure to mail writ   CCP §482.070
    Copy of writ of execution, failure to mail   CCP §699.550
    Manner of service, generally   CCP §684.120
    Public entity, collection from   CCP §708.770
    Sale of levied property, notice of   CCP §§701.530 to 701.550
Manufactured homes (See **MOBILEHOMES**)
Market value of property
    Redemption price, petition for court determination of disputed   CCP §729.070
Marriage
    Spouses (See within this heading, "**Spouses**")
Marshals
    Levying officer generally (See within this heading, "**Levying officer**")
Mechanics' liens affecting   CC §8468
Memoranda
    Costs memorandum   CCP §§685.070, 685.090
    Garnishee's memorandum (See **GARNISHMENT**)
Methods of levy
    Account receivable or general intangible   CCP §700.170
    Attachment (See **ATTACHMENT**)
    Bailee's possession, levy on goods in   CCP §700.060
    Chattel paper   CCP §700.100
    Contents of notice of levy   CCP §699.540
    Copy of original notice of levy or affidavit of identity sufficing as notice   CCP §699.545
    Crops, timber, or minerals   CCP §700.020
    Custody of levying officer, levy on personal property in   CCP §700.050
    Decedent's estate, levy on judgment debtor's interest in personal property of   CCP §700.200
    Deposit account (See within this heading, "**Deposit accounts**")
    Dwellings, levy on personal property used as   CCP §700.080
    Final money judgment   CCP §700.190
    General intangible or account receivable   CCP §700.170
    Going business of judgment debtor   CCP §700.070
    Instrument   CCP §700.110
    Negotiable document of title   CCP §700.120
    Pending action or proceedings, levy on property subject of   CCP §700.180
    Personal property
        Decedent's estate, levy on judgment debtor's interest in   CCP §700.200
        Dwellings, personal property used as   CCP §700.080
        Going business of judgment debtor   CCP §700.070
        Judgment debtor's control or possession, property in   CCP §700.030
        Levying officer, property in custody of   CCP §700.050
        Third persons control or possession, property in   CCP §700.040

ENFORCEMENT OF JUDGMENTS—Cont.
Methods of levy—Cont.
    Real property   CCP §700.015
    Safe-deposit box, levy on property in (See within this heading, **"Safe-deposit box"**)
    Security, method of levy on   CCP §700.130
    Service of papers pursuant to   CCP §700.010
    Vehicle or vessel   CCP §700.090
Minerals
    Crops, timber or minerals
        Attachment (See **ATTACHMENT**)
        Generally (See within this heading, **"Crops, timber or minerals"**)
Mobilehomes (See **MOBILEHOMES**)
Modification
    Judgment lien on real property affected by modified judgment   CCP §697.360
    Right to payment, modification of assignment of   CCP §708.560
    Trust beneficiaries, modification of orders concerning   Pro §15308
Money judgments, enforcement of   CCP §§695.010 to 709.030
    Attorney discipline
        Orders for payment of costs and for reimbursements to client security fund enforced as money judgment   CRC 9.23
Mortgages, foreclosure on (See **TRUST DEEDS AND MORTGAGES**)
Motor vehicles
    Attachment (See **ATTACHMENT**)
    Exemption claims   CCP §704.010
    Levy, method   CCP §700.090
Negotiable instruments
    Attachment (See **ATTACHMENT**)
    Instruments generally (See within this heading, **"Instruments"**)
    Judgment lien on personal property   CCP §697.530
Nonmoney judgment
    Public entity, enforceability of judgment against   CCP §712.070
    Writ of possession generally (See within this heading, **"Writ of possession"**)
    Writ of sale generally (See within this heading, **"Writ of sale"**)
Non-transferable property not subject to enforcement of money judgment   CCP §695.030
Notices
    Attachment (See **ATTACHMENT**)
    Judgment liens on personal property (See within this heading, **"Judgment lien on personal property"**)
    Opposition to exemption claim, notice of   CCP §§703.550 to 703.580
    Proof of service   CCP §§684.210, 684.220
    Publication, notice by (See within this heading, **"Posting or publication"**)
    Release of property levied upon   CCP §699.060
    Renewal of judgments (See within this heading, **"Renewal of judgments"**)
    Sales (See within this heading, **"Sales"**)
    State tax liability, enforcement pursuant to notice of levy for   CCP §§688.010 to 688.050
    Third party claims, hearing on   CCP §720.320
Objections and exceptions
    Attachment proceedings   CCP §§484.060, 484.110
    Exemption claims, notice of opposition in application for order determining   CCP §§703.550 to 703.580
    Third party claims (See within this heading, **"Third party claims"**)
    Undertakings
        Hearing on objections   CCP §§720.770, 922
    Wage garnishment law, contents of notice of opposition to claim of exemption under   CCP §706.128
Obligation of public entity to judgment debtor, application to satisfaction of judgment of (See within this heading, **"Public entities"**)
Operative date of provisions for   CCP §694.020
Organizations
    Corporations and associations
        Examination proceedings, appearance   CCP §708.150
        Order charging interest in partnership required for satisfaction against partner   CCP §§708.310, 708.320
Other states, judgments of (See **FOREIGN JUDGMENTS**)
Overpayment of tax, claims against public entities for   CCP §§708.730, 708.740, 708.780, 708.795
Partition, enforcement for unpaid costs of   CCP §874.140
Partnerships
    Examination proceedings, appearance   CCP §708.150
    Order charging interest in partnership required for satisfaction against partner   CCP §§708.310, 708.320
Pending action or proceedings
    Application of debtor's recovery to satisfaction of lien in   CCP §708.470
    Attachment (See **ATTACHMENT**)
    Entitlement to lien in   CCP §708.410
    Exemption determination re lien   CCP §708.450
    General provisions for enforcement of lien in   CCP §708.480

ENFORCEMENT OF JUDGMENTS—Cont.
Pending action or proceedings—Cont.
    Intervention
        Attachment action   CCP §491.430
        By judgment creditor, having obtained lien   CCP §708.430
    Levy on property that is subject of   CCP §700.180
    Notice of lien, contents of   CCP §708.420
    Procedure for obtaining lien in   CCP §708.410, CRC 3.1360
    Restrictions against enforcement of judgment entered in   CCP §708.440
    Statement of lien's existence endorsed upon judgment   CCP §708.460
    Stay of enforcement (See within this heading, **"Stay of enforcement"**)
    Termination of action, creditor's lien restricting   CCP §708.440
Periodic payment
    Public entities, judgments against   CRC 3.1804
Period of enforcement (See within this heading, **"Statutes of limitation"**)
Perishables   CCP §699.070
Permits (See within this heading, **"Licenses and permits"**)
Personal debt
    Exemption claims   CCP §§703.580, 703.610
    Retirement benefits   CCP §704.115
    Stay of enforcement   CCP §703.570
Personal property
    Defined   CCP §680.290
    Disposition of personal property on real property after execution of writ of possession   CCP §715.030
    Judgment for possession of property, enforcement of (See within this heading, **"Writ of possession"**)
    Judgment for sale of property, enforcement of (See within this heading, **"Writ of sale"**)
    Judgment liens (See within this heading, **"Judgment lien on personal property"**)
    Methods of levy generally (See within this heading, **"Methods of levy"**)
    Pending action or proceeding, levy on property subject of   CCP §700.180
    Registered process server, levy by   CCP §699.080
    Sale of levied property (See within this heading, **"Sales"**)
    Writ of possession, issuance and execution of   CCP §§714.010 to 714.030
Possession
    Custody of property generally (See within this heading, **"Custody of property"**)
    Levying officer's fees for taking immediate possession of property   Gov §26722
    Third party claim to ownership and possession (See within this heading, **"Third party claims"**)
    Writ of possession (See within this heading, **"Writ of possession"**)
Posting or publication
    Advertising sale of levied property   CCP §701.555
    Attachment lien affected by failure to post notice   CCP §488.120
    Copy of writ of execution, failure to post copy of   CCP §699.550
    Proof of service of   CCP §684.220
    Sale of levied property, notice of   CCP §§701.530 to 701.555
    Sheriff's fee for notice of publication   Gov §26729
Preferences and priorities
    Assignment of debtor's right to payment   CCP §708.530
    Attachment lien   CCP §488.500
    Default of highest bidder at sale   CCP §701.600
    Earnings assignment order for support (See **EARNINGS ASSIGNMENT FOR SUPPORT**)
    Earnings withholding orders (See **GARNISHMENT**)
    Execution lien, priority as between security interest and   CCP §701.040
    Judgment liens on personal property
        Insolvency proceedings, priority for proceeds of property in   CCP §697.620
        Proceeds of property   CCP §697.620
        Security interest, priority between judgment lien and   CCP §697.590
        Subsequent judgment liens, priority against   CCP §697.600
    Judgment liens on real property
        Generally   CCP §697.380
        Subordination of property subject to   CCP §697.370
        Transferred or encumbered property   CCP §697.390
    Labor claims, priority of   CCP §§1206 to 1208
    Liens, generally   CCP §697.020
    Security interest, priority of   CCP §§697.590, 701.040
    Subordination
        Personal property, judgment lien   CCP §697.650
        Real property, judgment lien   CCP §§697.370, 697.400
Preliminary injunction (See within this heading, **"Temporary injunctive relief"**)
Priorities (See within this heading, **"Preferences and priorities"**)
Prior law affecting provisions for   CCP §694.020
Private place, levy on personalty in   CCP §699.030
Probate Code governing enforcement following death of judgment debtor   CCP §686.020, Pro §§9300 to 9304

ENFORCEMENT OF JUDGMENTS—Cont.
Proceeds, distribution of
    Execution sale proceeds   CCP §§701.810 to 710.830
    Homestead sale   CCP §704.850
Process servers
    Attachment (See **ATTACHMENT**)
    Defined   CCP §680.330
    Liability of   CCP §§488.140, 687.040
    Writ of execution, levy under   CCP §699.080
    Writ of possession executed by   CCP §715.040
Proof of service   CCP §§684.210, 684.220
Property keeper fee   Gov §26726
Property subject to enforcement of judgment
    Levy under writ of execution, property subject to   CCP §699.710
    Money judgments   CCP §§695.010 to 695.070, 699.710, 699.720
    Personal property judgment lien, property attached by   CCP §697.530
    Real property judgment lien, property attached by   CCP §697.340
    Transitional provisions   CCP §694.040
Protective orders (See within this heading, **"Temporary injunctive relief"**)
Publication (See within this heading, **"Posting or publication"**)
Public entities
    Earnings assignment order as affecting retirement benefits   CCP §§704.110, 704.114
    Enforceability of money judgment against   CCP §695.050
    Exemptions
        Judgment debtor as creditor of public entity, claim of exemption by   CCP §708.770
        Retirement benefits   CCP §§704.110, 704.114
    Franchise (See within this heading, **"Franchise, enforcement against"**)
    Judgment debtor as creditor of
        Abstract or copy of judgment, filing of   CCP §§708.730, 708.740, 708.780, 708.785
        Applying public entity's obligation to satisfaction of judgment against judgment debtor   CCP §708.720
        Contractor on public work as judgment debtor, amount payable where   CCP §708.760
        Creation of lien   CCP §708.780
        Definitions   CCP §708.710
        Deposit by controller for discharge of claim   CCP §§708.740 to 708.770
        Exemption claim   CCP §708.770
        Lottery prize, procedure for enforcement of lien against   CCP §708.755
        Nonexempt portion of deposit, payment of   CCP §708.775
        Notice of support arrearage   CCP §§708.730, 708.780
        Officer or employee, liability of   CCP §708.790
        Public entities other than state, filing with   CCP §708.750
        State agencies, filing with   CCP §§708.730, 708.740
        Support arrearages, claims involving   CCP §§708.730, 708.740, 708.780
    Nonmoney judgment, enforceability of   CCP §712.070
    Ownership and possession claims by third party, public entity as judgment creditor affecting   CCP §720.160
    Period of enforcement and renewal provisions, applicability of   CCP §683.320
    Retirement benefits, exemption for   CCP §§704.110, 704.114
    Security interest or lien on personal property, third party claim of   CCP §720.260
    State tax liability, enforcement of
        Garnishment (See **GARNISHMENT**)
        Generally (See within this heading, **"State tax"**)
    Tax refund owed judgment debtor, claim filed against state for   CCP §§708.730, 708.740, 708.780, 708.795
Public officers' or employees' liability in action against public entity   CCP §708.790
Public works' contractor as judgment debtor, amount payable where   CCP §708.760
Real property
    Deed of sale (See within this heading, **"Sales"**)
    Defined   CCP §680.320
    Disposition of personal property on   CCP §715.030
    Health care provider or spousal and child support judgment liens   CCP §697.320
    Judgment for possession of property, enforcement of (See within this heading, **"Writ of possession"**)
    Judgment for sale of property, enforcement of (See within this heading, **"Writ of sale"**)
    Judgment liens (See within this heading, **"Judgment lien on real property"**)
    Method of levy   CCP §700.015
    Pending action or proceeding, levy on property subject of   CCP §700.180

ENFORCEMENT OF JUDGMENTS—Cont.
Real property—Cont.
    Registered process server, levy by   CCP §699.080
    Sale of levied property (See within this heading, **"Sales"**)
    Writ of possession, issuance and execution of   CCP §§715.010 to 715.040
Receivers
    Generally   CCP §§564, 708.610, 708.620
    Alcoholic beverage license applied to satisfaction of judgment, receivers appointed where   CCP §708.630
    Attachment proceedings   CCP §488.700
    Preservation of property value, appointment for   CCP §699.070
    Sale of property by   CCP §568.5
    Writ of possession or sale, appointment of receiver to enforce   CCP §712.060
Redemption (See **TRUST DEEDS AND MORTGAGES**)
Referees
    Attachment proceedings   CCP §491.130
    Examination proceedings   CCP §708.140
Registered process server (See within this heading, **"Process servers"**)
Release and discharge
    Attachments (See **ATTACHMENT**)
    Child support payments, real property deposited to secure   Fam §4641
    Extinguishment of lien, effect of   CCP §697.050
    Failure to claim property exemption within time provided by law   CCP §703.580
    Judgment lien on personal property   CCP §§697.650, 697.660
    Judgment lien on real property   CCP §§697.370, 697.400, 697.410
    Misidentified owner's right to release of   CCP §§697.410, 697.660
    Notice of release of property   CCP §699.060
    Procedure upon release of levied property   CCP §699.060
    Third party claims (See within this heading, **"Third party claims"**)
Remainder interest of judgment debtor applied to satisfaction of money judgment   CCP §709.020
Renewal of judgments
    Generally   CCP §683.110
    Application fees
        Superior court fees, specified services   Gov §70626
    Continuation of enforcement proceedings upon   CCP §683.200
    Definitions   CCP §683.110
    Entry of renewal by court clerk, contents of   CCP §683.150
    Family law judgments   Fam §§291, 4502
    General contents of application for   CCP §683.140
    Harassment, renewal of protection orders
        COVID-19, emergency rule   CRCAppx I Emer Rule 8
    Liens affected by   CCP §§683.180, 683.190
    Notices
        Application for renewal accompanying   CRC 3.1900
        Attachment of application   CRC 3.1900
        General notice for renewal   CCP §683.160
        Vacation of renewal   CCP §683.170
    Procedure for   CCP §683.120
    Statutes of limitation, commencement of running of   CCP §683.220
    Stay of enforcement affected by   CCP §683.210
    Support judgments   CCP §§683.130, 683.310, Fam §§291, 4502
    Time period for filing application for   CCP §§683.110, 683.130
    Transitional provisions for   CCP §694.030
    Vacation of renewal   CCP §683.170
Request for notice of sale   CCP §701.550
Restraining orders (See within this heading, **"Temporary injunctive relief"**)
Retirement benefits
    Personal debt   CCP §704.115
    Private retirement benefits, exemptions for   CCP §704.115
    Public retirement benefits, exemption for   CCP §§704.110, 704.114, Fam §17528
    Support obligations   Fam §17528
Return
    Attachment writ   CCP §488.130
    Execution writ, time for return of   CCP §699.560
    Wage garnishment law, contents of employer's return pursuant to   CCP §706.126
    Writ of possession or sale, return of   CCP §712.050
Review of law
    California law revision commission
        Continuing study, review, etc of provisions   CCP §681.035
Right to payment of debtor, assignment of (See within this heading, **"Assignments"**)
Safe-deposit box
    Attaching property in   CCP §§488.460, 488.465
    General method of levy on property in   CCP §700.150
    Registered process server, levy by   CCP §699.080
    Third person and debtor, levy where property in name of   CCP §700.160

ENFORCEMENT OF JUDGMENTS—Cont.
Salaries and wages
    Assignment of right to payment due judgment debtor   CCP §§708.510 to 708.560
    Attachment (See **ATTACHMENT**)
    Exempt amount   CCP §704.070
    Garnishment (See **GARNISHMENT**)
    Labor commissioner enforcement of judgment   CCP §§690.020 to 690.050
    Paid earnings defined   CCP §704.070
    Preference to wage claims   CCP §§1206 to 1208
Sales
    Attachment (See **ATTACHMENT**)
    Bidders at sale
        Default of highest bidder   CCP §701.600
        Homestead exemption, bid failing to exceed   CCP §704.800
        Minimum amount of bid   CCP §701.620
        Notice of sale containing clause for prospective bidders   CCP §701.547
    Binding effect of sale   CCP §701.680
    Certificate of sale of personal property   CCP §§701.650, 701.670
    Collection of property in lieu of   CCP §701.520
    Conducting property sale, sheriff's fees for   Gov §26730
    Declared homesteads, sale of (See **HOMESTEADS**)
    Deed of sale of real property
        Contents of   CCP §701.670
        Execution and delivery of   CCP §§262.4, 701.660
        Fees for execution and delivery   Gov §26741
        Redemption certificate, fees for   Gov §26740
    Default of highest bidder   CCP §701.600
    Distribution of proceeds   CCP §§701.810 to 701.830
    Escheat of decedent's estate   CCP §1423
    Foreclosure on deeds of trust (See **TRUST DEEDS AND MORTGAGES**)
    General provision re sale of levied property   CCP §701.510
    General requirements for purchase of property at   CCP §701.590
    Homesteads, sale of (See **HOMESTEADS**)
    Injury after sale, execution purchaser's right to damages for   CCP §746
    Interest acquired by purchaser   CCP §701.640
    Judgment on   CCP §491.360
    Liens extinguished upon sale of property   CCP §701.630
    Minimum amount of bid   CCP §701.620
    Notices
        Failure to give notice, effect of   CCP §701.560
        Mailing of notice   CCP §§701.530 to 701.550
        Personal property sales   CCP §701.530
        Prospective bidders, clause in notice of sale for   CCP §701.547
        Real property interest, sale of   CCP §§701.540, 701.545
        Request for notice of sale   CCP §701.550
    Perishables   CCP §699.070
    Possession of premises   CCP §1161a
    Postponement of sale
        Generally   CCP §701.580
        Sheriff's fees for   Gov §26730
    Procedural requirements for   CCP §701.570
    Proceeds, distribution of   CCP §§701.810 to 701.830
    Receivers selling   CCP §568.5
    Redemption (See **TRUST DEEDS AND MORTGAGES**)
    Released property not claimed, sale where   CCP §699.060
    Restriction on purchase by levying officer   CCP §701.610
    Sheriff's fees
        Generally   Gov §26725
        Additional notices   Gov §§26725.1, 26728.1
        Conducting or postponing property sales   Gov §26730
        Forced sale of personal property, notice of   Gov §§26728, 26728.1
    Third party claims generally (See within this heading, **"Third party claims"**)
    Transitional provisions for   CCP §694.050
    Unlawful detainer, holding over after execution sale as act constituting   CCP §1161a
    Writ of sale (See within this heading, **"Writ of sale"**)
Satisfaction
    Generally (See **SATISFACTION OF JUDGMENTS**)
    Distribution of proceeds (See within this heading, **"Distribution of proceeds"**)
    Foreign-money claims   CCP §§676 to 676.16
    Methods of levy generally (See within this heading, **"Methods of levy"**)
Secretary of State, judgment lien forms prescribed by   CCP §697.670
Securities and security interest
    Attachment (See **ATTACHMENT**)
    Definitions   CCP §§680.340 to 680.360, 697.590
    Disposition of property subject to   CCP §701.040
    Method of levy on   CCP §700.130

ENFORCEMENT OF JUDGMENTS—Cont.
Securities and security interest—Cont.
    Priority of security interest   CCP §§697.590, 701.040
    Third party claims generally (See within this heading, **"Third party claims"**)
Security bonds (See within this heading, **"Undertakings"**)
Separate maintenance as exempt property   CCP §704.111
Service
    Attachment (See **ATTACHMENT**)
    Attorney of creditor or debtor, provisions for service on   CCP §§684.010 to 684.050
    Commencement of levy, service of papers upon   CCP §700.010
    Copy of writ of execution, failure to serve   CCP §699.550
    Correct name and address of person to be served, judgment creditor specifying   CCP §684.130
    Costs
        General provisions regarding costs for service of writ   CCP §§685.095, 699.080
        Memorandum   CCP §§685.070, 685.090
    Creditor's suit, effect of service in   CCP §708.250
    Financial institutions, service on
        Central locations for service of process, designation by financial institution   CCP §684.115
        Manner of service   CCP §684.110
        Third-party agents, designation for service of process   CCP §684.115
    Garnishment (See **GARNISHMENT**)
    Hearing on enforcement, proof of service of notice of   CCP §684.210
    Interrogatories served on judgment debtor   CCP §§708.010 to 708.030
    Judgment liens on personal property, service of copy of   CCP §697.560
    Limited liability companies
        Notice of motion for order charging interest in   CCP §708.320
    Mail (See within this heading, **"Mail, service by"**)
    Manner of service, generally   CCP §684.110
    Partnership, notice of motion for order charging interest in   CCP §708.320
    Permission for service by person other than levying officer   CCP §684.140
    Posting or publication generally (See within this heading, **"Posting or publication"**)
    Process servers (See within this heading, **"Process servers"**)
    Proof of service   CCP §§684.210, 684.220
    Public entity, collection from   CCP §708.770
    Sale of levied property, notice of (See within this heading, **"Sales"**)
Setting aside
    Renewal of judgment vacated   CCP §683.170
    Right to payment
        Assignment, setting aside   CCP §708.560
Settlement, enforcement of terms of   CCP §§664.6, 664.7
Severability of provisions   CCP §681.050
Sheriff
    Levying officers generally (See within this heading, **"Levying officer"**)
Sheriff's deed (See within this heading, **"Sales"**)
Sheriff's fees
    Generally   Gov §§26725, 26746
    Additional notices   Gov §§26725.1, 26728.1
    Allocation of fees collected to special sheriff's fund   Gov §26731
    Cancellation of service or execution   Gov §26736
    Copy of service fees   Gov §26727
    Eviction under writ of possession   Gov §26733.5
    Execution and delivery, fees for   Gov §26741
    General fees for service of process   Gov §26721
    Not found returns   Gov §26738
    Other instruments, execution and delivery of   Gov §26742
    Personal property, levy on   Gov §26734
    Property keeper fee   Gov §26726
    Publication, notice of   Gov §26729
    Redemption certificate, execution and delivery of   Gov §26740
    Sales generally (See within this heading, **"Sales"**)
    Unlawful detainer action   Gov §26721.1
    Writs on real property, service of   Gov §§26725, 26725.1, 26746
Sheriff's sale (See within this heading, **"Sales"**)
Sister state judgments   CCP §§1710.10 to 1710.65 (See **FOREIGN JUDGMENTS**)
Small claims court (See **SMALL CLAIMS COURTS**)
Spendthrift trust subject to   CCP §§695.030, 709.010
Spouses
    Applicability of exemptions   CCP §§703.110, 703.140
        Amount of exemption, determination   CCP §703.150
    Bankruptcy proceedings, applicable exemptions in   CCP §703.140
        Amount of exemption, determination   CCP §703.150

ENFORCEMENT OF JUDGMENTS—Cont.
  Spouses—Cont.
    Deposit account in name of spouse and debtor, levy on   CCP §700.160
    Support judgments and orders, enforcement of (See **CHILD SUPPORT; SPOUSAL SUPPORT**)
    Support of debtor or family, exemption for (See within this heading, "**Support of debtor or family, exemption for**")
  State agencies (See within this heading, "**Public entities**")
  State tax
    Extinguishment of state tax lien   CCP §701.630
    Garnishment (See **GARNISHMENT**)
    Judgment for taxes, enforcement pursuant to   CCP §688.110
    Support arrearages claim filed against state for tax refund owed judgment debtor   CCP §§708.730, 708.740, 708.780
    Warrant or notice of levy, enforcement pursuant to   CCP §§688.010 to 688.050
  Statutes of limitation
    Generally   CCP §§683.010 to 683.050
    Offsetting cross-demand alleged as defense notwithstanding bar of   CCP §431.70
    Renewal of judgment, running of period following   CCP §683.220
    Suit by creditor   CCP §708.230
    Transitional provisions   CCP §§694.010 to 694.090
  Stay of enforcement
    Administrators and executors as appellants, discretionary application of security requirements to   CCP §919
    Attach order, appeal from   CCP §917.65
    Attorneys' fees or costs awarded
      Perfection of appeal in family code cases not to stay award   CCP §917.75
    Building as nuisance, appeal from judgment restricting use of   CCP §917.8
    Controlled substances nuisance abatement, appeal from order granted under   CCP §917.8
    Corporate records, appeal from judgment directing access for inspection of   CCP §917.8
    Costs, appeal from judgments awarding   CCP §917.1
    Custody of minor, appeal of judgments affecting   CCP §917.7
    Execution of instruments, appeal from judgment directing   CCP §917.3
    General discussion of stay on appeal   CCP §916
    Guardians and conservators as appellants, discretionary application of security requirements to   CCP §919
    Hazardous wastes, appeal from judgment or order re   CCP §917.15
    Liens, effect on   CCP §697.040
    Money judgments on appeal   CCP §917.1
    Pending action on disputed claim between judgment debtor and creditor   CCP §918.5
    Period of time for stay   CCP §918
    Personal debt   CCP §703.570
    Personal property, appeal from judgment directing assignment or delivery of   CCP §917.2
    Real property, appeal from judgment directing conveyance or delivery of   CCP §917.4
    Receiver, appeal from appointment of   CCP §917.5
    Red light abatement law, appeal from order granted under   CCP §917.8
    Renewal of judgment affected by   CCP §683.210
    Sterilization proceedings   Pro §1965
    Third party claims, stay pending outcome of proceedings for   CCP §720.380
    Trustees as appellants, discretionary application of security requirements to   CCP §919
    Two or more acts, appeal from judgment directing performance of   CCP §917.67
    Undertakings
      Attach order, appeal from   CCP §917.65
      Discretionary undertakings required by trial court   CCP §§917.9, 919
      Executors and administrators as appellants   CCP §919
      Guardians and conservators as appellants   CCP §919
      Insufficient undertakings, effect of   CCP §922
      Money judgments on appeal   CCP §917.1
      Personal property, appeal from judgment directing assignment or delivery of   CCP §917.2
      Real property, appeal from judgment directing conveyance or delivery of   CCP §917.4
      Receiver, appeal from appointment of   CCP §917.5
      Trustees as appellants   CCP §919
    Usurpation of public office, appeal from judgment re   CCP §917.8
  Studies
    California law revision commission
      Continuing study, review, etc of provisions   CCP §681.035
  Subject property (See within this heading, "**Property subject to enforcement of judgment**")

ENFORCEMENT OF JUDGMENTS—Cont.
  Subordination
    Personal property, judgment lien on   CCP §697.650
    Real property, judgments lien on   CCP §§697.370, 697.400
  Successor in interest
    Death of creditor, successor enforcing following   CCP §686.010
    Redemption by (See **TRUST DEEDS AND MORTGAGES**)
  Suit by creditor
    Generally   CCP §§708.210, 708.220
    Attachment proceedings   CCP §§491.310 to 491.370
    Costs, prohibition on recovery of   CCP §708.290
    Determinations made by court in   CCP §708.280
    Exemption claims
      Generally   CCP §708.260
      Determinations made by court on   CCP §708.280
    Jury trial, prohibition on right to   CCP §708.270
    Lien created by service of summons   CCP §708.250
    Statutes of limitation on   CCP §708.230
    Temporary injunctive relief   CCP §708.240
    Third person, action against   CCP §708.210
    Trust beneficiaries, claims against, generally (See within this heading, "**Trust assets**")
  Support judgments and orders, enforcement of (See **CHILD SUPPORT; SPOUSAL SUPPORT**)
  Support of debtor or family, exemption for
    Bankruptcy proceedings, applicable exemptions in   CCP §703.140
      Amount of exemption, determination   CCP §703.150
    Financial circumstances of judgment debtor, effect on exemption determination of change in   CCP §703.100
    Financial statement requirement for exemption claim   CCP §703.530
  Surety bond (See within this heading, "**Undertakings**")
  Tangible personal property
    Attachment (See **ATTACHMENT**)
    Defined   CCP §680.370
    General methods of levy (See within this heading, "**Methods of levy**")
    Personal property generally (See within this heading, "**Personal property**")
  Taxation (See within this heading, "**State tax**")
  Tax costs, judgment debtor's motion to   CCP §685.070
  Temporary injunctive relief
    Examination proceedings, availability of protective order for   CCP §708.200
    Suit by creditor   CCP §708.240
    Third party claims, relief pending outcome of proceedings for   CCP §720.380
  Termination of pending action, creditor's lien restricting   CCP §708.440
  Third parties
    Attachment (See **ATTACHMENT**)
    Claims by (See within this heading, "**Third party claims**")
    Control or possession by third party, levy on personal property in   CCP §700.040
    Deposit account in name of debtor and third party, levy on   CCP §700.160
    Duties and liabilities after levy
      Generally   CCP §701.010
      Account debtor on an account receivable, chattel paper, or general intangible, duties of   CCP §701.050
      Failure to deliver property or make payments   CCP §701.020
      Levying officer, payments made to   CCP §701.070
      Obligor under instrument, duties of   CCP §701.060
      Security interest, disposition of property subject to   CCP §701.040
    Examination proceedings (See within this heading, "**Examination proceedings**")
    Garnishment memorandum, liability of third party giving   CCP §488.620
    Safe-deposit box property in name of debtor and third party, levy on   CCP §700.160
    Satisfaction by order applying debtor's interest in property possessed or controlled by   CCP §708.205
    State tax liability, action to enforce   CCP §688.030
    Suit by creditor against   CCP §708.210
  Third party claims
    Apartment housekeeper's lien   CC §1861.25
    Appeal, right of   CCP §720.420
    Attachment (See **ATTACHMENT**)
    Burden of proof in hearings on   CCP §720.360
    Creditor's demand for claim by secured party or lienholder
      Generally   CCP §§720.510 to 720.530
      Failure to file timely claim, consequences of   CCP §720.550
      Prohibition against disposition of personal property   CCP §720.540
    Definitions   CCP §§720.010 to 720.030
    Dismissal of proceedings   CCP §720.370
    Findings, requirement for   CCP §720.400

ENFORCEMENT OF JUDGMENTS—Cont.
Third party claims—Cont.
    Hearings
        Dismissal of proceedings   CCP §720.370
        Jury trial, right to   CCP §720.410
        Notice of   CCP §720.320
        Papers filed   CCP §§720.330, 720.340
        Petition for   CCP §720.310
        Service of notice   CCP §720.320
        Time for service of notice of   CCP §1005
        Unlawful detainer action, right to possession claim in   CCP §1174.3
    Hotelkeeper's lien   CC §1861.25
    Judgment   CCP §720.390
    Objections to claims
        Ownership and possession claims   CCP §720.140
        Security interest or lien claims   CCP §§720.280, 720.340
        Third party claims of ownership and possession   CCP §720.140
        Undertaking by third party, release of property in absence of timely objection to   CCP §720.660
        Unlawful detainer action, right to possession claim in   CCP §1174.3
    Ownership and possession claims
        Generally   CCP §§720.110, 720.120
        Execution and contents of   CCP §720.130
        Failure to file claim, effect of   CCP §720.150
        General requirements for service of claim and other papers   CCP §720.140
        Public entity as judgment creditor   CCP §720.160
        Release of property   CCP §720.170
        Restriction on actions of levying officer on timely filing of   CCP §720.150
        Time for making objection   CCP §720.140
        Undertaking by judgment creditor affecting   CCP §720.160
        Unlawful detainer action, right to possession claim in   CCP §1174.3
    Petition for hearing   CCP §720.310
    Pleading, claim constitutes   CCP §720.350
    Proceeds of sale deposited with court where conflict of   CCP §701.830
    Release of property
        Objection to undertaking by third party not timely   CCP §720.660
        Ownership and possession claims   CCP §720.170
        Satisfaction of judgment, applied in   CCP §720.430
        Security interest or lien on personal property claims   CCP §720.270
    Security interest or lien on personal property
        Generally   CCP §§720.210, 720.220
        Creditor's claim   CCP §§720.280, 720.340, 720.350
        Deposit of creditor, acceptance or rejection of tender on payment of   CCP §720.290
        Execution and contents of claim   CCP §720.230
        Failure to file claim, effect of   CCP §720.250
        General requirements for service of claim and other papers   CCP §720.240
        Public entity as judgment creditor   CCP §720.260
        Release of property   CCP §720.270
        Restrictions on actions of levying officer upon timely filing of claim   CCP §720.250
        Undertaking by judgment creditor affecting   CCP §§720.240, 720.260, 720.280
    Stay of order of sale or enjoining other disposition of property   CCP §720.380
    Transitional provisions for   CCP §694.070
    Undertakings
        Contents and amount of   CCP §720.630
        Duties of levying officer on filing of   CCP §720.640
        Effective date of   CCP §720.650
        General discussion of undertaking to release property   CCP §§720.610, 720.620
        Objection to undertaking not timely, release of property where   CCP §720.660
        Security interest or lien, claim of   CCP §§720.240, 720.260, 720.280
        Third party claims of ownership and possession   CCP §720.160
    Unlawful detainer action, claim of right to possession in   CCP §1174.3
Timber
    Crops, timber or minerals
        Attachment (See **ATTACHMENT**)
        Generally (See within this heading, **"Crops, timber or minerals"**)
Time
    Creditor's demand for claim by secured party or lienholder, time for filing   CCP §720.520
    Exemption claims   CCP §703.030
    Extending and shortening time (See within this heading, **"Extending and shortening time"**)
    Interest on judgment accruing from time of entry   CCP §685.020

ENFORCEMENT OF JUDGMENTS—Cont.
Time—Cont.
    Notice of sale of real property   CCP §701.545
    Operative date of provisions for enforcement   CCP §694.020
    Renewal of judgments, filing of application for   CCP §§683.110, 683.130
    Return of writ of execution   CCP §699.560
    Statutes of limitation (See within this heading, **"Statutes of limitation"**)
    Tax lien pursuant to enforcement of state tax liability   CCP §688.050
    Third party claims, hearing on   CCP §720.310
    Trial of proceeding   CCP §1170.5
    When judgment becomes enforceable   CCP §683.010
Tracing of exempt fund   CCP §703.080
Transfer or encumbrance of property
    Attachment (See **ATTACHMENT**)
    Charging order, continuation of liens created by   CCP §697.920
    Creditor's suit, continuation of liens created by   CCP §697.920
    Examination proceedings, continuation of liens created by   CCP §697.920
    Execution lien, transferal or encumbering of property subject to   CCP §§697.720 to 697.750
    Ex parte application for transfer of property or title to levying officer   CCP §699.040
    Extension of judgment lien, transfer of property prior to   CCP §683.180
    General rule of enforceability of lien on transferred or encumbered property   CCP §695.070
    Homestead, encumbrance affecting sale of   CCP §704.810
    Judgment lien on personal property, effect of sale, exchange or other disposition of property subject to   CCP §697.610
    Judgment lien on real property, effect of transfer of property subject to   CCP §697.390
    Writ of possession   CCP §714.030
    Writ of sale   CCP §716.030
Transitional provisions   CCP §§694.010 to 694.090
Trust assets
    Generally   CCP §695.030, Pro §§15300, 15301
    Petition to apply judgment debtor's interest in trust to satisfaction of money judgment   CCP §709.010
    Statutes of limitation on enforcement of money judgment against judgment debtor's interest in trust   Pro §§15300 to 15309
Trust deeds, foreclosure on (See **TRUST DEEDS AND MORTGAGES**)
Undertakings
    Applicable law   CCP §720.710
    Attachment (See **ATTACHMENT**)
    Hearings on objections   CCP §§720.770, 922
    Manner of making objection   CCP §720.760
    Return of writ affecting   CCP §720.800
    Stay of enforcement (See within this heading, **"Stay of enforcement"**)
Unemployment compensation
    Child support enforcement against benefits   CCP §704.120, Fam §17518
    Exemption of unemployment compensation benefits   CCP §704.120
Uniform Foreign-Money Claims Act   CCP §§676 to 676.16
Unlawful detainer, holding over after execution sale as act constituting   CCP §1161a
Unvested interest of judgment debtor's property applied to satisfaction of money judgment   CCP §709.020
Use of property, effect on exemption determination of change in   CCP §703.100
Vacating and setting aside
    Renewal of judgment vacated   CCP §683.170
    Right to payment, setting aside assignment of   CCP §708.560
Value
    Effect on exemption determination of change in value of property   CCP §703.100
Venue
    Examination proceedings   CCP §708.160
    State tax liability, action to enforce   CCP §688.020
Vessels
    Attachment (See **ATTACHMENT**)
    General method of levy on   CCP §700.090
Wages
    Garnishment (See **GARNISHMENT**)
    Generally (See within this heading, **"Salaries and wages"**)
Waiver
    Attachment, waiver of defense to   CCP §484.110
    Exemption, considerations for waiver of   CCP §§703.040, 703.060
Warrant for enforcement of state tax liability   CCP §688.110
Witnesses
    Attachment proceedings   CCP §491.120
    Examination proceedings, appearance at   CCP §708.130
Workers' compensation
    Child support enforcement against benefits   CCP §704.160, Fam §17510
    Exemption for claim, award or payment of   CCP §704.160
    Judgment lien on real property based on award of   CCP §697.330

ENFORCEMENT OF JUDGMENTS—Cont.
Writ of execution
    Levy and execution generally (See within this heading, **"Levy and execution"**)
Writ of possession
    Application of judgment creditor for issuance of writ after entry of judgment for possession   CCP §712.010
    Contents   CCP §712.020
    Defined   CCP §680.380
    Delivery and execution   CCP §712.030
    Fees for issuance of writ
        Superior court fees, specified services   Gov §70626
    Immediate enforcement of   CCP §712.050
    Money judgment included in judgment for possession, enforcement for   CCP §712.040
    Personal property, issuance and execution of writ for   CCP §§714.010 to 714.030
    Real property, issuance and execution of writ of possession for   CCP §§715.010 to 715.030
    Receiver appointed for   CCP §712.060
    Registered process server, execution of writ by   CCP §715.040
    Return of   CCP §712.050
    Sheriff's fees generally (See within this heading, **"Sheriff's fees"**)
    Transfer of property or title to judgment creditor, order for   CCP §714.030
    Unlawful detainer (See **UNLAWFUL DETAINER**)
Writ of sale
    Application of judgment creditor for issuance of writ after entry of judgment for sale of property   CCP §712.010
    Contents   CCP §712.020
    Defined   CCP §680.380
    Delivery and execution   CCP §712.030
    Issuance and execution of   CCP §§716.010, 716.020
    Money judgment included in judgment for sale, enforcement for   CCP §712.040
    Receiver appointed to enforce   CCP §712.060
    Return of   CCP §712.050
    Sheriff's fees generally (See within this heading, **"Sheriff's fees"**)
    Transfer of possession or title, application for order directing   CCP §716.030

ENGAGEMENT GIFTS
Marriage refusal as basis for recovery of   CC §1590

ENGINEERING
Bond required to secure costs in action against engineers   CCP §1029.5
Certificate of merit in negligence action against engineer   CCP §§411.35, 430.10
Design professionals' liens   CC §§8300 to 8319 (See **LIENS**)
Indemnity agreements
    Hazardous materials identification   CC §2782.6
    Neglect inspections   CC §2782.2
    Public agencies, contracts with   CC §2782.8
Inverse condemnation action, engineer's fees in   CCP §1036
Latent deficiencies in planning or construction of improvement to real property, statutes of limitation on damages for   CCP §337.15
Late payment penalty in lieu of interest, contract provision for   CC §3319
Partition referees making contracts with engineers   CCP §873.110
Patent deficiencies in planning or construction of improvement to real property, statutes of limitation on actions for injury or death from   CCP §337.1
Public agencies, payment schedule for   CC §3320
Review committees, liability of   CC §43.7
Subcontractor design professionals, payments to   CC §3321
Withholding disputed amount   CC §§3320, 3321

ENGLISH LANGUAGE
Administrative adjudication   Gov §11435.20
Court trials in English   CCP §185, Ev §§750 to 757
Gender tax repeal act preventing charging different prices for services of similar or like kind based on gender
    Consumer affairs department pamphlet for affected businesses and other notice of requirements of provisions   CC §51.63
    Licensing authority notice of provisions to licensee upon issuance or renewal   CC §51.6
Interstate family support
    Convention support proceedings
        English translation of record filed in another language   Fam §5700.713
Judicial notice of English language   Ev §451
Judicial proceedings conducted and preserved in   CCP §185
Jury service, eligibility for   CCP §203
Membership camping contracts, language requirements for   CC §1812.303
Plain English defined   Gov §§11342, 11342.580

ENGLISH LANGUAGE—Cont.
Regulations affecting small business in plain English, drafting   Gov §11343.2
Summons, legend appearing on   CCP §412.20
Will written in foreign language, translation of   Pro §8002
Witnesses' knowledge of   Ev §701
Written proceedings to be in   CCP §185

ENHANCEMENT (See **SENTENCE AND PUNISHMENT**)

ENMITY
Challenge of juror for implied bias   CCP §229

ENOCH ARDEN STATUTE   Ev §§667, 1282

ENROLLMENT AGREEMENTS
Disaffirmance by minor of provisions purporting to waive rights or remedies arising out of sexual assault or battery of minor   CCP §1002.7

ENTAILED ESTATES
Abolished   CC §763

ENTERTAINMENT INDUSTRY
Athletics (See **ATHLETICS**)
Employer and employee
    Commercial online entertainment employment service providers
        Age information of subscribers, restriction on disclosure   CC §1798.83.5
Indecency and obscenity (See **INDECENCY AND OBSCENITY**)
Motion pictures (See **MOTION PICTURES**)

ENTICEMENT OF CHILD (See **PARENT AND CHILD**)

ENTRY ON LAND
Discovery, entry for purposes of (See **INSPECTION DEMANDS**)
Eminent domain, entry on property for activities related to acquisition of property   CCP §§1245.010 to 1245.060
Forcible entry and detainer (See **FORCIBLE ENTRY AND DETAINER**)
Mines and mining (See **MINES AND MINING**)
Notice required for mineral rights owner prior to   CC §848

ENTRY ON RECORD
Appellate rules
    Supreme court and courts of appeal (See **APPELLATE RULES, SUPREME COURT AND COURTS OF APPEAL**)
Judgments and decrees (See **JUDGMENTS**)

ENVIRONMENTAL HAZARDS
Attorney general
    Civil actions to enforce environmental provisions
        Fees and costs for attorney general   CCP §1021.8
    Copy of pleading provided to AG by party filing environmental pollution action   CCP §388
Automobile sales contract notifications regarding pollution control   CC §2982
Broker or seller's duty to inform transferee of known environmental hazards   CC §§2079.7, 2079.11
Complex litigation defined   CRC 3.400
Covenants   CC §1471
Dispute resolution for private parties
    Admissibility of commitment statement in subsequent proceedings   CC §853
    Commitment statement
        Generally   CC §851
        Acceptance by owner   CC §852
        Admissibility as evidence in subsequent proceedings   CC §853
        Damages in subsequent civil actions, limitation of   CC §852
        Form   CC §§852, 854
        Mediation following rejection of commitment statement   CC §852
        Stay of actions   CC §852
        Tolling of statutes of limitations   CC §852
    Damages available in actions after issuance of commitment statement, limitation of   CC §852
    Definitions   CC §850
    Effective date of requirements   CC §855
    Form of commitment statement
        General form   CC §854
        Notice   CC §852
    Indemnification of notice recipient   CC §853
    Mediation following rejection of commitment statement   CC §852
    Notice of potential liability
        Generally   CC §851
        Tolling of statutes of limitations   CC §852

ENVIRONMENTAL HAZARDS—Cont.
Dispute resolution for private parties—Cont.
- Release report
  - Generally   CC §851
  - Tolling of statutes of limitation   CC §852
- Stay of actions   CC §852
- Tolling of statutes of limitation   CC §852

Gasoline stations, air pollution standards for   CC §1952.8

Indemnification
- Dispute resolution procedures, indemnification under   CC §853
- Engineers and geologists identifying hazardous materials, indemnification agreements covering   CC §2782.6

Pipeline corporation's absolute liability for damages caused by discharge or leaking of oil   CC §3333.5

Referee, objection to appointment of   CCP §641.2

School districts, property acquired by (See **SCHOOL DISTRICTS**)

Secured lenders' rights and remedies for hazardous substance release on real property security (See **TRUST DEEDS AND MORTGAGES**)

Statutes of limitation
- Civil penalties and punitive damages, actions for   CCP §338.1
- Tolling of statutes under provisions for private dispute resolution   CCP §852

Stay of proceedings relating to   CCP §917.15

ENVIRONMENTAL IMPACT REPORTS

Capitol building annex project
- Judicial review of environmental impact report on building annex project
  - Petitions under environmental quality act, civil rules governing   CRC 3.2220 to 3.2240

Jobs and economic improvement through environmental leadership act of 2021
- Appellate review of CEQA cases   CRC 8.700 to 8.705
- Petitions under environmental quality act, civil rules governing   CRC 3.2220 to 3.2240

ENVIRONMENTAL QUALITY ACT

Appellate review of cases under public resources code   CRC 8.700 to CRC 8.705

Capital building annex project
- Petitions under environmental quality act, civil rules governing   CRC 3.2220 to 3.2237

Capital building annex project, expanded
- Appellate review of CEQA cases   CRC 8.700 to 8.705
  - Applicability of provisions   CRC 8.700, 8.702
  - Briefing   CRC 8.702
  - Civil appellate rules provisions, applicability   CRC 8.702
  - Costs in leadership projects, court of appeal   CRC 8.705
  - Cross appeals   CRC 8.702
  - Definitions   CRC 8.700
  - Electronic filing and service   CRC 8.701
  - Extensions of time   CRC 8.701, 8.702
  - New trial, motion   CRC 8.702
  - Notice of appeal   CRC 8.702
  - Oral arguments   CRC 8.702
  - Process and service of process   CRC 8.701
  - Reconsideration of appealable order, motion   CRC 8.702
  - Record on appeal   CRC 8.702
  - Superior court clerk duties   CRC 8.702
  - Vacation of judgment, motion   CRC 8.702
  - Writ proceedings   CRC 8.703
- Petitions under environmental quality act, civil rules governing   CRC 3.2220 to 3.2240
- Review of CEQA cases   CRC 8.700 to 8.705
- Writ proceedings   CRC 8.703

Civil rules governing petitions under act   CRC 3.2200 to 3.2240

Energy infrastructure projects
- Appellate review of CEQA cases
  - Court of appeal costs   CRC 8.705
- Petitions under environmental quality act, civil rules governing
  - Contents of petitions   CRC 3.2223
  - Trial court costs   CRC 3.2240

Environmental leadership development projects
- Appellate review of CEQA cases   CRC 8.700 to 8.705

Environmental leadership transit projects
- Appellate review of CEQA cases   CRC 8.700 to 8.705

Inglewood arena project
- Appellate review of CEQA cases   CRC 8.700 to 8.705
  - Applicability of provisions   CRC 8.700, 8.702
  - Briefing   CRC 8.702
  - Civil appellate rules provisions, applicability   CRC 8.702
  - Costs in leadership projects, court of appeal   CRC 8.705
  - Cross appeals   CRC 8.702
  - Definitions   CRC 8.700

ENVIRONMENTAL QUALITY ACT—Cont.

Inglewood arena project—Cont.
- Appellate review of CEQA cases—Cont.
  - Electronic filing and service   CRC 8.701
  - Extensions of time   CRC 8.701, 8.702
  - New trial, motion   CRC 8.702
  - Notice of appeal   CRC 8.702
  - Oral arguments   CRC 8.702
  - Process and service of process   CRC 8.701
  - Reconsideration of appealable order, motion   CRC 8.702
  - Record on appeal   CRC 8.702
  - Superior court clerk duties   CRC 8.702
  - Vacation of judgment, motion   CRC 8.702
  - Writ proceedings   CRC 8.703
- Petitions under environmental quality act, civil rules governing   CRC 3.2220 to 3.2240
- Review of CEQA cases   CRC 8.700 to 8.705

Jobs and economic improvement through environmental leadership act of 2011
- Writ proceedings   CRC 8.703

Jobs and economic improvement through environmental leadership act of 2021
- Appellate review of CEQA cases   CRC 8.700 to 8.705
  - Applicability of provisions   CRC 8.700, 8.702
  - Briefing   CRC 8.702
  - Civil appellate rules provisions, applicability   CRC 8.702
  - Costs in leadership projects, court of appeal   CRC 8.705
  - Cross appeals   CRC 8.702
  - Definitions   CRC 8.700
  - Electronic filing and service   CRC 8.701
  - Extensions of time   CRC 8.701, 8.702
  - New trial, motion   CRC 8.702
  - Notice of appeal   CRC 8.702
  - Oral arguments   CRC 8.702
  - Process and service of process   CRC 8.701
  - Reconsideration of appealable order, motion   CRC 8.702
  - Record on appeal   CRC 8.702
  - Superior court clerk duties   CRC 8.702
  - Vacation of judgment, motion   CRC 8.702
  - Writ proceedings   CRC 8.703
- Petitions under environmental quality act, civil rules governing   CRC 3.2220 to 3.2240
- Review of CEQA cases   CRC 8.700 to 8.705
- Writ proceedings   CRC 8.703

Oakland sports and mixed use project
- Appellate review of CEQA cases   CRC 8.700 to 8.705
  - Applicability of provisions   CRC 8.700, 8.702
  - Briefing   CRC 8.702
  - Civil appellate rules provisions, applicability   CRC 8.702
  - Costs in leadership projects, court of appeal   CRC 8.705
  - Cross appeals   CRC 8.702
  - Definitions   CRC 8.700
  - Electronic filing and service   CRC 8.701
  - Extensions of time   CRC 8.701, 8.702
  - New trial, motion   CRC 8.702
  - Notice of appeal   CRC 8.702
  - Oral arguments   CRC 8.702
  - Process and service of process   CRC 8.701
  - Reconsideration of appealable order, motion   CRC 8.702
  - Record on appeal   CRC 8.702
  - Superior court clerk duties   CRC 8.702
  - Vacation of judgment, motion   CRC 8.702
  - Writ proceedings   CRC 8.703
- Petitions under environmental quality act, civil rules governing   CRC 3.2220 to 3.2240
- Review of CEQA cases   CRC 8.700 to 8.705
- Writ proceedings   CRC 8.703

Old Town Center transit and transportation facilities project
- Appellate review of CEQA cases   CRC 8.700 to 8.705
  - Applicability of provisions   CRC 8.700, 8.702
  - Briefing   CRC 8.702
  - Civil appellate rules provisions, applicability   CRC 8.702
  - Costs in leadership projects, court of appeal   CRC 8.705
  - Cross appeals   CRC 8.702
  - Definitions   CRC 8.700
  - Electronic filing and service   CRC 8.701
  - Extensions of time   CRC 8.701, 8.702
  - New trial, motion   CRC 8.702
  - Notice of appeal   CRC 8.702
  - Oral arguments   CRC 8.702
  - Process and service of process   CRC 8.701
  - Reconsideration of appealable order, motion   CRC 8.702
  - Record on appeal   CRC 8.702

ENVIRONMENTAL QUALITY ACT—Cont.
  Old Town Center transit and transportation facilities project—Cont.
    Appellate review of CEQA cases —Cont.
      Superior court clerk duties   CRC 8.702
      Vacation of judgment, motion   CRC 8.702
      Writ proceedings   CRC 8.703
    Petitions under environmental quality act, civil rules governing   CRC 3.2220 to 3.2240
    Review of CEQA cases   CRC 8.700 to 8.705
    Writ proceedings   CRC 8.703
  Petitions under environmental quality act, civil rules governing   CRC 3.2200 to 3.2240
    Administrative record under CEQA
      Appendix of excerpts   CRC 3.2205
      Electronic format   CRC 3.2207
      Form   CRC 3.2205
      Format   CRC 3.2205, 3.2207, 3.2208
      Index   CRC 3.2205
      Jobs and economic improvement through environmental leadership act of 2011   CRC 3.2225
      Lodging of record   CRC 3.2206
      Organization of documents   CRC 3.2205
      Paper format   CRC 3.2208
      Sacramento downtown arena project, CEQA challenges   CRC 3.2225
      Service of record   CRC 3.2206
    Applicability of civil rules provisions   CRC 3.2200
    Capital building annex project
      Administrative record, lodging, service, etc   CRC 3.2225
      Applicability of provisions   CRC 3.2220
      Briefing   CRC 3.2227
      Case management conferences   CRC 3.2226
      Complex cases rules, exemption   CRC 3.2220
      Definitions   CRC 3.2220
      Electronic filing   CRC 3.2222
      Hearings   CRC 3.2227
      Initial case management conference   CRC 3.2226
      Judgments   CRC 3.2228
      Postjudgment motions   CRC 3.2231
      Process and service of process   CRC 3.2222
      Response to petition   CRC 3.2224
      Sanctions   CRC 3.2221
      Settlements, notice   CRC 3.2229
      Settlements, procedures   CRC 3.2230
      Statement of issues   CRC 3.2230
      Time, extensions   CRC 3.2221
    Capital building annex project, expanded
      Appellate review of CEQA cases   CRC 8.700 to 8.705
      Case management conferences   CRC 3.2226
      Contents of petitions   CRC 3.2223
      Electronic filing   CRC 3.2222
      Initial case management conference   CRC 3.2226
      Process and service of process   CRC 3.2222
      Review of CEQA cases   CRC 8.700 to 8.705
      Sanctions   CRC 3.2221
      Time, extensions   CRC 3.2221
    Energy infrastructure project
      Contents of petitions   CRC 3.2223
      Trial court costs   CRC 3.2240
    Environmental leadership transit projects
      Contents of petitions   CRC 3.2223
    Inglewood arena project   CRC 3.2220 to 3.2240
      Appellate review of CEQA cases   CRC 8.700 to 8.705
      Case management conferences   CRC 3.2226
      Contents of petitions   CRC 3.2223
      Electronic filing   CRC 3.2222
      Initial case management conference   CRC 3.2226
      Petitions under environmental quality act, civil rules governing   CRC 3.2220 to 3.2240
      Process and service of process   CRC 3.2222
      Review of CEQA cases   CRC 8.700 to 8.705
      Sanctions   CRC 3.2221
      Time, extensions   CRC 3.2221
      Trial court costs   CRC 3.2240
    Jobs and economic improvement through environmental leadership act of 2011
      Administrative record, lodging, service, etc   CRC 3.2225
      Briefing   CRC 3.2227
      Complex cases rules, exemption   CRC 3.2220
      Hearings   CRC 3.2227
      Judgments   CRC 3.2228
      Postjudgment motions   CRC 3.2231

ENVIRONMENTAL QUALITY ACT—Cont.
  Petitions under environmental quality act, civil rules governing —Cont.
    Jobs and economic improvement through environmental leadership act of 2011—Cont.
      Response to petition   CRC 3.2224
      Settlements, notice   CRC 3.2229
      Settlements, procedures   CRC 3.2230
      Statement of issues   CRC 3.2230
    Jobs and economic improvement through environmental leadership act of 2021   CRC 3.2220 to 3.2240
      Appellate review of CEQA cases   CRC 8.700 to 8.705
      Case management conferences   CRC 3.2226
      Contents of petitions   CRC 3.2223
      Electronic filing   CRC 3.2222
      Initial case management conference   CRC 3.2226
      Process and service of process   CRC 3.2222
      Review of CEQA cases   CRC 8.700 to 8.705
      Sanctions   CRC 3.2221
      Time, extensions   CRC 3.2221
    Oakland sports and mixed use project   CRC 3.2220 to 3.2240
      Case management conferences   CRC 3.2226
      Contents of petitions   CRC 3.2223
      Electronic filing   CRC 3.2222
      Initial case management conference   CRC 3.2226
      Process and service of process   CRC 3.2222
      Sanctions   CRC 3.2221
      Time, extensions   CRC 3.2221
      Trial court costs   CRC 3.2240
    Old Town Center transit and transportation facilities project   CRC 3.2220 to 3.2240
      Case management conferences   CRC 3.2226
      Contents of petitions   CRC 3.2223
      Electronic filing   CRC 3.2222
      Initial case management conference   CRC 3.2226
      Process and service of process   CRC 3.2222
      Sanctions   CRC 3.2221
      Time, extensions   CRC 3.2221
    Sacramento downtown arena project, CEQA challenges   CRC 3.2220 to 3.2240
      Administrative record, lodging, service, etc   CRC 3.2225
      Appellate review of CEQA cases   CRC 8.700 to 8.705
      Applicability of provisions   CRC 3.2220
      Applicable rules   CRC 3.2235
      Briefing   CRC 3.2227
      Case management conferences   CRC 3.2226
      Complex cases rules, exemption   CRC 3.2220
      Contents of petitions   CRC 3.2223
      Definitions   CRC 3.2220
      Electronic filing   CRC 3.2222
      Hearings   CRC 3.2227
      Initial case management conference   CRC 3.2226
      Judgments   CRC 3.2228
      Postjudgment motions   CRC 3.2231
      Process and service of process   CRC 3.2222
      Response to petition   CRC 3.2224
      Responsible parties, listing   CRC 3.2237
      Review of CEQA cases   CRC 8.700 to 8.705
      Sanctions   CRC 3.2221
      Service of petition   CRC 3.2236
      Settlements, notice   CRC 3.2229
      Settlements, procedures   CRC 3.2230
      Statement of issues   CRC 3.2230
      Time, extensions   CRC 3.2221
    Semiconductor or microelectronic project
      Contents of petitions   CRC 3.2223
      Trial court costs   CRC 3.2240
    Transfer of provisions to within civil rues   CRC 3.1365
    Water-related projects
      Contents of petitions   CRC 3.2223
      Trial court costs   CRC 3.2240
  Sacramento downtown arena project, CEQA challenges
    Appellate review of CEQA cases   CRC 8.700 to 8.705
      Applicability of provisions   CRC 8.700, 8.702
      Briefing   CRC 8.702
      Civil appellate rules provisions, applicability   CRC 8.702
      Costs in leadership projects, court of appeal   CRC 8.705
      Cross appeals   CRC 8.702
      Definitions   CRC 8.700
      Electronic filing and service   CRC 8.701
      Extensions of time   CRC 8.701, 8.702
      New trial, motion   CRC 8.702

ENVIRONMENTAL QUALITY ACT—Cont.
Sacramento downtown arena project, CEQA challenges—Cont.
    Appellate review of CEQA cases —Cont.
        Notice of appeal   CRC 8.702
        Oral arguments   CRC 8.702
        Process and service of process   CRC 8.701
        Reconsideration of appealable order, motion   CRC 8.702
        Record on appeal   CRC 8.702
        Superior court clerk duties   CRC 8.702
        Vacation of judgment, motion   CRC 8.702
        Writ proceedings   CRC 8.703
    Petitions under environmental quality act, civil rules governing   CRC 3.2220 to 3.2240
    Review of CEQA cases   CRC 8.700 to 8.705
Semiconductor or microelectronic projects
    Appellate review of CEQA cases
        Court of appeal costs   CRC 8.705
    Petitions under environmental quality act, civil rules governing
        Contents of petitions   CRC 3.2223
        Trial court costs   CRC 3.2240
Streamlined CEQA projects
    Petitions under environmental quality act, civil rules governing   CRC 3.2220 to 3.2240
    Review of CEQA cases   CRC 8.700 to 8.705
Water-related projects
    Appellate review of CEQA cases
        Court of appeal costs   CRC 8.705
    Petitions under environmental quality act, civil rules governing
        Contents of petitions   CRC 3.2223
        Trial court costs   CRC 3.2240

EPHEDRA AND RELATED SUBSTANCES
Minors, sales to
    Verification of age for sale of age-restricted products   CC §1798.99.1

EPINEPHRINE AUTO-INJECTORS
Anaphylaxis
    Epinephrine auto-injector administration for first aid
        Immunity from civil liability of lay rescuers, prehospital emergency medical care providers or authorized entities   CC §1714.23

EQUALIZATION, STATE BOARD OF
Burden of proof
    Tax evasion or fraud cases, penalty sought   Ev §524
Nondisclosure of name and address of registered or licensed persons by   CC §1798.69

EQUAL PROTECTION RIGHTS (See DISCRIMINATION)

EQUESTRIAN TRAILS
Closure of   CCP §731.5

EQUIPMENT
Attachment (See ATTACHMENT)
Seller assisted marketing plans   CC §§1812.200 to 1812.221
Serial number altered or destroyed prior to sale   CC §1710.1
Typewriters (See TYPEWRITERS AND TYPEWRITING)
Warranties   CC §§1790 to 1795.8

EQUIPMENT LEASES
Seller assisted marketing plan defined   CC §1812.201

EQUITABLE EXCUSAL
Attorney in fact
    Breach of duty   Pro §4231.5

EQUITABLE SERVITUDES
Common interest developments   CC §5975

EQUITY
Accounts and accounting (See ACCOUNTS AND ACCOUNTING)
Cancellation of instruments   CC §§3412 to 3415
Declaratory judgments (See DECLARATORY JUDGMENTS)
Injunctions (See INJUNCTIONS)
Judicial arbitration   CCP §§1141.13, 1141.16
Leases, relief under   CC §1951.8
Limited civil cases, cases in equity constituting   CCP §86
Reformation of instrument   CC §§3399 to 3402
Rescission (See RESCISSION)
Restitution (See RESTITUTION)

EQUITY—Cont.
Small claims court jurisdiction to grant equitable relief in lieu of or in addition to money damages   CCP §116.220
Specific performance (See SPECIFIC PERFORMANCE)

EQUITY SALES CONTRACTS (See HOME EQUITY SALES CONTRACTS)

ERISA
Certificate or license requirements on loan transactions   CC §1917.210
Estate tax liability on excess accumulations of individual retirement plans   Pro §20114
Usury laws, exemption from   CC §1917.220

EROSION (See also FLOODS)
Ownership of land after   CC §1015

ERRONEOUS EVIDENCE
Verdict, effect on   Ev §353

ERRORS (See MISTAKE)

ESCAPE
Juvenile wardship proceedings
    Detention of minor
        Escape from commitment   CRC 5.760

ESCHEAT
Generally   CCP §§1300 to 1305, 1420 to 1424
Abandoned property, escheat of   CCP §1476
Agreement to locate property   CCP §1582
Attorney general
    Generally   CCP §§1420 to 1423
    Proceedings subsequent to escheat   CCP §1355
    Title vesting in state   CCP §1410
Bank deposits   CCP §§1513, 1513.5
Business associations, escheat of unclaimed or abandoned property held by   CCP §§1511, 1513, 1516, 1520, 1520.5, 1542, 1581
Charges, deductibility of   CCP §1522
Claim of ownership
    Decedent's estate   CCP §§1354, 1420
    Payment to claimant, effect of   CCP §1335
    Third party claims   CCP §§1352, 1353
    Time limit for claim
        Generally   CCP §§1350, 1351, 1415, 1430
        Decedent's estate   CCP §1441, Pro §11903
        Proceedings subsequent to escheat   CCP §1355
Controller
    Accounts separated in unclaimed property fund by   CCP §§1314, 1319
    Actions against   CCP §1378
    Certified copy of court order received by   CCP §1312
    Contracts, limitations on   CCP §1377
    Destruction of property   CCP §1379
    Exempt transactions   CCP §1380
    Federal property   CCP §§1602, 1606
    Income credited to separate accounts by   CCP §§1319, 1320
    Known heirs and claimants, deposited property recorded to credit of   CCP §1316
    Notice received by   CCP §1311
    Powers of   CCP §1365
    Proceeds of sale, transactions on   CCP §§1390 to 1394
    Small estates   CCP §1415
    State custody of property delivered to   CCP §1361
    Title documents executed by   CCP §§1372, 1376, 1381
    Unclaimed property fund, ordering deposits into   CCP §1313
Credit balances   CC §1810.3
Decedent's estate
    Generally   Pro §§6800 to 6806
    Certified copy of court order furnished to controller   CCP §1312
    Claim against property on deposit   CCP §§1354, 1420
    Creditors of estate, escheat of deposit for absent   Pro §11428
    Disposition of unclaimed property   CCP §§1440 to 1449
    Distribution to state   Pro §§11900 to 11904
    Known heirs and claimants, deposited property recorded to credit of   CCP §1316
    Proceedings on behalf of state   CCP §§1420 to 1424
    Proceedings subsequent to escheat   CCP §1355
    Public administrator, funds deposited by   CCP §1449, Pro §§7643, 7644
    Recorded on controller's books to credit of estate or known heirs   CCP §§1315, 1316
Defined   CCP §1300

ESCHEAT—Cont.
Employee benefit plan distributions CCP §§1501, 1521, Pro §6806
Federal agencies, property held by CCP §§1600 to 1615
Fees for location of property CCP §§1522, 1582
Funeral trusts, preneed
    Unclaimed funds maintained in preneed funeral trust CCP §1518.5
        Reimbursement of holder upon submission of death certificate CCP §1560
Gift certificates CCP §1520.5
Income from permanently escheated property CCP §1320
Increase or decrease of amount of funds on deposit with holder
    Electronic transactions
        Debit or credit transactions, single or recurring CCP §1513
Infancy, effect on statutes of limitation due to CCP §§1415, 1430, 1441
Insurance rebate under Proposition 103, disposition of unclaimed CCP §1523
Insurers, property unclaimed following dissolution of CCP §1517
Intangibles
    Decedent's estate Pro §§6804, 6805
    General escheat provisions CCP §§1510, 1516, 1520, 1520.5
Interest income, permanently escheated property CCP §1320
Jurisdiction
    Generally CCP §§1353, 1420
    Title vesting in state CCP §1410
Limitations period for action concerning abandoned property, effect of CCP §1476
Mental illness
    Death of patient in mental hospital CCP §1447
    Statutes of limitation affected by CCP §§1415, 1430, 1441
Money orders CCP §§1511, 1513, 1542, 1581
Mortgage bond, funds remaining under CC §2941.7
Notice
    Banks and financial organizations, notice requirements for CCP §1513.5
    Business associations, notice requirement for CCP §1516
    Controller receiving CCP §1311
    Location of owner, notification program CCP §1531.5
    Pendency of action CCP §1410
    Property held in ordinary course of business CCP §1520
    Publication generally (See within this heading, "**Publication**")
    Savings bonds, war bonds or military awards
        Separate notice CCP §1531.6
    Small estates CCP §1415
    Title vesting in state CCP §1410
NOW accounts, funds in CCP §1513
Other states, property subject to escheat under CCP §1504
Partnerships, interests in and obligations of CCP §1516
Payment CCP §§1441 to 1445, 1449
Permanent escheat
    Defined CCP §1300
    Income from permanently escheated property CCP §1320
    Refunds of permanently escheated property CCP §1347
    Unclaimed Property Law, inapplicability under CCP §1501.5
    When property is permanently escheated CCP §§1430, 1441
Pleadings
    Decedent's estate CCP §§1354, 1420
    Proceedings subsequent to escheat CCP §1355
    Third party claims CCP §1353
    Title vesting in state CCP §1410
Prior law, property not subject to CCP §1503
Prisoners CCP §1446
Proceedings subsequent to escheat CCP §1355
Property determined to not be subject to escheat
    Holder's duties CCP §1532
Public administrator, funds deposited by CCP §1449, Pro §§7643, 7644
Publication
    Generally CCP §1531
    Decedent's estate, petition and notice re CCP §1420
    Location of owner, notification program CCP §1531.5
    Small estates CCP §1415
    Title vesting in state CCP §1410
Receivers appointed over decedents' estates CCP §1422
Recovery of unclaimed property, agreements to assist in CCP §1582
Refunds of permanently escheated property CCP §1347
Retirement funds (See **RETIREMENT**)
Safe deposit boxes CCP §§1514, 1532.1
Salaries and wages CCP §1513
Sale, proceeds from CCP §§1392 to 1394
Service
    Attorney general, petitions served to CCP §1355
    Proceedings subsequent to escheat CCP §1355
    Publication generally (See within this heading, "**Publication**")
$60,000 or less, unclaimed money or property of CCP §1352

ESCHEAT—Cont.
State custody of property CCP §1361
State held property under terms of express contract, applicability to CCP §1306
Statutes of limitation for actions concerning abandoned property, effect of CCP §1476
Third party claims of ownership CCP §§1352, 1353
Time limits for claim on escheated property (See within this heading, "**Claim of ownership**")
Title vesting in state CCP §§1410 to 1431
Traveler's checks CCP §§1511, 1513, 1542, 1581
Treasurer
    Cash deposited with CCP §1310
    Proceeds of sale delivered to CCP §§1390, 1391
    State custody of property delivered to CCP §1361
Trust deed bond, funds remaining under CC §2941.7
Trust funds CCP §1424, Pro §6806
Unclaimed Property Fund (See **UNCLAIMED PROPERTY**)
United States agencies, property held by CCP §§1600 to 1615
Venue for title vesting in state CCP §1410
Youth Authority inmate CCP §1448

ESCROW
Generally CC §1057
Agents
    Real estate sales
        Choice of agent lies with buyer CC §1103.22
    Regulations CC §1057.5
Conveyances (See **CONVEYANCES**)
Developers specifying escrow companies CC §2995
Impound accounts (See **IMPOUND ACCOUNTS**)
License name and name of license-issuing department, required statement in escrow instructions identifying CC §1057.7
Mechanic's liens
    Large projects, security for CC §§8700 to 8730
Membership camping contracts, payments for CC §1812.314
Notice to buyer in escrow transactions advising acquisition of title insurance CC §1057.6
Partition sales CCP §873.780
Rating services for escrow agents
    Actions by agents against service CC §1785.28
    Consumer credit reporting agency provisions, applicability CC §1785.28
    Personally identifiable information, safeguarding CC §1785.28
    Sunset of provisions CC §1785.28.6
Real estate sales
    Choice of escrow agent lies with buyer CC §1103.22
Return of deposited escrow account funds CC §1057.3
Seller assisted marketing plans, escrow accounts for CC §§1812.210, 1812.214
Sexual harassment, civil action for
    Construction or application of provisions in issue, solicitor general notified CC §51.1
Support judgment lien, demand statement needed to close escrow relating to CCP §697.360

ESTATES
Classes of CC §761
Conditional estates (See **CONDITIONAL ESTATES**)
Condominiums, estate interest in CC §783
Decedents' estates (See **DECEDENTS' ESTATES**)
Freehold estates CC §§765, 766
Grant limitations CCP §1971
Interests in CC §701
Judge, role of Pro §800
Minors, estates of (See **PARENT AND CHILD**)
Personal property CC §§765 to 767
Taxation (See **ESTATE TAX**)
Termination of estates
    Immigration or citizenship status irrelevant to liability or remedy CC §3339.10

ESTATES TAIL
Abolished CC §763

ESTATE TAX
Interpretation of will or trust provisions favoring elimination or reduction of federal estate tax liability Pro §21503
Marital deduction gifts (See **MARITAL DEDUCTION GIFTS**)
Power of attorney, powers under statutory form of Pro §4463
Proration
    Generally Pro §20110

ESTATE TAX—Cont.
Proration—Cont.
    Additions and reductions to taxable estate
        Allowances for   Pro §20112
        Qualified real property tax, additions to   Pro §20114
    Applicability of law   Pro §20101
    Definitions   Pro §20100
    Dispositions of trusts   Pro §20113
    Extensions on payments of federal estate tax, party liable for   Pro §20115
    Judicial proceedings
        Generally   Pro §20120
        Notice of hearing   Pro §20122
        Orders   Pro §§20123, 20124
        Out-of-state proration, enforcement of   Pro §20125
        Petition   Pro §20121
    Life estates, interests in property involving   Pro §20113
    Manner of   Pro §20111
    Personal representative
        Capacity to bring suit   Pro §20120
        Not in possession, tax liability for property where   Pro §20116
        Reimbursements, right to   Pro §20117
    Qualified real property   Pro §20114
    Reimbursement, right to   Pro §20117
    Retirement plans, excess accumulations of   Pro §§20114, 20114.5
    Tenancy for years, interests in property involving   Pro §20113
    Trusts, liability of   Pro §20113
Trusts
    Taxes (See **TRUSTS**)

ESTOPPEL
Alteration of instruments affecting   CC §1698
Mechanics' liens
    Statement purporting to release or waive lien, effect   CC §8126
Tenant denying landlord's title   Ev §624
Title marketability, effect on   CC §880.030
Voidable transactions   CC §3439.10

ETCHING CREAM
Minors, sale to
    Verification of age for sale of age-restricted products   CC §1798.99.1

ETCHINGS
Sales regulated   CC §§1740 to 1745

ETHICS
Attorneys
    Rules of professional conduct generally   ProfC 1.0 to 8.5 (See **ATTORNEY PROFESSIONAL CONDUCT**)
Judges
    Code of judicial ethics   CRCSupp JudEthicsCanons 1 to 6 (See **JUDGES**)
    Ethics opinions   CRC 9.80
        Committee on judicial ethics opinions, internal operating rules and procedures   CRCSupp JudEthicsOpinionsIOP 1 to CRCSupp JudEthicsOpinionsIOP 9
Judicial performance, commission on
    Members, ethical code   JudPerPolicy 6.1 to 6.5

ETHNIC GROUPS
Adoption proceedings (See **ADOPTION**)
Discrimination
    Damages, measure
        Lost earnings or impaired earning capacity, race, ethnicity or gender not to serve as basis for reduction in damages   CC §3361
    Judicial ethics code
        Administrative responsibilities of judge, impartial discharge   CRCSupp JudEthicsCanon 3
        Attorneys, judges to require to refrain from manifesting   CRCSupp JudEthicsCanon 3
        Bias, prejudice or harassment in performance of judicial duties   CRCSupp JudEthicsCanon 3
        Court personnel and staff under direction of judge, standards of conduct enforced by judge   CRCSupp JudEthicsCanon 3
        Membership in discriminatory organizations   CRCSupp JudEthicsCanon 2
Disqualification of judges, grounds for   CCP §170.2
Foster care placement   Fam §7950

EURO
As currency of participating member states of European Union   CC §1663

EUTHANASIA
Advance health care directives   Pro §§4670 to 4679

EUTHANASIA—Cont.
Medical decisions for adults lacking capacity   Pro §4653

EVICTION
Generally (See **LANDLORD AND TENANT**)
Demurrer
    Meet and confer prerequisite to filing
        Inapplicability of meet and confer requirement in forcible entry, forcible detainer or unlawful detainer cases   CCP §430.41
Floating home marinas   CC §800.70
Forms
    Judicial council legal forms   CRCAppx A
Hotel guests failing to depart by posted checkout time, eviction of   CC §1865
Mobilehome tenants (See **MOBILEHOMES**)
Nuisance as grounds
    Controlled substances unlawfully on property as basis for nuisance   CC §§3486, 3486.5
    Weapons or ammunition unlawfully on property as basis for nuisance   CC §3485
Recreational vehicle parks (See **RECREATIONAL VEHICLE PARKS**)
Special occupancy parks
    Overstaying guests   CC §1866
Unlawful detainer proceedings (See **UNLAWFUL DETAINER**)

EVIDENCE
Administrative adjudications
    Sympathy expressed to accident victim or family
        Inadmissibility   Gov §11440.45
Administrative Procedure Act (See **ADMINISTRATIVE PROCEDURE ACT**)
Admissible evidence (See **ADMISSIBILITY OF EVIDENCE**)
Adoption under Hague adoption convention
    Child residents of US
        Foreign country party to convention   CRC 5.490
Appellate rules, superior court appeals
    Evidence questions   Ev §§353, 354
Appellate rules, supreme court and courts of appeal
    Additional evidence on appeal, application for   CRC 8.252
    Costs, items recoverable as   CRC 8.278
Applicability of Evidence Code   Ev §300
Arbitration (See **ARBITRATION**)
Attorney professional conduct
    False evidence offered
        Candor towards the tribunal   ProfC 3.3
    Obstructing access to evidence, witness, etc
        Fairness to opposing party and counsel   ProfC 3.4
Best and secondary (See **BEST AND SECONDARY EVIDENCE**)
Beyond reasonable doubt (See **BEYOND REASONABLE DOUBT**)
Blood tests (See **BLOOD TESTS**)
Boundaries, evidence in dispute with state involving   CCP §2031.510, Ev §523
Burden of going forward (See **BURDEN OF GOING FORWARD**)
Burden of proof (See **BURDEN OF PROOF**)
Business records (See **BUSINESS RECORDS**)
Character and reputation (See **CHARACTER AND REPUTATION**)
Child support (See **CHILD SUPPORT**)
Clear and convincing evidence (See **CLEAR AND CONVINCING EVIDENCE**)
Code construction   Ev §§1 to 12
Common interest developments
    Alternative dispute resolution
        Applicability of evidence code   CC §5940
Computer information (See **COMPUTERS**)
Confessions (See **CONFESSIONS**)
Construction defects, actions for
    Residential construction standards, failure to meet   CC §942
Consumer privacy rights
    Violation of evidentiary privileges, businesses not to be compelled   CC §1798.145
Continuance of trial due to lack of   CCP §595.4
Coordination of actions, evidence at hearings   CRC 3.514
Court commissioner's power to take proof and make and report findings   CCP §259
Court reporters
    Reports as prima facie evidence of testimony and proceedings   CCP §273
Court to regulate order of proof   Ev §320
Creative expressions
    Admissibility   Ev §352.2
Cross examination (See **CROSS-EXAMINATION**)
Death penalty
    Electronic recordings presented or offered into evidence
        Pretrial proceedings   CRC 4.119
        Trial, additional requirements   CRC 4.230

EVIDENCE—Cont.
  Deceased child victims
    Sealing autopsy report and evidence   CCP §130
  Definitions   Ev §§105 to 260
  Dependent children, evidence at hearings
    Detention hearings   CRC 5.676
    Disposition hearings
      Nonminor disposition hearings   CRC 5.697
    Jurisdictional hearings   CRC 5.534, 5.682, 5.684
  Dependent persons
    Defined   Ev §177
  Depositions
    Generally (See **DEPOSITIONS**)
    Use of depositions as evidence   CCP §2025.620
  Direct evidence, generally   Ev §410
  Discovery (See **DISCOVERY**)
  Disqualification of judges, personal knowledge of evidentiary facts as grounds for   CCP §170.1
  District attorneys
    Exculpatory evidence
      Attorney professional conduct, prosecutor's duties   ProfC 3.8
  Documents (See **DOCUMENTARY EVIDENCE**)
  Domestic violence (See **DOMESTIC VIOLENCE**)
    Landlord and tenant
      Documentation or evidence of abuse or violence   CCP §1161.3
  Economic litigation procedures (See **ECONOMIC LITIGATION PROCEDURES**)
  Electronic recordings offered in evidence, provision of transcript   CRC 2.1040
  Eminent domain   CCP §1260.210, Ev §§810 to 822
  Exclusion of (See **ADMISSIBILITY OF EVIDENCE**)
  Exculpatory evidence
    Attorney professional conduct, prosecutor's duties   ProfC 3.8
  Exemplary damages, proof required for   CC §3295
  Exhibits (See **EXHIBITS**)
  Expedited jury trials
    Mandatory expedited jury trials, limited civil cases
      Applicability of evidentiary rules   CCP §630.25
      Objections   CRC 3.1552
      Rules of evidence, applicability   CCP §630.06
      Stipulations   CRC 3.1552
  Experts (See **EXPERT AND OPINION EVIDENCE**)
  Failure to explain or deny evidence, effect of   Ev §413
  Family rules
    Request for orders
      Evidence at hearings   CRC 5.111 to 5.115
  Findings (See **FINDINGS**)
  Forcible entry and detainer   CCP §1172
  Grants, evidence in dispute with state involving   CCP §2031.510, Ev §523
  Groundwater rights actions
    Long-term overdrafts   CCP §847
  Hearings, evidence at   CRC 3.1306
    Coordination of actions   CRC 3.514
    Detention hearings   CRC 5.676
  Hearsay evidence (See **HEARSAY**)
  Homestead declaration, effect of   CCP §704.940
  Human trafficking victims
    Prostitution or other commercial sex acts committed while victim
      Evidentiary significance   Ev §1161
  Innkeeper's lien, writ of possession on   CC §1861.9
  Insurance, admissibility of evidence of (See **INSURANCE**)
  Interrogatories
    Response
      Use of answer as evidence   CCP §2030.410
  Interstate family support
    Discovery assistance from tribunal of other state   Fam §5700.318
    Rules of evidence   Fam §5700.316
  Judges (See **JUDGES**)
  Judgment used as   CCP §1908.5
  Judicial arbitration   CCP §1282.2, CRC 3.823
  Judicial notice (See **JUDICIAL NOTICE**)
  Juvenile wardship proceedings
    Admissibility of evidence at jurisdictional hearings   CRC 5.780
    Disposition hearings, evidence considered   CRC 5.785
    Exculpatory evidence, duty to disclose   CRC 5.546
    Motion to suppress   CRC 5.544
    Transfer hearings, preponderance of evidence standard   CRC 5.770
  Landlord and tenant
    Domestic violence
      Documentation or evidence of abuse or violence   CCP §1161.3
    Sexual assault
      Documentation or evidence of abuse or violence   CCP §1161.3

EVIDENCE—Cont.
  Landlord and tenant—Cont.
    Stalking
      Documentation or evidence of abuse or violence   CCP §1161.3
  Law and motion hearing, evidence received at   CRC 3.1306
  Laying foundation
    Documents authenticated   Ev §§1400 to 1454
    Preliminary fact for admissibility, establishment of   Ev §§401 to 405
    Privileged matter, claim of   Ev §914
  Livestock service liens, sale under   CC §3080.08
  Marital property, will provision as evidence of transmutation of   Fam §853
  Mechanics' liens
    Public works, summary proceeding for release of funds
      Evidence at hearing   CC §9412
  Mental functions, deficit in   Pro §811
  Mining customs, usages or regulations, admission of evidence of established   CCP §748
  Missing person, administration of estate of   Pro §12406
  Motion pictures depicting cruelty, actions against   CC §3507.1
  Newly discovered evidence as grounds for new trial   CCP §657
  New trial (See **NEW TRIAL**)
  Nonjury trial   CCP §631.8
  Objections to evidence   CRC 3.1352
    Written objections   CRC 3.1354
  Official writings   Ev §§1530 to 1532
  Opinion testimony (See **EXPERT AND OPINION EVIDENCE**)
  Order of proof   Ev §320
  Original defined   Ev §255
  Parol evidence (See **PAROL EVIDENCE**)
  Patents, evidence in dispute with state involving   CCP §2031.510, Ev §523
  Polygraph evidence, exclusion of   Ev §351.1
  Prejudicial evidence, exclusion   Ev §352
    Creative expressions, admissibility   Ev §352.2
  Preliminary fact   Ev §§400 to 405
  Preponderance of (See **PREPONDERANCE OF EVIDENCE**)
  Preservation of evidence or perpetuation of testimony prior to filing action   CCP §§2035.010 to 2035.060
  Presumptions (See **PRESUMPTIONS**)
  Prior testimony   Ev §§1290 to 1293
  Privilege (See **PRIVILEGED COMMUNICATIONS**)
  Probative value   Ev §352
    Creative expressions, admissibility   Ev §352.2
  Probative value of   Ev §352
  Procedure for presenting   CCP §607
  Proffered evidence (See **ADMISSIBILITY OF EVIDENCE**)
  Proof defined   Ev §190
  Prostitution
    Extortion, serious felony, assault, domestic violence, human trafficking, sexual battery or stalking, victims or witnesses
      Inadmissibility of evidence of prostitution in prosecution for prostitution   Ev §1162
  Public improvement assessment, action to determine adverse interests in real property arising out of   CCP §801.11
  Public use of private lands   CC §1009
  Reasonable doubt (See **BEYOND REASONABLE DOUBT**)
  Relevant evidence, definition of   Ev §210
  Reputation (See **CHARACTER AND REPUTATION**)
  Requests for production (See **INSPECTION DEMANDS**)
  Self-incrimination (See **SELF-INCRIMINATION**)
  Sex offenses (See **SEX OFFENSES**)
  Sexual assault
    Landlord and tenant
      Documentation or evidence of abuse or violence   CCP §1161.3
  Small claims court (See **SMALL CLAIMS COURTS**)
  Spouse
    Registered domestic partner included in term   Ev §215
  Stalking
    Landlord and tenant
      Documentation or evidence of abuse or violence   CCP §1161.3
  Summary judgment motions
    Documentary evidence   CRC 3.1350
    Objections to evidence   CRC 3.1352
      Written objections   CRC 3.1354
    Supplemental briefs   CCP §437c
  Superior court reporters
    Reports as prima facie evidence of testimony and proceedings   CCP §273
  Suppression of (See **SUPPRESSION OF EVIDENCE**)
  Transcripts of recordings   CRC 2.1040
  Variance in pleading and proof (See **PLEADINGS**)
  Views, presentation of evidence at   CCP §651
  Weak evidence, generally   Ev §412

EVIDENCE—Cont.
Weight of evidence, generally   Ev §§410 to 413
Witnesses (See **WITNESSES**)

EVIDENCE SANCTION
Case questionnaires under economic litigation provisions for limited civil cases, failure to obey order compelling response to   CCP §93

EXAMINATION
Adoption proceedings (See **ADOPTION**)
Judgment debtor, examination of (See **ENFORCEMENT OF JUDGMENTS**)
Jurors (See **JURY**)
Witnesses, examination of (See **WITNESSES**)

EXCAVATIONS
Adjacent land owner, notice to   CC §832
Indemnity coverage   CC §2783
License to enter land of adjacent landowner   CC §832

EXCEPTIONS (See **OBJECTIONS AND EXCEPTIONS**)

EXCEPTIONS, BILL OF (See **BILL OF EXCEPTIONS**)

EXCESSIVE LEVY
Attachments   CCP §482.120

EXCHANGE OF PROPERTY
Administration of decedents' estates (See **ADMINISTRATION OF ESTATES**)
Advertising signs for exchange, display of   CC §§712, 713
Bonds, procedure for validation of authorization, issuance, sale or exchange of   CCP §349.4
Condemnation by   CCP §§1240.310 to 1240.350
Conservatorships   Pro §§2545, 2550, 2557
Deposit for exchange   CC §§1818, 1878
Eminent domain by   CCP §§1240.310 to 1240.350
Fraud in   CC §3343
Guardianships   Pro §§2545, 2550, 2557
Loan for exchange   CC §§1902 to 1906
Signs advertising property for exchange, display of   CC §§712, 713

EXCISE TAX (See **SALES AND USE TAX**)

EXCLUSION FROM COURTROOM
Witnesses   Ev §777

EXCUSABLE NEGLECT (See **MISTAKE**)

EXCUSES (See **JURY**)

EXECUTION OF INSTRUMENTS (See **SIGNATURES**)

EXECUTION OF PROCESS
Generally (See **PROCESS AND SERVICE OF PROCESS**)
Sheriffs generally (See **SHERIFF**)

EXECUTION ON JUDGMENTS (See **ENFORCEMENT OF JUDGMENTS**)

EXECUTIVE BRANCH
Attorney General (See **ATTORNEY GENERAL**)
Governor (See **GOVERNOR**)
Secretary of state (See **SECRETARY OF STATE**)

EXECUTORS AND ADMINISTRATORS (See also **ADMINISTRATION OF ESTATES; WILL PROBATE**)
Absconding representative   Pro §10953
Absent co-representative   Pro §9630
Accounting
    Generally   Pro §§1060 to 1064, 10900 to 10954
    Absconding personal representative, accounting required where   Pro §10953
    Allowance for necessary expenses   Pro §11004
    Attorney for absent or incapacitated personal representative, accounting rendered by   Pro §10953
    Attorneys' fees for defending actions   Pro §11003
    Cash in possession, duty to invest   Pro §9652
    Compelling account   Pro §§11050 to 11052
    Concealed or withheld property, hearing for accounting of   Pro §8873
    Conservators (See **CONSERVATORS**)
    Contempt for failure to file   Pro §§11050 to 11052
    Contents of   Pro §§1061 to 1063, 10900
    Contested accounts   Pro §11001
    Costs, award of   Pro §11003

EXECUTORS AND ADMINISTRATORS—Cont.
Accounting—Cont.
    Court-ordered accounting   Pro §10950
    Death of personal representative, accounting required where   Pro §10953
    Fees for defending actions   Pro §11003
    Final accounting
        Generally   Pro §§10951, 10954
        Notice of hearing   Pro §11000
        Supplemental accounting   Pro §11642
    Good faith, accounting for debts paid in   Pro §11005
    Guardianship (See **GUARDIAN AND WARD**)
    Hearings
        Generally   Pro §11002
        Notice of hearing   Pro §11000
    Improperly filed claims, payments by personal representative on   Pro §11005
    Incapacitated personal representative, accounting required where   Pro §10953
    Incorporation by reference of other fiduciary's accounting, personal representative's   Pro §10902
    Litigation expenses of administration   Pro §11003
    Notice of hearing   Pro §11000
    Partner surviving, accounting by   Pro §9761
    Resignation or removal of personal representative, accounting required where   Pro §10952
    Revocation of letters for failure to render   Pro §11052
    Settlement of accounts and distribution of estate   Pro §§11000 to 11005
    Special administrators   Pro §8546
    Supplemental accounting after final account rendered, reporting of   Pro §11642
    Supporting documents, production of   Pro §10901
    Vouchers filed with accounts, production of   Pro §10901
    Waiver of   Pro §10954
        Effect   CRC 7.550
    Writing requirements   Pro §1020
Acknowledgment of statement of duties and liabilities of office   CRC 7.150, Pro §8404
Actions maintained by   CCP §369
Address of nonresident executor, requirements for furnishing   Pro §8573
Administrators with will annexed (See **ADMINISTRATORS WITH WILL ANNEXED**)
Advice of proposed action (See **INDEPENDENT ADMINISTRATION OF ESTATES ACT**)
Ancillary administration (See **ANCILLARY ADMINISTRATION**)
Annuities, will instruction authorizing purchase of   Pro §9733
Annulment of letters (See within this heading, **"Revocation of letters"**)
Appeals
    Generally   CCP §904.1, Pro §§1300, 1303
    Reversal of order appointing fiduciary, effect of   Pro §1311
    Stay on appeal   Pro §1310
Appointment
    Administrators, appointment of   Pro §§8460 to 8469
    Administrators with will annexed (See **ADMINISTRATORS WITH WILL ANNEXED**)
    Ancillary administration, appointment for (See **ANCILLARY ADMINISTRATION**)
    Authority to administer estate prior to issuance of letters   Pro §8400
    Contest of (See within this heading, **"Contest of appointment"**)
    Decedent's pending claim against petitioner for letters, effect on   Pro §9605
    Executors, appointment of   Pro §§8420 to 8425
    Fee waivers   CRC 3.50 to 3.53, 7.5
    General provisions   Pro §§8400 to 8405
    Hearing
        Generally   Pro §8005
        Notice of   Pro §8003
        Order of   Pro §8006
        Time of   Pro §8003
    Letters
        Decedent's pending claim against petitioner for letters, effect of appointment on   Pro §9605
        Generally (See within this heading, **"Letters"**)
    Missing person presumed dead, appointment for estate of   Pro §12407
    Reversal on appeal of appointment order, effect of   Pro §1311
    Special administrators generally (See within this heading, **"Special administrators"**)
    Successor personal representative, appointment to vacancy in office of   Pro §§8520 to 8525
    Trust companies generally (See within this heading, **"Trust companies"**)
Appraisals of estate property (See **ADMINISTRATION OF ESTATES**)
Arbitration, submission of disputes to   Pro §9621

EXECUTORS AND ADMINISTRATORS—Cont.
Attorney for absent or incapacitated personal representative, accounting rendered by   Pro §10953
Attorney's death, practice administrator appointed by personal representative on   Pro §§9764, 17200
Attorneys' fees for defending actions   Pro §11003
Banks
   Corporate executor
      Trust companies generally (See within this heading, **"Trust companies"**)
   Savings accounts, withdrawal of   Pro §10201
Bonds
   Generally   Pro §8480
   Additional bond   Pro §8480
   Administrator with will annexed   Pro §§8480 to 8488
   Amount of bond required, determination of   Pro §8482
   Blocked account in lieu of   Pro §8483
   Bond and Undertaking Law, applicability of   Pro §8487
   Cost of bonds, amount allowed for   Pro §8486
   Damages arising from sale of estate assets, liability for   Pro §§10380, 10381
   Debt payments, liability on bond for failure to make   Pro §11424
   Delegating authority to name executor for service without bond   Pro §8422
   Former representative, maintaining action on bond of   Pro §9822
   Increase bond, duty to petition to   CRC 7.204
   Independent administrator   CRC 7.204, Pro §10453
   Inventory and appraisal, requirement for statement concerning sufficiency of bond in   CRC 7.501
   Joint and several liability under   Pro §8480
   Limitation on action against sureties   Pro §8488
   New bond   Pro §8480
   Notice to surety   Pro §1213
   Practice administrator appointed on death of attorney, bond posted by   Pro §9764
   Public administrators (See **PUBLIC ADMINISTRATORS**)
   Reduction of   Pro §§8483, 8484
   Release of surety   Pro §8485
   Sale of real property, requirements associated with   CRC 7.205, 7.206
   Special administrators   Pro §§8543, 8545
   Statement to show sufficiency or waiver of bond requirement in inventory and appraisal report   CRC 7.501
   Stay of order, bond requirements for   CCP §919, Pro §1310
   Substitution of sureties   Pro §8485
   Two or more representatives, separate bonds furnished by   CRC 7.202, Pro §8480
   Waiver of   Pro §8481
   Waiver of bond
      Will instrument waiving   CRC 7.201
Breach of duty
   Duty of care generally   Pro §§9600 to 9603
   Joint representatives, liability for breach   Pro §9631
Brokers
   Authority for employment of   CRC 7.453, Pro §10150
Brother of decedent, priority for appointment of   Pro §8461
Business interests continued by   Pro §9760
Cancellation of utility, cable, etc, services on behalf of deceased person
   In-person cancellation not to be required   Pro §217
Capacity to sue
   Generally   CCP §369, Pro §9820
   Partition action against cotenants of decedent   Pro §9823
   Surviving partner, action against   Pro §9763
Care, duty of   Pro §§9600 to 9603
   Joint representatives   Pro §9631
Cash in possession, duty to invest   Pro §9652
Chattel mortgages, authority for executing   Pro §9805
Children of decedent, priority for appointment of   Pro §8461
Claims against estates (See **CLAIMS AGAINST ESTATES**)
Closing estate administration, procedure for   Pro §§12200 to 12206
Coexecutors
   Co-representatives generally (See within this heading, **"Co-representatives"**)
Common trust funds, investment in   Pro §9730
Compensation
   Attorneys' fees
      Generally (See **ADMINISTRATION OF ESTATES**)
      Personal representative as attorney, compensation of   Pro §10804
      Practice administrator appointed on death of attorney, compensation for   Pro §9764
   Basis for   Pro §10800
   Co-representatives, apportionment for   Pro §10805
   Estate attorneys' fees (See **ADMINISTRATION OF ESTATES**)

EXECUTORS AND ADMINISTRATORS—Cont.
Compensation—Cont.
   Extraordinary services   Pro §§10801, 10832
   Failure to timely close estate, reduction of compensation for   Pro §12205
   Final accounting, compensation for all services rendered upon   Pro §10831
   Increase in compensation, validity of contract for   Pro §10803
   Partial allowance   Pro §10830
   Percentage allowed for   Pro §10800
   Practice administrator appointed on death of attorney, compensation for   Pro §9764
   Prior law   Pro §10850
   Probate rules
      Compensation of personal representatives and attorneys   CRC 7.700 to 7.707
   Public administrators (See **PUBLIC ADMINISTRATORS**)
   Reduction of compensation for failure to timely close estate, order for   Pro §12205
   Special administrators   Pro §8547
   Statutory compensation   Pro §10800
      In excess of statutory amount, validity of agreement for compensation where   Pro §10803
   Tax experts, employment of   Pro §10801
   Will provision for   Pro §10802
Compromise and settlement
   Generally   Pro §9830
   Accounting of settlement payments for less than full amount   Pro §9839
   Creditors' claims against decedent's estate   Pro §9831
   Debtors to decedent, authority to compromise claims of   Pro §9830
   Independent administrator, authority of   Pro §§10501, 10518, 10550
   Notice of hearing on   Pro §9837
   Order authorizing compromise or settlement of claim   Pro §9834
   Petition for authorization of   Pro §9837
   Real property, claims relating to   Pro §§9832, 9838
   Summary dispute determination
      Arbitration   Pro §9621
      Temporary judge, submission of disputes to   Pro §9620
   $25,000, authorization for compromise of matters in excess of   Pro §9833
   Wrongful death actions   Pro §§9835, 9836
Concealment
   Remedies available for wrongful concealment   Pro §859
   Third party, concealment of estate property by   Pro §§8870 to 8873
Conflict of interest   Pro §9880
Conservator, granting letters to   Pro §§8464, 8469
Contempt
   Accounts, failure to file accounts   Pro §§11050 to 11052
   Concealment of decedent's property, contempt for   Pro §§8870, 8873
   Removal from office, contempt as grounds for   Pro §8505
Contest of appointment
   Generally   Pro §8004
   Examination of witnesses   Pro §8005
   Findings, order of   Pro §8006
   Notice of   Pro §8004
Contracts affecting estate property, representative's interest in   Pro §9884
Co-representatives
   Absent co-representatives   Pro §9630
   Compensation   Pro §10805
   Liability for breach of duty   Pro §9631
   Majority consent of   Pro §9630
   Separate bonds required   CRC 7.202, 7.203, Pro §8480
   Vacancy in office   Pro §§8521, 8522
   Validity of action by one of   Pro §9630
Corporate representatives
   Trust companies generally (See within this heading, **"Trust companies"**)
Costs in actions prosecuted or defended by   CCP §1026
Court supervision
   Generally   Pro §9611
   Act or forbearance to act by personal representative, court order directing   Pro §9613
   Confirmation of acts performed by personal representative (See **ADMINISTRATION OF ESTATES**)
   Independent administrator (See **INDEPENDENT ADMINISTRATION OF ESTATES ACT**)
   Instructions from court   Pro §9611
      Independent administrator   Pro §§10500 to 10503
   Suspension of powers   Pro §9614
Creditors, priority for appointment of   Pro §8461
Criminal conviction, disqualification based on   Pro §8402
Cum testamento annexo (See **ADMINISTRATORS WITH WILL ANNEXED**)
Custody of will by executor   Pro §8200
Damages
   Generally   Pro §§9601 to 9606

EXECUTORS AND ADMINISTRATORS—Cont.
Damages—Cont.
  Sale of estate property   Pro §§10380, 10381
Death
  Accounting on death of administrator   Pro §10953
  Deceased professional fiduciary   Pro §9765
  Fact of death, proceedings to establish (See **FACT OF DEATH**)
  Requirements for proof of   Pro §8005
  Vacancy in office, successor personal representative where   Pro §§8520 to 8525
Debts
  Generally (See **ADMINISTRATION OF ESTATES**)
  Claims, duties concerning (See **CLAIMS AGAINST ESTATES**)
Dedication, authorization for   Pro §§9900, 9901
Deeds, execution of (See **ADMINISTRATION OF ESTATES**)
Defined   Pro §§58, 6203
Delegation of authority to appoint executor   Pro §8422
Delivery of decedent's property by third party immediately after death to personal representative   Pro §330
Digital assets, fiduciary access   Pro §§870 to 884 (See **FIDUCIARY ACCESS TO DIGITAL ASSETS**)
Discharge of personal representative
  Generally   Pro §§11753, 12250, 12251
  Final judgment or order, effect of   Pro §7250
  No property subject to administration, discharge where   Pro §12251
  Subsequent administration required after   Pro §12252
Disclaimer of estate interest
  Generally   Pro §§260 to 295
  Independent administrator, authority of   Pro §10519
Discovery
  Law and motion rules
    Applicable to discovery proceedings in probate   CRC 3.1100
Duties and liabilities
  General provisions   Pro §§9600 to 9604
  Statement of   CRC 7.150, Pro §8404
Duty of care
  General provisions   Pro §§9600 to 9603
  Joint representatives, liability of   Pro §9631
Easement rights to public entities, authorization of   Pro §§9900, 9901
Embezzlement, action for   Pro §§8870 to 8873
Equally entitled persons as administrators   Pro §8467
Exchange of property (See **ADMINISTRATION OF ESTATES**)
Extraordinary services, extra allowance for   Pro §§10801, 10832
Fact of death, proceedings to establish (See **FACT OF DEATH**)
Fees
  Compensation generally (See within this heading, "**Compensation**")
  Probate rules
    Compensation of personal representatives and attorneys   CRC 7.700 to 7.707
Fiduciaries
  Professional fiduciaries generally   Pro §§60.1, 2340, 2341
Fiduciary access to digital assets   Pro §§870 to 884 (See **FIDUCIARY ACCESS TO DIGITAL ASSETS**)
Foreign executors
  Ancillary administration (See **ANCILLARY ADMINISTRATION**)
  Mortgages on county records discharged by   CC §2939.5
  Nonresident executors   Pro §§8570 to 8577
  Non-United States citizen as personal representative, disqualification of   Pro §8402
Fraud (See **ADMINISTRATION OF ESTATES**)
Funeral expenses, payment of   Pro §8400
Grandchildren of decedent, priority for appointment of   Pro §8461
Guardian, granting letters to   Pro §§8464, 8469
Hearings
  Appointment, hearing on (See within this heading, "**Appointment**")
  Letters of administration, hearing on petition for   Pro §8005
  Notices generally (See within this heading, "**Notices**")
  Order of   Pro §8006
  Petitions generally (See within this heading, "**Petitions**")
  Report of status of administration, hearing on   Pro §12201
  Time of   Pro §8003
Heirs
  Partition
    Partition of real property act   CCP §§874.311 to 874.323 (See **PARTITION**)
Highways, transferring estate property for use as   Pro §§9900, 9901
Independent administration of estate (See **INDEPENDENT ADMINISTRATION OF ESTATES ACT**)
Infancy disqualification   Pro §8402
Instructions from court
  Generally   Pro §9611

EXECUTORS AND ADMINISTRATORS—Cont.
Instructions from court—Cont.
  Independent administrator   Pro §§10500 to 10503
Insurance (See **ADMINISTRATION OF ESTATES**)
Intention of testator in naming executor   Pro §8421
Inventory (See **ADMINISTRATION OF ESTATES**)
Investments (See **ADMINISTRATION OF ESTATES**)
Joint representatives (See within this heading, "**Co-representatives**")
Judges, service as   CRCSupp JudEthicsCanon 4
Law and motion rules
  Applicable to discovery proceedings in probate   CRC 3.1100
Leases (See **ADMINISTRATION OF ESTATES**)
Letters
  Annulment (See within this heading, "**Revocation of letters**")
  Appeals   Pro §§1303, 1310
  Collateral attack on order granting, limitation on   Pro §8007
  Contest of grant of   Pro §8004
  De bonis non administration, issuance of letters for purposes of   Pro §12252
  Defined   Pro §52
  Duties and liabilities statement   CRC 7.150, Pro §8404
  Fees for filing   Gov §70650
    Supplemental fees for first paper filing   Gov §§70602.5, 70602.6
  Foreign executors   CC §2939.5
  Form of   Pro §8405
  Form of notice of application for   Pro §8100
  Guardianship letters (See **GUARDIAN AND WARD**)
  Hearing on petition, time of   Pro §8005
  Judges in proceedings, disqualification of   Pro §7060
  Newly-discovered property after final settlement, issuance of new letters for administration of   Pro §12252
  Orders   Pro §§1046 to 1051
  Petition for   Pro §§8000, 8002
  Proof required before issuance of   Pro §8005
  Public administrators   Pro §7621
  Renunciation of letters by failure to file petition   Pro §8001
  Revocation (See within this heading, "**Revocation of letters**")
  Seal required for   Pro §8405
  Signature requirements   Pro §8405
  Special administrators   Pro §8542
  Successor trust company after merger, appointment of   Pro §8423
  Suspension of   Pro §9614
  Transfer of proceedings for grant of   Pro §§7070 to 7072
  Will annexed, form of letters for administrator with   Pro §8405
Liability insurance (See **ADMINISTRATION OF ESTATES**)
Liability of   Pro §§9600 to 9604
  Statement of duties and liabilities   CRC 7.150, Pro §8404
Marital deduction gifts (See **MARITAL DEDUCTION GIFTS**)
Medical information disclosures
  Authorization to employer to release   CC §56.21
  Personal representatives, disclosures to   CC §56.1007
Mental illness
  Accounting on incompetence of administrator   Pro §10953
  Disqualification because of   Pro §8402
Merger by corporate executor, appointment of successor trust company after   Pro §8423
Minority, disqualification based on   Pro §8402
Missing person presumed dead, appointment of personal representative for estate of   Pro §12407
Next of kin, priority for appointment of   Pro §8461
Nonresident executor   Pro §§8570 to 8577
Notices
  Generally (See **ADMINISTRATION OF ESTATES**)
  Accounts, settlement of   Pro §11000
  Contest of appointment   Pro §8004
  Form of application for letters   Pro §8100
  Independent administration, notice of hearing for   Pro §10451
  Nonresident decedents' estate, notice of proceedings for   Pro §12512
  Options, exercise of   Pro §9734
  Prior law, effect of   Pro §§3, 9645
  Service of   Pro §§8110 to 8113
  Special administrator, appointment of   Pro §8541
  Special notice request on filing of inventory and appraisement   Pro §§8803
  Status report in absence of distribution   Pro §12201
  Statutory form of notice of hearing   Pro §1211
  Surety, notice to   Pro §1213
Not named in will, appointing executor where   Pro §8421
Oath
  Generally   Pro §8403
  Appraisement, verification of   Pro §8905
  Inventory, verification of   Pro §8852

EXECUTORS AND ADMINISTRATORS—Cont.
Objections
    Appointment of administrator, contest of (See within this heading, **"Contest of appointment"**)
    Appraisement   Pro §8906
Parents of decedent, priority for appointment of   Pro §8461
Partition proceedings (See **ADMINISTRATION OF ESTATES**)
Partnership interests
    Appointment as administrator   Pro §8402
    Surviving partner   Pro §§9761, 9763
Partnerships
    Business partner, eligibility to serve as personal representative   Pro §8402
Petitions
    Compensation of personal representative, petition for   Pro §§10830, 10831
    Dedication of estate property to public   Pro §9901
    Filing fees   Gov §70650
        Supplemental fees for first paper filing   Gov §§70602.5, 70602.6
    Independent administration   Pro §10450
    Letters   Pro §§8000, 8002
    Partial allowance of executor or administrator's fees   Pro §10830
    Practice administrator for deceased attorney, petition for appointment of   Pro §§9764, 17200
    Prior law, effect of   Pro §§3, 9645
    Renunciation of letters by failure to file   Pro §8001
    Simultaneous death, proceedings regarding   Pro §§230 to 233
    Termination of further estate proceedings   Pro §12251
    Writing requirements   Pro §1020
Possession, right of   Pro §§9650, 9651
Powers of executor, testator limiting   Pro §12206
Practice administrator appointed on death of attorney   Pro §§9764, 17200
Priorities
    Administrator   Pro §§8461 to 8469
    Administrator with will annexed   Pro §8441
    Ancillary administration, personal representative for   Pro §12513
    Removal of appointed administrator, petition of person with higher priority for   Pro §8503
    Special administrator   Pro §8541
Prior law, effect of   Pro §§3, 9645
Probate, refusal of executor to petition for   Pro §8001
Probate rules
    Compensation of personal representatives and attorneys   CRC 7.700 to 7.707
Process
    Service
        Generally (See within this heading, **"Service of papers"**)
Profits from sales, liability for   Pro §§9657, 10005
Proxies, voting of
    Independent administrator, voting of stock   Pro §10560
    Voting of stock generally   Pro §9655
Public administrators (See **PUBLIC ADMINISTRATORS**)
Purchase of estate assets by personal representative, restrictions on (See **ADMINISTRATION OF ESTATES**)
Quieting title action   CCP §762.030, Pro §9654
Reduction of bond, application for   Pro §8484
Relatives, priority for appointment of   Pro §§8461, 8462
Release
    Discharge of personal representative generally (See within this heading, **"Discharge of personal representative"**)
Removal (See within this heading, **"Revocation of letters"**)
Rents, collection of   Pro §§9650, 9651
Repairs by   Pro §§9650, 10562
Report of status of administration   Pro §§12200 to 12202
Request for appointment of third party   Pro §8465
Residence
    Generally   Pro §8402
    Nonresident personal representatives   Pro §§8570 to 8577
Resignation of   Pro §§8520 to 8525
Revocation of letters
    Accounting, failure to render   Pro §11052
    Additional bond, failure to furnish   Pro §8480
    Cessation of authority   Pro §8501
    Contempt   Pro §8505
    Embezzlement   Pro §8502
    Examining personal representative in hearing for   Pro §8500
    Fraud as basis for   Pro §8502
    Grounds for   Pro §8502
    Independent administration   Pro §10454
    New will probated   Pro §8504
    Nonresident personal representative failing to furnish permanent address   Pro §8577
    Parties to proceeding for   Pro §8500

EXECUTORS AND ADMINISTRATORS—Cont.
Revocation of letters—Cont.
    Prior acts, validity of   Pro §8272
    Priority over appointed administrator, petition for removal by person asserting   Pro §8503
    Procedure for   Pro §8500
    Special administrator   Pro §8546
    Surety, notice to   Pro §1213
    Waste   Pro §8502
Revocation of probate as terminating powers of   Pro §8272
Sale of estate property (See **ADMINISTRATION OF ESTATES**)
Service of papers
    Application for letters, notice of proceedings   Pro §§8110 to 8113
    Claims against estates   Pro §9150
    Nonresident personal representatives   Pro §§8570 to 8577
Settlements
    Accounts, settlement of   Pro §§11000 to 11005
    Compromise of claims (See within this heading, **"Compromise and settlement"**)
Simultaneous death petition filed by   Pro §§230 to 234
Sister of decedent, priority for appointment of   Pro §8461
Special administrators
    Bond requirements   Pro §§8543, 8545
    Compensation   Pro §8547
    General powers and duties   Pro §8545
    Grounds for appointment   Pro §8540
    Letters, issuance of   Pro §8542
    Preference for appointment   Pro §8541
    Procedure for appointment   Pro §8541
    Special powers and duties   Pro §8544
    Termination of powers   Pro §8546
Special notice request on filing of inventory and appraisement   Pro §8803
Specific performance directed against   Pro §§850 to 859
Standard of care
    Duty of care generally   Pro §§9600 to 9603
    Joint representatives, liability   Pro §9631
Standing to sue (See within this heading, **"Capacity to sue"**)
Statement of duties and liabilities   CRC 7.150, Pro §8404
Status report   Pro §§12200 to 12202
Statute of frauds affecting promise of representative to pay claims against estate   Pro §9604
Stock voted by   Pro §9655
    Independent administrator   Pro §10560
Streets, transferring estate property for use as   Pro §§9900, 9901
Substitution
    Vacancy in office   Pro §§8520 to 8525
    Wartime, substitution during (See **FIDUCIARIES' WARTIME SUBSTITUTION LAW**)
Successor trust company as executor, appointment of   Pro §8423
Summary dispute determination
    Arbitration, submission of disputes to   Pro §9621
    Temporary judge, submission of disputes to   Pro §9620
Supervision of court (See within this heading, **"Court supervision"**)
Surety bonds (See within this heading, **"Bonds"**)
Survival of actions (See **SURVIVAL OF ACTIONS**)
Surviving partner
    Generally   Pro §§9761, 9763
    Appointment as administrator   Pro §8402
Surviving spouse, priority for appointment of   Pro §§8462, 8463
Suspension
    Generally   Pro §9614
    Surety, notice to   Pro §1213
Tax experts, compensation for employment of   Pro §10801
Tax liens and other federal liens, filing of notice of   CCP §2101
Temporary judges, summary determination of disputes by   Pro §9620
Third parties, request for appointment of   Pro §8465
Trust companies
    Generally   Pro §300
    Bond requirements   Pro §301
    Defined   Pro §83
    Recovery of money or property deposited, limitation of actions for   CCP §348
    Successor trust company as executor after merger, appointment of   Pro §8423
Trust deeds (See **ADMINISTRATION OF ESTATES**)
Trust funds, investment in   Pro §9730
Undue influence
    Definition of undue influence   Pro §86
Uniform Transfers to Minors Act, transfer under   Pro §3905
Unnamed executor, appointment where   Pro §8421
Vacancy in office   Pro §§8520 to 8525

EXECUTORS AND ADMINISTRATORS—Cont.
Venue of action against   CCP §395.1
Voting of stock
    Generally   Pro §9655
    Independent administrator   Pro §10560
Wartime substitution of (See **FIDUCIARIES' WARTIME SUBSTITUTION LAW**)
Waste
    Revocation of letters because of   Pro §8502
    Special administrators protecting from   Pro §8544
With will annexed, administrator (See **ADMINISTRATORS WITH WILL ANNEXED**)
Wrongful death actions, personal representatives maintaining   CCP §377.60

EXECUTORY INTERESTS
Judgment, executory interest of judgment debtor applied to satisfaction of   CCP §709.020

EXEMPLARY DAMAGES (See **DAMAGES**)

EXEMPLIFICATION OF RECORD
Superior court fees   Gov §70628

EXEMPTIONS
Assignment for benefit of creditors, property exempt from   CCP §1801
Attachment (See **ATTACHMENT**)
Credit reports, statutes affecting   CC §1785.4
Enforcement of judgments (See **ENFORCEMENT OF JUDGMENTS**)
Furniture (See **FURNITURE**)
Garnishment (See **GARNISHMENT**)
Homesteads (See **HOMESTEADS**)
Insurance policy, pleading exemption from liability under   CCP §431.50
Jury (See **JURY**)
Membership camping contracts, regulation of   CC §1812.305
Realty sales contracts exempt from Subdivision Map Act   CC §2985.51
Unclaimed deposits and payments, escheat of   CCP §§1502 to 1506, 1528

EXHIBITIONS (See **FAIRS AND EXPOSITIONS**)

EXHIBITS
Appeals, transmission of exhibits to reviewing court   CRC 8.224
Appellate rules, superior court appeals
    Infraction case appeals
        Record on appeal   CRC 8.921
    Misdemeanor appeals
        Record on appeal   CRC 8.870
Appellate rules, supreme court and courts of appeal (See **APPELLATE RULES, SUPREME COURT AND COURTS OF APPEAL**)
Binding together of document with exhibits   CRC 3.1110
Costs, prevailing party recovering expenses as   CCP §1033.5
Death penalty
    Lists of appearances, exhibits and motions   CRCAppx A
        Pretrial proceedings   CRC 4.119
        Trial, additional requirements   CRC 4.230
Deposition, use as exhibit   CRC 3.1116
Destruction   CCP §§1952 to 1952.3
Disposition of   CCP §§1952 to 1952.3
Exhibit references   CRC 3.1113
Foreign language, translation of exhibits written in   CRC 3.1110
Format for submission   CRC 3.1110
Judges
    Censure, removal, admonishment or retirement of judges
        Hearings, exhibits at   JudPerR 125.5
Law and motion rules
    Deposition testimony, format and filing of   CRC 3.1116
    Moving papers, exhibition references in   CRC 3.1113
Petition for Supreme Court review, exhibits   CRC 8.504
References to exhibits   CRC 3.1113
Retention of exhibits after trial   CCP §§1952, 1952.3
Return of   CRC 2.400
Superior courts (See **SUPERIOR COURTS**)
Translation of exhibits   CRC 3.1110
Transmission to reviewing court   CRC 8.224
Trial court rules
    Papers
        Inclusion of exhibits with papers   CRC 2.114
        Return of exhibits   CRC 2.400

EXIT (See **ACCESS**)

EXONERATION
Decedent's estate, exoneration of encumbered property of   Pro §21404

EXONERATION—Cont.
Notice of pendency of action, exoneration of undertaking for   CCP §405.37

EX PARTE PROCEDURE
Adoption
    Termination of parental rights
        Ex parte order terminating   Fam §7667
Appearance   CRC 3.1207
    Jurisdictional implications of appearance at hearing on ex parte application   CCP §418.11
    Telephone appearances   CRC 3.670, 3.672, 3.1207
Applicability of provisions   CRC 3.1200
Applications for ex parte orders
    Contents   CRC 3.1202
    Documents comprising request   CRC 3.1201
    Filing   CRC 3.1205
    Presentation   CRC 3.1205
    Service   CRC 3.1206
Arbitrators
    Judicial arbitration   CRC 3.820
Assignment of wages
    Termination of order   Fam §4324.5
Attachment (See **ATTACHMENT**)
Child support proceedings   Fam §§240 to 246, 4610, 4620
Claim and delivery (See **CLAIM AND DELIVERY**)
Court commissioner's powers to hear and determine ex parte motions   CCP §259
Custody of children (See **CUSTODY OF CHILDREN**)
Dependent child proceedings, ex parte restraining orders   CRC 5.630
    Firearm relinquishment procedures   CRC 5.630
        Forms for firearm relinquishment   CRCAppx A
Dissolution of marriage   Fam §§240 to 246, 2045
Domestic violence (See **DOMESTIC VIOLENCE**)
Fact of death, proceedings to establish   Pro §203
Factual showings
    Affirmative factual showing   CRC 3.1202
Family law mediators, evaluators, appointed counsel, etc
    Restrictions on ex parte communications   Fam §216
        Conciliation courts   Fam §1818
Family rules
    Request for emergency or ex parte orders   CRC 5.92, 5.151 to 5.170
Judicial arbitration
    Ex parte communications   CRC 3.820
Judicial ethics provision concerning judges' initiating or considering ex parte communications   CRCSupp JudEthicsCanon 3
Judicial performance, commission on
    Ethics code for commission members
        Ex parte contacts of members   JudPerPolicy 6.3
Livestock service liens, sale under   CC §3080.15
Local rules of court
    Preemption of local rules   CRC 3.20
Memorandum in support of request   CRC 3.1201
Notice to parties
    Contents   CRC 3.1204
    Declaration regarding notice   CRC 3.1204
    Shorter notice, explanation   CRC 3.1204
    Time   CRC 3.1203
Personal appearance   CRC 3.1207
Preemption of local rules   CRC 3.20
Probate proceedings
    Orders
        Ex parte applications for orders   CRC 7.55
    Restrictions on ex parte communications   Pro §1051
    Rule governing ex parte communications in probate proceedings   CRC 7.10
Receivers, bonds required on application for   CCP §566
Request for ex parte relief
    Contents   CRC 3.1201
    Form   CRC 3.1201
Service of papers
    Applications for ex parte orders   CRC 3.1206
Shorter notice
    Explanation   CRC 3.1204
Telephone appearances   CRC 3.670, 3.672, 3.1207
Uniform Parentage Act, proceedings under   Fam §§240 to 246, 7710
Unlawful detainer
    Notice to parties
        Time   CRC 3.1203

EXPECTANCY
Future interest, expectancy excluded from   CC §700

EXPEDITED JURY TRIALS CRC 3.1545 to 3.1553
Applicable provisions CRC 3.1545
Consent order
   Defined CRC 3.1545
   Proposed orders
      Content CRC 3.1547
      Submitting to court CRC 3.1547
Definitions CRC 3.1545
   Mandatory expedited jury trials, limited civil cases CCP §630.21
   Voluntary expedited jury trials CCP §630.01
Evidence
   Objections CRC 3.1552
   Stipulations CRC 3.1552
Expert and opinion evidence CRC 3.1548
Forms
   Judicial council legal forms CRCAppx A
Judicial council legal forms CRCAppx A
Judicial officers
   Assignment of officer to conduct CRC 3.1553
Mandatory expedited jury trials, limited civil cases CCP §§630.20 to 630.29
   Agreements as to pretrial and trial procedures CRC 3.1546
   Applicability of provisions and rules of court CCP §630.22
   Attorneys' fees
      Applicability of rules governing costs and attorney fees CCP §630.27
   Case management CRC 3.1546
   Composition of jury CCP §630.23
   Costs
      Applicability of rules governing costs and attorney fees CCP §630.27
   Court rules
      Judicial council duties CCP §630.28
   Definitions CCP §630.21
   Deliberations not time-limited CCP §630.24
   Effective date of provisions CCP §630.29
   Evidentiary rules, applicability CCP §630.25
      Objections CRC 3.1552
      Stipulations CRC 3.1552
   Forms
      Judicial council legal forms CRCAppx A
   Modification of rules by agreement CCP §630.23
   Opting out of expedited process CCP §630.20, CRC 3.1546
   Peremptory challenges CCP §630.23
   Presentation of case
      Exchange of items CRC 3.1551
      Methods CRC 3.1551
      Stipulations CRC 3.1551
      Time to present case CRC 3.1550
   Pretrial procedures CRC 3.1546
   Requirement of expedited procedure CCP §630.20
   Time granted for voir dire and presentation of case CCP §630.23
   Verdicts
      Number of votes required CCP §630.26
   Voir dire CRC 3.1549
Presentation of case
   Exchange of items CRC 3.1551
   Methods CRC 3.1551
   Stipulations CRC 3.1551
   Time to present case CRC 3.1550
Pretrial proceedings and exchanges CRC 3.1548
   Mandatory expedited jury trials, limited civil cases CRC 3.1546
Proof of service
   Judicial council legal forms CRCAppx A
Stipulations CRC 3.1551
   Evidentiary rules CRC 3.1552
Time to present case CRC 3.1550
Voir dire CRC 3.1549
Voluntary expedited jury trials CCP §§630.01 to 630.11
   Applicable provisions CCP §630.02
   Attorney's fees
      Applicable provisions CCP §630.10
      Post-trial motions CCP §630.09
   Challenges CCP §630.04
   Composition of jury CCP §630.04
   Consent order CCP §630.03
      Defined CRC 3.1545
      Proposed orders CRC 3.1547
   Costs
      Applicable provisions CCP §630.10
      Post-trial motions CCP §630.09
   Definitions CCP §630.01

EXPEDITED JURY TRIALS—Cont.
Voluntary expedited jury trials —Cont.
   Deliberation CCP §630.05
   Directed verdict
      Waiver of right to motions CCP §630.08
   Evidence
      Objections CRC 3.1552
      Rules of evidence, applicability CCP §630.06
      Stipulations CRC 3.1552
   Forms
      Judicial council legal forms CRCAppx A
   Fraud
      Post-trial motions CCP §630.09
   Judicial misconduct
      Post-trial motions CCP §630.09
   Misconduct of jury
      Post-trial motions CCP §630.09
   New trial
      Damage amount, waiver of motions concerning amount of damages CCP §630.08
      Permissible grounds CCP §630.09
   Participation
      Agreement to participate CCP §630.03
      Waiver of certain motions and rights CCP §§630.07 to 630.09
   Peremptory challenges CCP §630.04
   Post-trial motions
      Conditions CCP §630.09
   Presentation of case
      Exchange of items CRC 3.1551
      Methods CRC 3.1551
      Stipulations CRC 3.1551
      Time to present case CRC 3.1550
   Rules and forms
      Judicial council duties as to CCP §630.11
   Stipulations CRC 3.1551
      Evidentiary rules CRC 3.1552
   Subpoenas
      Applicable provisions CCP §630.06
   Verdict
      Binding effect CCP §630.07
   Voir dire CRC 3.1549

EXPENSES AND EXPENDITURES
Administration of decedents' estates
   Generally (See **ADMINISTRATION OF ESTATES**)
      Executors and administrators, allowance to Pro §10802
Administrative adjudication (See **ADMINISTRATIVE ADJUDICATION**)
Adoption proceedings Fam §8610
Bailment, property held under CC §§1956, 2078
Borrowed property, expenses for care of CC §1892
Business oversight commissioner, superior court hearings on sale of properties of savings and loan association whose business, properties and assets are in possession of CCP §73d
Change of venue CCP §396b
Coordination of actions CCP §404.8
Custody of children (See **CUSTODY OF CHILDREN**)
Delay, award of expenses incurred as result of bad-faith actions or tactics solely intended to cause (See **SANCTIONS**)
Domestic violence cases, order for restitution Fam §§6342, 7720
Escheat, deductibility of charges from property CCP §1522
Executors, allowance to Pro §10802
Family law matters, income and expense declaration defined Fam §95
Frivolous actions or tactics, award of expenses incurred as result of (See **SANCTIONS**)
Funeral expenses (See **FUNERALS**)
Guardian ad litem, payment of expenses of CCP §373.5
Last illness (See **LAST ILLNESS**)
Liens, expenditures concerning CC §2892
Medical records, inspection of Ev §1158
Mineral right preservation upon payment of litigation expenses, late notice of intention of CC §883.250
Partition (See **PARTITION**)
Receipt of summons by mail, liability for expenses incurred due to failure to acknowledge CCP §415.30
Receivers holding unknown persons' funds CCP §570
Repairs, manufacturer liable for cost of CC §§1793.3, 1793.6
Spousal support proceedings, expenses and fees charged to county Fam §4352
Summary judgment motion support or opposition presented in bad faith or solely for purposes of delay CCP §437c

EXPENSES AND EXPENDITURES—Cont.
Superior court appellate division, judges designated as members of   CCP §77
Support proceedings, income and expense declarations in (See **CHILD SUPPORT; SPOUSAL SUPPORT**)
Travel expenses (See **TRAVEL EXPENSES**)
Trusts (See **TRUSTS**)
Vexatious litigant, undertaking to assure payment of expenses incurred in connection with litigation instituted by   CCP §391

EXPERIMENTAL PROJECTS (See **PILOT AND DEMONSTRATION PROJECTS**)

EXPERT AND OPINION EVIDENCE
Appointment by court of expert witness   Ev §§722, 730 to 733
Background of witness   Ev §802
Basis for opinion   Ev §§802, 803
Battered woman or intimate partner battering effects, admissibility of expert testimony of   Ev §1107
Common experience, requirement that opinion be concerned with subject outside   Ev §801
Compensation of expert witnesses (See within this heading, "**Fees for expert witnesses**")
Compromise, costs of litigation charged to party refusing offer of   CCP §998
Conciliation Courts   Fam §1838
Cross-examination of expert witnesses   Ev §§721, 732
Demand for exchange of lists of expert witnesses
    Eminent domain proceedings   CCP §§1258.210, 1258.230
Deposition of listed expert witness   CCP §§2034.410 to 2034.470
    Time limits for witness examination   CCP §2025.290
Direct examination of expert witnesses   Ev §732
Discovery
    Eminent domain proceedings (See **EMINENT DOMAIN**)
    List of expert witnesses (See within this heading, "**Lists of expert witnesses**")
    Simultaneous information exchange, discovery by   CCP §§2034.010 to 2034.730
        Limitations on papers filed   CRC 3.250
        Methods of discovery   CCP §2019.010
    Time for completion of discovery   CCP §2024.030
Economic litigation provisions for limited civil cases, permissible forms of discovery under   CCP §94
Eminent domain proceedings (See **EMINENT DOMAIN**)
Exchange of witness lists (See within this heading, "**Lists of expert witnesses**")
Expedited jury trial   CRC 3.1548
Fees for expert witnesses
    Generally   Gov §68092.5
    Court-appointed witnesses   Ev §§730, 731, 733
    Parentage, genetic testing to determine   Fam §7553
    Prevailing party, recovery as costs by   CCP §1033.5
Groundwater rights actions
    Definition of expert witness   CCP §832
    Identity of experts and other disclosures   CCP §843
Handwriting   Ev §1416
Human trafficking victims
    Effect of human trafficking on victim, expert testimony   Ev §1107.5
Impeachment of expert
    Previously undesignated expert   CCP §2034.310
Insanity   Ev §870
Intimate partner battering effects, admissibility of expert testimony of   Ev §1107
Judicial notice based on expert consultants (See **JUDICIAL NOTICE**)
Juvenile court, inquiry into mental health of child before
    COVID-19, emergency rule   CRCAppx I Emer Rule 7
Juvenile rules
    Competence of child to cooperate with counsel   CRC 5.643
    Competence of minor subject to juvenile proceedings, doubt as to
        Evaluation of competence   CRC 5.645
Knowledge of witness   Ev §802
Layperson, opinion testimony of   Ev §800
Lists of expert witnesses
    Contents
        Eminent domain proceedings   CCP §1258.240
    Date of exchange
        Eminent domain proceedings   CCP §1258.220
    Demand for exchange
        Eminent domain proceedings   CCP §§1258.210, 1258.230
    Discovery by simultaneous information exchange   CCP §§2034.010 to 2034.730
        Methods of discovery   CCP §2019.010
    Incomplete lists
        Eminent domain proceedings   CCP §§1258.280, 1258.290

EXPERT AND OPINION EVIDENCE—Cont.
Lists of expert witnesses—Cont.
    Notice of changes
        Eminent domain proceedings   CCP §1258.270
Medical causation   Ev §801.1
Mental illness   Ev §870
Nonexpert testimony   Ev §800
Nonprofit or special use property where no relevant, comparable market value, method for determining value of   Ev §824
Number of expert witnesses   Ev §723
Opinion testimony based on opinion of another   Ev §804
Parentage
    Genetic tests to determine parentage
        Other expert evidence, right to produce   Fam §7557
Perception of witness in giving opinion evidence   Ev §800
Publications, cross examination regarding   Ev §721
Qualifications of expert witnesses   Ev §§720, 801
Sanity   Ev §870
Simultaneous information exchange about expert witnesses, discovery by means of   CCP §§2034.010 to 2034.730
    Augmenting or amending list or declaration   CCP §§2034.610 to 2034.630
        Conditions to grant leave   CCP §2034.620
        Court's authority to permit   CCP §2034.610
        Sanctions for unsuccessfully making or opposing motion to augment or amend   CCP §2034.630
    Content of information exchanged   CCP §2034.260
    Declaration   CCP §§2034.210, 2034.260, 2034.280
        Augmenting or amending list or declaration   CCP §§2034.610 to 2034.630
        Retention of demand, proof of service, lists and declaration   CCP §2034.290
    Demand for exchange   CCP §§2034.210 to 2034.310
        Content of information exchanged   CCP §2034.260
        Declaration   CCP §§2034.210, 2034.260, 2034.280, 2034.290
        Designations   CCP §2034.210
        Exclusion of expert testimony for failure to comply   CCP §2034.300
        Impeachment, use of witness not designated in order to impeach   CCP §2034.310
        Leave of court not required   CCP §2034.220
        Limitations on papers filed   CRC 3.250
        List exchange   CCP §2034.210
        Method of exchange   CCP §2034.260
        Previously undesignated witness, calling   CCP §2034.310
        Protective orders   CCP §2034.250
        Reports and writings discoverable   CCP §§2034.210, 2034.270
        Retention   CCP §2034.290
        Sanctions   CCP §2034.250
        Service of demand   CCP §2034.240
        Supplemental list, submission   CCP §2034.280
        Time for making demand   CCP §2034.220
        Written demand   CCP §2034.230
    Deposition of expert witness   CCP §§2034.410 to 2034.470
        Fees of expert for time at deposition   CCP §§2034.430 to 2034.470
        Notice for deposition accompanied by tender of fee, effect   CCP §2034.460
        Order setting fee, motion for   CCP §2034.470
        Place to take deposition   CCP §2034.420
        Production of materials called for by deposition notice   CCP §2034.415
        Right to depose listed witnesses   CCP §2034.410
        Tendering fees   CCP §2034.450
        Workers' compensation cases, fees   CCP §2034.430
    Eminent domain proceedings
        Exclusion from provisions   CCP §2034.010
    Exclusion of expert testimony for failure to comply   CCP §2034.300
    Impeachment, use of witness not designated in order to impeach   CCP §2034.310
    Limitations on papers filed   CRC 3.250
    Method of exchange   CCP §2034.260
    Methods of discovery   CCP §2019.010
    Retention of demand, proof of service, lists and declaration   CCP §2034.290
    Sanctions
        Augmenting or amending list or declaration   CCP §2034.630
        Demand for exchange   CCP §2034.250
        Tardy information submission   CCP §2034.730
    Supplemental list, submission   CCP §2034.280
    Tardy information submission   CCP §§2034.710 to 2034.730
        Conditions for granting leave   CCP §2034.720
        Court's authority to permit   CCP §2034.710

EXPERT AND OPINION EVIDENCE—Cont.
Simultaneous information exchange about expert witnesses, discovery by means of —Cont.
- Tardy information submission —Cont.
  - Sanctions for unsuccessfully making or opposing motion to submit CCP §2034.730

Small claims action, assistance and testimony in CCP §116.531

Trade secrets, misappropriation
- Costs recoverable, including for expert witness CC §3426.4

Ultimate issue, opinion testimony embracing Ev §805

Value of property
- Capitalized value of net rental value Ev §819
- Comparable property
  - Rental value of Ev §818
  - Sales price of Ev §816
- Eminent domain proceedings (See **EMINENT DOMAIN**)
- Improvements Ev §§820, 821
- Matters inadmissible and not proper basis for opinion testimony of Ev §822
- No comparable market value
  - Generally Ev §823
  - Nonprofit or special use property, method for Ev §824
- Rental value
  - Generally Ev §817
  - Capitalized value of net rental value Ev §819
  - Comparable rental property Ev §818
- Sale price
  - Generally Ev §815
  - Comparable property, value based on Ev §816

EXPLOSIVES
Landlord's duty to disclose danger of former explosive munitions in neighborhood area CC §1940.7
Seller's duty to disclose danger of former explosive munitions in neighborhood area CC §1102.15

EXPOSITIONS (See **FAIRS AND EXPOSITIONS**)

EXPRESS CONTRACTS (See **CONTRACTS AND AGREEMENTS**)

EXPUNGEMENT OF RECORDS
Attorney discipline records
- License fees, suspension for nonpayment
  - Bar recommendation for expungement CRC 9.8
Attorneys at law
- Continuing legal education, noncompliance leading to inactive status
  - Expungement of record of inactive enrollment CRC 9.31
Clearing records
- Proof of service
  - Forms, judicial council CRCAppx A
Forms, judicial council CRCAppx A
Pendency of actions, expungement (See **PENDENCY OF ACTIONS**)

EXTENSIONS OF TIME
Administration of decedents' estates (See **ADMINISTRATION OF ESTATES**)
Answer or demurrer, enlarging time for CCP §473
Appellate rules, superior court appeals CRC 8.810
- Limited civil cases in appellate division CRC 8.823
- Misdemeanor appeals
  - Statement on appeal as record CRC 8.869
- Polices and factors considered in determining CRC 8.811
- Rehearing
  - No extensions for granting or denying petition CRC 8.889
Appellate rules, supreme court and courts of appeal (See **APPELLATE RULES, SUPREME COURT AND COURTS OF APPEAL**)
Application
- Electronic filing, when required CRCSupp 1st AppDist
Attorneys (See **ATTORNEYS**)
Automobiles sales (See **AUTOMOBILES**)
Bill of exceptions CCP §§1054, 1054.1
Briefs, extension of time for filing CRC 10.1012
- Electronic filing, when required CRCSupp 1st AppDist
Change of venue, time to file petition for writ of mandate on grant or denial of motion for CCP §400
Complex case coordination CRC 3.503
Costs memorandum and motion to strike or tax costs, time to serve and file CRC 3.1700
Demurrer, enlarging time for CCP §473
Dissolution of marriage, final judgment of Fam §2339
Enforcement of judgments (See **ENFORCEMENT OF JUDGMENTS**)
Family law proceedings CRC 5.2

EXTENSIONS OF TIME—Cont.
Holiday, time in which act provided by law is to be done extended to next day which is not a CCP §12a
Homestead exemption CCP §704.830
New trial motions CCP §§659, 659a, 663.2
Parental custody and control, appeal from judgment freeing dependent child of juvenile court from CCP §45
Pleadings, acts relating to CCP §§1054, 1054.1
- Memorandum in support of application for order to extend not required CRC 3.1114
Rules of court CRC 1.10
- Application for order extending time
  - Electronic filing, when required CRCSupp 1st AppDist
- Trial court rules
  - Application for order extending time CRC 2.20
Service of notices CCP §§1054, 1054.1
Statutes of limitation (See **STATUTES OF LIMITATION**)
Traffic cases, extension of time for posting bail or paying fines CRC JudAdminStand 4.40
Trial court rules
- Application for order extending time CRC 2.20

EXTINGUISHING CONTRACTS (See **CONTRACTS AND AGREEMENTS**)

EXTORTION
Landlord and tenant
- Unduly influencing tenant to vacate CC §1940.2
Prostitution, evidence
- Extortion, serious felony, assault, domestic violence, human trafficking, sexual battery or stalking, victims or witnesses
  - Inadmissibility of evidence of prostitution in prosecution for prostitution Ev §1162
Real estate appraisal
- Improper influence of appraisal CC §1090.5

EXTRADITION
Interstate family support
- Criminal failure to provide support Fam §§5700.801, 5700.802

EXTRAORDINARY RELIEF
Contempt order stayed pending filing of petition for CCP §128

EXTRAORDINARY SERVICES
Personal representative, allowance of commissions to Pro §§10801, 10832

EXTRINSIC EVIDENCE (See **PAROL EVIDENCE**)

EYEGLASSES
Immunity from liability
- Nonprofit charitable organization and volunteer eye care professionals donating screening, eyeglasses, etc CC §1714.26

EYES
Vision care programs
- Minors, consent to vision care Fam §6922

EYE SPECIALIST (See **OPTICIANS AND OPTOMETRISTS**)

F

FABRICS
Warranties on sale of CC §§1790 to 1795.8

FACEBOOK
Child sexual abuse hosted on social media platform CC §§3273.65 to 3273.69
Commercial sexual exploitation of minor by social media platform CC §3345.1
Judicial ethics code
- Public confidence in judiciary
  - Electronic communications, care in using CRCSupp JudEthicsCanon 2

FACILITIES
Jury deliberation rooms CCP §216

FACSIMILES (See **COPIES; PHOTOGRAPHS AND PHOTOCOPIES**)

FACSIMILE TRANSMISSIONS
Attorney-client privilege for fax communications Ev §952
Filings, court CRC 2.300 to 2.306 (See **FAX FILING AND SERVICE**)
Service of process and papers CRC 2.300 to 2.306
- Levying officer electronic transactions act CCP §§263 to 263.7

FACSIMILE TRANSMISSIONS—Cont.
Trial court rules, fax number
    Papers, first page format and content   CRC 2.118
        Acceptance of noncomplying papers for filing   CRC 2.118
Trust deed or mortgage statement of unpaid balance by demand, delivery of   CC §2943

FACT OF DEATH
Generally   Pro §§200, 201
Administration of estate proceedings combined with fact of death proceedings   Pro §202
Hearing   Pro §203
Judgment   Pro §204
Medi-Cal beneficiary, notification of Health Services Department on death of   Pro §215
Notices
    Hearing, notice of   Pro §203
    Medi-Cal beneficiary, notification of Health Services Department on death of   Pro §215
    Prisoner as heir
        Director of victim compensation board, notice to   Pro §§216, 9202
    Prisoner, heir of decedent as   Pro §216
        Director of victim compensation and government claims board, notice to   Pro §9202
Prisoner as heir
    Notice of death to director of victim compensation board   Pro §§216, 9202
Recording evidence of   Ev §§1281 to 1283, Pro §§210 to 212

FACTORIES (See **MANUFACTURERS**)

FACTORS AND COMMISSION MERCHANTS
Agency relationship of   CC §§2367 to 2369
Consignment of property to   CC §2027
Defined   CC §§2026, 2367
Lien for services by   CC §3053
Sale of property by   CC §§2027 to 2030, 2368
Unclaimed property, sale of   CC §§2081.5, 2081.6

FACTORY-BUILT HOUSING
Sales of manufactured homes, disclosure requirements   CC §§1102 to 1102.18

FACTS
Disqualification of judges, personal knowledge of evidentiary facts as grounds for   CCP §170.1
Questions of fact (See **QUESTIONS OF LAW OR FACT**)

FAILURE OF CONSIDERATION
Rescission of contract because of   CC §1689

FAIR DEALERSHIP LAW   CC §§80 to 86

FAIR DEBT BUYING PRACTICES   CC §§1788.50 to 1788.66
Actions
    Bringing after expiration of statute of limitations
        Prohibited   CC §1788.56
    Complaints
        Contents   CC §1788.58
Charged-off consumer debt
    Defined   CC §1788.50
COVID-19 rental debt
    Sale or assignment
        Rental assistance recipients, prohibition on sale or assignment of debt   CC §1788.66
Credit services organizations
    Debt buyers
        Communication with credit services organizations about accounts   CC §1789.134
Debt buyers
    Defined   CC §1788.50
Default judgments against debtor   CC §1788.60
    Setting aside default and leave to defend
        Grounds   CC §1788.61
        Motion   CC §1788.61
        Notice of motion   CC §1788.61
Definitions   CC §1788.50
Dismissal of civil actions
    Consumer debt
        Plaintiff debt buyer failing to appear or prepare to proceed   CCP §581.5
Effective date of provisions   CC §1788.50

FAIR DEBT BUYING PRACTICES—Cont.
Forms
    Judicial council legal forms   CRCAppx A
Hospital debt
    Actions
        Contents of complaints   CC §1788.58
    Written statements to collect debt   CC §1788.52
Landlord and tenant
    COVID-19 rental debt
        Sale or assignment, prohibition on debt of rental assistance recipients   CC §1788.66
Limitation of actions
    Actions brought after expiration of statute of limitations
        Prohibited   CC §1788.56
Receipts for payments from debtors   CC §1788.54
Settlements
    Documentation   CC §1788.54
Violation of provisions   CC §1788.62
Waiver of provisions
    Void   CC §1788.64
Written statements to collect debt   CC §1788.52

FAIR DEBT COLLECTION PRACTICES   CC §§1788 to 1788.33 (See **CONSUMER DEBT COLLECTION**)

FAIR DEBT SETTLEMENT PRACTICES   CC §§1788.300 to 1788.307
Actions to enforce
    Consumer actions   CC §1788.305
Applicability of provisions   CC §1788.303
    Exemptions   CC §1788.304
Citation of provisions   CC §1788.300
Consumers
    Actions to enforce   CC §1788.305
    Defined   CC §1788.301
Contracts between providers and consumers   CC §1788.302
Creditors
    Defined   CC §1788.301
Debt
    Defined   CC §1788.301
Debt settlement providers   CC §1788.302
    Applicability of provisions   CC §1788.303
    Defined   CC §1788.301
    Duties   CC §1788.302
Debt settlement services
    Applicability of provisions   CC §1788.303
    Defined   CC §1788.301
Definitions   CC §1788.301
Exemptions from provisions   CC §1788.304
False, unfair, abusive, deceptive or misleading acts or practices
    Enumerated   CC §1788.302
Limitation of actions   CC §1788.305
Payment processing services
    Applicability of provisions   CC §1788.303
    Defined   CC §1788.301
Payment processors
    Defined   CC §1788.301
    Duties   CC §1788.302
Person
    Defined   CC §1788.301
Settlement accounts
    Defined   CC §1788.301
Severability of provisions   CC §1788.307
Short title   CC §1788.300
Termination of contracts between providers and consumers
    Consumer right   CC §1788.302
Waiver of provisions
    Void and unenforceable   CC §1788.306

FAIRS AND EXPOSITIONS
Guide dogs permitted in   CC §§54.2, 54.3
    Construction or application of provisions in issue, solicitor general notified   CC §55.2

FALLER
Lien of   CC §§3065 to 3065c

FALSE ARREST
Domestic violence protective orders, immunity for officers enforcing   Fam §6383
Liability of law enforcement officer for   Gov §820.4

FALSE CLAIMS
Case management of false claims act cases   CRC 2.573
Filing records under seal   CRC 2.570 to 2.573
    Access to sealed records   CRC 2.570
    Applicability   CRC 2.570
    Case management   CRC 2.573
    Confidentiality of records filed under act   CRC 2.570
    Custody of sealed records   CRC 2.571
    Definitions   CRC 2.570
    Extension of time, motions for   CRC 2.572
    Papers, filing under seal   CRC 2.571
    Procedures for filing records under seal   CRC 2.571
    Unsealing records   CRC 2.573

FALSE IMPRISONMENT
Domestic violence protective orders, immunity for officers enforcing   Fam §6383
Heir's false imprisonment of elderly or dependent decedent, effect on inheritance rights of   Pro §259
Invasion of privacy
    False imprisonment with intent to capture visual image or sound recording   CC §1708.8
Liability of law enforcement officer for   Gov §820.4
Limitation of actions   CCP §340

FALSE PERSONATION
Debt collectors   CC §1788.13

FALSE PRETENSES
Personal information from public records, wrongfully obtaining   CC §1798.56

FAMILY
Allowance (See **FAMILY ALLOWANCE**)
Conservatorships for support of family (See **CONSERVATORS**)
Counseling (See **MARRIAGE AND FAMILY COUNSELORS**)
Debt collectors communicating with   CC §1788.12
Domestic violence (See **DOMESTIC VIOLENCE**)
Dwelling
    Generally (See **DWELLING HOUSES**)
    Family home (See **FAMILY HOME**)
History (See **FAMILY HISTORY**)
Home (See **FAMILY HOME**)
Judges' actions on behalf of family members, Code of Judicial Ethics provisions concerning   CRCSupp JudEthicsCanon 2
Medical information disclosures to family members   CC §56.1007
Mobilehome park rates based on number in   CC §798.35
Parent-child relationship (See **PARENT AND CHILD**)
Warranties for goods sold for   CC §§1790 to 1795.8

FAMILY ALLOWANCE
Generally   Pro §§6540 to 6545
Appeals   Pro §§3103, 6545
Continuation of administration to pay allowance   Pro §12203
Defined   Pro §38
Dissolution of marriage proceedings   Fam §2337
Expenses of administration, payments charged as   Pro §6544
Independent administration, payment under   Pro §10535
Modification of   Pro §§6541, 6543
Other income, effect of   Pro §6540
Petition for   Pro §6541
Physical disability as basis for receiving   Pro §6540
Priority of family allowance payments for purposes of estate distribution   Pro §§11420, 11421
Quick sale of estate assets to provide for   Pro §§10252, 10259
Sale of personalty to provide for   Pro §§10252, 10259

FAMILY CODE
Amendments and additions to   Fam §§4, 7
Citation of code   Fam §1
Construction of code   Fam §§3, 6, 9 to 12
Continuation of existing law   Fam §2
Definitions   Fam §§50 to 155
Headings, effect of   Fam §5
Operative date of   Fam §4
Repeal of provisions   Fam §4
Restatement of existing law   Fam §2
Severability of provisions   Fam §13
Tense, construction of   Fam §9
Uniform act, construction of provisions drawn from   Fam §3

FAMILY CONCILIATION COURT LAW (See **CONCILIATION COURTS**)

FAMILY HISTORY
Generally   Ev §1310
Bible entries   Ev §1312
Church records concerning   Ev §1315
Community reputation concerning   Ev §1314
Crypts   Ev §1312
Friends, statements by   Ev §1311
Heirlooms   Ev §1312
Neighbor's testimony concerning   Ev §1314
Relative's statements   Ev §1311
Reputation among family members   Ev §1313
Tombstones   Ev §1312
Urns   Ev §1312

FAMILY HOME
Child support proceedings, rental value of family home for purposes of   Fam §4057
Deferred sale of family home, request of custodial parent for   Fam §§3800 to 3810
Excluding party from dwelling   Fam §§6321, 6340
Service of process at home of person being served   CCP §415.20
Surviving spouse's possession of family home pending administration of estate   Pro §§6500, 6501
Transient occupancy in single-family homes, recordkeeping required for accepting reservations or money for   CC §1864

FAMILY LAW FACILITATORS
Generally   Fam §§10000 to 10015
Coordination with family law information center   Fam §15010
Disclosures   CRCAppx A (CRCFL-940)
    Foreign language forms   CRCAppx A (CRCFL-940C to CRCFL-940V)
Guidelines for operation of family law facilitator offices   CRCAppx C
Standards for office of family law facilitator   CRC 5.430

FAMILY LAW FORMS   CRCAppx A (CRCFL-100 to CRCFL-985)
Adopted or approved forms by Judicial Council deemed adopted by rules of court   CRC 5.7
Assets and debts   CRCAppx A (CRCFL-142)
Assignment of wages   CRCAppxs A (CRCFL-430), (CRCFL-435), (CRCFL-455)
    Hearings
        Request for hearing   CRCAppx A (CRCFL-450)
Attorneys
    Limited scope representation
        Notice   CRCAppx A (CRCFL-950)
        Objection to application for relief from   CRCAppx A (CRCFL-956)
        Order deciding issue of relief   CRCAppx A (CRCFL-958)
        Relief as counsel, application   CRCAppx A (CRCFL-955)
    Withdrawal of attorney of record
        Notice of withdrawal   CRCAppx A (CRCFL-960)
Child custody and visitation
    Application attachment   CRCAppx A (CRCFL-311)
    Court-connected mediators or evaluators
        Declaration of evaluator concerning qualifications   CRCAppx A (CRCFL-325)
        Order appointing evaluator   CRCAppx A (CRCFL-327)
    Evaluators and investigators
        Declaration of private evaluator regarding qualifications   CRCAppx A (CRCFL-326)
        Order appointing evaluator   CRCAppx A (CRCFL-327)
    Holiday schedule attachment   CRCAppx A (CRCFL-341(C))
    Joint custody
        Attachment for joint legal custody   CRCAppx A (CRCFL-341(E))
    Petition for custody of minor children   CRCAppx A (CRCFL-260)
    Physical custody attachment   CRCAppx A (CRCFL-341(D))
    Registration of orders
        Out-of-state orders   CRCAppxs A (CRCFL-580), (CRCFL-585)
    Stipulation and order   CRCAppx A (CRCFL-355)
    Supervised visitation order   CRCAppx A (CRCFL-341(A))
Child support   CRCAppx A (CRCFL-380 to CRCFL-393)
    Delinquency and arrearages   CRCAppxs A (CRCFL-485), (CRCFL-490)
    Findings
        Nonguideline findings attachment   CRCAppx A (CRCFL-342(A))
    Information and order attachment   CRCAppx A (CRCFL-342)
    Modification
        Military service activation and deployment, notice of   CRCAppx A (CRCFL-398)
    Order attachment   CRCAppx A (CRCFL-343)
    Registration of order
        Statement of registration   CRCAppx A (CRCFL-440)
    Security deposit   CRCAppxs A (CRCFL-400), (CRCFL-401)

FAMILY LAW FORMS—Cont.
  Child support —Cont.
    Setting aside order
      Order deciding issues   CRCAppx A (CRCFL-367)
      Request for hearing   CRCAppx A (CRCFL-360)
      Responsive declaration   CRCAppx A (CRCFL-365)
    Simplified modification   CRCAppx A (CRCFL-390 to CRCFL-393)
    Stipulation to establish or modify   CRCAppx A (CRCFL-350)
  Commissioner, findings and recommendation of   CRCAppx A (CRCFL-665)
    Review   CRCAppx A (CRCFL-667)
  Contempt
    Affidavit of facts constituting   CRCAppxs A (CRCFL-411), (CRCFL-412)
    Findings and order   CRCAppx A (CRCFL-415)
    Order to show cause as to   CRCAppx A (CRCFL-410)
  Default, request and declaration for   CRCAppx A (CRCFL-165)
  Disclosure, declaration of   CRCAppxs A (CRCFL-140), (CRCFL-141)
  Divorce
    Property orders
      Attachments   CRCAppx A (CRCFL-344)
  Domestic relations, form of qualified order for support   CRCAppxs A (CRCFL-460), (CRCFL-461)
  Employee benefit plans
    Joinder
      Pleading on joinder   CRCAppx A (CRCFL-370)
  Family law and domestic violence, status of approved forms   CRC 5.7
  Family law facilitators
    Disclosures   CRCAppx A (CRCFL-940)
      Foreign language forms   CRCAppx A (CRCFL-940C to CRCFL-940V)
  Family law information centers
    Disclosures   CRCAppx A (CRCFL-945)
  Family support
    Order attachment   CRCAppx A (CRCFL-343)
    Simplified modification forms   CRCAppx A (CRCFL-390 to CRCFL-393)
  Financial declarations   CRCAppxs A (CRCFL-150), (CRCFL-155)
    Financial statement simplified form   CRCAppx A (CRCFL-155)
    Income and benefit information from employer
      Request   CRCAppx A (CRCFL-397)
  Findings after hearing   CRCAppx A (CRCFL-340)
  Guardians ad litem
    Appointment
      Application and order for appointment   CRCAppx A (CRCFL-935, CRCFL-936)
  Health insurance coverage   CRCAppxs A (CRCFL-470), (CRCFL-475)
  Injunctions and restraining orders, temporary restraining orders   CRCAppx A (CRCFL-305)
  Interstate family support
    Contest of income withholding order by obligor   CRC 5.335
    Determination of controlling support order, notice   CRCFL-571
    Discovery assistance request   CRCFL-559
    General testimony form   CRCFL-526
    Initial request for enforcement   CRCFL-505
    Judgments, parental responsibility   CRCAppx A (CRCFL-530), CRCFL-530
    Locate data sheet   CRCFL-558
    Nondisclosure order
      Ex parte application   CRCFL-511
    Party designation   CRC 5.370
    Registration of income-withholding and support orders   CRCFL-556
      Out-of-state orders, notice of registration   CRCAppx A (CRCFL-570), CRCFL-570
    Response to petition   CRCAppx A (CRCFL-520), CRCFL-520
    Show cause order   CRCFL-515
    Subsequent actions   CRCFL-557
    Summons   CRCAppx A (CRCFL-510), CRCFL-510
    Transfer of actions
      Ex parte application   CRCAppx A (CRCFL-560), CRCFL-560
    Uniform support petition   CRCFL-500
    Use of interstate forms   CRC 5.7
  Judgments   CRCAppx A (CRCFL-180)
    Abstract of support judgment   CRCAppx A (CRCFL-480)
    Default judgment   CRCAppx A (CRCFL-170)
    Final judgment of dissolution, request for   CRCAppx A (CRCFL-970)
    Income and expense declaration after   CRCAppx A (CRCFL-396)
    Notice of entry   CRCAppx A (CRCFL-180)
  Kidnapping and child abduction
    Orders to prevent
      Attachment   CRCAppx A (CRCFL-341(B))
      Request   CRCAppx A (CRCFL-312)
  List of Judicial Council forms   CRCAppx A

FAMILY LAW FORMS—Cont.
  Military service activation and deployment, notice of
    Support modifications   CRCAppx A (CRCFL-398)
  Motions
    Judicial council legal forms   CRCAppx A
  Name, restoration of   CRCAppx A (CRCFL-395)
  Nonfamily proceedings, applicability of forms in   CRC 5.7
  Notices
    Objection   CRCAppx A (CRCFL-666)
    Withdrawal of attorney of record   CRCAppx A (CRCFL-960)
  Orders
    Hearings, findings and orders after   CRCAppx A (CRCFL-340)
    Show cause orders   CRCAppxs A (CRCFL-300), (CRCFL-410)
  Parental obligations, supplemental forms for governmental enforcement   CRCAppx A (CRCFL-600 to CRCFL-697)
  Paternity   CRCAppx A (CRCFL-200 to CRCFL-290)
  Pension plans, joinder as party   CRCAppx A (CRCFL-372 to CRCFL-375)
  Petitions   CRCAppx A (CRCFL-100)
    Custody of minor children   CRCAppx A (CRCFL-260)
  Process and service of process
    Proof of personal service   CRCAppx A (CRCFL-330)
    Proof of service by mail   CRCAppx A (CRCFL-335)
  Property declaration   CRCAppx A (CRCFL-160)
  Property orders
    Attachments   CRCAppx A (CRCFL-344)
      Judgments, attachment to   CRCAppx A (CRCFL-345)
  Receipt of forms
    Notice and acknowledgment of receipt   CRCAppx A (CRCFL-117)
  Registration of orders
    Support order, request for hearing as to   CRCAppxs A (CRCFL-420), (CRCFL-421)
  Request for separate trial   CRCAppx A (CRCFL-170)
  Response   CRCAppx A (CRCFL-120)
  Show cause orders   CRCAppxs A (CRCFL-300), (CRCFL-410)
  Spousal support
    Modification
      Military service activation and deployment, notice of   CRCAppx A (CRCFL-398)
    Orders
      Attachment to orders   CRCAppx A (CRCFL-343)
      Registration of order, statement   CRCAppx A (CRCFL-440)
      Setting aside order   CRCAppx A (CRCFL-360 to CRCFL-367)
    Simplified modification   CRCAppx A (CRCFL-390 to CRCFL-393)
  Summary dissolution   CRCAppx A (CRCFL-800 to CRCFL-830)
  Summons
    Family law, generally   CRCAppx A (CRCFL-110)
    Petition for custody, uniform parentage   CRCAppx A (CRCFL-210)
    Proof of service   CRCAppx A (CRCFL-115)
  Supervised visitation order   CRCAppx A (CRCFL-341A)
  Support arrearages   CRCAppxs A (CRCFL-420), (CRCFL-421)
  Support orders
    Registration, request for hearing as to   CRCAppxs A (CRCFL-420), (CRCFL-421)
  Temporary restraining orders   CRCAppx A (CRCFL-305)
  Title IV-D support action   CRC 5.310
  Trial
    Separate trial
      Application for separate trial   CRCAppx A (CRCFL-315)
  Uniform child custody jurisdiction and enforcement act
    Declarations   CRCAppx A (CRCFL-105)
  Uniform parentage
    Default or uncontested judgment, declaration for   CRCAppx A (CRCFL-230)
    Judgment   CRCAppx A (CRCFL-250)
    Parental relationship, advisement and waiver of rights as to establishment   CRCAppx A (CRCFL-235)

FAMILY LAW INFORMATION CENTERS   Fam §§15000 to 15012
Disclosures   CRCAppx A (CRCFL-945)
Guidelines for operation of family law information centers   CRCAppx C

FAMILY LAW PILOT PROJECTS
Authorization in certain counties to conduct pilot projects   Fam §20001
Family law information centers for unrepresented low-income litigants   Fam §§15000 to 15012
Interpreters for child custody proceedings, public provision of   Fam §3032
Mediation proceedings
  San Mateo County, contested custody cases in   Fam §20019
  Santa Clara County, contested custody or visitation cases in   Fam §20038
San Mateo County
  Actions and proceedings subject to pilot project   Fam §20010

FAMILY LAW PILOT PROJECTS—Cont.
San Mateo County—Cont.
  Booklet describing family law program to public Fam §20016
  Contested cases
    Documents and papers required Fam §§20020, 20021
    Mediation proceedings for Fam §§20019, 20038
    Tax returns and paycheck stubs to be provided in Fam §20020
  Continuances Fam §20019
  District attorney in child custody cases involving welfare assistance Fam §20023
  Duration of pilot project Fam §20002
  Estimated savings upon implementation of pilot project Fam §20026
  Failure to submit documents, effect of Fam §20021
  Family law evaluator
    Availability at no cost Fam §20013
    Duties of Fam §20020
    Licensed attorney, qualification as Fam §20017
    Requirement to see evaluator when not represented by counsel Fam §20014
    Tax returns and paycheck stubs to be provided Fam §20020
  Guideline for temporary support orders to comply with state uniform guidelines Fam §20018
  Hearing on motion for temporary orders, time for Fam §20011
  Income tax returns
    Review by other party Fam §20022
    Submission to court Fam §20020
  Mediation in contested custody cases Fam §20019
  Protocol for hearing procedure, court to develop Fam §20015
  Service of papers Fam §20014
Santa Clara County
  Actions and proceedings subject to pilot project Fam §20031
  Attorney mediator, duties of Fam §20034
  Authorization for superior court to conduct pilot project Fam §§20001, 20030
  Booklet describing family law program for public, publishing of Fam §20040
  Contempt for failure to comply Fam §20032
  Continuances Fam §20032
  District attorney in child custody cases involving welfare assistance Fam §20037
  Documents required Fam §20032
  Duration of pilot project Fam §20002
  Estimated savings upon implementation of pilot project Fam §20043
  Exemption from pilot project requirements, motion for Fam §20036
  Existing programs to be coordinated and centralized Fam §20041
  Guidelines for temporary support orders to comply with state uniform guidelines Fam §20035
  Income and Expense declaration, suspending use of Fam §20033
  Mediation in contested custody or visitation cases Fam §20038
  Setting of hearing, time for Fam §20032
  Tax returns and paycheck stubs, production of Fam §20032
Support orders
  Expedited modification Fam §17441

FAMILY LAW PROCEEDINGS
Annulment (See **ANNULMENT**)
Change of venue where both parties moved from county rendering decree CCP §397.5
Discovery
  Postjudgment proceedings Fam §218
Dissolution of marriage (See **DISSOLUTION OF MARRIAGE**)
Enforcement of judgments (See **ENFORCEMENT OF JUDGMENTS**)
Family Conciliation Court Law (See **CONCILIATION COURTS**)
Legal separation (See **LEGAL SEPARATION**)
Procedural provisions Fam §§210 to 218
Rules (See **FAMILY RULES**)

FAMILY PLANNING
Consumer privacy rights
  Personal information restrictions of persons at or near family planning center CC §1798.99.90
Legally protected health care services CC §§1798.300 to 1798.308

FAMILY REUNIFICATION SERVICES CRC 5.695
Abused and neglected children CRC 5.695
Child custody or visitation rights proceedings Fam §3026
Continuation of case where additional services needed
  Subsequent permanency review hearing CRC 5.722
Denial of services CRC 5.695
Disqualification, findings CRC 5.695
Exceptions to required services CRC 5.695

FAMILY REUNIFICATION SERVICES—Cont.
Incarcerated father, reunification services with CRC 5.695
Missing parent or guardian, disposition in case of CRC 5.695
Neglected children CRC 5.695
Permanency review hearing CRC 5.720
Services, exceptions to requirement for provision of CRC 5.695
Sibling groups, failure of parent to participate in services regarding member of CRC 5.695
Termination of parental rights
  Failure to participate CRC 5.695
Termination of services
  For sibling, effect CRC 5.695
  Order for CRC 5.720
Visitation orders CRC 5.695
  Mandatory counseling orders Fam §§3190 to 3193
Voluntary relinquishment of child, exception to requirements CRC 5.695
Welfare department, services by CRC 5.695

FAMILY RULES CRC 5.1 to 5.500 (See also **DISSOLUTION OF MARRIAGE**)
Adoption
  Hague adoption convention, adoptions under CRC 5.490 to 5.492
  Intercountry adoptions CRC 5.490 to 5.493
  Native Americans
    Involuntary placements, rules governing CRC 5.480 to 5.488 (See **INDIAN CHILD WELFARE ACT INVOLUNTARY PLACEMENTS**)
  Postadoption contact agreements CRC 5.451
Alternate valuation date
  Bifurcation of issues
    Conditions when bifurcation appropriate CRC 5.390
Alternative relief, request for CRC 5.60
Annulment
  Domestic partnerships CRC 5.76
  Parties
    Husband and wife or domestic partners as parties CRC 5.16
  Statutes of limitation
    Quash, request for order CRC 5.63
  Title IV-D support enforcement
    Consolidation of support orders CRC 5.365
Appealable orders under Family Code proceedings, applicability of CCP provisions to CCP §904.1
Appearance CRC 5.62
  Emergency or ex parte orders, requests
    Appearance at hearing CRC 5.169
  General appearance, effect CRC 5.68
  Judicial Council form CRCAppx A CRCFL-130
  Telephone appearance CRC 3.672, 5.9
  Title IV-D support enforcement
    Local support agency appearance CRC 5.360
    Telephone appearance CRC 3.670, 5.324
Applicability CRC 5.2
Application
  Joinder CRC 5.24
Assignment of wages
  Forms CRCAppxs A (CRCFL-430), (CRCFL-435)
Attorney representation
  Limited scope representation CRC 5.425
  Service on attorney of record Fam §215
Attorneys, court-appointed
  Applicable guidelines for appointment CRC JudAdminStand 5.30
  Compensation CRC JudAdminStand 5.30
Attorneys' fees Fam §§270 to 274, 2030 to 2034
  Financial need basis CRC 5.427
Bifurcation of issues CRC 5.392
  Appeals Fam §2025
  Clerk of court
    Notice by clerk of decision of bifurcated issue CRC 5.390
  Conditions when bifurcation appropriate CRC 5.390
  Interlocutory appeal of order for CRC 5.392
  Modification of judgment or order
    Service of notice Fam §215
  Request for order to bifurcate CRC 5.390
  Termination of marriage or domestic partnership
    Joinder of pension plans as prerequisite for separate trial on termination CRC 5.390
  Briefs
    Setting trials and long-cause hearings
      Trial or hearing briefs CRC 5.394
  Child custody
    Attorneys, court appointment CRC 5.240 to 5.242

FAMILY RULES—Cont.
  Child custody—Cont.
    Children's participation and testimony CRC 5.250
    Declarations under uniform child custody jurisdiction and enforcement act (UCCJEA) CRC 5.52
    Domestic violence
      Communication protocol for domestic violence and child custody orders CRC 5.445
      Family court services protocol CRC 5.215
      Modification of orders in domestic violence prevention act cases CRC 5.381
    Evaluations CRC 5.220
    Indian Child Welfare Act, compliance with
      Involuntary placements CRC 5.480 to 5.488 (See **INDIAN CHILD WELFARE ACT INVOLUNTARY PLACEMENTS**)
    Investigators and evaluators
      Domestic violence training CRC 5.230
      Licensing, education, experience, and training standards CRC 5.225
    Judgments
      Entry of judgment CRC 5.413
      Notice of entry of judgment CRC 5.415
    Mediation CRC 5.210
      Training, education, etc., for mediator, mediation supervisor and family court services director CRC 5.210
    Modification of orders
      Domestic violence prevention act cases CRC 5.381
      Orders following termination of juvenile proceeding or probate court guardianship proceeding CRC 5.475
  Child support
    Case registry forms CRC 5.330
    Change of prior support orders
      Request CRC 5.260
    Child support commissioners, judicial education for CRC 5.340
    Computer software assisting in determining support CRC 5.275
    Deviations from child support guidelines CRC 5.260
    Financial declarations CRC 5.260
    Guidelines
      Certification of statewide uniform calculators CRC 5.275
    Interstate income withholding orders, hearings on CRC 5.335
    Judgment for support CRC 5.260
    Minimum training standards for court clerks CRC 5.355
    Modification of orders
      Domestic violence prevention act cases CRC 5.381
    Notice
      Child support agency, notice to CRC 5.260
    Title IV-D support enforcement CRC 5.300 to 5.375
    Waiver of fees and costs
      Repayment of waived fees in support actions CRC 5.45
  Civil rules
    Applicability in family, juvenile and probate cases in superior court CRC 3.10
    Generally CRC 1.4, 3.1 to 3.2240
  Claimant defined CRC 5.24
  Clerk of court
    Bifurcation of issues
      Notice by clerk of decision of bifurcated issue CRC 5.390
    Judgment, entry
      Notice of entry by clerk CRC 5.413
    Request for orders
      Filing papers in clerk's office CRC 5.96
    Title IV-D support enforcement
      Case registry form CRC 5.330
      Summons and complaint combined CRC 5.325
      Training of clerk and staff CRC 5.355
  Combined summons and complaint regarding parental obligations CRC 5.325
  Complaints
    Format CRC 5.60
    Proof of service CRC 5.66
  Conduct of party or attorney, sanctions based on Fam §271
  Conferences
    Family centered case resolution conferences CRC 5.83
  Conservators
    Indians, involuntary placements
      Indian Child Welfare Act, rules governing CRC 5.480 to 5.488
        (See **INDIAN CHILD WELFARE ACT INVOLUNTARY PLACEMENTS**)
  Consolidation of child support orders CRC 5.365
  Contempt Fam §2026
    Order to show cause as to CRCAppx A (CRCFL-410)
  Continuing jurisdiction of court CRC 5.68

FAMILY RULES—Cont.
  Coordination of court resources
    Child custody orders
      Court communication protocol CRC 5.445
    Domestic violence
      Court communication protocol CRC 5.445
    Related cases
      Confidentiality of information CRC 5.440
      Definition CRC 5.440
      Identification and management of related cases CRC 5.440
      Title IV-D cases CRC 5.440
  Costs Fam §§270 to 274, 2030 to 2034
    Financial need basis CRC 5.427
    Sanctions may include expenses for parties aggrieved by rules violation CRC 5.14
  Declarations
    Requests for orders
      Emergency or ex parte orders, requests CRC 5.151
      Supporting and responding to request CRC 5.111
    Temporary restraining orders
      Supporting temporary restraining orders issued without notice Fam §241
  Default
    Dissolution or legal separation
      Hearing on default judgments submitted on basis of declaration or affidavit CRC 5.409
      Review of default submitted on basis of declaration or affidavit CRC 5.407
    Employee benefit plan joined as party Fam §2065
    Entry of default CRC 5.401
    Form of request and declaration for CRCAppx A (CRCFL-165)
    Judgment on default
      Checklists for judgment CRC 5.405
      Disposition of all matters CRC 5.401
    Proof of facts CRC 5.401
    Request for default CRC 5.402
    Respondent's failure to respond CRC 5.401
    Service address requirement CRC 5.402
  Definitions CRC 5.2
    Pleadings CRC 5.74
  Demurrers
    No use of demurrers or summary judgment motions in family law actions CRC 5.74
  Dependent children
    Indian Child Welfare Act
      Involuntary placements, rules governing CRC 5.480 to 5.488 (See **INDIAN CHILD WELFARE ACT INVOLUNTARY PLACEMENTS**)
  Depositions
    Discovery CRC 5.12
  Discovery
    Code provisions applicable to discovery CRC 5.12
    Court rules provisions applicable to discovery CRC 5.12
    Law and motion rules
      Applicable to discovery proceedings in family law CRC 3.1100
  Dismissal of action
    Waiver of fees and costs
      Denial of waiver CRC 5.43
  Dissolution of marriage
    Bifurcation of issues
      Joinder of pension plans as prerequisite for separate trial on termination of marriage or domestic partnership CRC 5.390
    Default
      Hearing on default judgments submitted on basis of declaration or affidavit CRC 5.409
      Review of default submitted on basis of declaration or affidavit CRC 5.407
    Domestic partnerships CRC 5.76
    Family centered case resolution CRC 5.83
    Parties
      Husband and wife or domestic partners as parties CRC 5.16
    Residence requirements
      Quash, request for order, failure to meet residence requirements CRC 5.63
    Summary dissolution CRC 5.77
    Title IV-D support enforcement
      Consolidation of support orders CRC 5.365
  Domestic partnerships
    Dissolution, legal separation, or annulment CRC 5.76
      Default, hearing when submitted on basis of declaration or affidavit CRC 5.409

FAMILY RULES—Cont.
  Domestic partnerships—Cont.
    Dissolution, legal separation, or annulment —Cont.
      Default, review when submitted on basis of declaration or affidavit CRC 5.407
      Parties to proceeding   CRC 5.16
    Minor marriage or domestic partnership, request by minor
      Applicability of provision   CRC 5.448
      Family court services, duties   CRC 5.448
      Initial filings   CRC 5.448
      Judicial officers, duties   CRC 5.448
      Waiting period after order granting permission   CRC 5.448
    Support
      Change of prior support orders   CRC 5.260
      Financial declarations   CRC 5.260
      Judgment for support   CRC 5.260
  Domestic violence
    Child custody
      Communication protocol for domestic violence and child custody orders   CRC 5.445
      Family court services protocol   CRC 5.215
      Modification of orders in domestic violence prevention act cases   CRC 5.381
    Child support
      Modification of orders in domestic violence prevention act cases   CRC 5.381
    Confidentiality of minor's information in protective order proceedings
      Release of confidential information   CRC 5.382
      Request to make information confidential   CRC 5.382
    Parentage
      Agreement and judgment of parentage in domestic violence prevention act cases   CRC 5.380
    Parties in domestic violence prevention proceedings   CRC 5.16
    Protection orders
      Confidentiality of minor's information in protective order proceedings, request to make confidential   CRC 5.382
      Registration of foreign protection orders
        Tribal court orders   CRC 5.386
    Settlement service providers, court-connected   CRC 5.420
    Visitation
      Modification of orders in domestic violence prevention act cases   CRC 5.381
  Emergency or ex parte orders, requests   CRC 5.92, 5.151 to 5.170
    Appearance at hearing   CRC 5.169
    Applicability of provisions   CRC 5.151
    Contents of application and declaration   CRC 5.151
    Declarations
      Contents of application and declaration   CRC 5.151
    Documents to be included with request   CRC 5.151
    Notice of emergency hearing
      Contents of notice and declaration   CRC 5.151
      Court, notice to   CRC 5.165
      Matters not requiring notice to other parties   CRC 5.170
      Method of notice   CRC 5.165
      Parties, notice to   CRC 5.165
    Purpose of emergency request procedure   CRC 5.151
    Service of request and response   CRC 5.167
    Temporary emergency orders
      Service   CRC 5.167
  Exclusion of persons from courtroom during trial   Fam §214
  Extensions of time   CRC 5.2
  Facilitators, minimum standards for   CRC 5.430
  Family centered case resolution   CRC 5.83
  Family support
    Title IV-D support enforcement   CRC 5.300 to 5.375
  Fees for filing   CRC 5.40 to 5.46
    Additional fees   CRC 5.40
    Authority for fees
      Statutory authority   CRC 5.40
    Domestic violence
      Tribal court protection orders   CRC 5.386
    Summary dissolution of marriage   CRC 5.77
    Waiver of fees and costs   CRC 5.41
      Denial of waiver   CRC 5.43
      Support actions, repayment of waived fees   CRC 5.45
      Supreme court or court of appeal cases, applicable provisions   CRC 5.46
    When due   CRC 5.40
  Filing
    Joinder motion notice   CRC 5.24

FAMILY RULES—Cont.
  Financial declarations
    Attached to applications for order   CRC 5.401, 5.402
    Defaults, use in   CRC 5.401, 5.402
    Judicial Council forms   CRCAppxs A (CRCFL-150), (CRCFL-155), (CRCFL-397)
  Fines
    Sanctions   CRC 5.14
  Firearm relinquishment procedures
    Forms for firearm relinquishment   CRCAppx A
  Foreign country adoptions
    Hague adoption convention, adoptions under   CRC 5.490 to 5.492
    Intercountry adoptions generally   CRC 5.490 to 5.493
  Forms
    Local forms   CRC 5.4
    Use of forms   CRC 5.7
    Waiver of fees and costs   CRC 5.41
      Support actions, repayment of waived fees   CRC 5.45
  Foster care
    Indian children, involuntary placements
      Indian Child Welfare Act, rules governing   CRC 5.480 to 5.488 (See **INDIAN CHILD WELFARE ACT INVOLUNTARY PLACEMENTS**)
  General appearance, effect   CRC 5.68
  Guardianships
    Indian children
      Involuntary placements, rules governing   CRC 5.480 to 5.488 (See **INDIAN CHILD WELFARE ACT INVOLUNTARY PLACEMENTS**)
    Orders following termination of juvenile proceeding or probate court guardianship proceeding   CRC 5.475
  Hearing on temporary restraining order issued without notice   Fam §244
  Identity mistaken
    Title IV-D support enforcement
      Obligor motion regarding   CRC 5.375
  Immigration, juveniles
    Special immigrant juvenile findings, request for orders   CRC 5.130
      Forms, judicial council   CRCAppx A
  Implied procedures   CRC 5.2
  Income and expense declaration
    Attorneys' fees
      Financial need basis for fees   CRC 5.427
  Income withholding
    Title IV-D support enforcement
      Interstate income withholding orders   CRC 5.335
  Indians
    Involuntary placements
      Indian child welfare act involuntary placements   CRC 5.480 to 5.488 (See **INDIAN CHILD WELFARE ACT INVOLUNTARY PLACEMENTS**)
  Injunctions and restraining orders
    Individual restraining order   CRC 5.50
      Request for orders   CRC 5.91
    Judicial Council form   CRCAppx A (CRCFL-305)
    Persons not parties, injunctive relief against   CRC 5.18
    Standard family law restraining order   CRC 5.50
    Temporary restraining order   CRCAppx A (CRCFL-305)
  Interlocutory appeal of order bifurcating issues   CRC 5.392
  Joinder of parties   CRC 5.24, 5.29, CRCAppx A (CRCFL-371 to CRCFL-375), Fam §2021
    Application
      Form of application   CRC 5.24
    Claiming interest, joinder of persons   CRC 5.24
      Definition of claimant   CRC 5.24
    Determination on joinder   CRC 5.24
    Employee benefit plan joined as party   CRC 5.29, Fam §§2060 to 2074
      Pleading on joinder   CRCAppx A (CRCFL-370)
      Separate trial of termination of marriage or domestic partnership, joinder as prerequisite   CRC 5.390
    Mandatory joinder   CRC 5.24
    Permissive joinder   CRC 5.24
    Persons who may seek   CRC 5.24
    Pleading rules applicable   CRC 5.24
  Judges
    Assignment of judges   CRC JudAdminStand 5.30
    Education of judges   CRC 10.463
      Domestic violence issues   CRC 10.464
      Family law matters   CRC 10.463, CRC JudAdminStand 5.30
    Title IV-D support enforcement
      Hearings   CRC 5.305

FAMILY RULES—Cont.
Judgments
    Default judgment   CRCAppxs A (CRCFL-165), (CRCFL-170)
        Checklists for judgment   CRC 5.405
        Disposition of all matters   CRC 5.401
        Dissolution, legal separation, etc, review of default based on declaration or affidavit   CRC 5.407
    Defined   Fam §100
    Final judgment of dissolution, request for   CRCAppx A (CRCFL-970)
    Legal separation   CRC 5.413
        Notice of entry of judgment   CRC 5.415
    Modification of judgments, notice requirements   Fam §215
    Notice of entry of judgment   CRC 5.413, 5.415
    Quash, request for order
        Prior judgment   CRC 5.63
    Stipulated judgments   CRC 5.411
    Support   CRC 5.260
    Title IV-D support enforcement
        Proposed judgments and amended proposed judgments   CRC 5.325
Judicial notice
    Request for orders   CRC 5.115
Jurisdiction
    Generally   Fam §200
    Continuing jurisdiction   CRC 5.68
    Implied procedures   CRC 5.2
    Objections to   Fam §2012
    Reservation of jurisdiction   CRC 5.18
Law and motion rules
    Discovery
        Applicable to discovery proceedings in family law   CRC 3.1100
Legal capacity to sue
    Quash, request for order
        Lack of legal capacity to sue   CRC 5.63
Legal separation
    Default
        Hearing on default judgments submitted on basis of declaration or affidavit   CRC 5.409
        Review of default based on declaration or affidavit   CRC 5.407
    Domestic partnerships   CRC 5.76
    Judgment   CRC 5.413
        Notice of entry of judgment   CRC 5.415
    Parties
        Husband and wife or domestic partners as parties   CRC 5.16
    Title IV-D support enforcement
        Consolidation of support orders   CRC 5.365
Limited scope representation, attorneys
    Applicability of rule   CRC 5.425
    Definition   CRC 5.425
    Nondisclosure of attorney assistance in document preparation   CRC 5.425
    Noticed limited scope representation   CRC 5.425
    Relief as counsel upon completion   CRC 5.425
Live testimony
    Children's testimony   CRC 5.113
    Continuances
        Determination of whether necessary or desirable   CRC 5.113
    Court's questions   CRC 5.113
    Purpose of rule   CRC 5.113
    Refusal to receive
        Factors   CRC 5.113
        Findings   CRC 5.113
    Requirement to receive   CRC 5.113
    Witness lists   CRC 5.113
Local child support agencies, appearance by   CRC 5.360
Local rules and forms
    Compliance with family rules   CRC 5.4
Long-cause hearings
    Setting trials and long-cause hearings   CRC 5.393
Mandatory joinder of parties   CRC 5.24
Marriage
    Minor marriage or domestic partnership, request by minor
        Applicability of provision   CRC 5.448
        Family court services, duties   CRC 5.448
        Initial filings   CRC 5.448
        Judicial officers, duties   CRC 5.448
        Waiting period after order granting permission   CRC 5.448
Minor marriage or domestic partnership, request by minor
    Applicability of provision   CRC 5.448
    Family court services, duties   CRC 5.448
    Initial filings   CRC 5.448
    Judicial officers, duties   CRC 5.448
    Waiting period after order granting permission   CRC 5.448

FAMILY RULES—Cont.
Motions
    Appearance by filing notice of motion   CRC 5.62
    Attorney's fees and costs, application to modify award of   Fam §2031
    Bifurcation of issues, motion for (See within this heading, **"Bifurcation of issues"**)
    Joinder   CRC 5.24
    Quash, motion to or request for order   CRC 5.63, 5.401, Fam §2010
Native Americans
    Domestic violence
        Tribal court protection orders   CRC 5.386
    Involuntary placements
        Indian child welfare act involuntary placements   CRC 5.480 to 5.488
        (See **INDIAN CHILD WELFARE ACT INVOLUNTARY PLACEMENTS**)
Notice
    Emergency or ex parte orders, requests   CRC 5.151, 5.165
        Matters not requiring notice to other parties   CRC 5.170
    Joinder motion   CRC 5.24
    Judgment, entry of   CRC 5.413, 5.415
    Modification of judgment, service of notice requirements   Fam §215
    Sanctions   CRC 5.14
    Subsequent orders, service of notice requirements   Fam §215
    Subsequent proceedings, when notice required   CRC 5.62
    Support of child, spouse or domestic partner
        Child support agency, notice to   CRC 5.260
    Temporary restraining orders issued without notice   Fam §§240 to 246
Orders
    Request for orders   CRC 5.90 to 5.130
        Emergency or ex parte orders   CRC 5.92, 5.151 to 5.170
    Sanctions   CRC 5.14
    Show cause orders, forms for   CRCAppxs A (CRCFL-300), (CRCFL-410)
Parentage actions
    Confidential cover sheet   CRC 5.51
Parties
    Causes of action or claims for relief which may be asserted   CRC 5.17
    Designation   CRC 5.16
        Interstate and intrastate cases   CRC 5.370
        Title IV-D support enforcement   CRC 5.370
    Dissolution, legal separation or nullity
        Husband and wife or domestic partners as parties   CRC 5.16
    Emergency or ex parte orders, requests
        Notice of emergency hearing   CRC 5.165
    Joinder of   CRC 5.24, 5.29, CRCAppx A (CRCFL-371 to CRCFL-375)
        Employee benefit plans, joinder as prerequisite to separate trial of termination of marriage or domestic partnership   CRC 5.390
Paternity
    Actions to determine paternity
        Notice of entry of judgment   CRC 5.413, 5.415
        Parties   CRC 5.16
    Domestic violence prevention act
        Agreement and judgment of parentage in domestic violence prevention act cases   CRC 5.380
        Parties   CRC 5.16
    Title IV-D support enforcement
        Voluntary declaration of parentage or paternity, cancellation or setting aside   CRC 5.350
Pendency of proceedings
    Quash, request for order
        Action pending between same parties for same cause   CRC 5.63
Pension benefit plan, joinder   CRC 5.29
    Separate trial of termination of marriage or domestic partnership, joinder as prerequisite   CRC 5.390
Pension benefit plan, joinder of
    Judicial Council forms   CRCAppx A (CRCFL-372 to CRCFL-375)
    Pleading on joinder   CRCAppx A (CRCFL-370)
Permissive joinder of parties   CRC 5.24
Petitioner
    Default request   CRC 5.402
Petitions
    Alternative relief, request for   CRC 5.60
    Format   CRC 5.60
    Judicial Council form   CRCAppx A (CRCFL-100)
    Proof of service   CRC 5.66
    Service of process
        Manner of service   CRC 5.68
Pleadings   CRC 5.74
    Alternative relief   CRC 5.60
    Amendment to pleadings   CRC 5.74
    Definitions   CRC 5.74
    Format   CRC 5.60

FAMILY

FAMILY RULES—Cont.
  Pleadings —Cont.
    Forms of pleading   CRC 5.74
    Joinder of parties
      Pleading rules applicable   CRC 5.24
    Verification of   Fam §212
  Postadoption contact agreements   CRC 5.451
  Precedence for hearing and trial
    Support order issued without notice   Fam §244
    Temporary restraining orders issued without notice   Fam §244
  Private trial   Fam §214
  Protective orders
    Firearm relinquishment procedures
      Forms for firearm relinquishment   CRCAppx A
  Quash, motions to or requests for orders   CRC 5.63, 5.401, Fam §2012
  Related cases
    Coordination of court resources   CRC 5.440
  Relief   CRC 5.18, 5.60
  Request for orders   CRC 5.90 to 5.130
    Appearance   CRC 5.62
    Bifurcation of issues   CRC 5.390
    Clerk of court
      Filing papers in clerk's office   CRC 5.96
      Issuance of request for order   CRC 5.92
    Declarations supporting and responding to request
      Contents   CRC 5.111
      Form   CRC 5.111
      Format   CRC 5.111
      Length   CRC 5.111, 5.112.1
      Objections to declarations   CRC 5.111
      Page limitation, calculation   CRC 5.111, 5.112.1
    Discovery   CRC 5.12
    Document exchange at or before meet-and-confer   CRC 5.98
    Documents to be filed   CRC 5.92
    Emergency or ex parte orders   CRC 5.92, 5.151 to 5.170
    Evidence at hearings   CRC 5.111 to 5.115
    Ex parte orders   CRC 5.92, 5.151 to 5.170
    Failure to prepare proposed order   CRC 5.125
    Format of papers requesting   CRC 5.90
    Forms to use   CRC 5.92
    Individual restraining orders   CRC 5.91
    Judicial notice   CRC 5.115
    Jurisdiction
      Transfers of jurisdiction   CRC 5.97
    Juveniles
      Special immigrant juvenile findings, request   CRC 5.130
    Late filings   CRC 5.94
    Live testimony   CRC 5.113
    Meet-and-confer
      Requirements   CRC 5.98
    Memorandum of points and authorities
      When required   CRC 5.92
    Objections to proposed order   CRC 5.125
    Place for filing   CRC 5.96
    Preparation of order   CRC 5.125
    Procedure   CRC 5.92
    Proposed orders   CRC 5.125
    Quashing proceedings   CRC 5.63
    Reporting of proceedings   CRC 5.123
    Rescheduling hearings
      Failure to request rescheduling   CRC 5.94
      Request to reschedule hearing   CRC 5.95
    Responding papers   CRC 5.92
      Declarations supporting and responding to request   CRC 5.111
    Responsive declaration   CRC 5.92
    Sanctions   CRC 5.14
    Service of order after signature   CRC 5.125
    Service requirements   CRC 5.92
    Settlements affecting request
      Notice to court   CRC 5.96
    Shortening time requirements   CRC 5.92, 5.94
    Special immigrant juvenile findings, request   CRC 5.130
      Forms, judicial council   CRCAppx A
    Submission to court clerk
      Timely submission   CRC 5.94
    Temporary emergency orders   CRC 5.92, 5.151 to 5.170
      Continued hearing date   CRC 5.94
      Extension of temporary orders   CRC 5.94
      Late request   CRC 5.94
  Rescheduling hearings
    Definition of rescheduling the hearing   CRC 5.2

FAMILY RULES—Cont.
  Rescheduling hearings—Cont.
    Forms
      Judicial council forms   CRCAppx A
    Request for orders
      Failure to request   CRC 5.94
    Requesting to reschedule hearing   CRC 5.95
  Residence
    Quashing proceedings, request for order
      Failure to meet residence requirements   CRC 5.63
  Respondent
    Appearance at proceedings   CRC 5.62
    Default   CRC 5.401
    Defined   Fam §127
  Response
    Generally   Fam §213
    Alternative relief, request for   CRC 5.60
    Appearance, filing response as   CRC 5.62
    Emergency or ex parte orders, requests
      Service of request and response   CRC 5.167
    Judicial Council form   CRCAppx A (CRCFL-120)
    Proof of service   CRC 5.66
    Request for orders
      Declarations supporting and responding to request   CRC 5.111
      Responding papers   CRC 5.92
    Service of response
      Manner of service   CRC 5.68
    Time for filing   Fam §2020
  Retirement plans
    Generally (See **DISSOLUTION OF MARRIAGE**)
    Joinder of plan as party   CRC 5.29
      Separate trial of termination of marriage or domestic partnership, joinder as prerequisite   CRC 5.390
  Sanctions   CRC 5.14
    Award of attorney's fees and costs as   Fam §271
  Separate trial of certain issues   CRC 5.390
  Service of process
    General appearance as equivalent to personal service   CRC 5.68
    Joinder motion notice   CRC 5.24
    Manner of service   CRC 5.68
    Modification of judgments, notice requirements   Fam §215
    Proof of service   CRC 5.66
    Publication or posting, address unknown   CRC 5.72
    Request for orders
      Emergency or ex parte orders, requests   CRC 5.167
      Requirements for service   CRC 5.92
      Service of order after signature   CRC 5.125
    Setting trials and long-cause hearings
      Trial or hearing briefs   CRC 5.394
    Subsequent orders, notice requirements   Fam §215
    Title IV-D support enforcement
      Summons and process combined   CRC 5.325
  Setting trials and long-cause hearings
    Brief intervals when additional days must be scheduled   CRC 5.393
    Definitions   CRC 5.393
    Pretrial conference   CRC 5.393
    Sequential days, scheduling   CRC 5.393
    Trial or hearing briefs
      Contents   CRC 5.394
      Defined   CRC 5.393
      Service   CRC 5.394
  Settlements
    Domestic violence
      Court-connected settlement service providers   CRC 5.420
    Stipulated judgments   CRC 5.411
  Severance of disputed issues (See within this heading, **"Bifurcation of issues"**)
  Show cause orders
    Attorney's fees and costs, application to modify award of   Fam §2031
    Forms for   CRCAppxs A (CRCFL-300), (CRCFL-410)
    Support orders issued without notice   Fam §§240 to 246
    Temporary restraining orders issued without notice   Fam §§240 to 246
  Social Security Act Title IV-D support actions   CRC 5.300 to 5.375
  Spousal support
    Computer software assisting in determining support   CRC 5.275
  Statute of limitations
    Quash proceedings, request for order   CRC 5.63
  Stipulated judgments
    Disposition of all matters   CRC 5.411
    Format   CRC 5.411

FAMILY RULES—Cont.
Stipulations
    Rescheduling hearings
        Written agreements to reschedule   CRC 5.95
Summary dissolution   CRC 5.77, CRCAppx A (CRCFL-800 to CRCFL-830)
Summary judgment
    No use of demurrers or summary judgment motions in family law actions   CRC 5.74
Summons   CRC 5.50
    Combined summons and complaint
        Title IV-D support enforcement   CRC 5.325
    Form   CRCAppx A (CRCFL-110)
    Proof of service   CRC 5.66
    Quash, motion to   Fam §2012
    Service of process
        Manner of service   CRC 5.68
    Temporary restraining orders in   Fam §§231 to 235, 7700
Superior courts, family law proceedings in
    Civil rules
        Applicability in family, juvenile and probate cases in superior court   CRC 3.10
        Generally   CRC 1.4, 3.1 to 3.2240
Support obligor, mistaken identity   CRC 5.375
Support of child, spouse or domestic partner
    Change of prior support orders
        Request   CRC 5.260
    Deviations from child support guidelines   CRC 5.260
    Financial declarations   CRC 5.260
    Judgment for support   CRC 5.260
    Notice
        Child support agency, notice to   CRC 5.260
Telephone appearance   CRC 3.672, 5.9
    Child support, Title IV-D support actions   CRC 3.670, 3.672, 5.324
Temporary restraining orders   CRCAppx A (CRCFL-305)
    Issuance without notice   Fam §§240 to 246
    Request for orders
        Individual restraining orders   CRC 5.91
    Summons, orders in   CRC 5.50, Fam §§231 to 235, 7700
Termination of parental rights
    Indian children, involuntary placements
        Indian Child Welfare Act, rules governing   CRC 5.480 to 5.488
        (See **INDIAN CHILD WELFARE ACT INVOLUNTARY PLACEMENTS**)
Time
    Extensions   CRC 5.2
    Joinder motion notice filing   CRC 5.24
Title IV-D support enforcement   CRC 5.300 to 5.375
    Appearances
        Local support agency appearance   CRC 5.360
    Attorney of record   CRC 5.320
    Case registry form
        Procedure   CRC 5.330
    Child support commissioners
        Judicial education   CRC 5.340
    Clerk's training   CRC 5.355
    Consolidation of support orders   CRC 5.365
    Coordination of court resources
        Related cases   CRC 5.440
    Definitions   CRC 5.300
    Forms
        Case registry form, procedure for   CRC 5.330
        Existing forms   CRC 5.310
    Hearings   CRC 5.305
    Identity mistaken
        Obligor motion regarding   CRC 5.375
    Income withholding
        Interstate income withholding orders   CRC 5.335
    Indian child
        Transfer of title IV-D cases from tribal court   CRC 5.372
        Transfer of title IV-D cases to tribal court   CRC 5.372
    Motions, notice of   CRC 5.315
    Parentage or paternity, voluntary declaration
        Cancellation or setting aside   CRC 5.350
    Party designation
        Interstate and intrastate cases   CRC 5.370
    Promulgation of rules
        Authority   CRC 5.300
    Summons and complaint combined
        Clerk's handling   CRC 5.325
Title of rules   CRC 5.1, 5.2

FAMILY RULES—Cont.
Trial
    Separate trial of certain issues   CRC 5.390
    Setting trials and long-cause hearings   CRC 5.393
Unique role of family court   CRC JudAdminStand 5.30
Valuation date
    Bifurcation of issues
        Conditions when bifurcation appropriate   CRC 5.390
Verification of pleadings   Fam §212
Visitation
    Attorneys, court appointment   CRC 5.240 to 5.242
    Modification of orders
        Domestic violence prevention act cases   CRC 5.381
    Orders following termination of juvenile proceeding or probate court guardianship proceeding   CRC 5.475
Waiver of fees and costs   CRC 5.41
Wardship
    Indian children, involuntary placements   CRC 5.480 to 5.488 (See **INDIAN CHILD WELFARE ACT INVOLUNTARY PLACEMENTS**)
Welfare recipients, rules governing public enforcement of support rights of   CRC 5.300 to 5.375
Witnesses
    Live testimony   CRC 5.113

FAMILY SUPPORT
Assignment of wages (See **EARNINGS ASSIGNMENT FOR SUPPORT**)
Deduction from salaries and wages   Fam §4507
Defined   Fam §92
Enforcement of support orders (See **CHILD SUPPORT**)
Fees
    Title IV-D child support agency involved   Gov §70672
    Waiver of fees and costs
        Repayment of waived fees in support actions   CRC 5.45
Interest
    Accrual of interest   Fam §17433.5
Interstate family support   Fam §§5700.101 to 5700.903 (See **INTERSTATE FAMILY SUPPORT**)
Judgments
    Abstract of   Fam §4506
        Liens, digital form of lien record   Fam §17523.5
    Renewal requirements   CCP §§683.130, 683.310, Fam §§291, 4502
Liens
    Judgments, abstract of
        Digital form of lien record   Fam §17523.5
Modification of support orders   Fam §§3650 to 3694
Orders or stipulation designating support as family support   Fam §4066
Renewal of judgments   CCP §§683.130, 683.310, Fam §§291, 4502
Termination of support orders   Fam §§3650 to 3694
Title IV-D support enforcement   CRC 5.300 to 5.375
Welfare recipients (See **CHILD SUPPORT**)

FARES (See **TICKETS**)

FARM LABOR CONTRACTORS
Human trafficking or slavery
    Signs, businesses required to post notice concerning relief from slavery or human trafficking   CC §52.6

FARMS AND FARMERS
Animals (See **ANIMALS**)
Assignment for benefit of creditors, property exempt from   CCP §1801
Attachment of farm products (See **ATTACHMENT**)
Attorney's fees for trespass action, recovery of   CCP §1021.9
Barley (See **BARLEY**)
Claim and delivery   CCP §511.040
Common interest developments
    Personal agriculture by homeowner
        Unreasonable restrictions in governing documents, void   CC §4750
Dairies (See **DAIRIES AND DAIRY PRODUCTS**)
Disclosures incident to residential land transfers
    Right to farm notice   CC §1103.4
Eminent domain   CCP §1263.250
Enforcement of judgments (See **ENFORCEMENT OF JUDGMENTS**)
Fixtures, farm products as   CC §660
Irrigation (See **IRRIGATION**)
Landlord and tenant
    Personal agriculture by tenant   CC §1940.10
Lease restrictions   CC §717
Liens by farm workers   CC §§3061 to 3061.6
Nuisances
    Agricultural activities and operations in general, exclusion of   CC §3482.5

FARMS AND FARMERS—Cont.
Nuisances—Cont.
    Agricultural processing facilities, exclusion of   CC §3482.6
Owner's immunity for injury to person invited on premises to glean farm products for charitable purposes   CC §846.2
Repair of farm machinery, invoice requirements for   CC §1718
Right to farm
    Disclosures incident to residential land transfers   CC §1103.4
Small business action, costs in   CCP §1028.5

FAST TRACK RULES OF COURT (See TRIAL COURT DELAY REDUCTION)

FAX FILING AND SERVICE   CRC 2.300 to 2.306
Certification of documents and papers for court filing   CRC 2.303
Confidentiality requirements   CRC 2.303
    Juvenile court   CRC 5.522
Court proceedings and documents and papers subject to   CRC 2.300
Cover sheet   CRC 2.304
    Juvenile court   CRC 5.522
Credit card payment of fax filing charges   CCP §1010.5, CRC 2.304
Definitions   CRC 2.301
Direct filing   CRC 2.304
    Fees
        Courts, authority to set fees for products or services   CRC 10.815
Errors in fax transmission when unknown to sending party, effect of   CRC 2.304
Excluded documents and papers from   CRC 2.300
Fax filing agency
    Defined   CRC 2.301
    Duties of   CRC 2.303
Fees
    Accounts for filing fees   CRC 2.304
    Courts, authority to set fees for products or services   CRC 10.815
    Credit or debit card payments   CRC 2.304
1st Appellate District local rules   CRCSupp 1st AppDist
Inspection rights of other party to original signed document   CRC 2.305
Judicial Council to adopt rules governing filing of papers by facsimile transmission   CCP §1010.5
Judicial performance, commission on
    Censure, removal, admonishment or retirement of judges
        Filing with Commission   JudPerR 119.5
Juvenile court   CRC 5.522
Levying officer electronic transactions act   CCP §§263 to 263.7
Methods of filing   CCP §1013
    Direct filing   CRC 2.304
    Fax filing agency
        Defined   CRC 2.301
        Duties   CRC 2.303
Motion for order nunc pro tunc as judicial remedy for failure to file caused by errors unknown to sending party   CRC 2.304
Original document, sending party in possession or control of   CRC 2.305
Papers, form or format
    Documents for faxing to comply with provisions   CRC 2.302
Presumption of filing   CRC 2.304
Proof of service   CRC 2.306
Service, generally   CCP §1013, CRC 2.306
Service lists   CRC 2.306
Signature requirement   CRC 2.305
    Juvenile court   CRC 5.522
Small claims courts
    Claims, fax filing   CCP §116.320

FAX NUMBER
Change of number
    Service and filing notice of change   CRC 2.200
        Appeals   CRC 8.32, 8.816

FEDERAL COURTS
Automobile lease action previously filed in   CC §2989
Certification of state-law questions to California Supreme Court by federal appellate courts   CRC 8.548
Injunctions against proceedings in   CC §3423
Judicial notice of rules prescribed by   Ev §451
Notice of pendency of action on real property, applicability of state law in U.S.district courts for filing of   CCP §405.5
Statutes of limitation upon judgment or decree of   CCP §337.5
Time for response after remand from   CCP §430.90

FEDERAL ENCLAVES
Appropriation of water originating in   CC §1422

FEDERAL ENCLAVES—Cont.
Real property law of state, applicability of   CC §755

FEDERAL GOVERNMENT (See UNITED STATES)

FEDERAL LAW REFERENCED
15 USCS § 7001 et seq   Pro §16632
42 USCS § 1396p(d)(4)(A)   Pro §16610
Holocaust Expropriated Art Recovery Act   CCP §§338, 338.2

FEDERAL LIEN REGISTRATION ACT   CCP §§2100 to 2107
Fees for recording under act   Gov §27388.1

FEEBLE MINDED PERSONS (See DEVELOPMENTALLY DISABLED PERSONS)

FEED YARDS
Liens   CC §3051

FEES (See also COMPENSATION; COSTS)
Administrative adjudication (See ADMINISTRATIVE ADJUDICATION)
Administrators (See EXECUTORS AND ADMINISTRATORS)
Admitted surety insurer (See SURETYSHIP, BONDS AND UNDERTAKINGS)
Adoption (See ADOPTION)
Answers
    Filing fees (See ANSWERS)
Appellate rules, superior court appeals
    Costs
        Recoverable costs   CRC 8.891
        Limited civil cases in appellate division
            Notice of appeal   CRC 8.821
Appellate rules, supreme court and courts of appeal (See APPELLATE RULES, SUPREME COURT AND COURTS OF APPEAL)
Arbitration (See ARBITRATION)
Arrest
    Witnesses, arrest on bench warrant
        Fee for processing civil warrant   Gov §26744.5
Attachment (See ATTACHMENT)
Attorney general
    Civil actions enforcing public rights   CCP §1021.8
Attorneys' fees (See ATTORNEY'S FEES)
Burden of proof
    Evasion or fraud cases   Ev §524
Change of venue   CCP §399
Check for fees returned unpaid   CCP §411.20
Checks, court fees paid by   CCP §411.20
    Underpayment   CCP §411.21
Claims against public entities and employees
    State, claims against
        Filing fees   Gov §905.2
Clerks of court (See CLERKS OF COURT)
Complaints
    Filing generally (See COMPLAINTS)
Complex litigation
    Designation fee
        Permissible additional fees   Gov §70603
Conciliation court proceedings, filing of petition   Fam §1835
Confidential marriages, application for approval of notaries to authorize   Fam §536
Conservatorships (See CONSERVATORS)
Conveyances
    Transfer fees   CC §§1098, 1098.5
        Disclosures as to fees   CC §1102.6e
County clerks (See CLERKS OF COURT)
County recorders (See RECORDS AND RECORDING)
Court reporters (See COURT REPORTERS)
Credit card or debit card payments   CRC 3.100
Credit reports (See CREDIT REPORTING)
Debit card payments   CRC 3.100
Debt collectors   CC §1788.14
Depositions (See DEPOSITIONS)
Dissolution of marriage (See DISSOLUTION OF MARRIAGE)
Domestic violence protective orders, filing fees for (See DOMESTIC VIOLENCE)
Economically unable to pay
    Waiver of costs and fees   Gov §§68630 to 68641
        Bench warrants to secure attendance of witnesses, applicability of waiver   Gov §26744.5
        Civil rules governing waiver of fees and costs   CRC 3.50 to 3.58

FEES (—Cont.
Electronic filing and service rules
  Payment of filing fees   CRC 2.258
Employment agency fees (See **EMPLOYMENT AGENCIES**)
Employment counseling service fees (See **EMPLOYMENT COUNSELING SERVICES**)
Enforcement of judgments (See **ENFORCEMENT OF JUDGMENTS**)
Escheat, deduction of fees from property   CCP §1522
Escrow agents   CC §1057.5
Executors (See **EXECUTORS AND ADMINISTRATORS**)
Expert witnesses (See **EXPERT AND OPINION EVIDENCE**)
Family rules   CRC 5.40 to 5.46
Fax filing and service   CRC 2.304
Fee waiver
  Bench warrants to secure attendance of witnesses
    Fee for processing civil warrant, applicability of waiver   Gov §26744.5
  Civil rules governing waiver of fees and costs   CRC 3.50 to 3.58
  Economically unable to pay   Gov §§68630 to 68641
  Forms   CRCAppx A
Fine art, sale of   CC §986
Floating homes and floating home marinas (See **FLOATING HOMES**)
Grand jury (See **GRAND JURIES**)
High-frequency litigant fee   Gov §70616.5
Impound accounts maintained by banks   CC §§2954, 2954.8
Indigent persons, waiver of fees for (See **INDIGENT PERSONS**)
Information Practices Act, inspecting records under   CC §1798.33
Insufficient amount tendered for filing fee   CCP §411.21
Interpleader, initial filing by   Gov §§26826, 70612, 70614
  Supplemental fees for first paper filing   Gov §§70602.5, 70602.6
Intervenor, initial filing by   Gov §§70612, 70614
  Supplemental fees for first paper filing   Gov §§70602.5, 70602.6
Investigative agencies   CC §§1786.22, 1786.26
Job listing service fees (See **JOB LISTING SERVICES**)
Judgments, fees for service of notice of entry   CCP §1710.30
Jurors (See **JURY**)
Justice courts (See **JUSTICE COURTS**)
Kickbacks (See **KICKBACKS**)
Marriages (See **MARRIAGE**)
Medical records, inspection of   Ev §1158
Membership camping contracts   CC §§1812.302 to 1812.307
Mobilehome parks (See **MOBILEHOMES**)
Mortgages (See **TRUST DEEDS AND MORTGAGES**)
Notice, service of (See **NOTICES**)
Nurses' registry fees (See **NURSES**)
Personal records, inspection of   CC §1798.22
Personal representative (See **EXECUTORS AND ADMINISTRATORS**)
Petitions, filing fees for (See **PETITIONS**)
Pharmacies, provisions for study of fees of   CC §§2527, 2528
Probate proceedings   Gov §§70650 to 70663
Process, service of (See **PROCESS AND SERVICE OF PROCESS**)
Public administrator (See **PUBLIC ADMINISTRATORS**)
Public guardians (See **PUBLIC GUARDIANS**)
Rebates (See **REBATES**)
Reclassification of action, fees for   CCP §§403.050 to 403.060
Recording fees (See **RECORDS AND RECORDING**)
Referees (See **REFEREES**)
Reporters (See **COURT REPORTERS**)
Retail installment sales by third-party loan   CC §1801.6
Seller assisted marketing plans, annual disclosure statement filing fees for   CC §1812.203
Service of process (See **PROCESS AND SERVICE OF PROCESS**)
Sheriff's fees (See **SHERIFF**)
Small claims court (See **SMALL CLAIMS COURTS**)
State bar
  Suspension for nonpayment
    Expungement of suspension   CRC 9.6
Sterilization proceedings   Pro §1963
Tax liens, filing and recording of   CCP §2104
Telephone appearances   CRC 3.670
Transcripts
  Court reporters generally (See **COURT REPORTERS**)
Transfer fees for real property, limitation on   CC §1097
Transfer of action for lack of subject matter jurisdiction   CCP §396
Translators and interpreters (See **TRANSLATORS AND INTERPRETERS**)
Trust deeds (See **TRUST DEEDS AND MORTGAGES**)
Unclaimed property (See **UNCLAIMED PROPERTY**)
Underpayment of filing fees   CCP §411.21
Venue (See **VENUE**)

FEES (—Cont.
Waiver of costs and fees
  Appellate rules, supreme court and courts of appeal
    E-filing projects in supreme court and courts of appeal, eligibility for filing   CRC 8.76
  Bench warrants to secure attendance of witnesses
    Applicability of fee waiver provisions   Gov §26744.5
  Civil rules governing waiver of fees and costs   CRC 3.50 to 3.58
  Economically unable to pay   Gov §§68630 to 68641
  Family rules   CRC 5.41
    Denial of waiver   CRC 5.43
    Support actions, repayment of waived fees and cost   CRC 5.45
    Supreme court or court of appeal cases, applicable provisions   CRC 5.46
  Forms
    Judicial council legal forms   CRCAppx A
  Telephone appearances   CRC 3.670
Will probate (See **WILL PROBATE**)
Witnesses (See **WITNESSES**)

FEE SIMPLE
Definition   CC §762
Entailed estate as estate in   CC §763
Power of termination (See **TITLE AND OWNERSHIP**)
Presumption in transfer of real property   CC §1105
Statutes of limitation   CC §773

FELONY CONVICTIONS (See **CONVICTION OF CRIME**)

FENCES
Adjoining landowners
  Electrified security fences   CC §835
Adverse possession (See **ADVERSE POSSESSION**)
Construction defects, actions for
  Actionable defects   CC §896
Easement   CC §801
Electrified security fences   CC §835
Eminent domain compensation for   CCP §1263.450
Home improvement goods and services   CC §1689.8
Life tenant to repair   CC §840
Maintenance of   CC §841
Presumptions
  Adjoining landowners   CC §841
Spite fences as nuisances   CC §841.4

FESTIVALS (See **FAIRS AND EXPOSITIONS**)

FETUS
Abortion (See **ABORTIONS**)
Statute of limitations for personal injuries sustained during birth   CCP §340.4
Unborn child deemed existing person   CC §43.1

FICTITIOUS NAMES
False personation (See **FALSE PERSONATION**)
Levy on deposit account under fictitious business name   CCP §700.160
Small claims actions   CCP §116.430, CRC 3.2100
Unknown defendants (See **UNKNOWN PERSONS**)

FIDELITY BONDS (See **SURETYSHIP, BONDS AND UNDERTAKINGS**)

FIDUCIARIES
Access to digital assets   Pro §§870 to 884 (See **FIDUCIARY ACCESS TO DIGITAL ASSETS**)
Attorney in fact   Pro §4231.5
Community property (See **COMMUNITY PROPERTY**)
Conservator-conservatee relationship   Pro §§2101, 2113
Digital assets, access   Pro §§870 to 884 (See **FIDUCIARY ACCESS TO DIGITAL ASSETS**)
Guardian-ward relationship   Pro §2101
Husband and wife   Fam §721
Incapacitated professional fiduciary   Pro §2469
Judges, service as   CRCSupp JudEthicsCanon 4
Minor, service on   CCP §416.60
Mortgage brokers
  Fiduciary duty owed to borrower   CC §2923.1
Power of attorney (See **POWER OF ATTORNEY**)
Professional fiduciaries (See **PROFESSIONAL FIDUCIARIES**)
Trust decanting, uniform act
  Court involvement   Pro §19509
  Duties of fiduciary under provisions   Pro §19504
  Generally   Pro §§19501 to 19530

FIDUCIARIES—Cont.
  Trust decanting, uniform act—Cont.
    Liability and indemnification of trustee
      Exercise of decanting power Pro §19517
    Removal of authorized fiduciary
      Exercise of decanting power Pro §19518
    Special needs fiduciaries Pro §19513
      Exercise of decanting power, trust for beneficiary with a disability Pro §19513
  Trusts (See **TRUSTS**)
  Unclaimed deposits and payments escheated CCP §1518
  Uniform fiduciary income and principal act
    Applicability of provisions Pro §16322
      Place of administration as basis of applicability Pro §16323
    Generally Pro §§16320 to 16383
  Wartime substitution of (See **FIDUCIARIES' WARTIME SUBSTITUTION LAW**)

FIDUCIARIES' WARTIME SUBSTITUTION LAW
  Appointment of substitute fiduciary (See within this heading, **"Substitute fiduciary"**)
  Bond requirements for substitute fiduciary Pro §372
  Citation of act Pro §350
  Construction and interpretation
    Generally Pro §351
    Inconsistent provisions in wills or trusts, effect of Pro §361
  Consultant
    Defined Pro §352
    Delegation of powers
      Generally Pro §385
      By court Pro §386
      Cessation of Pro §387
      Liability for acts or omissions of delegate Pro §388
      Purely personal powers as non-delegable Pro §§385, 386
    Liability for acts or omissions of delegate Pro §388
    Purely personal power as non-delegable Pro §§385, 386
    Reinstatement of powers Pro §387
    Suspension of authority by court Pro §386
    War service defined Pro §356
  Definitions
    Consultant Pro §352
    Estate Pro §353
    Interested person Pro §354
    Original fiduciary Pro §355
    War service Pro §356
  Delegation of powers
    Authority of consultant (See within this heading, **"Consultant"**)
    Authority of fiduciary (See within this heading, **"Original fiduciary"**)
    Court-ordered delegation
      Consultant, substitution of Pro §386
      Original fiduciary, substitution of Pro §370
    Purely personal powers as non-delegable
      Consultant Pro §§385, 386
      Original fiduciary Pro §381
  Effective date of Act Pro §360
  Interpretation Pro §351
    Inconsistent provisions in wills or trusts, effect Pro §361
  Jurisdictional requirements for appointment of substitute fiduciary Pro §365
  Notice requirements Pro §366
  Original fiduciary
    Defined Pro §355
    Delegation of powers
      Generally Pro §380
      By court Pro §380
      Cessation of Pro §382
      Liability for act or omission of delegate fiduciary Pro §383
      Purely personal powers as non-delegable Pro §381
      Right of Pro §1702.2
    Liability for act or omission of delegate fiduciary Pro §383
    Purely personal powers as non-delegable Pro §381
    Reinstatement of powers and duties Pro §§373, 382
    Substitute fiduciary of (See within this heading, **"Substitute fiduciary"**)
    Suspension of powers and duties during war Pro §370
    War service defined Pro §356
  Purely personal powers
    Consultants, delegation of powers Pro §§385, 386
    Original fiduciary, delegation of powers Pro §381
  Substitute fiduciary
    Appointment
      Generally Pro §370
      Jurisdiction Pro §365

FIDUCIARIES' WARTIME SUBSTITUTION LAW—Cont.
  Substitute fiduciary—Cont.
    Appointment —Cont.
      Notice requirements Pro §366
    Bond requirements Pro §372
    Cessation of delegated powers Pro §382
    Discharge and removal of Pro §373
    Liability for act or omission of predecessor fiduciary Pro §374
    Powers of Pro §371

FIDUCIARY ACCESS TO DIGITAL ASSETS Pro §§870 to 884
  Accounts
    Contents of accounts of deceased user or settlor, disclosure
      Applicability of terms and conditions applicable to user or settlor Pro §883
    Defined Pro §871
    Termination
      Custodian's duties in complying with request Pro §881
  Agent
    Authority over content of electronic communications Pro §879.1
    Catalogue of electronic communications, disclosure to agent Pro §879.2
    Defined Pro §871
  Applicability of provisions Pro §872
  Carries
    Defined Pro §871
  Catalogue of electronic communications
    Agent, disclosure to Pro §879.2
    Defined Pro §871
    Disclosure to personal representative of estate Pro §877
    Trustee who is not original user of account, disclosure to Pro §879
  Conservator
    Access to digital assets of conservatee Pro §879.3
    Defined Pro §871
  Content of an electronic communication
    Agent's authority over Pro §879.1
    Defined Pro §871
    Disclosure of content of deceased user Pro §876
      Trustee who is not original user of account, disclosure to Pro §878
  Courts
    Defined Pro §871
  Custodians
    Defined Pro §871
  Definitions Pro §871
  Designated recipients
    Defined Pro §871
  Digital assets defined Pro §871
  Disclosure of digital assets
    Custodian's duties in complying with request Pro §881
    Custodian's rights when disclosing Pro §875
    Online tool
      Use to direct custodian Pro §873
  Effective date of provisions Pro §872
  Electronic
    Defined Pro §871
  Electronic communications
    Defined Pro §871
  Electronic communication services
    Defined Pro §871
  Electronic signatures in global and national commerce act
    Relationship between provisions and act Pro §882
  Executors and administrators
    Definition of personal representatives Pro §871
  Fiduciary defined Pro §871
  Information
    Defined Pro §871
  Management of digital assets
    Legal duties for management of tangible property
      Applicable to fiduciary management of digital assets Pro §880
  Online tools
    Defined Pro §871
  Person
    Defined Pro §871
  Personal representatives
    Defined Pro §871
  Power of attorney
    Defined Pro §871
  Principal
    Defined Pro §871
  Records
    Defined Pro §871

FIDUCIARY ACCESS TO DIGITAL ASSETS—Cont.
Remote-computing services
    Defined   Pro §871
Revised uniform fiduciary access to digital assets act
    Short title   Pro §870
Short title of provisions   Pro §870
Statutory construction
    Severability of provisions   Pro §884
Terms-of-service agreements
    Defined   Pro §871
    Rights under agreement not changed by provisions   Pro §874
Trustees
    Defined   Pro §871
Users
    Defined   Pro §871
Wills
    Defined   Pro §871

FIDUCIARY INCOME AND PRINCIPAL ACT   Pro §§16320 to 16383
Adjustments between income and principal
    Abuse of discretion
        Orders to remedy abuse   Pro §16326
    Disbursements, allocation   Pro §16366
    Factors considered by fiduciary   Pro §16327
    Powers of fiduciaries   Pro §§16325, 16327
Allocation of receipts   Pro §§16340 to 16355
Applicability of provisions   Pro §16322
    Place of administration as basis of applicability   Pro §16323
    Statutory construction   Pro §16382
Apportionment at beginning and end of income interest   Pro §§16375 to 16377
    Allocations of income receipt or disbursement   Pro §16376
    Asset becoming subject to trust
        Time   Pro §16375
    Time of entitlement to income   Pro §16375
    Undistributed income   Pro §16377
Asset-backed securities
    Receipts, allocation   Pro §16354
Beneficiaries
    Death of individual resulting in creation of estate or trust
        Beneficiary portion of net income   Pro §16371
    Distributions to beneficiaries
        Order of sources   Pro §16367
    Termination of income interest in trust
        Beneficiary portion of net income   Pro §16371
Compliance with trust or will
    Administration to comply notwithstanding provisions   Pro §16325
Conversions involving unitrust
    Abuse of discretion
        Orders to remedy abuse   Pro §16326
    Powers of fiduciaries   Pro §16325
Death of individual resulting in creation of estate or trust
    Distributions   Pro §16370
    Beneficiary portion of net income   Pro §16371
Decisions of fiduciaries
    Definition of fiduciary decision   Pro §16326
Definitions   Pro §16321
    Fiduciary decision defined   Pro §16326
    Receipts, allocation
        Marital trusts   Pro §16348
    Unitrust   Pro §16330
Depreciation
    Disbursements, allocation   Pro §16362
Disbursements, allocation   Pro §§16360 to 16367
    Adjustments between income and principal   Pro §16366
    Apportionment at beginning and end of income interest
        Allocations of income receipt or disbursement   Pro §16376
    Depreciation   Pro §16362
    Distributions to beneficiaries
        Order of sources   Pro §16367
    Income, disbursements from   Pro §16360
    Principal, charges to   Pro §16325
    Principal, disbursements from   Pro §16361
    Reimbursement of income   Pro §16363
    Reimbursement of principal   Pro §16364
    Taxes   Pro §16365
Discretion of fiduciary   Pro §16325
    Abuse of discretion
        Remedies   Pro §16326
Distributions
    Abuse of discretion
        Orders to remedy abuse   Pro §16326

FIDUCIARY INCOME AND PRINCIPAL ACT—Cont.
Distributions—Cont.
    Beneficiaries, distributions to
        Order of sources   Pro §16367
    Death of individual resulting in creation of estate or trust   Pro §16370
        Beneficiary portion of net income   Pro §16371
    Receipts, allocation   Pro §16341
        Entity distributions   Pro §16340
    Termination of income interest in trust   Pro §16370
        Beneficiary portion of net income   Pro §16371
Electronic signatures in global and national commerce act
    Effect of provisions on act   Pro §16381
Good faith   Pro §16325
Insurance proceeds
    Receipts, allocation   Pro §16346
Interest
    Receipts, allocation
        Income, allocation to   Pro §16345
Life insurance proceeds
    Receipts, allocation
        Principal, allocation to   Pro §16346
Marital deductions
    Receipts, allocation
        Effect of deduction   Pro §16352
Marital trusts
    Receipts, allocation   Pro §16348
Minerals, water or other natural resources, interests in
    Receipts, allocation   Pro §16350
Presumptions
    Fair and reasonable allocations, determinations or exercises of discretion   Pro §16325
Receipts, allocation   Pro §§16340 to 16355
    Accounting   Pro §16342
    Apportionment at beginning and end of income interest
        Allocations of income receipt or disbursement   Pro §16376
    Asset-backed securities   Pro §16354
    Derivatives   Pro §16353
    Distributions
        Income, allocation to   Pro §16341
    Entity distributions
        Income, allocation to   Pro §16340
    Financial instruments or arrangements not addressed by provisions
        Applicable provisions   Pro §16355
    Income, allocation to
        Distributions   Pro §16341
        Entity distributions   Pro §16340
        Insurance for income, profits from business, etc   Pro §16346
        Interest   Pro §16345
        Property rental amounts   Pro §16344
    Insubstantial allocation
        Reallocation of certain amounts to principal   Pro §16347
    Liquidating assets   Pro §16349
    Marital deductions, effect   Pro §16352
    Marital trusts   Pro §16348
    Minerals, water or other natural resources, interests in   Pro §16350
    Principal, allocation to   Pro §§16325, 16343
        Life insurance proceeds   Pro §16346
        Reallocation of certain amounts to principal   Pro §16347
        Sale, redemption, etc of obligation to pay fiduciary   Pro §16345
    Rentals
        Income, allocation to   Pro §16344
    Timber sales   Pro §16351
Reimbursement of income
    Disbursements, allocation   Pro §16363
Reimbursement of principal
    Disbursements, allocation   Pro §16364
Rentals
    Receipts, allocation
        Income, allocation to   Pro §16344
Severability of provisions   Pro §16383
Short title   Pro §16320
Standards for fiduciary administration   Pro §16325
Statutory construction
    Applicability of provisions   Pro §16382
    Severability of provisions   Pro §16383
    Uniformity among enacting states   Pro §16380
Taxes
    Disbursements, allocation   Pro §16365
Termination of income interest in trust
    Distributions   Pro §16370
        Beneficiary portion of net income   Pro §16371

FIDUCI INDEX

FIDUCIARY INCOME AND PRINCIPAL ACT—Cont.
Timber sales
    Receipts, allocation   Pro §16351
Unitrust   Pro §§16330 to 16338
    Abuse of discretion
        Orders to remedy abuse   Pro §16326
    Amount
        Definition of unitrust amount   Pro §16330
        Errors in calculating unitrust amount   Pro §16338
    Applicability of unitrust provisions   Pro §16331
    Beneficiary requests for fiduciary actions   Pro §16332
    Definitions   Pro §16330
    Distributions
        Plan methods and standards   Pro §16338
    Errors in calculating unitrust amount
        Plan methods and standards   Pro §16338
    Express unitrust
        Applicability of unitrust provisions   Pro §16331
        Defined   Pro §16330
    Income tax
        Plan methods and standards   Pro §16338
    Income trusts
        Applicability of unitrust provisions   Pro §16331
        Defined   Pro §16330
    Net fair market value of trust
        Defined   Pro §16330
    Notice requirements   Pro §16333
    Objections to proposed actions of fiduciary   Pro §16332
    Plan
        Compliance with unitrust plan   Pro §16334
        Contents of unitrust plan   Pro §16334
        Definition of unitrust plan   Pro §16330
    Powers of fiduciaries   Pro §§16325, 16332
    Rate
        Definition of unitrust rate   Pro §16330
        Fixed rates   Pro §16335
        Periodically determinable rates   Pro §16335
        Permissible rates   Pro §16335

FIFTH AMENDMENT (See **SELF-INCRIMINATION**)

FILING
Administrative law and procedure
    Adjudicative proceedings (See **ADMINISTRATIVE ADJUDICATION**)
    Rulemaking and regulatory procedure (See **ADMINISTRATIVE PROCEDURE ACT**)
Affidavits   CCP §2011
Appellate rules, superior court appeals   CRC 8.817
    Applications   CRC 8.806
    Motions   CRC 8.808
Appellate rules, supreme court and courts of appeal (See **APPELLATE RULES, SUPREME COURT AND COURTS OF APPEAL**)
Claims against estates (See **CLAIMS AGAINST ESTATES**)
Clerks of court (See **CLERKS OF COURT**)
Complaints (See **COMPLAINTS**)
Confession of judgment   CCP §1132
Costs (See **COSTS**)
Disclaimer of interest, requirements for filing   Pro §§279, 280
Electronic filing and service (See **ELECTRONIC FILING AND SERVICE**)
Enforcement of judgment, filing papers with levying officer   CCP §681.040
Family rules (See **FAMILY RULES**)
Fax filing of legal documents (See **FAX FILING AND SERVICE**)
Fees (See **FEES**)
Insufficient amount tendered for filing fee   CCP §411.21
Justice courts (See **JUSTICE COURTS**)
Law and motion practice (See **LAW AND MOTION PROCEEDINGS**)
Marriage (See **MARRIAGE**)
Motion, filing of notice of   CCP §1005.5
Partition (See **PARTITION**)
Personal data records   CC §1798.23
Privacy protection   CRC 1.20
Rules of court
    Determining when document filed   CRC 1.20
    Privacy protection   CRC 1.20
Superior courts (See **SUPERIOR COURTS**)
Supplemental pleadings   CCP §465
Surety bonds (See **SURETYSHIP, BONDS AND UNDERTAKINGS**)
Translator or interpreter, oath of   Ev §751
Voided filing
    Check for filing fees returned unpaid   CCP §411.20
    Underpayment of filing fee   CCP §411.21

FILING FEES
Family law cases   Gov §§70670 to 70676

FILLING STATIONS
Emission control standards   CC §1952.8

FILMS
Privacy
    Photographs, films, etc, exposing intimate body parts or sexual acts of another without permission, distribution
        Actions for injunctions, damages, etc   CC §1708.85
        Confidential information form   CRCAppx A

FINANCE CHARGES
Automobile sales   CC §§2981, 2981.7, 2981.8, 2982
Home improvement contracts   CC §§1805.6, 1810.10
Retail installment sales (See **RETAIL INSTALLMENT SALES**)
Small businesses
    Commercial financing transactions   CC §§1799.300 to 1799.304

FINANCE, DEPARTMENT OF (See **ADMINISTRATIVE PROCEDURE ACT**)

FINANCIAL ABUSE
Dependent or elder adults   Pro §259
    Attorney in fact
        Taking, concealing, etc property of principal   Pro §4231.5
    Remedies   Pro §859

FINANCIAL AID
Exempt property for purposes of enforcement of judgments   CCP §704.190

FINANCIAL CONDITION
Common interest developments (See **COMMON INTEREST DEVELOPMENTS**)
Exemplary damages, admissibility of evidence of financial condition of defendant for purposes of   CC §3295
Representation as to credit of another, writing required for   CCP §1974
Seller assisted marketing plans   CC §1812.206

FINANCIAL CONTRACTS
Statute of frauds   CC §1624

FINANCIAL INSTITUTIONS
Banks (See **BANKS AND BANKING**)
Identity theft in business entity filings   CC §§1798.200 to 1798.203
Savings and loans (See **SAVINGS AND LOANS**)

FINANCIAL INTERESTS
Defined   CCP §170.5
Disqualification of judges, grounds for   CCP §§170.1, 170.5

FINANCIAL PLANNERS (See **INVESTMENT ADVISERS**)

FINANCIAL RESOURCES
Unsoundness of mind presumed if unable to manage financial resources or resist fraud or undue influence   CC §39

FINDINGS
Attachment (See **ATTACHMENT**)
Claim and delivery proceedings   CCP §512.110
Court commissioner's power to take proof and make and report findings   CCP §259
Dependent children
    Approaching majority review hearings
        Transitional independent living case plan   CRC 5.707
Enforcement of judgments (See **ENFORCEMENT OF JUDGMENTS**)
Family rules
    Attorneys' fees
        Financial need basis for fees   CRC 5.427
Garnishment proceedings   CCP §706.106
Juvenile rules
    Termination of juvenile court jurisdiction
        Nonminor dependents or wards in foster care   CRC 5.555
Juvenile wardship
    Termination of jurisdiction   CRC 5.812
Partition action   CCP §§872.610 to 872.840
Statement of decision in lieu of   CCP §632

FINE ARTS (See **ART AND ARTISTS**)

FINES AND PENALTIES
Administrative adjudication (See **ADMINISTRATIVE ADJUDICATION**)

FINES AND PENALTIES—Cont.
  Age-appropriate design code
    Enforcement of provisions   CC §1798.99.35
  Age restricted products, sale
    Verification of age for sale of age-restricted products   CC §1798.99.11
  Animals
    Research, experimentation, use for biological products, etc
      Restrictions on shelters, dealers and research facilities   CC §1834.7
  Attorney General bringing action to recover   CC §3370.1
  Auction law violations   CC §§1812.604, 1812.607, 1812.608
  Autographed memorabilia, dealer's sale of   CC §1739.7
  Automobile sales contracts
    Document retention   CC §2984.5
  Automobile warranties
    Restitution or replacement actions   CCP §871.27
  Boats and boating
    Bail schedule   CRC 4.102
  Booking photographs
    Commercial use of booking photographs   CC §1798.91.1
  Check cashers operating without permit   CC §1789.37
  Checks to pay   CRC 10.821
  Child support (See **CHILD SUPPORT**)
  Civil rights violations   CC §§52, 52.1
  Claims against public entities and employees (See **CLAIMS AGAINST PUBLIC ENTITIES AND EMPLOYEES**)
  Commercial and industrial common interest developments
    Governing documents
      Noncompliance   CC §§6850, 6854
  Common interest developments
    Assembly by and communication among owners, guests, residents, etc
      Permitted activities   CC §4515
    Low water-using plants   CC §4735
  Conservators
    Abuse
      Civil penalty for abuse of conservatee   Pro §2112
  Consumer credit information, misuse or wrongful acquisition of   CC §1785.19
  Consumer privacy rights
    Businesses, service providers, contractors, etc
      Good faith of business, service provider, contractor, etc, consideration by agency   CC §1798.199.100
      Violation of provisions   CC §1798.199.90
    California privacy protection agency
      Actions to collect unpaid fines   CC §1798.199.75
      Enforcement of provisions   CC §1798.199.55
      Good faith of business, service provider, contractor, etc, consideration by agency   CC §1798.199.100
      Judgment to collect fines, application by agency for   CC §1798.199.80
      Judicial review of complaint or fine   CC §1798.199.85
    Penalties for noncompliance   CC §1798.155
  Contempt proceedings   CCP §1218
  Contracts
    Consumer goods or services, sale or lease
      Waiver of consumer rights to make statements about seller, lessor, goods or services, prohibited contract provisions   CC §1670.8
  Credit card number as condition of acceptance of negotiable instruments, use of   CC §1725
  Credit reports
    Discouraging or prohibiting consumer access to credit report   CC §1785.10.1
  Custody of child
    Reports on custody evaluations
      Confidentiality, breach   Fam §3111
  Customer records
    Disclosure of personal information of customer
      Remedies of customer   CC §1798.84
  Data broker registration
    Enforcement of registration requirement   CC §1798.99.82
  Debt collectors, illegal practices by   CC §§1788.30 to 1788.32
  Deposition officer, civil penalties for discovery violations by   CCP §2025.320
  Disabled persons, enhancement of civil fines for unfair and deceptive practices involving   CC §3345
  Discrimination, penal damages for   CC §52
    Dogs of law enforcement officers, firefighters or handlers of search and rescue dogs serving outside jurisdiction
      Lodging, eating, or transportation, prohibition on discrimination   CC §54.25
  Domestic violence
    Minor's information in protective order proceedings
      Confidentiality of minor's information in protective order proceedings, sanctions to enforce   Fam §6301.5

FINES AND PENALTIES—Cont.
  Dwelling units for hire, violations involving transient occupancy of   CC §1940.1
  Electronic Commerce Act, penalties for violation of   CC §1789.5
  Employment agencies, violations by   CC §1812.523
  Employment counseling services, violations by   CC §1812.523
  Equalization, state board
    Burden of proof
      Evasion or fraud cases   Ev §524
  Fair debt buying practices
    Violation of provisions   CC §1788.62
  Family rules
    Sanctions   CRC 5.14
  Fine print, violating sales provisions applicable to   CC §1745
  Firearm manufacturer liability
    CNC milling machine or 3-D printer, prohibited acts related to   CC §3273.62
    Digital firearm manufacturing codes
      Distribution to unauthorized persons   CC §3273.61
  Fish and game violations, penalty schedules for   CRC 4.102
  Foreclosure consultants, violations by   CC §2945.7
    Failure to register   CC §2945.45
  Foreclosure sales
    Residential property obtained at foreclosure sale
      Managing and maintaining vacant property   CC §2929.3
  Foreign country judgments
    Applicability of provisions   CCP §1715
  Forestry violations, penalty schedules for   CRC 4.102
  Gender neutral retail departments
    Gender neutral section or area for display of toys and childcare items, retailer duties   CC §55.8
  Genetic characteristics, disclosure of test results for   CC §56.17
  Genetic privacy
    Violations of provisions
      Punishments   CC §56.182
  Health care facility, obstructing person from entering or exiting
    Force, threat or other obstruction of access to facility   CC §1708.9
  Home equity sales contracts, violation of   CC §1695.8
  Hospitals
    Obstructing person from entering or exiting
      Force, threat or other obstruction of access to facility   CC §1708.9
  Hotels and motels
    Cancellation of reservations, refunds
      Action for violation of provisions   CC §1748.83
    Sex trafficking activity, hotel permitting or benefiting from
      Actions against hotel for sex trafficking activity   CC §52.65
  Identification documents
    Radio frequency identification (RFID) to remotely read identification document without knowledge or consent   CC §1798.79
  Information Practices Act, violation of   CC §1798.56
  Invasion of privacy to acquire video or sound recordings   CC §1708.8
  Invoices, solicitations appearing like   CC §1716
  Job listing services, violations by   CC §1812.523
  Judicial council, budgeting responsibilities
    Fee, fine and forfeiture revenue
      New revenue, allocation   CRC 10.105
  Jury summons, failure to respond to   CCP §209
    Motion to set aside sanctions imposed by default   CRC 2.1010
  Labor disputes, inciting violence during   CC §52
  Landlord and tenant
    Animals
      Declawing or devocalizing animals as condition of occupancy   CC §1942.7
    Unduly influencing tenant to vacate   CC §1940.2
  Landlord, termination of utility service by   CC §789.3
  Limitation of actions
    Corporations, actions against directors, shareholders or members   CCP §359
    Statutory penalties   CCP §340
  Low water-using plants, common interest developments   CC §4735
  Mandamus, disobedience of writ   CCP §1097
  Marital status, denial of credit because of   CC §1812.33
  Marriage (See **MARRIAGE**)
  Medical records, wrongful disclosure of   CC §56.36
  Mistake, inadvertence, surprise or excusable neglect, relief from default judgment based on   CCP §473
  Mobilehome park management (See **MOBILEHOMES**)
  Motion pictures depicting cruelty, violation of injunction against   CC §3507.3
  Notaries
    Failure of notary to obtain satisfactory evidence   CC §1185

FINES INDEX

FINES AND PENALTIES—Cont.
Obscene and harmful matter
    Electronic messages depicting obscene material
        Knowingly sending unsolicited messages   CC §1708.88
Online marketplaces
    Violation of provisions   CC §1749.8.4
Payment
    Form of payment   CRC 10.821
Price discrimination based on gender
    Price differences for substantially similar goods based on gender of marketing audience
        Enforcement of provisions   CC §51.14
Privacy
    Customer use data for electrical or natural gas usage   CC §1798.99
Private child support collectors   Fam §5615
Public utilities violations, penalty schedules for   CRC 4.102
Realty sales contracts requirements   CC §2985.51
Recreational vehicle park management, penalties for violation of statute by   CC §799.79
Retail installment sales provisions, violation of   CC §§1812.7, 1812.8
School grounds
    Force, threat or other obstruction of access to facility   CC §1708.9
Seller assisted marketing plans, violations of   CC §1812.217
Senior citizens, enhancement of civil fines for unfair and deceptive practices involving   CC §3345
Sexual exploitation
    Commercial sexual exploitation, minor or nonminor dependent victims   CC §3345.1
Short-term vacation rentals
    Cancellation of reservations, refunds
        Action for violation of provisions   CC §1748.83
Solicitations appearing like invoices   CC §1716
Specific performance of contract containing penalty provision   CC §3389
Statutes of limitation
    Corporation, actions against directors, shareholders or members of   CCP §359
    Statutory penalties   CCP §340
Subcutaneous implanting of identification device, requiring of another   CC §52.7
Subdivision Map Act, violation of   CC §2985.51
Subpoena disobeyed   CCP §1992
Timber, injury to   CC §3346
Traffic violations and regulations (See **TRAFFIC REGULATIONS AND VIOLATIONS**)
Trust deeds and mortgages
    Discharge certificate, refusal of   CC §2941.5
    Foreclosure consultants, violations by   CC §2945.7
    Modification or workout plan to avoid foreclosure
        Disabled person victim of prohibited acts, punishment   CC §2944.8
        Notice provided to borrower   CC §2944.6
        Prohibited acts   CC §2944.7
        Senior citizen victim of prohibited acts, punishment   CC §2944.8
        Statute of limitations to enforce protections   CC §2944.10
    Trustee's sale, interfering with bidding at   CC §2924h
Unclaimed deposits and payments   CCP §1576
Uniform Bail and Penalty Schedules   CRC 4.102
Unruh Civil Rights Act, violation of   CC §52
Venue in actions for recovery of   CCP §393
Violent video games   CC §1746.3
Witnesses, arrest to secure attendance
    Release of arrested witness
        Failure of released witness to appear   CCP §1993.2

FINGERPRINTING
Adoption proceedings (See **ADOPTION**)
Attorneys at law
    Active licensed attorneys   CRC 9.9.5
    Foreign countries, active attorney residing in   CRC 9.9.5
    Inactive status prior to becoming active status   CRC 9.9.5
    Special admissions attorneys   CRC 9.9.5
Electronic recording delivery systems
    Computer security auditors
        Eligibility to serve as   Gov §27395
Microphotographed files, records, photographs, etc., in custody of criminal justice agency
    Reproductions, admissibility   Ev §1550.1

FIREARM INDUSTRY STANDARDS OF CONDUCT   CC §§3273.50 to 3273.55
Actions against industry members for violation of standards   CC §3273.52
Compliance by industry members   CC §3273.51
Contents of standards   CC §3273.51

FIREARM INDUSTRY STANDARDS OF CONDUCT—Cont.
Definitions   CC §3273.50
Operative date of provisions   CC §3273.55
Statutory construction of provisions   CC §3273.54

FIREARMS AND OTHER WEAPONS
Actions and proceedings
    Regulation or restriction of firearms
        Recovery of attorney fees   CCP §1021.11
Aggravation, circumstances in   CRC 4.421
Ammunition
    Domestic violence
        Determining violation   Fam §6322.5
        Forms for firearm relinquishment   CRCAppx A
        Restrictions   Fam §§6304, 6389
    Firearm industry responsibility, industry standards of conduct
        Definition of ammunition   CC §3373.50
    Minors
        Verification of age for sale of age-restricted products   CC §1798.99.1
    Nuisance abatement
        Unlawful weapons or ammunition purpose   CC §3485
Attorneys' fees
    Actions to prevent enforcement of laws
        Recovery of attorney fees   CCP §1021.11
BB devices
    Sale to minor
        Verification of age for sale of age-restricted products   CC §1798.99.1
Defenses in civil actions
    Actions to prevent enforcement of laws
        What defenses not permitted   CCP §1021.11
Definitions
    Firearm industry responsibility, industry standards of conduct
        Definition of firearm   CC §3373.50
Dependent child of court proceedings
    Firearm relinquishment procedures   CRC 5.630
        Forms for firearm relinquishment   CRCAppx A
Domestic violence
    Confiscation
        Determining violation   Fam §6322.5
        Forms for firearm relinquishment   CRCAppx A
    Definition of firearms   Fam §6216
    Ex parte protective orders
        Possessed by restrained person of firearm or ammunition, determination whether in violation of order   Fam §6322.5
    Orders, hearings
        Determination whether subject of order has registered firearm prior to hearing   Fam §6306
    Ownership or possession by person subject to protective order
        Determining violation   Fam §6322.5
        Forms for firearm relinquishment   CRCAppx A
    Precursor part
        Definition of firearm precursor part   Fam §6216
    Prohibition on possession
        Determining violation   Fam §6322.5
        Judicial council forms   CRCAppx A
    Protective order, prohibition on firearm ownership or possession by person subject to   Fam §6389
    Relinquishment, records   Fam §6306
    Surrender of firearm
        Judicial council forms   CRCAppx A
    Taking temporary custody of firearms at scene of domestic violence incident
        Authority of peace officer at scene   Fam §6383
        Peace officers, authority at scene   Fam §6383
Felony convicts
    Relinquishment of firearms
        Forms for firearm relinquishment   CRCAppx A
Firearm industry responsibility act
    Industry standards of conduct   CC §§3273.50 to 3273.55 (See **FIREARM INDUSTRY STANDARDS OF CONDUCT**)
Firearm manufacturer liability   CC §§3273.60 to 3273.62
    CNC milling machine or 3-D printer, prohibited acts related to   CC §3273.62
    Definitions   CC §3273.60
    Digital firearm manufacturing codes
        Defined   CC §3273.60
        Distribution to unauthorized persons   CC §3273.61
Firearm precursor parts
    Firearm industry responsibility, industry standards of conduct
        Definition of firearm precursor part   CC §3373.50
Ghost guns
    Firearm manufacturer liability   CC §§3273.60 to 3273.62

FIREARMS AND OTHER WEAPONS—Cont.
Harassment, injunction or order prohibiting
    Address or location of complaining party or family, prohibition on enjoined party from obtaining   CCP §527.10
    Firearm purchases or possession while order in effect   CCP §527.6
        Court determination of possession of firearms in violation of restraining order   CCP §527.11
        COVID-19, emergency rule   CRCAppx I Emer Rule 8
    Firearm relinquishment and disposition
        Forms for firearm relinquishment   CRCAppx A
    Relinquishing and disposition of firearms   CCP §527.9
    Service of orders by peace officers   CCP §527.12
Industry standards of conduct   CC §§3273.50 to 3273.55 (See **FIREARM INDUSTRY STANDARDS OF CONDUCT**)
Less lethal weapons
    Sale to person under age of 18 years
        Verification of age for sale of age-restricted products   CC §1798.99.1
Manufacturers of firearms
    Firearm industry responsibility, industry standards of conduct (See **FIREARM INDUSTRY STANDARDS OF CONDUCT**)
    Firearm industry standards of conduct   CC §§3273.50 to 3273.55
    Firearm manufacturer liability   CC §§3273.60 to 3273.62
Minors
    Verification of age for sale of age-restricted products   CC §1798.99.1
Misdemeanor convicts
    Relinquishment of firearms
        Forms for firearm relinquishment   CRCAppx A
Nuisance
    Abatement
        Illegal weapons on real property   CC §3485
Parental liability for minors discharging   CC §1714.3
Parties to actions
    Actions to prevent enforcement of laws
        Recovery of attorney fees   CCP §1021.11
Postsecondary educational institutions
    Injunction against violence threatened on campus or facility
        Judicial council legal forms   CRCAppx A
    Orders against violence threatened on campus or facility
        Restrictions on firearm ownership by subjects of order   CRCAppx I Emer Rule 8
        Court determination of possession of firearms in violation of restraining order   CCP §527.11
        Service of orders by peace officers   CCP §527.12
Sale, lease or transfer of firearms
    Firearm industry standards of conduct   CC §§3273.50 to 3273.55
    Firearm manufacturer liability   CC §§3273.60 to 3273.62
    Manufacturers and importers, transfers between
        Firearm industry responsibility, industry standards of conduct (See **FIREARM INDUSTRY STANDARDS OF CONDUCT**)
        Firearm industry standards of conduct   CC §§3273.50 to 3273.55
School grounds, threats to commit violence using firearm or deadly weapon on   CC §48.8
Sentence and punishment
    Aggravation, circumstances in   CRC 4.421
Serial numbers of   CC §1710.1
Shooting range exemption from liability for noise pollution   CC §3482.1
Straw purchase
    Firearm industry responsibility, industry standards of conduct (See **FIREARM INDUSTRY STANDARDS OF CONDUCT**)
    Firearm industry standards of conduct   CC §§3273.50 to 3273.55
Stun guns and tasers
    Less lethal weapons
        Verification of age for sale of age-restricted products   CC §1798.99.1
Surrendered weapons
    Domestic violence
        Judicial council forms   CRCAppx A
Theft
    Firearm industry responsibility, industry standards of conduct (See **FIREARM INDUSTRY STANDARDS OF CONDUCT**)
    Firearm industry standards of conduct   CC §§3273.50 to 3273.55
3-D printed firearms
    Firearm manufacturer liability   CC §§3273.60 to 3273.62
Trafficking
    Firearm industry responsibility, industry standards of conduct (See **FIREARM INDUSTRY STANDARDS OF CONDUCT**)
    Firearm industry standards of conduct   CC §§3273.50 to 3273.55
Universities and colleges
    Protection orders against violence threatened on campus or facility
        Judicial council legal forms   CRCAppx A

FIREARMS AND OTHER WEAPONS—Cont.
Universities and colleges—Cont.
    Protection orders against violence threatened on campus or facility—Cont.
        Restrictions on firearm ownership by subjects of order   CCP §527.85, CRCAppx I Emer Rule 8
        Court determination of possession of firearms in violation of restraining order   CCP §527.11
    Service of orders by peace officers   CCP §527.12
Unlawful detainer actions
    Illegal weapons or ammunition on real property   CC §3485
Workplace violence or threats of violence, protection orders
    Address or location of complaining party or family, prohibition on enjoined party from obtaining   CCP §527.10
    Firearm possession or purchase by person subject to   CCP §527.8
        COVID-19, emergency rule   CRCAppx I Emer Rule 8
        Judicial council legal forms   CRCAppx A
    Firearm relinquishment and disposition
        Forms for firearm relinquishment   CRCAppx A
    Proof of sale or turning in of firearm
        Judicial council legal forms   CRCAppx A
    Relinquishing and disposition of firearms   CCP §527.9

FIRE DEPARTMENTS
Firefighters (See **FIREFIGHTERS**)

FIREFIGHTERS
Arbitration procedure under collective bargaining agreement (See **ARBITRATION**)
Contempt orders, stay of execution of   CCP §128
Dogs
    Assignment of firefighter to canine unit outside jurisdiction
        Discrimination in lodging, eating, or transportation due to dog   CC §54.25
Injuries willfully inflicted on firemen, responsibility for   CC §1714.9
Liability for costs of firefighting
    Attorney general, civil actions to enforce provisions
        Fees and costs for attorney general   CCP §1021.8
Public health and safety labor or service providers
    Logo or identifying mark of public agency, display   CC §3273
Public liability for injuries resulting from fire protection activities   Gov §§850 to 850.8
Resuscitative measures, requests regarding   Pro §§4780 to 4786
    Health care providers   Pro §4781
Volunteer firefighters
    Donations of fire protection apparatus to volunteer departments
        Immunity from liability of donators   CC §1714.11
Witnesses, firefighters subpoenaed as   Gov §§68097.1, 68907.2
Work-related death, health care benefits for survivors
    Continuity for survivors   Pro §13600

FIRE HYDRANTS
Junk dealers or recyclers
    Damages for wrongful possession of hydrants or fire department connections   CC §3336.5

FIRE MARSHAL
State agencies, approval of fire safety regulations adopted by   Gov §11359

FIREMEN (See **FIREFIGHTERS**)

FIRES
Appellate court procedures, emergency rule applicable to   CRC 8.66
Business records destroyed by   CCP §§1953.10 to 1953.13
Common interest developments
    Roofs, fire retardant roof coverings
        Restrictions on limitations, prohibitions   CC §4720
Construction defects, actions for
    Fire protection issues
        Actionable defects   CC §896
Court record destroyed by   CCP §§1953 to 1953.06
Destroyed land records relief law   CCP §§751.01 to 751.28
Hazards
    Disclosure to real estate buyers   CC §§1103 to 1103.15
Inspection warrants   CCP §1822.50
Maps destroyed by   CCP §§1953.10 to 1953.13
Mobilehomes and mobilehome parks
    Destruction of park by wildfire or other natural disaster and subsequent rebuilding
        Offers of renewed tenancy   CC §798.62
New trial, destroying bill of exceptions as grounds for   CCP §663.1

FIRES—Cont.
Nunc pro tunc filing where public records lost or destroyed   CCP §1046a
Prescribed burns
    Immunity from damages   CC §3333.8
Public liability for injuries resulting from fire protection activities   Gov §§850 to 850.8
Real estate sales, disclosures
    Fire hazard severity zones
        High or very high fire hazard severity zone, disclosure from seller to buyer   CC §1102.6f
        High or very high fire hazard severity zone, documentation of compliance with firebreak, vegetation management, etc, requirements   CC §1102.19
Repairs, fire destroying property left for   CC §1858.2
Sale of realty, hazard disclosure requirements for   CC §§1103 to 1103.15
Smoke detectors
    Real estate disclosure statements   CC §§1102.6, 1102.6d
State agencies, adoption of fire safety regulations by   Gov §11359
Will revoked by burning   Pro §§6120, 6121

FIREWORKS
Dangerous fireworks
    Minors, sale or delivery to
        Verification of age for sale of age-restricted products   CC §1798.99.1

FIRST AID
Anaphylaxis
    Epinephrine auto-injector administration for first aid
        Immunity from civil liability of lay rescuers, prehospital emergency medical care providers or authorized entities   CC §1714.23
Immunity from liability
    Drones or unmanned aircraft systems damaged by emergency responder
        Provision of emergency services by responder and interference with services by drone   CC §43.101
Personal injury liability of governmental agency for   CC §1714.5

FIRST AMENDMENT RIGHTS
Judicial review of permit or entitlement decision implicating First Amendment rights, expedited procedures for   CCP §1094.8
Landlord and tenant
    Political signs   CC §1940.4
Motion to strike causes of action with chilling effect on person's exercise of   CCP §§425.16, 425.17
    SLAPPback actions   CCP §425.18

FIRST DAY
Computation of time in which act provided by law is to be done   CCP §12

FISH AND FISHING
Easement rights   CC §§801, 802
Fish and wildlife laws
    Attorney general, civil actions to enforce provisions
        Fees and costs for attorney general   CCP §1021.8
Owner's liability for recreational land   CC §846
Statute of limitation in action commenced under Section 1603.1 or 5650.1 of Fish and Game Code   CCP §338

FISH AND GAME MANAGEMENT
Bail and penalty schedules for violations   CRC 4.102
Department of fish and wildlife
    Eminent domain taking by   CCP §1245.210
    Inspections   CCP §1822.58

FITNESS
Assistive devices, implied warranty of fitness   CC §1793.02
Consumer goods, implied warranty of fitness of   CC §1791.1
Professional persons, information concerning fitness of   CC §§43.7, 43.8

FIVE YEARS (See **STATUTES OF LIMITATION**)

FIXTURES
Generally   CC §§660, 1013, 1013.5
Attachment liens on   CCP §§488.375, 488.385
Home solicitation contracts, purchases under   CC §§1689.8, 1689.9
Installment purchase contract, venue of action on   CC §1812.10
Removal   CC §§1013.5, 1019
Trade fixtures   CC §1019

FLAGS
Commercial and industrial common interest developments
    United States flag displays
        Protected uses   CC §6702

FLAGS—Cont.
Common interest developments
    Display of US flag
        Restrictions on limitations, prohibitions   CC §4705
    Noncommercial signs, posters, flags or banners
        Restrictions on limitations, prohibitions   CC §4710
US flag
    Commercial and industrial common interest developments
        Protected uses   CC §6702
    Common interest developments
        Protected uses   CC §4705

FLAX
Storage regulations after sale of   CC §§1880 to 1881.2

FLOATING HOMES
Abandonment
    Marina-owned homes   CC §800.37
    Notice of belief of   CC §800.36
    Right of entry upon   CC §800.32
Advertising
    Condominium sales   CC §800.301
Attorney's fees, award of   CC §800.200
Buyer
    Financial or credit report, charges for   CC §800.85
    Prior approval of purchaser, management's right to
        Condominium sales   CC §800.304
        Floating home sales   CC §800.85
    Termination of tenancy for purposes of making berth available to new buyer, prohibition against   CC §800.73
Change of use
    Defined   CC §800.7
    Written notice to tenant concerning   CC §800.33
Citation of Act   CC §800
Club membership as condition for rental, prohibition against   CC §800.25
Common areas
    Failure to maintain
        Action against management   CC §800.91
        Public nuisance, improper maintenance as   CC §800.201
    Homeowner meetings, use of common area facilities for   CC §800.60
    Open hours of common area facilities, posting of   CC §800.30
    Public nuisance, improper maintenance of common area as   CC §800.201
Condominium sales
    Advertising for sale   CC §800.301
    Definitions   CC §800.300
    Listing for sale, homeowner's permission for   CC §800.302
    Prior approval of buyer, management's right to   CC §800.304
    Removal of floating home from marina   CC §800.303
    Waiver of buyer's statutory rights, prohibition against   CC §800.305
Definitions   CC §§800.1 to 800.9
Failure to maintain common areas
    Action against management   CC §800.91
    Public nuisance for improper maintenance   CC §800.201
Fees and charges
    Enforcement of marina rules and regulations, prohibition against charging fees for   CC §800.46
    Financial or credit report for prospective buyer, imposition of charges for   CC §800.85
    Guest fees   CC §800.44
    Hookup fees   CC §800.47
    Landscaping fees   CC §800.47
    Lien or security interest in floating home, acquisition by management of   CC §800.50
    Number of immediate family members of homeowner, prohibition against fees based on   CC §800.45
    Permissible fees   CC §800.41
    Pet fees   CC §800.43
    Security deposits   CC §800.49
    60-day notice required prior to imposition of fees not in rental agreement   CC §800.42
    30-day notice of rent increases   CC §§800.40, 800.40.5
    Transfer fees   CC §800.83
    Utility fees   CC §800.48
Floating home marina, sale of   CC §800.100
Foreclosure sales   CC §800.89
Governing law   CC §800.306
Guest fees   CC §800.44
Homeowner meetings
    Management-homeowners meetings   CC §800.61
    Use of common area facilities for   CC §800.60
Hookup fees   CC §800.47

FLOATING HOMES—Cont.
  Landscaping fees CC §800.47
  Liens
    Foreclosure sale by lienholder CC §800.89
    Management acquiring lien or security interest in floating home, validity of CC §800.50
  Listings for sale
    Condominiums, listing of CC §800.302
    Floating home marina, sale of CC §800.100
    Homeowner's permission for CC §800.82
    Used floating homes, listing of CC §800.90
  Management-homeowners meetings CC §800.61
  Management rules and regulations
    Amendment of CC §800.31
    Enforcement of rules and regulations, prohibition against charging fees for CC §800.46
    Entry rights of management, exercise of CC §800.35
    Name and address of floating home marina owner, disclosure of CC §800.34
    Open hours of common area facilities, posting of CC §800.30
    Right of entry CC §800.32
    Written notice requirements
      Notices generally (See within this heading, **"Notices"**)
  Notices
    Abandonment, belief of CC §800.36
    Amendment to management rules and regulations, written notice of CC §800.31
    Change of use, written notice concerning CC §800.33
    Copy of notices required by law, management to provide homeowners CC §800.20
    Eviction notices CC §800.70
    Failure to maintain common areas, notice of action against management for CC §800.91
    Floating home marina, notice to homeowner of sale of CC §800.100
    Management-homeowners meetings CC §800.61
    Name and address of floating home marina owner, disclosure of CC §800.34
    Open hours of common area facilities, posting of CC §800.30
    60-day notices
      Eviction notice CC §800.70
      Imposition of fees not in rental agreement CC §800.42
    Termination of tenancy CC §800.72
    30-day notice of rent increases CC §§800.40, 800.40.5
    oning matters, written notice concerning CC §800.33
  Open hours of common area facilities, posting of CC §800.30
  Personal representative of decedent's estate, sale by CC §800.88
  Pet fees CC §800.43
  Prior approval of buyer, management's right to
    Condominium sales CC §800.304
    Floating home sales CC §800.85
  Public nuisance, improper maintenance of common areas as CC §800.201
  Removal from marina after sale
    Generally CC §800.84
    Condominium sales to third party CC §800.303
  Rent
    Cap on rent or increases in rent CC §800.40.5
    Increases
      Cap on rent or increases in rent CC §800.40.5
  Rental agreement
    Club membership as condition for rental, prohibition against CC §800.25
    Defined CC §800.5
    Period of tenancy, terms for CC §800.23
    Permitted provisions CC §800.22
    Transfer of floating home remaining in marina, rental agreement required as condition to CC §800.86
    Waiver of tenant's statutory rights, prohibition against CC §800.24
    Written rental agreement to be furnished to prospective tenant CC §800.21
  Repair of common area facilities, failure of
    Action against management CC §800.91
    Public nuisance for improper maintenance CC §800.201
  Repossession of CC §800.89
  Right of entry CC §800.32
  Sales
    Advertising
      Condominium sales CC §800.301
    Condominium sales (See within this heading, **"Condominium sales"**)
    Floating home marina, sale of CC §800.100
    Foreclosure sales CC §800.89
    Heirs of owner, sale by CC §800.88
    Joint tenant, sale by CC §800.88
    Listings (See within this heading, **"Listings for sale"**)

FLOATING HOMES—Cont.
  Sales—Cont.
    Personal representative of decedent's estate, sale by CC §800.88
    Prior approval of buyer
      Condominium sales CC §800.304
      Floating home sales CC §800.85
    Removal of floating home from marina CC §800.84
      Condominium sales to third party CC §800.303
    Rental agreement as condition to transfer of floating home remaining in marina CC §800.86
    Transfer fees CC §800.83
    Unlawful occupant CC §800.86
    Waiver of homeowner's or buyer's statutory rights, prohibition against CC §800.87
  San Francisco Bay Conservation and Development Commission rules, applicability of CC §800.306
  Security deposits CC §800.49
  Security interest
    Foreclosure sale by lienholder CC §800.89
    Management acquiring lien or security interest in floating home, validity CC §800.50
  Senior citizens
    Club membership as condition for rental, prohibition against
      Applicability of prohibition to housing for elderly CC §800.25
  60-day notices
    Eviction notice CC §800.70
    Imposition of fees not in rental agreement, 60-day notice required before CC §800.42
  Tenant
    Club membership as condition for rental, prohibition against CC §800.25
    Copy of notice
      All notices required by law, management to provide CC §800.20
      Floating Home Residency Law, copy of CC §800.26
    Fees and charges generally (See within this heading, **"Fees and charges"**)
    Termination of tenancy (See within this heading, **"Termination of tenancy"**)
    Written rental agreement to be furnished to prospective tenant CC §800.21
  Termination of tenancy
    Eviction CC §800.70
    Grounds for CC §800.71
    Notice of termination
      By management CC §800.72
      By tenant CC §800.74
    Prohibition against termination for purposes of making berth available to new buyer CC §800.73
    60-day notice by vacating homeowner, requirement of CC §800.74
    Unlawful detainer action as remedy, availability of CC §800.75
  30-day notice of rent increases CC §§800.40, 800.40.5
  Transfers
    Sales generally (See within this heading, **"Sales"**)
  Unlawful detainer
    Defaulting tenant, action against CC §800.75
    Hold over by tenant after sale under execution or foreclosure, unlawful detainer action involving CCP §1161a
    New buyer as unlawful occupant CC §800.86
  Used floating homes, listing of CC §800.90
  Utility fees CC §800.48
  Waiver of rights
    Buyer's or homeowner's statutory rights, prohibition against waiver of CC §800.87
    Condominium buyer's statutory rights, prohibition against waiver of CC §800.305
    Tenant's statutory rights, prohibition against waiver of CC §800.24
  Zoning change, notice to tenant concerning CC §800.33

FLOODS
Boundary reestablishment CCP §§751.50 to 751.65
Destroyed land records relief law CCP §§751.01 to 751.28
Easement rights to flood land CC §801
Eminent domain to control floods, taking for CCP §1240.110
Flood control and water conservation facilities, public agency liability for injuries caused by Gov §§831.8, 831.9
Hazards, disclosure to real estate buyers CC §§1103 to 1103.15
Land carried away by flooding, reclaiming of CC §1015
Nunc pro tunc filing where public records lost or destroyed CCP §1046a
Property sales, disclosure of flood hazard CC §§1103 to 1103.15
Sale of realty, hazard disclosure requirements for CC §§1103 to 1103.15

FLOORS
Landlord's duty to repair CC §1941.1

FOOD

Food bank, injuries resulting from consumption of food distributed by   CC §1714.25
Jurors in criminal proceedings   CCP §217
Meals (See **MEALS**)
Trial court operations fund
     Food and lodging of jurors   CCP §217

FOOD AND AGRICULTURE DEPARTMENT

Mandamus proceedings for acts of   CCP §1085.5

FOOD BANKS

Injuries resulting from consumption of food distributed by   CC §1714.25

FORCE (See **DURESS**)

FORCIBLE ENTRY AND DETAINER (See also **UNLAWFUL DETAINER**)

Generally   CCP §§1159, 1160
Answer   CCP §§1167, 1167.3, 1170
Appeals   CCP §§1176, 1178
Boarding house occupants, protection for   CCP §1159
Complaint   CCP §§1166, 1166a, 1167.3, 1173
Cumulative remedies   CC §1952
Damages   CCP §§735, 1174
Default judgments   CCP §1169
Demurrer   CCP §1170
     Meet and confer prerequisite to filing
         Inapplicability of meet and confer requirement in forcible entry, forcible detainer or unlawful detainer cases   CCP §430.41
Discovery
     Motion for discovery   CCP §1170.8, CRC 3.1347
         Judicial council, rules as to   CCP §1170.9
     Time for completion of discovery   CCP §2024.040
Evidence   CCP §1172
Extensions of time to plead
     Judicial council, rules as to   CCP §1170.9
Forcible detainer defined   CCP §1160
Forcible entry defined   CCP §1159
Immigration or citizenship status irrelevant to issue of liability or remedy   CC §3339.10
Jury trial   CCP §1171
Motions for summary judgment   CRC 3.1351
     Judicial council, rules as to   CCP §1170.9
Notice requirements, exception to   CC §792
Practice rules governing   CCP §1177
Process, service of   CCP §§415.45, 415.47, 1167
Quashing service, motions for
     Judicial council, rules as to   CCP §1170.9
Quiet possession, defense of   CCP §1172
Rent default
     Untenantable premises, attorneys' fees and costs against landlord for initiating unlawful detainer   CCP §1174.21
Stay of proceedings   CCP §1176
Strike, motions to   CCP §1170
Summary judgment, motion for   CRC 3.1351
     Judicial council, rules as to   CCP §1170.9

FORECLOSURE

Auctions
     Prospective owner-occupant as bidder   CC §2924m
Avoiding foreclosure
     Discussing options to avoid
         Communication to borrower as to availability of alternatives after recordation of notice of default   CC §2924.9
         Contact of borrower by lender   CC §2923.5
         Injunction to enforce   CC §§2924.12, 2924.19
         Prior to recordation of notice of default   CC §2923.55
     Foreclosure prevention act generally   CC §2924
     Modification or workout plan   CC §2923.6
         Single point of contact   CC §2923.7
California foreclosure prevention act   CC §2924
Common interest developments
     Common area damage
         Limitation on foreclosure for penalties or damages   CC §5725
     Dispute resolution   CC §5705
     Limitation on foreclosure   CC §5720
     Sale under foreclosure   CC §5710
         Redemption after trustee sale   CC §5715
Consultants   CC §§2945 to 2945.11
     Contracts in Spanish or Asian languages   CC §1632
     Registration   CC §2945.45

FORECLOSURE—Cont.

Consultants —Cont.
     Regulation fund   CC §2945.45
COVID-19, emergency rule   CRCAppx I Emer Rule 2
Disability insurance claims, creditor remedies regarding   CC §1812.402
Execution of process by sheriff of new county in which subject property is situated   CCP §262.11
Holding over, unlawful detainer action
     Residential fixed term leases
         Possession until end of lease term   CCP §1161b
         Written notice to quit to tenant   CCP §1161b
Home equity sales contracts (See **HOME EQUITY SALES CONTRACTS**)
Liens (See **LIENS**)
Mortgage foreclosure consultants   CC §§2945 to 2945.11
Mortgages (See **TRUST DEEDS AND MORTGAGES**)
Notice   CC §2924.8
     Sale under power of sale   CC §2924f
Nuisance property
     Abatement assessment or lien
         Maximum amount   CC §2929.45
Prevention of foreclosure   CC §2924
     Communication to borrower as to availability of alternatives after recordation of notice of default   CC §2924.9
     Exploration of options prior to recordation of notice of default   CC §2923.55
Redemption
     Common interest developments
         Redemption after trustee sale   CC §5715
Removal of person holding over after
     Written notice to quit to tenant   CCP §1161b
Rescission of   CC §1695.14
Residential property obtained at foreclosure sale
     Managing and maintaining vacant property   CC §2929.3
Sale
     Attorney professional conduct
         Purchase by attorney of property at foreclosure or judicial sale   ProfC 1.8.9
     Common interest developments   CC §5710
         Redemption after trustee sale   CC §5715
     Eligible bidder as winning bidder
         Trustee's duties   CC §2924m
     Final sale
         Conditions for sale to be deemed final   CC §2924m
         Covenants for purchased property   CC §2924o
     Institution foreclosing on 175 or more residential properties
         Prospective owner-occupants and eligible bidders, first opportunity to purchase   CC §2924p
     Residential property obtained at foreclosure sale
         Managing and maintaining vacant property   CC §2929.3
Stay
     COVID-19, emergency rule   CRCAppx I Emer Rule 2
Street improvement assessment lien foreclosure, statute of limitations for   CCP §329
Trust deeds (See **TRUST DEEDS AND MORTGAGES**)
Unlawful detainer proceedings against persons holding over after
     Written notice to quit to tenant   CCP §1161b
Vacant property
     Failure to maintain vacant property
         Notice   CC §2929.4
     Nuisance property
         Abatement assessment or lien, maximum amount   CC §2929.45
     Residential property obtained at foreclosure sale
         Managing and maintaining vacant property   CC §2929.3
Venue in actions for foreclosure of liens and mortgages on real property   CCP §392

FORECLOSURE PREVENTION ACT   CC §2924

Alternatives
     Definition of foreclosure prevention alternatives   CC §2920.5
Application for prevention alternatives
     Denial   CC §2924.11
     Submission
         Effect   CC §§2924.11, 2924.12
Approval of preventive measures, effect   CC §§2924.11, 2924.12
Delayed notification of default and exercise of power of sale
     Requirements for filing and recording documents   CC §§2924.17, 2924.19
         Damages to enforce   CC §2924.12
         Injunction to enforce   CC §2924.12
Enforcement of preventive measures
     Actions for damages   CC §2924.12
     Injunctions   CC §2924.12

FORECLOSURE PREVENTION ACT—Cont.
Rulemaking to implement provisions   CC §2924.20

FOREIGN BODY
Health care providers, presence of foreign body tolling statute of limitation for actions against   CCP §340.5

FOREIGN CONSERVATORS (See CONSERVATORS)

FOREIGN CORPORATIONS
Attachment (See **ATTACHMENT**)
Attorney professional conduct
    Organization or entity as client   ProfC 1.13
Choice of law for purposes of jurisdiction in action or proceeding involving   CCP §410.40
Costs, bonds required to secure   CCP §1030

FOREIGN COUNTRIES
Acknowledgment of instruments   CC §§1183, 1183.5, 1189
Adoption
    Foreign country adoptions
        Intercountry adoptions generally   CRC 5.490 to 5.493, Fam §§8900 to 8925
Adoptions between countries (See **ADOPTION**)
Affidavits taking in   CCP §§2014, 2015
Aliens (See **ALIENS**)
Ancillary administration (See **ANCILLARY ADMINISTRATION**)
Attorneys at law
    Fingerprinting of active licensed attorney residing in foreign country   CRC 9.9.5
Conservators
    Interstate jurisdiction, transfer and recognition
        Foreign country considered as state for purposes of applicability of provisions   Pro §1983
Consuls and consulates (See **CONSULS AND CONSULATES**)
Corporations (See **FOREIGN CORPORATIONS**)
Depositions
    Interstate and international depositions and discovery act   CCP §§2029.100 to 2029.900 (See **DISCOVERY**)
    Taking depositions in foreign state or country   CCP §2027.010
Discovery
    Interstate and international depositions and discovery act   CCP §§2029.100 to 2029.900 (See **DISCOVERY**)
Family rules
    Service on person residing outside US
        Applicable provisions   CRC 5.68
Hague adoption convention, adoptions under   CRC 5.490 to 5.492
    Intercountry adoptions generally   CRC 5.490 to 5.493, Fam §§8900 to 8925
International commercial arbitration and conciliation (See **INTERNATIONAL COMMERCIAL ARBITRATION AND CONCILIATION**)
Judgments
    Money judgments, recognition   CCP §§1713 to 1725 (See **FOREIGN JUDGMENTS**)
Languages (See **LANGUAGE**)
Lapse of time for bringing action under laws of state or foreign country where action has arisen   CCP §361
Money judgments, recognition   CCP §§1713 to 1725 (See **FOREIGN JUDGMENTS**)
Organization of foreign nations, judicial notice of   Ev §§452, 454
Questions of law and fact as to foreign law   Ev §§310, 311
Records of captive persons in foreign countries, admissibility of   Ev §1283
Sealed documents presumed to be genuine   Ev §1452
Service of process outside United States   CCP §413.10
Signatures of officials presumed to be genuine   Ev §§1454, 1530
Uniform foreign country money judgments recognition act
    Citation of provisions   CCP §1713
    Generally (See **FOREIGN JUDGMENTS**)
Wills (See **WILLS**)

FOREIGNERS (See ALIENS)

FOREIGN EXECUTORS AND ADMINISTRATORS
Generally (See **EXECUTORS AND ADMINISTRATORS**)
Ancillary administration (See **ANCILLARY ADMINISTRATION**)

FOREIGN GUARDIANS (See GUARDIAN AND WARD)

FOREIGN JUDGMENTS   CCP §§1710.10 to 1710.65
Appeals
    Foreign country judgments   CCP §1720

FOREIGN JUDGMENTS—Cont.
Applicability of foreign country provisions   CCP §1715
Burden of proof
    Foreign country judgments   CCP §1715
Conclusiveness
    Foreign country judgments   CCP §1719
Construction and interpretation
    Foreign country judgment provisions   CCP §1722
Defamation judgments   CC §3425.4
    Declaratory relief   CCP §1725
    Denial of recognition   CCP §1725
Definitions
    Foreign country judgments   CCP §1714
    Sister state judgments   CCP §1710.10
Denial of recognition
    Foreign country judgments
        Exceptions   CCP §1717
        Grounds   CCP §1716
Dissolution of marriage
    Foreign country judgments
        Applicability   CCP §1715
Effective date of enactment
    Foreign country judgments   CCP §1724
Enforceability of judgments
    Foreign country judgments   CCP §1719
Execution on   CCP §1710.45
Fines
    Foreign country judgments
        Applicability of provisions   CCP §1715
Foreign countries
    Defined   CCP §1714
Foreign-country judgments
    Defined   CCP §1714
Indians
    Foreign countries defined
        Indian nation, tribe, etc included in definition   CCP §1714
    Tribal court civil money judgment act   CCP §§1730 to 1741
Jurisdiction, lack of
    Personal jurisdiction lacking
        Foreign country judgments   CCP §1717
Local enforcement of   CCP §§1710.10 to 1710.65
Money judgments
    Sister state money judgments   CCP §§1710.010 to 1710.65
    Uniform foreign country money judgments recognition act   CCP §§1713 to 1725
Notice   CCP §1710.30
Original actions
    Foreign country judgments
        Method of raising issue of recognition   CCP §1718
Parties bound by   CCP §§1913, 1914
Pending actions
    Foreign country judgments
        Method of raising issue of recognition   CCP §1718
Recognition of foreign country judgments
    Situations not covered by provisions   CCP §1723
Sister State Money-Judgments Act   CCP §§1710.10 to 1710.65
Slander action barred by   CC §3425.4
Statutes of limitation
    Federal courts or courts of other states   CCP §337.5
    Foreign country judgments   CCP §1721
Stay of proceedings   CCP §1710.50
    Foreign country judgment
        Appeal, stay on   CCP §1720
Support judgments
    Foreign country provisions
        Applicability   CCP §1715
Taxes
    Foreign country provisions
        Applicability   CCP §1715
Uniform Child Custody Jurisdiction Act (See **CUSTODY OF CHILDREN**)
Uniform Foreign-Money Claims Act   CCP §§676 to 676.16
Venue   CCP §1710.20

FOREIGN LANGUAGES
Consumer credit contracts
    Notice
        Foreign language translations of notice requirement   CC §1799.91
Courts
    Language access services for limited English proficient litigants
        Collaboration and technology to provide services   CRC 1.300

FOREIGN LANGUAGES—Cont.
Courts—Cont.
  Language access services for limited English proficient litigants —Cont.
    Court-ordered and court-provided programs, services and professionals   CRC 1.300
Fair debt buying practices
  Written statements to collect debt
    Use of language used in initial contract   CC §1788.52
Interpreters (See **TRANSLATORS AND INTERPRETERS**)
Jury service, persons not possessed of sufficient knowledge of English language ineligible for   CCP §203
Law and motion proceedings, translation of exhibits   CRC 3.1110

FOREIGN LAW
Conflict of laws (See **CONFLICT OF LAWS**)
Mistake as mistake of fact   CC §1579

FOREIGN LEGAL CONSULTANTS   CRC 9.44
Fingerprinting of special admission attorneys   CRC 9.9.5

FOREIGN STATES
Foreign countries (See **FOREIGN COUNTRIES**)
Sister states (See **OTHER STATES**)

FOREIGN WILLS (See **WILLS**)

FORENSIC SCIENCES
Medical records
  Forensic pathologists
    Disclosure of medical records to coroners, medical examiners or forensic pathologists   CC §56.10

FOREST FIRE PREVENTION AND CONTROL
Prescribed burns
  Immunity from damages   CC §3333.8
Realty located in forest fire hazard area, disclosure to purchaser   CC §§1103 to 1103.15

FORESTRY
Appropriation of water originating in national forest   CC §1422
Fines and penalties
  Bail schedule   CRC 4.102
Forestry and fire protection department
  Donations of apparatus to volunteer fire departments
    Immunity from liability   CC §1714.11
Logs and timbers (See **LOGS AND TIMBER**)

FORESTRY AND FIRE PROTECTION DEPARTMENT
Bail and penalty schedules for violating forestry regulations   CRC 4.102

FORESTS AND FORESTRY
Fiduciary income and principal act
  Receipts, allocation
    Timber sales   Pro §16351

FORFEITURES   CC §3275
Bail (See **BAIL**)
Corporate charter or right to do business (See **CORPORATIONS**)
Enforcement restrictions   CC §3369
Future interest defeated by   CC §741
Judicial council, budgeting responsibilities
  Fee, fine and forfeiture revenue
    New revenue, allocation   CRC 10.105
Leases (See **UNLAWFUL DETAINER**)
Liens, property subject to   CC §2889
Oil and gas liens on leasehold estates   CCP §1203.55
Statutes of limitation
  Action upon statute for forfeiture   CCP §340
  Against officer to recover damages for seizure of property for statutory forfeiture   CCP §340
  Corporation, actions against directors, shareholders or members of   CCP §359
Venue in actions for recovery of   CCP §393

FORGERY
Statutes of limitation for payment of forged or raised check   CCP §340
Trust deeds (See **TRUST DEEDS AND MORTGAGES**)

FORMA PAUPERIS
Application to proceed in forma pauperis
  Waiver of fees and costs
    Application   CRC 3.50 to 3.58 (See **CIVIL RULES**)

FORMA PAUPERIS—Cont.
Application to proceed in forma pauperis—Cont.
  Waiver of fees and costs—Cont.
    Bench warrants to secure attendance of witnesses, applicability of waiver   Gov §26744.5
    Generally   Gov §§68630 to 68641 (See **INDIGENT PERSONS**)

FORMATION (See **PUBLIC ENTITIES**)

FORMER ADJUDICATION (See **RES JUDICATA**)

FORMER NAME
Change of name, right at common law to   CCP §1279.5
Women using   CCP §1279.5

FORMER TESTIMONY
Admissibility of   Ev §§1290 to 1293

FORMS
Acknowledgments (See **ACKNOWLEDGMENTS**)
Administration of estates (See **ADMINISTRATION OF ESTATES**)
Adoption (See **ADOPTION**)
Alternative dispute resolution
  Judicial council legal forms   CRCAppx A
Annulment of marriage
  Judicial council legal forms   CRCAppx A
Appearances
  Notice to appear forms
    Judicial council legal forms   CRCAppx A
Appellate forms
  Judicial council legal forms   CRCAppx A
Approved forms, use of (See **JUDICIAL COUNCIL**)
Attorney in fact (See **POWER OF ATTORNEY**)
Automobiles (See **AUTOMOBILES**)
Bonds by party to action   CCP §995.330
Case management
  Judicial council legal forms   CRCAppx A
Case questionnaires under economic litigation provisions for limited civil cases, responsibility for development of   CCP §93
Child custody and visitation
  Judicial council legal forms   CRCAppx A
Child support
  Case registry forms   CRC 5.330
  Government support enforcement services
    Judicial council legal forms   CRCAppx A
Civil rules
  Waiver of fees and costs, application
    Forms for application   CRC 3.51
    Judicial council legal forms   CRCAppx A
Claim and delivery
  Generally (See **CLAIM AND DELIVERY**)
  Judicial council legal forms   CRCAppx A
Claims against estates (See **CLAIMS AGAINST ESTATES**)
Conciliation court, caption of petition filed in   Fam §1832
Construction-related accessibility claims
  Judicial council legal forms   CRCAppx A
Criminal law and procedure
  Judicial council legal forms   CRCAppx A
Decedent's estates
  Judicial council legal forms   CRCAppx A
  Notice to creditors to file claims against   Pro §9052
Deeds   CC §1092
Delinquent children
  Judicial council legal forms   CRCAppx A
Dependent child of court proceedings
  Judicial council legal forms   CRCAppx A
Destroyed land records relief law proceedings   CCP §§751.05, 751.23
Discovery
  Judicial council legal forms   CRCAppx A
Dissolution of marriage proceedings, forms of notice to insurance carriers in   Fam §§2050, 2051
Divorce
  Judicial council legal forms   CRCAppx A
Domestic violence
  Forms approved by Judicial Council
    List of judicial council legal forms   CRCAppx A
Donative transfers
  Presumption of fraud or undue influence
    Certificate of independent review   Pro §21384
Economic litigation procedures (See **ECONOMIC LITIGATION PROCEDURES**)

FORMS—Cont.
Elder abuse and neglect
    Judicial council legal forms   CRCAppx A
Electronic filing and service rules
    Judicial council forms   CRCAppx A
    Modification of judicial council forms   CRC 2.261
Emancipation of children (See **EMANCIPATION OF MINORS**)
Emergency protective orders
    Judicial council legal forms   CRCAppx A
Eminent domain valuation statements   CCP §1258.210
Enforcement of judgments (See **ENFORCEMENT OF JUDGMENTS**)
Executors and administrators (See **EXECUTORS AND ADMINISTRATORS**)
Family law proceedings (See **FAMILY RULES**)
Fax filing of legal documents (See **FAX FILING AND SERVICE**)
Fees
    Courts, authority to set fees for products or services   CRC 10.815
Forma pauperis, application for fee and cost waivers
    Forms for application   CRC 3.51
        Judicial council legal forms   CRCAppx A
Garnishment (See **GARNISHMENT**)
Grain sold in bulk, form of notice of   CC §1880.7
Guardian and ward (See **GUARDIAN AND WARD**)
Handwritten or handprinted forms   CRC 2.135
Harassment
    Judicial council legal forms   CRCAppx A
Home solicitation contract, cancellation of   CC §1689.7
Ignition interlock devices
    Judicial council legal forms   CRCAppx A
Insurers notified in dissolution of marriage proceedings   Fam §§2050, 2051
Interpreters
    Judicial council legal forms   CRCAppx A
Interrogatories
    Form interrogatories
        List of judicial council legal forms   CRCAppx A
Judge, peremptory challenge of   CCP §170.6
Judgments
    Judicial council legal forms   CRCAppx A
Judicial council forms   CRC 1.30 to 1.45
    Applicability of provisions   CRC 1.30
    Cause of action forms   CRC 1.45
    Current form, use   CRC 1.37
    Electronic filing and service rules   CRCAppx A
        Modification of judicial council forms to allow for electronic processing   CRC 2.261
    Electronic production   CRC 1.44
    Legibility   CRC 1.43
    List of legal forms   CRCAppx A
    Mandatory forms   CRC 1.30
        Alteration for form   CRC 1.31
        Colored forms   CRC 1.31
        Effect of mandatory status   CRC 1.31
        Identification   CRC 1.31
        List   CRC 1.31
        Orders not on mandatory form   CRC 1.31
        Probate form orders, electronic generation   CRC 7.101.5
    Optional forms   CRC 1.30
        Acceptance for filing   CRC 1.35
        Alteration of form   CRC 1.35
        Colored forms   CRC 1.35
        Identification   CRC 1.35
        List   CRC 1.35
        Use   CRC 1.35
    Pleading forms   CRC 1.45
    Probate forms
        Electronic generation of mandatory judicial council form orders   CRC 7.101.5
        Use of judicial council forms   CRC 7.101
    Proof of service on form   CRC 1.41
    Rejection of form
        Prohibited reasons for rejection   CRC 1.42
    Universities and colleges
        Violence prevention   CRCAppx A
Juvenile court proceedings   CRC 5.504
    Judicial council legal forms   CRCAppx A
Leases (See **LEASES**)
Legal separation
    Judicial council legal forms   CRCAppx A
Letters of administration   Pro §8405
Liens (See **LIENS**)
Local court forms   CRC 10.614
Marriage license   Fam §355

FORMS—Cont.
Medical malpractice arbitration clauses   CCP §1295
Merchandise offered for consumers, order forms for   CC §§1584.5, 1584.6
Military   CRCAppx A
Mortgages (See **TRUST DEEDS AND MORTGAGES**)
Name change
    Judicial council legal forms   CRCAppx A
Notarial acts by officers in armed services   CC §1183.5
Notice to appear forms
    Judicial council legal forms   CRCAppx A
Oaths (See **OATHS**)
Partition action, affidavit stating death of party to   CCP §872.530
Paternity
    Judicial council legal forms   CRCAppx A
Pleadings
    Judicial council legal forms   CRCAppx A
Power of attorney (See **POWER OF ATTORNEY**)
Probate
    Judicial council legal forms   CRCAppx A
        Electronic generation of mandatory judicial council form orders   CRC 7.101.5
Process (See **PROCESS AND SERVICE OF PROCESS**)
Protective orders
    California law enforcement telecommunications (CLETS) information form   CRCAppx A
        Confidentiality and use of information on form   CRC 1.51
    Emergency protective orders
        Judicial council legal forms   CRCAppx A
Receipt of summons, acknowledgment of   CCP §415.30
Receivers and receiverships
    Judicial council legal forms   CRCAppx A
Requests for admissions
    Form requests for admissions
        List of judicial council legal forms   CRCAppx A
Salaries (See **SALARIES AND WAGES**)
Service of process (See **PROCESS AND SERVICE OF PROCESS**)
Small claims actions, approval or adoption of claim form for   CCP §116.320
Statutory references on forms   CRC 1.40
Subpoenaed witness notified to call attorney   CCP §1985.2
Summary dissolution of marriage (See **SUMMARY DISSOLUTION OF MARRIAGE**)
Summons (See **PROCESS AND SERVICE OF PROCESS**)
Superior court records
    Judicial council legal forms   CRCAppx A
Superior courts (See **SUPERIOR COURTS**)
Surety bonds   CCP §995.330
Termination of parental rights
    Judicial council legal forms   CRCAppx A
Traffic violations, trial by written declaration   CRC 4.210
    List of judicial council legal forms   CRCAppx A
Transfer on death deeds
    Notice of deed   Pro §5681
    Statutory forms
        Revocable transfer on death (TOD) deed   Pro §5642
        Revocation of revocable transfer on death (TOD) deed   Pro §5644
Trial, notice of   CCP §594
Trust deeds (See **TRUST DEEDS AND MORTGAGES**)
Uniform Transfers to Minors Act, transfer under   Pro §3909
Universities and colleges
    Violence prevention
        Judicial council legal forms   CRCAppx A
Unlawful detainer (See **UNLAWFUL DETAINER**)
Wages (See **SALARIES AND WAGES**)
Waiver of fees and costs, application
    Forms for application   CRC 3.51
        Judicial council legal forms   CRCAppx A
Will, California statutory   Pro §§6240 to 6243
Workplace violence
    Judicial council legal forms   CRCAppx A

FORMS, MOLDS AND DIES
Ownership of   CC §1140

FOR SALE, LEASE, OR EXCHANGE SIGNS
Mobilehome condominiums, restrictions on   CC §799.1.5
Real property, sale of   CC §§712, 713

FORUM NON CONVENIENS (See **INCONVENIENT FORUM**)

FOSTER CARE HOMES
Adoption by foster parents (See **ADOPTION**)

FOSTER CARE HOMES—Cont.
Alienation of affection, cause of action against foster parent for   CC §43.56
Coerced debt   CC §§1798.97.1 to 1798.97.6
Community treatment facilities
    Placement review hearing   CRC 5.618
Definitions
    At risk of entering foster care   CRC 5.502
    Date child entered foster care   CRC 5.502
    Foster care   CRC 5.502
Delinquency jurisdiction
    Modification to transition jurisdiction, older than 17 years 5 months   CRC 5.811
Dependent child, placement in
    At risk of entering foster care defined   CRC 5.502
    Findings and orders of court, alternative dispositions
        Judicial council form for orders   CRCAppx A
    Hearings and continuances
        COVID-19, emergency rule   CRCAppx I Emer Rule 6
        Remote appearances   CRC 3.672
    Nonminor dependents, retention of jurisdiction   CRC 5.903
        Dismissal of dependency or transition jurisdiction and immediate resumption   CRC 5.570
        Disposition hearings   CRCAppx A
        Request for resumption of juvenile jurisdiction   CRC 5.906
    Out-of-county placements   CRC 5.614
        Judicial council legal forms   CRCAppx A
    Termination of juvenile court jurisdiction
        Nonminor dependents or wards in foster care   CRC 5.555
Discrimination in placement decision   Fam §7950
Education
    Change in placement affecting school of origin   CRC 5.651
    Educational and developmental services decisionmaking rights of children   CRC 5.651
Family finding and notice performed by social worker or probation officer   CRC 5.637
Foster family agency accountability   CCP §§1062.30 to 1062.34
    Applicability of provisions   CCP §1062.30
    Definitions   CCP §1062.32
    Indemnification void   CCP §1062.33
    Legislative findings   CCP §1062.31
    Liability   CCP §1062.33
    Public policy   CCP §1062.31
    Repeal of provisions   CCP §1062.34
Hearings and continuances
    COVID-19, emergency rule   CRCAppx I Emer Rule 6
Home study of prospective parents
    Interstate situations   Fam §§7901.1, 7906.5
Indian children
    Involuntary placements
        Indian Child Welfare Act, rules governing   CRC 5.480 to 5.488
        (See **INDIAN CHILD WELFARE ACT INVOLUNTARY PLACEMENTS**)
    Temporary custody of Indian child, agreement   CRCAppx A
Interstate Compact on Placement of Children   CRC 5.616, Fam §§7900 to 7913
    Children covered by compact   Fam §7907.5
    Home environment study request from another state   Fam §7901.1
        Interstate situations   Fam §7906.5
Intestate succession provisions, establishing parent-child relationship under   Pro §6454
Juvenile wardship proceedings
    Approaching majority   CRC 5.812
    Child at risk of entering foster care, notices to relatives
        Family finding and notice performed by social worker or probation officer   CRC 5.637
    Family-finding determination where risk of entry to foster care   CRC 5.790
    Termination of juvenile court jurisdiction
        Nonminor dependents or wards in foster care   CRC 5.555
Medi-Cal eligibility
    Specialty mental health services
        Judicial council legal forms   CRCAppx A
        Presumptive transfer of responsibility for services upon change of child placement, waiver proceedings   CRC 5.647
Minor's right to make statement regarding placement   Fam §7952
Out-of-state placements
    Intercounty placements generally   CRC 5.614
        Judicial council legal forms   CRCAppx A
    Out-of-county placements generally   CRC 5.614
        Judicial council legal forms   CRCAppx A
    Residential facilities   Fam §§7910, 7911
        Investigation of threats to child health or safety   Fam §7911.1
        Licensing of facilities   Fam §7911.1

FOSTER CARE HOMES—Cont.
Placement considerations
    Postpermanency status review hearings   CRC 5.810
Probation departments, county
    Reasonable efforts determinations
        COVID-19, emergency rule   CRCAppx I Emer Rule 7
Reasonable efforts determinations
    COVID-19, emergency rule   CRCAppx I Emer Rule 7
Relative, preference for placement with   Fam §7950
Review hearings
    Termination of jurisdiction   CRC 5.812
Security freezes, credit reports
    Protected consumer security freezes   CC §§1785.11.9 to 1785.11.11
Short term placements
    Residential therapeutic programs, short-term placements
        Placement review hearing   CRC 5.618
    Statutory criteria inapplicable   Fam §7951
Termination of parental rights
    Child in foster care for 15 of last 22 months   CRC 5.820
    Orders
        Judicial council form   CRCAppx A
Transition jurisdiction
    Modification from delinquency jurisdiction to transition jurisdiction, older than 17 years 5 months   CRC 5.811

FOUNDRIES
Lien of proprietor of   CC §3051

FOUR YEARS (See **STATUTES OF LIMITATION**)

FOWL (See **POULTRY**)

FRANCHISES
Discrimination by   CC §51.8
Eminent domain (See **EMINENT DOMAIN**)
Enforcement of judgments (See **ENFORCEMENT OF JUDGMENTS**)
Seller assisted marketing plans   CC §1812.201
Usurpation of franchise   CCP §§802 to 811

FRANCHISE TAX BOARD
Social security numbers
    Public posting or display
        Implementation of provisions   CC §1798.85

FRATERNAL ORGANIZATIONS
Charitable aid exempt for purposes of enforcement of judgments   CCP §704.170
Judge's office in organization not a financial interest for purposes of disqualification   CCP §170.5

FRAUD
Accrual of cause of action   CCP §338
Administrator (See **EXECUTORS AND ADMINISTRATORS**)
Agent, fraudulent acts by   CC §2306
Aircraft liens, loss by fraud   CCP §§1208.64, 1208.69
Annulment, grounds for   Fam §2210
Arbitration awards   CCP §1286.2
Attorney professional conduct
    Professional misconduct, conduct constituting   ProfC 8.4
Attorneys, participation in fraud
    Discovery of attorney work product
        Not protected   CCP §2018.050
Automobile, loss by fraud of possessory lien on   CC §3070
Claims against government, false
    Filing false claims act records under seal   CRC 2.570 to 2.573
Conservators
    Fraud detection investigations   Pro §2620.1
Consumer credit reporting
    Security alerts (See **CREDIT REPORTING**)
    Security freezes (See **CREDIT REPORTING**)
Contracts (See **CONTRACTS AND AGREEMENTS**)
Credit services organizations
    Personal information
        Protection of personal information   CC §1789.135
Damages
    Exemplary damages   CC §3294
    Liability for   CC §1709
    Measure of   CC §3343
Dance studio contracts   CC §1812.60
Dating services   CC §1694.4
Debts
    Coerced debt   CC §§1798.97.1 to 1798.97.6

FRAUD—Cont.
  Debts—Cont.
    Effect of fraud   CC §3431
  Decedent's estate, sale of assets of (See **EXECUTORS AND ADMINISTRATORS**)
  Deeds (See **DEEDS**)
  Discount buying services contracts   CC §§1812.100, 1812.106
  Donative transfers
    Presumption of fraud or undue influence   Pro §§21360 to 21392 (See **DONATIVE TRANSFERS**)
  Electronic recording delivery systems
    Action for relief from voidable transactions   Gov §27396
  Elements of actionable fraud   CC §1710
  Emancipation of minors, fraud in obtaining declaration of   Fam §7130
  Employment agencies, deceptive practices by   CC §§1812.508, 1812.523
  Employment counseling services, deceptive practices by   CC §§1812.513, 1812.523
  Equalization, state board
    Burden of proof
      Tax evasion or fraud cases   Ev §524
  Exculpatory provisions for   CC §1668
  Executor (See **EXECUTORS AND ADMINISTRATORS**)
  Expedited jury trials
    Post-trial motions   CCP §630.09
  Facts asserted, actionable fraud based on   CC §1710
  Fraudulent transfers (See **VOIDABLE TRANSACTIONS**)
  Guardian and ward
    Fraud detection investigations   Pro §2620.1
  Health care providers, proof of fraud tolling statutes of limitation for actions against   CCP §340.5
  Health studios services contracts   CC §1812.92
  Insurance (See **INSURANCE**)
  Intent to defraud
    Public, intent to defraud   CC §1711
    Serial numbers destroyed or altered for purpose of   CC §1710.1
  Involuntary trusts arising from   CC §§2223, 2224
    Attorney general actions
      Statute of limitations   CC §2224.5
  Job listing services, deceptive practices by   CC §§1812.520, 1812.523
  Judicial Council to develop and approve pleading forms   CCP §425.12
  Latent deficiencies in planning or construction of improvement to real property, applicability of statutes of limitation in actions arising from   CCP §337.15
  Limitation of actions (See within this heading, "**Statutes of limitation**")
  Marital privilege in proceedings involving   Ev §§956, 981
  Mechanics' liens
    Stop payment notices, false   CC §8504
    Public works   CC §9454
  Mortgage loans obtained by fraudulent conduct of borrower, action to recover   CCP §726
  Nonprofit corporations liable for fraudulent inducement of independent retailers to join cooperative association providing wholesale goods and services to members   CC §3343.7
  Nurses' registries, deceptive practices by   CC §§1812.523, 1812.533
  Parentage
    Voluntary declaration of parentage
      Challenge of declaration based on fraud, duress or material mistake of fact   Fam §7576
  Privileged communications
    Attorney referral service-client privilege
      Use of service to perpetrate fraud or crime   Ev §968
  Public employee's fraud, corruption or malice, indemnification of public entity for act or omission due to   Gov §825.6
  Public, intent to defraud   CC §1711
  Real Estate Fraud Prosecution Trust Fund distributions for purpose of prosecuting real estate fraud crimes   Gov §27388
  Rent control ordinances, fraudulent eviction of tenant based on owner's reoccupation of tenant's unit subject to   CC §1947.10
  Repayment to county of moneys fraudulently obtained, applicability of waiver provision to statutes of limitation on   CCP §340.5
  Rescission of contract grounded on   CC §1689, CCP §337
  Restoration of wife's former name denied on basis of   Fam §2081
  Return of property obtained without consent   CC §§1712, 1713
  Seller assisted marketing plans   CC §§1812.200 to 1812.221
  Serial number destroyed or altered for purpose of   CC §1710.1
  Small estates without administration (See **SMALL ESTATES WITHOUT ADMINISTRATION**)
  Specific performance (See **SPECIFIC PERFORMANCE**)
  Statute of frauds (See **STATUTE OF FRAUDS**)
  Statutes of limitation
    Decedent's estate, fraudulent sale of assets of   Pro §10382

FRAUD—Cont.
  Statutes of limitation—Cont.
    Health care providers, proof of fraud tolling statutes of limitation for actions against   CCP §340.5
    Latent deficiencies in planning or construction of improvement to real property   CCP §337.15
    Relief on grounds of fraud or mistake   CCP §338
    Repayment to county of moneys fraudulently obtained, applicability of waiver provision to   CCP §340.5
    Rescission of contract grounded on fraud or misrepresentation, running of statute of limitation for   CCP §337
  Transfer on death deeds
    Fraud, undue influence, etc, creation of deed
      Applicability of other provisions penalizing conduct   Pro §5698
  Tribal court civil money judgment act
    Objections
      Grounds for objection   CCP §1737
  Trust deed loans obtained by fraudulent conduct of borrower, action to recover   CCP §726
  Trusts (See **TRUSTS**)
  Unsoundness of mind presumed if unable to manage financial resources or resist fraud or undue influence   CC §39
  Voidable transactions (See **VOIDABLE TRANSACTIONS**)
  Weight loss programs   CC §1694.9

FRAUDS, STATUTE OF (See **STATUTE OF FRAUDS**)

FRAUDULENT TRANSFERS
Voidable transactions generally (See **VOIDABLE TRANSACTIONS**)

FREEDOM FROM PARENTAL CUSTODY AND CONTROL (See **TERMINATION OF PARENTAL RIGHTS**)

FREEDOM OF INFORMATION ACT (See **INFORMATION PRACTICES ACT**)

FREEDOM OF SPEECH (See **FIRST AMENDMENT RIGHTS**)

FREEWAYS (See **STREETS AND HIGHWAYS**)

FREIGHT
Generally (See **COMMON CARRIERS**)
Discount buying organization disclosing charges   CC §1812.106

FREIGHT MOTOR CARRIERS (See **MOTOR CARRIERS**)

FRIEND OF COURT, OFFICE OF
Child custody and visitation enforcement   Fam §§10101 to 10102

FRINGE BENEFITS
Attachment, exemption from   CCP §486.060
Retirement (See **RETIREMENT**)

FRIVOLOUS ACTIONS OR TACTICS
Appellate rules, superior court appeals
  Sanctions   CRC 8.891
Attorney professional conduct
  Probable cause to bring or defend claim   ProfC 3.1
Coerced debt
  Establishing debt as coerced, action or cross-complaint   CC §1798.97.3
Sanctions, award of (See **SANCTIONS**)
Vexatious litigant engaging in   CCP §391

FULL DISCLOSURE (See **DISCLOSURE**)

FULL FAITH AND CREDIT
Divorce obtained in other state by parties domiciled in California   Fam §2093
Marriage
  Valid out of state marriages recognized in California   Fam §308
Parentage
  Determinations   Fam §5604
  Voluntary declaration of parentage   Fam §7573
Uniform Child Custody Jurisdiction and Enforcement Act, provision of   Fam §3453

FUNDS AND FUNDING
Child support enforcement agencies   Fam §§17555, 17701 to 17714
Escheat of funds, exemption from   CCP §1502
Family mediation and conciliation services   Fam §1852
Institutional funds
  Uniform prudent management of institutional funds act   Pro §§18501 to 18510 (See **INSTITUTIONAL FUNDS MANAGEMENT**)

FUNDS AND FUNDING—Cont.
Public benefit trust fund   CC §3294.5
Unclaimed property fund (See **UNCLAIMED PROPERTY**)
Withdrawal of legal service agency attorney for indigent client when pubic funding reduced   CCP §285.2

FUNERALS
Administration of decedent's estate, priority of funeral expenses as debt of   Pro §§11420, 11421
Community property, funeral expenses as liability of   Pro §11446
Conservatorship as liable for funeral expenses   Pro §2631
Executor paying funeral expenses prior to appointment   Pro §8400
Guardianship as liable for funeral expenses   Pro §2631
Preneed contracts and trust funds
    Escheat of unclaimed funds maintained in preneed funeral trust   CCP §1518.5
        Reimbursement of holder upon submission of death certificate   CCP §1560
Public administrator (See **PUBLIC ADMINISTRATORS**)
Safe deposit box, access rights for removal of decedent's funeral instructions from   Pro §331
Trust estate of deceased settlor, claim for funeral expenses against   Pro §19326

FURNITURE
Apartment house keeper's lien, exemption from   CC §1861a
Attachments, use of furniture determining wrongful attachment   CCP §490.010
Lien for work on   CC §3066
Surviving spouse having possession of   Pro §6500
Unassembled furniture, advertising for   CC §1770
Waterbeds, tenants' possession of   CC §1940.5

FURTHERANCE OF JUSTICE (See **ENDS OF JUSTICE**)

FUTURE EARNINGS
Assignment for benefit of creditors, compensatory payments exempt from   CCP §1801

FUTURE ESTATES AND INTERESTS
Generally   CC §688
Accumulations   CC §§722 to 726
Alternative interests   CC §696
Conditional estates (See **CONDITIONAL ESTATES**)
Conditions precedent (See **CONDITIONS PRECEDENT**)
Conditions subsequent (See **CONDITIONS SUBSEQUENT**)
Contingency, effect of improbability of   CC §697
Creation of estate on contingency   CC §773
Definition   CC §690
Determinable interests   CC §§739 to 741
Easements, rights under   CC §808
Expectancy excluded   CC §700
Guardian ad litem appointed for unascertained persons legally or equitably interested in property   CCP §373.5
Heirs, taking by   CC §§698, 699
Income during suspended alienation   CC §733
Life estates (See **LIFE ESTATES**)
Notification requirements for beneficiaries with   Pro §15804
Partition costs, apportionment of   CCP §874.050
Perpetuities and restraints on alienation (See **PERPETUITIES AND RESTRAINTS ON ALIENATION**)
Possession taken at future time   CC §767
Possibility of reverter   CC §1045
Posthumous children   CC §§698, 739
Power of appointment affecting vesting of   CC §§781, 1387.1
Remainders (See **REMAINDERS**)
Restraints on alienation (See **PERPETUITIES AND RESTRAINTS ON ALIENATION**)
Reversion (See **REVERSION**)
Statutory recognition   CC §703
30 years after execution of instrument, invalidity of lease if possession does not commence within   CC §715
Time of creating   CC §749
Transfer   CC §699

G

GAMBLING
Inspection warrants, authorization for   CCP §1822.60
Native Americans
    Injunction to protect gaming rights   CCP §1811
Public nuisance, attorney's fees recoverable for enjoining use of building for illegal gambling as   CC §3496

GANG VIOLENCE
Decedent's sworn statement
    Administration and certification of oath   Ev §1231.2
    Admissibility under hearsay rule, generally   Ev §1231
    Jury instructions concerning unavailability of witness   Ev §1231.4
    Notice of intent to offer statement, requirement for   Ev §1231.1
    Peace officer testifying concerning statement, qualifications of   Ev §1231.3
Injunction for relief from   CCP §527.7
Shared gang databases
    Appeal of designation
        Proceedings for review   CRC 3.2300

GARAGES (See **PARKING FACILITIES**)

GARBAGE
Leases premises, disposal of garbage from   CC §§1941.1, 1941.2

GARNISHMENT
Accounting report from levying officer   CCP §706.026
Applicable law governing   CCP §706.020
Application for earnings withholding order
    Generally   CCP §706.102
    Contents of   CCP §706.121
    Process server, application for issuance of withholding order by   CCP §706.108
Child support
    Earnings assignment for support (See **EARNINGS ASSIGNMENT FOR SUPPORT**)
    Priority of withholding orders   CCP §706.030
    Withholding order for support (See within this heading, **"Withholding order for support"**)
Consumer Credit Protection Act of 1968 affecting   CCP §706.151
Costs
    Court order or memorandum of costs allowing additional costs as part of   CCP §685.090
    Final earnings withholding order to collect unsatisfied costs and interests   CCP §706.028
Court order for withholding order against earnings of spouse   CCP §706.109
Creation of lien on earnings   CCP §706.029
Definitions   CCP §706.011
Dismissal of employee, restrictions on   Pro §3088
Disposable earnings
    Defined   CCP §706.011
    Maximum amount of disposable earnings   CCP §706.050
Distribution when levy less than wage claims   CCP §1208
Duration of lien on earnings   CCP §706.029
Duties and instruction of employers
    Generally   CCP §§706.022, 706.104
    Form of instructions   CCP §706.127
    General requirements for service of documents on employer   CCP §706.103
    Violation of employer, failure to withhold or pay over constituting   CCP §§706.152 to 706.154
Duties of levying officer   CCP §706.026
Earnings assignment for support (See **EARNINGS ASSIGNMENT FOR SUPPORT**)
Earnings withholding order
    Amount required from employer to satisfy   CCP §706.024
    Application for (See within this heading, **"Application for earnings withholding order"**)
    Contents of   CCP §706.125
    Costs and interest, judgment creditor seeking additional earnings withholding order for   CCP §706.028
    Deduction for employer from payments under order   CCP §706.034
    Earnings assignment for support, priority of   CCP §706.031
    Elder and dependent adult abuse cases
        Judicial council forms   CRCAppx A
    Exemptions generally (See within this heading, **"Exemptions"**)
    Interest not collected, final earnings withholding order for   CCP §706.028
    Levy of execution effective on service of   CCP §706.021
    Lien upon earnings, creation and duration of   CCP §706.029
    Multiple orders, effect of service of   CCP §706.023
    Notice to employer
        Generally   CCP §706.024
        Contents of   CCP §706.122
        Satisfaction of judgment   CCP §706.027
    Return of order
        By employer to levying officer   CCP §706.032
        Contents of employer's return   CCP §706.126
        Supplemental return by levying officer   CCP §706.033
    Return of writ of execution, effect on   CCP §699.560

GARNISHMENT—Cont.
  Earnings withholding order—Cont.
    Service and issuance of orders and exemption claims   CCP §§706.101 to 706.109
    State taxes (See within this heading, **"Tax liability"**)
    Support, withholding order for (See within this heading, **"Withholding order for support"**)
    Termination of order
      Employment termination of judgment debtor, effect of   CCP §706.032
      Exemption claims   CCP §706.105
      Order or assignment with higher priority, earnings of judgment debtor subject to   CCP §706.032
      Satisfaction of judgment   CCP §706.027
      Supplemental return by levying officer   CCP §706.033
  Elder or dependent adult financial abuse
    Earnings withholding orders
      Defined   CCP §706.011
      Priorities   CCP §706.023, CRCAppx A
  Equitable division of judgment debtor's earnings, motion for   CCP §706.052
  Exemptions
    Attorneys' fees for certain purposes not subject to exemption   CCP §706.051
    Judgment debtor's exemption claim, contents of   CCP §706.123
    Office of levying officer, prescribed forms available at   CCP §706.129
    Opposition to exemption claim, contents of notice of   CCP §706.128
    Personal services, unavailability of exemption   CCP §706.051
    Procedure for claim of   CCP §706.105
    Support of debtor or family, earnings necessary for   CCP §706.051
    Tax orders from state, unavailability of exemption   CCP §706.051
    Termination or modification of order   CCP §706.105
    Time for service of notice of hearing for claim of exemption   CCP §1005
    Withholding order for support, earnings exempt from   CCP §706.052
  Financial statement of judgment debtor
    Contents of   CCP §706.124
    Office of levying officer, prescribed forms available at   CCP §706.129
  Findings, requirement for   CCP §706.106
  Foreign-money claims   CCP §676.11
  Forms
    Generally   CCP §706.120
    Application for issuance of earnings withholding order   CCP §706.121
    General contents of earnings withholding order   CCP §706.125
    Instructions to employer   CCP §706.127
    Judgment debtor's exemption claim, contents of   CCP §706.123
    Judicial Council forms, prescribed usage of   CCP §706.120
    List of judicial council legal forms   CRCAppx A
    Return of employer   CCP §706.126
    State tax liability, forms for collection of   CCP §706.081
  Inapplicable provisions   CCP §684.310
  Interest accrued, final earnings withholding order for   CCP §706.028
  Jeopardy withholding order for taxes   CCP §706.078
  Judicial Council forms, prescribed usage of   CCP §706.120
  Labor claims against garnishee, priority and processing of   CCP §§1206 to 1208
  Levy of execution upon earnings of employee made by service of earnings withholding order   CCP §706.021
  Lien on earnings, creation and duration of   CCP §706.029
  Memorandum of garnishee
    Request, service and contents of   CCP §§488.610, 701.030
    Third party, liability of   CCP §§488.620, 701.035
  Multiple withholding orders, service on employer of   CCP §706.023
  Notices
    Earnings withholding order (See within this heading, **"Earnings withholding order"**)
    Exemption, contents of notice of opposition to claim of   CCP §706.128
    Taxes, issuance of withholding order for   CCP §706.072
    Time for service of notice of hearing for claim of exemption   CCP §1005
  Payment of withheld wages to levying officer   CCP §§706.025, 706.026
  Preference to wage claims   CCP §1206
  Priorities
    Earnings assignment order for support, priority over any earnings withholding order of   CCP §706.031
    Labor claims against garnishee   CCP §§1206 to 1208
    Withholding order for support, priority over other earnings withholding orders of   CCP §706.030
    Withholding order for taxes, priority of   CCP §706.077
  Process server, issuance of withholding order by   CCP §706.108
  Return of employer, contents of   CCP §706.126
  Review of taxpayer's liability   CCP §706.082
  Rulemaking authority   CCP §706.100

GARNISHMENT—Cont.
  Service
    General requirements for service of withholding orders and related documents   CCP §§706.080, 706.101, 706.103
    Levy of execution effective upon service of earnings withholding order   CCP §706.021
    Memorandum of garnishee   CCP §§488.610, 701.030
    Multiple withholding orders   CCP §706.023
    Process server, issuance of withholding order by   CCP §706.108
    Sheriff's fees for service of wage garnishment orders   Gov §26750
    Time for service of notice of hearing for claim of exemption   CCP §1005
  Sheriff's fees for service of wage garnishment orders   Gov §26750
  Spouse of judgment debtor, issuance of withholding order against earnings of   CCP §706.109
  State issuance and service of earnings withholding orders   CCP §706.101
  Support of debtor and family, exemption of earnings needed for   CCP §706.051
  Tax liability
    Generally   CCP §§706.071 to 706.073
    Definition   CCP §706.070
    Documents to be served on employer and taxpayer   CCP §706.075
    Forms prescribed by state   CCP §706.081
    Jeopardy withholding order for taxes   CCP §706.078
    Method of service   CCP §706.080
    Notice of proposed issuance of withholding order for taxes   CCP §706.072
    Period for withholding   CCP §706.078
    Priority of withholding orders   CCP §706.077
    Review of tax liability   CCP §706.082
    Right of state to issue earnings withholding order   CCP §706.074
    State tax orders
      Unavailability of exemption   CCP §706.051
    Substitution of other documents for withholding order   CCP §706.084
    Warrant or notice of levy, enforcement pursuant to   CCP §§688.010 to 688.050
  Termination of earnings withholding order (See within this heading, **"Earnings withholding order"**)
  Termination of order on satisfaction of judgment   CCP §706.027
  Verified denial of wage claim   CCP §1207
  Violation by employer, failure to withhold or pay over constituting   CCP §§706.152 to 706.154
  Withholding order for support
    Generally   CCP §706.030
    Earnings exempt from   CCP §706.052
    Employment Development Department information reviewed by Department of Child Support Services to identify employed obligors subject to withholding orders   Fam §17509
    Local child support agency's issuance and enforcement of withholding order   CCP §706.030
    Priority of withholding orders   CCP §§706.030, 706.031
  Withholding period   CCP §706.022

GAS AND OIL (See **OIL AND GAS**)

GAS COMPANIES
  Credit cards
    Surcharge on credit card transaction, prohibition against
      Exception for electrical, gas or water corporation   CC §1748.1
  Debit cards
    Surcharge on debit card transaction, prohibition against
      Exception for electrical, gas or water corporation   CC §1748.1
  Diversion or tampering with gas services, action for   CC §§1882 to 1882.6
  Landlord and tenant (See **LANDLORD AND TENANT**)
  Privacy of customer electrical or natural gas usage data   CC §1798.98
    Actions and other remedies of customer   CC §1798.99
  Repairs or service during specified time period where subscriber's presence required, liability for failure to provide   CC §1722
  Unruh Civil Rights Act   CC §§51, 52

GASOLINE STATIONS
  Emission controls, standards for   CC §1952.8
  Unlawful detainer action against   CC §1754

GASOLINE TAX
  Decedent's estate, claims against   Pro §§9200 to 9205

GATED COMMUNITIES
  Service of papers or subpoena, access for   CCP §415.21

GAY MARRIAGE BAN
  Recognition of certain same sex marriages contracted in other jurisdictions
    Dissolution, annulment or legal separation, jurisdiction   Fam §2010
      Residence requirements   Fam §2320

GAY MARRIAGE BAN—Cont.
Repeal   Fam §300

GENDER
Change of gender, petition for
   Memorandum in support of petition not required   CRC 3.1114
Construction of words used in code   CCP §17
Damages, measure
   Lost earnings or impaired earning capacity
      Race, ethnicity or gender not to serve as basis for reduction in damages   CC §3361
Discrimination
   Judicial ethics code
      Administrative responsibilities of judge, impartial discharge   CRCSupp JudEthicsCanon 3
      Attorneys, judges to require to refrain from manifesting   CRCSupp JudEthicsCanon 3
      Bias, prejudice or harassment in performance of judicial duties   CRCSupp JudEthicsCanon 3
      Court personnel and staff under direction of judge, standards of conduct enforced by judge   CRCSupp JudEthicsCanon 3
      Membership in discriminatory organizations   CRCSupp JudEthicsCanon 2
   Notice
      Judicial council legal forms   CRCAppx A
Price differences for substantially similar goods based on gender of marketing audience   CC §51.14
Small business gender discrimination in pricing services   CC §§55.61 to 55.63
Jury service exemption based on sex, prohibition against   CCP §204

GENDER EXPRESSION
Child custody
   Best interest of child
      Prohibited considerations for best interest   Fam §§3011, 3020, 3040
Discrimination
   Judicial ethics code
      Administrative responsibilities of judge, impartial discharge   CRCSupp JudEthicsCanon 3
      Attorneys, judges to require to refrain from manifesting   CRCSupp JudEthicsCanon 3
      Bias, prejudice or harassment in performance of judicial duties   CRCSupp JudEthicsCanon 3
      Court personnel and staff under direction of judge, standards of conduct enforced by judge   CRCSupp JudEthicsCanon 3
      Membership in discriminatory organizations   CRCSupp JudEthicsCanon 2
Name change
   Conforming to gender identity   CCP §1277
      Objection to name change   CCP §1277.5
      Procedure   CCP §1277.5
      Publication of proceeding not required   CCP §1277.5
Uniform child custody jurisdiction and enforcement act
   Gender-affirming health care or mental health care
      Enforcement, effect of care   Fam §3453.5
      Jurisdiction, effect of care   Fam §§3421, 3424, 3427, 3428

GENDER IDENTITY
Child custody
   Best interest of child
      Prohibited considerations for best interest   Fam §§3011, 3020, 3040
Discrimination
   Judicial ethics code
      Administrative responsibilities of judge, impartial discharge   CRCSupp JudEthicsCanon 3
      Attorneys, judges to require to refrain from manifesting   CRCSupp JudEthicsCanon 3
      Bias, prejudice or harassment in performance of judicial duties   CRCSupp JudEthicsCanon 3
      Court personnel and staff under direction of judge, standards of conduct enforced by judge   CRCSupp JudEthicsCanon 3
      Membership in discriminatory organizations   CRCSupp JudEthicsCanon 2
Health care
   Medical information confidentiality
      Businesses organized to maintain medical information
         Limitation of access to information about gender affirming care, abortion, or contraception information   CC §56.101
      Gender-affirming health care or mental health care, restrictions on release of medical information   CC §56.109

GENDER IDENTITY—Cont.
Legally protected health care services   CC §§1798.300 to 1798.308
   Action for relief from abusive litigation infringing on protected activity   CC §1798.303
   Jurisdiction of court   CC §§1798.306, 1798.308
   Measure of damages   CC §1798.305
   Constitutional and statutory protections   CC §1798.301
   Definitions   CC §1798.300
   Foreign jurisdictions, interference with rights   CC §1798.302
   Laws governing   CC §1798.307
   Subpoena issued in connection with abusive litigation, motion to modify or quash   CC §1798.304
Medical information confidentiality
   Gender-affirming health care or mental health care
      Businesses organized to maintain medical information
         Limitation of access to information about gender affirming care, abortion, or contraception information   CC §56.101
      Restrictions on release of medical information   CC §56.109
Mental health care
   Medical information confidentiality
      Businesses organized to maintain medical information
         Limitation of access to information about gender affirming care, abortion, or contraception information   CC §56.101
      Gender-affirming health care or mental health care, restrictions on release of medical information   CC §56.109
Name change
   Conforming to gender identity   CCP §1277
      Objection to name change   CCP §1277.5
      Procedure   CCP §1277.5
      Publication of proceeding not required   CCP §1277.5
Uniform child custody jurisdiction and enforcement act
   Gender-affirming health care or mental health care
      Enforcement, effect of care   Fam §3453.5
      Jurisdiction, effect of care   Fam §§3421, 3424, 3427, 3428

GENDER NEUTRAL RETAIL DEPARTMENTS
Childcare items
   Gender neutral section or area for display, retailer duties   CC §55.8
Legislative findings and declarations   CC §55.7
Toys
   Gender neutral section or area for display, retailer duties   CC §55.8

GENDER TAX REPEAL ACT OF 1995
Prohibiting price differences for like services based solely on gender   CC §51.6

GENDER VIOLENCE
Civil rights action for damages   CC §52.4

GENERAL DENIAL
Answer containing general or specific denial of material allegations   CCP §431.30
Property not exceeding $1000, action involving   CCP §431.40

GENERAL OBLIGATION BONDS (See **BONDS**)

GENERAL POWER OF APPOINTMENT (See **POWER OF APPOINTMENT**)

GENERATION-SKIPPING TRANSFER TAX
Generally   Pro §20210
Additions and reductions to tax payable   Pro §20212
Applicability of law   Pro §20201
Capacity to bring suit   Pro §20220
Corpus of trust, payments from   Pro §20213
Definitions   Pro §20200
Income beneficiary, tax liability of   Pro §20213
Judicial proceedings
   Generally   Pro §20220
   Notice of hearing   Pro §20222
   Orders   Pro §§20223, 20224
   Out-of-state proration, enforcement of   Pro §20225
   Petition   Pro §20221
Life estates, interests in property involving   Pro §20213
Manner of proration of   Pro §20211
Reimbursements, trustee's right to   Pro §20215
Tenancy for years, interests in property involving   Pro §20213
Trustee
   Capacity to bring suit   Pro §20220
   Property not in possession, tax liability for   Pro §20214
   Reimbursement, right to   Pro §20215

GENETIC INFORMATION
Adoption proceedings, blood samples provided by biological parents in course of (See **ADOPTION**)
Disclosure of test results for genetic characteristics   CC §56.17
Discrimination based on genetic information prohibited   CC §51
Paternity actions (See **PATERNITY**)
Privacy
    Genetic privacy generally   CC §§56.18 to 56.186 (See **GENETIC PRIVACY**)
Uniform parentage act
    Right to genetic testing   Fam §7635.5
    Vacation or setting aside of judgment   Fam §7647.7
        Child support enforcement agency involvement, provision of genetic testing   Fam §7648.2
        Prior genetic testing, prohibition on vacating or setting aside judgment based on   Fam §7648.3
Wrongful life, no cause of action for   CC §43.6

GENETIC PRIVACY   CC §§56.18 to 56.186
Citation of provisions   CC §56.18
Conflict of laws
    Effect of provisions on other laws   CC §56.184
Definitions   CC §56.18
Direct-to-consumer genetic testing companies
    Defined   CC §56.18
    Express consent
        Requirement to obtain from consumer   CC §56.181
    Safeguarding privacy by companies
        Duties   CC §56.181
Severability of provisions   CC §56.186
Short title of provisions   CC §56.18
Statutory construction of provisions   CC §§56.184, 56.186
Violations of provisions
    Punishments   CC §56.182

GENOCIDE
Attorney's fees
    Assault and battery, wrongful death, etc constituting torture, genocide, crimes against humanity, etc   CCP §354.8
Statutes of limitations
    Assault and battery, wrongful death, etc constituting torture, genocide, crimes against humanity, etc   CCP §354.8

GENOCIDE REMEMBRANCE DAY
Judicial holidays, excluded from days designated as   CCP §135

GEOLOGISTS
Indemnity agreements for hazardous materials identification   CC §2782.6

GIFT CERTIFICATES
Defined   CC §1749.45
Escheat provisions, applicability of   CCP §1520.5
Expiration dates, prohibition against   CC §1749.5
    Waiver of protections
        Void   CC §1749.51
Ownership of value   CC §1749.6
Prepaid calling cards
    Applicability of provisions   CC §1749.45

GIFTS
Ademption   Pro §§21131 to 21139
Arbitrators
    Ethics standards
        Refusal of gifts   CRC ArbEthicsStand 11
Attorney in fact, authority of   Pro §4264
Attorney professional conduct
    Gifts from client
        Law firms, imputation to all members of firm of violations of certain provisions   ProfC 1.8.11
        Restrictions   ProfC 1.8.3
Community property (See **COMMUNITY PROPERTY**)
Death, gifts in view of (See **DEATH**)
Definition   CC §1146
Delivery   CC §1147
Dispositions under will (See **WILL CONSTRUCTION**)
Donative transfers
    Presumption of fraud or undue influence   Pro §§21360 to 21392 (See **DONATIVE TRANSFERS**)
Exoneration   Pro §§21131 to 21139
Judges
    Acceptance by judge or family members   CRCSupp JudEthicsCanon 4

GIFTS—Cont.
Judges—Cont.
        Limitations on acceptance of gifts by   CCP §170.9
Judicial council
    Administrative director
        Gifts, acceptance   CRC 10.102
Marital deduction gifts (See **MARITAL DEDUCTION GIFTS**)
Marriage refusal, recovery of gifts after   CC §1590
Mediation
    Standards of conduct for mediators
        Compensation and gifts   CRC 3.859
Minors (See **UNIFORM TRANSFERS TO MINORS ACT**)
Quieting title action, admissibility of evidence in   CCP §764.020
Revocation   CC §1148
Stock (See **CORPORATE SHARES AND SHAREHOLDERS**)
Uniform prudent management of institutional funds act   Pro §§18501 to 18510 (See **INSTITUTIONAL FUNDS MANAGEMENT**)
Uniform Transfers to Minors Act (See **UNIFORM TRANSFERS TO MINORS ACT**)
Unsolicited goods   CC §§1584.5, 1584.6

GLASSWARE
Common carrier's liability for   CC §2200

GLOBAL POSITIONING SYSTEMS
Consumer privacy rights
    Personal information restrictions of persons at or near family planning center   CC §1798.99.90

GOATS
Dogs injuring   CC §3341

GOING BUSINESS (See **BUSINESS**)

GOING FORWARD, BURDEN OF (See **BURDEN OF GOING FORWARD**)

GOLD
Common carrier's liability for transporting   CC §2200

GOLDEN STATE ENERGY
Action for acquisition of PG&E property   CCP §1240.655

GOOD CAUSE
Attorney or law firm appointed to represent indigent client without compensation   CCP §285.4
Defined   CCP §116.130

GOOD FAITH
Agreed case   CCP §1138
Attorney's fee award in actions not filed in good faith   CCP §1021.7
Bona fide purchasers (See **BONA FIDE PURCHASERS**)
Consumer privacy rights
    California privacy protection agency
        Consideration by agency of good faith of business, service provider, contractor, etc   CC §1798.199.100
Contracts, performance in good faith   CC §1493
Decedents' estates, payment of claims of   Pro §11005
Fiduciary income and principal act   Pro §16325
Improver of property of another (See **GOOD FAITH IMPROVER**)
Landlord, bad faith retention of deposits by   CC §1950.7
Marital deduction gift provisions, election in good faith by fiduciary regarding   Pro §21526
Minor's disaffirmance of contract   Fam §6713
Performance of contract   CC §1493
Public entities (See **PUBLIC ENTITIES**)
Settlement entered into by plaintiff and joint tortfeasor, contest of good faith of   CCP §877.6
Settlements in good faith (See **SETTLEMENT AND COMPROMISE**)
Small estates without administration, good faith purchaser of real property subject to   Pro §13203
Spouse called as adverse witness   Ev §971
Temporary restraining order, good faith attempt to notify party of   CCP §527
Trusts (See **TRUSTS**)
Unpleaded cause, permission to assert   CCP §426.50
Will probate proceedings, complying in good faith with notice requirements for   Pro §8122
Writ of execution, property incorrectly levied upon under   CCP §699.090

GOOD FAITH IMPROVER
Amount in controversy, action for relief treated as unlimited civil case regardless of   CCP §871.3
Authority to adjust rights, equities and interests   CCP §871.5

GOOD FAITH IMPROVER—Cont.
Burden to establish relief   CCP §871.3
Defined   CCP §871.1
Encroachment on adjoining land   CCP §871.6
Public entity or use, nonapplicability to   CCP §871.7
Removal of improvements as alternative remedy   CCP §871.4
Setoff
   Alternative remedy   CCP §871.4
   Withholding property, value of improvements set off against damages for   CCP §741
Statutes of limitation   CCP §340

GOODWILL
Ownership of   CC §655
Value   CCP §§1263.510 to 1263.530

GOUGING
Rent gouging
   Landlord and tenant
      Increase of gross rental rate on residential real property, limitations   CC §§1947.12, 1947.13

GOVERNMENTAL ENTITIES (See **PUBLIC ENTITIES**)

GOVERNMENT CLAIMS ACT (See **CLAIMS AGAINST PUBLIC ENTITIES AND EMPLOYEES**)

GOVERNOR
Administrative Procedure Act (See **ADMINISTRATIVE PROCEDURE ACT**)
Commissioners appointed by Governor acknowledging instruments   CC §§1182, 1183
Small claims advisory committee, appointments to   CCP §116.950
White Cane Safety Day, proclamation of   CC §54.5

GRAFFITI
Admissibility as evidence   Ev §1410.5
Aerosol paint containers sold to minor
   Verification of age for sale of age-restricted products   CC §1798.99.1

GRAIN
Barley (See **BARLEY**)
Bins   CC §§1880 to 1881.2
Oats (See **OATS**)
Storage in bulk after sale of   CC §§1880 to 1881.2

GRAIN ELEVATORS
Storage regulated   CC §§1880 to 1881.2

GRANDCHILDREN
Administrator, priority for serving as   Pro §8461
Support of grandchild   Fam §3930
Visitation rights   Fam §§3102 to 3104, 3171, 3176, 3185

GRAND JURIES
Applicability of Evidence Code   Ev §300
Demographic data on regular grand jurors, gathering and summarizing   CRC 10.625
Judicial council guidelines for selection of regular grand jury   CRC JudAdminStand 10.50
Jury service, persons serving as grand jurors ineligible for   CCP §203
Regular jurors
   Demographic data on regular grand jurors, gathering and summarizing   CRC 10.625
Selection of jurors   CRC JudAdminStand 10.50
Types of juries   CCP §193
Witness fees for attendance   Gov §68094

GRANDPARENTS
Visitation rights
   Dependent children   CRC 5.695

GRANTS OF LAND
Burden of proof in disputes involving state   Ev §523
Disclosure of written evidence in disputes involving state   CCP §2031.510
Statutes of limitation on actions for recovery of real property   CCP §§316, 317

GRANTS OF MONEY
Claims against public entities and employees
   Late payment by state agencies   Gov §927.1
Judicial council administering grants program   Fam §1850

GRAVEYARDS (See **CEMETERIES**)

GRAZING (See **PASTURES**)

GREAT BODILY INJURY OR HARM
Aggravation, circumstances in   CRC 4.421

GREENWAY EASEMENTS   CC §§816.50 to 816.66
Adjacent
   Defined   CC §816.52
Conflict of laws
   Effect of other provisions   CC §816.64
Definitions   CC §816.52
Duration of easement   CC §816.54
Enforcement of easement   CC §816.62
Entities permitted to acquire and hold easement   CC §816.56
Greenway defined   CC §816.52
Instruments creating or transferring easement
   Characteristics of easement specified in instrument   CC §816.54
   Recordation   CC §816.60
   Retention by grantor of interests not conveyed by instrument   CC §816.58
Interest in real property
   Nature of greenway easements   CC §816.54
Legislative findings and intent   CC §816.50
Local agency
   Defined   CC §816.52
Privity
   Enforcement of easement not affected by lack of privity   CC §816.62
Property tax assessments
   Enforceable restrictions, consideration in assessment
      Easement as enforceable restriction   CC §816.66
Tax exempt nonprofit organizations
   Entities permitted to acquire and hold easement   CC §816.56
Urbanized areas
   Defined   CC §816.52
Urban waterways
   Defined   CC §816.52

GREY MARKET GOODS
Advertising requirements for   CC §1797.82
Credit on purchase, buyer's right to   CC §1797.85
Definitions   CC §1797.8
Governing law   CC §1797.84
Language used for disclosures, reasonableness of   CC §1797.83
Refund, buyer's right to   CC §1797.85
Retail seller
   Disclosure requirements by   CC §1797.81
   Liability to buyer   CC §1797.85
   Unfair competition, violation by retail seller as   CC §1797.86
Unfair competition, violation by retail seller as   CC §1797.86

GROCERY STORES
Automatic checkout systems   CC §§7100 to 7106
Supermarket club cards
   Citation of Act   CC §1749.60
   Definitions   CC §1749.61
   Dissemination of personal identification information, restrictions on   CC §1749.65
   Driver's license number, prohibition against requirement in application for   CC §1749.64
   Marketing information, conditions for transfer or sale of   CC §1749.65
   Social security number, prohibition against requirement in application for   CC §1749.64
   Unfair competition, violations as   CC §1749.63
   Waiver of protections   CC §1749.66

GROUNDWATER RIGHTS ACTIONS   CCP §§830 to 852
Basins
   Defined   CCP §832
Boundaries of basin   CCP §841
Case management conference   CCP §840
Complaints
   Contact information of persons reporting extractions
      Plaintiff request of information following approval of notice   CCP §836.5
   Defined   CCP §832
   Notice   CCP §835
      Lodging other notice materials with court   CCP §836
Comprehensive adjudications
   Applicability of provisions   CCP §833
   Applicable provisions   CCP §831
   Complex actions
      Presumption that comprehensive adjudication is complex action   CCP §838
   Court's authority   CCP §834

GROUNDWATER RIGHTS ACTIONS—Cont.
Comprehensive adjudications—Cont.
    Defined   CCP §832
    Determination whether action is for comprehensive adjudication   CCP §838
    Intervention in comprehensive adjudication
        Local government intervention   CCP §837
        State intervention   CCP §837.5
    Notice of complaint   CCP §835
        Lodging other notice materials with court   CCP §836
    Parties
        Disclosures of parties appearing   CCP §842
    Physical solution
        Court's authority to impose   CCP §849
    Stay   CCP §848
Condition of long-term overdraft
    Defined   CCP §832
Definitions   CCP §832
Disqualification of judges   CCP §838
Expert witnesses
    Defined   CCP §832
    Identity of experts and other disclosures   CCP §843
Groundwater
    Defined   CCP §832
Groundwater extraction facilities
    Defined   CCP §832
Groundwater recharge
    Defined   CCP §832
Intervention in comprehensive adjudication
    Local government intervention   CCP §837
    State intervention   CCP §837.5
Judges   CCP §838
Judgments
    Binding nature of judgment on successors in interest   CCP §851
    Continuing jurisdiction to amend, modify, etc   CCP §852
    Findings by court   CCP §850
Legislative intent   CCP §830
Long-term overdrafts
    Evidence   CCP §847
    Injunctions   CCP §847
Masters
    Special masters
        Appointment   CCP §845
        Report of special master   CCP §846
Parties
    Disclosures of parties appearing   CCP §842
Person
    Defined   CCP §832
Physical solution
    Court's authority to impose   CCP §849
Plaintiffs
    Defined   CCP §832
Pleadings and papers
    Electronic service   CCP §839
Public water systems
    Defined   CCP §832
State small water systems
    Defined   CCP §832
Statutory construction   CCP §830
Sustainable groundwater management act
    Defined   CCP §832
Water resources department
    Definition of department   CCP §832
Written testimony by affidavit or declaration   CCP §844

GROUNDWATER SUSTAINABILITY AGENCIES
Groundwater rights actions
    Intervention in comprehensive adjudication   CCP §837

GUAM
Acknowledgment of instruments   CC §1183.5

GUARANTEED ASSET PROTECTION (GAP) INSURANCE
Automobile sales finance
    Conditional sales contracts
        Offer, sale, etc, of guaranteed asset protection waiver in connection with contract   CC §§2982.12, 2983.1
    Definition of guaranteed asset protection waiver   CC §2981
    Disclosures   CC §§2982, 2982.2

GUARANTORS (See **SURETYSHIP, BONDS AND UNDERTAKINGS**)

GUARANTY OF TITLE
Statutes of limitation on actions founded upon contract or obligation evidenced by CCP §339

GUARDIAN AD LITEM
Appearance of minor, conservatee or person lacking legal capacity   CCP §372
Appointment
    Application to appoint
        Form   CRCAppx A (CRCFL-935)
        Memorandum not required   CRC 3.1114
    Legal competence for decisions lacking, representation   CCP §§372, 373
    Order for appointment   CRCAppxs A (CRCFL-935), (CRCFL-935, CRCFL-936)
    Pseudonym, appointment under   CCP §372.5
Compromise claims, power to   CCP §§372, 373.5
Decedents' estates
    Accounting
        Waiver of accounting   CRC 7.550
    Disclosures   Pro §1003
Dependent children
    Child abuse prevention and treatment act (CAPTA) guardians ad litem   CRC 5.662
Disclaimer of interest   Pro §§260 to 295
Dissolution of marriage proceedings, representation of incapacitated spouse in   Fam §2332
Domestic violence
    Minors' appearances to obtain protective orders
        Appearance of minor under 12 to request or oppose temporary order   Fam §6229
Domestic violence protective order or injunction, minor party to proceedings for   CCP §§372, 374
Expenses of guardian ad litem, payment of   CCP §373.5
Harassment or violence, minor party to proceedings to restrain or enjoin   CCP §§372, 374
    Minors' appearances to obtain protective orders
        Appearance of minor under 12 to request or oppose temporary order   Fam §6229
Incapacity of spouse   Fam §2332
Parentage
    Actions to determine parent and child relationship   Fam §7635
Powers of   CCP §§372, 373.5
Procedure for appointment   CCP §373
Pseudonym, appointment under   CCP §372.5
Quieting title action   CCP §762.080
Small claims actions, appointment in   CCP §116.410
Trusts (See **TRUSTS**)
Unborn or unascertained persons, appointment for   CCP §373.5
Uniform parentage act
    Action to determine parent and child relationship   Fam §7635
    Vacation or setting aside of judgment
        Best interest of child, appointment to represent   Fam §7647.5

GUARDIAN AND WARD   Pro §§1400 to 1491, 2110 to 2113
Abuse of minor, screening guardian-nominee's name for prior referrals for   Pro §1516
Accounts of guardians   CRC 7.575, Pro §§1060 to 1064, 2620
    Account statement
        Format   Pro §2620
    Allowances to wards   Pro §2421
    Approval, petition for   Pro §1064
    Attorney presenting account of estate on death of guardian   Pro §2632
    Blocked accounts   Pro §2328
    Compensation, allowance for   Pro §2623
    Contents   Pro §§1061 to 1063
    Death of ward   Pro §§2620, 2630 to 2631
    Death or disability of guardian   Pro §§2630, 2632
    Exhausted estate   Pro §2626
    Expenses, allowance for   Pro §2623
    Failure to file   Pro §2620.2
    Final account or report
        Resignation or removal of guardian, service of copy after   CRC 7.1005
        Termination of guardianship, service of copy of   CRC 7.1006
    Form, development of   Pro §2620
        Judicial council forms   CRC 7.575, CRCAppx A
    Fraud detection investigations   Pro §2620.1
    Funeral expenses   Pro §2631
    Guardian defined   Pro §2600
    Incapacity of guardian   Pro §2632
    Jurisdiction retained for   Pro §2630
    Last illness, expenses of   Pro §2631

GUARDIAN AND WARD—Cont.
Accounts of guardians —Cont.
- Majority of ward   Pro §2627
- Notice re hearing on   Pro §2621
- Objections
  - Generally   Pro §§2622, 2622.5
  - Surety, notice to   Pro §1213
- Personal representative's incorporation by reference of guardian's accounting   Pro §10902
- Purchases, court review of   Pro §2625
- Reimbursement of guardians, allowance for   Pro §2623
- Remaining assets after death, transfer of   Pro §2631
- Salary of ward   Pro §2601
- Sales, court review of   Pro §2625
- Sanctions for bad-faith objections   Pro §2622.5
- Savings and loan associations
  - Definitions   Pro §1490
  - Deposit of funds generally (See within this heading, **"Deposit of funds"**)
  - Surety bond of guardian, funds in blocked account excluded in determining   Pro §2328
- Settlement and release by former minor   CRC 7.1007
- Small estates receiving public assistance   Pro §2628
- Supporting documentation   Pro §2620
- Temporary guardians   Pro §2256
- Termination of relationship   Pro §§2630 to 2633
- Transactions, court review of   Pro §2625
- Veterans Administration, notice requirement for   Pro §1461.5
- Waiver of accounting, request and order
  - Forms, judicial council   CRCAppx A
- Welfare payments, when estate consists of   Pro §2628

Accounts of ward
- Opening or changing name on accounts, responsibilities of guardian   CRC 7.1011

Actions by and against
- Fee waivers, civil actions on behalf of conservatee or ward   CRC 7.5
- Ward's behalf, guardian maintaining action   CCP §§372, 376

Administration of decedent's estate
- Appointment of guardian as administrator   Pro §§8464, 8469
- Service of notice on guardian   Pro §1210

Adoption
- Child free from parental custody and control
  - Proceeding to declare   Pro §1516.5
- Disclosure in guardianship petition concerning intention to adopt proposed ward   Pro §1510
- Investigative report for nonrelative guardianship   Pro §1543
- Petition for adoption   Fam §8802
- Termination of guardianship by adoption of ward   Pro §1600

Advance health care directive under Health Care Decisions Law, guardian or conservator nomination in   Pro §4672

Alcoholic beverages
- Social host liability for furnishing to person under 21   CC §1714

Allowances to wards   Pro §2421
Amending petition to reflect other proceedings   Pro §1512
Annual status reports   Pro §1513.2
- Confidential guardianship status report form   CRC 7.1003

Annuities   Pro §2459

Appeals
- Generally   Pro §§1300, 1301
- Reversal of appointment order, effect of   Pro §1311
- Stay on appeal   Pro §1310

Appearance of minor by guardian or guardian ad litem   CCP §372
Appearance of minor without guardian ad litem   CCP §372

Appellate court opinions
- Privacy, use of names in opinions   CRC 8.90

Appellate rules, superior court appeals
- Limited civil cases in appellate division
  - Compromise of claims, approval   CRC 8.825

Applicability of Probate Code provisions for legal guardianship   Pro §1517

Appointment
- Generally   Pro §§1510 to 1516
- Adoption of proposed ward, disclosure in guardianship petition concerning   Pro §1510
- Amending petition to disclose other proceedings   Pro §1512
- Best interests of child
  - Family court to provide relevant information   Pro §1514.5
- Capacity to petition for   Pro §1510
- Contents of petition for   Pro §1510
- Decedent's estate, appointment of guardian as administrator of   Pro §§8464, 8469
- Guidelines for   Pro §1514

GUARDIAN AND WARD—Cont.
Appointment—Cont.
- Investigator   Pro §1454
  - Education requirements   CRC 10.478
  - Qualifications   CRC 10.776, 10.777
- Joint guardians   Pro §2105
- Married minors   Pro §1515
- Money belonging to minor, guardian appointed for purposes of   Pro §3413
- Nonprofit charitable corporation, appointment of   Pro §2104
- Nonrelatives   Pro §§1540 to 1543
- Notice of hearing on   Pro §1511
- Patient of state institution, disclosure of proposed ward as   Pro §1510
- Petition
  - Forms available for use   CRC 7.101
- Public guardians as guardian (See **PUBLIC GUARDIANS**)
- Reversal on appeal of order appointing fiduciary, effect of   Pro §1311
- Screening of guardian prior to   Pro §1516
- Several wards, guardian for   Pro §2106
- Successor guardian   Pro §2670
- Temporary guardian   Pro §§2250 to 2258
  - Good cause exception to notice of hearing on petition for appointment   CRC 7.1012
- Trust companies as guardian   Pro §300
  - Oath and bond requirement   Pro §301
- Ward's participation and testimony in probate guardianship proceedings   CRC 7.1016
- Will, guardian nominated in   Pro §2108

Appointment of counsel for ward
- Financial eligibility guidelines for appointed counsel under guardianship-conservatorship law   CRCAppx E

Appointment of guardians
- Capacity to petition for   Pro §1510.1
  - Special immigrant juvenile status   CRC 7.1020, Pro §1510.1
- Dissolution of marriage proceedings, appointment for incapacitated spouse   Fam §2332
- Fee waivers   CRC 3.50 to 3.53, 7.5
- Nonprofit charitable corporations
  - Out-of-state corporations, guardianship of minor with special immigrant juvenile status   Pro §2104.1
- Petition   Pro §1510.1
  - Special immigrant juvenile status   CRC 7.1020, Pro §1510.1

Appraisals
- Assessor, copy to   Pro §2612
- Developmental services department, copy to   Pro §2611
- Failure to file   Pro §2614.5
- Fee schedule or other compensation
  - Professional fiduciary to file proposed hourly fee schedule or statement of proposed compensation   Pro §2614.7
- Guardian defined   Pro §2600
- Hearing on objections to   Pro §2614
- Independent   Pro §2614
- Later discovered property   Pro §2613
- Method for preparing   Pro §2610
- Petition to object to   Pro §2616
- Public guardians, appraisal by   Pro §2943
- State department of state hospitals, copy to   Pro §2611
- Supplemental   Pro §2613
- Temporary guardians   Pro §2255
- Termination, effect on   Pro §2633
- Time for filing   Pro §§2610, 2613

Arbitration of claims   Pro §§2405, 2406

Assets
- Personal property
  - Sales generally (See within this heading, **"Sales"**)

Attorneys
- Accounting of estate by attorney on death of guardian   Pro §2632
- Appointed counsel   CRC 7.1101 to 7.1105, Pro §§1470 to 1472
  - Alternatives to experience requirements   CRC 7.1102, 7.1103
  - Annual certification of attorney qualifications   CRC 7.1105
  - Certification of attorney qualifications   CRC 7.1105
  - Confidentiality of certifications, supporting documentations, etc   CRC 7.1105
  - Continuing education   CRC 7.1102, 7.1103
  - Disciplinary action against attorney, notification   CRC 7.1105
  - Experience requirements   CRC 7.1102, 7.1103
  - Financial eligibility determinations, guidelines   CRCAppx E
  - Initial certification of attorney qualifications   CRC 7.1105
  - Judicial council legal forms   CRCAppx A
  - Legal capacity of conservatee, proposed conservatee or person lacking, requirements for appointed attorney   CRC 7.1103
  - Local court administration   CRC 7.1104

GUARDIAN AND WARD—Cont.
  Attorneys—Cont.
    Appointed counsel —Cont.
      Qualifications   CRC 7.1101 to 7.1103
      Unqualified attorney appointed, grounds for exception to requirements   CRC 7.1104
    CASA programs   CRC 5.655
    Education of court-employed staff attorneys
      Rule of court implementing, judicial council duties   Pro §1456
    Fees (See within this heading, **"Attorneys' fees"**)
    Indians, proceedings for
      Inability to afford counsel   Pro §1474
    Probate attorneys
      Education requirements   CRC 10.478
      Qualifications   CRC 10.776, 10.777
    Withdrawal from representation of guardian, notice to surety required on   Pro §1213
  Attorneys' fees
    Accounting of estate by attorney on death of guardian, fee for   Pro §2632
    Contingency fee contract   Pro §2644
    Court-appointed counsel   Pro §§1470, 1472
      Financial eligibility determinations, guidelines   CRCAppx E
    Disclosure of relationships   Pro §2645
    Expense payable from principal and income of estate, general discussion of legal fees as   Pro §2430
    Guardian acting as attorney, court approval of legal fees for   Pro §2645
    Payment from estate   Pro §2647
    Periodic payment   Pro §2643
    Petitions
      By attorney   Pro §2642
      By guardian of estate   Pro §2640
      By guardian of person   Pro §2641
  Bank accounts
    Opening or changing name on accounts, responsibilities of guardian   CRC 7.1011
  Bankruptcy, actions in   Pro §2462
  Banks as trust companies (See within this heading, **"Trust companies"**)
  Blocked accounts, placing money or property in   Pro §2328
  Bond of guardian   CRC 7.207
    Generally   Pro §§2300, 2320 to 2330, 2333 to 2335
    Additional bond requirements   Pro §§2320.2, 2330, 2334
    Amount required   Pro §§2320, 2328
    Blocked accounts, exclusion of funds in   Pro §2328
    Ex parte application to increase amount of bond   Pro §2320.1
    Guardian of the person, requirement for   Pro §2322
    Insufficient bond   CRC 7.204, Pro §2334
    Inventory, failure to file   Pro §2615
    Joint guardians, rules re   CRC 7.203, Pro §2326
    Multiple wards, requirements for   Pro §2327
    Nonprofit charitable corporation, surety company for   Pro §2325
    Notice to surety   Pro §1213
    Public benefit payments, estates receiving   Pro §2323
    Public guardians (See **PUBLIC GUARDIANS**)
    Reduced amount   Pro §§2321, 2328, 2329
    Small estates, requirements for   Pro §2323
    Stay on appeal, bond requirement for   Pro §1310
    Substitution or discharge of surety   Pro §2335
    Temporary guardians   Pro §2251
    Trust companies, bond requirements for   Pro §301
    Waiver by person nominating guardian   Pro §2324
  Borrowing money   Pro §§2550 to 2552
  Breach of fiduciary duty
    Estate value, guardian's liability for   Pro §§2401.3, 2401.6
    Interest on loss, guardian's liability for   Pro §§2401.5, 2401.6
    Other remedies for   Pro §2401.7
  Care, custody, control, and education of ward
    Annual status reports   Pro §1513.2
      Confidential guardianship status report form   CRC 7.1003
    Permanent and stable home   Pro §1610
  Caregiver's authorization and affidavit for medical or dental treatment of minors in   Fam §§6550, 6552
  CASA advocacy   CRC 5.655
  Change of address
    Ward's residence, change   CRC 7.1013
  Change of name of ward   CCP §1276
  Charitable corporations as guardians   Pro §2104
    Out-of-state corporations, guardianship of minor with special immigrant juvenile status   Pro §2104.1
  Child custody and visitation
    Visitation
      Orders following termination of juvenile court or probate court proceedings   CRC 5.475

GUARDIAN AND WARD—Cont.
  Children's property, disposition where no guardianship
    Attorneys' fees for services to minors and persons with disability   CRC 7.955
    Trusts, payment into   CRC JudAdminStand 7.10
  Civil actions   Fam §6601, Pro §2462
  Claims
    Disputed claims   Pro §§2405, 2406
    Payment of   Pro §§2430, 2431
    Petition to determine claim to property, notice of hearing
      Form, judicial council   CRCAppx A
  Community property (See **COMMUNITY PROPERTY**)
  Compensation   Pro §§2430, 2640 to 2645
    Accounts for   Pro §2623
    Attorneys (See within this heading, **"Attorneys' fees"**)
    Fees payable from estate of conservatee, determination limited to   Pro §2646
    Just and reasonable compensation, standards for determining   CRC 7.756
    Probate rules
      Compensation for guardians, conservators and trustees   CRC 7.750 to 7.776
  Compromise (See within this heading, **"Settlement and compromise"**)
  Conduct of guardian
    Standards of conduct   Pro §2410
  Confidential Guardian Screening Form, use of   CRC 7.1001
  Confidential guardianship status report form   CRC 7.1003
  Confirmation of guardian's acts   Pro §§2359, 2403
  Consent
    Wards 19 or 20 years of age, extension of guardianship   CRC 7.1002.5
  Contempt for disobeying court order, removal for   Pro §2655
  Contracts
    Personal liability of guardian as fiduciary   Pro §2110
    Property, conveyance of   Pro §§2521 to 2528
  Control and regulation   Pro §2102
  Convulsive therapy   Pro §2356
  Costs in action prosecuted or defended by guardian   CCP §1026
  Court employees obtaining estate property, prohibition against   Pro §2111.5
  Court investigator
    Best interests of child
      Family court to provide relevant information   Pro §1514.5
    Defined   Pro §1419
    Education requirements   CRC 10.478
    Qualifications and appointment of   CRC 10.776, 10.777, Pro §1454
  Courts
    Court investigators, probate attorneys and probate examiners
      Education of judicial branch personnel   CRC 10.478
      Qualifications   CRC 10.776, 10.777
  Criminal history information records
    Public guardians   Pro §2920.5
  Custodial parent defined   Pro §1419.5
  Custodial property defined   Pro §3400
  Custody of children
    Drug or alcohol abuse as custody determination factor
      Testing for alcohol or controlled substance use ordered by court   Fam §3041.5
    Visitation
      Former legal guardians   Fam §3105, Pro §1602
  Damages for wrongful occupancy of land by guardian   CC §3335
  Death
    Accounting on death of guardian   Pro §§2630, 2632
    Accounting on death of ward   Pro §§2620, 2630 to 2631
    Duty on death of ward   Pro §2467
    Termination of guardianship on death of ward   Pro §1600
  Death of guardian
    Minor's death, termination of guardianship
      Final account, service   CRC 7.1006
  Debts
    Collecting   Pro §2451
    Payment of   Pro §§2430, 2431
  Decedent's estate, administration of
    Appointment of guardian as administrator   Pro §§8464, 8469
    Service of notice on guardian   Pro §1210
  Dedication of property   Pro §2556
  Deed to mortgaged property, acceptance of   Pro §2464
  Deficiency judgments on encumbered estate property   Pro §2551
  Definitions   Fam §6903, Pro §§1401 to 1446, 1490, 3004 to 3008
  Dependent children   CRC 5.730 to 5.740
    Investigation and recommendation concerning proposed guardianship   Pro §1513
  Dependents, support and maintenance of   Pro §§2420 to 2423

GUARDIAN AND WARD—Cont.
- Deposit of funds
  - Generally Pro §2453
  - Checks and drafts Pro §2452
  - Order authorizing deposit or withdrawal of money or property Pro §2456
  - Personal property Pro §2454
  - Public guardians Pro §2940
  - Securities Pro §2455
  - Trust companies (See within this heading, **"Trust companies"**)
- Developmental Services Department, notice to Pro §§1461, 1461.4, 1511
- Director of Social Services
  - Notice to Pro §§1516, 1542
  - Screening name of guardian-nominee for referrals for abuse of minor or neglect Pro §1516
- Disability of guardian, accounting on Pro §2632
- Discharge
  - Assets transferred out of state Pro §2808
  - Exhausted estate Pro §2626
  - Majority of ward Pro §2627
  - Temporary guardians Pro §2258
- Disclaimer of interest Pro §§260 to 295
- Dissolution of marriage proceedings, representation of incapacitated spouse Fam §2332
- Distributions of decedents' estate deposited with county treasurer for benefit of minor or ward without guardian Pro §§11850 to 11854
- Domestic violence
  - Victim representatives Fam §6228
- Drugs prohibited Pro §2356
- "Duties of Guardian" acknowledgment of receipt CRC 7.1002
- Easements Pro §2556
- Education
  - Appointment of person to make educational decisions for minor Pro §2662
- Emancipation of children (See **EMANCIPATION OF MINORS**)
- Employment of ward Pro §2601
- Enforcement of judgment against estate CCP §709.030
- Enticing ward from guardian CC §49
- Estate, guardianship of
  - Conflicts of interest CRC 7.1009
  - Forms available for use CRC 7.101
  - Management of guardianship estate
    - Standards of conduct CRC 7.1009, 7.1059
  - Powers of guardians, generally Pro §§2450 to 2469
  - Standards of conduct CRC 7.1009
- Estate less than $5,000, delivery of Pro §§3401, 3402
- Estate management powers Pro §§2450 to 2469
- Estate of the minor defined Pro §3400
- Examination of estate assets
  - Citation to appear, issuance of Pro §§2616, 2619
  - Interrogatories for Pro §2617
  - Petition for Pro §2616
  - Witnesses for Pro §2618
- Exchange of property Pro §§2545, 2550, 2557
- Expenses
  - Allowances for Pro §2623
  - Payments Pro §§2430, 2431
- Fees
  - Filing fees in probate proceedings generally Gov §§70650 to 70663
  - Waivers of fees in probate cases CRC 7.5
    - Appeals in supreme court and court of appeals CRC 8.26
    - Applicable provisions CRC 3.50
    - Application for waiver CRC 3.51
    - Determination of application CRC 3.52
    - Expiration CRC 7.5
    - Financial condition of ward, determination CRC 7.5
    - Grant of application unless acted on by court CRC 3.53
    - Judicial council forms CRCAppx A
    - Termination or modification of previously granted waivers CRC 7.5
- Fiduciary relationship Pro §2101
  - Professional fiduciaries generally Pro §§60.1, 2340, 2341
- Filing fees
  - Public guardian, etc., or State Mental Health Department employee, filing by Gov §70659
  - Riverside County
    - Courthouse seismic repair costs, additional filing fees authorized to defray Gov §70622
- Financial institutions
  - Deposit of funds generally (See within this heading, **"Deposit of funds"**)
  - Savings and loan associations (See within this heading, **"Savings and loan associations"**)
  - Trust companies (See within this heading, **"Trust companies"**)
- Foreclosure on estate property Pro §2551

GUARDIAN AND WARD—Cont.
- Foreign guardian
  - Defined Pro §2800
  - Recording letters of CC §2939.5
  - Removing property from state Pro §§3800 to 3803
- Forms
  - Confidential Guardian Screening Form CRC 7.1001
  - Judicial council legal forms CRCAppx A
  - Letters of guardianship Pro §2311
- Fraud detection investigations Pro §2620.1
- Funds for benefit of child
  - Orders by court Pro §1517
- Funeral expenses Pro §2631
- Gifts to minors (See **UNIFORM TRANSFERS TO MINORS ACT**)
- Governing law
  - Generally Pro §2100
  - Prior law, effect of Pro §3
- Hearings
  - Appointment of guardian, notice requirements Pro §1511
  - Appraisement of estate, objection to Pro §2614
  - Claims, disputed Pro §§2405, 2406
  - Disclaimer of interest Pro §277
  - Loans, authorization for Pro §§2550 to 2551
  - Notices generally (See within this heading, **"Notices"**)
  - Property disputes Pro §§2521 to 2528
  - Removal of guardians Pro §§2650 to 2654
  - Termination of guardianship Pro §1601
  - Transferring assets out of state Pro §§2800 to 2808
  - Venue change Pro §§2210 to 2217
- Home of ward Pro §§2457, 2571
  - Permanent and stable home Pro §1610
- Homestead property (See **HOMESTEADS**)
- Illegitimate children (See **PARENT AND CHILD**)
- Immigration
  - Special immigrant juvenile findings in guardianship proceedings CRC 7.1020
    - Appointment of guardians Pro §1510.1
- Incapacitated persons
  - Security freezes, credit reports
    - Protected consumer security freezes CC §§1785.11.9 to 1785.11.11
- Incapacitated professional fiduciary Pro §2469
- Independent exercise of powers Pro §§2408, 2590 to 2595
- Indian children
  - Applicability of Indian Child Welfare Act Pro §1459.5
  - Attorneys
    - Inability to afford counsel Pro §1474
  - Indian Child Welfare Act
    - Applicability CRC 7.1015
    - Involuntary placements, rules governing CRC 5.480 to 5.488 (See **INDIAN CHILD WELFARE ACT INVOLUNTARY PLACEMENTS**)
    - Notice when act may apply CRC 7.51
  - Investigation and report Pro §1513
  - Legislative findings and intent Pro §1459
  - Notices Pro §1511
    - Indian children as proposed ward Pro §1460.2
  - Petition, contents Pro §1510
  - Termination of guardianship Pro §1601
  - Ward's residence, change
    - Notice of change of personal residence CRC 7.1013
- Indigent persons
  - Waiver of fees CRC 7.5, Gov §68631
    - Appeals in supreme court and court of appeals CRC 8.26
    - Applicable provisions CRC 3.50
    - Application for waiver CRC 3.51
    - Definitions Gov §68631.5
    - Determination of application CRC 3.52
    - Expiration CRC 7.5
    - Financial condition of ward, determination CRC 7.5
    - Grant of application unless acted on by court CRC 3.53
    - Judicial council forms CRCAppx A
    - Termination or modification of previously granted waivers CRC 7.5
- Information Practices Act, obtaining information under CC §1798.24
- Instructions, petition for Pro §§1455, 2359, 2403
  - Vexatious litigants filing petitions regarding Pro §1611
- Insurance, guardians' powers re Pro §§2459, 2460
- Interested person defined Pro §1424
- Inventory
  - Appraisals generally (See within this heading, **"Appraisals"**)
  - Assessor, copy to Pro §2612
  - Contents of Pro §2610

GUARDIAN AND WARD—Cont.
  Inventory—Cont.
    Developmental Services Department, copy to   Pro §2611
    Failure to file   Pro §§2614.5, 2615
    Fee schedule or other compensation
      Professional fiduciary to file proposed hourly fee schedule or statement of proposed compensation   Pro §2614.7
    Guardian defined   Pro §2600
    Later discovered property   Pro §2613
    Liability for failure to file   Pro §2615
    Oath with   Pro §2610
    State department of state hospitals, copy to   Pro §2611
    Supplemental   Pro §2613
    Temporary guardians   Pro §2255
    Termination, effect of   Pro §2633
    Time for filing   Pro §2610
    Veterans Administration, notice requirement for   Pro §1461.5
  Investigations
    Generally   Pro §1513
    Adoption   Pro §1543
    Costs of investigation, assessment of   Pro §1513.1
    Court investigator (See within this heading, **"Court investigator"**)
    Education of investigators
      Rule of court implementing, judicial council duties   Pro §1456
    Fraud detection investigations   Pro §2620.1
    Security, sufficiency of   Pro §2334
  Investments
    Generally   Pro §§2547, 2570, 2573, 2574
    Powers of guardians   Pro §§2450 to 2469
    Public guardians   Pro §2940
  Joint guardians
    Generally   Pro §2105
    Bond requirements   Pro §2326
    Liability of   Pro §2105.5
    Terminal illness of custodial parent as grounds for appointing parent and parent's nominee as joint guardians   Pro §2105
  Joint purchase of real property   Pro §2572
  Judges
    Education as to conservatorship and guardianship matters
      Regularly assigned to probate cases   CRC 10.468
      Rule of court implementing, judicial council duties   Pro §1456
    Education of judges and subordinate judicial officers regularly assigned to probate cases
      Domestic violence issues   CRC 10.464
    Service as guardians   CRCSupp JudEthicsCanon 4
  Judgments
    Attorneys' fees for services to minors and incompetent persons   CRC 7.955
    Enforcement against estate   CCP §709.030
    Finality of   Pro §2103
    Payments pursuant to judgment in favor of minor or person with disabilities, disposition of   Pro §§3600 to 3613
      Definition of person with disability   Pro §3603
      Express consent of protected person to court orders, when required   Pro §3613
    Payments pursuant to judgment in favor of minor or person with disability, disposition of
      Trusts, payment into   CRC JudAdminStand 7.10
    Removing guardians   Pro §2653
  Jurisdiction
    Generally   Pro §2200
    Child custody and visitation proceedings   Pro §2205
      Communications between/among courts involved with custody, visitation and guardianship involving ward   CRC 7.1014
      More than one county, commencement of proceedings it   Pro §2204
    More than one county, commencement of proceedings in   Pro §2203
      Child custody or visitation proceedings   Pro §2204
      Communications between/among courts involved with custody, visitation and guardianship involving ward   CRC 7.1014
    Real property disputes   Pro §§2524 to 2526
    Settlement and compromise   Pro §2505
    Termination, retention after   Pro §2630
  Jury
    Generally   Pro §§825, 1452
    Challenge of juror for implied bias, relationships giving rise to   CCP §229
  Juvenile wardship
    Generally (See **JUVENILE WARDSHIP PROCEEDINGS**)
  Last illness, expenses of   Pro §2631
  Leases   Pro §§2553 to 2555
  Letters
    Generally   Pro §2310
    Administration   Pro §§8464, 8469

GUARDIAN AND WARD—Cont.
  Letters—Cont.
    Foreign guardians   CC §2939.5
    Form   Pro §2311
    Powers stated in   Pro §2594
    Public guardians   Pro §2922
    Revoking   Pro §§2650 to 2654
    Temporary guardianship   Pro §2251
  Liens on personalty, borrowing secured by   Pro §§2550 to 2552
  Limitation of actions
    Sold property, ward's action to recover   Pro §2548
    Surety, action against   Pro §2333
  Lis pendens, filing notice of   Pro §1004
  Loans   Pro §§2550 to 2552
  Location of property, duty to disclose   Pro §2529
  Mail, rules re use of   Pro §1467
  Majority of ward
    Accounts, settling of   Pro §2627
    Termination of guardianship on   Pro §1600
  Marriage
    Dissolution proceedings, appointment of guardian for incapacitated spouse   Fam §2332
  Medical information, authorization for release of   CC §56.10
  Medical treatment
    Consent, guardian giving   Pro §2353
    Existing or continuing condition, petition for order authorizing treatment for   Pro §2357
    Pre-employment physical, disclosure of information from   CC §56.10
  Mental health facility, placement of ward in   Pro §2356
  Mining leases   Pro §§2553 to 2555
  Money, depositing and withdrawing   Pro §§2453, 2456
  Mortgages
    Executing notes and   Pro §§2550 to 2552
    Foreign guardians satisfying   CC §2939.5
  Mutual funds
    Generally   Pro §2459
    Sale of mutual funds without beneficiary designation   Pro §2544.5
  Nature and location of property, duty to disclose   Pro §2529
  Neglect of child, name of guardian-nominee screened for prior referrals for   Pro §1516
  Negligence, suspension for   Pro §2334
  New trial motion   Pro §1453
  Nomination of guardian
    Generally   Pro §§1488, 1489, 1500 to 1502
    Consent to nomination   Pro §1500.1
    Parent's nomination in custody proceedings   Fam §3043
  Non-professional conservators or guardians
    Educational program   Pro §1457
  Nonprofit charitable corporations as guardians   Pro §2104
    Out-of-state corporations, guardianship of minor with special immigrant juvenile status   Pro §2104.1
  Nonrelative guardianships   Pro §§1540 to 1543
  Nonresident ward
    Generally   Pro §2107
    Foreign guardian (See within this heading, **"Foreign guardian"**)
    Removing property from state   Pro §§3800 to 3803
  Notices
    Generally   Pro §§1460 to 1469
    Accounts, hearings on   Pro §2621
    Additional notice, court requiring   Pro §1462
    Annual status reports
      Guardian to be notified of requirement to report   Pro §1513.2
    Appointment of guardian, hearing on   Pro §§1511, 1516
    Bond, reduction of   Pro §2329
    Change of residence   Pro §2352
    Decedent's estate proceedings, effect of guardian receiving notice of   Pro §1210
    Developmentally disabled persons, notice requirements involving   Pro §§1461, 1461.4, 1822
    Developmental Services Department   Pro §§1461, 1461.4, 1511
    Director of Social Services   Pro §§1516, 1542
    Disclaimer of interest, hearing regarding   Pro §277
    Financial institutions, conservator's taking possession of assets held by   Pro §§2890 to 2893
    Guardian, notice to   CRC 7.51
    Indian children as proposed ward   Pro §§1460.2, 1511
    Inventory and appraisal
      Mailing to family   Pro §2610
    Mailing, rules re   Pro §1467
    Nonrelative guardianship hearing   Pro §1542
    Persons entitled to   Pro §1511

GUARDIAN AND WARD—Cont.
  Notices—Cont.
    Property disputes, hearings on Pro §2521
    Removal of guardians Pro §2652
    Sales Pro §2543
    Shortening time requirement Pro §1462
    Special Pro §§2700 to 2702
    State hospital patient, ward as Pro §1461.4
        Ward or conservatee as patient, notice to state department of state hospitals Pro §§1461, 1511
    Surety, notice to Pro §1213
    Temporary guardians, petitions for Pro §2250
    Termination of guardianship Pro §1601
    Transferring assets out of state, hearing on Pro §2804
    12 years old, notice to child under Pro §1460.1
    Venue change hearing Pro §2214
    Veterans Administration, notice to Pro §1461.5
  Oaths
    Generally Pro §2300
    Temporary guardians Pro §2251
    Trust companies as guardian Pro §301
  Objections
    Accounts of guardians Pro §§2622, 2622.5
        Surety, notice to Pro §1213
    Transfer of assets out of state Pro §2805
  Orders
    Appeal from orders (See within this heading, **"Appeals"**)
    Blocked accounts, placing money or property in Pro §2328
    Compensation for services rendered, order for Pro §2643
    Deposit or withdraw money or property in trust companies Pro §2456
    Disclaimer of interest, filing of Pro §277
    Duties, failure to perform Pro §2404
    Finality of Pro §2103
    Independent exercise of powers Pro §§2590 to 2595
    Limiting powers Pro §2351
    Loans and security Pro §2551
    Removing guardians Pro §2653
    Transactions, authorizing or directing Pro §2111
    Transfer of property Pro §§2527, 2528
    Trust companies, deposit or withdraw money or property in Pro §2456
    Wage claims, failure to pay Pro §2431
  Other proceedings, amended petition to reflect Pro §1512
  Parental authority over minor child ceasing on appointment of guardian Fam §7505
  Partition (See **PARTITION**)
  Patient of state institution, disclosure of proposed ward as Pro §1510
  Permanent and stable home Pro §1610
  Personal liability on contracts by guardian as fiduciary Pro §2110
  Personal property
    Contracts to transfer personal property, court approval of Pro §§2521 to 2528
    Court employees obtaining estate property, prohibition against Pro §2111.5
    Depositing and withdrawing Pro §§2454, 2456
    Examination of estate assets (See within this heading, **"Examination of estate assets"**)
    Out-of-state transfer of assets Pro §§2800 to 2808
    Sales (See within this heading, **"Sales"**)
    Ward's assets
        Taking possession or control, responsibilities of guardian CRC 7.1011
  Person, guardianship Pro §§2350 to 2361
  Petition
    Accounts, approval of Pro §1064
    Additional security by guardian, request for Pro §2334
    Amendment to disclose other proceedings Pro §1512
    Appointment
        Form CRC 7.101
    Appraisement of estate, objection to Pro §2616
    Attorneys' fees (See within this heading, **"Attorneys' fees"**)
    Borrow money, authorization to Pro §2551
    Compensation for services rendered, petition for Pro §§2430, 2640 to 2647
    Defined Pro §1430
    Disclaimer of interest, order authorizing filing of Pro §277
    Duties, order to perform Pro §2404
    Examination of estate assets Pro §2616
    Forms available for use CRC 7.101
    Independent powers, grant of Pro §2592
    Medical treatment for existing or continuing condition, authorization for Pro §2357
    Nonrelative as guardian, appointment of Pro §§1540 to 1543

GUARDIAN AND WARD—Cont.
  Petition—Cont.
    Property transfers, authority re Pro §2526
    Removal of guardian Pro §2651
    Settlement and compromise, court approval of Pro §2506
    Temporary guardians Pro §2250
        Forms available for use CRC 7.101
    Termination of guardianship Pro §1601
    Transfer of assets out of state Pro §§2802, 2803
    Venue change Pro §§2211 to 2213
  Possession of disputed property Pro §§2521 to 2528
  Power of appointment released by guardian on behalf of minor donee Pro §662
  Power of attorney (See **POWER OF ATTORNEY**)
  Powers
    Generally Pro §§2350, 2351, 2450
    Annuities Pro §2459
    Bankruptcy Pro §2462
    Borrowing money Pro §§2550 to 2552
    Care plan, filing with court Pro §2351.2
    Checks, cashing and depositing Pro §2452
    Civil actions Pro §2462
    Contracts Pro §2451.5
    Death of ward Pro §2467
    Debt and benefit collection Pro §2451
    Dedication of property Pro §2556
    Deed to mortgaged property, acceptance of Pro §2464
    Easements, dedicating or granting Pro §2556
    Employment of professionals Pro §2451.5
    Encumbering personal property Pro §§2550 to 2552
    Exercise without court authorization Pro §2450
    Home for ward, maintenance of Pro §§2457, 2571
    Independent exercise of Pro §§2408, 2590 to 2595
    Insurance Pro §§2459, 2460
    Investments Pro §§2570 to 2574
    Joint guardians Pro §2109
    Leases Pro §§2550, 2552.5 to 2555
    Limits by court on Pro §§2351, 2450
    Loans Pro §§2550 to 2552
    Medical treatment, consent to Pro §2353
    Money, depositing and withdrawing Pro §§2453, 2456
    Nonresident wards Pro §2107
    Ownership rights, exercising Pro §2458
    Particular property, guardian nominated for Pro §2109
    Partition actions Pro §2463
    Personal property, depositing and withdrawing Pro §§2454, 2456
    Purchase of property Pro §2451.5
    Real property transactions Pro §2111
    Residence of ward, fixing place of Pro §2352
    Retirement plans, continuing Pro §2459
    Sales (See within this heading, **"Sales"**)
    Securities (See within this heading, **"Securities"**)
    Settlement and compromise (See within this heading, **"Settlement and compromise"**)
    Surrender during removal proceedings Pro §2654
    Taxes Pro §2461
    Temporary guardians Pro §2252
    Termination (See within this heading, **"Termination of guardianship"**)
    Transactions under court order Pro §2111
    Valueless property Pro §2465
    Welfare payments, acting as payee for Pro §2452
    Wills, guardians nominated in Pro §2108
    Withdrawal of independent powers Pro §2593
  Powers of appointment Pro §§600 to 695
  Pre-employment physical, disclosure of information from CC §56.10
  Presumptions favoring guardian Ev §§605, 606
  Prior law Pro §§1488 to 1490
  Private sale of assets Pro §2543
  Probate attorneys
    Education requirements CRC 10.478
    Qualifications CRC 10.776, 10.777
  Probate examiners
    Education requirements CRC 10.478
    Qualifications CRC 10.776, 10.777
  Probate referee, appraisal of estate by
    Appraisals generally (See within this heading, **"Appraisals"**)
  Probate rules
    Generally CRC 7.1 to 7.1105
  Process (See within this heading, **"Service of process"**)
  Professional fiduciaries
    Deceased professional fiduciary Pro §9765

GUARDIAN AND WARD—Cont.
Professional fiduciaries—Cont.
    Fee schedule or compensation, proposed
        Inventory and appraisal of estate   Pro §2614.7
        Submission of new schedule or statement   Pro §2614.8
    Periodic payments for services rendered by attorneys or fiduciaries
        Petition   Pro §2643.1
    Petition for guardianship
        Contents   Pro §1510
    Temporary guardians
        Petition for temporary guardian or conservator, contents   Pro §2250
Property disputes, procedure re   Pro §§2521 to 2528
Protection of family   CC §50
Public assistance (See within this heading, **"Welfare payments"**)
Public auctions   Pro §2543
Public defender, appointment and compensation   Pro §§1471, 1472
Public guardians (See **PUBLIC GUARDIANS**)
Purchases by guardian, accounting for   Pro §2625
Real property
    Generally   Pro §2111
    Contracts to convey real property, court approval of   Pro §§2521 to 2528
    Court employees obtaining estate property, prohibition against   Pro §2111.5
    Foreign jurisdictions, property in
        Determining ward's interests, standard of care   Pro §2401.1
    Interested persons, response to petition by   Pro §2522
    Joint purchase of   Pro §2572
    Jurisdiction for disputes involving   Pro §§2524 to 2526
    Lis pendens, filing notice of   Pro §1004
    Sales generally (See within this heading, **"Sales"**)
Recording real property transactions   Pro §2111
Referees
    Appraisal of estate by probate referee
        Appraisals generally (See within this heading, **"Appraisals"**)
    Disqualification as referee, guardian relationship as grounds for   CCP §641
Reimbursement of guardian   Pro §§2466, 2623
Removal
    Generally   Pro §§2650 to 2654
    Cause, removal for   Pro §2653
    Contempt for disobeying court order, removal for   Pro §2655
    Final account or report
        Service of copy after resignation or removal of guardian   CRC 7.1005
    Inventory or appraisal, failure to file   Pro §2614.5
    Professional fiduciaries, removal for cause
        Report to professional fiduciaries bureau   Pro §2653
    Surety, notice to   Pro §1213
    Surrendering estate during proceedings for   Pro §2654
    Temporary guardians   Pro §2258
    Ward's participation and testimony in probate guardianship proceedings   CRC 7.1016
Rent on leases arranged by   Pro §§2550, 2552.5 to 2555
Requests, procedure for   CRC 5.735
Residence of ward, guardian establishing   Pro §2352
    Change of residence   CRC 7.1013
    Ward's participation and testimony in probate guardianship proceedings   CRC 7.1016
Resignation
    Generally   Pro §2660
    Appointment of person to make educational decisions for minor   Pro §2662
    Final account or report
        Service of copy after resignation or removal of guardian   CRC 7.1005
    Temporary guardians   Pro §2258
Revocation of letters   Pro §§2650 to 2654
Safe deposit boxes
    Opening or changing name on accounts, responsibilities of guardian   CRC 7.1011
Salaries and wages
    Claims for wages, payment of   Pro §2431
    Guardian (See within this heading, **"Compensation"**)
    Ward's wages   Pro §2601
Sales
    Accounting and court review of   Pro §2625
    Appraisals   Pro §2543
    Bond requirements for sale of realty   Pro §2330
    Conduct of   Pro §2543
    Confirmation requirements   Pro §§2540, 2544 to 2545
    Exchanges   Pro §§2545, 2550, 2557
    Exclusive listing, contents of petition for approval of   CRC 7.453
    Joint purchase of real property   Pro §2572
    Mortgages and trust deeds   Pro §2542
    Mutual funds without beneficiary designation   Pro §2544.5

GUARDIAN AND WARD—Cont.
Sales—Cont.
    Notices of   Pro §§2540, 2543
    Permitted circumstances   Pro §2541
    Personal effects or furniture   Pro §2545
    Private sales   Pro §2543
    Proceeds, management of   Pro §§2547, 2570 to 2574
    Public auctions   Pro §2543
    Recovery action by ward   Pro §2548
    Refusal to show property to prospective buyers   CRC 7.451
    Securities   Pro §2544
    Tangible personalty under $5,000   Pro §2545
    Terms of   Pro §2542
Savings and loan associations
    Definitions   Pro §1490
    Funds deposited in (See within this heading, **"Deposit of funds"**)
    Surety bond of guardian, funds in blocked account excluded in determining   Pro §2328
Screening forms   CRC 7.1001
Screening name of guardian-nominee for abuse of minor or neglect   Pro §1516
Securities
    Deposits   Pro §§2455, 2456
    Sales   Pro §2544
    Shareholder rights, exercise of   Pro §2458
Separate property (See **COMMUNITY PROPERTY**)
Service of process
    Final account or report
        Resignation or removal of guardian, service of   CRC 7.1005
        Termination of guardianship, service of copy   CRC 7.1006
    Guardian, effect of notice of decedent's estate proceedings served on   Pro §1210
    Minor, service on   CCP §416.60
    Ward, service on   CCP §416.70
Settlement and compromise   Pro §§2500, 2507
    Accounts and accounting
        Settlement and release by former minor   CRC 7.1007
    Attorneys' fees for services to minors and incompetent persons   CRC 7.955
    Court approval for   Pro §§2500 to 2507
    Disposition of money or property paid pursuant to
        Trusts, payment into   CRC JudAdminStand 77.10
    Dispute between guardian and ward   Pro §2503
    Forms
        Judicial council forms   CRC 7.101
    Jurisdiction   Pro §2505
    Law governing   Pro §2507
    No guardian for minor, compromise of claims where   Pro §3500
        Hearings on petition for compromise   Pro §3505
    Notice of settlement of entire case
        Minor's or disabled person's claims involved   CRC 3.1385
    Payment pursuant to   Pro §§3600 to 3613
        Attorneys' fees for services to minors and persons with disability   CRC 7.955
        Express consent of protected person to court orders, when required   Pro §3613
        Trusts, payment into   CRC JudAdminStand 7.10
    Personal injury claims   Pro §2504
    Real property matters   Pro §2501
    Support and maintenance claims   Pro §2504
    Wrongful death claims   Pro §2504
Shares (See within this heading, **"Securities"**)
Small estates without administration   Pro §13051
Standards of conduct   Pro §2410
State hospital patients
    Ward or conservatee as patient
        Notice to state department of state hospitals   Pro §§1461, 1511
Status reports   Pro §1513.2
    Confidential guardianship status report form   CRC 7.1003
Statutes of limitation
    Sold property, ward's action to recover   Pro §2548
    Surety, action against   Pro §2333
Stay of proceedings, bond requirements for   CCP §919
Substitution of fiduciaries during wartime (See **FIDUCIARIES' WARTIME SUBSTITUTION LAW**)
Successor guardian   Pro §2670
Support of ward   Pro §§2420 to 2423
Sureties (See within this heading, **"Bond of guardian"**)
Surety bonds (See within this heading, **"Bond of guardian"**)
Surrendering estate during removal proceedings   Pro §2654
Suspension
    Removal of guardians, during proceedings for   Pro §2654
    Surety, notice to   Pro §1213

GUARDIAN AND WARD—Cont.
Suspension—Cont.
    Temporary guardians   Pro §2258
Taxation   Pro §2461
Temporary guardians   Pro §§2250 to 2258
    Forms available for use   CRC 7.101
    Good cause exception to notice of hearing on petition for appointment   CRC 7.1012
    Indian child, temporary guardianships or conservatorships   CRC 7.1015
Terminal illness of custodial parent as grounds for appointing parent and parent's nominee as joint guardians   Pro §2105
Termination of guardianship
    Generally   Pro §§1600, 1601
    Appraisals   Pro §2633
    Assets transferred out of state   Pro §2808
    Court order   CRC 7.1004
    Discharge (See within this heading, **"Discharge"**)
    Duty of guardian on termination   CRC 7.1004
    Exhausted estate   Pro §2626
    Final account
        Service of copy of final account on termination   CRC 7.1006
    Funeral expenses   Pro §2631
    Inventory   Pro §2633
    Jurisdiction retained following   Pro §2630
    Last illness, expenses of   Pro §2631
    Money as sole asset, guardianship of estate where   Pro §3412
    Operation of law   CRC 7.1004
    Order for   CRC 5.620
    Remaining assets after death of ward, transfer of   Pro §2631
    Removal of guardian (See within this heading, **"Removal"**)
    Revocation of letters   Pro §§2650 to 2654
    Temporary guardians   Pro §2257
    Vexatious litigants filing petitions regarding   Pro §1611
    Visitation rights of former guardian   Pro §1602
        Orders following termination of juvenile court or probate court proceedings   CRC 5.475
        Requests or orders   CRC 7.1008
    Ward's participation and testimony in probate guardianship proceedings   CRC 7.1016
Termination of parental rights, determination resulting in appointment of guardian for child   Fam §7893
Tort liability for acts of minor   CC §1714.1, CRCAppx B
Total estate of the minor defined   Pro §3400
Transfers
    Out of state, transfer of assets   Pro §§2800 to 2808
    Property, order transferring   Pro §§2527, 2528
Transitional provisions   Pro §§1488 to 1490
Trust companies
    Appointment as guardian
        Generally   Pro §300
        Oath and bond requirements   Pro §301
    Defined   Pro §83
    Deposit of funds
        Generally   Pro §2453
        Blocked accounts   Pro §2328
        Court supervision of   Pro §2456
        Interest rate   Pro §2453.5
        Securities, deposit of   Pro §2454
    Fiduciary duties, restriction on investments   Pro §2401
    Notice to court upon conservator's taking possession of assets held by financial institutions   Pro §§2890 to 2893
Trust deeds, executing notes and   Pro §§2550 to 2552
Uniform Parentage Act, judgments to determine existence of parent and child relationship   Fam §7637
Uniform Transfers to Minors Act (See **UNIFORM TRANSFERS TO MINORS ACT**)
Venue
    Action against guardian, venue of   CCP §395.1
    Change of venue   Pro §§2210 to 2217
    More than one county, commencement of proceedings in
        Child custody or visitation proceedings   Pro §2204
        Communications between/among courts involved with custody, visitation and guardianship involving ward   CRC 7.1014
    Resident ward, proceedings for   Pro §2201
Veterans Administration, notice to   Pro §§1461.5, 1511
Vexatious litigants   Pro §1611
Violent video games
    Reporting violations by parent, guardian, etc   CC §1746.4
Visitation rights
    Effect of appointment of temporary guardian on   Pro §2250

GUARDIAN AND WARD—Cont.
Visitation rights—Cont.
    Former legal guardian   Fam §3105
        Orders following termination of juvenile court or probate court proceedings   CRC 5.475
    Vexatious litigants filing petitions regarding   Pro §1611
    Ward's participation and testimony in probate guardianship proceedings   CRC 7.1016
Wages (See within this heading, **"Salaries and wages"**)
Ward of the court, juvenile courts (See **JUVENILE WARDSHIP PROCEEDINGS**)
Wards 19 or 20 years of age, extension of guardianship   CRC 7.1002.5
    Change of residence address, notice   CRC 7.1013
    Forms, judicial council   CRCAppx A
    Termination of guardianship   CRC 7.1004
Ward's participation and testimony in guardianship proceedings   CRC 7.1016
Wartime, substitution of fiduciaries during (See **FIDUCIARIES' WARTIME SUBSTITUTION LAW**)
Waste, actions for recovery of treble damages for   CCP §732
Welfare payments
    Accounting when estate consists of   Pro §2628
    Bond requirements for estates involving   Pro §2323
    Payee, guardian as   Pro §2452
Will probate proceedings
    Disclaimer of interest filed by guardian ad litem   Pro §§260 to 295
    Notice served on guardian, effect of   Pro §1210
Withdrawal
    Independent authority of guardian   Pro §2593
Witnesses
    Ward's participation and testimony in guardianship proceedings   CRC 7.1016

GUESTS
Alcoholic beverages served to guests, liability of host for   CC §1714
Mobilehome parks, guests of residents of   CC §798.34
Protection right   CC §50
Radio or television broadcast, libel by guest on   CC §48.5

GUIDE DOGS (See **DOGS**)

GUILTY PLEA
Appellate rules, supreme court and courts of appeal
    Appeal of conviction following guilty plea   CRC 8.304
Certificate of probable cause for appeal   CRC 8.304
Certification of case for superior court sentencing following   CRC 4.114
Evidence, admissibility in   Ev §1153
Probation officer, reference to   CRC 4.114
Punishment, specification in plea   CRC 4.412
Report to Justice Department concerning guilty pleas   CRC 4.320
Setting date for sentencing   CRC 4.114

GUN VIOLENCE RESTRAINING ORDERS
Emergency protective orders
    Form for firearms emergency protective order   CRCAppx A
Hearings
    Reschedule request and order   CRCAppx A
Notice and hearing, orders issued after
    Continuance of hearing
        Request to continue, form   CRCAppx A
    Forms   CRCAppx A
    New hearing date
        Form for notice   CRCAppx A
Petition
    Form   CRCAppx A
    Response form   CRCAppx A
Postsecondary educational institutions
    Orders against violence threatened on campus or facility
        Possession of firearms   CCP §527.11
Relinquishment of firearms
    Restraining orders
        Criminal rules   CRC 4.700
        Forms for firearm relinquishment   CRCAppx A
        Juvenile rules   CRC 5.630
Renewal of order
    Forms   CRCAppx A
Service of order on person restrained
    Mail
        Proof of service by mail   CRCAppx A
    Proof of personal service   CRCAppx A
Surrender of firearms and ammunition
    Proof of turning in, sale or storage
        Forms   CRCAppx A

GUN VIOLENCE RESTRAINING ORDERS—Cont.
Temporary emergency gun violence restraining orders
    Form   CRCAppx A
Termination of order during effective period
    Request for termination
        Forms   CRCAppx A
Universities and colleges
    Orders against violence threatened on campus or facility
        Possession of firearms   CCP §527.11
Workplace violence or threats of violence, injunctions or orders against
    Firearm possession or purchase by person subject to
        Determination of possession   CCP §527.11

H

HABEAS CORPUS
Appeals
    Death penalty cases
        Appeals from superior court decisions in habeas cases involving death penalty   CRC 8.390 to 8.398
    Supreme court or court of appeal granting writ, appeal from
        Filing decision   CRC 8.387
        Record on appeal   CRC 8.388
        Remittitur   CRC 8.387
Applicability of provisions   CRC 4.550
Attorney qualifications
    Appointed counsel, qualifications in noncapital cases   CRC 4.553
    Death penalty cases   CRC 4.562, 8.652
        Appeals from superior court decisions in habeas cases involving death penalty   CRC 8.391
        Forms, judicial council   CRCAppx A
Attorneys at law
    Death penalty cases
        Appointments   CRC 4.561, 4.562, 8.391, 8.605
        Forms, judicial council   CRCAppx A
        Ineffective assistance of trial counsel not raised prior to appeal from superior court habeas proceedings   CRC 8.397
Attorneys' fees, appointed counsel
    Indigent criminal appellants in supreme court, payment guidelines   CRCSupp PayGuideAppoint
Court of appeal
    Return of writ to reviewing court   CRC 8.385
        Decision in habeas proceedings   CRC 8.387
        Proceedings   CRC 8.386
Death penalty
    Appealability, certificate   CRC 4.576
    Appeals from superior court decisions in habeas cases involving death penalty   CRC 8.390 to 8.398
        Amici curiae briefs   CRC 8.396
        Appealability, certificate   CRC 8.392, 8.398
        Applicability of provisions   CRC 8.390
        Attorneys, appointment and qualifications   CRC 8.391
        Attorneys, ineffective assistance of trial counsel not previously raised   CRC 8.397
        Augmenting or correcting record   CRC 8.395
        Briefs   CRC 8.396
        Clerk's transcript   CRC 8.395
        Denial of certificate of appealability, finality   CRC 8.398
        Extension of time to prepare record   CRC 8.395
        Filing appeal   CRC 8.392
        Finality of decision   CRC 8.398
        Ineffective assistance of trial counsel not previously raised   CRC 8.397
        Judicial notice   CRC 8.395
        Notice of appeal   CRC 8.392
        Notification of filing of notice of appeal, distribution   CRC 8.392
        Record on appeal   CRC 8.395
        Reporter's transcript   CRC 8.395
        Service of briefs   CRC 8.396
        Stay of execution on appeal   CRC 8.394
        Successive petition cases, appeal of denial of relief   CRC 8.392
        Time for appeal   CRC 8.393
        Transcripts, partial   CRC 8.395
    Applicability of provisions   CRC 4.560
    Attorneys, appointment   CRC 4.561
        Appeals from superior court decisions in habeas cases involving death penalty   CRC 8.391
        Qualifications of attorneys, determination   CRC 4.562
        Recruitment of attorneys for appointment   CRC 4.562
        Regional habeas corpus panel committees   CRC 4.562

HABEAS CORPUS—Cont.
Death penalty—Cont.
    Attorneys, ineffective assistance
        Appeals from superior court decisions in habeas cases involving death penalty   CRC 8.397
    Briefing following order to show cause   CRC 4.574
    Compensation of attorney   CRCSupp SupCtPolicy
    Deadline extensions following order to show cause   CRC 4.574
    Death penalty-related proceedings in superior court   CRC 4.560 to 4.577
        Appeals from superior court decisions in habeas cases involving death penalty   CRC 8.390 to 8.398
    Denial following order to show cause   CRC 4.574
    Duty to investigate, attorney's   CRCSupp SupCtPolicy
    Evidentiary hearing following order to show cause   CRC 4.574
    Filing petition   CRC 4.571
    Fixed fee guidelines for appointed counsel in automatic appeals and related habeas corpus proceedings   CRCSupp FixedFeeAppoint
    Forms, judicial council   CRCAppx A
    Informal response and reply to petition   CRC 4.573
    Proceedings after filing of petition   CRC 4.573
    Proceedings after order to show cause   CRC 4.574
    Qualifications of counsel   CRC 8.652
    Return after order to show cause   CRC 4.574
    Ruling on petition   CRC 4.571, 4.574
    Service of petition   CRC 4.571
    Show cause, order   CRC 4.573, 4.574
    Statement of decision on petition   CRC 4.575
    Submission of cause for purposes of compensation of judges, determination   CRC 4.574
    Successive petitions   CRC 4.576
    Supreme court policies   CRCSupp SupCtPolicy
    Time for filing   CRCSupp SupCtPolicy
    Transfer of attorney files to appellate counsel for appeals taken   CRC 4.577
    Transfer of petition   CRC 4.572
Decision
    Filing decision   CRC 8.387
    Finality   CRC 8.387
Denial of petition
    Statement of reasons   CRC 4.551
Ex parte communications by court   CRC 4.551
Forms
    Judicial council legal forms   CRCAppx A
Hearing on return   CRC 4.551
    When required   CRC 4.551
Inappropriate court
    Petition filed in inappropriate court   CRC 8.385
Informal response   CRC 4.551, 8.385
Issuance of writ   CRC 4.551
Jurisdiction   CRC 4.552
Orders
    Shortening or extending time   CRC 4.551
    Show cause, issuance   CRC 4.551
    Show cause orders, issuance   CRC 8.385
Petition
    Appellate courts, original proceedings
        Attorney filing   CRC 8.384
    Inappropriate court, petition filed in   CRC 8.385
    Informal response   CRC 8.385
    Proceedings after filing   CRC 8.385
    Sealed or confidential records accompanying petition   CRC 8.380, 8.384
        Proceedings after petition   CRC 8.385
Remittitur   CRC 8.387
Request for ruling   CRC 4.551
Return of writ
    Denials   CRC 4.551
    Reviewing court, return ordered to   CRC 8.385
        Decision in habeas proceedings   CRC 8.387
        Proceedings   CRC 8.386
    Superior court, filing return in   CRC 8.385
    Time for   CRC 4.551
Ruling, notice and request for   CRC 4.551
Statute of limitations
    Felony offenses, damage actions based on commission
        Exception for those released via habeas corpus   CCP §340.3
Superior courts   CRC 4.551
    Applicability of provisions   CRC 4.550
    Court commissioner's powers   CCP §259
    Death penalty-related proceedings in superior court   CRC 4.560 to 4.577
    Denial   CRC 4.551
    Form of petition, requirements for   CRC 4.551
    Jurisdiction   CRC 4.552

HABEAS CORPUS—Cont.
Superior courts —Cont.
> Procedure   CRC 4.551

Supreme Court
> Application for recommendation   CRCSupp SupCtIOPP XIV
> Return of writ to reviewing court   CRC 8.385
>> Decision in habeas proceedings   CRC 8.387
>> Proceedings   CRC 8.386

Time for issuance of writ or order to show cause   CRC 4.551
Time for return of writ   CRC 4.551
Writs
> Issuance   CRC 4.551

HABIT
Admissible evidence to prove conduct   Ev §1105

HABITABLE PREMISES
Generally   CC §§1941 to 1942.5
Notice of pendency of action to declare building uninhabitable   CCP §405.7

HABITAT FOR HUMANITY
Sale of unit to nonprofit housing corporation after unit not purchased by income-qualifying person or family within time period   CC §714.7

HACKING
Data, illegally obtained or accessed
> Purchase by unauthorized person   CC §1724
> Sale   CC §1724

Security for connected devices   CC §§1798.91.04 to 1798.91.06

HAGUE CONVENTION
Acknowledgment in foreign countries affected by   CC §1183
Adoptions under Hague adoption convention   CRC 5.490 to 5.492
> Intercountry adoptions generally   CRC 5.490 to 5.493, Fam §§8900 to 8925
> Judicial council forms   CRCAppx A

Interstate family support
> Convention support proceedings   Fam §§5700.701 to 5700.713

Uniform Child Custody Jurisdiction and Enforcement Act, enforcement of Hague Convention on child abduction under   Fam §§3441, 3442, 3455

HAIRCUTS (See BARBERING AND COSMETOLOGY)

HALF-BLOOD
Inheritance by kindred of   Pro §6406

HANDICAPPED PERSONS (See DISABLED PERSONS)

HANDWRITING
Authentication of document   Ev §§1415 to 1419
Controlling words   CCP §1862
Holographic wills   Pro §6111
Proof of execution of instruments   CC §1198
Will admitted to probate on proof of   Pro §§8220, 8221

HANG GLIDING
Landowner's liability for injuries from   CC §846

HARASSMENT   CRC 3.1160
Appellate court opinions
> Privacy, use of names in opinions   CRC 8.90

Attorney professional conduct
> Prohibited discrimination, harassment and retaliation   ProfC 8.4.1

Businesses providing safe and welcoming environments for customers
> Pilot program to recognize   CC §51.17

Conservators
> Petitions
>> Unmeritorious petitions intended to annoy or harass   Pro §1970

Courts
> Workplace conduct policies
>> Courts' duties   CRC 10.351

COVID-19, emergency rule   CRCAppx I Emer Rule 8
Debt collectors, harassment by   CC §1788.11
Domestic violence (See DOMESTIC VIOLENCE)
Forms
> Judicial council legal forms   CRCAppx A

Guardian ad litem for minor seeking injunction against harassment or violence   CCP §§372, 374
> Appearance of minor under 12 to request or oppose temporary order   Fam §6229

Injunctive relief   CRC 3.1160
> Address or location of complaining party or family, prohibition on enjoined party from obtaining   CCP §527.10

HARASSMENT—Cont.
Injunctive relief —Cont.
> California law enforcement telecommunications (CLETS) information form, confidentiality and use of information   CRC 1.51, CRCAppx A
> COVID-19, emergency rule   CRCAppx I Emer Rule 8
> Dependency proceeding
>> Forms for firearm relinquishment   CRCAppx A
> Firearm relinquishment and disposition   CCP §527.9
>> Forms for firearm relinquishment   CRCAppx A
> Minor's appearance in proceedings to enjoin harassment or violence   CCP §§372, 374, 374.5
>> Appearance of minor under 12 to request or oppose temporary order   Fam §6229
> Minor's information confidentiality, request in civil harassment proceedings   CRC 3.1161, CRCAppx A
>> Release of minor's confidential information   CRC 3.1161
> Petition for
>> Memorandum in support of petition not required   CRC 3.1114
> Requests for protective orders   CRC 3.1160
> Translation of court orders into languages other than English   CCP §185

Judicial administration rules
> Workplace conduct policies
>> Courts' duties   CRC 10.351

Landlord and tenant
> Immigration or citizenship status of tenant, occupant, etc
>> Disclosures to immigration authorities with intent to intimidate or harass   CC §1940.35

Mail harassment protective orders
> Denial of petition for ex parte order, reasons to be provided   Fam §6320.5

Minors
> Appearance in proceedings to enjoin harassment or violence
>> Appearance of minor under 12 to request or oppose temporary order   Fam §6229
> Privacy protection
>> Forms, judicial council   CRCAppx A

Minor's appearance in proceedings to enjoin harassment or violence   CCP §§372, 374, 374.5
Phone harassment protective orders
> Denial of petition for ex parte order, reasons to be provided   Fam §6320.5

Protective orders   CCP §527.6
> Address or location of complaining party or family, prohibition on enjoined party from obtaining   CCP §527.10
> California law enforcement telecommunications (CLETS) information form, confidentiality and use of information   CRC 1.51, CRCAppx A
> COVID-19, emergency rule   CRCAppx I Emer Rule 8
> Denial of petition for ex parte order, reasons to be provided   Fam §6320.5
> Firearm relinquishment and disposition   CCP §527.9
>> Forms for firearm relinquishment   CRCAppx A
>> Procedures   CRC 4.700
> Forms
>> Judicial council legal forms   CRCAppx A
> Minor's information confidentiality, request in civil harassment proceedings   CRC 3.1161, CRCAppx A
>> Release of minor's confidential information   CRC 3.1161
> Possession of firearms   CCP §527.11
> Requests for protective orders   CRC 3.1160

Public officials, liability for harassment by   Gov §815.3
Sexual harassment (See SEXUAL HARASSMENT)
Small claims court judgment, award of attorney's fees on appeal from   CCP §116.790
Vexatious litigants   CCP §391.7
Witnesses protected from   Ev §765
Workplace harassment or discrimination
> Restrictions on nondisclosure agreements (NDAs) in certain cases   CCP §1001

Workplace Violence Safety Act
> COVID-19, emergency rule   CRCAppx I Emer Rule 8

HARBORS
Leasing of   CC §718

HARD-OF-HEARING PERSONS (See DEAF AND HARD OF HEARING PERSONS)

HARDSHIP
Child support (See CHILD SUPPORT)
Jury service, grounds for exemption from   CCP §204

HASTINGS COLLEGE OF LAW
Eminent domain taking by   CCP §1245.210

HATE CRIMES
Civil rights violations
    Construction or application of civil rights provisions in issue, solicitor general notified   CC §51.1
Misdemeanor hate crimes
    Sentencing considerations   CRC 4.330
Sentencing   CRC 4.427
    Aggravating circumstances   CRC 4.421
    Misdemeanor hate crimes, sentencing considerations   CRC 4.330
Violence
    Freedom from violence
        Waiver of right to freedom from violence, coerced or involuntary   CC §51.7

HAZARDOUS SUBSTANCES
Emergency response
    Public health and safety labor or service providers
        Logo or identifying mark of public agency, display   CC §3273
Enforcement of standards and regulations
    Civil actions   CCP §338.1
Exposure to hazardous materials or toxic substances
    Statutes of limitation   CCP §340.8
Underground storage
    Attorney general, civil actions to enforce provisions
        Fees and costs for attorney general   CCP §1021.8

HEALTH
Hearsay testimony showing   Ev §§1250 to 1252
Information Practices Act, information furnished under   CC §1798.24
Public health
    Medical information disclosures by providers
        Disease prevention or control   CC §56.10
Spousal support   Fam §4320

HEALTH, ACCIDENT, AND DISABILITY INSURANCE
Adoption
    Notice of reduced-cost options through California health benefit exchange or no-cost Medi-Cal
        Court notice to petitioners for adoption   Fam §8613.7
Advance health care directive as prerequisite for issuance of policy, prohibition on   Pro §4677
Annulment of marriage
    Notice of reduced-cost options through California health benefit exchange or no-cost Medi-Cal
        Court notice to parties upon filing for annulment, divorce, etc   Fam §2024.7
Benefits cards
    Radio frequency identification (RFID) to remotely read identification document without knowledge or consent   CC §1798.79
        Definitions   CC §1798.795
Child support (See **CHILD SUPPORT**)
Family law pilot project proceedings on health insurance matters (See **FAMILY LAW PILOT PROJECTS**)
Legal separation
    Notice of reduced-cost options through California health benefit exchange or no-cost Medi-Cal
        Court notice to parties upon filing for annulment, divorce, etc   Fam §2024.7
Medical claims data error correction   CC §57
Medical records, access to   CC §§56.10, 56.27
Power of attorney for health care as prerequisite for issuance of policy, prohibition on   Pro §4677
Punitive damages award, special notice of   CC §3296

HEALTH AIDS
Assignment for benefit of creditors, property exempt from   CCP §1801
Exempt property for purposes of enforcement of judgments   CCP §704.050

HEALTH BENEFIT EXCHANGE
Adoption
    Health insurance
        Notice of reduced-cost options through California health benefit exchange or no-cost Medi-Cal   Fam §8613.7
Annulment of marriage
    Health insurance
        Notice of reduced-cost options through California health benefit exchange or no-cost Medi-Cal   Fam §2024.7
Divorce
    Health insurance
        Notice of reduced-cost options through California health benefit exchange or no-cost Medi-Cal   Fam §2024.7

HEALTH BENEFIT EXCHANGE—Cont.
Legal separation
    Health insurance
        Notice of reduced-cost options through California health benefit exchange or no-cost Medi-Cal   Fam §2024.7

HEALTH CARE DECISIONS
Uniform Health Care Decisions Act   Pro §§4670 to 4679

HEALTH CARE DECISIONS LAW
Generally   Pro §§4600 to 4665
Admission to facility, prohibition against requiring advance health directive as prerequisite for   Pro §4677
Advance health care directives   Pro §§4670 to 4679
    Admission to facility, prohibition against requiring advance health care directive as prerequisite for   Pro §4677
    Appealable orders   Pro §1302.5
    Copy, effect of   Pro §4660
    Declarations under Natural Death Act as advance health care directives   Pro §4665
    Electronic directive or power of attorney   Pro §4673
    Forgery of health care directives   Pro §§4742, 4743
    Form of statutory advance health care directive   Pro §§4700, 4701
    Guardian or conservator nomination in advance health care directive   Pro §4672
    Individual health care instructions   Pro §4670
    Information about end of life decisions, advance directives, etc
        Development and communication   Pro §4806
    Insurance, prohibition against requiring advance health care directive as prerequisite for   Pro §4677
    Limitation of agent's authority   Pro §4753
    Medical records, right to inspect and consent to disclosure of   Pro §4678
    Mental health
        Psychiatric advance directives   Pro §4679
    Other jurisdictions, enforceability of directives executed in   Pro §4676
    Power of attorney for health care as advance health care directive   Pro §4665
    Psychiatric advance directives   Pro §4679
    Registration of advance health care directives   Pro §§4800 to 4806
        Identity card   Pro §4800
    Revocation   Pro §§4695 to 4698
    Sufficiency of directive   Pro §4673
    Witness requirements   Pro §§4674, 4675
Appealable orders   Pro §1302.5
Attorney's fees   Pro §4771
Conscientious objection, health care provider's right to decline to comply with health care decision based on   Pro §4734
Declarations under Natural Death Act as advance health care directives   Pro §4665
Decline to comply with health care decision, health care provider's right to   Pro §§4734 to 4736
Definitions   Pro §§4603 to 4643
Domestic partner, health care decisions for incapacitated partner by   Pro §4716
Euthanasia   Pro §4653
Forgery of health care directives   Pro §§4742, 4743
Form of statutory advance health care directive   Pro §§4700, 4701
Guardian or conservator nomination in advance health care directive   Pro §4672
Health care providers' duties and liabilities   Pro §§4730 to 4736, 4740, 4742
Homicide prosecution for hastening death by forging or concealing health care directives   Pro §4743
Immunities and liabilities   Pro §§4740 to 4743, 4782
Information about end of life decisions, advance directives, etc
    Development and communication   Pro §4806
Insurance, prohibition against requiring advance health care directive as prerequisite for   Pro §4677
Intentional violations   Pro §4742
Judicial proceedings
    Generally   Pro §§4750 to 4755
    Appealable orders   Pro §1302.5
    Attorney's fees   Pro §4771
    Jurisdiction   Pro §§4760 to 4762
    Petition and procedure on petition   Pro §§4765 to 4770
    Venue   Pro §4763
Jury trial as unavailable   Pro §4754
Medical records
    Agent's right to inspect and consent to disclosure of records in behalf of principal   Pro §4678
    Health care provider's duty to record   Pro §§4731, 4732
Mental health
    Psychiatric advance directives   Pro §4679
Ombudsman or advocate for patient in skilled nursing facility   Pro §4675

HEALTH CARE DECISIONS LAW—Cont.
Personal jurisdiction over agent or surrogate   Pro §4762
Petition and procedure on petition   Pro §§4765 to 4770
Power of attorney for health care (See **POWER OF ATTORNEY**)
Priority of legally recognized health care decisionmakers   Pro §4712
Psychiatric advance directives   Pro §4679
Registration of advance health care directives   Pro §§4800 to 4806
Resuscitative measures, request regarding   Pro §§4780 to 4786
Statutory form advance health care directive   Pro §§4700, 4701
Surrogates   Pro §4712
    Generally   Pro §§4711, 4714
    Disqualification   Pro §4715
    Domestic partner, health care decisions for incapacitated partner by   Pro §4716
    Hospital's duty to contact surrogate of patient incapable of communicating   Pro §4717
    Immunity from liability   Pro §4741
Temporary order prescribing care   Pro §4770
Venue   Pro §4763
Witness requirements for advance health care directives   Pro §§4674, 4675

HEALTH CARE FACILITIES
Pediatric care facilities
    Human trafficking or slavery
        Signs concerning relief from slavery or human trafficking, posting   CC §52.6

HEALTH CARE, GENERALLY (See **MEDICAL TREATMENT**)

HEALTH CARE POWERS OF ATTORNEY (See **POWER OF ATTORNEY**)

HEALTH CARE PROVIDERS
Commercial blockage tort affecting medical care facilities   CC §§3427 to 3427.4
Defined   CC §§3333.1, 3333.2, CCP §§340.5, 364, 667.7, 1295
Disciplinary proceedings against (See **ADMINISTRATIVE ADJUDICATION**)
Electronic medical records
    System requirements   CC §56.101
Health Care Decisions Law, duties and liabilities under   Pro §§4730 to 4736, 4740, 4742
Hospitals (See **HOSPITALS**)
Indemnification of   Gov §827
Liens, maximum amount recoverable   CC §3040
Medical claims data error correction   CC §57
Medical information corporation deemed as   CC §§56.06, 56.07
Medical records disclosure   CC §§56.10 to 56.16, 56.35 to 56.37, 56.101, 56.104
Power of attorney for health care, duties and liabilities with respect to   Pro §§4730 to 4736, 4740, 4742
Professional negligence (See **MALPRACTICE**)
Release of state from claim against   CC §1542.1
Resuscitative measures, liability for honoring request regarding   Pro §§4780 to 4786
Social security numbers, use of   CC §1798.85

HEALTH CARE SERVICE PLANS
Consultant under contract to Managed Health Care Department, immunity from prosecution of   CC §43.98
Duty of ordinary care to arrange for provision of medically necessary services, liability for breach of   CC §3428
Electronic medical records
    System requirements   CC §56.101
Genetic tests results, disclosure of   CC §56.17
Indemnification by health care provider for breach of duty by health care service plan, prohibition of   CC §3428
Liens, maximum amount recoverable   CC §3040
Medical claims data error correction   CC §57
Medical information
    Confidentiality
        Protection of confidentiality of medical information   CC §56.107
Medical records disclosure   CC §§56.10 to 56.17, 56.35 to 56.37, 56.101, 56.104
    Electronic medical records
        System requirements   CC §56.101
Punitive damages award, special notice of   CC §3296
Social security numbers, use of   CC §1798.85

HEALTH SERVICES DEPARTMENT
Claims against decedent's estate filed by (See **CLAIMS AGAINST ESTATES**)
Deceptive practice of charging unreasonable fees for assisting applicants of public social services   CC §1770
    Treble damages   CC §1780
Marriage (See **MARRIAGE**)
Medi-Cal recipients (See **MEDI-CAL**)

HEALTH SERVICES DEPARTMENT—Cont.
Special needs trust for minor or person with disability, notice of   Pro §§3602, 3605, 3611
    Definition of person with disability   Pro §3603
    Express consent of protected person to court orders, when required   Pro §3613

HEALTH STUDIO SERVICES CONTRACTS
Anabolic steroid warning, mandatory contract provision regarding   CC §1812.97 (Title 2.55 version of section)
Assignments of   CC §1812.88
Cancellation of   CC §§1812.85, 1812.89
Commencement of performance   CC §1812.85
Consideration requirements   CC §1812.86
Copy of contract, health studio customer receiving   CC §1812.82
Damages   CC §1812.94
Death of buyer, effect of   CC §1812.89
Defined   CC §1812.81
Disability of buyer, effect of   CC §1812.89
Duration of   CC §1812.84
Fraud, effect of   CC §1812.92
Money received prior to opening
    Trust account to hold money   CC §1812.96
Month-to-month contracts   CC §1812.98
Multiple contracts, effect of overlapping   CC §1812.83
New facilities
    Money received prior to opening
        Trust account to hold money   CC §1812.96
Noncompliance with act, effect of   CC §1812.91
Notes to third parties for health studio fees, execution of   CC §§1812.87, 1812.88
Pre-opening contracts
    Money held in trust   CC §1812.96
Public policy   CC §1812.80
Refunds   CC §§1812.85, 1812.89
Remedies, availability of   CC §1812.90
Severability clause of act   CC §1812.95
Waiver by buyer, effect of   CC §1812.93
Writing requirement   CC §1812.82

HEARING AIDS AND ACCESSORIES
Consumer warranty protection
    Extension of warranty period during service or repairs   CC §1795.6
    Return to seller for adjustment, replacement or refund   CC §1793.02

HEARING IMPAIRED PERSONS (See **DEAF AND HARD OF HEARING PERSONS**)

HEARINGS
Administration of decedents' estates
    Generally (See **ADMINISTRATION OF ESTATES**)
    Executors and administrators (See **EXECUTORS AND ADMINISTRATORS**)
    Independent administration   Pro §10451
Administrative hearings
    Adjudicative proceedings (See **ADMINISTRATIVE ADJUDICATION**)
    Rules and regulations (See **ADMINISTRATIVE PROCEDURE ACT**)
Adoption, authorization for, permanency planning hearing   CRC 5.706 to 5.740
Appellate review in civil cases
    Prehearing conferences   CRC 8.248
    Rehearings   CRC 8.268
        Supreme court   CRC 8.536
Appellate rules, supreme court and courts of appeal (See **APPELLATE RULES, SUPREME COURT AND COURTS OF APPEAL**)
Arbitration
    Generally (See **ARBITRATION**)
    Administrative adjudication proceedings (See **ADMINISTRATIVE ADJUDICATION**)
    International commercial arbitration (See **INTERNATIONAL COMMERCIAL ARBITRATION AND CONCILIATION**)
    Judicial arbitration (See **JUDICIAL ARBITRATION**)
Arraignments in superior court   CRC 4.100
Attachment (See **ATTACHMENT**)
Attorney discipline
    Testimony by judges   CRCSupp JudEthicsCanon 2
Business oversight commissioner, superior court hearings on sale of properties of savings and loan association whose business, properties and assets are in possession of   CCP §§73c, 73d
CARE act rules   CRC 7.2201 to 7.2303 (See **MENTAL DISABILITY**)
Chain of title, hearing on identity of party in   CCP §§770.060, 770.070

HEARINGS—Cont.
Change of names   CCP §1278
Child support (See **CHILD SUPPORT**)
Claim and delivery (See **CLAIM AND DELIVERY**)
Community assistance, recovery, and empowerment act
    CARE act rules   CRC 7.2201 to 7.2303 (See **MENTAL DISABILITY**)
Conciliation courts (See **CONCILIATION COURTS**)
Confession of judgments   CCP §1138
Conservators (See **CONSERVATORS**)
Coordination of actions
    Add-on cases   CRC 3.544
    Evidence   CRC 3.514
    Notice of hearing on petition   CRC 3.527
    Separate hearing on specified issues   CRC 3.528
Demurrers, notice of hearing   CRC 3.1320
Disclaimer of estate interest   Pro §277
Domestic violence protective order   Fam §§6340 to 6345
Emancipation of children (See **EMANCIPATION OF MINORS**)
Eminent domain (See **EMINENT DOMAIN**)
Enforcement of judgments (See **ENFORCEMENT OF JUDGMENTS**)
Executors of decedents' estates (See **EXECUTORS AND ADMINISTRATORS**)
Fact of death, hearing regarding establishment of   Pro §203
Family law rules (See **FAMILY RULES**)
Garnishment (See **GARNISHMENT**)
Guardianship (See **GUARDIAN AND WARD**)
Habeas corpus   CRC 4.551
Heirship determination proceedings   Pro §11704
Homesteads (See **HOMESTEADS**)
Independent administration of estate   Pro §10451
Indigent parents, adult child's petition to be relieved of obligation to support   Fam §§4412, 4414
Innkeeper's liens, writ of possession on   CC §§1861.6, 1861.8
International commercial arbitration and conciliation (See **INTERNATIONAL COMMERCIAL ARBITRATION AND CONCILIATION**)
Investment of funds of decedents estate   Pro §9732
Judges (See **JUDGES**)
Judicial arbitration (See **JUDICIAL ARBITRATION**)
Judicial notice
    Habeas corpus petition hearings   CRC 4.551
    Law and motion hearings   CRC 3.1306
Juvenile rules
    Termination of juvenile court jurisdiction
        Nonminor dependents or wards in foster care   CRC 5.555
Law and motion rules   CRC 3.1304, 3.1306
    Date, time and location of hearing, papers to specify   CRC 3.1110
    Demurrers   CRC 3.1320
    Evidence at hearing   CRC 3.1306
    Failure to appear, effect of   CRC 3.1304
    Injunctions   CRC 3.1160
    Telephone appearance at law and motion hearings   CRC 3.670
    Time for hearing   CRC 3.1304
Leases of city property, public hearings on   CC §719
Livestock service liens, sale under   CC §§3080.03 to 3080.22
Mandamus   CCP §§1094, 1094.5, 1094.6
Mechanic's lien, release from   CC §§8486, 8488
Mine co-owners failing to pay taxes   CCP §857
Missing persons (See **MISSING PERSONS**)
New trial motions   CCP §§660, 663.2
Office of Administrative Hearings (See **ADMINISTRATIVE PROCEDURE ACT**)
Partition (See **PARTITION**)
Power of attorney, notice of time and place of hearing on petitions involving   Pro §4544
Pretrial conferences (See **PRETRIAL CONFERENCES**)
Rehearings (See **REHEARINGS**)
Sentence and punishment hearings   CRC 4.433
Small claims court (See **SMALL CLAIMS COURTS**)
Sterilization proceedings (See **STERILIZATION**)
Superior court fees
    Motion, application or paper filed which would require hearing   Gov §70617
Surety bonds (See **SURETYSHIP, BONDS AND UNDERTAKINGS**)
Termination of parental rights
    Disposition hearings
        Setting hearing on termination   CRC 5.705
Transfer to another judge for hearing on motion   CCP §1006
Trusts (See **TRUSTS**)
Uniform Transfers to Minors Act, venue for hearing on petition filed under   Pro §3921
Validation proceedings   CCP §867

HEARINGS—Cont.
Vexatious litigant, motion to require security from   CCP §391.2
Will probate (See **WILL PROBATE**)

HEARSAY   Ev §§1200 to 1205
Administrative adjudicative proceedings   Gov §11513
Admissions   Ev §§1220, 1230
Ancient documents   Ev §1331
Arraignments, admissibility of hearsay evidence at   Ev §1203.1
Authorized statements, admissibility of   Ev §1222
Belief in truth of statement, admissibility upon establishment of   Ev §1221
Bill of sale, statements in   Ev §1330
Birth (See **BIRTH**)
Business records (See **BUSINESS RECORDS**)
Character (See **CHARACTER AND REPUTATION**)
Child abuse cases, admissibility in   Ev §§1228, 1253, 1293, 1360
Conspiracy to commit crime, admissible statements made while engaging in   Ev §1223
Constitutional inadmissibility of   Ev §1204
Contemporaneous statements, admissibility of   Ev §1241
Conviction record   Ev §452.5
Credibility of declarant attacked by hearsay evidence   Ev §§1202, 1235
Death (See **DEATH**)
Deeds, statements in   Ev §1330
Definition   Ev §§150, 1200
Dying declarations, admissibility of   Ev §1242
Elder abuse cases, admissibility of victim's videotaped statement in   Ev §1380
Emotional state of mind, evidence admissible concerning   Ev §§1250 to 1252
Exceptions   Ev §§1220 to 1390
Family history (See **FAMILY HISTORY**)
Former testimony, admissibility of   Ev §§1290 to 1294
Gang-related crimes, decedent's sworn statement concerning (See **GANG VIOLENCE**)
Identification of person aiding in crime, admissibility of hearsay evidence concerning   Ev §1238
Inconsistent statements   Ev §§1202, 1235, 1294
Judgments, admissibility of   Ev §§1300 to 1302
Kidnapping or murder of declarant to prevent arrest or prosecution of party against whom statement is offered, hearsay exception in cases of   Ev §1350
Liability of declarant, admissibility affected by   Ev §1224
Marriage (See **MARRIAGE**)
Mental state of mind, admissibility of evidence of   Ev §§1250 to 1252
Minors
    Child abuse cases, admissibility of minor's statement in   Ev §§1228, 1253, 1293, 1360
    Parent's action for injury to child, hearsay exception for child's statement against plaintiff in   Ev §1226
Missing persons (See **MISSING PERSONS**)
Murder or kidnapping of declarant to prevent arrest or prosecution of party against whom statement is offered, hearsay exception in cases of   Ev §1350
Official records and writings   Ev §§1280 to 1285
Physical injury or threat of physical injury to declarant, exception for statement concerning   Ev §1370
Physical state, admissibility of evidence of   Ev §§1250 to 1252
Public documents, generally   Ev §§1280, 1284
Records
    Official records and writings   Ev §§1280 to 1285
Reputation (See **CHARACTER AND REPUTATION**)
Res gestae   Ev §§1240, 1241
Sexually violent predators, commitment proceedings
    Statements admissible at hearing   Ev §1285
Spontaneous declarations, admissibility of   Ev §1240
Threat of physical injury to declarant, exception for statement concerning   Ev §1370
Title to property, admissibility of statements by declarant in proceedings for   Ev §1225
Trusts
    Establishment or amendment of revocable trust   Ev §1260
Unavailable as a witness
    Defined   Ev §240
    Wrongdoing to make witness unavailable
        Evidence of statements against wrongdoer as exception to hearsay   Ev §1390
Vital statistics records as admissible   Ev §1281
Wills, admissibility of evidence concerning   Ev §§1260, 1261, 1330
Writing previously made by witness   Ev §1237
Wrongful death action, deceased person's statements against plaintiff   Ev §1227

HEATING
Appurtenance   CC §662
Easement rights to   CC §801

HEATING—Cont.
Home improvement goods and services   CC §1689.8
Landlord terminating   CC §789.3
Solar energy used for   CC §801.5

HEIRLOOMS
Exempt property for purposes of enforcement of judgments   CCP §704.040

HEIRS
Abuse or neglect of elder or dependent adult by heir, effect of   Pro §259
Advancements (See **ADVANCEMENTS**)
Attorney General as party to heirship determination proceedings   Pro §11703
"By representation" property distribution to heirs   Pro §§240 to 246
Death of heir prior to distribution of estate   Pro §§11801, 11802
Deposit of funds with county treasurer for benefit of minor heir   Pro §§11850 to 11854
Deraignment of title proceedings
    Hearing   Pro §249
    Notice of hearing   Pro §248.5
    Petition for   Pro §248
Determination of heirship proceedings
    Attorney General as party   Pro §11703
    Hearing on   Pro §11704
    Judge, disqualification of   Pro §7060
    Notice of   Pro §11701
    Omission from testamentary instruments (See within this heading, "Omission from testamentary instruments")
    Orders   Pro §11705
    Petition for   Pro §11700
    Responsive pleadings   Pro §11702
Disclaimer of interest   Pro §§260 to 295
Eminent domain proceedings, heirs as parties to   CCP §1260.240
Escheat to state (See **ESCHEAT**)
Executors and administrators
    Determination of heirship
        Participation by personal representative   Pro §11704
Future interests taken by   CC §§698, 699
Hearings on heirship determination   Pro §11704
Homicide, effect of   Pro §§250 to 258
Identity of, petition and hearing procedure for determining   Pro §§248 to 249.8
    Conception of child after death of decedent
        Early distribution, petition for   Pro §249.8
        Effect on distribution   Pro §249.6
        Failure to provide timely notice   Pro §249.7
        Notice   Pro §§249.5 to 249.7
        Presumption of birth during lifetime of decedent   Pro §249.5
Intestate succession (See **INTESTATE SUCCESSION**)
Judges in proceedings, disqualification of   Pro §7060
Killing of ancestor by   Pro §§250 to 258
Marital privilege   Ev §984
Mobilehome park tenant, rights of heirs of   CC §798.78
Neglect or abuse of elder or dependent adult by heir, effect of   Pro §259
Notice of heirship determination proceedings   Pro §11701
Omission from testamentary instruments
    Generally   Pro §§21600, 21620
    Applicability of omitted child provisions   Pro §§21600, 21630
    Believed dead at time of execution of testamentary instruments, share of child   Pro §21622
    Definitions   Pro §21601
    Exceptions to omitted child's entitlement   Pro §21621
    Satisfaction of omitted child's share   Pro §21623
Orders in heirship determination proceedings   Pro §11705
Partition
    Generally (See **PARTITION**)
Partition of real property act   CCP §§874.311 to 874.323
Per capita property distribution to heirs   Pro §§245, 247
Per stirpes property distribution to heirs   Pro §§240 to 246
Petition for heirship determination   Pro §11700
Physician and patient privilege   Ev §1000
Posthumous children (See **POSTHUMOUS CHILDREN**)
Pretermitted heir (See within this heading, "Omission from testamentary instruments")
Prisoners
    Fact of death
        Notice when heir is prisoner   Pro §§216, 9202
Psychotherapist-patient privilege in claims by   Ev §1019
Shelley's case, modification of rule   CC §§779, 780
Statutes of limitation on actions to set aside sale of estate assets   Pro §10382
Uniform partition of heirs property act   CCP §§874.311 to 874.323
Unknown heirs
    Administration of estates
        Generally   Pro §§11850 to 11854

HEIRS—Cont.
Unknown heirs—Cont.
    Administration of estates —Cont.
        Public administrators, administration by   Pro §§7624, 7643, 7644, 7663
Wills
    Generally (See **WILLS**)
    Omitted child (See within this heading, "**Omission from testamentary instruments**")
Wrongful death actions, heirs maintaining   CCP §377.60

HIDES (See **LIVESTOCK**)

HIGH FIDELITY EQUIPMENT (See **PHONOGRAPHS AND PHONOGRAPH RECORDS**)

HIGH-FREQUENCY LITIGANTS
Construction-related accessibility claims
    Complaints
        Contents of complaint filed by high-frequency litigant   CCP §425.50
        Notice to defendant of rights to stay and early evaluation conference   CC §55.54
    Defined   CCP §425.55
Fees   Gov §70616.5

HIGH SCHOOLS (See **SCHOOLS**)

HIGHWAY PATROL
License plates
    Automated license plate recognition (ALPR) operators   CC §§1798.90.5 to 1798.90.55

HIGHWAYS (See **STREETS AND HIGHWAYS**)

HIKING
Owner's liability for recreational land   CC §846

HISTORY
Books, admissibility of   Ev §1341
Eminent domain statutes affecting historic sites   CCP §1240.680
Family history (See **FAMILY HISTORY**)
Information Practices Act, historical information furnished under   CC §1798.24
Reputation, community history as evidence of   Ev §1320
Statutes of limitation on actions for theft of articles of historic or artistic importance   CCP §338

HIV (See **ACQUIRED IMMUNE DEFICIENCY SYNDROME (AIDS)**)

HOBOS
Railroad, liability for injury   CC §1714.7

HOGS (See **LIVESTOCK**)

HOLIDAYS
As last day of time limitation period   CCP §12
Cesar Chavez Day, designation of   CCP §135
Computation of time for performance of act
    Generally   CC §10, CCP §§12 to 12b
    Judicial holidays excluded   CCP §134
Computation of time in which act provided by law is to be done   CC §10, CCP §§12 to 12b
Defined   CCP §12a
Designation of   CCP §10
Discovery, effect on time limits for   CCP §2016.060
Extension of time to next day which is not a holiday   CCP §12a
Judicial holidays
    Alternative days observed as   CCP §135
    Computation of time for performance of act, effect on   CCP §134
    Court calendar, effect on   CCP §136
    Courts closed for transaction of judicial business   CCP §134
    Days designated as   CCP §135
    Exceptions to nontransaction of judicial business   CCP §134
    Rules of court
        Saturday or Sunday, judicial holiday falling on   CRC 1.11
Optional bank holiday   CC §9
Performance
    Next business day, postponement to   CC §11, CCP §13
    Saturday, performance on   CCP §13b
    Special holiday, effect of performance on   CCP §13a
Postponing performance of act required by law or contract to next business day   CC §11, CCP §13
Public office closed for day, effect of   CCP §12b

HOLIDAYS—Cont.
Rules of court
  Computation of time   CRC 1.10
  Judicial holiday falling on Saturday or Sunday   CRC 1.11
Saturdays as   CCP §12a

HOLOCAUST (See **NAI GERMANY**)

HOLOGRAPHIC WILLS
Probate   Pro §8222
Validity of   Pro §6111

HOME APPLIANCES
Heating appliances or apparatus
  Construction defects, actions for
    Actionable defects   CC §896
Service contracts
  Retailers' duties under service contracts   CC §1794.45

HOME BREW (See **ALCOHOLIC BEVERAGES**)

HOME EQUITY LOAN DISCLOSURE ACT   CC §§2970 to 2971

HOME EQUITY SALES CONTRACTS
Cancellation, right of
  Generally   CC §1695.4
  Notice of cancellation, form of   CC §1695.5
  Return of contract to buyer   CC §1695.6
Contents of   CC §1695.3
Conveyance with option to repurchase by equity purchaser, presumptions regarding   CC §1695.12
Criminal penalties   CC §1695.8
Damages, recovery of   CC §1695.7
Definitions   CC §1695.1
Disclosure requirement in agreement regarding buyer's right to cancel   CC §1695.5
Legislative intent   CC §1695
Liability of equity purchaser
  Generally   CC §1695.15
  Limited liability, validity of provisions for   CC §1695.16
  Misrepresentation, liability for   CC §1695.6
Licensing requirements for agent or employee of equity purchaser   CC §1695.17
Misrepresentations, equity purchaser's liability for   CC §1695.6
Notices required   CC §§1695.3 to 1695.5
Option to repurchase
  Conveyance with option to repurchase by equity purchaser, presumptions regarding   CC §1695.12
  Prohibition against encumbering property subject to   CC §1695.6
Remedies available   CC §§1695.7, 1695.9
Requirements of   CC §1695.2
Rescission of foreclosure where unconscionable advantage of property owner   CC §1695.14
Return of contract on cancellation   CC §1695.6
Severability of unconstitutional provisions   CC §1695.11
Terms of   CC §1695.3
Unconscionable advantage of property owner
  Prohibition against transactions resulting from   CC §1695.13
  Rescission of foreclosure, action for   CC §1695.14
Waiver of contract provisions regulated by law as against public policy   CC §1695.10

HOME-FINDING SOCIETIES (See **ADOPTION**)

HOME HEALTH AGENCIES
Medical claims data error correction   CC §57

HOME IMPROVEMENT CONTRACTS
Broker or lender negotiating home improvement financing through contractor, unfair trade practice constituted by   CC §1770
Exempt property for purposes of enforcement of judgments   CCP §704.030
Finance charges   CC §§1805.6, 1810.10
Hazard insurance coverage imposed by lender, limitations on   CC §2955.5
Home solicitation contract encumbering real property   CC §§1689.8, 1770
Mechanics' liens   CC §§8000 to 9566 (See **MECHANICS' LIENS**)
Mortgage broker or lender negotiating home improvement financing through contractor, unfair trade practice constituted by   CC §1770
Roofing contracts (See **ROOFING WARRANTIES**)
Senior citizens
  Home improvement contract encumbering primary residence   CC §§1770, 1804.1

HOMELAND SECURITY DEPARTMENT, U.S
Detention
  Electronic testimony or participation in child custody proceedings allowed in cases of   Fam §3012

HOMELESS PERSONS
Hotels
  Interim homelessness programs, occupancy   CC §§1954.08 to 1954.092
Interim homelessness programs, occupancy   CC §§1954.08 to 1954.092
  Continuity of occupancy
    Requirements   CC §1954.09
    Tenant rights   CC §1954.091
  Definitions   CC §1954.08
  Duration of occupancy
    Tenant rights   CC §1954.091
  Nontransient hotel or motels
    Designation   CC §1954.092
    Termination policies   CC §1954.092
Landlord and tenant
  Persons at risk of homelessness
    Temporary residence by persons at risk of homelessness in dwelling unit of tenant   CC §1942.8
Misconduct by persons in transitional housing programs   CC §§1954.10 to 1954.18
Motels
  Interim homelessness programs, occupancy   CC §§1954.08 to 1954.092
Risk of homelessness, persons at
  Landlord and tenant
    Temporary residence by persons at risk of homelessness in dwelling unit of tenant   CC §1942.8
Shelters
  Interim homelessness programs, occupancy   CC §§1954.08 to 1954.092
Youth
  Intergenerational housing developments   CC §51.3.5
  Transition age youth
    Intergenerational housing developments   CC §51.3.5

HOMEOWNERS' ASSOCIATION
Common interest developments (See **COMMON INTEREST DEVELOPMENTS**)
Floating homes and floating home marinas (See **FLOATING HOMES**)

HOMEOWNER'S GUIDE TO EARTHQUAKE SAFETY   CC §§2079.8, 2079.11

HOMEOWNER'S PROPERTY TAX EXEMPTION (See **TAXATION**)

HOME SOLICITATION SALES CONTRACTS
Cancellation   CC §§1689.6, 1689.9
  Notice of right to cancel in contract   CC §1689.7
  Service and repair project contracts   CC §1689.15
Definitions   CC §1689.5
Disaster, contracts void within prescribed period from   CC §1689.14
Disclosure requirement in agreement or offer regarding buyer's right to cancel   CC §1689.7
Emergency repairs or services, applicability to   CC §1689.13
Fixtures   CC §§1689.8, 1689.9
Home improvement loan encumbering real property   CC §§1689.8, 1770
Immediately necessary repairs, inapplicability of requirements to   CC §1689.13
Notice of cancellation by buyer   CC §1689.6
Personal emergency response unit, canceling contract to purchase   CC §§1689.6, 1689.7
Refund of payments   CC §1689.10
Return of goods by buyer   CC §1689.11
Services rendered prior to cancellation of agreement, compensation for   CC §1689.11
Spanish language
  Language used in negotiation to be used in written contract   CC §1689.7
Telemarketing
  Unlawfulness of contracts generated by unlawful telemarketing   CC §1670.6
Waiver of contract provisions regulated by law as against public policy   CC §1689.12

HOMESTEADS
Abandonment of declared homesteads   CCP §§704.980, 704.990
Appeals
  Homestead exemption, appeal of   CCP §704.830
  Probate homestead, appeal of order setting aside   Pro §§1303, 1310
Application for order for sale of homestead   CCP §§704.750, 704.760
Attachment writs on declared homesteads   CCP §487.025

HOMESTEADS—Cont.

Bankruptcy proceedings, applicability of exemption in   CCP §703.140
    Amount of exemption, determination   CCP §703.150
Bid failing to exceed homestead exemption, consequences of   CCP §704.800
Claims against decedent's estate, liability of probate homestead for   Pro §6526
Conservatorship, management of homestead property subject to   Pro §§3000 to 3154
    Authorization of transaction, findings and order   Pro §3144
Costs, judgment creditor's recovery of   CCP §704.840
Death of declared homestead owner, protection from lien where   CCP §704.995
Debt liability on homestead property, prohibition against acceleration of   CCP §704.810
Declared homesteads
    Abandonment of   CCP §§704.980, 704.990
    Alienation of   CCP §704.940
    Attachment writ on   CCP §487.025
    Creation of   CCP §704.920
    Death of declared homestead owner, protection from lien where   CCP §704.995
    Definitions   CCP §704.910
    Evidentiary effect of declaration   CCP §704.940
    Judgment liens on   CCP §704.950
    Probate homesteads, effect on   Pro §6528
    Sale of homestead generally (See within this heading, "Sale of homestead")
Default, procedure requirement on   CCP §704.790
Exemption from enforcement of judgments
    Consumer debt, exemption of principal residence from execution of judgment lien   CCP §699.730
Governing law   Pro §6528
Hearing
    Conservatorship, homestead property subject to   Pro §3081
    Sale of homestead, hearing on application for   CCP §§704.770 to 704.790
Homestead exemption
    Generally   CCP §704.720
    Amount of   CCP §§704.730, 704.965
    Appeal, right to   CCP §704.830
    Bid failing to exceed homestead exemption, consequences of   CCP §704.800
    Declared homesteads generally (See within this heading, "Declared homesteads")
    Definition   CCP §704.710
    Extension of time, notice of   CCP §704.830
    Sale of homestead generally (See within this heading, "Sale of homestead")
    Transitional provisions   CCP §694.090
Joint tenancy, sale of homestead property owned in   CCP §704.820
Liens
    Acceleration of debt liability prohibited because of lien or encumbrance on homestead property   CCP §704.810
Modification of probate homesteads   Pro §6527
Notice of hearing
    Conservatorship, homestead property subject to   Pro §3081
    Probate homesteads   Pro §6525
Petition
    Conservatorship, homestead property subject to   Pro §§3120 to 3123
        Contents of petition   Pro §3121
    Probate homestead, petition to set apart   Pro §6525
Probate homesteads
    Appealable orders   Pro §§1303, 1310
    Claims against decedent's estate, liability for   Pro §6526
    Court discretion to set apart   Pro §6520
    Declaration of homestead, effect of   Pro §6528
    Defined   Pro §60
    Dissolution of marriage proceedings   Fam §2337
    Duration of   Pro §6524
    Factors for setting apart   Pro §6523
    Modification of   Pro §6527
    Notice of hearing   Pro §6525
    Persons entitled to   Pro §6521
    Petition to set apart   Pro §6525
    Priority of property subject to   Pro §6522
    Recordation of   Pro §7263
    Termination of   Pro §6527
    Time requirements for setting apart   Pro §6524
Recordation of probate homestead   Pro §7263
Sale of homestead
    Generally   CCP §704.720
    Application for order for   CCP §§704.750, 704.760
    Bid failing to exceed homestead exemption, consequences of   CCP §704.800
    Cost, recovery of judgment creditor's   CCP §704.840
    Distribution of proceeds   CCP §704.850

HOMESTEADS—Cont.

Sale of homestead—Cont.
    General requirements for   CCP §704.740
    Hearing on application for sale   CCP §§704.770 to 704.790
    Joint tenancy or tenancy in common, sale of dwelling owned in   CCP §704.820
    Lien or encumbrance on homestead, prohibition against acceleration of debt where   CCP §704.810
    Preservation of right of levy and sale   CCP §704.970
    Voluntary sale of declared homestead, exemption of proceeds from   CCP §704.960
Tenancy in common, sale of homestead property owned in   CCP §704.820

HOMICIDE

Advance health care directive, homicide prosecution for hastening death by forging or concealing   Pro §4743
Attempting or soliciting murder of spouse
    Damages for injuries to married person   Fam §782.5
    Spousal support
        Denial of support   Fam §4324
Hearsay exception for statement of declarant murdered or kidnapped to prevent arrest or prosecution of party against whom statement is offered   Ev §1350
Inheritance rights, effect on   Pro §§250 to 258
Juveniles tried as adults, sentencing upon conviction   CRC 4.510
Power of attorney for health care, prosecutable actions under   Pro §4743
Punitive damages for   CC §3294
Spouse
    Attempted murder of spouse (See **DOMESTIC VIOLENCE**)
    Custody and visitation determinations following one parent's murder by other parent   Fam §3030
Statutes of limitation
    Felony offenses, damage actions based on commission of   CCP §340.3
Trial court budget and fiscal management
    Cost reimbursement for homicide trials   CRC 10.811

HONORARIUM

Judges accepting   CCP §170.9

HONORARY TRUSTS   Pro §15211

HORSES

Auction, notice required at   CC §1834.8
Dogs injuring   CC §3341
Landowner's liability for injury from horseback riding on recreational land   CC §846
Liens
    Breeders   CC §§3062 to 3064.1
    Pasturage   CC §3051
Slaughter
    Notice that sale of horses for slaughter for human consumption constitutes felony   CC §1834.8

HORTICULTURE

Leasing land, limitations on   CC §717

HOSPICES

Medical claims data error correction   CC §57

HOSPITALS

Access to health facilities
    Force, threat or other obstruction of access to health facilities or school grounds   CC §1708.9
Adoption, release of child to be placed for   Fam §8607
Claims against public entities and employees (See **CLAIMS AGAINST PUBLIC ENTITIES AND EMPLOYEES**)
Commercial blockage tort affecting   CC §§3427 to 3427.4
Communication of information against doctors, action for damages concerning   CC §§43.7, 43.8
Confidentiality of medical information   CC §§56.101, 56.104, 56 to 56.37
Consumer debt collection
    Hospital debt
        Collection practices and required communications   CC §1788.14
        Complaints brought be debt collector   CC §1788.185
        Default judgments   CC §1788.185
Damages
    Hospital lien on personal injury award   CC §§3045.1 to 3045.6
    Malpractice (See **MALPRACTICE**)
Decedent's personal property to surviving spouse, delivery of   Pro §330
Electronic medical records
    System requirements   CC §56.101

HOSPITALS—Cont.

Emergency treatment, hospital lien on damages awarded to injured person in payment for   CC §§3045.1 to 3045.6
Fair debt buying practices
    Hospital debt
        Actions, contents of complaints   CC §1788.58
        Written statements to collect debt   CC §1788.52
Health care provider's professional negligence (See **MALPRACTICE**)
Health care surrogate for patient incapable of communicating, duty to make reasonable efforts in contacting   Pro §4717
Liens
    Damages awarded to injured party, hospital lien on   CC §§3045.1 to 3045.6
    Notice of sale for satisfaction of   CC §§1862.5, 3045.3
    Unclaimed personal property of patient, lien sale of   CC §1862.5
Limitation of actions
    Generally (See within this heading, "**Statutes of limitation**")
    Malpractice (See **MALPRACTICE**)
Loss of property, liability for   CC §§1859 to 1867
Mandamus for purpose of inquiry into validity of administrative action   CCP §1094.5
Medical claims data error correction   CC §57
Mental hospitals (See **MENTAL HOSPITALS**)
Minors (See **MINORS**)
Morbidity or mortality studies, admissibility of findings of   Ev §§1156, 1156.1
Nurses (See **NURSES**)
Nursing homes (See **NURSING HOMES**)
Periodic payment of damages   CCP §667.7
Physicians and surgeons (See **PHYSICIANS AND SURGEONS**)
Power of attorney for health care, prohibition on conditioning admission to hospital on execution of   Pro §4677
Professional review committees
    Discovery prohibition   Ev §§1157, 1157.5, 1157.7
    Liability   CC §§43.7, 43.8
Public administrator of death of patient, notification of   Pro §7600.5
Public liability (See **CLAIMS AGAINST PUBLIC ENTITIES AND EMPLOYEES**)
Recommendation of medical staff, limited immunity from liability for action taken on   CC §43.97
Release
    Adoption, child to be placed for   Fam §8607
Research findings, admissibility of   Ev §§1156, 1156.1
Review committees
    Discovery prohibition   Ev §§1157, 1157.5, 1157.7
    Liability of   CC §§43.7, 43.8
Sexual assaults
    Medically incapacitated patient, sexual battery against
        Statute of limitations on sexual assault damages   CCP §340.16
Statutes of limitation
    Lien, enforcement of   CC §3045.5
    Malpractice (See **MALPRACTICE**)
    Recovery or conversion of personal property left at   CCP §341a
    State or county hospitals, actions on accounts for support of patients at   CCP §345

HOSTILE POSSESSION (See **ADVERSE POSSESSION**)

HOSTS

Alcoholic beverages, social host's liability after serving   CC §1714

HOTELS AND MOTELS   CC §§1859 to 1867

Baggage
    Liability for loss or injury   CC §§1859 to 1867
Blind persons having equal rights to use of accommodations   CC §§54.1, 54.3, 54.4, 55
    Construction or application of provisions in issue, solicitor general notified   CC §55.2
    Touch screen devices for
        Self-service check-in at hotels or passenger transportation facilities   CC §54.9
Cancellation of reservations
    Refunds   CC §§1748.80 to 1748.84
Checkout time, eviction of guests failing to depart by   CC §1865
Children as guests, innkeeper's rights with respect to   CC §1865
Customer records
    Privacy
        Duties of innkeepers   CC §53.5
Disabled persons having equal rights to use of accommodations   CC §§54.1, 54.3, 54.4, 55
    Construction or application of provisions in issue, solicitor general notified   CC §55.2

HOTELS AND MOTELS—Cont.

Discrimination
    Law enforcement officer, firefighter or search and rescue dog handlers serving outside jurisdiction
        Lodging, eating or transportation, prohibition on discrimination   CC §54.25
Eviction of guests failing to depart by posted checkout time   CC §1865
Food service in hotels, status of   CC §1940
Guests
    Personal property, loss or injury   CC §§1859 to 1867
    Records, privacy
        Innkeeper duties   CC §53.5
Guide dogs
    Permitted in
        Construction or application of provisions in issue, solicitor general notified   CC §55.2
Guide dogs permitted in   CC §§54.1 to 54.4, 55
Homeless persons
    Interim homelessness programs, occupancy   CC §§1954.08 to 1954.092
Human trafficking or slavery
    Sex trafficking activity, hotel permitting or benefiting from
        Actions against hotel for sex trafficking activity   CC §52.65
    Signs, businesses required to post notice concerning relief from slavery or human trafficking   CC §52.6
Liens   CC §§1861 to 1861.28
Loss of property, liability for   CC §§1859, 1860
Minor guests, innkeeper's rights with respect to   CC §1865
Notices
    Eviction of guests failing to depart by posted checkout time   CC §1865
    Loss of property, notice as to liability for   CC §1860
    Rates, notices of   CC §1863
Occupancy, right to   CC §1940.1
Privacy
    Customer records
        Duties of innkeepers   CC §53.5
Prostitution prohibited
    Sex trafficking activity, hotel permitting or benefiting from
        Actions against hotel for sex trafficking activity   CC §52.65
Records
    Customer records
        Privacy, duties of innkeepers   CC §53.5
Refunds for canceled reservations   CC §§1748.80 to 1748.84
    Action for violation of provisions   CC §1748.83
    Definitions   CC §1748.80
    Exceptions to provisions   CC §1748.84
    Issuance of refund   CC §1748.82
    Time period for cancellation without penalty   CC §1748.81
Safe, liability limited to articles in   CC §1860
Sex trafficking activity, hotel permitting or benefiting from
    Actions against hotel for sex trafficking activity   CC §52.65
Statutes of limitation on actions for recovery or conversion of personal property left at   CCP §341a
Tenants, persons classified as   CC §1940
Unruh Civil Rights Act   CC §§51, 52

HOUSE CARS AND CAMPERS

Mobilehomes (See **MOBILEHOMES**)
Recreational vehicles (See **RECREATIONAL VEHICLES**)

HOUSEHOLD EXPENSES

Attachment, availability of   CCP §483.010

HOUSEHOLD FURNISHINGS AND APPLIANCES

Assignment for benefit of creditors, property exempt from   CCP §1801
Exempt property for purposes of enforcement of judgments   CCP §704.020

HOUSE OF REPRESENTATIVES (See **CONGRESS**)

HOUSES

Domestic violence cases, order for restitution of housing expenses in   Fam §§6342, 7720
Dwelling houses (See **DWELLING HOUSES**)
Family homes (See **FAMILY HOME**)
Public housing (See **PUBLIC HOUSING**)

HOUSE TRAILERS (See **MOBILEHOMES**)

HOUSING

Affordable housing developments
    Covenants, conditions, and restrictions
        Recorded restrictive covenants, unenforceability in face of approved and recorded restrictive covenant affordable housing modification document   CC §714.6

HOUSING—Cont.
Affordable housing developments—Cont.
    Covenants, conditions, and restrictions—Cont.
        Sale of unit to nonprofit housing corporation after unit not purchased by income-qualifying person or family within time period   CC §714.7
Affordable housing, shared appreciation loans
    Inoperative provisions   CC §§1917.010 to 1917.075, 1917.110 to 1917.175
Caregivers
    Intergenerational housing developments   CC §51.3.5
Covenants, conditions, and restrictions
    Affordable housing developments
        Recorded restrictive covenants, unenforceability in face of approved and recorded restrictive covenant affordable housing modification document   CC §714.6
        Sale of unit to nonprofit housing corporation after unit not purchased by income-qualifying person or family within time period   CC §714.7
Intergenerational housing developments   CC §51.3.5
Low-income housing
    Actions challenging priority housing development projects
        Special motion to strike   CCP §425.19
Shared appreciation loans
    Inoperative provisions   CC §§1917.010 to 1917.075, 1917.110 to 1917.175
Transition age youth
    Intergenerational housing developments   CC §51.3.5
Transitional housing
    Misconduct by participants   CC §§1954.10 to 1954.18

HOUSING COOPERATIVES AND HOUSING COOPERATIVE TRUSTS
CC §§817 to 817.4
Actions against boards and members
    Attorneys' fees and costs for successful plaintiffs   CC §817.4
Common interest developments
    Generally   CC §§4000 to 6150
Definitions   CC §817
Limited-equity housing cooperatives
    Defined   CC §817
    Dissolution   CC §817.2
Public funds accepted
    Restrictions on use of corporate funds   CC §817.4
Workforce housing cooperative trusts
    Defined   CC §§817, 817.1
    Dissolution   CC §817.2
    Sponsor organizations
        Standing as member   CC §817.3

HOUSING DEVELOPMENT LOANS
Acceleration of   CC §711.5
Injunction against project, undertaking for   CCP §529.2

HOUSING DISCRIMINATION
Attorney general, civil actions to enforce provisions
    Fees and costs for attorney general   CCP §1021.8
Common interest developments, restrictive covenants
    Unlawful restrictive covenants, deletion   CC §4225
Elderly persons, restrictions favoring
    Deed restrictions
        Applicability of prohibitions on restrictions to housing for elderly   CC §§782, 782.5
Restrictive covenants
    Common interest developments
        Unlawful restrictive covenants, deletion   CC §4225

HUMAN EMBRYOS
Unauthorized use or misuse of sperm, ova or embryo
    Civil action for damages   CC §1708.5.6

HUMAN IMMUNODEFICIENCY VIRUS (HIV) (See ACQUIRED IMMUNE DEFICIENCY SYNDROME (AIDS))

HUMAN TRAFFICKING
Access to domestic violence incident reports   Fam §6228
Actions   CC §52.5
Debts of victim attributable to human trafficking
    Findings as to   CC §52.5
Domestic violence incident reports
    Access to domestic violence incident reports   Fam §6228
Entertainment facility tickets   CC §52.66
Evidence
    Other crimes of defendant in sex offense prosecution, admissibility   Ev §1108

HUMAN TRAFFICKING—Cont.
Hotels and motels
    Sex trafficking activity, hotel permitting or benefiting from
        Actions against hotel for sex trafficking activity   CC §52.65
Landlord and tenant
    Restrictions on termination of tenancy   CCP §1161.3
    Victims of human trafficking
        Restrictions on termination of tenancy   CC §1946.7
Nuisance
    Attorney's fees recoverable for enjoining use of building for   CC §3496
Prostitution
    Victims forced to commit prostitution
        Evidentiary significance   Ev §1161
        Expunging arrest or vacating adjudication, form   CRCAppx A
        Extortion, serious felony, assault, domestic violence, human trafficking, sexual battery or stalking, victims or witnesses, inadmissibility of evidence of prostitution   Ev §1162
        Vacatur relief for arrests or convictions for nonviolent crimes while victim   CRC JudAdminStand 4.15
Real property used in offense
    Attorney's fees recoverable for enjoining use of building for   CC §3496
Sentence and punishment
    Human trafficking as mitigating circumstance   CRC 4.423
Signs
    Businesses required to post notice concerning relief from slavery or human trafficking   CC §52.6
Supply chains of certain businesses
    Disclosures by businesses of efforts to eradicate slavery and human trafficking in supply chain   CC §1714.43
Unlawful detainer
    Restrictions on termination of tenancy   CC §1946.7, CCP §1161.3
Victim-caseworker privilege   Ev §§1038 to 1038.3
    Child abuse reporting
        Duty to report not diminished by provisions   Ev §1038.3
    Compelling disclosure
        Grounds   Ev §1038.1
    Definitions   Ev §1038.2
    Eligibility to claim privilege   Ev §1038
    In chambers proceeding to determine ruling on privilege   Ev §1038.1
    Limitations on privilege
        Caseworker to notify victim   Ev §1038
    Waiver of privilege   Ev §912
Victims
    Expert testimony on effect of human trafficking on victim   Ev §1107.5
    Expunging arrest or vacating adjudication
        Judicial council legal forms   CRCAppx A
    Landlord and tenant
        Restrictions on termination of tenancy   CC §1946.7
    Prostitution or other commercial sex acts resulting from human trafficking
        Evidentiary significance   Ev §1161
    Sentences
        Mitigating factors   CRC 4.423
    Vacatur relief for arrests or convictions for nonviolent crimes while victim
        Procedure   CRC JudAdminStand 4.15

HUNTERS AND HUNTING
Easement rights   CC §§801, 802
Fines and penalties
    Bail schedule   CRC 4.102
Owner's liability for recreational land   CC §846

HUSBAND AND WIFE
Adoption proceedings (See ADOPTION)
Bigamy proceedings, admissibility of spousal testimony in   Ev §§972, 985
Blood tests to determine paternity   Fam §7541
Business transactions   Fam §721
Challenge of juror for implied bias, relationships giving rise to   CCP §229
Child support (See CHILD SUPPORT)
Community property (See COMMUNITY PROPERTY)
Conciliation courts (See CONCILIATION COURTS)
Conservatorship of spouse lacking legal capacity (See CONSERVATORS)
Contracts altering spouses' legal relations   Fam §1620
Criminal conversation (See CRIMINAL CONVERSATION)
Custody (See CUSTODY OF CHILDREN)
Defending own and spouse's rights   CCP §370
Defined   Fam §11
    Registered domestic partner included in term spouse   CC §14, CCP §17, Ev §215, Fam §143, Pro §72

HUSBAND AND WIFE—Cont.
Dissolution of marriage
    Generally (See **DISSOLUTION OF MARRIAGE**)
    Annulment (See **ANNULMENT**)
    Summary dissolution of marriage (See **SUMMARY DISSOLUTION OF MARRIAGE**)
Domestic violence (See **DOMESTIC VIOLENCE**)
False representation as spouse, sexual acts performed by person making
    Statute of limitations
        Civil damages   CCP §340.16
Fidelity, obligation of   Fam §720
Fiduciary relationship   Fam §721
Formerly married persons, reference to spouse to include   Fam §11
Homesteads (See **HOMESTEADS**)
Homicide
    Attempted murder (See **DOMESTIC VIOLENCE**)
    Custody and visitation determinations following one parent's murder by other parent   Fam §3030
Interstate family support   Fam §§5700.101 to 5700.903 (See **INTERSTATE FAMILY SUPPORT**)
Joint credit accounts, regulation of   CC §1812.30
Joint tenancy, holding property in   Fam §750
Married persons may sue or be sued without spouse being joined   CCP §370
Mutual obligations of   Fam §720
Name of spouse
    Dissolution of marriage, restoration of former name   Fam §§2080 to 2082, 2401
    Prohibition against refusal to engage in business with person using birth or former name regardless of marital status   CCP §1279.6
Negligence
    Concurrent negligence of spouse   Fam §783
    Imputed negligence   Fam §1000
    Married person causing injury to spouse   Fam §782
    Personal injury damages (See **COMMUNITY PROPERTY**)
    Third person causing injury to spouse   Fam §783
Parentage
    Actions to challenge parentage   Fam §7541
    Blood tests to determine   Fam §7541
    Presumption   Fam §§7540, 7611
        Actions to challenge parentage   Fam §7541
Partition (See **PARTITION**)
Personal injury damages (See **COMMUNITY PROPERTY**)
Predeceased spouse
    Defined   Pro §59
Presumption of paternity   Fam §§7540, 7611
    Actions to challenge parentage   Fam §7541
Privileged communications
    Marital privilege (See **MARITAL PRIVILEGE**)
Probate rules
    Spousal property petitions   CRC 7.301
Protection of spouse   CC §50
Putative spouse   Fam §§2251, 2252
Quasi-community property (See **COMMUNITY PROPERTY**)
Reconciliation (See **CONCILIATION COURTS**)
Relation of spouses   Fam §§720, 721
Rule against perpetuities, effect of (See **PERPETUITIES AND RESTRAINTS ON ALIENATION**)
Separate property (See **COMMUNITY PROPERTY**)
Specific performance of contract to obtain spouse's consent   CC §3390
Spousal property petitions   CRC 7.301
Spousal rape
    Statute of limitations on sexual assault damages   CCP §340.16
Spousal support (See **SPOUSAL SUPPORT**)
Summary dissolution of marriage (See **SUMMARY DISSOLUTION OF MARRIAGE**)
Support and maintenance
    Interstate family support   Fam §§5700.101 to 5700.903 (See **INTERSTATE FAMILY SUPPORT**)
Support proceedings, marital privilege   Fam §3551
Surviving spouse (See **SURVIVING SPOUSE**)
Third parties, transactions with   Fam §721
Transactions with each other   Fam §721
Value of property, spouse testifying on   Ev §813

HUSBAND AND WIFE PRIVILEGE   Ev §§980 to 987 (See **MARITAL PRIVILEGE**)

HYPNOSIS
Witnesses, hypnosis of   Ev §795

I

ICWA
Indian child welfare act involuntary placements   CRC 5.480 to 5.488 (See **INDIAN CHILD WELFARE ACT INVOLUNTARY PLACEMENTS**)

IDENTIFICATION
Acknowledgment, identification of party making   CC §§1185, 1196, 1197
Adoption, disclosure of identity of birth parents   Fam §§8702, 8818, 9203
Apartment house owner, procedure for identifying   CC §§1961 to 1962.7
Cards (See **IDENTIFICATION CARDS**)
Check cashers   CC §1789.35
Child support orders, mistaken identity cases   CRC 5.375
Conservators
    Photographs
        Conservatee, annual photograph   Pro §2360
Contract, identification of parties to   CC §1558
Credit card holder, prohibition against vendor eliciting personal information concerning   CC §1747.08
Credit card number, prohibited use of   CC §1725
Credit report information, identification of party requesting (See **CREDIT REPORTING**)
Electronic court records, remote access
    Government entities, access by
        Identity verification and management   CRC 2.541
    Parties, designees, attorneys, court-appointed persons or persons working in legal organization or qualified legal services project, access by
        Identity verification and management   CRC 2.523
Emancipated minors, identification cards for   Fam §§7140 to 7143
Escrow agent rating service
    Personally identifiable information, safeguarding   CC §§1785.28, 1785.28.6
Hearsay testimony concerning   Ev §1238
Judgment lien on property of misidentified owner, release of   CCP §§697.410, 697.660
Marriage
    Remote licensing and solemnization
        Photo identification   Fam §552
Marriage license applicants   Fam §354
Missing person, disputed identity of reappearing   Pro §12408
Mortgage unpaid balance, proving identity of party requesting   CC §2943
Owner of property, procedure for identifying   CC §§1961 to 1962.7
Process and service of process
    Levying officer electronic transactions act
        Identifiers, exclusion or redaction   CCP §263.7
Quieting title action, identity of person in chain of title for   CCP §§770.010 to 770.080
Radio frequency identification (RFID)
    Use to remotely read identification document without knowledge or consent   CC §1798.79
        Definitions   CC §1798.795
Serial numbers (See **SERIAL NUMBERS**)
Small estates without administration, identification of affiant collecting property under   Pro §13104
Subcutaneous implanting of identification device, requiring of another   CC §52.7
Theft of identity (See **IDENTITY THEFT**)
Trainers of seeing eye dogs to carry   CC §§54.1 to 54.4, 55
Trust deed unpaid balance, proving identity of party requesting   CC §2943
Weapons (See **FIREARMS AND OTHER WEAPONS**)

IDENTIFICATION CARDS
Age-restricted products, sales
    Verification of age for sale of age-restricted products
        Government-issued identification   CC §1798.99.1
Driver's license (See **DRIVER'S LICENSES**)
Emancipated minors   Fam §§7140 to 7143
Radio frequency identification (RFID)
    Use to remotely read identification document without knowledge or consent   CC §1798.79
        Definitions   CC §1798.795

IDENTITY THEFT   CC §1798.93
Business entity filings   CC §§1798.200 to 1798.203
    Definitions   CC §1798.200
    Disclaimers of proper authority   CC §1798.203
    Order for alleged perpetrator to show cause
        Contents of orders   CC §1798.202
        Findings   CC §1798.202
        Form   CRCAppx A
        Hearing on petition   CC §1798.202

IDENTITY THEFT—Cont.
Business entity filings —Cont.
    Order for alleged perpetrator to show cause—Cont.
        Petition   CC §1798.201
Certificate of Identity: Judicial Determination of Factual Innocence (CR-150) forms, access to   CRC 4.601
    Judicial council forms   CRCAppx A
Change of address requests
    Credit card issuers and telephone account businesses
        Notice to customer of requests   CC §1799.1b
Collection agencies
    Duties upon notice from victim of identity theft   CC §1788.18
Common interest developments
    Record inspection
        Withholding or redacting information from records   CC §5215
Consumer credit reporting, security alerts or security freezes for (See **CREDIT REPORTING**)
Continuing jurisdiction of action   CC §1798.95
Credit card application using person's name by unauthorized person   CC §1748.95
Credit reports
    Address verification by users of credit reports   CC §1785.20.3
    Blocking access to fraudulent data   CC §1785.15
    Fees for security freezes for victims prohibited   CC §1785.15
    Security alerts or freezes   CC §§1785.11.1 to 1785.11.11
    Victims to be provided information as to statutory rights   CC §1785.15.3
Credit services organizations
    Personal information
        Protection of personal information   CC §1789.135
Debt collectors
    Duties upon notice from victim of identity theft   CC §1788.18
Definitions   CC §1798.92
Escrow agent rating service
    Personally identifiable information, safeguarding   CC §§1785.28, 1785.28.6
Joinder of claimants against victim of identity theft   CC §1798.94
Perpetrator of identity theft, claimant's rights and remedies against   CC §1798.97
Process and service of process
    Levying officer electronic transactions act
        Identifiers, exclusion or redaction   CCP §263.7
Radio frequency identification (RFID)
    Use to remotely read identification document without knowledge or consent   CC §1798.79
        Definitions   CC §1798.795
Social security number confidentiality   CC §§1798.85 to 1798.89
Statute of limitations   CC §1798.96
Victim service providers, personal information protection   CC §§1798.79.8 to 1798.79.95

IGNITION INTERLOCK DEVICES
Forms
    Judicial council legal forms   CRCAppx A
Orders, guidelines   CRC 4.325

ILLEGITIMATE CHILDREN (See PARENT AND CHILD; PATERNITY)

ILLNESS
Child support, illness of obligor   Fam §4726
Contagious diseases (See **CONTAGIOUS DISEASES**)
Contempt, effect on person under arrest for   CCP §1221
Cotrustee, illness as grounds for incapacity of   Pro §15622
Genetic information generally (See **GENETIC INFORMATION**)
Inspection warrants for purposes of eradication of (See **INSPECTION WARRANTS**)
Juror, procedure in event of illness of   CCP §233
Last illness (See **LAST ILLNESS**)
Preference, motion for   CCP §36
Telegrams, priority for transmitting   CC §2207
Witnesses unavailable due to   Ev §240

IMMATERIAL ALLEGATIONS
Defined   CCP §431.10

IMMIGRATION
Child custody
    Effect of immigration status   Fam §3040
    Special immigrant juvenile status   CCP §155
        Nonprofit charitable corporations, guardianship of minor with special immigrant juvenile status   Pro §2104.1

IMMIGRATION—Cont.
Consultants
    Attorney general, civil actions to enforce provisions
        Fees and costs for attorney general   CCP §1021.8
    Foreign legal consultants   CRC 9.44
Contracts
    Local government or law enforcement agency contracts to detain noncitizens for civil immigration custody
        Prohibition   CC §1670.9
Criminal law and procedure
    Disclosure of immigration status in open court   Ev §351.4
Damages
    Children and minors
        Immigration status irrelevant   CC §3339.5
Disclosure in open court of immigration status
    Civil actions   Ev §351.3
    Criminal cases   Ev §351.4
Discrimination prohibited   CC §51
Evidence of immigration status
    Disclosure in open court
        Civil actions   Ev §351.3
    Tort or wrongful death cases
        Inadmissibility   Ev §351.2
Family rules
    Request for orders
        Special immigrant juvenile findings, request   CRC 5.130
Forcible entry and detainer
    Immigration or citizenship status irrelevant to issue of liability or remedy   CC §3339.10
Guardianships
    Special immigrant juvenile status
        Appointment of guardians   Pro §1510.1
        Findings   CRC 7.1020
Interpreters
    Juveniles
        Determination of special immigrant juvenile status   Ev §757
Juvenile courts
    Special immigrant juvenile status
        Findings   CRCAppx A
        Guardianships by nonprofit charitable corporation   Pro §2104.1
        Interpreters in proceedings to determine special immigrant juvenile status   Ev §757
        Request for orders, family rules   CRC 5.130
Juvenile status
    Special immigrant juvenile status   CCP §155
        Forms, judicial council   CRCAppx A
        Guardianships by nonprofit charitable corporation   Pro §2104.1
        Request for orders, family rules   CRC 5.130
Landlord and tenant
    Immigration or citizenship status of persons
        Actions to recover possession, restrictions on landlord actions based in immigration or citizenship status   CCP §1161.4
        Definition of immigration or citizenship status   CC §1940.05
        Involuntary quit by tenant, restrictions on landlord actions based in immigration or citizenship status   CCP §1161.4
        Prohibited acts based on   CC §§1940.3, 1940.35
        Retaliation against tenant by reporting or threatening to report to immigration authorities   CC §1942.5
        Unduly influencing tenant to vacate by threatening disclosures relating to immigration or citizenship status   CC §1940.2
Minors
    Actions for damages
        Discovery into immigration status prohibited   CC §3339.5
        Immigration status irrelevant   CC §3339.5
Superior court
    Jurisdiction
        Child custody, etc, determinations   CCP §155
Torts
    Evidence of immigration status
        Inadmissibility of evidence in tort or wrongful death cases   Ev §351.2
Wages, hours and working conditions
    Deductions from wages for costs of transport to US
        Void contracts   CC §1670.7
Wrongful death
    Evidence of immigration status
        Inadmissibility of evidence in tort or wrongful death cases   Ev §351.2

IMMIGRATION CONSULTANTS
Foreign legal consultants
    Fingerprinting of special admission attorneys   CRC 9.9.5

IMMUNITY
Anaphylaxis
> Epinephrine auto-injector administration for first aid
>> Immunity from civil liability of lay rescuers, prehospital emergency medical care providers or authorized entities   CC §1714.23

Ancillary administration, immunity of sister state personal representative taking small estate property without   Pro §12573

Animals trapped in unattended vehicles
> Rescue of animal trapped in closed vehicle, immunity from civil or criminal liability for damage to vehicle   CC §43.100

Arbitrators   CCP §1297.119
Automated external defibrillators, use   CC §1714.21
Cardiopulmonary resuscitation (See **CARDIOPULMONARY RESUSCITATION**)
Civil rights, actions to enforce
> Peace officer or custodial officer defendants
>> State immunity provisions, inapplicability   CC §52.1

Claims against public entities and employees (See **CLAIMS AGAINST PUBLIC ENTITIES AND EMPLOYEES**)
Crime reports, persons or organizations making   CC §48.9
Death of person committing felony on property, immunity of landowner for   CC §847
Defibrillator, immunity from liability associated with emergency care using   CC §1714.21
Dependent children   CRC 5.548
Drones   Gov §§853 to 853.5
Drug take-back bins, secure
> Liability of collector, limitation   CC §1714.24

Emergencies
> Drones or unmanned aircraft systems damaged by emergency responder
>> Provision of emergency services by responder and interference with services by drone   CC §43.101
> Vehicles   CC §43.102

Epinephrine auto-injector administration for first aid
> Immunity from civil liability of lay rescuers, prehospital emergency medical care providers or authorized entities   CC §1714.23

Eyeglasses
> Nonprofit charitable organization and volunteer eye care professionals donating screening, eyeglasses, etc   CC §1714.26

Farm owner's immunity for injury to person invited on premises to glean farm products for charitable purposes   CC §846.2
Firefighters
> Volunteer firefighters
>> Donators of fire protection apparatus to volunteer departments   CC §1714.11

Health Care Decisions Law   Pro §§4740 to 4743, 4782
Health care service plans, immunity of consultant to Managed Health Care Department overseeing statutory compliance of   CC §43.98
International commercial conciliators   CCP §§1297.431, 1297.432
Interstate family support
> Employer complying with income withholding order   Fam §5700.504
> Limited immunity of complainant   Fam §5700.314

Juvenile court proceedings, witnesses in   CRC 5.548
Juvenile court social workers and child protection workers, extent of civil immunity of   Gov §820.21
Libel (See **LIBEL AND SLANDER**)
Motor vehicles
> Animals trapped in unattended vehicles
>> Rescue of animal trapped in closed vehicle, immunity from civil or criminal liability for damage to vehicle   CC §43.100
> Records, false information in   Fam §7142

National Influenza Program, immunity of public entity or employee participating in   Gov §856.6
911 emergency services
> Telecommunications services providing   CC §1714.55

Ophthalmologists
> Nonprofit charitable organization and volunteer eye care professionals donating screening, eyeglasses, etc   CC §1714.26

Optometrists
> Nonprofit charitable organization and volunteer eye care professionals donating screening, eyeglasses, etc   CC §1714.26

Personal injuries to person committing felony on property, immunity of landowner for   CC §847
Power of attorney for health care   Pro §§4740, 4741
Prescribed burns   CC §3333.8
Professional societies   CC §§43.7, 43.91, 43.95, 43.97
Psychotherapist's failure to protect from or predict violent behavior   CC §43.92
Rescue of child from vehicle
> Immunity from liability for damage or trespass to vehicle   CC §43.102

Residential building permit reviewers   CC §43.99

IMMUNITY—Cont.
Secure drug take-back bins
> Liability of collector, limitation   CC §1714.24

Settlement of dispute, immunity for communicating information to assist in   CC §43.9
Slander (See **LIBEL AND SLANDER**)
Space flight liability and immunity   CC §§2210 to 2212
Telecommunications
> 911 emergency services, telecommunications services providing   CC §1714.55

Vision screening
> Nonprofit charitable organization and volunteer eye care professionals donating screening, eyeglasses, etc   CC §1714.26

IMPARTIALITY
Change of venue, grounds for   CCP §397
Judges (See **JUDGES**)

IMPEACHMENT OF VERDICT   Ev §1150

IMPERSONATION (See **FALSE PERSONATION**)

IMPLANTS
Subcutaneous implanting of identification device, requiring of another   CC §52.7

IMPLIED CONTRACTS (See **CONTRACTS AND AGREEMENTS**)

IMPLIED REPEALS
Privileged communications provisions   Ev §920

IMPOTENCY
Annulment of marriage   Fam §2210
Slander   CC §46

IMPOUND ACCOUNTS
Deposits by borrower or vendee, requirement for   CC §2954.1
Interest on   CC §2954.8
Trust deeds and mortgages   CC §§2954, 2955

IMPRISONMENT (See also **PRISONERS**)
Adverse possession, disabilities tolling statutes of limitation in actions for   CCP §328
Appellate rules, superior court appeals
> Filing
>> Timeliness of documents mailed from custodial institutions   CRC 8.817

Appellate rules, supreme court and courts of appeal
> Filing
>> Timeliness   CRC 8.25

Conditions of confinement, applicability of provision tolling statutes of limitation on action arising from   CCP §352
Contempt of court   CCP §1219
Debts, imprisonment for   CCP §501
Habeas corpus (See **HABEAS CORPUS**)
Mandamus, imprisonment for disobedience of writ   CCP §1097
Tolling statutes of limitation   CCP §352
Torts, imprisonment for   CCP §501

IMPROVEMENT DISTRICTS (See **PUBLIC ENTITIES**)

IMPROVEMENTS
Adverse possession (See **ADVERSE POSSESSION**)
Architects (See **ARCHITECTS**)
Asian language contracts, translations   CC §1632
Condominium, right to improve separate interest in   CC §4760
> Architectural review and decisionmaking, standards when required   CC §4765

Construction of improvements to real property (See **BUILDING CONSTRUCTION**)
Eminent domain (See **EMINENT DOMAIN**)
Engineers (See **ENGINEERING**)
Excavation (See **EXCAVATIONS**)
Family home, order specifying responsibility for maintenance of   Fam §3806
Fixtures (See **FIXTURES**)
Good faith improver (See **GOOD FAITH IMPROVER**)
Hazard insurance coverage imposed by lender, limitations on   CC §2955.5
Home improvements (See **HOME IMPROVEMENT CONTRACTS**)
Landlord entering to make   CC §1954
Lien claims
> Arbitration rights, lien claim affecting   CCP §1281.5
> Mechanics' liens (See **MECHANICS' LIENS**)
> Public improvements (See **PUBLIC CONTRACTS AND WORKS**)

Mobilehome parks (See **MOBILEHOMES**)
Public improvements (See **PUBLIC CONTRACTS AND WORKS**)

IMPROVEMENTS—Cont.
Realty sales contracts requirements   CC §2985.51
Spanish language contract requirements, applicability of   CC §1632
Support from adjacent property for   CC §832
Surveyors (See **SURVEYS AND SURVEYORS**)
Taxation (See **TAXATION**)
Trust property   Pro §16229

IMPUTED NEGLIGENCE (See **NEGLIGENCE**)

INADVERTENCE (See **MISTAKE**)

IN CAMERA PROCEEDINGS
Sealed records   CRC 2.585

INCARCERATION
Jury summons, failure to respond to   CCP §209

INCEST
Annulment of marriage   Fam §2200
Aunts and nephews, invalidity of marriage between   Fam §2200
Siblings, invalidity of marriage between   Fam §2200
Uncles and nieces, invalidity of marriage between   Fam §2200

INCOME
Accumulations   CC §§722 to 726
Blind persons, income considered when renting housing accommodations to   CC §§54.1, 54.3, 54.4, 55
Decedent's estate (See **ADMINISTRATION OF ESTATES**)
Disabled persons, income considered when renting housing accommodations to   CC §§54.1, 54.3, 54.4, 55
Family law matters, income and expense declaration defined   Fam §95
Support proceedings, income and expense declarations in (See **CHILD SUPPORT; SPOUSAL SUPPORT**)
Trust income (See **TRUSTS**)
Unclaimed property fund, separate accounts in   CCP §1319
Will (See **WILLS**)

INCOME AND EXPENSE DECLARATION
Child support (See **CHILD SUPPORT**)
Spousal support (See **SPOUSAL SUPPORT**)

INCOME TAX
Child support (See **CHILD SUPPORT**)
Community property
　Joint income tax liability   Fam §2628
Decedent's estate, tax claims against   Pro §§9200 to 9205
Declaratory judgments in action by nonresident   CCP §1060.5
Dissolution of marriage
　Division of community property   Fam §2628
Fiduciary income and principal act
　Unitrust
　　Plan methods and standards   Pro §16338
Liens by federal government, Uniform Registration Act for   CCP §§2100 to 2107
　Fees for recording under act   Gov §27388.1
Power of attorney, powers under statutory form of   Pro §4463
Public entity's liability for tax law administration   Gov §§860 to 860.4
Returns
　Child support delinquency
　　Use of return data to collect delinquency   Fam §17452
Support proceedings   Fam §§3552, 3665, 3667, 4320

INCOMPETENCE (See **MENTAL DISABILITY**)

INCONSISTENT STATEMENTS (See **WITNESSES**)

INCONVENIENCE
Damages recoverable for   CC §3333.2

INCONVENIENT FORUM
Generally   CCP §§410.30, 410.40
Choice of law (See **CHOICE OF LAW**)
Stay or dismissal of action, motion for   CCP §§410.30, 418.10
Tribal court civil money judgment act
　Objections
　　Grounds for objection   CCP §1737
Uniform Child Custody Jurisdiction and Enforcement Act, inconvenient forum determination under   Fam §3427

INCORPORATION BY REFERENCE
Fictitious mortgage or trust deed, provisions of   CC §2952
Will construction (See **WILL CONSTRUCTION**)

INCRIMINATION (See **SELF-INCRIMINATION**)

INDECENCY AND OBSCENITY
Children and minors
　Commercial sexual exploitation of minor by social media platform   CC §3345.1
　Distribution of unauthorized obscene material
　　Actions   CC §52.8
　Offenses against
　　Statute of limitations on sexual assault damages   CCP §340.16
　Settlement of civil cases
　　Confidentiality agreements, restrictions   CCP §1002
Debt collectors using obscene language   CC §1788.11
Electronic messages depicting obscene material
　Knowingly sending unsolicited messages
　　Actions   CC §1708.88
Public nuisance, attorney's fees recoverable for enjoining commercial sale or distribution of obscene matter as   CC §3496
Unauthorized obscene material
　Actions for distribution   CC §52.8

INDEMNITY
Acceptance of contract   CC §2795
Agents covered by   CC §2775
Attorneys' fees   CCP §1021.6
Bailment, loss from property held under   CC §§1893, 1894
Borrowed property, defects in   CC §1893
Cartage contracts   CC §2784.5
Claims against public entities and employees (See **CLAIMS AGAINST PUBLIC ENTITIES AND EMPLOYEES**)
Community property as consideration for indemnity contract   Fam §782
Conditional liability   CC §§2806 to 2808
Construction contracts   CC §§2782 to 2784
　January 1, 2013, contracts on or after   CC §2782.05
　Subcontractor's defense or indemnity obligation   CC §2782.05
　Void or unenforceable provisions, insertion   CC §2782.05
Costs of action   CC §2778, CCP §1038
Damages, reimbursement for   CC §2779
Defined   CC §2772
Deposits, requirements for   CC §1833
Design professionals
　Public agencies, contracts with   CC §2782.8
Engineers (See **ENGINEERING**)
Foster family agency accountability
　Indemnification void   CCP §1062.33
Good faith of settlement, contest of   CCP §877.6
Hauling contracts   CC §2784.5
Hazardous materials identification, indemnity agreements concerning   CC §2782.6
Health care service plan, prohibition against indemnification by health care provider for breach of duty by   CC §3428
Hospitals, public
　Medical or mental facilities (See **CLAIMS AGAINST PUBLIC ENTITIES AND EMPLOYEES**)
Interpretation of contract   CC §§2778, 2782
Joint and several liability   CC §2777
Joint tortfeasors, effect of settlement by one of   CCP §877.6
Judgment admissible from earlier action   Ev §1301
Judicial administration rules
　Contracts with courts   CRC 10.203
Latent deficiencies in planning or construction of improvement to real property, limitation of actions for damages for   CCP §337.15
Multiple tortfeasors, effect of settlement by one of   CCP §877.6
Negligence   CC §2784.5
Notices
　Attorneys' fees in indemnity action   CCP §1021.6
　Default notice   CC §§2807, 2808
Past conduct   CC §2774
Public employees, indemnification of (See **PUBLIC OFFICERS AND EMPLOYEES**)
Public officer bonds (See **BONDS OF PUBLIC OFFICIALS**)
Public works
　Wrap-up insurance, construction contracts   CC §2782.96
Repairs, contract for   CC §2783
Residential construction contracts   CC §2782
　Wrap-up insurance, construction contracts   CC §2782.9
　　Private residential improvement covered   CC §2782.95
Retail installment sales financed by third-party loans   CC §1801.6
Retail seller's right against manufacturer   CC §1792
Rules of construction of indemnity agreements   CC §2778
Spouse's act of negligence causing injury to other spouse   Fam §782
Trucking contracts   CC §2784.5
Two or more persons covered by   CC §2776

INDEMNITY—Cont.
Unclaimed deposits and payments escheated, indemnity of holder of   CCP §1561
Unclaimed property, delivery of   CCP §1321
Unlawful conduct, exclusion of   CC §2773
Willful misconduct   CC §2784.5
Witness, public entity defending or indemnifying   Gov §995.9
Wrap-up insurance, construction contracts
    Public works   CC §2782.96
    Residential construction   CC §2782.9
        Private residential improvements   CC §2782.95

INDEPENDENT ADMINISTRATION OF ESTATES ACT
Actions not requiring court supervision   Pro §§10550 to 10564
Allowing claims against estate, personal representative's authority for   Pro §§10501, 10518, 10550
Bond of representative   CRC 7.204
Bond requirement   Pro §10453
Citation of Act   Pro §10400
Claims against estate, acting on
    Court's action on   CRC 7.402
    Personal representatives' action on claim   CRC 7.401
Compromise of claims   Pro §§10501, 10518, 10550
Contracts, authority to make   Pro §10532
Conveyances
    Completion of decedent's contract to convey property, authority for   Pro §10517
    Option in will, authority to transfer property pursuant to   Pro §10516
Court supervision
    Generally   Pro §§10500 to 10503
    Actions not requiring court supervision   Pro §§10550 to 10565
    Defined   Pro §10401
    Notice of proposed action   Pro §§10580 to 10592
Disclaimers, power to make   Pro §10519
Exchange of property   Pro §10537
Full authority defined   Pro §10402
Governing law   Pro §§10406, 10530
Limited authority
    Defined   Pro §10403
    General provision   Pro §9640
    Petition to limit powers of personal representative   Pro §10454
Management and control of estate property   Pro §10531
Notice of hearing on petition for independent administration   Pro §10451
Notice of proposed action   CRC 7.250, Pro §§10580 to 10592
Objections   Pro §10452
Options
    Granting option to purchase realty, authority of   Pro §10515
    Transfer or convey property, effect of option in will to   Pro §10516
Petition for revocation of authority for continued administration   Pro §10454
Powers of independent administrator   Pro §10502
Preliminary distributions   Pro §§10520, 11623
Removal of personal representative   Pro §10592
Report of actions taken without court supervision   CRC 7.250
Revocation of authority for continued administration, petition for   Pro §10454
Sale of property
    Generally   Pro §§10503, 10511
    Bond requirement for   CRC 7.204, Pro §10453
    Exclusive right to sell property, power to grant or deny   Pro §10538
    Personal property sales   Pro §10537
Settlement of claims   Pro §§10501, 10518, 10550
Special administrators   Pro §10405
Statutory limitations on independent administrator   Pro §9140
Third party claims, determining merit of   Pro §10518
Will prohibiting independent administration, effect of   Pro §10404

INDEPENDENT ADOPTION OF CHILDREN (See **ADOPTION**)

INDEPENDENT CONTRACTORS
Consumer privacy rights
    Communications or transactions, applicability of rights   CC §1798.145
    Personnel records, applicability of rights   CC §1798.145
Public entity's liability for tortious act of   Gov §815.4
Small claims courts advisors   CCP §116.940

INDEPENDENT WHOLESALE SALES REPRESENTATIVES (See **WHOLESALE SALES REPRESENTATIVES**)

INDEX
Appellate rules, superior court appeals
    Limited civil cases in appellate division
        Record on appeal   CRC 8.838

INDEX—Cont.
Fees for filing and indexing unspecified papers   Gov §26850
Tax liens, fee for filing and indexing of   CCP §2104

INDIAN CHILD WELFARE ACT INVOLUNTARY PLACEMENTS   CRC 5.480 to 5.488
Active efforts to prevent family breakup   CRC 5.485
Adoption
    Confidentiality, affidavit
        Providing to bureau of Indian affairs   CRC 5.488
    Decree
        Copies   CRC 5.488
Appearances
    Discretionary tribal participation   CRC 5.530
    Tribal appearance by telephone or other remote means   CRC 3.672, 5.482
Applicability of act, determination by court   CRC 5.482
Applicability of provisions   CRC 5.480
Commencement of proceedings
    Time for commencement   CRC 5.482
Conservatorship proceedings
    Applicable provisions   CRC 7.1015
    Notice requirements   CRC 7.51
Continuances   CRC 5.482
    Dispositional hearings when court knows or has reason to know Indian child involved
        Limits on continuances   CRC 5.550
Dismissal
    Tribal court having exclusive jurisdiction   CRC 5.483
Emergency proceedings involving Indian child   CRC 5.484
Evidence
    Placement, evidence for   CRC 5.485
    Termination of parental rights   CRC 5.486
Family finding and notice performed by social worker or probation officer   CRC 5.637
Forms
    Judicial council   CRCAppx A
Guardianship proceedings
    Applicable provisions   CRC 7.1015
    Notice requirements   CRC 7.51
Inquiry as to Indian status of child   CRC 5.481
    Guardianship and conservatorship proceedings   CRC 7.1015
Intervention by tribe or by Indian custodian   CRC 5.482
Invalidation of placement
    Petitions   CRC 5.487
Notice
    Judicial council forms   CRCAppx A
    Proof of notice   CRC 5.482
    Requirements when Indian child involved   CRC 5.481
    Time interval between notice and commencement of proceedings   CRC 5.482
Preferences as to placement
    Applicable provisions   CRC 5.482, 5.485
    Change in placement, analysis and consideration of placement preferences   CRC 5.485
    Consultation with tribe   CRC 5.482
    Deviation from preferences   CRC 5.485
Prevention of family breakup
    Active efforts to prevent family breakup   CRC 5.485
Proceedings to which applicable   CRC 5.480
Proof of notice   CRC 5.482
Reason to know child is Indian child
    Criteria   CRC 5.481
Records
    Adoption records   CRC 5.488
Removal
    Emergency proceedings involving Indian child
        Standards for removal   CRC 5.484
Return of custody of child
    Emergency proceedings involving Indian child
        End of emergency, return of child   CRC 5.484
    Request to return   CRC 5.487
Termination of parental rights
    Findings   CRC 5.486
    Refusal to order termination
        Grounds   CRC 5.486
    Selection of permanent plan   CRC 5.725
Time limitation
    Emergency proceedings, duration   CRC 5.484
Transfer of case to tribal court
    Advisement when transfer order granted   CRC 5.483

INDIAN CHILD WELFARE ACT INVOLUNTARY PLACEMENTS—Cont.
Transfer of case to tribal court—Cont.
  Mandatory transfers
    Circumstances requiring   CRC 5.483
  Orders   CRC 5.483
    Advisement when transfer order granted   CRC 5.483
  Presumptive transfers   CRC 5.483
  Proceedings after transfer ordered   CRC 5.483
  Request to transfer
    Burden of establishing cause to deny request   CRC 5.483
    Denial, grounds   CRC 5.483
    Documentation   CRC 5.483
    Factors considered in determining   CRC 5.483
Tribal participation
  Discretionary tribal participation   CRC 5.530
  Request, form   CRCAppx A

INDIANS (See **NATIVE AMERICANS**)

INDICTMENT, INFORMATION AND COMPLAINT
Agent's duty to furnish information to principal   CC §2020
Credit reports (See **CREDIT REPORTING**)
Nuisance, maintenance of   CC §§3491, 3492
Setting aside
  Motion for   CRC 4.111
Time for filing information   CRC 4.110

INDIGENT AID
Statutes of limitation, waiver of   CCP §360.5

INDIGENT PERSONS
Appeals
  Notice of appeal, filing   CCP §936.1
  Payment guidelines for appointed counsel in Supreme Court   CRCSupp PayGuideAppoint
  Settled statement in lieu of reporter's transcript, use of   CRC 8.137
  Supreme court and courts of appeal
    Waiver of fees   CRC 8.26
Appointment of attorney (See within this heading, **"Court-appointed attorney"**)
Attorneys
  Civil legal representation   Gov §§68650, 68651
  Court-appointed attorney (See within this heading, **"Court-appointed attorney"**)
  Indian children as proposed wards or conservatees   Pro §1474
  Withdrawal of legal service agency attorney for indigent client   CCP §§285.2 to 285.4
Child to support indigent parent   Fam §§4400 to 4414
Civil legal representation   Gov §§68650, 68651
Costs and fees   CRC 3.50 to 3.58, Gov §§68630 to 68641 (See within this heading, **"Waiver of fees"**)
Court-appointed attorney
  Criminal appeals   CRC 8.300
  Custody and visitation cases, counsel for child
    Inability of party to pay   CRC 5.241
  Fixed fee appointments   CRCSupp FixedFeeAppoint
  Supreme court, payment guidelines   CRCSupp PayGuideAppoint
  Termination of parental rights, appointment of counsel for indigent appellant   Fam §7895
  Without compensation, appointment of attorney or law firm to represent indigent client   CCP §285.4
Court fees and costs
  Waiver
    Applicants defined   Gov §68631.5
    Conservatorships and guardianships   Gov §68631
    Petitioners defined   Gov §68631.5
    Probate cases   CRC 3.50 to 3.53, 7.5
  Waiver of fees   CRC 3.50 to 3.58, Gov §§68630 to 68641
    Bench warrants to secure attendance of witnesses, applicability of waiver   Gov §26744.5
Criminal trials
  Electronic filing and service of documents
    Fees not chargeable in some criminal actions   CRC 2.255
Emancipation of minors, rescission of declaration of minor for   Fam §7130
Fee waiver
  Appeals in supreme court or court of appeals   CRC 8.26
  Generally   CRC 3.50 to 3.58, Gov §§68630 to 68641 (See within this heading, **"Waiver of fees"**)
Forma pauperis
  Civil rules governing application for waiver of fees and costs   CRC 3.50 to 3.58

INDIGENT PERSONS—Cont.
Forma pauperis—Cont.
  Waiver of fees generally   Gov §§68630 to 68641
    Bench warrants to secure attendance of witnesses, applicability of waiver   Gov §26744.5
In forma pauperis
  Civil rules governing waiver of fees and costs   CRC 3.50 to 3.58
  Waiver of fees generally   Gov §§68630 to 68641
    Bench warrants to secure attendance of witnesses, applicability of waiver   Gov §26744.5
Mobilehomes, waiver of surety bond requirement after default of sales contract for   CCP §515.020
Sheriff's fees for service of process, waiver of   Gov §26720.5
Termination of parental rights, appointment of counsel for indigent appellant   Fam §7895
Waiver of fees   Gov §§68630 to 68641
  Abstract of judgment or writ of execution
    Payment of waived fees   Gov §68638
  Appellate rules, superior court appeals   CRC 8.818
  Appellate rules, supreme court and courts of appeal   CRC 8.26
  Application for initial fee waiver   Gov §68633
    Civil rules governing waiver of fees and costs   CRC 3.50
  Bench warrants to secure attendance of witnesses, applicability of waiver   Gov §26744.5
  Change in financial circumstances
    Person granted waiver, notice   Gov §68636
  Civil rules governing waiver of fees and costs   CRC 3.50 to 3.58
    Applicability of rules   CRC 3.50
    Definitions   CRC 3.50
  Confidentiality of application
    Civil rules governing   CRC 3.54
  Conservatorships and guardianships   Gov §68631
  Court clerk copying fees   Gov §70676
  Definitions
    Civil rules governing waiver of fees and costs   CRC 3.50
  Determining application for waiver
    Procedure, civil rules governing   CRC 3.52
  Expiration of initial fee waiver   Gov §68639
  Family law case
    Payment of waived fees   Gov §68637
  Form with which to apply for waiver
    Civil rules governing waiver of fees and costs   CRC 3.51
    Judicial council legal forms   CRCAppx A
  Granting initial fee waiver   Gov §68631
    Presumed grant of application unless court acts, civil rules governing   CRC 3.53
  Hearing on eligibility for waiver   Gov §68636
  Initial fee waivers   Gov §68631
    Defined, civil rules governing waiver of fees and costs   CRC 3.50
  Installment payments
    Rules allowing payment   Gov §68640
  Judicial Council application form
    Application for initial fee waiver   Gov §68633
  Legislative findings and declarations   Gov §68630
  Lien for waived costs and fees   CRC 3.57
  List of fees and costs waived   CRC 3.55
    Additional fees and costs waived   CRC 3.56
  Notice of right to apply for waiver   CRC 3.58
  Payment of waived fees by party against whom judgment entered
    Trial court fees   Gov §68637
  Person granted waiver not entitled   Gov §68636
  Persons granted permission to proceed without paying   Gov §68632
  Persons sentenced to state prison or county jail
    Trial court fees   Gov §68635
  Probate cases   CRC 3.50 to 3.53, 7.5
    Judicial council forms   CRCAppx A
  Processing and determination of application for waiver
    Appellate courts   Gov §68634.5
    Trial courts   Gov §68634
  Recovery of waived fees or costs   Gov §68636
  Rules, adoption   Gov §§68640, 68641
  Settlement, compromise, award or other recovery
    Payment of fees from   Gov §68637
  Sheriff's fees   Gov §26720.5
  Trial courts fees   Gov §§68635, 68637
    Determination of waiver   Gov §68634
Withdrawal of legal service agency attorney for indigent client   CCP §§285.2 to 285.4

INDIVIDUAL RETIREMENT ACCOUNTS
Disclaimer of estate interest   Pro §§260 to 295

INDIVIDUAL RETIREMENT ACCOUNTS—Cont.
Dissolution of marriage
    Deferred distribution, preservation by means of assignment   Fam §2337

INDUSTRIAL ACCIDENTS DIVISION
Administrative adjudication, generally (See **ADMINISTRATIVE ADJUDICATION**)
Medical records, disclosure of   CC §56.25

INDUSTRIAL BANKS
Conservators
    Opening or changing name on conservatee's account, responsibilities of conservator   CRC 7.1061
Guardians
    Opening or changing name on accounts, responsibilities of guardian   CRC 7.1011

INDUSTRIAL COMMON INTEREST DEVELOPMENTS
Commercial and industrial common interest developments generally   CC §§6500 to 6876 (See **COMMERCIAL AND INDUSTRIAL COMMON INTEREST DEVELOPMENTS**)

INDUSTRIAL LOAN COMPANIES
Late payment charges   CC §2954.4
Recovery of money or property deposited, statutes of limitation on actions for   CCP §348
Retail installment sales, financing of   CC §1801.7

INDUSTRIES (See **MANUFACTURERS**)

INFANTS (See **MINORS**)

INFECTIOUS DISEASE (See **CONTAGIOUS DISEASES**)

INFERENCE
Defined   Ev §600

INFERIOR LIENS (See **LIENS**)

INFERTILITY TREATMENT
Sperm, ova or embryos, written consent for use of
    Unauthorized use or misuse of sperm, ova or embryo
        Civil action for damages   CC §1708.5.6

INFORMANTS (See **INFORMERS**)

IN FORMA PAUPERIS
Application to proceed in forma pauperis
    Waiver of fees and costs   Gov §§68630 to 68641
        Application   CRC 3.50 to 3.58 (See **CIVIL RULES**)
Indigent persons generally (See **INDIGENT PERSONS**)

INFORMATION
Juror personal information (See **JURY**)
Jury commissioner, information acquired by   CCP §196
Marriage information brochures   Fam §358
Parent's right to access records of child   Fam §3025
Statistical information (See **STATISTICAL INFORMATION**)

INFORMATION BOOKLETS
Small claims court rules and procedures, publications describing   CCP §116.930

INFORMATION PRACTICES ACT
Generally   CC §§1798, 1798.1
Access to records   CC §§1798.30 to 1798.44
Accounting requirements for information furnished   CC §§1798.25 to 1798.28
Accuracy requirements
    Corrections generally (See within this heading, "**Corrections**")
Addresses
    Generally   CC §1798.3
    Professional persons, disclosure of name and address of   CC §1798.61
    Removal of names from lists   CC §1798.62
    Restriction on furnishing   CC §1798.60
    State Board of Equalization, release of name and address of registered or licensed persons by   CC §1798.69
Administrative safeguards, establishment of   CC §§1798.20, 1798.21
Adoption information   CC §1798.24
Amendment of record
    Corrections generally (See within this heading, "**Corrections**")
Applicability of Act   CC §1798.43
Attorneys' fees
    Generally   CC §1798.48

INFORMATION PRACTICES ACT—Cont.
Attorneys' fees—Cont.
    Exemplary damages, award on recovery of   CC §1798.53
    Record, compelling production of   CC §1798.46
Automobile registration disclosures   CC §1798.26
Citation   CC §1798
Compliance with statute, agency responsibility for   CC §1798.22
Computerized data owned or licensed by agency
    Breach of security system causing release of personal information
        Disclosures to persons affected   CC §1798.29
Concessionaires, disclosure of criminal background to city or county agencies screening   CC §1798.24a
Consent for disclosing information   CC §1798.24
Construction and interpretation of   CC §§1798.63, 1798.70 to 1798.78
Contracting for maintenance of records   CC §1798.19
Copies of records, furnishing of   CC §1798.34
Corrections
    Action to compel   CC §§1798.45 to 1798.51
    Agency responsibility   CC §1798.18
    Refusal of   CC §1798.36
    Request for   CC §1798.35
    Time for   CC §§1798.28, 1798.35
Costs in action under   CC §§1798.46, 1798.47
Crimes
    Enforcement agency receiving information   CC §1798.24
    False pretenses, obtaining information by   CC §1798.56
    Judicial decisions, interference with   CC §1798.76
    Privacy of information acquired during investigation   CC §1798.40
Cumulative remedies   CC §§1798.49, 1798.53
Damages, recovery of   CC §§1798.48, 1798.53, 1798.77
Definitions   CC §1798.3
Deletion by agency of exempt information   CC §1798.43
Deposit of records   CC §1798.64
Destruction of requested information   CC §1798.77
Determination of confidentiality   CC §§1798.40, 1798.41
Developmental Disabilities Patients' Rights Protection Agency, disclosure to   CC §1798.24b
Disagreement with record, statement of   CC §§1798.36, 1798.37
Disclosing information   CC §§1798.24, 1798.24a, 1798.24b
District attorneys
    Disclosures to   CC §1798.68
    Injunctions against agencies in noncompliance prosecuted by   CC §1798.47
Employees of agency, unauthorized disclosures by   CC §1798.55
Employment qualifications, information concerning   CC §§1798.38, 1798.40
Examination of records   CC §§1798.30 to 1798.44
Federal agencies, furnishing information to   CC §1798.24
Fees for examining records   CC §1798.33
General services department, records stored by   CC §1798.64
Government agencies, furnishing information to   CC §1798.24
Inaccuracies
    Corrections generally (See within this heading, "**Corrections**")
Injunctions
    Enjoining agencies in noncompliance with confidentiality requirements   CC §1798.47
    Record wrongfully withheld   CC §1798.46
Inspection of records   CC §§1798.30 to 1798.44
Institutional review boards
    Agreements with boards   CC §1798.24
Intergovernmental transfer of information   CC §1798.17
Jurisdiction of actions under   CC §1798.49
Justice Department review of records   CC §1798.23
Legislators, disclosures to   CC §1798.24
Licenses for professional practice, applicants for   CC §1798.61
Liens, information creating   CC §1798.67
Magnetic tape, extension of time for records on   CC §1798.66
Mailing lists
    Addresses (See within this heading, "**Addresses**")
Maintenance of records   CC §§1798.14, 1798.19
Medical or psychiatric records, liability for wrongful disclosure of   CC §1798.57
Mental health digital services
    Confidentiality of records
        Businesses organized to maintain medical information, data breach reporting   CC §56.251
Mental illness patients' rights protection agency, disclosure to   CC §1798.24b
Mistakes in record
    Corrections generally (See within this heading, "**Corrections**")
Modifying information to avoid statutory compliance   CC §1798.77
Motor Vehicles Department, disclosure procedures of   CC §1798.26
Noncompliance by agency, remedy for   CC §1798.77
Nondisclosure of information exempt from   CC §1798.43

INFORMATION PRACTICES ACT—Cont.
Notice
    Error or disputed information, notice as to   CC §1798.28
    Existence of record, notice as to   CC §1798.32
    Request for information, contents of notice showing   CC §1798.17
Opinion as to inaccuracy of record   CC §1798.50
Parties entitled to information   CC §1798.24
Penalties
    Employees of agency, unauthorized disclosure by   CC §1798.55
    False pretenses, obtaining information by   CC §1798.56
    Wrongful disclosure, penalties for   CC §§1798.53, 1798.57
Personal information released by breach of security system
    Disclosures to persons affected   CC §1798.29
Prescription drug monitoring program information
    Data sharing   CC §1798.24
Professional persons, names and addresses of   CC §1798.61
Promotion in employment, information concerning   CC §1798.38
Protecting personal information   CC §§1798.3, 1798.40, 1798.42, 1798.43
Public agencies, information to   CC §1798.24
Publishing information   CC §1798.24
Relevant personal information, requirements of   CC §§1798.14, 1798.15
Reputation, information injuring   CC §1798.38
Right of access to records   CC §§1798.30 to 1798.44
Rules authorized   CC §§1798.20, 1798.30
Search warrants, compliance with   CC §1798.24
Security system breached causing release of personal data
    Disclosures to persons affected   CC §1798.29
Source of information
    Generally   CC §1798.16
    Property rights, information affecting   CC §1798.39
    Protection for   CC §1798.38
State Board of Equalization, release of name and address of registered or licensed persons by   CC §1798.69
Statistical research, disclosure for   CC §1798.24
Statutes of limitation   CC §1798.49
Storage of records   CC §1798.64
Subpoenas, information furnished pursuant to   CC §1798.24
Technical safeguards, establishment of   CC §1798.21
Telephone listings, privacy of   CC §1798.3
Third parties
    Protecting information concerning   CC §1798.42
    Wrongful disclosure by   CC §1798.53
Time
    Confidentiality, time for review of determination of   CC §1798.41
    Correction of records   CC §§1798.28, 1798.35
    Extension of time for notice of records   CC §1798.66
    Inspection of record   CC §1798.34
    Maintenance of records   CC §1798.27
    Review of information   CC §1798.23
    Updating of information   CC §1798.18
Universities, disclosures to   CC §1798.24
Updating of records   CC §1798.18
Venue of action   CC §1798.49
Wrongful disclosure of information   CC §§1798.53, 1798.57

INFORMED CONSENT
Dependent children
    Disposition hearings
        Nonminor disposition hearings   CRC 5.697
Minors   Fam §§6920 to 6930
Reproductive practice, diversion of sperm or ova
    Unauthorized use or misuse of sperm, ova or embryo
        Civil action for damages   CC §1708.5.6

INFORMERS
Identity, disclosure of   Ev §§1040 to 1042
Privileged communications protecting identity of   Ev §§915, 1040, 1041

INFRACTION CASE APPEALS
Appellate rules, superior court appeals   CRC 8.900 to 8.929 (See **APPELLATE RULES, SUPERIOR COURT APPEALS**)

INFRACTIONS
Ability to pay program
    Appearances
        Alternatives to personal appearance   Gov §68645.1
    Clerk making ability to pay determinations   Gov §68645.3
    Funding estimate   Gov §68645.7
    Online tool for adjudication of infraction violations   Gov §68645
        Deadline for offering tool   Gov §68645.2
        Electronic verification of public benefits   Gov §68645.3

INFRACTIONS—Cont.
Ability to pay program—Cont.
    Online tool for adjudication of infraction violations—Cont.
        Establishing inability to pay   Gov §68645.2
        Languages available when using tool   Gov §68645.2
        Payment recommendations   Gov §68645.2
    Online trial   Gov §68645.4
    Report by judicial council to legislature   Gov §68645.5
Criminal rules
    Ability-to-pay determinations   CRC 4.335
        Confidential can't afford to pay fine form   CRC 4.336, CRCAppx A
    Installment payment agreements   CRC 4.108
    Notice to appear
        Failure to appear or failure to pay for notice to appear   CRC 4.106
        Mandatory reminder notices   CRC 4.107
Failure to appear or failure to pay for notice to appear   CRC 4.106
Installment payment plan   CRC 4.108
    Failure to pay or make payment under installment payment plan   CRC 4.106
Notice to appear
    Ability-to-pay determinations   CRC 4.335
        Confidential can't afford to pay fine form   CRC 4.336, CRCAppx A
    Failure to appear or failure to pay   CRC 4.106
    Mandatory reminder notices   CRC 4.107
Reminder notices
    Mandatory reminder notices for notice to appear   CRC 4.107

INGLEWOOD ARENA PROJECT
Environmental quality act
    Petitions under environmental quality act, civil rules governing   CRC 3.2220 to 3.2240
Review of CEQA cases   CRC 8.700 to 8.705

INHERENTLY UNSAFE PRODUCTS
Availability of products liability action for injury caused by   CC §1714.45

INHERITANCE
Heirs (See **HEIRS**)
Intestate succession (See **INTESTATE SUCCESSION**)
Testamentary succession (See **WILLS**)

INHERITANCE TAX
Appeals   Pro §1312
Homestead, appraisal of   Pro §6523
Power of attorney, powers under statutory form of   Pro §4463
Unclaimed property fund appropriations for transfer   CCP §1325

INITIATIVE AND REFERENDUM
Tax limitation initiative (See **TAXATION**)

INJUNCTIONS
Generally   CC §§3420 to 3423
Adequate remedy at law, absence of   CC §3422, CCP §526
Affidavits regarding grounds for   CCP §527
Answers   CCP §528
Appeals   CCP §§904.1, 904.2
Arbitration agreements, effect of injunctive relief filed by party subject to   CCP §1281.8
Artwork
    Integrity of artwork, injunctive relief to preserve or restore   CC §989
    Sale of fine prints, injunctive relief involving   CC §1745.5
Attachment provisions affecting grant of   CCP §482.020
Auction law, enjoining violations of   CC §1812.602
Blind persons, violation of equal rights of   CC §55
Bonds
    Construction projects   CCP §529.1
    Housing development projects   CCP §529.2
    Undertakings (See within this heading, **"Undertakings"**)
    Water diversion cases   CCP §532
Cities, prevention of legislation by   CCP §526
Civil rights violations   CC §52.1
    Construction or application of civil rights provisions in issue, solicitor general notified   CC §51.1
    Gender violence   CC §52.4
Claim and delivery, effect of   CCP §516.050
Coerced debt
    Establishing debt as coerced, action or cross-complaint   CC §1798.97.3
Commercial financing transactions with small businesses
    Prohibited fees
        Remedies for violations   CC §1799.303

INJUNCTIONS—Cont.
  Common interest developments
    Board meetings
      Actions for declaratory or equitable relief to enforce provisions   CC §4955
    Member elections
      Action for declaratory or equitable relief to enforce   CC §5145
  Complaint, injunction granted at any time prior to judgment on   CCP §527
  Conservation easements, impairment of   CC §815.7
  Construction projects   CCP §529.1
  Consumer privacy rights
    Actions for damages, injunctions, declaratory relief, etc
      Security practices and procedures not in place   CC §1798.150
    Businesses, service providers, contractors, etc
      Violation of provisions   CC §1798.199.90
  Consumer protection   CC §1782
  Continuous conduct   CCP §526
  Contracts, preventing breach of   CC §3423, CCP §526
  Corporations, suspending business of   CCP §531
  Court proceedings, stay of   CCP §526
  COVID-19 small landlord and homeowner relief act
    Action by borrower harmed by violation of provisions   CC §3273.15
  Credit reporting   CC §1785.31
  Credit services organization, action against   CC §1789.21
  Damages
    Inadequacy or difficulty in ascertaining amount of compensation as grounds for issuance of injunction   CC §3422, CCP §526
    Undertaking or bond required as security for damages sustained by enjoined party   CCP §529
  Data broker registration
    Injunction to enforce registration   CC §1798.99.82
  Deeds of trust and mortgages
    Enforcement of foreclosure prevention   CC §2924.12
  Defined   CCP §525
  Dependent adult abuse
    Protective orders to prevent
      Requests for protective orders   CRC 3.1160
  Dependent child, ex parte injunction against parent, guardian or household member of
    Firearm relinquishment procedures
      Forms for firearm relinquishment   CRCAppx A
  Disabled persons, violation of equal rights of   CC §§55, 55.1
  Discount buying organization officer subject to   CC §1812.106
  Discrimination, injunctive relief for   CC §52.1
    Construction or application of civil rights provisions in issue, solicitor general notified   CC §51.1
  Dissolution of injunction   CC §3424, CCP §533
  Domestic violence, order to prevent (See **DOMESTIC VIOLENCE**)
  Dwelling house, excluding from (See **DOMESTIC VIOLENCE**)
  Easements, injunction for protection of   CRC 3.1151
  Elder abuse
    Protective orders to prevent
      Requests for protective orders   CRC 3.1160
  Employer's action for injunctive relief against threats of violence towards employees
    Possession of firearms   CCP §527.11
    Service of order   CCP §527.12
  Employer's action for orders against threats of violence towards employees   CCP §527.8
    Address or location of complaining party or family, prohibition on enjoined party from obtaining   CCP §527.10
    California law enforcement telecommunications (CLETS) information form, confidentiality and use of information   CRC 1.51, CRCAppx A
    COVID-19, emergency rule   CRCAppx I Emer Rule 8
    Firearm relinquishment and disposition   CCP §527.9
      Forms for firearm relinquishment   CRCAppx A
    Judicial council legal forms   CRCAppx A
    Memorandum in support of petition for order not required   CRC 3.1114
    Requests for protective orders   CRC 3.1160
  Employment agencies, violations by   CC §1812.523
  Employment counseling services, violations by   CC §1812.523
  Enforcement of judgments (See **ENFORCEMENT OF JUDGMENTS**)
  Fair debt settlement practices
    Consumers
      Actions to enforce   CC §1788.305
  Final or permanent injunction   CC §§3420, 3422, 3424
  Fine prints
    Integrity of artwork
      Injunctive relief to preserve or restore   CC §989
    Sale of fine print
      Injunctive relief involving   CC §1745.5

INJUNCTIONS—Cont.
  Firearms and other weapons
    Firearm industry standards of conduct
      Actions against industry members for violation of standards   CC §3273.52
  Gang violence, injunction for relief from   CCP §527.7
  Gender violence   CC §52.4
  Greenway easements
    Enforcement of easement   CC §816.62
  Grounds for granting or denying issuance of   CC §§3422, 3423, CCP §526
  Groundwater rights actions
    Long-term overdrafts   CCP §847
  Harassment
    Civil   CRC 3.1160
    Prevention
      COVID-19, emergency rule   CRCAppx I Emer Rule 8
      Generally (See **HARASSMENT**)
      Minor's information confidentiality, request in civil harassment proceedings   CRC 3.1161, CRCAppx A
      Possession of firearms   CCP §527.11
  Health facilities
    Force, threat or other obstruction of access to facility   CC §1708.9
  Hospitals
    Force, threat or other obstruction of access to facility   CC §1708.9
  Housing projects, challenge of   CCP §529.2
  Human trafficking   CC §52.5
  Identity theft, injunctive relief in actions involving   CC §1798.93
  Information Practices Act (See **INFORMATION PRACTICES ACT**)
  Interpleader as basis for enjoining other proceedings   CCP §386
  Irreparable injury   CCP §526
  Irrigation, preventing water diversion   CCP §§530, 532, 534
  Job listing services, violations by   CC §1812.523
  Judgments
    Enforcement of (See **ENFORCEMENT OF JUDGMENTS**)
    Interference by injunction   CCP §526
  Judicial holiday, issuance on   CCP §134
  Labor disputes   CRC 3.1151
  Landlord and tenant
    Action by tenant against landlord   CC §789.3
    Immigration or citizenship status of tenant, occupant, etc
      Disclosures to immigration authorities with intent to intimidate or harass   CC §1940.35
  Law and motion rules   CRC 3.1150 to 3.1161
  Legally protected health care services
    Action for relief from abusive litigation infringing on protected activity   CC §1798.303
  Limitation of time for commencement of action stayed by injunction or statutory prohibition   CCP §356
  Limited civil cases, unavailability in   CCP §580
  Low-income housing project   CCP §529.2
  Marital status, denial of credit because of   CC §§1812.32, 1812.33
  Mobilehome park homeowner meetings, management enjoined from denying right to assemble at   CC §798.52
  Moderate-income housing project   CCP §529.2
  Modification or dissolution of   CC §3424, CCP §533
  Mortgage foreclosure, preventing waste pending   CCP §745
  Motion pictures depicting cruelty to animals   CC §3507
  Multiplicity of suits, prevention of   CC §§3422, 3423, CCP §526
  Municipalities, enjoining acts of   CC §3423, CCP §526
  Notice
    Corporations, suspending business of   CCP §531
    Grant of preliminary injunction without notice   CCP §527
    Water, preventing diversion of   CCP §530
  Nuisances   CC §3496, CCP §731
  Obscene matter, attorneys' fees and costs awarded for injunction in action involving   CC §3496
  Oil wells, secondary recovery operations   CCP §731c
  Order to show cause, use of TRO   CRC 3.1150
  Other states, staying proceedings in   CCP §526
  Partition action, injunctions during   CCP §872.130
  Permanent or final injunction   CC §§3420, 3422, 3424
  Perpetual injunction   CCP §526
  Personal services, enforcement of contracts for   CCP §526
  Picketing (See **DEMONSTRATIONS, PARADES AND MEETINGS**)
  Postsecondary educational institutions
    Protection orders against violence threatened on campus or facility   CCP §527.85
      California law enforcement telecommunications (CLETS) information form, confidentiality and use of information   CRC 1.51, CRCAppx A
      COVID-19, emergency rule   CRCAppx I Emer Rule 8

INJUNCTIONS—Cont.
  Postsecondary educational institutions—Cont.
    Protection orders against violence threatened on campus or facility —Cont.
      Judicial council legal forms   CRCAppx A
      Memorandum in support of petition not required   CRC 3.1114
      Requests for protective orders   CRC 3.1160
  Precedence to hearing on preliminary injunction granted without notice   CCP §527
  Preliminary injunctions   CCP §527, CRC 3.1150
    Arbitration agreements, effect on party subject to   CCP §1281.8
    Class actions   CCP §527
    Innkeeper's lien   CC §§1861.16, 1861.23
    Local rules of court
      Preemption of local rules   CRC 3.20
    Noticed motion or order to show cause   CRC 3.1150
    Order to show cause   CRC 3.1150
    Precedence to hearing on injunction granted without notice   CCP §527
    Proposed order and undertaking, time for presentation   CRC 3.1150
    Undertakings   CRC 3.1150
  Price discrimination based on gender
    Price differences for substantially similar goods based on gender of marketing audience   CC §51.14
  Privacy
    Photographs, films, etc, exposing intimate body parts or sexual acts of another without permission, distribution
      Actions for injunctions, damages, etc   CC §1708.85
  Procedure for   CCP §527
  Protective orders (See within this heading, **"Temporary restraining orders"**)
  Public contracts   CCP §526a
  Public improvement or utility, damages for wrongfully enjoining   CCP §526b
  Public officers, restraint on   CC §3423, CCP §526
  Public trails, closure of   CCP §731.5
  Rental passenger vehicle transactions
    Actions for violation of provisions   CC §1939.25
  Riparian rights   CCP §§530, 532, 534
  School grounds
    Force, threat or other obstruction of access to facility   CC §1708.9
  Sexually explicit depiction of individual, creation or disclosure   CC §1708.86
  Sexual orientation violence
    Civil actions   CC §52.45
  Small claims court jurisdiction   CCP §116.220
  Statutes, enjoining execution of   CC §3423, CCP §526
  Student borrower bill of rights
    Enforcement of compliance with rights   CC §1788.103
  Subcutaneous implanting of identification device, requiring of another   CC §52.7
  Surety bonds (See within this heading, **"Undertakings"**)
  Temporary restraining orders   CRC 3.1150
    Arbitration agreements, effect on party subject to   CCP §1281.8
    Child removed from state without consent or court order   Fam §§233, 2030
    Civil rights violations   CC §52.1
      Construction or application of civil rights provisions in issue, solicitor general notified   CC §51.1
    Claim and delivery proceedings   CCP §§512.120, 513.010, 513.020
    Class actions   CCP §527
    Custody proceedings (See **CUSTODY OF CHILDREN**)
    Day upon which order is made returnable   CCP §527
    Dissolution of marriage (See **DISSOLUTION OF MARRIAGE**)
    Domestic violence, prevention of (See **DOMESTIC VIOLENCE**)
    Employer's action against threats of violence towards employee   CCP §527.8, CRC 3.1160
      Address or location of complaining party or family, prohibition on enjoined party from obtaining   CCP §527.10
      California law enforcement telecommunications (CLETS) information form, confidentiality and use of information   CRC 1.51, CRCAppx A
      COVID-19, emergency rule   CRCAppx I Emer Rule 8
      Firearm relinquishment and disposition   CCP §527.9
      Forms for firearm relinquishment   CRCAppx A
      Judicial council legal forms   CRCAppx A
      Memorandum in support of petition for order not required   CRC 3.1114
      Possession of firearms   CCP §527.11
      Requests for protective orders   CRC 3.1160
      Service of order   CCP §527.12
    Failure to serve defendant   CCP §527
    Family law rules (See **FAMILY RULES**)
    Harassment, prevention of (See **HARASSMENT**)
    Innkeeper's lien   CC §§1861.15 to 1861.17, 1861.21, 1861.23
    Modification or dissolution of   CCP §533
    Notice requirements   CCP §527

INJUNCTIONS—Cont.
  Temporary restraining orders —Cont.
    Order to show cause   CRC 3.1150
    Partition actions   CCP §872.130
    Postsecondary educational institutions, orders against violence threatened on campus or facility
      Possession of firearms   CCP §527.11
      Service of order   CCP §527.12
    Postsecondary educational institutions, protection order against violence threatened on campus or facility   CCP §527.85
      California law enforcement telecommunications (CLETS) information form, confidentiality and use of information   CRC 1.51, CRCAppx A
      COVID-19, emergency rule   CRCAppx I Emer Rule 8
      Judicial council legal forms   CRCAppx A
      Memorandum in support of petition not required   CRC 3.1114
      Requests for protective orders   CRC 3.1160
    Precedence to hearing on preliminary injunction granted without notice   CCP §527
    Reissue of   CCP §527
    Undertakings   CRC 3.1150
    Workplace violence, employer's action against   CCP §527.8, CRC 3.1160
      Address or location of complaining party or family, prohibition on enjoined party from obtaining   CCP §527.10
      California law enforcement telecommunications (CLETS) information form, confidentiality and use of information   CRC 1.51, CRCAppx A
      COVID-19, emergency rule   CRCAppx I Emer Rule 8
      Firearm relinquishment and disposition   CCP §527.9
      Forms for firearm relinquishment   CRCAppx A
      Hearing to renew restraining order
        Reschedule request and order   CRCAppx A
      Judicial council legal forms   CRCAppx A
      Memorandum in support of petition for order not required   CRC 3.1114
      Possession of firearms   CCP §527.11
      Requests for protective orders   CRC 3.1160
      Service of order   CCP §527.12
  Trade secret, injunctive relief from misappropriation of   CC §3426.2
  Transitional housing program misconduct
    Injunctions or temporary restraining orders   CC §§1954.13 to 1954.16
  Trials enjoined   CC §3423, CCP §526
  Trusts   CC §3422, CCP §526
  Undertakings
    Generally   CCP §529
    Construction projects   CCP §529.1
    Housing development projects   CCP §529.2
    Preliminary injunction, undertaking for   CRC 3.1150
  United States courts, staying proceedings in   CC §3423, CCP §526
  Universities and colleges
    Protection orders against violence threatened on campus or facility   CCP §527.85
      California law enforcement telecommunications (CLETS) information form, confidentiality and use of information   CRC 1.51, CRCAppx A
      COVID-19, emergency rule   CRCAppx I Emer Rule 8
      Judicial council legal forms   CRCAppx A
      Memorandum in support of petition not required   CRC 3.1114
      Requests for protective orders   CRC 3.1160
  Unruh Civil Rights Act violations   CC §52.1
    Construction or application of civil rights provisions in issue, solicitor general notified   CC §51.1
  Victim service providers, personal information protection
    Sexual assault victims, domestic violence victims, stalking victims, etc, protecting information   CC §1798.79.95
  Waste, prevention of   CCP §526
  Water, preventing diversion of   CCP §§530, 532, 534
  Workplace violence, employer's action to prevent   CCP §527.8, CRC 3.1160
    Address or location of complaining party or family, prohibition on enjoined party from obtaining   CCP §527.10
    California law enforcement telecommunications (CLETS) information form, confidentiality and use of information   CRC 1.51, CRCAppx A
    COVID-19, emergency rule   CRCAppx I Emer Rule 8
    Firearm relinquishment and disposition   CCP §527.9
      Forms for firearm relinquishment   CRCAppx A
    Judicial council legal forms   CRCAppx A
    Memorandum in support of petition for order not required   CRC 3.1114
    Possession of firearms   CCP §527.11
    Requests for protective orders   CRC 3.1160
    Service of order   CCP §527.12

INJURIES
Basis for civil actions CCP §25
Personal injuries (See **PERSONAL INJURIES**)
Types of CCP §§27 to 29

INNOCENT PURCHASERS FOR VALUE (See **BONA FIDE PURCHASERS**)

INNS AND INNKEEPERS (See **HOTELS AND MOTELS**)

IN PROPRIA PERSONA
Vexatious litigant defined CCP §391

INQUESTS (See **JURIES OF INQUEST**)

INQUIRIES
Jury commissioner inquiry into qualification of prospective jurors CCP §196

IN REM PROCEEDINGS
Boundaries reestablished after earthquake CCP §§751.50 to 751.65
Service in CCP §415.50

INSANITY
Mental disability generally (See **MENTAL DISABILITY**)

INSANITY DEFENSE
Appealability of commitment order
    Procedure for appeal from order of civil commitment CRC 8.483
Commitment after insanity finding
    Appealability of order
        Procedure for appeal from order of civil commitment CRC 8.483
    Remote proceedings
        Conditions for proceeding through use of remote technology CCP §367.76

INSANITY PROCEEDINGS
Court reporter taking down and transcribing at cost of county CCP §274a

INSOLVENCY (See also **BANKRUPTCY**)
Ancillary administration, effect of insolvency of decedent's estate in sister state on property distributed under Pro §12542
Assignment for benefit of creditors (See **ASSIGNMENT FOR BENEFIT OF CREDITORS**)
Banks in process of liquidation, statutes of limitation for recovery of money or property deposited applicable to CCP §348
Enforcement of judgments (See **ENFORCEMENT OF JUDGMENTS**)
Family allowance, insolvency of estate as placing limitation on Pro §§6540 to 6543
Fraudulent transfers (See **VOIDABLE TRANSACTIONS**)
Wage claims, preference for CCP §§1204 to 1204.5

INSPECTION
Administrative Procedure Act, inspection of rulemaking file for proposed regulation under Gov §11347.3
Adoption records (See **ADOPTION**)
Automobiles (See **AUTOMOBILES**)
Brokers (See **BROKERS**)
Buildings
    Exterior elevated elements
        Landlord entry of building to comply with provisions CC §1954
Business records (See **BUSINESS RECORDS**)
Common interest developments
    Record inspection CC §§5200 to 5240
    Reserve funds, planning
        Exterior elevated elements, visual inspection CC §5551
        Inspection of premises and components CC §5550
Construction defects, actions for
    Prelitigation procedures CC §916
Construction-related accessibility claims
    Certified access specialists (CASp)
        Duties CC §55.53
Court records
    Public access to judicial administration records CRC 10.500
Credit report files (See **CREDIT REPORTING**)
Discovery by inspection, demand for (See **INSPECTION DEMANDS**)
Information Practices Act, inspection of records under CC §§1798.30 to 1798.44
Judgment liens on personal property, inspection of filed notices of CCP §697.580
Juvenile court records (See **JUVENILE COURTS**)
Landlord and tenant
    Bed bug infestations
        Entry by landlord to inspect CC §1954.604

INSPECTION—Cont.
Medical records, authorization for attorney inspecting CCP §1985.7, Ev §1158
Membership camping contracts contingent on inspection of camp site CC §1812.304
Police reports on juveniles CRC 5.546
Real estate sales
    Disclosures regarding electrical inspections CC §1102.6i
Structural pest control inspection report prior to transfer of title to real property CC §1099
Subpoena duces tecum (See **SUBPOENA DUCES TECUM**)
Termination of parental rights, inspection of petition and reports Fam §7805
Warrants (See **INSPECTION WARRANTS**)

INSPECTION DEMANDS CCP §§2031.010 to 2031.510
Attorney work product
    Electronically stored information
        Privilege claimed or attorney work product protection requested CCP §2031.285
Boundary of land granted by state
    Duty to disclose CCP §2031.510
Civil rules
    Limitation on papers filed CRC 3.250
Complete or partial compliance with demand
    Statement as to CCP §2031.220
Contents of demand CCP §2031.030
Defendants
    Making demand at any time CCP §2031.020
Documents produced to respond
    Form CCP §2031.280
    Organization CCP §2031.280
Economic litigation provisions for limited civil cases, permissible forms of discovery under CCP §94
Electronically stored information (ESI) CCP §2031.010
    Form of information, specifying CCP §2031.030
    Objections CCP §2031.240
    Privilege claimed or attorney work product protection requested CCP §2031.285
    Protective orders CCP §2031.060
    Response, form of information furnished CCP §2031.280
    Sanctions for failure to provide, circumstances avoiding CCP §§2031.300, 2031.320
    Unreasonably inaccessible
        Burden of proof CCP §2031.060
        Compelling discovery despite burden of providing CCP §2031.310
        Details as to inaccessible information as part of response CCP §2031.210
Extension of time to serve response CCP §2031.270
Failure to serve timely response CCP §2031.300
Fax filing, inspection of original signed document where subject of CRC 2.305
Format of demand CCP §2031.030
Identification by set and number CCP §2031.030, CRC 3.1000, 3.1345
    Response to demand CCP §2031.210
Inability to comply CCP §2031.230
Land patents or grants
    Duty to disclose CCP §2031.510
Limitation on papers filed CRC 3.250
Methods of discovery CCP §§2019.010, 2031.010
Motion to compel
    Response to demand CCP §2031.300
        Failure to permit inspection in accord with demand CCP §2031.320
        Further response, motion to compel CCP §2031.310
    Separate document setting forth item to which further response, answer or production is requested CRC 3.1345
Numbering demands CCP §2031.030
Objections
    Response to demand
        Statement regarding demands objectionable in whole or in part CCP §2031.240
Partial compliance with demand
    Statement as to CCP §2031.220
Plaintiffs
    When plaintiff may make demand CCP §2031.020
Privileges
    Electronically stored information
        Privilege claimed or attorney work product protection requested CCP §2031.285
Protective orders and sanctions CCP §2031.060
Response to demand CCP §§2031.210 to 2031.320
    Attorney work product claimed
        Electronically stored information CCP §2031.285

INSPECTION DEMANDS—Cont.
Response to demand —Cont.
    Complete or partial compliance with demand
        Statement as to   CCP §2031.220
    Contents   CCP §2031.210
    Documents produced to respond
        Form   CCP §2031.280
        Organization   CCP §2031.280
    Failure to permit inspection in accord with demand   CCP §2031.320
    Further response
        Motion to compel further response   CCP §2031.310, CRC 3.1345
    Identification and sequence of responses   CRC 3.1000
    Inability to comply   CCP §2031.230
    Motion to compel   CCP §2031.300, CRC 3.1345
    Objections
        Statement regarding demands objectionable in whole or in part   CCP §2031.240
    Privilege claimed
        Electronically stored information   CCP §2031.285
    Retention of demand, proof of service and response   CCP §2031.290
    Separate response   CCP §2031.210
    Signature   CCP §2031.250
    Time to serve response   CCP §2031.260
        Extension of time to serve response   CCP §2031.270
        Failure to serve timely response   CCP §2031.300
Retention of demand, proof of service and response   CCP §2031.290
Right to discovery by   CCP §2031.010
Sanctions
    Protective orders
        Unsuccessfully making or opposing motion for protective order   CCP §2031.060
    Response to demand
        Failure to file timely response   CCP §2031.300
        Failure to permit inspection in accord with demand   CCP §2031.320
        Further response, motion to compel   CCP §2031.310
Sequence of responses   CRC 3.1000
Service of demand   CCP §2031.040
    Retention of demand, proof of service and response   CCP §2031.290
Signature
    Response to demand   CCP §2031.250
Supplemental inspection demands   CCP §2031.050, CRC 3.1000
Time to serve response   CCP §2031.260
    Extension of time to serve response   CCP §2031.270
    Failure to serve timely response   CCP §2031.300
Unlawful detainer
    Time to serve response   CCP §2031.260
    When demand may be made   CCP §2031.020

INSPECTION WARRANTS
Affidavit for   CCP §1822.51
Aquaculture, warrant for inspection of storage location of   CCP §1822.58
Authorized or required by state or local law or regulation, order to conduct inspection   CCP §1822.50
Cause, determination for   CCP §§1822.51 to 1822.54
Defined   CCP §1822.50
Description requirements
    Generally   CCP §1822.54
    Geographical area description requirements   CCP §1822.59
Gambling Control, warrant for inspection by   CCP §1822.60
Refusal to permit inspection   CCP §1822.57
Time of service   CCP §§1822.55, 1822.56

INSTALLMENTS
Costs and filing fees
    Indigent persons
        Rules allowing installment payment   Gov §68640
Dating services (See **DATING SERVICES**)
Infractions   CRC 4.108
    Failure to pay or make payment under installment payment plan   CRC 4.106
Judgments (See **JUDGMENTS**)
Land sales contracts (See **REAL PROPERTY SALES CONTRACTS**)
Retail installment sales (See **RETAIL INSTALLMENT SALES**)
Weight loss program (See **WEIGHT LOSS PROGRAMS**)

INSTANT MESSAGING
Statute of frauds
    Insufficiency of text message or instant message format communications to constitute contract to convey realty   CC §1624

INSTITUTIONAL FUNDS MANAGEMENT   Pro §§18501 to 18510
Accumulations   Pro §18504

INSTITUTIONAL FUNDS MANAGEMENT—Cont.
Applicability of provisions   Pro §18508
Appropriations   Pro §18504
Citation of provisions   Pro §18501
Compliance with provisions   Pro §18507
Considerations in managing and investing funds   Pro §18503
Definitions   Pro §18502
Delegation of management or investment function   Pro §18505
Effective date of provisions   Pro §18508
Electronic signatures in global and national commerce act
    Effect of provisions on federal act   Pro §18509
Investments
    Considerations in managing and investing funds   Pro §18503
    Delegation of management or investment function   Pro §18505
Restrictions in gift instruments
    Release   Pro §18506
Uniform construction of provisions   Pro §18510
Uniform prudent management of institutional funds act   Pro §§18501 to 18510

INSTRUCTIONS
Attachment proceedings (See **ATTACHMENT**)
Court reporters to take down all statements, remarks and instructions given by judge   CCP §269
Disregard of nonprejudicial error   CCP §475
Executors and administrators of decedents' estates, court instructions to (See **EXECUTORS AND ADMINISTRATORS**)
Garnishment proceedings (See **GARNISHMENT**)
Jury instructions (See **JURY**)
Trust administration, instructions for   Pro §16001

INSTRUCTIONS TO JURY (See **JURY**)

INSTRUMENTS
Court commissioner's power to take acknowledgments and proof of   CCP §259

INSULTS
Protection from   CC §43

INSURANCE
Administration of decedents' estates
    Generally (See **ADMINISTRATION OF ESTATES**)
    Claims against decedents' estate (See **CLAIMS AGAINST ESTATES**)
Admissibility of evidence of insurance
    Collateral source rule   CC §3333.1
    Negligence or wrongdoing, admissibility of evidence of insurance to prove   Ev §1155
Admitted surety insurer (See **SURETYSHIP, BONDS AND UNDERTAKINGS**)
Application
    Denials based on information from investigative consumer reporting agencies or other sources
        Information as to reports given rejected applicant   CC §1786.40
Arbitration of liability coverage disputes
    Agreements to arbitrate   CCP §1784
    Amount in controversy   CCP §1777
    Court-ordered mediation or arbitration, relief from obligation to participate in   CCP §1780
    Definitions   CCP §1776
    Presumption of insurer's good faith   CCP §§1778, 1779
    Removal from arbitration   CCP §1779
    Requests for arbitration   CCP §1777
    Tolling of limitations periods and suspension of case-management requirements   CCP §1780
Armenian genocide victims, jurisdiction and limitation period for actions against insurers by   CCP §354.4
Attorney professional conduct
    Communications with clients
        Malpractice insurance lacking, duty to inform client   ProfC 1.4.2
Attorneys
    Independent counsel, insurance defense cases requiring representation of insured by   CC §2860
    Liability of attorney as member of insurance underwriting committee   CC §43.7
Automobile insurance (See **AUTOMOBILE INSURANCE**)
Child support (See **CHILD SUPPORT**)
Claims
    Settlements
        Time-limited demands   CCP §§999 to 999.5
Claims against decedent's estate (See **CLAIMS AGAINST ESTATES**)
Collateral source rule   CC §3333.1
Commercial and industrial common interest developments
    Common areas, coverage   CC §6840
Common interest developments (See **COMMON INTEREST DEVELOPMENTS**)

INSURANCE—Cont.
Companies
    Filings with secretary of state
        Identity theft in business entity filings   CC §§1798.200 to 1798.203
Complex litigation defined   CRC 3.400
Conflict of interests in insurance defense cases requiring representation of insured by independent counsel   CC §2860
Conservators
    Assets of ward
        Taking possession or control, responsibilities of guardian   CRC 7.1061
Credit disability insurance (See **CREDIT DISABILITY INSURANCE**)
Credit reports (See **CREDIT REPORTING**)
Discovery of insurance coverage
    Scope of discovery   CCP §2017.210
Dissolution of insurer, disposition of unclaimed property following   CCP §1517
Dissolution of marriage proceedings (See **DISSOLUTION OF MARRIAGE**)
Emancipated minors, contracts by   Fam §7051
Exemptions from liability, pleadings for   CCP §431.50
Fiduciary income and principal act
    Receipts, allocation   Pro §16346
Guardianships
    Assets of ward
        Taking possession or control, responsibilities of guardian   CRC 7.1011
Hazard insurance coverage imposed by lender, limitations on   CC §2955.5
Health, accident, and disability insurance (See **HEALTH, ACCIDENT, AND DISABILITY INSURANCE**)
Holocaust victims, jurisdiction and limitation period for actions against insurers by   CCP §354.5
Hospital lien notice transmitted to   CC §3045.3
Identity theft in business entity filings   CC §§1798.200 to 1798.203
Independent counsel, conflict of interests in insurance defense cases requiring representation by   CC §2860
Investigative consumer reporting agencies (See **INVESTIGATIVE CONSUMER REPORTING AGENCIES**)
Judgment debtor, assignment of right to payment due   CCP §§708.510 to 708.560
Life insurance (See **LIFE INSURANCE**)
Medical information, release of   CC §§56.15, 56.27
Mortgages (See **TRUST DEEDS AND MORTGAGES**)
Northridge earthquake of 1994, revival of cause of action for damages arising out of   CCP §340.9
Pleadings for liability exemption   CCP §431.50
Power of attorney (See **POWER OF ATTORNEY**)
Premiums
    Increase based on information from investigative consumer reporting agencies or other sources
        Information as to reports given to policy holder   CC §1786.40
Professional liability insurance (See **PHYSICIANS AND SURGEONS**)
Proposition 103 rebate, disposition of unclaimed   CCP §1523
Public entities, insurance considerations in claims against   Gov §§989 to 991.2
Punitive damages award against insurer, special notice of   CC §3296
Real property sales contract, insurance payments received under   CC §2985.4
Rebate under Proposition 103, disposition of unclaimed   CCP §1523
Repairs, protecting property left for   CC §§1858 to 1858.3
Rescission of policy
    Generally   CC §1689
    Statute of limitation for rescission based on misrepresentation   CCP §337
Retail installment sales (See **RETAIL INSTALLMENT SALES**)
Shared mobility devices
    Agreements with or permits from local government   CC §2505
    Study and report to legislature on insurance issues   CC §2505.5
Small claims court, appearance of insurers in (See **SMALL CLAIMS COURTS**)
Third-party cause of action for unfair claims settlement practices by liability insurers   CC §§2870, 2871
Trust deeds (See **TRUST DEEDS AND MORTGAGES**)
Trusts (See **TRUSTS**)
Unclaimed deposits and payments
    Demutualization
        Property distributable as part of demutualization   CCP §1515.5
Underwriting committees' liability for evaluations pursuant to   CC §§43.7, 43.8
Unfair claims settlement practices by liability insurers, third-party cause of action for   CC §§2870, 2871
Uniform parentage act
    Vacation or setting aside of judgment
        Payments made in good faith by estate, trustees, insurers, etc., based on paternity judgment   Fam §7649.5
Volunteer health professionals, insurance for   Gov §990.9
Workers' compensation (See **WORKERS' COMPENSATION**)

INTENT
Contracts, construction of   CC §§1636, 1637, 1648 to 1650
Creditors, voidable transactions   CC §3439.04
Expedited jury trials
    Mandatory expedited jury trials, limited civil cases
        Opting out of expedited process   CCP §630.20
Fraud, class of persons, intended for   CC §1711
Infants (See **MINORS**)
Ordinary consequences from voluntary acts, presumption of intent for   Ev §665
Pleadings, objection to   CCP §§430.10, 430.20
Presumption of unlawful intent arising from doing unlawful act   Ev §668
Trusts, creation of   Pro §15201
Voidable transactions   CC §§3439.04, 3439.07
    Actual intent to hinder, delay or defraud creditors   CC §3439.04
Waters, intent for appropriation of   CC §1415
Wills (See **WILLS**)

INTERCOUNTRY ADOPTION OF CHILDREN (See **ADOPTION**)

INTERESTED PERSONS
Process shown to   CCP §262.2

INTEREST IN OUTCOME
Challenge of juror for implied bias   CCP §229

INTEREST ON INVESTMENTS
Interpleader deposits   CCP §386.1

INTEREST ON MONEY
Adjustable rate mortgages (See **TRUST DEEDS AND MORTGAGES**)
Administration of decedents' estates
    Generally (See **ADMINISTRATION OF ESTATES**)
    Claims against decedents' estates (See **CLAIMS AGAINST ESTATES**)
Annual interest rates
    Credit card holders' right to request annual report concerning finance charges   CC §1748.5
    Presumptions   CC §1916
Annuities, accrual of interest on   Pro §12004
Child support judgment or support order   CCP §695.211
Claims against public entities and employees
    Judgments   Gov §965.5
Contracts
    Award for breach of   CC §3288
    Rate of interest   CC §1916.12-1
Damages (See **DAMAGES**)
Deposit in lieu of surety bond where no proceedings pending, payment of interest on   CCP §995.740
Earnings withholding order, interest included in   CCP §706.028
Eminent domain compensation award acquiring   CCP §§1263.015, 1268.310 to 1268.360
Employee Retirement Income Security Act (See **ERISA**)
Enforcement of judgments (See **ENFORCEMENT OF JUDGMENTS**)
Fiduciary income and principal act
    Receipts, allocation
        Income, allocation to   Pro §16345
Housing loans by public entities, assumption of   CC §711.5
Impound accounts   CC §2954.8
Income of property   CC §748
International commercial arbitration award, interest on   CCP §1297.317
Inverse condemnation, computation of interest award in action for   CCP §1268.311
Judgments
    Enforcement of judgments (See **ENFORCEMENT OF JUDGMENTS**)
    Inclusion in interest in   CRC 3.1802
Legacies by will, interest on (See **WILLS**)
Legal rate of interest   CC §1916.12-1
Mechanics' liens
    Stop payment notices, enforcement of claim stated
        Interest included in award   CC §8560
Offer to perform as terminating   CC §1504
Partition referees contracts providing for   CCP §873.150
Permanently escheated property   CCP §1320
Political items, illegal sale of   CC §1739.4
Precomputed interest   CC §1799.5
    Waiver of protections   CC §1799.6
Prejudgment interest, award of   CC §3291
Presumption of loan on interest   CC §§1914 to 1916.5
Public entity defendant, interest on liquidated claim against   Gov §926.10
Public entity loans for purchase or rehabilitation of realty   CC §711.5
Public retirement system loans, exemption from usury laws for   CC §1916.2

INTEREST ON MONEY—Cont.
Real estate brokers, interest on loans by CC §1916.1
Shared appreciation loans (See **SHARED APPRECIATION LOANS**)
Small claims courts
    Judgment CCP §116.820
Trust deeds and mortgages, loans secured by (See **TRUST DEEDS AND MORTGAGES**)
Trusts (See **TRUSTS**)
Unclaimed property
    Generally (See **UNCLAIMED PROPERTY**)
    Deposits unclaimed CCP §§1513, 1513.5, 1516
Usury (See **USURY**)
Variable interest rate loans (See **TRUST DEEDS AND MORTGAGES**)
Waiver of CC §3290
Wills, interest on legacies by (See **WILLS**)

INTERESTS OF JUSTICE
Attorney's fee award to prevailing party in action resulting in enforcement of right affecting public interest CCP §1021.5
Disqualification of judges, grounds for CCP §170.1
Preference, discretion of court to grant motion for CCP §36
Stay or dismissal of action that should be heard in forum outside state CCP §410.30

INTERGENERATIONAL HOUSING DEVELOPMENTS CC §51.3.5

INTERLOCUTORY JUDGMENT
Family law rules (See **FAMILY RULES**)
Partition action CCP §§872.720, 872.810

INTERMENT (See **CEMETERIES**)

INTERNAL REVENUE DEPARTMENT
Estate tax (See **ESTATE TAX**)
Income tax (See **INCOME TAX**)
Marital deduction gifts (See **MARITAL DEDUCTION GIFTS**)
Will construction, application of Internal Revenue Code provisions to (See **WILL CONSTRUCTION**)

INTERNATIONAL COMMERCIAL ARBITRATION AND CONCILIATION
Applicability of provisions
    Uniformity CCP §1297.20
Appointment
    Arbitrators
        Challenges (See within this heading, **"Challenges to arbitrator"**)
    Conciliators CCP §§1297.341 to 1297.343
        Arbitrator, appointment as CCP §1297.393
Appointment of arbitrators
    Challenge to (See within this heading, **"Challenges to arbitrator"**)
    Conciliator as arbitrator, appointment of CCP §1297.393
    Court action
        Appealability of CCP §1297.117
        Enforcement of appointment procedure CCP §1297.116
        Factors for appointing arbitrator CCP §1297.118
    Failure to agree on CCP §§1297.114, 1297.115
    Nationality requirements CCP §1297.111
    Procedure for appointing tribunal CCP §1297.112
    Substitute arbitrator, appointment of CCP §1297.152
Arbitration agreement
    Defined CCP §1297.71
    Writing requirements of CCP §§1297.72, 1297.73
Awards
    Additional award
        Generally CCP §§1267.335, 1297.334
        Extension of time for requesting CCP §1297.336
        Form and content of CCP §1297.337
    Correction or interpretation
        Generally CCP §§1297.331 to 1297.333
        Extension of time for requesting CCP §1297.336
        Form and content of CCP §1297.337
    Costs CCP §1297.318
    Delivery of copy to parties CCP §1297.315
    Enforcement of CCP §1297.316
    Interest, award of CCP §1297.317
    Interim award CCP §1297.316
    Settlement, effect of CCP §§1297.303, 1297.304
    Statement of date and place of arbitration CCP §1297.314
    Statement of reasons CCP §1297.313
    Termination of proceedings on final award CCP §1297.321
    Writing requirements CCP §1297.311

INTERNATIONAL COMMERCIAL ARBITRATION AND CONCILIATION—Cont.
Challenges to arbitrator
    Decision
        Superior court, decision of CCP §§1297.134 to 1297.136
        Tribunal, decision of CCP §1297.133
    Disclosure obligation of arbitrators (See within this heading, **"Disclosure requirements"**)
    Grounds for CCP §§1297.124, 1297.125
    Impartiality of arbitrators, disclosure of matters affecting CCP §1297.121
    Procedure
        Absence of agreement CCP §1297.132
        Agreement of parties to CCP §1297.131
Choice of law CCP §1297.283
Conciliation
    Appointment of conciliators
        Generally CCP §§1297.341 to 1297.343
        Arbitrator, appointment as CCP §1297.393
    Confidentiality of proceedings CCP §1297.371
    Costs CCP §§1297.411, 1297.412
    Enforcement of written conciliation agreement CCP §1297.401
    Immunity of conciliators CCP §§1297.431, 1297.432
    Jurisdiction of superior court, effect of CCP §1297.421
    Nonwaiver of rights during CCP §1297.394
    Report of conciliators CCP §§1267.362, 1297.361
    Representation of parties CCP §1297.351
    Stay of arbitration or judicial proceedings during CCP §1297.381
    Termination of CCP §§1297.391, 1297.392
    Tolling of statutes of limitation CCP §1297.382
Confidentiality of conciliation proceedings CCP §1297.371
Conflict of laws CCP §1297.282
Consolidation of arbitration CCP §§1297.272, 1297.273
Construction and interpretation CCP §§1297.21 to 1297.24
Contract terms, decision-making process to include CCP §1297.285
Costs
    Arbitration proceedings CCP §1297.318
    Conciliation proceedings CCP §§1297.411, 1297.412
Customs and usage of trade, decision-making process to include CCP §1297.285
Date of commencement of proceedings CCP §1297.211
Decision of tribunal
    Ex aequo et bono or as amiable compositeur, decision based on CCP §1297.284
    Majority of arbitrators, decision by CCP §1297.291
    Procedural questions, decision of presiding arbitrator on CCP §1297.291
Defaulting party
    Appearance at hearing or produce documentary evidence, failure to CCP §1297.253
    Statement of claim, failure to communicate CCP §1297.251
    Statement of defense, failure to communicate CCP §1297.252
Definitions CCP §1297.21
Delivery of written communications CCP §§1297.31 to 1297.32
Disclosure requirements
    Continuing nature of disclosure obligation CCP §1297.123
    Matters affecting impartiality of arbitrators, disclosure of CCP §1297.121
    Nonwaiver of disclosure obligation CCP §1297.122
Equal treatment of parties CCP §1297.181
Expert witnesses
    Appointment of CCP §1297.261
    Oral hearings, appearance at CCP §1297.262
Failure or impossibility to act as arbitrator CCP §§1297.141 to 1297.144
General principles of law CCP §1297.20
Hearings
    Generally CCP §1297.241
    Communication of evidence to opposing party CCP §1297.244
    Default by party failing to appear CCP §1297.253
    Expert witnesses, appearance of CCP §1297.262
    In camera proceedings CCP §1297.245
    Notice of CCP §1297.243
    Oral hearings, party requesting CCP §1297.242
Interest, award of CCP §1297.317
Interim protective measures
    Superior court, interim measures of (See within this heading, **"Superior court"**)
    Tribunal, interim measures of CCP §§1297.171 to 1297.180
        Authority to award CCP §1297.171
        Conditions CCP §1297.172
        Disclosures CCP §1297.177
        Liability for costs and damages CCP §1297.178
        Modification, suspension, or termination CCP §1297.175
        Notice CCP §1297.179
        Preliminary orders CCP §1297.174

INTERNATIONAL COMMERCIAL ARBITRATION AND CONCILIATION—Cont.
Interim protective measures—Cont.
    Tribunal, interim measures of —Cont.
        Recognition as final and binding order   CCP §1297.179
            Refusal   CCP §1297.180
        Requests   CCP §1297.173
        Security   CCP §1297.176
Judicial intervention, restrictions on   CCP §1297.51
Jurisdiction
    Conciliation proceedings, effect of   CCP §1297.421
    Superior court, jurisdiction of   CCP §1297.61
    Tribunal, jurisdiction of (See within this heading, **"Tribunal"**)
Language requirements   CCP §§1297.221 to 1297.224
Manner and conduct of proceedings   CCP §§1297.181 to 1297.224
Notice of hearing   CCP §1297.243
Place of arbitration   CCP §§1297.201 to 1297.203
Procedural rules   CCP §§1297.191 to 1297.193
Receipt of written communications   CCP §§1297.31 to 1297.33
Replacement of arbitrator (See within this heading, **"Substitute arbitrator"**)
Report of conciliators   CCP §§1267.362, 1297.361
Scope of application   CCP §§1297.11 to 1297.17
Settlement
    Award on agreed terms   CCP §§1297.303, 1297.304
    Procedures for   CCP §1297.301
    Termination of proceedings on   CCP §1297.302
Signature of arbitrators   CCP §§1297.311, 1297.312
Statement of claims and defenses   CCP §§1297.231 to 1297.233
Statutes of limitation, tolling of   CCP §1297.382
Statutory construction
    General principles of law   CCP §1297.20
Stay of proceedings
    Application for court order for stay of judicial proceedings   CCP §1297.81
    Conciliation proceedings, stay of arbitration or judicial proceedings pending   CCP §1297.381
    Grant of court order for stay of judicial proceedings   CCP §1297.82
Substitute arbitrator
    Appointment of   CCP §1297.152
    Prior hearings, effect of   CCP §1297.153
    Prior orders, effect of   CCP §1297.154
Superior court
    Appointment of arbitrators
        Court action (See within this heading, **"Appointment of arbitrators"**)
    Evidence taking, tribunal requesting court assistance in   CCP §1297.271
    Failure or impossibility to act as arbitrator   CCP §§1297.141 to 1297.144
    Functions performed by   CCP §1297.61
    Interim protective measures
        Authority to issue   CCP §1297.91
        Availability of   CCP §1297.90
        Enforcement of   CCP §1297.92
        Factors for granting   CCP §1297.94
        Pending objection to tribunal's jurisdiction, effect on   CCP §1297.95
        Permissible interim measures   CCP §1297.93
    Jurisdiction of   CCP §1297.61
    Stay of proceedings generally (See within this heading, **"Stay of proceedings"**)
Termination of proceedings
    Arbitration
        Agreement of parties to terminate   CCP §1297.151
        Final arbitration award, termination on   CCP §1297.321
        Mandate of tribunal, termination of   CCP §1297.323
        Other circumstances   CCP §1297.322
        Substitute arbitrator (See within this heading, **"Substitute arbitrator"**)
        Withdrawal of mandate   CCP §1297.151
    Conciliation, termination of   CCP §§1297.391, 1297.392
Tribunal
    Appointment of arbitrators (See within this heading, **"Appointment of arbitrators"**)
    Decision of (See within this heading, **"Decision of tribunal"**)
    Designating applicable laws for arbitrating dispute   CCP §1297.283
    Evidence taking, tribunal requesting court assistance in   CCP §1297.271
    Jurisdiction
        Challenges to   CCP §1297.162
        Exceeding scope of authority   CCP §1297.163
        Late permits, power to permit   CCP §1297.164
        Ruling on jurisdiction by tribunal   CCP §§1297.161, 1297.165
    Number of arbitrators   CCP §1297.101
    Pending objection in superior court to tribunal's jurisdiction, effect of   CCP §1297.95
    Superior court decision on   CCP §§1297.166, 1297.167

INTERNATIONAL COMMERCIAL ARBITRATION AND CONCILIATION—Cont.
Waiver of objection to application of arbitration procedure by failure to timely object   CCP §§1297.41, 1297.42

INTERNATIONAL LAW
Statutes of limitations
    Taking property in violation of international law   CCP §354.8

INTERNET
Accessibility violations
    Attorney complaint or demand letter
        Duties of attorney upon sending or serving   CC §55.32
Administrative Procedure Act (See **ADMINISTRATIVE PROCEDURE ACT**)
Appellate rules, supreme court and courts of appeal
    E-filing in supreme court and courts of appeal   CRC 8.70 to 8.79
        Supreme court-specific rules   CRCSupp SuprCtE-file 1 to CRCSupp SuprCtE-file 13
Arbitration and arbitrators
    Reports
        Data collection and reports available on web site   CCP §1281.96
Blind and visually impaired persons
    Internet website-related accessibility claims   CC §55.33
California Code of Regulations, legislature's intent to establish Internet access to   Gov §§11340.1, 11344
Child sexual abuse hosted on social media platform   CC §§3273.65 to 3273.69
Commercial sexual exploitation of minor by social media platform   CC §3345.1
Digital equity bill of rights   CC §§3120 to CC 3123
Human trafficking
    Supply chains of certain businesses
        Disclosures by businesses of efforts to eradicate slavery and human trafficking in supply chain   CC §1714.43
Investigative consumer reporting agencies
    Privacy practices   CC §1786.20
    Procuring report
        Notice to consumer   CC §1786.16
Judicial ethics opinions
    Committee contact information   CRC 9.80
Neutrality   CC §§3100 to 3104
Notaries public
    Online notarizations   CC §1181.1
Online violence prevention   CC §§1798.99.20 to 1798.99.23
Privacy policies
    Consumer privacy rights
        Conflict with other provisions   CC §1798.175
Public agencies maintaining Internet websites, electronic publication or distribution by   Gov §§11340.9, 11340.85
    Participation in government by public
        Decisions and pending opportunities for public participation link on homepage   Gov §§11364, 11365
Social security numbers, restrictions to transmission of   CC §1798.85
    Waiver of protections   CC §1798.86
Things, internet of
    Security for connected devices   CC §§1798.91.04 to 1798.91.06
Violence prevention
    Online violence prevention   CC §§1798.99.20 to 1798.99.23
Vlogging, minors engaged in the work of   Fam §§6650 to 6656 (See **VLOGGING**)

INTERNET NEUTRALITY   CC §§3100 to 3104

INTERNET OF THINGS
Security for connected devices   CC §§1798.91.04 to 1798.91.06

INTERPLEADER
Actions to compel claimants to interplead and litigate conflicting claims   CCP §386
Attorney's fees   CCP §386.6
Contract, actions based on   CCP §386
Costs and attorney's fees, allowance for   CCP §386.6
Deposits in court
    Amount of   CCP §386
    Costs and attorney's fees   CCP §386.6
    Deficiency determination   CCP §386
    Dismissal of stakeholder   CCP §386.5
    Investment in interest-bearing account   CCP §386.1
Dismissal of stakeholder   CCP §386.5
Filing fees
    Generally   Gov §§70612, 70614
    Riverside County
        Courthouse seismic repair costs, additional filing fees authorized to defray   Gov §70622

INTERPLEADER—Cont.
Filing fees—Cont.
 Supplemental fees for first paper filing   Gov §§70602.5, 70602.6
Injunctions against other proceedings   CCP §386
Triable by court   CCP §386

INTERPRETATION (See **CONSTRUCTION AND INTERPRETATION**)

INTERPRETERS (See **TRANSLATORS AND INTERPRETERS**)

INTERROGATORIES   CCP §§2030.010 to 2030.410
Additional interrogatories with supporting declaration   CCP §2030.040
 Format of declaration   CCP §2030.050
Amended answer   CCP §2030.310
Continuance of trial proceedings includes   CCP §595.1
Depositions generally (See **DEPOSITIONS**)
Economic litigation provisions for limited civil cases, permissible forms of discovery under   CCP §94
Enforcement of money judgments   CCP §§708.010 to 708.030
Evidence
 Use of answer as evidence   CCP §2030.410
Extension of time for response   CCP §2030.270
Format of interrogatories   CCP §2030.060
Form interrogatories
 Judicial Council development of   CCP §2033.710
  Advisory committees, consultation with   CCP §2033.730
  Nontechnical language, use in drafting   CCP §2033.730
 List of judicial council legal forms   CRCAppx A
 Optional use   CCP §2033.740
 Restitution for victims not paid
  Development of form interrogatories for   CCP §2033.720
Identification by set and number   CRC 3.1000, 3.1345
Judgment debtors   CCP §§708.010 to 708.030
Limitations on papers filed   CRC 3.250
Methods of discovery   CCP §2019.010
Motion to compel
 Response or further response, motion to compel   CCP §2030.300
 Separate document setting forth item to which further response, answer or production is requested   CRC 3.1345
Number   CCP §2030.030
 Additional interrogatories with supporting declaration   CCP §2030.040
  Format of declaration   CCP §2030.050
Numbering of interrogatories   CCP §2030.060
Objections to
 Limitations on papers filed   CRC 3.250
 Response
  Unobjectionable portion, response to   CCP §2030.240
Propounding   CCP §§2030.010 to 2030.090
 Additional interrogatories with supporting declaration   CCP §2030.040
  Format of declaration   CCP §2030.050
 Electronic format for inquiries   CCP §2030.210
 Format of interrogatories   CCP §2030.060
 Number   CCP §2030.030
  Additional interrogatories with supporting declaration   CCP §§2030.040, 2030.050
 Numbering of interrogatories   CCP §2030.060
 Protective orders   CCP §2030.090
 Service of interrogatories   CCP §2030.080
 Style   CCP §2030.060
 Supplemental interrogatory to get later-acquired information   CCP §2030.070
 Use of interrogatory for discovery   CCP §2030.010
 When propounded   CCP §2030.020
Protective orders
 Propounding interrogatories   CCP §2030.090
Reference to other responses   CRC 3.1345
Requests for admission generally (See **REQUEST FOR ADMISSION**)
Response   CCP §§2030.210 to 2030 to 310
 Amended answer   CCP §2030.310
 Completeness of responses   CCP §2030.220
 Electronic format for responses, objections, etc   CCP §2033.210
 Evidence, use as   CCP §2030.410
 Identification and sequence of responses   CRC 3.1000
 Initial response
  Motion to make binding   CCP §2030.310
 Limitation on papers filed   CRC 3.250
 Motion to compel further response   CCP §2030.300
 Motion to compel response or further response   CRC 3.1345
 Number to which party must respond   CCP §2030.030
 Objections   CCP §2030.240
 References to other responses   CRC 3.1345

INTERROGATORIES—Cont.
Response —Cont.
 Reference to writings from which answer could be derived   CCP §2030.230
 Retention   CCP §2030.280
 Signature   CCP §2030.250
 Time for response   CCP §2030.260
  Extension   CCP §2030.270
  Failure to serve timely response   CCP §2030.290
 Unobjectionable portion, answer to   CCP §2030.240
 Written responses   CCP §2030.210
Retention of interrogatory, response, and proof of service   CCP §2030.280
Sanctions
 Generally (See **DISCOVERY**)
 Propounding interrogatories
  Protective orders, unsuccessfully making or opposing motion for   CCP §2030.090
 Response
  Amended responses, unsuccessfully making or opposing motion to make initial response binding   CCP §2030.310
  Failure to serve timely response   CCP §2030.290
  Motion to compel further response, unsuccessfully making or opposing   CCP §2030.300
Sequence of responses   CRC 3.1000
Signature of responses   CCP §2030.250
Style   CCP §2030.060
Summary judgments, answer in interrogatories in support or opposition of motion for   CCP §437c
Supplemental and further discovery, format of   CRC 3.1000
Supplemental interrogatories
 Later-acquired information, eliciting   CCP §2030.070
Time for response   CCP §2030.260
 Extension   CCP §2030.270
 Failure to serve timely response   CCP §2030.290
Unlawful detainer
 Propounding, time for   CCP §2030.020
 Response
  Time for response   CCP §2030.260
Use of interrogatory for discovery   CCP §2030.010
When propounded   CCP §2030.020

INTERSTATE AND INTERNATIONAL DEPOSITIONS AND DISCOVERY ACT   CCP §§2029.100 to 2029.900 (See **DISCOVERY**)

INTERSTATE COMPACT ON PLACEMENT OF CHILDREN   CRC 5.616, Fam §§7900 to 7913
Children covered by compact   Fam §7907.5
Home environment study request from another state   Fam §7901.1
 Custody of child in requesting state   Fam §7906.5
Indian children, applicability of compact   Fam §7907.3

INTERSTATE FAMILY SUPPORT   Fam §§5700.101 to 5700.903
Applicability of provisions   Fam §5700.105
 Convention support proceedings   Fam §5700.702
 General applicability   Fam §5700.301
 Nonresident subject to personal jurisdiction   Fam §5700.210
 Prospective applicability   Fam §5700.902
 Responding tribunal, application of state law   Fam §5700.303
 Uniform application and construction   Fam §5700.901
Attorneys employed as private counsel   Fam §5700.309
Child support services department
 Convention support proceedings
  Initiation of support proceeding   Fam §5700.704
  Relation to United States central authority   Fam §5700.703
 State information agency   Fam §5700.310
Citation of chapter   Fam §5700.101
Commencement of proceedings   Fam §5700.301
 Convention support proceedings
  Child support services department   Fam §5700.704
  Direct request for establishment or modification of order   Fam §5700.705
  Direct request for recognition and enforcement of foreign support agreements   Fam §5700.710
Costs and fees   Fam §5700.313
Discovery assistance   Fam §5700.318
Duties of initiating tribunal   Fam §5700.304
Duties of responding tribunal   Fam §5700.305
Duties of support enforcement agency   Fam §5700.307
Inappropriate tribunal   Fam §5700.306
Limited immunity of complainant   Fam §5700.314
Nonparentage as defense, prohibition   Fam §5700.315

INTERSTATE FAMILY SUPPORT—Cont.
  Commencement of proceedings —Cont.
    Pleadings and accompanying documents   Fam §5700.311
    Private counsel   Fam §5700.309
    Rules of evidence and procedure   Fam §5700.316
  Communication between tribunals   Fam §5700.317
  Confidentiality of identifying information   Fam §5700.312
  Confirmation of registered order   Fam §5700.608
  Construction and interpretation of provisions
    Prospective applicability   Fam §5700.902
    Severability of provisions   Fam §5700.903
    Uniform application and construction   Fam §5700.901
  Contest of validity of income withholding order   Fam §5700.506
    Convention support orders   Fam §5700.707
  Contest of validity or enforcement of registered support order   Fam §5700.606
    Defenses and burdens of proof applicable   Fam §5700.607
  Convention support proceedings   Fam §§5700.701 to 5700.713
    Applicability of provisions   Fam §5700.702
    Child support services department
      Initiation of support proceeding   Fam §5700.704
      Relation to United States central authority   Fam §5700.703
    Contest of registered order   Fam §5700.707
    Definitions   Fam §5700.701
    Direct request for establishment or modification of order   Fam §5700.705
    Direct request for recognition and enforcement of foreign support agreements   Fam §5700.710
    English translation of record filed in another language   Fam §5700.713
    Foreign support agreements
      Recognition and enforcement   Fam §5700.710
    Initiation of support proceeding
      Child support services department   Fam §5700.704
      Direct request   Fam §5700.705
    Modification of convention child support order   Fam §5700.711
    Partial enforcement   Fam §5700.709
    Personal information protection   Fam §5700.712
    Recognition and enforcement of registered order   Fam §5700.708
    Registration of convention support order   Fam §5700.706
      Contest of registered order   Fam §5700.707
      Recognition and enforcement of registered order   Fam §5700.708
    Severability of orders, partial enforcement   Fam §5700.709
  Cumulation of remedies   Fam §5700.104
  Definitions   Fam §5700.102
    Convention support proceedings   Fam §5700.701
  Discovery assistance   Fam §5700.318
    Request form   CRCFL-559
  Enforcement of support orders   Fam §5700.402
    Administrative enforcement   Fam §5700.507
    Contest of validity   Fam §5700.506
    Continuing jurisdiction   Fam §5700.206
    Credit for payments collected   Fam §5700.209
    Determination of controlling support order   Fam §5700.207
      Notice   CRCFL-571
    Income withholding orders of another state
      Administrative enforcement   Fam §5700.507
      Contest of order by obligor   CRC 5.335
      Employer compliance with order   Fam §§5700.502 to 5700.505
      Immunity, employer compliance with order   Fam §5700.504
      Penalties for employer noncompliance with order   Fam §5700.505
      Receipt of order by employer   Fam §5700.501
      Terms of order   Fam §5700.502
      Two or more orders   Fam §5700.503
    Multiple obligees   Fam §5700.208
    Nonregistered orders
      Contest of income-withholding order by obligor   CRC 5.335
    Party designation   CRC 5.370
    Receipt and disbursement of payments   Fam §5700.319
    Registration for enforcement   Fam §5700.616
  Establishment of support order   Fam §5700.401
  Evidentiary rules   Fam §5700.316
  Extradition for criminal failure to provide support   Fam §§5700.801, 5700.802
  Fees and costs   Fam §5700.313
  Foreign support proceedings, applicability of provisions   Fam §5700.105
  Forms
    Contest of income withholding order by obligor   CRC 5.335
    Determination of controlling support order, notice   CRCFL-571
    Discovery assistance request   CRCFL-559
    General testimony form   CRCFL-526
    Initial request for enforcement   CRCFL-505
    Judgments, parental responsibility   CRCAppx A (CRCFL-530)
    Locate data sheet   CRCFL-558

INTERSTATE FAMILY SUPPORT—Cont.
  Forms—Cont.
    Nondisclosure order
      Ex parte application   CRCFL-511
    Party designation   CRC 5.370
    Registration of income-withholding and support orders   CRCFL-556
      Out-of-state orders, notice of registration   CRCAppx A (CRCFL-570)
    Response to petition   CRCAppx A (CRCFL-520)
    Show cause order   CRCFL-515
    Subsequent actions   CRCFL-557
    Summons   CRCAppx A (CRCFL-510)
    Transfer of actions
      Ex parte application   CRCAppx A (CRCFL-560), CRCFL-560
    Uniform support petition   CRCFL-500
    Use of interstate forms   CRC 5.7
  Forms, use of interstate   CRC 5.7
  Governor, rendition of person failing to provide support   Fam §§5700.801, 5700.802
  Immunity of employer complying with income withholding order   Fam §5700.504
  Immunity of petitioner from service
    Limited immunity of complainant   Fam §5700.314
  Inappropriate tribunal
    Transfer of case   Fam §17404.2
  Income withholding
    Employer receipt of out-of-state income withholding order   Fam §5700.501
  Interstate rendition   Fam §§5700.801, 5700.802
  Issuance of support order   Fam §5700.401
  Jurisdiction   Fam §§5700.201 to 5700.211
    Applicability of provisions to nonresident subject to personal jurisdiction   Fam §5700.210
    Basis for jurisdiction over nonresident   Fam §5700.201
    Child support order enforcement   Fam §5700.206
    Continuing exclusive jurisdiction
      Child support orders   Fam §§5700.202, 5700.205
      Spousal support order modification   Fam §5700.211
    Credit for payments collected   Fam §5700.209
    Determination of controlling support order   Fam §5700.207
    Duration of personal jurisdiction   Fam §5700.202
    Initiating tribunal of state   Fam §5700.203
    Modification of orders
      Foreign country orders   Fam §5700.615
    Multiple obligees   Fam §5700.208
    Responding tribunal of state   Fam §5700.203
    Simultaneous proceedings   Fam §5700.204
  Minor parents, instituting proceedings   Fam §5700.302
  Modification of child support orders   Fam §§5700.609 to 5700.614
    Continuing exclusive jurisdiction   Fam §5700.205
    Convention support orders   Fam §5700.711
    Effect   Fam §5700.610
    Foreign country orders
      Jurisdiction to modify   Fam §5700.615
      Registration for modification   Fam §5700.616
    Individual parties residing in state   Fam §5700.613
    Notice to issuing tribunal of modification   Fam §5700.614
    Out-of-state orders   Fam §5700.611
    Procedures   Fam §5700.609
    Recognition of order modified in another state   Fam §5700.612
  Modification of support orders
    Party designation   CRC 5.370
    Spousal support orders
      Continuing exclusive jurisdiction   Fam §5700.211
  Multiple support orders
    Determination of controlling support order   Fam §5700.207
  New actions, party designation   CRC 5.370
  Nonexclusivity of remedies   Fam §5700.104
  Party designation   CRC 5.370
  Paternity determinations
    Nonparentage as defense, prohibition   Fam §5700.315
    Proceedings to determine   Fam §5700.402
  Payments
    Receipt and disbursement   Fam §5700.319
  Pleadings and accompanying documents   Fam §5700.311
  Procedural rules   Fam §5700.316
  Registration for enforcement   Fam §§5700.601 to 5700.616
    Choice of laws   Fam §5700.604
    Confirmation of registered order   Fam §5700.608
    Contest of validity or enforcement of registered order   Fam §5700.606
      Confirmation of registered order   Fam §5700.608
      Convention support orders   Fam §5700.707

INTERSTATE FAMILY SUPPORT—Cont.
Registration for enforcement —Cont.
    Contest of validity or enforcement of registered order —Cont.
        Defenses and burdens of proof applicable   Fam §5700.607
        Notice of registration   Fam §5700.605
        Stay of enforcement pending   Fam §5700.607
    Convention support orders   Fam §5700.706
        Contest of registered order   Fam §5700.707
        Recognition and enforcement of registered order   Fam §5700.708
    Duties of support enforcement agency requesting   Fam §5700.307
    Effect of registration   Fam §5700.603
    Governing law   Fam §5700.604
    Multiple orders in effect   Fam §5700.602
        Notice of registration   Fam §5700.605
    Notice of registration   Fam §5700.605
    Orders subject to registration   Fam §5700.601
    Procedures   Fam §5700.602
    Records to be sent to tribunal   Fam §5700.602
    Vacation of registration, seeking   Fam §5700.607
    When order considered registered   Fam §5700.603
Registration for modification of child support order   Fam §§5700.609 to 5700.616
    Effect   Fam §5700.610
    Foreign country orders
        Jurisdiction to modify   Fam §5700.615
        Registration for modification   Fam §5700.616
    Individual parties residing in state   Fam §5700.613
    Notice to issuing tribunal of modification   Fam §5700.614
    Out-of-state order, modification   Fam §5700.611
    Procedures   Fam §5700.609
    Recognition of order modified in another state   Fam §5700.612
Remedies cumulative   Fam §5700.104
Rendition for criminal failure to support   Fam §§5700.801, 5700.802
Self-incrimination, privilege against
    Adverse inference from refusal to testify   Fam §5700.316
Service of process
    Limited immunity of complainant   Fam §5700.314
    Summons form   CRCAppx A (CRCFL-510)
Severability of provisions   Fam §5700.903
Show cause orders   Fam §17404.1
    Form   CRCFL-515
State information agency
    Duties   Fam §5700.310
Summons
    Forms
        Judicial council forms   CRCAppx A
Support enforcement agency
    Administrative enforcement of orders   Fam §5700.507
    Commencement of proceedings, duties   Fam §5700.307
    Convention support proceedings
        Initiation of support proceeding   Fam §5700.704
        Relation of office to United States central authority   Fam §5700.704
    Designation   Fam §5700.103
    Duties of state officials, compelling performance   Fam §5700.308
    Receipt and disbursement of payments   Fam §5700.319
Temporary support orders
    Continuing exclusive jurisdiction not created   Fam §5700.205
Title of provisions   Fam §5700.101
Transfer of case   Fam §17404.2
    Ex parte application, form   CRCAppx A (CRCFL-560)
Tribunals of state   Fam §5700.103
    Communication between tribunals   Fam §5700.317
    Determination of controlling support order   Fam §5700.207
    Inappropriate tribunal   Fam §5700.306
    Initiating tribunal
        Acting as   Fam §5700.203
        Duties   Fam §5700.304
    Responding tribunal
        Acting as   Fam §5700.203
        Application of state law   Fam §5700.303
        Duties   Fam §5700.305
        Powers   Fam §5700.305
    Simultaneous proceedings, restrictions on jurisdiction   Fam §5700.204

INTERVENING CAUSE (See PROXIMATE CAUSE)

INTERVENTION
Administrative adjudication   Gov §11440.50
Application to intervene in action or proceeding   CCP §387
Arbitration proceedings   CCP §1281.2

INTERVENTION—Cont.
Attorney General's intervention in appeal when state law ruled unconstitutional   CCP §§664.5, 902.1
Eminent domain action   CCP §1250.230
Enforcement of judgments (See **ENFORCEMENT OF JUDGMENTS**)
Examination for purposes of enforcement of judgments   CCP §708.190
Filing fees
    Generally   Gov §§70612, 70614
    Riverside County
        Courthouse seismic repair costs, additional filing fees authorized to defray   Gov §70622
    Supplemental fees for first paper filing   Gov §§70602.5, 70602.6
Groundwater rights actions
    Intervention in comprehensive adjudication
        Local government intervention   CCP §837
        State intervention   CCP §837.5
Indian child welfare act involuntary placements
    Tribe or Indian custodian, intervention by   CRC 5.482
Interest in property or transaction subject to action   CCP §387
Judges
    Temporary judges
        Motion for leave to file complaint for intervention   CRC 2.835
Referees
    Motion for leave to file complaint for intervention   CRC 3.932

INTERVIEWS
Adoption proceedings (See **ADOPTION**)

INTESTATE SUCCESSION
Abuse or neglect of elder or dependent adult by heir, effect of   Pro §259
Adoption, effect of (See **ADOPTION**)
Advancements (See **ADVANCEMENTS**)
Advertising, heritable property rights in use of deceased personality's name or likeness in   CC §3344.1
Alien, inheritance by   Pro §6411
American Indian tribal custom, recognition of   Fam §295
Appeals   Pro §§1303, 1310
Application of governing statutes   Pro §§6400, 6414, 6455
Brothers, inheritance by   Pro §§6402, 6402.5
Collateral kindred, claims of   Pro §§6402, 6402.5
Contracts regarding succession   Pro §21700
Debts owed to decedent   Pro §6410
Disclaimer of estate interest   Pro §§260 to 295
Escheat of estate property (See **ESCHEAT**)
Foster parents, determining succession from or through   Pro §6454
General discussion of order of succession and intestate shares   Pro §§6401 to 6402
Half-blood, inheritance by kindred of   Pro §6406
Heirs
    Partition
        Partition of real property act   CCP §§874.311 to 874.323
Homicide, effect of   Pro §§250 to 258
Joint tenancy, property acquired by   Pro §§6401 to 6402.5
Manslaughter, inheritance by person committing   Pro §§250 to 258
Marital deduction gifts (See **MARITAL DEDUCTION GIFTS**)
Neglect or abuse of elder or dependent adult by heir, effect of   Pro §259
Next of kin, taking by   Pro §§6402, 6402.5
Non-citizens or non-nationals, inheritance by   Pro §6411
Notices   Pro §§1200 to 1266
    Known heirs or devisees, notice to   Pro §1206
    Predeceased spouse, notice to issue of   Pro §6402.5
Parent-child relationship
    Parent inheriting from child based on relationship
        Situations preventing inheritance   Pro §6452
Parent-child relationship, determination of   Pro §§6450 to 6455
Partition
    Partition of real property act   CCP §§874.311 to 874.323
Posthumous children   Pro §§240, 6407
    Conception after death of decedent   Pro §6453
Predeceased heirs   Pro §6403
Predeceased spouse, issue of   Pro §§6402, 6402.5
Prior law, effect of   Pro §6414
Real property acquired through   CC §1000
Representation, distribution by right of   Pro §§240 to 241, 6401 to 6402.5
Separate property, inherited property as   Pro §§6400 to 6402.5
Severance of matters associated with proceedings and actions under Probate Code   Pro §801
Simultaneous death (See **SIMULTANEOUS DEATH**)
Sisters, inheritance by   Pro §§6402, 6402.5
Stepparents
    Adoption by stepparents   Fam §9004, Pro §6451

INTESTATE SUCCESSION—Cont.
Stepparents—Cont.
    Establishing parent-child relationship in absence of adoption   Pro §6454
Surviving spouse, rights of   Pro §§6401 to 6402.5
Time period required for heirs to survive decedent   Pro §6403
Two lines of blood, persons related to decedent through   Pro §6413
Undue influence
    Definition of undue influence   Pro §86
Uniform Parentage Act governing determination of natural parent and child relationship   Pro §6453

INTIMATE PARTNER BATTERING EFFECTS
Expert testimony   Ev §1107

INTIMIDATION
Civil rights, deprivation by
    Waiver of right to freedom from violence, coerced or involuntary   CC §51.7
Health care facilities
    Intimidation
        Force, threat or other obstruction of access to health facilities or school grounds   CC §1708.9
Landlord and tenant
    Immigration or citizenship status of tenant, occupant, etc
        Disclosures to immigration authorities with intent to intimidate or harass   CC §1940.35
Sexual orientation, intimidation based on
    Waiver of right to freedom from violence, coerced or involuntary   CC §51.7

INTOXICATED PERSONS (See **SUBSTANCE ABUSE**)

INTOXICATING BEVERAGES (See **ALCOHOLIC BEVERAGES**)

INVASION OF PRIVACY
Generally   CC §1798.53
Advertising, unauthorized use of name or likeness in   CC §§3344, 3344.1
Assault with intent to capture visual image or sound recording   CC §1708.8
Constructive invasion of privacy   CC §1708.8
Credit reporting (See **CREDIT REPORTING**)
Damages
    Advertising, unauthorized use of name or likeness in   CC §§3344, 3344.1
    Information Practices Act   CC §1798.53
    Visual image or sound recording or other physical impression of plaintiff engaged in personal or familial activity, attempt to capture   CC §1708.8
Eavesdropping and wiretapping (See **EAVESDROPPING AND WIRETAPPING**)
False imprisonment with intent to capture visual image or sound recording   CC §1708.8
Information Practices Act (See **INFORMATION PRACTICES ACT**)
Personal information, protection for (See **INFORMATION PRACTICES ACT**)
Photographs (See within this heading, "**Visual images and sound recordings**")
Public employees, liability of   CC §1798.53
Right of protection from   CC §43
Sound recordings
    Generally (See within this heading, "**Visual images and sound recordings**")
    Eavesdropping and wiretapping (See **EAVESDROPPING AND WIRETAPPING**)
Visual images and sound recordings
    Advertising, unauthorized use of name or likeness in   CC §§3344, 3344.1
    Exposing intimate body parts or sexual acts of another without permission, distribution of photos, etc
        Actions for injunctions, damages, etc   CC §1708.85
        Confidential information form   CRCAppx A
    Personal or familial activity, attempt to capture visual image or sound recording or other physical impression of plaintiff engaged in   CC §1708.8

INVENTIONS (See **PATENT OF INVENTION**)

INVENTORY
Administration of decedents' estates
    Generally (See **ADMINISTRATION OF ESTATES**)
    Small estates without administration (See **SMALL ESTATES WITHOUT ADMINISTRATION**)
Attachment (See **ATTACHMENT**)
Claim and delivery   CCP §511.050
Conservators (See **CONSERVATORS**)
Family allowance payments, effect on   Pro §6541
Guardianship (See **GUARDIAN AND WARD**)

INVENTORY—Cont.
Homesteads, filing inventory affecting possession of   Pro §§6510, 6520
Life tenant furnishing inventory to personal representative   Pro §11752
Receiver's inventory, law and motion rule of court regarding   CRC 3.1181
Small estates without administration (See **SMALL ESTATES WITHOUT ADMINISTRATION**)
Veterans Administration, notice requirement for   Pro §1461.5

INVERSE CONDEMNATION (See **EMINENT DOMAIN**)

INVESTIGATIONS
Adoption proceedings (See **ADOPTION**)
Agencies (See **INVESTIGATIVE CONSUMER REPORTING AGENCIES**)
Child custody proceedings (See **CUSTODY OF CHILDREN**)
Conservators (See **CONSERVATORS**)
Credit report disputes   CC §1785.25
Guardianship (See **GUARDIAN AND WARD**)
Judges
    Facts of case   CRCSupp JudEthicsCanon 3
Missing person, administrator of estate seeking   Pro §12406
Sterilization proceedings   Pro §1955
Surveyors investigating boundaries   CC §846.5
Termination of parental rights   Fam §§7850 to 7852

INVESTIGATIVE CONSUMER REPORTING AGENCIES
Access to report, consumer's   CC §1786.11
Accuracy of information supplied, procedures to ensure   CC §1786.20
Adverse information
    Disclosure to consumer of   CC §§1786.10, 1786.28
    Subsequent reports, inclusion of adverse information in   CC §1786.30
Arrest information, restrictions on disclosure of   CC §1786.18
Attorney-client privilege
    Law not changed by provisions   CC §1786.55
Attorneys' fees, action for   CC §1786.50
Bankruptcy information, restrictions on   CC §1785.18
Certification of users' lawful purpose and compliance with relevant requirements, requirement for   CC §1786.20
Charges to consumer   CC §§1786.22, 1786.26
Citations of statutes affecting   CC §1786.1
Codes explained   CC §1786.22
Conditions for procuring report   CC §1786.16
Consumer privacy rights
    Relation between records of agencies and obligations imposed under consumer privacy provisions   CC §1798.145
Consumer reports
    Personal information protection
        Software updates and other measures by consumer credit reporting agencies to address security vulnerability   CC §1798.81.6
Conviction of crime, restrictions on disclosure of   CC §1786.18
Corrected records   CC §1786.24
Costs, action for   CC §1786.50
Court order, furnishing of report in compliance with   CC §1786.12
Damages action   CC §1786.50
Definitions   CC §1786.2
Deletion of information   CC §1786.24
Disclosures by reporting entities not using agencies   CC §1786.53
Disputed information   CC §1786.24
Employers gathering information without use of agencies   CC §1786.55
Federal statutes, action under   CC §1786.52
Fees charged to consumers   CC §§1786.22, 1786.26
Furnishing of report, circumstances warranting   CC §§1786.12, 1786.14
Governmental agencies, information to   CC §1786.14
Identification of prospective users   CC §§1786.20, 1786.22
Indictment information, restrictions on   CC §1786.18
Inspection of files by consumers   CC §§1786.10, 1786.22
Insurance denials based on information reported by agency
    Information given to rejected applicant   CC §1786.40
Invasion of privacy action   CC §1786.52
Libel and slander action   CC §1786.52
Medical information   CC §§1786.2, 1786.12
New investigations   CC §1786.24
Notice
    Disputed information, notices in connection with   CC §1786.24
    Procuring of report, notice to consumer of   CC §1786.16
    Rights and obligations of recipient of report, notice of   CC §1786.29
Old information   CC §1786.18
Personal information protection
    Consumer credit reporting agencies
        Software updates and other measures to address security vulnerability   CC §1798.81.6

INVESTIGATIVE CONSUMER REPORTING AGENCIES—Cont.
Person providing consumer information but not using investigative consumer reporting agency, disclosure requirements by   CC §1786.53
Public policy affecting   CC §1786
Records of violations, disclosure of   CC §1786.54
Reinvestigation   CC §1786.24
Removal of information   CC §1786.24
Res judicata   CC §1786.52
Restrictions on information in report   CC §1786.18
Separability clause   CC §1786.56
7-year-old information   CC §1786.18
Sources   CC §1786.28
Statutes of limitation on action against   CC §1786.52
Subpoenas   CC §1786.12
Subsequent reports, inclusion of adverse information in   CC §1786.30
Tax liens, restrictions on disclosure of   CC §1786.18
Telephones, information disclosure over   CC §1786.22
United States statutes, action under   CC §1786.52
Unlawful detainer actions, prohibition on information concerning   CC §1786.18
Verification of adverse information   CC §1786.28
Waiver of protections   CC §1786.57

INVESTMENT ADVISERS
Generally   CC §3372
Conservator
    Opening or changing name on conservatee's account, responsibilities of conservator   CRC 7.1061
Guardians
    Assets of ward
        Taking possession or control, responsibilities of guardian   CRC 7.1011
Sexual harassment, civil action for
    Construction or application of provisions in issue, solicitor general notified   CC §51.1

INVESTMENT CERTIFICATES
Decedents' estates, sale of certificates held by   Pro §10200

INVESTMENT COMPANIES
Conservators
    Opening or changing name on conservatee's account, responsibilities of conservator   CRC 7.1061
Guardians and conservators
    Assets of ward
        Taking possession or control, responsibilities of guardian   CRC 7.1011

INVESTMENTS
Administration of decedents' estates (See ADMINISTRATION OF ESTATES)
Advisers, regulations on   CC §3372
Charitable investments or loans
    Uniform prudent management of institutional funds act   Pro §§18501 to 18510 (See INSTITUTIONAL FUNDS MANAGEMENT)
Conservators, investment of funds by (See CONSERVATORS)
Consumer credit contracts, restrictions concerning investment property pledged as collateral on   CC §1799.103
Endowments
    Uniform prudent management of institutional funds act   Pro §§18501 to 18510 (See INSTITUTIONAL FUNDS MANAGEMENT)
Guardians, investment of funds by (See GUARDIAN AND WARD)
Impound accounts for payment of taxes or insurance premiums on mortgaged property   CC §2955
Institutional funds management
    Uniform prudent management of institutional funds act   Pro §§18501 to 18510 (See INSTITUTIONAL FUNDS MANAGEMENT)
Interpleader deposits, investment of   CCP §386.1
Judge's ownership in mutual or common investment fund not a financial interest for purposes of disqualification   CCP §170.5
Trusts (See TRUSTS)
Unclaimed deposits and payments   CCP §1562
Uniform prudent management of institutional funds act   Pro §§18501 to 18510 (See INSTITUTIONAL FUNDS MANAGEMENT)

INVESTMENT SECURITIES
Electronic transactions
    Exceptions to applicability of electronic transactions provisions   CC §1633.3

INVITEES
Personal injury   CC §846

INVOICES
Farm machinery repairs, invoice requirements for   CC §1718
Payment solicited for goods not ordered   CC §1716

INVOLUNTARY MANSLAUGHTER (See MANSLAUGHTER)

INVOLUNTARY TRUSTS (See CONSTRUCTIVE TRUSTS)

IRREPARABLE INJURY
Injunctions against   CCP §526

IRRIGATION
Appeals in mandamus proceedings   CCP §1110a
Construction defects, actions for
    Irrigation systems
        Actionable defects   CC §896
Government tort liability
    Injuries caused by condition of canals, conduits or drains   Gov §831.8
Injunctions to prevent diversion of water   CCP §§530, 532, 534

ISLANDS
Changes in river channels, ownership of islands formed by   CC §1018
Ownership of islands in rivers and streams   CC §§1016, 1017

ISSUANCE
Bonds, procedure for validation of authorization, issuance, sale or exchange of   CCP §349.4

ISSUES
Fact issues for jury, referee or court   CCP §592
Joinder of issues (See JOINDER OF ISSUES)
Law, issues of   CCP §591
Notice of trial   CCP §594
Referees determining   CCP §638
Strike, motion to   CCP §589

ISSUE SANCTION
Case questionnaires under economic litigation provisions for limited civil cases, failure to obey order compelling response to   CCP §93

IUDS
Dalkon Shield claimants, extension of limitations statute in action for   CCP §340.7

J

JAILS
Child support
    Suspension of orders or judgments
        Incarceration or institutionalization of obligee   Fam §4007.5
City jails
    Social security numbers of inmates
        Release with consent and upon request from department of veterans affairs   CC §1798.85
County jail
    Small claims action, appearance of incarcerated plaintiff   CCP §116.540
    Social security numbers of inmates
        Release with consent and upon request from department of veterans affairs   CC §1798.85
Gender changes of those incarcerated
    Rights to name and gender change   CCP §1279.5
Jury service
    Ineligible to serve as juror   CCP §203
Name changes of those incarcerated   CCP §1279.5
Prisoners generally (See PRISONERS)
Sentencing for certain felonies to county jail
    Mandatory supervision, suspension of portion of sentence
        Criteria affecting mandatory supervision   CRC 4.415
Social security numbers of inmates
    Release with consent and upon request from department of veterans affairs   CC §1798.85

JBSIS
Judicial branch statistical information system   CRC 10.400

JENKINS ACT
Claims
    Attorneys' fees and costs   CCP §1021.10

JEOPARDY WITHHOLDING ORDER
Taxes, earnings withholding orders for   CCP §706.078

JEWELRY AND JEWELERS
Assignment for benefit of creditors, property exempt from CCP §1801
Common carrier's liability for transporting jewelry CC §2200
Exempt property for purposes of enforcement of judgments CCP §704.040
Lien for work performed in shops CC §3052a

JOBBERS
Wholesale sales representatives, contractual relations with (See **WHOLESALE SALES REPRESENTATIVES**)

JOB LISTING SERVICES (See also **EMPLOYMENT AGENCIES; EMPLOYMENT COUNSELING SERVICES**)
Advertising requirements of CC §1812.520
Bonding requirements CC §1812.515
Defined CC §1812.501
Exempt activities CC §1812.502
Fees
    Refund of fees to jobseeker CC §§1812.516, 1812.518, 1812.523
    Schedule of job listing service fees CC §1812.517
Fraud and misrepresentation, liability for CC §§1812.520, 1812.523
Job orders CC §1812.519
Minors, job placement for CC §1812.521
Nurses' registries (See **NURSES**)
Recordkeeping requirements CC §1812.522
Refund of fees to jobseeker CC §§1812.516, 1812.518, 1812.523
Remedies available CC §1812.523
Service agreements with jobseeker, requirements of CC §1812.516
Union contract or labor troubles at jobsite, notice to jobseeker of CC §1812.521

JOB RECRUITMENT CENTERS
Human trafficking or slavery
    Signs, businesses required to post notice concerning relief from slavery or human trafficking CC §52.6

JOINDER OF ACTIONS
Cross-complaints (See **CROSS-COMPLAINTS**)
Exceptions to compulsory joinder requirement CCP §426.40
Mechanics' liens
    Stop payment notices, enforcement of claim stated
        Joinder of multiple claimants or actions CC §§8552, 9506
Permissive joinder of causes of action CCP §427.10
Wrongful death (See **WRONGFUL DEATH**)

JOINDER OF CAUSES (See **JOINDER OF ACTIONS**)

JOINDER OF ISSUES
Generally CCP §588
Demurrer, law issues joined on CCP §589
Fact issues joined on answer CCP §590
Motion to strike, effect of CCP §589

JOINDER OF PARTIES
Answer alleging defect of CCP §430.10
Arbitration proceedings CCP §1281.2
CARE act rules
    Local government entity, joinder CRC 7.2240
Compulsory joinder CCP §389
Costs in absence of CCP §1022
Creditor's action against third person, joinder of judgment debtor in CCP §708.220
Cross-complaints, joinder of parties in (See **CROSS-COMPLAINTS**)
Demurrer alleging defect of CCP §430.10
Dependent child or ward of court proceedings, joinder of government agency or private service provider in CRC 5.575
Dismissal of action where person subject to compulsory joinder cannot be joined CCP §389
Dissolution of marriage (See **DISSOLUTION OF MARRIAGE**)
Doubt as to person from whom plaintiff is entitled to redress CCP §379
Eminent domain action CCP §1250.240
Enforcement of judgments (See **ENFORCEMENT OF JUDGMENTS**)
Family law proceedings CRC 5.24, 5.29
    Employee benefit plans, joinder as prerequisite to separate trial of termination of marriage or domestic partnership CRC 5.390
Family law rules (See **FAMILY RULES**)
Identity theft, action involving CC §1798.94
Interest in property, joinder of persons claiming CCP §389.5
Interpleader CCP §386
Intervention CCP §387
Mechanics' liens
    Stop payment notices, enforcement of claim stated
        Joinder of multiple claimants or actions CC §§8552, 9506

JOINDER OF PARTIES—Cont.
Parent of injured child CCP §376
Partition action CCP §§872.510 to 872.550
Partnership or other unincorporated association, joinder of member as party in action against CCP §369.5
Permissive joinder
    Defendants CCP §379
    Plaintiffs CCP §378
Quieting title action CCP §762.040
Quo warranto proceedings, defendants in CCP §808
Separate trials CCP §379.5
Surety bonds, joinder of surety and principal in action to enforce liability on CCP §996.430
Unwilling plaintiff made defendant CCP §382
Venue, improper joinder to fix CCP §395
Ward of court proceedings
    Joinder of government agency or private service provider in CRC 5.575

JOINT ACCOUNTS (See **MULTIPLE-PARTY ACCOUNTS**)

JOINT AND SEVERAL LIABILITY CC §§1430 to 1432
Benefits under contract CC §1659
Bond furnished by estate representative Pro §8480
Common interest development, liability based on interest in common area CC §5805
Contribution among joint tortfeasors CCP §§875 to 880
Covenant not to sue, effect on liability of joint tortfeasor CCP §877
Dismissal of suit, effect on liability of joint tortfeasor CCP §877
Execution of contract by several persons CC §1660
Indemnity contract CC §2777
Jurisdiction over persons liable on contract CCP §410.70
Motion pictures depicting cruelty, liability of distributor for CC §3507.4
Parent's liability for torts of children CC §1714.1, CRCAppx B
Performance by one party CC §1474
Release, effect on liability of joint tortfeasor by CCP §§875 to 880
Surety bonds (See **SURETYSHIP, BONDS AND UNDERTAKINGS**)

JOINT AUTHORITY
Public officers and employees CC §12

JOINT CUSTODY (See **CUSTODY OF CHILDREN**)

JOINT DEBTORS
After judgment proceedings against joint debtors not originally served CCP §§989 to 994
Contribution between (See **CONTRIBUTION**)
Jurisdiction to proceed against such defendants as are served CCP §410.70
Proceeding against defendants served
    After judgment proceedings against joint debtors not originally served CCP §§989 to 994
    Jurisdiction to proceed against such defendants as are served CCP §410.70
Release of one, effect of CCP §1543

JOINT INTERESTS
Defined CC §683
Title held by CC §682

JOINT STOCK COMPANY
Service of process CCP §416.30

JOINT TENANCY
Bank deposits CC §683
Consent, severance of interest without CC §683.2
Defined CC §683
Descent of joint tenancy property Pro §§6401, 6402.5
Disclaimer of interest Pro §285
Division of property on dissolution of marriage Fam §§2580, 2581, 2650
Homestead, sale of CCP §704.820
Husband and wife holding property in Fam §750
Mobilehome joint tenant, rights of CC §798.78
Multiple-party accounts (See **MULTIPLE-PARTY ACCOUNTS**)
Nonprobate transfers (See **NONPROBATE TRANSFERS**)
Partition (See **PARTITION**)
Personal property CC §683
Presumption for purpose of division of property in dissolution proceedings Fam §2581
Safe deposit boxes CC §683.1
Severance of interest CC §683.2
Simultaneous death Pro §223
Spouses holding property as joint tenants Fam §750
Waste, actions for recovery of treble damages for CCP §732

JOURNALISTS
Contempt for failure to testify, findings of court required to hold journalist in CCP §1986.1
Court proceedings, restrictions on media coverage of   CRC 1.150
Interfering with trial   CCP §1209
Privilege against disclosing sources   Ev §1070

JOURNALS (See NEWSPAPERS AND MAGAZINES)

JUDGE ADVOCATE
Legal representation by   CRC 9.41

JUDGES
Acknowledgment of instruments   CC §§1180 to 1183
Adjournment for absence of   CCP §139
Administer oaths, power to   CCP §177
Administration of decedent's estate, disqualification for (See **ADMINISTRATION OF ESTATES**)
Administrative law judges (See **ADMINISTRATIVE PROCEDURE ACT**)
Admonishment (See within this heading, "Censure, removal, admonishment or retirement of judges")
Advertising, use of judge's name in   CRCSupp JudEthicsCanon 4
Affidavit, judicial officer's power to take and certify   CCP §179
Alternative Dispute Resolution programs (See **ALTERNATIVE DISPUTE RESOLUTION**)
Answer (See within this heading, "Censure, removal, admonishment or retirement of judges")
Appellate rules
    Superior court appellate division proceedings
        Appellate division assignments   CCP §77, CRC 10.1100
    Supreme court and courts of appeal
        Justices (See **APPELLATE RULES, SUPREME COURT AND COURTS OF APPEAL**)
Appointments
    Commission on judicial appointments (See **JUDICIAL APPOINTMENTS, COMMISSION ON**)
    Conduct during campaigns and appointment process   CRCSupp JudEthicsCanon 5
    Extrajudicial, acceptance of   CRCSupp JudEthicsCanon 5
Arbitrator, serving as   CRCSupp JudEthicsCanon 5
Assignment
    Administrative law judges   Gov §11370.3
    Appellate division of superior court   CRC 10.1100
    Disqualified judge, replacement for   CCP §170.8
    Juvenile courts, Judicial Council standards for judges assigned to   CRC JudAdminStand 5.40
    Reciprocal assignment orders, reporting   CRC 10.630
Attorney professional conduct
    Appointment to judicial office, lawyer seeking   ProfC 8.2
    Candidates for judicial office
        Applicable provisions   ProfC 8.2
    Contacts with judges, jurors, tribunal officials or employees, etc   ProfC 3.5
    False statements as to qualifications or integrity   ProfC 8.2
    Former judges, arbitrators, mediators, etc
        Restrictions on representation of clients   ProfC 1.12
    Professional misconduct, conduct constituting
        Assisting, inducing, etc, judge to violate judicial ethics, code of judicial conduct, etc   ProfC 8.4
    Service as temporary judge, referee or court-appointed arbitrator
        Judicial ethics canon 6D, when applicable   ProfC 2.4.1
Attorneys
    Censure, removal, retirement or admonishment, right to representation by counsel in proceedings for   JudPerR 106, 126
    Discipline
        Factual information in state bar disciplinary proceedings, code of judicial ethics   JudEthicsCanon 2
    Private practice of law defined   CCP §170.5
    Relationship to judge, disqualification based on   CCP §170.1
    Restriction on waiver of disqualification   CCP §170.3
    Served as lawyer in proceeding or for party, disqualification of judge having   CCP §170.1
Bias and prejudice
    Appointments by court, nondiscrimination in   CRC 1.6, 10.611, CRC JudAdminStand 10.21
    Code of Judicial Ethics provision   CRCSupp JudEthicsCanon 3
    Drafting laws, effect of participation in   CCP §170.2
    Grounds for disqualification   CCP §170.1
    Judicial administration standards
        Appointments by court, nondiscrimination in   CRC JudAdminStand 10.21
        Duty of court to prevent bias   CRC JudAdminStand 10.20

JUDGES—Cont.
Bias and prejudice—Cont.
    Peremptory challenge   CCP §§170.6, 170.7
    Prevention, court's duty   CRC JudAdminStand 10.20
    Restriction on waiver of disqualification   CCP §170.3
Briefs in proceedings against judges (See within this heading, "Censure, removal, admonishment or retirement of judges")
Business dealings   CRCSupp JudEthicsCanons 4, 5
Campaign contributions
    Disqualification from case, contribution as grounds   CCP §170.1
Canons of judicial ethics   CRCSupp JudEthicsCanons 1 to 6
Capacity to be impartial (See within this heading, "Bias and prejudice")
Case management and delay reduction of trial, consideration of   CRC JudAdminStand 2.1
Censure, removal, admonishment or retirement of judges
    Additional evidence   JudPerR 133
    Advisory letter to judge
        Preliminary investigation   JudPerR 111
    Amendment to pleadings   JudPerR 128
    Amicus curiae briefs   JudPerR 131
    Answer
        Generally   JudPerR 104, 119
        Amendments to   JudPerR 128
        Extension of time for   JudPerR 108, 119
    Appearance before commission
        Masters' report, appearance after   JudPerR 132
        Notice of intended private admonishment, appearance after   JudPerR 114
    Attorney representing judge   JudPerR 106, 126
    Briefs   JudPerR 130
        Amicus curiae briefs   JudPerR 131
        Review of commission's censure recommendation   CRC 9.60
    Commencement of commission action   JudPerR 109
    Commission member's participation prohibited in proceedings involving own censure, removal or admonishment   JudPerR 101
    Commission's own motion, staff inquiry or preliminary investigation on   JudPerR 109
    Confidentiality of proceedings   JudPerR 102, 122
    Conflicts of interest
        Disqualification of commission member unless quorum prevented by disqualification   JudPerR 134.5
    Consent
        Amicus curiae briefs, consent to submission of   JudPerR 131
        Discipline by consent   JudPerR 127
        One master to hear case, judge's consent to appointment of   JudPerR 121
    Conservator, appointment of   JudPerR 126
    Construction of rules governing   JudPerR 138
    Defamatory material   JudPerR 103
    Defending against charges, opportunity for   JudPerR 126
    Definitions   JudPerR 138
    Depositions, taking of   JudPerR 122
    Dereliction of duty   JudPerR 109
    Disclosures concerning proceedings   JudPerR 102
    Discovery   JudPerR 122
        Extension of time   JudPerR 108
    Dismissal of charge by examiner   JudPerR 128
    Dismissal of proceedings   JudPerR 134
    Disqualification pending further proceedings or appeal   JudPerR 120
    Drugs, use of   JudPerR 109
    Duty to cooperate   JudPerR 104
    Evidence
        Additional evidence, hearing for taking of   JudPerR 133
        Hearings, evidence admissible at   JudPerR 123, 125
        Prior proceedings, testimony concerning   Ev §703.5
    Extension of time in proceedings   JudPerR 108, 119
        Private admonishment procedure   JudPerR 114
    Failure to appear at hearing   JudPerR 123
    Filing with Commission   JudPerR 119.5
    Finality of commission determination   JudPerR 136
    Hearings
        Additional evidence   JudPerR 133
        Confidentiality   JudPerR 102
        Evidence at   JudPerR 123, 125
        Failure by judge to appear at   JudPerR 123
        Intended private admonishment, appearance to object to   JudPerR 114
        Media coverage   JudPerR 124
        Number of commission members required to attend hearing   JudPerR 123
        Procedural rights of judge   JudPerR 126

JUDGES—Cont.
Censure, removal, admonishment or retirement of judges—Cont.
    Interested party serving on commission   JudPerR 101
    Intoxicants, use of   JudPerR 109
    Judicial performance commission generally (See **JUDICIAL PERFORMANCE, COMMISSION ON**)
    Legal error reflecting bad faith, bias, abuse of authority, etc
        Basis for discipline   JudPerR 111.4
    Masters, hearing before and report of
        Additional evidence   JudPerR 133
        Extension of time   JudPerR 108
        Objections to report   JudPerR 130
        Preparation of report   JudPerR 129
        Setting for hearing   JudPerR 121
    Media coverage of hearings   JudPerR 124
    Medical examination, submission to   JudPerR 105
    Monitoring, deferring termination of investigation for   JudPerR 112
    Notice
        Advisory letter to judge   JudPerR 111
        Appointment of masters   JudPerR 121
        Determination by commission   JudPerR 135
        Disqualification pending formal proceedings   JudPerR 120
        Formal proceedings for censure or removal, institution of   JudPerR 118
        Hearing before commission or masters   JudPerR 121, 132, 133
        Intended private admonishment   JudPerR 107, 113
        Intended public admonishment   JudPerR 107
        Judge's request, notification of disposition at   JudPerR 109
        Preliminary investigation, notice of   JudPerR 107, 109, 111
        Staff inquiry, notice of   JudPerR 107
        Transcript filed with recommendation for censure, removal or retirement   CRC 9.60
    Objections
        Intended private admonishment, objections to   JudPerR 114
    Observation and review, deferring termination of investigation for   JudPerR 112
    Perpetuation of testimony by deposition   JudPerR 122
    Petition for review of commission recommendation or proceeding   CRC 9.60
    Pleadings   JudPerR 119, 128
    Preliminary investigation
        Confidentiality   JudPerR 102
        Determination whether formal proceedings should be instituted   JudPerR 109
        Letter   JudPerR 111
        Negotiated settlements during preliminary investigation or disciplinary proceeding   JudPerR 116.5
        Notice to judge   JudPerR 107, 109, 111
        Termination of   JudPerR 111
    Prior disciplinary action, receiving evidence of   JudPerR 125
    Prior proceedings, testimony concerning   Ev §703.5
    Private admonishment procedure, generally   JudPerR 113, 114
    Privilege
        Defamation, protection from liability for   JudPerR 103
        Discovery   JudPerR 122
        Judge's exercise of privilege at hearing   JudPerR 104, 123
    Proceedings involving   CRC 9.61
    Record of proceedings
        Generally   JudPerR 135
        Use and retention of records of complaints against judges   JudPerR 117
    Representation of judge by counsel   JudPerR 106
    Response to commission   JudPerR 104
    Retention and use of records of complaints against judges   JudPerR 117
    Retroactivity of discipline provisions   JudPerR 137
    Review of commission recommendation
        Censure, removal or retirement   CRC 9.60, 9.61
        Private admonishment   CRC 9.61
    Rights of judge in proceedings   JudPerR 126
    Self-incrimination, protection against   JudPerR 104
    Service
        Formal proceedings, notice of institution of   JudPerR 118
        Masters' report   JudPerR 129
        Petition for review of commission recommendation   CRC 9.60
    Setting for hearing   JudPerR 121
    Settlements
        Negotiated settlements during preliminary investigation or disciplinary proceeding   JudPerR 116.5
    Staff inquiry into judicial misconduct   JudPerR 107
    State Bar Court judges   CRC 9.11
    Subpoenas, right to issuance of   JudPerR 126

JUDGES—Cont.
Censure, removal, admonishment or retirement of judges—Cont.
    Supreme court
        Justice of supreme court, proceedings involving admonishment, censure, removal, or retirement of   CRC 9.61
        Review of recommendation of commission for admonishment, censure, removal, or retirement   CRC 9.60, 9.61
    Suspension   JudPerR 120.5
    Temporary disqualification pending formal proceedings   JudPerR 120
    Temporary judges
        Presiding judges, authority to remove or discontinue   CRC 10.741
    Termination of suspension   JudPerR 120.5
    Testimony, failure of judge to offer   JudPerR 123
    Time
        Amendments to pleadings   JudPerR 128
        Answer to charges   JudPerR 119
        Discovery requests   JudPerR 122
        Extension of time   JudPerR 108, 114, 119
        Formal proceedings, notice of institution of   JudPerR 118
        Masters' report   JudPerR 129
        Petition to review recommendation for censure, removal or admonishment   CRC 9.60
    Transcript
        Generally   JudPerR 135
        Available for use by judge   JudPerR 126
        Masters, proceedings before   JudPerR 129
        Supreme court filing with recommendation for censure, removal or retirement   CRC 9.60
    Tribunal of court of appeals judges for proceedings involving censure or removal of supreme court judge   CRC 9.61
    Vote of commission   JudPerR 134
    Witnesses
        Perpetuation of testimony by deposition   JudPerR 122
Center for judicial education and research
    Advisory committee   CRC 10.50
Challenge to judge
    Disqualification (See **JUDGES, DISQUALIFICATION OF**)
Chambers, powers and duties of judges at   CCP §§165, 166
Character witnesses, Code of Judicial Ethics provisions concerning judges testifying as   CRCSupp JudEthicsCanon 2
Civic and charitable activities, Code of Judicial Ethics provisions concerning judges' participation in   CRCSupp JudEthicsCanon 4
Claims against estates (See **CLAIMS AGAINST ESTATES**)
Clerk's duties, performance by judge of   CCP §167
Code of judicial ethics
    Administrative law judges, application to   Gov §§11475.20 to 11475.70
    Appearance of impropriety, avoiding   CRCSupp JudEthicsCanon 2
    Appointment to judicial office
        Conduct during campaigns and appointment process   CRCSupp JudEthicsCanon 5
    Arbitrators
        Court-appointed arbitrators, applicability of Code to   CRCSupp JudEthicsCanon 6
        Private arbitrator or mediator, service as   CRCSupp JudEthicsCanon 4
    Attorney discipline
        Factual information in state bar disciplinary proceedings   JudEthicsCanon 2
    Business dealings   CRCSupp JudEthicsCanon 4
    Campaign contributions
        Disclosures of campaign contributions   CRCSupp JudEthicsCanon 3
    Character witness, testimony as   CRCSupp JudEthicsCanon 2
    Civic and charitable activities, participation in   CRCSupp JudEthicsCanon 4
    Compliance provisions   CRCSupp JudEthicsCanon 6
    Corrective action when Code of Judicial Ethics or Rules of Professional Conduct violated, judge's responsibility for   CRCSupp JudEthicsCanon 3
    Criminal charge or conviction, duty of charged or convicted judge to report   CRCSupp JudEthicsCanon 3
    Definitions   CRCSupp JudEthicsTerminology
    Diligence in performance of judicial duties   CRCSupp JudEthicsCanon 3
    Disciplinary responsibilities   CRCSupp JudEthicsCanon 3
    Discrimination
        Administrative responsibilities of judge, impartial discharge   CRCSupp JudEthicsCanon 3
        Attorneys, judges to require to refrain from manifesting   CRCSupp JudEthicsCanon 3
        Court personnel and staff under direction of judge, standards of conduct enforced by judge   CRCSupp JudEthicsCanon 3

JUDGES

JUDGES—Cont.
Code of judicial ethics—Cont.
   Discrimination—Cont.
      Membership in discriminatory organizations   CRCSupp JudEthicsCanon 2
   Disqualification provisions   CRCSupp JudEthicsCanon 3
      Temporary judges   CRC 2.818, 2.819
   Electronic communications
      Public confidence in judiciary   CRCSupp JudEthicsCanon 2
   Ex parte communications   CRCSupp JudEthicsCanon 3
   Extra-judicial activities and judicial obligations, minimizing risk of conflict between   CRCSupp JudEthicsCanon 4
   Facts not part of record not to be considered   CRCSupp JudEthicsCanon 3
   Family members, actions in behalf of   CRCSupp JudEthicsCanon 2
   Fiduciary activities   CRCSupp JudEthicsCanon 4
   Gifts, acceptance of   CRCSupp JudEthicsCanon 4
   Governmental committees or commissions, appointment to   CRCSupp JudEthicsCanon 4
   Honorarium, acceptance of   CRCSupp JudEthicsCanon 4
   Impartiality and diligence in performing judicial duties   CRCSupp JudEthicsCanon 3
   Integrity and independence of judiciary, duty to uphold   CRCSupp JudEthicsCanon 1
   Investigation of facts   CRCSupp JudEthicsCanon 3
   Judicial performance commission
      Communications with commission   JudEthicsCanon 2
      Responsiveness   JudEthicsCanon 3
   Magistrates
      Applicability of code   CRCSupp JudEthicsCanon 6
   Membership in organizations   CRCSupp JudEthicsCanon 2
   Parole
      Communications concerning parole   CRCSupp JudEthicsCanon 2
   Political activity   CRCSupp JudEthicsCanon 5
      Leave, applicability of code to judge on leave to pursue election to other office   CRCSupp JudEthicsCanon 6
      Solicitation of contributions or endorsements for personal campaign or for judicial campaigns of others   CRCSupp JudEthicsCanon 5
   Practice of law, prohibition on   CRCSupp JudEthicsCanon 4
   Probation department
      Communications initiated by judge with sentencing judge or probation department representatives   CRCSupp JudEthicsCanon 2
   Publication of judges' writings   CRCSupp JudEthicsCanons 2, 4
   Public comment on pending litigation, restrictions on   CRCSupp JudEthicsCanon 3
   Quasi-judicial activities and judicial obligations, minimizing risk of conflict between   CRCSupp JudEthicsCanon 4
   Recusal   CRCSupp JudEthicsCanon 3
   Referees, provisions applicable to   CRCSupp JudEthicsCanon 6
   References or recommendations, service as   JudEthicsCanon 2
   Retired judges, provisions applicable to   CRCSupp JudEthicsCanon 6
   Sentencing judge
      Communications initiated by judge with sentencing judge or probation department representatives   CRCSupp JudEthicsCanon 2
   Settlement conferences
      Participation in efforts to resolve disputes   CRCSupp JudEthicsCanon 3
   Statements committing judge on upcoming cases, issues, etc   CRCSupp JudEthicsCanon 2
      Disqualification   CRCSupp JudEthicsCanon 3
   Temporary judges, provisions applicable to   CRCSupp JudEthicsCanon 6
      Disclosure obligations incumbent on temporary judge   CRC 2.817
      Disqualification   CRC 2.818, 2.819
Comments by court
   Pending cases, comments on   CRCSupp JudEthicsCanon 3
   Verdict or mistrial, comments on   CRC JudAdminStand 2.30
Commission on judicial appointments (See **JUDICIAL APPOINTMENTS, COMMISSION ON**)
Commission on Judicial Nominees Evaluation, recommendations to   CRCSupp JudEthicsCanon 2
Commission on Judicial Performance
   Policy declarations of   JudPerPolicy 1.1 to 6.5
   Proceedings before (See within this heading, **"Censure, removal, admonishment or retirement of judges"**)
Committee on judicial ethics opinions   CRC 9.80
   Authority of committee   CRCSupp JudEthicsOpinionsIOP 1
   Composition   CRCSupp JudEthicsOpinionsIOP 1
   Conferences   CRCSupp JudEthicsOpinionsIOP 3
   Confidentiality   CRCSupp JudEthicsOpinionsIOP 5
   Definitions   CRCSupp JudEthicsOpinionsIOP 2
   Distribution of opinions   CRCSupp JudEthicsOpinionsIOP 8

JUDGES—Cont.
Committee on judicial ethics opinions—Cont.
   Informal responses issued by CJA
      Delivery to CJEO   CRCSupp JudEthicsOpinionsIOP 9
   Internal operating rules and procedures   CRCSupp JudEthicsOpinionsIOP 1 to CRCSupp JudEthicsOpinionsIOP 9
   Meetings   CRCSupp JudEthicsOpinionsIOP 3
   Purpose   CRCSupp JudEthicsOpinionsIOP 1
   Referrals to CJA committee on judicial ethics   CRCSupp JudEthicsOpinionsIOP 4
   Requests for opinions
      Consideration of requests   CRCSupp JudEthicsOpinionsIOP 7
      Procedure for requesting   CRCSupp JudEthicsOpinionsIOP 6
      Response to request   CRCSupp JudEthicsOpinionsIOP 7
Compel obedience to lawful orders, power to   CCP §177
Compensation of judges and justices   CRCSupp JudEthicsCanons 3, 4
   Quasi-judicial and extrajudicial activities   CRCSupp JudEthicsCanon 6
   Temporary judges
      Request by parties for temporary judge   CRC 2.832
Complaint filed
   Temporary judges
      Procedure for complaints   CRC 10.746
Conciliation courts   Fam §§1811 to 1813
Confidentiality of removal or censure proceedings   JudPerR 102, 122
Conflicts of interest   CRCSupp JudEthicsCanons 3, 4
   Basis for disqualification of
      Employment or prospective employment as a dispute resolution neutral as basis for disqualification of   CCP §§170.1, 1281.9
Consent in proceedings against judge (See within this heading, **"Censure, removal, admonishment or retirement of judges"**)
Conservators
   Appointment of conservators in proceedings against   JudPerR 126
   Education as to conservatorship and guardianship matters
      Regular assignment to probate cases, education of judges and subordinate judicial officers   CRC 10.468
      Rule of court implementing, judicial council duties   Pro §1456
   Education of judges and subordinate judicial officers regularly assigned to probate cases
      Domestic violence issues   CRC 10.464
Contempt
   Competency to testify as to statement or conduct that gave rise to   Ev §703.5
   Power to punish for   CCP §178
Conveyance of real property, judicial officer's power to take and certify proof and acknowledgment of   CCP §179
Conviction of crime
   Suspension of judges   JudPerR 120.5
Coordination of actions (See **COORDINATION OF ACTIONS**)
Court executive officer, duties of   CRC 10.610
Courthouse access
   Prohibition of activities threatening access to courthouses and court proceedings
      Authority of judge   CCP §177
Court operations costs, salaries and benefits included as   CRC 10.810
Court reporters to take down all statements, remarks and instructions given by   CCP §269
Courts of Appeal
   Appellate rules, supreme court and courts of appeal
      Justices (See **APPELLATE RULES, SUPREME COURT AND COURTS OF APPEAL**)
   Chambers, powers and duties at   CCP §165
Criminal charges or convictions, reports to Commission on Judicial Performance   CRCSupp JudEthicsCanon 3
Deaf or hard of hearing judges
   Assistive listening systems   CC §54.8
Death penalty
   Education
      Additional education recommendations for certain judicial assignments   CRC 10.469
   Record on appeal
      Preliminary proceedings   CRC 8.613
Decedents' estates
   Education of judges and subordinate judicial officers regularly assigned to probate cases
      Conservatorship and guardianship matters   CRC 10.468
      Domestic violence issues   CRC 10.464
Declaration, judicial officer's power to take and certify   CCP §179
Defamation liability (See **LIBEL AND SLANDER**)
Defined   JudPerR 138
Delay reduction of trial, consideration of   CRC JudAdminStand 2.1
Dignified conduct   CRCSupp JudEthicsCanon 3

JUDGES—Cont.

Disability retirement applications, Commission on Judicial Performance policy declarations   JudPerPolicy 5.1 to 5.6
Disciplinary action against   CRCSupp JudEthicsCanons 1 to 6
    State Bar Court judges   CRC 9.11
Disciplinary responsibilities   CRCSupp JudEthicsCanon 3
Discipline of judges
    Censure, removal, admonishment or retirement of judges (See within this heading, **"Censure, removal, admonishment or retirement of judges"**)
    Code of Judicial Ethics (See within this heading, **"Code of judicial ethics"**)
Disclosures of nonpublic information   CRCSupp JudEthicsCanon 3
Discovery in proceedings against judges   JudPerR 122
    Extension of time   JudPerR 108
Discrimination
    Bias and prejudice   CRCSupp JudEthicsCanon 3
    Membership in discriminatory organizations   CRCSupp JudEthicsCanon 2
Disqualification (See **JUDGES, DISQUALIFICATION OF**)
Dissolution of marriage cases, duration of assignment of judges to   Fam §2330.3
Duties (See within this heading, **"Powers and duties"**)
Education
    Judicial branch education   CRC 10.451 to 10.493
    Trial Court Delay Reduction Act, training program under   Gov §68610
Elections and election proceedings
    Campaign contributions
        Disclosures   CRCSupp JudEthicsCanon 3
        Disqualification from case, contribution as grounds   CCP §170.1
    Code of judicial ethics
        Ethical obligations of candidates   CRCSupp JudEthicsCanon 6
        Leave, applicability of code to judge on leave to pursue election to other office   CRCSupp JudEthicsCanon 6
    Judicial elections
        Political activities by judges   CRCSupp JudEthicsCanon 5
    Judicial performance, commission on
        Ethics code for commission members   JudPerPolicy 6.4
Electronic filing and service
    Signatures by court or judicial officer   CRC 2.257
Employment or prospective employment as a dispute resolution neutral as basis for disqualification of   CCP §§170.1, 1281.9
Estate planning, authority in   Pro §800
Ethical conduct, code of   CRCSupp JudEthicsCanons 1 to 6
Ethics opinions   CRC 9.80
    Committee on judicial ethics opinions
        Internal operating rules and procedures   CRCSupp JudEthicsOpinionsIOP 1 to CRCSupp JudEthicsOpinionsIOP 9
Ethics orientation for judicial branch employees   CRC 10.455
Ethnic group as grounds for disqualification   CCP §170.2
Evidence (See within this heading, **"Censure, removal, admonishment or retirement of judges"**)
Excusing witnesses   Ev §778
Executive committee   CRC 10.605
Ex parte communications
    Code of Judicial Ethics provisions concerning   CRCSupp JudEthicsCanon 3
Expedited jury trials
    Judicial misconduct
        Post-trial motions   CCP §630.09
Expert advice, seeking   CRCSupp JudEthicsCanon 3
Extrajudicial activities   CRCSupp JudEthicsCanon 4
Failure of judge to perform duties
    Notification of judicial performance commission   CRC 10.1016
Family and social relationships, influence of   CRCSupp JudEthicsCanon 2
Family history, judge's certificates as evidence of   Ev §1316
Family law assignments   CRC JudAdminStand 5.30
    Duration   Fam §2330.3
    Education for family law judges   CRC 10.463, CRC JudAdminStand 5.30
    Judicial administration standards for judicial assignments to family court   CRC JudAdminStand 5.30
Family law judges, judicial education programs   CRC 10.463, CRC JudAdminStand 5.30
Federal crime, judge's conviction of, report to Judicial Performance Commission   CRCSupp JudEthicsCanon 3
Felonies
    Conviction of crime
        Suspension of judges   JudPerR 120.5
Fiduciary capacity, serving in   CRCSupp JudEthicsCanon 4
Financial and business dealings   CRCSupp JudEthicsCanon 4
Financial interest in case   CRCSupp JudEthicsCanon 3
Financial interest in proceeding, disqualification for   CCP §§170.1, 170.5
Former judges or justices
    Oaths, administration   CCP §2093
Form of affidavit for peremptory challenge   CCP §170.6

JUDGES—Cont.

Fund raising by   CRCSupp JudEthicsCanon 5
Gifts to judges   CCP §170.9, CRCSupp JudEthicsCanon 4
Groundwater rights actions   CCP §838
Guardian and ward
    Education of judges and subordinate judicial officers regularly assigned to probate cases
        Conservatorship and guardianship matters   CRC 10.468, Pro §1456
        Domestic violence issues   CRC 10.464
Handwriting comparison by   Ev §1417
Hearings (See within this heading, **"Censure, removal, admonishment or retirement of judges"**)
Honorarium, acceptance of   CCP §170.9, CRCSupp JudEthicsCanon 4
Impartiality (See within this heading, **"Bias and prejudice"**)
Impeachment (See within this heading, **"Censure, removal, admonishment or retirement of judges"**)
Implied powers to effectuate conferred powers   CCP §187
Impropriety, avoidance of   CRCSupp JudEthicsCanon 2
Independence of judiciary, upholding   CRCSupp JudEthicsCanon 1
Integrity, standards of   CRCSupp JudEthicsCanons 1, 2
Interlocutory orders
    Powers of judges   CCP §166.1
Investigations
    Facts of case   CRCSupp JudEthicsCanon 3
Investments and investment advice   CRCSupp JudEthicsCanon 5
Judicial branch education   CRC 10.451 to 10.493
Judicial Council (See **JUDICIAL COUNCIL**)
Jury (See **JURY**)
Law practice   CRCSupp JudEthicsCanon 4
    Rules governing law practice, attorneys and judges   CRC 9.0 to 9.90
        Attorney discipline   CRC 9.10 to 9.23
        Authority for rules   CRC 9.0
        Continuing legal education   CRC 9.31
        Definitions   CRC 9.1
        Legal specialists, certification   CRC 9.35
        Non-bar members, appearances and practice by   CRC 9.40 to 9.49.1
        Oath taken upon admission to practice   CRC 9.7
        Title of rules   CRC 9.0
        Unaccredited law schools, study in   CRC 9.30
Lecturing   CRCSupp JudEthicsCanons 4, 5
Libel and slander liability (See **LIBEL AND SLANDER**)
Loans to   CRCSupp JudEthicsCanon 4
Marriage ceremony   Fam §400
Masters (See within this heading, **"Censure, removal, admonishment or retirement of judges"**)
Medical examination upon showing of good cause, submission to   JudPerR 105
Money sanctions for violations of lawful court orders, power to impose   CCP §177.5
Moral turpitude
    Suspension for crimes involving moral turpitude   JudPerR 120.5
Not disqualified, duty to decide proceeding in which   CCP §170
Notice
    Censure, removal, admonishment or retirement of judges (See within this heading, **"Censure, removal, admonishment or retirement of judges"**)
    Recusal, notification of   CCP §170.3
    Temporary judges
        Disqualification   CRC 2.818
        Request by parties for temporary judge, notice of proceedings   CRC 2.834
        Stipulations as to use of temporary judge   CRC 2.816
Oaths, administering   CCP §2093
Objections
    Intended private admonishment, objections to   JudPerR 114
Open hearing
    Censure, removal, etc, of judges
        Hearings generally (See within this heading, **"Censure, removal, admonishment or retirement of judges"**)
Order and decorum
    Maintaining   CRCSupp JudEthicsCanon 3
Order, power to preserve and enforce   CCP §177
Other office or employment
    Extrajudicial activities   CRCSupp JudEthicsCanon 4
    Practice of law   CRCSupp JudEthicsCanon 4
    Public office, running for   CRCSupp JudEthicsCanon 5
Parole
    Communications concerning parole   CRCSupp JudEthicsCanon 2
Participation in drafting laws, effect of   CCP §170.2
Partition referees, partners of judge as   CCP §873.050
Part-time judges, compliance with ethical rules   CRCSupp JudEthicsCanon 6
Peremptory challenge   CCP §§170.6, 170.7
Personal knowledge of evidentiary facts, disqualification for   CCP §170.1

JUDGES — INDEX

JUDGES—Cont.

Petition for review of recommendation or proceeding for censure, removal or admonishment   CRC 9.60

Physical examinations in connection with removal or censure hearings   JudPerR 105

Physical impairment as grounds for disqualification   CCP §170.1

Pleadings in proceedings against judges   JudPerR 119, 128

Policy declarations of Commission on Judicial Performance   JudPerPolicy 1.1 to 6.5

Political activities   CRCSupp JudEthicsCanon 5
- Leave, applicability of code to judge on leave to pursue election to other office   CRCSupp JudEthicsCanon 6
- Solicitation of contributions or endorsements for personal campaign or for judicial campaigns of others   CRCSupp JudEthicsCanon 5

Powers and duties   CRC 10.608
- All judges   CRC 10.608
- At chambers   CCP §166
- Clerk's duties, judge may perform   CCP §167
- Interlocutory orders   CCP §166.1
- Not disqualified, duty to decide proceeding in which   CCP §170
- Out of court   CCP §166

Practicing law   CRCSupp JudEthicsCanon 4
- Rules governing law practice, attorneys and judges   CRC 9.0 to 9.90
  - Attorney discipline   CRC 9.10 to 9.23
  - Authority for rules   CRC 9.0
  - Continuing legal education   CRC 9.31
  - Definitions   CRC 9.1
  - Legal specialists, certification   CRC 9.35
  - Non-bar members, appearances and practice by   CRC 9.40 to 9.49.1
  - Oath taken upon admission to practice   CRC 9.7
  - Title of rules   CRC 9.0
  - Unaccredited law schools, study in   CRC 9.30

Preliminary investigation (See within this heading, "Censure, removal, admonishment or retirement of judges")

Presiding judges
- Appellate division of superior court   CRC 10.1104
- Authority   CRC 10.603
- Coordination of actions   CCP §404
- Criminal cases, duties in   CRC 10.950, 10.951
- Criminal departments, designation of   CRC 10.950
- Duties   CRC 10.603
- Education of judicial officers
  - Duties of presiding judges   CRC 10.452
- Executive committee   CRC 10.605
- Selection and term   CRC 10.602
- Signing of judgment when trial judge unavailable   CCP §635
- Subordinate judicial officers, review of complaints against   CRC 10.703
- Superior courts (See **SUPERIOR COURTS**)
- Term   CRC 10.602
- Vexatious litigant, order permitting filing of litigation by   CCP §391.7

Presumption that judges act in lawful exercise of jurisdiction   Ev §666

Private admonishment
- Censure, removal, admonishment, etc, of judges generally (See within this heading, "Censure, removal, admonishment or retirement of judges")

Privilege
- Censure, removal, admonishment or retirement of judges (See within this heading, "Censure, removal, admonishment or retirement of judges")
- Ruling on claim of privilege, disclosure required for purposes of   Ev §915

Probate cases, judges and subordinate judicial officers regularly assigned to
- Education   CRC 10.468
  - Domestic violence issues   CRC 10.464

Probation department
- Communications initiated by judge with sentencing judge or probation department representatives   CRCSupp JudEthicsCanon 2

Prompt disposition of cases   CRCSupp JudEthicsCanon 3

Public admonishment
- Censure, removal, admonishment, etc, of judges (See within this heading, "Censure, removal, admonishment or retirement of judges")

Public comments re pending proceedings   CRCSupp JudEthicsCanon 3

Public hearings, appearances at   CRCSupp JudEthicsCanon 4

Public office, running for   CRCSupp JudEthicsCanon 5

Racial group as grounds for disqualification   CCP §170.2

Reciprocal assignment orders, reporting   CRC 10.630

Records in proceedings against judges   JudPerR 135
- Use and retention of records of complaints against judges   JudPerR 117

Recusal
- Disqualification generally (See **JUDGES, DISQUALIFICATION OF**)

Referees on order of   CCP §639

References or recommendations
- Code of judicial ethics   JudEthicsCanon 2

Relationship to party as grounds for disqualification   CCP §170.1

JUDGES—Cont.

Religion
- Grounds for disqualification   CCP §170.2
- Religious activities   CRCSupp JudEthicsCanon 4

Remote proceedings
- Judicial officers presiding over remote proceeding from location other than courtroom   CRC 10.635
  - Judicial council to adopt rules   CCP §367.10

Removal (See within this heading, "Censure, removal, admonishment or retirement of judges")

Reporting of ethical violations, duties re   CRCSupp JudEthicsCanon 3

Report of masters (See within this heading, "Censure, removal, admonishment or retirement of judges")

Retired judges
- Application of ethical rules to   CRCSupp JudEthicsCanon 6
- Arbitration panels, appointment to   CRC 3.814
- Assignment of retired judges
  - Code of Judicial Ethics provisions, applicability of   CRCSupp JudEthicsCanon 6
- Ethics rules applicable to   CRCSupp JudEthicsCanon 6
- Petition for review of recommendation or proceeding for censure, removal or admonishment   CRC 9.60
- Proceedings involving censure, removal, admonishment or retirement   CRC 9.61
- Temporary judges, service of retired judicial officers as
  - Court-appointed temporary judges   CRC 2.810 to 2.819

Retirement
- Assignment of retired judges
  - Criminal case, stipulation that retired judge is not qualified to try   CCP §170.65
- Removal of judge (See within this heading, "Censure, removal, admonishment or retirement of judges")

Review of commission on judicial performance recommendation or proceeding   CRC 9.60, 9.61

Robes   CRC 10.505

Rules on appeal
- Superior court appellate division proceedings
  - Appellate division assignments   CCP §77, CRC 10.1100
- Supreme court and courts of appeal
  - Justices (See **APPELLATE RULES, SUPREME COURT AND COURTS OF APPEAL**)

Sabbaticals
- Judicial sabbatical pilot program   CRC 10.502

Sanctions for violations of lawful court orders, power to impose   CCP §177.5

Satisfaction of judgment, judicial officer's power to take and certify acknowledgment of   CCP §179

Sentencing judge
- Communications initiated by judge with sentencing judge or probation department representatives   CRCSupp JudEthicsCanon 2

Service of process
- Censure, removal, admonishment or retirement of judges (See within this heading, "Censure, removal, admonishment or retirement of judges")
- Party's address unknown, papers served on judge when no clerk   CRC 3.252

Settlement conferences
- Participation in efforts to resolve disputes   CRCSupp JudEthicsCanon 3

Small claims court (See **SMALL CLAIMS COURTS**)

Solicitation of funds for charitable or civic organizations   CRCSupp JudEthicsCanon 5

Speechmaking   CRCSupp JudEthicsCanons 4, 5

State Bar Court judges   CRC 9.11

State bar, testimony before   Ev §703.5

Statements committing judge on upcoming cases, issues, etc   CRCSupp JudEthicsCanon 2
- Disqualification   CRCSupp JudEthicsCanon 3

Subordinate judicial duty   CCP §482.060

Subordinate judicial officers
- Complaints against   CRC 10.703
- Education of judicial branch employees   CRC 10.451 to 10.493
  - Additional education recommendations for certain judicial assignments   CRC 10.469
  - Trial court subordinate judicial officers   CRC 10.462
- Investigation   JudPerR 109
- Law practice   CRC 10.702
- Notice to commission on judicial performance of complaints against   CRC 10.703
- Qualifications and education   CRC 10.701
- Role   CRC 10.700

Superior court appellate division
- Assignments in appellate division   CCP §77, CRC 10.1100

Superior courts (See **SUPERIOR COURTS**)

JUDGES—Cont.
Supervisorial responsibilities   CRCSupp JudEthicsCanon 3
Supreme Court
   Appellate rules, supreme court and courts of appeal (See **APPELLATE RULES, SUPREME COURT AND COURTS OF APPEAL**)
   Censure, removal, admonishment or retirement of judges
      Justices of supreme court   CRC 9.61
      Review of commission recommendations   CRC 9.60, 9.61
   Chambers, powers and duties at   CCP §165
Suspension from office (See within this heading, **"Censure, removal, admonishment or retirement of judges"**)
Teaching, engaging in   CRCSupp JudEthicsCanons 4, 5
Temporary judges   CRC 2.830 to 2.835
   Administration of decedent's estate, temporary judge summarily determining disputes to   Pro §9620
   Administrator of temporary judge program   CRC 10.743
   Application for appointment   CRC 10.744
   Appointment
      Application for appointment   CRC 10.744
      Conditions   CRC 10.742
      Oaths   CRC 2.814
      Order   CRC 2.814
      Presiding judge, authority as to   CRC 10.742
      Purpose   CRC 2.811
      Qualifications of attorneys   CRC 2.812
      Trial court appointment   CRC 2.810
   Attorney professional conduct
      Service as temporary judge, referee or court-appointed arbitrator, applicability of judicial ethics canon 6D   ProfC 2.4.1
   Compensation
      Request by parties for temporary judge   CRC 2.832
   Complaints against   CRC 10.703
      Procedure   CRC 10.746
   Compliance with Code of Judicial Ethics   CRCSupp JudEthicsCanon 6
   Continuing education   CRC 2.815
   Court commissioners acting as   CCP §259
   Disclosures to parties required of judges incumbent on temporary judge   CRC 2.817
      Continuing duty   CRC 2.819
      Request by parties for temporary judge   CRC 2.831
   Discontinuance
      Presiding judges, authority to remove or discontinue   CRC 10.741
   Disqualification   CRC 2.818
      Continuing duty   CRC 2.819
      Request by parties for temporary judge   CRC 2.831
   Ethical rules, compliance with   CRCSupp JudEthicsCanon 6
   Exhibits, custody of   CRC 2.400
   Expedited jury trials
      Assignment of judicial officer to conduct   CRC 3.1553
   Limitations on service   CRC 2.818
   Nondiscriminatory application and selection procedure   CRC 10.741
   Performance monitoring and review   CRC 10.745
   Presiding judges
      Administrator of temporary judge program, appointment   CRC 10.743
      Appointment of temporary judges, duties as to   CRC 2.811
      Responsibility of presiding judges   CRC 10.741, 10.742
   Publicizing opportunity to serve as temporary judge   CRC 10.741
   Removal
      Presiding judges, authority to remove or discontinue   CRC 10.741
   Request by parties for temporary judge
      Applicability of provisions   CRC 2.830
      Assignment   CRC 2.831
      Compensation   CRC 2.832
      Court facilities, use   CRC 2.834
      Disclosures   CRC 2.831
      Disqualification   CRC 2.831
      Intervention, motion for leave to file complaint for   CRC 2.835
      Notice of proceedings   CRC 2.834
      Oaths   CRC 2.831
      Open proceedings   CRC 2.834
      Orders   CRC 2.831
      Privately compensated, defined   CRC 2.830
      Sealing records, motion   CRC 2.835
      Site for hearing, appropriateness   CRC 2.834
      Stipulation   CRC 2.831
   Responsibility of courts using   CRC 10.740
   Retired judicial officers
      Education and training requirements   CRC 2.812
   Small claims court   CCP §116.240, CRC 2.816
   Stipulation as to temporary judge   CRC 2.816

JUDGES—Cont.
Temporary judges —Cont.
   Subordinate judicial officers serving as   CRC 10.700
   Training programs   CRC 2.813
      Continuing education   CRC 2.815
   Trial court appointment   CRC 2.810
      Application for appointment   CRC 10.744
      Conditions   CRC 10.742
      Oaths   CRC 2.814
      Orders   CRC 2.814
      Presiding judge, authority as to   CRC 10.742
      Purpose   CRC 2.811
      Qualifications of attorneys   CRC 2.812
Testify, power to compel attendance of persons to   CCP §177
Time
   Case management and delay reduction   CRC JudAdminStand 2.1
   Censure, removal or admonishment (See within this heading, **"Censure, removal, admonishment or retirement of judges"**)
Title, use of in communications   CRCSupp JudEthicsCanon 2
Transcript (See within this heading, **"Censure, removal, admonishment or retirement of judges"**)
Travel expense reimbursement   CRC 10.106
Travel, gift of   CCP §170.9
Trial court delay reduction programs (See **TRIAL COURT DELAY REDUCTION**)
Trial court, judicial branch education
   Executive officers   CRC 10.473
   Judges   CRC 10.462
   Managers, supervisors and personnel   CRC 10.474
   Subordinate judicial officers   CRC 10.462
      Additional education recommendations for certain judicial assignments   CRC 10.469
Trial court presiding judges advisory committee   CRC 10.46
Trial management, judge's responsibilities   CRC JudAdminStand 2.20
Trusts
   Education of judges and subordinate judicial officers regularly assigned to probate cases   CRC 10.468
      Domestic violence issues   CRC 10.464
Undue influence, exercise of   CRCSupp JudEthicsCanon 4
Vacancy involving all or any judges or justices, effect of   CCP §184
Venue in criminal proceedings
   Change of venue
      Selection of court and trial judge   CRC 4.152
Views, presence at   CCP §651
Vote of Commission on Judicial Performance to recommend judge's removal, censure or retirement   JudPerR 134
Wedding gifts, acceptance of   CCP §170.9
Will, beneficiary under   Pro §7060
Witness
   Censure, removal or admonishment of judge, proceedings for   JudPerR 126
   Disqualification based on personal knowledge of evidentiary facts   CCP §170.1
   Effect of judges testifying as   Ev §§703, 703.5
   Interrogation of   Ev §§765, 775
   Judges as witnesses
      Character witness   CRCSupp JudEthicsCanon 2
   Restriction on waiver of disqualification   CCP §170.3
Workers' compensation
   Judicial branch workers' compensation program advisory committee   CRC 10.67

JUDGES, DISQUALIFICATION OF   CRCSupp JudEthicsCanon 3
Administration of decedent's estate proceedings (See **ADMINISTRATION OF ESTATES**)
Answer to statement of   CCP §170.3
Appellate division of superior court exempt from peremptory challenge provision   CCP §170.7
Assignment of judge by Judicial Council   CCP §170.8
Campaign contributions
   Disqualification from case, contribution as grounds   CCP §170.1
Code of Judicial Ethics provisions   CRCSupp JudEthicsCanon 3
Conflicts of interest as basis for disqualification
   Employment or prospective employment as a dispute resolution neutral as basis for disqualification of   CCP §§170.1, 1281.9
Consent to   CCP §170.3
Coordinated actions   CRC 3.516
Coordination proceedings   CRC 3.516
Definitions   CCP §170.5
Determination of question of disqualification   CCP §170.3
Elections and election proceedings
   Campaign contributions
      Disqualification from case, contribution as grounds   CCP §170.1

JUDGES, DISQUALIFICATION OF—Cont.
Employment or prospective employment as a dispute resolution neutral as basis for disqualification of judges   CCP §§170.1, 1281.9
Filing statement of disqualification   CCP §170.3
Form of affidavit for peremptory challenge   CCP §170.6
Grounds for   CCP §§170.1, 170.2
Groundwater rights actions   CCP §838
No legal grounds for disqualification, effect of statement disclosing   CCP §170.4
Notification of recusal   CCP §170.3
Peremptory challenge   CCP §§170.6, 170.7
Power of judge to act, effect of disqualification proceedings on   CCP §170.4
Recusal   CRCSupp JudEthicsCanon 3
Removal or retirement determination by Commission on Judicial Performance, disqualification pending finalization of or appeal from   JudPerR 120
Review of determination   CCP §170.3
Striking statement of disqualification   CCP §170.4
Temporary disqualification pending formal proceedings before Commission on Judicial Performance   JudPerR 120
Temporary judges   CRC 2.818
    Continuing duty   CRC 2.819
    Request by parties for temporary judge   CRC 2.830 to 2.835
Time
    After commencement of trial or hearing, statement filed   CCP §170.4
    Consent or answer, time for filing   CCP §170.3
    Filing statement of disqualification, generally   CCP §170.3
    Peremptory challenge   CCP §170.6
    Review of determination   CCP §170.3
    Untimely filing of statement of disqualification, effect of   CCP §170.4
Trial court delay reduction program, challenge to judge as not constituting ground for removal of case from   Gov §68607.5
Waiver of   CCP §170.3
Will probate proceedings   Pro §7060

JUDGMENT CREDITORS
Creditor's suit (See ENFORCEMENT OF JUDGMENTS)
Defined   CCP §116.130

JUDGMENT DEBTORS
Contribution (See CONTRIBUTION)
Defined   CCP §116.130
Examination proceedings (See ENFORCEMENT OF JUDGMENTS)
Foreign judgments
    Foreign country money judgments   CCP §§1713 to 1725 (See FOREIGN JUDGMENTS)
    Sister state money judgments   CCP §§1710.10 to 1710.65 (See FOREIGN JUDGMENTS)
Small claims court judgments (See SMALL CLAIMS COURTS)

JUDGMENT NOTWITHSTANDING VERDICT   CCP §629
Appellate rules, superior court appeals
    Limited civil cases in appellate division
        Motion for judgment notwithstanding verdict extending time to appeal   CRC 8.823

JUDGMENT ON THE PLEADINGS   CCP §438
Meet and confer prior to moving for judgment on the pleadings   CCP §439
    Forms
        Judicial council legal forms   CRCAppx A

JUDGMENT ROLLS
Contents of   CCP §670

JUDGMENTS   CCP §§577 to 599
Abstract of judgment (See ABSTRACT OF JUDGMENT)
Administration of estates (See ADMINISTRATION OF ESTATES)
Admission of erroneous evidence   Ev §353
Adverse possession by person claiming title founded on judgment or decree   CCP §§322, 323
Affirmance of judgment (See AFFIRMANCE OF JUDGMENT)
Agreed case   CCP §1139
Alternatives to entry in judgment book   CCP §668.5
Annulment of marriage (See ANNULMENT)
Appellate division of superior court
    Statement of reasons for judgment   CCP §77
Appellate rules
    Superior court appeals (See APPELLATE RULES, SUPERIOR COURT APPEALS)
    Supreme court and courts of appeal (See APPELLATE RULES, SUPREME COURT AND COURTS OF APPEAL)

JUDGMENTS—Cont.
Arbitration awards
    Entry as judgment   CRC 3.827
    Generally (See ARBITRATION)
Argument, reserving case for   CCP §665
Assignment of judgment, recording   CCP §673
Attorneys (See ATTORNEYS)
Certiorari   CCP §1077
Child support (See CHILD SUPPORT)
Claims against decedent's estate (See CLAIMS AGAINST ESTATES)
Claims against public entities and employees (See CLAIMS AGAINST PUBLIC ENTITIES AND EMPLOYEES)
Class actions   CRC 3.771
    Jurisdiction retained to enforce   CRC 3.769
    Settlement of class actions   CRC 3.769
Clerical errors in judgments, correction of   CCP §473
Coerced debt
    Establishing debt as coerced, action or cross-complaint   CC §1798.97.3
Confession of judgments (See CONFESSION OF JUDGMENTS)
Conformity with pleadings, requirement that relief granted be in   CCP §580
Consumer privacy rights
    California privacy protection agency
        Fines, judgments to collect   CC §1798.199.80
Contempt (See CONTEMPT)
Contribution among joint tortfeasors   CCP §§875 to 880
Contribution, judgment for   CCP §878
Control of action, parties having   CCP §1908
Coordination of complex actions   CRC 3.545
Costs
    Generally (See COSTS)
    Motion for judgment, granting costs on   CCP §1038
Court's power to compel obedience to   CCP §128
Criminal proceedings
    Juvenile ward of court proceedings
        Deferred entry of judgment proceedings against child subject to petition alleging felony offense   CRC 5.800
    Probation reports
        Statement of views in lieu of   CRC 4.480
        Statement of views for forwarding to corrections and rehabilitation department   CRC 4.480
Cross-complaint claim exceeding demand of opposing party   CCP §666
Death (See DEATH)
Decision, statement of (See STATEMENT OF DECISION)
Declaratory (See DECLARATORY JUDGMENTS)
Default (See DEFAULT JUDGMENTS)
Deficiency (See DEFICIENCY JUDGMENTS)
Defined   CCP §§577, 1064, Fam §100
Destroyed land records relief law proceedings   CCP §§751.15 to 751.17
Dismissal orders constituting judgments   CCP §581d
Disregard of nonprejudicial error   CCP §475
Dissolution of marriage (See DISSOLUTION OF MARRIAGE)
Dollars and cents, judgment amount in   CCP §577.5
Domestic violence protective orders included in   Fam §§2049, 6360, 6361
Earnings for credit purposes established by   CC §1812.30
Earthquakes, boundary reestablishment after   CCP §§751.60 to 751.63
Electronic filing and service
    Orders, judgments and other documents prepared by court   CRC 2.252
Eminent domain (See EMINENT DOMAIN)
Enforcement of (See ENFORCEMENT OF JUDGMENTS)
Entry of judgment
    After verdict, time of entry of judgment   CCP §664
    Agreed case   CCP §1139
    Alternatives to entry in judgment book   CCP §668.5
    Confession of judgments   CCP §1132
    Contribution, judgment for   CCP §878
    Fee for service of notice of   CCP §1710.30
    Foreign judgments   CCP §1710.25
    Judgment book   CCP §668
    Judicial arbitration   CCP §1141.23, CRC 3.827
    Notice of entry of judgments, generally   CCP §664.5
    Reviewing court, clerk of trial court recording judgment of   CCP §912
    Sister State Money-Judgment Act (See SISTER STATE MONEY-JUDGMENT ACT)
    Small claims actions (See SMALL CLAIMS COURTS)
Environmental quality act
    Petitions under environmental quality act, civil rules governing
        Jobs and economic improvement through environmental leadership act of 2011   CRC 3.2228
        Sacramento downtown arena project, CEQA challenges   CRC 3.2228
Escheated property, recording notice of action for   CCP §1410
Evidence, use in   CCP §1908.5

JUDGMENTS—Cont.
- Exclusion of evidence, effect of   Ev §354
- Excusable neglect, relief from   CCP §473
- Fact of death, decree establishing   Pro §204
- Fair debt buying practices
  - Default judgments against debtor   CC §1788.60
- Family law rules (See **FAMILY RULES**)
- Family support (See **FAMILY SUPPORT**)
- Fees for service of notice of entry   CCP §1710.30
- Filing   CRC 3.1590
- Final discharge of personal representative   Pro §§11753, 12250, 12251
- Final judgment, effect of   CCP §1908
- Fire destroying   CCP §§1953 to 1953.06
- Foreign judgments
  - Foreign country money judgments   CCP §§1713 to 1725 (See **FOREIGN JUDGMENTS**)
  - Sister state money judgments   CCP §§1710.10 to 1710.65 (See **FOREIGN JUDGMENTS**)
- Forms
  - Judicial council legal forms   CRCAppx A
- Garnishment (See **GARNISHMENT**)
- Government tort liability
  - Periodic payment of judgments against public entities   CRC 3.1804
- Groundwater rights actions
  - Binding nature of judgment on successors in interest   CCP §851
  - Continuing jurisdiction to amend, modify, etc   CCP §852
  - Findings by court   CCP §850
- Hearsay rule affecting admissibility of   Ev §§1300 to 1302
- Heirs, order establishing existence of   Pro §11705
- Indians
  - Money judgments
    - Tribal court civil money judgment act   CCP §§1730 to 1741
- Injunctions (See **INJUNCTIONS**)
- Innkeeper's liens   CC §1861
- Installment judgments
  - Enforcement (See **ENFORCEMENT OF JUDGMENTS**)
  - Limited civil cases   CCP §582.5
  - Small claims court judgments   CCP §116.620
- Interest
  - Calculating interest and amount owed on judgment
    - Judicial council legal forms   CRCAppx A
  - Enforcement of judgments (See **ENFORCEMENT OF JUDGMENTS**)
  - Inclusion in judgment   CRC 3.1802
- Interlocutory judgment (See **INTERLOCUTORY JUDGMENT**)
- Inter se rights of parties   CCP §§578, 579
- Interstate family support act
  - Parental responsibility   CRCAppx A (CRCFL-530)
- Joint debtors, proceedings after judgment against   CCP §§989 to 994
- Judges (See **JUDGES**)
- Judgment book   CCP §668
- Judgment liens
  - Abstract of judgment   CCP §674
  - Claims against estates (See **CLAIMS AGAINST ESTATES**)
  - Enforcement of judgments (See **ENFORCEMENT OF JUDGMENTS**)
  - Foreclosure on   CCP §726
  - Garnishment (See **GARNISHMENT**)
- Judgment on the pleadings   CCP §438
  - Meet and confer prior to moving for judgment on the pleadings   CCP §439
  - Judicial council legal forms   CRCAppx A
- Judgment roll (See **JUDGMENT ROLLS**)
- Judicial arbitration
  - Entry of award as judgment   CRC 3.827
  - Vacating judgment on award   CRC 3.828
- Legal separation (See **LEGAL SEPARATION**)
- Letter of credit supporting secured obligations   CCP §580.5
- Liens
  - Abstract of judgment   CCP §674
  - Claims against decedents' estates (See **CLAIMS AGAINST ESTATES**)
  - Enforcement of judgments (See **ENFORCEMENT OF JUDGMENTS**)
  - Foreclosure on   CCP §726
  - Garnishment (See **GARNISHMENT**)
- Mandamus   CCP §1094
- Marriage
  - Annulment proceedings (See **ANNULMENT**)
  - Dissolution of (See **DISSOLUTION OF MARRIAGE**)
- Merits, rendering judgment on   CCP §582
- Mine co-owners failing to pay taxes   CCP §858
- Mining leases, termination of right of entry   CCP §§772.040, 772.050
- Minor or disabled person, judgment in favor of
  - Attorneys' fees for services to minors and person with disability   CRC 7.955

JUDGMENTS—Cont.
- Minor or disabled person, judgment in favor of—Cont.
  - Disposition of proceeds, court approval
    - Expedited approval, petition   CRC 7.950.5
    - Petition   CRC 7.950, 7.950.5
  - Trusts, payment into   CRC JudAdminStand 7.10
- Mistake, inadvertence, surprise or excusable neglect, relief from   CCP §473
- Modification of judgment (See **MODIFICATION OF JUDGMENT**)
- Money judgments
  - Defined   CCP §680.270
  - Discovery
    - Civil discovery act, effect on enforcement of money judgments   CCP §2016.070
  - Dollars and cents, judgments stated in   CCP §577.5
  - Enforcement of   CCP §§695.010 to 709.030
    - Attorney discipline involving orders for payments or reimbursement   CRC 9.23
    - Civil discovery act, effect on enforcement of money judgments   CCP §2016.070
  - Foreign country money judgments   CCP §§1713 to 1725 (See **FOREIGN JUDGMENTS**)
  - Letter of credit supporting secured obligations   CCP §580.5
  - Real property lien, judgment secured by   CCP §580a
  - Recovery of money granted   CCP §667
  - Sister state money judgments   CCP §§1710.10 to 1710.65 (See **FOREIGN JUDGMENTS**)
  - Stay of proceedings on payment of   CCP §917.1
  - Tribal court civil money judgment act   CCP §§1730 to 1741
- Mortgages (See **TRUST DEEDS AND MORTGAGES**)
- Motion for judgment
  - Costs of defense on granting motion for judgment, award of   CCP §1038
  - Judgment on the pleadings   CCP §438
    - Judicial council legal forms   CRCAppx A
    - Meet and confer prior to moving for judgment on the pleadings   CCP §439
  - Nonjury trials, motion for judgment in   CCP §631.8
- Motions to vacate judgment   CCP §663a
- Natural disaster destroying   CCP §§1953 to 1953.06
- Nonjury trial, motion for judgment in   CCP §631.8
- Notices
  - Determination, notice of   CRC 3.1109
  - Enforcement of judgments (See **ENFORCEMENT OF JUDGMENTS**)
  - Family law
    - Notice of entry in family law proceeding   CRC 5.413, 5.415
  - Renewal of judgments (See **ENFORCEMENT OF JUDGMENTS**)
- Objection to proposed judgment   CRC 3.1590
- Oil and gas lease, termination of right of entry   CCP §§772.040, 772.050
- One defendant, judgment for or against   CCP §§578, 579
- Opening
  - Vacation
    - Adoption (See **ADOPTION**)
    - Attachment (See **ATTACHMENT**)
    - Default judgments (See **DEFAULT JUDGMENTS**)
    - Enforcement of judgments (See **ENFORCEMENT OF JUDGMENTS**)
    - Generally (See within this heading, "**Vacation of judgment**")
    - Small claims (See **SMALL CLAIMS COURTS**)
- Parentage
  - Agreement and judgment of parentage in domestic violence prevention act cases
    - Notice of entry of judgment   CRC 5.380
  - Vacating or setting aside judgments   Fam §§7645 to 7649.5
- Partition, action for (See **PARTITION**)
- Partners, judgment based on personal liability of   CCP §369.5
- Periodic payment
  - Public entities, judgments against   CRC 3.1804
- Pleadings
  - Allegations of judgment or judicial action   CCP §§456, 1908.5
  - Conformity with pleadings, requirement that relief granted be in   CCP §580
  - Judgment on the pleadings, motion for   CCP §438
    - Judicial council legal forms   CRCAppx A
    - Meet and confer prior to moving for judgment on the pleadings   CCP §439
- Possession, recovery of   CCP §667
- Preparation of, requests for   CRC 3.1590
- Presumed to set forth parties' rights   Ev §639
- Private student loan collections reform
  - Requirements for judgments against debtor   CC §1788.206
- Proof of execution of instruments   CC §1204
- Proposed judgments
  - Law and motion proceedings   CRC 3.1113

JUDGMENTS—Cont.
Proposed judgments—Cont.
    Objection to proposed judgment   CRC 3.1590
Public improvement assessment, action to determine adverse interests in real property arising out of   CCP §§801.12, 801.14
Quieting title action   CCP §§764.010 to 764.070
Quo warranto proceedings   CCP §§805, 809
Receivers on enforcement of   CCP §564
Recordation of   CCP §§668, 668.5, 674
Records and recordation
    Abstract of judgment (See **ABSTRACT OF JUDGMENT**)
    Alternative entry of individual judgments   CCP §668.5
    Judgment book   CCP §668
Referee's decisions as basis for   CCP §644
Renewal of judgments (See **ENFORCEMENT OF JUDGMENTS**)
Replevin, alternative judgment in   CCP §667
Respective liabilities, judgment given against one or more defendants according to their   CCP §379
Respective right to relief, judgment given to one or more plaintiffs according to their   CCP §378
Restitution judgments awarded in felony convictions, trust assets used in satisfaction of   Pro §15305.5
Reversal of judgment (See **REVERSAL OF JUDGMENT**)
Satisfaction of judgments (See **SATISFACTION OF JUDGMENTS**)
Setting aside
    Vacation
        Adoption (See **ADOPTION**)
        Attachment (See **ATTACHMENT**)
        Default judgments (See **DEFAULT JUDGMENTS**)
        Enforcement of judgments (See **ENFORCEMENT OF JUDGMENTS**)
        Generally (See within this heading, "**Vacation of judgment**")
        Small claims (See **SMALL CLAIMS COURTS**)
Settlement, judgment entered pursuant to terms of (See **SETTLEMENT AND COMPROMISE**)
Several judgment   CCP §579
Signature   CRC 3.1590
    Trial judge not available   CCP §635
Sister State Money-Judgment Act (See **SISTER STATE MONEY-JUDGMENT ACT**)
Small claims courts (See **SMALL CLAIMS COURTS**)
Specie judgment   CCP §667
Spousal support proceedings (See **SPOUSAL SUPPORT**)
Statement of decision (See **STATEMENT OF DECISION**)
Stipulated judgments (See **SETTLEMENT AND COMPROMISE**)
Summary dissolution of marriage (See **SUMMARY DISSOLUTION OF MARRIAGE**)
Summary judgments (See **SUMMARY JUDGMENTS**)
Superior court appellate division (See **APPELLATE RULES, SUPERIOR COURT APPEALS**)
Superior courts (See **SUPERIOR COURTS**)
Surety's liability effected by creditor recovering judgment   CC §2838
Surprise, relief from   CCP §473
Tentative decisions not constituting judgment   CRC 3.1590
Termination of parental rights   Fam §7894
Third parties
    Earlier action against third parties, admissibility of judgment in   Ev §1302
    Enforcement of judgments (See **ENFORCEMENT OF JUDGMENTS**)
Tribal court civil money judgment act   CCP §§1730 to 1741
Trust deeds (See **TRUST DEEDS AND MORTGAGES**)
Trusts (See **TRUSTS**)
Uniform Parentage Act (See **UNIFORM PARENTAGE ACT**)
Uniform Transfers to Minors Act, transfer of funds from judgment under   Pro §§3602, 3611
Unincorporated association, judgment based on personal liability of member of   CCP §369.5
Unlawful detainer (See **UNLAWFUL DETAINER**)
Vacation of judgment
    Administrative adjudication decision   Gov §11520
    Adoption orders (See **ADOPTION**)
    Attachment (See **ATTACHMENT**)
    Default judgments (See **DEFAULT JUDGMENTS**)
    Employee benefit plan joined as party in family law proceeding   Fam §2074
    Enforcement of judgments (See **ENFORCEMENT OF JUDGMENTS**)
    Grounds for   CCP §§662 to 663
    Loss of transcription of trial   CCP §914
    Mediation, vacation of judgment on grounds of irregular reference to   CCP §1775.12, Ev §1128
    Motion to vacate   CCP §663a
        Effect on time for appeal   CRC 8.108

JUDGMENTS—Cont.
Vacation of judgment—Cont.
    Motion to vacate —Cont.
        Hearing   CRC 3.1602
    New trial motion   CCP §§662 to 663
    Notice of appeal
        Effect of motion to vacate judgment on time for filing   CRC 8.108
    Service of motions for   CCP §663a
    Small claims court (See **SMALL CLAIMS COURTS**)
    Summary dissolution of marriage   Fam §2405
    Time for service of motions for   CCP §663a
    Uniform Parentage Act
        Court authority as to   Fam §7642
        Generally   Fam §§7645 to 7649.5
Validation proceedings   CCP §870
Will probate proceedings (See **WILL PROBATE**)
Written obligation to pay money, notation of judgment on face of   CRC 3.1806

JUDGMENTS NOTWITHSTANDING THE VERDICT
Appellate rules
    Notice of appeal, time to file   CRC 8.108
Notice of appeal, effect of motion for judgment notwithstanding verdict on time for filing   CRC 8.108

JUDICIAL ADMINISTRATION RULES   CRC 10.1 to 10.1108
Administrative director
    Role   CRC 10.101
Alternative dispute resolution programs   CRC 10.780 to 10.783
Appellate court administration, superior court appellate division   CRC 10.1100 to 10.1108
    Assignments to appellate division   CRC 10.1100
    Judicial assignments to appellate division   CRC 10.1100
    Presiding judge of division   CRC 10.1104
    Sessions of appellate division   CRC 10.1108
Appellate court administration, supreme court and courts of appeal   CRC 10.1000 to 10.1030
    Administrative presiding judge, court of appeals   CRC 10.1004
    Attorney misconduct triggering notification to state bar
        Justice's duties   CRC 10.1017
    Clerk/executive officer, role and duties of   CRC 10.1020
        Education, minimum   CRC 10.471
        Education of judicial branch, duties as to   CRC 10.452
    Divisions of court of appeals
        Assignment of cases to balance workload   CRC 10.1008
    Judicial duties, failure to perform   CRC 10.1016
    Local rules of courts of appeal   CRC 10.1030
    Minutes
        Court of appeal minutes   CRC 10.1024
    Progress of appeals, supervision   CRC 10.1012
    Records
        Preservation and destruction of court of appeals records   CRC 10.1028
        Signing, subscribing or verifying documents   CRC 10.1028
    Signing, subscribing or verifying documents   CRC 10.1028
    Transfer of causes   CRC 10.1000
Automation standards
    Trial court automation   CRC 10.870
Budgeting
    Administrative director's role   CRC 10.101
    Contracts
        Former employees, limitations on contracting with   CRC 10.104
        Intrabranch contracting   CRC 10.103
    Fee, fine and forfeiture revenue
        Allocation   CRC 10.105
    Financial policies and procedures, superior courts   CRC 10.804
    Gifts, acceptance   CRC 10.102
    Judicial council role   CRC 10.101
    Superior court budgeting   CRC 10.800, 10.801
        Checks and other negotiable paper to pay court fees, fines, etc   CRC 10.821
        Court operations   CRC 10.810
        Credit card payments of fees   CRC 10.820
        Fees set by courts   CRC 10.815
        Homicide trials, cost reimbursements   CRC 10.811
        Information maintained by superior court   CRC 10.501
        Public access to budget information   CRC 10.803
        Surplus property, disposal   CRC 10.830
    Travel expense reimbursement for judicial branch   CRC 10.106
    Trial court budgeting   CRC 10.800, 10.801
        Checks and other negotiable paper to pay court fees, fines, etc   CRC 10.821

JUDICIAL ADMINISTRATION RULES—Cont.
  Budgeting—Cont.
    Trial court budgeting —Cont.
      Court operations CRC 10.810
      Credit card payments of fees CRC 10.820
      Fees set by courts CRC 10.815
      Homicide trials, cost reimbursements CRC 10.811
      Information maintained by superior court CRC 10.501
      Public access to budget information CRC 10.803
      Surplus property, disposal CRC 10.830
  Civil case management, trial courts CRC 10.900 to 10.910
    Assigned cases, trial or dismissal CRC 10.910
    Calendaring system CRC 10.900
    Case management and calendaring system CRC 10.900
    Internal management procedures CRC 10.901
    Judicial council legal forms CRCAppx A
  Complaints against subordinate judicial officers CRC 10.703
  Contents of rules of court CRC 1.4
  Continuing education
    Education of judicial officers
      Delivery methods to satisfy continuing education requirements CRC 10.493
  Contracts
    Former employees
      Limitations on contracting with CRC 10.104
    Indemnification CRC 10.203
    Intrabranch contracting
      Limitations CRC 10.103
  Court employee labor relations CRC 10.650 to 10.660
  Court facilities standards CRC 10.180
    Smoking in court facilities CRC 10.504
  Criminal case management, trial courts CRC 10.950 to 10.953
    Calendars
      Master calendar department CRC 10.950
    Criminal divisions
      Role CRC 10.950
    Judicial council legal forms CRCAppx A
    Meetings concerning criminal court system, designating judges to attend CRC 10.952
    Preliminary hearings
      Disposition of cases prior to preliminary hearing, procedures CRC 10.953
    Presiding judges
      Role CRC 10.950
    Supervising judges
      Duties CRC 10.951
      Role CRC 10.950
  Cross-complaints CRC 3.812
  Discrimination
    Workplace conduct policies
      Courts' duties CRC 10.351
  Education of judicial officers CRC 10.451 to 10.493
    Additional education recommendations for certain assignments CRC 10.469
    Administrative presiding justices
      Duties CRC 10.452
    Capital case assignments
      Additional education recommendations for certain assignments CRC 10.469
    Clerk/executive officer
      Duties of justices, clerk/administrators, managing attorneys and supervisors CRC 10.452
      Minimum requirements CRC 10.471
    Content-based education requirement
      Temporary extension and reduction of education requirements, content-based and hours-based requirements CRC 10.492
    Course criteria
      Approved course criteria CRC 10.481
    Court of appeal justices
      Minimum education requirements CRC 10.461
      Delivery methods to satisfy continuing education requirements CRC 10.493
    Domestic violence issues CRC 10.464
    Ethics orientation for those required to file statement of economic interest CRC 10.455
    Executive officers
      Duties CRC 10.452
      Trial court executive officers CRC 10.473
    Fairness and access education
      Additional education recommendations for certain assignments CRC 10.469

JUDICIAL ADMINISTRATION RULES—Cont.
  Education of judicial officers —Cont.
    Fairness and access education—Cont.
      Recommendations for appellate and trial court personnel CRC 10.479
    Hours-based education requirement
      Temporary extension and reduction of education requirements, content-based and hours-based requirements CRC 10.492
    Judges CRC 10.462
    Judicial council
      Ethics orientation for those required to file statement of economic interest CRC 10.455
      Staff of council, minimum education requirements CRC 10.491
    Jury trial assignments
      Additional education recommendations for certain assignments CRC 10.469
      Treatment of jurors, recommendations for appellate and trial court personnel CRC 10.479
    Justices
      Duties of justices, clerk/executive officers, managing attorneys and supervisors CRC 10.452
    Juvenile dependency cases
      Additional education recommendations for certain assignments CRC 10.469
    Managers
      Duties of justices, clerk/executive officer, managing attorneys and supervisors CRC 10.452
      Minimum education requirements for managing attorneys, supervisors, etc CRC 10.472
      Trial court managers, supervisors and personnel CRC 10.474
    Minimum requirements, expectations and recommendations CRC 10.452
    Objectives of education CRC 10.451
    Presiding judges
      Duties CRC 10.452
    Probate court investigators, probate attorneys and probate examiners CRC 10.478
    Probate judges and subordinate judicial officers CRC 10.468
      Domestic violence issues CRC 10.464
    Providers
      Approved providers CRC 10.481
    Purpose of provisions CRC 10.451
    Quality service to court users
      Recommendations for appellate and trial court personnel CRC 10.479
    Recommendations for appellate and trial court personnel CRC 10.479
    Supervisors
      Duties of justices, clerk/executive officers, managing attorneys and supervisors CRC 10.452
      Minimum education requirements for managing attorneys, supervisors, etc CRC 10.472
      Trial court managers, supervisors and personnel CRC 10.474
    Supreme court justices
      Minimum education requirements CRC 10.461
    Temporary extension and reduction of education requirements, content-based and hours-based requirements CRC 10.492
    Trial courts
      Executive officers CRC 10.473
      Managers, supervisors and personnel CRC 10.474
      Recommendations for appellate and trial court personnel CRC 10.479
      Subordinate judicial officers CRC 10.462
  Finance director
    Budget, duties CRC 10.101
  Former employees
    Limitations on contracting with CRC 10.104
  Grand jury
    Demographic data on regular grand jurors, gathering and summarizing CRC 10.625
  Harassment
    Workplace conduct policies
      Courts' duties CRC 10.351
  Human resources management CRC 10.350, 10.351
  Indemnification
    Contracts with courts CRC 10.203
  Interpreters
    Cross-assignments for court interpreter employees CRC 10.762
    Regional court interpreter employment relations CRC 10.761
  Intrabranch contracting
    Limitations CRC 10.103
  Judicial branch education CRC 10.451 to 10.493
  Judicial Council (See **JUDICIAL COUNCIL**)

JUDICIAL ADMINISTRATION RULES—Cont.
Judicial sabbatical pilot program   CRC 10.502
Management of claims and litigation   CRC 10.201 to 10.203
    Claims and litigation management generally   CRC 10.202
    Contracts
        Indemnification   CRC 10.203
    Procedure   CRC 10.201
Records management
    Public access to judicial administrative records   CRC 10.500
    Trial court management   CRC 10.850 to 10.856
Regional court interpreter employment relations   CRC 10.761
Retaliation
    Workplace conduct policies
        Courts' duties   CRC 10.351
Sabbaticals
    Judicial sabbatical pilot program   CRC 10.502
Smoking in court facilities   CRC 10.504
Subordinate judicial officers
    Complaints against subordinate judicial officers   CRC 10.703
    Education of judicial branch employees   CRC 10.451 to 10.493
    Law practice   CRC 10.702
    Qualifications and education   CRC 10.701
    Role of subordinate judicial officers   CRC 10.700
Surplus property of courts
    Disposal of surplus personal property   CRC 10.830
Temporary judges   CRC 10.740 to 10.746
Trial court management   CRC 10.601 to 10.960
    Administrative decisions of trial courts
        Public access   CRC 10.620
    Alternative dispute resolution programs   CRC 10.780 to 10.783
    Attorney misconduct triggering notification of state bar
        Judge's duties   CRC 10.609
    Automation standards for trial courts   CRC 10.870
    Budgeting   CRC 10.800, 10.801
        Court operations   CRC 10.810
    Civil case management   CRC 10.900 to 10.910
        Assigned cases, trial or dismissal   CRC 10.910
        Calendaring system   CRC 10.900
        Case management and calendaring system   CRC 10.900
        Internal management procedures   CRC 10.901
        Judicial council legal forms   CRCAppx A
    Claim and litigation management   CRC 10.202
    Claim and litigation procedure   CRC 10.201
    Court executive officer, duties   CRC 10.610
    Court self-help centers   CRC 10.960
    Credit cards for payment, acceptance   CRC 10.820
    Criminal case management   CRC 10.950 to 10.953
        Criminal divisions   CRC 10.950
        Judicial council legal forms   CRCAppx A
        Master calendar department   CRC 10.950
        Meetings concerning criminal court system, designating judges to attend   CRC 10.952
        Preliminary hearings, disposition of cases prior to   CRC 10.953
        Presiding judges   CRC 10.950
        Supervising judges   CRC 10.950, 10.951
    Discrimination in court appointments   CRC 10.611
    Executive committees of courts   CRC 10.605
    Fees set by courts   CRC 10.815
    Financial policies and procedures, superior courts   CRC 10.804
    Gender-neutral language in rules, forms, etc   CRC 10.612
    Grand jury
        Demographic data on regular grand jurors, gathering and summarizing   CRC 10.625
    Homicide trials
        Cost reimbursements   CRC 10.811
    Interpreters
        Cross-assignments for court interpreter employees   CRC 10.762
        Regional court interpreter employment relations   CRC 10.761
    Judges
        Duties and powers   CRC 10.608
    Labor relations, court employees   CRC 10.650 to 10.660
    Litigation management program to resolve disputes against trial courts   CRC 10.202
    Local court forms   CRC 10.614
    Local court rules   CRC 10.613
    Notice of change in court-county relationship   CRC 10.805
    Personnel plans   CRC 10.670
    Presiding judges
        Authority and duties   CRC 10.603
        Education of judicial officers, duties of presiding judges   CRC 10.452
        Selection and term   CRC 10.602

JUDICIAL ADMINISTRATION RULES—Cont.
Trial court management —Cont.
    Probate court
        Court investigators, probate attorneys and probate examiners, qualifications   CRC 10.478, 10.776, 10.777
    Public access to management information
        Information access disputes, writ petitions   CRC 10.803
        Information maintained by superior court   CRC 10.501
    Reciprocal assignment orders, reporting   CRC 10.630
    Records management   CRC 10.850 to 10.856
        Definition of court records   CRC 10.850
        Indexes   CRC 10.851
        Sampling program   CRC 10.855
        Standards and guidelines   CRC 10.854
        Trial Court Records Manual as standard   CRC 10.854
    Remote proceedings
        Judicial officers presiding over remote proceeding from location other than courtroom   CRC 10.635
    Self-help centers   CRC 10.960
    Subordinate judicial officers   CRC 10.700 to 10.703
        Education of judicial branch employees   CRC 10.451 to 10.493
    Superior courts   CRC 10.601 to 10.953
    Surplus court personal property, disposal   CRC 10.830
    Temporary judges   CRC 10.740 to 10.746
Workers' compensation program
    Judicial council workers' compensation program for trial courts   CRC 10.350
Workplace conduct policies
    Courts' duties   CRC 10.351

JUDICIAL ADMINISTRATION STANDARDS   CRC JudAdminStand 2.1 to CRC JudAdminStand 10.80
Alternative dispute resolution programs
    Committees to oversee ADR programs   CRC JudAdminStand 10.71
    Coordination of ADR programs, Judicial Council guidelines for   CRC JudAdminStand 10.70
    Criteria for referring cases to ADR providers   CRC JudAdminStand 10.72
Appearance by telephone, procedure for   CRC JudAdminStand 3.1
Appointment of counsel
    Nondiscrimination standard   CRC JudAdminStand 10.21
Bias
    Appointments by court, nondiscrimination in   CRC JudAdminStand 10.21
    Duty of court to prevent bias   CRC JudAdminStand 10.20
Case management and delay reduction procedures   CRC JudAdminStand 2.1
    Judicial council legal forms   CRCAppx A
    Time goals   CRC JudAdminStand 2.2
Child abuse and neglect
    Resource guidelines for child abuse and neglect cases   CRC JudAdminStand 5.45
Children's waiting room in courthouses, recommendation for   CRC JudAdminStand 10.24
Community outreach by judiciary   CRC JudAdminStand 10.5
Complex litigation, judicial management of   CRC JudAdminStand 3.10
Contents of rules of court   CRC 1.4
Court employees, standards concerning (See **COURT OFFICERS AND EMPLOYEES**)
Court records management standards   CRC JudAdminStand 10.80
Court sessions conducted near state penal institutions   CRC JudAdminStand 10.41
Criminal case standards   CRC JudAdminStand 4.10 to CRC JudAdminStand 4.42
    Drug diversion programs   CRC JudAdminStand 4.10
    Sentencing
        Risk/needs assessments, court use at sentencing   CRC JudAdminStand 4.35
    Traffic infraction procedures   CRC JudAdminStand 4.40 to CRC JudAdminStand 4.42
        Bail schedule adherence   CRC JudAdminStand 4.40
        Extensions of time   CRC JudAdminStand 4.40
        Scheduling trials   CRC JudAdminStand 4.42
    Voir dire of potential jurors   CRC JudAdminStand 4.30
Disabilities, court personnel with
    Reasonable accommodation   CRC JudAdminStand 10.25
Education of judges (See **JUDGES**)
Ethics code for court employees   CRC JudAdminStand 10.16
Family court matters   CRC JudAdminStand 5.30
Grand juries, guidelines for selection   CRC JudAdminStand 10.50
Interpreters   CRC JudAdminStand 2.10, CRC JudAdminStand 2.11
Judicial comments on verdict or mistrial, propriety of   CRC JudAdminStand 2.30
Judicial education (See **JUDGES**)

JUDICIAL ADMINISTRATION STANDARDS—Cont.
Juror complaints
    Receiving and responding to complaints   CRC JudAdminStand 10.51
Jury (See **JURY**)
Jury selection
    Master jury list, updating   CRC JudAdminStand 10.31
    Uninterrupted jury selection   CRC JudAdminStand 2.25
Juvenile court matters (See **JUVENILE COURTS**)
Mediation
    Alternative dispute resolution programs
        Committees to oversee ADR programs   CRC JudAdminStand 10.71
        Coordination of ADR programs, judicial council guidelines for   CRC JudAdminStand 10.70
Memorandum opinions by courts of appeal   CRC JudAdminStand 8.1
Mistrial
    Judicial comments on verdict or mistrial, propriety of   CRC JudAdminStand 2.30
Sentencing
    Risk/needs assessments, court use at sentencing   CRC JudAdminStand 4.35
Telephones (See **TELEPHONES AND TELEGRAPHS**)
Traffic infraction procedures   CRC JudAdminStand 4.40 to CRC JudAdminStand 4.42
    Bail schedule adherence   CRC JudAdminStand 4.40
    Extensions of time   CRC JudAdminStand 4.40
    Scheduling trials   CRC JudAdminStand 4.42
Trial court performance standards   CRC JudAdminStand 10.17
Trial management standards   CRC JudAdminStand 2.20
Trusts
    Settlements or judgments in civil cases involving minors or persons with disabilities   CRC JudAdminStand 7.10
Verdict
    Judicial comments on verdict or mistrial, propriety of   CRC JudAdminStand 2.30
Waste reduction and recycling programs for courts   CRC JudAdminStand 10.55

JUDICIAL APPOINTMENTS, COMMISSION ON
Broadcasting of hearings   CRCSupp JudAppointGuide 5
Chairperson, powers of   CRCSupp JudAppointGuide 3
Commission on Judicial Nominees Evaluation, recommendations   CRCSupp JudAppointGuide 4
Communications with commission   CRCSupp JudAppointGuide 4
Conference before confirmation hearing   CRCSupp JudAppointGuide 5
Confirmation hearings, scheduling   CRCSupp JudAppointGuide 4
Decisions, announcement   CRCSupp JudAppointGuide 5
Definitions   CRCSupp JudAppointGuide 1
Files, access to   CRCSupp JudAppointGuide 7
Headquarters of commission   CRCSupp JudAppointGuide 1
Hearings
    Absence of commission member at   CRCSupp JudAppointGuide 5
    Procedures   CRCSupp JudAppointGuide 5
    Public attendance and broadcasting   CRCSupp JudAppointGuide 5
    Records   CRCSupp JudAppointGuide 5
Membership   CRCSupp JudAppointGuide 2
Nominees
    Notice to   CRCSupp JudAppointGuide 4
    Witness lists, presentation of   CRCSupp JudAppointGuide 4
Notice to nominee   CRCSupp JudAppointGuide 4
Official records   CRCSupp JudAppointGuide 5
Post-hearing procedures   CRCSupp JudAppointGuide 7
Pre-hearing procedures   CRCSupp JudAppointGuide 4
Publication and distribution of guidelines   CRCSupp JudAppointGuide 8
Public attendance at hearings   CRCSupp JudAppointGuide 5
Record of hearing   CRCSupp JudAppointGuide 5
Requests to testify   CRCSupp JudAppointGuide 4
Secretary to commission   CRCSupp JudAppointGuide 6
Speakers and communications, release of lists of   CRCSupp JudAppointGuide 4
Staff to commission   CRCSupp JudAppointGuide 6
Testimony, permissible   CRCSupp JudAppointGuide 4
Web site of official guidelines   CRCSupp JudAppointGuide 8
Witnesses
    List
        Presentation of nominee's witness list   CRCSupp JudAppointGuide 4
    Order of hearing   CRCSupp JudAppointGuide 5
Written presentations   CRCSupp JudAppointGuide 4

JUDICIAL ARBITRATION   CRC 3.810 to 3.830
Absence of party   CRC 3.821
Actions subject to   CCP §§1141.11, 1141.12, CRC 3.811
Administrative costs, parties liable for payment of   CCP §1141.28

JUDICIAL ARBITRATION—Cont.
ADR administrator
    Designation   CRC 3.813
ADR committee
    Duties   CRC 3.813
    Panels
        Duties of committee as to   CRC 3.814
Amount in controversy   CCP §§1141.11, 1141.12, CRC 3.811
    Awards in excess of   CCP §1141.26
    Determination of   CCP §1141.16
Applicability of rules   CRC 3.810
Appointments by court, nondiscrimination standard for   CRC 10.611, CRC JudAdminStand 10.21
Arbitration generally (See **ARBITRATION**)
Arbitration under an agreement not in conformity to rules of   CRC 3.830
Arbitrator's fees   CCP §§1141.18, 1141.28, CRC 3.819
Assignment of cases   CRC 3.815
Assignment to arbitration   CRC 3.812
Attorney professional conduct
    Former judges, arbitrators, mediators, etc, restrictions on representation of clients   ProfC 1.12
    Service as temporary judge, referee or court-appointed arbitrator, applicability of judicial ethics canon 6D   ProfC 2.4.1
    Service by attorney as third-party neutral   ProfC 2.4
Attorney, representation by   CRC 3.821
Authority of arbitrators   CRC 3.824
Awards   CCP §1141.20, CRC 3.825
    Amount in controversy, effect of awards in excess of   CCP §1141.26
    Small claims court jurisdiction   CCP §116.220
    Vacation of awards   CCP §1141.22, CRC 3.827
Bad-faith actions or tactics, award of expenses and attorney's fees incurred as result of   CCP §128.5
Case management conference   CRC 3.812
    Telephone appearance at case management conferences   CRC 3.670
Class actions
    Exemption from arbitration   CRC 3.811
Communications with arbitrator   CRC 3.820
Compensation of arbitrators   CCP §§1141.18, 1141.28, CRC 3.819
Conduct of hearing   CRC 3.824
Conferences   CCP §1141.16
Conflicts of interest   CRC 3.816
    Judges' employment or prospective employment as a dispute resolution neutral as basis for disqualification of judges   CCP §§170.1, 1281.9
Construction of statute   CCP §1141.30
Continuances   CRC 3.818
Costs
    Administrative costs, parties liable for payment of   CCP §1141.28
    Salaries and benefits of administrator included as court operations costs   CRC 10.810
Counties
    Administrative costs, liability for   CCP §1141.28
    Salaries and benefits of administrator included as court operations costs   CRC 10.810
Court-appointed arbitrators, compliance with Code of Judicial Ethics   CRCSupp JudEthicsCanon 6
Court Commissioners, retired, appointment as arbitrators   CRC 3.814
Declining by arbitrator to serve   CRC 3.815
Default by defendant   CRC 3.821
Depositions   CRC 3.823
Discovery   CRC 3.822
    Post-award discovery, prohibition against   CCP §1141.24
    Profits and financial condition of defendant, court approval for discovery of evidence re   CCP §1141.19.5
    Time for completion of discovery   CCP §2024.040
Dismissal for delay in bringing action to trial, effect on   CCP §1141.17
Disqualification of arbitrators   CCP §1141.18, CRC 3.816
    Cause, disqualification for   CRC 3.816
    Judges' employment or prospective employment as a dispute resolution neutral as basis for disqualification of judges   CCP §§170.1, 1281.9
Distinguished from general arbitration agreements   CCP §1141.30
Election
    Filing of   CCP §1141.12, CRC 3.812
    Trial de novo   CCP §1141.20, CRC 3.826
Entry of judgment   CCP §1141.23, CRC 3.827
Equitable relief   CCP §§1141.13, 1141.16
Ethics code for judges as applied to court-appointed arbitrators   CRCSupp JudEthicsCanon 6
Evidence, rules of   CRC 3.823
Exceptions to   CCP §§1141.13, 1141.15, CRC 3.811
Exempt cases   CRC 3.811
Ex parte communications   CRC 3.820

JUDICIAL ARBITRATION—Cont.

Fees of arbitrator   CCP §§1141.18, 1141.28, CRC 3.819
Finality of award   CCP §1141.20
Financial condition of defendant, prerequisites for requiring production of evidence re   CCP §1141.19.5
Frivolous actions or tactics, award of expenses and attorney's fees incurred as result of   CCP §128.5
Functional budget categories   CRC 10.810
Hearings
    Conduct of   CRC 3.824
    Continuances   CRC 3.818
    Evidentiary rules   CRC 3.823
    Location   CRC 3.817
    Notice of   CRC 3.817
    Subpoena of witnesses   CRC 3.823
Judge serving as arbitrator   CRCSupp JudEthicsCanon 6
Judgment and award   CCP §1141.23
Judgment, entry of award as   CRC 3.827
Judicial Council rules governing procedure   CCP §§1141.14, 1141.31
Local court rules   CCP §1141.11, CRC 3.811
Mediation as alternative   CCP §§1175.3, 1175.4
Multiple causes of action, exemption for   CRC 3.811
New trial (See within this heading, **"Trial de novo"**)
Notices
    Hearing, notice of   CRC 3.817
    Settlement of case, notice of   CRC 3.829, 3.1385
Panels of arbitrators   CRC 3.814
    Composition   CRC 3.814
    Lists   CRC 3.814
Personal notes of arbitrator   CRC 3.824
Powers of arbitrators   CCP §1141.19, CRC 3.824
Profits and financial condition of defendant, prerequisites for requiring production of evidence re   CCP §1141.19.5
Public entity, actions involving   CCP §1141.27
Purpose of   CCP §1141.10
Qualifications of arbitrators   CCP §1141.18
Record of proceedings   CRC 3.824
Rejection by parties of arbitrator   CRC 3.815
Rules
    Judicial Council rules   CCP §§1141.14, 1141.31
    Local court rules   CCP §1141.11
Salaries and benefits of administrator, court operations costs to include   CRC 10.810
Selection of arbitrators   CCP §1141.18, CRC 3.814, 3.815
    Declining by arbitrator to serve   CRC 3.815
    Local rules   CRC 3.815
    Rejection by parties   CRC 3.815
Settlement of case
    Disclosure of settlement offers to arbitrator   CRC 3.820
    Neutral
        Notice to neutral of settlement of case   CRC 3.1385
    Notice   CRC 3.829, 3.1385
Signature on award   CCP §1141.23
Small claims
    Exemption from arbitration   CRC 3.811
Stipulations   CCP §§1141.12, 1141.16, CRC 3.812
    Non-attorneys as arbitrators   CCP §1141.18
Subpoena of witnesses   CRC 3.823
Time
    Conferences   CCP §1141.16
    Election, filing of   CCP §1141.12, CRC 3.812
    Submission of action to arbitration   CCP §1141.17
Trial de novo   CRC 3.826
    Amount of recovery in   CCP §1141.26
    Election   CCP §1141.20, CRC 3.826
    Priority   CCP §1141.20, CRC 3.826
    References to arbitration at trial, prohibition against   CCP §1141.25, CRC 3.826
    Request for new trial   CCP §1141.20
    Submission of action to arbitration, computation of time pending   CCP §1141.17
Unlawful detainer
    Exemption from arbitration   CRC 3.811
Vacation of award   CCP §1141.22, CRC 3.828
Witnesses   CRC 3.823

JUDICIAL BRANCH STATISTICAL INFORMATION SYSTEM (JBSIS)
CRC 10.400

JUDICIAL BRANCH WORKERS' COMPENSATION PROGRAM ADVISORY COMMITTEE   CRC 10.67

JUDICIAL BUSINESS
When transacted   CCP §133

JUDICIAL COUNCIL
Ability to pay program   Gov §§68645 to 68645.7 (See **ABILITY TO PAY PROGRAM**)
Access and fairness, advisory committee on providing   CRC 10.55
Administrative director   CRC 10.80
    Budget responsibilities   CRC 10.101
    Education requirements, director's responsibilities   CRC 10.491
    Gifts, acceptance   CRC 10.102
    Governance policies   CRCAppx D
    Secretary of judicial council   CRC 10.2
Administrative office of the courts
    Ethics training for members   CRC 10.455
    References to administrative office of courts   CRC 10.81
Administrative presiding justices advisory committee   CRC 10.52
Advisory bodies, working groups and task forces   CRC 10.30 to 10.70
    Access and fairness, advisory committee on providing   CRC 10.55
    Administrative presiding justices advisory committee   CRC 10.52
    Appellate advisory committee   CRC 10.40
    Audits and financial accountability for the judicial branch   CRC 10.63
    Center for judicial education and research (CJER), advisory committee   CRC 10.50
    Civil and small claims advisory committee   CRC 10.41
    Collaborative justice courts advisory committee   CRC 10.56
    Court executives advisory committee   CRC 10.48
    Court facilities advisory committee   CRC 10.62
    Court interpreters advisory panel   CRC 10.51
    Court security advisory committee   CRC 10.61
    Creation of committees   CRC 10.30
    Criminal law advisory committee   CRC 10.42
    Data analytics advisory committee   CRC 10.68
    Duties and responsibilities   CRC 10.34
    Establishment of task forces and other advisory bodies   CRC 10.70
    Family and juvenile law advisory committee   CRC 10.43
    Functions of advisory bodies   CRC 10.30
    Functions of committees   CRC 10.30
    Governance policies   CRCAppx D
    Information technology advisory committee   CRC 10.53
    Internal operation   CRC 10.31
    Jury instructions
        Civil jury instructions, advisory committee on   CRC 10.58
        Criminal jury instructions, advisory committee on   CRC 10.59
    Meetings   CRC 10.33, 10.75
    Membership and terms   CRC 10.31
    Nominations and appointments of committee members   CRC 10.32
    Oversight by internal committees   CRC 10.10
        Technology committee duties   CRC 10.16
    Probate and mental health advisory committee   CRC 10.44
    Proposals to change rules
        Review by appropriate committee   CRC 10.21
    Reappointments to membership   CRC 10.31
    Restrictions on membership   CRC 10.2
    Staff of committee   CRC 10.30
    Subcommittees   CRC 10.30
    Terms   CRC 10.31
    Traffic advisory committee   CRC 10.54
    Trial court budget advisory committee   CRC 10.64
    Trial court facility modification advisory committee   CRC 10.65
    Trial court presiding judges advisory committee   CRC 10.46
    Tribal court-state court forum   CRC 10.60
    Workers' compensation
        Judicial branch workers' compensation program advisory committee   CRC 10.67
    Workload assessment advisory committee   CRC 10.66
Agenda for council meetings   CRC 10.5
Amended rules, standards, or forms, proposals for   CRC 10.20
    General public, proposals from   CRC 10.21
Appellate advisory committee   CRC 10.40
Appointments to Judicial Council   CRC 10.4
Arbitrators, adoption of ethics standards for   CCP §1281.85
Audits and financial accountability for the judicial branch
    Advisory committee   CRC 10.63
Authority, duty, and goals of Judicial Council   CRC 10.1
Broadcasting of meetings   CRC 10.6
Budgeting responsibilities of judicial council   CRC 10.101
    Budget and management information
        Maintenance of information by council staff   CRC 10.501
    Fee, fine and forfeiture revenue
        New revenue, allocation   CRC 10.105

JUDICIAL COUNCIL—Cont.
   Budgeting responsibilities of judicial council —Cont.
      Judicial branch budget committee   CRC 10.15, CRCAppx D
      Travel expense reimbursement for judicial branch   CRC 10.106
   Budget meetings   CRC 10.5
      Presenting information   CRC 10.6
   Care plan submission rules   Pro §1456.5
   Center for judicial education and research
      Advisory committee   CRC 10.50
   Child support
      Statewide registry of support orders
         Forms, judicial council duties   Fam §§17392, 17393
   Child support proceedings (See **CHILD SUPPORT**)
   Circulating orders   CRC 10.5
   Civil and small claims advisory committee   CRC 10.41
   Closed sessions   CRC 10.6
   Collaborative justice courts advisory committee   CRC 10.56
   Committees of Judicial Council
      Advisory bodies (See within this heading, "**Advisory bodies, working groups and task forces**")
      Executive and planning committee   CRC 10.11
         Governance policies   CRCAppx D
      Internal committees   CRC 10.10
      Judicial branch budget committee   CRC 10.15, CRCAppx D
      Legislation committee   CRC 10.12
         Governance policies   CRCAppx D
      Litigation management committee   CRC 10.14
         Governance policies   CRCAppx D
      Policy coordination and liaison committee   CRC 10.12
         Governance policies   CRCAppx D
      Rules and projects committee   CRC 10.13
         Governance policies   CRCAppx D
      Rules committee   CRC 10.13
         Governance policies   CRCAppx D
      Technology committee   CRC 10.16, CRCAppx D
   Community assistance, recovery, and empowerment act
      CARE act rules   CRC 7.2201 to 7.2303 (See **MENTAL DISABILITY**)
   Conciliation proceedings, duties respecting   Fam §§1850 to 1852
   Conservators
      Educational requirements for court staff, court rule concerning   Pro §1456
      Interstate jurisdiction, transfer and recognition
         Judicial council to develop rules and forms   Pro §2023
      Non-professional conservators or guardians, educational program   Pro §1457
   Conservatorship alternatives program
      Establishment   Pro §1836
   Conservatorships, rules regarding
      Effectiveness of court in conservatorship cases
         Study, reporting by judicial council   Pro §1458
   Constitutional duties   CRC 10.1
   Contracting with former employees   CRC 10.104
   Coordination of actions, assignment of judge   CCP §§404, 404.3
   Court executives advisory committee   CRC 10.48
   Court facilities
      Acquisition, space planning, construction and design   CRC 10.184
      Advisory committee   CRC 10.62
      Operation and maintenance of facilities   CRC 10.182
      Recommendations for policies, procedures and standards   CRC 10.181
      Standards   CRC 10.180
      Transfer of responsibilities to judicial council   CRC 10.183
   Court interpreters advisory panel   CRC 10.51
   Court operations, list of approved costs for   CRC 10.810
   Court records
      Remote access to electronic records
         Governance policies   CRCAppx D
   Court security
      Court security advisory committee   CRC 10.61
      Court security committees   CRC 10.173
      Plans for court security   CRC 10.172
   Criminal law advisory committee   CRC 10.42
   Data analytics advisory committee   CRC 10.68
   Discovery
      Interstate and international depositions and discovery act
         Subpoenas, forms to be developed by council   CCP §2029.390
   Disqualification, assignment in case of   CCP §170.8
   Education of judicial officers
      Ethics orientation for those required to file statement of economic interest   CRC 10.455
      Generally   CRC 10.451 to 10.493
   Electronic court records, remote access
      Governance policies   CRCAppx D

JUDICIAL COUNCIL—Cont.
   Email
      Advisory body meetings
         Action by email between meetings   CRC 10.75
   Ethics training for members   CRC 10.455
   Executive and planning committee
      Duties   CRC 10.11
      Governance policies   CRCAppx D
   Executives, managers, supervisors, etc, education requirements   CRC 10.491
      Temporary extension and reduction of education requirements, content-based and hours-based requirements   CRC 10.492
   Expedited jury trials
      Mandatory expedited jury trials, limited civil cases
         Rules and forms, judicial council duties   CCP §630.28
      Rules and forms
         Duties of council as to   CCP §630.11
   Family and juvenile law advisory committee   CRC 10.43
   Family law proceedings (See **FAMILY LAW PROCEEDINGS**)
   Family law rules (See **FAMILY RULES**)
   Forms   CRC 1.30 to 1.45
      Applicability of provisions   CRC 1.30
      Cause of action forms   CRC 1.45
      Current form, use   CRC 1.37
      Destruction of superior court records   CRC 10.856
      Electronic production   CRC 1.44
      Family law and domestic violence forms
         Nonfamily law proceedings, use in   CRC 5.7
         Status   CRC 5.7
      Handwritten or handprinted forms   CRC 2.135
      Juvenile court actions, use of general mandatory forms   CRC 5.502
      Legal forms   CRCAppx A
      Legibility   CRC 1.43
      Listing of legal forms   CRCAppx A
      Mandatory forms   CRC 1.30
         Alteration for form   CRC 1.31
         Colored forms   CRC 1.31
         Effect of mandatory status   CRC 1.31
         Identification   CRC 1.31
         List   CRC 1.31
         Orders not on mandatory form   CRC 1.31
         Probate form orders, electronic generation   CRC 7.101.5
      Optional forms   CRC 1.30
         Acceptance for filing   CRC 1.35
         Alteration of form   CRC 1.35
         Colored forms   CRC 1.35
         Identification   CRC 1.35
         List   CRC 1.35
         Use   CRC 1.35
      Pleading forms   CRC 1.45
      Probate proceedings   CRC 7.101
      Proof of service on form   CRC 1.41
      Rejection of form
         Prohibited reasons for rejection   CRC 1.42
   Goals of judicial branch   CRC 10.1
      Governance policies   CRCAppx D
   Governance policies   CRCAppx D
      Contents of rules   CRC 1.4
      Description of contents of policies   CRC 10.1
   Government tort liability
      Actions against judicial branch entities
         Settlement of claims   Gov §948.1
      Claims against judicial branch entity
         Adjustment and payment of claims   Gov §935.8
         Rules of court to determine action on claim   Gov §912.7
   Guardian and ward
      Educational requirements for court staff, court rule concerning   Pro §1456
      Non-professional conservators or guardians, educational program   Pro §1457
   Information technology advisory committee   CRC 10.53
   Internal committees   CRC 10.10
      Chairs and vice chairs   CRC 10.2
      Governance policies   CRCAppx D
   Interpreter services for courts
      Reimbursement to courts for services of court interpreter   Ev §756
   Interrogatories
      Form interrogatories
         Development by judicial council   CCP §§2033.710 to 2033.740
   Inventory and appraisal, rules regarding filing   Pro §1456.5
   Judicial branch budget committee   CRC 10.15, CRCAppx D
   Judicial branch statistical information system (JBSIS)   CRC 10.400
   Judicial branch workers' compensation program advisory committee   CRC 10.67

JUDICIAL COUNCIL—Cont.
Jury instructions
    Civil jury instructions, advisory committee on   CRC 10.58
    Criminal jury instructions, advisory committee on   CRC 10.59
    Judicial council jury instructions   CRC 2.1050
Jury trial
    Peremptory challenges
        Reduction in number, study and report   CCP §231
Legislation committee   CRC 10.12
    Governance policies   CRCAppx D
List of forms   CRCAppx A
Litigation management committee   CRC 10.14
    Governance policies   CRCAppx D
Local court rules
    Filed with council   CRC 10.613
Long-Range Strategic Plan   CRC 10.1
Meetings
    Advisory bodies, committees and task forces
        Meetings of advisory bodies   CRC 10.75
    Agenda   CRC 10.5
    Broadcasting   CRC 10.6
    Budget meetings   CRC 10.5
        Presenting information   CRC 10.6
    Notice and agenda   CRC 10.5
    Parliamentary procedures for judicial council   CRCAppx G
        Contents of California rules of court   CRC 1.4
    Photographing   CRC 10.6
    Requests to speak by members of public   CRC 10.6
    Video recording   CRC 10.6
Membership and terms   CRC 10.2 to 10.4
    Ethics training for members   CRC 10.455
    Role of members   CRC 10.2
        Governance policies   CRCAppx D
Motion to be relieved as counsel, use of Judicial Council form   CRC 3.1362
New rules, standards, or forms, proposals for   CRC 10.20
No judge qualified to hear action or proceeding, assignment of judge by council where   CCP §170.8
Nomination procedures   CRC 10.4
Nonvoting members   CRC 10.3
Notice of council meetings   CRC 10.5
Officers, employees, and committees
    Chair and vice chair   CRC 10.2
        Governance policies   CRCAppx D
    Governance policies   CRCAppx D
    Internal committees
        Chairs and vice chairs   CRC 10.2
    Secretary   CRC 10.2
        Governance policies   CRCAppx D
Open-meeting policy   CRC 10.6
Parliamentary procedures for judicial council   CRCAppx G
    Contents of California rules of court   CRC 1.4
Photographing of meetings   CRC 10.6
Policy coordination and liaison committee   CRC 10.12
    Governance policies   CRCAppx D
Policymaking by council
    Governance policies   CRCAppx D
Probate and Mental Health Advisory Committee   CRC 10.44
Probate rules
    Mandatory judicial council form orders
        Electronic generation   CRC 7.101.5
Proposals for new or amended rules, standards, or forms   CRC 10.20
    General public proposals   CRC 10.21
    Rule-making procedures   CRC 10.22
Purpose   CRC 10.1
    Governance policies   CRCAppx D
Records
    Public access to judicial administrative records   CRC 10.500
Referees and references by trial court, adoption and implementation of court rules pertaining to   CCP §645.2
Requests for admissions
    Form requests
        Development by judicial council   CCP §§2033.710 to 2033.740
Responsibilities of council
    Governance policies   CRCAppx D
Rule-making procedures   CRC 10.22
Rules committee   CRC 10.13
    Governance policies   CRCAppx D
    Review of new and amended proposals   CRC 10.20
Rules of court
    Authority to adopt rules   CRC 1.3

JUDICIAL COUNCIL—Cont.
Rules of court—Cont.
    Preemptive effect   CRC 3.20
Small claims court (See **SMALL CLAIMS COURTS**)
Staff of judicial council
    Administrative director   CRC 10.80
    Duties of staff   CRC 10.81
    Education requirements   CRC 10.491
        Temporary extension and reduction of education requirements, content-based and hours-based requirements   CRC 10.492
    Ethics orientation for those required to file statement of economic interest   CRC 10.455
    Management by administrative director   CRC 10.81
    References to administrative office of courts   CRC 10.81
    Relationship between staff and council   CRCAppx D
    Role of staff   CRC 10.1
Standards of administration (See **JUDICIAL ADMINISTRATION STANDARDS**)
Strategic and tactical technology plans   CRC 10.16
Task forces
    Advisory bodies, working groups and task forces   CRC 10.30 to 10.70
Technology committee   CRC 10.16, CRCAppx D
Telephone appearances and teleconferencing by counsel
    Fees   CCP §367.6
Traffic advisory committee   CRC 10.54
Transitional housing program misconduct
    Injunctions or temporary restraining orders
        Forms and instructions to implement provisions, judicial council duties   CC §1954.16
Travel expense reimbursement for judicial branch   CRC 10.106
Trial court budgeting
    Advisory committee   CRC 10.64
    Trial court budget and fiscal management
        Information access disputes, writ petitions   CRC 10.803
        Information maintained by superior court   CRC 10.501
Trial court delay reduction, standards for (See **TRIAL COURT DELAY REDUCTION**)
Trial court facility modification
    Advisory committee   CRC 10.65
Trial court improvement fund
    Fee, fine and forfeiture revenue
        Allocation of revenue in fund   CRC 10.105
Trial court presiding judges advisory committee   CRC 10.46
Vexatious litigants subject to prefiling orders, records of   CCP §391.7
    Vacating order and removing name from list   CCP §391.8
Video recording of meetings   CRC 10.6
Workers' compensation
    Judicial branch workers' compensation program advisory committee   CRC 10.67
    Judicial council workers' compensation program for trial courts   CRC 10.350
Workload assessment advisory committee   CRC 10.66

JUDICIAL DISTRICT
Defined   CCP §§17, 38

JUDICIAL ETHICS, CODE OF (See **JUDGES**)

JUDICIAL HOLIDAYS (See **HOLIDAYS**)

JUDICIAL NOTICE
Generally   Ev §450
Administrative Procedure Act, judicial notice of agency regulations filed under   Ev §451, Gov §§11343.6, 11344.6
Appeals court   Ev §459
Appellate rules
    Briefs
        Capital case   CRC 8.630
    Death penalty appeals
        Habeas corpus, appeals from superior court decisions in habeas cases involving death penalty   CRC 8.395
    Motion requesting in court of appeal or supreme court   CRC 8.252
        Habeas corpus   CRC 8.386
    Requests for judicial notice
        4th Appellate District local rules   CRCSupp 4th AppDist Misc Order 15-16, 4th AppDist Misc Order 16-16, 4th AppDist Misc Order 17-16, 4th AppDist Misc Order 18-16
        E-filing in supreme court and courts of appeal, format of electronic documents   CRC 8.74
    Superior court appeals   CRC 8.809
Attorneys, rules of conduct governing   Ev §451

JUDICIAL NOTICE—Cont.
Common knowledge, facts within   Ev §§451, 452
Computer-generated official court records relating to criminal convictions   Ev §452.5
Demurrer   CCP §§430.30, 430.70
Denial by court to take judicial notice   Ev §456
English language   Ev §451
Expert consultants
    Generally   Ev §§454, 455, 459
    Appointment by court   Ev §460
Family rules
    Request for orders   CRC 5.115
Habeas corpus
    Petition hearings   CRC 4.551
    Return of writ to reviewing court   CRC 8.386
Jury, instructions to   Ev §457
Law and motion rules
    Hearing, evidence at   CRC 3.1306
    Moving papers, request associated with   CRC 3.1113
Legislative history materials
    3rd Appellate District local rules   CRCSupp 3rd AppDist
Mandatory judicial notice   Ev §§451, 453
Parentage determinations   CRC 5.635
Permissive judicial notice   Ev §§452, 453
Propriety of court taking judicial notice, determination of   Ev §§454, 455
Requests for   CRC 8.252, Ev §§453, 456
    1st Appellate District local rules   CRCSupp 1st AppDist
    Habeas corpus   CRC 8.386
Restrictive covenants in recorded instruments   CC §53
Review courts, judicial notice by   Ev §459
Secretary of state, judicial notice of agency regulations filed with   Ev §451, Gov §§11343.6, 11344.6
Submission of arguments prior to court decision for taking   Ev §455
Subsequent proceedings of trial, effect on   Ev §458
Summary judgments, support or opposition of motion for   CCP §437c
Supreme court or court of appeal, motion for judicial notice in case pending before   CRC 8.252
    Habeas corpus   CRC 8.386

JUDICIAL OFFICERS (See JUDGES)

JUDICIAL PERFORMANCE, COMMISSION ON
Censure, removal, admonishment or retirement of judges
    Additional evidence   JudPerR 133
    Advisory letter to judge
        Negotiated settlements during preliminary investigation or disciplinary proceeding   JudPerR 116.5
        Notice of tentative advisory letter to judge   JudPerR 107, 113
        Objection to tentative advisory letter   JudPerPolicy 2.1
        Preliminary investigation   JudPerR 111
        Procedure   JudPerR 114
    Amendment to pleadings   JudPerR 128
    Amicus curiae briefs   JudPerR 131
    Answer   JudPerR 104, 119
        Amendments   JudPerR 128
        Extension of time for   JudPerR 108, 119
    Appearance before commission
        Masters' report, appearance after   JudPerR 132
        Modification of decision after formal proceedings   JudPerPolicy 2.6
        Notice of tentative discipline, appearance after   JudPerR 114
    Attorney representing judge   JudPerR 106, 126
    Briefs   JudPerR 130
        Amicus curiae briefs   JudPerR 131
    Characteristics of misconduct
        Factors relevant to sanctions   JudPerPolicy 7.1
    Commencement of commission action   JudPerR 109
    Commission member's participation prohibited in proceedings involving own censure, removal or admonishment   JudPerR 101
    Commission's own motion, staff inquiry or preliminary investigation on   JudPerR 109
    Confidentiality of proceedings   JudPerR 102, 122
    Conflicts of interest
        Disqualification of commission member unless quorum prevented by disqualification   JudPerR 134.5
    Consent
        Amicus curiae briefs, consent to submission of   JudPerR 131
        Discipline by   JudPerPolicy 2.4
        Discipline by consent   JudPerR 127
        One master to hear case, judge's consent to appointment of   JudPerR 121

JUDICIAL PERFORMANCE, COMMISSION ON—Cont.
Censure, removal, admonishment or retirement of judges—Cont.
    Conservator
        Appointment   JudPerR 126
    Construction of rules governing   JudPerR 138
    Cooperation, duty of
        Factors relevant to sanctions   JudPerPolicy 7.1
    Defamatory material   JudPerR 103
    Defending against charges, opportunity for   JudPerR 126
    Definitions   JudPerR 138
    Demeanor of judge
        Factors relevant to sanctions   JudPerPolicy 7.1
    Depositions   JudPerR 122
    Dereliction of duty   JudPerR 109
    Disclosures concerning proceedings   JudPerR 102
    Discovery   JudPerR 122
        Extension of time   JudPerR 108
    Dishonesty
        Factors relevant to sanctions   JudPerPolicy 7.1
    Dismissal of charge by examiner   JudPerR 128
    Dismissal of proceedings   JudPerR 134
    Disqualification pending further proceedings or appeal   JudPerR 120
    Drug use   JudPerR 109
    Duty to cooperate   JudPerR 104
    Evidence
        Additional evidence, hearing for taking   JudPerR 133
        Hearings, evidence admissible at   JudPerR 123, 125
    Exhibits at hearings   JudPerR 125.5
    Extension of time in proceedings   JudPerR 108, 119
        Private tentative discipline   JudPerR 114
    Failure to appear at hearing   JudPerR 123
    Filing with Commission   JudPerR 119.5
    Finality of commission determination   JudPerR 136
    Formal proceedings
        Disclosures in compliance with discovery obligations, protection of confidentiality   JudPerR 102
        Extension of time to file answer   JudPerR 108
        Filing with commission during formal proceedings   JudPerR 119.5
    Former judges
        Barring assignments to former judges   JudPerPolicy 2.5
    Hearings
        Additional evidence   JudPerR 133
        Confidentiality   JudPerR 102
        Evidence at   JudPerR 125
        Exhibits at hearings   JudPerR 125.5
        Failure by judge to appear at   JudPerR 123
        Media coverage   JudPerR 124
        Number of commission members required to attend hearing   JudPerR 123
        Procedural rights of judge   JudPerR 126
        Tentative private discipline, appearance to object   JudPerR 114
    Injury to others
        Factors relevant to sanctions   JudPerPolicy 7.1
    Intent involved in misconduct
        Factors relevant to sanctions   JudPerPolicy 7.1
    Interested party serving on commission   JudPerR 101
    Intoxicant use   JudPerR 109
    Investigation, preliminary
        Extension of time to respond to preliminary investigation letter   JudPerR 108
    Legal error reflecting bad faith, bias, abuse of authority, etc
        Basis for discipline   JudPerR 111.4
    Length of service
        Factors relevant to sanctions   JudPerPolicy 7.1
    Masters, hearing before and report of
        Additional evidence   JudPerR 133
        Extension of time   JudPerR 108
        Objections to report   JudPerR 130
        Preparation of report   JudPerR 129
        Setting for hearing   JudPerR 121
    Media coverage of hearings   JudPerR 124
    Medical examination, submission to   JudPerR 105
    Monitoring, deferring termination of investigation for   JudPerR 112
    Nature of misconduct
        Factors relevant to sanctions   JudPerPolicy 7.1
    Notice
        Advisory letter to judge   JudPerR 107, 110, 111, 113
        Appointment of masters   JudPerR 121
        Determination by commission   JudPerR 135
        Disqualification pending formal proceedings   JudPerR 120

JUDICIAL PERFORMANCE, COMMISSION ON—Cont.
Censure, removal, admonishment or retirement of judges—Cont.
    Notice—Cont.
        Formal proceedings for censure or removal, institution of   JudPerR 118
        Hearing before commission or masters   JudPerR 121, 132, 133
        Judge's request, notification of disposition at   JudPerR 109
        Preliminary investigation, notice of   JudPerR 107, 109, 111
        Tentative private admonishment   JudPerR 107, 113
        Tentative public admonishment   JudPerR 107, 113
    Number of acts
        Factors relevant to sanctions   JudPerPolicy 7.1
    Objections
        Tentative private discipline, objections to   JudPerR 114
    Observation and review, deferring termination of investigation for   JudPerR 112
    Official nature of misconduct
        Factors relevant to sanctions   JudPerPolicy 7.1
    Perpetuation of testimony by deposition   JudPerR 122
    Pleadings   JudPerR 119, 128
    Preliminary investigation
        Confidentiality   JudPerR 102
        Determination whether formal proceedings should be instituted   JudPerR 109
        Letter   JudPerR 111
        Negotiated settlements during preliminary investigation or disciplinary proceeding   JudPerR 116.5
        Notice to judge   JudPerR 107, 109, 111
        Termination of   JudPerR 111
    Prior disciplinary action, receiving evidence of   JudPerR 125
    Private admonishment
        Negotiated settlements during preliminary investigation or disciplinary proceeding   JudPerR 116.5
    Private admonishment procedure, generally   JudPerR 113, 114
    Privilege
        Defamation, protection from liability for   JudPerR 103
        Discovery   JudPerR 122
        Judge's exercise of privilege at hearing   JudPerR 104, 123
    Public admonishment   JudPerR 114
        Negotiated settlements during preliminary investigation or disciplinary proceeding   JudPerR 116.5
    Public admonishment or reproval   JudPerR 113
    Record of proceedings   JudPerR 135
        Use and retention of records of complaints against judges   JudPerR 117
    Representation of judge by counsel   JudPerR 106
    Reputation for fairness, impartiality and dignified performance
        Factors relevant to sanctions   JudPerPolicy 7.1
    Response to commission   JudPerR 104
    Retention and use of records of complaints against judges   JudPerR 117
    Retroactivity of discipline provisions   JudPerR 137
    Rights of judge in proceedings   JudPerR 126
    Sanctions
        Factors relevant to sanctions   JudPerPolicy 7.1
    Self-incrimination, protection against   JudPerR 104
    Seriousness of misconduct
        Factors relevant to sanctions   JudPerPolicy 7.1
    Service
        Formal proceedings, notice of institution of   JudPerR 118
        Masters' report   JudPerR 129
    Setting for hearing   JudPerR 121
    Settlements
        Discussions of settlements, evidence at hearings   JudPerR 125
        Negotiated settlements during preliminary investigation or disciplinary proceeding   JudPerR 116.5
    Staff inquiry into judicial misconduct   JudPerR 107
    Subpoenas, production of documents   JudPerR 122
    Subpoenas, right to issuance of   JudPerR 126
    Supreme court
        Justice of supreme court, proceedings involving admonishment, censure, removal, retirement or disqualification   CRC 9.61
    Suspension   JudPerR 120.5
    Temporary disqualification pending formal proceedings   JudPerR 120
    Tentative admonishments
        Notice of tentative private admonishment   JudPerR 107, 113
        Notice of tentative private admonishment, appearance after   JudPerR 114
        Notice of tentative public admonishment   JudPerR 107, 113
        Objections to   JudPerPolicy 2.1
    Tentative advisory letter
        Notice of tentative discipline   JudPerR 113

JUDICIAL PERFORMANCE, COMMISSION ON—Cont.
Censure, removal, admonishment or retirement of judges—Cont.
    Tentative advisory letter—Cont.
        Objection to   JudPerPolicy 2.1
    Termination of suspension   JudPerR 120.5
    Testimony, failure of judge to offer   JudPerR 123
    Time
        Amendments to pleadings   JudPerR 128
        Answer to charges   JudPerR 119
        Discovery requests   JudPerR 122
        Extension of time   JudPerR 108, 114, 119
        Formal proceedings, notice of institution of   JudPerR 118
        Masters' report   JudPerR 129
    Transcript   JudPerR 135
        Available for use by judge   JudPerR 126
        Masters, proceedings before   JudPerR 129
    Vote of commission   JudPerR 134
    Witnesses
        Oath, statements under   JudPerPolicy 1.13
        Perpetuation of testimony by deposition   JudPerR 122
        Record of witness statements   JudPerPolicy 1.11
Complaints
    Reconsideration of closed complaints   JudPerPolicy 1.1.5
Conflicts of interest   JudPerR 101
    Censure, removal, admonishment or retirement of judges
        Disqualification of commission member unless quorum prevented by disqualification   JudPerR 134.5
    Ethics code for commission members
        Recusal, conditions requiring   JudPerPolicy 6.1
    Recusal of commission staff   JudPerPolicy 3.13
Decisions
    Citation of commission decisions   JudPerPolicy 2.7
    Modification of decision following formal proceedings   JudPerPolicy 2.6
Ethics code for commission members   JudPerPolicy 6.1 to 6.5
    Bias, prejudice, impropriety or appearance of impropriety   JudPerPolicy 6.5
    Confidentiality of proceedings   JudPerPolicy 6.2
    Ex parte contacts of members   JudPerPolicy 6.3
    Judicial elections
        Restrictions on member activities   JudPerPolicy 6.4
    Recusal
        Conditions requiring   JudPerPolicy 6.1
Ethics code, judges
    Communications by judge with commission   JudEthicsCanon 2
    Responsiveness of judge   JudEthicsCanon 3
Former judges
    Barring assignments to former judges   JudPerPolicy 2.5
    Certification to administer oaths or affirmation, confidentiality of application   JudPerPolicy 3.14
Policy declarations   JudPerPolicy 1.1 to 6.5
    Administration   JudPerPolicy 3.1 to 3.14
    Advisory letter to judge
        Objection to tentative advisory letter   JudPerPolicy 2.1
    Agreed statement   JudPerPolicy 2.4
    Anonymous complaints   JudPerPolicy 1.1
    Character letters, submission   JudPerPolicy 1.14
    Citation of commission decisions   JudPerPolicy 2.7
    Complaints
        Reconsideration of closed complaints   JudPerPolicy 1.1.5
    Date of hearing   JudPerPolicy 2.2
    Depositions
        Transcripts   JudPerPolicy 2.3.5
    Disability retirement applications   JudPerPolicy 5.1 to 5.6
    Discipline by consent   JudPerPolicy 2.4
    Disclosure of information   JudPerPolicy 4.1 to 4.6
    Ethics code for commission members   JudPerPolicy 6.1 to 6.5
    Former judges
        Barring assignments to former judges   JudPerPolicy 2.5
        Certification to administer oaths or affirmation, confidentiality of application   JudPerPolicy 3.14
    Information, disclosure of   JudPerPolicy 4.1 to 4.6
    Interviewers, admonishments to   JudPerPolicy 1.9
    Investigations, preliminary   JudPerPolicy 1.4 to 1.9
    Legal advisor to commissioners   JudPerPolicy 3.9
    Modification of decision following formal proceedings   JudPerPolicy 2.6
    Prehearing conference   JudPerPolicy 2.3
    Prehearing status report   JudPerPolicy 2.3
    Process for drafting declarations or amendments, etc   JudPerPolicy 3.6
    Reconsideration of closed complaints   JudPerPolicy 1.1.5
    Records, disclosure   JudPerPolicy 4.3, 4.4
    Removal from active calendar   JudPerPolicy 1.8

JUDICIAL PERFORMANCE, COMMISSION ON—Cont.
Policy declarations —Cont.
    Rules of commission
        Review   JudPerPolicy 3.5
    Sanctions
        Factors relevant to sanctions   JudPerPolicy 7.1
    Subpoenas, investigation   JudPerPolicy 1.12
    Tentative admonishments, objections to   JudPerPolicy 2.1
    Transcripts
        Deposition transcripts   JudPerPolicy 2.3.5
    Witness statements   JudPerPolicy 1.10 to 1.13
Process and service of process
    Manner of service   JudPerR 126
Records   JudPerPolicy 4.1 to 4.6
Recusal of commission staff   JudPerPolicy 3.13
Rules of commission
    Review   JudPerPolicy 3.5
Sanctions
    Censure, removal, etc
        Factors relevant to sanctions   JudPerPolicy 7.1
        Generally (See within this heading, **"Censure, removal, admonishment or retirement of judges"**)
Subordinate judicial officers
    Investigation   JudPerR 109

JUDICIAL PROCEEDINGS
English language, papers and proceedings to be in   CCP §185

JUDICIAL RECORDS
Defined   CCP §1904

JUDICIAL REMEDIES
Classification of   CCP §21
Defined   CCP §20

JUDICIAL SABBATICAL PILOT PROGRAM   CRC 10.502

JUDICIAL SALES (See **ENFORCEMENT OF JUDGMENTS**)

JUNIOR ACCESSORY DWELLING UNITS
Common interest developments
    Construction or use on single-family residential lot
        Restrictions prohibited   CC §4751
Covenants, conditions, and restrictions
    Unenforceability of accessory dwelling unit prohibitions   CC §714.3

JUNIOR LIENS (See **LIENS**)

JUNK YARDS
Fire hydrants or fire department corrections
    Damages for wrongful possession by junk dealers or recyclers   CC §3336.5

JURIES OF INQUEST
Defined   CCP §194
Function of   CCP §236
Selection, compensation and obligation   CCP §235
Types of juries   CCP §193
Witness fees   Gov §68095

JURISDICTION
Administration of estates (See **ADMINISTRATION OF ESTATES**)
Adoption   Fam §§8714, 9210
    Interstate adoptions   Fam §9212
Amount in controversy (See **AMOUNT IN CONTROVERSY**)
Annulment   Fam §§2010 to 2013
    Same sex marriages
        Residence requirements   Fam §2320
Answer alleging lack of   CCP §430.10
Appearance (See **APPEARANCE**)
Arbitration proceedings   CCP §§86, 1292.4 to 1293
Assisted reproduction
    Gestational carriers, agreements   Fam §7620
Attorney's practice, court's assumption of jurisdiction over (See **ATTORNEYS**)
Cause, jurisdiction over   CCP §1917
Certiorari   CCP §1068
Change of names   CCP §1275
Child custody
    Exclusive jurisdiction of juvenile court   CRC 5.510
    Generally (See **CUSTODY OF CHILDREN**)
Child support
    Interstate family support   Fam §§5700.201 to 5700.211
Child support proceedings (See **CHILD SUPPORT**)
Choice of law (See **CHOICE OF LAW**)

JURISDICTION—Cont.
Civil rights actions   CC §52.2
Community property (See **COMMUNITY PROPERTY**)
Conciliation court proceedings (See **CONCILIATION COURTS**)
Conservators
    California conservatorship jurisdiction act
        Judicial council legal forms   CRCAppx A
    Generally (See **CONSERVATORS**)
    Interstate jurisdiction, transfer and recognition
        Generally   Pro §§1980 to 2033 (See **CONSERVATORS**)
        Judicial council legal forms   CRCAppx A
Constitution   CCP §410.10
Continuing jurisdiction   CCP §410.50
Contract, persons liable on   CCP §410.70
Coordination of actions   CRC 3.540 to 3.545
Corporations forfeiting charter, jurisdiction over trustees and stockholders of   CCP §410.60
Courts of appeal, original jurisdiction
    Habeas corpus   CRC 8.380 to 8.398
    Mandate, certiorari and prohibition in supreme court or court of appeal   CRC 8.485 to 8.493
Custody of children (See **CUSTODY OF CHILDREN**)
Defined as to court authority   CCP §410.10
Demurrer alleging lack of   CCP §430.10
Destroyed land records relief law proceedings   CCP §751.11
Dissolution of marriage (See **DISSOLUTION OF MARRIAGE**)
Earthquakes, boundary reestablishment after   CCP §751.55
Eminent domain action   CCP §1250.010
Enforcement of judgments (See **ENFORCEMENT OF JUDGMENTS**)
Escheat (See **ESCHEAT**)
Family law   Fam §200
Foreign country judgments
    Personal jurisdiction lacking
        Circumstances allowing for recognition   CCP §1717
Forum non conveniens (See **INCONVENIENT FORUM**)
Guardianship (See **GUARDIAN AND WARD**)
Habeas corpus proceedings   CRC 4.551
Impeachment of record for absence of   CCP §1916
Implied powers to effectuate conferred powers   CCP §187
Inconvenient forum doctrine (See **INCONVENIENT FORUM**)
Information Practices Act, proceedings under   CC §1798.49
International commercial arbitration and conciliation (See **INTERNATIONAL COMMERCIAL ARBITRATION AND CONCILIATION**)
Interstate family support   Fam §§5700.201 to 5700.211
Judges   Pro §800
Judge's power to act, effect of proceedings for disqualification on   CCP §170.4
Judgment on the pleadings, jurisdiction as basis of motion for   CCP §438
Juvenile courts, exclusive jurisdiction of   CRC 5.510, 5.620
    Harassment or domestic violence proceedings brought against or initiated by minor, jurisdiction over   CCP §374.5
    Termination of juvenile court jurisdiction
        Nonminor dependents or wards in foster care   CRC 5.555
Labor disputes, limitation on enjoining acts relating to   CCP §527.3
Legally protected health care services
    Action for relief from abusive litigation infringing on protected activity   CC §§1798.306, 1798.308
Legal separation   Fam §§2010 to 2013
    Same sex marriages
        Residence requirements   Fam §2320
Limited civil cases
    Generally   CCP §85
    Amount in controversy   CCP §85
    Jurisdictional classification defined   CCP §32.5
    Long-Term Care, Health, Safety and Security Act, jurisdiction in actions brought pursuant to   CCP §86.1
    Original jurisdiction   CCP §86
    Reclassification generally (See within this heading, **"Reclassification of action"**)
    Small claims division   CCP §87
    Statutes relating to court's authority in limited and unlimited civil cases   CCP §89
    Unlimited civil case defined   CCP §88
Mandate
    Writs of mandate, certiorari and prohibition in supreme court or court of appeal   CCP §1085, CRC 8.485 to 8.493
Missing persons' estate, administration of   Pro §12403
Motions   CCP §1004
Motion to quash service of summons on ground of lack of   CCP §418.10, Fam §2012
Nazi regime, actions by victims of (See **NAI GERMANY**)

JURISDICTION—Cont.
Objection to jurisdiction CCP §§418.10, 418.11
Other states (See **OTHER STATES**)
Over parties
    Extends from service through subsequent proceedings CCP §410.50
    Record, jurisdiction sufficient to sustain CCP §1917
Particular persons, jurisdiction over
    Contract, persons liable on CCP §410.70
    Trustees and stockholders of corporation forfeiting charter CCP §410.60
Parties
    Extension of jurisdiction over parties from service to subsequent proceedings CCP §410.50
    Record, jurisdiction sufficient to sustain CCP §1917
Partition (See **PARTITION**)
Paternity actions
    Juvenile court jurisdiction CRC 5.510
Power of attorney, jurisdiction in actions involving (See **POWER OF ATTORNEY**)
Presumption of lawful exercise of Ev §666
Prohibition writs CCP §1103
Property settlement Fam §§2010 to 2013
Public administrators Pro §7601
Quieting title action CCP §760.040
Reclassification of action
    Appearance, filing for reclassification constituting CCP §1014
    Applicability of reclassification provisions CCP §403.010
    Commencement of reclassified action, deemed time of CCP §403.070
    Fees CCP §§403.050 to 403.060
    Procedure for reclassifying actions CCP §§403.020 to 403.040
    Review of reclassification order, writ of mandate for CCP §403.080
    Rules for reclassification, Judicial Council's authority to prescribe CCP §403.090
Related causes of action CCP §§426.30, 426.40
Severance of trial or action CRC 3.529
Simultaneous death, establishment of Pro §232
Small claims court (See **SMALL CLAIMS COURTS**)
Spousal support proceedings (See **SPOUSAL SUPPORT**)
Sufficiency of jurisdiction to sustain record CCP §1917
Superior courts CCP §86
    Appellate division jurisdiction on appeal CCP §77
    Child custody and care determinations
        Immigration and nationality act decisions CCP §155
    Limited civil cases CCP §§85 to 89
Support proceedings Fam §§2010 to 2013
    Child support (See **CHILD SUPPORT**)
    Spousal support (See **SPOUSAL SUPPORT**)
Surety bonds, jurisdiction for enforcement of liability on CCP §§996.420, 996.430
Tribal court civil money judgment act
    Objections
        Grounds for objection CCP §1737
Trusts (See **TRUSTS**)
Uniform Parentage Act Fam §7620
Uniform Transfers to Minors Act (See **UNIFORM TRANSFERS TO MINORS ACT**)
Unlawful detainer
    Motions to quash service for lack of jurisdiction CRC 3.1327
Unlimited civil case defined CCP §88
Unlimited civil cases
    Jurisdictional classification defined CCP §32.5
Validation proceedings CCP §862
Wages, hours, and working conditions
    Judgments, enforcement by labor commissioner
        Superior court jurisdiction CCP §690.020
Wholesale sales representatives, contract actions involving CC §1738.14
Will probate (See **WILL PROBATE**)

JURISPRUDENCE MAXIMS CC §§3509 to 3548

JURY
Additional instructions CCP §614
Additional jurors
    Selection and role CCP §234
    Substitution of alternate juror CCP §233
Addresses of jurors, disclosure of (See within this heading, "**Personal juror information**")
Adjournment of court during deliberations by CCP §617
Administration of estates, cases involving Pro §825
Admonishment CCP §611
Alternate jurors
    Selection and role CCP §234

JURY—Cont.
Alternate jurors—Cont.
    Substitution of CCP §233
Appellate rules, superior court appeals
    Misdemeanor appeals
        Record on appeal, juror-identifying information CRC 8.871
Applicability of chapter CCP §192
Attachment of juror CCP §209
Attendance
    Compelling attendance CCP §209
    One-hour notice by telephone, jurors to attend on CCP §213
    Per diem fee allowed for attendance CCP §215
Attorney professional conduct
    Contacts with judges, jurors, tribunal officials or employees, etc ProfC 3.5
Attorneys (See **ATTORNEYS**)
Availability of jurors on one-hour notice CCP §213
Bench trials (See **NONJURY TRIALS**)
Bias and prejudice
    Challenges to prospective jurors (See within this heading, "**Challenges**")
    Voir dire examination calculated to discover CCP §222.5
Blind persons
    Disabled persons generally (See within this heading, "**Disabled persons**")
Burden of proof, instructions on Ev §502
Capital punishment cases
    Challenge for cause based on conscientious objections to death penalty CCP §229
    Peremptory challenges
        Number CCP §231
Cause, challenges for (See within this heading, "**Challenges**")
Challenges CCP §§225 to 231.7
    Bias
        Actual bias CCP §225
        Prohibition against use of peremptory challenge CCP §231.7
    Death penalty cases
        Challenge for cause based on conscientious objections to death penalty CCP §229
        Peremptory challenges, number CCP §231
    Defined CCP §225
    Disability as grounds for CCP §228
    Expedited jury trials CCP §630.04
    For cause
        Actual bias CCP §225
        General disqualification, challenges for CCP §§225, 228
        Implied bias CCP §§225, 229
        Issue of challenge, court trying CCP §230
        Order of challenges CCP §227
    General disqualification of juror, challenges for CCP §§225, 228
    Implied bias CCP §§225, 229
    Individual jurors CCP §§225 to 231.7
        Procedure for challenge to CCP §226
    Order of challenges CCP §§226, 227
    Panel, challenge to CCP §225
    Peremptory challenges
        Alternate jurors CCP §234
        Expedited jury trials CCP §630.04
        Number of CCP §231
        Prohibited use of CCP §§231.5, 231.7
    Right of counsel to examine prospective jurors CCP §222.5
    Types and classes of CCP §225
Charge (See within this heading, "**Instructions**")
Citizenship, jury service as obligation of CCP §191
Closing argument (See **CLOSING ARGUMENT**)
Communications with jury or jurors
    Inclusion in record CRC 2.1030
    Post-trial discussions regarding deliberation or verdict CCP §206
    Telephone communications (See within this heading, "**Telephone communications**")
    With judge, preservation and inclusion in record CRC 2.1030
Compelling attendance CCP §209
Compensation and fees
    Advance jury fees CCP §631
    Alternate jurors CCP §234
    Appropriations for payment of fees CCP §215
    Court's general funds, payment of jury fees from CCP §631.2
    Demanding party, liability for jurors' fees by CCP §631.2
    Deposit of fees, notice
        Limitation on papers filed CRC 3.250
    Eminent domain cases CCP §631.5
    Functional budget categories CRC 10.810
    Juries of inquest CCP §235

JURY—Cont.
  Compensation and fees—Cont.
    Low-income jurors
      San Francisco low-income juror pilot program   CCP §240
    Mileage rate allowed   CCP §215
    Nonrefundable fee from parties to offset state's costs   CCP §631.1
      Settlement, continuance or waiver of jury not to affect obligation for fee   CCP §631.3
    One-hour notice, jurors required to attend on   CCP §213
    Per diem fee allowed for attendance   CCP §215
    Pilot program to study impact on juror diversity and participation   CCP §241
    Public transit, use of service   CCP §215
    Recovery as costs by prevailing party   CCP §1033.5
    Refunding when case settled or continued   CCP §631.3
    Standard jury fee   CCP §215
    Summons by sheriff   Gov §26745
    Waiver of trial by jury, failure to deposit as   CCP §631
  Complaints by jurors, receipt and response mechanism   CRC JudAdminStand 10.51
  Complex civil cases
    Notebooks
      Preparation for benefit of jurors   CRC 2.1032
  Conflict of interests
    Challenges generally (See within this heading, **"Challenges"**)
  Conservator and conservatee relationship, effect of (See **CONSERVATORS**)
  Conversation with third parties
    Contempt for violation   CCP §1209
  Coroner's inquest jury (See **JURIES OF INQUEST**)
  Costs
    Compensation and fees generally (See within this heading, **"Compensation and fees"**)
  Court defined   CCP §194
  Court officers and personnel
    Education of judicial branch
      Treatment of jurors, recommendations for appellate and trial court personnel   CRC 10.479
  Creation of master and qualified juror lists   CCP §198
  Creditor's suit   CCP §708.270
  Criminal trials
    Applicability of chapter   CCP §192
    Appropriations for payment of fees   CCP §215
    Challenges generally (See within this heading, **"Challenges"**)
    Death penalty cases
      Challenge for cause based on conscientious objections to death penalty   CCP §229
      Number of peremptory challenges   CCP §231
    Examination of prospective jurors   CCP §223
    Food and lodging for jurors   CCP §217
    Judges
      Comments on performance of jury   CRCSupp JudEthicsCanon 3
    Judicial administration standards   CRC JudAdminStand 4.30
    Number of peremptory challenges   CCP §231
    Peace officers as jurors, exclusion of   CCP §219
    Personal juror information, defendant's request for (See within this heading, **"Personal juror information"**)
    Post-trial discussion of deliberation or verdict with juror   CCP §206
    Pre-voir dire conference in criminal cases   CRC 4.200
    Unreasonable contact with juror   CCP §206
    Voir dire   CCP §223, CRC 4.201, CRC JudAdminStand 4.30
      Judicial administration standards of Judicial Council   CRC JudAdminStand 4.30
      Opening statement by counsel to panel   CRC 4.202
      Pre-voir dire conference   CRC 4.200
      Supplemental questioning   CRC 4.201
      Uninterrupted jury selection, judicial administration standards   CRC JudAdminStand 2.20
  Deaf and hard of hearing persons
    Assistive listening systems for hard-of-hearing persons   CC §54.8
    Eligibility for service   CCP §§203, 228
    Interpreters and other assistance   CC §54.8, CCP §224
  Death penalty cases
    Challenge for cause based on conscientious objections to death penalty   CCP §229
    Number of peremptory challenges   CCP §231
  Defective verdict, correction of   CCP §619
  Deferral of jury service   CCP §194, CRC 2.1008
    Scheduling accommodations   CRC 2.1004
  Definitions   CCP §194
  Deliberation
    Generally   CCP §613

JURY—Cont.
  Deliberation—Cont.
    Exhibits taken for use in   CCP §612
    Expedited jury trials   CCP §630.05
    Food and lodging for jurors   CCP §217
    Further information, return to court for   CCP §614
    Instructions to jury, availability of   CCP §612.5
    Judicial holiday, instructions given on   CCP §134
    Post-trial discussions with jurors regarding   CCP §206
    Provision and design of deliberation rooms   CCP §216
    Service provider for disabled juror during jury deliberations, presence of   CCP §224
    Verdict (See **VERDICT**)
  Demand for   CCP §631
  Department of Motor Vehicles list of licensed drivers and identification cardholders as source for selection of jurors   CCP §197
  Disabled persons
    Assistive listening systems for hard-of-hearing persons, use of   CC §54.8
    Challenges to   CCP §228
    Disability as ground for excuse   CRC 2.1008
      Permanent medical excuse from jury service   CRC 2.1009
    Eligibility of   CCP §203
    Service provider for disabled jurors, use of   CCP §224
  Discharge
    Discussion of deliberation or verdict with juror following   CCP §206
    Judicial holiday, discharge on   CCP §134
    Procedure when juror becomes ill or otherwise unable to perform duties   CCP §233
    Substitution of alternate juror   CCP §233
  Discriminatory basis for exclusion of juror   CCP §231.7
  Discussion of deliberation or verdict with juror prior to or following discharge of jury   CCP §206
  Disqualification of juror
    Challenges generally (See within this heading, **"Challenges"**)
  Dissemination of information
    Admonishment against conducting research, dissemination of information and conversation   CCP §611
      Contempt for violation   CCP §1209
  Documents taken to jury room   CCP §612
  Drawing and selection
    Lists (See within this heading, **"Juror lists"**)
    Uninterrupted jury selection, judicial policy of   CRC JudAdminStand 2.25
  Education of judicial branch
    Judges
      Additional education recommendations for certain judicial assignments   CRC 10.469
    Treatment of jurors, recommendations for appellate and trial court personnel   CRC 10.479
  Eligibility for jury service (See within this heading, **"Qualifications"**)
  Enforcement of judgments (See **ENFORCEMENT OF JUDGMENTS**)
  Examination of jurors
    Voir dire
      Criminal trials (See within this heading, **"Criminal trials"**)
      Generally (See within this heading, **"Voir dire"**)
  Exclusion of particular groups   CCP §231.7
  Excuse and exemption from service   CCP §204, CRC 2.1008
    Breastfeeding   CRC 2.1006
    Excused jurors defined   CCP §194
    Hardship   CRC 2.1008
    Jury commissioner shall hear excuses of jurors summoned   CCP §218
    Medical excuse
      Permanent medical excuse from jury service   CRC 2.1009
    Mother breastfeeding child, one-year deferral from jury service for   CRC 2.1006
    Standards for   CRC 2.1008
    Undue hardship   CCP §204, CRC 2.1008
    Writing and signed by juror, excuses shall be in   CCP §218
  Expedited jury trials
    Generally   CRC 3.1545 to 3.1553 (See **EXPEDITED JURY TRIALS**)
    Mandatory expedited jury trials (See **EXPEDITED JURY TRIALS**)
    Voluntary expedited jury trials   CCP §§630.01 to 630.11 (See **EXPEDITED JURY TRIALS**)
  Expedited jury trials, civil   CRC 3.1545 to 3.1553
  Fact issues determined by   CCP §592
  Failure to respond to jury commissioner inquiry, effect of   CCP §196
  Fees (See within this heading, **"Compensation and fees"**)
  Felons currently on parole, probation, etc
    Ineligibility to serve as juror   CCP §203
  Fines for failure to attend
    Motion to set aside sanctions imposed by default   CRC 2.1010
  Food and lodging for jurors   CCP §217

JURY—Cont.
Forcible entry and detainer CCP §1171
Formation of jury (See within this heading, **"Selection and formation"**)
Forms
    Expedited jury trial
        Judicial council legal forms CRCAppx A
    Questionnaires
        Judicial council legal forms CRCAppx A
Functional budget categories CRC 10.810
General disqualification of juror, challenges for CCP §§225, 228
Grand juries (See **GRAND JURIES**)
Guardian and ward relationship, effect of (See **GUARDIAN AND WARD**)
Guardianship (See **GUARDIAN AND WARD**)
Handicapped jurors (See within this heading, **"Disabled persons"**)
Hardship
    Excuse from jury duty CRC 2.1008
Health Care Decision Law, unavailability of jury trial under Pro §4754
Hearing-impaired
    Disabled persons generally (See within this heading, **"Disabled persons"**)
Identifying information, redaction of from documents in criminal appeal records CRC 8.332
    Death penalty appeals CRC 8.610, 8.611
    Misdemeanor appeals CRC 8.871
Illness of juror, procedure in event of CCP §233
Immediate summons, service and attachment of persons for completion of jury panel CCP §211
Impasse
    Assisting jury at impasse CRC 2.1036
Implied bias
    Challenges generally (See within this heading, **"Challenges"**)
Information requests concerning juror (See within this heading, **"Personal juror information"**)
Inquest, juries of (See **JURIES OF INQUEST**)
Instructions CCP §608
    Additional instructions CCP §614
    Citation of authorities supporting proposed instructions CRC 2.1055
    Civil cases, applicable rules CRC 3.1580
    Copy of instructions, jury request for CCP §612.5
    Counsel serving CCP §607a
    Form of proposed instruction CRC 2.1055
    Gender-neutral language, use of CRC 2.1058
    Impasse
        Assisting jury at impasse CRC 2.1036
    Judge receiving copy of CCP §607a
    Judicial council jury instructions CRC 2.1050
        Advisory committee on civil jury instructions CRC 10.58
    Judicial holiday, instructions given on CCP §134
    Opposing counsel, service on CCP §607a
    Preinstruction CRC 2.1035
    Proposed instructions CCP §607a, CRC 2.1055
    Service provider for disabled jurors, court instructions concerning CCP §224
    Special instructions CCP §609
        Proposed instructions CRC 2.1055
Instructions, criminal cases
    Citation of authorities supporting proposed instructions CRC 2.1055
    Death penalty
        Lists of appearances, exhibits, motions and jury instructions CRC 4.230, CRCAppx A
    Form of proposed instruction CRC 2.1055
    Gang-related crimes, instruction concerning unavailability as witness of decedent who gave sworn statement concerning Ev §1231.4
    Gender-neutral language, use of CRC 2.1058
    Judicial council jury instructions CRC 2.1050
        Advisory committee on criminal jury instructions CRC 10.59
    Proposed instructions CRC 2.1055
    Special jury instructions
        Proposed instructions CRC 2.1055
Issues of law and fact in jury trials CCP §592, Ev §312
Jails
    Ineligible to serve as juror CCP §203
Judges
    Comments by on performance of jury CRCSupp JudEthicsCanon 3
    Communications between jury and judge, preservation and inclusion in record CRC 2.1030
    Discuss deliberation and verdict, informing jurors of right to CCP §206
    Education of judicial branch
        Additional education recommendations for certain judicial assignments CRC 10.469
    Initial examination of prospective jurors CCP §222.5
    Jury commissioner, appointment of CCP §195

JURY—Cont.
Judges—Cont.
    Reading of testimony previously received in evidence, presence of judge during CCP §614.5
    Separate panel for each judge CCP §201
    Stipulation to examine prospective jurors outside judge's presence CCP §222.5
Judicial administration standards
    Complaints from jurors, receiving and responding to CRC JudAdminStand 10.51
    Master jury list, updating CRC JudAdminStand 10.31
    Voir dire
        Civil cases CRC JudAdminStand 3.25
        Criminal cases CRC JudAdminStand 4.30
        Uninterrupted jury selection, recommendation of CRC JudAdminStand 2.20
Judicial notice, instructions Ev §457
Juror lists
    Counties where superior court sessions held in place other than county seat CCP §198.5
    Creation of master and qualified juror lists CCP §198
    Definitions CCP §194
    Updating master jury list CRC JudAdminStand 10.31
Juror orientation CCP §214
Juror panels
    Challenge to CCP §225
    Immediate summons, service and attachment of persons for completion of CCP §211
    Perjury acknowledgment and agreement CCP §232
    Random selection of CCP §219
    Separate panel for each judge CCP §201
    Trial jury panel defined CCP §194
Juror pools
    Defined CCP §194
Juror questions CRC 2.1033
Jury assembly facilities CCP §216
Jury commissioner (See **JURY COMMISSIONER**)
Jury lists
    Exclusion of particular groups CCP §231.7
Length of jury service CRC 2.1002
Liability issue, trial of CCP §598
Low-income jurors
    San Francisco low-income juror pilot program CCP §240
Mandamus proceedings CCP §1090
Master jury lists
    Defined CCP §194
    Updating CRC JudAdminStand 10.31
Mechanical device, selection by CCP §202
Media coverage of trial, restrictions on CRC 1.150
Mental health
    Information provided to jurors CCP §242
Mistrial for failure to reach verdict by CCP §616
Mother breastfeeding child, one-year deferral from jury service for CRC 2.1006
Motion to set aside sanctions imposed by default
    Failure to respond to jury summons CRC 2.1010
Name and address of juror (See within this heading, **"Personal juror information"**)
New trial, jury misconduct as grounds for CCP §657
Nonjury trials (See **NONJURY TRIALS**)
Notebooks
    Complex civil cases, preparation for benefit of jurors CRC 2.1032
Note-taking
    Permitted CRC 2.1031
Notice
    Challenge to jury panel CCP §225
    One-hour notice by telephone, jurors to attend on CCP §213
    Summons (See within this heading, **"Summoning jurors"**)
    Unsealing of juror information records, notice to former juror of hearing on petition for CCP §237
Number of jurors CCP §220
Number of peremptory challenges CCP §231
Number of votes required CCP §613
Oath sworn by jurors CCP §232
Objections to juror
    Challenges generally (See within this heading, **"Challenges"**)
One-day/one-trial rule for length of jury service CRC 2.1002
One-hour notice by telephone, jurors to attend on CCP §213
Opening statements
    Voir dire CCP §222.5
Orientation of jurors CCP §214
Panels (See within this heading, **"Juror panels"**)

JURY—Cont.
  Peace officers
    Criminal proceedings, exclusion as jurors in   CCP §219
    Scheduling accommodations   CRC 2.1004
      Judicial council to provide rule for   CCP §219.5
  Penalty for failure to respond to jury summons   CCP §209
    Motion to set aside sanctions imposed by default   CRC 2.1010
  Peremptory challenges (See within this heading, "**Challenges**")
  Personal juror information
    Post-trial request by defendant for   CCP §206
    Public disclosure of names of qualified jurors   CCP §237
    Sealing court records on juror information, procedure for   CCP §237
  Photographing of jurors   CRC 1.150
  Polling jury   CCP §618
  Potential jurors
    Defined   CCP §194
    Sealing of record of identifying information   CRC 8.332
      Death penalty appeals, protection of juror information   CRC 8.610, 8.611
  Power of attorney (See **POWER OF ATTORNEY**)
  Preinstruction   CRC 2.1035
  Pre-voir dire conference in criminal cases   CRC 4.200
  Prior service as juror or witness in previous action as grounds for challenge
    Excuse based on prior service   CRC 2.1008
  Prisoners
    Ineligible to serve as juror   CCP §203
  Probate proceedings (See **WILL PROBATE**)
  Proposed instructions   CCP §607a, CRC 2.1055
  Prospective juror defined   CCP §194
  Public officers and employees
    Compensation of public employee at regular rate
    Fee for juror service not paid   CCP §215
  Qualifications
    Alternate jurors   CCP §234
    Challenge for general disqualification of juror   CCP §§225, 228
    Disabled persons (See within this heading, "**Disabled persons**")
    Eligibility generally   CCP §203
    Exceptions to eligibility   CCP §203
    Failure to respond to jury commissioner inquiry, effect of   CCP §196
    Jury commissioner inquiry into   CCP §196
  Qualified juror
    Defined   CCP §194
    Public disclosure of names of   CCP §237
  Questionnaires
    Format
      Civil cases   CRC JudAdminStand 3.25
    Forms
      Judicial council legal forms   CRCAppx A
    Jury commissioner's inquiries into qualifications   CCP §196
    Master jury list used for purpose of mailing   CCP §198
    Qualifying prospective jurors and for management of jury system, use for   CCP §205
    Voir dire process, use to assist in   CCP §205
      Time to evaluate responses   CCP §222.5
  Questions from jurors   CRC 2.1033
  Questions of fact
    Determination by jury   CCP §592, Ev §312
    Pleadings, question of fact not put in issue by   CCP §309
  Random selection
    Creation of master and qualified juror lists   CCP §198
    Juror panels   CCP §219
    Policy of state   CCP §191
    Random defined   CCP §194
    Sources for selection   CCP §197
    Voir dire, random selection for   CCP §222
  Referees, previous service as juror as grounds for disqualification of   CCP §641
  Registered voters list as source for selection of jurors   CCP §197
  Replevin, finding value in   CCP §627
  Request for special findings by   CRC 3.1580
  Research
    Admonishment against conducting research, dissemination of information and conversation   CCP §611
      Contempt for violation   CCP §1209
  Retrial of action where jury discharged without rendering verdict   CCP §616
  Sealing court records on juror information, procedure for   CCP §237
  Selection and formation
    Alternate jurors   CCP §234
    Applicability of chapter   CCP §192
    Disabled persons (See within this heading, "**Disabled persons**")

JURY—Cont.
  Selection and formation—Cont.
    Examination of prospective jurors
      Voir dire, criminal trials (See within this heading, "**Criminal trials**")
      Voir dire generally (See within this heading, "**Voir dire**")
    Juries of inquest   CCP §235
    Juror lists (See within this heading, "**Juror lists**")
    Mechanical device, selection by   CCP §202
    Panels (See within this heading, "**Juror panels**")
    Questionnaires (See within this heading, "**Questionnaires**")
    Random selection (See within this heading, "**Random selection**")
    Representative cross section of population, selection from   CCP §§197, 205
    Sources for selection   CCP §197
    Summons (See within this heading, "**Summoning jurors**")
    Voir dire
      Criminal trials (See within this heading, "**Criminal trials**")
      Generally (See within this heading, "**Voir dire**")
  Separate panel for each judge   CCP §201
  Service provider for disabled jurors, use of   CCP §224
  Sex offender registration
    Ineligibility for jury service   CCP §203
  Sheriff's inquest jury (See **JURIES OF INQUEST**)
  Show cause orders as to disobedience of summonses   CCP §209
    Motion to set aside sanctions imposed by default   CRC 2.1010
  Sliding scale recovery agreements disclosed to   CCP §877.5
  Smoking in court facilities   CRC 10.504
  Stipulation to examine prospective jurors outside judge's presence   CCP §222.5
  Submitting special issue to jury   CCP §309
  Summoning jurors
    Contents   CCP §210
    Failure to respond, penalty for   CCP §209
    Fees for   Gov §26745
    General procedure   CCP §208
    Immediate summons for completion of jury panel   CCP §211
    Motion to set aside sanctions imposed by default   CRC 2.1010
    Orders for   CCP §§209, 211
    Postponement option for breast-feeding mothers, Judicial Council standardized jury summons with   CCP §210.5
    Response to jury commissioner concerning   CCP §196
    Summons list defined   CCP §194
    Time for mailing   CCP §208
  Tax filers list as source for selection of jurors   CCP §197
  Telephone communications
    Modification of date, time or place of appearance   CCP §208
    One-hour notice by telephone, jurors to attend on   CCP §213
    Summons directing jurors to call for instructions for appearance   CCP §210
  Telephone directories as source for selection of jurors   CCP §197
  Third parties, conversations with   CCP §611
  Time period for jury service, limitations on   CRC 2.1002
  Travel expenses   CCP §§215, 631, 631.5
  Trial court operations fund
    Food and lodging of jurors   CCP §217
  Trial jurors defined   CCP §194
  Trial jury panels
    Challenges to panel generally   CCP §225
    Defined   CCP §194
    Juror panels generally (See within this heading, "**Juror panels**")
  Trusts, right to jury trial in disputes involving   Pro §825
  Types of juries   CCP §193
  Undue hardship
    Grounds for exemption from jury service   CCP §204
    What constitutes   CRC 2.1008
  Uninterrupted selection of jury, judicial policy of   CRC JudAdminStand 2.20
  Unlawful detainer trials   CCP §1171
  Unreasonable contact with juror   CCP §206
  Utility company lists as source for selection of jurors   CCP §197
  Verdict (See **VERDICT**)
  View, presence of trier of fact at   CCP §651
  Voir dire   CCP §222.5, CRC 3.1540
    Bias and prejudice, examination calculated to discover   CCP §222.5
    Criminal trials, voir dire at (See within this heading, "**Criminal trials**")
    Discretion of court, exercise of   CCP §§222.5, 223
    Eminent domain cases   CRC JudAdminStand 3.25
    Examination by counsel and court
      Civil cases   CRC JudAdminStand 3.25
    Expedited jury trials   CRC 3.1549
    Improper question   CCP §222.5
    Judicial administration standards of judicial council
      Civil cases   CRC JudAdminStand 3.25
      Criminal cases   CRC JudAdminStand 4.30

JURY—Cont.
Voir dire —Cont.
    Judicial administration standards of judicial council—Cont.
        Uninterrupted jury selection, recommendation of   CRC JudAdminStand 2.20
    Jury fees, liability of party demanding trial by jury for payment of   CCP §631.2
    Opening statements   CCP §222.5
    Order provided by panel list, seating prospective jurors in   CCP §222
    Perjury acknowledgment and agreement   CCP §232
    Pre-voir dire conference
        Civil cases   CRC JudAdminStand 3.25
    Questionnaires   CCP §205
        Time to evaluate responses   CCP §222.5
    Random selection for   CCP §222
    Stipulation to examine prospective jurors outside judge's presence   CCP §222.5
Waiver of jury trial
    Generally   CCP §631
Will probate, contest of   Pro §825
Witnesses
    Calling juror to testify at present trial, procedure for   Ev §704
    Challenge, juror as witness in previous action as grounds for   CCP §229

JURY CHALLENGES (See JURY)

JURY COMMISSIONER
Appointment of   CCP §195
Authority of   CCP §195
Challenges to jury panel, services of legal counsel in connection with   CCP §225
Court operations costs, salaries and benefits as   CRC 10.810
Creation of master and qualified juror lists   CCP §198
Deputy jury commissioners   CCP §195
Duties and powers   CCP §196
Excuses of jurors summoned, jury commissioner shall hear   CCP §218
Failure to respond to inquiry, effect of   CCP §196
Grand jury
    Demographic data on regular grand jurors
        Gathering and summarizing, duties of commissioner   CRC 10.625
Information acquired by   CCP §196
Juries of inquest, provides prospective jurors for   CCP §235
Juror orientation   CCP §214
Oaths, power to administer   CCP §196
Qualifications of potential jurors, inquiry into   CCP §196
Random selection of names of prospective jurors   CCP §198
Recordkeeping requirements   CCP §207
Response to inquiry or summons   CCP §196
Responsibility for management of jury systems   CCP §§191, 195
Salary   CCP §195
Superior court administrator or executive officer serving as ex officio jury commissioner   CCP §195
Travel expenses allowed   CCP §196

JURY INSTRUCTIONS (See JURY)

JURY LISTS (See JURY)

JUSTICE COURTS
Chambers, powers and duties of judges at   CCP §167
Contempt orders (See CONTEMPT)
Costs
    Generally (See COSTS)
Fax machines, use of (See FAX FILING AND SERVICE)
Filing
    Fax machines, use of (See FAX FILING AND SERVICE)
Jury (See JURY)
Law and motion proceedings (See LAW AND MOTION PROCEEDINGS)
Local rules
    Sanctions for noncompliance   CCP §575.2
Small claims courts (See SMALL CLAIMS COURTS)
Transcripts
    Court reporters generally (See COURT REPORTERS)

JUSTICE, DEPARTMENT OF
Check cashers, registration of   CC §1789.37
Conviction of crime, report by courts concerning   CRC 4.320
Domestic violence protective orders, notification of   Fam §§6380, 6385
Information Practices Act procedures   CC §1798.23

JUSTICE OF THE PEACE
Generally (See JUSTICE COURTS)

JUSTICES
Courts of appeal (See COURTS OF APPEAL)
Supreme Court (See SUPREME COURT, CALIFORNIA)

JUVENILE COURTS   CCP §917.7
Adoption of child
    Interstate compact on placement of children   Fam §§7900 to 7913
        Children covered by compact   Fam §7907.5
    Juvenile rules (See JUVENILE RULES)
    Orders
        Judicial council form   CRCAppx A
    Relative adoptions
        Generally   Fam §8714.5
        Kinship adoption agreement with birth parent   CRC 5.451
        Kinship adoption agreement with siblings   CRC 5.451
        Postadoption contact agreement with birth parent   Fam §8616.5
    Relinquishment by birth parent of child subject to dependency proceedings, notice of   Fam §8700
    Reports submitted to court   Fam §8715
    Statewide exchange system, registration of approved family with   Fam §8710.3
Appeals
    Extraordinary writ, petition for review by   CRC 8.454, 8.456
    Juvenile case appeals   CRC 5.585 to 5.595
        Supreme court and courts of appeal   CRC 8.400 to 8.474
    Limited rights to appeal
        Access to juvenile records, judicial council forms   CRCAppx A
Arrest
    Sealing of arrest records
        Forms, judicial council   CRCAppx A
        Order on prosecutor request for access   CRCAppx A
        Prosecuting attorney request to access sealed juvenile case files   CRC 5.860
Attorneys
    Delinquency proceedings
        Responsibility of children's counsel in delinquency proceedings   CRC 5.663
    Dependency proceedings, collection for reimbursement of appointed attorneys
        Guidelines for juvenile dependency counsel collections program   CRCAppx F
    Discrimination, prohibition against in appointments   CRC JudAdminStand 5.40
    Representation and compensation standards   CRC JudAdminStand 5.40
Certification to juvenile court
    Superior court to juvenile court   CRC 4.116
Child protection workers, extent of immunity of   Gov §820.21
Child welfare services case plan, effect of parent signing or accepting services under   Ev §1228.1
Claims against public agencies (See CLAIMS AGAINST PUBLIC ENTITIES AND EMPLOYEES)
Competence inquiry
    COVID-19, emergency rule   CRCAppx I Emer Rule 7
Computer access to juvenile court records
    Research
        Release of case file information for research   CRC 5.552
Continuances
    Educational and developmental services decisionmaking rights of children   CRC 5.651
Court-appointed counsel
    Child's counsel, responsibilities in delinquency proceedings   CRC 5.663
Court reporters   CCP §274a
Criminal prosecutions, certification to juvenile court   CRC 4.116
Custody of child
    Juvenile rules (See JUVENILE RULES)
Dependent child of court proceedings (See DEPENDENT CHILDREN)
Detention
    Dependency (See DEPENDENT CHILDREN)
    Wardship (See JUVENILE WARDSHIP PROCEEDINGS)
Disposition hearings
    Dependency (See DEPENDENT CHILDREN)
    Wardship (See JUVENILE WARDSHIP PROCEEDINGS)
Domestic violence proceedings involving minor party, jurisdiction over   CCP §374.5
Educational rights of children   CRC JudAdminStand 5.40
    Educational rights holders
        Judicial council forms   CRCAppx A
Ethics code for court employees, adoption of   CRC JudAdminStand 10.16
Expert witnesses by court-appointment, compensation of   Ev §731
Fitness hearings
    Wardship (See JUVENILE WARDSHIP PROCEEDINGS)

JUVENILE COURTS—Cont.
Forms
    Judicial council legal forms   CRCAppx A
Guardians
    Termination of   CRC 5.620
Harassment proceedings brought against or initiated by minor, jurisdiction over   CCP §374.5
Health of minor
    Administration of psychotropic medication to ward of court
        Forms, judicial council   CRCAppx A
Hearing officers
    Law practice of subordinate judicial officers   CRC 10.702
        Ethical provisions   CRCSupp JudEthicsCanon 6
    Qualifications and education of subordinate judicial officers   CRC 10.701
Hearings
    Educational and developmental services decisionmaking rights of children   CRC 5.651
    Juvenile rules (See **JUVENILE RULES**)
Immigration status
    Special immigrant juvenile status
        Forms, judicial council   CRCAppx A
        Interpreters in proceedings to determine special immigrant juvenile status   Ev §757
        Request for orders, family rules   CRC 5.130
Immunity of social workers and child protection workers, extent of   Gov §820.21
Initial hearing
    Dependency (See **DEPENDENT CHILDREN**)
Injunction against parent, guardian or other member of child's household
    Firearm relinquishment procedures
        Forms for firearm relinquishment   CRCAppx A
Judges
    Education of judges and subordinate judicial officers
        Domestic violence issues   CRC 10.464
    Judicial administration standards for judges assigned to   CRC JudAdminStand 5.40
Judicial administration standards
    Assignment of judges, guidelines for   CRC JudAdminStand 5.40
    Attorney representation, guidelines for   CRC JudAdminStand 5.40
    Resource guidelines of National Council of Juvenile and Family Court Judges, recommendation of   CRC JudAdminStand 5.45
Jurisdiction
    Transition jurisdiction
        Forms, judicial council   CRCAppx A
Jurisdiction hearings
    Dependency (See **DEPENDENT CHILDREN**)
    Wardship (See **JUVENILE WARDSHIP PROCEEDINGS**)
Modification of orders
    Removal of minor from parental custody, hearing requirements for
        Notice   CRC 5.565
Orders and decrees
    Stay of   CCP §917.7
Out-of-county placement   CRC 5.614
    Judicial council legal forms   CRCAppx A
Out-of-state placement
    Out-of-county placements generally   CRC 5.614
        Judicial council legal forms   CRCAppx A
Performance measurement
    Dependency court performance   CRC 5.505
Permanency planning
    Dependency (See **DEPENDENT CHILDREN**)
Petition
    Dependency (See **DEPENDENT CHILDREN**)
    Juvenile rules (See **JUVENILE RULES**)
    Sealing of records
        Forms, judicial council   CRCAppx A
    Wardship (See **JUVENILE WARDSHIP PROCEEDINGS**)
Placement facilities
    Community treatment facilities
        Hearings, review, etc, of placement   CRC 5.618
    Out-of-county placements   CRC 5.614
        Judicial council legal forms   CRCAppx A
    Short-term residential therapeutic program
        Hearings, review, etc, of placement   CRC 5.618
Polygraph evidence, exclusion of   Ev §351.1
Priority of juvenile appeals   CCP §45
Probation officers
    Family finding and notice performed by social worker or probation officer   CRC 5.637
    Records of juvenile court, disclosure of
        Research, release of case file information   CRC 5.552

JUVENILE COURTS—Cont.
Psychiatric residential treatment facility, admission to
    Forms, judicial council   CRCAppx A
Psychotropic medication, administration to ward of court
    Forms, judicial council   CRCAppx A
Records
    Criminal court convictions
        Order on prosecutor request for access   CRCAppx A
        Prosecuting attorney request to access sealed juvenile case files   CRC 5.860
    Research, release of case file information   CRC 5.552
    Sealing
        Access to sealed juvenile files   CRCAppx A
        Order on prosecutor request for access   CRCAppx A
        Prosecuting attorney request to access sealed juvenile case files   CRC 5.860
Referees and referee proceedings
    Juvenile rules (See **JUVENILE RULES**)
    Law practice of subordinate judicial officers   CRC 10.702
        Ethical provisions   CRCSupp JudEthicsCanon 6
    Qualifications and education of subordinate judicial officers   CRC 10.701
Relatives
    Adoption by relatives (See, within this heading, "**Adoption of child**")
Removal from parental custody
    Court-ordered removal, placement following
        Out-of-county placements   CRC 5.614, CRCAppx A
    Modification of removal orders, hearing requirements for
        Notice   CRC 5.565
    Out-of-county placement on   CRC 5.614
        Judicial council legal forms   CRCAppx A
    Return to custody   CRC 5.684
Reporters   CCP §274a
Resource guidelines, child abuse and neglect cases   CRC JudAdminStand 5.45
Rightfully present parties
    Presence of child   CRC 5.534
Role of court   CRC JudAdminStand 5.40
Rules of court
    Juvenile rules generally   CRC 5.500 to 5.840, CRC JudAdminStand 2.20 (See **JUVENILE RULES**)
Service of papers
    Request for sheriff to serve papers   CRCAppx A
Social workers
    Immunity, extent of   Gov §820.21
Stay of order or judgment   CCP §917.7
Superior courts (See **SUPERIOR COURTS**)
Temporary custody
    Probation officer, duty of
        Family finding and notice performed by social worker or probation officer   CRC 5.637
Termination of parental rights
    Juvenile rules (See **JUVENILE RULES**)
Transcripts   CCP §274a
Visitation rights
    Adoption by relatives
        Kinship agreement in conjunction with   CRC 5.451
        Postadoption contact agreement in conjunction with   Fam §8616.5
Writs and levies
    Special instructions, form of attachment   CRCAppx A

JUVENILE DELINQUENCY
Attorneys at law
    Juvenile court rules
        Responsibilities of children's counsel in delinquency proceedings   CRC 5.663
        Training requirements for children's counsel   CRC 5.664
Forms
    Judicial council legal forms   CRCAppx A
Hearings
    COVID-19, emergency rule   CRCAppx I Emer Rule 7
Judges
    Education of judges and subordinate judicial officers
        Domestic violence issues   CRC 10.464
Juvenile probation officer (See **PROBATION**)
Marital privilege, waiver   Ev §972
Orders
    COVID-19, emergency rule   CRCAppx I Emer Rule 7
Placement of delinquent children in institution in another state   Fam §7908
Placement under Interstate Compact   CRC 5.616
Transition jurisdiction
    Modification to transition jurisdiction, older than 17 years 5 months   CRC 5.811
Ward of court (See **JUVENILE WARDSHIP PROCEEDINGS**)

JUVENILE FACILITIES
Child support
    Suspension of orders or judgments
        Incarceration or institutionalization of obligee   Fam §4007.5
Commitment to
    Dangerous persons, extensions of commitment
        Appeal from order of civil commitment   CRC 8.483
Dangerous offender
    Extending detention beyond sentenced time
        Appeal from order of civil commitment   CRC 8.483
Detention in juvenile halls and other facilities
    Grounds   CRC 5.676
    Hearings   CRC 5.670, 5.672
    Indian children
        Active efforts   CRC 5.678
        Evidence required for detention of Indian child   CRC 5.676
        Findings necessary for detention   CRC 5.674, 5.678
        Placement preferences   CRC 5.678
    Marital privilege, waiver   Ev §§972, 986
    Prerequisites   CRC 5.674
    Rehearings   CRC 5.678
    Sealing arrest records of juvenile delinquents
        Forms, judicial council   CRCAppx A
        Order on prosecutor request for access   CRCAppx A
        Prosecuting attorney request to access sealed juvenile case files   CRC 5.860
Diagnostic and treatment centers
    Temporary commitment   CRC 5.782
Escheat of assets after death of inmate   CCP §1448
Exemption for funds of incarcerated judgment debtors   CCP §704.090
Extended detention of dangerous persons
    Appeal from order of civil commitment   CRC 8.483
Psychiatric residential treatment facility, admission to
    Form, judicial council   CRCAppx A
Psychotropic medication, standards for administration
    Forms, judicial council   CRCAppx A
Remittitur to   CRC 8.272
Secure youth treatment facilities   CRC 5.804 to 5.808
    Adjusting baseline term   CRC 5.806
    Baseline term   CRC 5.804, 5.806
    Commitment to facility
        Adjusting baseline term   CRC 5.806
        Baseline term   CRC 5.804, 5.806
        Grounds   CRC 5.804
        Individualized rehabilitation plans   CRC 5.804
        Maximum term of confinement   CRC 5.804
        Offense-based classification matrix   CRC 5.806
    Discharge from facility   CRC 5.808
    Offense-based classification matrix   CRC 5.806
    Progress review hearing   CRC 5.804
        Adjusting baseline term   CRC 5.806
        Process for progress review   CRC 5.807
    Transfers
        Less restrictive programs   CRC 5.807

JUVENILE HALL
Superior court holding session in judicial district in which juvenile hall located   CCP §73e

JUVENILE OFFENDERS
Aerosol paint containers, offenses involving
    Verification of age for sale of age-restricted products   CC §1798.99.1
Appeals
    Advisement of rights   CRC 5.590
    Stay pending appeal
        Conditions   CRC 5.595
Attorneys
    Children's counsel, responsibilities in delinquency cases   CRC 5.663
Competence inquiry
    COVID-19, emergency rule   CRCAppx I Emer Rule 7
Criminal proceedings, suspension of and certification to juvenile court   CRC 4.116
Disposition hearing after conviction as adult   CRC 4.510
Prosecution as adult
    Postconviction fitness hearing   CRC 4.510
    Sentencing upon conviction   CRC 4.510
Reverse remand of juvenile convicted as adult   CRC 4.510
Sex offender registration
    Sealing of records
        Order on prosecutor request for access   CRCAppx A

JUVENILE OFFENDERS—Cont.
Sex offender registration—Cont.
    Sealing of records—Cont.
        Prosecuting attorney request to access sealed juvenile case files   CRC 5.860

JUVENILE RULES   CRC 5.500 to 5.840
Admission of petition allegations
    Dependent child of court proceedings   CRC 5.674
    Ward of court proceedings   CRC 5.754, 5.778
Adoption of child   CRC 5.706 to 5.740
    Counsel for child, CASA programs   CRC 5.655
    Dependent children   CRC 5.706 to 5.740
    Hague adoption convention, adoptions under   CRC 5.490 to 5.492
    Intercountry adoptions   CRC 5.490 to 5.493
    Interstate Compact on Placement of Children   CRC 5.616
    Native Americans
        Involuntary placements, rules governing   CRC 5.480 to 5.488 (See **INDIAN CHILD WELFARE ACT INVOLUNTARY PLACEMENTS**)
    Postadoption contact agreements   CRC 5.451
    Prospective adoptive parents
        Designation   CRC 5.726
        Emergency removal   CRC 5.728
        Removal from, proposed   CRC 5.727
    Review hearings on adoption   CRC 5.740
    Wards for adoption, procedure for freeing   CRC 5.825
Appeals   CRC 5.585 to 5.595
    Adoption of child
        Prospective adoptive parents, removal from   CRC 5.727
    Representation of child on appeal   CRC 5.661
    Review by appeal   CRC 5.585
    Right to appeal
        Notice of rights   CRC 5.590
    Stay pending appeal
        Conditions   CRC 5.595
Appearance
    Citation to appear, issuance of   CRC 5.526
    Persons entitled to appear   CRC 5.530
    Subpoena powers   CRC 5.526
    Telephone appearances   CRC 3.672, 5.531
        Nonminor dependents, retention of jurisdiction   CRC 3.672, 5.900
Applicability of provisions   CRC 5.501
Appointment
    CASA volunteers, requirements   CRC 5.655
    Court-appointed attorney   CRC 5.534
    Referees, appointment of   CRC 5.536
Approaching majority review hearings   CRC 5.707
Arrest warrants, issuance of   CRC 5.526
Attorneys at law
    Appeals
        Representation of child on appeal   CRC 5.661
    Delinquency proceedings
        Responsibilities of children's counsel in delinquency proceedings   CRC 5.663
        Training requirements for children's counsel   CRC 5.664
    Electronic service
        Consent by child, consultation with and notification by attorney   CRC 5.523
Bailiffs, presence at proceedings   CRC 5.530
CASA programs, requirements   CRC 5.655
Child abuse and neglect
    Witnesses, immunity   CRC 5.548
Child custody
    Domestic violence
        Communication protocol for domestic violence and child custody orders   CRC 5.445
    Exclusive jurisdiction of juvenile court   CRC 5.510
    Orders   CRC 5.620
        Termination of juvenile proceeding or probate court guardianship proceeding, orders following   CRC 5.475
    Termination of jurisdiction
        Orders as to custody or visitation   CRC 5.700
    Visitation   CRC 5.695
    Wardship, disposition hearings
        Orders determining custody or visitation   CRC 5.790
Citation to appear   CRC 5.526
Civil rules
    Applicability in family, juvenile and probate cases in superior court   CRC 3.10
    Generally   CRC 1.4, 3.1 to 3.2240

JUVENILE RULES—Cont.
  Clerical errors, correction of CRC 5.560
  Commencement of proceedings CRC 5.510 to 5.526
  Commitment orders, hearing on CRC 5.580
  Community treatment facility placements
    Hearings, review, etc CRC 5.618
  Competence of child before court, inquiry into CRC 5.643
    Evaluation as to competence CRC 5.645
  Condition of sentence CRC 5.790
  Confidentiality of records CRC 5.552
    Adoption of child, prospective adoptive parent proceedings
      Designations CRC 5.726
      Emergency removals from prospective adoptive parents CRC 5.728
      Removal from prospective adoptive parents CRC 5.727
    Deceased child, release of juvenile case file CRC 5.553
  Consent
    Electronic service, consent by child CRC 5.523
  Conservators
    Indians, involuntary placements
      Indian Child Welfare Act, rules governing CRC 5.480 to 5.488
      (See **INDIAN CHILD WELFARE ACT INVOLUNTARY PLACEMENTS**)
  Construction of provisions CRC 5.501
  Continuances CRC 5.550
    Educational and developmental services decisionmaking rights of children CRC 5.651
    Restraining orders
      Dependent child of court proceedings CRC 5.630
  Counsel
    Appeals
      Representation of child on appeal CRC 5.661
    CASA programs CRC 5.655
    Competency standards, dependency proceedings CRC 5.660
    Doubt as to child's capacity to cooperate with counsel CRC 5.643
    Right to and appointment of counsel CRC 5.534
  County counsel, appearance by CRC 5.530
  Court-appointed special advocates (CASA) CRC 5.655
  Court reporters CRC 5.532
  Criminal history information records CRC 5.552
  Cross-examination, right to CRC 5.534
    Detention hearing in dependent child of court proceedings CRC 5.674
  Custody of children
    Indian Child Welfare Act, compliance with
      Involuntary placements CRC 5.480 to 5.488 (See **INDIAN CHILD WELFARE ACT INVOLUNTARY PLACEMENTS**)
  Deceased child
    Juvenile case file of deceased child, release CRC 5.553
  De facto parents
    Defined CRC 5.502
    Presence of CRC 5.534
  Definitions CRC 5.502
  Delinquent children
    Attorneys in delinquency cases
      Responsibilities of children's counsel in delinquency proceedings CRC 5.663
      Training requirements for children's counsel CRC 5.664
    Modification to transition jurisdiction, older than 17 years 5 months CRC 5.811
      Forms, judicial council CRCAppx A
    Placement under interstate compact CRC 5.616
  Dependent children
    Indian Child Welfare Act
      Involuntary placements, rules governing CRC 5.480 to 5.488 (See **INDIAN CHILD WELFARE ACT INVOLUNTARY PLACEMENTS**)
  Discovery CRC 5.546
  Disposition
    Dependency proceedings CRC 5.690 to 5.705
    Wardship proceedings CRC 5.785 to 5.808
  District attorney
    Appearance CRC 5.530
    Dependency proceedings, district attorney representing petitioner in CRC 5.530
    Discretion whether to file petition CRC 5.520
    Mandatory referrals CRC 5.514
  Domestic violence
    Child custody
      Communication protocol for domestic violence and child custody orders CRC 5.445

JUVENILE RULES—Cont.
  Education
    Educational and developmental services decisionmaking rights of children CRC 5.651
    Educational rights holders
      Appointment CRC 5.650, 5.790
      Defined CRC 5.502
      Identification of holder CRC 5.649
      Orders concerning rights holder and educational decisionmaking CRC 5.649
      Powers and duties of holders CRC 5.650
      Qualifications CRC 5.650
      Training CRC 5.650
      Transfer of parent's or guardian's educational rights to rights holder CRC 5.650
    Limitations on parental control CRC 5.790
      Educational rights holder CRC 5.502, 5.534, 5.650
      Identification of holder CRC 5.649
      Orders concerning rights holder and educational decisionmaking CRC 5.649
    Truancy
      Records of pupil, access CRC 5.652
  Electronic filing CRC 5.522
  Electronic service CRC 5.523
    Address for electronic service to be provided to court on first appearance CRC 5.534
  Emancipation petition CRC 3.1370, 5.605
  Emotional distress of child as ground for court intervention CRC 5.678
  Family finding and notice performed by social worker or probation officer CRC 5.637
  Family maintenance review hearings CRC 5.706
  Fax filing CRC 5.522
  Felonies, wardship proceedings
    Declaration of offense as misdemeanor after hearing CRC 5.795
    Finding offense as misdemeanor or felony CRC 5.790
  Firearm relinquishment procedures
    Forms for firearm relinquishment CRCAppx A
  Foreign country adoptions
    Hague adoption convention, adoptions under CRC 5.490 to 5.492
    Intercountry adoption CRC 5.490 to 5.493
  Forms
    Implementation of use CRC 5.504
    Use of judicial council forms CRC 5.524
  Foster care CRC 5.720, 5.725
    Change in placement affecting school of origin CRC 5.651
    Family-finding determination where risk of entry to foster care CRC 5.790
    Indian children, involuntary placements
      Indian Child Welfare Act, rules governing CRC 5.480 to 5.488
      (See **INDIAN CHILD WELFARE ACT INVOLUNTARY PLACEMENTS**)
    Review hearing on CRC 5.740
    Specialty mental health services
      Judicial council legal forms CRCAppx A
      Presumptive transfer of responsibility for services upon change of child placement, waiver proceedings CRC 5.647
  General public, exclusion of CRC 5.530
  Guardianships
    Attorneys, CASA programs CRC 5.655
    Dependent children CRC 5.730 to 5.740
    Indian children
      Involuntary placements, rules governing CRC 5.480 to 5.488 (See **INDIAN CHILD WELFARE ACT INVOLUNTARY PLACEMENTS**)
    Orders CRC 5.620
      Termination of juvenile proceeding or probate court guardianship proceeding, orders following CRC 5.475
      Ward of court proceedings CRC 5.625
    Requests, procedure for CRC 5.735
    Wardship proceedings
      Legal guardians for wards of court CRC 5.815
  Hearings
    Adoption
      Authorization for, permanency planning hearing CRC 5.706 to 5.740
      Prospective adoptive parent designation CRC 5.726
    Commitment orders, hearing on CRC 5.580
    Community treatment facilities, placements
      Hearings, review, etc CRC 5.618
    Conduct of CRC 5.534
    Educational and developmental services decisionmaking rights of children CRC 5.651

JUVENILE RULES—Cont.
Hearings—Cont.
- Joinder of government agency or private service provider for failure to meet legal obligations to child   CRC 5.575
- Modification of order, hearing on   CRC 5.560, 5.570
- Notice   CRC 5.565
- Petition for modification hearing   CRC 5.560, 5.570
- Pre-hearing motions   CRC 5.544
- Public, exclusion of   CRC 5.530
- Referees, hearings conducted by   CRC 5.536
- Short-term residential therapeutic program, placements
  - Hearings, review, etc   CRC 5.618
- Stayed commitment orders, hearing on   CRC 5.560
- Subsequent petition, hearing on   CRC 5.565
- Supplemental petition, hearing on   CRC 5.565
- Termination of parental rights
  - Setting termination hearing at disposition hearing   CRC 5.705
- Transfer hearings in wardship proceedings   CRC 5.766 to 5.770
- Transfer-in hearings   CRC 5.612
  - Date   CRC 5.610
  - Nonminor dependents   CRC 5.613
- Transfer-out hearings   CRC 5.610
  - Nonminor dependents   CRC 5.613

Husband and wife, inapplicability of marital communications privilege in dependency proceedings   CRC 5.684
Immunity of witnesses from prosecution   CRC 5.548
Indians
- Child
  - Definition of Indian child   CRC 5.502
- Dependency proceedings, tribal rights in   CRC 5.534
  - Tribal information form   CRCAppx A
- Dependent children, placement under Indian Child Welfare Act   CRC 5.565, 5.570
- Involuntary placements
  - Indian child welfare act involuntary placements   CRC 5.480 to 5.488
  - (See **INDIAN CHILD WELFARE ACT INVOLUNTARY PLACEMENTS**)
- Psychotropic medication for treatment of psychiatric disorder or illness, authorization of
  - Forms, judicial council   CRCAppx A
  - Notice to Indian child's tribe   CRC 5.640
  - Release of psychotropic medication prescription information to medical board, authorization   CRC 5.642
- Tribe
  - Definition of Indian child's tribe   CRC 5.502

Informal supervision programs
- Guidelines for   CRC 5.514
- Relevant factors   CRC 5.516

Information, disclosure of   CRC 5.546
Initial appearance, wardship   CRC 5.752 to 5.764
Initial hearings, dependency   CRC 5.667 to 5.678
Inspection of reports
- Deceased child, release of juvenile case file   CRC 5.553
- Petition for disclosure of juvenile court records   CRC 5.552
- Police reports on juveniles   CRC 5.546
- Prehearing discovery   CRC 5.546
- Ward of court proceedings, detention hearing in   CRC 5.756

Intake program   CRC 5.514
- Settlement at intake   CRC 5.516

Intercounty transfers
- Interstate compact on placement of children
  - Applicability   CRC 5.616
- Nonminor dependents   CRC 5.613
- Transfer-in hearings   CRC 5.612
  - Date of transfer-in hearing   CRC 5.610
  - Nonminor dependents   CRC 5.613
- Transfer-out hearings   CRC 5.610
  - Nonminor dependents   CRC 5.613

Joinder of government agency or private service provider for failure to meet legal obligations to child   CRC 5.575
Joint assessment procedure   CRC 5.512
Judicial notice, parentage determinations   CRC 5.635
Jurisdiction   CRC 5.510
- Child custody and visitation   CRC 5.510
- General jurisdiction
  - Defined   CRC 5.502
- Paternity issues   CRC 5.510
- Termination of juvenile court jurisdiction
  - Nonminor dependents or wards in foster care   CRC 5.555

Jurisdiction hearings
- Dependency proceedings   CRC 5.682, 5.684

JUVENILE RULES—Cont.
Jurisdiction hearings—Cont.
- Wardship proceedings   CRC 5.774 to 5.782

Juvenile facilities
- Diagnostic and treatment centers, temporary commitment   CRC 5.782
- Secure youth treatment facilities   CRC 5.804 to 5.805

Juvenile facilities commitment
- Disposition orders   CRC 5.790
- 90-day observation   CRC 5.782

Local rules of court, right to counsel in dependency proceedings   CRC 5.660
Mental health of child before court
- Competence of minor subject to juvenile proceedings, doubt as to
  - Evaluation of competence   CRC 5.645
- Foster care
  - Judicial council legal forms   CRCAppx A
  - Specialty mental health services, proceedings upon waiver of presumptive transfer of responsibility for services upon change of child placement   CRC 5.647
- Inquiry into   CRC 5.643

Misdemeanors, wardship proceedings
- Declaration of offense as misdemeanor after hearing   CRC 5.795
- Finding offense as misdemeanor or felony   CRC 5.790

Modification hearings   CRC 5.560, 5.570
- Guardianship orders   CRC 5.620, 5.625

Native Americans
- Indians generally (See within this heading, "**Indians**")
- Involuntary placements
  - Indian Child Welfare Act, rules governing   CRC 5.480 to 5.488
  - (See **INDIAN CHILD WELFARE ACT INVOLUNTARY PLACEMENTS**)

No contest pleas
- Dependent child of court proceedings, initial hearing in   CRC 5.674

Nonminor dependents, retention of jurisdiction   CRC 5.900 to 5.906
- Applicability   CRC 5.900
- Definition of nonminor and nonminor dependent   CRC 5.502
- Disposition hearings
  - Judicial council forms   CRCAppx A
- Educational rights holders
  - Appointment of continuation of appointment   CRC 5.650
  - Powers and duties of holders   CRC 5.650
- Hearings   CRC 5.900
- Legal status of nonminor dependents   CRC 5.900
- Resumption of jurisdiction
  - Petition to resume jurisdiction   CRC 5.570
  - Request by nonminor for juvenile jurisdiction   CRC 5.906
- Status review hearings   CRC 5.903
- Telephone appearances   CRC 3.672, 5.900

Notice of hearing   CRC 5.524
- Adoption of child, prospective adoptive parent proceedings
  - Designation hearing   CRC 5.726
  - Emergency removals from prospective adoptive parents   CRC 5.728
  - Removal from prospective adoptive parents   CRC 5.727
- Caregivers
  - Notice of proceedings to current caregivers   CRC 5.534
- Commitment orders, notice of hearing on   CRC 5.580
- Modification of order, notice of hearing on   CRC 5.570

Oral notice of proceedings   CRC 5.524
Orders and decrees
- Appeal of   CRC 5.585 to 5.595
- Clerical errors, correction of   CRC 5.560
- Commitment orders, hearing on   CRC 5.580
- Stayed commitment orders   CRC 5.560
- Transfer hearings   CRC 5.770
- Transfer of proceedings, order for   CRC 5.610

Out-of-county placements   CRC 5.614
- Judicial council legal forms   CRCAppx A

Parentage   CRC 5.635
- Actions to determine paternity, jurisdiction   CRC 5.510
- Dependent children, paternity inquiry at commencement of hearing   CRC 5.668
- Juvenile court proceedings, findings of paternity   CRC 5.534

Perjury   CRC 5.548
Permanency planning hearings   CRC 5.810
Persons entitled to appear   CRC 5.530
Persons present at proceedings   CRC 5.530
Petition   CRC 5.516
- Access to juvenile court records   CRC 5.552
- Amendment of   CRC 5.524
- Application for petition   CRC 5.520
- Content   CRC 5.524
- Disclosure of juvenile court records   CRC 5.552

JUVENILE RULES—Cont.
  Petition —Cont.
    Filing   CRC 5.516, 5.520
    Forms to be used   CRC 5.524
    Modification hearing, petition for   CRC 5.560, 5.570
    Petitioner defined   CRC 5.502
    Probation officer, filing by   CRC 5.514, 5.516
    Prosecuting attorney, filing by   CRC 5.514, 5.516
    Social worker, filing by   CRC 5.516
    Subsequent and supplemental petitions   CRC 5.560 to 5.580
  Police reports, inspection of   CRC 5.546
  Pre-hearing motions, wardship proceedings   CRC 5.544
  Preliminary provisions   CRC 5.501
  Prisoners
    Children of prisoners, family reunification services   CRC 5.695
  Privileged communications, inapplicability of marital privilege in dependency proceedings   CRC 5.684
  Probation officer
    Defined   CRC 5.502
    Informal supervision programs, guidelines for   CRC 5.514
    Intake programs, guidelines for   CRC 5.514
    Petition, filing of   CRC 5.514, 5.516
  Probation reports
    Commitment order, hearing on   CRC 5.580
    Disclosure of   CRC 5.546
    Fitness hearings   CRC 5.768
  Protective custody warrant, issuance of   CRC 5.526
  Protective orders
    Firearm relinquishment procedures
      Forms for firearm relinquishment   CRCAppx A
  Psychiatric residential treatment facility, admission to
    Forms, judicial council   CRCAppx A
  Psychotropic medication for treatment of psychiatric disorder or illness, authorization of   CRC 5.640
    Forms, judicial council   CRCAppx A
    Prescriptions
      Release of psychotropic medication prescription information to medical board, authorization   CRC 5.642
  Public records
    Confidentiality   CRC 5.552
    Deceased child, release of juvenile case file   CRC 5.553
    Petition for access   CRC 5.552
    Request for disclosure   CRC 5.552
  Records
    Confidentiality   CRC 5.552
    Deceased child, release of juvenile case file   CRC 5.553
    Petition for access   CRC 5.552
    Request for disclosure   CRC 5.552
  Referees and referee proceedings   CRC 5.536 to 5.542
    Appeal rights   CRC 5.538, 5.542
    Appointment of referee   CRC 5.536
    Approval of judge
      Orders requiring   CRC 5.540
    Findings and orders   CRC 5.538, 5.540
    Orders
      Issuance of   CRC 5.540
    Procedural requirements for   CRC 5.538
    Recording   CRC 5.532, 5.538
    Rehearing of proceeding conducted by referee, right to   CRC 5.542
    Rehearings   CRC 5.542
    Temporary judge, referee as   CRC 5.536
  Referrals to prosecuting attorney   CRC 5.514
  Rehearings
    Referee, rehearing of proceeding conducted by   CRC 5.542
  Remote filing   CRC 5.522
  Removal of juvenile from home
    Family finding and notice performed by social worker or probation officer   CRC 5.637
  Reporters   CRC 5.532
  Reports
    Disclosure   CRC 5.546
    Permanent plan, petitioner's report on   CRC 5.740
    Police reports, inspection   CRC 5.546
    6-month review hearing
      Dependency proceedings   CRC 5.710
      Ward of court proceedings   CRC 5.810
    Transcripts   CRC 5.532
    12-month review hearing, petitioner's report for   CRC 5.715
  Representation of child   CRC 5.655 to 5.663
  Residence
    Children and minors   CRC 5.510

JUVENILE RULES—Cont.
  Residence—Cont.
    Parent or guardian subject to juvenile proceedings, notice as to address   CRC 5.534
  Restraining orders
    Dependent child of court proceedings   CRC 5.620, 5.630
      Firearm relinquishment procedures   CRC 5.630
      Forms for firearm relinquishment   CRCAppx A
  Review hearings
    Approaching majority, status review hearing   CRC 5.812
    Dependency proceedings   CRC 5.706 to 5.740
    Foster care, termination of jurisdiction   CRC 5.812
    Wardship proceedings   CRC 5.810
  Sealing of records   CRC 5.830
    Forms, judicial council   CRCAppx A
    Prosecuting attorney request to access sealed juvenile case files   CRC 5.860
      Order on prosecutor request for access   CRCAppx A
  Secure youth treatment facilities   CRC 5.804 to 5.808
    Adjusting baseline term   CRC 5.806
    Baseline term   CRC 5.804, 5.806
    Commitment to facility
      Adjusting baseline term   CRC 5.806
      Baseline term   CRC 5.804, 5.806
      Grounds   CRC 5.804
      Individualized rehabilitation plans   CRC 5.804
      Maximum term of confinement   CRC 5.804
      Offense-based classification matrix   CRC 5.806
    Discharge from facility   CRC 5.808
    Offense-based classification matrix   CRC 5.806
    Progress review hearing   CRC 5.804
      Adjusting baseline term   CRC 5.806
      Process for progress review   CRC 5.807
    Transfers
      Less restrictive programs   CRC 5.807
  Self-incrimination, privilege against   CRC 5.534, 5.548
    Dependency proceedings   CRC 5.534, 5.682
    Detention hearings   CRC 5.674, 5.756
    Wardship proceedings   CRC 5.534, 5.778
    Witnesses, testimony of   CRC 5.548
  Separate sessions of court, juvenile proceedings conducted in   CRC 5.530
  Service of papers
    Citation to appear, issuance of   CRC 5.526
    Educational rights holders
      Orders, service   CRC 5.650
    Electronic service   CRC 5.523
      Address for electronic service to be provided to court on first appearance   CRC 5.534
    Notice of hearing   CRC 5.524
    Pre-hearing motions   CRC 5.544
    Restraining orders
      Dependency cases   CRC 5.630
  Settlement at intake, relevant factors   CRC 5.516
  Short-term residential therapeutic program, placements
    Hearings, review, etc   CRC 5.618
  6-month review
    Dependency proceedings   CRC 5.612, 5.710
    Ward of court proceedings   CRC 5.810
  Social studies
    Defined   CRC 5.502
    Dependent child of court proceedings   CRC 5.684
      Disposition hearings   CRC 5.690
    Ward of court proceedings   CRC 5.785
  Social workers
    Defined   CRC 5.502
    Petition, filing of   CRC 5.520
  Special education needs
    Limitations on parental control   CRC 5.790
  Special or separate sessions   CRC 5.530
  Standing to sue or contest, de facto parents   CRC 5.534
  Stays
    Commitment orders, hearing on   CRC 5.560
    Educational and developmental services decisionmaking rights of children   CRC 5.651
  Subpoenas, issuance of   CRC 5.526
  Subsequent petition
    Contents of   CRC 5.565
    Filing of   CRC 5.560
    Hearing on   CRC 5.565

JUVENILE RULES—Cont.

Superior courts, juvenile court proceedings in
    Civil rules
        Applicability in family, juvenile and probate cases in superior court CRC 3.10
        Generally   CRC 1.4, 3.1 to 3.2240
Supplemental petition
    Contents of   CRC 5.565
    Filing of   CRC 5.560
    Hearing on   CRC 5.565
Surrogate parent appointment
    Special education needs   CRC 5.650
Telephone appearances   CRC 3.672, 5.531
    Nonminor dependents, retention of jurisdiction   CRC 3.672, 5.900
Temporary judge
    Attorney as   CRC 5.536
    Referee as   CRC 5.536
Termination of parental rights   CRC 5.725
    Counsel, appointment of   CRC 5.655, 5.660
    18-month review hearing, termination hearing ordered at   CRC 5.720
    Family reunification services, failure to participate   CRC 5.695
    Foster care for 15 of last 22 months   CRC 5.820
    Hearings
        Setting hearing on termination at disposition hearing   CRC 5.705
    Indian children, involuntary placements
        Indian Child Welfare Act, rules governing   CRC 5.480 to 5.488
        (See **INDIAN CHILD WELFARE ACT INVOLUNTARY PLACEMENTS**)
    One parent, conditions to termination of rights of
        Disposition hearings generally   CRC 5.690 to 5.705
    Only one parent, restrictions on setting hearing for termination of rights of   CRC 5.705, 5.725
    Orders   CRC 5.725
    6-month review hearing, termination hearing ordered at   CRC 5.710
    12-month review hearing, termination hearing ordered at   CRC 5.715
Title of rules   CRC 5.1, 5.500
Transcripts   CRC 5.532
Transfer hearings   CRC 5.610 to 5.616
    Wardship proceedings   CRC 5.766 to 5.770
Transition jurisdiction
    Defined   CRC 5.502
    Hearings   CRC 5.812
    Modification to transition jurisdiction   CRC 5.813
        Age of ward between 17 years 5 months and 18   CRC 5.811, 5.814
        Forms, judicial council   CRCAppx A
    Transition dependent defined   CRC 5.502
Truancy
    Records of pupil, access   CRC 5.652
Venue   CRC 5.510
    Intercounty transfer of proceedings   CRC 5.610
Visitation rights
    Custody or visitation orders following termination of juvenile court or probate court proceedings   CRC 5.475
    Orders   CRC 5.620
    Termination of jurisdiction
        Orders as to custody or visitation   CRC 5.700
    Wardship, disposition hearings
        Orders determining custody or visitation   CRC 5.790
Waiver of service of papers   CRC 5.524
Wardship
    Generally (See **JUVENILE WARDSHIP PROCEEDINGS**)
    Indian children, involuntary placements   CRC 5.480 to 5.488 (See **INDIAN CHILD WELFARE ACT INVOLUNTARY PLACEMENTS**)
Warrants of arrest, issuance of   CRC 5.526
Witnesses
    Cross-examination of witness, right to   CRC 5.534
    Immunity, grant of   CRC 5.548
    Self-incrimination, privilege against   CRC 5.548
    Subpoenas   CRC 5.526
Youth
    Defined   CRC 5.502

JUVENILE WARDSHIP PROCEEDINGS

Admission of allegations   CRC 5.754
Adoption of wards   CRC 5.825
Advice of hearing rights   CRC 5.534, 5.754, 5.778
Age
    Misrepresentation of   CRC 5.752
Amendment of petitions   CRC 5.524
Appeals   CRC 5.585 to 5.595
    Advisement of rights   CRC 5.590

JUVENILE WARDSHIP PROCEEDINGS—Cont.

Appeals —Cont.
    Forms, judicial council   CRCAppx A
    Right to appeal, notification of   CRC 5.590
    Stay pending appeal
        Conditions   CRC 5.595
    Transfer of case between counties   CRC 5.610
    Transfer orders, review   CRC 5.770
Appearance
    Remote appearances   CRC 3.672
        COVID-19, emergency rule   CRCAppx I Emer Rule 7
    Telephone appearances   CRC 3.672, 5.531
        Nonminor dependents, retention of jurisdiction   CRC 3.672, 5.900
Approaching majority
    Dispositional hearings   CRC 5.812
    Status review hearings   CRC 5.812
    Termination of jurisdiction   CRC 5.812
Arrest of minors, warrants for   CRC 5.526
Assessments
    Joint assessment procedure   CRC 5.512
Attendance at proceedings   CRC 5.530
Attorneys
    Advice of right and appointment for minor   CRC 5.534
    Appointment by court   CRC 5.534
    Capacity to cooperate with counsel, inquiry into child's   CRC 5.643
    Compensation   CRC JudAdminStand 5.40
    Conflict of interest between parent and child   CRC 5.534
    Continuance to obtain   CRC 5.776
    Discrimination, prohibition against in appointments   CRC JudAdminStand 5.40
    Doubt as to child's capacity to cooperate with   CRC 5.643
    Fitness hearings   CRC 5.534
    Jurisdictional hearing   CRC 5.534, 5.778
    Liability for cost of services   CRC 5.534
    Modification of order, notice of petition   CRC 5.570
    Presence at proceedings   CRC 5.530
    Prosecuting attorney   CRC 5.520, 5.530
    Right to representation, requirement for notification of   CRC 5.534
    Service of petition on   CRC 5.524
    Standards of representation and compensation   CRC JudAdminStand 5.40
CASA volunteers, requirements   CRC 5.655
Change of name   CCP §§1276, 1277
Citation to appear   CRC 5.526
Commencement of proceedings   CRC 5.510 to 5.526
    Certification after suspension of criminal proceedings   CRC 4.116
    Investigation by probation officer   CRC 5.514
    Mandatory referrals to prosecuting attorney   CRC 5.514
    Notice, issuance by clerk on filing of petition   CRC 5.524
    Service of notice and petition   CRC 5.524
    Supervision of minor in lieu of filing petition   CRC 5.514
    Venue   CRC 5.510
Community treatment facilities
    Placement review hearing   CRC 5.618
Competence inquiry   CRC 5.643
    COVID-19, emergency rule   CRCAppx I Emer Rule 7
    Evaluation of competence   CRC 5.645
Conditions, deferred entry of judgment   CRC 5.800
Conditions of probation   CRC 5.790
Confinement period   CRC 5.795
Confrontation rights   CRC 5.534
    Jurisdictional hearings   CRC 5.778
Constitutional rights, advice of   CRC 5.534
Contested hearings   CRC 5.780
Continuances   CRC 5.550
    Availability of witness   CRC 5.776
    Confession or admission, obtaining witnesses for   CRC 5.776
    Counsel, to obtain   CRC 5.776
    COVID-19, emergency rule   CRCAppx I Emer Rule 7
    Disposition hearing   CRC 5.782
    Educational and developmental services decisionmaking rights of children   CRC 5.651
    Good cause showing   CRC 5.550
    Jurisdictional hearings   CRC 5.776
    Prima facie hearing   CRC 5.764
    Transfer hearings   CRC 5.770
Control of minor by parent or guardian
    Limitation by court after adjudication as ward   CRC 5.790
County institutions
    Supplemental petition for confinement in   CRC 5.580
Court-Appointed Special Advocate (CASA) program   CRC 5.655
Court order, violation as grounds for detention   CRC 5.760

JUVENILE WARDSHIP PROCEEDINGS—Cont.
  Criminal proceedings against minor
    Suspension of and certification to juvenile court   CRC 4.116, 5.516
  Cross-examination rights   CRC 5.534
  Custody
    Disposition hearings
      Orders determining custody or visitation   CRC 5.790
    Orders   CRC 5.752
    Time limits   CRC 5.752
  De facto parents, participation in proceedings   CRC 5.534
    Definition of de facto parent   CRC 5.502
  Deferred entry of judgment   CRC 5.800
  Delinquency jurisdiction
    Modification to transition jurisdiction   CRC 5.811
      Forms, judicial council   CRCAppx A
  Detention hearing   CRC 5.752 to 5.764
    Admission of petition allegations   CRC 5.754
    Appearance of minor, parent, or guardian, order for   CRC 5.526
    Attorneys   CRC 5.534
    Commencement of hearing   CRC 5.754
    Conduct of hearing   CRC 5.756
    Continuances   CRC 5.550
    COVID-19, emergency rules   CRCAppx I Emer Rule 7
    Evidence requirements   CRC 5.756, 5.762
    Examination by court   CRC 5.756
    Findings required   CRC 5.758, 5.760
    Grounds for detention   CRC 5.760
    No contest plea   CRC 5.754
    Prima facie hearing   CRC 5.764
    Rehearings   CRC 5.762
    Restraining order as condition of release or detention on home supervision   CRC 5.760
    Right to inspect documents   CRC 5.756
    Setting of detention hearing   CRC 5.752
    Time limit on detention before hearing   CRC 5.752
    Violation of probation   CRC 5.580
    Visitation orders   CRC 5.670
  Detention of minor
    Disposition order, detention pending execution of   CRC 5.790
    Escape from commitment   CRC 5.760
    Grounds   CRC 5.760
    Written detention report   CRC 5.760
  Discharge from detention or restriction after hearing   CRC 5.780
    Secure youth treatment facilities
      Discharge from facility   CRC 5.808
  Discovery rights   CRC 5.534, 5.546
  Dismissal of petition   CRC 5.774
  Disposition hearing   CRC 5.785 to 5.808
    Confinement period   CRC 5.795
    Continuances   CRC 5.782
    De facto parents, participation as parties   CRC 5.534
    Detention of child pending   CRC 5.782
    Evidence   CRC 5.785
    Felony or misdemeanor, determination of   CRC 5.795
    15-day review   CRC 5.790
    Findings   CRC 5.790, 5.795
    Judgment and orders   CRC 5.790, 5.795
    Juvenile facilities commitment   CRC 5.795
      Observation and diagnosis   CRC 5.782
    Orders   CRC 5.790
    Secure youth treatment facilities   CRC 5.804 to 5.808
    Sentencing in adult court upon conviction of crime   CRC 4.510
    Social studies   CRC 5.785
  District attorney
    Appearance on behalf of People   CRC 5.530
    Discretion whether to file petition   CRC 5.520
    Mandatory referrals   CRC 5.514
  Diversion services
    Satisfactory completion
      Determination   CRC 5.850
      Sealing of records upon satisfactory completion of informal supervision, diversion, etc   CRC 5.850
    Unsatisfactory completion
      Review by juvenile court   CRC 5.850
  Domestic violence proceedings involving minor party, jurisdiction over   CCP §374.5
  Dual status as dependent and ward
    Modification of jurisdiction   CRC 5.812
  Duration of confinement, maximum   CRC 5.752
    Protective custody or prevention of flight   CRC 5.760

JUVENILE WARDSHIP PROCEEDINGS—Cont.
  Education
    Educational and developmental services decisionmaking rights of children   CRC 5.651
      Principals guiding juvenile court   CRC JudAdminStand 5.40
    Educational rights holders
      Appointment   CRC 5.650, 5.790
      Judicial council forms   CRCAppx A
      Powers and duties of holders   CRC 5.650
      Qualifications   CRC 5.650
      Training   CRC 5.650
      Transfer of parent's or guardian's educational rights to rights holder   CRC 5.650
    Special education needs   CRC 5.650
      Educational rights holders   CRC 5.650
      Juvenile court proceedings   CRC 5.502, 5.524, 5.650
  Emancipation of dependents and wards of court, rules of court for   CRC 3.1370, 5.605
  Emergency medical, dental, or surgical care
    COVID-19, emergency rule   CRCAppx I Emer Rule 7
  Evidence
    Detention hearing   CRC 5.756
    Disposition hearings   CRC 5.785
    Exculpatory evidence, duty to disclose   CRC 5.546
    Jurisdiction hearing   CRC 5.780
    Motion to suppress   CRC 5.544
    Transfer hearing   CRC 5.770
  Exclusion of public   CRC 5.530
  Ex parte injunction against parent or guardian or member of child's household
    Firearm relinquishment procedures
      Forms for firearm relinquishment   CRCAppx A
  Factors to be considered   CRC 5.760
  Felonies
    Declaration of offense after hearing   CRC 5.795
  Findings
    Detention hearing   CRC 5.758, 5.760
    Disposition hearing   CRC 5.790, 5.795
    Jurisdictional hearing   CRC 5.778, 5.780
    Offense as felony or misdemeanor   CRC 5.790
  Flight, likelihood as grounds for detention   CRC 5.760
  Forms
    Judicial council legal forms   CRCAppx A
  Foster care
    Approaching majority   CRC 5.812
    At risk of entering defined   CRC 5.502
    Postpermanency status review hearings   CRC 5.810
    Termination of juvenile court jurisdiction
      Nonminor dependents or wards in foster care   CRC 5.555
  Grounds for detention   CRC 5.760
  Guardians
    Legal guardians for wards   CRC 5.815
  Harassment proceedings brought against or initiated by minor, jurisdiction over   CCP §374.5
  Hearings
    Community treatment facilities
      Placement review hearing   CRC 5.618
    Contested issues   CRC 5.780
    Educational and developmental services decisionmaking rights of children   CRC 5.651
    Persons entitled to attend   CRC 5.530, 5.534
    Prosecuting witness and family members, attendance by   CRC 5.530
    Short-term residential therapeutic program
      Placement review hearing   CRC 5.618
    Transfer of case, hearing by receiving court   CRC 5.612
      Date of transfer-in hearing   CRC 5.610
    Victim and support persons, attendance by   CRC 5.530
    Victim's presence   CRC 5.530
  Immunity, grants of   CRC 5.548
  Indian Child Welfare Act
    Involuntary placements, rules governing   CRC 5.480 to 5.488 (See **INDIAN CHILD WELFARE ACT INVOLUNTARY PLACEMENTS**)
  Informal supervision   CRC 5.514
    Satisfactory completion
      Dismissal of petition, sealing and destruction of records   CRC 5.840
  Initial appearance
    Admission of petition allegations   CRC 5.754
    Commencement of hearing   CRC 5.754
    Continuances   CRC 5.550
    COVID-19, emergency rule   CRCAppx I Emer Rule 7
    Evidence requirements in detention cases   CRC 5.756, 5.762
    Examination by court in detention cases   CRC 5.756

JUVENILE WARDSHIP PROCEEDINGS—Cont.
Initial appearance—Cont.
- Findings required in detention cases   CRC 5.758, 5.760
- Grounds for detention   CRC 5.760
- No contest plea   CRC 5.754
- Prima facie hearing in detention cases   CRC 5.764
- Rehearings   CRC 5.762
- Restraining order as condition of release or detention on home supervision   CRC 5.760
- Right to inspect documents in detention cases   CRC 5.756
- Setting of initial hearing   CRC 5.752

Intake program   CRC 5.514
Intercounty transfers   CRC 5.610 to 5.616
- Interstate Compact on Placement of Children   CRC 5.616
Interpreters   CRC 2.890
Interstate Compact on Placement of Children   CRC 5.616, Fam §§7900 to 7913
Joint assessment procedure   CRC 5.512
Judgment, deferred entry of   CRC 5.800
Judgment on disposition of minor found to be ward   CRC 5.790, 5.795
Jurisdictional hearing   CRC 5.774 to 5.782
- Admissions   CRC 5.778
- Allegations of petition, explanation of   CRC 5.778
- Attorney, right to   CRC 5.534, 5.778
- Contested hearing   CRC 5.780
- Continuances   CRC 5.776
- Dismissal   CRC 5.774
- Evidence   CRC 5.780
- Explanation of proceeding   CRC 5.778
- Findings   CRC 5.778, 5.780
- 90-day observation period   CRC 5.782
- No contest plea   CRC 5.778
- Pre-hearing motions   CRC 5.544
- Termination of juvenile court jurisdiction
  - Nonminor dependents or wards in foster care   CRC 5.555
- Trial rights, advice of   CRC 5.778
- Waiver   CRC 5.774

Juvenile court rules, definitions   CRC 5.502
Legal guardians for wards   CRC 5.815
Medical care and treatment
- Psychotropic medications, administration
  - Forms, judicial council   CRCAppx A
Mental health of child before court, inquiry into   CRC 5.643
- Competence of minor to face juvenile proceedings, doubt as to
  - Evaluation of competence   CRC 5.645
Misdemeanors
- Declaration of offense as after hearing   CRC 5.795
- Detention hearing after warrantless arrest, time for
  - COVID-19, emergency rule   CRCAppx I Emer Rule 7
Modification of orders and judgments
- Commitment or placement order   CRC 5.580
- Denial of petition   CRC 5.570
- Grounds for grant of petition   CRC 5.570
- Hearings   CRC 5.570
- Notice of petition for modification   CRC 5.570
- Petitions   CRC 5.570
- Previously established wardship   CRC 5.625
Modification of previously established wardship   CRC 5.625
Name of juvenile
- Change of name   CCP §§1276, 1277
No contest pleas
- Initial hearing   CRC 5.754
- Jurisdiction hearing   CRC 5.778
Nonminor wards
- Termination of juvenile court jurisdiction
  - Nonminor dependents or wards in foster care   CRC 5.555
Notices
- Hearings   CRC 5.524
  - Fitness hearing   CRC 5.766
- Issuance on filing of petition   CRC 5.524
Orders   CRC 5.625
- Judicial council form   CRCAppx A
Parentage
- Declarations   CRC 5.635
- Determinations   CRC 5.534, 5.635
- Inquiry   CRC 5.635
- Voluntary declaration   CRC 5.635
Parents or guardians
- Address, notice of   CRC 5.534
- Arrest, warrant for   CRC 5.526
- Citation directing appearance at hearing   CRC 5.526
- De facto parents   CRC 5.502, 5.534

JUVENILE WARDSHIP PROCEEDINGS—Cont.
Parents or guardians—Cont.
- Guardianship   CRC 5.625
- Inspection and copying of documents   CRC 5.756
- Limitations on parental control   CRC 5.790
- Modification or setting aside order, petition for   CRC 5.570
- Petition and notice, issuance and service   CRC 5.524
- Removal of child from physical custody after adjudication as ward   CRC 5.790, 5.795
- Subpoenas, request for issuance   CRC 5.526
- Surrogate parents, appointment for children with special needs
  - Juvenile court proceedings   CRC 5.650

Permanency planning hearings
- Selection of permanent plan   CRC 5.725
Petition to commence proceedings
- Amendment   CRC 5.524
- Discretion whether to file petition   CRC 5.520
- Judicial council forms   CRCAppx A
- Reading of at hearing   CRC 5.778
- Service of petition   CRC 5.524
Police reports, inspection and copying   CRC 5.546
- Detention hearings   CRC 5.756
Prehearing discovery   CRC 5.534, 5.546
Prehearing motions   CRC 5.544
Prima facie case   CRC 5.758
Prima facie hearings   CRC 5.764
Probation
- Report after remand following conviction as adult   CRC 4.510
- Satisfactory completion of probation
  - Dismissal of petition, sealing and destruction of records   CRC 5.840
- Violation of   CRC 5.580
Probation officers
- Application to commence proceedings   CRC 5.520
- Discretion whether to file petition   CRC 5.514, 5.516
- Fitness reports   CRC 5.768
- Investigation of minor's circumstances   CRC 5.516, 5.520
- Reports   CRC 5.768
- Violation of probation, notice of   CRC 5.580
Process and service of process
- Petition and notice of hearing   CRC 5.524
- Subpoenas   CRC 5.526
Prosecuting attorney
- Appearance   CRC 5.530
- Petition, filing of   CRC 5.520
Protection of minor or others, detention on grounds of   CRC 5.760
Protection of property, detention on grounds of   CRC 5.760
Psychotropic medications, administration   CRC 5.640
- COVID-19, emergency rule   CRCAppx I Emer Rule 7
- Forms, judicial council   CRCAppx A
- Prescriptions
  - Release of psychotropic medication prescription information to medical board, authorization   CRC 5.642
Punishment defined   CRC 5.502
Rehearings   CRC 5.762
Relatives
- Presence at hearings   CRC 5.534
Release of minor after temporary custody
- Time for   CRC 5.752
Relocation of family unit
- Interstate compact on placement of children   CRC 5.616
Remand from conviction as adult, probation report   CRC 4.510
Removal from custody of parent or guardian   CRC 5.790, 5.795
- Judicial council forms   CRCAppx A
- Permanency planning hearings   CRC 5.810
- Postpermanency planning hearings   CRC 5.810
- Postpermanency status review hearings   CRC 5.810
- Six-month review hearing   CRC 5.810
Requirements for detention   CRC 5.758
Residence, determination of   CRC 5.510, 5.610
Restraining orders   CRC 5.625
- Release or detention on home supervision, condition of   CRC 5.760
Reverse remand after prosecution as adult   CRC 4.510
Role of juvenile court   CRC JudAdminStand 5.40
Sealing of records   CRC 5.830
- Access to or inspection
  - Judicial council forms   CRCAppx A
  - Order on prosecutor request for access   CRCAppx A
  - Prosecuting attorney request to access sealed juvenile case files   CRC 5.860
- Former wards, records of
  - Order on prosecutor request for access   CRCAppx A

JUVENILE WARDSHIP PROCEEDINGS—Cont.
  Sealing of records —Cont.
    Former wards, records of—Cont.
      Prosecuting attorney request to access sealed juvenile case files CRC 5.860
    Forms, judicial council   CRCAppx A
    Satisfactory completion of informal program of supervision
      Dismissal of petition, sealing and destruction of records   CRC 5.840
      Order on prosecutor request for access   CRCAppx A
      Procedures to seal records   CRC 5.850
      Prosecuting attorney request to access sealed juvenile case files   CRC 5.860
  Secure youth treatment facilities
    Adjusting baseline term   CRC 5.806
    Baseline term   CRC 5.804, 5.806
    Commitment to facility
      Adjusting baseline term   CRC 5.806
      Baseline term   CRC 5.804, 5.806
      Grounds   CRC 5.804
      Individualized rehabilitation plans   CRC 5.804
      Maximum term of confinement   CRC 5.804
      Offense-based classification matrix   CRC 5.806
    Discharge from facility   CRC 5.808
    Offense-based classification matrix   CRC 5.806
    Progress review hearing   CRC 5.804
      Adjusting baseline term   CRC 5.806
      Process for progress review   CRC 5.807
    Transfers
      Less restrictive programs   CRC 5.807
  Self-incrimination, privilege against   CRC 5.534
  Jurisdictional hearings   CRC 5.778
  Sentencing in adult court upon conviction of crime   CRC 4.510
  Separate sessions of juvenile court   CRC 5.530
  Short-term residential therapeutic program
    Placement review hearing   CRC 5.618
  6-month review hearing   CRC 5.810
  Social studies   CRC 5.785
  Special education needs
    Educational and developmental services decisionmaking rights of children   CRC 5.651
    Educational rights holders, appointment   CRC 5.650
      Powers and duties of holders   CRC 5.650
    Juvenile court proceedings   CRC 5.502, 5.534, 5.650
    Surrogate parent appointment   CRC 5.650
  Special sessions of juvenile court   CRC 5.530
  Status review hearings
    Approaching majority   CRC 5.812
    Termination of jurisdiction   CRC 5.812
  Stays
    Educational and developmental services decisionmaking rights of children   CRC 5.651
  Subpoenas   CRC 5.526
  Supervision
    In lieu of filing petition   CRC 5.514
    Sealing of records upon satisfactory completion of informal supervision, diversion, etc   CRC 5.850
  Surrogate parents, appointment for children with special needs
    Juvenile court proceedings   CRC 5.650
  Telephone appearances   CRC 3.672, 5.531
    Nonminor dependents, retention of jurisdiction   CRC 3.672, 5.900
  Temporary custody and detention
    COVID-19, emergency rule   CRCAppx I Emer Rule 7
    Escape from commitment, grounds for detention   CRC 5.760
    Family finding and notice performed by social worker or probation officer   CRC 5.637
    Likelihood of flight, grounds for detention   CRC 5.760
    Maximum time for custody absent petition   CRC 5.752
  Termination of juvenile court jurisdiction
    Nonminor dependents or wards in foster care   CRC 5.555
    Orders as to custody or visitation   CRC 5.700
  Termination of parental rights, when required
    Foster care for child during 15 of last 22 months   CRC 5.820
  Transcription of testimony   CRC 5.532
  Transfer hearing   CRC 5.766 to 5.770
    After remand from trial as adult   CRC 4.510
    Appellate review   CRC 5.770
    Burden of proof   CRC 5.770
    Continuance to obtain stay   CRC 5.770
    Conviction as adult, hearing after   CRC 4.510
    Counsel, representation by   CRC 5.534
    Criteria for determination   CRC 5.770

JUVENILE WARDSHIP PROCEEDINGS—Cont.
  Transfer hearing —Cont.
    Evidentiary requirements   CRC 5.770
    Findings and orders   CRC 5.770
    Notice   CRC 5.766
    Orders   CRC 5.770
    Pleas
      Postponement of plea prior to transfer hearing   CRC 5.770
    Preponderance of evidence standard   CRC 5.770
    Prima facie showing   CRC 5.766
    Probation reports   CRC 5.768
    Report and recommendation by probation officer   CRC 5.768
    Review of determination   CRC 5.770
    Section 707 hearings, conduct   CRC 5.770
    Sentencing in adult court upon conviction of crime   CRC 4.510
    Statement of basis for decision   CRC 5.770
    Time limits   CRC 5.766
  Transfers to county of residence   CRC 5.610 to 5.616
    Appeal from order   CRC 5.610
    Order for   CRC 5.610
  Transition age youth
    Intergenerational housing developments   CC §51.3.5
  Transition jurisdiction
    Defined   CRC 5.502
    Hearings   CRC 5.812
    Modification to transition jurisdiction   CRC 5.813
      Age of ward between 17 years 5 months and 18   CRC 5.814
      Delinquency jurisdiction, transition from   CRC 5.811
      Forms, judicial council   CRCAppx A
    Transition dependent defined   CRC 5.502
  Venue for proceedings   CRC 5.510
  Verification
    Petition to commence proceedings   CRC 5.524
  Violation of probation
    Dismissal of notice   CRC 5.580
    Hearing following   CRC 5.580
  Wards of court
    Placement under Interstate Compact   CRC 5.616
  Warrant for arrest
    COVID-19, emergency rule   CRCAppx I Emer Rule 7
    Minors   CRC 5.526
    Parents or guardians   CRC 5.526
  Witnesses
    Continuance for unavailability   CRC 5.776
    Immunity, granting of   CRC 5.548
  Youth
    Removal from custody of parent or guardian
      Postpermanency status review hearings   CRC 5.810

K

KARNETTE RENTAL-PURCHASE ACT   CC §§1812.620 to 1812.650

KEENE HEALTH CARE AGENT ACT (See **POWER OF ATTORNEY**)

KEEPER OF THE ARCHIVES
Spanish title papers prepared by keeper as admissible   Ev §1605

KEYS
Parking facilities' liability when keys required to remain with car   CC §1630.5

KICKBACKS
Automobile leases   CC §2986.12
Mortgage or trust deed sales   CC §2924d

KIDNAPPING AND CHILD ABDUCTION
Custody of children (See **CUSTODY OF CHILDREN**)
Hearsay exception for statement of declarant murdered or kidnapped to prevent prosecution of party against whom statement is offered   Ev §1350
Juveniles tried as adults, sentencing upon conviction   CRC 4.510
Orders to prevent
  Attachment   CRCAppx A (CRCFL-341(B))
  Request   CRCAppx A (CRCFL-312)
Visitation orders
  Risk of abduction findings and preventative measures   Fam §3048

KINDRED (See **RELATIVES**)

KINSHIP ADOPTION AGREEMENTS (See **POSTADOPTION CONTACT AGREEMENTS**)

KNOWLEDGE
Authentication based on facts known only to writer Ev §1421
Disqualification of judges, personal knowledge of evidentiary facts as grounds for CCP §170.1
Expert witnesses Ev §802
Preliminary fact as within personal knowledge of witness Ev §403
Value of property in eminent proceedings, knowledge of witness as basis for opinion testimony on Ev §813
Witness' personal knowledge of matters testified to Ev §702

KOREAN LANGUAGE
Contracts in Chinese, Tagalog, Vietnamese or Korean languages CC §1632
 Consumer credit contracts
  Federal notice requirement CC §1799.96
  Foreign language translations of notice requirement CC §1799.91
Gender tax repeal act preventing charging different prices for services of similar or like kind based on gender
 Consumer affairs department pamphlet for affected businesses and other notice of requirements of provisions CC §51.63
 Licensing authority notice of provisions to licensee upon issuance or renewal CC §51.6
Mortgages of residential property, foreign language summaries of terms CC §1632.5

L

LABOR AND LABOR UNIONS
Arbitration proceedings under collective bargaining agreement CCP §1282.4
Arbitration proceedings under collective bargaining agreement, representation by non-attorney in CCP §1282.4
Braceros
 Actions to recover savings fund amounts CCP §354.7
Child support enforcement services, obligation of labor organizations to cooperate with Fam §17512
Consumer privacy rights
 Communications or transactions, applicability of rights CC §1798.145
 Personnel records, applicability of rights CC §1798.145
Court employee labor relations CRC 10.650 to 10.660
Employment agencies to notify jobseeker of union contract or labor troubles at jobsite CC §1812.509
Injunctions against picketing CCP §527.3
Job listing services to notify jobseeker of union contract or labor troubles at jobsite CC §1812.521
Nazi regime during Second World War, actions to recover compensation for slave or forced labor under CCP §354.6
Picketing
 Petition for injunction to limit picketing, description of premises in CRC 3.1151
 Protection from injunction of CCP §527.3
Violence during labor disputes, protection from CC §§51.7, 52
 Construction or application of provisions in issue, solicitor general notified CC §51.1
 Waiver of right to freedom from violence, coerced or involuntary CC §51.7

LABORATORY
Bioanalysts' records, attorney's authorized inspection of CCP §1985.7, Ev §1158
Clinical laboratory technologists (See **CLINICAL LABORATORY TECHNOLOGISTS**)
Genetic defects, actions involving CC §43.6
Parentage
 Genetic testing to determine parentage
  Accreditation of laboratories Fam §7552

LABORATORY TECHNOLOGISTS (See **CLINICAL LABORATORY TECHNOLOGISTS**)

LABOR COMMISSIONER
Judgments, enforcement by labor commissioner CCP §§690.020 to 690.050

LABOR STANDARDS ENFORCEMENT DIVISION
Judgments, enforcement
 Labor commissioner enforcement of judgments CCP §§690.020 to 690.050

LACE
Common carrier's liability for CC §2200

LACHES
Child support arrears, defenses by obligor
 Laches as to portion owed to state Fam §291

LACHES—Cont.
Community property, action for breach of fiduciary duty between spouses involving Fam §1101
Title, effect on marketability of CC §880.030

LADING, BILL OF (See **BILL OF LADING**)

LAKES
Ownership of CC §670
Title
 Border land CC §830
 State CC §670
Venue in action for recovery of penalty imposed for offense committed on CCP §393

LAND (See **REAL PROPERTY**)

LAND GRANTS (See **GRANTS OF LAND**)

LANDLORD AND TENANT CC §§1940 to 1954.07 (See also **RENT**)
Abandoned property after termination of tenancy, disposition of CC §§1980 to 1991
 Applicability of provisions CC §1980.5
 Commercial real property
  Generally CC §§1993 to 1993.09 (See within this heading, "**Commercial real property tenancies**")
  Inapplicability of provisions CC §1980.5
Abandonment by lessee
 Commercial real property
  Belief of abandonment, lessor's notice CC §1951.35
Access to tenant, landlord preventing CC §789.3
Actions
 COVID-19 rental debt, actions to recover CCP §§871.10 to 871.12
Adverse possession by tenant CCP §326
Agriculture
 Personal agriculture by tenant CC §1940.10
Aliens
 Immigration or citizenship status of persons
  Definition of immigration or citizenship status CC §1940.05
  Prohibited acts based on CC §§1940.3, 1940.35
  Retaliation against tenant by reporting or threatening to report to immigration authorities CC §1942.5
  Unduly influencing tenant to vacate by threatening disclosures relating to immigration or citizenship status CC §1940.2
Amount of deposits CC §1950.5
Animals
 Abandoned CC §1981
 Declawing or devocalizing animals
  Discouraging or denying application for occupancy for refusal of animal owner to declaw or devocalize animal CC §1942.7
Apartments (See **APARTMENTS**)
Applicant screening
 Fee CC §1950.6
 Reusable tenant screening report CC §1950.1
Assignments
 Commercial real property leases, transfer of (See **LEASES**)
 Subrogation, right of
  Lessee's remedies against assigns of lessor for breach CC §823
  Lessor's remedies against assignee of lessee for breach CC §822
 Trust deeds and mortgages, assignment of rents and leases in connection with (See **TRUST DEEDS AND MORTGAGES**)
Assisted housing developments
 Rent
  Forwarding of payment information to nationwide consumer reporting agency, election of tenant CC §1954.06
  Increase of gross rental rate on residential real property, limitations CC §1947.12
  Initial unassisted rental rate, establishment CC §1947.13
Association of tenants CC §1942.5
Attorneys' fees
 Action against landlord CC §789.3
 COVID-19
  Rental debt, action to recover CCP §871.11
 Immigration or citizenship status of tenant, occupant, etc
  Disclosures to immigration authorities with intent to intimidate or harass CC §1940.35
 Rent control litigation CC §1947.15
 Retaliatory eviction, liability CC §1942.5
Attornment of tenant to stranger CC §1948
Bed bug infestations CC §§1954.600 to §CC 1954.605
 Current infestation
  Showing, renting or leasing of premises prohibited CC §1954.602

LANDLORD AND TENANT—Cont.
  Bed bug infestations —Cont.
    Information on bed bugs provided to prospective tenants   CC §1954.603
    Inspections
      Entry by landlord to inspect   CC §1954.604
      Findings, notice to tenant   CC §1954.605
    Legislative findings and intent   CC §1954.600
    Notice by tenant of suspected infestation
      Retaliatory eviction or other retaliatory actions, prohibitions   CC §1942.5
    Pest control operators
      Defined   CC §1954.601
  Blind persons, housing accommodations for   CC §§54.1, 54.3, 54.4, 55
    Construction or application of provisions in issue, solicitor general notified   CC §55.2
  Cash payments
    Requiring cash payments   CC §1947.3
  Challenge of juror for implied bias, relationships giving rise to   CCP §229
  Charging stations for electric vehicles
    Commercial leases
      Lease terms prohibiting or restricting, void   CC §1952.7
    Installation by lessee, approval by landlord   CC §1947.6
  Citizenship status of persons
    Definition of immigration or citizenship status   CC §1940.05
    Prohibited acts based on   CC §§1940.3, 1940.35
    Retaliation against tenant by reporting or threatening to report to immigration authorities   CC §1942.5
    Unduly influencing tenant to vacate by threatening disclosures relating to immigration or citizenship status   CC §1940.2
  Cleaning deposits   CC §1950.5
  Clotheslines
    Tenant use clothesline or drying rack in private areas   CC §1940.20
  Commercial real property tenancies
    Abandonment by lessee
      Belief of abandonment, lessor's notice   CC §1951.35
    Construction-related accessibility standards
      Certified access specialist (CASp) inspections, statements, inspection certificates and inspection reports   CC §1938
    Disposition of property remaining upon termination   CC §§1993 to 1993.09
      Applicable provisions   CC §1993.01
      Contents of notice   CC §1993.04
      Definitions   CC §1993
      Form of notice   CC §1993.04
      Inapplicability of provisions   CC §1980.5
      Liability of landlord   CC §1993.08
      Nontenants, notice to   CC §1993.05
      Notice   CC §§1993.03 to 1993.05, 1993.07
      Optional nature of procedure   CC §1993.02
      Public sale   CC §1993.07
      Released property, liability   CC §1993.08
      Retention by landlord if resale value less than threshold amount   CC §1993.07
      Scope of provisions   CC §1993
      Service of notice   CC §1993.03
      Statutory construction in relation to notice of abandonment provision   CC §1993.09
      Storage of property   CC §1993.06
    Fees to recover building operating costs   CC §1950.9
    Leases generally (See **LEASES**)
    Unlawful detainer
      Notice to quit   CCP §1162
  Common interest developments (See **COMMON INTEREST DEVELOPMENTS**)
  Condominiums (See **COMMON INTEREST DEVELOPMENTS**)
  Consumer credit report used in screening of rental applicants   CC §1950.6
  Consumer reports regarding rent payments   CC §1954.07
  Controlled substance activities, abatement
    Nuisances involving controlled substances
      Unlawful detainer   CC §§3486, 3486.5
  Court or government order to vacate property
    Termination of tenancy
      Year's continuous, lawful occupation, no-fault just cause for termination   CC §1946.2
  COVID-19
    Fair debt buying practices, COVID-19 rental debt
      Sale or assignment, prohibition for debt of rental assistance recipients   CC §1788.66
    Rental debt, action to recover   CCP §§871.10 to 871.12
      Attorneys' fees   CCP §871.11
      Breach of contract actions filed before October 2020   CCP §871.10

LANDLORD AND TENANT—Cont.
  COVID-19—Cont.
    Rental debt, action to recover —Cont.
      Good faith effort by plaintiff to seek rental assistance   CCP §871.10
      Reduction in damages for refusal to obtain rental assistance   CCP §871.10
      Small claims court jurisdiction   CCP §116.223
      Sunset of provisions   CCP §871.12
      Time to commence action   CCP §871.10
      Unlawful detainer actions, applicability of provisions   CCP §871.10
    Rental debt, fees or service reductions   CC §1942.9
    Rental debt, negative use in evaluating housing applications
      Prohibition on housing providers, tenant screening companies, etc   CC §1785.20.4
    Rental housing recovery act   CCP §§1179.08 to 1179.15 (See **UNLAWFUL DETAINER**)
    Small landlord and homeowner relief act   CC §§3273.01 to 3273.16 (See **TRUST DEEDS AND MORTGAGES**)
    Tenant relief act   CCP §§1179.01 to 1179.07 (See **UNLAWFUL DETAINER**)
  Criminal activity on residential real property
    Termination of tenancy
      Just cause for termination after year's continuous, lawful occupation   CC §1946.2
  Damages
    Access, landlord preventing   CC §789.3
    Demand for return of tenant's property, landlord's failure to comply with   CC §1965
    Immigration or citizenship status of persons
      Disclosures to immigration authorities with intent to intimidate or harass   CC §1940.35
      Irrelevant to liability or remedy   CC §3339.10
    Prior recovery, effect of   CC §1952
    Retaliatory eviction   CC §1942.5
    Utilities, termination of   CC §789.3
    Wrongful occupancy   CC §§3334, 3335
  Dead-bolt locks, duty to install and maintain   CC §1941.3
  Death, rent recovery after   CC §825
  Declawing or devocalizing animals
    Discouraging or denying application for occupancy for refusal of animal owner to declaw or devocalize animal   CC §1942.7
  Deduct, repair and   CC §1942
  Demand for return of tenant's property after vacating premises   CC §1965
  Demolition of residential dwellings
    Notice of application to demolish   CC §1940.6
    Termination of tenancy
      Year's continuous, lawful occupation, no-fault just cause for termination   CC §1946.2
  Dependent adult abuse
    Termination of tenancy, restrictions   CC §1946.7, CCP §1161.3
  Deposits by tenant   CC §§1950.5, 1950.7
  Disabilities, persons with
    Modifications to premises to afford full enjoyment   CC §54.1
    Rent control units
      Moving tenant with permanent physical disability to accessible floor of property   CC §1954.53
  Discrimination in housing (See **DISCRIMINATION**)
  Domestic violence
    Documentation or evidence of abuse or violence   CCP §1161.3
    Termination of tenancy
      Victims of domestic violence, sexual assault or stalking   CC §1946.7, CCP §1161.3
  Drying racks
    Tenant use clothesline or drying rack in private areas   CC §1940.20
  Duress
    Unduly influencing tenant to vacate   CC §1940.2
  Duties   CC §§1941.1, 1941.2
  E-bikes or scooters
    Personal micromobility devices
      Rights of tenants   CC §1940.41
  Elder abuse
    Termination of tenancy, restrictions   CC §1946.7, CCP §1161.3
  Electricity (See within this heading, "**Utilities**")
  Electric vehicle charging stations
    Commercial leases
      Lease terms prohibiting or restricting, void   CC §1952.7
    Installation by lessee, approval by landlord   CC §1947.6
  Electronic funds transfers
    Alternative forms of payment   CC §1947.3

LANDLORD AND TENANT—Cont.
Emergencies
    Landlord entering because of emergency   CC §1954
    Lease provision penalizing good faith summoning of law enforcement or emergency assistance   CC §1946.8
Entry by landlord, requirements   CC §1954
    Bed bug infestations
        Inspections   CC §1954.604
    Termination of tenancy
        Just cause for termination after year's continuous, lawful occupation   CC §1946.2
    Violation of access rights
        Unduly influencing tenant to vacate   CC §1940.2
    Water service in multifamily residential rental buildings   CC §1954.211
Eviction
    Generally   CC §§789 to 793
    Floating home marinas   CC §800.70
    Forms
        Judicial council legal forms   CRCAppx A
    Mobilehome tenants (See **MOBILEHOMES**)
    Rent control ordinances, eviction of tenant based on owner's reoccupation of tenant's unit where subject to   CC §1947.10
    Retaliatory eviction   CC §1942.5
    Screening of tenants
        Reusable tenant screening report   CC §1950.1
Explosive munitions in neighborhood, notice to tenant of   CC §1940.7
Extortion
    Unduly influencing tenant to vacate   CC §1940.2
Firearms and other weapons
    Nuisances involving illegal weapons or ammunition
        Unlawful detainer   CC §3485
Fitness for occupancy, landlord's duty   CC §1941
Fixtures (See **FIXTURES**)
Forcible entry and detainer (See **FORCIBLE ENTRY AND DETAINER**)
Forms
    Judicial council legal forms   CRCAppx A
Freedom of speech
    Political signs
        Restrictions on prohibition   CC §1940.4
Gardens
    Personal agriculture by tenant   CC §1940.10
Gasoline stations   CC §1754
Gas service (See within this heading, **"Utilities"**)
Guide dogs, service dogs, and signal dogs
    Construction or application of provisions in issue, solicitor general notified   CC §55.2
Habitability, standards of   CC §§1941 to 1942.5
Harassment of tenants
    Immigration or citizenship status of tenant, occupant, etc
        Disclosures to immigration authorities with intent to intimidate or harass   CC §1940.35
Hold over tenants   CC §3335
    Foreclosure sale
        Written notice to quit to tenant   CCP §1161b
    Residential fixed term leases
        Foreclosure, possession through end of term   CCP §1161b
Homelessness
    Temporary residence by persons at risk of homelessness in dwelling unit of tenant   CC §1942.8
Human trafficking
    Restrictions on termination of tenancy   CCP §1161.3
    Victims of human trafficking
        Restrictions on termination of tenancy   CC §1946.7
Identification of property owner, procedure for   CC §§1961 to 1962.7
Immigration status of persons
    Actions to recover possession
        Restrictions on landlord actions based in immigration or citizenship status   CCP §1161.4
    Definition of immigration or citizenship status   CC §1940.05
    Involuntary quit by tenant, landlord causing
        Restrictions on landlord actions based in immigration or citizenship status   CCP §1161.4
    Prohibited acts based on   CC §§1940.3, 1940.35
    Retaliation against tenant by reporting or threatening to report to immigration authorities   CC §1942.5
    Unduly influencing tenant to vacate by threatening disclosures relating to immigration or citizenship status   CC §1940.2
Improvements, entry by landlord for   CC §1954
Injunctions against landlord   CC §789.3
Inspection upon termination   CC §1950.5
    Access by landlord to premises   CC §1954

LANDLORD AND TENANT—Cont.
Interactive computer system authorized to prepare standardized pro per court documents   CCP §1062.20
Intimidation of tenants
    Immigration or citizenship status of tenant, occupant, etc
        Disclosures to immigration authorities with intent to intimidate or harass   CC §1940.35
Karnette Rental-Purchase Act for rental-purchase contracts   CC §§1812.620 to 1812.650
Law enforcement officers
    Lease provisions penalizing good faith summoning of law enforcement or emergency assistance   CC §1946.8
Leases (See **LEASES**)
Locks, duty to install and maintain   CC §1941.3
    Change when requested by eligible tenant   CC §1941.5
    Change when requested by protected tenant   CC §1941.6
Lodgers
    Homelessness
        Temporary residence by persons at risk of homelessness in dwelling unit of tenant, rights of person at risk as lodger   CC §1942.8
Mail receptacles
    Locking mail receptacles
        Untenantable if lacking   CC §1941.1
Military service members
    Deposits, limitations   CC §1950.5
Mobilehomes (See **MOBILEHOMES**)
Mold
    Dilapidation relating to mold
        Repair obligation dependent on notice   CC §1941.7
Month-to-month tenancy, presumption of   CC §1943
Mortgagees, entry by landlord to exhibit dwelling unit to   CC §1954
Narcotics and dangerous drugs
    Unlawful detainer
        Nuisances involving controlled substances   CC §3486, CCP §1161
Notices
    Abandoned personal property of tenant, notice for disposition of   CC §§1983 to 1985
    Abandonment of real property, notice of belief of
        Commercial tenancies   CC §1951.35
    Bed bug infestations
        Information on bed bugs provided to prospective tenants   CC §1954.603
        Inspection findings, notice to tenant   CC §1954.605
    Commercial real property tenancies
        Disposition of property remaining upon termination   CC §§1993.03 to 1993.05, 1993.07
        Quit, notice to   CCP §1162
    Explosive munitions in neighborhood, notice to tenant of   CC §1940.7
    Fees prohibited   CCP §1161
    Leases (See **LEASES**)
    Locks, deficient   CC §1941.3
    Notice to quit, holding over after service
        Foreclosure sale situations, written notice to quit to tenant   CCP §1161b
    Quit notice
        Foreclosure sale situations, written notice to quit to tenant   CCP §1161b
    Rent
        Increase of gross rental rate on residential real property, limitations   CC §1947.12
    Repairs   CC §§1941.3, 1942
    Sale of building, notification of tenant   CC §1950.5
    Security deposit, disposition of   CC §1950.5
    Structural pest control notice   CC §1940.8
    Subsidized rent, notice to tenant of termination of landlord's contract with government agency providing   CC §1954.535
    Termination of tenancy
        Landlord's notice   CC §789
        Victims of domestic violence, sexual assault or stalking   CC §1946.7
    Third party claim for property, tenant receiving notice of   CC §1949
    Waiver of tenant's right to   CC §1953
Nuisances
    Termination of tenancy
        Just cause for termination after year's continuous, lawful occupation   CC §1946.2
Occupancy, tenant's right to   CC §1940.1
Oral notice of need for repairs   CC §1942
Owner of property, procedure for identification of   CC §§1961 to 1962.7
Owner's intent to occupy premises
    Termination of tenancy
        Year's continuous, lawful occupation, no-fault just cause for termination   CC §1946.2

LANDLORD AND TENANT—Cont.
- Parking, unbundling from price of rent   CC §1947.1
- Penalties for rent collection for untenantable dwelling   CC §1942.4
  - Attorneys' fees and cost of suit, landlord liability   CCP §1174.21
- Personal agriculture by tenant   CC §1940.10
- Personal injuries to tenant, waiver of landlord's duty to prevent   CC §1953
- Personal micromobility devices
  - Rights of tenants   CC §1940.41
- Pest control notice from landlord   CC §1940.8
- Pesticides
  - Notice requirements   CC §1940.8.5
- Political signs
  - Restrictions on prohibition   CC §1940.4
- Possessory notices of third party, tenant's duty to notify landlord of receipt of   CC §1949
- Preparation fees for lease or rental agreements, prohibition against   CC §1950.8
- Presumptions
  - Habitability requirements, landlord's breach of   CC §1942.3
  - Repairs, reasonable time of tenant for   CC §1942
- Pro per court documents, interactive computer system authorized to prepare standardized   CCP §1062.20
- Protected tenants
  - Locks, change upon request   CC §1941.6
- Religious items displayed on dwelling entry
  - Restrictions unenforceable   CC §1940.45
- Relocation assistance
  - Termination of tenancy
    - Year's continuous, lawful occupation, no-fault just cause for termination   CC §1946.2
- Rent
  - Assisted housing developments
    - Forwarding of payment information to nationwide consumer reporting agency, election of tenant   CC §1954.06
    - Increase of gross rental rate on residential real property, limitations   CC §1947.12
    - Initial unassisted rental rate, establishment   CC §1947.13
  - Consumer reports regarding payments   CC §1954.07
  - COVID-19 rental debt, action to recover
    - Small claims court jurisdiction   CCP §116.223
  - Homelessness
    - Temporary residence by persons at risk of homelessness in dwelling unit of tenant, adjustment of rent   CC §1942.8
  - Increase of gross rental rate on residential real property, limitations   CC §1947.12
    - Expiration of limitations, limitation of rent upon   CC §1947.13
  - Notice of increase
    - Increase of gross rental rate on residential real property, limitations   CC §1947.12
  - Parking, unbundling from price of rent   CC §1947.1
  - Payment
    - Presumption arising from receipt   Ev §636
    - Third party payment of rent   CC §1947.3
  - Public utility payments
    - Deductions from rent   CC §1942.2
  - Rent-to-own transactions   CC §§1812.620 to 1812.650
  - Termination of tenancy
    - Just cause for termination after year's continuous, lawful occupation   CC §1946.2
  - Third party payment of rent   CC §1947.3
  - Value recoverable by landlord   CC §1954.05
- Rental-purchase contracts, Karnette Rental-Purchase Act   CC §§1812.620 to 1812.650
- Rent control (See **RENT CONTROL**)
- Repairs
  - Deduct cost of repairs, tenant's right to   CC §1942
  - Deposits by tenants   CC §1950.5
  - Duty of landlord, generally   CC §1941
  - Entry by landlord for making   CC §1954
  - Locks, duty to install and maintain   CC §1941.3
  - Mold, dilapidation
    - Repair obligation dependent on notice   CC §1941.7
  - Vacate, tenant's right to   CC §1942
- Repairs and maintenance
  - Water service in multifamily residential rental buildings
    - Entry by landlord   CC §1954.211
    - Fixtures   CC §1954.210
    - Water-saving devices   CC §1954.210
- Retaliatory eviction   CC §1942.5
- Return of tenant's personal property left on premises   CC §1965
- Sale of building
  - Notifying tenant of sale of building by mail   CC §1950.5

LANDLORD AND TENANT—Cont.
- Sale of personal property abandoned by tenant   CC §1988
- Scooters
  - Personal micromobility devices, rights of tenants   CC §1940.41
- Screening fee for rental applications, landlord's right to impose   CC §1950.6
- Screening of tenants
  - COVID-19 rental debt, negative use in evaluating housing applications
    - Prohibition on housing providers, tenant screening companies, etc   CC §1785.20.4
  - Prior abuse or violence   CC §1946.9
  - Reusable tenant screening report   CC §1950.1
- Security deposits
  - Generally   CC §§1950.5, 1950.7
  - Cash payments
    - Requiring cash payments   CC §1947.3
  - Electronic funds transfers
    - Alternative forms of payment   CC §1947.3
  - Waterbeds, additional security deposit for tenants possessing   CC §1940.5
- Sexual assault
  - Documentation or evidence of abuse or violence   CCp §1161.3
  - Termination of tenancy
    - Victims of domestic violence, sexual assault or stalking   CC §1946.7, CCP §1161.3
- Small landlord and homeowner relief act   CC §§3273.01 to 3273.16
- Smoking
  - Prohibition by landlord   CC §1947.5
- Stalking
  - Documentation or evidence of abuse or violence   CCP §1161.3
  - Termination of tenancy
    - Victims of domestic violence, sexual assault or stalking   CC §1946.7, CCP §1161.3
- Storage
  - Abandoned property   CC §§1986 to 1990, CCP §1174
  - Liability for costs of storage of personal property after vacating premises   CC §1965
- Subleases (See **LEASES**)
- Subrogation rights
  - Lessee's remedies against assigns of lessor for breach   CC §823
  - Lessor's remedies against assignee of lessee for breach   CC §822
- Substandard conditions of rental housing in receivership   CCP §§568.2, 568.3
- Substantial remodeling of residential property
  - Termination of tenancy
    - Year's continuous, lawful occupation, no-fault just cause for termination   CC §1946.2
- Surrender of tenant's property left on premises   CC §1965
- Telephone services
  - Duty of landlord to install telephone jack and wiring   CC §1941.1
  - Liability of landlord for willful interruption or termination of   CC §789.3
- Tenant defined   CC §1940
- Termination of tenancy
  - Generally   CC §§789 to 793
  - Commercial real property tenancies
    - Disposition of property remaining upon termination   CC §§1993 to 1993.09
  - Demand for surrender of tenant's property left on premises   CC §1965
  - Homelessness
    - Temporary residence by persons at risk of homelessness in dwelling unit of tenant, grounds for termination of residence of person at risk   CC §1942.8
  - Mobilehome parks (See **MOBILEHOMES**)
  - Notices
    - Forcible entry and unlawful detainer complaints, detailing service of notices of termination   CCP §1166
  - Security deposit, disposition of   CC §1950.5
  - Victims of domestic violence, sexual assault, stalking and dependent or elder adult abuse
    - Restrictions on termination   CC §1946.7, CCP §1161.3
  - Water service in multifamily residential rental buildings
    - Nonpayment of bill   CC §1954.213
  - Year's continuous, lawful occupation
    - Just cause for termination, conduct constituting   CC §1946.2
    - Limitations on termination   CC §1946.2
    - No-fault just cause for termination   CC §1946.2
    - Notice from landlord to tenant of content of provisions   CC §1946.2
    - Relocation assistance in no-fault just cause situations   CC §1946.2
- Theft
  - Unduly influencing tenant to vacate   CC §1940.2
- Third party payment of rent   CC §1947.3
- Threats
  - Unduly influencing tenant to vacate   CC §1940.2
- Title of landlord, tenant denying   Ev §624

LANDLORD AND TENANT—Cont.
Trespass, entry on property to provide tenants' rights information or to participate in tenants' association as not constituting   CC §1942.6
Unlawful detainer (See **UNLAWFUL DETAINER**)
Unlawful use of premises
    Termination of tenancy
        Just cause for termination after year's continuous, lawful occupation   CC §1946.2
Unsafe conditions of rental housing in receivership   CCP §568.2
Untenantable premises   CC §§1941 to 1942.5
Use restrictions in commercial real property leases (See **LEASES**)
Utilities
    Habitability standards   CC §1941.1
    Payments to utilities
        Deductions from rent   CC §1942.2
    Separate meters, landlord's liability for failure to provide   CC §1940.9
    Termination, landlord's liability for   CC §789.3
Vacating dwelling
    Unduly influencing tenant to vacate   CC §1940.2
Victims of abuse or crime
    Lease provisions penalizing good faith summoning of law enforcement or emergency assistance   CC §1946.8
Waterbeds, tenants' possession of   CC §1940.5
Water service in multifamily residential rental buildings   CC §§1954.201 to 219
    Applicability   CC §1954.216
    Billing
        Allowable charges   CC §1954.205
        Calculations   CC §§1954.205, 1954.212
        Cycle   CC §1954.206
        Final reading and billing   CC §1954.207
        Information as to billing methodologies   CC §1954.209
        Initial reading and billing   CC §1954.207
        Monthly reading unavailable, calculations   CC §1954.212
        Statement   CC §1954.206
    Definitions   CC §1954.202
    Fees incurred by landlord from purveyors, billing agents or for penalties assessed against landlord
        Tenants not to be charged for landlord's penalties or fees   CC §1954.208
    Late fees   CC §1954.213
    Legislative findings and intent   CC §1954.201
    Nonpayment of bill
        Termination of tenancy   CC §1954.213
    Operative date of provisions   CC §1954.218
    Ordinances adopted prior to 1/1/2013
        Applicability, continuation   CC §1954.214
    Partial payments
        Crediting   CC §1954.213
    Repairs
        Entry by landlord   CC §1954.211
        Fixtures   CC §1954.210
        Water-saving devices   CC §1954.210
    Shutting off of or other interference with water service by landlord
        Prohibition   CC §1954.213
    Submeters   CC §1954.203
        Disclosures to tenants   CC §1954.204
        Entry by landlord to install, repair, etc   CC §1954.211
        Final reading and billing   CC §1954.207
        Information as to maintenance   CC §1954.209
        Initial reading and billing   CC §1954.207
        Maintenance   CC §1954.209
        Monthly reading unavailable, calculations for billing   CC §1954.212
        Portion of unit's usage metered, applicability of provisions   CC §1954.217
        When required   CC §1954.219
    Waiver of provisions prohibited   CC §1954.215
Withdrawal of property from rental market
    Termination of tenancy
        Year's continuous, lawful occupation, no-fault just cause for termination   CC §1946.2

LAND SALES CONTRACTS (See **REAL PROPERTY SALES CONTRACTS**)

LANDSCAPERS
Bond required to secure costs in action against   CCP §1029.5
Water conservation
    Commercial and industrial common interest developments
        Water-efficient landscaping, protected interest   CC §6712
    Common interest developments
        Artificial turf, architectural guidelines not to prohibit   CC §4735

LANDSCAPERS—Cont.
Water conservation—Cont.
    Common interest developments—Cont.
        Low water-using plants, architectural guidelines not to prohibit   CC §4735

LAND SURVEYORS
Design professionals' liens   CC §§8300 to 8319 (See **LIENS**)
Generally (See **SURVEYS AND SURVEYORS**)

LAND TITLES (See **TITLE AND OWNERSHIP**)

LANGUAGE
Descriptions (See **DESCRIPTIONS**)
English (See **ENGLISH LANGUAGE**)
Home solicitation sales contracts
    Cancellation
        Notice of right to cancel in contract in same language as language of negotiation   CC §1689.7
International commercial arbitration and conciliation   CCP §§1297.221 to 1297.224
Spanish (See **SPANISH**)
Translators (See **TRANSLATORS AND INTERPRETERS**)

LANTERMAN-PETRIS-SHORT ACT
Conservatorship for gravely disabled persons
    Remote proceedings
        Conditions for proceeding through use of remote technology   CCP §367.76
Involuntary treatment
    Remote proceedings
        Conditions for proceeding through use of remote technology   CCP §367.76

LARCENY (See **THEFT**)

LAST DAY
Computation of time in which act provided by law is to be done   CCP §12

LAST ILLNESS
Community property, last illness expense liability of   Pro §11446
Conservatorship, last illness expense liability of   Pro §2631
Guardianship, last illness expense liability of   Pro §2631
Priority for payment of last illness expenses by decedent's estate   Pro §§11420, 11421
Trust estate of deceased settlor, claim for last illness expenses against   Pro §19326

LATENT DEFECTS
Statutes of limitation on actions for damages for deficiencies in planning or construction of improvement to real property   CCP §337.15

LATERAL SUPPORT FROM ADJOINING PROPERTY
Right to   CC §832

LAUNDRIES
Gender
    Prohibition against charging different price for services of similar or like kind based solely on   CC §51.6
    Small business gender discrimination in pricing services compliance act   CC §§55.61 to 55.63
Lien for services of   CC §§3051, 3066

LAW
Generally   CCP §1895
Constitution and statutes, law expressed by   CC §22.1
Organic law   CCP §1897
Unwritten law   CCP §§1895, 1899
Written laws   CCP §1896

LAW AND FACT QUESTIONS (See **QUESTIONS OF LAW OR FACT**)

LAW AND MOTION PROCEEDINGS   CRC 3.1100 to 3.1372
Administrative mandate cases, lodging of record in   CRC 3.1140
Advancing case set for trial
    Motion or application to advance, specially set or reset   CRC 3.1335
Amended pleadings   CRC 3.1324
Appendices
    Papers, etc, in support of motion   CRC 3.1112
Applicability   CRC 3.1100, 3.1103
Arbitration, motions concerning   CRC 3.1330
Attachments to notice of motion   CRC 3.1113

LAW AND MOTION PROCEEDINGS—Cont.
Attorneys
    Relief as counsel, motion for   CRC 3.1362
Binding together of document with exhibits   CRC 3.1110
Bonds and undertakings   CRC 3.1130
Captions
    Declaration or affidavit   CRC 3.1115
    Demurrers   CRC 3.1320
Case citation format
    Memorandum in support of motion   CRC 3.1113
Change of venue, motion for   CRC 3.1326
Civil petitions
    Emancipation of minors   CRC 3.1370
    Environmental quality act   CRC 3.1365
    Military service
        Financial obligations during service, relief   CRC 3.1372
Clerk, material lodged with   CRC 3.1302
Combined summons and complaint regarding parental obligations   CRC 5.325
Continuance, motion for   CRC 3.1332
Copies of authorities   CRC 3.1113
Counsel, motion to be relieved as   CRC 3.1362
Date, time and location of hearing, papers to specify   CRC 3.1110
Declarations in support of motion   CRC 3.1112
Definitions and construction   CRC 3.1103
Demurrers   CRC 3.1320
Depositions
    Use as exhibits   CRC 3.1116
Determination of submitted matters, notice of   CRC 3.1109
Discovery   CRC 3.1100
Dismissal of actions
    Delay in prosecution   CRC 3.1342
    Motions to dismiss   CRC 3.1340
Driving license suspension, stay of   CRC 3.1142
Emancipation of minors   CRC 3.1370
Environmental quality act   CRC 3.1365
    Petitions under environmental quality act   CRC 3.2200 to 3.2240
Evidence at hearings   CRC 3.1306
Exhibits
    Format for submission   CRC 3.1110
    Papers, etc, in support of motion   CRC 3.1112
    References   CRC 3.1113
Ex parte applications and orders   CRC 3.1200 to 3.1207
Foreign language, translation of exhibits written in   CRC 3.1110
Format and filing of papers   CRC 3.1110 to 3.1116
General format requirements   CRC 3.1110
Hearings   CRC 3.1304, 3.1306
    Telephone appearance at law and motion hearings   CRC 3.670
Injunctions   CRC 3.1150 to 3.1161
In limine motions
    Format of motion papers   CRC 3.1112
Judicial notice of material   CRC 3.1306
Late filing of papers   CRC 3.1300
Length of memorandum in support of motion   CRC 3.1113
Lien on cause of action, motion to grant   CRC 3.1360
Memorandum in support of motion   CRC 3.1113
    Summary judgment or adjudication   CRC 3.1350
    When memorandum not required   CRC 3.1114
Military service
    Financial obligations during service, relief   CRC 3.1372
Motions
    Required elements of   CRC 3.1112
    Strike, motions to   CRC 3.1322
Motions in limine   CRC 3.1112
Moving and supporting papers   CRC 3.1112
    Date, time and location of hearing, papers shall specify   CRC 3.1110
    Late papers, effect of filing   CRC 3.1300
    Memorandum in support of motion   CRC 3.1113
        When memorandum not required   CRC 3.1114
    Place and manner of filing   CRC 3.1302
    Preparation of court orders by prevailing party   CRC 3.1312
    Proof of service, time for filing   CRC 3.1300
    Proposed order, electronic submission   CRC 3.1312
    Reference to previously filed papers   CRC 3.1110
    Time for filing and serving   CRC 3.1300
Nonappearance of parties   CRC 3.1304
Noticed motions   CRC 3.1300 to 3.1312
Notices
    Attorney, notice of motion to be relieved as   CRC 3.1362
    Matter not to be heard, duty to notify if   CRC 3.1304
    Motions   CRC 3.1110
    Nonappearance at law and motion hearing   CRC 3.1304

LAW AND MOTION PROCEEDINGS—Cont.
Oral testimony   CRC 3.1306
Orders
    Proposed order, preparation by prevailing party   CRC 3.1312
        Electronic submission of proposed order   CRC 3.1312
    Shortening time   CRC 3.1300
    Show cause, application for   CRC 3.1150
Page limits
    Memorandum in support of motion   CRC 3.1113
Place and manner of filing papers   CRC 3.1300, 3.1302
Preliminary injunctions, application or noticed motion and service   CRC 3.1150
Preparation of court orders by prevailing party   CRC 3.1312
    Electronic submission of proposed order   CRC 3.1312
Procedural motions   CRC 3.1330 to 3.1335
Proof of service, time for filing   CRC 3.1300
Proposed orders or judgments   CRC 3.1113
Provisional and injunctive relief   CRC 3.1130 to 3.1184
    Bonds, surety   CRC 3.1130
    Receivers   CRC 3.1175 to 3.1184
    Writs
        Administrative mandate cases, lodging of record   CRC 3.1140
        Driving license suspension, stay of   CRC 3.1142
Receivers   CRC 3.1175 to 3.1184
Reference to previously filed papers   CRC 3.1110
Reporting of proceedings   CRC 3.1310
Resetting trial date
    Motion or application to advance, specially set or reset   CRC 3.1335
Schedule of hearings   CRC 3.1304
Service of papers
    Harassment, enjoining   CRC 3.1160
Setting trial date
    Motion or application to advance, specially set or reset   CRC 3.1335
Strike, motion to   CRC 3.1322
Style of memorandum in support of motion   CRC 3.1113
Submission of cause
    Without hearing   CRC 3.1304
Summary adjudication   CRC 3.1350
    Memorandum in support of motion
        Page limits   CRC 3.1113
    Objections to evidence   CRC 3.1352
        Written objections   CRC 3.1354
    Unlawful detainer
        Motions for summary judgment   CRC 3.1351
Support actions under Social Security Act Title IV-D, notice   CRC 5.315
Supporting papers   CRC 3.1112
Telephone appearances   CRC 3.670
Temporary restraining order, application for order to show cause   CRC 3.1150
Tentative rulings   CRC 3.1308
    Procedure for issuance of   CRC 3.1306
Time
    Filing and service of papers   CRC 3.1300
    Hearing, time of   CRC 3.1304
    Motions to strike   CRC 3.1322
    Moving and supporting papers, filing and serving   CRC 3.1300
    Preparation of court orders by prevailing party   CRC 3.1312
    Proof of service, time for filing   CRC 3.1300
    Shortening time, application for order   CRC 3.1300
    Venue, moving to strike, demur or plead following denial of motion to transfer   CRC 3.1326
Transcript of law and motion proceedings, availability of   CRC 3.1310
Trial date
    Motion or application to advance, specially set or reset   CRC 3.1335
Unlawful detainer
    Quash or stay, motions in summary proceedings involving real property possession   CRC 3.1327
Venue, motion for change of   CRC 3.1326
Writs
    Administrative mandate cases, lodging of record   CRC 3.1140
    Driving license suspension, stay of   CRC 3.1142

LAW BOOKS
Presumptions of accuracy of   Ev §645

LAW CLERKS
Small claims court judges, law clerks assisting   CCP §116.270

LAW ENFORCEMENT AGENCIES
Consumer privacy rights
    Compliance or cooperation by business with law enforcement direction to retain information   CC §1798.145
Domestic violence orders (See **DOMESTIC VIOLENCE**)

LAW ENFORCEMENT AGENCIES—Cont.
Electronic court records, remote access
  Government entities, access by
    List of government entities which may be authorized to receive access CRC 2.540
Harassment, enforcing protective orders against CCP §527.6
  California law enforcement telecommunications (CLETS) information form, confidentiality and use of information CRC 1.51, CRCAppx A
  COVID-19, emergency rule CRCAppx I Emer Rule 8
Immigration and naturalization
  Contracts by local government or law enforcement agency to detain noncitizens for civil immigration custody
    Prohibition CC §1670.9
Real Estate Fraud Prosecution Trust Fund, procedures for distributions from Gov §27388

LAW ENFORCEMENT OFFICERS
Arbitration procedure in collective bargaining agreement
  Firefighters and law enforcement officers (See **ARBITRATION**)
Arrest (See **ARREST**)
Civil rights, actions to enforce against peace officer or custodial officer
  Immunity
    Inapplicability of state immunity provisions CC §52.1
Claims against public entities and employees (See **CLAIMS AGAINST PUBLIC ENTITIES AND EMPLOYEES**)
Contempt orders, stay of execution of CCP §128
Deaf or hard of hearing victims
  Interpreter services Ev §754
Decedent's tangible personal property to surviving spouse, delivery of Pro §330
Defamation action brought by CC §47.5
Deprivation of individual's constitutionally protected rights, privileges or immunities, prohibition against CC §52.3
Dogs
  Assignment of officer to canine unit outside jurisdiction
    Discrimination in lodging, eating, or transportation due to dog CC §54.25
Domestic violence prevention orders (See **DOMESTIC VIOLENCE**)
Firearms and other weapons
  Domestic violence, taking temporary custody of firearms at scene of incident
    Authority of peace officer at scene Fam §6383
Harassment, serving and enforcing protective orders against CCP §527.6
  California law enforcement telecommunications (CLETS) information form, confidentiality and use of information CRC 1.51, CRCAppx A
  COVID-19, emergency rule CRCAppx I Emer Rule 8
Immunity (See **CLAIMS AGAINST PUBLIC ENTITIES AND EMPLOYEES**)
Injuries willfully inflicted on peace officers, responsibility for CC §1714.9
Jury duty
  Criminal proceedings, exclusion as juror CCP §219
  Scheduling accommodations CCP §219.5, CRC 2.1004
Landlord and tenant
  Lease provisions penalizing good faith summoning of law enforcement or emergency assistance CC §1946.8
Lost property, duties as to CC §§2080.1 to 2080.5
Missing persons, search for Pro §12406
Resuscitative measures, requests regarding Pro §§4780 to 4786
  Health care providers Pro §4781
Sexual assault by officer
  Claims against public entities and employees
    Presentation of claims arising from sexual assault by officer, requirements Gov §945.9
Supervisorial officers
  Excessive force allegations, motion for disclosure of information
    Records of officers not present, exceptions to nondisclosure Ev §1047
Transitional housing program misconduct
  Injunctions or temporary restraining orders
    Notice to law enforcement of order or injunction CC §1954.14
Unemployment insurance administration, right to disclosure of information obtained through Ev §1040
Warrants for arrest (See **ARREST**)
Witnesses, peace officers as (See **WITNESSES**)
Work-related death, health care benefits for survivors
  Continuity for survivors Pro §13600

LAW LIBRARIES
State Law Library, civil filing fees, deposit into Special Account Gov §68926.3

LAW REVISION COMMISSION
Enforcement of judgments and orders
  Continuing study, review, etc of provisions CCP §681.035

LAW REVISION COMMISSION—Cont.
Transfer on death deeds
  Study of effect of revocable transfer on death deed by law revision commission Pro §5605

LAW SCHOOLS
Certified law students
  Practice under supervision CRC 9.42
Examining committee, schools unaccredited with CRC 9.30
Judges, teaching by CRCSupp JudEthicsCanon 4
Legal services programs
  Attorney professional conduct
    Limited legal services programs, service in ProfC 6.5
    Membership in legal services organization ProfC 6.3
  Registered legal aid attorneys CRC 9.45
    Fingerprinting of special admission attorneys CRC 9.9.5
Provisional licensing of 2020 law school graduates CRC 9.49
  Pathway to full licensure, provisional licensure with CRC 9.49.1
Small claims courts, law students assisting litigants in CCP §116.940, CRC 3.2120
Unaccredited schools CRC 9.30
  Study in unaccredited law schools CRC 9.30

LAW STUDENTS
Certified law student program CRC 9.42
Provisional licensing of 2020 law school graduates CRC 9.49
  Pathway to full licensure, provisional licensure with CRC 9.49.1
Small claims courts, law students assisting litigants in CCP §116.940, CRC 3.2120
Unaccredited law schools, study in CRC 9.30

LAWYERS (See **ATTORNEYS**)

LAYAWAY PLANS CC §§1749 to 1749.4
Defined CC §1749.1

LAYING FOUNDATION (See **EVIDENCE**)

LAYOFFS
Discrimination
  Discounts or benefits for loss of or reduction in employment not considered discrimination CC §51.13

LEAD PAINT ABATEMENT
Nuisances
  Participating properties in abatement program not considered nuisances CC §3494.5
Participating properties in abatement program
  Immunity from liability CC §3494.5
  Not considered nuisances CC §3494.5
  Not considered substandard building CC §3494.5
  Not considered untenantable CC §3494.5

LEASES
Abandonment by lessee CC §§1951 to 1951.7, 1954, CCP §415.47
Administration of estates (See **ADMINISTRATION OF ESTATES**)
Agricultural land, limitations on leasing CC §717
Arbitration under CC §§1942.1, 1942.5
Asian language contracts, translations CC §1632
Assignment of lease
  Termination of tenancy
    Just cause for termination after year's continuous, lawful occupation CC §1946.2
  Assignments
    Assignee for benefit of creditor, right to occupy business premises CC §1954.05
    Commercial real property leases, transfer of (See within this heading, "**Commercial real property leases**")
    Subrogation, right of
      Lessee's remedies against assigns of lessor for breach CC §823
      Lessor's remedies against assignee of lessee for breach CC §822
    Trust deed or mortgage, assignment in connection with (See **TRUST DEEDS AND MORTGAGES**)
Attachments on CCP §487.010
Automobiles (See **AUTOMOBILES**)
Blanket encumbrance, required notice to purchaser or lessee of CC §1133
Blind persons, right to lease housing accommodations CC §§54.1, 54.3, 54.4, 55
  Construction or application of provisions in issue, solicitor general notified CC §55.2
Breach of lease, statutes of limitations on action involving
  Parol lease CCP §339.5

LEASES—Cont.
 Breach of lease, statutes of limitations on action involving—Cont.
  Written lease   CCP §337.2
 Broker's duty to inspect premises   CC §§2079 to 2079.5
 Change of term of lease period   CC §827
 City property, lease of   CC §719
 Commercial real property leases
  Abandonment
   Belief of abandonment, lessor's notice   CC §1951.35
  Definitions   CC §1995.020
  Disposition of property remaining upon termination of tenancy   CC §§1993 to 1993.09 (See **LANDLORD AND TENANT**)
  Effective date of governing law   CC §1995.030
  Implied renewal of lease
   Termination, notice requirements   CC §1946.1
  Notice of change of terms of lease   CC §827
  Restrictions on transfers
   Absence of restrictive lease provisions   CC §1995.210
   Ambiguities in restrictive lease provisions   CC §1995.220
   Breach and remedies   CC §§1995.300 to 1995.340
   Express standard or condition, validity of transfer subject to   CC §1995.240
   Landlord's consent, validity of transfer requiring   CC §§1995.250, 1995.260
   Legislative findings regarding   CC §1995.270
   Remedies of landlord and tenant   CC §§1995.300 to 1995.340
   Subsequent transfer, effect of breach upon tenant   CC §1995.340
  Scope of law   CC §1995.010
  Trust deed or mortgage, assignment of rents and leases in connection with (See **TRUST DEEDS AND MORTGAGES**)
  Unlawful detainer actions   CCP §1161.1
  Use restrictions
   Generally   CC §§1997.010 to 1997.050
   Absolute prohibition on change in use   CC §1997.230
   Ambiguity in   CC §1997.220
   Computation of rental loss   CC §1997.040
   Consent required of landlord   CC §§1997.250, 1997.260
   Continuation after breach and abandonments   CC §1997.040
   Express standard or condition   CC §1997.240
   Scope of law   CC §1997.270
   Validity of use   CC §1997.210
 Common interest developments
  Governing documents not to prohibit   CC §§4740, 4741
 Community property (See **COMMUNITY PROPERTY**)
 Consumer warranty protection for leased goods   CC §§1791, 1795.4
 Covenants   CC §§1469, 1470
 Damages
  Generally   CC §3308
  Automobile lease violations (See **AUTOMOBILES**)
  Liquidated damages in action on real property leases   CC §1951.5
 Decedents' estates (See **ADMINISTRATION OF ESTATES**)
 Deeds of trust and mortgages
  Foreclosure
   Notification of foreclosure   CC §2924b
 Destruction of property by lessee   CC §1941.2
 Disabled persons, rights to lease housing accommodations   CC §§54.1, 54.3, 54.4, 55
  Construction or application of provisions in issue, solicitor general notified   CC §55.2
 Discriminatory clauses in real property leases   CC §§53, 782, 782.5
 Electricity furnished under   CC §§1941.1, 1941.2
 Eminent domain (See **EMINENT DOMAIN**)
 Enforcement of judgment against lessee's property interests   CCP §695.035
 Equity relief in   CC §1951.8
 Floors, repair of   CC §1941.1
 Forcible entry and unlawful detainer complaints, residential property
  Copy of lease included with complaint   CCP §1166
 Forfeiture (See **UNLAWFUL DETAINER**)
 For lease signs, regulation of   CC §§712, 713
 Forms
  Belief of abandonment, notice of   CC §1951.3
   Commercial tenancies   CC §1951.35
  Reclaiming abandoned property, notice of rights in   CC §§1984, 1985
 Garbage, disposal of   CC §§1941.1, 1941.2
 Gasoline stations, emission standards affecting leases for   CC §1952.8
 Guardianship (See **GUARDIAN AND WARD**)
 Heat, requirements for furnishing   CC §1941.1
 Heavy equipment rentals
  Personal property tax
   Addition of estimated personal property tax reimbursement to rental price   CC §1656.5

LEASES—Cont.
 Husband and wife having leasehold interest in property, characterization of property   Fam §700
 Implied renewal of lease agreement   CC §1945
  Termination, notice requirements   CC §1946.1
 Increase of rent
  Notice in intent to increase rent   CC §827
 Inspection of residential property, broker's duty of   CC §§2079 to 2079.5
 Karnette Rental-Purchase Act for rental-purchase contracts   CC §§1812.620 to 1812.650
 Life leases, rent recovery under   CC §824
 Limitation of actions
  Parol lease   CCP §339.5
  Written lease   CCP §337.2
 Mail
  City property, notice of   CC §719
  Termination notice   CC §1946
 Mineral rights (See **MINERALS AND MINERAL RIGHTS**)
 Mortgage default, notification of   CC §2924b
 Municipal corporations (See **CITIES AND MUNICIPALITIES**)
 Notices
  Abandonment notice, form of   CC §§1951.3, 1984, 1985
   Commercial tenancies, belief by lessor of abandonment   CC §1951.35
  Advance payment of rent on reletting   CC §1951.7
  Blanket encumbrance   CC §1133
  Changing terms of lease period   CC §827
  City property, leases of   CC §719
  Forfeiture, relief from   CCP §1179
  Landlord and tenant (See **LANDLORD AND TENANT**)
  Mailing of
   City property   CC §719
   Termination notice   CC §1946
  Mortgages, foreclosure of   CC §2924b
  Registered sex offenders, notification concerning statewide database of locations of   CC §2079.10a
  Repairs, tenant's notice for   CC §1942
  Termination notice   CC §1946
  Trust deeds, foreclosure of   CC §2924b
 Oil and gas (See **OIL AND GAS**)
 Partition action involving   CCP §872.540
 Personal property   CC §§1925 to 1935
  Rent-to-own transactions   CC §§1812.620 to 1812.650
 Plumbing requirements under   CC §§1941.1, 1941.2
 Registered sex offenders, notification concerning statewide database of locations of   CC §2079.10a
 Renewal of lease
  Implied renewal of lease
   Generally   CC §1945
   Termination, notice requirements   CC §1946.1
  Provisions in lease agreement   CC §1945.5
 Rental-purchase contracts, Karnette Rental-Purchase Act for   CC §§1812.620 to 1812.650
 Rent control on real property leases (See **RENT CONTROL**)
 Retaliatory eviction   CC §1942.5
 Retroactive operation of provisions governing   CC §1952.2
 Sanitation requirements   CC §§1941.1, 1941.2
 Spanish language, leases written in   CC §1632
 Stairways, repair of   CC §1941.1
 State of California (See **STATE OF CALIFORNIA**)
 Statute of frauds   CC §1624, CCP §1971
 Statutes of limitation
  Parol lease, period for action after breach of   CCP §339.5
  Written lease, period for action after breach of   CCP §337.2
 Subleases
  Lessor's remedies for abandoned lease subject to lessee's right to sublet property, availability of   CC §1951.4
  Termination of tenancy
   Just cause for termination after year's continuous, lawful occupation   CC §1946.2
 Subrogation rights
  Lessee's remedies against assigns of lessor for breach   CC §823
  Lessor's remedies against assignee of lessee for breach   CC §822
 Surrender, landlord entering after   CC §1954
 Termination of lease
  Inspection by landlord   CC §1950.5
  Notice requirements   CC §1946.1
  Rights of parties after   CC §§1951 to 1951.7
  Statutes of limitation
   Parol lease   CCP §339.5
   Written lease   CCP §337.2

LEASES—Cont.
Termination of lease—Cont.
- Victims of domestic violence, sexual assault, stalking and dependent or elder adult abuse
  - Restrictions on termination of tenancy   CC §1946.7, CCP §1161.3

30 years after execution of instrument, invalidity of lease if possession does not commence within   CC §715
Trusts (See **TRUSTS**)
Unclaimed property (See **UNCLAIMED PROPERTY**)
Unlawful detainer (See **UNLAWFUL DETAINER**)
Use restrictions (See within this heading, "**Commercial real property leases**")
Vacation of premises, rights of parties after   CC §§1951 to 1951.7
Voidable transactions statute, exemption of lease-back transactions to   CC §3440.1
Waiver
- Clause in lease, requirements for   CC §1953
- Restrictions on right to   CC §1942.1

Warranty protection for leased goods   CC §§1791, 1795.4
Water supply, requirements for furnishing   CC §1941.1
Weather, protecting from   CC §1941.1
Writing requirements   CC §1624, CCP §1971

LEASES AND RENTAL AGREEMENTS   CC §§1941 to 1954.07

LEGAL AID
Registered legal aid attorneys   CRC 9.45
- Fingerprinting of special admission attorneys   CRC 9.9.5

LEGAL DISABILITIES (See **STATUTES OF LIMITATION**)

LEGAL ESTATES PRINCIPAL AND INCOME LAW
Administrative expenses, allocation of   CC §731.15
Animals, allocation of receipts for   CC §731.10
Applicability of Act   CC §§731.02, 731.04
Bonds, allocation of   CC §731.08
Citation of Act   CC §731
Construction and interpretation   CC §731.05
Continuation of business, use of principal for   CC §731.09
Corporate assets, distribution of   CC §731.07
Death of tenant, effect of   CC §731.06
Definitions   CC §731.03
Delayed income, allocation of   CC §731.13
Depletion, allocation of property subject to   CC §731.12
Management expenses, allocation of   CC §731.15
Mortgage payments, apportionment of   CC §731.14
Natural resources, allocation of receipts for   CC §731.11
Sale of property, allocation of gain on   CC §731.14
Saving clause of Act   CC §731.01
Termination of tenant's right to income   CC §731.06

LEGAL MALPRACTICE (See **MALPRACTICE**)

LEGAL RESEARCH
Small claims court judges, law clerks assisting   CCP §116.270

LEGAL SEPARATION   Fam §2000
Action for breach of fiduciary duty between spouses   Fam §1101
Affidavit, proof of grounds by   Fam §2336
Animals
- Pet animals
  - Division of property   Fam §2605

Assets and liabilities, disclosure of   Fam §§2100 to 2113
Attorney's fees and costs   Fam §§270 to 274, 2010, 2030 to 2034, 2040
- Allocation of fees and costs   Fam §§2032, 2034
- Financial need basis   CRC 5.427

Concealment of property   Fam §§2040 to 2045
Conciliation petition affecting stay on filing petition for separation   Fam §1840
Consent required for judgment   Fam §2345
Contempt   CCP §1218
Conversion of proceeding to dissolution proceeding   Fam §2321
Date of separation
- Defined   Fam §2321

Decision of court on   Fam §2338
Declaration of assets and liabilities   Fam §§2100 to 2113
Default judgment
- Declaration for default or uncontested dissolution or legal separation
  - Judicial council forms   CRCAppx A
- Procedure for   Fam §§2335.5, 2338.5
- Proof required for   Fam §2336
- Waiver of final declaration of financial disclosure   Fam §2110

Disclosure of assets and liabilities   Fam §§2100 to 2113

LEGAL SEPARATION—Cont.
Division of property
- Income tax liability, joint   Fam §2628
- Pet animals   Fam §2605
- Retirement benefits
  - Tribal court orders, payments pursuant to   Fam §2611

Domestic partnerships   CRC 5.76
Earnings and accumulations while living separate and apart are separate property   Fam §§771, 772
Encumbering property, restrictions on   Fam §§754, 2040 to 2045
Expenses and income, disclosure of   Fam §§2100 to 2113
Extension of time   Fam §2339
Family centered case resolution   CRC 5.83, Fam §§2450 to 2452
Family law information centers for unrepresented low-income litigants   Fam §§15000 to 15012
Family rules
- Default
  - Hearing on default judgments submitted on basis of declaration or affidavit   CRC 5.409
  - Review of default based on declaration or affidavit   CRC 5.407
- Domestic partnerships
  - Dissolution, legal separation, or annulment   CRC 5.76
- Parties
  - Husband and wife or domestic partners as parties   CRC 5.16
- Title IV-D support enforcement
  - Consolidation of support orders   CRC 5.365

Fees
- Filing fees in family law cases   Gov §§70670 to 70676
- Superior court fees
  - First paper, filing   Gov §§70602.5, 70602.6, 70670

Financial assets and liabilities
- Sealing pleadings concerning financial assets and liabilities   Fam §2024.6

Forms
- Judicial council legal forms   CRCAppx A

Grounds for   Fam §2310
Health insurance
- Notice of reduced-cost options through California health benefit exchange or no-cost Medi-Cal
  - Court notice to parties upon filing for annulment, divorce, etc   Fam §2024.7

Incapacity
- Legal incapacity to make decisions
  - Effect on support obligation   Fam §2313
  - Grounds for dissolution   Fam §2310
  - Proof   Fam §2312

Income and expenses, disclosure of   Fam §§2100 to 2113
Income tax liability, joint   Fam §2628
Joinder of parties   Fam §2021
Joint petition for dissolution of marriage or for legal separation   Fam §2330
- Procedure   Fam §2342.5
  - Rulemaking   Fam §2342.5.1
- Service deemed upon filing   Fam §2331

Judgments   CRC 5.413, Fam §2338
- Consent required for   Fam §2345
- Final   Fam §§2339, 2342
- Notice of entry of judgment   CRC 5.415
- Protective orders included in   Fam §§2049, 6360, 6361
- Relief from   Fam §§2120 to 2129
- Subsequent judgment for dissolution not barred by   Fam §2347

Jurisdiction   Fam §§2010 to 2013
- Same sex marriage
  - Residence   Fam §2320

Military personnel, waiver of respondent's filing fees for   Gov §70673
Notice of entry of judgment   CRC 5.413, 5.415
Notice to parties advising review of wills, insurance policies, etc   Fam §2024
Pendency of proceeding, recording notice of   Fam §754
Pet animals
- Division of property   Fam §2605

Petitions
- Generally   Fam §2330
- Amendment to convert proceeding to dissolution proceeding   Fam §2321
- Contents of   Fam §2330
- Financial assets and liabilities
  - Sealing pleadings concerning financial assets and liabilities   Fam §2024.6
- Service on other spouse   Fam §2331
- Social security numbers
  - Redaction to ensure privacy   Fam §2024.5

Power of attorney, termination of   Pro §3722
Protective and restraining orders
- Ex parte orders   Fam §§240 to 246, 2045

LEGAL SEPARATION—Cont.
Protective and restraining orders—Cont.
    Judgment, orders in   Fam §§2049, 6360, 6361
    Notice and hearing, orders after   Fam §2047
    Summons, inclusion of restraining order in   Fam §§231 to 235, 2040, 2041
Residency requirements   Fam §2321
    Same sex marriages   Fam §2320
Responsive pleading, time for filing   Fam §2020
Same sex marriage
    Residency requirements   Fam §2320
Social security numbers
    Confidentiality of persons involved in annulment, dissolution or legal separation
        Redaction of numbers from documents   Fam §2024.5
Specific acts of misconduct, admissibility of   Fam §2335
Statistical information collected by Judicial Council and reported to legislature   Fam §2348
Summons, inclusion of temporary restraining order in   Fam §§231 to 235, 2040 to 2041
Transferring property during pendency of action   Fam §§754, 2040 to 2045
Uncontested cases
    Declaration for default or uncontested dissolution or legal separation
        Judicial council forms   CRCAppx A
Withdrawal of attorney in domestic relations matters   CCP §285.1

LEGAL SERVICES AGENCIES
Attorney professional conduct
    Limited legal services programs, service in   ProfC 6.5
    Membership in legal services organization   ProfC 6.3
Attorneys
    Registered legal aid attorneys   CRC 9.45
        Fingerprinting of special admission attorneys   CRC 9.9.5
Withdrawal of legal service agency attorney for indigent client   CCP §§285.2 to 285.4

LEGAL SERVICES FOR INDIGENTS
Attorney professional conduct
    Limited legal services programs, service in   ProfC 6.5
    Membership in legal services organization   ProfC 6.3
Attorneys
    Registered legal aid attorney   CRC 9.45
        Fingerprinting of special admission attorneys   CRC 9.9.5
Civil legal counsel
    Sargent Shriver civil counsel act   Gov §§68650, 68651
Fee waiver
    Civil rules governing waiver of fees and costs   CRC 3.50 to 3.58
    Economically unable to pay   Gov §§68630 to 68641
Registered legal aid attorney   CRC 9.45
    Fingerprinting of special admission attorneys   CRC 9.9.5

LEGATEES (See **WILLS**)

LEGISLATION
Judge's participation in drafting laws, effect on impartiality of   CCP §170.2

LEGISLATIVE INTENT (See **CONSTRUCTION AND INTERPRETATION**)

LEGISLATURE
Administrative Procedure Act (See **ADMINISTRATIVE PROCEDURE ACT**)
Attorney professional conduct
    Nonadjudicative proceedings
        Advocacy in nonadjudicative proceedings   ProfC 3.9
Attorneys attending legislature, time extension for   CCP §1054.1
Claims against public entities and employees (See **CLAIMS AGAINST PUBLIC ENTITIES AND EMPLOYEES**)
Code effect, time of   CC §23
Continuance of trials when participants members of   CCP §595
Information Practices Act, obtaining disclosures under   CC §1798.24
Judicial notice of acts by   Ev §§451, 452
Jury service and selection, policy statement re   CCP §191
Libel and slander action, privilege from   CC §47
Marriage, legislators as authorized to solemnize   Ev §400
Privileged communications rule applicable to hearings   CC §47, Ev §901
Small claims
    Advisory committee, appointments to   CCP §116.950
    Legislative findings and declarations regarding small claims division   CCP §116.120

LEGITIMACY OF CHILDREN
Parentage
    Generally   Fam §§7540 to 7581 (See **PATERNITY**)
    Genetic testing to determine parentage   Fam §§7550 to 7562 (See **PATERNITY**)

LEMON LAW (See **AUTOMOBILES**)

LESSER INCLUDED OFFENSES
Multiple punishment for same act   CRC 4.412

LETTERS
Administration of decedent's estate, letters of (See **EXECUTORS AND ADMINISTRATORS**)
Adoption agency releasing personal property upon request of adoptee and others   Fam §9206
Answer admissible as evidence after letter read   Ev §356
Conservators (See **CONSERVATORS**)
Employment recommendation, protecting source of letters for   CC §1798.26
Guardianship (See **GUARDIAN AND WARD**)
Presumption of receiving properly addressed and mailed letter   Ev §641
Response as authenticated writing   Ev §1420
Title to   CC §985

LETTERS OF CREDIT
Electronic transactions
    Exceptions to applicability of electronic transactions provisions   CC §1633.3
Mechanics' liens
    Large projects, security for   CC §§8700 to 8730
Secured obligations, letters of credit supporting   CCP §580.5
Specified loan transactions, unenforceability of letter in   CCP §580.7
Suretyship obligation not including   CC §2787

LETTERS PATENT
Limitation of actions for recovery of real property   CCP §§316, 317

LEVY AND LEVYING OFFICERS
Attachment (See **ATTACHMENT**)
Claim and delivery (See **CLAIM AND DELIVERY**)
Enforcement of judgments (See **ENFORCEMENT OF JUDGMENTS**)
Garnishment (See **GARNISHMENT**)

LEWDNESS (See **INDECENCY AND OBSCENITY**)

LIABILITY INSURANCE (See **INSURANCE**)

LIBEL AND SLANDER
Generally   CC §44
Attorneys' fees   CCP §1021.7
Candidates for office (See **CANDIDATES FOR OFFICE**)
Child abuse report   CC §48.7
Complaint
    Extrinsic facts, alleging   CCP §460
    Mitigating circumstances alleged to reduce damages   CCP §461
    Time for answer to   CCP §§460.5, 460.7
    Truth alleged to reduce damages   CCP §461
Constitutional right to petition and free speech on public issues, motion to strike causes of action having chilling effect on   CCP §§425.16, 425.17
    SLAPPback actions   CCP §425.18
Contagious diseases   CC §46
Continuously published, affidavit stating alleged defamatory matter has been   CCP §460.5
Correction demand for libel by newspaper or radio   CC §48a
Credit reporting (See **CREDIT REPORTING**)
Damages recoverable from newspaper or radio broadcast   CC §48a
Definitions   CC §§45, 46
Elective office or by candidate, preference on appeal of actions by person holding   CCP §44
Evidence necessary for damage action   CC §45a
Extrinsic facts   CC §45a
Foreign judgments
    Bar to action, foreign judgment as   CC §3425.4
    Declaratory relief   CCP §1725
    Denial of recognition   CCP §1725
Immunities
    Privileges generally (See within this heading, "**Privileges**")
Innuendo   CC §45a
Joint actions for   CC §§3425.1 to 3425.5
Judges
    Censure or removal proceedings against judge, protection from defamation liability for statements in   JudPerR 103

LIBEL AND SLANDER—Cont.
Judges—Cont.
    Comments of judges as privileged   CC §47
Limitation of actions   CCP §340
    Slander to title   CCP §338
Malice   CC §§47, 48, 48a
Mitigation of damages for   CCP §461
Motion to strike causes of action having chilling effect on constitutional right to petition and free speech on public issues   CCP §§425.16, 425.17
    SLAPPback actions   CCP §425.18
Peace officer bringing defamation action   CC §47.5
Photographs   CC §45
Physicians and surgeons, peer review committees for   CC §§43.7, 43.8
Pleadings (See within this heading, **"Complaint"**)
Priority of action   CCP §460.5
Privileges
    Dissolution of marriage proceedings, publication of   CC §47
    Doctors, investigation of   CC §§43.7, 43.8
    Employer and employee relations   CC §§47, 48
    Exceptions to   CC §47
    Job performance communications by employer to prospective employer   CC §47
    Journals   CC §47
    Judges
        Censure or removal proceedings, protection from defamation liability for statements   JudPerR 103
        Comments as judges as privileged   CC §47
    Legislative proceedings   CC §47
    Medical personnel, complaints from public about   CC §43.96
    Meetings   CC §47
    Pleadings   CC §47
    Professional persons, investigation of   CC §§43.7, 43.8
    Sexual assault, harassment, or discrimination
        Communications made without malice regarding incidents   CC §47.1
Publication
    Malice   CC §48a
    Single publication rule   CC §§3425.1 to 3425.5
Radio (See **RADIO AND TELEVISION**)
Retraction, demand for   CC §48a
Right of protection from   CC §43
Shortening time to respond   CCP §§460.5, 460.7
Slander to title, statutes of limitation on action for   CCP §338
Special damages, evidence necessary for proof of   CC §45a
Statutes of limitation
    Generally   CCP §340
    Slander to title, actions for   CCP §338
Television (See **RADIO AND TELEVISION**)

LIBRARIES
Cards
    Radio frequency identification (RFID) to remotely read identification document without knowledge or consent   CC §1798.79
        Definitions   CC §1798.795
Court archives, maintenance   CRC 10.855
Telephone information library   CC §43.95

LICENSED PROFESSIONAL CLINICAL COUNSELORS
Immunity from liability
    Communications to licensing board, hospital, medical staff, etc   CC §43.8
    Professional standards committees   CC §43.7
    Referral services   CC §43.95
Peer review or discipline
    Discovery of records, proceedings, etc
        Restrictions   Ev §1157
Privileged communications
    Psychotherapist-patient privilege
        Status of counselors for purpose of privilege   Ev §1010
Sexual contact by psychotherapist   CC §43.93

LICENSED VOCATIONAL NURSES
Blood test, affidavit of technique of taking   Ev §712

LICENSE PLATE RECOGNITION SYSTEMS
Automated license plate recognition systems (ALPR)
    Data security   CC §§1798.90.5 to 1798.90.55

LICENSES AND PERMITS
Administrative adjudication involving holder of (See **ADMINISTRATIVE ADJUDICATION**)
Adoption agencies (See **ADOPTION**)
Associate real estate licensees (See **BROKERS**)

LICENSES AND PERMITS—Cont.
Attorneys' fees in action between licensee and regulatory agency   CCP §1028.5
Automobile (See **AUTOMOBILES**)
Carpenter-Katz Small Business Equal Access to Justice Act   CCP §1028.5
Check cashers   CC §1789.37
Child custody evaluators   CRC 5.225
Child support obligation, suspension or denial of licenses and permits for noncompliance with   Fam §§17520, 17521
Driver's licenses (See **DRIVER'S LICENSES**)
Enforcement of judgments (See **ENFORCEMENT OF JUDGMENTS**)
ERISA pension funds, licenses for loans of   CC §1917.210
Escrow agents, required statement in escrow instructions identifying license name and name of license-issuing department of   CC §1057.7
Fees for recording or registering licenses and certificates   Gov §26851
    Superior court fees, specified services   Gov §70626
Home equity purchaser, licensing requirements for   CC §1695.17
Identification documents
    Radio frequency identification (RFID) to remotely read identification document without knowledge or consent   CC §1798.79
        Definitions   CC §1798.795
Immunity of public entity or employee from decisions involving   Gov §§818.4, 821.2
Marriage (See **MARRIAGE**)
Membership camping facility, disclosure of operating license for   CC §1812.302
Mobilehome parks, change of use of   CC §798.56
Mortgage foreclosure consultants, licensing requirements for   CC §2945.11
Professional license applicant, disclosure of information about   CC §1798.61
Professional licensing boards, communication of information to   CC §§43.8, 43.96
Radio frequency identification (RFID)
    Use to remotely read identification document without knowledge or consent   CC §1798.79
        Definitions   CC §1798.795
Recording or registering licenses and certificates, fees for   Gov §26851
    Superior court fees, specified services   Gov §70626
State agencies, adjudicatory proceedings of (See **ADMINISTRATIVE ADJUDICATION**)
Support obligation, suspension or denial of licenses and permits for noncompliance with   Fam §§17520, 17521
Surety bonds (See **SURETYSHIP, BONDS AND UNDERTAKINGS**)
Unlicensed person, action for injury caused by   CCP §1029.8

LICENSES IN REALTY
Personal injury   CC §846

LIE DETECTOR (See **POLYGRAPH**)

LIENS
Absence of recordation of, certification   CCP §2103
Administration of decedents' estates
    Generally (See **ADMINISTRATION OF ESTATES**)
    Claims against decedents' estates (See **CLAIMS AGAINST ESTATES**)
After-acquired property covered by   CC §2883
Aircraft and aviation (See **AIRCRAFT AND AVIATION**)
Alternative lien-sale procedure for charges not exceeding $150   CC §3052b
Animals   CCP §1208.5
Apartment housekeeper's lien   CC §1861a
Artisans' liens   CC §§3051, 3051a
Assignment for benefit of creditors (See **ASSIGNMENT FOR BENEFIT OF CREDITORS**)
Attachment (See **ATTACHMENT**)
Auctioned items, disclosure of liens on   CC §1812.607
Automobiles (See **AUTOMOBILES**)
Bankers' liens   CC §3054
Bankruptcy affecting   CCP §§493.030 to 493.050
Blanket encumbrances, required notice to purchaser or lessee of   CC §1133
Blanket liens, priority of   CC §2899
Boarding houses   CC §§1861 to 1861.28
Bottomry lien regulations applicable to   CC §2877
Breeders' liens   CC §§3062 to 3064.1
Carriers' liens (See **COMMON CARRIERS**)
Cause of action, lien on   CRC 3.1360
Child support (See **CHILD SUPPORT**)
Civil rules
    Waiver of fees
        Amount of lien   CRC 3.57
Claims against decedents' estates (See **CLAIMS AGAINST ESTATES**)
Cleaners' lien   CC §3066
Commercial and industrial common interest developments
    Assessments
        Common areas, damage   CC §6824

LIENS—Cont.
  Commercial and industrial common interest developments—Cont.
    Assessments —Cont.
      Contents   CC §6814
      Enforcement of lien   CC §6820
      Governing documents, no lien for noncompliance   CC §6824
      Noncompliance with procedures for liens   CC §6819
      Pre-lien notice to owner   CC §6812
      Priority   CC §6816
      Release of lien   CC §6818
      Sale to enforce lien   CC §§6820, 6822
    Scope of liens   CC §6658
  Common carriers' liens (See **COMMON CARRIERS**)
  Common interest developments
    Condominiums, contractor's lien
      Transfer restrictions   CC §4615
    Generally (See **COMMON INTEREST DEVELOPMENTS**)
  Concurrent liens, priority between   CC §2899
  Construction liens   CC §§8000 to 9566 (See **MECHANICS' LIENS**)
  Contract, creation by   CC §2881
  Conversion extinguishing   CC §2910
  Damages for conversion   CC §3338
  Defined   CC §2872, CCP §1180
  Deposits (See **DEPOSITS**)
  Design professionals' liens   CC §§8300 to 8319
    Availability of other remedies   CC §8314
    Conditions for lien   CC §8304
    Conversion to mechanics lien   CC §8319
    Creation of lien   CC §§8302, 8306
    Definition of design professional   CC §8300
    Expiration   CC §8306
    Mechanics' liens
      Relationship between different lien provisions   CC §8310
    Priority of lien   CC §8316
    Provisions of part applicable   CC §8308
    Recordation   CC §8306
      Time to record   CC §8312
    Residences
      Single-family owner-occupied residence, applicability of provisions   CC §8318
  Disclosures on purchase money liens on residential property   CC §§2956 to 2968
  Discriminatory clauses in lien instruments, prohibition against   CC §§53, 782
  Earnings assignment for support   Fam §5242
  Eminent domain (See **EMINENT DOMAIN**)
  Enforcement of judgments (See **ENFORCEMENT OF JUDGMENTS**)
  Expenditures concerning lien, recovery of   CC §2892
  Factors   CC §3053
  Family law attorney's real property lien   Fam §§2033, 2034
  Family support
    Judgments, abstract of
      Digital form of lien record   Fam §17523.5
  Farm workers, liens by   CC §§3061 to 3061.6
  Federal Lien Registration Act   CCP §§2100 to 2107
    Fees for recording under act   Gov §27388.1
  Fixtures   CC §1013.5
  Floating homes (See **FLOATING HOMES**)
  Foreclosure
    Generally   CCP §726
    Apartment housekeepers' lien   CC §1861a
    Appraisal on   CCP §726
    Attorneys' fees   CCP §730
    Boarding housekeeper's liens   CC §1861
    Deficiency judgments   CCP §726
    Deposit, lien for   CC §1857
    Hospital liens   CC §1862.5
    Hotelkeeper's liens   CC §1861
    Judgments   CCP §726
    Mortgage foreclosure prevention   CC §2924
    Nuisance property
      Abatement assessment or lien, maximum amount   CC §2929.45
    Partial sales   CCP §728
    Stay of proceedings   CCP §917.2
    Surplus on   CCP §727
  Forfeiture agreement, validity of   CC §2889
  Forms
    Service dealer lien notice   CC §3052.5
    Wages, liens securing   CC §§3061.5, 3061.6
  Future act secured by   CC §2884
  Garnishment proceedings (See **GARNISHMENT**)
  General liens defined   CC §§2873, 2874
  Harvester's liens   CC §§3061.5, 3061.6

LIENS—Cont.
  Health care liens   CC §3040
  Home equity loans   CC §§2970 to 2971
  Homesteads (See **HOMESTEADS**)
  Horses (See **HORSES**)
  Hospital liens (See **HOSPITALS**)
  Implied obligations   CC §2890
  Improvements (See **IMPROVEMENTS**)
  Income tax (federal), registration act for   CCP §§2100 to 2107
    Fees for recording under act   Gov §27388.1
  Indigent persons
    Waiver of fees
      Amount of lien   CRC 3.57
  Inferior liens
    Dwelling, lienholder served with notice of removal of occupant from   CCP §700.080
    Mobilehomes (See **MOBILEHOMES**)
    Priorities   CC §§2897 to 2899
    Redemption   CC §2904
  Information Practices Act, disclosure under   CC §1798.67
  Jewelers' liens   CC §3052a
  Judgment liens (See **JUDGMENTS**)
  Junior liens
    Generally (See within this heading, "**Inferior liens**")
    Mobilehomes (See **MOBILEHOMES**)
  Labor performed   CC §§3051, 3051a, 3052
  Law and motion rule of court regarding motion to grant lien on cause of action   CRC 3.1360
  Livestock (See **LIVESTOCK**)
  Loggers   CC §§3065 to 3065c
  Lottery prize, procedure for enforcement of lien against   CCP §708.755
  Mechanics' liens   CC §§8000 to 9566 (See **MECHANICS' LIENS**)
  Mining liens   CC §3060
  Mobilehomes (See **MOBILEHOMES**)
  Mortgage forcclosure consultants taking   CC §2945.4
  Mortgages (See **TRUST DEEDS AND MORTGAGES**)
  Oil and gas (See **OIL AND GAS**)
  Operation of law, creation by   CC §§2881, 2882
  Option granted to secured party, priority of   CC §2906
  Original obligation, security limited to   CC §2891
  Parking facilities   CC §§3067 to 3074
  Partial performance, effect of   CC §2912
  Partition (See **PARTITION**)
  Pending actions or proceedings, liens in   CRC 3.1360
  Performance of main obligation, effect of   CC §§2909, 2912
  Personal services secured by   CC §3051
  Pledge transactions, lien regulations applicable to   CC §2877
  Possession, lien dependent on   CC §§2913, 3051
  Postponed property taxes, notice of default on property subject to lien for   CC §2924b
  Priorities
    Generally   CC §§2897 to 2899
    Commercial and industrial common interest developments
      Assessments   CC §6816
    Design professionals' liens   CC §8316
    Option granted to secured party, priority of   CC §2906
  Protective ex parte order determining payment of liens   Fam §6324
  Publication of notice of   CC §3052.5
  Public improvements (See **PUBLIC CONTRACTS AND WORKS**)
  Purchase money liens on residential property, disclosures on   CC §§2956 to 2968
  Recreational vehicle parks (See **RECREATIONAL VEHICLE PARKS**)
  Redemption
    Effectiveness of redemption, terms of   CC §2906
    Inferior liens   CC §2904
    Procedure for   CC §2905
    Restraining right of   CC §2889
    Right of   CC §2903
  Registration under Uniform Federal Lien Registration Act   CCP §§2100 to 2107
    Fees for recording under act   Gov §27388.1
  Repairs   CC §§3051, 3052.5
  Respondentia lien regulations applicable to   CC §2877
  Retail installment sales contracts, limitation under   CC §1804.3
  Sales
    Alternative lien-sale procedure for charges not exceeding $150   CC §3052b
    Extinguishing liens by   CC §2910
    Required notice of   CC §§3052.5, 3052a
    Satisfaction of liens by   CC §3052
  Savings and loan associations   CC §3054
  Secured transactions, provisions applicable to   CC §2914
  Service dealers' liens   CC §3052.5
  Shared appreciation loans (See **SHARED APPRECIATION LOANS**)

LIENS—Cont.
Special liens defined   CC §§2873, 2875
Spousal support
    Judgments, abstract of
        Digital form of lien record   Fam §17523.5
Statutes of limitation on action for enforcement of   CC §2911
Storage liens   CC §§3051, 3051a, 3052
Streets (See **STREETS AND HIGHWAYS**)
Subrogation rights   CC §2876
Support and maintenance
    Judgments, abstract of
        Digital form of lien record   Fam §17523.5
    Service of order for earnings assignment for   Fam §5242
Tax liens (See **TAXATION**)
Third party claim of lien on property levied upon   CCP §§720.210 to 720.290, 720.510 to 720.550
Threshers   CC §3061
Time of creation of   CC §2882
Title, effect on   CC §2888
Trust deeds and mortgages (See **TRUST DEEDS AND MORTGAGES**)
Trusts (See **TRUSTS**)
Unclaimed property fund appropriations for payment of   CCP §1325
Uniform Federal Lien Registration Act   CCP §§2100 to 2107
    Fees for recording under act   Gov §27388.1
Venue in actions for foreclosure of liens and mortgages on real property   CCP §392
Wages (See **SALARIES AND WAGES**)
Warehouses
    Mobilehome park management enforcement of warehouse lien resulting in acquisition of mobilehome
        Disposal, notice   CC §798.56a
Watch repairs   CC §3052a
Will deposited for safekeeping, viability of attorney lien against   Pro §714

LIFE ESTATES
Buildings, duty of life tenant to repair   CC §840
Eminent domain compensation for loss of   CCP §1265.420
Fences, duty of life tenant to repair   CC §840
Fiduciary income and principal act
    Applicability of provisions   Pro §16322
        Place of administration as basis of applicability   Pro §16323
    Generally   Pro §§16320 to 16383
Inventory furnished by party receiving   Pro §11752
Partition (See **PARTITION**)
Principal and income allocations   CC §§731 to 731.15
Taxes and assessments, life tenant to pay   CC §840
Term of years, interest created on   CC §773
Third party, estate for life of   CC §766
Transfer of estate greater than   CC §1108
Use of   CC §818
Waste, actions for recovery of treble damages for   CCP §732

LIFE INSURANCE
Assignment for benefit of creditors, property exempt from   CCP §1801
Beneficiaries
    Disclaimer of estate interest   Pro §§260 to 295
    Physician-patient privileges, beneficiaries claiming   Ev §996
    Simultaneous death with insured   Pro §224
    Trustee named in will designated as   Pro §§6321 to 6330
Disclaimer of estate interest   Pro §§260 to 295
Exempt property for purposes of enforcement of judgments   CCP §704.100
Fiduciary income and principal act
    Receipts, allocation
        Principal, allocation to   Pro §16346
Medical information, disclosure of   CC §56.15
Pour-over provisions   Pro §§6321 to 6330
Punitive damages award against insurer, special notice of   CC §3296
Simultaneous death of insured and beneficiary   Pro §224
Spousal support, life insurance to provide for continued   Fam §4360
Trusts (See **TRUSTS**)
Unclaimed deposits and payments escheated   CCP §1515

LIFE TENANTS (See **LIFE ESTATES**)

LIGHTS AND LIGHTING
Appurtenance   CC §662

LIGHTS AND LIGHTING—Cont.
Easement rights to   CC §801
Landlord terminating   CC §789.3

LIMITATION OF ACTIONS (See **STATUTES OF LIMITATION**)

LIMITATION OF LIABILITY
Baggage (See **BAGGAGE**)
Construction contracts, agreements involving   CC §2782.5
Easement holder's liability for recreational use of property   CC §846
Sliding scale recovery agreements for   CCP §877.5

LIMITED CIVIL CASES
Appellate review
    Forms for unlimited civil cases   CRCAppx A
Appellate rules, superior court appeals
    Limited civil cases in appellate division   CRC 8.820 to 8.845 (See **APPELLATE RULES, SUPERIOR COURT APPEALS**)
Appendix as record
    Election
        Judicial council form   CRCAppx A
Caption requirements   CCP §422.30
Case questionnaire
    Forms
        Judicial council legal forms   CRCAppx A
Delay reduction program   Gov §68620
Economic litigation procedures (See **ECONOMIC LITIGATION PROCEDURES**)
Expedited jury trials
    Mandatory expedited jury trials, limited civil cases   CCP §§630.20 to 630.29
Fees in superior courts
    Reclassification to unlimited civil case   Gov §70619
Installment judgments   CCP §582.5
Jurisdiction (See **JURISDICTION**)
Jury trial
    Expedited jury trials
        Mandatory expedited jury trials, limited civil cases   CCP §§630.20 to 630.29
Reclassification to unlimited civil case
    Fees in superior courts   Gov §70619
Relief granted, restrictions on   CCP §580
Superior court fees
    Appeal, notice of to appellate division   Gov §70621
        Supplemental fees for first paper filing   Gov §§70602.5, 70602.6
Trial court rules
    Amount demanded
        Papers, first page format and content   CRC 2.111

LIMITED CONSERVATORSHIP (See **CONSERVATORS**)

LIMITED ENGLISH PROFICIENT LITIGANTS
Language access services
    Collaboration and technology to provide services   CRC 1.300
    Court-ordered and court-provided programs, services and professionals   CRC 1.300

LIMITED INTEREST   CC §§688, 692

LIMITED LIABILITY COMPANIES
Attorney professional conduct
    Organization or entity as client   ProfC 1.13
Charging orders
    Enforcement of judgment against members' interests   CCP §§708.310, 708.320
Claim and delivery actions involving   CCP §155.070
Eminent domain actions involving   CCP §1235.160
Enforcement of judgments against   CCP §680.279
Oil and gas actions involving   CCP §1203.51
Probate purposes, definition for   Pro §56
Small claims court, actions in   CCP §116.130
Tax liens and other federal liens, filing of notice of   CCP §2101
Unclaimed property, actions involving   CCP §1601
Wage garnishment actions involving   CCP §706.011

LIMITED PARTNERSHIPS
Attorney professional conduct
    Organization or entity as client   ProfC 1.13

LIQUIDATION
Banks in process of liquidation, statutes of limitation for recovery of money or property deposited applicable to   CCP §348

LIQUOR (See ALCOHOLIC BEVERAGES)

LIS PENDENS (See PENDENCY OF ACTIONS)

LISTENING DEVICES (See EAVESDROPPING AND WIRETAPPING)

LISTING AGENTS (See BROKERS)

LISTS, JUROR (See JURY)

LITERARY PROPERTY (See also BOOKS)
Compositions (See COMPOSITIONS)
Felon's story, trust established for proceeds from sale of   CC §2225
Indecency and obscenity (See INDECENCY AND OBSCENITY)
Infringement, action for   CCP §429.30
Letters and private writings, publication of   CC §985
Ownership
    Generally   CC §980
    Proportion of   CC §981
    Publication, dedication by   CC §983
    Right of reproduction, transfer of   CC §982

LITHOGRAPHS
Sales regulated   CC §§1740 to 1745

LIVERY STABLES
Liens   CC §3051

LIVESTOCK
Attachment proceedings   CCP §481.110
Claim and delivery   CCP §511.040
Defined   CC §3080
Dogs injuring   CC §3341
Liens
    Breeders   CC §§3062 to 3064.1
    Service liens   CC §§3080 to 3080.22
    Veterinary services   CC §3051
Pastures (See PASTURES)

LIVING WILLS
Advance health care directives   Pro §§4670 to 4679 (See HEALTH CARE DECISIONS LAW)

LOANS
Acceleration of (See ACCELERATION OF LOANS)
Adjustable rate loans (See TRUST DEEDS AND MORTGAGES)
Administration of estates (See ADMINISTRATION OF ESTATES)
Animals loaned, treatment of   CC §1887
Asian language contracts   CC §1632
    Mortgages of residential property, foreign language summaries of terms   CC §1632.5
Automobile sales (See AUTOMOBILES)
Conditional sales (See CONDITIONAL SALES)
Contract for loan of money   CC §§1912 to 1916.5
Credit cards for obtaining (See CREDIT CARDS)
Creditors (See CREDITORS)
Credit rating regulated   CC §§1785.1 to 1785.4
Debts (See DEBTS)
Decedents' estates (See ADMINISTRATION OF ESTATES)
Due-on-sale clause re real property secured loans   CC §711.5
Employee Retirement Income Security Act (See ERISA)
Exchange, loan for   CC §§1902 to 1906
Home Equity Loan Disclosure Act   CC §§2970 to 2971
Home equity sales contract construed as loan transaction   CC §1695.12
Housing loans, assumption of subsequent purchaser of   CC §711.5
Impound accounts   CC §§2954, 2954.8, 2955
Injuries resulting from use of money loaned, liability for   CC §3434
Interest
    Precomputed interest
        Waiver of protections   CC §1799.6
Loans of money, generally   CC §§1912 to 1916
Mechanics' liens
    Construction lenders generally (See MECHANICS' LIENS)
    Deed securing loan
        Designation as construction trust deed required   CC §8174
    Large projects, security for
        Copy of loan documentation to be provided   CC §8710
    Stop payment notices to construction lenders   CC §§8530 to 8538

LOANS—Cont.
Mechanics' liens—Cont.
    Stop work notices to construction lenders   CC §8836
Mortgage loans (See TRUST DEEDS AND MORTGAGES)
Option to extend term of   CC §1916.5
Power of attorney (See POWER OF ATTORNEY)
Precomputed interest
    Waiver of protections   CC §1799.6
Prepayments (See PREPAYMENTS)
Private student loan collections reform   CC §§1788.200 to 1788.211
Public entity loans for purchase or rehabilitation of realty   CC §711.5
Public retirement systems loans, exemption from usury laws for   CC §1916.2
Rehabilitation housing loans, assumption of   CC §711.5
Renegotiable-rate mortgages   CC §§1916.8, 1916.9
Repairs, lender not liable for injuries resulting from   CC §3434
Respondentia, loans upon (See LOANS UPON RESPONDENTIA)
Retail installment sales (See RETAIL INSTALLMENT SALES)
Shared appreciation loans (See SHARED APPRECIATION LOANS)
Shift-in-land-use loans, sale of decedent's land for   Pro §10207
Spanish language   CC §1632
    Mortgages of residential property, foreign language summaries of terms   CC §1632.5
Student loan collection
    Private student loan collections reform   CC §§1788.200 to 1788.211 (See PRIVATE STUDENT LOAN COLLECTIONS REFORM)
Trusts (See TRUSTS)
Truth-in-lending (See TRUTH-IN-LENDING ACT)
Use of loan   CC §§1884 to 1896
Usury (See USURY)
Variable interest rate loans (See TRUST DEEDS AND MORTGAGES)

LOAN SHARKING
Usury generally (See USURY)

LOANS UPON RESPONDENTIA
Discharge provisions applicable to mortgages, exception to   CC §2942
Lien statutes applicable to   CC §2877
Priority rule, exception from   CC §2897

LOBBYISTS
Sexual harassment, civil action for   CC §51.9

LOCAL AGENCIES
Adjudicative proceedings (See ADMINISTRATIVE ADJUDICATION)
Attorney professional conduct
    Organization or entity as client   ProfC 1.13
Greenway easements
    Definition of local agency   CC §816.52
Public entities, generally (See PUBLIC ENTITIES)
Rules and regulations, procedural requirements for adoption of (See ADMINISTRATIVE PROCEDURE ACT)
Unclaimed property
    Claim not required for controller to transfer property to state or local agencies   CCP §1540
Venue in actions by or against   CCP §394

LOCAL OR SPECIAL LAWS
Judicial arbitration proceedings, local rules governing   CCP §1141.11
Pleading as to   CCP §459
Public laws distinguished   CCP §1898

LOCAL RULES OF COURT   CCP §575.1, CRC 10.613
Adopting, filing, and distribution procedures   CRC 10.613
Attorneys for parties in dependency proceedings   CRC 5.660
Civil rules
    Preemption of local rules   CRC 3.20
Coordination of actions   CRC 3.504
Coordination of complex actions
    Specification of applicable local rules   CRC 3.504
Courts of appeals
    Administration of appellate courts
        Local rules of courts of appeal   CRC 10.1030
Dependency proceedings, right to counsel in   CRC 5.660
Differential case management rules   CRC 3.711
Electronic filing and service rules
    Close of business, filing by
        Local rule providing for receipt by midnight as being filed on that day   CRC 2.259
    Criminal trials   CRC 2.251
        Permissive electronic filing by local rule   CRC 2.253
    Permissive electronic filing by local rule   CRC 2.253

LOCAL RULES OF COURT—Cont.
Electronic filing and service rules—Cont.
    Requiring electronic service by local rule or court order   CRC 2.251
Family rules
    Compliance with family rules   CRC 5.4
Gender-neutral language in rules, forms, etc   CRC 10.612
Inspection
    Deposit and maintenance of rules statewide for inspection   CRC 10.613
Judicial arbitration proceedings, local rules governing   CRC 3.811
Mediation in custody proceedings   Fam §3163
Periodic review   CRC 10.613
Preemption by Judicial Council   CRC 3.20
Preemption of local rules   CRC 3.20
Proposed rules
    Comment period   CRC 10.613
Publication   CRC 10.613
Remote appearances
    Local court rules for remote proceedings   CRC 3.672
Sanctions for noncompliance   CCP §575.2
Superior courts (See **SUPERIOR COURTS**)
Trial Court Delay Reduction Act (See **TRIAL COURT DELAY REDUCTION**)

LOCKS
Landlord's duty to install and maintain   CC §1941.3
    Change of lock upon request by eligible tenant   CC §1941.5
    Change of lock upon request by protected tenant   CC §1941.6

LODGERS
Boardinghouses generally (See **BOARDINGHOUSES**)
Hotels and motels generally (See **HOTELS AND MOTELS**)
Jurors in criminal proceedings   CCP §217
Landlord and tenant
    Applicability of provisions to   CC §§1940, 1940.1
    Homelessness
        Temporary residence by persons at risk of homelessness in dwelling unit of tenant, rights of person at risk as lodger   CC §1942.8
    Termination of room rental   CC §1946.5
Statutes of limitation on actions for recovery or conversion of personal property left at lodging house   CCP §341a

LOGS AND TIMBER
Attachment (See **ATTACHMENT**)
Damages, liability for   CC §3346, CCP §§733, 734
Damages recoverable for taking   CCP §§733, 734
Easement rights   CC §§801, 802
Enforcement of provisions
    Civil or administrative enforcement
        Statute of limitations   CCP §338
Fiduciary income and principal act
    Receipts, allocation
        Timber sales   Pro §16351
Lien for loggers   CC §§3065 to 3065c
Principal and income allocations   CC §731.11
Recording of contracts for   CC §§1220, 3065 to 3065c
Saw mills, liens against   CC §§3065 to 3065c
Voidable transactions provisions, applicability to sale of   CC §3440

LOITERING
Prostitution offenses, loitering for
    Condoms
        Evidence of possession of condoms, inadmissibility   Ev §782.1

LONG ARM STATUTE
Service of process   CCP §§413.10, 413.20, 415.40, 417.20

LONG BEACH, CITY OF
Unlawful detainer actions
    Firearms or weapons as nuisances
        Applicability of provisions   CC §3485

LONG-DISTANCE HAULING TRUCKERS (See **MOTOR CARRIERS**)

LONG-TERM CARE FACILITIES (See **NURSING HOMES**)

LONG-TERM CARE, HEALTH, SAFETY, AND SECURITY ACT
Jurisdiction for actions under   CCP §86.1

LOS ANGELES, CITY OF
Unlawful detainer actions
    Controlled substances as nuisance
        Applicability of provisions   CC §3486

LOS ANGELES, CITY OF—Cont.
Unlawful detainer actions—Cont.
    Firearms or weapons as nuisances
        Applicability of provisions   CC §3485

LOS ANGELES COUNTY
Groundwater recharge, reporting requirements for injuries during and claims based on   Gov §831.9
Jury (See **JURY**)
Mediation of civil actions, pilot project for   CCP §1730
Small estates, giving notice of escheat of   CCP §1415
Unlawful detainer actions
    Controlled substances as nuisance
        Applicability of provisions   CC §3486
    Firearms or weapons as nuisances
        Applicability of provisions   CC §3485

LOST INSTRUMENTS
Credit cards   CC §1747.20
Damages   CC §3356
Deposit of estate-planning documents with attorney (See **TRUSTS; WILLS**)
Destroyed land records relief law   CCP §§751.01 to 751.28
Maps replaced   CCP §1855
Marriage certificates (See **MARRIAGE**)
Nunc pro tunc filing where public records lost or destroyed   CCP §1046a
Oral evidence of contents of lost writing, admissibility of   Ev §1523
Photographic copies as evidence   Ev §1551
Restoration, action for   CC §3415
Secondary evidence of contents of lost writing   Ev §§1523, 1551
Trust documents deposited with attorney (See **TRUSTS**)
Wills (See **WILLS**)

LOST PROPERTY
California state university
    Care and disposition of property   CC §2080.8
Deposited property   CC §§1838, 2080
Landlord protecting property of tenant   CCP §1174
Police, duties of   CC §§2080.1 to 2080.5
Possession, taking of   CC §2080
Unclaimed property   CC §§2080.3 to 2080.8 (See **UNCLAIMED PROPERTY**)
Unknown owner   CC §2080.1
Unlawful detainer   CCP §1174

LOTS (See **SUBDIVISIONS**)

LOTTERY
Procedure for enforcement of lien against lottery prize   CCP §708.755
Support arrearages claim filed against state for winnings owed judgment debtor   CCP §§708.30, 708.740

LOW-FLOW TOILETS, FAUCETS AND SHOWER HEADS
Water conserving plumbing retrofits   CC §§1101.1 to 1101.9

LOW INCOME HOUSING
Acceleration of loans   CC §711.5
Injunctions against projects   CCP §529.2

LUGGAGE (See **BAGGAGE**)

LUMBER (See **LOGS AND TIMBER**)

LUNACY (See **MENTAL DISABILITY**)

LUNAR NEW YEAR
Judicial holidays, excluded from days designated as   CCP §135

LUNCHROOMS (See **RESTAURANTS**)

LUXURY CRUISERS (See **VESSELS**)

M

MACHINERY
Eminent domain compensation for   CCP §§1263.205, 1263.620
Mining machinery, records of sale of   CC §1631

MADE IN CALIFORNIA PROGRAM
Unfair competition or deceptive trade practices   CC §1770

MAGAZINES (See **NEWSPAPERS AND MAGAZINES**)

MAGISTRATES
Judicial ethics, code of
    Applicability   CRCSupp JudEthicsCanon 6

MAGISTRATES—Cont.
Marriage ceremony   Fam §400

MAGNETIC RECORD DEVICES (See RECORDING OF SOUND)

MAIDEN NAME
Refusal to do business with person using   CCP §1279.6

MAIDS (See PERSONAL SERVICES)

MAIL AND MAILING
Administration of decedents' estates (See **ADMINISTRATION OF ESTATES**)
Administrative adjudicative proceedings (See **ADMINISTRATIVE ADJUDICATION**)
Authentication of document   Ev §1420
Automobile repossession notice, regulating mailing of   CC §§2982, 2983.2, 2983.3
Certified mail
    Electronic service not authorized when certified or registered mail required   CCP §1020
    Probate proceedings, sufficiency of notice in   Pro §5
    Registered mail, certified mail in lieu of   CC §17, CCP §11
Conservatorship proceedings   Pro §1467
Credit reports, copy of   CC §1785.15
Defined   CCP §116.130
Dies, molds and forms, notice of termination of customer's title to   CC §1140
Eminent domain taking notice   CCP §1245.235
Enforcement of judgments (See **ENFORCEMENT OF JUDGMENTS**)
Executor as nonresident, mailing process to   Pro §§8574, 8575
Express mail
    Summary judgment, notice of motion
        Time limits, effect of express or other overnight mail delivery   CCP §437c
Fees
    Courts, authority to set fees for products or services   CRC 10.815
Filing fees
    Notice of return of check for   CCP §411.20
    Underpayment, notice   CCP §411.21
Groundwater rights actions
    Notice of complaint   CCP §835
Guardianship proceedings   Pro §1467
Hospital lien notice transmitted by   CC §3045.3
Jury summons   CCP §208
Landlord and tenant
    Locking mail receptacles
        Untenantable if lacking   CC §1941.1
    Notifying tenant of sale of building by   CC §1950.5
Lease notices (See **LEASES**)
Mechanic's lien, notice of
    Method of giving   CC §8106
    Notice of cessation or completion
        Copy to be mailed to person giving preliminary notice by county clerk   CC §8214
    Requirements when notice mailed   CC §8110
Merchandise offered to consumers   CC §§1584.5, 1584.6
Missing person, notice of administration of estate of   Pro §12405
Motion, service by mail of notices of (See **MOTIONS**)
Notice of pendency, service of   CCP §§405.22, 405.23
Presumption of receipt of letters correctly addressed and posted   Ev §641
Probate proceedings
    Delivery of notice
        Methods   Pro §1215
Proof of service by mail   CCP §1013a
Public entities and employees, manner of mailing claim against   Gov §915.2
Registered mail, certified mail in lieu of   CC §17, CCP §11
    Electronic service not authorized when certified or registered mail required   CCP §1020
Sale by (See **MAIL ORDER SALES**)
Service of process (See **PROCESS AND SERVICE OF PROCESS**)
Small claims court (See **SMALL CLAIMS COURTS**)
Social security numbers
    Visible display on mail   CC §1786.60
Tax lien, notice to state tax debtor of   CC §2885
Trial notice served through   CCP §594
Unconditional gifts   CC §§1584.5, 1584.6
Unlawful detainer process, service of   CCP §415.45
Unsolicited goods sent by   CC §§1584.5, 1584.6
Will probate proceedings (See **WILL PROBATE**)

MAILING LISTS
Information Practices Act (See **INFORMATION PRACTICES ACT**)

MAILING LISTS—Cont.
Jurors, sources for selection of   CCP §197

MAIL ORDER SALES
Assistive devices   CC §1793.02
Autographed memorabilia, sale of   CC §1739.7
Fine prints, sale of   CC §§1742 to 1744
Place of business defined   CC §1791
Retail installment sales provisions applicable   CC §1803.8
Unsolicited goods sent by   CC §§1584.5, 1584.6
Warranties   CC §1792.4

MAINTENANCE
Recordkeeping (See **RECORDS AND RECORDING**)
Repairs (See **REPAIRS**)
Spousal support (See **SPOUSAL SUPPORT**)

MAJORITY
Joint authority, effect of grant of   CCP §15

MAJORITY OF WARD (See GUARDIAN AND WARD)

MALFEASANCE
Jury service, exceptions to eligibility for   CCP §203
Notary public, statutes of limitation on actions upon bond of   CCP §338

MALICE
Construction, damages for malicious destruction of property under   CC §3294
Damages awarded   CC §3294
Exemplary damages for   CC §3294
Libel and slander   CC §§47, 48, 48a

MALICIOUS PROSECUTION (See VEXATIOUS LITIGANTS)

MALPRACTICE
Arbitration
    Health care providers
        General arbitration provisions inapplicable   CCP §§1281.2, 1281.3
Architects (See **ARCHITECTS**)
Attorney professional conduct
    Communications with clients
        Malpractice insurance lacking, duty to inform client   ProfC 1.4.2
    Limitation of attorney liability to client
        Prohibitions   ProfC 1.8.8
Attorneys
    Action for wrongful act or omission arising in performance of professional services   CCP §340.6
    Referrals by professional society, immunity from liability for   CC §43.95
Compromise and settlement of claims
    Time-limited demands   CCP §§999 to 999.5
Damages
    Health care providers (See within this heading, "**Health care providers**")
    Unlicensed person, treble damages for injury caused by   CCP §1029.8
Engineers (See **ENGINEERING**)
Health care providers
    Arbitration
        Contracts for medical services providing for arbitration of professional negligence of provider   CCP §1295
        General arbitration provisions inapplicable   CCP §§1281.2, 1281.3
        Medical services contract, arbitration provision in   CCP §1295
    Collateral benefits, admissible evidence of source of   CC §3333.1
    Contempt of court, physicians failing to pay future damages held in   CCP §667.7
    Damages
        Collateral benefits, admissible evidence of source of   CC §3333.1
        Future damages, periodic payment of   CCP §667.7
        Insurer, special notice of punitive damages award against   CC §3296
        Noneconomic losses, liability for   CC §3333.2
        Punitive damage claims against   CCP §425.13
    Death of judgment creditor, modification of periodic payments on   CCP §667.7
    Declaration of rights of insurers   CCP §1062.5
    Defined   CCP §§340.5, 364
    Failure to comply with notice requirement   CCP §365
    Form for arbitration clause in medical services contract   CCP §1295
    Indemnification by state   Gov §827
    Insurance
        Arbitration, applicability of   CCP §1295
        Declaration of rights of professional liability insurer   CCP §1062.5
        Indemnification   Gov §827
        Punitive damages award against insurer, special notice of   CC §3296

MALPRACTICE—Cont.
Health care providers—Cont.
- Insurance—Cont.
  - Third-party cause of action for unfair claims settlement practices, applicability of provisions for   CC §2871
- Judgment liens against   CCP §§697.320, 697.350, 697.380 to 697.400
- Multiphasic screening units, patients referred by   CC §43.9
- Noneconomic losses, recovery for   CC §3333.2
- Notice
  - Arbitration clause in medical services contract   CCP §1295
  - Insurer, special notice of punitive damages award against   CC §3296
  - Intention to commence action   CCP §364
- Periodic payment of future damages   CCP §667.7
- Preference, setting for trial on grant of motion for   CCP §36
- Professional negligence defined   CCP §364
- Punitive damages, claim for   CCP §425.13
- Recommendation of medical staff, limited immunity from liability for action taken on   CC §43.97
- Release of state from claim against   CC §1542.1
- Separate trial of defense of statutes of limitation   CCP §597.5
- Sexual harassment, civil action for
  - Construction or application of provisions in issue, solicitor general notified   CC §51.1
- Statutes of limitation
  - Actions for injury or death   CCP §340.5
  - Punitive damages, time for filing amended pleading for   CCP §425.13
  - Separate trial of defense of statutes of limitation   CCP §597.5
- Undertaking to secure costs in action against   CCP §1029.6

Indemnification of health care providers by state   Gov §827
Insurance (See within this heading, **"Health care providers"**)
Legal malpractice
- Action for wrongful act or omission arising in performance of professional services   CCP §340.6
- Communications with clients
  - Malpractice insurance lacking, duty to inform client   ProfC 1.4.2
- Limitation of attorney liability to client
  - Prohibitions   ProfC 1.8.8
- Prospectively limiting attorney's liability to client for professional malpractice   ProfC 3-400

Medical malpractice (See within this heading, **"Health care providers"**)
Professional negligence defined   CCP §§340.5, 364
Release of state from claim against health care provider   CC §1542.1
Statutes of limitation
- Architects (See **ARCHITECTS**)
- Engineers (See **ENGINEERING**)
- Health care providers (See within this heading, **"Health care providers"**)
- Legal malpractice   CCP §340.6
- Surveyors (See **SURVEYS AND SURVEYORS**)

Surveyors (See **SURVEYS AND SURVEYORS**)
Unlicensed person, treble damages for injury caused by   CCP §1029.8

MANAGED HEALTH CARE (See HEALTH CARE SERVICE PLANS)

MANAGEMENT
Agent managing business   CC §2319
Apartment houses, requirements for notice of manager of   CC §§1961 to 1962.5
Common interest developments (See **COMMON INTEREST DEVELOPMENTS**)
Mobilehome parks   CC §798.2
Trustee   Pro §16227

MANDAMUS
Abuse of discretion, administrative body   CCP §1094.5
Adequacy of other remedy   CCP §1086
Administrative orders or decision, review of (See **ADMINISTRATIVE ADJUDICATION**)
Alternative writs   CCP §§1087, 1088
Answer   CCP §§1089, 1089.5
Change of venue, petition for writ of mandate on grant or denial of motion for   CCP §400
Claims against public entities and employees (See **CLAIMS AGAINST PUBLIC ENTITIES AND EMPLOYEES**)
Contents of writ   CCP §1087
Coordination of actions   CCP §404.6
Costs   CCP §§1094.5, 1095
Countervailing return   CCP §1091
Damages, recovery of   CCP §1095
Default judgments   CCP §§585, 586
Default, prohibition against granting writ by   CCP §1088
Defined   CCP §1084
Demurrer   CCP §1089

MANDAMUS—Cont.
Disobedience of writ   CCP §1097
Disqualification of judge, review of determination re   CCP §170.3
Emancipation of minors, petition for   Fam §7123
Eminent domain proceedings   CCP §1245.255
Food and Agriculture Department, special procedures for mandamus proceedings against   CCP §1085.5
Hearings   CCP §§1094, 1094.5, 1094.6
Irrigation cases, appeal from   CCP §1110a
Judgment on peremptory writ   CCP §1094
Jurisdiction (See **JURISDICTION**)
Jury, trial by   CCP §1090
Local agency decisions   CCP §1094.6
New trial, motion for   CCP §1092
Notice
- Application on notice   CCP §1088
- Argument of application   CCP §1093

Notice of pendency of action (See **PENDENCY OF ACTIONS**)
Peremptory writs   CCP §§1087, 1088, 1097
Pest control and eradication, special procedure for   CCP §1085.5
Petition   CCP §1086
Public entity, damages and costs where respondent is officer of   CCP §1095
Reclassification of action, review of order granting or denying   CCP §403.080
Record of proceedings
- Local agency decisions, review of   CCP §1094.6
- Retention or destruction of   CCP §1094.5

Return of writ   CCP §§1089, 1108
Service
- Petition, service of   CCP §1088
- Prerogative writs, service of application for   CCP §1107
- Proof of service of petition   CCP §1088.5
- Writ, service of   CCP §1096

Settlement in good faith, review of determination of   CCP §877.6
Stay of proceedings
- Administrative order or decision stayed pending judgment   CCP §1094.5
- When appeal does not stay   CCP §§1110a, 1110b

Summons, quashing service of   CCP §418.10
Time
- Local agency decision, filing petition to review   CCP §1094.6
- Return and hearing   CCP §1108

Transcripts
- Record of proceedings
  - Local agency decisions, review   CCP §1094.6
  - Retention or destruction   CCP §1094.5

Verdict, forwarding of   CCP §1093

MANDATE, WRIT OF   CRC 8.485 to 8.493
Administrative mandamus
- Filing of record below   CRC 3.1140

Amicus briefs   CRC 8.487
Appeals
- Appellate division of superior court
  - Judgment involving mandamus or prohibition directed to superior court   CCP §904.3
  - Small claims courts, writ petitions   CRC 8.970 to 8.977
  - Writ proceedings within original jurisdiction of appellate division   CRC 8.930 to 8.936
- Appellate rules, supreme court and court of appeal
  - Opposition   CRCSupp 4th AppDist
  - Writ proceedings in supreme court or court of appeal   CRC 8.485 to 8.493
    - Environmental quality act cases under public resources code   CRC 8.703

Applicability of provisions   CRC 8.485
Attorney general amicus brief   CRC 8.487
Briefs   CRC 8.487
Certificate of interested entities or persons   CRC 8.488
- Electronic filing, when required   CRCSupp 1st AppDist

Costs
- Award and recovery   CRC 8.493

Decisions   CRC 8.490
Denial
- Time to file responsive pleading in trial court   CRC 8.491

Environmental quality act cases under public resources code
- Writ proceedings   CRC 8.703

Filing of decision   CRC 8.490
Finality of decision   CRC 8.490
Judicial Council rules   CRC 8.485 to 8.493
Jurisdiction   CRC 8.485 to 8.493
- Original jurisdiction   CRC 8.485 to 8.493

Law and motion rules, applicability   CRC 3.1103
Modification of decision   CRC 8.490

MANDATE, WRIT OF—Cont.
Notices
    Issuance of writ   CRC 8.489
    Sanctions sought   CRC 8.492
Opposition   CRC 8.487
    Sanctions   CRC 8.492
Oral argument
    Sanctions   CRC 8.492
Original writs in reviewing courts
    Mandate, certiorari and prohibition in supreme court or court of appeal   CRC 8.485 to 8.493
        Environmental quality act cases under public resources code   CRC 8.703
Petitions
    Contents   CRC 8.486
    Denial of petition for writ
        Time to file responsive pleading in trial court   CRC 8.491
    Supporting documents   CRC 8.486
Record of proceedings
    Lodging of record from administrative case for subsequent mandamus hearing   CRC 3.1140
Rehearings   CRC 8.490
Remittitur   CRC 8.490
Rules of practice and procedure   CRC 8.485 to 8.493
    Environmental quality act cases under public resources code
        Writ proceedings   CRC 8.703
Sanctions   CRC 8.492
Sealed or confidential records   CRC 8.486
Service
    Petition, service of   CRC 8.486
    Supporting documents, service of   CRC 8.486
Small claims courts
    Petition for extraordinary relief relating to act of small claims division   CCP §116.798
    Writ petitions   CRC 8.970 to 8.977
Superior court appellate division
    Writ proceedings within original jurisdiction of appellate division   CRC 8.930 to 8.936
Writs of mandate, certiorari and prohibition in supreme court or court of appeal   CRC 8.485 to 8.493
    Environmental quality act cases under public resources code   CRC 8.703

MANDATORY ARBITRATION (See JUDICIAL ARBITRATION)

MANNER OF SERVICE (See PROCESS AND SERVICE OF PROCESS)

MANSLAUGHTER
Inheritance rights, effect on   Pro §§250 to 258

MANUALS
Small claims court rules and procedures, publications describing   CCP §116.930

MANUFACTURED HOMES
Covenants restricting use of prefabricated modular homes, validity of   CC §714.5
Mobilehomes (See MOBILEHOMES)
Sales, disclosure requirements   CC §§1102 to 1102.18
Unlawful detainer proceedings   CCP §§1161a, 1166a
Warranties   CC §§1797.1 to 1797.7

MANUFACTURERS
Automobile manufacturers, transporters, dealers and sales professionals
    Restitution, licensee ordered to pay
        Effect of order for restitution   Gov §11519.1
Defined   CC §1791
Guns (See FIREARMS AND OTHER WEAPONS)
Mobilehome warranties   CC §§1797.2, 1797.3
Nameplate removed from articles   CC §1710.1
Nuisance charges against   CCP §731a
Products liability (See PRODUCTS LIABILITY)
Repair of goods sold under warranty   CC §§1793.1 to 1795.8
Warranty of goods sold   CC §§1790 to 1795.8
Wholesale sales representatives, contractual relations with (See WHOLESALE SALES REPRESENTATIVES)

MAPS AND PLATS
Admissibility of   Ev §1341
Description conflicting with   CCP §2077
Destroyed maps, replacement of   CCP §1855
Fires, destruction by   CCP §§1953.10 to 1953.13
Natural disaster, destruction by   CCP §§1953.10 to 1953.13

MAPS AND PLATS—Cont.
Realty sales contracts, requirements for   CC §2985.51
Recordings (See RECORDS AND RECORDING)
Replacement of destroyed maps   CCP §1855
Subdivisions (See SUBDIVISIONS)

MARCHING (See DEMONSTRATIONS, PARADES AND MEETINGS)

MARIJUANA
Attorney-client privilege
    Advice as to conflict between state and federal law required to maintain privilege   Ev §956
Contracts and agreements
    Medical cannabis/marijuana
        Commercial activity in relation to marijuana as lawful object of contract   CC §1550.5
    Retail marijuana
        Commercial activity in relation to marijuana as lawful object of contract   CC §1550.5
Juvenile possession cases
    Request to reduce juvenile marijuana offenses
        Judicial council forms   CRCAppx A
Possession and possession for sale
    Recall or dismissal of sentence, petition
        Judicial council forms   CRCAppx A

MARINES (See MILITARY)

MARITAL AGREEMENTS (See PROPERTY SETTLEMENT AGREEMENTS)

MARITAL DEDUCTION GIFTS
Generally   Pro §21522
Application of law trust gifts   Pro §21521
Defined   Pro §21520
Liability of fiduciary   Pro §21526
Maximum allowable deduction   Pro §21523
Survivorship requirements   Pro §21525
Trusts
    Generally   Pro §21524
    Application of law   Pro §21521

MARITAL DISPUTES (See DOMESTIC VIOLENCE)

MARITAL PRIVILEGE   Ev §§970, 980, 987
Abandonment proceedings   Ev §§972, 985
Adverse party, spouse called as witness by   Ev §971
Aiding in commission of crime   Ev §§956, 981
Arrest
    Effect of prior criminal charges or   Ev §972
Bigamy
    Admissibility of spousal testimony in proceedings for   Ev §§972, 985
Defendant as spouse offering communication   Ev §987
Dependency proceedings   CRC 5.684
Estate, testifying as to   Ev §984
Exception to privilege
    Grounds   Ev §972
Fraud   Ev §§956, 981
Inheritances, testifying as to   Ev §984
Juvenile delinquency proceedings   Ev §§972, 986
Mental illness, testifying as to   Ev §§972, 982, 983
Party claiming   Ev §§912, 918
Personal injuries against spouse   Ev §§972, 985
Property of spouse or third party, crimes against   Ev §§972, 985
Support proceedings, testimony in   Fam §3551
Waiver of privilege   Ev §§912, 973

MARITAL PROPERTY
Generally (See COMMUNITY PROPERTY)
Joint tenancy, holding property in   Fam §750
Leasehold interests   Fam §700
Premarital agreements affecting (See PROPERTY SETTLEMENT AGREEMENTS)

MARKETABILITY OF RECORD TITLE (See TITLE AND OWNERSHIP)

MARKETING INFORMATION
Credit card holder's right to prohibit release of marketing information, notice of   CC §1748.12
Medical information used for direct marketing   CC §1798.91
Supermarket club card holders, conditions for sale or transfer of marketing information concerning   CC §1749.65

MARKETPLACE SALES AND SELLERS
Commercial relationships, terms and conditions   CC §1749.7
Payments to influence search results
    Commercial relationships, terms and conditions   CC §1749.7
Termination or suspension of marketplace seller
    Commercial relationships, terms and conditions   CC §1749.7

MARKET VALUE (See VALUE)

MARKS
Definition of signature or subscription to include   CCP §17
Signature by   CCP §17
Witnesses to signature by mark   CCP §17

MARRIAGE
Action to establish validity of marriage   Fam §309
Adoption
    Stepparent adoption
        Birth of child during marriage, domestic partnership, etc   Fam §9000.5
Affidavit for marriage license   Fam §§355, 505
    Identification of applicants
        Use of affidavit in lieu of photo identification   Fam §354
Age requirements   Fam §301
AIDS, information on   Fam §358
American Indians   Fam §295
Annulment (See **ANNULMENT**)
Bible entries as evidence   Ev §1312
Bigamous marriages   Fam §2201
Bigamy (See **BIGAMY**)
Blood tests (See **BLOOD TESTS**)
Breach of promise of marriage, action for   CC §43.5
Brochure on marriage   Fam §358
Capacity to marry
    Age requirement   Fam §301
    Conservatees (See **CONSERVATORS**)
    Judicial determination regarding   Pro §§810 to 812
    Minors   Fam §302
Ceremony requirements
    Solemnization generally (See within this heading, "**Solemnization of marriage**")
Certificates
    Additional fees   Gov §§26840.3, 26840.8
    Change of name on marriage licenses, certificates, etc
        Application to change name on California marriage license, etc   CCP §1276
    Copy fees   Gov §27365
    Declaration of marriage   Fam §425
    Filing fees   Gov §26840.1
    License becomes marriage certificate upon registration   Fam §300
        Confidential marriage   Fam §500.5
    Returning certificates   Fam §506
    Search fees   Gov §27369
Change of name
    Amendment to correct clerical errors   Fam §306.5
    Election to change name   Fam §306.5
    Marriage license to allow for   Fam §355
    Permissible names   Fam §306.5
Church records as evidence of   Ev §1315
Clergypersons authorized to perform marriage   Fam §400
Clerks of court
    Ceremony, fee for performing   Gov §26861
    Certificates generally (See within this heading, "**Certificates**")
    Commissioner of Civil Marriages   Fam §§400, 401
    Confidential marriage certificates   Fam §511
    Duties of   Fam §357
    Remote licensing and solemnization
        Guidance on process by county clerk   Fam §558
        Physical location of license applicants, solemnizer, witnesses and county clerk   Fam §554
        Transmission of license to county clerk   Fam §556
    Cohabitants
        Confidential marriage of   Fam §500
        Fraudulent promise, damages for   CC §43.4
Commissioner of Civil Marriages   Fam §§400, 401
Community property (See **COMMUNITY PROPERTY**)
Conciliation courts (See **CONCILIATION COURTS**)
Conditions based on restraints of   CC §710
Confidential marriages
    Generally   Fam §§500 to 511

MARRIAGE—Cont.
Confidential marriages—Cont.
    Change of name on confidential marriage licenses, certificates, etc
        Application to change name on California confidential marriage license, etc   CCP §1276
    Notaries public
        Issuance of confidential marriage licenses   Fam §§530 to 536
    Remote licensing and solemnization
        Issuance of license using remote technology   Fam §550
Congress member authorized to perform marriage   Fam §400
Conscientious refusal to solemnize marriage contrary to faith's tenets   Fam §400
Consent
    Generally   Fam §§300 to 305
    Parent's consent to marriage of minor   Fam §302
Conservatee's right to marry (See **CONSERVATORS**)
Consummation of   Fam §§301, 302
County recorder, duties of   Fam §357
    Registration of license with county recorder   Fam §300
Credit accounts, married women entitled to   CC §§1812.30, 1812.31
Custody of children (See **CUSTODY OF CHILDREN**)
Date of separation
    Defined   Fam §70
Declarant unavailable, admissibility of statement of   Ev §1310
Defined   Fam §300
Discrimination based on marital status   CC §51
    Judicial ethics code
        Administrative responsibilities of judge, impartial discharge   CRCSupp JudEthicsCanon 3
        Attorneys, judges to require to refrain from manifesting   CRCSupp JudEthicsCanon 3
        Court personnel and staff under direction of judge, standards of conduct enforced by judge   CRCSupp JudEthicsCanon 3
Dissolution (See **DISSOLUTION OF MARRIAGE**)
Domestic partnership
    Equal rights, protections and benefits for domestic partnership   Fam §297.5
Domestic violence information disseminated to marriage license applicants   Fam §358
Dowry recoverable   CC §1590
Duplicate of lost, damaged or destroyed license   Fam §360
    Confidential marriage licenses   Fam §510
Emancipation of minor on entering into valid marriage   Fam §7002
Evidence
    Consent, proof of   Fam §305
    Identification of applicants for marriage license   Fam §354
Family friends, statements concerning marriage by   Ev §1311
Fees
    Certificate fees
        Certificates generally (See within this heading, "**Certificates**")
    License fees (See within this heading, "**License requirements**")
    Marriage licenses (See within this heading, "**License requirements**")
Filing and returning documents
    Confidential marriage license   Fam §506
Foreign marriages, validity of   Fam §308
Forms
    Judicial council legal forms   CRCAppx A
Fraudulent promise, action for damages for   CC §43.4
Full faith and credit
    Out of state marriages
        Valid marriage recognized in California   Fam §308
Gay marriage ban
    Repeal   Fam §300
Gifts in contemplation of marriage, recovery of   CC §1590
Illegitimate children (See **PARENT AND CHILD**)
Imputed negligence   Fam §1000
Incestuous marriages   Fam §2200
Informational brochure available to applicants for marriage license   Fam §358
Installment purchases by married women   CC §§1812.30, 1812.31
Intoxicated persons   Fam §352
Judges authorized to perform   Fam §400
Judicial determination that person lacks legal capacity to marry   Pro §§810 to 812
Legal separation (See **LEGAL SEPARATION**)
Legislator authorized to perform marriage   Fam §400
License requirements   Fam §§300, 306, 350
    Address options   Fam §§351.5, 351.6
    Change of name on marriage licenses, certificates, etc
        Allowing for in license   Fam §355
        Application to change name on California marriage license, etc   CCP §1276
    Completion by person solemnizing marriage   Fam §359
    Confidential marriages   Fam §§501 to 505

MARRIAGE—Cont.
　License requirements —Cont.
　　Contents of license　　Fam §§351, 359
　　　Address options　　Fam §§351.5, 351.6
　　Copies of license
　　　Confidential marriage license　　Fam §§508, 509
　　Damaged licenses　　Fam §360
　　　Confidential marriage licenses　　Fam §510
　　Denial of license　　Fam §352
　　Destroyed licenses　　Fam §360
　　　Confidential marriage licenses　　Fam §510
　　Expiration of license　　Fam §356
　　Identification of applicants　　Fam §354
　　Issuance fees
　　　Generally　　Gov §§26840, 26840.2
　　　Additional fees　　Gov §§26840.7 to 26840.11
　　　Alameda county　　Gov §26840.10
　　　Solano county　　Gov §26840.11
　　Lost licenses　　Fam §360
　　　Confidential marriage licenses　　Fam §510
　　Noncompliance, effect of　　Fam §306
　　Preparation of license　　Fam §359
　　Presentation to person solemnizing　　Fam §359
　　Registration of license　　Fam §300
　　　Confidential marriage　　Fam §500.5
　　Remote licensing and solemnization　　Fam §§550 to 560
　　Return of license　　Fam §§359, 423
　　　Confidential marriage license　　Fam §506
　　Statement of person solemnizing marriage　　Fam §§422, 423
　　Unrecorded marriages　　Fam §425
　　Witness requirement　　Fam §359
　Living together, solemnizing marriage after　　Fam §500
　Local government officials
　　Solemnization, authority　　Fam §400
　Lost licenses　　Fam §360
　　Confidential marriage licenses　　Fam §510
　Magistrates authorized to perform　　Fam §400
　Marriage certificates
　　Certificates generally (See within this heading, **"Certificates"**)
　Military personnel
　　Overseas personnel
　　　Attorney-in-fact, appearance on behalf of personnel stationed overseas to solemnize marriage　　Fam §420
　Minister authorized to perform　　Fam §400
　Minors　　Fam §302
　　Court order consenting to issuance of license　　Fam §303
　　Court order for marriage of　　Fam §302
　　Emancipated minors　　Fam §7002
　　Family rule governing minor's request to marry　　CRC 5.448
　　Gender of parties
　　　Recording　　Fam §304
　　Information provided to parties upon order permitting marriage　　Fam §304
　　Interview of parties and parents/guardians　　Fam §304
　　Nullity based on incapacity　　Fam §2210
　　Parental authority ceasing on marriage of　　Fam §7505
　　Premarital counseling　　Fam §304
　　Solemnizing marriages
　　　Court order permitting marriage included with license　　Fam §423
　　Surviving spouse, married minor waiving rights as　　Pro §§142, 146
　Narcotic drugs, persons under influence of　　Fam §352
　Native Americans　　Fam §295
　Neighbor's testimony concerning　　Ev §1314
　Noncompliance with procedural requirements, effect of　　Fam §306
　Nonprofit religious institutions, officials of　　Fam §402
　Opposite sex requirement
　　Recognition of certain same sex marriages contracted in other jurisdictions
　　　Dissolution, annulment or legal separation, jurisdiction　　Fam §§2010, 2320
　　Repeal　　Fam §300
　Parent's consent to marriage of minor　　Fam §302
　Parties authorized to perform　　Fam §§400 to 402
　Physical inability to appear at marriage　　Fam §502
　Polygamous marriages　　Fam §2201
　Powers of attorney
　　Military personnel, overseas
　　　Attorney-in-fact, appearance on behalf of personnel stationed overseas to solemnize marriage　　Fam §420
　Premarital counseling of minors　　Fam §304
　Presumption of validity of　　Ev §663
　Priest authorized to perform　　Fam §400
　Privileged communications (See **MARITAL PRIVILEGE**)

MARRIAGE—Cont.
　Prohibited degrees of relationships　　Fam §2200
　Property settlement agreements (See **PROPERTY SETTLEMENT AGREEMENTS**)
　Public health department
　　Informational brochures published by　　Fam §358
　　Statement required by　　Fam §307
　Putative spouse　　Fam §§2251, 2252, 2254
　Rabbi authorized to perform　　Fam §400
　Rape of spouse
　　Statute of limitations on sexual assault damages　　CCP §340.16
　Recordation
　　Official records as proof of marriage　　Ev §1281
　Refusal to solemnize marriage contrary to faith's tenets　　Fam §400
　Registration
　　License becomes marriage certificate upon registration　　Fam §300
　　　Confidential marriage　　Fam §500.5
　Relatives
　　Degrees of relationship prohibited　　Fam §2200
　　Evidence from relatives concerning marriage　　Ev §1311
　Religious ceremonies　　Fam §400
　Religious society or denomination not having clergy, members of　　Fam §307
　Remote licensing and solemnization　　Fam §§550 to 560
　　Definition of remote technology　　Fam §560
　　Documentary proof of identity　　Fam §552
　　Guidance on process by county clerk　　Fam §558
　　Issuance of license using remote technology　　Fam §550
　　Photo identification　　Fam §552
　　Physical location of license applicants, solemnizer, witnesses and county clerk　　Fam §554
　　Signatures on license　　Fam §556
　　Transmission of license to county clerk　　Fam §556
　Reputation as evidence for　　Ev §§1313, 1314
　Returning certificates
　　Confidential marriage license　　Fam §506
　Same sex
　　Ban on same sex marriage
　　　Repeal　　Fam §300
　　Recognition of certain same sex marriages contracted in other jurisdictions
　　　Dissolution, annulment or legal separation, jurisdiction　　Fam §§2010, 2320
　Separate property (See **COMMUNITY PROPERTY**)
　Separation
　　Date of separation
　　　Defined　　Fam §70
　　Legal separation (See **LEGAL SEPARATION**)
　Siblings, invalidity of marriage between　　Fam §2200
　Solemnization of marriage
　　Generally　　Fam §420
　　Correctness of facts stated in license　　Fam §421
　　County clerk's fee for performing　　Gov §26861
　　License
　　　Duties of person solemnizing as to　　Fam §§359, 506
　　Minors
　　　Court order permitting marriage included with license　　Fam §423
　　Noncompliance, effect of　　Fam §306
　　Officiating persons　　Fam §400
　　Presumption of valid marriage where conducted under　　Ev §663
　　Proof of　　Fam §305
　　Religious society or denomination not having clergy, members of　　Fam §307
　　Remote licensing and solemnization　　Fam §§550 to 560
　　Requirements for　　Fam §300
　　Statement of person solemnizing marriage　　Fam §§422, 423
　　Unconventional religious denominations　　Fam §307
　Spousal rape
　　Statute of limitations on sexual assault damages　　CCP §340.16
　Spouses (See **HUSBAND AND WIFE**)
　Summary dissolution of (See **SUMMARY DISSOLUTION OF MARRIAGE**)
　Surviving spouse (See **SURVIVING SPOUSE**)
　Trusts
　　Fiduciary income and principal act
　　　Allocation of receipts involving marital trusts　　Pro §16348
　Two consenting persons　　Fam §300
　Unrecorded marriages　　Fam §425
　Validity
　　Limit to man and woman marriages
　　　Repeal　　Fam §300
　　Only marriage between man and woman as valid in California
　　　Repeal　　Fam §300

MARRIAGE—Cont.
Validity of marriage
- Action to establish validity of marriage   Fam §309
- Ceremony as valid, presumption of   Ev §663
- Foreign marriages   Fam §308
- Only marriage between man and woman as valid in California   Fam §300
  - Dissolution, annulment or legal separation involving out of state same sex marriage recognized in California, jurisdiction   Fam §§2010, 2320

Void or voidable marriage
- Annulment (See **ANNULMENT**)
- Attorney's fees and costs   Fam §2255
- Bigamous or polygamous marriages   Fam §2201
- Custody of children   Fam §2253
- Incestuous marriages   Fam §2200
- Premarital contracts, effect of void marriage on   Fam §1616
- Putative spouse   Fam §§2251, 2252
- Quasi-marital property   Fam §§2251, 2252
- Withdrawal by attorney in domestic relations matters   CCP §285.1
- Wrongful death actions, putative spouse and children of putative spouse as heirs for purposes of   CCP §377.60

Witnesses
- Remote licensing and solemnization
  - Physical location of license applicants, solemnizer, witnesses and county clerk   Fam §554

MARRIAGE AND FAMILY COUNSELORS
Discovery of records of health care professional review committees   Ev §1157
Peer review and professional reporting
- Liability for communication of information to evaluate, immunity   CC §43.8
Privileges (See **PRIVILEGED COMMUNICATIONS**)
Professional standards committees
- Immunity form liability   CC §43.7
Review committees
- Immunity form liability   CC §43.7
Sexual harassment, civil action for
- Construction or application of provisions in issue, solicitor general notified   CC §51.1

MARRIAGE AND FAMILY THERAPISTS
Child custody proceedings, court-ordered counseling   Fam §§3190 to 3193

MARRIAGE SETTLEMENT AGREEMENTS (See **PROPERTY SETTLEMENT AGREEMENTS**)

MARSHALING ASSETS   CC §3433

MARSHALS
Enforcement of judgments (See **ENFORCEMENT OF JUDGMENTS**)
Sheriff defined to include   CCP §17
Witnesses, marshals as (See **WITNESSES**)

MASSAGE PARLORS
Human trafficking or slavery
- Signs, businesses required to post notice concerning relief from slavery or human trafficking   CC §52.6

MASS CARE CENTERS
Personal injury liability of governmental agency to parties using   CC §1714.5

MASS MEDIA
Court proceedings, broadcasting, photographing, or recording   CRC 1.150

MASTER AND SERVANT (See **EMPLOYER AND EMPLOYEE**)

MASTER CALENDAR
Superior courts (See **SUPERIOR COURTS**)

MASTERS
Discrimination, prohibition against in court appointments   CRC 10.611, CRC JudAdminStand 10.21
Ethics rules, compliance with   CRCSupp JudEthicsCanon 6
Family law proceedings
- Appointment of masters
  - Applicable guidelines for appointment   CRC JudAdminStand 5.30
Special masters
- Groundwater rights actions
  - Appointment of special master   CCP §845
  - Report of special master   CCP §846

MASTURBATION
Sexual battery
- Statute of limitations on sexual assault damages   CCP §340.16

MATERIAL ALLEGATIONS (See **PLEADINGS**)

MATERIALMEN   CC §§8000 to 9566

MAXIMS OF JURISPRUDENCE   CC §§3509 to 3548

MAYHEM
Damages recoverable for   CC §3333.2
Malpractice of physician causing mayhem, recovery for   CC §3333.2

MCENERNEY ACT
Destroyed land records, reestablishment of   CCP §§751.01 to 751.28

MEALS
Jurors in criminal proceedings   CCP §217

MEASURE OF DAMAGES (See **DAMAGES**)

MECHANICS' LIENS   CC §§8000 to 9566
Action to enforce lien   CC §§8460 to 8470
- Contractor defenses   CC §8470
- Costs awarded to claimant   CC §8464
- Deduction from amount owed to direct contractor
  - Judgment against owner   CC §8470
- Deficiency of proceeds, entry of deficiency judgment   CC §8466
- Dismissal for want of prosecution   CC §8462
- Effect of judgment   CC §8468
- Limitations period   CC §8460
- Recording notice of pendency   CC §8461
- Release of property from claim of lien
  - Joinder of petition with pending action   CC §8480
- Removal of claim of lien from record   CC §§8490, 8494
- Stop payment notices
  - Enforcement of claim stated in notice   CC §§8550 to 8560
  - Public works   CC §§9362, 9500 to 9510
- Withholding payment from direct contractor during pendency of action   CC §8470

Agents
- Scope of agency and authority of agents   CC §8066
Amount of lien   CC §§8430 to 8434
- Generally   CC §8430
- Liens of other claimants to be deducted   CC §8434
- Single claim for multiple works of improvement   CC §8446
- Work not included in contract, restrictions   CC §8432
Applicability of provisions
- Bond and undertaking law   CC §8150
- Exclusions   CC §8054
- Governing law for actions taken prior to July 1, 2012   CC §8052
- Large projects, security for
  - Conditions for applicability   CC §8700
  - Excluded owners   CC §8704
  - Excluded works of improvement   CC §8702
- Private works of improvement generally   CC §8160
- Public works   CC §9000
- Retention payments   CC §8810
  - Exception regarding construction loan agreements   CC §8822
- Rules of practice in proceedings   CC §8056
- Stop work notices   CC §8848
Architects
- Design professionals   CC §§8300 to 8319 (See **LIENS**)
Assignment of funds, effect
- Public works   CC §9456
Attachment, availability of writ of   CC §8468
Authorization for improvement work   CC §8404
Bonds   CC §§8150 to 8154
- Applicability of bond and undertaking law   CC §8150
- Conditions not releasing surety   CC §§8152, 8154
- Construction of bond   CC §8154
- Large projects, security for   CC §§8700 to 8730
- Payment bonds   CC §§8600 to 8614 (See within this heading, "**Payment bonds**")
- Public works, payment bonds   CC §§9550 to 9566
- Release bonds   CC §8424
  - Stop payment notices   CC §§8510, 9364
- Sole condition of recovery on bond   CC §8154
Building permits
- Requirements   CC §8172

MECHANICS' LIENS—Cont.
Code provisions applicable   CC §3059
Commercial and industrial common interest developments
    Claim of lien served on association   CC §8119
        Notice by association to owners   CC §6660
Common interest developments
    Association served with claim of lien   CC §8119
        Notice to members   CC §4620
    Labor or material furnished to owner   CC §4615
Completion, notice of   CC §§8180 to 8190
    When work considered complete   CC §8180
Condominiums (See **COMMON INTEREST DEVELOPMENTS**)
Construction documents   CC §§8170 to 8174
Construction lenders
    Retention payments
        Exception to provisions regarding construction loan agreements   CC §8822
    Stop payment notices to   CC §§8530 to 8538
    Stop work notices to   CC §8836
Construction trust deed, security instrument to bear designation   CC §8174
Contract documents
    Amount of lien
        Work not included in contract, restrictions   CC §8432
    Direct contract, written
        Information required   CC §8170
County recorder, duties of   CC §8060
Definitions   CC §§8000 to 8050, 8058
Design professionals   CC §§8300 to 8319 (See **LIENS**)
Direct contract document
    Information required   CC §8170
Direct performance of contract
    Acts of owner in good faith not to prevent   CC §8062
Enforcement of lien
    Actions for enforcement   CC §§8460 to 8470 (See within this heading, **"Action to enforce lien"**)
    Claim of lien, document requirements   CC §8416
        Erroneous information, effect   CC §8422
    Conditions   CC §§8410 to 8424
    Notice of lien   CC §8416
        Erroneous information, effect   CC §8422
    Owner dispute as to correctness or validity, obtaining release bond   CC §8424
    Preliminary notice requirement   CC §8410
    Property subject to lien   CC §§8440 to 8448
    Recordation required   CC §§8412, 8414
    Removal of claim of lien from record   CC §§8490, 8494
    Stop payment notices
        Enforcement of claim stated in notice   CC §§8550 to 8560
        Public works   CC §§9362, 9500 to 9510
Engineers
    Design professionals   CC §§8300 to 8319 (See **LIENS**)
Entitlement to lien   CC §§8400, 8402
Estoppel
    Statement purporting to release or waive lien, effect   CC §8126
Final payment
    Conditional waiver and release on final payment   CC §8136
    Unconditional waiver and release on final payment   CC §8138
Fraud
    Stop payment notices, false   CC §8054
        Public works   CC §9454
Governing law
    Actions taken prior to July 1, 2012   CC §8052
    Rules of practice in proceedings   CC §8056
    Stop payment notices   CC §8500
        Public works   CC §9350
Large projects, security for   CC §§8700 to 8730
    Amount of security   CC §8730
    Applicability of chapter
        Conditions for applicability   CC §8700
        Excluded owners   CC §8704
        Excluded works of improvement   CC §8702
    Approved forms of security   CC §8720
    Bond requirements   CC §8722
    Copy of loan documentation to be provided   CC §8710
    Effect of provisions on other laws   CC §8716
    Escrow account requirements   CC §8726
        Deposit to or disbursement from account   CC §8728
    Letter of credit requirements   CC §8724
    Notice demanding security   CC §8712
    Public works payment bonds   CC §§9550 to 9566
    Required security by owner   CC §8710

MECHANICS' LIENS—Cont.
Large projects, security for —Cont.
    Waiver of provisions prohibited   CC §8714
Limitation period for enforcement action   CC §8460
    Payment bonds
        Public works, action to enforce liability on bond   CC §9558
        Recording prior to completion of work, action to enforce liability on bond   CC §8610
        Reduction of limitations period via provision in bond, restrictions   CC §8609
    Stop payment notices, enforcement of claim stated   CC §8550
        Public works   CC §§9362, 9502
Loan, deed securing
    Designation as construction trust deed required   CC §8174
Mortgages, priority of   CC §§8452 to 8456
Notice of cessation
    Copies to be delivered   CC §8190
    Ineffective notice   CC §8190
    Recordation   CC §8188
        Public works   CC §9202
Notice of completion   CC §§8180 to 8190
    Cessation notice   CC §8188
        Public works   CC §9202
    Contents required   CC §8182
    Copies to be delivered   CC §8190
    Ineffective notice   CC §8190
    Portion of work covered by direct contract   CC §8186
    Public works   CC §§9200 to 9208
        Payment bonds, notice of completion as prerequisite to enforcement   CC §9560
    Recordation
        Acceptance for recording   CC §8184
        Portion of work covered by a direct contract, completion of   CC §8186
        Public works   CC §§9202 to 9208
        When notice may be recorded   CC §8182
    Retention payments
        Notice of completion of disputed work   CC §8816
    When work considered complete   CC §8180
        Public works   CC §9200
Notice of lien   CC §8416
    Erroneous information, effect   CC §8422
Notice of nonresponsibility   CC §8444
Notices
    Cessation
        Copies to be delivered   CC §8190
        Ineffective notice   CC §8190
        Public works   CC §9202
        Recordation   CC §8188
    Claim of lien   CC §8416
        Erroneous information, effect   CC §8422
    Commercial and industrial common interest developments
        Delivery of or service of notice on association   CC §8119
    Common interest developments
        Delivery of or service of notice on association   CC §8119
    Completion   CC §§8180 to 8190
        Generally (See within this heading, **"Notice of completion"**)
    Contents   CC §8102
    Effective, when notice deemed to be   CC §8116
    Enforcement of claim stated in stop payment notice
        Notice of commencement of action   CC §§8550, 9504
    Failure to pay laborer full compensation, notice required   CC §8104
    Governing law for actions taken prior to July 1, 2012   CC §8052
    Information required   CC §8102
    Large projects, security for
        Notice demanding security   CC §8712
    Lis pendens   CC §8461
    Mailing   CC §§8106, 8110
    Method of giving notice   CC §8106
        Place of notice   CC §8108
    Nonresponsibility, notice of   CC §8444
    Payment bonds
        Notice of compliance   CC §8614
    Personal delivery   CC §8106
    Place of giving notice   CC §8108
    Posting of notice   CC §8114
    Preliminary notice   CC §§8104, 8200 to 8216 (See within this heading, **"Preliminary notice"**)
    Proof of notice   CC §8118
    Release bond, notice of recording   CC §8424

MECHANICS' LIENS—Cont.
  Notices—Cont.
    Release of property from claim of lien   CC §8482
      Hearing notice   CC §8486
    Stop payment notices   CC §§8500 to 8560 (See within this heading, **"Stop payment notices"**)
    Stop work notices   CC §§8830 to 8848 (See within this heading, **"Stop work notices"**)
    Time notice deemed complete   CC §8116
    Writing requirement   CC §8100
  Owner
    Acts of owner in good faith not to exonerate surety or prevent direct performance of contract   CC §8062
    Agent of owner, scope of authority   CC §8066
    Co-owners, acts on behalf of   CC §8064
    Large projects, security for
      Excluded owners   CC §8704
    Retention payments withheld by owner   CC §§8810 to 8822
    Stop payment notices to owner   CC §§8520, 8522
  Payment bonds   CC §§8600 to 8614
    Acts of owner in good faith not to exonerate surety   CC §8062
    Bond or other security allowed as protection   CC §8602
    Claimant entitled to recover on   CC §8606
    Compliance with provisions, notice of   CC §8614
    Conditioned for payment in full of claims of all claimants   CC §8606
    Direct contract with bond of at least 50% of price stated
      Restriction of lien enforcement   CC §8600
    Large projects, security for   CC §§8700 to 8730
    Lending institutions, objections   CC §8604
    Preliminary notice as prerequisite to enforcement action   CC §8612
      Public works   CC §9560
    Priority of mortgage upon recording of bond   CC §8452
    Public works   CC §§9550 to 9566
    Recording prior to completion of work
      Limitations period for action to enforce liability on bond   CC §8610
    Reduction of limitations period via provision in bond, restrictions   CC §8609
    Waiver and release, requirements   CC §8124
    Work to have been provided, prerequisite to recovery   CC §8608
      Public works   CC §9566
  Performance bonds
    Acts of owner in good faith not to exonerate surety   CC §8062
  Preliminary 20-day notices
    Additional recording fees   Gov §27361.9
  Preliminary notice   CC §§8200 to 8216
    Construction loan obtained after commencement
      Information to person who has given notice   CC §8210
    Contents required   CC §8202
      Public works   CC §9303
    Design professionals   CC §8204
    Enforcement of lien, notice as condition of   CC §8410
    Failure to give notice, effect   CC §8216
    Failure to pay laborer full compensation, notice required   CC §8104
    Filing and recordation   CC §8214
    Information to be available to person giving notice   CC §8208
    Multiple subcontractors, separate notices required   CC §8206
    Notice of cessation or completion
      Copy to be mailed to person giving preliminary notice by county clerk   CC §8214
    Number of notices required   CC §8206
    Payment bonds
      Preliminary notice as prerequisite to enforcement action   CC §§8612, 9560
    Public works   CC §§9300 to 9306
    Purpose of document   CC §8214
    Recordation   CC §8214
    Requirements generally   CC §8200
      Public works   CC §9302
    Statement required to be included   CC §8202
    Time for delivery   CC §8204
    Waiver of rights as void   CC §8212
  Price in contract greater than one million dollars
    Large projects, security for   CC §§8700 to 8730
  Priorities   CC §§8450 to 8458
    Contract for site improvement separate from contract for construction   CC §8454
    Generally   CC §8450
    Mortgage for original commitment of lender   CC §8456
    Payment bond, priority of mortgage upon recording of   CC §8452
    Site improvement, lien for   CC §8458

MECHANICS' LIENS—Cont.
  Priorities—Cont.
    Stop payment notice, effect
      Public works   CC §9456
    Unrecorded liens   CC §8450
  Progress payments
    Conditional waiver and release, form   CC §8132
    Direct contractor, payment due to   CC §8800
    Public utility contract with direct contractor
      Payment to subcontractor   CC §8802
    Unconditional waiver and release, form   CC §8134
  Property subject to lien   CC §§8440 to 8448
    Interests in real property   CC §8442
    Notice of nonresponsibility   CC §8444
    Release of property from claim of lien   CC §§8480 to 8494
    Separate residential units   CC §8448
    Single claim for multiple works of improvement   CC §8446
    Work of improvement and site of work   CC §8440
  Public works   CC §§9000 to 9566
    Applicability of provisions   CC §9000
    Bonds   CC §§8150 to 8154
      Payment bonds   CC §§9550 to 9566
    Definitions   CC §§8000 to 8050
    Direct performance of contract
      Acts of owner in good faith not to prevent   CC §8062
    Enforcement of payment of claim stated in stop payment notice   CC §§9500 to 9510
      Cessation of notice and release of funds   CC §9510
      Commencement of action   CC §9502
      Conditions prerequisite to commencing action   CC §9500
      Dismissal for want of prosecution   CC §9508
      Joinder of multiple claimants or actions   CC §9506
      Limitation of actions   CC §§9362, 9502
      Notice of commencement of action   CC §9504
      Notices prerequisite to commencing action   CC §9500
    Exclusions from provisions   CC §8054
    Filing and recordation of documents   CC §8060
    Governing law
      Actions taken prior to July 1, 2012   CC §8052
      Rules of practice in proceedings   CC §8056
    Notice of cessation
      Recording   CC §9202
    Notice of completion
      Payment bonds, prerequisite to enforcement   CC §9560
      Recording notice of cessation   CC §9202
      Recording notice of completion   CC §§9204, 9208
      Requirements   CC §9204
      When completion occurs   CC §9200
    Notices generally (See within this heading, **"Notices"**)
    Payment bonds   CC §§9550 to 9566
      Action to enforce liability on bond   CC §§9558, 9564
      Amount   CC §9554
      Bids to state whether bond required   CC §9550
      Failure to provide and approve   CC §9552
      Notice compliance requirements generally   CC §9562
      Notice of completion as prerequisite   CC §9560
      Preliminary notice as prerequisite   CC §9560
      Requirements   CC §9554
      Terms and conditions   CC §9554
      When required   CC §9550
      Work provided, prerequisite to right of claimant to recover   CC §9566
    Preliminary notice   CC §§9300 to 9306
      Contents   CC §9303
      Prerequisite to other actions   CC §9300
      Recipients   CC §9300
      Requirements generally   CC §9302
      Stop payment notice, when given in relation to preliminary notice   CC §9304
      Subcontractor duties to give   CC §9306
    Release bond   CC §9364
    Release of funds, summary proceeding   CC §§9400 to 9414
      Action for declaration of rights   CC §9408
      Burden of proof at hearing   CC §9410
      Counter-affidavit of claimant   CC §9406
      Court order containing final determination   CC §9412
      Evidence at hearing   CC §9412
      Grounds for obtaining release   CC §9400
      Motion for determination of rights after action commenced   CC §9408
      Other actions not barred by determination   CC §9414
      Pleadings, affidavits to constitute   CC §9410

MECHANICS' LIENS—Cont.
  Public works —Cont.
    Release of funds, summary proceeding —Cont.
      Service of affidavit on claimant   CC §9404
      Service of affidavit on public entity   CC §9402
      Service of order on public entity   CC §9412
    Release of lien   CC §§8120 to 8138 (See within this heading, **"Release of lien"**)
    Stop payment notices   CC §§9350 to 9510
      Action to enforce payment, limitations period   CC §§9362, 9502
      Chapter as governing law   CC §9350
      Compliance with general notice requirements   CC §9354
      Contents required   CC §9352
      Distribution of funds withheld   CC §§9450 to 9456
      Effectiveness, time requirements   CC §9356
      Enforcement of payment of claim stated   CC §§9500 to 9510
      False stop payment notice   CC §9454
      Insufficient funds, priority of distribution   CC §9450
      Payments not prohibited   CC §9360
      Persons entitled to give   CC §9100
      Priorities   CC §9456
      Procedure for giving   CC §9354
      Release bond   CC §9364
      Release of funds, summary proceeding   CC §§9400 to 9414
      Right to recover deficits not impaired   CC §9452
      Signature and verification   CC §9352
      Validity, conditions for   CC §9356
      Withholding of funds to pay claims   CC §9358
  Recordation
    Action to enforce lien pending, notice of pendency   CC §8461
    Construction trust deed   CC §8174
    Co-owners, acts on behalf of   CC §8064
    County recorder
      Duties   CC §8060
    Enforcement of lien, prerequisites   CC §§8412, 8414
    Filing and recordation generally   CC §8060
    Notice of cessation   CC §8188
    Notice of completion
      Acceptance for recording   CC §8184
      Portion of work covered by a direct contract, completion of   CC §8186
      Public works   CC §§9202 to 9208
      When notice may be recorded   CC §8182
    Preliminary notice   CC §8214
  Release bonds
    Stop payment notices   CC §8510
      Public works   CC §9364
  Release of lien   CC §§8120 to 8138
    Accord and satisfaction, effect of waiver and release provisions   CC §8130
    Applicability of provisions   CC §8120
    Bonds   CC §8424
      Stop payment notices   CC §§8510, 9364
    Conditional waiver and release on final payment   CC §8136
    Conditional waiver and release on progress payments   CC §8132
    Execution of waiver and release required   CC §8122
    Payment bonds, requirements for waiver and release   CC §8124
    Settlement agreement, effect of waiver and release provisions   CC §8130
    Statement purporting to release, effect   CC §8126
    Stop payment notice, reduction or release   CC §8128
    Unconditional waiver and release on final payment   CC §8138
    Unconditional waiver and release on progress payments   CC §8134
  Release of property from claim of lien   CC §§8480 to 8494
    Allegations required in petition   CC §8484
    Attorneys' fees for prevailing party   CC §8488
    Hearing
      Burden of production of evidence and proof   CC §8488
      Date and notice of hearing   CC §8486
      Issues to be decided   CC §8488
    Joinder of petition with pending action   CC §8480
    Judgment in favor of petitioner, effect   CC §8488
    Notice requirement   CC §8482
    Other causes of action not barred   CC §8480
    Petition for release   CC §8480
    Removal of claim of lien from record   CC §§8490, 8494
    Verification of petition   CC §8484
  Removal of claim of lien from record   CC §§8490, 8494
  Retention payments   CC §§8810 to 8822
    Acceptance or rejection of disputed work   CC §8816
    Applicability of provisions   CC §8810
      Exception regarding construction loan agreements   CC §8822
    Contractor withholding funds from subcontractor   CC §8814

MECHANICS' LIENS—Cont.
  Retention payments —Cont.
    Failure to make   CC §8818
    Notice of completion of disputed work   CC §8816
    Owner withholding funds from direct contractor   CC §8812
    Waiver of provisions prohibited   CC §8820
    Work to become part of public entity
      Condition of payment on acceptance of work by public entity   CC §8812
  Right to   CC §§8400, 8402
  Security for large projects   CC §§8700 to 8730
    Public works payment bonds   CC §§9550 to 9566
  Service of notice
    Preliminary notice   CC §8204
    Public works, summary proceeding for release of funds
      Affidavit, service on claimant   CC §9404
      Affidavit, service on public entity   CC §9402
      Counter-affidavit of claimant   CC §9406
      Service of order on public entity   CC §9412
  Site improvements
    Priority of lien   CC §8458
  Stop payment notices   CC §§8500 to 8560
    Amount claimed   CC §8502
    Architect to receive   CC §8506
    Compliance with general notice requirements   CC §8502
      Public works   CC §9354
    Construction lenders   CC §§8530 to 8538
      Claimant notice   CC §8532
      Election not to withhold funds   CC §8538
      Objection to sufficiency of sureties on bond   CC §8534
      Person entitled to give notice   CC §8530
      Request for notice of election not to withhold funds   CC §8538
      To whom delivered   CC §8506
      Withholding of funds   CC §8536
    Contents   CC §8502
      Public works   CC §9352
    Enforcement of claim stated in notice   CC §§8550 to 8560
      Attorneys' fees and costs   CC §8558
      Commencement of action   CC §8550
      Determination of prevailing party   CC §8558
      Dismissal for want of prosecution   CC §§8554, 9508
      Effect of dismissal   CC §8556
      Interest included in award   CC §8560
      Joinder of multiple claimants or actions   CC §§8552, 9506
      Notice of commencement of action   CC §8550
      Public works   CC §§9362, 9500 to 9510
    False or fraudulent notice   CC §8504
      Public works   CC §9454
    Governing law   CC §8500
      Public works   CC §9350
    Owner, notice to   CC §§8520, 8522
    Prerequisites for validity   CC §8508
    Priority of rights to funds withheld   CC §§8540 to 8544
      Amount recoverable   CC §8542
      Assignment of funds, effect on rights of claimant   CC §8544
      Distribution of funds   CC §8540
      Pro rata distribution   CC §8540
      Public works   CC §9456
    Public works   CC §§9350 to 9510 (See within this heading, **"Public works"**)
    Reduction or release   CC §8128
    Release bond   CC §8510
      Public works   CC §9364
    Rights governed by chapter   CC §8500
    Validity, conditions for   CC §8508
      Public works   CC §9356
    Withholding of amount due to direct contractor   CC §8520
      Public works   CC §9358
  Stop work notices   CC §§8830 to 8848
    Additional notices   CC §8834
    Applicability of provisions   CC §8848
    Cancellation of claim, notice   CC §8840
    Copy provided to construction lenders   CC §8836
    Copy provided to subcontractors   CC §8834
    Definition   CC §8830
    Expedited court proceeding to determine liability   CC §8844
    Judicial determination of liability   CC §8844
    Liability of contractor, subcontractor or sureties   CC §8838
    Resolution of claim, notice   CC §8840
    Supplemental nature of right   CC §8842
    Waiver of provisions prohibited   CC §8846

MECHANICS' LIENS—Cont.
Stop work notices —Cont.
When given   CC §8832
Subcontractors
Preliminary notice, subcontractor duties to give
Public works   CC §9306
Progress payments
Public utility contract with direct contractor   CC §8802
Retention payments withheld by direct contractor   CC §§8810 to 8822 (See within this heading, **"Retention payments"**)
Stop work notices
Copy provided to subcontractors   CC §8834
Liability of contractor, subcontractor or sureties   CC §8838
Sureties
Acts of owner in good faith not to exonerate surety of performance or payment bond   CC §8062
Conditions not releasing surety on bond   CC §§8152, 8154
Payment bonds generally (See within this heading, **"Payment bonds"**)
Release bonds
Public works   CC §9364
Stop payment notices   CC §8510
Stop payment notice to construction lender
Objection to sufficiency of sureties on bond   CC §8534
Stop work notices
Liability of contractor, subcontractor or sureties   CC §8838
Waiver
Release of lien   CC §§8120 to 8138 (See within this heading, **"Release of lien"**)
Release of property from claim of lien   CC §§8480 to 8494
Release of property from claim of lien generally (See within this heading, **"Release of property from claim of lien"**)

MEDIA
Attorney professional conduct
Trial publicity   ProfC 3.6
Court proceedings, coverage of   CRC 1.150
Radio and television generally (See **RADIO AND TELEVISION**)

MEDIATION
Administrative adjudication provisions, confidentiality of mediation under   Gov §11420.30
Admonishing of mediator
Complaints about court-program mediators
Permissible actions on complaints   CRC 3.870
Appearances at mediation sessions   CRC 3.894
Telephone, appearance by
Fees   CCP §367.6
Hearing on status of arbitration or mediation   CCP §367.5
Appointments by court, nondiscrimination standard for   CRC 10.611, CRC JudAdminStand 10.21
Arbitration (See **ARBITRATION**)
Attorney professional conduct
Former judges, arbitrators, mediators, etc
Restrictions on representation of clients   ProfC 1.12
Service by attorney as third-party neutral   ProfC 2.4
Attorneys at law
Confidentiality of communications, admissions, etc, in mediation proceedings
Disclosure by attorney to client of confidentiality requirements   Ev §1129
Civil action mediation   CCP §§1775, 1775.15, CRC 3.890 to 3.898
1st appellate district rules of court   CRCSupp 1st AppDist
3rd appellate district local rules   CRCSupp 3rd AppDist
5th appellate district   CRCSupp 5th AppDist
6th appellate district local rules   CRCSupp 6th AppDist
ADR program information   CRC 10.781
Amount in controversy, limit on   CCP §1775.5, CRC 3.891
Appearance at mediation sessions   CCP §1737, CRC 3.894
Applicability of provisions for civil action mediation   CCP §§1775.2 to 1775.5, CRC 3.890, 3.891
Applicability of rules   CRC 3.835
Attendance   CRC 3.894
Confidentiality of communications in course of mediation (See within this heading, **"Confidentiality"**)
Costs   CCP §1775.8
Court list of ADR neutrals   CRC 10.781
Definitions   CCP §1775.1
Discovery
Right to obtain discovery as unaffected by participation in mediation   CCP §§1741, 1775.11

MEDIATION—Cont.
Civil action mediation —Cont.
Dismissal of action for delay in prosecution, tolling of time periods for   CCP §§1740, 1775.7
Educational materials concerning ADR processes, courts' provision of   CRC 3.878, 3.898
Election by court to apply mediation provisions to eligible actions   CCP §1775.2
Fifth appellate district   CRCSupp 5th AppDist
First appellate district rules of court   CRCSupp 1st AppDist
Lists of mediation participants
Filing   CRC 3.894
Mandatory mediation (See within this heading, **"Mandatory mediation"**)
Mediation statements
Request for submission   CRC 3.894
Mediator panels, establishment of   CCP §1735, CRC 3.892
Mediators
Compensation   CCP §§1735, 1775.8
Complaints about court-program mediators   CRC 3.865 to 3.872
Qualifications of mediators in general civil cases   CRC 10.781
Selection   CCP §§1735, 1775.6, CRC 3.893
Standards of conduct   CRC 3.850 to 3.860
Mutual exclusion of judicial arbitration and civil action mediation   CCP §1775.4
Nonagreement, statement of   CCP §§1739, 1775.9, CRC 3.895
Form   CRC 3.845
Preemption of other alternative resolution dispute programs   CCP §1775.13
Privilege to serve as neutral   CRC 10.781
Public entity as party to mediation   CCP §1775.3
Reporting requirements for courts   CCP §1775.14
Reports or statements of mediator
Form   CRC 3.845
Statement of agreement or nonagreement   CCP §§1739, 1775.9, CRC 3.895
Form   CRC 3.845
Stipulation to mediation   CRC 3.891
3rd Appellate District rules of court   CRCSupp 3rd AppDist
Trial court delay reduction provisions, requirements under   CRC 3.896
Common interest developments
Alternative dispute resolution (See **COMMON INTEREST DEVELOPMENTS**)
Complaints about court-program mediators   CRC 3.865 to 3.872
Acknowledgment of complaint   CRC 3.869
Applicability of provisions   CRC 3.865
Complainants
Defined   CRC 3.866
Complaint committee
Defined   CRC 3.866
Complaint coordinator
Defined   CRC 3.866
Designation   CRC 3.867
Identification   CRC 3.867
Process for handling complaints   CRC 3.869
Complaints defined   CRC 3.866
Confidentiality of proceedings   CRC 3.871
Conflicts of interest
Participation in proceeding, disqualification from adjudicating underlying dispute   CRC 3.872
Counseling, admonishing or reprimanding mediator
Permissible actions on complaints   CRC 3.870
Court-program mediators
Defined   CRC 3.866
Definitions   CRC 3.866
Inquiry
Defined   CRC 3.866
Local rule to establish complaint procedure   CRC 3.868
Mediation communication
Confidentiality, preservation   CRC 3.871
Defined   CRC 3.866
No action
Permissible actions on complaints   CRC 3.870
Notice
Final action   CRC 3.869
Participation in proceeding
Disqualification from adjudicating underlying dispute   CRC 3.872
Permissible actions on complaints   CRC 3.870
Preliminary review and disposition   CRC 3.869
Procedure
Definition of complaint procedure   CRC 3.866
General requirements   CRC 3.869
Local rule to establish complaint procedure   CRC 3.868

MEDIATION—Cont.
  Complaints about court-program mediators —Cont.
    Proceedings
      Confidentiality   CRC 3.871
      Definition of complaint proceeding   CRC 3.866
      General requirements   CRC 3.869
    Prompt handling   CRC 3.869
    Purpose of provisions   CRC 3.865
    Record of complaints   CRC 3.869
    Referral of complaints   CRC 3.869
    Removal from panel or list
      Permissible actions on complaints   CRC 3.870
    Rules of conduct
      Defined   CRC 3.866
    Submission of complaints   CRC 3.869
    Suspension from panel or list
      Permissible actions on complaints   CRC 3.870
    Training
      Imposition of additional training, permissible actions on complaints   CRC 3.870
  Conciliation courts (See **CONCILIATION COURTS**)
  Conduct of mediators, standards   CRC 3.850 to 3.860
    Complaints about court-program mediators   CRC 3.865 to 3.872
  Confidentiality
    Generally   CCP §§1775.10, 1775.12, Ev §§1116 to 1117, 1119 to 1120
    Administrative adjudication provisions, mediation under   Gov §11420.30
    Attorney disclosure to client of confidentiality standards in mediation proceedings   Ev §1129
    Attorney fees and costs awarded against party attempting to compel mediator to testify or produce writing   Ev §1127
    Complaints about court-program mediators   CRC 3.871
    Complaints about mediator conduct
      Disclosures concerning proceedings   CRC 3.860
    Conditions for disclosure
      Generally   Ev §1122
      Oral agreement   Ev §1124
      Report of mediator   Ev §1121
      Settlement agreement   Ev §1123
    Definitions   Ev §§1115, 1118
    Disclosure notification and acknowledgment
      Form, judicial council   CRCAppx A
    End of mediation
      Continuing confidentiality   Ev §1126
      Defined   Ev §1125
    Mandatory mediation   CCP §1738
    New trial or hearing, reference to mediation in subsequent proceedings as grounds for   CCP §1775.12, Ev §1128
    Report of mediator, conditions for subsequent use of   Ev §1121
    Standards of conduct for mediators
      Complaints about court-program mediators   CRC 3.871
    Vacation or modification of decision in subsequent proceeding, reference to mediation as grounds for   CCP §1775.12, Ev §1128
  Conflicts of interest
    Complaints about court-program mediators   CRC 3.865 to 3.872
      Participation in proceeding, disqualification from adjudicating underlying dispute   CRC 3.872
  Construction defects, actions for
    Prelitigation procedures
      Offer to mediate   CC §919
      Undergoing mediation   CC §928
  Counseling of mediators
    Complaints about court-program mediators
      Permissible actions on complaints   CRC 3.870
  Court officers and employees
    Labor relations
      Mediation of labor disputes   CRC 10.659
  Custody of children (See **CUSTODY OF CHILDREN**)
  Definitions   CRC 3.800
  Discovery
    Right to obtain discovery as unaffected by participation in mediation   CCP §1775.11
  Discrimination, prohibition against in court appointments of mediators   CRC 10.611, CRC JudAdminStand 10.21
  Domestic violence (See **DOMESTIC VIOLENCE**)
  Eminent domain disputes, referral of   CCP §1250.420
  Ethical standards for conduct of mediators   CRC 3.850 to 3.860
    Complaints about court-program mediators   CRC 3.865 to 3.872
  Evidence
    Confidentiality requirements
      Attorney disclosure to client of confidentiality standards in mediation proceedings   Ev §1129

MEDIATION—Cont.
  Evidence—Cont.
    Discovery
      Confidentiality, attorney disclosure to client of confidentiality standards in mediation proceedings   Ev §1129
    Inadmissibility as evidence of oral or written communications by mediation participants
      Attorney disclosure to client of confidentiality standards in mediation proceedings   Ev §1129
  Family law
    Conciliation (See **CONCILIATION COURTS**)
    Custody of children (See **CUSTODY OF CHILDREN**)
    Domestic violence (See **DOMESTIC VIOLENCE**)
    Judicial Council duties   Fam §§1850 to 1852
    Mediators and evaluators
      Appointment, applicable guidelines   CRC JudAdminStand 5.30
      Ex parte communications   Fam §216
  1st Appellate District rules of court   CRCSupp 1st AppDist
  Inquiries
    Complaints about court-program mediators   CRC 3.865 to 3.872
  Judges, service as mediators   CRCSupp JudEthicsCanons 3, 4
  Judicial administration standards
    Alternative dispute resolution programs
      Committees to oversee ADR programs   CRC JudAdminStand 10.71
      Coordination of ADR programs, judicial council guidelines for   CRC JudAdminStand 10.70
  Juvenile court dependency mediation program
    Court-connected dependency mediation   CRC 5.518
  Lists of mediators
    Complaints about court-program mediators
      Removal from panel or list, permissible actions on complaints   CRC 3.870
      Suspension from panel or list, permissible actions on complaints   CRC 3.870
  Mandatory mediation
    Appearance at mediation sessions   CCP §1737
    Application of provisions   CCP §1732
    Confidentiality of mediation   CCP §1738
    Definitions   CCP §1731
    Discovery
      Discoverability of evidence of mediation   CCP §1738
      Right to obtain discovery as unaffected by participation in mediation   CCP §1741
    Exemption from other judicially ordered arbitration or mediation   CCP §1733
    Fees   CCP §1735
    Mediators   CCP §1735
    Pilot programs   CCP §1730
    Repealer   CCP §1743
    Statement of nonagreement   CCP §1739
    Status conference   CCP §1734
      Telephone appearance at status conferences   CRC 3.670
    Time limits
      Mediation   CCP §1736
      Status conference   CCP §1734
      Tolling of time limits for prosecuting civil actions   CCP §1740
  Mediation communications
    Confidentiality, preservation
      Complaints about court-program mediators   CRC 3.871
    Defined
      Complaints about court-program mediators   CRC 3.866
  Mediators
    Attorney professional conduct
      Former judges, arbitrators, mediators, etc, restrictions on representation of clients   ProfC 1.12
      Service by attorney as third-party neutral   ProfC 2.4
    Civil action mediation (See within this heading, **"Civil action mediation"**)
    Complaints about court-program mediators   CRC 3.865 to 3.872
    Conciliation courts   Fam §§1816, 3160, 3164
    Contempt, competency to testify as to act that gave rise to   Ev §703.5
    Counseling, admonishing or reprimanding mediator
      Permissible actions on complaints   CRC 3.870
    No action on complaint
      Permissible actions on complaints   CRC 3.870
    Selection   CRC 3.893
    Standards of conduct   CRC 3.850 to 3.860
      Complaints about court-program mediators   CRC 3.865 to 3.872
    Training
      Imposition of additional training, permissible actions on complaints   CRC 3.870

MEDIATION—Cont.
New trial, reference to mediation proceedings in subsequent trial as grounds for CCP §1775.12, Ev §1128
Offer to compromise as inadmissible evidence   CCP §1775.10
Panels of mediators   CRC 3.892
    Complaints about court-program mediators
        Removal from panel or list, permissible actions on complaints   CRC 3.870
        Suspension from panel or list, permissible actions on complaints   CRC 3.870
Pilot mediation programs   CCP §1730
Privileged communication
    Confidentiality generally (See within this heading, **"Confidentiality"**)
Reprimand of mediator
    Complaints about court-program mediators
        Permissible actions on complaints   CRC 3.870
Settlement agreements
    Conditions for disclosure of   Ev §1123
    Standards of conduct for mediators   CRC 3.857
Standards of conduct for mediators   CRC 3.850 to 3.860
    Applicability of provisions   CRC 3.851
    Attendance sheet
        Participant duties as to   CRC 3.860
    Background
        Truthful representations   CRC 3.856
    Combination of mediation with other ADR processes   CRC 3.857
    Compensation   CRC 3.859
    Competence   CRC 3.856
    Complaints about court-program mediators   CRC 3.865 to 3.872
    Confidentiality   CRC 3.854
        Complaints about court-program mediators   CRC 3.871
    Conflicts of interest   CRC 3.855
    Contingent fees   CRC 3.859
    Definitions   CRC 3.852
    Diligence of mediator   CRC 3.857
    Discipline
        Complaints about court-program mediators   CRC 3.865 to 3.872
        Disclosures   CRC 3.855
    Disclosures   CRC 3.855
        Complaints about mediator conduct, disclosures concerning proceedings   CRC 3.860
        Disciplinary history   CRC 3.856
    Discretionary termination and withdrawal   CRC 3.857
    Explaining process to participants   CRC 3.857
    Fairness   CRC 3.857
    Favors   CRC 3.859
    Gifts   CRC 3.859
    Impartiality   CRC 3.855
    Marketing   CRC 3.858
    Nonparticipant interests   CRC 3.857
    Professional services of mediator   CRC 3.857
    Punctuality of mediator   CRC 3.857
    Purpose of provisions   CRC 3.850
    Quality of mediation process   CRC 3.857
    Recommendations for other services   CRC 3.857
    Self-determination by participants in mediation   CRC 3.853
    Settlements   CRC 3.857
    Skill level assessment   CRC 3.856
    Soliciting business   CRC 3.858
    Termination
        Discretionary termination and withdrawal   CRC 3.857
    Voluntary participation in mediation   CRC 3.853
    Withdrawal   CRC 3.855
        Discretionary termination and withdrawal   CRC 3.857
        Skill level inadequate   CRC 3.856
Statement by mediator, filing of   CRC 3.895
    Form   CRC 3.845
Vacation of judgment in subsequent trial, reference to mediation as grounds for CCP §1775.12, Ev §1128

MEDI-CAL
Adoption
    Health insurance
        Notice of reduced-cost options through California health benefit exchange or no-cost Medi-Cal   Fam §8613.7
Annulment of marriage
    Health insurance
        Notice of reduced-cost options through California health benefit exchange or no-cost Medi-Cal   Fam §2024.7
Divorce
    Health insurance
        Notice of reduced-cost options through California health benefit exchange or no-cost Medi-Cal   Fam §2024.7

MEDI-CAL—Cont.
Legal separation
    Health insurance
        Notice of reduced-cost options through California health benefit exchange or no-cost Medi-Cal   Fam §2024.7
Recipients
    Claim against estate by Director of Health Services   Pro §9202
    Eligibility of child   Fam §8903
    Late payment of Medi-Cal claims   Gov §927.5
    Notification of Health Services Department on death of beneficiary   Pro §215
Specialty mental health services
    Foster care
        Presumptive transfer of responsibility for services upon change of child placement, waiver proceedings   CRC 5.647

MEDICAL BOARD OF CALIFORNIA   Gov §§11371 to 11373.3

MEDICAL CANNABIS/MARIJUANA
Attorney-client privilege
    Advice as to conflict between state and federal law required to maintain privilege   Ev §956
Contracts
    Commercial activity in relation to marijuana as lawful object of contract   CC §1550.5
Physician recommendation of medical cannabis/marijuana
    Confidentiality of medical information, obligations   CC §56.06

MEDICAL CARE AND TREATMENT
Sexual battery against medically incapacitated person
    Statute of limitations on sexual assault damages   CCP §340.16

MEDICAL CONDITION
Preference, motion for   CCP §36

MEDICAL EXAMINATIONS (See **MENTAL EXAMINATIONS; PHYSICAL EXAMINATIONS**)

MEDICAL EXPENSES
Communication of debts, authority for   CC §1788.12
Domestic violence cases, order for restitution   Fam §§6342, 7720
Last illness (See **LAST ILLNESS**)

MEDICAL FACILITIES (See **HOSPITALS**)

MEDICAL INFORMATION
Direct marketing, use of medical information for   CC §1798.91
Disclosures by providers
    Caregivers, disclosure to   CC §56.1007
    Domestic partners, disclosure to   CC §56.1007
    Family members, disclosure to   CC §56.1007
    Friends, disclosure to   CC §56.1007
    Minors
        Coordination of health care services and treatment   CC §56.103
    Personal representatives, disclosure to   CC §56.1007

MEDICAL MALPRACTICE (See **MALPRACTICE**)

MEDICAL QUALITY HEARING PANEL
Generally   Gov §11371
Interim orders issued by   Gov §11529

MEDICAL RECORDS
Abortion
    Restrictions on release of medical information related to abortion   CC §§56.108, 56.110
Administrators, use and disclosure by   CC §56.26
Admissibility of   Ev §§1156 to 1158
Adoption proceedings, furnishing medical information in (See **ADOPTION**)
Assisted reproduction, consent required for   Fam §7613
Attorneys, inspection of records by   CCP §1985.7, Ev §1158
Confidentiality   CC §§56.101, 56.104, 56 to 56.37
    Abortion
        Restrictions on release of medical information related to abortion   CC §§56.108, 56.110
    Age-appropriate design code
        Applicability of code provisions in light of confidentiality of medical information act   CC §1798.99.40
    Confidential communications request
        Defined   CC §56.05
        Written or electronic requests   CC §56.107

MEDICAL RECORDS—Cont.
  Confidentiality —Cont.
    Consumer privacy rights
      Applicability of provisions   CC §1798.146
      Reidentification of deidentified information, prohibitions   CC §1798.148
      Relation between medical records confidentiality and obligations imposed under consumer privacy provisions   CC §1798.145
    Defenses to actions for wrongful release   CC §56.36
    Gender-affirming health care or mental health care
      Businesses organized to maintain medical information
        Limitation of access to information about gender affirming care, abortion, or contraception information   CC §56.101
      Restrictions on release of medical information   CC §56.109
    Health care service plans
      Protection of confidentiality of medical information   CC §56.107
    Marketing
      Defined   CC §56.05
      Disclosure of information for use in marketing   CC §56.10
    Minors
      Removal from physical custody of parent or guardian, protection of mental health records from release   CC §56.106
    Pharmaceutical company requiring disclosure as condition of receiving pharmaceuticals   CC §56.102
    Software or hardware providers of information-sharing products
      Health care providers for purposes of confidentiality provisions   CC §56.06
  Costs of inspection, authorizing party charged for   Ev §1158
  Criminal liability for wrongful disclosure   CC §§56.36, 1798.57
  Damages for wrongful disclosure   CC §§56.35, 56.36, 1798.57
  Disclosure
    Criminal liability for wrongful disclosure   CC §1798.57
    Damages for wrongful disclosure   CC §§56.35, 56.36, 1798.57
    Defenses to actions for wrongful disclosure   CC §56.36
    Employer release   CC §56.21
    Employers, disclosure by   CC §§56.20 to 56.25, 56.27
    Exceptions to confidentiality requirements   CC §§56.27 to 56.31
    Fines and penalties for wrongful disclosure   CC §56.36
    Genetic characteristics, test results for   CC §56.17
    Health care providers and contractors, disclosure by   CC §§56.10 to 56.16, 56.35 to 56.37, 56.101, 56.104
    Health care service plans, disclosure by   CC §§56.10 to 56.17, 56.35 to 56.37, 56.101, 56.104
    HIV status of workers, limited confidentiality of   CC §56.31
    Information Practices Act (See **INFORMATION PRACTICES ACT**)
    Insurance underwriters   CC §56.265
    Liability for wrongful disclosure   CC §§56.35 to 56.37
    Marketing
      Defined   CC §56.05
      Disclosure of information for use in marketing   CC §56.10
    Medical information corporation, disclosure by   CC §56.06
    Misdemeanor, violations as   CC §56.36
    Pharmaceutical company requiring disclosure as condition of receiving pharmaceuticals   CC §56.102
    Physician-patient privilege, effect of disclosure on   Ev §1156
    Psychotherapy, authorized disclosure concerning   CC §56.104, Ev §1158
    Third party administrators, disclosure by   CC §56.26
  Discovery procedure (See **DISCOVERY**)
  Electronic medical records
    Attorney inspection of records
      Requirements for situations where records kept electronically   Ev §1158
    System requirements   CC §56.101
  Employers, disclosure by   CC §§56.20 to 56.25, 56.27
  Excited delirium
    Term not to be admitted in civil action   Ev §1156.5
  Fines for wrongful disclosure   CC §56.36
  Forensic pathologists
    Disclosure of medical records to coroners, medical examiners or forensic pathologists   CC §56.10
  Forms
    Authorization for release   Ev §1158
  Gender-affirming health care or mental health care
    Businesses organized to maintain medical information
      Limitation of access to information about gender affirming care, abortion, or contraception information   CC §56.101
    Restrictions on release of medical information   CC §56.109
  Genetic characteristics, disclosure of test results for   CC §56.17
  Health Care Decisions Law (See **HEALTH CARE DECISIONS LAW**)
  Health care providers and contractors, disclosure by   CC §§56.10 to 56.16, 56.35 to 56.37, 56.101, 56.104

MEDICAL RECORDS—Cont.
  Health care service plans, disclosure by   CC §§56.10 to 56.17, 56.35 to 56.37, 56.101, 56.104
  HIV status of workers, limited confidentiality of   CC §56.31
  Information Practices Act (See **INFORMATION PRACTICES ACT**)
  Information Practices Act, protection under   CC §§56.29, 1798.3
  Inspection by authorized attorney   CCP §1985.7, Ev §1158
  Insurance companies' access to   CC §§56.10, 56.27
  Insurance underwriters, restrictions on   CC §56.265
  Investigative agencies having medical information   CC §§1786.2, 1786.12
  Medical examiners
    Disclosure of medical records to coroners, medical examiners or forensic pathologists   CC §56.10
  Medical information corporations, access to medical information maintained by   CC §§56.06, 56.07
  Mental health digital services
    Software or hardware providers of information-sharing products
      Health care providers for purposes of confidentiality provisions   CC §56.06
  Minors, disclosure of mental health records of
    Removal from physical custody of parent or guardian, protection of mental health records from release   CC §56.106
  Noncustodial parent's right to   Fam §3025
  Parent's right to access records of child   Fam §3025
  Penalties for wrongful disclosure   CC §56.36
  Physician-patient privilege, effect of disclosure on   Ev §1156
  Police officers   Ev §1044
  Prisoners
    Mental health records
      Release   CC §56.10
  Psychotherapy, authorized disclosure concerning   CC §56.104, Ev §1158
  Release, requirements for   CC §§56.101, 56.104, 56 to 56.37
    Employer release   CC §56.21
  Reproductive or sexual health digital services
    Software or hardware providers of information-sharing products
      Health care providers for purposes of confidentiality provisions   CC §56.06
      Limitation of access to information about gender affirming care, abortion, or contraception information   CC §56.101
  Review committees, admissibility of research findings of   Ev §§1156, 1156.1
  School-linked services coordinator
    Release of records   CC §56.10
  Third party administrators, use and disclosure by   CC §56.26
  Wrongful disclosure
    Disclosure generally (See within this heading, "**Disclosure**")

MEDICAL RESEARCH
Animal experimentation
  Traditional and nontraditional test methods, when used   CC §1834.9
Animal testing, restrictions against
  Pesticides or chemical substances
    Canine and feline toxicological experiments   CC §1834.9.3

MEDICAL SOCIETIES (See **PROFESSIONAL SOCIETIES**)

MEDICAL TREATMENT
Capacity determinations
  Conservators   Pro §§1880 to 1898, 2354, 2355
  Health care decisions for adult with conservator   Pro §§3200 to 3212
  Judicial determinations, generally   Pro §§810 to 813, 3200 to 3212
  Primary physician making capacity determinations under Health Care Decisions Law   Pro §4658
Capacity to consent to medical treatment, generally   Pro §813
Conservatorship (See **CONSERVATORS**)
Emergencies (See **EMERGENCIES**)
Guardian and ward (See **GUARDIAN AND WARD**)
Health Care Decisions Law (See **HEALTH CARE DECISIONS LAW**)
Health care power of attorney (See **POWER OF ATTORNEY**)
Health care providers (See **HEALTH CARE PROVIDERS**)
Health care service plans (See **HEALTH CARE SERVICE PLANS**)
Hospitals (See **HOSPITALS**)
Malpractice (See **MALPRACTICE**)
Medical records (See **MEDICAL RECORDS**)
Minors (See **MINORS**)
Power of attorney for health care (See **POWER OF ATTORNEY**)
Prohibited treatment involving adult patient without conservator   Pro §3211
Prosthetics (See **PROSTHETICS**)
Psychotropic medication to major neurocognitive conservatees   Pro §2356.5
Spiritual means of treatment, right to choose   Pro §3212
Sterilization (See **STERILIZATION**)

MEDICINES (See **PHARMACISTS AND PHARMACIES**)

MEET-AND-CONFER REQUIREMENT
Civil rules
    Case management   CRC 3.724
        Complex cases   CRC 3.750
        Telephone appearance at case management conferences   CRC 3.670
    Forms
        Judicial council legal forms   CRCAppx A
Common interest developments
    Dispute resolution for disputes between association and member
        Meet and confer procedure   CC §5915
Demurrer
    Forms
        Judicial council legal forms   CRCAppx A
    Prerequisite to filing demurrer   CCP §430.41
Family rules
    Request for orders   CRC 5.98

MEETINGS
Common interest developments (See **COMMON INTEREST DEVELOPMENTS**)
Demonstrations (See **DEMONSTRATIONS, PARADES AND MEETINGS**)
Libel and slander action, public meetings privileged from   CC §47
Mobilehome tenants (See **MOBILEHOMES**)
Public entities
    Participation by public
        Decisions and pending opportunities for public participation link on homepage   Gov §§11364, 11365
Quorum (See **QUORUM**)

MEMBERS
Associations and clubs (See **ASSOCIATIONS**)
Camping contracts, regulation of membership   CC §§1812.300 to 1812.309
Discount buying services   CC §§1812.100 to 1812.129

MEMORABILIA
Autographed memorabilia   CC §1739.7

MEMORANDUM
Costs (See **COSTS**)
Enforcement of judgments (See **ENFORCEMENT OF JUDGMENTS**)
Garnishment memorandum (See **GARNISHMENT**)
Points and authorities (See **POINTS AND AUTHORITIES**)

MENACE (See also **DURESS**)
Contracts, consent for   CC §§1567, 1570
Debt collection by use of   CC §1788.10
Forcible detainer   CCP §1160
Rescission of contract because of   CC §1689
Wills, general discussion of effect on   Pro §6104

MENTAL DISABILITY (See also **MENTAL HOSPITALS**)
Administrators (See **EXECUTORS AND ADMINISTRATORS**)
Adoption (See **ADOPTION**)
Advance health care directives
    Psychiatric advance directives   Pro §4679
Adverse possession, disabilities tolling statutes of limitation on actions for   CCP §328
Annulment, grounds for   Fam §2210
Appearance of person lacking legal capacity by conservator or guardian ad litem   CCP §372
Appellate court opinions
    Privacy, use of names in opinions   CRC 8.90
Attorney-client privilege   Ev §959
Attorneys' fees
    Services to minors and incompetent persons   CRC 7.955
Burden of proof   Ev §522
CARE act rules   CRC 7.2201 to 7.2303
    Accountability hearing   CRC 7.2301
    Definitions   CRC 7.2205
    Forms
        Judicial council forms   CRCAppx A
    Hearing notices   CRC 7.2235
    Joinder
        Local government entity   CRC 7.2240
    Local rules   CRC 7.2210
    Notices
        Appearance, initial   CRC 7.2235
        Order for report to augment petition   CRC 7.2235
        Other hearings   CRC 7.2235
        Service
            Method   CRC 7.2235

MENTAL DISABILITY—Cont.
CARE act rules —Cont.
    Order to show cause
        Accountability hearing   CRC 7.2301
        Joinder of local government entity   CRC 7.2240
    Persons who may file petition   CRC 7.2225
    Petition
        Contents   CRC 7.2221
        Copy to counsel for respondent   CRC 7.2230
        Filing   CRC 7.2221
        Persons who may file   CRC 7.2225
        Report to augment petition, order   CRC 7.2235
    Purpose of rules   CRC 7.2201
    Records
        Access   CRC 7.2210
    Referral under Penal code §1370.01   CRC 7.2225
    Respondent
        Appointment of counsel   CRC 7.2230
            Substitution   CRC 7.2230
    Transfer   CRC 7.2223
    Venue   CRC 7.2223
Child custody
    Best interest of child
        Effect of mental illness of parent, guardian, or relative on best interest determination   Fam §3040
Children and minors, treatment
    Juvenile court, inquiry into mental health of child before   CRC 5.643
        Competence evaluations   CRC 5.645
Community assistance, recovery, and empowerment act
    Rules of court   CRC 7.2201 to 7.2303 (See within this heading, "**CARE act rules**")
Community property, disposition of   Fam §1103
Competence to stand trial generally   CRC 4.130
Compromise and settlement of claims
    Attorneys' fees for services to minors and incompetent persons   CRC 7.955
    Conservatorship (See **CONSERVATORS**)
    Court approval of compromise of incompetent's claims
        Attendance at hearing by petitioner and claimant   CRC 7.952
        Deposit of funds   CRC 3.1384, 7.953, 7.954
        Disclosure of attorney's interest   CRC 7.951
        Expedited approval, petition   CRC 7.950.5
        Memorandum in support of petition not required   CRC 3.1114
        Petition   CRC 3.1384, 7.101, 7.950, 7.950.5
        Withdrawal of deposited funds   CRC 7.954
    Payments pursuant to settlement, disposition of   Pro §§3600 to 3613
        Definition of person with disability   Pro §3603
        Express consent of protected person to court orders, when required   Pro §3613
        Trusts, payment into   CRC JudAdminStand 7.10
Confidentiality of records   CC §§56.101, 56.104, 56 to 56.37
    Businesses organized to maintain medical information
        Mental health digital services offered to consumers   CC §56.06
Conservators (See **CONSERVATORS**)
Contracts, mentally impaired persons making   CC §§38 to 40, 1556, 1557, 1587
Criminal trials, case management
    Mental health case protocols   CRC 10.951
Dangerous patient, disclosing condition of   Ev §1024
Decedents' estates
    Compromise and settlement of claims
        Attorneys' fees for services to minors and incompetent persons   CRC 7.955
        Trusts, payment into   CRC JudAdminStand 7.10
    Judgments in favor of persons with disability, disposition of payments pursuant to
        Attorneys' fees for services to minors and persons with disability   CRC 7.955
        Trusts, payment into   CRC JudAdminStand 7.10
Developmentally disabled persons (See **DEVELOPMENTALLY DISABLED PERSONS**)
Dissolution of marriage (See **DISSOLUTION OF MARRIAGE**)
Distributions from decedent's estate deposited with county treasurer for benefit of incompetent person   Pro §§11850 to 11854
Diversion
    Pretrial diversion of individuals with mental disorders
        Mental competency proceedings   CRC 4.130
        Reinstatement of felony proceedings   CRC 4.130
Equal access rights to public facilities   CC §54
    Construction or application of provisions in issue, solicitor general notified   CC §55.2
Escheat (See **ESCHEAT**)
Executors (See **EXECUTORS AND ADMINISTRATORS**)

MENTAL DISABILITY—Cont.
Gender-affirming mental health care
    Legally protected health care services   CC §§1798.300 to 1798.308
    Medical information confidentiality
        Businesses organized to maintain medical information
            Limitation of access to information about gender affirming care, abortion, or contraception information   CC §56.101
            Restrictions on release of medical information   CC §56.109
Guardian ad litem (See **GUARDIAN AD LITEM**)
Guardianship (See **GUARDIAN AND WARD**)
Hearsay testimony showing mental condition   Ev §§1250 to 1252
Heirs incompetent, deposit of shares for   Pro §11850
Information Practices Act, disclosure to patients' rights protection agency under   CC §1798.24b
Judges, proceedings for removal of   JudPerR 126
Judgments in favor of persons with disabilities, disposition of payments pursuant to   Pro §§3600 to 3613
    Attorneys' fees for services to minors and person with disability   CRC 7.955
    Definition of person with disability   Pro §3603
    Express consent of protected person to court orders, when required   Pro §3613
    Trusts, payment into   CRC JudAdminStand 7.10
Judicial council, probate and mental health advisory committee   CRC 10.44
Judicial determination that person lacks legal capacity based on evidence of deficit in mental functions rather than diagnosis of mental disorder   Pro §§810 to 813
Juvenile court, inquiry into mental health of child before   CRC 5.643
    COVID-19, emergency rule   CRCAppx I Emer Rule 7
    Evaluation of competence   CRC 5.645
Legally protected health care services
    Gender-affirming mental health care   CC §§1798.300 to 1798.308
Marital privilege, waiver   Ev §§972, 982, 983
Medi-Cal
    Specialty mental health services
        Foster care, proceedings upon waiver of presumptive transfer of responsibility for services upon change of child placement   CRC 5.647
        Judicial council legal forms   CRCAppx A
Medical privilege in proceedings to determine competence   Ev §§1004, 1005, 1023 to 1025
Mentally retarded persons (See **DEVELOPMENTALLY DISABLED PERSONS**)
Minors, treatment of (See **MINORS**)
Mitigating circumstances   CRC 4.423
Opinion testimony, admissibility of   Ev §870
Outpatient care
    Appeal from order of civil commitment   CRC 8.483
Parent and child relationship affected by   Fam §§7826, 7827
Psychotherapist-patient privilege (See **PRIVILEGED COMMUNICATIONS**)
Psychotherapists (See **PSYCHOTHERAPISTS**)
Public facilities, right to equal access to   CC §54
    Construction or application of provisions in issue, solicitor general notified   CC §55.2
Retarded persons (See **DEVELOPMENTALLY DISABLED PERSONS**)
Rules of court
    Community assistance, recovery, and empowerment act rules   CRC 7.2201 to 7.2303 (See within this heading, **"CARE act rules"**)
Sentences
    Mitigating factors   CRC 4.423
Sex and other offenses against mentally incompetent persons
    Rape
        Statute of limitations   CCP §340.16
    Sodomy
        Statute of limitations   CCP §340.16
Sex offender (See **SEX OFFENSES**)
Sheriff's fee for transporting insane person to state hospital   Gov §26749
Small claims cases (See **SMALL CLAIMS COURTS**)
Sodomy against mentally ill person
    Statute of limitations
        Civil damages   CCP §340.16
Special needs trusts (See **SPECIAL NEEDS TRUSTS**)
Spousal support
    Legal incapacity of spouse to make decisions   Fam §2313
Support of adult child   Fam §3910
Termination of parental rights
    Circumstances where proceedings may be brought   Fam §§7826, 7827
Tolling statutes of limitation   CCP §352
Tort liability   CC §41
Trial of competency issue   CRC 4.130

MENTAL DISABILITY—Cont.
Trusts
    Revocation of trust
        Incompetence of person holding power to revoke trust   Pro §15800
Uniform child custody jurisdiction and enforcement act
    Gender-affirming health care or mental health care
        Enforcement, effect of care   Fam §3453.5
        Jurisdiction, effect of care   Fam §§3421, 3424, 3427, 3428
Veterans in need of services
    Orders for dismissal
        Judicial council legal forms   CRCAppx A
Wills, competency to make   Pro §§6100, 6100.5
Witness unavailable because of   Ev §240

MENTAL EXAMINATIONS (See also **PHYSICAL EXAMINATIONS**)
Administrative adjudication, language assistance provided in (See **ADMINISTRATIVE ADJUDICATION**)
Discovery procedure   CCP §§2032.010 to 2032.650
    Applicability of provisions   CCP §2032.010
    Attorney presence   CCP §2032.530
    Conduct of examination   CCP §§2032.510 to 2032.530
    Failure to produce another for examination
        Sanctions   CCP §2032.420
    Failure to submit
        Sanctions   CCP §2032.410
    Limitations on papers filed   CRC 3.250
    Methods of discovery   CCP §2019.010
    Motions for examinations   CCP §§2032.310, 2032.320
        Grounds for granting   CCP §2032.320
        Leave of court   CCP §2032.310
    Psychologists performing   CCP §2032.020
    Recording examination   CCP §2032.530
    Reports of examination   CCP §§2032.610 to 2032.650
        Attorney work product waived for demand for report   CCP §§2032.610, 2032.630
        Demanding report   CCP §2032.610
        Existing and later reports of same condition, demand recipient's right to   CCP §§2032.640, 2032.650
        Failure to timely deliver   CCP §2032.620
        Motion to compel   CCP §§2032.620, 2032.650
    Right to discovery   CCP §2032.020
    Sexual abuse of minor
        Duration of examination of minor aged 14 years or less   CCP §2032.340
        Qualifications of examiner for examinee aged 14 or less   CCP §2032.020
Economic litigation provisions for limited civil cases, permissible forms of discovery under   CCP §94
Judges, proceedings for removal of   JudPerR 105
Sterilization proceedings   Pro §1955

MENTAL FUNCTIONS
Judicial determination regarding capacity to perform specific acts   Pro §§810 to 813

MENTAL HEALTH
Juries and jurors
    Information provided to jurors   CCP §242

MENTAL HEALTH DEPARTMENT
Special needs trust for minor or person with disability, notice of
    Definition of person with disability   Pro §3603
    Express consent of protected person to court orders, when required   Pro §3613

MENTAL HEALTH DIGITAL SERVICES
Confidentiality of records
    Businesses organized to maintain medical information   CC §56.06
        Data breach reporting   CC §56.251
Defined   CC §56.05

MENTAL HEALTH PRACTITIONERS (See **PSYCHOTHERAPISTS**)

MENTAL HOSPITALS (See also **MENTAL DISABILITY**)
Admissibility of hospital records   Ev §§1156.1, 1157.6
Child support
    Suspension of orders or judgments for incarcerated or involuntarily institutionalized   Fam §4007.5
Claims against public entities and employees (See **CLAIMS AGAINST PUBLIC ENTITIES AND EMPLOYEES**)
Conservatee, mental health facility placement of   Pro §2356

MENTAL HOSPITALS—Cont.
Convulsive therapy, consent required for treatment of minor using   Fam §6924
Escheat of patient's assets   CCP §1447
Judicial commitments
    Remote proceedings
        Conditions for proceeding through use of remote technology   CCP §367.76
Psychiatric residential treatment facilities
    Children and minors
        Voluntary admission   CRC 5.619
Psychosurgery, consent required for treatment of minor using   Fam §6924
Restoration to capacity (See **MENTAL DISABILITY**)
Review committees, admissibility of research findings of   Ev §1156.1
Sexual battery against medically incapacitated patients
    Statute of limitations on sexual assault damages   CCP §340.16
Sheriff's fees for transporting patients to   Gov §26749
Statutes of limitation for recovery or conversion of personal property left at   CCP §341a
Ward, mental health facility placement of   Pro §2356

MENTAL ILLNESS (See **MENTAL DISABILITY**)

MENTALLY DISORDERED OFFENDERS
Commitment
    Appeal from order of civil commitment   CRC 8.483
Commitment to state department of state hospitals
    Appeal from order of civil commitment   CRC 8.483
Discharged prisoners
    Remote proceedings
        Conditions for proceeding through use of remote technology   CCP §367.76
Outpatient status
    Appeal from order of civil commitment   CRC 8.483
    Remote proceedings
        Conditions for proceeding through use of remote technology   CCP §367.76

MENTALLY DISORDERED SEX OFFENDERS
Commitments to nonpenal institutions
    Appeal of commitment order
        Procedure for appeal from order of civil commitment   CRC 8.483

MENTALLY RETARDED PERSONS (See **DEVELOPMENTALLY DISABLED PERSONS**)

MERCHANDISE
Clubs for sale of   CC §§1584.5, 1584.6
Unsolicited goods   CC §§1584.5, 1584.6

MERCHANTABILITY
Warranty of   CC §1791.1

MERCHANTS (See **STORES AND STOREKEEPERS**)

MERGER
Civil and criminal actions, merger of   CCP §32

MERITORIOUS CAUSE OF ACTION
Architect, engineer or surveyor, certificate of merit requirement in action based on professional negligence of   CCP §§411.35, 430.10
Sexual abuse of minor, certificate of merit requirement in action for   CCP §340.1
Summary judgment motion where action is without merit or defense   CCP §437c
Vexatious litigant defined   CCP §391

MESNE PROFITS
Statutes of limitation   CCP §336

MESOTHELIOMA
Depositions
    Time limits for witness examination
        Actions involving mesothelioma or silicosis   CCP §2025.295

MIA-POWS (See **MILITARY**)

MICROFICHE
Fees
    Courts, authority to set fees for products or services   CRC 10.815

MICROFILM
Business records for evidence   Ev §1550
Certified copies of documents recorded on   CCP §1985

MICROFILM—Cont.
Conciliation court records and documents   Fam §1819
Indexes accessible by   CRC 10.851
Judgments recorded on   CCP §668.5
Lost or destroyed writings   Ev §1551

MIDWIVES
Communications to review committees, etc
    Immunity for communications in aid of evaluation   CC §43.8
Professional standards committees
    Discovery of proceedings, limitation   Ev §1157
    Immunity from liability   CC §43.7

MILEAGE
Depositions (See **DEPOSITIONS**)
Subpoena duces tecum, mileage costs for   Ev §1563

MILITARY
Absentees
    Fiduciaries substituted during wartime (See **FIDUCIARIES' WARTIME SUBSTITUTION LAW**)
    Missing persons generally (See within this heading, "**Missing persons**")
Acknowledgment of instruments   CC §1183.5
Adoption proceedings, absence of adoptive parent serving in military   Fam §8613
Annulment of marriage or legal separation, waiver of respondent's filing fees in action for   Gov §70673
Attack shelters, governmental liability   CC §1714.5
Attorney practice
    Registered military spouse attorney   CRC 9.41.1
Attorney representation by military counsel   CRC 9.41
Child support
    Arrears collection
        Compromise of arrears program   Fam §17560
    Modification of support
        Active duty   Fam §§3651, 3653
        Government support enforcement services   Fam §17440
        Notice of activation and deployment   CRCAppx A (CRCFL-398)
Consumer warranty protection
    Motor vehicle purchased in US   CC §1791.8
Custody of children
    Absence or relocation of parent from family residence as consideration for court in awarding custody or visitation
        Active service in military   Fam §3047
Discharge from service records, waiver of recording fees for   Gov §27381
Dissolution of marriage or legal separation, waiver of respondent's filing fees in action for   Gov §70673
Dogs used in police work, injuries inflicted by   CC §§3342, 3342.5
Escheated property, military awards and decorations
    Separate notice for savings bonds, war bonds and military awards   CCP §1531.6
Family support
    Modification of support
        Active duty   Fam §§3651, 3653
Fiduciaries substituted during wartime (See **FIDUCIARIES' WARTIME SUBSTITUTION LAW**)
Financial obligations during service, relief
    Petitions for relief   CRC 3.1372
Forms   CRCAppx A
Infants (See **PARENT AND CHILD**)
Investigative agencies, military identification card as identification   CC §1786.22
Judge advocate, appearance in state court   CRC 9.41
Judges   CRCSupp JudEthicsCanon 2
Landlord and tenant
    Deposits, limitations for military service members   CC §1950.5
Marriage
    Overseas personnel
        Attorney-in-fact, appearance on behalf of personnel stationed overseas to solemnize marriage   Fam §420
Minor's enlistment in armed forces   Fam §6950
Missing persons
    Generally   Pro §3700
    Agency, revocation of   CC §2357
    Fiduciaries substituted during wartime (See **FIDUCIARIES' WARTIME SUBSTITUTION LAW**)
    Judicial proceedings to set aside personal property of   Pro §§3701 to 3708
    Management of personal property without court proceeding   Pro §§3710 to 3712
    Power of attorney   Pro §§3720 to 3722
Paternity suit, waiver of filing fees for defendant in   Gov §70673

MILITARY—Cont.
  POWs
    Missing persons generally (See within this heading, **"Missing persons"**)
  Small claims actions, appearance in   CCP §116.540
  Spousal support
    Modification of support
      Active duty   Fam §§3651, 3653
      Notice of activation and deployment   CRCAppx A (CRCFL-398)
  Spouse
    Attorney practice
      Registered military spouse attorney   CRC 9.41.1
  Statutory violations in caring out orders of military commander   CC §1714.6
  Unclaimed property
    Notice
      Separate notice for savings bonds, war bonds or military awards   CCP §1531.6
  Veterans Administration (See **VETERANS ADMINISTRATION**)
  Warranties
    Consumer warranty protection
      Motor vehicle purchased in US   CC §1791.8

MILK (See **DAIRIES AND DAIRY PRODUCTS**)

MINERALS AND MINERAL RIGHTS
Abandonment of mineral rights
  Generally   CC §883.130
  Lessee's responsibility after   CC §883.140
Applicability of chapter   CC §§883.120, 883.270
Attachment (See **ATTACHMENT**)
Attorneys' fees in actions involving preservation of   CC §883.250
Definitions   CC §883.110
Dormant mineral rights
  Termination generally (See within this heading, **"Termination of mineral rights"**)
Easement rights   CC §§801, 802
Enforcement of judgments (See **ENFORCEMENT OF JUDGMENTS**)
Expenses of litigation, late notice of intent to preserve mineral rights upon payment of   CC §883.250
Fiduciary income and principal act
  Receipts, allocation
    Minerals, water or other natural resources, interests in   Pro §16350
Gas (See **OIL AND GAS**)
Municipal land leased for production of mineral   CC §§718, 718f
Notices
  Entry on land by mineral rights owner, notice of   CC §848
  Preservation of mineral rights   CC §§883.230, 883.240
Oil (See **OIL AND GAS**)
Preservation of mineral rights
  General notice of intent to preserve mineral rights   CC §883.230
  Late notice of intent to preserve mineral rights upon payment of litigation expenses   CC §883.250
Principal and income allocations of investments in   CC §731.11
Termination of mineral rights
  Generally   CC §§883.210, 883.240
  Abandonment   CC §883.130
    Lessee's responsibility after   CC §883.140
  Conditions for dormant mineral right   CC §883.220
  Unenforceability of terminated mineral right   CC §883.260
Trust assets (See **TRUSTS**)

MINES AND MINING
Administration of estate (See **ADMINISTRATION OF ESTATES**)
Bill of sale for mining machinery   CC §1631
Continuance of trial concerning claims on   CCP §595.3
Co-owners failing to pay taxes   CCP §§853 to 859
Customs, usages or regulations, admission of evidence of established   CCP §748
Entry on land
  Right of entry on mining lease, action to terminate   CCP §§772.010 to 772.060
  To conduct survey   CCP §§742, 743
Hearings for co-owners failing to pay taxes   CCP §857
Judgments on co-owners failing to pay taxes   CCP §858
Liens by miners   CC §3060
Machinery, sales of   CC §1631
Minerals and mineral rights (See **MINERALS AND MINERAL RIGHTS**)
Notice of mining operations
  Disclosures incident to residential property transfers   CC §1103.4
Notice to co-owners failing to pay taxes   CCP §857
Petition to co-owners failing to pay taxes   CCP §§855, 858
Quarries (See **QUARRIES**)
Quieting title action   CCP §§742, 743

MINES AND MINING—Cont.
Real estate sales
  Mining operations, disclosures incident to residential property transfers   CC §1103.4
Taxes
  Co-owners failing to pay   CCP §§853 to 859
    Hearings   CCP §857
    Judgment   CCP §858
    Notice of failure to pay   CCP §853
    Petition   CCP §855
    Recordation of certified copy of decree   CCP §859
    Service of notice   CCP §854
    Venue when mine located in multiple counties   CCP §856
Mining claim
  Co-owners, actions against   CCP §§853 to 859
Tenant's use of mines   CC §819

MINING (See **MINES AND MINING**)

MINISTERS (See **CLERGYPERSONS**)

MINORITIES
Political structure equal protection   CC §53.7

MINORS (See also **PARENT AND CHILD**)
Abortion, consent required for   Fam §6925
Abuse of children (See **CHILD ABUSE**)
Action for injury to child, parents maintaining   CCP §376
Actions for damages
  Immigration status irrelevant   CC §3339.5
Administrator, disqualification for serving as   Pro §8402
Adoption (See **ADOPTION**)
Adult defined   Fam §6501
Adverse possession, disabilities tolling statutes of limitation on actions for   CCP §328
Aerosol paint containers sold to
  Verification of age for sale of age-restricted products   CC §1798.99.1
Age-appropriate design code   CC §§1798.99.28 to 1798.99.40
Age of majority, effect on parental authority on reaching   Fam §7505
Age of minority   Fam §§6500, 6502
Aggravation, inducing minor to commit or assist in commission of crime as circumstance in   CRC 4.421
Alcohol abuse counseling   Fam §6929
Appearance of minor by guardian or guardian ad litem   CCP §372
Appellate court opinions
  Privacy, use of names in opinions   CRC 8.90
Appellate rules, supreme court and courts of appeal
  Compromise of case   CRC 8.244
  Supersedeas writ   CRC 8.112
Armed forces, enlistment in   Fam §6950
Attorney's fees
  Contract made by or on behalf of minor for   Fam §6602
Bank accounts of (See **BANKS AND BANKING**)
Birth-related injuries, statutes of limitation for   CCP §340.4
Body branding, safe body art act
  Verification of age for sale of age-restricted products   CC §1798.99.1
Calculation of period of minority   Fam §§6500, 6502
California hope, opportunity, perseverance, and empowerment (HOPE) for children trust account act
  Enforcement of judgments and orders
    Exemption claims   CCP §704.235
Change of names   CCP §1276
Childhood sexual abuse (See **SEX OFFENSES**)
Children born out of wedlock (See **PARENT AND CHILD; PATERNITY**)
Child support (See **CHILD SUPPORT**)
Cigarettes or tobacco
  Sale to persons under age 21
    Verification of age for sale of age-restricted products   CC §1798.99.1
Civil actions by   Fam §6601
Civil liability   Fam §6600
Claims against public entities (See **CLAIMS AGAINST PUBLIC ENTITIES AND EMPLOYEES**)
Commercial exploitation of child
  Sexual exploitation hosted on social media platform   CC §3345.1
Communicable disease, treatment of   Fam §6926
Compromise and settlement   Pro §3500
  Attorneys' fees for services to minors and persons with disability   CRC 7.955
  Court approval of compromise of minor's claims
    Appellate court opinions, privacy protection as to use of names in opinions   CRC 8.90

MINORS

MINORS—Cont.
Compromise and settlement —Cont.
   Court approval of compromise of minor's claims—Cont.
      Attendance at hearing by petitioner and claimant   CRC 7.952
      Deposit of funds   CRC 3.1384, 7.953, 7.954
      Disclosure of attorney's interest   CRC 7.951
      Expedited approval, petition   CRC 7.950.5
      Forms, use of judicial council forms   CRC 7.101
      Memorandum in support of petition not required   CRC 3.1114
      Notice of settlement   CRC 3.1385
      Petition   CRC 3.1384, 7.101, 7.950, 7.950.5
      Withdrawal of deposited funds   CRC 7.954
   Disposition of funds awarded
      Express consent of protected person to court orders, when required   Pro §3613
      Procedure where no guardian or conservator   Pro §§3610 to 3612
   Disposition of funds or property   Pro §§3601, 3602
      Trusts, payments into   CRC JudAdminStand 7.10
   Electronic court records
      Courthouse electronic access   CRC 2.503
   Governing law   Pro §3600
   Jurisdiction over   Pro §§3500, 3612
   Order of approval   Pro §3601
      Express consent of protected person to court orders, when required   Pro §3613
   Parent's right to compromise child's claim
      Hearings on petition for compromise   Pro §3505
   Settlement agreements   Fam §1501
   Trusts, payment into   CRC JudAdminStand 7.10
Conciliation courts (See **CONCILIATION COURTS**)
Consent to medical treatment (See within this heading, **"Medical treatment"**)
Conservatorship for minor who is or has been married, establishment of   Pro §1800.3
Consumer privacy rights
   Sale or sharing of personal information
      Restrictions on sale or disclosure   CC §1798.120
Contempt
   Imprisonment or physical confinement
      Circumstances where imprisonment barred   CCP §1219
   Refusal to testify   CCP §1219.5
Contracts of minors (See **CONTRACTS AND AGREEMENTS**)
Courthouse waiting room for children, surcharge on filing fees to fund   Gov §70640
Cruelty to children (See **CHILD ABUSE**)
Custody of child proceedings (See **CUSTODY OF CHILDREN**)
Damages
   Exemplary damages, liability for   Fam §6600
   Imputed liability for willful misconduct of minor   CC §1714.1, CRCAppx B
   Injuries to minor child, actions by parents for   CCP §376
   Wrongful occupancy of land by representative of infant   CC §3335
Decedents' estates
   Powers of appointment, release of power on behalf of minor powerholder   Pro §662
Definition   Fam §6500
Dental care
   Defined   Fam §6901
   Medical treatment generally (See within this heading, **"Medical treatment"**)
Dentists, consent to treatment by   Fam §§6920 to 6930
Deposit accounts (See **BANKS AND BANKING**)
Deposit of funds with county treasurer for benefit of minor heirs   Pro §§11850 to 11854
Developmentally disabled person (See **DEVELOPMENTALLY DISABLED PERSONS**)
Discovery, mental examinations
   Sexual abuse of minor
      Duration of examination of minor aged 14 years or less   CCP §2032.340
Distribution of estate, deposit of minor's share from   Pro §§11850 to 11854
Domestic partnership
   Age requirement   Fam §297
      Younger than minimum age, order of court granting permission   Fam §297.1
   Children of domestic partner
      Equal rights and obligations as to   Fam §297.5
   Family rule governing minor's request to establish domestic partnership   CRC 5.448
Domestic violence
   Minor's appearance in proceedings to restrain or enjoin   CCP §§372, 374, 374.5
      Appearance of minor under 12 to request or oppose temporary order   Fam §6229

MINORS—Cont.
Domestic violence—Cont.
   Protective orders
      Confidentiality of minor's information in protective order proceedings, release   CRC 5.382
      Confidentiality of minor's information in protective order proceedings, request to make confidential   CRC 5.382, Fam 6301.5
      Minor's information, confidentiality   CRCAppx A
Drug abuse counseling   Fam §6929
Earnings (See **PARENT AND CHILD**)
Education (See **EDUCATION**)
Electronic cigarettes
   Verification of age for sale of age-restricted products   CC §1798.99.1
Emancipation (See **EMANCIPATION OF MINORS**)
Employment
   Generally   Fam §6700
   Arts, entertainment, and professional sports, contracts for employment in   Fam §§6750 to 6753
   Employment agencies, job placement for minors by   CC §1812.509
   Job listing services, job placement for minors by   CC §1812.521
   Pre-employment physical, disclosure of information from   CC §§56.10, 212
Employment agencies, job placement for minors by   CC §1812.509
Ephedra and related substances
   Sales to minors
      Verification of age for sale of age-restricted products   CC §1798.99.1
Escheat, statutes of limitation on   CCP §§1415, 1430, 1441
Establishment of parent-child relationship (See **PARENT AND CHILD**)
Estate of minor, control of (See **PARENT AND CHILD**)
Etching cream
   Sale to minors
      Verification of age for sale of age-restricted products   CC §1798.99.1
Evidence concerning (See **HEARSAY**)
Executor, disqualification for serving as   Pro §8402
Family allowance (See **FAMILY ALLOWANCE**)
Fireworks, dangerous
   Sale or delivery to minors
      Verification of age for sale of age-restricted products   CC §1798.99.1
Foster care (See **FOSTER CARE HOMES**)
Freedom from parental custody
   Emancipation (See **EMANCIPATION OF MINORS**)
   Termination of parental rights (See **TERMINATION OF PARENTAL RIGHTS**)
Gender neutral retail departments
   Gender neutral section or area for display of childcare items and toys, retailer duties   CC §55.8
Gifts (See **UNIFORM TRANSFERS TO MINORS ACT**)
Guardians
   Generally (See **GUARDIAN AND WARD**)
   Guardian ad litem (See **GUARDIAN AD LITEM**)
Harassment or violence
   Minor's appearance in proceedings to enjoin or restrain   CCP §§372, 374, 374.5
      Appearance of minor under 12 to request or oppose temporary order   Fam §6229
   Protection orders
      Confidentiality of minor's information   CCP §527.6, CRC 3.1161, CRCAppx A
      COVID-19, emergency rule   CRCAppx I Emer Rule 8
      Release of minor's confidential information   CRC 3.1161
Health care (See within this heading, **"Medical treatment"**)
Hearsay evidence involving (See **HEARSAY**)
Homesteads (See **HOMESTEADS**)
Hospitals (See within this heading, **"Medical treatment"**)
Hotel guests, innkeeper's rights with respect to minor   CC §1865
Illegitimate children (See **PARENT AND CHILD; PATERNITY**)
Indian children
   Custody   Fam §§170 to 185
Informed consent
   Minor's capacity to consent   Fam §§6920 to 6930
Interstate family support
   Generally   Fam §§5700.101 to 5700.903 (See **INTERSTATE FAMILY SUPPORT**)
   Minor parents, instituting proceedings   Fam §5700.302
Intimate partner violence
   Victim 12 or older
      Consent to medical care   Fam §6930
Job listing services, job placement for minors by   CC §1812.521
Judgments in favor of minor or disabled person   Pro §§3600 to 3613
   Attorneys' fees for services to minors and person with disability   CRC 7.955

MINORS—Cont.
  Judgments in favor of minor or disabled person —Cont.
    Disposition of proceeds, court approval
      Expedited approval, petition   CRC 7.950.5
        Petition   CRC 7.950, 7.950.5
      Express consent of protected person to court orders, when required   Pro §3613
      Person with disability defined   Pro §3603
      Trusts, payment into   CRC JudAdminStand 7.10
  Jury service, exceptions to eligibility for   CCP §203
  Juvenile courts (See **JUVENILE COURTS**)
  Juvenile delinquents (See **JUVENILE DELINQUENCY**)
  Limitation of actions (See within this heading, **"Statutes of limitation"**)
  Marital agreements by   Fam §1501
  Marriage (See **MARRIAGE**)
  Medical information disclosures
    Coordination of health care services and treatment   CC §56.103
  Medical records confidentiality
    Mental health records   CC §56.103
      Removal from physical custody of parent or guardian, protection of mental health records from release   CC §56.106
  Medical treatment
    Alcohol treatment   Fam §6929
    Caregiver's authorization and affidavit for   Fam §§6550, 6552
    Communicable disease, treatment of   Fam §6926
    Consent
      Court authorization   Fam §6911
      Minor's consent   Fam §§6920 to 6929
      Parent or guardian or relative/caregiver, consent by   Fam §6910
    Definitions   Fam §§6900 to 6903
    Drug treatment   Fam §6929
    Emancipated minors   Fam §7050
    Mental health treatment, minor's consent to   Fam §6924
    Pre-employment physical, disclosure of information from   CC §56.10
    Pregnancy, care related to   Fam §6925
    Rape, treatment for   Fam §6927
    Release of information, authorization for   CC §56.10
    Sexually assaulted minors   Fam §6928
    Statutes of limitation on actions against health care providers   CCP §340.5
    Vision care, definition   Fam §6904
  Mental examinations, discovery procedures
    Sexual abuse of minor
      Duration of examination of minor aged 14 years or less   CCP §2032.340
  Mental health
    Consent to counseling   Fam §6924
  Military (See **PARENT AND CHILD**)
  Multiple-party accounts, payments to minors from   Pro §5407
  Negligence liability of parent (See **PARENT AND CHILD**)
  Oath requirements for children under 10 years old   Ev §710
  Paraphernalia
    Drug use, sale of paraphernalia for
      Verification of age for sale of age-restricted products   CC §1798.99.1
    Tobacco and tobacco products, sale of paraphernalia
      Verification of age for sale of age-restricted products   CC §1798.99.1
  Parent-child relationship (See **PARENT AND CHILD**)
  Parties to actions   CCP §372
  Partition (See **PARTITION**)
  Paternity (See **PATERNITY**)
  Powers of appointment, release of power on behalf of minor powerholder   Pro §662
  Pre-employment physical, disclosure of information from   CC §56.10
  Preference in action for wrongful death or personal injury   CCP §36
  Premarital agreements by   Fam §1501
  Prisoners (See **PRISONERS**)
  Probate proceedings
    Notice to minor   CRC 7.51
  Psychotropic medication, consent to administration of
    Forms, judicial council   CRCAppx A
  Residence of child, parent to determine   Fam §7501
  Residential shelter services, minor's consent to   Fam §6924
  Runaway houses   Fam §6924
  Salaries (See **PARENT AND CHILD**)
  Sale of age-restricted products
    Verification of age for sale of age-restricted products   CC §1798.99.1
  Sales by minors (See **SALES**)
  Security freezes, credit reports
    Protected consumer security freezes   CC §§1785.11.9 to 1785.11.11
  Seduction of minor, statutes of limitation on actions for   CCP §340

MINORS—Cont.
  Sentencing
    Mitigating circumstances
      Juvenile when committing offense   CRC 4.423
  Service of process on   CCP §416.60
  Sex offenses (See **SEX OFFENSES**)
  Sexual abuse hosted on social media platform   CC §§3273.65 to 3273.69
  Sexually transmitted disease, consent to treatment of   Fam §6926
  Small claims court (See **SMALL CLAIMS COURTS**)
  Small estates of minors (See **PARENT AND CHILD**)
  Special occupancy parks
    Conditions for minors staying   CC §1866
  Spray paint containers sold to
    Verification of age for sale of age-restricted products   CC §1798.99.1
  Statutes of limitation
    Birth-related injuries   CCP §340.4
    Health care providers, actions against   CCP §340.5
    Heir's action to set aside sale of estate assets   Pro §10382
    Minority tolling statute   CCP §352
    Recovery of real property, tolling statute in actions for   CCP §328
    Seduction of minor, actions for   CCP §340
    Sexual abuse
      Childhood sexual abuse   CCP §340.35
    Sexual assault, actions for recovery of damages for   CCP §§340.1, 340.11
  Sterilization of   Fam §6925
  Subpoena served on   CCP §1987
  Superior courts (See **SUPERIOR COURTS**)
  Tanning facilities
    Verification of age for sale of age-restricted products   CC §1798.99.1
  Termination of parental rights (See **TERMINATION OF PARENTAL RIGHTS**)
  Tort liability of parent (See **PARENT AND CHILD**)
  Transfers to minors (See **UNIFORM TRANSFERS TO MINORS ACT**)
  Transition age youth
    Intergenerational housing developments   CC §51.3.5
  Trusts (See **TRUSTS**)
  Unborn child deemed existing person   CC §43.1
  Undue influence
    Wrongful taking, concealment, etc of property of conservatee, minor, elder, dependent adult, etc   Pro §859
  Uniform Parentage Act, minor children as parties to actions brought under   Fam §7635
  Uniform Transfers to Minors Act (See **UNIFORM TRANSFERS TO MINORS ACT**)
  Violent video games
    Definition of minor   CC §1746
    Sale or rental to minor   CC §1746.1
  Vision care, consent to treatment   Fam §6922
  Wages (See **PARENT AND CHILD**)
  Welfare (See **WELFARE**)
  Wills
    Disclaimer of estate interest on behalf of minor   Pro §277
    Emancipated minors   Fam §7050
    Testator, capacity of minor as   Pro §6100
    Uniform Transfers to Minors Act, devise under (See **UNIFORM TRANSFERS TO MINORS ACT**)
  Wrongful death (See **WRONGFUL DEATH**)
  Wrongful taking, concealment, etc of property of conservatee, minor, elder, dependent adult, etc   Pro §859

MINUTE ORDERS
Date of entry for purposes of appeal   CRC 8.104
Juvenile court, sealing
  Prosecuting attorney request to access sealed juvenile case files   CRC 5.860
    Order on prosecutor request for access   CRCAppx A

MINUTES
Decedents' estates, entry of orders affecting   Pro §1048
Verdict entered in   CCP §628

MIRANDA RULE
Generally (See **SELF-INCRIMINATION**)

MISAPPROPRIATION
Division of property upon dissolution of marriage   Fam §2602

MISDEMEANORS
Appellate rules, superior court appeals
  Misdemeanor appeals   CRC 8.850 to 8.874 (See **APPELLATE RULES, SUPERIOR COURT APPEALS**)

MISDEMEANORS—Cont.
Firearms and other weapons
    Relinquishment of firearms
        Forms for firearm relinquishment   CRCAppx A
Juvenile wardship proceedings
    Declaration of offense as misdemeanor after hearing   CRC 5.795
    Misdemeanor or felony, finding of offense as   CRC 5.790
Minors
    Sealing of records
        Order on prosecutor request for access   CRCAppx A
        Prosecuting attorney request to access sealed juvenile case files   CRC 5.860
    Warrantless arrest, time for release or detention hearing
        COVID-19, emergency rule   CRCAppx I Emer Rule 7
Sealing of record of minors
    Prosecuting attorney request to access sealed juvenile case files   CRC 5.860
        Order on prosecutor request for access   CRCAppx A

MISFEASANCE
Notary public, statutes of limitation upon bond of   CCP §338

MISREPRESENTATION (See **FRAUD**)

MISSING IN ACTION (See **MILITARY**)

MISSING PERSONS (See also **UNKNOWN PERSONS**)
Administration of estate of missing person presumed dead
    Court-ordered search   Pro §12406
    Executor or administrator, appointment of   Pro §12407
    5-year absence, presumption of death after   Ev §667, Pro §12401
    Governing law   Pro §12402
    Hearing
        Generally   Pro §12406
        Notice of   Pro §12405
    Jurisdiction for   Pro §12403
    Missing person defined   Pro §12400
    Notices
        Hearing, notice of   Pro §12405
        Whereabouts of missing person, notice requesting   Pro §12406
    Petition
        Generally   Pro §12404
        Reappearing person, recovery of estate by   Pro §12408
    Reappearing person, estate of   Pro §12408
Artists, money owed to   CC §986
Children as missing persons   Fam §§3140, 7603
Community estate, division where one spouse cannot be located   Fam §2604
Conservators for (See **CONSERVATORS**)
Custody of children (See **CUSTODY OF CHILDREN**)
Death of missing person, presumption of
    Federal Missing Persons Act, presumption under   Ev §1282
    5-year absence, presumption of death after   Ev §667, Pro §12401
Distributee under decedent's estate, whereabouts unknown for   Pro §11603
Earnings assignment for support   Fam §5280
Executor or administrator, appointment of   Pro §12407
Federal personnel
    Generally   Pro §§3700 to 3712
    Agency, revocation of   CC §2357
    Death, presumption of   Ev §1282
    Military (See **MILITARY**)
    Power of attorney   Pro §§3720 to 3722
5-year absence, presumption of death after   Ev §667, Pro §§11603, 12401
Hearings
    Conservator, proposed appointment of   Pro §§1461.7, 1847
    Estate administration of missing person presumed dead   Pro §12406
        Notice of hearing   Pro §12405
Identity of reappearing person, dispute regarding   Pro §12408
Investigator employed by administrator of estate   Pro §12406
Jurisdiction for administration of estate   Pro §12403
Military personnel (See **MILITARY**)
Notices
    Conservators (See **CONSERVATORS**)
    Hearing on petition   Pro §12405
    Search for persons   Pro §12406
Petitions
    Administration of decedent's estate   Pro §12404
        Reappearing person, recovery of estate   Pro §12408
    Conservators (See **CONSERVATORS**)
Power of attorney for federal absentees   Pro §§3720 to 3722
POWs (See **MILITARY**)
Reappearing person, estate of   Pro §12408

MISSING PERSONS—Cont.
Records of missing persons admissible in evidence   Ev §1283
Service by publication on   CCP §1250.125

MISTAKE
Administrative adjudication decision, mistake or clerical error in   Gov §11518.5
Attorney's affidavit of fault, award of costs and fees based on   CCP §473
Child support agency's erroneous enforcement action, remediation of   Fam §§17433, 17530
Clerical errors (See **CLERICAL ERRORS**)
Contracts (See **CONTRACTS AND AGREEMENTS**)
Credit card billing errors   CC §§1747.50 to 1747.65
Default judgments, relief from   CCP §473
Electronic transaction, error in record of   CC §1633.10
Information Practices Act, correcting under (See **INFORMATION PRACTICES ACT**)
Involuntary trust resulting from
    Attorney general actions
        Statute of limitations   CC §2224.5
Judgment lien on property of misidentified owner, release of   CCP §§697.410, 697.660
Judgments, grounds for relief from   CCP §473
Liens
    Judgment lien on property of misidentified owner, release of   CCP §§697.410, 697.660
Membership camping contract, error in   CC §1812.306
Merits, affidavit of   CCP §473
Nonprejudicial error, disregard of   CCP §475
Parentage
    Voluntary declaration of parentage
        Challenge of declaration based on fraud, duress or material mistake of fact   Fam §7576
Parol evidence showing   CCP §1856
Pleadings (See **PLEADINGS**)
Return of property, effect on duty for   CC §1713
Small claims court, incorrect or erroneous legal basis as grounds for vacating judgment of   CCP §116.725
Specific performance (See **SPECIFIC PERFORMANCE**)
Statutes of limitation for relief on grounds of fraud or mistake   CCP §338
Time to apply for relief   CCP §473
Trust relationship arising for property acquired by   CC §§2223, 2224
    Attorney general actions
        Statute of limitations   CC §2224.5
Unpleaded cause, permission to assert   CCP §426.50
Verdict, correction of   CCP §§618, 619

MISTRIAL
Comments by court   CRC JudAdminStand 2.30
Judge testifying as witness as grounds for   Ev §703
Juror testifying at trial as grounds for   Ev §704
Retrial of action where jury discharged without rendering verdict   CCP §616
Short cause cases, case management   CRC 3.735
Verdict, failure of jury to reach   CCP §616

MITIGATING EVIDENCE (See **EVIDENCE**)

MITIGATION OF DAMAGES
Libel and slander, pleading mitigating circumstances in actions for   CCP §461

MIXING OF GOODS
Sales contracts   CC §1497

MOBILEHOME PARKS (See **MOBILEHOMES**)

MOBILEHOMES   CC §§798 to 799.11 (See also **RECREATIONAL VEHICLES**)
Abandoned mobilehomes, sale of   CC §798.61
Advertising restrictions on sale or rent of   CC §§798.70, 799.1.5
Age requirements
    Condominiums, cooperatives, subdivisions, and resident-owned parks
        Adults-only rule   CC §799.5
        Family member requiring live-in care supervision, exceptions to age requirements   CC §799.9
    Mobilehome parks
        Generally   CC §798.76
        Family member requiring live-in care or supervision, exception for   CC §798.34
        Owners and employees of park, applicability of age requirements to   CC §798.23
Alteration of new vehicles into housecars, effect on warranties upon   CC §1793.05

MOBILEHOMES—Cont.
  Amendment to rules   CC §798.25
  Animals as pets, fees for   CC §798.33
  Application for residency, request for
    Information provided to prospective homeowners   CC §798.74.5
  Approval of mobilehome purchaser by park owner   CC §798.74
    Condominiums, cooperatives or subdivisions   CC §799.4
  Asian language contracts, translations   CC §1632
  Attachment (See **ATTACHMENT**)
  Attorneys' fees in actions concerning   CC §§798.39.5, 798.85
  Buyer
    Right to prior approval of purchaser by mobilehome park owner
      Condominiums, cooperatives or subdivisions   CC §799.4
      Mobilehome parks   CC §798.74
  California Alternate Rates for Energy (CARE) program, assistance to low-income persons under   CC §798.431
  Change of use of park
    Defined   CC §798.10
    Notice of   CC §798.56
  Common areas, access to   CC §798.24
    Meetings of homeowners
      Cleaning deposits   CC §798.51
  Companions
    Additional resident in mobilehome, rights and restrictions   CC §798.34
  Condominiums, cooperatives, subdivisions, and resident-owned parks   CC §§799 to 799.11
    Age restrictions
      Adults-only rule   CC §799.5
      Family member requiring live-in care or supervision, exception for   CC §799.9
    Applicability of article   CC §799.1
    Caregiver or family member requiring care, senior homeowner's right to share home with   CC §799.9
    Definitions   CC §799
    "For sale or rent" signs, restrictions on   CC §799.1.5
    Interruption of utility services, advance notice of   CC §799.7
    Listing for sale or showing mobilehome to buyers, owner's written authorization required for   CC §799.2
    Removal of mobilehome upon sale to third party   CC §799.3
    Right of entry by ownership or management   CC §799.2.5
    Right to prior approval of buyer by management upon notice of sale   CC §799.4
    Waiver of statutory rights by purchaser, prohibition against   CC §799.6
  Consent to entry   CC §798.26
    Condominiums, cooperatives, subdivisions, and resident-owned parks
      Ownership or management, right to entry by   CC §799.2.5
  Constructive eviction, protection from   CC §798.55
  Contractors
    Warranty responsibilities generally (See within this heading, **"Warranties"**)
  Contracts
    Rental agreements (See within this heading, **"Rental agreements"**)
  Controlled substances use on premises, tenancy terminated for conviction of   CC §798.56
  Cooperatives   CC §§799 to 799.11 (See within this heading, **"Condominiums, cooperatives, subdivisions, and resident-owned parks"**)
  Costs in actions   CC §798.85
  Credit report on prospective buyer, fees for   CC §798.74
  Damages
    Actions concerning   CC §798.86
    Park, awards against
      Rent increases for prohibited   CC §798.39.5
  Dealers
    Warranty responsibilities generally (See within this heading, **"Warranties"**)
  Death of homeowner-resident, rights of heirs of   CC §798.78
  Deficiency judgment under conditional sales agreement   CC §2983.8
  Definitions   CC §§798.1 to 798.12, 799
  Disabled persons
    Installation of ramps, handrails and other accommodations, permission of homeowner   CC §798.29.6
    Subdivisions, cooperatives and condominiums   CC §799.11
  Disasters
    Destruction of park by wildfire or other natural disaster and subsequent rebuilding
      Offers of renewed tenancy   CC §798.62
  Disclosures
    Name, address, and telephone number of park owner   CC §798.28
    Sales (See within this heading, **"Sales"**)
    Transfer, disclosures on   CC §§1102 to 1102.18
    Utility charges for common areas, disclosure to homeowner of   CC §798.43
  Discrimination   CC §798.20

MOBILEHOMES—Cont.
  Disposal of mobilehomes
    Abandoned mobilehomes   CC §798.61
    Acquisition of mobilehome by lien   CC §798.56a
  Driveways
    Maintenance and upkeep of   CC §798.37.5
    Vehicle removal from driveway or designated parking space   CC §798.28.5
  Earthquake hazard disclosure requirements   CC §§1103 to 1103.15
  Employees of park, rules and regulations applicable to   CC §798.23
  Enclosed accessory structures
    Consent to entry   CC §798.26
  Enforcement
    Attachment (See **ATTACHMENT**)
    Fees for enforcing mobile park rules   CC §798.36
    Levy procedure   CCP §§700.080, 700.090
    Sales agreement, recording requirement of   CCP §1062.10
  Eviction   CC §§798.55 to 798.62
    Injunction to stop recurring or continuing violation of park rules   CC §798.88
    Reasons for termination   CC §798.56
    Removal of unauthorized vehicles   CC §798.28.5
    Termination of tenancy to enable purchase or rental of unit from park owner prohibited   CC §798.58
    Unlawful occupants   CC §798.75
  Failure to maintain park in good and working order, action for   CC §798.84
  Family members, rates based on number of   CC §798.35
  Fees
    Amendment to park rules or regulations, prohibition against creating new fee by   CC §798.25
    Attorneys' fees   CC §798.85
    California Alternate Rates for Energy (CARE) program, assistance to low-income persons under   CC §798.431
    Credit rating report on prospective buyer, collection of fee for   CC §798.74
    Enforcement of park rules and regulation, imposition of fees for   CC §798.36
    Family members, imposition of fees based on number of   CC §798.35
    Fines and penalties against management, prohibition of fees or rent increases reflecting cost of   CC §798.39.5
    Guests, fee exclusion for   CC §798.34
    Hookup fees   CC §798.37
    Incidental services, fees for   CC §798.31
    Landscaping fees   CC §798.37
    Leases, imposition of fees on   CC §798.31
    Liens as security for charges, imposition of   CC §798.38
    Local government assessments   CC §798.49
    Management's cost from fine, forfeiture, or penalty, passing on to tenants   CC §798.39.5
    Pet fees   CC §798.33
    Rent control ordinances   CC §798.17
    Security deposits   CC §798.39
    Senior homeowner, fee exclusion for persons providing care to or receiving care from   CC §§798.34, 799.9
    Separate billing, requirement of
      Generally   CC §798.32
      Local government assessments   CC §798.49
      Utility service fees   CC §798.41
    60-day notice required before imposition of fees not listed in rental agreement   CC §798.32
    Transfer fees   CC §798.72
  Fines and penalties
    Maximum penalty for willful violation by management   CC §798.86
    Rent increases or fees to offset fines and penalties against management, prohibition of   CC §798.39.5
  Fire hazard disclosure requirements   CC §§1103 to 1103.15
  Flood hazard disclosure requirements   CC §§1103 to 1103.15
  Foreclosure by lienholder   CC §798.79
  Gas sold to mobilehome owners and park residents by park management, limitation on price of liquefied petroleum   CC §798.44
  Guests of park residents   CC §798.34
  Heirs of homeowner, rights of   CC §798.78
  Homeowner meetings
    Generally   CC §798.51
    Injunctive relief, right to   CC §798.52
    Legislative intent   CC §798.50
    Management-homeowner meetings   CC §798.53
  Hookup fees   CC §798.37
  Improper maintenance of physical improvements as public nuisance   CC §798.87
  Improvements
    Maintenance generally (See within this heading, **"Maintenance of park"**)
  Increase in rent, notice of   CC §798.30

MOBILEHOMES—Cont.
- Injunctions
  - Management enjoined for preventing right to assemble at homeowner meetings   CC §798.88
  - Recurring or continuing violation of park rules, injunction against   CC §798.88
- Joint homeowner's rights on death of homeowner   CC §798.78
- Junior lienholders
  - Liens generally (See within this heading, **"Liens"**)
- Landscaping fees   CC §§798.37, 798.37.5
- Leases
  - Rental agreement provisions generally   CC §798.15
- Liens
  - Foreclosure by lienholder   CC §798.79
  - Inapplicability of law   CC §3067.2
  - Levy procedure   CCP §§700.080, 700.090
  - Notice to management regarding election of options of lienholder or legal owner on receipt of notice of termination   CC §798.56a
  - Rent, imposition of security for   CC §798.38
- Liquefied petroleum gas, sale to owners and residents   CC §798.44
- Listings
  - Permission of owner for   CC §§798.71, 799.2
  - Used mobilehomes, listing sale of   CC §798.81
- Live-in care, persons requiring or providing   CC §§798.34, 799.9
- Living-alone homeowner's right to share occupancy with one person   CC §798.34
- Local government assessments, rental inclusion of   CC §798.49
- Maintenance of park
  - Failure to maintain park in good and working order, action for   CC §798.84
  - Fees for   CC §§798.15, 798.36
  - Interruption of utility services, advance notice of   CC §§798.42, 799.7
  - Removal of mobilehome from park, limitation on homeowner's liability for repairs or improvements to park space or property when management requires   CC §798.73
  - Sale or transfer of mobilehome within park
    - Limitation on homeowner's liability for repairs or improvements to park space or property   CC §798.83
    - Management, repairs or improvements to mobilehome remaining in park required by   CC §798.73.5
  - Sudden or unforeseeable deterioration of improvements, repair following   CC §798.15
- Management
  - Applicability of park rules to management to same extent as residents and guests   CC §798.23
- Management-homeowner meetings   CC §798.53
- Manufacturers
  - Warranty responsibilities generally (See within this heading, **"Warranties"**)
- Medical situation of homeowner
  - Subleasing or renting residence
    - Medical situation justifying   CC §798.23.5
- Meetings
  - Homeowner meetings (See within this heading, **"Homeowner meetings"**)
  - Management-homeowner meetings   CC §798.53
- Membership camping areas distinguished from mobilehome parks   CC §1812.300
- Mobilehome assistance center
  - Signs, posting by housing and community development department   CC §798.29
- Name, address, and telephone number of park owner disclosed at homeowner request   CC §798.28
- New construction
  - Defined   CC §798.7
  - Exemption from rent control ordinances for   CC §798.45
- New mobilehome park construction
  - Defined   CC §798.7
  - Exemption from rent control ordinances   CC §798.45
- 90-day notices of rent increases   CC §798.30
- Nonprofit mutual benefit corporations
  - Parks owned and operated by   CC §799.1
- Notices
  - Abandonment, belief of   CC §798.61
  - Amendment of rules   CC §798.25
  - California Alternate Rates for Energy (CARE) program, assistance to low-income persons under   CC §798.431
  - Change of use of park   CC §798.56
  - Combining notices into single notice   CC §798.14
  - Curing default   CC §798.56
  - Delivery of   CC §798.14
  - Failure to maintain park in good and working order   CC §798.84
  - Fees   CC §§798.15, 798.32, 798.36
  - Increase in rent   CC §798.30

MOBILEHOMES—Cont.
- Notices—Cont.
  - Interruption of utility services, advance notice of   CC §§798.42, 799.7
  - Law regulating rights and responsibilities involved with mobilehomes   CC §798.15
  - 90-day notices of rent increases   CC §798.30
  - Rent control exemptions   CC §§798.17, 798.21
  - Rent not paid
    - Warning notice   CC §798.56
  - 60-day notice requirements (See within this heading, **"60-day notices"**)
  - Termination of tenancy   CC §§798.55, 798.56a, 798.59
  - 3-day notice to cure default   CC §798.56
  - Unlawful detainer proceedings   CCP §§1161a, 1166a
  - Waiver of written notice requirement for repeated rules violations   CC §798.56
  - Warranty on sale   CC §1797.5
  - Zoning changes   CC §798.27
- Nuisance, improper maintenance of physical improvements as   CC §798.87
- Number in family, rates based on   CC §798.35
- Onsite employees of management, housing
  - Applicability of park rules to management to same extent as residents and guests   CC §798.23
- Parents as family members, rates based on   CC §798.35
- Parking spaces
  - Vehicle removal from driveway or designated parking space   CC §798.28.5
- Penalties
  - Maximum penalty for willful violation by management   CC §798.86
  - Rent increases of fees to offset fines, etc, against management
    - Prohibition   CC §798.39.5
- Permit for change of use of park   CC §798.56
- Personal property of homeowner or resident
  - Removal of personal property to comply with park rules or statutory provisions   CC §798.36
- Petroleum gas sold to mobilehome owners and park residents by park management, limitation on price of liquefied   CC §798.44
- Pets   CC §798.33
- Possession, writ for   CCP §§515.010, 515.020, 1166a
- Prostitution on premises, tenancy terminated for conviction of   CC §798.56
- Public utility (See within this heading, **"Utility services"**)
- Recordation of sales agreements   CCP §1062.10
- Recreational vehicles
  - Generally (See **RECREATIONAL VEHICLE PARKS**)
  - Restrictions on rental of mobilehome park space to   CC §798.22
- Re-entry right   CC §§790, 791
- Rejection of mobilehome purchaser by park owner
  - Statement of reasons   CC §798.74
- Removal of mobilehome
  - From condominiums, cooperative or subdivisions   CC §799.3
  - From mobilehome parks   CC §798.73
  - Unauthorized vehicles   CC §798.28.5
- Renewal of tenancies
  - Destruction of park by wildfire or other natural disaster and subsequent rebuilding
    - Offers of renewed tenancy   CC §798.62
- Rental agreements
  - Copy returned to homeowner   CC §798.16
  - Defined   CC §798.8
  - Duration of   CC §798.18
  - First refusal rights granted to management upon sale of home
    - Prohibition of provisions in rental agreements   CC §798.19.5
  - Gross rental rate
    - Restrictions on rates for tenancy in qualified park   CC §798.30.5
  - Increases
    - Notice of increase   CC §798.30
    - Restrictions   CC §798.30.5
  - Liens, imposition of   CC §798.38
  - Other provisions   CC §798.16
  - Rent control ordinances   CC §798.17
  - Sale or transfer of mobilehome remaining in park, rental agreement with buyer upon   CC §§798.75, 798.75.5
  - Subleasing
    - Medical situation justifying   CC §798.23.5
  - Waiver of rights in   CC §§798.19, 798.77, 799.6
  - Written rental agreement, requirement of prospective buyer to be furnished   CC §798.15
- Rental fees
  - Fees generally (See within this heading, **"Fees"**)
- Rent control ordinances
  - Generally   CC §§798.17, 798.21
  - New construction, exemption of   CC §798.45

MOBILEHOMES—Cont.
  Renting or subleasing restrictions
    Applicability of park rules to management to same extent as residents and guests CC §798.23
  Repairs
    Maintenance generally (See within this heading, **"Maintenance of park"**)
  Replacement of mobilehome or manufactured home
    Requirement of use of specific broker, dealer, etc
      Prohibited CC §798.71
  Repossessed mobilehome, sale of CC §798.79
  Resident-owned parks CC §§799 to 799.11 (See within this heading, **"Condominiums, cooperatives, subdivisions, and resident-owned parks"**)
  Right of entry CC §798.26
    Condominiums, cooperatives, subdivisions, and resident-owned parks
      Ownership or management, right to entry by CC §799.2.5
  Roofing contracts and warranties (See **ROOFING WARRANTIES**)
  Rules and regulations of park
    Generally CC §798.23
    Amendment to rules or regulations CC §798.25
    Void and unenforceable rules CC §§798.25, 798.25.5
  Sale or lease of mobilehome
    Notice of sale of mobilehome that will remain in park CC §798.74
    Purchaser approval by management, requirements and process CC §798.74
  Sales
    Abandoned mobilehomes CC §798.61
    Advertising, restrictions on CC §§798.70, 799.1.5
    Credit report on prospective buyers, fees for CC §798.74
    Disclosures CC §§1102 to 1102.18
      Delivery of disclosure statement CC §1102.3a
      Form of disclosure statement CC §§1102.6d, 1103.2
      Natural hazard disclosure requirements CC §§1103 to 1103.15
      Rental agreement, park owner's disclosures in connection with CC §798.75.5
      Transfer disclosure requirements CC §798.74.4
    Enforcement of sales agreements CCP §1062.10
    First refusal rights of management upon sale of home
      Rental agreements, prohibited provisions CC §798.19.5
    "For sale or rent" signs, restrictions on CC §799.1.5
    Joint surviving tenant, sale by CC §798.78
    Listings
      Permission of owner CC §§798.71, 799.2
    Personal representative of decedent's estate, sale by CC §798.78
    Prohibited practices by park management CC §798.81
    Prospective homeowners
      Information provided to prospective homeowners CC §798.74.5
    Recordation of sales agreements CCP §1062.10
    Rental agreement provisions generally CC §798.15
    Rental agreement with park owner in connection with sale or transfer of mobilehome CC §§798.75, 798.75.5
    Repairs or improvements upon sale of mobilehome within park
      Limitation on homeowner's liability for CC §798.83
      Management, repairs to mobilehome remaining in park after sale or transfer required by CC §798.73.5
    Repossessed mobilehome CC §798.79
    Right to prior approval of purchaser
      Condominiums, cooperatives or subdivisions CC §799.4
      Mobilehome parks CC §798.74
    Surety bonds after default under sales contract CCP §§515.010, 515.020
    Transfer fees on CC §798.72
    Used homes sold within park CC §798.81
    Warranties (See within this heading, **"Warranties"**)
  School facilities fee, disclosure that manufactured home or mobile home subject to CC §§198.82, 199.8
  Security deposits CC §798.39
  Senior homeowners
    Age restrictions (See within this heading, **"Age requirements"**)
    Caregiver, right to share home with CC §§798.34, 799.9
    Discrimination effected by requiring membership in restrictive club
      Applicability of prohibition in housing for elderly CC §798.20
  Share occupancy with one other person, homeowner otherwise living alone as entitled to CC §798.34
  Signs
    Mobilehome assistance center
      Posting sign by housing and community development department CC §798.29
    Placement CC §§798.70, 799.1.5
    Political campaign signs CC §§798.51, 799.10
  60-day notices
    Fees not included in rental agreement, notice of CC §798.32

MOBILEHOMES—Cont.
  60-day notices—Cont.
    Lienholder or legal owner to notify park management regarding option elected against homeowner in default CC §798.56a
    Recreational facilities regulations, amendment of CC §798.25
    Termination of tenancy, notice of CC §§798.55, 798.59
  Smoke detectors
    Real estate disclosure statements CC §1102.6d
  Solar energy systems CC §§798.44.1, 799.12
  Spanish language, rental contract in CC §1632
  State employee housing, exemption for CC §798.13
  Subdivisions (See within this heading, **"Condominiums, cooperatives, subdivisions, and resident-owned parks"**)
  Subleasing
    Applicability of park rules to management to same extent as residents and guests CC §798.23
    Medical situation justifying CC §798.23.5
  Surety bonds after default under sales contract CCP §§515.010, 515.020
  Taxation
    Property taxation
      Rental agreement provisions CC §798.15
  Termination of tenancy CC §§798.55 to 798.62
    Eviction (See within this heading, **"Eviction"**)
    Homeowner's notice to management before vacating tenancy CC §798.59
  Term of lease, notice of changes in CC §798.27
  Transfer fees CC §798.72
  Tree planting and maintenance CC §798.37.5
  TROs against recurring or continuing violation of park rules CC §798.88
  Unauthorized vehicles, removal of CC §798.28.5
  Unlawful detainer proceedings CCP §§1161a, 1166a
  Unlawful occupants, eviction from mobilehome park of CC §798.75
  Used mobilehomes, sale of CC §798.81
  Utility services
    Generally CC §798.31
    California Alternate Rates for Energy (CARE) program, assistance to low-income persons under CC §798.431
    Disclosure to homeowner of utility charges for common areas CC §798.43
    Interruption of utility services, advance notice of CC §§798.42, 799.7
    Rate schedule, posting of CC §798.40
    Separate billing for CC §798.41
    Third party billing services
      Contact information for service on resident bills CC §798.40
    Water service
      Separate billing of water service to homeowners CC §798.40
  Void and unenforceable rules CC §§798.25, 798.25.5
  Waiver
    Rental agreement, waiver of rights under CC §§798.19, 798.77, 799.6
    Surety bond requirements after default on sales contract, waiver of CCP §515.020
    Written notice requirement waived for repeated rules violations CC §798.56
  Warehouse liens
    Management enforcement resulting in acquisition of mobilehome
      Disposal, notice CC §798.56a
  Warranties
    Generally CC §1797.2
    Alteration of new vehicles into housecars CC §1793.05
    Applicability of chapter CC §1797
    Definitions CC §1797.1
    Maintenance records required CC §1797.6
    Notice, display of CC §1797.5
    Period for completion of warranty service CC §1797.7
    Roofing warranties (See **ROOFING WARRANTIES**)
    Terms of CC §1797.3
    Waiver of CC §1797.4
  Water service
    Separate billing of water service to homeowners CC §798.40
  Wildfires or other natural disasters
    Destruction of park by wildfire or other natural disaster and subsequent rebuilding
      Offers of renewed tenancy CC §798.62
  Zoning changes, notice of CC §798.27

MODERATE INCOME HOUSING
Injunctions against CCP §529.2

MODIFICATION
Contracts (See **CONTRACTS AND AGREEMENTS**)
Forgery (See **FORGERY**)
Homestead, modification of probate right to Pro §6527

MODIFICATION—Cont.

Information Practices Act, agency modifying information to avoid compliance with   CC §1798.77
Injunctions   CC §3424, CCP §533
Judgments (See **MODIFICATION OF JUDGMENT**)
Power of attorney (See **POWER OF ATTORNEY**)
Temporary restraining orders   CCP §533
Trusts (See **TRUSTS**)

MODIFICATION OF JUDGMENT

Authority of Supreme Court and Courts of Appeal to affirm, reverse or modify judgment or order appealed from   CCP §43
Consent to modification of judgment   CRC 8.264
Costs on appeal   CRC 8.278
Custody of children (See **CUSTODY OF CHILDREN**)
Earnings assignment order for support   Fam §5272
Employee benefit plan joined as party in family law proceeding   Fam §2074
Entering judgment of reviewing court in records of trial court   CCP §912
Family law proceedings   Fam §215
General powers of reviewing court   CCP §906
Indigent parents, order for support of   Fam §4405
Restitution of rights on   CCP §908
Support orders
    Child support (See **CHILD SUPPORT**)
    Spousal support (See **SPOUSAL SUPPORT**)
Uniform Parentage Act, judgment in action brought under   Fam §7642

MOLD

Landlord and tenant
    Dilapidation relating to mold
        Repair obligation dependent on notice   CC §1941.7

MOLDS, FORMS AND DIES

Ownership of   CC §1140

MONEY

Attorney's authority to receive money claimed by client   CCP §283
Check cashers (See **CHECK CASHERS**)
Contract for loan of   CC §§1912 to 1916.5
Euro as currency of participating member states of European Union   CC §1663
Judgments
    Foreign money judgments (See **FOREIGN JUDGMENTS**)
    Money judgments (See **JUDGMENTS**)
Minors, protective proceedings for money or property belonging to (See **PARENT AND CHILD**)
Orders for money (See **MONEY ORDERS**)
Presumptions   Ev §631
Uniform Foreign-Money Claims Act   CCP §§676 to 676.16
Uniform Transfers to Minors Act (See **UNIFORM TRANSFERS TO MINORS ACT**)
Verdict determining amount of recovery   CCP §626

MONEYCHANGERS (See **VENDING MACHINES**)

MONEY JUDGMENTS (See **JUDGMENTS**)

MONEY ORDERS

Check cashers (See **CHECK CASHERS**)
Court clerks, payments to   CRC 10.821
Escheat of   CCP §§1511, 1513, 1542, 1581

MONTH

Defined   CCP §17

MONUMENTS (See **BOUNDARIES**)

MORAL TURPITUDE

Expedited jury trials
    Mandatory expedited jury trials, limited civil cases
        Opting out of expedited process   CCP §630.20
Judges
    Suspension for crimes involving moral turpitude   JudPerR 120.5

MORTGAGE FORECLOSURE CONSULTANTS   CC §§2945 to 2945.11

MORTGAGES (See **TRUST DEEDS AND MORTGAGES**)

MOTELS (See **HOTELS AND MOTELS**)

MOTION PICTURES

Actors (See **ACTORS AND ACTRESSES**)

MOTION PICTURES—Cont.

Age
    Commercial online entertainment employment service providers
        Age information of subscribers, restriction on disclosure   CC §1798.83.5
Animals, film depicting cruelty to   CC §§3504 to 3508.2
Child star contracts   Fam §§6750 to 6753
Employer and employee
    Commercial online entertainment employment service providers
        Age information of subscribers, restriction on disclosure   CC §1798.83.5
Human beings, film depicting cruelty to   CC §§3504 to 3508.2
Indecency and obscenity (See **INDECENCY AND OBSCENITY**)
Killings, depiction of   CC §§3504 to 3508.2
Pornography (See **INDECENCY AND OBSCENITY**)

MOTIONS

Appeals   CRC 8.54
    Electronic copies of paper documents   CRC 8.44
    Number of copies filed   CRC 8.44
    Superior court appeals   CRC 8.808
        Attorneys, withdrawal   CRC 8.814
        Judicial notice   CRC 8.809
        Parties, substitution   CRC 8.814
    Supreme court and courts of appeal, appellate rules (See **APPELLATE RULES, SUPREME COURT AND COURTS OF APPEAL**)
Attachment (See **ATTACHMENT**)
Blood tests to determine paternity, motion for   Fam §7541
Calendar preference for trial, motion for (See **PRIORITIES AND PREFERENCES**)
Clerical errors in judgments, correction of   CCP §473
Compel, motion to
    Depositions (See **DEPOSITIONS**)
    Inspection of documents (See **INSPECTION DEMANDS**)
    Interrogatories (See **INTERROGATORIES**)
    Requests for admissions (See **REQUEST FOR ADMISSION**)
Computation of time
    Holidays (See **HOLIDAYS**)
    Limitation of actions (See **STATUTES OF LIMITATION**)
Consolidation of cases   CRC 3.350
Contribution, entry of judgment for   CCP §878
Coordination of cases
    Noncomplex actions
        Transfer and consolidation of noncomplex common-issue actions filed in different courts   CRC 3.500
Costs, motion to tax (See **COSTS**)
Death penalty
    Lists of appearances, exhibits and motions   CRCAppx A
        Pretrial proceedings   CRC 4.119
        Trial, additional requirements   CRC 4.230
Default judgments, setting aside (See **DEFAULT JUDGMENTS**)
Defined   CCP §§116.130, 1003
Directed verdict   CCP §630
Discovery
    Civil rules   CRC 3.1345 to 3.1348
Dismissal of case (See **DISMISSAL**)
Failure to file memorandum in support of motion, effect   CRC 3.1113
Family law rules (See **FAMILY RULES**)
Forms
    Judicial council legal forms   CRCAppx A
Frivolous actions
    Inapplicability to discovery motions   CCP §128.5
Good faith settlement, motion for determination of   CRC 3.1382
Judgment lien on property of misidentified owner, release of   CCP §§697.410, 697.660
Judgment, motion for (See **JUDGMENTS**)
Jurisdiction for   CCP §1004
Justice courts (See **JUSTICE COURTS**)
Law and motion proceedings
    Generally   CRC 3.1100 to 3.1372 (See **LAW AND MOTION PROCEEDINGS**)
Low-income housing
    Actions challenging priority housing development projects
        Special motion to strike   CCP §425.19
Mailing notice of motions (See within this heading, "Notice of motion")
New trial (See **NEW TRIAL**)
Notice of motion
    Failure to file memorandum in support of motion, effect   CRC 3.1113
    Family law
        Responsive declaration   CRCAppx A (CRCFL-320)
    Format   CRC 3.1110

MOTIONS—Cont.
Notice of motion—Cont.
  Mail, service by
    Generally CCP §1012
    Procedure for CCP §1013
    Proof of service CCP §1013a
  Memorandum in support of motion CRC 3.1113
  Motion deemed made on service and filing of CCP §1005.5
  Service
    Generally CCP §§1005, 1010
    Appearance by defendant, effect of CCP §1014
    Attorney, service on CCP §§1011, 1015
    Method and place of CCP §1011
    Nonresidents, service on CCP §1015
    Time limitations for CCP §§1005, 1013
  Taxing costs CRC 3.1700
  Time limitations
    Mail, service by CCP §§1005, 1013
    Personal delivery CCP §1005
Notice of pendency, motion to expunge CCP §405.30
Opposing motion, service of papers CCP §1005
Order granting or denying motion
  Reconsideration, motion for CCP §1008
  Service of notice of CCP §1019.5
Preference, motion for (See **PRIORITIES AND PREFERENCES**)
Probation
  Out-of-county transfers CRC 4.530
Quash, motion to (See **QUASH, MOTION TO**)
Reconsideration of grant or denial of order, motion for CCP §1008
Reply papers, time for service of CCP §1005
Sealing and unsealing of record, motion for CRC 2.551
Service of notices
  Motions to quash service CCP §418.10
  Notice of motion (See within this heading, "**Notice of motion**")
  Order granting or denying motion, service of notice of CCP §1019.5
Stay of proceedings (See **STAY OF PROCEEDINGS**)
Strike, motion to (See **MOTION TO STRIKE**)
Summary judgment, motion for CCP §437c
  Unlawful detainer CRC 3.1351
Superior court fees
  Hearings, filing motion, application or paper filed which would require Gov §70617
Superior courts (See **SUPERIOR COURTS**)
Taxing costs, motion for (See **COSTS**)
Transfer to another judge for hearing on motion CCP §1006
Trial calendar, motion for preference in (See **CALENDAR**)
Vacate judgment (See **JUDGMENTS**)
Venue, change of CCP §396b, CRC 3.1326
  Criminal cases CRC 4.151
Vexatious litigants (See **VEXATIOUS LITIGANTS**)
Where made CCP §1004
Written notice, motions requiring CCP §§1005, 1010

MOTION TO COMPEL
Depositions (See **DEPOSITIONS**)
Inspection of documents (See **INSPECTION DEMANDS**)
Interrogatories (See **INTERROGATORIES**)
Requests for admissions (See **REQUEST FOR ADMISSION**)

MOTION TO STRIKE CCP §§435 to 437
Amendment of pleading
  Right to amend pleadings CCP §472
Appeal, order for partial striking as open on CCP §472c
Appearance by filing CCP §1014
Constitutional right to petition and free speech in discussion of public issues, motion to strike causes of action having chilling effect on CCP §§425.16, 425.17
  SLAPPback actions CCP §425.18
Default judgments CCP §§585, 586
Discretion to grant leave to amend pleadings where motion to strike granted CCP §472a
Dismissal based on CCP §581
Economic litigation provisions for limited civil cases CCP §92
Exceptions to order striking or refusing to strike out pleading CCP §647
Forcible entry and detainer CCP §1170
Grounds CCP §§436, 437
Issue of law arising upon CCP §589
Judgment roll, records constituting CCP §670
Law and motion rules of court regarding CRC 3.1322
Leave to amend pleadings where motion to strike granted CCP §472a
Local rules of superior court, failure to comply with CCP §575.2

MOTION TO STRIKE—Cont.
Low-income housing
  Actions challenging priority housing development projects
    Special motion to strike CCP §425.19
Meet and confer prior to moving to strike pleadings
  Amendment of pleadings, effect CCP §435.5
    Judicial council legal forms CRCAppx A
Portions to be stricken, designation of CRC 3.1322
Public issues, motion to strike causes of action having chilling effect on right of free speech in public discussion of CCP §§425.16, 425.17
  SLAPPback actions CCP §425.18
Remand from federal court, time to move to strike after CCP §430.90
Sexual assault of minor, failure to comply with certificate of merit requirement in action for CCP §340.1
SLAPPback actions CCP §425.18
Time requirements CRC 3.1322
Unlawful detainer CCP §1170

MOTION TO VACATE (See **JUDGMENTS**)

MOTORBOATS (See **VESSELS**)

MOTOR CARRIERS
Baggage, liability for loss of CC §2205
Buses (See **BUSES**)
Cargo tank vehicles traveling through tunnels, immunity of public entity from liability for failure to prohibit or restrict Gov §821.5
Construction trucking services brokers
  Transportation charges, payment CC §3322
Indemnity agreements CC §2784.5

MOTOR VEHICLES (See **AUTOMOBILES**)

MOTOR VEHICLES DEPARTMENT
Access to public databases for service of process purposes CCP §415.50
Attachment notices filed with CCP §488.385
Emancipated minors, identification cards for Fam §§7140 to 7143
Information Practices Act, disclosure procedures under CC §1798.26
Jurors, list of licensed drivers and identification cardholders as source for selection of CCP §197
Lease regulations, authority for adopting CC §2989.6
Liability for injury to lienholder or good faith purchaser of vehicle Gov §818.5
Lien sale notices to CC §§3067.1, 3071 to 3073
Records and reports
  Access to public databases for service of process purposes CCP §415.50
  Sealed records of wards of court, access to
    Order on prosecutor request for access CRCAppx A
    Prosecuting attorney request to access sealed juvenile case files CRC 5.860

MOVIES (See **MOTION PICTURES**)

MUG SHOTS
Commercial use of booking photographs CC §1798.91.1

MULTIDISTRICT LITIGATION (See **COORDINATION OF ACTIONS**)

MULTIFAMILY DWELLINGS
Service of papers or subpoena, access to covered multifamily dwelling CCP §415.21

MULTIPHASIC SCREENING UNITS
Malpractice immunity for physicians from patients referred by CC §43.9

MULTIPLE LIABILITY
Interpleader CCP §386

MULTIPLE LISTING SERVICE CC §§1086 to 1089.5

MULTIPLE PARTIES
Small claims court (See **SMALL CLAIMS COURTS**)

MULTIPLE-PARTY ACCOUNTS
Community property Pro §§5305, 5307
Definitions Pro §§5120 to 5152
Disclaimer of estate interest in Pro §§260 to 295
Excess withdrawal by party
  Claim for recovery Pro §5301
  Proportional ownership interest in other parties Pro §5301
General provisions Pro §§5100, 5201, 5202
Minors, payments to Pro §5407
Ownership of Pro §§5301 to 5307

MULTIPLE-PARTY ACCOUNTS—Cont.
Payments from   Pro §§5401 to 5407
Power of attorney   Pro §5204
Protection of financial institution   Pro §§5401 to 5407
Right of survivorship   Pro §§5301 to 5306
Small estates without administration, exclusions for   Pro §13050
Types of account created by terms used in bank signature cards   Pro §5203

MULTIPLICITY OF SUITS
Injunction preventing   CC §§3422, 3423, CCP §526

MULTIUNIT DWELLING STRUCTURES (See APARTMENTS)

MUNICIPAL BONDS (See BONDS)

MUNICIPAL CORPORATIONS (See CITIES AND MUNICIPALITIES)

MUNICIPAL COURTS
Superior courts generally (See SUPERIOR COURTS)

MUNICIPALITIES (See CITIES AND MUNICIPALITIES)

MUNICIPAL UTILITIES (See PUBLIC UTILITIES)

MURDER (See HOMICIDE)

MUSEUMS   CC §§1899 to 1899.11

MUSIC
Child star contracts   Fam §§6750 to 6753
Infringement, action for   CCP §429.30

MUSICAL INSTRUMENTS
Apartment housekeeper's lien, exemption from   CC §1861a
Hotelkeeper's lien, exemption from   CC §1861
Pianos (See PIANOS)

MUSIC MACHINES (See VENDING MACHINES)

MUTUAL BENEFIT CORPORATIONS, NONPROFIT
Attorney professional conduct
    Organization or entity as client   ProfC 1.13
Commercial and industrial common interest developments
    Associations
        Exercise by association of powers granted to nonprofit mutual benefit corporations   CC §6752
Mobilehome parks owned and operated by   CC §799.1

MUTUAL FUNDS
Conservatorship (See CONSERVATORS)
Guardianship (See GUARDIAN AND WARD)
Judge's ownership in mutual or common investment fund not a financial interest for purposes of disqualification   CCP §170.5

MUTUAL INSURANCE COMPANIES
Disqualification of judges, proprietary interest of policyholder as financial interest for purposes of   CCP §170.5

MUTUALITY OF CONTRACT   CC §1580

MUTUAL MISTAKE
Specific performance   CC §3399

MUTUAL SAVINGS ASSOCIATIONS
Disqualification of judges, proprietary interest of depositor as financial interest for purposes of   CCP §170.5

MUTUAL WILLS   Pro §21700

N

NAILS
Fixtures attached to real property with   CC §660

NAIL SALONS
Human trafficking
    Signs, businesses required to post notice concerning relief from slavery or human trafficking   CC §52.6

NAMEPLATES
Manufacturer's nameplate removed from articles   CC §1710.1

NAMES
Adoption proceedings (See ADOPTION)

NAMES—Cont.
Advertising, unauthorized use of name or likeness in   CC §§3344, 3344.1
Annulment, restoration of former name in proceedings for   Fam §§2080 to 2082
Attorney professional conduct
    Firm names and trade names   ProfC 7.5
Change of (See CHANGE OF NAMES)
Commercial blockage tort, pseudonyms used in civil proceedings for   CC §3427.3
Complaint, names of parties in title   CCP §422.40
Deeds (See DEEDS)
Dissolution of marriage, restoration of former name in proceedings for   Fam §2401
Doe defendants, generally (See UNKNOWN PERSONS)
Fictitious names (See FICTITIOUS NAMES)
Former name
    Restoration on dissolution of marriage   CRCAppx A (CRCFL-395)
Guardians ad litem
    Pseudonym, appointment under   CCP §372.5
Invasion of privacy, unauthorized use of name or likeness in advertising as   CC §§3344, 3344.1
Judgment lien on property of misidentified owner, release of   CCP §§697.410, 697.660
Juror personal information (See JURY)
Owner of property (See TITLE AND OWNERSHIP)
Pleadings, amendment of   CCP §473
Prohibition against refusal to engage in business with person using birth or former name regardless of marital status   CCP §1279.6
Restoration of former name   Fam §§2080 to 2082, 2401
Small claims court (See SMALL CLAIMS COURTS)
True name of defendant designated as unknown, amendment to add   CCP §474

NARCOTICS AND DANGEROUS DRUGS
Abuse of (See SUBSTANCE ABUSE)
Custody of children
    Substance abuse as custody determining factor
        Testing for alcohol or controlled substance use ordered by court   Fam §3041.5
Guardian and ward, custody of child
    Substance abuse as custody determining factor
        Testing for alcohol or controlled substance use ordered by court   Fam §3041.5
Marriage license denied to persons under influence of   Fam §352
Mobilehome tenancy terminated for conviction of use on premises   CC §798.56
Nuisance actions (See NUISANCES)
Pharmacists and pharmacies (See PHARMACISTS AND PHARMACIES)
Secure drug take-back bins
    Liability of collector, limitation   CC §1714.24
Unlawful detainer proceedings based on tenant's drug-selling on premises   CCP §1161
    Nuisance, termination of leases for   CC §§3486, 3486.5

NATIONAL BANKS (See BANKS AND BANKING)

NATIONAL INFLUENZA PROGRAM
Public entity or employee participating in program, immunity of   Gov §856.6

NATIONAL ORIGIN
Adoption proceedings, prohibited discrimination in   Fam §8708
Discrimination   CC §§51 to 53
    Judicial ethics code
        Administrative responsibilities of judge, impartial discharge   CRCSupp JudEthicsCanon 3
        Attorneys, judges to require to refrain from manifesting   CRCSupp JudEthicsCanon 3
        Court personnel and staff under direction of judge, standards of conduct enforced by judge   CRCSupp JudEthicsCanon 3
        Membership in discriminatory organizations   CRCSupp JudEthicsCanon 2
Equal protection
    Political structure equal protection   CC §53.7
Foster care placement   Fam §7950
Jury service exemption not allowed based on   CCP §204
Political structure equal protection   CC §53.7

NATIONAL PARKS
Appropriation of water originating in   CC §1422

NATIVE AMERICANS
Abandoned children
    Transfer by parent of care, custody and control to Indian custodian as not constituting abandonment   Fam §7822
Adoption (See ADOPTION)

NATIVE AMERICANS—Cont.
- Child custody
  - Temporary custody of Indian child, agreement   CRCAppx A
- Child support
  - Title IV-D support actions
    - Transfer of title IV-D cases from tribal court   CRC 5.372
    - Transfer of title IV-D cases to tribal court   CRC 5.372
- Conservation easements held by tribes   CC §815.3
- Conservatorship proceedings for Indian children
  - Applicability of Indian Child Welfare Act   Pro §1459.5
  - Attorneys
    - Inability to afford counsel   Pro §1474
  - Interstate jurisdiction, transfer and recognition
    - Generally   Pro §§1980 to 2033
    - Judicial council legal forms   CRCAppx A
    - Provisions specific to federally recognized Indian tribes   Pro §§2031 to 2033
  - Involuntary placements
    - Indian Child Welfare Act, rules governing   CRC 5.480 to 5.487
    - (See **INDIAN CHILD WELFARE ACT INVOLUNTARY PLACEMENTS**)
  - Legislative findings and intent   Pro §1459
  - Notice
    - Indian children as proposed conservatee   Pro §1460.2
  - Notice requirements
    - Indian Child Welfare Act applicability   CRC 7.51
  - Registration and recognition of orders from other states
    - Tribal courts (California tribes), applicability of provisions   Pro §2019
  - Transfers of conservatorships
    - Tribal courts (California tribes), transfers to or from   Pro §2003
  - Tribal membership of conservatee
    - Petition, contents   Pro §§1821, 1826
- Custody of children (See **CUSTODY OF CHILDREN**)
- Dependency matters
  - Appearances
    - Telephone or computerized remote appearances by tribe   CRC 3.672, 5.531
  - Detention hearing
    - Active efforts   CRC 5.678
    - Evidence required for detention of Indian child   CRC 5.676
    - Findings necessary to detain   CRC 5.674, 5.678
    - Placement preferences   CRC 5.678
  - Emergency removal
    - Hearing for return of custody when emergency ends   CRC 5.678
  - Generally (See **DEPENDENT CHILDREN**)
  - Inquiry as to Indian status at first appearance   CRC 5.668
  - Intake process
    - Purposes of intake process   CRC 5.510
  - Notice under Indian Child Welfare Act   CRC 5.725
  - Orders
    - Judicial council form   CRCAppx A
  - Placement under Indian Child Welfare Act   CRC 5.565, 5.570
    - Out-of-county placements   CRC 5.614, CRCAppx A
    - Rules governing involuntary placements   CRC 5.480 to 5.488 (See **INDIAN CHILD WELFARE ACT INVOLUNTARY PLACEMENTS**)
  - Reunification services, requirement
    - Termination of reunification services, findings   CRC 5.570
  - Telephone or computerized remote appearances by tribe   CRC 3.672, 5.531
  - Termination of juvenile court jurisdiction
    - Nonminor dependents or wards in foster care   CRC 5.555
  - Tribal rights in   CRC 5.534
    - Tribal information form   CRCAppx A
- Divorces, validity of   Fam §295
- Electronic court records, remote access
  - Government entities, access by
    - List of government entities which may be authorized to receive access   CRC 2.540
- Family rules
  - Domestic violence
    - Tribal court protection orders   CRC 5.386
  - Involuntary placements
    - Indian child welfare act involuntary placements   CRC 5.480 to 5.488
    - (See **INDIAN CHILD WELFARE ACT INVOLUNTARY PLACEMENTS**)
  - Title IV-D support actions
    - Transfer of title IV-D cases from tribal court   CRC 5.372
    - Transfer of title IV-D cases to tribal court   CRC 5.372

NATIVE AMERICANS—Cont.
- Foreign judgments
  - Foreign countries defined
    - Indian nation, tribe, etc included in definition   CCP §1714
  - Tribal court civil money judgment act   CCP §§1730 to 1741
- Foster placements
  - Involuntary placements
    - Indian Child Welfare Act, rules governing   CRC 5.480 to 5.488
    - (See **INDIAN CHILD WELFARE ACT INVOLUNTARY PLACEMENTS**)
- Gaming rights
  - Injunction to protect   CCP §1811
- Greenway easements
  - Entities permitted to acquire and hold easement   CC §816.56
- Guardianship proceedings for Indian children
  - Applicability of Indian Child Welfare Act   Pro §1459.5
  - Attorneys
    - Inability to afford counsel   Pro §1474
  - Investigation and report   Pro §1513
  - Involuntary placements
    - Indian Child Welfare Act, rules governing   CRC 5.480 to 5.488
    - (See **INDIAN CHILD WELFARE ACT INVOLUNTARY PLACEMENTS**)
  - Legislative findings and intent   Pro §1459
  - Notice requirements
    - Indian Child Welfare Act applicability   CRC 7.51
  - Notices
    - Indian children as proposed ward   Pro §§1460.2, 1511
  - Petition, contents   Pro §1510
  - Termination of guardianship   Pro §1601
  - Ward's residence, change
    - Notice of change of personal residence   CRC 7.1013
- Indian Child Welfare Act
  - Involuntary placements, rules governing   CRC 5.480 to 5.488 (See **INDIAN CHILD WELFARE ACT INVOLUNTARY PLACEMENTS**)
- Interstate compact on placement of children
  - Applicability to Indian children   Fam §7907.3
- Interstate family support   Fam §§5700.101 to 5700.903 (See **INTERSTATE FAMILY SUPPORT**)
- Intestate succession   Fam §295
- Judgments
  - Money judgments
    - Notice of application for recognition and entry of tribal court money judgment   CRCAppx A
    - Tribal court civil money judgment act   CCP §§1730 to 1741
- Judicial council
  - Tribal court-state court forum   CRC 10.60
- Juvenile wardship proceedings
  - Involuntary placements, rules governing   CRC 5.480 to 5.488 (See **INDIAN CHILD WELFARE ACT INVOLUNTARY PLACEMENTS**)
  - Termination of juvenile court jurisdiction
    - Nonminor dependents or wards in foster care   CRC 5.555
- Marriage, validity of   Fam §295
- Money judgments
  - Tribal court civil money judgment act   CCP §§1730 to 1741
- Property division
  - Retirement benefits
    - Tribal court orders, payments pursuant to   Fam §2611
- Psychotropic medication for treatment of psychiatric disorder or illness, authorization
  - Notice to Indian child's tribe   CRC 5.640
    - Forms, judicial council   CRCAppx A
  - Prescriptions
    - Release of psychotropic medication prescription information to medical board, authorization   CRC 5.642
- Termination of parental rights
  - Indian children   Fam §7892.5
    - Involuntary placements   CRC 5.480 to 5.488 (See **INDIAN CHILD WELFARE ACT INVOLUNTARY PLACEMENTS**)
  - Permanent plan selection   CRC 5.725
- Tribal courts
  - Judicial council
    - Tribal court-state court forum   CRC 10.60
  - Money judgments
    - Tribal court civil money judgment act   CCP §§1730 to 1741
  - Title IV-D support actions
    - Transfer of title IV-D cases from tribal court   CRC 5.372
    - Transfer of title IV-D cases to tribal court   CRC 5.372

NATURAL CATASTROPHES
Appellate courts
- E-filing in supreme court and courts of appeal
  - Documents subject to e-filing in Supreme Court, modifications in light of emergencies   CRCSupp SuprCtE-file 2

Boundary reestablishment   CCP §§751.50 to 751.65
Business records destroyed by   CCP §§1953.10 to 1953.13
Common interest developments
- Board meetings
  - Emergencies or disasters, meetings entirely by teleconference   CC §5450

Contract performance prevented by   CC §1511
Court record destroyed by   CCP §§1953 to 1953.06
Destroyed land records relief law   CCP §§751.01 to 751.28
Disaster relief organizations, medical information disclosed to   CC §57.10
Earthquakes (See **EARTHQUAKES**)
Emergencies (See **EMERGENCIES**)
Fires (See **FIRES**)
Floods (See **FLOODS**)
Home solicitation sales contracts void within prescribed period from   CC §1689.14
Maps destroyed by   CCP §§1953.10 to 1953.13
Mobilehomes and mobilehome parks
- Destruction of park by wildfire or other natural disaster and subsequent rebuilding
  - Offers of renewed tenancy   CC §798.62

New trial, destroying bill of exceptions as grounds for   CCP §663.1
Nunc pro tunc filing where public records lost or destroyed   CCP §1046a
Personal injuries to persons using emergency facilities, governmental liability for   CC §1714.5
Supreme court e-filing rules
- Emergency situations, modifications to rules governing documents subject to electronic filing   CRCSupp SuprCtE-file 2

NATURAL DEATH ACT
Declarations under Natural Death Act as advance health care directives under Health Care Decisions Law   Pro §4665

NATURAL DISASTERS (See **NATURAL CATASTROPHES**)

NATURAL GAS FIXTURES
Habitability including   CC §1941.1

NATURAL HAZARDS DISCLOSURE   CC §§1103 to 1103.15

NATURAL PARENTS
Adoption (See **ADOPTION**)

NATURAL RESOURCES (See **MINERALS AND MINERAL RIGHTS; WATERS**)

NATURE STUDY
Landowner liability for   CC §846

NAVIGABLE WATERS
Public entity's liability for injury on   Gov §831.6

NAVY (See **MILITARY**)

NAZI GERMANY
Artwork
- Action to recover Holocaust-era artwork   CCP §354.3
  - Limitation of actions   CCP §338

Insurance actions by holocaust victims, jurisdiction and limitation period for   CCP §354.5
Slave or forced labor under Nazi regime, actions to recover compensation for   CCP §354.6

NECESSARIES
Asian language contracts, translations   CC §1632
Child support, third person providing necessaries for   Fam §3950
Married person's liability for debts incurred by spouse   Fam §914
Minor's contract for   Fam §6712
Spanish language contracts for purchase of   CC §1632
Support of parents, promise of child to pay for necessaries   Fam §4401
Unsound mind, liability of persons with   CC §38

NEGLECT
Inheritance rights, effect of heir's neglect or abuse on   Pro §259
Mistake, inadvertence, surprise or excusable neglect (See **MISTAKE**)

NEGLIGENCE
Generally   CC §§1708, 1714

NEGLIGENCE—Cont.
Agents   CC §§2338, 2339
Alcoholic beverages, social host's liability after serving   CC §1714
Automobile insurance coverage inadmissible evidence to prove   Ev §1155
Bailment, degree of care for property held under   CC §§1888, 1928, 2078
Blind or partially blind person failing to carry white cane or use guide dog   CC §54.4
Cardiopulmonary resuscitation   CC §§1714.2, 1714.21
Common carriers (See **COMMON CARRIERS**)
Common interest developments (See **COMMON INTEREST DEVELOPMENTS**)
Contract exempting from liability for willful injury, validity of   CC §1668
Credit reports as basis for action   CC §§1785.31, 1785.32
Dalkon Shield claimants, extension of limitations statute in action for   CCP §340.7
Defibrillator, use of   CC §1714.21
Deposits (See **DEPOSITS**)
Food bank, injuries resulting from consumption of food distributed by   CC §1714.25
Guns (See **FIREARMS AND OTHER WEAPONS**)
Health care providers (See **MALPRACTICE**)
Husband and wife (See **HUSBAND AND WIFE**)
Imputed negligence
- Husband and wife   Fam §1000
- Parent, child's negligence imputed to   CC §1714.1

Indemnity   CC §2784.5
Liability insurance coverage inadmissible to prove   Ev §1155
Military commanders, carrying out orders of   CC §1714.6
Nonprofit corporations, negligence actions against non-compensated officers and directors of   CCP §425.15
Parents maintaining action for injury of child   CCP §376
Precautionary evidence   Ev §1151
Professional negligence (See **MALPRACTICE**)
Public entities and employees, claims against (See **CLAIMS AGAINST PUBLIC ENTITIES AND EMPLOYEES**)
Referral services of professional societies, liability arising from   CC §43.95
Repairs inadmissible as evidence to prove   Ev §1151
Res ipsa loquitur presumption   Ev §646
Social host's liability after serving alcoholic beverages   CC §1714
Statutes of limitation, generally   CCP §335.1
Telegrams, transmission of   CC §2162
Venue   CCP §395
Violation of statute as failure to exercise due care   Ev §§669, 669.1
Wrongful death (See **WRONGFUL DEATH**)

NEGOTIABLE INSTRUMENTS
Assignees, action by   CCP §368
Attachment (See **ATTACHMENT**)
Bill of lading (See **BILL OF LADING**)
Bills and notes (See **BILLS AND NOTES**)
Bills of exchange (See **BILLS OF EXCHANGE**)
Bonds (See **BONDS**)
Checks (See **CHECKS**)
Electronic transactions
- Exceptions to applicability of electronic transactions provisions   CC §1633.3

Enforcement of judgments (See **ENFORCEMENT OF JUDGMENTS**)
Money orders (See **MONEY ORDERS**)
Nonnegotiable instruments (See **NONNEGOTIABLE INSTRUMENTS**)
Traveler's checks (See **TRAVELER'S CHECKS**)
Warehouse receipts (See **WAREHOUSE RECEIPTS**)

NEIGHBORS
Family history, reputation among neighbors concerning   Ev §1314

NET NEUTRALITY   CC §§3100 to 3104
Blocking
- Fixed internet service providers
  - Prohibited conduct   CC §3101

Definitions   CC §3100
Emergency communications
- Obligation of service providers   CC §3103

Fixed internet service providers
- Defined   CC §3100
- Emergency communications
  - Obligation of service providers   CC §3103
- Prohibited conduct   CC §§3101, 3102

Impairing or degrading internet content
- Definitions   CC §3100
- Fixed internet service providers
  - Prohibited conduct   CC §3101

NET NEUTRALITY—Cont.
ISP traffic exchange
    Defined   CC §3100
    Fixed internet service providers
        Prohibited conduct   CC §3101
Mobile internet service providers
    Defined   CC §3100
    Emergency communications
        Obligation of service providers   CC §3103
Network management practices
    Definition of reasonable network management practices   CC §3100
    Fixed internet service providers
        Prohibited conduct   CC §3101
Paid prioritization
    Defined   CC §3100
    Fixed internet service providers
        Prohibited conduct   CC §3101
Services other than internet delivered over same last-mile connections to either evade provisions or negatively affect internet performance
    Fixed internet service providers
        Prohibited conduct   CC §3102
Waiver of provisions
    Barred   CC §3104
Zero-rating
    Defined   CC §3100
    Fixed internet service providers
        Prohibited conduct   CC §3101

NEUTRALITY, INTERNET   CC §§3100 to 3104

NEWLY DISCOVERED EVIDENCE
New trial because of   CCP §657

NEWS MEDIA
Newspapers and magazines (See **NEWSPAPERS AND MAGAZINES**)
Radio and television (See **RADIO AND TELEVISION**)

NEWSPAPERS AND MAGAZINES
Administration of decedent's estate, publication of notice of petition for   Pro §8121
Attorney professional conduct
    Trial publicity   ProfC 3.6
Contempt
    Disruption of proceedings   CCP §1209
    Journalist in contempt for failure to testify, findings of court required for holding   CCP §1986.1
    Privilege against disclosure of sources   Ev §1070
Court proceedings, media coverage   CRC 1.150
Indecency and obscenity (See **INDECENCY AND OBSCENITY**)
Journalists (See **JOURNALISTS**)
Judges' writings, Code of Judicial Ethics provisions concerning   CRCSupp JudEthicsCanons 2, 4
Levied property, advertising sale of   CCP §701.545
Libel
    Correction demands   CC §48a
    Fair comment doctrine   CC §47
    Official proceedings published   CC §47
Missing person, notice of search for   Pro §12406
Official proceedings, privilege attaching report on   CC §47
Pornography (See **INDECENCY AND OBSCENITY**)
Presumption regarding publications purporting to be newspapers or periodicals   Ev §645.1
Privilege against disclosure of sources   Ev §1070
Seller assisted marketing plan defined   CC §1812.201
Telegrams for publication in newspapers, priority for transmitting   CC §2207
Trials
    Court proceedings, restrictions on media coverage of   CRC 1.150

NEWSREELS (See **MOTION PICTURES**)

NEW TRIAL
Administration of estates proceedings   Pro §7220
Affidavits
    Grounds for new trial requiring filing of supporting affidavit   CCP §658
    Motion for new trial, affidavit in support of   CCP §659a
    Time for service of   CCP §659a
Appeals   CCP §906
    Order on motion for, appeal from
        Extension of time   CRC 8.108
    Superior courts, limited civil cases in appellate division
        Motion for new trial   CRC 8.823

NEW TRIAL—Cont.
Appeals —Cont.
    Supreme court and courts of appeal
        Notice of appeal, extension of time to file   CRC 8.108
Bifurcated trial, motion following   CRC 3.1591
Bill of exceptions, loss of   CCP §663.1
Court reporter
    Death or disability, effect   CCP §§657.1, 914
    Hearings on new trial motion, transcripts   CCP §660
Courts of appeal authorized to direct   CCP §43
Damages
    Excessive or inadequate damages   CCP §662.5
    Grounds for new trial   CCP §657
    Reduction of   CCP §662.5
Death or disability of court reporter as grounds for   CCP §§657.1, 914
Defined   CCP §656
Denial of motion, extension of time for appeal   CRC 8.108
Discretion abuse as ground for   CCP §657
Dismissal actions regarding   CCP §583.320
Dismissal for delay in prosecution following granting of new trial motion
    COVID-19, emergency rule   CRCAppx I Emer Rule 10
Dissolution of marriage (See **DISSOLUTION OF MARRIAGE**)
Environmental quality act
    Jobs and economic improvement through environmental leadership act of 2021
        Appellate review of CEQA cases   CRC 8.702
    Sacramento downtown arena project, CEQA challenges
        Appellate review of CEQA cases   CRC 8.702
Evidence
    Grounds for new trial   CCP §657
    Motions, evidence supporting   CCP §660
Expedited jury trials
    Permissible grounds   CCP §630.09
    Waiver of motions concerning amount of damages   CCP §630.08
Extensions of time   CCP §§659, 659a
Fire destroying bill of exceptions   CCP §663.1
Grounds for   CCP §657
Hearings   CCP §§660, 663.2
Judicial arbitration (See **JUDICIAL ARBITRATION**)
Jury misconduct as grounds for new trial   CCP §657
Law errors as grounds for   CCP §657
Mandamus   CCP §1092
Mandatory time to bring action to trial
    Generally   CCP §583.320
    Computation of   CCP §583.340
    Extension of time   CCP §§583.330, 583.350
    Failure to obtain action within time limit, effect of   CCP §583.360
Mediation, new trial on grounds of irregular reference to   CCP §1775.12, Ev §1128
Motion for new trial
    Affidavit in support of new trial motion   CCP §659a
    Bifurcated trial, motion following   CRC 3.1591
    Evidence considered on   CCP §660
    Hearings on   CCP §§660, 663.2
    Memorandum in support of   CRC 3.1600
    Notice of   CCP §659
    Ruling on motion, alternatives   CCP §662
    Time for filing   CCP §659
    Trial judge determining   CCP §661
Natural catastrophe destroying bill of exceptions   CCP §663.1
Newly-discovered evidence as ground for   CCP §657
Nonjury cases   CCP §662
Reporter
    Death or disability of court reporter, effect of   CCP §§657.1, 914
    Hearings on new trial motion, use of transcripts at   CCP §660
Reviewing court's authority to order new trial   CCP §906
Ruling on motion, alternatives   CCP §662
Service of papers
    Motion for new trial   CCP §659
    Supporting affidavit for new trial   CCP §659a
Special proceedings   CCP §1110
Supreme Court authorized to direct   CCP §43
Surprise as grounds for   CCP §657
Time
    Vacation of judgment
        Notice of motion, time for   CCP §663a
        Ruling on motion, time for   CCP §663a
Trial court rules
    Notice of intention to move for
        Memorandum in support of   CRC 3.1600
Unlawful detainer   CCP §1178

NEW TRIAL—Cont.
Will probate proceedings   Pro §7220

NEXT BUSINESS DAY
Extension of time to next day which is not a holiday   CCP §12a
Postponing performance from holiday to   CCP §13

NIGHT SESSIONS
Small claims court sessions   CCP §116.250

911 EMERGENCY LINE
Immunity from liability, telecommunications services providing   CC §1714.55

99-YEAR LEASE
Validity of   CC §§718, 718f

NO CONTEST CLAUSES (See WILL PROBATE)

NOISE
Eminent domain to prevent noise pollution, taking for   CCP §1240.110
Shooting range exemption from liability for noise pollution   CC §3482.1

NOLO CONTENDERE PLEAS
Appellate rules, supreme court and courts of appeal
    Appeal of conviction following plea of nolo contendere   CRC 8.304
Certificate of probable cause for appeal   CRC 8.304
Certification for superior court sentencing following plea of   CRC 4.114
Judgment based on plea of nolo contendere, admissibility of   Ev §1300
Punishment
    Specification in plea   CRC 4.412
Report to Justice Department concerning nolo contendere plea   CRC 4.320
Setting date for sentencing and reference of case to probation officer   CRC 4.114

NOMINAL DAMAGES   CC §3360

NON-DOMICILIARIES
Jury service, exceptions to eligibility for   CCP §203

NONJUDICIAL REMEDIES
Administrative hearings, procedure for (See **ADMINISTRATIVE ADJUDICATION**)
Arbitration (See **ARBITRATION**)

NONJURY TRIALS
Appeals   CCP §909
Default judgments   CCP §636
Evidence   CCP §631.8
Fact issues   CCP §592
Liability issue, trial of   CCP §598
Motion for judgment in   CCP §631.8
New trial, motion for   CCP §661
Order of   CCP §631.7
Rebuttal of evidence after motion for judgment   CCP §631.8
Rendition of judgment   CCP §636
Statement of decision   CCP §632
Waiver of jury trial   CCP §631
Witnesses, rehabilitation of   CCP §631.8

NONMARITAL RELATIONSHIPS (See COHABITATION)

NONNEGOTIABLE INSTRUMENTS
Endorsement of   CC §1459
Transfer of   CC §955

NONPROBATE TRANSFERS
Community property
    Execution of provision for nonprobate transfer without consent of spouse, validity of   Pro §5020
    Fraud, undue influence, duress or mistake, validity of consent procured by   Pro §5015
    Holder of community property under nonprobate instrument, effect on   Pro §5012
    Limitations on parties' community property rights   Pro §5011
    Modification of provision for nonprobate transfer   Pro §5023
    Revocation of consent
        Generally   Pro §5030
        Holder's authority to transfer property, effect on   Pro §5031
        Manner of revocation   Pro §5031
        Passage of property after   Pro §5032
    Right of survivorship without administration pursuant to terms of written instrument   CC §682.1
    Scope of law   Pro §5014

NONPROBATE TRANSFERS—Cont.
Community property—Cont.
    Set-aside proceeding for nonprobate transfer   Pro §5021
    Transmutation of consenting spouse's interest, effect of spousal consent on   Fam §853, Pro §5022
    Waiver of surviving spouse's rights, effect on   Pro §5013
    Written consent, written joinder by parties to provisions of instrument interpreted as   Pro §5010
Dissolution of marriage
    Beneficiary designation
        Summary dissolution of marriage proceedings, court order to designate   Fam §2337
Former spouse, transfers to   Pro §§5040 to 5048
    Bona fide purchaser or encumbrancer, effect on rights of   Pro §5044
    Continuing authority over parties by court   Pro §5046
    Effective date of act   Pro §5048
    Joint tenant property   Pro §§5042, 5046
Grounds for holder of property not complying with written provisions for nonprobate transfer upon death   Pro §5002
Liability of person complying with provisions of nonprobate instrument for transfer of property upon death   Pro §5003
Notice requirements   Pro §5003
Protection of holder of property complying with provisions of nonprobate instrument for transfer of property upon death   Pro §5003
Validity of nonprobate transfer upon death by written instrument lacking formalities of execution of will   Pro §5000

NONPROFIT CORPORATIONS AND ASSOCIATIONS
Attorney professional conduct
    Organization or entity as client   ProfC 1.13
Conservation easements held by   CC §§815 to 816
Conservator, appointment of nonprofit charitable corporation as   Pro §2104
Emancipated minor holding membership in   Fam §7052
Eminent domain proceedings (See **EMINENT DOMAIN**)
Fraudulent inducement of independent retailers to join cooperative association providing wholesale goods and services to members, liability for   CC §3343.7
Greenway easements
    Tax exempt nonprofit organizations
        Entities permitted to acquire and hold easement   CC §816.56
Guardian, appointment of nonprofit charitable corporation as   Pro §2104
Lease abandonment provisions, applicability of   CC §1952.6
Marriage ceremony by officials of nonprofit religious institutions   Fam §402
Trustee, appointment of nonprofit charitable corporation as   Pro §15604
Uniform prudent management of institutional funds act   Pro §§18501 to 18510
    (See **INSTITUTIONAL FUNDS MANAGEMENT**)
Vision screenings, eyeglasses, etc
    Immunity from liability
        Nonprofit charitable organization and volunteer eye care professionals donating screening, eyeglasses, etc   CC §1714.26
Volunteer officers and directors, action against   CCP §425.15

NONRESIDENTS
Administration of decedents' estates
    Generally (See **ADMINISTRATION OF ESTATES**)
    Executor or administrator, nonresident as   Pro §§8570 to 8577
Administrator with will annexed, nonresident as   Pro §§8570 to 8577
Attachment (See **ATTACHMENT**)
Choice of law for purposes of jurisdiction in action or proceeding involving   CCP §410.40
Conservators (See **CONSERVATORS**)
Costs, bonds required to secure   CCP §1030
Executor of decedent's estate, nonresident as   Pro §§8570 to 8577
Guardian and ward (See **GUARDIAN AND WARD**)
Interstate family support   Fam §§5700.101 to 5700.903
Jury service, exceptions to eligibility for   CCP §203
Service of papers on nonresidents   CCP §1015
Small claims court (See **SMALL CLAIMS COURTS**)
Wholesale sales representatives, contract actions involving   CC §1738.14

NONSUIT
Generally   CCP §581c
Costs on   CCP §1038

NOTARIES PUBLIC
Acknowledgment of instruments   CC §§1181 to 1183.5
    Scope of certification   CC §1189
        Proof of execution, certificate of proof   CC §1195
Armed forces officers, notarial acts performed by   CC §1183.5
Confidential marriages
    Issuance of confidential marriage licenses   Fam §§530 to 536
    Request for issuance of license for confidential marriage   Fam §503

NOTARIES PUBLIC—Cont.

Electronic transaction, satisfaction of notarization requirements with respect to CC §1633.11
Failure of notary to obtain satisfactory evidence   CC §1185
Fees for filing bonds   Gov §26849.1
Identification of person making acknowledgment   CC §§1185, 1196, 1197
Oaths, administering   CCP §2093
Online notarization   CC §1181.1
Sealed documents presumed to be genuine   Ev §1452
Signatures presumed to be genuine   Ev §§1452, 1453
Statutes of limitation upon bond of   CCP §338
Suspending or revoking registration of   Fam §535
Transfer on death deeds
   Execution of instrument
      Effective, when   Pro §5624

NOTES (See BILLS AND NOTES)

NOTICE OF MOTION   CRC 3.1112

Attachments to notice   CRC 3.1113
Attorneys' fees, notice of motion to claim   CRC 3.1702
Family law
   Appearance by filing notice of motion   CRC 5.62
Memorandum in support of motion, attachment of   CRC 3.1113
Striking of pleadings   CRC 3.1322

NOTICE OF PROPOSED ACTION

Administrative regulations of state agencies, procedural requirements for adoption of (See **ADMINISTRATIVE PROCEDURE ACT**)
Independent administration of decedent's estate   Pro §§10580 to 10592

NOTICES

Abandoned property of tenant, notice for disposition of   CC §§1983 to 1985
Acknowledgment defects in recorded documents   CC §1207
Address change
   Electronic filing, when required   CRCSupp 1st AppDist
   Trial court rules   CRC 2.200
Address, parent subject to juvenile proceedings   CRC 5.534
Administration of decedents' estates
   Generally (See **ADMINISTRATION OF ESTATES**)
   Ancillary administration (See **ANCILLARY ADMINISTRATION**)
   Claims against decedents' estates (See **CLAIMS AGAINST ESTATES**)
   Executors and administrators (See **EXECUTORS AND ADMINISTRATORS**)
Administrative Procedure Act
   Adjudicative proceedings (See **ADMINISTRATIVE ADJUDICATION**)
   Rulemaking and regulations (See **ADMINISTRATIVE PROCEDURE ACT**)
Adoption proceedings (See **ADOPTION**)
Affidavit for proof of service of   CCP §1013a
Aircraft liens   CCP §1208.62
Ancillary administration (See **ANCILLARY ADMINISTRATION**)
Animals, notice as to abandonment of   CC §1834.5
Annulment of marriage, notice of entry of judgment   CRC 5.413, 5.415
Apartment house owner, requirements for notice as to   CC §§1961 to 1962.5
Appeals
   Indigent appeal   CCP §936.1
   Small claims court (See **SMALL CLAIMS COURTS**)
   Superior court, rules on appeal to (See **APPELLATE RULES, SUPERIOR COURT APPEALS**)
   Supreme court and courts of appeal, rules on appeal to (See **APPELLATE RULES, SUPREME COURT AND COURTS OF APPEAL**)
   Withdrawal of legal service agency attorney for indigent client, effect on time limitations of   CCP §285.3
Appearances
   Criminal cases
      Electronic citation forms   CRC 4.103
      Notice to appear forms   CRC 4.103
   Remote appearances, technology use   CCP §367.75
   Service on party making   CCP §1014
Arbitration (See **ARBITRATION**)
Arbitrators
   Ethics standards
      Future professional relationships, notice of offers in consumer arbitrations   CRC ArbEthicsStand 12
Arrest (See **ARREST**)
Attachment (See **ATTACHMENT**)
Attorneys (See **ATTORNEYS**)
Automobiles (See **AUTOMOBILES**)
Bail and recognizance (See **BAIL**)
Bailed property, notice of expenditures on   CC §1957

NOTICES—Cont.

Bonds, procedure for validation of authorization, issuance, sale or exchange of CCP §349.4
CARE act rules
   Notices under   CRC 7.2235
Certified mail, sufficiency of notice by   Pro §5
Chain of title, hearing to identify party in   CCP §770.060
Change of address
   Electronic filing, when required   CRCSupp 1st AppDist
   Trial court rules   CRC 2.200
Change of venue, notice of transmittal of papers and pleadings pursuant to order for   CCP §399
   Time frames for transferring jurisdiction
      Family law actions or proceedings   CRC 5.97
Charitable trusts
   Disposal of all or substantially all of charitable assets
      Trustee notice to attorney general prior to disposal   Pro §16110
Child support (See **CHILD SUPPORT**)
Citation to appear (See **CITATION TO APPEAR**)
City property, leases of   CC §719
Claim and delivery (See **CLAIM AND DELIVERY**)
Claims against decedents' estates (See **CLAIMS AGAINST ESTATES**)
Claims against public entities and employees (See **CLAIMS AGAINST PUBLIC ENTITIES AND EMPLOYEES**)
Clerk, proof of service by   CCP §1013a
Common carriers (See **COMMON CARRIERS**)
Conciliation court proceedings   Fam §1836
Conditional sales contracts, notice of cosigner's liability on   CC §§1799.90 to 1799.96
Conservators (See **CONSERVATORS**)
Construction and interpretation   CCP §1865
Constructive notice for inquiry   CC §19
Consumer privacy rights
   Actions for damages, injunctions, declaratory relief, etc
      Security practices and procedures not in place   CC §1798.150
Credit cards (See **CREDIT CARDS**)
Credit denial notice   CC §§1787.1 to 1787.3
   Waiver of protections   CC §1787.4
Credit reports (See **CREDIT REPORTING**)
Cross-appeals   CRC 8.100, 8.108
Custodial institutions, late notices mailed from
   Appellate rules, superior court appeals
      Filing, timeliness   CRC 8.817
   Appellate rules, supreme court and courts of appeal
      Filing, timeliness   CRC 8.25
Custody of children (See **CUSTODY OF CHILDREN**)
Dance studio contracts, notice for cancellation of   CC §1812.54
Default judgments, setting aside (See **DEFAULT JUDGMENTS**)
Definition   CC §18
Demurrers, notice of hearing   CRC 3.1320
Depositions, notice of (See **DEPOSITIONS**)
Deposits (See **DEPOSITS**)
Destroyed land records relief law proceedings   CCP §§751.23 to 751.26
Dies, molds and forms, notice of termination of customer's title to   CC §1140
Disability insurance claims   CC §1812.402
Dismissal of civil action, notice of entry of dismissal   CRC 3.1390
Dissolution of marriage (See **DISSOLUTION OF MARRIAGE**)
District attorney (See **DISTRICT ATTORNEY**)
Domestic violence (See **DOMESTIC VIOLENCE**)
Donative transfers
   Presumption of fraud or undue influence
      Contested instrument, notice of   Pro §21388
Earnings assignment for support (See **EARNINGS ASSIGNMENT FOR SUPPORT**)
Electronic filing and service
   Orders, judgments and other documents prepared by court   CRC 2.252
Emancipation of children (See **EMANCIPATION OF MINORS**)
Eminent domain taking   CCP §1245.235
   Conservation easements
      Acquisition of property subject to conservation easement   CCP §1240.055
Enforcement of judgments (See **ENFORCEMENT OF JUDGMENTS**)
Entry of judgment (See **JUDGMENTS**)
Escheat (See **ESCHEAT**)
Executors (See **EXECUTORS AND ADMINISTRATORS**)
Ex parte proceedings
   Contents of notice   CRC 3.1204
   Declaration regarding notice   CRC 3.1204
   Shorter notice, explanation   CRC 3.1204
   Time for notice   CRC 3.1203

NOTICES—Cont.

Extensions of time for service of notices   CCP §§1054, 1054.1
Fact of death proceedings (See **FACT OF DEATH**)
Fair debt settlement practices
     Termination of contracts between providers and consumers
         Consumer right to terminate with notice   CC §1788.302
Family law rules (See **FAMILY RULES**)
Federal tax lien registration act   CCP §§2100 to 2107
     Fees for recording under act   Gov §27388.1
Fees
     Filing fees
         Return of check for   CCP §411.20
         Underpayment   CCP §411.21
     Sheriff's fee for service of notice (See **SHERIFF**)
Fictitious name, requirements for entry of default against person sued under CCP §474
Fiduciaries' Wartime Substitution Law (See **FIDUCIARIES' WARTIME SUBSTITUTION LAW**)
Fiduciary income and principal act
     Unitrust
         Notice requirements   Pro §16333
Filing fees
     Return of check for   CCP §411.20
     Underpayment   CCP §411.21
Floating homes and floating home marinas (See **FLOATING HOMES**)
Forms, molds and dies, notice of termination of customer's title to   CC §1140
Garnishment (See **GARNISHMENT**)
Gender tax repeal act preventing charging different prices for services of similar or like kind based on gender
     Consumer affairs department pamphlet for affected businesses and other notice of requirements of provisions   CC §51.63
     Licensing authority notice of provisions to licensee upon issuance or renewal   CC §51.6
Grain sold in bulk, posting notice of   CC §1880.7
Guardianship (See **GUARDIAN AND WARD**)
Harassment, protection orders
     Notice of hearing or petition   CCP §527.6
         COVID-19, emergency rule   CRCAppx I Emer Rule 8
         Requests for protective orders   CRC 3.1160
Health care provider's professional negligence, notice of intention to commence action based on   CCP §364
Heirship determination proceedings   Pro §11701
Home equity sales contracts   CC §§1695.3 to 1695.5
Home improvement contracts, notice to buyer under   CC §1804.3
Homesteads (See **HOMESTEADS**)
Horses sold at auction
     Sale for slaughter for human consumption as felony, notice of   CC §1834.8
Hospital lien, notice of sale for satisfaction of   CC §§1862.5, 3045.3
Hotels (See **HOTELS AND MOTELS**)
Indemnity (See **INDEMNITY**)
Indian child welfare act involuntary placements
     Proof of notice   CRC 5.482
     Requirements when Indian child involved   CRC 5.481
     Time interval between notice and commencement of proceedings   CRC 5.482
Indigent parents, adult child's petition to be relieved of obligation to support   Fam §§4412, 4413
Information Practices Act (See **INFORMATION PRACTICES ACT**)
Injunctions (See **INJUNCTIONS**)
Innkeeper's lien, writ of possession on   CC §§1861.8, 1861.19, 1861.23
Insurer, special notice of punitive damages award against   CC §3296
Interstate family support
     Enforcement of support orders
         Contest of validity   Fam §5700.506
     Modification of registered child support order   Fam §5700.614
     Registration for enforcement   Fam §5700.605
Intestate succession (See **INTESTATE SUCCESSION**)
Investigative agencies (See **INVESTIGATIVE CONSUMER REPORTING AGENCIES**)
Judges (See **JUDGES**)
Judgments (See **JUDGMENTS**)
Judicial arbitration hearing   CRC 3.817
Judicial council, notice of meetings   CRC 10.5
Judicial notice (See **JUDICIAL NOTICE**)
Jury (See **JURY**)
Justice courts (See **JUSTICE COURTS**)
Juvenile court hearing   CRC 5.524
Landlord and tenant (See **LANDLORD AND TENANT**)
Law and motion proceedings (See **LAW AND MOTION PROCEEDINGS**)
Leases (See **LEASES**)
Legal separation, notice of entry of judgment   CRC 5.413, 5.415

NOTICES—Cont.

Lemon Law Buyback   CC §§1793.23, 1793.24
Letters of administration, application for   Pro §8100
Libel or slander by newspaper or radio broadcast, written notice of   CC §48a
Liens (See **LIENS**)
Lis pendens (See **PENDENCY OF ACTIONS**)
Local rules of superior court
     Sanctions for failure to comply with rules   CCP §575.2
Lost property, disposition of   CC §§2080.1 to 2080.8
Mail (See **MAIL AND MAILING**)
Mechanics' liens (See **MECHANICS' LIENS**)
Mediation
     Complaints about court-program mediators
         Final action, notice of   CRC 3.869
Membership camping contracts, notice of cancellation of   CC §§1812.303, 1812.304, 1812.314
Mine co-owners failing to pay taxes   CCP §857
Mineral rights (See **MINERALS AND MINERAL RIGHTS**)
Missing persons (See **MISSING PERSONS**)
Mobilehomes (See **MOBILEHOMES**)
Molds, forms, and dies, notice of termination of customer's title to   CC §1140
Money sanctions for violations of lawful court orders, judicial officer's power to impose   CCP §177.5
Mortgages (See **TRUST DEEDS AND MORTGAGES**)
Motions, generally (See **LAW AND MOTION PROCEEDINGS**)
Multiphasic screening units notifying patient to consult physician   CC §43.9
New trial motions   CCP §659
Nonprobate transfer of property on death   Pro §5003
Nuisances, removal   CC §3503
     Illegal weapons on real property   CC §3485
Oil and gas lien claims   CCP §1203.59
Parentage actions
     Alleged parents, notice to   CRC 5.635
     Entry of judgment, notice of   CRC 5.413, 5.415
Partition (See **PARTITION**)
Paternity
     Actions to determine parent and child relationship   Fam §7630
Pendency of actions (See **PENDENCY OF ACTIONS**)
Personal delivery, service by   CCP §1011
Physicians and surgeons (See **PHYSICIANS AND SURGEONS**)
Postsecondary educational institutions
     Protection orders against violence threatened on campus or facility   CCP §527.85
         COVID-19, emergency rule   CRCAppx I Emer Rule 8
         Requests for protective orders   CRC 3.1160
Power of attorney, notice of time and place of hearings regarding petitions on   Pro §4544
Probation
     Out-of-county transfers   CRC 4.530
Proposed action, notice of (See **NOTICE OF PROPOSED ACTION**)
Protective orders
     Domestic violence
         Terminating or modifying order, motion made by person other than protected party   Fam §6345
     Harassment, prevention
         Requests for protective orders   CRC 3.1160
         Terminating or modifying order, motion made by person other than party   CCP §527.6, CRCAppx I Emer Rule 8
     University or other postsecondary school students, protection
         Requests for protective orders   CRC 3.1160
         Terminating or modifying order, motion made by person other than protected party   CCP §527.85, CRCAppx I Emer Rule 8
     Workplace violence and threats, prevention
         Requests for protective orders   CRC 3.1160
         Terminating or modifying order, motion made by person other than party   CCP §527.8, CRCAppx I Emer Rule 8
Psychotropic medication for children   CRC 5.640
     Forms, judicial council   CRCAppx A
Publication, notice by (See **PUBLICATION**)
Public contracts and works (See **PUBLIC CONTRACTS AND WORKS**)
Public easement rights to private land   CC §813
Public entities
     Participation by public
         Decisions and pending opportunities for public participation link on homepage   Gov §§11364, 11365
Public officer's bonds, action on   CCP §1055
Public records, notice of destruction
     Superior court records   CRC 10.856
Public use of private property   CC §§813, 1008
Record on appeal, date of filing   CRC 8.150
Recreational vehicle parks (See **RECREATIONAL VEHICLE PARKS**)

NOTICES—Cont.

Referees
    Proceedings, notice and information about   CRC 3.931
Registered mail, certified mail in lieu of   CCP §11
Related case pending   CRC 3.300
Remote appearances
    Local court rules for remote proceedings   CRC 3.672
Renegotiable interest rates   CC §1916.8
Repairs (See **REPAIRS**)
Reporting services, notice of unavailability   CRC 2.956
Rescission of contract   CC §1691
Retail installment sales contracts, notice of cosigner's liability on   CC §§1799.90 to 1799.96, 1803.2
Sale and leaseback, recordation of notice of   CC §3440
Sanctions for frivolous actions or delaying tactics, notice of motion for   CCP §§128.5, 128.7
Service of (See **SERVICE OF PAPERS**)
Simultaneous death, hearing as to   Pro §233
Sister state judgment, notice of entry of   CCP §1710.30
Slaughter
    Horses sold for slaughter for human consumption as felony, notices detailing   CC §1834.8
Small estates without administration (See **SMALL ESTATES WITHOUT ADMINISTRATION**)
Social services department (See **SOCIAL SERVICES DEPARTMENT**)
Spousal support proceedings (See **SPOUSAL SUPPORT**)
Stay of proceedings, notice of   CRC 3.650
Sterilization proceedings   Pro §1953
Stranger, giving notice of death of   Pro §7600.5
Strike, notice of motion to (See **MOTION TO STRIKE**)
Striking of pleadings, notice of motion   CRC 3.1322
Submitted matters, notice of determination   CCP §309, CRC 3.1109
Subordinate judicial officers, notice of action on complaints   CRC 10.703
Subpoena (See **SUBPOENA**)
Subpoena duces tecum (See **SUBPOENA DUCES TECUM**)
Substitution of attorney   CCP §284
Summary dissolution of marriage, revocation of petition for   Fam §2402
Summary judgment, notice of motion for   CCP §437c
Superior courts
    Generally (See **SUPERIOR COURTS**)
    Appellate rules (See **APPELLATE RULES, SUPERIOR COURT APPEALS**)
Support actions under Social Security Act Title IV-D   CRC 5.315
Sureties, notice for terminating liability of   CCP §§2819 to 2825
Tax liens by federal government   CC §2885, CCP §§2100 to 2107
    Fees for recording under act   Gov §27388.1
Telephone appearances, notice of intent   CRC 3.670
Time extension for service by mail   CCP §1013
Title IV-D support enforcement cases
    Tribal court
        Transfer of case to tribal court   CRC 5.372
Title of case   CCP §1046
Traffic regulations and violations (See **TRAFFIC REGULATIONS AND VIOLATIONS**)
Trial notice   CCP §594
Tribal court civil money judgment act
    Objections
        Grounds for objection   CCP §1737
Trust decanting, uniform act
    Exercise of decanting power
        Notice of intent to exercise   Pro §19507
    Representation
        Effect of notice   Pro §19508
Trust deeds (See **TRUST DEEDS AND MORTGAGES**)
Trusts (See **TRUSTS**)
Type size requirements   CCP §1019
Unconstitutionality of regulation, notice of judgment of   CRC 2.1100
Unlawful detainer (See **UNLAWFUL DETAINER**)
Voidable transactions   CC §1228
Warranties, notice of rights to independent dealers   CC §1793.3
Waters, appropriation of use of   CC §§1415, 1418
Will probate proceedings (See **WILL PROBATE**)
Witnesses
    Arrest of
        Failure to appear notice prior to warrant of arrest for failure to appear   CCP §1993
    Fees and mileage, notice of entitlement   CCP §2065
Workplace violence, protection orders   CCP §527.8
    COVID-19, emergency rule   CRCAppx I Emer Rule 8
    Requests for protective orders   CRC 3.1160
Writing requirements   CCP §1010

NOTICE TO QUIT   CCP §§1161 to 1162

NOVATION

Alteration of instruments affecting   CC §1698
Definition   CC §1530
New obligation created   CC §1531
Rescission   CC §1533
Rules governing   CC §1532

NOW ACCOUNTS

Escheat of   CCP §1513

NO WILL CONTEST CLAUSES (See **WILL PROBATE**)

NUISANCES

Generally   CC §3479
Abatement
    Past damages, effect of abatement on right to recover   CC §3484
    Private nuisances (See within this heading, **"Private nuisances"**)
    Public nuisances (See within this heading, **"Public nuisances"**)
    Standing to sue   CCP §731
    Substandard conditions of rental dwelling, order to landlord to abate nuisance or to repair   CC §1942.4
    Successive owners of property failing to abate continuing nuisance, liability of   CC §3483
    Weapons or ammunition unlawfully on real property   CC §3485
Agricultural activities and operations (See **FARMS AND FARMERS**)
Airport zones   CCP §§731a, 731b
Alcoholic liquor, attorney's fees recoverable for enjoining unlawful sales or distribution of   CC §3496
Animal fighting
    Dog or cock fighting, property used for   CC §3482.8
        Unlawful detainer   CCP §1161
Attorney's fees recoverable for enjoining public nuisances   CC §3496
Brokers
    Industrial use zoning, disclosure of nuisances caused by   CC §1102.17
Cockfighting, property used for   CC §3482.8
    Unlawful detainer   CCP §1161
Commercial zones   CCP §731a
Continuing nuisance, liability of successive landowner for   CC §3483
Controlled substances
    Definition of nuisance   CC §3479
    Injunction against using building for unlawful sale or distribution of controlled substances
        Attorney's fees recoverable in action for   CC §3496, CCP §917.8
    Unlawful detainer proceedings, nuisance committed by tenant as grounds for   CC §§3486, 3486.5, CCP §1161
Destruction of   CC §3492
Dog fighting, property used for   CC §3482.8
    Unlawful detainer   CCP §1161
Domestic violence
    Unlawful detainer proceedings, nuisance committed by tenant as grounds
        Presumption of nuisance   CCP §1161
Drugs (See within this heading, **"Controlled substances"**)
Farming operations (See **FARMS AND FARMERS**)
Floating home marinas, public nuisance where improper maintenance of common areas of   CC §800.201
Foreclosure
    Nuisance property
        Abatement assessment or lien, maximum amount   CC §2929.45
Gambling, attorney's fees recoverable for enjoining use of building for   CC §3496
Indictment or information for maintaining public nuisances   CC §§3491, 3492
Landlord and tenant
    Termination of tenancy
        Just cause for termination after year's continuous, lawful occupation   CC §1946.2
Lead paint abatement program, participation
    Not evidence that participating property is nuisance   CC §3494.5
Manufacturing zones   CCP §731a
Mobilehome parks, public nuisance where improper maintenance of   CC §798.87
Motion pictures depicting cruelty to animals and humans   CC §§3504 to 3508.2
Obscene matter as public nuisance, attorney's fees recoverable for enjoining commercial sale or distribution of   CC §3496
Pest control inspection report prior to transfer of title   CC §1099
Prescriptive right claims for existing nuisances   CC §3490
Private nuisances
    Abatement
        Generally   CC §3501
        Notice requirement   CC §3503

NUISANCES—Cont.
  Private nuisances—Cont.
    Abatement—Cont.
      Removal or destruction of nuisance, abatement by   CC §3502
        Standing to sue   CCP §731
    Agricultural activities (See **FARMS AND FARMERS**)
    Defined   CC §3481
  Private suits, complaints against public nuisances based on   CC §3493
  Prostitution, attorney's fees recoverable for enjoining use of building for   CC §3496
  Public nuisances
    Abatement
      Airports   CCP §§731a, 731b
      Private abatement   CC §3495
      Public abatement   CC §3494
      Standing to sue   CCP §731
    Agricultural activities (See **FARMS AND FARMERS**)
    Alcoholic liquor, enjoining unlawful sales or distribution of   CC §3496
    Controlled substances, enjoining use of building for unlawful sale or distribution of   CC §3496
    Defined   CC §3480
    Floating home marinas, public nuisance where improper maintenance of common areas of   CC §800.201
    Gambling, enjoining use of building for   CC §3496
    Human trafficking, enjoining use of building for   CC §3496
    Indictment or information maintaining   CC §§3491, 3492
    Lead paint abatement program, participation
      Not evidence that participating property is nuisance   CC §3494.5
    Mobilehome park, public nuisance where improper maintenance of   CC §798.87
    Obscene matter, action to enjoin commercial sale or distribution of   CC §3496
    Prescriptive right claims for existing nuisances   CC §3490
    Private suits, complaints against public nuisances based on   CC §3493
    Prostitution, enjoining use of building for   CC §3496
  Public trails, enjoining closure of   CCP §731.5
  Sexual assault
    Unlawful detainer proceedings, nuisance committed by tenant as grounds
      Presumption of nuisance   CCP §1161
  Shooting range exemption from liability for noise pollution   CC §3482.1
  Spite fences   CC §841.4
  Stalking
    Unlawful detainer proceedings, nuisance committed by tenant as grounds
      Presumption of nuisance   CCP §1161
  Statutes, exclusion of acts authorized by   CC §3482
  Substandard conditions of rental dwelling, order to landlord to abate nuisance or to repair   CC §1942.4
  Unlawful detainer proceedings, nuisance committed by tenant as grounds for   CCP §1161
    Controlled substances, illegal conduct involving   CC §§3486, 3486.5
    Weapons or ammunition unlawfully on real property as basis of nuisance   CC §3485
  Weapons as
    Illegal weapons or ammunition on real property   CC §3485

NULLITY OF MARRIAGE (See **ANNULMENT**)

NUMBERS AND NUMBERING
Jury (See **JURY**)
Small claims court (See **SMALL CLAIMS COURTS**)
Use in legal papers   CCP §186

NUNC PRO TUNC ENTRY
Dissolution of marriage judgments   Fam §2346
Lost or destroyed records   CCP §1046a

NURSES
Blood test technique of nurse as admissible evidence   Ev §712
Definitions   CC §1812.524
Immunity for action taken on recommendation of medical staff   CC §43.97
Malpractice (See **MALPRACTICE**)
Medical records, attorney's authorized inspection of   CCP §1985.7, Ev §1158
Psychotherapists, status of registered nurses as   Ev §1010
Registries
  Advertising by   CC §§1812.523, 1812.533
  Bonding requirements   CC §1812.525
  Contracts with private duty nurses   CC §1812.526
  Definitions   CC §1812.524
  Deposit in lieu of bond   CC §1812.525
  Fraud and misrepresentation, liability for   CC §§1812.523, 1812.533
  Log sheets and records, maintenance of   CC §1812.529

NURSES—Cont.
  Registries—Cont.
    Refund of fees   CC §§1812.523, 1812.532
    Restriction on fees   CC §1812.530
    Schedule of fees   CC §1812.527
    Service agreements, requirements of   CC §1812.526
    Splitting fees, prohibition against   CC §1812.531
    Verification of work experience and licensing of jobseeker by   CC §1812.528

NURSING HOMES
Death of patient as terminating contract with   CC §1934.5
Employment agencies, referrals from
  Advertisements, required recordkeeping of   CC §1812.544
  Certified nurse assistants, statement of qualifications of   CC §1812.541
  Complaint procedure for referrals from employment agencies   CC §1812.544
  Definitions   CC §1812.540
  Licensed nurses or psychiatric technicians, statement of qualifications of   CC §1812.542
  Prevention of patient abuse, policies and procedures of employment agency for   CC §1812.543
Ombudsman or advocate for patient in skilled nursing facility, Health Care Decisions Law provision for   Pro §4675
Public administrator of death of patient, notification of   Pro §7600.5
Sexual battery against incapacitated person
  Statute of limitations on sexual assault damages   CCP §340.16
Statutes of limitation for recovery or conversion of personal property left at   CCP §341a

O

OAKLAND, CITY OF
Unlawful detainer actions
  Controlled substances as nuisance
    Pilot program   CC §3486.5
  Firearms or weapons as nuisances
    Applicability of provisions   CC §3485

OAKLAND SPORTS AND MIXED USE PROJECT
Environmental quality act
  Petitions under environmental quality act, civil rules governing   CRC 3.2220 to 3.2240
Review of CEQA cases   CRC 8.700 to 8.705

OATHS
Generally   CCP §§2015.6, 2093 to 2094
Administrative Procedure Act (See **ADMINISTRATIVE PROCEDURE ACT**)
Administrators (See **EXECUTORS AND ADMINISTRATORS**)
Arbitration   CCP §1282.8
  Judicial arbitration   CRC 3.824
Attachment (See **ATTACHMENT**)
Claims and delivery possession writ, application for   CCP §512.010
County recorder's fees for administering or certifying   Gov §27379
Declaration or certification of written instrument executed under penalty of perjury   CCP §2015.5
Dependent persons   Ev §710
Depositions
  Oath of deponent   CCP §2025.330
Executors (See **EXECUTORS AND ADMINISTRATORS**)
Form of   CCP §2094
Inclusions in definition   CCP §17
Innkeeper's liens, writ of possession on   CC §1861.5
Judges
  Temporary judges   CRC 2.814
    Request by parties for temporary judge   CRC 2.831
Jurors, oath sworn by   CCP §232
Jury commissioner's power to administer   CCP §196
Manner of administering oath or affirmation   CCP §2094
Parties administering   CCP §2093
Penalty of perjury, declaration or certification of written instrument executed under   CCP §2015.5
Power of court to administer   CCP §128
Power of judge to administer   CCP §177
Proofs of execution of instruments, officers administering oaths for   CC §1201
Public guardians appointed as guardian or conservator, oaths required for   Pro §2922
Receivers, faithful performance of   CCP §567
Shorthand reporters at deposition proceedings, oaths administered by   CCP §2093
State agency proceedings (See **ADMINISTRATIVE PROCEDURE ACT**)

OATHS—Cont.
Statutory requirement   Ev §710
Temporary restraining order, certification of attempt to notify party of   CCP §527
Translators and interpreters in court proceedings   Ev §751
Witnesses   Ev §710

OATS
Storage regulations after sale of   CC §§1880 to 1881.2

OBJECTIONS AND EXCEPTIONS
Administrators of decedents' estates (See **EXECUTORS AND ADMINISTRATORS**)
Answers, objection to allegations in   CCP §430.20
Appealable orders deemed excepted to   CCP §647
Arbitration (See **ARBITRATION**)
Blood test, submission of evidence on technique of taking   Ev §712
Complaints, objection to allegations in   CCP §§430.10, 430.30
Conservatorship proceedings (See **CONSERVATORS**)
Court reporters to take down all objections and exceptions made   CCP §269
Cross-complaints, objection to allegations in   CCP §§430.10, 430.30
Demurrers (See **DEMURRERS**)
Economic litigation provision excluding evidence or witness not included in statement   CCP §97
Eminent domain, objections to right to take in   CCP §§1250.350 to 1250.370, 1260.110, 1260.120
Enforcement of judgments (See **ENFORCEMENT OF JUDGMENTS**)
Evidence erroneously admitted   Ev §353
Exception defined   CCP §646
Executors of decedents' estates (See **EXECUTORS AND ADMINISTRATORS**)
Guardian and ward (See **GUARDIAN AND WARD**)
Interlocutory orders deemed excepted to   CCP §647
Judges (See **JUDGES**)
Judicial arbitration, exceptions to   CCP §§1141.13, 1141.15
Jurisdiction, objection to   CCP §§418.10, 418.11
Orders and rulings, exceptions to   CCP §§646, 647
Pleadings, objections to   CCP §§430.10 to 430.80
Referee's statement of decision   CCP §645
Reversed without exceptions, orders and rulings   CCP §647
Sterilization proceedings, objections by party to be sterilized in   Pro §1958
Striking out or refusing to strike out pleading   CCP §647
Summary judgment hearing, waiver of objections not raised in   CCP §437c
Superior courts (See **SUPERIOR COURTS**)
Surety and fidelity bonds (See **SURETYSHIP, BONDS AND UNDERTAKINGS**)
Time to except   CCP §646
Verdicts deemed excepted to   CCP §647

OBLIGATIONS
Abstaining from injuring person or property of another   CC §1708
Civil actions, obligations as basis for   CCP §26

OBSCENITY AND INDECENCY (See **INDECENCY AND OBSCENITY**)

OCCUPANCY (See **ADVERSE POSSESSION**)

OCCUPATION
Jury service exemption not allowed based on   CCP §204

ODOMETERS
Vehicle history reports
  Contents   CC §1784.1

OFFAL (See **GARBAGE**)

OFFENSES (See **CRIMINAL ACTIONS AND PROCEEDINGS**)

OFFER
Contracts (See **CONTRACTS AND AGREEMENTS**)
Settlement offers (See **SETTLEMENT AND COMPROMISE**)
Tender, refused offer as   CCP §2074

OFFICE
Service of process at office of person being served   CCP §415.20

OFFICE OF ADMINISTRATIVE LAW (See **ADMINISTRATIVE PROCEDURE ACT**)

OFFICE OF INFORMATION PRACTICES (See **INFORMATION PRACTICES ACT**)

OFFICERS
Police officers (See **LAW ENFORCEMENT OFFICERS**)
Probation officers (See **PROBATION OFFICERS AND DEPUTIES**)
Public officers and employees (See **PUBLIC OFFICERS AND EMPLOYEES**)

OFFICIAL BONDS (See **BONDS OF PUBLIC OFFICIALS**)

OIL AND GAS
Administration of estates (See **ADMINISTRATION OF ESTATES**)
Discharge or leaking, absolute liability for damages caused by pipeline   CC §3333.5
Indemnity coverage for construction, repair, renovation, maintenance or demolition of lines   CC §2783
Injunctions, secondary recovery operations   CCP §731c
Liens
  Assignments of   CCP §1203.64
  Bonds for release of   CCP §1203.60
  Citation of statute   CCP §1203.50
  Drilling defined   CCP §1203.51
  Enforcement of   CCP §1203.61
  Forfeiture of leasehold estates   CCP §1203.55
  Labor liens, preference of   CCP §1203.57
  Notice of lien claims   CCP §1203.59
  Owner defined   CCP §1203.51
  Parties entitled to   CCP §1203.52
  Perfection of   CCP §1203.65
  Personal action for debt, right to   CCP §1203.62
  Priority   CCP §1203.56
  Record of   CCP §1203.58
  Services defined   CCP §1203.51
  Statutory construction   CCP §1203.66
  Subcontractor's liens   CCP §1203.54
  Time of   CCP §1203.53
  Waiver of   CCP §1203.63
Mineral rights (See **MINERALS AND MINERAL RIGHTS**)
Mobilehome park management, limitation on price of liquefied petroleum gas sold to mobilehome owners and park residents by   CC §798.44
Municipal land, leasing of   CC §§718, 718f
Partition action involving leases   CCP §872.540
Pipelines
  Discharge or leaking, absolute liability for damages caused by   CC §3333.5
  Indemnity coverage for construction, repair, renovation, maintenance or demolition of lines   CC §2783
Quieting title on lease   CCP §§772.010 to 772.060
Recordation
  Leases   CC §1219
  Liens   CC §1203.58
Restraints on alienation (See **PERPETUITIES AND RESTRAINTS ON ALIENATION**)
Right of entry, action to terminate   CCP §§772.010 to 772.060
Secondary oil recovery operations causing damages   CCP §731c
Termination of lease   CC §1952.4
Trust assets   Pro §16232
Unlawful detainer action brought by petroleum distributor against gasoline dealer   CCP §1174

OLD PERSONS (See **SENIOR CITIZENS**)

OLD TOWN CENTER TRANSIT AND TRANSPORTATION FACILITIES PROJECT
Environmental quality act
  Petitions under environmental quality act, civil rules governing   CRC 3.2220 to 3.2240
Review of CEQA cases   CRC 8.700 to 8.705

OMBUDSMAN
Health Care Decisions Law provision for ombudsman or advocate for patient in skilled nursing facility   Pro §4675

ONE YEAR (See **STATUTES OF LIMITATION**)

ONLINE ACCESS AND SERVICES
Privacy policies
  Consumer privacy rights
    Conflict with other provisions   CC §1798.175

ONLINE MARKETPLACES   CC §§1749.8 to 1749.8.9
Consumer products
  Defined   CC §1749.8
  Inapplicability of provisions to damages caused by product   CC §1749.8.5
Definitions   CC §1749.8

ONLINE MARKETPLACES—Cont.
High-volume third-party sellers
    Defined   CC §1749.8
    Information provided to online marketplace   CC §1749.8.1
        Gross revenue greater than certain amount, additional information and disclosure   CC §1749.8.2
        Redaction   CC §1749.8.3
        Retention   CC §1749.8.3
        Security   CC §1749.8.3
Suspension
    Failure to provide information   CC §§1749.8.1, 1749.8.2
Suspicious activity by seller
    Reporting mechanism   CC §1749.8.2
Reports regarding third-party sellers selling stolen goods   CC §1749.8.9
Verification
    Definition of verify   CC §1749.8.1
    High-volume third-party sellers
        Information provided to online marketplace   CC §1749.8.1
Violation of provisions
    Fines, penalties, etc   CC §1749.8.4

ONLINE VIOLENCE PREVENTION   CC §§1798.99.20 to 1798.99.23
Applicability of provisions
    Size of social media platform, applicability based on   CC §1798.99.23
Definitions   CC §1798.99.20
Violent posts
    Defined   CC §1798.99.20
    Removal
        Action to remove violent post   CC §1798.99.22
    Reporting mechanism   CC §1798.99.21

OOCYTES
Parent-child relationship, effect of donation of ova   Fam §7613

OPEN ACCOUNT (See ACCOUNTS AND ACCOUNTING)

OPEN-END CREDIT (See CREDIT CARDS)

OPENING DEFAULT (See DEFAULT JUDGMENTS)

OPEN MEETING LAWS
Agenda
    Judicial council
        Advisory body meetings   CRC 10.75
Closed sessions
    Judicial council
        Advisory body meetings   CRC 10.75
Judicial council
    Advisory body meetings   CRC 10.75
Notice of meeting
    Judicial council
        Advisory body meetings   CRC 10.75

OPEN-SPACE EASEMENTS
Greenway easements generally   CC §§816.50 to 816.66 (See GREENWAY EASEMENTS)
Property tax assessments
    Greenway easements as enforceable restriction   CC §816.66

OPEN SPACE LAND
Conservation easements for   CC §§815 to 816

OPERATION OF LAW
Civil actions, obligations arising from operation of law as basis for   CCP §26

OPHTHALMOLOGISTS
Immunity from liability
    Nonprofit charitable organization and volunteer eye care professionals donating screening, eyeglasses, etc   CC §1714.26

OPIATES (See NARCOTICS AND DANGEROUS DRUGS)

OPINION AND BELIEF
Challenge of juror for implied bias   CCP §229

OPINION EVIDENCE (See EXPERT AND OPINION EVIDENCE)

OPINIONS
Appellate opinions, publication   CRC 8.1100 to 8.1125 (See PUBLICATION OF OPINIONS)
Appellate rules, supreme court and courts of appeal
    Privacy in opinions
        Names, use in court opinions   CRC 8.90

OPINIONS—Cont.
Information Practices Act, personal opinion as basis for recovery under   CC §1798.50
Judicial ethics opinions   CRC 9.80
Referee, disqualification of   CCP §641

OPIOID OVERDOSES
Emergency medical care
    Naloxone hydrochloride
        Immunity for administering   CC §1714.22
Minors
    Consent to treatment for opioid use disorder   Fam §§6929, 6929.1

OPPOSING PARTIES (See ADVERSE PARTY)

OPTICIANS AND OPTOMETRISTS
Bond required to secure costs in action against   CCP §1029.6
Damages (See DAMAGES)
Malpractice (See MALPRACTICE)
Medical records, attorney's authorized inspection of   CCP §1985.7, Ev §1158
Review committees, liability of   CC §§43.7, 43.8
Vision screening
    Immunity from liability
        Nonprofit charitable organization and volunteer eye care professionals donating screening, eyeglasses, etc   CC §1714.26
Volunteers
    Immunity from liability
        Nonprofit charitable organization and volunteer eye care professionals donating screening, eyeglasses, etc   CC §1714.26

OPTIONS
Administration of decedents' estates, options rights subject to (See ADMINISTRATION OF ESTATES)
Eminent domain, option price of property taken by   Ev §822
Employee benefit plan including stock options   Fam §80
Home equity sales contracts, option to repurchase in (See HOME EQUITY SALES CONTRACTS)
Lien on property, priority of option where   CC §2906
Loans, extension of term of   CC §1916.5
Marketability of title (See TITLE AND OWNERSHIP)
Power of attorney, statutory form   Pro §4454
Title and ownership (See TITLE AND OWNERSHIP)
Trustee, exercise of options by   Pro §16233
Unexercised options (See TITLE AND OWNERSHIP)
Wills, enforcement of options granted by (See ADMINISTRATION OF ESTATES)

OPTOMETRISTS (See OPTICIANS AND OPTOMETRISTS)

ORAL COPULATION
Divorce
    Violent sexual felony by spouse against spouse
        Consequences in divorce proceedings   Fam §4324.5
Prisoners
    Offenses by
        Statute of limitations   CCP §340.16

ORANGE COUNTY
Appellate rules, supreme court and courts of appeal
    Juvenile case appeals   CRC 8.416

ORDERS
Administration of estates (See ADMINISTRATION OF ESTATES)
Administrative adjudicative proceedings (See ADMINISTRATIVE ADJUDICATION)
Adoption proceedings (See ADOPTION)
Appealable orders
    Extensions of time   CRC 8.108
Change of venue   CCP §399
    Time frames for transferring jurisdiction
        Family law actions or proceedings   CRC 5.97
Child support (See CHILD SUPPORT)
Claims against estates (See CLAIMS AGAINST ESTATES)
Computation of time
    Holidays (See HOLIDAYS)
    Limitation of actions (See STATUTES OF LIMITATION)
Conciliation Courts   Fam §1839
Conservators (See CONSERVATORS)
Contempt
    Show cause orders
        Dissolution of marriage   CRCAppx A (CRCFL-410)

ORDERS—Cont.
  Contempt—Cont.
    Show cause orders —Cont.
      Family law cases   CRCAppx A (CRCFL-410)
      Preliminary injunction, obtaining order by   CRC 3.1150
  Contempt for violation of requirements for subsequent application upon different state of facts   CCP §1008
  Coordination proceedings   CCP §404.4
    Grant or denial of coordination   CRC 3.529
    Stay orders, motions for   CRC 3.515
  Court's power to compel obedience to   CCP §128
  Custody of children (See **CUSTODY OF CHILDREN**)
  Defined   CCP §1003, Fam §100
  Dependent children   CRC 5.620
    Appeals from orders   CRC 5.585 to 5.595
    Approaching majority review hearings   CRC 5.707
    Court orders   CRC 5.695
    Modification of judgments and orders   CRC 5.560 to 5.580
    Restraining orders   CRC 5.534, 5.630
      Firearm relinquishment procedures   CRC 5.630
        Forms for firearm relinquishment   CRCAppx A
    Termination of jurisdiction   CRC 5.812
  DNA
    Genetic tests, juvenile court orders for   CRC 5.635
  Domestic violence (See **DOMESTIC VIOLENCE**)
  Domestic violence, restraining orders in dependency proceedings
    Firearm relinquishment   CRC 5.630
      Forms for firearm relinquishment   CRCAppx A
  Earnings assignment for support (See **EARNINGS ASSIGNMENT FOR SUPPORT**)
  Electronic filing and service
    Orders, judgments and other documents prepared by court   CRC 2.252
  Exceptions to orders and rulings   CCP §§646, 647
  Ex parte proceedings
    Local rules of court
      Preemption of local rules   CRC 3.20
  Extensions of time, orders for
    Trial court rules   CRC 2.20
  Family allowance (See **FAMILY ALLOWANCE**)
  Family centered case resolution orders   CRC 5.83
  Family reunification services, visitation orders   CRC 5.695
  Family rules
    Request for orders   CRC 5.90 to 5.130
      Emergency or ex parte orders   CRC 5.92, 5.151 to 5.170
    Sanctions   CRC 5.14
  Family support   Fam §4066
  Fire destroying   CCP §§1953 to 1953.06
  Genetic tests, juvenile court orders for   CRC 5.635
  Guardianship (See **GUARDIAN AND WARD**)
  Habeas corpus
    Order shortening or extending time   CRC 4.551
    Show cause order, issuance   CRC 4.551
  Harassment, civil proceedings
    Minor's information confidentiality, request in civil harassment proceedings
      Order on request   CRC 3.1161
        Release of minor's confidential information   CRC 3.1161
  Ignition interlock orders, guidelines   CRC 4.325
  Indigent parents, adult child's petition to be relieved of obligation to support   Fam §§4410 to 4414
  Injunctions (See **INJUNCTIONS**)
  Interlocutory orders
    Powers of judges   CCP §166.1
  Interstate family support   Fam §§5700.101 to 5700.903
  Judge's power to compel obedience to   CCP §177
  Judgment lien on property of misidentified owner, release of   CCP §§697.410, 697.660
  Judicial council, circulating orders   CRC 10.5
  Juvenile rules
    Termination of juvenile court jurisdiction
      Nonminor dependents or wards in foster care   CRC 5.555
  Juvenile wardship proceedings   CRC 5.625
    Disposition hearings, judgment and orders   CRC 5.790, 5.795
    Modification of orders   CRC 5.560 to 5.580
    Restraining orders   CRC 5.620, 5.625
    Sibling visitation   CRC 5.670
    Termination of jurisdiction   CRC 5.812
    Transfer hearings, findings and orders   CRC 5.770
    Visitation orders   CRC 5.670
  Minors, marriage of (See **MARRIAGE**)
  Minute orders, date of entry for appeal purposes   CRC 8.104

ORDERS—Cont.
  Money sanctions for violations of lawful court orders, requirements for order imposing   CCP §177.5
  Natural disaster destroying   CCP §§1953 to 1953.06
  Notice of determination   CRC 3.1109
  Notice of pendency, order expunging (See **PENDENCY OF ACTIONS**)
  Objections to orders and rulings   CCP §§646, 647
  Partition (See **PARTITION**)
  Presumption under   CCP §1909
  Proposed orders
    Electronic filing and service
      Orders, judgments and other documents prepared by court   CRC 2.252
    Electronic submission   CRC 3.1312
    Preparation by prevailing party   CRC 3.1312
  Protective orders (See **PROTECTIVE ORDERS**)
  Publication and depublication orders by Supreme Court   CRC 8.1105
  Reader privacy act
    Court order, required for disclosures   CC §1798.90
  Reconsideration of order   CCP §1008
  Refereed juvenile court proceedings   CRC 5.540
  Restraining orders
    Family rules
      Individual restraining order   CRC 5.50
      Request for individual restraining order   CRC 5.91
      Standard family law restraining order   CRC 5.50
      Judicial Council form   CRCAppx A (CRCFL-305)
      Requirements in certain cases   CRC 3.1151
      Temporary restraining order   CRCAppx A (CRCFL-305)
  Revocation of order made on subsequent application   CCP §1008
  Sales, order of
    Superior court fees, specified services   Gov §70626
  Show cause orders (See **SHOW CAUSE ORDERS**)
  Simultaneous death, order establishing   Pro §234
  Small claims courts
    Requests for court order   CRC 3.2107
  Small estates without administration (See **SMALL ESTATES WITHOUT ADMINISTRATION**)
  Spousal support (See **SPOUSAL SUPPORT**)
  State bar court, effective date of orders   CRC 9.18
  Sterilization proceedings (See **STERILIZATION**)
  Subsequent application upon alleged different state of facts   CCP §1008
  Superior courts (See **SUPERIOR COURTS**)
  Surety bond, order for waiver of   CCP §995.240
  Telegraph, execution of orders transmitted by   CCP §1017
  Temporary restraining orders
    Form   CRCAppx A (CRCFL-305)
    Injunctions generally (See **INJUNCTIONS**)
    Order to show cause, use of   CRC 3.1150
  Termination of parental rights   CRC 5.725
  Trial, orders during (See **TRIAL**)
  Trusts (See **TRUSTS**)
  Vacation of orders made on subsequent application   CCP §1008
  Venue in criminal proceedings
    Change of venue
      Order upon change   CRC 4.153
  Vexatious litigant prohibited from filing new litigation   CCP §391.7
    Vacating prefiling order and removing name from list   CCP §391.8
  Will probate proceedings (See **WILL PROBATE**)

ORDER TO APPEAR
Small claims court   CCP §116.330

ORDER TO SHOW CAUSE
Application for order   CRC 3.1150
CARE act rules
  Accountability hearing   CRC 7.2301
  Joinder of local government entity   CRC 7.2240
Contempt
  Dissolution of marriage   CRCAppx A (CRCFL-410)
  Family law cases   CRCAppx A (CRCFL-410)
  Preliminary injunction, obtaining order by   CRC 3.1150
Family law cases   CRCAppx A (CRCFL-410)
  Contempt   CRCAppx A (CRCFL-410)
  Forms   CRCAppxs A (CRCFL-300), (CRCFL-410), (CRCFL-575)
Habeas corpus   CRC 4.551
Interstate family support act
  Form   CRCFL-515
Preliminary injunction, obtaining OTC by   CRC 3.1150
Temporary restraining order
  Application for show cause order   CRC 3.1150

ORDER TO SHOW CAUSE—Cont.
Temporary restraining order—Cont.
 Use CRC 3.1150

ORDINANCES
Advertising realty for sale, restrictions on CC §713
Equal protection
 Political structure equal protection CC §53.7
Human trafficking or slavery
 Effect of local ordinances preventing CC §52.6
Leases of city property subject to CC §719
Lost property, providing for disposition of CC §2080.4
Pleading CCP §459
Political structure equal protection CC §53.7
Rent control ordinances (See **RENT CONTROL**)

ORGANIZATIONS AND CLUBS (See **ASSOCIATIONS**)

ORIENTATION
Juror orientation CCP §214

ORIGINAL PROCEEDINGS IN APPELLATE COURTS
Habeas corpus CRC 8.380 to 8.398
Mandate, certiorari and prohibition in supreme court or court of appeal CRC 8.485 to 8.493
 Environmental quality act cases under public resources code CRC 8.703

ORIGINAL WRIT (See **ATTACHMENT**)

ORNAMENTS
Fixtures removable CC §1019

ORPHANS
Abandoned children (See **PARENT AND CHILD**)
Adoption (See **ADOPTION**)

OSTEOPATHS
Bond required to secure costs in action against CCP §1029.6
Malpractice (See **MALPRACTICE**)
Mandamus for review of administrative order of agency issuing licenses CCP §1094.5
Medical records, attorney's authorized inspection of CCP §1985.7, Ev §1158

OTHER STATES
Abortion laws of other states
 Confidentiality of medical information
  Restrictions on release of medical information related to abortion CC §§56.108, 56.110
 Legally protected health care services
  Foreign jurisdictions, interference with rights CC §1798.302
  Jurisdiction over state resident in out-of-state forum CC §1798.308
Acknowledgment of instruments CC §§1182, 1189
Adoption (See **ADOPTION**)
Affidavits taking in CCP §§2013, 2015
Ancillary administration (See **ANCILLARY ADMINISTRATION**)
Attachment (See **ATTACHMENT**)
Attorney professional conduct
 Multijurisdictional practice of law ProfC 5.5
Attorneys (See **ATTORNEYS**)
Certification of state-law questions to California Supreme Court by courts of last resort in other states and territories CRC 8.548
Community property (See **COMMUNITY PROPERTY**)
Conflict of laws (See **CONFLICT OF LAWS**)
Conservators
 Interstate jurisdiction, transfer and recognition Pro §§1980 to 2033
  Judicial council legal forms CRCAppx A
Conservatorship proceedings (See **CONSERVATORS**)
Cum testamento annexo (See **ADMINISTRATORS WITH WILL ANNEXED**)
Custody proceedings (See **CUSTODY OF CHILDREN**)
Declaration or certification of written instrument executed under penalty of perjury CCP §2015.5
Depositions
 Generally (See **DEPOSITIONS**)
 Interstate and international depositions and discovery act CCP §§2029.100 to 2029.900 (See **DISCOVERY**)
Discovery
 Interstate and international depositions and discovery act CCP §§2029.100 to 2029.900 (See **DISCOVERY**)
Divorce obtained in other state by parties domiciled in California Fam §§2090 to 2093

OTHER STATES—Cont.
Domestic partnership
 Legal unions formed in other jurisdiction
  Recognition of legal unions as domestic partnership Fam §299.2
Earnings assignments for support (See **EARNINGS ASSIGNMENT FOR SUPPORT**)
Escheat of property subject to CCP §1504
Gender-affirming health care or mental health care
 Legally protected health care services
  Foreign jurisdictions, interference with rights CC §1798.302
  Jurisdiction over state resident in out-of-state forum CC §1798.308
 Medical information confidentiality
  Restrictions on release of medical information CC §56.109
Inconvenient forum as grounds for stay or dismissal of action CCP §§410.30, 418.10
Injunctions staying proceedings in CCP §526
Interstate compact on placement of children CRC 5.616, Fam §§7900 to 7913
 Children covered by compact Fam §7907.5
 Home environment study request from another state Fam §7901.1
  Custody of child in requesting state Fam §7906.5
Judgments (See **FOREIGN JUDGMENTS**)
Limitation of actions
 Lapse of time for bringing action under laws of state where action has arisen, effect CCP §361
 Upon judgment or decree of court of sister state CCP §337.5
Marriages, validity of foreign Fam §308
 Same sex marriages
  Dissolution, annulment or legal separation of recognized same sex marriages, jurisdiction Fam §§2010, 2320
Nonresidents (See **NONRESIDENTS**)
Paternity determinations (See **PATERNITY**)
Penalty of perjury, declaration or certification of written instrument executed under CCP §2015.5
Power of attorney (See **POWER OF ATTORNEY**)
Process, service of (See **PROCESS AND SERVICE OF PROCESS**)
Retail installment sales contracts CC §1802.19
Sentence running consecutively or concurrently with sentence imposed in CRC 4.451
Service of process (See **PROCESS AND SERVICE OF PROCESS**)
Statutes of limitation
 Lapse of time for bringing action under laws of state where action has arisen, effect of CCP §361
 Upon judgment or decree of court of sister state CCP §337.5
Stay or dismissal, inconvenient forum as grounds for CCP §§410.30, 418.10
Trusts (See **TRUSTS**)
Unclaimed property (See **UNCLAIMED PROPERTY**)
Uniform Divorce Recognition Act Fam §§2090 to 2093
Witnesses (See **WITNESSES**)

OUSTER
Cotenant's right to establish CC §843

OUTPATIENT SETTINGS
Medical claims data error correction CC §57

OVA
Unauthorized use or misuse of sperm, ova or embryo
 Civil action for damages CC §1708.5.6

OVERDOSES
Minors
 Consent to treatment for opioid use disorder Fam §§6929, 6929.1

OWNERSHIP (See **TITLE AND OWNERSHIP**)

P

PACIFIC GAS AND ELECTRIC COMPANY
Eminent domain action by Golden State Energy for acquisition of PG&E property CCP §1240.655
Receivership CCP §568.6

PAIN AND SUFFERING
Assignment for benefit of creditors, compensatory payments exempt from CCP §1801
Damages for pain and suffering CC §3333.2
 Voir dire examination re CRC JudAdminStand 3.25
Rape by threat to inflict
 Statute of limitations
  Civil damages CCP §340.16

PAIN AND SUFFERING—Cont.
  Sodomy, force by threat to inflict
    Statute of limitations
      Civil damages   CCP §340.16

PAINT
  Aerosol containers
    Verification of age for sale of age-restricted products   CC §1798.99.1
  Lead paint abatement
    Nuisances
      Participating properties in abatement program not considered nuisances   CC §3494.5
    Participating properties in abatement program
      Immunity from liability   CC §3494.5
      Not considered nuisances   CC §3494.5
      Not considered substandard building   CC §3494.5
      Not considered untenantable   CC §3494.5

PAINTINGS
  Commissions for sale of   CC §986
  Infringement, action for   CCP §429.30

PANAMA CANAL ZONE
  Acknowledgment of instruments   CC §1183.5

PANDEMICS
  COVID-19 (See **COVID-19**)

PANELS
  Juror panels (See **JURY**)

PAPARAZZI
  Invasion of privacy to capture visual image or sound recording   CC §1708.8

PAPERS (See **DOCUMENTS AND PAPERS**)

PARACHUTING
  Owner's liability for recreational use of land for   CC §846

PARADES (See **DEMONSTRATIONS, PARADES AND MEETINGS**)

PARALEGALS
  Small claims courts, assisting litigants in   CCP §116.940, CRC 3.2120

PARAMEDICS
  Contempt orders, stay of execution of   CCP §128

PARAPHERNALIA
  Drug use, paraphernalia for
    Sale
      Verification of age for sale of age-restricted products   CC §1798.99.1
  Tobacco and tobacco products
    Sales to persons under 21
      Verification of age for sale of age-restricted products   CC §1798.99.1

PARDONS
  Credibility attack for prior conviction, pardon affecting right of   Ev §788
  Statute of limitations
    Felony offenses, damage actions based on commission of   CCP §340.3

PARENTAGE
  Paternity generally (See **PATERNITY**)
  Uniform parentage act generally   Fam §§7600 to 7730 (See **UNIFORM PARENTAGE ACT**)

PARENT AND CHILD   Fam §§7540 to 7581 (See also **MINORS**)
  Abandonment
    Generally   Fam §3010
    Adult child's duty to support parent relieved by   Fam §§4410 to 4414
    Indian children, transfer by parent of care, custody and control to Indian custodian as not constituting abandonment   Fam §7822
    Intestate succession
      Desertion with intent to abandon as situation preventing inheritance by parent   Pro §6452
    Relief from duty to support parent who abandoned child   Fam §§4410 to 4414
    Relinquishment of control and earnings of child, abandonment as   Fam §7504
    Termination of parental rights
      Circumstances where proceedings may be brought   Fam §7822
  Abortion performed on minor child   Fam §6925
  Abuse of child (See **CHILD ABUSE**)

PARENT AND CHILD—Cont.
  Administrator, priority for serving as   Pro §8461
  Adoption
    Generally (See **ADOPTION**)
    Termination of parental rights by   Fam §§7660 to 7671
  Adult child supported by parent, right to compensation when   Fam §7506
  Age of majority, effect on parental authority on reaching   Fam §7505
  Alcoholic beverages
    Social host liability for furnishing to person under 21   CC §1714
  Artificial insemination, parentage of child conceived by
    Forms for assisted reproduction   Fam §7613.5
  Authority over child, termination of   Fam §7505
  Bible entries as evidence of parent-child relationship   Ev §1312
  Breast-feeding in public
    Jury service, deferral from   CCP §210.5, CRC 2.1006
    Right to breastfeed in public and private places where mother and child are otherwise authorized to be present   CC §43.3
  Challenge of juror for implied bias, relationships giving rise to   CCP §229
  Child care (See **CHILD CARE**)
  Children born out of wedlock
    Action for injury to child, parent maintaining   CCP §376
    Paternity generally (See **PATERNITY**)
  Child support (See **CHILD SUPPORT**)
  Church records as evidence of parent-child relationship   Ev §1315
  Compromise of minor's claims (See **MINORS**)
  Contracts
    Consent of parent or guardian
      Minor's representation that parent or guardian has consented not considered consent   CC §1568.5
  Cruelly treated child, proceeding to free child from parental custody and control   Fam §7823
  Custody of children (See **CUSTODY OF CHILDREN**)
  De facto parents, participation in juvenile court proceedings   CRC 5.534
    Definition of de facto parent   CRC 5.502
  Definitions
    Child   Pro §26
    Parent   Fam §6903, Pro §54
    Parent and child relationship   Fam §7601
  Department of child support services   Fam §§17000 to 17325
  Descent and distribution, determining parent-child relationship for purpose of   Pro §§6450 to 6455
  Earnings of child
    Characterization of property of spouses living separate and apart   Fam §771
    Child stars, trust funds for earnings of   Fam §§6752, 6753
    Court order to set aside net earnings of minor in trust fund or savings plan   Fam §§6752, 6753
    Deposit of   Fam §§6752, 6753
    Emancipated minors   Fam §7050
    Extras, background performers, etc.
      Trusts for percentage of earnings, exceptions to requirements   Fam §6752
    Parents' right to   Fam §7500
    Payment of earnings directly to minor   Fam §7503
    Relinquishment by parent of control of   Fam §7504
    Unmarried minor child, parent's right to earnings of   Fam §3010
  Education
    Generally (See **EDUCATION**)
  Educational rights holder for special education programs
    Appointment   CRC 5.534, 5.650
    Definition of educational rights holder   CRC 5.502
    Educational and developmental services decisionmaking rights of children   CRC 5.651
    Identification of holder   CRC 5.649
    Orders concerning rights holder and educational decisionmaking   CRC 5.649
    Qualifications   CRC 5.650
    Training   CRC 5.650
    Transfer of parent or guardian's educational rights to rights holder   CRC 5.650
  Emancipation of child (See **EMANCIPATION OF MINORS**)
  Enticement   CC §49
  Establishment of parent-child relationship
    Generally   Fam §7610
    Definitions   Fam §7601
    Evidence of parent-child relationship   Ev §§1310 to 1316
    Intestate succession, establishment for purpose of   Pro §§6450 to 6455
    Marital status of parents   Fam §7602
    Paternity (See **PATERNITY**)
  Estate of minors
    Small estates (See within this heading, **"Small estate of minors"**)

PARENT AND CHILD—Cont.
  Evidence of parent-child relationship, admissibility of   Ev §§1310 to 1316
  Family friends, statements concerning parent-child relationship by   Ev §1311
  Firearms, parental liability for child discharging   CC §1714.3
  Fitness of parent (See **CUSTODY OF CHILDREN**)
  Foster care
    Alienation of affection, action against foster parent   CC §43.56
    At risk of entering defined   CRC 5.502
  Freedom from parental custody, proceedings for (See **TERMINATION OF PARENTAL RIGHTS**)
  Genetic defects, cause of action for   CC §43.6
  Gifts to minors (See **UNIFORM TRANSFERS TO MINORS ACT**)
  Guardianship, effect of   Fam §7505
  Hearsay evidence of parent-child relationship, admissibility of   Ev §§1310 to 1316
  Heirs (See **HEIRS**)
  Illegitimate children
    Action for injury to child, parent maintaining   CCP §376
    Paternity generally (See **PATERNITY**)
  Indian children (See **NATIVE AMERICANS**)
  Indigent parents, support of   Fam §§4400 to 4414
  Injury to child, parents maintaining action for   CCP §376
  Interstate family support   Fam §§5700.101 to 5700.903 (See **INTERSTATE FAMILY SUPPORT**)
  Intestate succession
    Parent inheriting from child based on relationship
      Situations preventing inheritance   Pro §6452
  Intestate succession, determining parent-child relationship for purpose of   Pro §§6450 to 6455
  Judgments in favor of minors, disposition of payments pursuant to   Pro §§3600 to 3613
    Attorneys' fees for services to minors and persons with disability   CRC 7.955
    Trusts, payment into   CRC JudAdminStand 7.10
  Jury service, deferral for breastfeeding mother from   CCP §210.5, CRC 2.1006
  Juvenile rules, definitions   CRC 5.502
  Legitimacy
    Establishment of relationship generally (See within this heading, "**Establishment of parent-child relationship**")
    Paternity generally (See **PATERNITY**)
  Limitations on parental control
    Juvenile court proceedings   CRC 5.695, 5.790
  Marital status of parent, relationship not dependent on   Fam §7602
  Marriage of minor (See **MARRIAGE**)
  Medical treatment of minors   Fam §§6900 to 6930 (See **MINORS**)
  Military service, effect of   Fam §§6950, 7002
  Missing child   Fam §§3140, 7603
  Money or property belonging to minor
    Compromise and settlement of minor's claims (See **MINORS**)
    Parent's control over   Fam §§7502 to 7504
    Small estates (See within this heading, "**Small estate of minors**")
  More than 2 parents
    Court may find more than 2 persons with claim to parentage   Fam §7612
    Parent and child relationship   Fam §7601
  Natural parents
    Adoption (See **ADOPTION**)
    Defined   Fam §7601
    Establishing natural parent and child relationship   Fam §7610
    Presumption of parentage   Fam §7611
    Uniform Parentage Act (See **UNIFORM PARENTAGE ACT**)
  Neglected child, proceeding to free child from parental custody and control   Fam §7823
  Negligence
    Tort liability generally (See within this heading, "**Tort liability**")
  Paternity (See **PATERNITY**)
  Posthumous children (See **POSTHUMOUS CHILDREN**)
  Pre-employment physical, disclosure of information from   CC §56.10
  Prisoners (See **PRISONERS**)
  Probate proceedings
    Compromise of minor's claim by parent
      Attorneys' fees for services to minors and incompetent persons   CRC 7.955
      Hearings on petition for compromise   Pro §3505
      Trusts, payment into   CRC JudAdminStand 7.10
    Judgments in favor of minors, disposition of payments pursuant to
      Attorneys' fees for services to minors and persons with disability   CRC 7.955
      Trusts, payment into   CRC JudAdminStand 7.10
  Property
    Compromise and settlement of minor's claims (See **MINORS**)

PARENT AND CHILD—Cont.
  Property—Cont.
    Parental control   Fam §§7502 to 7504
    Small estates of minors (See within this heading, "**Small estate of minors**")
  Protection of family   CC §50
  Relative's statements concerning parent-child relationship, admissibility of   Ev §1311
  Removal of child from home
    Family finding and notice performed by social worker or probation officer   CRC 5.637
  Reputation among family members concerning parent-child relationship, admissibility of   Ev §1313
  Residence of child, parents' right to change   Fam §7501
  Rights of parents   Fam §§7500 to 7507
  Service of child, parents' right to   Fam §7500
  Service of process
    Injured child's parent not joined as plaintiff, service of summons on   CCP §376
    Service on minor, generally   CCP §416.60
  Settlement of disputed claims of minor
    Compromise (See **MINORS**)
  Small estate of minors
    Generally   Pro §3410
    Accounting of minor's property by parent   Pro §3300
    Appointment of guardian of estate, order for   Pro §3413
    Delivery to parent of money or property belonging to minor, requirements for   Pro §§3401, 3402
    Disposition of funds   Pro §3413
    Petition for instructions   Pro §3411
    Termination of guardianship of estate, order for   Pro §3412
    Total estate of minor defined   Pro §3400
  Special needs trusts (See **SPECIAL NEEDS TRUSTS**)
  Suitability of parent (See **CUSTODY OF CHILDREN**)
  Support
    Abandonment of child, relief from duty to support parent where   Fam §§4410 to 4414
    Child support (See **CHILD SUPPORT**)
    Indigent parents, adult child to support   Fam §§4400 to 4414
  Surrogacy or donor facilitators   Fam §§7960, 7961
  Surrogate parents for special education programs
    Juvenile court proceedings   CRC 5.650
  Termination of parental authority
    Generally   Fam §§7505, 7800 to 7895 (See **TERMINATION OF PARENTAL RIGHTS**)
    Adoption proceedings (See **ADOPTION**)
    Emancipation of children (See **EMANCIPATION OF MINORS**)
    Indian children   Fam §7892.5
    Small estate of minor, order of termination of guardianship of   Pro §3412
  Tort liability
    Generally   Fam §§6600 to 6602
    Emancipated child   Fam §7050
    Imputed liability for willful misconduct of minor   CC §1714.1, CRCAppx B
    Limits of parent or guardian   CRCAppx B
    Weapons fired by minor   CC §1714.3
  Transfers to minors (See **UNIFORM TRANSFERS TO MINORS ACT**)
  Trust funds for child stars   Fam §§6752, 6753
    Extras, background performers, etc
      Trusts for percentage of earnings, exceptions to requirements   Fam §6752
  Uniform Parentage Act (See **UNIFORM PARENTAGE ACT**)
  Uniform Transfers to Minors Act (See **UNIFORM TRANSFERS TO MINORS ACT**)
  Violent video games
    Reporting violations by parent, guardian, etc   CC §1746.4
  Visitation rights
    Supervised visitation
      Administration of programs   Fam §3201.5
      Compliance with provisions   Fam §3202
      Declaration of provider, form   CRCAppx A
      Family law division, administration of programs and counseling   Fam §3203
      Grant funds, administration   Fam §3204
      Providers, standards   Fam §3200.5
      Superior courts as supervised visitation and exchange locations   Fam §3200
    Virtual visitation, presence of third person   Fam §3100
  Weapons, parental liability for child discharging   CC §1714.3
  Wrongful life, cause of action against parent for   CC §43.6

PARENT LOCATOR SERVICE AND CENTRAL REGISTRY   Fam §17506

PARENT LOCATOR SERVICES Fam §5280

PARENT'S ACCOUNTABILITY AND CHILD PROTECTION ACT CC §1798.99.1

PARKING FACILITIES
Contracts for parking motor vehicles CC §§1630, 1630.5
Indemnity coverage for construction of CC §2783
Keys left in stolen vehicle, liability affected by CC §1630.5
Landlord and tenant
    Rent, unbundling parking from price of CC §1947.1
Liens CC §§3067 to 3074
Limitation on liability CC §1630
Mobilehome parks (See **MOBILEHOMES**)
Shared mobility devices
    Agreements with or permits from local government CC §2505

PARKS AND PLAYGROUNDS
Blind persons having equal rights for use of CC §§54.1, 54.3, 54.4, 55
    Construction or application of provisions in issue, solicitor general notified CC §55.2
Caves (See **CAVES**)
Disabled persons having equal rights for use of CC §§54.1, 54.3, 54.4, 55
    Construction or application of provisions in issue, solicitor general notified CC §55.2
Eminent domain (See **EMINENT DOMAIN**)
Fines and penalties
    Bail schedule CRC 4.102
Guide dogs permitted in CC §§54.2, 54.3, 54.7
    Construction or application of provisions in issue, solicitor general notified CC §55.2
Leasing limitations CC §718
Mobilehome park (See **MOBILEHOMES**)
National parks, appropriation of water originating in CC §1422
Trailer courts (See **MOBILEHOMES**)

PARKS AND RECREATION DEPARTMENT
Unclaimed deposits and payments escheated CCP §1567

PAROLE
Aggravation, circumstance in CRC 4.421
Judges, ethics
    Communications concerning parole CRCSupp JudEthicsCanon 2
Juvenile offenders
    Dangerous persons, extended detention by juvenile facilities
        Appeal from order of civil commitment CRC 8.483
    Extended detention of dangerous persons
        Appeal from order of civil commitment CRC 8.483
Name-change restrictions CCP §1279.5
Notice
    Release, notice of
        Name change proceedings under address confidentiality program CRC 2.575 to 2.577
Postrelease community supervision
    Revocation procedure
        Supervising agency reports as to compliance with provisions CRC 4.541
Public entity's liability for injury resulting from parole determinations Gov §§845.8, 856
Stalking offenders
    Name change proceedings under address confidentiality program CRC 2.575 to 2.577
Statute of limitations
    Felony offenses, damage actions based on commission of CCP §340.3

PAROL EVIDENCE
Generally CCP §1856
Best and secondary evidence (See **BEST AND SECONDARY EVIDENCE**)
Business records (See **BUSINESS RECORDS**)
Inconsistent statements Ev §770
Statute of frauds (See **STATUTE OF FRAUDS**)
Surrounding circumstances, proof of CCP §§1856, 1860
Technical meaning of words used, proof of CCP §1861
Validity of contracts CC §§1622, 1697

PARTIAL TAKING (See **EMINENT DOMAIN**)

PARTICULAR PERSONS, JURISDICTION OVER (See **JURISDICTION**)

PARTIES
Address change
    Service and filing notice
        Trial court rules CRC 2.200
Administration of decedents' estates (See **ADMINISTRATION OF ESTATES**)
Adverse parties (See **ADVERSE PARTY**)

PARTIES—Cont.
Affidavits CCP §§2012 to 2015.5
Aiding and abetting
    Rape, punishment for aiding in
        Statute of limitations on sexual assault damages CCP §340.16
Appeals
    Definition of party CRC 8.10
    Electronic court records, public access
        Party access CRC 8.81
    Extension of time
        Notice to party of extension of time CRC 8.60
    Substitution of party CRC 8.36
    Superior court appeals
        Address and telephone number of record CRC 8.816
        Substitution of party CRC 8.814
Assignees, action by CCP §368
Assignments (See **ASSIGNMENTS**)
Bad faith actions, assessment of expenses and attorney's fees incurred as result of (See **SANCTIONS**)
Challenge of juror for implied bias, relationships giving rise to CCP §229
Class actions CCP §382
Complaint, names in CCP §422.40
Contracts (See **CONTRACTS AND AGREEMENTS**)
Control of action, judgment binding parties having CCP §1908
Convenience of (See **CONVENIENCE**)
Coordination of actions, request by all parties for CCP §404
Covenants binding CC §1465
Credit reports, parties entitled to CC §§1785.11, 1785.12
Deceased persons, bringing action for or against (See **SURVIVAL OF ACTIONS**)
Defendant (See **DEFENDANT**)
Delaying tactics, assessment of expenses and attorney's fees incurred as result of (See **SANCTIONS**)
Delay or undue expense, court may make orders to prevent CCP §379.5
Deposition proceedings (See **DEPOSITIONS**)
Designation of parties CCP §308
Disability of party during pending action or proceeding, effect of CCP §375
Disclosure, claiming privilege of Ev §§911 to 916
Disqualification of judges, grounds for CCP §170.1
Electronic court records
    Access by attorneys and parties CRC 2.501
    Remote access
        Parties, designees, attorneys, court-appointed persons or persons working in legal organization or qualified legal services project, access by CRC 2.515 to 2.528
Electronic filing and service
    Service by parties CRC 2.251
Embarrassment, delay or undue expense, court may make orders to prevent CCP §379.5
Eminent domain action CCP §§1250.210 to 1250.240
Executors and administrators CCP §369
Family rules
    Causes of action or claims for relief which may be asserted CRC 5.17
    Designation CRC 5.16
        Interstate and intrastate cases CRC 5.370
        Title IV-D support enforcement CRC 5.370
    Dissolution, legal separation or nullity
        Husband and wife or domestic partners as parties CRC 5.16
    Emergency or ex parte orders, requests
        Notice of emergency hearing CRC 5.165
    Joinder of parties CRC 5.24, 5.29
        Employee benefit plans, joinder as prerequisite to separate trial of termination of marriage or domestic partnership, joinder as prerequisite CRC 5.390
Firearms and other weapons
    Actions to prevent enforcement of laws
        Recovery of attorney fees CCP §1021.11
Frivolous actions, assessment of expenses and attorney's fees incurred as result of (See **SANCTIONS**)
Guardian ad litem CCP §§372 to 373.5
Guardian and ward (See **GUARDIAN AND WARD**)
Information Practices Act, parties receiving information under CC §1798.24
Interpleader (See **INTERPLEADER**)
Intervention CCP §387
Joinder of parties (See **JOINDER OF PARTIES**)
Judgments determining inter se rights of CCP §§578, 579
Jurisdiction (See **JURISDICTION**)
Legislative continuance CCP §595
List of parties and addresses CRC 3.254
Married persons CCP §370
Missing persons (See **MISSING PERSONS**)
Nonresidents (See **NONRESIDENTS**)

PARTIES—Cont.
Notice
    Served on   CCP §1011
Notice to produce
    Limitation on papers filed   CRC 3.250
Oil and gas liens, right to   CCP §1203.52
Parentage
    Actions to determine parent and child relationship   Fam §7635
Parents maintaining action for injury of child   CCP §376
Partition (See **PARTITION**)
Plaintiffs (See **PLAINTIFFS**)
Probate rules
    Ex parte communications
        Prohibition on communications   CRC 7.10
Protected persons
    Confidentiality requirements for protected party in civil proceeding   CCP §367.3
        Judicial council forms   CRCAppx A
Quieting title action   CCP §§762.010 to 762.090
Real party in interest, action prosecuted in name of   CCP §367
Revocation of letters of administration   Pro §8500
Settlements
    Waiver in contract or settlement of right to testify concerning criminal conduct or sexual harassment   CC §1670.11
Small claims court (See **SMALL CLAIMS COURTS**)
Sodomy
    Force, violence, etc, to commit sodomy
        Statute of limitations for sexual assault damages   CCP §340.16
Special administrator maintaining actions for estate   Pro §8544
Specific performance decree, parties bound by   CC §3395
Substitution of parties
    Appeal, substitution on   CRC 8.36
    Disability of party during pending action or proceeding   CCP §375
    Transfer of interests, substitution of successor in interest as party in action where   CCP §368.5
Successor in interest as party in action, standing of (See **SUCCESSOR IN INTEREST**)
Survival of actions (See **SURVIVAL OF ACTIONS**)
Transfer of interests, continuance of action by original party or by successor in interest where   CCP §368.5
Trustees   CCP §369
Unborn or unascertained persons   CCP §373.5
Undue expense, court may make orders to prevent   CCP §379.5
Unknown parties (See **UNKNOWN PERSONS**)
Unlawful detainer proceedings   CCP §§1164, 1165
Unwilling plaintiff made defendant   CCP §382
Vexatious litigants   CCP §§391 to 391.8 (See **VEXATIOUS LITIGANTS**)
Voidable marriage, proceeding for nullity of   Fam §2211
Will probate (See **WILL PROBATE**)
Wrongful death actions   CCP §377.60

PARTITION
Administration of estates (See **ADMINISTRATION OF ESTATES**)
Answer   CCP §§872.410 to 872.430
Appraisal, partition by   CCP §§873.910 to 873.980
Attorneys
    Fees (See within this heading, **"Attorney's fees"**)
    Purchasers, attorneys as   CCP §873.690
    Referees making contracts with   CCP §§873.110, 873.120, 873.150
    Sale notice, inspection of   CCP §873.650
Attorney's fees
    Allowance and apportionment of costs   CCP §§874.010 to 874.050
    Payment of costs   CCP §§874.110 to 874.130
    Resale of property, action involving   CCP §873.760
Auctions
    Determination of type of sale   CCP §§873.520, 873.530
    Location of   CCP §873.670
    Referees making contracts for   CCP §§873.110, 873.140
Civil actions generally, applicability of statutes and rules governing practice in   CCP §872.030
Commercial and industrial common interest developments
    Common areas
        Prohibition on partition   CC §6656
    Entire project   CC §6656
Common interest developments
    Condominiums
        Transfer restrictions   CC §4600
Complaint
    Contents   CCP §872.230
    Death of party, complaint stating   CCP §872.530
    Joinder of all parties claiming interest   CCP §872.550

PARTITION—Cont.
Complaint—Cont.
    Title report availability designated in   CCP §872.220
Compliance with property laws   CCP §872.040
Concurrent interests   CCP §872.710
Condominiums
    Transfer restrictions   CC §4610
Consent
    Appointment of referee   CCP §873.040
    Sale, consent of parties to   CCP §§872.820, 873.600
Conservator
    Generally   Pro §2463
    Purchasers, conservators as   CCP §873.690
    Referee, consent on appointment of   CCP §873.040
Contribution
    Answer including claims for   CCP §872.430
    Orders for   CCP §872.140
Conveyances
    Binding and conclusive, conveyances as   CCP §874.240
    Deeds   CCP §873.230
    Referees executing   CCP §§873.750, 873.790
Costs
    Allowance and apportionment of costs   CCP §§874.010 to 874.050
    Attorneys' fees generally (See within this heading, **"Attorney's fees"**)
    Common benefit, cost of other actions necessarily incurred by party for   CCP §874.020
    Decedent's estate proceedings   Pro §11955
    Liens   CCP §§874.120, 874.130
    Orders for apportionment of   CCP §§874.050, 874.110
    Payment of costs   CCP §§874.110 to 874.130
    Real property partition
        Apportionment of costs   CCP §874.321.5
    Resale of property, action involving   CCP §873.760
    Sale proceeds for payment of   CCP §873.820
Decedents' estates (See **ADMINISTRATION OF ESTATES**)
Deeds   CCP §873.230
Depreciable property   CCP §873.660
Description
    Appraisal agreement including   CCP §873.920
    Complaint including   CCP §872.230
    Publication of process, description in   CCP §872.320
    Report by referee including   CCP §873.280
    Sale reports including   CCP §§873.650, 873.710
Determinations in actions for   CCP §§872.610 to 872.840
Division
    In accordance with interests determined in interlocutory judgment   CCP §§872.210, 872.810
    Procedures, generally   CCP §§873.210 to 873.290
Easements   CC §807, CCP §873.710
Engineers, referee contracting with   CCP §873.110
Expenses
    Referees   CCP §873.010
    Sale expenses   CCP §873.820
    Surveyors   CCP §§873.110, 873.130, 873.150, 874.020
    Title report   CCP §874.010
Filing
    Appraisal agreement for partition   CCP §873.920
    Death of party, statement of   CCP §872.530
    Interim accounts of referee   CCP §873.010
    Notice of pendency   CCP §872.250
    Report of referee   CCP §§873.280, 873.290
Form of affidavit stating death of party   CCP §872.530
Guardian
    Purchasers, guardians as   CCP §873.690
    Referee, consent on appointment of   CCP §873.040
Hearings
    Generally   CCP §872.120
    Appraisal agreements   CCP §873.960
    Modification of referee's report   CCP §873.290
    Proceeds of sale, continuation of action to determine respective claims to   CCP §873.850
    Sales, hearings to confirm or set aside   CCP §§873.730 to 873.790
Heirs
    Appraisal agreements as binding on   CCP §873.970
    Joinder   CCP §872.530
    Partition of real property act   CCP §§874.311 to 874.323
Improvements, effect of   CCP §873.220
Injunctions and temporary restraining orders   CCP §872.130
Judgments
    Generally   CCP §§872.120, 874.210 to 874.240
    Binding and conclusive   CCP §§874.210, 874.225

PARTITION—Cont.
　Judgments—Cont.
　　　Costs included in　CCP §874.110
　　　Distribution, decree before　Pro §11953
　　　Failure to appear, judgments based on　CCP §872.330
　　　Interlocutory judgments　CCP §§872.720, 872.810
　Jurisdiction
　　　Generally　CCP §872.110
　　　Purchaser's failure to pay, effect of　CCP §873.760
　Leases, action involving　CCP §872.540
　Liens
　　　Answer including　CCP §872.420
　　　Costs as　CCP §§874.120, 874.130
　　　Decedent's estate proceedings, lien for expenses of　Pro §11955
　　　Definition　CCP §872.010
　　　Division of property affecting　CCP §873.260
　　　Priorities
　　　　　Court determination of priority　CCP §872.630
　　　　　Sales for benefit of lienholders, priorities during　CCP §874.130
　　　Purchaser as lienholder　CCP §873.770
　　　Sale requirements　CCP §§873.710, 873.770, 873.820
　Life estates
　　　Cash proceeds, taking land in lieu of　CCP §873.830
　　　Parties to action, owners of life estates as　CCP §872.210
　　　Sales involving　CCP §§873.830, 873.840
　Lots, division of　CCP §873.240
　Minors
　　　Compensation requirements from　CCP §873.250
　Notices
　　　Appraisal agreement　CCP §§873.930, 873.950
　　　Decedent's estate, notice of distribution of　Pro §11952
　　　Report of referee, notice of modification of　CCP §873.290
　　　Sales, notice of　CCP §§873.640, 873.650
　One action for partition of real and personal property　CCP §872.240
　Orders
　　　Closing of sale　CCP §873.780
　　　Contributions, orders for　CCP §872.140
　　　Costs, apportionment of　CCP §§874.050, 874.110
　　　Trust property, orders for sale of　CCP §872.840
　　　Unit sale of personalty and realty　CCP §873.620
　Partial sale with division of remainder　CCP §872.830
　Parties
　　　Generally　CCP §872.210
　　　Appraisal agreement, parties to　CCP §873.910
　　　Consent to appointment of referee　CCP §873.040
　　　Death of　CCP §872.530, Pro §9823
　　　Joinder of parties　CCP §§872.510 to 872.550
　　　Petition, filing of　Pro §11951
　　　Setting aside of sale by　CCP §873.720
　　　Unknown persons generally (See within this heading, **"Unknown persons"**)
　Partition of real property act　CCP §§874.311 to 874.323
　　　Applicability　CCP §874.313
　　　Broker offering property for open market sale, report requirement　CCP §874.321
　　　Conflict of laws　CCP §874.313
　　　Costs, apportionment　CCP §874.321.5
　　　Cotenant option to buy interest　CCP §874.317
　　　Definitions　CCP §874.312
　　　Electronic signature in global and national commerce act, effect of uniform act on　CCP §874.323
　　　In kind partition　CCP §§874.312, 874.318, 874.319
　　　Open-market sale　CCP §§874.320, 874.321
　　　Prejudicial result from in kind partition, determination　CCP §874.319
　　　Referees　CCP §874.315
　　　Sale, partition by　CCP §§874.312, 874.317
　　　Service of complaint　CCP §874.314
　　　Short title　CCP §874.311
　　　Valuation of property　CCP §874.316
　Partnership accounting and dissolution, applicability of partition provisions to　CCP §872.730
　Pendency, recordation of notice of　CCP §872.250
　Perishable or depreciable property　CCP §873.660
　Personal property
　　　Generally　CCP §872.020
　　　Auctions (See within this heading, **"Auctions"**)
　　　Description of personalty in complaint　CCP §872.230
　　　Infants, compensation required of　CCP §873.250
　　　Jurisdiction　CCP §872.110
　　　One action for partition of real and personal property　CCP §872.240

PARTITION—Cont.
　Personal property—Cont.
　　　Sales
　　　　　Auctions (See within this heading, **"Auctions"**)
　　　　　Generally (See within this heading, **"Sales"**)
　　　Unit, personalty sold with realty as　CCP §873.620
　Priorities
　　　Court determining priority of lien　CCP §872.630
　　　Sales for benefit of lienholders, priorities during　CCP §874.130
　Private sales
　　　Commissions of agents　CCP §873.745
　　　Determination of type of sale　CCP §873.520
　　　Notice of　CCP §873.650
　　　Time for　CCP §873.680
　Process
　　　Court directing issuance of　CCP §872.630
　　　Service　CCP §§872.310 to 872.330
　　　　　Publication　CCP §§872.310 to 872.330
　Property interests determined　CCP §§872.610, 872.640
　Public improvement assessment, action to determine adverse interests in real property arising out of　CCP §801.13
　Real property
　　　Applicability　CCP §872.020
　　　Partition of real property act　CCP §§874.311 to 874.323
　Referees
　　　Appointment of　CCP §§872.630, 873.010 to 873.050
　　　Appraisal agreements　CCP §§873.940, 873.950
　　　Authority of　CCP §873.060
　　　Bond requirements　CCP §873.010
　　　Contracts for services by　CCP §§873.110 to 873.160
　　　Conveyance, execution of　CCP §§873.750, 873.790
　　　Distribution or deposit of sale proceeds　CCP §873.750
　　　Liability for contracts by　CCP §873.160
　　　Lienholder, receipt from purchaser as　CCP §873.770
　　　Notice of sale, inspection of　CCP §873.650
　　　Persons prohibited as　CCP §873.050
　　　Petition for instructions　CCP §873.070
　　　Purchasers, referees as　CCP §873.690
　　　Real property, partition
　　　　　Appointment of referees　CCP §874.315
　　　Reports
　　　　　Appraisal agreements　CCP §873.940
　　　　　Filing　CCP §§873.280, 873.290
　　　Setting aside of sale　CCP §873.720
　　　Status and priority of liens, determination of　CCP §872.630
　　　Three referees　CCP §873.030
　　　Value of property, responsibility for　CCP §873.660
　Reports
　　　Appraisal agreements　CCP §873.940
　　　Filing of　CCP §§873.280, 873.290
　Right to partition, determination of　CCP §872.710
　Roads, designation of portion of property as　CCP §§873.080, 873.710
　Sales
　　　Agreement of parties to　CCP §§872.820, 873.600
　　　As more equitable than division　CCP §§872.820, 872.830
　　　Auctions (See within this heading, **"Auctions"**)
　　　Bona fide purchasers　CCP §873.690
　　　Closing　CCP §873.780
　　　Commissions of agents　CCP §873.745
　　　Complaints seeking　CCP §872.230
　　　Confirmation of　CCP §§873.720, 873.730
　　　Credit, sales on　CCP §873.630
　　　Description requirements　CCP §§873.650, 873.710
　　　Disposition of proceeds　CCP §§873.810 to 873.850
　　　Distribution or deposit of sale proceeds　CCP §873.750
　　　Escrow　CCP §873.780
　　　Hearings to confirm or set aside　CCP §§873.730 to 873.790
　　　Lien claimants, sale of property for benefit of　CCP §874.130
　　　Liens, effect on　CCP §§873.710, 873.770, 873.820
　　　Life estates　CCP §§873.830, 873.840
　　　Manner of sale　CCP §873.510
　　　Notice of　CCP §§873.640, 874.650
　　　Partial sale with division of remainder　CCP §872.830
　　　Perishable or depreciable property　CCP §873.660
　　　Private sales (See within this heading, **"Private sales"**)
　　　Procedure　CCP §§873.600 to 873.690
　　　Purchaser's failure to pay, effect of　CCP §873.760
　　　Referees generally (See within this heading, **"Referees"**)
　　　Report of sale to court　CCP §873.710
　　　Securities　CCP §873.660

PARTITION—Cont.
Sales—Cont.
    Setting aside of sale   CCP §§873.720 to 873.740
    Trusts (See within this heading, **"Trusts"**)
    Unit, sales of realty and personalty as   CCP §873.620
    Unknown persons, proceeds to   CCP §873.850
    Vacation of   CCP §§873.720 to 873.740
Securities   CCP §873.660
Service of process
    Generally   CCP §§872.310 to 872.330
    Publication   CCP §§872.310 to 872.330
Single action for partition of real and personal property   CCP §872.240
State has interest, action for partition in which   Gov §956
Streets, designation of portion of property as   CCP §§873.080, 873.710
Successive estates   CCP §872.710
Surveyors   CCP §§873.110, 873.130, 873.150, 874.020
Survival of actions   CCP §872.530, Pro §9823
Temporary restraining orders   CCP §872.130
Time
    Appraisal agreements, modification of   CCP §873.950
    Private sales   CCP §873.680
    Setting aside of sale, motion for   CCP §873.720
Title report
    Generally   CCP §872.220
    Expenses for   CCP §874.010
Title, state of   CCP §872.620
Trial   CCP §§872.610 to 872.840
Trusts
    Life estate proceeds placed in   CCP §873.840
    Orders for sale of trust property   CCP §872.840
    Proceeds from sales placed in   CCP §§873.810, 873.840
Unequal division   CCP §873.250
Uniform partition of heirs property act   CCP §§874.311 to 874.323
Unknown persons
    Combined interests of unknown persons, portion of property allocated to   CCP §873.270
    Compensation requirements from   CCP §873.250
    Determination of interests of   CCP §872.640
    Joinder of   CCP §872.520
    Judgments affecting   CCP §874.210
    Publication of process for   CCP §§872.310 to 872.330
    Sale proceeds for   CCP §873.850
Venue   CCP §872.110
Witnesses
    Appraisal agreement hearings   CCP §873.960
    Court compelling attendance of   CCP §872.630
    Sales, hearings to confirm or set aside   CCP §873.730

PARTITION OF REAL PROPERTY ACT   CCP §§874.311 to 874.323 (See **PARTITION**)

PARTNERSHIPS
Administration of decedents' estates
    Generally (See **ADMINISTRATION OF ESTATES**)
    Executors and administrators, surviving partner as (See **EXECUTORS AND ADMINISTRATORS**)
Appellate rules, supreme court and courts of appeal
    Briefs
        Certificate of interested entities or persons   CRC 8.208, 8.361, 8.488, CRCSupp 1st AppDist
Assignment for benefit of creditors affecting   CCP §1800
Attachments, property subject to   CCP §487.010
Attorney professional conduct
    Organization or entity as client   ProfC 1.13
Attorneys
    Registered in-house counsel   CRC 9.46
        Fingerprinting of special admission attorneys   CRC 9.9.5
Capacity to sue or be sued   CCP §369.5
Challenge of juror for implied bias, relationships giving rise to   CCP §229
Common interest developments (See **COMMON INTEREST DEVELOPMENTS**)
Death of partner, continuation of business after   Pro §§9762, 9763
Decedent's estate, disposition of partnership interest in (See **ADMINISTRATION OF ESTATES**)
Decedent's interest
    Sale   Pro §10204
Dissolution
    Affidavit of publication of notice
        Superior court fees, specified services   Gov §70626
Eminent domain, partners giving evidence for valuation under   Ev §813
Enforcement of judgments (See **ENFORCEMENT OF JUDGMENTS**)

PARTNERSHIPS—Cont.
Escheat of interests and obligations   CCP §1516
Executors and administrators
    Business partner, eligibility to serve as personal representative   Pro §8402
Foreign partnerships, attaching assets of   CCP §492.010
In-house counsel
    Registered in-house counsel   CRC 9.46
        Fingerprinting of special admission attorneys   CRC 9.9.5
Judgment based on personal liability of member   CCP §369.5
Marital status, denial of credit because of   CC §1812.32
Partition provisions applicable to partnership accounting and dissolution   CCP §872.730
Process
    Generally   CCP §412.30
    Default notice   CCP §412.30
    Service of process (See within this heading, **"Service of process"**)
Receivers protecting assets of   CCP §564
Referees, disqualification of   CCP §641
Registered in-house counsel   CRC 9.46
    Fingerprinting of special admission attorneys   CRC 9.9.5
Service of process
    Generally   CCP §416.40
    Manner of service of business organizations
        Leaving summons and complaint at office, mailing copy   CCP §415.95
    Partner as an individual, service on   CCP §§369.5, 412.30
Small claims court (See **SMALL CLAIMS COURTS**)
Tax liens and other federal lines, filing of notice of   CCP §2101
Title held by   CC §§682, 684
Voidable transactions, insolvency for purposes of   CC §3439.02

PASSENGER CHARTER-PARTY CARRIERS
Carrier of passengers act   CC §§2213 to 2218
    Applicability   CC §§2215, 2217
    Civil actions and penalties   CC §2216
    Definitions   CC §2214
    Severability   CC §2218

PASSENGERS ON COMMON CARRIERS (See **COMMON CARRIERS**)

PASSENGER VEHICLE RENTALS
Rental passenger vehicle transactions generally   CC §§1939.01 to 1939.39 (See **RENTAL PASSENGER VEHICLE TRANSACTIONS**)

PASSPORTS
Age-restricted products, sales
    Verification of age for sale of age-restricted products
        Government-issued identification   CC §1798.99.1

PASTORS
Conciliation Courts   Fam §1838

PASTURES
Attorney's fees for trespass action, recovery of   CCP §1021.9
Easement rights   CC §§801, 802
Executor authorized to sell land to pasture associations   Pro §10207
Grazing, right to farm
    Disclosures incident to residential land transfers   CC §1103.4
Lien for   CC §3051
Shift-in-land use loans   Pro §10207

PATENT DEFECTS
Statutes of limitation for damages for deficiencies in planning or construction of improvement to real property   CCP §337.1

PATENT OF INVENTION
Generally   CC §980
Judgment debtor, assignment of right to payment due   CCP §§708.510 to 708.560
Proportion of ownership   CC §981
Publication, dedication by   CC §983
Transfer of ownership or right of reproduction   CC §982

PATENT OF LAND
Burden of proof in dispute involving state   Ev §523
Disclosure of written evidence in dispute involving state   CCP §2031.510

PATERNITY   Fam §§7540 to 7581
Action for injury to child born out of wedlock, prior acknowledgment of paternity by father maintaining   CCP §376
Actions to challenge parentage   Fam §7541

PATERNITY—Cont.
  Actions to determine parent and child relationship Fam §§7630 to 7644
    Fees and costs Fam §7640
    Guardian ad litem Fam §7635
    Judgments and orders Fam §§7636, 7637
    Jurisdiction and venue CRC 5.510, Fam §7620
    Notice of entry of judgment CRC 5.413, 5.415
    Parties CRC 5.16, Fam §7635
    Venue CCP §395
    Voluntary declaration of parentage
      Actions based on declaration Fam §7644
    Who may bring action Fam §7630
  Adoption, termination of parental rights Fam §§7660 to 7671
    Unknown father Fam §§7662 to 7671
  Agreement and judgment of parentage in domestic violence prevention act cases CRC 5.380
  Artificial insemination Fam §7613.5
  Assisted reproduction Fam §7613
    Surrogacy or donor facilitators Fam §§7960, 7961
  Blood tests
    Genetic testing to determine parentage Fam §§7550 to 7562
  Child support
    Duty to inquire in dependency or wardship proceedings CRC 5.635
  Child support agencies, paternity determinations in enforcement actions prosecuted by Fam §§17404, 17406, 17410 to 17416
    Genetic testing to determine parentage Fam §7558
  Child support services department, determination of paternity Fam §§17000 to 17325
  Closed court
    Hearings in closed court Fam §7643.5
  Confidentiality of papers and records
    Confidential cover sheet for parentage actions CRC 5.51
  Custody or visitation rights (See **CUSTODY OF CHILDREN**)
  Declarations of parentage Fam §§7570 to 7581
    Hearing procedure to cancel or set aside voluntary declarations of parentage or paternity CRC 5.350
  Dependent child hearings
    Commencement of hearing, paternity inquiry at CRC 5.668
    Duty to inquire CRC 5.635
  Domestic violence (See **DOMESTIC VIOLENCE**)
  Family law information centers for unrepresented low-income litigants Fam §§15000 to 15012
  Fees
    Title IV-D child support agency involved Gov §70672
  Forms
    Judicial council legal forms CRCAppx A
  Full faith and credit accorded to other states' paternity determinations Fam §5604
  Genetic testing to determine parentage Fam §§7550 to 7562
    Actions to determine parent and child relationship
      Costs of genetic testing Fam §7640
    Advance payment of cost of initial genetic testing Fam §7559
    Child support enforcement
      Administrative order for genetic testing Fam §7558
    Cohabiting husband and wife Fam §7541
    Cost
      Advance payment of cost of initial genetic testing Fam §7559
    Criminal law and procedure
      Applicability to criminal proceedings Fam §7556
    Deceased persons, testing Fam §7562
    Definitions Fam §7550.5
    Discovery
      Inapplicability of discovery provisions CCP §2032.010
    Expert and opinion evidence
      Fees and mileage Fam §7553
      Right to produce other expert evidence Fam §7557
    Facilitation Fam §7551.5
    Findings of parentage
      Criteria to find parentage Fam §7554
    Identification as genetic parent
      Challenge to identification Fam §7555
      Criteria Fam §7555
      Multiple persons identified Fam §7555
      Order for additional testing upon challenge to identification Fam §7560
    In utero testing not to be ordered Fam §§7551, 7558
    Juvenile court orders for genetic tests CRC 5.635
    Laboratories
      Accreditation Fam §7552
    Objections to relationship index calculations Fam §7552

PATERNITY—Cont.
  Genetic testing to determine parentage—Cont.
    Orders to submit to genetic testing Fam §7551
      Challenge to genetic identification, additional testing ordered Fam §7560
    Prohibited uses of testing Fam §7551
    Refusal to comply with order
      Effect Fam §7551
    Service of genetic test results Fam §7552.5
    Standards for testing Fam §7552
    Voluntary declaration of paternity
      Rescission Fam §7575
  Interstate family support
    Nonparentage as defense, prohibition Fam §5700.315
    Proceedings to determine paternity Fam §5700.402
  Intestate succession
    Parent inheriting from child based on relationship
      Acknowledgment of paternity not given, situations preventing inheritance Pro §6452
  Judgment
    Agreement and judgment of parentage in domestic violence prevention act cases CRC 5.380
    Judicial council forms CRCAppx A
    Setting aside or vacating judgment of parentage Fam §§7645 to 7649.5
  Judicial Council forms CRCAppx A (CRCFL-200 to CRCFL-290)
  Juvenile court determinations CRC 5.635
    Findings of parentage CRC 5.534
  Military personnel, waiver of filing fees in paternity suit against Gov §70673
  Modification of judgment or order after entry of judgment, notice requirements for Fam §215
  More than 2 parents
    Court may find more than 2 persons with claim to parentage Fam §7612
  Notice to alleged fathers CRC 5.635
  Other states
    Full faith and credit for paternity determinations of other states Fam §4846
  Pendente lite relief Fam §7604
  Presumed natural father ordered to pay child support in domestic violence proceeding Fam §6341
    Agreement and judgment of parentage in domestic violence prevention act cases CRC 5.380
  Presumptions
    Generally Fam §§7611 to 7612
    Child of marriage Fam §§7540, 7541, 7611
      Actions to challenge parentage Fam §7541
    Rape, child conceived as result of Fam §7611.5
    Voluntary declaration of parentage
      Minor signatories, effect of declaration Fam §7580
      Pre-1977 declarations Fam §7581
      Rebuttal Fam §7612
  Records
    Inspection or copying of records pertaining to action Fam §7643.5
  Service of genetic test results Fam §7552.5
  Summons, inclusion of temporary restraining order in Fam §§233 to 235
  Supplemental complaint for Fam §2330.1
  Surrogacy or donor facilitators Fam §§7960, 7961
  Temporary restraining order included in summons Fam §§233 to 235
  Uniform Act on Blood Tests to Determine Paternity
    Genetic testing to determine parentage Fam §§7550 to 7562
  Uniform parentage act
    Generally Fam §§7600 to 7730 (See **UNIFORM PARENTAGE ACT**)
  Venue in proceedings to determine CCP §395
    Temporary support, attorney fees, custody and visitation issues determined prior to determination of motion for transfer of CCP §396b
  Voluntary declaration of parentage CRC 5.635, Fam §§7570 to 7581
    Actions for determination of parent and child relationship based on declaration Fam §7644
    Challenge by nonsignatories of declaration Fam §7577
      Birth certificate replacement in light of ruling Fam §7578
      Burden of proof Fam §7578
      Signatories to be parties Fam §7578
    Challenge of declaration based on fraud, duress or material mistake of fact Fam §7576
    Child support enforcement
      Effect of declaration Fam §17412
    Constitutional rights of alleged father, notice concerning Fam §7572
    Contents of declaration Fam §7574
    Costs of filing paternity declaration, district attorney's payment of Fam §7571
    Distribution of declaration forms Fam §7571
    Effective date of declaration Fam §7573

PATERNITY—Cont.
Voluntary declaration of parentage —Cont.
    Effect of declaration   Fam §7573
        Minor signatories   Fam §7580
    Effect of refusal to sign   Fam §7612
    Hearings to cancel or set aside declaration of parentage or paternity   CRC 5.350
    Informational and training materials   Fam §7572
    Legislative findings and intent   Fam §7570
    Minor signatories
        Effect of voluntary declaration   Fam §7580
    Other state, declaration from
        Full faith and credit   Fam §7573
    Petition to set aside voluntary declaration   Fam §7612
    Presumption of parentage
        Minor signatories   Fam §7580
        Pre-1977 declarations   Fam §7581
        Rebuttal   Fam §7612
    Rescission or motion to set aside
        Minor signatories   Fam §7580
    Signature
        Persons authorized to sign   Fam §7573
    Support enforcement actions, declaration in   Fam §§17410 to 17414
    Void declarations
        Actions to determine that declaration void   Fam §7573.5
        Factors making declaration void   Fam §7573.5
Wardship proceedings, duty to inquire   CRC 5.635
Witnesses
    Live testimony
        When received   CRC 5.113, Fam §217

PATIENTS' RIGHTS
Sexual battery against incapacitated person
    Statute of limitations on sexual assault damages   CCP §340.16

PAYMENT BONDS
Mechanics' liens   CC §§8600 to 8614
    Public works   CC §§9550 to 9566

PAYMENTS
Admitted amount, payment of   CC §1525
Agent authorized to receive   CC §§2325, 2326
Child support (See **CHILD SUPPORT**)
Claim and delivery bonds, in lieu of   CCP §515.020
Claims against decedent's estate (See **CLAIMS AGAINST ESTATES**)
Claims against public entities and employees (See **CLAIMS AGAINST PUBLIC ENTITIES AND EMPLOYEES**)
Continuing contract, payments on account of principal or interest sufficient acknowledgment or promise of   CCP §360
Contractual obligation   CC §§1478, 1479
Decedent's estate, claims against (See **CLAIMS AGAINST ESTATES**)
Deposit in bank as constituting   CC §1500
Enforcement of judgments (See **ENFORCEMENT OF JUDGMENTS**)
Evidence to prove invalidity of claim   Ev §1154
Filing fees (See **FEES**)
Garnished wages, payment of   CCP §§706.025, 706.026
Lien foreclosures, surplus on   CCP §727
Mortgages (See **TRUST DEEDS AND MORTGAGES**)
Multiple-party accounts   Pro §§5401 to 5407
Preexisting debt, proof of payment of   Ev §1152
Preferences in payment of debts   CC §3432
Prepayments (See **PREPAYMENTS**)
Receipts (See **RECEIPTS**)
Renewing liability, payments on account of principal or interest sufficient acknowledgment or promise for purposes of   CCP §360
Rent installment payment presumed from receipt   Ev §636
Retail installment sales   CC §§1803.2, 1806.1 to 1806.4
Spousal support (See **SPOUSAL SUPPORT**)
Tender (See **TENDER**)
Time for performance of contract requiring   CC §1657
Trust deeds (See **TRUST DEEDS AND MORTGAGES**)
Unsolicited goods, statements for payment of   CC §§1584.5, 1584.6

PEACE OFFICERS (See **LAW ENFORCEMENT OFFICERS**)

PECULIAR VALUE
Damages, effect on   CC §3355

PECUNIARY DEVISES (See **WILLS**)

PEDESTRIANS
Blind pedestrians
    Construction or application of provisions in issue, solicitor general notified   CC §55.2
Shared mobility devices
    Agreements with or permits from local government
        Insurance for injuries to pedestrians   CC §2505

PEDESTRIAN TRAILS
Closure of   CCP §731.5

PEDIGREE
Stud purposes, false pedigree advertised in connection with   CC §3064.1

PEER REVIEW COMMITTEES
Generally   CC §§43.7, 43.8
Physicians and surgeons (See **PHYSICIANS AND SURGEONS**)

PENAL INSTITUTIONS (See **PRISONERS**)

PENALTIES (See **FINES AND PENALTIES**)

PENDENCY OF ACTIONS
Actual notice
    Expungement orders, effect of   CCP §§405.60, 405.61
    Withdrawal of notice of pendency, effect of   CCP §§405.60, 405.61
Answer alleging simultaneous action   CCP §430.10
Appeals   CCP §405.39
Attachment (See **ATTACHMENT**)
Attorneys
    Attorneys' fees and costs, award of   CCP §405.38
    Signature required on notice of pendency for recordation purposes   CCP §405.21
Attorneys' fees and costs, award of   CCP §405.38
Civil Code, effect on action or proceeding commenced prior to enactment of   CC §6
Claimant defined   CCP §405.1
Claims against decedent's estate (See **CLAIMS AGAINST ESTATES**)
Conciliation proceeding, pendency of other family law proceedings affecting   Fam §1840
Constructive notice
    Generally   CCP §405.24
    Expungement order, effect of   CCP §§405.60, 405.61
    Withdrawal of notice of pendency, effect of   CCP §§405.60, 405.61
Continuation of action
    Disability of party during pending action, effect of   CCP §375
    Survival of actions (See **SURVIVAL OF ACTIONS**)
    Transfer of interests, effect on pending action by   CCP §368.5
Decedent's estate, claims against (See **CLAIMS AGAINST ESTATES**)
Definitions   CCP §§405 to 405.4
Demurrer alleging simultaneous action   CCP §430.10
Destroyed land records, action for reestablishment of   CCP §751.13
Disability of party during pending action, effect of   CCP §375
Duration of   CCP §1049
Effect of code on pending actions   CCP §8
Eminent domain proceedings (See **EMINENT DOMAIN**)
Enforcement of judgments (See **ENFORCEMENT OF JUDGMENTS**)
Exoneration of undertaking requirements   CCP §405.37
Expiration of title, effect on   CC §880.260
Expunging notice of pendency
    Actual or constructive notice, effect on   CCP §§405.60, 405.61
    Attorneys' fees and costs   CCP §405.38
    Burden of proof   CCP §405.30
    Effective date of expungement orders   CCP §405.35
    Motion to expunge   CCP §405.30
    No real property claim in pleading as grounds for   CCP §405.31
    Presumption of actual knowledge of action, effect on   CCP §405.61
    Probable validity of real property claims in pleading not established as grounds for   CCP §405.32
    Second notice after expungement, court approval required for recordation of   CCP §405.36
    Time for service of notice of motion   CCP §1005
    Time restrictions on recordation of expungement orders   CCP §405.35
    Transferability of property, effect on   CCP §405.61
    Undertaking posted by moving party as adequate relief to indemnify claimant as grounds for   CCP §405.33
    Writ of mandate to review order granting or denying motion to expunge   CCP §405.35
Federal courts, applicability of state law governing notice of pendency of action to   CCP §405.5
Judgment creditor's lien (See **ENFORCEMENT OF JUDGMENTS**)
Lis pendens (See within this heading, **"Notice of pendency"**)

PENDENCY OF ACTIONS—Cont.
Mandamus writ   CCP §405.39
   Expungement orders   CCP §405.35
Mechanics' liens
   Action to enforce lien, notice of pendency   CC §8461
Modification of undertaking requirements   CCP §405.37
Notice of pendency
   Generally   CCP §405.20
   Actual notice of
      Expungement orders, effect   CCP §§405.60, 405.61
      Withdrawal of notice, effect   CCP §§405.60, 405.61
   Annulment of marriage, effect of notice on disposition of property   Fam §754
   Constructive notice (See within this heading, "**Constructive notice**")
   Contents of   CCP §405.20
   Defined   CCP §405.2
   Dissolution of marriage, effect of notice on disposition of property   Fam §754
   Effect of recordation   CCP §405.24
   Escheated property, recording notice of action for   CCP §1410
   Expunging notice of pendency (See within this heading, "**Expunging notice of pendency**")
   Legal separation, effect of notice on disposition of property   Fam §754
   Partition action   CCP §872.250
   Place of recordation   CCP §405.20
   Public improvement assessment, action to determine adverse interests in real property arising out of   CCP §801.5
   Quiet title action   CCP §§761.010, 761.045
   Second notice after expungement, court approval required for recordation of   CCP §405.36
   Service by mail   CCP §405.22
   Service of notice
      Generally (See within this heading, "**Service of notice**")
   Signature of attorney or party required for recordation purposes   CCP §405.21
   Undertaking posted by claimant as condition of maintaining notice of pendency in record title   CCP §405.34
   Uninhabitable, action to declare building   CCP §405.7
   United States district courts, actions pending in   CCP §405.5
   Withdrawal of (See within this heading, "**Withdrawal of notice of pendency**")
Other actions for relief on real property claims, effect of state recordation statute on party to action seeking   CCP §405.8
Probable validity
   Defined   CCP §405.3
   Failure to establish probable validity of real property claim in pleading as grounds for expunging notice   CCP §405.32
Real property claim defined   CCP §405.4
Related cases   CRC 3.300
Second notice of pendency following expungement, court approval required for recordation of   CCP §405.36
Separate trial of special defense   CCP §597
Service of notice
   Generally   CCP §405.22
   Actual notice
      Expungement orders, effect   CCP §§405.60, 405.61
      Withdrawal of notice of pendency, effect of   CCP §§405.60, 405.61
   Party not served, invalidity of notice of pendency as to   CCP §405.23
   Writ of mandate, petition for   CCP §405.39
Transferability of property after expungement or withdrawal of notice of pendency   CCP §405.61
Transfer of interests, continuation of action where   CCP §368.5
Undertakings
   Exoneration or modification of   CCP §405.37
   Expunging notice, undertaking posted by moving party as grounds for   CCP §405.33
   Maintaining notice of pendency, undertaking posted by claimant as condition of   CCP §405.34
Uninhabitable, notice of pendency of action to declare building   CCP §405.7
Withdrawal of notice of pendency
   Generally   CCP §405.50
   Actual or constructive notice, effect of withdrawal on   CCP §§405.60, 405.61
   Presumption of actual knowledge of action, effect on   CCP §405.61
   Transferability of property, effect on   CCP §405.61
Writ of mandate
   Generally   CCP §405.39
   Expungement orders, effect of filing petition for writ of mandate on   CCP §405.35

PENITENT (See **PRIVILEGED COMMUNICATIONS**)

PENSIONS (See **RETIREMENT**)

PER DIEM ALLOWANCE
Superior court appellate division, judges designated as members of   CCP §77

PEREMPTORY CHALLENGE
Disqualification of judge   CCP §§170.6, 170.7
Expedited jury trials   CCP §630.04
   Mandatory expedited jury trials, limited civil cases   CCP §630.23
Jurors challenged peremptorily (See **JURY**)

PEREMPTORY WRITS
Summary judgment proceeding, review of determination in   CCP §437c

PERFORMANCE
Contracts (See **CONTRACTS AND AGREEMENTS**)
Holidays, performance on (See **HOLIDAYS**)

PERFORMANCE BONDS (See **SURETYSHIP, BONDS AND UNDERTAKINGS**)

PERFORMANCE OF CONTRACT (See **CONTRACTS AND AGREEMENTS**)

PERIODICALS (See **NEWSPAPERS AND MAGAZINES**)

PERISHABLE AND DEPRECIABLE PROPERTY
Attachment (See **ATTACHMENT**)
Claim and delivery   CCP §514.030
Common carriers, sale by   CC §2204
Damages for delay in delivery of   CC §3317
Decedents' estates, sale of assets of   Pro §§10252, 10259
Depository, sale by   CC §1837
Enforcement of money judgment by writ of execution, property subject to   CCP §699.070
Innkeeper's lien   CC §1861.19
Partition sale of   CCP §873.660
Special administrator protecting   Pro §8544

PERJURY
Aggravation, suborning perjury as circumstance in   CRC 4.421
Appellate rules, supreme court and courts of appeal
   E-filing in supreme court and courts of appeal
      Signatures of documents under penalty of perjury   CRC 8.76
Coordination of actions
   Judicial Council
      Electronic submission of documents to council, signature under penalty of perjury   CRC 3.512
Electronic filing and service rules
   Documents filed under penalty of perjury   CRC 2.257
Jurors' perjury acknowledgment and agreement   CCP §232
Juvenile court proceedings   CRC 5.548
Tribal court civil money judgment act
   Application for recognition and entry of judgment
      Execution of application under penalty of perjury   CCP §1734

PERMISSIVE JOINDER (See **JOINDER OF PARTIES**)

PERMISSIVE USE
Public using private property   CC §§813, 1007, 1009

PERMITS (See **LICENSES AND PERMITS**)

PERPETUAL INTEREST   CC §§688, 691

PERPETUITIES AND RESTRAINTS ON ALIENATION
Generally   Pro §21205
Birth of child to individual after individual's death, effect on nonvested interest by possibility of   Pro §21208
Citation of Act   Pro §21200
Common law rule, applicability of   Pro §21201
Community property, spouse's right to exercise power with respect to   Pro §21211
Conditions restraining alienation where repugnant to interest created, validity of   CC §711
Cy pres doctrine   Pro §21220
Exclusions to statutory rule against perpetuities   Pro §21225
"For sale" signs, validity of prohibition against use of   CC §§712, 713
General rule   Pro §21205
Husband and wife
   Community property, spouse's exercise of power with respect to   Pro §21211
   Measuring life, spouse as deemed to be alive for purposes of   Pro §21231
Income accrued pending suspension of power of alienation, right to   CC §733

PERPETUITIES AND RESTRAINTS ON ALIENATION—Cont.
Interests subject to statutory rule against perpetuities   Pro §21201
Judicial proceedings, effect of statutory rule against perpetuities to interests determined in   Pro §21202
Limitation of language in perpetuities saving clause, validity of   Pro §21209
Measuring life
    Limitations on   Pro §21230
    Spouse as deemed alive at time of creation of interest   Pro §21231
Municipal leases of property   CC §§718, 719
Nondonative transfer of property, applicability of statutory rule against perpetuities to   Pro §21225
Oil and gas leases
    Municipal property   CC §§718, 719
    99-year oil and gas leases   CC §718f
Power of appointment
    Applicability of statutory rule against perpetuities   Pro §690
    Birth of child to individual after individual's death, effect of possibility of   Pro §21208
    General power of appointment subject to conditions precedent, validity of   Pro §21206
    General testamentary power of appointment, validity of   Pro §21207
    Limitation of language in perpetuities saving clause, validity of   Pro §21209
    Nongeneral power of appointment, validity of   Pro §21207
Reformation of transferor's plan of distribution, petition for   Pro §21220
Settlement proceedings, effect of statutory rule against perpetuities to interests determined in   Pro §21202
Spouses
    Community property
        Spouse's exercise of power   Pro §21211
    Measuring life
        Spouse ad deemed to be alive for purposes of measurement   Pro §21231
Time of creation of interest
    General rule   Pro §21210
    Previously funded trust, transfer of property to   Pro §21212
    Unqualified owner of nonvested interest, creation of interest on termination of power to become   Pro §21211
Trust decanting, uniform act
    Second trust, duration
        Applicability of maximum perpetuity provisions   Pro §19520
Trusts (See **TRUSTS**)

PERSON
Defined   Fam §105

PERSONAL EFFECTS
Exempt property for purposes of enforcement of judgments   CCP §704.020

PERSONAL EMERGENCY RESPONSE UNIT
Cancellation of purchase contract   CC §§1689.6, 1689.7

PERSONAL INFORMATION
Customer records (See **CUSTOMER RECORDS**)
Information Practices Act (See **INFORMATION PRACTICES ACT**)
Reader privacy act   CC §1798.90

PERSONAL INJURIES
Administrative adjudication, generally (See **ADMINISTRATIVE ADJUDICATION**)
Alcoholic beverages, social host's liability after serving   CC §1714
Arbitration clause in real estate contract, applicability of   CCP §1298.7
As basis for civil actions   CCP §§25, 29
Assignment for benefit of creditors, compensatory payments exempt from   CCP §1801
Attachments, grounds for issuing writ in ex parte procedure   CCP §485.010
Birth-related injuries, action on behalf of minor for   CCP §340.4
Claims against decedents' estates   Pro §9000
Claims against governmental entities (See **CLAIMS AGAINST PUBLIC ENTITIES AND EMPLOYEES**)
Common interest developments, limited liability of volunteer officer or director of   CC §5800
Community property, personal injury damages as (See **COMMUNITY PROPERTY**)
Complaints   CCP §§425.10 to 425.12
Damages
    Community property (See **COMMUNITY PROPERTY**)
    Community property liable for (See **COMMUNITY PROPERTY**)
    Pleading   CCP §425.10
    Request for statement of damages   CCP §§425.11, 425.12

PERSONAL INJURIES—Cont.
Damages—Cont.
    Reservation of right to seek punitive damages on default   CCP §§425.12, 425.115
Default judgment, reservation of right to seek punitive damages on   CCP §§425.12, 425.115
Employee interfering with work   CC §49
Exemption for personal injury cause of action, settlement or award of judgment debtor   CCP §704.140
Farm owner's immunity for injury to person invited on premises to glean farm products for charitable purposes   CC §846.2
Guns (See **FIREARMS AND OTHER WEAPONS**)
Immunity of landowner for personal injuries to person committing felony   CC §847
Indemnity against damages from   CC §2784.5
Infant's statements concerning injury, admissibility of   Ev §1226
Invitees   CC §846
Labor disputes, causing injuries during   CC §52
Landowner's immunity for personal injuries to person committing felony   CC §847
Limitation of actions (See within this heading, "**Statutes of limitation**")
Malpractice (See **MALPRACTICE**)
Marital privilege, waiver   Ev §§972, 985
Married persons, imputed negligence   Fam §1000
Mayhem (See **MAYHEM**)
Nonsuit motion in action involving   CCP §581c
Parents maintaining action for injury of child   CCP §376
Patent deficiencies in planning or construction of improvement to real property, limitation of actions for injury from   CCP §337.1
Public entities, collateral source payments in claims against   Gov §985
Request for statement of damages being sought   CCP §§425.11, 425.12
Reservation of right to seek punitive damages on default   CCP §§425.12, 425.115
Right of protection   CC §43
Social host's liability after serving alcoholic beverages   CC §1714
Statement of damages being sought, request for   CCP §§425.11, 425.12
Statutes of limitation
    Asbestos, actions based on exposure to   CCP §340.2
    Birth-related injuries, action on behalf of minor for   CCP §340.4
    Health care provider's professional negligence, actions based on   CCP §340.5
    Injury caused by wrongful or negligent act   CCP §335.1
    Patent deficiencies in planning or construction of improvement to real property, injury from   CCP §337.1
Summary judgment in actions involving   CCP §437c
Unborn child, action on behalf of   CCP §340.4
Under age of 14, entitlement to preference of party who is   CCP §36
Venue   CCP §395
Waiver of landlord's duty to prevent personal injuries to tenant   CC §1953

PERSONAL PROPERTY
Accession   CC §§1025 to 1033
Action to recover   CC §§3379, 3380
Administration of decedents' estates (See **ADMINISTRATION OF ESTATES**)
Adoption agency releasing personal property upon request of adoptee and others   Fam §9206
Article made from material of another   CC §1028
Attachment (See **ATTACHMENT**)
Bailment of (See **BAILMENT**)
Bill of sale (See **BILL OF SALE**)
Chattel mortgages (See **CHATTEL MORTGAGES**)
Claim and delivery (See **CLAIM AND DELIVERY**)
Classification of interests   CC §702
Common ownership   CC §§1029, 1030
Community property, management and control of   Fam §1100
Conditional sales contracts, use of household goods and personal property as collateral in   CC §1799.100
Conservators (See **CONSERVATORS**)
Court surplus personal property, disposal procedure for   CRC 10.830
Definition   CC §663, Ev §180
Delivery (See **DELIVERY**)
Deposits (See **DEPOSITS**)
Destruction (See **DESTRUCTION OF PROPERTY**)
Domestic violence
    Use, possession and control of real or personal property
        Orders determining   Fam §6342.5
Domicile of owner, applicability of law of   CC §946
Embezzlement (See **EMBEZLEMENT**)
Eminent domain, valuation of property for   Ev §811
Enforcement of judgments (See **ENFORCEMENT OF JUDGMENTS**)
Escheat (See **ESCHEAT**)

PERSONAL PROPERTY—Cont.
Estates in   CC §§765 to 767
Fraudulent transfers (See **VOIDABLE TRANSACTIONS**)
Freehold estates   CC §§765, 766
Gifts (See **GIFTS**)
Guardian and ward (See **GUARDIAN AND WARD**)
Hotel, apartment, lodging or hospital, limitation of action for recovery or conversion of personal property left at   CCP §341a
Inclusions in definition   CCP §17
Interpleader in actions for   CCP §386
Inventions   CC §§980, 981
Joinder of persons claiming interest in property   CCP §389.5
Joint ownership   CC §1029
Joint tenancy   CC §683
Letters   CC §985
Liens (See **LIENS**)
Literary property (See **LITERARY PROPERTY**)
Loan for use, title not transferred by   CC §1885
Lost property (See **LOST PROPERTY**)
Material used without permission   CC §§1031 to 1033
Minor, money or property belonging to (See **PARENT AND CHILD**)
Missing military persons, petition to set aside property of   Pro §§3700 to 3720
Online marketplaces   CC §§1749.8 to 1749.8.9
Ownership (See **TITLE AND OWNERSHIP**)
Partition (See **PARTITION**)
Power of attorney (See **POWER OF ATTORNEY**)
Principal ownership of   CC §1025
Property defined to include   CCP §17
Quieting title (See **QUIETING TITLE**)
Receivers selling   CCP §568.5
Safekeeping by public agency, procedures for temporary   CC §2080.10
Small estates without administration (See **SMALL ESTATES WITHOUT ADMINISTRATION**)
Statute of frauds
    Records required to enforce   CC §1624.5
Statutory form power of attorney, powers under   Pro §§4452 to 4454
Temporary safekeeping by public agency, procedures for   CC §2080.10
Trusts (See **TRUSTS**)
Unclaimed (See **UNCLAIMED PROPERTY**)
United goods   CC §§1025 to 1027
Unlawful detainer action, landlord disposing of personalty in   CCP §1174
Value (See **VALUE**)
Venue (See **VENUE**)
Voidable transactions (See **VOIDABLE TRANSACTIONS**)
Wills, disposition by   Pro §6132

PERSONAL PROPERTY BROKERS
Late payment charges   CC §2954.4

PERSONAL PROPERTY TAXATION
Heavy equipment rentals
    Addition of estimated personal property tax reimbursement to rental price   CC §1656.5
Reimbursement law
    Heavy equipment rentals, addition of estimated personal property tax reimbursement to rental price   CC §1656.5
Small claims court jurisdiction to enforce payment of delinquent unsecured personal property taxes   CCP §116.220

PERSONAL REPRESENTATIVES (See **EXECUTORS AND ADMINISTRATORS**)

PERSONAL SERVICE OF PROCESS (See **PROCESS AND SERVICE OF PROCESS**)

PERSONAL SERVICES
Birth name use   CCP §1279.6
Injunctions to prevent breach of contract   CCP §526
Lien for   CC §3051
Specific performance, denial of   CC §3390
Wage claims, preferences for   CCP §1206

PERSONNEL BOARD
Judicial notice of regulations   Ev §451

PEST CONTROL
Common interest developments
    Notice of pesticide application when not applied by licensed pest control operator   CC §4777
    Termites   CC §4780
        Temporary removal of occupant   CC §4785

PEST CONTROL—Cont.
Landlord and tenant
    Notice requirements   CC §1940.8.5

PESTICIDES
Animal testing, restrictions against
    Pesticides or chemical substances
        Canine and feline toxicological experiments   CC §1834.9.3
Claims against public entities and employees for use of   Gov §862
Landlord and tenant
    Notice requirements   CC §1940.8.5

PESTS (See **TERMITES AND PESTS**)

PETITION FOR REDRESS OF GRIEVANCE
Motion to strike causes of action having chilling effect on protected constitutional right to petition   CCP §§425.16, 425.17
    SLAPPback actions   CCP §425.18

PETITIONS
Administration of decedents' estates
    Generally (See **ADMINISTRATION OF ESTATES**)
    Executors and administrators (See **EXECUTORS AND ADMINISTRATORS**)
    Notice of petition to administer estate
        Publication   CRC 7.54
Administrative Procedure Act (See **ADMINISTRATIVE PROCEDURE ACT**)
Adoption (See **ADOPTION**)
Adult child requesting release from duty to support parent who abandoned him as minor   Fam §§4410 to 4414
Ancillary administration proceedings (See **ANCILLARY ADMINISTRATION**)
Annulment, petition for judgment of   Fam §2250
Appellate rules
    Superior courts (See **APPELLATE RULES, SUPERIOR COURT APPEALS**)
    Supreme court and courts of appeal (See **APPELLATE RULES, SUPREME COURT AND COURTS OF APPEAL**)
Arbitration (See **ARBITRATION**)
Certiorari   CCP §1069
Change of names   CCP §1276
Community property (See **COMMUNITY PROPERTY**)
Conciliation courts (See **CONCILIATION COURTS**)
Conservators (See **CONSERVATORS**)
Custody of children, petition for temporary custody   Fam §3060
Decedents' estates
    Administration of estates generally (See **ADMINISTRATION OF ESTATES**)
    Executors and administrators (See **EXECUTORS AND ADMINISTRATORS**)
    Notice of petition to administer estate   CRC 7.54
Disclaimer of estate interest, order authorizing personal representative to file   Pro §277
Dissolution of marriage (See **DISSOLUTION OF MARRIAGE**)
Emancipation of children (See **EMANCIPATION OF MINORS**)
Escheat (See **ESCHEAT**)
Executors of decedents' estates (See **EXECUTORS AND ADMINISTRATORS**)
Fact of death (See **FACT OF DEATH**)
Family law rules (See **FAMILY RULES**)
Filing fees
    Amendment of complaint or other subsequent pleadings
        Effect on filing fee   Gov §70613.5
    Conservatorship petitions (See **CONSERVATORS**)
    Guardianship petitions (See **GUARDIAN AND WARD**)
    Initial filing fees   Gov §§70611, 70613
        Permissible additional fees   Gov §70603
        Supplemental fees for first paper filing   Gov §§70602.5, 70602.6
    Probate petitions (See **WILL PROBATE**)
    Riverside County
        Courthouse seismic repair costs, additional filing fees authorized to defray   Gov §70622
Grandparental visitation rights   Fam §§3103, 3104
Guardian and ward (See **GUARDIAN AND WARD**)
Heirship proceedings (See **HEIRS**)
Homesteads (See **HOMESTEADS**)
Indigent parents, adult child's petition to be relieved of obligation to support   Fam §§4410 to 4414
Legal separation (See **LEGAL SEPARATION**)
Letters of administration, petition for   Pro §§8000, 8002
Mandamus   CCP §1086
Maps replaced   CCP §1855

PETITIONS—Cont.
Military service
  Financial obligations during service, relief   CRC 3.1372
Missing persons (See **MISSING PERSONS**)
Power of attorney (See **POWER OF ATTORNEY**)
Quieting title action (See **QUIETING TITLE**)
Simultaneous death, establishment of   Pro §§230 to 233
Small estates without administration (See **SMALL ESTATES WITHOUT ADMINISTRATION**)
State agency proceedings (See **ADMINISTRATIVE PROCEDURE ACT**)
Sterilization proceedings (See **STERILIZATION**)
Summary dissolution of marriage (See **SUMMARY DISSOLUTION OF MARRIAGE**)
Termination of parental rights   Fam §§7840, 7841
  Superior court fees   Gov §70633
Trusts (See **TRUSTS**)
Uniform Transfers to Minors Act (See **UNIFORM TRANSFERS TO MINORS ACT**)
Will probate (See **WILL PROBATE**)

PETIT JURY (See **JURY**)

PETS
Commercial and industrial common interest developments
  Protected uses   CC §6706
Divorce
  Division of property   Fam §2605
Domestic violence
  Protective orders on behalf of animals   Fam §6320
    California law enforcement telecommunications (CLETS) information form, confidentiality and use of information   CRC 1.51, CRCAppx A
    Denial of petition for ex parte order, reasons to be provided   Fam §6320.5
Harassment, protection orders
  Permissible orders regarding animal of petitioner   CCP §527.6
Legal separation
  Division of property   Fam §2605
Trusts for care of pets or domestic animals   Pro §15212

PEW
Easement rights for   CC §§801, 802

PHARMACISTS AND PHARMACIES
Bond required to secure costs in action against pharmacists   CCP §1029.6
Electronic medical records
  System requirements   CC §56.101
Malpractice (See **MALPRACTICE**)
Medical records
  Confidentiality to be maintained   CC §56.101
    Minors' records, disclosure to accomplish coordination of health care services and treatment   CC §56.103
    Pharmaceutical company requiring disclosure as condition of receiving pharmaceuticals   CC §56.102
    Waiver of confidentiality not to be required by companies   CC §56.05
  Electronic medical records
    System requirements   CC §56.101
Pharmaceutical companies
  Medical records
    Confidentiality to be maintained   CC §56.101
    Definition of pharmaceutical company   CC §56.05
    Pharmaceutical company requiring disclosure as condition of receiving pharmaceuticals   CC §56.102
    Waiver of confidentiality not to be required by companies   CC §56.05
Review committees, liability   CC §§43.7, 43.8
  Records of pharmacy review boards
    Discovery prohibition   Ev §1157
Study of fees charged for pharmaceutical services   CC §§2527, 2528

PHONOGRAPHS AND PHONOGRAPH RECORDS
Apartment housekeeper's lien, exemption from   CC §1861a
Serial number destroyed or altered prior to sale   CC §1710.1

PHOTOGRAPHS AND PHOTOCOPIES (See also **COPIES**)
Adoption agency releasing personal property upon request of adoptee and others   Fam §9206
Adoption proceedings, photo-listing service   Fam §8707
Advertising, unauthorized use of name or likeness in   CC §§3344, 3344.1
Apartment housekeeper's lien, exemption from   CC §1861a
Booking photographs
  Commercial use of booking photographs   CC §1798.91.1

PHOTOGRAPHS AND PHOTOCOPIES—Cont.
Business records photographed for evidence   Ev §1550
Conservators
  Conservatee, annual photograph   Pro §2360
Court indexes   CRC 10.851
Court proceedings, photographic recording of   CRC 1.150
Dead bodies
  Reproduction of photographs or video   CCP §129
Dependent adults or persons, abuse
  Domestic violence reports
    Inclusion of photographs   Fam §6228
Domestic violence
  Incident reports, inclusion of photographs   Fam §6228
Duplicates defined   Ev §260
Elderly persons, abuse and neglect
  Domestic violence reports
    Inclusion of photographs   Fam §6228
Eminent domain, preliminary photographs for   CCP §1245.010
Evidence, use as
  Microphotographed files, records, photographs, etc., in custody of criminal justice agency
    Reproductions, admissibility   Ev §1550.1
Fax transmissions (See **FACSIMILE TRANSMISSIONS**)
Fine prints, regulating sale of   CC §§1740 to 1745
Human trafficking
  Domestic violence incident reports
    Inclusion of photographs   Fam §6228
Invasion of privacy (See **INVASION OF PRIVACY**)
Jurors, photographing or other media coverage   CRC 1.150
Libel and slander   CC §45
Lost or destroyed writings   Ev §1551
Marriage
  Remote licensing and solemnization
    Photo identification   Fam §552
Medical records, attorney's written authorization to copy   Ev §1158
Original as evidence   Ev §255
Pornography (See **INDECENCY AND OBSCENITY**)
Postmortem examination or autopsy, restriction on reproducing photograph or video taken at scene of death or in course of   CCP §129
Privacy
  Photographs, films, etc., exposing intimate body parts or sexual acts of another without permission, distribution
    Actions for injunctions, damages, etc   CC §1708.85
    Confidential information form   CRCAppx A
Rape and other sex offenses
  Domestic violence incident reports
    Inclusion of photographs   Fam §6228
Stalking
  Domestic violence incident reports
    Inclusion of photographs   Fam §6228
Wills, photographic copies of (See **WILL PROBATE**)

PHYSICAL DISABILITIES (See **DISABLED PERSONS**)

PHYSICAL EXAMINATIONS (See also **MENTAL EXAMINATIONS**)
Administrative adjudication, language assistance provided in (See **ADMINISTRATIVE ADJUDICATION**)
Child abuse cases, admissibility of minor's statements made for purposes of medical diagnosis or treatment in   Ev §1253
Discovery procedure   CCP §§94, 2032.010 to 2032.650
  Applicability of provisions   CCP §2032.010
  Attorney attendance   CCP §2032.510
  Conduct of examination   CCP §§2032.510 to 2032.530
  Failure to produce another for examination
    Sanctions   CCP §2032.420
  Failure to submit
    Sanctions   CCP §2032.410
  Limitations on papers filed   CRC 3.250
  Methods of discovery   CCP §2019.010
  Monitoring examination   CCP §2032.510
  Motions for examination   CCP §§2032.310, 2032.320, CRC 3.1345
    Grounds for granting   CCP §2032.320
    Leave of court   CCP §2032.310
  Physician performing   CCP §2032.020
  Plaintiffs, personal injury cases   CCP §§2032.210 to 2032.260
    Conditions for examination   CCP §2032.220
    Definitions   CCP §2032.210
    Failure to timely respond   CCP §2032.240
    Grounds for seeking examination   CCP §2032.220
    Motion for compliance with demand   CCP §2032.250
    Response to demand   CCP §2032.230

PHYSICAL EXAMINATIONS—Cont.
Discovery procedure —Cont.
Plaintiffs, personal injury cases —Cont.
Retention of demand, proof of service and response   CCP §2032.260
Sanctions   CCP §§2032.240, 2032.250
Protective orders
Suspension of examination pending motion   CCP §2032.510
Recording examination   CCP §2032.510
Reports of examination   CCP §§2032.610 to 2032.650
Attorney work product waived for demand for report   CCP §§2032.610, 2032.630
Demanding report   CCP §2032.610
Existing and later reports of same condition, demand recipient's right to   CCP §§2032.640, 2032.650
Failure to timely deliver   CCP §2032.620
Motion to compel   CCP §§2032.620, 2032.650
Right to discovery   CCP §2032.020
Economic litigation provisions for limited civil cases, permissible forms of discovery under   CCP §94
Interpreter during
Generally   Ev §755.5
Administrative adjudication (See **ADMINISTRATIVE ADJUDICATION**)
Judges, proceedings for removal of   JudPerR 105
Juvenile court, authorization of psychotropic medication for treatment of psychiatric disorder or illness of dependent child   CRC 5.640
Forms, judicial council   CRCAppx A
Prescriptions
Release of psychotropic medication prescription information to medical board, authorization   CRC 5.642
Sterilization proceedings   Pro §1955

PHYSICAL IMPAIRMENT
Disqualification of judges, grounds for   CCP §170.1

PHYSICALLY CHALLENGED PERSONS (See **DISABLED PERSONS**)

PHYSICAL THERAPISTS
Bond required to secure costs in action against therapists   CCP §1029.6
Malpractice (See **MALPRACTICE**)
Medical records, attorney's authorized inspection of   CCP §1985.7, Ev §1158

PHYSICIANS AND SURGEONS
Abortions (See **ABORTIONS**)
Administrative law proceedings (See **ADMINISTRATIVE ADJUDICATION**)
Assisted reproduction, consent required for   Fam §7613
Bond required to secure costs in action against   CCP §1029.6
Chiropractors (See **CHIROPRACTORS**)
Commercial blockage tort affecting medical care facilities   CC §§3427 to 3427.4
Complaints from public   CC §43.96
Conciliation court proceedings, testimony in   Fam §1838
Confidentiality of medical information   CC §§56.101, 56.104, 56 to 56.37
Electronic medical records
System requirements   CC §56.101
Disciplinary proceedings (See **ADMINISTRATIVE ADJUDICATION**)
Discovery of medical records (See **DISCOVERY**)
Infants, treatment of (See **MINORS**)
Insurance
Malpractice (See **MALPRACTICE**)
Underwriting committee, liability of physician member of   CC §§43.7, 43.8
Intimate partner violence, minor victims 12 or older
Reports by health practitioner
Duties of reporting practitioner   Fam §6930
Libel of physicians by communicating proceedings of peer review committees   CC §§43.7, 43.8
Life sustaining procedures
Physician orders for life sustaining treatment form   Pro §4780
Conflicting instructions   Pro §4781.4
Duties of health care providers to apply   Pro §4781.2
Limitation of actions (See **MALPRACTICE**)
Malpractice (See **MALPRACTICE**)
Medical Board of California
Psychotropic medication
Release of information to medical board, judicial council forms   CRCAppx A
Medical claims data error correction   CC §57
Medical treatment (See **MEDICAL TREATMENT**)
Minors, treatment of (See **MINORS**)
Morbidity and mortality studies, admissibility of   Ev §§1156, 1156.1

PHYSICIANS AND SURGEONS—Cont.
Multiphasic screening units, immunity from liability for patients referred by   CC §43.9
Opticians and optometrists (See **OPTICIANS AND OPTOMETRISTS**)
Osteopaths (See **OSTEOPATHS**)
Peer review committees
Disclosure of medical information to   CC §56.10
Discovery or testimony, prohibition relating to   Ev §§1157, 1157.5
Liability of members of   CC §§43.7, 43.8
Physical examinations
Discovery procedure
By whom performed   CCP §2032.020
Physical therapists (See **PHYSICAL THERAPISTS**)
Privileged communications (See **PRIVILEGED COMMUNICATIONS**)
Professional review committee (See within this heading, **"Peer review committees"**)
Professional societies (See **PROFESSIONAL SOCIETIES**)
Psychotherapists (See **PSYCHOTHERAPISTS**)
Recommendation of medical staff, limited immunity from liability for action taken on   CC §43.97
Records of (See **MEDICAL RECORDS**)
Referral of complaints to appropriate board   CC §43.96
Review committee (See within this heading, **"Peer review committees"**)
Sexual misconduct
Assault on incapacitated person
Statute of limitations on sexual assault damages   CCP §340.16
University of California
Physician employed by or with privileges at university facility
Statute of limitations on sexual assault or other inappropriate action by physician   CCP §340.16
Wrongful death caused by physician (See **MALPRACTICE**)

PHYSICIAN'S PROFESSIONAL NEGLIGENCE (See **MALPRACTICE**)

PIANOS
Serial number destroyed or altered prior to sale   CC §1710.1

PICKETING (See **DEMONSTRATIONS, PARADES AND MEETINGS**)

PICNICS
Landowner liability for picnickers   CC §846

PICTURES
Motion pictures (See **MOTION PICTURES**)
Photographs (See **PHOTOGRAPHS AND PHOTOCOPIES**)

PIERS (See **WHARVES**)

PILOT AND DEMONSTRATION PROJECTS
Alternative dispute resolution   CCP §1775
Family law pilot projects (See **FAMILY LAW PILOT PROJECTS**)
Mediation of civil actions   CCP §§1730, 1775
Small claims courts, public entity as party in   CCP §116.232

PIPELINES
Gas pipelines
Real estate sales, residential property disclosures
Gas and hazardous liquid transmission pipelines   CC §2079.10.5
Hazardous liquid pipelines
Real estate sales, residential property disclosures
Gas and hazardous liquid transmission pipelines   CC §2079.10.5
Indemnity coverage for construction, repair, renovation, maintenance or demolition of lines   CC §2783
Real estate sales, residential property disclosures
Gas and hazardous liquid transmission pipelines   CC §2079.10.5

PISTOLS (See **FIREARMS AND OTHER WEAPONS**)

PLACE
Conciliation courts, place of hearings   Fam §1837
Inspection of personal records of state agency   CC §§1798.21, 1798.22
Process, place for service of   CCP §413.10

PLACEMENT PREFERENCE RULES (See **ADOPTION; FOSTER CARE HOMES**)

PLACE OF BUSINESS
Service of process at   CCP §415.20

PLAINTIFFS
Designation of parties   CCP §308

PLAINTIFFS—Cont.
Groundwater rights actions
    Definition of plaintiffs   CCP §832
Permissive joinder   CCP §§378, 427.10
Unwilling plaintiff made defendant   CCP §382
Vexatious litigants (See **VEXATIOUS LITIGANTS**)

PLANNED DEVELOPMENTS
Common interest developments
    Commercial and industrial common interest developments generally   CC §§6500 to 6876 (See **COMMERCIAL AND INDUSTRIAL COMMON INTEREST DEVELOPMENTS**)
    Generally   CC §§4000 to 6150 (See **COMMON INTEREST DEVELOPMENTS**)

PLANTS
Eminent domain statutes affecting property reserved for protection of   CCP §1240.670
Inspection warrants (See **INSPECTION WARRANTS**)

PLASTER
Fixtures attached to real property by   CC §660

PLASTIC FABRICATORS
Mechanics' liens by   CC §3051

PLATS (See **MAPS AND PLATS**)

PLAYGROUNDS (See **PARKS AND PLAYGROUNDS**)

PLEA BARGAINING   CCP §33
Guilty plea
    Punishment, specification in plea   CRC 4.412

PLEADINGS
Accounts alleged   CCP §454
Affidavit, verification by   CCP §446
Ambiguity   CCP §§430.10, 430.20
Amendment   CRC 3.1324
    Alterations on face of pleading   CRC 3.1324
    Contents of motion to amend   CRC 3.1324
    Court to which action transferred, amended or supplemental pleadings necessary for determination in   CCP §399
    Demurrer sustained, discretion to grant leave to amend pleadings where   CCP §472a
    Designation of pages and line numbers of deleted or added allegations   CRC 3.1324
    Discretion to allow   CCP §473
    Health care providers, amended pleadings for punitive damages against   CCP §425.13
    Immaterial variance in pleading and proof   CCP §470
    Judge allowing   CCP §576
    Judgment on the pleadings
        Leave to amend pleadings   CCP §438
        Meet and confer prior to moving for judgment on the pleadings
            Effect of amendment to pleadings   CCP §439
            Judicial council legal forms   CRCAppx A
    Law and motion proceedings   CRC 3.1324
    Material variance in pleading and proof   CCP §469
    Mistakes as grounds for   CCP §473
    Motion to strike granted, discretion to grant leave to amend pleadings where   CCP §472a
    Names, discretion to allow party to add, strike or correct   CCP §473
    Orders deemed excepted to   CCP §647
    Postponement of trial   CCP §473
    Striking of pleadings, motion
        Meet and confer prior to moving to strike pleadings
            Effect of amendment to pleadings   CCP §435.5
            Judicial council legal forms   CRCAppx A
        Right to amend pleadings   CCP §472
    Supplemental pleadings generally (See within this heading, "**Supplemental pleadings**")
    Supporting declaration   CRC 3.1324
    Time limitations to amend pleadings by party in action   CCP §472
    Transferred causes, amendment of pleadings in
        Time frames for transferring jurisdiction in family law actions or proceedings   CRC 5.97
    True name of defendant designated as unknown   CCP §474
    Unpleaded cause, permission to assert   CCP §426.50
Answers (See **ANSWERS**)
Attorneys, verification by   CCP §446

PLEADINGS—Cont.
Bar of statutes of limitation, pleading   CCP §458
Captions   CCP §422.30
    Affidavits or declarations   CRC 3.1115
    Class actions   CRC 3.761
    Demurrers   CRC 3.1320
Case cover sheets   CRC 3.220
Certainty, absence of   CCP §§430.10, 430.20
Change of venue, transfer of pleadings and papers on   CCP §399
    Time frames for transferring jurisdiction
        Family law actions or proceedings   CRC 5.97
Cities, verification by   CCP §446
Complaints (See **COMPLAINTS**)
Construction of   CCP §452
Contracts
    Conditions precedent, allegations as to   CCP §457
    Written contract, alleging uncertainty of   CCP §§430.10, 430.20
Corporations, verification by   CCP §446
Counties, verification by   CCP §446
Cover sheet requirement for first paper filed in action or proceeding   CRC 3.220
Cross-complaints (See **CROSS-COMPLAINTS**)
Defined   CCP §420
Demurrers (See **DEMURRERS**)
Depositions (See **DEPOSITIONS**)
Deposits in court   CCP §572
Disregard of nonprejudicial error   CCP §475
Dissolution of marriage (See **DISSOLUTION OF MARRIAGE**)
Districts, verification by   CCP §446
Economic litigation provisions for limited civil cases   CCP §92
Eminent domain (See **EMINENT DOMAIN**)
English language, papers and proceedings to be in   CCP §185
Environmental pollution action, Attorney General to be provided copy of pleading by party filing   CCP §388
Escheat (See **ESCHEAT**)
Extension of time for acts relating to   CCP §§1054, 1054.1
    Electronic filing, when required   CRCSupp 1st AppDist
    Memorandum in support of application for order to extend not required   CRC 3.1114
Facts, alleging lack of sufficiency of   CCP §430.10
Family law rules (See **FAMILY RULES**)
Forms
    Judicial council legal forms   CRCAppx A
    Preemption of local rules   CRC 3.20
General rules of pleading   CCP §§452 to 465
Good faith settlement, motion for dismissal of pleading or part of pleading on basis of   CRC 3.1382
Governing law   CCP §421
Groundwater rights actions
    Electronic service of pleadings and papers   CCP §839
Immaterial allegation defined   CCP §431.10
Indictment (See **INDICTMENT, INFORMATION AND COMPLAINT**)
Insurance liability exemptions   CCP §431.50
Intelligibility, objection based on absence of   CCP §§430.10, 430.20
Interpleader (See **INTERPLEADER**)
Interstate family support
    Commencement of proceedings   Fam §5700.311
Issues joined   CCP §§588 to 590
Judges (See **JUDGES**)
Judgments (See **JUDGMENTS**)
Jury to try question of fact not put in issue by   CCP §309
Law and motion proceedings
    Motions concerning pleading and venue   CRC 3.1320 to 3.1326
Libel and slander action (See **LIBEL AND SLANDER**)
Liberal construction   CCP §452
Livestock service liens, sale under   CC §3080.08
Local laws, allegations as to   CCP §459
Local rules of court
    Preemption of local rules for form and format   CRC 3.20
Lost pleadings, copies replacing   CCP §1045
Material allegation
    Admission by failure to respond   CCP §§431.20, 431.30
    Defined   CCP §431.10
Mistakes
    Amended pleadings   CCP §473
    Demurrer (See **DEMURRERS**)
    Disregard of nonprejudicial error   CCP §475
    Variance in pleading and proof (See within this heading, "**Variance**")
Motion to strike (See **MOTION TO STRIKE**)
Nonprejudicial error, disregard of   CCP §475
Objections to pleadings   CCP §§430.10 to 430.80
Permissible pleadings   CCP §422.10

PLEADINGS—Cont.
Preemption of local rules for form and format CRC 3.20
Privacy protection CRC 1.201
Probate rules
    Definitions CRC 7.3
    Execution and verification of amended or supplemental pleadings CRC 7.104
    Notice of hearing
        Amended or supplemental pleadings CRC 7.53
        Description of pleadings in notice of hearing CRC 7.50
    Signature CRC 7.103
    Verification CRC 7.103
Process and service of process
    Time for service CRC 3.110
Real property, recovery of CCP §455
Related cases, notice to judge of CRC 3.300
Relief from judgment application accompanied by pleading proposed to be filed therein CCP §473
School districts, verification by CCP §446
State, verification by CCP §446
Statute of limitation, alleging cause of action barred by CCP §458
Striking motion (See **MOTION TO STRIKE**)
Striking of pleadings
    Amendment of pleading
        Following grant of motion CCP §472a
Superior courts (See **SUPERIOR COURTS**)
Supplemental pleadings
    Court to which action transferred, amended or supplemental pleadings necessary for determination in CCP §399
    Filing and service of CCP §465
    Motion for CCP §464
Third party pleadings CCP §428.70
Time after cross-complaint CCP §432.10
Transfer of causes, forwarding of pleadings
    Time frames for transferring jurisdiction
        Family law actions or proceedings CRC 5.97
Unlawful detainer CC §1952.3, CCP §§425.12, 1166
    Forms
        Judicial council legal forms CRCAppx A
Unpleaded cause, permission to assert CCP §426.50
Variance
    Distinguished from failure of proof CCP §471
    Immaterial variance CCP §470
    Material variance in pleading and proof CCP §469
Venue changes, transfer of pleadings for
    Time frames for transferring jurisdiction
        Family law actions or proceedings CRC 5.97
Verification of pleadings (See **VERIFICATION**)
Voided filing
    Check for filing fees returned unpaid CCP §411.20
    Underpayment of filing fees CCP §411.21

PLEAS
Court reporters to take down all arraignments, pleas and sentences in felony cases CCP §269
Domestic violence
    Judicial council forms CRCAppx A
Guilty plea (See **GUILTY PLEA**)
Judicial council forms CRCAppx A

PLEDGES
Common interest developments
    Collection of assessments
        Assignment or pledge of right to collect CC §5735
Distinguishing between pledge and mortgage CC §2924
Lien statutes applicable to CC §2877

PLUMBERS AND PLUMBING
Inspection warrants to determine violations CCP §1822.50
Water conserving plumbing retrofits CC §§1101.1 to 1101.9

PLURAL
Construction of words used in code CCP §17
Family code Fam §10

P.O.D ACCOUNTS (See **MULTIPLE-PARTY ACCOUNTS**)

PODIATRY AND PODIATRISTS
Administrative law disciplinary proceedings (See **ADMINISTRATIVE ADJUDICATION**)
Bond required to secure costs in action against podiatrists CCP §1029.6

PODIATRY AND PODIATRISTS—Cont.
Communication of information, liability for CC §43.8
Complaints from public CC §43.96
Discovery prohibitions Ev §1157
Malpractice (See **MALPRACTICE**)
Medical records, attorney's authorized inspection of CCP §1985.7, Ev §1158
Referral of complaints to appropriate board CC §43.96
Review committees, liability of CC §§43.7, 43.8

POINTS AND AUTHORITIES
Attachment CCP §§484.070, 484.350, 484.360
Claim and delivery hearings CCP §512.050
Innkeeper's lien, writ of possession on CC §1861.9
New trial, memorandum of points and authorities for (See **NEW TRIAL**)

POLICE OFFICERS (See **LAW ENFORCEMENT OFFICERS**)

POLITICAL AFFILIATION
Discrimination based on political affiliation CC §§51.7, 52
    Construction or application of provisions in issue, solicitor general notified CC §51.1
    Judicial ethics code
        Administrative responsibilities of judge, impartial discharge CRCSupp JudEthicsCanon 3
        Attorneys, judges to require to refrain from manifesting CRCSupp JudEthicsCanon 3
        Court personnel and staff under direction of judge, standards of conduct enforced by judge CRCSupp JudEthicsCanon 3
    Violence or intimidation, freedom from
        Waiver of right to freedom from violence, coerced or involuntary CC §51.7

POLITICAL CAMPAIGN FUNDS
Judges
    Campaign contributions
        Disqualification from case, contribution as grounds CCP §170.1
    Solicitation of contributions or endorsements for personal campaign or for judicial campaigns of others CRCSupp JudEthicsCanon 5

POLITICAL CAMPAIGNS
Advertising
    Superimposition of photographs
        Precedence of proceedings involving elections CCP §35

POLITICAL SUBDIVISIONS
Bonds issued by (See **BONDS**)
Presentation of claims as prerequisite to commencement of actions against governmental agencies CCP §313
Service of process on CCP §416.50

POLITICS
Sale of political items CC §§1739 to 1739.4

POLLING JURY CCP §618

POLLUTION (See **ENVIRONMENTAL HAZARDS**)

POLYGRAPH
Exclusion of polygraph evidence Ev §351.1

POOLS
Juror pools (See **JURY**)

POOR PERSONS (See **INDIGENT PERSONS**)

POPULAR NAMES OF ACTS (See **CITATION OF ACTS**)

PORCELAIN PAINTING
Fine art, defined as CC §997

PORTER-COLOGNE WATER QUALITY CONTROL ACT
Limitation of actions CCP §338

POSSESSION
Action to recover for CC §§3375, 3379, 3380
Administrator having right of Pro §§9650, 9651
Adverse possession (See **ADVERSE POSSESSION**)
Attachment (See **ATTACHMENT**)
Bailment contract, transfer under CC §1925
Bonds
    Corporate executors, bond requirements for Pro §301
    Trust companies Pro §301
Claim and delivery (See **CLAIM AND DELIVERY**)

POSSESSION—Cont.
Contempt for re-entry after removal from   CCP §1210
Damages for wrongful possession   CC §§3334 to 3336
Domestic violence protective orders determining   Fam §6324
Easement, rights under   CC §810
Eminent domain
    Orders for possession
        After judgment   CCP §§1268.210 to 1268.240
        Prior to judgment   CCP §§1255.410 to 1255.480
Enforcement of judgments (See **ENFORCEMENT OF JUDGMENTS**)
Executor having right of   Pro §§9650, 9651
Future time, possession at   CC §767
Homestead   Pro §6520
Innkeeper's lien   CC §§1861 to 1861.28
Judgment granting recovery of   CCP §667
Lien dependent on possession   CC §§2913, 3051
Lost property, liability and duties of finder of   CC §2080
Mobilehomes, writ of possession for   CCP §§515.010, 515.020
Mortgages (See **TRUST DEEDS AND MORTGAGES**)
Ouster, cotenant's right to establish   CC §843
Ownership presumed from   Ev §637
Quieting title (See **QUIETING TITLE**)
Receivers   CCP §568
Recovery of real property, seisin or possession within five years of commencement of action for   CCP §318
Renewal of lease presumed   CC §1945
Retail installment sales, finance charge assessed after buyer's possession of goods   CC §§1805.6, 1810.10
Risk of loss under sales contract after transfer of   CC §1662
Room, tenant's right to possession of   CC §1950
Special administrators having possession of estate assets   Pro §8544
Specific relief, award of   CC §3367
Stay of judgment for delivery of   CCP §917.4
Third party claim of right of possession of property levied upon   CCP §§720.110 to 720.170
Title to real property, seisin or possession within five years of commencement of action arising out of   CCP §319
Unlawful detainer (See **UNLAWFUL DETAINER**)
Voidable transaction presumed in absence of   CC §3440
Wills (See **WILLS**)

POSSIBILITY OF REVERTER
Conveyances   CC §1045

POSTADOPTION CONTACT AGREEMENTS   CRC 5.451, Fam §§8616.5, 8714, 8714.5

POSTAL SERVICE (See **MAIL AND MAILING**)

POSTERS
Political posters, sale of   CC §1739.1

POSTHUMOUS CHILDREN
Conception after death of decedent
    Heirs, identity and distributions   Pro §§249.5 to 249.8
        Early distribution, petition for   Pro §249.8
        Effect on distribution   Pro §249.6
        Failure to provide timely notice   Pro §249.7
        Intestate descent   Pro §6453
        Presumption of birth during lifetime of decedent   Pro §249.5
Future interests   CC §§698, 739
Intestate descent   Pro §§240, 6407

POSTING
Administration of estates (See **ADMINISTRATION OF ESTATES**)
Apartment house owner, posting notice of   CC §1962.5
Decedents' estates (See **ADMINISTRATION OF ESTATES**)
Destroyed land records relief law proceedings, service in   CCP §751.08
Earthquakes, boundary reestablishment after   CCP §751.54
Electronic court records
    Privacy policy, posting   CRC 2.504
Enforcement of judgments (See **ENFORCEMENT OF JUDGMENTS**)
Grain sold in bulk, posting notice of   CC §1880.7
Hotel rights, notice of   CC §1863
Human trafficking
    Businesses required to post notice concerning relief from slavery or human trafficking   CC §52.6
Letters of administration, notice of hearing for   Pro §8003
Mobilehome parks
    Mobilehome assistance center
        Signs, posting by housing and community development department   CC §798.29

POSTING—Cont.
Parking facilities' limitation of liability, posting contract for   CC §1630
Process (See **PROCESS AND SERVICE OF PROCESS**)
Quieting title action   CCP §763.020
Unlawful detainer actions, service in   CCP §415.45

POSTMORTEM EXAMINATIONS
Restriction on reproducing photograph or video taken in course of   CCP §129

POSTPONEMENT
Continuances (See **CONTINUANCES**)
Holiday postponing performance of act required by law or contract   CCP §13
Small claims court (See **SMALL CLAIMS COURTS**)

POSTRELEASE COMMUNITY SUPERVISION
Jury service
    Felons currently on parole, probation, etc
        Ineligibility to serve as juror   CCP §203
Revocation
    Sentencing upon revocation   CRC 4.435
Revocation procedure
    Supervising agency reports as to compliance with provisions   CRC 4.541
Risk/needs assessment, court use in sentencing   CRC JudAdminStand 4.35

POSTSECONDARY EDUCATION
Debt collection
    Educational debt collection practices   CC §§1788.90 to 1788.94
        Definitions   CC §1788.92
        Legislative findings and intent   CC §1788.91
        Prohibited debt collection practices by schools   CC §1788.93
        Short title of act   CC §1788.90
        Transcript used as leverage to collect debt, prohibition   CC §1788.93
        Waivers   CC §1788.94
Students
    Violence threatened on campus or facility
        Orders against violence threatened on campus or facility   CRCAppx I Emer Rule 8
Violence threatened on campus or facility
    Orders against violence threatened on campus or facility
        COVID-19, emergency rule   CRCAppx I Emer Rule 8

POST-TRAUMATIC STRESS DISORDER (PTSD)
Veterans in need of services
    Sentence and punishment, alternate commitment for combat veterans
        Orders for dismissal, judicial council legal forms   CRCAppx A

POULTRY
Dogs injuring   CC §3341
Statute of limitation against veterinarians or persons boarding or feeding   CCP §340

POUR-OVER PROVISIONS
Life insurance   Pro §§6321 to 6330
Trusts (See **TRUSTS**)
Wills (See **WILLS**)

POWER OF APPOINTMENT   Pro §§600 to 695
Common law rules, applicability of   Pro §600
Contract to make appointment by donee, validity of   Pro §660
Creating instruments
    Required to create power   Pro §621
Creation
    Generally   Pro §620
    Requirements   Pro §621
    Revocability   Pro §695
Creditors' rights
    Donor
        Ability of donor to nullify or alter rights of powerholder's creditors   Pro §680
        General power of appointment in favor of donor, claims against property subject to   Pro §683
    General power of appointment
        Donor, claims against property subject to power in favor of   Pro §683
        Powerholder, claims against property subject to power exercised by   Pro §682
    Special power of appointment, claims against property subject to   Pro §681
    Support obligations of powerholder   Pro §684
Death
    Ineffective appointment resulting from death of appointee where powers exercisable only on powerholder's death   Pro §673
    Powerholder, exercise of power on death of   Pro §§634, 671

POWER OF APPOINTMENT—Cont.
Death—Cont.
  Special power of appointment, effect of death of appointee before exercise of   Pro §674
Definitions   Pro §§610 to 613
Disclaimer of estate interest   Pro §§260 to 295
Discretionary power of appointment
  Defined   Pro §613
  Failure of appointment, release of powers or failure to exercise by powerholder as grounds for   Pro §672
Exercise of power by powerholder   Pro §625
  Capacity of powerholder   Pro §625
Exercise of powers
  Generally   Pro §630
  Consent of donor or other third party   Pro §633
  Discretionary power of court to excuse failure to comply with formal requirements   Pro §631
  Intent required of power holder   Pro §§640 to 642
    Creation of power, intent required   Pro §621
  Judicial relief for defective imperative powers   Pro §635
  Legal capacity of powerholder   Pro §625
  Manner, time, and conditions for   Pro §630
  Revocability of   Pro §695
  Specific reference to power of appointment, requirement that exercising instrument contain   Pro §632
  Two or more powerholders, effect of powers created in favor of   Pro §634
  Who may exercise powers   Pro §625
Failure of appointment
  Exercise of power more than permitted by terms of power, validity of   Pro §670
  Imperative powers, defective exercise or failure to exercise   Pro §671
Future estate, effect on vesting of   CC §781
General power of appointment
  Creditors' claims
    Donor, claims against property subject to power in favor of   Pro §683
    Powerholder, claims against property subject to power exercised by   Pro §682
  Defined   Pro §611
  Ineffective appointment by powerholder resulting in implied alternative appointment to powerholder's estate   Pro §672
Governing law   Pro §601
Imperative power of appointment
  Defective power, effect of   Pro §635
  Defined   Pro §613
  Failure of appointment, defective exercise or failure to exercise as grounds for   Pro §671
Intent required of powerholder   Pro §§640 to 642
  Required to create power   Pro §621
Minor powerholder
  Exercise of power during minority   Pro §625
  Release on behalf of by guardian   Pro §662
Postponed powers of appointment   Pro §612
Powerholders
  Adult, requirement that powerholder exercising power be   Pro §625
  Capacity   Pro §625
  Death   Pro §§634, 671
  Intent to exercise power, circumstances manifesting   Pro §§640 to 642
  Legal capacity   Pro §625
  Minor   Pro §§625, 662
  Release of one of several powerholders, effect   Pro §634
  Scope of authority   Pro §§630 to 635
  Several powerholders, exercise of power by   Pro §634
  Types of general power appointments   Pro §650
  Types of special power appointments   Pro §§651, 652
Presently executable   Pro §612
Presently exercisable   Pro §660
Release
  Generally   Pro §661
  Discretionary powers, effect of powerholder's release   Pro §672
  Minor powerholder, release of power by guardian or trustee on behalf of   Pro §662
  Revocability of   Pro §695
Revocation of   Pro §695
Rule against perpetuities (See **PERPETUITIES AND RESTRAINTS ON ALIENATION**)
Special power of appointment
  Creditors' claims   Pro §681
  Defined   Pro §611
  Exclusion of appointees by powerholder   Pro §651
Support obligations of powerholder, effect of claims involving   Pro §684

POWER OF APPOINTMENT—Cont.
Surviving issue
  Special power of appointment, surviving issue of appointee   Pro §674
  Testamentary power of appointment, surviving issue of appointee   Pro §673
Testamentary power of appointment   Pro §612
Transfer of appointive power
  Required to create power   Pro §621
Trusts subject to (See **TRUSTS**)
Two or more powerholders, effect of powers created in favor of   Pro §634
Voidable powers
  Exercise of power in excess of terms in power   Pro §670
  Imperative powers, defective exercise or failure to exercise   Pro §671
Wills
  Existing power of appointment at donee's death but created after execution of donee's will, effect on exercise of powers by   Pro §642
  General residuary clause as grounds for exercising powers, applicability of   Pro §641

POWER OF ATTORNEY
Generally   Pro §§4000 to 4034
Absentee principal   Pro §§3720 to 3722
Accounts of transactions, duty to maintain   Pro §4236
Affidavit regarding good faith action without knowledge of death or incapacity of principal   Pro §4305
Aged persons, health care power of attorney for (See within this heading, **"Health care power of attorney"**)
Agency law, applicability of   Pro §4051
Annuity transactions, powers under statutory form power of attorney for   Pro §4457
Appeals from orders   Pro §§1302, 1302.5, 1310
Applicability of agency law   Pro §4051
Applicability of power of attorney provisions   Pro §§4050, 4100, 4101
Attorney in fact
  Breach of duty   Pro §4231.5
  Capacity to act as   Pro §4200
  Compensation of   Pro §4204
  Equitable excusal   Pro §4231.5
  Exercise authority, duty to   Pro §4230
  Grant of authority   Pro §§4260 to 4266
  Health care (See within this heading, **"Health care power of attorney"**)
  Mechanical acts, power to delegate authority for   Pro §4205
  More than one attorney in fact, designation of   Pro §4202
  Nondurable power of attorney, termination of authority under   Pro §4155
  Personal jurisdiction, attorney in fact subject to   Pro §4522
  Redesignation of   Pro §4207
  Remedy for bad faith wrongful act   Pro §4231.5
  Revocation of authority   Pro §4153
  Separate and distinct, duty to keep principal's property as   Pro §4233
  Sole interest of principal, duty of attorney in fact to act in   Pro §4232
  Standard of care in dealing with principal's property   Pro §4231
  Successor attorneys in fact, designation of one or more   Pro §4203
  Termination of authority under nondurable power of attorney   Pro §4155
  Undue influence to take, conceal, etc property of principal   Pro §4231.5
  Unqualified person, effect of designating   Pro §5201
Attorney's fees
  Award of   Pro §4545
  Health care power of attorney, action on   Pro §4771
  Liability in action to confirm authority of attorney in fact against third persons   Pro §4306
  Statutory power of attorney, compelling third person to honor agent's authority under   Pro §4406
Authority granted by   Pro §4123
Bad faith of attorney in fact   Pro §4231.5
Banks
  Financial institutions (See within this heading, **"Financial institutions"**)
  Loans
    Authority to perform act regarding   Pro §4264
    No requirement for financial institution to make loan when prior relationship with principal   Pro §4310
Beneficiaries
  General authority to perform act regarding designation of   Pro §4264
  Statutory form power of attorney, powers under   Pro §4458
Bond transactions, statutory form power of attorney regarding   Pro §4453
Business operating transactions, authority under statutory form power of attorney for   Pro §4456
Capacity to execute power of attorney   Pro §4120
Certified copy of power of attorney, effect of   Pro §4307
Claims and litigation, powers under statutory form power of attorney as to   Pro §4459
Commencement of proceedings under petition   Pro §4542

POWER OF ATTORNEY—Cont.
Commodity and option transactions, statutory form powers regarding   Pro §4454
Communication with principal, duty for   Pro §4234
Compensation of attorney in fact   Pro §4204
Conservators and guardians
   Accountability of attorney in fact to   Pro §4206
   Nomination of   Pro §§4126, 4127
Consultants for carrying out duties, designation of   Pro §4235
Copy of records, persons entitled to make   Pro §4236
Cumulative remedies   Pro §4501
Deeds of trust and mortgages
   Modification or workout plan to avoid foreclosure
      Disabled person victim of prohibited acts, punishment   CC §2944.8
      Prohibited acts   CC §2944.7
      Senior citizen victim of prohibited acts, punishment   CC §2944.8
      Statute of limitations to enforce protections   CC §2944.10
Definitions for purposes of   Pro §§4014 to 4034
Delivery of property and records on termination of authority, duty for   Pro §4238
Dismissal of petitions   Pro §4543
Dissolution of marriage
   Generally   Pro §§3722, 4154
   Health care power of attorney   Pro §4697
Durable power of attorney
   Defined   Pro §§4018, 4124
   Effect of acts done by   Pro §4125
   Fiduciary or conservator's power to revoke or amend durable power of attorney   Pro §4206
   Health care (See within this heading, **"Health care power of attorney"**)
   Printed form of durable power for use without advice of counsel   Pro §4128
   Statutory form power of attorney (See within this heading, **"Statutory form power of attorney"**)
Effective date of law   Pro §4054
Elderly persons, health care power of attorney for (See within this heading, **"Health care power of attorney"**)
Employees, effect of power of attorney on third person conducting activities through   Pro §4308
Estate transactions, powers under statutory form power of attorney for   Pro §4458
Euthanasia   Pro §4653
Examination of records, persons entitled to   Pro §4236
Exercise authority, duty of attorney in fact to   Pro §4230
Express statement, limiting application of power by   Pro §4101
Family maintenance, powers under statutory form power of attorney regarding   Pro §4460
Fiduciaries
   Conservators and guardians
      Accountability of attorney in fact to   Pro §4206
      Nomination   Pro §§4125, 4126
Financial institutions
   Loans
      Authority to perform act regarding   Pro §4264
      No requirement for financial institution to make loan when prior relationship with principal   Pro §4310
      Previous relationship with principal, obligation to open accounts or make loans in absence of   Pro §4310
   Special power of attorney applicable to transactions with   Pro §5204
   Statutory form power of attorney, powers under   Pro §4455
Form, statutory form power of attorney
   Applicability of provisions   Pro §4407
General authority without limitations, authority of attorney in fact under grant of   Pro §4261
General procedural provisions of Probate Code, application of   Pro §4505
Gift, authority to perform act regarding   Pro §4264
Good faith reliance on power of attorney, liability of third person acting on   Pro §4303
Governmental programs, powers under statutory form power of attorney regarding   Pro §4461
Gross negligence of attorney in fact   Pro §4231.5
Guardians
   Accountability of attorney in fact to   Pro §4206
   Nomination   Pro §§4126, 4127
Health care power of attorney   Pro §§4680 to 4691
   Generally   Pro §4671
   Admission to facility, prohibition on requiring health care directive as prerequisite to   Pro §4677
   Advance health care directives under Health Care Decisions Law, durable powers of attorney as   Pro §4665
      Electronic directive or power of attorney   Pro §4673
   Agent's authority, generally   Pro §§4682 to 4688
   Appealable orders   Pro §1302.5

POWER OF ATTORNEY—Cont.
Health care power of attorney —Cont.
   Attorneys' fees in action on power of attorney   Pro §4771
   Conflict between attorney in fact and principal, resolution of   Pro §4689
   Consultation with others in event of principal's incapacitation   Pro §4690
   Death of principal
      Notice   Pro §4691
   Definitions   Pro §§4603 to 4643
   Dissolution of marriage between principal and agent, effect of   Pro §4697
   Electronic directive or power of attorney   Pro §4673
   Eligibility for agency   Pro §4659
   Euthanasia   Pro §4653
   Forgery of health care directives   Pro §§4742, 4743
   General provisions of Health Care Decisions Law   Pro §§4600 to 4665
   Health care providers' duties and liabilities   Pro §§4730 to 4736, 4740, 4742
   Homicide prosecution for hastening death by concealing or forging health care directive   Pro §4743
   Immunity from liability   Pro §§4740, 4741
   Information and medical records, right of attorney in fact to receive   Pro §4678
   Insurance, prohibition on requiring advance health care directive as prerequisite to   Pro §4677
   Judicial proceedings
      Generally   Pro §§4750 to 4755
      Appealable orders   Pro §1302.5
      Attorneys' fees   Pro §4771
      Jurisdiction   Pro §§4760 to 4762
      Petition and procedure on petition   Pro §§4765 to 4770
      Venue   Pro §4763
   Jurisdiction for actions on   Pro §§4760 to 4762
   Jury trial as unavailable   Pro §4754
   Legal sufficiency of writing   Pro §4680
   Limitation on authority
      Express statement in power of attorney, limitation by   Pro §§4681, 4753
      Statutory limitation on consent in behalf of principal   Pro §4652
   Personal jurisdiction over agent   Pro §4762
   Petition and procedure on petition   Pro §§4765 to 4770
   Principal
      Notice of death   Pro §4691
   Priority of attorney in fact over other persons   Pro §4685
   Registration of advance health care directives   Pro §§4800 to 4806
   Resuscitative measures, request regarding   Pro §§4780 to 4786
   Revocation   Pro §§4695 to 4698
   Statutory form advance health care directive   Pro §§4700, 4701
   Temporary orders prescribing health care of principal   Pro §4770
   Termination by revocation of advance directives   Pro §§4695 to 4698
   Venue in actions on powers of attorney   Pro §4763
   Witnesses to durable power of attorney for health care   Pro §4674
Homicide, actions regarding durable power of attorney that are considered   Pro §4743
Hospital admission conditioned on execution of durable power of attorney for health care, prohibition on   Pro §4677
Identification of attorney in fact, right of third person to require   Pro §4302
Income tax matters, powers under statutory form power of attorney regarding   Pro §4463
Inconsistent authority granted by principal, controlling authority where   Pro §4130
Incorporation of powers by reference to other statutes, grant of authority by   Pro §4263
Instructions of principal, duty to follow   Pro §4234
Insurance
   Medical insurance conditioned on execution of durable power of attorney for health care, prohibition on   Pro §4677
   Statutory form power of attorney, powers under   Pro §4457
Intentional wrongdoing of attorney in fact   Pro §4231.5
Judges, service as attorney in fact   CRCSupp JudEthicsCanon 4
Judicial intervention, exercise of power of attorney free of   Pro §4500
Jurisdiction
   Generally   Pro §§4520 to 4522
   Health care power of attorney, actions involving   Pro §§4760 to 4762
Jury trial, unavailability of
   Generally   Pro §4504
   Health care power of attorney   Pro §4754
Legal separation from principal by attorney in fact, effect of   Pro §3722
Legal sufficiency of power of attorney, requirements for   Pro §4121
Liability of third person acting in reliance on power of attorney   Pro §4303
Limitation in power of attorney
   Generally   Pro §§4101, 4262

POWER OF ATTORNEY—Cont.
  Limitation in power of attorney—Cont.
    Health care power of attorney
      Express statement in power of attorney, limitation by   Pro §§4681, 4753
      Statutory limitation on consent in behalf of principal   Pro §4652
    Judicial proceedings, authority in   Pro §§4502, 4503
  Loans
    Authority to perform act regarding   Pro §4264
    Financial institution not required to make loan where no prior relationship with principal   Pro §4310
  Marriage
    Military personnel
      Overseas personnel
        Attorney-in-fact, appearance on behalf of personnel stationed overseas to solemnize marriage   Fam §420
  Mechanical acts, power of attorney in fact to delegate authority for   Pro §4205
  Medical treatment (See within this heading, **"Health care power of attorney"**)
  Mercy killing   Pro §4653
  Military missing persons   Pro §§3720 to 3722
  Missing persons   Pro §§3720 to 3722
  Modification
    Generally   Pro §4150
    Durable power of attorney   Pro §4206
  Mortgages, execution of   CC §§2933, 2945.4
  Multiple-party accounts   Pro §5204
  Murder, actions under durable power of attorney for health care considered as   Pro §4743
  Nondurable power of attorney, termination of authority of attorney in fact under   Pro §4155
  Other jurisdiction, execution of health care power of attorney in   Pro §4053
  Personal and family maintenance, powers under statutory form power of attorney regarding   Pro §4460
  Petitions
    Capacity to file   Pro §4540
    Commencement of proceedings under   Pro §4542
    Dismissal of   Pro §4543
    Health care power of attorney   Pro §§4765 to 4770
    Limiting authority for   Pro §4503
    Notice of time and place of hearings regarding petitions   Pro §4544
    Purpose of petition regarding power of attorney   Pro §4541
  Printed form of durable power of attorney   Pro §4102
  Recordation of revocation of power of attorney   CC §1216
  Records of transactions, duty to maintain   Pro §4236
  Redesignation of attorney in fact   Pro §4207
  Reference in law, effect of   Pro §4052
  Refusal to engage in transaction with attorney in fact, right of third person for   Pro §4309
  Remarriage to former spouse, revival of designation on   Pro §4154
  Restrictions on limiting application of   Pro §4101
  Resuscitative measures, request regarding   Pro §§4780 to 4786
  Retirement plan transactions, powers under statutory form power of attorney regarding   Pro §4462
  Revocation
    Generally   Pro §4151
    Attorney in fact, authority of   Pro §4153
    Fiduciary or conservator's power to revoke or amend durable power of attorney   Pro §4206
    Health care power of attorney   Pro §§4695 to 4698
    Recordation of revocation of power of attorney   CC §1216
  Separate and distinct, duty to keep principal's property as   Pro §4233
  Short form power of attorney, validity of   Pro §4409
  Sole interest of principal, duty of attorney in fact to act in   Pro §4232
  Special power of attorney applicable to transactions with financial organizations   Pro §5204
  Special skills, duty of attorney in fact to apply   Pro §4237
  Springing power of attorney
    Contingency, designation of person with power to determine event of   Pro §4129
    Defined   Pro §4030
  Standard of care in dealing with principal's property   Pro §§4231, 4231.5
  Statutes governing   CC §2400
  Statutory form power of attorney
    Generally   Pro §§4400, 4401
    Applicability of provisions   Pro §4407
    Attorney's fees in action to compel honoring of authority under   Pro §4406
    Beneficiaries
      Powers of agent as to   Pro §4458
    Claims and litigation, powers regarding   Pro §4459
    Commodity and option transactions, powers regarding   Pro §4454

POWER OF ATTORNEY—Cont.
  Statutory form power of attorney—Cont.
    Estate transactions
      Powers of agent as to   Pro §4458
    Event or contingency, effectiveness on occurrence of   Pro §4405
    Execution, powers unaffected by location of   Pro §4464
      Express grant of power required   Pro §4465
    Family maintenance, powers under statutory form power of attorney regarding   Pro §4460
    Financial institutions, powers regarding   Pro §4455
    Governmental programs, powers regarding   Pro §4461
    Health care powers generally (See within this heading, **"Health care power of attorney"**)
    Initialing line providing for all listed powers in   Pro §4403
    Insurance and annuity transactions, powers granted to agent   Pro §4457
    Legal sufficiency of   Pro §4402
    Location of property, powers unaffected by   Pro §4464
      Express grant of power required   Pro §4465
    Particular subject granted to agent, powers regarding   Pro §4459
    Personal and family maintenance, powers regarding   Pro §4460
    Personal property, powers regarding   Pro §§4452 to 4454
    Real property transactions, powers regarding   Pro §4451
    Retirement plan transactions, powers regarding   Pro §4462
    Short form power of attorney, validity of   Pro §4409
    Stock and bond transactions, powers regarding   Pro §4453
    Tax matters, powers regarding   Pro §4463
    Time interest in acquired, powers unaffected by   Pro §4464
      Express grant of power required   Pro §4465
    Trusts, modification or revocation
      Powers of agent as to   Pro §4458
  Stay on appeal   Pro §1310
  Stock and bond transactions, statutory form power of attorney regarding   Pro §4453
  Successor attorneys in fact, designation of one or more   Pro §4203
  Survivorship interest, authority to perform act regarding   Pro §4264
  Tax matters, powers under statutory form power of attorney regarding   Pro §4463
  Termination
    Generally   Pro §4152
    Death or incapacity of principal, effect of third person acting without knowledge of   Pro §4304
    Delivery of property and records on termination of authority, duty for   Pro §4238
    Dissolution of marriage or legal separation as grounds for   Pro §§3722, 4154
    Health care power of attorney
      Revocation of advance directive, termination by   Pro §§4695 to 4698
    Nondurable power of attorney, termination of authority of attorney in fact under   Pro §4155
    Revocation generally (See within this heading, **"Revocation"**)
  Third persons
    Affidavit regarding good faith action without knowledge of death or incapacity of principal   Pro §4305
    Attorney's fees generally (See within this heading, **"Attorney's fees"**)
    Bank not required to open deposit account where no previous relationship with principal   Pro §4310
    Death or incapacity of principal, effect of third person acting without knowledge of   Pro §4304
    Employees, effect of power of attorney on third person conducting activities through   Pro §4308
    Identification of attorney in fact, right to require   Pro §4302
    Liability of third person acting in reliance on power of attorney   Pro §4303
    Refusal of third person to accept authority of attorney in fact   Pro §4306
    Refusal to engage in transaction with attorney in fact, right of third person for   Pro §4309
    Rights and privileges accorded by   Pro §4300
    Specific authorization, actions by third persons without regard to   Pro §4301
    Statutory form power of attorney, compelling third person to honor authority under   Pro §4406
  Transfer of property   CC §1095
  Trusts
    General authority to perform act regarding   Pro §4264
    Statutory form power of attorney, powers under   Pro §4458
  Undue influence or financial abuse of elder or dependent adult to take, conceal, etc, property of principal
    Liability of attorney in fact for attorney fees   Pro §4231.5
  Uniform statutory form power of attorney (See within this heading, **"Statutory form power of attorney"**)
  Venue
    Generally   Pro §4523

POWER OF ATTORNEY—Cont.
Venue—Cont.
    Health care power of attorney   Pro §4763
Will, authority to act regarding   Pro §4265
Witnesses
    Generally   Pro §4122
    Health care, witnesses to durable power of attorney for   Pro §4674

POWER OF SALE (See TRUST DEEDS AND MORTGAGES)

POWER OF TERMINATION (See TITLE AND OWNERSHIP)

POWERS
Executors, testator limiting administrative powers of   Pro §12206
Judges (See JUDGES)
Judicial arbitrators   CCP §1141.19
Receivers   CCP §568

POWS (See MILITARY)

PRACTICE ADMINISTRATORS (See ATTORNEYS)

PRACTICE OF LAW (See ATTORNEYS)

PRECEDENCE (See PRIORITIES AND PREFERENCES)

PREEXISTING DEBT
Promise to pay as admissible evidence of   Ev §1152

PREFABRICATED HOUSING (See MANUFACTURED HOMES)

PREFERENCES (See PRIORITIES AND PREFERENCES)

PREFILING ORDERS
Vexatious litigants subject to   CCP §391.7
    Vacating prefiling order and removing name from list   CCP §391.8

PREGNANCY
Abortion (See ABORTIONS)
Assisted reproduction
    Consent required for   Fam §7613
    Parentage of child conceived by   Fam §7613
        Forms for assisted reproduction   Fam §7613.5
    Unauthorized use or misuse of sperm, ova or embryo
        Civil action for damages   CC §1708.5.6
Birth (See BIRTH)
Birth control
    Abortion (See ABORTIONS)
    Sterilization (See STERILIZATION)
Minors
    Consent to medical care   Fam §6925
    Requests by minor to marry or establish domestic partnership
        Waiting period after order granting request not required in cases of pregnancy   CRC 5.448
Parentage
    Voluntary declaration   Fam §§7570 to 7581
Sperm, ova or embryos, written consent for use of
    Unauthorized use or misuse of sperm, ova or embryo
        Civil action for damages   CC §1708.5.6

PREJUDICE (See BIAS AND PREJUDICE)

PRELIMINARY EXAMINATION OR HEARING
Disposition of cases prior to, procedures for   CRC 10.953
Evidence
    Creative expressions
        Admissibility determined in limine   Ev §352.2
Readiness conferences (See SUPERIOR COURTS)

PRELIMINARY FACT
Admissibility, preliminary fact proved for purpose of   Ev §§400 to 405

PRELIMINARY INJUNCTIONS (See INJUNCTIONS)

PRELIMINARY INVESTIGATION (See JUDGES)

PRELIMINARY PROVISIONS
Code of Civil Procedure   CCP §§2 to 32

PREMARITAL AGREEMENTS
Uniform premarital agreement act (See PROPERTY SETTLEMENT AGREEMENTS)

PREMISES LIABILITY
Common interest development, liability based on interest in common area   CC §5805
Farm owner's immunity for injury to person invited on premises to glean farm products for charitable purposes   CC §846.2
Felony, immunity of landowner for personal injuries to person committing   CC §847
Judicial Council to develop and approve forms   CCP §425.12
Public property (See CLAIMS AGAINST PUBLIC ENTITIES AND EMPLOYEES)
Recreational users
    Generally   CC §846
    Attorney's fees in recreational user's action against public entity or private owner contractually related to public or nonprofit agency, administrative claim for recovery of   CC §846.1

PREMIUM COUPONS
Gift certificates, expiration dates
    Bankruptcy of issuer, duty to honor   CC §1749.6
    Waiver of protections   CC §1749.51

PRE-NUPS (PREMARITAL AGREEMENTS)
Premarital agreements   Fam §§1600 to 1620

PREPAID CALLING CARDS
Gift certificate provisions inapplicable   CC §1749.45

PREPAID DEBIT CARDS
Consumer refunds offered by prepaid debit card
    Alternative method of receiving refund required to be offered   CC §1748.41
    Definitions   CC §1748.40

PREPAYMENTS
Automobiles purchased under conditional sales contract   CC §2982
Real property sales contracts, right under   CC §2985.6
Single family dwellings, prepayment charges on loans secured by mortgage or deed of trust   CC §2954.9
Trust deeds and mortgages (See TRUST DEEDS AND MORTGAGES)

PREPONDERANCE OF EVIDENCE
Burden of proof required in proceedings except where higher degree of proof otherwise required by law   Ev §115
Jury instructions on   Ev §502
Sentencing procedure, applicability to   CRC 4.420

PRESCRIBED BURNS
Immunity for damages   CC §3333.8

PRESCRIPTIONS
Default judgment for recovery of realty   CCP §585
Easements   CC §§813, 1008
Medical information disclosures
    Minors
        Coordination of health care services and treatment   CC §56.103
Nuisances, prescriptive rights for   CC §3490
Opioid antagonists   CC §1714.22
Psychotropic medication
    Juvenile rules
        Release of psychotropic medication prescription information to medical board, authorization   CRC 5.642
Public easement on private land   CC §813
Secure drug take-back bins
    Liability of collector, limitation   CC §1714.24
Take-back bins
    Secure drug take-back bins
        Liability of collector, limitation   CC §1714.24
Title by   CC §§813, 1007 to 1009

PRESERVATION OF INTEREST
Easements (See EASEMENTS)
Mineral rights (See MINERALS AND MINERAL RIGHTS)
Records and recordings (See RECORDS AND RECORDING)

PRESIDING JUDGES (See JUDGES)

PRESUMED FATHER (See PATERNITY)

PRESUMPTIONS
Administrative Procedure Act (See ADMINISTRATIVE PROCEDURE ACT)
Adverse possession (See ADVERSE POSSESSION)
Ancient documents   Ev §643

PRESUMPTIONS—Cont.
  Appeals
    Record on appeal
      Limited civil cases in appellate division CRC 8.830
      Presumption from record CRC 8.163
  Attorney professional conduct
    Communications concerning lawyer's services
      Development of standards as to presumptively violative communications ProfC 7.1
  Authentication of documents Ev §1450
  Boarding house tenancy, presumed duration of CC §1944
  Books, printing or publishing of Ev §644
  Burden of producing evidence, effect on Ev §§603, 604, 630
  Burden of proof, effect on Ev §§601, 605, 606, 660 to 669.5
  Ceremonial marriages presumed valid Ev §663
  Check payments, presumption involving disputes concerning Ev §670
  Child support (See **CHILD SUPPORT**)
  Classification Ev §601
  Community property (See **COMMUNITY PROPERTY**)
  Conclusive presumptions Ev §601
  Construction-related accessibility claims
    Technical violations CC §55.56
  Creditor possessing obligation as presumption of money owed Ev §635
  Criminal prosecutions Ev §607
  Death of missing persons Ev §§667, 1282, Pro §12401
  Dedication for public improvement CCP §§771.010, 771.020
  Definition Ev §600
  Delivery, presumption concerning Ev §632
  Documentary evidence (See **DOCUMENTARY EVIDENCE**)
  Donative transfers
    Presumption of fraud or undue influence Pro §§21360 to 21392 (See **DONATIVE TRANSFERS**)
  Due care, statutory violation as failure to exercise Ev §§669, 669.1
  Duty regularly performed Ev §664
  Eminent domain proceedings (See **EMINENT DOMAIN**)
  Fax filing and service
    Filing, presumption of CRC 2.304
  Fee-simple title CC §1105
  Fences
    Adjoining landowners CC §841
  Fiduciary income and principal act
    Fair and reasonable allocations, determinations or exercises of discretion Pro §16325
  Filing fees
    Nonpayment of CCP §411.20
    Underpayment CCP §411.21
  Firearm industry standards of conduct
    Reasonable controls, failure to establish, implement and enforce CC §3273.52
  Firearm manufacturer liability
    CNC milling machine or 3-D printer, prohibited acts related to CC §3273.62
    Digital firearm manufacturing codes
      Distribution to unauthorized persons CC §3273.61
  Gifts
    Donative transfers
      Presumption of fraud or undue influence Pro §§21360 to 21392 (See **DONATIVE TRANSFERS**)
  Gifts in view of death Pro §5703
  Grain stored in bulk, presumed ownership of CC §1880.9
  Groundwater rights actions
    Comprehensive adjudication as complex action CCP §838
  Interest on loans CC §§1914 to 1916.5
  Interstate family support
    Self-incrimination, privilege invoked
      Adverse inference from refusal to testify Fam §5700.316
  Joint custody of children Fam §3080
  Judgments presumed to set forth parties' rights Ev §639
  Jurisdiction, lawful exercise of Ev §666
  Landlord and tenant (See **LANDLORD AND TENANT**)
  Law books, presumptions of accuracy of Ev §645
  Legitimacy of children Ev §605
  Letter correctly addressed presumed to be received Ev §641
  Limitation of actions (See **STATUTES OF LIMITATION**)
  Marriage, presumption of validity of Ev §663
  Missing person, presumption of death of Ev §§667, 1282, Pro §12401
  Money paid to another as presumed owed Ev §631
  Month-to-month tenancy presumed CC §1943
  Mother of child
    Child in utero upon death of mother
      Woman presumed to be natural mother Fam §7650

PRESUMPTIONS—Cont.
  Motor vehicles under express warranty, presumption regarding buyer's attempt to resolve disputes concerning repair of CC §1793.22
  Multiple-party accounts law, community property presumption in Pro §5305
  Negligence, statutory violation as evidence of Ev §669
  Newspapers and periodicals, presumption regarding publications purporting to be Ev §645.1
  Note, possession as presumption of payment Ev §634
  Obligations delivered to debtor as presumed paid Ev §633
  Official reports, existence of Ev §1530
  Orders, presumptions under CCP §1909
  Ordinary consequences of voluntary acts Ev §665
  Ownership Ev §§638, 662
  Parent of injured child not joined as plaintiff, service by mail on CCP §376
  Paternity disputes
    Generally as to parentage presumptions (See **PATERNITY**)
    Voluntary declaration of parentage
      Pre-1977 declarations Fam §7581
      Rebuttal Fam §7612
  Police officers performing official duties in regular manner Ev §664
  Possession of things presumed to be owned by possessor Ev §637
  Prejudice, presumption against CCP §475
  Prima facie evidence establishing rebuttable presumption Ev §602
  Privilege not to testify, effect of prior exercise of Ev §913
  Process server's return creating Ev §647
  Public improvement assessment, action to determine adverse interests in real property arising out of CCP §801.11
  Public officers and employees (See **PUBLIC OFFICERS AND EMPLOYEES**)
  Rebuttable presumptions, generally Ev §§601, 630
  Recitals in written instruments Ev §622
  Rent installment payments presumed from receipt Ev §636
  Res ipsa loquitur Ev §646
  Sales tax added to purchase price of personalty CC §1656.1
  Sealed documents Ev §1452
  Sentencing for felonies
    Mandatory supervision of concluding portion
      Criteria affecting imposition of mandatory supervision CRC 4.415
  Small claims court judgment, presumption of full or partial payment of CCP §116.850
  Spousal support proceedings, presumption affecting jurisdiction over Fam §4336
  Tenant repairing and deducting, presumption of reasonable time for CC §1942
  Title and ownership Ev §§605, 638, 662
  Transcripts presumed correct CCP §273
  Trial court rules
    Sealing records
      Openness of records presumed CRC 2.550
  Trusts
    Donative transfers
      Presumption of fraud or undue influence Pro §§21360 to 21392 (See **DONATIVE TRANSFERS**)
    Generally (See **TRUSTS**)
  Unlawful detainer, nuisance as grounds
    Sexual assault, stalking or domestic violence against tenant
      Nuisance presumed CCP §1161
  Unlawful intent Ev §668
  Unsoundness of mind presumed if unable to manage financial resources or resist fraud or undue influence CC §39
  Wills
    Donative transfers
      Presumption of fraud or undue influence Pro §§21360 to 21392 (See **DONATIVE TRANSFERS**)
  Writing presumed truly dated Ev §640

PRETERMITTED HEIRS (See **HEIRS**)

PRETRIAL ARBITRATION (See **JUDICIAL ARBITRATION**)

PRETRIAL CONFERENCES CRC 3.722, 3.723
Additional case management conferences CRC 3.723
Amendment of orders CCP §576
Case management conferences CRC 3.722, 3.723
  Complex cases CRC 3.750
  Environmental quality act
    Petitions under environmental quality act, civil rules governing CRC 3.2226
  Groundwater rights actions CCP §840
  Setting trial date CRC 3.729
  Subjects considered CRC 3.727
  Telephone appearances CRC 3.670

PRETRIAL CONFERENCES—Cont.
Class actions
    Case conference   CRC 3.762
        Conference order   CRC 3.763
Complex cases
    Case management conferences   CRC 3.750
        Telephone appearance at case management conferences   CRC 3.670
Construction-related accessibility claims
    Stay and early evaluation conference
        Notice to defendant of rights to   CC §55.54
Coordinated actions   CRC 3.541
Criminal cases
    Readiness conference   CRC 4.112
Expedited jury trials   CRC 3.1548
Family centered case resolution conferences   CRC 5.83
Initial case management conference   CRC 3.722
    Complex cases   CRC 3.750
    Environmental quality act
        Petitions under environmental quality act, civil rules governing   CRC 3.2226
    Telephone appearance at case management conferences   CRC 3.670
Judge allowing amended order   CCP §576
Judicial arbitration   CCP §1141.16, CRC 3.812
Judicial Council rules authorized   CCP §575
Management of trial, judge's responsibilities   CRC JudAdminStand 2.20
Mediation, mandatory   CCP §1734
Postponement of   CCP §595.1
Superior courts (See **SUPERIOR COURTS**)
Telephone appearances   CRC 3.670, CRC JudAdminStand 10.21
Trial date
    Setting trial date   CRC 3.729
        Telephone appearances   CCP §367.6
Voir dire
    Pre-voir dire conference in criminal cases   CRC 4.200

PRETRIAL DIVERSION OF MISDEMEANOR OFFENDERS
Mental disorders, individuals with
    Mental competency proceedings   CRC 4.130

PREVENTION OF DOMESTIC VIOLENCE (See **DOMESTIC VIOLENCE**)

PREVENTIVE RELIEF
Generally   CC §§3368, 3369
Injunctions (See **INJUNCTIONS**)

PREVIOUS WILLS (See **WILLS**)

PRICE
Gender, prohibition against charging different price for services of similar or like kind based solely on   CC §51.6
Partition sales   CCP §873.710
Real property (See **VENDOR AND PURCHASER**)
Scanners
    Automatic checkout systems   CC §§7100 to 7106
Unassembled furniture, advertising price for   CC §1770

PRICE DISCRIMINATION BASED ON GENDER
Price differences for substantially similar goods based on gender of marketing audience   CC §51.14
Small business gender discrimination in pricing services compliance act   CC §§55.61 to 55.63

PRIESTS (See **CLERGYPERSONS**)

PRIMA FACIE EVIDENCE
Generally   Ev §602
Transcripts as prima facie evidence of testimony and proceedings   CCP §273

PRINCIPAL AND AGENT (See **AGENCY**)

PRINCIPAL AND INCOME
Legal Estates Principal and Income Law (See **LEGAL ESTATES PRINCIPAL AND INCOME LAW**)
Trusts (See **TRUSTS**)

PRINTERS AND PRINTING
Administrative Procedure Act, official publications under (See **ADMINISTRATIVE PROCEDURE ACT**)
Affidavit of printer as evidence of publication   CCP §2010
Presumptions of printing of books   Ev §644
Type size (See **TYPE SIZE**)
Writing defined to include printing   CCP §17

PRINTERS AND PRINTING—Cont.
Written part of document controlling   CCP §1862

PRIOR CONVICTIONS (See **CONVICTION OF CRIME**)

PRIOR INCONSISTENT STATEMENTS (See **WITNESSES**)

PRIORITIES AND PREFERENCES
Administration of estates
    Abatement of bequests (See **ADMINISTRATION OF ESTATES**)
    Claims against estates, payment of   Pro §§11420, 11421
    Executors and administrators (See **EXECUTORS AND ADMINISTRATORS**)
Adoption placement preference rules (See **ADOPTION**)
Affidavit in support of motion for preference   CCP §36.5
Appeal, motion for calendar preference   CRC 8.240
Arbitration proceedings   CCP §1291
Assignment for benefit of creditors (See **ASSIGNMENT FOR BENEFIT OF CREDITORS**)
Attachment (See **ATTACHMENT**)
Child support (See **CHILD SUPPORT**)
Commission of felony, precedence where damages caused during   CCP §37
Common carriers   CC §§2170, 2171
Concurrent liens   CC §2899
Continuances, effect of grant of motion for preference on   CCP §36
Custody proceedings (See **CUSTODY OF CHILDREN**)
Debt payments   CC §3432
Decedents' estates
    Abatement of bequests (See **ADMINISTRATION OF ESTATES**)
    Claims against estates, payment of   Pro §§11420, 11421
    Executors and administrators (See **EXECUTORS AND ADMINISTRATORS**)
Declaratory relief   CCP §1062.3
Earnings assignment for support (See **EARNINGS ASSIGNMENT FOR SUPPORT**)
Elections proceedings, precedence to cases involving   CCP §§35, 44
Eminent domain proceedings   CCP §1260.010
Enforcement of judgments (See **ENFORCEMENT OF JUDGMENTS**)
Family law rules (See **FAMILY RULES**)
First in time   CC §2897
Foster care placement (See **FOSTER CARE HOMES**)
Garnishment claims (See **GARNISHMENT**)
Illness or condition raising substantial medical doubt of survival of party   CCP §36
Interests of justice served by granting preference, discretion of court to grant motion where   CCP §36
Issues, order of trial of   CCP §598
Juvenile appeals, priority of   CCP §45
Landlord, deposits by tenant to   CC §1950.7
Libel, action for   CCP §460.5
Liens (See **LIENS**)
Livestock service liens   CC §3080.01
Mechanics' liens   CC §§8450 to 8458
    Public works, stop payment notices   CC §9456
Messages transmitted by carriers   CC §§2207 to 2209
Mortgage liens (See **TRUST DEEDS AND MORTGAGES**)
Nonjury trials, priority of   CCP §598
Oil and gas liens   CCP §§1203.56, 1203.57
Over age of 70 years, motion for preference of party who is   CCP §36
Parental rights of alleged father, action to terminate   Fam §7667
Partition (See **PARTITION**)
Preliminary injunctions granted without notice, precedence to hearing on   CCP §527
Purchase money mortgage or trust deed   CC §2898
Recording instruments   CC §1214
Related cases   CRC 3.300
Satisfaction of money judgments, priorities for crediting money received in   CCP §§695.220, 695.221
Setting for trial   CCP §36
Settlement in good faith, review of determination of   CCP §877.6
Slander, action for   CCP §460.5
Subordinate liens   CC §2899
Termination of parental rights, proceedings for   Fam §7870
Transportation of persons or goods   CC §§2170, 2171
Under age of 14, preference in wrongful death or personal injury action to party   CCP §36
Unlawful detainer cases   CCP §1179a
Validation proceedings   CCP §867
Wage assignment for support, priority of   CCP §706.031

PRIORITIES AND PREFERENCES—Cont.
Wage claims, preference to   CCP §§1204 to 1208

PRISONERS (See also **IMPRISONMENT**)
Acknowledgments
    Identification   CC §1185
Adverse possession, disabilities tolling statute of limitation in actions for   CCP §328
Appellate rules, superior court appeals
    Filing
        Timeliness of documents mailed from custodial institutions   CRC 8.817
Appellate rules, supreme court and courts of appeal
    Filing
        Timeliness   CRC 8.25
Children of prisoners
    Family reunification services   CRC 5.695
Child support
    Suspension of orders or judgments
        Incarceration or institutionalization of obligee   Fam §4007.5
Contracts, incapacity of prisoners to make   CC §1556
Court sessions conducted near state penal institutions   CRC JudAdminStand 10.41
Credit on term
    Probation report, inclusion of information regarding   CRC 4.411.5
Crimes by prisoners
    Sodomy or oral copulation
        Statute of limitations   CCP §340.16
Custodial officers
    Personnel records, disclosure   Ev §1043
        Inclusions and exclusions from disclosure   Ev §1045
        Officer not present for alleged conduct   Ev §1047
Decedents
    Fact of death
        Heir of decedent in prison, notice   Pro §§216, 9202
Dependent child of court proceedings
    Incarcerated parents, participation   CRC 5.530
Depositions of prisoners   CCP §§1995 to 1997
Escheat of assets of prisoner   CCP §1446
Exempt property for purposes of enforcement of judgments   CCP §704.090
Gender changes
    Rights of prisoners   CCP §1279.5
Habeas corpus (See **HABEAS CORPUS**)
Jury service
    Ineligible to serve as juror   CCP §203
Medical care, liability of public entity for failure to provide   Gov §845.6
Name change, application for   CCP §1279.5
Pardons (See **PARDONS**)
Probation (See **PROBATION**)
Public entity's liability for injuries to (See **CLAIMS AGAINST PUBLIC ENTITIES AND EMPLOYEES**)
Release of prisoners
    Name change proceedings under address confidentiality program   CRC 2.575 to 2.577
Reunification services, right of incarcerated fathers to   CRC 5.695
Severely mentally disordered prisoners, disposition of
    Remote proceedings
        Conditions for proceeding through use of remote technology   CCP §367.76
Sheriff's fees for transportation of prisoners (See **SHERIFF**)
Small claims court (See **SMALL CLAIMS COURTS**)
Social security numbers of inmates
    Release with consent and upon request from department of veterans affairs   CC §1798.85
Sodomy or oral copulation while incarcerated
    Statute of limitations
        Civil damages   CCP §340.16
Stalking offenses
    Name change proceedings under address confidentiality program   CRC 2.575 to 2.577
Statutes of limitation, imprisonment tolling   CCP §§328.5, 352.1
Witnesses, prisoners as   CCP §§1995 to 1997

PRISONERS OF WAR (See **MILITARY**)

PRIVACY
Abortion medical records
    Restrictions on release of medical information related to abortion   CC §§56.108, 56.110
Address confidentiality
    Reproductive health care service providers, employees, volunteers and patients   Gov §§6215 to 6218.5

PRIVACY—Cont.
Address confidentiality—Cont.
    Victims of certain crimes   Gov §§6205 to 6211
        Actions, confidentiality requirements for protected persons in civil proceeding   CCP §367.3
        Judicial council forms   CRCAppx A, Fam §6226.5
        Name change proceedings under address confidentiality program   CRC 2.575 to 2.577
Adoption records, confidentiality   Fam §§9200 to 9209
Age-appropriate design code
    Data protection impact assessment
        Online services, products or features likely to be accessed by children   CC §1798.99.31
    Generally   CC §§1798.99.28 to 1798.28
Appellate rules, supreme court and courts of appeal
    Electronic court records, public access
        Posting of privacy policy   CRC 8.84
    Opinions
        Names, use in court opinions   CRC 8.90
    Protection of privacy in documents and records   CRC 1.201, 8.41
Arbitrators
    Ethics standards
        Confidentiality   CRC ArbEthicsStand 15
Blind and visually impaired persons
    Touch screen devices for self-service check-in at hotels or passenger transportation facilities   CC §54.9
Buses
    Private or charter bus transportation companies
        Duties of companies   CC §53.5
Business records (See **BUSINESS RECORDS**)
California privacy protection agency   CC §§1798.199.10 to 1798.199.100
Change of name
    Gender identity, conforming name
        Publication of proceedings not required   CCP §1277.5
    Witness Protection Program or domestic violence address confidentiality program
        Trial court rules   CRC 2.575 to 2.577
Commercial blockage tort, privacy of civil proceedings for   CC §3427.3
Constructive invasion of privacy   CC §1708.8
Consumer privacy rights   CC §§1798.100 to 1798.199.100 (See **CONSUMER PRIVACY RIGHTS**)
Court-appointed special advocates (CASA)
    Confidentiality of case information, records, etc
        Plan   CRC 5.655
Custody of child
    Psychological evaluation of child involved in custody or visitation proceedings   Fam §3025.5
    Reports on custody evaluations
        Confidentiality   Fam §3111
Customer records (See **CUSTOMER RECORDS**)
Data broker registration   CC §§1798.99.80 to 1798.99.89
Dissolution of marriage, legal separation, or annulment proceedings
    Financial assets and liabilities
        Sealing pleadings concerning financial assets and liabilities   Fam §2024.6
Domestic violence protection orders
    Minor's information, confidentiality   Fam §6301.5
        Release of confidential information   CRC 5.382
        Request to make information confidential   CRC 5.382
Domestic violence victims
    Address confidentiality
        Actions, confidentiality requirements for protected persons in civil proceeding   CCP §367.3
        Judicial council forms   CRCAppx A
        Name change proceedings under address confidentiality program   CRC 2.575 to 2.577
Driver's licenses
    Encoded information use   CC §1798.90.1
Electricity
    Customer electrical or natural gas usage data   CC §1798.98
        Actions and other remedies of customer   CC §1798.99
Electronic court records
    Posting privacy policy   CRC 2.504
    Remote access
        Government entities, access by   CRC 2.542
        Parties, designees, attorneys, court-appointed persons or persons working in legal organization or qualified legal services project, access by   CRC 2.524
Factual innocence
    Certificate of Identity: Judicial Determination of Factual Innocence (CR-150) forms, access to   CRC 4.601

PRIVACY—Cont.

False claims act
  Filing records under seal   CRC 2.570 to 2.573
Family planning
  Personal information restrictions of persons at or near family planning center   CC §1798.99.90
Filings
  Protection of privacy   CRC 1.201
    Appellate rules, supreme court and courts of appeal   CRC 8.41
Genetic privacy   CC §§56.18 to 56.186
Harassment protection orders
  Minor's information, confidentiality   CCP §527.6
    COVID-19, emergency rule   CRCAppx I Emer Rule 8
    Release of minor's confidential information   CRC 3.1161
    Request in civil harassment proceedings   CRC 3.1161, CRCAppx A
Hotels, inns, lodginghouses, etc
  Customer records
    Duties of innkeepers   CC §53.5
Information Practices Act, privacy under (See **INFORMATION PRACTICES ACT**)
Internet
  Privacy policies
    Consumer privacy rights, conflict with other provisions   CC §1798.175
Interpreters maintaining confidentiality   CRC JudAdminStand 2.11
Invasion of (See **INVASION OF PRIVACY**)
Invasion of privacy
  Visual images and sound recordings
    Exposing intimate body parts or sexual acts of another without permission, distribution of photos, etc, confidential information form   CRCAppx A
Mediation
  Complaints about court-program mediators
    Confidentiality   CRC 3.871
  Standards of conduct for mediators
    Confidentiality   CRC 3.854
Medical information
  Direct marketing, use of medical information for   CC §1798.91
  Genetic privacy   CC §§56.18 to 56.186
Names
  Change of name
    Address confidentiality program, change of name under   CRC 2.575 to 2.577
    Confidentiality of information   CCP §1277
    Gender identity conformity, publication of proceedings not required   CCP §1277
Natural gas
  Customer electrical or natural gas usage data   CC §1798.98
    Actions and other remedies of customer   CC §1798.99
Photographs, films, etc, exposing intimate body parts or sexual acts of another without permission, distribution
  Actions for injunctions, damages, etc   CC §1708.85
  Confidential information form   CRCAppx A
Private student loan collections reform
  Actions to collect
    Complaints not to include confidential information   CC §1788.205
Reader privacy act   CC §§1798.90, 1798.90.05
Settlements
  Nondisclosure agreements (NDAs) as part of settlement
    Restrictions   CCP §1001
  Sex offense prosecutable as felony, confidential settlement of civil action
    Prohibition   CCP §1002
Sexual assault victims
  Actions, confidentiality requirements for protected persons in civil proceeding   CCP §367.3
    Judicial council forms   CRCAppx A
  Name change proceedings under address confidentiality program   CRC 2.575 to 2.577
Social security numbers, confidentiality
  Untruncated social security numbers, filing documents that will be public containing   CC §1798.89
Stalking victims
  Address confidentiality
    Actions, confidentiality requirements for protected persons in civil proceeding   CCP §367.3
    Judicial council forms   CRCAppx A
    Name change proceedings under address confidentiality program   CRC 2.575 to 2.577
Subcutaneous implanting of identification device, requiring of another   CC §52.7

PRIVACY—Cont.

Subpoenas duces tecum
  Personally identifying information sought in free speech exercise context   CCP §§1987.1, 1987.2
Victims of crime
  Victim service providers, personal information protection   CC §§1798.79.8 to 1798.79.95

PRIVATE ADMONISHMENT OF JUDGES (See **JUDGES**)

PRIVATE BULK GRAIN STORAGE LAW   CC §§1880 to 1881.2

PRIVATE FOUNDATION TRUSTS (See **TRUSTS**)

PRIVATE LAWS (See **LOCAL OR SPECIAL LAWS**)

PRIVATE NUISANCES (See **NUISANCES**)

PRIVATE POSTSECONDARY AND CAREER TECHNICAL INSTITUTIONS

Violence threatened on campus or facility
  Appellate court opinions
    Privacy, use of names in opinions   CRC 8.90
  Orders against violence threatened on campus or facility
    COVID-19, emergency rule   CRCAppx I Emer Rule 8
    Judicial council legal forms   CRCAppx A

PRIVATE RESIDENCE RENTALS

Cancellation of reservations, refunds   CC §§1748.80 to 1748.84
  Action for violation of provisions   CC §1748.83
  Definitions   CC §1748.80
  Exceptions to provisions   CC §1748.84
  Issuance of refund   CC §1748.82
  Time period for cancellation without penalty   CC §1748.81

PRIVATE RIGHTS

One form of civil actions for enforcement or protection of   CCP §307

PRIVATE SCHOOLS

Enrollment agreements
  Disaffirmance by minor of provisions purporting to waive rights or remedies arising out of sexual assault or battery of minor   CCP §1002.7

PRIVATE STATUTES

Distinguished from public statutes   CCP §1898
Enactment of code, effect on existing statutes of   CCP §18
Pleading   CCP §459

PRIVATE STUDENT LOAN COLLECTIONS REFORM   CC §§1788.200 to 1788.211

Actions against creditor, lender or collector for violations of provisions   CC §1788.208
Actions to collect
  Complaints   CC §1788.205
Citation of provisions   CC §1788.200
Class actions
  Actions against creditor, lender or collector for violations of provisions   CC §1788.208
Creditors
  Actions against creditor, lender or collector for violations of provisions   CC §1788.208
Default judgments against debtor
  Actions against creditor, lender or collector for violations of provisions   CC §1788.208
  Actual notice not provided
    Motion to set aside default   CC §1788.207
  Requirements   CC §1788.206
Definitions   CC §1788.201
Judgments against debtor
  Requirements   CC §1788.206
Limitation of actions
  Actions against creditor, lender or collector for violations of provisions   CC §1788.208
  Effect of statute of limitations   CC §1788.204
Operative date of provisions   CC §1788.211
Private education lenders
  Actions against creditor, lender or collector for violations of provisions   CC §1788.208
Private education loan collectors
  Actions against creditor, lender or collector for violations of provisions   CC §1788.208

PRIVATE STUDENT LOAN COLLECTIONS REFORM—Cont.
Process and service of process
    Actual notice not provided
        Motion to set aside default   CC §1788.207
Settlements
    Acceptance of settlement agreement as payment in full   CC §1788.203
Severability of provisions   CC §1788.210
Short title   CC §1788.200
Statement to debtor by lender or loan collector
    Information required prior to statement   CC §1788.202
Waiver of provisions
    Void and unenforceable   CC §1788.209

PRIVATE WRONGS
One form of civil actions for redress or prevention of private wrongs   CCP §307

PRIVILEGE AGAINST SELF-INCRIMINATION
Interstate family support
    Adverse inference from refusal to testify   Fam §5700.316

PRIVILEGED COMMUNICATIONS
Generally   Ev §§910 to 920
Administrative adjudication
    Alternative dispute resolution in administrative adjudication, communications during   Gov §11420.30
    Applicability of privilege in   Ev §901, Gov §§11420.30, 11513
Applicant for employment, communications concerning job performance of   CC §47
Arbitrators
    Ethics standards
        Confidentiality   CRC ArbEthicsStand 15
Attorney-client privilege
    Breach of duty   Ev §958
        Discovery of attorney work product   CCP §2018.080
    Cellular telephone conversations   Ev §952
    Certificate of meritorious cause   CCP §411.35
    Certified law student program, privilege under (See **LAW STUDENTS**)
    Client's confidential information
        Professional duty of attorney   ProfC 1.6
    Crime, disclosure of information to prevent   Ev §956.5
    Definitions   Ev §§950 to 953
        Client   Ev §951
        Confidential communications between client and lawyer   Ev §952
        Holder of privilege   Ev §953
        Lawyer   Ev §950
    Documents   Ev §§959 to 961
    Exceptions   Ev §§956 to 962
    Fax communications   Ev §952
    Investigative consumer reporting agencies
        Law on privilege not changed by provisions   CC §1786.55
    Marijuana, medical or adult-use
        Advice as to conflict between state and federal law required to maintain privilege   Ev §956
    Parties claiming   Ev §§954, 955
    Two or more clients represented by same attorney   Ev §962
    Waiver of   Ev §912
    Wills   Ev §§959 to 961
Attorney professional conduct
    Client's confidential information   ProfC 1.6
    Prospective clients
        Duties to prospective clients   ProfC 1.18
Attorney referral service-client privilege   Ev §§965 to 968
    Clients
        Defined   Ev §965
    Confidential communication between client and lawyer referral service
        Defined   Ev §965
    Crimes
        Use of service to perpetrate fraud or crime   Ev §968
    Definitions   Ev §965
    Description of privilege   Ev §966
    Fraud
        Use of service to perpetrate fraud or crime   Ev §968
    Holder of the privilege
        Defined   Ev §965
    Lawyer-referral service
        Defined   Ev §965
    Waiver of   Ev §912
    Who may claim   Ev §966
        When service must claim privilege   Ev §967
Brokers societies   CC §43.91
Burden of proving absence of confidence   Ev §917

PRIVILEGED COMMUNICATIONS—Cont.
Clergy-penitent privilege
    Definitions   Ev §§1030 to 1032
    Parties asserting   Ev §§1033, 1034
    Waiver of   Ev §912
Client-attorney privilege (See within this heading, "**Attorney-client privilege**")
Clinical social worker
    Psychotherapist-patient privilege generally (See within this heading, "**Psychotherapist-patient privilege**")
Common interest development action against builder, pretrial communications required in   CC §6000
Consumer privacy rights
    Violation of evidentiary privileges, businesses not to be compelled   CC §1798.145
Court records
    Public access to judicial administrative records
        Exemptions from requirement to provide access   CRC 10.500
Crimes
    Attorney-client privilege   Ev §956.5
    Husband and wife privilege (See **MARITAL PRIVILEGE**)
    Physician-patient privileges   Ev §§998, 999
    Psychotherapist (See within this heading, "**Psychotherapist-patient privilege**")
Deaf persons, privileged communications involving interpreters for   Ev §754.5
Disclosure
    Consent of   Ev §912
    Forced disclosure   Ev §919
    Hospital research findings   Ev §§1156, 1156.1
    Judges' chambers, disclosure in   Ev §915
Domestic partners   Ev §980
Domestic violence counselor-victim privilege
    Child abuse, effect on obligation to report   Ev §1037.3
    Court order to compel disclosure by domestic violence counselor   Ev §1037.2
    Definitions
        Confidential communication   Ev §1037.2
        Domestic violence   Fam §6211
        Domestic violence counselor   Ev §1037.1
        Domestic violence victim service organizations   Ev §1037.1
        Holder of privilege   Ev §1037.4
        Victim   Ev §1037
    Limits to confidentiality, notice   Ev §1037.8
    Parties asserting   Ev §§1037.5, 1037.6
    Waiver of privilege   Ev §912
Educational psychologists
    Psychotherapist-patient privilege
        Applicability to educational psychologists   Ev §1010.5
        Generally (See within this heading, "**Psychotherapist-patient privilege**")
Employment, communications concerning job performance of applicant for   CC §47
Forced disclosure of privileged information, inadmissibility of   Ev §919
Hospital research findings   Ev §§1156, 1156.1
Human trafficking victim-caseworker privilege   Ev §§1038 to 1038.3
    Child abuse reporting
        Duty to report not diminished by provisions   Ev §1038.3
    Compelling disclosure
        Grounds   Ev §1038.1
    Definitions   Ev §1038.2
    Eligibility to claim privilege   Ev §1038
    In chambers proceeding to determine ruling on privilege   Ev §1038.1
    Limitations on privilege
        Caseworker to notify victim   Ev §1038
    Waiver   Ev §912
Husband and wife privilege (See **MARITAL PRIVILEGE**)
Indian child welfare act involuntary placements
    Adoption
        Affidavit of confidentiality to bureau of Indian affairs   CRC 5.488
Informer, protecting identity of   Ev §§915, 1040, 1041
Inspection demands
    Electronically stored information
        Privilege claimed or attorney work product protection requested   CCP §2031.285
Job applicant, communications concerning job performance of   CC §47
Joint holders   Ev §912
Judges (See **JUDGES**)
    Committee on judicial ethics opinions
        Confidentiality of communications to and from committee   CRC 9.80
Lawyer-client privilege (See within this heading, "**Attorney-client privilege**")
Marital communications (See **MARITAL PRIVILEGE**)

PRIVILEGED COMMUNICATIONS—Cont.
Marriage counselor
    Psychotherapist-patient privilege generally (See within this heading, **"Psychotherapist-patient privilege"**)
Mediation (See **MEDIATION**)
Mediation proceedings
    Attorney disclosure to client of confidentiality standards in mediation proceedings   Ev §1129
    Standards of conduct for mediators   CRC 3.854
Newsmen refusing to reveal source of information   Ev §1070
Official information   Ev §§1040 to 1042
Parties claiming privilege   Ev §§911 to 916
Paternity suits
    Confidential cover sheet for parentage actions   CRC 5.51
    Confidentiality of papers and records   Fam §7643
Physician-patient privilege
    Attorney inspecting records, authorizations for   CCP §1985.7, Ev §1158
    Breach of duty   Ev §1001
    Conduct of patient, privilege in action for damages for   Ev §999
    Definitions   Ev §§990 to 993
    Exceptions to privilege   Ev §§996 to 1007
    Heirs   Ev §1000
    Mental condition of client   Ev §§1004, 1005
    Parties claiming   Ev §§993 to 995
    Public entities, proceedings by   Ev §1007
    Reports to public employee   Ev §§1006, 1007
    Research findings affecting   Ev §§1156, 1156.1
    Waiver of   Ev §912
    Wills, determining validity of   Ev §§1002, 1003
Preliminary determination of privilege   Ev §914
Prior hearing, exercise of privilege in   Ev §913
Psychiatrists (See within this heading, **"Psychotherapist-patient privilege"**)
Psychologists (See within this heading, **"Psychotherapist-patient privilege"**)
Psychotherapist-patient privilege
    Aid in committing crime   Ev §1018
    Breach of duty   Ev §1020
    Court appointed   Ev §1017
    Crimes   Ev §§1017, 1018
    Dangerous patient, disclosing condition of   Ev §1024
    Definitions   Ev §§1010 to 1013
    Educational psychologists, application to   Ev §1010.5
    Exceptions to privilege   Ev §§1016 to 1026
    Heirs, testimony by   Ev §1019
    Parties claiming   Ev §§1014, 1015
    Reports to public agencies   Ev §1026
    Research findings affecting   Ev §1156.1
    Sanity hearing   Ev §§1023 to 1025
    Waiver of   Ev §912
    Wills, determining validity of   Ev §§1021, 1022
Rape victim-counselor privilege (See within this heading, **"Sexual assault counselor-victim privilege"**)
Real estate brokers societies   CC §43.91
School psychologists
    Psychotherapist-patient privilege
        Educational psychologists, applicability   Ev §1010.5
        Generally (See within this heading, **"Psychotherapist-patient privilege"**)
Sexual assault counselor-victim privilege
    Definitions
        Confidential communications   Ev §1035.4
        Holder of privilege   Ev §1035.6
        Sexual assault   Ev §1036.2
        Sexual assault counselor   Ev §1035.2
        Victim   Ev §1035
    Name change proceedings under address confidentiality program   CRC 2.575 to 2.577
    Parties asserting   Ev §§1035.8, 1036
    Qualification requirements for sexual assault counselor   Ev §1035.2
    Waiver of   Ev §912
Spousal communications privilege   Ev §§980 to 987 (See **MARITAL PRIVILEGE**)
Trade secrets
    Closed criminal proceedings, procedure for   Ev §1062
    Definitions   Ev §1061
    Disclosure in judge's chambers to determine claim of privilege   Ev §915
    Protective orders   Ev §1061
    Requests to seal articles, procedure for   Ev §1063
    Unauthorized, intentional disclosure to competitor as not privileged communication   CC §3426.11
Vote in public election   Ev §1050

PRIVILEGED COMMUNICATIONS—Cont.
Waiver of privilege   Ev §§912, 919

PRIVILEGES (See **IMMUNITY**)

PROBABLE CAUSE
Appeal in criminal case   CRC 8.304
Attorney professional conduct
    Prosecutor's responsibilities
        Requirement of probable cause to institute or continue prosecution   ProfC 3.8
Competence to stand trial
    Hearing on determination of probable cause
        Procedure   CRC 4.131
Juvenile wardship proceedings
    Detention hearing
        COVID-19, emergency rule   CRCAppx I Emer Rule 7

PROBATE OF WILL (See **WILL PROBATE**)

PROBATE REFEREES
Appointment
    Generally   Pro §400
    Decedents' estates   Pro §§8920 to 8922
    Eligibility requirements   Pro §401
    Prior law, effect of appointment under   Pro §408
    Qualification examinations for   Pro §402
        Eligibility period for appointment   Pro §401
    Revocation of (See within this heading, **"Revocation of appointment"**)
    Term of office   Pro §403
Appraisals
    Conservatorship estates (See **CONSERVATORS**)
    Decedent's estates (See **ADMINISTRATION OF ESTATES**)
    Guardianship estates (See **GUARDIAN AND WARD**)
Decedents' estates (See **ADMINISTRATION OF ESTATES**)
Discrimination prohibited in appointment of   Pro §401
Petition for orders in support of or against subpoena of witnesses by   Pro §453
Political activity of   Pro §407
Powers
    Appraisal of decedent's estate (See **ADMINISTRATION OF ESTATES**)
    General powers   Pro §450
    Subpoena powers
        Production of documents   Pro §452
        Witnesses generally (See within this heading, **"Witnesses"**)
Production of documents by subpoena   Pro §452
Qualification examinations
    Generally   Pro §402
    Eligibility period for appointment   Pro §401
Revocation of appointment
    Generally   Pro §405
    Decedents' estates   Pro §8924
    Governing law   Pro §408
    Noncompliance with standards as grounds for   Pro §404
    Political activity as grounds for   Pro §407
Standards   Pro §404
Subpoenas
    Production of documents   Pro §452
    Witnesses generally (See within this heading, **"Witnesses"**)
Termination
    Generally   Pro §406
    Revocation of appointment (See within this heading, **"Revocation of appointment"**)
    Term of office   Pro §403
Term of office   Pro §403
Witnesses
    Compelling appearance by subpoena   Pro §451
    Examination of   Pro §452
    Petition for orders in support of or against subpoenaing of   Pro §453

PROBATE RULES   CRC 7.1 to 7.1105
Accounting
    Compensation for guardians and conservators
        Ordering accounting prior to allowing compensation   CRC 7.752
    Conservators   CRC 7.575
        Final account of conservator of estate   CRC 7.576
    Guardians   CRC 7.575
    Waiver   CRC 7.550
Administration of estates
    Notice of petition to administer estate
        Publication   CRC 7.54

PROBATE RULES—Cont.
  Administrators
    Acknowledgment of receipt of duties and liabilities statement   CRC 7.150
    Compensation of personal representatives and attorneys   CRC 7.700 to 7.707
  Applicability of rules   CRC 7.2
  Attorneys
    Compensation of personal representatives and attorneys   CRC 7.700 to 7.707
    Minors or incompetent persons, services to
      Attorneys' fees for services to minors or incompetents   CRC 7.955
  Bonding
    Conservators   CRC 7.207
    Guardians   CRC 7.207
    Increase of bond   CRC 7.204
    Inventory and appraisal to show sufficiency of bond   CRC 7.501
    Multiple personal representatives   CRC 7.202
    Real property, bond increase as to sales   CRC 7.205, 7.206
    Separate bonds for individuals   CRC 7.203
    Waiver in will   CRC 7.201
  Children or minors
    Attorneys' fees for services to minors or incompetents   CRC 7.955
  Civil rules
    Applicability in family, juvenile and probate cases in superior court   CRC 3.10
    Fee waivers in probate cases   CRC 3.50
    Generally   CRC 1.4, 3.1 to 3.2240
  Compensation for guardians, conservators and trustees   CRC 7.750 to 7.776
    Accounting
      Ordering accounting prior to allowing compensation   CRC 7.752
    Advance payments   CRC 7.755
    Applicability of provisions   CRC 7.750
    Attorneys for guardians or conservators
      Advance payments   CRC 7.755
      Contingency fee agreements   CRC 7.753
      Petitions for orders to allow compensation   CRC 7.751
    Contingency fee agreements   CRC 7.753
    Just and reasonable compensation for conservators and guardians
      Standards for determining   CRC 7.756
    Paralegals used to perform legal services   CRC 7.754
    Petitions for orders to allow compensation   CRC 7.751
  Compensation for trustees   CRC 7.776
  Compensation of personal representatives and attorneys   CRC 7.700 to 7.707
    Advance payments   CRC 7.700
    Allowances
      Statutory compensation   CRC 7.701
    Applicability of provisions   CRC 7.707
    Attorney serving as personal representative   CRC 7.706
    Contingency fees
      Extraordinary legal services   CRC 7.703
    Extraordinary compensation
      Justification   CRC 7.703
      Petition   CRC 7.702
    Paralegals
      Extraordinary services, use in   CRC 7.703
    Statutory compensation
      Allowances   CRC 7.701
      Apportionment   CRC 7.704
      Calculation   CRC 7.705
  Conservatorships
    Accounts of conservators and guardians   CRC 7.575
      Final account of conservator of estate   CRC 7.576
    Attorneys, court appointment   CRC 7.1101 to 7.1105
      Alternatives to experience requirements   CRC 7.1102, 7.1103
      Annual certification of attorney qualifications   CRC 7.1105
      Certification of attorney qualifications   CRC 7.1105
      Confidentiality of certifications, supporting documentations, etc   CRC 7.1105
      Continuing education   CRC 7.1102, 7.1103
      Disciplinary action against attorney, notification   CRC 7.1105
      Experience requirements   CRC 7.1102, 7.1103
      Initial certification of attorney qualifications   CRC 7.1105
      Legal capacity of conservatee, proposed conservatee or person lacking, requirements for appointed attorney   CRC 7.1103
      Local court administration   CRC 7.1104
      Qualifications of appointees   CRC 7.1101 to 7.1103
      Unqualified attorney appointed, grounds for exception to requirements   CRC 7.1104
    Bonding   CRC 7.207
    Change of address
      Residence of conservatee, change   CRC 7.1063

PROBATE RULES—Cont.
  Conservatorships—Cont.
    Compensation for guardians, conservators and trustees   CRC 7.750 to 7.776
      Just and reasonable compensation, standards for determining   CRC 7.756
    Court investigators   CRC 7.1060
    "Duties of Conservator" acknowledgment of receipt of   CRC 7.1051
    Estates, conservators of
      Management of conservatorship estate   CRC 7.1059
      Standards of conduct   CRC 7.1059
    Indians, proceedings for
      Applicability of Indian Child Welfare Act   CRC 7.1015
      Involuntary placements   CRC 5.480 to 5.488 (See **INDIAN CHILD WELFARE ACT INVOLUNTARY PLACEMENTS**)
    Just and reasonable compensation, standards for determining   CRC 7.756
    Screening forms   CRC 7.1050
    Temporary conservators
      Good cause exception to notice of hearing on petition for appointment   CRC 7.1062
    Termination of conservatorship
      Appointment of counsel   Pro §1816.5
  Construction   CRC 7.2
  Contested probate proceedings
    Electronic filing and service   CRC 7.802
  Creditors' claims   CRC 7.401 to 7.403
    Court's action   CRC 7.402
    Final report, listing of claims   CRC 7.403
    Personal representative's action   CRC 7.401
  Definitions   CRC 7.3
  Disabilities, persons with
    Minors or persons with disability, claims   CRC 7.950 to 7.955
  Distribution
    Character of property
      Allegations in petition   CRC 7.652
    Petition
      Property description in petition for distribution   CRC 7.651
    Testamentary trusts, decree establishing   CRC 7.650
  Executors
    Acknowledgment of receipt of duties and liabilities statement   CRC 7.150
    Compensation of personal representatives and attorneys   CRC 7.700 to 7.707
  Ex parte applications for orders   CRC 7.55
  Ex parte communications   CRC 7.10
    Attorneys
      Prohibition on communications   CRC 7.10
    Definitions   CRC 7.10
    Parties
      Prohibition on communications   CRC 7.10
    When received and considered   CRC 7.10
  Forms
    Judicial council legal forms   CRCAppx A
      Electronic generation of mandatory judicial council form orders   CRC 7.101.5
      Use   CRC 7.101
  Guardianships
    Accounts of conservators and guardians   CRC 7.575
    Attorneys, court appointment   CRC 7.1101 to 7.1105
      Alternatives to experience requirements   CRC 7.1102, 7.1103
      Annual certification of attorney qualifications   CRC 7.1105
      Certification of attorney qualifications   CRC 7.1105
      Confidentiality of certifications, supporting documentations, etc   CRC 7.1105
      Continuing education   CRC 7.1102, 7.1103
      Disciplinary action against attorney, notification   CRC 7.1105
      Experience requirements   CRC 7.1102, 7.1103
      Initial certification of attorney qualifications   CRC 7.1105
      Legal capacity of conservatee, proposed conservatee or person lacking, requirements for appointed attorney   CRC 7.1103
      Local court administration   CRC 7.1104
      Qualifications of appointees   CRC 7.1101 to 7.1103
      Unqualified attorney appointed, grounds for exception to requirements   CRC 7.1104
    Bonding   CRC 7.207
    Change of address
      Ward's residence, change   CRC 7.1013
    Compensation for guardians, conservators and trustees   CRC 7.750 to 7.776
      Just and reasonable compensation, standards for determining   CRC 7.756

PROBATE RULES—Cont.
Guardianships—Cont.
   Consent
      Wards 19 or 20 years of age, extension of guardianship   CRC 7.1002.5
   "Duties of Guardian" acknowledgment of receipt   CRC 7.1002
   Estate, guardianship of
      Management of guardianship estate   CRC 7.1009, 7.1059
      Standards of conduct   CRC 7.1009
   Indian child welfare act in guardianship proceedings   CRC 7.1015
   Just and reasonable compensation, standards for determining   CRC 7.756
   Petitions
      Forms available for use   CRC 7.101
   Removal of guardian
      Final account or report, service after resignation or removal   CRC 7.1005
   Resignation of guardian
      Final account or report, service after resignation or removal   CRC 7.1005
   Screening forms   CRC 7.1001
   Settlement of accounts and release by former minor   CRC 7.1007
   Status reports   CRC 7.1003
   Temporary guardians
      Good cause exception to notice of hearing on petition for appointment   CRC 7.1012
   Termination of guardianship   CRC 7.1004
      Final account, service upon termination   CRC 7.1006
      Visitation by former guardian   CRC 7.1008
   Venue of guardianship
      Communications between/among courts involved with custody, visitation and guardianship involving ward   CRC 7.1014
   Wards 19 or 20 years of age, extension of guardianship   CRC 7.1002.5
      Change of residence address, notice   CRC 7.1013
      Forms, judicial council   CRCAppx A
      Termination of guardianship   CRC 7.1004
   Ward's participation and testimony in guardianship proceedings   CRC 7.1016
Incompetent persons
   Attorneys' fees for services to minors or incompetents   CRC 7.955
Independent administration of estates, report   CRC 7.250
Inventory and appraisal to show sufficiency of bond   CRC 7.501
Judges
   Education of judges
      Conservatorship and guardianship issues   CRC 10.468
      Domestic violence issues   CRC 10.464
Judicial council
   Forms, use of   CRC 7.101
   Probate and mental health advisory committee   CRC 10.44
Jurisdiction
   Effect of rules on court jurisdiction   CRC 7.2
Minors or persons with disability, claims   CRC 7.950 to 7.955
   Attorney fees for services   CRC 7.955
   Compromise of claim, petition for approval   CRC 7.950
      Attendance at hearing on petition   CRC 7.952
      Attorney's interest in petition to compromise, disclosure   CRC 7.951
      Expedited approval, petition   CRC 7.950.5
      Forms, use of judicial council form   CRC 7.101
   Deposit of funds
      Order for deposit   CRC 7.953
      Withdrawal   CRC 7.954
Notice of hearing
   Pleadings
      Amended or supplemental pleadings   CRC 7.53
      Description in notice of hearing   CRC 7.50
   Service   CRC 7.51
      Address unknown   CRC 7.52
Notice of petition to administer estate
   Publication   CRC 7.54
Objections   CRC 7.801
Orders
   Ex parte applications for orders   CRC 7.55
   Form orders
      Electronic generation of judicial council form orders   CRC 7.101.5
   Titles for   CRC 7.102
Personal representatives
   Acknowledgment of receipt of duties and liabilities statement   CRC 7.150
   Compensation of personal representatives and attorneys   CRC 7.700 to 7.707
Pleadings
   Amended pleadings
      Defined   CRC 7.3

PROBATE RULES—Cont.
Pleadings—Cont.
   Amended pleadings —Cont.
      Execution and verification   CRC 7.104
      Notice of hearing   CRC 7.53
   Amendment to a pleading
      Defined   CRC 7.3
      Execution and verification   CRC 7.104
      Notice of hearing   CRC 7.53
   Definitions   CRC 7.3
   Execution and verification of amended or supplemental pleadings   CRC 7.104
   Notice of hearing
      Amended or supplemental pleadings   CRC 7.53
      Description of pleadings in notice of hearing   CRC 7.50
   Signature   CRC 7.103
   Supplements to pleadings
      Defined   CRC 7.3
      Execution and verification   CRC 7.104
      Notice of hearing   CRC 7.53
   Titles for   CRC 7.102
   Use of Judicial Council forms   CRC 7.101
   Verification   CRC 7.103
Property sales   CRC 7.451 to 7.454
   Confirmation hearing, attendance at   CRC 7.452
   Exclusive listing, petition for   CRC 7.453
   Personal property
      Ex parte application for order authorizing   CRC 7.454
   Refusal to show property, effect   CRC 7.451
Purpose of provisions   CRC 7.2
Responses   CRC 7.801
Service of process
   Notice of hearing   CRC 7.51
      Address unknown   CRC 7.52
Spousal property petitions   CRC 7.301
Superior courts, probate cases in
   Civil rules
      Applicability in family, juvenile and probate cases in superior court   CRC 3.10
      Generally   CRC 1.4, 3.1 to 3.2240
   Fee waivers in probate cases   CRC 3.50
Telephone appearances   CRC 3.670
Testamentary trusts, decree establishing   CRC 7.650
Title of rules   CRC 7.1
Trusts
   Accounts of trustees   CRC 7.901
   Beneficiaries listed in petitions and accounts   CRC 7.902
   Compensation for trustees   CRC 7.776
   Court orders, trusts funded by   CRC 7.903
      Judicial administration standards   CRC JudAdminStand 7.10
Verification of pleadings   CRC 7.103
   Amended and supplemented pleadings   CRC 7.104
Waiver of bond in will   CRC 7.201
Waiver of rules   CRC 7.4

PROBATION
Adult probation officer (See **PROBATION OFFICERS AND DEPUTIES**)
Aggravating and mitigating factors
   Circumstance in aggravation   CRC 4.421
Appellate review
   Conditions of probation
      Limited normal record for certain cases   CRC 8.867
   Revocation after admitting violation   CRC 8.304
Conditions of probation
   Appellate rules, superior court appeals
      Limited normal record for certain cases   CRC 8.867
   Ignition Interlock Devices
      Guidelines for orders   CRC 4.325
Contempt, punishment   CCP §1218
County probation departments
   Access to juvenile delinquency case files
      Research, release of case file information   CRC 5.552
   Electronic court records, remote access
      Government entities, access by   CRC 2.540
Criteria considered in granting   CRC 4.414
District attorney (See **DISTRICT ATTORNEY**)
Eligibility for probation
   Aggravating and mitigating factors   CRC 4.414
   Presumptively ineligible defendant, granting probation   CRC 4.413
      Risk/needs assessment, court use in sentencing   CRC JudAdminStand 4.35

PROBATION—Cont.
Factors considered in granting   CRC 4.414
Hearings   CRC 4.433
Interests of justice, criteria where special showing required   CRC 4.413
    Risk/needs assessment, court use in sentencing   CRC JudAdminStand 4.35
Judges, nonsentencing, interference in process by   CRCSupp JudEthicsCanon 2
Jury service
    Felons currently on parole, probation, etc
        Ineligibility to serve as juror   CCP §203
Juvenile wardship
    Satisfactory completion of probation
        Dismissal of petition, sealing and destruction of records   CRC 5.840
Name-change restrictions   CCP §1279.5
Officers (See **PROBATION OFFICERS AND DEPUTIES**)
Out-of-county transfers   CRC 4.530
    Restitution
        Effect of transfer on outstanding restitution obligation   CRC 4.530
Presentence investigation reports   CRC 4.411, 4.411.5
Presumptively ineligible defendant
    Granting probation   CRC 4.413
        Risk/needs assessment, court use in sentencing   CRC JudAdminStand 4.35
Reports (See **PROBATION REPORTS**)
Restitution as condition of probation   CRC 4.411.5
    Recommendation by probation officer   CRC 4.411.5
    Transfer of probation cases to other counties
        Effect of transfer on outstanding fees   CRC 4.430
Revocation   CRC 4.435
    Admission of violation, appealability   CRC 8.304
    Appeal   CRC 8.304
        Notification of appeal rights   CRC 4.305, 4.306
    Certificate of probable cause for appeal   CRC 8.304
    Sentencing upon   CRC 4.435
    Supervising agency petitions   CRC 4.541
Suitability for probation
    Aggravating and mitigating factors, consideration   CRC 4.414
Supervision
    Mandatory supervision
        Revocation of probation, sentencing upon   CRC 4.435
        Risk/needs assessment, court use in sentencing   CRC JudAdminStand 4.35
    Risk/needs assessment, court use in sentencing   CRC JudAdminStand 4.35
Supervision responsibilities of probation officers
    Mandatory supervision
        Revocation procedure   CRC 4.541
        Transfers of cases   CRC 4.530
Termination   CRC 4.435
Transfer of probation cases to other counties   CRC 4.530

PROBATION OFFICERS AND DEPUTIES
Conciliation Courts   Fam §1817
Custody proceedings, investigations for   Fam §§3110 to 3116
Guilty pleas, reference to probation officer   CRC 4.114
Judges, nonsentencing, communications with probation officers   CRCSupp JudEthicsCanon 2
Juvenile rules
    Removal of juvenile from home
        Family finding and notice performed by social worker or probation officer   CRC 5.637
Nolo contendere pleas, setting date for sentencing and reference of case to probation officer   CRC 4.114
Probation reports   CCP §1131.3, CRC 4.411, 4.411.5
Removal of juvenile from home
    Family finding and notice performed by social worker or probation officer   CRC 5.637
Restitution
    Recommendation by probation officer   CRC 4.411.5
    Transfer of probation and mandatory supervision cases
        Effect of transfer on outstanding restitution obligation   CRC 4.530
    Victims of crime, recommendation by probation officer as to restitution to   CRC 4.411.5
Termination of parental rights, investigation and report concerning petition for   Fam §§7850 to 7852
Terms and conditions of probation, furnishing of   CCP §131.1
Violation or breach of terms and conditions of probation, requirement to report   CCP §131.1
Witnesses, subpoenaed as   Gov §§68097.1, 68907.2

PROBATION REPORTS   CCP §1131.3, CRC 4.411, 4.411.5
Appellate rules, superior court appeals
    Misdemeanor appeals
        Record on appeal, clerk's transcript   CRC 8.861, 8.862

PROBATION REPORTS—Cont.
Appellate rules, supreme court and courts of appeal
    Probation violation
        Appeal after admission   CRC 8.304
        Preparing, certifying and sending record   CRC 8.336
Contents   CRC 4.411.5
Crime victims, inclusion of statements by   CRC 4.411.5
Recommendations by probation officer   CRC 4.411.5
Restitution, recommendation regarding   CRC 4.411.5
Sentencing decisions, generally   CRC 4.411, 4.411.5
Supplemental reports   CRC 4.411
Victims of crime
    Statements by, inclusion   CRC 4.411.5

PROCESS AND SERVICE OF PROCESS
Abandonment of leased property   CCP §415.47
Address of party unknown   CRC 3.252
Admissions, service proved by   CCP §§417.10, 417.20
Adoption
    Termination of parental rights
        Alleged fathers, notice requirements for mother relinquishing child for adoption   Fam §7666
Affidavit
    Manner of showing proof of service   CCP §417.10
Answers
    Time for service   CRC 3.110
Appearances
    Motions to quash service   CCP §418.10
Appellate rules   CRC 8.25
    Address and telephone number change   CRC 8.32
        Electronic filing, when required   CRCSupp 1st AppDist
    Attorney general or other nonparty officer or agency, service on   CRC 8.29
    Attorneys
        Electronic filing for substitution, when required   CRCSupp 1st AppDist
        Substitution   CRC 8.36
        Withdrawal   CRC 8.36
    Briefs
        Certificate of interested entities or persons   CRC 8.208, 8.361, 8.488, CRCSupp 1st AppDist
        New authorities discovered after brief, letter to court   CRC 8.254
    Certiorari, mandate and prohibition
        Service of petition and supporting documents   CRC 8.486
    E-filing in supreme court and courts of appeal   CRC 8.70 to 8.79
        Supreme court-specific rules   CRCSupp SuprCtE-file 1 to CRCSupp SuprCtE-file 13
    Juvenile case appeals
        Briefs   CRC 8.412
        Orders setting hearing in termination cases, writ petition to review   CRC 8.452
    Parties, substitution   CRC 8.36
    Superior court appeals   CRC 8.817
        Applications   CRC 8.806
        Briefs   CRC 8.882, 8.927
        Limited civil cases in appellate division, appendix   CRC 8.845
        Motions   CRC 8.808
    Supreme court and courts of appeal
        Elder and dependent adult civil protection act, expedited appeals process   CRC 8.711
Associations (See **ASSOCIATIONS**)
Attachment proceedings   CCP §§482.070, 484.040
Attorneys
    Service on attorney   CRC 1.21
Bank officers accepting service   CCP §416.10
Boards   CCP §416.50
CARE act rules   CRC 7.2235
Certiorari writ
    Certificate of interested entities or persons   CRC 8.488
        Electronic filing, when required   CRCSupp 1st AppDist
Child custody
    Court-ordered evaluations
        Report, service   CRC 5.220
Child placement
    Out-of-county placements   CRC 5.614
Child support
    Combined summons and complaint, filing by clerks   CRC 5.325
    Enforcement services, action brought by   CRC 5.325
Claim and delivery   CCP §512.030
Claims against public entities and employees (See **CLAIMS AGAINST PUBLIC ENTITIES AND EMPLOYEES**)

PROCESS AND SERVICE OF PROCESS—Cont.

Clerks accepting
    Party's address unknown, papers served on clerk   CRC 3.252

Clerk signing   CCP §412.20

Commissions   CCP §416.50

Common interest developments
    Alternative dispute resolution
        Request for resolution   CC §5935

Compensation
    Fees generally (See within this heading, **"Fees"**)

Complaints
    Time for service   CRC 3.110

Complex cases
    Coordination   CRC 3.510
        Memoranda and declarations   CRC 3.513
    Electronic service   CRC 3.751

Conservators (See **CONSERVATORS**)

Construction-related accessibility claims
    Mandatory evaluation conference
        Service of application and notice   CRC 3.682
    Stay and early evaluation conference
        Service of notice   CRC 3.680

Contents of summons   CCP §412.20

Coroner (See **CORONER**)

Corporations (See **CORPORATIONS**)

Costs
    Fees generally (See within this heading, **"Fees"**)

Counties (See **COUNTIES**)

Court directing manner of service in absence of statute   CCP §413.30

Court's power to control   CCP §128

Criminal trials
    Electronic filing and service of documents   CRC 2.251, 2.252
        Electronic summons, issuance   CRC 2.259
        Fees not chargeable in some criminal actions   CRC 2.255

Cross-complaints
    Papers to be served on cross-defendants   CRC 3.222
    Time for service   CRC 3.110

Date of service, entry of   CCP §415.10

Debt collectors, applicability to   CC §1788.15

Decision of court
    Tentative decisions   CRC 3.1590

Default judgment, summons not timely served as grounds to set aside   CCP §473.5

Defendant, summons directed to   CCP §412.20

Defined   CCP §17

Depositions
    Subpoenas
        Service of deposition subpoena   CCP §2020.220

Destroyed land records relief law proceedings   CCP §§751.05 to 751.10

Discovery
    Evidence, preservation prior to filing action
        Service of notice of petition   CCP §2035.040
    Mail or fax, service by   CCP §2016.050

Dismissal of civil actions
    Notice of entry, service and filing   CRC 3.1390

Districts   CCP §416.50

Domestic violence
    Service of papers (See **DOMESTIC VIOLENCE**)

Dwelling house of person subject to summons, service at   CCP §415.20

Earthquakes boundary reestablishment after   CCP §751.54

Elections Code, service under   CCP §416.80

Electronic filing and service
    Generally (See **ELECTRONIC FILING AND SERVICE**)
    Issuance of electronic summons   CRC 2.259
    Proof of service   CCP §1013b
        Probate cases   Pro §1265
    Registered or certified mail required
        Electronic service not available when registered or certified mail required   CCP §1020
    Rules   CRC 2.250 to 2.261

Elisor, execution of process by   CCP §§262.8 to 262.10

Eminent domain (See **EMINENT DOMAIN**)

Enforcement of judgments (See **ENFORCEMENT OF JUDGMENTS**)

Environmental quality act
    Administrative record under CEQA
        Service of record   CRC 3.2206
    Appellate review of CEQA cases
        Jobs and economic improvement through environmental leadership act of 2021   CRC 8.701
        Sacramento downtown arena project, CEQA challenges   CRC 8.701

PROCESS AND SERVICE OF PROCESS—Cont.

Environmental quality act—Cont.
    Petitions under environmental quality act, civil rules governing
        Jobs and economic improvement through environmental leadership act of 2021   CRC 3.2222
        Sacramento downtown arena project, CEQA challenges   CRC 3.2222, 3.2236

Escheat (See **ESCHEAT**)

Execution of
    Coroner, execution of process by   CCP §§262.6, 262.10
    Directions of party re   CCP §262
    Elisor, execution of process by   CCP §§262.8 to 262.10
    Levying officer electronic transactions act   CCP §§263 to 263.7
    Liability of sheriff for   CCP §262
    New county, effect of creation of   CCP §262.11
    Regular on its face, sheriff to execute process   CCP §262.1
    Successors in office, execution by   CCP §262.3

Executors and administrators (See **EXECUTORS AND ADMINISTRATORS**)

Ex parte orders
    Application or written opposition   CRC 3.1206
    Temporary restraining orders   Fam §§242, 243

Expenses incurred due to failure to acknowledge receipt of summons by mail, liability for   CCP §415.30

Expert and opinion evidence
    Simultaneous information exchange about expert witnesses, discovery by means of
        Demand for exchange, service   CCP §2034.240

Facsimile transmissions   CRC 2.306
    Service by   CRC 2.300 to 2.306

Fair debt buying practices
    Default judgments against debtor
        Setting aside default and leave to defend premised on failure to receive actual notice   CC §1788.61

Family law
    Forms   CRCAppxs A (CRCFL-110), (CRCFL-115)
    Proof of personal service   CRCAppx A (CRCFL-330)
    Proof of service by mail   CRCAppx A (CRCFL-335)

Family rules
    General appearance as equivalent to personal service   CRC 5.68
    Manner of service   CRC 5.68
    Parental obligations, combined summons and complaint regarding   CRC 5.325
    Proof of service of papers   CRC 5.66
    Publication or posting, address unknown   CRC 5.72
    Request for orders
        Emergency or ex parte orders, requests   CRC 5.167
        Service of order after signature   CRC 5.125

Fees
    Indigent party, fee waived for   Gov §26720.5
    Issuance of summons, payment of fees prior to   CCP §412.10
    Recovery as costs by prevailing party   CCP §1033.5
    Sheriff's fees for service of process (See **SHERIFF**)

Fictitious name, notice requirement for entry of default against person sued under   CCP §474

Forcible detainer   CCP §1167

Forcible entry   CCP §§415.45, 415.47, 1167

Foreign language, legend appearing in   CCP §412.20

Forms
    Acknowledgment of receipt   CCP §415.30
    Destroyed land records relief law proceedings, summons in   CCP §751.05
    Judicial council forms   CCP §§412.20, 415.30, CRCAppx A
    Mail, notice re service by   CCP §415.30

Gang database removal, appeal proceedings
    Petition   CRC 3.2300

Gated community, access to   CCP §415.21

General appearance equivalent to personal service   CCP §410.50

Groundwater rights actions
    Parties
        Disclosures of parties appearing   CCP §842
    Pleadings and papers
        Electronic service   CCP §839

Guardian (See **GUARDIAN AND WARD**)

Guardian and ward (See **GUARDIAN AND WARD**)

Harassment
    Protective orders   CCP §527.6

Household member of party to action, service of summons involving   CCP §415.20

Indigent party, fee waived for   Gov §26720.5

Innkeeper's lien, writ of possession on   CC §1861.6

In rem actions   CCP §415.50

PROCESS AND SERVICE OF PROCESS—Cont.
- Inspection demands
  - Service of demand   CCP §2031.040
    - Retention of demand, proof of service and response   CCP §2031.290
- Interested persons, process shown to   CCP §262.2
- Interrogatories
  - Service of interrogatories   CCP §2030.080
- Interstate family support act
  - Form   CRCAppx A (CRCFL-510), CRCFL-510
- Issuance of summons   CCP §412.10
- Joint-debtor proceedings   CCP §990
- Joint debtors (See **JOINT DEBTORS**)
- Joint stock company   CCP §416.30
- Judicial Council approved forms, use of   CCP §§412.20, 415.30
- Jury summons   CCP §209
- Juvenile courts
  - Request for sheriff to serve papers   CRCAppx A
- Juvenile rules
  - Citation to appear, issuance   CRC 5.526
  - Educational rights holders
    - Orders, service   CRC 5.650
  - Electronic service   CRC 5.523
    - Address for electronic service to be provided to court on first appearance   CRC 5.534
  - Notice of hearing   CRC 5.524
  - Pre-hearing motions   CRC 5.544
  - Restraining orders
    - Dependency cases   CRC 5.630
- Landlord-tenant cases
  - Commercial real property tenancies
    - Disposition of property remaining upon termination, notice   CC §1993.03
- Legend appearing on summons   CCP §412.20
- Levying officer electronic transactions act   CCP §§263 to 263.7
  - Citation of provisions   CCP §263
  - Definitions   CCP §263.1
  - Electronic records as substitute for paper   CCP §§263.1, 263.4
  - Execution writs, retention of original or electronic copy   CCP §263.6
  - Facsimile transmissions   CCP §§263.1, 263.3
  - Identifiers, exclusion or redaction   CCP §263.7
  - Information processing systems   CCP §§263.1, 263.2
  - Legislative intent   CCP §263
  - Technical problems, effect on filing day   CCP §263.2
- Limitation of actions   CCP §583.210
- Mail
  - Failure to acknowledge receipt by mail, liability for expenses incurred due to   CCP §415.30
  - General procedure for service by   CCP §415.30
  - Office or home, service by leaving summons at   CCP §415.20
  - Persons outside state, service on   CCP §415.40
  - Proof of service by   CCP §417.10
  - Publication, service by   CCP §415.50
  - Time limit not extended for service by   CCP §413.20
  - Unlawful detainer actions   CCP §415.45
- Mandate
  - Certificate of interested entities or persons   CRC 8.488
    - Electronic filing, when required   CRCSupp 1st AppDist
  - Quashing service of summons   CCP §418.10
- Mandatory electronic service   CCP §1010.6
- Mandatory time for service of summons
  - Generally   CCP §583.210
  - Computation of   CCP §583.240
  - Extension of time   CCP §583.230
  - Failure to obtain action within time limit, result of   CCP §583.250
  - Filing of pleading following denial of dismissal motion   CCP §472a
  - Nonapplicability of   CCP §583.220
- Manner of service of summons
  - Business organizations
    - Leaving summons and complaint at office, mailing copy   CCP §415.95
  - Home or office, service at   CCP §415.20
  - Mail, service by   CCP §415.30
  - Out-of-state person, service on   CCP §§413.10, 415.40
    - Publication in newspaper   CCP §415.50
  - Personal service   CCP §415.10
  - Persons not otherwise specified   CCP §416.90
  - Publication, service of summons by   CCP §415.50
  - Unlawful detainer actions, service in   CCP §§415.45 to 415.47
- Mechanics' liens
  - Preliminary notice   CC §8204

PROCESS AND SERVICE OF PROCESS—Cont.
- Mechanics' liens—Cont.
  - Public works, summary proceeding for release of funds
    - Affidavit, service on claimant   CC §9404
    - Affidavit, service on public entity   CC §9402
    - Counter-affidavit of claimant   CC §9406
    - Service of order on public entity   CC §9412
- Military service
  - Financial obligations during service, relief
    - Petitions for relief   CRC 3.1372
- Mines and mining
  - Taxes, co-owners failing to pay
    - Service of notice   CCP §854
- Minors   CCP §416.60
- Mortgage trustee, effect of service of process on   CC §2937.7
- Motions to quash   CCP §418.10
- Municipal corporations   CCP §416.50
- Newspapers (See **PUBLICATION**)
- Nonparty deponent, service of papers on   CRC 3.1346
- Office of person subject to summons, service at   CCP §415.20
- Order to show cause or temporary restraining order, supporting papers   CRC 3.1150
- Other states
  - Persons outside state, service on   CCP §§413.10, 415.40
  - Proof of service outside state   CCP §417.20
- Papers to be served   CRC 3.220 to 3.222
  - Clerk
    - Party's address unknown, service of papers on clerk   CRC 3.252
- Parentage
  - Genetic testing to determine parentage
    - Service of genetic test results   Fam §7552.5
- Parent of injured child not joined as plaintiff, service of summons on   CCP §376
- Partition
  - Generally (See **PARTITION**)
  - Real property
    - Service of complaint   CCP §874.314
- Partnerships (See **PARTNERSHIPS**)
- Personal service
  - Generally   CCP §415.10
  - Persons not otherwise specified   CCP §416.90
  - Proof of   CCP §§417.10 to 417.40
- Persons not otherwise specified, service on   CCP §416.90
- Place for   CCP §413.10
- Pleadings
  - Time for service   CRC 3.110
- Posting
  - Family rules
    - Publication or posting, address unknown   CRC 5.72
  - Proof of service by   CCP §§417.10, 417.20
  - Unlawful detainer actions, service in   CCP §415.45
- Preliminary injunction, service of noticed motion for   CRC 3.1150
- Presumption of facts stated in return of service, effect on burden of producing evidence by   Ev §647
- Probate proceedings
  - Notice of hearing
    - Address unknown   CRC 7.52
    - Service   CRC 7.51
- Prohibition writs
  - Certificate of interested entities or persons   CRC 8.488
    - Electronic filing, when required   CRCSupp 1st AppDist
- Proof of service   CCP §417.10, CRC 1.21
  - Affidavit
    - Manner of showing proof of service   CCP §417.10
  - Computer-generated or typewritten proof of service forms, requirements for   CRC 2.150
  - Construction-related accessibility claims
    - Mandatory evaluation conference   CRC 3.682
    - Stay and early evaluation conference   CRC 3.680
  - Coordination of complex actions   CRC 3.510
  - Electronic filing and service rules   CCP §1013b, CRC 2.251
    - Probate cases   Pro §1265
  - Family law forms
    - Mail, proof of service by   CRCAppx A (CRCFL-335)
    - Personal service, proof of   CRCAppx A (CRCFL-330)
  - Family rules   CRC 5.66
  - Fax filing and service   CRC 2.306
  - Forms
    - Judicial council forms   CRCAppx A
  - Out-of-state service   CCP §417.20
  - Registered process server, requirements for   CCP §417.40
  - Return of   CCP §417.30

PROCESS AND SERVICE OF PROCESS—Cont.
Proof of service —Cont.
    Typewritten proof of service forms, requirements for   CRC 2.150
Protective orders   Fam §§6383, 6384
    Alternative service where respondent evades service   Fam §6340
    Harassment   CCP §527.6
    Requests for protective orders   CRC 3.1160
Publication
    Generally   CCP §415.50
    Family rules
        Publication or posting, address unknown   CRC 5.72
    Proof of service by   CCP §417.10
Public databases
    Access to databases for service of process purposes   CCP §415.50
Public improvement assessment, action to determine adverse interests in real property arising out of   CCP §801.8
Public improvement assessments, actions to determine adverse interests in real property arising out of   CCP §§801.6 to 801.8
Quash, motion to   CCP §418.10
Quieting title (See **QUIETING TITLE**)
Regents of University of California   CCP §416.50
Registered process server, violating requirements for   CCP §413.40
Related case
    Notice of related case   CRC 3.300
Remote appearances, service for
    Restraining orders   CRC 3.1162, 5.496
Rental passenger vehicle transactions
    Foreign renters
        Service of complaint by foreign renters   CC §1939.33
Request for admission
    Service of request   CCP §2033.070
        Retention of request, proof of service, and response   CCP §2033.270
Return of summons   CCP §417.30
    Presumption of facts stated in return of service, effect on burden of producing evidence by   Ev §647
    Proof of service
        Generally (See within this heading, "Proof of service")
Rules of court
    Attorney to be served   CRC 1.21
    Proof of service   CRC 1.21
Seal of court   CCP §412.20
Serve and file
    Requirement to serve and file
        Defined   CRC 1.21
Servers
    Generally   CCP §414.10
    Attachment (See **ATTACHMENT**)
    Enforcement of judgments (See **ENFORCEMENT OF JUDGMENTS**)
    Garnishment actions, issuance of withholding order in   CCP §706.108
    Presumption of facts stated in return of service, effect on burden of producing evidence by   Ev §647
    Proof of service   CCP §417.40
    Registration requirements, violation of   CCP §413.40
    Sheriff, service by (See **SHERIFF**)
Sheriff
    Service by (See **SHERIFF**)
Small claims courts   CRC 3.2102
    Writ petitions
        Pro se petitions   CRC 8.972
Spanish, legend in   CCP §412.20
State of California   CCP §416.50
Statute of limitation   CCP §583.210
Statute, proof of service in manner prescribed by   CCP §417.10
Stay of proceedings
    Notice of court and others of stay
        Duty of party requesting   CRC 3.650
Substituted service
    Small claims courts   CRC 3.2102
Summons and complaint
    Commercial mail receiving agencies
        Leaving copy of summons and complaint with agency   CCP §415.20
    Electronic filing and service
        Issuance of electronic summons   CRC 2.259
    Forms   CRCAppx A
    Jury summons   CCP §209
Superior courts, process extending throughout state   CCP §71
Telegraph, service of summons by   CCP §1017
Time
    Date of service, entry of   CCP §415.10

PROCESS AND SERVICE OF PROCESS—Cont.
Time—Cont.
    Mailing summons   CCP §413.20
    Mandatory time for service of summons (See within this heading, "**Mandatory time for service of summons**")
    Motion to quash service of process   CCP §418.10
Transferred causes
    Superior court appellate division case transferred to court of appeal
        Briefs   CRC 8.1012
Trial court rules
    Proof of service
        Computer-generated or typewritten proof of service forms, requirements for   CRC 2.150
Tribal court civil money judgment act
    Application for recognition and entry of judgment
        Notice of filing   CCP §1735
    Objections
        Time for service and filing   CCP §1737
Unlawful detainer (See **UNLAWFUL DETAINER**)
Validation proceedings   CCP §§861, 861.1, 863
Will probate proceedings (See **WILL PROBATE**)

PRODUCTION DEMANDS (See **INSPECTION DEMANDS**)

PRODUCTION OF EVIDENCE
Burden of going forward (See **BURDEN OF GOING FORWARD**)
Consumer privacy rights
    California privacy protection agency
        Authority of agency   CC §1798.199.65
Demand for production for inspection of documents, tangible things, land or other property (See **INSPECTION DEMANDS**)
Depositions, production at (See **DEPOSITIONS**)
Expedited jury trials
    Applicable provisions   CCP §630.06
Subpoena duces tecum (See **SUBPOENA DUCES TECUM**)

PRODUCTS LIABILITY
Animal experimentations, inadmissibility of evidence in products liability actions involving motor vehicles based on   Ev §1159
Compromise or settlement of claim by personal representative
    Time-limited demands   CCP §§999 to 999.5
Inherently unsafe products, availability of products liability action for injury caused by   CC §1714.45
Judicial council development and approval of pleading forms   CCP §425.12

PROFESSIONAL CONDUCT
Attorney professional conduct   ProfC 1.0 to 8.5 (See **ATTORNEY PROFESSIONAL CONDUCT**)
Interpreters   CRC 2.890

PROFESSIONAL CORPORATIONS
Privileged communications
    Psychotherapist-patient privilege   Ev §1014
Small claims court, exceptions to restriction on representation by attorneys in   CCP §116.530

PROFESSIONAL FIDUCIARIES
Bureau
    Removal of professional fiduciaries from conservatorship or guardianship for cause
        Report to professional fiduciaries bureau   Pro §2653
Deceased professional fiduciary   Pro §9765
Defined   Pro §60.1
Fees
    Fee schedule or other compensation
        Filing proposed hourly fee schedule or statement of proposed compensation   Pro §§2614.7, 2614.8
Licenses   Pro §2340
Periodic payments for services rendered by attorneys or fiduciaries
    Petition   Pro §2643.1
Petition for guardianship or conservatorship
    Contents   Pro §1510
Removal of professional fiduciaries from conservatorship or guardianship for cause
    Report to professional fiduciaries bureau   Pro §2653
Temporary guardians or conservators
    Petition for temporary guardian or conservator, contents   Pro §2250

PROFESSIONAL MALPRACTICE (See **MALPRACTICE**)

PROFESSIONAL SOCIETIES
Dental committee records subject to discovery   Ev §§1156, 1157

PROFESSIONAL SOCIETIES—Cont.
Immunity from liability of   CC §§43.7, 43.91, 43.95

PROFESSIONS
Exemption for purposes of enforcement of judgments of property used in   CCP §704.060

PROFFERED EVIDENCE (See ADMISSIBILITY OF EVIDENCE)

PROFITS
Executors of decedents' estates liable for profits from sale of estate property   Pro §§9657, 10005
Limitation of actions (See STATUTES OF LIMITATION)
Trust deeds and mortgages (See TRUST DEEDS AND MORTGAGES)
Unclaimed deposits and payments escheated   CCP §1516

PROFIT-SHARING
Employee pension benefit plan defined   Fam §80

PRO HAC VICE
Application to appear as counsel pro hac vice   CRC 9.40
    Filing fee   Gov §70617

PROHIBITION, WRIT OF   CRC 8.485 to 8.493
Alternative writs   CCP §1104
Amicus briefs   CRC 8.487
Appeals
    Appellate division of superior court
        Judgment involving mandamus or prohibition directed to superior court   CCP §904.3
        Small claims courts, writ petitions   CRC 8.970 to 8.977
        Writ proceedings within original jurisdiction of appellate division   CRC 8.930 to 8.936
Appellate rules, supreme court and court of appeal
    Opposition   CRCSupp 4th AppDist
Applicability of code   CCP §1105
Applicability of provisions   CRC 8.485
Attorney general amicus brief   CRC 8.487
Briefs   CRC 8.487
Certificate of interested entities or persons   CRC 8.488
    Electronic filing, when required   CRCSupp 1st AppDist
Costs
    Award and recovery   CRC 8.493
Decisions   CRC 8.490
Defined   CCP §1102
Environmental quality act cases under public resources code
    Writ proceedings   CRC 8.703
Fees for issuance of writ
    Superior court fees, specified services   Gov §70626
Filing of decision   CRC 8.490
Finality of decision   CRC 8.490
Judicial holiday, issuance on   CCP §134
Jurisdiction of issuing writs   CCP §1103
Law and motion rules, applicability of   CRC 3.1103
Modification of decision   CRC 8.490
Notice if writ issues   CRC 8.489
Notice of sanctions   CRC 8.492
Opposition   CRC 8.487
    Sanctions   CRC 8.492
Oral argument
    Sanctions   CRC 8.492
Original writs in reviewing courts   CRC 8.485 to 8.493
    Environmental quality act cases under public resources code   CRC 8.703
Peremptory writs   CCP §1104
Petition
    Contents   CRC 8.486
    Supporting documents   CRC 8.486
Rehearings   CRC 8.490
Remittitur   CRC 8.490
Returns   CCP §1108
Sanctions   CRC 8.492
Service   CCP §1107
    Petition and supporting documents   CRC 8.486
Small claims courts
    Petition for extraordinary relief relating to act of small claims division   CCP §116.798
    Writ petitions   CRC 8.970 to 8.977
Statute of limitation for commencement of action stayed by   CCP §356
Superior court appellate division
    Writ proceedings within original jurisdiction of appellate division   CRC 8.930 to 8.936

PROHIBITION, WRIT OF—Cont.
Writs
    Mandate, certiorari and prohibition in supreme court or court of appeal   CRC 8.485 to 8.493
        Environmental quality act cases under public resources code   CRC 8.703

PROMISES
Renewing liability, acknowledgment or promise   CCP §360

PROMISSORY NOTES (See NEGOTIABLE INSTRUMENTS)

PROMOTING ENDS OF JUSTICE (See ENDS OF JUSTICE)

PROOF, BURDEN OF (See BURDEN OF PROOF)

PROOF OF EXECUTION (See ACKNOWLEDGMENTS)

PROOF OF SERVICE
Administration of estates proceedings (See ADMINISTRATION OF ESTATES)
Enforcement of judgments (See ENFORCEMENT OF JUDGMENTS)
Mail, proof of service of papers by   CCP §1013a
Nonresident personal representatives   Pro §8575
Process (See PROCESS AND SERVICE OF PROCESS)
Will probate proceedings (See WILL PROBATE)

PROPERTY
After-acquired property (See AFTER-ACQUIRED PROPERTY)
Attachment (See ATTACHMENT)
Classification   CC §657
Defined   Ev §185, Fam §113
Division in dissolution and related proceedings (See DISSOLUTION OF MARRIAGE)
Enforcement of judgment, property subject to (See ENFORCEMENT OF JUDGMENTS)
Immovable   CC §657
Inclusions in definition   CCP §17
Literary property (See LITERARY PROPERTY)
Minor's money and property (See PARENT AND CHILD)
Movable   CC §657
Parent's right to control property of child   Fam §7502
Personalty (See PERSONAL PROPERTY)
Realty (See REAL PROPERTY)
Title (See TITLE AND OWNERSHIP)

PROPERTY DAMAGE
Injury to property as basis for civil actions   CCP §§25, 28
Judicial Council to develop and approve pleading forms   CCP §425.12
Latent deficiencies in planning or construction of improvement to real property, statute of limitation for damages for   CCP §337.15
Nonsuit motion in action involving   CCP §581c
Patent deficiencies in planning or construction of improvement to real property, statute of limitation for injury from   CCP §337.1
Statute of limitation   CCP §338
Venue   CCP §395

PROPERTY INTERESTS
Compulsory joinder of persons claiming interest relating to subject of action   CCP §389
Intervention in action by person claiming interest in subject property or transaction   CCP §387
Joinder of persons claiming interest in property   CCP §389.5
Partition proceeding, determination in   CCP §§872.610, 872.640
Quieting title proceedings, appearance in   CCP §762.050

PROPERTY SETTLEMENT AGREEMENTS
Attorney professional conduct
    Contingent fees
        Circumstances where contingent fee agreement impermissible   ProfC 1.5
Bankruptcy, effect of discharge in   Fam §3592
Child support provisions   Fam §§3585 to 3587
Effect of   Fam §1500
Jurisdiction   Fam §§2010 to 2013
Law applicable to agreements made before 1986   Fam §1503
Minors, marital agreements by   Fam §1501
Recording of agreements   Fam §1502
Spousal support provisions severable from   Fam §§3590 to 3593
Undue influence
    Definition of undue influence   Pro §86
Uniform Premarital Agreement Act
    Generally   Fam §§1600, 1601

PROPERTY SETTLEMENT AGREEMENTS—Cont.
Uniform Premarital Agreement Act—Cont.
    Amendment of agreement   Fam §1614
    Child support affected by   Fam §1612
    Citation of act   Fam §1600
    Consideration   Fam §1611
    Definitions   Fam §1610
    Effective date of agreement   Fam §1613
    Enforceability of agreement, conditions for
        Generally   Fam §1615
        Spousal support provisions   Fam §1612
    Execution of agreement
        Generally   Fam §1611
        Voluntarily executed, conditions for finding   Fam §1615
    Independent counsel, representation by   Fam §1612
    Revocation of agreement   Fam §1614
    Statute of limitations   Fam §1617
    Subject matter of agreement   Fam §1612
    Unconscionability of agreement   Fam §1615
    Void marriage, effect of   Fam §1616
Wills, effect upon   Fam §1612, Pro §§140 to 147

PROPERTY TAXES
Adverse possession, establishment of   CCP §325
Personal property (See **PERSONAL PROPERTY TAXATION**)
Real property taxes (See **TAXATION**)

PROPOSALS (See **CONTRACTS AND AGREEMENTS**)

PROPOSED INSTRUCTIONS TO JURY (See **JURY**)

PROSECUTING ATTORNEY (See **DISTRICT ATTORNEY**)

PRO SE LITIGANTS
Change of address or other contact information
    Serving and filing notice of change   CRC 2.200
Court self-help centers   CRC 10.960
Judicial council
    Access and fairness, advisory committee on providing   CRC 10.55
Small claims courts
    Writ petitions
        Pro se petitions   CRC 8.972

PROSTHETICS
Apartment housekeeper's lien, exemption from   CC §1861a
Hotel keeper's lien, exemption from   CC §1861
Warranties on assistive devices   CC §§1791, 1791.1, 1792.2, 1793.02

PROSTITUTION
AIDS
    Repeat offenses by person testing positive
        Vacating disposition and dismissal of adjudication, forms   CRCAppx A
Condoms
    Evidence of possession of condoms
        Inadmissibility   Ev §782.1
Evidence in prosecution
    Condoms
        Inadmissibility of evidence of possession of condom   Ev §782.1
    Extortion, serious felony, assault, domestic violence, human trafficking, sexual battery or stalking, victims or witnesses
        Inadmissibility of evidence of prostitution in prosecution for prostitution   Ev §1162
    Human trafficking victims, commercial sex acts
        Evidentiary significance   Ev §1161
Hotels and motels
    Sex trafficking activity, hotel permitting or benefiting from
        Actions against hotel for sex trafficking activity   CC §52.65
Human trafficking victims forced to commit prostitution
    Evidentiary significance   Ev §1161
    Expunging arrest or vacating adjudication
        Judicial council legal forms   CRCAppx A
    Vacatur relief for arrests or convictions for nonviolent crimes while victim
        Procedure   CRC JudAdminStand 4.15
Loitering in public place with intent
    Condoms
        Evidence of possession of condoms, inadmissibility   Ev §782.1
Mobilehome tenancy terminated on conviction of prostitution on premises   CC §798.56
Multiple convictions combined with positive test for AIDS
    Vacating disposition and dismissal of adjudication
        Judicial council legal forms   CRCAppx A

PROSTITUTION—Cont.
Public nuisance, attorney's fees recoverable for enjoining use of building for prostitution as   CC §3496
Victims and victims' rights
    Extortion, serious felony, assault, domestic violence, human trafficking, sexual battery or stalking, victims or witnesses
        Inadmissibility of evidence of prostitution in prosecution for prostitution   Ev §1162
Witnesses
    Extortion, serious felony, assault, domestic violence, human trafficking, sexual battery or stalking, victims or witnesses
        Inadmissibility of evidence of prostitution in prosecution for prostitution   Ev §1162

PROTECTIVE ORDERS
Animals
    Domestic violence cases, orders on behalf of animals   Fam §6320
        California law enforcement telecommunications (CLETS) information form, confidentiality and use of information   CRC 1.51, CRCAppx A
        Denial of petition for ex parte order, reasons to be provided   Fam §6320.5
Attachment (See **ATTACHMENT**)
Campus safety, threat to   Fam §6250.5
COVID-19, emergency rule   CRCAppx I Emer Rule 8
Denial
    Ex parte order, denial of petition
        Reasons to be provided   Fam §6320.5
        Statement of reasons   Fam §6340
Dependent adult abuse, protective orders to prevent
    Requests for protective orders   CRC 3.1160
Dependent child proceedings
    Firearm relinquishment procedures
        Forms for firearm relinquishment   CRCAppx A
Discovery
    Unsuccessfully making or opposing motion for protective order   CCP §2017.020
Dissolution of marriage (See **DISSOLUTION OF MARRIAGE**)
Domestic violence (See **DOMESTIC VIOLENCE**)
Dwelling exclusion orders
    Firearm relinquishment procedures
        Forms for firearm relinquishment   CRCAppx A
Emergency protective orders
    Forms
        Judicial council legal forms   CRCAppx A
Enforcement of judgments (See **ENFORCEMENT OF JUDGMENTS**)
Examination for purposes of enforcement of judgments   CCP §708.200
Exemplary damages, proof required for   CC §3295
Ex parte orders
    Denial of petition for ex parte order, reasons to be provided   Fam §6320.5
    Domestic violence   Fam §§6320 to 6327
        Electronic submission of petitions   Fam §§6306.5, 6307
        Remote appearance of party, support person or witness   Fam §6308
        Self-help services, posting information on services on superior court website   Fam §6306.6
    Notice not required   Fam §6326
Family Law matters
    Ex parte temporary restraining orders
        Electronic submission of petitions   Fam §§6306.5, 6307
Family rules
    Tribal court protective orders   CRC 5.386
Firearms
    Emergency protective order   CRCAppx A
    Relinquishment
        Forms for firearm relinquishment   CRCAppx A
        Procedures   CRC 4.700
Forms
    California law enforcement telecommunications (CLETS) information form   CRCAppx A
        Confidentiality and use of information on form   CRC 1.51
    Emergency protective orders
        Judicial council legal forms   CRCAppx A
Harassment   CCP §527.6
    Address or location of complaining party or family, prohibition on enjoined party from obtaining   CCP §527.10
    California law enforcement telecommunications (CLETS) information form, confidentiality and use of information   CRC 1.51, CRCAppx A
    COVID-19, emergency rule   CRCAppx I Emer Rule 8
    Denial of petition for ex parte order, reasons to be provided   Fam §6320.5
    Firearm relinquishment and disposition   CCP §527.9
        Forms for firearm relinquishment   CRCAppx A

PROTECTIVE ORDERS—Cont.
  Harassment —Cont.
    Firearm relinquishment and disposition —Cont.
      Procedures   CRC 4.700
    Minor's information confidentiality, request in civil harassment proceedings   CRC 3.1161, CRCAppx A
      Release of minor's confidential information   CRC 3.1161
    Requests for protective orders   CRC 3.1160
  Insurance
    Changing, canceling, cashing in, etc
      Ex parte orders restraining   Fam §6325.5
  Minors' rights to
    Appearance of minor under 12 to request or oppose temporary order   Fam §6229
  Notice and hearing, orders issuable following
    Service
      Alternative service where respondent evades service   Fam §6340
  Postsecondary educational institutions
    Orders against violence threatened on campus or facility
      COVID-19, emergency rule   CRCAppx I Emer Rule 8
      Possession of firearms   CCP §527.11
      Service of order   CCP §527.12
  Requests for protective orders   CRC 3.1160
  Stalking, protective orders against
    Firearm relinquishment procedures   CRC 4.700
      Forms for firearm relinquishment   CRCAppx A
    Name change proceedings under address confidentiality program   CRC 2.575 to 2.577
  Temporary restraining or protective orders
    COVID-19, emergency rule   CRCAppx I Emer Rule 8
  Totality of circumstances considered   Fam §6301
  Universities and colleges
    Orders against violence threatened on campus or facility   CCP §527.85
      California law enforcement telecommunications (CLETS) information form, confidentiality and use of information   CRC 1.51, CRCAppx A
      COVID-19, emergency rule   CRCAppx I Emer Rule 8
      Judicial council legal forms   CRCAppx A
      Memorandum in support of petition not required   CRC 3.1114
      Possession of firearms   CCP §527.11
      Requests for protective orders   CRC 3.1160
      Service of order   CCP §527.12
  Workplace violence or threats of violence, injunctions or orders against
    Firearm possession or purchase by person subject to
      Determination of possession   CCP §527.11
      Service of order   CCP §527.12
  Workplace violence or threats of violence, orders against   CCP §527.8
    Address or location of complaining party or family, prohibition on enjoined party from obtaining   CCP §527.10
    California law enforcement telecommunications (CLETS) information form, confidentiality and use of information   CRC 1.51, CRCAppx A
    Firearm possession or purchase by person subject to
      Court determination of possession of firearms in violation of restraining order   CCP §527.11
      COVID-19, emergency rule   CRCAppx I Emer Rule 8
    Firearm relinquishment and disposition   CCP §527.9
      Forms for firearm relinquishment   CRCAppx A
    Judicial council legal forms   CRCAppx A
    Memorandum in support of petition for order not required   CRC 3.1114
    Requests for protective orders   CRC 3.1160
    Service of orders by peace officers   CCP §527.12

PROVISIONAL REMEDIES
Attachment (See **ATTACHMENT**)
Claim and delivery (See **CLAIM AND DELIVERY**)
Deposits in court (See **DEPOSITS IN COURT**)
Domestic violence, prevention of (See **DOMESTIC VIOLENCE**)
Injunctions (See **INJUNCTIONS**)
Nonimprisonment in civil action for debt or tort   CCP §501
Receivers (See **RECEIVERS AND RECEIVERSHIP**)

PROXIES
Estate representative exercising (See **EXECUTORS AND ADMINISTRATORS**)

PROXIMATE CAUSE
Damages, recovery of   CC §§3300, 3333
Insurance liability exemptions, pleadings for   CCP §431.50

PRUDENT INVESTOR RULE   Pro §§16045 to 16054

PRUDENT MANAGEMENT OF INSTITUTIONAL FUNDS ACT   Pro §§18501 to 18510 (See **INSTITUTIONAL FUNDS MANAGEMENT**)

PSEUDONYMS
Commercial blockage tort, privacy of civil proceedings for   CC §3427.3

PSYCHIATRISTS (See **PSYCHOTHERAPISTS**)

PSYCHOLOGISTS (See **PSYCHOTHERAPISTS**)

PSYCHOTHERAPISTS
Bond required to secure costs in action against   CCP §1029.6
Childhood sexual assault, certificate of merit required in action for   CCP §§340.1, 340.11
Counseling (See **COUNSELING**)
Damages (See **DAMAGES**)
Malpractice (See **MALPRACTICE**)
Medical records, disclosure of   CC §56.104, Ev §1158
  Preventing or lessening serious threat to foreseeable victim   CC §56.10
Mental examinations
  Discovery procedure
    By whom performed   CCP §2032.020
Privileged communication (See **PRIVILEGED COMMUNICATIONS**)
Protection of third persons
  Duty to protect
    Immunity from liability   CC §43.92
    Psychotherapist-patient privilege, applicability   Ev §1024
Registered psychologists
  Psychotherapist-patient privilege
    Registered psychologist as psychotherapist   Ev §1010
Review committees, liability of   CC §§43.7, 43.8
Sex offenses, cause of action against psychotherapist for   CC §43.93
Sexual harassment, civil action for
  Construction or application of provisions in issue, solicitor general notified   CC §51.1

PSYCHOTROPIC MEDICATION
Child welfare services
  Forms, judicial council   CRCAppx A
Dependent children   CRC 5.640
  Prescriptions
    Release of psychotropic medication prescription information to medical board, authorization   CRC 5.642
Forms
  Juvenile forms   CRCAppx A
Group homes for children
  Forms, judicial council   CRCAppx A
Juvenile wardship proceedings
  Administration of psychotropic medication to ward of court
    Authorization, procedure   CRC 5.640
    COVID-19, emergency rule   CRCAppx I Emer Rule 7
    Forms, judicial council   CRCAppx A
    Release of psychotropic medication prescription information to medical board, authorization   CRC 5.642
Major neurocognitive dementia conservatorships, medication consents under   Pro §2356.5
Medical board of California
  Release of information to medical board
    Judicial council forms   CRCAppx A
Minors, consent to administration to
  Forms, judicial council   CRCAppx A
Prescriptions
  Juvenile rules
    Release of psychotropic medication prescription information to medical board, authorization   CRC 5.642

PTSD (POST-TRAUMATIC STRESS DISORDER)
Veterans
  Orders for dismissal
    Judicial council legal forms   CRCAppx A
  Petition for resentencing, form   CRCAppx A

PUBLIC ADMINISTRATORS
Abandonment of unclaimed money, presumption of   Pro §7644
Additional compensation   Pro §7623
Administration of estate, applicability of general rules governing   Pro §7622
Attorney for public administrator, compensation for services of   Pro §7622
Banks
  Surrender of decedent's property to public administrator   Pro §7603
  Unclaimed money deposited by public administrator, distribution   Pro §7644

PUBLIC INDEX

PUBLIC ADMINISTRATORS—Cont.
Bonds
    Generally   Pro §7621
    Liability on   Pro §7624
Burial instructions, search for   Pro §7602
Claims against estates, payment of   Pro §7662
Compensation
    Generally   Pro §7622
    Additional compensation   Pro §7623
    Attorney for public administrator, services of   Pro §7622
    Small estates, compensation for summary disposition of   Pro §7666
Continuing education   Pro §7605
Convalescent hospitals' duty to notify public administrator of death of patient   Pro §7600.5
Costs of estate administration
    Generally   Pro §7621
    Small estates, summary disposition of   Pro §§7662, 13114
    Subsequent personal representative, costs recoverable on appointment of   Pro §7604
Delivery of decedent's tangible personal property to surviving spouse   Pro §330
Deposit of funds
    Generally   Pro §7640
    County treasurer, funds deposited with   Pro §7643
    Interest on money deposited   Pro §7642
    State treasurer, deposit with   Pro §7644
    Unclaimed deposits   Pro §§7624, 7643, 7644, 7663
    Withdrawal by public administrator for estate administration   Pro §7641
Electronic court records, remote access
    Government entities, access by   CRC 2.540
English language, judicial proceedings preserved and published in   CCP §185
Escheat of assets held by   CCP §1449, Pro §§7643, 7644
Fees
    Additional compensation   Pro §7623
    Costs and expenses for small estate administration   Pro §§7662, 13114
    Probate proceedings, filing fees payable by public administrator as petitioner in   Gov §70659
Final distribution of estate, money remaining after   Pro §§7624, 7663
Financial institutions
    Surrender of decedent's property to public administrator   Pro §7603
    Unclaimed money deposited by public administrator, distribution of   Pro §7644
Funds, refusal to surrender   Pro §7624
Funeral director's duty to notify public administrator of unclaimed body   Pro §7600.6
Funeral instructions, search for   Pro §7602
Hospitals' duty to notify public administrator of death of patient   Pro §7600.5
Interest on money deposited, disposition of   Pro §7642
Jurisdiction of   Pro §7601
Letters issued to   Pro §7621
Petition for appointment as personal representative   Pro §7620
Possession and control of decedent's property subject to loss or waste   Pro §§7601, 7602
Priority of appointment   Pro §8461
Probate proceedings, filing fees payable by public administrator as petitioner in   Gov §70659
Public employees' duty to notify public administrator of decedent's property subject to loss or waste   Pro §7600
Safe deposit box of decedent, right to access to   Pro §7603
Savings and loans
    Surrender of decedent's property to public administrator   Pro §7603
    Unclaimed money deposited by public administrator, distribution   Pro §7644
Small claims court law and procedures, publications describing   CCP §116.930
Small estates, summary disposition of (See **SMALL ESTATES WITHOUT ADMINISTRATION**)
State treasurer, deposit of unclaimed funds with   Pro §7644
Stranger, administering estate of   Pro §§7600.5, 7601
Summary disposition of small estates (See **SMALL ESTATES WITHOUT ADMINISTRATION**)
Surety
    Bonds   Pro §7621
        Liability on bond   Pro §7624
Trustees
    Public administrators as trustees   Pro §15660.5
        Compensation   Pro §15688
Unclaimed property, disposition of   Pro §§7624, 7643, 7644, 7663
Waste, prevention of   Pro §§7601, 7602
Wills, search for   Pro §7602
Withdrawal of money deposited by public administrator for estate administration   Pro §7641

PUBLIC ADMINISTRATORS—Cont.
Written certifications, collection of property by   Pro §7603

PUBLIC ASSISTANCE (See **WELFARE**)

PUBLICATION
Administration of estates (See **ADMINISTRATION OF ESTATES**)
Administrative Procedure Act (See **ADMINISTRATIVE PROCEDURE ACT**)
Affidavit, proof by   CCP §2010
Appellate opinions, publication of (See **APPELLATE RULES, SUPREME COURT AND COURTS OF APPEAL**)
Change of name proceedings, publication requirement in   CCP §1277
Claims against decedent's estate, notice for filing   Pro §9001
Contempt charge for refusing to reveal source of information   Ev §1070
Continuous defamatory publication, shortening time to respond for   CCP §460.5
Decedents' estates (See **ADMINISTRATION OF ESTATES**)
Default judgment after service by   CCP §585
Destroyed land records relief law proceedings, service in   CCP §751.06
Earthquakes, boundary reestablishment after   CCP §751.54
Eminent domain summons served by   CCP §1250.125
Enforcement of judgments (See **ENFORCEMENT OF JUDGMENTS**)
Escheat (See **ESCHEAT**)
Lease of city property, notice of   CC §719
Libel and slander (See **LIBEL AND SLANDER**)
Liens by service dealers   CC §3052.5
Local rules   CCP §575.1
Lost property, notice of   CC §§2080.3 to 2080.8
Newspapers (See **NEWSPAPERS AND MAGAZINES**)
Opinions (See **PUBLICATION OF OPINIONS**)
Partition action, Service of process in   CCP §§872.310 to 872.330
Presumptions of publication of books   Ev §644
Process (See **PROCESS AND SERVICE OF PROCESS**)
Quieting title action, service in   CCP §§763.010 to 763.040
Sale and leaseback, notices required   CC §3440
Service dealers' liens   CC §3052.5
Service of process (See **PROCESS AND SERVICE OF PROCESS**)
Sexually explicit depiction of individual, creation or disclosure
    Actions for damages   CC §1708.86
Trust deed or mortgage, notice of sale under power of sale in   CC §2924f
Type size requirements   CCP §1019
Unclaimed deposits and payments escheated, publication of notices of   CCP §1531
Unclaimed property, notice for   CC §§2080.3, 2080.4
Unknown persons' funds, notice of   CCP §570
Validation proceedings, summons in   CCP §861
Voidable transactions, publication of notice of intended transfer   CC §3440
Will probate (See **WILL PROBATE**)

PUBLICATION OF OPINIONS   CRC 8.1100 to 8.1125
Assignments for preparation of opinions   CRCSupp SupCtIOPP VIII
Authority for rules governing   CRC 8.1100
Circulation of opinions   CRCSupp SupCtIOPP IX
Citation   CRC 8.1115
Computer-based source of decisional law   CRC 8.1115
Depublication   CRC 8.1125
Dismissal after supreme court grant of review   CRC 8.528
Filing of opinions   CRCSupp SupCtIOPP X
Memorandum opinions by courts of appeal   CRC JudAdminStand 8.1
Partial publication   CRC 8.1110
Publication and depublication orders by Supreme Court   CRC 8.1105
Request for depublication of published opinion   CRC 8.1125
Request for publication of unpublished opinion   CRC 8.1120
Review of published opinion granted   CRC 8.1115
Standards for publication   CRC 8.1105
Unpublished opinions
    Citation   CRC 8.1115
    Effect   CRC 8.1115
    Request for publication of unpublished opinion   CRC 8.1120

PUBLIC AUCTIONS (See **AUCTIONS**)

PUBLIC BENEFIT CORPORATIONS, NONPROFIT
Attorney professional conduct
    Organization or entity as client   ProfC 1.13

PUBLIC BENEFIT TRUST FUND
Creation   CC §3294.5
Punitive damage awards
    Allocation of punitive damage awards to fund   CC §3294.5

PUBLIC BUILDINGS
Accessibility of buildings and facilities
    Attorney general, civil actions to enforce
        Fees and costs for attorney general   CCP §1021.8
Blind persons having equal rights to use of   CC §§54, 54.3, 54.4, 55
    Construction or application of provisions in issue, solicitor general notified   CC §55.2
Disabled persons having equal rights to use of   CC §§54, 54.3, 54.4, 55
    Construction or application of provisions in issue, solicitor general notified   CC §55.2
Lease abandonment provisions, applicability of   CC §1952.6

PUBLIC CONSERVATORS
Continuing education   Pro §1456.2
Fees
    Probate proceedings, filing fees payable by public conservator as petitioner in   Gov §70659

PUBLIC CONTRACTS AND WORKS
Arbitration of   CC §1670, CCP §§1281.5, 1296
Assessments for public improvements (See **TAXATION**)
Bond requirements   CCP §995.311
Construction contracts
    Indemnity
        Wrap-up insurance   CC §2782.96
Design professionals, contracts with   CC §§3320, 3321
False claims for payment, civil liability
    Filing false claims act records under seal   CRC 2.570 to 2.573
Indemnity
    Wrap-up insurance   CC §2782.96
Injunction against   CCP §526a
Judgment debtor as contractor on   CCP §708.760
Liens
    Assessments for public improvements, lien claims based on (See **TAXATION**)
Mechanic's liens   CC §§9000 to 9566 (See **MECHANICS' LIENS**)
Private property used as public land   CC §1009
Subcontractor payment within 15 days, contractor's duty to make   CC §3321
Validation proceedings   CCP §§860 to 870

PUBLIC DEFENDER
Conservatorship proceedings   Pro §§1471, 1472
Death penalty cases
    Attorneys for capital cases generally (See **CAPITAL PUNISHMENT**)
    Qualifications of counsel
        Appellate counsel   CRC 8.605
        Habeas counsel   CRC 8.652
Electronic court records, remote access
    Government entities, access by
        List of government entities which may be authorized to receive access   CRC 2.540
Indigent criminal appellants, Supreme Court guidelines for compensation of attorneys representing   CRCSupp PayGuideAppoint

PUBLIC EMPLOYEES' RETIREMENT SYSTEM
Community property interests in benefits
    Tribal court orders, payments pursuant to   Fam §2611

PUBLIC EMPLOYMENT RELATIONS BOARD
Review of decisions   CRC 8.728

PUBLIC ENTITIES
Administrative law proceedings, generally (See **ADMINISTRATIVE PROCEDURE ACT**)
Agreements between public entities, tort liability under   Gov §§895 to 895.8
Appellate briefs
    Attorney general representing public officer or agency, service of brief on   CRC 8.29
    Service of briefs on public officers or agencies   CRC 8.212
Attorney professional conduct
    Organization or entity as client   ProfC 1.13
Boundaries
    Limitation of actions to contest change of   CCP §349.1
    Validation procedure for change in   CCP §349.4
Carpenter-Katz Small Business Equal Access to Justice Act   CCP §1028.5
Claims against public entities and employees (See **CLAIMS AGAINST PUBLIC ENTITIES AND EMPLOYEES**)
Conservation easement held by   CC §815.3
Consolidation
    Contesting consolidation, limitation of actions for   CCP §349.1
    Validation procedure   CCP §349.4

PUBLIC ENTITIES—Cont.
Constitutionality of funding statute, limitation of action by public entity against state to challenge   CCP §341.5
Decedent's estate, claims against   Pro §§9200 to 9205
Definition   Ev §200
Dissolution
    Contesting dissolution, limitation of actions for   CCP §349.1
    Validation procedure   CCP §349.4
Employees of (See **PUBLIC OFFICERS AND EMPLOYEES**)
Enforcement of judgments (See **ENFORCEMENT OF JUDGMENTS**)
Formation
    Contesting formation, limitation of actions for   CCP §349.1
    Validation procedure   CCP §349.4
Funding statute, limitation of action by public entity against state to challenge constitutionality of   CCP §341.5
Good faith
    Claims against public entities and employees (See **CLAIMS AGAINST PUBLIC ENTITIES AND EMPLOYEES**)
    Good faith improver provisions, applicability of   CCP §871.7
Information Practices Act, disclosure under   CC §1798.24
Judicial arbitration of actions involving   CCP §1141.27
Leases, applicability of remedies for breach of   CC §1952.6
Loans for purchase or rehabilitation of realty   CC §711.5
Mediation of civil actions, party to   CCP §1775.3
Officials of (See **PUBLIC OFFICERS AND EMPLOYEES**)
Participation by public
    Decisions and pending opportunities for public participation link on homepage   Gov §§11364, 11365
Presentation of claims as prerequisite to commencement of actions against   CCP §313
Public health and safety labor or service providers
    Logo or identifying mark of public agency, display restrictions   CC §3273
Public interest issues, fee awards in actions based on   CCP §1021.5
Public officers and employees (See **PUBLIC OFFICERS AND EMPLOYEES**)
Rent subsidy (See **RENT**)
Reorganization
    Contesting reorganization, limitation of actions for   CCP §349.1
    Validation procedure   CCP §349.4
Safekeeping of personal property, procedures for temporary   CC §2080.10
Service of process on   CCP §416.50
Shared appreciation loans, use of   CC §1917.006
Small business and regulatory agency, attorneys' fees in action between   CCP §1028.5
Small claims courts, preferential scheduling of hearing for   CCP §116.330
Statutes of limitation
    Actions against public entity   CCP §342
    Boundaries, actions to contest change of   CCP §349.1
    Contesting formation, dissolution, consolidation or change of organization   CCP §349.1
    Tolling statute, applicability of provision re   CCP §352
Support cases, payment claims against public entity in   CCP §§708.710 to 708.795
Temporary safekeeping of personal property, procedures for   CC §2080.10
Termination of parental rights, petition by state or county agency   Fam §7840
Tort Claims Act (See **CLAIMS AGAINST PUBLIC ENTITIES AND EMPLOYEES**)
Trust estate, filing claims against (See **TRUSTS**)
Unclaimed property
    Claim not required for controller to transfer property to state or local agencies   CCP §1540
Validation proceedings   CCP §§860 to 870
Venue in actions by or against   CCP §394

PUBLIC FINANCE
Bonds (See **BONDS**)
General obligation bonds, action upon   CCP §§337.5, 337.6

PUBLIC GUARDIANS
Administration of estate
    Appraisal of property   Pro §2943
    Attorneys
        Employment of attorney   Pro §2941
        Fees as administrative expense   Pro §2942
    Bond fees, liability for   Pro §2942
    Compensation for services rendered, claims for   Pro §2942
    Deposit or investment of funds   Pro §2940
    Mentally impaired elders, financial abuse of (See **SENIOR CITIZENS**)
    Reasonable expenses, liability for   Pro §2942
Appointment as guardian or conservator
    Application of public guardian for   Pro §2920
    Background checks   Pro §2920.5

PUBLIC GUARDIANS—Cont.
Appointment as guardian or conservator—Cont.
- Bond requirements   Pro §2922
    - Amount charged against estate as administrative expense   Pro §2942
- Consent of Mental Health Department or Developmental Services Department required for   Pro §2922
- Letters of guardianship or conservatorship, issuance of   Pro §2922
- Oath requirements   Pro §2922

Appraisal of property   Pro §2943

Attorneys
- Employment of   Pro §2941
- Fees as administrative expense   Pro §2942

Bond requirements
- Generally   Pro §2922
- Amount charged against estate of ward or conservatee as administrative expense   Pro §2942

Certification for taking possession and control of property   Pro §2901

Consent to appointment as guardian or conservator required of Mental Health Department or Developmental Services Department   Pro §2922

Continuing education   Pro §2923

Control of property by (See within this heading, **"Temporary possession or control of property"**)

Costs and fees
- Administrative expenses, liability for   Pro §2942
- Probate proceedings, filing fees payable by public guardian as petitioner in Gov §70659
- Temporary possession or control of property   Pro §2902

Deposit or investment of funds   Pro §2940

Developmental services department
- Consent for public guardianship for persons under department jurisdiction Pro §2921

Disclosure of information to public guardian concerning property owned by ward or conservatee   Pro §2901

Electronic court records, remote access
- Government entities, access by
    - List of government entities which may be authorized to receive access CRC 2.540

Fees (See within this heading, **"Costs and fees"**)

Immunity from liability for failure to take possession or control of property   Pro §2944

Investigations
- Prefiling investigations   Pro §§2910, 2911

Letters of guardianship or conservatorship, issuance of   Pro §2922

Liability
- Immunity of public guardian for failing to take possession or control of property   Pro §2944
- Surrender of property to public guardian, written certification discharging liability of third party for   Pro §2901

Loss, injury, waste, or misappropriation, public guardian taking temporary possession or control of property subject to   Pro §2900

Mentally impaired elders, financial abuse of (See **SENIOR CITIZENS**)

Oath required on appointment as guardian or conservator   Pro §2922

Prefiling investigations   Pro §§2910, 2911

Recordation of written certification authorizing possession of real property   Pro §2901

State hospitals, state department
- Consent for public guardianship for persons under department jurisdiction Pro §2921

Surrender of property to public guardian   Pro §2901

Temporary possession or control of property
- Generally   Pro §2900
- Costs and fees   Pro §2902
- Governing law, effective date of   Pro §2903
- Grounds for authority to take possession or control   Pro §2900
- Immunity for failing to take possession or control of property   Pro §2944
- Residence of intended ward or conservatee, procedure for removing occupant from   Pro §2900
- Restraints on transfer, encumbrance, disposition, etc, of property   Pro §2900
    - Certification entitling guardian or conservator to restrain   Pro §2901.5
- Written certification for   Pro §2901

Trustee, public guardian as (See **TRUSTS**)

Written certifications   Pro §§2901, 2952

PUBLIC HOUSING
Leasing of land by municipalities   CC §718c
Shared appreciation loans, use of   CC §1917.006
State agencies, adoption of housing regulations by (See **ADMINISTRATIVE PROCEDURE ACT**)

PUBLIC IMPROVEMENTS
Assessments (See **TAXATION**)
Dedication (See **DEDICATION**)
Public contracts and works (See **PUBLIC CONTRACTS AND WORKS**)

PUBLIC INDECENCY (See INDECENCY AND OBSCENITY)

PUBLIC INTEREST
Attorney's fee award to prevailing party in action resulting in enforcement of right affecting   CCP §1021.5
Motion to strike causes of action having chilling effect on free speech rights in public discussion of public issues   CCP §§425.16, 425.17
- SLAPPback actions   CCP §425.18

PUBLIC LANDS
Generally   CC §§669, 670
Appropriation of water originating on   CC §1422
Claims against public entities and employees (See **CLAIMS AGAINST PUBLIC ENTITIES AND EMPLOYEES**)
Leasing of   CC §718
Ownership of   CC §670
Prescriptive use   CC §1007
Reputation as evidence of   Ev §§1321 to 1323

PUBLIC NUISANCES (See NUISANCES)

PUBLIC OFFICERS AND EMPLOYEES
Abolishment of office by repeal of statutes, effect on officeholders of   CCP §§6, 7
Appellate briefs
- Attorney general representing public officer or agency, service of brief on CRC 8.29
- Service of briefs on public officers or agencies   CRC 8.212

Attorney General (See **ATTORNEY GENERAL**)
Attorney professional conduct
- Conflicts of interest
    - Former and current government officials or employees   ProfC 1.11

Bank superintendent   CC §1916.5
Bonds
- Exemption from bond requirement in actions or proceedings   CCP §995.220
- Indemnity rights, bond as basis for   CCP §1055
- Official bonds, generally (See **BONDS OF PUBLIC OFFICIALS**)

Certificate as to official capacity of public officials, fee for   Gov §26852
Change of venue of actions by or against state officers   CCP §401
Claims against public entities and employees (See **CLAIMS AGAINST PUBLIC ENTITIES AND EMPLOYEES**)
Clerks of court (See **CLERKS OF COURT**)
Commissioners (See **COMMISSIONERS**)
Conflict of interests (See **CONFLICT OF INTERESTS**)
Controller (See **CONTROLLER**)
County board of supervisors (See **SUPERVISORS**)
County counsel   CC §1181
Court employees (See **COURT OFFICERS AND EMPLOYEES**)
Credit report on public officer or employee, restrictions on   CC §1785.135
District attorney (See **DISTRICT ATTORNEY**)
Documents prepared by public officials, general provision concerning admissibility of   Ev §1280
Due care, presumption of violation of employee standard of conduct as failure to exercise   Ev §669.1
Emancipation of minor, liability for false information on DMV records   Fam §7142
Employee defined   Ev §195
Enforcement of judgments   CCP §708.790
Firefighters (See **FIREFIGHTERS**)
Governor (See **GOVERNOR**)
Indemnity
- Claims against public entities and employees (See **CLAIMS AGAINST PUBLIC ENTITIES AND EMPLOYEES**)
- Surety, indemnification of   CCP §1055

Information Practices Act, violation of   CC §1798.55
Information privilege   Ev §§1040 to 1042
Injunctions against   CC §3423, CCP §526
Joint authority
- Effect of grant of   CCP §15
- Joint authority statute   CC §12

Judges
- Generally (See **JUDGES**)
- Service by   CRCSupp JudEthicsCanon 4

Judicial arbitration of actions involving   CCP §1141.27
Jurors (See **JURY**)
Law enforcement officers (See **LAW ENFORCEMENT OFFICERS**)
Legislators (See **LEGISLATURE**)

PUBLIC OFFICERS AND EMPLOYEES—Cont.
Libel and slander action on comments   CC §47
Mandamus, damages and costs where respondent is officer of public entity   CCP §1095
Medical reports, authorization for disclosure of   Ev §§1006, 1007
Mental examination disclosed   Ev §1026
Notaries public (See **NOTARIES PUBLIC**)
Personnel board (See **PERSONNEL BOARD**)
Police officers (See **LAW ENFORCEMENT OFFICERS**)
Postal service employees (See **MAIL AND MAILING**)
Presumptions
    Due care, statutory violation as failure to exercise   Ev §669.1
    Official duty regularly performed   Ev §664
Probation officers and deputies (See **PROBATION OFFICERS AND DEPUTIES**)
Promotion in employment, information concerning   CC §1798.38
Psychotherapists, employees functioning as   Ev §1010
Public administrators (See **PUBLIC ADMINISTRATORS**)
Public defender in conservatorship proceedings   Pro §§1471, 1472
Public Employment Relations Board, judicial review of decisions   CRC 8.728
Public guardians (See **PUBLIC GUARDIANS**)
Quieting title to improperly encumbered property of public officer or employee, proceedings for   CCP §§765.010 to 765.060
    Counsel for officer or employee supplied by employer   CCP §765.060
    Financial institution claims
        Applicability of provisions   CCP §765.050
    Order striking lien or encumbrance   CCP §765.030
    Penalty for filing for lien or encumbrance designed to hinder or harass   CCP §765.040
    Petition to strike lien or incumbrance   CCP §765.010
        Affidavit in support of petition   CCP §765.020
        Contents   CCP §765.020
    Prohibition on filing lawsuit, lien, etc, to harass or hinder officers and employees   CCP §765.010
Quo warranto   CCP §§802 to 811, 917.8
Rape committed by public official by threatening to use authority
    Statute of limitations on sexual assault damages   CCP §340.16
Referee (See **REFEREES**)
Sealed documents presumed to be genuine   Ev §1452
Seal of (See **SEAL**)
Secretary of State (See **SECRETARY OF STATE**)
Sexual acts performed under threat by person claiming to be
    Statute of limitations
        Civil damages   CCP §340.16
Sexual harassment, civil action for
    Elected officials   CC §51.9
Sheriff (See **SHERIFF**)
Signatures presumed to be genuine   Ev §§1453, 1454, 1530
Supervisors (See **SUPERVISORS**)
Surveyor general   Ev §1605
Tenure (See **TERMS OF OFFICE**)
Tort Claims Act (See **CLAIMS AGAINST PUBLIC ENTITIES AND EMPLOYEES**)
Treasurer (See **TREASURER**)
Undertakings
    Exemption from bond requirement in actions or proceedings   CCP §995.220
    Indemnity rights, bond as basis   CCP §1055
    Official bonds generally (See **BONDS OF PUBLIC OFFICIALS**)
Usurpation of office   CCP §§802 to 811, 917.8
Venue in actions against   CCP §393
Witnesses, compensation of public employee as   Gov §68097.2

PUBLIC OFFICES
Holiday for purposes of computing time if public office closed   CCP §12b
Quo warranto   CCP §§802 to 811, 917.8
Usurpation of office   CCP §§802 to 811, 917.8

PUBLIC POLICY
Acceleration of loan provisions, waiver of   CC §2924.6
Automobile leases   CC §2988
Conservation easements   CC §815
Credit reports   CC §1785.1
Custody of children   Fam §3020
Dance studio contracts, regulation of   CC §1812.50
Disclosure of public information   Ev §§1040 to 1042
Discount buying services contracts   CC §1812.127
Exemptions from enforcement of judgments, waiver of   CCP §703.040
Health studio services contracts   CC §1812.80
Jury service and selection   CCP §191
Layaway provisions, buyer waiving   CC §1749.2

PUBLIC POLICY—Cont.
Retail installment sales provisions, waiver of   CC §1801
Seller assisted marketing plans, regulation of   CC §1812.200
Warranties on consumer goods, waiver of   CC §1790.1

PUBLIC RESTROOMS
Disabled persons' right to use of   CC §55

PUBLIC SAFETY EMPLOYEES
Contempt orders, stay of execution of   CCP §128

PUBLIC SALES (See **AUCTIONS**)

PUBLIC SITTINGS
Court sittings   CCP §124

PUBLIC TRAILS
Enjoining closure of   CCP §731.5

PUBLIC TRANSPORTATION (See **COMMON CARRIERS**)

PUBLIC UTILITIES
Bail and penalty schedules for misdemeanor cases involving   CRC 4.102
Cancellation of utility, cable, etc, services on behalf of deceased person
    In-person cancellation not to be required   Pro §217
Consumer's personal records, subpoena of   CCP §1985.3
Damages
    Diversion or tampering with gas or electric utility services, action for   CC §§1882 to 1882.6
    Repairs or service during specified time period where subscriber's presence required, failure to provide   CC §1722
Diversion of gas or electricity, damages for   CC §§1882 to 1882.6
Electricity (See **ELECTRICITY AND ELECTRIC COMPANIES**)
Eminent domain (See **EMINENT DOMAIN**)
Fines and penalties
    Bail schedule   CRC 4.102
Gas companies (See **GAS COMPANIES**)
Jurors, source for selection of   CCP §197
Landlord and tenant (See **LANDLORD AND TENANT**)
Mineral rights owner, notice of intent to enter on land for excavation by   CC §848
Mobilehome parks (See **MOBILEHOMES**)
Penalty schedules for misdemeanor cases involving   CRC 4.102
Pipeline corporation's absolute liability for damages caused by discharge or leaking   CC §3333.5
Repairs or service during specified time period where subscriber's presence required, liability for failure to provide   CC §1722
Wrongfully enjoining public improvement or utility, damages for   CCP §526b

PUBLIC UTILITIES COMMISSION
Administrative Procedure Act, applicability of rulemaking provisions of   Gov §11351
Judicial review of decisions   CRC 8.724
    Procedural provisions   CRC 8.724
    Supreme Court review   CRC 8.724
Petition for review   CRC 8.724

PUBLIC WATER SYSTEMS
Groundwater rights actions
    Definition of public water systems   CCP §832

PUBLIC WORKS
Generally (See **PUBLIC CONTRACTS AND WORKS**)
Mechanics' liens   CC §§9000 to 9566 (See **MECHANICS' LIENS**)

PUBLIC WORKS DEPARTMENT
Eminent domain taking by   CCP §1245,210

PUERTO RICO
Acknowledgment of instruments   CC §1183.5

PUNITIVE DAMAGES
Doxing victims' recourse   CC §1708.89
Exemplary damages (See **DAMAGES**)

PURCHASER OF REALTY (See **VENDOR AND PURCHASER**)

PURCHASER'S LIEN
Generally   CC §§3048, 3050

PUTATIVE SPOUSE
Generally   Fam §§2251, 2252

PUTATIVE SPOUSE—Cont.
Defined   CCP §377.60
Wrongful death actions, assertion of   CCP §377.60

Q

QUALIFICATIONS
Congress of United States (See **CONGRESS**)
Jurors (See **JURY**)
Personal sureties, affidavit of qualifications by   CCP §995.520
Small claims advisors   CCP §116.920
Witnesses   Ev §§700, 701

QUARRIES
Tenant's use of quarries   CC §819

QUASH, MOTION TO
Administrative adjudication proceeding, motion to quash subpoena in   Gov §11450.30
Appeals from   CCP §§904.1 to 904.2
Appearance of defendant at ex parte hearings, effect of   CCP §418.11
Attachment (See **ATTACHMENT**)
Default judgments   CCP §§585, 586
Earnings assignment for support (See **EARNINGS ASSIGNMENT FOR SUPPORT**)
Family rules   CRC 5.401
    Request for order to quash   CRC 5.63
Forcible entry and detainer
    Judicial council, rules as to   CCP §1170.9
Health insurance coverage for supported child, motion to quash assignment of   Fam §§3764, 3765
Innkeeper's lien, writ of possession on   CC §1861.6
Service of summons, motion to quash   CCP §418.10
Subpoena (See **SUBPOENA**)
Subpoena duces tecum   CCP §1987.1
Support modification, request for income information from employer in proceedings for   Fam §3664
Time for service of motion   CCP §1005
Unlawful detainer actions   CCP §1167.4
    Judicial council rules as to   CCP §1170.9
    Motions to quash service   CRC 3.1327

QUASI-COMMUNITY PROPERTY (See **COMMUNITY PROPERTY**)

QUESTIONNAIRES
Economic litigation provisions for limited civil cases   CCP §93
Family law rules (See **FAMILY RULES**)
Jury questionnaires (See **JURY**)

QUESTIONS OF LAW OR FACT
Coordination of actions   CCP §§404, 404.1
Court determining questions of law   Ev §§310, 311
Foreign law   Ev §310
Fraud in contracts   CC §1574
Jury (See **JURY**)
Notice of trial   CCP §594
Referees determining   CCP §§638, 639

QUICK SALE
Decedents' estates, assets of   Pro §§10252, 10259

QUIET ENJOYMENT
Bailment, property held under   CC §1955
Damages for breach of covenant of   CC §3304

QUIETING TITLE (See also **ADVERSE POSSESSION**)
Action to establish title against adverse claims   CCP §760.020
Answers   CCP §761.030
Appearance at proceedings   CCP §762.050
Chain of title, identity of person in   CCP §§770.010 to 770.080
Civil actions in general, applicability of statutes and rules governing practice in   CCP §760.060
Complaints   CCP §§761.010, 761.020
Cross complaints   CCP §761.040
Cumulative remedy   CCP §760.030
Damages for withholding property   CCP §§740, 741
Deceased defendant   CCP §762.030
Decedent's estate   CCP §762.030, Pro §9654
Dedication of property   CCP §§771.010, 771.020
Default judgments   CCP §764.010
Defendants in action   CCP §§762.010 to 762.090

QUIETING TITLE—Cont.
Definitions   CCP §760.010
Destroyed instruments   CCP §1046a
Earthquakes, reestablishing title after   CCP §§751.01 to 751.28
Encumbrancer, rights of   CCP §764.060
Guardian ad litem, appointment of   CCP §762.080
Hearing in action to identify party in chain of title   CCP §§770.060, 770.070
Identity of person in chain of title   CCP §§770.010 to 770.080
Joinder of parties   CCP §762.040
Judgments   CCP §§764.010 to 764.070
Jurisdiction   CCP §760.040
Limited civil cases, unavailability of title determinations in   CCP §580
Lost instruments   CCP §1046a
Notice of pendency   CCP §§761.010, 761.045
Notice on hearing for identity of party in chain of title   CCP §770.060
Occupancy, effect of title by   CC §1006
Oil and gas leases, right of entry or occupation under   CCP §§772.010 to 772.060
Parties   CCP §§762.010 to 762.090
Petitions
    Identify person in chain of title, petition to   CCP §§770.040 to 770.060
    Public officer or employee, petition to strike and release improper lien or encumbrance on property of   CCP §§765.010 to 765.060
Process (See within this heading, "Service")
Publication, service by   CCP §§763.010 to 763.040
Public improvement liens, effect of   CCP §§801.1 to 801.15
Public officer or employee, proceedings to strike and release improper lien or encumbrance on property of   CCP §§765.010 to 765.060
Purchaser, rights of   CCP §764.060
Remedies available   CCP §760.030
Service
    Generally   CCP §§763.010 to 763.040
    Survey order   CCP §743
    Unknown defendant   CCP §762.070
State as party   CCP §§762.090, 764.070
State Lands Commission, land subject to boundary line or exchange agreements with   CCP §§760.020, 764.080
Surveys   CCP §§742, 743
Title reports required   CCP §762.040
Unknown defendants   CCP §§762.020, 762.060, 762.070
Venue   CCP §760.050
Will, actions involving validity of gift, devise, bequest or trust under   CCP §764.020

QUITCLAIM DEEDS
Damages for breach of agreement to execute   CC §3306a
Power of termination, effect of   CC §885.060

QUORUM
Judges' removal or censure hearings   JudPerR 123
Referees   CCP §1053

QUO WARRANTO
Generally   CCP §§802 to 811
Attorney general bringing   CCP §803
Complaint   CCP §804
Costs of proceedings   CCP §810
Joinder of defendants   CCP §808
Judgments   CCP §§805, 809
Stay of proceedings   CCP §917.8

R

RABBIS (See **CLERGYPERSONS**)

RACE
Adoption proceedings (See **ADOPTION**)
Bible entries as evidence   Ev §1312
Church records as evidence of   Ev §1315
Damages, measure
    Lost earnings or impaired earning capacity
        Race, ethnicity or gender not to serve as basis for reduction in damages   CC §3361
Discrimination
    Generally (See **DISCRIMINATION**)
    Judicial ethics code
        Administrative responsibilities of judge, impartial discharge   CRCSupp JudEthicsCanon 3
        Attorneys, judges to require to refrain from manifesting   CRCSupp JudEthicsCanon 3

RACE—Cont.
 Discrimination—Cont.
  Judicial ethics code—Cont.
   Court personnel and staff under direction of judge, standards of conduct enforced by judge   CRCSupp JudEthicsCanon 3
   Membership in discriminatory organizations   CRCSupp JudEthicsCanon 2
 Disqualification of judges, grounds for   CCP §170.2
 Equal protection
  Political structure equal protection   CC §53.7
 Family friends, statements concerning race by   Ev §1311
 Foster care placement   Fam §7950
 Hearsay evidence, acceptance of   Ev §1310
 Jury service exemption not allowed based on   CCP §204
 Political structure equal protection   CC §53.7
 Relative's statements concerning   Ev §1311
 Reputation among family members concerning   Ev §1313

RACIAL DISCRIMINATION
 Sentencing
  Mitigating circumstances
   Enhancement could result in discriminatory racial impact   CRC 4.423

RADAR
 Traffic lights and signs, automated enforcement systems
  Evidentiary effect of printed representations of computer information
   Applicability to systems   Ev §1552
  Evidentiary effect of printed representations of images stored on video or digital medium
   Applicability to systems   Ev §1552

RADIO AND TELEVISION
 Administrative adjudication proceedings conducted by television (See **ADMINISTRATIVE ADJUDICATION**)
 Age
  Commercial online entertainment employment service providers
   Age information of subscribers, restriction on disclosure   CC §1798.83.5
 Apartment housekeeper's lien, exemption from   CC §1861a
 Attorney professional conduct
  Trial publicity   ProfC 3.6
 Cable television companies (See **CABLE TELEVISION COMPANIES**)
 Child star contracts   Fam §§6750 to 6753
 Common interest developments
  Antennas or dishes
   Restrictions on installation or use of antennas or satellite dishes   CC §4725
 Contempt charge for newsmen refusing to reveal source of information   Ev §1070
 Court proceedings, broadcasting, photographing, or recording of   CRC 1.150
 Employer and employee
  Commercial online entertainment employment service providers
   Age information of subscribers, restriction on disclosure   CC §1798.83.5
 Judges, media coverage of Judicial Performance Commission proceedings against   JudPerR 124
 Libel and slander
  Generally   CC §46
  Correction demands   CC §48a
  Guest, defamation of character by   CC §48.5
  Privileged broadcasts and exceptions   CC §47
  Retraction   CC §48a
  Third parties, statements by   CC §48.5
 Privileged broadcasts and exceptions under defamation law   CC §47
 Satellite dish restrictions in common interest developments
  Restrictions on limitations, prohibitions   CC §4725
 Schools, sales to   CC §998
 Serial number destroyed or altered prior to sale   CC §1710.1
 Trials
  Court proceedings, restrictions on media coverage of   CRC 1.150

RADIO FREQUENCY IDENTIFICATION (RFID) DEVICES
 Identification documents
  Use to remotely read identification document without knowledge or consent   CC §1798.79
   Definitions   CC §1798.795
 Subcutaneous implanting of identification device, requiring of another   CC §52.7

RAILROADS
 Blind person having equal right to use of trains   CC §§54.1, 54.3, 54.4, 55
  Construction or application of provisions in issue, solicitor general notified   CC §55.2

RAILROADS—Cont.
 Child support payments made pursuant to Railroad Retirement Act   Fam §4504
 Disabled persons having equal right to use of trains   CC §§54.1, 54.3, 54.4, 55
  Construction or application of provisions in issue, solicitor general notified   CC §55.2
 Easements
  Generally   CC §801.7
  Repairs   CC §845
  Stopping trains   CC §801
 Grade crossings
  Automated enforcement systems
   Evidentiary effect of printed representations of computer information   Ev §1552
   Evidentiary effect of printed representations of images stored on video or digital medium   Ev §1552
 Guide dogs permitted on trains   CC §§54.2, 54.3
  Construction or application of provisions in issue, solicitor general notified   CC §55.2
 Hobos, liability for personal injury to   CC §1714.7
 Indemnity contract for construction of   CC §2783
 Intercity rail stations
  Human trafficking or slavery
   Signs, businesses required to post notice concerning relief from slavery or human trafficking   CC §52.6
 Moving train, injuries to party boarding   CC §1714.7
 Passengers and passenger service
  Human trafficking or slavery
   Signs, businesses required to post notice concerning relief from slavery or human trafficking   CC §52.6
 Stations
  Human trafficking or slavery
   Signs, businesses required to post notice concerning relief from slavery or human trafficking   CC §52.6
 Street railways (See **STREET RAILWAYS**)

RAIN
 Water appropriation construction, effect of rain on time for completion of   CC §1416

RALPH CIVIL RIGHTS ACT OF 1976
 Freedom from violence, remedies   CC §51.7

RANDOM SELECTION
 Jurors (See **JURY**)

RAPE (See **SEX OFFENSES**)

RATIFICATION
 Agent, acts of   CC §§2307, 2310 to 2314
 Contacts voidable for want of consent   CC §1588

READER PRIVACY ACT   CC §§1798.90, 1798.90.05

READINESS CONFERENCES   CRC 4.112, 10.951

REAL ESTATE BROKERS (See **BROKERS**)

REAL ESTATE CONTRACT ARBITRATION
 Generally   CCP §1298
 Claims for bodily injury or wrongful death, effect of arbitration provision on   CCP §1298.7
 Effective date of Act   CCP §1298.8
 Nonwaiver of arbitration rights   CCP §1298.5

REAL ESTATE DEVELOPERS (See **BUILDING CONSTRUCTION**)

REAL ESTATE DEVELOPMENTS
 Common interest developments
  Commercial and industrial common interest developments generally   CC §§6500 to 6876 (See **COMMERCIAL AND INDUSTRIAL COMMON INTEREST DEVELOPMENTS**)
  Generally   CC §§4000 to 6150 (See **COMMON INTEREST DEVELOPMENTS**)

REAL ESTATE FRAUD PROSECUTION TRUST FUND
 Distributions for purpose of prosecuting real estate fraud crimes   Gov §27388

REAL ESTATE SALES
 Agency
  Acknowledgment of receipt of disclosure form   CC §2079.14

REAL ESTATE SALES—Cont.
  Buyer's agents
    Disclosure
      Acknowledgment of receipt of disclosure form   CC §2079.14
  Buyer's choice act   CC §§1103.20 to 1103.22
  Common interest developments
    Commercial and industrial common interest developments generally   CC §§6500 to 6876 (See **COMMERCIAL AND INDUSTRIAL COMMON INTEREST DEVELOPMENTS**)
    Generally   CC §§4000 to 6150 (See **COMMON INTEREST DEVELOPMENTS**)
  Disclosures   CC §§1102 to 1103.15
    Agency
      Acknowledgment of receipt of disclosure form   CC §2079.14
    AIDS disclosures   CC §1710.2
    Amendment of disclosure   CC §§1102.9, 1103.9
    Applicability of provisions   CC §§1102, 1102.18, 1103.15
    Appraisals
      Unbiased appraisal and complaint process   CC §1102.6g
    Completion of duty to disclose   CC §1103.5
    Delivery of disclosure statements   CC §§1102.2, 1102.3, 1103.3
    Electrical inspections   CC §1102.6i
    Energy rating   CC §2079.10
    Errors or omissions, liability   CC §§1102.4, 1102.5, 1103.4
    Escrow and escrow agents, requirements for   CC §1102.11
    Fire hazards   CC §§1103 to 1103.15
      Forest fire hazard area   CC §§1103 to 1103.15
      High or very high fire hazard severity zone, documentation of compliance with firebreak, vegetation management, etc, requirements   CC §1102.19
      High or very high fire hazard severity zone, notice by seller to buyer   CC §§1102.6f, 1103.2
    Flood hazard area   CC §§1103 to 1103.15
    Forest fire hazard area   CC §§1103 to 1103.15
    Forms   CC §1102.6
      Local requirements, form of statement reflecting   CC §1102.6a
      Natural hazards, disclosure concerning   CC §1103.2
    Gas powered appliances   CC §1102.6j
    Legislative intent   CC §1102.1
    Mello-Roos Community Facilities Act, disclosure regarding special tax liens on transfer of property pursuant to   CC §1102.6b
    Mobile home sales   CC §§1102 to 1102.18
    Other laws, effect   CC §1103.8
    Purchase money liens on residential property   CC §§2956 to 2968
    Residential property   CC §§1102 to 1103.15
      Gas and hazardous liquid transmission pipelines   CC §2079.10.5
    Room additions, structural modifications, repairs, etc performed by contractor   CC §1102.6h
    Taxation
      Supplemental property tax bills   CC §1102.6c
    Water conservation programs   CC §2079.10
    Water conserving plumbing retrofits
      Noncompliant plumbing fixtures, disclosures upon sale or transfer   CC §1102.155
    Water storage tank disclosures   CC §1102.156
  Earthquake hazards disclosures
    Dwellings   CC §§1103 to 1103.15
  Fire hazard disclosures   CC §§1103 to 1103.15
  Flood hazard disclosure   CC §§1103 to 1103.15
  Forest fire hazard area, disclosure to prospective purchaser   CC §§1103 to 1103.15
  Gas lines
    Residential property, disclosures
      Gas and hazardous liquid transmission pipelines   CC §2079.10.5
  Hazardous liquid transmission pipelines
    Residential property, disclosures
      Gas and hazardous liquid transmission pipelines   CC §2079.10.5
  Karnette Rental-Purchase Act for rental-purchase contracts   CC §§1812.620 to 1812.650
  Listing agreements
    Exclusive listing agreements, restrictions   CC §1670.12
  Multiple listing services   CC §§1086 to 1089.5
  Natural hazard disclosure statements   CC §§1103 to 1103.15
  Purchase money liens on residential property, disclosures on   CC §§2956 to 2968
  Record retention for listings   CC §1088
  Rental-purchase contracts, Karnette Rental-Purchase Act for   CC §§1812.620 to 1812.650
  Seller's agents
    Acknowledgment of receipt of disclosure form   CC §2079.14
  Transfer disclosure statements   CC §§1102 to 1102.18

REAL ESTATE SALES—Cont.
  Transfer fees
    New transfer fees banned   CC §1098.6
  Water storage tank disclosures   CC §1102.156

REAL PARTY IN INTEREST
Action to sue   CCP §367

REAL PROPERTY
Accession   CC §§1013 to 1019
Acquisition   CC §§1000, 1001
Adverse possession (See **ADVERSE POSSESSION**)
Appraisal (See **APPRAISALS**)
Appurtenances
  Covenants   CC §1460
  Definition   CC §662
  Easements (See **EASEMENTS**)
Associate real estate licensees (See **BROKERS**)
Assumption of loan by subsequent purchaser of   CC §711.5
Attachment (See **ATTACHMENT**)
Auctions
  Real property auctions
    Bids intended only to increase sale price   CC §1812.610
Boundaries (See **BOUNDARIES**)
Brokers (See **BROKERS**)
Buyer's choice act   CC §§1103.20 to 1103.22
Child support, assets deposited to secure future payments of   Fam §4617
Claims against public entities and employees (See **CLAIMS AGAINST PUBLIC ENTITIES AND EMPLOYEES**)
Classification of interests   CC §702
Common interest developments
  Commercial and industrial common interest developments generally   CC §§6500 to 6876 (See **COMMERCIAL AND INDUSTRIAL COMMON INTEREST DEVELOPMENTS**)
  Generally   CC §§4000 to 6150 (See **COMMON INTEREST DEVELOPMENTS**)
Community apartment projects (See **COMMON INTEREST DEVELOPMENTS**)
Community property (See **COMMUNITY PROPERTY**)
Condominiums (See **COMMON INTEREST DEVELOPMENTS**)
Conservation easements   CC §§815 to 816
Conservators
  Foreign jurisdictions, property in
    Determining conservatee's interests, standard of care   Pro §2401.1
Conveyances of (See **CONVEYANCES**)
Cotenancy (See **COTENANCY**)
Covenants (See **COVENANTS AND CONDITIONS**)
Death of person committing felony, immunity of landowner for   CC §847
Default judgment in action affecting   CCP §585
Defined   CC §§658, 659, Ev §205
Deraignment of title to general class of heirs (See **HEIRS**)
Description of property
  Trial court rules
    Papers, single spacing permitted   CRC 2.108
Description of property in complaint for recovery of   CCP §455
Destroyed land records, reestablishment of   CCP §§751.01 to 751.28
Developers (See **BUILDING CONSTRUCTION**)
Domestic violence
  Use, possession and control of real or personal property
    Orders determining   Fam §6342.5
Easements (See **EASEMENTS**)
Eminent domain (See **EMINENT DOMAIN**)
Encroachments, petitions for injunctions to restrain   CRC 3.1151
Enforcement of judgments (See **ENFORCEMENT OF JUDGMENTS**)
Escheat   Pro §6801
Estate interests   CC §701
Exchange of property (See **EXCHANGE OF PROPERTY**)
Fee simple (See **FEE SIMPLE**)
Fixtures (See **FIXTURES**)
Forcible entry and detainer (See **FORCIBLE ENTRY AND DETAINER**)
Fraud crimes, distributions from Real Estate Fraud Prosecution Trust Fund for purpose of deterring   Gov §27388
Future interests (See **FUTURE ESTATES AND INTERESTS**)
Good faith improver (See **GOOD FAITH IMPROVER**)
Guardian and ward
  Foreign jurisdictions, property in
    Determining ward's interests, standard of care   Pro §2401.1
Homesteads (See **HOMESTEADS**)
Improvements (See **IMPROVEMENTS**)
Inclusions in definition   CCP §17
Joinder of persons claiming interest in property   CCP §389.5

REAL PROPERTY—Cont.
Judgment liens
    Health care provider or spousal and child support judgment liens   CCP §697.320
Judicial Council to develop and approve forms damages to   CCP §425.12
Karnette Rental-Purchase Act for rental-purchase contracts   CC §§1812.620 to 1812.650
Law governing   CC §755
Leases (See **LEASES**)
Liens (See **LIENS**)
Limitation of actions (See **STATUTES OF LIMITATION**)
Limited interest   CC §§688, 692
Lis pendens (See **PENDENCY OF ACTIONS**)
Mechanics' liens
    Generally (See **MECHANICS' LIENS**)
    Property subject to lien   CC §§8440 to 8448
    Release of property from claim of lien   CC §§8480 to 8494
Mortgages (See **TRUST DEEDS AND MORTGAGES**)
Notice of pendency (See **PENDENCY OF ACTIONS**)
Options (See **OPTIONS**)
Ownership (See **TITLE AND OWNERSHIP**)
Partition
    Partition of real property act   CCP §§874.311 to 874.323 (See **PARTITION**)
Permissive use of   CC §§813, 1007, 1009
Perpetual interest   CC §§688, 691
Perpetuities and restraints on alienation (See **PERPETUITIES AND RESTRAINTS ON ALIENATION**)
Power of appointment (See **POWER OF APPOINTMENT**)
Power of attorney (See **POWER OF ATTORNEY**)
Power of termination (See **TITLE AND OWNERSHIP**)
Precomputed finance charge contracts
    Waiver of protections   CC §1799.85
Present interest   CC §688
Property defined to include   CCP §17
Public entity loans for purchase or rehabilitation of   CC §711.5
Public lands (See **PUBLIC LANDS**)
Purchaser's lien   CC §§3048, 3050
Quasi-community property (See **COMMUNITY PROPERTY**)
Quiet enjoyment (See **QUIET ENJOYMENT**)
Real Estate Fraud Prosecution Trust Fund, procedures for distributions from   Gov §27388
Receivers (See **RECEIVERS AND RECEIVERSHIP**)
Recording of transfers (See **RECORDS AND RECORDING**)
Recovery of real property
    Adverse possession (See **ADVERSE POSSESSION**)
    Default judgment   CCP §585
    Description of property in complaint   CCP §455
    Time of commencing actions for   CCP §§315 to 330
    Venue   CCP §392
Reestablishment of destroyed land records, action for   CCP §§751.01 to 751.28
Rehabilitation loans, assumption of   CC §711.5
Rent control of residential real property (See **RENT CONTROL**)
Restrictions defined   CC §784
Rule against perpetuities (See **PERPETUITIES AND RESTRAINTS ON ALIENATION**)
Sales
    Generally (See **SALE OF REALTY; VENDOR AND PURCHASER**)
    Decedents' estates (See **ADMINISTRATION OF ESTATES**)
    Installments (See **REAL PROPERTY SALES CONTRACTS**)
    Partition (See **PARTITION**)
Small claims court (See **SMALL CLAIMS COURTS**)
Small estates without administration (See **SMALL ESTATES WITHOUT ADMINISTRATION**)
Spanish title papers   Ev §1605
Spouse of owner testifying on value of   Ev §813
Statutes of limitation (See **STATUTES OF LIMITATION**)
Statutory form power of attorney, powers under   Pro §4451
Stock cooperatives (See **COMMON INTEREST DEVELOPMENTS**)
Streets (See **STREETS AND HIGHWAYS**)
Subleases (See **LEASES**)
Tenancy in common (See **TENANCY IN COMMON**)
Testamentary dispositions (See **WILL CONSTRUCTION**)
Time for enjoyment   CC §707
Title and ownership (See **TITLE AND OWNERSHIP**)
Transfers (See **CONVEYANCES**)
Trees (See **TREES**)
Trespass on land (See **TRESPASS ON LAND**)
Trust deeds (See **TRUST DEEDS AND MORTGAGES**)
Trusts (See **TRUSTS**)
Unlawful detainer (See **UNLAWFUL DETAINER**)
Value (See **VALUE**)

REAL PROPERTY—Cont.
Voidable transactions   CC §§1227 to 1231
Waste (See **WASTE**)
Water conserving plumbing retrofits   CC §§1101.1 to 1101.9
Water storage tank disclosures   CC §1102.156

REAL PROPERTY SALES CONTRACTS
Generally   CC §§2985 to 2985.6
Arbitration clause (See **REAL ESTATE CONTRACT ARBITRATION**)
Definition of   CC §2985
Discriminatory clauses, prohibition against   CC §§53, 782
Division of property requirements   CC §2985.51
Family residence property, itemized accounting for   CC §2954.2
Fees for transfer of contract   CC §2985.1
Recordation requirement of   CCP §1062.10
Taxes, payment of   CC §§2985.4, 2985.5
Text message or instant message format communications, insufficiency to constitute contract to convey realty   CC §1624
Unperformed contract for sale of realty (See **TITLE AND OWNERSHIP**)

REAL PROPERTY TAXES (See **TAXATION**)

REASONABLE CAUSE
Attorney's fee award in actions filed without   CCP §1021.7

REASONABLE DOUBT (See **BEYOND REASONABLE DOUBT**)

REBATES
Automobile leases   CC §2986.12
Mortgage or trust deed sales   CC §2924d

RECALL
Witnesses, recall of   Ev §778

RECEIPTS
Appeals, receipts for payments of fees for   CRC 8.100
Parties entitled to   CCP §2075
Repairs, property left for purpose of   CC §§1858 to 1858.3
Uniform Transfers to Minors Act, receipt from custodian acknowledging transfer under   Pro §3908
Written receipts, requirements for   CC §1499

RECEIVABLES (See **ACCOUNTS AND ACCOUNTING**)

RECEIVERS AND RECEIVERSHIP
Accounting and reports
    Final accounting   CRC 3.1184
    Monthly reports   CRC 3.1182
    Objections to receiver's interim accounting and reports   CRC 3.1183
Agent of court, receiver as   CRC 3.1179
Appointment
    Confirmation of ex parte appointment   CRC 3.1176
    Escheat of decedents' estates   CCP §1422
    Ex parte appointment   CRC 3.1175, 3.1176
    Grounds for   CCP §564
    Law and motion rules, applicability of   CRC 3.1103
    Nomination of receivers   CRC 3.1177
    Nondiscrimination standard for appointments by court   CRC 10.611, CRC JudAdminStand 10.21
    Role and duties of receiver   CRC 3.1179
Arbitration agreements, rights of party on appointment of receiver under   CCP §1281.8
Attorney, employment of   CRC 3.1180
    Compensation
        Claim for compensation of attorney in final account   CRC 3.1184
Bank accounts, deposit of funds in   CCP §569
Bonds
    Amount of undertaking   CRC 3.1178
    Deposits by receiver   CCP §568.1
    Ex parte application   CCP §566
    State, bonds executed to   CCP §567
Compensation
    Claim for compensation in final account   CRC 3.1184
Consent for appointments   CCP §566
Corporate dissolutions   CCP §§564, 565
Deposits
    Bonds deposited in securities depositories   CCP §568.1
    Funds deposited in interest-bearing accounts   CCP §569
Discrimination, prohibition against in court appointments of receivers   CRC 10.611, CRC JudAdminStand 10.21
Enforcement of judgments (See **ENFORCEMENT OF JUDGMENTS**)
Ex parte appointment   CRC 3.1175, 3.1176

RECEIVERS AND RECEIVERSHIP—Cont.
Expenses of holding unknown persons' funds CCP §570
Family law proceedings Fam §290
    Appointment of receivers
        Applicable guidelines for appointment CRC JudAdminStand 5.30
Fees for services rendered by receiver, court approval of CRC 3.1183
Forms
    Judicial council legal forms CRCAppx A
Hazardous substance releases, receiver appointed for secured lender with authority to inspect real property security for CCP §564
Interim reports CRC 3.1183
Inventory of property CRC 3.1181
Judgments, enforcement of CCP §564
Law and motion proceedings, rules governing CRC 3.1175 to 3.1184
Liens, termination of CCP §493.040
Mortgages (See **TRUST DEEDS AND MORTGAGES**)
Nomination CRC 3.1177
Notice of unknown persons' funds published by CCP §570
Oaths for faithful performance CCP §567
Pacific Gas and Electric Company CCP §568.6
Partnership assets CCP §564
Possession by CCP §568
Powers of CCP §568
Prohibited contractual arrangements of receiver CRC 3.1179
Publication of notice of unknown persons' funds CCP §570
Real property
    Sale of CCP §568.5
    Substandard conditions of rental housing CCP §§568.2, 568.3
    Unsafe conditions of rental housing CCP §568.2
Rules of court governing receiverships CRC 3.1175 to 3.1184
Sales by CCP §568.5
    Attorney professional conduct
        Purchase by attorney of property at foreclosure or judicial sale ProfC 1.8.9
Securities deposited by CCP §568.1
Stay of proceedings CCP §917.5
Stipulations
    Accounting and final report CRC 3.1184
Substandard conditions of rental housing, abatement of CCP §§568.2, 568.3
Time for hearing on order to show cause re ex parte appointment CRC 3.1176
Trust deeds and mortgages (See **TRUST DEEDS AND MORTGAGES**)
Unclaimed property, holding of CCP §570
Unknown persons' funds, holding of CCP §570
Unlawful detainers CCP §564
Unsafe conditions of rental housing, abatement of CCP §568.2
Voidable transactions vacated CCP §564
Wage claims CCP §§1204 to 1204.5

RECESSES
Adjournments construed as CCP §42
Superior court adjournments construed as recesses CCP §74

RECIPROCAL ENFORCEMENT OF SUPPORT
Declaration of state reciprocity by attorney general Fam §17407.5
Interstate family support Fam §§5700.101 to 5700.903

RECLAMATION
Eminent domain taking by CCP §1245.210

RECLASSIFICATION OF ACTIONS (See **JURISDICTION**)

RECOGNIZANCE (See **BAIL**)

RECOMMENDATION BY JUDGE (See **JUDGES**)

RECONCILIATION OF PARTIES (See **CONCILIATION COURTS; DISSOLUTION OF MARRIAGE**)

RECONSIDERATION
Administrative adjudicative decision (See **ADMINISTRATIVE ADJUDICATION**)
Motion for reconsideration of grant or denial of order CCP §1008

RECORDATION OF DOCUMENTS (See **RECORDS AND RECORDING**)

RECORDING DEVICES (See **EAVESDROPPING AND WIRETAPPING**)

RECORDING OF SOUND
Court proceedings, recording of CRC 2.950 to 2.954
    Media coverage CRC 1.150
Fees
    Courts, authority to set fees for products or services CRC 10.815

RECORDING OF SOUND—Cont.
Invasion of privacy through attempt to capture visual image or sound recording or other physical impression of plaintiff engaged in personal or familial activity CC §1708.8
Ownership
    Generally CC §980
    Proportion of CC §981
    Publication, dedication by CC §983
    Transfer of right of reproduction CC §982
Phonographs and phonograph records (See **PHONOGRAPHS AND PHONOGRAPH RECORDS**)
Royalty audits CC §§2500, 2501
Transcripts
    Court reporters generally (See **COURT REPORTERS**)
    Recording, transcript of offered as evidence CRC 2.1040

RECORDKEEPING REQUIREMENTS (See **RECORDS AND RECORDING**)

RECORDS AND RECORDING
Generally CC §1213
Abstract of judgment (See **ABSTRACT OF JUDGMENT**)
Acknowledgment of instruments
    Generally CC §1185
    Fees for Gov §27375
Address confidentiality for victims of domestic violence, sexual assault and stalking
    Actions, confidentiality requirements for protected persons in civil proceeding CCP §367.3
Administration of estates (See **ADMINISTRATION OF ESTATES**)
Administrative law and procedure
    Adjudicative proceedings (See **ADMINISTRATIVE PROCEDURE ACT**)
    Rulemaking and regulations (See **ADMINISTRATIVE PROCEDURE ACT**)
Affirmations, fees for administering or certifying Gov §27379
Ancient mortgages and trust deeds (See **TITLE AND OWNERSHIP**)
Appellate rules
    Superior court appeals
        Record on appeal (See **APPELLATE RULES, SUPERIOR COURT APPEALS**)
    Supreme court and courts of appeal
        Record on appeal (See **APPELLATE RULES, SUPREME COURT AND COURTS OF APPEAL**)
        Records of court of appeals CRC 10.1028
Armed services discharge records, waiver of fees for Gov §27381
Assignment of interest in mortgage or trust deed (See **TRUST DEEDS AND MORTGAGES**)
Assignment of judgment CCP §673
Attachment (See **ATTACHMENT**)
Attorney professional conduct
    Trust accounts
        Safekeeping of funds and property of clients ProfC 1.15
Attorneys
    Proof of compliance in disciplinary action involving attorney CRC 9.20
Best and secondary evidence Ev §§1530 to 1532
Birth certificates
    Copy fees Gov §27365
    Custody proceedings involving missing party or child Fam §3140
    Search fees Gov §27369
    Uniform Parentage Act, judgment at variance with birth certificate Fam §7639
Bona fide purchaser, priority of CC §1214
Breeders' lien CC §3063
Building Homes and Jobs Trust Fund, fees remitted to Gov §27388.1
Business records (See **BUSINESS RECORDS**)
Certificate under seal, fees for Gov §27364
Child support, deposit of real property to secure future payments of Fam §4617
Commercial and industrial common interest developments
    Change in member information CC §6756
    Condominium plans
        Consent to recordation of plan, signature requirements CC §6626
    Creation of common interest development CC §6580
Common interest developments
    Assessment liens
        Decision to record as board decision CC §§5673, 5690
    Condominium plans CC §4290
    Deeds of trust and mortgages
        Power of sale under, transfer of property in CID CC §2924.1
Community property (See **COMMUNITY PROPERTY**)

RECORDS AND RECORDING—Cont.
  Confidentiality
    Domestic violence, sexual assault and stalking victims
      Actions, confidentiality requirements for protected persons in civil proceeding   CCP §367.3
  Conservatorships (See **CONSERVATORS**)
  Constructive notice
    Generally   CC §§1213, 1215
    Bona fide purchaser or judgment creditor, effect on   CC §1214
    Copies in outside counties   CC §§1213, 1218
    Oil and gas leases   CC §1219
    Power of attorney, revocation of   CC §1216
    Timber, sale of   CC §1220
  Convictions   CRC 4.320
  Copies
    Generally   CCP §1950
    Admissibility of   CCP §1950
    Birth certificates, fees for   Gov §27365
    Constructive notice, copies in outside counties as   CC §§1213, 1218
    Death certificates, fees for   Gov §27365
    Marriage certificates, fees for   Gov §27365
    Other instruments, fees for   Gov §27366
  County recorder   Gov §§27201 to 27388.1
    Acknowledgment of instruments   CC §1181
    Deposit of instrument with   CC §1170
    Duties   CC §1172
    Electronic recording delivery systems   Gov §§27390 to 27399 (See **ELECTRONIC RECORDING DELIVERY SYSTEMS**)
    Fees generally (See within this heading, **"Fees"**)
    Situs of property affected   CC §1169
  Court indexes   CRC 10.851
  Court of appeal records
    Destruction   CRC 10.1028
    Preservation   CRC 10.1028
    Public access to judicial administrative records   CRC 10.500
  Court records
    Judicial administration standards
      Court records management standards   CRC JudAdminStand 10.80
    Public access to judicial administrative records   CRC 10.500
  Covenants   CC §1468
    Affordable housing developments
      Recorded restrictive covenants, unenforceability in face of approved and recorded restrictive covenant affordable housing modification document   CC §714.6
  Credit report violations, exception from   CC §1785.35
  Custody of children (See **CUSTODY OF CHILDREN**)
  Death
    Certificates
      Copy fees   Gov §27365
      Search fees   Gov §27369
    Evidence establishing fact of   Ev §§1281 to 1283, Pro §§210 to 212
  Deferred sale of family home, order for   Fam §3804
  Design professionals' liens, recordation of   CC §§8306, 8312
  Dimensions of page   Gov §§27361.5, 27361.6
  Electronic court records   CRC 2.500 to 2.545
  Electronic recording delivery systems   Gov §§27390 to 27399 (See **ELECTRONIC RECORDING DELIVERY SYSTEMS**)
  Employment agencies, recordkeeping requirements of   CC §1812.522
  Enforcement liens   CCP §996.540
  Escheated property, recording notice of action for   CCP §1410
  Evidence
    Microphotographed files, records, photographs, etc., in custody of criminal justice agency
      Reproductions, admissibility   Ev §1550.1
  Exemplification of record
    Superior court fees   Gov §70628
  Fact of death, evidence establishing   Ev §§1281 to 1283, Pro §§210 to 212
  Fees   Gov §§27360 to 27388.2
    Abstract of judgment, filing of   Gov §27387
    Acknowledgment of instruments   Gov §27375
    Affirmations or oaths, administering or certifying   Gov §27379
    Armed services discharge records, waiver of fees for   Gov §27381
    Birth certificates (See within this heading, **"Birth certificates"**)
    Certificate under seal   Gov §27364
    Death certificates
      Copy fees   Gov §27365
      Search fees   Gov §27369
    Documentary transfer tax
      Effect of tax on additional fees   Gov §27388
    Indexing fees   Gov §§27361, 27388
    Licenses and associated certificates   Gov §26851

RECORDS AND RECORDING—Cont.
  Fees —Cont.
    Maps and plats   Gov §27371
      Subdivision maps   Gov §27372
    Marriages (See **MARRIAGE**)
    Mechanic's lien preliminary 20-day notice, additional fees for filing   Gov §27361.9
    Micrographics, additional fee to defray conversion of county records to   Gov §27361.4
    Multiple instruments attached   Gov §27361.1
    Notice of filing of deed or quitclaim or trust deed with Los Angeles county recorder, additional fee for processing   Gov §27387.1
    Political subdivisions, waiver of fees for   Gov §27383
    Real Estate Fraud Prosecution Trust Fund, fees funding   Gov §27388
    Reference to previously recorded documents, fees charged for   Gov §27361.2
    Release of lien or notice by political subdivision   Gov §27361.3
    State agencies, waiver of fees for   Gov §27383
    Tax liens by federal government   CCP §2104
    Truncation of social security numbers, program for
      Funding of program   Gov §27361
    20-day notice for mechanic's lien, additional filing fees for   Gov §27361.9
  First page of real estate instrument, paper or notice
    Additional fee for recording first page   Gov §27388.2
  Foreign executors recording letters   CC §2939.5
  Form of notice to preserve interest   CC §880.340
  Greenway easements
    Instruments creating or transferring easement   CC §816.60
  Handwritten copies   Gov §27361.7
  Homesteads   Pro §7263
  Identification of person acknowledging instrument, records officer requiring   CC §1185
  Illegible documents   Gov §§27361.6, 27361.7
  Indexing fees   Gov §§27361, 27361.8
  Indian child welfare act involuntary placements
    Adoption records   CRC 5.488
  Information Practices Act (See **INFORMATION PRACTICES ACT**)
  Inquiry, sufficient for   CC §19
  Inspection of records (See **INSPECTION**)
  Instruments not required to be recorded, filing fees for   Gov §27380
  Job listing services, recordkeeping requirements of   CC §1812.522
  Judges (See **JUDGES**)
  Judgment creditor, priority of   CC §1214
  Judgments (See **JUDGMENTS**)
  Judicial administration rules
    Public access to judicial administrative records   CRC 10.500
  Judicial notice of court records   Ev §452
  Jury commissioner   CCP §207
  Licenses and associated certificates, fees for recording   Gov §26851
    Superior court fees, specified services   Gov §70626
  Liens
    Design professionals' liens   CC §8306
      Time to record   CC §8312
  Lis pendens (See **PENDENCY OF ACTIONS**)
  Logging contract   CC §§1220, 3065 to 3065c
  Maps and plats
    Generally   CCP §1855
    Fees
      Generally   Gov §27371
      Subdivision maps   Gov §27372
  Marketability of title (See **TITLE AND OWNERSHIP**)
  Marriage (See **MARRIAGE**)
  Mechanics' liens (See **MECHANICS' LIENS**)
  Mediation
    Complaints about court-program mediators
      Record of complaints   CRC 3.869
  Medical records as evidence   Ev §§1156 to 1158
  Micrographics, additional fee to defray conversion of county records to   Gov §27361.4
  Microphotographed files, records, photographs, etc., in custody of criminal justice agency
    Reproductions, admissibility   Ev §1550.1
  Military discharge records, waiver of fees for   Gov §27381
  Mines and mining
    Taxes, co-owners failing to pay
      Recordation of certified copy of decree   CCP §859
  Mining machinery, sale of   CC §1631
  Mobilehome sales agreements   CCP §1062.10
  Mortgages (See **TRUST DEEDS AND MORTGAGES**)
  Nunc pro tunc filing   CCP §1046a
  Nurses' registries, duty to maintain log sheets and records by   CC §1812.529

RECORDS AND RECORDING—Cont.
Oaths, fees for administering or certifying   Gov §27379
Official records
    Social security number truncation program   Gov §§27300 to 27307 (See **SOCIAL SECURITY**)
Oil and gas (See **OIL AND GAS**)
Other counties, instruments recorded in   CC §§1213, 1218
Ownership (See **TITLE AND OWNERSHIP**)
Pendency of actions (See **PENDENCY OF ACTIONS**)
Plats (See within this heading, "**Maps and plats**")
Political subdivisions, waiver of fees for   Gov §27383
Power of attorney (See **POWER OF ATTORNEY**)
Premarital agreements   Fam §1502
Preservation of interest
    Contents of notice for   CC §880.330
    Form of notice to preserve interest   CC §880.340
    Grace period for recording notice   CC §880.370
    Intent to preserve interest, notice of   CC §880.310
    Manner of recording notice of intent   CC §880.350
    Person having capacity to preserve interest   CC §880.320
    Place to record notice of intent   CC §880.350
    Slander of title, recording interest with intent for   CC §880.360
Priority of recording   CC §1214
Private child support collectors   Fam §5614
Production of (See **SUBPOENA DUCES TECUM**)
Proof of execution, following   CC §1204
Property settlement agreements   Fam §1502
Public guardians (See **PUBLIC GUARDIANS**)
Public records
    Access to databases for service of process purposes   CCP §415.50
    Address confidentiality for victims of domestic violence, sexual assault and stalking
        Judicial council forms   CRCAppx A
        Name change proceedings under address confidentiality program   CRC 2.575 to 2.577
    Domestic violence, sexual assault and stalking victims
        Judicial council forms   CRCAppx A
    Social security number truncation program   Gov §§27300 to 27307 (See **SOCIAL SECURITY**)
    Unlawful detainer filings   CCP §1161.2
        COVID-19 rental debt recovery actions, access to case records   CCP §1161.2.5
Real property sales contracts   CCP §1062.10
Reestablishment of destroyed land records, action for   CCP §§751.01 to 751.28
Rescission of foreclosure   CC §1695.14
Sale and leaseback, notice of   CC §3440
Size of paper   Gov §§27361.5, 27361.6
Slander of title, recording notice of preservation of interest for purpose of   CC §880.360
Small estates without administration (See **SMALL ESTATES WITHOUT ADMINISTRATION**)
Social security numbers
    Truncation program
        Generally   Gov §§27300 to 27307 (See **SOCIAL SECURITY**)
        Untruncated social security numbers, filing documents that will be public containing   CC §1798.89
State agencies, waiver of fees for   Gov §27383
Subdivision maps, fees for   Gov §27372
Superior courts
    Destruction, notice   CRC 10.856
    Forms
        Judicial council legal forms   CRCAppx A
    Indexes   CRC 10.851
    Sampling program   CRC 10.855
Surety bond, certified copy used for recording of   CCP §995.260
Tax liens by federal government   CCP §§2100 to 2107
    Fees for recording under act   Gov §27388.1
Termination, power of   CC §885.060
Timber, contracts for   CC §§1220, 3065 to 3065c
Title (See **TITLE AND OWNERSHIP**)
Transfer fees in conveyance   CC §1098.5
    New transfer fees banned   CC §1098.6
Translator's or interpreter's oath, record of   Ev §751
Trial court records
    Electronic trial court records   CRC 2.500 to 2.545
Trial courts   CRC 2.400, CRC JudAdminStand 10.17
Truncation of social security numbers, program for
    Generally   Gov §§27300 to 27307 (See **SOCIAL SECURITY**)
Trust deeds (See **TRUST DEEDS AND MORTGAGES**)
Trusts   Pro §15210
    Certification of trust   Pro §18100.5

RECORDS AND RECORDING—Cont.
Trusts —Cont.
    Change of trustee, recordation of affidavit   Pro §§18105 to 18108
Typewritten copies   Gov §27361.7
Unclaimed deposits and payments, controller examining records of   CCP §1571
Unexercised options (See **TITLE AND OWNERSHIP**)
Validity of unrecorded instruments   CC §1217
Vessels, transfers of   CC §1173
Vexatious litigants subject to prefiling orders, records of   CCP §391.7
    Vacating prefiling order and removing name from list   CCP §391.8
Voidable transactions, notice of transfer as affecting claim of   CC §3440
Water appropriation   CC §§1415, 1421
Wills, recordation requirements for   Pro §8225

RECOVERY OF PROPERTY
Claim and delivery (See **CLAIM AND DELIVERY**)
Real property, recovery of (See **REAL PROPERTY**)

RECREATIONAL VEHICLE PARKS
Abandoned possessions, disposition of   CC §799.75
Attorney's fees awarded to prevailing party in actions involving   CC §799.78
Citation of Act   CC §799.20
Defaulting occupant
    Abandoned possessions, disposition of   CC §799.75
    Defined   CC §799.22
    Liens for charges due   CC §799.75
    Nonmotorized vehicle, removal of   CC §799.56
    Physically incapacitated occupant, removal of vehicle belonging to   CC §799.56
    Reasonable and ordinary care in removing vehicle to storage area, management's duty of   CC §799.59
    Service of notice   CC §799.56
    72-hour notice
        Statement required concerning removal and storage of vehicle   CC §799.57
        Written notice requirement prior to removal of vehicle   CC §799.55
    Sheriff or police, removal of vehicle by   CC §799.58
    Special occupancy parks
        Eviction of overstaying guests   CC §1866
Defaulting resident
    Abandoned possessions, disposition of   CC §799.75
    Defined   CC §799.23
    Eviction of   CC §799.71
    Liens for charges due   CC §799.75
    Termination or refusal to renew right of occupancy, grounds for management's right of   CC §799.70
Defaulting tenant
    Abandoned possessions, disposition of   CC §799.75
    Defined   CC §799.24
    Eviction of   CC §799.67
    Liens for charges due   CC §799.75
    Nonpayment of rent or other charges, termination by management for   CC §799.65
    Refusal to renew right of occupancy other than nonpayment of rent or other charges, grounds for termination by management by   CC §799.66
Definitions   CC §§799.20 to 799.32
Disabled occupant, removal of vehicle belonging to   CC §799.56
Eviction from park
    Defaulting tenants generally (See within this heading, "**Defaulting tenant**")
    Occupant, eviction of   CC §799.67
    Resident   CC §799.71
    Tenant   CC §799.67
Fines and penalties against park management for violation of statute   CC §799.79
General provisions   CC §§799.40 to 799.46
Guests defined   CC §799.25
Liens for charges due   CC §799.75
Manufactured homes, provisions governing recreational vehicles as inapplicable to   CC §799.41
Mobilehomes, provisions governing recreational vehicles as inapplicable to   CC §799.41
Nonmotorized vehicle, removal of   CC §799.56
Notices
    72-hour notice for removal of vehicle
        Statement concerning removal and storage of vehicle   CC §799.57
        Written notice requirement before removal   CC §799.55
    Termination
        Defaulting residents   CC §799.70
        Defaulting tenants generally (See within this heading, "**Defaulting tenant**")

RECREATIONAL VEHICLE PARKS—Cont.
Physically incapacitated occupant in default, removal of vehicle belonging to   CC §799.56
Registration agreement
   Form and content of   CC §799.43
   Occupancy in excess of 30 consecutive days, validity of rental agreements for   CC §799.45
   Park rules and regulations, furnishing copy of   CC §799.44
   Reregistration of occupant, tenant or resident   CC §799.47
   Waiver of tenant's rights in rental agreement prohibited   CC §799.46
Remedial statutory rights as cumulative to other relief available to parties   CC §799.40
Removal of vehicle
   Defaulting occupant
     Generally (See within this heading, **"Defaulting occupant"**)
   Defaulting resident   CC §799.71
   Defaulting tenant   CC §799.67
   Sign posted at park entrance warning of removal of vehicle for nonpayment, requirement of   CC §799.46
72-hour notice
   Statement required in 72-hour notice concerning removal and storage of vehicle   CC §799.57
   Written notice requirement before removal of vehicle   CC §799.55
Special occupancy parks
   Danger imminent, requiring guests to move   CC §1867
   Eviction of overstaying guests   CC §1866
   Minors
     Conditions for minors staying   CC §1866
Termination
   Defaulting resident   CC §799.70
   Defaulting tenant
     Generally (See within this heading, **"Defaulting tenant"**)
Waiver of tenant's rights in rental agreement, prohibition against   CC §799.42

RECREATIONAL VEHICLES (See also **MOBILEHOMES**)
Alteration of new vehicles into housecars, effect on warranties upon   CC §1793.05
Recreational vehicle parks (See **RECREATIONAL VEHICLE PARKS**)
Warranties on new vehicles altered into house cars   CC §1793.05

RECREATION AREAS
Camps (See **CAMPING**)
Caves (See **CAVES**)
Easement holder's liability   CC §846
Eminent domain (See **EMINENT DOMAIN**)
Landowner's liability for recreation activities   CC §846
Parks (See **PARKS AND PLAYGROUNDS**)
Public entity's liability for injuries on unpaved roads or trails providing access to   Gov §831.4

RECROSS EXAMINATION (See **CROSS-EXAMINATION**)

RECUSAL OF JUDGES
Disqualification (See **JUDGES, DISQUALIFICATION OF**)

RECYCLED PRODUCTS
Appeals
   Transcripts   CRC 8.144
Fire hydrants or fire department corrections
   Damages for wrongful possession by junk dealers or recyclers   CC §3336.5
Judicial Council policy regarding waste reduction and recycling programs for local courts   CRC JudAdminStand 10.55
Trial court rules
   Forms   CRC 2.131

RED CROSS (See **AMERICAN RED CROSS**)

REDELIVERY
Conveyances   CC §1058

REDEMPTION
Enforcement of judgments (See **ENFORCEMENT OF JUDGMENTS**)
Execution sales   CCP §701.680
Liens (See **LIENS**)
Mortgages (See **TRUST DEEDS AND MORTGAGES**)

REDIRECT EXAMINATION
Definition   Ev §762
Leading questions   Ev §767

RED LIGHT ABATEMENT LAW
Enforcement of judgments
   Stay of enforcement
     Appeal from order granted under   CCP §917.8

REES-LEVERING MOTOR VEHICLES SALES AND FINANCE ACT
CC §§2981 to 2984.5 (See **AUTOMOBILES**)

REFEREES
Accounts, fact questions on   CCP §639
Administration of decedents' estates (See **ADMINISTRATION OF ESTATES**)
Advisory decisions by referee, effect of   CCP §644
Affinity, disqualification   CCP §641
Agency relationship as ground for disqualification of   CCP §641
Agreement, reference by   CRC 3.900 to 3.907
   Documents and exhibits, applicable provisions   CRC 3.930
   Intervention, motion for leave to file complaint   CRC 3.932
   Notice by and contact information for referee   CRC 3.931
   Open proceedings   CRC 3.931
   Sealing of records, motion or application   CRC 3.932
   Site for proceedings   CRC 3.931
Appellate rule for production of additional evidence on appeal   CRC 8.252
Appointment   CCP §640
   Agreement, reference by   CRC 3.901
   Court-ordered reference   CRC 3.921
   Nondiscrimination standard for court appointments   CRC 10.611, CRC JudAdminStand 10.21
   Objection to   CCP §§641.2, 642
     Agreement, reference by   CRC 3.905
   Order appointing
     Agreement, reference by   CRC 3.902
     Court-ordered reference   CRC 3.922
   Partition referees   CCP §§872.630, 873.010 to 873.050
   Probate referees (See **PROBATE REFEREES**)
   Stipulation
     Agreement, reference by   CRC 3.901
     Withdrawal of stipulation in agreed reference   CRC 3.906
Attorney professional conduct
   Service as temporary judge, referee or court-appointed arbitrator, applicability of judicial ethics canon 6D   ProfC 2.4.1
Bond executed by   CCP §571
Certification by referee
   Agreement, reference by   CRC 3.904
   Court-ordered reference   CRC 3.924
Child support matters (See **CHILD SUPPORT**)
Code of Judicial Ethics, compliance with   CRCSupp JudEthicsCanon 6
Conflict of interest as grounds for disqualification of   CCP §641
   Disclosures by referee
     Agreement, reference by   CRC 3.904
     Court-ordered reference   CRC 3.924
Consanguinity as ground for disqualification of   CCP §641
Consensual general referee decisions, effect of   CCP §644
Consent of parties
   Generally   CCP §638
   Partition referee, consent to appointment of   CCP §873.040
Conservatorship (See **CONSERVATORS**)
Contact information for referee   CRC 3.931
Court operations costs, salaries and benefits as   CRC 10.810
Court-ordered reference   CCP §639, CRC 3.920 to 3.926
   Documents and exhibits, applicable provisions   CRC 3.930
   Intervention, motion for leave to file complaint   CRC 3.932
   Notice by and contact information for referee   CRC 3.931
   Open proceedings   CRC 3.931
   Sealing of records, motion or application   CRC 3.932
   Site for proceedings   CRC 3.931
Court records, management of   CRC 2.400
Decedents' estates, administration of (See **ADMINISTRATION OF ESTATES**)
Decisions by
   Statement of decision (See within this heading, **"Statement of decision"**)
Deficiency judgment proceeding on foreclosure of mortgages   CCP §§580a, 726
Disciplinary actions
   Censure and removal procedures, applicability of   JudPerR 138
   Complaints against subordinate judicial officers, procedures for   CRC 10.703
Disclosures by referee
   Agreement, reference by   CRC 3.904
   Court-ordered reference   CRC 3.924
Discovery referees   CCP §639
   Court-ordered reference   CRC 3.920
   Report to legislature regarding practice and costs   CCP §640.5
Discrimination, prohibition against in court appointments   CRC 10.611, CRC JudAdminStand 10.21
Disqualification
   Affidavits and evidence   CCP §642
   Definitions for CCP 170–170.5   CCP §170.5
   Discovery matters, motion to disqualify appointed referee in   CCP §639

REFEREES—Cont.
Disqualification—Cont.
  Filing of disqualification statement   CCP §170.4
  Grounds for   CCP §641
  Notification of recusal   CCP §170.3
  Objections to appointment
    Generally   CCP §§641, 642
  Peremptory challenges   CCP §170.6
  Powers of disqualified judge   CCP §170.4
Documents and exhibits   CRC 2.400, 3.930
Education of judicial officers
  Subordinate judicial officers, qualifications and education   CRC 10.701
    Additional education recommendations for certain judicial assignments   CRC 10.469
Eminent domain (See **EMINENT DOMAIN**)
Employer relationship as ground for disqualification of   CCP §641
Enforcement of judgments (See **ENFORCEMENT OF JUDGMENTS**)
Ethics programs   CRC JudAdminStand 10.16
Exhibits, custody of   CRC 2.400, 3.930
Facilities
  Use of court facilities
    Agreement, reference by   CRC 3.907
    Court-ordered reference   CRC 3.926
Fact questions determined   CCP §§638, 639
Family law
  Appointment of referees
    Applicable guidelines for appointment   CRC JudAdminStand 5.30
Fees
  Generally   CCP §§645.1, 1023
  Apportionment of referral fees
    Court-ordered reference   CRC 3.922
Foreclosure, deficiency judgment proceeding on   CCP §§580a, 726
Guardian and ward (See **GUARDIAN AND WARD**)
Incompetency as ground for disqualification   CCP §641
Intervention in cause before referee
  Motion for leave to file complaint for intervention   CRC 3.932
Judgment, referee's statement of decision as basis for   CCP §644
Judicial ethics code, applicability of   CRCSupp JudEthicsCanon 6
Jury service as ground for disqualification of   CCP §641
Juvenile court proceedings (See **JUVENILE COURTS**)
Law practice of subordinate judicial officers   CRC 10.702
Law questions determined   CCP §638
Notice
  Proceedings, notice and information about   CRC 3.931
Objections
  Appointment
    Agreement, reference by   CRC 3.905
  Decision, objection to   CCP §645
  Reference, objection to
    Court-ordered reference   CRC 3.925
Open proceedings   CRC 3.931
Opinion formed, disqualification because of   CCP §641
Orders
  Appointment of referee
    Agreement, reference by   CRC 3.902
    Court-ordered reference   CRC 3.922
Partition (See **PARTITION**)
Partnership relationship as grounds for disqualification of   CCP §641
Pollution action, objection to referee appointed in   CCP §641.2
Privately compensated referees
  Proceedings before   CRC 3.907
Probate referees (See **PROBATE REFEREES**)
Purpose of reference
  Agreement, reference by   CRC 3.900
  Court-ordered reference   CRC 3.920
Qualifications
  Agreement, reference by   CRC 3.903
  Court-ordered reference   CRC 3.923
  Subordinate judicial officers, education and qualifications   CRC 10.701
Quorum of   CCP §1053
Relatives, disqualification of   CCP §641
Residence of   CCP §640
Sealing of records
  Motion or application to seal   CRC 3.932
Selection
  Agreement, reference by   CRC 3.903
  Court-ordered reference   CRC 3.923
Site for proceedings
  Appropriate and accessible hearing site   CRC 3.931
Special proceedings   CCP §639
Special verdict, statement of decision having effect of   CCP §645

REFEREES—Cont.
Statement of decision
  Advisory decisions by referee, effect of   CCP §644
  Consensual general referee decision, effect of   CCP §644
  Judgment of court standing on   CCP §644
  Objections to referee's decision   CCP §645
  Special verdict, referee's decision as having effect of   CCP §645
  Time for filing report of   CCP §643
Stipulation
  Appointment of referee
    Agreement, reference by   CRC 3.901
    Withdrawal of stipulation in agreed reference   CRC 3.906
Subordinate judicial officers, complaints against   CRC 10.703
Surety relationship, disqualification for   CCP §641
Time for filing referee's report on statement of decision   CCP §643
Triable issues   CCP §592
Trial court rules
  Papers, first page format and content   CRC 2.111
Withdrawal of stipulation
  Agreement, reference by   CRC 3.906

REFERENCE OF DISPUTED ISSUES (See **REFEREES**)

REFERRAL SERVICES
Professional societies, liability of   CC §43.95

REFORMATION OF INSTRUMENTS
Action for   CC §§3399 to 3402
Small claims court jurisdiction to grant equitable relief in lieu of or in addition to money damages   CCP §116.220
Transfer on death deeds
  Cy pres doctrine to reform deed   Pro §5658
  Error or ambiguity in deed   Pro §5659

REFRIGERATION (See **AIR CONDITIONING**)

REFUNDS
Assistive devices, sale of   CC §1793.02
Automobiles (See **AUTOMOBILES**)
Dance studios contracts   CC §1812.57
Dating services contracts   CC §1694.4
Debit cards, prepaid
  Consumer refunds offered by prepaid debit card
    Alternative method of receiving refund to be provided   CC §1748.41
    Definitions   CC §1748.40
Discount buying services contracts   CC §§1812.116, 1812.118, 1812.121
Employment agency fees, refund of   CC §§1812.504, 1812.506, 1812.523
Escheated property   CCP §1347
Grey market goods, buyer's right to refund on return of   CC §1797.85
Health studios, contracts with   CC §§1812.85, 1812.89
Home solicitation contracts, rescission of   CC §1689.10
Hotel and private residence rentals
  Cancellation of reservations   CC §§1748.80 to 1748.84
Job listing service fees, refund of   CC §§1812.516, 1812.518, 1812.523
Jury fees when case settled or continued   CCP §631.3
Membership camping contracts   CC §1812.306
Nurses' registries, refund of fees to jobseeker by   CC §§1812.523, 1812.532
Retail installment sales, payment in advance   CC §§1803.2, 1806.3
Retail sellers, sign displaying refund policy of   CC §1723
Seminar sales solicitation contracts, buyer's right to refund on cancellation of   CC §1689.20
Tax refunds owed judgment debtor, filing claim against public entities for   CCP §§708.730, 708.740, 708.780, 708.795
Tenant's deposits, right to refund of   CC §1950.5
Unclaimed property
  Appropriations for payment of   CCP §1325
  Controller, refunds by   CCP §1561
  Court or public agency, business association refunds ordered by   CCP §1519.5
Weight loss programs   CC §1694.9

REFUSE (See **GARBAGE**)

REGISTERED FOREIGN LEGAL CONSULTANTS   CRC 9.44
Fingerprinting of special admission attorneys   CRC 9.9.5

REGISTERED MAIL
Certified mail in lieu of   CC §17
Electronic service not authorized when certified or registered mail required   CCP §1020

REGISTERED SEX OFFENDERS (See **SEX OFFENSES**)

REGISTER OF ACTIONS (See **CLERKS OF COURT**)

REGISTRATION
Advance health care directives Pro §§4800 to 4808
Conservators (See **CONSERVATORS**)
Guardians (See **GUARDIAN AND WARD**)
Liens for taxes by federal government CCP §§2100 to 2107
Support orders (See **CHILD SUPPORT**)
Surety bonds (See **SURETYSHIP, BONDS AND UNDERTAKINGS**)
Tax liens by federal government CCP §§2100 to 2107
Trustees (See **TRUSTS**)
Voter registration
    Action to compel registration
        Fees, clerk not to charge Gov §70633

REGISTRATION OF DATA BROKERS CC §§1798.99.80 to 1798.99.89
(See **DATA BROKER REGISTRATION**)

REGULATIONS
Administrative Procedure Act (See **ADMINISTRATIVE PROCEDURE ACT**)

REGULATION Z (See **TRUTH-IN-LENDING ACT**)

REHEARINGS
Appellate rules, superior court appeals CRC 8.880, 8.889
Appellate rules, supreme court and courts of appeal
    Certiorari, mandate and prohibition CRC 8.490
    Electronic filings CRCSupp 1st AppDist
    Petition and answer
        Form CRCSupp 6th AppDist
Arbitration awards CCP §1287

REIMBURSEMENT
Child support (See **CHILD SUPPORT**)
Community property contributions (See **COMMUNITY PROPERTY**)
Generation-skipping transfer tax, right to reimbursement for payments of Pro §20215
Sales and use tax (See **SALES AND USE TAX**)
Surety, right of (See **SURETYSHIP, BONDS AND UNDERTAKINGS**)
Trustee for expenditures, reimbursement of (See **TRUSTS**)
Uniform Transfers to Minors Act, reimbursement to custodian under Pro §3915

REJECTED CLAIMS AGAINST ESTATES (See **CLAIMS AGAINST ESTATES**)

RELATED CAUSE OF ACTION
Answer to complaint alleging CCP §426.30
Cross-complaint alleging CCP §426.30
Defined CCP §426.10
Failure to allege related cause of action in cross-complaint, effect of CCP §426.30

RELATIVES
Administrators, priority for appointment as Pro §§8461, 8462
Adoption proceedings (See **ADOPTION**)
Ancestry, statements concerning Ev §1311
Birth, statements concerning Ev §1311
Brothers (See **BROTHERS AND SISTERS**)
Consanguinity (See **CONSANGUINITY**)
Conservators (See **CONSERVATORS**)
Death, statements concerning Ev §1311
Dissolution of marriage, statements concerning Ev §1311
Escheat in absence of (See **ESCHEAT**)
Family (See **FAMILY**)
Foster care placement with relative, preference for Fam §7950
Grandparents (See **GRANDCHILDREN**)
Intestate succession (See **INTESTATE SUCCESSION**)
Judges' actions in behalf of relatives, Code of Judicial Ethics provisions concerning CRCSupp JudEthicsCanon 2
Legitimacy, statements concerning Ev §1311
Marriage (See **MARRIAGE**)
Name change, listing in petition for CCP §1276
Partition referees, relatives as CCP §873.050
Protecting from harm CC §§43, 49, 50
Race, statements concerning Ev §1311
Referees, disqualification of CCP §641
Sisters (See **BROTHERS AND SISTERS**)
Testate succession to (See **WILLS**)

RELEASE
Appellate rules, superior court appeals
    Misdemeanor appeals
        Release on appeal CRC 8.854
Attachment (See **ATTACHMENT**)

RELEASE—Cont.
Child support payments, deposit of real property to secure future Fam §4641
Consideration for CC §1541
Construction defects, actions for
    Defenses of builder CC §945.5
Contribution, effect of
    Joint debtors CC §1543
    Joint tortfeasors CCP §§875 to 880
Effect of valid release CC §1541
Enforcement of judgments (See **ENFORCEMENT OF JUDGMENTS**)
Executors (See **EXECUTORS AND ADMINISTRATORS**)
General release, limitations on effect of CC §1542
Health care provider, release of state from claim against CC §1542.1
Joint debtor, effect of release of CC §1543
Joint tortfeasors CCP §§875 to 880
Judgment liens (See **ENFORCEMENT OF JUDGMENTS**)
Later-discovered claims, effect on CC §1542
Livestock service liens CC §3080.20
Mechanic's liens
    Release bonds
        Public works CC §9364
        Stop payment notices CC §8510
    Release of property from claim of lien CC §§8480 to 8494
    Release or waiver of lien CC §§8120 to 8138 (See **MECHANICS' LIENS**)
Medical records, release of CC §§56.101, 56.104, 56 to 56.37
Oral release must be supported by new consideration CC §1541
Power of appointment (See **POWER OF APPOINTMENT**)
Sureties (See **SURETYSHIP, BONDS AND UNDERTAKINGS**)
Trustee, release of liability of Pro §16464
Unknown claims CC §1542
Written release with or without consideration CC §1541

RELEVANT EVIDENCE
Admissible evidence Ev §§350, 351, 355
Definition Ev §210

RELIGION
Adoption, placement for Fam §8709
Churches (See **CHURCHES**)
Common interest developments
    Religious items displayed on dwelling entry
        Governing documents not to restrict CC §4706
        Restrictions unenforceable CC §1940.45
Credibility of witness not subject to attack for religious beliefs Ev §789
Credit card issuance CC §1747.80
Crimes based on
    Freedom from violence, right to
        Construction or application of provisions in issue, solicitor general notified CC §51.1
        Waiver of right to freedom from violence, coerced or involuntary CC §51.7
Discrimination CC §§51 to 53
    Judicial ethics code
        Administrative responsibilities of judge, impartial discharge CRCSupp JudEthicsCanon 3
        Attorneys, judges to require to refrain from manifesting CRCSupp JudEthicsCanon 3
        Court personnel and staff under direction of judge, standards of conduct enforced by judge CRCSupp JudEthicsCanon 3
        Membership in discriminatory organizations CRCSupp JudEthicsCanon 2
Disqualification of judges, grounds for CCP §170.2
Exemplary damages claims against religious corporations CCP §425.14
Judges
    Disqualification of judges
        Prohibited grounds for disqualification CRCSupp JudEthicsCanon 3
        Membership in discriminatory organizations CRCSupp JudEthicsCanon 2
        Office in religious organization not a financial interest for purposes of disqualification CCP §170.5
Jury service exemption not allowed based on CCP §204
Landlord and tenant
    Religious items displayed on dwelling entry
        Restrictions unenforceable CC §1940.45
Marriage ceremony Fam §§307, 400
Security interest, religious materials as CC §1799.97
Uniform prudent management of institutional funds act Pro §§18501 to 18510
(See **INSTITUTIONAL FUNDS MANAGEMENT**)
Witness's credibility, religious belief as grounds for attacking Ev §789

RELINQUISHMENT OF CHILD (See **ADOPTION**)

RELOCATION BENEFITS
Exempt property for purposes of enforcement of judgments   CCP §704.180
Landlord and tenant
    Termination of tenancy
        Year's continuous, lawful occupation, no-fault just cause for termination   CC §1946.2

REMAINDERS
Action to injury of inheritance   CC §826
Attornment on transfer of   CC §1111
Conditional estates   CC §764
Contingency limitation   CC §778
Death of first taker   CC §780
Definition   CC §769
Easements, effect of   CC §808
Estates tail abolished   CC §763
Inventory by holder of life estate, remainderman receiving   Pro §11752
Judgment, remainder interest of judgment debtor applied to satisfaction of   CCP §709.020
Partition proceedings   CCP §873.840
Principal and income allocations   CC §§731 to 731.15
Remainderman, definition of   CC §731.03
Shelley's case, modification of rule in   CC §§779, 780

REMARRIAGE (See DISSOLUTION OF MARRIAGE)

REMITTITUR
Certiorari, mandate and prohibition   CCP §1076
    Modification of decision   CRC 8.490
Damages
    Consent to remission on appeal   CRC 8.264
Habeas corpus   CRC 8.387
Judgment
    Appellate rules   CRC 8.272
Small claims courts
    Writ petitions   CRC 8.976
Superior court appeals   CRC 8.880, 8.890
    Writ proceedings within original jurisdiction of appellate division   CRC 8.935
Supreme court and courts of appeal (See **APPELLATE RULES, SUPREME COURT AND COURTS OF APPEAL**)

REMOTE APPEARANCES   CCP §367.75
Child support
    Title IV-D support actions
        Telephone appearances   CRC 3.672, 5.324
Civil cases   CRC 3.672
Competence to stand trial
    Conditions for proceeding through use of remote technology   CCP §367.76
Conservatorship for gravely disabled persons
    Conditions for proceeding through use of remote technology   CCP §367.76
Contempt
    Conditions for proceeding through use of remote technology   CCP §367.76
COVID-19, emergency rule   CRCAppx I Emer Rule 3
Dependency proceedings
    Emergency orders
        COVID-19, emergency rule   CRC 3.672, CRCAppx I Emer Rule 6
    Telephone appearances   CRC 3.672, 5.531
        Nonminor dependents, retention of jurisdiction   CRC 3.672, 5.900
Depositions
    Oral deposition by telephone, videoconference or other remote electronic means   CRC 3.1010
Domestic violence restraining order
    Remote appearance of party, support person or witness   Fam §6308
Duration of case
    Notice of intent to appear remotely for duration of case   CRC 3.672
Encouragement of remote appearance   CRC 3.672
Equal and fair access to justice
    Working group for statewide framework for remote proceedings   CCP §367.9
Evidentiary hearing or trial   CRC 3.672
Ex parte applications, consideration without appearance by applicant or counsel   CRC 3.672, 3.1207
Family rules
    Telephone appearance   CRC 3.672, 5.9
Fees
    Remote appearance fees   CRC 3.672
Forms
    Judicial council forms   CRCAppx A
Foster care and foster care facilities
    Dependent child, placement in
        Hearings and continuances   CRC 3.672, CRCAppx I Emer Rule 6

REMOTE APPEARANCES—Cont.
Indian child, dependency matters
    Tribal appearance by telephone or other remote means   CRC 3.672, 5.531
Indian child welfare act involuntary placements
    Tribal appearance by telephone or other remote means   CRC 3.672, 5.482
In-person appearance
    Court discretion to require   CRC 3.672
Insanity defense
    Commitment after insanity finding
        Conditions for proceeding through use of remote technology   CCP §367.76
Involuntary treatment for gravely disabled persons
    Conditions for proceeding through use of remote technology   CCP §367.76
Judicial commitments, persons subject to
    Conditions for proceeding through use of remote technology   CCP §367.76
Judicial officers presiding over remote proceeding from location other than courtroom   CRC 10.635
    Judicial council to adopt rules   CCP §367.10
Juvenile rules
    Telephone appearances   CRC 3.672, 5.531
        Nonminor dependents, retention of jurisdiction   CRC 3.672, 5.900
Juvenile wardship proceedings
    Telephone appearances   CRC 3.672, 5.531
        COVID-19, emergency rule   CRCAppx I Emer Rule 7
        Nonminor dependents, retention of jurisdiction   CRC 3.672, 5.900
Local court rules for remote proceedings   CRC 3.672
Marriage, remote licensing and solemnization   Fam §§550 to 560 (See **MARRIAGE**)
Mentally disordered offender proceedings
    Conditions for proceeding through use of remote technology   CCP §367.76
Outpatient status
    Conditions for proceeding through use of remote technology   CCP §367.76
Open court proceedings
    Limiting public access when remote access available
        Restrictions on limiting public access   CCP §124
Proceedings other than evidentiary hearing or trial   CRC 3.672
Report on use of remote technology   CCP §367.8
Service requirements
    Restraining orders   CRC 3.1162, 5.496
State hospitals
    Involuntary medication and treatment hearings
        Conditions for proceeding through use of remote technology   CCP §367.76
Superior courts
    Reports on use of remote technology in civil actions   CCP §367.8

REMOVAL
Attorney's removal, appointment of new attorney on   CCP §286
Good faith improvements to property of another   CCP §871.4
Judges (See **JUDGES**)
Trusts (See **TRUSTS**)

REMOVAL OF CAUSE (See TRANSFER OF ACTIONS)

RENEWAL
Harassment, renewal of protection order   CCP §527.6
Judgments, renewal of (See **ENFORCEMENT OF JUDGMENTS**)
Leases   CC §§1945, 1945.5

RENOVATIONS (See HOME IMPROVEMENT CONTRACTS)

RENT (See also LANDLORD AND TENANT)
Abandonment of lease by lessee   CC §§1951 to 1951.7
Administrators collecting   Pro §§9650, 9651
Amount of deposits   CC §1950.5
Apartment housekeeper's lien for   CC §1861a
Assignment of rents in connection with secured obligations (See **TRUST DEEDS AND MORTGAGES**)
Attornment, transfer in absence of   CC §1111
Blind persons having equal rights to rent housing accommodations   CC §§54.1, 54.3, 54.4, 55
    Construction or application of provisions in issue, solicitor general notified   CC §55.2
Boarding house keeper's lien for   CC §1861
Cash payments
    Requiring cash payments   CC §1947.3
Changing terms of lease period   CC §827
Commercial rental control (See **RENT CONTROL**)
Consumer credit report used in screening of rental applicants   CC §1950.6
Control of rent (See **RENT CONTROL**)

RENT (—Cont.)
  Death, rent recovery after CC §825
  Deposits
    Generally CC §§1950.5, 1950.7
    Attachment, rent deposits affecting CCP §483.020
  Disabled persons having equal rights to rent housing accommodations CC §§54.1, 54.3, 54.4, 55
    Construction or application of provisions in issue, solicitor general notified CC §55.2
  Easement right to collect CC §§802, 808
  Electronic funds transfers
    Alternative forms of payment CC §1947.3
  Eminent domain proceedings, rental value of property as basis for opinion testimony in Ev §§817 to 819, 822
  Executors collecting Pro §§9650, 9651
  Fiduciary income and principal act
    Receipts, allocation
      Income, allocation to Pro §16344
  Floating homes and floating home marinas (See **FLOATING HOMES**)
  Gouging
    Increase of gross rental rate on residential real property, limitations CC §1947.12
      Expiration of limitations, limitation of rent upon CC §1947.13
  Grantee recovering CC §821
  Hotel keeper's lien for CC §1861
  Income of property CC §748
  Installment payment, presumption of Ev §636
  Judgment debtor, assignment of right to payment due CCP §§708.510 to 708.560
  Karnette Rental-Purchase Act for rental-purchase contracts CC §§1812.620 to 1812.650
  Life leases, rent recovery under CC §824
  Limitation of actions (See **STATUTES OF LIMITATION**)
  Mobilehomes (See **MOBILEHOMES**)
  Nursing home, death of patient terminating rent obligation to CC §1934.5
  Preparation fees for lease or rental agreements, prohibition against CC §1950.8
  Principal and income allocations CC §731.05
  Redemption of mortgaged property (See **TRUST DEEDS AND MORTGAGES**)
  Renewal of lease presumed from acceptance of CC §1945
  Rental-purchase contracts, Karnette Rental-Purchase Act for CC §§1812.620 to 1812.650
  Repairs by tenant as deductible from CC §1942
  Screening fee for rental applications, landlord's right to impose CC §1950.6
  Security deposits
    Generally CC §§1950.5, 1950.7
    Floating homes CC §800.49
    Mobilehomes CC §798.39
    Rental-purchase contracts CC §1812.625
  Skimming
    Generally CC §891
    Affirmative defenses CC §893
    Applicability of law CC §894
    Criminal penalties CC §892
    Definitions CC §890
  Special administrator collecting Pro §8544
  Stabilization of rent (See **RENT CONTROL**)
  Subsidized rent (See **RENT CONTROL**)
  Substandard conditions of rental housing in receivership CCP §§568.2, 568.3
  Third party payment of rent CC §1947.3
  Time for payment, usage controlling CC §1947
  Unlawful detainer (See **UNLAWFUL DETAINER**)
  Unsafe conditions of rental housing in receivership CCP §568.2
  Untenantable premises, penalties for rent collection for CC §1942.4
    Attorneys' fees and cost of suit, landlord liability CCP §1174.21
  Utility payments
    Deductions from rent CC §1942.2
  Victims of domestic violence, sexual assault or stalking
    Termination of tenancy, liability for rent CC §1946.7

RENTAL PASSENGER VEHICLE TRANSACTIONS CC §§1939.01 to 1939.39
  Actions
    Theft CC §1939.27
    Violation of provisions CC §1939.25
  Additional mandatory charges
    Defined CC §1939.01
    Imposition CC §1939.19
    Unfair practices, exception CC §1939.20
  Customer facility charge
    Collection of charge or alternative customer facility charge by rental company CC §1939.17

RENTAL PASSENGER VEHICLE TRANSACTIONS—Cont.
  Customer facility charge—Cont.
    Defined CC §1939.01
  Damage waivers CC §1939.09
    Contents CC §1939.09
    Defined CC §1939.01
    Disclosures CC §1939.09
      Membership programs of rental companies, disclosure requirements CC §1939.31
    Exclusions
      Permitted exclusions CC §1939.09
    Purchase of damage waiver or optional insurance
      Prohibited practices to induce purchase CC §1939.13
    Sale
      Rates CC §1939.09
  Definitions CC §1939.01
  Drivers' license requirements
    Membership agreements allowing remote access to vehicle
      Exceptions to drivers' license requirements of vehicle code CC §1939.37
  Electronic communications between company and renter
    Agreement by renter in rental or lease agreement CC §1939.22
  Electronic surveillance technology
    Activation
      Time when activation permitted CC §1939.23
    Defined CC §1939.01
    Restrictions on use CC §1939.23
  Foreign renters
    Service of complaint by foreign renters CC §1939.33
  Mechanical damage
    Recovery by rental company
      Prohibited means of recovery CC §1939.15
    Renter responsibilities for rented vehicle CC §1939.03
      Claim against renter for damage or loss CC §1939.07
      Damage waivers CC §§1939.09, 1939.13
      Insurance coverage for renter CC §1939.07
      Mitigation of damages by rental company CC §1939.07
      Total amount of renter liability CC §1939.05
  Membership program of rental company
    Disclosure obligations, compliance CC §1939.31
    Drivers' license requirements
      Remote access to vehicle permitted under program, exceptions to drivers' license requirements of vehicle code CC §1939.37
  Personal vehicle sharing programs
    Airports, regulation of access and fees at airport facilities CC §1939.38
    Defined CC §1939.01
    Tax certifications required prior making vehicle available for rental CC §1939.39
  Physical damage
    Recovery by rental company
      Prohibited means of recovery CC §1939.15
    Renter responsibilities for rented vehicle CC §1939.03
      Claim against renter for damage or loss CC §1939.07
      Damage waivers CC §§1939.09, 1939.13
      Insurance coverage for renter CC §1939.07
      Mitigation of damages by rental company CC §1939.07
      Total amount of renter liability CC §1939.05
  Quotes
    Business program sponsor, renters of
      Separate quotation and imposition of additional charges CC §1939.21
    Contents CC §1939.19
    Defined CC §1939.01
    Unfair practices, exception CC §1939.20
  Renter responsibilities for rented vehicle CC §1939.03
    Claim against renter for damage or loss CC §1939.07
    Damage waivers CC §§1939.09, 1939.13
    Insurance coverage for renter CC §1939.07
    Mitigation of damages by rental company CC §1939.07
    Recovery by rental company
      Prohibited means of recovery CC §1939.15
    Total amount of renter liability CC §1939.05
  Theft
    Action for loss due to theft CC §1939.27
    Electronic surveillance technology
      Activation, when permitted CC §1939.23
      Restrictions on use CC §1939.23
    Recovery by rental company
      Prohibited means of recovery CC §1939.15
    Renter responsibilities for rented vehicle CC §1939.03
      Claim against renter for damage or loss CC §1939.07

RENTAL PASSENGER VEHICLE TRANSACTIONS—Cont.
Theft—Cont.
    Renter responsibilities for rented vehicle —Cont.
        Damage waivers   CC §§1939.09, 1939.13
        Insurance coverage for renter   CC §1939.07
        Mitigation of damages by rental company   CC §1939.07
        Total amount of renter liability   CC §1939.05
Vandalism
    Recovery by rental company
        Prohibited means of recovery   CC §1939.15
    Renter responsibilities for rented vehicle   CC §1939.03
        Claim against renter for damage or loss   CC §1939.07
        Damage waivers   CC §§1939.09, 1939.13
        Insurance coverage for renter   CC §1939.07
        Mitigation of damages by rental company   CC §1939.07
        Recovery by rental company, prohibited means of recovery   CC §1939.15
        Total amount of renter liability   CC §1939.05
Vans
    Advisories for 15-passenger van renters   CC §1939.35
Waivers
    Damage waivers   CC §§1939.09, 1939.13
    Provisions of chapter, restrictions on waiver   CC §1939.29

RENTAL-PURCHASE CONTRACTS
Acquiring ownership
    Consumer right as to   CC §1812.632
Cash price
    Maximums, calculation   CC §1812.644
Contents   CC §1812.623
Definitions   CC §1812.622
Electronic devices
    Defined   CC §1812.622
    Geophysical location tracking, monitoring and remote assistance technology
        Disclosures to consumers   CC §1812.650
        Restrictions on lessor/seller use of information   CC §1812.650
Form   CC §1812.623
Income reduction
    Consumer protection   CC §1812.632
Job loss
    Consumer protection   CC §1812.632
Karnette Rental-Purchase Act   CC §§1812.620 to 1812.650
Notice of consumer right to acquire ownership   CC §1812.632
Payoff
    Calculation of payoff   CC §1812.632
Prohibited provisions   CC §1812.624
Recordkeeping by lessor   CC §1812.644
Total of payments
    Maximums   CC §1812.644

RENT CONTROL
Commercial rental control
    Generally   CC §1954.27
    Definitions   CC §1954.26
    Findings of legislature regarding effects of local rent control practices   CC §1954.25
    Governing law   CC §1954.28
    Notices on termination of commercial lease   CC §1954.31
    Powers of public entity, effect on   CC §§1954.29, 1954.30
Disabled persons
    Moving tenant with permanent physical disability to accessible floor of property   CC §1954.53
Mobilehome parks (See **MOBILEHOMES**)
Mobilehomes and mobilehome parks
    Gross rental rate
        Restrictions on rates for tenancy in qualified park   CC §798.30.5
Residential real property
    Confidentiality of tenant information disclosed for purposes of establishing compliance   CC §1947.7
    Costa-Hawkins Rental Housing Act   CC §§1954.50 to 1954.53
    Damages
        Fraudulent eviction of tenant   CC §1947.10
        Refund excess rent, failure to   CC §1947.11
    Definitions   CC §1954.51
    Establishment and certification of permissible rent levels   CC §1947.8
    Eviction of tenant based on owner's reoccupation of tenant's unit   CC §1947.10
    Expenses and fees in calculating fair return   CC §1947.15
    Refund of excess rent   CC §1947.11
    Rental unit exceptions   CC §1954.53
    Requirements for setting rates   CC §1954.52

RENT CONTROL—Cont.
Residential real property—Cont.
    Subletting, effect of   CC §1954.53
    Substantial compliance with local rent control ordinances, limitations on penalties for landlords in   CC §1947.7
San Francisco, city and county
    Temporary displacement of tenant household
        Compensation levels   CC §1947.9
Subsidized rent
    Adjustment
        Adjustment to rent following termination of contract with government to provide rent limitation, restrictions concerning   CC §1954.53
        Notice to tenant of termination of landlord's contract with government agency providing for rent limitation   CC §1954.535

RENT SKIMMING (See **RENT**)

REORGANIZATION (See **PUBLIC ENTITIES**)

REPAIRS
Aircraft liens   CCP §1208.61
Arbitration, proof of costs of repairs in   CRC 3.823
Automobiles (See **AUTOMOBILES**)
Bailment, property held under   CC §§1889, 1929
Borrowed property   CC §1889
Boundaries, landowners' duty to maintain   CC §841
Building contractors
    Contracts for service and repair
        Commencement of work, effect on contract   CC §1689.15
        Rescission   CC §1689.15
Common interest developments   CC §4775
    Communications wiring access   CC §4790
    Religious items displayed on dwelling entry
        Temporary removal to accommodate repair   CC §4706
    Termites   CC §4780
        Temporary removal of occupant   CC §4785
Construction defects, actions for
    Defenses of builder   CC §945.5
    Prelitigation procedures
        Accepting offer   CC §918
        Access to information about repair   CC §923
        Failure to offer   CC §920
        Observation   CC §922
        Offer to repair   CC §917
        Scheduling and effecting repair   CC §921
        Undertaking some but not all repairs   CC §924
        Unsuccessful repairs   CC §933
        Untimely repairs   CC §925
        Waiver or release from provisions   CC §926
Consumer goods
    Installation or becoming affixed preventing repair of goods
        Replacement and installation of goods or reimbursement of buyer   CC §1793.2
Covenants binding for   CC §1468
Decedent's estate, property of   Pro §§9650, 10562
Definition of service facilities   CC §1791
Deposits by tenant for   CC §1950.5
Easements, owner's duty to repair   CC §845
Emergency repairs   CC §1689.13
    Void contracts   CC §1689.14
Eminent domain acquired to enter upon adjacent or nearby property for   CC §1002, CCP §1245.326
Exempt property for purposes of enforcement of judgments   CCP §704.030
Expenses, manufacturer liable for   CC §§1793.3, 1793.6
Facilities for service and repair by manufacturer
    Out-of-state facilities   CC §§1793.03, 1793.4 to 1793.6
    Within state facilities   CC §§1793.2, 1793.3
Failure to commence repairs within specified four-hour period, retailer's liability for   CC §1722
Family home, order specifying responsibility for maintenance of   Fam §3806
Farm machinery repairs, invoice requirements for   CC §1718
Fences, landowners' duty to maintain   CC §841
Financial institutions making health and building code repairs to foreclosed residential property   CC §2932.6
Fire destroying property left for   CC §1858.2
Foreclosed residential property, financial institutions making Health and Building Code repairs to   CC §2932.6
Home solicitation sales contracts for (See **HOME SOLICITATION SALES CONTRACTS**)
Indemnity contract covering   CC §2783
Insurance coverage for property left for   CC §§1858 to 1858.3
Landlord and tenant (See **LANDLORD AND TENANT**)

REPAIRS—Cont.
Lien for   CC §§3051, 3052.5
Loan funds used in repairs, liability for injuries from   CC §3434
Manufacturers
    Facilities for service and repair
        Out-of-state facilities   CC §§1793.03, 1793.4 to 1793.6
        Within state facilities   CC §§1793.2, 1793.3
    Warranties for repairs
        Automobiles (See **AUTOMOBILES**)
        Generally (See within this heading, **"Warranties"**)
        Roofs (See **ROOFING WARRANTIES**)
Mobilehome parks (See **MOBILEHOMES**)
Monuments, landowners' duty to maintain   CC §841
Negligence, inadmissible evidence to prove   Ev §1151
Notice
    Nonconformity notice of goods purchased under warranty   CC §1793.1
    Tenant's notice for repairs   CC §1942
Receipt for property left for   CC §§1858 to 1858.3
Rental-purchase contracts, repairs under   CC §§1812.633 to 1812.635
Retail installment sales contracts   CC §1805.8
Roofs (See **ROOFING WARRANTIES**)
Service contracts
    Damages, recovery of   CC §§1794, 1794.1
    Defined   CC §1791
    In lieu of or in addition to warranties, requirements for service contracts   CC §§1794.4, 1794.41
    Rental-purchase agreements, service contracts offered for sale in conjunction with   CC §1812.635
    Retailers' duties under service contracts   CC §1794.45
Theft of property left for   CC §1858.2
Trust property   Pro §16229
Unclaimed property fund appropriations for   CCP §1325
Warranties
    Generally   CC §§1793.1 to 1793.3, 1793.4, 1794.3
    Automobiles (See **AUTOMOBILES**)
    Damages, recovery of   CC §§1794, 1794.1
    Independent servicemen, liability of manufacturer to   CC §§1793.6, 1794.1
    Rental-purchase contracts, transfer of warranties on transfer of ownership under   CC §1812.635
    Retail seller, liability of manufacturer to   CC §§1793.5, 1794.1, 1795.7
    Roofs (See **ROOFING WARRANTIES**)
    Service and repair facilities
        Out-of-state facilities   CC §§1793.03, 1793.4 to 1793.6
        Within state facilities   CC §§1793.2, 1793.3
    Service contracts in addition to or in lieu of warranties, requirements for   CC §§1794.4, 1794.41
        Retailers' duties under service contracts   CC §1794.45
    Standards for warranty work   CC §§1796, 1796.5
    Suggestions of service or repair by manufacturer, effect of   CC §1794.5
    Tolling period of warranty   CC §1795.6
    Used consumer goods   CC §§1795.4, 1795.5

REPAIRS AND MAINTENANCE
Real estate sales
    Disclosures
        Room additions, structural modifications, repairs, etc performed by contractor   CC §1102.6h

REPAIR SERVICES BUREAU
Liens by dealers registered with   CC §3052.5

REPEAL
Abolishment of office by repeal of statutes, effect on officeholders of   CCP §§6, 7
Administrative rules and regulations (See **ADMINISTRATIVE PROCEDURE ACT**)
Enactment of code, effect on existing statutes of   CCP §18
Exemptions applicable to procedures for enforcement of judgments   CCP §703.060
General repeals   CC §20
State agency regulations, repeal procedure for (See **ADMINISTRATIVE PROCEDURE ACT**)

REPEAT OFFENDERS
Sentencing
    Sex offenders   CRC 4.426

REPLEVIN (See **CLAIM AND DELIVERY**)

REPORTER OF DECISIONS
Opinions on appeals transmitted to   CRC 8.1105

REPORTERS
Court reporters (See **COURT REPORTERS**)
Journalists (See **JOURNALISTS**)

REPORTS
Administration of decedents' estates
    Executors, status report by   Pro §§12200 to 12202
    Final distribution, status report   Pro §§12200 to 12202
    Sale, report of   Pro §§10260, 10308, 10351
Adoption proceedings (See **ADOPTION**)
Appraisals (See **APPRAISALS**)
Automobile leases, requirements for   CC §2989.5
Child custody proceedings (See **CUSTODY OF CHILDREN**)
Credit card company's obligation to report finance charges annually at cardholder's request   CC §1748.5
Credit reports (See **CREDIT REPORTING**)
Crime reports, immunity for persons or organizations making   CC §48.9
Decedents' estates
    Final distribution, status report   Pro §§12200 to 12202
    Sale, report of   Pro §§10260, 10308, 10351
Executors' report on status of administration   Pro §§12200 to 12202
International commercial conciliators, report of   CCP §§1267.362, 1297.361
Investigative agencies (See **INVESTIGATIVE CONSUMER REPORTING AGENCIES**)
Partition (See **PARTITION**)
Police reports (See **LAW ENFORCEMENT OFFICERS**)
Postrelease community supervision
    Revocation procedure
        Supervising agency reports as to compliance with provisions   CRC 4.541
Probation (See **PROBATION**)
State agency reporting requirement, appeal from certification of   Gov §11380
Sterilization proceedings, reports of examiners in   Pro §1955
Title reports (See **TITLE REPORTS**)
Transcript
    Court reporters generally (See **COURT REPORTERS**)
Trusts (See **TRUSTS**)
Unclaimed deposits and payments escheated, controller receiving reports of   CCP §1530
    Interest payable on property not reported   CCP §1577
    Postponement of date for filing report   CCP §1532

REPOSSESSORS
Rental-purchase contracts
    Electronic devices with geophysical location tracking, monitoring and remote assistance technology
        Restrictions on lessor/seller use of information   CC §1812.650

REPRESENTATIVE SUITS (See CLASS ACTIONS)

REPRIEVES (See PARDONS)

REPRODUCTIONS
Postmortem examination or autopsy, restriction on reproducing photograph or video taken at scene of death or in course of   CCP §129

REPRODUCTIVE COERCION
Domestic violence
    Ex parte protective orders
        Restraining disturbing peace of other party   Fam §6320

REPRODUCTIVE MEDICINE
Legally protected health care services   CC §§1798.300 to 1798.308
Medical records confidentiality
    Businesses organized to maintain medical information
        Digital services offered to consumers   CC §56.06
            Limitation of access to information about gender affirming care, abortion, or contraception information   CC §56.101
Unauthorized use or misuse of sperm, ova or embryo
    Civil action for damages   CC §1708.5.6

REPUTATION (See CHARACTER AND REPUTATION)

REQUEST FOR ADMISSION   CCP §§2033.010 to 2033.420
Amendment of response   CCP §2033.300
Attorney's fees
    Failure to admit
        Expense incurred to prove matters not admitted   CCP §2033.420
Declaration for additional discovery   CCP §2033.040
    Form   CCP §2033.050
Depositions generally (See **CORPORATE SHARES AND SHAREHOLDERS**)

REQUEST FOR ADMISSION—Cont.
Documents, genuineness
    Form of request   CCP §2033.060
    Unlimited number of requests   CCP §2033.030
Economic litigation provisions for limited civil cases, permissible forms of discovery under   CCP §94
Effect of admissions   CCP §§2033.410, 2033.420
    Pending actions, effect on   CCP §2033.410
Extension of time for response   CCP §2033.260
Failure to admit
    Expense incurred to prove matters not admitted   CCP §2033.420
Form admissions requests, Judicial Council development of   CCP §2033.710
    Advisory committees, consultation with   CCP §2033.730
    Nontechnical language, use in drafting   CCP §2033.730
    Optional use of form request   CCP §2033.740
Format of request   CCP §2033.060
Interrogatories generally (See **INTERROGATORIES**)
Methods of discovery   CCP §2019.010
Motion to compel
    Further response   CCP §2033.290
Motion to deem matters admitted
    Failure to timely respond to request   CCP §2033.280
Number permitted   CCP §2033.030
    Increase when request accompanied by declaration   CCP §2033.040
        Form of declaration   CCP §2033.050
Objections
    Response to request   CCP §2033.230
Order deeming matters admitted   CCP §2033.290
Pending actions, effect on   CCP §2033.410
Protective orders   CCP §2033.080
Response to request   CCP §§2033.210 to 2033.300
    Amendment of response   CCP §2033.300
    Completeness   CCP §2033.220
    Failure to timely serve response   CCP §2033.280
    Format of response   CCP §2033.210
    Further response
        Motion to compel   CCP §2033.290
    Motion to deem matters admitted   CCP §2033.280
    Objections   CCP §2033.230
    Reasonable inquiry to formulate response   CCP §2033.220
    Retention   CCP §2033.270
    Signature   CCP §2033.240
    Time for service of response   CCP §2033.250
        Extension of time for response   CCP §2033.260
    Withdrawal of admission   CCP §2033.300
    Written response   CCP §2033.210
Restriction to combining other discovery methods with   CCP §2033.010
Retention of request, proof of service, and response   CCP §2033.270
Sanctions
    Generally (See **DISCOVERY**)
    Protective orders
        Unsuccessfully making or opposing motion for protective order   CCP §2033.080
    Response to request
        Failure to timely respond   CCP §2033.280
        Further response, failure to provide   CCP §2033.290
Scope   CCP §2033.010
Service of request   CCP §2033.070
    Retention of request, proof of service, and response   CCP §2033.270
Signature of response   CCP §2033.240
Style of request   CCP §2033.060
Time for service of response   CCP §2033.250
    Extension of time for response   CCP §2033.260
Time limitations for   CCP §2033.020
Unlawful detainer
    Time for service of process   CCP §2033.250
    Time limitations for   CCP §2033.020
Withdrawal of admission   CCP §2033.300

REQUEST FOR PRODUCTION (See **INSPECTION DEMANDS**)

REQUEST FOR STATEMENT OF DAMAGES   CCP §§425.11, 425.12

REQUESTS FOR ADMISSIONS
Civil rules
    Limitation on papers filed   CRC 3.250
Form requests for admissions
    List of judicial council legal forms   CRC Appx A
Identification   CRC 3.1000, 3.1345
Limitation on papers filed   CRC 3.250

REQUESTS FOR ADMISSIONS—Cont.
Motion to compel
    Separate document setting forth item to which further response, answer or production is requested   CRC 3.1345
Objections to
    Limitations on papers filed   CRC 3.250
Response to request
    Further response
        Motion to compel   CRC 3.1345
    Identification and sequence of responses   CRC 3.1000
    Limitations on papers filed   CRC 3.250
Sequence of responses   CRC 3.1000
Supplemental and further discovery, format of   CRC 3.1000

RESCISSION
Generally (See **CONTRACTS AND AGREEMENTS**)
Adoption agency, relinquishment of child to   Fam §8700
    Revocation of right to relinquish, waiver   Fam §8700.5
Agency, rescinding ratification of acts of   CC §2314
Contracts (See **CONTRACTS AND AGREEMENTS**)
Emancipation of minors, declaration of   Fam §§7130, 7132 to 7135
Health studio services contracts
    Cancellation of   CC §§1812.85, 1812.89
Home solicitation sales contracts
    Cancellation   CC §§1689.6, 1689.9
        Notice of right to cancel in contract   CC §1689.7
        Service and repair project contracts   CC §1689.15
Small claims court jurisdiction to grant equitable relief in lieu of or in addition to money damages   CCP §116.220
Trust deeds (See **TRUST DEEDS AND MORTGAGES**)

RESCUE WORKERS
Anaphylaxis
    Epinephrine auto-injector administration for first aid
        Immunity from civil liability of lay rescuers, prehospital emergency medical care providers or authorized entities   CC §1714.23
Prehospital emergency medical care personnel
    Discovery, review committee records exempt from   Ev §1157
Public health and safety labor or service providers
    Logo or identifying mark of public agency, display   CC §3273

RESEARCH
Animal shelter sign stating use of animals for   CC §1834.7
Hospital mortality studies, admissibility of   Ev §§1156, 1156.1
Medical information disclosed for purposes of   CC §§56.15, 56.16

RESERVE POLICE OFFICERS (See **LAW ENFORCEMENT OFFICERS**)

RESERVOIRS (See **DAMS**)

RES GESTAE
Hearsay evidence, admissibility of   Ev §§1240, 1241

RESIDENCE
Assignment for benefit of creditors, property exempt from   CCP §1801
Children and minors   CRC 5.510
    Parent subject to juvenile proceedings, notice of address   CRC 5.534
Conservatee, restrictions on changing residence of   Pro §§2253, 2254, 2352
    Least restrictive appropriate residence   Pro §2352.5
Conveyance of residential property (See **CONVEYANCES**)
Custody of children (See **CUSTODY OF CHILDREN**)
Debt collectors and   CC §1788.15
Deferred sale of family home, request of custodial parent for   Fam §§3800 to 3810
Dissolution of marriage   Fam §§2320 to 2322
Domicile (See **DOMICILE**)
Excluding party from dwelling   Fam §§5552, 6321, 6340
Executors (See **EXECUTORS AND ADMINISTRATORS**)
Guardian subject to juvenile proceedings, notice of address   CRC 5.534
Legal separation proceeding   Fam §2321
Missing person's estate, jurisdiction for administration of   Pro §12403
Parent's right to determine residence of minor child   Fam §7501
Parent subject to juvenile proceedings, notice of address   CRC 5.534
Referees   CCP §640
Same sex marriage
    Dissolution of marriage, annulment or legal separation   Fam §2320
Senior citizen housing developments, generally   CC §§51.2 to 51.4
Small claims court hearing, effect of residence of defendant on scheduling case for   CCP §116.330
Support, duty of   Fam §3550

RESIDENCE—Cont.
Transfer of causes
    Family Law Act proceedings, subsequent to final judgment   CCP §397.5
    Retention of jurisdiction to issue protective orders   CCP §399
    Time frames for transferring jurisdiction
        Family law actions or proceedings   CRC 5.97
Transfer of residential property (See **CONVEYANCES**)
Venue in county of residence of defendant   CCP §395
Ward, guardian establishing residence of   Pro §2352

RESIDENTIAL HOTELS (See **HOTELS AND MOTELS**)

RESIDUAL RIGHTS
Artworks, residual rights of artist in   CC §986
Unclaimed residuals, escheat of   CCP §§1501, 1521

RESIDUARY CLAUSE (See **WILLS**)

RESIGNATION
Guardianship (See **GUARDIAN AND WARD**)
Personal representative of decedent's estate   Pro §§8520 to 8525
Trustees (See **TRUSTS**)

RES IPSA LOQUITUR
Certificate of meritorious cause   CCP §411.35
Presumptions   Ev §646
Public property, applicability to dangerous condition of   Gov §830.5

RES JUDICATA   CCP §§1908 to 1911
Credit reports   CC §1785.34
Foreign judgments   CCP §§1913, 1914
Investigative agencies   CC §1786.52
Separate trial of special defense   CCP §597
Uniform Child Custody Jurisdiction and Enforcement Act, effect of custody determinations under   Fam §3406
Unpublished opinion, reliance on   CRC 8.1115

RESOLUTIONS
Eminent domain (See **EMINENT DOMAIN**)

RESORTS
Blind persons having equal rights to visit   CC §§54.1, 54.3, 54.4, 55
    Construction or application of provisions in issue, solicitor general notified   CC §55.2
Disabled persons having equal rights to visit   CC §§54.1, 54.3, 54.4, 55
    Construction or application of provisions in issue, solicitor general notified   CC §55.2

RESPONDEAT SUPERIOR (See **AGENCY**)

RESPONDENT
Definitions   Fam §127

RESPONDENTIA, LOANS UPON (See **LOANS UPON RESPONDENTIA**)

RESPONSES
Generally (See **ANSWERS**)
Administrative adjudicative proceedings (See **ADMINISTRATIVE ADJUDICATION**)
Arbitration (See **ARBITRATION**)
Dissolution of marriage (See **DISSOLUTION OF MARRIAGE**)
Economic litigation procedures for limited civil cases, time for response to request for statement identifying witnesses and evidence under   CCP §96
Family law rules (See **FAMILY RULES**)
Jury commissioner inquiry or summons   CCP §196

REST AREAS
Human trafficking or slavery
    Signs, businesses required to post notice concerning relief from slavery or human trafficking   CC §52.6

RESTAURANTS
Discrimination
    Law enforcement officer, firefighter or search and rescue dog handlers serving outside jurisdiction
        Lodging, eating or transportation, prohibition on discrimination   CC §54.25
Unruh Civil Rights Act   CC §§51, 52

REST HOMES (See **NURSING HOMES**)

RESTITUTION
Administrative adjudication order for restitution   Gov §11519

RESTITUTION—Cont.
Assignment for benefit of creditors, crime victim's compensatory payments exempt from   CCP §1801
Automobile manufacturers, transporters, dealers and sales professionals
    Licensees
        Effect of order for restitution   Gov §11519.1
Automobile warranties
    Restitution or replacement actions   CCP §§871.20 to 871.28
    Restitution under   CC §1793.2
Criminal proceedings
    Recommendation by probation officer   CRC 4.411.5
    Transfer of probation and mandatory supervision cases
        Effect of transfer on outstanding restitution obligation   CRC 4.530
Defendant, restitution by   CRC 4.423
Domestic violence cases, order for restitution   Fam §§6342, 7720
Felony convictions
    Damage actions based on commission of felony   CCP §340.3
Forms
    Criminal forms   CRCAppx A
Incarcerated judgment debtor, exempt funds of   CCP §704.090
Interrogatories for victim who has not received full restitution
    Form interrogatories
        Development by judicial council   CCP §2033.720
        Judicial council forms   CRCAppx A
Juvenile courts
    Records sealing
        Order on prosecutor request for access   CRCAppx A
        Prosecuting attorney request to access sealed juvenile case files   CRC 5.860
Limitations period, effect of order for restitution on running of   CCP §352.5
Mitigating circumstances   CRC 4.423
Price discrimination based on gender
    Price differences for substantially similar goods based on gender of marketing audience
        Enforcement of provisions   CC §51.14
Private student loan collections reform
    Actions against creditor, lender or collector for violations of provisions   CC §1788.208
Probation   CRC 4.411.5
    Reports, recommendation regarding restitution   CRC 4.411.5
    Transfer of probation
        Effect of transfer on outstanding restitution obligation   CRC 4.530
Small claims court jurisdiction to grant equitable relief in lieu of or in addition to money damages   CCP §116.220
Small estates without administration (See **SMALL ESTATES WITHOUT ADMINISTRATION**)
Student borrower bill of rights
    Enforcement of compliance with rights   CC §1788.103
Subcutaneous implanting of identification device, requiring of another   CC §52.7
Victims of crime
    Interrogatories
        Judicial council forms   CRCAppx A
    Recommendation by probation officer as to restitution to victim   CRC 4.411.5
    Transfer of probation or mandatory supervision
        Effect of transfer on outstanding restitution obligation   CRC 4.530

RESTORATION TO MENTAL HEALTH (See **MENTAL DISABILITY**)

RESTRAINING ORDERS (See **INJUNCTIONS**)

RESTRAINTS OF TRADE
Antitrust litigation
    Complex litigation defined   CRC 3.400
Unfair competition (See **UNFAIR COMPETITION**)

RESTRAINTS ON ALIENATION (See **PERPETUITIES AND RESTRAINTS ON ALIENATION**)

RESTRICTIVE COVENANTS (See **COVENANTS AND CONDITIONS**)

RESTROOMS (See **PUBLIC RESTROOMS**)

RESULTING TRUSTS
Applicability of Trust Law provisions to   Pro §15003

RETAIL FOOD FACILITIES
Supermarket club cards, restrictions as to
    Waiver of protections   CC §1749.66

RETAIL INSTALLMENT SALES
Generally   CC §§1801 to 1802.20

RETAIL INSTALLMENT SALES—Cont.
Acceptance of retail installment account agreement by buyer   CC §1810
Add-on sales   CC §§1808.1 to 1808.5
Advance payment of full amount   CC §§1803.2, 1806.1 to 1806.4
Advertisements clearly stating period rate   CC §1803.11
Affidavit filed with complaint in action on contract   CC §1812.10
Aircraft, exclusion of   CC §1801.4
Asian language contracts, translations   CC §1632
Assignments
    Authority for   CC §1809.1
    Defenses against assignee   CC §1804.2
    Discount buying services contracts   CC §1812.114
    Limitation on liability to purchaser   CC §1804.2
    Notes, defense against holders of   CC §1810.7
    Seller, buyer's defenses against   CC §1804.2
Attorneys' fees
    Generally   CC §1811.1
    Contract provision as to   CC §1810.4
    Provision for recovering   CC §§1810.4, 1811.1
    Repossession proceedings   CC §1812.4
Automobiles (See **AUTOMOBILES**)
Billing cycle, statement of account furnished for   CC §1810.3
Boats   CC §1801.4
Catalog sales   CC §1803.8
Collection charges   CC §1810.12
Condition of buyer obtaining financing   CC §1803.9
Conditions of sale, customer furnished with statement of   CC §1810.1
Consolidation of several contracts   CC §§1808.1 to 1808.5
Construction of provisions   CC §1802
Contracts
    Assignments generally (See within this heading, **"Assignments"**)
    Blanks contained in   CC §1803.4
    Content requirements   CC §§1803.2, 1803.3
    Copy for buyer   CC §1803.7
    Cosigner's liability   CC §§1799.90 to 1799.103
    Default under   CC §§1812.2 to 1812.5
    Defined   CC §1802.6
    Delinquency charges under   CC §1803.6
    Delivery to buyer after full payment   CC §1806.4
    Discount buying services   CC §§1812.100 to 1812.129
    Insurance, statement as to   CC §1803.5
    Prohibited provisions   CC §§1804.1 to 1804.4
    Security interest agreements (See within this heading, **"Security interest agreements"**)
    Signature requirements   CC §1803.4
    Single document requirement for   CC §1803.2
    Subsequent purchases covered by   CC §§1808.1 to 1808.5
    Type size required for   CC §1803.1
    Venue of action on   CC §1812.10, CCP §396a
Cosigner's liability   CC §§1799.90 to 1799.103
Costs, provisions for recovering   CC §§1810.4, 1811.1
Credit balance, refund of   CC §1810.3
Credit cards (See **CREDIT CARDS**)
Credit reports (See **CREDIT REPORTING**)
Criminal liability   CC §1812.6
Damages
    Generally   CC §1812.9
    Denial of credit, failure to comply with notification requirements for   CC §1787.3
    Rate of interest as   CC §3289.5
Deferred payment   CC §§1802.21, 1807.1
Deficiency recovery   CC §1812.5
Definitions governing construction   CC §§1802.1 to 1802.21
Delinquency charges   CC §§1803.6, 1806.3, 1810.12
Delivery of goods and repair services requiring consumer's presence during specified 4-hour period, retailer's liability for failure of   CC §1722
Denial of credit, notice of   CC §1787.2
Discount buying services   CC §§1812.100 to 1812.129
Dishonored check or negotiable instrument, charge for   CC §1805.4
Down payment   CC §1803.3
Expenses of loan, finance charge including   CC §§1805.4, 1810.4
Extending time of loan   CC §§1807.1 to 1807.3
Extinguishing obligation under contract   CC §1806.1
Finance charge
    Add-on sales   CC §§1808.1 to 1808.5
    Advertisements clearly stating period rate   CC §1803.11
    Buyer's possession of goods   CC §§1805.6, 1810.10
    Consolidated payments   CC §1808.5
    Deferred payments, effect of   CC §1807.1
    Defined   CC §1802.10
    Dishonored check or negotiable instrument, charge for   CC §1805.4

RETAIL INSTALLMENT SALES—Cont.
Finance charge—Cont.
    Expenses of loan, inclusion of   CC §§1805.4, 1810.4
    Information furnished customer prior to sale   CC §1810.1
    Insurance contracts   CC §1805.8
    Maximum charge   CC §1810.2
    Notice to buyer   CC §§1803.2, 1810.3
    Permissible rates   CC §1805.1
    Precomputed basis   CC §§1799.8, 1802.21, 1803.2, 1803.3, 1805.1
        Waiver of protections   CC §1799.85
    Prepayment   CC §1806.3
    Preservation of goods or security interest   CC §1805.8
    Refinancing charge   CC §1807.2
    Repairs   CC §1805.8
    Request for statement of finance charges assessed during preceding year   CC §1810.11
    Several bases for   CC §1805.9
    Simple interest basis   CC §§1802.20, 1803.2, 1803.3, 1805.7
    Statutory violations affecting recovery of   CC §§1812.7, 1812.8
    360-day basis   CC §1802.20
    365-day basis   CC §§1802.20, 1803.3
Financing
    Particular source, designation of   CC §1812.20
    Third party loans   CC §§1801.6, 1801.7, 1803.9
Full payment before maturity, buyer's right to make   CC §1806.3
Future event, rebate based on happening of   CC §1803.10
Indemnity, seller's obligation to third-party lender   CC §1801.6
Industrial loan company, financing by   CC §1801.7
Inquiry by debtor, time for answering   CC §1720
Insurance
    Contract statement concerning   CC §1803.5
    Finance charge   CC §1805.8
    Requirements   CC §1803.5
    Separate charge, procedure for   CC §1810.5
Investment property pledged as collateral on consumer credit contract, restrictions concerning   CC §1799.103
Later purchasers   CC §§1808.1 to 1808.5
Layaway provisions, effect of   CC §1749.2
Liens, limitation on   CC §1804.3
Mail, sales by   CC §1803.8
Married women, credit accounts by   CC §§1812.30, 1812.31
Maximum finance charge   CC §1810.2
Membership camping contracts   CC §§1812.300 to 1812.309
Monthly statements, requirements for   CC §1810.3
Notes, defenses against holders of   CC §1810.7
Notices
    Generally   CC §§1799.90 to 1799.93, 1803.2
    Denial of credit, notice of   CC §1787.2
Out-of-state contracts   CC §§1802.19, 1803.10
Payment   CC §§1803.2, 1806.1 to 1806.4
Penalties for violating statute   CC §§1812.7, 1812.8
Prepayment   CC §§1803.2, 1806.3
Redemption of collateral   CC §1806.3
Referral fees for loan   CC §1801.6
Refinancing loan   CC §§1807.1 to 1807.3
Refund after full payment in advance   CC §§1803.2, 1806.3
Regulation Z
    Automobile conditional sales   CC §2981
    Defined   CC §1802.18
    Information conforming with   CC §1801.5
Religious materials as security interest   CC §1799.97
Rent-to-own transactions   CC §§1812.620 to 1812.650
Repair contracts   CC §1805.8
Reports of financial rating, regulation of   CC §§1785.1 to 1785.4
Repossessing goods   CC §§1806.3, 1812.2 to 1812.5
Rescission if buyer unable to obtain financing   CC §1803.9
Schedule of installments   CC §1805.2
Security interest agreements
    Generally   CC §§1803.2, 1810.6
    Home improvement contract with buyer over age 65, prohibition on provision for security interest in home in   CC §1804.1
    Religious materials as security interest   CC §1799.97
Ships   CC §1801.4
Single document, contract in   CC §1803.2
Small claims court, holder filing in   CCP §116.420
Spanish-language contracts   CC §1632
Statement of account mailed to customer   CC §1810.3
Subsequent purchases   CC §§1808.1 to 1808.5
Surrender of collateral   CC §1806.3
Telephone sales   CC §1803.8
Third party loans   CC §§1801.6, 1801.7, 1803.9

RETAIL INSTALLMENT SALES—Cont.
Time balance defined   CC §1802.12
Transfer of contracts (See within this heading, **"Assignments"**)
Truth in lending (See within this heading, **"Regulation äd;"**)
Unpaid balance
    Defined   CC §1802.11
    Statement furnished on request   CC §1806.2
Unruh act   CC §§1801 to 1802.20
Venue of actions on contract   CC §1812.10, CCP §396a
Vessels   CC §1801.4
Waiver of provisions   CC §1801.1

RETAIL MARIJUANA
Attorney-client privilege
    Advice as to conflict between state and federal law required to maintain privilege   Ev §956
Bureau of cannabis control
    Enforcement
        Limitation of actions to enforce licensing requirement   CCP §338
Commercial marijuana activity
    License required
        Limitation of actions to enforce licensing requirement   CCP §338
Contracts
    Commercial activity in relation to marijuana as lawful object of contract   CC §1550.5
Enforcement
    Limitation of actions to enforce licensing requirement   CCP §338
Licensing
    Medical information received by licensees from identification cards or physician recommendations
        Confidentiality of medical information, obligations   CC §56.06
    Requirement of license for commercial marijuana activity
        Penalties for unlicensed commercial cannabis activity, limitation of actions   CCP §338

RETAIL SALES
Costs in small business action   CCP §1028.5
Credit cards (See **CREDIT CARDS**)
Discounts (See **DISCOUNTS**)
Failure to deliver merchandise requiring consumer's presence during specified 4-hour period, liability for   CC §1722
Fraudulent inducement of independent retailers to join cooperative association providing wholesale goods and services to members, liability for   CC §3343.7
Gift certificates, prohibition against expiration dates on   CC §1749.5
Grey market goods, sale of (See **GREY MARKET GOODS**)
Grocery stores (See **GROCERY STORES**)
Installment sales (See **RETAIL INSTALLMENT SALES**)
Pricing, improper   CC §§7100 to 7106
Products liability (See **PRODUCTS LIABILITY**)
Refund policy of retailer, sign displaying   CC §1723
Sales tax reimbursement schedules   CC §1656.1
Stores (See **STORES AND STOREKEEPERS**)
Supermarkets (See **GROCERY STORES**)
Warranties (See **WARRANTIES**)

RETALIATORY DISCRIMINATION
Attorney professional conduct
    Prohibited discrimination, harassment and retaliation   ProfC 8.4.1
Consumer privacy rights
    Consumer exercise of rights   CC §1798.125
Courts
    Workplace conduct policies
        Courts' duties   CRC 10.351
Harassment
    Settlements
        Restrictions on nondisclosure agreements (NDAs) in certain cases   CCP §1001
Judicial administration rules
    Workplace conduct policies
        Courts' duties   CRC 10.351
Sex discrimination
    Settlements
        Restrictions on nondisclosure agreements (NDAs) in certain cases   CCP §1001
Sex offenses
    Future retaliation, threat of
        Statute of limitations on sexual assault damages   CCP §340.16

RETALIATORY EVICTION   CC §1942.5

RETARDATION (See **DEVELOPMENTALLY DISABLED PERSONS**)

RETIREMENT
Abandonment
    Escheat of retirement funds   CCP §§1513, 1518, Pro §6806
    Employee benefit plan distribution   CCP §§1501, 1521
Assignment for benefit of creditors, property exempt from   CCP §1801
Beneficiary under retirement plan, trustee named in will as   Pro §§6320 to 6330
Community property (See **COMMUNITY PROPERTY**)
Disclaimer of estate interest   Pro §§260 to 295
Dissolution of marriage
    Employee benefit plans (See **DISSOLUTION OF MARRIAGE**)
Earnings assignment for support (See **EARNINGS ASSIGNMENT FOR SUPPORT**)
Employee pension benefit plan defined   Fam §80
Employee Retirement Income Security Act (See **ERISA**)
Enforcement of judgment on retirement benefits (See **ENFORCEMENT OF JUDGMENTS**)
Escheat of retirement funds
    Generally   CCP §§1513, 1518, Pro §6806
    Employee benefit plan distribution   CCP §§1501, 1521
Estate tax liability on excess accumulations of retirement plans   Pro §§20114, 20114.5
Family law proceedings
    Joinder of pension and retirement systems   CRC 5.29
        Separate trial of termination of marriage or domestic partnership, joinder as prerequisite   CRC 5.390
Judges (See **JUDGES**)
Legislators (See **LEGISLATURE**)
Loans from public retirement systems, exemption from usury laws for   CC §1916.2
Marriage dissolution (See **DISSOLUTION OF MARRIAGE**)
Murder
    Attempting or soliciting murder of spouse
        Damages for injuries to married person   Fam §782.5
Nonprobate transfer provisions in retirement plans (See **NONPROBATE TRANSFERS**)
Power of attorney under statutory form, powers regarding retirement transactions under   Pro §4462
Public retirement system loans, exemption from usury laws for   CC §1916.2
Request for joinder, Judicial Council forms   CRCAppx A (CRCFL-372 to CRCFL-375)
Self-employed beneficiary as trustee named in will   Pro §§6320 to 6330
Trusts (See **TRUSTS**)
Usury law exemptions for pension funds (See **USURY**)

RETRACTION
Libel and slander   CC §48a

RETROACTIVE LAWS
Acknowledgments of instruments   CC §§1205, 1206
Artists consigning works to art dealers affected by   CC §1738.9
Civil Code   CC §3
Code of Civil Procedure   CCP §3
Eminent domain   CCP §§1230.065, 1230.070
Fine art, sale of   CC §§986, 1738.9
Leases, provisions governing   CC §1952.2
Uniform Single Publication Act   CC §3425.5
Uniform voidable transactions act   CC §3439.14

RETROACTIVE OPERATION
Child support proceedings (See **CHILD SUPPORT**)
Code of Civil Procedure   CCP §3
Spousal support orders   Fam §4333

RETROSPECTIVE LAWS (See **RETROACTIVE LAWS**)

RETURN OF PROPERTY
Duty for   CC §§1712, 1713

RETURN OF SUMMONS (See **PROCESS AND SERVICE OF PROCESS**)

REVERSAL OF JUDGMENT
Authority of Supreme Court and Courts of Appeal to affirm, reverse or modify judgment or order appealed from   CCP §43
Costs on appeal   CRC 8.278
Entering judgment of reviewing court in records of trial court   CCP §912
General powers of reviewing court   CCP §906
Restitution of rights on   CCP §908
Review by supreme court, decision of cause on   CRC 8.528
Statute of limitation, extension of   CCP §355

REVERSE MORTGAGES (See **TRUST DEEDS AND MORTGAGES**)

REVERSION
Action for injury to estate CC §826
Attornment on transfer of CC §1111
Definition CC §768
Power of termination, applicability of CC §885.015

REVIEW, WRIT OF CRC 8.720 to 8.730
Certiorari
    Writs of mandate, certiorari and prohibition in supreme court or court of appeal CRC 8.485 to 8.493
        Environmental quality act cases under public resources code CRC 8.703
Decisions
    Filing CRC 8.730
    Finality CRC 8.730
    Modification CRC 8.730
Miscellaneous writs CRC 8.720 to 8.730
    Agricultural Labor Relations Board
        Judicial review of cases CRC 8.728
    Decisions CRC 8.730
    Environmental quality act cases under public resources code CRC 8.703
    Public Utilities Commission cases CRC 8.724
    Remittitur CRC 8.730
    Workers compensation appeals board cases, review of CRC 8.720
Remittitur CRC 8.730
Small claims courts
    Petition for extraordinary relief relating to act of small claims division CCP §116.798

REVISED UNIFORM FIDUCIARY ACCESS TO DIGITAL ASSETS ACT
Pro §§870 to 884 (See **FIDUCIARY ACCESS TO DIGITAL ASSETS**)

REVOCABLE TRANSFER ON DEATH DEEDS Pro §§5600 to 5698 (See **TRANSFER ON DEATH DEEDS**)

REVOCABLE TRUSTS (See **TRUSTS**)

REVOCATION
Administrators (See **EXECUTORS AND ADMINISTRATORS**)
Adoption (See **ADOPTION**)
Agency CC §2356
Conservator's letters (See **CONSERVATORS**)
Contract offer CC §§1586, 1587
Executors (See **EXECUTORS AND ADMINISTRATORS**)
Gifts CC §1148
Guardian's letters (See **GUARDIAN AND WARD**)
Independent Administration of Estates Act, revoking authority for continued administration under Pro §10454
Letters of administration (See **EXECUTORS AND ADMINISTRATORS**)
Notaries public, registration of Fam §535
Orders made on subsequent application CCP §1008
Personal representative's letters (See **EXECUTORS AND ADMINISTRATORS**)
Power of attorney (See **POWER OF ATTORNEY**)
Premarital agreements Fam §1614
Probate referees, revocation of authority of (See **PROBATE REFEREES**)
Summary dissolution of marriage, revocation of joint petition for Fam §§2342, 2401
Trusts (See **TRUSTS**)
Wills (See **WILLS**)

REVOLVERS (See **FIREARMS AND OTHER WEAPONS**)

RICE
Storage regulations after sale of CC §§1880 to 1881.2

RIGHT OF SURVIVORSHIP
Joint tenancy (See **JOINT TENANCY**)
Multiple-party accounts Pro §§5301 to 5306

RIGHT OF WAY (See **EASEMENTS**)

RIGHTS OF ACCUSED
Appeal rights, notification of CRC 4.305, 4.306

RIGHT TO COUNSEL
Appointment of counsel
    Indigent criminal appellants in supreme court, payment guidelines
        Habeas corpus proceedings CRCSupp PayGuideAppoint

RIGHT TO DIE
Advance health care directives Pro §§4670 to 4679

RIGHT TO PRIVACY (See **INVASION OF PRIVACY**)

RIPARIAN RIGHTS (See **WATERS**)

RIVERS AND STREAMS
Appropriation (See **WATERS**)
Appurtenances CC §662
Boundary, center of stream as CCP 2077
Declaratory judgments determining natural flow of CCP §1060
Easement rights to flow of water over land CC §801
Easements
    Greenway easements generally CC §§816.50 to 816.66 (See **GREENWAY EASEMENTS**)
Flooding (See **FLOODS**)
Greenway easements generally CC §§816.50 to 816.66 (See **GREENWAY EASEMENTS**)
Injunction to prevent diversion of water CCP §§530, 532, 534
Ownership of CC §670
Title
    Accretion CC §§1014 to 1017
    Border land CC §830
    Erosion CC §1015
    Islands CC §§1016 to 1018
    Nonnavigable streams CCP §2077
    Reclaiming land carried away by flooding CC §1015
    State CC §670
Venue in action for recovery of penalty imposed for offense committed on CCP §393

RIVERSIDE COUNTY
Senior citizen housing requirements CC §§51.10 to 51.12

ROADS (See **STREETS AND HIGHWAYS**)

ROBES
Judges' robes CRC 10.505

ROCKS
Owner's liability for recreational land used for rock collecting CC §846
Real property, part of CC §659

ROOFING WARRANTIES
Duration or warranty, disclosure requirements for CC §1797.93
New homes CC §1797.95
Residences subject to warranty law CC §1797.90
Standardized warranties for multistate use CC §1797.94
Subsequent purchaser, enforceability by CC §§1797.92, 1797.94
Writing requirement CC §1797.91

ROOMS
Tenant's possession of room rented CC §1950

ROSENTHAL FAIR DEBT COLLECTION PRACTICES ACT CC §§1788 to 1788.32

ROSENTHAL-ROBERTI ITEM PRICING ACT CC §§7100 to 7106

ROYALTIES
Artists CC §986
Judgment debtor, assignment of right to payment due CCP §§708.510 to 708.560
Sound recordings
    Audits of royalty reporting parties CC §§2500, 2501

RUBBISH (See **GARBAGE**)

RULE AGAINST PERPETUITIES (See **PERPETUITIES AND RESTRAINTS ON ALIENATION**)

RULE, PUTTING WITNESSES UNDER Ev §777

RULES
Coordination of actions CCP §404.7
Small claims court (See **SMALL CLAIMS COURTS**)
State agencies, rules and regulations of (See **ADMINISTRATIVE PROCEDURE ACT**)

RULES OF COURT
Appearance
    Remote appearances, technology use
        COVID-19, emergency rule CRCAppx I Emer Rule 3

RULES OF COURT—Cont.
  Appearance—Cont.
    Remote appearances, technology use—Cont.
      Service requirements
        Restraining orders   CRC 3.1162, 5.496
  Appellate rules   CRC 8.1 to 8.1125
    Contents of rules   CRC 1.4
    Superior court appellate division proceedings   CRC 8.800 to 8.936 (See **APPELLATE RULES, SUPERIOR COURT APPEALS**)
    Supreme court and courts of appeal   CRC 8.1 to 8.642 (See **APPELLATE RULES, SUPREME COURT AND COURTS OF APPEAL**)
  Appendices
    Contents of rules of court   CRC 1.4
  Arbitration
    Ethics standards for neutral arbitrators in contract arbitrations
      Contents of rules of court   CRC 1.4
  Attorneys
    Generally (See **ATTORNEYS**)
    Law practice and judges, rules relating to   CRC 9.0 to 9.90
  Authority for rules   CRC 1.3
  Bail (See **BAIL**)
  Bluebook citations   CRC 1.200
  California Style Manual
    Citations, format   CRC 1.200
  Citations
    Format   CRC 1.200
  Civil rules
    Contents of rules   CRC 1.4
    Generally   CRC 3.1 to 3.2240
  Clerk (See **CLERKS OF COURT**)
  Construction of rules and standards   CRC 1.5
  Contents of rules   CRC 1.4
  Coordination proceedings (See **COORDINATION OF ACTIONS**)
  Coronavirus
    Emergency rules related to COVID-19   CRCAppx I Emer Rules 1 to 13
  Courts of Appeal, rules on appeal to
    Supreme court and courts of appeal   CRC 8.1 to 8.642 (See **APPELLATE RULES, SUPREME COURT AND COURTS OF APPEAL**)
  COVID-19
    Emergency rules related to COVID-19   CRCAppx I Emer Rules 1 to 13
  Criminal rules
    Appellate rules, supreme court and courts of appeal   CRC 8.300 to 8.398
    Contents of rules   CRC 1.4
    Generally   CRC 4.1 to 4.601 (See **CRIMINAL RULES**)
  Definitions   CRC 1.6
  Dependent child proceedings
    Juvenile rules generally   CRC 5.500 to 5.840
  Disabled or handicapped persons
    Accommodation by courts of persons with disability   CRC 1.100
  Dismissal (See **DISMISSAL**)
  Dissolution of marriage (See **FAMILY RULES**)
  Family and juvenile rules
    Contents of rules   CRC 1.4
    Generally   CRC 5.1 to 5.500 (See **FAMILY RULES**)
  Filing
    Determining when document filed   CRC 1.20
    Mandatory forms
      Acceptance for filing   CRC 1.31
    Optional forms
      Acceptance for filing   CRC 1.35
    Privacy protection   CRC 1.201
      Appellate rules, supreme court and courts of appeal   CRC 8.41
  Forms
    Applicability of provisions   CRC 1.30
    Cause of action forms   CRC 1.45
    Electronic production   CRC 1.44
    Judicial council forms   CRC 1.30 to 1.45
      Listing   CRCAppx A
    Legibility   CRC 1.43
    Mandatory forms   CRC 1.30
      Alteration for form   CRC 1.31
      Colored forms   CRC 1.31
      Effect of mandatory status   CRC 1.31
      Identification   CRC 1.31
      List   CRC 1.31
      Orders not on mandatory form   CRC 1.31
    Optional forms   CRC 1.30
      Acceptance for filing   CRC 1.35
      Alteration of form   CRC 1.35
      Colored forms   CRC 1.35
      Identification   CRC 1.35

RULES OF COURT—Cont.
  Forms—Cont.
    Optional forms—Cont.
      List   CRC 1.35
      Use   CRC 1.35
    Pleading forms   CRC 1.45
    Proof of service on form   CRC 1.41
    Rejection of form
      Prohibited reasons for rejection   CRC 1.42
    Statutory references on forms   CRC 1.40
  Gender
    Construction of additional terms   CRC 1.5
  Holidays
    Computation of time   CRC 1.10
    Judicial holiday falling on Saturday or Sunday   CRC 1.11
  Judges, censure, removal or admonishment of (See **JUDGES**)
  Judicial administration rules
    Contents of rules   CRC 1.4
    Generally   CRC 10.1 to 10.1108
  Judicial administration standards
    Contents of rules   CRC 1.4
    Generally   CRC JudAdminStand 2.1 to CRC JudAdminStand 10.80 (See **JUDICIAL ADMINISTRATION STANDARDS**)
  Judicial arbitration (See **JUDICIAL ARBITRATION**)
  Judicial council
    Generally   CRC 10.1 to 10.81 (See **JUDICIAL COUNCIL**)
  Judicial notice of   Ev §§451, 452
  Juvenile rules
    Generally   CRC 5.500 to 5.840
  Language access services   CRC 1.300
  Law and motion proceedings (See **LAW AND MOTION PROCEEDINGS**)
  Local rules of court (See **LOCAL RULES OF COURT**)
  May
    Construction of terminology   CRC 1.5
  May not
    Construction of terminology   CRC 1.5
  Media coverage of court proceedings   CRC 1.150
  Minors
    Damages, imputed liability for willful misconduct of minor
      Calculations   CRCAppx B
    Psychiatric residential treatment facilities
      Voluntary admission   CRC 5.619
  Must
    Construction of terminology   CRC 1.5
  Newspapers
    Media coverage of court proceedings   CRC 1.150
  Number
    Construction of additional terms   CRC 1.5
  Photographs
    Media coverage of court proceedings   CRC 1.150
  Plural
    Construction of additional terms   CRC 1.5
  Probate rules   CRC 7.1 to 7.1105
    Contents of rules   CRC 1.4
  Psychiatric residential treatment facilities
    Children and minors
      Voluntary admission   CRC 5.619
  Public health emergencies
    COVID-19
      Emergency rules related to COVID-19   CRCAppx I Emer Rules 1 to 13
  Radio
    Media coverage of court proceedings   CRC 1.150
  Remote appearances
    Service requirements
      Restraining orders   CRC 3.1162, 5.496
    Technology use for remote appearances
      COVID-19, emergency rule   CRCAppx I Emer Rule 3
  Rules applicable to all courts   CRC 1.1 to 1.201
  Rules on appeal
    Appellate rules   CRC 8.1 to 8.1125
      Contents of rules   CRC 1.4
      Superior court appellate division proceedings   CRC 8.800 to 8.936 (See **APPELLATE RULES, SUPERIOR COURT APPEALS**)
      Supreme court and courts of appeal   CRC 8.1 to 8.642 (See **APPELLATE RULES, SUPREME COURT AND COURTS OF APPEAL**)
  Sanctions for noncompliance
    Media coverage of court proceedings, restrictions   CRC 1.150
    Trial court rules
      Civil cases   CRC 2.30

RULES — INDEX

RULES OF COURT—Cont.
Saturdays
    Computation of time   CRC 1.10
    Judicial holiday falling on Saturday or Sunday   CRC 1.11
Schedules (See **SCHEDULES**)
Sentencing rules for superior courts (See **SENTENCE AND PUNISHMENT**)
Service
    Attorney to be served   CRC 1.21
    Proof of service   CRC 1.21
Should
    Construction of terminology   CRC 1.5
Singular
    Construction of additional terms   CRC 1.5
Standards
    Construction of terminology   CRC 1.5
Sundays
    Computation of time   CRC 1.10
    Judicial holiday falling on Saturday or Sunday   CRC 1.11
Superior court cases
    Appellate rules   CRC 8.800 to 8.936 (See **APPELLATE RULES, SUPERIOR COURT APPEALS**)
    Sentencing rules (See **SENTENCE AND PUNISHMENT**)
    Trial rules (See **SUPERIOR COURTS**)
Supreme court
    Appellate rules   CRC 8.1 to 8.642 (See **APPELLATE RULES, SUPREME COURT AND COURTS OF APPEAL**)
    Authority to adopt rules   CRC 1.3
    Capital punishment (See **CAPITAL PUNISHMENT**)
Television
    Media coverage of court proceedings   CRC 1.150
Tenses
    Construction of additional terms   CRC 1.5
Time
    Computation of time   CRC 1.10
    Extending or shortening   CRC 1.10
        Trial court rules   CRC 2.20
Title of rules   CRC 1.1, 1.2
Traffic violations (See **TRAFFIC VIOLATIONS**)
Trial (See **TRIAL**)
Trial court rules
    Contents of rules   CRC 1.4
    Generally   CRC 2.1 to 2.1100
Venue (See **VENUE**)
Vessels (See **VESSELS**)
Will
    Construction of terminology   CRC 1.5

RULES OF PROFESSIONAL CONDUCT   ProfC 1.0 to 8.5 (See **ATTORNEY PROFESSIONAL CONDUCT**)

RULES OF THE ROAD (See **TRAFFIC REGULATIONS AND VIOLATIONS**)

RULINGS OF COURT
Court reporters to take down all   CCP §269

S

SACRAMENTO
Downtown arena
    Petitions under environmental quality act, civil rules governing
        Sacramento downtown arena project, CEQA challenges   CRC 3.2220 to 3.2240
Small estates escheating, giving notice for   CCP §1415

SACRAMENTO AND SAN JOAQUIN DRAINAGE DISTRICT
Eminent domain taking by   CCP §1245.210

SACRAMENTO COUNTY
Change of venue of actions by or against state   CCP §401
Unlawful detainer actions
    Controlled substances as nuisance
        Pilot program   CC §3486.5
    Firearms or weapons as nuisances
        Applicability of provisions   CC §3485
Venue of actions by or against state   CCP §401

SAFE AT HOME PROGRAM
Common interest developments
    Record inspection
        Duties of association concerning safe at home program participants   CC §5216

SAFE AT HOME PROGRAM—Cont.
Confidentiality for victims of certain crimes
    Actions, confidentiality requirements for protected persons in civil proceeding   CCP §367.3
        Judicial council forms   CRCAppx A

SAFE BODY ART ACT
Minors
    Verification of age for sale of age-restricted products   CC §1798.99.1

SAFES
Innkeeper's liability limited to articles kept in   CC §1860
Serial number altered or destroyed prior to sale   CC §1710.1

SAFETY DEPOSIT BOXES
Attachment of property in   CCP §§488.460, 488.465
Conservator's taking possession of assets of conservatee held by financial institutions   Pro §§2890 to 2893
    Opening or changing name on account, responsibilities of conservator   CRC 7.1061
Enforcement of judgments
    General method of levy on property in box   CCP §700.150
Escheat   CCP §§1514, 1532.1
Funeral instructions, access for removal of   Pro §331
Guardian's taking possession of assets of ward held by financial institutions   Pro §§2890 to 2893
    Opening or changing name on accounts, responsibilities of guardian   CRC 7.1011
Joint tenancy in   CC §683.1
Notice
    Escheat of property   CCP §1514
Opening
    Sheriff's fees   Gov §26723
Public administrators, right to access by   Pro §7603
Sheriffs
    Opening
        Fees for opening   Gov §26723
Trust instruments, access for removal of   Pro §331
Unclaimed contents of   CCP §§1514, 1532.1
Will instruments, access for removal of   Pro §331

SAFE WORKING PLACE
Medical information on job-related accidents   CC §56.26
Violence toward employee, employer's action to prevent   CCP §527.8, CRC 3.1160
    Address or location of complaining party or family, prohibition on enjoined party from obtaining   CCP §527.10
    California law enforcement telecommunications (CLETS) information form, confidentiality and use of information   CRC 1.51, CRCAppx A
    COVID-19, emergency rule   CRCAppx I Emer Rule 8
    Firearm relinquishment and disposition   CCP §527.9
        Forms for firearm relinquishment   CRCAppx A
    Judicial council legal forms   CRCAppx A
    Memorandum in support of petition for order not required   CRC 3.1114
    Requests for protective orders   CRC 3.1160

SALARIES AND WAGES
Agricultural labor, liens securing wages for   CC §§3061.5, 3061.6
Assignment of wages
    Generally (See **ASSIGNMENT OF WAGES**)
    Support orders, enforcement of (See **EARNINGS ASSIGNMENT FOR SUPPORT**)
Assignment of wages, family support forms   CRCAppxs A (CRCFL-430), (CRCFL-435), (CRCFL-455)
Attachment of (See **ATTACHMENT**)
Attorneys' fees in action for wages for labor performed   CCP §1031
Braceros
    Actions to recover savings fund amounts withheld from wages   CCP §354.7
Bulk sales, preferred liens on   CCP §1205
Child's earnings (See **PARENT AND CHILD**)
Child stars, establishing trust funds or savings plans for   Fam §§6752, 6753
Child support payments (See **CHILD SUPPORT**)
Conservatee, assignment of wages for support of   Pro §3088
Court operations costs, list of court personnel included in   CRC 10.810
Creditor considering   CC §1812.30
Damages
    Measure of damages for lost earnings or impaired earning capacity
        Race, ethnicity or gender not to serve as basis for reduction in damages   CC §3361

SALARIES AND WAGES—Cont.
Deductions from wages
  Transportation costs for transporting immigrant to US
    Void contracts   CC §1670.7
Enforcement of judgments (See **ENFORCEMENT OF JUDGMENTS**)
Fees (See **FEES**)
Form for lien securing wages   CC §§3061.5, 3061.6
Garnishment (See **GARNISHMENT**)
Guardianship (See **GUARDIAN AND WARD**)
Immigrants
  Deductions from wages for costs of transport to US
    Void contracts   CC §1670.7
Judgment debtors
  Assignment of right to payment due   CCP §§708.510 to 708.560
Judgments, enforcement by labor commissioner   CCP §§690.020 to 690.050
  Jurisdiction in superior court   CCP §690.020
  Levy on property
    Exemptions of debtor   CCP §690.040
    Performance by commissioner of duties of levying officer   CCP §690.050
    Third party claims   CCP §690.040
  Remedies available to commissioner to enforce   CCP §690.030
  Venue   CCP §690.030
Jury commissioner   CCP §195
Liens
  Generally   CC §3051, CCP §§1204 to 1208
  Farm workers   CC §§3061.5, 3061.6
  Garnishment (See **GARNISHMENT**)
Minor's earnings (See **PARENT AND CHILD**)
Mortgage foreclosure consultants, prohibition against assignment of wages by   CC §2945.4
Payment of wages
  Judgment for nonpayment, labor commissioner enforcement   CCP §§690.020 to 690.050
Personal services, preference for liens covering   CCP §1206
Preference to wage claims   CCP §§1204 to 1208
Small estates without administration (See **SMALL ESTATES WITHOUT ADMINISTRATION**)
Spousal support (See **SPOUSAL SUPPORT**)
Spousal support, assignments of wages forms   CRCAppxs A (CRCFL-430), (CRCFL-435)
Support of children (See **CHILD SUPPORT**)
Unclaimed deposits and payments
  Escheat   CCP §1513
Wage claims
  Attachment
    Priorities and preferences   CCP §§1206 to 1208
  Conservators
    Payment of wage claims   Pro §2431
    Definitions   Pro §11402
  Garnishment
    Distribution when levy less than wage claims   CCP §1208
    Preference to wage claims   CCP §1206
    Verified denial of wage claim   CCP §1207
  Guardianships
    Payment of wage claims   Pro §2431
  Priorities   CCP §§1204, 1204.5
  Receivers and receiverships   CCP §1204
  Small claims courts
    Costs of suit   CCP §1031

SALE OF GOODS
Delivery of goods
  Financing agency's rights respecting   UCC §2506
Financing agency, rights of   UCC §2506
Online marketplaces   CC §§1749.8 to 1749.8.9

SALE OF REALTY (See also **VENDOR AND PURCHASER**)
Buyer's choice act   CC §§1103.20 to 1103.22
  Escrow agents
    Choice of escrow agent lies with buyer   CC §1103.22
    Legislative findings and intent   CC §1103.21
    Short title   CC §1103.20
  Title insurers
    Choice of insurer lies with buyer   CC §1103.22
Contracts for sale of realty
  Generally   CC §§2985 to 2985.6 (See **REAL PROPERTY SALES CONTRACTS**)
Deferred sale of family home, request of custodial parent for   Fam §§3800 to 3810

SALE OF REALTY—Cont.
Foreclosure sales
  Residential property obtained at foreclosure sale
    Managing and maintaining vacant property   CC §2929.3
Judgment lien on real property, effect on   CCP §697.390
Judicial officer's power to take and certify proof and acknowledgment of conveyance   CCP §179
Karnette Rental-Purchase Act for rental-purchase contracts   CC §§1812.620 to 1812.650
Notice of pendency of action (See **PENDENCY OF ACTIONS**)
Rental-purchase contracts, Karnette Rental-Purchase Act for   CC §§1812.620 to 1812.650
Sheriff, conveyances on sale of real estate by   CCP §262.4
Text message or instant message format communications, insufficiency to constitute contract to convey realty   CC §1624

SALES
Abandoned property of tenant, landlord selling   CC §1988
Administration of estates (See **ADMINISTRATION OF ESTATES**)
Aerosol paint containers
  Verification of age for sale of age-restricted products   CC §1798.99.1
Aircraft liens, satisfaction of   CCP §§1208.65 to 1208.68
Artworks, residual rights of artist in   CC §986
"As is" sales   CC §§1790 to 1795.8
Attachment (See **ATTACHMENT**)
Auctions (See **AUCTIONS**)
Autographed memorabilia, sale   CC §1739.7
Automobile manufacturers, transporters, dealers and sales professionals
  Restitution, licensee ordered to pay
    Effect of order for restitution   Gov §11519.1
Automobiles (See **AUTOMOBILES**)
Bill of sale (See **BILL OF SALE**)
Birth name use   CCP §1279.6
Bonds, procedure for validation of authorization, issuance, sale or exchange of   CCP §349.4
Bulk sales (See **BULK SALES**)
Catalogs (See **MAIL ORDER SALES**)
Child support, sale of assets deposited to secure future payment   Fam §§4616, 4630 to 4632
Clubs for periodic sale   CC §§1584.5, 1584.6
Commingling of goods   CC §1497
Community property (See **COMMUNITY PROPERTY**)
Conditional sales (See **CONDITIONAL SALES**)
Confession of judgments for debts arising from   CCP §1132
Conservators (See **CONSERVATORS**)
Consumer protection (See **CONSUMER PROTECTION**)
Credit cards (See **CREDIT CARDS**)
Damages (See **DAMAGES**)
Delivery of merchandise purchased under retail sales contract within specified 4-hour period   CC §1722
Delivery requirements   CC §1496
Deposits (See **DEPOSITS**)
Discount buying services   CC §§1812.100 to 1812.129
Door-to-door sales (See **HOME SOLICITATION SALES CONTRACTS**)
Electronic commercial services (See **ELECTRONIC COMMERCIAL SERVICES**)
Enforcement of judgments (See **ENFORCEMENT OF JUDGMENTS**)
Factors, sale of property by   CC §§2027 to 2030
Family use, warranty of goods sold for   CC §§1790 to 1795.8
Felon's story, trust established for proceeds from sale of   CC §2225
Fine prints, regulating sale of   CC §§1740 to 1745.5
Fitness warranty   CC §1791.1
Grey market goods (See **GREY MARKET GOODS**)
Guardianship (See **GUARDIAN AND WARD**)
Home solicitation sales contracts (See **HOME SOLICITATION SALES CONTRACTS**)
Homesteads, sale of (See **HOMESTEADS**)
Independent Administration of Estates Act, sale of property under (See **INDEPENDENT ADMINISTRATION OF ESTATES ACT**)
Innkeeper's lien   CC §§1861.19, 1861.24
Installments (See **RETAIL INSTALLMENT SALES**)
Judicial sales (See **ENFORCEMENT OF JUDGMENTS**)
Landlord and tenant
  Commercial real property tenancies
    Disposition of property remaining upon termination, public sale   CC §1993.07
Liens (See **LIENS**)
Livestock service liens, sale under   CC §§3080.02 to 3080.22
Lost property not claimed   CC §§2080.4 to 2080.8
Mail order sales (See **MAIL ORDER SALES**)

SALES — INDEX

SALES—Cont.
Marketplace sales and sellers
    Commercial relationships, terms and conditions   CC §1749.7
Membership camping contracts   CC §§1812.300 to 1812.309
Merchandise sales by clubs   CC §§1584.5, 1584.6
Merchantability, warranty of   CC §1791.1
Mining machinery   CC §1631
Mixing of goods   CC §1497
Mobilehomes (See **MOBILEHOMES**)
Nonconforming goods, notice of   CC §1793.1
Order of sale
    Superior court fees, specified services   Gov §70626
Paintings, resale of   CC §986
Partition (See **PARTITION**)
Periodic ordering of merchandise   CC §§1584.5, 1584.6
Political items   CC §§1739 to 1739.4
Products liability (See **PRODUCTS LIABILITY**)
Real property (See **SALE OF REALTY; VENDOR AND PURCHASER**)
Receivers selling personal property   CCP §568.5
Rental-purchase contracts, Karnette Rental-Purchase Act   CC §§1812.620 to 1812.650
Repairs for goods sold under warranty   CC §§1793.1 to 1795.8
Retail installment sales (See **RETAIL INSTALLMENT SALES**)
Serial number destroyed or altered prior to   CC §1710.1
Social security numbers
    Prohibition of sale, advertising for sale or offering for sale of number of another   CC §1798.85
Spray paint containers
    Verification of age for sale of age-restricted products   CC §1798.99.1
Stay of proceedings pending appeal   CCP §§917.2, 917.4
Tax (See **SALES AND USE TAX**)
Trust deeds (See **TRUST DEEDS AND MORTGAGES**)
Trusts (See **TRUSTS**)
Unclaimed property (See **UNCLAIMED PROPERTY**)
Unsolicited goods   CC §§1584.5, 1584.6
Warranties (See **WARRANTIES**)
Wholesale sales representatives (See **WHOLESALE SALES REPRESENTATIVES**)

SALES AND USE TAX
Automobile sales warranties, manufacturer's reimbursement for sales or use tax refunded to new buyer for restitution under   CC §1793.25
Decedent's estate, tax claims against   Pro §§9200 to 9205
Schedules for reimbursement of retail sales tax   CC §1656.1

SAME SEX MARRIAGE BAN
Recognition of certain same sex marriages contracted in other jurisdictions
    Dissolution, annulment or legal separation of recognized same sex marriages, jurisdiction   Fam §2010
        Residence requirements   Fam §2320
Repeal   Fam §300

SANCTIONS
Administrative adjudication (See **ADMINISTRATIVE ADJUDICATION**)
Appeal as frivolous action or tactic, sanction based on   CCP §907, CRC 8.276
Appeal of sanction orders or judgments   CCP §904.1
Appellate rules, superior court appeals   CRC 8.891
    Infraction case appeals
        Record on appeal, failure to procure   CRC 8.924
    Limited civil cases in appellate division
        Record on appeal, failure to procure   CRC 8.842
    Misdemeanor appeals
        Record on appeal, failure to procure   CRC 8.874
Appellate rules, supreme court and courts of appeal
    Briefs
        Failure to file brief   CRC 8.220
    Certiorari, mandate and prohibition   CRC 8.492
    Frivolous actions or tactics   CRC 8.276
        Criminal appeals   CRC 8.366
    Grounds for sanctions   CRC 8.276
        Criminal appeals   CRC 8.366
    Procedure   CRC 8.276
        Criminal appeals   CRC 8.366
    Record on appeal
        Failure of party to procure   CRC 8.140
Bad faith actions (See within this heading, "**Frivolous actions or delaying tactics**")
Case questionnaires under economic litigation provisions for limited civil cases, failure to answer or obey order compelling response to   CCP §93
Child abuse or neglect, false accusations of   Fam §3027.1

SANCTIONS—Cont.
Child support, incomplete and inaccurate income and expense declarations
    Fam §3667
Delay, appeal taken for purposes of   CRC 8.276
Discovery abuse (See **DISCOVERY ABUSES, SANCTIONS FOR**)
Environmental quality act
    Petitions under environmental quality act, civil rules governing
        Jobs and economic improvement through environmental leadership act of 2021   CRC 3.2221
Family law proceedings   CRC 5.14
    Award of attorney's fees and costs as   Fam §271
Frivolous actions or delaying tactics
    Generally   CCP §128.7
    Administrative adjudicative proceeding, expenses awarded in   Gov §11455.30
    Costs on appeal, award of   CCP §907, CRC 8.276
        Criminal appeals   CRC 8.366
    Defined   CCP §128.5
    Reconsideration motions   CCP §1008
Judicial officer's power to impose money sanctions for violations of lawful court orders   CCP §177.5
Judicial performance, commission on
    Censure, etc of judge (See **JUDICIAL PERFORMANCE, COMMISSION ON**)
Jury summons
    Failure to respond to summons   CCP §209
Local rules of court, noncompliance with   CCP §575.2
Media coverage of court proceedings, violations of restrictions on   CRC 1.150
Small claims court judgment, sanctions for failure to disclose assets for purposes of enforcement of   CCP §116.830
Summary judgment motion support or opposition presented in bad faith or solely for purposes of delay   CCP §437c
Television and radio coverage of court proceedings, violations of restrictions on   CRC 1.150
Unreasonable contact with juror   CCP §206

SAN DIEGO COUNTY
Appellate rules, supreme court and courts of appeal
    Juvenile case appeals   CRC 8.416
Cedar fire
    Reconstruction contracts
        Construction defects actions, incorporation of statutory provisions in contracts   CC §945.6

SAN FRANCISCO BAY CONSERVATION AND DEVELOPMENT COMMISSION
Attorney general, civil actions to enforce provisions
    Fees and costs for attorney general   CCP §1021.8
Floating homes   CC §800.306
Review of regulatory provisions and administrative record of proceeding   Gov §11354.1
Vendor and purchaser
    Disclosures in conjunction with real property transactions
        Jurisdiction of commission   CC §1103.4

SAN FRANCISCO, CITY AND COUNTY OF
Jurors
    Low-income jurors
        San Francisco low-income juror pilot program   CCP §240
Rent control
    Temporary displacement of tenant household
        Compensation levels   CC §1947.9
Small claims court pilot project, participation in   CCP §116.232
Small estates, giving notice of escheat of   CCP §1415

SANITARIUMS (See **MENTAL HOSPITALS**)

SAN MATEO COUNTY
Family law pilot projects (See **FAMILY LAW PILOT PROJECTS**)

SANTA CLARA COUNTY
Family law pilot projects (See **FAMILY LAW PILOT PROJECTS**)

SARGENT SHRIVER CIVIL COUNSEL ACT   Gov §§68650, 68651

SATELLITE TELEVISION
Commercial and industrial common interest developments
    Dishes, protected uses   CC §6708

SATISFACTION
Accord and satisfaction (See **ACCORD AND SATISFACTION**)
Judgment, satisfaction of (See **SATISFACTION OF JUDGMENTS**)

SATISFACTION OF JUDGMENTS
Generally   CCP §724.010
Acknowledgment
   Generally   CCP §724.030
   Abstract of judgment, obligation for acknowledgment upon recording of   CCP §724.040
   Assignment of judgment, effect of filing acknowledgment of   CC §954.5
   Attorneys' fees, recoverability of   CCP §724.080
   Conditions for acknowledgment, liability of creditor establishing   CCP §724.070
   Contents of   CCP §724.060
   Damages recovered, effect on entitlement to other damages where   CCP §724.090
   Installment judgment, acknowledgment of satisfaction of matured installments under   CCP §§724.210 to 724.260
   Judgment lien on personal property, acknowledgment of satisfaction of   CCP §697.640
   Judgment lien on real property released upon recording   CCP §697.400
   Matured installments under installment judgment, acknowledgment of satisfaction of   CCP §§724.210 to 724.260
   Partial satisfaction, acknowledgment of   CCP §§724.110, 724.120
   Written demand for   CCP §724.050
Alcoholic beverage license applied to satisfaction of judgment, receivers appointed where   CCP §708.630
Appeals
   Payment in satisfaction of money judgment
      Effect of payment on right to appeal   CCP §695.215
Attorney's fees
   Acknowledgment of satisfaction, proceedings for   CCP §724.080
   Matured installments under installment judgment, acknowledgment of satisfaction of   CCP §724.260
Certificate of satisfaction, issuance and contents of   CCP §724.100
Child support judgments, crediting of money received pursuant to   CCP §695.221
Conditions on acknowledgment of satisfaction, liability of creditor establishing   CCP §724.070
Crediting of money received, priorities for   CCP §§695.220, 695.221
Earnings withholding order, termination of   CCP §706.027
Entry of satisfaction of money judgment   CCP §724.020
Fees for issuance of writ
   Superior court fees, specified services   Gov §70626
Judicial officer's power to take and certify acknowledgment of   CCP §179
Limited liability companies
   Satisfaction by order charging interest in   CCP §§708.310, 708.320
Marital status of judgment debtors affecting applicability of exemptions   CCP §703.110
Matured installments under installment judgment, acknowledgment of satisfaction of   CCP §§724.210 to 724.260
Partial satisfaction, acknowledgment of   CCP §§724.110, 724.120
Partnership, satisfaction by order charging interest in   CCP §§708.310, 708.320
Payment in satisfaction of money judgment
   Effect on right to appeal   CCP §695.215
Person indebted to judgment debtor, satisfaction by   CCP §699.020
Preferences and priorities for crediting money received in satisfaction of money judgment   CCP §§695.220, 695.221
Redemption action   CCP §729.080
Small claims court (See **SMALL CLAIMS COURTS**)
Surety bond withdrawn for   CCP §995.430

SATURDAYS
As holidays for purpose of computing time   CCP §12a
Banks, holidays on Saturdays affecting   CC §9
Discovery, effect on time limits for   CCP §2016.060
Judicial holidays falling on   CCP §135
   Rules of court   CRC 1.11
Performance of act required by law   CCP §13b
Rules of court
   Computation of time   CRC 1.10
   Judicial holiday falling on Saturday or Sunday   CRC 1.11
Small claims court sessions   CCP §§116.250, 134

SAVINGS AND LOAN ASSOCIATIONS
Conservators
   Opening or changing name on conservatee's account, responsibilities of conservator   CRC 7.1061
Guardians and conservators
   Opening or changing name on accounts, responsibilities of guardian   CRC 7.1011
Joint tenancy accounts
   Excess withdrawal by party
      Claim for recovery   Pro §5301

SAVINGS AND LOAN ASSOCIATIONS—Cont.
Joint tenancy accounts—Cont.
   Excess withdrawal by party —Cont.
      Proportional ownership interest in other parties   Pro §5301

SAVINGS AND LOANS
Attachment (See **ATTACHMENT**)
Blocked accounts (See **BLOCKED ACCOUNTS**)
Business oversight commissioner, superior court hearings on sale of association properties in possession of   CCP §§73c, 73d
Conservatorship (See **CONSERVATORS**)
Creditors, deposit of money due   CC §1500
Decedents' estates, sale of shares held by   Pro §10200
Deposits
   Attachment (See **ATTACHMENT**)
   Blocked accounts (See **BLOCKED ACCOUNTS**)
   Child stars, savings plans for   Fam §§6752, 6753
   Child support security deposits   CC §710
   Decedents' estates, funds of   Pro §§8401, 9700 to 9705
   Definitions   Pro §§23, 46
   Gifts of deposit to minors (See **UNIFORM TRANSFERS TO MINORS ACT**)
   Lien on   CC §3054
   Multiple-party accounts (See **MULTIPLE-PARTY ACCOUNTS**)
Federal institutions, rules applicable to   CC §1916.12
Guardianship (See **GUARDIAN AND WARD**)
Interest on impound accounts   CC §2954.8
Liens by   CC §3054
Multiple-party accounts (See **MULTIPLE-PARTY ACCOUNTS**)
Option to extend term of loan   CC §1916.5
Public administrators (See **PUBLIC ADMINISTRATORS**)
Recovery of money or property deposited, limitation of actions for   CCP §348
Shared appreciation loans (See **SHARED APPRECIATION LOANS**)
Totten trust accounts   Pro §§5404, 5406
Trustee, financial institutions as   Pro §16015

SAVINGS BONDS
Unclaimed property
   Notice
      Separate notice for savings bonds, war bonds or military awards   CCP §1531.6

SAW MILL
Liens   CC §§3065 to 3065c

SCANNERS
Computers   CC §§7100 to 7106
Grocery stores
   Price scanners
      Automatic checkout systems   CC §§7100 to 7106

SCAVENGERS (See **GARBAGE**)

SCHEDULES
Sales tax reimbursement   CC §1656.1

SCHOOL DISTRICTS
Administrative Procedure Act (See **ADMINISTRATIVE PROCEDURE ACT**)
Construction-related accessibility claims
   Attorney prelitigation letter to education entities   CC §54.27
Design professionals
   Indemnification, public agencies   CC §2782.8
Hazardous substances on property acquired by
   Abandonment of proceedings   CCP §1263.750
   Application of article   CCP §1263.770
   Appraisal of property   CCP §1263.740
   Cost of required action   CCP §§1263.720, 1263.730
   Definitions   CCP §§1263.710, 1263.711
   Offer to purchase property   CCP §1263.760
   Presence of hazardous material, required action on   CCP §1263.720
   Remedies available   CCP §1263.750
Pleadings verification by   CCP §446
State agency regulations (See **ADMINISTRATIVE PROCEDURE ACT**)
Unclaimed deposits and payments escheated   CCP §1519
Validation proceedings   CCP §§860 to 870

SCHOOLS
Access to buildings
   Construction-related accessibility claims
      Prelitigation letters to education entities, attorney duties   CC §54.27

SCHOOLS—Cont.

Access to school premises
    Force, threat or other obstruction of access to health facilities or school grounds   CC §1708.9

Caregiver's authorization and affidavit for medical or dental treatment of minors in Fam §§6550, 6552

Claims against public entities and employees (See **CLAIMS AGAINST PUBLIC ENTITIES AND EMPLOYEES**)

Computers leased or sold to   CC §998

Construction-related accessibility claims
    Attorneys at law
        Prelitigation letters to education entities   CC §54.27

Consumer privacy rights
    Deletion of personal information related to student grades, scores, etc, inapplicability of provisions   CC §1798.145
    Student grades, educational scores or test results
        Limits on obligations on businesses   CC §1798.145

Controlled substances violation, liability of schools for publication or reports or photographs of persons convicted of   Gov §818.7

Districts (See **SCHOOL DISTRICTS**)

Education (See **EDUCATION**)

Eminent domain, generally (See **EMINENT DOMAIN**)

Enrollment agreements
    Disaffirmance by minor of provisions purporting to waive rights or remedies arising out of sexual assault or battery of minor   CCP §1002.7

Escheat of funds   CCP §1528

Foster homes
    Change in placement affecting school of origin   CRC 5.651

Hazardous substances on property acquired by (See **SCHOOL DISTRICTS**)

Institutional funds
    Uniform prudent management of institutional funds act   Pro §§18501 to 18510 (See **INSTITUTIONAL FUNDS MANAGEMENT**)

Juvenile court schools
    Educational rights holders
        Judicial council forms   CRCAppx A

Law students (See **LAW STUDENTS**)

Medical or dental treatment of minors, caregiver's authorization and affidavit for Fam §§6550, 6552

Mobilehome or manufactured home subject to school facilities fee, disclosure that CC §§198.82, 199.8

Parent's right to access records of child   Fam §3025

Safety
    Access to school premises
        Force, threat or other obstruction of access to health facilities or school grounds   CC §1708.9

Services coordinator, school-linked
    Medical records
        Release of records   CC §56.10

Sexual harassment, civil action for
    Construction or application of provisions in issue, solicitor general notified CC §51.1

Student records, Information Practices Act affecting disclosure of   CC §1798.74

Teachers, disclosure of information affecting employment of   CC §1798.38

Telecommunications, goods and services for   CC §998

Threats to commit violence using firearm or deadly weapon   CC §48.8

Uniform prudent management of institutional funds act   Pro §§18501 to 18510 (See **INSTITUTIONAL FUNDS MANAGEMENT**)

Violence prevention
    Forms
        Judicial council legal forms   CRCAppx A

SCIENCE
Books, admissibility of   Ev §1341

SCIRE FACIAS
Abolishment of   CCP §802

SCOOTERS
Landlord and tenant
    Personal micromobility devices, rights of tenants   CC §1940.41
Shared mobility devices   CC §§2505 to 2506

SCOPE OF EMPLOYMENT (See **AGENCY**)

SCREWS
Fixtures attached to real property by   CC §660

SCULPTURE
Commissions for sale of   CC §986
Infringement, action for   CCP §429.30

SEAL
Generally   CCP §§1929 to 1934
Acknowledgment of instruments (See **ACKNOWLEDGMENTS**)
Affidavit taken in foreign state   CCP §2015
Authentication of documents under   Ev §1452
Contracts   CC §§1628, 1629
Corporations (See **CORPORATIONS**)
Court commissioners   CCP §259
Defined   CCP §14
Documents that must be sealed   CCP §153
Foreign official's seals on documents presumed to be genuine   Ev §1454
Letters of administration, requirements for   Pro §8405
Process   CCP §412.20

SEALED RECORDS   CRC 2.550, 2.551
Appellate rules, superior court appeals
    Applicable rules   CRC 8.819
Appellate rules, supreme court and courts of appeal   CRC 8.46
    Briefs conditionally under seal   CRC 8.212
    Certiorari, mandate and prohibition   CRC 8.486
    Criminal appeals
        Capital cases   CRC 8.610
    E-filing in supreme court and courts of appeal
        Format of electronic documents   CRC 8.74
    Juror-identifying information in record on criminal appeal, sealing of
        Capital cases   CRC 8.610
    Sealed and confidential records generally   CRC 8.45 to 8.47
Applicability of provisions   CRC 2.550
Application to seal   CRC 2.551
Arrest records
    Forms
        Judicial council legal forms   CRCAppx A
        Prosecuting attorney request to access sealed juvenile case files   CRC 5.860
        Order on prosecutor request for access   CRCAppx A
Attachment
    Prejudgment attachment
        Delayed public disclosure, request for   CRC 2.580
Confidential in-camera proceedings   CRC 2.585
Custody of sealed records   CRC 2.551
    Voluminous records   CRC 2.551
Deceased child victims
    Sealing autopsy report and evidence   CCP §130
Definitions   CRC 2.550
Delayed public disclosure, request for   CRC 2.580
Dissolution of marriage, legal separation, or annulment proceedings
    Financial assets and liabilities
        Sealing pleadings concerning financial assets and liabilities   Fam §2024.6
Factual findings necessary to seal   CRC 2.550
False claims act
    Filing records under seal   CRC 2.570 to 2.573
Filing records under seal
    Court approval   CRC 2.551
    False claims act   CRC 2.570 to 2.573
    Procedures   CRC 2.551
Forms
    Judicial council legal forms   CRCAppx A
In camera proceedings
    Confidential in camera proceedings   CRC 2.585
Judges
    Temporary judges
        Motion to seal records   CRC 2.835
Juror-identifying information
    Record on criminal appeal, sealing of   CRC 8.332
        Death penalty appeals   CRC 8.610, 8.611
Juror information records, unsealing of   CCP §237
Juvenile courts
    Access to sealed juvenile case file
        Judicial council forms   CRCAppx A
        Order on prosecutor request for access   CRCAppx A
        Prosecuting attorney request to access sealed juvenile case files   CRC 5.860
    Arrest records of juvenile delinquents
        Order on prosecutor request for access   CRCAppx A
        Prosecuting attorney request to access sealed juvenile case files   CRC 5.860
    Forms, judicial council   CRCAppx A
    Juvenile wardship proceedings   CRC 5.830
        Access to or inspection
            Judicial council forms   CRCAppx A

SEALED RECORDS—Cont.
Juvenile wardship proceedings —Cont.
    Access to or inspection—Cont.
        Order on prosecutor request for access   CRCAppx A
        Prosecuting attorney request to access sealed juvenile case files   CRC 5.860
    Former wards, records
        Order on prosecutor request for access   CRCAppx A
        Prosecuting attorney request to access sealed juvenile case files   CRC 5.860
    Forms, judicial council   CRCAppx A
    Satisfactory completion of informal program of supervision
        Dismissal of petition, sealing and destruction of records   CRC 5.840
        Order on prosecutor request for access   CRCAppx A
        Procedure for sealing   CRC 5.850
        Prosecuting attorney request to access sealed juvenile case files   CRC 5.860
Lodging of records   CRC 2.551
    Definition of lodged   CRC 2.550
Minors
    Arrest records
        Order on prosecutor request for access   CRCAppx A
        Prosecuting attorney request to access sealed juvenile case files   CRC 5.860
    Criminal court convictions
        Order on prosecutor request for access   CRCAppx A
        Prosecuting attorney request to access sealed juvenile case files   CRC 5.860
    Juvenile court records   CRC 5.830
        Access   CRCAppx A
        Forms, judicial council   CRCAppx A
        Order on prosecutor request for access   CRCAppx A
        Prosecuting attorney request to access sealed juvenile case files   CRC 5.860
    School's right of access to   CRC 5.552
    Ward of court proceedings
        Order on prosecutor request for access   CRCAppx A
        Prosecuting attorney request to access sealed juvenile case files   CRC 5.860
Motion to seal or unseal record   CRC 2.551
Order to seal records
    Clerk's duties   CRC 2.551
    Content   CRC 2.550
    Scope   CRC 2.550
Petition to unseal   CRC 2.551
Presumption of evidence as to   Ev §1452
Presumptions
    Openness of court records   CRC 2.550
Procedures for filing   CRC 2.551
Proof of service in criminal record clearing requests
    Forms, judicial council   CRCAppx A
Public records
    Nonpublic material in public record, references to   CRC 2.551
Referees
    Motion or application to seal   CRC 3.932
Sexual conduct evidence to attack credibility of complaining witness
    Affidavit containing offer of proof   Ev §782
Trial court rules   CRC 2.550, 2.551
    Name changes
        Address confidentiality program for victims of certain crimes, proceedings for   CRC 2.577
Unsealing records
    Motion, application or petition to unseal   CRC 2.551
Verdicts, sealed   CCP §617
Voluminous records
    Custody   CRC 2.551

SEARCH AND SEIZURE
Business records
    Criminal cases, custody of business that is nonparty and was not scene of crime
        Compliance with warrant   Ev §1560
Dogs
    Handlers of search and rescue dogs serving outside jurisdiction
        Lodging, eating or transportation, prohibition on discrimination   CC §54.25
Informer, identity of   Ev §§1040 to 1042
Inspection warrants (See **INSPECTION WARRANTS**)
Warrants
    Accounting companies disclosing information pursuant to   CC §1799.1

SEARCH AND SEIZURE—Cont.
Warrants—Cont.
    Information Practices Act, disclosures under   CC §1798.24
    Inspection (See **INSPECTION WARRANTS**)
    Personal information furnished under   CC §1798.24
    Reader privacy act, required for disclosures   CC §1798.90.05

SEARCH WARRANTS (See **SEARCH AND SEIZURE**)

SEATS
Common carriers required to furnish   CC §2185

SECONDARY EVIDENCE (See **BEST AND SECONDARY EVIDENCE**)

SECONDARY SCHOOLS (See **SCHOOLS**)

SECOND USE, TAKING FOR (See **EMINENT DOMAIN**)

SECRETARIES
Conciliation courts, secretary to assist in   Fam §1814

SECRETARY OF STATE
Administrative Procedure Act (See **ADMINISTRATIVE PROCEDURE ACT**)
Administrators with will annexed, service for   Pro §8574
Business entity filings
    Identity theft   CC §§1798.200 to 1798.203
Commercial and industrial common interest developments
    Associations
        Information filed with secretary of state   CC §6760
Commissions appointed by secretary acknowledging instruments   CC §§1182, 1183
Domestic partnership
    Statistics on domestic partnerships
        Document regarding, preparation   Fam §298.8
Executor as nonresident, accepting service for   Pro §8574
Federal tax liens, accepting service for   CCP §2101
Identity theft
    Business entity filings   CC §§1798.200 to 1798.203
International wills registry   Pro §6389
Judgment lien forms prescribed by   CCP §697.670
Judicial notice of regulations filed with   Ev §451, Gov §§11343.6, 11344.6
Seller assisted marketing plans   CC §§1812.203, 1812.214

SECURE DRUG TAKE-BACK BINS
Liability of collector, limitation   CC §1714.24

SECURED TRANSACTIONS (See also **CHATTEL MORTGAGES; CONDITIONAL SALES**)
Apartment keeper's lien, priority over   CC §1861a
Applicability of lien provisions   CC §2914
Asian language contracts   CC §1632
    Mortgages of residential property, foreign language summaries of terms   CC §1632.5
Attachment (See **ATTACHMENT**)
Automobiles (See **AUTOMOBILES**)
Coerced debt
    Inapplicability of provisions to secured debt   CC §1798.97.4
Discharge of instrument, applicability of provisions regulating   CC §2944
Electronic transactions
    Exceptions to applicability of electronic transactions provisions   CC §1633.3
Enforcement of judgments (See **ENFORCEMENT OF JUDGMENTS**)
Home Equity Loan Disclosure Act   CC §§2970 to 2971
Investment property pledged as collateral on consumer credit contract, restrictions concerning   CC §1799.103
Letters of credit supporting   CCP §580.5
Mortgages (See **TRUST DEEDS AND MORTGAGES**)
Retail installment sales (See **RETAIL INSTALLMENT SALES**)
Spanish-language contracts   CC §1632
    Mortgages of residential property, foreign language summaries of terms   CC §1632.5
Statutory liens
    Certification of nonrecordation   CCP §2103
    Civil Code provisions, exemption from   CC §2914
Stay of foreclosure   CCP §917.2
Sureties, security for obligations guaranteed by (See **SURETYSHIP, BONDS AND UNDERTAKINGS**)
Trust deeds (See **TRUST DEEDS AND MORTGAGES**)
Unlawful detainer, holding over after sale pursuant to default provisions as act constituting   CCP §1161a

SECURITIES
Generally (See **CORPORATE SHARES AND SHAREHOLDERS**)

INDEX

SECURITIES—Cont.
Complex litigation defined   CRC 3.400
Seller assisted marketing plans as   CC §1812.201

SECURITY AGREEMENTS
Small claims court, holder filing in   CCP §116.420

SECURITY BOND (See SURETYSHIP, BONDS AND UNDERTAKINGS)

SECURITY DEPOSITS (See RENT)

SECURITY FOR CONNECTED DEVICES   CC §§1798.91.04 to 1798.91.06
(See CONNECTED DEVICES, SECURITY)

SECURITY FREEZES, CREDIT REPORTS   CC §1785.11.2
Generally   CC §1785.11.2
Check services company, exemption of   CC §1785.11.6
Deposit account information service company, exemption of   CC §1785.11.6
Effect of freeze on obligations of reporting agency   CC §1785.15
Fees assessed for placing, removing, etc   CC §1785.11.2
    Identity theft victims, prohibition on fees   CC §1785.15
Fraud prevention services, exemption   CC §1785.11.6
Free copy of consumer's credit report   CC §1785.11.3
Placing alerts and freezes in report   CC §§1785.11.1 to 1785.11.11
Protected consumer security freezes   CC §§1785.11.9 to 1785.11.11
    Applicability of provisions   CC §1785.11.10
    Definitions   CC §1785.11.9
    Exceptions to provisions   CC §1785.11.10
    Placement, requirements   CC §1785.11.11
    Removal, procedure   CC §1785.11.11
Reseller of credit information, exemption of   CC §1785.11.4

SECURITY INTERESTS
Third party claim of security interest in property levied upon   CCP §§720.210 to 720.290, 720.510 to 720.550

SEDUCTION
Action for seducing person of legal age   CC §43.5
Forbidden   CC §49
Statute of limitation   CCP §340

SEEING EYE DOGS (See DOGS)

SEGREGATION OF GOODS
Sales contracts   CC §1497

SEISIN
Damages for breach of covenant of   CC §3304
Recovery of real property, seisin or possession within five years of commencement of action for   CCP §318
Title to real property, seisin or possession within five years of commencement of action arising from   CCP §319

SEIZURE OF PROPERTY
Search and seizure (See SEARCH AND SEIZURE)
Statutory forfeiture, limitation of actions against officer to recover damages for seizure of property for   CCP §340
Tax collector, limitation of action to recover goods seized by   CCP §341

SELECTION OF JURY (See JURY)

SELF-INCRIMINATION   Ev §940
Dependent child proceedings   CRC 5.534, 5.682
Judges
    Censure, removal or admonishment
        Protection against self-incrimination   JudPerR 104
Juvenile wardship proceedings   CRC 5.534
    Detention hearings   CRC 5.756
    Jurisdictional hearings   CRC 5.778
Preliminary determination of claim of   Ev §404
Report to Justice Department concerning waiver of self-incrimination privilege   CRC 4.320
Witness, calling defendant as   Ev §§930, 940

SELLER ASSISTED MARKETING PLANS   CC §§1812.200 to 1812.221

SELLER OF REALTY (See VENDOR AND PURCHASER)

SEMINAR SALES SOLICITATION CONTRACTS
Definitions   CC §1689.24
Disclosure requirement in agreement regarding buyer's right to cancel   CC §1689.21

SEMINAR SALES SOLICITATION CONTRACTS—Cont.
General discussion of buyer's right to cancel   CC §1689.20
Refund of payments on cancellation by buyer   CC §1689.20
Return of goods by buyer on cancellation   CC §1689.23
Services rendered prior to cancellation, compensation for   CC §1689.23

SENATE (See CONGRESS)

SENIOR CITIZENS
Abuse and neglect
    Arbitration, appeals
        Expedited process   CCP §1294.4, CRC 8.710 to 8.717
    Domestic violence reports
        Access to domestic violence incident reports   Fam §6228
    Emergency protective orders
        COVID-19, emergency rule   CRCAppx I Emer Rule 8
        Forms for firearm relinquishment   CRCAppx A
    Forms
        Judicial council legal forms   CRCAppx A
    Garnishment
        Elder or dependent adult financial abuse, earnings withholding orders   CCP §§706.011, 706.023
    Protective orders to prevent
        Appellate court opinions, privacy protection as to use of names in opinions   CRC 8.90
        Judicial council forms   CRCAppx A
        Memorandum in support of petition not required   CRC 3.1114
    Unlawful detainer
        Restrictions on termination of tenancy   CC §1946.7, CCP §1161.3
Caregivers
    Housing
        Intergenerational housing developments   CC §51.3.5
Consumer protection provisions, remedies for senior citizens under   CC §§1780, 3445
Deeds of trust and mortgages
    Modification or workout plan to avoid foreclosure
        Senior citizen victim of prohibited acts, punishment   CC §2944.8
        Statute of limitations to enforce protections   CC §2944.10
Dependent adults
    Discovery
        Elder abuse and dependent adult civil protection act   CCP §§2017.310, 2017.320
Elder abuse
    Discovery
        Elder abuse and dependent adult civil protection act   CCP §§2017.310, 2017.320
    Emergency protective order   Fam §§6250 to 6257
    Inheritance rights, effect on   Pro §259
    Other acts of elder abuse committed by defendant, admissibility of evidence of   Ev §1109
    Public guardian for mentally impaired elders (See within this heading, "**Public guardian for mentally impaired elders**")
    Victim's videotaped statement, admissibility under hearsay rule of   Ev §1380
Emergency protective orders
    COVID-19, emergency rule   CRCAppx I Emer Rule 8
    Firearm relinquishment procedures
        Forms for firearm relinquishment   CRCAppx A
Financial abuse
    Attorney in fact
        Taking, concealing, etc property of principal   Pro §4231.5
    Mentally impaired elders (See within this heading, "**Public guardian for mentally impaired elders**")
Floating homes
    Club membership as condition for rental, prohibition against
        Applicability of prohibition to housing for elderly   CC §800.25
Health care durable power of attorney (See POWER OF ATTORNEY)
Home improvement contracts
    Limitations on liens on real property under   CC §1804.1
Housing
    Age discrimination in housing, generally   CC §51.2
    Deed restrictions
        Applicability of prohibition on unlawful restrictions to housing for older persons   CC §§782, 782.5
    Intergenerational housing developments   CC §51.3.5
    Mobilehome parks (See MOBILEHOMES)
    Riverside County senior citizen housing requirements   CC §§51.10 to 51.12
    Senior citizen housing requirements, generally   CC §§51.3 to 51.4
Landlord and tenant
    Abuse and neglect of elderly or dependent adults
        Restrictions on termination of tenancy   CC §1946.7, CCP §1161.3

SENIOR CITIZENS—Cont.
Mobilehomes and mobilehome parks
  Discrimination effected by requiring membership in restrictive club
    Applicability of prohibition in housing for elderly   CC §798.20
Power of attorney for health care (See **POWER OF ATTORNEY**)
Protective orders
  Abuse and neglect
    Memorandum in support of petition not required   CRC 3.1114
  COVID-19, emergency rule   CRCAppx I Emer Rule 8
  Requests for protective orders   CRC 3.1160
Public guardian for mentally impaired elders
  Compensable costs incurred by   Pro §2953
  Conditions for taking possession or control of elder's property   Pro §2952
  Declaration form issued by peace officer   Pro §2954
  Definitions   Pro §2951
  Mandated programs   Pro §2950
  Other undertakings authorized by law   Pro §2955
Shared appreciation loans for   CC §§1917.320 to 1917.714
Supportive care organizations
  Medical information disclosures   CC §56.10
Trial calendar preference for (See **CALENDAR**)
Undue influence
  Wrongful taking, concealment, etc of property of conservatee, minor, elder, dependent adult, etc   Pro §859
Wrongful taking, concealment, etc of property of conservatee, minor, elder, dependent adult, etc   Pro §859

SENTENCE AND PUNISHMENT   CRC 4.305 to 4.480
Additional criteria used in   CRC 4.408
Adoption of sentencing rules for superior courts, authority for   CRC 4.401
Aggravating circumstances   CRC 4.421
  Hate crimes   CRC 4.427
  Statement in aggravation, submission of   CRC 4.437
Aggregate terms for multiple felonies   CRC 4.447
Agreement by defendant to sentence choice, effect of   CRC 4.412
Base term, selection of   CRC 4.420
Battered wife syndrome, consideration in mitigation   CRC 4.423
Bodily injury inflicted   CRC 4.414, 4.421
Certification of case for sentencing on plea of guilty or no contest   CRC 4.114
Civil rights, violation of   CC §52
Combining of prior consecutive determinate sentences   CRC 4.452
Consecutive or concurrent sentences   CRC 4.424, 4.425
  Combining of prior consecutive determinate sentences   CRC 4.452
  Factors determining   CRC 4.424, 4.425
  Indeterminate term, sentence running consecutive to or concurrent with   CRC 4.451
  Multiple convictions   CRC 4.425
  Other jurisdiction, sentence running consecutively with or concurrently to sentence in   CRC 4.451
Construction of sentencing rules of superior courts   CRC 4.405
Contempt proceedings   CCP §1218
Court reporters to take down all arraignments, pleas and sentences in felony cases   CCP §269
Credit for time served   CRC 4.310, 4.472
  Probation report, inclusion of information regarding   CRC 4.411.5
Deadly weapon, use of   CRC 4.421
Definitions   CRC 4.405
Determinate sentencing   CRC 4.401 to 4.480
  Aggravation
    Circumstances in aggravation   CRC 4.421
    Statements in aggravation and mitigation   CRC 4.437
  Applicability of sentencing rules   CRC 4.403
  Base term of imprisonment   CRC 4.420
  Concurrent or consecutive sentences
    Factors affecting determination   CRC 4.425
    Foreign jurisdiction, sentence consecutive to or concurrent with term in   CRC 4.451
    Indeterminate term, sentence consecutive to or concurrent with   CRC 4.451
    Multiple punishment, applicability of prohibition against multiple punishments   CRC 4.424
    Prior determinate sentence, determinate sentence consecutive to   CRC 4.452
  Definitions   CRC 4.405
  Double jeopardy
    Agreement to punishment as abandonment of claim   CRC 4.412
    Concurrent or consecutive sentences, applicability of prohibition against multiple punishments   CRC 4.424
  Enhancements
    Dismissing   CRC 4.428
    Factors affecting imposition   CRC 4.428

SENTENCE AND PUNISHMENT—Cont.
Determinate sentencing —Cont.
  Enhancements—Cont.
    Hate crimes   CRC 4.427
    Stay of execution on excessive or prohibited portion of sentence resulting from enhancement   CRC 4.447
    Striking   CRC 4.428
  Factors listed in rules
    Not exhaustive   CRC 4.408
    Relevant factors, mandatory consideration   CRC 4.409
  Hate crimes   CRC 4.427
  Hearing
    Matters considered at time set for sentencing   CRC 4.433
  Lesser included offenses
    Agreement to punishment as abandonment of claim   CRC 4.412
  Mandatory supervision
    Criteria affecting imposition   CRC 4.415
    Revocation, sentencing upon   CRC 4.435
  Mitigation
    Circumstances in mitigation   CRC 4.423
    Statements in aggravation and mitigation   CRC 4.437
  Objectives in sentencing   CRC 4.410
  Presentence custody time credit   CRC 4.472
  Presentence investigations and reports   CRC 4.411
    Probation officer's report   CRC 4.411.5
  Probation
    Criteria affecting   CRC 4.414
    Presumptively ineligible defendant, granting probation   CRC 4.413, CRC JudAdminStand 4.35
    Revocation, sentencing upon   CRC 4.435
  Reasons for sentence choice   CRC 4.406
  Repeat offenders
    Violent sex crimes   CRC 4.426
  Reporting of sentencing proceedings   CRC 4.431
  Sex crimes
    Violent sex crimes   CRC 4.426
  Statement of views of judge and district attorney   CRC 4.480
  Statutory authority for rules   CRC 4.401
  Supervision
    Mandatory supervision, criteria affecting imposition   CRC 4.415
Documentary evidence produced on hearing for   CRC 4.437
Dual use of facts   CRC 4.420
Employment history   CRC 4.414
Enhancement
  Aggravation, circumstances in   CRC 4.421
  Base term of imprisonment, selection of   CRC 4.420
  Dismissing   CRC 4.428
  Excessive term of imprisonment, effect of   CRC 4.447
  Factors affecting imposition   CRC 4.428
  Hate crimes   CRC 4.427
  Multiple enhancements   CRC 4.447
  Striking   CRC 4.428, 4.447
  Unlawful sentence resulting from enhancement   CRC 4.447
Factors for discretionary sentencing decisions
  Listing of factors in rules not considered to be exhaustive   CRC 4.408
  Relevant factors, mandatory consideration   CRC 4.409
Family, providing for   CRC 4.423
Felonies
  Applicability of sentencing rules to offenses punishable as   CRC 4.403
  Imprisonment where term not specified
    Mandatory supervision of concluding portion, criteria affecting imposition   CRC 4.415
  Jail sentence for certain felonies, mandatory supervision
    Criteria affecting mandatory supervision   CRC 4.415
Great provocation for criminal conduct   CRC 4.423
Guilty or nolo plea
  Specification of punishment in   CRC 4.412
Hate crimes   CRC 4.427
  Aggravating circumstances   CRC 4.421
  Misdemeanor hate crimes, sentencing considerations   CRC 4.330
Hearing   CRC 4.433
Judges
  Nonsentencing, interference in process by   CRCSupp JudEthicsCanon 2
  Statement under Penal Code 1203.01 regarding person convicted and crime committed   CRC 4.480
Judicial administration standards
  Risk/needs assessments, court use at sentencing   CRC JudAdminStand 4.35
Judicial Council
  Sentencing rules, adoption of   CRC 4.401 to 4.480

SENTENCE AND PUNISHMENT—Cont.
Lower term
    Imposition of   CRC 4.420
    Statement of reasons for sentence choice   CRC 4.406, 4.420
    When justified   CRC 4.420
Matters to be considered at time for sentencing   CRC 4.433
Mental condition of defendant, consideration of   CRC 4.423
    Veterans, alternate commitment for combat veterans
        Orders for dismissal, judicial council legal forms   CRCAppx A
Middle term, imposition of   CRC 4.420
Minors
    Conviction as adult   CRC 4.510
    Induced to commit or assist in commission of crime   CRC 4.421
Mitigating circumstances   CRC 4.423
    Battered wife syndrome   CRC 4.423
    Statement in mitigation, submission of   CRC 4.437
    Veterans suffering from specified conditions
        Petition for resentencing, form   CRCAppx A
Motions
    Disposition of   CRC 4.437
Multiple punishment for same act   CRC 4.412
    Prohibition against   CRC 4.424
Notice of additional evidence on hearing for   CRC 4.437
Objection to proposed sentencing, lack of   CRC 4.412
Objectives of sentencing   CRC 4.410
Other states
    Sentence running consecutively with or concurrently to sentence in   CRC 4.451
Passive participant   CRC 4.423
Personal life of defendant, consideration of   CRC 4.414
Physical condition of defendant, consideration of   CRC 4.423
Premeditation   CRC 4.421
Presentence custody time credit   CRC 4.310, 4.472
Presentence investigations and reports   CRC 4.411, 4.411.5
Presumption as to consideration of criteria for   CRC 4.409
Probation (See **PROBATION**)
Purpose of sentencing   CRC 4.410
Reasons for sentence choice, statement by court   CRC 4.406, 4.420
Recall of sentence
    Veterans serving for felony conviction, mitigating factors
        Petition for resentencing, form   CRCAppx A
Recording of proceedings   CRC 4.431
Repeat offenders
    Prior felony conviction   CRC 4.421
    Sex offenders   CRC 4.426
Reporting of proceedings   CRC 4.431
Resentencing
    Forms
        Judicial council legal forms   CRCAppx A
Risk/needs assessments
    Court use at sentencing   CRC JudAdminStand 4.35
Seller assisted marketing plans, noncompliance with   CC §1812.217
Separate sentencing provisions, same act punishable by   CRC 4.412
Sex offenders   CRC 4.426
Statement in aggravation or mitigation   CRC 4.406, 4.420
    Contents   CRC 4.437
    Filing and serving of   CRC 4.437
Stay of prohibited portion of term   CRC 4.447
Stay of sentence affecting time for commencement of actions for damages resulting from commission of felony offense   CCP §340.3
Striking an enhancement or prior conviction, reasons required for   CRC 4.406
Supervision or incarceration
    Combining of prior consecutive determinate sentences
        Determination whether sentence served in custody or under mandatory supervision   CRC 4.452
Suspended sentence   CRC 4.433
Term of imprisonment
    Selection of term   CRC 4.420
Uniformity of sentences   CRC 4.410
Upper term
    Imposition   CRC 4.420
    Judicial Council sentencing rules   CRC 4.420
    Statement of reasons for sentence choice   CRC 4.406, 4.420
    When justified   CRC 4.420
Veterans
    Mitigating factors
        Petition for resentencing, form   CRCAppx A
    Orders for dismissal
        Judicial council legal forms   CRCAppx A
Victims and victims' rights
    Initiator of crime, victim as   CRC 4.423

SENTENCE AND PUNISHMENT—Cont.
Violent conduct, defendant showing pattern of   CRC 4.421
Violent sex offenses   CRC 4.426

SEPARABILITY CLAUSE
Consumers Legal Remedies Act containing   CC §1753
Dance studio contracts, provision regulating   CC §1812.68
Discount buying services contracts   CC §1812.128
Enforcement of judgments, severability of provisions governing   CCP §681.050
Family code   Fam §13
Health studio contracts, provision regulating   CC §1812.95
Home equity sales contracts   CC §§1695.11, 2945.8
Investigative agencies, statutes affecting   CC §1786.56
Probate Code   Pro §11
Retail installment sales provisions   CC §1801.2
Seller assisted marketing plans   CC §1812.220

SEPARATE PROPERTY (See **COMMUNITY PROPERTY**)

SEPARATE TRIAL (See **SEVERANCE**)

SEPARATION AGREEMENTS (See **PROPERTY SETTLEMENT AGREEMENTS**)

SEPARATION OF SPOUSES (See **LEGAL SEPARATION**)

SEPTEMBER 11, 2001 TERRORIST ATTACKS
Statute of limitations   CCP §340.10

SERIAL NUMBERS
Sale of articles after destruction or alteration of   CC §1710.1

SERVICE CONTRACTS (See **REPAIRS**)

SERVICE DEALERS
Liens by   CC §3052.5

SERVICE DOGS
Disabled persons using   CC §§54.1, 54.2

SERVICE OF PAPERS
Address of party unknown
    Generally   CCP §1011
Administrative law and procedure
    Adjudicative proceedings (See **ADMINISTRATIVE ADJUDICATION**)
    Rulemaking and regulations (See **ADMINISTRATIVE PROCEDURE ACT**)
Administrators (See **EXECUTORS AND ADMINISTRATORS**)
Administrators with will annexed (See **ADMINISTRATORS WITH WILL ANNEXED**)
Amended complaint   CCP §471.5
Appellate rules
    Superior court appeals
        Applications   CRC 8.806
        Briefs   CRC 8.882, 8.927
    Supreme court and court of appeals (See **APPELLATE RULES, SUPREME COURT AND COURTS OF APPEAL**)
Arbitration (See **ARBITRATION**)
Attachment (See **ATTACHMENT**)
Attorneys (See **ATTORNEYS**)
Certified rather than registered mail, notice by   CCP §11
Certiorari writ   CCP §§1073, 1107
Child support (See **CHILD SUPPORT**)
Citation to appear (See **CITATION TO APPEAR**)
Complaints (See **PROCESS AND SERVICE OF PROCESS**)
Corporations (See **CORPORATIONS**)
Cross-complaints (See **CROSS-COMPLAINTS**)
Dismissal for delay in (See **DISMISSAL**)
Dissolution of marriage (See **DISSOLUTION OF MARRIAGE**)
Domestic violence (See **DOMESTIC VIOLENCE**)
Economic litigation procedures for limited civil cases, time for service and response to request for statement identifying witnesses and evidence under CCP §96
Electronic filing and service (See **ELECTRONIC FILING AND SERVICE**)
Eminent domain (See **EMINENT DOMAIN**)
Enforcement of judgments (See **ENFORCEMENT OF JUDGMENTS**)
Escheat (See **ESCHEAT**)
Executors (See **EXECUTORS AND ADMINISTRATORS**)
Extensions of time for service of notices   CCP §§1054, 1054.1
Family law rules (See **FAMILY RULES**)
Fax filing and service (See **FAX FILING AND SERVICE**)
Garnishment (See **GARNISHMENT**)

SERVICE OF PAPERS—Cont.
Genetic test results in paternity action Fam §7552.5
Guardians (See **GUARDIAN AND WARD**)
Health care provider's professional negligence, notice of intention to commence action based on CCP §364
Innkeeper's lien, writ of possession on CC §§1861.6, 1861.7, 1861.9, 1861.18, 1861.20
Intervention, complaint in CCP §387
Judges (See **JUDGES**)
Judgment vacation motions CCP §663a
Jury instructions, proposed CCP §607a
Jury summons CCP §208
Law and motion proceedings (See **LAW AND MOTION PROCEEDINGS**)
Lease termination notice CC §1946
Letters of administration, notice of application for Pro §8003
Livestock service liens, actions based on CC §3080.03
Mandate, writ of (See **MANDAMUS**)
Mechanics' liens (See **MECHANICS' LIENS**)
Motions (See **MOTIONS**)
New trial, motion for (See **NEW TRIAL**)
Nonresidents CCP §1015
Party, general procedure for service of notice on CCP §1011
Pendency, notice of CCP §§405.22, 405.23
Process (See **PROCESS AND SERVICE OF PROCESS**)
Prohibition writ CCP §1107
Quieting title (See **QUIETING TITLE**)
Recreational vehicle park, notice to occupants of (See **RECREATIONAL VEHICLE PARKS**)
Residents appearing by attorney CCP §1015
Sheriff, service on CCP §262.5
Simultaneous death hearing, notice of Pro §233
Small claims actions (See **SMALL CLAIMS COURTS**)
Sterilization proceedings, notice of Pro §1953
Subpoenas (See **SUBPOENA**)
Summons, service of (See **PROCESS AND SERVICE OF PROCESS**)
Superior court appellate division
    Applications CRC 8.806
    Briefs CRC 8.882, 8.927
Superior courts (See **SUPERIOR COURTS**)
Supplemental pleading CCP §465
Surety bonds (See **SURETYSHIP, BONDS AND UNDERTAKINGS**)
Survey order in quiet title action CCP §743
Termination of parental rights, service of citation to appear Fam §§7880 to 7882
Trial, notice of CCP §594
Unlawful detainer proceedings, service of notice to quit in CCP §1162
Will probate (See **WILL PROBATE**)
Wills (See **WILLS**)

SERVICE OF PROCESS (See **PROCESS AND SERVICE OF PROCESS**)

SERVICE STATIONS
Emission control standards CC §1952.8

SESSIONS OF COURT
Small claims court CCP §116.250
Superior court holding session in judicial district in which juvenile hall located CCP §73e

SET-OFFS
Assignees, action by CCP §368
Good faith improver (See **GOOD FAITH IMPROVER**)
Statute of limitation, offsetting money cross-demands notwithstanding bar of CCP §431.70

SETTING ASIDE (See **JUDGMENTS**)

SETTLED STATEMENT
Appellate rules
    Supreme court and courts of appeal (See **APPELLATE RULES, SUPREME COURT AND COURTS OF APPEAL**)

SETTLEMENT AND COMPROMISE
Administrative adjudication (See **ADMINISTRATIVE ADJUDICATION**)
Administrators of decedent's estate (See **EXECUTORS AND ADMINISTRATORS**)
Admissibility of evidence of settlement negotiations, generally Ev §1152
Alternative dispute resolution programs (See **ALTERNATIVE DISPUTE RESOLUTION**)
Appellate rules, superior court appeals
    Limited civil cases in appellate division
        Guardian or conservator compromise, approval CRC 8.825

SETTLEMENT AND COMPROMISE—Cont.
Appellate rules, superior court appeals—Cont.
    Limited civil cases in appellate division —Cont.
        Notice of settlement CRC 8.825
Appellate rules, supreme court and courts of appeal
    1st Appellate District local rules CRCSupp 1st AppDist
    Civil settlement conference procedures
        4th Appellate District local rules CRCSupp 4th AppDist
    Notice to court of settlement following filing of notice of appeal CRC 8.244
Arbitration
    Notice to neutral of settlement of case CRC 3.1385
Attorney discipline
    Sex offense cases, civil case settlements
        Confidentiality agreements, discipline of attorneys insisting on agreement contrary to legal restrictions CCP §1002
Attorney professional conduct
    Aggregate settlements involving multiple clients ProfC 1.8.7
        Law firms, imputation to all members of firm of violations of certain provisions ProfC 1.8.11
    Client's decision to settle
        Attorney to abide ProfC 1.2
    Communications with clients
        Prompt communication of settlement offers ProfC 1.4.1
    Limitation of attorney liability to client
        Law firms, imputation to all members of firm of violations of certain provisions ProfC 1.8.11
        Prohibitions ProfC 1.8.8
Attorneys' fees
    Attorney professional conduct
        Financial and other arrangements with nonattorneys ProfC 5.4
Child support
    Government support enforcement services
        Statewide compromise of arrears program Fam §17560
Claims against decedent's estate
    Generally (See **EXECUTORS AND ADMINISTRATORS**)
    Trust property of deceased settlor, claims against (See **TRUSTS**)
Claims against public entities and employees (See **CLAIMS AGAINST PUBLIC ENTITIES AND EMPLOYEES**)
Class actions, settlement of CRC 3.769
Collections cases
    Civil case management CRC 3.741
Commercial and industrial common interest developments
    Construction defects litigation
        Settlement agreements CC §6874
Common interest development, disclosure to association members of settlement agreement with builder of CC §6100
Confidential settlement agreements
    Restrictions on nondisclosure agreements (NDAs) in certain cases CCP §1001
    Sex offense prosecutable as felony as basis of action
        Prohibition of confidential settlement CCP §1002
Conflict of laws
    Time-limited demands CCP §999.4
Conservatorship (See **CONSERVATORS**)
Construction defects, actions for
    Prelitigation procedures
        Cash settlements CC §929
Construction-related accessibility claims
    Demand letters
        Allegation of construction-related accessibility claim CC §55.31
Contribution among joint tortfeasors, effect on CCP §§877, 877.6
Coordinated actions CRC 3.545
    Standards CCP §404.1
Costs of litigation charged to party refusing offer of compromise CCP §998
Damage or loss, inadmissible evidence to prove liability for Ev §1152
Debt settlements
    Fair debt settlement practices CC §§1788.300 to 1788.307
Decedent's estates, claims against (See **EXECUTORS AND ADMINISTRATORS**)
Dismissal of civil actions after settlement CRC 3.1385
Dismissal of pleading or part of pleading, motion for CRC 3.1382
Employment disputes
    Prohibited terms in agreements settling employment disputes CCP §1002.5
Enforcement of judgment pursuant to terms of settlement CCP §§664.6, 664.7
Environmental quality act
    Petitions under environmental quality act, civil rules governing
        Jobs and economic improvement through environmental leadership act of 2011 CRC 3.2229, 3.2230

SETTLEMENT AND COMPROMISE—Cont.
  Environmental quality act—Cont.
    Petitions under environmental quality act, civil rules governing —Cont.
      Sacramento downtown arena project, CEQA challenges   CRC 3.2229, 3.2230
  Executors of decedent's estate (See **EXECUTORS AND ADMINISTRATORS**)
  Expert witness costs charged to party refusing offer of compromise   CCP §998
  Fair debt buying practices   CC §1788.54
  Fair debt settlement practices   CC §§1788.300 to 1788.307
  Family rules
    Domestic violence
      Court-connected settlement service providers   CRC 5.420
    Request for orders
      Notice to court of settlement   CRC 5.96
    Stipulated judgments   CRC 5.411
  Good faith settlement
    Dismissal of pleading or part of pleading, motion for   CRC 3.1382
    Hearing to determine   CCP §877.6
    Time for service of papers concerning   CCP §§877.6, 1005
  Guardian ad litem's power to compromise claims   CCP §§372, 373.5
  Guardianship (See **GUARDIAN AND WARD**)
  Incompetent persons
    Payments pursuant to settlement, disposition of   Pro §§3600 to 3613
    Definition of person with disability   Pro §3603
    Express consent of protected person to court orders, when required   Pro §3613
    Trusts, payment into   CRC JudAdminStand 7.10
    Petition for approval of compromise of claim   CRC 3.1384, 7.950
      Attendance at hearing on petition   CRC 7.952
      Attorney interest in petition   CRC 7.951
      Deposit of funds, order   CRC 7.953
      Expedited approval, petition   CRC 7.950.5
      Forms, use of judicial council form   CRC 7.101
      Memorandum in support of petition not required   CRC 3.1114
      Withdrawal of deposited funds   CRC 7.954
  International commercial arbitration and conciliation (See **INTERNATIONAL COMMERCIAL ARBITRATION AND CONCILIATION**)
  Judges
    Censure, removal, admonishment or retirement of judges
      Negotiated settlements during preliminary investigation or disciplinary proceeding   JudPerR 116.5
    Code of judicial ethics
      Participation in efforts to resolve disputes   CRCSupp JudEthicsCanon 3
  Judgment by stipulation (See within this heading, **"Stipulated judgments"**)
  Judicial administrative records
    Public access to judicial administrative records   CRC 10.500
  Judicial arbitration cases   CRC 3.829, 3.1385
    Neutral
      Notice to neutral of settlement of case   CRC 3.1385
    Notice   CRC 3.829
    Offer of settlement, disclosure to arbitrator   CRC 3.820
  Judicial performance, commission on
    Censure, removal, admonishment or retirement of judges
      Discussions of settlements, evidence at hearings   JudPerR 125
      Negotiated settlements during preliminary investigation or disciplinary proceeding   JudPerR 116.5
  Jury fees refunded   CCP §631.3
  Mechanics' liens
    Settlement agreement, effect of waiver and release provisions   CC §8130
  Mediation
    Conditions for disclosure of settlement agreement reached in   Ev §1123
    Standards of conduct for mediators   CRC 3.857
  Mentally disabled persons, compromise of claims of (See **MENTAL DISABILITY**)
  Minors, compromise of claims of (See **PARENT AND CHILD**)
  Minors or persons with disabilities entering into
    Attorneys' fees for services to minors and persons with disabilities   CRC 7.955
    Court approval
      Appellate court opinions, privacy protection as to use of names in opinions   CRC 8.90
      Forms, use of judicial council forms   CRC 7.101
      Notice of settlement   CRC 3.1385
      Reviewing courts   CRC 8.244
      Small claims appeals   CRC 8.963
    Disposition of money or property
      Trusts, payment into   CRC JudAdminStand 7.10
    Electronic court records
      Courthouse electronic access   CRC 2.503

SETTLEMENT AND COMPROMISE—Cont.
  Minors or persons with disabilities entering into—Cont.
    Parent's right to compromise child's claim
      Hearings on petition for compromise   Pro §3505
    Petition for approval of compromise of claim   CRC 3.1384, 7.950
      Attendance at hearing on petition   CRC 7.952
      Attorney interest in petition   CRC 7.951
      Deposit of funds, order   CRC 7.953
      Expedited approval, petition   CRC 7.950.5
      Forms, use of judicial council forms   CRC 7.101
      Memorandum in support of petition not required   CRC 3.1114
      Withdrawal of deposited funds   CRC 7.954
  Motion for determination of good faith settlement   CRC 3.1382
  Multiple tortfeasors, good faith settlement by one of   CCP §877.6
  Notice of proceedings   Pro §1200
  Notification of court   CRC 3.1385
  Offers to compromise
    Generally   CCP §998
    Admissibility as evidence   Ev §1152
    Costs of litigation assessed against party refusing offer and failing to obtain more favorable judgment   CCP §998
  Offers to settle or compromise
    Limitation on papers filed   CRC 3.250
  Parent, compromise of minor's claims by (See **PARENT AND CHILD**)
  Parent's right to compromise child's claim
    Hearings on petition for compromise   Pro §3505
  Parties
    Waiver in contract or settlement of right to testify concerning criminal conduct or sexual harassment   CC §1670.11
  Police officers as expert witnesses for purposes of settlement costs provision   CCP §998
  Private student loan collections reform
    Acceptance of settlement agreement as payment in full   CC §1788.203
  Retaliation
    Harassment or discrimination based on sex
      Restrictions on nondisclosure agreements (NDAs) in certain cases   CCP §1001
  Seal, absence of   CCP §1934
  Several tortfeasors, good faith settlement by one of   CCP §877.6
  Sex discrimination
    Restrictions on nondisclosure agreements (NDAs) in certain cases   CCP §1001
  Sex offense prosecutable as felony as basis of action
    Confidential settlement agreements, prohibition   CCP §§1001, 1002
  Sexual assault
    Employment disputes, prohibited terms in settlement agreements   CCP §1002.5
  Sexual harassment
    Employment disputes, prohibited terms in settlement agreements   CCP §1002.5
    Restrictions on nondisclosure agreements (NDAs) in certain cases   CCP §1001
    Waiver of right to testify concerning criminal conduct or sexual harassment   CC §1670.11
  Sliding scale recovery agreement   CCP §877.5
  Statutory offers
    Offers generally (See within this heading, **"Offers to compromise"**)
  Stipulated judgments
    Generally   CCP §664.6
    Construction defect actions, stipulated judgments in   CCP §664.7
    Family rules   CRC 5.411
  Superior courts (See **SUPERIOR COURTS**)
  Time-limited demands   CCP §§999 to 999.5
    Applicability of chapter   CCP §§999.4, 999.5
    Conflict of laws   CCP §999.4
    Definitions   CCP §999
    Delivery requirements   CCP §999.2
    Demand acceptance   CCP §999.3
    Public policy   CCP §999
    Written requirements   CCP §999.1
  Trusts, claims against (See **TRUSTS**)
  Uniform Transfers to Minors Act, transfer of funds from settlement under   Pro §§3602, 3611
  Unlawful detainer settlement opportunities   CRC 3.2005
  Witnesses
    Waiver in contract or settlement of right to testify concerning criminal conduct or sexual harassment   CC §1670.11

SETTLEMENT CONFERENCES
  1st Appellate District rules of court   CRCSupp 1st AppDist
  2nd Appellate District rules of court   CRCSupp 2nd AppDist

SETTLEMENT CONFERENCES—Cont.
3rd Appellate District rules of court   CRCSupp 3rd AppDist
4th Appellate District rules of court   CRCSupp 4th AppDist
Judge's power to act, effect of proceedings for disqualification on   CCP §170.4

SETTLORS (See TRUSTS)

70 YEARS OR OLDER
Preference, motion for   CCP §36

SEVERABILITY CLAUSE (See SEPARABILITY CLAUSE)

SEVERAL LIABILITY (See JOINT AND SEVERAL LIABILITY)

SEVERAL OWNERSHIP
Definition   CC §681

SEVERANCE
Authority for   CCP §1048
Child support, separate trial on issue of   Fam §4003
Custody of children   Fam §3023
Discretionary separation of issues for trial   CCP §598
Dissolution of marriage proceedings, severance of disputed issues in (See **DISSOLUTION OF MARRIAGE**)
Economy purposes, separate trial for   CCP §598
Family law rules (See **FAMILY RULES**)
International commercial arbitration and conciliation   CCP §§1297.272, 1297.273
Joined parties, separate trials for   CCP §379.5
Joint tenancy, severance of   CC §683.2
Jurisdiction   CRC 3.529
Membership camping contracts, severance of provisions governing   CC §1812.308
Motion of court for bifurcation   CCP §§597, 597.5
Probate code provisions, separate civil actions for matters associated with proceedings and actions under   Pro §801
Special defense, trial of   CCP §597
Statute of limitations, separate trial of defense on   CCP §§597, 597.5

SEWAGE FACILITIES
Eminent domain takings for   CCP §1240.125
Indemnity coverage for construction, repair, renovation, maintenance or demolition of lines   CC §2783
Inspection warrants   CCP §1822.50

SEWING MACHINES
Serial number destroyed or altered prior to sale   CC §1710.1

SEX (See GENDER)

SEX DISCRIMINATION
Child custody
    Best interest of child
        Prohibited considerations for best interest   Fam §§3011, 3020, 3040
Courts, prevention of bias based on gender or sexual orientation   CRC JudAdminStand 10.20
Judicial ethics code
    Administrative responsibilities of judge, impartial discharge   CRCSupp JudEthicsCanon 3
    Attorneys, judges to require to refrain from manifesting   CRCSupp JudEthicsCanon 3
    Court personnel and staff under direction of judge, standards of conduct enforced by judge   CRCSupp JudEthicsCanon 3
    Membership in discriminatory organizations   CRCSupp JudEthicsCanon 2
Jury instructions, gender-neutral language in   CRC 2.1055
Price differences for substantially similar goods based on gender of marketing audience   CC §51.14
Settlement
    Restrictions on nondisclosure agreements (NDAs) in certain cases   CCP §1001
Small business gender discrimination in pricing services   CC §§55.61 to 55.63

SEX OFFENDER REGISTRATION
Juvenile offenders
    Sealing of records
        Order on prosecutor request for access   CRCAppx A
        Prosecuting attorney request to access sealed juvenile case files   CRC 5.860
Termination of registration
    Forms   CRCAppx A

SEX OFFENSES
Access to domestic violence incident reports   Fam §6228
Address of victim
    Confidentiality for victims of domestic violence, sexual assault and stalking
        Actions, confidentiality requirements for protected persons in civil proceeding   CCP §367.3
        Judicial council forms   CRCAppx A
        Name change proceedings under address confidentiality program   CRC 2.575 to 2.577
Admissibility of evidence
    Evidence generally (See within this heading, "**Evidence**")
Adults in position of authority over minors
    Conduct of victim, admissibility of evidence   Ev §1106
    Consent not deemed defense in civil actions   CC §1708.5.5
Aiding or abetting rape
    Statute of limitations on sexual assault damages   CCP §340.16
Battery, sexual
    Statute of limitations on sexual assault damages   CCP §340.16
Childhood sexual abuse
    Civil actions
        Government tort liability   Gov §905
        Settlement, confidentiality agreements   CCP §1002
    Minors generally (See within this heading, "**Minors**")
Civil actions
    Conduct of victim, admissibility of evidence   Ev §1106
    Consent not deemed defense in cases of adults in position of authority over minors   CC §1708.5.5
Commercial sexual exploitation of minor by social media platform   CC §3345.1
Contempt orders against victim of sexual assault   CCP §§128, 1219
Controlled substance, victim's resistance prevented by administration of
    Statute of limitations
        Civil damages   CCP §340.16
Custody and visitation, prohibition of (See **CUSTODY OF CHILDREN**)
Defendant as victim of sexual abuse, mitigation of sentence based on   CRC 4.423
Defenses in civil actions
    Consent not deemed defense in cases of adults in position of authority over minors   CC §1708.5.5
Discovery regarding plaintiff's or complainant's sexual conduct (See **DISCOVERY**)
Divorce
    Violent sexual felony by spouse against spouse
        Consequences in divorce proceedings   Fam §4324.5
Domestic violence (See **DOMESTIC VIOLENCE**)
Elderly persons, offenses against, reporting
    Settlement of civil cases
        Confidentiality agreements, restrictions   CCP §1002
Enhancement of punishment
    Prior determinate sentence, determinate sentence consecutive to   CRC 4.452
Enrollment agreements
    Disaffirmance by minor of provisions purporting to waive rights or remedies arising out of sexual assault or battery of minor   CCP §1002.7
Evidence
    Address and telephone number of victim, exclusion of   Ev §352.1
    Hearsay exceptions applicable to statements of minor victim   Ev §§1228, 1253, 1293, 1360
    Other sexual offense, evidence of commission of   Ev §1108
    Reputation or prior bad acts (See **CHARACTER AND REPUTATION**)
False representations inducing consent by
    Statute of limitations
        Civil damages   CCP §340.16
Foreign or unknown object, penetration by
    Statute of limitations
        Civil damages   CCP §340.16
Fraudulent representation
    Penetration represented as having professional purpose
        Statute of limitations on sexual assault damages   CCP §340.16
    Sodomy
        Penetration represented as having professional purpose
            Statute of limitations for sexual assault damages   CCP §340.16
    Statute of limitations for sexual assault damages   CCP §340.16
    Touching represented as having professional purpose
        Statute of limitations on sexual assault damages   CCP §340.16
Future retaliation, threat of
    Statute of limitations on sexual assault damages   CCP §340.16
Injunctions and protective orders
    Address or location of complaining party or family, prohibition on enjoined party from obtaining   CCP §527.10
    California law enforcement telecommunications (CLETS) information form, confidentiality and use of information   CRC 1.51, CRCAppx A

SEX OFFENSES—Cont.
Injunctions and protective orders—Cont.
- COVID-19, emergency rule CRCAppx I Emer Rule 8
- Waiver of fees CCP §527.6

Juvenile offenders
- Trial as adult
  - Sentencing upon conviction CRC 4.510

Landlord and tenant
- Documentation or evidence of abuse or violence
  - Victims of domestic violence, sexual assault or stalking CCP §1161.3
- Termination of tenancy
  - Victims of domestic violence, sexual assault or stalking CC §1946.7, CCP §1161.3
- Unlawful detainer proceedings, nuisance committed by tenant as grounds
  - Presumption of nuisance CCP §1161
  - Restrictions on termination of tenancy CC §1946.7, CCP §1161.3

Law enforcement officers
- Sexual assault by officer, claims against public entities and employees
  - Presentation of claims arising from sexual assault by officer, requirements Gov §945.9

Medical treatment of minor victims Fam §§6927, 6928

Mentally incompetent persons
- Sex offense victims as
  - Statute of limitations CCP §340.16

Minors
- Adults in position of authority over minors
  - Conduct of victim, admissibility of evidence Ev §1106
  - Consent not deemed defense in civil actions CC §1708.5.5
- Certificate of merit required in action for childhood sexual assault CCP §§340.1, 340.11
- Childhood sexual abuse, civil actions
  - Government tort liability Gov §905
  - Settlement, confidentiality agreements CCP §1002
- Childhood sexual assault, civil actions
  - After attaining age of majority CCP §340.1
- Childhood sexual assault, civil actions after attaining age of majority CCP §340.11
- Civil actions
  - Consent not deemed defense in cases of adults in position of authority over minors CC §1708.5.5
  - Limitation CCP §§340.1, 340.11
  - Settlements
    - Confidentiality agreements, restrictions CCP §1002
- Contempt
  - Refusal to testify CCP §1219.5
- Contract for payment to minor victim of unlawful sex act as void CC §§1169.5, 1169.7
- Custody and visitation (See **CUSTODY OF CHILDREN**)
- Damage action by victim after attaining age of majority CCP §340.11
- Definitions
  - Sexual assault CCP §§340.1, 340.11
- Enrollment agreements
  - Disaffirmance by minor of provisions purporting to waive rights or remedies arising out of sexual assault or battery of minor CCP §1002.7
- Government tort liability
  - Childhood sexual abuse damage claims, presentation of claims Gov §905
- Injunctions and protective orders
  - California law enforcement telecommunications (CLETS) information form, confidentiality and use of information CRC 1.51, CRCAppx A
  - COVID-19, emergency rule CRCAppx I Emer Rule 8
  - Waiver of fees CCP §527.6
- Juveniles tried as adults, sentencing upon conviction CRC 4.510
- Limitation of actions CCP §§340.1, 340.11
- Medical care for victims Fam §§6927, 6928
- Reasonable and meritorious cause for filing action CCP §§340.1, 340.11
- Revival of actions
  - Sexual assault of a minor, damages actions based on commission of CCP §340.11
- Settlement of civil cases
  - Confidentiality agreements, restrictions CCP §1002
- Sexual exploitation
  - Settlement of civil case
    - Confidentiality agreements, restrictions CCP §1002
- Social media platform, hosted on CC §§3273.65 to 3273.69
- Sodomy
  - Statute of limitations, civil damages CCP §340.16

SEX OFFENSES—Cont.
Minors—Cont.
- Statute of limitations CCP §340.35
  - Sexual assault damages CCP §340.16

Name changes
- Sex offenders
  - Restrictions on sex offenders CCP §1279.5
- Victims of sexual assault CCP §1277

Paternity presumptions, effect of rape on Fam §7611.5

Penetration
- Causing another person to penetrate
  - Statute of limitations CCP §340.16
- Foreign object
  - Statute of limitations CCP §340.16
- Fraudulent representation
  - Sodomy
    - Statute of limitations CCP §340.16

Privileged communications between sexual assault victim and counselor (See **PRIVILEGED COMMUNICATIONS**)

Psychotherapists, cause of action against CC §43.93

Public officials
- Sexual acts performed by person claiming to be
  - Statute of limitations CCP §340.16
- Threat of authority of
  - Statute of limitations
    - Civil damages CCP §340.16

Public officials, liability for sexual battery by Gov §815.3

Punishment CRC 4.426
- Enhancements
  - Prior determinate sentence, determinate sentence consecutive to CRC 4.452
- Multiple offenses CRC 4.426
- Repeat sex offenders CRC 4.426

Real property sale or lease, notification concerning statewide database of locations of registered sex offenders in connection with CC §2079.10a

Registered sex offenders
- Custody and visitation
  - Denial of Fam §3030
  - Household membership of or permitting contact by registered sex offender Fam §3030
  - Modification or termination of order upon commission of offense requiring registration by custodian or member of household Fam §3030.5
- Jury service
  - Ineligibility for jury service CCP §203
- Real property sale or lease, notification concerning statewide database of locations of registered sex offenders in connection with CC §2079.10a

Retaliation in future, threat of
- Statute of limitations
  - Civil damages CCP §340.16

Sentencing criteria for multiple violent sex offenders CRC 4.426

Settlement in civil case
- Employment dispute settlement agreements
  - Prohibited terms in settlement agreements CCP §1002.5
- Sex offense prosecutable as felony
  - Confidential settlement prohibited CCP §§1001, 1002

Settlement of civil action
- Restrictions on nondisclosure agreements (NDAs) in certain cases CCP §1001

Sexual battery
- Action for CC §1708.5
- Discovery
  - Sexual conduct of plaintiff CCP §2017.220
- Prostitution, evidence
  - Extortion, serious felony, assault, domestic violence, human trafficking, sexual battery or stalking, victims or witnesses, restrictions on admissibility of evidence of prostitution Ev §1162
- Statute of limitations on sexual assault damages CCP §340.16
- Stealthing or nonconsensual condom removal CC §1708.5

Sodomy
- Disabled persons as victims of
  - Statute of limitations, civil damages CCP §340.16
- False representation as spouse or public official, perpetrator making
  - Statute of limitations, civil damages CCP §340.16
- Foreign-object offenses
  - Statute of limitations, civil damages CCP §340.16
- Fraudulent representation
  - Penetration represented as having professional purpose, statute of limitations CCP §340.16
- Mentally ill person, crime against
  - Statute of limitations, civil damages CCP §340.16

SEX OFFENSES—Cont.
Sodomy—Cont.
Minors
Statute of limitation, civil damages   CCP §340.16
Prison inmates, offenses by
Statute of limitations   CCP §340.16
Public official or impostor as perpetrator
Statute of limitations, civil damages   CCP §340.16
Statute of limitations
Civil damages   CCP §340.16
Threats of future violence or harm, perpetration by
Statute of limitations, civil damages   CCP §340.16
Unconscious to nature of act, sodomy of person who is
Statute of limitations, civil damages   CCP §340.16
Violent sexual felony by spouse against spouse
Divorce proceedings, consequences   Fam §4324.5
Spousal rape
Acting in concert
Statute of limitations on sexual assault damages   CCP §340.16
Alcoholic beverage or anesthetic, use to accomplish
Statute of limitations on sexual assault damages   CCP §340.16
Statute of limitations on sexual assault damages   CCP §340.16
Statute of limitations
Childhood sexual abuse
Certificate of merit   CCP §§340.1, 340.11
Damages   CCP §340.35
Sexual assault damages   CCP §340.16
Unconscious to nature of act, rape of person who is
Statute of limitations
Civil damages   CCP §340.16
Unlawful detainer proceedings
Limitations on termination of or refusal to renew tenancy of victims   CC §1946.7, CCP §1161.3
Nuisance committed by tenant as grounds
Presumption of nuisance   CCP §1161
Sexual assault victims
Abuse or violence against tenant, remedies   CCP §1174.27
Victims and victims' rights
Name change proceedings under address confidentiality program   CCP §1277
Victim service providers, personal information protection   CC §§1798.79.8 to 1798.79.95
Definitions   CC §1798.79.8
Disclosing personal information
Grants, requiring disclosure as condition   CC §1798.79.9
Injunctions to prevent   CC §1798.79.95
Prohibited   CC §1798.79.9
Name change proceedings under address confidentiality program   CRC 2.575 to 2.577

SEXUAL ASSAULT VICTIM-COUNSELOR PRIVILEGE (See **PRIVILEGED COMMUNICATIONS**)

SEXUAL EXPLOITATION
Child victims
Settlement of civil cases involving childhood sexual exploitation
Confidentiality agreements, restrictions   CCP §1002
Commercial sexual exploitation
Minor or nonminor dependent victims
Actions   CC §3345.1

SEXUAL HARASSMENT
Administrative adjudication proceedings alleging sexual harassment, assault or battery, evidence in   Gov §11440.40
Civil cause of action created
Construction or application of provisions in issue, solicitor general notified   CC §51.1
Contracts
Waiver of right to testify concerning criminal conduct or sexual harassment   CC §1670.11
Defamation, privileges
Communications made without malice regarding incidents   CC §47.1
Job performance communications by employer to prospective employer
Complaints of sexual harassment included within privilege   CC §47
Discovery
Sexual conduct of plaintiff   CCP §2017.220
Elements of cause of action for sexual harassment   CC §51.9
Judges   CRCSupp JudEthicsCanon 3
Settlements
Employment disputes, prohibited terms   CCP §1002.5

SEXUAL HARASSMENT—Cont.
Settlements—Cont.
Restrictions on nondisclosure agreements (NDAs) in certain cases   CCP §1001
Waiver of right to testify concerning criminal conduct or sexual harassment   CC §1670.11

SEXUALLY EXPLICIT DEPICTION OF INDIVIDUAL
Creation or disclosure
Actions   CC §1708.86
Damages   CC §1708.86

SEXUALLY-ORIENTED BUSINESSES
Human trafficking or slavery
Signs, businesses required to post notice concerning relief from slavery or human trafficking   CC §52.6

SEXUALLY TRANSMITTED DISEASES
Sex offenses
Statute of limitations for sexual assault damages   CCP §340.16

SEXUALLY VIOLENT PREDATORS
Commitment proceedings
Appeal from order of civil commitment   CRC 8.483
Forms
Judicial council legal forms   CRCAppx A
Hearsay rule
Statements admissible at hearing   Ev §1285
Judicial commitment to mental health facility
Remote proceedings
Conditions for proceeding through use of remote technology   CCP §367.76

SEXUAL ORIENTATION
Child custody
Best interest of child
Prohibited considerations for best interest   Fam §§3011, 3020, 3040
Discrimination   CC §51
Judicial ethics code
Membership in discriminatory organizations   CRCSupp JudEthicsCanon 2
Disqualification of judges, grounds for   CCP §170.2
Equal protection
Political structure equal protection   CC §53.7
Intimidation based on
Construction or application of provisions in issue, solicitor general notified   CC §51.1
Waiver of right to freedom from violence, coerced or involuntary   CC §51.7
Judges, membership in discriminatory organizations   CRCSupp JudEthicsCanon 2
Marriage, opposite sex requirement
Recognition of certain same sex marriages contracted in other jurisdictions
Dissolution, annulment or legal separation of recognized same sex marriages, jurisdiction   Fam §§2010, 2320
Repeal   Fam §300
Political structure equal protection   CC §53.7
Sexual orientation violence
Civil actions   CC §52.45
Violence against victim based on
Freedom from, right to
Construction or application of provisions in issue, solicitor general notified   CC §51.1
Waiver of right to freedom from violence, coerced or involuntary   CC §51.7
Waiver of right to freedom from violence, coerced or involuntary   CC §51.7

SEXUAL PENETRATION
Divorce
Violent sexual felony by spouse against spouse
Consequences in divorce proceedings   Fam §4324.5

SEXUAL RELATIONS
Discoverability of sexual conduct (See **DISCOVERY**)

SHARED APPRECIATION LOANS
Generally   CC §§1917 to 1917.006
ERISA pension funds
Inoperative provisions   CC §§1917.010 to 1917.075
Senior citizens, shared appreciation loans for   CC §§1917.320 to 1917.714

SHARED APPRECIATION LOANS—Cont.
State facilitation of shared appreciation loans
    Inoperative provisions   CC §§1917.110 to 1917.175

SHARED MOBILITY DEVICES   CC §§2505 to 2506
Agreements with or permits from local government   CC §2505
Definitions   CC §2505
Disclosures to customers
    Insurance coverage, disclosures as to   CC §2505
Identification sign of service provider on devices   CC §2506
Insurance   CC §2505
    Study and report to legislature on insurance issues   CC §2505.5

SHAREHOLDERS (See CORPORATE SHARES AND SHAREHOLDERS)

SHEEP
Dogs injuring   CC §3341

SHELLEY'S CASE
Heirs of body, remainder limited to   CC §§779, 780

SHELTER, ANIMAL (See ANIMALS)

SHERIFF
Attachment (See ATTACHMENT)
Bench warrants, fees for service and execution of   Gov §26744
Certificate
    Generally   CCP §§2015.3, 2015.5
    Redemption, certificate or deed of   Gov §26740
Contempt   CCP §1209
Conveyances on sale of real estate by sheriff   CCP §262.4
Court operations costs, salaries and benefits included as   CRC 10.810
Deeds on sale of real estate by (See ENFORCEMENT OF JUDGMENTS)
Deposits in court, sheriff receiving   CCP §574
Electronic court records, remote access
    Government entities, access by
        List of government entities which may be authorized to receive access   CRC 2.540
Enforcement of judgments (See ENFORCEMENT OF JUDGMENTS)
Execution of process
    Directions of party re   CCP §262
    Liability of sheriff for   CCP §262
    New county, effect of creation of   CCP §262.11
    Party to action, execution of process where sheriff is   CCP §§262.6, 262.8
    Regular on its face, sheriff to execute process   CCP §262.1
    Successors in office, execution by   CCP §262.3
Fees   Gov §26720.9
    Generally   Gov §26720
    Attachment (See ATTACHMENT)
    Bench warrants, service and execution of   Gov §26744
    Collection
        Generally   Gov §26720
        Additional fees collectible   Gov §§26746, 26748
    Conducting or postponing property sales, fees for   Gov §26730
    Copy fees   Gov §26727
    Deed of sale, execution and delivery of   Gov §26741
    Earnings withholding orders, fee for serving   Gov §26750
    Emergency protective orders   Gov §26721
    Eviction   Gov §26733.5
    Execution, writ of (See ENFORCEMENT OF JUDGMENTS)
    Indigent party, waiver of fee for   Gov §26720.5
    In forma pauperis, waiver of fee where   Gov §26720.5
    Insane persons transported to state hospital   Gov §26749
    Jury summons, fee for   Gov §26745
    Mental hospitals, transportation of insane persons to   Gov §26749
    Other instruments, executing and delivering of   Gov §26742
    Possession, writ of (See ENFORCEMENT OF JUDGMENTS)
    Prisoners, transportation of
        To county jail   Gov §26747
        To state prison   Gov §26749
    Property keeper fee
        Generally   Gov §26726
        Additional fees, collection of   Gov §26748
    Real property, writs on   Gov §§26725, 26725.1, 26726
    Redemption, execution and delivery of certificate of   Gov §26740
    Repossessed automobiles, notice of   Gov §26751
    Safe deposit box, opening   Gov §26723
    Sale, writ of (See ENFORCEMENT OF JUDGMENTS)
    Service of process   Gov §26720.9
        Generally   Gov §26721
        Cancellation of service, fee charged for   Gov §26736

SHERIFF—Cont.
Fees —Cont.
    Service of process —Cont.
        Copy of service, fee for   Gov §26727
        Earnings withholding orders   Gov §26750
        Emergency protective orders   Gov §26721
        Forced sale of personal property, fee for notice of   Gov §§26728, 26728.1
        Indigent party, fee waived for   Gov §26720.5
        Not found returns, fee for   Gov §26738
        Publication, fee for notice of   Gov §§26729, 26732
        Real property, writs related to   Gov §§26725, 26725.1
        Superior court summons   Gov §26721.2
        Unlawful detainer action   Gov §26721.1
    Superior court summons   Gov §26721.2
    Wage garnishment orders, fees for service of   Gov §26750
    Witnesses, subpoena of   Gov §26743
Inclusions in definition   CCP §17
Inquest jury (See JURIES OF INQUEST)
Interested persons, process shown to   CCP §262.2
Levying officer electronic transactions act   CCP §§263 to 263.7
Lost property, duties as to   CC §§2080.1 to 2080.5
Marriage
    Local government officials, authority to solemnize   Fam §400
Motor vehicle certificate of correction, special county fund for fees collected by sheriff's inspection for proof of   Gov §26746.1
Prisoners, fee for transporting
    To county jail   Gov §26747
    To state prison   Gov §26749
Process, service of (See within this heading, "Service of process")
Property keeper fee   Gov §26746
    Additional fees, collection   Gov §26748
Redemption, execution and delivery of certificate of   Gov §26740
Salaries and benefits as court operations costs   CRC 10.810
Sales by sheriff (See ENFORCEMENT OF JUDGMENTS)
Service of papers on   CCP §262.5
Service of process
    Action against sheriff   CCP §262.7
    Fees (See within this heading, "Fees")
    Juvenile court papers, request for service of   CRCAppx A
    Levying officer electronic transactions act   CCP §§263 to 263.7
        Citation of provisions   CCP §263
        Definitions   CCP §263.1
        Electronic records as substitute for paper   CCP §§263.1, 263.4
        Execution writs, retention of original or electronic copy   CCP §263.6
        Facsimile transmissions   CCP §§263.1, 263.3
        Identifiers, exclusion or redaction   CCP §263.7
        Information processing systems   CCP §§263.1, 263.2
        Legislative intent   CCP §263
        Technical problems, effect on filing day   CCP §263.2
    Subpoenas, service of
        Concealed witness   CCP §1988
        Fees for service   Gov §26743
Special sheriff's fund
    Allocation of sheriff's fees collected to   Gov §26731
    Motor vehicle certificate of correction, deposit of fees collected from sheriff's inspection for   Gov §26746.1
Statute of limitation against   CCP §339
Subpoenas
    Concealed witness, service by sheriff on   CCP §1988
    Fees for service of   Gov §26743
Successors in office, execution of process by   CCP §262.3
Wage garnishment orders, fees for service of   Gov §26750
Warrants (See ARREST)
Witnesses, sheriffs as (See WITNESSES)

SHIPMENT
Bill of lading (See BILL OF LADING)
Common carriers (See COMMON CARRIERS)

SHIPS (See VESSELS)

SHOOTING RANGES
Noise pollution liability, exemption from   CC §3482.1

SHOP BOOK RULE (See BOOK ACCOUNTS)

SHORT CAUSES
Case management   CRC 3.735

SHORTENING TIME
Administration of decedents' estates (See ADMINISTRATION OF ESTATES)

SHORTENING TIME—Cont.
Appellate court rules   CRC 8.68
    Superior court appeals   CRC 8.813
Complex case coordination   CRC 3.503
Continuous defamatory publication, shortening time to respond for   CCP §460.5
Election campaign, shortening of time to respond to complaint in action for libel alleged to have occurred during   CCP §460.7
Enforcement of judgments (See **ENFORCEMENT OF JUDGMENTS**)
Law and motion rule   CRC 3.1300
Rules of court   CRC 1.10
Will probate proceedings, shortening time for giving notice in   Pro §1203

SHORTHAND REPORTERS
Oath at deposition proceedings, administration of   CCP §2093

SHORT-TERM VACATION RENTALS
Cancellation of reservations, refunds   CC §§1748.80 to 1748.84
    Action for violation of provisions   CC §1748.83
    Definitions   CC §1748.80
    Exceptions to provisions   CC §1748.84
    Issuance of refund   CC §1748.82
    Time period for cancellation without penalty   CC §1748.81

SHOTGUNS (See **FIREARMS AND OTHER WEAPONS**)

SHOW CAUSE ORDERS
Child abuse or neglect, motion for sanctions for false accusation of   Fam §3027.1
Custody of children (See **CUSTODY OF CHILDREN**)
Domestic violence (See **DOMESTIC VIOLENCE**)
Family law rules (See **FAMILY RULES**)
Marital disputes, granting temporary restraining order in   CCP §527
Surety bonds, sufficiency of (See **SURETYSHIP, BONDS AND UNDERTAKINGS**)
Transfer to another judge for hearing on   CCP §1006

SHOWERS
Water conserving plumbing retrofits   CC §§1101.1 to 1101.9

SHOWS (See **FAIRS AND EXPOSITIONS**)

SHRUBS   CC §660

SIBLINGS (See **BROTHERS AND SISTERS**)

SIDEWALKS
Blind persons having equal rights to use of   CC §§54, 54.3, 54.4, 55
    Construction or application of provisions in issue, solicitor general notified   CC §55.2
Construction defects, actions for
    Actionable defects   CC §896
Disabled persons having equal rights to use of   CC §§54, 54.3, 54.4, 55
    Construction or application of provisions in issue, solicitor general notified   CC §55.2

SIGHTLESS PERSONS (See **BLIND PERSONS**)

SIGHTSEEING
Owner's liability for recreational land   CC §846

SIGNAL DOGS
Deaf persons' right to   CC §§54.1, 54.2
    Construction or application of provisions in issue, solicitor general notified   CC §55.2

SIGNATURES
Acknowledgment and proof of execution of instruments (See **ACKNOWLEDGMENTS**)
Advertising, unauthorized use of name or likeness in   CC §§3344, 3344.1
Appellate court administration, supreme court and courts of appeal
    Signing, subscribing or verifying documents   CRC 10.1028
Appellate rules, superior court appeals
    Electronically filed documents
        Signatures on electronically filed documents   CRC 8.804
Appellate rules, supreme court and courts of appeal
    E-filing in supreme court and courts of appeal   CRC 8.75
    Entry of appealable order determined by   CRC 8.104
    Multiple parties' signatures required   CRC 8.42
        E-filed documents   CRC 8.75
    Notice of appeal   CRC 8.100
Assignment of judgment, acknowledgment of   CCP §673
Authentication of documents   Ev §§1453, 1454, 1530
Automobile conditional sales contracts   CC §2982

SIGNATURES—Cont.
Campaign advertisements, action for damages for use of unauthorized signatures in   CC §3344.5
Confession of judgment, attorneys signing certificates for   CCP §1132
Contracts (See **CONTRACTS AND AGREEMENTS**)
Coordination of actions
    Judicial Council
        Electronic submission of documents to council, signature under penalty of perjury   CRC 3.512
Declaration or certification of written instrument executed under penalty of perjury   CCP §2015.5
Electronic filing and service rules   CRC 2.257
Electronic signatures
    Child support
        Government support enforcement services, electronic filing of pleadings signed by agent of local child support agency   Fam §17400
    Defined   CCP §17
    Effectiveness   CCP §34
    Electronic filing and service rules   CRC 2.257
Electronic transactions (See **ELECTRONIC TRANSACTIONS**)
Emergency protective orders   Fam §6270
Family law rules (See **FAMILY RULES**)
Fax filing and service
    Signature requirement   CRC 2.305
Inclusions in definition   CCP §17
Inspection demand
    Response to demand   CCP §2031.250
Interrogatories
    Response to interrogatories   CCP §2030.250
Invasion of privacy, unauthorized use of signature in advertising as   CC §§3344, 3344.1
Judicial arbitration award   CCP §1141.23
Jurors, excuses of   CCP §218
Letters of administration   Pro §8405
Limitation of actions (See **STATUTES OF LIMITATION**)
Liquidated damages clauses   CC §1677
Mark, signature by   CCP §17
Marriage
    Remote licensing and solemnization
        Signatures on license   Fam §556
Medical information, authorization for release of   CC §§56.10, 56.11
Memorabilia
    Sale of autographed memorabilia   CC §1739.7
Penalty of perjury, declaration or certification of written instrument under   CCP §2015.5
Premarital agreements   Fam §1611
Presiding judge signing judgment when trial judge unavailable   CCP §635
Pretrial arbitration award   CCP §1141.23
Probate rules
    Pleadings
        Signature   CRC 7.103
Public entities, signatures on claims against   Gov §910.2
Receipts   CCP §2075
Request for admission
    Response to request   CCP §2033.240
Retail installment sale contracts   CC §1803.4
Stay of orders   CCP §917.3
Stipulated judgment   CCP §664.6
Summons   CCP §412.20
Superior courts (See **SUPERIOR COURTS**)
Transfer on death deeds
    Execution of instrument
        Effective, when   Pro §5624
Trust decanting, uniform act
    Exercise of decanting power
        Writing and other formalities for exercise   Pro §19510
Verification of papers (See **VERIFICATION**)
Wills (See **WILLS**)

SIGN LANGUAGE INTERPRETERS (See **TRANSLATORS AND INTERPRETERS**)

SIGNS AND BILLBOARDS
Animal shelter sign stating use of animals for research   CC §1834.7
Commercial and industrial common interest developments
    Noncommercial signage display
        Protected uses   CC §6704
Common interest developments
    For sale signs on property
        Provisions outside of common interest development law limiting association's regulation of member's separate interest   CC §4700

SIGNS

SIGNS AND BILLBOARDS—Cont.
Common interest developments—Cont.
    Noncommercial signs, posters, flags or banners
        Restrictions on limitations, prohibitions   CC §4710
Courts
    No-smoking signs in court facilities   CRC 10.504
For sale signs, display of   CC §§712, 713
Human trafficking
    Businesses required to post notice concerning relief from slavery or human trafficking   CC §52.6
        Training for employees who might interact with victims   CC §52.6
Landlord and tenant
    Political signs
        Restrictions on prohibition   CC §1940.4
Mobilehome parks   CC §§798.70, 799.1.5
    Mobilehome assistance center
        Posting sign by housing and community development department   CC §798.29
    Signs, placement of
        Political campaign signs   CC §§798.51, 799.10
Ownership, subject to   CC §655
Public entity, liability of (See **CLAIMS AGAINST PUBLIC ENTITIES AND EMPLOYEES**)
Retail sellers, sign displaying refund policy of   CC §1723
Slavery
    Businesses required to post notice concerning relief from slavery or human trafficking   CC §52.6
        Training for employees who might interact with victims   CC §52.6

SILICOSIS
Depositions
    Time limits for witness examination
        Actions involving mesothelioma or silicosis   CCP §2025.295

SILK
Common carrier's liability for   CC §2200

SILVER
Common carrier's liability for transporting   CC §2200

SIMULTANEOUS DEATH
Generally   Pro §220
Applicability of law   Pro §226
Community property, effect on   Pro §§103, 6402
Division of property after   Pro §222
Failure of heirs to survive decedent   Pro §§6211, 6403
Hearing on issue of   Pro §§230 to 234
Insurance proceeds, disposition of   Pro §224
Joint tenancy property   Pro §223
Jurisdiction of proceedings establishing   Pro §232
Life insurance   Pro §224
Notice of hearing to establish   Pro §233
Order   Pro §234
Petition for establishment of   Pro §§230 to 234
Survival of actions (See **SURVIVAL OF ACTIONS**)
Time period required for heirs to survive decedent   Pro §§6211, 6403
Trusts affected by provisions regulating   Pro §221
Wills, effect of statutory regulations on   Pro §221
Wrongful death action (See **WRONGFUL DEATH**)

SINGULAR
Construction of words used in code   CCP §17
Family code   Fam §10

SISTERS (See **BROTHERS AND SISTERS**)

SISTER STATE MONEY-JUDGMENT ACT
Generally   CCP §§1710.55, 1710.60
Applicability of chapter   CCP §1710.35
Applications for   CCP §§1710.15, 1710.20
Definitions   CCP §1710.10
Entry of judgment
    Generally   CCP §§1710.25, 1710.65
    Notice, service of   CCP §1710.30
Notice, service of   CCP §1710.30
Stay of enforcement   CCP §1710.50
Vacation of judgment   CCP §1710.40
Writ of execution, issuance of   CCP §1710.45

SISTER STATES (See **OTHER STATES**)

SIT-INS (See **DEMONSTRATIONS, PARADES AND MEETINGS**)

SITTING OF COURT
Judicial holidays falling on day appointed for   CCP §136
Public, sittings open to   CCP §124

SITUS
Venue determination   CCP §392

SIX MONTHS (See **STATUTES OF LIMITATION**)

SIX YEARS (See **STATUTES OF LIMITATION**)

SKILLED NURSING FACILITIES
Medical claims data error correction   CC §57

SLANDER (See **LIBEL AND SLANDER**)

SLANDER OF TITLE
Preservation of interest notice recorded with intent to slander title   CC §880.360

SLAPPBACK ACTIONS   CCP §425.18

SLAPP SUITS (See **STRATEGIC LAWSUITS AGAINST PUBLIC PARTICIPATION**)

SLAVERY
Actions for relief based on human trafficking   CC §52.5
Human trafficking
    Nuisance
        Attorney's fees recoverable for enjoining use of building for   CC §3496
    Prostitution, victims forced to commit
        Evidentiary significance   Ev §1161
    Real property used in offense
        Attorney's fees recoverable for enjoining use of building for   CC §3496
    Signs
        Businesses required to post notice concerning relief from slavery or human trafficking   CC §52.6
    Supply chains of certain businesses
        Disclosures by businesses of efforts to eradicate slavery and human trafficking in supply chain   CC §1714.43
    Victim-caseworker privilege
        Waiver of privilege   Ev §912
    Victims
        Prostitution or other commercial sex acts committed by victims, evidentiary significance   Ev §1161
Human trafficking victim-caseworker privilege   Ev §§1038 to 1038.2
    Compelling disclosure
        Grounds   Ev §1038.1
    Definitions   Ev §1038.2
    Eligibility to claim privilege   Ev §1038
    In chambers proceeding to determine ruling on privilege   Ev §1038.1
    Limitations on privilege
        Caseworker to notify victim   Ev §1038
Nazi regime during Second World War, actions to recover compensation for slave or forced labor under   CCP §354.6

SLIDES
Boundary reestablishment   CCP §§751.50 to 751.65

SLIDING SCALE RECOVERY AGREEMENTS
Disclosure requirement   CCP §877.5

SMALL BUSINESS
Administrative Procedure Act (See **ADMINISTRATIVE PROCEDURE ACT**)
Commercial financing transactions
    Applicability of provisions   CC §1799.301
    Definitions   CC §1799.300
    Prohibited fees   CC §1799.302
        Remedies for violations   CC §1799.303
    Waiver of provisions as void   CC §1799.304
Costs in action involving   CCP §1028.5
Defined   CCP §1028.5, Gov §§11342, 11342.610
Gender discrimination in pricing services   CC §§55.61 to 55.63

SMALL BUSINESS GENDER DISCRIMINATION IN PRICING SERVICES COMPLIANCE ACT   CC §§55.61 to 55.63
Complaints
    Contents   CC §55.62
Definitions   CC §55.62
Demand letter
    Contents   CC §55.62

SMALL BUSINESS GENDER DISCRIMINATION IN PRICING SERVICES COMPLIANCE ACT—Cont.
Demand letter—Cont.
    Defined   CC §55.62
Pamphlet or other information for use by certain businesses
    Consumer affairs department duties   CC §55.63
Short title of provisions   CC §55.61
Written advisory notice to defendant
    Contents of demand letter or complaint   CC §55.62
    Form   CC §55.62

SMALL CLAIMS COURTS
Acknowledgment of satisfaction of judgment   CCP §116.850
Active duty in armed forces, submission of evidence by plaintiff in   CCP §116.540
Adjacent counties, joint advisory services of   CCP §116.940
Administration
    Advisory service generally (See within this heading, **"Advisory service"**)
    Judicial Council (See within this heading, **"Judicial council"**)
    Publications describing small claims court law and procedures   CCP §116.930
Advisory service   CRC 3.2120
    Adjacent counties, joint advisory services of   CCP §116.940
    Availability of individual assistance to advise small claims litigants   CCP §116.260
    Conflict of interest   CCP §116.940, CRC 3.2120
    Contracting with third party to provide   CCP §116.940
    Department of Consumer Affairs, input of   CCP §§116.920, 116.950
    Establishment and composition of advisory committee   CCP §116.950
    Immunity of advisors and other court employees   CCP §116.940
    Individual personal advisory service, availability of   CCP §116.940
    Law students as small claims advisors   CCP §116.940
    Local needs and conditions   CCP §116.940
    Manual or information booklet on rules and procedures   CCP §116.930
    Minimum advisory services, election to provide   CCP §116.940
    Nonadvocacy rule   CCP §116.940
    Notice of availability of   CCP §116.920, CRC 3.2120
    Paralegals as small claims advisors   CCP §116.940
    Qualifications of advisors   CCP §116.920, CRC 3.2120
    Telephone services, availability of   CCP §116.940
    Topics covered   CCP §116.940
    Training standards for advisors   CCP §116.920
    Volunteers as small claims advisors   CCP §116.940
Amendment
    Judgment, terms and conditions for payment of   CCP §116.620
    Party's names
        Motion to amend name of party   CCP §§116.560, 116.630
Amount in controversy
    Claim in excess of jurisdictional limit (See within this heading, **"Claim in excess of jurisdictional limit"**)
    Jurisdictional limits based on   CCP §116.220
        Natural persons, actions by   CCP §116.221
Appeal   CCP §§116.710 to 116.798, CRC 8.950 to 8.966
    Abandonment   CRC 8.963
    Applicability of rules   CRC 8.950
    Attorney participation   CCP §116.770
    Attorney's fees
        Generally   CCP §116.780
        Bad-faith appeals   CCP §116.790
    Bad-faith appeals   CCP §116.790
    Claim form notice re right of   CCP §116.320
    Compromise of case involving wards or conservatees, approval   CRC 8.963
    Conduct of hearing   CCP §116.770
    Continuance   CRC 8.960
    Definitions   CRC 8.952
    Dismissal   CRC 8.963
        Delay in bringing case to trial   CCP §116.795, CRC 8.963
        Enforcement of judgment   CCP §116.810
        Failure to appear   CCP §116.795
        Jurisdiction, effect on   CCP §116.795
        Lack of timely prosecution   CCP §116.795
        Notice   CRC 8.963
        Request for   CRC 8.963
        Stipulation for   CRC 8.963
    Examination and cross examination   CRC 8.966
    Failure to appear, dismissal for   CCP §116.795
    Fee for   CCP §116.760
    Finality of superior court judgment   CCP §116.780
    Force and effect of superior court judgment   CCP §116.780
    Governing law   CCP §904.5

SMALL CLAIMS COURTS—Cont.
Appeal —Cont.
    Insurer's appeal   CCP §116.710
    Judgment debtor's assets, effect of appeal on time for disclosure of   CCP §116.830
    Lack of timely prosecution, dismissal for   CCP §116.795
    Motion to vacate judgment, appeal on denial of   CCP §116.730
    No right to trial by jury   CCP §116.770
    Notice of appeal   CRC 8.954
        Appeal taken by filing   CCP §116.750
        Motion to vacate judgment, denial of   CCP §116.730
        Time for filing   CCP §116.750
    Notice of hearing, time for   CCP §116.770
    Record on appeal   CCP §116.770, CRC 8.957
    Restrictions on right of appeal   CCP §116.710
    Scheduling hearing   CCP §116.770
    Setting time for hearing   CCP §116.770
    Suspension of judgment enforcement pending   CCP §116.810
    Transmitting record   CRC 8.957
    Writ petitions   CRC 8.970 to 8.977
        Applicability of provisions   CRC 8.970
        Attorney filing for party   CRC 8.973
        Costs   CRC 8.977
        Decisions   CRC 8.976
        Definitions   CRC 8.971
        Notice to small claims court   CRC 8.975
        Opposition   CRC 8.974
        Pro se petitions   CRC 8.972
        Remittitur   CRC 8.976
        Return or opposition   CRC 8.974
        Telephone notice to small claims court   CRC 8.975
Appearance
    Active duty in armed forces, plaintiff in   CCP §116.540
    Appeal dismissed for failure to appear   CCP §116.795
    Commercial and industrial common interest developments
        Associations managing development   CCP §116.540
    Common interest developments
        Associations managing development   CCP §116.540
    Corporations   CCP §116.540
    Defendant's failure to appear, presentation of evidence on   CCP §116.520
    Employee appearing for plaintiff   CCP §116.540
    Guardian ad litem, minor or incompetent person appear by   CCP §116.410
    Husband and wife on joint claims   CCP §116.540
    Incarcerated plaintiff   CCP §116.540
    Issuance of order to appear   CCP §116.330
    Minors
        Guardian ad litem, appearance by   CCP §116.410
    Motion to vacate judgment for lack of appearance   CCP §116.720
    Nonresident owner of real property   CCP §116.540
    Party other than corporation or natural person   CCP §116.540
    Personal appearance of parties not required, conditions   CCP §116.540
    Property manager appearing for owner of rental property   CCP §116.540
    Service of order to appear (See within this heading, **"Service of claim and order to appear"**)
    Spouse on joint claims   CCP §116.540
Attorneys
    Appeal, participation in hearing on   CCP §116.770
    Exceptions to restriction on representation by   CCP §116.530
    Fees (See within this heading, **"Attorney's fees"**)
    Notice in claim form re representation by   CCP §116.320
    Restriction on representation by   CCP §116.530
    Small claims advisors   CCP §116.940
    Writ petitions
        Attorney filing for party   CRC 8.973
Attorney's fees
    Appeal   CCP §116.780
        Bad-faith appeals   CCP §116.790
    Arbitration award in fee dispute, jurisdiction to confirm, correct or vacate   CCP §116.220
    Judgment debtor's assets, sanction for failure to disclose   CCP §116.830
    Transfer of action when cross-claim in excess of jurisdictional limit, award of costs incurred in   CCP §116.390
Automobiles (See within this heading, **"Motor vehicles"**)
Bonds and undertakings
    Jurisdiction   CCP §116.220
Burden of proof on defendant's failure to appear   CCP §116.520
Check on insufficient funds, damages for passing   CC §1719
Civil rights actions   CC §52.2
Claim
    Approval or adoption of claim form   CCP §116.320
    Assignee filing claim, restrictions on   CCP §116.420

SMALL CLAIMS COURTS—Cont.
  Claim—Cont.
    Contents of   CCP §116.320
    Defendants filing   CRC 3.2104
    Filing   CCP §§116.320, 116.330
    Initiating action   CCP §116.310
    Number of claims filed
      Claims exceeding $2500, restrictions on filing   CCP §116.231
      Minimum advisory services, election to provide   CCP §116.940
    Service on defendant (See within this heading, **"Service of claim and order to appear"**)
  Claim in excess of jurisdictional limit
    Defendant's claim in excess of jurisdictional limit   CCP §116.390
    Filing restrictions on claims in excess of $2500   CCP §116.231
    Waiver of excess amount   CCP §116.220
  Clerk, assistance to litigants   CRC 3.2110
  Consumer protection laws
    Availability of bench book describing   CCP §116.930
    Selection of forum outside of state
      Contracts for personal, family or household purposes   CCP §116.225
  Continuances
    Appeals   CRC 8.960
  Corporate officers and employees
    Appearing for corporation   CCP §116.540
    Exception to restriction on representation by attorneys   CCP §116.530
  Costs
    Attorney's fees generally (See within this heading, **"Attorney's fees"**)
    Enforcement of judgment   CCP §116.820
    Fees generally (See within this heading, **"Fees"**)
    Limited civil case resulting in judgment for less than small claims jurisdictional amount, recovery of costs in   CCP §1033
    Payment to court in which judgment entered, procedure for   CCP §116.860
    Prevailing party entitled to   CCP §116.610
    Transfer of action when cross-claim in excess of jurisdictional limit, award of costs incurred in   CCP §116.390
    Wage claims for labor performed, attorneys' fees in   CCP §1031
  Court clerk's role in assisting litigants   CRC 3.2110
  Creation of small claims division   CCP §116.210
  Cross-claim
    Applicability of cross-complaint provisions   CCP §426.60
    Filing   CCP §116.360
    Service   CCP §116.360
    Transfer of action when defendant's claim is in excess of jurisdictional limit   CCP §116.390
  Cross-complaints
    Filing   CRC 3.2104
  Cross examination on appeal   CRC 8.966
  Declaration
    Appear for party, declaration stating individual authorized to   CCP §116.540
    Defined   CCP §116.130
    Fictitious business name laws, compliance with   CCP §116.430, CRC 3.2100
    Motion to vacate (See within this heading, **"Motion to vacate"**)
    Number of claims in excess of $2500 filed in calendar year   CCP §116.231
    Presumption of full or partial payment of judgment   CCP §116.850
    Submission of evidence by   CCP §116.540
    Transfer of action when cross-claim in excess of jurisdictional limit   CCP §116.390
  Defendant defined   CCP §116.130
  Definitions   CCP §116.130
    Appellate rules   CRC 8.952
  Delay
    Award of attorney's fees on finding that appeal taken for purposes of   CCP §116.790
    Entry of satisfaction of judgment, type of payment delaying   CCP §116.860
  Department of Consumer Affairs, input of   CCP §§116.920, 116.930, 116.950
  Department of corrections and rehabilitation
    Participation by department via employee   CCP §116.541
  Direct and cross-examination
    Appeals, trial of   CRC 8.966
  Discovery procedure not permitted in   CCP §116.310
  Dismissal
    Appeal (See within this heading, **"Appeal"**)
    Fictitious business name laws, failure to comply with   CCP §116.430
    Improper venue   CCP §116.370
  Driver's license suspension for failure to satisfy small claims judgment   CCP §§116.870 to 116.880
  Electronic filing of claims   CCP §116.320
  Emancipated minor as party   CCP §116.410

SMALL CLAIMS COURTS—Cont.
  Enforcement of judgment
    Appeal, suspension of judgment enforcement pending   CCP §116.810
    Applicable provisions   CCP §116.820
    Costs and interest   CCP §116.820
    Fees   CCP §116.820
    Judgment debtor's assets, disclosure of   CCP §116.830
    Motion to vacate judgment, enforcement suspended pending determination of   CCP §116.740
    Payment of judgment, generally   CCP §116.840
    Payment to court in which judgment entered, procedure for   CCP §116.860
    Satisfaction of judgment generally (See within this heading, **"Satisfaction of judgment"**)
    Suspension of driving privilege   CCP §§116.870 to 116.880
  Equitable relief   CRC 3.2108
    In lieu of or in addition to money damages   CCP §116.220
  Ethics code for court employees   CRC JudAdminStand 10.16
  Evidence
    Active duty in armed forces, submission of evidence by plaintiff in   CCP §116.540
    Business record, evidence of an account that constitutes   CCP §116.540
    Defendant's failure to appear, effect of   CCP §116.520
    Incarcerated plaintiff, submission of evidence by   CCP §116.540
    Nonresident owner of real property   CCP §116.540
    Right to offer   CCP §116.520
  Examination and cross examination on appeal   CRC 8.966
  Experts, assistance and testimony of   CCP §116.531
  Fax filing of claim   CCP §116.320
  Fees
    Appeal, fee for   CCP §116.760
    Disposition   CCP §116.230
    Enforcement of judgment   CCP §116.820
    Filing fees   CCP §116.230
    Mail service, cost of   CCP §116.232
    Motion to vacate   CCP §116.745
    Payment to court in which judgment entered, procedure for   CCP §116.860
    Postponement and rescheduling of hearing date, request for   CCP §116.570
    Suspension of judgment debtor's driving privilege, notice requesting   CCP §116.880
    Waiver of filing fees and fees for serving claim   CCP §116.320
  Fictitious business name
    Compliance with fictitious business name law   CCP §116.430
    Correct legal name of party, amendment of claim to state   CCP §§116.560, 116.630
    Statement of compliance with law   CRC 3.2100
  Filing restrictions on claims in excess of $2500   CCP §116.231
  Finality of superior court judgment after hearing on appeal   CCP §116.780
  Good cause defined   CCP §116.130
  Guarantors
    Jurisdiction over   CCP §116.220
    Service in action against principal and guaranty or surety   CCP §116.340
  Guardian ad litem, minor or incompetent person appear by   CCP §116.410
  Hearing
    Appearance generally (See within this heading, **"Appearance"**)
    Attorney representation restricted   CCP §116.530
    Evidence, generally   CCP §116.520
    Expert testimony   CCP §116.531
    Manner of conducting hearing   CCP §116.510
    Motion to vacate judgment for lack of appearance   CCP §116.720
    Order to appear, issuance and service of   CCP §116.330
    Scheduling case for   CCP §116.330
    Witnesses   CCP §116.520
  Hotelkeeper or innkeeper's liens, writ of possession issued for property subject to   CCP §116.220
  Immunity for small claims court advisors   CCP §116.940, Gov §818.9
  Incarcerated participants
    Department of corrections and rehabilitation
      Participation by department via employee   CCP §116.541
  Incompetent persons
    Approval of compromise of case on appeal   CRC 8.963
    Guardian ad litem, minor or incompetent person appear by   CCP §116.410
  Individual defined   CCP §116.130
  Insurers
    Appeals by   CCP §116.710
    Assistance by representatives of   CCP §116.531
  Judges
    Bench books, availability   CCP §116.930
    Composition of small claims advisory committee   CCP §116.950
    Consumer protection laws, availability of bench book describing   CCP §116.930
    Law clerks, assistance of   CCP §116.270

SMALL CLAIMS COURTS—Cont.
Judges—Cont.
- Temporary
  - Qualifications of and training program for   CRC 2.812, 2.813
  - Stipulation to   CRC 2.816
  - Use of   CCP §116.240
- Training standards   CCP §116.920

Judgment   CRC 3.2108
- Appeal (See within this heading, **"Appeal"**)
- Costs, prevailing party entitled to   CCP §116.610
- Damages and/or equitable relief   CCP §116.610, CRC 3.2108
- Enforcement (See within this heading, **"Enforcement of judgment"**)
- Examination of judgment debtor
  - Fee for application for order for examination   CCP §116.820
- Interest on money   CCP §116.820
- Motion to vacate judgment (See within this heading, **"Motion to vacate"**)
- Motor vehicle accident, determination whether judgment resulted from   CCP §116.610
- Name of party, motion to amend   CCP §§116.560, 116.630
- Notice of entry of
  - Generally   CCP §116.610
  - Judgment debtor's assets, time for disclosure of   CCP §116.830
  - Motion to vacate, time for filing   CCP §§116.720, 116.730
  - Notice of appeal, time for filing   CCP §116.750
- Payment of judgment   CCP §116.840
- Presumption of full or partial payment of judgment   CCP §116.850
- Rendering judgment   CCP §116.610
- Satisfaction of judgment (See within this heading, **"Satisfaction of judgment"**)
- Several defendants, action against   CCP §116.610
- Suspension of driving privilege for failure to satisfy judgment   CCP §§116.870 to 116.880
- Vacation   CCP §§116.710 to 116.798

Judgment creditor defined   CCP §116.130

Judgment debtor
- Assets, disclosure of   CCP §116.830
- Defined   CCP §116.130
- Payment to court in which judgment entered, procedure for   CCP §116.860
- Suspension of driving privilege   CCP §§116.870 to 116.880

Judicial arbitration
- Exemption from arbitration   CRC 3.811
- Legislative purpose and intent   CCP §1141.10

Judicial council
- Appeals, rulemaking authority with regard to practice and procedure for   CCP §116.770
- Appointments to small claims advisory committee   CCP §116.950
- Claim form, approval or adoption of   CCP §116.320
- Forms
  - Approval   CCP §116.920
  - List of judicial council legal forms   CRCAppx A
  - Writ proceedings   CRCAppx A
- General rulemaking authority   CCP §116.920
- Judgment debtor's assets, approval of form for disclosure of   CCP §116.830
- Request to make payment to court in which judgment entered, approval of form for   CCP §116.860

Jurisdiction   CCP §116.220
- Amount in controversy, jurisdictional limits based on   CCP §116.220
  - Automobile accidents causing bodily injury   CCP §116.114
  - Natural persons, actions by   CCP §116.221
- Automobile accidents causing bodily injury   CCP §116.114
- Claim in excess of jurisdictional limit (See within this heading, **"Claim in excess of jurisdictional limit"**)
- COVID-19 rental debt, action to recover   CCP §116.223
- Dismissal of appeal, effect of   CCP §116.795
- Guarantors, jurisdiction over   CCP §116.220
- Incarcerated plaintiff, action filed by   CCP §116.220
- Limited civil cases   CCP §87
- Natural persons, actions by   CCP §116.221
- Selection of forum outside of state
  - Contracts for personal, family or household purposes   CCP §116.225

Juvenile facilities division
- Participation via employee   CCP §116.541

Legislative findings and declarations   CCP §116.120

Limited civil cases   CCP §87

Location of actions
- Venue   CCP §116.370

Mail
- Claim filed by   CCP §116.320
- Defined   CCP §116.130
- Fee to cover cost of service by mail   CCP §116.232

SMALL CLAIMS COURTS—Cont.
Mail—Cont.
- Notice of appeal, mailing notice of entry of judgment not extending time for filing   CCP §116.750
- Notice of entry of judgment   CCP §116.610
- Service on defendant   CCP §116.340

Mandate, writ of
- Petition for extraordinary relief relating to act of small claims division   CCP §116.798

Minors
- Compromise of case on appeal, approval of   CRC 8.963
- Guardian ad litem, appearance by   CCP §116.410

Motion defined   CCP §116.130

Motions filed in small claims cases
- Memorandum in support of motion not required   CRC 3.1114

Motion to vacate   CCP §§116.710 to 116.798
- Appeal on denial of   CCP §116.730
- Clerical errors as grounds for   CCP §116.725
- Defendant's motion
  - Improper service, motion to vacate for   CCP §116.740
  - Lack of appearance   CCP §116.730
- Filing fee   CCP §116.745
- Improper service, motion to vacate for   CCP §116.740
- Incorrect or erroneous legal basis as grounds for   CCP §116.725
- Judgment debtor's assets, effect of motion on time for disclosure of   CCP §116.830
- Plaintiff who did not appear at hearing, motion of   CCP §116.720
- Time
  - Defendant's motion to vacate for lack of appearance, filing   CCP §116.730
  - Improper service, filing defendant's motion to vacate for   CCP §116.740
  - Notice of appeal on denial of motion, filing   CCP §116.730
  - Plaintiff's motion to vacate for lack of appearance, filing   CCP §116.720

Motor vehicles
- Accidents
  - Bodily injury, jurisdiction   CCP §116.114
  - Judgment to include determination concerning   CCP §116.610
  - Conditional sale contract, standing to file claim based on   CCP §116.420
  - Suspension of judgment debtor's driving privilege for failure to satisfy judgment   CCP §§116.870 to 116.880

Multiple defendants
- Appeals   CCP §116.770
- Date of appearance, setting   CCP §116.330
- Judgment   CCP §116.610

Names
- After judgment, amendment of party's names   CCP §116.630
- Fictitious business names, use of   CCP §116.430, CRC 3.2100
- Motion to amend name of party   CCP §§116.560, 116.630

Natural persons, action by
- Jurisdiction   CCP §116.221

Night sessions   CCP §116.250

Nonresidents
- Motor vehicle involved in accident in California, service on nonresident owner or operator of   CCP §116.340
- Real property owners
  - Appearance and submission of evidence   CCP §116.540
  - Service on   CCP §116.340

Notice of appeal (See within this heading, **"Appeal"**)
Notice of entry of judgment (See within this heading, **"Judgment"**)
Notice of motion requirements, limitations on   CCP §116.140

Number of claims filed
- Claims in excess of $2500, restriction on filing   CCP §116.231
- Minimum advisory services, election to provide   CCP §116.940

Orders of court
- Appearance
  - Order to appear, issuance and service   CCP §116.330
- Requests for order   CRC 3.2107

Parties
- Generally   CCP §116.410
- Amendment of party's names
  - Names generally (See within this heading, **"Names"**)
- Appearance generally (See within this heading, **"Appearance"**)
- Assignee filing claim, restrictions on   CCP §116.420
- Defined   CCP §116.130
- Incompetent persons   CCP §116.410
- Minors   CCP §116.410
- Multiple defendants (See within this heading, **"Multiple defendants"**)
- Nonresidents (See within this heading, **"Nonresidents"**)
- Order to appear, issuance and service of   CCP §116.330

SMALL CLAIMS COURTS—Cont.
Parties—Cont.
- Public entities   CCP §116.330
- Temporary judge, consent to use of   CCP §116.240

Partnerships
- Appearance by persons representing   CCP §116.540
- Exception to restriction on representation by attorneys   CCP §116.530

Personal property taxes, jurisdiction to enforce payment of delinquent unsecured   CCP §116.220
Person defined   CCP §116.130
Plaintiff defined   CCP §116.130
Postponement of hearing   CCP §116.570
Posttrial requests for court orders   CRC 3.2107
Prejudgment attachment procedures, inapplicability of   CCP §116.140
Presumption of full or partial payment of judgment   CCP §116.850
Pretrial requests for court orders   CRC 3.2107

Prisoners
- Department of corrections and rehabilitation
  - Participation by department via employee   CCP §116.541

Prohibition, writ of
- Petition for extraordinary relief relating to act of small claims division   CCP §116.798

Proof of service of claim and order   CCP §116.340
Publications describing small claims court law and procedures   CCP §116.930
Public entities, preferential scheduling of hearing for   CCP §116.330
Representation by attorney, restriction on   CCP §116.530
Residence of defendant affecting scheduling case for hearing   CCP §116.330

Review, writ of
- Petition for extraordinary relief relating to act of small claims division   CCP §116.798

Rulemaking authority
- Judicial council generally (See within this heading, **"Judicial council"**)

Satisfaction of judgment
- Acknowledgment of   CCP §116.850
- Entry of   CCP §116.840
- Failure to acknowledge   CCP §116.850
- Installments, payment by   CCP §116.620
- Payment to court in which judgment entered, procedure for   CCP §116.860
- Presumption of full or partial payment of judgment   CCP §116.850
- Suspension of driving privilege   CCP §§116.870 to 116.880
- Terms and conditions for payment of judgment   CCP §116.620

Saturday sessions   CCP §§116.250, 134
Scheduling case for hearing   CCP §116.330

Service of claim and order to appear
- Generally   CCP §116.330
- Cross-claim, service of   CCP §116.360
- Fee to cover cost of service by mail   CCP §116.232
- Methods of   CCP §116.340
- Motion to vacate judgment for improper service   CCP §116.740
- Nonresident owner of real estate, service on   CCP §116.340
- Principal and guaranty or surety, service in action against   CCP §116.340
- Proof of service   CCP §116.340
- Substituted service   CCP §116.340, CRC 3.2102
- Time for   CCP §116.340

Service of process and papers   CRC 3.2102
Sessions of court   CCP §116.250
Substituted service   CCP §116.340, CRC 3.2102
Superior court, appeals to (See within this heading, **"Appeal"**)

Sureties
- Jurisdiction of guarantors   CCP §116.220
- Service in action against principal and guaranty or surety   CCP §116.340

Suspension of judgment debtor's driving privilege for failure to satisfy judgment   CCP §§116.870 to 116.880
Telephone advisory services, availability of   CCP §116.940

Temporary judges
- Qualifications of and training program for   CRC 2.812, 2.813
- Stipulations by party litigant to   CRC 2.816
- Use of   CCP §116.240

Time
- Hearing on appeal, time for notice of   CCP §116.770
- Judgment debtor's assets, disclosure of   CCP §116.830
- Motion to vacate (See within this heading, **"Motion to vacate"**)
- Notice of appeal, filing   CCP §116.750
- Postponement of hearing date   CCP §116.570
- Scheduling case for hearing   CCP §116.330
- Service of claim and order to appear, time for   CCP §116.340

Title   CCP §116.110

Transfer of actions
- Defendant's claim in excess of jurisdictional limit   CCP §116.390
- Service not completed on principal, transfer of action where   CCP §116.340

SMALL CLAIMS COURTS—Cont.
Trial Court Delay Reduction Act   Gov §68620
- Case disposition time goals   CRC JudAdminStand 2.2

Unlawful detainer   CCP §116.220
Vacation of judgment (See within this heading, **"Motion to vacate"**)
Venue   CCP §116.370, CRC 3.2106
- Selection of forum outside of state
  - Contracts for personal, family or household purposes   CCP §116.225

Wage claims for labor performed, attorneys' fees in   CCP §1031

Waiver
- Filing fees and fees for serving claim, waiver of   CCP §116.320
- Jurisdictional limit, waiver of amount of claim in excess of   CCP §116.220

Writ of possession for property subject to hotelkeeper or innkeeper's liens, issuance of   CCP §116.220

Writ petitions   CRC 8.970 to 8.977
- Applicability of provisions   CRC 8.970
- Attorney filing for party   CRC 8.973
- Costs   CRC 8.977
- Decisions   CRC 8.976
- Definitions   CRC 8.971
- Filing of decisions   CRC 8.976
- Finality of decisions   CRC 8.976
- Forms   CRCAppx A
- Issuance of writ
  - Notice to small claims court   CRC 8.975
- Modification of decisions   CRC 8.976
- Notice to small claims court   CRC 8.975
- Opposition   CRC 8.974
- Preliminary opposition   CRC 8.974
- Pro se petitions   CRC 8.972
- Remittitur   CRC 8.976
- Return or opposition   CRC 8.974
- Service
  - Pro se petitions   CRC 8.972
- Supporting documents
  - Pro se petitions   CRC 8.972
- Telephone notice to small claims court   CRC 8.975

SMALL ESTATES
Administration not required (See **SMALL ESTATES WITHOUT ADMINISTRATION**)
Escheat of   CCP §1415

SMALL ESTATES WITHOUT ADMINISTRATION
Affidavit procedure
- Ancillary administration (See **ANCILLARY ADMINISTRATION**)
- Personal property, collection of (See within this heading, **"Personal property collection"**)
- Real property of small value, procedure for (See within this heading, **"Real property succession"**)
- Salaries and earnings, collection of
  - Contents of affidavit   Pro §13601
  - Good faith reliance on affidavit   Pro §13603

Amount of estate   Pro §§6602, 13100
Ancillary administration (See **ANCILLARY ADMINISTRATION**)
Appeal of order setting aside small estate   Pro §§1303, 1310

Appraisement
- Generally (See within this heading, **"Inventory and appraisement"**)
- Real property succession
  - Inventory and appraisement (See within this heading, **"Real property succession"**)

Attorney's fees
- Confirmation of property proceedings   Pro §13660
- Personal property collection, action for   Pro §13105
- Real property succession, action for   Pro §13157
- Salaries and earnings owed to decedent, action for   Pro §13604
- Set-aside proceedings for small estates   Pro §6613

Automobiles excluded from decedent's estate   Pro §13050
Boats excluded from decedent's estate   Pro §13050
Bond requirements for transfers of personal property   Pro §13102

Claims against estate
- Personal property (See within this heading, **"Personal property collection"**)

Confirmation of property
- Attorney's fees   Pro §13660
- Business property, effect of creditors' claims to   Pro §13658
- Contents of petition   Pro §13651
- Filing of petition
  - Generally   Pro §13650
  - Joint filing with petition for probate   Pro §13653
  - Pending probate proceedings, filing petition where   Pro §13652

SMALL ESTATES WITHOUT ADMINISTRATION—Cont.
  Confirmation of property—Cont.
    Filing of petition—Cont.
      Subsequent probate proceedings, effect of filing petition on   Pro §13654
    Inventory and appraisement
      Generally   Pro §13659
      Business property   Pro §13658
    Joint filing with petition for probate proceedings   Pro §13653
    Notice of hearing   Pro §13655
    Orders
      Generally   Pro §13656
      Finality of   Pro §13657
    Pending probate proceedings, filing petition where   Pro §13652
    Subsequent probate proceedings, effect of filing petition on   Pro §13654
  Conservator acting on behalf of conservatee, authority of   Pro §13051
  Coroner's fees for property found on decedent, payment of   Pro §13114
  Creditors (See within this heading, **"Debt liability"**)
  Damages
    Personal property   Pro §§13110, 13111
    Real property   Pro §13206
  Debt liability
    Liability for decedent's unsecured debts   Pro §13109
    Personal property collection (See within this heading, **"Personal property collection"**)
    Public administrator, liability of distributee to estate administered by   Pro §7664
    Real property succession (See within this heading, **"Real property succession"**)
    Set-aside proceedings, liability for decedent's debts in   Pro §6611
    Successor's liability
      Real property, collection of   Pro §§13156, 13204
    Surviving spouse
      Generally   Pro §13550
      Business interests of creditors, protection of   Pro §13658
      Commencement of administration of estate proceedings, effect of   Pro §13552
      Enforcement against   Pro §13554
      Limitations on liability   Pro §13551
      No liability if all property administered   Pro §13553
    Transferee liability   Pro §§13109.5, 13204.5
  Decedent's property defined   Pro §13005
  Definitions   Pro §§13000 to 13007
  Election of surviving spouse
    Administration of estate, election for   Pro §13502
    Trustee, election to transfer property to   Pro §13503
  Exclusion from decedent's estate, property subject to   Pro §13050
  Forms
    Judicial council forms   CRCAppx A
  Fraud
    Personal property collection   Pro §§13110, 13111
      Remedies for fraud   Pro §13113
    Real property succession
      Damages   Pro §13206
      Liability of affiant   Pro §13205
    Salaries and earnings owed to decedent, fraudulent collection of   Pro §13605
    Surviving spouse, liability of   Pro §13564
  Fraudulent transfers   Pro §§13100 to 13117
  Good faith purchaser of real property   Pro §13203
  Governing law   Pro §§13053, 13054
  Guardian acting on behalf of ward, authority of   Pro §13051
  Health insurance
    Survivors of firefighters and peace officers, continuance   Pro §13600
  Holder of decedent's property   Pro §13002
  Identity of affiant for collection of personal property, proof of   Pro §13104
  Inventory and appraisement
    Date of valuation   Pro §13052
    Personal property collection   Pro §13103
    Real property (See within this heading, **"Real property succession"**)
    Set-aside proceedings   Pro §6608
  Joint tenancy property excluded from decedent's estate   Pro §13050
  Limitation of actions
    Personal property, actions involving   Pro §§13110, 13111
    Real property, actions involving   Pro §13205
  Limitations on liability
    Surviving spouse   Pro §13563
    Debts of decedent   Pro §13551
  Military service compensation excluded from decedent's estate   Pro §13050
  Mobilehomes excluded from decedent's estate   Pro §13050
  Multiple-party accounts excluded from decedent's estate   Pro §13050

SMALL ESTATES WITHOUT ADMINISTRATION—Cont.
  Notices
    Generally (See **ADMINISTRATION OF ESTATES**)
    Confirmation of property, notice of hearing on   Pro §13655
    Interest in real property for sale by surviving spouse, notice of   Pro §13541
    Set-aside proceedings, notice of hearing for   Pro §6607
    Succession of real property, notice of hearing on   Pro §13153
  Orders
    Confirmation of property   Pro §13656
      Finality of orders   Pro §13657
    Real property succession   Pro §13154
      Finality of orders   Pro §13155
    Set-aside proceedings (See within this heading, **"Set-aside proceedings"**)
  Pecuniary devises or fractional interests passing to surviving spouse, administration of   Pro §13502.5
  Pending litigations, generally   Pro §13107.5
  Periodic adjustment of dollar amounts   Pro §890
  Personal property collection   Pro §§13100 to 13117
    Generally   Pro §13100
    Affidavit procedure   Pro §§13100 to 13117
      Good faith reliance of holder regarding   Pro §13106
      Ownership of decedent, evidence of   Pro §13102
      Scope of   Pro §13116
    Ancillary administration (See **ANCILLARY ADMINISTRATION**)
    Appraisement of decedent's estate   Pro §13103
    Attorney's fees   Pro §13105
    Bond requirements   Pro §13102
    Claims against estate
      Deceased heir of decedent, filing claims on behalf of   Pro §13107
      Substitution of successor for decedent as party in pending action   Pro §13107.5
    Damages   Pro §§13110, 13111
    Debts of decedent
      Liability for decedent's unsecured debts   Pro §13109
      Real property lien, debt secured by   Pro §13106.5
    Discharge of holder's liability   Pro §13106
    Fair market value defined   Pro §§13110, 13111
    Fraud
      Generally   Pro §§13110, 13111
      Remedies for   Pro §13113
    Identity of affiant, proof of   Pro §13104
    Increase or decrease in value of property   Pro §13113.5
    Inventory of decedent's estate   Pro §13103
    Other estates in probate, claims involving   Pro §13107
    Pending and subsequent probate proceedings, effect of   Pro §13108
    Public administrator generally (See within this heading, **"Public administrator"**)
    Real property
      Appraisal included in affidavit   Pro §13103
      Collection procedure as inapplicable to   Pro §13115
      Debts secured by lien on   Pro §13106.5
      Recording of affidavit where debts secured by real property lien   Pro §13106.5
    Refusal to deliver by holder   Pro §13105
    Remedies available   Pro §13113
    Restitution of property by transferee   Pro §13111
    Salaries and earnings (See within this heading, **"Salaries and earnings, collection of"**)
    Successor
      Liability for decedent's unsecured debts   Pro §13109
      Transfers to   Pro §13105
    Superior rights to decedent's estate, transferee's liability to person having   Pro §13110
    Tax liability of holder   Pro §13106
    Transferee liability   Pro §13109.5
    Voluntary return of transferred property   Pro §13110.5
  Petitions
    Confirmation of property generally (See within this heading, **"Confirmation of property"**)
    Real property succession
      Content of petition   Pro §13152
      Filing of petition   Pro §13151
    Set-aside proceedings generally (See within this heading, **"Set-aside proceedings"**)
  Property of decedent defined   Pro §13005
  Public administrator
    Claims against estate, payment of   Pro §7662
    Compensation of   Pro §7666
    Costs of administration   Pro §§7662, 13114
    Debt liability of distributee   Pro §7664
    Distribution of property   Pro §7663

SMALL ESTATES WITHOUT ADMINISTRATION—Cont.
  Public administrator—Cont.
    General requirements for summary disposition Pro §7660
    Liquidation of assets Pro §7661
    Statement of disposition, filing of Pro §7665
  Real property
    Personal property collection (See within this heading, "Personal property collection")
    Sale of
      Generally (See within this heading, "Sale of real property")
      Public administrator generally (See within this heading, "Public administrator")
    Succession (See within this heading, "Real property succession")
  Real property succession
    Generally Pro §§13150, 13151
    Affidavit procedure Pro §§13200 to 13211
      Certified copy Pro §13202
      Filing fee Pro §13201
      Fraudulent affidavit, liability for Pro §13205
      Prerequisite requirements for use of Pro §13210
      Superior court fees Gov §70626
      Unsecured debt of decedent, affiant's liability for Pro §13204
    Attorney's fees Pro §13157
    Certified copy, issuance and recording of Pro §13202
    Damages for Pro §13206
    Debts of decedent, successor's liability for Pro §§13156, 13204
    Fair market value defined Pro §§13205, 13206
    Fraud
      Damages Pro §13206
      Liability of affiant Pro §13205
    Good faith purchaser, rights of Pro §13203
    Increase or decrease in value of property Pro §13208.5
    Interest, excuse from liability Pro §13211
    Inventory and appraisement
      Generally Pro §13152
      Affidavit procedure for property of small value Pro §13200
      Personal property collection requiring real property appraisement Pro §13103
    Limitation of actions Pro §13205
    Notice of hearing Pro §13153
    Orders
      Generally Pro §13154
      Finality of Pro §13155
    Petition
      Contents of Pro §13152
      Filing of Pro §13151
    Primary residence of decedent Pro §§13151, 13152, 13154
    Recording
      Certified copy of affidavit Pro §13202
      Debts secured by real property lien Pro §13106.5
      Effect of Pro §13203
      Surviving spouse, notice of interest in property for sale by Pro §13541
    Remedies available Pro §13208
    Restitution of property Pro §13206
    Return of transferred property Pro §13209
    Successor's liability for unsecured debts of decedent Pro §§13156, 13204
    Superior rights to property, successor's liability to person having Pro §13205
    Transferee liability Pro §13204.5
    Unsecured debt of decedent, liability for Pro §13156
    Voluntary return of transferred property Pro §13205.5
  Recording (See within this heading, "Real property succession")
  Restitution of property
    Personal property Pro §13111
    Real property of small value Pro §13206
    Surviving spouse Pro §13562
  Revocable trusts
    Community property held in revocable trust, disposition of Pro §13504
    General exclusion from estate of revocable trust property Pro §13050
  Salaries and earnings, collection of
    Generally Pro §13600
    Affidavit
      Contents of Pro §13601
      Good faith reliance on Pro §13603
    Attorney's fees Pro §13604
    Employer, payments by
      Good faith, liability for payments made in Pro §13603
      Refusal to pay Pro §13604
      Requirements for Pro §13602
    Fraud liability for Pro §13605

SMALL ESTATES WITHOUT ADMINISTRATION—Cont.
  Salaries and earnings, collection of—Cont.
    Other collection procedures, applicability of Pro §13606
    Superior right to payments made, liability to party with Pro §13605
  Sale of real property
    Notice of interest in property for sale by surviving spouse Pro §13541
    Prior law, effect of Pro §13542
    Public administrator generally (See within this heading, "Public administrator")
    Rights of surviving spouse Pro §13540
  Securities registered in name of surviving spouse Pro §13545
  Set-aside proceedings
    Generally Pro §6600
    Applicability of law Pro §§6614, 6615
    Attorney's fees Pro §6613
    Capacity of party to bring action Pro §6606
    Contents of petition Pro §6604
    Debts of decedent, liability for Pro §6611
    Definitions Pro §§6600, 6601
    Denial of order for Pro §6612
    Filing
      Generally Pro §6605
      Inventory and appraisement Pro §6608
      Joint filing with petition for will probate, effect of Pro §§6607, 6612
    Finality of orders Pro §6610
    Inventory and appraisement, filing of Pro §6608
    Issuance of orders Pro §6609
    Joint filing with petition for will probate, effect of Pro §§6607, 6612
    Notice of hearing Pro §6607
    Orders
      Denial of Pro §6612
      Finality of Pro §6610
      Issuance of Pro §6609
    Statutory amount of estate subject to Pro §6602
    Venue Pro §6603
  Sister state personal representative to act on behalf of beneficiaries, authority of Pro §13051
  Small value, affidavit procedure for real property of (See within this heading, "Real property succession")
  Statutes of limitation
    Personal property, actions on Pro §§13110, 13111
    Real property, actions on Pro §13205
  Successor
    Debts of decedent, successor's liability for
      Real property Pro §§13156, 13204
    Defined Pro §13006
    Personal property collection
      Transfers to successor Pro §13105
    Substitution of successor for decedent as party in pending action Pro §13107.5
  Superior rights, party with
    Personal property, effect on Pro §13110
    Real property succession, effect on Pro §13205
    Surviving spouse, liability of Pro §13561
  Surviving spouse
    Generally Pro §§13500, 13501
    Elections
      Administration of estate, election for Pro §13502
      Trustee, election to transfer property to Pro §13503
    Governing law Pro §§13505, 13506
    Interest, excuse from liability Pro §13565
    Liability of
      Debts of decedent (See within this heading, "Debt liability")
      Decedent's property defined Pro §13560
      Fraud, remedies for Pro §13564
      Limitations on liability Pro §13563
      Restitution of property Pro §13562
      Superior rights, liability to person having Pro §13561
    Limitations on liability
      Generally Pro §13563
      Debts of decedent Pro §13551
    Pecuniary devises or fractional interests passing to surviving spouse, administration of Pro §13502.5
    Restitution of property Pro §13562
    Sale of real property
      Right of surviving spouse Pro §13540
    Securities registered in name of Pro §13545
    Trusts
      Election to transfer property to trustee Pro §13503
      Revocable trust property, law applicable to Pro §13504
  Transferred property Pro §13114.5

SMALL ESTATES WITHOUT ADMINISTRATION—Cont.
Trustee
    Authority for acting on behalf of inter vivos trust   Pro §13051
    Surviving spouse transferring property to   Pro §13503
Trusts
    Revocable trust property as excluded from estate   Pro §13050
    Surviving spouse
        Election to transfer property to trustee   Pro §13503
        Revocable trust property, law applicable to   Pro §13504
    Trustee
        Authority for acting on behalf of inter vivos trust   Pro §13051
        Surviving spouse transferring property to   Pro §13503
Uniform Transfers to Minors Act, bequest under   Pro §13051
Value limitation   Pro §§6602, 13100
Voidable transfers   Pro §§13100 to 13117
Voluntary return of transferred property   Pro §§13110.5, 13205.5

SMART PHONES
Security for connected devices   CC §§1798.91.04 to 1798.91.06

SMOKELESS TOBACCO NONSALE DISTRIBUTION
Attorney general, civil actions to enforce provisions
    Fees and costs for attorney general   CCP §1021.8

SMOKING
Cigarette tax claim against decedent's estate, filing of   Pro §§9200 to 9205
Court facilities   CRC 10.504
Electronic cigarettes
    Verification of age for sale of age-restricted products   CC §1798.99.1
Inherently unsafe products, applicability of statutory restrictions on products liability actions against manufacturers and distributors of   CC §1714.45
Landlord and tenant
    Prohibition by landlord   CC §1947.5
Minors
    Sale of tobacco to persons under 21
        Verification of age for sale of age-restricted products   CC §1798.99.1
    Verification of age for sale of age-restricted products   CC §1798.99.1
Paraphernalia
    Sales of tobacco, paraphernalia, etc, to persons under 21
        Verification of age for sale of age-restricted products   CC §1798.99.1
Sales and distribution of tobacco products
    Attorney general, civil actions to enforce provisions
        Fees and costs for attorney general   CCP §1021.8

SNOW
Easements, snow removal from right-of-way on   CC §845
Water appropriation construction, effect of snow on completion of   CC §1416

SNOWMOBILES
Landowner liability for snowmobilers   CC §846

SNUFF FILMS   CC §§3504 to 3508.2

SOCIAL HOSTS
Alcoholic beverages, liability after serving   CC §1714

SOCIAL MEDIA
Child sexual abuse hosted on social media platform   CC §§3273.65 to 3273.69
    Definitions   CC §3273.65
    Duties of social media platform   CC §3273.66
        Failure to comply   CC §3273.67
    Liability for failure to comply   CC §3273.67
    Reporting of material
        Social media platform to provide reporting mechanism   CC §3273.66
    Severability of provisions   CC §3273.69
    Waiver of provisions as void   CC §3273.68
Commercial sexual exploitation of minor by social media platform   CC §3345.1
Judicial ethics code
    Public confidence in judiciary
        Electronic communications, care in using   CRCSupp JudEthicsCanon 2
Online violence prevention   CC §§1798.99.20 to 1798.99.23
Sexual conduct evidence, use to attack credibility of witness
    Definition of evidence of sexual conduct   Ev §782

SOCIAL SECURITY
Abstracts of judgment requiring Social Security number   CCP §674
Annulment of marriage proceedings
    Social security numbers
        Redaction from documents to ensure privacy   Fam §2024.5
Assignment for benefit of creditors, property exempt from   CCP §1801
Child support payment made by government pursuant to   Fam §4504

SOCIAL SECURITY—Cont.
Confidentiality
    Financial institutions, continued use   CC §1786.60
    Social security numbers
        Businesses   CC §1798.85
        Financial institutions, continued use   CC §1786.60
        Redaction from documents to ensure privacy   Fam §2024.5
        Truncation program   Gov §§27300 to 27307
        Untruncated social security numbers, filing documents that will be public containing   CC §1798.89
        Waiver of protections   CC §1798.86
Dissolution of marriage proceedings   Fam §2337
    Social security numbers
        Redaction from documents to ensure privacy   Fam §2024.5
Earnings, Social Security payments as   CC §1812.30
Enforcement of judgments, payments for (See **ENFORCEMENT OF JUDGMENTS**)
Financial institutions
    Continued use   CC §1786.60
Investigative agencies, Social Security number as identification   CC §1786.22
Legal separation proceedings
    Social security numbers
        Redaction from documents to ensure privacy   Fam §2024.5
Malpractice suits against physicians, evidence in   CC §3333.1
Prohibiting posting or display to general public of social security numbers   CC §1798.85
    Waiver of protections   CC §1798.86
Sale of social security numbers
    Prohibition of sale, advertising for sale or offering for sale of number of another   CC §1798.85
Truncation of social security numbers, program for   Gov §§27300 to 27307
    County recorder
        Due diligence   Gov §27302
        Duties   Gov §27301
        Implementation of provisions, powers as to   Gov §27307
    DD214 official record
        Copy upon request, criteria   Gov §27303.5
    Definitions   Gov §27300
    Establishment of program   Gov §27301
    Funding of program   Gov §§27304, 27361
    Legislature, report to   Gov §27305
    Public record version of official records   Gov §27301
        Disclosures   Gov §27303

SOCIAL SERVICES DEPARTMENT
Adoption proceedings (See **ADOPTION**)
Deceptive practice of charging unreasonable fees to assist applicants for public social services   CC §1770
    Treble damages   CC §1780
Enforcement of judgment, filing with department for   CCP §§708.730, 708.740
Medical information, release of   CC §56.25
Unreasonable fees to assist applicants for public social services
    Deceptive practices   CC §1770
    Treble damages   CC §1780

SOCIAL WORKERS
Discovery of records of health care professional review committees   Ev §1157
Juvenile rules
    Removal of juvenile from home
        Family finding and notice performed by social worker or probation officer   CRC 5.637
Privileged communications (See **PRIVILEGED COMMUNICATIONS**)
Psychotherapists, psychiatric social workers as   Ev §1010
Removal of juvenile from home
    Family finding and notice performed by social worker or probation officer   CRC 5.637
Sexual harassment, civil action for
    Construction or application of provisions in issue, solicitor general notified   CC §51.1

SODOMY (See **SEX OFFENSES**)

SOFTWARE (See **COMPUTERS**)

SOIL
Real property, part of   CC §659

SOLAR ENERGY
Common interest developments, restrictions in   CC §714.1
    Approvals
        Determinations of applications   CC §714

SOLAR ENERGY—Cont.
Common interest developments, restrictions in —Cont.
    Common areas, exclusive use grants   CC §4600
    Protected uses of separate interests
        Solar energy systems on multifamily common area roofs   CC §4746
        Provisions outside of common interest development law limiting association's regulation of member's separate interest   CC §4700
Covenants prohibiting use of solar energy systems, invalidity of   CC §714
Easements   CC §§801, 801.5
Mobilehome parks   CC §§798.44.1, 799.12

SOLDIERS (See MILITARY)

SOLE PROXIMATE CAUSE (See PROXIMATE CAUSE)

SOLICITATION
Advertising (See ADVERTISING)
Arbitration
    Disclosure   CCP §1281.9
    Not to be made party to   CCP §1281.93
Arbitrators
    Ethics standards
        Soliciting business   CRC ArbEthicsStand 17
Attorney professional conduct
    Clients, solicitation of   ProfC 7.3
Home solicitation sales contracts (See HOME SOLICITATION SALES CONTRACTS)
Mediation
    Standards of conduct for mediators
        Marketing   CRC 3.858
Murder
    Attempting or soliciting murder of spouse
        Damages for injuries to married person   Fam §782.5
        Spousal support, denial   Fam §4324
Seminar sales solicitation contracts (See SEMINAR SALES SOLICITATION CONTRACTS)
Telemarketing
    Unlawfulness of contracts generated by unlawful telemarketing   CC §1670.6
Transient occupancy in common interest developments, apartment buildings or single-family homes, recordkeeping required for accepting reservations or money for   CC §1864

SOLID WASTE RECOVERY AND RECYCLING
Fire hydrants or fire department corrections
    Damages for wrongful possession by junk dealers or recyclers   CC §3336.5

SONG-BEVERLY CONSUMER WARRANTY ACT   CC §§1790 to 1795.8 (See WARRANTIES)

SONG-BEVERLY CREDIT CARD ACT   CC §§1747 to 1748.95 (See CREDIT CARDS)

SORGHUM
Storage regulations after sale of   CC §§1880 to 1881.2

SOUND RECORDINGS (See RECORDING OF SOUND)

SOURCE OF INFORMATION (See INFORMATION PRACTICES ACT)

SOVEREIGN IMMUNITY (See CLAIMS AGAINST PUBLIC ENTITIES AND EMPLOYEES)

SPACE
Real property, part of   CC §659

SPACE FLIGHT LIABILITY AND IMMUNITY   CC §§2210 to 2212
Definitions   CC §2210
Entity liability   CC §2212
Warning and acknowledgment statements   CC §2211

SPANISH
Attorneys' fees, translation requirements in contracts for   CC §1632
Consumer credit contracts, notice of liability of cosigners
    Foreign language translations of notice requirement
        Federal notice requirement   CC §1799.96
Contracts written in   CC §§1632, 2991
Cosigners of consumer credit contracts, notice of liability of   CC §1799.91
Gender tax repeal act preventing charging different prices for services of similar or like kind based on gender
    Consumer affairs department pamphlet for affected businesses and other notice of requirements of provisions   CC §51.63
Gender tax repeal act preventing charging different prices for services of similar or like kind based on gender—Cont.
    Licensing authority notice of provisions to licensee upon issuance or renewal   CC §51.6
Home solicitation sales contracts
    Language used in negotiation to be used in written contract   CC §1689.7
Membership camping contracts, language requirements for   CC §1812.303
Mortgages of residential property, foreign language summaries of terms   CC §1632.5
Summons, legend appearing on   CCP §412.20
Title papers in Spanish relating to land claims, admissible evidence of   Ev §1605

SPECIAL ADMINISTRATORS (See EXECUTORS AND ADMINISTRATORS)

SPECIAL AGENT (See AGENCY)

SPECIAL APPEARANCE (See APPEARANCE)

SPECIAL DEFENSE
Separate trial of   CCP §597

SPECIAL DISTRICTS (See PUBLIC ENTITIES)

SPECIAL EDUCATION
Educational rights holder
    Appointment   CRC 5.650
    Identification of holder   CRC 5.649
    Juvenile court proceedings   CRC 5.502, 5.534, 5.650
        Educational and developmental services decisionmaking rights of children   CRC 5.651
    Orders concerning rights holder and educational decisionmaking   CRC 5.649
    Qualifications   CRC 5.650
    Training   CRC 5.650
    Transfer of parent or guardian's educational rights to representative   CRC 5.650
Limitations on parental control
    Juvenile court proceedings   CRC 5.695, 5.790
Surrogate parents
    Juvenile court proceedings   CRC 5.650

SPECIAL ISSUE
Jury, submitting special issue to   CCP §309

SPECIAL LAWS (See LOCAL OR SPECIAL LAWS)

SPECIAL NEEDS TRUSTS
Claims of government agencies against   Pro §3605
Court supervision of   Pro §3604
Disposition of funds to   Pro §§3602, 3611
    Express consent of protected person to court orders, when required   Pro §3613
Parental duty to maintain incapacitated child   Fam §3910

SPECIAL OCCUPANCY PARKS
Danger imminent, requiring guests to move   CC §1867
Eviction of overstaying guests   CC §1866
Minors
    Conditions for minors staying   CC §1866

SPECIAL POWER OF APPOINTMENT (See POWER OF APPOINTMENT)

SPECIAL PROCEEDINGS
Agreed case (See AGREED CASE)
As class of judicial remedy   CCP §21
Confession of judgments (See CONFESSION OF JUDGMENTS)
Defined   CCP §23
Forcible entry and detainer (See FORCIBLE ENTRY AND DETAINER)
Judgment creditor's lien (See ENFORCEMENT OF JUDGMENTS)
Judicial arbitration (See JUDICIAL ARBITRATION)
Limitation periods prescribed, applicability of   CCP §363
Mandamus (See MANDAMUS)
Prohibition, writ of (See PROHIBITION, WRIT OF)
Referees, appointment of   CCP §639
Unlawful detainer (See UNLAWFUL DETAINER)
Writ of review (See CERTIORARI)

SPECIAL VERDICT (See VERDICT)

SPECIFIC DEVISES (See WILLS)

SPECIFIC PERFORMANCE
Adequate remedy at law, absence of CC §3387
Authority for action CC §3384
Conditions precedent, performance of CC §3392
Consideration, requirements for adequacy of CC §3391
Damages
    Inadequate damages CC §3387
    Liquidated damage provision CC §3389
Decedents' estates, conveyance or transfer of property in Pro §§850 to 859
Defenses to action for CC §§3390 to 3394
Denial of relief, grounds for CC §3390
Fraud
    Generally CC §3399
    Defense based on CC §3391
Good and sufficient title, requirements for CC §3394
Liquidated damages clauses affecting CC §1680
Mistake
    Defense to actions CC §3391
    Mutual mistakes CC §3399
Mutuality CC §3386
Parties bound by decree of CC §3395
Part performance CC §§3386, 3388, CCP §1972
Penalties provided in contract CC §3389
Reasonableness of contract, requirements for CC §3391
Reformation of instruments CC §§3399 to 3402
Revision of contract CC §§3399 to 3402
Small claims court jurisdiction to grant equitable relief in lieu of or in addition to money damages CCP §116.220
Stay of CCP §917.6
Third party, denial of relief in actions involving CC §3390
Title requirements CC §3394

SPECIFIC RELIEF
Generally CC §§3366 to 3369
Specific performance (See **SPECIFIC PERFORMANCE**)

SPELUNKING
Personal injuries CC §846

SPENDTHRIFT TRUSTS
Disclaimer of interest, right to file Pro §286
Enforcement of judgment against CCP §§695.030, 709.010

SPERM
Use and implantation of sperm, ova, or embryo without authorization
    Civil action for damages CC §1708.5.6

SPITE FENCE ACT CC §841.4

SPLIT-INTEREST TRUSTS (See **TRUSTS**)

SPONTANEOUS DECLARATION
Hearsay evidence, admissibility of Ev §1240

SPORT FISHING
Fines and penalties, bail schedule CRC 4.102

SPORTS (See **ATHLETICS**)

SPOUSAL PRIVILEGE Ev §§980 to 987 (See **MARITAL PRIVILEGE**)

SPOUSAL SUPPORT
Generally Fam §4300
Acceleration of loan, restrictions on CC §2924.6
Action to enforce spouse's right to support Fam §4303
Age of parties Fam §4320
Agreement providing for support, court order based on Fam §§3590 to 3593
Annuity, purchase of Fam §4360
Annulment of marriage Fam §2254
Appeals
    Generally CCP §904.1, Fam §3554
    Attorney General's appeal in case brought by child support agency Fam §17407
Assignment for benefit of creditors, effect of CCP §§1800, 1801
Assignment of wages (See **EARNINGS ASSIGNMENT FOR SUPPORT**)
Attachment
    Judicial council forms CRCAppx A
Attempted murder
    Attorney fees and costs awarded to victim Fam §274
    Award of support or benefits to convicted spouse
        Prohibition Fam §4324
Attorney obligors CRC 9.22

SPOUSAL SUPPORT—Cont.
Attorney professional conduct
    Contingent fees
        Circumstances where contingent fee agreement impermissible ProfC 1.5
Attorney's fees
    Generally Fam §§270 to 274, 2010, 2030 to 2034
    Financial need basis CRC 5.427
    Modification of support orders Fam §3652
    Murder attempt, awarded to victim of Fam §274
    Temporary orders for award of Fam §2031
Bankruptcy, effect of discharge of obligations in Fam §3592
Care of dependent children as consideration Fam §4320
Changed circumstances Fam §4336
    Child support termination as change in circumstances justifying modification of spousal support Fam §4326
Child support
    Generally (See **CHILD SUPPORT**)
Circumstances considered by court Fam §4320
Cohabitation, effect of Fam §4323
Community property liable for Fam §4338
Computers
    Software used to determine support amount CRC 5.275, Fam §3830
    System authorized to provide standardized information CCP §1062.20
Conciliation Courts, orders of Fam §1839
Contempt, limitations period in action for CCP §1218.5
Contingent period of time, support for Fam §4334
Contributions to marriage of supported spouse Fam §4320
Costs
    Financial need basis CRC 5.427
    Modification of support orders Fam §3652
    Murder attempt, awarded to victim of Fam §274
    Order for payment of Fam §§270 to 274, 2010, 2030 to 2034
County, expenses and fees charged to Fam §4352
County officer
    As designated payee Fam §§4350 to 4352
    Forwarding of support payment to designated payee Fam §3555
Court commissioner's powers to hear and report findings and conclusions in preliminary matters including petitions for CCP §259
Crediting money judgments for support CCP §695.221
Creditor, order of payments directly to Fam §2023
Custody of children, denial of support based on Fam §4321
Death of party
    Generally Fam §4337
    Annuity, life insurance, or trust to benefit supported spouse Fam §4360
    Earnings assignment for support, termination of order Fam §5240
Defenses
    Laches as to portion owed to state Fam §291
Definitions Fam §§142, 3500, 3515
Denial of support, reasons for Fam §§4321, 4322
Discovery
    Law and motion rules applicable to CRC 3.1100
    Modification of support order Fam §§3660 to 3668
    Termination of support order Fam §§3660 to 3668
Domestic duties, effect on employment of supported spouse Fam §4320
Domestic violence (See **DOMESTIC VIOLENCE**)
Duration of marriage Fam §§4320, 4336
Duty of support Fam §4300
Earning capacity Fam §4320
Earnings and accumulations
    Generally Fam §4338
    Assignment of wages (See **EARNINGS ASSIGNMENT FOR SUPPORT**)
    Denial of support, reasons for Fam §§4321, 4322
Education needed for employment of spouse Fam §4320
Enforcement
    Generally Fam §§4303, 4500
    Appeals CCP §904.1, Fam §3554
        Attorney general's appeal in case brought by child support agency Fam §17407
    Assignment of wages (See **EARNINGS ASSIGNMENT FOR SUPPORT**)
    Child support enforcement agencies, general provisions concerning enforcement of spousal support by Fam §§17000, 17604
    Employee benefit plan, enforcement for support against Fam §5103
    Execution, writ of Fam §§5100 to 5104
    Garnishment proceedings (See **GARNISHMENT**)
    Parent Locator Service and Central Registry Fam §17506
    Possession or sale of property Fam §§291, 4502
    Referral to local child support agency for enforcement Fam §§4351, 4352
Enforcement of judgments
    Levy and execution
        Application for writ of execution, priority CCP §699.510

SPOUSAL SUPPORT—Cont.
Exemption from execution   CCP §704.111
Ex parte protective orders   Fam §2045
Expenses charged to county   Fam §4352
Family allowance (See **FAMILY ALLOWANCE**)
Family law facilitators for unrepresented parties   Fam §§10000 to 10015
Family law information centers for unrepresented low-income litigants   Fam §§15000 to 15012
Family rules
    Computer software assisting in determining support   CRC 5.275
Family support defined   Fam §92
Fees
    Title IV-D child support agency involved   Gov §70672
Fixed period of time, support for   Fam §4335
Foreign country judgments
    Applicability of provisions   CCP §1715
Garnishment proceedings (See **GARNISHMENT**)
Guardian (See **GUARDIAN AND WARD**)
Guidelines
    Certification of statewide uniform calculators   CRC 5.275
Health of parties   Fam §4320
Incapacity of spouse
    Legal incapacity to make decisions
        Effect on support obligation   Fam §2313
Income and benefit information provided by employer admissible in proceeding to modify or terminate support   Ev §1567
Income and expense declaration
    Defined   Fam §95
    Employer, request for information from   Fam §3664
    Request for   Fam §3664
    Sanctions for incomplete or inaccurate   Fam §3667
Income withholding
    Form   CRCAppx A
Interstate family support   Fam §§5700.101 to 5700.903 (See **INTERSTATE FAMILY SUPPORT**)
Judgments
    Abstract of   Fam §4506
        Liens, digital form of lien record   Fam §17523.5
    Interest
        Accrual of interest   Fam §17433.5
    Relief from   Fam §§2120 to 2129, 3690 to 3693, 17432
    Renewal of   CCP §683.310, Fam §§291, 4502
Judicial Council forms   CRCAppx A, Fam §3668
Jurisdiction   Fam §§2010 to 2013
    Retention of   Fam §4336
Law and motion rules
    Discovery
        Applicable to discovery proceedings in family law   CRC 3.1100
Liens
    Judgments, abstract of
        Digital form of lien record   Fam §17523.5
Life insurance on life of spouse making support payments   Fam §4360
Living separate, duty of support when   Fam §4302
Marital privilege   Fam §3551
Marketable skills of supported party   Fam §4320
Missing military personnel (See **MILITARY**)
Modification
    Generally   Fam §§3650 to 3654
    Admissibility of income and benefit information provided by employer   Ev §1567
    Child support termination as change in circumstances   Fam §4326
    Discovery procedures   Fam §§3660 to 3668
    Effective dates for modification and requests for modification   CRCAppx I Emer Rule 13
    Military service activation and deployment, notice of   CRCAppx A (CRCFL-398)
    Retroactivity of   Fam §3653
    Support agreement, authority to modify   Fam §3591
    Temporary support orders   Fam §3603
Murder attempt
    Attorney fees and costs awarded to victim   Fam §274
    Award of support or benefits to convicted spouse prohibited   Fam §4324
Mutual obligations of husband and wife   Fam §720
Obligee   Fam §3550
Obligor   Fam §3550
Orders
    Generally   Fam §§4330 to 4338
    Attachment to orders   CRCAppx A (CRCFL-343)
    Defined   Fam §155
    Modification (See within this heading, "**Modification**")

SPOUSAL SUPPORT—Cont.
Orders—Cont.
    Registration of order
        Statement of registration   CRCAppx A (CRCFL-440)
    Retroactivity of   Fam §4333
    Setting aside order
        Order deciding issues   CRCAppx A (CRCFL-367)
        Request for hearing   CRCAppx A (CRCFL-360)
        Responsive declaration   CRCAppx A (CRCFL-365)
    Subsequent orders, rights with respect to   Fam §3604
    Temporary support (See within this heading, "**Temporary support**")
    Vocational training consultant, examination by   Fam §4331
Parent Locator Service and Central Registry   Fam §17506
Pendente lite support (See within this heading, "**Temporary support**")
Pilot projects (See **FAMILY LAW PILOT PROJECTS**)
Presumption of duration of marriage   Fam §4336
Probate proceedings
    Power of appointment, claims against powerholder's property subject to   Pro §684
Property settlement agreements, support provisions severable from   Fam §§3590 to 3593
Public entity's obligation to judgment debtor, application to satisfaction on money judgment of   CCP §§708.710 to 708.795
Putative spouse   Fam §2254
Qualified order for support, form   CRCAppxs A (CRCFL-460), (CRCFL-461)
Quasi-community property liable for   Fam §4338
Reconciliation of parties, effect of   Fam §3602
Relief from judgment or order   Fam §§2120 to 2129, 3690 to 3693, 17432
Remarriage, effect of   Fam §4337
Residence of obligor   Fam §3550
Satisfaction of money judgment for support, crediting of   CCP §695.221
Security for payment   Fam §4339
Self-help materials   Fam §291
Self-supporting within reasonable time, goal that recipient become   Fam §§4320, 4330
Separate property   Fam §§915, 4301, 4320 to 4322, 4338
Separation agreement, provisions for support in   Fam §3580
Software used to determine support amount   Fam §3830
Standard of living   Fam §§4320, 4330, 4332
Summary dissolution of marriage, effect of judgment of   Fam §2404
Support factors
    Judicial Council forms   CRCAppx A
Support order defined   Fam §155
Surviving spouse (See within this heading, "**Death of party**")
Tax consequences of   Fam §4320
Tax returns of parties   Fam §§3552, 3665, 3667
Temporary support
    Generally   Fam §3600
    Termination of   Fam §§3601, 3603
    Transfer of venue, determining support issues prior to determination of motion for   CCP §§396b, 397
Termination
    Generally   Fam §§3650 to 3654
    Admissibility of income and benefit information provided by employer   Ev §1567
    Changed circumstances   Fam §4336
    Contingent period of time, support for   Fam §4334
    Discovery procedures   Fam §§3660 to 3668
    Effective dates for termination and requests for termination   CRCAppx I Emer Rule 13
    Relief from support judgment or order   Fam §§2120 to 2129, 3690 to 3693, 17432
    Retroactivity of   Fam §3653
    Support agreement, authority to terminate   Fam §3591
    Temporary support   Fam §§3601, 3603
Transfer of venue, determining support issues prior to determination of motion for   CCP §§396b, 397
Trust to provide for support   Fam §4360
Unemployment periods of spouse devoting time to domestic duties   Fam §4320
Vocational training   Fam §§4320, 4331
Welfare recipients, enforcement in behalf of   Fam §4351
Workers' compensation temporary disability benefits in satisfaction of support judgment, assignment of   CCP §704.160

SPOUSES (See **HUSBAND AND WIFE**)

SPRAY PAINT CONTAINERS
Minors, sale to
    Verification of age for sale of age-restricted products   CC §1798.99.1

SPRINGING POWER OF ATTORNEY (See **POWER OF ATTORNEY**)

SPRINGING USE CC §773

STABLES (See **BOARDING FACILITIES AND STABLES**)

STADIUMS AND ARENAS
Sacramento downtown arena
    Petitions under environmental quality act, civil rules governing
        Sacramento downtown arena project, CEQA challenges   CRC 3.2220 to 3.2240

STAINED GLASS ARTISTRY
Fine art, defined as   CC §997

STAIRWAYS
Landlord's duty to repair   CC §1941.1

STALKING
Access to domestic violence incident reports   Fam §6228
Address confidentiality for victims
    Actions, confidentiality requirements for protected persons in civil proceeding   CCP §367.3
        Judicial council forms   CRCAppx A
    Name change proceedings under address confidentiality program   CRC 2.575 to 2.577
Damages   CC §1708.7
Ex parte order enjoining   Fam §§6274, 6320
    California law enforcement telecommunications (CLETS) information form, confidentiality and use of information   CRC 1.51, CRCAppx A
    Denial of petition for ex parte order, reasons to be provided   Fam §6320.5
Injunctions
    COVID-19, emergency rule   CRCAppx I Emer Rule 8
    Dependency proceeding
        Forms for firearm relinquishment   CRCAppx A
    Ex parte order enjoining
        Denial of petition for ex parte order, reasons to be provided   Fam §6320.5
Landlord and tenant
    Documentation or evidence of abuse or violence
        Victims of domestic violence, sexual assault or stalking   CCP §1161.3
    Termination of tenancy
        Victims of domestic violence, sexual assault or stalking   CC §1946.7, CCP §1161.3
    Unlawful detainer proceedings, nuisance committed by tenant as grounds
        Presumption of nuisance   CCP §1161
        Restrictions on termination of tenancy   CC §1946.7, CCP §1161.3
Name change to avoid stalking   CCP §1277
Postsecondary educational institutions
    Injunction against violence threatened on campus or facility
        Judicial council legal forms   CRCAppx A
    Orders against violence threatened on campus or facility
        COVID-19, emergency rule   CRCAppx I Emer Rule 8
Prostitution, evidence
    Extortion, serious felony, assault, domestic violence, human trafficking, sexual battery or stalking, victims or witnesses
        Inadmissibility of evidence of prostitution in prosecution for prostitution   Ev §1162
Protective orders
    Address or location of complaining party or family, prohibition on enjoined party from obtaining   CCP §527.10
    California law enforcement telecommunications (CLETS) information form, confidentiality and use of information   CRC 1.51, CRCAppx A
    COVID-19, emergency rule   CRCAppx I Emer Rule 8
    Firearm relinquishment and disposition
        Forms for firearm relinquishment   CRCAppx A
        Procedures   CRC 4.700
    Name change proceedings under address confidentiality program   CRC 2.575 to 2.577
    Requests for protective orders   CRC 3.1160
    Waiver of fees   CCP §527.6
Public records
    Address confidentiality for victims
        Actions, confidentiality requirements for protected persons in civil proceeding   CCP §367.3
        Judicial council forms   CRCAppx A
        Name change proceedings under address confidentiality program   CRC 2.575 to 2.577
Universities and colleges
    Injunction against violence threatened on campus or facility
        Requests for protective orders   CRC 3.1160

STALKING—Cont.
Universities and colleges—Cont.
    Protection orders against violence threatened on campus or facility   CCP §527.85
        California law enforcement telecommunications (CLETS) information form, confidentiality and use of information   CRC 1.51, CRCAppx A
        Memorandum in support of petition not required   CRC 3.1114
Unlawful detainer proceedings
    Abuse or violence against tenant, remedies   CCP §1174.27
    Limitations on termination of or refusal to renew tenancy of victims   CC §1946.7, CCP §1161.3
    Nuisance committed by tenant as grounds
        Presumption of nuisance   CCP §1161
Victim service providers, personal information protection   CC §§1798.79.8 to 1798.79.95
    Definitions   CC §1798.79.8
    Disclosing personal information
        Grants, requiring disclosure as condition   CC §1798.79.9
        Injunctions to prevent   CC §1798.79.95
        Prohibited   CC §1798.79.9
Workplace Violence Safety Act
    COVID-19, emergency rule   CRCAppx I Emer Rule 8

STANDARD OF LIVING
Spousal support   Fam §§4320, 4330, 4332

STANDING TO SUE (See **CAPACITY TO SUE**)

STANISLAUS COUNTY
Small claims court pilot project, participation in   CCP §116.232

STATE
Inclusions in definition   CCP §17
Superior court fees
    Services to local, state and federal governments   Gov §70633

STATE AGENCIES (See **PUBLIC ENTITIES**)

STATE BAR
Appellate briefs, inclusion of State Bar membership number   CRC 8.204
Attorney discipline generally (See **ATTORNEY DISCIPLINE**)
Bar examination (See **BAR EXAMINATION**)
Board of trustees
    Appointment
        Nominating committee   CRC 9.90
        Qualifications for appointment   CRC 9.90
    Nomination and election of members
        Committee for nominations   CRC 9.90
        Evaluation of applicants   CRC 9.90
Certified law student program   CRC 9.42
Child support, suspension of membership for failure to pay   CRC 9.22
Class action awards, collection of unpaid residue of   CCP §384
Criminal history information records, provision to
    Fingerprinting of attorneys   CRC 9.9.5
Damages, liability of legal professional societies for   CC §§43.7, 43.95
Discovery abuses, sanctions for
    Reporting sanction to state bar   CCP §2023.050
Fingerprinting of attorneys   CRC 9.9.5
Information practices, disclosure of breach of security
    Applicability to state bar   CC §1798.29
In-house counsel
    Registered in-house counsel   CRC 9.46
        Fingerprinting of special admission attorneys   CRC 9.9.5
Law students
    Certified law student program   CRC 9.42
    Provisional licensure of 2020 law school graduates   CRC 9.49
        Pathway to full licensure, provisional licensure with   CRC 9.49.1
Lawyer referral service, immunity from liability for referrals by   CC §43.95
Legal aid attorneys
    Registered legal aid attorneys   CRC 9.45
        Fingerprinting of special admission attorneys   CRC 9.9.5
New attorney training   CRC 9.32
Out-of-state attorney arbitration counsel program   CRC 9.43
Registered foreign legal consultant program   CRC 9.44
Roll of attorneys admitted to practice   CRC 9.8
Rules of professional conduct   ProfC 1.0 to 8.5 (See **ATTORNEY PROFESSIONAL CONDUCT**)
Small claims advisors   CCP §116.940
Small claims advisory committee, appointments to   CCP §116.950

STATE BAR—Cont.
Temporarily in California
    Litigation, presence as part of   CRC 9.47
    Nonlitigation services, providing   CRC 9.48
Training for new attorneys   CRC 9.32
Unaccredited law schools, study in   CRC 9.30

STATE BAR COURT
Authority   CRC 9.10
Effective date of orders   CRC 9.18
Judges   CRC 9.11
    Applicant evaluation and nomination committee   CRC 9.11
    Code of judicial ethics, applicability   CRCSupp JudEthicsCanon 6
    Disciplinary action against   CRC 9.11
Notice to interested parties   CRC 9.20
Orders, effective date of   CRC 9.18
Probation proceedings, stipulations, approval   CRC 9.10
Public or private reprovals, conditions   CRC 9.19
Review department
    Independent review of record by   CRC 9.12
Review of decisions   CRC 9.13 to 9.15
    Bar member petition for review   CRC 9.13
    Chief trial counsel, petition for review   CRC 9.14
    Standard of review for   CRC 9.12
    State bar petition for review   CRC 9.15
Rule 9.20 proceedings
    Compliance enforcement   CRC 9.10
Standard of review for   CRC 9.12
Stay of suspension order   CRC 9.10
Supreme court review   CRC 9.13
    Chief trial counsel, petitions by   CRC 9.14
    Denial of review as final determination on the merits   CRC 9.16
    Effective date of orders and decisions   CRC 9.18
    Grounds for review   CRC 9.16
    Interim decision, review of   CRC 9.13
    Petition   CRC 9.13
        Chief trial counsel, petitions by   CRC 9.14
    Remand with instructions   CRC 9.17
    State bar court, petitions by   CRC 9.13

STATE BOARD OF EQUALIZATION (See TAXATION)

STATE BONDS (See BONDS)

STATE HOSPITALS
Involuntary medication and treatment hearings
    Remote proceedings
        Conditions for proceeding through use of remote technology   CCP §367.76
Mental hospitals (See MENTAL HOSPITALS)
Special needs trust for minor or person with disability, notice of
    State department of state hospitals to be notified   Pro §§3602, 3605, 3611
Statute of limitation on accounts for support of patients at   CCP §345

STATE HOSPITALS DEPARTMENT
Probate proceedings, filing fees payable by department employee as petitioner in   Gov §70659

STATE LANDS COMMISSION
Eminent domain taking by   CCP §1245.210
Quiet title action involving land subject to boundary line or exchange agreements with   CCP §§760.020, 764.080

STATE LOTTERY
Support arrearages claim filed against state for winnings owed judgment debtor   CCP §§708.30, 708.740

STATEMENT OF DECISION
Generally   CCP §632
Ambiguity of   CCP §634
Arbitration proceedings   CCP §1291
Referees (See REFEREES)
Requirements for   CCP §632
Sterilization proceedings, requirements for   Pro §1962

STATEMENTS
Administrative Procedure Act (See ADMINISTRATIVE PROCEDURE ACT)
Damages, request for statement of   CCP §§425.11, 425.12
Decision, statement of (See STATEMENT OF DECISION)
Executors and administrators, statement of duties and liabilities of   Pro §8404
Foster placement, minor's right to make statement regarding   Fam §7952

STATEMENTS—Cont.
Indirect contempt proceedings, statement of facts by judicial officer in   CCP §§1211, 1211.5

STATEMENTS OF DECISIONS
Announcement of tentative decision, statement of decision and judgment   CRC 3.1590
Bifurcated trial, request following   CRC 3.1591
Preparation and submission   CRC 3.1590
Proposed contents   CRC 3.1590
Request for statement of decision   CRC 3.1590
Service of   CRC 3.1590
Tentative decisions   CRC 3.1590
Time limitations   CRC 3.1590

STATE OF CALIFORNIA
Agencies of (See PUBLIC ENTITIES)
Appellate briefs
    Attorney general representing public officer or agency, service of brief on   CRC 8.29
Bonds issued by (See BONDS)
Change of venue of actions by or against   CCP §401
Claim and delivery   CCP §511.100
Common carriers giving preferential treatment to   CC §2171
Conservation easements held by   CC §815.3
Costs, liability for   CCP §1028
Decedent's estate (See ADMINISTRATION OF ESTATES)
Defined   Fam §145
Governmental liability (See CLAIMS AGAINST PUBLIC ENTITIES AND EMPLOYEES)
Greenway easements
    Entities permitted to acquire and hold easement   CC §816.56
Groundwater rights actions
    Intervention in comprehensive adjudication   CCP §837.5
Judicial notice of statutory laws   Ev §§451, 452
Leases
    Abandonment provisions, applicability of   CC §1952.6
    Limitations on   CC §718
Partition sale proceeds invested in government obligations   CCP §873.810
Pleadings verified by   CCP §446
Presentation of claims as prerequisite to commencement of actions against governmental agencies   CCP §313
Quieting title   CCP §§762.090, 764.070
Real property, time limitations with respect to state action for recovery of   CCP §315
Service of process on   CCP §416.50
Statute of limitation applicable to actions brought in name of or for benefit of   CCP §345
Telegrams for state business, priority for transmitting   CC §2207
Unclaimed deposits and payments escheated   CCP §1519
Unclaimed property, disposition of   CC §2080.6
Validation proceedings   CCP §§860 to 870
Venue of actions by or against   CCP §401
Wills, taking under   Pro §6102

STATE OF EMERGENCY
Deeds of trust and mortgages
    Property within geographic limits of declared state of emergency
        Information to be provided regarding repair of property   CC §2968

STATE OFFICES
Holiday for purposes of computing time if public office closed   CCP §12b

STATES OF THE UNITED STATES
Full faith and credit (See FULL FAITH AND CREDIT)

STATE TAX LIABILITY
Enforcement of judgments (See ENFORCEMENT OF JUDGMENTS)
Garnishment (See GARNISHMENT)

STATE TREASURER (See TREASURER)

STATE TREASURY (See TREASURY)

STATEWIDE UNIFORM GUIDELINES (See CHILD SUPPORT)

STATIONS (See RAILROADS)

STATISTICAL INFORMATION
Family law cases, Judicial Council's collection of data and report to legislature concerning   Fam §2348
Information Practices Act, disclosures under   CC §§1798.3, 1798.24

STATISTICAL INFORMATION—Cont.
Judicial Branch Statistical Information System (JBSIS)   CRC 10.400

STATUS CONFERENCES
Pretrial conferences generally (See **PRETRIAL CONFERENCES**)

STATUTE OF FRAUDS
Generally   CC §1624
Alteration of instruments   CC §1698
Credit of third person, representations as to   CCP §1974
Decedents' estates, representative's promise to pay claims against   Pro §9604
Financial contracts   CC §1624
Instant message format communications
    Insufficiency of text message or instant message format communications to constitute contract to convey realty   CC §1624
Personal property
    Records required to enforce   CC §1624.5
Real property, grant or conveyance of   CC §1624, CCP §1971
Suretyship agreements   CC §§1624, 2794
Testamentary dispositions   CCP §1972
Text messaging
    Insufficiency of text message or instant message format communications to constitute contract to convey realty   CC §1624
Trust instruments, applicability to   Pro §15206

STATUTES
Constitutionality of statutes
    Briefs, questioning in
        Attorney general to be served copy of brief   CRC 8.29
    Judgment of unconstitutionality
        Attorney general, notice to   CRC 2.1100
Due care, statutory violation as evidence of absence of   Ev §669
Injunction against execution of   CC §3423, CCP §526
Judgment of unconstitutionality, notice to Attorney General   CRC 2.1100
Nuisance arising from compliance with   CC §3482
Service of process, proof of   CCP §417.10
Statute of limitation upon liability created by   CCP §338
Unconstitutional, judgment of
    Attorney general, notice to   CRC 2.1100

STATUTES OF LIMITATION   CCP §§312, 335, 350 to 363
Absence from state, effect of defendant's   CCP §351
Accounts (See **ACCOUNTS AND ACCOUNTING**)
Adoption order, vacation of   Fam §9102
Adverse possession (See **ADVERSE POSSESSION**)
Air quality enforcement   CCP §338
Animals, actions against persons boarding or feeding   CCP §340
Annulment of marriage   Fam §2211
    Quash, request for order   CRC 5.63
Applicability of periods prescribed in title unless different limitation prescribed by statute   CCP §312
Armenian genocide victims
    Banks' failure to pay deposited or looted assets to victim or heir, claims for   CCP §354.45
    Insurance claims against insurers by   CCP §354.4
Artists, money owed to   CC §986
Artwork
    Holocaust-era artwork
        Action to recover Holocaust-era artwork   CCP §354.3
Art works, action for defacement or destruction of   CC §987
Asbestos, actions based on exposure to   CCP §340.2
Assault and battery   CCP §335.1
    Torture, genocide, crimes against humanity, etc   CCP §354.8
Attorneys (See **ATTORNEYS**)
Automobile warranty disputes
    Restitution or replacement actions   CCP §871.21
Banks and banking (See **BANKS AND BANKING**)
Blood tests to determine paternity, filing of motion for   Fam §7541
Bonds (See **BONDS**)
Braceros
    Actions to recover savings fund amounts   CCP §354.7
Childhood sexual assault, adults' actions for   CCP §§340.1, 340.11
Child support (See **CHILD SUPPORT**)
Cities (See **CITIES AND MUNICIPALITIES**)
Claims against estates (See **CLAIMS AGAINST ESTATES**)
Claims against public entities and employees
    Judgments
        Time limit for enforcement   Gov §965.5
Coerced debt
    Establishing debt as coerced, action or cross-complaint   CC §1798.97.3
Commencement of actions, generally   CCP §350

STATUTES OF LIMITATION—Cont.
Common interest developments
    Alternative dispute resolution
        Tolling statute of limitations   CC §5945
    Declarants, developers or builders, legal proceedings against
        Limitations of actions not extended   CC §5986
Community property, spouse's action for breach of fiduciary duty involving   Fam §1101
Conservatorship (See **CONSERVATORS**)
Construction defects, actions for   CC §941
    Prelitigation procedures
        Tolling statute of limitations   CC §927
Construction of improvements to real property (See **BUILDING CONSTRUCTION**)
Consumer debt collection
    Time-barred debt, attempts to collect
        Communications with debtor   CC §1788.14
Consumer privacy rights
    California privacy protection agency
        Administrative actions   CC §1798.199.70
Contracts (See **CONTRACTS AND AGREEMENTS**)
Conversion (See **CONVERSION**)
Coroner's official act or omission to act   CCP §339
Corporate bonds, notes or debentures, action upon   CCP §336a
Corporate directors or shareholders, actions against   CCP §359
Counties (See **COUNTIES**)
Credit denial because of marital status, action for   CC §1812.35
Credit reporters, actions against (See **CREDIT REPORTING**)
Dalkon Shield claimants, extension of limitations statute in action for   CCP §340.7
Data broker registration
    Administrative actions, time for bringing   CC §1798.99.89
Death
    Survival of action after death of party   CCP §§366.1 to 366.3
    Wrongful death (See **WRONGFUL DEATH**)
Decedents' estates, claims against (See **CLAIMS AGAINST ESTATES**)
Deficiency judgments
    COVID-19, emergency rule   CRCAppx I Emer Rule 2
Detinue   CCP §338
Directed trusts
    Breach of trust actions   Pro §16622
Disabilities
    Existence when cause of action accrued, requirement of   CCP §357
    Tacking disabilities   CCP §358
    Tolling statute generally (See within this heading, **"Tolling statute"**)
Discrimination
    Violence based on prejudice, right of all persons to be free of   CC §52, CCP §338
Districts (See **DISTRICTS**)
Domestic violence, civil action based on   CCP §340.15
Embezzlement (See **EMBEZLEMENT**)
Enactment of code affecting limitation of time prescribed in existing statute   CCP §9
Enforcement of judgments (See **ENFORCEMENT OF JUDGMENTS**)
Escheat (See **ESCHEAT**)
Escheat proceedings, effect of statutes of limitation on   CCP §1476
Excluding first day   CCP §12
Execution of documents
    Writing and execution
        Renewing liability, acknowledgment or promise   CCP §360
        Waiver of limitation period   CCP §360.5
Expropriated art
    Holocaust   CCP §338
    Political persecution   CCP §338.2
Extensions
    Death of party   CCP §§366.1, 366.2
    Health care provider's professional negligence, notice of intent to commence action on   CCP §364
    Holiday, extension of time to next day which is not a   CCP §12a
    Plaintiff's attorney, court assuming jurisdiction over practice of   CCP §353.1
    Reversed on appeal, judgment for plaintiff   CCP §355
    Survival of actions   CCP §§366.1 to 366.3
Fair debt buying practices
    Actions brought after expiration of statute of limitations
        Prohibited   CC §1788.56
    Violation of provisions
        Enforcement of liability under provisions   CC §1788.62
Fair debt settlement practices   CC §1788.305
False advertising   CCP §338
False imprisonment   CCP §340

STATUTES OF LIMITATION—Cont.
Family rules
    Quashing proceedings, request for order   CRC 5.63
Felony offense, limitation of actions for damages against person based on commission of   CCP §340.3
Fine prints sale, limitation for action involving   CC §1745
Fines and penalties (See **FINES AND PENALTIES**)
Five years
    Adverse possession (See **ADVERSE POSSESSION**)
    Entry upon real estate deemed sufficient or valid as claim   CCP §320
    Hazardous waste control law violations, actions for penalties and punitive damages for   CCP §338.1
    Mesne profits, action for   CCP §336
    Seisin or possession within five years of commencement of action   CCP §§318, 319
    Void letters patent or grant, action for recovery of property conveyed by   CCP §317
Foreclosure
    COVID-19, emergency rule   CRCAppx I Emer Rule 2
Foreign judgments
    Federal courts or courts of other states   CCP §337.5
    Foreign country judgments   CCP §1721
Forfeitures (See **FORFEITURES**)
Forged or raised check, action against bank for payment of   CCP §340
Four years
    Actions not otherwise provided for   CCP §343
    Attorney's performance of professional services, actions arising out of   CCP §340.6
    Contracts, actions upon   CCP §337
    Patent deficiencies in planning or construction of improvement to real property, injury or death from   CCP §337.1
    State or county hospitals, actions on accounts for support of patients at   CCP §345
    Waivers, time limit on   CCP §360.5
Fraud (See **FRAUD**)
Fraudulently or illegally obtained money to be repaid to county, applicability of waiver provision to   CCP §360.5
Good faith improver of property owned by another, action by   CCP §340
Governmental agencies, presentation of claims as prerequisite to commencement of actions against   CCP §313
Governmental entities (See **PUBLIC ENTITIES**)
Grants or letters patent
    Real property
        Grantee or patentee, action by   CCP §316
Guardianship (See **GUARDIAN AND WARD**)
Hazardous or toxic substances or materials exposures   CCP §340.8
Hazardous waste control law violations, actions for civil penalties and punitive damages for   CCP §338.1
Health care providers, actions against   CCP §340.5
Holidays and computation of time   CCP §§12 to 12b
Holocaust-era artwork
    Action to recover Holocaust-era artwork   CCP §354.3
Hospitals (See **HOSPITALS**)
Hotels
    Conversion of personalty   CCP §341a
    Sex trafficking activity permitted by or benefiting hotel
        Actions against hotel   CC §52.65
Human trafficking   CC §52.5
Identity theft, action involving   CC §1798.96
Imprisonment tolling statute   CCP §§328.5, 352.1
Improvement districts (See **PUBLIC ENTITIES**)
Including last day   CCP §12
Indigent aid repayment, applicability of waiver provision to   CCP §360.5
Information Practices Act, proceeding under   CC §1798.49
Injunction or statutory prohibition, commencement of action stayed by   CCP §356
Injury caused by wrongful or negligent act   CCP §335.1
International law
    Taking property in violation of international law   CCP §354.8
Involuntary trusts
    Attorney general actions   CC §2224.5
IUDs, extension of limitations statute in action involving   CCP §340.7
Law enforcement officer, criminal charges as tolling statutes of limitation for actions against   Gov §945.3
Laws of state or foreign country where action has arisen, lapse of time for bringing action under   CCP §361
Leases (See **LEASES**)
Legal capacity lacking
    Tolling of statute   CCP §352
Legal disabilities
    Existence when cause accrued, requirement   CCP §357

STATUTES OF LIMITATION—Cont.
Legal disabilities—Cont.
    Tacking disabilities   CCP §355
    Tolling generally (See within this heading, "**Tolling statute**")
Legally protected health care services
    Action for relief from abusive litigation infringing on protected activity   CC §1798.303
Letters patent
    Real property
        Grantee or patentee, action by   CCP §316
Libel (See **LIBEL AND SLANDER**)
Liens, enforcement of   CC §2911
Logs and timber
    Civil or administrative enforcement   CCP §338
Mechanics' liens
    Payment bonds
        Public works, action to enforce liability on bond   CC §9558
        Recording prior to completion of work, action to enforce liability on bond   CC §8610
        Reduction of limitations period via provision in bond, restrictions   CC §8609
    Stop payment notices, enforcement of claim stated   CC §8550
        Public works   CC §§9362, 9502
Mesne profits of real property, action for   CCP §336
Minority tolling statute   CCP §352
Minors (See **MINORS**)
Mistake, action for relief on ground of   CCP §338
Mortgages (See **TRUST DEEDS AND MORTGAGES**)
Motor vehicle warranty disputes   CC §1793.22
Nazi regime, actions by victims of (See **NAZI GERMANY**)
Negligence   CCP §335.1
Northridge earthquake of 1994, extended limitation period for insurance claims arising out of   CCP §340.9
Notary public, actions upon bond of   CCP §338
Offsetting cross-demands for money notwithstanding bar of statute of limitations   CCP §431.70
Oil wells, wrongful use   CCP §349.5
One year
    Animals, actions against persons boarding or feeding   CCP §340
    Asbestos, actions based on exposure to   CCP §340.2
    Attorney's performance of professional services, actions arising out of   CCP §340.6
    Entry upon real estate deemed sufficient or valid as claim   CCP §320
    Fair debt buying practices
        Violation of provisions, enforcement of liability   CC §1788.62
    False imprisonment   CCP §340
    Forged or raised check, action against bank for payment of   CCP §340
    Good faith improver of property owned by another   CCP §340
    Libel and slander   CCP §340
    Reversal on appeal, extension applicable on   CCP §355
    Seduction of minor   CCP §340
    Seizure of property for statutory forfeiture, action against officer for damages arising from   CCP §340
    Statutory penalty or forfeiture   CCP §340
    Streets improvements, foreclosure of lien for   CCP §329
    Torts   CCP §340
    Veterinarians, actions against   CCP §340
Other states (See **OTHER STATES**)
Paternity
    Voluntary declaration of parentage
        Challenge by nonsignatories of declaration   Fam §7577
        Challenge of declaration based on fraud, duress or material mistake of fact   Fam §7576
Payments on account as sufficient acknowledgment of continuing contract   CCP §360
Penalties (See **FINES AND PENALTIES**)
Pending causes excepted   CCP §362
Personal injuries (See **PERSONAL INJURIES**)
Physicians and surgeons (See **MALPRACTICE**)
Planning or construction of improvements to real property (See **BUILDING CONSTRUCTION**)
Pleadings alleging cause of action barred by   CCP §458
Police officer, criminal charges as tolling statutes of limitation for actions against   Gov §945.3
Political items, illegal sale of   CC §1739.4
Premarital contracts, claims brought under   Fam §1617
Presumptions
    Adverse possession (See **ADVERSE POSSESSION**)
    Streets improvements, lien for   CCP §329
Prints, violating sales provisions applicable to   CC §1745
Prisoners, tolling of statute for   CCP §§328.5, 352.1

STATUTES OF LIMITATION—Cont.
  Private student loan collections reform
    Actions against creditor, lender or collector for violations of provisions   CC §1788.208
    Effect of statute of limitations   CC §1788.204
  Process, mandatory time for service of   CCP §583.210
  Profits (See within this heading, **"Rents and profits"**)
  Property damage   CCP §338
  Public entities (See **PUBLIC ENTITIES**)
  Real property
    Adverse possession (See **ADVERSE POSSESSION**)
    Certificate, abstract or guaranty of title, actions founded upon contract or obligation evidenced by   CCP §339
    Disabilities tolling statute   CCP §328
    Entry upon real estate deemed sufficient or valid as claim   CCP §320
    Good faith improver of property owned by another   CCP §340
    Grantee or patentee, action by   CCP §316
    Imprisonment tolling statute in action for recovery of   CCP §328.5
    Latent deficiencies in planning or construction of improvement to real property, damages for   CCP §337.15
    Legal capacity lacking
      Tolling of statute   CCP §328
    Mesne profits, action for   CCP §336
    Mortgages and trust deeds (See **TRUST DEEDS AND MORTGAGES**)
    Parol lease, period for action after breach of   CCP §339.5
    Patent deficiencies in planning or construction of improvement to real property, injury or death from   CCP §337.1
    Recovery of real property, time of commencing actions for   CCP §§315 to 330
    Restrictions on use of land, actions for violation of   CCP §336
    Seisin or possession within five years of commencement of action   CCP §§318, 319
    State, suit for or in respect to real property brought by   CCP §315
    Streets improvements, foreclosure of lien for   CCP §329
    Trespass   CCP §338
    Void letters patent or grant, action for recovery of property conveyed by   CCP §317
    Written lease, period for action after breach of   CCP §337.2
  Recovery of money or property deposited with bank, actions for   CCP §348
  Recovery of real property, time of commencing actions for   CCP §§315 to 330
  Renewing liability, acknowledgment or promise   CCP §360
  Rents and profits
    Disabilities tolling statute   CCP §328
    Mesne profits, action for   CCP §336
    Mortgagor's action to redeem   CCP §346
    Seisin or possession within five years of commencement of action arising out of title to   CCP §319
    State, suit for or in respect to real property brought by   CCP §315
    Tenant, adverse possession by   CCP §326
  Rescission of contract, action based on   CCP §§337, 339
  Restitution, effect of order for   CCP §352.5
  Retail marijuana
    Licenses
      Penalties for unlicensed commercial cannabis activity   CCP §338
  Reversed on appeal, judgment for plaintiff   CCP §355
  Revival of actions
    Childhood sexual abuse, damages actions based on commission of   CCP §340.35
    Childhood sexual assault, damages actions based on commission of   CCP §§340.1, 340.11
    Felony offenses, damage actions based on commission of   CCP §340.3
    Sexual abuse of a minor, damages actions based on commission of   CCP §340.35
    Sexual assault of a minor, damages actions based on commission of   CCP §§340.1, 340.11
  Saturdays as holidays for purpose of computing time   CCP §12a
  Seduction of minor   CCP §340
  Seizure of property (See **SEIZURE OF PROPERTY**)
  Separate trial of special defense   CCP §597
  Seven years
    Human trafficking   CC §52.5
  Sex offenses involving children   CCP §§340.1, 340.11, 340.35
  Sex trafficking activity permitted by or benefiting hotel
    Actions against hotel   CC §52.65
  Sexual abuse
    Childhood sexual abuse   CCP §340.35
  Sexual assault
    Childhood sexual assault   CCP §340.1
    Damages actions   CCP §340.16
  Sexual assault suffered in childhood   CCP §§340.1, 340.11
  Sexually explicit depiction of individual, creation or disclosure   CC §1708.86

STATUTES OF LIMITATION—Cont.
  Sexual orientation violence
    Civil actions   CC §52.45
  Sheriff's official act or omission to act   CCP §339
  Six months
    Bonds, contest of validity of   CCP §349.2
    Court's assumption of jurisdiction over attorney's practice, extension applicable on   CCP §353.1
    Dissolved corporation, action to set aside any action taken by trustees of   CCP §341
    Formation, dissolution or other change of organization of city, county, district or other public entity   CCP §349.1
    Stock sale   CCP §341
    Territorial boundaries, contest of change of   CCP §349.1
    Wrongful levy   CCP §341
  Slander (See **LIBEL AND SLANDER**)
  Small estates without administration (See **SMALL ESTATES WITHOUT ADMINISTRATION**)
  Special districts (See **PUBLIC ENTITIES**)
  Special proceeding of civil nature, action as used in title construed as including   CCP §363
  Spouse's action for breach of fiduciary duty by other spouse   Fam §1101
  State, applicability of limitations prescribed to actions brought in the name of or for the benefit of   CCP §345
  State of war, effect of existence of   CCP §354
  Statute, action upon liability created by   CCP §338
  Statutory prohibition, commencement of action stayed by   CCP §356
  Street improvement assessment lien foreclosure   CCP §329
  Student borrower bill of rights
    Enforcement of compliance with rights   CC §1788.103
  Subcutaneous implanting of identification device, requiring of another   CC §52.7
  Successive waivers   CCP §360.5
  Summons, mandatory time for service of   CCP §583.210
  Sureties, actions against (See **SURETYSHIP, BONDS AND UNDERTAKINGS**)
  Survival of actions   CCP §§366.1 to 366.3
  Tacking disabilities   CCP §358
  Tax assessments, actions concerning (See **TAXATION**)
  Ten years
    Judgments or decrees of federal courts or courts of other states, limitation of actions upon   CCP §337.5
    Latent deficiencies in planning or construction of improvement to real property, damages for   CCP §337.15
    Sexual assault, damages actions   CCP §340.16
    State and general obligation bonds, action upon   CCP §337.5
    State, suit for or in respect to real property brought by   CCP §315
  Terrorism
    September 11, 2001 terrorist attacks   CCP §340.10
  Theft of articles of historic or artistic importance   CCP §338
  Three months
    Trover against owner of hotel, apartment, lodging or hospital   CCP §341a
  Three years
    Air quality enforcement   CCP §338
    Bond of public official, action upon   CCP §338
    Conversion   CCP §338
    Corporate directors or shareholders, actions against   CCP §359
    Detinue   CCP §338
    Discrimination
      Violence based on prejudice, right of all persons to be free of   CC §52, CCP §338
    False advertising   CCP §338
    Fraud or mistake, action for relief on ground of   CCP §338
    Health care providers, actions against   CCP §340.5
    Notary public, actions upon bond of   CCP §338
    Property damage   CCP §338
    Section 1603.1 or 5650.1 of Fish and Game Code, action commenced under   CCP §338
    Sexual abuse of minor, civil action based upon   CCP §340.1
    Sexually explicit depiction of individual, creation or disclosure   CC §1708.86
    Slander to title   CCP §338
    Statute, action upon liability created by   CCP §338
    Theft of articles of historic or artistic importance   CCP §338
    Trespass   CCP §338
    Water Quality Control Act, actions commenced under   CCP §338
  Title and ownership (See **TITLE AND OWNERSHIP**)
  Tolling statute
    Absence from state, defendant's   CCP §351
    Adverse possession, disabilities tolling statute of limitations in actions for   CCP §328
    Attorneys' fees, dispute resolution   CCP §340.6

STATUTES OF LIMITATION—Cont.
Tolling statute—Cont.
    Attorney's performance of professional services, actions arising out of CCP §340.6
    Childhood sexual assault, damages actions based on commission of CCP §§340.1, 340.11
    COVID-19, emergency rule CRCAppx I Emer Rule 9
    Death of plaintiff or defendant CCP §§366.1 to 366.3
    Deficiency judgments
        COVID-19, emergency rule CRCAppx I Emer Rule 2
    Existence of disability when cause of action accrued CCP §357
    Felony offenses, damage actions based on commission of CCP §340.3
    Foreclosure
        COVID-19, emergency rule CRCAppx I Emer Rule 2
    Health care providers, actions against CCP §340.5
    Human trafficking CC §52.5
    Injunction or statutory prohibition, commencement of action stayed by CCP §356
    Legal capacity lacking CCP §352
    Minority CCP §352
    Payments on account as sufficient acknowledgment of continuing contract CCP §360
    Public entities or employees, actions against CCP §352
    Recovery of real property, disabilities tolling statute of limitations for CCP §328
    Restitution, effect of order for CCP §352.5
    Sexual assault of a minor, damages actions based on commission of CCP §§340.1, 340.11
    State of war, existence of CCP §354
    Stay of sentence tolling time for commencement of action for damages against felon CCP §340.3
    Survival of actions CCP §§366.1 to 366.3
    Tacking disabilities CCP §358
Torts CCP §§335.1, 340
Trade secret, limitations statute for actions regarding CC §3426.6
Trespass, generally CCP §338
Tribal court civil money judgment act
    Time for action to recognize CCP §1739
Trust deeds and mortgages
    Balance due after exercise of power of sale, action for money judgment for CCP §337
    Corporate obligations CCP §336a
    Modification or workout plan to avoid foreclosure
        Prohibited acts, statute of limitations to enforce CC §2944.10
    Mortgagor's action to redeem, generally CCP §346
    Reverse mortgage, lender's action on CC §1923.2
Trusts and trustees, claims against (See **TRUSTS**)
Two years
    Assault and battery CCP §335.1
    Attorney's performance of professional services, actions arising out of
        Factual innocence to criminal charge as element of claim CCP §340.6
    Certificate, abstract or guaranty of title, actions founded upon contract or obligation evidenced by CCP §339
    Hazardous or toxic substances or materials exposures CCP §340.8
    Injury caused by wrongful or negligent act CCP §335.1
    Official acts or omission to act by sheriff or coroner CCP §339
    Parol contracts, actions upon CCP §339
    Streets improvements, foreclosure of lien for CCP §329
    Torts CCP §335.1
    Wrongful death CCP §335.1
Unfair competition, action based on CC §§1770, 1783
Uniform Parentage act
    Vacation or setting aside of judgment
        Limitation on bringing action to vacate or set aside Fam §7646
University of Southern California
    Sexual assault at student health center
        Revival of actions otherwise barred by statute of limitations claiming damages for sexual assault at student health center CCP §340.16
Validation proceedings, time limit for answering party to file action after dismissal by public agency of CCP §867.5
Validation suit CCP §860
Veterinarians, actions against CCP §340
Voidable transactions CC §3439.09
    Personal property, transfers involving CC §3440.6
Waiver of limitations period CCP §360.5
War, effect of existence of state of CCP §354
Water Quality Control Act, actions commenced under CCP §338
Will probate, contest of (See **WILL PROBATE**)
Withdrawal of legal service agency attorney for indigent client, effect of CCP §285.3

STATUTES OF LIMITATION—Cont.
Writing and execution
    Renewing liability, acknowledgment or promise CCP §360
    Waiver of limitations period CCP §360.5
Wrongful death (See **WRONGFUL DEATH**)

STATUTORY CONSTRUCTION (See **CONSTRUCTION AND INTERPRETATION**)

STAY OF EXECUTION
Administrative adjudication (See **ADMINISTRATIVE ADJUDICATION**)
Appellate rules, superior court appeals
    Infraction case appeals CRC 8.903
    Misdemeanor appeals CRC 8.854
Contempt order stayed pending filing of petition for extraordinary relief CCP §128
Earnings assignment for support orders (See **EARNINGS ASSIGNMENT FOR SUPPORT**)
Enforcement of judgments (See **ENFORCEMENT OF JUDGMENTS**)
Unlawful detainer actions CCP §1176

STAY OF PROCEEDINGS
Adoption
    Termination of parental rights
        Alleged fathers, petitions Fam §7662
Appellate papers
    Notation of request for stay on cover CRC 8.116
Appellate rules, superior court appeals
    Limited civil cases in appellate division
        Supersedeas CRC 8.824
Appellate rules, supreme court and court of appeals (See **APPELLATE RULES, SUPREME COURT AND COURTS OF APPEAL**)
Arbitration (See **ARBITRATION**)
Authority for CCP §923
Bond requirements CCP §§917.9 to 922
Capital cases
    Supreme court policies CRCSupp SupCtPolicy
Certiorari CCP §1072
Change of venue, petition for writ of mandate on grant or denial of motion for CCP §400
Civil rules
    Notice of court and others of stay
        Duty of party requesting CRC 3.650
Complex actions, coordination CRC 3.515
Conciliation petition affecting stay on filing petition for dissolution of marriage Fam §1840
Construction-related accessibility claims
    Stay and early evaluation conference
        Notice to defendant of rights to CC §55.54
Coordination of actions
    Effect of stay CCP §404.5
Criminal appeals, stay of execution pending CRC 8.312
Custody of minor children CCP §917.7
Default judgments CCP §§585, 586
Deficiency judgments
    COVID-19, emergency rule CRCAppx I Emer Rule 2
Delivery
    Personal property CCP §917.2
    Real property CCP §917.4
Discovery
    Interstate and international depositions and discovery act
        Choice of law to resolve disputes, appeal for extraordinary writ CCP §2029.650
Execution of instruments CCP §917.3
Felony offense, effect of stay of sentence or judgment on time for commencement of actions for damages resulting from commission of CCP §340.3
Forcible entry and detainer CCP §1176
Foreclosure proceedings CCP §917.2
    COVID-19, emergency rule CRCAppx I Emer Rule 2
Foreign country judgments
    Appeal, stay on CCP §1720
Groundwater rights actions
    Comprehensive adjudications CCP §848
Hazardous waste CCP §917.15
Inconvenient forum doctrine (See **INCONVENIENT FORUM**)
International commercial arbitration and conciliation (See **INTERNATIONAL COMMERCIAL ARBITRATION AND CONCILIATION**)
Interstate family support
    Contest of validity or enforcement of registered order
        Stay of enforcement pending Fam §5700.607

STAY OF PROCEEDINGS—Cont.
Juvenile case appeals
  Order designating specific placement of dependent child, writ petition to review   CRC 8.456
  Orders setting hearing in termination cases, writ petition to review   CRC 8.452
Mandamus proceedings   CCP §§1094.5, 1110a, 1110b
Modification of stay
  Notice   CRC 3.650
Money judgments, enforcement of   CCP §917.1
Notice of stay, filing of   CRC 3.650
Perfecting of appeal, effect of   CCP §§916 to 917.9
Quo warranto   CCP §917.8
Receivers appointed   CCP §917.5
Sale of personalty   CCP §§917.2, 917.4
Service of process
  Notice of court and others of stay
    Duty of party requesting   CRC 3.650
Specific performance   CCP §917.6
Supersedeas, writ of   CRC 8.112, 8.116
Supreme court
  Application for recommendation   CRCSupp SupCtIOPP XIV
Termination of parental rights   Fam §7807
Termination of stay
  Notice   CRC 3.650
Two or more acts, judgment directing   CCP §917.6
Unlawful detainer actions
  Venue
    Stay or dismissal of action for inconvenient forum   CRC 3.1327
Vacation of stay
  Notice   CRC 3.650
Vexatious litigants (See **VEXATIOUS LITIGANTS**)

STEALTHING
Sexual battery
  Damages for sexual battery   CC §1708.5
  Nonconsensual condom removal as sexual battery   CC §1708.5

STEPPARENTS
Adoption   Fam §§9000 to 9007 (See **ADOPTION**)
Intestate succession (See **INTESTATE SUCCESSION**)
Visitation rights   Fam §§3101, 3171, 3176, 3185

STEREO EQUIPMENT (See **PHONOGRAPHS AND PHONOGRAPH RECORDS**)

STERILIZATION
Appeals   Pro §1962
  Conservatee sterilization, judgment authorizing conservator to consent   CRC 8.482
  Stay of order pending appeal   Pro §1965
Appearance by party to be sterilized required at hearing   Pro §1956
Appointments
  Attorney, appointment of   Pro §1954
  Facilitator, appointment of   Pro §1954.5
  Limited conservators   Pro §1960
    Petition for appointment   Pro §1952
Attorneys
  Appointment of   Pro §1954
  Fees   Pro §1963
Attorney's fees   Pro §1963
Castrations, applicability of sterilization proceedings for procuring   Pro §1961
Consent
  Generally   Pro §1951
  Minor's consent   Fam §6925
  Rights of developmentally disabled persons capable of consent   Pro §1969
Conservators
  Limited conservators   Pro §1960
    Petition for appointment   Pro §1952
Costs   Pro §1963
Definitions   Pro §1951
Determinations by court for authorizing   Pro §§1958, 1959
Facilitators
  Generally   Pro §1954.5
  Fees   Pro §1963
Fees   Pro §1963
Hearing
  Appearance by party to be sterilized required at   Pro §1956
  Notice of   Pro §1953
Hysterectomies, applicability of sterilization proceedings for procuring   Pro §1961

STERILIZATION—Cont.
Interpreters
  Facilitators   Pro §1954.5
    Fees   Pro §1963
Investigations conducted by court   Pro §1955
Legislative intent   Pro §1950
Liability of parties   Pro §1967
Limited conservators
  Generally   Pro §1960
  Petition for appointment of   Pro §1952
Mental examinations of party to be sterilized   Pro §1955
Minor, consent required for sterilization of   Fam §6925
Notice of hearing   Pro §1953
Objections by party to be sterilized   Pro §1958
Orders
  Generally   Pro §1962
  Duration of   Pro §1964
  Stay of order pending appeal   Pro §1965
Other medical procedures resulting in sterilization, application of law to   Pro §1968
Petition
  Generally   Pro §1952
  Re-filing of petition after denial, grounds for   Pro §1966
Physical examinations of party to be sterilized   Pro §1955
Proof of findings beyond reasonable doubt, requirement of   Pro §1958
Reports by examiners   Pro §1955
Service of papers   Pro §1953
Statement of decision, requirement of   Pro §1962
Stay of order pending appeal   Pro §1965
Translators
  Facilitators   Pro §1954.5
    Fees   Pro §1963
Witnesses
  Generally   Pro §1955
  Party to be sterilized, views of   Pro §1957

STEROIDS (See **ANABOLIC STEROIDS**)

STIPULATED JUDGMENTS (See **SETTLEMENT AND COMPROMISE**)

STIPULATIONS
Appellate rules, superior court appeals
  Attorneys
    Substitution   CRC 8.814
  Infraction case appeals
    Limited record on appeal   CRC 8.910
  Misdemeanor appeals
    Limited record on appeal   CRC 8.860
Appellate rules, supreme court and courts of appeal (See **APPELLATE RULES, SUPREME COURT AND COURTS OF APPEAL**)
Arbitration (See **ARBITRATION**)
Change of venue   CCP §398
Child support award, stipulated agreement for   Fam §§4057, 4065
Dissolution of marriage, stipulation for retention of jurisdiction   Fam §2343
Expedited jury trials   CRC 3.1551
  Evidentiary rules   CRC 3.1552
Family rules
  Judgments
    Stipulated judgments   CRC 5.411
Family support   Fam §4066
Judgment by stipulation (See **SETTLEMENT AND COMPROMISE**)
Judgment reversal by stipulation of parties, appeal court's findings required for   CCP §128
Judicial arbitration (See **JUDICIAL ARBITRATION**)
Jurors, examination outside of judge's presence of   CCP §222.5
Reclassification of action, fees for   CCP §403.050
Retired judge not qualified to try criminal case, stipulation that   CCP §170.65
Reversal by stipulation of parties, appeal court's findings required for   CCP §128
Surety bonds (See **SURETYSHIP, BONDS AND UNDERTAKINGS**)

STOCK (See **CORPORATE SHARES AND SHAREHOLDERS**)

STOCK BONUS PLANS
Employee pension benefit plan defined   Fam §80

STOCK COOPERATIVES
Generally (See **COMMON INTEREST DEVELOPMENTS**)
Defined   CC §783.1

STOLEN PROPERTY
Marketplace sales and sellers
    Reports regarding third-party sellers selling stolen goods   CC §1749.8.9

STOP PAYMENT AND STOP WORK NOTICES (See MECHANICS' LIENS)

STOPPING AND STOP SIGNS
Automated enforcement systems
    Evidentiary effect of printed representations of computer information
        Applicability to automated traffic enforcement systems   Ev §1552
    Evidentiary effect of printed representations of images stored on video or digital medium
        Applicability to automated traffic enforcement systems   Ev §1552

STORAGE
Aircraft liens   CCP §1208.61
Electronic recording reels for court proceedings   CRC 2.952
Landlord and tenant
    Commercial real property tenancies
        Disposition of property remaining upon termination, storage of property   CC §1993.06
    Landlord's removal and storage of tenant's personal property (See LANDLORD AND TENANT)
Warehouses (See WAREHOUSES)

STORES AND STOREKEEPERS
Attachment proceedings   CCP §481.120
Birth name use   CCP §1279.6
Consumer protection (See CONSUMER PROTECTION)
Credit cards (See CREDIT CARDS)
Credit reports, regulation of   CC §§1785.1 to 1785.4
Gift certificates, expiration dates
    Bankruptcy of issuer, duty to honor   CC §1749.6
    Waiver of protections   CC §1749.51
Grey market goods, sale of (See GREY MARKET GOODS)
Grocery stores (See GROCERY STORES)
Pricing policies   CC §§7100 to 7106
Products liability (See PRODUCTS LIABILITY)
Retail installment sales (See RETAIL INSTALLMENT SALES)
Supermarket club cards, restrictions as to
    Waiver of protections   CC §1749.66
Supermarkets (See GROCERY STORES)
Unruh Act (See RETAIL INSTALLMENT SALES)
Unruh Civil Rights Act   CC §§51, 52
Warranties (See WARRANTIES)

STRATEGIC LAWSUITS AGAINST PUBLIC PARTICIPATION
Motion to strike causes of action having chilling effect on public discussion of public issues   CCP §§425.16, 425.17
    SLAPPback actions   CCP §425.18

STREAMS (See RIVERS AND STREAMS)

STREET RAILWAYS
Blind persons having equal right to use of streetcars   CC §§54.1, 54.3, 54.4, 55
    Construction or application of provisions in issue, solicitor general notified   CC §55.2
Disabled persons having equal right to use of streetcars   CC §§54.1, 54.3, 54.4, 55
    Construction or application of provisions in issue, solicitor general notified   CC §55.2
Guide dogs permitted on streetcars   CC §§54.2, 54.3
    Construction or application of provisions in issue, solicitor general notified   CC §55.2
Overcrowding, applicability of carrier provisions as to   CC §§2184, 2185

STREETS AND HIGHWAYS
Adjacent landowners
    Boundaries of   CC §831, CCP §2077
    Title grants of   CC §1112
Blind persons having equal access rights to use of   CC §§54, 54.3, 54.4, 55
    Construction or application of provisions in issue, solicitor general notified   CC §55.2
Boundary lines of bordering land   CC §831, CCP §2077
Decedent's estate, transfer of property from   Pro §§9900, 9901
Disabled persons having equal access rights to use of   CC §§54, 54.3, 54.4, 55
    Construction or application of provisions in issue, solicitor general notified   CC §55.2
Earthquakes, change of boundaries after   CCP §751.58

STREETS AND HIGHWAYS—Cont.
Eminent domain
    Federal Aid Highway Act, taking pursuant to   CCP §1240.250
    Governing body defined   CCP §1245.210
    Park or open-space land for highways, acquisition of   CCP §§1240.690, 1240.700
Indemnity contracts covering construction work on   CC §2783
Liens, limitation for enforcement of   CC §2911
Ownership of bordering land as including   CC §1112
Partition referee designating portion of property as public or private way, road or street   CCP §§873.080, 873.710
Public entities, liability of (See CLAIMS AGAINST PUBLIC ENTITIES AND EMPLOYEES)
Signs and billboards (See SIGNS AND BILLBOARDS)
Statute of limitation for street improvement assessment lien foreclosure   CCP §329
Timber used to repair highway, damages for   CC §3346
Title grants to bordering land as including   CC §1112

STRIKES AND OTHER TRADE DISPUTES
Injunctions and restraining orders   CRC 3.1151
Picketing
    Injunctions and restraining orders   CRC 3.1151

STRIKING OF PLEADINGS
Motion to strike (See MOTION TO STRIKE)
    Sexual assault of minor, failure to comply with certificate of merit requirement in action for   CCP §340.11

STRUCTURAL PEST CONTROL OPERATORS
Termite work
    Common interest developments, liability for termite damages in   CC §4780
    Temporary removal of occupant   CC §4785

STUDENT AID COMMISSION
Social security numbers
    Public posting or display
        Implementation of provisions   CC §1798.85

STUDENT DEBT
Educational debt collection practices   CC §§1788.90 to 1788.94
    Definitions   CC §1788.92
    Legislative findings and intent   CC §1788.91
    Short title   CC §1788.90
    Transcript used as leverage to collect, prohibition   CC §1788.93
    Waivers   CC §1788.94

STUDENT FINANCIAL AID
Borrower bill of rights
    California student loan ombudsman   CC §1788.104
    Definitions   CC §1788.100
    Enforcement of compliance with rights   CC §1788.103
    Highlighting student loan industry practices   CC §1788.105
    Monitoring for risks to consumers   CC §1788.105
    Prohibited acts by servicers   CC §1788.101
    Rules of the road for student loan industry   CC §1788.102
    Waivers   CC §1788.106
California student loan ombudsman   CC §1788.104
Golden State Scholarshare Trust Act
    Exemptions from execution   CCP §704.105
Private student loan collections reform   CC §§1788.200 to 1788.211 (See PRIVATE STUDENT LOAN COLLECTIONS REFORM)
Student aid commission
    Social security numbers
        Public posting or display   CC §1798.85
Student loan collection
    Private student loan collections reform   CC §§1788.200 to 1788.211 (See PRIVATE STUDENT LOAN COLLECTIONS REFORM)

STUDENT LOAN SERVICING ACT
Borrower bill of rights
    California student loan ombudsman   CC §1788.104
    Definitions   CC §1788.100
    Enforcement of compliance with rights   CC §1788.103
    Highlighting student loan industry practices   CC §1788.105
    Monitoring for risks to consumers   CC §1788.105
    Prohibited acts by servicers   CC §1788.101
    Rules of the road for student loan industry   CC §1788.102
    Waivers   CC §1788.106

STUN GUNS AND TASERS
Less lethal weapons
    Sale to person under age of 18 years
        Verification of age for sale of age-restricted products   CC §1798.99.1

SUBCUTANEOUS IMPLANTING OF IDENTIFICATION DEVICE
Requiring implant in another   CC §52.7

SUBDIVISIONS
Blanket encumbrance, required notice to purchaser or lessee of   CC §1133
Common interest developments (See **COMMON INTEREST DEVELOPMENTS**)
Community apartment projects (See **COMMON INTEREST DEVELOPMENTS**)
Condominiums (See **COMMON INTEREST DEVELOPMENTS**)
Escrow companies specified by developer   CC §2995
Mobilehome subdivisions (See **MOBILEHOMES**)
Partition of lots   CCP §873.240
Penal damages for Subdivision Map Act violation   CC §2985.51
Real property sales contracts, lots transferred under   CC §§2985 to 2985.6
Recording fees for subdivision maps   Gov §27372
Trustee creating   Pro §16230

SUBJECT MATTER JURISDICTION (See **JURISDICTION**)

SUBMERGED LANDS (See **TIDELANDS**)

SUBMISSION OF CAUSE
Generally   CCP §1138
Appellate rules, superior court appeals   CRC 8.886
   Applicability of provisions   CRC 8.880
Appellate rules, supreme court and courts of appeal (See **APPELLATE RULES, SUPREME COURT AND COURTS OF APPEAL**)
Uncontested matters, submission in superior court of   CCP §75
Uncontested matters, submission of   CCP §75

SUBORDINATE JUDICIAL OFFICERS
Investigation   JudPerR 109
Judicial administration rules covering   CRC 10.700 to 10.703
   Education of judicial branch employees   CRC 10.451 to 10.493
      Additional education recommendations for certain judicial assignments   CRC 10.469
   Trial court subordinate judicial officers   CRC 10.462

SUBORDINATION OF CLAIMS
Assignment for benefit of creditors, claims under   CCP §1204.5
Judgment liens, subordination of (See **ENFORCEMENT OF JUDGMENTS**)
Trust deeds (See **TRUST DEEDS AND MORTGAGES**)

SUBPOENA
Administrative adjudication proceeding (See **ADMINISTRATIVE ADJUDICATION**)
Agreement to change time of appearance   CCP §1985.1
Arbitration   CCP §1282.6
   Attendance of witnesses   CRC 3.823
Attorneys' fees, award of   CCP §1987.2
Bench warrant (See **ARREST**)
Civil rules
   Limitation on papers filed   CRC 3.250
Concealed witness, service of   CCP §1988
Consumer privacy rights
   California privacy protection agency
      Authority of agency   CC §1798.199.65
   Compliance with subpoenas
      Exemptions on businesses to comply with subpoenas   CC §1798.145
Contempt for disobedience   CCP §§1985.1, 1991 to 1992
Dependency proceedings   CRC 5.526
Deposition subpoena (See **DEPOSITIONS**)
Electronically stored information   CCP §1985.8
Expedited jury trials
   Applicable provisions   CCP §630.06
Fees and mileage   CCP §§1986.5, 2020
Forms
   Judicial council forms   CRCAppx A
Gated community, access to
   Service of subpoena or summons   CCP §415.21
Judges, proceedings against   JudPerR 126
Judicial arbitration, attendance of witnesses   CRC 3.823
Juvenile proceedings
   Dependency proceedings, issuance in   CRC 5.526
   Wardship proceedings, issuance in   CRC 5.526
Juvenile wardship proceedings   CRC 5.526
Limitation on papers filed   CRC 3.250
Minors, subpoena of   CCP §1987
Modification, motion and order for   CCP §§1987.1, 1987.2
Motion and order to quash, modify, or comply   CCP §§1987.1, 1987.2

SUBPOENA—Cont.
Nonresident witness   CCP §1989
Notice   CCP §1985.2
   Administrative adjudication proceeding, notice in lieu of subpoena in   Gov §11450.50
   In lieu of subpoena, notice to appear   CCP §1987
Journalists, effect of subpoena on privilege as to news source   CCP §1986.1
Obtaining subpoena   CCP §1986
Peace officers   Gov §68097.1
Penalty for disobedience   CCP §1992
Probate referees, subpoena powers of   Pro §451
Quash, motion to   CCP §§1987.1, 1987.2
   Administrative adjudication   Gov §11450.30
Subpoena duces tecum (See **SUBPOENA DUCES TECUM**)
Service
   Generally   CCP §1987
   Administrative adjudication   Gov §11450.20
   Concealed witness served by sheriff   CCP §1988
Sheriff (See **SHERIFF**)
State employees   Gov §68097.1
Trial court employees   Gov §68097.1
Warrants (See **ARREST**)

SUBPOENA DUCES TECUM   CCP §1985, Ev §§1560 to 1566
Administrative adjudication (See **ADMINISTRATIVE ADJUDICATION**)
Affidavits
   Affidavit forming basis of subpoena, requirement for serving copy of   CCP §1987.5
   Custodian of records, affidavit of   Ev §§1561, 1562
Agreement to change time of appearance   CCP §1985.1
Civil rules
   Limitation on papers filed   CRC 3.250
Concealed witness, service of   CCP §1988
Consumer privacy rights
   California privacy protection agency
      Authority of agency   CC §1798.199.65
Consumer records   CCP §§1985.3, 1985.4
Contempt for disobedience   CCP §§1985.1, 1991 to 1992
Copies
   Business records, copies of   Ev §§1560, 1564
   Service of copy of affidavit and designation of materials   CCP §1987.5
Custodian of records
   Administrative adjudication   Gov §11450.10
   Affidavit of   Ev §§1561, 1562
   Multiple subpoena duces tecum, custodian receiving   Ev §1565
   Personal attendance of   Ev §1564
Disobedience of subpoena   CCP §§1985.1, 1991 to 1992
Economic litigation provisions for limited civil cases, permissible forms of discovery under   CCP §94
Electronically stored information (ESI)
   Lost, damaged, etc, information caused by good faith operation of electronic information system
      No sanctions for failure to provide information   CCP §1987.2
   Quash, motion to   CCP §1987.1
   Requiring production of ESI   CCP §1985
      Employment records defined to include ESI   CCP §1985.6
      Objection to form of production   CCP §1985.8
      Personal records defined to include ESI   CCP §1985.3
   Witness subpoena may include request to bring ESI and other things   CCP §1987
Employment records   CCP §1985.6
Fees and mileage   CCP §1986.5, Ev §1563
Judicial performance, commission on
   Censure, removal, admonishment or retirement of judges   JudPerR 122
Limitation on papers filed   CRC 3.250
Modification, motion and order for   CCP §§1987.1, 1987.2
Motion to quash or modify   CCP §§1987.1, 1987.2, CRC 3.1345
Nonresident witness   CCP §1989
Notice
   Generally   CCP §1985.2
   Administrative adjudication proceeding, notice in lieu of subpoena in   Gov §11450.50
   In lieu of subpoena, notice to appear   CCP §1987
Obtaining subpoena   CCP §1986
Original records, production of   Ev §1564
Penalty for disobedience   CCP §1992
Personal attendance of custodian   Ev §1564
Personal records of consumer   CCP §§1985.3, 1985.4
Probate referees, subpoena powers of   Pro §452
Quash, motion to   CCP §§1987.1, 1987.2, CRC 3.1345
   Administrative adjudication   Gov §11450.30

SUBPOENA DUCES TECUM—Cont.
Quash, motion to —Cont.
    Consumer records, subpoena seeking   CCP §1985.3
    Employment records, subpoena seeking   CCP §1985.6
Service
    Generally   CCP §1987
    Administrative adjudication   Gov §11450.20
    Copy of affidavit and designation of materials   CCP §1987.5
Sheriff (See **SHERIFF**)

SUBPOENAS
Legally protected health care services
    Subpoena issued in connection with abusive litigation, motion to modify or quash   CC §1798.304

SUBROGATION
Assignments for benefit of creditors   CCP §493.060
Landlord-tenant relationship (See **LANDLORD AND TENANT**)
Liens, rights under   CC §2876
Sureties (See **SURETYSHIP, BONDS AND UNDERTAKINGS**)

SUBSCRIBING WITNESSES
Generally (See **WILLS**)
Acknowledged instruments   CC §§1195 to 1199
Defined   CCP §1935

SUBSTANCE ABUSE
Commercial motor vehicle employer for vehicle accident caused by employee under the influence, damages recoverable from   CC §3333.7
Court-ordered programs
    Proof of enrollment or completion
        Forms, judicial council   CRCAppx A
Custody of children (See **CUSTODY OF CHILDREN**)
Ignition interlock orders   CRC 4.325
Judges, unfitness of   JudPerR 109
Minors
    Consent to treatment for opioid use disorder   Fam §§6929, 6929.1
Minor's consent to treatment for   Fam §6929
Proof of enrollment in or completion of program
    Form   CRCAppx A
Veterans
    Sentence and punishment
        Petition for resentencing, form   CRCAppx A

SUBSTITUTED SERVICE
Small claims court claim and order to appear   CCP §116.340

SUBSTITUTION
Appellate rules, supreme court and courts of appeal
    Attorney   CRC 8.36
        Electronic filing, when required   CRCSupp 1st AppDist
    Parties   CRC 8.36
Attorneys (See **ATTORNEYS**)
Child support, recordation of substitution of payee for   Fam §§4506.2, 4506.3
Executors (See **EXECUTORS AND ADMINISTRATORS**)
Interpleader   CCP §386
Party in action, substitution of (See **PARTIES**)
Sureties, release and substitution of   CCP §§996.110 to 996.150
Trust deeds, substitution of trustees for   CC §§2934a, 2941.7
Uniform Transfers to Minors Act, substitution of custodian under   Pro §3918

SUCCESSION (See **INHERITANCE**)

SUCCESSOR CONSERVATORS (See **CONSERVATORS**)

SUCCESSOR GUARDIANS
Appointment of   Pro §2670

SUCCESSOR IN INTEREST
Party to action involving transfer of interests, successor in interest as   CCP §368.5

SUCCESSORS IN OFFICE
Execution of process by sheriff's successors in office   CCP §262.3

SUITCASES (See **BAGGAGE**)

SUMMARY ADMINISTRATION OF SMALL ESTATES (See **SMALL ESTATES WITHOUT ADMINISTRATION**)

SUMMARY CRIMINAL HISTORY
Subsequent arrests, notification of
    Attorneys, fingerprinting   CRC 9.9.5

SUMMARY DISSOLUTION OF MARRIAGE
Brochure describing proceedings   Fam §2406
Commencing proceedings   CRC 5.77, Fam §2400
Disclosure of income and expenses   Fam §2109
Domestic partnerships   CRC 5.76
Entry of judgment   Fam §§2403, 2404
Former name of spouse restored   Fam §2401
Forms
    Judicial council legal forms   CRCAppx A
Judgments
    Entry of   Fam §§2403, 2404
Notice of revocation of petition   Fam §2402
Petition
    Generally   Fam §2401
    Fee for filing   CRC 5.77
    Filing   CRC 5.77
    Revocation of   Fam §§2342, 2402
Revocation of petition   Fam §§2342, 2401
Setting aside judgment, action for   Fam §2405
Termination of proceeding   Fam §2402

SUMMARY JUDGMENTS   CRC 3.1350
Additional motions   CCP §437c
Agreed cases   CCP §437c
Appeal or review of determination   CCP §437c
Coordinated actions   CRC 3.545
Costs on   CCP §1038
Documents in opposition or support of motion   CRC 3.1350
Evidence   CRC 3.1350
    Written objections to   CRC 3.1354
Family rules
    No use of demurrers or summary judgment motions in family law actions   CRC 5.74
Format for separate statements   CRC 3.1350
General procedure   CCP §437c
Judgment on the pleadings
    Meet and confer prior to moving for judgment on the pleadings   CCP §439
    Judicial council legal forms   CRCAppx A
Law and motion rules   CRC 3.1350
    Length of memorandum in support of motion   CRC 3.1113
    Objections to evidence in support of or in opposition to summary judgment motion   CRC 3.1352, 3.1354
Objections to evidence   CRC 3.1352
    Written objections   CRC 3.1354
Opposition to motion   CCP §437c, CRC 3.1350
Pleadings, judgment on
    Meet and confer prior to moving for judgment on the pleadings   CCP §439
    Judicial council legal forms   CRCAppx A
Separate statement of undisputed material facts   CRC 3.1350
Stipulations   CCP §437c
Summary adjudication of issues, claims, causes, etc, within action   CCP §437c
Time limits and requirements for motion   CCP §437c
Unlawful detainer action   CCP §1170.7, CRC 3.1351
    Judicial council rules as to   CCP §1170.9

SUMMARY PROCEEDINGS
Administration of small estates (See **SMALL ESTATES WITHOUT ADMINISTRATION**)
Agreed case (See **AGREED CASE**)
Confession of judgments (See **CONFESSION OF JUDGMENTS**)
Dissolution of marriages (See **SUMMARY DISSOLUTION OF MARRIAGE**)
Forcible entry and detainer (See **FORCIBLE ENTRY AND DETAINER**)
Judicial arbitration (See **JUDICIAL ARBITRATION**)
Unlawful detainer (See **UNLAWFUL DETAINER**)

SUMMONS
Dismissal of action for delay in service (See **DISMISSAL**)
Dissolution of marriage proceedings, temporary restraining order included in summons   Fam §§231 to 235, 2030, 2031
Family law rules (See **FAMILY RULES**)
Forcible entry and unlawful detainer complaints
    Issuance of summons upon filing complaint   CCP §1166
Forms
    Judicial council forms   CRCAppx A
Jury duty (See **JURY**)
Process, generally (See **PROCESS AND SERVICE OF PROCESS**)
Seal of court, documents requiring   CCP §153
Service (See **PROCESS AND SERVICE OF PROCESS**)
Uniform Parentage Act, summons containing temporary restraining order in proceeding under   Fam §7700

SUNDAYS
As holidays   CC §7
Discovery, effect on time limits for   CCP §2016.060
Judicial holidays falling on   CCP §135
Performance on   CC §§7, 10, 11
Rules of court
   Computation of time   CRC 1.10
   Judicial holiday falling on Saturday or Sunday   CRC 1.11
White Cane Safety Day, observance of   CC §54.5

SUNLIGHT (See SOLAR ENERGY)

SUPERINTENDENT OF PUBLIC INSTRUCTION (See SCHOOLS)

SUPERIOR COURT APPELLATE DIVISION (See APPELLATE DIVISION OF SUPERIOR COURT)

SUPERIOR COURTS
Adjournments construed as recesses   CCP §74
Administrative judge
   Presiding judge generally (See within this heading, **"Presiding judge"**)
Adoption hearings (See ADOPTION)
Affidavit, judicial officer's power to take and certify   CCP §179
Appellate provisions
   Appellate division
      Administration of appellate division   CRC 10.1100 to 10.1108
      Generally (See **APPELLATE DIVISION OF SUPERIOR COURT**)
      Rules governing appellate division proceedings   CRC 8.800 to 8.966 (See **APPELLATE RULES, SUPERIOR COURT APPEALS**)
   Fees
      Administrative agency decisions, appeals to superior court   Gov §70615
      Certification fees   Gov §70620
   Gangs and gang violence
      Shared gang databases, appeal of designation   CRC 3.2300
   Jurisdiction of superior court   CCP §77
   Mandamus
      Judgment involving mandamus or prohibition directed to superior court   CCP §904.3
   Prohibition, writ of
      Judgment involving mandamus or prohibition directed to superior court   CCP §904.3
Applications
   Amendment of complaint or other subsequent pleadings
      Effect on filing fee   Gov §70613.5
   Incompetent person, court approval of compromise of claims involving   CRC 3.1384
      Attendance at hearing on petition   CRC 7.952
      Attorney interest in petition   CRC 7.951
      Deposit of funds, order   CRC 7.953
      Petition for approval   CRC 7.950
      Withdrawal of deposited funds   CRC 7.954
   Initial filing fees   Gov §§70611, 70613
   Permissible additional fees   Gov §70603
   Supplemental fees for first paper filing   Gov §§70602.5, 70602.6
   Minors, court approval for compromise of claim involving   CRC 3.1384
      Attendance at hearing on petition   CRC 7.952
      Attorney interest in petition   CRC 7.951
      Deposit of funds, order   CRC 7.953
      Petition for approval   CRC 7.950
      Withdrawal of deposited funds   CRC 7.954
Arbitration
   Generally (See **ARBITRATION**)
   International commercial arbitration (See **INTERNATIONAL COMMERCIAL ARBITRATION AND CONCILIATION**)
   Judicial arbitration (See **JUDICIAL ARBITRATION**)
Assignment of cases
   Trial or dismissal of assigned cases   CRC 10.910
Audio taping
   Broadcasting, photographing or recording of court proceedings   CRC 1.150
   Transcripts
      Court reporter fees (See **COURT REPORTERS**)
      Court reporter generally (See **COURT REPORTERS**)
      Generally (See within this heading, **"Transcripts"**)
Automation standards for trial courts   CRC 10.870
Automobile conditional sales contract enforced in   CC §2984.4
Budget, court
   Appropriations   CRC 10.810
   Checks and other negotiable paper to pay court fees, fines, etc   CRC 10.821

SUPERIOR COURTS—Cont.
Budget, court—Cont.
   Court operations   CRC 10.810
   Credit card payments of fees   CRC 10.820
   Fees set by courts   CRC 10.815
   Functional budget categories   CRC 10.810
   Homicide trials, cost reimbursements   CRC 10.811
   Judicial Administration Rules (See **JUDICIAL ADMINISTRATION RULES**)
   Maintenance of budget and management information   CRC 10.501
   Procedures for budgeting   CRC 10.800, 10.801
   Public access to budget information
      Information access disputes, writ petitions   CRC 10.803
   Surplus property, disposal   CRC 10.830
   Trial court budget advisory committee   CRC 10.64
Business oversight commissioner, hearings on sale of properties of savings and loan association whose business, properties and assets are in possession of   CCP §§73c, 73d
Calendars
   Case disposition time standards   CRC JudAdminStand 2.2
   Case-flow management and court delay reduction   CRC JudAdminStand 2.2
   Civil case management
      Calendaring system   CRC 10.900
   Master calendar
      Criminal case assignment   CRC 4.115
Capital punishment cases (See **CAPITAL PUNISHMENT**)
Case management
   Civil case management   CRC 10.900 to 10.910
   Criminal case management   CRC 10.950 to 10.953
   Judicial council legal forms   CRCAppx A
Chambers, powers and duties of judges at   CCP §167
Change of venue, petition for writ of mandate on grant or denial of motion for   CCP §400
Child custody
   Superior courts as supervised visitation and exchange locations   Fam §3200
Children's waiting rooms
   Fees in superior courts
      Allocations from fees   Gov §70640
Child star contracts, approval of   Fam §§6750 to 6753
Civil case management   CRC 10.900 to 10.910
   Assignment of cases
      Trial or dismissal of assigned cases   CRC 10.910
   Calendaring system   CRC 10.900
   Case management and calendaring system   CRC 10.900
   Internal management procedures   CRC 10.901
   Judicial council legal forms   CRCAppx A
Civil rules   CRC 1.4, 3.1 to 3.2240 (See **CIVIL RULES**)
Clerk
   Filing requirements
      Abandonment of appeal   CRC 8.224
Collections performed in enforcement of court orders, costs of   CRC 10.810
Compensation of judges   CRC 10.810
Complaints (See **COMPLAINTS**)
Compromise (See within this heading, **"Settlement and compromise"**)
Conferences
   Arbitration status conferences   CCP §1141.16
      Telephone appearance at status conferences   CRC 3.670
   Case management generally (See within this heading, **"Case management"**)
   Pre-voir dire conferences   CRC 4.200
Conservatorship alternatives program
   Self-help centers   Pro §1836
Continuances
   Trial court delay reduction program (See **TRIAL COURT DELAY REDUCTION**)
Conveyance of real property, judicial officer's power to take and certify proof and acknowledgment of   CCP §179
Coordination of actions sharing common issues of law or fact   CCP §§404, 404.3
Coordination of trial courts (See **JUDICIAL ADMINISTRATION STANDARDS**)
Copies
   Local rules of court, distribution   CRC 10.613
Costs
   Generally (See **COSTS**)
   Court operations   CRC 10.810
   Functional budget categories   CRC 10.810
   General county services, costs reported as   CRC 10.810
Court commissioners (See **COURT COMMISSIONERS**)
Court employees (See **COURT OFFICERS AND EMPLOYEES**)
Court executive officer, duties of   CRC 10.610

SUPERIOR COURTS—Cont.
  Court operations   CRC 10.810
  Court records
    Computer-generated records (See **COMPUTERS**)
    Destruction, notice   CRC 10.856
    Historic court records preservation program   CRC 10.855
    Indexes   CRC 10.851
    Storage   CRC 10.855
    Transcripts
      Court reporter generally (See **COURT REPORTERS**)
      Generally (See within this heading, "Transcripts")
  Court reporters
    Cost of county, matters reported at   CCP §274a
    Duties of   CCP §269
    Functional budget categories   CRC 10.810
    Generally (See **COURT REPORTERS**)
    Reports as prima facie evidence of testimony and proceedings   CCP §273
    Transcripts
      Generally (See within this heading, "Transcripts")
  Criminal cases
    Case disposition standards   CRC JudAdminStand 2.2
    Criminal rules generally   CRC 4.1 to 4.601
    Death penalty cases (See **CAPITAL PUNISHMENT**)
    Fees in superior courts   Gov §70633
    Management of criminal cases   CRC 10.950 to 10.953
      Meetings concerning criminal court system, designating judges to attend   CRC 10.952
      Supervising judges, duties   CRC 10.951
      Three or more judges in court, organization   CRC 10.950
    Sentencing (See **SENTENCE AND PUNISHMENT**)
    Time
      Standards for case disposition   CRC JudAdminStand 2.2
  Cross-complaints (See **CROSS-COMPLAINTS**)
  Death penalty cases (See **CAPITAL PUNISHMENT**)
  Declaration, judicial officer's power to take and certify   CCP §179
  Delay in prosecution   CCP §§583.410 to 583.430
  Delay reduction of trial, Judicial Council standards for   CRC JudAdminStand 2.2
  Determinate sentencing rules   CRC 4.401 to 4.480
  Dismissal   CCP §§581, 581d
    Assigned cases, trial or dismissal   CRC 10.910
    Delay in prosecution   CCP §§583.410 to 583.430
    Failure to comply with local rules   CCP §575.2
  Electronic recordings
    Broadcasting, photographing or recording of court proceedings   CRC 1.150
    Transcripts
      Court reporter generally (See **COURT REPORTERS**)
      Generally (See within this heading, "Transcripts")
  Employees of court (See **COURT OFFICERS AND EMPLOYEES**)
  Enhancement of punishment
    Disabled persons, fines enhanced for deceptive consumer sales practices resulting in injury to   CC §3345
    Senior citizens, fines enhanced for deceptive consumer sales practices resulting in injury to   CC §3345
  Exhibits
    Transmission to or from reviewing court   CRC 8.224
  Extensions of time
    Habeas corpus procedure   CRC 4.551
  Facility modification
    Trial court facility modification advisory committee   CRC 10.65
  Facsimile transmission of documents for court filing (See **FAX FILING AND SERVICE**)
  Failure to comply with rules or orders, sanctions for   CCP §575.2
  Family law pilot projects (See **FAMILY LAW PILOT PROJECTS**)
  Family law proceedings   Fam §200
    Civil rules
      Applicability in family, juvenile and probate cases in superior court   CRC 3.10
      Generally   CRC 1.4, 3.1 to 3.2240
    Fees in superior courts   Gov §§70670 to 70678
      Supplemental fees for first paper filing   Gov §§70602.5, 70602.6
  Fax filing and service (See **FAX FILING AND SERVICE**)
  Fees in superior courts   Gov §§70600 to 70678
    Additional fees   Gov §70603
    Administrative agency decisions
      Appeals to superior court   Gov §70615
    Adoption proceedings   Gov §70633
    Amendment of complaint or other subsequent pleadings
      Effect on filing fee   Gov §70613.5
    Appeal certificates   Gov §70620

SUPERIOR COURTS—Cont.
  Fees in superior courts —Cont.
    Applications
      Hearings, filing motion, application or paper filed which would require   Gov §70617
    Authentication of documents
      Court order, authentication pursuant to   Gov §70629
    Comparing originals with copies   Gov §70627
    Copies   Gov §70627
    Criminal cases   Gov §70633
    Exemplification of record   Gov §70628
    Family law matters   Gov §§70670 to 70678
      Certified copies of dissolution of marriage or domestic partnership records   Gov §70674
      Child custody and visitation   Gov §70678
      First paper, filing   Gov §§70602.5, 70602.6, 70670, 70671
      Hearings, subsequent filings causing need for   Gov §70677
      Indigent petitioners, fee waivers   Gov §70676
      Military personnel, waiver of certain fees   Gov §70673
      Papers, construction of term   Gov §70671
      Parentage, title IV-D child support agency involved   Gov §70672
      Supplemental fees for first paper filing   Gov §§70602.5, 70602.6
      Support, title IV-D child support agency involved   Gov §70672
    Governments
      Services to local, state and federal governments   Gov §70633
    Hearings
      Motion, application or paper filed which would require hearing   Gov §70617
    Increases
      Moratorium   Gov §70601
    Initial filing   Gov §70611
      Defendant's first filing   Gov §70612
      Limited civil case   Gov §§70602.5, 70602.6, 70613, 70614
      Supplemental fees for first paper filing   Gov §§70602.5, 70602.6
    Limited civil cases
      Appeal, notice of to appellate division   Gov §§70602.5, 70602.6, 70621
      First filing   Gov §§70602.5, 70602.6, 70613, 70614
      Reclassification to unlimited civil case   Gov §70619
    Motions
      Hearings, filing motion, application or paper filed which would require   Gov §70617
    Orders
      Request for order authorizing service of summons   Gov §70617
    Papers
      Hearings, filing motion, application or paper filed which would require   Gov §70617
    Probate proceedings   Gov §§70650 to 70661
      Advance health care directives   Gov §§70602.5, 70602.6, 70655
      Capacity determinations and health care decisions for adult without conservator   Gov §70655
      Clerks of court, documents transferred to   Gov §§70660, 70661
      Combined petitions, applications, objections or other opposition   Gov §70658.5
      Community property held with incompetent spouse, transactions involving   Gov §§70602.5, 70602.6, 70655
      Conservators, appointment   Gov §§70602.5, 70602.6, 70653
      Developmental disabilities department employees   Gov §70659
      Fact of death   Gov §§70602.5, 70602.6, 70655
      Guardians, appointment   Gov §§70602.5, 70602.6, 70653, 70654
      Hearings, subsequent filings requiring   Gov §70657
      Letters, petitions for   Gov §70650
      Mental health department employees   Gov §70659
      Minor's claim, compromise   Gov §§70602.5, 70602.6, 70655
      Objections or papers in opposition, filing   Gov §70651
      Orders, opposition to petition for   Gov §§70602.5, 70602.6, 70658
      Petitions, applications, objections or other objections   Gov §70657.5
      Powers of attorney   Gov §§70602.5, 70602.6, 70655
      Public administrators, guardians, conservators, etc   Gov §70659
      Small estates, setting aside   Gov §§70602.5, 70602.6, 70656
      Succession to real property   Gov §§70602.5, 70602.6, 70655
      Supplemental fees for first paper filing   Gov §§70602.5, 70602.6
      Survivors, confirmation of property passing to   Gov §§70602.5, 70602.6, 70655
      Trusts, compromise or approval of claims   Gov §§70602.5, 70602.6, 70655
      Trusts, internal affairs   Gov §70652
    Reductions in certain distributions   Gov §70603
    Riverside County
      Surcharges on various fees for courthouse repair   Gov §70622
    Search of records   Gov §70627

SUPERIOR COURTS—Cont.
  Fees in superior courts —Cont.
    Service fees
      Specified services   Gov §70626
      Unspecified services   Gov §70631
    Statewide applicability   Gov §70603
    Supplemental fees for first paper filings   Gov §§70602.5, 70602.6
    Surcharges for certain localities   Gov §§70622 to 70625
    Termination of parental rights   Gov §70633
    Trust, funds held in   Gov §70632
    Uniform fees
      Legislative intent   Gov §70600
    Unspecified services   Gov §70631
    Venue
      Change of venue   Gov §70618
    Videoconferencing   Gov §70630
    Waiting rooms for children
      Allocations from fees   Gov §70640
  Filing
    Abandonment of appeal   CRC 8.244
    Fax machines, use of (See **FAX FILING AND SERVICE**)
    Filing fees, generally (See **FEES**)
  Findings (See **STATEMENT OF DECISION**)
  Functional budget categories   CRC 10.810
  Funds held in trust
    Fees in superior courts   Gov §70632
  Grand jury
    Demographic data on regular grand jurors, gathering and summarizing   CRC 10.625
  Habeas corpus (See **HABEAS CORPUS**)
  Hearing
    Age of person charged, hearing to determine   CRC 4.116
    Habeas corpus petition   CRC 4.551
  Historic court records preservation program   CRC 10.855
  Incompetent person, petition for court approval of compromise of claims involving   CRC 3.1384
    Deposit of funds, order   CRC 7.953
    Petition   CRC 7.950
      Attendance at hearing on petition   CRC 7.952
      Attorney interest in petition   CRC 7.951
      Expedited approval, petition   CRC 7.950.5
      Forms, use of judicial council form   CRC 7.101
    Withdrawal of deposited funds   CRC 7.954
  Indigent persons (See **INDIGENT PERSONS**)
  International commercial arbitration and conciliation (See **INTERNATIONAL COMMERCIAL ARBITRATION AND CONCILIATION**)
  Interpreters, use of (See **TRANSLATORS AND INTERPRETERS**)
  Judges
    Duties and powers   CRC 10.608
      Generally   CCP §166
      Interlocutory orders   CCP §166.1
    Functional budget categories   CRC 10.810
    Master calendar
      Criminal case assignment   CRC 4.115
    Presiding judge (See within this heading, "**Presiding judge**")
    Record on appeal, lack of authority to extend time for any act involving   CRC 8.60
    Salaries and benefits as court operations costs   CRC 10.810
    Subordinate judicial officers
      Complaints against   CRC 10.703
      Education of judicial branch employees   CRC 10.451 to 10.493
      Law practice   CRC 10.702
      Qualifications   CRC 10.701
      Role   CRC 10.700
    Temporary judges   CRC 2.810 to 2.834
      Subordinate judicial officers serving as   CRC 10.700
  Judicial administration rules (See **JUDICIAL ADMINISTRATION RULES**)
  Judicial administration standards (See **JUDICIAL ADMINISTRATION STANDARDS**)
  Judicial arbitration (See **JUDICIAL ARBITRATION**)
  Judicial Branch Statistical Information System (JBSIS)   CRC 10.400
  Jurisdiction
    Child custody and care determinations
      Immigration and nationality act decisions   CCP §155
  Jury (See **JURY**)
  Jury commissioner, superior court administrator or executive officer serving as   CCP §195
  Juvenile court proceedings
    Certification to juvenile court   CRC 4.116

SUPERIOR COURTS—Cont.
  Juvenile court proceedings—Cont.
    Civil rules
      Applicability in family, juvenile and probate cases in superior court   CRC 3.10
      Generally   CRC 1.4, 3.1 to 3.2240
    Juvenile rules generally   CRC 5.500 to 5.840
  Juvenile courts
    Juvenile rules generally   CRC 5.500 to 5.840
  Juvenile hall located, court holding session in judicial district in which   CCP §73e
  Law and motion proceedings (See **LAW AND MOTION PROCEEDINGS**)
  Limited civil cases
    Appeal, notice of to appellate division
      Superior court fees   Gov §§70602.5, 70602.6, 70621
    Delay reduction program   Gov §68620
    Jurisdiction   CCP §396a
  Local rules   CCP §575.1, CRC 10.613
    Mediation in custody proceedings   Fam §3162
    Sanctions for noncompliance   CCP §575.2
  Mandamus   CCP §1085
  Mandatory arbitration (See **JUDICIAL ARBITRATION**)
  Master calendar
    Criminal case assignment   CRC 4.115
  Minors
    Certification to juvenile court   CRC 4.116
    Compromise of claims of   CRC 3.1384
      Attendance at hearing on petition   CRC 7.952
      Attorney interest in petition   CRC 7.951
      Deposit of funds, order   CRC 7.953
      Expedited approval, petition   CRC 7.950.5
      Petition   CRC 7.101, 7.950, 7.950.5
      Withdrawal of deposited funds   CRC 7.954
    Waiting rooms for children
      Fees in superior courts, allocations for waiting rooms   Gov §70640
  Motions
    Dismiss, motion to
      Dismissal generally (See within this heading, "**Dismissal**")
    Law and motion proceedings generally (See **LAW AND MOTION PROCEEDINGS**)
  Notices
    Abandonment of appeal   CRC 8.244
  Pilot and demonstration projects (See **PILOT AND DEMONSTRATION PROJECTS**)
  Presiding judge
    Duties   CRC 10.603
    Education of judicial branch
      Duties of presiding judge   CRC 10.452
    Executive committee   CRC 10.605
    Family court's role   CRC JudAdminStand 5.30
    Selection of   CRC 10.602
  Pretrial arbitration (See **JUDICIAL ARBITRATION**)
  Pretrial conferences
    Case management generally (See within this heading, "**Case management**")
  Pre-voir dire conferences in criminal cases   CRC 4.200
  Probate jurisdiction
    Civil rules
      Applicability in family, juvenile and probate cases in superior court   CRC 3.10
      Generally   CRC 1.4, 3.1 to 3.2240
    Probate rules generally   CRC 7.1 to 7.1105
  Probate proceedings, fees   Gov §§70650 to 70661
    Supplemental fees for first paper filing   Gov §§70602.5, 70602.6
  Process extends throughout state   CCP §71
  Prohibition, writ of   CCP §1103
  Records
    Budget and management information   CRC 10.501
    Destruction, notice   CRC 10.856
    Forms
      Judicial council legal forms   CRCAppx A
    Indexes   CRC 10.851
    Public access to judicial administrative records   CRC 10.500
    Sampling program   CRC 10.855
    Storage   CRC 10.855
  Referees (See **REFEREES**)
  Remote appearances
    Reports on use of remote technology in civil actions   CCP §367.8
  Residence of defendants
    Venue   CCP §395
  Retail installment sales actions   CC §1812.10
  Rules for sentencing (See **SENTENCE AND PUNISHMENT**)

SUPERIOR COURTS—Cont.
Rules of court
    Civil rules   CRC 1.4, 3.1 to 3.2240 (See **CIVIL RULES**)
    Juvenile rules   CRC 5.500 to 5.840 (See **JUVENILE RULES**)
    Probate rules   CRC 7.1 to 7.1105 (See **PROBATE RULES**)
    Trial court rules   CRC 2.1 to 2.1100 (See **TRIAL COURT RULES**)

Rules on appeal
    Superior court appellate division proceedings   CRC 8.800 to 8.936 (See **APPELLATE RULES, SUPERIOR COURT APPEALS**)

Sanctions (See **SANCTIONS**)

Satisfaction of judgment, judicial officer's power to take and certify acknowledgment of   CCP §179

Sealed records   CRC 8.46

Security
    Court security committees   CRC 10.173
    Memorandum of understanding
        Disputes related to MOU, petition   CRC 10.174

Sentencing
    Determinate sentencing rules   CRC 4.401 to 4.480

Sentencing rules for superior courts
    Generally (See **SENTENCE AND PUNISHMENT**)

Settlement and compromise
    Incompetent persons, proceedings involving   CRC 3.1384
        Attendance at hearing on petition   CRC 7.952
        Attorney interest in petition   CRC 7.951
        Deposit of funds, order   CRC 7.953
        Expedited approval, petition   CRC 7.950.5
        Petition for approval   CRC 7.101, 7.950, 7.950.5
        Withdrawal of deposited funds   CRC 7.954
    Minors, proceedings involving   CRC 3.1384
        Attendance at hearing on petition   CRC 7.952
        Attorney interest in petition   CRC 7.951
        Expedited approval, petition   CRC 7.950.5
        Petition for approval   CRC 7.101, 7.950, 7.950.5

Small claims division (See **SMALL CLAIMS COURTS**)

Smoking policy for   CRC 10.504

Statement of decision (See **STATEMENT OF DECISION**)

Subordinate judicial officers
    Complaints against   CRC 10.703
    Education of judicial branch employees   CRC 10.451 to 10.493
        Additional education recommendations for certain judicial assignments   CRC 10.469
        Trial court subordinate judicial officers   CRC 10.462
    Law practice   CRC 10.702
    Qualifications   CRC 10.701
    Role   CRC 10.700

Superior Court Appellate Division (See **APPELLATE DIVISION OF SUPERIOR COURT**)

Support staff ethics program   CRC JudAdminStand 10.16

Temporary judges   CRC 2.810 to 2.835
    Subordinate judicial officers serving as   CRC 10.700

Time
    Calendars generally (See within this heading, "**Calendars**")
    Case disposition, time standards for   CRC JudAdminStand 2.2
    Criminal cases
        Standards for case disposition   CRC JudAdminStand 2.2
    Extensions of time
        Habeas corpus procedure   CRC 4.551
    Habeas corpus procedure   CRC 4.551
    Record on appeal, lack of authority to extend time for any act involving   CRC 8.60

Transcripts
    Court reporter
        Fees (See **COURT REPORTERS**)
        Generally (See **COURT REPORTERS**)
    Felony case, preparation of record on appeal for   CCP §269
    Preparation of   CCP §269
    Settlement with respect to omissions or errors, submission by reviewing court for   CRC 8.155
    Superior court file in lieu of clerk's transcript, stipulation for inclusion in record on appeal of   CRC 8.128
        Content of record on appeal   CRC 8.120

Transfer of cases
    Generally   CCP §402
    Limited civil cases   CCP §396a
    Wrong court, appeal or petition filed in   CCP §396

Translators, use of (See **TRANSLATORS AND INTERPRETERS**)

Trial
    Case management generally (See within this heading, "**Case management**")
    Jury trial (See **JURY**)

SUPERIOR COURTS—Cont.
Trial—Cont.
    Master calendar
        Criminal case assignment   CRC 4.115

Trial court delay reduction program (See **TRIAL COURT DELAY REDUCTION**)

Trial court employment protection and governance, writ petitions in labor relations disputes   CRC 10.660

Trial court management   CRC 10.601 to 10.953

Trial court rules   CRC 2.1 to 2.1100 (See **TRIAL COURT RULES**)

Trial courts, optional state funding of
    Change in court-county relationship, notice   CRC 10.805

Uncontested matters, submission of   CCP §75

Uniform civil fees and standard fee schedule act of 2005   Gov §§70600 to 70678
    Supplemental fees for first paper filing   Gov §§70602.5, 70602.6
    Surcharges for certain localities   Gov §§70622 to 70625

Venue
    Contracts, actions founded on   CCP §395
    Generally   CCP §402
    Injury to person or personal property   CCP §395
    Real property actions   CCP §392
    Transfer of cases   CCP §402

Videotaping
    Broadcasting, photographing or recording of court proceedings   CRC 1.150
    Transcripts
        Court reporters generally (See **COURT REPORTERS**)
        Generally (See within this heading, "**Transcripts**")

Waiting rooms for children
    Fees in superior courts
        Allocations from fees   Gov §70640

SUPERMARKETS (See **GROCERY STORES**)

SUPERSEDEAS, WRIT OF   CRC 8.112, 8.116
Appellate rules, superior court appeals
    Limited civil cases in appellate division   CRC 8.824

Petition   CRC 8.112, 8.116

SUPERVISED FINANCIAL ORGANIZATION (See **RETAIL INSTALLMENT SALES**)

SUPERVISORS
Acknowledgment of instruments   CC §1181

Contempt orders against county governing board members for failure to perform duties   CCP §128

SUPPLEMENTAL PLEADINGS (See **PLEADINGS**)

SUPPLIES
Lien for furnishing   CC §3051

SUPPORT
Child support (See **CHILD SUPPORT**)

Defenses
    Laches as to portion owed to state   Fam §291

Defined   Fam §150

Family support
    Generally (See **FAMILY SUPPORT**)

Fees
    Waiver of fees and costs
        Repayment of waived fees in support actions   CRC 5.45

Foreign country judgments
    Applicability of provisions   CCP §1715

Forms
    Judicial council forms   CRCAppx A

Income and expense declaration defined   Fam §95

Interstate family support   Fam §§5700.101 to 5700.903 (See **INTERSTATE FAMILY SUPPORT**)

Modification of support orders
    Effective dates for modification and requests for modification   CRCAppx I Emer Rule 13

Orders or stipulation designating support as family support
    Attachment to orders   CRCAppx A (CRCFL-343)

Self-help materials   Fam §291

Separate maintenance
    Exemption from execution   CCP §704.111

Social Security Act Title IV-D support actions, rules for   CRC 5.300 to 5.375

Spousal support (See **SPOUSAL SUPPORT**)

Support order defined   Fam §155

Termination of support orders
    Effective dates for termination and requests for termination   CRCAppx I Emer Rule 13

SUPPORT—Cont.
Title IV-D support enforcement   CRC 5.300 to 5.375

SUPPRESSION OF EVIDENCE   Ev §413
Appellate rules, superior court appeals
   Misdemeanor appeals
      Limited normal record   CRC 8.867
Discretion of court
   Creative expressions, admissibility   Ev §352.2
Juvenile wardship proceedings
   Pre-hearing motions   CRC 5.544
Misleading evidence, exclusion
   Creative expressions, admissibility   Ev §352.2
Motion to suppress   CRC 4.111
Pharmacist review board records   Ev §1157
Prejudicial evidence, exclusion
   Creative expressions, admissibility   Ev §352.2
Probative value *vs.* **prejudicial effect**
   Creative expressions, admissibility   Ev §352.2
Time for motion   CRC 4.111

SUPREME COURT, CALIFORNIA
Acknowledgment of instruments
   Justices, retired justices or clerk/executive officer   CC §1180
Adjournments construed as recesses   CCP §42
Affidavit, justice's power to take and certify   CCP §179
Amicus briefs   CRC 8.520
Amicus curiae letters, review of   CRC 8.500
Appellate rules relating to supreme court   CRC 8.1 to 8.642 (See **APPELLATE RULES, SUPREME COURT AND COURTS OF APPEAL**)
Attorney General, filing of amicus curiae brief   CRC 8.520
Attorneys
   Admission to practice
      Supreme Court inherent power   CRC 9.3
   Communications in pending cases   CRCSupp SupCtIOPP XVI
   Criminal cases, appointments in   CRCSupp SupCtIOPP XV
   Practice of law
      Inherent jurisdiction of Supreme Court   CRC 9.3
Authority to affirm, reverse or modify judgment or order appealed from   CCP §43
Bar examination
   Approval by supreme court   CRC 9.6
Briefs   CRC 8.520
   Service   CRC 8.212
Calendar
   Memoranda   CRCSupp SupCtIOPP VI
   Sessions
      Oral argument   CRCSupp SupCtIOPP V
Certified questions, request procedure and answers to   CRC 8.548
Chief Justice
   Acting Chief Justice   CRCSupp SupCtIOPP I
   Appellate rules (See **APPELLATE RULES, SUPREME COURT AND COURTS OF APPEAL**)
   Education of judicial branch
      Additional education recommendations for certain judicial assignments   CRC 10.469
      Duties of chief judge   CRC 10.452
   Judicial Council chair   CRC 10.2
Clemency
   Application for recommendation for executive clemency   CRCSupp SupCtIOPP XIV
Clerk/executive officer
   Acknowledgment of instruments
      Justices, retired justices or clerk/executive officer   CC §1180
   Appellate rules (See **APPELLATE RULES, SUPREME COURT AND COURTS OF APPEAL**)
Conferences
   Memorandum   CRCSupp SupCtIOPP IV
   Regular conferences   CRCSupp SupCtIOPP III
   Special conferences   CRCSupp SupCtIOPP III
   Temporary absence of justice   CRCSupp SupCtIOPP XII
Contested election cases, preference to   CCP §44
Conveyance of real property, justice's power to take and certify proof and acknowledgment of   CCP §179
Costs on appeal   CRC 8.544
Court of appeal decisions, review of   CRC 8.500
   Dismissal and remand   CRC 8.528
   Specification of issues   CRC 8.516
COVID-19
   Supreme court e-filing rules
      Emergency situations, modifications to rules governing documents subject to electronic filing   CRCSupp SuprCtE-file 2
Death penalty cases (See **CAPITAL PUNISHMENT**)

SUPREME COURT, CALIFORNIA—Cont.
Decisions
   Disposition of causes   CRC 8.528
   Finality   CRC 8.532
      Habeas corpus   CRC 8.387
Declaration, justice's power to take and certify   CCP §179
Deferral of action pending disposition of other case   CRC 8.512
Disciplinary action against judges
   Supreme court justice, proceedings involving   CRC 9.61
Education of judicial branch   CRC 10.451 to 10.493
   Recommendations for appellate and trial court personnel   CRC 10.479
E-filing in supreme court and courts of appeal
   Generally   CRC 8.70 to 8.79
   Supreme court-specific rules   CRCSupp SuprCtE-file 1 to CRCSupp SuprCtE-file 13
      Applicability of rules   CRCSupp SuprCtE-file 1
      Capital matter notation   CRCSupp SuprCtE-file 10
      Confidential records, privacy protection   CRCSupp SuprCtE-file 11
      Documents subject to e-filing   CRCSupp SuprCtE-file 2 to CRCSupp SuprCtE-file 4
      Emergency situations, modifications to rules governing documents subject to electronic filing   CRCSupp SuprCtE-file 2
      Excuse from electronic filing   CRCSupp SuprCtE-file 6
      Fees   CRCSupp SuprCtE-file 12
      Format of electronically filed documents   CRCSupp SuprCtE-file 10
      Mandatory electronic filing   CRCSupp SuprCtE-file 3
      Paper copies filed with electronically filed documents   CRCSupp SuprCtE-file 5
      Personal identifiers, privacy protection   CRCSupp SuprCtE-file 11
      Privacy protection   CRCSupp SuprCtE-file 11
      Registration of electronic filers   CRCSupp SuprCtE-file 7
      Sealed records, privacy protection   CRCSupp SuprCtE-file 11
      Service   CRCSupp SuprCtE-file 9
      Signatures   CRCSupp SuprCtE-file 8
      Size of electronically filed documents   CRCSupp SuprCtE-file 10
      Technical failure of system   CRCSupp SuprCtE-file 13
      Voluntary electronic filing   CRCSupp SuprCtE-file 4
Emergencies
   Supreme court e-filing rules
      Emergency situations, modifications to rules governing documents subject to electronic filing   CRCSupp SuprCtE-file 2
Ethics
   Code for court employees, adoption of   CRC JudAdminStand 10.16
   Training for judicial branch employees   CRC 10.455
Family rules
   Waiver of fees and costs in supreme court and court of appeal   CRC 5.46
Filing fees
   Waiver
      Judicial council legal forms   CRCAppx A
Finality of decisions   CRC 8.532
   Habeas corpus   CRC 8.387
Internal operating practices and procedures   CRCSupp SupCtIOPP I to CRCSupp SupCtIOPP XVII
   Acting chief justice   CRCSupp SupCtIOPP I
   Attorneys
      Communications in pending cases   CRCSupp SupCtIOPP XVI
      Criminal cases, appointments in   CRCSupp SupCtIOPP XV
   Calendar
      Memoranda   CRCSupp SupCtIOPP VI
      Oral argument   CRCSupp SupCtIOPP V
   Clemency
      Application for recommendation for executive clemency   CRCSupp SupCtIOPP XIV
   Conferences
      Memorandum   CRCSupp SupCtIOPP IV
      Regular conferences   CRCSupp SupCtIOPP III
      Special conferences   CRCSupp SupCtIOPP III
      Temporary absence of justice   CRCSupp SupCtIOPP XII
   Habeas corpus
      Application for recommendation   CRCSupp SupCtIOPP XIV
   Judicial performance commission
      Review of determinations   CRCSupp SupCtIOPP XI
   Justices
      Court of appeals justices assisting court upon disqualification of justice   CRCSupp SupCtIOPP XIII
      Disqualification or otherwise unavailable for case   CRCSupp SupCtIOPP XIII
      Retired justices, continuing with case after retirement   CRCSupp SupCtIOPP XIII
      Temporary absence   CRCSupp SupCtIOPP XII

SUPREME COURT, CALIFORNIA—Cont.
Internal operating practices and procedures —Cont.
- Opinions
  - Assignments for preparation of opinions   CRCSupp SupCtIOPP VIII
  - Circulation   CRCSupp SupCtIOPP IX
  - Filing   CRCSupp SupCtIOPP X
- Oral argument
  - Calendar sessions   CRCSupp SupCtIOPP V
- Stays
  - Application for recommendation   CRCSupp SupCtIOPP XIV
- Submission of cause   CRCSupp SupCtIOPP VII
- Suspension of internal operating practices and procedures   CRCSupp SupCtIOPP XVII
- Transfer of causes   CRCSupp SupCtIOPP II
- Judges
- Justices
  - Appellate rules (See **APPELLATE RULES, SUPREME COURT AND COURTS OF APPEAL**)
  - Generally (See within this heading, "**Justices**")
- Judicial notice   Ev §459
  - Motion requesting   CRC 8.252
  - Habeas corpus   CRC 8.386
- Judicial performance commission
  - Review of determinations   CRCSupp SupCtIOPP XI
- Justices
  - Appellate rules (See **APPELLATE RULES, SUPREME COURT AND COURTS OF APPEAL**)
  - Censure, removal or retirement of supreme court justice, proceedings for   CRC 9.61
  - Chambers, powers and duties at   CCP §165
  - Disqualification or otherwise unavailable for case   CRCSupp SupCtIOPP XIII
  - Court of appeals justices assisting court upon disqualification of justice   CRCSupp SupCtIOPP XIII
  - Proceedings for censure, removal, retirement or disqualification of supreme court justice   CRC 9.61
  - Education of judicial branch
    - Additional education recommendations for certain judicial assignments   CRC 10.469
    - Duties of justices, clerk/executive officers, managing attorneys and supervisors   CRC 10.452
    - Minimum education requirements   CRC 10.461
  - Failure to perform duties   CRC 10.1016
  - Retired justices
    - Continuation with case after retirement   CRCSupp SupCtIOPP XIII
  - Temporary absence   CRCSupp SupCtIOPP XII
- Libel or slander actions by person holding elective office or by candidate, preference to   CCP §44
- Managing attorneys
  - Education of judicial branch
    - Minimum education requirements for managing attorneys, supervisors, etc   CRC 10.472
- Natural disasters
  - Supreme court e-filing rules
    - Emergency situations, modifications to rules governing documents subject to electronic filing   CRCSupp SuprCtE-file 2
- New trial, authority to direct   CCP §43
- Opinions
  - Assignments for preparation of opinions   CRCSupp SupCtIOPP VIII
  - Circulation   CRCSupp SupCtIOPP IX
  - Filing   CRCSupp SupCtIOPP X
- Oral argument   CRC 8.524
  - Calendar sessions   CRCSupp SupCtIOPP V
  - Habeas corpus   CRC 8.386
- Original writs, procedural rules
  - Habeas corpus   CRC 8.380 to 8.398
  - Mandate, certiorari and prohibition in supreme court or court of appeal   CRC 8.485 to 8.493
    - Environmental quality act cases under public resources code   CRC 8.703
- Petitions for review   CRC 8.500 to 8.512
  - Answer and reply   CRC 8.500 to 8.512
  - Exhibits or appendices   CRC 8.504
  - Finality of order denying petition   CRC 8.532
    - Habeas corpus   CRC 8.387
  - Issues which may be raised   CRC 8.516
  - Length limits   CRC 8.504
  - Proof of service   CRC 8.500
  - Time for granting   CRC 8.512, 8.552
- Probate proceedings, preference to   CCP §44

SUPREME COURT, CALIFORNIA—Cont.
- Publication of opinions
  - Appellate opinions, publication generally   CRC 8.1100 to 8.1125
  - Depublication orders by Supreme Court   CRC 8.1105
  - Dismissal after supreme court grant of review   CRC 8.528
- Public utilities commission cases
  - Judicial review   CRC 8.724
- Records
  - Public access to judicial administrative records   CRC 10.500
- Rehearings   CRC 8.536
  - Habeas corpus   CRC 8.387
- Remittitur, issuance and recall   CRC 8.540
- Request for publication of opinions   CRC 8.1120
- Rules of court
  - Authority to adopt rules   CRC 1.3
- Rules on appeal   CRC 8.1 to 8.642 (See **APPELLATE RULES, SUPREME COURT AND COURTS OF APPEAL**)
- Satisfaction of judgment, justice's power to take and certify acknowledgment of   CCP §179
- State bar court, review of decisions of   CRC 9.12 to 9.15
- Stays
  - Application for recommendation   CRCSupp SupCtIOPP XIV
- Submission of cause   CRC 8.524, CRCSupp SupCtIOPP VII
  - Habeas corpus   CRC 8.386
- Supervisors
  - Education of judicial branch
    - Minimum education requirements for managing attorneys, supervisors, etc   CRC 10.472
- Support staff ethics program   CRC JudAdminStand 10.16
- Suspension of internal operating practices and procedures   CRCSupp SupCtIOPP XVII
- Time
  - Appellate rules (See **APPELLATE RULES, SUPREME COURT AND COURTS OF APPEAL**)
  - Transact business at any time, courts may   CCP §41
- Transfer of causes   CRC 10.1000, CRCSupp SupCtIOPP II
  - Pending court of appeal case   CRC 8.552
  - Transfer on disposition   CRC 8.528
  - Wrong court, appeal or petition filed in   CCP §396
- Travel expense reimbursement for judicial officers and employees   CRC 10.106
- Tribunal in disciplinary proceedings against supreme court justice   CRC 9.61
- Vacancy in office of all or any justices, effect on proceedings of   CCP §184

SURETYSHIP, BONDS AND UNDERTAKINGS
- Generally   CCP §§995.010 to 995.050
- Additional, new and supplemental bonds
  - Generally   CCP §§996.010, 996.020, 996.210 to 996.230
  - Effective date for liability of   CCP §996.240
  - Joint and several liability of original and   CCP §§996.250, 996.360
  - License suspension, new bond requirement following   CCP §996.340
  - Withdrawal of surety, new bond following   CCP §§996.340, 996.350
- Administrator's bond (See **EXECUTORS AND ADMINISTRATORS**)
- Admitted surety insurer   CCP §§995.610, 995.620, CRC 3.1130
  - Approval requirements   CCP §§995.630, 995.660
  - Certificate of authority
    - Generally   CCP §995.640
    - Fee for   Gov §26855.3
  - Defined   CCP §995.120
  - Documents and papers
    - Approval of bond or on objection to sufficiency, documents submitted by admitted surety insurer for   CCP §995.660
    - Party objecting to sufficiency, documents to be filed by   CCP §995.650
  - Financial statement, filing fees for   Gov §26855.2
  - Objection to sufficiency of   CCP §§995.650, 995.660
  - Power of attorney, fee for filing or canceling   Gov §26855.1
  - Public entities, further bonding requirements imposed by   CCP §§995.670, 995.675
  - Public works contracts, required on   CCP §995.311
- Affidavit of qualifications for personal surety   CCP §995.520
- Alteration of obligation   CC §§2819 to 2821
- Alternate dispositions following determination at hearing on sufficiency   CCP §§995.960, 996.010
- Apparent principal shown as surety   CC §2832
- Approval
  - Generally   CCP §§995.410, 995.420
  - Admitted surety insurer   CCP §§995.630, 995.660
- Arbitration award against principal, effect of   CC §2855
- Architects, undertaking required to secure costs in action against   CCP §1029.5
- Assignment of cause of action for enforcement of liability on   CCP §996.430
- Attachment (See **ATTACHMENT**)

SURETYSHIP, BONDS AND UNDERTAKINGS—Cont.
  Auctioneers, surety bonds maintained by   CC §1812.600
  Bail (See **BAIL**)
  Blocked accounts, effect of (See **BLOCKED ACCOUNTS**)
  Bonding company (See within this heading, "**Admitted surety insurer**")
  Building contractors (See **BUILDING CONTRACTORS**)
  Cancellation (See within this heading, "**Withdrawal**")
  Cash deposit in lieu of bond   CCP §995.710
  Certificate of authorization for admitted surety insurer   CCP §995.640
  Challenge of juror for implied bias, relationships giving rise to   CCP §229
  Change of obligation   CC §§2819 to 2821
  Child support payments   Fam §§4012, 4615
  Claim and delivery (See **CLAIM AND DELIVERY**)
  Class of persons, beneficiary seeking enforcement consisting of   CCP §996.410
  Commissioner handling property or money   CCP §571
  Conditional liability   CC §§2806 to 2808
  Consent requirements   CC §2788
  Conservators (See **CONSERVATORS**)
  Consideration requirements   CC §2792
  Construction contractors (See **BUILDING CONTRACTORS**)
  Construction of agreement   CC §§2799 to 2802, 2837
  Consumer contract, seller's obligation to furnish guarantor with copy of   CC §1799.206
  Contents of bond   CCP §995.320
  Continuing liability   CC §§2814, 2815
  Contract of suretyship   CC §§2792 to 2795
  Contribution
     Generally   CC §2848
     Waiver of right to   CC §2856
  Corporate sureties
     Admitted surety insurers (See within this heading, "**Admitted surety insurer**")
  Costs
     Award following judgment including bond-related costs   CCP §§995.250, 1033.5
     Enforcement of liability, costs of independent action for   CCP §996.480
  Court commissioner's power to take and approve bonds and undertakings in actions and proceedings   CCP §259
  Creditor's duty to pursue remedies   CC §§2823, 2845
  Credit services organizations (See **CREDIT SERVICES ORGANIZATIONS**)
  Dance studios furnishing bond   CC §§1812.64 to 1812.67, 1812.69
  Default, notice absence of   CC §§2807, 2808
  Defect in   CCP §995.380
  Definitions   CC §2787, CCP §§995.110 to 995.190
  Departure of principal from state, effect of   CC §2802
  Deposit in lieu of bond   CCP §§995.710 to 995.770
     Auctioneers   CC §1812.600
     Credit service organizations   CC §§1789.24, 1789.26
     Discount buying services   CC §§1812.105, 1812.129
     Employment agencies   CC §1812.503
     Employment counseling services   CC §1812.510
     Job listing services   CC §1812.515
     Nurses' registries   CC §1812.525
  Deposit of money, agreement with surety for   CC §2811
  Designers, undertaking required to secure costs in action against   CCP §1029.5
  Disability of principal, effect of   CC §2810
  Discount buying services furnishing bond or deposit in lieu of bond   CC §§1812.103 to 1812.105, 1812.129
  Duration
     Generally   CCP §995.430
     Licenses and permits, bonds for   CCP §995.440
  Employment agencies, bond requirements for   CC §1812.503
  Employment counseling services, bond requirements for   CC §1812.510
  Enforcement of judgments (See **ENFORCEMENT OF JUDGMENTS**)
  Enforcement of liability
     Generally   CCP §§996.460, 996.495
     Class of persons, beneficiary as   CCP §996.410
     Good faith payments without awaiting enforcement   CCP §§996.480, 996.490
     Independent action necessitated by sureties' nonpayment   CCP §996.480
     Joint and several liability
        Original and new bonds   CCP §§996.250, 996.360
        Principal and surety, enforcement against   CCP §996.460
     Jurisdiction for   CCP §§996.420, 996.430
     Liens, enforcement   CCP §§996.510 to 996.560
     Limited liability of principal and surety   CCP §§996.470, 996.475
     Procedural consideration in motion for   CCP §996.440
  Engineers, undertaking required to secure costs in action against   CCP §1029.5
  Excessive bonds
     Generally (See within this heading, "**Insufficient and excessive bonds**")
     Objections generally (See within this heading, "**Objections**")

SURETYSHIP, BONDS AND UNDERTAKINGS—Cont.
  Execution
     Generally   CCP §995.310
     Admitted surety insurers, execution by   CCP §995.620
     Personal sureties   CCP §§995.510, 995.520
     State of California as beneficiary   CCP §§995.810 to 995.850
  Executor's bond (See **EXECUTORS AND ADMINISTRATORS**)
  Exemption of public agencies and employees from posting   CCP §995.220
  Expiration of term   CCP §995.430
  Extensions of time   CCP §995.050
  Extinguishing liability   CC §§2819 to 2825, 2839
  Filing   CCP §§995.340, 995.350
     Defect in   CCP §995.380
     Withdrawal from file and return to principal   CCP §§995.360, 995.430
  Form of bond or undertaking   CCP §995.330
  Good faith payments without awaiting enforcement   CCP §§996.480, 996.490
  Guarantor, abolishing distinction as to   CC §2787
  Guardianship (See **GUARDIAN AND WARD**)
  Hearings
     Market value of deposit, hearing to determine   CCP §995.720
     Objections to bond   CCP §995.950
  Housing projects, action to enjoin   CCP §529.2
  Hypothecation of surety's property with property of principal, order of application to discharge of debt in case of   CC §2850
  Indemnified officer's or person's rights   CCP §1055
  Independent action to enforce liability   CCP §§996.440, 996.480
  Injunctions (See **INJUNCTIONS**)
  Innkeeper's lien, writ of possession on   CC §§1861.21 to 1861.23
  Insufficient and excessive bonds
     Court determination
        Excessive, bond as   CCP §996.030
        Insufficient, bond as   CCP §§996.010, 996.020
     Objection to bonds as insufficient (See within this heading, "**Objections**")
     Reduction of excessive bond   CCP §996.030
     Show cause order
        Beneficiary served with show cause order where excessive bond alleged   CCP §996.030
        Principal served with show cause order where insufficiency alleged   CCP §996.020
  Interchangeability of bonds and undertakings   CCP §995.210
  Interpretation of contract   CC §2837
  Job listing services, bond requirements for   CC §1812.515
  Joinder of parties, costs in absence of   CCP §1022
  Joinder of principal and surety in action to enforce liability on bond   CCP §996.430
  Joint and several liability
     Original and new bonds   CCP §§996.250, 996.360
     Principal and surety, enforcement against   CCP §996.460
  Judgment, creditor recovering   CC §2838
  Jurisdiction for enforcement of liability   CCP §§996.420, 996.430
  Latent deficiencies in planning or construction of improvement to real property, statute of limitation for damages for   CCP §337.15
  Letters of credit not suretyship obligations   CC §2787
  Licenses and permits
     Duration of bonds for   CCP §995.440
     Suspension of license or registration, new bond required following   CCP §996.340
  Liens, enforcement   CCP §§996.510 to 996.560
  Limitation of actions   CCP §359.5
     Guardian's or conservator's bond   Pro §2333
  Limited liability of principal and surety   CCP §§996.470, 996.475
  Livestock service liens, actions on   CC §§3080.09 to 3080.11
  Low-income housing projects, action to enjoin   CCP §529.2
  Market value of property
     Bearer bonds or notes   CCP §995.720
     Deposit in lieu of bond   CCP §995.710
     Objection to insufficiency of bond amount   CCP §995.940
  Mechanics' liens (See **MECHANICS' LIENS**)
  Medical services, undertaking required to secure costs in action alleging negligence in performance of   CCP §1029.5
  Mobilehomes, bonds after default under sales contract for   CCP §§515.010, 515.020
  Moderate-income housing projects, action to enjoin   CCP §529.2
  Mortgages
     Security generally (See within this heading, "**Security**")
  New bonds (See within this heading, "**Additional, new and supplemental bonds**")
  Notice for termination of liability   CC §§2819 to 2825
  Notice of pendency of action (See **PENDENCY OF ACTIONS**)
  Nurses' registries, bond requirements for   CC §1812.525

SURETYSHIP, BONDS AND UNDERTAKINGS—Cont.
Objections
    Generally   CCP §§995.910 to 995.930
    Additional, new and supplemental bonds   CCP §996.230
    Hearing on   CCP §995.950
    Market value of property
        Objection to insufficiency of bond amount   CCP §995.940
Official bonds (See **BONDS OF PUBLIC OFFICIALS**)
Oil and gas liens, release of   CCP §1203.60
Partial satisfaction of obligation   CC §2822
Partition referees requiring   CCP §873.010
Payment (See within this heading, "Enforcement of liability")
Performance   CC §§2839, 2846
Permits
    Bonds, duration   CCP §995.440
    Suspension, new bond required following   CCP §996.340
Personal sureties   CCP §§995.510, 995.520
Premiums as part of costs, recovery of   CCP §§995.250, 1033.5
Procedural considerations in motion to enforce liability on   CCP §996.440
Professional persons, bonds required to secure costs in actions against   CCP §§1029.5, 1029.6
Public administrators (See **PUBLIC ADMINISTRATORS**)
Public entities, further bonding requirements imposed by   CCP §§995.670, 995.675
Public guardians (See **PUBLIC GUARDIANS**)
Public officials' bonds (See **BONDS OF PUBLIC OFFICIALS**)
Public works contracts, bond requirement on   CCP §995.311
Receivers (See **RECEIVERS AND RECEIVERSHIP**)
Recording, certified copy for   CCP §995.260
Reduction or waiver of bond
    Beneficiary giving written consent for   CCP §995.230
    Excessive bond, reduction of   CCP §996.030
    Indigent principal, waiver of bond for   CCP §995.240
    Obligation of surety reducible in proportion to principal obligation   CC §2809
Referees
    Bond requirement for   CCP §571
    Disqualification for surety relationship   CCP §641
Registration
    Bonds, duration   CCP §995.440
    Suspension, new bond required following   CCP §996.340
Reimbursement rights
    Generally   CC §2847
    Waiver of   CC §2856
Release
    Payment of liability on bond constituting full discharge   CCP §996.490
    Principal, effect of release of   CC §§2824, 2825
    Substitution and release   CCP §§996.110 to 996.150
Return
    Deposit made in lieu of security bond   CCP §995.770
    Withdrawal, return to principal following   CCP §§995.360, 995.430
Satisfaction of judgments affecting   CCP §995.430
Secondary oil recovery operations causing damages, undertaking in lieu of injunction against   CCP §731c
Security
    Release of mortgage lien, corporate bond for   CC §2941.7
    Resort to security
        Creditor's resort to security given surety   CC §2854
        Surety's resort to security given creditor   CC §2849
    Waiver of surety's rights and defenses stemming from real property security for principal's obligation   CC §2856
Seller assisted marketing plans   CC §§1812.204, 1812.206, 1812.214
Service
    Generally   CCP §995.030
    Copy of bond   CCP §995.370
    Market value of deposit, action to determine   CCP §995.720
Shortening time for commencement of enforcement proceedings, validity of bond provisions concerning   CCP §996.450
Show cause orders
    Beneficiary served with show cause order where excessive bond alleged   CCP §996.030
    Principal served with show cause order where insufficiency alleged   CCP §996.020
Small claims court, action against guarantors in (See **SMALL CLAIMS COURTS**)
Small estates without administration   Pro §13102
Spousal support, security for payment   Fam §4339
State of California as beneficiary   CCP §§995.810 to 995.850
Statute of frauds   CC §1624, CCP §1971
Statutes of limitation for actions against sureties
    Generally   CCP §359.5

SURETYSHIP, BONDS AND UNDERTAKINGS—Cont.
Statutes of limitation for actions against sureties—Cont.
    Guardian's or conservator's bond   Pro §2333
Stay of proceedings   CCP §§917.9 to 922
Stipulations
    Limited liability of principal and surety   CCP §996.470
    Market value of deposit   CCP §995.720
Subrogation rights
    Generally   CC §2848
    Waiver of   CC §2856
Substitution following release of   CCP §§996.110 to 996.150
Supplemental bond (See within this heading, "Additional, new and supplemental bonds")
Surveyors, undertaking required to secure costs in action against   CCP §1029.5
Term   CCP §995.430
    Licenses, permits, registration, etc, duration of bonds   CCP §995.440
Terminating liability of surety   CC §§2819 to 2825, 2839
Third parties, answering for obligations of   CC §2794
Time
    Generally   CC §2846
    Duration   CCP §995.430
        Licenses, permits, registrations, etc, bond duration   CCP §995.440
    Enforcement of liability   CCP §§996.440, 996.450
    Extensions of time   CCP §995.050
    General effective date of bond   CCP §995.420
    New bond, effective date for liability of   CCP §996.240
    Withdrawal of surety, effective date of   CCP §996.330
Trust deeds, satisfaction of   CC §2941.7
Trusts (See **TRUSTS**)
Unclaimed property fund appropriations for indemnity payments   CCP §1325
Unlawful detainer action   CCP §1166a
Vexatious litigation (See **VEXATIOUS LITIGANTS**)
Voidable transactions, undertaking and action to set aside   CC §§3445 to 3449 (See **VOIDABLE TRANSACTIONS**)
Void and voidable bonds   CCP §995.380
Waiver
    Bond, waiver of (See within this heading, "Reduction or waiver of bond")
    Rights and defenses of sureties, waiver of   CCP §995.230
Wartime substitution of fiduciary, bond requirements for   Pro §372
Withdrawal   CCP §996.310, CRC 3.1130
    Effective date of   CCP §996.330
    Liability of bond after   CCP §996.360
    New bond, replacement with   CCP §§996.340, 996.350
    Notice   CCP §996.320
    Principal, withdrawal from file and return to   CCP §995.360

SURGEONS (See **PHYSICIANS AND SURGEONS**)

SURGERY (See **MEDICAL TREATMENT**)

SURPLUS PROPERTY
Courts
    Disposal of surplus personal property   CRC 10.830

SURPRISE
Mistake, inadvertence, surprise or excusable neglect (See **MISTAKE**)
New trial, ground for   CCP §657

SURRENDER
Landlord entering dwelling unit after   CC §1954

SURROGACY OR DONOR FACILITATORS   Fam §§7960, 7961
Definitions   Fam §7960
Deposit of client funds   Fam §7961
Gestational carriers
    Assisted reproduction agreements for gestational carriers   Fam §7962
    Jurisdiction   Fam §7620
    Venue   Fam §7620

SURROGATES FOR HEALTH CARE (See **HEALTH CARE DECISIONS LAW**)

SURROUNDING CIRCUMSTANCES
Parol evidence proving   CCP §§1856, 1860

SURVEYOR-GENERAL
Spanish title papers authenticated by Surveyor-General as admissible   Ev §1605

SURVEYS AND SURVEYORS
Bond required to secure costs in action against surveyors   CCP §1029.5
Boundaries, rights to investigate   CC §846.5
Certificate of merit in negligence action against surveyor   CCP §§411.35, 430.10

SURVEYS AND SURVEYORS—Cont.
Eminent domain, preliminary surveys for CCP §1245.010
Indemnity agreements
    Public agencies, contracts with CC §2782.8
Latent deficiencies in planning or construction of improvement to real property, limitation of actions for damages for CCP §337.15
Late payment penalty in lieu of interest, contract provision for CC §3319
Monuments (See **BOUNDARIES**)
Notice requirement for entry on land CC §846.5
Partition action CCP §§873.110, 873.130, 873.150, 874.020
Patent deficiencies in planning or construction of improvement to real property, limitation of actions for injury or death from CCP §337.1
Public agencies, payment schedule for CC §3320
Quiet title action CCP §§742, 743
Subcontractor design professionals, payments to CC §3321
Withholding disputed amount CC §§3320, 3321

SURVIVAL OF ACTIONS
Generally CCP §377.20
Actions against decedent's estate
    Damages recoverable CCP §377.42
    Effective date of law governing CCP §377.43
    Motions to allow continuation of pending action or proceeding CCP §377.41
    Party to action, decedent's personal representative or successor in interest as CCP §377.40
    Time limitations CCP §366.2
Actions for decedent's estate
    Affidavit or declaration of decedent's successor in interest CCP §377.32
    Damages recoverable CCP §377.34
    Effective date of law governing CCP §377.35
    Jurisdiction and powers of court CCP §377.33
    Motions to allow continuation of pending action or proceeding CCP §377.31
    Party to action, decedent's personal representative or successor in interest as CCP §377.30
    Special administrator or guardian ad litem, appointment of CCP §377.33
    Time limitations CCP §§366.1 to 366.3
Affidavit or declaration of decedent's successor in interest as party to action CCP §377.32
Assignability of causes of action CCP §377.22
"Beneficiaries of decedent's estate" for purposes of CCP §377.10
Commencement of action
    Actions against decedent's estate generally (See within this heading, "**Actions against decedent's estate**")
    Actions for decedent's estate generally (See within this heading, "**Actions for decedent's estate**")
    Continuation of pending action or proceeding CCP §377.21
        Actions against decedent's estate (See within this heading, "**Actions against decedent's estate**")
Continuation of pending action of decedent
    Generally CCP §377.21
    Actions against decedent's estate generally (See within this heading, "**Actions against decedent's estate**")
Creditor claims, generally (See within this heading, "**Actions against decedent's estate**")
Damages recoverable
    Action brought for decedent's estate CCP §377.34
    Actions against decedent's estate CCP §377.42
    Punitive damages where death resulted from homicide CC §3294
Definitions CCP §§377.10, 377.11
Insurance claims, actions to establish decedent's liability for purposes of CCP §377.50, Pro §550
Partition proceedings CCP §872.530, Pro §9823
Pending action or proceeding
    Continuation of pending action of decedent CCP §377.21
        Actions against decedent's estate generally (See within this heading, "**Actions against decedent's estate**")
Successor in interest
    Actions against decedent's estate generally (See within this heading, "**Actions against decedent's estate**")
    Actions for decedent's estate generally (See within this heading, "**Actions for decedent's estate**")
    Defined CCP §377.11
Time limitations CCP §§366.1 to 366.3
Wrongful death actions (See **WRONGFUL DEATH**)

SURVIVING DOMESTIC PARTNERS
Equal rights, benefits and protections Fam §297.5
Health insurance
    Survivors of firefighters and peace officers, continuance Pro §13600

SURVIVING SPOUSE
Acceleration of loan, absence of CC §2924.6
Administrator, priority for serving as Pro §§8461, 8463
Advertising, property rights in use of deceased personality's name or likeness for CC §3344.1
Claims against decedent's estate (See **CLAIMS AGAINST ESTATES**)
Clothing, possession of Pro §6500
Community property CC §682.1
    Generally Pro §§100, 105
    Confirmation of small estate without administration (See **SMALL ESTATES WITHOUT ADMINISTRATION**)
    Descent of intestate interest Pro §§6401 to 6402.5
    Funeral expenses, liability for Pro §11446
    Inventory for decedent's estate, inclusion of community property in Pro §8850
    Last illness, payment for expenses of Pro §11446
    Nonprobate transfers of property (See **NONPROBATE TRANSFERS**)
    Quasi-community property
        Generally Pro §§101, 102
        Defined Pro §66
    Small estates without administration (See **SMALL ESTATES WITHOUT ADMINISTRATION**)
    Wills Pro §6101
Revocable trust, community property in Pro §§104, 104.5
Simultaneous death, effect of Pro §§103, 6402
Small estates without administration (See **SMALL ESTATES WITHOUT ADMINISTRATION**)
Wills
    General provisions regarding disposition by Pro §6101
    Nonprobate transfers of property (See **NONPROBATE TRANSFERS**)
    Transmutation of marital property, admissibility of statement in will as evidence of Fam §853
Confirmation of small estate without administration (See **SMALL ESTATES WITHOUT ADMINISTRATION**)
Consideration, spouse recovering property transferred in absence of Pro §102
Debts of decedent' estate, liability of surviving spouse for (See **CLAIMS AGAINST ESTATES**)
Defined Pro §78
Delivery of decedent's property by third party immediately after death to surviving spouse Pro §330
Descent of intestate interest to Pro §§6401 to 6402.5
Exempt property, petition to set aside Pro §§6510, 6511
Family allowance (See **FAMILY ALLOWANCE**)
Family home during administration of estate, petition for possession of Pro §§6500, 6501
Funeral expenses, liability for Pro §11446
Furniture, possession of Pro §6500
Health insurance
    Survivors of firefighters and peace officers, continuance Pro §13600
Homesteads (See **HOMESTEADS**)
Intestate succession by Pro §§6401 to 6402.5
Inventory for decedent's estate, inclusion of community property in Pro §8850
Last illness, payment of expenses of Pro §11446
Nondomiciliary decedent, surviving spouse's right of election in California real property of Pro §120
Nonprobate transfers of property (See **NONPROBATE TRANSFERS**)
Omitted from testamentary instruments
    Generally Pro §§21600, 21610
    Applicability of omitted spouse provisions Pro §§21600, 21630
    Definitions Pro §21601
    Exceptions to omitted spouse's entitlement Pro §21611
    Satisfaction of omitted spouse's share Pro §21612
Passage of estate property to without administration
    Property of deceased spouse, liability for Pro §§13560 to 13565
Simultaneous death, effect of Pro §§103, 6402
Small estates without administration (See **SMALL ESTATES WITHOUT ADMINISTRATION**)
Support (See **SPOUSAL SUPPORT**)
Third party, delivery to surviving spouse of decedent's property in possession of Pro §330
Trust property of deceased settlor, claims against (See **TRUSTS**)
Waiver of rights
    "All rights," definition of Pro §145
    Alteration, amendment or revocation of Pro §146
    Definition Pro §140
    Enforcement of
        Generally Pro §§143, 146
        Discretion of court for Pro §144
    Exceptions to enforcement of Pro §143

SURVIVING SPOUSE—Cont.
Waiver of rights—Cont.
Instrument in writing and signed by surviving spouse, requirement of Pro §142
Nonprobate transfers, effect on surviving spouse's rights in Pro §5013
Rights of surviving spouse subject to waiver Pro §141
Transmutation of marital property, effect of waiver as evidence of Fam §853
Validity of Pro §147
Wills
Community property
Disposition Pro §6101
Nonprobate transfers generally (See **NONPROBATE TRANSFERS**)
Transmutation of marital property, admissibility of statement in will as evidence Fam §853

SURVIVORSHIP
Attorney in fact, authority of Pro §4264
Deposits delivered to survivor CC §1828
Marital deduction gifts, survivorship requirements for Pro §21525
Right of survivorship (See **RIGHT OF SURVIVORSHIP**)

SUSPENSION
Attorney's suspension, appointment of new attorney on CCP §286
Conservators (See **CONSERVATORS**)
Driving privilege (See **AUTOMOBILES**)
Executors and administrators (See **EXECUTORS AND ADMINISTRATORS**)
Guardians (See **GUARDIAN AND WARD**)
Notaries public, registration of Fam §535

SUSTAINABLE GROUNDWATER MANAGEMENT ACT
Groundwater rights actions
Definitions of sustainable groundwater management act CCP §832

SWEARING (See **OATHS**)

SYPHILIS
Minor's consent to treatment Fam §6926

T

TAGALOG
Contracts in Chinese, Tagalog, Vietnamese or Korean languages CC §1632
Consumer credit contracts
Federal notice requirement CC §1799.96
Foreign language translations of notice requirement CC §1799.91
Gender tax repeal act preventing charging different prices for services of similar or like kind based on gender
Consumer affairs department pamphlet for affected businesses and other notice of requirements of provisions CC §51.63
Licensing authority notice of provisions to licensee upon issuance or renewal CC §51.6
Mortgages of residential property, foreign language summaries of terms CC §1632.5

TAGS
Baggage, tagging requirements for CC §2205

TAILORS
Gender, prohibition against charging different price for services of similar or like kind based solely on CC §51.6
Small business gender discrimination in pricing services compliance act CC §§55.61 to 55.63

TAKING (See **EMINENT DOMAIN**)

TANGIBLE THINGS, INSPECTION OF (See **INSPECTION DEMANDS**)

TANNING FACILITIES
Minors
Verification of age for sale of age-restricted products CC §1798.99.1

TAX ASSESSMENTS (See **TAXATION**)

TAXATION
Assessments
Adverse interests in real property arising out of public improvement assessment, action to determine CCP §§801.1 to 801.15
Adverse possession, payment of taxes to establish CCP §325
Auction of land subject to assessment lien, time limit for public official's CCP §330

TAXATION—Cont.
Assessments—Cont.
Chartered city, action to contest validity of levy by CCP §329.5
Condemnation proceedings, assessment liens in CCP §§1250.250, 1265.250
Covenants requiring payment of CC §1468
Definition of encumbrance CC §1114
Eminent domain proceedings
Basis for value of property, tax assessments establishing Ev §822
Encumbered by tax lien, acquisition of property CCP §§1250.250, 1265.250
Environmental constraints on use of land, consideration of
Greenway easements as enforceable restriction CC §816.66
Life tenant to pay CC §840
Mello-Roos Community Facilities Act, disclosure regarding special tax liens on transfer of property pursuant to CC §1102.6b
Quieting title to real property subject to public improvement assessment, action to CCP §§801.1 to 801.15
Restricted property valuations
Greenway easements as enforceable restriction CC §816.66
Special assessment liens
Eminent domain, encumbered property acquired by CCP §1265.250
Mello-Roos Community Facilities Act, disclosure regarding special tax liens on transfer of property pursuant to CC §1102.6b
Statute of limitation for bringing action to challenge validity of levy CCP §338
Statutes of limitation
Chartered city, action to contest validity of levy by CCP §329.5
Special assessment, action challenging validity of CCP §338
Street improvement assessment, action on lien securing CCP §329
Street improvement assessment, action on lien securing CCP §329
Supplemental property tax bills
Disclosures upon transfer of real property CC §1102.6c
Auction of land subject to assessment lien, time limit for public official's CCP §330
Child support (See **CHILD SUPPORT**)
Claims against decedents' estates Pro §§9200 to 9205
Costs, motion to tax (See **COSTS**)
Disclosure of information
By bookkeeping services CC §1799.1a
By Franchise Tax Board CC §1798.28
Dissolution of marriage proceedings Fam §2337
Distribution of estates, payment of taxes prior to Pro §9650
Eminent domain (See **EMINENT DOMAIN**)
Enforcement of judgments (See **ENFORCEMENT OF JUDGMENTS**)
Estate tax (See **ESTATE TAX**)
Fiduciary income and principal act
Disbursements, allocation Pro §16365
Foreign country judgments
Applicability of provisions CCP §1715
Garnishment proceedings (See **GARNISHMENT**)
Generation-skipping transfer tax (See **GENERATION-SKIPPING TRANSFER TAX**)
Impound accounts (See **IMPOUND ACCOUNTS**)
Income tax (See **INCOME TAX**)
Inheritance tax (See **INHERITANCE TAX**)
Internal revenue department
Estate tax (See **ESTATE TAX**)
Income tax (See **INCOME TAX**)
Marital deduction gifts (See **MARITAL DEDUCTION GIFTS**)
Will construction, application of Internal Revenue Code provisions to (See **WILL CONSTRUCTION**)
Liens
Assessments generally (See within this heading, "**Assessments**")
Credit reports (See **CREDIT REPORTING**)
Federal tax lien registration CCP §§2100 to 2107
Fees for recording under act Gov §27388.1
State tax lien, notice of CC §2885
Mello-Roos Community Facilities Act, disclosure regarding special tax liens on transfer of property pursuant to CC §1102.6b
Mine co-owners failing to pay CCP §§853 to 859
Mortgages (See **TRUST DEEDS AND MORTGAGES**)
Motion to tax costs (See **COSTS**)
Postponed property taxes, notice of default on property subject to lien for CC §2924b
Power of attorney, powers under statutory form of Pro §4463
Principal and income allocations CC §731.14, Pro §§6371, 6374, 6375
Public entity's liability for tax law administration Gov §§860 to 860.4
Quiet title to real property subject to public improvement assessment, action to CCP §§801.1 to 801.15
Real property sales contract, payments received under CC §2985.4

TAXATION—Cont.
  Rental passenger vehicle transactions
    Personal vehicle sharing programs
      Tax certifications required prior making vehicle available for rental   CC §1939.39
  Sales tax (See **SALES AND USE TAX**)
  Special assessments
    Assessments generally (See within this heading, "**Assessments**")
    Statutes of limitation on actions based on assessments (See within this heading, "**Assessments**")
  Trust decanting, uniform act
    Exercise of decanting power
      Tax-related limitations   Pro §19519
  Trust deeds (See **TRUST DEEDS AND MORTGAGES**)
  Trusts (See **TRUSTS**)
  Unclaimed property fund appropriations for payment   CCP §1325
  Validation proceedings on bonds for which tax revenue has been pledged by agency other than agency imposing tax, notice requirements for   CCP §870.5

TAX COLLECTOR
  Limitation of actions to recover goods seized by   CCP §341

TAXING COSTS (See **COSTS**)

TAXIS
  Blind persons having equal rights to use of   CC §§54.1, 54.3, 54.4, 55
    Construction or application of provisions in issue, solicitor general notified   CC §55.2
  Disabled persons having equal rights to use of   CC §§54.1, 54.3, 54.4, 55
    Construction or application of provisions in issue, solicitor general notified   CC §55.2
  Guide dogs permitted in   CC §§54.2, 54.3
    Construction or application of provisions in issue, solicitor general notified   CC §55.2

TAXPAYERS' SUITS
  Public contracts enjoined   CCP §526a

TEACHERS (See **SCHOOLS**)

TEACHERS' RETIREMENT SYSTEM
  Community property rights
    Tribal court orders, payments pursuant to   Fam §2611

TEAR GAS AND TEAR GAS WEAPONS
  Nuisance abatement
    Unlawful weapons or ammunition purpose   CC §3485
  Unlawful detainer actions
    Illegal weapons or ammunition on real property   CC §3485

TEARING
  Will revoked by   Pro §§6120, 6121

TECHNICAL LANGUAGE (See **CONSTRUCTION AND INTERPRETATION**)

TELECOMMUNICATIONS
  Common interest developments
    Board meetings
      Remote meeting by teleconference   CC §4926
  Electronic commercial services (See **ELECTRONIC COMMERCIAL SERVICES**)
  911 emergency services
    Immunity from liability, telecommunications services providing   CC §1714.55
  Radio and television (See **RADIO AND TELEVISION**)
  Telephones and telegraphs (See **TELEPHONES AND TELEGRAPHS**)

TELEGRAPHS (See **TELEPHONES AND TELEGRAPHS**)

TELEMARKETING
  Contracts
    Unlawfulness of contracts generated by unlawful telemarketing   CC §1670.6

TELEPHONE INFORMATION LIBRARY
  Professional society referral service, liability of   CC §43.95

TELEPHONES AND TELEGRAPHS
  Accounts
    Change of address requests
      Notice to account holder   CC §1799.1b
  Administrative adjudication proceedings conducted by telephone (See **ADMINISTRATIVE ADJUDICATION**)

TELEPHONES AND TELEGRAPHS—Cont.
  Adoption
    Appearance by remote electronic means   Fam §8613.5
  Appeals courts
    Certiorari, mandate and prohibition
      Notice by telephone   CRC 8.489
  Appearance of counsel by (See **APPEARANCE**)
  Attorney-client privilege for cellular phone conversations   Ev §952
  Cancellation of utility, cable, etc, services on behalf of deceased person
    In-person cancellation not to be required   Pro §217
  Cellular telephone conversations, attorney-client privilege for   Ev §952
  Change of number
    Appeals
      Service and filing notice of change   CRC 8.32
  Child support
    Title IV-D support actions
      Appearance by telephone   CRC 3.670, 3.672, 5.324
  Coin-operated telephone (See **VENDING MACHINES**)
  Commercial and industrial common interest developments
    Wiring
      Maintenance   CC §6722
  Common interest developments, access to telephone wiring in
    Communications wiring access   CC §4790
  Court appearances by telephone   CRC 3.670
    Conference call provider, designation of   CRC 3.670
    Hardware and procedure   CRC JudAdminStand 3.1
    Juvenile rules   CRC 3.672, 5.531
      Nonminor dependents, retention of jurisdiction   CRC 3.672, 5.900
    Unlawful detainer   CRC 3.670
    Waiver of fees   CRC 3.670
  Credit reports, copies of   CC §1785.15
  Deaf or disabled persons
    Equal access rights
      Construction or application of provisions in issue, solicitor general notified   CC §55.2
  Debt collectors using telephones, regulation on   CC §1788.11
  Delivery of telegrams   CC §2161
  Depositions
    Remote electronic means of taking depositions   CCP §2025.310, CRC 3.1010
  Disabled persons, use of telephones by   CC §54.1
    Construction or application of provisions in issue, solicitor general notified   CC §55.2
  Ex parte order enjoining annoying telephone calls   Fam §6320
    California law enforcement telecommunications (CLETS) information form, confidentiality and use of information   CRC 1.51, CRCAppx A
    Denial of petition for ex parte order, reasons to be provided   Fam §6320.5
  Family rules
    Request for orders
      Meet-and-confer   CRC 5.98
      Telephone appearances   CRC 3.672, 5.9
  Fax filing of legal documents (See **FAX FILING AND SERVICE**)
  Harassing calls, protective orders
    Denial of petition for ex parte order, reasons to be provided   Fam §6320.5
  Information library, professional society operating   CC §43.95
  Information Practices Act, privacy of telephone listings under   CC §1798.3
  Injunctions
    Ex parte order enjoining annoying telephone calls
      Denial of petition for ex parte order, reasons to be provided   Fam §6320.5
  Judicial administration standards
    Appearance by telephone   CRC JudAdminStand 3.1
  Judicial ethics opinions
    Committee contact information   CRC 9.80
  Jury (See **JURY**)
  Juvenile rules
    Appearance by telephone appearances   CRC 3.672, 5.531
      Nonminor dependents, retention of jurisdiction   CRC 3.672, 5.900
  Landlord, duties and liabilities of (See **LANDLORD AND TENANT**)
  Negligence   CC §2162
  Notice of intent to appear by telephone   CRC 3.670
  Obscenity and obscene calls
    Domestic violence protective orders
      Denial of petition for ex parte order, reasons to be provided   Fam §6320.5
  Oral argument before appeals court via teleconference system   CRCSupp 5th AppDist
  Orders transmitted by telegraph   CCP §1017
  Priority of transmission   CC §§2207 to 2209
  Repair service telephone number for goods sold under warranty, requirements for furnishing   CC §1793.1

TELEPHONES AND TELEGRAPHS—Cont.
Retail installment sale provisions applicable to sale by telephone   CC §1803.8
Service of summons, telegraphic transmission of   CCP §1017
Sex offenses, exclusion of victim's telephone number in trial for   Ev §352.1
Small claims court advisory services   CCP §116.940
Solicitation
   Telemarketing
      Unlawfulness of contracts generated by unlawful telemarketing   CC §1670.6
Unsolicited prerecorded telephone messages, prohibition against businesses disseminating   CC §1770
Writs, telegraphic transmission of   CCP §1017

TELEVISION (See **RADIO AND TELEVISION**)

TEMPORARY CUSTODY OF CHILDREN (See **CUSTODY OF CHILDREN**)

TEMPORARY DETENTIONS
Records
   Sealing or destruction
      Order on prosecutor request for access   CRCAppx A
      Prosecuting attorney request to access sealed juvenile case files   CRC 5.860

TEMPORARY INJUNCTIONS (See **INJUNCTIONS**)

TEMPORARY JUDGES (See **JUDGES**)

TEMPORARY PROTECTIVE ORDERS
Attachment (See **ATTACHMENT**)
Dissolution of marriage (See **DISSOLUTION OF MARRIAGE**)
Domestic violence (See **DOMESTIC VIOLENCE**)

TEMPORARY RESTRAINING ORDERS (See **INJUNCTIONS**)

TEMPORARY SUPPORT (See **CHILD SUPPORT; SPOUSAL SUPPORT**)

TENANCY BY ENTIRETY
Husband and wife holding property as   Fam §§2580, 2581

TENANCY IN COMMON
Acceleration of loan, absence of   CC §2924.6
Division of property on dissolution of marriage   Fam §2650
Homestead, sale of   CCP §704.820
Husband and wife holding property as   Fam §§2580, 2581
Multiple-party accounts   Pro §5306
Partition (See **PARTITION**)
Spouses holding property as tenants in common
   Husband and wife holding property as   Fam §750
Title held by   CC §§682, 685
Waste, actions for recovery of treble damages for   CCP §732

TENANT (See **LANDLORD AND TENANT**)

TENDER
Objection to   CCP §2076
Offer refused treated as tender   CCP §2074

TENSE
Construction of words used in code   CCP §17
Family code   Fam §9

TENTATIVE DECISIONS   CRC 3.1590

TENURE (See **TERMS OF OFFICE**)

TEN YEARS (See **STATUTES OF LIMITATION**)

TERMINATING SANCTION
Case questionnaires under economic litigation provisions for limited civil cases, failure to answer or obey order compelling response to   CCP §93

TERMINATION
Child support (See **CHILD SUPPORT**)
Conservators (See **CONSERVATORS**)
Credit cards, termination of third party use of   CC §1747.02(f)
Earnings assignment order for support   Fam §5240
Guardianship (See **GUARDIAN AND WARD**)
Homestead, termination of probate right to   Pro §6527
Indigent parents, order for support of   Fam §4405
International commercial arbitration and conciliation (See **INTERNATIONAL COMMERCIAL ARBITRATION AND CONCILIATION**)

TERMINATION—Cont.
Judgment creditor's lien restricting termination of pending action   CCP §708.440
Landlord and tenant (See **LANDLORD AND TENANT**)
Lodger, termination by   CC §1946.5
Mineral rights (See **MINERALS AND MINERAL RIGHTS**)
Mobilehome tenancy (See **MOBILEHOMES**)
Power of attorney (See **POWER OF ATTORNEY**)
Spousal support (See **SPOUSAL SUPPORT**)
Summary dissolution of marriage proceeding   Fam §2402
Trusts (See **TRUSTS**)

TERMINATION OF PARENTAL RIGHTS   Fam §§7800 to 7895
Abandoned child   Fam §7822
Adoption   Fam §§7660 to 7671
   Exception to requirement of parental consent   Fam §8606
   Orders
      Judicial council form   CRCAppx A
   Referral for   Fam §7893
   Termination of parental rights in adoption proceedings (See **ADOPTION**)
Alcoholic parent   Fam §7824
Appeals
   Juvenile case appeals   CRC 8.400 to 8.474
   Orders setting hearing, writ petition to review   CRC 8.452
   Parents' rights   Fam §§7893 to 7895
Appointment of counsel   CRC 5.660, Fam §§7860 to 7864
   CASA programs   CRC 5.655
   Indigent appellant, appointment of counsel for   Fam §7895
Appointment of person to act on child's behalf   Fam §7804
Child's wishes, consideration of   Fam §§7890, 7891
Circumstances where proceeding may be brought   Fam §§7820 to 7827
Citation requiring attendance at hearing   Fam §§7880 to 7883
Clear and convincing evidence   Fam §7821
Closed to public, proceedings as   Fam §7884
Contempt   Fam §7883
Continuance   Fam §7871
   Appointment of counsel   Fam §7864
Conviction of felony   Fam §7825
Counsel, appointment of   CRC 5.660, Fam §§7860 to 7864
   CASA programs   CRC 5.655
   Indigent appellant, appointment of counsel for   Fam §7895
Court fees   Fam §7806
Court reporters
   Payment by county   Gov §69952
Cruelly treated child   Fam §7823
Declaration, effect of   Fam §7803
Dependent child of juvenile court   Fam §7808
   One parent's rights terminated
      Disposition hearings generally   CRC 5.690 to 5.705
   Orders
      Judicial council form   CRCAppx A
Disability of parent due to alcohol or drugs   Fam §7824
Fees
   Superior court fees   Gov §70633
Forms
   Judicial council legal forms   CRCAppx A
Foster care and foster care facilities
   Child in foster care during 15 of last 22 months   CRC 5.820
Grounds   Fam §§7820 to 7827
Guardian for child, appointment of   Fam §7893
Hearings
   Setting termination hearing at disposition hearing   CRC 5.705
Indian children
   Involuntary placements
      Indian Child Welfare Act, rules governing   CRC 5.480 to 5.488
      (See **INDIAN CHILD WELFARE ACT INVOLUNTARY PLACEMENTS**)
   Permanent plan selection   CRC 5.725
Indigent appellant, appointment of counsel for   Fam §7895
Inspection of petition and reports   Fam §7805
Interstate compact on placement of children   Fam §§7900 to 7913
Intestate succession
   Parent inheriting from child based on relationship
      Situations preventing inheritance   Pro §6452
Investigation and report   Fam §§7850 to 7852
Judgment or order   Fam §7894
Juvenile courts
   Appellate review
      Appeal from termination of parental rights   CRC 8.416
      Extraordinary writ, petition for   CRC 8.454, 8.456

TERMINATION OF PARENTAL RIGHTS—Cont.
Juvenile courts—Cont.
    Appellate review —Cont.
        Juvenile case appeals in supreme court and courts of appeal   CRC 8.400 to 8.474
        Order designating specific placement of dependent child, writ petition to review   CRC 8.454, 8.456
        Orders setting hearing, writ petition to review   CRC 8.450
    Orders
        Judicial council form   CRCAppx A
    Juvenile probation officer, investigation and report by   Fam §§7850 to 7852
    Mentally ill parent   Fam §§7826, 7827
    Moral depravity of parent   Fam §7824
    Neglected child   Fam §7823
    Non-contested proceeding
        Orders may be issued based on pleadings and evidence offered   Fam §7870
    Noncustodial parent, placement with
        Out-of-county placements   CRC 5.614
            Judicial council legal forms   CRCAppx A
    One parent, conditions to termination of rights of
        Disposition hearings generally   CRC 5.690 to 5.705
    Order for   CRC 5.725
    Other states (See **UNIFORM CHILD CUSTODY JURISDICTION AND ENFORCEMENT ACT**)
    Petition
        Adoption agency, petition by   Fam §7840
        Both parents, single petition to free from custody   Fam §7842
        Interested person, petition by   Fam §7841
        Public agency, petition by   Fam §7840
        Superior court fees   Gov §70633
    Precedence over other matters   Fam §7870
    Procedure   Fam §§7840, 7841
    Service of citation   Fam §§7880 to 7882
    Statute of limitations for bringing action   Fam §7823
    Stay of proceedings   Fam §7807
    Substance abuse of parent   Fam §7824
    Testimony of child in chambers   Fam §§7891, 7892
    Time for hearing   Fam §7870
    Transcripts   Fam §7895
    Unknown parents   Fam §7882
    Venue   Fam §7845
    Whereabouts of parent unknown   Fam §7882

TERMITES AND PESTS
Commercial and industrial common interest developments
    Termites or other wood-destroying pests
        Forced vacation of separate or common interest   CC §6720
        Responsibility for maintenance   CC §6718
Common interest developments
    Termite damage, liability for   CC §4780
        Temporary removal of occupant   CC §4785
Conveyance of real property, requirement of pest control inspection report prior to   CC §1099
Home improvement goods and services   CC §1689.8
Inspection warrants for purposes of eradication of (See **INSPECTION WARRANTS**)
Landlord's duty to provide notice of pest control inspection to new tenant   CC §1099
Mandamus in actions involving state pest control and eradication, issuance of   CCP §1085.5
Structural pest control inspection
    Landlord's duty to provide notice of pest control inspection to new tenant   CC §1099
    Transfer of title, delivery to transferee of pest inspection report prior to   CC §1099

TERMS OF OFFICE
Congress of United States (See **CONGRESS**)
Probate referees   Pro §403

TERRORISM
Construction defects, actions for
    Unforeseen act of nature
        Defenses of builder   CC §945.5
September 11, 2001 terrorist attacks
    Statute of limitations   CCP §340.10

TESTAMENTARY DISPOSITIONS (See **WILL CONSTRUCTION**)

TESTAMENTARY TRUSTS (See **TRUSTS**)

TESTATORS (See **WILLS**)

TESTIFY
Inclusions in definition   CCP §17

TESTIMONY (See **EVIDENCE; WITNESSES**)

TESTS (See **BLOOD TESTS**)

TEXTILE GOODS
Warranties   CC §§1790 to 1795.8

TEXT MESSAGING
Judicial ethics code
    Public confidence in judiciary
        Electronic communications, care in using   CRCSupp JudEthicsCanon 2
Obscene and harmful matter
    Electronic messages depicting obscene material
        Knowingly sending unsolicited messages   CC §1708.88
Statute of frauds
    Insufficiency of text message or instant message format communications to constitute contract to convey realty   CC §1624

TEXTURE COATING
Home improvement goods and services   CC §1689.8

THEATERS (See **MOTION PICTURES**)

THEFT (See also **EMBEZLEMENT**)
Attachments, real property destroyed   CCP §488.060
Automobile theft (See **AUTOMOBILE THEFT**)
Credit cards   CC §1747.20
False pretenses (See **FALSE PRETENSES**)
Fur-bearing animals   CC §996
Identity theft (See **IDENTITY THEFT**)
Landlord and tenant
    Unduly influencing tenant to vacate   CC §1940.2
Public employee's liability for theft of money for employee's official custody   Gov §822
Rental passenger vehicle transactions
    Action for loss due to theft   CC §1939.27
    Electronic surveillance technology
        Activation, when permitted   CC §1939.23
        Restrictions on use   CC §1939.23
    Recovery by rental company
        Prohibited means of recovery   CC §1939.15
    Renter responsibilities for rented vehicle   CC §1939.03
        Claim against renter for damage or loss   CC §1939.07
        Damage waivers   CC §§1939.09, 1939.13
        Insurance coverage for renter   CC §1939.07
        Mitigation of damages by rental company   CC §1939.07
        Total amount of renter liability   CC §1939.05
Repairs, theft of property deposited for   CC §1858.2
Statute of limitation for theft of articles of historic or artistic importance   CCP §338

THEFT AND LARCENY
Firearms and other weapons
    Firearm industry responsibility, industry standards of conduct (See **FIREARM INDUSTRY STANDARDS OF CONDUCT**)
    Firearm industry standards of conduct   CC §§3273.50 to 3273.55

THERAPY
Marriage and family counselors (See **MARRIAGE AND FAMILY COUNSELORS**)
Physical therapists (See **PHYSICAL THERAPISTS**)
Psychotherapists (See **PSYCHOTHERAPISTS**)

THING IN ACTION (See **CHOSE IN ACTION**)

THIRD PARTIES
Administrators, request for appointment as   Pro §8465
Adverse claims by   CCP §1050
Alcoholic beverages, social host's liability to third party after serving   CC §1714
Arbitration (See **ARBITRATION**)
Attachment (See **ATTACHMENT**)
Claim of property after levy   CCP §514.050
Contracts (See **CONTRACTS AND AGREEMENTS**)
Credit cards, termination of third party use of   CC §1747.02
Enforcement of judgments (See **ENFORCEMENT OF JUDGMENTS**)
Escheat, claims of ownership to prevent   CCP §§1352, 1353
Escrow (See **ESCROW**)

THIRD PARTIES—Cont.
Estate for life of   CC §766
Garnishment (See **GARNISHMENT**)
Genetic defects of child, action involving   CC §43.6
Husband and wife having transactions with   Fam §721
Improvements on land of another   CCP §§871.1 to 871.7
Information Practices Act (See **INFORMATION PRACTICES ACT**)
Judgments (See **JUDGMENTS**)
Jury conversing with   CCP §611
Necessaries for child, recovery for   Fam §6712
Ownership or right of possession of property levied upon, third party claim of   CCP §§720.110 to 720.170
Power of attorney (See **POWER OF ATTORNEY**)
Promise to answer for obligations of   CC §2794
Retail installment sales pursuant to loans by   CC §§1801.6, 1801.7, 1803.9
Security interest in or lien on property levied upon, third party claim of   CCP §§720.210 to 720.290, 720.510 to 720.550
Social host's liability after serving alcoholic beverages   CC §1714
Specific performance of contract to obtain consent of   CC §3390
Trusts (See **TRUSTS**)
Written contract to answer for default of   CC §1624

THIRD PARTY BENEFICIARIES (See **CONTRACTS AND AGREEMENTS**)

THREATS
Debts
    Coerced debt   CC §§1798.97.1 to 1798.97.6
Domestic violence protection orders
    COVID-19, emergency rule   CRCAppx I Emer Rule 8
    Denial of petition for ex parte order, reasons to be provided   Fam §6320.5
Duress (See **DURESS**)
Health care facilities
    Force, threat or other obstruction of access to health facilities or school grounds   CC §1708.9
Landlord and tenant
    Unduly influencing tenant to vacate   CC §1940.2
Online violence prevention   CC §§1798.99.20 to 1798.99.23
Protective orders
    Firearm relinquishment and disposition
        Forms for firearm relinquishment   CRCAppx A
        Procedures   CRC 4.700
Rape accomplished by threat of future retaliation
    Statute of limitations
        Civil damages   CCP §340.16
Schools
    Force, threat or other obstruction of access to health facilities or school grounds   CC §1708.9
    Grounds, threats to commit violence using firearm or deadly weapon on   CC §48.8
Sodomy perpetrated by
    Statute of limitations
        Civil damages   CCP §340.16
Stalking
    Name change proceedings under address confidentiality program   CRC 2.575 to 2.577

THREE MONTHS (See **STATUTES OF LIMITATION**)

THREE YEARS (See **STATUTES OF LIMITATION**)

THRESHING MACHINES
Lien for use of   CC §3061

TICKETS
Common carrier limiting liability by provisions in   CC §2176
Entertainment facilities
    Notice regarding human trafficking   CC §52.66
Railroads (See **RAILROADS**)
Vessels (See **VESSELS**)

TIDELANDS
Eminent domain, taking for   CCP §1240.110
Highwater mark as boundary   CCP §2077
Leasing of   CC §718
Ownership of   CC §670
Public entity's liability for injury on   Gov §831.6
Public lands, private property used as   CC §1009
Title to
    Border land   CC §830

TIDELANDS—Cont.
Title to—Cont.
    State   CC §670

TIMBER (See **LOGS AND TIMBER**)

TIME
Administration of decedents' estates
    Generally (See **ADMINISTRATION OF ESTATES**)
    Claims against decedents' estates (See **CLAIMS AGAINST ESTATES**)
Administrative law and procedure
    Adjudicative proceedings (See **ADMINISTRATIVE ADJUDICATION**)
    Rulemaking and regulation (See **ADMINISTRATIVE PROCEDURE ACT**)
Annulment proceedings, time for filing responsive pleading   Fam §2020
Appellate rules
    Superior court appeals
        Extensions of time (See **APPELLATE RULES, SUPERIOR COURT APPEALS**)
    Supreme court and courts of appeal (See **APPELLATE RULES, SUPREME COURT AND COURTS OF APPEAL**)
Appropriation of waters, time for completion of work for   CC §1416
Arbitration awards   CCP §1283.8
Attachment (See **ATTACHMENT**)
Attorneys (See **ATTORNEYS**)
Blood test, submission of affidavit stating technique in taking   Ev §712
Change of venue, time to file petition for writ of mandate on grant or denial of motion for   CCP §400
Civil Code takes effect   CC §2
Claim and delivery, return of possession writs to court   CCP §514.040
Claims against decedents' estates (See **CLAIMS AGAINST ESTATES**)
Commencing actions, time for (See **STATUTES OF LIMITATION**)
Common carriers, time schedules required for   CC §§2170, 2172
Community property, valuation of   Fam §2552
Computation of time
    Holidays (See **HOLIDAYS**)
    Limitation of actions (See **STATUTES OF LIMITATION**)
Conciliation court hearings   Fam §1837
Consent for contract agreement, time for   CC §1583
Courts of appeal (See **COURTS OF APPEAL**)
Cross-complaints (See **CROSS-COMPLAINTS**)
Custody investigation, time for filing reports of   Fam §3111
Default judgments (See **DEFAULT JUDGMENTS**)
Demurrers   CCP §§430.40, 432.10, 471.5, 472a, 472b
Discovery
    Saturday, Sunday or holiday, deadline falling on   CCP §2016.060
Dismissal of action (See **DISMISSAL**)
Disqualification of judges (See **JUDGES, DISQUALIFICATION OF**)
Dissolution of marriage proceedings, time for filing responsive pleadings   Fam §2020
Effect of codes   CC §23
Enforcement of judgments (See **ENFORCEMENT OF JUDGMENTS**)
Enjoyment of real property   CC §707
Environmental quality act
    Petitions under environmental quality act, civil rules governing
        Extensions of time   CRC 3.2221
Evidence excluded on undue consumption of   Ev §352
Exceptions   CCP §646
Extensions of time (See **EXTENSIONS OF TIME**)
Family law rules (See **FAMILY RULES**)
Forms, molds and dies, notice of termination of customer's title to   CC §1140
Groundwater rights actions
    Notice of complaint   CCP §835
Harassment, duration of protection order   CCP §527.6
    COVID-19, emergency rule   CRCAppx I Emer Rule 8
Health care provider's professional negligence, notice of intention to commence action based on   CCP §364
Information Practices Act (See **INFORMATION PRACTICES ACT**)
Judges (See **JUDGES**)
Judgments, entry of   CCP §664
Judicial arbitration (See **JUDICIAL ARBITRATION**)
Jury instructions, time for decision on proposed   CCP §607a
Jury summons, time for mailing   CCP §208
Last day to perform act before hearing date
    Computation   CCP §12c
Limitation of actions (See **STATUTES OF LIMITATION**)
Mandamus   CCP §§1094.6, 1108
Mechanics' liens (See **MECHANICS' LIENS**)
Missing persons (See **MISSING PERSONS**)
Mistake, inadvertence, surprise or excusable neglect, time to apply for relief from judgment based on   CCP §473

TIME—Cont.

Molds, forms and dies, notice of termination of customer's title to   CC §1140
Motion, service of notice of   CCP §§1005, 1013
Motions to strike   CRC 3.1322
Motor vehicle warranties, actions involving   CC §1793.22
New trial motion   CCP §§659, 659a, 661
Notices served by mail   CCP §1013
Oil and gas liens, duration of   CCP §1203.53
Pending litigation (See **PENDENCY OF ACTIONS**)
Process (See **PROCESS AND SERVICE OF PROCESS**)
Protective orders, expiration of   CCP §486.090
Receiver, hearing on order to show cause re ex parte appointment of   CRC 3.1176
Referee's report of statement of decision, filing of   CCP §643
Rent, payment of   CC §1947
Rules of court
 Computation of time   CRC 1.10
 Extending or shortening time   CRC 1.10
  Trial court rules   CRC 2.20
Service of process (See **PROCESS AND SERVICE OF PROCESS**)
Service of summons (See **PROCESS AND SERVICE OF PROCESS**)
Setting for trial (See **TRIAL**)
Settlements
 Request for additional time to complete   CRC 3.1385
Shortened time (See **SHORTENING TIME**)
Small claims court (See **SMALL CLAIMS COURTS**)
Stay of enforcement of judgment, duration of   CCP §918
Subpoena duces tecum, delivery pursuant to   Ev §1560
Summary dissolution of marriage, time for entry of judgment in   Fam §2403
Summary judgments, motion for   CCP §437c
Summons, service of (See **PROCESS AND SERVICE OF PROCESS**)
Sundays and holidays in time computation   CC §§10, 12, 12a
Superior courts (See **SUPERIOR COURTS**)
Supreme Court (See **SUPREME COURT, CALIFORNIA**)
Surety bonds (See **SURETYSHIP, BONDS AND UNDERTAKINGS**)
Temporary restraining orders, day upon which order is made returnable   CCP §527
Termination of parental rights, hearings   Fam §7870
Trial court rules
 Extension of time
  Application for order to extend time   CRC 2.20
Uniform Transfers to Minors Act (See **UNIFORM TRANSFERS TO MINORS ACT**)
Unlawful detainer (See **UNLAWFUL DETAINER**)
Vacate judgment
 Ruling on motion   CCP §663a
 Service of motion   CCP §663a
Venue change (See **VENUE**)
Will probate (See **WILL PROBATE**)
Withdrawal of legal service agency attorney for indigent client, effect on time limitations of   CCP §285.3

TIME-SHARES

Common interest developments
 Generally   CC §§4000 to 6150

TISSUE BANKS

Medical information disclosed to   CC §56.10

TITLE AND OWNERSHIP   CC §§659, 699, 829 to 835

Abandoned easements   CC §§887.010 to 887.090
Absolute ownership defined   CC §§678, 679
Abstract of title
 Lost or destroyed documents, abstract as proof of existence of   Ev §1601
 Partition (See **PARTITION**)
 Statute of limitation founded upon contract or obligation evidenced by   CCP §339
 Unclaimed property fund appropriations for title searches   CCP §1325
Accessions   CC §732
Administration of estates (See **ADMINISTRATION OF ESTATES**)
Adverse possession (See **ADVERSE POSSESSION**)
Alien's rights to own land   CC §671
Ancient trust deeds
 Generally   CC §882.020
 Enforcement of expired security   CC §882.030
 Prior recorded security interest, effect of   CC §882.040
Animals (See **ANIMALS**)
Apartment building owner, requirements for identifying   CC §§1961 to 1962.5
Art and artists (See **ART AND ARTISTS**)
Beneficiaries under will, title passing to   Pro §§7000, 7001
Bill of sale (See **BILL OF SALE**)

TITLE AND OWNERSHIP—Cont.

Borrowed property, title to   CC §1885
Campground owner (See **CAMPING**)
Certificate of title, limitation of actions founded upon contract or obligation evidenced by   CCP §339
Citizen's rights to own land   CC §671
Community property (See **COMMUNITY PROPERTY**)
Condition precedent, title vesting on performance of   CC §1110
Conveyance (See **CONVEYANCES**)
Cotenancy (See **COTENANCY**)
Covenants and conditions (See **COVENANTS AND CONDITIONS**)
Creditor receiving title   CC §1502
Death
 Deraignment of title to general class of heirs (See **HEIRS**)
 Multiple-party accounts   Pro §§5302, 5405
 Prior owner's death, procedure for establishing (See **FACT OF DEATH**)
 Transfer of title at time of   Pro §§7000, 7001
Decedents' estates (See **ADMINISTRATION OF ESTATES**)
Dedicated land   CC §670
Deeds   CC §994
Default judgment recovering   CCP §585
Definitions   CC §§678 to 701
Deposit for exchange as transferring title   CC §1878
Destroyed land records, action for reestablishment of   CCP §§751.01 to 751.28
Dies, molds and forms   CC §1140
Discrimination in ownership of real property   CC §§53, 782, 782.5
Earthquake, ownership determination after   CCP §§751.50 to 750.65
Easements (See **EASEMENTS**)
Escheated property   CCP §§1410 to 1431, Pro §§6404, 6800
Exchange, title to property loaned for   CC §1904
Exercise of ownership as presumption of ownership   Ev §638
Expiration of title
 Generally   CC §880.240
 Ancient mortgages and trust deeds   CC §882.020
 Limitations statute, tolling of   CC §880.250
 Lis pendens, effect of   CC §880.260
 Power of termination, effect of expiration of   CC §885.030
 Unperformed contracts for sale of realty, effect on   CC §886.030
Forms, molds and dies   CC §1140
Guaranty of title, limitation of actions founded upon contract or obligation evidenced by   CCP §339
Hearsay statements as to title   Ev §1225
Highways, grants bordering on   CC §1112
Homesteads (See **HOMESTEADS**)
Improvements by third party   CCP §§871.1 to 871.7
Intestate succession to title (See **INTESTATE SUCCESSION**)
Inventions (See **PATENT OF INVENTION**)
Joint interests   CC §682
Laches affecting marketability of   CC §880.030
Lakes (See **LAKES**)
Legal title owner presumed to be full beneficial title owner   Ev §662
Liens affecting   CC §2888
Life tenant's use of land   CC §818
Limitation of actions
 Adverse possession generally (See **ADVERSE POSSESSION**)
 Generally (See within this heading, "Statutes of limitation")
Lis pendens (See **PENDENCY OF ACTIONS**)
Literary property (See **LITERARY PROPERTY**)
Marketability of title
 Abandoned easements   CC §§887.010 to 887.090
 Ancient trust deeds generally (See within this heading, "**Ancient trust deeds**")
 Equitable principles as   CC §880.030
 Expiration of title (See within this heading, "**Expiration of title**")
 Limitations statute
  Adverse possession generally (See **ADVERSE POSSESSION**)
  Generally (See within this heading, "**Statutes of limitation**")
 Power of termination generally (See within this heading, "**Power of termination**")
 Public policy on   CC §880.020
 Unexercised options generally (See within this heading, "**Unexercised options**")
 Unperformed contract for sale of realty (See within this heading, "**Unperformed contract for sale of realty**")
McEnerney Act   CCP §§751.01 to 751.28
Mobilehome park owner, disclosure of   CC §798.28
Molds, forms and dies   CC §1140
Multiple-party accounts   Pro §§5301 to 5306
Names of owners
 Change of name   CC §1096
 Unnamed party in deed   CC §1085

TITLE AND OWNERSHIP—Cont.
Occupancy of land, title by   CC §§1006, 1007
Options
    Unexercised (See within this heading, **"Unexercised options"**)
Partition action, determination of state of title in   CCP §872.620
Partnership interests   CC §§682, 684
Patent of invention (See **PATENT OF INVENTION**)
Pendency of actions (See **PENDENCY OF ACTIONS**)
Possibility of reverter, power of termination affecting   CC §885.020
Power of termination
    Abolishment of fee simple   CC §885.020
    Defined   CC §885.010
    Expiration
        Generally   CC §885.030
        Obsolete power as expired   CC §885.040
        Unenforceability of expired power   CC §885.060
    Limitations statute on exercise of   CC §885.050
    Nonapplicability of chapter to certain powers of termination   CC §885.015
    Obsolete power   CC §885.040
    Prior recordation, effect of   CC §885.070
    Quitclaim, requirement for   CC §885.060
    Reclassification of fee simple   CC §885.020
    Recordation of termination   CC §885.060
Prescription, title by   CC §§813, 1007, 1009
Preservation of interest (See **RECORDS AND RECORDING**)
Presumptions of   Ev §§605, 638, 662
Property rights regardless of citizenship status   CC §671
Public lands   CC §670
Qualified ownership   CC §§678, 680
Quieting title (See **QUIETING TITLE**)
Quitclaim deed affecting power of termination   CC §885.060
Records and recordings
    Ancient trust deeds generally (See within this heading, **"Ancient trust deeds"**)
    Destroyed land records, action for reestablishment of   CCP §§751.01 to 751.28
    Preservation of interest (See **RECORDS AND RECORDING**)
    Unexercised options
        Prior recorded option, grace period   CC §884.030
Return of property to owner, requirements for   CC §§1712, 1713
Rivers and streams (See **RIVERS AND STREAMS**)
Roads as boundaries   CCP §2077
Sale of realty (See **VENDOR AND PURCHASER**)
Seisin or possession within five years of commencement of action arising from   CCP §319
Several ownership   CC §681
Slander of title (See **SLANDER OF TITLE**)
Sole ownership defined   CC §681
Sound recordings (See **RECORDING OF SOUND**)
Spanish title papers   Ev §1605
Statutes of limitation
    Generally   CC §880.250
    Adverse possession (See **ADVERSE POSSESSION**)
    Certificate, abstract or guaranty of title, actions founded upon contract or obligation evidenced by   CCP §339
    Power of termination, exercise of   CC §885.050
    Unperformed contract for sale of realty   CC §886.030
Statutory rights   CC §655
Streams (See **RIVERS AND STREAMS**)
Streets, grants bordering on   CC §1112
Surveyor's rights   CC §846.5
Tenancy in common   CC §§682, 685
Tenant's denial of landlord's title   Ev §624
Things subject to ownership   CC §655
Third party claim of ownership of property levied upon   CCP §§720.110 to 720.170
Tidelands (See **TIDELANDS**)
Totten trust accounts   Pro §§5301, 5302
Transfers (See **BILL OF SALE; CONVEYANCES**)
Trees   CC §§660, 833, 834
Trustee to unclaimed property, State of California as   CCP §1424
Unclaimed property fund appropriations for title searches   CCP §1325
Unexercised options
    Effect of expired unexercised option   CC §884.020
    Expiration of   CC §884.010
    Prior recorded option, grace period for   CC §884.030
Unperformed contract for sale of realty
    Defined   CC §886.010
    Expired recorded contract, effect of   CC §§886.030, 886.040
    Prior recorded contract, applicability of chapter two   CC §886.050
    Release of contract of failure to satisfy conditions   CC §886.020

TITLE AND OWNERSHIP—Cont.
Vessels, transferring title to   CC §1135
Wills (See **WILLS**)

TITLE INSURANCE
Destroyed land records relief law   CCP §§751.01 to 751.28
Notice to buyer in escrow transactions advising acquisition of title insurance   CC §1057.6
Real estate sales
    Choice of insurer lies with buyer   CC §1103.22
Statute of limitation founded upon contract or obligation evidenced by policy of   CCP §339

TITLE IV-D ACTIONS
Child support (See **CHILD SUPPORT**)
Family rules   CRC 5.300 to 5.375

TITLE REPORTS
Quieting title action, requirement for   CCP §762.040

TITLES AND DIVISION OF CODES
Acts, citation of (See **CITATION OF ACTS**)
Civil Code   CC §1
Code of Civil Procedure   CCP §1
Conflicting titles in codes   CC §23.3

TITLE TO OFFICE (See **PUBLIC OFFICERS AND EMPLOYEES**)

TOBACCO (See **SMOKING**)

TOD DEEDS
Revocable transfer on death deeds   Pro §§5600 to 5698 (See **TRANSFER ON DEATH DEEDS**)

TOD SECURITY REGISTRATION ACT   Pro §§5500 to 5512

TOLL BRIDGE AUTHORITY
Eminent domain taking by   CCP §1245.210

TOLLING STATUTES OF LIMITATION (See **STATUTES OF LIMITATION**)

TOLL ROADS (See **STREETS AND HIGHWAYS**)

TOLLS
Easement right to collect   CC §802

TOM BANE CIVIL RIGHTS ACT
Injunctive or other equitable relief to protect exercise or enjoyment of legal rights   CC §52.1

TOMBSTONES
Family history   Ev §1312

TOOLS
Assignment for benefit of creditors, property exempt from   CCP §1801
Dies, molds and forms, ownership of   CC §1140
Exempt property for purposes of enforcement of judgments   CCP §704.060

TORT CLAIMS ACT (See **CLAIMS AGAINST PUBLIC ENTITIES AND EMPLOYEES**)

TORTS
Generally   CC §§1708, 1714
Abstaining from injuring person or property of another
    Obligation to abstain   CC §1708
Administrative adjudicative proceedings (See **ADMINISTRATIVE ADJUDICATION**)
Agreement between tortfeasors   CCP §877.5
Children
    Liability limits of parent or guardian for torts of   CRCAppx B
Claims against decedents' estates   Pro §9000
Claims against governmental entities (See **CLAIMS AGAINST PUBLIC ENTITIES AND EMPLOYEES**)
Commercial blockage tort affecting medical care facilities   CC §§3427 to 3427.4
Common interest developments
    Limitation of member liability   CC §5805
    Limited liability of volunteer officer or director of   CC §5800
Community property, liability of   Fam §2627
Contribution among joint tortfeasors   CCP §§875 to 880
Dissolution of marriage, assignment of liabilities on   Fam §2627
Domestic violence   CC §1708.6

TORTS—Cont.
Emancipated minor's torts   Fam §7050
Exculpatory provisions re intentional torts   CC §1668
Guardian liability, torts of children   CC §1714.1, CRCAppx B
Imprisonment because of   CCP §§501, 748
Invitees injured   CC §846
Licensees   CC §846
Minors (See **PARENT AND CHILD**)
Negligence (See **NEGLIGENCE**)
Nonimprisonment in civil action for debt or tort   CCP §501
Parental liability, torts of children   CRCAppx B
Parent and child (See **PARENT AND CHILD**)
Physician's services aiding in commission of tort, adherence of privilege where   Ev §997
Products liability (See **PRODUCTS LIABILITY**)
Psychotherapist's services aiding in commission of tort, absence of privilege where   Ev §1018
Public entities and employees, claims against (See **CLAIMS AGAINST PUBLIC ENTITIES AND EMPLOYEES**)
Sliding scale recovery agreements   CCP §877.5
Space flight liability and immunity   CC §§2210 to 2212
State agency adjudicative proceedings (See **ADMINISTRATIVE ADJUDICATION**)
Statutes of limitation   CCP §§335.1, 340

TORTURE
Attorney's fees
    Assault and battery, wrongful death, etc constituting torture, genocide, crimes against humanity, etc   CCP §354.8
Statutes of limitations
    Assault and battery, wrongful death, etc constituting torture, genocide, crimes against humanity, etc   CCP §354.8

TOTTEN TRUST ACCOUNTS
Defined   Pro §80
Disclaimer of estate interest in   Pro §§260 to 295
Ownership of   Pro §§5301, 5302
Payments on account by financial institutions   Pro §§5404 to 5407

TOWING AUTOMOBILES (See **AUTOMOBILES**)

TOXIC SUBSTANCES EXPOSURES
Statutes of limitation   CCP §340.8

TOYS
Gender neutral retail departments
    Gender neutral section or area for display, retailer duties   CC §55.8

TRACING FUNDS
Exempt funds for purposes of enforcement of judgments   CCP §703.080

TRACKING DEVICES
Buy-here-pay-here auto dealers
    Automobile sales finance
        Restrictions on installing electronic tracking technology   CC §2983.37

TRADEMARKS AND TRADE NAMES
Attorney professional conduct
    Firm names and trade names   ProfC 7.5
Ownership, subject to   CC §655
Seller assisted marketing plan   CC §§1812.201, 1812.204

TRADES
Exemption for purposes of enforcement of judgments of property used in   CCP §704.060

TRADE SECRETS
Applicability of Act   CC §§3426.7, 3426.9, 3426.10
Attorneys' fees for claim of misappropriation made in bad faith   CC §3426.4
Citation of Act   CC §3426
Costs in misappropriation cases
    Expert witness and other recoverable costs   CC §3426.4
Court records
    Public access to judicial administrative records
        Exemptions from requirement to provide access   CRC 10.500
Damages for loss caused by misappropriation of   CC §3426.3
Definitions   CC §3426.1
Discovery actions concerning
    Method and sequence of discovery   CCP §2019.210
Injunctive relief from misappropriation of   CC §3426.2

TRADE SECRETS—Cont.
Preservation of secrecy by court   CC §3426.5
Privileged communications (See **PRIVILEGED COMMUNICATIONS**)
Purpose of Act   CC §3426.8
Statute of limitation for bringing action   CC §3426.6

TRADE UNIONS (See **LABOR AND LABOR UNIONS**)

TRAFFIC REGULATIONS AND VIOLATIONS
Appellate division of superior court, traffic cases as exception to requirement for participation of three judges in   CCP §77

TRAFFIC SCHOOL
Ability to pay program
    Traffic violator school eligibility   Gov §68645.15
Eligibility to attend   CRC 4.104
Substance abuse
    Effect on eligibility for school   CRC 4.104

TRAFFIC SIGNS, SIGNALS, AND MARKINGS
Automated enforcement systems
    Evidentiary effect of printed representations of computer information
        Applicability to systems   Ev §1552
    Evidentiary effect of printed representations of images stored on video or digital medium
        Applicability to systems   Ev §1552

TRAFFIC VIOLATIONS
Appearances
    Bail
        Appearance without deposit of bail in traffic infraction cases   CRC 4.105
Bail
    Appearance without deposit of bail in traffic infraction cases   CRC 4.105
    Deposit of bail, when required   CRC 4.105
    Extensions of time for payment   CRC JudAdminStand 4.40
    Infraction trials
        Appearance without deposit of bail in traffic infraction cases   CRC 4.105
        Deposit of bail, when required   CRC 4.105
    Schedules   CRC 4.102
Fines and penalties
    Schedules   CRC 4.102
    Trial by written declaration, imposition in   CRC 4.210
Forms
    Judicial council legal forms   CRCAppx A
    Trial by written declaration   CRC 4.210
Infractions
    Installment payment agreements   CRC 4.108
    Notice to appear   CRC 4.106
        Mandatory reminder notices for notice to appear   CRC 4.107
Judges
    Temporary judges
        Attorney serving as temporary judge in traffic cases   CRC 2.812
Judicial Council
    Forms for trial by written declaration   CRC 4.210
    Traffic advisory committee   CRC 10.54
Traffic school
    Ability to pay program
        Traffic violator school eligibility   Gov §68645.15
    Eligibility for   CRC 4.104
Trial
    Infractions
        Scheduling   CRC JudAdminStand 4.42
        Written declaration, trial by   CRC 4.106
    Written declaration, trial by   CRC 4.210
Uniform Bail and Penalty Schedule   CRC 4.102
Written declaration, trial of infractions by   CRC 4.210

TRAILERS
House cars and campers
    Mobilehomes (See **MOBILEHOMES**)
    Recreational vehicles (See **RECREATIONAL VEHICLES**)

TRAILS
Enjoining closure of   CCP §731.5

TRAINS (See **RAILROADS**)

TRANSCRIPTS
Agreed statement   CRC 8.134
    Content of record on appeal   CRC 8.120

TRANSCRIPTS—Cont.
- Appendix designated as record on appeal   CRC 8.124
  - Content of record on appeal   CRC 8.120
- Arbitration
  - Certified shorthand reporters
    - Party's right   CCP §1282.5
- Audiotapes offered as evidence   CRC 2.1040
- Availability of reporting services   CRC 2.956
- Clerk's transcript   CRC 8.122, 8.144
  - Appellate rules, superior court appeals
    - Infraction case appeals, record on appeal   CRC 8.912, 8.913
    - Limited civil cases in appellate division, record on appeal   CRC 8.832
    - Misdemeanor appeals, record on appeal   CRC 8.861, 8.862
  - Appendix instead of   CRC 8.124
  - Content of record on appeal   CRC 8.120
  - Criminal appeals
    - Sealed or confidential records, form of record on appeal   CRC 8.336
  - Sealed or confidential records
    - Criminal appeals, form of record on appeal   CRC 8.336
    - Form of record, compliance with sealed or confidential records provisions   CRC 8.144
  - Superior court file instead of, stipulation   CRC 8.128
- Correction   CRC 8.155
- Court reporters generally (See **COURT REPORTERS**)
- Criminal appeals
  - Sealed or confidential records, form of record on appeal   CRC 8.336
- Death penalty cases
  - Appeals
    - Delivery date of transcript   CRC 8.608
  - Review daily by counsel during trial
    - Trial, additional requirements   CRC 4.230
- Debt collection
  - Educational debt collection practices
    - Transcript used as leverage to collect debt, prohibition   CC §1788.93
- Electronic recordings   CRC 2.952
  - Delivery of transcript in electronic form   CCP §271
  - Limited civil cases in appellate division, record on appeal
    - Transcript from electronic recording of proceedings   CRC 8.835
- Indexes   CRC 8.144
- Jurors, redaction of identifying information from transcripts   CRC 8.332
- Death penalty appeals   CRC 8.610, 8.611
- Juvenile court proceedings   CRC 5.532
- Paper transcripts
  - Grounds for providing paper in lieu of electronic transcript   CCP §271
  - Searchable PDF copy to be provided when paper transcript delivered   CCP §271
- Prima facie evidence   CCP §273
- Record on appeal
  - Content of record on appeal   CRC 8.120
  - Designation of documents   CRC 8.122
  - Sealed or confidential records
    - Form of record, compliance with sealed or confidential records provisions   CRC 8.144
- Recycled paper   CRC 8.144
- Reimbursement fund   CRC 8.130
- Reporter's transcript   CRC 8.130, 8.144
  - Appellate rules, superior court appeals
    - Infraction case appeals, record on appeal   CRC 8.918, 8.919
    - Limited civil cases in appellate division, record on appeal   CRC 8.834
    - Misdemeanor appeals, record on appeal   CRC 8.864 to 8.866
  - Content of record on appeal   CRC 8.120
  - Criminal appeals
    - Sealed or confidential records, form of record on appeal   CRC 8.336
  - Deposit of approximate cost   CRC 8.130
  - Electronic recordings   CRC 2.952
    - Delivery of transcript in electronic form   CCP §271
  - Extension of time for preparation   CRC 8.130
  - Multi-reporter cases   CRC 8.130
  - Sealed or confidential records
    - Criminal appeals, form of record on appeal   CRC 8.336
    - Form of record, compliance with sealed or confidential records provisions   CRC 8.144
  - Settled statement instead of   CRC 8.137
    - Content of record on appeal   CRC 8.120
  - Superior court reporters
    - Rough draft transcripts
      - Limitations on use   CCP §273
    - Visual display of testimony or proceedings
      - Limitations on use of instant visual display   CCP §273

TRANSCRIPTS—Cont.
- Video offered as evidence   CRC 2.1040

TRANSFER OF ACTIONS   CRC 3.500
- Appearance by filing motion for   CCP §1014
- Appellate rules, superior court appeals
  - Transfers from superior court appellate division to court of appeal   CRC 8.1000 to 8.1018
- Appellate rules, supreme court and courts of appeal
  - Generally (See **APPELLATE RULES, SUPREME COURT AND COURTS OF APPEAL**)
  - Transfers from superior court appellate division to court of appeal   CRC 8.1000 to 8.1018 (See **APPELLATE RULES, SUPREME COURT AND COURTS OF APPEAL**)
- CARE act rules, transfer under   CRC 7.2223
- Change of venue (See **VENUE**)
- Common issue actions filed in different courts   CRC 3.500
- Conciliation courts   Fam §§1812, 1841, 1842
- Coordination of actions (See **COORDINATION OF ACTIONS**)
- Long-Term Care, Health, Safety and Security Act, actions brought pursuant to   CCP §86.1
- Small claims court (See **SMALL CLAIMS COURTS**)
- Superior Court Appellate Division, transfer to Court of Appeals from   CCP §911
- Superior courts   CCP §402
  - Limited civil cases   CCP §396a
- Supreme court   CRC 10.1000
  - Pending court of appeal case   CRC 8.552
  - Transfer on disposition   CRC 8.528
- Venue (See **VENUE**)
- Wrong court, appeal or petition filed in   CCP §396

TRANSFER OF REALTY (See **SALE OF REALTY**)

TRANSFER OF VENUE (See **VENUE**)

TRANSFER ON DEATH DEEDS   Pro §§5600 to 5698
- Ambiguity describing property or designating beneficiary
  - Effect   Pro §5659
- Applicability of provisions   Pro §§5600 to 5605
  - Conveyance of real property by other methods   Pro §5602
  - Definitions   Pro §5606
  - Nonprobate transfers on death   Pro §5604
- Contest of transfer   Pro §§5690 to 5698
  - Applicability of principles of fraud, undue influence, etc., or other invalidating causes   Pro §5696
  - Disqualification of a beneficiary, action for   Pro §5690
  - Dual recordation same property
    - Claim of inoperative deed brought as contest   Pro §5660
  - Fraud, undue influence, etc, creation of deed
    - Applicability of other provisions penalizing conduct   Pro §5698
  - Types of court relief   Pro §5694
  - Validity of transfer of property   Pro §5690
  - When action may be brought   Pro §5692
- Creditors' rights   Pro §§5670 to 5678
  - Administration of the transferor's estate   Pro §5674
  - Beneficiary's personal liability for unsecured debts of transferor   Pro §5677
  - Personal liability of beneficiary   Pro §§5672, 5674
  - Priority right against property   Pro §5670
  - Voluntary return of property to estate for administration   Pro §5678
- Cy pres doctrine to reform deed   Pro §5658
- Definitions   Pro §§5606 to 5616
- Effect of transfer   Pro §§5650 to 5668
  - Community property with right of survivorship   Pro §§5664, 5666, 5668
  - Conveyance of any right, title or interest in the property   Pro §5650
  - Dual recordation same property, effect   Pro §§5628, 5660
  - General provisions   Pro §§5650 to 5656
  - Holder of rights under that instrument, enforcement of rights   Pro §5652
  - Legal or equitable right in the beneficiary   Pro §5650
  - Other instruments and forms of tenure   Pro §§5660 to 5668
  - Ownership rights of the transferor   Pro §5650
  - Property held in joint tenancy   Pro §5664
  - Property taxation and documentary transfer tax provisions
    - Change of ownership, time of death   Pro §5656
  - State department of health care services
    - Subject to claims of department   Pro §5654
  - Transferor's interest in the property on the transferor's death   Pro §5652
- Error describing property or designating beneficiary
  - Effect   Pro §5659
- Execution of instrument   Pro §§5620 to 5628
  - Beneficiary, identity in document   Pro §5622
  - Capacity to contract   Pro §5620

TRANSFER ON DEATH DEEDS—Cont.
  Execution of instrument —Cont.
    Effective, when   Pro §5624
    Recordation   Pro §§5626, 5628
      Common questions portions of basic form not required to be recorded   Pro §5626
      Dual recordation same property, effect   Pro §§5628, 5660
      Time period   Pro §5626
    Witnesses   Pro §§5624, 5625
  Forms
    Notice of deed   Pro §5681
    Statutory forms   Pro §§5642, 5644
      Revocable transfer on death (TOD) deed   Pro §5642
      Revocation of revocable transfer on death (TOD) deed   Pro §5644
  Fraud, undue influence, etc, creation of deed
    Applicability of other provisions penalizing conduct   Pro §5698
  Notice of deed   Pro §5681
  Real property
    Defined   Pro §5610
    Revocable transfer on death deed
      Use of deed   Pro §5614
  Reformation
    Cy pres doctrine to reform deed   Pro §5658
    Error or ambiguity in deed   Pro §5659
  Relations with beneficiary   Pro §§5680, 5682
    Filing the change in ownership statement   Pro §5680
    Liability for prorated estate and generation-skipping transfer taxes   Pro §5680
    Notice to the director of health care services   Pro §5680
    Order for distribution of the transferor's estate   Pro §5682
  Return of property
    Voluntary return of property to estate for administration   Pro §5678
  Revocable TOD deeds
    Defined   Pro §69
  Revocable transfer on death deeds
    Defined   Pro §69
  Revocation of instrument   Pro §§5630, 5632
    Revocable transfer on death (TOD) deed
      Statutory form   Pro §5644
    Who may revoke   Pro §5630
  Statutory forms   Pro §§5642, 5644
    Revocable transfer on death (TOD) deed   Pro §5642
    Revocation of revocable transfer on death (TOD) deed   Pro §5644
  Stock cooperatives
    Defined   Pro §5614.5
    Effect of transfer   Pro §5652
  Study of effect of revocable transfer on death deed by law revision commission   Pro §5605
  Voluntary return of property to estate for administration   Pro §5678

TRANSFERS OF INTEREST
Abatement of pending action, effect of transfer of interest on   CCP §368.5
Assignments (See **ASSIGNMENTS**)
Attachment (See **ATTACHMENT**)
Bill of exchange (See **BILLS OF EXCHANGE**)
Bill of lading (See **BILL OF LADING**)
Bill of sale (See **BILL OF SALE**)
Chose in action   CC §954
Common interest developments (See **COMMON INTEREST DEVELOPMENTS**)
Definition   CC §1039
Enforcement of judgments (See **ENFORCEMENT OF JUDGMENTS**)
Gifts (See **GIFTS**)
Guardian and ward (See **GUARDIAN AND WARD**)
Marital property (See **COMMUNITY PROPERTY**)
Minors (See **UNIFORM TRANSFERS TO MINORS ACT**)
Real property (See **CONVEYANCES**)
Sales (See **SALES**)
Substitution of parties in pending action involving   CCP §368.5
Trusts (See **TRUSTS**)
Uniform Transfers to Minors Act (See **UNIFORM TRANSFERS TO MINORS ACT**)
Voluntary transfer defined   CC §1040

TRANSIENT OCCUPANCY
Generally (See **HOTELS AND MOTELS**)
Recordkeeping required for accepting reservations or money for transient occupancy in common interest developments, apartment buildings or single-family homes   CC §1864

TRANSITIONAL HOUSING PROGRAM MISCONDUCT   CC §§1954.10 to 1954.18
Definitions   CC §1954.12

TRANSITIONAL HOUSING PROGRAM MISCONDUCT—Cont.
  Exclusion from site
    Clear and convincing evidence for order   CC §1954.13
    Contempt of order, modification to exclude participant   CC §1954.14
    Recovery of dwelling
      Participant's property, reasonable opportunity to recover   CC §1954.18
      Program operator's taking of possession   CC §1954.17
  Forms
    Judicial council legal forms   CRCAppx A
  Injunctions or temporary restraining orders   CC §§1954.13 to 1954.16
    Affidavits   CC §1954.13
    Exclusion from site
      Clear and convincing evidence for order   CC §1954.13
      Contempt of order, modification to exclude participant   CC §1954.14
      Recovery of dwelling   CC §§1954.17, 1954.18
    Forms and instructions to implement provisions
      Judicial council duties   CC §1954.16
    Notice   CC §1954.13
      Law enforcement notified of order or injunction   CC §1954.14
    Petitions by program operators   CC §1954.13
    Violation of order
      Unlawful detainer, effect of violation of order   CC §1954.15
      Willful disobedience as misdemeanor   CC §1954.14
  Legislative findings and intent   CC §1954.11
  Short title of provisions   CC §1954.10

TRANSLATORS AND INTERPRETERS   Ev §§750 to 757
Administrative law proceedings (See **ADMINISTRATIVE ADJUDICATION**)
Appointments   CRC 2.893, CRCSupp JudEthicsCanon 3
Certification
  Criminal and juvenile delinquency proceedings, appointment of noncertified interpreters for   CRC 2.894
  Deaf persons, guidelines for programs certifying interpreters for   CRC 2.892
Confidentiality of information   CRC 2.890
Conflicts of interest, avoidance of   CRC 2.890
Continuing education requirements   CRC 2.890
Costs
  Court interpreter fees   CCP §1033.5
Court interpreters
  Advisory panel   CRC 10.51
  Appointments by judges   CRC 2.893, CRCSupp JudEthicsCanon 3
  Certification and professional conduct   CRC 2.890 to 2.895
  Certified or registered interpreters
    Statements on record   CRC 2.893
  Court interpreters advisory panel   CRC 10.51
  Credential review
    Request for court interpreter credential review   CRC 2.891
  Determination of need   CRC JudAdminStand 2.10
  Disciplinary procedures
    Credential review, requests   CRC 2.891
  Examination to determine need   CRC JudAdminStand 2.10
  Instructions to counsel   CRC JudAdminStand 2.11
  Instructions to interpreters   CRC JudAdminStand 2.11
  Intermediary interpreters when two non-English languages involved   CRC 2.893
  Legislative intent   Gov §68092.1
  Noncertified or nonregistered interpreters
    Statements on record   CRC 2.893
    When permitted   CRC 2.893
  Preappearance interview, good cause for   CRC JudAdminStand 2.10
  Provisionally qualified interpreters
    Criteria for provisional qualification   CRC 2.893
    Limitation on repeat appointments   CRC 2.893
  Provision of interpreter regardless of income of parties   Gov §68092.1
  Record of examination to determine need   CRC JudAdminStand 2.10
  Temporary interpreters
    Findings on record   CRC 2.893
    When permitted   CRC 2.893
Court operations costs, salaries and benefits of court personnel as   CRC 10.810
Court proceedings   Ev §§750 to 757
Credential review
  Request for court interpreter credential review   CRC 2.891
Cross-assignments for court interpreter employees   CRC 10.762
Custody of children, public provision of interpreters for proceedings to determine   Fam §3032
Deaf persons
  Administrative adjudicative proceeding   Gov §11435.10
  Court-appointed interpreters for   Ev §754
  Privileged communications of   Ev §754.5

TRANSLATORS AND INTERPRETERS—Cont.
Disciplinary procedures
    Credential review, requests   CRC 2.891
Domestic violence cases (See **DOMESTIC VIOLENCE**)
Ethical violations, duty to report   CRC 2.890
Fees   Ev §752
    Administrative adjudicative proceeding (See **ADMINISTRATIVE ADJUDICATION**)
    Deaf persons, interpreter fees for   Ev §754
    Payment of   Gov §68092
    Translators, when required   Ev §753
Filing oath of translator or interpreter   Ev §751
Forms
    Judicial council legal forms   CRCAppx A
Functional budget categories   CRC 10.810
Harassment, translation of court orders concerning   CCP §185
Hard-of-hearing persons (See within this heading, "**Deaf persons**")
Immigrants
    Juveniles
        Determination of special immigrant juvenile status   Ev §757
Instructions for   CRC JudAdminStand 2.11
Intermediary interpreters, court appointment of   Ev §754
Judicial Council standards for   CRC JudAdminStand 2.10, CRC JudAdminStand 2.11
Juror with physical disability, use of service provider for   CCP §224
Labor and employment relations
    Cross-assignments for court interpreter employees   CRC 10.762
    Regional court interpreter employment relations   CRC 10.761
Language assistance service providers
    Forms   CRCAppx A
Medical examination
    Generally   Ev §755.5
    Administrative law proceedings (See **ADMINISTRATIVE ADJUDICATION**)
Noncertified or nonregistered spoken language interpreters
    Forms
        Judicial council official forms   CRCAppx A
Notice by attorney if party requesting interpreter will not be appearing   CRC 2.895
Oath of   Ev §751
Privileged communications of hearing-impaired persons, use of interpreters facilitating   Ev §754.5
Professional conduct   CRC 2.890
Proof of execution of instruments, officers calling interpreters for   CC §1201
Qualified interpreters, court appointment of   Ev §754
Record of translator's or interpreter's oath   Ev §751
Reimbursement to courts for services of court interpreter   Ev §756
Requests for interpreters
    Forms, judicial council   CRCAppx A
    Procedures for handling requests   CRC 2.895
    Tracking requests   CRC 2.895
Right to use   Ev §§752 to 757
Sign language interpreters generally
    Deaf persons generally (See within this heading, "**Deaf persons**")
State agency adjudicative proceedings (See **ADMINISTRATIVE ADJUDICATION**)
Sterilization proceedings, facilitator in (See **STERILIZATION**)
Will written in foreign language   Pro §8002
Workplace violence, translation of court orders concerning   CCP §185
Written materials
    Translators, when required   Ev §753

TRANSMITTERS
Subcutaneous implanting of identification device, requiring of another   CC §52.7

TRANSMUTATION OF MARITAL PROPERTY (See **COMMUNITY PROPERTY**)

TRANSPORTATION
Aircraft and aviation (See **AIRCRAFT AND AVIATION**)
Automobiles (See **AUTOMOBILES**)
Bicycles (See **BICYCLES**)
Buses (See **BUSES**)
Common carriers (See **COMMON CARRIERS**)
Elevators (See **ELEVATORS**)
Motor carriers (See **MOTOR CARRIERS**)
Public Utilities Commission regulating (See **PUBLIC UTILITIES COMMISSION**)
Street railways (See **STREET RAILWAYS**)
Taxis (See **TAXIS**)
Trains (See **RAILROADS**)
Vessels (See **VESSELS**)

TRANSPORTATION DEPARTMENT
Eminent domain taking by   CCP §1245.210

TRASH (See **GARBAGE**)

TRAUMATIC BRAIN INJURY
Veterans
    Orders for dismissal
        Judicial council legal forms   CRCAppx A
    Petition for resentencing, form   CRCAppx A

TRAVELER'S CHECKS
Court clerks, payments to   CRC 10.821
Credit card number notation as condition of acceptance for negotiable instruments, prohibited use of   CC §1725
Escheat   CCP §§1511, 1513, 1542, 1581

TRAVEL EXPENSES
Business oversight commissioner, hearings on sale of savings and loan association properties in possession of   CCP §73d
Jury   CCP §§215, 631, 631.5
Jury commissioner   CCP §196
Superior court appellate division, judges designated as members of   CCP §77
Visitation of child, travel expenses for   Fam §4062

TREASURER
Administration of decedent's estate (See **ADMINISTRATION OF ESTATES**)
Common carrier selling unclaimed property, disposition of proceeds   CC §2081.3
Credit denied because of marital status, distribution of fines for   CC §1812.33
Escheat (See **ESCHEAT**)
Public administrator depositing funds with   Pro §§7640 to 7644

TREASURY
Artists, deposit of money owed to   CC §986
Deposits in court
    Deposit with treasury   CCP §573
Eminent domain compensation deposited in   CCP §1255.070
Expert testimony, payment of costs of   Ev §731

TREBLE DAMAGES
Buyer's choice act
    Choice of escrow agent and title insurer lies with buyer   CC §1103.22
Child support, assisting obligor in avoiding payment   CC §§1714.4, 1714.41
Deeds of trust and mortgages
    Foreclosure prevention
        Enforcement   CC §2924.12
Fire hydrants
    Junk dealers or recyclers
        Wrongful possession of hydrants or fire department connections   CC §3336.5
Forcible entry   CCP §735
Human trafficking   CC §52.5
Public social services
    Unreasonable fees to assist applicants for public social services as deceptive practice   CC §1780
Sexual exploitation
    Commercial sexual exploitation, minor or nonminor dependent victims   CC §3345.1
Trees or timber, liability for injuries to   CCP §§733, 734
Unfair trade practices actions
    Public social services
        Unreasonable fees to assist applicants for public social services as deceptive practice   CC §1780
Unlawful detainer   CCP §735
Unlicensed person, action for injury caused by   CCP §1029.8
Usury   CC §1916.12-3
Waste, actions for recovery of treble damages for   CCP §732

TREES
Generally   CC §660
Damages for injury to   CC §3346, CCP §733
Damages recoverable for taking   CCP §§733, 734
Logs and timber (See **LOGS AND TIMBER**)
Ownership of   CC §§660, 833, 834

TRESPASS ON LAND
Attorney's fees for trespass of land under agricultural use   CCP §1021.9
Eminent domain, entry on premises for preliminary studies for   CCP §§1245.010 to 1245.060
Fur-bearing animals   CC §996

TRESPASS ON LAND—Cont.
Invasion of privacy
Unauthorized entry onto land or airspace above land to capture visual image or sound recording or other physical impression of plaintiff engaged in personal or familial activity   CC §1708.8
Statutes of limitation
Generally   CCP §338
Tenants' rights information dissemination or participation in tenants' association, entry on property for purpose of   CC §1942.6

TRESPASS TO TRY TITLE (See **QUIETING TITLE**)

TRIAL
Ability to pay program
Infractions
Online trial   Gov §68645.4
Absence of party, notice of trial where   CCP §594
Adjournment (See **ADJOURNMENTS**)
Administration of estates (See **ADMINISTRATION OF ESTATES**)
Appearance at (See **APPEARANCE**)
Arbitration, request for trial after   CCP §1141.20
Judicial arbitration   CRC 3.826
Arguments, time for presenting   CCP §607
Assistive listening systems for hard-of-hearing persons, courtroom use of   CC §54.8
Attorney professional conduct
Trial publicity   ProfC 3.6
Attorneys (See **ATTORNEYS**)
Audio taping
Broadcasting, photographing or recording of court proceedings   CRC 1.150
Bench trials (See **NONJURY TRIALS**)
Bifurcated trials
Dismissal of petition, when not appropriate   CCP §583.161
Broadcast coverage (See **RADIO AND TELEVISION**)
Calendar (See **CALENDAR**)
Case management rules (See **TRIAL COURT DELAY REDUCTION**)
Charging the jury
Instructions to jury (See **JURY**)
Conservatees, right to jury trial by   Pro §§1452, 1453, 1823, 1826 to 1828, 1863
Consolidation (See **CONSOLIDATION**)
Contempt, trial for   CCP §1217
Continuances (See **CONTINUANCES**)
Coordination proceedings   CRC 3.500 to 3.550
Costs (See **COSTS**)
Date
Setting trial date
Civil case management   CRC 3.729
Decedents' estates, trial procedure for issues involving   Pro §§1000 to 1051
Delay in prosecution, dismissal for (See **DISMISSAL**)
Delay reduction rules (See **TRIAL COURT DELAY REDUCTION**)
De novo (See **NEW TRIAL**)
Depositions (See **DEPOSITIONS**)
Differential case management rules (See **TRIAL COURT DELAY REDUCTION**)
Dismissal (See **DISMISSAL**)
Electronic recordings
Broadcasting, photographing or recording of court proceedings   CRC 1.150
English language, proceedings to be in   CCP §185
Evidence (See **EVIDENCE**)
Exhibits (See **EXHIBITS**)
Expedited jury trials, civil   CRC 3.1545 to 3.1553
Generally (See **EXPEDITED JURY TRIALS**)
Mandatory expedited jury trial (See **EXPEDITED JURY TRIALS**)
Voluntary expedited jury trials   CCP §§630.01 to 630.11 (See **EXPEDITED JURY TRIALS**)
Family law forms
Separate trial
Application for separate trial   CRCAppx A (CRCFL-315)
Family rules
Separate trial of certain issues   CRC 5.390
Findings (See **FINDINGS**)
Form of notice of trial   CCP §594
Guardian ad litem (See **GUARDIAN AD LITEM**)
Heirship proceedings, rules of   Pro §§11700 to 11705
Infractions
Ability to pay program
Online trial   Gov §68645.4
Injunction against trial of case   CC §3423, CCP §526
Instructions to jury (See **JURY**)
Interpleader   CCP §386

TRIAL—Cont.
Issues of law   CCP §591
Judges (See **JUDGES**)
Judicial administration standards for trial management   CRC JudAdminStand 2.20
Judicial arbitration (See **JUDICIAL ARBITRATION**)
Jurisdiction (See **JURISDICTION**)
Jury trial (See **JURY**)
Management of trial, judge's responsibilities   CRC JudAdminStand 2.20
Media coverage of court proceedings   CRC 1.150
Mistrial (See **MISTRIAL**)
Modification of award   CCP §1141.22
Newspapers and magazines covering trials (See **NEWSPAPERS AND MAGAZINES**)
New trial (See **NEW TRIAL**)
Nonjury trials (See **NONJURY TRIALS**)
Nonsuit   CCP §581c
Notice of   CCP §594
Order of proceedings   CCP §607
Partition   CCP §§872.610 to 872.840
Photographic recording of   CRC 1.150
Pleading (See **PLEADINGS**)
Preference in setting for trial (See **PRIORITIES AND PREFERENCES**)
Pretrial arbitration (See **JUDICIAL ARBITRATION**)
Pretrial conferences (See **PRETRIAL CONFERENCES**)
Priority on calendar (See **PRIORITIES AND PREFERENCES**)
Publicity activities by attorneys
Attorney professional conduct   ProfC 3.6
Radio and television coverage (See **RADIO AND TELEVISION**)
Related cause of action (See **RELATED CAUSE OF ACTION**)
Remote appearances
Evidentiary hearing or trial   CRC 3.672
Retrial of action where jury discharged without rendering verdict   CCP §616
Rules of court
Trial court rules generally   CRC 2.1 to 2.1100 (See **TRIAL COURT RULES**)
Service of notice of trial   CCP §594
Setting for trial
Date for trial
Civil case management   CRC 3.729
Judge's power to act, effect of proceedings for disqualification on   CCP §170.4
Motion to advance, reset, or specially set   CRC 3.1335
Preference, setting for trial on grant of motion for   CCP §36
Small claims court, hearing in   CCP §116.330
Superior courts (See **SUPERIOR COURTS**)
Severance (See **SEVERANCE**)
Special defenses   CCP §597
Special findings by jury, request for   CRC 3.1580
Statement of decision (See **STATEMENT OF DECISION**)
Submission of cause   CRC 2.900
Superior courts (See **SUPERIOR COURTS**)
Television and radio coverage (See **RADIO AND TELEVISION**)
Time limits for bringing case to trial
COVID-19, emergency rule   CRCAppx I Emer Rule 10
Transcripts
Court reporters generally (See **COURT REPORTERS**)
Trial court delay reduction rules (See **TRIAL COURT DELAY REDUCTION**)
Trial de novo (See **NEW TRIAL**)
Unlawful detainer (See **UNLAWFUL DETAINER**)
Venue change (See **VENUE**)
Will probate proceedings (See **WILL PROBATE**)
Written declaration, trial by for Vehicle Code infractions   CRC 4.210

TRIAL COURT COORDINATION PLAN (See **JUDICIAL ADMINISTRATION STANDARDS**)

TRIAL COURT DELAY REDUCTION
Applicability of Act   Gov §§68605.5, 68608
Authorization for delay reduction programs   Gov §§68600, 68603
Case disposition time standards   CRC JudAdminStand 2.2
Case management, civil   CRC 3.700 to 3.771
Case-management plans   Gov §68603
Challenge to judge, prohibition on removal of case from program for   Gov §68607.5
Civil action mediation
Coordination   CRC 3.896
Civil Action Mediation Act, coordination with   CCP §1775.15
Civil case disposition time goals
Judicial administration standards   CRC JudAdminStand 2.2

TRIAL COURT DELAY REDUCTION—Cont.
Continuances
    Judges' obligation to discourage continuances   Gov §68607
    Stipulated continuances   Gov §§68604, 68616
Contracting out of Judicial Council duties under Act   Gov §68615
Disposition time standards   CRC JudAdminStand 2.2
Domestic relations cases as exempted from assignment to program   Gov §68608
Effective dates   Gov §§68603, 68605.5
Exceptional criminal cases
    Case disposition time goals   CRC JudAdminStand 2.2
Felony cases
    Case disposition time goals   CRC JudAdminStand 2.2
    Preliminary examinations
        Case disposition time goals   CRC JudAdminStand 2.2
    Superior court cases, case-disposition time standards for   CRC JudAdminStand 2.2
Filing of standards, policies, and procedures   Gov §68612
Funding of programs   Gov §68613
Goal of programs   CRC JudAdminStand 2.1, CRC JudAdminStand 2.2
    Generally   Gov §68603
    Case-disposition time standards   CRC JudAdminStand 2.2
Individual case management
    Case disposition time goals   CRC JudAdminStand 2.2
Judges
    Challenge to judge, prohibition on removal of case from program for   Gov §68607.5
    Responsibilities under act   CRC JudAdminStand 2.1, Gov §68607
    Sanctions, power to impose   Gov §68608
    Training program   Gov §68610
Juvenile cases as exempted from assignment to program   Gov §68608
Limited civil cases
    Case disposition time goals   CRC JudAdminStand 2.2
Local rules
    Obstructive   CRC JudAdminStand 2.1
    Review of local rules by Judicial Council   Gov §68619
Mediation submissions, coordination with   CRC 3.896
Minimum time periods for procedures   Gov §68616
Misdemeanor cases
    Case disposition time goals   CRC JudAdminStand 2.2
Probate cases as exempted from assignment to program   Gov §68608
Publication
    Standards, policies, and procedures   Gov §68612
    Statistics   Gov §68604
Removal of case from court's control
    Computation of time, exclusion from case disposition time   CRC JudAdminStand 2.2
Sanctions, judges' power to impose   Gov §68608
Small claims cases   Gov §68620
    Case disposition time goals   CRC JudAdminStand 2.2
Standards
    Case-disposition time standards   CRC JudAdminStand 2.2
    Minimum time periods for procedures   Gov §68616
Statement of principles   CRC JudAdminStand 2.1
Statistics, compilation and publication of   Gov §68604
Stipulated continuances   Gov §§68604, 68616
Superior courts   Gov §68620
Uniform Delay Reduction Rules, Judicial Council adoption of   Gov §68619
Uninsured motorist cases   Gov §68609.5
Unlawful detainer cases   Gov §68620
    Case disposition time goals   CRC JudAdminStand 2.2
Unlimited civil cases
    Case disposition time goals   CRC JudAdminStand 2.2

TRIAL COURT EMPLOYEES
Witnesses, trial court employees as
    Fees   Gov §68097.2
    Subpoena   Gov §68097.1

TRIAL COURT, JUDICIAL BRANCH EDUCATION
Executive officers   CRC 10.473
Judges   CRC 10.462
Managers, supervisors and personnel   CRC 10.474
Subordinate judicial officers   CRC 10.462
    Additional education recommendations for certain judicial assignments   CRC 10.469

TRIAL COURT MANAGEMENT (See **JUDICIAL ADMINISTRATION RULES**)

TRIAL COURT OPERATIONS FUND
Food and lodging of jurors   CCP §217

TRIAL COURT RECORDS   CRC 2.400
Electronic court records   CRC 2.500 to 2.545

TRIAL COURT RULES   CRC 2.1 to 2.1100
Access to electronic court records   CRC 2.500 to 2.545
Address of attorneys
    Change of address
        Service and filing of notice   CRC 2.200
    Papers, first page format and content   CRC 2.111
Amount demanded
    Papers, first page format and content   CRC 2.111
Applicability   CRC 2.2
Attorneys
    Name, address, telephone number, bar membership number, etc
        Papers, first page format and content   CRC 2.111
Bar membership number
    Papers, first page format and content   CRC 2.111
Case management
    Sealing records
        False claims act, filing records under seal   CRC 2.573
Character of action or proceeding
    Papers, first page format and content   CRC 2.111
Civil trial court management rules
    Management duties   CRC 10.901
Court interpreters   CRC 2.890 to 2.895
Court reporting
    Civil cases
        Availability of reporter services   CRC 2.956
    Fees   CRC 2.956
Cover sheets
    Sealing records
        False claims act, filing records under seal   CRC 2.571
Definitions   CRC 2.3
Documents
    Duplicates for temporary judge or referee   CRC 2.400
    Original documents filed with clerk   CRC 2.400
    Removal of court records   CRC 2.400
Electronic court records   CRC 2.500 to 2.545
Electronic filing and service rules   CRC 2.250 to 2.261
Electronic recordings offered as evidence
    Transcript to be included   CRC 2.1040
Email address
    Papers, first page format and content   CRC 2.118
        Acceptance of noncomplying papers for filing   CRC 2.118
Exhibits
    Electronic filing of papers
        Applicable rule   CRC 2.114
    Papers
        Inclusion of exhibits with papers   CRC 2.114
    Return   CRC 2.400
Extending time
    Orders extending   CRC 2.20
    Sealing records
        False claims act, filing records under seal   CRC 2.572
False claims act, filing records under seal   CRC 2.570 to 2.573
Fax filing and service   CRC 2.300 to 2.306
Fax number
    Papers, first page format and content   CRC 2.118
        Acceptance of noncomplying papers for filing   CRC 2.118
Filing
    Acceptance of papers for filing   CRC 2.118
    Change of address of party or attorney
        Notice, service and filing   CRC 2.200
    Drop box   CRC 2.210
    Electronic filing and service rules   CRC 2.250 to 2.261
    False claims act, filing under seal   CRC 2.570 to 2.573
    Fax filing and service   CRC 2.300 to 2.306
    Local court forms   CRC 10.614
    Seal, filing records under   CRC 2.551
Forms
    Applicability of provisions   CRC 2.130, 2.140, 2.150
    Handwritten or handprinted forms   CRC 2.135
    Hole punching   CRC 2.133
    Judicial council forms
        Applicability of provisions   CRC 2.130, 2.140
    Local court forms   CRC 2.141, 10.614
        Applicability of provisions   CRC 2.130, 2.150
    Multiple page forms   CRC 2.134
    Papers
        Inapplicability of provisions to judicial council forms, local forms or juvenile dependence forms   CRC 2.119

TRIAL COURT RULES—Cont.
  Forms—Cont.
    Proof of service of summons and complaint
      Computer-generated or typewritten forms   CRC 2.150
    Recycled paper   CRC 2.131
    True copy
      Filing as certification that form is true copy   CRC 2.132
    Handwritten or handprinted forms   CRC 2.135
  In-camera proceedings
    Sealing records
      Confidential in-camera proceedings   CRC 2.585
  Interpreters   CRC 2.890 to 2.895
    Accurate translation   CRC 2.890
    Appointment in court proceedings   CRC 2.893
    Certification
      Approval of certification programs   CRC 2.892
      Reports on appointment of certified/registered interpreters   CRC 2.894
    Complete translation   CRC 2.890
    Confidentiality   CRC 2.890
    Conflicts of interest   CRC 2.890
    Credential review
      Request for court interpreter credential review   CRC 2.891
    Disciplinary procedures
      Credential review, requests   CRC 2.891
    Noncertified interpreters
      Reports on appointment of noncertified/nonregistered interpreters   CRC 2.894
    Notice by attorney if party requesting interpreter will not be appearing   CRC 2.895
    Professional conduct   CRC 2.890
    Requests for interpreters
      Forms, judicial council   CRCAppx A
      Procedures for handling requests   CRC 2.895
      Tracking requests   CRC 2.895
  Judges
    Name of judge to which cause assigned
      Papers, first page format and content   CRC 2.111
    Robes   CRC 10.505
    Temporary judges   CRC 2.810 to 2.835
  Jury
    Breastfeeding
      Deferral from jury service   CRC 2.1006
    Communications with or from
      Record, inclusion within   CRC 2.1030
    Excuse from jury service   CRC 2.1008
      Medical excuse, permanent   CRC 2.1009
    Impasse
      Assisting jury at impasse   CRC 2.1036
    Instructions to jury
      Civil cases, applicable rules   CRC 3.1580
      Gender neutral language   CRC 2.1058
      Impasse, assisting jury   CRC 2.1036
      Judicial council jury instructions   CRC 2.1050
      Preinstruction   CRC 2.1035
      Proposed jury instructions   CRC 2.1055
    Length of service   CRC 2.1002
    Medical excuse   CRC 2.1008
      Permanent medical excuse from jury service   CRC 2.1009
    Motion to set aside sanctions imposed by default   CRC 2.1010
    Notebooks
      Complex civil cases, preparation for benefit of jurors   CRC 2.1032
    Note-taking
      Permitted   CRC 2.1031
    Preinstruction   CRC 2.1035
    Questions from jurors   CRC 2.1033
    Scheduling accommodations for jurors
      One-time deferral   CRC 2.1004
  Limited civil cases
    Amount demanded
      Papers, first page format and content   CRC 2.111
  Local court forms   CRC 2.141, 10.614
    Applicability of provisions   CRC 2.130, 2.150
  Management
    Civil trial court management rules
      Management duties   CRC 10.901
    False claims act, filing records under seal
      Case management   CRC 2.573
  Name changes
    Address confidentiality program for victims of certain crimes, proceedings for   CRC 2.575 to 2.577
      Applicability   CRC 2.575

TRIAL COURT RULES—Cont.
  Name changes—Cont.
    Address confidentiality program for victims of certain crimes, proceedings for —Cont.
      Cover sheets   CRC 2.575
      Current name, confidentiality   CRC 2.575, 2.576
      Definitions   CRC 2.575
      Lodging petition, sealed cases   CRC 2.577
      Procedures to obtain access   CRC 2.576
      Proposed name, confidentiality   CRC 2.575
      Seal, proceedings under   CRC 2.577
      Termination of confidentiality   CRC 2.576
  Nature of paper
    Papers, first page format and content   CRC 2.111
  Number of case
    Papers, first page format and content   CRC 2.111
  Papers
    Acceptance for filing   CRC 2.118
    Binding   CRC 2.113
    Changes to contents
      Noting and initialing by clerk or judge   CRC 2.116
    Color
      Font color   CRC 2.106
      White paper only   CRC 2.103
    Copies
      Conformity to originals   CRC 2.117
    Electronic format of papers
      Applicable rule   CRC 2.100
    Exhibits   CRC 2.114
    False claims act, filing under seal   CRC 2.571
    Fax filing and service
      Documents for faxing to comply with provisions   CRC 2.302
      Generally   CRC 2.300 to 2.306
    First page format and content   CRC 2.111
    Fonts   CRC 2.105
      Footers   CRC 2.110
      Size   CRC 2.104
    Footers   CRC 2.110
    Footnotes   CRC 2.108
    Form and format requirements
      Applicable rules   CRC 2.100
    Forms
      Inapplicability of provisions to judicial council forms, local forms or juvenile dependence forms   CRC 2.119
    Hole punching   CRC 2.115
    Local court forms   CRC 10.614
    Local rules on form and format of papers
      Preemption   CRC 2.100
    Margins   CRC 2.107
    Noncomplying papers
      Acceptance for filing   CRC 2.118
    Numbering of lines   CRC 2.108
    Numbering of pages   CRC 2.109
    One side only   CRC 2.102
    Page numbering   CRC 2.109
    Quality of paper   CRC 2.103
    Quotations   CRC 2.108
    Separate causes, counts and defenses
      Contents   CRC 2.112
    Size   CRC 2.103
    Spacing of lines   CRC 2.108
    Weight of paper   CRC 2.103
  Parties
    Address, change
      Service and filing of notice   CRC 2.200
  Process and service of process
    Change of address of party or attorney
      Notice, service and filing   CRC 2.200
    Electronic filing and service rules   CRC 2.250 to 2.261
    Fax filing and service   CRC 2.300 to 2.306
    Proof of service, forms
      Computer-generated or typewritten forms for proof of summons and complaint   CRC 2.150
  Reclassified proceedings
    Papers, first page format and content   CRC 2.111
  Record of proceedings
    Jury communications
      Inclusion in record   CRC 2.1030
  Records of court   CRC 2.400
    Electronic court records   CRC 2.500 to 2.545
    Sealing records   CRC 2.550, 2.551

TRIAL

TRIAL COURT RULES—Cont.
Recycled paper
    Forms   CRC 2.131
Referees
    Papers, first page format and content   CRC 2.111
Sanctions
    Civil cases   CRC 2.30
Scope of rules   CRC 2.10
Sealing records   CRC 2.550, 2.551
    Applicability of provisions   CRC 2.550
    Definitions   CRC 2.550
    Delayed public disclosure
        Request   CRC 2.580
    Factual findings necessary to seal   CRC 2.550
    False claims act, filing records under seal   CRC 2.570 to 2.573
        Access to records   CRC 2.570
        Applicability   CRC 2.570
        Case management   CRC 2.573
        Confidentiality of records filed under act   CRC 2.570
        Cover sheet   CRC 2.571
        Custody of sealed records   CRC 2.571
        Definitions   CRC 2.570
        Extension of time, motion for   CRC 2.572
        Multiple filing locations, procedure   CRC 2.571
        Order not required   CRC 2.571
        Procedures for filing   CRC 2.571
        Unsealing records   CRC 2.573
    Filing records under seal
        Court approval   CRC 2.551
        False claims act, filing records under seal   CRC 2.570 to 2.573
        Motion to seal   CRC 2.551
    Findings
        Express findings required   CRC 2.550
    In-camera proceedings
        Confidential proceedings   CRC 2.585
    Lodging records requested to be sealed   CRC 2.551
        Definition of lodged   CRC 2.550
    Name changes
        Address confidentiality program for victims of certain crimes, proceedings for   CRC 2.577
    Nonpublic material
        Referral to nonpublic material in public records   CRC 2.551
    Order sealing records   CRC 2.551
        Content   CRC 2.550
        Scope of order sealing   CRC 2.550
    Prejudgment attachment
        Delayed public disclosure, request for   CRC 2.580
    Presumption of openness of records   CRC 2.550
    Scope of order sealing   CRC 2.550
    Temporary judges
        Motion to seal records   CRC 2.835
Submission of cause in trial court   CRC 2.900
Temporary judges   CRC 2.810 to 2.835
Time
    Extending or shortening
        Application for order extending   CRC 2.20
        False claims act, filing records under seal, extension   CRC 2.572
Title of case
    Papers, first page format and content   CRC 2.111
Title of court
    Papers, first page format and content   CRC 2.111
Title of set of rules   CRC 2.1
Transcripts
    Electronic recordings offered as evidence
        Transcript to be included   CRC 2.1040
Unconstitutionality of statute or regulation declared
    Attorney general, notice to   CRC 2.1100

TRIAL DE NOVO (See **NEW TRIAL**)

TRIAL JURY SELECTION AND MANAGEMENT ACT   CCP §§190 to 236

TRIAL SETTING CONFERENCE
Superior courts (See **SUPERIOR COURTS**)
Telephone, appearance by   CCP §367.5
    Fees   CCP §367.6

TRIBAL COURT CIVIL MONEY JUDGMENT ACT   CCP §§1730 to 1741
Appeals
    Stay of enforcement   CCP §1738

TRIBAL COURT CIVIL MONEY JUDGMENT ACT—Cont.
Applicability of provisions   CCP §1731
    Effective date   CCP §1741
Application for recognition and entry of judgment   CCP §1733
    Attachments   CCP §1734
    Contents   CCP §1734
    Joint application by parties to tribal court proceeding   CCP §1733.1
    Notice of filing   CCP §1735
    Perjury
        Execution of application under penalty of perjury   CCP §1734
    Process for application   CCP §1733.1
Communications by superior court with tribal court   CCP §1740
Definitions   CCP §1732
Family law
    Property division
        Retirement benefits, payments pursuant to tribal court order   Fam §2611
Objections
    Grounds for objection   CCP §1737
    Lack of objections   CCP §1736
    Time for service and filing   CCP §1737
Recognition of tribal court judgments
    Procedure   CCP §1731
Short title of provisions   CCP §1730
Statute of limitations
    Time for action to recognize   CCP §1739
Stay of enforcement   CCP §1738
Uniform foreign-country money judgments recognition act
    Pending actions, applicability   CCP §1741
Venue
    Application for recognition and entry of judgment   CCP §1733

TRIER OF FACT
Definition   Ev §235

TROVER
Claim and delivery (See **CLAIM AND DELIVERY**)
Conversion (See **CONVERSION**)

TRUANTS
Juvenile rules
    Access to pupil records   CRC 5.652
Records of pupil
    Access to pupil records   CRC 5.652
Truancy mediation program, disclosure of pupil records for
    Juvenile court proceedings   CRC 5.652

TRUCKERS (See **MOTOR CARRIERS**)

TRUCK STOPS
Human trafficking or slavery
    Signs, businesses required to post notice concerning relief from slavery or human trafficking   CC §52.6

TRUNKS (See **BAGGAGE**)

TRUST ACCOUNTS (See **TOTTEN TRUST ACCOUNTS**)

TRUST COMPANIES
Conservators (See **CONSERVATORS**)
Executors and administrators (See **EXECUTORS AND ADMINISTRATORS**)
Guardian and ward (See **GUARDIAN AND WARD**)

TRUST DECANTING, UNIFORM ACT   Pro §§19501 to 19530
Animal trusts
    Defined   Pro §19523
    Exercise of decanting power
        Care of animals   Pro §19523
Applicability of provisions   Pro §§19503, 19505
Appointive property
    Defined   Pro §19502
Ascertainable standard
    Defined   Pro §19502
Authorized fiduciary
    Defined   Pro §19502
Beneficiary
    Defined   Pro §19502
Beneficiary with disability
    Defined   Pro §19513
    Trust for beneficiary with disability   Pro §19513
Breach of trust
    Liability and indemnification of trustee
        Exercise of decanting power   Pro §19517

TRUST DECANTING, UNIFORM ACT—Cont.
  Charitable interest
    Defined   Pro §19502
    Protection of charitable interest   Pro §19514
  Charitable organization
    Defined   Pro §19502
  Compensation of trustee, change
    Exercise of decanting power   Pro §19516
  Court
    Defined   Pro §19502
    Involvement of court   Pro §19509
  Court involvement   Pro §19509
  Current beneficiary
    Defined   Pro §19502
  Decanting power
    Defined   Pro §19502
    Exercise of decanting power
      Animals, trust care   Pro §19523
      Charitable interest, protection   Pro §19514
      Compensation of trustee, change   Pro §19516
      Court involvement   Pro §19509
      Distributions, need to not required   Pro §19521
      Expanded distributive discretion   Pro §19511
      Later-discovered property, effect   Pro §19526
      Liability and indemnification of trustee for breach   Pro §19517
      Limitation in trust on decanting   Pro §19515
      Limited distributive discretion   Pro §19512
      Notice of intent to exercise   Pro §19507
      Removal of authorized fiduciary   Pro §19518
      Second trust not in compliance with provisions, saving provision   Pro §19522
      Special needs fiduciaries exercising for beneficiary with disability   Pro §19513
      Tax-related limitations   Pro §19519
      Writing and other formalities for exercise   Pro §19510
  Definitions   Pro §19502
    Animal trusts   Pro §19523
    Beneficiary with disability   Pro §19513
    Exercise of decanting power, expanded distributive discretion   Pro §19511
    Governmental benefits   Pro §19513
    Grantor trust   Pro §19519
    Limited distributive discretion   Pro §19512
    Nongrantor trusts   Pro §19519
    Protector   Pro §19523
    Qualified benefits property   Pro §19519
    Special needs fiduciaries   Pro §19513
    Special needs trusts   Pro §19513
  Determinable charitable interest
    Defined
      Charitable interest protection   Pro §19514
  Exercise of decanting power
    Animals, trust care   Pro §19523
    Approval
      Court involvement   Pro §19509
    Charitable interest, protection   Pro §19514
    Compensation of trustee, change   Pro §19516
    Distributions, need to not required   Pro §19521
    Expanded distributive discretion   Pro §19511
    Ineffective exercise, determination
      Court involvement   Pro §19509
    Later-discovered property
      Effect of later-discovered property   Pro §19526
    Liability and indemnification of trustee for breach
      Restrictions on power   Pro §19517
    Limitation in trust on decanting   Pro §19515
    Limited distributive discretion   Pro §19512
    Notice of intent to exercise   Pro §19507
    Removal of authorized fiduciary   Pro §19518
    Second trust not in compliance with provisions
      Saving provision   Pro §19522
    Special needs fiduciaries exercising for beneficiary with disability   Pro §19513
    Tax-related limitations   Pro §19519
    Writing and other formalities for exercise   Pro §19510
  Expanded distributive discretion
    Defined   Pro §19502
    Exercise of decanting power   Pro §19511
  Fiduciaries
    Court involvement   Pro §19509
    Duties under provisions   Pro §19504

TRUST DECANTING, UNIFORM ACT—Cont.
  Fiduciaries—Cont.
    Liability and indemnification of trustee
      Exercise of decanting power   Pro §19517
    Removal of authorized fiduciary
      Exercise of decanting power   Pro §19518
    Special needs fiduciaries   Pro §19513
      Exercise of decanting power, trust for beneficiary with a disability   Pro §19513
  First trust
    Defined   Pro §19502
  First trust instrument
    Defined   Pro §19502
  General power of appointment
    Defined   Pro §19502
  Governing law   Pro §19505
  Grantor trust
    Defined   Pro §19519
  Involvement of court   Pro §19509
  Later-discovered property
    Exercise of decanting power
      Effect of later-discovered property   Pro §19526
  Limitation in trust on decanting   Pro §19515
  Limited distributive discretion
    Defined   Pro §19512
  Noncontingent rights
    Defined
      Exercise of decanting power, expanded distributive discretion   Pro §19511
  Nongrantor trusts
    Defined   Pro §19519
  Notice
    Exercise of decanting power
      Notice of intent to exercise   Pro §19507
    Representation
      Effect of notice   Pro §19508
  Obligations enforceable against first trust enforceable on second or subsequent trusts   Pro §19527
  Petitions by trustee for instructions   Pro §19529
  Powerholders
    Defined   Pro §19502
  Presently exercisable power of appointment
    Defined   Pro §19502
  Presumptive remainder beneficiary
    Defined
      Exercise of decanting power, expanded distributive discretion   Pro §19511
  Protectors
    Defined   Pro §19523
  Qualified beneficiary
    Defined   Pro §19502
  Qualified benefits property
    Defined   Pro §19519
  Reasonably definite standard
    Defined   Pro §19502
  Scope of provisions   Pro §§19503, 19505
  Second trust
    Defined   Pro §19502
    Duration   Pro §19520
    Exercise of decanting power
      Second trust not in compliance with provisions, saving provision   Pro §19522
    Petitions by trustee for instructions   Pro §19529
    Settlor's intent
      Determination of intent   Pro §19525
    Trust instrument or terms of trusts
      References in probate code include second trusts under provisions   Pro §19524
  Second trust instrument
    Defined   Pro §19502
  Settlor
    Defined   Pro §19502
    First trust's settlor deemed to be settlor of second trust   Pro §19525
    Intent of settlor of second trust
      Determination of intent   Pro §19525
  Severability of provisions   Pro §19530
  Short title   Pro §19501
  Special needs fiduciaries
    Defined   Pro §19513
  Special needs trusts
    Defined   Pro §19513

TRUST DECANTING, UNIFORM ACT—Cont.
State
    Defined   Pro §19502
Statutory construction
    Severability of provisions   Pro §19530
Successor beneficiaries
    Defined
        Exercise of decanting power, expanded distributive discretion   Pro §19511
Taxation
    Exercise of decanting power
        Tax-related limitations   Pro §19519
Terms of the trust
    Defined   Pro §19502
The decanting power
    Defined   Pro §19502
Trust instrument
    Defined   Pro §19502
    References in probate code to trust instrument include second trusts under provisions   Pro §19524
Unconditional
    Defined
        Charitable interest protection   Pro §19514
Vested interests
    Defined
        Exercise of decanting power, expanded distributive discretion   Pro §19511

TRUST DEEDS AND MORTGAGES   CC §§2872 to 2968
Generally   CC §§2872 to 2877
Acceleration clauses   CC §§2924.5 to 2924.7, 2954.10
Accounting   CC §§2943, 2954, 2954.2
Account of rents and profits
    In action to redeem   CCP §346
    Proportionate to interest in mortgaged premises   CCP §347
Acknowledgment requirements   CC §2952
Adjustable rate mortgage loans
    Generally   CC §1916.7
    Information to prospective borrowers, requirements for   CC §1921
Administration of decedents' estates
    Generally (See **ADMINISTRATION OF ESTATES**)
Advertising for sale, restrictions on   CC §712
Agent for collection, notice requirements for   CC §2924.3
Ancient trust deeds (See **TITLE AND OWNERSHIP**)
Appraisals for purposes of deficiency judgments   CCP §§580a to 580e, 726
Asian languages
    Foreign language summaries of terms   CC §1632.5
    Reverse mortgages
        Asian language negotiations and contracts   CC §1632
Assignments
    Foreclosure
        Notification of assignees   CC §2924b
        Power of sale under assigned mortgage   CC §2932.5
    Forgery of trust deed, assignee's action for damages for   CCP §749.5
    General rule that assignment of debt carries security with it   CC §2936
    Leases, rents, issues, or profits
        Assignment, generally   CC §2938
        Receiver, appointment of   CC §2938, CCP §564
    Receivers, appointment of
        Generally   CCP §564
        Leases, rents, issues, or profits, assignment of   CC §2938, CCP §564
    Recording
        Generally   CC §2934
        Debtor, recordation as not constituting notice to   CC §2935
        Leases, rents, issues, or profits of real property, assignment of interest in   CC §2938
        Requirements for filing and recording documents   CC §§2924.12, 2924.17, 2924.19
Assumption of loans made by public entity   CC §711.5
Attachment, availability of (See **ATTACHMENT**)
Attorneys' fees associated with foreclosure   CC §2924d, CCP §§580c, 730
Auction
    Foreclosure (See within this heading, **"Foreclosure"**)
Avoiding foreclosure   CC §2924
    Approved alternative, effect   CC §2924.18
        Enforcement of provisions   CC §2924.19
    Communication by lender with borrower   CC §2923.5
        Damages to enforce   CC §2924.12
        Injunction to enforce   CC §§2924.12, 2924.19
    Communication to borrower as to availability of alternatives after recordation of notice of default   CC §2924.9

TRUST DEEDS AND MORTGAGES—Cont.
Avoiding foreclosure —Cont.
    First lien loan modification   CC §2923.6
        Acknowledging receipt of application or documentation   CC §2924.10
        Pending application, effect   CC §§2924.18, 2924.19
    Modification or workout plan   CC §2923.6
    Rulemaking to implement provisions   CC §2924.20
    Single point of contact   CC §2923.7
Balance due after exercise of power of sale, limitation of action for money judgment for   CCP §337
Balloon payments
    Generally   CC §2924i
    Purchase money liens on residential property   CC §§2957, 2966
Beneficiary
    Equity lines of credit
        Suspending and closing line, borrower's instruction   CC §2943.1
    Statements   CC §2943
Bonds authorized by financial protection and innovation commissioner   CC §2924c
Bonds on satisfaction of   CC §2941.7
Borrowers
    Defined   CC §2920.5
Business, transportation and housing agency secretary, authority of   CC §1918.5
Cancellation of private mortgage insurance or mortgage guaranty insurance, borrower's right to   CC §2954.6
Certificate of discharge   CC §§2939, 2940 to 2941.7
Chattel mortgages (See **CHATTEL MORTGAGES**)
Claims against estates (See **CLAIMS AGAINST ESTATES**)
Collection agent, notice requirement for   CC §2924.3
Commercial Code, applicability of foreclosure proceedings to security interest in personal property or fixtures subject to   CCP §730.5
Commercial Code, exemption of transactions and security interests governed by   CC §2944
Conflicting claims
    Notice to parties   CC §2924j
    State of California as party   CC §2931a
Construction trust deeds   CC §8174
Contracts written for assumption of debts under   CC §1624
Copies of notices of sale and default, procedure for obtaining   CC §2924b
Corporate bonds on satisfaction of   CC §2941.7
Costs and fees
    Discharge certificate, issuance of   CC §2941
    Foreclosure   CC §2924d
    Prepayment fees, restrictions on   CC §2954.10
    Reconveyance fees   CC §2941.1
    Reverse mortgages   CC §1923.2
    Unpaid balance statement   CC §2943
COVID-19
    Small landlord and homeowner relief act   CC §§3273.01 to 3273.16
        Action by borrower harmed by violation of provisions   CC §3273.15
        Applicability of provisions   CC §3273.2
        Communications about forbearance options   CC §3273.14
        Compliance with federal guidance regarding borrower options   CC §3273.11
        Definitions   CC §3273.1
        Denial of forbearance request by mortgage servicer   CC §3273.10
        Legislative intent   CC §3273.12
        Title of provisions   CC §3273.01
        Waiver of provisions prohibited   CC §3273.16
Criminal liability
    Discharge certificate, refusal of   CC §2941.5
    Foreclosure consultants, violations by   CC §2945.7
    Modification or workout plan to avoid foreclosure
        Notice provided to borrower   CC §2944.6
        Prohibited acts   CC §2944.7
    Trustee's sale, interfering with bidding at   CC §2924h
Decedents' estates
    Administration (See **ADMINISTRATION OF ESTATES**)
Declaration of satisfaction of   CC §2941.7
Defamation liability, default notice as privileged against   CC §2924
Default
    First lien loan modification   CC §2923.6
        Acknowledging receipt of application or documentation   CC §2924.10
        Approved alternative, effect   CC §§2924.18, 2924.19
        Pending application, effect   CC §§2924.18, 2924.19
    Modification or workout plan
        Single point of contact   CC §2923.7

TRUST DEEDS AND MORTGAGES—Cont.
  Default—Cont.
    Notice   CC §§2924.3, 2924b, 2924c
      Approval of foreclosure prevention measures, effect   CC §§2924.11, 2924.12
      Foreclosure avoidance options to be discussed prior to filing   CC §§2923.5, 2924.12, 2924.19
      Modification or workout plan   CC §2923.6
      Recorded notice of default   CC §§2923.3, 2923.55, 2924, 2924.26
      Requirements for filing and recording documents   CC §§2924.12, 2924.17, 2924.19
      Rescission of notice of default   CC §2924.11
      Timing   CC §§2923.5, 2924.12, 2924.15, 2924.19
      Title company immunity for recording notice of default or sale   CC §2924.26
Deficiency judgments   CCP §§580a to 580e, 726
Definitions   CC §§2920, 2920.5, 2924, 2957
Delinquency charges, notice of   CC §2954.5
Discharge of   CC §§2939 to 2941.7
Disclosures
  Adjustable rate mortgage loans   CC §1921
  General provisions concerning purchase money liens on residential property   CC §§2956 to 2968
  Purchase money liens on residential property   CC §§2956 to 2968
    Emergency declaration, property within geographic limits of declared area
      Information to be provided regarding repair of property   CC §2968
  Reverse mortgages (See within this heading, **"Reverse mortgages"**)
  Variable interest rate loans   CC §§1916.5, 1916.8, 1920
Discriminatory clauses in written instruments, prohibition against   CC §§53, 782
Due-on-sale clauses   CC §2954.10
Eminent domain compensation for impairment of security   CCP §§1265.210 to 1265.240
Enforcement of judgments (See **ENFORCEMENT OF JUDGMENTS**)
Environmental damage to real property security
  Action by secured lender against borrower for breach of environmental provisions relating to real property security   CCP §736
  Election of remedies of secured lender against defaulting borrower for   CCP §726.5
  Receivers, as grounds for appointment of   CCP §564
  Right of entry and inspection on land by secured lender   CC §2929.5, CCP §726.5
Equity lines of credit
  Suspending and closing line, borrower's instruction   CC §2943.1
Equity sales contracts (See **HOME EQUITY SALES CONTRACTS**)
Escheat of funds under bond   CC §2941.7
Family residence property, itemized accounting for   CC §2954.2
Fax machines, transmittal of statement of unpaid balance by   CC §2943
Fees
  Costs and fees generally (See within this heading, **"Costs and fees"**)
Fictitious trust deeds   CC §2952
Fiduciary duties of mortgage brokers   CC §2923.1
Fines and penalties
  Discharge certificate, refusal of   CC §2941.5
  Foreclosure consultants, violations by   CC §2945.7
  Modification or workout plan to avoid foreclosure
    Notice provided to borrower   CC §2944.6
    Prohibited acts   CC §2944.7
  Trustee's sale, interfering with bidding at   CC §2924h
First lien modification application
  Approval
    Damages to enforce   CC §2924.12
    Injunction to enforce   CC §§2924.12, 2924.19
  Definition for first lien   CC §2920.5
  Denial   CC §2924.11
Forbearances
  Modification or workout plan to avoid foreclosure   CC §2923.6
    Acknowledging receipt of application or documentation for first lien loan modification   CC §2924.10
    Approval of alternative, effect   CC §§2924.18, 2924.19
    First lien loan modification   CC §2923.6
    Pending application, effect   CC §§2924.18, 2924.19
    Single point of contact   CC §2923.7
    Notice provided to borrower   CC §2944.6
    Prohibited acts   CC §2944.7
      Disabled person victim of prohibited acts, punishment   CC §2944.8
      Senior citizen victim of prohibited acts, punishment   CC §2944.8
      Statute of limitations to enforce protections   CC §2944.10
Foreclosure   CCP §726
  Agent for collection, notice requirements of   CC §2924.3

TRUST DEEDS AND MORTGAGES—Cont.
  Foreclosure —Cont.
    Appraisals   CCP §726
    Assignment
      Notification of assignees   CC §2924b
      Power of sale under assigned mortgage   CC §2932.5
    Attachment in conjunction with foreclosure, viability of   CCP §483.012
    Attorneys
      Auctioneer, as   CC §2924a
    Attorneys' fees   CC §2924d, CCP §§580c, 730
    Auctions
      Generally   CC §§2924g, 2924h
      Attorney as auctioneer   CC §2924a
      State bids on real property   CC §2931b
    Certificate of sale   CCP §729.040
    Commercial Code, applicability of foreclosure proceedings to security interest in personal property or fixtures subject to   CCP §730.5
    Conflicting claims to proceeds of sale   CC §2924j
    Copies of notices of default and sale   CC §2924b
    Costs and fees, generally   CC §2924d
    COVID-19, emergency rule   CRCAppx I Emer Rule 2
    Deficiency judgments   CCP §§580a to 580e, 726
    Distribution of proceeds from sale   CC §2924k
    Environmental damage (See within this heading, **"Environmental damage to real property security"**)
    Environmentally impaired real property, secured lender's options regarding   CCP §726.5
    Financial institutions making Health and Building Code repairs to foreclosed residential property   CC §2932.6
    Fraud, lender's action against borrower for   CCP §726
    Health and Building Code repairs to foreclosed residential property, financial institutions making   CC §2932.6
    Home equity sales contracts (See **HOME EQUITY SALES CONTRACTS**)
    Injury to property pending foreclosure, restraint of   CCP §745
    Judgments   CCP §726
    Lessees notified of   CC §2924b
    Loss mitigation options
      Availability   CC §2923.4
    Mortgage foreclosure consultants   CC §§2945 to 2945.11
    Notice requirements   CC §§2924, 2924.3, 2924b, 2924c, 2924f
    Partial sales   CCP §728
    Place of sale   CC §2924g
    Possession, right to   CCP §744
    Postponement of sale   CC §2924g
    Power of sale   CC §§2924, 2932
      Common interest developments   CC §2924.1
      Conducting sale under power   CC §2924a
      Exercise of power of sale   CC §2924
      Notice of sale   CC §§2924, 2924f
      Postponement of sale   CC §§2924, 2924.15
    Prevention of foreclosures
      Application, effect of submission   CC §§2924.11, 2924.12
      Approval of preventive measures, effect   CC §§2924.11, 2924.12
      Communication to borrower as to availability of alternatives after recordation of notice of default   CC §2924.9
      Definition of foreclosure prevention alternatives   CC §2920.5
      Denial of application for prevention   CC §2924.11
      Enforcement by injunction and damages   CC §2924.12
      Exploration of options prior to recordation of notice of default   CC §2923.55
      Generally   CC §2924
      Loss mitigation options   CC §2923.4
      Rulemaking to implement provisions   CC §2924.20
    Processing fees   CCP §580c
    Public utility property   CC §2924
    Purchaser notified of   CC §2924b
    Purchaser's rights prior to redemption   CCP §729.090
    Receivers on   CCP §564
    Recovery   CCP §§580a to 580e
    Redemption (See within this heading, **"Redemption"**)
    Reinstatement prior to   CC §2924c
    Rescission generally (See within this heading, **"Rescission"**)
    Series of notes secured by same property or note secured by property equivalent to series transaction, beneficiaries' agreement to be governed by majority interest in   CC §2941.9
    Sheriff's fees for deed or certificate of redemption   Gov §26740
    Special administrator protecting from   Pro §8544
    Standing to sue, generally   CCP §725a
    State as party, action by   CC §§2931a to 2931c

TRUST DEEDS AND MORTGAGES—Cont.
Foreclosure —Cont.
    Stay
        COVID-19, emergency rule   CRCAppx I Emer Rule 2
    Successor in interest
        Bringing suit   CCP §725a
        Notification of   CC §2924b
    Surplus proceeds, disposal of   CCP §727
        Foreclosure consultant contract to assist in gaining release of surplus funds   CC §§2945.3, 2945.4
    Tax liens affecting   CC §§2931a to 2931c
    Trustee fees   CC §§2924c, 2924f
    Unlawful detainer, holding over after foreclosure sale as act constituting   CCP §1161a
    Waste enjoined   CCP §745
Foreclosure consultants   CC §§2945 to 2945.11
Foreign language summaries of terms   CC §1632.5
Forgery of trust deed
    Action for damages, generally   CCP §749
    Assignee or successor, action for damages by   CCP §749.5
Forms
    Curing of default, notice for   CC §2924c
    Request for notice of default   CC §2924b
    Statutory trust deeds   CC §2948
    Subordination agreement notices   CC §§2953.2, 2953.3
Fraud, lender's action against borrower for   CCP §726
Guardianship (See **GUARDIAN AND WARD**)
Hazard insurance coverage imposed by lender, limitations on   CC §2955.5
Hazardous substance releases (See within this heading, **"Environmental damage to real property security"**)
Home equity sales contracts (See **HOME EQUITY SALES CONTRACTS**)
Home improvement financing, unfair trade practice constituted by mortgage broker or lender negotiating through contractor to arrange   CC §1770
Impound accounts   CC §§2954, 2954.1, 2954.8, 2955
Insurance
    Acceleration of payments for failure to pay insurance premiums   CC §2924.7
    Continuous period with no expiration date, prohibition on refusal to accept policy for   CC §2944.5
    Hazard insurance coverage required by lender, limitations on   CC §2955.5
    Impound accounts   CC §§2954, 2954.1, 2954.8, 2955
    Private mortgage and mortgage guaranty insurance (See within this heading, **"Private mortgage and mortgage guaranty insurance"**)
Interest on loan
    Accrual of interest on secured promissory note   CC §2948.5
    Adjustable rate mortgages   CC §1916.7
        Information to prospective borrowers   CC §1921
    Balloon payments   CC §2924i
        Purchase money liens on residential property   CC §§2957, 2966
    Foreclosure consultants charging interest   CC §2945.4
    Modification or workout plan to avoid foreclosure
        Disabled person victim of prohibited acts, punishment   CC §2944.8
        Prohibited acts   CC §2944.7
        Senior citizen victim of prohibited acts, punishment   CC §2944.8
        Statute of limitations to enforce protections   CC §2944.10
    Reverse mortgages   CC §1923.2
    Variable interest rates (See within this heading, **"Variable interest rate loans"**)
Judgments and decrees
    Deficiency judgment on foreclosure   CCP §§580a to 580e, 726
    Enforcement of (See **ENFORCEMENT OF JUDGMENTS**)
Junior mortgage on single-family dwelling, default claimed because of   CC §2949
Kickback of fees, prohibition against   CC §2924d
Landlords
    Entry to exhibit dwelling unit to mortgagees   CC §1954
Late payment charges on loan secured by mortgage or trust deed   CC §§2954.4, 2954.5
Leases, rents, issues, or profits of real property, assignment of   CC §2938
    Receiver, appointment   CC §2938, CCP §564
Letters of credit supporting   CCP §580.5
Lien on property
    Modification or workout plan to avoid foreclosure
        Disabled person victim of prohibited acts, punishment   CC §2944.8
        Prohibited acts   CC §2944.7
        Senior citizen victim of prohibited acts, punishment   CC §2944.8
        Statute of limitations to enforce protections   CC §2944.10
Limitation of actions (See within this heading, **"Statutes of limitation"**)
Majority action by beneficiaries of series of notes secured by same property or note secured by property equivalent to series transaction   CC §2941.9
Marketability of title (See **TITLE AND OWNERSHIP**)

TRUST DEEDS AND MORTGAGES—Cont.
Mechanic's liens, priority as to   CC §§8452 to 8456
Modification or workout plan to avoid foreclosure   CC §2923.6
    Approved alternative, effect   CC §2924.18
        Enforcement of provisions   CC §2924.19
    Availability of loss mitigation options   CC §2923.4
    First lien loan modification   CC §2923.6
        Acknowledging receipt of application or documentation   CC §2924.10
        Pending application, effect   CC §§2924.18, 2924.19
    Foreign language summaries of terms   CC §1632.5
    Notice provided to borrower   CC §2944.6
    Prohibited acts   CC §2944.7
        Disabled person victim of prohibited acts, punishment   CC §2944.8
        Senior citizen victim of prohibited acts, punishment   CC §2944.8
        Statute of limitations to enforce   CC §2944.10
    Single point of contact   CC §2923.7
New servicing agent, notice to borrower of transfer of debt instrument to   CC §2937
Nonacceptance, recording notice of   CC §1058.5
Nonmonetary status declaration filed by trustee named in proceeding solely in its capacity as trustee   CC §2924l
Nonprobate transfer of property provisions (See **NONPROBATE TRANSFERS**)
Notices
    Adjustable rate mortgage loans, disclosure notice requirements for   CC §1916.7
    Agent for collection, notice requirement for   CC §2924.3
    Assignees notified of foreclosure   CC §2924b
    Assignment of interest, recordation as constructive notice of   CC §2934
    Balloon payment loans   CC §2924i
    Change of servicing agent, notice to borrower of   CC §2937
    Conflicting claims to proceeds of sale, notice of   CC §2924j
    Curing of default   CC §2924c
    Default notice   CC §§2924.3, 2924b, 2924c
        Approval of foreclosure prevention measures, effect   CC §§2924.11, 2924.12
        Foreclosure avoidance options to be discussed prior to filing   CC §§2923.5, 2924.12, 2924.19
        Recorded notice of default   CC §§2923.55, 2924, 2924.26
        Requirements for filing and recording documents   CC §§2924.12, 2924.17, 2924.19
        Rescission of notice of default   CC §2924.11
        Timing   CC §§2923.5, 2924.12, 2924.15, 2924.19
        Title company immunity for recording notice of default or sale   CC §2924.26
    Delinquency charges   CC §2954.5
    Fictitious instruments, notice of provisions of   CC §2952
    Foreclosure   CC §§2924, 2924.3, 2924b, 2924c, 2924f
        Posting notice of sale, required contents   CC §2924.8
        Requirements for filing and recording documents   CC §§2924.12, 2924.17, 2924.19
    Lessees notified of foreclosure   CC §2924b
    Majority action by beneficiaries of series of notes secured by same property or note secured by property equivalent to series transaction   CC §2941.9
    Nonacceptance, recording notice of   CC §1058.5
    Postponement of sale   CC §2924g
    Private mortgage and mortgage guaranty insurance, notice of borrower's right to cancel   CC §2954.6
    Purchaser notified of foreclosure   CC §2924b
    Redemption, judgment debtor served with notice of right of   CCP §729.050
    Renegotiable interest rates   CC §1916.8
    Rescission, recording notice of   CC §1058.5
    Sale, notice of   CC §§2924, 2924.8, 2924f
        Approval of foreclosure prevention measures, effect   CC §§2924.11, 2924.12
    Sale of property under power of sale, publication of   CC §2924.8
    Servicing agent, notice requirements for change of   CC §2937
    Subordination agreement   CC §§2953.2, 2953.3
    Substitution of trustees   CC §2934a
    Successor in interest, notice of default to   CC §2924b
    Transfer of debt instrument to new servicing agent, notice to borrower of   CC §2937
Payoff demand statements
    Equity lines of credit
        Suspending and closing line, borrower's instruction   CC §2943.1
Penalties
    Criminal liability generally (See within this heading, **"Criminal liability"**)
Personal liability under   CC §2928
Possession
    Generally   CC §§2923, 2927
    Foreclosure, possession after   CCP §744

TRUST DEEDS AND MORTGAGES—Cont.
Postponement of sale   CC §2924g
Power of attorney for executing   CC §2933
Power of sale   CC §§2924, 2932
   Common interest developments
      Transfer of property in CID, recording   CC §2924.1
   Compliance with applicable laws   CC §2924n
   Conducting sale under power   CC §2924a
   Exercise of power of sale   CC §2924
   Notice of sale   CC §§2924, 2924.8, 2924f
   Postponement of sale   CC §2924
   Prospective owner-occupant as bidder   CC §2924m
Prepayment
   Generally   CC §2954.9
   Due-on-sale clauses, prepayment under   CC §2954.10
   Installment loans   CC §2954.11
Principal and income allocations   CC §§731.14, 731.15
Priority of liens
   Generally   CC §2898
   Reverse mortgages   CC §1923.3
Private mortgage and mortgage guaranty insurance
   Future insurance payments, conditions for terminating   CC §§2954.7, 2954.12
   Notice of borrower's right to cancel   CC §2954.6
   Refund of unused premium after cancellation   CC §2954.65
   Requirement as condition of loan secured by deed of trust   CC §2954.6
Probate proceedings
   Small estates
      Transferee liability   Pro §13204.5
      Voluntary return of transferred property   Pro §13205.5
Profits
   Account of rents and profits
      Action to redeem   CCP §d346
      Proportionate to interest in mortgaged premises   CCP §d347
   Assignment   CC §2938
      Receiver, appointment   CC §2938, CCP §564
Proof of execution   CC §2952
Publication of notice of sale of property under power of sale   CC §2924.8
Purchase money liens on residential property, disclosures on   CC §§2956 to 2968
Rebate of fees, prohibition against   CC §2924d
Receivers, appointment of
   Generally   CCP §564
   Assignment   CCP §564
   Leases, rents, issues or profits   CC §2938, CCP §564
Reconveyance   CC §§2941, 2941.5, 2941.7
Reconveyance fees   CC §2941.1
Recording
   Assignment of interests (See within this heading, **"Assignments"**)
   Bond on satisfaction of trust deed   CC §2941.7
   Certificate of discharge   CC §§2941, 2941.5
   Default notice   CC §§2924.3, 2924b
      Approval of foreclosure prevention measures, effect   CC §§2924.11, 2924.12
      Recorded notice of default   CC §§2923.3, 2923.55, 2924
      Requirements for filing and recording documents   CC §§2924.12, 2924.17, 2924.19
   Defeasance, effect of recordation of   CC §2950
   Fictitious instruments   CC §2952
   Majority action affidavit where majority interest acts for all beneficiaries under trust deed   CC §2941.9
   Nonacceptance, recording notice of   CC §1058.5
   Power of sale   CC §2932.5
   Reconveyance   CC §§2941, 2941.5, 2941.7
   Recorder's duties (See **RECORDS AND RECORDING**)
   Refusal of trustee to accept appointment   CC §2934a
   Request for notice of default   CC §2924b
   Requirements for filing and recording documents   CC §§2924.17, 2924.19
      Injunction to enforce   CC §2924.12
   Rescission, recording notice of   CC §1058.5
   Resignation of trustee   CC §2934a
   Sales, notice
      Approval of foreclosure prevention measures, effect   CC §§2924.11, 2924.12
      Recorded notice of sale   CC §§2923.3, 2924
   Substitution of trustee   CC §2934a
Redemption
   Generally   CC §2931, CCP §729.010
   Account of rents and profits   CCP §§346, 347
   By judgment debtor or successor in interest   CCP §§729.020, 729.060
   Certificate of sale   CCP §729.040

TRUST DEEDS AND MORTGAGES—Cont.
Redemption—Cont.
   Common interest developments
      Foreclosure by association for nonpayment of assessments   CCP §729.035
   Disputed price, petition for court determination of   CCP §729.070
   Enforcement of judgments
      Equitable right of redemption   CCP §701.680
   Failure to deposit redemption price, effect of   CCP §729.080
   Limitation of actions   CCP §346
   Notice of right of redemption served on judgment debtor   CCP §729.050
   Period of redemption restricted   CCP §729.030
   Persons barred from redeeming, interests of   CCP §347
   Price   CCP §729.060
   Procedure for   CCP §729.060
   Purchaser's rights prior to   CCP §729.090
   Sheriff's fees for deed or certificate of redemption   Gov §26740
   Tender of deposit to purchaser, procedure on acceptance or refusal of   CCP §729.080
Referees to appraise property for purposes of deficiency judgments   CCP §§580a, 726
Refinancing
   Appraisal
      Disclosure as to unbiased appraisal and complaint process   CC §1102.6g
Refusal of trustee of appointment   CC §2934a
Reinstatement after default in payments   CC §2924c
Renegotiable-rate mortgages   CC §§1916.8, 1916.9
Rents and profits
   Accounting
      Proportionate to interest in mortgaged premises   CCP §347
      Redemption, action   CCP §346
   Assignment   CC §2938
      Receiver, appointment   CC §2938, CCP §564
Repairs to residential property acquired by foreclosure, financial institutions making   CC §2932.6
Rescission
   Failure of consideration, trustee's sale subject to rescission for   CC §2924h
   Foreclosure in violation of home equity sales contract, rescission of   CC §1695.14
   Home equity sales contracts, rescission of foreclosure where violation of   CC §1695.14
   Mortgage, declared default on   CC §2924c
   Recording notice of   CC §1058.5
Resignation of trustee   CC §2934a
Reverse mortgages
   Advances to borrower   CC §1923.2
   Annuity as condition for mortgage   CC §1923.2
   Asian language negotiations and contracts   CC §§1632, 1923.2
   Checklist of issues for discussion with financial counselor   CC §1923.5
   Counseling prior to acceptance of application   CC §1923.2
      Checklist of issues for discussion   CC §1923.5
      Disclosures   CC §1923.5
   Defined   CC §1923
   Disclosure
      Loan application, disclosure statement in conjunction with   CC §1923.5
      Presumption of satisfaction of disclosure obligation   CC §1923.6
      Trust deed, notice on   CC §1923.2
   Due and payable, when mortgage loan is   CC §1923.2
   Effective date of statutes   CC §1923.10
   Fees   CC §1923.2
   Interest rates   CC §1923.2
   Lien against property   CC §1923.3
   Means-tested programs, classification of payments to borrower and undisbursed funds for purposes of eligibility for   CC §1923.9
   Noncompliance of lender, effect of   CC §1923.7
   Owner-occupied, classification of mortgaged property as   CC §1923.4
   Prepayment without penalty   CC §1923.2
   Priority of lien created by reverse mortgage   CC §1923.3
   Spanish language negotiations and contracts   CC §§1632, 1923.2
   Statute of limitations for lender's action   CC §1923.2
   Worksheet guide to determine appropriateness   CC §1923.5
RRM's   CC §§1916.8, 1916.9
Sales
   Attorney professional conduct
      Purchase by attorney of property at foreclosure or judicial sale   ProfC 1.8.9
   Cancellation of trustee's sale
      Foreclosure prevention measures, execution   CC §2924.11

TRUST DEEDS AND MORTGAGES—Cont.
  Sales—Cont.
    Damages
      Enforcement of foreclosure prevention   CC §2924.12
    Injunctions
      Enforcement of foreclosure prevention   CC §§2924.12, 2924.19
    Notice of sale
      Approval of foreclosure prevention measures, effect   CC §§2924.11, 2924.12
      Recorded notice of sale   CC §2923.3
    Postponement   CC §§2924, 2924.15
  Sales under power of sale (See within this heading, **"Foreclosure"**)
  Satisfaction of   CC §§2941 to 2941.5
  Second trust deed, default claimed because of   CC §2949
  Service of process on trustee, effect of   CC §2937.7
  Servicing agent, notice requirements for change of   CC §2937
  Shared appreciation loans (See **SHARED APPRECIATION LOANS**)
  Short-pay agreements   CC §2943
  Short-pay demand statements   CC §2943
  Short-pay requests   CC §2943
  Single family dwellings
    Junior mortgages, default claimed because of   CC §2949
    Prepayment charges   CC §2954.9
  Small estates
    Transferee liability   Pro §13204.5
    Voluntary return of transferred property   Pro §13205.5
  Spanish language
    Foreign language summaries of terms   CC §1632.5
    Reverse mortgages
      Spanish language negotiations and contracts   CC §1632
  Special administrators, authority of   Pro §8544
  Statement of unpaid balance and related information in demand   CC §2943
  State of California as party to action   CC §§2931a to 2931c
  Statute of frauds   CC §1624
  Statutes of limitation
    Balance due after exercise of power of sale, action for money judgment for   CCP §337
    Corporate obligations   CCP §336a
    Mortgagor's action to redeem, generally   CCP §346
    Reverse mortgage, lender's action on   CC §1923.2
  Subordination clauses
    Generally   CC §§2953.1 to 2953.3
    Default, notification of   CC §2924b
  Substitution of trustees   CC §§2934a, 2941.7
    Recording
      Requirements for filing and recording documents   CC §§2924.12, 2924.17, 2924.19
  Surety bonds on satisfaction of   CC §2941.7
  Taxes
    Generally   CC §§2931a to 2931c
    Acceleration of payments for failure to pay taxes   CC §2924.7
    Impound account for   CC §§2954, 2954.1, 2954.8
    Liens, effect of   CC §§2931a to 2931c
  Transfer of debt instrument to new servicing agent, notice to borrower of   CC §2937
  Trustees
    Fees   CC §§2924c, 2924f
    Nonmonetary status, filing declaration of   CC §2924l
    Service of process on   CC §2937.7
    Substitution of   CC §§2934a, 2941.7
    Vacation of office of   CC §2934b
  Trust property, description of trust deed as requirement for filing claims against   Pro §19152
  Type of property subject to   CC §2947
  Unclaimed property fund appropriations for payment of   CCP §1325
  Unlawful detainer, holding over after foreclosure sale as act constituting   CCP §1161a
  Unpaid balance, rendering statement of   CC §2943
  Variable interest rate loans
    Generally   CC §§1916.5, 1920
    Business, transportation and housing agency secretary, authority of   CC §1918.5
    5-year intervals between rate-adjustments, instruments offering   CC §1916.6
    Renegotiable-rate mortgages   CC §§1916.8, 1916.9
  Venue in actions for foreclosure of liens and mortgages on real property   CCP §392
  Waiver of rights, prohibition against   CC §2953
  Writing required   CC §2922

TRUST DEEDS AND MORTGAGES—Cont.
  Written contracts for assumption of debts under   CC §1624

TRUSTEES (See **TRUST DEEDS AND MORTGAGES**; **TRUSTS**)

TRUSTS
Abuse or neglect of elder or dependent settlor by beneficiary, effect of   Pro §259
Acceptance
  Attorney's acceptance of documents for deposit   Pro §713
  Trustee's acceptance of trust   Pro §15600
Accounting
  Generally   Pro §§1060 to 1064, 16062
  Compelling trustee to account   Pro §16064
  Contents of   Pro §§1061 to 1063, 16063
  Contest of account, sanctions for bad faith in prosecuting or defending   Pro §17211
  Exceptions to duty to report   Pro §§16064, 16069
  Filing fees of trustee   Gov §70652
    Supplemental fees for first paper filing   Gov §§70602.5, 70602.6
  General duty to report to beneficiaries   Pro §§16060, 16061
  Names and addresses of vested and contingent beneficiaries to be listed in petitions and accounts   CRC 7.902
  Objections to items in accounts
    Release of trustee upon failure to object   Pro §16461
  Period covered by account   CRC 7.901
  Principal and income allocations generally (See within this heading, **"Principal and income allocations"**)
  Totten trust accounts (See **TOTTEN TRUST ACCOUNTS**)
Acquisition of property by trustee   Pro §16226
Additions to trust
  Governing law   Pro §§6300 to 6303
  Trustee accepting   Pro §16221
Administration
  Generally   Pro §16000
  Combining similar trusts   Pro §15411
  Dividing trust into separate trusts   Pro §15412
  Duties of trustees   Pro §§16000 to 16110
  Instructions for   Pro §16001
  Judicial intervention in   Pro §17209
  Liens generally (See within this heading, **"Liens"**)
  Loyalty, duty of   Pro §16002
  Place of trust administration   Pro §17002
  Powers of trustees
    Proposed actions, notice of   Pro §§16500 to 16504
  Principal and income allocations generally (See within this heading, **"Principal and income allocations"**)
  Sales generally (See within this heading, **"Sales"**)
  Testamentary trust administration (See within this heading, **"Testamentary trusts under continuing jurisdiction"**)
  Transferred trusts, administration of   Pro §17457
  Uniform fiduciary income and principal act
    Applicability of provisions   Pro §16322
    Generally   Pro §§16320 to 16383
    Place of administration as basis of applicability   Pro §16323
Affidavits
  Claims against estate
    Claim filed, supporting affidavit   Pro §19151
    Publication of notice   Pro §19040
Allowance of claims filed against estate (See within this heading, **"Claims against estate"**)
Annuity beneficiary designated as trustee named in will   Pro §§6320 to 6330
Appeals
  Generally   Pro §1304
  Insurance or employee benefits, trusts for   Pro §6327
  Stay on appeal   Pro §1310
Appointment of trustees (See within this heading, **"Trustees"**)
Approval of claims filed against estate (See within this heading, **"Claims against estate"**)
Attachment of deposit account of beneficiary of   CCP §488.455
Attorney General
  Charitable trusts, jurisdiction over
    Beneficiaries' rights, enforcement of   Pro §17210
    Civil enforcement, fees and costs for attorney general   CCP §1021.8
    Service of notice on Attorney General   Pro §8111
    Settlement of claims involving   Pro §§19024, 19030
  Involuntary trusts
    Actions by attorney general, statute of limitations   CC §2224.5
  Revocable trust beneficiary, limitations on rights applicable to Attorney General as   Pro §15805
Attorney professional conduct
  Trust accounts
    Safekeeping of funds and property of clients   ProfC 1.15

TRUSTS—Cont.
- Attorneys at law
  - Probate attorneys
    - Education requirements   CRC 10.478
    - Qualifications   CRC 10.776, 10.777
  - Trust accounts, state bar client trust account protection program   CRC 9.8.5
- Attorneys' fees
  - Trustees and associates of trustees, restrictions on legal fees for   Pro §15687
- Beneficiaries
  - Generally   Pro §15205
  - Abuse or neglect of elder or dependent settlor by beneficiary, effect of   Pro §259
  - Acceleration of loan, restrictions on   CC §2924.6
  - Attachment of deposit account of   CCP §488.455
  - Charitable trusts, Attorney General's jurisdiction to enforce rights of beneficiaries of   Pro §17210
  - Claims against estate, distributee liability for (See within this heading, "**Claims against estate**")
  - Class of beneficiaries
    - Court determination of   Pro §15404
    - Presumption of fertility for determining   Pro §15406
  - Consent of (See within this heading, "**Consent requirement**")
  - Creditors of
    - Enforcement of judgment against beneficiary (See within this heading, "**Enforcement of judgment against beneficiary**")
    - Lifetime of settlor of revocable trust, creditor's rights during   Pro §§18200, 18201
    - Protection of creditors and other third persons   Pro §§18100 to 18108
  - Disclaimer of interest by   Pro §§260 to 295, 15309
  - Distributions to
    - Claims against estate, distributee liability (See within this heading, "**Claims against estate**")
    - Enforcement of judgment against beneficiary (See within this heading, "**Enforcement of judgment against beneficiary**")
  - Doctrine of merger, applicability of   Pro §15209
  - Enforcement of judgment against beneficiary (See within this heading, "**Enforcement of judgment against beneficiary**")
  - Felon's story, beneficiary of proceeds from sale of   CC §2225
  - Future interests (See **FUTURE ESTATES AND INTERESTS**)
  - Jurisdiction over   Pro §17003
  - Loans to   Pro §16244
  - Loyalty, trustee's duty of   Pro §16002
  - Modification, generally (See within this heading, "**Modification**")
  - Multiple-party accounts (See **MULTIPLE-PARTY ACCOUNTS**)
  - Names and addresses of vested and contingent beneficiaries to be listed in petitions and accounts   CRC 7.902
  - No contest clause   Pro §§21300 to 21322
  - Notice, generally (See within this heading, "**Notices**")
  - Objection by beneficiary to proposed action by trustee   Pro §16503
  - Objections to items in accounts
    - Release of trustee upon failure to object   Pro §16461
  - Omitted child (See **HEIRS**)
  - Omitted spouse (See **SURVIVING SPOUSE**)
  - Power of appointment, rights of holder of   Pro §15803
  - Renunciation of interest, effect of   Pro §15309
  - Restitution judgment awarded in felony conviction of beneficiary, trust assets used in satisfaction of   Pro §15305.5
  - Revocable trusts (See within this heading, "**Revocable trusts**")
  - Special notice
    - Beneficiary or interested person requesting   Pro §17204
  - Termination, generally (See within this heading, "**Termination**")
  - Trustee's duty of impartiality in dealings with   Pro §16003
  - Waiver of trustee liability as condition of receiving distribution
    - Trustee not to require   Pro §16004.5
- Bond requirements for trustees   Pro §§15602, 15604
- Breach of trust
  - Generally   Pro §16400
  - Damages, measure of (See within this heading, "**Damages, measure of**")
  - Remedies for   Pro §§16420, 16421
- Business interests
  - Change in form of business
    - Generally   Pro §16222
    - Consent requirements   Pro §16236
  - Continuation of business by trustee   Pro §16222
- Certification of trustees
  - Court clerk's certification   Pro §15603
  - Trustee's certificate of trust   Pro §18100.5
- Changed circumstances, effect of   Pro §15409
- Charitable nonprofit corporation as trustee   Pro §15604

TRUSTS—Cont.
- Charitable trusts
  - Decanting of trusts, uniform act   Pro §§19501 to 19530 (See **TRUST DECANTING, UNIFORM ACT**)
  - Generally (See **CHARITABLE TRUSTS**)
- Child stars, setting aside earnings of minor in trust fund   Fam §§6752, 6753
- Child support payments, liability for   Pro §§15302, 15305 to 15306.5
- Citation of act   Pro §15000
- Claims against estate
  - Actual notice to creditors
    - Generally   Pro §19050
    - Distributee liability in absence of   Pro §19401
    - Exceptions to notice requirements   Pro §19054
    - Form of   Pro §19052
    - Immunity of trustee for giving or failing to give notice   Pro §19053
    - Time requirements   Pro §19051
  - Affidavits
    - Claims filed, affidavit in support of   Pro §19151
    - Publication of notice, affidavit of   Pro §19040
  - Allocation of debts
    - Agreement by interested parties for   Pro §19324
    - Apportionment of debts in absence of agreement   Pro §19324
    - Characterization of debts as separate or community   Pro §19324
    - Funeral expenses   Pro §19326
    - Last illness expenses   Pro §19326
    - Notice of hearing   Pro §19323
    - Order by court   Pro §19325
    - Petition for   Pro §§19320, 19321
    - Valuation of surviving spouse's property, show cause order for   Pro §19322
  - Allowance or rejection of claim
    - Generally   Pro §19250
    - Authority and powers of trustee for   Pro §19005
    - Bringing action on rejected claim   Pro §19255
    - Compromise of claim   Pro §§19005, 19252
    - Contents of   Pro §19251
    - Failure of trustee to act on claim   Pro §19254
    - Failure to timely file action on rejected claim   Pro §19253
    - Judicial Council form, use of   Pro §19251
    - Statute of limitations   Pro §19253
    - Trustee or trustee's attorney as creditor   Pro §19252
    - Writing requirement   Pro §19251
  - Amended claims, filing of   Pro §19104
  - Applicability of provisions governing claims against revocable trust of deceased settlor   Pro §19002
  - Attachment lien into judgment lien, conversion of   Pro §19304
  - Bona fide purchaser, rights of   Pro §19403
  - Bringing action on rejected claim   Pro §19255
  - Costs, award of   Pro §19255
  - Defects in claim, waiver of   Pro §19154
  - Definitions   Pro §19000
  - Disclosure of existence or contents of trust to beneficiary or creditor   Pro §19009
  - Distributee liability
    - Actual notice to creditors, liability in absence of   Pro §19401
    - Administration of decedent's estate, liability in absence of   Pro §19400
    - Bona fide purchaser, rights of   Pro §19403
    - Defenses to action involving   Pro §19402
    - Limited liability of distributee   Pro §19402
    - Proposed notice to creditors, liability in absence of   Pro §19400
    - Public entities, liability of distributees to claims filed by   Pro §19203
  - Execution liens on trust property   Pro §19303
  - Failure of trustee to act on claim   Pro §19254
  - Failure to file proposed notice to creditors, trustee's liability for   Pro §19008
  - Failure to timely file action on rejected claim   Pro §19253
  - Family exemption   Pro §19304
  - Filing requirements
    - Affidavit in support of claim   Pro §19151
    - Amended claims, filing of   Pro §19104
    - Attachment of written instrument on which claim is based   Pro §19152
    - Defects in claim, waiver of   Pro §19154
    - Judicial Council forms, use of   Pro §19153
    - Late filing   Pro §19103
    - Manner of filing   Pro §19150
    - Mortgage, trust deed or lien on which claim is based, description of   Pro §19152
    - Timely filed but not acted on before expiration of filing period, effect on claim where   Pro §19102

TRUSTS INDEX

TRUSTS—Cont.
Claims against estate—Cont.
    Filing requirements—Cont.
        Time periods for claim filing   Pro §19100
        Vacant office of trustee, effect of claim filed before expiration of filing period where   Pro §19101
        Who may file   Pro §19150
    Funeral expenses   Pro §19326
    Governing law   Pro §19012
    Health care services department, notification of death of settlor to   Pro §19202
    Judgment claims
        Attachment lien into judgment lien, conversion of   Pro §19304
        Execution liens on trust property, enforcement of   Pro §19303
        Family exemption   Pro §19304
        Money judgments, payment of   Pro §§19300, 19301
        Possession or sale of trust property   Pro §19302
    Judicial Council forms
        Allowance or rejection of claim   Pro §19251
        Filing claims in general   Pro §19153
        Proposed notice to creditors   Pro §19011
    Last illness expenses   Pro §19326
    Liens
        Attachment lien into judgment lien, conversion of   Pro §19304
        Description of lien on which claim is based   Pro §19152
        Execution liens on trust property   Pro §19303
    Money judgments, payment of   Pro §§19300, 19301
    Mortgage or trust deed on which claim is based, description of   Pro §19152
    No duty by trustee to initiate notice proceedings   Pro §19010
    Other trusts by deceased settlor
        Liability as between other trusts of settlor   Pro §19007
        Notice to creditors, effect of filing   Pro §19006
    Payment of claim by trustee   Pro §19005
    Petition
        Allocation of debts, petition for   Pro §§19320, 19321
        Late claim, petition to file   Pro §19103
    Possession or sale of trust property, judgment for   Pro §19302
    Proposed notice to creditors
        Generally   Pro §19003
        Distributee liability in absence of   Pro §19400
        Failure to file, trustee's liability for   Pro §19008
        No duty by trustee to initiate notice proceedings   Pro §19010
        Other trusts of deceased settlor, effect of notice filing on   Pro §19006
        Time and place for filing of   Pro §19003
        Timely claims filing required after filing of   Pro §19004
    Publication of notice
        Generally   Pro §19040
        Affidavit of   Pro §19040
        Form of   Pro §19040
        Good faith compliance, requirements for   Pro §19041
    Public entities, claims filed by
        Distributee liability after early distribution   Pro §19203
        Filing period for   Pro §19200
        Illegally acquired sums, applicability to   Pro §19205
        Notification of health care services department on death of settlor   Pro §19202
        Priority for debt payments, effect on   Pro §19204
        Public entity defined   Pro §19200
        Restitution of amounts acquired by fraud, applicability to   Pro §19205
        Statute, claims arising from   Pro §19201
    Right to recover debts payable from probate assets but paid from trust   Pro §19006
    Settlement of (See within this heading, **"Settlement of claims"**)
    Statute of limitations   Pro §19253
    Surviving spouse
        Action on liability of   Pro §19330
        Allocation of debts   Pro §§19320 to 19325
    Timely filing of claims after notice to creditors   Pro §19004
    Trust property subject to   Pro §19001
    Waiver of defects in claim filed   Pro §19154
Class of beneficiaries
    Court determination   Pro §15404
    Presumption of fertility for determining   Pro §15406
Collection of trust property   Pro §16220
Combining similar trusts   Pro §15411
Common law rules, applicability of   Pro §15002
Community property held in revocable trusts   Fam §761, Pro §§104, 104.5, 13504

TRUSTS—Cont.
Compensation
    Deposit of documents with attorney, charge for   Pro §714
        Transfer of documents to second attorney   Pro §732
    Guardian ad litem   Pro §1003
    Trustee (See within this heading, **"Trustees"**)
Conflicts of interest   Pro §§16004, 16005
Consent requirement
    Business, trustee's consent to change in form of   Pro §16236
    Liability of trustee, effect of consent of beneficiaries on   Pro §16463
    Modification or termination of trust   Pro §15404
    Revocable trust, action to be taken on   Pro §15801
Consideration requirement   Pro §15208
Construction
    Generally (See **WILL CONSTRUCTION**)
    Charitable lead trusts   Pro §21541
    Charitable remainder trusts   Pro §21540
    No contest clause   Pro §§21310 to 21315
Constructive trusts (See **CONSTRUCTIVE TRUSTS**)
Contest of wills, trusts, etc
    No contest clause   Pro §§21310 to 21315
Continuation of business by trustee   Pro §16222
Conveyance by trustee, presumption of   Ev §642
Corporate stock
    Generally   Pro §16234
    Calls and assessments, payments of   Pro §16235
    Custody of securities   Pro §16238
    Deposit of securities   Pro §16239
    Subscriptions of stock   Pro §16236
    Voting trusts   Pro §16237
Corpus
    Claims against trust property of deceased settlor
        Claims against estate generally (See within this heading, **"Claims against estate"**)
    General requirement   Pro §15202
Costs
    Actions prosecuted or defended by trustee, recovery of costs in   CCP §1026
    Claims against estate   Pro §19255
    Removal of trustee, action for   Pro §15645
Cotrustees (See within this heading, **"Trustees"**)
Court investigators
    Education requirements   CRC 10.478
Court orders, trusts funded by   CRC 7.903
    Judicial administration standards   CRC JudAdminStand 7.10
Creation of trust
    Generally   CCP §§1971, 1972
    Intent requirement   Pro §15201
    Methods of   Pro §15200
    Recordation of   Pro §15210
Creditors' rights
    Beneficiaries, enforcement of judgment against (See within this heading, **"Enforcement of judgment against beneficiary"**)
    Deceased settlor of revocable trust
        Claims against estate generally (See within this heading, **"Claims against estate"**)
    Lifetime of settlor of revocable trust, creditors' rights during   Pro §§18200, 18201
    Protection of creditors and other third persons   Pro §§18100 to 18108
Cy pres doctrine   Pro §21220
    Institutional funds management
        Restrictions in gift instruments, release   Pro §18506
Damages, measure of
    Generally   Pro §16440
    Exemplary damages   Pro §16442
    Interest on money   Pro §§16440, 16441
    Wrongful concealment or taking of trust property   Pro §16249
Decanting   Pro §§19501 to 19530
Decedent's estate
    Claims against (See within this heading, **"Claims against estate"**)
    Distribution decree establishing testamentary trust   CRC 7.650
    Investment of money from estate pending settlement of   Pro §9730
Declaration of settlor
    Generally   Pro §15200
    Intent requirement   Pro §15201
    Oral trust of personal property   Pro §15207
Dedication of property to public use   Pro §16230
Definitions   Pro §§82, 83
Delivery of property to successor trustee   Pro §15644
Deposit of documents with attorney
    Acceptance by attorney, effect of   Pro §713
    Acknowledgment of terms by depositor   Pro §715

TRUSTS—Cont.
  Deposit of documents with attorney—Cont.
    Compensation
      Generally   Pro §714
      Transfer of documents to second attorney   Pro §732
    Death of attorney, termination of deposit on   Pro §735
    Death of depositor, termination of deposit on   Pro §734
    Definitions   Pro §§701 to 704
    Incapacity of attorney, termination of deposit on   Pro §735
    Lien in favor of attorney, viability of   Pro §714
    Loss or destruction of documents
      Liability of attorney   Pro §712
      Notice to depositor   Pro §711
      Standard of care   Pro §§710, 716
    Notice to depositor
      General notice of terms   Pro §715
      Loss or destruction of documents   Pro §711
    Notice to state Bar of transfer for termination of deposit   Pro §733
    Standards of care   Pro §§710, 716
    Termination of deposit
      By attorney   Pro §§730 to 735
      By depositor   Pro §720
  Deposits of trust funds   Pro §16225
  Destruction or loss of documents deposited with attorney (See within this heading, "**Deposit of documents with attorney**")
  Directed trusts   Pro §§16600 to 16632
    Breach of trust actions   Pro §16622
  Disabled beneficiaries, distributions to   Pro §15306
  Disclaimer of interest by beneficiary   Pro §§260 to 295, 15309
  Discount buying organization establishing   CC §1812.116
    Affiliates, exemptions from trust account provisions   CC §1812.117
  Discretionary powers of trustee (See within this heading, "**Trustees**")
  Distribution
    Generally   Pro §§16245, 16246
    Claims against estate, distributee liability for (See within this heading, "**Claims against estate**")
    Enforcement of judgment against beneficiary generally (See within this heading, "**Enforcement of judgment against beneficiary**")
    In-kind distributions   Pro §16246
    Legal disability, distribution to beneficiary under   Pro §16245
    Principal and income allocations (See within this heading, "**Principal and income allocations**")
    Private foundation trusts   Pro §16101
    Restitution judgment awarded in felony conviction of beneficiary, trust assets used in satisfaction of   Pro §15305.5
    Waiver of trustee liability as condition of beneficiary receiving distribution
      Trustee not to require   Pro §16004.5
  Dividing trust into separate trust   Pro §15412
  Donative transfers
    Presumption of fraud or undue influence   Pro §§21360 to 21392 (See **DONATIVE TRANSFERS**)
  Educational trusts, effect of money judgments against beneficiary on   Pro §15302
  Employee benefits plans (See within this heading, "**Retirement benefits plans**")
  Enforcement of judgment against beneficiary
    Generally   CCP §695.030, Pro §§15300, 15301
    Child and spousal support, liability for   Pro §§15302, 15305 to 15306.5
    Disabled beneficiaries, distribution to   Pro §15306
    Disclaimer of interest, effect of   Pro §15309
    Discretionary powers of trustee, effect on   Pro §15303
    Educational trusts, effect on   Pro §15302
    Excess income subject to creditors' claims   Pro §15307
    Modification of orders   Pro §15308
    Petition to apply judgment debtor's interest in trust to satisfaction of money judgment   CCP §709.010
    Public support, liability for   Pro §15306
    Restitution judgment awarded in felony conviction of beneficiary, satisfaction of   Pro §15305.5
    Satisfaction of money judgment against beneficiary, order directing   Pro §15306.5
    Settlor as beneficiary, effect of distribution to   Pro §15304
    Trustees
      Third party, trustee's liability to
        Enforcement of judgment against beneficiary generally (See within this heading, "**Enforcement of judgment against beneficiary**")
  Escheat to state
    Health and welfare trust funds, prohibition against escheat of   Pro §6806
    Unclaimed retirement benefits   CCP §1521

TRUSTS—Cont.
  Estate tax
    Taxes
      Generally (See within this heading, "**Taxes**")
      Generation-skipping transfer tax (See **GENERATION-SKIPPING TRANSFER TAX**)
      Marital deduction gifts (See **MARITAL DEDUCTION GIFTS**)
      Private foundation trusts generally (See within this heading, "**Private foundation trusts**")
  Execution of instruments to accomplish trust   Pro §16248
  Executors investing funds in   Pro §9730
  Expenditures
    General discussion of reimbursement of trustee for   Pro §15684
    Lien on trust property by trustee for reimbursement of   Pro §15685
  Extinguishment (See within this heading, "**Termination**")
  Felon's story, involuntary trust established for proceeds from sale of   CC §2225
  Fertility, presumption of   Pro §15406
  Fiduciary duties of trustees   Pro §§16000 to 16110
  Fiduciary income and principal act
    Applicability of provisions   Pro §16322
      Place of administration as basis of applicability   Pro §16323
    Generally   Pro §§16320 to 16383
  Financial institutions as trustee, actions by   Pro §16015
  Fraud
    Independent review to determine whether designated trustee should be removed   Pro §15642
    Involuntary trust arising from   CC §§2223, 2224
      Attorney general actions, statute of limitations   CC §2224.5
    Public entities, claims against trusts filed by   Pro §19205
  Funeral trusts, preneed
    Escheat of unclaimed funds maintained in preneed funeral trust   CCP §1518.5
      Reimbursement of holder upon submission of death certificate   CCP §1560
  Future interests (See **FUTURE ESTATES AND INTERESTS**)
  Generation-skipping transfer tax (See **GENERATION-SKIPPING TRANSFER TAX**)
  Good faith in third party transactions (See within this heading, "**Third parties**")
  Governing law   Pro §§15001 to 15004
  Guardian ad litem
    Generally   CCP §373.5, Pro §1003
    Modification or termination of trust, consent to   Pro §15405
    Settlement of claims proceedings, appointment in   Pro §19029
  Guardians ad litem
    Disclosures   Pro §1003
  Health care services department, notification of death of settlor to   Pro §19202
  Health studio services contracts
    Pre-opening contracts
      Money held in trust   CC §1812.96
  Hearing
    Jury trial   Pro §17006
    Notice of generally (See within this heading, "**Notices**")
    Transfer of trust
      From other state   Pro §§17452, 17454
      To other state   Pro §17403
  Hearsay
    Establishment or amendment of revocable trust   Ev §1260
  Honorary trusts   Pro §15211
  Housing cooperative trusts generally   CC §§817 to 817.4
  Impartiality in dealings with beneficiaries, trustee's duty of   Pro §16003
  Implication, creation by   CCP §1972
  Improvements to property   Pro §16229
  Incapacity of cotrustees   Pro §15622
  Income and principal allocation (See within this heading, "**Principal and income allocations**")
  Independent review to determine whether designated trustee should be removed   Pro §15642
  Injunctions   CC §3422, CCP §526
  Instructions for administration   Pro §16001
  Insurance
    Liability insurance on trust property   Pro §16240
    Life insurance trusts (See within this heading, "**Insurance trusts**")
  Insurance trusts
    Appeals   Pro §6327
    Application of law   Pro §§6329, 6330
    Benefits payable or transferable to trustee   Pro §6323
    Debts of designator, effect of   Pro §6324
    Definitions   Pro §6320
    Designation of trustee   Pro §§6320 to 6322
    Jurisdiction for administration of   Pro §§6325, 6326
    Personal representative of designator, right to payments by   Pro §6328

TRUSTS INDEX

TRUSTS—Cont.
Intent to create trusts Pro §15201
Interest
    Damages for breach of trust, liability of trustee for interest on Pro §§16440, 16441
Interpretation
    Construction
        Generally (See within this heading, "Construction")
        Will construction generally (See WILL CONSTRUCTION)
Investments
    Compliance with prudent investor rule Pro §§16051, 16053
    Costs and expenses Pro §16050
    Delegation of investment and management functions Pro §§16012, 16052
    Deposits in interest-bearing accounts Pro §16225
    Diversification Pro §16048
    Government obligations Pro §16224
    Impartiality, trustee's duty of Pro §16003
    Initial review and implementation of investment strategy Pro §16049
    Language in trust provisions deemed to require compliance with prudent investor rule Pro §16053
    Money market funds Pro §16224
    Powers of trustees Pro §16200
        Proposed actions, notice of Pro §§16500 to 16504
    Principal and income allocations generally (See within this heading, "Principal and income allocations")
    Prudent investor rule Pro §§16045 to 16054
    Prudent management of institutional funds Pro §§18501 to 18510 (See INSTITUTIONAL FUNDS MANAGEMENT)
Involuntary trusts
    Mistake or wrongful acts as grounds for
        Attorney general actions, statute of limitations CC §2224.5
Irrevocable trusts
    Consent of all beneficiaries, modification or termination of trust by Pro §15403
    Notification obligations Pro §16061.7
    Reformation
        Trust decanting, uniform act Pro §§19501 to 19530
    Trustee's reporting obligations Pro §§16060.5, 16061.5 to 16061.8
    Waivers as against public policy Pro §16068
Judges
    Education of judges and subordinate judicial officers regularly assigned to probate cases CRC 10.468
        Domestic violence issues CRC 10.464
Judgments
    Action on claims against estate (See within this heading, "Claims against estate")
    Enforcement against beneficiary (See within this heading, "Enforcement of judgment against beneficiary")
Judicial Council forms for claims against trust property of deceased settlor (See within this heading, "Claims against estate")
Judicial determination that person lacks legal capacity to execute Pro §§810 to 812
Judicial intervention, management in absence of Pro §17209
Judicial proceedings
    Generally Pro §17001
    Administration of trust, judicial intervention in Pro §17209
    Attorney General's enforcement of beneficiaries' rights in charitable trusts Pro §17210
    Contest of trustee's account, sanctions for bad faith in prosecuting or defending Pro §17211
    Guardian ad litem, court appointment of Pro §1003
    Jurisdiction (See within this heading, "Jurisdiction")
    Necessary orders, power of court to issue Pro §17206
    Notice generally (See within this heading, "Notices")
    Petitions
        Claims against estate (See within this heading, "Claims against estate")
        Generally (See within this heading, "Petitions")
        Settlement of claims (See within this heading, "Settlement of claims")
    Temporary trustee, court appointment of Pro §17206
Jurisdiction
    Generally Pro §§17000, 17004
    Beneficiaries, jurisdiction over Pro §17003
    General jurisdiction, superior court powers as court of Pro §17001
    Insurance trusts, administration of Pro §§6325, 6326
    Other state jurisdiction, transfer of trust to (See within this heading, "Transfer of trust")
    Place of trust administration, effect of Pro §17002
    Retirement benefits plans, administration of Pro §§6325, 6326
    Testamentary trusts (See within this heading, "Testamentary trusts under continuing jurisdiction")

TRUSTS—Cont.
Jurisdiction—Cont.
    Trustees, jurisdiction over Pro §17004
    Venue Pro §17005
Jury trial, right to Pro §825
Leases
    Generally Pro §16231
    Mineral leases Pro §16232
Legal capacity to execute trusts, judicial determination regarding Pro §§810 to 812
Liens
    Generally Pro §16228
    Claims against trust property (See within this heading, "Claims against estate")
    Deposited documents, viability of attorney lien on Pro §714
    Presumptions regarding Pro §18104
    Reimbursement of expenditures, trustee's lien for Pro §15685
    Tax liens by federal government, registration of CCP §2101
Limitation of actions (See within this heading, "Statutes of limitation")
Loans
    Beneficiaries
        Trustees loaning to beneficiary Pro §16244
    Trustee borrowing money Pro §16241
Loss or destruction of documents deposited with attorney (See within this heading, "Deposit of documents with attorney")
Loyalty, trustee's duty of Pro §16002
Management of trust property Pro §16227
Marital deduction gifts in trust (See MARITAL DEDUCTION GIFTS)
Marital trusts
    Fiduciary income and principal act
        Receipts, allocation Pro §16348
Merger doctrine, exception to Pro §15209
Methods of creation of trusts Pro §15200
Mineral leases Pro §16232
Minors
    Disclaimer of estate interest on behalf of Pro §277
    Power of appointment released by trustee on behalf of minor powerholder Pro §662
    Uniform Transfers to Minors Act (See UNIFORM TRANSFERS TO MINORS ACT)
Mistake, involuntary trusts arising from CC §§2223, 2224
    Attorney general actions
        Statute of limitations CC §2224.5
Modification
    Generally Pro §15404
    Changed circumstances, effect of Pro §15409
    Combining similar trusts Pro §15411
    Dividing trust into separate trusts Pro §15412
    Guardian ad litem, consent by Pro §15405
    Irrevocable trusts, modification by consent of all beneficiaries of Pro §15403
    Money judgment orders against beneficiaries, modification of Pro §15308
    Revocation by settlor as Pro §15402
    Underproductive property as grounds for Pro §15408
Money judgment against beneficiary, trustee's liability for
    Enforcement against beneficiary generally (See within this heading, "Enforcement of judgment against beneficiary")
Mortgage description as requirement for filing claims against trust property Pro §19152
Multiple-party accounts (See MULTIPLE-PARTY ACCOUNTS)
Natural resources Pro §16232
Neglect or abuse of elder or dependent settlor by beneficiary, effect of Pro §259
No contest clause Pro §§21300 to 21322
Notices
    Generally Pro §1208
    Additional notice, requirements of Pro §17105
    Attorney General, notification of
        Charitable trusts, jurisdiction over Pro §8111
    Charitable trusts Pro §8111
    Deposit of documents with attorney
        Loss or destruction of documents, notice to depositor Pro §711
        Terms and conditions Pro §715
    Future interests, beneficiaries with Pro §15804
    General notice requirements for hearing Pro §17203
    Governing law Pro §17100
    Irrevocable trusts, notice of changes to Pro §16061.7
    Parties to be noticed Pro §§17105, 17203
    Proposed actions of trustee, notice of Pro §§16500 to 16504
    Revocable trusts Pro §§15802, 15804
    Settlement of claims
        Hearing, notice Pro §§19023, 19024

TRUSTS—Cont.
- Notices—Cont.
    - Special notice
        - Beneficiary or interested person requesting   Pro §17204
    - Transfer of trust
        - From other state   Pro §17454
        - To other state   Pro §17403
- Omitted child (See **HEIRS**)
- Omitted spouse (See **SURVIVING SPOUSE**)
- Option agreements by trustee   Pro §16233
- Oral trust of personal property   Pro §15207
- Other state jurisdiction (See within this heading, "**Transfer of trust**")
- Partition (See **PARTITION**)
- Pension plans (See within this heading, "**Retirement benefits plans**")
- Per capita defined   Pro §§245, 247
- Per stirpes defined   Pro §§245, 246
- Petitions
    - Claims against estate
        - Allocation of debts   Pro §§19320, 19321
        - Late claim, petition to file   Pro §19103
        - Settlement of (See within this heading, "**Settlement of claims**")
    - Contents of petitions   Pro §17201
    - Copies of   Pro §17205
    - Discovery   Pro §17201.1
    - Dismissal of petition, grounds for   Pro §17202
    - Filing of   Pro §17201
    - Grounds for   Pro §17200
    - Names and addresses of vested and contingent beneficiaries to be listed in petition   CRC 7.902
    - Satisfaction of money judgment, petition to apply judgment debtor's interest in trust to   CCP §709.010
    - Settlement of claims against estate (See within this heading, "**Settlement of claims**")
    - Transfer of trust
        - From other state   Pro §17453
        - To other state   Pro §17402
    - Trustees as petitioners   Pro §17200
    - Trustee's fee, review of increase in   Pro §15686
- Pets or domestic animals, trust for care of   Pro §15212
- Pour-over provisions
    - Generally   Pro §§6300 to 6303
    - Insurance   Pro §§6321 to 6330
- Power of appointment
    - Release of powers on behalf of minor powerholder by trustee   Pro §662
    - Revocable trusts subject to   Pro §15803
- Power of attorney
    - Generally (See **POWER OF ATTORNEY**)
    - Deposit of signed power (See within this heading, "**Deposit of documents with attorney**")
- Preservation of property   Pro §§15600, 16006
- Presumptions
    - Conveyance by trustee   Ev §642
    - Fertility, presumption of   Pro §15406
    - Revocability of trust   Pro §15400
    - Undue influence presumed in transactions between trustee and beneficiary   Pro §16004
- Pretermitted heirs (See **HEIRS**)
- Principal and income allocations   CRC 7.901, Pro §16320
    - Fiduciary income and principal act
        - Applicability of provisions   Pro §16322
        - Generally   Pro §§16320 to 16383
        - Place of administration as basis of applicability   Pro §16323
    - Notice of proposed action by trustee   CRC 7.901, Pro §§16500 to 16504
    - Objection to proposed action, beneficiary's procedure for   Pro §16337
- Private foundation trusts
    - Defined   Pro §16100
    - Distributions under   Pro §16101
    - Proceedings under Tax Reform Act, procedure for   Pro §16105
    - Restrictions   Pro §16102
    - Statutory provisions   Pro §16104
- Private trusts and foundations
    - Trustees' duties   Pro §§16100 to 16110
- Probate attorneys
    - Education requirements   CRC 10.478
    - Qualifications   CRC 10.776, 10.777
- Probate examiners
    - Education requirements   CRC 10.478
    - Qualifications   CRC 10.776, 10.777
- Probate rules
    - Compensation for trustees   CRC 7.776
    - Generally   CRC 7.1 to 7.1105

TRUSTS—Cont.
- Proceedings
    - Discovery   Pro §17201.1
- Profit-sharing plan beneficiary designated as trustee, named in will   Pro §§6320 to 6330
- Property in trust
    - Claims against estate generally (See within this heading, "**Claims against estate**")
    - Corpus, general requirements   Pro §15202
- Prudent investor rule   Pro §§16045 to 16054
- Public administrators as trustees   Pro §15660.5
    - Compensation   Pro §15688
- Public entities filing claims against trusts (See within this heading, "**Claims against estate**")
- Public guardian as trustee (See within this heading, "**Trustees**")
- Public support payments to beneficiary, liability for reimbursement of   Pro §15306
- Purpose of   Pro §§15203, 15204
- Quieting title action involving   CCP §764.020
- Real property transactions
    - Third parties
        - Omission in trust instrument, effect   Pro §18103
        - Undisclosed beneficiaries, effect of transactions involving   Pro §18104
- Recording requirements   Pro §15210
- Registration of trustees, county filing by private professional trustees
    - Charitable nonprofit corporation as trustee   Pro §15604
    - Prerequisite to appointment   Pro §§2340, 2341
- Reimbursement of expenditures, generally (See within this heading, "**Expenditures**")
- Rejection of claims against estate
    - Allowance or rejection (See within this heading, "**Claims against estate**")
- Rejection of trust by trustee   Pro §§15600, 15601
- Release of trustee's liability by beneficiaries   Pro §16464
- Remedies for breach of trust   Pro §§16420, 16421
- Removal
    - Testamentary trusts under continuing jurisdiction   Pro §§17303, 17350 to 17354
    - Trustee (See within this heading, "**Trustees**")
- Renunciation of interest by beneficiary, effect of   Pro §15309
- Repair of trust property by trustee   Pro §16229
- Reports
    - Accounting generally (See within this heading, "**Accounting**")
- Representation, right of   Pro §§245, 246
- Resignation of trustee (See within this heading, "**Trustees**")
- Restitution judgments awarded in felony conviction of beneficiary, trust assets used in satisfaction of   Pro §15305.5
- Resulting trusts (See **RESULTING TRUSTS**)
- Retirement benefits plans
    - Appeals   Pro §6327
    - Application of law   Pro §§6329, 6330
    - Benefits payable or transferable to trustee   Pro §6323
    - Debts of designator, effect of   Pro §6324
    - Designation of trustee   Pro §§6320 to 6322
    - Escheat of unclaimed benefit payments   CCP §1521
    - Estate tax liability on excess accumulations of   Pro §20114.5
    - Jurisdiction for administration of   Pro §§6325, 6326
    - Personal representative of designator, right to payments by   Pro §6328
- Revocable trusts
    - Generally   Pro §15400
    - Administration, generally (See within this heading, "**Administration**")
    - Beneficiaries
        - Attorney General as revocable trust beneficiary, rights of   Pro §15805
        - Consent by beneficiaries on action to be taken   Pro §15801
        - Rights of, generally   Pro §15800
    - Claims against trust of deceased settlor
        - Claims against estate generally (See within this heading, "**Claims against estate**")
    - Community property held in   Fam §761, Pro §§104, 104.5, 13504
    - Irrevocable, trustees' reporting duties concerning revocable trusts becoming   Pro §§16060.5, 16061.5 to 16061.8
    - Methods of revocation by settlor   Pro §15401
    - Modification as revocation of trust   Pro §15402
    - Notice requirements   Pro §§15802, 15804
    - Power of appointment or withdrawal, rights of holder of   Pro §15803
    - Small estates without administration (See **SMALL ESTATES WITHOUT ADMINISTRATION**)
- Revocation of trust
    - Power to revoke, person holding
        - Incompetency of person holding power   Pro §15800
        - Trustee duties owed to person holding power   Pro §15800

TRUSTS — INDEX

TRUSTS—Cont.
Rule against perpetuities
    Petition for termination of trust continuing after expiration of statutory perpetuities period   Pro §15414
    Validity of trust provision prohibiting termination after expiration of statutory perpetuities period   Pro §15413
Safe deposit box, access rights for removal of decedent's trust instruments from   Pro §331
Sales
    Generally   Pro §16226
    Felon's story, involuntary trust established for proceeds from sale of   CC §2225
    Loyalty, duty of   Pro §16002
Service of notification of changes to trust   Pro §§16061.7 to 16061.9
Settlement of claims
    Attorney General
        Notice of hearing   Pro §19024
        Petition, filing of   Pro §19030
    Commencement of proceedings   Pro §19022
    Debt payments, judicial discretion as to   Pro §19027
    Failure of creditor to timely file written pleading upon notice, effect of   Pro §19025
    Guardian ad litem, appointment of   Pro §19029
    Judicial discretion   Pro §19027
    Notice of hearing
        Other interested parties, mailing to   Pro §19024
        Service on creditors   Pro §19023
    Orders
        Debt payments, order for   Pro §19027
        Finality of   Pro §19025
    Petition
        Attorney General, filing by   Pro §19030
        Contents of   Pro §19022
        Dismissal of   Pro §19026
        Failure of creditor to timely file written pleading upon notice   Pro §19025
        Judicial discretion   Pro §19027
        Place of filing   Pro §19021
        Time of filing   Pro §19020
    Powers of trustee for   Pro §§19005, 19252
    Surviving spouse, action on liability of   Pro §19330
Settlor
    Abuse or neglect of elder or dependent settlor by beneficiary, effect of   Pro §259
    Claims against deceased settlor
        Claims against estate generally (See within this heading, **"Claims against estate"**)
    Declaration of (See within this heading, **"Declaration of settlor"**)
    Designation of trustee consistent with settlor's intent and not product of fraud, menace, duress or undue influence   Pro §15642
    Intent requirements of   Pro §15201
    Money judgment, trust liability for settlor as beneficiary subject to   Pro §15304
    Prudent investor rule, right to expand or restrict   Pro §16046
    Revocable trusts, generally (See within this heading, **"Revocable trusts"**)
Severance of matters associated with proceedings and actions under Probate Code   Pro §801
Simultaneous death statute, effect of   Pro §221
Small estate without administration (See **SMALL ESTATES WITHOUT ADMINISTRATION**)
Special needs trust for minor (See **PARENT AND CHILD**)
Spendthrift trusts (See **SPENDTHRIFT TRUSTS**)
Split-interest trusts
    Defined   Pro §16100
    Proceedings under Tax Reform Act, procedure for   Pro §16105
    Restrictions   Pro §§16102, 16103
    Statutory provisions for   Pro §16104
Spousal support payments, liability for   Fam §4360, Pro §§15302, 15305 to 15306.5
Standard of care
    Deposit of documents with attorney   Pro §§710, 716, 730
    Trustees   Pro §16040
        Compensation, effect   Pro §16041
Statute of frauds   Pro §15206
Statutes of limitation
    Involuntary trusts
        Attorney general actions   CC §2224.5
    Trustees, claims against   Pro §16460
    Trust estates, claims against   Pro §19253
Stay of order, bond requirements for   CCP §919
Stock (See within this heading, **"Corporate stock"**)

TRUSTS—Cont.
Subdivision of property by trustee   Pro §16230
Successor trustees (See within this heading, **"Trustees"**)
Superior court fees
    Funds held by court in trust   Gov §70632
Surety bonds   Pro §§15602, 15604
Surviving spouse's liability in claims against estate
    Action on liability   Pro §19330
    Allocation of debts   Pro §§19320 to 19325
Taxes
    Federal tax liens, registration of   CCP §2101
    Generation-skipping transfer tax (See **GENERATION-SKIPPING TRANSFER TAX**)
    Interpretation of will or trust provisions favoring elimination or reduction of federal estate tax liability   Pro §21503
    Marital deduction (See **MARITAL DEDUCTION GIFTS**)
    Private foundation trusts
        Generally (See within this heading, **"Private foundation trusts"**)
    Proration provisions for estates taxes   Pro §20113
    Split-interest trusts
        Proceedings under tax reform act   Pro §16105
Termination
    Generally   Pro §§15404, 15407
    Changed circumstances, effect of   Pro §15409
    Disposition of trust property   Pro §15410
    Doctrine of merger, effect of   Pro §15209
    Guardian ad litem, consent by   Pro §15405
    Irrevocable trusts, termination by consent of all beneficiaries of   Pro §15403
    Rule against perpetuities
        Petition for termination of trust continuing after expiration of statutory perpetuities period   Pro §15414
        Validity of trust provision prohibiting termination after expiration of statutory perpetuities period   Pro §15413
    Underproductive property as grounds for   Pro §15408
Testamentary trusts under continuing jurisdiction   Pro §§17300 to 17302
    Different county, transfer of trust to   Pro §17304
    Distribution decree establishing testamentary trust   CRC 7.650
    Electronic transactions
        Exceptions to applicability of electronic transactions provisions   CC §1633.3
    Removal   Pro §§17303, 17350 to 17354
Third parties
    Change of trustee, recordation of affidavit   Pro §§18105 to 18108
    Contract liability of trustee to   Pro §18000
    Creditors' rights
        Enforcement of judgment against beneficiary (See within this heading, **"Enforcement of judgment against beneficiary"**)
        Lifetime of settlor of revocable trust, creditor rights during   Pro §§18200, 18201
        Notice to creditors, effect of filing   Pro §19006
        Protection of creditors and other third persons   Pro §§18100 to 18108
    Determination of liability between trustee and trust estate   Pro §18005
    Dissenting cotrustee's liability to   Pro §18003
    Good faith transactions
        Generally   Pro §18100
        Certification of trust by trustee   Pro §18100.5
        Claims against estate, third party liability in   Pro §19403
        Delivery to trustee, effect of   Pro §18101
        Former trustee, transactions with   Pro §18102
    Ownership or control of trust property, trustee's personal liability arising from   Pro §18001
    Protection of creditors and other third parties   Pro §§18100 to 18108
    Real property transactions
        Omission in trust instrument, effect of   Pro §18103
        Undisclosed beneficiaries, effect of transactions involving   Pro §18104
    Representative capacity, liability of trustee in   Pro §18004
    Restitution judgment awarded in felony conviction of beneficiary, satisfaction of   Pro §15305.5
    Tort liability of trustee   Pro §18002
Title to unclaimed property vested in State of California   CCP §1424
Totten trust accounts (See **TOTTEN TRUST ACCOUNTS**)
Transfer of property
    Disclaimer of interest by beneficiary, effect of   Pro §15309
    Enforcement of judgment against beneficiary (See within this heading, **"Enforcement of judgment against beneficiary"**)
Transfer of trust
    From other state
        Generally   Pro §17451
        Administration of transferred trusts   Pro §17457

TRUSTS—Cont.
  Transfer of trust—Cont.
    From other state —Cont.
      Application of law   Pro §17450
      Notice and hearing requirements   Pro §17454
      Order for transfer   Pro §§17455, 17456
      Petition   Pro §17453
      Venue   Pro §17452
    Testamentary trusts   Pro §17304
    To other state
      Generally   Pro §17401
      Application of law   Pro §17400
      Discharge of trustee resulting from   Pro §17405
      Manner of transfer   Pro §17405
      Notice and hearing requirements   Pro §17403
      Order for transfer   Pro §17404
      Petition   Pro §17402
  Trust deed description as requirement for filing claims against trust property   Pro §19152
  Trustees
    "Absolute," "sole," or "uncontrolled" powers, restrictions on exercise of   Pro §16081
    Abuse or neglect of elder or dependent settlor as disqualifying potential fiduciary   Pro §259
    Acceptance of trust by   Pro §15600
    Accounting by (See within this heading, "Accounting")
    Acquisition of property   Pro §16226
    Additions to trust, acceptance of   Pro §16221
    Administration of trusts   Pro §§16000 to 16110
    Affirmation of trustee's acts by beneficiary, effect of   Pro §16465
    Agents, liability for acts of   Pro §16401
    Appointment of trustee
      Generally   Pro §15660
      Nonprofit charitable corporation, appointment of   Pro §15604
      Private professional trustee, appointment of   Pro §§2340, 2341
      Temporary trustee, court appointment of   Pro §17206
    Attorneys' fees for trustees and associates of trustees, restrictions concerning   Pro §15687
    Bond requirements   CRC 7.203, Pro §§15602, 15604
    Borrow money, power to   Pro §16241
    Breach of trust generally (See within this heading, "Breach of trust")
    Business interests, generally (See within this heading, "Business interests")
    Capacity to sue or be sued   CCP §369, Pro §§16011, 16249
    Certification
      Court clerk's certification of trustee   Pro §15603
      Trustee's certificate of trust   Pro §18100.5
    Change of trustee, recordation of affidavit   Pro §18105
      Evidentiary effect   Pro §18107
      Indexing   Pro §18106
      Presumptions   Pro §18107
      Requirements for recordation   Pro §18106
      Trust provisions concerning successor trustee, attachment to affidavit   Pro §18108
    Charitable nonprofit corporation as trustee   Pro §15604
    Charitable trusts, trustee duties   Pro §§16100 to 16110
    Claims against estate, generally (See within this heading, "Claims against estate")
    Collection of property   Pro §16220
    Compensation   Pro §§15680 to 15687, 16243
      Attorneys' fees for trustees and associates of trustees, restrictions concerning   Pro §15687
      Cotrustees   Pro §15683
      Increase in trustee's fee   Pro §15686
      Probate rules   CRC 7.776
      Public administrator as trustee   Pro §15688
      Public guardian as trustee   Pro §15688
      Standard of care, effect on   Pro §16041
    Conflicts of interest   Pro §§16004, 16005
    Consent (See within this heading, "Consent requirement")
    Contested claims, disposition of   Pro §16242
    Corporate stock, generally (See within this heading, "Corporate stock")
    Costs, award of   Pro §15645
    Cotrustees
      Generally   Pro §16013
      Compensation of   Pro §15683
      Dissenting cotrustee, liability of   Pro §18003
      Incapacity of   Pro §15622
      Liability of   Pro §16402
      Unanimous action, requirement of   Pro §15620
      Vacancy in office   Pro §15621
  Damages for wrongful occupancy of land by   CC §3335

TRUSTS—Cont.
  Trustees—Cont.
    Dedication of property to public use   Pro §16230
    Deeds of trust (See **TRUST DEEDS AND MORTGAGES**)
    Defense of claims by   CCP §369, Pro §§16011, 16249
    Defined   Pro §84
    Delegation of duties to others   Pro §16012
    Deposits of trust funds   Pro §16225
    Designation consistent with settlor's intent and not product of fraud, menace, duress or undue influence   Pro §15642
    Digital assets, fiduciary access   Pro §§870 to 884
    Directed trusts   Pro §§16600 to 16632
    Discretionary powers
      "Absolute," "sole," or "uncontrolled" powers, restrictions on exercise of   Pro §16081
      Legal obligations of trustee, prohibition on exercise of discretionary power to discharge   Pro §16082
      Money judgments against beneficiary, effect of   Pro §15303
      Reasonable exercise of   Pro §16080
    Disposition of property   Pro §16226
    Distribution, generally (See within this heading, "Distribution")
    Duties   Pro §§16000 to 16110
    Employee benefit plan beneficiary designated as trustee named in will   Pro §§6320 to 6330
    Endowment beneficiary designated as trustee named in will   Pro §§6321 to 6330
    Enforcement of claims by   Pro §16010
    Enforcement of judgment against beneficiary generally (See within this heading, "Enforcement of judgment against beneficiary")
    Exculpatory trust provisions, applicability of   Pro §16461
    Execution and delivery of instruments to accomplish trust   Pro §16248
    Exoneration of   Pro §§16461, 16462
    Expenditures generally (See within this heading, "Expenditures")
    Fiduciary access to digital assets   Pro §§870 to 884
    Financial institutions as trustee, acts of   Pro §16015
    General powers of   Pro §§16200 to 16202
      Proposed actions of trustee, notice of   Pro §§16500 to 16504
    Generation-skipping transfer tax (See **GENERATION-SKIPPING TRANSFER TAX**)
    Governing law
      Generally   Pro §15001
      Prior law, effect of   Pro §§3, 16203
    Hire, power to   Pro §16247
    Honorary trusts   Pro §15211
    Impartiality in dealings with beneficiaries, duty of   Pro §16003
    Improvements to property   Pro §16229
    Incapacity of cotrustees   Pro §15622
    Independent review to determine whether designated trustee should be removed   Pro §15642
    Insurance on trust property   Pro §16240
    Investments generally (See within this heading, "Investments")
    Irrevocable trusts, reporting duties concerning   Pro §§16060.5, 16061.5 to 16061.8
      Waivers as against public policy   Pro §16068
    Judges, appointment as   CRCSupp JudEthicsCanon 4
    Jurisdiction over   Pro §17004
    Lease agreements generally (See within this heading, "Leases")
    Liens, generally (See within this heading, "Liens")
    Limitation of actions on claims against   Pro §16460
    Loans
      Beneficiary, making loans to   Pro §16244
      Borrowing money by trustee   Pro §16241
    Loyalty, duty of   Pro §16002
    Management of property   Pro §16227
    No contest clause unenforceable on grounds that designated trustee subject to removal   Pro §21306
    Nonprofit charitable corporation as trustee   Pro §15604
    Notices, generally (See within this heading, "Notices")
    Objection by beneficiary to proposed action   Pro §16503
    Option agreements   Pro §16233
    Pets or domestic animals, trust for care of   Pro §15212
    Powers and duties, generally   Pro §§16000 to 16110
      Proposed actions of trustee, notice of   Pro §§16500 to 16504
    Power to prosecute or defend actions   Pro §16249
    Preservation of property   Pro §§15600, 16006
    Presumptions favoring   Ev §§605, 606
    Prior law governing trustee's powers, applicability of   Pro §§3, 16203
    Private foundations, trustee duties   Pro §§16100 to 16110
    Probate rules   CRC 7.755, 7.756
    Proceedings for transfer of trust property   Pro §17200.1
    Productive trust property, duty to make   Pro §16007

TRUSTS—Cont.
Trustees—Cont.
    Professional fiduciaries generally   Pro §§60.1, 2340, 2341
    Proposed actions, notice of   Pro §§16500 to 16504
        Circumstances authorizing notice   Pro §16501
        Consent to action   Pro §16501
        Content of notice   Pro §16502
        Method for notice   Pro §16501
        Objection to proposed action   Pro §16503
        Permissive nature of provisions   Pro §16504
        Principal and income allocations   Pro §16337
        Prohibition, circumstances   Pro §16501
        Recipients of notice   Pro §16501
        Scope of provisions   Pro §16500
    Prosecution of claims by   CCP §369
    Prudent management of institutional funds   Pro §§18501 to 18510 (See **INSTITUTIONAL FUNDS MANAGEMENT**)
    Public administrators as trustees   Pro §15660.5
        Compensation   Pro §15688
    Public guardian as trustee   Pro §15660.5
        Compensation   Pro §15688
        Deposit of trust funds in custody of public guardian   Pro §16042
    Registration of trustees, county filing by private professional trustees   Pro §15604
    Rejection of trust by   Pro §§15600, 15601
    Release of liability by beneficiary, effect of   Pro §16464
        Failure of beneficiary to object to items in account   Pro §16461
    Removal
        Generally   Pro §15642
        Delivery of trust property to successor trustee on   Pro §15644
        No contest clause unenforceable on grounds that designated trustee subject to   Pro §21306
    Repair of trust property, duty of   Pro §16229
    Report to beneficiaries
        Accounting generally (See within this heading, **"Accounting"**)
        Exceptions to duties to account, provide trust or requested information   Pro §16069
        General duty to report information to beneficiaries   Pro §16060
        Irrevocable trusts   Pro §§16060.5, 16061.5 to 16061.8
        On request, duty to provide information   Pro §16061
        Terms of trust provided to beneficiaries   Pro §16060.7
        Waivers as against public policy   Pro §16068
    Resignation
        Delivery of property to successor trustee   Pro §15644
        Liability of trustee   Pro §15641
        Methods of   Pro §15640
    Restitution judgment awarded in felony conviction of beneficiary, trust assets used in satisfaction of   Pro §15305.5
    Revocable trusts
        Waivers as against public policy   Pro §16068
    Self-dealing by   Pro §16004
    Separation and identification of trust property   Pro §16009
    Settlement of claims   Pro §16242
    Special skills, use of   Pro §16014
    Split-interest trusts, generally (See within this heading, **"Split-interest trusts"**)
    Standard of care
        Generally   Pro §16040
        Compensation, effect of   Pro §16041
    Standing to sue   CCP §369
    Subdivision of trust property by   Pro §16230
    Substitution during wartime (See **FIDUCIARIES' WARTIME SUBSTITUTION LAW**)
    Successor trustees
        Appointment of   Pro §15660
        Change of trustee, recordation of affidavit   Pro §§18105 to 18108
        Delivery of property to   Pro §15644
        Liability of   Pro §16403
    Tax liability, payment of   Pro §16243
    Temporary trustee, court appointment of   Pro §17206
    Testamentary trust established by distribution decree   CRC 7.650
    Third party, trustee's liability to
        Creditor's rights generally (See within this heading, **"Creditors' rights"**)
        Generally (See within this heading, **"Third parties"**)
    Transfer of trust, discharge of trustee resulting from   Pro §17405
    Trustee's accounts   CRC 7.901
    Undue influence
        Involuntary trusts, creation of   CC §2224.5
        Presumption of undue influence in transactions between trustee and beneficiary   Pro §16004

TRUSTS—Cont.
Trustees—Cont.
    Uniform prudent management of institutional funds act   Pro §§18501 to 18510 (See **INSTITUTIONAL FUNDS MANAGEMENT**)
    Uniform Transfers to Minors Act, transfer under   Pro §3905
    Vacancy in office
        Generally   Pro §15643
        Appointment of successor trustee   Pro §15660
        Cotrustee   Pro §15621
        Delivery of property to successor trustee   Pro §15644
        Removal or discharge   Pro §15642
    Venue of action against   CCP §395.1
    Voting trusts   Pro §16237
    Waiver of trustee liability as condition of beneficiary receiving distribution
        Trustee not to require   Pro §16004.5
    Waivers as against public policy   Pro §16068
    Wartime substitution of (See **FIDUCIARIES' WARTIME SUBSTITUTION LAW**)
    Wrongful detention of property, involuntary trust arising from
        Attorney general actions, statute of limitations   CC §2224.5
Trustor (See within this heading, **"Settlor"**)
Two or more trusts, order for combining   Pro §15411
Unclaimed deposits and payments of employee benefit plans, escheat of   CCP §§1501, 1521
Underproductive property   Pro §15408
Undue influence
    Definition of undue influence   Pro §86
    Independent review to determine whether designated trustee should be removed   Pro §15642
    Involuntary trusts, creation of   CC §2224
    Presumption of   Pro §16004
    Wrongful taking, concealment, etc of property of conservatee, minor, elder, dependent adult, etc   Pro §859
Uniform directed trust act   Pro §§16600 to 16632
Uniform Parentage act
    Vacation or setting aside of judgment
        Payments made in good faith by estate, trustees, insurers, etc., based on paternity judgment   Fam §7649.5
Uniform Principal and Income Act (See within this heading, **"Principal and income allocations"**)
Uniform prudent management of institutional funds act   Pro §§18501 to 18510 (See **INSTITUTIONAL FUNDS MANAGEMENT**)
Uniform Testamentary Additions to Trusts Act   Pro §§6300 to 6303
Uniform Transfers to Minors Act (See **UNIFORM TRANSFERS TO MINORS ACT**)
Unitrust
    Fiduciary income and principal act   Pro §§16330 to 16338
Validity of trust, effect of doctrine of merger on   Pro §15209
Venue   CCP §395.1, Pro §17005
Vlogging, trust accounts for minors engaged in the work of   Fam §6653
Voting trusts   Pro §16237
Waiver of defects in claims filed against trust property of deceased settlor   Pro §19154
Writing
    Generally   CCP §§1971, 1972
    Statute of frauds   Pro §15206
Wrongful detention of property, involuntary trust arising from   CC §§2223, 2224
Wrongful taking, concealment, etc of property of conservatee, minor, elder, dependent adult, etc   Pro §859

TRUTH
Hearsay statements admissible upon establishment of belief in   Ev §1221
Libel and slander, alleging truth in action for   CCP §461
Witnesses (See **WITNESSES**)

TRUTH-IN-LENDING ACT
Automobile sales contracts   CC §2982
Balloon payment loans   CC §2924i
Retail installment sales (See **RETAIL INSTALLMENT SALES**)
Song-Beverly Credit Card Act, relation to   CC §1747.01

TUNNELS
Cargo tank vehicles traveling through tunnels, immunity of public entity from liability for failure to prohibit or restrict   Gov §821.5

TWENTY YEARS (See **STATUTES OF LIMITATION**)

TWITTER
Judicial ethics code
    Public confidence in judiciary
        Electronic communications, care in using   CRCSupp JudEthicsCanon 2

TWO YEARS (See **STATUTES OF LIMITATION**)

TYPE SIZE
Invoices, solicitations appearing like   CC §1716
Leases, automatic renewal clauses   CC §1945.5
Liquidated damages clauses   CC §1677
Notices, requirements for   CCP §1019
Retail installment sales contracts   CC §1803.1

TYPEWRITERS AND TYPEWRITING
Instructions to jury   CCP §607a
Serial number destroyed or altered prior to sale of typewriter   CC §1710.1
Writing defined to include   CCP §17

U

UNAUTHORIZED PRACTICE OF LAW   ProfC 5.5

UNBORN CHILDREN
Generally (See **POSTHUMOUS CHILDREN**)
Fetus (See **FETUS**)

UNCERTAINTY (See **CERTAINTY**)

UNCLAIMED PROPERTY
Generally   CCP §§1300 to 1615
Abandoned property
     Claims, time limit for commencement of actions for   CCP §1476
     Delivery to treasurer or controller   CCP §1449
     Intentional abandonment   CC §2080.7
Administration of estates
     Generally   Pro §§11850 to 11854
     Public administrators, administration by   Pro §§7624, 7643, 7644, 7663
Agreement to locate   CCP §1582
Annuities   CCP §1515
Attorneys at law
     Interest on lawyers trust accounts (IOLTA)
         Administration of funds escheated from IOLTA accounts   CCP §1564.5
Auctions
     Sales generally (See within this heading, "**Sales**")
Banks   CCP §§1513, 1513.5
Bills of sale by controller   CCP §§1372, 1376, 1563
Board of control, approval by   CCP §§1352, 1370 to 1382
Bona fide purchasers   CCP §§1381, 1430, 1441
Bonds, indemnity, recovery of expenses incurred by controller   CCP §1325
Canceled warrants, transfer of amounts of to general fund   CCP §1317
Cash transmitted to treasurer   CCP §1310
Certificates as to interests in intangible property, issuance of duplicate   CCP §1532
Certification
     Federal custody, regarding property held in   CCP §1605
     Right or title to property   CCP §1353
Citation of statute   CCP §1500
City property   CCP §1519
Claims
     California voluntary compliance program   CCP §1577.5
     Payment   CCP §§1540 to 1543
     Streamlining secure payment of claims   CCP §1543
Common carriers, sale of property by   CC §§2081 to 2081.4
Contracts
     Agreement to locate property   CCP §1582
     Controller's action on unclaimed property   CCP §1377
     State as party to   CCP §1306
Controller
     Generally (See **ESCHEAT**)
     Abandoned property account   CCP §1564
     Actions brought up by   CCP §1572
     Auctions by   CCP §1563
     California voluntary compliance program   CCP §1577.5
     Claims   CCP §§1540 to 1543
     Delivery of escheated property to   CCP §1532
     General fund, depositing investments in   CCP §1562
     Indemnification of holder by   CCP §1561
     Investments deposited in general fund by   CCP §1562
     Notices
         Apparent owners of escheated property, notice to   CCP §1531
         Decision on claim, notice to claimant of   CCP §1540
         Location of owner, notification program   CCP §1531.5
     Other states claims   CCP §1542
     Parks and recreation director examining property delivered to   CCP §1567
     Payments   CCP §1540
     Publication of notices of escheat caused by   CCP §1531

UNCLAIMED PROPERTY—Cont.
Controller—Cont.
     Records examination by   CCP §1571
     Refund by   CCP §1561
     Regulations formed by   CCP §1580
     Reimbursement by   CCP §1560
     Report of escheat sent to   CCP §1530
         Interest payable on property not reported   CCP §1577
         Postponement of time for fling of report   CCP §1532
     Rules formed by   CCP §1580
     Securities sold by   CCP §1563
     Suit by claimant against   CCP §1566
     Tangible property excluded by   CCP §1533
     Time expiration by statute, effect of   CCP §1570
     Worthless property, disposing of   CCP §1565
County property   CCP §1519
Damages, indemnity from liability for   CCP §1321
Deeds executed by controller   CCP §1376
Definitions   CCP §§1300, 1501
Delivery of escheated property to controller   CCP §1532
Delivery or payment
     Claims to property paid or delivered to controller   CCP §§1540 to 1543
Dissolution of business associations   CCP §1517
Districts' property   CCP §1519
Dividend payments   CCP §1516
Employee benefit trust plans   CCP §§1501, 1521
Escheat (See **ESCHEAT**)
Exemptions from escheat   CCP §§1502 to 1506, 1528
Expenditures from funds   CCP §1325
Federal agencies, property held by   CCP §§1600 to 1615
Fees
     Disposition of property   CC §2082
     Locating property, compensation for   CCP §1582
Fiduciary property   CCP §1518
Fines on violating statutes on   CCP §1576
Fund (See within this heading, "**Unclaimed property fund**")
Funeral trusts, preneed
     Escheat of unclaimed funds maintained in preneed funeral trust   CCP §1518.5
         Reimbursement of holder upon submission of death certificate   CCP §1560
Indemnity for party surrendering possession of   CCP §1321
Insurance rebate under Proposition 103, disposition of unclaimed   CCP §1523
Insurers
     Demutualization
         Property distributable as part of demutualization   CCP §1515.5
     Dissolution, property unclaimed following   CCP §1517
Intangible personalty   CCP §§1510, 1516, 1520, 1520.5
Interest   CCP §§1513, 1513.5, 1516
     Controller, waiver of interest payable   CCP §1577
     Crediting   CCP §§1318 to 1320
     Failure to deliver unclaimed property, interest rate imposed for   CCP §1577
     Failure to file substantially compliant report, imposition of interest   CCP §1577
     Indemnity against liability for   CCP §1321
     Not paid   CCP §1540
Interest on lawyers trust accounts (IOLTA)
     Administration of funds escheated from IOLTA accounts   CCP §1564.5
Investments deposited in unclaimed property fund   CCP §1562
Leases
     Controller executing   CCP §1376
     Personal property   CCP §1370
     Proceeds, disposition of   CCP §§1390 to 1394
     Real property   CCP §§1373, 1375
Liability
     California voluntary compliance program   CCP §1577.5
Liability for escheated property   CCP §1560
Life insurance funds   CCP §1515
Liquidation of business associations   CCP §1517
Location of property, agreement for determining of   CCP §1582
Lost property not claimed   CC §§2080.3 to 2080.8
Military history artifacts, storage in lieu of sale   CCP §1563
Money orders   CCP §§1511, 1513, 1542, 1581
Municipal corporation property   CCP §1519
Museums, unclaimed property in hands of   CC §§1899 to 1899.11
Notice
     Banks and financial organizations, notice requirements for   CCP §1513.5
     Business associations, notice requirement for   CCP §1516
     Controller, notices by (See within this heading, "**Controller**")
     Escheat generally (See **ESCHEAT**)

UNCLAI INDEX 572

UNCLAIMED PROPERTY—Cont.
Notice—Cont.
    Expansive notification program
        Legislative intent   CCP §1501.5
        Location of owner, notification program   CCP §1531.5
    Savings bonds, war bonds or military awards
        Separate notice   CCP §1531.6
Other states
    Absence of law escheating intangible property to state   CCP §1510
    Actions by attorney generals of   CCP §1574
    Agreement for valuation information with   CCP §1573
    Attorney general, duties of   CCP §§1574, 1575
    Claim of ownership by   CCP §1542
    Information for valuation, agreement for   CCP §1573
    Property escheated under laws of   CCP §1504
    Reciprocal enforcement of unclaimed property laws, agreements as to   CCP §§1574, 1575
Parks and recreation director examining property delivered to controller   CCP §1567
Penalties on violating statutes on   CCP §1576
Postponement of date for payment or delivery   CCP §1532
Prior law, property not subject to   CCP §1503
Profits   CCP §1516
Property determined to not be subject to escheat
    Holder's duties   CCP §1532
Public agencies, disposition of property held by   CC §2080.6
Publication of notice by Controller   CCP §1531
    Location of owner, notification program   CCP §1531.5
Receivers   CCP §§570, 1422
Refunds
    Appropriations for payment of   CCP §1325
    Controller, refunds by   CCP §1561
    Court or public agency, business association refunds ordered by   CCP §1519.5
Residuals   CCP §§1501, 1521
Retirement funds (See **RETIREMENT**)
Safety deposit boxes   CCP §§1514, 1532.1
Salaries and wages
    Escheat   CCP §1513
Sales   CC §§2080.3 to 2080.8
    Common carriers, property held by   CC §§2081.1, 2081.6
    Controller, sale by   CCP §§1373, 1374, 1563
    Lost property not claimed   CC §§2080.3 to 2080.8
    Military history artifacts, storage in lieu of sale   CCP §1563
    Proceeds, disposition of   CCP §§1390 to 1394
    Stock   CCP §§1371, 1563
    Time for sale   CCP §1563
    Unclaimed Property Fund, property held by   CCP §1382
    Warehouseman, sale by   CC §§2081.5, 2081.6
School district property   CCP §1519
Small claims court judgment entered, unclaimed payment to court in which   CCP §116.860
State held property under terms of express contract, applicability to   CCP §1306
State property   CCP §1519
Time   CCP §§1540 to 1543
    Expiration by statute, effect   CCP §1570
Traveler's checks   CCP §§1511, 1513, 1542, 1581
Treasurer
    Cash deposited with   CCP §1310
    Proceeds of sale delivered to   CCP §§1390, 1391
    State custody of property delivered to   CCP §1361
Unclaimed property fund
    Abandoned property account in   CCP §1564
    Accounts separated by controller in   CCP §§1314, 1319
    Advertising, appropriations for   CCP §1325
    Appraisal of title, appropriations for   CCP §1325
    Controller ordering deposits into   CCP §1313
    Creation of   CCP §1313
    Decedents' estates, claims to   CCP §1354
    Escheated property deposited into   CCP §1313
    Income credited to separate accounts   CCP §1319
    Indemnity bonds, appropriations for   CCP §1325
    Inheritance tax fund, appropriations for transfer to   CCP §1325
    Investments deposited in   CCP §1562
    Liens, appropriations for   CCP §1325
    Mortgages, appropriations for   CCP §1325
    Permanent escheat   CCP §1431
    Proceeds of sale deposited into   CCP §1390
    Refund   CCP §1345
    Repairs, appropriations for   CCP §1325
    Sale of property held by   CCP §1382

UNCLAIMED PROPERTY—Cont.
Unclaimed property fund—Cont.
    Taxes, appropriations for   CCP §1325
    Title searches, appropriations for   CCP §1325
    Trust deeds, appropriations for   CCP §1325
United States agencies, property held by   CCP §§1600 to 1615
Universities and colleges, disposition by   CC §2080.8
Violations of statutes on   CCP §1576

UNCONSCIONABLE ATTORNEYS' FEES
Attorney professional conduct   ProfC 1.5

UNCONSCIONABLE CONTRACTS (See **CONTRACTS AND AGREEMENTS**)

UNCONTESTED ACTIONS
Court commissioner's powers   CCP §259

UNCONVENTIONAL RELIGIOUS MARRIAGES (See **MARRIAGE**)

UNDERGROUND STORAGE OF HAZARDOUS MATERIALS
Attorney general, civil actions to enforce provisions
    Fees and costs for attorney general   CCP §1021.8

UNDERPASSES
Eminent domain compensation for   CCP §1263.450

UNDERTAKINGS (See **SURETYSHIP, BONDS AND UNDERTAKINGS**)

UNDISCLOSED PRINCIPAL (See **AGENCY**)

UNDUE EXPENSE
Court orders to prevent   CCP §379.5

UNDUE HARDSHIP
Jury service, grounds for exemption from   CCP §204

UNDUE INFLUENCE
Contracts   CC §1575
Debts
    Coerced debt   CC §§1798.97.1 to 1798.97.6
Donative transfers
    Presumption of fraud or undue influence   Pro §§21360 to 21392 (See **DONATIVE TRANSFERS**)
Involuntary trust resulting from undue influence   CC §2224
    Attorney general actions
        Statute of limitations   CC §2224.5
Judge's exercise of   CRCSupp JudEthicsCanon 4
Power of attorney
    Attorney in fact
        Undue influence to take, conceal, etc property of principal   Pro §4231.5
Probate code
    Definition of undue influence   Pro §86
Transfer on death deeds
    Fraud, undue influence, etc, creation of deed
        Applicability of other provisions penalizing conduct   Pro §5698
Trustee and beneficiary transactions, presumption of undue influence in   Pro §16004
Unsoundness of mind presumed if unable to manage financial resources or resist fraud or undue influence   CC §39
Wills, general discussion of effect on   Pro §6104

UNEMPLOYMENT
Child support obligations (See **CHILD SUPPORT**)
Spousal support, consideration of unemployment periods because of domestic duties   Fam §4320

UNEMPLOYMENT COMPENSATION
Assignment for benefit of creditors, property exempt from   CCP §1801
Attachment, exemption   CCP §486.060
Decedent's estate, claims against   Pro §§9200 to 9205
Disclosure of information obtained through unemployment compensation administration   Ev §1040
Enforcement of judgments (See **ENFORCEMENT OF JUDGMENTS**)
Escheat, exception to requirements for   Pro §6806
Mortgage foreclosure proceedings, enforcement of lien in   CC §2931c
Trust deed foreclosure, enforcement of lien   CC §2931c

UNEXERCISED OPTIONS (See **TITLE AND OWNERSHIP**)

UNFAIR CLAIMS SETTLEMENT PRACTICES BY LIABILITY INSURERS
Third-party cause of action   CC §§2870, 2871

UNFAIR COMPETITION
Advertising regulated   CC §1770
Complex litigation defined   CRC 3.400
Deceptive practices prohibited   CC §1770
Grey market goods in violation of law as unfair competition, sale of   CC §1797.86
Public social services
    Unreasonable fees to assist applicants for public social services as deceptive practice   CC §1770
        Treble damages   CC §1780
Statute of limitation for unfair competition   CC §§1770, 1783
Supermarket club cards, unfair competition constituted by violation of provisions for   CC §1749.63
Veterans benefits or entitlements
    Workshops, presentations, events, etc regarding veterans benefits or entitlements
        Advertising or promoting without certain disclosures as unfair or deceptive practice   CC §1770

UNIFORM BAIL AND PENALTY SCHEDULES   CRC 4.102

UNIFORM BUSINESS RECORDS AS EVIDENCE ACT   Ev §§1270 to 1272

UNIFORM CHILD CUSTODY JURISDICTION AND ENFORCEMENT ACT
Adoption, inapplicability of Act to   Fam §3403
Affidavit or initial pleading, information to be furnished in   Fam §3429
Appeals from enforcement actions   Fam §3454
Appearance
    Generally   Fam §3430
    Enforcement hearing, order to appear at   Fam §3448
    Evidentiary hearing, order to appear at   Fam §3412
    Immunity from personal jurisdiction in other proceedings despite appearance in custody proceeding   Fam §3409
Application of Act   Fam §§3403 to 3405, 3461, 3465
Binding force of custody determinations   Fam §3406
Citation of Act   Fam §3400
Communication between courts of different states   Fam §§3410, 3424
Construction of Act   Fam §3461
Contemporaneous proceedings   Fam §3426
    Enforcement and modification proceedings   Fam §§3426, 3447
Contesting registration of other state's order, procedure for   Fam §3445
Custody evaluations   Fam §3412
Declarations
    Family rules   CRC 5.52
    Form   CRCAppx A (CRCFL-105)
Declination of jurisdiction when jurisdiction established by unjustifiable conduct on part of party seeking to invoke jurisdiction   Fam §3428
Definitions   Fam §§3402, 3442
Depositions of witnesses in other state   Fam §3411
Dismissal of proceedings
    Commencement of proceedings in another state, determination of   Fam §3426
    Declination of jurisdiction on ground of unjustifiable conduct on part of party seeking to invoke jurisdiction   Fam §3428
District attorney's role   Fam §§3135, 3455, 3457
Documentary evidence transmitted from other state   Fam §3411
Emergency medical care, inapplicability of Act to   Fam §3403
Emergency temporary jurisdiction   Fam §3424
Enforcement of custody orders
    Generally   Fam §3443
    Appeals   Fam §3454
    Contesting registration of other state's order   Fam §3445
    Costs award   Fam §§3450, 3452
    Defenses to enforcement   Fam §3450
    Definitions   Fam §3442
    District attorney's role   Fam §§3135, 3455, 3457
    Full faith and credit accorded other state's orders   Fam §3453
    Gender-affirming health care or mental health care, removal of child based on
        Other state laws authorizing removal unenforceable   Fam §3453.5
    Hague Convention on Civil Aspects of International Child Abduction, enforcement of order for return of child under   Fam §§3441, 3442, 3455
    Hearings   Fam §§3445, 3448
    Law enforcement officers' assistance in locating missing party or child   Fam §3456
    Petition requirements   Fam §§3448, 3449
    Privileges against testifying, applicability of   Fam §3450
    Registration of other state's order   Fam §§3445, 3446
    Service of petition   Fam §3449

UNIFORM CHILD CUSTODY JURISDICTION AND ENFORCEMENT ACT—Cont.
Enforcement of custody orders—Cont.
    Simultaneous modification and enforcement proceedings in different states   Fam §§3426, 3447
    Temporary order enforcing other state's visitation provisions when court lacks jurisdiction to modify custody   Fam §3444
    Warrant to take physical custody of child   Fam §3451
Evidence, procedures for gathering   Fam §§3411, 3412
Exclusive and continuing jurisdiction   Fam §3422
Expenses
    Dismissal for unjustifiable conduct, assessment of costs against offending party after   Fam §3428
    District Attorney's expenses   Fam §3457
    Enforcement hearing, cost award in   Fam §§3450, 3452
Foreign country's custody determination, applicability of Act to   Fam §3405
Full faith and credit accorded other state's orders   Fam §3453
Gender-affirming health care or mental health care
    Jurisdiction
        Presence of child in state for care, effect on jurisdiction   Fam §3421
        Temporary emergency jurisdiction   Fam §3424
        Unjustifiable misconduct determinations, taking of child to obtain gender-affirming care not considered as   Fam §3428
    Removal of child based on gender-affirming care
        Other state laws authorizing removal unenforceable   Fam §3453.5
Hague Convention on Civil Aspects of International Child Abduction, enforcement of order for return of child under   Fam §§3441, 3442, 3455
Hearings
    Contesting registration of other state's order   Fam §3445
    Evidentiary hearings   Fam §3412
    Petition for enforcement, hearing on   Fam §3448
Immigrants
    Juvenile immigrants
        Request for special findings   CRCAppx A
        Special findings   CRCAppx A
Immunity from personal jurisdiction in other proceedings despite appearance in custody proceedings   Fam §3409
Inconvenient forum determination   Fam §3427
Indian children, applicability of Act to proceedings involving   Fam §3404
Intervene, right to   Fam §3425
Joinder of parties   Fam §3425
Jurisdiction to make custody determinations, generally   Fam §3421
Law enforcement officers' assistance in locating missing party or child   Fam §3456
Modification of custody determination
    Other state's determination, jurisdiction and grounds for modifying   Fam §3423
    Simultaneous enforcement and modification proceedings in different states   Fam §§3426, 3447
Native American children, applicability of Act to proceedings involving   Fam §3404
Notice requirements   Fam §§3408, 3425
Pleading or attached affidavit, information to be furnished in   Fam §3429
Priority on calendar for challenge to jurisdiction   Fam §3407
Proof of service   Fam §3408
Records
    Communication between courts, record of   Fam §3410
    Preservation of records   Fam §3412
Registration of other state's order   Fam §§3445, 3446
Res judicata effect of custody determinations   Fam §3406
Severability of provisions   Fam §3462
Simultaneous proceedings
    Generally   Fam §3426
    Enforcement and modification proceedings   Fam §§3426, 3447
Stay of proceedings
    Commencement of proceedings in another state, stay on determination of   Fam §3426
    Declination of jurisdiction based on unjustifiable conduct of party seeking to invoke jurisdiction   Fam §3428
    Inconvenient forum determination   Fam §3427
    Information to be furnished in initial pleading, failure to provide   Fam §3429
Temporary emergency jurisdiction   Fam §3424
Temporary order enforcing other state's visitation provisions when court lacks jurisdiction to modify custody   Fam §3444
Testimony of witnesses in other state   Fam §3411
Unjustifiable conduct on part of party seeking to invoke jurisdiction, declination of jurisdiction when jurisdiction established by   Fam §3428
Visitation provisions of other state, temporary order enforcing   Fam §3444
Warrant to take physical custody of child   Fam §3451

UNIFORM COMMERCIAL CODE
Electronic transactions
    Exceptions to applicability of electronic transactions provisions   CC §1633.3

UNIFORM DIRECTED TRUST ACT   Pro §§16600 to 16632

UNIFORM DIVORCE RECOGNITION ACT   Fam §§2090 to 2093

UNIFORM DURABLE POWER OF ATTORNEY (See **POWER OF ATTORNEY**)

UNIFORM ELECTRONIC TRANSACTIONS ACT (See **ELECTRONIC TRANSACTIONS**)

UNIFORM FEDERAL LIEN REGISTRATION ACT   CCP §§2100 to 2107
Fees for recording under act   Gov §27388.1

UNIFORM FIDUCIARY ACCESS TO DIGITAL ASSETS ACT   Pro §§870 to 884 (See **FIDUCIARY ACCESS TO DIGITAL ASSETS**)

UNIFORM FIDUCIARY INCOME AND PRINCIPAL ACT   Pro §§16320 to 16383

UNIFORM FOREIGN COUNTRY MONEY JUDGMENTS RECOGNITION ACT   CCP §§1713 to 1725

UNIFORM FOREIGN-MONEY CLAIMS ACT   CCP §§676 to 676.16

UNIFORM GIFTS TO MINORS ACT (See **UNIFORM TRANSFERS TO MINORS ACT**)

UNIFORM HEALTH CARE DECISIONS ACT   Pro §§4670 to 4743

UNIFORM INTERNATIONAL WILLS ACT   Pro §§6380 to 6390

UNIFORM INTERSTATE DEPOSITIONS AND DISCOVERY ACT   CCP §§2029.100 to 2029.900
California version of uniform act described   CCP §2029.700
Generally (See **DISCOVERY**)

UNIFORM INTERSTATE ENFORCEMENT OF DOMESTIC VIOLENCE PROTECTION ORDERS ACT (See **DOMESTIC VIOLENCE**)

UNIFORM INTERSTATE FAMILY SUPPORT ACT   Fam §§5700.101 to 5700.903 (See **INTERSTATE FAMILY SUPPORT**)

UNIFORM PARENTAGE ACT   Fam §§7600 to 7730
Adoption proceedings   Fam §§7660 to 7671
Agreement between alleged father or presumed parent with other parent
    Effect   Fam §7632
Appearance by minor without guardian ad litem   CCP §372
Assisted reproduction   Fam §7613
    Defined   Fam §7606
    Forms for assisted reproduction   Fam §7613.5
    Jurisdiction based on conception caused by   Fam §7620
    Vacation or setting aside of judgment
        Effect of provisions on paternity determinations   Fam §7648.9
Assisted reproduction agreements
    Defined   Fam §7606
    Parent-child relationship
        Parties to agreement bringing action to establish   Fam §7630
Attorney's fees   Fam §7640
Birth certificate, issuance of new   Fam §7639
Change of name of child   Fam §7638
Child support
    Local child support agency
        Action to determine paternity   Fam §7634
Citation of act   Fam §7600
Closed court
    Hearings in closed court   Fam §7643.5
Confidentiality
    Hearings and records   Fam §7643
    Promise to furnish support   Fam §7614
Consideration as not required for enforcement of promise to furnish support   Fam §7614
Contempt for failure to obey judgment   Fam §7641
Costs of litigation   Fam §7640
Costs of pregnancy and childbirth, admissible evidence concerning   Fam §7604.5
Custody of children   Fam §§6323, 6346, 7604, 7637
Default judgment of parentage
    Reconsideration   Fam §7646

UNIFORM PARENTAGE ACT—Cont.
Definitions   Fam §7601
Descent and distribution, application to   Pro §6453
DNA
    Right to genetic testing   Fam §7635.5
    Vacation or setting aside of judgment   Fam §7647.7
        Child support enforcement agency involvement, provision of genetic testing   Fam §7648.2
        Prior genetic testing, prohibition on vacating or setting aside judgment based on   Fam §7648.3
Domestic violence
    Agreement and judgment of parentage in domestic violence prevention act cases   CRC 5.380
    Protective orders   Fam §§7710 to 7730
    Temporary custody and visitation privileges   Fam §§6323, 6346
Establishing parent and child relationship   Fam §§7610 to 7614
Ex parte orders   Fam §7710
Fees
    Title IV-D child support agency involved   Gov §70672
Forms
    Judicial council forms   CRCAppx A
Genetic testing
    Right to genetic testing   Fam §7635.5
    Vacation or setting aside of judgment   Fam §7647.7
        Child support enforcement agency involvement, provision of genetic testing   Fam §7648.2
        Prior genetic testing, prohibition on vacating or setting aside judgment based on   Fam §7648.3
Intestate succession, application to   Pro §6453
In vitro fertilization   Fam §7613
    Forms for assisted reproduction   Fam §7613.5
Judgments
    Effect of   Fam §7636
    Enforcement of   Fam §7641
    Modification or setting aside of   Fam §7642
        Vacating or setting aside generally   Fam §§7645 to 7649.5
    Other provisions of judgment including support, custody, etc   Fam §7637
    Protective orders included in   Fam §§6360, 6361, 7730
    Vacating or setting aside   Fam §§7645 to 7649.5
Jurisdiction   Fam §7620
Minor children as parties to action
    Appearance by minor without guardian ad litem   CCP §372
More than 2 parents
    Court may find more than 2 persons with claim to parentage   Fam §7612
    Parent and child relationship   Fam §7601
Mother and child relationship, action to determine   Fam §7650
Name changes   Fam §7638
Natural parent
    Defined   Fam §7601
    Presumption of parentage   Fam §7611
Parent and child relationship
    Defined   Fam §7601
    Determination   Fam §§7630 to 7644
        Forms   CRCAppx A
Parties in actions under   Fam §7635
Paternity generally (See **PATERNITY**)
Paternity presumptions   Fam §§7611 to 7612
Pre-born children, action to establish paternity of   Fam §7633
Presumption of paternity   Fam §§7611 to 7612
Promise to furnish support, consideration as not required for enforcement of   Fam §7614
Protective orders   Fam §§7710 to 7730
Records
    Inspection or copying of records pertaining to action   Fam §7643.5
Summons, temporary restraining order in   Fam §7700
Support provisions of judgment   Fam §7637
Temporary custody orders   Fam §§6323, 6346, 7604
Temporary restraining orders   Fam §7700
Termination of parental rights   Fam §§7660 to 7671
Vacation or setting aside of judgment   Fam §§7645 to 7649.5
    Adoption
        Effect of provisions on   Fam §7648.5
    Artificial insemination, conception by
        Effect of provisions on paternity determinations   Fam §7648.9
    Child
        Defined   Fam §7645
    Child support enforcement agency involvement
        Genetic testing provided   Fam §7648.2
    Child support orders vacated   Fam §7648.4
    Construction and interpretation   Fam §7649
    Definitions   Fam §7645

UNIFORM PARENTAGE ACT—Cont.
Vacation or setting aside of judgment —Cont.
    Denial of motion
        Best interests of child as grounds   Fam §§7648, 7648.1
    Genetic testing   Fam §7647.7
        Child support enforcement agency involvement, provision of genetic testing   Fam §7648.2
        Prior genetic testing, prohibition on vacating or setting aside judgment based on   Fam §7648.3
        Time to set aside   Fam §7635.5
    Good faith payments made by estate, trustee, insurer, etc., based on paternity judgment   Fam §7649.5
    Grounds   Fam §7647
    Guardian ad litem
        Best of interest of child, appointment to represent   Fam §7647.5
    Judgment defined   Fam §7645
    Motions
        Contents   Fam §7647
    Out of state order
        Prohibition on vacating or setting aside   Fam §7648.3
    Previously established father
        Defined   Fam §7645
    Previously established mother
        Defined   Fam §7645
    Prohibition of vacating or setting aside   Fam §7648.3
    Statute of limitation to bring action to vacate or set aside   Fam §7646
Venue   Fam §7620
    Temporary support, attorney fees, custody and visitation issues determined prior to determination of motion for transfer of   CCP §396b
Voluntary declaration of parentage   Fam §7644

UNIFORM PREMARITAL AGREEMENT ACT (See PROPERTY SETTLEMENT AGREEMENTS)

UNIFORM PRUDENT INVESTOR ACT   Pro §§16045 to 16054

UNIFORM PRUDENT MANAGEMENT OF INSTITUTIONAL FUNDS ACT   Pro §§18501 to 18510 (See **INSTITUTIONAL FUNDS MANAGEMENT**)

UNIFORM RECOGNITION AND ENFORCEMENT OF CANADIAN DOMESTIC VIOLENCE PROTECTION ORDERS ACT   Fam §§6450 to 6460

UNIFORM SIMULTANEOUS DEATH ACT   Pro §§103, 220 to 232, 6402

UNIFORM SINGLE PUBLICATION ACT   CC §§3425.1 to 3425.5

UNIFORM STATUTORY FORM POWER OF ATTORNEY (See POWER OF ATTORNEY)

UNIFORM STATUTORY RULE AGAINST PERPETUITIES   Pro §§21200 to 21231

UNIFORM TESTAMENTARY ADDITIONS TO TRUSTS ACT   Pro §§6300 to 6303

UNIFORM TOD SECURITY REGISTRATION ACT   Pro §§5500 to 5512

UNIFORM TRADE SECRETS ACT (See TRADE SECRETS)

UNIFORM TRANSFERS TO MINORS ACT
Generally   Pro §§3903 to 3907, 3909
Accounting by custodian, petition for   Pro §3919
Applicability of Act   Pro §§3303, 3902, 3922, 6349
Bequest under act
    Will provisions generally (See within this heading, **"Will provisions"**)
Citation   Pro §3900
Compensation of custodian   Pro §3915
Definitions   Pro §3901
Delay in transfer of custodial property to minor   Pro §3920.5
Delivery of property to minor   Pro §3914
Devise under act
    Will provisions generally (See within this heading, **"Will provisions"**)
Disclaimer by custodian   Pro §3918
Duties of custodian   Pro §3912
Executors and administrators, transfer by   Pro §3905
Form of transfer   Pro §3909
Hearing on petition filed under Act, venue for   Pro §3921
Judgment for minor, disposition of funds obtained from   Pro §§3602, 3611
Jurisdiction
    Generally   Pro §3902

UNIFORM TRANSFERS TO MINORS ACT—Cont.
Jurisdiction—Cont.
    Will provisions for transfer, jurisdiction where   Pro §6348
Liability of custodian and minor   Pro §3917
Limits of transfer   Pro §3910
Nomination of custodian   Pro §3903
Payments to minor   Pro §3914
Prior law, effect of   Pro §3923
Purpose of Act   Pro §3925
Receipt from custodian acknowledging transfer   Pro §3908
Reimbursement to custodian   Pro §3915
Replacement of custodian   Pro §3918
Rights of custodian   Pro §3913
Settlement and compromise, disposition of funds obtained from   Pro §§3602, 3611
Substitution of custodian   Pro §3918
Third person dealing with custodian   Pro §3916
Time
    Delay in transfer of custodial property to minor   Pro §3920.5
    General provisions regarding transfer of custodial property to minor   Pro §3920
Trustees, transfer by   Pro §3905
Unauthorized transfer to custodian   Pro §3906
Validity and effect of transfer   Pro §3911
Venue for hearing on petition filed under   Pro §3921
Will provisions
    Generally   Pro §§6206, 6341
    Applicability of law regarding   Pro §6349
    Custodians, provisions regarding   Pro §§6345, 6347
    Jurisdiction of court   Pro §6348

UNIFORM TRUST DECANTING ACT   Pro §§19501 to 19530

UNIFORM VENDOR AND PURCHASER RISK ACT   CC §1662

UNIFORM VOIDABLE TRANSACTIONS ACT   CC §§3439 to 3439.14 (See **VOIDABLE TRANSACTIONS**)

UNINCORPORATED ASSOCIATIONS (See ASSOCIATIONS)

UNINSURED MOTORIST COVERAGE
Arbitration of disputes
    Differential case management rules, applicability   CRC 3.712

UNIONS (See LABOR AND LABOR UNIONS)

UNITED STATES
Acknowledgment of instruments by officers in foreign countries   CC §1183
Administration of decedents' estates (See **ADMINISTRATION OF ESTATES**)
Civil procedure, judicial notice of federal rules of   Ev §451
Claims by federal agency against credits owing to State by debtor   Gov §926.8
Common carriers giving preferential treatment to   CC §2171
Courts (See **FEDERAL COURTS**)
Credit reports, statutes affecting   CC §1785.34
Criminal procedure, judicial notice of rules of   Ev §451
Decedents' estates (See **ADMINISTRATION OF ESTATES**)
Escheat of unclaimed property   CCP §§1502, 1600 to 1615
Federal enclaves (See **FEDERAL ENCLAVES**)
Information Practices Act, furnishing information under   CC §1798.24
Internal revenue department
    Estate tax (See **ESTATE TAX**)
    Income tax (See **INCOME TAX**)
    Marital deduction gifts (See **MARITAL DEDUCTION GIFTS**)
    Will construction, application of Internal Revenue Code provisions to (See **WILL CONSTRUCTION**)
Judicial notice of federal laws   Ev §§451, 452
Military personnel (See **MILITARY**)
Missing federal personnel (See **MISSING PERSONS**)
Partition sale proceeds invested in government obligations   CCP §873.810
Retail installment sales, compliance with federal statutes as sufficient under statute regulating   CC §1799.96
Sealed documents presumed to be genuine   Ev §1452
Signatures of public employees presumed to be genuine   Ev §1453
Superior court fees
    Services to local, state and federal governments   Gov §70633
Telegrams for federal agencies, priority in transmitting   CC §2207
Unclaimed property, escheat of   CCP §§1502, 1600 to 1615
Wills
    Dispositions by will to United States   Pro §6102

UNITED STATES—Cont.
Wills—Cont.
    Probate proceedings, government agencies as interested persons in   Pro §7280

UNITED STATES CONGRESS (See **CONGRESS**)

UNITED STATES COURTS (See **FEDERAL COURTS**)

UNITED STATES TERRITORIES
State defined to include   CCP §17

UNITRUST
Fiduciary income and principal act   Pro §§16330 to 16338

UNIT SALES
Decedents' estates, sale of assets of   Pro §10004

UNIVERSAL KNOWLEDGE
Judicial notice   Ev §§451, 452

UNIVERSITIES AND COLLEGES
Computers leased or sold to   CC §998
Consumer privacy rights
    Deletion of personal information related to student grades, scores, etc, inapplicability of provisions   CC §1798.145
Debt collection
    Educational debt collection practices   CC §§1788.90 to 1788.94
        Definitions   CC §1788.92
        Legislative findings and intent   CC §1788.91
        Prohibited debt collection practices by schools   CC §1788.93
        Short title of act   CC §1788.90
        Transcript used as leverage to collect debt, prohibition   CC §1788.93
        Waivers   CC §1788.94
Emergency protective order issued in response to threat to campus safety   Fam §6250.5
Employment qualifications, notifying as to information concerning   CC §1798.38
Escheat of scholarship funds, exemption from   CCP §1528
Information Practices Act, disclosure under   CC §1798.24
Orders against violence threatened on campus or facility
    COVID-19, emergency rule   CRCAppx I Emer Rule 8
Protection orders against violence threatened on campus or facility   CCP §527.85
    California law enforcement telecommunications (CLETS) information form, confidentiality and use of information   CRC 1.51, CRCAppx A
    Judicial council legal forms   CRCAppx A
    Memorandum in support of petition not required   CRC 3.1114
    Requests for protective orders   CRC 3.1160
Sexual assault
    Counselors
        Privileged communications, sexual assault counselor-victim privilege   Ev §1035.2
    Victims
        Privileged communications, sexual assault counselor-victim privilege   Ev §1035.2
Students
    Orders against violence threatened on campus or facility
        COVID-19, emergency rule   CRCAppx I Emer Rule 8
Telecommunications goods and services for   CC §998
Unclaimed property, disposition of   CC §2080.8
Uniform prudent management of institutional funds act   Pro §§18501 to 18510
    (See **INSTITUTIONAL FUNDS MANAGEMENT**)
University of California (See **UNIVERSITY OF CALIFORNIA**)
Victims and victims' rights
    Sexual assault
        Privileged communications, sexual assault counselor-victim privilege   Ev §1035.2
Violence
    Protection orders against violence threatened on campus or facility   CCP §527.85
        California law enforcement telecommunications (CLETS) information form, confidentiality and use of information   CRC 1.51, CRCAppx A
        COVID-19, emergency rule   CRCAppx I Emer Rule 8
        Judicial council legal forms   CRCAppx A
        Memorandum in support of petition not required   CRC 3.1114
        Requests for protective orders   CRC 3.1160

UNIVERSITY OF CALIFORNIA
Asbestos claims against   Gov §905.6

UNIVERSITY OF CALIFORNIA—Cont.
Attachment proceedings   CCP §481.200
Claim and delivery   CCP §511.100
Construction of actions against   Gov §943
Construction-related accessibility claims
    Attorney prelitigation letter to education entities   CC §54.27
Eminent domain taking by   CCP §1245.210
Information Practices Act, disclosures under   CC §1798.24
Physician employed by or with privileges at university facility
    Statute of limitations on sexual assault or other inappropriate action by physician   CCP §340.16
Service of process on regents of   CCP §416.50
Sexual assault
    Statute of limitations on sexual assault or other inappropriate action by physician employed by or with privileges at university facility   CCP §340.16
Social security numbers
    Public posting or display
        Implementation of provisions   CC §1798.85
Unclaimed property, disposition of   CC §2080.8
    Claim not required for controller to transfer property to state or local agencies   CCP §1540

UNIVERSITY OF SOUTHERN CALIFORNIA
Student health center
    Sexual assault
        Actions claiming damages for sexual assault at student health center, revival when otherwise barred by statute of limitations   CCP §340.16

UNKNOWN CLAIMS
Release affecting   CC §1542

UNKNOWN PERSONS (See also **MISSING PERSONS**)
Adoption proceedings
    Termination of unknown biological father's parental rights   Fam §7665
Amendment to add true name of defendant designated as unknown   CCP §474
Complaint   CCP §474
Death of unknown person, giving notice of   Pro §7600.5
Default judgments   CCP §474
Distributee under decedent's estate, whereabouts unknown for   Pro §11603
Eminent domain proceedings   CCP §1260.240
Guardian ad litem appointed for   CCP §373.5
Lost property, unknown owners of   CC §2080.1
Mortgagee   CC §2941.7
Partition (See **PARTITION**)
Publication of notice of funds by receiver   CCP §570
Public improvement assessments, actions to determine adverse interests in real property arising out of   CCP §§801.4, 801.9, 801.10
Quieting title action, defendant in   CCP §§762.020, 762.060, 762.070
Receivers holding funds of   CCP §570
Trust deed, obligor under   CC §2941.7
Unclaimed property (See **UNCLAIMED PROPERTY**)

UNLAWFUL DETAINER (See also **FORCIBLE ENTRY AND DETAINER**)
Access to court records, restrictions on   CCP §1161.2
    COVID-19 rental debt recovery actions   CCP §1161.2.5
    Superior court fees
        Permissible additional fees   Gov §70603
Acts constituting   CCP §§1161, 1161a
Affirmative defense of habitability, effect of   CCP §1174.2
Answer or demurrer
    Generally   CCP §1170
    Forms
        Judicial council legal forms   CRCAppx A
    Time for   CCP §§1167, 1167.3
Appeals
    Generally   CCP §§1176, 1178
    New trial   CCP §1178
    Stay of execution pending   CCP §1176
Attachment, writ of   CCP §483.020
Claim of right to possession
    Claim of occupant   CCP §1174.25
    Form   CCP §1174.3
    Objection to enforcement of judgment against occupant by filing   CCP §1174.3
    Prejudgment claim of right to possession, service on occupant of   CCP §415.46
Commercial real property, unlawful detainer of   CCP §1161.1
Commercial tenants
    Notice to quit   CCP §1162

UNLAWFUL DETAINER—Cont.
Complaints
    Generally   CCP §§425.12, 1166
    Amendment of   CC §1952.3, CCP §1173
    Contents of   CCP §1166
    Immediate possession on filing   CCP §1166a
    Judicial Council development and approval of pleading forms   CCP §425.12
    Possession no longer in issue   CC §1952.3
    Verification of   CCP §1166
Conditional sales contract, holding over after sale pursuant to default provisions of CCP §1161a
Controlled substances, use by tenants
    Nuisances involving controlled substances   CC §3486.5
Costs
    Award to prevailing party   CCP §1174.2
    Default judgment, costs on   CCP §1169
    Nuisances
        Controlled substances activities   CC §§3486, 3486.5
        Weapons or ammunition on real property   CC §3485
    Rent default as basis of unlawful detainer complaint
        Untenantable dwellings, landlord liability for costs and attorney fees   CCP §1174.21
    Supplemental costs bill, filing of   CCP §1034.5, CRC 3.2000
    Warranty of habitability as affirmative defense, award of costs in action involving   CCP §1174.2
Court records, restricted access to   CCP §1161.2
    COVID-19 rental debt recovery actions   CCP §1161.2.5
    Superior court fees
        Permissible additional fees   Gov §70603
COVID-19
    Emergency rule   CRCAppx I Emer Rule 1
    Financial distress, declaration
        Judicial council form   CRCAppx A
    Rental debt recovery actions
        Access to case records   CCP §1161.2.5
        Applicability of provisions   CCP §871.10
    Rental housing recovery act
        Definitions   CCP §1179.09
        Dismissal of actions if criteria for summons not met   CCP §1179.14
        Forfeiture of lease or rental agreement, prevention by court and restoration to former status   CCP §1179.13
        Governmental rental assistance programs, application determination information   CCP §1179.12
        Governmental rental assistance programs, verification of application status   CCP §1179.12
        Notice to vacate, property requiring recovery of COVID-19 recovery period rental debt   CCP §1179.10
        Short title of act   CCP §1179.08
        Summons on complaint for unlawful detainer based on accumulation of COVID-19 rental debt, plaintiff duties prior to issuance   CCP §§1179.11, 1179.14
        Sunset of provisions   CCP §1179.15
    Tenant relief act   CCP §§1179.01 to 1179.07
        Agreements purporting to waive statutory provisions   CCP §1179.06
        Cover sheet for unlawful detainer actions   CCP §1179.01.5, CRCAppx A
        Definitions   CCP §§1179.02, 1179.02.5
        Findings required for determination of unlawful detainer   CCP §1179.03.5
        High-income tenants   CCP §1179.02.5
        Legislative intent   CCP §1179.01.5
        Local provisions to protect tenants from eviction, requirements   CCP §1179.05
        Monthly rental payments, application to COVID-19 rental debt   CCP §1179.04.5
        Notice demanding payment of COVID-19 rental debt   CCP §1179.03
        Notice from landlord for tenants defaulting on one or more rental payments   CCP §1179.04
        Prohibited actions by courts   CCP §1179.01.5
        Security deposit, application to COVID-19 rental debt   CCP §1179.04.5
        Sunset of statutory provisions   CCP §1179.07
        Title of chapter   CCP §1179.01
Credit reporting (See **CREDIT REPORTING**)
Cumulative remedies   CC §1952
Damages
    Generally   CCP §1174
    Possession, damages after delivery of   CC §1952.3
    Treble damages   CCP §735
Deed of receiver or levying officer, service or exhibition of   CCP §1162a

UNLAWFUL DETAINER—Cont.
Default judgments   CCP §1169
Defaults
    COVID-19
        Emergency rule   CRCAppx I Emer Rule 1
        Financial distress, declaration   CRCAppx A
        Tenant relief act   CCP §§1179.01 to 1179.07
Defenses
    Immigration or citizenship status as motivator of landlord action   CCP §1161.4
    Lease provisions penalizing good faith summoning of law enforcement or emergency assistance   CC §1946.8
Delivery of possession, effect of   CC §1952.3
Demurrer   CCP §1170
    Meet and confer prerequisite to filing
        Inapplicability of meet and confer requirement in forcible entry, forcible detainer or unlawful detainer cases   CCP §430.41
Depositions
    Notice of deposition
        Time for taking deposition   CCP §2025.270
Discovery
    Motion for discovery   CCP §1170.8, CRC 3.1347
    Judicial council, rules as to   CCP §1170.9
Dismissal
    Service of summons
        Proof not timely filed   CCP §1167.1
Dismissal, time for motion for   CCP §1167.4
    Judicial council rules as to   CCP §1170.9
Domestic violence victims
    Abuse or violence against tenant, remedies   CCP §1174.27
    Limitations on termination of or refusal to renew tenancy   CC §1946.7, CCP §1161.3
    Nuisance committed by tenant as grounds
        Presumption of notice   CCP §1161
Drug-selling by tenant as grounds for unlawful detainer proceedings   CCP §1161
    Nuisances involving controlled substances   CC §3486.5
Emergencies
    COVID-19
        Emergency rule   CRCAppx I Emer Rule 1
        Financial distress, declaration   CRCAppx A
        Tenant relief act   CCP §§1179.01 to 1179.07
Execution sale, holding over after   CCP §1161a
Ex parte proceedings
    Notice to parties
        Time   CRC 3.1203
Extension of time
    Generally   CCP §§1167.4, 1167.5
    Judicial council rules as to   CCP §1170.9
    Trial of proceeding, extension of period for   CCP §1170.5
Filings, public access to   CCP §1161.2
    COVID-19 rental debt recovery actions   CCP §1161.2.5
Financial distress, declaration
    COVID-19
        Judicial council form   CRCAppx A
Firearms or other weapons
    Nuisance, termination of leases for
        Weapons or ammunition unlawfully on real property as basis of nuisance   CC §3485
Five-day stay   CCP §1174
Floating homes and floating home marinas (See **FLOATING HOMES**)
Forcible entry and detainer (See **FORCIBLE ENTRY AND DETAINER**)
Foreclosure sale, holding over after   CCP §1161a
Forfeiture of lease
    Conditions nullifying declaration of   CCP §1161.5
    Judgment restoring premises and forfeiting lease   CCP §1174
    Relief from   CCP §1179
Forms
    Claim of right to possession   CCP §1174.3
    Interrogatories
        Form interrogatories   CRCAppx A
    Judicial council legal forms   CRCAppx A
    Pleadings
        Judicial council legal forms   CRCAppx A
    Prejudgment claim of right to possession   CCP §415.46
Franchises of gasoline dealer, termination of   CCP §1174
Gas companies, action against   CC §1754
Habitability requirements
    Breach of warranty of habitability as affirmative defense, remedies of prevailing party involving   CCP §1174.2
    Presumption of landlord's breach of   CC §1942.3

UNLAWFUL DETAINER—Cont.
Holding over after sale pursuant to writ of execution, foreclosure or default provisions of conditional sales or security agreement   CCP §1161a
Human trafficking
    Restrictions on termination of tenancy   CC §1946.7, CCP §1161.3
Immediate possession, order for   CCP §1166a
Inspection demands
    Time to serve response   CCP §2031.260
    When demand may be made   CCP §2031.020
Interrogatories
    Propounding, time for   CCP §2030.020
    Response
        Time for response   CCP §2030.260
Involuntary trusts resulting from
    Attorney general actions
        Statute of limitations   CC §2224.5
Judgment
    Default judgment   CCP §1169
    Forfeiture of lease   CCP §1174
    Forms, judicial council   CRCAppx A
    Habitability defense, effect of   CCP §1174.2
    Possession of premises, assessing damages and disposition of property   CCP §1174
    Relief from   CCP §1179
Judicial arbitration
    Unlawful detainer
        Exemption from arbitration   CRC 3.811
Jurisdiction lacking
    Motions to quash service for lack of jurisdiction   CRC 3.1327
Jury trial   CCP §1171
Law and motion proceedings
    Quash or stay, motions in summary proceedings involving real property possession   CRC 3.1327
Lease, breach of   CC §§1952, 1952.3
Liability of lessee upon forfeiture of lease   CCP §1174.5
Lost property by   CCP §1174
Mail, service of process by   CCP §415.45
Mandatory settlement conference statement deadline, exception   CRC 3.2005
Manufactured homes
    Holding over after sale   CCP §1161a
    Immediate possession on filing complaint, when may have   CCP §1166a
Mobilehomes
    Holding over after sale   CCP §1161a
    Immediate possession on filing complaint, when may have   CCP §1166a
    Termination of tenancy, generally (See **MOBILEHOMES**)
Motion to quash service of summons   CCP §§418.10, 1167.4, CRC 3.1327
    Judicial council rules as to   CCP §1170.9
Narcotics and dangerous drugs
    Unlawful detainer proceedings based on tenant's drug-selling on premises   CC §3486, CCP §1161
Necessary parties   CCP §§1164, 1165
New trial   CCP §1178
Notice
    Commercial tenants   CCP §1162
    Content of notice   CCP §1161.2
    COVID-19 tenant relief act
        Notice demanding payment of COVID-19 rental debt   CCP §1179.03
        Notice from landlord for tenants defaulting on one or more rental payments   CCP §1179.04
    Exception   CC §792
    Extension of time to plead   CCP §1167.4
        Judicial council rules as to   CCP §1170.9
    Filing of complaint and restrictions on access to court records, notice to defendants of   CCP §1161.2
    Forfeiture of lease or rental agreement, conditions nullifying declaration of   CCP §1161.5
    Illegal weapons on real property   CC §3485
    Quash summons or dismiss, notice of motion to   CCP §1167.4
        Judicial council rules as to   CCP §1170.9
    Quit, notice to   CCP §§1161 to 1162
        Foreclosure sale situations, written notice to quit to tenant   CCP §1161b
    Service of notice to quit   CCP §1162
    Termination of tenancies   CC §§789, 1946
    3-day notice to quit   CC §791, CCP §1161
    Trial   CCP §594
Nuisance, termination of leases for
    Controlled substances, illegal conduct involving   CC §3486.5
    Narcotics, illegal conduct involving   CC §3486
    Nuisance as grounds for unlawful detainer proceedings   CCP §1161

UNLAWFUL DETAINER—Cont.
Nuisance, termination of leases for—Cont.
    Weapons or ammunition unlawfully on real property as basis of nuisance   CC §3485
Parties to proceedings   CCP §§1164, 1165
Personal property left on premises   CCP §1174
Petroleum distributor against gasoline dealer, action for unlawful detainer brought by   CCP §1174
Pleadings
    Forms
        Judicial council legal forms   CRCAppx A
Possession
    Claim of right to (See within this heading, **"Claim of right to possession"**)
    Delivery of possession affecting action for damages   CC §1952.3
    Holding over after sale   CCP §1161a
    Writ of possession (See within this heading, **"Writ of possession"**)
Posting, service by   CCP §415.45
Practice rules governing   CCP §1177
Prejudgment claim of right to possession
    Form   CCP §415.46
    Service of occupant with   CCP §415.46
Priority of cases   CCP §1179a
Process
    Abandonment of real property lease, service in action involving   CCP §415.47
    Posting   CCP §415.45
    Prejudgment claim of right to possession, service upon occupant of   CCP §415.46
    Proof of service   CCP §§417.10, 417.20
    Publication of   CCP §§415.50, 1167
    Quash, motion to   CCP §§418.10, 1167.4, CRC 3.1327
        Judicial council rules as to   CCP §1170.9
    Response, effect on time for filing   CCP §1167
    Sheriff's fees   Gov §26721.1
    Specified form for summons   CCP §1167
    Summonses
        COVID-19, emergency rule   CRCAppx I Emer Rule 1
        Proof of service of summons   CCP §1167.1
    Unnamed occupants, duty of process server to ascertain identity of   CCP §415.46
Public access to new filings   CCP §1161.2
    COVID-19 rental debt recovery actions   CCP §1161.2.5
Publication, service of summons by   CCP §§415.50, 1167
Quash, motions to   CCP §1167.4
    Judicial council rules as to   CCP §1170.9
Real estate contract arbitration clause, effect of   CCP §1298.5
Receivers   CCP §564
Reentry as contempt   CCP §1210
Renewal of tenancy of victims of domestic violence
    Limitations on denial of renewal   CC §1946.7, CCP §1161.3
Rent
    Attachment, amount of   CCP §483.020
    Default in payment
        Complaint stating amount of   CCP §1166
        Untenantable premises, attorneys' fees and costs against landlord for initiating unlawful detainer   CCP §1174.21
    Judgment assessing rent due   CCP §1174
    Untenantable dwelling, penalty for rent collection for   CC §1942.4
        Attorneys' fees and cost of suit, landlord liability   CCP §1174.21
Rental payments
    COVID-19 tenant relief act
        Monthly rental payments, application to COVID-19 rental debt   CCP §1179.04.5
Request for admission
    Response to request
        Time for service of response   CCP §2033.250
    Time limitations for   CCP §2033.020
Response
    Answer or demurrer   CCP §1170
        Time for answer or demurrer   CCP §§1167, 1167.3
Retaliatory eviction, defense of   CC §1942.5
Rules of practice   CCP §1177
Sale of property, holding over after   CCP §1161a
Security agreement, holding over after sale pursuant to default provisions of   CCP §1161a
Security deposits
    COVID-19 tenant relief act
        Application of security deposit to COVID-19 rental debt   CCP §1179.04.5
Service
    Notice to quit   CCP §1162

UNLAWFUL DETAINER—Cont.
Service—Cont.
Receiver's or levying officer's deed   CCP §1162a
Service of process
Process generally (See within this heading, **"Process"**)
Service of process and papers
Victims of certain crimes
Address confidentiality program   CCP §1167
Service stations, actions re termination of franchises   CCP §1174
Settlement opportunities   CRC 3.2005
Sexual assault victims
Abuse or violence against tenant, remedies   CCP §1174.27
Sheriff's deed, service of   CCP §§415.45, 415.47, 1162a, 1167
Sheriff's fees   Gov §26721.1
Small claims court jurisdiction   CCP §116.220
Stalking victims
Abuse or violence against tenant, remedies   CCP §1174.27
Stay of judgment   CCP §§1174, 1176
Stays of action   CRC 3.1327
Storage of personalty   CCP §1174
Strike, motions to   CCP §1170
Subtenants
Summary judgment
Judicial council rules as to   CCP §1170.9
Motions   CRC 3.1351
Summary judgment, motion for   CCP §1170.7, CRC 3.1351
Judicial council rules as to   CCP §1170.9
Summary proceedings   CC §792, CCP §1166a
Summons
COVID-19, emergency rule   CRCAppx I Emer Rule 1
Forms
Judicial council legal forms   CRCAppx A
Proof of service of summons   CCP §1167.1
Supplemental costs   CRC 3.2000
Supplemental costs bill, filing of   CCP §1034.5
Surety bond required for order of immediate possession   CCP §1166a
Telephone appearances   CRC 3.670
Termination of tenancy of victims of domestic violence
Limitations   CC §1946.7, CCP §1161.3
Time
Amendment of complaint for damage action   CC §§1952, 1952.3
COVID-19, emergency rule   CRCAppx I Emer Rule 1
Dismissal, motion for   CCP §1167.4
Judicial council rules as to   CCP §1170.9
Extension of time (See within this heading, **"Extension of time"**)
Rental unit, removal from   CCP §1166a
Response, time for filing   CCP §1167
Title transferred   CCP §1161a
Transitional housing program misconduct
Injunctions or temporary restraining orders
Violation of order, effect   CC §1954.15
Trial
Notice of   CCP §594
Summary judgment motion   CCP §1170.7, CRC 3.1351
Judicial council rules as to   CCP §1170.9
Time considerations for   CCP §1170.5
COVID-19, emergency rule   CRCAppx I Emer Rule 1
Trial Court Delay Reduction Act   Gov §68620
Trial court delay reduction
Case disposition time goals   CRC JudAdminStand 2.2
Unnamed occupants, duty of process server to serve prejudgment claim of right to possession upon   CCP §415.46
Venue   CCP §396a
Location nearest or most accessible to real property involved   CCP §392
Stay or dismissal of action for inconvenient forum   CRC 3.1327
Verification
Rental assistance
Form for landlord verification   CRCAppx A
Victims and victims' rights
Service of process and papers
Address confidentiality program   CCP §1167
Warrant of habitability   CC §§1941, 1942.3, CCP §1174.2
Writ of possession
Claim of right to possession, filing of   CCP §1174.3
Five-day stay   CCP §1174
Immediate possession, obtaining   CCP §1166a
Judgment for possession of premises, enforcement of   CCP §1174

UNMANNED AIRCRAFT   Gov §§853 to 853.5
Emergency response
Drones or unmanned aircraft systems damaged by emergency responder
Provision of emergency services by responder and interference with services by drone, immunity from liability for damage to drone or system   CC §43.101

UNPAID BALANCE (See **RETAIL INSTALLMENT SALES**)

UNPERFORMED CONTRACT FOR SALE OF REALTY (See **TITLE AND OWNERSHIP**)

UNRUH ACT
Retail installment sales   CC §§1801 to 1802.20 (See **RETAIL INSTALLMENT SALES**)

UNRUH CIVIL RIGHTS ACT   CC §51

UNSOLICITED GOODS   CC §§1584.5, 1584.6

URBAN WATERFRONT RESTORATION
Greenway easements generally   CC §§816.50 to 816.66

URGENT CARE CENTERS
Human trafficking or slavery
Signs, businesses required to post notice concerning relief from slavery or human trafficking   CC §52.6

USAGE (See **CUSTOM AND USAGE**)

USE
Loan for use   CC §§1884 to 1896

USED CARS
Consumer warranty protection
Buy-here-pay-here dealers' obligations   CC §1795.51

USE TAX (See **SALES AND USE TAX**)

USURY   CC §§1916.12-1 to 1916.12-5
Actions
Payment of illegal interest
Rights of person paying   CC §1916.12-3
Brokers, exemption re   CC §1916.1
Civil code provisions concerning interest rates
Repeal   CC §1916.12-4
Compound interest   CC §1916.12-2
Contract rate of interest   CC §1916.12-1
Limitations   CC §1916.12-2
Payment of illegal interest
Rights of person paying   CC §1916.12-3
Penalties for violating   CC §1916.12-3
Criminal penalties   CC §1916.12-3
ERISA, exemption re pension funds governed by   CC §1917.220
Legal rate of interest   CC §1916.12-1
Payment of illegal interest
Rights of person paying   CC §1916.12-3
Penalties for violating   CC §1916.12-3
Payment of illegal interest
Rights of person paying   CC §1916.12-3
Pension fund exemptions
ERISA   CC §1917.220
Public retirement systems   CC §1916.2
Public retirement system funds, exemption re   CC §1916.2
Repeal of certain civil code provisions   CC §1916.12-4
Shared appreciation loan transactions, exemption re   CC §§1917 to 1917.006
Short title of provisions   CC §1916.12-5
Treble damages for violations   CC §1916.12-3
Writing, when required   CC §1916.12-1

UTILITIES (See **PUBLIC UTILITIES**)

V

VACANCIES IN OFFICE
Congress of United States (See **CONGRESS**)
Executor and administrator, vacancy in office of   Pro §§8520 to 8525
Judges or justices, effect on proceedings of vacancy in office of all or any   CCP §184
Trustees (See **TRUSTS**)

VACATION CREDITS
Employee benefit plan including   Fam §80

VACATION CREDITS—Cont.
Exempt property for purposes of enforcement of judgments CCP §704.113

VACATION OF JUDGMENTS (See JUDGMENTS)

VALIDATION PROCEEDINGS
Generally CCP §§860 to 870.5
Annexation CCP §349.4
Appeals CCP §870
Authorization and existence of bonds, warrants, contracts, date of CCP §864
Bonds (See **BONDS**)
Boundaries of city, county, district or other public entity, change in CCP §349.4
Consolidation of actions CCP §865
Contracts CCP §§860 to 870
Costs CCP §868
Dismissal of validation action by public agency, time limit for answering party to file action following CCP §867.5
Exclusiveness of remedy CCP §869
Formation, dissolution or other change of organization of city, county, district or other public entity CCP §349.4
Hearings CCP §867
Judgments in CCP §870
Jurisdiction CCP §862
Publication, summons by CCP §861
Service of process CCP §§861, 861.1, 863
Summons CCP §§861, 861.1
Taxes pledged as security by agency other than agency imposing tax, notice requirements concerning CCP §870.5
Time limit for answering party to file action after dismissal of validation action by public agency CCP §867.5

VALISE (See BAGGAGE)

VALUE
Administration of estates, valuation for (See **ADMINISTRATION OF ESTATES**)
Advancements Pro §6409
Appraisals (See **APPRAISALS**)
Common carrier's liability for loss of valuable goods CC §§2177, 2200
Community estate, valuation in dissolution of marriage proceedings Fam §2552
Community property Fam §2552
Damages, measure of (See **DAMAGES**)
Deposit in lieu of surety bonds (See **SURETYSHIP, BONDS AND UNDERTAKINGS**)
Eminent domain, exchange of valuation data for CCP §§1258.210 to 1258.300, Ev §§810 to 822
Enforcement of judgments (See **ENFORCEMENT OF JUDGMENTS**)
Evidence rules for ascertaining value of property (See **EXPERT AND OPINION EVIDENCE**)
Expert testimony of (See **EXPERT AND OPINION EVIDENCE**)
Form for exchange of valuation data in eminent domain action CCP §1258.210
Opinion testimony of (See **EXPERT AND OPINION EVIDENCE**)
Ownership, value as affecting CC §§1027, 1028, 1032
Peculiar value CC §3355
Small estates distributed without administration, value limitation Pro §§6602, 13100
Spouse of owner, testimony by Ev §813
Surety bonds (See **SURETYSHIP, BONDS AND UNDERTAKINGS**)

VANDALISM
Aerosol paint containers
    Sale to minor of
        Verification of age for sale of age-restricted products CC §1798.99.1
Graffiti as evidence of vandalism, admissibility of Ev §1410.5
Rental passenger vehicle transactions
    Recovery by rental company
        Prohibited means of recovery CC §1939.15
    Renter responsibilities for rented vehicle CC §1939.03
        Claim against renter for damage or loss CC §1939.07
        Damage waivers CC §§1939.09, 1939.13
        Insurance coverage for renter CC §1939.07
        Mitigation of damages by rental company CC §1939.07
        Total amount of renter liability CC §1939.05
Spray paint containers
    Minors, sale to
        Verification of age for sale of age-restricted products CC §1798.99.1

VARIABLE INTEREST RATE LOANS (See TRUST DEEDS AND MORTGAGES)

VARIANCE (See PLEADINGS)

VAULTS (See SAFES)

VEHICLE LEASING ACT (See AUTOMOBILES)

VEHICLES
Automobiles (See **AUTOMOBILES**)
Bicycles (See **BICYCLES**)
Buses (See **BUSES**)
Mobilehomes (See **MOBILEHOMES**)
Recreational vehicles (See **RECREATIONAL VEHICLES**)
Street railways (See **STREET RAILWAYS**)

VENDING MACHINES
Seller assisted marketing plans CC §§1812.200 to 1812.221

VENDOR AND PURCHASER (See also SALE OF REALTY)
AIDS, liability of owner regarding occupant afflicted with CC §1710.2
Blanket encumbrance, required notice to purchaser or lessee of CC §1133
Brokers (See **BROKERS**)
Buyer's choice act CC §§1103.20 to 1103.22
    Escrow agents
        Choice of escrow agent lies with buyer CC §1103.22
    Legislative findings and intent CC §1103.21
    Short title CC §1103.20
    Title insurers
        Choice of insurer lies with buyer CC §1103.22
Consideration, measure of damages based on CC §3353
Contracts
    Administrator's contract for purchase of estate property (See **ADMINISTRATION OF ESTATES**)
    Construction of CC §1662
    Damages for breach of contract CC §§3306 to 3307
    Decedent's estate, contract to purchase realty from (See **ADMINISTRATION OF ESTATES**)
    Installment contracts (See **REAL PROPERTY SALES CONTRACTS**)
    Liquidated damages clauses CC §§1675 to 1681
    Written contracts for sale CC §1624
Decedents' estates, sale of realty of (See **ADMINISTRATION OF ESTATES**)
Destruction of property, party bearing loss from CC §1662
Disclosure requirements
    AIDS, disclosures regarding occupant afflicted with CC §1710.2
    Earthquake hazard
        Consumer information booklets CC §§2079.8, 2079.9, 2079.11
    Environmental hazards, compliance with requirements to inform transferee of CC §§2079.7, 2079.11
    Explosive munitions in neighborhood area, written notice of CC §1102.15
    Home energy ratings, information regarding CC §2079.10
    Industrial use zoning CC §1102.17
    Mello-Roos Community Facilities Act, disclosure regarding special tax liens on transfer of property pursuant to CC §1102.6b
    Purchase money liens on residential property CC §§2956 to 2968
    Registered sex offenders, notification concerning statewide database of locations of CC §2079.10a
    Statements (See within this heading, "Disclosure statements")
    Taxation
        Supplemental property tax bills CC §1102.6c
    Water conservation CC §2079.10
        Plumbing retrofits, disclosures as to noncompliant plumbing fixtures CC §§1101.4, 1102.155
    Window security bars and safety release mechanism CC §1102.16
Disclosure statements
    Amendment of CC §§1102.9, 1103.9
    Applicability of requirement CC §§1102 to 1102.2, 1103
    Condominiums, newly converted CC §1134
    Damages for noncompliance CC §1102.13
    Delivery of CC §§1102.3, 1102.10, 1103.3, 1103.10, 1103.12
    Errors or omissions, liability for CC §§1102.4, 1102.5, 1103.4
    Escrow agents, effect on CC §1102.11
    Forms
        General form of transfer disclosure statement CC §1102.6
        Local requirements, form of statement reflecting CC §1102.6a
        Natural hazards, form of disclosure concerning CC §1103.2
    Good faith requirement CC §§1102.7, 1103.7
    Legislative intent CC §1102.1
    Other laws, effect of CC §§1102.8, 1103.8
Earthquake hazard
    Disclosure requirements
        Consumer information booklets CC §§2079.8, 2079.9, 2079.11
Eminent domain, alternative to CCP §1240.120
Enforcement liens CCP §§996.510 to 996.560
Environmental hazards, compliance with requirements to inform transferee of CC §§2079.7, 2079.11
Equity sales contracts (See **HOME EQUITY SALES CONTRACTS**)
Escrow (See **ESCROW**)
Explosive munitions in neighborhood area, disclosure of CC §1102.15

VENDOR AND PURCHASER—Cont.
Fraud   CC §3343
Guardian (See **GUARDIAN AND WARD**)
Home energy ratings, disclosure of information regarding   CC §2079.10
Home equity sales contracts (See **HOME EQUITY SALES CONTRACTS**)
Homesteads (See **HOMESTEADS**)
Industrial use zoning, disclosure of   CC §1102.17
Installment sales contracts (See **REAL PROPERTY SALES CONTRACTS**)
Listing agents (See **BROKERS**)
Marketability of title (See **TITLE AND OWNERSHIP**)
Mello-Roos Community Facilities Act, disclosure regarding special tax liens on transfer of property pursuant to   CC §1102.6b
Mortgages (See **TRUST DEEDS AND MORTGAGES**)
Multiple listing services   CC §§1086 to 1089.5
Options (See **OPTIONS**)
Partition (See **PARTITION**)
Prepayment of balance due   CC §2985.6
Purchase money liens on residential property, disclosures on   CC §§2956 to 2968
Purchaser's lien   CC §§3048, 3050
Real property sales contracts
    Generally (See **REAL PROPERTY SALES CONTRACTS**)
    Unperformed (See **TITLE AND OWNERSHIP**)
Receivers selling real property   CCP §568.5
Recording of instruments (See **RECORDS AND RECORDING**)
Registered sex offenders, notification concerning statewide database of locations of   CC §2079.10a
Risk of loss, uniform act governing   CC §1662
Shared appreciation loans (See **SHARED APPRECIATION LOANS**)
Signs on property for sale   CC §§712, 713
Stay of judgment for sale of realty   CCP §917.4
Structural pest control report, requirements for   CC §1099
Taxation
    Supplemental property tax bills
        Disclosures upon transfer of real property   CC §1102.6c
Title and ownership (See **TITLE AND OWNERSHIP**)
Transfer of ownership (See **CONVEYANCES**)
Trust deeds (See **TRUST DEEDS AND MORTGAGES**)
Unperformed contract for sale of realty (See **TITLE AND OWNERSHIP**)
Vendor's liens   CC §§3046 to 3048
Water conserving plumbing retrofits
    Definition of sale or transfer   CC §1101.3
    Disclosures as to noncompliant plumbing fixtures   CC §§1101.4, 1102.155
Window security bars and safety release mechanism   CC §1102.16

VENDOR'S LIEN   CC §§3046 to 3048

VENUE
Administration of decedent's estate, proceedings for (See **ADMINISTRATION OF ESTATES**)
Adoption
    Adult adoptions   Fam §9321.5
    Agency adoptions
        Request for adoption   Fam §8714
    Independent adoptions
        Request for adoption   Fam §8802
    International adoption or readoption requests   Fam §8912
    Nondependent minors
        Request for filing request for adoption or readoption of nondependent minor, locations for filing   Fam §8609.5
Affidavit stating facts showing action commenced in proper court   CCP §396a
Ancillary administration proceedings   Pro §12511
Annulment of marriage   CCP §395
Arbitration proceedings   CCP §§1292, 1292.2
Assisted reproduction
    Gestational carriers, agreements   Fam §7620
Associations, action against   CCP §395.5
Automobile sales, actions involving   CC §2984.4, CCP §396a
Booking photographs
    Commercial use of booking photographs
        Actions to enforce prohibition   CC §1798.91.1
CARE act rules   CRC 7.2223
Change of venue
    Conservatorships   Pro §§2210 to 2217
    Costs and fees, payment of   CCP §399
    County, city or local agency, actions by or against   CCP §394
    Criminal proceedings
        Appeals following change   CRC 4.150
        Applicable rules   CRC 4.150
        Costs, reimbursement guidelines   CRC 4.155
        Motion for change   CRC 4.151
        Order upon change   CRC 4.153

VENUE—Cont.
Change of venue—Cont.
    Criminal proceedings—Cont.
        Receiving court, proceedings in   CRC 4.154
        Reimbursement of costs in change of venue, guidelines for   CRC 4.155
        Rules for transfers   CRC 4.150 to 4.155
        Selection of court and trial judge   CRC 4.152
        Transfer   CRC 4.150 to 4.155
        Transferring courts, proceedings in   CRC 4.150
    Decedent's estate proceedings   Pro §§7070 to 7072
    Designation of place of change   CCP §398
    Eminent domain action   CCP §1250.040
    Exercise of jurisdiction by court to which action is transferred   CCP §399
    Expenses and attorney's fees to prevailing party   CCP §396b
    Family law proceedings
        Both parties moved from county rendering decree   CCP §397.5
        Retention of jurisdiction to issue protective orders   CCP §399
        Time frames for transferring jurisdiction   CRC 5.97
    Family law proceedings where both parties moved from county rendering decree   CCP §397.5
    Fees
        Children's waiting room in courthouse, surcharge to fund   Gov §70640
        Filing fees   Gov §70618
        Payment of   CCP §399
    Grounds for   CCP §397
    Guardianships   Pro §§2210 to 2217
    Law and motion rule   CRC 3.1326
    Motions   CCP §396b, CRC 3.1326
    Motion to transfer action to appropriate court   CCP §396b
    Nonconsenting party, award of costs of   CCP §394
    Order changing   CCP §399
    Petition for writ of mandate on grant or denial of motion   CCP §400
    Pleadings and papers, transfer of   CCP §399
    State, actions by or against   CCP §401
    Stipulations   CCP §398
    Time for defendant to move to strike, demur or plead following denial of motion to transfer   CRC 3.1326
    Time frames for transferring jurisdiction
        Family law actions or proceedings   CRC 5.97
    Transmittal of papers and pleadings   CCP §399
    Wrong venue, transfer of action or proceeding to proper court where commenced in   CCP §396b
Child support, actions to enforce   CCP §395
City or local agency, actions by or against   CCP §394
Claims against public entities and employees (See **CLAIMS AGAINST PUBLIC ENTITIES AND EMPLOYEES**)
Complaint stating facts showing action commenced in proper court   CCP §396a
Consent to keeping action in court where commenced   CCP §§396a, 396b
Conservatorships (See **CONSERVATORS**)
Consumer goods and services, venue in action founded on obligation for   CCP §§395, 396a
Consumer protection actions   CC §1780
Contracts, actions founded on   CCP §395
Coordination of actions, judge's power to determine venue   CRC 3.541, 3.543
Corporations, action against   CCP §395.5
Costs
    Change of venue
        Fees (See within this heading, "**Change of venue**")
        Payment of costs   CCP §399
County, city or local agency, actions by or against   CCP §394
Criminal proceedings
    Juvenile court proceedings   CRC 5.510
Dependent child proceedings   CRC 5.510
Dissolution of marriage (See **DISSOLUTION OF MARRIAGE**)
Eminent domain action   CCP §§1250.020 to 1250.040
Enforcement of judgments (See **ENFORCEMENT OF JUDGMENTS**)
Executor, venue in action against   CCP §395.1
Family law proceedings
    Both parties moved from county rendering decree   CCP §397.5
    Retention of jurisdiction to issue protective orders   CCP §399
    Time frames for transferring jurisdiction
        Family law actions or proceedings   CRC 5.97
Fees (See within this heading, "**Change of venue**")
Foreclosure of liens and mortgages on real property   CCP §392
Foreign judgments   CCP §1710.20
Guardianship (See **GUARDIAN AND WARD**)
Health Care Decision Law, actions under   Pro §4763
Improper joinder to fix venue   CCP §395
Information Practices Act, action under   CC §1798.49

VENUE—Cont.

Juvenile court proceedings   CRC 5.510
Juvenile wardship proceedings   CRC 5.510
Lake, river or stream, recovery of penalty imposed for offense committed on   CCP §393
Law and motion proceedings
    Motions concerning pleading and venue   CRC 3.1320 to 3.1326
Local agencies, actions by or against   CCP §394
Mines and mining
    Taxes, co-owners failing to pay
        Venue when mine located in multiple counties   CCP §856
Negligence   CCP §395
Parental relationship, proceedings to determine   CCP §395
Partition, action for   CCP §872.110
Penalty or forfeiture imposed by statute, actions for recovery of   CCP §393
Personal, family or household use, action founded on obligation for goods or services intended primarily for   CCP §§395, 396a
Personal injury actions   CCP §395
Petition for writ of mandate on grant or denial of motion for change of   CCP §400
Power of attorney, venue in actions involving (See POWER OF ATTORNEY)
Property damage, actions for   CCP §395
Public entities and employees, claims against (See CLAIMS AGAINST PUBLIC ENTITIES AND EMPLOYEES)
Public officers, actions against   CCP §393
Quieting title action   CCP §760.050
Recovery of real property, action for   CCP §392
Rental-purchase contracts, actions involving   CC §1812.645
Residence of defendant   CCP §395
Retail installment sales contract, action on   CC §1812.10, CCP §396a
Situs of subject matter   CCP §392
Small claims courts   CCP §116.370, CRC 3.2106
State, actions by or against   CCP §401
Support obligation, actions to enforce   CCP §395
Termination of parental rights, petition for   Fam §7845
Time
    Moving to strike, demur or plead following denial of motion to transfer venue   CRC 3.1326
Title vesting in state   CCP §1410
Transfer of causes
    CARE act rules   CRC 7.2223
    Family Law Act
        Subsequent to final judgment   CCP §397.5
Transfer of venue (See within this heading, "Change of venue")
Tribal court civil money judgment act
    Application for recognition and entry of judgment   CCP §1733
Trustee, venue in action against   CCP §395.1
Trust estate   CCP §395.1, Pro §17005
Uniform Parentage Act   Fam §7620
Uniform Transfers to Minors Act, venue for hearing on petition filed under   Pro §3921
Unincorporated association, action against   CCP §395.2
Unlawful detainer actions   CCP §396a
    Location nearest or most accessible to real property involved   CCP §392
    Stay or dismissal of action for inconvenient forum   CRC 3.1327
Wages, hours, and working conditions
    Judgments, enforcement by labor commissioner   CCP §690.030
Where cause of action arose   CCP §393
Will probate proceedings (See WILL PROBATE)
Wrong court, appeal or petition filed in
    Transfer to appropriate court   CCP §396
Wrongful death action   CCP §395
Wrong venue, transfer of action or proceeding to proper court where commenced in   CCP §396b

VERDICT

Admission of erroneous evidence   Ev §353
Conflict with special verdict   CCP §625
Defective verdict, correction of   CCP §619
Directed verdict
    Generally   CCP §630
    Costs on   CCP §1038
    Expedited jury trials
        Waiver of right to motions   CCP §630.08
Entry in minutes   CCP §628
Exceptions, reserved without   CCP §647
Exclusion of evidence, effect of   Ev §354
Expedited jury trials   CCP §630.07
    Mandatory expedited jury trials, limited civil cases
        Number of votes required   CCP §630.26
General verdict   CCP §624

VERDICT—Cont.

Impeachment of   Ev §1150
Judgment notwithstanding   CCP §629
Judicial comments on verdict   CRC JudAdminStand 2.30
Judicial holiday, receiving verdict on   CCP §134
Mandamus   CCP §1093
Minutes, entry in   CCP §628
Mistake, correction of   CCP §§618, 619
Mistrial for jury failing to reach   CCP §616
Money recovery, determining amount of   CCP §626
Number of jurors required by   CCP §613
Polling jury   CCP §618
Post-trial discussions with jurors regarding   CCP §206
Punitive damages action   CCP §625
Receiving verdict   CCP §618
Retrial of action where jury discharged without rendering verdict   CCP §616
Sealed verdict   CCP §617
Special verdict   CCP §624
    Civil cases   CRC 3.1580
    Entry   CCP §628
    General verdict, control over   CCP §625
    Referee's decision   CCP §645
Writing requirements   CCP §618

VERIFICATION

Accounts, pleadings alleging   CCP §454
Administration of estates (See ADMINISTRATION OF ESTATES)
Administrative adjudicative proceedings (See ADMINISTRATIVE ADJUDICATION)
Affidavits, use of   CCP §2009
Appellate court administration, supreme court and courts of appeal
    Signing, subscribing or verifying documents   CRC 10.1028
Eminent domain action   CCP §1250.330
Family law proceedings, verification of pleadings in   Fam §212
Pleadings, in general   CCP §446
Quieting title complaint   CCP §761.020
Will probate proceedings (See WILL PROBATE)

VESSELS

Attachment (See ATTACHMENT)
Bail and penalty schedules   CRC 4.102
Bill of lading (See BILL OF LADING)
Bill of sale   CC §1135
Blind persons having equal rights to use of   CC §§54.1, 54.3, 54.4, 55
    Construction or application of provisions in issue, solicitor general notified   CC §55.2
Bottomry (See BOTTOMRY)
Charter-party agreement   CC §1959
Disabled persons having equal rights to use of   CC §§54.1, 54.3, 54.4, 55
    Construction or application of provisions in issue, solicitor general notified   CC §55.2
Enforcement of judgments (See ENFORCEMENT OF JUDGMENTS)
Fines and civil penalties
    Bail schedule   CRC 4.102
Floating homes (See FLOATING HOMES)
Guide dogs permitted on   CC §§54.2, 54.3
    Construction or application of provisions in issue, solicitor general notified   CC §55.2
Loans upon respondentia (See LOANS UPON RESPONDENTIA)
Penalties for violations
    Bail and penalty schedules   CRC 4.102
Recording transfers   CC §1173
Respondentia (See LOANS UPON RESPONDENTIA)
Retail installment sales of   CC §1801.4
Unruh Act, exclusion from coverage under   CC §1801.4
Voidable transactions provisions, applicability to vessel cargo   CC §3440

VETERANS

Consumer protection provisions
    Remedies for veterans under   CC §3345
Family code, proceedings under
    Resources for self-identified veterans in proceedings under family code   Fam §211.5
Sentence and punishment
    Mitigating factors
        Petition for resentencing, form   CRCAppx A
    Orders for dismissal
        Judicial council legal forms   CRCAppx A
Sexual trauma
    Sentence and punishment
        Petition for resentencing, form   CRCAppx A

VETERANS—Cont.
Traumatic brain injury
  Sentence and punishment
    Petition for resentencing, form   CRCAppx A

VETERANS ADMINISTRATION
Accounts, notice of   Pro §1461.5
Conservatorship proceedings involving proposed conservatee entitled to VA benefits, notice of   Pro §§1461.5, 1822
Guardianship proceedings involving proposed ward entitled to VA benefits, notice of   Pro §§1461.5, 1511
Inventory, notice of   Pro §1461.5

VETERANS' BENEFITS
Assignment for benefit of creditors, property exempt from   CCP §1801
Attachment of veterans' federal disability benefits
  Exemptions from attachment and other legal process   CCP §483.013
Workshops, presentations, events, etc regarding veterans benefits or entitlements
  Advertising or promoting without certain disclosures as unfair or deceptive practice   CC §1770

VETERINARIANS AND VETERINARY TECHNICIANS
Abandoned animals   CC §1834.5
Lien for services   CC §3051
Professional standards review committees   CC §§43.7, 43.8
Review committees, liability of   CC §§43.7, 43.8
Statute of limitations
  Injury to animals by parties practicing veterinary medicine   CCP §340
  Negligence actions   CCP §§340, 340.5, 597.5

VEXATIOUS LITIGANTS   CCP §§391 to 391.8
Attorney professional conduct
  Probable cause to bring or defend claim   ProfC 3.1
Conservators
  Petitions
    Unmeritorious petitions intended to annoy or harass   Pro §1970
Costs   CCP §1038
Definitions   CCP §391
Dismissal
  Grounds for granting motion to dismiss   CCP §391.3
  Motion to dismiss   CCP §391.1
  Prefiling order, dismissal of litigation filed by vexatious litigant subject to   CCP §391.7
  Security not furnished   CCP §391.4
Forms
  Judicial council legal forms   CRCAppx A
Guardian and ward
  Unmeritorious petitioning regarding visitation, termination of guardianship or instructions to guardian   Pro §1611
In propria persona, litigant acting   CCP §391
Judicial Council records of vexatious litigants subject to prefiling orders   CCP §391.7
  Vacating prefiling order and removing name from list   CCP §391.8
List of vexatious litigants
  Application for removal
    Form   CRCAppx A
  Judicial council to maintain   CCP §391.7
  Vacating prefiling order and removing name from list   CCP §391.8
Motions
  Prohibit filing of new litigation, motion to   CCP §391.7
  Security required by vexatious litigant, motion for   CCP §§391 to 391.8
Orders
  Permitting filing   CCP §391.7
  Prohibiting filing   CCP §391.7
    Vacating order and removing litigant's name from list   CCP §391.8
  Vacation of prefiling order, application
    Form   CRCAppx A
Prohibit filing of new litigation, order to   CCP §391.7
Security
  Defined   CCP §391
  Dismissal if security not furnished   CCP §391.4
  Hearing   CCP §391.2
  Motion to require   CCP §§391 to 391.8
  Order to furnish   CCP §391.3
  Stay of proceeding on filing of motion for   CCP §391.6
SLAPPback actions   CCP §425.18
Stay of proceedings
  Prefiling order, stay of litigation filed by vexatious litigant subject to   CCP §391.7
  Security, stay of proceedings on filing motion for   CCP §391.6

VEXATIOUS LITIGANTS—Cont.
Undertaking
  Security generally (See within this heading, "Security")

VICARIOUS LIABILITY
Local public officials   Gov §820.9

VICIOUSNESS
Dogs, liability of owner of   CC §§3341, 3342, 3342.5

VICTIMS AND VICTIMS' RIGHTS
Address confidentiality for victims of domestic violence, sexual assault, stalking, human trafficking, child abduction, and elder or dependent adult abuse
  Forms   CRCAppx A, Fam §6226.6
Appellate court opinions
  Privacy, use of names in opinions   CRC 8.90
Child victims
  Consent to medical treatment
    Intimate partner violence, victim 12 or older   Fam §6930
  Intimate partner violence, victim 12 or older
    Consent to medical care   Fam §6930
Claims against public entities and employees
  Presentation of claim
    State, claims against   Gov §905.2
Compensation of victims
  Direct loss requirement   Gov §13964
Deaf persons
  Interpreter services for deaf or hard of hearing victims   Ev §754
Dependent adults or persons
  Abuse of elder or dependent adult
    Coerced debt   CC §§1798.97.1 to 1798.97.6
Director of victim compensation and government claims board
  Notice of death of decedent with imprisoned heir   Pro §9202
Domestic violence
  Coerced debt   CC §§1798.97.1 to 1798.97.6
Human trafficking
  Expert and opinion evidence
    Effect of human trafficking on victim, expert testimony   Ev §1107.5
  Expunging arrest or vacating adjudication
    Judicial council legal forms   CRCAppx A
  Prostitution or other commercial sex acts resulting from human trafficking
    Evidentiary significance   Ev §1161
  Vacatur relief for arrests or convictions for nonviolent crimes while victim
    Procedure   CRC JudAdminStand 4.15
  Victim-caseworker privilege   Ev §§1038 to 1038.3
    Waiver of privilege   Ev §912
Human trafficking victim-caseworker privilege   Ev §§1038 to 1038.2
Landlord and tenant
  Documentation or evidence of abuse or violence
    Domestic violence, sexual assault, stalking, dependent adult or elder abuse victims   CCP §1161.3
  Termination of tenancy
    Domestic violence, sexual assault, stalking, dependent adult or elder abuse victims   CC §1946.7, CCP §1161.3
  Victims of abuse or crime
    Lease provisions penalizing good faith summoning of law enforcement or emergency assistance   CC §1946.8
Prisoner as heir
  Notice of death to director of board   Pro §§216, 9202
Privacy rights of victims
  Victim service providers, personal information protection   CC §§1798.79.8 to 1798.79.95
Prostitution
  Extortion, serious felony, assault, domestic violence, human trafficking, sexual battery or stalking, victims or witnesses
    Inadmissibility of evidence of prostitution in prosecution for prostitution   Ev §1162
Release of stalking or domestic violence offender, warning to victim
  Name change proceedings under address confidentiality program   CRC 2.575 to 2.577
Restitution
  Forms
    Criminal forms   CRCAppx A
Service of process and papers
  Unlawful detainer
    Address confidentiality program   CCP §1167
Sexual assault
  Privileged communications
    Sexual assault counselor-victim privilege   Ev §1035.2
Sexual exploitation
  Commercial sexual exploitation
    Minor or nonminor dependent victims, actions   CC §3345.1

VICTIMS AND VICTIMS' RIGHTS—Cont.
Universities and colleges
    Sexual assault
        Privileged communications, sexual assault counselor-victim privilege   Ev §1035.2
Unlawful detainer
    Service of process and papers
        Address confidentiality program   CCP §1167

VIDEOCONFERENCING
Adoption
    Appearance by remote electronic means   Fam §8613.5
Appellate rules, superior court appeals
    Oral argument by videoconference   CRC 8.885
        Infraction case appeals   CRC 8.929
Depositions
    Remote electronic means of taking oral depositions   CRC 3.1010
Remote appearances, technology use
    COVID-19, emergency rule   CRCAppx I Emer Rule 3
    Service requirements
        Restraining orders   CRC 3.1162, 5.496
Superior courts
    Fees in superior courts   Gov §70630

VIDEO GAMES
Age
    Commercial online entertainment employment service providers
        Age information of subscribers, restriction on disclosure   CC §1798.83.5
Employer and employee
    Commercial online entertainment employment service providers
        Age information of subscribers, restriction on disclosure   CC §1798.83.5
Violent video games   CC §§1746 to 1746.5
    Definitions   CC §1746
    Fines   CC §1746.3
    Labeling   CC §1746.2
    Minors
        Defined   CC §1746
        Sale or rental to minor   CC §1746.1
    Prosecution of violations   CC §1746.4
    Reporting violations   CC §1746.4
    Severability of provisions   CC §1746.5

VIDEO RECORDINGS
Coroners', copying   CCP §129
Court proceedings, recording of
    Notice
        Limitation on papers filed   CRC 3.250
Court reporting and transcriptions
    Court reporters generally (See **COURT REPORTERS**)
Depositions (See **DEPOSITIONS**)
Elder abuse
    Victim's videotaped statement, admissibility under hearsay rule of   Ev §1380
Fees
    Courts, authority to set fees for products or services   CRC 10.815
Invasion of privacy   CC §1708.8
Printed representation of images stored on video or digital medium
    Presumption of accuracy of   Ev §1553
Privacy
    Commercial invasion by use of video   CC §3344
    Photographs, films, etc, exposing intimate body parts or sexual acts of another without permission, distribution
        Actions for injunctions, damages, etc   CC §1708.85
        Confidential information form   CRCAppx A
Superior court reporters
    Visual display of testimony or proceedings
        Limitations on use of instant visual display   CCP §273
Transcripts of videotapes offered as evidence   CRC 2.1040
Trial court proceedings, reporters records   CRC 2.958
Vendors of video recordings for sale or rent, nondisclosure of personal information in business records maintained by   CC §1799.3

VIETNAMESE LANGUAGE
Contracts in Chinese, Tagalog, Vietnamese or Korean languages   CC §1632
    Consumer credit contracts
        Federal notice requirement   CC §1799.96
        Foreign language translations of notice requirement   CC §1799.91
Gender tax repeal act preventing charging different prices for services of similar or like kind based on gender
    Consumer affairs department pamphlet for affected businesses and other notice of requirements of provisions   CC §51.63

VIETNAMESE LANGUAGE—Cont.
Gender tax repeal act preventing charging different prices for services of similar or like kind based on gender—Cont.
    Licensing authority notice of provisions to licensee upon issuance or renewal   CC §51.6
Mortgages of residential property, foreign language summaries of terms   CC §1632.5

VIEW OF PREMISES
Jury as trier of fact, view of premises by   CCP §651
Value determination in eminent domain proceedings   Ev §813

VINES   CC §660

VIOLATIONS
Criminal violations (See **CRIMINAL ACTIONS AND PROCEEDINGS**)
Presumption of failure to exercise due care, violation of statute establishing   Ev §§669, 669.1
Probation, requirement to report violations of   CCP §131.1

VIOLENCE PREVENTION
Freedom from violence or intimidation based on sex, race, religion, etc
    Coerced or involuntary waiver of rights   CC §51.7
Online violence prevention   CC §§1798.99.20 to 1798.99.23
Postsecondary educational institutions, protection orders against violence threatened on campus or facility   CCP §527.85
    California law enforcement telecommunications (CLETS) information form, confidentiality and use of information   CRC 1.51, CRCAppx A
    COVID-19, emergency rule   CRCAppx I Emer Rule 8
    Judicial council legal forms   CRCAppx A
    Memorandum in support of petition not required   CRC 3.1114
    Requests for protective orders   CRC 3.1160
Workplace violence
    Appellate court opinions
        Privacy, use of names in opinions   CRC 8.90
    Employer's action to prevent   CCP §527.8
        Address or location of complaining party or family, prohibition on enjoined party from obtaining   CCP §527.10
        California law enforcement telecommunications (CLETS) information form, confidentiality and use of information   CRC 1.51, CRCAppx A
        COVID-19, emergency rule   CRCAppx I Emer Rule 8
        Judicial council legal forms   CRCAppx A
        Requests for protective orders   CRC 3.1160

VIOLENT VIDEO GAMES   CC §§1746 to 1746.5
Definitions   CC §1746
Fines   CC §1746.3
Labeling   CC §1746.2
Minors
    Defined   CC §1746
    Sale or rental to minor   CC §1746.1
Prosecution of violations   CC §1746.4
Reporting violations   CC §1746.4
Severability of provisions   CC §1746.5

VIRGIN ISLANDS
Acknowledgment of instruments   CC §1183.5

VISION SCREENING
Immunity from liability
    Nonprofit charitable organization and volunteer eye care professionals donating screening, eyeglasses, etc   CC §1714.26

VISITATION RIGHTS   CRC 5.695
Application attachment   CRCAppx A (CRCFL-311)
Appointment of attorney for child   CRC 5.240 to 5.242, Fam §§3114, 3150 to 3153
Child custody proceedings, visitation in   CRC 5.695
Custody of children (See **CUSTODY OF CHILDREN**)
Dependent children
    Detained child, visitation with   CRC 5.670
    Grandparents' visitation rights   CRC 5.695
    Parents' or guardians' visitation rights   CRC 5.695
    Sibling visitation   CRC 5.670
Family reunification services, visitation orders   CRC 5.695
Forms
    Judicial council legal forms   CRCAppx A
Guardianships
    Jurisdiction   Pro §2205

VISITATION RIGHTS—Cont.
  Guardianships—Cont.
    Venue, multiple counties with pending proceedings Pro §2204
      Communications between/among courts involved with custody, visitation and guardianship involving ward CRC 7.1014
      Ward's participation and testimony in probate guardianship proceedings CRC 7.1016
  Holiday schedule attachment CRCAppx A (CRCFL-341(C))
  Juvenile court, exclusive jurisdiction of CRC 5.510
    Termination of jurisdiction
      Orders as to custody or visitation CRC 5.700
  Modification of orders
    Domestic violence prevention act proceedings CRC 5.381
  Physical custody attachment CRCAppx A (CRCFL-341(D))
  Reasons for no or for supervised visitation
    Form CRCAppx A
  Stipulation and order CRCAppx A (CRCFL-355)
  Supervised visitation
    Declaration of provider
      Form CRCAppx A
    Order CRCAppx A (CRCFL-341(A))
    Reasons for no or for supervised visitation
      Form CRCAppx A
  Supervised visitation, child abuse and neglect cases CRC JudAdminStand 5.20

VISUALLY HANDICAPPED PERSONS (See **BLIND PERSONS**)

VITAL STATISTICS
Birth (See **BIRTH**)
Records admissible in evidence Ev §§1281 to 1283

VLOGGING
Minors engaged in the work of Fam §6651
  Applicability of part Fam §§6655, 6656
  Compensation of minor Fam §6653
  Damages for violations Fam §6654
  Definitions Fam §6650
  Enforcement Fam §6654
  Parent or guardian, contract for vlogging services between minor and Fam §6656
  Records required Fam §6652
  Trust accounts for Fam §6653

VOCATIONAL TRAINING
Spousal support, order for examination by vocational training consultant Fam §4331

VOICES
Invasion of privacy, unauthorized use of voice in advertising as CC §§3344, 3344.1

VOIDABLE TRANSACTIONS CC §§1227, 3439 to 3439.14, 3440, 3440.3
Actual intent to hinder, delay or defraud creditors CC §3439.04
Agency, application of rules relating to law of CC §3439.12
Antecedent debt, property received to secure CC §3439.03
Assignee of assignment for benefit of creditors, rights and remedies CC §3439.07
Attachment against asset transferred or its proceeds CC §3439.07
Avoidance of obligation as remedy CC §3439.07
Bona fide purchasers as affected by CC §3439.08
Bond in action to set aside CC §§3445 to 3449
Cause of action, when extinguished CC §3439.09
Citation of act CC §3439
Coercion, application of rules as to effect of CC §3439.12
Consideration CC §§3439.03, 3439.04
  Value given CC §3439.04
Construction of statute CC §§3439.12, 3440.9
Damages, recovery of CC §3439.08
Debts, fraudulent incurring of CC §§3439.04, 3439.05
Decedent's estate, recovering property for creditors of Pro §9653
Definitions CC §§3439.01, 3445
Defraud or delay creditors, transaction made with intent to CC §3439.04
Delivery requirements CC §3440
Discount buying organization officer CC §1812.106
Duress, application of rules CC §3439.12
Equity rules, application CC §3439.12
Execution
  Property, execution on CC §3439.07
Exemptions
  Generally CC §§3440.1, 3440.2

VOIDABLE TRANSACTIONS—Cont.
Exemptions—Cont.
  Secured party, interest from transferee or successor acquired by CC §3440.5
Former law, transfers made under CC §3439.14
Fraud, application of rules CC §3439.12
Good faith takers for value CC §3439.08
Hinder creditors, transaction made with intent to CC §3439.04
Injunctive relief CC §3439.07
Innocent purchasers
  Delivery, purchase of personal property without CC §§3440.3, 3440.4
  Real property CC §§1227, 1228
  Remedies of creditors CC §3439.07
  Rights of good faith purchasers CC §§3439.08, 3440.4
Insolvency
  Application of rules CC §3439.12
  Defined CC §3439.02
  Partnership, determination of insolvency of CC §3439.02
  Transaction resulting in, as fraudulent CC §3439.05
Intent to defraud CC §3439.04
Law merchant, application CC §3439.12
Limitation of actions CC §3439.09
Marital property, fraudulent transmutation of Fam §851
Multiple-party accounts law, effect Pro §5202
Nonvoidable transfers or obligations CC §3439.08
Notices requirements CC §§1228, 3440.1
Obligations
  Fraudulently incurred CC §§3439.04, 3439.05
  Nonvoidable CC §3439.08
  When incurred CC §3439.06
Partnership, insolvency of CC §3439.02
Possession not transferred CC §3440
Principal and agent, application of law CC §3439.12
Purchasers' rights
  Good faith purchasers
    Innocent purchasers generally (See within this heading, "**Innocent purchasers**")
  Secured party, interest from transferee or successor acquired by CC §3440.5
Purpose of provisions CC §3439.13
Receivers
  Actions for vacation CCP §564
  Appointment CC §3439.07
Remedies of creditors CC §3439.07
Retroactive nature of Uniform Voidable Transactions Act CC §3439.14
Secured party, interest from transferee or successor acquired by CC §3440.5
Small estate dispositions without administration Pro §§13100 to 13117
Statutes of limitation
  Personal property, transfers involving CC §3440.6
  Uniform Voidable Transactions Act, action under CC §3439.09
Subsequent transferees for value CC §3439.08
Time of transfer of property, determination CC §3439.06
Transfers
  Nonvoidable CC §3439.08
  Rights of transferees CC §3439.08
  When made CC §3439.06
Trust beneficiary's disclaimer of interest, effect Pro §283
Undertaking CC §§3445 to 3449
  Amount CC §3448
  Condition CC §3447
  Effect CC §3446
  Effective date CC §3449
Uniform act CC §§3439 to 3439.14
Value, when given CC §3439.03
Water supply property
  Personal property conveyed without delivery
    Exception to provisions CC §3440.1

VOID FILING
Check for filing fees
  Returned unpaid CCP §411.20
  Underpayment CCP §411.21

VOID OR VOIDABLE MARRIAGES (See **ANNULMENT; MARRIAGE**)

VOIR DIRE (See **JURY**)

VOLCANIC ACTIVITY
State's immunity from liability for prediction of Gov §955.1

VOLUNTARY MANSLAUGHTER (See **MANSLAUGHTER**)

VOLUNTEERS
Court-appointed special advocates (CASA)
    Appointment of volunteers   CRC 5.655
    Oath   CRC 5.655
    Prohibited activities   CRC 5.655
    Removal, resignation or termination   CRC 5.655
    Screening of volunteers   CRC 5.655
    Supervision, support, etc   CRC 5.655
    Training   CRC 5.655
Small claims advisors   CCP §116.940
Vision screening
    Immunity from liability
        Nonprofit charitable organization and volunteer eye care professionals donating screening, eyeglasses, etc   CC §1714.26

VOTER REGISTRATION
Jurors, list of registered voters as source for selection of   CCP §197
Precedence to cases involving elections proceedings   CCP §35

VOTES AND VOTING
Administrative adjudicative proceedings (See **ADMINISTRATIVE ADJUDICATION**)
Conservatee's right to vote   Pro §§1823, 1828, 1851
Elections (See **ELECTIONS AND ELECTIONS PROCEEDINGS**)
Initiative and referendum
    Tax limitation initiative (See **TAXATION**)
Judges participating in political activities, Code of Judicial Ethics provisions regarding   CRCSupp JudEthicsCanon 5
Recall of elective officer (See **RECALL**)
Rights
    Report of findings and orders affecting   CRC 10.970, CRCAppx A
Voting rights
    Report of findings and orders affecting   CRC 10.970, CRCAppx A

VOTING TRUSTS
Participation in voting trusts by trustee   Pro §16237

VOUCHERS
Administration of estates (See **ADMINISTRATION OF ESTATES**)
Claims against decedent's estate, vouchers filed in support of   Pro §9151

W

WAGE ASSIGNMENTS FOR SUPPORT (See **EARNINGS ASSIGNMENT FOR SUPPORT**)

WAGERING (See **GAMBLING**)

WAGES (See **SALARIES AND WAGES**)

WAIVER
Acceleration of loan provisions, waiver of   CC §2924.6
Administration of decedents' estates (See **ADMINISTRATION OF ESTATES**)
Administrative adjudication provisions, waiver of rights under   Gov §11415.40
Adoption proceedings, waiver of confidentiality in   Fam §§9204, 9205
    Sibling contact
        Request for sibling contact information   CRC 5.460
Adoption, waiver of right to revoke consent to   Fam §8814.5
Alteration of instruments affecting   CC §1698
Appearances
    Personal appearance waivers
        COVID-19, emergency rule   CRCAppx I Emer Rule 5
Arbitration, waiver of (See **ARBITRATION**)
Artists waiving rights to art dealers   CC §1738.8
Assistive devices, warranty on sale of   CC §1793.02
Attachment proceedings, waiver of defense in   CCP §484.110
Attorney-client privilege   Ev §912
Automobile conditional sales contract, prohibited provision in   CC §2983.7
Child sexual abuse hosted on social media platform
    Waiver of provisions as void   CC §3273.68
Claim and delivery possession writs   CCP §512.100
Claims against decedent's estate, effect of personal representative waiving defects in filing   Pro §9154
Clergyman-penitent privilege   Ev §912
Confession of judgment, attorneys advising defendant of waiver of rights in   CCP §1132
Conservators
    Accounting
        Order waiving accounting   CRC 7.575
Consumer credit organization, waiver of rights by buyer using   CC §1789.19

WAIVER—Cont.
Consumer goods or services, contract for sale or lease
    Statements by consumer about seller, lessor, goods or services
        Prohibited contract provisions   CC §§1670.8, 1670.8.5
Consumer privacy rights
    Waiver or limitation of consumer rights
        Contracts or agreements void   CC §1798.192
Contract rights   CC §3268
Court fees and costs
    Bench warrants to secure attendance of witnesses, applicability of waiver   Gov §26744.5
    Civil rules governing waiver of fees and costs   CRC 3.50 to 3.58
    Court reporters
        Request for reporter if granted fee waiver   CRC 2.956
    Economically unable to pay   Gov §§68630 to 68641
    Forms, judicial council   CRCAppx A
Court reporters
    Request for reporter if granted fee waiver
        Judicial council form   CRCAppx A
Criminal conduct
    Contract or settlement waiving right to testify concerning criminal conduct or sexual harassment   CC §1670.11
Dance studio contracts, provisions regulating   CC §1812.61
Demurrer (See **DEMURRERS**)
Disability insurance provisions, effect of waiver of   CC §1812.408
Disclaimer of estate interest, waiver of right to file   Pro §284
Domestic violence counselor-victim privilege   Ev §912
Enforcement of judgments (See **ENFORCEMENT OF JUDGMENTS**)
Fair debt settlement practices
    Void and unenforceable   CC §1788.306
Floating homes and floating home marinas (See **FLOATING HOMES**)
Foster care
    Specialty mental health services
        Judicial council legal forms   CRCAppx A
        Presumptive transfer of responsibility for services upon change of child placement, proceedings upon request for waiver   CRC 5.647
Guardianships
    Accounting
        Order waiving accounting   CRC 7.575
Health studio services contracts, effect of buyer waiving rights under   CC §1812.93
Home equity sales contracts   CC §1695.10
Indigent persons (See **INDIGENT PERSONS**)
Innkeeper's lien, writ of possession on   CC §1861.13
Interest   CC §3290
Judges, waiver of disqualification of   CCP §1170.3
Jury trial   CCP §631
Landlord and tenant
    Rent increase limitations for residential real property
        Void nature of waiver   CC §1947.12
    Water service in multifamily residential rental buildings
        Waiver of provisions prohibited   CC §1954.215
Layaway provisions, buyer waiving   CC §1749.2
Leases (See **LEASES**)
Limitation, statutes of   CCP §360.5
Livestock service liens, sale under   CC §3080.08
Marital privilege   Ev §§912, 973
Merchantability warranty   CC §1792.3
Mobilehomes (See **MOBILEHOMES**)
Mortgage foreclosure consultant provisions   CC §2945.5
Mortgages, rights under statute governing   CC §2953
Net neutrality
    Barring waiver of provisions   CC §3104
Objections to pleadings   CCP §430.80
Oil and gas liens   CCP §1203.63
Oral argument   CRC 8.885
Pension claimants, affidavit fees waived for   Gov §26858
Physician-patient privilege   Ev §912
Private student loan collections reform
    Void and unenforceable   CC §1788.209
Privileged communication   Ev §§912, 919
Psychotherapist-patient privilege   Ev §912
Realty sales contract waiving provisions of Subdivision Map Act   CC §2985.51
Rental passenger vehicle transactions
    Damage waivers   CC §1939.09
        Defined   CC §1939.01
        Purchase of damage waiver or optional insurance, prohibited practices to induce   CC §1939.13
    Provisions of chapter, restrictions on waiver   CC §1939.29
Retail installment sales provisions   CC §1801.1
Seller assisted marketing plans, rights of purchaser   CC §1812.216

WAIVER—Cont.
Sexual harassment
 Contract or settlement waiving right to testify concerning criminal conduct or sexual harassment CC §1670.11
Small claims court (See **SMALL CLAIMS COURTS**)
Statutes of limitation CCP §360.5
Subrogation, guarantor waiving rights of CC §2856
Sureties and suretyship (See **SURETYSHIP, BONDS AND UNDERTAKINGS**)
Surviving spouse, rights of (See **SURVIVING SPOUSE**)
Tender, objection to CCP §2076
Title, effect on marketability of CC §880.030
Trust deeds, rights under statute governing CC §2953
Trust estate, waiver of defects in claims filed against Pro §19154
Violence
 Freedom from violence or intimidation based on sex, race, religion, etc
  Coerced or involuntary waiver of rights CC §51.7
Warranties on consumer goods CC §1790.1
Will probate proceedings, waiver of notice in Pro §1204

WALLS
Generally CC §660
Easement rights to CC §801

WAR
Construction defects, actions for
 Unforeseen act of nature
  Defenses of builder CC §945.5
Emergency care centers, governmental liability for injuries to parties using CC §1714.5
Fiduciaries substituted during wartime (See **FIDUCIARIES' WARTIME SUBSTITUTION LAW**)
Prisoners of war (See **MILITARY**)
Statutes of limitation, effect on running of CCP §354

WAR BONDS
Unclaimed property
 Notice
  Separate notice for savings bonds, war bonds or military awards CCP §1531.6

WAR CRIMES
Attorney's fees
 Assault and battery, wrongful death, etc constituting torture, genocide, crimes against humanity, etc CCP §354.8
Statutes of limitations
 Assault and battery, wrongful death, etc constituting torture, genocide, crimes against humanity, etc CCP §354.8

WARD
Generally (See **GUARDIAN AND WARD**)
Juvenile ward of the court (See **JUVENILE WARDSHIP PROCEEDINGS**)

WAREHOUSE RECEIPTS
Storage in bulk CC §§1880.4, 1880.5

WAREHOUSES
Grain storage in bulk CC §§1880 to 1881.2
Receipts (See **WAREHOUSE RECEIPTS**)
Small business action, costs in CCP §1028.5
Tenant's abandoned personalty, storage of CC §§1986 to 1990, CCP §1174
Unclaimed property, sale of CC §§2081.5, 2081.6

WARES (See **MERCHANDISE**)

WARNING
Recreational landowner's duty to give warning of hazardous conditions CC §846

WARRANTIES
Appliances CC §§1790 to 1795.8
Assistive devices CC §§1791, 1791.1, 1792.2, 1793.02
Autographed memorabilia CC §1739.7
Automobiles (See **AUTOMOBILES**)
Collateral warranties, abolishment of CC §1115
Construction defects, actions for CC §900
 Enhanced protection agreements generally CC §§902 to 906
Consumer goods, regulating warranties on CC §§1790 to 1795.8
Damages for violation of CC §§1794 to 1794.1
Definitions CC §1791
Express warranties defined CC §1791.2
Extension of CC §1793.1
Grey market goods (See **GREY MARKET GOODS**)

WARRANTIES—Cont.
Habitability, warrant of CC §§1941, 1942.3, CCP §1174.2
Hearing aids and accessories
 Consumer warranty protection
  Extension of warranty period during service or repairs CC §1795.6
  Return to seller for adjustment, replacement or refund CC §1793.02
Implied warranties defined CC §1791.1
Indemnification of retail seller by manufacturer CC §1792
Judgment admissible from earlier action for breach of Ev §1301
Leased goods, consumer warranty protection for CC §§1791, 1795.4
Lineal warranties, abolishment of CC §1115
Magnuson-Moss Warranty Federal Trade Commission Improvement Act CC §1793.1
Manufactured homes CC §§1797.1 to 1797.7
Memorabilia
 Autographed memorabilia CC §1739.7
Military personnel
 Motor vehicle purchased in US
  Applicability of California warranty protections CC §1791.8
Mobilehomes (See **MOBILEHOMES**)
Motor vehicles (See **AUTOMOBILES**)
Notice of rights to independent dealer CC §1793.3
Rental-purchase contracts, transfer of warranties under CC §1812.634
Repairs (See **REPAIRS**)
Roofs (See **ROOFING WARRANTIES**)
Service contracts (See **REPAIRS**)
Song-Beverly consumer warranty act CC §§1790 to 1795.8
Tolling of warranties on goods sold CC §§1795.6, 1795.7
Used vehicles
 Buy-here-pay-here dealers' obligations CC §1795.51
Wheelchairs CC §1793.025
Work orders, requirements for CC §1793.3

WARRANTS
Arrest (See **ARREST**)
Child unlawfully detained or concealed, protective custody warrant for recovery of Fam §3134.5
Inspection warrants (See **INSPECTION WARRANTS**)
Request and order forms CRCAppx A
Search warrants (See **SEARCH AND SEIZURE**)
Validation proceedings, date of authorization and existence for purposes of CCP §864
Witnesses, bench warrants to secure attendance of CCP §§1993, 1994
 Fee for processing civil warrant Gov §26744.5
 Release of arrested witness CCP §1993.1
  Failure of released witness to appear CCP §1993.2

WASHING MACHINES
Serial number destroyed or altered prior to sale CC §1710.1

WASTE
Administrators (See **EXECUTORS AND ADMINISTRATORS**)
Damages recoverable for CCP §732
Executors (See **EXECUTORS AND ADMINISTRATORS**)
Grantee, rights of CC §821
Guardian, action against CCP §732
Hazardous waste (See **ENVIRONMENTAL HAZARDS**)
Injunction against CCP §526
Joint tenants, action against CCP §732
Judicial Council policy regarding waste reduction and recycling programs for local courts CRC JudAdminStand 10.55
Life tenant, action against CCP §732
Mortgage foreclosure proceedings, enjoining waste pending CCP §745
Partition actions, injunctions preventing waste during CCP §872.130
Pharmaceutical waste
 Secure drug take-back bins
  Liability of collector, limitation CC §1714.24
Public administrators preventing Pro §§7601, 7602
Remainder interest, action by party having CC §826
Reversionary interest, action by party having CC §826
Special administrator protecting from Pro §8544
Tenants in common, action against CCP §732

WATCHES
Common carrier's liability for transporting CC §2200
Lien for repairs CC §3052a
Serial number destroyed or altered prior to sale CC §1710.1

WATER APPROPRIATION CC §§1414 to 1422

WATERBEDS
Tenants' possession of CC §1940.5

WATER COMMISSION
Eminent domain taking by   CCP §1245.210

WATER CONSERVATION
Common interest developments
    Restrictions on water efficiency measures prohibited   CC §4735
Disclosure requirements   CC §2079.10
    Plumbing retrofits, disclosures as to noncompliant plumbing fixtures   CC §§1101.4, 1102.155
Government tort liability
    Injuries caused by condition of facilities   Gov §831.8
Landscaping
    Commercial and industrial common interest developments
        Water-efficient landscaping, protected interest   CC §6712
    Common interest developments
        Artificial turf, architectural guidelines not to prohibit   CC §4735
        Low water-using plants, architectural guidelines not to prohibit   CC §4735
Plumbing retrofits   CC §§1101.1 to 1101.9

WATER CONSERVING PLUMBING RETROFITS
Applicability of provisions   CC §§1101.2, 1101.7
Commercial real property
    Defined   CC §1101.3
    Replacement of noncompliant plumbing fixtures   CC §1101.5
Construction date
    Applicability of provisions   CC §1101.2
Definitions   CC §1101.3
Demolition of building
    Effect on replacement requirements   CC §1101.6
Historical sites
    Applicability of provisions   CC §1101.7
Legislative findings and intent   CC §1101.1
Local government ordinances
    Grandfathering of existing ordinances   CC §1101.9
    Permissible ordinances   CC §1101.8
Multifamily residential real property
    Defined   CC §1101.3
    Replacement of noncompliant plumbing fixtures   CC §1101.5
Noncompliant plumbing fixtures
    Commercial real property, replacements   CC §1101.5
    Defined   CC §1101.3
    Disclosures upon sale or transfer   CC §1101.4
    Multifamily residential property, replacements   CC §1101.5
    Replacement as condition of permits for alterations, improvements, etc   CC §1101.4
    Schedule for replacement   CC §1101.4
    Single-family residential property, replacements   CC §1101.4
Permanently disconnected water service
    Applicability of provisions   CC §1101.7
Sale or transfer
    Defined   CC §1101.3
Single-family residential real property
    Defined   CC §1101.3
    Replacement of noncompliant plumbing fixtures   CC §1101.4
Technically not feasible
    Applicability of provisions   CC §1101.7
Water-conserving plumbing fixtures
    Defined   CC §1101.3

WATER CORPORATIONS
Cancellation of utility, cable, etc, services on behalf of deceased person
    In-person cancellation not to be required   Pro §217
Credit cards
    Surcharge on credit card transaction, prohibition against
        Exception for electrical, gas or water corporation   CC §1748.1
Debit cards
    Surcharge on debit card transaction, prohibition against
        Exception for electrical, gas or water corporation   CC §1748.1
Indemnity coverage for construction, repair, renovation, maintenance or demolition of lines   CC §2783

WATERCRAFT (See VESSELS)

WATER QUALITY (See ENVIRONMENTAL HAZARDS)

WATER RESOURCES CONTROL BOARD
Review of administrative regulations of (See **ADMINISTRATIVE PROCEDURE ACT**)

WATER RESOURCES DEPARTMENT
Eminent domain taking by   CCP §1245.210

WATER RIGHTS
Attorney general civil enforcement
    Fees and costs for attorney general   CCP §1021.8
Fiduciary income and principal act
    Receipts, allocation
        Minerals, water or other natural resources, interests in   Pro §16350

WATERS
Accretion (See **ACCRETION**)
Appropriation of
    Loss of   CC §1419
    Notice of intent   CC §§1415, 1418
    Prior claims, statute effect on   CC §1420
    Priority   CC §1414
    Public lands, appropriation of water originating on   CC §1422
    Recordation of requirements   CC §§1415, 1421
    Time for completion of work   CC §1416
Dams (See **DAMS**)
Drinking water (See **WATER SUPPLY**)
Easement rights   CC §§801, 802
Eminent domain taking for facilities for   CCP §§1240.110, 1240.125
Erosion (See **EROSION**)
Federal water pollution control act enforcement
    Attorney general, civil actions to enforce provisions
        Fees and costs for attorney general   CCP §1021.8
Injunctions to prevent diversion of   CCP §§530, 532, 534
Lakes (See **LAKES**)
Rivers and streams
    Generally (See **RIVERS AND STREAMS**)
    Appropriation generally (See within this heading, "**Appropriation of**")

WATER SERVICE
Landlord and tenant
    Water service in multifamily residential rental buildings   CC §§1954.201 to 219 (See **LANDLORD AND TENANT**)

WATER SPORTS
Owner's liability for recreational land   CC §846

WATER SUPPLY
Appeals in mandamus proceedings   CCP §1110a
Flood control and water conservation facilities, liability for injuries caused by   Gov §831.8
Landlord and tenant
    Termination by landlord   CC §789.3
Unauthorized diversion or use
    Attorney general, civil actions to enforce provisions
        Fees and costs for attorney general   CCP §1021.8
Voidable transactions
    Personal property conveyed without delivery
        Exception to provisions for water supply property   CC §3440.1
Waste or unreasonable use
    Attorney general, civil actions to enforce provisions
        Fees and costs for attorney general   CCP §1021.8

WATER WELLS
Groundwater rights actions   CCP §§830 to 852 (See **GROUNDWATER RIGHTS ACTIONS**)

WEALTH (See FINANCIAL CONDITION)

WEAPONS (See FIREARMS AND OTHER WEAPONS)

WEARING APPAREL (See CLOTHING)

WEIGHT LOSS PROGRAMS
Cancellation of agreement
    Buyer's right to   CC §1694.6
    Noncompliance with statute   CC §1694.7
Damages recoverable   CC §1694.9
Death or disability of buyer, effect of   CC §1694.8
Definition   CC §1694.5
False and misleading advertisement, liability for   CC §1694.9
Installment payments
    Generally   CC §1694.7
    Refund or credit, buyer's right to   CC §1694.9
Refund or credit of payments, buyer's right to   CC §1694.9
Relocation of buyer's residence, effect of   CC §1694.8
Terms of agreement   CC §1694.7
Void and unenforceable contracts, grounds for   CC §1694.9

WELFARE
Assignment for benefit of creditors, property exempt from CCP §1801
Child support (See **CHILD SUPPORT**)
Custody of children (See **CUSTODY OF CHILDREN**)
Decedent's estate, claims against Pro §§9200 to 9205
Emancipated minor Fam §7111
Enforcement of judgments against deposit accounts (See **ENFORCEMENT OF JUDGMENTS**)
Guardian and ward (See **GUARDIAN AND WARD**)
Indigent parents, duty to support Fam §§3550, 3555, 4400 to 4405
Missing person, search for Pro §12406
Spousal support enforcement in behalf of welfare recipients Fam §§4351, 17000, 17604
Supportive care organizations
    Medical information disclosures CC §56.10

WHARVES
Indemnity coverage for construction of CC §2783
Leasing of CC §718

WHEELCHAIRS
Warranty and disclosure requirements CC §1793.025

WHEREABOUTS UNKNOWN (See **MISSING PERSONS; UNKNOWN PERSONS**)

WHISKEY (See **ALCOHOLIC BEVERAGES**)

WHITE CANES (See **BLIND PERSONS**)

WHOLESALE SALES REPRESENTATIVES
Alcohol Beverage Control Act, exemption from contract in writing requirement for persons licensed under CC §1738.17
Attorneys' fees, award to prevailing party CC §1738.16
Citation of Act CC §1738.11
Court costs, award to prevailing party CC §1738.16
Damages recoverable by CC §1738.15
Definitions CC §1738.11
Legislative findings and intent CC §1738.10
Nonresident manufacturer, jobber or distributor doing business in this state, personal jurisdiction over CC §1738.14
Written contract with manufacturer, jobber or distributor, requirement of CC §1738.13

WIFE (See **HUSBAND AND WIFE**)

WIFE-BEATING (See **DOMESTIC VIOLENCE**)

WILD ANIMAL PARKS
Guide dogs allowed in CC §54.7

WILDFIRES
Mobilehomes and mobilehome parks
    Destruction of park by wildfire or other natural disaster and subsequent rebuilding
        Offers of renewed tenancy CC §798.62
Prescribed burns
    Immunity from damages CC §3333.8

WILDLIFE CONSERVATION BOARD
Eminent domain taking by CCP §1245.210

WILL CONSTRUCTION
Ademption by satisfaction Pro §21135
Adopted persons included in class for disposition Pro §21115
After-acquired property passed by will, disposition of Pro §21105
Ambiguities Pro §21121
Annuities, gifts of Pro §21117
At-death transfers
    Annuities Pro §21117
    Anti-lapse Pro §21110
    Class gifts Pro §21114
    Defined Pro §21104
    Demonstrative gifts Pro §21117
    Failure of transfer, treatment Pro §21111
    General gifts Pro §21117
    General pecuniary gifts Pro §21117
    Lifetime gifts in satisfaction of at-death transfer Pro §21135
    Residuary gifts Pro §§21111, 21117
    Rules, intent Pro §21139
    Securities Pro §21132

WILL CONSTRUCTION—Cont.
At-death transfers—Cont.
    Specific gifts Pro §§21117, 21133
        Transfer of encumbrance of specific gift, rights of transferee Pro §21134
    Survival of transferee Pro §21109
California statutory wills Pro §§6200 to 6211
Classification of testamentary gift Pro §21117
Conflict of laws Pro §§6113, 6141
Consanguinity
    Degrees of kinship and consanguinity Pro §13
Contests
    No contest clause Pro §§21310 to 21315
Definitions Pro §§20 to 88, 6200 to 6211
Demonstrative gifts Pro §21117
Dispositions
    Generally Pro §21101
    Ademption by satisfaction Pro §21135
    After-acquired property passed by will, disposition of Pro §21105
    Choice of law Pro §21103
    Class descriptions Pro §§21114, 21115
    Classification of testamentary gift Pro §21117
    Conservator's sale or encumbrance of property subject to specific gift, effect of Pro §21134
    Converted real property, treatment of Pro §21107
    Exoneration, no right to Pro §21131
    Failure of transfer Pro §21111
    Federal law, applicability of Pro §21501
    Halfbloods and adopted persons included in class Pro §21115
    Intent of transferor as controlling Pro §21102
    Issue of deceased transferee taking under instrument Pro §21110
    Language used in instrument, meaning of Pro §§21120 to 21122
    Property subject to Pro §§6101, 6102
    Reference to death with or without issue, effect of Pro §21112
    Time for applicability of sections on Pro §21140
    Valuation of property Pro §21118
    Worthier title rule, abolishment of Pro §21108
Estate tax liability, interpretation of will or trust provisions favoring elimination or reduction of Pro §21503
Extrinsic evidence, admissibility of Pro §6111.5
Federal law
    Generally Pro §21500
    Distributions, applicability to Pro §21501
    Estate tax liability, interpretation of will or trust provisions favoring elimination or reduction of Pro §21503
    Incorporation by reference, effect of Pro §21502
    Marital deduction gifts (See **MARITAL DEDUCTION GIFTS**)
Future interests
    Failure Pro §21111
General gifts Pro §21117
Governing law Pro §§6 to 13, 20
Halfbloods and adopted persons included in class for disposition Pro §21115
Incorporation by reference
    Generally Pro §6130
    Federal law, effect on applicability of Pro §21502
    Statutory provisions Pro §§7, 241
Independent significance, reference to acts of Pro §6131
Intent
    Generally Pro §6140
    General construction and interpretation Pro §21120
    Statutory provisions, intent of testator controlling over Pro §12000
Internal Revenue Code
    Federal law
        Generally (See within this heading, "**Federal law**")
International wills Pro §6387
Kinship
    Degrees of kinship and consanguinity Pro §13
Language used in instrument, meaning of Pro §§21120 to 21122
No contest clauses Pro §§21300 to 21308, 21310 to 21315, 21320 to 21322
120-hour survival requirement Pro §6211
Pecuniary gifts Pro §21117
Per capita Pro §§245, 247
Per stirpes Pro §§245, 246
Representation, right of Pro §§245, 246
Residuary gifts Pro §§21111, 21117
Several instruments, interpretation of Pro §§6120, 6123
Two or more instruments, interpretation of Pro §§6120, 6123
Undue influence
    Definition of undue influence Pro §86
Valuation of property Pro §21118
Worthier title, abolishment of rule of Pro §21108

WILLFUL INJURY
Contract exempting from liability, validity of CC §1668

WILLFUL MISCONDUCT
Latent deficiencies in planning or construction of improvement to real property, applicability of statute of limitation in actions arising from CCP §337.15

WILLING AND ABLE PERSONS
Performance of contract CC §1495

WILL PROBATE (See also ADMINISTRATION OF ESTATES; EXECUTORS AND ADMINISTRATORS)
Additional or further notice, requirements of Pro §1202
Admission
    Conclusiveness of admission Pro §8226
    Prior admission of another will, effect of Pro §8226
    Recordation of Pro §8225
Affidavits, admissibility of Pro §§1022, 8220, 8221
Ancillary administration (See ANCILLARY ADMINISTRATION)
Appeals
    Generally Pro §1303
    Costs on CRC 8.278, Pro §1002
    Stay on appeal Pro §1310
Attorney General, notice to Pro §§1209, 8111
Beneficiaries
    No contest clauses (See within this heading, "**No contest clauses**")
    Subscribing witnesses as Pro §6112
Citations, issuance of Pro §§1240 to 1242
Clerk of court, delivery of will to Pro §8200
Clerk of court, fees for documents transferred to Gov §§70660, 70661
Collateral attack on jurisdiction Pro §8007
Conditional wills Pro §6105
Conservator as interested person for purposes of Pro §1210
Construction of will provisions (See WILL CONSTRUCTION)
Contested wills
    After probate (See within this heading, "**Revocation of probate**")
    Before probate Pro §§8250 to 8254
    Burden of proof Pro §8252
    Costs Pro §1002
    Demurrer Pro §8251
    Examination of witnesses Pro §8005
    Findings, order of Pro §8006
    Judgment, order of Pro §8254
    Jury trial, right to Pro §825
    Limitations period
        Before probate Pro §8250
        Revocation of probate Pro §8270
    New trial, motion for Pro §7220
    No contest clauses Pro §§21300 to 21308, 21310 to 21315, 21320 to 21322
    Parties to action Pro §1044
    Responsive pleadings Pro §§1043, 8251
    Revocation of probate (See within this heading, "**Revocation of probate**")
    Subscribing witnesses (See within this heading, "**Subscribing witnesses**")
Continuances
    Generally Pro §1045
    Notice of continued or postponed hearing Pro §1205
Copies
    Admissibility of copy where original will detained outside California Pro §8202
    Photographic copies (See within this heading, "**Photographic copies**")
Costs Pro §1002
    Appeals, cost of CRC 8.278, Pro §1002
County treasurer, copy of decree of distribution to Pro §11853
Court reporter taking down and transcribing at cost of county CCP §274a
Declaratory relief
    Construction of writing CCP §1060
    No contest clauses Pro §§21320 to 21322
Decrees (See within this heading, "**Orders and decrees**")
Definitions Pro §§20 to 88, 6200 to 6211
Delivery of will for purpose of Pro §§8200 to 8203
Demurrer in will contest Pro §8251
Destroyed instrument Pro §8223
Disclaimer of interest Pro §§260 to 295
Discovery
    Law and motion rules
        Applicable to discovery proceedings in probate CRC 3.1100
Dispositions under wills (See WILL CONSTRUCTION)
Entry and filing of orders Pro §1048
Execution of will, proof of Pro §§8220, 8221

WILL PROBATE—Cont.
Ex parte communications
    Restrictions Pro §1051
Fact of death, proceedings to establish (See FACT OF DEATH)
Fees
    Clerk of court fees for transferred documents Gov §§70660, 70661
    Delivery of will to clerk Pro §8200
    Filing (See within this heading, "**Filing fees**")
Filing fees Gov §§70650 to 70663
    Children's waiting room in courthouse, surcharge to fund Gov §70640
    Initial petition for probate Gov §70650
    Supplemental fees for first paper filing Gov §§70602.5, 70602.6
    Public administrator, etc., or Mental Health Department employee as petitioner, filing fees payable by Gov §70659
    Riverside County
        Courthouse seismic repair costs, additional filing fees authorized to defray Gov §70622
Foreign wills (See ANCILLARY ADMINISTRATION)
General personal representative
    Defined Pro §§42, 58
Good faith attempt to comply with notice requirements, sufficiency of Pro §8122
Guardian as interested person for purposes of Pro §1210
Handwriting of testator, proof of Pro §8221
Hearings
    Generally Pro §8005
    Clerk, matter set for hearing by Pro §1041
    Continuance or postponement of Pro §1045
    Notices generally (See within this heading, "**Notices**")
    Order of Pro §8006
    Petition for probate Pro §8005
    Rules of procedure for Pro §1040
    Time of Pro §8003
    Trials (See within this heading, "**Trial**")
Holographic wills Pro §8222
Homesteads (See HOMESTEADS)
Income received during probate, distribution of Pro §12006
Interactive computer system authorized to prepare standardized pro per court documents CCP §1062.20
Interpretation of terms (See WILL CONSTRUCTION)
Judge, disqualification of Pro §7060
Judgment roll of proceedings Pro §1050
Judgments
    Orders and decrees generally (See within this heading, "**Orders and decrees**")
Jurisdiction
    Generally Pro §§7050, 7051
    Collateral attack on Pro §8007
Jury trial, right to Pro §825
Known heirs or devisees, notice to Pro §§1206, 8110
Law and motion rules
    Discovery
        Applicable to discovery proceedings in probate CRC 3.1100
Limitations period
    Before probate Pro §8250
    Revocation of probate Pro §8270
Lost instruments Pro §8223
Mail
    General requirements for mailing notices Pro §§1215, 1217
    Hearings, mailing notice of Pro §1220
    Proof of mailing of notice Pro §1261
Missing persons' estates (See MISSING PERSONS)
Multiple-party accounts (See MULTIPLE-PARTY ACCOUNTS)
New trial motion Pro §7220
No contest clauses Pro §§21300 to 21308, 21310 to 21315, 21320 to 21322
    Applicability of provisions Pro §§21314, 21315
    Common law governing no contest clauses Pro §§21301, 21313
    Declaratory relief Pro §§21320 to 21322
    Definitions Pro §§21300, 21310
    Enforcement Pro §21311
    Intent of transferor
        Strict construction of clause Pro §21312
    Witness or will drafter as beneficiaries, effect on party contesting will provision providing for Pro §6112
Nonprobate transfers (See NONPROBATE TRANSFERS)
Notices
    Additional or further notice requirements Pro §1202
    Address unknown, procedure for notice where Pro §1212
    Attorney as proper recipient of notices to parties Pro §1214
    Attorney General, notice to Pro §§1209, 8111
    Conservators, service of notice on Pro §1210

WILL PROBATE—Cont.
  Notices—Cont.
    Continued or postponed hearings, notice of   Pro §1205
    Delivery of notice
      Methods of delivery   Pro §1215
    Electronic delivery
      Proof of electronic delivery   Pro §1265
    Evidence at hearing of proof of notice   Pro §1266
    Exceptions
      Parent-child relationships   Pro §1207
      Petitioners in action   Pro §1201
    Good faith attempt to comply with notice requirements, sufficiency of   Pro §8122
    Governing law, application of   Pro §1200
    Guardians, service of notice on   Pro §1210
    Known heirs or devisees, notice to   Pro §§1206, 8110
    Mailing of (See within this heading, **"Mail"**)
    Methods of delivery
      Delivery of notice   Pro §1215
    Parent-child relationship, giving notice where   Pro §1207
    Personal delivery
      Proof of   Pro §1264
    Petitioner in proceedings, notice to   Pro §1201
    Posting or publication of (See within this heading, **"Posting or publication"**)
    Postponed hearings, notice of   Pro §1205
    Proof of notice
      Evidence at hearing   Pro §1266
      Hearing, proof of notice of   Pro §1260
      Mailing of   Pro §1261
      Personal delivery   Pro §1264
    Service of notice
      Generally   Pro §§8003, 8110
      Attorney General, notice to   Pro §§1209, 8111
    Shortening time for giving notice   Pro §1203
    Special notice   Pro §§1250 to 1252
    Statutory form of notice of hearing   Pro §1211
    Trust beneficiaries, notice to   Pro §1208
    Waiver of   Pro §1204
  Objections to petition   Pro §§1043, 8251
  Orders and decrees
    Generally   Pro §1046
    Contents of   Pro §1047
    County treasurer, copy of decree of distribution to   Pro §11853
    Enforcement of   Pro §1049
    Entry and filing of   Pro §1048
    Judgment roll   Pro §1050
    Production of will, order for   Pro §8201
    Recital of jurisdictional facts in   Pro §1047
    Recording requirements for orders affecting real property   Pro §7263
    Rules of procedure governing   Pro §1040
  Other state, probate of will after probate in   Pro §§12520 to 12524
  Parties
    Generally   Pro §8000
    After probate   Pro §§8270, 8271
    Before probate   Pro §8250
    Conservator as interested person   Pro §1210
    Control of action   CCP §1908
    Guardian as interested person   Pro §1210
    United States as interested person   Pro §7280
  Personal delivery of notice
    Proof   Pro §1264
  Personal representative defined   Pro §58
  Petition
    Generally   Pro §8000
    Contents of   Pro §8002
    Disclaimer, petition for order authorizing   Pro §277
    Filing fees generally (See within this heading, **"Filing fees"**)
    Form of notice of petition to administer estate   Pro §8100
    Hearing on petition for probate   Pro §8005
    Lost instrument   Pro §8223
    Objections to   Pro §§1043, 8251
    Response to   Pro §§1043, 8251
    Titles of petition or pleading papers to identify relief sought or granted   CRC 7.102
    Verification   Pro §1021
      Evidentiary use of verified petition   Pro §1022
  Photographic copies
    Admission to probate of   Pro §8202
    Petition for probate, attaching photographic copy of will to   Pro §8002
    Proof of original will by examination of   Pro §8220

WILL PROBATE—Cont.
  Posting or publication
    Notice of hearing, posting of   Pro §1230
    Proof of posting   Pro §1263
    Proof of publication   Pro §1262
  Postponements   Pro §1045
    Notice of continued or postponed hearing   Pro §1205
  Preference in hearing in Courts of Appeal and Supreme Court   CCP §44
  Probate rules generally   CRC 7.1 to 7.1105
  Process
    Notice, service of   Pro §§8003, 8110
      Attorney general, notice to   Pro §§1209, 8111
    Summons
      Contested will proceedings   Pro §8250
      Revocation of probate proceedings   Pro §8271
  Production of will
    Admissibility of photographic copy of will detained out of state   Pro §8202
    Court ordering   Pro §8201
    Delivery to clerk of court or executor   Pro §§8200 to 8203
    Transfer of will instrument to county where proceeding is pending, petition and order for   Pro §8203
  Proof of notice (See within this heading, **"Notices"**)
  Proof of will
    Generally   Pro §§8220, 8221
    Former testimony of subscribing witnesses in subsequent will contests, admissibility of   Pro §8224
    Holographic wills   Pro §8222
    Lost or destroyed wills   Pro §8223
  Pro per court documents, interactive computer system authorized to prepare standardized   CCP §1062.20
  Publication
    Notices generally (See within this heading, **"Notices"**)
  Recording requirements
    Admission of will to probate, recordation of   Pro §8225
    Orders affecting real property   Pro §7263
  Response to petition for   Pro §§1043, 8251
  Revocation of probate
    Judgment, order of   Pro §8272
    Limitations period   Pro §8270
    Petition for   Pro §8270
    Statute of limitation   Pro §8270
    Summons, service of   Pro §8271
  Search of will stored with clerk of court, fees for   Gov §70661
  Service of papers
    Notices, service   Pro §§8003, 8110
      Attorney general, notice to   Pro §§1209, 8111
  Severance of matters associated with proceedings and actions under Probate Code   Pro §801
  Shortening time for giving notice   Pro §1203
  Small estates (See **SMALL ESTATES WITHOUT ADMINISTRATION**)
  Special notice, request for   Pro §§1250 to 1252
  Statutes of limitation
    Before probate   Pro §8250
    Revocation of probate   Pro §8270
  Subscribing witnesses
    Beneficiaries as   Pro §6112
    No contest clause, effect of will provision benefiting witnesses contested by party subject to forfeiture under   Pro §6112
    Production and examination of   Pro §8253
    Proof of will by   Pro §§8220, 8224
  Summons
    Contested will proceedings   Pro §8250
    Revocation of probate, proceedings for   Pro §8271
  Surviving spouse (See **SURVIVING SPOUSE**)
  Time
    Limitations period
      Before probate   Pro §8250
      Revocation of probate   Pro §8270
    Will contest, time for   Pro §§8250, 8270
  Titles of petition or pleading papers to identify relief sought or granted   CRC 7.102
  Transferee defined   Pro §81.5
  Transfer of documents to clerk of court, fees for   Gov §§70660, 70661
  Trial   Pro §§1000 to 1051
    Costs   Pro §1002
    Jury trial, right of   Pro §825
    New trial motions   Pro §7220
    Procedural rules of practice governing   Pro §§1000, 1001
  Trusts (See **TRUSTS**)
  Undue influence
    Definition of undue influence   Pro §86

WILL PROBATE—Cont.
United States as interested person for purposes of   Pro §7280
Venue
    Generally   Pro §7051
    Nondomiciliary decedent, venue for   Pro §7052
Verification
    Generally   Pro §1021
    Evidentiary use of verified petition   Pro §1022
Waiver of notice requirements   Pro §1204
Witnesses
    Subscribing witnesses (See within this heading, "**Subscribing witnesses**")

WILLS
Abatement of bequests (See **ADMINISTRATION OF ESTATES**)
Abuse or neglect of elder or dependent testator by beneficiary, effect of   Pro §259
Acceptance of documents for deposit, effect on attorney of   Pro §713
Accounts defined   Pro §§21 to 23, 46
Acknowledgment
    Subscribing witnesses generally (See within this heading, "**Subscribing witnesses**")
Ademption   Pro §§6409, 21131 to 21139
Administration of estates (See **ADMINISTRATION OF ESTATES**)
Administrators of (See **EXECUTORS AND ADMINISTRATORS**)
Advancements (See **ADVANCEMENTS**)
Advertising, transferable property rights in use of deceased personality's name or likeness for   CC §3344.1
After-born heirs (See **POSTHUMOUS CHILDREN**)
Annuities, interest on   Pro §12004
Annulment of marriage
    Dissolution generally (See within this heading, "**Dissolution of marriage**")
Appellate rules, supreme court and courts of appeal
    Construction of term will   CRC 8.10
    Will probate cases, costs on appeal of   CRC 8.278, Pro §1002
Applicability of law   Pro §6103
At-death transfers
    Annuities   Pro §21117
    Anti-lapse   Pro §21110
    Class gifts   Pro §21114
    Classification of gifts   Pro §21117
    Defined   Pro §21104
    Demonstrative gifts   Pro §21117
    Failure of transfer, treatment   Pro §21111
    General gifts   Pro §21117
    General pecuniary gifts   Pro §21117
    Lifetime gifts in satisfaction of at-death transfer   Pro §21135
    Residuary gifts   Pro §§21111, 21117
    Rules, intent   Pro §21139
    Securities   Pro §21132
    Specific gifts   Pro §§21117, 21133
        Transfer or encumbrance of specific gift, rights of transferee   Pro §21134
    Survival of transferee   Pro §21109
Attesting witnesses (See within this heading, "**Subscribing witnesses**")
Attorney in fact, authority of   Pro §4265
Attorney professional conduct
    Gifts from client
        Restrictions   ProfC 1.8.3
Attorneys' fees for deposit of documents
    Compensation generally   Pro §714
    Transfer of documents to second attorney   Pro §732
Beneficiaries
    Abatement of bequests (See **ADMINISTRATION OF ESTATES**)
    Advancements (See **ADVANCEMENTS**)
    Defined   Pro §§24, 44
    Disclaimer of interest   Pro §§260 to 295
    Donative transfers
        Presumption of fraud or undue influence   Pro §§21360 to 21392 (See **DONATIVE TRANSFERS**)
    Escheat for failure to claim distribution   Pro §§11900 to 11904
    Governmental agencies   Pro §6102
    Homicide, effect of   Pro §§250 to 258
    Judge as beneficiary   Pro §7060
    Neglect or abuse of elder or dependent testator by beneficiary, effect of   Pro §259
    Omitted child (See **HEIRS**)
    Omitted spouse (See **SURVIVING SPOUSE**)
    Posthumous children (See **POSTHUMOUS CHILDREN**)
    Preliminary distribution to   Pro §§11620 to 11624
    Representation, taking by   Pro §§245 to 246
    Service of probate notice on   Pro §8110
    Settlement of accounts, distribution after   Pro §11641

WILLS—Cont.
Beneficiaries—Cont.
    Title passing to   Pro §§7000, 7001
    Uniform Transfers to Minors Act, devise under (See **UNIFORM TRANSFERS TO MINORS ACT**)
Bonding of personal representatives
    Waiver of bond in will   CRC 7.201
California statutory will
    Definitions   Pro §§6200 to 6211
    Form of   Pro §§6240 to 6243
    General provisions   Pro §§6220 to 6227
Capacity to make wills   Pro §§810 to 812, 6100, 6100.5
Certificate of execution of international will   Pro §§6384, 6385
Codicil, amendment of California statutory will by   Pro §6225
Community property (See **COMMUNITY PROPERTY**)
Compensation
    Deposit of documents with attorney, charge for   Pro §714
        Transfer of documents to second attorney   Pro §732
    Executor, will provisions for compensation of   Pro §10802
Conditional wills   Pro §6105
Conflicting instruments   Pro §6120
Conservators
    Generally (See **CONSERVATORS**)
    Deposit of nomination with attorney generally (See within this heading, "**Deposit of documents with attorney**")
    Making will for conservatee   Pro §§6100, 6100.5, 6110
Construction (See **WILL CONSTRUCTION**)
Contest of probate
    No contest clauses   Pro §§21300 to 21308, 21310 to 21315, 21320 to 21322
Conveyance by   CCP §1972
Declaratory judgments determining rights under   CCP §1060
Definitions   Pro §§20 to 88, 6200 to 6211
Delivery to clerk of superior court
    Superior court fees for specified services   Gov §70626
Deposition by subscribing witnesses   Pro §8220
Deposit of documents with attorney
    Acceptance by attorney, effect of   Pro §713
    Acknowledgment of terms by depositor   Pro §715
    Compensation
        Generally   Pro §714
        Transfer of documents to second attorney   Pro §732
    Death of attorney, termination of deposit on   Pro §735
    Death of depositor, termination of deposit on   Pro §734
    Definitions   Pro §§701 to 704
    Incapacity of attorney, termination of deposit on   Pro §735
    Lien in favor of attorney, viability of   Pro §714
    Loss or destruction of document
        Liability of attorney   Pro §712
        Notice to depositor   Pro §711
        Standard of care   Pro §§710, 716
    Notice to depositor
        General notice of terms   Pro §715
        Loss or destruction of document   Pro §711
    Notice to state Bar of transfer for termination of deposit   Pro §733
    Standards of care   Pro §§710, 716
    Termination of deposit
        By attorney   Pro §§730 to 735
        By depositor   Pro §720
Destruction of wills
    Deposited with attorney (See within this heading, "**Deposit of documents with attorney**")
    Probate procedure for lost or destroyed wills   Pro §8223
    Revocation, testator destroying instrument for purposes of   Pro §§6120, 6121
Disclaimer of interest   Pro §§260 to 295
Dispositions under will (See **WILL CONSTRUCTION**)
Dissolution of marriage
    Generally   Pro §§140 to 147, 6122, 6226
    Notice of effect of judgment on will provisions   Fam §2024
    Property settlement agreement affecting wills   Pro §§140 to 147
Domestic partnership, testamentary effect upon termination of   Pro §6122.1
Duress, fraud, or undue influence   Pro §6104
    Definition of undue influence   Pro §86
Earlier wills
    Revocation
        Generally (See within this heading, "**Revocation**")
        Prior will, revocation   Pro §6120
Election to take against
    Disclaimer of interest   Pro §§260 to 295
    Restoration of expectancy, effect on   Pro §102

WILLS—Cont.
- Electronic transactions
  - Exceptions to applicability of electronic transactions provisions   CC §1633.3
- Estate tax (See **ESTATE TAX**)
- Execution of
  - California statutory will   Pro §6221
  - Extrinsic evidence, admissibility of   Pro §6111.5
  - Foreign wills   Pro §6113
  - Signature (See within this heading, "**Signature**")
  - Subscribing witnesses (See within this heading, "**Subscribing witnesses**")
- Executors of (See **EXECUTORS AND ADMINISTRATORS**)
- Exoneration, no right to   Pro §21131
- Extrinsic evidence admissible where unclear meaning   Pro §6111.5
- Fact of death, proceedings to establish (See **FACT OF DEATH**)
- Fax filing and service
  - Excluded documents and papers from   CRC 2.300
- Fees
  - Delivery of will to clerk   Pro §8200
- Fiduciary income and principal act
  - Applicability of provisions   Pro §16322
    - Place of administration as basis of applicability   Pro §16323
  - Generally   Pro §§16320 to 16383
- Foreign wills
  - Ancillary administration of (See **ANCILLARY ADMINISTRATION**)
  - Domicile, applicability of law of   Pro §6113
  - Taking under   Pro §6102
  - Translation of   Pro §8002
  - Uniform International Wills Act (See within this heading, "**International wills**")
  - Validity of   Pro §6113
- Form of California statutory will   Pro §§6240 to 6246
- Fraud against testator, general discussion of effect of   Pro §6104
- Future interests
  - Failure   Pro §21111
- General devises, interest on   Pro §12003
- General personal representatives
  - Defined   Pro §§42, 58
- Gifts in view of impending death (See **DEATH**)
- Guardian ad litem, disclaimer of interest by   Pro §§260 to 295
- Guardian, disclaimer of interest by   Pro §§260 to 295
- Hearsay evidence concerning   Ev §§1260, 1261, 1330
- Heirs at law
  - Class gift to   Pro §21114
- Holographic wills (See **HOLOGRAPHIC WILLS**)
- Inclusions in definition   CCP §17
- Income earned during administration, right to   Pro §12006
- Inconsistent instruments   Pro §6120
- Intent
  - Executor where not named in will, intent of testator as to regarding   Pro §8421
  - Interpretation (See **WILL CONSTRUCTION**)
  - Revocation of will   Pro §§6120, 6124
- Interest on legacies
  - Annuities   Pro §12004
  - General pecuniary devises   Pro §12003
  - Maintenance, devise for   Pro §12005
  - Rate of interest   Pro §12001
  - Residuary devises   Pro §12006
  - Specific devises   Pro §12002
  - Transitional provision   Pro §12007
- International wills
  - Authorized person to supervise execution of   Pro §6388
  - Certification requirements   Pro §§6285, 6384
  - Definitions   Pro §6380
  - Governing law   Pro §§6387, 6390
  - Registry system for   Pro §6389
  - Revocation of   Pro §6386
  - Signature requirements   Pro §§6382, 6383
  - Validity of   Pro §6381
  - Witnesses   Pro §§6283, 6382
- Interpretation (See **WILL CONSTRUCTION**)
- Judicial determination that person lacks legal capacity to execute wills   Pro §§810 to 812
- Lien by attorney against documents deposited for safekeeping, viability of   Pro §714
- Lost documents
  - Deposited with attorney (See within this heading, "**Deposit of documents with attorney**")
  - Probate procedures for lost or destroyed wills   Pro §8223
- Marital deduction gifts (See **MARITAL DEDUCTION GIFTS**)

WILLS—Cont.
- Marital property, will provision as evidence of transmutation of   Fam §853
- Menace against testator, general discussion of effect of   Pro §6104
- Mental capacity to make wills   Pro §§810 to 812, 6100, 6100.5
- Minors (See **MINORS**)
- Mutual will   Pro §21700
- Neglect or abuse of elder or dependent testator by beneficiary, effect of   Pro §259
- No contest clauses   Pro §§21300 to 21308, 21310 to 21315, 21320 to 21322
- Nonprobate transfers (See **NONPROBATE TRANSFERS**)
- Omitted child (See **HEIRS**)
- Omitted spouse (See **SURVIVING SPOUSE**)
- 120-hour survival requirement   Pro §6211
- Pecuniary devises
  - Annuities, interest on   Pro §12004
  - Interest on   Pro §12003
  - Surviving spouse, administration of pecuniary devise or fractional interest passing to   Pro §13502.5
- Personal property
  - Writing disposing of personal property
    - Reference in will to writing   Pro §6132
- Personal representative defined   Pro §58
- Petition for order authorizing filing of disclaimer   Pro §277
- Posthumous children (See **POSTHUMOUS CHILDREN**)
- Pour-over provisions
  - Generally   Pro §§6300 to 6303
  - Life insurance   Pro §§6321 to 6330
- Power of appointment (See **POWER OF APPOINTMENT**)
- Preliminary distribution under   Pro §§11620 to 11624
- Presumption of fraud or undue influence   Pro §§21360 to 21392 (See **DONATIVE TRANSFERS**)
- Presumptions of authenticity   Ev §643
- Pretermitted heirs (See **HEIRS**)
- Previous wills, revocation of
  - Revocation generally (See within this heading, "**Revocation**")
- Privilege claims concerning property interest   Ev §§959 to 961, 1002, 1003, 1021, 1022
- Probate (See **WILL PROBATE**)
- Production of   Pro §§8200 to 8203
- Property settlement agreement, dissolution of marriage affecting provisions in   Pro §§140 to 147
- Public administrator, search by   Pro §7602
- Quiet title actions involving validity of gift, devise, bequest or trust under   CCP §764.020
- Real property acquired through   CC §1000
- Residuary gifts or devises   Pro §21111
  - Debts satisfied from property transferred from   Pro §§21400, 21402
  - Interest on   Pro §12006
- Revocation
  - California statutory wills   Pro §§6225, 6226
  - Destruction of instrument   Pro §§6120, 6121
  - Dissolution of marriage   Pro §§140 to 147, 6122, 6226
  - Domestic partnership, testamentary effect upon termination of   Pro §6122.1
  - Inconsistent instruments   Pro §6120
  - Intent of testator as to   Pro §§6120, 6124
  - International will   Pro §6386
  - Mutual will   Pro §21700
  - Presumption of   Pro §6124
  - Prior wills   Pro §6120
  - Revival of earlier instrument   Pro §6123
  - Written instrument of   Pro §6120
- Safe deposit box, access rights for removal of decedent's will from   Pro §331
- Sale of estate assets under direction of   Pro §§10000, 10002
- Severance of matters associated with proceedings and actions under Probate Code   Pro §801
- Signature
  - Generally   Pro §6221
  - International will requirements   Pro §§6382, 6383
  - Procedure for   Pro §6110
  - Third party signing for testator   Pro §6110
- Simultaneous death (See **SIMULTANEOUS DEATH**)
- Small estates (See **SMALL ESTATES WITHOUT ADMINISTRATION**)
- Specific devises
  - Abatement, order of (See **ADMINISTRATION OF ESTATES**)
  - Interest on   Pro §12002
- Statutory will
  - Domestic partnership termination, revocation of will by   Pro §6227
- Subscribing witnesses
  - Generally   Pro §6110
  - Affidavits, admissibility of   Pro §8220
  - California statutory will, execution of   Pro §§6221, 6221.5

WILLS—Cont.
Subscribing witnesses—Cont.
- Competency of   Pro §6112
- Depositions, admissibility of   Pro §8220
- Former testimony of subscribing witnesses in subsequent will contests, admissibility of   Pro §8224
- Interested witnesses, presumptions involving   Pro §6112
- International wills, affidavit requirements for   Pro §§6382, 6383
- Judges   Pro §7060
- Number of   Pro §6110
- Probate proceedings, proof of will by evidence of subscribing witnesses in   Pro §§8220, 8224

Survival requirement, 120-hour period   Pro §6211
Surviving spouse (See **SURVIVING SPOUSE**)
Testators
- Generally   Pro §§6100, 6102
- Defined   Pro §6201
- Homicide, effect of   Pro §§250 to 258
- Intent
  - Executor where not named in will, intent of testator   Pro §8421
  - Interpretation (See **WILL CONSTRUCTION**)
  - Revocation of will   Pro §§6120, 6124
- International will requirements   Pro §§6382, 6383
- Mental capacity of   Pro §§810 to 812, 6100, 6100.5
- Neglect or abuse of elder or dependent testator by beneficiary, effect of   Pro §259
- Signature (See within this heading, "**Signature**")

Translation into English language   Pro §8002
Undue influence exercised on testator, general discussion of effect of   Pro §6104
Uniform International Wills Act (See within this heading, "**International wills**")
Uniform Transfers to Minors Act, devise under (See **UNIFORM TRANSFERS TO MINORS ACT**)
United States, dispositions by will to   Pro §6102
Witnesses
- Subscribing witnesses (See within this heading, "**Subscribing witnesses**")
- Writing directing disposition of personal property
  - Reference in will to writing   Pro §6132
Written contracts for making   CC §1624, Pro §21700

WINDOWS
Forcible entry by breaking   CCP §1159

WINDOW SECURITY BARS
Disclosure requirements   CC §1102.16

WINE (See **ALCOHOLIC BEVERAGES**)

WIRETAPPING (See **EAVESDROPPING AND WIRETAPPING**)

WITH ALL FAULTS SALES   CC §§1790 to 1795.8

WITHDRAWAL
Administrative Procedure Act (See **ADMINISTRATIVE PROCEDURE ACT**)
Attorneys
- Generally (See **ATTORNEYS**)
- Indigent clients (See **INDIGENT PERSONS**)

Conservatorship money or property, withdrawal of (See **CONSERVATORS**)
Economic litigation provisions, withdrawal of actions from   CCP §91
Guardianship money or property, withdrawal of (See **GUARDIAN AND WARD**)
Notice of pendency (See **PENDENCY OF ACTIONS**)
State agency, withdrawal of proposed regulation by (See **ADMINISTRATIVE PROCEDURE ACT**)
Sureties (See **SURETYSHIP, BONDS AND UNDERTAKINGS**)

WITHHOLDING ORDERS (See **GARNISHMENT**)

WITHOUT MERIT
Small claims court judgment, award of attorney's fees on appeal from   CCP §116.790

WITNESSES
Generally   Ev §§700, 701
Absence of   Ev §240
Acknowledgment of instrument   CC §1185
Administrative adjudicative proceedings (See **ADMINISTRATIVE ADJUDICATION**)
Adverse party
- Called as witness   Ev §776
- Spouse called as witness by   Ev §971

Aggravation
- Threatening witnesses   CRC 4.421

WITNESSES—Cont.
Appeals
- Perpetuation of testimony pending appeal   CCP §§2036.010 to 2036.050

Arbitration (See **ARBITRATION**)
Arrest of   CCP §§1993, 1994
- Fee for processing civil warrant   Gov §26744.5
- Release of arrested witness   CCP §1993.1
  - Failure of released witness to appear   CCP §1993.2

Attendance
- Court's power to compel   CCP §128
- Duties of witnesses   CCP §2064
- Judge's power to compel   CCP §177
- Means of compelling (See **SUBPOENA**)

Attorney professional conduct
- Attorney as witness   ProfC 3.7
- Obstructing access to evidence, witness, etc
  - Fairness to opposing party and counsel   ProfC 3.4

Authentication of document, testimony concerning   Ev §§1411 to 1413
Bench trial, rehabilitation of witness in   CCP §631.8
Bench warrant to secure attendance of   CCP §§1993, 1994
- Fee for processing civil warrant   Gov §26744.5
- Release of arrested witness   CCP §1993.1
  - Failure of released witness to appear   CCP §1993.2

Building inspector as witness   Gov §§68907.1, 68907.2
Character and reputation (See **CHARACTER AND REPUTATION**)
Child abuse and neglect
- Child witnesses, waiting room   CRC JudAdminStand 10.24
- Juvenile court proceedings   CRC 5.548

Child support
- Live testimony
  - When received   CRC 5.113, Fam §217

Child witnesses
- Waiting room   CRC JudAdminStand 10.24

City employees as witness, reimbursement of salary and expenses of   Gov §68096.1
Concealment by   CCP §1988
Conflicting statements (See within this heading, "**Inconsistent statements**")
Confrontation, right of   Ev §711
Conservators
- Interstate jurisdiction, transfer and recognition
- Other state, testimony in   Pro §1986

Consumer privacy rights
- California privacy protection agency
  - Subpoenas, agency authority   CC §1798.199.65

Continuance of trial, deposition of witness for adversary on   CCP §596
Contracts
- Waiver in contract or settlement of right to testify concerning criminal conduct or sexual harassment   CC §1670.11

Convenience of (See **CONVENIENCE**)
Coroner's jury, witness fee at   Gov §68095
County employee as witness   Gov §§68907.1, 68907.2
County employees as witness, reimbursement of salary and expenses of   Gov §68096.1
Court presence without subpoena   CCP §1990
Court reporters to take down all testimony   CCP §269
- Reports as prima facie evidence of testimony and proceedings   CCP §273

Court's power to compel attendance of   CCP §128
Credibility of witnesses
- Generally   Ev §§780, 785
- Admissibility of evidence on issue of   Ev §406
- Character traits   Ev §§780, 782, 786, 787, 790
- Consistent statements   Ev §791
- Eminent domain
  - Deposit reports   CCP §1255.060
- Good character references   Ev §790
- Hearsay evidence admissible for attacking   Ev §§1202, 1235
- Inconsistent statements (See within this heading, "**Inconsistent statements**")
- Prior felony convictions   Ev §788
- Rape prosecution, evidence admissible in   Ev §§782, 1103
- Religious beliefs as inadmissible for attack on   Ev §789
- Sexual conduct evidence   Ev §§782, 783, 1103

Cross-examination
- Small claims appeals   CRC 8.966

Custodian of records (See **SUBPOENA DUCES TECUM**)
Custody of children
- Child as witness   Fam §3042
  - Children's participation and testimony in family court proceedings   CRC 5.250
- Live testimony
  - When received   CRC 5.113, Fam §217

WITNESSES—Cont.
- Death, unavailable witness because of   Ev §240
- Defendant in criminal case   Ev §§930, 940
- Defined   CCP §1878
- Depositions (See **DEPOSITIONS**)
- Direct examination
  - Small claims appeals   CRC 8.966
- Disqualified persons   Ev §701
- Dissolution of marriage
  - Live testimony
    - When received   CRC 5.113, Fam §217
- Distance of travel by   CCP §1989
- District attorney inspector as witness   Gov §§68907.1, 68907.2
- Enforcement of judgments (See **ENFORCEMENT OF JUDGMENTS**)
- Examination
  - Generally   Ev §§765 to 778
  - Cross-examination (See **CROSS-EXAMINATION**)
  - Direct examination (See **DIRECT EXAMINATION**)
  - Inconsistent statements (See within this heading, "**Inconsistent statements**")
- Exclusion of
  - Courtroom, exclusion from   Ev §777
  - Economic litigation provisions for limited civil cases   CCP §97
- Excusing witnesses by court   Ev §778
- Expert witnesses (See **EXPERT AND OPINION EVIDENCE**)
- Failure to appear notice
  - Required prior to issuance of arrest warrant for failure to appear   CCP §1993
- Family law proceedings
  - Live testimony
    - When received   CRC 5.113, Fam §217
- Fees
  - Generally   CCP §1986.5, Gov §68093
  - Advance compensation, demand for   Gov §68097
  - Arbitration proceedings   CCP §1283.2
  - City employees as witness, reimbursement of salary and expenses of   Gov §68096.1
  - Coroner's jury witness fee   Gov §68095
  - County employees as witness, reimbursement of salary and expenses of   Gov §68096.1
  - Crimes against humanity
    - Assault and battery, wrongful death, etc constituting torture, genocide, crimes against humanity, etc   CCP §354.8
  - Criminal cases, county funds chargeable in   Gov §68098
  - Depositions   CCP §2020.230
  - Expert witnesses (See **EXPERT AND OPINION EVIDENCE**)
  - Genocide
    - Assault and battery, wrongful death, etc constituting torture, genocide, crimes against humanity, etc   CCP §354.8
  - Grand jury witness fee   Gov §68094
  - Local agency employees as witness, reimbursement of salary and expenses of   Gov §68096.1
  - Notice of entitlement to   CCP §2065
  - Peace officers
    - Compensation (See within this heading, "**Peace officers**")
  - Production of business records   Ev §1563
  - Public employee witnesses   Gov §68097.2
  - Public safety employee as witness, generally
    - Compensation (See within this heading, "**Peace officers**")
  - Recovery of costs by prevailing party   CCP §1033.5
  - Sheriff's fees for subpoenaing witness   Gov §26743
  - Torture
    - Assault and battery, wrongful death, etc constituting torture, genocide, crimes against humanity, etc   CCP §354.8
  - Trial court employees   Gov §68097.2
  - War crimes
    - Assault and battery, wrongful death, etc constituting torture, genocide, crimes against humanity, etc   CCP §354.8
- Firefighters subpoenaed as witnesses   Gov §§68097.1, 68907.2
- Former testimony admissible   Ev §§1290 to 1293
- Guardian and ward
  - Ward's participation and testimony in guardianship proceedings   CRC 7.1016
- Hearsay evidence (See **HEARSAY**)
- Hiding   CCP §1988
- Highway Patrol (See within this heading, "**Peace officers**")
- Human trafficking victims
  - Impeachment of witnesses
    - Prostitution or other commercial sex acts committed while victim, evidentiary significance   Ev §1161
- Husband and wife privileged communications (See **MARITAL PRIVILEGE**)

WITNESSES—Cont.
- Hypnosis of   Ev §795
- Illness, unavailable because of   Ev §240
- Impeachment
  - Credibility of witnesses generally (See within this heading, "**Credibility of witnesses**")
- Impeachment and credibility
  - Human trafficking victims
    - Prostitution or other commercial sex acts committed while victim, evidentiary significance   Ev §1161
- Inconsistent statements
  - Generally   Ev §769
  - Extrinsic evidence   Ev §770
  - Hearsay rule, effect of   Ev §§1202, 1235, 1236
- Informer as material witness   Ev §1042
- Judges (See **JUDGES**)
- Judicial performance, commission on
  - Censure, removal, admonishment or retirement of judges
    - Oath, witness statements under   JudPerPolicy 1.13
    - Perpetuation of testimony by deposition   JudPerR 122
    - Record of witness statements   JudPerPolicy 1.11
- Jurors (See **JURY**)
- Juvenile court proceedings   CRC 5.548
- Legislative continuance   CCP §595
- Letters of administration, compelling attendance of witnesses at hearing for   Pro §8005
- Local agency employees as witness, reimbursement of salary and expenses of   Gov §68096.1
- Mark, witnesses to signature by   CCP §17
- Marriage
  - Remote licensing and solemnization
    - Physical location of license applicants, solemnizer, witnesses and county clerk   Fam §554
- Medical causation
  - Expert and opinion evidence   Ev §801.1
- Mileage costs (See **MILEAGE**)
- Nonjury trial, rehabilitation of witness in   CCP §631.8
- Notice of entitlement to fees and mileage   CCP §2065
- Number of witnesses necessary for proof of fact   Ev §411
- Oaths (See **OATHS**)
- Opinion evidence (See **EXPERT AND OPINION EVIDENCE**)
- Partition (See **PARTITION**)
- Paternity
  - Live testimony
    - When received   CRC 5.113, Fam §217
- Peace officers
  - Compensation
    - Generally   Gov §68097.2
    - Costs, taxable by prevailing party as   Gov §68097.8
    - Highway Patrol members   Gov §68097.4
    - Subsequent appearances, advance payment for   Gov §68097.5
    - Waiver of deposit or payment of   Gov §68097.55
  - Depositions of   Gov §68097.6
  - Gang-related crimes, qualifications of peace officer testifying about sworn statement of decedent concerning   Ev §1231.3
  - Settlement cost provision, police officers as expert witnesses for purpose of   CCP §998
  - Subpoena as witness
    - Generally   Gov §68097.1
    - Depositions   Gov §68097.6
    - Highway Patrol members   Gov §§68097.1, 68097.3
- Perpetuation of testimony
  - Actions, prior to filing   CCP §§2035.010 to 2035.060
  - Appeal pending   CCP §§2036.010 to 2036.050
- Personal knowledge necessary for testifying   Ev §702
- Police officers (See within this heading, "**Peace officers**")
- Power of attorney (See **POWER OF ATTORNEY**)
- Presence of parties for questioning of   Ev §711
- Prior inconsistent statements (See within this heading, "**Inconsistent statements**")
- Prisoners as   CCP §§1995 to 1997
- Privileged communications (See **PRIVILEGED COMMUNICATIONS**)
- Probate referees, subpoena by (See **PROBATE REFEREES**)
- Probation officer as witness   Gov §§68907.1, 68907.2
- Prostitution
  - Extortion, serious felony, assault, domestic violence, human trafficking, sexual battery or stalking, victims or witnesses
    - Inadmissibility of evidence of prostitution in prosecution for prostitution   Ev §1162
- Public employee as witness, compensation of   Gov §68097.2
- Public entity defending or indemnifying   Gov §995.9
- Public safety employees as witnesses (See within this heading, "**Peace officers**")

WITNESSES—Cont.

Qualifications of   Ev §§700, 701
Rape, testimony in prosecution of   Ev §§782, 1103
Refusal to testify
    Unavailability as witness   Ev §240
Rehabilitation of witness in nonjury trial   CCP §631.8
Religion (See **RELIGION**)
Rule, putting under   Ev §777
Self-incrimination (See **SELF-INCRIMINATION**)
Settlement and compromise
    Waiver in contract or settlement of right to testify concerning criminal conduct or sexual harassment   CC §1670.11
Sheriff
    Fee for subpoenaing witnesses   Gov §26743
    Witnesses, sheriffs as (See within this heading, **"Peace officers"**)
Small claims actions   CCP §116.520
State agency adjudicative proceedings (See **ADMINISTRATIVE ADJUDICATION**)
State employees as witnesses   Gov §§68097.1, 68907.2
Sterilization proceedings (See **STERILIZATION**)
Subpoena duces tecum (See **SUBPOENA DUCES TECUM**)
Subpoenas (See **SUBPOENA**)
Subscribing witnesses (See **SUBSCRIBING WITNESSES**)
Superior court reporters
    Reports as prima facie evidence of testimony and proceedings   CCP §273
Time for appearance, agreement changing   CCP §1985.1
Transfer on death deeds
    Contest of transfer
        Subscribing witnesses produced and examined   Pro §5690
    Execution of instrument
        Effective, when   Pro §5624
        Qualifications of witnesses   Pro §5625
Translators and interpreters (See **TRANSLATORS AND INTERPRETERS**)
Trauma from crime, unavailable because of   Ev §240
Trial court employees
    Compensation   Gov §68097.2
    Subpoena   Gov §68097.1
Truthfulness
    Attack on credibility   Ev §780
    Understanding duty for   Ev §701
Unavailable witnesses (See **HEARSAY**)
Views by trier of fact, presence at   CCP §651
Wills (See **WILLS**)
Witness Protection Program, change of name for participating witness in   CCP §1277

WITNESS PROTECTION PROGRAM

Change of name for participating witness   CCP §1277

WOLFE V SHELLEY (See **SHELLEY'S CASE**)

WOMEN

Judges, membership in discriminatory organizations   CRCSupp JudEthicsCanon 2

WOOD

Logs (See **LOGS AND TIMBER**)

WOODCUTS

Sales regulated   CC §§1740 to 1745

WOOL

Attachment proceedings   CCP §481.110
Claim and delivery   CCP §511.040

WORD PROCESSING (See **COMPUTERS**)

WORDS AND PHRASES (See **DEFINITIONS**)

WORK-AT-HOME

Seller assisted marketing plans   CC §§1812.200 to 1812.221

WORKERS' COMPENSATION

Administrative Procedure Act, applicability of rulemaking provision of   Gov §11351
Appeals board (WCAB)
    Judicial review of decisions   CRC 8.720
    Review of orders and awards   CRC 8.720
Attachment, exemption from   CCP §486.060
Award
    Filing and entering
        Superior court fees, specified services   Gov §70626

WORKERS' COMPENSATION—Cont.

Claims against public entities and employees, no implied repeals by sections affecting   Gov §814.2
Claims procedures
    Review of orders and awards   CRC 8.720
Enforcement of judgments (See **ENFORCEMENT OF JUDGMENTS**)
Expert witnesses
    Deposition of expert witness
        Fees   CCP §2034.430
HIV status of workers, limited confidentiality of   CC §56.31
Judicial branch workers' compensation program advisory committee   CRC 10.67
Judicial council workers' compensation program for trial court   CRC 10.350
Malpractice suits against physicians, evidence in   CC §3333.1

WORKING DAYS

Civil Code statute   CC §§9, 11

WORKMANSHIP

Ownership, workmanship as deciding   CC §1028

WORKPLACE SAFETY (See **SAFE WORKING PLACE**)

WORKPLACE VIOLENCE

Appellate court opinions
    Privacy, use of names in opinions   CRC 8.90
Forms
    Judicial council legal forms   CRCAppx A
Injunctive relief against violence or threat of violence toward employee
    Possession of firearms   CCP §527.11
    Service of order   CCP §527.12
Protection orders against violence or threat of violence toward employee   CCP §527.8, CRC 3.1160
    Address or location of complaining party or family, prohibition on enjoined party from obtaining   CCP §527.10
    California law enforcement telecommunications (CLETS) information form, confidentiality and use of information   CRC 1.51, CRCAppx A
    COVID-19, emergency rule   CRCAppx I Emer Rule 8
    Firearm relinquishment and disposition   CCP §527.9
        Forms for firearm relinquishment   CRCAppx A
    Judicial council legal forms   CRCAppx A
    Memorandum in support of petition for order not required   CRC 3.1114
    Requests for protective orders   CRC 3.1160

WORK PRODUCT DOCTRINE

Coordination of actions, standards for   CCP §404.1
Discovery
    Attorney work product generally   CCP §§2018.010 to 2018.080
Electronically stored information
    Inspection demands
        Privilege claimed or attorney work product protection requested   CCP §2031.285
Subpoenas
    Applicability of privilege   CCP §1985.8

WORKS OF IMPROVEMENT

Construction contracts (See **CONSTRUCTION CONTRACTS**)
Contractors (See **CONTRACTORS**)
Mechanics' liens   CC §§8000 to 9566 (See **MECHANICS' LIENS**)
Public works (See **PUBLIC CONTRACTS AND WORKS**)

WRITERS (See **AUTHORS**)

WRITINGS (See also **DOCUMENTS AND PAPERS**)

Contracts (See **CONTRACTS AND AGREEMENTS**)
Conveyances (See **CONVEYANCES**)
Definitions   Ev §250
Documentary evidence (See **DOCUMENTARY EVIDENCE**)
Electronic transactions, satisfaction of writing requirements in   CC §§1633.7, 1633.8
Evidence
    Microphotographed files, records, photographs, etc., in custody of criminal justice agency
        Reproductions, admissibility   Ev §1550.1
Graffiti   Ev §1410.5
Handwriting (See **HANDWRITING**)
Inclusions in definition   CCP §17
Interpretation
    Translators, when required   Ev §753
Jurors, excuses of   CCP §218
Libel and slander (See **LIBEL AND SLANDER**)
Medical records, authorization for release of   CC §§56.10, 56.11

WRITINGS—Cont.
Motions requiring notice in writing   CCP §§1005, 1010
Release   CC §1541
Statute of frauds (See **STATUTE OF FRAUDS**)
Statutes of limitation (See **STATUTES OF LIMITATION**)
Trusts (See **TRUSTS**)
Verdict   CCP §618
Wills   CC §1624, Pro §21700

WRIT OF ATTACHMENT (See **ATTACHMENT**)

WRIT OF EXECUTION
Enforcement of judgments (See **ENFORCEMENT OF JUDGMENTS**)
Levying officer electronic transactions act
    Retention of original or electronic copy   CCP §263.6
Unlawful detainer, holding over after execution sale as act constituting   CCP §1161a

WRIT OF POSSESSION
Claim and delivery (See **CLAIM AND DELIVERY**)
Enforcement of judgments (See **ENFORCEMENT OF JUDGMENTS**)
Small claims court, writ of possession issued by   CCP §116.220

WRIT OF PROHIBITION (See **PROHIBITION, WRIT OF**)

WRITS
Attachment, writ of (See **ATTACHMENT**)
Certiorari, writ of (See **CERTIORARI**)
Defined   CCP §17
Discovery
    Interstate and international depositions and discovery act
        Choice of law to resolve disputes, appeal for extraordinary writ   CCP §2029.650
Execution, writ of (See **WRIT OF EXECUTION**)
Habeas corpus, writ of (See **HABEAS CORPUS**)
Juvenile courts
    Special instructions for writs and levies, form of attachment   CRCAppx A
Mandamus, writ of (See **MANDAMUS**)
Original proceedings in reviewing courts, procedural rules
    Habeas corpus   CRC 8.380 to 8.398
    Mandate, certiorari and prohibition in supreme court or court of appeal   CRC 8.485 to 8.493
        Environmental quality act cases under public resources code   CRC 8.703
Petitions
    Copies   CRCSupp 1st AppDist, 6th AppDist
Possession, writ of (See **WRIT OF POSSESSION**)
Prohibition, writ of (See **PROHIBITION, WRIT OF**)
Quo warranto, writ of (See **QUO WARRANTO**)
Review, writ of (See **CERTIORARI**)
Sale, writ of (See **ENFORCEMENT OF JUDGMENTS**)
Seal of court, documents requiring   CCP §153
Writ of review (See **CERTIORARI**)

WRITTEN CONFESSIONS (See **CONFESSIONS**)

WRITTEN INSTRUMENTS
Adverse possession by person claiming title founded on written instrument   CCP §§322, 323
Attorney's performance of professional services, running of statute of limitation for actions arising out of   CCP §340.6
Parol evidence (See **PAROL EVIDENCE**)

WRITTEN INTERROGATORIES (See **INTERROGATORIES**)

WRONGFUL ATTACHMENT (See **ATTACHMENT**)

WRONGFUL DEATH
Administrative adjudicative proceedings, generally (See **ADMINISTRATIVE ADJUDICATION**)
Arbitration clause in real estate contract, applicability of   CCP §1298.7
Asbestos, limitation of actions based on exposure to   CCP §340.2
Assignment for benefit of creditors, compensatory payments exempt from   CCP §1801
Common interest developments, limited liability of volunteer officer or director of   CC §5800
Complaints for   CCP §§425.10 to 425.12
Compromise or settlement of claim by personal representative
    Time-limited demands   CCP §§999 to 999.5

WRONGFUL DEATH—Cont.
Consolidation
    Action arising out of same wrongful act or neglect   CCP §377.61
    Minor child, actions for injury and for wrongful death of   CCP §376
Damages
    Medical malpractice
        Limitation on damages   CC §3333.2
Damages recoverable
    Generally   CCP §377.61
    Complaint or cross-complaint, demand for judgment in   CCP §425.10
    Punitive damages (See within this heading, **"Punitive damages"**)
    Request for statement of damages   CCP §§425.11, 425.12
Deceased person's statements against plaintiff   Ev §1227
Default judgment, reservation of right to seek punitive damages on   CCP §§425.12, 425.115
Domestic partners
    Eligibility to bring action for wrongful death   CCP §377.60
Exemption for purposes of enforcement of judgment of cause of action or award for   CCP §704.140
Health care provider's professional negligence, limitation of actions based on   CCP §340.5
Heirs maintaining action for   CCP §377.60
Homicide
    Benefit from wrongful death action, homicide slayer not expected to   Pro §258
    Punitive damages   CC §3294
Immigration status
    Evidence, inadmissibility   Ev §351.2
Joinder of actions
    Consolidation
        Action arising out of same wrongful act or neglect   CCP §377.61
        Minor child, actions for injury and for wrongful death   CCP §376
Legal guardian of decedent, damages action by   CCP §377.60
Married person liable for damages caused by other spouse   Fam §1000
Medical malpractice
    Damages
        Limitation on damages   CC §3333.2
Medical malpractice, death by (See **PHYSICIANS AND SURGEONS**)
Minors
    Consolidation of actions for wrongful death and injury to minor child   CCP §376
    Heirs for purposes of maintaining wrongful death action   CCP §377.60
Parent's liability for acts of minor child   CC §§1714.1, 1714.3
Patent deficiencies in planning or construction of improvement to real property, limitation of actions for death from   CCP §337.1
Personal representatives maintaining action for   CCP §377.60
Physician-patient privilege, applicability of   Ev §996
Public entities, collateral source payments in claims against   Gov §985
Punitive damages
    Default judgment, reservation of right to seek punitive damages on   CCP §§425.12, 425.115
    Homicide   CC §3294
Putative spouse and children of putative spouse as heirs   CCP §377.60
Request for statement of damages being sought   CCP §§425.11, 425.12
Reservation of right to seek punitive damages on default   CCP §§425.12, 425.115
Statement of damages being sought, request for   CCP §§425.11, 425.12
Statutes of limitation
    Generally   CCP §335.1
    Asbestos, actions based on exposure to   CCP §340.2
    Health care provider's professional negligence, actions based on   CCP §340.5
    Patent deficiencies in planning or construction of improvement to real property, actions for death from   CCP §337.1
    Torture, genocide, crimes against humanity, etc   CCP §354.8
Under age of 14, entitlement to preference of party who is   CCP §36
Venue   CCP §395

WRONGFUL LIFE
Parent, cause of action against   CC §43.6

Y

YEAR 2000 PROBLEM
Dissemination of information concerning Year 2000 Problem, liability for   CC §§3269 to 3271

YOUTH AUTHORITY
Juvenile facilities generally (See **JUVENILE FACILITIES**)

Z

ZONES AND ZONING
Commercial and industrial common interest developments
    Like structures, lots, etc, to be treated alike
        Local zoning requirements   CC §6510
Common interest developments (See **COMMON INTEREST DEVELOPMENTS**)
Eminent domain valuation data for   CCP §1258.260

ZONES AND ZONING—Cont.
Floating homes and floating home marinas, zoning change for   CC §800.33
Industrial use zoning, residential property seller's obligation to disclose   CC §1102.17
Inspection warrants to determine violations   CCP §1822.50
Mobilehome parks (See **MOBILEHOMES**)

ZOOS
Eminent domain statutes affecting property reserved for   CCP §1240.670
Guide dogs allowed in   CC §54.7